SCOTT

What's new for 2021 Scott Standard Volume 6?

Another catalog season is upon us as we continue the journey of the 152-year history of the Scott catalogs. The 2021 volumes are the 177th edition of the Scott *Standard Postage Stamp Catalogue*. Vol. 6A includes listings for countries of the world San Marino through Tete. Listings for countries of the world Thailand through Z can be found in Vol. 6B.

VOL. 6A

The country of Saudi Arabia received a thorough review with more than 2,000 value changes made, largely slight decreases. For example, the 1966 set of five stamps issued to publicize the Eighth Congress of the Arab Telecommunications Union, Riyadh, decreased from $16.30 unused to $15.25.

The stamps of Sharjah, one of six Persian Gulf sheikdoms to join the United Arab Emirates in 1971, were reviewed with 174 value changes noted, mostly slight decreases. One exception was the first set of 15 Sheik Saqr bin Sultan al Qasimi, Flag and Map stamps (Scott 1-15). The movement of the value changes was mixed in that set; the unused value decreased from $18.20 to $7.70, and the used value increased from $6.65 to $28.80.

A careful review of Singapore took place, with approximately 450 changes made. Value changes were mixed with slight drops in value for post-1980s stamps. Editorially, the modern dated definitive varieties were double-checked, and a couple of additions were made. See the Number Additions, Deletions & Changes list in the catalog for the specific items added. One increase to note was the 1970 set of four Sea Shells stamps (Scott 112-115), which went from $18.50 to $20.50 unused. Also the souvenir sheet of these four stamps (115a) moved from $30 to $35.

South Sudan overprints from 2017 were reviewed, and increases were made for 12 values. For example, the £75-on-£2 Bearded Vultures surcharged stamp went from $7 unused and used to $11 both ways. The values are in italics because this stamp is challenging to value and does not trade frequently.

Singapore's 1970 set of four Sea Shells stamps (Scott 112-115) increased from $18.50 to $20.50 in unused condition. The souvenir sheet of those four stamps also increased from $30 to $35 in unused condition.

A line-by-line review of Spain took place with a mixed amount of increases and decreases. The set of 1876 King Alfonso XII stamps (Scott 222-230) increased from $366.75 in unused condition to $436.75. The used value for the set stayed at $320.95. Many of the values that changed for Spain's post-2008 stamp issues reflected slight increases, especially for stamps in used condition. For example, the used value for the 2010 Cathedrals of Plasencia souvenir sheet (3702) was changed to match the $7.50 unused value.

Sweden from 1920 to date was thoroughly reviewed. The result was approximately 4,600 value changes, with decreases outweighing increases. The most sizeable decreases were noted for booklet panes of stamps. Additionally, values for recent used stamps were adjusted to reflect what they are selling for.

The United Arab Emirates 2017 National Program for Happiness and Positivity souvenir sheet (Scott 1160) changed from $8.75 to $20 in unused condition and used condition.

The Scott catalog editors added a minor variety for Switzerland Scott 232b. The catalog now pictures Type I and Type II varieties of the 1936 20-centime carmine St. Gotthard Railroad stamp that have distinct visual differences.

The 1913-14 stamps of the Portuguese colonial district of Tete were reviewed, and a handful of value changes were made for the 40 major Scott numbers listed. Overall increases were noted throughout those changes, including the 7½-centavo-on-75-real Vasco da Gama stamp (Scott 14), which moved from $4 unused to $5.

VOL. 6B

The stamps of the United Arab Emirates were reviewed, with a mix of increases and decreases among the more than 1,300 value changes. One larger increase was for the 2017 National Program for Happiness and Positivity souvenir sheet (Scott 1160), which moved from $8.75 to $20 in both unused condition and used condition.

Uruguay was reviewed, with almost 2,000 value changes made. The first stamp of Uruguay, the 60-centavo blue El Sol de Mayo (Scott 1), increased in unused condition from $450 to $650. The Scott editors also upgraded footnoted date varieties of a couple of the 1997 definitive stamps that show a children's painting and the bird of prey Geranoaetus melanoleucus (Scott 1674-1675).

And lastly, we encourage you to pay special attention to the Number Additions, Deletions & Changes in this volume. We also suggest reading the catalog introduction, which includes an abundance of useful information.

Best wishes in your stamp collecting pursuits!

Jay Bigalke, Scott catalog editor-in-chief

Acknowledgments

Our appreciation and gratitude go to the following individuals who have assisted us in preparing information included in this year's Scott Catalogues. Some helpers prefer anonymity. These individuals have generously shared their stamp knowledge with others through the medium of the Scott Catalogue.

Those who follow provided information that is in addition to the hundreds of dealer price lists and advertisements and scores of auction catalogues and realizations that were used in producing the catalogue values. It is from those noted here that we have been able to obtain information on items not normally seen in published lists and advertisements. Support from these people goes beyond data leading to catalogue values, for they also are key to editorial changes.

A special acknowledgment to Liane and Sergio Sismondo of The Classic Collector for their assistance and knowledge sharing that have aided in the preparation of this year's Standard and Classic Specialized Catalogues.

Clifford J. Alexander (Carriers and Locals Society)
Roland Austin
Michael & Cecilia Ball (A to Z Stamps)
Jim Bardo (Bardo Stamps)
John Birkinbine II
James A. Booth
Les Bootman
Roger S. Brody
Keith & Margie Brown
Tina & John Carlson (JET Stamps)
Carlson Chambliss
Bob Coale
Tony L. Crumbley (Carolina Coin and Stamp, Inc.)
Christopher Dahle
Markand Dave
Tony Davis
Bob and Rita Dumaine (Sam Houston Duck Co.)
Mark Eastzer
Paul G. Eckman
Steve Farago
Mike Farrell
Robert Finder (Korea Stamp Society)
Jeffrey M. Forster
Ernest E. Fricks (France & Colonies Philatelic Society)
Bob Genisol (Sultan Stamp Center)
Henning Gmerek
Stan Goldfarb
Marc E. Gonzales
Daniel Grau
Dan Harding
Sy Harvell
Bruce Hecht (Bruce L. Hecht Co.)
Armen Hovsepian (ArmenStamp)
Robert Jack
Eric Jackson
Peter C. Jeannopoulos
William A. (Bill) Jones
Allan Katz (Ventura Stamp Co.)
Jon Kawaguchi (Ryukyu Philatelic Specialist Society)
Han Ki Klm
John R. Lewis (The William Henry Stamp Co.)
Ignacio Llach (Filatelia Llach, S.L.)
Nicolas Mallosetti
William K. McDaniel
Pat McElroy
Gary Morris (Pacific Midwest Co.)
Peter Mosiondz, Jr.
Phillip Moulay
Bruce M. Moyer (Moyer Stamps & Collectables)
Richard H. Muller (Richard's Stamps)
Scott Murphy
Leonard Nadybal
Dr. Tiong Tak Ngo
Nik & Lisa Oquist
Nicholas Pertwee
Don Peterson (International Philippine Philatelic Society)
Stanley M. Piller (Stanley M. Piller & Associates)
Dr. Charles Posner
Peter W. W. Powell
Siddique Mahmudur Rahman (Bangladesh Institute of Philatelic Studies)
Ghassan D. Riachi
Omar Rodriguez
Mehrdad Sadri (Persiphila)
Alex Schauss (Schauss Philatelics)
Joyce & Chuck Schmidt
Guy Shaw (Mexico-Elmhurst Philatelic Society International)
J. Randall Shoemaker (Philatelic Stamp Authenication and Grading, Inc.)
Jeff Siddiqui (Pakistan Philatelic Study Circle)
Sergio & Liane Sismondo (The Classic Collector)
Jay Smith
Telah Smith
Scott R. Trepel (Siegel Auction Galleries, Inc.)
Steven Unkrich
Herbert R. Volin
Philip T. Wall
Yong S. Yi (Korea Stamp Society)
Ralph Yorio
Dr. Michal Zika (Album)
Alfonso G. Zulueta, Jr.

Addresses, Telephone Numbers, Web Sites, E-Mail Addresses of General & Specialized Philatelic Societies

Collectors can contact the following groups for information about the philately of the areas within the scope of these societies, or inquire about membership in these groups. Aside from the general societies, we limit this list to groups that specialize in particular fields of philately, particular areas covered by the Scott Standard Postage Stamp Catalogue, and topical groups. Many more specialized philatelic society exist than those listed below. These addresses are updated yearly, and they are, to the best of our knowledge, correct and current. Groups should inform the editors of address changes whenever they occur. The editors also want to hear from other such specialized groups not listed. Unless otherwise noted all website addresses begin with http://

General Societies

American Philatelic Society
100 Match Factory Place
Bellefonte, PA 16823-1367
(814) 933-3803
https://stamps.org
apsinfo@stamps.org

International Society of Worldwide Stamp Collectors
Joanne Murphy, M.D.
P.O. Box 19006
Sacramento, CA 95819
www.iswsc.org
executivedirector@iswsc.org

Royal Philatelic Society of Canada
P.O. Box 69080
St. Clair Post Office
Toronto, ON M4T 3A1
CANADA
(888) 285-4143
www.rpsc.org
info@rpsc.org

Royal Philatelic Society London
15 Abchurch Lane
London EX4N 7BW
UNITED KINGDOM
+44 (0) 20 7486 1044
www.rpsl.org.uk
secretary@rpsl.org.uk

Libraries, Museums, and Research Groups

American Philatelic Research Library
Scott Tiffney
100 Match Factory Place
Bellefonte, PA 16823
(814) 933-3803
www.stamplibrary.org
library@stamps.org

V. G. Greene Philatelic Research Foundation
P.O. Box 69100
St. Clair Post Office
Toronto, ON M4T 3A1
CANADA
(416) 921-2073
info@greenefoundation.ca

Aero/Astro Philately

American Air Mail Society
Stephen Reinhard
P.O. Box 110
Mineola, NY 11501
www.americanairmailsociety.org
sreinhard1@optonline.net

Postal History

Auxiliary Markings Club
Jerry Johnson
6621 W. Victoria Ave.
Kennewick, WA 99336
www.postal-markings.org
membership-2010@postal-markings.org

Postage Due Mail Study Group
Bob Medland
Camway Cottage
Nanny Hurn's Lane
Cameley, Bristol BS39 5AJ
UNITED KINGDOM
01761 45959
www.postageduemail.org.uk
secretary.pdmsg@gmail.com

Postal History Society
Yamil Kouri
405 Waltham St. #347
Lexington, MA 02421
www.postalhistorysociety.org
yhkouri@massmed.org

Post Mark Collectors Club
Bob Milligan
7014 Woodland Oaks Drive
Magnolia, TX 77354
(281) 259-2735
www.postmarks.org
bob.milligan@gmail.com

U.S. Cancellation Club
Roger Curran
18 Tressler Blvd.
Lewisburg, PA 17837
rdcnrc@ptd.net

Revenues & Cinderellas

American Revenue Association
Lyman Hensley
473 E. Elm St.
Sycamore, IL 60178-1934
www.revenuer.org
ilrno2@netzero.net

Christmas Seal & Charity Stamp Society
John Denune, Jr.
234 E. Broadway
Granville, OH 43023
(740) 814-6031
www.seal-society.org

National Duck Stamp Collectors Society
Anthony J. Monico
P.O. Box 43
Harleysville, PA 19438-0043
www.ndscs.org
ndscs@ndscs.org

State Revenue Society
Kent Gray
P.O. Box 67842
Albuquerque, NM 87193
www.staterevenue.org
srssecretary@comcast.net

Thematic Philately

Americana Unit
Dennis Dengel
17 Peckham Road
Poughkeepsie, NY 12603-2018
www.americanaunit.org
ddengel@americanaunit.org

American Topical Association
Jennifer Miller
P.O. Box 2143
Greer, SC 29652-2143
(618) 985-5100
www.americantopicalassn.org
americantopical@msn.com

Astronomy Study Unit
Leonard Zehr
1009 Treverton Crescent
Windsor, ON N8P 1K2
CANADA
(416) 833-9317
www.astronomystudyunit.net
lenzehr@gmail.com

Bicycle Stamps Club
Corey Hjalseth
1102 Broadway, Suite 200
Tacoma, WA 98402
(253) 318-6222
www.bicyclestampsclub.org
coreyh@evergreenhomeloans.com

Biology Unit
Chris Dahle
1401 Linmar Drive NE
Cedar Rapids, IA 52402-3724
www.biophilately.org
chris-dahle@biophilately.org

Bird Stamp Society
Mr. S. A. H. (Tony) Statham
Ashlyns Lodge
Chesham Road
Berkhamsted, Herts HP4 2ST
UNITED KINGDOM
www.bird-stamps.org/bss
tony.statham@sky.com

Captain Cook Society
Jerry Yucht
8427 Leale Ave.
Stockton, CA 95212
www.captaincooksociety.com
us@captaincooksociety.com

The CartoPhilatelic Society
Marybeth Sulkowski
2885 Sanford Ave., SW, #32361
Grandville, MI 49418-1342
www.mapsonstamps.org
secretary@mapsonstamps.org

Casey Jones Railroad Unit
Jeff Lough
2612 Redbud Land, Apt. C
Lawrence, KS 66046
www.uqp.de/cjr
jeffydplaugh@gmail.com

Cats on Stamps Study Unit
Robert D. Jarvis
2731 Teton Lane
Fairfield, CA 94533
www.catstamps.info
catmews1@yahoo.com

Chemistry & Physics on Stamps Study Unit
Dr. Roland Hirsch
13830 Metcalf Ave., Apt. 15218
Overland Park, KS 66223-8017
(301) 792-6296
www.cpossu.org
rfhirsch@cpossu.org

Chess on Stamps Study Unit
Barry Keith
511 1st St. N., Apt. 106
Charlottesville, VA 22902
www.chessonstamps.org
keithfam@embarqmail.com

Cricket Philatelic Society
A. Melville-Brown
11 Weppons, Ravens Road
Shorham-by-Sea
West Sussex BN43 5AW
UNITED KINGDOM
www.cricketstamp.net
mel.cricket.100@googlemail.com

Earth's Physical Features Study Group
Fred Klein
515 Magdalena Ave.
Los Altos, CA 94024
http://epfsu.jeffhayward.com
epfsu@jeffhayward.com

Ebony Society of Philatelic Events and Reflections (ESPER)
Don Neal
P.O. Box 5245
Somerset, NJ 08875-5245
www.esperstamps.org
esperdon@verizon.net

Europa Study Unit
Tonny E. Van Loij
3002 S. Xanthia St.
Denver, CO 80231-4237
(303) 752-0189
www.europastudyunit.org
tvanloij@gmail.com

Fire Service in Philately
John Zaranek
81 Hillpine Road
Cheektowaga, NY 14227-2259
(716) 668-3352
jczaranek@roadrunner.com

Gastronomy on Stamps Study Unit
David Wolfersburger
5062 NW 35th Lane Road
Ocala, FL 34482
(314) 494-3795
www.gastronomystamps.org

Gay & Lesbian History on Stamps Club
Joe Petronie
P.O. Box 190842
Dallas, TX 75219-0842
www.glhsonline.org
glhsc@aol.com

Gems, Minerals & Jewelry Study Unit
Fred Haynes
10 Country Club Drive
Rochester, NY 14618-3720
fredmhaynes55@gmail.com

Graphics Philately Association
Larry Rosenblum
1030 E. El Camino Real
PMB 107
Sunnyvale, CA 94087-3759
www.graphics-stamps.org
larry@graphics-stamps.org

Journalists, Authors and Poets on Stamps
Christopher D. Cook
7222 Hollywood Rd.
Berrien Springs, MI 49103
cdcook2@gmail.com

Lighthouse Stamp Society
Dalene Thomas
1805 S. Balsam St., #106
Lakewood, CO 80232
(303) 986-6620
www.lighthousestampsociety.org
dalene@lighthousestampsociety.org

Lions International Stamp Club
David McKirdy
s-Gravenwetering 248
3062 SJ Rotterdam
NETHERLANDS
31(0) 10 212 0313
www.lisc.nl
davidmckirdy@aol.com

Masonic Study Unit
Gene Fricks
25 Murray Way
Blackwood, NJ 08012-4400
genefricks@comcast.net

Medical Subjects Unit
Dr. Frederick C. Skvara
P.O. Box 6228
Bridgewater, NJ 08807
fcskvara@optonline.net

Napoleonic Age Philatelists
Ken Berry
4117 NW 146th St.
Oklahoma City, OK 73134-1746
(405) 748-8646
www.nap-stamps.org
krb4117@att.net

Old World Archaeological Study Unit
Caroline Scannell
14 Dawn Drive
Smithtown, NY 11787-1761
www.owasu.org
editor@owasu.org

Petroleum Philatelic Society International
Feitze Papa
922 Meander Drive
Walnut Creek, CA 94598-4239
www.ppsi.org.uk
oildad@astound.net

Rotary on Stamps Fellowship
Gerald L. Fitzsimmons
105 Calle Ricardo
Victoria, TX 77904
www.rotaryonstamps.org
glfitz@suddenlink.net

Scouts on Stamps Society International
Woodrow (Woody) Brooks
498 Baldwin Road
Akron, OH 44312
(330) 612-1294
www.sossi.org
secretary@sossi.org

Ships on Stamps Unit
Erik Th. Matzinger
Voorste Havervelden 30
4822 AL Breda
NETHERLANDS
www.shipsonstamps.org
erikships@gmail.com

Space Topic Study Unit
David Blog
P.O. Box 174
Bergenfield, NJ 07621
www.space-unit.com
davidblognj@gmail.com

Stamps on Stamps Collectors Club
Michael Merritt
73 Mountainside Road
Mendham, NJ 07945
www.stampsonstamps.org
stampsonstamps@yahoo.com

Windmill Study Unit
Walter J. Hallien
607 N. Porter St.
Watkins Glenn, NY 14891-1345
(607) 229-3541
www.windmillworld.com

Wine On Stamps Study Unit
David Wolfersburger
5062 NW 35th Lane Road
Ocala, FL 34482
(314) 494-3795
www.wine-on-stamps.org

United States

American Air Mail Society
Stephen Reinhard
P.O. Box 110
Mineola, NY 11501
www.americanairmailsociety.org
sreinhard1@optonline.net

American First Day Cover Society
Douglas Kelsey
P.O. Box 16277
Tucson, AZ 85732-6277
(520) 321-0880
www.afdcs.org
afdcs@afdcs.org

Auxiliary Markings Club
Jerry Johnson
6621 W. Victoria Ave.
Kennewick, WA 99336
www.postal-markings.org
membership-2010@postal-markings.org

American Plate Number Single Society
Rick Burdsall
APNSS Secretary
P.O. BOX 1023
Palatine, IL 60078-1023
www.apnss.org
apnss.sec@gmail.com

American Revenue Association
Lyman Hensley
473 E. Elm St.
Sycamore, IL 60178-1934
www.revenuer.org
ilrno2@netzero.net

American Society for Philatelic Pages and Panels
Ron Walenciak
P.O. Box 1042
Washington Township, NJ 07676
www.asppp.org
rwalenciak@aol.com

Canal Zone Study Group
Mike Drabik
P.O. Box 281
Bolton, MA 01740
www.canalzonestudygroup.com
czsgsecretary@gmail.com

Carriers and Locals Society
John Bowman
14409 Pentridge Drive
Corpus Christi, TX 78410
(361) 933-0757
www.pennypost.org
jbowman@stx.rr.com

Christmas Seal & Charity Stamp Society
John Denune, Jr.
234 E. Broadway
Granville, OH 43023
(740) 814-6031
www.seal-society.org
john@christmasseals.net

Confederate Stamp Alliance
Patricia A. Kaufmann
10194 N. Old State Road
Lincoln, DE 19960-3644
(302) 422-2656
www.csalliance.org
trishkauf@comcast.net

Error, Freaks, and Oddities Collectors Club
Scott Shaulis
P.O. Box 549
Murrysville, PA 15668-0549
(724) 733-4134
www.efocc.org
scott@shaulisstamps.com

National Duck Stamp Collectors Society
Anthony J. Monico
P.O. Box 43
Harleysville, PA 19438-0043
www.ndscs.org
ndscs@ndscs.org

Plate Number Coil Collectors Club (PNC3)
Gene Trinks
16415 W. Desert Wren Court
Surprise, AZ 85374
(623) 322-4619
www.pnc3.org
gctrinks@cox.net

Post Mark Collectors Club
Bob Milligan
7014 Woodland Oaks Drive
Magnolia, TX 77354
(281) 259-2735
www.postmarks.org
bob.milligan@gmail.com

Souvenir Card Collectors Society
William V. Kriebel
1923 Manning St.
Philadelphia, PA 19103-5728
www.souvenircards.org
kriebewv@drexel.edu

United Postal Stationery Society
Dave Kandziolka
404 Sundown Drive
Knoxville, TN 37934
www.upss.org
membership@upss.org

U.S. Cancellation Club
Roger Curran
18 Tressler Blvd.
Lewisburg, PA 17837
rdcnrc@ptd.net

U.S. Philatelic Classics Society
Rob Lund
2913 Fulton St.
Everett, WA 98201-3733
www.uspcs.org
membershipchairman@uspcs.org

US Possessions Philatelic Society
Daniel F. Ring
P.O. Box 113
Woodstock, IL 60098
http://uspps.tripod.com
danielfring@hotmail.com

United States Stamp Society
Rod Juell
P.O. Box 3508
Joliet, IL 60434-3508
www.usstamps.org
execsecretary@usstamps.org

Africa

Bechuanalands and Botswana Society
Otto Peetoom
Roos
East Yorkshire HU12 0LD
UNITED KINGDOM
44(0)1964 670239
www.bechuanalandphilately.com
info@bechuanalandphilately.com

Egypt Study Circle
Mike Murphy
11 Waterbank Road
Bellingham
London SE6 3DJ
UNITED KINGDOM
(44) 0203 6737051
www.egyptstudycircle.org.uk
secretary@egyptstudycircle.org.uk

Ethiopian Philatelic Society
Ulf Lindahl
21 Westview Place
Riverside, CT 06878
(203) 722-0769
https://ethiopianphilatelicsociety.weebly.com
ulindahl@optonline.net

Liberian Philatelic Society
P.O. Box 1570
Parker, CO 80134
www.liberiastamps.org
liberiastamps@comcast.net

Orange Free State Study Circle
J. R. Stroud, RDPSA
24 Hooper Close
Burnham-on-sea
Somerset TA8 1JQ
UNITED KINGDOM
44 1278 782235
www.orangefreestatephilately.org.uk
richard@richardstroud.plus.com

Philatelic Society for Greater Southern Africa
Alan Hanks
34 Seaton Drive
Aurora, ON L4G 2K1
CANADA
www.psgsa.org
alan.hanks@sympatico.ca

Rhodesian Study Circle
William R. Wallace
P.O. Box 16381
San Francisco, CA 94116
(415) 564-6069
www.rhodesianstudycircle.org.uk
bwall8rscr@earthlink.net

Society for Moroccan and Tunisian Philately
S.P.L.M.
206, Bld Pereire
75017 PARIS
FRANCE
http://splm-philatelie.org
splm206@aol.com

South Sudan Philatelic Society
William Barclay
1370 Spring Hill Road
South Londonderry, VT 05155
barclayphilatelics@gmail.com

Sudan Study Group
Andy Neal
Bank House, Coedway
Shrewsbury SY5 9AR
UNITED KINGDOM
www.sudanstamps.org
andywneal@gmail.com

Transvaal Study Circle
c/o 9 Meadow Road
Gravesend, Kent DA11 7LR
UNITED KINGDOM
www.transvaalstamps.org.uk
transvaalstudycircle@aol.co.uk

West Africa Study Circle
Martin Bratzel
1233 Virginia Ave.
Windsor, ON N8S 2Z1
CANADA
www.wasc.org.uk
marty_bratzel@yahoo.ca

Asia

Aden & Somaliland Study Group
Gary Brown
P.O. Box 106
Briar Hill, VIC 3088
AUSTRALIA
www.stampdomain.com/aden
garyjohn951@optushome.com.au

Burma (Myanmar) Philatelic Study Circle
Michael Whittaker
1, Ecton Leys, Hillside
Rugby
Warwickshire CV22 5SL
UNITED KINGDOM
https://burmamyanmarphilately.wordpress.com/burma-myanmar-philatelic-study-circle
manningham8@mypostoffice.co.uk

Ceylon Study Circle
Rodney W. P. Frost
42 Lonsdale Road
Cannington
Bridgwater, Somerset TA5 2JS
UNITED KINGDOM
01278 652592
www.ceylonsc.org
rodney.frost@tiscali.co.uk

China Stamp Society
H. James Maxwell
1050 W. Blue Ridge Blvd.
Kansas City, MO 64145-1216
www.chinastampsociety.org
president@chinastampsociety.org

Hong Kong Philatelic Society
John Tang
G.P.O. Box 446
HONG KONG
www.hkpsociety.com
hkpsociety@outlook.com

Hong Kong Study Circle
Robert Newton
www.hongkongstudycircle.com/index.html
newtons100@gmail.com

India Study Circle
John Warren
P.O. Box 7326
Washington, DC 20044
(202) 488-7443
https://indiastudycircle.org
jw-kbw@earthlink.net

International Philippine Philatelic Society
James R. Larot, Jr.
4990 Bayleaf Court
Martinez, CA 94553
(925) 260-5425
www.theipps.info
jlarot@ccwater.com

International Society for Japanese Philately
William Eisenhauer
P.O. Box 230462
Tigard, OR 97281
(503) 496-2634
www.isjp.org
secretary@isjp.org

Iran Philatelic Study Circle
Nigel Gooch
Marchwood, 56, Wickham Ave.
Bexhill-on-Sea
East Sussex TN39 3ER
UNITED KINGDOM
www.iranphilately.org
nigelmgooch@gmail.com

Korea Stamp Society
Peter Corson
1109 Gunnison Place
Raleigh, NC 27609
(919) 787-7611
https://koreastampsociety.org
pbcorson@aol.com

Nepal & Tibet Philatelic Study Circle
Colin Hepper
12 Charnwood Close
Peterborough, Cambs PE2 9BZ
UNITED KINGDOM
http://fuchs-online.com/ntpsc
ntpsc@fuchs-online.com

Pakistan Philatelic Study Circle
Jeff Siddiqui
P.O. Box 7002
Lynnwood, WA 98046
jeffsiddiqui@msn.com

Society of Indo-China Philatelists
Ron Bentley
2600 N. 24th St.
Arlington, VA 22207
(703) 524-1652
www.sicp-online.org
ron.bentley@verizon.net

Society of Israel Philatelists, Inc.
Sarah Berezenko
100 Match Factory Place
Bellefonte, PA 16823-1367
(814) 933-3803 ext. 212
www.israelstamps.com
israelstamps@gmail.com

Australasia and Oceana

Australian States Study Circle of the Royal Sydney Philatelic Club
Ben Palmer
G.P.O. 1751
Sydney, NSW 2001
AUSTRALIA
http://club.philas.org.au/states

Fellowship of Samoa Specialists
Trevor Shimell
18 Aspen Drive, Newton Abbot
Devon TQ12 4TN
UNITED KINGDOM
www.samoaexpress.org
trevor.shimell@gmail.com

Malaya Study Group
Michael Waugh
151 Roker Lane
Pudsey
Leeds LS28 9ND
UNITED KINGDOM
http://malayastudygroup.com
mawpud43@gmail.com

New Zealand Society of Great Britain
Michael Wilkinson
121 London Road
Sevenoaks
Kent TN13 1BH
UNITED KINGDOM
01732 456997
www.nzsgb.org.uk
mwilkin799@aol.com

Pacific Islands Study Circle
John Ray
24 Woodvale Ave.
London SE25 4AE
UNITED KINGDOM
www.pisc.org.uk
secretary@pisc.org.uk

Papuan Philatelic Society
Steven Zirinsky
P.O. Box 49, Ansonia Station
New York, NY 10023
(718) 706-0616
www.papuanphilatelicsociety.com
szirinsky@cs.com

Pitcairn Islands Study Group
Dr. Everett L. Parker
207 Corinth Road
Hudson, ME 04449-3057
(207) 573-1686
www.pisg.net
eparker@hughes.net

Ryukyu Philatelic Specialist Society
Laura Edmonds
P.O. Box 240177
Charlotte, NC 28224-0177
(336) 509-3739
www.ryukyustamps.org
secretary@ryukyustamps.org

Society of Australasian Specialists / Oceania
Steve Zirinsky
P.O. Box 230049
New York, NY 10023-0049
www.sasoceania.org
president@sosoceania.org

Sarawak Specialists' Society
Stephen Schumann
2417 Cabrallo Drive
Hayward, CA 94545
(510) 785-4794
www.britborneostamps.org.uk
vpnam@s-s-s.org.uk

Western Australia Study Group
Brian Pope
P.O. Box 423
Claremont, WA 6910
AUSTRALIA
(61) 419 843 943
www.wastudygroup.com
wastudygroup@hotmail.com

Europe

American Helvetia Philatelic Society
Richard T. Hall
P.O. Box 15053
Asheville, NC 28813-0053
www.swiss-stamps.org
secretary2@swiss-stamps.org

American Society for Netherlands Philately
Hans Kremer
50 Rockport Court
Danville, CA 94526
(925) 820-5841
www.asnp1975.com
hkremer@usa.net

Andorran Philatelic Study Circle
David Hope
17 Hawthorn Drive
Stalybridge
Cheshire SK15 1UE
UNITED KINGDOM
www.andorranpsc.org.uk
andorranpsc@btinternet.com

Austria Philatelic Society
Ralph Schneider
P.O. Box 978
Iowa Park, TX 76376
(940) 213-5004
www.austriaphilatelicsociety.com
rschneiderstamps@gmail.com

Channel Islands Specialists Society
Richard Flemming
Burbage, 64 Falconers Green
Hinckley
Leicestershire LE102SX
UNITED KINGDOM
www.ciss1950.org.uk
secretary@ciss1950.org.uk

Cyprus Study Circle
Rob Wheeler
47 Drayton Ave.
London W13 0LE
UNITED KINGDOM
www.cyprusstudycircle.org
robwheeler47@aol.com

Danish West Indies Study Unit of Scandinavian Collectors Club
Arnold Sorensen
7666 Edgedale Drive
Newburgh, IN 47630
(812) 480-6532
www.scc-online.org
valbydwi@hotmail.com

Eire Philatelic Association
John B. Sharkey
1559 Grouse Lane
Mountainside, NJ 07092-1340
www.eirephilatelicassoc.org
jsharkeyepa@me.com

Faroe Islands Study Circle
Norman Hudson
40 Queen's Road
Vicar's Cross
Chester CH3 5HB
UNITED KINGDOM
www.faroeislandssc.org
jntropics@hotmail.com

France & Colonies Philatelic Society
Edward Grabowski
111 Prospect St., 4C
Westfield, NJ 07090
(908) 233-9318
www.franceandcolsps.org
edjjg@alum.mit.edu

Germany Philatelic Society
P.O. Box 6547
Chesterfield, MO 63006-6547
www.germanyphilatelicusa.org
info@germanyphilatelicsocietyusa.org

Gibraltar Study Circle
Susan Dare
22, Byways Park, Strode Road
Clevedon
North Somerset BS21 6UR
UNITED KINGDOM
www.gibraltarstudycircle.wordpress.com
smldare@yahoo.co.uk

International Society for Portuguese Philately
Clyde Homen
1491 Bonnie View Road
Hollister, CA 95023-5117
www.portugalstamps.com
ispp1962@sbcglobal.net

Italy and Colonies Study Circle
Richard Harlow
7 Duncombe House
8 Manor Road
Teddington, Middlesex TW118BE
UNITED KINGDOM
44 208 977 8737
www.icsc-uk.com
richardharlow@outlook.com

Liechtenstudy USA
Paul Tremaine
410 SW Ninth St.
Dundee, OR 97115-9731
(503) 538-4500
www.liechtenstudy.org
tremaine@liechtenstudy.org

Lithuania Philatelic Society
Audrius Brazdeikis
9915 Murray Landing
Missouri City, TX 77459
(281) 450-6224
www.lithuanianphilately.com/lps
audrius@lithuanianphilately.com

Luxembourg Collectors Club
Gary B. Little
7319 Beau Road
Sechelt, BC V0N 3A8
CANADA
(604) 885-7241
http://lcc.luxcentral.com
gary@luxcentral.com

Plebiscite-Memel-Saar Study Group of the German Philatelic Society
Clayton Wallace
100 Lark Court
Alamo, CA 94507
claytonwallace@comcast.net

Polonus Polish Philatelic Society
Daniel Lubelski
P.O. Box 2212
Benicia, CA 94510
(419) 410-9115
www.polonus.org
info@polonus.org

Rossica Society of Russian Philately
Alexander Kolchinsky
1506 Country Lake Drive
Champaign, IL 61821-6428
www.rossica.org
alexander.kolchinsky@rossica.org

Scandinavian Collectors Club
Steve Lund
P.O. Box 16213
St. Paul, MN 55116
www.scc-online.org
steve88h@aol.com

Society for Czechoslovak Philately
Tom Cossaboom
P.O. Box 4124
Prescott, AZ 86302
(928) 771-9097
www.csphilately.org
klfckl@aol.com

Society for Hungarian Philately
Alan Bauer
P.O. Box 4028
Vineyard Haven, MA 02568
(617) 645-4045
www.hungarianphilately.org
alan@hungarianstamps.com

Spanish Study Circle
Edith Knight
www.spaincircle.wixsite.com/spainstudycircle
spaincircle@gmail.com

Ukrainian Philatelic & Numismatic Society
Martin B. Tatuch
5117 8th Road N.
Arlington, VA 22205-1201
www.upns.org
treasurer@upns.org

Vatican Philatelic Society
Joseph Scholten
1436 Johnston St. SE
Grand Rapids, MI 49507-2829
www.vaticanphilately.org
jscholten@vaticanphilately.org

Yugoslavia Study Group
Michael Chant
1514 N. Third Ave.
Wausau, WI 54401
208-748-9919
www.yugosg.org
membership@yugosg.org

Interregional Societies

American Society of Polar Philatelists
Alan Warren
P.O. Box 39
Exton, PA 19341-0039
(610) 321-0740
www.polarphilatelists.org
alanwar@att.net

First Issues Collector's Club
Kurt Streepy
3128 E. Mattatha Drive
Bloomington, IN 47401
www.firstissues.org
secretary@firstissues.org

Former French Colonies Specialist Society
Col.fra
BP 628
75367 PARIS Cedex 08
FRANCE
www.colfra.org
postmaster@colfra.org

France & Colonies Philatelic Society
Edward Grabowski
111 Prospect St., 4C
Westfield, NJ 07090
(908) 233-9318
www.franceandcolsps.org
edjjg@alum.mit.edu

Joint Stamp Issues Society
Richard Zimmermann
29A, Rue Des Eviats
67220 LALAYE
FRANCE
www.philarz.net
richard.zimmermann@club-internet.fr

The King George VI Collectors Society
Brian Livingstone
21 York Mansions
Prince of Wales Drive
London SW11 4DL
UNITED KINGDOM
www.kg6.info
livingstone484@btinternet.com

International Society of Reply Coupon Collectors
Peter Robin
P.O. Box 353
Bala Cynwyd, PA 19004
peterrobin@verizon.net

Italy and Colonies Study Circle
Richard Harlow
7 Duncombe House
8 Manor Road
Teddington, Middlesex TW118BE
UNITED KINGDOM
44 208 977 8737
www.icsc-uk.com
richardharlow@outlook.com

St. Helena, Ascension & Tristan Da Cunha Philatelic Society
Dr. Everett L. Parker
207 Corinth Road
Hudson, ME 04449-3057
(207) 573-1686
www.shatps.org
eparker@hughes.net

United Nations Philatelists
Blanton Clement, Jr.
P.O. Box 146
Morrisville, PA 19067-0146
www.unpi.com
bclemjunior@gmail.com

Latin America

Asociación Filatélica de Panamá
Edward D. Vianna B
ASOFILPA
0819-03400
El Dorado, Panama
PANAMA
http://asociacionfilatelicadepanama.blogspot.com
asofilpa@gmail.com

Asociacion Mexicana de Filatelia (AMEXFIL)
Alejandro Grossmann
Jose Maria Rico, 129
Col. Del Valle
3100 Mexico City, DF
MEXICO
www.amexfil.mx
amexfil@gmail.com

Associated Collectors of El Salvador
Joseph D. Hahn
301 Rolling Ridge Drive, Apt. 111
State College, PA 16801-6149
www.elsalvadorphilately.org
joehahn100@hotmail.com

Association Filatelic de Costa Rica
Giana Wayman (McCarty)
#SJO 4935
P.O. Box 025723
Miami, FL 33102-5723
011-506-2-228-1947
scotland@racsa.co.cr

Brazil Philatelic Association
William V. Kriebel
1923 Manning St.
Philadelphia, PA 19103-5728
www.brazilphilatelic.org
info@brazilphilatelic.org

Canal Zone Study Group
Mike Drabik
P.O. Box 281
Bolton, MA 01740
www.canalzonestudygroup.com
czsgsecretary@gmail.com

Colombia-Panama Philatelic Study Group
Thomas P. Myers
P.O. Box 522
Gordonsville, VA 22942
www.copaphil.org
tpmphil@hotmail.com

Falkland Islands Philatelic Study Groups
Morva White
42 Colton Road
Shrivenham
Swindon SN6 8AZ
UNITED KINGDOM
44(0) 1793 783245
www.fipsg.org.uk
morawhite@supanet.com

Federacion Filatelica de la Republica de Honduras
Mauricio Mejia
Apartado Postal 1465
Tegucigalpa, D.C.
HONDURAS
504 3399-7227
www.facebook.com/filateliadehonduras
ffrh@hotmail.com

International Cuban Philatelic Society (ICPS)
Ernesto Cuesta
P.O. Box 34434
Bethesda, MD 20827
(301) 564-3099
www.cubafil.org
ecuesta@philat.com

International Society of Guatemala Collectors
Jaime Marckwordt
449 St. Francis Blvd.
Daly City, CA 94015-2136
(415) 997-0295
www.guatemalastamps.com
president@guatamalastamps.com

Mexico-Elmhurst Philatelic Society International
Eric Stovner
P.O. Box 10097
Santa Ana, CA 92711-0097
www.mepsi.org
treasurer@mepsi.org

Nicaragua Study Group
Erick Rodriguez
11817 S. W. 11th St.
Miami, FL 33184-2501
nsgsec@yahoo.com

North America (excluding United States)

British Caribbean Philatelic Study Group
Bob Stewart
7 West Dune Lane
Long Beach Township, NJ 08008
(941) 379-4108
www.bcpsg.com
bcpsg@comcast.net

British North America Philatelic Society
Andy Ellwood
10 Doris Ave.
Gloucester, ON K1T 3W8
CANADA
www.bnaps.org
secretary@bnaps.org

British West Indies Study Circle
Steve Jarvis
5 Redbridge Drive
Andover
Hants SP10 2LF
UNITED KINGDOM
01264 358065
www.bwisc.org
info@bwisc.org

Bermuda Collectors Society
John Pare
405 Perimeter St.
Mount Horeb, WI 53572
(608) 852-7358
www.bermudacollectorssociety.com
pare16@mhtc.net
john@christmasseals.net

Haiti Philatelic Society
Ubaldo Del Toro
5709 Marble Archway
Alexandria, VA 22315
www.haitiphilately.org
u007ubi@aol.com

Hawaiian Philatelic Society
Gannon Sugimura
P.O. Box 10115
Honolulu, HI 96816-0115
www.stampshows.com/hps.html
hiphilsoc@gmail.com

Stamp Dealer Associations

American Stamp Dealers Association, Inc.
P.O. Box 692
Leesport, PA 19553
(800) 369-8209
www.americanstampdealer.com
asda@americanstampdealer.com

National Stamp Dealers Association
Sheldon Ruckens, President
3643 Private Road 18
Pinckneyville, IL 62274-3426
(618) 357-5497
www.nsdainc.org
nsda@nsdainc.org

Youth Philately

Young Stamp Collectors of America
100 Match Factory Place
Bellefonte, PA 16823
(814) 933-3803
https://stamps.org/stamps.org/Learn/youth-in-philately
ysca@stamps.org

Expertizing Services

The following organizations will, for a fee, provide expert opinions about stamps submitted to them. Collectors should contact these organizations to find out about their fees and requirements before submiting philatelic material to them. The listing of these groups here is not intended as an endorsement by Amos Media Co.

General Expertizing Services

American Philatelic Expertizing Service (a service of the American Philatelic Society)
100 Match Factory Place
Bellefonte PA 16823-1367
(814) 237-3803
www.stamps.org/stamp-authentication
apex@stamps.org
Areas of Expertise: Worldwide

BPA Expertising, Ltd.
P.O. Box 1141
Guildford, Surrey, GU5 0WR
UNITED KINGDOM
www.bpaexpertising.com
sec@bpaexpertising.org
Areas of Expertise: British Commonwealth, Great Britain, Classics of Europe, South America and the Far East

Philatelic Foundation
22 E. 35th St., 4th Floor
New York NY 10016
(212) 221-6555
www.philatelicfoundation.org
philatelicfoundation@verizon.net
Areas of Expertise: U.S. & Worldwide

Philatelic Stamp Authentication and Grading, Inc.
P.O. Box 41-0880
Melbourne FL 32941-0880
(305) 345-9864
www.psaginc.com
info@psaginc.com
Areas of Expertise: U.S., Canal Zone, Hawaii, Philippines, Canada & Provinces

Professional Stamp Experts
P.O. Box 539309
Henderson NV 89053-9309
(702) 776-6522
www.gradingmatters.com
www.psestamp.com
info@gradingmatters.com
Areas of Expertise: Stamps and covers of U.S., U.S. Possessions, British Commonwealth

Royal Philatelic Society London Expert Committee
15 Abchurch Lane
London, EX4N 7BW
UNITED KINGDOM
www.rpsl.limited/experts.aspx
experts@rpsl.limited
Areas of Expertise: Worldwide

Expertizing Services Covering Specific Fields or Countries

China Stamp Society Expertizing Service
1050 W. Blue Ridge Blvd.
Kansas City MO 64145
(816) 942-6300
hjmesq@aol.com
Areas of Expertise: China

Confederate Stamp Alliance Authentication Service
C/O Stefan T. Jaronski
P.O. Box 232
Sidney, MT 59270-0232
www.csalliance.org/CSAAS.shtml
authentication@csalliance.org
Areas of Expertise: Confederate stamps and postal history

Errors, Freaks and Oddities Collectors Club Expertizing Service
138 East Lakemont Drive
Kingsland GA 31548
(912) 729-1573
Areas of Expertise: U.S. errors, freaks and oddities

Hawaiian Philatelic Society Expertizing Service
P.O. Box 10115
Honolulu HI 96816-0115
www.stampshows.com/hps.html
hiphilsoc@gmail.com
Areas of Expertise: Hawaii

Hong Kong Stamp Society Expertizing Service
P.O. Box 206
Glenside PA 19038
Areas of Expertise: Hong Kong

International Association of Philatelic Experts United States Associate members:

Paul Buchsbayew
119 W. 57th St.
New York NY 10019
(212) 977-7734
Areas of Expertise: Russia, Soviet Union

William T. Crowe
P.O. Box 2090
Danbury CT 06813-2090
wtcrowe@aol.com
Areas of Expertise: United States

John Lievsay
(see American Philatelic Expertizing Service and Philatelic Foundation)
Areas of Expertise: France

Robert W. Lyman
P.O. Box 348
Irvington on Hudson NY 10533
(914) 591-6937
Areas of Expertise: British North America, New Zealand

Robert Odenweller
P.O. Box 401
Bernardsville NJ 07924-0401
(908) 766-5460
Areas of Expertise: New Zealand, Samoa to 1900

Sergio Sismondo
The Regency Tower, Suite 1109
770 James St.
Syracuse NY 13203
(315) 422-2331
Areas of Expertise: British East Africa, Camerouns, Cape of Good Hope, Canada, British North America

International Society for Japanese Philately Expertizing Committee
132 North Pine Terrace
Staten Island NY 10312-4052
(718) 227-5229
Areas of Expertise: Japan and related areas, except WWII Japanese Occupation issues

International Society for Portuguese Philately Expertizing Service
P.O. Box 43146
Philadelphia PA 19129-3146
(215) 843-2106
s.s.washburne@worldnet.att.net
Areas of Expertise: Portugal and Colonies

Mexico-Elmhurst Philatelic Society International Expert Committee
Expert Committee Administrator
Marc E. Gonzales
P.O. Box 29040
Denver CO 80229-0040
www.mepsi.org/expert_committeee.htm
expertizations@mepsi.org
Areas of Expertise: Mexico

Ukrainian Philatelic & Numismatic Society Expertizing Service
30552 Dell Lane
Warren MI 48092-1862
Areas of Expertise: Ukraine, Western Ukraine

V. G. Greene Philatelic Research Foundation
P.O. Box 69100
St. Clair Post Office
Toronto, ON M4T 3A1
CANADA
(416) 921-2073
www.greenefoundation.ca
info@greenefoundation.ca
Areas of Expertise: British North America

Information on Catalogue Values, Grade and Condition

Catalogue Value

The Scott Catalogue value is a retail value; that is, an amount you could expect to pay for a stamp in the grade of Very Fine with no faults. Any exceptions to the grade valued will be noted in the text. The general introduction on the following pages and the individual section introductions further explain the type of material that is valued. The value listed for any given stamp is a reference that reflects recent actual dealer selling prices for that item.

Dealer retail price lists, public auction results, published prices in advertising and individual solicitation of retail prices from dealers, collectors and specialty organizations have been used in establishing the values found in this catalogue. Amos Media Co. values stamps, but Amos Media is not a company engaged in the business of buying and selling stamps as a dealer.

Use this catalogue as a guide for buying and selling. The actual price you pay for a stamp may be higher or lower than the catalogue value because of many different factors, including the amount of personal service a dealer offers, or increased or decreased interest in the country or topic represented by a stamp or set. An item may occasionally be offered at a lower price as a "loss leader," or as part of a special sale. You also may obtain an item inexpensively at public auction because of little interest at that time or as part of a large lot.

Stamps that are of a lesser grade than Very Fine, or those with condition problems, generally trade at lower prices than those given in this catalogue. Stamps of exceptional quality in both grade and condition often command higher prices than those listed.

Values for pre-1900 unused issues are for stamps with approximately half or more of their original gum. Stamps with most or all of their original gum may be expected to sell for more, and stamps with less than half of their original gum may be expected to sell for somewhat less than the values listed. On rarer stamps, it may be expected that the original gum will be somewhat more disturbed than it will be on more common issues. Post-1900 unused issues are assumed to have full original gum. From breakpoints in most countries' listings, stamps are valued as never hinged, due to the wide availability of stamps in that condition. These notations are prominently placed in the listings and in the country information preceding the listings. Some countries also feature listings with dual values for hinged and never-hinged stamps.

Grade

A stamp's grade and condition are crucial to its value. The accompanying illustrations show examples of Very Fine stamps from different time periods, along with examples of stamps in Fine to Very Fine and Extremely Fine grades as points of reference. When a stamp seller offers a stamp in any grade from fine to superb without further qualifying statements, that stamp should not only have the centering grade as defined, but it also should be free of faults or other condition problems.

FINE stamps (illustrations not shown) have designs that are quite off center, with the perforations on one or two sides very close to the design but not quite touching it. There is white space between the perforations and the design that is minimal but evident to the unaided eye. Imperforate stamps may have small margins, and earlier issues may show the design just touching one edge of the stamp design. Very early perforated issues normally will have the perforations slightly cutting into the design. Used stamps may have heavier than usual cancellations.

FINE-VERY FINE stamps will be somewhat off center on one side, or slightly off center on two sides. Imperforate stamps will have two margins of at least normal size, and the design will not touch any edge. For perforated stamps, the perfs are well clear of the design, but are still noticeably off center. *However, early issues of a country may be printed in such a way that the design naturally is very close to the edges. In these cases, the perforations may cut into the design very slightly.* Used stamps will not have a cancellation that detracts from the design.

VERY FINE stamps will be just slightly off center on one or two sides, but the design will be well clear of the edge. The stamp will present a nice, balanced appearance. Imperforate stamps will be well centered within normal-sized margins. *However, early issues of many countries may be printed in such a way that the perforations may touch the design on one or more sides. Where this is the case, a boxed note will be found defining the centering and margins of the stamps being valued.* Used stamps will have light or otherwise neat cancellations. This is the grade used to establish Scott Catalogue values.

EXTREMELY FINE stamps are close to being perfectly centered. Imperforate stamps will have even margins that are slightly larger than normal. Even the earliest perforated issues will have perforations clear of the design on all sides.

Amos Media Co. recognizes that there is no formally enforced grading scheme for postage stamps, and that the final price you pay or obtain for a stamp will be determined by individual agreement at the time of transaction.

Condition

Grade addresses only centering and (for used stamps) cancellation. *Condition* refers to factors other than grade that affect a stamp's desirability.

Factors that can increase the value of a stamp include exceptionally wide margins, particularly fresh color, the presence of selvage, and plate or die varieties. Unusual cancels on used stamps (particularly those of the 19th century) can greatly enhance their value as well.

Factors other than faults that decrease the value of a stamp include loss of original gum, regumming, a hinge remnant or foreign object adhering to the gum, natural inclusions, straight edges, and markings or notations applied by collectors or dealers.

Faults include missing pieces, tears, pin or other holes, surface scuffs, thin spots, creases, toning, short or pulled perforations, clipped perforations, oxidation or other forms of color changelings, soiling, stains, and such man-made changes as reperforations or the chemical removal or lightening of a cancellation.

Grading Illustrations

On the following two pages are illustrations of various stamps from countries appearing in this volume. These stamps are arranged by country, and they represent early or important issues that are often found in widely different grades in the marketplace. The editors believe the illustrations will prove useful in showing the margin size and centering that will be seen on the various issues.

In addition to the matters of margin size and centering, collectors are reminded that the very fine stamps valued in the Scott catalogues also will possess fresh color and intact perforations, and they will be free from defects.

Examples shown are computer-manipulated images made from single digitized master illustrations.

Stamp Illustrations Used in the Catalogue

It is important to note that the stamp images used for identification purposes in this catlaogue may not be indicative of the grade of stamp being valued. Refer to the written discussion of grades on this page and to the grading illustrations on the following two pages for grading information.

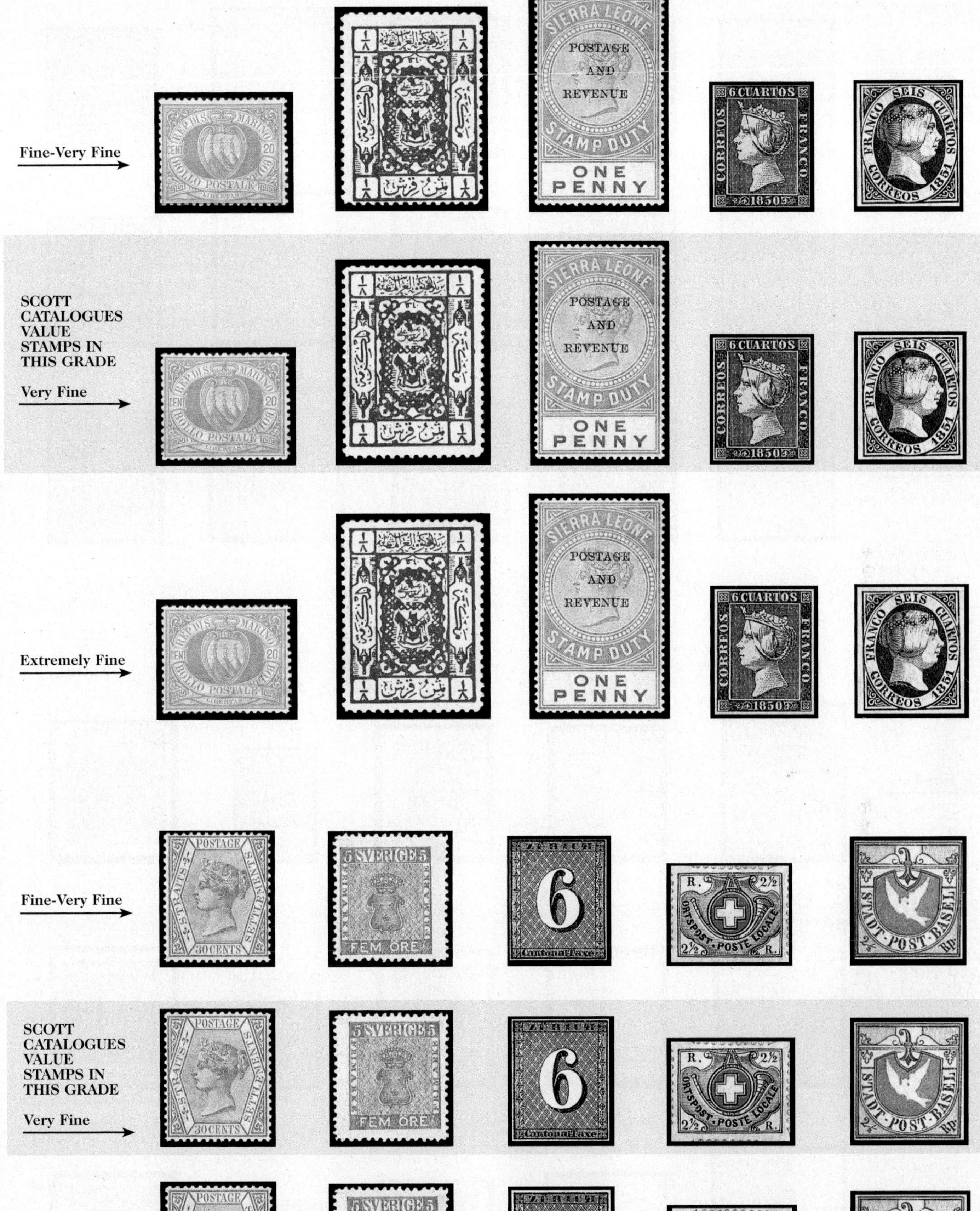

Fine-Very Fine
SCOTT CATALOGUES VALUE STAMPS IN THIS GRADE
Very Fine
Extremely Fine
Fine-Very Fine
SCOTT CATALOGUES VALUE STAMPS IN THIS GRADE
Very Fine
Extremely Fine

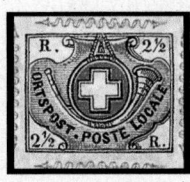

Fine-Very Fine →

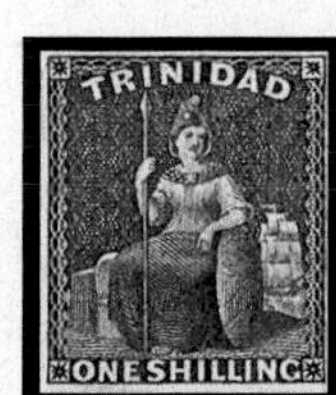

SCOTT CATALOGUES VALUE STAMPS IN THIS GRADE

Very Fine →

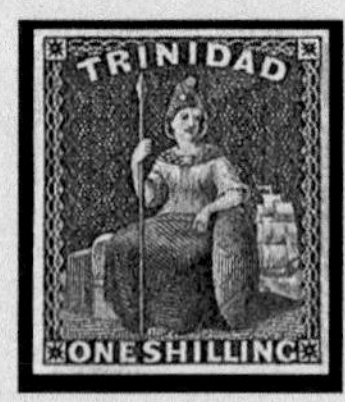

Extremely Fine →

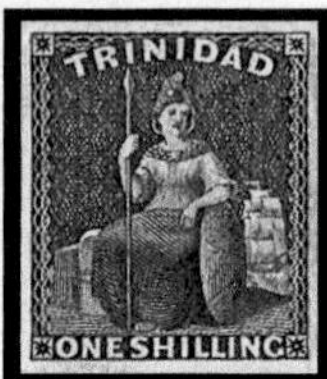

Fine-Very Fine →

SCOTT CATALOGUES VALUE STAMPS IN THIS GRADE

Very Fine →

Extremely Fine →

For purposes of helping to determine the gum condition and value of an unused stamp, Scott presents the following chart which details different gum conditions and indicates how the conditions correlate with the Scott values for unused stamps. Used together, the Illustrated Grading Chart on the previous pages and this Illustrated Gum Chart should allow catalogue users to better understand the grade and gum condition of stamps valued in the Scott catalogues.

Gum Categories:	MINT N.H.	ORIGINAL GUM (O.G.)				NO GUM
	 **Mint Never Hinged** *Free from any disturbance*	 **Lightly Hinged** *Faint impression of a removed hinge over a small area*	 **Hinge Mark or Remnant** *Prominent hinged spot with part or all of the hinge remaining*	 **Large part o.g.** *Approximately half or more of the gum intact*	**Small part o.g.** *Approximately less than half of the gum intact*	**No gum** *Only if issued with gum*
Commonly Used Symbol:	★★	★	★	★	★	(★)
Pre-1900 Issues (Pre-1881 for U.S.)	*Very fine pre-1900 stamps in these categories trade at a premium over Scott value*			Scott Value for "Unused"		Scott "No Gum" listings for selected unused classic stamps
From 1900 to breakpoints for listings of never-hinged stamps	Scott "Never Hinged" listings for selected unused stamps	Scott Value for "Unused" (Actual value will be affected by the degree of hinging of the full o.g.)				
From breakpoints noted for many countries	Scott Value for "Unused"					

Never Hinged (NH; ★★): A never-hinged stamp will have full original gum that will have no hinge mark or disturbance. The presence of an expertizer's mark does not disqualify a stamp from this designation.

Original Gum (OG; ★): Pre-1900 stamps should have approximately half or more of their original gum. On rarer stamps, it may be expected that the original gum will be somewhat more disturbed than it will be on more common issues. Post-1900 stamps should have full original gum. Original gum will show some disturbance caused by a previous hinge(s) which may be present or entirely removed. The actual value of a post-1900 stamp will be affected by the degree of hinging of the full original gum.

Disturbed Original Gum: Gum showing noticeable effects of humidity, climate or hinging over more than half of the gum. The significance of gum disturbance in valuing a stamp in any of the Original Gum categories depends on the degree of disturbance, the rarity and normal gum condition of the issue and other variables affecting quality.

Regummed (RG; (★)): A regummed stamp is a stamp without gum that has had some type of gum privately applied at a time after it was issued. This normally is done to deceive collectors and/or dealers into thinking that the stamp has original gum and therefore has a higher value. A regummed stamp is considered the same as a stamp with none of its original gum for purposes of grading.

Understanding the Listings

On the opposite page is an enlarged "typical" listing from this catalogue. Below are detailed explanations of each of the highlighted parts of the listing.

1 Scott number — Scott catalogue numbers are used to identify specific items when buying, selling or trading stamps. Each listed postage stamp from every country has a unique Scott catalogue number. Therefore, Germany Scott 99, for example, can only refer to a single stamp. Although the Scott catalogue usually lists stamps in chronological order by date of issue, there are exceptions. When a country has issued a set of stamps over a period of time, those stamps within the set are kept together without regard to date of issue. This follows the normal collecting approach of keeping stamps in their natural sets.

When a country issues a set of stamps over a period of time, a group of consecutive catalogue numbers is reserved for the stamps in that set, as issued. If that group of numbers proves to be too few, capital-letter suffixes, such as "A" or "B," may be added to existing numbers to create enough catalogue numbers to cover all items in the set. A capital-letter suffix indicates a major Scott catalogue number listing. Scott generally uses a suffix letter only once. Therefore, a catalogue number listing with a capital-letter suffix will seldom be found with the same letter (lower case) used as a minor-letter listing. If there is a Scott 16A in a set, for example, there will seldom be a Scott 16a. However, a minor-letter "a" listing may be added to a major number containing an "A" suffix (Scott 16Aa, for example).

Suffix letters are cumulative. A minor "b" variety of Scott 16A would be Scott 16Ab, not Scott 16b.

There are times when a reserved block of Scott catalogue numbers is too large for a set, leaving some numbers unused. Such gaps in the numbering sequence also occur when the catalogue editors move an item's listing elsewhere or have removed it entirely from the catalogue. Scott does not attempt to account for every possible number, but rather attempts to assure that each stamp is assigned its own number.

Scott numbers designating regular postage normally are only numerals. Scott numbers for other types of stamps, such as air post, semi-postal, postal tax, postage due, occupation and others have a prefix consisting of one or more capital letters or a combination of numerals and capital letters.

2 Illustration number — Illustration or design-type numbers are used to identify each catalogue illustration. For most sets, the lowest face-value stamp is shown. It then serves as an example of the basic design approach for other stamps not illustrated. Where more than one stamp use the same illustration number, but have differences in design, the design paragraph or the description line clearly indicates the design on each stamp not illustrated. Where there are both vertical and horizontal designs in a set, a single illustration may be used, with the exceptions noted in the design paragraph or description line.

When an illustration is followed by a lower-case letter in parentheses, such as "A2(b)," the trailing letter indicates which overprint or surcharge illustration applies.

Illustrations normally are 70 percent of the original size of the stamp. Oversized stamps, blocks and souvenir sheets are reduced even more. Overprints and surcharges are shown at 100 percent of their original size if shown alone, but are 70 percent of original size if shown on stamps. In some cases, the illustration will be placed above the set, between listings or omitted completely. Overprint and surcharge illustrations are not placed in this catalogue for purposes of expertizing stamps.

3 Paper color — The color of a stamp's paper is noted in italic type when the paper used is not white.

4 Listing styles — There are two principal types of catalogue listings: major and minor.

Major listings are in a larger type style than minor listings. The catalogue number is a numeral that can be found with or without a capital-letter suffix, and with or without a prefix.

Minor listings are in a smaller type style and have a small-letter suffix or (if the listing immediately follows that of the major number) may show only the letter. These listings identify a variety of the major item. Examples include perforation and shade differences, multiples (some souvenir sheets, booklet panes and se-tenant combinations), and singles of multiples.

Examples of major number listings include 16, 28A, B97, C13A, 10N5, and 10N6A. Examples of minor numbers are 16a and C13Ab.

5 Basic information about a stamp or set — Introducing each stamp issue is a small section (usually a line listing) of basic information about a stamp or set. This section normally includes the date of issue, method of printing, perforation, watermark and, sometimes, some additional information of note. *Printing method, perforation and watermark apply to the following sets until a change is noted.* Stamps created by overprinting or surcharging previous issues are assumed to have the same perforation, watermark, printing method and other production characteristics as the original. Dates of issue are as precise as Scott is able to confirm and often reflect the dates on first-day covers, rather than the actual date of release.

6 Denomination — This normally refers to the face value of the stamp; that is, the cost of the unused stamp at the post office at the time of issue. When a denomination is shown in parentheses, it does not appear on the stamp. This includes the non-denominated stamps of the United States, Brazil and Great Britain, for example.

7 Color or other description — This area provides information to solidify identification of a stamp. In many recent cases, a description of the stamp design appears in this space, rather than a listing of colors.

8 Year of issue — In stamp sets that have been released in a period that spans more than a year, the number shown in parentheses is the year that stamp first appeared. Stamps without a date appeared during the first year of the issue. Dates are not always given for minor varieties.

9 Value unused and Value used — The Scott catalogue values are based on stamps that are in a grade of Very Fine unless stated otherwise. Unused values refer to items that have not seen postal, revenue or any other duty for which they were intended. Pre-1900 unused stamps that were issued with gum must have at least most of their original gum. Later issues are assumed to have full original gum. From breakpoints specified in most countries' listings, stamps are valued as never hinged. Stamps issued without gum are noted. Modern issues with PVA or other synthetic adhesives may appear ungummed. Unused self-adhesive stamps are valued as appearing undisturbed on their original backing paper. Values for used self-adhesive stamps are for examples either on piece or off piece. For a more detailed explanation of these values, please see the "Catalogue Value," "Condition" and "Understanding Valuing Notations" sections elsewhere in this introduction.

In some cases, where used stamps are more valuable than unused stamps, the value is for an example with a contemporaneous cancel, rather than a modern cancel or a smudge or other unclear marking. For those stamps that were released for postal and fiscal purposes, the used value represents a postally used stamp. Stamps with revenue cancels generally sell for less.

Stamps separated from a complete se-tenant multiple usually will be worth less than a pro-rated portion of the se-tenant multiple, and stamps lacking the attached labels that are noted in the listings will be worth less than the values shown.

10 Changes in basic set information — Bold type is used to show any changes in the basic data given for a set of stamps. These basic data categories include perforation gauge measurement, paper type, printing method and watermark.

11 Total value of a set — The total value of sets of three or more stamps issued after 1900 are shown. The set line also notes the range of Scott numbers and total number of stamps included in the grouping. The actual value of a set consisting predominantly of stamps having the minimum value of 25 cents may be less than the total value shown. Similarly, the actual value or catalogue value of se-tenant pairs or of blocks consisting of stamps having the minimum value of 25 cents may be less than the catalogue values of the component parts.

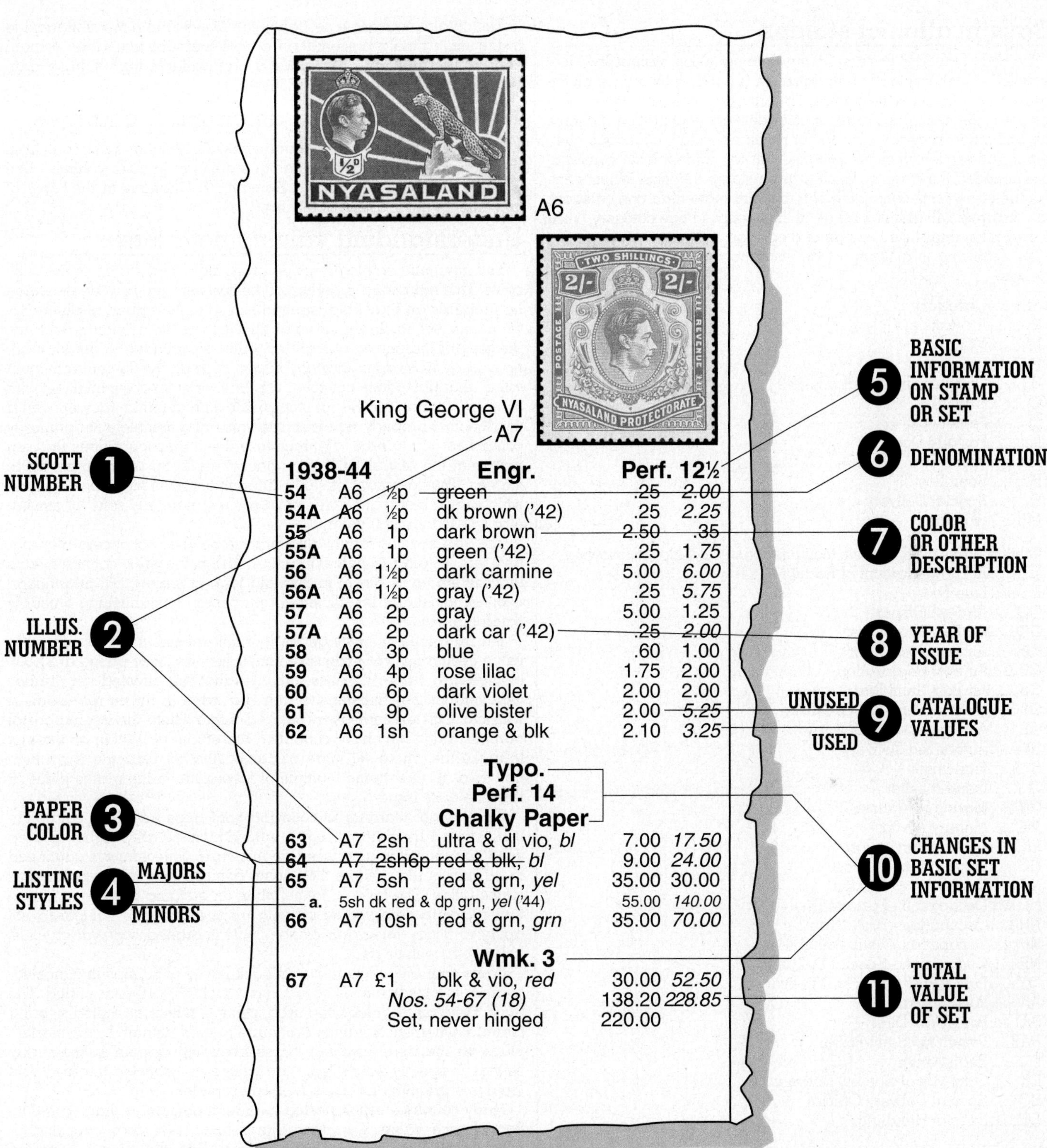

1938-44 Engr. Perf. 12½

54	A6	½p	green	.25	*2.00*
54A	A6	½p	dk brown ('42)	.25	*2.25*
55	A6	1p	dark brown	2.50	.35
55A	A6	1p	green ('42)	.25	1.*75*
56	A6	1½p	dark carmine	5.00	*6.00*
56A	A6	1½p	gray ('42)	.25	*5.75*
57	A6	2p	gray	5.00	1.25
57A	A6	2p	dark car ('42)	.25	*2.00*
58	A6	3p	blue	.60	1.00
59	A6	4p	rose lilac	1.75	2.00
60	A6	6p	dark violet	2.00	2.00
61	A6	9p	olive bister	2.00	*5.25*
62	A6	1sh	orange & blk	2.10	*3.25*

Typo.
Perf. 14
Chalky Paper

63	A7	2sh	ultra & dl vio, *bl*	7.00	*17.50*
64	A7	2sh6p	red & blk, *bl*	9.00	*24.00*
65	A7	5sh	red & grn, *yel*	35.00	30.00
a.			5sh dk red & dp grn, *yel* ('44)	55.00	*140.00*
66	A7	10sh	red & grn, *grn*	35.00	*70.00*

Wmk. 3

67	A7	£1	blk & vio, *red*	30.00	*52.50*
			Nos. 54-67 (18)	138.20	*228.85*
			Set, never hinged	220.00	

Special Notices

Classification of stamps

The *Scott Standard Postage Stamp Catalogue* lists stamps by country of issue. The next level of organization is a listing by section on the basis of the function of the stamps. The principal sections cover regular postage, semi-postal, air post, special delivery, registration, postage due and other categories. Except for regular postage, catalogue numbers for all sections include a prefix letter (or number-letter combination) denoting the class to which a given stamp belongs. When some countries issue sets containing stamps from more than one category, the catalogue will at times list all of the stamps in one category (such as air post stamps listed as part of a postage set).

The following is a listing of the most commonly used catalogue prefixes.

Prefix .... Category
C......... Air Post
M........ Military
P......... Newspaper
N......... Occupation - Regular Issues
O........ Official
Q........ Parcel Post
J.......... Postage Due
RA...... Postal Tax
B......... Semi-Postal
E......... Special Delivery
MR...... War Tax

Other prefixes used by more than one country include the following:
H......... Acknowledgment of Receipt
I.......... Late Fee
CO...... Air Post Official
CQ...... Air Post Parcel Post
RAC.... Air Post Postal Tax
CF...... Air Post Registration
CB...... Air Post Semi-Postal
CBO... Air Post Semi-Postal Official
CE...... Air Post Special Delivery
EY....... Authorized Delivery
S......... Franchise
G........ Insured Letter
GY...... Marine Insurance
MC..... Military Air Post
MQ..... Military Parcel Post
NC...... Occupation - Air Post
NO...... Occupation - Official
NJ........ Occupation - Postage Due
NRA.... Occupation - Postal Tax
NB...... Occupation - Semi-Postal
NE...... Occupation - Special Delivery
QY...... Parcel Post Authorized Delivery
AR...... Postal-fiscal
RAJ..... Postal Tax Due
RAB.... Postal Tax Semi-Postal
F......... Registration
EB....... Semi-Postal Special Delivery
EO...... Special Delivery Official
QE...... Special Handling

New issue listings

Updates to this catalogue appear each month in the *Linn's Stamp News* monthly magazine. Included in this update are additions to the listings of countries found in the *Scott Standard Postage Stamp Catalogue* and the *Specialized Catalogue of United States Stamps and Covers*, as well as corrections and updates to current editions of this catalogue.

From time to time there will be changes in the final listings of stamps from the *Linn's Stamp News* magazine to the next edition of the catalogue. This occurs as more information about certain stamps or sets becomes available.

The catalogue update section of the *Linn's Stamp News* magazine is the most timely presentation of this material available. Annual subscriptions to *Linn's Stamp News* are available from Linn's Stamp News, Box 4129, Sidney, OH 45365-4129.

Number additions, deletions & changes

A listing of catalogue number additions, deletions and changes from the previous edition of the catalogue appears in each volume. See Catalogue Number Additions, Deletions & Changes in the table of contents for the location of this list.

Understanding valuing notations

The *minimum catalogue value* of an individual stamp or set is 25 cents. This represents a portion of the cost incurred by a dealer when he prepares an individual stamp for resale. As a point of philatelic-economic fact, the lower the value shown for an item in this catalogue, the greater the percentage of that value is attributed to dealer mark up and profit margin. In many cases, such as the 25-cent minimum value, that price does not cover the labor or other costs involved with stocking it as an individual stamp. The sum of minimum values in a set does not properly represent the value of a complete set primarily composed of a number of minimum-value stamps, nor does the sum represent the actual value of a packet made up of minimum-value stamps. Thus a packet of 1,000 different common stamps — each of which has a catalogue value of 25 cents — normally sells for considerably less than 250 dollars!

The *absence of a retail value* for a stamp does not necessarily suggest that a stamp is scarce or rare. A dash in the value column means that the stamp is known in a stated form or variety, but information is either lacking or insufficient for purposes of establishing a usable catalogue value.

Stamp values in *italics* generally refer to items that are difficult to value accurately. For expensive items, such as those priced at $1,000 or higher, a value in italics indicates that the affected item trades very seldom. For inexpensive items, a value in italics represents a warning. One example is a "blocked" issue where the issuing postal administration may have controlled one stamp in a set in an attempt to make the whole set more valuable. Another example is an item that sold at an extreme multiple of face value in the marketplace at the time of its issue.

One type of warning to collectors that appears in the catalogue is illustrated by a stamp that is valued considerably higher in used condition than it is as unused. In this case, collectors are cautioned to be certain the used version has a genuine and contemporaneous cancellation. The type of cancellation on a stamp can be an important factor in determining its sale price. Catalogue values do not apply to fiscal, telegraph or non-contemporaneous postal cancels, unless otherwise noted.

Some countries have released back issues of stamps in canceled-to-order form, sometimes covering as much as a 10-year period. The Scott Catalogue values for used stamps reflect canceled-to-order material when such stamps are found to predominate in the marketplace for the issue involved. Notes frequently appear in the stamp listings to specify which items are valued as canceled-to-order, or if there is a premium for postally used examples.

Many countries sell canceled-to-order stamps at a marked reduction of face value. Countries that sell or have sold canceled-to-order stamps at *full* face value include United Nations, Australia, Netherlands, France and Switzerland. It may be almost impossible to identify such stamps if the gum has been removed, because official government canceling devices are used. Postally used examples of these items on cover, however, are usually worth more than the canceled-to-order stamps with original gum.

Abbreviations

Scott uses a consistent set of abbreviations throughout this catalogue to conserve space, while still providing necessary information.

COLOR ABBREVIATIONS

amb. amber	crim. crimson	ol ..... olive
anil.. aniline	cr ..... cream	olvn . olivine
ap.... apple	dk .... dark	org... orange
aqua aquamarine	dl ..... dull	pck .. peacock
az .... azure	dp.... deep	pnksh pinkish
bis ... bister	db.... drab	Prus. Prussian
bl ..... blue	emer emerald	pur... purple
bld... blood	gldn. golden	redsh reddish
blk... black	gryshgrayish	res ... reseda
bril... brilliant	grn... green	ros ... rosine
brn... brown	grnsh greenish	ryl .... royal
brnsh brownish	hel ... heliotrope	sal ... salmon
brnz. bronze	hn .... henna	saph sapphire
brt.... bright	ind... indigo	scar. scarlet
brnt . burnt	int .... intense	sep .. sepia
car... carmine	lav ... lavender	sien . sienna
cer ... cerise	lem .. lemon	sil..... silver
chlky chalky	lil ..... lilac	sl...... slate
chamchamois	lt ...... light	stl .... steel
chnt . chestnut	mag. magenta	turq.. turquoise
choc chocolate	man. manila	ultra ultramarine
chr... chrome	mar.. maroon	Ven.. Venetian
cit .... citron	mv ... mauve	ver ... vermilion
cl...... claret	multi multicolored	vio ... violet
cob .. cobalt	mlky milky	yel ... yellow
cop .. copper	myr .. myrtle	yelsh yellowish

When no color is given for an overprint or surcharge, black is the color used. Abbreviations for colors used for overprints and surcharges include: "(B)" or "(Blk)," black; "(Bl)," blue; "(R)," red; and "(G)," green.

Additional abbreviations in this catalogue are shown below:

Adm. ....Administration
AFL...............American Federation of Labor
Anniv. ....Anniversary
APS ....American Philatelic Society
Assoc. ....Association
ASSR. ....Autonomous Soviet Socialist Republic
b. ....Born
BEP...............Bureau of Engraving and Printing
Bicent. ....Bicentennial
Bklt. ....Booklet
Brit................British
btwn. ....Between
Bur.................Bureau
c. or ca..........Circa
Cat. ....Catalogue
Cent. ....Centennial, century, centenary
CIO ....Congress of Industrial Organizations
Conf. ....Conference
Cong. ....Congress
Cpl. ....Corporal
CTO ....Canceled to order
d. ....Died
Dbl. ....Double
EDU..............Earliest documented use
Engr. ....Engraved
Exhib. ....Exhibition
Expo. ....Exposition
Fed. ....Federation
GB ....Great Britain
Gen. ....General
GPO ....General post office
Horiz. ....Horizontal
Imperf. ....Imperforate
Impt...............Imprint
Intl.................International
Invtd.............Inverted
L ....Left
Lieut., lt.........Lieutenant
Litho.............Lithographed
LL ....Lower left
LR..................Lower right
mm................Millimeter
Ms. ....Manuscript
Natl. ....National
No..................Number
NY ....New York
NYC ....New York City
Ovpt. ....Overprint
Ovptd. ....Overprinted
P ....Plate number
Perf...............Perforated, perforation
Phil. ....Philatelic
Photo.............Photogravure
PO ....Post office
Pr. ....Pair
P.R.................Puerto Rico
Prec. ....Precancel, precanceled
Pres. ....President
PTT ....Post, Telephone and Telegraph
R....................Right
Rio.................Rio de Janeiro
Sgt.................Sergeant
Soc. ....Society
Souv. ....Souvenir
SSR...............Soviet Socialist Republic, see ASSR
St...................Saint, street
Surch. ....Surcharge
Typo. ....Typographed
UL..................Upper left
Unwmkd. ......Unwatermarked
UPU..............Universal Postal Union
UR ....Upper Right
US ....United States
USPOD ....United States Post Office Department
USSR ....Union of Soviet Socialist Republics
Vert...............Vertical
VP..................Vice president
Wmk..............Watermark
Wmkd. ....Watermarked
WWI ....World War I
WWII............World War II

Examination

Amos Media Co. will not comment upon the genuineness, grade or condition of stamps, because of the time and responsibility involved. Rather, there are several expertizing groups that undertake this work for both collectors and dealers. Neither will Amos Media Co. appraise or identify philatelic material. The company cannot take responsibility for unsolicited stamps or covers sent by individuals.

All letters, E-mails, etc. are read attentively, but they are not always answered due to time considerations.

How to order from your dealer

When ordering stamps from a dealer, it is not necessary to write the full description of a stamp as listed in this catalogue. All you need is the name of the country, the Scott catalogue number and whether the desired item is unused or used. For example, "Japan Scott 422 unused" is sufficient to identify the unused stamp of Japan listed as "422 A206 5y brown."

Catalogue Listing Policy

It is the intent of Amos Media Co. to list all postage stamps of the world in the *Scott Standard Postage Stamp Catalogue*. The only strict criteria for listing is that stamps be decreed legal for postage by the issuing country and that the issuing country actually have an operating postal system. Whether the primary intent of issuing a given stamp or set was for sale to postal patrons or to stamp collectors is not part of our listing criteria. Scott's role is to provide basic comprehensive postage stamp information. It is up to each stamp collector to choose which items to include in a collection.

It is Scott's objective to seek reasons why a stamp should be listed, rather than why it should not. Nevertheless, there are certain types of items that will not be listed. These include the following:

1. Unissued items that are not officially distributed or released by the issuing postal authority. If such items are officially issued at a later date by the country, they will be listed. Unissued items consist of those that have been printed and then held from sale for reasons such as change in government, errors found on stamps or something deemed objectionable about a stamp subject or design.

2. Stamps "issued" by non-existent postal entities or fantasy countries, such as Nagaland, Occusi-Ambeno, Staffa, Sedang, Torres Straits and others. Also, stamps "issued" in the names of legitimate, stamp-issuing countries that are not authorized by those countries.

3. Semi-official or unofficial items not required for postage. Examples include items issued by private agencies for their own express services. When such items are required for delivery, or are valid as prepayment of postage, they are listed.

4. Local stamps issued for local use only. Postage stamps issued by governments specifically for "domestic" use, such as Haiti Scott 219-228, or the United States non-denominated stamps, are not considered to be locals, since they are valid for postage throughout the country of origin.

5. Items not valid for postal use. For example, a few countries have issued souvenir sheets that are not valid for postage. This area also includes a number of worldwide charity labels (some denominated) that do not pay postage.

6. Egregiously exploitative issues such as stamps sold for far more than face value, stamps purposefully issued in artificially small quantities or only against advance orders, stamps awarded only to a selected audience such as a philatelic bureau's standing order customers, or stamps sold only in conjunction with other products. All of these kinds of items are usually controlled issues and/or are intended for speculation. These items normally will be included in a footnote.

7. Items distributed by the issuing government only to a limited group, club, philatelic exhibition or a single stamp dealer or other private company. These items normally will be included in a footnote.

8. Stamps not available to collectors. These generally are rare items, all of which are held by public institutions such as museums. The existence of such items often will be cited in footnotes.

The fact that a stamp has been used successfully as postage, even on international mail, is not in itself sufficient proof that it was legitimately issued. Numerous examples of so-called stamps from non-existent countries are known to have been used to post letters that have successfully passed through the international mail system.

There are certain items that are subject to interpretation. When a stamp falls outside our specifications, it may be listed along with a cautionary footnote.

A number of factors are considered in our approach to analyzing how a stamp is listed. The following list of factors is presented to share with you, the catalogue user, the complexity of the listing process.

Additional printings — "Additional printings" of a previously issued stamp may range from an item that is totally different to cases where it is impossible to differentiate from the original. At least a minor number (a small-letter suffix) is assigned if there is a distinct change in stamp shade, noticeably redrawn design, or a significantly different perforation measurement. A major number (numeral or numeral and capital-letter combination) is assigned if the editors feel the "additional printing" is sufficiently different from the original that it constitutes a different issue.

Commemoratives — Where practical, commemoratives with the same theme are placed in a set. For example, the U.S. Civil War Centennial set of 1961-65 and the Constitution Bicentennial series of 1989-90 appear as sets. Countries such as Japan and Korea issue such material on a regular basis, with an announced, or at least predictable, number of stamps known in advance. Occasionally, however, stamp sets that were released over a period of years have been separated. Appropriately placed footnotes will guide you to each set's continuation.

Definitive sets — Blocks of numbers generally have been reserved for definitive sets, based on previous experience with any given country. If a few more stamps were issued in a set than originally expected, they often have been inserted into the original set with a capital-letter suffix, such as U.S. Scott 1059A. If it appears that many more stamps than the originally allotted block will be released before the set is completed, a new block of numbers will be reserved, with the original one being closed off. In some cases, such as the U.S. Transportation and Great Americans series, several blocks of numbers exist. Appropriately placed footnotes will guide you to each set's continuation.

New country — Membership in the Universal Postal Union is not a consideration for listing status or order of placement within the catalogue. The index will tell you in what volume or page number the listings begin.

"No release date" items — The amount of information available for any given stamp issue varies greatly from country to country and even from time to time. Extremely comprehensive information about new stamps is available from some countries well before the stamps are released. By contrast some countries do not provide information about stamps or release dates. Most countries, however, fall between these extremes. A country may provide denominations or subjects of stamps from upcoming issues that are not issued as planned. Sometimes, philatelic agencies, those private firms hired to represent countries, add these later-issued items to sets well after the formal release date. This time period can range from weeks to years. If these items were officially released by the country, they will be added to the appropriate spot in the set. In many cases, the specific release date of a stamp or set of stamps may never be known.

Overprints — The color of an overprint is always noted if it is other than black. Where more than one color of ink has been used on overprints of a single set, the color used is noted. Early overprint and surcharge illustrations were altered to prevent their use by forgers.

Personalized Stamps — Since 1999, the special service of personalizing stamp vignettes, or labels attached to stamps, has been offered to customers by postal administrations of many countries. Sheets of these stamps are sold, singly or in quantity, only through special orders made by mail, in person, or through a sale on a computer website with the postal administrations or their agents for which an extra fee is charged, though some countries offer to collectors at face value personalized stamps having generic images in the vignettes or on the attached labels. It is impossible for any catalogue to know what images have been chosen by customers. Images can be 1) owned or created by the customer, 2) a generic image, or 3) an image pulled from a library of stock images on the stamp creation website. It is also impossible to know the quantity printed for any stamp having a particular image. So from a valuing standpoint, any image is equivalent to any other image for any personalized stamp having the same catalogue number. Illustrations of personalized stamps in the catalogue are not always those of stamps having generic images.

Personalized items are listed with some exceptions. These include:

1. Stamps or sheets that have attached labels that the customer cannot personalize, but which are nonetheless marketed as "personalized," and are sold for far more than the franking value.
2. Stamps or sheets that can be personalized by the customer, but where a portion of the print run must be ceded to the issuing country for sale to other customers.
3. Stamps or sheets that are created exclusively for a particular commercial client, or clients, including stamps that differ from any similar stamp that has been made available to the public.
4. Stamps or sheets that are deliberately conceived by the issuing authority that have been, or are likely to be, created with an excessive number of different face values, sizes, or other features that are changeable.
5. Stamps or sheets that are created by postal administrations using the same system of stamp personalization that has been put in place for use by the public that are printed in limited quantities and sold above face value.
6. Stamps or sheets that are created by licensees not directly affiliated or controlled by a postal administration.

Excluded items may or may not be footnoted.

Se-tenants — Connected stamps of differing features (se-tenants) will be listed in the format most commonly collected. This includes pairs, blocks or larger multiples. Se-tenant units are not always symmetrical. An example is Australia Scott 508, which is a block of seven stamps. If the stamps are primarily collected as a unit, the major number may be assigned to the multiple, with minors going to each component stamp. In cases where continuous-design or other unit se-tenants will receive significant postal use, each stamp is given a major Scott number listing. This includes issues from the United States, Canada, Germany and Great Britain, for example.

Basic Stamp Information

A stamp collector's knowledge of the combined elements that make a given stamp issue unique determines his or her ability to identify stamps. These elements include paper, watermark, method of separation, printing, design and gum. On the following pages each of these important areas is briefly described.

Paper

Paper is an organic material composed of a compacted weave of cellulose fibers and generally formed into sheets. Paper used to print stamps may be manufactured in sheets, or it may have been part of a large roll (called a web) before being cut to size. The fibers most often used to create paper on which stamps are printed include bark, wood, straw and certain grasses. In many cases, linen or cotton rags have been added for greater strength and durability. Grinding, bleaching, cooking and rinsing these raw fibers reduces them to a slushy pulp, referred to by paper makers as "stuff." Sizing and, sometimes, coloring matter is added to the pulp to make different types of finished paper.

After the stuff is prepared, it is poured onto sieve-like frames that allow the water to run off, while retaining the matted pulp. As fibers fall onto the screen and are held by gravity, they form a natural weave that will later hold the paper together. If the screen has metal bits that are formed into letters or images attached, it leaves slightly thinned areas on the paper. These are called watermarks.

When the stuff is almost dry, it is passed under pressure through smooth or engraved rollers - dandy rolls - or placed between cloth in a press to be flattened and dried.

Wove | Laid | Granite

Quadrille | Oblong Quadrille | Laid Batonne

Stamp paper falls broadly into two types: wove and laid. The nature of the surface of the frame onto which the pulp is first deposited causes the differences in appearance between the two. If the surface is smooth and even, the paper will be of fairly uniform texture throughout. This is known as *wove paper*. Early papermaking machines poured the pulp onto a continuously circulating web of felt, but modern machines feed the pulp onto a cloth-like screen made of closely interwoven fine wires. This paper, when held to a light, will show little dots or points very close together. The proper name for this is "wire wove," but the type is still considered wove. Any U.S. or British stamp printed after 1880 will serve as an example of wire wove paper.

Closely spaced parallel wires, with cross wires at wider intervals, make up the frames used for what is known as *laid paper*. A greater thickness of the pulp will settle between the wires. The paper, when held to a light, will show alternate light and dark lines. The spacing and the thickness of the lines may vary, but on any one sheet of paper they are all alike. See Russia Scott 31-38 for examples of laid paper.

Batonne, from the French word meaning "a staff," is a term used if the lines in the paper are spaced quite far apart, like the printed ruling on a writing tablet. Batonne paper may be either wove or laid. If laid, fine laid lines can be seen between the batons.

Quadrille is the term used when the lines in the paper form little squares. *Oblong quadrille* is the term used when rectangles, rather than squares, are formed. Grid patterns vary from distinct to extremely faint. See Mexico-Guadalajara Scott 35-37 for examples of oblong quadrille paper.

Paper also is classified as thick or thin, hard or soft, and by color. Such colors may include yellowish, greenish, bluish and reddish.

Brief explanations of other types of paper used for printing stamps, as well as examples, follow.

Colored — Colored paper is created by the addition of dye in the paper-making process. Such colors may include shades of yellow, green, blue and red. *Surface-colored papers*, most commonly used for British colonial issues in 1913-14, are created when coloring is added only to the surface during the finishing process. Stamps printed on surface-colored paper have white or uncolored backs, while true colored papers are colored through. See Jamaica Scott 71-73.

Pelure — Pelure paper is a very thin, hard and often brittle paper that is sometimes bluish or grayish in appearance. See Serbia Scott 169-170.

Native — This is a term applied to handmade papers used to produce some of the early stamps of the Indian states. Stamps printed on native paper may be expected to display various natural inclusions that are normal and do not negatively affect value. Japanese paper, originally made of mulberry fibers and rice flour, is part of this group. See Japan Scott 1-18.

Manila — This type of paper is often used to make stamped envelopes and wrappers. It is a coarse-textured stock, usually smooth on one side and rough on the other. A variety of colors of manila paper exist, but the most common range is yellowish-brown.

Silk — Introduced by the British in 1847 as a safeguard against counterfeiting, silk paper contains bits of colored silk thread scattered throughout. The density of these fibers varies greatly and can include as few as one fiber per stamp or hundreds. U.S. revenue Scott R152 is a good example of an easy-to-identify silk paper stamp.

Silk-thread paper has uninterrupted threads of colored silk arranged so that one or more threads run through the stamp or postal stationery. See Great Britain Scott 5-6 and Switzerland Scott 14-19.

Granite — Filled with minute cloth or colored paper fibers of various colors and lengths, granite paper should not be confused with either type of silk paper. Austria Scott 172-175 and a number of Swiss stamps are examples of granite paper.

Chalky — A chalk-like substance coats the surface of chalky paper to discourage the cleaning and reuse of canceled stamps, as well as to provide a smoother, more acceptable printing surface. Because the designs of stamps printed on chalky paper are imprinted on what is often a water-soluble coating, any attempt to remove a cancellation will destroy the stamp. *Do not soak these stamps in any fluid.* To remove a stamp printed on chalky paper from an envelope, wet the paper from underneath the stamp until the gum dissolves enough to release the stamp from the paper. See St. Kitts-Nevis Scott 89-90 for examples of stamps printed on this type of chalky paper.

India — Another name for this paper, originally introduced from China about 1750, is "China Paper." It is a thin, opaque paper often used for plate and die proofs by many countries.

Double — In philately, the term double paper has two distinct meanings. The first is a two-ply paper, usually a combination of a thick and a thin sheet, joined during manufacture. This type was used experimentally as a means to discourage the reuse of stamps.

The design is printed on the thin paper. Any attempt to remove a cancellation would destroy the design. U.S. Scott 158 and other Banknote-era stamps exist on this form of double paper.

The second type of double paper occurs on a rotary press, when the end of one paper roll, or web, is affixed to the next roll to save time feeding the paper through the press. Stamp designs are printed over the joined paper and, if overlooked by inspectors, may get into post office stocks.

Goldbeater's Skin — This type of paper was used for the 1866 issue of Prussia, and was a tough, translucent paper. The design was printed in reverse on the back of the stamp, and the gum applied over the printing. It is impossible to remove stamps printed on this type of paper from the paper to which they are affixed without destroying the design.

Ribbed — Ribbed paper has an uneven, corrugated surface made by passing the paper through ridged rollers. This type exists on some copies of U.S. Scott 156-165.

Various other substances, or substrates, have been used for stamp manufacture, including wood, aluminum, copper, silver and gold foil, plastic, and silk and cotton fabrics.

Watermarks

Watermarks are an integral part of some papers. They are formed in the process of paper manufacture. Watermarks consist of small designs, formed of wire or cut from metal and soldered to the surface of the mold or, sometimes, on the dandy roll. The designs may be in the form of crowns, stars, anchors, letters or other characters or symbols. These pieces of metal - known in the paper-making industry as "bits" - impress a design into the paper. The design sometimes may be seen by holding the stamp to the light. Some are more easily seen with a watermark detector. This important tool is a small black tray into which a stamp is placed face down and dampened with a fast-evaporating watermark detection fluid that brings up the watermark image in the form of dark lines against a lighter background. These dark lines are the thinner areas of the paper known as the watermark. Some watermarks are extremely difficult to locate, due to either a faint impression, watermark location or the color of the stamp. There also are electric watermark detectors that come with plastic filter disks of various colors. The disks neutralize the color of the stamp, permitting the watermark to be seen more easily.

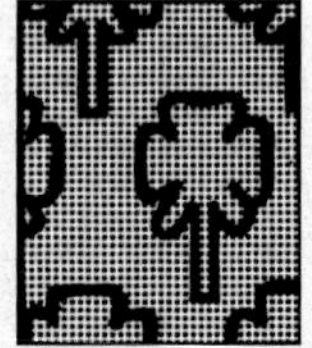

Multiple watermarks of Crown Agents and Burma

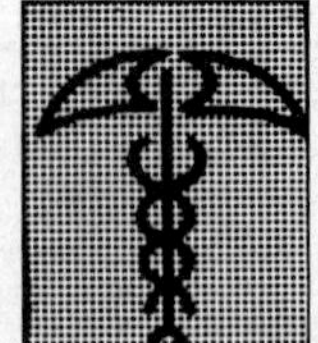

Watermarks of Uruguay, Vatican City and Jamaica

WARNING: Some inks used in the photogravure process dissolve in watermark fluids (Please see the section on Soluble Printing Inks). Also, see "chalky paper."

Watermarks may be found normal, reversed, inverted, reversed and inverted, sideways or diagonal, as seen from the back of the stamp. The relationship of watermark to stamp design depends on the position of the printing plates or how paper is fed through the press. On machine-made paper, watermarks normally are read from right to left. The design is repeated closely throughout the sheet in a "multiple-watermark design." In a "sheet watermark," the design appears only once on the sheet, but extends over many stamps. Individual stamps may carry only a small fraction or none of the watermark.

"Marginal watermarks" occur in the margins of sheets or panes of stamps. They occur on the outside border of paper (ostensibly outside the area where stamps are to be printed). A large row of letters may spell the name of the country or the manufacturer of the paper, or a border of lines may appear. Careless press feeding may cause parts of these letters and/or lines to show on stamps of the outer row of a pane.

Soluble Printing Inks

WARNING: Most stamp colors are permanent; that is, they are not seriously affected by short-term exposure to light or water. Many colors, especially of modern inks, fade from excessive exposure to light. There are stamps printed with inks that dissolve easily in water or in fluids used to detect watermarks. Use of these inks was intentional to prevent the removal of cancellations. Water affects all aniline inks, those on so-called safety paper and some photogravure printings - all such inks are known as fugitive colors. *Removal from paper of such stamps requires care and alternatives to traditional soaking.*

Separation

"Separation" is the general term used to describe methods used to separate stamps. The three standard forms currently in use are perforating, rouletting and die-cutting. These methods are done during the stamp production process, after printing. Sometimes these methods are done on-press or sometimes as a separate step. The earliest issues, such as the 1840 Penny Black of Great Britain (Scott 1), did not have any means provided for separation. It was expected the stamps would be cut apart with scissors or folded and torn. These are examples of imperforate stamps. Many stamps were first issued in imperforate formats and were later issued with perforations. Therefore, care must be observed in buying single imperforate stamps to be certain they were issued imperforate and are not perforated copies that have been altered by having the perforations trimmed away. Stamps issued imperforate usually are valued as singles. However, imperforate varieties of normally perforated stamps should be collected in pairs or larger pieces as indisputable evidence of their imperforate character.

PERFORATION

The chief style of separation of stamps, and the one that is in almost universal use today, is perforating. By this process, paper between the stamps is cut away in a line of holes, usually round, leaving little bridges of paper between the stamps to hold them together. Some types of perforation, such as hyphen-hole perfs, can be confused with roulettes, but a close visual inspection reveals that paper has been removed. The little perforation bridges, which project from the stamp when it is torn from the pane, are called the teeth of the perforation.

As the size of the perforation is sometimes the only way to differentiate between two otherwise identical stamps, it is necessary to be able to accurately measure and describe them. This is done with a perforation gauge, usually a ruler-like device that has dots or graduated lines to show how many perforations may be counted in the space of two centimeters. Two centimeters is the space universally adopted in which to measure perforations.

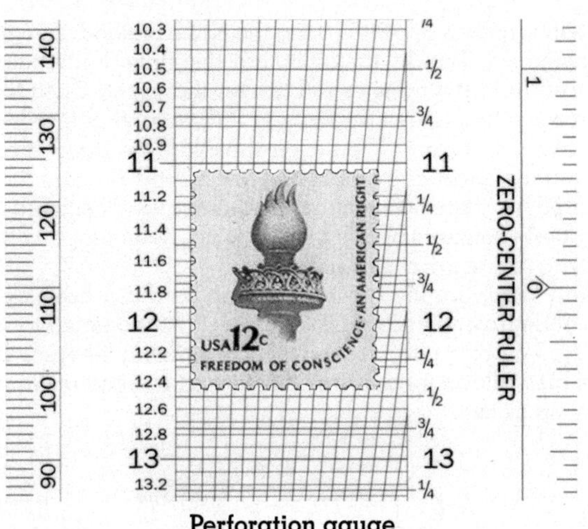

Perforation gauge

To measure a stamp, run it along the gauge until the dots on it fit exactly into the perforations of the stamp. If you are using a graduated-line perforation gauge, simply slide the stamp along the surface until the lines on the gauge perfectly project from the center of the bridges or holes. The number to the side of the line of dots or lines that fit the stamp's perforation is the measurement. For example, an "11" means that 11 perforations fit between two centimeters. The description of the stamp therefore is "perf. 11." If the gauge of the perforations on the top and bottom of a stamp differs from that on the sides, the result is what is known as *compound perforations*. In measuring compound perforations, the gauge at top and bottom is always given first, then the sides. Thus, a stamp that measures 11 at top and bottom and 10½ at the sides is "perf. 11 x 10½." See U.S. Scott 632-642 for examples of compound perforations.

Stamps also are known with perforations different on three or all four sides. Descriptions of such items are clockwise, beginning with the top of the stamp.

A perforation with small holes and teeth close together is a "fine perforation." One with large holes and teeth far apart is a "coarse perforation." Holes that are jagged, rather than clean-cut, are "rough perforations." *Blind perforations* are the slight impressions left by the perforating pins if they fail to puncture the paper. Multiples of stamps showing blind perforations may command a slight premium over normally perforated stamps.

The term *syncopated perfs* describes intentional irregularities in the perforations. The earliest form was used by the Netherlands from 1925-33, where holes were omitted to create distinctive patterns. Beginning in 1992, Great Britain has used an oval perforation to help prevent counterfeiting. Several other countries have started using the oval perfs or other syncopated perf patterns.

A new type of perforation, still primarily used for postal stationery, is known as microperfs. Microperfs are tiny perforations (in some cases hundreds of holes per two centimeters) that allows items to be intentionally separated very easily, while not accidentally breaking apart as easily as standard perforations. These are not currently measured or differentiated by size, as are standard perforations.

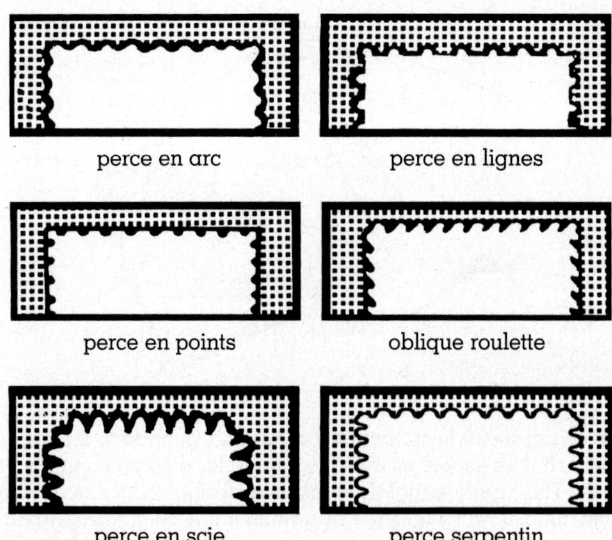

ROULETTING

In rouletting, the stamp paper is cut partly or wholly through, with no paper removed. In perforating, some paper is removed. Rouletting derives its name from the French roulette, a spur-like wheel. As the wheel is rolled over the paper, each point makes a small cut. The number of cuts made in a two-centimeter space determines the gauge of the roulette, just as the number of perforations in two centimeters determines the gauge of the perforation.

The shape and arrangement of the teeth on the wheels varies. Various roulette types generally carry French names:

Perce en lignes - rouletted in lines. The paper receives short, straight cuts in lines. This is the most common type of rouletting. See Mexico Scott 500.

Perce en points - pin-rouletted or pin-perfed. This differs from a small perforation because no paper is removed, although round, equidistant holes are pricked through the paper. See Mexico Scott 242-256.

Perce en arc and *perce en scie* - pierced in an arc or saw-toothed designs, forming half circles or small triangles. See Hanover (German States) Scott 25-29.

Perce en serpentin - serpentine roulettes. The cuts form a serpentine or wavy line. See Brunswick (German States) Scott 13-18.

Once again, no paper is removed by these processes, leaving the stamps easily separated, but closely attached.

DIE-CUTTING

The third major form of stamp separation is die-cutting. This is a method where a die in the pattern of separation is created that later cuts the stamp paper in a stroke motion. Although some standard stamps bear die-cut perforations, this process is primarily used for self-adhesive postage stamps. Die-cutting can appear in straight lines, such as U.S. Scott 2522, shapes, such as U.S. Scott 1551, or imitating the appearance of perforations, such as New Zealand Scott 935A and 935B.

Printing Processes

ENGRAVING (Intaglio, Line-engraving, Etching)

Master die — The initial operation in the process of line engraving is making the master die. The die is a small, flat block of softened steel upon which the stamp design is recess engraved in reverse.

Master die

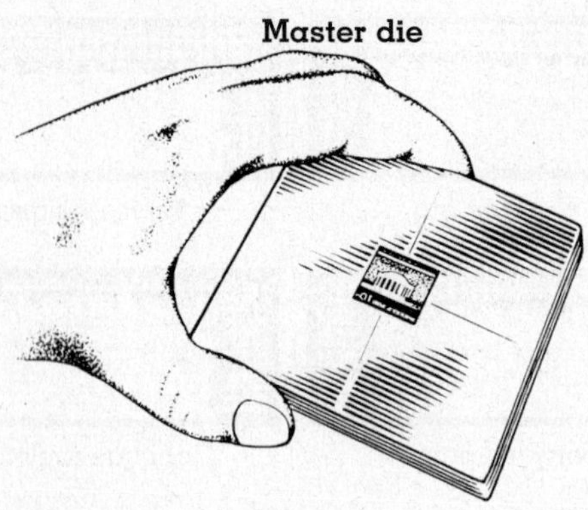

Photographic reduction of the original art is made to the appropriate size. It then serves as a tracing guide for the initial outline of the design. The engraver lightly traces the design on the steel with his graver, then slowly works the design until it is completed. At various points during the engraving process, the engraver hand-inks the die and makes an impression to check his progress. These are known as progressive die proofs. After completion of the engraving, the die is hardened to withstand the stress and pressures of later transfer operations.

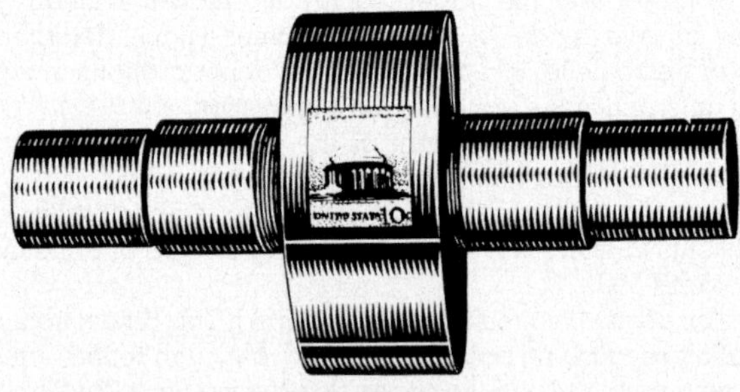

Transfer roll

Transfer roll — Next is production of the transfer roll that, as the name implies, is the medium used to transfer the subject from the master die to the printing plate. A blank roll of soft steel, mounted on a mandrel, is placed under the bearers of the transfer press to allow it to roll freely on its axis. The hardened die is placed on the bed of the press and the face of the transfer roll is applied to the die, under pressure. The bed or the roll is then rocked back and forth under increasing pressure, until the soft steel of the roll is forced into every engraved line of the die. The resulting impression on the roll is known as a "relief" or a "relief transfer." The engraved image is now positive in appearance and stands out from the steel. After the required number of reliefs are "rocked in," the soft steel transfer roll is hardened.

Different flaws may occur during the relief process. A defective relief may occur during the rocking in process because of a minute piece of foreign material lodging on the die, or some other cause. Imperfections in the steel of the transfer roll may result in a breaking away of parts of the design. This is known as a relief break, which will show up on finished stamps as small, unprinted areas. If a damaged relief remains in use, it will transfer a repeating defect to the plate. Deliberate alterations of reliefs sometimes occur. "Altered reliefs" designate these changed conditions.

Plate — The final step in pre-printing production is the making of the printing plate. A flat piece of soft steel replaces the die on the bed of the transfer press. One of the reliefs on the transfer roll is positioned over this soft steel. Position, or layout, dots determine the correct position on the plate. The dots have been lightly marked on the plate in advance. After the correct position of the relief is determined, the design is rocked in by following the same method used in making the transfer roll. The difference is that this time the image is being transferred from the transfer roll, rather than to it. Once the design is entered on the plate, it appears in reverse and is recessed. There are as many transfers entered on the plate as there are subjects printed on the sheet of stamps. It is during this process that double and shifted transfers occur, as well as re-entries. These are the result of improperly entered images that have not been properly burnished out prior to rocking in a new image.

Modern siderography processes, such as those used by the U.S. Bureau of Engraving and Printing, involve an automated form of rocking designs in on preformed cylindrical printing sleeves. The same process also allows for easier removal and re-entry of worn images right on the sleeve.

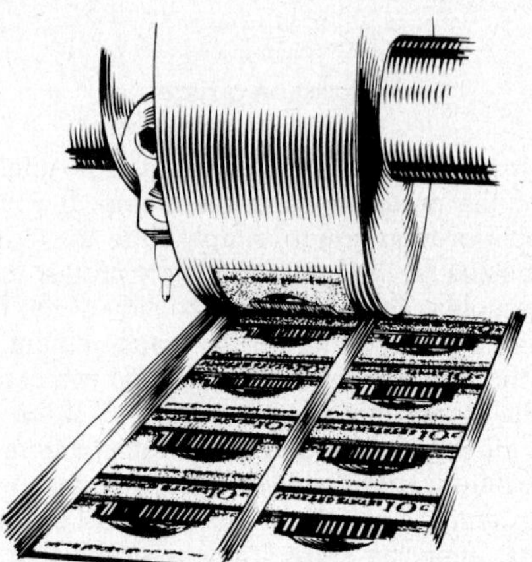

Transferring the design to the plate

Following the entering of the required transfers on the plate, the position dots, layout dots and lines, scratches and other markings generally are burnished out. Added at this time by the siderographer are any required *guide lines, plate numbers* or other *marginal markings*. The plate is then hand-inked and a proof impression is taken. This is known as a plate proof. If the impression is approved, the plate is machined for fitting onto the press, is hardened and sent to the plate vault ready for use.

On press, the plate is inked and the surface is automatically wiped clean, leaving ink only in the recessed lines. Paper is then forced under pressure into the engraved recessed lines, thereby receiving the ink. Thus, the ink lines on engraved stamps are slightly raised, and slight depressions (debossing) occur on the back of the stamp. Prior to the advent of modern high-speed presses and more advanced ink formulations, paper had to be dampened before receiving the ink. This sometimes led to uneven shrinkage by the time the stamps were perforated, resulting in improperly perforated stamps, or misperfs. Newer presses use drier paper, thus both *wet* and *dry printings* exist on some stamps.

Rotary Press — Until 1914, only flat plates were used to print engraved stamps. Rotary press printing was introduced in 1914, and slowly spread. Some countries still use flat-plate printing.

After approval of the plate proof, older *rotary press plates* require additional machining. They are curved to fit the press cylinder. "Gripper slots" are cut into the back of each plate to receive the "grippers," which hold the plate securely on the press. The plate is then hardened. Stamps printed from these bent rotary press plates are longer or wider than the same stamps printed from flat-plate presses. The stretching of the plate during the curving process is what causes this distortion.

Re-entry — To execute a re-entry on a flat plate, the transfer roll is re-applied to the plate, often at some time after its first use on the press. Worn-out designs can be resharpened by carefully burnishing out the original image and re-entering it from the transfer roll. If the original impression has not been sufficiently removed and the transfer roll is not precisely in line with the remaining impression, the resulting double transfer will make the re-entry obvious. If the registration is true, a re-entry may be difficult or impossible to distinguish. Sometimes a stamp printed from a successful re-entry is identified by having a much sharper and clearer impression than its neighbors. With the advent of rotary presses, post-press re-entries were not possible. After a plate was curved for the rotary press, it was impossible to make a re-entry. This is because the plate had already been bent once (with the design distorted).

However, with the introduction of the previously mentioned modern-style siderography machines, entries are made to the preformed cylindrical printing sleeve. Such sleeves are dechromed and softened. This allows individual images to be burnished out and re-entered on the curved sleeve. The sleeve is then rechromed, resulting in longer press life.

Double Transfer — This is a description of the condition of a transfer on a plate that shows evidence of a duplication of all, or a portion of the design. It usually is the result of the changing of the registration between the transfer roll and the plate during the rocking in of the original entry. Double transfers also occur when only a portion of the design has been rocked in and improper positioning is noted. If the worker elected not to burnish out the partial or completed design, a strong double transfer will occur for part or all of the design.

It sometimes is necessary to remove the original transfer from a plate and repeat the process a second time. If the finished re-worked image shows traces of the original impression, attributable to incomplete burnishing, the result is a partial double transfer.

With the modern automatic machines mentioned previously, double transfers are all but impossible to create. Those partially doubled images on stamps printed from such sleeves are more than likely re-entries, rather than true double transfers.

Re-engraved — Alterations to a stamp design are sometimes necessary after some stamps have been printed. In some cases, either the original die or the actual printing plate may have its "temper" drawn (softened), and the design will be re-cut. The resulting impressions from such a re-engraved die or plate may differ slightly from the original issue, and are known as "re-engraved." If the alteration was made to the master die, all future printings will be consistently different from the original. If alterations were made to the printing plate, each altered stamp on the plate will be slightly different from each other, allowing specialists to reconstruct a complete printing plate.

Dropped Transfers — If an impression from the transfer roll has not been properly placed, a dropped transfer may occur. The final stamp image will appear obviously out of line with its neighbors.

Short Transfer — Sometimes a transfer roll is not rocked its entire length when entering a transfer onto a plate. As a result, the finished transfer on the plate fails to show the complete design, and the finished stamp will have an incomplete design printed. This is known as a "short transfer." U.S. Scott No. 8 is a good example of a short transfer.

TYPOGRAPHY (Letterpress, Surface Printing, Flexography, Dry Offset, High Etch)

Although the word "Typography" is obsolete as a term describing a printing method, it was the accepted term throughout the first century of postage stamps. Therefore, appropriate Scott listings in this catalogue refer to typographed stamps. The current term for this form of printing, however, is "letterpress."

As it relates to the production of postage stamps, letterpress printing is the reverse of engraving. Rather than having recessed areas trap the ink and deposit it on paper, only the raised areas of the design are inked. This is comparable to the type of printing seen by inking and using an ordinary rubber stamp. Letterpress includes all printing where the design is above the surface area, whether it is wood, metal or, in some instances, hardened rubber or polymer plastic.

For most letterpress-printed stamps, the engraved master is made in much the same manner as for engraved stamps. In this instance, however, an additional step is needed. The design is transferred to another surface before being transferred to the transfer roll. In this way, the transfer roll has a recessed stamp design, rather than one done in relief. This makes the printing areas on the final plate raised, or relief areas.

For less-detailed stamps of the 19th century, the area on the die not used as a printing surface was cut away, leaving the surface area raised. The original die was then reproduced by stereotyping or electrotyping. The resulting electrotypes were assembled in the required number and format of the desired sheet of stamps. The plate used in printing the stamps was an electroplate of these assembled electrotypes.

Once the final letterpress plates are created, ink is applied to the raised surface and the pressure of the press transfers the ink impression to the paper. In contrast to engraving, the fine lines of letterpress are impressed on the surface of the stamp, leaving a debossed surface. When viewed from the back (as on a typewritten page), the corresponding line work on the stamp will be raised slightly (embossed) above the surface.

PHOTOGRAVURE (Gravure, Rotogravure, Heliogravure)

In this process, the basic principles of photography are applied to a chemically sensitized metal plate, rather than photographic paper. The design is transferred photographically to the plate through a halftone, or dot-matrix screen, breaking the reproduction into tiny dots. The plate is treated chemically and the dots form depressions, called cells, of varying depths and diameters, depending on the degrees of shade in the design. Then, like engraving, ink is applied to the plate and the surface is wiped clean. This leaves ink in the tiny cells that is lifted out and deposited on the paper when it is pressed against the plate.

Gravure is most often used for multicolored stamps, generally using the three primary colors (red, yellow and blue) and black. By varying the dot matrix pattern and density of these colors, virtually any color can be reproduced. A typical full-color gravure stamp will be created from four printing cylinders (one for each color). The original multicolored image will have been photographically separated into its component colors.

Modern gravure printing may use computer-generated dot-matrix screens, and modern plates may be of various types including metal-coated plastic. The catalogue designation of Photogravure (or "Photo") covers any of these older and more modern gravure methods of printing.

For examples of the first photogravure stamps printed (1914), see Bavaria Scott 94-114.

LITHOGRAPHY (Offset Lithography, Stone Lithography, Dilitho, Planography, Collotype)

The principle that oil and water do not mix is the basis for lithography. The stamp design is drawn by hand or transferred from engraving to the surface of a lithographic stone or metal plate in a greasy (oily) substance. This oily substance holds the ink, which will later be transferred to the paper. The stone (or plate) is wet with an acid fluid, causing it to repel the printing ink in all areas not covered by the greasy substance.

Transfer paper is used to transfer the design from the original stone or plate. A series of duplicate transfers are grouped and, in turn, transferred to the final printing plate.

Photolithography — The application of photographic processes to lithography. This process allows greater flexibility of design, related to use of halftone screens combined with line work. Unlike photogravure or engraving, this process can allow large, solid areas to be printed.

Offset — A refinement of the lithographic process. A rubber-covered blanket cylinder takes the impression from the inked lithographic plate. From the "blanket" the impression is *offset* or transferred to the paper. Greater flexibility and speed are the principal reasons offset printing has largely displaced lithography. The term "lithography" covers both processes, and results are almost identical.

EMBOSSED (Relief) Printing

Embossing, not considered one of the four main printing types, is a method in which the design first is sunk into the metal of the die. Printing is done against a yielding platen, such as leather or linoleum. The platen is forced into the depression of the die, thus forming the design on the paper in relief. This process is often used for metallic inks.

Embossing may be done without color (see Sardinia Scott 4-6); with color printed around the embossed area (see Great Britain Scott 5 and most U.S. envelopes); and with color in exact registration with the embossed subject (see Canada Scott 656-657).

HOLOGRAMS

For objects to appear as holograms on stamps, a model exactly the same size as it is to appear on the hologram must be created. Rather than using photographic film to capture the image, holography records an image on a photoresist material. In processing, chemicals eat away at certain exposed areas, leaving a pattern of constructive and destructive interference. When the photoresist is developed, the result is a pattern of uneven ridges that acts as a mold. This mold is then coated with metal, and the resulting form is used to press copies in much the same way phonograph records are produced.

A typical reflective hologram used for stamps consists of a reproduction of the uneven patterns on a plastic film that is applied to a reflective background, usually a silver or gold foil. Light is reflected off the background through the film, making the pattern present on the film visible. Because of the uneven pattern of the film, the viewer will perceive the objects in their proper three-dimensional relationships with appropriate brightness.

The first hologram on a stamp was produced by Austria in 1988 (Scott 1441).

FOIL APPLICATION

A modern technique of applying color to stamps involves the application of metallic foil to the stamp paper. A pattern of foil is applied to the stamp paper by use of a stamping die. The foil usually is flat, but it may be textured. Canada Scott 1735 has three different foil applications in pearl, bronze and gold. The gold foil was textured using a chemical-etch copper embossing die. The printing of this stamp also involved two-color offset lithography plus embossing.

THERMOGRAPHY

In the 1990s stamps began to be enhanced with thermographic printing. In this process, a powdered polymer is applied over a sheet that has just been printed. The powder adheres to ink that lacks drying or hardening agents and does not adhere to areas where the ink has these agents. The excess powder is removed and the sheet is briefly heated to melt the powder. The melted powder solidifies after cooling, producing a raised, shiny effect on the stamps. See Scott New Caledonia C239-C240.

COMBINATION PRINTINGS

Sometimes two or even three printing methods are combined in producing stamps. In these cases, such as Austria Scott 933 or Canada 1735 (described in the preceding paragraph), the multiple-printing technique can be determined by studying the individual characteristics of each printing type. A few stamps, such as Singapore Scott 684-684A, combine as many as three of the four major printing types (lithography, engraving and typography). When this is done it often indicates the incorporation of security devices against counterfeiting.

INK COLORS

Inks or colored papers used in stamp printing often are of mineral origin, although there are numerous examples of organic-based pigments. As a general rule, organic-based pigments are far more subject to varieties and change than those of mineral-based origin.

The appearance of any given color on a stamp may be affected by many aspects, including printing variations, light, color of paper, aging and chemical alterations.

Numerous printing variations may be observed. Heavier pressure or inking will cause a more intense color, while slight interruptions in the ink feed or lighter impressions will cause a lighter appearance. Stamps printed in the same color by water-based and solvent-based inks can differ significantly in appearance. This affects several stamps in the U.S. Prominent Americans series. Hand-mixed ink formulas (primarily from the 19th century) produced under different conditions (humidity and temperature) account for notable color variations in early printings of the same stamp (see U.S. Scott 248-250, 279B, for example). Different sources of pigment can also result in significant differences in color.

Light exposure and aging are closely related in the way they affect stamp color. Both eventually break down the ink and fade colors, so that a carefully kept stamp may differ significantly in color from an identical copy that has been exposed to light. If stamps are exposed to light either intentionally or accidentally, their colors can be faded or completely changed in some cases.

Papers of different quality and consistency used for the same stamp printing may affect color appearance. Most pelure papers, for example, show a richer color when compared with wove or laid papers. See Russia Scott 181a, for an example of this effect.

The very nature of the printing processes can cause a variety of differences in shades or hues of the same stamp. Some of these shades are scarcer than others, and are of particular interest to the advanced collector.

Luminescence

All forms of tagged stamps fall under the general category of luminescence. Within this broad category is fluorescence, dealing with forms of tagging visible under longwave ultraviolet light, and phosphorescence, which deals with tagging visible only under shortwave light. Phosphorescence leaves an afterglow and fluorescence does not. These treated stamps show up in a range of different colors when exposed to UV light. The differing wavelengths of the light activates the tagging material, making it glow in various colors that usually serve different mail processing purposes.

Intentional tagging is a post-World War II phenomenon, brought about by the increased literacy rate and rapidly growing mail volume. It was one of several answers to the problem of the need for more automated mail processes. Early tagged stamps served the purpose of triggering machines to separate different types of mail. A natural outgrowth was to also use the signal to trigger machines that faced all envelopes the same way and canceled them.

Tagged stamps come in many different forms. Some tagged stamps have luminescent shapes or images imprinted on them as a form of security device. Others have blocks (United States), stripes, frames (South Africa and Canada), overall coatings (United States), bars (Great Britain and Canada) and many other types. Some types of tagging are even mixed in with the pigmented printing ink (Australia Scott 366, Netherlands Scott 478 and U.S. Scott 1359 and 2443).

The means of applying taggant to stamps differs as much as the intended purposes for the stamps. The most common form of tagging is a coating applied to the surface of the printed stamp. Since the taggant ink is frequently invisible except under UV light, it does not interfere with the appearance of the stamp. Another common application is the use of phosphored papers. In this case the paper itself either has a coating of taggant applied before the stamp is printed, has taggant applied during the papermaking process (incorporating it into the fibers), or has the taggant mixed into the coating of the paper. The latter method, among others, is currently in use in the United States.

Many countries now use tagging in various forms to either expedite mail handling or to serve as a printing security device against counterfeiting. Following the introduction of tagged stamps for public use in 1959 by Great Britain, other countries have steadily joined the parade. Among those are Germany (1961); Canada and Denmark (1962); United States, Australia, France and Switzerland (1963); Belgium and Japan (1966); Sweden and Norway (1967); Italy (1968); and Russia (1969). Since then, many other countries have begun using forms of tagging, including Brazil, China, Czechoslovakia, Hong Kong, Guatemala, Indonesia, Israel, Lithuania, Luxembourg, Netherlands, Penrhyn Islands, Portugal, St. Vincent, Singapore, South Africa, Spain and Sweden to name a few.

In some cases, including United States, Canada, Great Britain and Switzerland, stamps were released both with and without tagging. Many of these were released during each country's experimental period. Tagged and untagged versions are listed for the aforementioned countries and are noted in some other countries' listings. For at least a few stamps, the experimentally tagged version is worth far more than its untagged counterpart, such as the 1963 experimental tagged version of France Scott 1024.

In some cases, luminescent varieties of stamps were inadvertently created. Several Russian stamps, for example, sport highly fluorescent ink that was not intended as a form of tagging. Older stamps, such as early U.S. postage dues, can be positively identified by the use of UV light, since the organic ink used has become slightly fluorescent over time. Other stamps, such as Austria Scott 70a-82a (varnish bars) and Obock Scott 46-64 (printed quadrille lines), have become fluorescent over time.

Various fluorescent substances have been added to paper to make it appear brighter. These optical brightners, as they are known, greatly affect the appearance of the stamp under UV light. The brightest of these is known as Hi-Brite paper. These paper varieties are beyond the scope of the Scott Catalogue.

Shortwave UV light also is used extensively in expertizing, since each form of paper has its own fluorescent characteristics that are impossible to perfectly match. It is therefore a simple matter to detect filled thins, added perforation teeth and other alterations that involve the addition of paper. UV light also is used to examine stamps that have had cancels chemically removed and for other purposes as well.

Gum

The Illustrated Gum Chart in the first part of this introduction shows and defines various types of gum condition. Because gum condition has an important impact on the value of unused stamps, we recommend studying this chart and the accompanying text carefully.

The gum on the back of a stamp may be shiny, dull, smooth, rough, dark, white, colored or tinted. Most stamp gumming adhesives use gum arabic or dextrine as a base. Certain polymers such as polyvinyl alcohol (PVA) have been used extensively since World War II.

The *Scott Standard Postage Stamp Catalogue* does not list items by types of gum. The *Scott Specialized Catalogue of United States Stamps and Covers* does differentiate among some types of gum for certain issues.

Reprints of stamps may have gum differing from the original issues. In addition, some countries have used different gum formulas for different seasons. These adhesives have different properties that may become more apparent over time.

Many stamps have been issued without gum, and the catalogue will note this fact. See, for example, United States Scott 40-47. Sometimes, gum may have been removed to preserve the stamp. Germany Scott B68, for example, has a highly acidic gum that eventually destroys the stamps. This item is valued in the catalogue with gum removed.

Reprints and Reissues

These are impressions of stamps (usually obsolete) made from the original plates or stones. If they are valid for postage and reproduce obsolete issues (such as U.S. Scott 102-111), the stamps are *reissues*. If they are from current issues, they are designated as *second, third,* etc., *printing*. If designated for a particular purpose, they are called *special printings*.

When special printings are not valid for postage, but are made from original dies and plates by authorized persons, they are *official reprints*. *Private reprints* are made from the original plates and dies by private hands. An example of a private reprint is that of the 1871-1932 reprints made from the original die of the 1845 New Haven, Conn., postmaster's provisional. *Official reproductions* or imitations are made from new dies and plates by government authorization. Scott will list those reissues that are valid for postage if they differ significantly from the original printing.

The U.S. government made special printings of its first postage stamps in 1875. Produced were official imitations of the first two stamps (listed as Scott 3-4), reprints of the demonetized pre-1861 issues (Scott 40-47) and reissues of the 1861 stamps, the 1869 stamps and the then-current 1875 denominations. Even though the official imitations and the reprints were not valid for postage, Scott lists all of these U.S. special printings.

Most reprints or reissues differ slightly from the original stamp in some characteristic, such as gum, paper, perforation, color or watermark. Sometimes the details are followed so meticulously that only a student of that specific stamp is able to distinguish the reprint or reissue from the original.

Remainders and Canceled to Order

Some countries sell their stock of old stamps when a new issue replaces them. To avoid postal use, the *remainders* usually are canceled with a punch hole, a heavy line or bar, or a more-or-less regular-looking cancellation. The most famous merchant of remainders was Nicholas F. Seebeck. In the 1880s and 1890s, he arranged printing contracts between the Hamilton Bank Note Co., of which he was a director, and several Central and South American countries. The contracts provided that the plates and all remainders of the yearly issues became the property of Hamilton. Seebeck saw to it that ample stock remained. The "Seebecks," both remainders and reprints, were standard packet fillers for decades.

Some countries also issue stamps *canceled-to-order (CTO),* either in sheets with original gum or stuck onto pieces of paper or envelopes and canceled. Such CTO items generally are worth less than postally used stamps. In cases where the CTO material is far more prevalent in the marketplace than postally used examples, the catalogue value relates to the CTO examples, with postally used examples noted as premium items. Most CTOs can be detected by the presence of gum. However, as the CTO practice goes back at least to 1885, the gum inevitably has been soaked off some stamps so they could pass as postally used. The normally applied postmarks usually differ slightly from standard postmarks, and specialists are able to tell the difference. When applied individually to envelopes by philatelically minded persons, CTO material is known as *favor canceled* and generally sells at large discounts.

Cinderellas and Facsimiles

Cinderella is a catch-all term used by stamp collectors to describe phantoms, fantasies, bogus items, municipal issues, exhibition seals, local revenues, transportation stamps, labels, poster stamps and many other types of items. Some cinderella collectors include in their collections local postage issues, telegraph stamps, essays and proofs, forgeries and counterfeits.

A *fantasy* is an adhesive created for a nonexistent stamp-issuing authority. Fantasy items range from imaginary countries (Occusi-Ambeno, Kingdom of Sedang, Principality of Trinidad or Torres Straits), to non-existent locals (Winans City Post), or nonexistent transportation lines (McRobish & Co.'s Acapulco-San Francisco Line).

On the other hand, if the entity exists and could have issued stamps (but did not) or was known to have issued other stamps, the items are considered *bogus* stamps. These would include the Mormon postage stamps of Utah, S. Allan Taylor's Guatemala and Paraguay inventions, the propaganda issues for the South Moluccas and the adhesives of the Page & Keyes local post of Boston.

Phantoms is another term for both fantasy and bogus issues.

Facsimiles are copies or imitations made to represent original stamps, but which do not pretend to be originals. A catalogue illustration is such a facsimile. Illustrations from the Moens catalogue of the last century were occasionally colored and passed off as stamps. Since the beginning of stamp collecting, facsimiles have been made for collectors as space fillers or for reference. They often carry the word "facsimile," "falsch" (German), "sanko" or "mozo" (Japanese), or "faux" (French) overprinted on the face or stamped on the back. Unfortunately, over the years a number of these items have had fake cancels applied over the facsimile notation and have been passed off as genuine.

Forgeries and Counterfeits

Forgeries and counterfeits have been with philately virtually from the beginning of stamp production. Over time, the terminology for the two has been used interchangeably. Although both forgeries and counterfeits are reproductions of stamps, the purposes behind their creation differ considerably.

Among specialists there is an increasing movement to more specifically define such items. Although there is no universally accepted terminology, we feel the following definitions most closely mirror the items and their purposes as they are currently defined.

Forgeries (also often referred to as *Counterfeits*) are reproductions of genuine stamps that have been created to defraud collectors. Such spurious items first appeared on the market around 1860, and most old-time collections contain one or more. Many are crude and easily spotted, but some can deceive experts.

An important supplier of these early philatelic forgeries was the Hamburg printer Gebruder Spiro. Many others with reputations in this craft included S. Allan Taylor, George Hussey, James Chute, George Forune, Benjamin & Sarpy, Julius Goldner, E. Oneglia and L.H. Mercier. Among the noted 20th-century forgers were Francois Fournier, Jean Sperati and the prolific Raoul DeThuin.

Forgeries may be complete replications, or they may be genuine stamps altered to resemble a scarcer (and more valuable) type. Most forgeries, particularly those of rare stamps, are worth only a small fraction of the value of a genuine example, but a few types, created by some of the most notable forgers, such as Sperati, can be worth as much or more than the genuine. Fraudulently produced copies are known of most classic rarities and many medium-priced stamps.

In addition to rare stamps, large numbers of common 19th- and early 20th-century stamps were forged to supply stamps to the early packet trade. Many can still be easily found. Few new philatelic forgeries have appeared in recent decades. Successful imitation of well-engraved work is virtually impossible. It has proven far easier to produce a fake by altering a genuine stamp than to duplicate a stamp completely.

Counterfeit (also often referred to as *Postal Counterfeit* or *Postal Forgery*) is the term generally applied to reproductions of stamps that have been created to defraud the government of revenue. Such items usually are created at the time a stamp is current and, in some cases, are hard to detect. Because most counterfeits are seized when the perpetrator is captured, postal counterfeits, particularly used on cover, are usually worth much more than a genuine example to specialists. The first postal counterfeit was of Spain's 4-cuarto carmine of 1854 (the real one is Scott 25). Apparently, the counterfeiters were not satisfied with their first version, which is now very scarce, and they soon created an engraved counterfeit, which is common. Postal counterfeits quickly followed in Austria, Naples, Sardinia and the Roman States. They have since been created in many other countries as well, including the United States.

An infamous counterfeit to defraud the government is the 1-shilling Great Britain "Stock Exchange" forgery of 1872, used on telegraph forms at the exchange that year. The stamp escaped detection until a stamp dealer noticed it in 1898.

Fakes

Fakes are genuine stamps altered in some way to make them more desirable. One student of this part of stamp collecting has estimated that by the 1950s more than 30,000 varieties of fakes were known. That number has grown greatly since then. The widespread existence of fakes makes it important for stamp collectors to study their philatelic holdings and use relevant literature. Likewise, collectors should buy from reputable dealers who guarantee their stamps and make full and prompt refunds should a purchased item be declared faked or altered by some mutually agreed-upon authority. Because fakes always have some genuine characteristics, it is not always possible to obtain unanimous agreement among experts regarding specific items. These students may change their opinions as philatelic knowledge increases. More than 80 percent of all fakes on the philatelic market today are regummed, reperforated (or perforated for the first time), or bear forged overprints, surcharges or cancellations.

Stamps can be chemically treated to alter or eliminate colors. For example, a pale rose stamp can be re-colored to resemble a blue shade of high market value. In other cases, treated stamps can be made to resemble missing color varieties. Designs may be changed by painting, or a stroke or a dot added or bleached out to turn an ordinary variety into a seemingly scarcer stamp. Part of a stamp can be bleached and reprinted in a different version, achieving an inverted center or frame. Margins can be added or repairs done so deceptively that the stamps move from the "repaired" into the "fake" category.

Fakers have not left the backs of the stamps untouched either. They may create false watermarks, add fake grills or press out genuine grills. A thin India paper proof may be glued onto a thicker backing to create the appearance an issued stamp, or a proof printed on cardboard may be shaved down and perforated to resemble a stamp. Silk threads are impressed into paper and stamps have been split so that a rare paper variety is added to an otherwise inexpensive stamp. The most common treatment to the back of a stamp, however, is regumming.

Some in the business of faking stamps have openly advertised fool-proof application of "original gum" to stamps that lack it, although most publications now ban such ads from their pages. It is believed that very few early stamps have survived without being hinged. The large number of never-hinged examples of such earlier material offered for sale thus suggests the widespread extent of regumming activity. Regumming also may be used to hide repairs or thin spots. Dipping the stamp into watermark fluid, or examining it under longwave ultraviolet light often will reveal these flaws.

Fakers also tamper with separations. Ingenious ways to add margins are known. Perforated wide-margin stamps may be falsely represented as imperforate when trimmed. Reperforating is commonly done to create scarce coil or perforation varieties, and to eliminate the naturally occurring straight-edge stamps found in sheet margin positions of many earlier issues. Custom has made straight-edged stamps less desirable. Fakers have obliged by perforating straight-edged stamps so that many are now uncommon, if not rare.

Another fertile field for the faker is that of overprints, surcharges and cancellations. The forging of rare surcharges or overprints began in the 1880s or 1890s. These forgeries are sometimes difficult to detect, but experts have identified almost all. Occasionally, overprints or cancellations are removed to create non-overprinted stamps or seemingly unused items. This is most commonly done by removing a manuscript cancel to make a stamp resemble an unused example. "SPECIMEN" overprints may be removed by scraping and repainting to create non-overprinted varieties. Fakers use inexpensive revenues or pen-canceled stamps to generate unused stamps for further faking by adding other markings. The quartz lamp or UV lamp and a high-powered magnifying glass help to easily detect removed cancellations.

The bigger problem, however, is the addition of overprints, surcharges or cancellations - many with such precision that they are very difficult to ascertain. Plating of the stamps or the overprint can be an important method of detection.

Fake postmarks may range from many spurious fancy cancellations to a host of markings applied to transatlantic covers, to adding normally appearing postmarks to definitives of some countries with stamps that are valued far higher used than unused. With the increased popularity of cover collecting, and the widespread interest in postal history, a fertile new field for fakers has come about. Some have tried to create entire covers. Others specialize in adding stamps, tied by fake cancellations, to genuine stampless covers, or replacing less expensive or damaged stamps with more valuable ones. Detailed study of postal rates in effect at the time a cover in question was mailed, including the analysis of each handstamp used during the period, ink analysis and similar techniques, usually will unmask the fraud.

Restoration and Repairs

Scott bases its catalogue values on stamps that are free of defects and otherwise meet the standards set forth earlier in this introduction. Most stamp collectors desire to have the finest copy of an item possible. Even within given grading categories there are variances. This leads to a controversial practice that is not defined in any universal manner: stamp *restoration*.

There are broad differences of opinion about what is permissible when it comes to restoration. Carefully applying a soft eraser to a stamp or cover to remove light soiling is one form of restoration, as is washing a stamp in mild soap and water to clean it. These are fairly accepted forms of restoration. More severe forms of restoration include pressing out creases or removing stains caused by tape. To what degree each of these is acceptable is dependent upon the individual situation. Further along the spectrum is the freshening of a stamp's color by removing oxide build-up or the effects of wax paper left next to stamps shipped to the tropics.

At some point in this spectrum the concept of *repair* replaces that of restoration. Repairs include filling thin spots, mending tears by reweaving or adding a missing perforation tooth. Regumming stamps may have been acceptable as a restoration or repair technique many decades ago, but today it is considered a form of fakery.

Restored stamps may or may not sell at a discount, and it is possible that the value of individual restored items may be enhanced over that of their pre-restoration state. Specific situations dictate the resultant value of such an item. Repaired stamps sell at substantial discounts from the value of sound stamps.

Terminology

Booklets — Many countries have issued stamps in small booklets for the convenience of users. This idea continues to become increasingly popular in many countries. Booklets have been issued in many sizes and forms, often with advertising on the covers, the panes of stamps or on the interleaving.

The panes used in booklets may be printed from special plates or made from regular sheets. All panes from booklets issued by the United States and many from those of other countries contain stamps that are straight edged on the sides, but perforated between. Others are distinguished by orientation of watermark or other identifying features. Any stamp-like unit in the pane, either printed or blank, that is not a postage stamp, is considered to be a *label* in the catalogue listings.

Scott lists and values booklet panes. Modern complete booklets also are listed and valued. Individual booklet panes are listed only when they are not fashioned from existing sheet stamps and, therefore, are identifiable from their sheet stamp counterparts.

Panes usually do not have a used value assigned to them because there is little market activity for used booklet panes, even though many exist used and there is some demand for them.

Cancellations — The marks or obliterations put on stamps by postal authorities to show that they have performed service and to prevent their reuse are known as cancellations. If the marking is made with a pen, it is considered a "pen cancel." When the location of the post office appears in the marking, it is a "town cancellation." A "postmark" is technically any postal marking, but in practice the term generally is applied to a town cancellation with a date. When calling attention to a cause or celebration, the marking is known as a "slogan cancellation." Many other types and styles of cancellations exist, such as duplex, numerals, targets, fancy and others. See also "precancels," below.

Coil Stamps — These are stamps that are issued in rolls for use in dispensers, affixing and vending machines. Those coils of the United States, Canada, Sweden and some other countries are perforated horizontally or vertically only, with the outer edges imperforate. Coil stamps of some countries, such as Great Britain and Germany, are perforated on all four sides and may in some cases be distinguished from their sheet stamp counterparts by watermarks, counting numbers on the reverse or other means.

Covers — Entire envelopes, with or without adhesive postage stamps, that have passed through the mail and bear postal or other markings of philatelic interest are known as covers. Before the introduction of envelopes in about 1840, people folded letters and wrote the address on the outside. Some people covered their letters with an extra sheet of paper on the outside for the address, producing the term "cover." Used airletter sheets, stamped envelopes and other items of postal stationery also are considered covers.

Errors — Stamps that have some major, consistent, unintentional deviation from the normal are considered errors. Errors include, but are not limited to, missing or wrong colors, wrong paper, wrong watermarks, inverted centers or frames on multicolor printing, inverted or missing surcharges or overprints, double impressions, missing perforations, unintentionally omitted tagging and others. Factually wrong or misspelled information, if it appears on all examples of a stamp, are not considered errors in the true sense of the word. They are errors of design. Inconsistent or randomly appearing items, such as misperfs or color shifts, are classified as freaks.

Color-Omitted Errors — This term refers to stamps where a missing color is caused by the complete failure of the printing plate to deliver ink to the stamp paper or any other paper. Generally, this is caused by the printing plate not being engaged on the press or the ink station running dry of ink during printing.

Color-Missing Errors — This term refers to stamps where a color or colors were printed somewhere but do not appear on the finished stamp. There are four different classes of color-missing errors, and the catalog indicates with a two-letter code appended to each such listing what caused the color to be missing. These codes are used only for the United States' color-missing error listings.

FO = A *foldover* of the stamp sheet during printing may block ink from appearing on a stamp. Instead, the color will appear on the back of the foldover (where it might fall on the back of the selvage or perhaps on the back of the stamp or another stamp). FO also will be used in the case of foldunders, where the paper may fold underneath the other stamp paper and the color will print on the platen.

EP = When the extraneous paper is removed, an unprinted area of stamp paper remains and may show a color or colors to be totally missing on the finished stamp..

CM = A misregistration of the printing plates during printing will result in a *color misregistration*, and such a misregistraion may result in a color not appearing on the finished stamp.

PS = *A perforation shift* after printing may remove a color from the finished stamp. Normally, this will occur on a row of stamps at the edge of the stamp pane.

Measurements – When measurements are given in the Scott catalogues for stamp size, grill size or any other reason, the first measurement given is always for the top and bottom dimension, while the second measurement will be for the sides (just as perforation gauges are measured). Thus, a stamp size of 15mm x 21mm will indicate a vertically oriented stamp 15mm wide at top and bottom, and 21mm tall at the sides. The same principle holds for measuring or counting items such as U.S. grills. A grill count of 22x18 points (B grill) indicates that there are 22 grill points across by 18 grill points down.

Overprints and Surcharges — Overprinting involves applying wording or design elements over an already existing stamp. Overprints can be used to alter the place of use (such as "Canal Zone" on U.S. stamps), to adapt them for a special purpose ("Porto" on Denmark's 1913-20 regular issues for use as postage due stamps, Scott J1-J7) or to commemorate a special occasion (United States Scott 647-648).

A *surcharge* is a form of overprint that changes or restates the face value of a stamp or piece of postal stationery.

Surcharges and overprints may be handstamped, typeset or, occasionally, lithographed or engraved. A few hand-written overprints and surcharges are known.

Personalized Stamps — In 1999, Australia issued stamps with se-tenant labels that could be personalized with pictures of the customer's choice. Other countries quickly followed suit, with some offering to print the selected picture on the stamp itself within a frame that was used exclusively for personalized issues. As the picture used on these stamps or labels vary, listings for such stamps are for any picture within the common frame (or any picture on a se-tenant label), be it a "generic" image or one produced especially for a customer, almost invariably at a premium price.

Precancels — Stamps that are canceled before they are placed in the mail are known as precancels. Precanceling usually is done to expedite the handling of large mailings and generally allow the affected mail pieces to skip certain phases of mail handling.

In the United States, precancellations generally identified the point of origin; that is, the city and state. This information appeared across the face of the stamp, usually centered between parallel lines. More recently, bureau precancels retained the parallel lines, but the city and state designations were dropped. Recent coils have a service inscription that is present on the original printing plate. These show the mail service paid for by the stamp. Since these stamps are not intended to receive further cancellations when used as intended, they are considered precancels. Such items often do not have parallel lines as part of the precancellation.

In France, the abbreviation *Affranchts* in a semicircle together with the word *Postes* is the general form of precancel in use. Belgian precancellations usually appear in a box in which the name of the city appears. Netherlands precancels have the name of the city enclosed between concentric circles, sometimes called a "lifesaver." Precancellations of other countries usually follow these patterns, but may be any arrangement of bars, boxes and city names.

Precancels are listed in the Scott catalogues only if the precancel changes the denomination (Belgium Scott 477-478); if the precanceled stamp is different from the non-precanceled version (such as untagged U.S. precancels); or if the stamp exists only precanceled (France Scott 1096-1099, U.S. Scott 2265).

Proofs and Essays — Proofs are impressions taken from an approved die, plate or stone in which the design and color are the same as the stamp issued to the public. Trial color proofs are impressions taken from approved dies, plates or stones in colors that vary from the final version. An essay is the impression of a design that differs in some way from the issued stamp. "Progressive die proofs" generally are considered to be essays.

Provisionals — These are stamps that are issued on short notice and intended for temporary use pending the arrival of regular issues. They usually are issued to meet such contingencies as changes in government or currency, shortage of necessary postage values or military occupation.

During the 1840s, postmasters in certain American cities issued stamps that were valid only at specific post offices. In 1861, postmasters of the Confederate States also issued stamps with limited validity. Both of these examples are known as "postmaster's provisionals."

Se-tenant — This term refers to an unsevered pair, strip or block of stamps that differ in design, denomination or overprint.

Unless the se-tenant item has a continuous design (see U.S. Scott 1451a, 1694a) the stamps do not have to be in the same order as shown in the catalogue (see U.S. Scott 2158a).

Specimens — The Universal Postal Union required member nations to send samples of all stamps they released into service to the International Bureau in Switzerland. Member nations of the UPU received these specimens as samples of what stamps were valid for postage. Many are overprinted, handstamped or initial-perforated "Specimen," "Canceled" or "Muestra." Some are marked with bars across the denominations (China-Taiwan), punched holes (Czechoslovakia) or back inscriptions (Mongolia).

Stamps distributed to government officials or for publicity purposes, and stamps submitted by private security printers for official approval, also may receive such defacements.

The previously described defacement markings prevent postal use, and all such items generally are known as "specimens."

Tete Beche — This term describes a pair of stamps in which one is upside down in relation to the other. Some of these are the result of intentional sheet arrangements, such as Morocco Scott B10-B11. Others occurred when one or more electrotypes accidentally were placed upside down on the plate, such as Colombia Scott 57a. Separation of the tete-beche stamps, of course, destroys the tete beche variety.

Pronunciation Symbols

ə .... banana, collide, abut

ˈə, ˌə .... humdrum, abut

ə .... immediately preceding \l\, \n\, \m\, \ŋ\, as in battle, mitten, eaten, and sometimes open \ˈō-pᵊm\, lock and key \-ᵊŋ-\; immediately following \l\, \m\, \r\, as often in French table, prisme, titre

ər .... further, merger, bird

ˈər-, ˈə-r .... as in two different pronunciations of hurry \ˈhər-ē, ˈhə-rē\

a .... mat, map, mad, gag, snap, patch

ā .... day, fade, date, aorta, drape, cape

ä .... bother, cot, and, with most American speakers, father, cart

ȧ .... father as pronounced by speakers who do not rhyme it with *bother*; French patte

au̇ .... now, loud, out

b .... baby, rib

ch .... chin, nature \ˈnā-chər\

d .... did, adder

e .... bet, bed, peck

ˈē, ˌē .... beat, nosebleed, evenly, easy

ē .... easy, mealy

f .... fifty, cuff

g .... go, big, gift

h .... hat, ahead

hw .... whale as pronounced by those who do not have the same pronunciation for both *whale* and *wail*

i .... tip, banish, active

ī .... site, side, buy, tripe

j .... job, gem, edge, join, judge

k .... kin, cook, ache

k̲ .... German ich, Buch; one pronunciation of loch

l .... lily, pool

m .... murmur, dim, nymph

n .... no, own

ⁿ .... indicates that a preceding vowel or diphthong is pronounced with the nasal passages open, as in French *un bon vin blanc* \œⁿ -bōⁿ -vaⁿ -bläⁿ\

ŋ .... sing \ˈsiŋ\, singer \ˈsiŋ-ər\, finger \ˈfiŋ-gər\, ink \ˈiŋk \

ō .... bone, know, beau

ȯ .... saw, all, gnaw, caught

œ .... French boeuf, German Hölle

œ̄ .... French feu, German Höhle

ȯi .... coin, destroy

p .... pepper, lip

r .... red, car, rarity

s .... source, less

sh .... as in shy, mission, machine, special (actually, this is a single sound, not two); with a hyphen between, two sounds as in *grasshopper* \ˈgras-ˌhä-pər\

t .... tie, attack, late, later, latter

th .... as in thin, ether (actually, this is a single sound, not two); with a hyphen between, two sounds as in *knighthood* \ˈnīt-ˌhu̇d\

t̲h̲ .... then, either, this (actually, this is a single sound, not two)

ü .... rule, youth, union \ˈyün-yən\, few \ˈfyü\

u̇ .... pull, wood, book, curable \ˈkyu̇r-ə-bəl\, fury \ˈfyu̇r-ē\

ue .... German füllen, hübsch

ue̅ .... French rue, German fühlen

v .... vivid, give

w .... we, away

y .... yard, young, cue \ˈkyü\, mute \ˈmyüt\, union \ˈyün-yən\

ʸ .... indicates that during the articulation of the sound represented by the preceding character the front of the tongue has substantially the position it has for the articulation of the first sound of *yard*, as in French *digne* \dēnʸ\

z .... zone, raise

zh .... as in vision, azure \ˈa-zhər\ (actually, this is a single sound, not two); with a hyphen between, two sounds as in *hogshead* \ˈhȯgz-ˌhed, ˈhägz-\

\ .... slant line used in pairs to mark the beginning and end of a transcription: \ˈpen\

ˈ .... mark preceding a syllable with primary (strongest) stress: \ˈpen-mən-ˌship\

ˌ .... mark preceding a syllable with secondary (medium) stress: \ˈpen-mən-ˌship\

- .... mark of syllable division

( ) .... indicate that what is symbolized between is present in some utterances but not in others: *factory* \ˈfak-t(ə-)rē\

÷ .... indicates that many regard as unacceptable the pronunciation variant immediately following: *cupola* \ˈkyü-pə-lə, ÷-ˌlō\

Currency Conversion

Country	Dollar	Pound	S Franc	Yen	HK $	Euro	Cdn $	Aus $
Australia	1.5528	1.9457	1.6130	0.0146	0.2003	1.7045	1.1072	–
Canada	1.4024	1.7572	1.4567	0.0131	0.1809	1.5394	–	0.9031
European Union	0.9110	1.1415	0.9463	0.0085	0.1175	–	0.6496	0.5867
Hong Kong	7.7521	9.7130	8.0525	0.0727	–	8.5094	5.5277	4.9923
Japan	106.66	133.64	110.79	–	13.759	117.08	76.055	68.689
Switzerland	0.9627	1.2063	–	0.0090	0.1242	1.0568	0.6865	0.6200
United Kingdom	0.7981	–	0.8290	0.0075	0.1030	0.8761	0.5691	0.5140
United States	–	1.2530	1.0387	0.0094	0.1290	1.0977	0.7131	0.6440

Country	Currency	U.S. $ Equiv.
San Marino	euro	1.0977
Saudi Arabia	riyal	.2667
Senegal	Community of French Africa (CFA) franc	.0017
Serbia	dinar	.0093
Seychelles	rupee	.0568
Sierra Leone	leone	.0001
Singapore	dollar	.7069
Slovakia	euro	1.0977
Slovenia	euro	1.0977
Solomon Islands	dollar	.1214
Somalia	shilling	.0017
South Africa	rand	.0532
S. Georgia & S. Sandwich Isls	British pound	1.2530
South Sudan	pound	.0181
Spain	euro	1.0977
Sri Lanka	rupee	.0052
Sudan	pound	.0181
Surinam	dollar	.1341
Swaziland	emalangeni	.0532
Sweden	krona	.1020
Switzerland	franc	1.0387
Syria	pound	.0019
Tajikistan	somoni	.0976
Tanzania	shilling	.0004

Source: ***xe.com*** *May 1, 2020. Figures reflect values as of May 1, 2020.*

COMMON DESIGN TYPES

Pictured in this section are issues where one illustration has been used for a number of countries in the Catalogue. Not included in this section are overprinted stamps or those issues which are illustrated in each country. Because the location of Never Hinged breakpoints varies from country to country, some of the values in the listings below will be for unused stamps that were previously hinged.

EUROPA

Europa, 1956

The design symbolizing the cooperation among the six countries comprising the Coal and Steel Community is illustrated in each country.

Belgium	*496-497*
France	*805-806*
Germany	*748-749*
Italy	*715-716*
Luxembourg	*318-320*
Netherlands	*368-369*

Nos. 496-497 (2)	9.00	.50
Nos. 805-806 (2)	5.25	1.00
Nos. 748-749 (2)	7.40	1.10
Nos. 715-716 (2)	9.25	1.25
Nos. 318-320 (3)	65.50	42.00
Nos. 368-369 (2)	25.75	1.50
Set total (13) Stamps	122.15	47.35

Europa, 1958

"E" and Dove — CD1

European Postal Union at the service of European integration.

1958, Sept. 13

Belgium	527-528
France	889-890
Germany	790-791
Italy	750-751
Luxembourg	341-343
Netherlands	375-376
Saar	317-318

Nos. 527-528 (2)	3.75	.60
Nos. 889-890 (2)	1.65	.55
Nos. 790-791 (2)	2.95	.60
Nos. 750-751 (2)	1.05	.60
Nos. 341-343 (3)	1.35	.90
Nos. 375-376 (2)	1.25	.75
Nos. 317-318 (2)	1.05	2.30
Set total (15) Stamps	13.05	6.30

Europa, 1959

6-Link Enless Chain — CD2

1959, Sept. 19

Belgium	536-537
France	929-930
Germany	805-806
Italy	791-792
Luxembourg	354-355
Netherlands	379-380

Nos. 536-537 (2)	1.55	.60
Nos. 929-930 (2)	1.40	.80
Nos. 805-806 (2)	1.35	.60
Nos. 791-792 (2)	.80	.50
Nos. 354-355 (2)	2.65	1.00
Nos. 379-380 (2)	2.10	1.85
Set total (12) Stamps	9.85	5.35

Europa, 1960

19-Spoke Wheel CD3

First anniversary of the establishment of C.E.P.T. (Conference Europeenne des Administrations des Postes et des Telecommunications.) The spokes symbolize the 19 founding members of the Conference.

1960, Sept.

Belgium	553-554
Denmark	379
Finland	376-377
France	970-971
Germany	818-820
Great Britain	377-378
Greece	688
Iceland	327-328
Ireland	175-176
Italy	809-810
Luxembourg	374-375
Netherlands	385-386
Norway	387
Portugal	866-867
Spain	941-942
Sweden	562-563
Switzerland	400-401
Turkey	1493-1494

Nos. 553-554 (2)	1.25	.55
No. 379 (1)	.55	.50
Nos. 376-377 (2)	1.70	1.80
Nos. 970-971 (2)	.50	.50
Nos. 818-820 (3)	1.90	1.35
Nos. 377-378 (2)	8.00	5.00
No. 688 (1)	4.25	1.75
Nos. 327-328 (2)	1.30	1.85
Nos. 175-176 (2)	47.50	27.50
Nos. 809-810 (2)	.50	.50
Nos. 374-375 (2)	1.00	.80
Nos. 385-386 (2)	2.00	2.00
No. 387 (1)	1.00	.80
Nos. 866-867 (2)	3.00	1.75
Nos. 941-942 (2)	1.50	.75
Nos. 562-563 (2)	1.05	.55
Nos. 400-401 (2)	1.75	.75
Nos. 1493-1494 (2)	2.10	1.35
Set total (34) Stamps	80.85	50.05

Europa, 1961

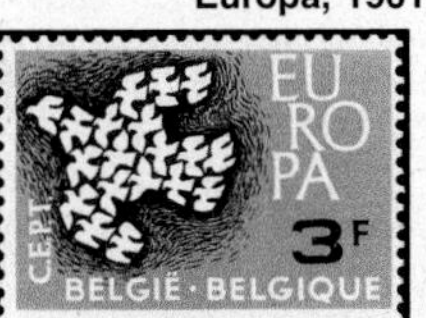

19 Doves Flying as One — CD4

The 19 doves represent the 19 members of the Conference of European Postal and Telecommunications Administrations C.E.P.T.

1961-62

Belgium	572-573
Cyprus	201-203
France	1005-1006
Germany	844-845
Great Britain	382-384
Greece	718-719
Iceland	340-341
Italy	845-846
Luxembourg	382-383
Netherlands	387-388
Spain	1010-1011
Switzerland	410-411
Turkey	1518-1520

Nos. 572-573 (2)	.75	.50
Nos. 201-203 (3)	*2.10*	*1.20*
Nos. 1005-1006 (2)	.50	.50
Nos. 844-845 (2)	.60	.75
Nos. 382-384 (3)	.75	.75
Nos. 718-719 (2)	.80	.50
Nos. 340-341 (2)	1.10	1.60
Nos. 845-846 (2)	.50	.50
Nos. 382-383 (2)	.55	.55
Nos. 387-388 (2)	.50	.50
Nos. 1010-1011 (2)	.60	.50
Nos. 410-411 (2)	1.90	.60
Nos. 1518-1520 (3)	1.55	.90
Set total (29) Stamps	12.20	9.35

Europa, 1962

Young Tree with 19 Leaves CD5

The 19 leaves represent the 19 original members of C.E.P.T.

1962-63

Belgium	582-583
Cyprus	219-221
France	1045-1046
Germany	852-853
Greece	739-740
Iceland	348-349
Ireland	184-185
Italy	860-861
Luxembourg	386-387
Netherlands	394-395
Norway	414-415
Switzerland	416-417
Turkey	1553-1555

Nos. 582-583 (2)	.65	.65
Nos. 219-221 (3)	*76.25*	*6.75*
Nos. 1045-1046 (2)	.60	.50
Nos. 852-853 (2)	.65	.75
Nos. 739-740 (2)	2.00	1.15
Nos. 348-349 (2)	.85	.85
Nos. 184-185 (2)	2.00	.50
Nos. 860-861 (2)	1.00	.55
Nos. 386-387 (2)	.75	.55
Nos. 394-395 (2)	1.35	.90
Nos. 414-415 (2)	1.75	1.70
Nos. 416-417 (2)	1.65	1.00
Nos. 1553-1555 (3)	*2.05*	1.10
Set total (28) Stamps	91.55	16.95

Europa, 1963

Stylized Links, Symbolizing Unity — CD6

1963, Sept.

Belgium	598-599
Cyprus	229-231
Finland	419
France	1074-1075
Germany	867-868
Greece	768-769
Iceland	357-358
Ireland	188-189
Italy	880-881
Luxembourg	403-404
Netherlands	416-417
Norway	441-442
Switzerland	429
Turkey	1602-1603

Nos. 598-599 (2)	1.60	.55
Nos. 229-231 (3)	*64.00*	*9.40*
No. 419 (1)	1.25	.55
Nos. 1074-1075 (2)	.60	.50
Nos. 867-868 (2)	.50	.55
Nos. 768-769 (2)	4.65	1.65
Nos. 357-358 (2)	1.20	1.20
Nos. 188-189 (2)	4.75	3.25
Nos. 880-881 (2)	.50	.50
Nos. 403-404 (2)	.75	.55
Nos. 416-417 (2)	1.30	1.00
Nos. 441-442 (2)	2.60	2.40
No. 429 (1)	.90	.60
Nos. 1602-1603 (2)	1.20	.50
Set total (27) Stamps	85.80	23.20

Europa, 1964

Symbolic Daisy — CD7

5th anniversary of the establishment of C.E.P.T. The 22 petals of the flower symbolize the 22 members of the Conference.

1964, Sept.

Austria	738
Belgium	614-615
Cyprus	244-246
France	1109-1110
Germany	897-898
Greece	801-802
Iceland	367-368
Ireland	196-197
Italy	894-895
Luxembourg	411-412
Monaco	590-591
Netherlands	428-429
Norway	458
Portugal	931-933
Spain	1262-1263
Switzerland	438-439
Turkey	1628-1629

No. 738 (1)	1.20	.80
Nos. 614-615 (2)	1.40	.60
Nos. 244-246 (3)	*32.25*	*5.10*
Nos. 1109-1110 (2)	.50	.50
Nos. 897-898 (2)	.50	.50
Nos. 801-802 (2)	4.15	1.55
Nos. 367-368 (2)	1.40	1.15
Nos. 196-197 (2)	17.00	4.25
Nos. 894-895 (2)	.50	.50
Nos. 411-412 (2)	.75	.55
Nos. 590-591 (2)	2.50	.70
Nos. 428-429 (2)	.75	.60
No. 458 (1)	3.50	3.50
Nos. 931-933 (3)	*10.00*	*2.00*
Nos. 1262-1263 (2)	1.15	.80
Nos. 438-439 (2)	1.65	.50
Nos. 1628-1629 (2)	2.00	.80
Set total (34) Stamps	81.20	24.40

Europa, 1965

Leaves and "Fruit" CD8

1965

Belgium	636-637
Cyprus	262-264
Finland	437
France	1131-1132
Germany	934-935
Greece	833-834
Iceland	375-376
Ireland	204-205
Italy	915-916
Luxembourg	432-433
Monaco	616-617
Netherlands	438-439
Norway	475-476
Portugal	958-960
Switzerland	469
Turkey	1665-1666

Nos. 636-637 (2)	.50	.50
Nos. 262-264 (3)	*25.35*	*6.00*
No. 437 (1)	1.25	.55
Nos. 1131-1132 (2)	.70	.55
Nos. 934-935 (2)	.50	.50
Nos. 833-834 (2)	2.25	1.15
Nos. 375-376 (2)	2.50	1.75
Nos. 204-205 (2)	16.00	3.35
Nos. 915-916 (2)	.50	.50
Nos. 432-433 (2)	.75	.55
Nos. 616-617 (2)	3.25	1.65
Nos. 438-439 (2)	.55	.50
Nos. 475-476 (2)	2.40	1.90
Nos. 958-960 (3)	*10.00*	*2.75*
No. 469 (1)	1.15	.50
Nos. 1665-1666 (2)	2.00	1.25
Set total (32) Stamps	69.65	23.95

Europa, 1966

Symbolic Sailboat — CD9

1966, Sept.

Andorra, French	172
Belgium	675-676
Cyprus	275-277
France	1163-1164
Germany	963-964

Greece ... 862-863
Iceland ... 384-385
Ireland ... 216-217
Italy ... 942-943
Liechtenstein ... 415
Luxembourg ... 440-441
Monaco ... 639-640
Netherlands ... 441-442
Norway ... 496-497
Portugal ... 980-982
Switzerland ... 477-478
Turkey ... 1718-1719

No. 172 (1)	3.00	3.00
Nos. 675-676 (2)	.80	.50
Nos. 275-277 (3)	4.75	2.75
Nos. 1163-1164 (2)	.55	.50
Nos. 963-964 (2)	.50	.55
Nos. 862-863 (2)	2.10	1.05
Nos. 384-385 (2)	4.50	3.50
Nos. 216-217 (2)	6.75	2.00
Nos. 942-943 (2)	.50	.50
No. 415 (1)	.40	.35
Nos. 440-441 (2)	.70	.55
Nos. 639-640 (2)	2.00	.65
Nos. 441-442 (2)	.85	.50
Nos. 496-497 (2)	2.35	2.15
Nos. 980-982 (3)	9.75	2.25
Nos. 477-478 (2)	1.40	.60
Nos. 1718-1719 (2)	3.35	1.75
Set total (34) Stamps	44.25	23.15

Europa, 1967

Cogwheels
CD10

1967

Andorra, French ... 174-175
Belgium ... 688-689
Cyprus ... 297-299
France ... 1178-1179
Germany ... 969-970
Greece ... 891-892
Iceland ... 389-390
Ireland ... 232-233
Italy ... 951-952
Liechtenstein ... 420
Luxembourg ... 449-450
Monaco ... 669-670
Netherlands ... 444-447
Norway ... 504-505
Portugal ... 994-996
Spain ... 1465-1466
Switzerland ... 482
Turkey ... B120-B121

Nos. 174-175 (2)	10.75	6.25
Nos. 688-689 (2)	1.05	.55
Nos. 297-299 (3)	4.25	2.50
Nos. 1178-1179 (2)	.55	.50
Nos. 969-970 (2)	.55	.55
Nos. 891-892 (2)	3.05	.85
Nos. 389-390 (2)	3.00	2.00
Nos. 232-233 (2)	5.90	2.30
Nos. 951-952 (2)	.60	.50
No. 420 (1)	.45	.40
Nos. 449-450 (2)	1.00	.70
Nos. 669-670 (2)	2.75	.70
Nos. 444-447 (4)	2.70	2.05
Nos. 504-505 (2)	2.00	1.80
Nos. 994-996 (3)	9.50	1.85
Nos. 1465-1466 (2)	.50	.50
No. 482 (1)	.60	.30
Nos. B120-B121 (2)	2.50	2.00
Set total (38) Stamps	51.70	26.30

Europa, 1968

Golden Key
with
C.E.P.T.
Emblem
CD11

1968

Andorra, French ... 182-183
Belgium ... 705-706
Cyprus ... 314-316
France ... 1209-1210
Germany ... 983-984
Greece ... 916-917
Iceland ... 395-396
Ireland ... 242-243
Italy ... 979-980
Liechtenstein ... 442
Luxembourg ... 466-467
Monaco ... 689-691
Netherlands ... 452-453
Portugal ... 1019-1021
San Marino ... 687
Spain ... 1526
Switzerland ... 488
Turkey ... 1775-1776

Nos. 182-183 (2)	16.50	10.00
Nos. 705-706 (2)	1.25	.50
Nos. 314-316 (3)	2.90	2.50
Nos. 1209-1210 (2)	.85	.55
Nos. 983-984 (2)	.50	.55
Nos. 916-917 (2)	3.10	1.45
Nos. 395-396 (2)	3.00	2.20
Nos. 242-243 (2)	3.30	2.25
Nos. 979-980 (2)	.50	.50
No. 442 (1)	.45	.40
Nos. 466-467 (2)	.80	.70
Nos. 689-691 (3)	5.40	.95
Nos. 452-453 (2)	1.05	.70
Nos. 1019-1021 (3)	9.75	2.10
No. 687 (1)	.55	.35
No. 1526 (1)	.25	.25
No. 488 (1)	.40	.25
Nos. 1775-1776 (2)	2.50	1.25
Set total (35) Stamps	53.05	27.45

Europa, 1969

"EUROPA"
and "CEPT"
CD12

Tenth anniversary of C.E.P.T.

1969

Andorra, French ... 188-189
Austria ... 837
Belgium ... 718-719
Cyprus ... 326-328
Denmark ... 458
Finland ... 483
France ... 1245-1246
Germany ... 996-997
Great Britain ... 585
Greece ... 947-948
Iceland ... 406-407
Ireland ... 270-271
Italy ... 1000-1001
Liechtenstein ... 453
Luxembourg ... 475-476
Monaco ... 722-724
Netherlands ... 475-476
Norway ... 533-534
Portugal ... 1038-1040
San Marino ... 701-702
Spain ... 1567
Sweden ... 814-816
Switzerland ... 500-501
Turkey ... 1799-1800
Vatican ... 470-472
Yugoslavia ... 1003-1004

Nos. 188-189 (2)	18.50	12.00
No. 837 (1)	.65	.30
Nos. 718-719 (2)	.75	.50
Nos. 326-328 (3)	3.00	2.25
No. 458 (1)	.75	.75
No. 483 (1)	3.50	.75
Nos. 1245-1246 (2)	.55	.50
Nos. 996-997 (2)	.70	.50
No. 585 (1)	.25	.25
Nos. 947-948 (2)	4.00	1.25
Nos. 406-407 (2)	4.20	2.40
Nos. 270-271 (2)	3.50	2.00
Nos. 1000-1001 (2)	.50	.50
No. 453 (1)	.45	.45
Nos. 475-476 (2)	.95	.50
Nos. 722-724 (3)	10.50	2.00
Nos. 475-476 (2)	1.35	1.00
Nos. 533-534 (2)	2.20	1.95
Nos. 1038-1040 (3)	17.75	2.40
Nos. 701-702 (2)	.90	.90
No. 1567 (1)	.25	.25
Nos. 814-816 (3)	4.00	2.85
Nos. 500-501 (2)	1.85	1.00
Nos. 1799-1800 (2)	2.50	1.65
Nos. 470-472 (3)	.75	.75
Nos. 1003-1004 (2)	4.00	4.00
Set total (51) Stamps	88.30	43.65

Europa, 1970

Interwoven
Threads
CD13

1970

Andorra, French ... 196-197
Belgium ... 741-742
Cyprus ... 340-342
France ... 1271-1272
Germany ... 1018-1019
Greece ... 985, 987
Iceland ... 420-421
Ireland ... 279-281
Italy ... 1013-1014
Liechtenstein ... 470
Luxembourg ... 489-490
Monaco ... 768-770
Netherlands ... 483-484
Portugal ... 1060-1062
San Marino ... 729-730
Spain ... 1607
Switzerland ... 515-516
Turkey ... 1848-1849
Yugoslavia ... 1024-1025

Nos. 196-197 (2)	20.00	8.50
Nos. 741-742 (2)	1.10	.55
Nos. 340-342 (3)	2.70	2.75
Nos. 1271-1272 (2)	.65	.50
Nos. 1018-1019 (2)	.60	.50
Nos. 985,987 (2)	6.35	1.60
Nos. 420-421 (2)	6.00	4.00
Nos. 279-281 (3)	7.50	2.50
Nos. 1013-1014 (2)	.50	.50
No. 470 (1)	.45	.45
Nos. 489-490 (2)	.80	.55
Nos. 768-770 (3)	6.35	2.10
Nos. 483-484 (2)	1.30	1.15
Nos. 1060-1062 (3)	9.75	2.35
Nos. 729-730 (2)	.90	.55
No. 1607 (1)	.25	.25
Nos. 515-516 (2)	1.85	.70
Nos. 1848-1849 (2)	2.50	1.50
Nos. 1024-1025 (2)	.80	.80
Set total (40) Stamps	70.35	31.80

Europa, 1971

"Fraternity,
Cooperation,
Common
Effort"
CD14

1971

Andorra, French ... 205-206
Belgium ... 803-804
Cyprus ... 365-367
Finland ... 504
France ... 1304
Germany ... 1064-1065
Greece ... 1029-1030
Iceland ... 429-430
Ireland ... 305-306
Italy ... 1038-1039
Liechtenstein ... 485
Luxembourg ... 500-501
Malta ... 425-427
Monaco ... 797-799
Netherlands ... 488-489
Portugal ... 1094-1096
San Marino ... 749-750
Spain ... 1675-1676
Switzerland ... 531-532
Turkey ... 1876-1877
Yugoslavia ... 1052-1053

Nos. 205-206 (2)	20.00	7.75
Nos. 803-804 (2)	1.30	.55
Nos. 365-367 (3)	2.60	3.25
No. 504 (1)	5.00	.75
No. 1304 (1)	.45	.40
Nos. 1064-1065 (2)	.60	.50
Nos. 1029-1030 (2)	4.00	1.80
Nos. 429-430 (2)	5.00	3.75
Nos. 305-306 (2)	4.50	1.50
Nos. 1038-1039 (2)	.65	.50
No. 485 (1)	.45	.45
Nos. 500-501 (2)	1.00	.65
Nos. 425-427 (3)	.80	.80
Nos. 797-799 (3)	15.00	2.80
Nos. 488-489 (2)	1.20	.95
Nos. 1094-1096 (3)	9.75	1.75
Nos. 749-750 (2)	.65	.55
Nos. 1675-1676 (2)	.75	.55
Nos. 531-532 (2)	1.85	.65
Nos. 1876-1877 (2)	2.50	1.25
Nos. 1052-1053 (2)	.50	.50
Set total (43) Stamps	78.55	31.65

Europa, 1972

Sparkles, Symbolic
of Communications
CD15

1972

Andorra, French ... 210-211
Andorra, Spanish ... 62
Belgium ... 825-826
Cyprus ... 380-382
Finland ... 512-513
France ... 1341
Germany ... 1089-1090
Greece ... 1049-1050
Iceland ... 439-440
Ireland ... 316-317
Italy ... 1065-1066
Liechtenstein ... 504
Luxembourg ... 512-513
Malta ... 450-453
Monaco ... 831-832
Netherlands ... 494-495
Portugal ... 1141-1143
San Marino ... 771-772
Spain ... 1718
Switzerland ... 544-545
Turkey ... 1907-1908
Yugoslavia ... 1100-1101

Nos. 210-211 (2)	21.00	7.00
No. 62 (1)	60.00	60.00
Nos. 825-826 (2)	.95	.55
Nos. 380-382 (3)	5.95	4.25
Nos. 512-513 (2)	7.00	1.40
No. 1341 (1)	.50	.35
Nos. 1089-1090 (2)	1.10	.50
Nos. 1049-1050 (2)	2.00	1.55
Nos. 439-440 (2)	2.90	2.65
Nos. 316-317 (2)	13.00	4.50
Nos. 1065-1066 (2)	.55	.50
No. 504 (1)	.45	.45
Nos. 512-513 (2)	.95	.65
Nos. 450-453 (4)	1.05	1.40
Nos. 831-832 (2)	5.00	1.40
Nos. 494-495 (2)	1.20	.90
Nos. 1141-1143 (3)	9.75	1.50
Nos. 771-772 (2)	.70	.50
No. 1718 (1)	.50	.40
Nos. 544-545 (2)	1.65	.60
Nos. 1907-1908 (2)	4.00	2.00
Nos. 1100-1101 (2)	1.20	1.20
Set total (44) Stamps	141.40	94.25

Europa, 1973

Post Horn
and Arrows
CD16

1973

Andorra, French ... 219-220
Andorra, Spanish ... 76
Belgium ... 839-840
Cyprus ... 396-398
Finland ... 526
France ... 1367
Germany ... 1114-1115
Greece ... 1090-1092
Iceland ... 447-448
Ireland ... 329-330
Italy ... 1108-1109
Liechtenstein ... 528-529
Luxembourg ... 523-524
Malta ... 469-471
Monaco ... 866-867
Netherlands ... 504-505
Norway ... 604-605
Portugal ... 1170-1172
San Marino ... 802-803
Spain ... 1753
Switzerland ... 580-581
Turkey ... 1935-1936
Yugoslavia ... 1138-1139

Nos. 219-220 (2)	20.00	11.00
No. 76 (1)	1.25	.85
Nos. 839-840 (2)	1.00	.65
Nos. 396-398 (3)	4.25	3.85
No. 526 (1)	1.25	.55
No. 1367 (1)	1.25	.75
Nos. 1114-1115 (2)	.85	.50
Nos. 1090-1092 (3)	2.10	1.40
Nos. 447-448 (2)	6.65	3.35

Nos. 329-330 (2)	5.25	2.00
Nos. 1108-1109 (2)	.50	.50
Nos. 528-529 (2)	.60	.60
Nos. 523-524 (2)	.90	.75
Nos. 469-471 (3)	.90	1.20
Nos. 866-867 (2)	15.00	2.40
Nos. 504-505 (2)	1.20	.95
Nos. 604-605 (2)	4.00	1.80
Nos. 1170-1172 (3)	*13.00*	2.15
Nos. 802-803 (2)	*1.00*	.60
No. 1753 (1)	.35	.25
Nos. 580-581 (2)	1.55	.60
Nos. 1935-1936 (2)	4.15	2.25
Nos. 1138-1139 (2)	1.15	1.10
Set total (46) Stamps	88.15	40.05

Europa, 2000

CD17

2000

Albania....................2621-2622
Andorra, French....................522
Andorra, Spanish....................262
Armenia....................610-611
Austria....................1814
Azerbaijan....................698-699
Belarus....................350
Belgium....................1818
Bosnia & Herzegovina (Moslem)....358
Bosnia & Herzegovina (Serb)........111-112
Croatia....................428-429
Cyprus....................959
Czech Republic....................3120
Denmark....................1189
Estonia....................394
Faroe Islands....................376
Finland....................1129
Aland Islands....................166
France....................2771
Georgia....................228-229
Germany....................2086-2087
Gibraltar....................837-840
Great Britain (Jersey)....................935-936
Great Britain (Isle of Man)....................883
Greece....................1959
Greenland....................363
Hungary....................3699-3700
Iceland....................910
Ireland....................1230-1231
Italy....................2349
Latvia....................504
Liechtenstein....................1178
Lithuania....................668
Luxembourg....................1035
Macedonia....................187
Malta....................1011-1012
Moldova....................355
Monaco....................2161-2162
Poland....................3519
Portugal....................2358
Portugal (Azores)....................455
Portugal (Madeira)....................208
Romania....................4370
Russia....................6589
San Marino....................1480
Slovakia....................355
Slovenia....................424
Spain....................3036
Sweden....................2394
Switzerland....................1074
Turkey....................2762
Turkish Rep. of Northern Cyprus....500
Ukraine....................379
Vatican City....................1152

Nos. 2621-2622 (2)	11.00	11.00
No. 522 (1)	2.00	1.00
No. 262 (1)	1.75	.80
Nos. 610-611 (2)	4.75	4.75
No. 1814 (1)	1.40	1.40
Nos. 698-699 (2)	6.00	6.00
No. 350 (1)	1.75	1.75
No. 1818 (1)	1.40	.60
No. 358 (1)	4.75	4.75
Nos. 111-112 (2)	110.00	110.00
Nos. 428-429 (2)	6.25	6.25
No. 959 (1)	2.10	1.40
No. 3120 (1)	1.20	.40
No. 1189 (1)	3.50	2.25
No. 394 (1)	1.25	1.25
No. 376 (1)	2.40	2.40
No. 1129 (1)	2.00	.60
No. 166 (1)	2.00	1.10
No. 2771 (1)	1.25	.40
Nos. 228-229 (2)	9.00	9.00
Nos. 2086-2087 (2)	4.35	2.10
Nos. 837-840 (4)	5.50	5.30
Nos. 935-936 (2)	2.40	2.40
No. 883 (1)	1.75	1.75
No. 363 (1)	1.90	1.90
Nos. 3699-3700 (2)	6.50	2.50
No. 910 (1)	1.60	1.60
Nos. 1230-1231 (2)	4.35	4.35
No. 2349 (1)	1.50	.40
No. 504 (1)	5.00	2.40
No. 1178 (1)	2.25	1.75
No. 668 (1)	1.50	1.50
No. 1035 (1)	1.40	.85
No. 187 (1)	3.00	3.00
Nos. 1011-1012 (2)	4.35	4.35
No. 355 (1)	3.50	3.50
Nos. 2161-2162 (2)	2.80	1.40
No. 3519 (1)	1.25	.75
No. 2358 (1)	1.25	.65
No. 455 (1)	1.25	.50
No. 208 (1)	1.25	.50
No. 4370 (1)	2.50	1.25
No. 6589 (1)	4.00	.85
No. 1480 (1)	1.00	1.00
No. 355 (1)	1.60	.80
No. 424 (1)	3.25	3.25
No. 3036 (1)	1.00	.40
No. 2394 (1)	3.00	1.50
No. 1074 (1)	2.10	1.05
No. 2762 (1)	2.75	2.00
No. 500 (1)	2.50	2.50
No. 379 (1)	4.50	3.00
No. 1152 (1)	1.25	1.25
Set total (68) Stamps	263.85	229.40

The Gibraltar stamps are similar to the stamp illustrated, but none have the design shown above. All other sets listed above include at least one stamp with the design shown, but some include stamps with entirely different designs. Bulgaria Nos. 4131-4132, Guernsey Nos. 802-803 and Yugoslavia Nos. 2485-2486 are Europa stamps with completely different designs.

PORTUGAL & COLONIES
Vasco da Gama

Fleet Departing CD20

Fleet Arriving at Calicut — CD21

Embarking at Rastello CD22

Muse of History CD23

San Gabriel, da Gama and Camoens CD24

Archangel Gabriel, the Patron Saint CD25

Flagship San Gabriel — CD26

Vasco da Gama — CD27

Fourth centenary of Vasco da Gama's discovery of the route to India.

1898

Azores....................93-100
Macao....................67-74
Madeira....................37-44
Portugal....................147-154
Port. Africa....................1-8
Port. Congo....................75-98
Port. India....................189-196
St. Thomas & Prince Islands...170-193
Timor....................45-52

Nos. 93-100 (8)	113.50	73.50
Nos. 67-74 (8)	138.75	91.75
Nos. 37-44 (8)	60.55	37.25
Nos. 147-154 (8)	155.00	50.25
Nos. 1-8 (8)	35.00	23.50
Nos. 75-98 (24)	52.15	41.65
Nos. 189-196 (8)	25.25	15.50
Nos. 170-193 (24)	56.30	43.00
Nos. 45-52 (8)	39.75	27.25
Set total (104) Stamps	676.25	403.65

Pombal
POSTAL TAX
POSTAL TAX DUES

Marquis de Pombal — CD28

Planning Reconstruction of Lisbon, 1755 — CD29

Pombal Monument, Lisbon — CD30

Sebastiao Jose de Carvalho e Mello, Marquis de Pombal (1699-1782), statesman, rebuilt Lisbon after earthquake of 1755. Tax was for the erection of Pombal monument. Obligatory on all mail on certain days throughout the year. Postal Tax Dues are inscribed "Multa."

1925

Angola.............RA1-RA3, RAJ1-RAJ3
Azores...........RA9-RA11, RAJ2-RAJ4
Cape Verde......RA1-RA3, RAJ1-RAJ3
Macao.............RA1-RA3, RAJ1-RAJ3
Madeira............RA1-RA3, RAJ1-RAJ3
Mozambique.....RA1-RA3, RAJ1-RAJ3
Nyassa.............RA1-RA3, RAJ1-RAJ3
Portugal........RA11-RA13, RAJ2-RAJ4
Port. Guinea.....RA1-RA3, RAJ1-RAJ3
Port. India........RA1-RA3, RAJ1-RAJ3
St. Thomas & Prince Islands.............RA1-RA3, RAJ1-RAJ3
Timor...............RA1-RA3, RAJ1-RAJ3

Nos. RA1-RA3,RAJ1-RAJ3 (6)	6.60	6.60
Nos. RA9-RA11,RAJ2-RAJ4 (6)	6.60	6.60
Nos. RA1-RA3,RAJ1-RAJ3 (6)	4.50	3.90
Nos. RA1-RA3,RAJ1-RAJ3 (6)	21.25	13.20
Nos. RA1-RA3,RAJ1-RAJ3 (6)	7.95	*14.70*
Nos. RA1-RA3,RAJ1-RAJ3 (6)	2.40	2.55
Nos. RA1-RA3,RAJ1-RAJ3 (6)	63.00	63.00
Nos. RA11-RA13,RAJ2-RAJ4 (6)	5.95	5.20
Nos. RA1-RA3,RAJ1-RAJ3 (6)	5.10	4.65
Nos. RA1-RA3,RAJ1-RAJ3 (6)	3.45	3.45
Nos. RA1-RA3,RAJ1-RAJ3 (6)	4.50	4.50
Nos. RA1-RA3,RAJ1-RAJ3 (6)	2.10	3.90
Set total (72) Stamps	133.40	132.25

Vasco da Gama CD34

Mousinho de Albuquerque CD35

Dam CD36

Prince Henry the Navigator CD37

Affonso de Albuquerque CD38

Plane over Globe CD39

1938-39

Angola....................274-291, C1-C9
Cape Verde....................234-251, C1-C9
Macao....................289-305, C7-C15
Mozambique....................270-287, C1-C9
Port. Guinea....................233-250. C1-C9
Port. India....................439-453, C1-C8
St. Thomas & Prince Islands ... 302-319, 323-340, C1-C18
Timor....................223-239, C1-C9

Nos. 274-291,C1-C9 (27)	129.40	22.85
Nos. 234-251,C1-C9 (27)	87.00	27.15
Nos. 289-305,C7-C15 (26)	495.70	149.20
Nos. 270-287,C1-C9 (27)	63.45	11.20
Nos. 233-250,C1-C9 (27)	130.20	49.15
Nos. 439-453,C1-C8 (23)	82.75	30.95
Nos. 302-319,323-340,C1-C18 (54)	467.70	244.80
Nos. 223-239,C1-C9 (26)	193.55	94.50
Set total (237) Stamps	1,650.	629.80

Lady of Fatima

Our Lady of the Rosary, Fatima, Portugal — CD40

1948-49

Angola....................315-318
Cape Verde....................266
Macao....................336
Mozambique....................325-328
Port. Guinea....................271
Port. India....................480
St. Thomas & Prince Islands..........351
Timor....................254

Nos. 315-318 (4)	68.00	17.25
No. 266 (1)	8.50	4.50
No. 336 (1)	42.50	12.00
Nos. 325-328 (4)	73.25	16.85
No. 271 (1)	6.50	3.50
No. 480 (1)	4.50	3.00
No. 351 (1)	8.50	7.00
No. 254 (1)	6.00	6.00
Set total (14) Stamps	217.75	70.10

A souvenir sheet of 9 stamps was issued in 1951 to mark the extension of the 1950 Holy Year. The sheet contains: Angola No. 316, Cape Verde No. 266, Macao No. 336, Mozambique No. 325, Portuguese Guinea No. 271, Portuguese India Nos. 480, 485, St. Thomas & Prince Islands No. 351, Timor No. 254. The sheet also contains a portrait of Pope Pius XII and is inscribed "Encerramento do

Ano Santo, Fatima 1951." It was sold for 11 escudos.

Holy Year

Church Bells and Dove CD41

Angel Holding Candelabra CD42

Holy Year, 1950.

1950-51

Angola 331-332
Cape Verde 268-269
Macao 339-340
Mozambique 330-331
Port. Guinea 273-274
Port. India 490-491, 496-503
St. Thomas & Prince Islands 353-354
Timor 258-259

Nos. 331-332 (2)	7.60	1.35
Nos. 268-269 (2)	5.50	3.50
Nos. 339-340 (2)	60.00	14.00
Nos. 330-331 (2)	3.00	1.10
Nos. 273-274 (2)	11.25	3.50
Nos. 490-491,496-503 (10)	10.40	4.95
Nos. 353-354 (2)	7.75	4.90
Nos. 258-259 (2)	8.00	4.00
Set total (24) Stamps	113.50	37.30

A souvenir sheet of 8 stamps was issued in 1951 to mark the extension of the Holy Year. The sheet contains: Angola No. 331, Cape Verde No. 269, Macao No. 340, Mozambique No. 331, Portuguese Guinea No. 275, Portuguese India No. 490, St. Thomas & Prince Islands No. 354, Timor No. 258, some with colors changed. The sheet contains doves and is inscribed 'Encerramento do Ano Santo, Fatima 1951.' It was sold for 17 escudos.

Holy Year Conclusion

Our Lady of Fatima — CD43

Conclusion of Holy Year. Sheets contain alternate vertical rows of stamps and labels bearing quotation from Pope Pius XII, different for each colony.

1951

Angola 357
Cape Verde 270
Macao 352
Mozambique 356
Port. Guinea 275
Port. India 506
St. Thomas & Prince Islands 355
Timor 270

No. 357 (1)	5.25	1.50
No. 270 (1)	1.50	1.25
No. 352 (1)	45.00	10.00
No. 356 (1)	2.25	1.00
No. 275 (1)	1.75	.90
No. 506 (1)	2.50	1.00
No. 355 (1)	3.00	2.00
No. 270 (1)	5.75	2.40
Set total (8) Stamps	67.00	20.05

Medical Congress

CD44

First National Congress of Tropical Medicine, Lisbon, 1952. Each stamp has a different design.

1952

Angola 358
Cape Verde 287
Macao 364
Mozambique 359
Port. Guinea 276
Port. India 516
St. Thomas & Prince Islands 356
Timor 271

No. 358 (1)	1.50	.50
No. 287 (1)	.75	.60
No. 364 (1)	10.00	6.00
No. 359 (1)	1.25	.55
No. 276 (1)	1.00	.45
No. 516 (1)	5.50	2.00
No. 356 (1)	.35	.30
No. 271 (1)	2.50	1.30
Set total (8) Stamps	22.85	11.70

Postage Due Stamps

CD45

1952

Angola J37-J42
Cape Verde J31-J36
Macao J53-J58
Mozambique J51-J56
Port. Guinea J40-J45
Port. India J47-J52
St. Thomas & Prince Islands J52-J57
Timor J31-J36

Nos. J37-J42 (6)	4.30	2.55
Nos. J31-J36 (6)	2.80	2.30
Nos. J53-J58 (6)	17.45	6.85
Nos. J51-J56 (6)	1.80	1.55
Nos. J40-J45 (6)	2.55	2.55
Nos. J47-J52 (6)	6.10	6.10
Nos. J52-J57 (6)	3.85	3.85
Nos. J31-J36 (6)	6.20	3.50
Set total (48) Stamps	45.05	29.25

Sao Paulo

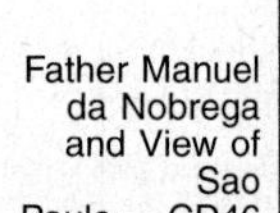

Father Manuel da Nobrega and View of Sao Paulo — CD46

Founding of Sao Paulo, Brazil, 400th anniv.

1954

Angola 385
Cape Verde 297
Macao 382
Mozambique 395
Port. Guinea 291
Port. India 530
St. Thomas & Prince Islands 369
Timor 279

No. 385 (1)	.80	.50
No. 297 (1)	.70	.60
No. 382 (1)	15.00	6.00
No. 395 (1)	.40	.30
No. 291 (1)	.35	.25
No. 530 (1)	.80	.40
No. 369 (1)	.70	.50
No. 279 (1)	3.00	1.25
Set total (8) Stamps	21.75	9.80

Tropical Medicine Congress

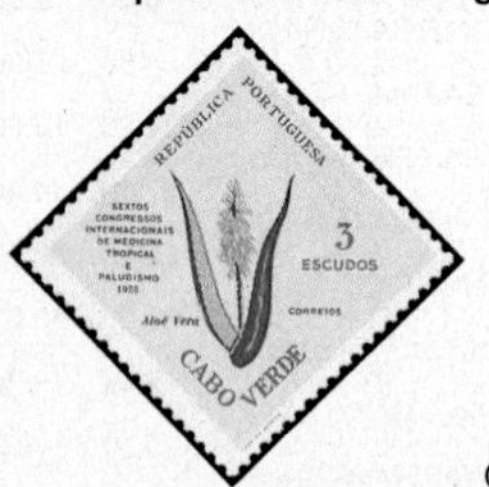

CD47

Sixth International Congress for Tropical Medicine and Malaria, Lisbon, Sept. 1958. Each stamp shows a different plant.

1958

Angola 409
Cape Verde 303
Macao 392
Mozambique 404
Port. Guinea 295
Port. India 569
St. Thomas & Prince Islands 371
Timor 289

No. 409 (1)	3.50	1.10
No. 303 (1)	5.50	2.10
No. 392 (1)	10.00	5.00
No. 404 (1)	2.50	.85
No. 295 (1)	3.00	1.10
No. 569 (1)	1.75	.75
No. 371 (1)	2.75	2.00
No. 289 (1)	3.50	2.75
Set total (8) Stamps	32.50	15.65

Sports

CD48

Each stamp shows a different sport.

1962

Angola 433-438
Cape Verde 320-325
Macao 394-399
Mozambique 424-429
Port. Guinea 299-304
St. Thomas & Prince Islands 374-379
Timor 313-318

Nos. 433-438 (6)	5.50	3.20
Nos. 320-325 (6)	15.25	5.20
Nos. 394-399 (6)	68.65	14.60
Nos. 424-429 (6)	5.70	2.45
Nos. 299-304 (6)	6.00	3.00
Nos. 374-379 (6)	6.75	3.20
Nos. 313-318 (6)	9.15	5.05
Set total (42) Stamps	117.00	36.70

Anti-Malaria

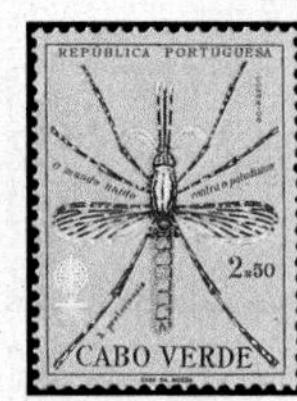

Anopheles Funestus and Malaria Eradication Symbol — CD49

World Health Organization drive to eradicate malaria.

1962

Angola 439
Cape Verde 326
Macao 400
Mozambique 430
Port. Guinea 305
St. Thomas & Prince Islands 380
Timor 319

No. 439 (1)	1.75	.90
No. 326 (1)	1.40	.90
No. 400 (1)	7.00	2.25
No. 430 (1)	1.40	.40
No. 305 (1)	1.25	.45
No. 380 (1)	2.25	1.25
No. 319 (1)	1.50	1.00
Set total (7) Stamps	16.55	7.15

Airline Anniversary

Map of Africa, Super Constellation and Jet Liner — CD50

Tenth anniversary of Transportes Aereos Portugueses (TAP).

1963

Angola 490
Cape Verde 327
Mozambique 434
Port. Guinea 318
St. Thomas & Prince Islands 381

No. 490 (1)	1.00	.35
No. 327 (1)	1.10	.70
No. 434 (1)	.40	.25
No. 318 (1)	.65	.35
No. 381 (1)	.80	.50
Set total (5) Stamps	3.95	2.15

National Overseas Bank

Antonio Teixeira de Sousa — CD51

Centenary of the National Overseas Bank of Portugal.

1964, May 16

Angola 509
Cape Verde 328
Port. Guinea 319
St. Thomas & Prince Islands 382
Timor 320

No. 509 (1)	.90	.30
No. 328 (1)	1.10	.75
No. 319 (1)	.65	.40
No. 382 (1)	.70	.50
No. 320 (1)	1.50	.85
Set total (5) Stamps	4.85	2.80

ITU

ITU Emblem and the Archangel Gabriel — CD52

International Communications Union, Cent.

1965, May 17

Angola 511
Cape Verde 329
Macao 402
Mozambique 464
Port. Guinea 320
St. Thomas & Prince Islands 383
Timor 321

No. 511 (1)	1.25	.65
No. 329 (1)	2.10	1.40
No. 402 (1)	6.00	2.25
No. 464 (1)	.45	.25
No. 320 (1)	1.90	.75
No. 383 (1)	2.00	1.00
No. 321 (1)	1.50	.90
Set total (7) Stamps	15.20	7.20

National Revolution

CD53

40th anniv. of the National Revolution. Different buildings on each stamp.

1966, May 28

Angola 525
Cape Verde 338
Macao 403
Mozambique 465
Port. Guinea 329
St. Thomas & Prince Islands 392
Timor 322

No. 525 (1)	.50	.25
No. 338 (1)	.60	.45
No. 403 (1)	9.00	2.25
No. 465 (1)	.50	.30
No. 329 (1)	.55	.35
No. 392 (1)	.85	.50
No. 322 (1)	1.75	.95
Set total (7) Stamps	13.70	5.05

Navy Club

CD54

Centenary of Portugal's Navy Club. Each stamp has a different design.

1967, Jan. 31

Angola	527-528
Cape Verde	339-340
Macao	412-413
Mozambique	478-479
Port. Guinea	330-331
St. Thomas & Prince Islands	393-394
Timor	323-324

Nos. 527-528 (2)	1.75	.75
Nos. 339-340 (2)	2.00	1.40
Nos. 412-413 (2)	11.25	4.00
Nos. 478-479 (2)	1.40	.65
Nos. 330-331 (2)	1.20	.90
Nos. 393-394 (2)	3.30	1.30
Nos. 323-324 (2)	4.65	1.90
Set total (14) Stamps	25.55	10.90

Admiral Coutinho

CD55

Centenary of the birth of Admiral Carlos Viegas Gago Coutinho (1869-1959), explorer and aviation pioneer. Each stamp has a different design.

1969, Feb. 17

Angola	547
Cape Verde	355
Macao	417
Mozambique	484
Port. Guinea	335
St. Thomas & Prince Islands	397
Timor	335

No. 547 (1)	.85	.35
No. 355 (1)	.50	.25
No. 417 (1)	5.00	1.75
No. 484 (1)	.25	.25
No. 335 (1)	.35	.25
No. 397 (1)	.60	.35
No. 335 (1)	2.50	1.05
Set total (7) Stamps	10.05	4.25

Administration Reform

Luiz Augusto Rebello da Silva — CD56

Centenary of the administration reforms of the overseas territories.

1969, Sept. 25

Angola	549
Cape Verde	357
Macao	419
Mozambique	491
Port. Guinea	337
St. Thomas & Prince Islands	399
Timor	338

No. 549 (1)	.35	.25
No. 357 (1)	.50	.25
No. 419 (1)	6.00	1.00
No. 491 (1)	.25	.25
No. 337 (1)	.25	.25
No. 399 (1)	.45	.45
No. 338 (1)	1.25	.50
Set total (7) Stamps	9.05	2.95

Marshal Carmona

CD57

Birth centenary of Marshal Antonio Oscar Carmona de Fragoso (1869-1951), President of Portugal. Each stamp has a different design.

1970, Nov. 15

Angola	563
Cape Verde	359
Macao	422
Mozambique	493
Port. Guinea	340
St. Thomas & Prince Islands	403
Timor	341

No. 563 (1)	.45	.25
No. 359 (1)	.55	.35
No. 422 (1)	2.00	1.00
No. 493 (1)	.40	.25
No. 340 (1)	.35	.25
No. 403 (1)	.75	.40
No. 341 (1)	1.00	.35
Set total (7) Stamps	5.50	2.85

Olympic Games

CD59

20th Olympic Games, Munich, Aug. 26-Sept. 11. Each stamp shows a different sport.

1972, June 20

Angola	569
Cape Verde	361
Macao	426
Mozambique	504
Port. Guinea	342
St. Thomas & Prince Islands	408
Timor	343

No. 569 (1)	.65	.25
No. 361 (1)	.85	.30
No. 426 (1)	4.25	1.00
No. 504 (1)	.30	.25
No. 342 (1)	.45	.25
No. 408 (1)	.45	.25
No. 343 (1)	1.60	.80
Set total (7) Stamps	8.55	3.10

Lisbon-Rio de Janeiro Flight

CD60

50th anniversary of the Lisbon to Rio de Janeiro flight by Arturo de Sacadura and Coutinho, March 30-June 5, 1922. Each stamp shows a different stage of the flight.

1972, Sept. 20

Angola	570
Cape Verde	362
Macao	427
Mozambique	505
Port. Guinea	343
St. Thomas & Prince Islands	409
Timor	344

No. 570 (1)	.35	.25
No. 362 (1)	1.50	.30
No. 427 (1)	22.50	8.50
No. 505 (1)	.25	.25
No. 343 (1)	.25	.25
No. 409 (1)	.50	.25
No. 344 (1)	1.40	.60
Set total (7) Stamps	26.75	10.40

WMO Centenary

WMO Emblem — CD61

Centenary of international meterological cooperation.

1973, Dec. 15

Angola	571
Cape Verde	363
Macao	429
Mozambique	509
Port. Guinea	344
St. Thomas & Prince Islands	410
Timor	345

No. 571 (1)	.45	.25
No. 363 (1)	.65	.30
No. 429 (1)	6.00	1.75
No. 509 (1)	.30	.25
No. 344 (1)	.45	.35
No. 410 (1)	.60	.50
No. 345 (1)	4.25	2.50
Set total (7) Stamps	12.70	5.90

FRENCH COMMUNITY

Upper Volta can be found under Burkina Faso in Vol. 1
Madagascar can be found under Malagasy in Vol. 3

Colonial Exposition

People of French Empire CD70

Women's Heads CD71

France Showing Way to Civilization CD72

"Colonial Commerce" CD73

International Colonial Exposition, Paris.

1931

Cameroun	213-216
Chad	60-63
Dahomey	97-100
Fr. Guiana	152-155
Fr. Guinea	116-119
Fr. India	100-103
Fr. Polynesia	76-79
Fr. Sudan	102-105
Gabon	120-123
Guadeloupe	138-141
Indo-China	140-142
Ivory Coast	92-95
Madagascar	169-172
Martinique	129-132
Mauritania	65-68
Middle Congo	61-64
New Caledonia	176-179
Niger	73-76
Reunion	122-125
St. Pierre & Miquelon	132-135
Senegal	138-141
Somali Coast	135-138
Togo	254-257
Ubangi-Shari	82-85
Upper Volta	66-69
Wallis & Futuna Isls.	85-88

Nos. 213-216 (4)	23.00	18.25
Nos. 60-63 (4)	22.00	22.00
Nos. 97-100 (4)	26.00	26.00
Nos. 152-155 (4)	22.00	22.00
Nos. 116-119 (4)	19.75	19.75
Nos. 100-103 (4)	18.00	*18.00*
Nos. 76-79 (4)	30.00	30.00
Nos. 102-105 (4)	19.00	19.00
Nos. 120-123 (4)	17.50	17.50
Nos. 138-141 (4)	19.00	19.00
Nos. 140-142 (3)	12.00	11.50
Nos. 92-95 (4)	22.50	22.50
Nos. 169-172 (4)	9.25	6.50
Nos. 129-132 (4)	21.00	21.00
Nos. 65-68 (4)	22.00	22.00
Nos. 61-64 (4)	20.00	18.50
Nos. 176-179 (4)	24.00	24.00
Nos. 73-76 (4)	20.50	20.50
Nos. 122-125 (4)	22.00	22.00
Nos. 132-135 (4)	24.00	24.00
Nos. 138-141 (4)	20.00	20.00
Nos. 135-138 (4)	22.00	22.00
Nos. 254-257 (4)	22.00	22.00
Nos. 82-85 (4)	21.00	21.00
Nos. 66-69 (4)	19.00	19.00
Nos. 85-88 (4)	31.00	35.00
Set total (103) Stamps	548.50	543.00

Paris International Exposition Colonial Arts Exposition

"Colonial Resources"
CD74 CD77

Overseas Commerce CD75

Exposition Building and Women CD76

"France and the Empire" CD78

Cultural Treasures of the Colonies CD79

Souvenir sheets contain one imperf. stamp.

1937

Cameroun	217-222A
Dahomey	101-107
Fr. Equatorial Africa	27-32, 73
Fr. Guiana	162-168
Fr. Guinea	120-126
Fr. India	104-110
Fr. Polynesia	117-123
Fr. Sudan	106-112
Guadeloupe	148-154
Indo-China	193-199
Inini	41
Ivory Coast	152-158
Kwangchowan	132
Madagascar	191-197
Martinique	179-185
Mauritania	69-75
New Caledonia	208-214
Niger	77-83
Reunion	167-173
St. Pierre & Miquelon	165-171
Senegal	172-178
Somali Coast	139-145
Togo	258-264
Wallis & Futuna Isls.	89

Nos. 217-222A (7)	18.80	20.30
Nos. 101-107 (7)	23.60	27.60
Nos. 27-32, 73 (7)	28.10	32.10
Nos. 162-168 (7)	22.50	24.50
Nos. 120-126 (7)	24.00	28.00
Nos. 104-110 (7)	21.15	36.50
Nos. 117-123 (7)	58.50	75.00
Nos. 106-112 (7)	23.60	27.60
Nos. 148-154 (7)	19.55	21.05
Nos. 193-199 (7)	17.70	19.70
No. 41 (1)	21.00	27.50
Nos. 152-158 (7)	22.20	26.20
No. 132 (1)	9.25	11.00
Nos. 191-197 (7)	19.25	21.75
Nos. 179-185 (7)	19.95	21.70
Nos. 69-75 (7)	20.50	24.50
Nos. 208-214 (7)	39.00	50.50
Nos. 73-83 (11)	40.60	45.10
Nos. 167-173 (7)	21.70	23.20
Nos. 165-171 (7)	49.60	64.00
Nos. 172-178 (7)	21.00	23.80
Nos. 139-145 (7)	25.60	32.60
Nos. 258-264 (7)	20.40	20.40
No. 89 (1)	19.00	37.50
Set total (154) Stamps	606.55	742.10

Curie

Pierre and Marie Curie CD80

40th anniversary of the discovery of radium. The surtax was for the benefit of the Intl. Union for the Control of Cancer.

1938

Cameroun	B1
Cuba	B1-B2
Dahomey	B2
France	B76
Fr. Equatorial Africa	B1
Fr. Guiana	B3
Fr. Guinea	B2
Fr. India	B6
Fr. Polynesia	B5
Fr. Sudan	B1
Guadeloupe	B3
Indo-China	B14
Ivory Coast	B2
Madagascar	B2
Martinique	B2
Mauritania	B3
New Caledonia	B4
Niger	B1
Reunion	B4
St. Pierre & Miquelon	B3
Senegal	B3
Somali Coast	B2
Togo	B1

No. B1 (1)	10.00	10.00
Nos. B1-B2 (2)	12.00	3.35
No. B2 (1)	9.50	9.50
No. B76 (1)	21.00	12.50
No. B1 (1)	24.00	24.00
No. B3 (1)	13.50	13.50
No. B2 (1)	8.75	8.75
No. B6 (1)	10.00	10.00
No. B5 (1)	20.00	20.00
No. B1 (1)	12.50	12.50
No. B3 (1)	11.00	10.50
No. B14 (1)	12.00	12.00
No. B2 (1)	11.00	7.50
No. B2 (1)	11.00	11.00
No. B2 (1)	13.00	13.00
No. B3 (1)	7.75	7.75
No. B4 (1)	16.50	17.50
No. B1 (1)	16.50	16.50
No. B4 (1)	14.00	14.00
No. B3 (1)	21.00	22.50
No. B3 (1)	10.50	10.50
No. B2 (1)	7.75	7.75
No. B1 (1)	20.00	20.00
Set total (24) Stamps	313.25	294.60

Caillie

Rene Caillie and Map of Northwestern Africa — CD81

Death centenary of Rene Caillie (1799-1838), French explorer. All three denominations exist with colony name omitted.

1939

Dahomey	108-110
Fr. Guinea	161-163
Fr. Sudan	113-115
Ivory Coast	160-162
Mauritania	109-111
Niger	84-86
Senegal	188-190
Togo	265-267

Nos. 108-110 (3)	1.20	3.60
Nos. 161-163 (3)	1.20	3.20
Nos. 113-115 (3)	1.20	3.20
Nos. 160-162 (3)	1.05	2.55
Nos. 109-111 (3)	1.05	3.80
Nos. 84-86 (3)	2.35	2.35
Nos. 188-190 (3)	1.05	2.90
Nos. 265-267 (3)	1.05	3.30
Set total (24) Stamps	10.15	24.90

New York World's Fair

Natives and New York Skyline CD82

1939

Cameroun	223-224
Dahomey	111-112
Fr. Equatorial Africa	78-79
Fr. Guiana	169-170
Fr. Guinea	164-165
Fr. India	111-112
Fr. Polynesia	124-125
Fr. Sudan	116-117
Guadeloupe	155-156
Indo-China	203-204
Inini	42-43
Ivory Coast	163-164
Kwangchowan	133-134
Madagascar	209-210
Martinique	186-187
Mauritania	112-113
New Caledonia	215-216
Niger	87-88
Reunion	174-175
St. Pierre & Miquelon	205-206
Senegal	191-192
Somali Coast	179-180
Togo	268-269
Wallis & Futuna Isls.	90-91

Nos. 223-224 (2)	2.80	2.40
Nos. 111-112 (2)	1.60	3.20
Nos. 78-79 (2)	1.60	3.20
Nos. 169-170 (2)	2.60	2.60
Nos. 164-165 (2)	1.60	3.20
Nos. 111-112 (2)	3.00	*8.00*
Nos. 124-125 (2)	4.80	4.80
Nos. 116-117 (2)	1.60	3.20
Nos. 155-156 (2)	2.50	2.50
Nos. 203-204 (2)	2.05	2.05
Nos. 42-43 (2)	7.50	9.00
Nos. 163-164 (2)	1.50	3.00
Nos. 133-134 (2)	2.50	2.50
Nos. 209-210 (2)	1.50	2.50
Nos. 186-187 (2)	2.35	2.35
Nos. 112-113 (2)	1.40	2.80
Nos. 215-216 (2)	3.35	3.35
Nos. 87-88 (2)	1.60	2.80
Nos. 174-175 (2)	2.80	2.80
Nos. 205-206 (2)	4.80	6.00
Nos. 191-192 (2)	1.40	2.80
Nos. 179-180 (2)	1.40	2.80
Nos. 268-269 (2)	1.40	2.80
Nos. 90-91 (2)	5.00	6.00
Set total (48) Stamps	62.65	86.65

French Revolution

Storming of the Bastille CD83

French Revolution, 150th anniv. The surtax was for the defense of the colonies.

1939

Cameroun	B2-B6
Dahomey	B3-B7
Fr. Equatorial Africa	B4-B8, CB1
Fr. Guiana	B4-B8, CB1
Fr. Guinea	B3-B7
Fr. India	B7-B11
Fr. Polynesia	B6-B10, CB1
Fr. Sudan	B2-B6
Guadeloupe	B4-B8
Indo-China	B15-B19, CB1
Inini	B1-B5
Ivory Coast	B3-B7
Kwangchowan	B1-B5
Madagascar	B3-B7, CB1
Martinique	B3-B7
Mauritania	B4-B8
New Caledonia	B5-B9, CB1
Niger	B2-B6
Reunion	B5-B9, CB1
St. Pierre & Miquelon	B4-B8
Senegal	B4-B8, CB1
Somali Coast	B3-B7
Togo	B2-B6
Wallis & Futuna Isls.	B1-B5

Nos. B2-B6 (5)	60.00	60.00
Nos. B3-B7 (5)	47.50	47.50
Nos. B4-B8,CB1 (6)	120.00	120.00
Nos. B4-B8,CB1 (6)	79.50	79.50
Nos. B3-B7 (5)	47.50	47.50
Nos. B7-B11 (5)	28.75	*32.50*
Nos. B6-B10,CB1 (6)	122.50	122.50
Nos. B2-B6 (5)	50.00	50.00
Nos. B4-B8 (5)	50.00	50.00
Nos. B15-B19,CB1 (6)	85.00	85.00
Nos. B1-B5 (5)	80.00	100.00
Nos. B3-B7 (5)	43.75	43.75
Nos. B1-B5 (5)	46.25	46.25
Nos. B3-B7,CB1 (6)	65.50	65.50
Nos. B3-B7 (5)	52.50	52.50
Nos. B4-B8 (5)	42.50	42.50
Nos. B5-B9,CB1 (6)	101.50	101.50
Nos. B2-B6 (5)	60.00	60.00
Nos. B5-B9,CB1 (6)	87.50	87.50
Nos. B4-B8 (5)	67.50	72.50
Nos. B4-B8,CB1 (6)	56.50	56.50
Nos. B3-B7 (5)	45.00	45.00
Nos. B2-B6 (5)	42.50	42.50
Nos. B1-B5 (5)	80.00	110.00
Set total (128) Stamps	1,562.	1,621.

Plane over Coastal Area CD85

All five denominations exist with colony name omitted.

1940

Dahomey	C1-C5
Fr. Guinea	C1-C5
Fr. Sudan	C1-C5
Ivory Coast	C1-C5
Mauritania	C1-C5
Niger	C1-C5
Senegal	C12-C16
Togo	C1-C5

Nos. C1-C5 (5)	4.00	4.00
Nos. C1-C5 (5)	4.00	4.00
Nos. C1-C5 (5)	4.00	4.00
Nos. C1-C5 (5)	3.80	3.80
Nos. C1-C5 (5)	3.50	3.50
Nos. C1-C5 (5)	3.50	3.50
Nos. C12-C16 (5)	3.50	3.50
Nos. C1-C5 (5)	3.15	3.15
Set total (40) Stamps	29.45	29.45

Defense of the Empire

Colonial Infantryman — CD86

1941

Cameroun	B13B
Dahomey	B13
Fr. Equatorial Africa	B8B
Fr. Guiana	B10
Fr. Guinea	B13
Fr. India	B13
Fr. Polynesia	B12
Fr. Sudan	B12
Guadeloupe	B10
Indo-China	B19B
Inini	B7
Ivory Coast	B13
Kwangchowan	B7
Madagascar	B9
Martinique	B9
Mauritania	B14
New Caledonia	B11
Niger	B12
Reunion	B11
St. Pierre & Miquelon	B8B
Senegal	B14
Somali Coast	B9
Togo	B10B
Wallis & Futuna Isls.	B7

No. B13B (1)	1.60
No. B13 (1)	1.20
No. B8B (1)	3.50
No. B10 (1)	1.40
No. B13 (1)	1.40
No. B13 (1)	1.25
No. B12 (1)	3.50
No. B12 (1)	1.40
No. B10 (1)	1.00
No. B19B (1)	3.00
No. B7 (1)	1.75
No. B13 (1)	1.25
No. B7 (1)	.85
No. B9 (1)	1.50
No. B9 (1)	1.40
No. B14 (1)	.95
No. B12 (1)	1.40
No. B11 (1)	1.60
No. B8B (1)	4.50
No. B14 (1)	1.25
No. B9 (1)	1.60
No. B10B (1)	1.10
No. B7 (1)	1.75
Set total (23) Stamps	40.15

Each of the CD86 stamps listed above is part of a set of three stamps. The designs of the other two stamps in the set vary from country to country. Only the values of the Common Design stamps are listed here.

Colonial Education Fund

CD86a

1942

Cameroun	CB3
Dahomey	CB4
Fr. Equatorial Africa	CB5
Fr. Guiana	CB4
Fr. Guinea	CB4
Fr. India	CB3
Fr. Polynesia	CB4
Fr. Sudan	CB4
Guadeloupe	CB3
Indo-China	CB5
Inini	CB3
Ivory Coast	CB4
Kwangchowan	CB4
Malagasy	CB5
Martinique	CB3
Mauritania	CB4
New Caledonia	CB4
Niger	CB4
Reunion	CB4
St. Pierre & Miquelon	CB3
Senegal	CB5
Somali Coast	CB3
Togo	CB3
Wallis & Futuna	CB3

No. CB3 (1)	1.10	
No. CB4 (1)	.80	5.50
No. CB5 (1)	.80	
No. CB4 (1)	1.10	
No. CB4 (1)	.40	5.50
No. CB3 (1)	.90	
No. CB4 (1)	2.00	
No. CB4 (1)	.40	5.50
No. CB3 (1)	1.10	
No. CB5 (1)	2.00	
No. CB3 (1)	1.25	
No. CB4 (1)	1.00	5.50
No. CB4 (1)	1.00	
No. CB5 (1)	.65	
No. CB3 (1)	1.00	
No. CB4 (1)	.80	
No. CB4 (1)	2.25	
No. CB4 (1)	.35	
No. CB4 (1)	.90	
No. CB3 (1)	7.00	
No. CB5 (1)	.80	6.50
No. CB3 (1)	.70	
No. CB3 (1)	.35	
No. CB3 (1)	2.00	
Set total (24) Stamps	30.65	28.50

Cross of Lorraine & Four-motor Plane CD87

1941-5

Cameroun	C1-C7
Fr. Equatorial Africa	C17-C23
Fr. Guiana	C9-C10
Fr. India	C1-C6
Fr. Polynesia	C3-C9
Fr. West Africa	C1-C3
Guadeloupe	C1-C2
Madagascar	C37-C43

Martinique C1-C2
New Caledonia C7-C13
Reunion C18-C24
St. Pierre & Miquelon C1-C7
Somali Coast C1-C7

Nos. C1-C7 (7)	6.30	6.30
Nos. C17-C23 (7)	10.40	6.35
Nos. C9-C10 (2)	3.80	3.10
Nos. C1-C6 (6)	9.30	*15.00*
Nos. C3-C9 (7)	13.75	10.00
Nos. C1-C3 (3)	9.50	3.90
Nos. C1-C2 (2)	3.75	2.50
Nos. C37-C43 (7)	5.60	3.80
Nos. C1-C2 (2)	3.00	1.60
Nos. C7-C13 (7)	8.85	7.30
Nos. C18-C24 (7)	7.05	5.00
Nos. C1-C7 (7)	11.60	9.40
Nos. C1-C7 (7)	13.95	11.10
Set total (71) Stamps	106.85	85.35

Somali Coast stamps are inscribed "Djibouti".

Transport Plane CD88

Caravan and Plane CD89

1942

Dahomey C6-C13
Fr. Guinea C6-C13
Fr. Sudan C6-C13
Ivory Coast C6-C13
Mauritania C6-C13
Niger C6-C13
Senegal C17-C25
Togo C6-C13

Nos. C6-C13 (8)	7.15
Nos. C6-C13 (8)	5.75
Nos. C6-C13 (8)	8.00
Nos. C6-C13 (8)	11.15
Nos. C6-C13 (8)	9.75
Nos. C6-C13 (8)	6.20
Nos. C17-C25 (9)	9.45
Nos. C6-C13 (8)	6.75
Set total (65) Stamps	64.20

Red Cross

Marianne CD90

The surtax was for the French Red Cross and national relief.

1944

Cameroun B28
Fr. Equatorial Africa B38
Fr. Guiana B12
Fr. India B14
Fr. Polynesia B13
Fr. West Africa B1
Guadeloupe B12
Madagascar B15
Martinique B11
New Caledonia B13
Reunion B15
St. Pierre & Miquelon B13
Somali Coast B13
Wallis & Futuna Isls. B9

No. B28 (1)	2.00	1.60
No. B38 (1)	1.60	1.20
No. B12 (1)	1.75	1.25
No. B14 (1)	1.50	1.25
No. B13 (1)	2.00	1.60
No. B1 (1)	6.50	4.75
No. B12 (1)	1.40	1.00
No. B15 (1)	.90	.90
No. B11 (1)	1.20	1.20
No. B13 (1)	1.50	1.50
No. B15 (1)	1.60	1.10
No. B13 (1)	2.60	2.60
No. B13 (1)	1.75	2.00
No. B9 (1)	3.00	3.00
Set total (14) Stamps	29.30	24.95

Eboue

CD91

Felix Eboue, first French colonial administrator to proclaim resistance to Germany after French surrender in World War II.

1945

Cameroun 296-297
Fr. Equatorial Africa 156-157
Fr. Guiana 171-172
Fr. India 210-211
Fr. Polynesia 150-151
Fr. West Africa 15-16
Guadeloupe 187-188
Madagascar 259-260
Martinique 196-197
New Caledonia 274-275
Reunion 238-239
St. Pierre & Miquelon 322-323
Somali Coast 238-239

Nos. 296-297 (2)	2.40	1.95
Nos. 156-157 (2)	2.55	2.00
Nos. 171-172 (2)	2.45	2.00
Nos. 210-211 (2)	2.20	1.95
Nos. 150-151 (2)	3.60	2.85
Nos. 15-16 (2)	2.40	2.40
Nos. 187-188 (2)	2.05	1.60
Nos. 259-260 (2)	2.00	1.45
Nos. 196-197 (2)	2.05	1.55
Nos. 274-275 (2)	3.40	3.00
Nos. 238-239 (2)	2.40	2.00
Nos. 322-323 (2)	4.40	3.45
Nos. 238-239 (2)	2.45	2.10
Set total (26) Stamps	34.35	28.30

Victory

Victory — CD92

European victory of the Allied Nations in World War II.

1946, May 8

Cameroun C8
Fr. Equatorial Africa C24
Fr. Guiana C11
Fr. India C7
Fr. Polynesia C10
Fr. West Africa C4
Guadeloupe C3
Indo-China C19
Madagascar C44
Martinique C3
New Caledonia C14
Reunion C25
St. Pierre & Miquelon C8
Somali Coast C8
Wallis & Futuna Isls. C1

No. C8 (1)	1.60	1.20
No. C24 (1)	1.60	1.25
No. C11 (1)	1.75	1.25
No. C7 (1)	1.00	4.00
No. C10 (1)	2.75	2.00
No. C4 (1)	1.60	1.20
No. C3 (1)	1.25	1.00
No. C19 (1)	1.00	.55
No. C44 (1)	1.00	.35
No. C3 (1)	1.30	1.00
No. C14 (1)	1.50	1.25
No. C25 (1)	1.10	.90
No. C8 (1)	2.10	2.10
No. C8 (1)	1.75	1.40
No. C1 (1)	2.25	1.90
Set total (15) Stamps	23.55	21.35

Chad to Rhine

Leclerc's Departure from Chad — CD93

Battle at Cufra Oasis — CD94

Tanks in Action, Mareth — CD95

Normandy Invasion — CD96

Entering Paris — CD97

Liberation of Strasbourg — CD98

"Chad to the Rhine" march, 1942-44, by Gen. Jacques Leclerc's column, later French 2nd Armored Division.

1946, June 6

Cameroun C9-C14
Fr. Equatorial Africa C25-C30
Fr. Guiana C12-C17
Fr. India C8-C13
Fr. Polynesia C11-C16
Fr. West Africa C5-C10
Guadeloupe C4-C9
Indo-China C20-C25
Madagascar C45-C50
Martinique C4-C9
New Caledonia C15-C20
Reunion C26-C31
St. Pierre & Miquelon C9-C14
Somali Coast C9-C14
Wallis & Futuna Isls. C2-C7

Nos. C9-C14 (6)	12.05	9.70
Nos. C25-C30 (6)	14.70	10.80
Nos. C12-C17 (6)	12.65	10.35
Nos. C8-C13 (6)	12.80	*15.00*
Nos. C11-C16 (6)	17.55	13.40
Nos. C5-C10 (6)	16.05	11.95
Nos. C4-C9 (6)	12.00	9.60
Nos. C20-C25 (6)	6.40	6.40
Nos. C45-C50 (6)	10.30	8.40
Nos. C4-C9 (6)	8.85	7.30
Nos. C15-C20 (6)	13.40	11.90
Nos. C26-C31 (6)	10.25	6.55
Nos. C9-C14 (6)	17.30	14.35
Nos. C9-C14 (6)	18.10	12.65
Nos. C2-C7 (6)	13.75	10.45
Set total (90) Stamps	196.15	158.80

UPU

French Colonials, Globe and Plane — CD99

Universal Postal Union, 75th anniv.

1949, July 4

Cameroun C29
Fr. Equatorial Africa C34
Fr. India C17
Fr. Polynesia C20
Fr. West Africa C15
Indo-China C26
Madagascar C55
New Caledonia C24
St. Pierre & Miquelon C18
Somali Coast C18
Togo C18
Wallis & Futuna Isls. C10

No. C29 (1)	8.00	4.75
No. C34 (1)	16.00	12.00
No. C17 (1)	11.50	8.75
No. C20 (1)	20.00	15.00
No. C15 (1)	12.00	8.75
No. C26 (1)	4.75	4.00
No. C55 (1)	4.00	2.75
No. C24 (1)	7.50	5.00
No. C18 (1)	20.00	12.00
No. C18 (1)	14.00	10.50
No. C18 (1)	8.50	7.00
No. C10 (1)	11.00	8.25
Set total (12) Stamps	137.25	98.75

Tropical Medicine

Doctor Treating Infant CD100

The surtax was for charitable work.

1950

Cameroun B29
Fr. Equatorial Africa B39
Fr. India B15
Fr. Polynesia B14
Fr. West Africa B3
Madagascar B17
New Caledonia B14
St. Pierre & Miquelon B14
Somali Coast B14
Togo B11

No. B29 (1)	7.25	5.50
No. B39 (1)	7.25	5.50
No. B15 (1)	6.00	4.00
No. B14 (1)	10.50	8.00
No. B3 (1)	9.50	7.25
No. B17 (1)	5.50	5.50
No. B14 (1)	6.75	5.25
No. B14 (1)	16.00	15.00
No. B14 (1)	7.75	6.25
No. B11 (1)	5.00	3.50
Set total (10) Stamps	81.50	65.75

Military Medal

Medal, Early Marine and Colonial Soldier — CD101

Centenary of the creation of the French Military Medal.

1952

Cameroun 322
Comoro Isls. 39
Fr. Equatorial Africa 186

Fr. India....................233
Fr. Polynesia....................179
Fr. West Africa....................57
Madagascar....................286
New Caledonia....................295
St. Pierre & Miquelon....................345
Somali Coast....................267
Togo....................327
Wallis & Futuna Isls. 149

No. 322 (1)	7.25	3.25
No. 39 (1)	45.00	37.50
No. 186 (1)	8.00	5.50
No. 233 (1)	5.50	7.00
No. 179 (1)	13.50	10.00
No. 57 (1)	8.75	6.50
No. 286 (1)	3.75	2.50
No. 295 (1)	6.50	6.00
No. 345 (1)	16.00	15.00
No. 267 (1)	9.00	8.00
No. 327 (1)	5.50	4.75
No. 149 (1)	7.25	7.25
Set total (12) Stamps	136.00	113.25

Liberation

Allied Landing, Victory Sign and Cross of Lorraine — CD102

Liberation of France, 10th anniv.

1954, June 6

Cameroun....................C32
Comoro Isls. C4
Fr. Equatorial Africa....................C38
Fr. India....................C18
Fr. Polynesia....................C22
Fr. West Africa....................C17
Madagascar....................C57
New Caledonia....................C25
St. Pierre & Miquelon....................C19
Somali Coast....................C19
Togo....................C19
Wallis & Futuna Isls. C11

No. C32 (1)	7.25	4.75
No. C4 (1)	32.50	19.00
No. C38 (1)	12.00	8.00
No. C18 (1)	11.00	8.00
No. C22 (1)	10.00	8.00
No. C17 (1)	12.00	5.50
No. C57 (1)	3.25	2.00
No. C25 (1)	7.50	5.00
No. C19 (1)	19.00	12.00
No. C19 (1)	10.50	8.50
No. C19 (1)	7.00	5.50
No. C11 (1)	11.00	8.25
Set total (12) Stamps	143.00	94.50

FIDES

Plowmen CD103

Efforts of FIDES, the Economic and Social Development Fund for Overseas Possessions (Fonds d' Investissement pour le Developpement Economique et Social). Each stamp has a different design.

1956

Cameroun....................326-329
Comoro Isls. 43
Fr. Equatorial Africa....................189-192
Fr. Polynesia....................181
Fr. West Africa....................65-72
Madagascar....................292-295
New Caledonia....................303
St. Pierre & Miquelon....................350
Somali Coast....................268-269
Togo....................331

Nos. 326-329 (4)	6.90	3.20
No. 43 (1)	2.25	1.60
Nos. 189-192 (4)	3.20	1.65
No. 181 (1)	4.00	2.00
Nos. 65-72 (8)	16.00	6.35
Nos. 292-295 (4)	2.25	1.20
No. 303 (1)	1.90	1.10
No. 350 (1)	6.00	4.00
Nos. 268-269 (2)	5.35	3.15
No. 331 (1)	4.25	2.10
Set total (27) Stamps	52.10	26.35

Flower

CD104

Each stamp shows a different flower.

1958-9

Cameroun....................333
Comoro Isls. 45
Fr. Equatorial Africa....................200-201
Fr. Polynesia....................192
Fr. So. & Antarctic Terr. 11
Fr. West Africa....................79-83
Madagascar....................301-302
New Caledonia....................304-305
St. Pierre & Miquelon....................357
Somali Coast....................270
Togo....................348-349
Wallis & Futuna Isls. 152

No. 333 (1)	1.60	.80
No. 45 (1)	5.25	4.25
Nos. 200-201 (2)	3.60	1.60
No. 192 (1)	6.50	4.00
No. 11 (1)	8.75	7.50
Nos. 79-83 (5)	10.45	5.60
Nos. 301-302 (2)	1.60	.60
Nos. 304-305 (2)	8.00	3.00
No. 357 (1)	4.50	2.25
No. 270 (1)	4.25	1.40
Nos. 348-349 (2)	1.10	.50
No. 152 (1)	3.25	3.25
Set total (20) Stamps	58.85	34.75

Human Rights

Sun, Dove and U.N. Emblem CD105

10th anniversary of the signing of the Universal Declaration of Human Rights.

1958

Comoro Isls. 44
Fr. Equatorial Africa....................202
Fr. Polynesia....................191
Fr. West Africa....................85
Madagascar....................300
New Caledonia....................306
St. Pierre & Miquelon....................356
Somali Coast....................274
Wallis & Futuna Isls. 153

No. 44 (1)	9.00	9.00
No. 202 (1)	2.40	1.25
No. 191 (1)	13.00	8.75
No. 85 (1)	2.40	2.00
No. 300 (1)	.80	.40
No. 306 (1)	2.00	1.50
No. 356 (1)	3.50	2.50
No. 274 (1)	3.50	2.10
No. 153 (1)	4.50	4.50
Set total (9) Stamps	41.10	32.00

C.C.T.A.

CD106

Commission for Technical Cooperation in Africa south of the Sahara, 10th anniv.

1960

Cameroun....................339
Cent. Africa....................3
Chad....................66
Congo, P.R. 90
Dahomey....................138
Gabon....................150
Ivory Coast....................180
Madagascar....................317
Mali....................9
Mauritania....................117
Niger....................104
Upper Volta....................89

No. 339 (1)	1.60	.75
No. 3 (1)	1.60	.75
No. 66 (1)	1.75	.50
No. 90 (1)	1.00	1.00
No. 138 (1)	.50	.25
No. 150 (1)	1.25	1.10
No. 180 (1)	1.10	.50
No. 317 (1)	.60	.30
No. 9 (1)	1.20	.50
No. 117 (1)	.75	.40
No. 104 (1)	.85	.45
No. 89 (1)	.65	.40
Set total (12) Stamps	12.85	6.90

Air Afrique, 1961

Modern and Ancient Africa, Map and Planes — CD107

Founding of Air Afrique (African Airlines).

1961-62

Cameroun....................C37
Cent. Africa....................C5
Chad....................C7
Congo, P.R. C5
Dahomey....................C17
Gabon....................C5
Ivory Coast....................C18
Mauritania....................C17
Niger....................C22
Senegal....................C31
Upper Volta....................C4

No. C37 (1)	1.00	.50
No. C5 (1)	1.00	.65
No. C7 (1)	1.00	.25
No. C5 (1)	1.75	.90
No. C17 (1)	.80	.40
No. C5 (1)	11.00	6.00
No. C18 (1)	2.00	1.25
No. C17 (1)	2.40	1.25
No. C22 (1)	1.75	.90
No. C31 (1)	.80	.30
No. C4 (1)	3.50	1.75
Set total (11) Stamps	27.00	14.15

Anti-Malaria

CD108

World Health Organization drive to eradicate malaria.

1962, Apr. 7

Cameroun....................B36
Cent. Africa....................B1
Chad....................B1
Comoro Isls. B1
Congo, P.R. B3
Dahomey....................B15
Gabon....................B4
Ivory Coast....................B15
Madagascar....................B19
Mali....................B1
Mauritania....................B16
Niger....................B14
Senegal....................B16
Somali Coast....................B15
Upper Volta....................B1

No. B36 (1)	1.00	.45
No. B1 (1)	1.40	1.40
No. B1 (1)	1.00	.50
No. B1 (1)	3.50	3.50
No. B3 (1)	1.40	1.00
No. B15 (1)	.75	.75
No. B4 (1)	1.00	1.00
No. B15 (1)	1.25	1.25
No. B19 (1)	.75	.50
No. B1 (1)	1.25	.60
No. B16 (1)	.50	.50
No. B14 (1)	.75	.75
No. B16 (1)	1.10	.65
No. B15 (1)	7.00	7.00
No. B1 (1)	.75	.70
Set total (15) Stamps	23.40	20.55

Abidjan Games

CD109

Abidjan Games, Ivory Coast, Dec. 24-31, 1961. Each stamp shows a different sport.

1962

Cent. Africa....................19-20, C6
Chad....................83-84, C8
Congo, P.R. 103-104, C7
Gabon....................163-164, C6
Niger....................109-111
Upper Volta....................103-105

Nos. 19-20,C6 (3)	4.15	2.85
Nos. 83-84,C8 (3)	5.80	1.55
Nos. 103-104,C7 (3)	3.85	1.80
Nos. 163-164,C6 (3)	5.00	3.00
Nos. 109-111 (3)	2.60	1.25
Nos. 103-105 (3)	2.80	1.75
Set total (18) Stamps	24.20	12.20

African and Malagasy Union

Flag of Union CD110

First anniversary of the Union.

1962, Sept. 8

Cameroun....................373
Cent. Africa....................21
Chad....................85
Congo, P.R. 105
Dahomey....................155
Gabon....................165
Ivory Coast....................198
Madagascar....................332
Mauritania....................170
Niger....................112
Senegal....................211
Upper Volta....................106

No. 373 (1)	2.00	.75
No. 21 (1)	1.25	.75
No. 85 (1)	1.25	.25
No. 105 (1)	1.50	.50
No. 155 (1)	1.25	.90
No. 165 (1)	1.60	1.25
No. 198 (1)	2.10	.75
No. 332 (1)	.80	.80
No. 170 (1)	.75	.50
No. 112 (1)	.80	.50
No. 211 (1)	.80	.50
No. 106 (1)	1.10	.75
Set total (12) Stamps	15.20	8.20

Telstar

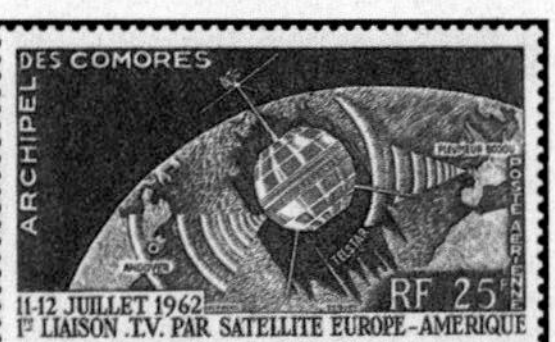

Telstar and Globe Showing Andover and Pleumeur-Bodou — CD111

First television connection of the United States and Europe through the Telstar satellite, July 11-12, 1962.

1962-63

Andorra, French....................154
Comoro Isls. C7
Fr. Polynesia....................C29
Fr. So. & Antarctic Terr. C5
New Caledonia....................C33
St. Pierre & Miquelon....................C26
Somali Coast....................C31
Wallis & Futuna Isls. C17

No. 154 (1)	2.00	1.60
No. C7 (1)	4.50	2.75
No. C29 (1)	11.50	8.00

No. C5 (1)	29.00	21.00
No. C33 (1)	25.00	18.50
No. C26 (1)	7.25	4.50
No. C31 (1)	1.00	1.00
No. C17 (1)	3.75	3.75
Set total (8) Stamps	84.00	61.10

Freedom From Hunger

World Map and Wheat Emblem CD112

U.N. Food and Agriculture Organization's "Freedom from Hunger" campaign.

1963, Mar. 21

Cameroun	B37-B38
Cent. Africa	B2
Chad	B2
Congo, P.R.	B4
Dahomey	B16
Gabon	B5
Ivory Coast	B16
Madagascar	B21
Mauritania	B17
Niger	B15
Senegal	B17
Upper Volta	B2

Nos. B37-B38 (2)	2.25	.75
No. B2 (1)	1.25	1.25
No. B2 (1)	1.10	.50
No. B4 (1)	1.40	1.00
No. B16 (1)	.80	.80
No. B5 (1)	1.00	1.00
No. B16 (1)	1.50	1.50
No. B21 (1)	.60	.45
No. B17 (1)	.60	.60
No. B15 (1)	.75	.75
No. B17 (1)	.80	.50
No. B2 (1)	.75	.70
Set total (13) Stamps	12.80	9.80

Red Cross Centenary

CD113

Centenary of the International Red Cross.

1963, Sept. 2

Comoro Isls.	55
Fr. Polynesia	205
New Caledonia	328
St. Pierre & Miquelon	367
Somali Coast	297
Wallis & Futuna Isls.	165

No. 55 (1)	7.50	6.00
No. 205 (1)	15.00	12.00
No. 328 (1)	8.00	6.75
No. 367 (1)	12.00	5.50
No. 297 (1)	6.25	6.25
No. 165 (1)	4.00	4.00
Set total (6) Stamps	52.75	40.50

African Postal Union, 1963

UAMPT Emblem, Radio Masts, Plane and Mail CD114

Establishment of the African and Malagasy Posts and Telecommunications Union.

1963, Sept. 8

Cameroun	C47
Cent. Africa	C10
Chad	C9
Congo, P.R.	C13
Dahomey	C19
Gabon	C13
Ivory Coast	C25
Madagascar	C75
Mauritania	C22
Niger	C27
Rwanda	36
Senegal	C32
Upper Volta	C9

No. C47 (1)	2.25	1.00
No. C10 (1)	1.90	.90
No. C9 (1)	1.80	.60
No. C13 (1)	1.40	.75
No. C19 (1)	.75	.25
No. C13 (1)	1.90	.80
No. C25 (1)	2.50	1.50
No. C75 (1)	1.25	.80
No. C22 (1)	1.50	.60
No. C27 (1)	1.25	.60
No. 36 (1)	1.00	.75
No. C32 (1)	1.75	.50
No. C9 (1)	1.50	.75
Set total (13) Stamps	20.75	9.80

Air Afrique, 1963

Symbols of Flight — CD115

First anniversary of Air Afrique and inauguration of DC-8 service.

1963, Nov. 19

Cameroun	C48
Chad	C10
Congo, P.R.	C14
Gabon	C18
Ivory Coast	C26
Mauritania	C26
Niger	C35
Senegal	C33

No. C48 (1)	1.25	.40
No. C10 (1)	1.80	.60
No. C14 (1)	1.60	.60
No. C18 (1)	1.25	.65
No. C26 (1)	1.00	.50
No. C26 (1)	.70	.25
No. C35 (1)	1.00	.55
No. C33 (1)	2.00	.65
Set total (8) Stamps	10.60	4.20

Europafrica

Europe and Africa Linked — CD116

Signing of an economic agreement between the European Economic Community and the African and Malagasy Union, Yaounde, Cameroun, July 20, 1963.

1963-64

Cameroun	402
Cent. Africa	C12
Chad	C11
Congo, P.R.	C16
Gabon	C19
Ivory Coast	217
Niger	C43
Upper Volta	C11

No. 402 (1)	2.25	.60
No. C12 (1)	2.50	1.75
No. C11 (1)	1.60	.50
No. C16 (1)	1.60	1.00
No. C19 (1)	1.25	.75
No. 217 (1)	1.10	.35
No. C43 (1)	.85	.50
No. C11 (1)	1.50	.80
Set total (8) Stamps	12.65	6.25

Human Rights

Scales of Justice and Globe CD117

15th anniversary of the Universal Declaration of Human Rights.

1963, Dec. 10

Comoro Isls.	56
Fr. Polynesia	206
New Caledonia	329
St. Pierre & Miquelon	368
Somali Coast	300
Wallis & Futuna Isls.	166

No. 56 (1)	7.50	6.00
No. 205 (1)	15.00	12.00
No. 329 (1)	7.00	6.00
No. 368 (1)	7.00	3.50
No. 300 (1)	8.50	8.50
No. 166 (1)	7.00	7.00
Set total (6) Stamps	52.00	43.00

PHILATEC

Stamp Album, Champs Elysees Palace and Horses of Marly CD118

Intl. Philatelic and Postal Techniques Exhibition, Paris, June 5-21, 1964.

1963-64

Comoro Isls.	60
France	1078
Fr. Polynesia	207
New Caledonia	341
St. Pierre & Miquelon	369
Somali Coast	301
Wallis & Futuna Isls.	167

No. 60 (1)	4.00	3.50
No. 1078 (1)	.25	.25
No. 206 (1)	15.00	10.00
No. 341 (1)	6.50	6.50
No. 369 (1)	11.00	8.00
No. 301 (1)	7.75	7.75
No. 167 (1)	3.00	3.00
Set total (7) Stamps	47.50	39.00

Cooperation

CD119

Cooperation between France and the French-speaking countries of Africa and Madagascar.

1964

Cameroun	409-410
Cent. Africa	39
Chad	103
Congo, P.R.	121
Dahomey	193
France	1111
Gabon	175
Ivory Coast	221
Madagascar	360
Mauritania	181
Niger	143
Senegal	236
Togo	495

Nos. 409-410 (2)	2.50	.50
No. 39 (1)	.90	.50
No. 103 (1)	1.00	.25
No. 121 (1)	.90	.35
No. 193 (1)	.80	.35
No. 1111 (1)	.25	.25
No. 175 (1)	.90	.60
No. 221 (1)	1.10	.35
No. 360 (1)	.60	.25
No. 181 (1)	.60	.35
No. 143 (1)	.80	.40
No. 236 (1)	1.60	.85
No. 495 (1)	.70	.25
Set total (14) Stamps	12.65	5.25

ITU

Telegraph, Syncom Satellite and ITU Emblem CD120

Intl. Telecommunication Union, Cent.

1965, May 17

Comoro Isls.	C14
Fr. Polynesia	C33
Fr. So. & Antarctic Terr.	C8
New Caledonia	C40
New Hebrides	124-125
St. Pierre & Miquelon	C29
Somali Coast	C36
Wallis & Futuna Isls.	C20

No. C14 (1)	18.00	9.00
No. C33 (1)	80.00	52.50
No. C8 (1)	200.00	160.00
No. C40 (1)	10.00	8.00
Nos. 124-125 (2)	32.25	27.25
No. C29 (1)	24.00	11.50
No. C36 (1)	15.00	9.00
No. C20 (1)	16.00	16.00
Set total (9) Stamps	395.25	293.25

French Satellite A-1

Diamant Rocket and Launching Installation — CD121

Launching of France's first satellite, Nov. 26, 1965.

1965-66

Comoro Isls.	C16a
France	1138a
Reunion	359a
Fr. Polynesia	C41a
Fr. So. & Antarctic Terr.	C10a
New Caledonia	C45a
St. Pierre & Miquelon	C31a
Somali Coast	C40a
Wallis & Futuna Isls.	C23a

No. C16a (1)	9.00	9.00
No. 1138a (1)	.65	.65
No. 359a (1)	3.50	3.00
No. C41a (1)	14.00	14.00
No. C10a (1)	29.00	24.00
No. C45a (1)	7.00	7.00
No. C31a (1)	14.50	14.50
No. C40a (1)	7.00	7.00
No. C23a (1)	8.50	8.50
Set total (9) Stamps	93.15	87.65

French Satellite D-1

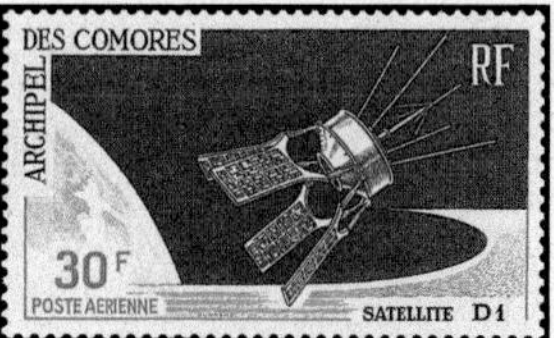

D-1 Satellite in Orbit — CD122

Launching of the D-1 satellite at Hammaguir, Algeria, Feb. 17, 1966.

1966

Comoro Isls.	C17
France	1148

Fr. Polynesia........................C42
Fr. So. & Antarctic Terr. C11
New Caledonia........................C46
St. Pierre & Miquelon........................C32
Somali Coast........................C49
Wallis & Futuna Isls. C24

No. C17 (1)	4.00	4.00
No. 1148 (1)	.25	.25
No. C42 (1)	7.00	4.75
No. C11 (1)	57.50	40.00
No. C46 (1)	2.25	2.00
No. C32 (1)	9.00	6.00
No. C49 (1)	4.25	2.75
No. C24 (1)	3.50	3.50
Set total (8) Stamps	87.75	63.25

Air Afrique, 1966

Planes and Air Afrique Emblem — CD123

Introduction of DC-8F planes by Air Afrique.

1966

Cameroun........................C79
Cent. Africa C35
Chad........................C26
Congo, P.R.........................C42
Dahomey........................C42
Gabon........................C47
Ivory Coast........................C32
Mauritania........................C57
Niger........................C63
Senegal C47
Togo........................C54
Upper Volta........................C31

No. C79 (1)	.80	.25
No. C35 (1)	1.00	.50
No. C26 (1)	.85	.25
No. C42 (1)	1.00	.25
No. C42 (1)	.75	.25
No. C47 (1)	.90	.35
No. C32 (1)	1.00	.60
No. C57 (1)	.60	.30
No. C63 (1)	.70	.35
No. C47 (1)	.80	.30
No. C54 (1)	.80	.25
No. C31 (1)	.75	.50
Set total (12) Stamps	9.95	4.15

African Postal Union, 1967

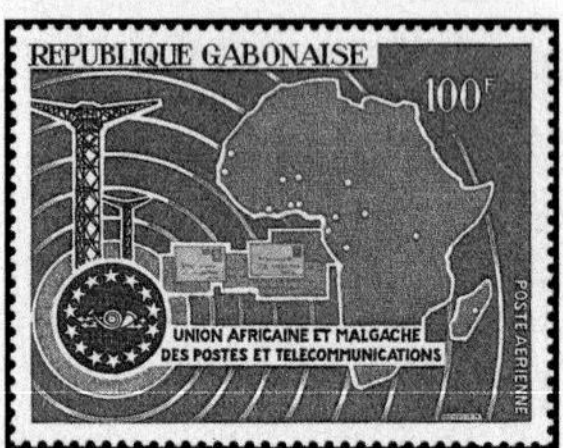

Telecommunications Symbols and Map of Africa — CD124

Fifth anniversary of the establishment of the African and Malagasy Union of Posts and Telecommunications, UAMPT.

1967

Cameroun........................C90
Cent. Africa C46
Chad........................C37
Congo, P.R.........................C57
Dahomey C61
Gabon........................C58
Ivory Coast........................C34
Madagascar........................C85
Mauritania........................C65
Niger........................C75
Rwanda C1-C3
Senegal C60
Togo........................C81
Upper Volta........................C50

No. C90 (1)	2.40	.65
No. C46 (1)	2.25	.85
No. C37 (1)	2.00	.60
No. C57 (1)	1.60	.60
No. C61 (1)	1.75	.95
No. C58 (1)	2.00	.85
No. C34 (1)	3.50	1.50
No. C85 (1)	1.25	.60
No. C65 (1)	1.25	.60
No. C75 (1)	1.40	.60
Nos. C1-C3 (3)	2.30	1.25
No. C60 (1)	1.75	.50
No. C81 (1)	1.90	.30
No. C50 (1)	1.80	.70
Set total (16) Stamps	27.15	10.55

Monetary Union

Gold Token of the Ashantis, 17-18th Centuries — CD125

West African Monetary Union, 5th anniv.

1967, Nov. 4

Dahomey........................244
Ivory Coast........................259
Mauritania........................238
Niger........................204
Senegal 294
Togo........................623
Upper Volta........................181

No. 244 (1)	.65	.65
No. 259 (1)	.85	.40
No. 238 (1)	.45	.25
No. 204 (1)	.55	.25
No. 294 (1)	.60	.25
No. 623 (1)	.60	.25
No. 181 (1)	.65	.35
Set total (7) Stamps	4.35	2.40

WHO Anniversary

Sun, Flowers and WHO Emblem CD126

World Health Organization, 20th anniv.

1968, May 4

Afars & Issas........................317
Comoro Isls. 73
Fr. Polynesia........................241-242
Fr. So. & Antarctic Terr. 31
New Caledonia........................367
St. Pierre & Miquelon........................377
Wallis & Futuna Isls. 169

No. 317 (1)	3.00	3.00
No. 73 (1)	2.40	1.75
Nos. 241-242 (2)	22.00	12.75
No. 31 (1)	62.50	47.50
No. 367 (1)	4.00	2.25
No. 377 (1)	12.00	9.00
No. 169 (1)	5.75	5.75
Set total (8) Stamps	111.65	82.00

Human Rights Year

Human Rights Flame — CD127

1968, Aug. 10

Afars & Issas........................322-323
Comoro Isls. 76
Fr. Polynesia........................243-244
Fr. So. & Antarctic Terr. 32
New Caledonia........................369
St. Pierre & Miquelon........................382
Wallis & Futuna Isls. 170

Nos. 322-323 (2)	6.75	4.00
No. 76 (1)	3.25	3.25
Nos. 243-244 (2)	24.00	14.00
No. 32 (1)	55.00	47.50
No. 369 (1)	2.75	1.50
No. 382 (1)	8.00	5.50
No. 170 (1)	3.25	3.25
Set total (9) Stamps	103.00	79.00

2nd PHILEXAFRIQUE

CD128

Opening of PHILEXAFRIQUE, Abidjan, Feb. 14. Each stamp shows a local scene and stamp.

1969, Feb. 14

Cameroun........................C118
Cent. Africa C65
Chad........................C48
Congo, P.R.........................C77
Dahomey C94
Gabon........................C82
Ivory Coast........................C38-C40
Madagascar........................C92
Mali........................C65
Mauritania........................C80
Niger........................C104
Senegal C68
Togo........................C104
Upper Volta........................C62

No. C118 (1)	3.25	1.25
No. C65 (1)	1.75	1.75
No. C48 (1)	2.40	1.00
No. C77 (1)	2.00	1.75
No. C94 (1)	2.25	2.25
No. C82 (1)	2.00	2.00
Nos. C38-C40 (3)	14.50	14.50
No. C92 (1)	1.75	.85
No. C65 (1)	1.75	1.00
No. C80 (1)	1.90	.75
No. C104 (1)	3.00	1.90
No. C68 (1)	2.00	1.40
No. C104 (1)	2.25	.45
No. C62 (1)	4.00	3.25
Set total (16) Stamps	44.80	34.10

Concorde

Concorde in Flight CD129

First flight of the prototype Concorde supersonic plane at Toulouse, Mar. 1, 1969.

1969

Afars & Issas........................C56
Comoro Isls. C29
France........................C42
Fr. Polynesia........................C50
Fr. So. & Antarctic Terr. C18
New Caledonia........................C63
St. Pierre & Miquelon........................C40
Wallis & Futuna Isls. C30

No. C56 (1)	26.00	16.00
No. C29 (1)	18.00	12.00
No. C42 (1)	.75	.35
No. C50 (1)	55.00	35.00
No. C18 (1)	55.00	37.50
No. C63 (1)	27.50	20.00
No. C40 (1)	32.50	11.00
No. C30 (1)	15.00	10.00
Set total (8) Stamps	229.75	141.85

Development Bank

Bank Emblem — CD130

African Development Bank, fifth anniv.

1969

Cameroun........................499
Chad........................217
Congo, P.R.........................181-182
Ivory Coast........................281
Mali........................127-128
Mauritania........................267
Niger........................220
Senegal 317-318
Upper Volta........................201

No. 499 (1)	.80	.25
No. 217 (1)	.90	.25
Nos. 181-182 (2)	1.00	.50
No. 281 (1)	.70	.40
Nos. 127-128 (2)	1.00	.50
No. 267 (1)	.60	.25
No. 220 (1)	.70	.30
Nos. 317-318 (2)	1.55	.50
No. 201 (1)	.65	.30
Set total (12) Stamps	7.90	3.25

ILO

ILO Headquarters, Geneva, and Emblem — CD131

Intl. Labor Organization, 50th anniv.

1969-70

Afars & Issas........................337
Comoro Isls. 83
Fr. Polynesia........................251-252
Fr. So. & Antarctic Terr. 35
New Caledonia........................379
St. Pierre & Miquelon........................396
Wallis & Futuna Isls. 172

No. 337 (1)	2.75	2.00
No. 83 (1)	1.25	.75
Nos. 251-252 (2)	24.00	12.50
No. 35 (1)	15.00	10.00
No. 379 (1)	2.25	1.10
No. 396 (1)	10.00	5.50
No. 172 (1)	2.75	2.75
Set total (8) Stamps	58.00	34.60

ASECNA

Map of Africa, Plane and Airport CD132

10th anniversary of the Agency for the Security of Aerial Navigation in Africa and Madagascar (ASECNA, Agence pour la Securite de la Navigation Aerienne en Afrique et a Madagascar).

1969-70

Cameroun........................500
Cent. Africa 119
Chad........................222
Congo, P.R.........................197
Dahomey 269
Gabon........................260
Ivory Coast........................287
Mali........................130
Niger........................221
Senegal 321
Upper Volta........................204

No. 500 (1)	2.00	.60
No. 119 (1)	2.00	.80
No. 222 (1)	1.00	.25
No. 197 (1)	2.00	.40
No. 269 (1)	.90	.55
No. 260 (1)	1.75	.75
No. 287 (1)	.90	.40
No. 130 (1)	.90	.40
No. 221 (1)	1.40	.70
No. 321 (1)	1.60	.50
No. 204 (1)	1.75	1.00
Set total (11) Stamps	16.20	6.35

U.P.U. Headquarters

CD133

New Universal Postal Union headquarters, Bern, Switzerland.

1970

Afars & Issas ... 342
Algeria ... 443
Cameroun ... 503-504
Cent. Africa ... 125
Chad ... 225
Comoro Isls. ... 84
Congo, P.R. ... 216
Fr. Polynesia ... 261-262
Fr. So. & Antarctic Terr. ... 36
Gabon ... 258
Ivory Coast ... 295
Madagascar ... 444
Mali ... 134-135
Mauritania ... 283
New Caledonia ... 382
Niger ... 231-232
St. Pierre & Miquelon ... 397-398
Senegal ... 328-329
Tunisia ... 535
Wallis & Futuna Isls. ... 173

No. 342 (1)	2.50	1.40
No. 443 (1)	1.10	.40
Nos. 503-504 (2)	2.60	.55
No. 125 (1)	1.75	.70
No. 225 (1)	1.20	.25
No. 84 (1)	5.50	2.00
No. 216 (1)	1.00	.25
Nos. 261-262 (2)	20.00	10.00
No. 36 (1)	40.00	27.50
No. 258 (1)	.90	.55
No. 295 (1)	1.10	.50
No. 444 (1)	.55	.25
Nos. 134-135 (2)	1.05	.50
No. 283 (1)	.60	.30
No. 382 (1)	3.00	1.50
Nos. 231-232 (2)	1.50	.60
Nos. 397-398 (2)	34.00	16.25
Nos. 328-329 (2)	1.55	.55
No. 535 (1)	.60	.25
No. 173 (1)	3.25	3.25
Set total (26) Stamps	123.75	67.55

De Gaulle

CD134

First anniversary of the death of Charles de Gaulle, (1890-1970), President of France.

1971-72

Afars & Issas ... 356-357
Comoro Isls. ... 104-105
France ... 1325a
Fr. Polynesia ... 270-271
Fr. So. & Antarctic Terr. ... 52-53
New Caledonia ... 393-394
Reunion ... 380a
St. Pierre & Miquelon ... 417-418
Wallis & Futuna Isls. ... 177-178

Nos. 356-357 (2)	12.50	7.50
Nos. 104-105 (2)	9.00	5.75
No. 1325a (1)	3.00	2.50
Nos. 270-271 (2)	51.50	29.50
Nos. 52-53 (2)	40.00	29.50
Nos. 393-394 (2)	23.00	11.75
No. 380a (1)	9.25	8.00
Nos. 417-418 (2)	56.50	31.00
Nos. 177-178 (2)	20.00	16.25
Set total (16) Stamps	224.75	141.75

African Postal Union, 1971

UAMPT Building, Brazzaville, Congo — CD135

10th anniversary of the establishment of the African and Malagasy Posts and Telecommunications Union, UAMPT. Each stamp has a different native design.

1971, Nov. 13

Cameroun ... C177
Cent. Africa ... C89
Chad ... C94
Congo, P.R. ... C136
Dahomey ... C146
Gabon ... C120
Ivory Coast ... C47
Mauritania ... C113
Niger ... C164
Rwanda ... C8
Senegal ... C105
Togo ... C166
Upper Volta ... C97

No. C177 (1)	2.00	.50
No. C89 (1)	2.25	.85
No. C94 (1)	1.50	.50
No. C136 (1)	1.60	.75
No. C146 (1)	1.75	.80
No. C120 (1)	1.75	.70
No. C47 (1)	2.00	1.00
No. C113 (1)	1.10	.65
No. C164 (1)	1.25	.60
No. C8 (1)	2.75	2.50
No. C105 (1)	1.60	.50
No. C166 (1)	1.25	.40
No. C97 (1)	1.50	.70
Set total (13) Stamps	22.30	10.45

West African Monetary Union

African Couple, City, Village and Commemorative Coin — CD136

West African Monetary Union, 10th anniv.

1972, Nov. 2

Dahomey ... 300
Ivory Coast ... 331
Mauritania ... 299
Niger ... 258
Senegal ... 374
Togo ... 825
Upper Volta ... 280

No. 300 (1)	.65	.25
No. 331 (1)	1.00	.50
No. 299 (1)	.75	.25
No. 258 (1)	.65	.30
No. 374 (1)	.50	.30
No. 825 (1)	.60	.25
No. 280 (1)	.60	.25
Set total (7) Stamps	4.75	2.10

African Postal Union, 1973

Telecommunications Symbols and Map of Africa — CD137

11th anniversary of the African and Malagasy Posts and Telecommunications Union (UAMPT).

1973, Sept. 12

Cameroun ... 574
Cent. Africa ... 194
Chad ... 294
Congo, P.R. ... 289
Dahomey ... 311
Gabon ... 320
Ivory Coast ... 361
Madagascar ... 500
Mauritania ... 304
Niger ... 287
Rwanda ... 540
Senegal ... 393
Togo ... 849
Upper Volta ... 297

No. 574 (1)	1.75	.40
No. 194 (1)	1.25	.75
No. 294 (1)	1.75	.40
No. 289 (1)	1.60	.50
No. 311 (1)	1.25	.55
No. 320 (1)	1.40	.75
No. 361 (1)	2.50	1.00
No. 500 (1)	1.10	.35
No. 304 (1)	1.10	.40
No. 287 (1)	.90	.60
No. 540 (1)	4.00	2.00
No. 393 (1)	1.60	.50
No. 849 (1)	1.00	.35
No. 297 (1)	1.25	.70
Set total (14) Stamps	22.45	9.25

Philexafrique II — Essen

CD138

CD139

Designs: Indigenous fauna, local and German stamps. Types CD138-CD139 printed horizontally and vertically se-tenant in sheets of 10 (2x5). Label between horizontal pairs alternately commemoratives Philexafrique II, Libreville, Gabon, June 1978, and 2nd International Stamp Fair, Essen, Germany, Nov. 1-5.

1978-1979

Benin ... C286a
Central Africa ... C201a
Chad ... C239a
Congo Republic ... C246a
Djibouti ... C122a
Gabon ... C216a
Ivory Coast ... C65a
Mali ... C357a
Mauritania ... C186a
Niger ... C292a
Rwanda ... C13a
Senegal ... C147a
Togo ... C364a

No. C286a (1)	9.00	8.50
No. C201a (1)	7.50	7.50
No. C239a (1)	7.50	4.00
No. C246a (1)	7.00	7.00
No. C122a (1)	6.50	6.50
No. C216a (1)	6.50	4.00
No. C65a (1)	9.00	9.00
No. C357a (1)	5.00	3.00
No. C186a (1)	5.50	5.00
No. C292a (1)	6.00	6.00
No. C13a (1)	4.00	4.00
No. C147a (1)	10.00	4.00
No. C364a (1)	3.00	1.50
Set total (13) Stamps	86.50	70.00

BRITISH COMMONWEALTH OF NATIONS

The listings follow established trade practices when these issues are offered as units by dealers. The Peace issue, for example, includes only one stamp from the Indian state of Hyderabad. The U.P.U. issue includes the Egypt set. Pairs are included for those varieties issued with bilingual designs se-tenant.

Silver Jubilee

Windsor Castle and King George V CD301

Reign of King George V, 25th anniv.

1935

Antigua ... 77-80
Ascension ... 33-36
Bahamas ... 92-95
Barbados ... 186-189
Basutoland ... 11-14
Bechuanaland Protectorate ... 117-120
Bermuda ... 100-103
British Guiana ... 223-226
British Honduras ... 108-111
Cayman Islands ... 81-84
Ceylon ... 260-263
Cyprus ... 136-139
Dominica ... 90-93
Falkland Islands ... 77-80
Fiji ... 110-113
Gambia ... 125-128
Gibraltar ... 100-103
Gilbert & Ellice Islands ... 33-36
Gold Coast ... 108-111
Grenada ... 124-127
Hong Kong ... 147-150
Jamaica ... 109-112
Kenya, Uganda, Tanzania ... 42-45
Leeward Islands ... 96-99
Malta ... 184-187
Mauritius ... 204-207
Montserrat ... 85-88
Newfoundland ... 226-229
Nigeria ... 34-37
Northern Rhodesia ... 18-21
Nyasaland Protectorate ... 47-50
St. Helena ... 111-114
St. Kitts-Nevis ... 72-75
St. Lucia ... 91-94
St. Vincent ... 134-137
Seychelles ... 118-121
Sierra Leone ... 166-169
Solomon Islands ... 60-63
Somaliland Protectorate ... 77-80
Straits Settlements ... 213-216
Swaziland ... 20-23
Trinidad & Tobago ... 43-46
Turks & Caicos Islands ... 71-74
Virgin Islands ... 69-72

The following have different designs but are included in the omnibus set:

Great Britain ... 226-229
Offices in Morocco (Sp. Curr.) ... 67-70
Offices in Morocco (Br. Curr.) ... 226-229
Offices in Morocco (Fr. Curr.) ... 422-425
Offices in Morocco (Tangier) ... 508-510
Australia ... 152-154
Canada ... 211-216
Cook Islands ... 98-100
India ... 142-148
Nauru ... 31-34
New Guinea ... 46-47
New Zealand ... 199-201
Niue ... 67-69
Papua ... 114-117
Samoa ... 163-165
South Africa ... 68-71
Southern Rhodesia ... 33-36
South-West Africa ... 121-124

Nos. 77-80 (4)	20.25	*23.25*
Nos. 33-36 (4)	58.50	*127.50*
Nos. 92-95 (4)	25.00	*46.00*
Nos. 186-189 (4)	30.00	50.30
Nos. 11-14 (4)	11.60	*21.25*
Nos. 117-120 (4)	15.75	*36.00*
Nos. 100-103 (4)	16.80	*58.50*
Nos. 223-226 (4)	22.35	35.50
Nos. 108-111 (4)	15.25	*16.35*
Nos. 81-84 (4)	21.60	*24.50*
Nos. 260-263 (4)	10.40	21.60
Nos. 136-139 (4)	39.75	*34.40*
Nos. 90-93 (4)	18.85	19.85
Nos. 77-80 (4)	55.00	14.75
Nos. 110-113 (4)	20.25	34.00
Nos. 125-128 (4)	13.05	*25.25*
Nos. 100-103 (4)	28.75	42.75
Nos. 33-36 (4)	36.80	*67.00*
Nos. 108-111 (4)	25.75	*78.10*
Nos. 124-127 (4)	16.70	*40.60*
Nos. 147-150 (4)	59.00	18.75
Nos. 109-112 (4)	17.00	39.00
Nos. 42-45 (4)	8.75	*11.00*
Nos. 96-99 (4)	35.75	49.60
Nos. 184-187 (4)	22.00	33.70
Nos. 204-207 (4)	44.60	58.25
Nos. 85-88 (4)	10.25	*30.25*
Nos. 226-229 (4)	17.50	12.05
Nos. 34-37 (4)	17.50	*70.00*
Nos. 18-21 (4)	17.00	15.00
Nos. 47-50 (4)	39.75	*80.25*
Nos. 111-114 (4)	31.15	*36.50*
Nos. 72-75 (4)	10.80	*18.65*
Nos. 91-94 (4)	16.00	*20.80*
Nos. 134-137 (4)	9.45	*21.25*
Nos. 118-121 (4)	15.75	*40.00*
Nos. 166-169 (4)	23.60	*50.35*
Nos. 60-63 (4)	29.00	38.00
Nos. 77-80 (4)	17.00	*48.25*
Nos. 213-216 (4)	15.00	*25.10*
Nos. 20-23 (4)	6.80	18.25
Nos. 43-46 (4)	14.05	27.75
Nos. 71-74 (4)	8.40	14.50
Nos. 69-72 (4)	25.00	55.25
Nos. 226-229 (4)	5.15	*4.40*

Nos. 67-70 (4)	14.35	26.10
Nos. 226-229 (4)	8.20	28.90
Nos. 422-425 (4)	3.90	2.00
Nos. 508-510 (3)	18.80	23.85
Nos. 152-154 (3)	49.50	45.35
Nos. 211-216 (6)	23.85	13.35
Nos. 98-100 (3)	9.65	12.00
Nos. 142-148 (7)	28.85	14.00
Nos. 31-34 (4)	9.90	9.90
Nos. 46-47 (2)	4.35	1.70
Nos. 199-201 (3)	23.00	28.50
Nos. 67-69 (3)	11.80	26.50
Nos. 114-117 (4)	9.20	17.50
Nos. 163-165 (3)	4.40	6.50
Nos. 68-71 (4)	57.50	153.00
Nos. 33-36 (4)	27.75	45.25
Nos. 121-124 (4)	13.00	36.10
Set total (245) Stamps	1,337.	2,145.

Coronation

Queen Elizabeth and King George VI CD302

1937

Aden....13-15
Antigua....81-83
Ascension....37-39
Bahamas....97-99
Barbados....190-192
Basutoland....15-17
Bechuanaland Protectorate....121-123
Bermuda....115-117
British Guiana....227-229
British Honduras....112-114
Cayman Islands....97-99
Ceylon....275-277
Cyprus....140-142
Dominica....94-96
Falkland Islands....81-83
Fiji....114-116
Gambia....129-131
Gibraltar....104-106
Gilbert & Ellice Islands....37-39
Gold Coast....112-114
Grenada....128-130
Hong Kong....151-153
Jamaica....113-115
Kenya, Uganda, Tanzania....60-62
Leeward Islands....100-102
Malta....188-190
Mauritius....208-210
Montserrat....89-91
Newfoundland....230-232
Nigeria....50-52
Northern Rhodesia....22-24
Nyasaland Protectorate....51-53
St. Helena....115-117
St. Kitts-Nevis....76-78
St. Lucia....107-109
St. Vincent....138-140
Seychelles....122-124
Sierra Leone....170-172
Solomon Islands....64-66
Somaliland Protectorate....81-83
Straits Settlements....235-237
Swaziland....24-26
Trinidad & Tobago....47-49
Turks & Caicos Islands....75-77
Virgin Islands....73-75

The following have different designs but are included in the omnibus set:

Great Britain....234
Offices in Morocco (Sp. Curr.)....82
Offices in Morocco (Fr. Curr.)....439
Offices in Morocco (Tangier)....514
Canada....237
Cook Islands....109-111
Nauru....35-38
Newfoundland....233-243
New Guinea....48-51
New Zealand....223-225
Niue....70-72
Papua....118-121
South Africa....74-78
Southern Rhodesia....38-41
South-West Africa....125-132

Nos. 13-15 (3)	2.70	5.65
Nos. 81-83 (3)	1.85	8.00
Nos. 37-39 (3)	2.75	2.75
Nos. 97-99 (3)	1.05	3.05
Nos. 190-192 (3)	1.10	1.95
Nos. 15-17 (3)	1.15	3.00
Nos. 121-123 (3)	.95	3.35
Nos. 115-117 (3)	1.25	5.00
Nos. 227-229 (3)	1.45	3.05
Nos. 112-114 (3)	1.20	2.40
Nos. 97-99 (3)	1.10	2.70
Nos. 275-277 (3)	8.25	10.35
Nos. 140-142 (3)	3.75	6.50
Nos. 94-96 (3)	.85	2.40
Nos. 81-83 (3)	2.90	2.30
Nos. 114-116 (3)	1.35	5.75
Nos. 129-131 (3)	.85	3.95
Nos. 104-106 (3)	2.25	6.45
Nos. 37-39 (3)	.85	2.15
Nos. 112-114 (3)	3.10	10.00
Nos. 128-130 (3)	1.00	.85
Nos. 151-153 (3)	23.00	12.50
Nos. 113-115 (3)	1.25	1.25
Nos. 60-62 (3)	1.00	2.35
Nos. 100-102 (3)	1.55	4.00
Nos. 188-190 (3)	1.25	1.60
Nos. 208-210 (3)	1.75	3.50
Nos. 89-91 (3)	1.00	3.35
Nos. 230-232 (3)	7.00	2.80
Nos. 50-52 (3)	3.25	8.50
Nos. 22-24 (3)	.95	2.25
Nos. 51-53 (3)	1.05	1.30
Nos. 115-117 (3)	1.45	2.05
Nos. 76-78 (3)	.95	2.15
Nos. 107-109 (3)	1.05	2.05
Nos. 138-140 (3)	.80	4.75
Nos. 122-124 (3)	1.20	1.90
Nos. 170-172 (3)	1.95	5.65
Nos. 64-66 (3)	.90	2.00
Nos. 81-83 (3)	1.10	3.50
Nos. 235-237 (3)	3.25	1.60
Nos. 24-26 (3)	.75	2.70
Nos. 47-49 (3)	1.00	1.00
Nos. 75-77 (3)	1.30	1.15
Nos. 73-75 (3)	2.20	6.90

No. 234 (1)	.25	.25
No. 82 (1)	.80	.80
No. 439 (1)	.35	.25
No. 514 (1)	.55	.55
No. 237 (1)	.35	.25
Nos. 109-111 (3)	.85	.80
Nos. 35-38 (4)	1.10	5.50
Nos. 233-243 (11)	41.90	30.40
Nos. 48-51 (4)	1.40	7.90
Nos. 223-225 (3)	1.75	2.25
Nos. 70-72 (3)	.80	2.05
Nos. 118-121 (4)	1.60	5.25
Nos. 74-78 (5)	7.60	9.35
Nos. 38-41 (4)	3.55	15.50
Nos. 125-132 (8)	5.00	8.40
Set total (189) Stamps	170.50	261.90

Peace

King George VI and Parliament Buildings, London CD303

Return to peace at the close of World War II.

1945-46

Aden....28-29
Antigua....96-97
Ascension....50-51
Bahamas....130-131
Barbados....207-208
Bermuda....131-132
British Guiana....242-243
British Honduras....127-128
Cayman Islands....112-113
Ceylon....293-294
Cyprus....156-157
Dominica....112-113
Falkland Islands....97-98
Falkland Islands Dep....1L9-1L10
Fiji....137-138
Gambia....144-145
Gibraltar....119-120
Gilbert & Ellice Islands....52-53
Gold Coast....128-129
Grenada....143-144
Jamaica....136-137
Kenya, Uganda, Tanzania....90-91
Leeward Islands....116-117
Malta....206-207
Mauritius....223-224
Montserrat....104-105
Nigeria....71-72
Northern Rhodesia....46-47
Nyasaland Protectorate....82-83
Pitcairn Islands....9-10
St. Helena....128-129
St. Kitts-Nevis....91-92
St. Lucia....127-128
St. Vincent....152-153
Seychelles....149-150
Sierra Leone....186-187
Solomon Islands....80-81
Somaliland Protectorate....108-109
Trinidad & Tobago....62-63
Turks & Caicos Islands....90-91
Virgin Islands....88-89

The following have different designs but are included in the omnibus set:

Great Britain....264-265
Offices in Morocco (Tangier)....523-524
Aden
Kathiri State of Seiyun....12-13
Qu'aiti State of Shihr and Mukalla....12-13
Australia....200-202
Basutoland....29-31
Bechuanaland Protectorate....137-139
Burma....66-69
Cook Islands....127-130
Hong Kong....174-175
India....195-198
Hyderabad....51-53
New Zealand....247-257
Niue....90-93
Pakistan-Bahawalpur....O16
Samoa....191-194
South Africa....100-102
Southern Rhodesia....67-70
South-West Africa....153-155
Swaziland....38-40
Zanzibar....222-223

Nos. 28-29 (2)	.95	2.50
Nos. 96-97 (2)	.50	.80
Nos. 50-51 (2)	.80	2.00
Nos. 130-131 (2)	.50	1.40
Nos. 207-208 (2)	.50	1.10
Nos. 131-132 (2)	.55	.55
Nos. 242-243 (2)	1.05	1.40
Nos. 127-128 (2)	.50	.50
Nos. 112-113 (2)	.80	.80
Nos. 293-294 (2)	.60	2.10
Nos. 156-157 (2)	.90	.70
Nos. 112-113 (2)	.50	.50
Nos. 97-98 (2)	.90	1.35
Nos. 1L9-1L10 (2)	1.30	1.00
Nos. 137-138 (2)	.75	1.75
Nos. 144-145 (2)	.50	.95
Nos. 119-120 (2)	.75	1.00
Nos. 52-53 (2)	.50	1.10
Nos. 128-129 (2)	1.85	3.75
Nos. 143-144 (2)	.50	.95
Nos. 136-137 (2)	.80	12.50
Nos. 90-91 (2)	.65	.65
Nos. 116-117 (2)	.50	1.50
Nos. 206-207 (2)	.65	2.00
Nos. 223-224 (2)	.50	1.05
Nos. 104-105 (2)	.50	.50
Nos. 71-72 (2)	.70	2.75
Nos. 46-47 (2)	1.25	2.00
Nos. 82-83 (2)	.50	.50
Nos. 9-10 (2)	1.40	1.40
Nos. 128-129 (2)	.65	.70
Nos. 91-92 (2)	.50	.50
Nos. 127-128 (2)	.50	.60
Nos. 152-153 (2)	.50	.50
Nos. 149-150 (2)	.55	.50
Nos. 186-187 (2)	.50	.50
Nos. 80-81 (2)	.50	1.50
Nos. 108-109 (2)	.70	.50
Nos. 62-63 (2)	.50	.50
Nos. 90-91 (2)	.50	.50
Nos. 88-89 (2)	.50	.50

Nos. 264-265 (2)	.50	.50
Nos. 523-524 (2)	1.50	3.00
Nos. 12-13 (2)	.50	.90
Nos. 12-13 (2)	.50	1.25
Nos. 200-202 (3)	1.60	1.25
Nos. 29-31 (3)	2.10	2.60
Nos. 137-139 (3)	2.05	4.75
Nos. 66-69 (4)	1.50	1.25
Nos. 127-130 (4)	2.00	1.85
Nos. 174-175 (2)	6.75	3.15
Nos. 195-198 (4)	5.60	5.50
Nos. 51-53 (3)	1.50	1.70
Nos. 247-257 (11)	3.35	3.65
Nos. 90-93 (4)	1.70	2.20
No. O16 (1)	5.50	7.00
Nos. 191-194 (4)	2.05	1.00
Nos. 100-102 (3)	1.00	3.25
Nos. 67-70 (4)	1.40	1.75
Nos. 153-155 (3)	1.85	3.25
Nos. 38-40 (3)	2.40	5.50
Nos. 222-223 (2)	.65	1.00
Set total (151) Stamps	74.55	114.15

Silver Wedding

King George VI and Queen Elizabeth

CD304 CD305

1948-49

Aden....30-31
Kathiri State of Seiyun....14-15
Qu'aiti State of Shihr and Mukalla....14-15
Antigua....98-99
Ascension....52-53
Bahamas....148-149
Barbados....210-211
Basutoland....39-40
Bechuanaland Protectorate....147-148
Bermuda....133-134
British Guiana....244-245
British Honduras....129-130
Cayman Islands....116-117
Cyprus....158-159
Dominica....114-115
Falkland Islands....99-100
Falkland Islands Dep....1L11-1L12
Fiji....139-140
Gambia....146-147
Gibraltar....121-122
Gilbert & Ellice Islands....54-55
Gold Coast....142-143
Grenada....145-146
Hong Kong....178-179
Jamaica....138-139
Kenya, Uganda, Tanzania....92-93
Leeward Islands....118-119
Malaya
Johore....128-129
Kedah....55-56
Kelantan....44-45
Malacca....1-2
Negri Sembilan....36-37
Pahang....44-45
Penang....1-2
Perak....99-100
Perlis....1-2
Selangor....74-75
Trengganu....47-48
Malta....223-224
Mauritius....229-230
Montserrat....106-107
Nigeria....73-74
North Borneo....238-239
Northern Rhodesia....48-49
Nyasaland Protectorate....85-86
Pitcairn Islands....11-12
St. Helena....130-131
St. Kitts-Nevis....93-94
St. Lucia....129-130
St. Vincent....154-155
Sarawak....174-175
Seychelles....151-152
Sierra Leone....188-189
Singapore....21-22
Solomon Islands....82-83
Somaliland Protectorate....110-111
Swaziland....48-49
Trinidad & Tobago....64-65
Turks & Caicos Islands....92-93
Virgin Islands....90-91
Zanzibar....224-225

The following have different designs but are included in the omnibus set:

Great Britain....267-268
Offices in Morocco (Sp. Curr.)....93-94
Offices in Morocco (Tangier)....525-526
Bahrain....62-63
Kuwait....82-83
Oman....25-26
South Africa....106
South-West Africa....159

Nos. 30-31 (2)	40.40	56.50
Nos. 14-15 (2)	17.85	16.00
Nos. 14-15 (2)	18.55	12.50
Nos. 98-99 (2)	13.55	15.75
Nos. 52-53 (2)	55.55	50.45
Nos. 148-149 (2)	45.25	40.30
Nos. 210-211 (2)	18.35	13.55
Nos. 39-40 (2)	52.80	55.25
Nos. 147-148 (2)	42.85	47.75
Nos. 133-134 (2)	47.75	55.25
Nos. 244-245 (2)	24.25	28.45
Nos. 129-130 (2)	25.25	53.20
Nos. 116-117 (2)	25.25	33.50
Nos. 158-159 (2)	58.50	78.05
Nos. 114-115 (2)	25.25	32.75
Nos. 99-100 (2)	112.10	76.10
Nos. 1L11-1L12 (2)	4.25	6.00
Nos. 139-140 (2)	18.20	11.50
Nos. 146-147 (2)	21.25	21.25
Nos. 121-122 (2)	61.00	78.00
Nos. 54-55 (2)	14.25	26.25
Nos. 142-143 (2)	35.25	48.20
Nos. 145-146 (2)	21.75	21.75
Nos. 178-179 (2)	283.50	96.50
Nos. 138-139 (2)	27.85	60.25
Nos. 92-93 (2)	50.25	67.75
Nos. 118-119 (2)	7.00	8.25
Nos. 128-129 (2)	29.25	53.25
Nos. 55-56 (2)	35.25	50.25
Nos. 44-45 (2)	35.75	62.75
Nos. 1-2 (2)	35.40	49.75
Nos. 36-37 (2)	28.10	38.20
Nos. 44-45 (2)	28.00	38.05
Nos. 1-2 (2)	40.50	37.80

Nos. 99-100 (2)	27.80	*37.75*
Nos. 1-2 (2)	33.50	*58.00*
Nos. 74-75 (2)	30.25	25.30
Nos. 47-48 (2)	32.75	*61.75*
Nos. 223-224 (2)	40.55	45.25
Nos. 229-230 (2)	19.25	*45.25*
Nos. 106-107 (2)	8.75	*17.25*
Nos. 73-74 (2)	17.85	*22.80*
Nos. 238-239 (2)	35.30	*45.75*
Nos. 48-49 (2)	100.30	90.25
Nos. 85-86 (2)	18.25	*30.25*
Nos. 11-12 (2)	44.75	48.50
Nos. 130-131 (2)	32.80	*42.80*
Nos. 93-94 (2)	11.25	10.50
Nos. 129-130 (2)	22.25	*40.25*
Nos. 154-155 (2)	27.75	*30.25*
Nos. 174-175 (2)	50.40	*52.90*
Nos. 151-152 (2)	16.25	*48.25*
Nos. 188-189 (2)	25.25	*29.75*
Nos. 21-22 (2)	116.00	45.40
Nos. 82-83 (2)	13.40	13.40
Nos. 110-111 (2)	8.40	*8.75*
Nos. 48-49 (2)	40.30	*47.75*
Nos. 64-65 (2)	32.75	*38.25*
Nos. 92-93 (2)	11.25	*16.25*
Nos. 90-91 (2)	16.25	22.25
Nos. 224-225 (2)	29.60	38.00
Nos. 267-268 (2)	30.40	25.25
Nos. 93-94 (2)	20.10	25.35
Nos. 525-526 (2)	23.10	29.25
Nos. 62-63 (2)	38.50	*57.75*
Nos. 82-83 (2)	69.50	45.50
Nos. 25-26 (2)	41.00	*42.50*
No. 106 (1)	.80	1.00
No. 159 (1)	1.10	.35
Set total (136) Stamps	2,488.	2,681.

U.P.U.

Mercury and Symbols of Communications — CD306

Plane, Ship and Hemispheres — CD307

Mercury Scattering Letters over Globe CD308

U.P.U. Monument, Bern CD309

Universal Postal Union, 75th anniversary.

1949

Aden 32-35
Kathiri State of Seiyun....16-19
Qu'aiti State of Shihr and Mukalla 16-19
Antigua 100-103
Ascension 57-60
Bahamas 150-153
Barbados 212-215
Basutoland....41-44
Bechuanaland Protectorate....149-152
Bermuda 138-141
British Guiana....246-249
British Honduras....137-140
Brunei 79-82
Cayman Islands....118-121
Cyprus 160-163
Dominica....116-119
Falkland Islands 103-106
Falkland Islands Dep....1L14-1L17
Fiji 141-144
Gambia 148-151
Gibraltar....123-126
Gilbert & Ellice Islands....56-59
Gold Coast 144-147
Grenada....147-150
Hong Kong 180-183
Jamaica 142-145
Kenya, Uganda, Tanzania 94-97
Leeward Islands 126-129
Malaya
Johore 151-154
Kedah....57-60
Kelantan 46-49
Malacca....18-21
Negri Sembilan 59-62
Pahang....46-49
Penang....23-26
Perak....101-104
Perlis 3-6
Selangor....76-79
Trengganu 49-52
Malta....225-228
Mauritius....231-234
Montserrat 108-111
New Hebrides, British 62-65
New Hebrides; French 79-82
Nigeria 75-78
North Borneo....240-243
Northern Rhodesia....50-53
Nyasaland Protectorate....87-90
Pitcairn Islands....13-16
St. Helena 132-135
St. Kitts-Nevis....95-98
St. Lucia 131-134
St. Vincent....170-173
Sarawak....176-179
Seychelles 153-156
Sierra Leone....190-193
Singapore 23-26
Solomon Islands....84-87
Somaliland Protectorate....112-115
Southern Rhodesia 71-72
Swaziland 50-53
Tonga....87-90
Trinidad & Tobago 66-69
Turks & Caicos Islands 101-104
Virgin Islands....92-95
Zanzibar....226-229

The following have different designs but are included in the omnibus set:

Great Britain....276-279
Offices in Morocco (Tangier) 546-549
Australia....223
Bahrain 68-71
Burma....116-121
Ceylon 304-306
Egypt....281-283
India....223-226
Kuwait....89-92
Oman....31-34
Pakistan-Bahawalpur 26-29, O25-O28
South Africa....109-111
South-West Africa 160-162

Nos. 32-35 (4)	5.85	*8.45*
Nos. 16-19 (4)	2.75	*16.00*
Nos. 16-19 (4)	2.60	8.00
Nos. 100-103 (4)	3.60	*7.70*
Nos. 57-60 (4)	11.10	9.00
Nos. 150-153 (4)	5.35	9.30
Nos. 212-215 (4)	4.40	*14.85*
Nos. 41-44 (4)	4.75	*10.00*
Nos. 149-152 (4)	3.35	*7.25*
Nos. 138-141 (4)	4.75	6.15
Nos. 246-249 (4)	2.75	4.20
Nos. 137-140 (4)	3.30	6.35
Nos. 79-82 (4)	9.50	8.45
Nos. 118-121 (4)	3.60	*7.25*
Nos. 160-163 (4)	4.60	*10.70*
Nos. 116-119 (4)	2.30	5.65
Nos. 103-106 (4)	14.00	17.10
Nos. 1L14-1L17 (4)	14.60	14.50
Nos. 141-144 (4)	3.35	15.75
Nos. 148-151 (4)	2.75	7.10
Nos. 123-126 (4)	5.90	*8.75*
Nos. 56-59 (4)	4.30	*13.00*
Nos. 144-147 (4)	2.55	*10.35*
Nos. 147-150 (4)	2.15	3.55
Nos. 180-183 (4)	57.25	18.25
Nos. 142-145 (4)	2.25	2.45
Nos. 94-97 (4)	2.90	3.40
Nos. 126-129 (4)	3.05	*9.60*
Nos. 151-154 (4)	4.70	8.90
Nos. 57-60 (4)	4.80	12.00
Nos. 46-49 (4)	4.25	12.65
Nos. 18-21 (4)	4.25	*17.30*
Nos. 59-62 (4)	3.50	10.75
Nos. 46-49 (4)	3.00	7.25
Nos. 23-26 (4)	5.10	11.75
Nos. 101-104 (4)	3.65	10.75
Nos. 3-6 (4)	3.95	14.25
Nos. 76-79 (4)	4.90	12.30
Nos. 49-52 (4)	5.55	12.25
Nos. 225-228 (4)	4.50	4.85
Nos. 231-234 (4)	3.70	7.05
Nos. 108-111 (4)	3.30	4.35
Nos. 62-65 (4)	1.60	*4.25*
Nos. 79-82 (4)	15.40	*22.00*
Nos. 75-78 (4)	2.80	*9.25*
Nos. 240-243 (4)	7.15	6.50
Nos. 50-53 (4)	5.00	*6.50*
Nos. 87-90 (4)	4.05	4.05
Nos. 13-16 (4)	18.50	16.50
Nos. 132-135 (4)	4.85	7.10
Nos. 95-98 (4)	3.35	5.55
Nos. 131-134 (4)	2.55	*3.85*
Nos. 170-173 (4)	2.20	*5.05*
Nos. 176-179 (4)	8.15	10.85
Nos. 153-156 (4)	3.00	5.15
Nos. 190-193 (4)	2.90	*9.15*
Nos. 23-26 (4)	19.00	13.70
Nos. 84-87 (4)	4.05	4.90
Nos. 112-115 (4)	3.95	8.70
Nos. 71-72 (2)	1.95	*2.25*
Nos. 50-53 (4)	2.80	4.65
Nos. 87-90 (4)	3.00	*5.25*
Nos. 66-69 (4)	3.15	3.15
Nos. 101-104 (4)	2.70	4.10
Nos. 92-95 (4)	2.60	5.90
Nos. 226-229 (4)	5.45	13.50
Nos. 276-279 (4)	1.35	1.00
Nos. 546-549 (4)	3.20	*10.15*
No. 223 (1)	.40	.40
Nos. 68-71 (4)	4.75	*16.50*
Nos. 116-121 (6)	7.30	5.35
Nos. 304-306 (3)	3.35	4.25
Nos. 281-283 (3)	5.75	2.70
Nos. 223-226 (4)	27.25	10.50
Nos. 89-92 (4)	6.10	10.25
Nos. 31-34 (4)	8.00	15.75
Nos. 26-29,O25-O28 (8)	2.00	*42.00*
Nos. 109-111 (3)	2.00	2.70
Nos. 160-162 (3)	3.00	5.50
Set total (313) Stamps	453.35	718.40

University

Arms of University College CD310

Alice, Princess of Athlone CD311

1948 opening of University College of the West Indies at Jamaica.

1951

Antigua 104-105
Barbados 228-229
British Guiana....250-251
British Honduras....141-142
Dominica....120-121
Grenada....164-165
Jamaica 146-147
Leeward Islands 130-131
Montserrat 112-113
St. Kitts-Nevis....105-106
St. Lucia 149-150
St. Vincent....174-175
Trinidad & Tobago 70-71
Virgin Islands....96-97

Nos. 104-105 (2)	1.35	*3.75*
Nos. 228-229 (2)	1.75	2.65
Nos. 250-251 (2)	1.10	*1.25*
Nos. 141-142 (2)	1.40	2.20
Nos. 120-121 (2)	1.40	*1.75*
Nos. 164-165 (2)	1.20	*1.60*
Nos. 146-147 (2)	.90	.70
Nos. 130-131 (2)	1.35	4.00
Nos. 112-113 (2)	.85	*2.00*
Nos. 105-106 (2)	.90	2.25
Nos. 149-150 (2)	1.40	1.50
Nos. 174-175 (2)	1.00	*2.15*
Nos. 70-71 (2)	.75	.75
Nos. 96-97 (2)	1.50	*3.75*
Set total (28) Stamps	16.85	30.30

Coronation

Queen Elizabeth II — CD312

1953

Aden 47
Kathiri State of Seiyun....28
Qu'aiti State of Shihr and Mukalla 28
Antigua 106
Ascension....61
Bahamas 157
Barbados 234
Basutoland....45
Bechuanaland Protectorate....153
Bermuda....142
British Guiana....252
British Honduras....143
Cayman Islands....150
Cyprus 167
Dominica....141
Falkland Islands 121
Falkland Islands Dependencies 1L18
Fiji....145
Gambia 152
Gibraltar....131
Gilbert & Ellice Islands....60
Gold Coast 160
Grenada....170
Hong Kong 184
Jamaica 153
Kenya, Uganda, Tanzania 101
Leeward Islands 132
Malaya
Johore 155
Kedah....82
Kelantan 71
Malacca....27
Negri Sembilan 63
Pahang....71
Penang....27
Perak....126
Perlis 28
Selangor....101
Trengganu 74
Malta....241
Mauritius....250
Montserrat 127
New Hebrides, British 77
Nigeria 79
North Borneo....260
Northern Rhodesia....60
Nyasaland Protectorate....96
Pitcairn Islands....19
St. Helena 139
St. Kitts-Nevis....119
St. Lucia 156
St. Vincent....185
Sarawak....196
Seychelles 172
Sierra Leone....194
Singapore....27
Solomon Islands....88
Somaliland Protectorate....127
Swaziland....54
Trinidad & Tobago 84
Tristan da Cunha....13
Turks & Caicos Islands 118
Virgin Islands....114

The following have different designs but are included in the omnibus set:

Great Britain....313-316
Offices in Morocco (Tangier) 579-582
Australia....259-261
Bahrain 92-95
Canada....330
Ceylon 317
Cook Islands 145-146
Kuwait....113-116
New Zealand 280-284
Niue 104-105
Oman....52-55
Samoa....214-215
South Africa....192
Southern Rhodesia 80
South-West Africa 244-248
Tokelau Islands....4

No. 47 (1)	1.25	1.25
No. 28 (1)	.75	*1.50*
No. 28 (1)	1.10	.60
No. 106 (1)	.40	*.75*
No. 61 (1)	1.25	2.75
No. 157 (1)	1.40	.75
No. 234 (1)	1.00	.25
No. 45 (1)	.50	*.60*
No. 153 (1)	.75	.35
No. 142 (1)	.85	.50
No. 252 (1)	.45	.25
No. 143 (1)	.60	.40
No. 150 (1)	.40	*1.75*
No. 167 (1)	1.60	.75
No. 141 (1)	.40	.40
No. 121 (1)	.90	1.50
No. 1L18 (1)	1.80	1.40
No. 145 (1)	1.00	.60
No. 152 (1)	.50	.50
No. 131 (1)	.50	.50
No. 60 (1)	.65	*2.25*
No. 160 (1)	1.00	.25

No. 170 (1)	.30	.25
No. 184 (1)	6.00	.35
No. 153 (1)	.70	.25
No. 101 (1)	.40	.25
No. 132 (1)	1.00	2.25
No. 155 (1)	1.40	.30
No. 82 (1)	2.25	.60
No. 71 (1)	1.60	1.60
No. 27 (1)	1.10	1.50
No. 63 (1)	1.40	.65
No. 71 (1)	2.25	.25
No. 27 (1)	1.75	.30
No. 126 (1)	1.60	.25
No. 28 (1)	1.75	4.00
No. 101 (1)	1.75	.25
No. 74 (1)	1.50	1.00
No. 241 (1)	.50	.25
No. 250 (1)	1.10	.25
No. 127 (1)	.60	.45
No. 77 (1)	.75	.60
No. 79 (1)	.45	.25
No. 260 (1)	1.75	1.00
No. 60 (1)	.70	.25
No. 96 (1)	.75	.75
No. 19 (1)	2.25	2.25
No. 139 (1)	1.25	1.25
No. 119 (1)	.35	.25
No. 156 (1)	.70	.35
No. 185 (1)	.50	.30
No. 196 (1)	2.00	1.75
No. 172 (1)	.80	.80
No. 194 (1)	.40	.40
No. 27 (1)	2.50	.40
No. 88 (1)	1.00	1.00
No. 127 (1)	.40	.25
No. 54 (1)	.30	.25
No. 84 (1)	.25	.25
No. 13 (1)	1.00	1.75
No. 118 (1)	.40	1.10
No. 114 (1)	.40	1.00
Nos. 313-316 (4)	16.35	5.95
Nos. 579-582 (4)	7.40	5.20
Nos. 259-261 (3)	3.60	2.75
Nos. 92-95 (4)	15.25	12.75
No. 330 (1)	.25	.25
No. 317 (1)	1.40	.25
Nos. 145-146 (2)	2.65	2.65
Nos. 113-116 (4)	16.00	8.50
Nos. 280-284 (5)	3.30	4.55
Nos. 104-105 (2)	1.60	1.60
Nos. 52-55 (4)	14.25	6.50
Nos. 214-215 (2)	2.50	.80
No. 192 (1)	.45	.30
No. 80 (1)	7.25	7.25
Nos. 244-248 (5)	3.00	2.35
No. 4 (1)	2.75	2.75
Set total (106) Stamps	164.90	115.45

Separate designs for each country for the visit of Queen Elizabeth II and the Duke of Edinburgh.

Royal Visit 1953

1953

Aden	62
Australia	267-269
Bermuda	163
Ceylon	318
Fiji	146
Gibraltar	146
Jamaica	154
Kenya, Uganda, Tanzania	102
Malta	242
New Zealand	286-287

No. 62 (1)	.65	4.00
Nos. 267-269 (3)	2.75	2.05
No. 163 (1)	.50	.25
No. 318 (1)	1.00	.25
No. 146 (1)	.65	.35
No. 146 (1)	.50	.30
No. 154 (1)	.50	.25
No. 102 (1)	.50	.25
No. 242 (1)	.35	.25
Nos. 286-287 (2)	.50	.50
Set total (13) Stamps	7.90	8.45

West Indies Federation

Map of the Caribbean CD313

Federation of the West Indies, April 22, 1958.

1958

Antigua	122-124
Barbados	248-250
Dominica	161-163
Grenada	184-186
Jamaica	175-177
Montserrat	143-145
St. Kitts-Nevis	136-138
St. Lucia	170-172
St. Vincent	198-200
Trinidad & Tobago	86-88

Nos. 122-124 (3)	5.80	3.80
Nos. 248-250 (3)	1.60	2.90
Nos. 161-163 (3)	1.95	1.85
Nos. 184-186 (3)	1.50	1.20
Nos. 175-177 (3)	2.65	3.45
Nos. 143-145 (3)	2.35	1.35
Nos. 136-138 (3)	3.00	3.10
Nos. 170-172 (3)	2.05	2.80
Nos. 198-200 (3)	1.50	1.75
Nos. 86-88 (3)	.75	.90
Set total (30) Stamps	23.15	23.10

Freedom from Hunger

Protein Food CD314

U.N. Food and Agricultural Organization's "Freedom from Hunger" campaign.

1963

Aden	65
Antigua	133
Ascension	89
Bahamas	180
Basutoland	83
Bechuanaland Protectorate	194
Bermuda	192
British Guiana	271
British Honduras	179
Brunei	100
Cayman Islands	168
Dominica	181
Falkland Islands	146
Fiji	198
Gambia	172
Gibraltar	161
Gilbert & Ellice Islands	76
Grenada	190
Hong Kong	218
Malta	291
Mauritius	270
Montserrat	150
New Hebrides, British	93
North Borneo	296
Pitcairn Islands	35
St. Helena	173
St. Lucia	179
St. Vincent	201
Sarawak	212
Seychelles	213
Solomon Islands	109
Swaziland	108
Tonga	127
Tristan da Cunha	68
Turks & Caicos Islands	138
Virgin Islands	140
Zanzibar	280

No. 65 (1)	1.50	1.75
No. 133 (1)	.35	.35
No. 89 (1)	1.00	.50
No. 180 (1)	.65	.65
No. 83 (1)	.50	.25
No. 194 (1)	.50	.50
No. 192 (1)	1.00	.50
No. 271 (1)	.45	.25
No. 179 (1)	.60	.25
No. 100 (1)	3.25	2.25
No. 168 (1)	.55	.30
No. 181 (1)	.30	.30
No. 146 (1)	10.50	2.50
No. 198 (1)	3.50	2.25
No. 172 (1)	.50	.25
No. 161 (1)	4.00	2.25
No. 76 (1)	1.40	.40
No. 190 (1)	.30	.25
No. 218 (1)	47.50	7.50
No. 291 (1)	2.00	2.00
No. 270 (1)	.45	.25
No. 150 (1)	.55	.35
No. 93 (1)	.60	.25
No. 296 (1)	1.90	.75
No. 35 (1)	10.00	4.50
No. 173 (1)	2.25	1.10
No. 179 (1)	.40	.40
No. 201 (1)	.90	.50
No. 212 (1)	1.60	1.75
No. 213 (1)	.85	.35
No. 109 (1)	3.00	.85
No. 108 (1)	.50	.50
No. 127 (1)	.60	.35
No. 68 (1)	.75	.35
No. 138 (1)	.50	.25
No. 140 (1)	.50	.50
No. 280 (1)	1.50	.80
Set total (37) Stamps	107.20	39.05

Red Cross Centenary

Red Cross and Elizabeth II CD315

1963

Antigua	134-135
Ascension	90-91
Bahamas	183-184
Basutoland	84-85
Bechuanaland Protectorate	195-196
Bermuda	193-194
British Guiana	272-273
British Honduras	180-181
Cayman Islands	169-170
Dominica	182-183
Falkland Islands	147-148
Fiji	203-204
Gambia	173-174
Gibraltar	162-163
Gilbert & Ellice Islands	77-78
Grenada	191-192
Hong Kong	219-220
Jamaica	203-204
Malta	292-293
Mauritius	271-272
Montserrat	151-152
New Hebrides, British	94-95
Pitcairn Islands	36-37
St. Helena	174-175
St. Kitts-Nevis	143-144
St. Lucia	180-181
St. Vincent	202-203
Seychelles	214-215
Solomon Islands	110-111
South Arabia	1-2
Swaziland	109-110
Tonga	134-135
Tristan da Cunha	69-70
Turks & Caicos Islands	139-140
Virgin Islands	141-142

Nos. 134-135 (2)	1.00	2.00
Nos. 90-91 (2)	6.75	3.35
Nos. 183-184 (2)	2.30	2.80
Nos. 84-85 (2)	1.20	.90
Nos. 195-196 (2)	.95	.85
Nos. 193-194 (2)	3.00	2.80
Nos. 272-273 (2)	.85	.60
Nos. 180-181 (2)	1.00	2.50
Nos. 169-170 (2)	1.10	3.00
Nos. 182-183 (2)	.70	1.05
Nos. 147-148 (2)	18.00	5.50
Nos. 203-204 (2)	3.25	2.80
Nos. 173-174 (2)	.75	1.00
Nos. 162-163 (2)	6.25	5.40
Nos. 77-78 (2)	2.00	3.50
Nos. 191-192 (2)	.80	.50
Nos. 219-220 (2)	35.00	7.35
Nos. 203-204 (2)	.75	1.65
Nos. 292-293 (2)	2.50	4.75
Nos. 271-272 (2)	.85	.50
Nos. 151-152 (2)	1.00	.75
Nos. 94-95 (2)	1.00	.50
Nos. 36-37 (2)	6.50	5.50
Nos. 174-175 (2)	1.70	2.30
Nos. 143-144 (2)	.90	.90
Nos. 180-181 (2)	1.25	1.25
Nos. 202-203 (2)	.90	.90
Nos. 214-215 (2)	1.00	1.50
Nos. 110-111 (2)	1.25	1.15
Nos. 1-2 (2)	1.25	1.25
Nos. 109-110 (2)	1.10	1.10
Nos. 134-135 (2)	1.00	1.25
Nos. 69-70 (2)	1.15	.80
Nos. 139-140 (2)	.85	.75
Nos. 141-142 (2)	.80	1.25
Set total (70) Stamps	110.65	73.95

Shakespeare

Shakespeare Memorial Theatre, Stratford-on-Avon — CD316

400th anniversary of the birth of William Shakespeare.

1964

Antigua	151
Bahamas	201
Bechuanaland Protectorate	197
Cayman Islands	171
Dominica	184
Falkland Islands	149
Gambia	192
Gibraltar	164
Montserrat	153
St. Lucia	196
Turks & Caicos Islands	141
Virgin Islands	143

No. 151 (1)	.35	.25
No. 201 (1)	.60	.35
No. 197 (1)	.35	.35
No. 171 (1)	.35	.30
No. 184 (1)	.35	.35
No. 149 (1)	1.60	.50
No. 192 (1)	.35	.25
No. 164 (1)	.65	.55
No. 153 (1)	.35	.25
No. 196 (1)	.45	.25
No. 141 (1)	.40	.25
No. 143 (1)	.45	.45
Set total (12) Stamps	6.25	4.10

ITU

ITU Emblem CD317

Intl. Telecommunication Union, cent.

1965

Antigua	153-154
Ascension	92-93
Bahamas	219-220
Barbados	265-266
Basutoland	101-102
Bechuanaland Protectorate	202-203
Bermuda	196-197
British Guiana	293-294
British Honduras	187-188
Brunei	116-117
Cayman Islands	172-173
Dominica	185-186
Falkland Islands	154-155
Fiji	211-212
Gibraltar	167-168
Gilbert & Ellice Islands	87-88
Grenada	205-206
Hong Kong	221-222
Mauritius	291-292
Montserrat	157-158
New Hebrides, British	108-109
Pitcairn Islands	52-53
St. Helena	180-181
St. Kitts-Nevis	163-164
St. Lucia	197-198
St. Vincent	224-225
Seychelles	218-219
Solomon Islands	126-127
Swaziland	115-116
Tristan da Cunha	85-86
Turks & Caicos Islands	142-143
Virgin Islands	159-160

Nos. 153-154 (2)	1.45	1.35
Nos. 92-93 (2)	1.90	1.30
Nos. 219-220 (2)	1.35	1.50
Nos. 265-266 (2)	1.50	1.25
Nos. 101-102 (2)	.85	.65
Nos. 202-203 (2)	1.10	.75
Nos. 196-197 (2)	2.15	2.25
Nos. 293-294 (2)	.50	.50
Nos. 187-188 (2)	.75	.75
Nos. 116-117 (2)	1.75	1.75
Nos. 172-173 (2)	1.00	.85
Nos. 185-186 (2)	.55	.55
Nos. 154-155 (2)	6.75	3.15
Nos. 211-212 (2)	2.00	1.05
Nos. 167-168 (2)	9.00	5.95
Nos. 87-88 (2)	.85	.60
Nos. 205-206 (2)	.50	.50
Nos. 221-222 (2)	24.50	3.80
Nos. 291-292 (2)	1.10	.50
Nos. 157-158 (2)	1.05	1.15
Nos. 108-109 (2)	.65	.50
Nos. 52-53 (2)	6.25	4.30
Nos. 180-181 (2)	.80	.60
Nos. 163-164 (2)	.60	.60
Nos. 197-198 (2)	1.25	1.25
Nos. 224-225 (2)	.80	.90
Nos. 218-219 (2)	.75	.60
Nos. 126-127 (2)	.70	.55
Nos. 115-116 (2)	.70	.70
Nos. 85-86 (2)	1.00	.65
Nos. 142-143 (2)	.75	.50
Nos. 159-160 (2)	.85	.85
Set total (64) Stamps	75.70	42.15

Intl. Cooperation Year

ICY Emblem CD318

1965

Antigua....155-156
Ascension....94-95
Bahamas....222-223
Basutoland....103-104
Bechuanaland Protectorate....204-205
Bermuda....199-200
British Guiana....295-296
British Honduras....189-190
Brunei....118-119
Cayman Islands....174-175
Dominica....187-188
Falkland Islands....156-157
Fiji....213-214
Gibraltar....169-170
Gilbert & Ellice Islands....104-105
Grenada....207-208
Hong Kong....223-224
Mauritius....293-294
Montserrat....176-177
New Hebrides, British....110-111
New Hebrides, French....126-127
Pitcairn Islands....54-55
St. Helena....182-183
St. Kitts-Nevis....165-166
St. Lucia....199-200
Seychelles....220-221
Solomon Islands....143-144
South Arabia....17-18
Swaziland....117-118
Tristan da Cunha....87-88
Turks & Caicos Islands....144-145
Virgin Islands....161-162

Nos. 155-156 (2)	.55	.50
Nos. 94-95 (2)	1.30	1.40
Nos. 222-223 (2)	.65	1.90
Nos. 103-104 (2)	.75	.85
Nos. 204-205 (2)	.85	1.00
Nos. 199-200 (2)	2.05	1.25
Nos. 295-296 (2)	.55	.50
Nos. 189-190 (2)	.60	.55
Nos. 118-119 (2)	.85	.85
Nos. 174-175 (2)	1.00	.75
Nos. 187-188 (2)	.55	.55
Nos. 156-157 (2)	6.00	1.65
Nos. 213-214 (2)	1.95	1.25
Nos. 169-170 (2)	1.25	*2.75*
Nos. 104-105 (2)	.85	.60
Nos. 207-208 (2)	.50	.50
Nos. 223-224 (2)	22.00	3.10
Nos. 293-294 (2)	.65	.50
Nos. 176-177 (2)	.80	.65
Nos. 110-111 (2)	.50	.50
Nos. 126-127 (2)	12.00	12.00
Nos. 54-55 (2)	6.35	4.50
Nos. 182-183 (2)	.95	.50
Nos. 165-166 (2)	.80	.60
Nos. 199-200 (2)	.55	.55
Nos. 220-221 (2)	.80	.60
Nos. 143-144 (2)	.70	.60
Nos. 17-18 (2)	1.20	.50
Nos. 117-118 (2)	.75	.75
Nos. 87-88 (2)	1.05	.65
Nos. 144-145 (2)	.65	.50
Nos. 161-162 (2)	.65	.50
Set total (64) Stamps	70.65	43.85

Churchill Memorial

Winston Churchill and St. Paul's, London, During Air Attack CD319

1966

Antigua....157-160
Ascension....96-99
Bahamas....224-227
Barbados....281-284
Basutoland....105-108
Bechuanaland Protectorate....206-209
Bermuda....201-204
British Antarctic Territory....16-19
British Honduras....191-194
Brunei....120-123
Cayman Islands....176-179
Dominica....189-192
Falkland Islands....158-161
Fiji....215-218
Gibraltar....171-174
Gilbert & Ellice Islands....106-109
Grenada....209-212
Hong Kong....225-228
Mauritius....295-298
Montserrat....178-181
New Hebrides, British....112-115
New Hebrides, French....128-131
Pitcairn Islands....56-59
St. Helena....184-187
St. Kitts-Nevis....167-170
St. Lucia....201-204
St. Vincent....241-244
Seychelles....222-225
Solomon Islands....145-148
South Arabia....19-22
Swaziland....119-122
Tristan da Cunha....89-92
Turks & Caicos Islands....146-149
Virgin Islands....163-166

Nos. 157-160 (4)	3.05	3.05
Nos. 96-99 (4)	10.00	6.40
Nos. 224-227 (4)	2.30	*3.20*
Nos. 281-284 (4)	3.00	4.95
Nos. 105-108 (4)	2.80	3.25
Nos. 206-209 (4)	2.50	2.50
Nos. 201-204 (4)	4.00	*4.75*
Nos. 16-19 (4)	41.20	18.00
Nos. 191-194 (4)	2.45	1.30
Nos. 120-123 (4)	7.65	6.55
Nos. 176-179 (4)	3.10	3.65
Nos. 189-192 (4)	1.15	1.15
Nos. 158-161 (4)	12.75	9.55
Nos. 215-218 (4)	4.40	3.00
Nos. 171-174 (4)	3.05	5.30
Nos. 106-109 (4)	1.50	1.30
Nos. 209-212 (4)	1.10	1.10
Nos. 225-228 (4)	52.50	11.40
Nos. 295-298 (4)	3.70	3.75
Nos. 178-181 (4)	1.60	1.55
Nos. 112-115 (4)	2.30	1.00
Nos. 128-131 (4)	8.35	8.35
Nos. 56-59 (4)	11.00	6.75
Nos. 184-187 (4)	1.85	1.95
Nos. 167-170 (4)	1.50	1.70
Nos. 201-204 (4)	1.50	1.50
Nos. 241-244 (4)	1.50	1.75
Nos. 222-225 (4)	3.20	4.35
Nos. 145-148 (4)	1.50	1.60
Nos. 19-22 (4)	2.95	2.20
Nos. 119-122 (4)	1.70	2.55
Nos. 89-92 (4)	5.95	2.70
Nos. 146-149 (4)	1.60	1.75
Nos. 163-166 (4)	1.90	1.90
Set total (136) Stamps	210.60	135.75

Royal Visit, 1966

Queen Elizabeth II and Prince Philip CD320

Caribbean visit, Feb. 4 - Mar. 6, 1966.

1966

Antigua....161-162
Bahamas....228-229
Barbados....285-286
British Guiana....299-300
Cayman Islands....180-181
Dominica....193-194
Grenada....213-214
Montserrat....182-183
St. Kitts-Nevis....171-172
St. Lucia....205-206
St. Vincent....245-246
Turks & Caicos Islands....150-151
Virgin Islands....167-168

Nos. 161-162 (2)	3.50	2.60
Nos. 228-229 (2)	3.05	3.05
Nos. 285-286 (2)	3.00	2.00
Nos. 299-300 (2)	2.35	.85
Nos. 180-181 (2)	3.45	1.80
Nos. 193-194 (2)	3.00	.60
Nos. 213-214 (2)	.80	.50
Nos. 182-183 (2)	2.00	1.00
Nos. 171-172 (2)	.90	.75
Nos. 205-206 (2)	1.50	1.35
Nos. 245-246 (2)	2.75	1.35
Nos. 150-151 (2)	1.20	.55
Nos. 167-168 (2)	1.75	1.75
Set total (26) Stamps	29.25	18.15

World Cup Soccer

Soccer Player and Jules Rimet Cup CD321

World Cup Soccer Championship, Wembley, England, July 11-30.

1966

Antigua....163-164
Ascension....100-101
Bahamas....245-246
Bermuda....205-206
Brunei....124-125
Cayman Islands....182-183
Dominica....195-196
Fiji....219-220
Gibraltar....175-176
Gilbert & Ellice Islands....125-126
Grenada....230-231
New Hebrides, British....116-117
New Hebrides, French....132-133
Pitcairn Islands....60-61
St. Helena....188-189
St. Kitts-Nevis....173-174
St. Lucia....207-208
Seychelles....226-227
Solomon Islands....167-168
South Arabia....23-24
Tristan da Cunha....93-94

Nos. 163-164 (2)	.80	.85
Nos. 100-101 (2)	2.50	2.00
Nos. 245-246 (2)	.65	.65
Nos. 205-206 (2)	1.75	1.75
Nos. 124-125 (2)	1.30	1.25
Nos. 182-183 (2)	.75	.65
Nos. 195-196 (2)	1.20	.75
Nos. 219-220 (2)	1.70	.60
Nos. 175-176 (2)	1.85	1.75
Nos. 125-126 (2)	.70	.60
Nos. 230-231 (2)	.65	*.95*
Nos. 116-117 (2)	1.00	1.00
Nos. 132-133 (2)	7.00	7.00
Nos. 60-61 (2)	5.50	5.00
Nos. 188-189 (2)	1.25	.60
Nos. 173-174 (2)	.85	.80
Nos. 207-208 (2)	1.15	.90
Nos. 226-227 (2)	.85	.75
Nos. 167-168 (2)	1.10	1.10
Nos. 23-24 (2)	1.90	.55
Nos. 93-94 (2)	1.25	.80
Set total (42) Stamps	35.70	30.30

WHO Headquarters

World Health Organization Headquarters, Geneva — CD322

1966

Antigua....165-166
Ascension....102-103
Bahamas....247-248
Brunei....126-127
Cayman Islands....184-185
Dominica....197-198
Fiji....224-225
Gibraltar....180-181
Gilbert & Ellice Islands....127-128
Grenada....232-233
Hong Kong....229-230
Montserrat....184-185
New Hebrides, British....118-119
New Hebrides, French....134-135
Pitcairn Islands....62-63
St. Helena....190-191
St. Kitts-Nevis....177-178
St. Lucia....209-210
St. Vincent....247-248
Seychelles....228-229
Solomon Islands....169-170
South Arabia....25-26
Tristan da Cunha....99-100

Nos. 165-166 (2)	1.15	.55
Nos. 102-103 (2)	6.60	3.35
Nos. 247-248 (2)	.80	.80
Nos. 126-127 (2)	1.35	1.35
Nos. 184-185 (2)	2.25	1.20
Nos. 197-198 (2)	.75	.75
Nos. 224-225 (2)	4.70	3.30
Nos. 180-181 (2)	6.50	4.50
Nos. 127-128 (2)	.80	.70
Nos. 232-233 (2)	.80	.50
Nos. 229-230 (2)	11.25	2.30
Nos. 184-185 (2)	1.00	1.00
Nos. 118-119 (2)	.75	.50
Nos. 134-135 (2)	8.50	8.50
Nos. 62-63 (2)	7.25	6.50
Nos. 190-191 (2)	3.50	1.50
Nos. 177-178 (2)	.60	.60
Nos. 209-210 (2)	.80	.80
Nos. 247-248 (2)	1.15	1.05
Nos. 228-229 (2)	1.25	.65
Nos. 169-170 (2)	.95	.80
Nos. 25-26 (2)	2.10	.70
Nos. 99-100 (2)	1.90	1.25
Set total (46) Stamps	66.70	43.15

UNESCO Anniversary

"Education" — CD323

"Science" (Wheat ears & flask enclosing globe). "Culture" (lyre & columns). 20th anniversary of the UNESCO.

1966-67

Antigua....183-185
Ascension....108-110
Bahamas....249-251
Barbados....287-289
Bermuda....207-209
Brunei....128-130
Cayman Islands....186-188
Dominica....199-201
Gibraltar....183-185
Gilbert & Ellice Islands....129-131
Grenada....234-236
Hong Kong....231-233
Mauritius....299-301
Montserrat....186-188
New Hebrides, British....120-122
New Hebrides, French....136-138
Pitcairn Islands....64-66
St. Helena....192-194
St. Kitts-Nevis....179-181
St. Lucia....211-213
St. Vincent....249-251
Seychelles....230-232
Solomon Islands....171-173
South Arabia....27-29
Swaziland....123-125
Tristan da Cunha....101-103
Turks & Caicos Islands....155-157
Virgin Islands....176-178

Nos. 183-185 (3)	1.90	*2.50*
Nos. 108-110 (3)	11.00	5.80
Nos. 249-251 (3)	2.35	2.35
Nos. 287-289 (3)	2.35	2.15
Nos. 207-209 (3)	3.80	*3.90*
Nos. 128-130 (3)	4.65	5.40
Nos. 186-188 (3)	2.50	1.50
Nos. 199-201 (3)	1.60	.75
Nos. 183-185 (3)	6.50	3.25
Nos. 129-131 (3)	2.50	*2.45*
Nos. 234-236 (3)	1.10	1.20
Nos. 231-233 (3)	69.50	17.50
Nos. 299-301 (3)	2.10	1.50
Nos. 186-188 (3)	2.40	2.40
Nos. 120-122 (3)	1.90	1.90
Nos. 136-138 (3)	7.75	7.75
Nos. 64-66 (3)	7.10	4.75
Nos. 192-194 (3)	5.25	3.65
Nos. 179-181 (3)	.90	.90
Nos. 211-213 (3)	1.15	1.15
Nos. 249-251 (3)	2.30	1.35
Nos. 230-232 (3)	2.40	2.40
Nos. 171-173 (3)	2.00	1.50
Nos. 27-29 (3)	5.50	5.50
Nos. 123-125 (3)	1.40	1.40
Nos. 101-103 (3)	2.00	1.40
Nos. 155-157 (3)	1.05	.90
Nos. 176-178 (3)	1.40	1.30
Set total (84) Stamps	156.35	88.50

Silver Wedding, 1972

Queen Elizabeth II and Prince Philip — CD324

Designs: borders differ for each country.

1972

Anguilla....161-162
Antigua....295-296
Ascension....164-165
Bahamas....344-345
Bermuda....296-297
British Antarctic Territory....43-44
British Honduras....306-307
British Indian Ocean Territory....48-49

Brunei 186-187
Cayman Islands 304-305
Dominica 352-353
Falkland Islands 223-224
Fiji 328-329
Gibraltar 292-293
Gilbert & Ellice Islands 206-207
Grenada 466-467
Hong Kong 271-272
Montserrat 286-287
New Hebrides, British 169-170
New Hebrides, French 188-189
Pitcairn Islands 127-128
St. Helena 271-272
St. Kitts-Nevis 257-258
St. Lucia 328-329
St.Vincent 344-345
Seychelles 309-310
Solomon Islands 248-249
South Georgia 35-36
Tristan da Cunha 178-179
Turks & Caicos Islands 257-258
Virgin Islands 241-242

Nos. 161-162 (2) 1.10 *1.50*
Nos. 295-296 (2) .50 .50
Nos. 164-165 (2) .70 .70
Nos. 344-345 (2) .60 .60
Nos. 296-297 (2) .50 *.65*
Nos. 43-44 (2) 6.50 5.65
Nos. 306-307 (2) .80 .80
Nos. 48-49 (2) 2.00 1.00
Nos. 186-187 (2) .70 .70
Nos. 304-305 (2) .75 .75
Nos. 352-353 (2) .65 .65
Nos. 223-224 (2) 1.00 1.15
Nos. 328-329 (2) .70 .70
Nos. 292-293 (2) .50 .50
Nos. 206-207 (2) .50 .50
Nos. 466-467 (2) .70 .70
Nos. 271-272 (2) 1.70 1.50
Nos. 286-287 (2) .50 .50
Nos. 169-170 (2) .50 .50
Nos. 188-189 (2) 1.25 1.25
Nos. 127-128 (2) .90 .85
Nos. 271-272 (2) .60 1.20
Nos. 257-258 (2) .65 .50
Nos. 328-329 (2) .75 .75
Nos. 344-345 (2) .55 .55
Nos. 309-310 (2) .90 .90
Nos. 248-249 (2) .50 .50
Nos. 35-36 (2) 1.40 1.40
Nos. 178-179 (2) .70 .70
Nos. 257-258 (2) .50 .50
Nos. 241-242 (2) .50 .50
Set total (62) Stamps 30.10 29.15

Princess Anne's Wedding

Princess Anne and Mark Phillips — CD325

Wedding of Princess Anne and Mark Phillips, Nov. 14, 1973.

1973

Anguilla 179-180
Ascension 177-178
Belize 325-326
Bermuda 302-303
British Antarctic Territory 60-61
Cayman Islands 320-321
Falkland Islands 225-226
Gibraltar 305-306
Gilbert & Ellice Islands 216-217
Hong Kong 289-290
Montserrat 300-301
Pitcairn Islands 135-136
St. Helena 277-278
St. Kitts-Nevis 274-275
St. Lucia 349-350
St. Vincent 358-359
St. Vincent Grenadines 1-2
Seychelles 311-312
Solomon Islands 259-260
South Georgia 37-38
Tristan da Cunha 189-190
Turks & Caicos Islands 286-287
Virgin Islands 260-261

Nos. 179-180 (2) .55 .55
Nos. 177-178 (2) .60 .60
Nos. 325-326 (2) .50 .50
Nos. 302-303 (2) .50 .50
Nos. 60-61 (2) 1.10 1.10
Nos. 320-321 (2) .50 .50
Nos. 225-226 (2) .70 .60
Nos. 305-306 (2) .55 .55
Nos. 216-217 (2) .50 .50
Nos. 289-290 (2) 2.65 2.00
Nos. 300-301 (2) .55 .55
Nos. 135-136 (2) .70 .60
Nos. 277-278 (2) .50 .50
Nos. 274-275 (2) .50 .50
Nos. 349-350 (2) .50 .50
Nos. 358-359 (2) .50 .50
Nos. 1-2 (2) .50 .50
Nos. 311-312 (2) .65 .65
Nos. 259-260 (2) .70 .70
Nos. 37-38 (2) .75 .75
Nos. 189-190 (2) .50 .50
Nos. 286-287 (2) .50 .50
Nos. 260-261 (2) .50 .50
Set total (46) Stamps 15.50 14.65

Elizabeth II Coronation Anniv.

CD326

CD327

CD328

Designs: Royal and local beasts in heraldic form and simulated stonework. Portrait of Elizabeth II by Peter Grugeon. 25th anniversary of coronation of Queen Elizabeth II.

1978

Ascension 229
Barbados 474
Belize 397
British Antarctic Territory 71
Cayman Islands 404
Christmas Island 87
Falkland Islands 275
Fiji 384
Gambia 380
Gilbert Islands 312
Mauritius 464
New Hebrides, British 258
New Hebrides, French 278
St. Helena 317
St. Kitts-Nevis 354
Samoa 472
Solomon Islands 368
South Georgia 51
Swaziland 302
Tristan da Cunha 238
Virgin Islands 337

No. 229 (1) 2.00 2.00
No. 474 (1) 1.35 1.35
No. 397 (1) 1.40 1.75
No. 71 (1) 6.00 6.00
No. 404 (1) 2.00 2.00
No. 87 (1) 3.50 *4.00*
No. 275 (1) 4.00 5.50
No. 384 (1) 1.75 1.75
No. 380 (1) 1.50 1.50
No. 312 (1) 1.25 1.25
No. 464 (1) 2.10 2.10
No. 258 (1) 1.75 1.75
No. 278 (1) 3.50 3.50
No. 317 (1) 1.75 1.75
No. 354 (1) 1.00 1.00
No. 472 (1) 2.10 2.10
No. 368 (1) 2.50 2.50
No. 51 (1) 3.00 3.00
No. 302 (1) 1.60 1.60
No. 238 (1) 1.50 1.50
No. 337 (1) 1.80 1.80
Set total (21) Stamps 47.35 49.70

Queen Mother Elizabeth's 80th Birthday

CD330

Designs: Photographs of Queen Mother Elizabeth. Falkland Islands issued in sheets of 50; others in sheets of 9.

1980

Ascension 261
Bermuda 401
Cayman Islands 443
Falkland Islands 305
Gambia 412
Gibraltar 393
Hong Kong 364
Pitcairn Islands 193
St. Helena 341
Samoa 532
Solomon Islands 426
Tristan da Cunha 277

No. 261 (1) .40 .40
No. 401 (1) .45 .75
No. 443 (1) .40 .40
No. 305 (1) .40 .40
No. 412 (1) .40 .50
No. 393 (1) .35 .35
No. 364 (1) 1.10 1.25
No. 193 (1) .60 .60
No. 341 (1) .50 .50
No. 532 (1) .55 .55
No. 426 (1) .50 .50
No. 277 (1) .45 .45
Set total (12) Stamps 6.10 6.65

Royal Wedding, 1981

Prince Charles and Lady Diana — CD331

CD331a

Wedding of Charles, Prince of Wales, and Lady Diana Spencer, St. Paul's Cathedral, London, July 29, 1981.

1981

Antigua 623-627
Ascension 294-296
Barbados 547-549
Barbuda 497-501
Bermuda 412-414
Brunei 268-270
Cayman Islands 471-473
Dominica 701-705
Falkland Islands 324-326
Falkland Islands Dep. 1L59-1L61
Fiji 442-444
Gambia 426-428
Ghana 759-764
Grenada 1051-1055
Grenada Grenadines 440-443
Hong Kong 373-375
Jamaica 500-503
Lesotho 335-337
Maldive Islands 906-909
Mauritius 520-522
Norfolk Island 280-282
Pitcairn Islands 206-208
St. Helena 353-355
St. Lucia 543-549
Samoa 558-560
Sierra Leone 509-518
Solomon Islands 450-452
Swaziland 382-384
Tristan da Cunha 294-296
Turks & Caicos Islands 486-489
Caicos Island 8-11
Uganda 314-317
Vanuatu 308-310
Virgin Islands 406-408

Nos. 623-627 (5) 6.55 2.55
Nos. 294-296 (3) 1.00 1.00
Nos. 547-549 (3) .90 .90
Nos. 497-501 (5) 10.95 10.95
Nos. 412-414 (3) 2.00 2.00
Nos. 268-270 (3) 2.15 *4.50*
Nos. 471-473 (3) 1.20 1.30
Nos. 701-705 (5) 8.35 2.35
Nos. 324-326 (3) 1.65 1.70
Nos. 1L59-1L61 (3) 1.45 1.45
Nos. 442-444 (3) 1.35 1.35
Nos. 426-428 (3) .80 .80
Nos. 759-764 (9) 6.20 6.20
Nos. 1051-1055 (5) 9.85 1.85
Nos. 440-443 (4) 2.35 2.35
Nos. 373-375 (3) 3.05 2.85
Nos. 500-503 (4) 1.45 1.35
Nos. 335-337 (3) .90 .90
Nos. 906-909 (4) 1.55 1.55
Nos. 520-522 (3) 2.15 2.15
Nos. 280-282 (3) 1.75 1.75
Nos. 206-208 (3) 1.10 1.10
Nos. 353-355 (3) .85 .85
Nos. 543-549 (5) 7.00 7.00
Nos. 558-560 (3) .85 .85
Nos. 509-518 (10) 15.50 15.50
Nos. 450-452 (3) 1.25 1.25
Nos. 382-384 (3) 1.30 1.25
Nos. 294-296 (3) .90 .90
Nos. 486-489 (4) 2.20 2.20
Nos. 8-11 (4) 5.00 5.00
Nos. 314-317 (4) 3.30 3.00
Nos. 308-310 (3) 1.15 1.15
Nos. 406-408 (3) 1.10 1.10
Set total (131) Stamps 109.10 92.95

Princess Diana

CD332

CD333

Designs: Photographs and portrait of Princess Diana, wedding or honeymoon photographs, royal residences, arms of issuing country. Portrait photograph by Clive Friend. Souvenir sheet margins show family tree, various people related to the princess. 21st birthday of Princess Diana of Wales, July 1.

1982

Antigua 663-666
Ascension 313-316
Bahamas 510-513
Barbados 585-588
Barbuda 544-547
British Antarctic Territory 92-95
Cayman Islands 486-489
Dominica 773-776
Falkland Islands 348-351
Falkland Islands Dep. 1L72-1L75
Fiji 470-473
Gambia 447-450
Grenada 1101A-1105
Grenada Grenadines 485-491
Lesotho 372-375
Maldive Islands 952-955
Mauritius 548-551
Pitcairn Islands 213-216
St. Helena 372-375
St. Lucia 591-594
Sierra Leone 531-534
Solomon Islands 471-474
Swaziland 406-409
Tristan da Cunha 310-313
Turks and Caicos Islands 531-534
Virgin Islands 430-433

Nos. 663-666 (4) 8.25 7.35
Nos. 313-316 (4) 3.50 3.50
Nos. 510-513 (4) 6.00 3.85
Nos. 585-588 (4) 3.40 3.25
Nos. 544-547 (4) 9.75 7.70
Nos. 92-95 (4) 4.25 3.45
Nos. 486-489 (4) *4.75* *2.70*
Nos. 773-776 (4) 7.05 7.05
Nos. 348-351 (4) 2.95 2.95
Nos. 1L72-1L75 (4) 2.50 2.60
Nos. 470-473 (4) 3.25 2.95
Nos. 447-450 (4) 2.85 2.85
Nos. 1101A-1105 (7) 16.05 15.55

Nos. 485-491 (7)	17.65	17.65
Nos. 372-375 (4)	4.00	4.00
Nos. 952-955 (4)	5.50	3.90
Nos. 548-551 (4)	5.00	5.00
Nos. 213-216 (4)	2.15	2.15
Nos. 372-375 (4)	2.00	2.00
Nos. 591-594 (4)	8.70	8.70
Nos. 531-534 (4)	7.20	7.20
Nos. 471-474 (4)	2.90	2.90
Nos. 406-409 (4)	3.85	2.25
Nos. 310-313 (4)	3.65	1.45
Nos. 486-489 (4)	2.20	2.20
Nos. 430-433 (4)	3.00	3.00
Set total (110) Stamps	142.35	128.15

250th anniv. of first edition of Lloyd's List (shipping news publication) & of Lloyd's marine insurance.

CD335

Designs: First page of early edition of the list; historical ships, modern transportation or harbor scenes.

1984

Ascension....351-354
Bahamas....555-558
Barbados....627-630
Cayes of Belize....10-13
Cayman Islands....522-526
Falkland Islands....404-407
Fiji....509-512
Gambia....519-522
Mauritius....587-590
Nauru....280-283
St. Helena....412-415
Samoa....624-627
Seychelles....538-541
Solomon Islands....521-524
Vanuatu....368-371
Virgin Islands....466-469

Nos. 351-354 (4)	2.90	2.55
Nos. 555-558 (4)	4.15	2.95
Nos. 627-630 (4)	6.10	5.15
Nos. 10-13 (4)	2.65	2.65
Nos. 522-526 (5)	9.30	8.45
Nos. 404-407 (4)	3.50	3.65
Nos. 509-512 (4)	5.30	4.90
Nos. 519-522 (4)	4.20	4.30
Nos. 587-590 (4)	9.40	9.40
Nos. 280-283 (4)	2.40	2.35
Nos. 412-415 (4)	2.40	2.40
Nos. 624-627 (4)	2.55	2.35
Nos. 538-541 (4)	5.00	5.00
Nos. 521-524 (4)	4.65	3.95
Nos. 368-371 (4)	2.40	2.40
Nos. 466-469 (4)	4.25	4.25
Set total (65) Stamps	71.15	66.70

Queen Mother 85th Birthday

CD336

Designs: Photographs tracing the life of the Queen Mother, Elizabeth. The high value in each set pictures the same photograph taken of the Queen Mother holding the infant Prince Henry.

1985

Ascension....372-376
Bahamas....580-584
Barbados....660-664
Bermuda....469-473
Falkland Islands....420-424
Falkland Islands Dep....1L92-1L96
Fiji....531-535
Hong Kong....447-450
Jamaica....599-603
Mauritius....604-608
Norfolk Island....364-368
Pitcairn Islands....253-257
St. Helena....428-432
Samoa....649-653
Seychelles....567-571
  Zil Elwannyen Sesel....101-105
Solomon Islands....543-547
Swaziland....476-480
Tristan da Cunha....372-376
Vanuatu....392-396

Nos. 372-376 (5)	4.65	4.65
Nos. 580-584 (5)	7.70	6.45
Nos. 660-664 (5)	8.00	6.70
Nos. 469-473 (5)	9.40	9.40
Nos. 420-424 (5)	7.35	6.65
Nos. 1L92-1L96 (5)	8.00	8.00
Nos. 531-535 (5)	6.15	6.15
Nos. 447-450 (4)	9.50	8.50
Nos. 599-603 (5)	6.15	7.00
Nos. 604-608 (5)	11.30	11.30
Nos. 364-368 (5)	5.00	5.00
Nos. 253-257 (5)	5.25	5.95
Nos. 428-432 (5)	5.25	5.25
Nos. 649-653 (5)	8.40	7.55
Nos. 567-571 (5)	8.70	8.70
Nos. 101-105 (5)	6.60	6.60
Nos. 543-547 (5)	3.95	3.95
Nos. 476-480 (5)	7.75	7.25
Nos. 372-376 (5)	5.40	5.40
Nos. 392-396 (5)	5.25	5.25
Set total (99) Stamps	139.75	135.70

Queen Elizabeth II, 60th Birthday

CD337

1986, April 21

Ascension....389-393
Bahamas....592-596
Barbados....675-679
Bermuda....499-503
Cayman Islands....555-559
Falkland Islands....441-445
Fiji....544-548
Hong Kong....465-469
Jamaica....620-624
Kiribati....470-474
Mauritius....629-633
Papua New Guinea....640-644
Pitcairn Islands....270-274
St. Helena....451-455
Samoa....670-674
Seychelles....592-596
  Zil Elwannyen Sesel....114-118
Solomon Islands....562-566
South Georgia....101-105
Swaziland....490-494
Tristan da Cunha....388-392
Vanuatu....414-418
Zambia....343-347

Nos. 389-393 (5)	2.80	3.30
Nos. 592-596 (5)	2.75	*3.70*
Nos. 675-679 (5)	3.25	3.10
Nos. 499-503 (5)	4.65	*5.15*
Nos. 555-559 (5)	4.55	5.60
Nos. 441-445 (5)	3.95	*4.95*
Nos. 544-548 (5)	3.00	3.00
Nos. 465-469 (5)	8.75	6.75
Nos. 620-624 (5)	2.75	2.70
Nos. 470-474 (5)	2.10	2.10
Nos. 629-633 (5)	3.50	3.50
Nos. 640-644 (5)	4.10	4.10
Nos. 270-274 (5)	2.70	2.70
Nos. 451-455 (5)	2.50	3.05
Nos. 670-674 (5)	2.55	2.55
Nos. 592-596 (5)	2.70	2.70
Nos. 114-118 (5)	2.15	2.15
Nos. 562-566 (5)	2.90	2.90
Nos. 101-105 (5)	3.30	3.65
Nos. 490-494 (5)	2.15	2.15
Nos. 388-392 (5)	3.00	3.00
Nos. 414-418 (5)	3.10	3.10
Nos. 343-347 (5)	1.75	1.75
Set total (115) Stamps	74.95	77.65

Royal Wedding

Marriage of Prince Andrew and Sarah Ferguson
CD338

1986, July 23

Ascension....399-400
Bahamas....602-603
Barbados....687-688
Cayman Islands....560-561
Jamaica....629-630
Pitcairn Islands....275-276
St. Helena....460-461
St. Kitts....181-182
Seychelles....602-603
  Zil Elwannyen Sesel....119-120
Solomon Islands....567-568
Tristan da Cunha....397-398
Zambia....348-349

Nos. 399-400 (2)	1.60	1.60
Nos. 602-603 (2)	2.75	2.75
Nos. 687-688 (2)	2.00	1.25
Nos. 560-561 (2)	1.70	*2.35*
Nos. 629-630 (2)	1.35	1.35
Nos. 275-276 (2)	2.40	2.40
Nos. 460-461 (2)	1.05	1.05
Nos. 181-182 (2)	1.50	2.25
Nos. 602-603 (2)	2.50	2.50
Nos. 119-120 (2)	2.30	2.30
Nos. 567-568 (2)	1.00	1.00
Nos. 397-398 (2)	1.40	1.40
Nos. 348-349 (2)	1.10	1.30
Set total (26) Stamps	22.65	23.50

Queen Elizabeth II, 60th Birthday

Queen Elizabeth II & Prince Philip, 1947 Wedding Portrait — CD339

Designs: Photographs tracing the life of Queen Elizabeth II.

1986

Anguilla....674-677
Antigua....925-928
Barbuda....783-786
Dominica....950-953
Gambia....611-614
Grenada....1371-1374
Grenada Grenadines....749-752
Lesotho....531-534
Maldive Islands....1172-1175
Sierra Leone....760-763
Uganda....495-498

Nos. 674-677 (4)	8.00	8.00
Nos. 925-928 (4)	5.50	6.20
Nos. 783-786 (4)	23.15	23.15
Nos. 950-953 (4)	7.25	7.25
Nos. 611-614 (4)	8.25	7.90
Nos. 1371-1374 (4)	6.80	6.80
Nos. 749-752 (4)	6.75	6.75
Nos. 531-534 (4)	5.25	5.25
Nos. 1172-1175 (4)	6.25	6.25
Nos. 760-763 (4)	5.25	5.25
Nos. 495-498 (4)	8.50	8.50
Set total (44) Stamps	90.95	91.30

Royal Wedding, 1986

CD340

Designs: Photographs of Prince Andrew and Sarah Ferguson during courtship, engagement and marriage.

1986

Antigua....939-942
Barbuda....809-812
Dominica....970-973
Gambia....635-638
Grenada....1385-1388
Grenada Grenadines....758-761
Lesotho....545-548
Maldive Islands....1181-1184
Sierra Leone....769-772
Uganda....510-513

Nos. 939-942 (4)	7.00	*8.75*
Nos. 809-812 (4)	14.55	14.55
Nos. 970-973 (4)	7.25	7.25
Nos. 635-638 (4)	7.80	7.80
Nos. 1385-1388 (4)	8.30	8.30
Nos. 758-761 (4)	9.00	9.00
Nos. 545-548 (4)	7.45	7.45
Nos. 1181-1184 (4)	8.45	8.45
Nos. 769-772 (4)	5.35	5.35
Nos. 510-513 (4)	9.25	10.00
Set total (40) Stamps	84.40	86.90

Lloyds of London, 300th Anniv.

CD341

Designs: 17th century aspects of Lloyds, representations of each country's individual connections with Lloyds and publicized disasters insured by the organization.

1986

Ascension....454-457
Bahamas....655-658
Barbados....731-734
Bermuda....541-544
Falkland Islands....481-484
Liberia....1101-1104
Malawi....534-537
Nevis....571-574
St. Helena....501-504
St. Lucia....923-926
Seychelles....649-652
  Zil Elwannyen Sesel....146-149
Solomon Islands....627-630
South Georgia....131-134
Trinidad & Tobago....484-487
Tristan da Cunha....439-442
Vanuatu....485-488

Nos. 454-457 (4)	5.00	5.00
Nos. 655-658 (4)	8.90	4.95
Nos. 731-734 (4)	12.50	8.35
Nos. 541-544 (4)	8.00	*6.60*
Nos. 481-484 (4)	5.45	3.85
Nos. 1101-1104 (4)	4.25	4.25
Nos. 534-537 (4)	11.00	7.85
Nos. 571-574 (4)	8.35	8.35
Nos. 501-504 (4)	8.70	7.15
Nos. 923-926 (4)	8.80	8.80
Nos. 649-652 (4)	12.85	12.85
Nos. 146-149 (4)	11.25	11.25
Nos. 627-630 (4)	7.00	4.45
Nos. 131-134 (4)	6.30	3.70
Nos. 484-487 (4)	10.25	6.35
Nos. 439-442 (4)	7.60	7.60
Nos. 485-488 (4)	5.90	5.90
Set total (68) Stamps	142.10	117.25

Moon Landing, 20th Anniv.

CD342

Designs: Equipment, crew photographs, spacecraft, official emblems and report profiles created for the Apollo Missions. Two stamps in each set are square in format rather than like the stamp shown; see individual country listings for more information.

1989

Ascension....468-472
Bahamas....674-678
Belize....916-920
Kiribati....517-521
Liberia....1125-1129
Nevis....586-590
St. Kitts....248-252
Samoa....760-764
Seychelles....676-680
  Zil Elwannyen Sesel....154-158
Solomon Islands....643-647
Vanuatu....507-511

Nos. 468-472 (5)	9.40	8.60
Nos. 674-678 (5)	23.00	19.70
Nos. 916-920 (5)	22.85	18.10
Nos. 517-521 (5)	12.50	12.50
Nos. 1125-1129 (5)	8.50	8.50
Nos. 586-590 (5)	7.50	7.50

Nos. 248-252 (5)	8.00	8.25
Nos. 760-764 (5)	9.85	9.30
Nos. 676-680 (5)	16.05	16.05
Nos. 154-158 (5)	26.85	26.85
Nos. 643-647 (5)	9.00	6.75
Nos. 507-511 (5)	9.90	9.90
Set total (60) Stamps	163.40	152.00

Queen Mother, 90th Birthday

CD343

CD344

Designs: Portraits of Queen Elizabeth, the Queen Mother. See individual country listings for more information.

1990

Ascension....491-492
Bahamas....698-699
Barbados....782-783
British Antarctic Territory....170-171
British Indian Ocean Territory....106-107
Cayman Islands....622-623
Falkland Islands....524-525
Kenya....527-528
Kiribati....555-556
Liberia....1145-1146
Pitcairn Islands....336-337
St. Helena....532-533
St. Lucia....969-970
Seychelles....710-711
Zil Elwannyen Sesel....171-172
Solomon Islands....671-672
South Georgia....143-144
Swaziland....565-566
Tristan da Cunha....480-481

Nos. 491-492 (2)	4.75	4.75
Nos. 698-699 (2)	5.25	5.25
Nos. 782-783 (2)	4.00	3.70
Nos. 170-171 (2)	6.00	6.00
Nos. 106-107 (2)	18.00	18.50
Nos. 622-623 (2)	4.00	*5.50*
Nos. 524-525 (2)	4.75	4.75
Nos. 527-528 (2)	7.00	7.00
Nos. 555-556 (2)	4.75	4.75
Nos. 1145-1146 (2)	3.25	3.25
Nos. 336-337 (2)	4.25	4.25
Nos. 532-533 (2)	5.25	5.25
Nos. 969-970 (2)	4.60	4.60
Nos. 710-711 (2)	6.60	6.60
Nos. 171-172 (2)	8.25	8.25
Nos. 671-672 (2)	5.00	*5.30*
Nos. 143-144 (2)	5.50	6.50
Nos. 565-566 (2)	4.10	4.10
Nos. 480-481 (2)	5.60	5.60
Set total (38) Stamps	110.90	113.90

Queen Elizabeth II, 65th Birthday, and Prince Philip, 70th Birthday

CD345

CD346

Designs: Portraits of Queen Elizabeth II and Prince Philip differ for each country. Printed in sheets of 10 + 5 labels (3 different) between. Stamps alternate, producing 5 different triptychs.

1991

Ascension....506a
Bahamas....731a
Belize....970a
Bermuda....618a
Kiribati....572a
Mauritius....734a
Pitcairn Islands....349a
St. Helena....555a
St. Kitts....319a
Samoa....791a
Seychelles....724a
Zil Elwannyen Sesel....178a
Solomon Islands....689a
South Georgia....150a
Swaziland....587a
Vanuatu....541a

No. 506a (1)	3.50	3.75
No. 731a (1)	4.00	4.00
No. 970a (1)	3.75	3.75
No. 618a (1)	3.50	*4.00*
No. 572a (1)	4.00	4.00
No. 734a (1)	4.00	4.00
No. 349a (1)	3.25	3.25
No. 555a (1)	2.75	2.75
No. 319a (1)	3.00	3.00
No. 791a (1)	3.75	3.75
No. 724a (1)	5.00	5.00
No. 178a (1)	6.25	6.25
No. 689a (1)	3.75	3.75
No. 150a (1)	4.75	7.00
No. 587a (1)	4.00	4.00
No. 541a (1)	2.50	2.50
Set total (16) Stamps	61.75	64.75

Royal Family Birthday, Anniversary

CD347

Queen Elizabeth II, 65th birthday, Charles and Diana, 10th wedding anniversary: Various photographs of Queen Elizabeth II, Prince Philip, Prince Charles, Princess Diana and their sons William and Henry.

1991

Antigua....1446-1455
Barbuda....1229-1238
Dominica....1328-1337
Gambia....1080-1089
Grenada....2006-2015
Grenada Grenadines....1331-1340
Guyana....2440-2451
Lesotho....871-875
Maldive Islands....1533-1542
Nevis....666-675
St. Vincent....1485-1494
St. Vincent Grenadines....769-778
Sierra Leone....1387-1396
Turks & Caicos Islands....913-922
Uganda....918-927

Nos. 1446-1455 (10)	21.70	20.05
Nos. 1229-1238 (10)	125.00	119.50
Nos. 1328-1337 (10)	30.20	30.20
Nos. 1080-1089 (10)	24.65	24.40
Nos. 2006-2015 (10)	25.45	22.10
Nos. 1331-1340 (10)	23.85	23.35
Nos. 2440-2451 (12)	21.40	21.15
Nos. 871-875 (5)	13.55	13.55
Nos. 1533-1542 (10)	28.10	28.10
Nos. 666-675 (10)	23.65	23.65
Nos. 1485-1494 (10)	26.75	25.90
Nos. 769-778 (10)	25.40	25.40
Nos. 1387-1396 (10)	26.35	26.35
Nos. 913-922 (10)	27.50	25.30
Nos. 918-927 (10)	26.60	26.60
Set total (147) Stamps	470.15	455.60

Queen Elizabeth II's Accession to the Throne, 40th Anniv.

CD348

Various photographs of Queen Elizabeth II with local Scenes.

1992

Antigua....1513-1518
Barbuda....1306-1311
Dominica....1414-1419
Gambia....1172-1177
Grenada....2047-2052
Grenada Grenadines....1368-1373
Lesotho....881-885
Maldive Islands....1637-1642
Nevis....702-707
St. Vincent....1582-1587
St. Vincent Grenadines....829-834
Sierra Leone....1482-1487
Turks and Caicos Islands....978-987
Uganda....990-995
Virgin Islands....742-746

Nos. 1513-1518 (6)	15.00	*15.10*
Nos. 1306-1311 (6)	125.25	83.65
Nos. 1414-1419 (6)	12.50	12.50
Nos. 1172-1177 (6)	14.95	14.85
Nos. 2047-2052 (6)	15.95	15.95
Nos. 1368-1373 (6)	17.00	15.35
Nos. 881-885 (5)	11.90	11.90
Nos. 1637-1642 (6)	17.55	17.55
Nos. 702-707 (6)	13.55	13.55
Nos. 1582-1587 (6)	14.40	14.40
Nos. 829-834 (6)	19.65	19.65
Nos. 1482-1487 (6)	22.50	22.50
Nos. 913-922 (10)	27.50	25.30
Nos. 990-995 (6)	19.50	19.50
Nos. 742-746 (5)	15.50	15.50
Set total (92) Stamps	362.70	317.25

CD349

1992

Ascension....531-535
Bahamas....744-748
Bermuda....623-627
British Indian Ocean Territory....119-123
Cayman Islands....648-652
Falkland Islands....549-553
Gibraltar....605-609
Hong Kong....619-623
Kenya....563-567
Kiribati....582-586
Pitcairn Islands....362-366
St. Helena....570-574
St. Kitts....332-336
Samoa....805-809
Seychelles....734-738
Zil Elwannyen Sesel....183-187
Solomon Islands....708-712
South Georgia....157-161
Tristan da Cunha....508-512
Vanuatu....555-559
Zambia....561-565

Nos. 531-535 (5)	6.10	6.10
Nos. 744-748 (5)	6.90	4.70
Nos. 623-627 (5)	7.40	*7.55*
Nos. 119-123 (5)	22.75	19.25
Nos. 648-652 (5)	7.60	6.60
Nos. 549-553 (5)	5.95	5.90
Nos. 605-609 (5)	5.15	*5.50*
Nos. 619-623 (5)	5.10	5.25
Nos. 563-567 (5)	9.10	9.10
Nos. 582-586 (5)	3.85	3.85
Nos. 362-366 (5)	5.35	5.35
Nos. 570-574 (5)	5.70	5.70
Nos. 332-336 (5)	6.60	5.50
Nos. 805-809 (5)	7.85	5.90
Nos. 734-738 (5)	10.55	10.55
Nos. 183-187 (5)	9.40	9.40
Nos. 708-712 (5)	5.00	5.30
Nos. 157-161 (5)	5.60	5.90
Nos. 508-512 (5)	8.75	8.30
Nos. 555-559 (5)	3.65	3.65
Nos. 561-565 (5)	5.60	5.60
Set total (105) Stamps	153.95	144.95

Royal Air Force, 75th Anniversary

CD350

1993

Ascension....557-561
Bahamas....771-775
Barbados....842-846
Belize....1003-1008
Bermuda....648-651
British Indian Ocean Territory....136-140
Falkland Is.....573-577
Fiji....687-691
Montserrat....830-834
St. Kitts....351-355

Nos. 557-561 (5)	15.60	14.60
Nos. 771-775 (5)	24.65	21.45
Nos. 842-846 (5)	14.15	12.85
Nos. 1003-1008 (6)	16.55	16.50
Nos. 648-651 (4)	9.65	*10.45*
Nos. 136-140 (5)	16.10	16.10
Nos. 573-577 (5)	10.85	10.85
Nos. 687-691 (5)	17.75	17.40
Nos. 830-834 (5)	14.10	14.10
Nos. 351-355 (5)	22.80	23.55
Set total (50) Stamps	162.20	157.85

Royal Air Force, 80th Anniv.

Design CD350 Re-inscribed

1998

Ascension....697-701
Bahamas....907-911
British Indian Ocean Terr....198-202
Cayman Islands....754-758
Fiji....814-818
Gibraltar....755-759
Samoa....957-961
Turks & Caicos Islands....1258-1265
Tuvalu....763-767
Virgin Islands....879-883

Nos. 697-701 (5)	16.10	16.10
Nos. 907-911 (5)	13.60	12.65
Nos. 136-140 (5)	16.10	16.10
Nos. 754-758 (5)	15.25	15.25
Nos. 814-818 (5)	14.00	12.75
Nos. 755-759 (5)	9.70	9.70
Nos. 957-961 (5)	15.70	14.90
Nos. 1258-1265 (2)	27.50	27.50
Nos. 763-767 (5)	9.75	9.75
Nos. 879-883 (5)	15.00	15.00
Set total (47) Stamps	152.70	149.70

End of World War II, 50th Anniv.

CD351

CD352

1995

Ascension....613-617
Bahamas....824-828
Barbados....891-895
Belize....1047-1050
British Indian Ocean Territory....163-167
Cayman Islands....704-708
Falkland Islands....634-638
Fiji....720-724
Kiribati....662-668
Liberia....1175-1179
Mauritius....803-805
St. Helena....646-654
St. Kitts....389-393
St. Lucia....1018-1022
Samoa....890-894
Solomon Islands....799-803
South Georgia....198-200
Tristan da Cunha....562-566

Nos. 613-617 (5)	21.50	21.50

Nos. 824-828 (5)	22.00	18.70
Nos. 891-895 (5)	14.20	11.90
Nos. 1047-1050 (4)	6.05	5.90
Nos. 163-167 (5)	16.25	16.25
Nos. 704-708 (5)	17.65	13.95
Nos. 634-638 (5)	18.65	17.15
Nos. 720-724 (5)	17.50	14.50
Nos. 662-668 (7)	16.30	16.30
Nos. 1175-1179 (5)	15.25	11.15
Nos. 803-805 (3)	7.50	7.50
Nos. 646-654 (9)	26.10	26.10
Nos. 389-393 (5)	16.40	16.40
Nos. 1018-1022 (5)	12.25	10.15
Nos. 890-894 (5)	15.25	14.50
Nos. 799-803 (5)	14.75	14.75
Nos. 198-200 (3)	14.50	15.50
Nos. 562-566 (5)	20.10	20.10
Set total (91) Stamps	292.20	272.30

UN, 50th Anniv.

CD353

1995

Bahamas	839-842
Barbados	901-904
Belize	1055-1058
Jamaica	847-851
Liberia	1187-1190
Mauritius	813-816
Pitcairn Islands	436-439
St. Kitts	398-401
St. Lucia	1023-1026
Samoa	900-903
Tristan da Cunha	568-571
Virgin Islands	807-810

Nos. 839-842 (4)	7.15	6.40
Nos. 901-904 (4)	7.00	5.75
Nos. 1055-1058 (4)	4.70	4.70
Nos. 847-851 (5)	5.40	5.45
Nos. 1187-1190 (4)	9.65	9.65
Nos. 813-816 (4)	4.55	4.55
Nos. 436-439 (4)	8.15	8.15
Nos. 398-401 (4)	6.15	7.15
Nos. 1023-1026 (4)	7.50	7.25
Nos. 900-903 (4)	9.35	8.20
Nos. 568-571 (4)	13.50	13.50
Nos. 807-810 (4)	7.45	7.45
Set total (49) Stamps	90.55	88.20

Queen Elizabeth, 70th Birthday

CD354

1996

Ascension	632-635
British Antarctic Territory	240-243
British Indian Ocean Territory	176-180
Falkland Islands	653-657
Pitcairn Islands	446-449
St. Helena	672-676
Samoa	912-916
Tokelau	223-227
Tristan da Cunha	576-579
Virgin Islands	824-828

Nos. 632-635 (4)	5.30	5.30
Nos. 240-243 (4)	9.45	8.15
Nos. 176-180 (5)	11.50	11.50
Nos. 653-657 (5)	13.55	11.20
Nos. 446-449 (4)	8.60	8.60
Nos. 672-676 (5)	12.45	12.70
Nos. 912-916 (5)	10.50	10.50
Nos. 223-227 (5)	10.50	10.50
Nos. 576-579 (4)	8.35	8.35
Nos. 824-828 (5)	11.30	11.30
Set total (46) Stamps	101.50	98.10

Diana, Princess of Wales (1961-97)

CD355

1998

Ascension	696
Bahamas	901A-902
Barbados	950
Belize	1091
Bermuda	753
Botswana	659-663
British Antarctic Territory	258
British Indian Ocean Terr.	197
Cayman Islands	752A-753
Falkland Islands	694
Fiji	819-820
Gibraltar	754
Kiribati	719A-720
Namibia	909
Niue	706
Norfolk Island	644-645
Papua New Guinea	937
Pitcairn Islands	487
St. Helena	711
St. Kitts	437A-438
Samoa	955A-956
Seycelles	802
Solomon Islands	866-867
South Georgia	220
Tokelau	252B-253
Tonga	980
Niuafo'ou	201
Tristan da Cunha	618
Tuvalu	762
Vanuatu	718A-719
Virgin Islands	878

No. 696 (1)	5.25	5.25
Nos. 901A-902 (2)	5.30	5.30
No. 950 (1)	6.25	6.25
No. 1091 (1)	5.00	5.00
No. 753 (1)	5.00	5.00
Nos. 659-663 (5)	8.25	8.80
No. 258 (1)	5.50	5.50
No. 197 (1)	5.50	5.50
Nos. 752A-753 (3)	7.40	7.40
No. 694 (1)	5.00	5.00
Nos. 819-820 (2)	5.25	5.25
No. 754 (1)	4.75	4.75
Nos. 719A-720 (2)	4.85	4.85
No. 909 (1)	1.75	1.75
No. 706 (1)	5.50	5.50
Nos. 644-645 (2)	5.60	5.60
No. 937 (1)	6.25	6.25
No. 487 (1)	4.75	4.75
No. 711 (1)	4.25	4.25
Nos. 437A-438 (2)	5.15	5.15
Nos. 955A-956 (2)	7.00	7.00
No. 802 (1)	6.25	6.25
Nos. 866-867 (2)	5.40	5.40
No. 220 (1)	4.50	5.00
Nos. 252B-253 (2)	6.00	6.00
No. 980 (1)	5.75	5.75
No. 201 (1)	6.50	6.50
No. 618 (1)	5.00	5.00
No. 762 (1)	4.00	4.00
Nos. 718A-719 (2)	8.00	8.00
No. 878 (1)	4.50	4.50
Set total (46) Stamps	169.45	170.50

Wedding of Prince Edward and Sophie Rhys-Jones

CD356

1999

Ascension	729-730
Cayman Islands	775-776
Falkland Islands	729-730
Pitcairn Islands	505-506
St. Helena	733-734
Samoa	971-972
Tristan da Cunha	636-637
Virgin Islands	908-909

Nos. 729-730 (2)	4.50	4.50
Nos. 775-776 (2)	4.95	4.95
Nos. 729-730 (2)	14.00	14.00
Nos. 505-506 (2)	7.00	7.00
Nos. 733-734 (2)	5.00	5.00
Nos. 971-972 (2)	5.00	5.00
Nos. 636-637 (2)	7.50	7.50
Nos. 908-909 (2)	7.50	7.50
Set total (16) Stamps	55.45	55.45

1st Manned Moon Landing, 30th Anniv.

CD357

1999

Ascension	731-735
Bahamas	942-946
Barbados	967-971
Bermuda	778
Cayman Islands	777-781
Fiji	853-857
Jamaica	889-893
Kirbati	746-750
Nauru	465-469
St. Kitts	460-464
Samoa	973-977
Solomon Islands	875-879
Tuvalu	800-804
Virgin Islands	910-914

Nos. 731-735 (5)	12.80	12.80
Nos. 942-946 (5)	14.10	14.10
Nos. 967-971 (5)	9.45	8.25
No. 778 (1)	9.00	9.00
Nos. 777-781 (5)	9.25	9.25
Nos. 853-857 (5)	9.25	8.45
Nos. 889-893 (5)	8.30	7.18
Nos. 746-750 (5)	8.85	8.85
Nos. 465-469 (5)	9.25	8.00
Nos. 460-464 (5)	11.35	11.65
Nos. 973-977 (5)	12.60	12.45
Nos. 875-879 (5)	7.50	7.50
Nos. 800-804 (5)	7.45	7.45
Nos. 910-914 (5)	11.75	11.75
Set total (66) Stamps	140.90	136.68

Queen Mother's Century

CD358

1999

Ascension	736-740
Bahamas	951-955
Cayman Islands	782-786
Falkland Islands	734-738
Fiji	858-862
Norfolk Island	688-692
St. Helena	740-744
Samoa	978-982
Solomon Islands	880-884
South Georgia	231-235
Tristan da Cunha	638-642
Tuvalu	805-809

Nos. 736-740 (5)	15.50	15.50
Nos. 951-955 (5)	13.75	12.65
Nos. 782-786 (5)	8.35	8.35
Nos. 734-738 (5)	30.00	28.25
Nos. 858-862 (5)	12.80	13.25
Nos. 688-692 (5)	9.50	9.50
Nos. 740-744 (5)	16.15	16.15
Nos. 978-982 (5)	12.50	12.10
Nos. 880-884 (5)	7.50	7.00
Nos. 231-235 (5)	29.75	30.00
Nos. 638-642 (5)	18.00	18.00
Nos. 805-809 (5)	8.65	8.65
Set total (60) Stamps	182.45	179.40

Prince William, 18th Birthday

CD359

2000

Ascension	755-759
Cayman Islands	797-801
Falkland Islands	762-766
Fiji	889-893
South Georgia	257-261
Tristan da Cunha	664-668
Virgin Islands	925-929

Nos. 755-759 (5)	15.50	15.50
Nos. 797-801 (5)	11.15	10.90
Nos. 762-766 (5)	24.60	22.50
Nos. 889-893 (5)	12.90	12.90
Nos. 257-261 (5)	29.00	28.75
Nos. 664-668 (5)	21.50	21.50
Nos. 925-929 (5)	14.50	14.50
Set total (35) Stamps	129.15	126.55

Reign of Queen Elizabeth II, 50th Anniv.

CD360

2002

Ascension	790-794
Bahamas	1033-1037
Barbados	1019-1023
Belize	1152-1156
Bermuda	822-826
British Antarctic Territory	307-311
British Indian Ocean Territory	239-243
Cayman Islands	844-848
Falkland Islands	804-808
Gibraltar	896-900
Jamaica	952-956
Nauru	491-495
Norfolk Island	758-762
Papua New Guinea	1019-1023
Pitcairn Islands	552
St. Helena	788-792
St. Lucia	1146-1150
Solomon Islands	931-935
South Georgia	274-278
Swaziland	706-710
Tokelau	302-306
Tonga	1059
Niuafo'ou	239
Tristan da Cunha	706-710
Virgin Islands	967-971

Nos. 790-794 (5)	14.10	14.10
Nos. 1033-1037 (5)	15.25	15.25
Nos. 1019-1023 (5)	12.90	12.90
Nos. 1152-1156 (5)	12.65	12.25
Nos. 822-826 (5)	18.00	18.00
Nos. 307-311 (5)	23.00	23.00
Nos. 239-243 (5)	19.40	19.40
Nos. 844-848 (5)	13.25	13.25
Nos. 804-808 (5)	23.00	22.00
Nos. 896-900 (5)	6.65	6.65
Nos. 952-956 (5)	16.65	16.65
Nos. 491-495 (5)	17.75	17.75
Nos. 758-762 (5)	15.90	15.90
Nos. 1019-1023 (5)	14.50	14.50
No. 552 (1)	9.25	9.25
Nos. 788-792 (5)	19.75	19.75
Nos. 1146-1150 (5)	12.25	12.25
Nos. 931-935 (5)	12.40	12.40
Nos. 274-278 (5)	28.00	28.50
Nos. 706-710 (5)	12.50	12.50
Nos. 302-306 (5)	14.50	14.50
No. 1059 (1)	8.50	8.50
No. 239 (1)	8.75	8.75
Nos. 706-710 (5)	18.50	18.50
Nos. 967-971 (5)	16.50	16.50
Set total (113) Stamps	383.90	383.00

Queen Mother Elizabeth (1900-2002)

CD361

2002

Ascension 799-801
Bahamas 1044-1046
Bermuda..................................834-836
British Antarctic Territory..........312-314
British Indian Ocean Territory 245-247
Cayman Islands........................857-861
Falkland Islands 812-816
Nauru.....................................499-501
Pitcairn Islands........................561-565
St. Helena 808-812
St. Lucia 1155-1159
Seychelles 830
Solomon Islands......................945-947
South Georgia 281-285
Tokelau 312-314
Tristan da Cunha......................715-717
Virgin Islands..........................979-983

Nos. 799-801 (3)	8.85	8.85
Nos. 1044-1046 (3)	9.10	9.10
Nos. 834-836 (3)	12.25	12.25
Nos. 312-314 (3)	18.75	18.75
Nos. 245-247 (3)	17.35	17.35
Nos. 857-861 (5)	15.00	15.00
Nos. 812-816 (5)	28.50	28.50
Nos. 499-501 (3)	14.00	14.00
Nos. 561-565 (5)	15.25	15.25
Nos. 808-812 (5)	12.00	12.00
Nos. 1155-1159 (5)	12.00	12.00
No. 830 (1)	6.50	6.50
Nos. 945-947 (3)	9.25	9.25
Nos. 281-285 (5)	19.50	19.50
Nos. 312-314 (3)	11.85	11.85
Nos. 715-717 (3)	16.25	16.25
Nos. 979-983 (5)	23.50	23.50
Set total (63) Stamps	249.90	249.90

Head of Queen Elizabeth II

CD362

2003

Ascension 822
Bermuda..865
British Antarctic Territory.................322
British Indian Ocean Territory 261
Cayman Islands...............................878
Falkland Islands 828
St. Helena 820
South Georgia 294
Tristan da Cunha.............................731
Virgin Islands................................1003

No. 822 (1)	12.50	12.50
No. 865 (1)	50.00	50.00
No. 322 (1)	9.50	9.50
No. 261 (1)	11.00	11.00
No. 878 (1)	14.00	14.00
No. 828 (1)	9.00	9.00
No. 820 (1)	9.00	9.00
No. 294 (1)	8.50	8.50
No. 731 (1)	10.00	10.00
No. 1003 (1)	10.00	10.00
Set total (10) Stamps	143.50	143.50

Coronation of Queen Elizabeth II, 50th Anniv.

CD363

2003

Ascension 823-825
Bahamas 1073-1075
Bermuda..................................866-868
British Antarctic Territory..........323-325
British Indian Ocean Territory 262-264
Cayman Islands........................879-881
Jamaica 970-972
Kiribati 825-827
Pitcairn Islands........................577-581
St. Helena 821-823
St. Lucia 1171-1173
Tokelau 320-322
Tristan da Cunha......................732-734
Virgin Islands........................1004-1006

Nos. 823-825 (3)	12.50	12.50
Nos. 1073-1075 (3)	13.00	13.00
Nos. 866-868 (2)	14.25	14.25
Nos. 323-325 (3)	23.00	23.00
Nos. 262-264 (3)	28.00	28.00
Nos. 879-881 (3)	19.25	19.25
Nos. 970-972 (3)	10.00	10.00
Nos. 825-827 (3)	13.50	13.50
Nos. 577-581 (5)	14.40	14.40
Nos. 821-823 (3)	7.25	7.25
Nos. 1171-1173 (3)	8.75	8.75
Nos. 320-322 (3)	17.25	17.25
Nos. 732-734 (3)	16.75	16.75
Nos. 1004-1006 (3)	25.00	25.00
Set total (43) Stamps	222.90	222.90

Prince William, 21st Birthday

CD364

2003

Ascension 826
British Indian Ocean Territory 265
Cayman Islands........................882-884
Falkland Islands 829
South Georgia 295
Tokelau 323
Tristan da Cunha.............................735
Virgin Islands........................1007-1009

No. 826 (1)	7.25	7.25
No. 265 (1)	8.00	8.00
Nos. 882-884 (3)	6.95	6.95
No. 829 (1)	13.50	13.50
No. 295 (1)	8.50	8.50
No. 323 (1)	7.25	7.25
No. 735 (1)	6.00	6.00
Nos. 1007-1009 (3)	10.00	10.00
Set total (12) Stamps	67.45	67.45

British Commonwealth of Nations

Dominions, Colonies, Territories, Offices and Independent Members

Comprising stamps of the British Commonwealth and associated nations.

A strict observance of technicalities would bar some or all of the stamps listed under Burma, Ireland, Kuwait, Nepal, New Republic, Orange Free State, Samoa, South Africa, South-West Africa, Stellaland, Sudan, Swaziland, the two Transvaal Republics and others but these are included for the convenience of collectors.

1. Great Britain

Great Britain: Including England, Scotland, Wales and Northern Ireland.

2. The Dominions, Present and Past

AUSTRALIA

The Commonwealth of Australia was proclaimed on January 1, 1901. It consists of six former colonies as follows:

New South Wales
Queensland
South Australia
Victoria
Tasmania
Western Australia

The following islands and territories are, or have been, administered by Australia: Australian Antarctic Territory, Christmas Island, Cocos (Keeling) Islands, Nauru, New Guinea, Norfolk Island, Papua.

CANADA

The Dominion of Canada was created by the British North America Act in 1867. The following provinces were former sepa- rate colonies and issued postage stamps:

British Columbia and Vancouver Island
New Brunswick
Newfoundland
Nova Scotia
Prince Edward Island

FIJI

The colony of Fiji became an independent nation with dominion status on Oct. 10, 1970.

GHANA

This state came into existence Mar. 6, 1957, with dominion status. It consists of the former colony of the Gold Coast and the Trusteeship Territory of Togoland. Ghana became a republic July 1, 1960.

INDIA

The Republic of India was inaugurated on January 26, 1950. It succeeded the Dominion of India which was proclaimed August 15, 1947, when the former Empire of India was divided into Pakistan and the Union of India. The Republic is composed of about 40 predominantly Hindu states of three classes: governor's provinces, chief commissioner's provinces and princely states. India also has various territories, such as the Andaman and Nicobar Islands.

The old Empire of India was a federation of British India and the native states. The more important princely states were autonomous. Of the more than 700 Indian states, these 43 are familiar names to philatelists because of their postage stamps.

CONVENTION STATES

Chamba
Faridkot
Gwalior
Jhind
Nabha
Patiala

FEUDATORY STATES

Alwar
Bahawalpur
Bamra
Barwani
Bhopal
Bhor
Bijawar
Bundi
Bussahir
Charkhari
Cochin
Dhar
Dungarpur
Duttia
Faridkot (1879-85)
Hyderabad
Idar
Indore
Jaipur
Jammu
Jammu and Kashmir
Jasdan
Jhalawar
Jhind (1875-76)
Kashmir
Kishangarh
Kotah
Las Bela
Morvi
Nandgaon
Nowanuggur
Orchha
Poonch
Rajasthan
Rajpeepla
Sirmur
Soruth
Tonk
Travancore
Wadhwan

NEW ZEALAND

Became a dominion on September 26, 1907. The following islands and territories are, or have been, administered by New Zealand:

Aitutaki
Cook Islands (Rarotonga)
Niue
Penrhyn
Ross Dependency
Samoa (Western Samoa)
Tokelau Islands

PAKISTAN

The Republic of Pakistan was proclaimed March 23, 1956. It succeeded the Dominion which was proclaimed August 15, 1947. It is made up of all or part of several Moslem provinces and various districts of the former Empire of India, including Bahawalpur and Las Bela. Pakistan withdrew from the Commonwealth in 1972.

SOUTH AFRICA

Under the terms of the South African Act (1909) the self-governing colonies of Cape of Good Hope, Natal, Orange River Colony and Transvaal united on May 31, 1910, to form the Union of South Africa. It became an independent republic May 3, 1961.

Under the terms of the Treaty of Versailles, South-West Africa, formerly German South-West Africa, was mandated to the Union of South Africa.

SRI LANKA (CEYLON)

The Dominion of Ceylon was proclaimed February 4, 1948. The island had been a Crown Colony from 1802 until then. On May 22, 1972, Ceylon became the Republic of Sri Lanka.

3. Colonies, Past and Present; Controlled Territory and Independent Members of the Commonwealth

Abu Dhabi
Aden
Aitutaki
Alderney
Anguilla
Antigua
Ascension
Australia
Bahamas
Bahrain
Bangladesh
Barbados
Barbuda
Basutoland
Batum
Bechuanaland
Bechuanaland Prot.
Belize
Bermuda
Botswana
British Antarctic Territory
British Central Africa
British Columbia and Vancouver Island
British East Africa
British Guiana

British Honduras
British Indian Ocean Territory
British New Guinea
British Solomon Islands
British Somaliland
Brunei
Burma
Bushire
Cameroons
Canada
Cape of Good Hope
Cayman Islands
Christmas Island
Cocos (Keeling) Islands
Cook Islands
Crete,
British Administration
Cyprus
Dominica
East Africa & Uganda
Protectorates
Egypt
Falkland Islands
Fiji
Gambia
German East Africa
Ghana
Gibraltar
Gilbert Islands
Gilbert & Ellice Islands
Gold Coast
Grenada
Griqualand West
Guernsey
Guyana
Heligoland
Hong Kong
Indian Native States
(see India)
Ionian Islands
Jamaica
Jersey
Jordan
Kenya

Kenya, Uganda & Tanzania
Kiribati
Kuwait
Labuan
Lagos
Leeward Islands
Lesotho
Madagascar
Malawi
Malaya
Federated Malay States
Johore
Kedah
Kelantan
Malacca
Negri Sembilan
Pahang
Penang
Perak
Perlis
Selangor
Singapore
Sungei Ujong
Trengganu
Malaysia
Maldive Islands
Malta
Man, Isle of
Mauritius
Mesopotamia
Montserrat
Mozambique
Muscat
Namibia
Natal
Nauru
Nevis
New Britain
New Brunswick
Newfoundland
New Guinea
New Hebrides
New Republic
New South Wales

New Zealand
Niger Coast Protectorate
Nigeria
Niue
Norfolk Island
North Borneo
Northern Nigeria
Northern Rhodesia
North West Pacific Islands
Nova Scotia
Nyasaland Protectorate
Oman
Orange River Colony
Pakistan
Palestine
Papua New Guinea
Penrhyn Island
Pitcairn Islands
Prince Edward Island
Qatar
Queensland
Rhodesia
Rhodesia & Nyasaland
Ross Dependency
Rwanda
Sabah
St. Christopher
St. Helena
St. Kitts
St. Kitts-Nevis-Anguilla
St. Lucia
St. Vincent
Samoa
Sarawak
Seychelles
Sierra Leone
Singapore
Solomon Islands
Somaliland Protectorate
South Africa
South Arabia
South Australia
South Georgia
Southern Nigeria

Southern Rhodesia
South-West Africa
Sri Lanka
Stellaland
Straits Settlements
Sudan
Swaziland
Tanganyika
Tanzania
Tasmania
Tobago
Togo
Tokelau Islands
Tonga
Transvaal
Trinidad
Trinidad and Tobago
Tristan da Cunha
Trucial States
Turks and Caicos
Turks Islands
Tuvalu
Uganda
United Arab Emirates
Vanuatu
Victoria
Virgin Islands
Western Australia
Zambia
Zanzibar
Zimbabwe
Zululand

POST OFFICES IN FOREIGN COUNTRIES

Africa
East Africa Forces
Middle East Forces
Bangkok
China
Morocco
Turkish Empire

Colonies, Former Colonies, Offices, Territories Controlled by Parent States

Belgium

Belgian Congo
Ruanda-Urundi

Denmark

Danish West Indies
Faroe Islands
Greenland
Iceland

Finland

Aland Islands

France

COLONIES PAST AND PRESENT, CONTROLLED TERRITORIES

Afars & Issas, Territory of
Alaouites
Alexandretta
Algeria
Alsace & Lorraine
Anjouan
Annam & Tonkin
Benin
Cambodia (Khmer)
Cameroun
Castellorizo
Chad
Cilicia
Cochin China
Comoro Islands
Dahomey
Diego Suarez
Djibouti (Somali Coast)
Fezzan
French Congo
French Equatorial Africa
French Guiana
French Guinea
French India
French Morocco
French Polynesia (Oceania)
French Southern & Antarctic Territories
French Sudan
French West Africa
Gabon
Germany
Ghadames
Grand Comoro
Guadeloupe
Indo-China
Inini
Ivory Coast
Laos
Latakia
Lebanon
Madagascar
Martinique
Mauritania
Mayotte
Memel
Middle Congo
Moheli
New Caledonia
New Hebrides
Niger Territory
Nossi-Be
Obock
Reunion
Rouad, Ile
Ste.-Marie de Madagascar
St. Pierre & Miquelon
Senegal
Senegambia & Niger
Somali Coast
Syria
Tahiti
Togo
Tunisia
Ubangi-Shari
Upper Senegal & Niger
Upper Volta
Viet Nam
Wallis & Futuna Islands

POST OFFICES IN FOREIGN COUNTRIES

China
Crete
Egypt
Turkish Empire
Zanzibar

Germany

EARLY STATES

Baden
Bavaria
Bergedorf
Bremen
Brunswick
Hamburg
Hanover
Lubeck
Mecklenburg-Schwerin
Mecklenburg-Strelitz
Oldenburg
Prussia
Saxony
Schleswig-Holstein
Wurttemberg

FORMER COLONIES

Cameroun (Kamerun)
Caroline Islands
German East Africa
German New Guinea
German South-West Africa
Kiauchau
Mariana Islands
Marshall Islands
Samoa
Togo

Italy

EARLY STATES

Modena
Parma
Romagna
Roman States
Sardinia
Tuscany
Two Sicilies
  Naples
  Neapolitan Provinces
  Sicily

FORMER COLONIES, CONTROLLED TERRITORIES, OCCUPATION AREAS

Aegean Islands
  Calimno (Calino)
  Caso
  Cos (Coo)
  Karki (Carchi)
  Leros (Lero)
  Lipso
  Nisiros (Nisiro)
  Patmos (Patmo)
  Piscopi
  Rodi (Rhodes)
  Scarpanto
  Simi
  Stampalia
Castellorizo
Corfu
Cyrenaica
Eritrea
Ethiopia (Abyssinia)
Fiume
Ionian Islands
  Cephalonia
  Ithaca
  Paxos
Italian East Africa
Libya
Oltre Giuba
Saseno
Somalia (Italian Somaliland)
Tripolitania

POST OFFICES IN FOREIGN COUNTRIES

"ESTERO"*
Austria
China
  Peking
  Tientsin
Crete
Tripoli
Turkish Empire
  Constantinople
  Durazzo
  Janina
Jerusalem
Salonika
Scutari
Smyrna
Valona

*Stamps overprinted "ESTERO" were used in various parts of the world.

Netherlands

Aruba
Caribbean Netherlands
Curacao
Netherlands Antilles (Curacao)
Netherlands Indies
Netherlands New Guinea
St. Martin
Surinam (Dutch Guiana)

Portugal

COLONIES PAST AND PRESENT, CONTROLLED TERRITORIES

Angola
Angra
Azores
Cape Verde
Funchal
Horta
Inhambane
Kionga
Lourenco Marques
Macao
Madeira
Mozambique
Mozambique Co.
Nyassa
Ponta Delgada
Portuguese Africa
Portuguese Congo
Portuguese Guinea
Portuguese India
Quelimane
St. Thomas & Prince Islands
Tete
Timor
Zambezia

Russia

ALLIED TERRITORIES AND REPUBLICS, OCCUPATION AREAS

Armenia
Aunus (Olonets)
Azerbaijan
Batum
Estonia
Far Eastern Republic
Georgia
Karelia
Latvia
Lithuania
North Ingermanland
Ostland
Russian Turkestan
Siberia
South Russia
Tannu Tuva
Transcaucasian Fed. Republics
Ukraine
Wenden (Livonia)
Western Ukraine

Spain

COLONIES PAST AND PRESENT, CONTROLLED TERRITORIES

Aguera, La
Cape Juby
Cuba
Elobey, Annobon & Corisco
Fernando Po
Ifni
Mariana Islands
Philippines
Puerto Rico
Rio de Oro
Rio Muni
Spanish Guinea
Spanish Morocco
Spanish Sahara
Spanish West Africa

POST OFFICES IN FOREIGN COUNTRIES

Morocco
Tangier
Tetuan

Dies of British Colonial Stamps

DIE A:

1. The lines in the groundwork vary in thickness and are not uniformly straight.

2. The seventh and eighth lines from the top, in the groundwork, converge where they meet the head.

3. There is a small dash in the upper part of the second jewel in the band of the crown.

4. The vertical color line in front of the throat stops at the sixth line of shading on the neck.

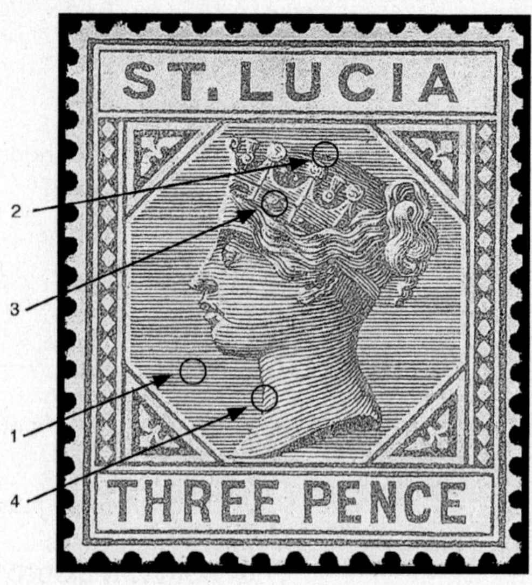

DIE B:

1. The lines in the groundwork are all thin and straight.

2. All the lines of the background are parallel.

3. There is no dash in the upper part of the second jewel in the band of the crown.

4. The vertical color line in front of the throat stops at the eighth line of shading on the neck.

DIE I:

1. The base of the crown is well below the level of the inner white line around the vignette.

2. The labels inscribed "POSTAGE" and "REVENUE" are cut square at the top.

3. There is a white "bud" on the outer side of the main stem of the curved ornaments in each lower corner.

4. The second (thick) line below the country name has the ends next to the crown cut diagonally.

DIE Ia.
1 as die II.
2 and 3 as die I.

DIE Ib.
1 and 3 as die II.
2 as die I.

DIE II:

1. The base of the crown is aligned with the underside of the white line around the vignette.

2. The labels curve inward at the top inner corners.

3. The "bud" has been removed from the outer curve of the ornaments in each corner.

4. The second line below the country name has the ends next to the crown cut vertically.

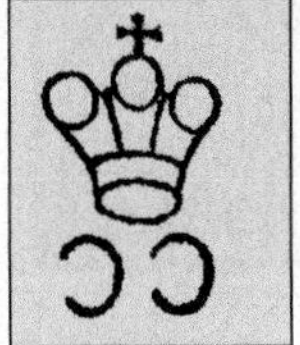

Wmk. 1
Crown and C C

Wmk. 2
Crown and C A

Wmk. 3
Multiple Crown and C A

Wmk. 4
Multiple Crown and Script C A

Wmk. 4a

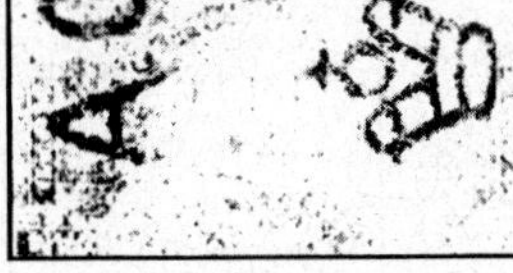

Wmk. 46

Wmk. 314
St. Edward's Crown and C A Multiple

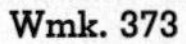

Wmk. 373

Wmk. 384

Wmk. 406

British Colonial and Crown Agents Watermarks

Watermarks 1 to 4, 314, 373, 384 and 406, common to many British territories, are illustrated here to avoid duplication.

The letters "CC" of Wmk. 1 identify the paper as having been made for the use of the Crown Colonies, while the letters "CA" of the others stand for "Crown Agents." Both Wmks. 1 and 2 were used on stamps printed by De La Rue & Co.

Wmk. 3 was adopted in 1904; Wmk. 4 in 1921; Wmk. 46 in 1879; Wmk. 314 in 1957; Wmk. 373 in 1974; Wmk. 384 in 1985; Wmk 406 in 2008.

In Wmk. 4a, a non-matching crown of the general St. Edwards type (bulging on both sides at top) was substituted for one of the Wmk. 4 crowns which fell off the dandy roll. The non-matching crown occurs in 1950-52 printings in a horizontal row of crowns on certain regular stamps of Johore and Seychelles, and on various postage due stamps of Barbados, Basutoland, British Guiana, Gold Coast, Grenada, Northern Rhodesia, St. Lucia, Swaziland and Trinidad and Tobago. A variation of Wmk. 4a, with the non-matching crown in a horizontal row of crown-CA-crown, occurs on regular stamps of Bahamas, St. Kitts-Nevis and Singapore.

Wmk. 314 was intentionally used sideways, starting in 1966. When a stamp was issued with Wmk. 314 both upright and sideways, the sideways varieties usually are listed also – with minor numbers. In many of the later issues, Wmk. 314 is slightly visible.

Wmk. 373 is usually only faintly visible.

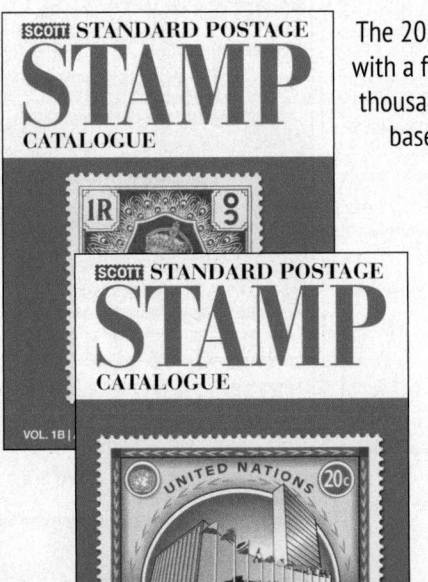

SAN MARINO

ˌsan mə-ˈrē-ˌnō

LOCATION — Eastern Italy, about 20 miles inland from the Adriatic Sea
GOVT. — Republic
AREA — 24.1 sq. mi.
POP. — 25,061 (1999 est.)
CAPITAL — San Marino

100 Centesimi = 1 Lira
100 Cents = 1 Euro (2002)

Catalogue values for unused stamps in this country are for Never Hinged items, beginning with Scott 412 in the regular postage section, Scott B39 in the semi-postal section, Scott C97 in the airpost section, Scott E26 in the special delivery section, and Scott Q40 in the parcel post section.

Watermarks

Wmk. 140 — Crown

Wmk. 174 — Coat of Arms

Wmk. 217 — Three Plumes

Wmk. 277 — Winged Wheel

Wmk. 303 — Multiple Stars

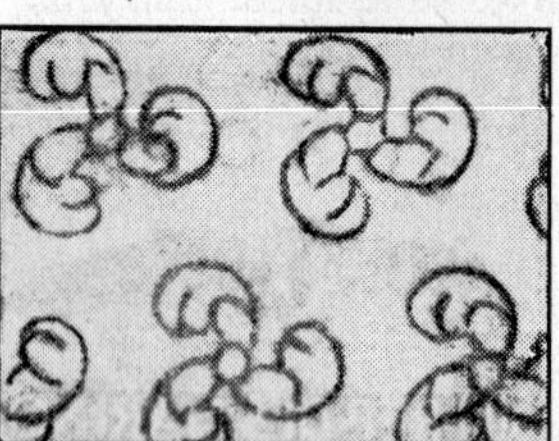

Wmk. 339 — Triskelion

Nos. 1-28 were spaced very narrowly on the plates, so that perforations often cut into the design on one or two sides. Values are for stamps with perforations clear of the design. Examples with perfs cutting in the design sell for less, while examples with four clear, full margins sell for substantially more than the values shown.

Numeral — A1

Coat of Arms — A2

Coat of Arms — A3

1877-99 Typo. Wmk. 140 ***Perf. 14***

No.	Type	Description	Unused	Used
1	A1	2c green	37.50	19.00
2	A1	2c blue ('94)	15.00	19.00
3	A1	2c claret ('95)	13.50	19.00
4	A2	5c orange ('90)	180.00	50.00
5	A2	5c olive grn ('92)	9.00	9.25
6	A2	5c green ('99)	9.25	14.00
7	A2	10c ultra	350.00	115.00
a.		10c blue ('90)	3,600.	300.00
8	A2	10c dk green ('92)	9.25	11.00
9	A2	10c claret ('99)	9.25	13.50
10	A2	15c claret ('94)	170.00	120.00
11	A2	20c vermilion	45.00	19.00
12	A2	20c lilac ('95)	9.25	19.00
13	A2	25c maroon ('90)	150.00	90.00
14	A2	25c blue ('99)	9.25	17.00
15	A2	30c brown	925.00	125.00
16	A2	30c org yel ('92)	9.25	19.00
17	A2	40c violet	925.00	125.00
18	A2	40c dk brn ('92)	9.25	19.00
19	A2	45c gray grn ('92)	9.25	19.00
20	A2	65c red brn ('92)	9.25	19.00
21	A3	1 l car & yel ('92)	1,825.	950.00
22	A3	1 l lt blue ('95)	1,675.	750.00
23	A3	2 l brn & yel ('94)	90.00	120.00
24	A3	5 l vio & grn ('94)	225.00	450.00

Nos. 7a, 15, 11 Surcharged in Black

1892

No.	Type	Description	Unused	Used
25	A2	5c on 10c blue	90.00	26.00
a.		Inverted surcharge	110.00	34.00
b.		5c on 10c ultramarine	*50,000.*	*12,000.*
c.		As "b," inverted surch.	—	—
d.		Double surcharge, one inverted	—	
e.		Pair, one without surcharge	2,250.	
f.		Pair, one without surcharge, surcharge inverted	2,250.	
26	A2	5c on 30c brn	300.00	135.00
a.		Inverted surcharge	375.00	170.00
b.		Double surch., one inverted	375.00	210.00
c.		Double invtd. surcharge	375.00	210.00
27	A2	10c on 20c ver	67.50	15.00
a.		Inverted surcharge	75.00	22.50
b.		Double surch., one inverted	82.50	30.00
c.		Double surcharge	82.50	30.00

Ten to twelve varieties of each surcharge.

No. 11 Surcharged

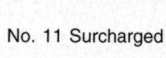

No.	Type	Description	Unused	Used
28	A2	10c on 20c ver	300.00	19.00

Government Palace and Portraits of Regents, Tonnini and Marcucci
A6 A7

Portraits of Regents and View of Interior of Palace — A8

Wmk. 174

1894, Sept. 30 Litho. ***Perf. 15½***

No.	Type	Description	Unused	Used
29	A6	25c blue & dk brn	7.50	3.00
30	A7	50c dull red & dk brn	45.00	9.50
31	A8	1 l green & dk brown	35.00	11.50
		Nos. 29-31 (3)	87.50	24.00

Opening of the new Government Palace and the installation of the new Regents.

Statue of Liberty — A9

Wmk. 140

1899-1922 Typo. ***Perf. 14***

No.	Type	Description	Unused	Used
32	A9	2c brown	3.75	1.90
33	A9	2c claret ('22)	.75	.75
34	A9	5c brown org	7.50	4.50
35	A9	5c olive grn ('22)	.75	.75
36	A9	10c brown org ('22)	.75	.75
37	A9	20c dp brown ('22)	.75	.75
38	A9	25c ultra ('22)	1.50	1.50
39	A9	45c red brown ('22)	3.00	3.00
		Nos. 32-39 (8)	18.75	13.90

Numeral of Value — A10

Mt. Titano — A11

1903-25 ***Perf. 14, 14½x14***

No.	Type	Description	Unused	Used
40	A10	2c reddish lilac	22.50	12.00
41	A10	2c org brn ('21)	1.50	1.10
42	A11	5c blue grn	11.00	7.50
43	A11	5c olive grn ('21)	1.50	1.10
a.		Imperforate	85.00	
44	A11	5c red brn ('25)	.75	.75
45	A11	10c claret	11.50	7.50
46	A11	10c brown org ('21)	1.50	1.20
47	A11	10c olive grn ('25)	.75	.75
48	A11	15c blue grn ('22)	1.50	1.10
49	A11	15c brown vio ('25)	.75	.75
50	A11	20c brown orange	150.00	60.00
51	A11	20c brown ('21)	1.50	1.20
52	A11	20c blue grn ('25)	.75	.75
53	A11	25c blue	27.50	12.00
54	A11	25c gray ('21)	1.50	1.10
55	A11	25c violet ('25)	.75	.75
56	A11	30c brown red	12.00	*18.50*
57	A11	30c claret ('21)	1.50	1.20
58	A11	30c orange ('25)	22.50	3.75
59	A11	40c orange red	22.50	18.50
60	A11	40c dp rose ('21)	1.50	1.20
61	A11	40c brown ('25)	.75	.75
62	A11	45c yellow	16.50	18.50
63	A11	50c brown vio ('23)	3.00	3.00
64	A11	50c gray blk ('25)	.75	.75
65	A11	60c brown red ('25)	1.50	.75
66	A11	65c chocolate	17.00	18.50
67	A11	80c blue ('21)	6.00	6.00
68	A11	90c brown ('23)	6.00	6.00
69	A11	1 l olive green	60.00	30.00
70	A11	1 l ultra ('21)	6.00	6.00
71	A11	1 l lt blue ('25)	1.50	.75
72	A11	2 l violet	1,000.	425.00
73	A11	2 l orange ('21)	22.50	27.00
74	A11	2 l lt green ('25)	7.50	7.50
75	A11	5 l slate	275.00	300.00
76	A11	5 l ultra ('25)	16.50	19.00
		Nos. 40-76 (37)	1,736.	1,022.

For overprints and surcharges see Nos. 77, 93-96, 103, 107, 188-189, B1-B2, E2, E4.

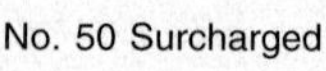

No. 50 Surcharged

1905, Sept. 1

No.	Type	Description	Unused	Used
77	A11	15c on 20c brown org	15.00	10.50
a.		Large 5 in 1905 on level with 9	92.50	45.00

Coat of Arms
A12 A13

Two types:
I — Width 18½mm.
II — Width 19mm.

1907-10 Unwmk. Engr. ***Perf. 12***

No.	Type	Description	Unused	Used
78	A12	1c brown, II ('10)	8.00	2.00
a.		Type I	16.00	3.00
79	A13	15c gray, I	37.50	6.00
a.		Imperforate	140.00	140.00
b.		Type II ('10)	300.00	32.50
c.		As "b," imperfórate	600.00	600.00

No. 79b Surcharged in Brown

1918, Mar. 15

No.	Type	Description	Unused	Used
80	A13	20c on 15c gray	6.00	3.75

St. Marinus — A14

Perf. 14½x14, 14x14½

1923, Aug. 11 Typo. Wmk. 140

No.	Type	Description	Unused	Used
81	A14	30c dark brown	.75	.75

San Marino Intl. Exhib. of 1923. Proceeds from the sale of this stamp went to a mutual aid society.

Imperforate examples on chalky paper are proofs. Value, $175.

Italian Flag and Views of Arbe and Mt. Titano A15

1923, Aug. 6

No.	Type	Description	Unused	Used
82	A15	50c olive green	.75	.75
a.		Reverse printing omitted	215.00	

Presentation to San Marino of the Italian flag which had flown over the island of Arbe, the birthplace of the founder of San Marino. Inscribed on back: "V. Moraldi dis. Blasi inc. Petiti impr.-Roma."

Imperfroate examples on chalky paper are proofs. Value, $175.

Mt. Titano and Sword — A16

1923, Sept. 29 *Perf. 14x14½*

No.	Type	Description	Unused	Used
83	A16	1 l dark brown	22.50	22.50

In honor of the San Marino Volunteers who were killed or wounded in WWI.

Giuseppe Garibaldi A17

Allegory-San Marino Sheltering Garibaldi A18

1924, Sept. 25 *Perf. 14*

No.	Type	Description	Unused	Used
84	A17	30c dark violet	3.75	4.00
85	A17	50c olive brown	3.75	4.00
86	A17	60c dull red	5.00	5.00
87	A18	1 l deep blue	9.00	9.00
88	A18	2 l gray green	11.00	11.00
		Nos. 84-88 (5)	32.50	33.00

75th anniv. of Garibaldi's taking refuge in San Marino.

No. B8 Surcharged in Black

1924, Oct. 9

No.	Type	Description	Unused	Used
89	SP1	30c on 45c yel brn & blk	3.00	3.00

Nos. B9-B11 Surcharged

No.	Type	Description	Unused	Used
90	SP2	60c on 1 l bl grn & blk	10.50	10.50
91	SP2	1 l on 2 l vio & blk	29.00	29.00
92	SP2	2 l on 3 l claret & blk	22.00	22.00
		Nos. 89-92 (4)	64.50	64.50

Nos. 67 and 68 Surcharged in Black or Red

1926, July 1

No.	Type	Description	Unused	Used
93	A11	75c on 80c blue	2.25	2.50
94	A11	1.20 l on 90c brown	2.25	2.50
95	A11	1.25 l on 90c brn (R)	3.75	3.75
96	A11	2.50 l on 80c blue (R)	8.00	8.00
		Nos. 93-96 (4)	16.25	16.75

Antonio Onofri — A19

Unwmk.

1926, July 29 Engr. *Perf. 11*

No.	Type	Description	Unused	Used
97	A19	10c dk blue & blk	.75	.75
98	A19	20c olive grn & blk	1.50	1.50
99	A19	45c dk vio & blk	.75	.75
100	A19	65c, green & blk	.75	.75
101	A19	1 l orange & blk	5.50	5.50
102	A19	2 l red vio & blk	5.50	5.50
		Nos. 97-102 (6)	14.75	14.75

For surcharges see Nos. 104-106, 181-182.

Special Delivery Stamp No. E2 Surcharged

Perf. 14½x14

1926, Nov. 25 Wmk. 140

No.	Type	Description	Unused	Used
103	A11	1.85 l on 60c violet	.80	.80

Nos. 101 and 102 Surcharged

1927, Mar. 10 Unwmk. *Perf. 11*

No.	Type	Description	Unused	Used
104	A19	1.25 l on 1 l	9.50	9.50
105	A19	2.50 l on 2 l	19.00	19.00
106	A19	5 l on 2 l	55.00	55.00
		Nos. 104-106 (3)	83.50	83.50

Type of Special Delivery Stamp of 1923 Surcharged

1927, Sept. 15 Wmk. 140 *Perf. 14*

No.	Type	Description	Unused	Used
107	A11	1.75 l on 50c on 25c vio	1.25	1.25

The 50c on 25c violet was not issued without 1.75-lire surcharge.

War Memorial A21

Unwmk.

1927, Sept. 28 Engr. *Perf. 12*

No.	Type	Description	Unused	Used
108	A21	50c brown violet	2.25	2.25
109	A21	1.25 l blue	3.25	3.25
110	A21	10 l gray	27.50	27.50
		Nos. 108-110 (3)	33.00	33.00

Erection of a cenotaph in memory of the San Marino volunteers in WWI.

Capuchin Church and Convent A22

Design: 2.50 l, 5 l, Death of St. Francis.

1928, Jan. 2

No.	Type	Description	Unused	Used
111	A22	50c red	25.00	10.00
112	A22	1.25 l dp blue	12.00	12.00
113	A22	2.50 l dk brown	12.00	12.00
114	A22	5 l dull violet	35.00	32.50
		Nos. 111-114 (4)	84.00	66.50

7th centenary of the death of St. Francis of Assisi.

For surcharges see Nos. 183-184.

The Rocca (State Prison) A24

Government Palace A25

Statue of Liberty — A26

1929-35 Wmk. 217

No.	Type	Description	Unused	Used
115	A24	5c vio brn & ultra	1.50	.75
116	A24	10c grnsh blue & red vio	2.00	1.25
117	A24	15c dp org & emer	1.50	.75
118	A24	20c dk bl & org red	1.50	.75
119	A24	25c grn & gray blk	1.50	.75
120	A24	30c gray brn & red	1.50	.75
121	A24	50c red vio & ol gray	1.50	.75
122	A24	75c dp red & gray blk	1.50	.75
123	A25	1 l dk brn & emer	1.50	.75
124	A25	1.25 l dk blue & blk	1.50	.75
125	A25	1.75 l green & org	4.00	2.00
126	A25	2 l bl gray & red	2.00	1.25
127	A25	2.50 l car rose & ultra	2.00	1.25
128	A25	3 l dp org & bl	2.00	1.25
129	A25	3.70 l ol blk & red brn ('35)	2.00	1.25
130	A26	5 l dk vio & dk grn	4.00	3.75
131	A26	10 l bis brn & dk bl	16.00	15.00
132	A26	15 l grn & red vio	75.00	*90.00*
133	A26	20 l dk bl & red	325.00	325.00
		Nos. 115-133 (19)	447.50	448.75

General Post Office — A27

1932, Feb. 4

No.	Type	Description	Unused	Used
134	A27	20c blue green	27.50	21.00
135	A27	50c dark red	35.00	25.00
136	A27	1.25 l dark blue	225.00	175.00
137	A27	1.75 l dark brown	140.00	75.00
138	A27	2.75 l dark violet	70.00	42.50
		Nos. 134-138 (5)	497.50	338.50

Opening of new General Post Office.

For surcharges see Nos. 151-160.

San Marino-Rimini Electric Railway — A28

1932, June 11

No.	Type	Description	Unused	Used
139	A28	20c deep green	4.25	4.25
140	A28	50c dark red	7.00	7.00
141	A28	1.25 l dark blue	17.50	17.50
142	A28	5 l deep brown	100.00	100.00
		Nos. 139-142 (4)	128.75	128.75

Opening of the new electric railway between San Marino and Rimini.

Giuseppe Garibaldi — A29

Garibaldi's Arrival at San Marino — A30

1932, July 30

No.	Type	Description	Unused	Used
143	A29	10c violet brown	10.00	4.25
144	A29	20c violet	10.00	4.25
145	A29	25c green	10.00	4.25
146	A29	50c yellow brn	14.00	8.50
147	A30	75c dark red	35.00	17.50
148	A30	1.25 l dark blue	42.50	25.00
149	A30	2.75 l brown org	85.00	50.00
150	A30	5 l olive green	325.00	*400.00*
		Nos. 143-150 (8)	531.50	513.75

Garibaldi (1807-1882), Italian patriot.

Nos. 138 and 137 Surcharged

1933, May 27

No.	Type	Description	Unused	Used
151	A27	25c on 2.75 l	14.00	14.00
152	A27	50c on 1.75 l	27.50	27.50
153	A27	75c on 2.75 l	55.00	55.00
154	A27	1.25 l on 1.75 l	400.00	400.00
		Nos. 151-154 (4)	496.50	496.50

Convention of philatelists, San Marino, May 28.

Nos. 134-137 Surcharged in Black

1934, Apr. 12

155	A27	25c on 1.25 l	2.75	2.75
156	A27	50c on 1.75 l	4.25	4.25
157	A27	75c on 50c	10.00	10.00
158	A27	1.25 l on 20c	35.00	35.00
		Nos. 155-158 (4)	52.00	52.00

San Marino's participation (with a philatelic pavilion) in the 15th annual Trade Fair at Milan, Apr. 12-27.

Nos. 136 and 138 Surcharged Wheel and New Value

1934, Apr. 12

159	A27	3.70 l on 1.25 l	67.50	67.50
160	A27	3.70 l on 2.75 l	77.50	77.50

Ascent to Mt. Titano A31

Unwmk.

1935, Feb. 7 Engr. *Perf. 14*

161	A31	5c choc & blk	.70	.70
162	A31	10c dk vio & blk	.70	.70
163	A31	20c orange & blk	.70	.70
164	A31	25c green & blk	.70	.70
165	A31	50c olive bis & blk	.70	.70
166	A31	75c brown red & blk	2.75	2.75
167	A31	1.25 l blue & blk	5.50	5.50
		Nos. 161-167 (7)	11.75	11.75

12th anniv. of the founding of the Fascist Movement.

Melchiorre Delfico — A32

Statue of Delfico — A33

1935, Apr. 15 Wmk. 217 *Perf. 12*

Center in Black

169	A32	5c brown lake	2.10	2.10
170	A32	7½c lt brown	2.10	2.10
171	A32	10c dk blue grn	2.10	2.10
172	A32	15c rose carmine	42.50	25.00
173	A32	20c orange	3.00	2.50
174	A32	25c green	3.00	2.50
175	A33	30c dull violet	3.00	2.50
176	A33	50c olive green	4.25	4.25
177	A33	75c red	12.50	12.50
178	A33	1.25 l dark blue	3.50	3.50
179	A33	1.50 l dk brown	57.50	*62.50*
180	A33	1.75 l brown org	85.00	*97.50*
		Nos. 169-180 (12)	220.55	219.05

Melchiorre Delfico (1744-1835), historian.
For surcharges see Nos. 202, 277.

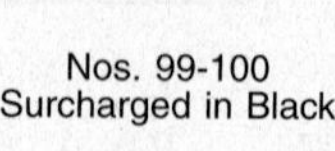

Nos. 99-100 Surcharged in Black

Nos. 112-113 Surcharged in Black

1936 Unwmk. *Perf. 11*

181	A19	80c on 45c dk vio & blk	3.50	3.50
182	A19	80c on 65c grn & blk	3.50	3.50

Perf. 12

183	A22	2.05 l on 1.25 l	8.50	8.50
184	A22	2.75 l on 2.50 l	20.00	20.00
		Nos. 181-184 (4)	35.50	35.50

Issued: Nos. 181-182, 4/14; Nos. 183-184, 8/23.

Souvenir Sheet

Design from Base of Roman Column — A34

1937, Aug. 23 Engr. Wmk. 217

185	A34	5 l steel blue	15.00	12.50

Unveiling of the Roman Column at San Marino. The date "1636 d. F. R." means the 1,636th year since the founding of the republic.

No. 185 was privately surcharged "+ 10 L 1941."

Souvenir Sheets

Abraham Lincoln — A35

1938, Apr. 7 Wmk. 217 *Perf. 13*

186	A35	3 l dark blue	2.75	2.75
187	A35	5 l rose red	18.00	18.00

Dedication of a Lincoln bust, Sept. 3, 1937.

No. 49 & Type of 1925 Surcharged in Black

1941 Wmk. 140 *Perf. 14*

188	A11	10c on 15c brown vio	.50	.50
189	A11	10c on 30c brown org	.90	.90

Flags of Italy and San Marino — A36

Harbor of Arbe A37

1942 Photo.

190	A36	10c yel brn & brn org	.30	.30
191	A36	15c brn & red brn	.30	.30
192	A36	20c gray grn & gray blk	.30	.30
193	A36	25c green & blue	.30	.30
194	A36	50c brn red & brn	.30	.30
195	A36	75c red & gray blk	.30	.30
196	A37	1.25 l bl & gray bl	.30	.30
197	A37	1.75 l brn & grnsh blk	.30	.30
198	A37	2.75 l bis brn & gray bl	.70	.70
199	A37	5 l green & brown	3.50	3.50
		Nos. 190-199 (10)	6.60	6.60

Return of the Italian flag to Arbe.

No. 190 Surcharged in Black

1942, July 30

200	A36	30c on 10c	.30	.30

Rimini-San Marino Stamp Day, Aug. 3.

No. 192 Surcharged in Black

1942, Sept. 14

201	A36	30c on 20c	.30	.30

No. 177 Surcharged with New Value in Black

1942, Sept. 28 Wmk. 217 *Perf. 12*

202	A33	20 l on 75c red & blk	17.50	17.50

Printing Press and Newspaper A38

Newspapers A39

Wmk. 140

1943, Apr. 12 Photo. *Perf. 14*

203	A38	10c deep green	.30	.30
204	A38	15c bister	.30	.30
205	A38	20c dk orange brn	.30	.30
206	A38	30c dk rose vio	.30	.30
207	A38	50c blue black	.30	.30
208	A38	75c red orange	.30	.30
209	A39	1.25 l blue	.30	.30
210	A39	1.75 l deep violet	.30	.30
211	A39	5 l slate	1.10	1.10
212	A39	10 l dark brown	3.00	3.00
		Nos. 203-212 (10)	6.50	6.50

Nos. 206 and 207 Overprinted in Red

1943, July 1

213	A38	30c dk rose vio	.25	.25
214	A38	50c blue black	.25	.25

Rimini-San Marino Stamp Day, July 5.

A40

A41

Overprinted in Black: "28 LVGLIO 1943 1642 F. R."

1943, Aug. 27

215	A40	5c brown	.30	.30
216	A40	10c orange red	.30	.30
217	A40	20c ultra	.30	.30
218	A40	25c deep green	.30	.30
219	A40	30c brown carmine	.30	.30
220	A40	50c deep violet	.30	.30
221	A40	75c car rose	.30	.30
222	A41	1.25 l sapphire	.30	.30
223	A41	1.75 l red org	.30	.30
224	A41	2.75 l dk red brn	1.00	1.00
225	A41	5 l green	1.40	1.40
226	A41	10 l violet	2.10	2.10
227	A41	20 l slate blue	5.75	5.75
		Nos. 215-227,C26-C33 (21)	24.95	24.95

This series was prepared for the 20th anniv. of fascism, but as Mussolini was overthrown July 25, 1943, it was overprinted for the downfall of fascism.

Overprint on Nos. 222-227 adds "d." before "F.R."

Exist without overprint. Value of set $55.

A42

A43

Overprinted "Governo Provvisorio" in Black

1943, Aug. 27

No.	Type	Description	Unused	Used
228	A42	5c brown	.30	.30
229	A42	10c orange red	.30	.30
230	A42	20c ultra	.30	.30
231	A42	25c deep green	.30	.30
232	A42	30c brown carmine	.30	.30
233	A42	50c deep violet	.30	.30
234	A42	75c carmine rose	.30	.30
235	A43	1.25 l sapphire	.30	.30
236	A43	1.75 l red orange	.30	.30
237	A43	5 l green	.70	.70
238	A43	20 l slate blue	1.75	1.75
		Nos. 228-238,C34-C39 (17)	10.20	10.20

Souvenir Sheets

A44

Perf. 14, Imperf.

1945, Mar. 15 Photo. Unwmk.

No.	Type	Description	Unused	Used
239	A44	Sheet of 3	70.00	65.00
		Never hinged	115.00	
a.		10 l dull blue	20.00	20.00
b.		15 l dull green	20.00	20.00
c.		25 l dull red brown	20.00	20.00

Sheets contain a papermaker's watermark, "Hammermill Bond, Made in U.S.A."

Nos. 239, 241 and C40 were issued to commemorate the 50th anniv. of the reconstruction of the Government Palace.

Government Palace — A45

1945, Mar. 15 Wmk. 140 *Perf. 14*

No.	Type	Description	Unused	Used
241	A45	25 l brown violet	5.75	5.75
		Never hinged	11.50	

Coat of Arms of Faetano — A46

Coats of Arms: 20c, 60c, 25 l, Montegiardino. 40c, 5 l, 50 l, San Marino. 80c, 2 l-4 l, Fiorentino. 10 l, Borgomaggiore. 20 l, Serravalle.

1945-46 Wmk. 277

No.	Type	Description	Unused	Used
242	A46	10c dark blue	.25	.25
243	A46	20c vermilion	.25	.25
244	A46	40c deep orange	.25	.25
245	A46	60c slate black	.25	.25
246	A46	80c dark green	.25	.25
247	A46	1 l dk car rose	.25	.25
248	A46	1.20 l deep violet	.25	.25
249	A46	2 l chestnut	.25	.25
250	A46	3 l dp blue ('46)	.25	.25
250A	A46	4 l red org ('46)	.25	.25
251	A46	5 l dark brown	.25	.25
251A	A46	15 l dp blue ('46)	1.75	*2.25*

Lithographed and Engraved

No.	Type	Description	Unused	Used
252	A46	10 l brt red & brn	1.75	*2.25*
253	A46	20 l brt red & ultra	5.00	3.00
254	A46	20 l org brn & ultra ('46)	10.00	3.25
a.		Vert. pair, imperf. btwn.	625.00	
		Never hinged	1,250.	
255	A46	25 l hn brn & ultra ('46)	8.50	7.00

Size: 22x27mm

No.	Type	Description	Unused	Used
256	A46	50 l ol brn & ultra ('46)	16.00	11.00
		Nos. 242-256 (17)	45.75	31.50
		Set, never hinged	87.50	

Nos. 252-256 are in sheets of 10 (2x5). Values: Nos. 252, 254-255, $90 each. No. 253, $125, No. 256, $300.

For surcharges see Nos. 258-259, B26.

"Dawn of New Hope" — A52

Engr. & Litho.

1946 Unwmk. *Perf. 14*

No.	Type	Description	Unused	Used
257	A52	100 l dull yel & brn vio	7.75	7.75
		Never hinged	15.50	
j.		Vert. pair, imperf. btwn.	950.00	
		Never hinged	1,950.	

UN Relief and Rehabilitation Administration. Sheets of 10 with blue coat of arms in top margin.

Franklin D. Roosevelt and Flags of San Marino and US — A52a

Designs: 1 l, 50 l, Quotation on Liberty, from Franklin D. Roosevelt. 2 l, 100 l, Roosevelt portrait, vert. 5 l, 15 l, Roosevelt and flags (as shown).

Wmk. 277

1947, May 3 Photo. *Perf. 14*

No.	Type	Description	Unused	Used
257A	A52a	1 l bister & brn	.25	.25
257B	A52a	2 l blue & sepia	.25	.25
257C	A52a	5 l violet & multi	.25	.25
257D	A52a	15 l green & multi	.25	.25
257E	A52a	50 l ver & brn	.70	.70
257F	A52a	100 l violet & sepia	1.10	1.10
		Nos. 257A-257F,C51A-C51H (14)	26.70	21.95
		Set, never hinged	60.00	

For surcharges see Nos. 257G-257I, C51I-C51K.

Nos. 257A-257C Surcharged with New Value

1947, June 16

No.	Type	Description	Unused	Used
257G	A52a	3 l on 1 l	.35	.35
257H	A52a	4 l on 2 l	.35	.35
257I	A52a	6 l on 5 l	.35	.35
		Nos. 257G-257I,C51I-C51K (6)	2.25	2.25
		Set, never hinged	4.75	

No. 250A Surcharged with New Value in Black

1947, June 16 Wmk. 277

No.	Type	Description	Unused	Used
258	A46	6(l) on 4 l red org	.25	.25
		Never hinged	.35	

No. 250A Surcharged in Black

No.	Type	Description	Unused	Used
259	A46	21 l on 4 l red org	.80	*1.10*
		Never hinged	1.60	

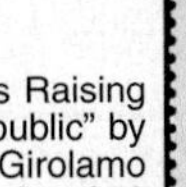

"St. Marinus Raising the Republic" by Girolamo Batoni — A53

Wmk. 217

1947, July 18 Engr. *Perf. 12*

No.	Type	Description	Unused	Used
260	A53	1 l brt grn & vio	.25	.30
261	A53	2 l purple & olive	.25	.30
262	A53	4 l vio brn & dk bl grn	.25	.30
263	A53	10 l org & bl blk	.25	.30
264	A53	25 l carmine & purple	.70	.70
265	A53	50 l dk bl grn & brn	17.00	17.00
		Nos. 260-265,C52-C53 (8)	22.70	22.65
		Set, never hinged	55.00	

For overprints and surcharges see Nos. 294-295, B27-B38, C56.

United States 1847 Stamp — A54

United States Stamps of 1847 and 1869 — A55

A56

Wmk. 277

1947, Dec. 24 Photo. *Perf. 14*

No.	Type	Description	Unused	Used
266	A54	2 l red vio & dk brn	.30	.30
267	A55	3 l sl gray, dp ultra & car	.30	.30
268	A54	6 l dp bl & dk gray grn	.30	.30
269	A56	15 l vio, dp ultra & car	.35	.70
270	A55	35 l dk brn, dp ultra & car	1.40	1.40
271	A56	50 l sl grn, dp ultra & car	1.40	1.40
		Nos. 266-271,C55 (7)	14.05	14.40
		Set, never hinged	35.00	

1st United States postage stamps, cent.

Laborer and San Marino Flag — A57

1948, June 3

No.	Type	Description	Unused	Used
272	A57	5 l brown	2.75	1.75
273	A57	8 l green	2.75	1.75
274	A57	30 l crimson	3.50	1.75
275	A57	50 l red brn & rose lil	5.00	4.50

Engr.

No.	Type	Description	Unused	Used
276	A57	100 l dk bl & dp vio	45.00	*60.00*
		Nos. 272-276 (5)	59.00	69.75
		Set, never hinged	125.00	

See Nos. 373-374.

No. 172 Surcharged with New Value and Ornaments in Black

1948 Wmk. 217 *Perf. 12*

No.	Type	Description	Unused	Used
277	A32	100 l on 15c	50.00	50.00
		Never hinged	100.00	

Government Palace — A58

Mt. Titano, Distant View — A59

Various Views of San Marino.

1949-50 Wmk. 277 Photo. *Perf. 14*

No.	Type	Description	Unused	Used
278	A58	1 l black & blue	.35	.25
279	A58	2 l violet & car	.35	.25
280	A58	3 l violet & ultra	.35	.25
281	A58	4 l black & vio	.35	.25
282	A58	5 l violet & brn	.35	.25
283	A58	6 l dp blue & sep	1.10	.70
284	A59	8 l blk brn & yel brn	.70	.25
285	A59	10 l brn blk & bl	1.10	.25
286	A58	12 l brt rose & vio	2.10	1.40
287	A58	15 l vio & brt rose	7.00	1.40
288	A58	20 l dp bl & brn ('50)	21.00	2.10
289	A58	35 l green & violet	10.50	10.50
290	A58	50 l brt rose & yel brn	7.00	2.10
291	A58	55 l dp bl & dl grn ('50)	60.00	35.00

Perf. 14x13½

Engr.

No.	Type	Description	Unused	Used
292	A59	100 l blk brn & dk grn	70.00	55.00
293	A59	200 l dp blue & brn	70.00	90.00
		Nos. 278-293 (16)	252.25	199.95
		Set, never hinged	525.00	

Nos. 260 and 261 Overprinted in Black

1949, June 28 Wmk. 217

No.	Type	Description	Unused	Used
294	A53	1 l brt green & vio	.35	.35
295	A53	2 l purple & olive	.35	.35
		Set, never hinged	1.40	

San Marino-Riccione Stamp Day, June 28.

Francesco Nullo — A60

1 l, 20 l, Francesco Nullo. 2 l, 5 l, Anita Garibaldi. 3 l, 50 l, Giuseppe Garibaldi. 4 l, 15 l, Ugo Bassi.

Wmk. 277

1949, July 31 Photo. *Perf. 14*

Size: 22x28mm

No.	Type	Description	Unused	Used
296	A60	1 l bl blk & car	.25	.25
297	A60	2 l red brn & blue	.25	.25
298	A60	3 l red & dk grn	.25	.25
299	A60	4 l violet & dk brn	.25	.25

Size: 26½x36½mm

No.	Type	Description	Unused	Used
300	A60	5 l purple & dk brn	.25	.25
301	A60	15 l car lake & gray bl	.70	.70
302	A60	20 l violet & car lake	1.40	1.40
303	A60	50 l red brn & violet	12.50	12.50
		Nos. 296-303,C57-C61 (13)	31.50	27.50
		Set, never hinged	65.00	

Centenary of Garibaldi's escape to San Marino.

See Nos. C57-C61, 404-410.

Stagecoach on Road from San Marino — A61

1949, Dec. 29 **Engr.**

304 A61 100 l bl & gray vio 10.00 10.00
Never hinged 20.00
Sheet of 6 200.00 200.00
Never hinged 300.00

UPU, 75th anniversary.

A62

A63

A63a

Perf. 13½x14, 14x13½

1951, Mar. 15 **Engr.** **Wmk. 277**

Sky and Cross in Carmine

305 A62 25 l dk brn & red vio 5.75 6.25
306 A63 75 l org brn & dk brn 8.75 8.75
307 A63a 100 l dk brn & gray blk 11.00 11.00
Nos. 305-307 (3) 25.50 26.00
Set, never hinged 55.00

Issued to honor the San Marino Red Cross.

Christopher Columbus A64

Designs: 2 l, 25 l, Columbus on his ship. 3 l, 10 l, 20 l, Landing of Columbus. 4 l, 15 l, 80 l, Pioneers trading with Indians. 5 l, 200 l, Columbus and map of Americas.

1952, Jan. 28 **Photo.** ***Perf. 14***

308 A64 1 l brn org & dk grn .30 .25
309 A64 2 l dk brn & vio .30 .25
310 A64 3 l vio & dk brn .30 .25
311 A64 4 l bl & org brn .30 .25
312 A64 5 l grn & dk bl grn .35 .35
313 A64 10 l dk brn & blk .55 .55
314 A64 15 l carmine & blk .70 .70

Engr.

315 A64 20 l dp bl & dk bl grn 1.10 1.10
316 A64 25 l vio brn & blk brn 6.25 6.25
317 A64 60 l choc & vio bl 7.75 7.75
318 A64 80 l gray & blk 24.50 24.50
319 A64 200 l Prus grn & dp ultra 42.50 42.50
Nos. 308-319,C80 (13) 112.40 112.20
Set, never hinged 230.00

Issued to honor Christopher Columbus.

Type of 1952 in New Colors Overprinted in Black or Red

1952, June 29 **Photo.**

320 A64 1 l vio & dk brn .25 .25
321 A64 2 l carmine & blk .25 .25
322 A64 3 l grn & dk bl grn (R) .25 .25
323 A64 4 l dk brn & blk .25 .25
324 A64 5 l purple & vio .30 .30
325 A64 10 l bl & org brn (R) .65 .70
326 A64 15 l org brn & blue 2.40 *2.50*
Nos. 320-326,C81 (8) 39.35 39.50
Set, never hinged 75.00

4th Intl. Sample Fair of Trieste.

Discobolus — A65

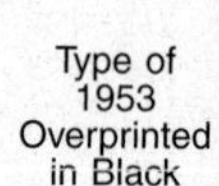

Tennis A66

Model Airplane — A67

Designs: 3 l, Runner. 4 l, Cyclist. 5 l, Soccer. 25 l, Shooting. 100 l, Roller skating.

1953, Apr. 20 **Wmk. 277** ***Perf. 14***

327 A65 1 l dk brn & blk .25 .25
328 A66 2 l black & brown .25 .25
329 A65 3 l blk & grnsh bl .25 .25
330 A66 4 l blk & brt bl .25 .25
331 A66 5 l dk brn & sl grn .25 .25
332 A67 10 l dp blue & crim .35 .35
333 A67 25 l blk & dk brn 2.00 2.00
334 A66 100 l dk brn & slate 6.25 6.25
Nos. 327-334,C90 (9) 54.85 54.85
Set, never hinged 125.00

See No. 438.

Type of 1953 Overprinted in Black

1953, Aug. 24

335 A66 100 l grn & dk bl grn 14.00 14.00
Never hinged 30.00

San Marino-Riccione Stamp Day, Aug. 24.

Narcissus A68

Flowers: 2 l, Tulips. 3 l, Oleanders. 4 l, Cornflowers. 5 l, Carnations. 10 l, Irises. 25 l, Cyclamen. 80 l, Geraniums. 100 l, Roses.

1953, Dec. 28 **Photo.**

336 A68 1 l multicolored .25 .25
337 A68 2 l multicolored .25 .25
338 A68 3 l multicolored .25 .25
339 A68 4 l multicolored .25 .25
340 A68 5 l multicolored .25 .25
341 A68 10 l multicolored .25 .25
342 A68 25 l multicolored 1.75 1.75
343 A68 80 l multicolored 12.50 12.50
344 A68 100 l multicolored 19.00 19.00
Nos. 336-344 (9) 34.75 34.75
Set, never hinged 67.50

Walking Racer — A69

Fencing A70

Sports: 3 l, Boxing. 4 l, 200 l, 250 l, Gymnastics. 5 l, Motorcycling. 8 l, Javelin-throwing. 12 l, Automobiling. 25 l, Wrestling. 80 l, Walk racer.

1954-55 **Photo.** **Wmk. 277**

345 A69 1 l violet & cer .25 .25
346 A70 2 l dk grn & vio .25 .25
347 A70 3 l brn & brn org .25 .25
348 A69 4 l dk bl & brt bl .25 .25
349 A70 5 l dk grn & dk brn .25 .25
350 A70 8 l lil rose & pur .25 .25
351 A70 12 l black & crim .25 .25
352 A69 25 l bl & dk bl grn .35 .35
353 A69 80 l dk bl & bl grn 1.75 1.00
354 A69 200 l violet & brn 5.00 4.00

Perf. 12½x13

Engr.

355 A69 250 l multi ('55) 28.00 28.00
Sheet of 4 (#355) 250.00 250.00
Nos. 345-355 (11) 36.85 35.10
Set, never hinged 75.00

A71

Liberty statue and Government palace.

1954, Dec. 16 **Photo.** ***Perf. 13x13½***

356 A71 20 l choc & blue .35 .35
357 A71 60 l car & dk grn .70 .70
Nos. 356-357,C92 (3) 2.15 2.15
Set, never hinged 4.50

A72

1955, Aug. 27 **Wmk. 303** ***Perf. 14***

358 A72 100 l gray blk & bl 2.50 2.50
Never hinged 5.00

7th San Marino-Riccione Stamp Fair. See No. 385.

Murata Nuova Bridge — A73

View of La Rocca — A74

Design: 15 l, Government Palace.

Size: 22x27½mm; 27½x22mm

1955, Nov. 15 ***Perf. 14***

359 A73 5 l blue & brown .25 .25
360 A74 10 l org & bl grn .25 .25
361 A74 15 l Prus grn & car .25 .25
362 A73 25 l dk brn & vio .25 .25
363 A74 35 l vio & red car .35 .25
Nos. 359-363 (5) 1.35 1.25
Set, never hinged 1.40

See Nos. 386-388, 636-638.

Ice Skater — A75

Skier A76

3 l, 50 l, Tobogganing. 4 l, Skier going downhill. 5 l, 100 l, Ice Hockey player. 10 l, Girl ice skater.

1955, Dec. 15 **Wmk. 303** ***Perf. 14***

364 A75 1 l brown & yellow .25 .25
365 A76 2 l brt blue & red .25 .25
366 A76 3 l blk brn & lt brn .25 .25
367 A75 4 l brown & green .25 .25
368 A76 5 l ultra & sal pink .25 .25
369 A75 10 l ultra & pink .25 .25
370 A76 25 l gray blk & red .45 .45
371 A76 50 l brown & indigo 1.60 1.60
372 A76 100 l blk & Prus grn 4.25 4.25
Nos. 364-372,C95 (10) 25.30 25.30
Set, never hinged 47.50

7th Winter Olympic Games at Cortina d'Ampezzo, Jan. 26-Feb. 5, 1956.
For surcharge see No. C96.

Type of 1948 Inscribed: "50th Anniversario Arengo 25 Marzo 1906"

1956, Mar. 24 **Wmk. 303** ***Perf. 14***

373 A57 50 l sapphire 4.25 *5.50*
Never hinged 8.50

50th anniv. of the meeting of the heads of families (Arengo), the beginning of the democratic era in San Marino.

Type of 1948 inscribed: "Assistenza Invernale"

1956, Mar. 24 **Photo.**

374 A57 50 l dark green 4.25 *5.50*
Never hinged 8.50

Issued to publicize the Winterhelp charity.

Pointer and Arms A77

Dogs: 2 l, Russian greyhound. 3 l, Sheep dog. 4 l, English greyhound. 5 l, Boxer. 10 l, Great Dane. 25 l, Irish setter. 60 l, German shepherd. 80 l, Scotch collie. 100 l, Hunting hound.

1956, June 8 Wmk. 303 *Perf. 14*

375 A77 1 l ultra & brown .25 .25
376 A77 2 l car lake & bl gray .25 .25
377 A77 3 l ultra & brown .25 .25
378 A77 4 l grnsh bl & gray vio .25 .25
379 A77 5 l car lake & dk brn .25 .25
380 A77 10 l ultra & brown .25 .25
381 A77 25 l dk blue & multi .80 *.90*
382 A77 60 l car lake & multi 5.25 4.50
383 A77 80 l dk blue & multi 6.50 4.50
384 A77 100 l car lake & multi 9.50 7.50
Nos. 375-384 (10) 23.55 18.90
Set, never hinged 47.50

Sailboat Type of 1955

1956 Wmk. 303 *Perf. 14*

385 A72 100 l brown & bl grn 1.00 *1.75*
Never hinged 2.50

8th San Marino-Riccione Stamp Fair.

Types of 1955 with added inscription: "Congresso Internaz. Periti Filatelici San Marino-Salsomaggiore 6-8 Ottobre 1956."

Designs: 20 l, La Rocca. 80 l, Murata Nuova Bridge. 100 l, Government palace.

1956, Oct. 6 *Perf. 14*
Size: 26x36mm; 36x26mm

386 A74 20 l blue & brown .70 .70
387 A73 80 l vio & red car 1.25 *2.10*
388 A74 100 l org & bl grn 2.25 *4.50*
Nos. 386-388 (3) 4.20 7.30
Set, never hinged 9.00

Intl. Philatelic Cong., San Marino, 10/6-8.

Street and Borgo Maggiore Church — A78

Hospital Street — A79

Views: 3 l, Gate tower. 20 l, Covered Market of Borgo Maggiore. 125 l, View from South Bastion.

1957, May 9 Photo. Wmk. 303

389 A78 2 l dk grn & rose red .25 .25
390 A78 3 l blue & brown .25 .25
391 A78 20 l dk blue green .25 .25
392 A79 60 l brn & blue vio .90 *1.50*

Engr.

393 A78 125 l dk blue & blk .35 .25
Nos. 389-393 (5) 2.00 2.50
Set, never hinged 3.00

See Nos. 473-476, 633-635.

Daisies and View of San Marino — A80

Flowers: 2 l, Primrose. 3 l, Lily. 4 l Orchid. 5 l, Lily of the Valley. 10 l, Poppy. 25 l, Pansy. 60 l, Gladiolus. 80 l, Wild Rose. 100 l, Anemone.

Wmk. 303
1957, Aug. 31 Photo. *Perf. 14*
Flowers in Natural Colors

394 A80 1 l dk vio blue .25 .25
395 A80 2 l dk vio blue .25 .25
396 A80 3 l dk vio blue .25 .25
397 A80 4 l dk vio blue .25 .25
398 A80 5 l dk vio blue .25 .25
399 A80 10 l blue, buff & lilac .25 .25
400 A80 25 l blue, yel & lilac .25 .25
401 A80 60 l blue, yel & dl red brn .35 *.50*
402 A80 80 l blue & dl red brn .70 *1.40*
403 A80 100 l bl, yel & dl red brn 1.00 *1.75*
Nos. 394-403 (10) 3.80 5.40
Set, never hinged 6.25

Type of 1949 Inscribed: "Commemorazione 150 Nascita G. Garibaldi."

Portraits: 2 l, 50 l, Anita Garibaldi. 3 l, 25 l, Francesco Nullo. 5 l, 100 l, Giuseppe Garibaldi. 15 l, Ugo Bassi.

1957, Dec. 12 Wmk. 303 *Perf. 14*
Size: 22x28mm

404 A60 2 l vio & dull bl .25 .25
405 A60 3 l lake & dk grn .25 .25
406 A60 5 l brn & ol gray .25 .25

Size: 26½x37mm

407 A60 15 l blue & vio .25 .25
408 A60 25 l green & dk gray .25 .25
409 A60 50 l violet & brn 1.00 *1.50*
410 A60 100 l brown & vio 1.00 *1.50*
Nos. 404-410 (7) 3.25 4.25
Set, never hinged 5.50

Nos. 409-410 are printed se-tenant.
Birth of Giuseppe Garibaldi, 150th anniv.

Panoramic View A81

1958, Feb. 27 Engr. *Perf. 14*

411 A81 500 l green & blk 62.50 62.50
Never hinged 90.00
Sheet of 6 500.00 525.00
Never hinged 750.00

Catalogue values for unused stamps in this section, from this point to the end of the section, are for Never Hinged items.

Fair Emblem and San Marino Peaks — A82

1958, Apr. 12 Photo. *Perf. 14*

412 A82 40 l yel green & brn .25 .25
413 A82 60 l brt blue & mar .55 .55

World's Fair, Brussels, Apr. 17-Oct. 19.

Madonna and Fair Entrance A83

Design: 60 l, View of Fair Grounds.

1958, Apr. 12

414 A83 15 l yellow, grn & bl .25 .25
415 A83 60 l green & rose red .60 .50
Nos. 414-415,C97 (3) 4.10 4.00

San Marino's 10th participation in the Milan Fair.

Wheat — A84

Designs: 2 l, 125 l, Corn. 3 l, 80 l, Grapes. 4 l, 25 l, Peaches. 5 l, 40 l, Plums.

1958, Aug. 30 Wmk. 303 *Perf. 14*

416 A84 1 l dk blue & yel org .25 .25
417 A84 2 l dk grn & red org .25 .25
418 A84 3 l blue & ocher .25 .25
419 A84 4 l grn & rose car .25 .25
420 A84 5 l blue, yel & grn .25 .25
421 A84 15 l ultra & brn org .25 .25
422 A84 25 l multicolored .25 .25
423 A84 40 l multicolored .75 .50
424 A84 80 l multicolored 1.10 .60
425 A84 125 l bl, grn & org ver 4.50 3.00
Nos. 416-425 (10) 8.10 5.85

Bay and Stamp of Naples A85

1958, Oct. 8 Photo.

426 A85 25 l lilac & red brn .25 .25

Cent. of the stamps of Naples. See No. C100.

Pierre de Coubertin — A86

Portraits: 3 l, Count Alberto Bonacossa. 5 l, Avery Brundage. 30 l, Gen. Carlo Montu. 60 l, J. Sigfrid Edstrom. 80 l, Henri de Baillet Latour.

1959, May 19 Wmk. 303 *Perf. 14*

427 A86 2 l brn org & blk .25 .25
428 A86 3 l lilac & gray brn .25 .25
429 A86 5 l blue & dk grn .25 .25
430 A86 30 l violet & blk .25 .25
431 A86 60 l dk grn & gray brn .25 .25
432 A86 80 l car rose & dp grn .25 .25
Nos. 427-432,C106 (7) 6.00 4.75

Leaders of the Olympic movement; 1960 Olympic Games, Rome.
See Nos. 1060-1062.

Lincoln and his Praise of San Marino, May 7, 1861 A87

Lincoln Portraits and: 10 l, Map of San Marino. 15 l, Government palace. 70 l, San Marino peaks, vert.

1959, July 1 *Perf. 14*

433 A87 5 l brown & blk .25 .25
434 A87 10 l blue grn & ultra .25 .25
435 A87 15 l gray & green .25 .25

Perf. 13x13½
Engr.

436 A87 70 l violet .45 .45
Nos. 433-436,C108 (5) 6.95 6.20

Birth sesquicentennial of Abraham Lincoln.

Arch of Augustus, Rimini, and Romagna ½b Stamp A88

1959, Aug. 29 Photo. *Perf. 14*

437 A88 30 l black & brown .25 .25

Centenary of the first stamps of Romagna. See No. C109.

Type of 1953 Inscribed: "Universiade Torino"

1959, Aug. 29 Wmk. 303 *Perf. 14*

438 A65 30 l red orange .75 .50

Turin University Sports Meet, 8/27-9/6.

Messina Cathedral Portal and Stamp of Sicily 1859 — A89

Stamp of Sicily and: 2 l, Greek temple, Selinus. 3 l, Erice Church. 4 l, Temple of Concordia, Agrigento. 5 l, Ruins of Castor and Pollux Temple, Agrigento. 25 l, San Giovanni degli Eremiti Church. 60 l, Greek theater, Taormina, horiz.

1959, Oct. 16

439 A89 1 l ocher & dk brn .25 .25
440 A89 2 l olive & dk red .25 .25
441 A89 3 l blue & slate .25 .25
442 A89 4 l red & brown .25 .25
443 A89 5 l dull bl & rose lil .25 .25
444 A89 25 l multicolored .25 .25
445 A89 60 l multicolored .25 .25
Nos. 439-445,C110 (8) 4.25 4.00

Centenary of stamps of Sicily.

Golden Oriole A90

Nightingale — A91

Birds: 3 l, Woodcock. 4 l, Hoopoe. 5 l, Red-legged partridge. 10 l, Goldfinch. 25 l, European Kingfisher. 60 l, Ringnecked pheasant. 80 l, Green woodpecker. 110 l, Red-breasted flycatcher.

1960, Jan. 28 Photo. *Perf. 14*
Centers in Natural Colors

446 A90 1 l blue .25 .25
447 A91 2 l green & red .25 .25
448 A90 3 l green & red .25 .25
449 A91 4 l dk green & red .25 .25
450 A90 5 l dark green .25 .25
451 A91 10 l blue & red .25 .25
452 A91 25 l grnsh blue .75 .40
453 A90 60 l blue & red 2.25 1.50
454 A91 80 l Prus blue & red 4.50 3.00
455 A91 110 l blue & red 5.50 4.50
Nos. 446-455 (10) 14.50 10.90

Shot Put — A92

Sports: 2 l, Gymnastics. 3 l, Walking. 4 l, Boxing. 5 l, Fencing, horiz. 10 l, Bicycling. 15 l, Hockey, horiz. 25 l, Rowing, horiz. 60 l, Soccer. 110 l, Equestrian, horiz.

1960, May 23 Wmk. 303 *Perf. 14*

456 A92 1 l car rose & vio .25 .25
457 A92 2 l gray & org .25 .25
458 A92 3 l brn ol & pur .25 .25
459 A92 4 l rose red & brn .25 .25
460 A92 5 l brown & blue .25 .25
461 A92 10 l red brn & bl .25 .25
462 A92 15 l green & lilac .25 .25
463 A92 25 l bl grn & org .25 .25
464 A92 60 l dp grn & org .25 .25
465 A92 110 l emer, red & blk .30 .25
Set of 3 souvenir sheets, imperf. 11.00 11.00
Nos. 456-465,C111-C114 (14) 3.65 3.50

17th Olympic Games, Rome, 8/25-9/11.

Souvenir sheets are: (1.) Sheet of 4, one each of 1 l, 2 l, 3 l and 60 l, all printed in deep green and brown. (2.) Sheet of 4, one each of 4 l and 10 l plus a 20 l and 40 l in designs of Nos. C111-C112 but without "Posta Aerea" inscribed-all 4 printed in rose red and brown. (3.) Sheet of 6, one each of 5 l, 15 l, 25 l and 110 l plus an 80 l and 125 l in designs of Nos. C113-C114 but without "Posta Aerea"- all 6 printed in emerald and brown.

Mt. Titano — A93

Founder Melvin Jones and Lions Headquarters — A94

60 l, Government Palace and statue of Liberty. 115 l, Clarence L. Sturm, president. 150 l, Finis E. Davis, vice president.

1960, July 1 Photo. Wmk. 303

466	A93	30 l red brn & dk bl	.25	.25
467	A94	45 l bl vio & bis brn	.50	.50
468	A93	60 l dull rose & bl	.25	.25
469	A94	115 l green & blk	.50	.50
470	A94	150 l brn & dk bl	2.75	2.75
		Nos. 466-470,C115 (6)	11.75	11.75

Lions Intl.; founding of the Lions Club of San Marino.

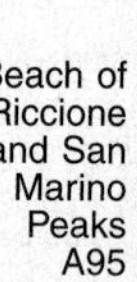

Beach of Riccione and San Marino Peaks A95

1960, Aug. 27 ***Perf. 14***

471	A95	30 l multicolored	.30	.25

12th San Marino-Riccione Stamp Day, Aug. 27. See No. C116.

Boy with Basket of Fruit, by Caravaggio — A96

1960, Dec. 29 Wmk. 303 ***Perf. 14***

472	A96	200 l multicolored	9.00	8.50

350th anniversary of the death of Michelangelo da Caravaggio (Merisi), painter.

Types of 1957

Views: 1 l, Hospital street. 4 l, Government building. 30 l, Gate tower. 115 l, Covered market of Borgo Maggiore.

1961, Feb. 16 ***Perf. 14***

473	A79	1 l dk blue grn	.25	.25
474	A78	4 l dk blue & blk	.25	.25
475	A78	30 l brt vio & brn	.60	.40
476	A78	115 l brown & blue	.60	.40
		Nos. 473-476 (4)	1.70	1.30

Hunting Roebuck A97

Hunting Scenes (16th-18th century): 2 l, Falconer, vert. 3 l, Wild boar hunt. 4 l, Duck shooting with crossbow. 5 l, Stag hunt. 10 l, Mounted falconer, vert. 30 l, Hunter with horn and dogs. 60 l, Hunter with rifle and dog, vert. 70 l, Hunter and beater. 115 l, Duck hunt.

Wmk. 303

1961, May 4 Photo. ***Perf. 14***

477	A97	1 l lil rose & vio bl	.25	.25
478	A97	2 l gray, dk red & blk	.25	.25
479	A97	3 l red org, brn & blk	.25	.25
480	A97	4 l lt bl, red & blk	.25	.25
481	A97	5 l yellow grn & brn	.25	.25
482	A97	10 l org, blk, brn & vio	.25	.25
483	A97	30 l yel, bl & dk grn	.25	.25
484	A97	60 l ocher, brn, blk & red	.25	.25
485	A97	70 l green, blk & car	.25	.25
486	A97	115 l brt pink, blk & dk bl	.50	.50
		Nos. 477-486 (10)	2.75	2.75

Mt. Titano and Cancelled Stamp of Sardinia, 1862 — A98

Photogravure and Embossed

1961, Sept. 5 Wmk. 303 ***Perf. 13***

487	A98	30 l multicolored	.50	.50
488	A98	70 l multicolored	.70	.70
489	A98	200 l multicolored	.75	.75
		Nos. 487-489 (3)	1.95	1.95

Cent. of Independence Phil. Exhib., Turin, 1961.

Europa Issue

View of San Marino A99

Wmk. 339

1961, Oct. 20 Photo. ***Perf. 13***

490	A99	500 l brn & blue grn	*30.00*	*15.00*
		Sheet of 6	*225.00*	*150.00*

King Enzo's Palace and Neptune Fountain, Bologna — A100

Views of Bologna: 70 l, Loggia dei Mercanti. 100 l, Two Towers.

1961, Nov. 25 Wmk. 339 ***Perf. 14***

491	A100	30 l grnsh bl & blk	.25	.25
492	A100	70 l dk ol grn & blk	.25	.25
493	A100	100 l red brn & blk	.25	.25
		Nos. 491-493 (3)	.75	.75

Bophilex, philatelic exhibition, Bologna.

Duryea, 1892 A101

Automobiles (pre-1910): 2 l, Panhard-Levassor. 3 l, Peugeot. 4 l, Daimler. 5 l, Fiat, vert. 10 l, Decauville. 15 l, Wolseley. 20 l, Benz. 25 l, Napier. 30 l, White, vert. 50 l, Oldsmobile. 70 l, Renault, vert. 100 l, Isotta Fraschini. 115 l, Bianchi. 150 l, Alfa.

1962, Jan. 23 Wmk. 303 ***Perf. 14***

494	A101	1 l red brn & bl	.25	.25
495	A101	2 l ultra & org brn	.25	.25
496	A101	3 l black, brn & org	.25	.25
497	A101	4 l gray & dk red	.25	.25
498	A101	5 l violet & org	.25	.25
499	A101	10 l black & org	.25	.25
500	A101	15 l black & ver	.25	.25
501	A101	20 l black & ultra	.25	.25
502	A101	25 l gray & org	.25	.25
503	A101	30 l black & ocher	.25	.25
504	A101	50 l black & brt pink	.25	.25
505	A101	70 l black, gray & grn	.25	.25
506	A101	100 l black, yel & car	.30	.30
507	A101	115 l blk, org & bl grn	.40	.40
508	A101	150 l multicolored	.50	.50
		Nos. 494-508 (15)	4.20	4.20

Wright Plane, 1904 A102

Historic Planes (1907-1910): 2 l, Ernest Archdeacon. 3 l, Albert and Emile Bonnet-Labranche. 4 l, Glenn Curtiss. 5 l, Farman. 10 l, Louis Bleriot. 30 l, Hubert Latham. 60 l, Alberto Santos Dumont. 70 l, Alliott Verdon Roe. 115 l, Faccioli.

Wmk. 339

1962, Apr. 4 Photo. ***Perf. 14***

509	A102	1 l blk & dull yel	.25	.25
510	A102	2 l red brn & grn	.25	.25
511	A102	3 l red brn & gray grn	.25	.25
512	A102	4 l brown & blk	.25	.25
513	A102	5 l magenta & blue	.25	.25
514	A102	10 l ocher & bl grn	.25	.25
515	A102	30 l ocher & ultra	.25	.25
516	A102	60 l black & ocher	.30	.30
517	A102	70 l dp orange & blk	.35	.35
518	A102	115 l blk, grn & ocher	.70	.70
		Nos. 509-518 (10)	3.10	3.10

Mountaineer Descending A103

Designs: 2 l, View of Sassolungo. 3 l, Mt. Titano. 4 l, Three Peaks of Lavaredo. 5 l, Matterhorn. 15 l, Skier on downhill run. 30 l, Climbing an overhang. 40 l, Cutting steps in ice. 85 l, Giant's Tooth. 115 l, Mt. Titano.

1962, June 14 Wmk. 339 ***Perf. 14***

519	A103	1 l bis brn & blk	.25	.25
520	A103	2 l Prus grn & blk	.25	.25
521	A103	3 l lilac & blk	.25	.25
522	A103	4 l brt bl & blk	.25	.25
523	A103	5 l dp org & blk	.25	.25
524	A103	15 l org yel & blk	.25	.25
525	A103	30 l carmine & blk	.25	.25
526	A103	40 l grnsh bl & blk	.25	.25
527	A103	85 l lt green & blk	.25	.25
528	A103	115 l vio bl & blk	.40	.40
		Nos. 519-528 (10)	2.65	2.65

Hunter with Dog A104

Modern Hunting Scenes: 2 l, Hound master on horseback, vert. 3 l, Duck hunt. 4 l, Stag hunt. 5 l, Partridge hunt. 15 l, Lapwing (hunt). 50 l, Wild duck hunt. 70 l, Duck hunt from boat. 100 l, Boar hunt. 150 l, Pheasant hunt, vert.

1962, Aug. 25 Photo. ***Perf. 14***

529	A104	1 l brown & yel grn	.25	.25
530	A104	2 l dk bl & org	.25	.25
531	A104	3 l blk & Prus bl	.25	.25
532	A104	4 l black & brown	.25	.25
533	A104	5 l brn & yel grn	.25	.25
534	A104	15 l blk & org brn	.25	.25
535	A104	50 l brn, dp grn & blk	.25	.25
536	A104	70 l grn, sal pink & blk	.25	.25
537	A104	100 l blk, brick red & sep	.25	.25
538	A104	150 l grn, lil & blk	.40	.40
		Nos. 529-538 (10)	2.65	2.65

Europa Issue

Mt. Titano and "Europa" A105

1962, Oct. 25 Wmk. 339

539	A105	200 l gray & car	*1.40*	*1.25*
		Sheet of 6	*9.50*	*9.50*

Egyptian Cargo Ship A106

Ancient Ships: 2 l, Greece, 2nd Cent. B.C. 3 l, Roman galley. 4 l, Vikings, 10th Cent. 5 l, "Santa Maria," 1492. 10 l, Cypriote galleon, vert. 30 l, Galley, 1600. 60 l, "Sovereign of the Seas," 1637, vert. 70 l, Danish ship, 1750, vert. 115 l, Frigate, 1850.

1963, Jan. 10

540	A106	1 l blue & org yel	.25	.25
541	A106	2 l mag, tan & brn	.25	.25
542	A106	3 l brown & lil rose	.25	.25
543	A106	4 l vio brn & gray	.25	.25
544	A106	5 l brown & yellow	.25	.25
545	A106	10 l brn & brt yel grn	.25	.25
546	A106	30 l blk, bl & sep	.60	.60
547	A106	60 l lt vio bl & yel grn	.60	.60
548	A106	70 l blk, gray & dl red	.95	.95
549	A106	115 l blk, brn & gray bl	1.50	1.50
		Nos. 540-549 (10)	5.15	5.15

Lady with Veil, by Raphael — A107

Paintings by Raphael: 70 l, Self-portrait. 100 l, St. Barbara from Sistine Madonna. 200 l, Portrait of a Young Woman (Maddalena Strozzi).

Size: 26½x37mm

Wmk. 339

1963, Mar. 28 Photo. ***Perf. 14***

550	A107	30 l multicolored	.35	.35
551	A107	70 l multicolored	.25	.25
552	A107	100 l multicolored	.30	.25

Size: 26½x44mm

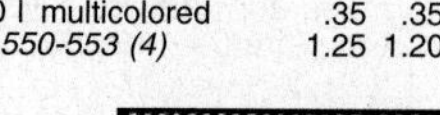

553	A107	200 l multicolored	.35	.35
		Nos. 550-553 (4)	1.25	1.20

Jousting with "Saracen," Arezzo — A108

Medieval "Knightly Games": 2 l, French knights, horiz. 3 l, Crossbow contest. 4 l, English knight receiving lance, horiz. 5 l, Tournament, Florence. 10 l, Jousting with "Quintana," Ascoli Piceno. 30 l, "Quintana," Foligno, horiz. 60 l, Race through Siena. 70 l, Tournament, Malpaga, horiz. 115 l, Knights challenging.

1963, June 22 Wmk. 339 *Perf. 14*

No.	Type	Value	Color	Unused	Used
554	A108	1 l	lilac rose	.25	.25
555	A108	2 l	slate	.25	.25
556	A108	3 l	black	.25	.25
557	A108	4 l	violet	.25	.25
558	A108	5 l	rose violet	.25	.25
559	A108	10 l	dull green	.25	.25
560	A108	30 l	red brown	.25	.25
561	A108	60 l	Prus green	.25	.25
562	A108	70 l	brown	.25	.25
563	A108	115 l	black	.25	.25
			Nos. 554-563 (10)	2.50	2.50

Butterfly — A109

Various butterflies. 70 l, 115 l, horiz.

Wmk. 339

1963, Aug. 31 Photo. *Perf. 14*

No.	Type	Value	Color	Unused	Used
564	A109	25 l	multicolored	.25	.25
565	A109	30 l	multicolored	.25	.25
566	A109	60 l	multicolored	.25	.25
567	A109	70 l	multicolored	.30	.30
568	A109	115 l	multicolored	.45	.45
			Nos. 564-568 (5)	1.50	1.50

St. Marinus Statue, Government Palace — A110

1963, Aug. 31

No.	Type	Value	Description	Unused	Used
569	A110	100 l	shown	.25	.25
570	A110	100 l	Modern fountain	.25	.25

San Marino-Riccione Stamp Fair.

Europa Issue

Flag and "E" — A111

1963, Sept. 21 Wmk. 339 *Perf. 14*

No.	Type	Value	Color	Unused	Used
571	A111	200 l	blue & brn org	*.60*	.50

Women's Hurdles A112

Sports: 2 l, Pole vaulting, vert. 3 l, Women's relay race. 4 l, Men's high jump. 5 l, Soccer. 10 l, Women's high jump. 30 l, Women's discus throw, vert. 60 l, Women's javelin throw. 70 l, Water polo. 115 l, Hammer throw.

1963, Sept. 21

No.	Type	Value	Color	Unused	Used
572	A112	1 l	org & red brn	.25	.25
573	A112	2 l	lt grn & dk brn	.25	.25
574	A112	3 l	bl & dk brn	.25	.25
575	A112	4 l	dp bl & dk brn	.25	.25
576	A112	5 l	red & dk brn	.25	.25
577	A112	10 l	lil rose & claret	.25	.25
578	A112	30 l	gray & red brn	.25	.25
579	A112	60 l	brt yel & dk brn	.25	.25
580	A112	70 l	brt bl & dk brn	.25	.25
581	A112	115 l	grn & dk brn	.25	.25
			Nos. 572-581 (10)	2.50	2.50

Publicity for 1964 Olympic Games.

Modern Pentathlon A113

Designs: 1 l, Runner, vert. 2 l, Woman gymnast, vert. 3 l, Basketball, vert. 5 l, Dual rowing. 15 l, Broad jumper. 30 l, Swimmer in racing dive. 70 l, Woman sprinter. 120 l, Bicycle racers, vert. 150 l, Fencers, vert.

Inscribed "Tokio, 1964"

1964, June 25 Wmk. 339 *Perf. 14*

No.	Type	Value	Color	Unused	Used
582	A113	1 l	brn & yel grn	.25	.25
583	A113	2 l	blk & red brn	.25	.25
584	A113	3 l	blk & brown	.25	.25
585	A113	4 l	blk & org red	.25	.25
586	A113	5 l	blk & brt bl	.25	.25
587	A113	15 l	dk brn & org	.25	.25
588	A113	30 l	dk vio & bl	.25	.25
589	A113	70 l	red brn & grn	.25	.25
590	A113	120 l	brn & brt bl	.25	.25
591	A113	150 l	blk & crimson	.25	.25
			Nos. 582-591 (10)	2.50	2.50

18th Olympic Games, Tokyo, Oct. 10-25.

Same Inscribed "Verso Tokio"

1964, June 25 Photo.

No.	Type	Value	Color	Unused	Used
592	A113	30 l	indigo & lilac	.25	.25
593	A113	70 l	brn & Prus grn	.25	.25

"Verso Tokyo" Stamp Exhibition at Rimini, Italy, June 25-July 6.

Murray-Blenkinsop Locomotive, 1812 — A114

History of Locomotive: 2 l, Puffing Billy, 1813. 3 l, Locomotion I, 1825. 4 l, Rocket, 1829. 5 l, Lion, 1838. 15 l, Bayard, 1839. 20 l, Crampton, 1849. 50 l, Little England, 1851. 90 l, Spitfire, c. 1860. 110 l, Rogers, c. 1865.

1964, Aug. 29 Wmk. 339 *Perf. 14*

No.	Type	Value	Color	Unused	Used
594	A114	1 l	blk & buff	.25	.25
595	A114	2 l	blk & green	.25	.25
596	A114	3 l	blk & rose lilac	.25	.25
597	A114	4 l	blk & yellow	.25	.25
598	A114	5 l	blk & salmon	.25	.25
599	A114	15 l	blk & yel grn	.25	.25
600	A114	20 l	blk & dp pink	.25	.25
601	A114	50 l	blk & pale bl	.25	.25
602	A114	90 l	blk & yel org	.25	.25
603	A114	110 l	blk & brt bl	.35	.35
			Nos. 594-603 (10)	2.60	2.60

Baseball Players A115

1964, Aug. 29 Photo.

No.	Type	Value	Description	Unused	Used
604	A115	30 l	shown	.30	.30
605	A115	70 l	Pitcher	.30	.30

8th European Baseball Championship, Milan.

Europa Issue

"E" and Globe A116

1964, Oct. 15 Wmk. 339 *Perf. 14*

No.	Type	Value	Color	Unused	Used
606	A116	200 l	dk blue & red	*1.50*	*1.00*

President John F. Kennedy (1917-1963) — A117

130 l, Kennedy and American flag, vert.

1964, Nov. 22 Photo. *Perf. 14*

No.	Type	Value	Color	Unused	Used
607	A117	70 l	multicolored	.25	.25
608	A117	130 l	multicolored	.25	.25

Start of Bicycle Race from Government Palace — A118

Designs: 70 l, Cyclists (going right) and view of San Marino. 200 l, Cyclists (going left) and view of San Marino.

1965, May 15 Photo. Wmk. 339

No.	Type	Value	Color	Unused	Used
609	A118	30 l	sepia	.25	.25
610	A118	70 l	deep claret	.25	.25
611	A118	200 l	rose red	.25	.25
			Nos. 609-611 (3)	.75	.75

48th Bicycle Tour of Italy.

Brontosaurus — A119

Dinosaurs: 2 l, Brachiosaurus, vert. 3 l, Pteranodon. 4 l, Elasmosaurus. 5 l, Tyrannosaurus. 10 l, Stegosaurus. 75 l, Thaumatosaurus victor. 100 l, Iguanodon. 200 l, Triceratops.

1965, June 30 Wmk. 339 *Perf. 14*

No.	Type	Value	Color	Unused	Used
612	A119	1 l	dk brn & emer	.25	.25
613	A119	2 l	blk & sl bl	.25	.25
614	A119	3 l	sl grn, ol grn & yel	.25	.25
615	A119	4 l	brn & slate bl	.25	.25
616	A119	5 l	claret & grn	.25	.25
617	A119	10 l	claret & grn	.25	.25
618	A119	75 l	dk bl & bl grn	.25	.25
619	A119	100 l	green & claret	.40	.40
620	A119	200 l	brown & grn	.50	.50
			Nos. 612-620 (9)	2.65	2.65

Europa Issue

Rooks on Chessboard A120

1965, Aug. 28 Photo. *Perf. 14*

No.	Type	Value	Color	Unused	Used
621	A120	200 l	brown & multi	*1.10*	.65

Dante by Gustave Doré A121

Doré's Illustrations for Divina Commedia: 90 l, Charon ferrying boat across Acheron. 130 l, Eagle carrying Dante from Purgatory to Paradise. 140 l, Dante with Beatrice examined by Sts. Peter, James and John on faith.

Perf. 14x14½

1965, Nov. 20 Engr. Wmk. 339

Center in Brown Black

No.	Type	Value	Color	Unused	Used
622	A121	40 l	indigo	.25	.25
623	A121	90 l	car rose	.25	.25
624	A121	130 l	red brown	.25	.25
625	A121	140 l	ultra	.25	.25
			Nos. 622-625 (4)	1.00	1.00

Dante Alighieri (1265-1321), poet.

Stylized Peaks, Flags of Italy and San Marino A122

1965, Nov. 25 Photo. *Perf. 14*

No.	Type	Value	Color	Unused	Used
626	A122	115 l	grn, red, ocher & bl	.30	.30

Visit of Giuseppe Saragat, president of Italy.

Trotter A123

Horses: 20 l, Cross Country, vert. 40 l, Hurdling. 70 l, Gallop. 90 l, Steeplechase. 170 l, Polo, vert.

Perf. 14x13, 13x14

1966, Feb. 28 Photo. Wmk. 339

No.	Type	Value	Color	Unused	Used
627	A123	10 l	multicolored	.25	.25
628	A123	20 l	multicolored	.25	.25
629	A123	40 l	multicolored	.25	.25
630	A123	70 l	multicolored	.25	.25
631	A123	90 l	multicolored	.25	.25
632	A123	170 l	multicolored	.25	.25
			Nos. 627-632 (6)	1.50	1.50

Scenic Types of 1955-57

5 l, Hospital Street. 10 l, Gate tower. 15 l, View from South Bastion. 40 l, Murata Nuova Bridge. 90 l, View of La Rocca. 140 l, Government Palace.

1966, Mar. 29 Wmk. 339 *Perf. 14*

No.	Type	Value	Color	Unused	Used
633	A79	5 l	blue & brn	.25	.25
634	A78	10 l	dk sl grn & bl grn	.25	.25
635	A78	15 l	dk brn & vio	.25	.25
636	A73	40 l	dk pur & brick red	.25	.25
637	A74	90 l	blk & dull bl	.25	.25
638	A74	140 l	violet & org	.25	.25
			Nos. 633-638 (6)	1.50	1.50

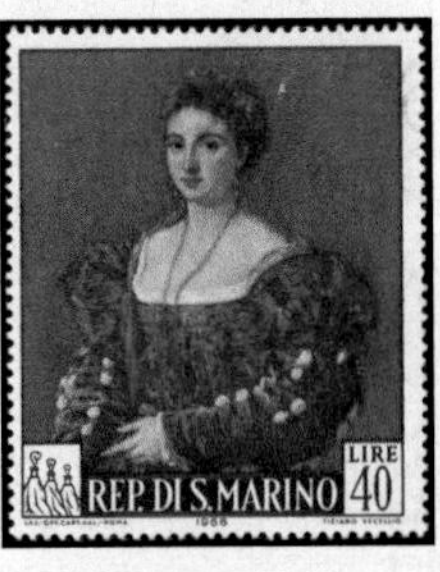

"Bella" by Titian A124

Titian Paintings: 90 l, 100 l, Details from "The Education of Love." 170 l, Detail from "Sacred and Profane Love."

1966, June 16 Wmk. 339 *Perf. 14*

No.	Type	Value	Color	Unused	Used
639	A124	40 l	multicolored	.25	.25
640	A124	90 l	multicolored	.25	.25
641	A124	100 l	multicolored	.25	.25
642	A124	170 l	multicolored	.25	.25
			Nos. 639-642 (4)	1.00	1.00

Stone Bass
A125

Fish: 2 l, Cuckoo wrasse. 3 l, Dolphin. 4 l, John Dory. 5 l, Octopus, vert. 10 l, Orange scorpionfish. 40 l, Electric ray, vert. 90 l, Jellyfish, vert. 115 l, Sea Horse, vert. 130 l, Dentex.

Perf. 14x13½, 13½x14

1966, Aug. 27 Photo. Wmk. 339

643	A125	1 l	multicolored	.25	.25
644	A125	2 l	multicolored	.25	.25
645	A125	3 l	multicolored	.25	.25
646	A125	4 l	multicolored	.25	.25
647	A125	5 l	multicolored	.25	.25
648	A125	10 l	multicolored	.25	.25
649	A125	40 l	multicolored	.25	.25
650	A125	90 l	multicolored	.25	.25
651	A125	115 l	multicolored	.25	.25
652	A125	130 l	multicolored	.25	.25
			Nos. 643-652 (10)	2.50	2.50

Europa Issue

Our Lady of Europe
A126

1966, Sept. 24 Wmk. 339 *Perf. 14*

653	A126	200 l	multicolored	.45	.35

Peony and Mt. Titano — A127

Flowers and Various Views of Mt. Titano: 10 l, Bell flowers. 15 l, Pyrenean poppy. 20 l, Purple nettle. 40 l, Day lily. 140 l, Gentian. 170 l, Thistle.

Wmk. 339

1967, Jan. 12 Photo. *Perf. 14*

654	A127	5 l	multicolored	.25	.25
655	A127	10 l	multicolored	.25	.25
656	A127	15 l	multicolored	.25	.25
657	A127	20 l	multicolored	.25	.25
658	A127	40 l	multicolored	.25	.25
659	A127	140 l	multicolored	.25	.25
660	A127	170 l	multicolored	.25	.25
			Nos. 654-660 (7)	1.75	1.75

St. Marinus — A128

The Return of the Prodigal Son — A129

Design: 170 l, St. Francis. The paintings are by Giovanni Francesco Barbieri (1591-1666).

Wmk. 339

1967, Mar. 16 Photo. *Perf. 14*

661	A128	40 l	multicolored	.25	.25
662	A128	170 l	multicolored	.25	.25
663	A129	190 l	multicolored	.25	.25
a.			Strip of 3, #661-663	.75	.75

Europa Issue

Map Showing Members of CEPT — A130

1967, May 5 Wmk. 339 *Perf. 14*

664	A130	200 l	sl grn & brn org	*.75*	.45

Amanita Caesarea — A131

Various Mushrooms.

1967, June 15 Photo. *Perf. 14*

665	A131	5 l	multicolored	.25	.25
666	A131	15 l	multicolored	.25	.25
667	A131	20 l	multicolored	.25	.25
668	A131	40 l	multicolored	.25	.25
669	A131	50 l	multicolored	.25	.25
670	A131	170 l	multicolored	.25	.25
			Nos. 665-670 (6)	1.50	1.50

Amiens Cathedral
A132

Designs: 40 l, Siena Cathedral. 80 l, Toledo Cathedral. 90 l, Salisbury Cathedral. 170 l, Cologne Cathedral.

Wmk. 339

1967, Sept. 21 Engr. *Perf. 14*

671	A132	20 l	dk vio, *bister*	.25	.25
672	A132	40 l	slate grn, *bis*	.25	.25
673	A132	80 l	slate bl, *bis*	.25	.25
674	A132	90 l	sepia, *bis*	.25	.25
675	A132	170 l	deep plum, *bis*	.25	.25
			Nos. 671-675 (5)	1.25	1.25

Crucifix of Santa Croce, by Cimabue
A133

1967, Dec. 5 Wmk. 339 *Perf. 15*

676	A133	300 l	brn & vio blue	.60	.60

The Crucifix of Santa Croce, by Giovanni Cimabue (1240-1302), was severely damaged in the Florentine flood of Nov. 1966.

Coat of Arms — A134

Coats of Arms: 3 l, Penna Rossa. 5 l, Fiorentino. 10 l, Montecerreto. 25 l, Serravalle. 35 l, Montegiardino. 50 l, Faetano. 90 l, Borgo Maggiore. 180 l, Montelupo. 500 l, State arms of San Marino.

Perf. 13x13½

1968, Mar. 14 Litho. Wmk. 339

677	A134	2 l	multi	.25	.25
678	A134	3 l	multi	.25	.25
679	A134	5 l	multi	.25	.25
680	A134	10 l	multi	.25	.25
681	A134	25 l	multi	.25	.25
682	A134	35 l	multi	.25	.25
683	A134	50 l	multi	.25	.25
684	A134	90 l	multi	.25	.25
685	A134	180 l	multi	.25	.25
686	A134	500 l	multi	.45	.25
			Nos. 677-686 (10)	2.70	2.50

Common Design Types pictured following the introduction.

Europa Issue, 1968
Common Design Type

1968, Apr. 29 Engr. *Perf. 14x13½*
Size: 37x27½mm

687	CD11	250 l	claret brown	*.55*	.35

"Battle of San Romano" (Detail), by Paolo Uccello — A135

Designs: Details from "The Battle of San Romano," by Paolo Uccello (1397-1475).

Photogravure and Engraved

1968, June 14 Wmk. 339 *Perf. 14*

688	A135	50 l	pale lil & blk	.25	.25
689	A135	90 l	pale lil & blk, vert.	.25	.25
690	A135	130 l	pale lil & blk	.25	.25
691	A135	230 l	pale pink & blk	.25	.25
			Nos. 688-691 (4)	1.00	1.00

The Mystic Nativity, by Botticelli, Detail
A136

Wmk. 339

1968, Dec. 5 Engr. *Perf. 14*

692	A136	50 l	dark blue	.25	.25
693	A136	90 l	deep claret	.25	.25
694	A136	180 l	sepia	.25	.25
			Nos. 692-694 (3)	.75	.75

Christmas.

"Peace" by Lorenzetti
A137

Designs: 80 l, "Justice." 90 l, "Moderation." 180 l, View of Siena, 14th century, horiz. All designs are from the "Good Government" frescoes by Ambrogio Lorenzetti in the Town Hall of Siena.

Wmk. 339

1969, Feb. 13 Engr. *Perf. 14*

695	A137	50 l	dark blue	.25	.25
696	A137	80 l	brown	.25	.25
697	A137	90 l	dk blue vio	.25	.25
698	A137	180 l	magenta	.25	.25
			Nos. 695-698 (4)	1.00	1.00

Young Soldier, by Bramante — A138

Designs: 90 l, Old Soldier, by Bramante. Designs are from murals in the Pinakotheke of Brear, Milan.

1969, Apr. 28 Photo. *Perf. 14*

699	A138	50 l	multicolored	.25	.25
700	A138	90 l	multicolored	.25	.25

Bramante (1444-1514), Italian architect and painter.

Europa Issue
Common Design Type

1969, Apr. 28 Engr. *Perf. 14x13*
Size: 37x27mm

701	CD12	50 l	dull green	*.45*	*.45*
702	CD12	180 l	rose claret	*.45*	*.45*

Charabanc
A139

Coaches, 19th Century: 10 l, Barouche. 25 l, Private drag. 40 l, Hansom cab. 50 l, Curricle. 90 l, Wagonette. 180 l, Spider phaeton.

Perf. 14½x14

1969, June 25 Photo. Unwmk.

703	A139	5 l	blk, ocher & dk bl	.25	.25
704	A139	10 l	blk, grn & pur	.25	.25
705	A139	25 l	dk grn, pink & brn	.25	.25
706	A139	40 l	ind, lil & lt brn	.25	.25
707	A139	50 l	blk, dl yel & dk bl	.25	.25
708	A139	90 l	blk, yel grn & brn	.25	.25
709	A139	180 l	multi	.25	.25
			Nos. 703-709 (7)	1.75	1.75

Pier at Rimini
A140

Paintings by R. Viola: 20 l, Mt. Titano. 200 l, Pier at Riccione, horiz.

1969, Sept. 17 Unwmk. *Perf. 14*

710	A140	20 l multicolored	.25	.25
711	A140	180 l multicolored	.25	.25
712	A140	200 l multicolored	.30	.30
		Nos. 710-712 (3)	.80	.80

"Faith" by Raphael — A141

Designs: 180 l, "Hope" by Raphael. 200 l, "Charity" by Raphael.

Perf. 13½x14

1969, Dec. 10 Engr. Wmk. 339

713	A141	20 l dl pur & sal	.25	.25
714	A141	180 l dl pur & lt grn	.25	.25
715	A141	200 l dp pur & bis	.25	.25
		Nos. 713-715 (3)	.75	.75

Signs of the Zodiac A142

Perf. 14x13½

1970, Feb. 18 Photo. Unwmk.

716	A142	1 l Aries	.25	.25
717	A142	2 l Taurus	.25	.25
718	A142	3 l Gemini	.25	.25
719	A142	4 l Cancer	.25	.25
720	A142	5 l Leo	.25	.25
721	A142	10 l Virgo	.25	.25
722	A142	15 l Libra	.25	.25
723	A142	20 l Scorpio	.25	.25
724	A142	70 l Sagittarius	.25	.25
725	A142	90 l Capricorn	.25	.25
726	A142	100 l Aquraius	.25	.25
727	A142	180 l Pisces	.30	.30
		Nos. 716-727 (12)	3.05	3.05

Fleet in Bay of Naples, by Peter Brueghel, the Elder — A143

Unwmk.

1970, Apr. 30 Photo. *Perf. 14*

728	A143	230 l multi	.40	.40

10th Europa Phil. Exhib., Naples, May 2-10.

Europa Issue

Common Design Type

1970, Apr. 30 *Perf. 14x13½*

Size: 36x27mm

729	CD13	90 l brt yel grn & red	*.45*	.25
730	CD13	180 l ocher & red	*.45*	.30

St. Francis' Gate and Rotary Emblem — A144

220 l, Rocca (State Prison) and Rotary emblem.

1970, June 25 Photo. *Perf. 13½x14*

731	A144	180 l multi	.25	.25
732	A144	220 l multi	.45	.45

65th anniv. of Rotary Intl.; 10th anniv. of the San Marino Rotary Club.

Woman with Mandolin, by Tiepolo — A145

Paintings by Tiepolo: 180 l, Woman with Parrot. 220 l, Rinaldo and Armida Surprised, horiz.

Size: 26½x37½mm

1970, Sept. 10 Unwmk. *Perf. 14*

733	50 l multi	.25	.25
734	180 l multi	.25	.25

Size: 56x37½mm

735	220 l multi	.25	.25
a.	A145 Strip of 3, #733-735	1.00	1.00

Giambattista Tiepolo (1696-1770), Venetian painter.

Black Pete — A146

Walt Disney and Jungle Book Scene A147

Disney Characters: 2 l, Gyro Gearloose. 3 l, Pluto. 4 l, Minnie Mouse. 5 l, Donald Duck. 10 l, Goofy. 15 l, Scrooge McDuck. 50 l, Huey, Louey and Dewey. 90 l, Mickey Mouse.

Perf. 13x14, 14x13

1970, Dec. 22 Photo.

736	A146	1 l multi	.25	.25
737	A146	2 l multi	.25	.25
738	A146	3 l multi	.25	.25
739	A146	4 l multi	.25	.25
740	A146	5 l multi	.25	.25
741	A146	10 l multi	.25	.25
742	A146	15 l multi	.25	.25
743	A146	50 l multi	.30	.30
744	A146	90 l multi	.75	.75
745	A147	220 l multi	5.25	5.25
		Nos. 736-745 (10)	8.05	8.05

Walt Disney (1901-66), cartoonist & film maker.

Customhouse Dock, by Canaletto — A148

Paintings by Canaletto: 180 l, Grand Canal between Balbi Palace and Rialto Bridge. 200 l, St. Mark's and Doges' Palace.

1971, Mar. 23 Unwmk. *Perf. 14*

746	A148	20 l multi	.25	.25
747	A148	180 l multi	.40	.40
748	A148	200 l multi	.40	.40
		Nos. 746-748 (3)	1.05	1.05

Save Venice campaign.

Europa Issue, 1971

Common Design Type

1971, May 29 *Perf. 13½x14*

Size: 27½x23mm

749	CD14	50 l org & blue	.25	.25
750	CD14	90 l blue & org	.40	.30

Congress Emblem and Hall, San Marino Flag — A149

Design: 90 l, Detail from Government Palace door, Congress and San Marino emblems, vert.

1971, May 29 Photo. *Perf. 12*

751	A149	20 l violet & multi	.25	.25
752	A149	90 l olive & multi	.25	.25
753	A149	180 l multi	.25	.25
		Nos. 751-753 (3)	.75	.75

Italian Philatelic Press Union Congress, San Marino, May 29-30.

Duck-shaped Jug with Flying Lasa — A150

Etruscan Art, 6th-3rd Centuries B.C.: 80 l, Head of Mercury, vert. 90 l, Sarcophagus of a married couple, vert. 180 l, Chimera.

Photo. & Engr.

1971, Sept. 16 *Perf. 14*

754	A150	50 l blk & org	.25	.25
755	A150	80 l blk & lt grn	.25	.25
756	A150	90 l blk & lt bl	.25	.25
757	A150	180 l blk & org	.35	.35
		Nos. 754-757 (4)	1.10	1.10

Tiger Lily — A151

1971, Dec. 2 Photo. *Perf. 11½*

758	A151	1 l shown	.25	.25
759	A151	2 l Phlox	.25	.25
760	A151	3 l Carnations	.25	.25
761	A151	4 l Globe flowers	.25	.25
762	A151	5 l Thistles	.25	.25
763	A151	10 l Peonies	.25	.25
764	A151	15 l Hellebore	.25	.25
765	A151	50 l Anemones	.25	.25
766	A151	90 l Gaillardia	.25	.25
767	A151	220 l Asters	.25	.25
		Nos. 758-767 (10)	2.50	2.50

Venus, by Botticelli — A152

Details from La Primavera, by Sandro Botticelli: 180 l, Three Graces. 220 l, Spring.

Sizes: 50 l, 220 l, 21x37mm; 180 l, 27x37mm

1972, Feb. 23 *Perf. 14, 13x14 (180 l)*

768	A152	50 l gold & multi	.25	.25
769	A152	180 l gold & multi	.50	.50
770	A152	220 l gold & multi	.50	.50
		Nos. 768-770 (3)	1.25	1.25

Europa Issue

Common Design Type

1972, Apr. 27 *Perf. 11½*

Granite Paper

Size: 22½x33mm

771	CD15	50 l org & multi	.30	.25
772	CD15	90 l lt bl & multi	.40	.25

St. Marinus Taming Bear A153

Designs: 55 l, Donna Felicissima asking St. Marinus for mercy for her sons. 100 l, St. Marinus turning archers to stone. 130 l, Felicissima giving mountains to St. Marinus to establish Republic.

Photo. & Engr.

1972, Apr. 27 *Perf. 14*

773	A153	25 l dl yel & blk	.25	.25
774	A153	55 l sal pink & blk	.25	.25
775	A153	100 l dl bl & blk	.25	.25
776	A153	130 l citron & blk	.25	.25
		Nos. 773-776 (4)	1.00	1.00

Allegories of San Marino after 16th century paintings.

Italian House Sparrow — A154

2 l, Firecrest. 3 l, Blue tit. 4 l, Ortolan bunting. 5 l, White-spotted bluethroat. 10 l, Bullfinch. 25 l, Linnet. 50 l, Black-eared wheater. 90 l, Sardinian warbler. 220 l, Greenfinch.

1972, June 30 Photo. *Perf. 11½*

Granite Paper

777	A154	1 l shown	.25	.25
778	A154	2 l multicolored	.25	.25
779	A154	3 l multicolored	.25	.25
780	A154	4 l multicolored	.25	.25
781	A154	5 l multicolored	.25	.25
782	A154	10 l multicolored	.25	.25
783	A154	25 l multicolored	.25	.25
784	A154	50 l multicolored	.25	.25
785	A154	90 l multicolored	.25	.25
786	A154	220 l multicolored	.25	.25
		Nos. 777-786 (10)	2.50	2.50

Young Man, Heart, Emblem — A155

Design: 90 l, Heart disease victim, horiz.

Perf. 13½x14, 14x13½

1972, Aug. 26

787	A155	50 l lt bl & multi	.25	.25
788	A155	90 l ocher & multi	.25	.25

World Heart Month.

Italian Philatelic Federation Emblem — A156

1972, Aug. 26 ***Perf. 13½x14***

789 A156 25 l gold & ultra .25 .25

Honoring veterans of Philately.

5c Coin, 1864 A157

Coins: 10 l, 10c coin, 1935. 15 l, 1 lira, 1906. 20 l, 5 lire, 1898. 25 l, 5 lire, 1937. 50 l, 10 lire, 1932. 55 l, 20 lire, 1938. 220 l, 20 lire, 1925.

1972, Dec. 15 **Litho.** ***Perf. 12½x13***

790 A157 5 l gray, blk & brn .25 .25
791 A157 10 l org, blk & sil .25 .25
792 A157 15 l brt rose, blk & sil .25 .25
793 A157 20 l lil, blk & sil .25 .25
794 A157 25 l vio, blk & sil .25 .25
795 A157 50 l brt bl, blk & sil .25 .25
796 A157 55 l ocher, blk & sil .25 .25
797 A157 220 l emer, blk & gold .25 .25
Nos. 790-797 (8) 2.00 2.00

New York, 1673 — A158

300 l, View of New York from East River, 1973.

1973, Mar. 9 **Photo.** ***Perf. 11½***
Granite Paper

798 200 l bis, och & ol grn .40 .40
799 300 l bl, lil & blk .75 .75
a. A158 Pair, #798-799 1.50 1.50

New York, 300th anniv. Printed checkerwise.

Rotary Press, San Marino Towers — A159

1973, May 10 **Photo.** ***Perf. 13x14***

800 A159 50 l multi .25 .25

Tourist Press Congress, San Marino.

Gymnasts and Olympic Rings — A160

1973, May 10 **Unwmk.**

801 A160 100 l grn & multi .25 .25

5th Youth Games.

Europa Issue
Common Design Type

1973, May 10 ***Perf. 11½***
Size: 32½x23mm

802 CD16 20 l salmon & multi *.40* .25
803 CD16 180 l lt bl & multi *.60* .35

Grapes — A161

1973, July 11 **Photo.** ***Perf. 11½***

804 A161 1 l shown .25 .25
805 A161 2 l Tangerines .25 .25
806 A161 3 l Apples .25 .25
807 A161 4 l Plums .25 .25
808 A161 5 l Strawberries .25 .25
809 A161 10 l Pears .25 .25
810 A161 25 l Cherries .25 .25
811 A161 50 l Pomegranate .25 .25
812 A161 90 l Apricots .25 .25
813 A161 220 l Peaches .25 .25
Nos. 804-813 (10) 2.50 2.50

Arc-en-Ciel, France — A162

Famous Aircraft: 55 l, Macchi Castoldi, Italy. 60 l, Antonov, USSR. 90 l, Spirit of St. Louis, US. 220 l, Handley Page, Great Britain.

1973, Aug. 31 **Photo.** ***Perf. 14x13½***

814 A162 25 l ocher, vio bl & gold .25 .25
815 A162 55 l gray, vio bl & gold .25 .25
816 A162 60 l rose, vio bl & gold .25 .25
817 A162 90 l lem, vio bl & gold .25 .25
818 A162 220 l org, vio bl & gold .35 .35
Nos. 814-818 (5) 1.35 1.35

Crossbowman, Serravalle Castle — A163

Designs: 10 l, Crossbowman, Pennarossa Castle. 15 l, Drummer, Montegiardino Castle. 20 l, Trumpeter, Fiorentino Castle. 30 l, Crossbowman, Borga Maggiore Castle. 50 l, Trumpeter, Guaita Castle. 80 l, Crossbowman, Faetano Castle. 200 l, Crossbowman, Montelupo Castle.

1973, Nov. 7 **Photo.** ***Perf. 13½***

819 A163 5 l black & multi .25 .25
820 A163 10 l black & multi .25 .25
821 A163 15 l black & multi .25 .25
822 A163 20 l black & multi .25 .25
823 A163 30 l black & multi .25 .25
824 A163 40 l black & multi .25 .25
825 A163 50 l black & multi .25 .25
826 A163 80 l black & multi .25 .25
827 A163 200 l black & multi .30 .30
Nos. 819-827 (9) 2.30 2.30

San Marino victories in the Crossbow Tournament, Massa Marittima, July 15, 1973.

Attendants, by Gentile Fabriano — A164

Christmas: Details from Adoration of the Kings, by Gentile Fabriano (1370-1427).

1973, Dec. 19 **Photo.** ***Perf. 11½***

828 A164 5 l shown .25 .25
829 A164 30 l King .25 .25
830 A164 115 l King .25 .25
831 A164 250 l Horses .30 .30
Nos. 828-831 (4) 1.05 1.05

Shield, 16th Century A165

16th Century Armor: 5 l, Round shield. 10 l, German full armor. 15 l, Helmet with intricate etching. 20 l, Horse's head armor "Massimiliano." 30 l, Decorated helmet with Sphinx statuette on top. 50 l, Pommeled sword and gauntlets. 80 l, Sparrow-beaked helmet. 250 l, Sforza round shield.

Engr. & Litho.

1974, Mar. 12 ***Perf. 13***

832 A165 5 l blk, lt grn & buff .25 .25
833 A165 10 l blk, buff & bl .25 .25
834 A165 15 l blk, bl & ultra .25 .25
835 A165 20 l blk, tan & ultra .25 .25
836 A165 30 l blk & lt bl .25 .25
837 A165 50 l blk, rose & ultra .25 .25
838 A165 80 l blk, gray & grn .25 .25
839 A165 250 l blk & yel .35 .35
Nos. 832-839 (8) 2.10 2.10

Head of Woman, by Emilio Greco — A166

Europa: 200 l, Nude, by Emilio Greco (head shown on 100 l).

Engr. & Litho.

1974, May 9 ***Perf. 13x14***

840 A166 100 l buff & blk *.45* *.40*
841 A166 200 l pale grn & blk *.65* *.50*

Yachts at Riccione and San Marino Peaks A167

1974, July 18 **Photo.** ***Perf. 11½***
Granite Paper

842 A167 50 l ultra & multi .25 .25

26th San Marino-Riccione Stamp Day.

Arms of Lucia — A168

Coats of arms of participating cities.

1974, July 18 ***Perf. 12***

843 A168 15 l shown .50 .50
844 A168 20 l Massa Marittima .50 .50
845 A168 50 l San Marino .50 .50
846 A168 115 l Gubbio .75 .75
847 A168 300 l Lucca .75 .75
a. Strip of 5, #843-847 4.00 4.00

9th Crossbow Tournament, San Marino.

UPU Emblem — A169

1974, Oct. 9 **Photo.** ***Perf. 11½***
Granite Paper

848 A169 50 l multi .25 .25
849 A169 90 l grn & multi .30 .30

Centenary of Universal Postal Union.

Mt. Titano and Hymn by Tommaseo A170

Niccolo Tommaseo A171

1974, Dec. 12 **Photo.** ***Perf. 13½x14***

850 A170 50 l lt grn, blk & red .30 .30
851 A171 150 l yel, grn & blk .30 .30

Tommaseo (1802-1874), Italian writer.

Virgin and Child, 14th Century Wood Panel — A172

1974, Dec. 12 ***Perf. 11½***

852 A172 250 l gold & multi .50 .50

Christmas.

"Refuge in San Marino" — A173

1975, Feb. 20 **Photo.** ***Perf. 13½x14***

853 A173 50 l multi .25 .25

Flight of 100,000 refugees from Romagna to San Marino, 30th anniversary.

Musicians, from Leopard Tomb, Tarquinia — A174

Etruscan Art: 30 l, Chariot race, from Tomb on the Hill, Chiusi. 180 l, Achilles and Troilus, from Bulls' Tomb, Tarquinia. 220 l, Dancers, from Triclinium Tomb, Tarquinia.

Litho. & Engr.

1975, Feb. 20 ***Perf. 14***

854 A174 20 l multi .25 .25
855 A174 30 l multi .25 .25
856 A174 180 l multi .25 .25
857 A174 220 l multi .30 .30
Nos. 854-857 (4) 1.05 1.05

Europa Issue

St. Marinus, by Guercino (Francesco Barbieri)
A175 A176

1975, May 14 Photo. ***Perf. 11½***

Granite Paper

858 A175 100 l multi .55 .25
859 A176 200 l multi .75 .35

The Lamentation, by Giotto — A177

Frescoes by Giotto (details): 40 l, Mary and Jesus (Flight into Egypt). 50 l, Heads of four angels (Flight into Egypt). 100 l, Mary Magdalene (Noli Me Tangere), horiz. 500 l, Angel and the elect (Last Judgment), horiz.

1975, July 10 Photo. ***Perf. 11½***

Granite Paper

860 A177 10 l gold & multi .25 .25
861 A177 40 l gold & multi .25 .25
862 A177 50 l gold & multi .25 .25
863 A177 100 l gold & multi .25 .25
864 A177 500 l gold & multi .65 .65
Nos. 860-864 (5) 1.65 1.65

Holy Year.

Tokyo, 1835, Woodcut by Hiroshige — A178

300 l, Tokyo, Business District, 1975.

1975, Sept. 5 Photo. ***Perf. 11½***

Granite Paper

865 A178 200 l multi .35 .35
866 A178 300 l multi .35 .35
a. Pair, #865-866 1.10 1.10

Printed checkerwise.

Aphrodite A179

1975, Sept. 19 Photo. ***Perf. 11½***

867 A179 50 l vio, blk & gray .30 .30

Europa '75 Philatelic Exhibition, Naples.

Multiple Crosses A180

1975, Sept. 19

868 A180 100 l blk, dp org & vio .30 .30

EUROCOPHAR Intl. Pharmaceutical Cong.

Christmas — A181

Christmas: Paintings by Michelangelo: 50 l, Angel. 100 l, Head of Virgin. 250 l, Doni Madonna.

1975, Dec. 3 Photo. ***Perf. 11½***

Granite Paper

869 50 l multi .25 .25
870 100 l multi .30 .30
871 250 l multi .30 .30
a. A181 Strip of 3, #869-871 1.25 1.25

Woman on Balcony, by Gentilini — A183

Two Women, by Gentilini A184

230 l, Woman (same as right head on 150 l) & IWY emblem, by Franco Gentilini.

1975, Dec. 3 **Granite Paper**

872 A183 70 l bl & multi .25 .25
873 A184 150 l multi .50 .50
874 A183 230 l multi .50 .50
Nos. 872-874 (3) 1.25 1.25

International Women's Year.

Modesty, by Emilio Greco — A185

"Civic Virtues": 20 l, Temperance. 50 l, Fortitude. 100 l, Altruism. 150 l, Hope. 220 l, Prudence. 250 l, Justice. 300 l, Faith. 500 l, Honesty. 1000 l, Industry. Designs show drawings of women's heads by Emilio Greco.

1976, Mar. 4 Photo. ***Perf. 11½***

Granite Paper

875 A185 10 l buff & blk .25 .25
876 A185 20 l pink & blk .25 .25
877 A185 50 l grnsh & blk .25 .25
878 A185 100 l salmon & blk .25 .25
879 A185 150 l lilac & blk .25 .25
880 A185 220 l gray & blk .25 .25
881 A185 250 l yel & multi .25 .25
882 A185 300 l gray & blk .30 .30
883 A185 500 l yel & blk .40 .40
884 A185 1000 l gray & blk 1.00 1.00
Nos. 875-884 (10) 3.45 3.45

See Nos. 900-905, 931-933.

Capitol, Washington, D.C. — A186

Arms of San Marino and: 150 l, Statue of Liberty. 180 l, Independence Hall, Philadelphia.

1976, May 29 Photo. ***Perf. 11½***

885 A186 70 l multi .25 .25
886 A186 150 l multi .25 .25
887 A186 180 l multi .30 .30
Nos. 885-887 (3) .80 .80

American Bicentennial.

Montreal Olympic Games Emblem A187

1976, May 29

888 A187 150 l crimson & blk .30 .30

21st Olympic Games, Montreal, Canada, 7/17-8/1.

Decorated Plate — A188

Europa: 180 l, Seal of San Marino.

1976, July 8 Photo. ***Perf. 11½***

Granite Paper

889 A188 150 l multi .40 .40
890 A188 180 l bl, sil & blk .60 .60

"Unity" — A189

1976, July 8 ***Perf. 13½x14***

891 A189 150 l vio blk, yel & red .25 .25

United Mutual Aid Society, centenary.

"Peaks of San Marino" — A190

1976, Oct. 14 Photo. ***Perf. 13x14***

892 A190 150 l blk & multi .30 .30

ITALIA 76 Intl. Phil. Exhib., Milan, 10/14-24.

Children and UNESCO Emblem A191

1976, Oct. 14 ***Perf. 11½***

Granite Paper

893 A191 180 l multi .25 .25
894 A191 220 l multi .25 .25

UNESCO, 30th anniv.

Christmas — A192

Design: 150 l, Annunciation (detail), by Titian. 300 l, Virgin and Child, by Titian.

Litho. & Engr.

1976, Dec. 15 ***Perf. 13x14***

895 150 l multi .30 .30
896 300 l multi .50 .50
a. A192 Pair, #895-896 1.00 1.00

Exhibition Emblem A193

1977, Jan. 28 Photo. ***Perf. 11½***

Granite Paper

897 A193 80 l grn, ol grn & red .25 .25
898 A193 170 l pur, blue, yel .25 .25
899 A193 200 l blue, lt bl & org .30 .30
Nos. 897-899,C133 (4) 1.10 1.10

San Marino 77 Phil. Exhib.
See. No. C133.

Civic Virtues Type of 1976

70 l, Fortitude. 90 l, Prudence. 120 l, Altruism. 160 l, Temperance. 170 l, Hope. 320 l, Faith.

1977, Apr. 14 Photo. ***Perf. 11½***

Granite Paper

900 A185 70 l pink & blk .25 .25
901 A185 90 l buff & blk .25 .25
902 A185 120 l lt bl & blk .25 .25
903 A185 160 l lt grn & blk .25 .25
904 A185 170 l cream & blk .25 .25
905 A185 320 l lil & blk .35 .35
Nos. 900-905 (6) 1.60 1.60

EUROPA 77
SAN MARINO 170

San Marino, after Ghirlandaio A194

Europa: 200 l, San Marino, detail from painting by Guercino.

1977, Apr. 14 **Granite Paper**

906 A194 170 l multi *.50* .35
907 A194 200 l multi *.50* .35

Vertical Flying Machine, by da Vinci — A195

Litho. & Engr.

1977, June 6 ***Perf. 13x14***

908 A195 120 l multi .30 .30

Centenary of Enrico Forlanini's experiments with vertical flight.

University Square, Bucharest, 1877 — A196

Design: 400 l, National Theater and Intercontinental Hotel, 1977.

1977, June 6 **Photo.** ***Perf. 11½***
Granite Paper

909 200 l bis & multi .35 .35
910 400 l lt bl & multi .50 .50
a. A196 Pair, #909-910 1.25 1.25

Centenary of Romanian independence. Printed checkerwise.

Type A2 of 1877 — A197

1977, June 15 **Engr.** ***Perf. 15x14½***

911 A197 40 l slate grn .25 .25
912 A197 70 l deep blue .25 .25
913 A197 170 l red .25 .25
914 A197 500 l brown .40 .40
915 A197 1000 l purple 1.00 1.00
Nos. 911-915 (5) 2.15 2.15

Centenary of San Marino stamps.

Souvenir Sheet

St. Marinus, by Retrosi — A198

1977, Aug. 28 **Photo.** ***Perf. 11½***
Granite Paper

916 Sheet of 5 9.00 9.00
a. A198 1000 l single stamp 1.75 1.75

Centenary of San Marino stamps; San Marino '77 Phil. Exhib., Aug. 28-Sept. 4.

Medicinal Plants — A199

1977, Oct. 19 **Photo.** ***Perf. 11½***

917 A199 170 l multi .30 .30

Congress of Italian Pharmacists' Union. Design shows high mallow, tilia, camomile, borage, centaury and juniper.

Woman Attacked by Octopus, Emblem A200

1977, Oct. 19

918 A200 200 l multi .30 .30

World Rheumatism Year.

Virgin Mary — A201

Christmas: 230 l, Palm, olive and star. 300 l, Angel.

1977, Dec. 5 **Photo.** ***Perf. 11½***

919 A201 170 l sil, gray & blk .25 .25
920 A201 230 l sil, gray & blk .30 .30
921 A201 300 l sil, gray & blk .40 .40
a. Strip of 3, #919-921 1.10 1.10

San Francisco Gate — A202

Europa: 200 l, Ripa Gate.

1978, May 30 **Photo.** ***Perf. 11½***

922 A202 170 l lt bl & dk bl *.50* .40
923 A202 200 l buff & brn *.50* .50

Baseball Player and Diamond — A203

1978, May 30

924 A203 90 l multi .25 .25
925 A203 120 l multi .25 .25

World Baseball Championships.

Feather, WHO Emblem — A204

1978, May 30

926 A204 320 l multi .50 .50

Fight against hypertension.

ITU Emblem, Waves Coming from 3 Peaks — A205

1978, July 26 **Photo.** ***Perf. 11½***

927 A205 10 l car & yel .25 .25
928 A205 200 l vio bl & lt bl .25 .25

Membership in ITU.

Seagull and Falcon, 3 Peaks A206

1978, July 26

929 A206 120 l multi .25 .25
930 A206 170 l multi .30 .30

30th San Marino-Riccione Stamp Day.

Civic Virtues Type of 1976

Drawings by Emilio Greco: 5 l, Wisdom. 35 l, Love. 2000 l, Faithfulness.

1978, Sept. 28 **Photo.** ***Perf. 11½***
Granite Paper

931 A185 5 l lt vio & blk .25 .25
932 A185 35 l gray & blk .25 .25
933 A185 2000 l yel & blk 2.00 2.00
Nos. 931-933 (3) 2.50 2.50

Christmas A207

1978, Dec. 6 **Photo.** ***Perf. 14x13½***

941 A207 10 l Holly leaves .25 .25
942 A207 120 l Stars .25 .25
943 A207 170 l Snowflakes .25 .25
Nos. 941-943 (3) .75 .75

Globe and Woman Holding Torch — A208

1978, Dec. 6 ***Perf. 11½x12***

944 A208 200 l multi .30 .30

Universal Declaration of Human Rights, 30th anniversary.

First San Marino Autobus, 1915 A209

Europa: 220 l, Mail coach, 1895.

1979, Mar. 29 **Photo.** ***Perf. 11½x12***

945 A209 170 l multi *1.25* .75
946 A209 220 l multi *1.75* *1.00*

Albert Einstein (1879-1955), Theoretical Physicist — A210

1979, Mar. 29 ***Perf. 11½***

947 A210 120 l gray, lt & dk brn .40 .40

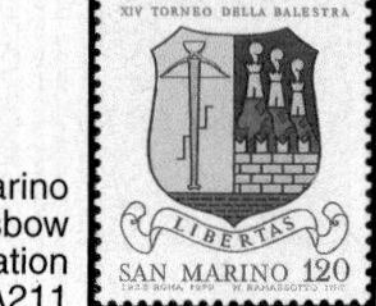
San Marino Crossbow Federation Emblem — A211

1979, July 12 **Litho.** ***Perf. 14x13***

948 A211 120 l multi .25 .25

14th Crossbow Tournament.

Maigret — A212

Fictional Detectives: 80 l, Perry Mason. 150 l, Nero Wolfe. 170 l, Ellery Queen. 220 l, Sherlock Holmes.

Litho. & Engr.

1979, July 12 ***Perf. 13x14***

949 A212 10 l multi .25 .25
950 A212 80 l multi .25 .25
951 A212 150 l multi .25 .25
952 A212 170 l multi .25 .25
953 A212 220 l multi .25 .25
Nos. 949-953 (5) 1.25 1.25

Girl Holding Book — A213

IYC Emblem, Paintings by Marina Busignani: 120 l, 170 l, 220 l, Children and birds, diff. 350 l, Mother nursing child.

1979, Sept. 6 **Litho.** ***Perf. 11½***

954 A213 20 l multi .25 .25
955 A213 120 l multi .25 .25
956 A213 170 l multi .25 .25
957 A213 220 l multi .25 .25
958 A213 350 l multi .35 .35
Nos. 954-958 (5) 1.35 1.35

St. Apollonia, 15th Century Woodcut — A214

1979, Sept. 6 **Photo.**

959 A214 170 l multi	.25	.25

13th Biennial Intl. Congress of Stomatology.

Waterskier A215

1979, Sept. 6

960 A215 150 l multi	.25	.25

European Waterskiing Championship.

Chestnut Tree, Deer — A216

Protected Trees and Animals or Birds: 10 l, Cedar of Lebanon, falcon. 35 l, Dogwood, racoon. 50 l, Banyan, tiger. 70 l, Umbrella pine, hoopoe. 90 l, Siberian spruce, marten. 100 l, Eucalyptus, koala bear. 120 l, Date palm, camel. 150 l, Sugar maple, beaver. 170 l, Adansonia, elephant.

1979, Oct. 25 **Photo.** ***Perf. 11½***

961 A216 5 l multi	.25	.25
962 A216 10 l multi	.25	.25
963 A216 35 l multi	.25	.25
964 A216 50 l multi	.25	.25
965 A216 70 l multi	.25	.25
966 A216 90 l multi	.25	.25
967 A216 100 l multi	.25	.25
968 A216 120 l multi	.25	.25
969 A216 150 l multi	.25	.25
970 A216 170 l multi	.25	.25
Nos. 961-970 (10)	2.50	2.50

Holy Family, by Antonio Alberto de Ferrara, 15th Century Fresco A217

Christmas (de Ferrara Fresco): 80 l, St. Joseph. 170 l, Infant Jesus. 220 l, One of the Three Kings.

1979, Dec. 6 **Photo.** ***Perf. 12***

971 A217 80 l multi	.25	.25
972 A217 170 l multi	.25	.25
973 A217 220 l multi	.30	.30
974 A217 320 l multi	.50	.50
Nos. 971-974 (4)	1.30	1.30

Disturbing Muses, by Giorgio de Chirico — A218

1979, Dec.

975 A218 40 l shown	.25	.25
976 A218 150 l Ancient horses	.25	.25
977 A218 170 l Self-portrait	.25	.25
Nos. 975-977 (3)	.75	.75

Giorgio de Chirico, Italian surrealist painter.

St. Benedict, 15th Century Fresco — A219

Granite Paper

1980, Mar. 27 **Photo.** ***Perf. 12x11½***

978 A219 170 l multi	.35	.35

St. Benedict of Nursia, 1500th birth anniversary.

Fight Against Cigarette Smoking — A220

Designs: Sketches of smokers and cigarettes by Giuliana Consilivio.

1980, Mar. 27

979 A220 120 l multi	.25	.25
980 A220 220 l multi	.30	.30
981 A220 520 l multi	.50	.50
Nos. 979-981 (3)	1.05	1.05

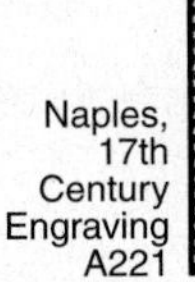
Naples, 17th Century Engraving A221

1980, Mar. 27 ***Perf. 14x13½***

982 A221 170 l multi	.30	.30

20th Intl. Phil. Exhib., Europa '80, Naples, Apr. 26-May 4.

View of London, 1850 — A222

400 l, London, 1980.

1980, May 8 ***Perf. 11½x12***

983 200 l multicolored	.30	.30
984 400 l multicolored	.50	.50
a. A222 Pair, #983-984	1.25	1.25

London 1980 Intl. Stamp Exhib., May 6-14. Printed checkerwise.

See Nos. 1001-1002, 1032-1033, 1054-1055, 1069-1070, 1098-1099, 1110-1111, 1141-1142, 1339-1340.

A223

Europa: 170 l, Giovanbattista Belluzzi (1506-54), military architect. 220 l, Antonio Orafo (1460-1552), goldsmith and jeweler.

1980, May 8 ***Perf. 11½***

985 A223 170 l multi	*.90*	*.60*
986 A223 220 l multi	*1.00*	*.85*

A224

Granite Paper

1980, July 7 **Photo.** ***Perf. 11½***

987 A224 70 l Bicycling	.25	.25
988 A224 90 l Basketball	.25	.25
989 A224 170 l Running	.25	.25
990 A224 350 l Gymnast	.35	.35
991 A224 450 l High jump	.55	.55
Nos. 987-991 (5)	1.65	1.65

22nd Summer Olympic Games, Moscow, July 19-Aug. 3.

Ancient Fortifications A225

Photogravure and Engraved

1980, Sept. 18 ***Perf. 13½x14***

992 A225 220 l multi	.35	.35

World Tourism Conf., Manila, Sept. 27.

Weight Lifting — A226

1980, Sept. 18 **Photo.** ***Perf. 14x13½***

993 A226 170 l multi	.30	.30

European Junior Weight Lifting Championship, Sept.

Robert Stolz, "Philatelic Waltz" Score A227

Photo. & Engr.

1980, Sept. 18 ***Perf. 14***

994 A227 120 l lt bl & blk	.30	.30

Robert Stolz (1880-1975) composer.

Madonna of the Harpies, by Andrea Del Sarto — A228

Annunciation by Del Sarto (Details): 250 l, Virgin Mary. 500 l Angel.

1980, Dec. 11 ***Perf. 13½***

995 A228 180 l multi	.30	.30
996 A228 250 l multi	.35	.35
997 A228 500 l multi	.85	.85
Nos. 995-997 (3)	1.50	1.50

Christmas; 450th death anniv. of Del Sarto.

Europa Issue

St. Joseph's Eve Bonfire — A229

300 l, San Marino Day fireworks.

1981, Mar. 24 **Photo.** ***Perf. 12***

Granite Paper

998 A229 200 l shown	*.55*	*.40*
999 A229 300 l multicolored	*1.50*	*.55*

Intl. Year of the Disabled — A230

1981, May 15 **Photo.** ***Perf. 11½***

Granite Paper

1000 A230 300 l multi	.40	.40

Exhibition Type of 1980

St. Charles' Square, Vienna, by Jakob Alt: 200 l Vienna, 1817. 300 l, Vienna, 1981.

1981, May 15 **Granite Paper**

1001 A222 200 l multicolored	.30	.30
1002 A222 300 l multicolored	.40	.40
a. Pair, #1001-1002	1.00	1.00

WIPA '81 Intl. Phil. Exhib., Vienna, 5/22-31.

Woman Playing Flute — A232

Drawings based on Roman sculptures.

1981, July 10 **Photo.** ***Perf. 11½***

Granite Paper

1003 A232 300 l shown	.35	.35
1004 A232 550 l Soldier	.60	.60
1005 A232 1500 l Shepherd	1.75	1.70
a. Souv. sheet of 3, #1003-1005	4.50	4.50

Virgil's death bimillennium. No. 1005a has continuous design.

Grand Prix Motorcycle Race — A233

1981, July 10 Litho. *Perf. 14x15*

1006 A233 200 l multi .30 .30

Natl. Urban Development Plan (Housing) — A234

1981, Sept. 22 Photo.

Granite Paper

1007 A234 20 l shown .25 .25
1008 A234 80 l Parks .25 .25
1009 A234 400 l Energy plants .40 .40
Nos. 1007-1009 (3) .90 .90

European Junior Judo Championship, Oct. 30-Nov. 1 — A235

1981, Sept. 22 Photo. *Perf. 11½*

Granite Paper

1010 A235 300 l multi .40 .40

World Food Day — A236

1981, Oct. 23 Granite Paper

1011 A236 300 l multi .50 .50

A237

Designs: 150 l, Child Holding a Dove, by Pablo Picasso (1881-1973). 200 l, Homage to Picasso, by Renato Guttuso.

1981, Oct. 23 Granite Paper

1012 A237 150 l multi .25 .25
1013 A237 200 l multi .40 .40

A238

Christmas; 500th Birth Anniv. of Benvenuto Tisi da Garofalo Adoration of the Kings and St. Bartholomew): 200 l, One of the Three Kings with Goblet, by Garafalo. 300 l, King with a Jar. 600 l, Virgin and Child.

Photo. & Engr.

1981, Dec. 15 *Perf. 13½*

1014 A238 200 l multi .25 .25
1015 A238 300 l multi .40 .40
1016 A238 600 l multi .75 .75
Nos. 1014-1016 (3) 1.40 1.40

Postal Stationery Centenary A239

1982, Feb. 19 Photo. *Perf. 12*

1017 A239 200 l multi .30 .30

Savings Bank Centenary A240

1982, Feb. 19

1018 A240 300 l multi .40 .40

Europa 1982 — A241

Designs: 300 l, Convocation of the Assembly of Heads of Families, 1906. 450 l, Napoleons's Treaty of Friendship offer, 1797.

1982, Apr. 21 Photo. *Perf. 11½*

Granite Paper

1019 A241 300 l multi *2.00 1.25*
1020 A241 450 l multi *3.25 1.50*

Archimedes — A242

30 l, Copernicus. 40 l, Newton. 50 l, Lavoisier. 60 l, Marie Curie. 100 l, Robert Koch. 200 l, Thomas Edison. 300 l, Guglielmo Marconi. 450 l, Hippocrates. 5000 l, Galileo.

1982, Apr. 21 Photo. *Perf. 14x13½*

1021 A242 20 l shown .25 .25
1022 A242 30 l lt blue & blk .25 .25
1023 A242 40 l yel brn & blk .25 .25
1024 A242 50 l grn & blk .25 .25
1025 A242 60 l red org & blk .25 .25
1026 A242 100 l brn blk & blk .25 .25

Litho. & Engr.

1027 A242 200 l sepia & blk .25 .25
1028 A242 300 l yel olive & blk .25 .25
1029 A242 450 l car rose & blk .45 .45

Engr.

1030 A242 5000 l gray blue & ultra 5.00 5.00
Nos. 1021-1030 (10) 7.45 7.45

See Nos. 1041-1046.

800th Birth Anniv. of St. Francis of Assisi — A243

1982, June 10 Photo.

1031 A243 200 l multi .30 .30

Exhibition Type of 1980

1982, June 10

1032 A222 300 l Notre Dame, 1806 .35 .35
1033 A222 450 l 1982 .55 .55
a. Pair, #1032-1033 1.25 1.25

PHILEXFRANCE '82 Stamp Exhibition, Paris, June 11-21.

Visit of Pope John Paul II — A245

1982, Aug. 29 Litho. *Perf. 13½x14*

1034 A245 900 l multi 1.10 1.10

Natl. Flags of ASCAT Members — A246

Granite Paper

1982, Sept. 1 Photo. *Perf. 11½*

1035 A246 300 l multi .40 .40

Inaugural Meeting of ASCAT (Assoc. of Editors of Philatelic Catalogues), 1977.

A247

1982, Sept. 1 Unwmk.

1036 A247 700 l blk & red .85 .85

15th Amnesty Intl. Congress, Rimini, Italy, Sept. 9-15.

A248

Christmas: Paintings by Gregorio Sciltian (1900-85).

Photo. & Engr.

1982, Dec. 15 *Perf. 13½*

1037 A248 200 l Angel .30 .30
1038 A248 300 l Virgin and Child .40 .40
1039 A248 450 l Angel, diff. .55 .55
Nos. 1037-1039 (3) 1.25 1.25

Secondary School Centenary A249

1983, Feb. 24 Photo. *Perf. 13½x14*

1040 A249 300 l Begni Building .45 .45

Scientist Type of 1982

150 l, Alexander Fleming. 250 l, Alessandro Volta. 350 l, Evangelista Torricelli. 400 l, Carolus Linnaeus. 1000 l, Pythagoras. 1400 l, Leonardo da Vinci.

1983, Apr. 21 *Perf. 14x13½*

1041 A242 150 l multi .25 .25
1042 A242 250 l multi .30 .30
1043 A242 350 l multi .35 .35
1044 A242 400 l multi .50 .50
1045 A242 1000 l multi 1.00 1.00
1046 A242 1400 l multi 1.50 1.50
Nos. 1041-1046 (6) 3.90 3.90

3rd Formula One Grand Prix A250

1983, Apr. 20 Photo. *Perf. 14x13½*

1047 A250 50 l multi .25 .25
1048 A250 350 l multi .70 .70

Auguste Piccard — A251

1983, Apr. 20 *Perf. 12x11½*

Granite Paper

1049 A251 400 l Aerostat *1.75 1.10*
1050 A251 500 l Bathyscaph *2.50 1.75*

Europa. Piccard (1884-1962), Swiss scientist.

World Communications Year — A252

400 l, Ham radio operator. 500 l, Mailman.

1983, Apr. 28 Engr. *Perf. 14x13*

1051 A252 400 l multicolored .65 .65
1052 A252 500 l multicolored .80 .80

Manned Flight Bicentenary A253

500 l, Montgolfiere, 1783.

Lithographed and Engraved

1983, May 22 *Perf. 13½x14*

1053 A253 500 l multicolored .65 .65

Exhibition Type of 1980

Designs: Botafogo Bay and Monte Corcovado, Rio de Janeiro.

1983, July 29 Photo. *Perf. 11½x12*
Granite Paper

1054	A222	400 l 1845	.40	.40
1055	A222	1400 l 1983	1.50	1.50
a.		Pair, #1054-1055	2.75	2.75

BRASILIANA '83 Intl. Stamp Show, Rio de Janeiro, July 29-Aug. 7.

20th Anniv. of World Food Program A255

1983, Sept. 29 Photo. *Perf. 14x13½*

1056	A255	500 l multi	.70	.70

Christmas A256

Paintings, Raphael (1483-1520): 300 l, Our Lady of the Grand Duke. 400 l, Our Lady of the Goldfinch. 500 l, Our Lady of the Chair.

Photo. & Engr.
1983, Dec. 1 *Perf. 13½*

1057	A256	300 l multi	.35	.35
1058	A256	400 l multi	.45	.45
1059	A256	500 l multi	.65	.65
a.		Strip of 3, #1057-1059	2.00	2.00

Olympic Type of 1959

IOC Presidents: 300 l, Demetrius Vikelas, 1894-96. 400 l, Lord Killanin. 550 l, Antonio Samaranch, 1984.

1984, Feb. 8 Photo. *Perf. 14x13½*

1060	A86	300 l multi	.45	.45
1061	A86	400 l multi	.55	.55
1062	A86	550 l multi	1.00	1.00
		Nos. 1060-1062 (3)	2.00	2.00

Flag-wavers Group, 2nd Anniv. — A257

Litho. & Engr.
1984, Apr. 27 *Perf. 13x14*

1063	A257	300 l Flag	.40	.40
1064	A257	400 l Flags	.60	.60

Europa (1959-1984) A258

1984, Apr. 27 Photo. *Perf. 11½*
Granite Paper

1065	A258	400 l multi	*1.75*	*1.00*
1066	A258	550 l multi	*2.50*	*1.50*

A259

1984, June 14 Photo. *Perf. 13½x14*

1067	A259	450 l multi	.70	.70

Motorcross Grand Prix, Baldasserona.

Souvenir Sheet

A260

1984, June 14 Litho. *Perf. 13x14*

1068	A260	Sheet of 2	3.00	3.00
a.		550 l Man	.60	.60
b.		1000 l Woman	1.20	1.20

1984 Summer Olympics.

Exhibition Type of 1980

Ausipex '84: Views of Melbourne. Se-tenant.

1984, Sept. 21 Photo. *Perf. 11½*
Granite Paper

1069	A222	1500 l 1839	1.75	1.75
1070	A222	2000 l 1984	2.25	2.25
a.		Pair, #1069-1070	4.75	4.75

Visit of Italian Pres. Pertini A262

1984, Oct. 20 Photo. *Perf. 14x13½*

1071	A262	1950 l multi	2.75	2.75

School and Philately — A263

Sketches by Jacovitti.

1984, Oct. 30 *Perf. 13½x14*

1072	A263	50 l Universe	.25	.25
1073	A263	100 l Evolution	.25	.25
1074	A263	150 l Environment	.25	.25
1075	A263	200 l Mankind	.25	.25
1076	A263	450 l Science	.55	.55
1077	A263	550 l Philosophy	.65	.65
		Nos. 1072-1077 (6)	2.20	2.20

Christmas — A264

Details of Madonna of San Girolamo by Correggio, 1527.

1984, Dec. 5 Litho. *Perf. 13½x14*

1078		400 l multi	.55	.55
1079		450 l multi	.75	.75
1080		550 l multi	.85	.85
a.	A264	Strip of 3, #1078-1080	2.75	2.75

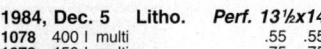

Composers and Music — A265

Europa: 450 l, Johann Sebastian Bach (1685-1750), Toccata and Fugue. 600 l, Vincenzo Bellini (1801-1835), Norma.

1985, Mar. 18 Photo. *Perf. 12*

1081	A265	450 l ocher & gray blk	*1.75*	*.90*
1082	A265	600 l yel grn & gray blk	*2.25*	*1.40*

Olympiad of the Small States, May 23-26 — A266

Sportphilex '85: Natl. Olympic Committee and Sportphilex '85 emblems, flags of Andorra, Cyprus, Iceland, Liechtenstein, Luxembourg, Malta, Monaco, San Marino.

1985, May 16 Litho. *Perf. 13½x14*

1083	A266	50 l Diving	.25	.25
1084	A266	350 l Running	.45	.45
1085	A266	400 l Rifle shooting	.55	.55
1086	A266	450 l Cycling	.60	.60
1087	A266	600 l Basketball	.90	.90
		Nos. 1083-1087 (5)	2.75	2.75

Emigration A267

1985, May 16

1088	A267	600 l Birds migrating	1.00	1.00

Intl. Youth Year — A268

1985, June 24 Photo. *Perf. 12*
Granite Paper

1089	A268	400 l Boy, dove	.50	.50
1090	A268	600 l Girl, dove, horse	1.00	1.00

Helsinki Conference, 10th Anniv. — A269

600 l, Sapling, sunburst, clouds.

1985, June 24 *Perf. 13½x14*

1091	A269	600 l multicolored	.80	.80

City Hall, by Renzo Bonelli, Camera Lens. — A270

1985, June 24 *Perf. 13½x14½*

1092	A270	450 l multi	.75	.75

Intl. Fed. of Photographic Art, 18th Congress.

World Angling Championships, Arno River, Florence, Sept. 14-15 — A271

1985, Sept. 11 Photo. *Perf. 14½x15*

1093	A271	600 l Hooked fish	1.00	1.00

Alessandro Manzoni (1785-1873), Novelist & Poet — A272

19th century engravings from Manzoni's I Promessi Sposi (1825-27): 400 l, Don Abbondio encounters Don Rodrigo's henchmen. 450 l, The attempt to force the curate to perform a dubious marriage ceremony. 600 l, The Plague at Milan.

1985, Sept. 11 Engr. *Perf. 14x13½*

1094	A272	400 l multi	.50	.50
1095	A272	450 l multi	.60	.60
1096	A272	600 l multi	.90	.90
		Nos. 1094-1096 (3)	2.00	2.00

Intl. Feline Fed. Congress A273

Mosaic detail: Cat, Natl. Museum, Naples.

1985, Oct. 25 Photo. *Perf. 12*
Granite Paper

1097	A273	600 l multi	1.00	1.00

Exhibition Type of 1980

ITALIA '85: Views of the Colosseum, Rome.

1985, Oct. 25 *Perf. 11½x12*
Granite Paper

1098	A222	1000 l multi	1.10	1.10
1099	A222	1500 l multi	1.90	1.90
a.		Pair, #1098-1099	4.00	4.00

Christmas A275

400 l, Angel in air. 450 l, Mother and Child. 600 l, Angel seated.

Photo. & Engr.

1985, Dec. 3 ***Perf. 14***

1100 A275 400 l multi .80 .80
1101 A275 450 l multi 1.25 1.25
1102 A275 600 l multi 1.50 1.50
a. Strip of 3, #1100-1102 4.25 4.25

Hospital, Cailungo A276

1986, Mar. 6 Photo. ***Perf. 12x11½***

1103 A276 450 l multi .60 .60
1104 A276 650 l multi .85 .85

Natl. social security org., ISS, 30th anniv., and World Health Day.

Halley's Comet — A277

Designs: 550 l, Giotto space probe. 1000 l, Adoration of the Magi, by Giotto (1276-1337).

1986, Mar. 6 ***Perf. 11½x12***

1105 A277 550 l multi 1.00 1.00
1106 A277 1000 l multi 1.50 1.50

Europa Issue

Deer — A278

1986, May 22 Photo. ***Perf. 13½x14***

1107 A278 550 l shown *8.50 7.00*
1108 A278 650 l Falcon *10.00 8.00*

3rd Veterans World Table Tennis Championships A279

1986, May 22 **Engr.**

1109 A279 450 l multicolored .80 .80

AMERIPEX '86, Chicago, May 22-June 1 — A280

Views of Old Water Tower, Chicago: 2000 l, Lithograph, 1870, by Charles Shober. 3000 l, Photograph, 1986.

Perf. 11½x12

1986, May 22 Photo. Unwmk.

1110 2000 l multi 2.25 2.25
1111 3000 l multi 3.25 3.25
a. A280 Pair, #1110-1111 7.00 7.00

Intl. Peace Year — A281

1986, July 10 Photo. ***Perf. 11½x12***

1112 A281 550 l multi .75 .75

Souvenir Sheet

Terra Cotta Statuary, Tomb of Emperor Qin Shi Huang Di (259-210 B.C.) — A282

Litho. & Engr.

1986, July 10 ***Perf. 13½***

1113 A282 Sheet of 3 5.00 5.00
a. 550 l Bearded man .90 .90
b. 650 l Horse, horiz. 1.25 1.25
c. 2000 l Bearded man, diff. 2.00 2.00

Normalization of diplomatic relations with the People's Republic of China, 15th anniv.

UNICEF, 40th Anniv. — A283

1986, Sept 16 Photo. ***Perf. 12***

1114 A283 650 l multi .90 .90

European Boccie Championships A284

1986, Sept. 16 ***Perf. 14x15***

1115 A284 550 l multi .75 .75

Choral Society, 25th Anniv. — A285

Painting (detail): Apollo Dancing with the Muses, by Giulio Romano (1492-1546).

1986, Sept. 16

1116 A285 450 l multi .70 .70

Christmas A286

Oil on wood triptych, 15th cent., by Hans Memling (1435-1494), Kunsthistorisches Museum, Vienna: 450 l, St. John the Baptist. 550 l, Virgin and Child. 650 l, St. John the Evangelist.

Photo. & Engr.

1986, Nov. 26 ***Perf. 14***

1117 A286 450 l multi .85 .85
1118 A286 550 l multi 1.00 1.00
1119 A286 650 l multi 1.25 1.25
a. Strip of 3, #1117-1119 3.75 3.75

Europa Issue

Our Lady of Consolation Church, Borgomaggiore A287

Church designed by Giovanni Michelucci, architect: 600 l, Architect's sketch of interior. 700 l, Actual interior.

1987, Mar. 12 Photo. ***Perf. 12***

1120 A287 600 l multi *7.50 4.00*
1121 A287 700 l multi *10.00 5.00*

Motoring Events A288

Designs: 500 l, 80th anniv., Peking-Paris Race. 600 l, 15th San Marino Rally. 700 l, Mille Miglia Race, 60th anniv.

1987, Mar. 12 ***Perf. 11½***

1122 A288 500 l multi .70 .70
1123 A288 600 l multi .85 .85
1124 A288 700 l multi 1.00 1.00
Nos. 1122-1124 (3) 2.55 2.55

Sculptures, Open-air Museum — A289

Perf. 14½x13½

1987, June 13 **Photo.**

1125 A289 50 l Reffi Busignani .25 .25
1126 A289 100 l Bini .25 .25
1127 A289 200 l Guguianu .30 .30
1128 A289 300 l Berti .50 .50
1129 A289 400 l Crocetti .60 .60
1130 A289 500 l Berti, diff. .80 .80
1131 A289 600 l Messina 1.00 1.00
1132 A289 1000 l Minguzzi 1.25 1.25
1133 A289 2200 l Greco 3.25 3.25
1134 A289 10000 l Sassu 15.00 15.00
Nos. 1125-1134 (10) 23.20 23.20

Seventh Natl. Art Biennale — A290

Abstract works: 500 l, Dal Diario del Brasileforesta Vergine, by Emilio Vedova. 600 l, Invenzione Cromatica con Brio, by Corrado Cagli.

Granite Paper

1987, June 13 ***Perf. 11½***

1135 A290 500 l multi .70 .70
1136 A290 600 l multi .80 .80

Air Club of San Marino Ultralightweight Aircraft — A291

1987, June 13 **Granite Paper**

1137 A291 600 l multi 1.00 1.00

Mahatma Gandhi A292

500 l, Gandhi Square, bust.

1987, Aug. 2 Photo. ***Perf. 14x13½***

1138 A292 500 l multicolored .85 .85

Olympic Emblem, Athlete — A293

1987, Aug. 29 ***Perf. 12***

Granite Paper

1139 A293 600 l multi 1.00 1.00

OLYMPHILEX '87, Rome.

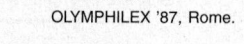

A294

1987, Aug. 29 **Granite Paper**

1140 A294 700 l ultra, blk & red 1.10 1.10

First Representation of San Marino at the Mediterranean Games, Syria, Sept. 11-15.

Exhibition Type of 1980

HAFNIA '87: Views of Copenhagen (1836-1986), as seen from the Round Tower.

1987, Oct. 16 Photo. ***Perf. 11½x12***

Granite Paper

1141 A222 1200 l multi 1.90 1.90
1142 A222 2200 l multi, diff. 2.75 2.75
a. Pair, #1141-1142 6.00 6.00

Christmas A296

Details from Triptych of Cortona and The Annunciation, by Fra Angelico (c. 1400-1455), Diocesan Museum of Cortona: No. 1143, Angel. No. 1144, Madonna and child. No. 1145, Saint. Printed se-tenant.

Photo. & Engr.

1987, Nov. 12 *Perf. 13½*

1143 A296 600 l multi 1.10 1.10
1144 A296 600 l multi 1.10 1.10
1145 A296 600 l multi 1.10 1.10
a. Strip of 3, #1143-1145 4.25 4.25

Europa Issue

High Speed Train — A297

Granite Paper

1988, Mar. 17 **Photo.** *Perf. 12*

1146 A297 600 l shown *5.00 3.50*
1147 A297 700 l Fiber optics *6.50 4.00*

Promote Stamp Collecting A298

Stamps, cancellations, covers: 50 l, Nos. 81, B25 and 859. 150 l, No. C11. 300 l, Nos. 349 and 1006. 350 l, Nos. 944 and 1031. 1000 l, Nos. 303, 1081 and 308.

1988, Mar. 17 *Perf. 11½*

Granite Paper

1148 A298 50 l multi .25 .25
1149 A298 150 l multi .25 .25
1150 A298 300 l multi .45 .45
1151 A298 350 l multi .60 .60
1152 A298 1000 l multi 1.50 1.50
Nos. 1148-1152 (5) 3.05 3.05

See Nos. 1179-1183, 1225-1229.

Bologna University, 900th Anniv. — A299

Historic sites and distinguished professors: 550 l, Carlo Malagola. 650 l, Pietro Ellero. 1300 l, Giosue Carducci (1835-1907), professor of literary history, 1861-1904, and Nobel Prize winner for literature, 1906. 1700 l, Giovanni Pascoli (1855-1912), lyric poet, Pascoli's successor as professor at Bologna.

1988, May 7 **Photo.** *Perf. 13½x14*

1153 A299 550 l multi .75 .75
1154 A299 650 l multi .90 .90
1155 A299 1300 l multi 1.60 1.60
1156 A299 1700 l multi 2.25 2.25
Nos. 1153-1156 (4) 5.50 5.50

A300

Posters from Fellini Films: 300 l, La Strada. 900 l, La Dolce Vita. 1200 l, Amarcord.

1988, July 8 **Photo.** *Perf. 13½x14*

1157 A300 300 l multi .40 .40
1158 A300 900 l multi 1.25 1.25
1159 A300 1200 l multi 1.75 1.75
Nos. 1157-1159 (3) 3.40 3.40

Federico Fellini, Italian film director and winner of the 1988 San Marino Prize.

See Nos. 1187-1189, 1202-1204.

Mt. Titano and Sand Dunes of the Adriatic Coast A301

1988, July 8 *Perf. 14x13½*

1160 A301 750 l multi 1.00 1.00

40th Stamp Fair, Riccione.

Souvenir Sheet

1988 Summer Olympics, Seoul — A302

1988, Sept. 19 **Photo.** *Perf. 13½x14*

1161 A302 Sheet of 3 3.75 3.75
a. 650 l Running .80 .80
b. 750 l Hurdles .90 .90
c. 1300 l Gymnastics 1.25 1.25

Intl. AIDS Congress, San Marino, Oct. 10-14 A303

1988, Sept. 19 *Perf. 14x13½*

1162 A303 250 l shown .45 .45
1163 A303 350 l "AIDS" .55 .55
1164 A303 650 l Virus, knot 1.00 1.00
1165 A303 1000 l Newspaper 1.60 1.60
Nos. 1162-1165 (4) 3.60 3.60

Kurhaus Scheveningen, The Hague — A304

1988, Oct. 18 **Photo.** *Perf. 11½x12*

Granite Paper

1166 1600 l Lithograph, c. 1885 2.25 2.25
1167 3000 l 1988 4.25 4.25
a. A304 Pair, #1166-1167 7.25 7.25

FILACEPT '88, Holland.

See Nos. 1190-1191.

Christmas — A305

Paintings by Melozzo da Forli (1438-1494): No. 1168, Angel with Violin, Vatican Art Gallery. No. 1169, Angel of the Annunciation, Uffizi Gallery, Florence. No. 1170, Angel with Lute, Vatican Art Gallery.

1988, Dec. 9 **Photo.** *Perf. 13½*

Size of No. 1169: 21x40mm

1168 650 l multi 1.25 1.25
1169 650 l multi 1.25 1.25
1170 650 l multi 1.25 1.25
a. A305 Strip of 3, #1168-1168 4.50 4.50

Europa Issue

Souvenir Sheet

Children's Games — A306

1989, Mar. 31 **Photo.** *Perf. 13½x14*

1171 A306 Sheet of 2 *18.00 15.00*
a. 650 l Sledding *5.00 5.00*
b. 750 l Hopscotch *5.00 5.00*

Nature Conservation — A307

Illustrations by contest-winning youth: 200 l, Federica Sparagna. 500 l, Giovanni Monteduro. 650 l, Rosa Mannarino.

1989, Mar. 31 *Perf. 14x13½*

1172 A307 200 l multi .35 .35
1173 A307 500 l multi .75 .75
1174 A307 650 l multi .90 .90
Nos. 1172-1174 (3) 2.00 2.00

Sporting Anniversaries and Events — A308

1989, May 13 **Photo.** *Perf. 12*

Granite Paper

1175 A308 650 l Olympics .80 .80
1176 A308 750 l Soccer .90 .90
1177 A308 850 l Tennis 1.00 1.00
1178 A308 1300 l Car racing 1.50 1.50
Nos. 1175-1178 (4) 4.20 4.20

Natl. Olympic Committee, 30th anniv. (650 l); admission of San Marino Soccer Federation to the UEFA and FIFA (750 l); San Marino '89, the tennis grand prix (850 l); Grand Prix of San Marino, Imola (1300 l).

Stamp Collecting Type of 1988

Covers and canceled stamps (postal history): 100 l, No. 916a with Iserravalle cancel, Sept. 1, 1977. 200 l, No. 1151 with Montegiardino cancel, May 3, 1986. 400 l, Italy No. 47 canceled on San Marino parcel card #422, 1895. 500 l, Type SP3 essay proposed by Martin Riester di Parigi, March 1865. 1000 l, Stampless cover, 1862.

1989, May 13 *Perf. 12*

Granite Paper

1179 A298 100 l multi .30 .30
1180 A298 200 l multi .40 .40
1181 A298 400 l multi .60 .60
1182 A298 500 l multi .90 .90
1183 A298 1000 l multi 1.25 1.25
Nos. 1179-1183 (5) 3.45 3.45

French Revolution, Bicent. — A309

700 l, The Tennis Court Oath. 1000 l, Arrest of Louis XVI. 1800 l, Napoleon.

1989, July 7 **Litho.** *Perf. 12½x13*

1184 A309 700 l multicolored .90 .90
1185 A309 1000 l multicolored 1.50 1.50
1186 A309 1800 l multicolored 1.75 1.75
Nos. 1184-1186 (3) 4.15 4.15

Show Business Type of 1988

Scenes from: 1200 l, *Marguerite et Armand.* 1500 l, *Apollon Musagete.* 1700 l, *Valentino.*

1989, Sept. 18 **Photo.** *Perf. 13½x14*

1187 A300 1200 l multi 1.50 1.50
1188 A300 1500 l multi 2.00 2.00
1189 A300 1700 l multi 2.50 2.50
Nos. 1187-1189 (3) 6.00 6.00

Rudolf Nureyev, Russian ballet dancer and winner of the 1989 San Marino Prize.

Exhibition Type of 1988

Views of The Capitol, Washington, DC.: 2000 l, In 1850. 2500 l, In 1989.

1989, Nov. 17 **Photo.** *Perf. 11½*

Granite Paper

1190 A304 2000 l multi 2.50 2.50
1191 A304 2500 l multi 3.25 3.25
a. Pair, #1190-1191 7.00 7.00

World Stamp Expo '89.

Christmas — A310

Panels from a Polyptych, c. 1540, by Coda Studio of Rimini, in the Church of the Servants of Mary, Valdragone.

Size of No. 1193: 50x40mm

1989, Nov. 17 **Granite Paper**

1192 650 l Angel 1.00 1.00
1193 650 l Holy family 1.00 1.00
1194 650 l Praying Madonna 1.00 1.00
a. A310 Strip of 3, #1192-1194 3.75 3.75

Palazzeto delle Poste, 1842 — A311

Europa — Post offices: 800 l, Dogana.

1990, Feb. 22 **Photo.** *Perf. 13½x14*

1195 A311 700 l multicolored *1.50 1.10*
1196 A311 800 l multicolored *2.00 1.40*

A312

Design: *The Martyrdom of Saint Agatha,* by Giambattista Tiepolo, and occupation force departing by the Porta del Loco.

1990, Feb. 22 ***Perf. 12***

Granite Paper

1197 A312 3500 l multicolored 6.25 5.00

Liberation from Cardinal Alberoni's occupation force, 250th anniv.

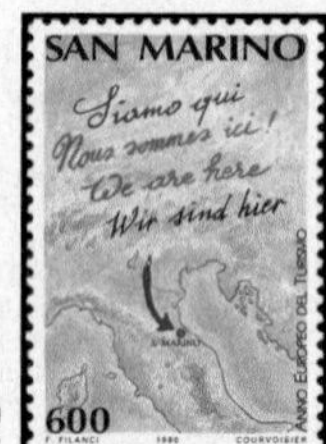

European Tourism Year — A313

No. 1198, The republic pinpointed on a map of Italy. No. 1199, San Marino atop Mt. Titano in proximity to other cities in the region. No. 1200, Rocca Guaita, San Marino.

1990, Mar. 23 **Photo.** ***Perf. 11½x12***

Granite Paper

1198 A313 600 l shown .75 .75
1199 A313 600 l multicolored .75 .75
1200 A313 600 l multicolored .75 .75
Nos. 1198-1200 (3) 2.25 2.25

See Nos. 1209a, 1260-1262.

Souvenir Sheet

1990 World Cup Soccer Championships, Italy — A314

Various athletes: a, Germany. b, Italy. c, Great Britain. d, Uruguay. e, Brazil. f, Argentina.

1990, Mar. 23 ***Perf. 13½x14***

1201 A314 Sheet of 6 6.25 6.25
a.-f. 700 l any single .80 .80

Show Business Type of 1988

Scenes from: 600 l, *Hamlet.* 700 l, *Richard III.* 1500 l, *Marathon Man.*

1990, May 3 **Photo.** ***Perf. 13½x14***

1202 A300 600 l multi 1.00 1.00
1203 A300 700 l multi 1.25 1.25
1204 A300 1500 l multi 2.75 2.75
Nos. 1202-1204 (3) 5.00 5.00

Sir Laurence Olivier (1907-1989), British actor, winner of the 1990 San Marino Prize. Name misspelled "Lawrence" on the stamps.

President of Italy, State Visit A315

1990, June 11 **Litho.** ***Perf. 13x12½***

1205 A315 600 l multicolored .90 .90

Statue of Saint Marinus — A316

No. 1207, Liberty statue. No. 1208, Government Palace. No. 1209, Flag of San Marino.

Granite Paper

Booklet Stamps

1990, June 11 **Photo.** ***Perf. 11½***

1206 A316 50 l multicolored .25 .25
1207 A316 50 l multicolored .25 .25
1208 A316 50 l multicolored .25 .25
1209 A316 50 l multicolored .25 .25
a. Bklt. pane of 7, #1198-1200, perf. 11½ vert., #1206-1209 4.00
Nos. 1206-1209 (4) 1.00 1.00

See Nos. 1256-1259.

Discovery of America, 500th Anniv. (in 1992) A317

1500 l, Artifacts, map. 2000 l, Native plants, map.

1990, Sept. 6 **Litho.** ***Perf. 13x12½***

1210 A317 1500 l multicolored 2.25 2.25
1211 A317 2000 l multicolored 3.00 3.00

See Nos. 1230-1231.

Pinocchio, by Carlo Collodi (1826-1890) A318

Cartoon style drawings from Pinocchio.

1990, Sept. 6 **Photo.** ***Perf. 11½x12***

Granite Paper

1212 A318 250 l shown .40 .40
1213 A318 400 l Geppetto .55 .55
1214 A318 450 l Blue fairy .60 .60
1215 A318 600 l Cat & wolf 1.25 1.25
Nos. 1212-1215 (4) 2.80 2.80

Flora and Fauna — A319

Designs: 200 l, Papilio machaon, Ephedra major. 300 l, Apoderus coryli, Corylus avellana. 500 l, Eliomys quercinus, Quercus ilex. 1000 l, Lacerta viridis, Ophrys bertolonii. 2000 l, Regulus ignicapillus, Pinus nigra.

1990, Oct. 31 **Photo.** ***Perf. 14x13½***

1216 A319 200 l multicolored .30 .30
1217 A319 300 l multicolored .50 .50
1218 A319 500 l multicolored .90 .90
1219 A319 1000 l multicolored 1.50 1.50
1220 A319 2000 l multicolored 2.75 2.75
Nos. 1216-1220 (5) 5.95 5.95

A320

Christmas: Cuciniello Crib, San Martino Museum of Naples.

1990, Oct. 31 ***Perf. 11½***

Granite Paper

1221 750 l shown 1.25 1.25
1222 750 l Nativity, diff. 1.25 1.25
a. A320 Pair, #1221-1222 3.25 3.25

Europa — A321

1991, Feb. 12 **Photo.** ***Perf. 13½x14***

1223 A321 750 l Ariane 4 rocket *3.75 3.75*
1224 A321 800 l ERS-1 satellite *3.75 3.75*

Stamp Collecting Type of 1988

Areas of philately: 100 l, Stamp store. 150 l, Clubs. 200 l, Exhibitions. 450 l, Albums, catalogues. 1500 l, Magazines, books.

1991, Feb. 12 ***Perf. 12***

Granite Paper

1225 A298 100 l multicolored .25 .25
1226 A298 150 l multicolored .25 .25
1227 A298 200 l multicolored .35 .35
1228 A298 450 l multicolored .75 .75
1229 A298 1500 l multicolored 2.00 2.00
Nos. 1225-1229 (5) 3.60 3.60

Italian Philatelic Press Union, 25th anniv. (No. 1229).

Discovery of America Type

750 l, Map, instruments. 3000 l, Columbus' fleet.

1991, Mar. 22 **Litho.** ***Perf. 13x12½***

1230 A317 750 l multicolored 1.25 1.25
1231 A317 3000 l multicolored 4.75 4.75

1992 Summer Olympics, Barcelona A323

Olympic torch relay.

1991, Mar. 22 ***Perf. 15x14***

1232 A323 400 l Athens .60 .60
1233 A323 600 l San Marino .80 .80
1234 A323 2000 l Barcelona 3.00 3.00
Nos. 1232-1234 (3) 4.40 4.40

Basketball, Cent. — A324

Designs: 750 l, James Naismith (1861-1939), creator of basketball, players.

1991, June 4 **Photo.** ***Perf. 13½x14***

1235 A324 650 l multicolored 1.00 1.00
1236 A324 750 l multicolored 1.25 1.25

Fauna — A325

500 l, House cat. 550 l, Hamster on wheel. 750 l, Great Dane, poodle. 1000 l, Tropical fish. 1200 l, Birds in cage.

1991, June 4 ***Perf. 14x13½***

1237 A325 500 l multi .75 .75
1238 A325 550 l multi .80 .80
1239 A325 750 l multi 1.10 1.10
1240 A325 1000 l multi 1.50 1.50
1241 A325 1200 l multi 1.75 1.75
Nos. 1237-1241 (5) 5.90 5.90

See Nos. 1251-1255.

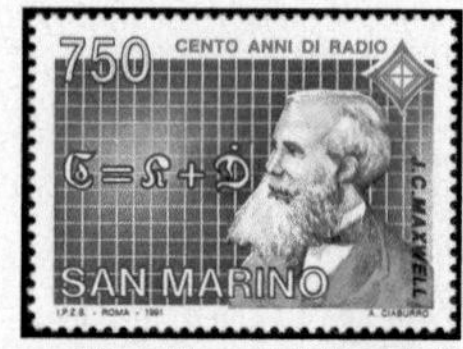

James Clerk Maxwell (1831-1879), Physicist — A326

1991, Sept. 24 **Photo.** ***Perf. 14x13½***

1242 A326 750 l multicolored 1.00 1.00

Radio, cent. (in 1995).

See Nos. 1263, 1279, 1300.

Souvenir Sheet

Birth of New Europe — A327

Designs: No. 1243a, Dove, broken chains, Brandenburg Gate. b, Pres. Gorbachev, rainbow, Pres. Bush. c, Flower, broken barbed wire, map.

1991, Sept. 24 **Litho.**

1243 A327 1500 l Sheet of 3, #a.-c. 7.00 7.00

La Rocca Fortress — A328

Christmas: Diff. winter views of 10th cent.

1991, Nov. 13 **Litho.** ***Perf. 14½***

1244 A328 600 l multicolored 1.00 1.00
1245 A328 750 l multicolored 1.25 1.25
1246 A328 1200 l multicolored 1.75 1.75
Nos. 1244-1246 (3) 4.00 4.00

No. 1246 is airmail.

Gioacchino Rossini (1792-1868), Composer — A329

Designs: 750 l, Bianca e Falliero, Rossini opera festival 1989. 1200 l, The Barber of Seville, La Scala 1982-83.

1992, Feb. 3 Photo. ***Perf. 14x13½***

1247 A329 750 l multicolored 1.25 1.25
1248 A329 1200 l multicolored 1.75 1.75

Discovery of America, 500th Anniv. A330

Designs: 1500 l, Columbus, ships at anchor, natives. 2000 l, Map of voyages.

1992, Feb. 3 Litho. ***Perf. 12***

1249 A330 1500 l multicolored 2.10 2.10
1250 A330 2000 l multicolored 3.25 3.25

Fauna Type of 1991

Flora.

1992, Mar. 26 Litho. ***Perf. 13½***

1251 A325 50 l Roses .25 .25
1252 A325 200 l House plant .30 .30
1253 A325 300 l Orchids .40 .40
1254 A325 450 l Cacti .60 .60
1255 A325 5000 l Geraniums 6.00 6.00
Nos. 1251-1255 (5) 7.55 7.55

Tourism Types of 1990

Designs: No. 1256, Crossbowman. No. 1257, Tennis player. No. 1258, Motorcyclist. No. 1259, Race car. No. 1260, Couple in moonlight. No. 1261, Man in restaurant. No. 1262, Woman reading beneath umbrella.

1992, Mar. 26 ***Perf. 14½x13½***

Booklet Stamps

1256 A316 50 l multicolored .25 .25
1257 A316 50 l multicolored .25 .25
1258 A316 50 l multicolored .25 .25
1259 A316 50 l multicolored .25 .25

Perf. 13½ Vert.

1260 A313 600 l multicolored 1.00 1.00
1261 A313 600 l multicolored 1.00 1.00
1262 A313 600 l multicolored 1.00 1.00
a. Bklt. pane of 7, #1256-1262+label 4.00

Physicist Type of 1991

Design: Heinrich Rudolf Hertz (1857-94).

1992, Mar. 26 Photo. ***Perf. 14x13½***

1263 A326 750 l multicolored 1.00 1.00

Radio, cent. (in 1995).

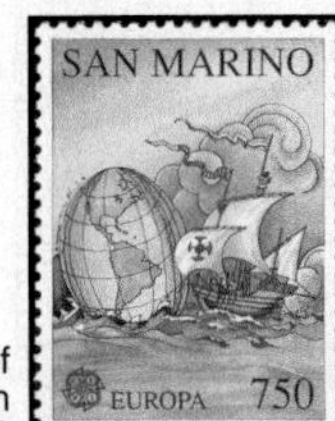

Discovery of America, 500th Anniv. — A331

750 l, Globe, ship at sea. 850 l, Ship in egg.

1992, May 22 Photo. ***Perf. 12x11½***

Granite Paper

1264 A331 750 l multi *1.75 1.75*
1265 A331 850 l multi *2.25 2.25*

Europa.

Souvenir Sheet

1992 Summer Olympics, Barcelona — A332

a, Soccer. b, Shooting. c, Swimming. d, Running.

1992, May 22 Litho. ***Perf. 14***

1266 A332 1250 l Sheet of 4, #a.-d. 7.25 7.25

Mushrooms — A333

Designs: Nos. 1267, Poisonous mushrooms. No. 1268a, Edible mushrooms in bowl. No. 1268b, Edible mushrooms on table.

1992, Sept. 18 Photo. ***Perf. 11½x12***

Granite Paper

1267 A333 Pair 1.25 1.25
a.-b. 250 l any single .55 .55
1268 A333 Pair 1.50 1.50
a.-b. 350 l any single .70 .70

Admission to the UN — A334

Designs: a, Arms of San Marino, buildings. b, UN emblem, buildings.

1992, Sept. 18 Litho. ***Perf. 12x12½***

1269 A334 Pair 2.50 2.50
a.-b. 1000 l any single 1.00 1.00

The Sacred Conversation, by Piero della Francesca (1420-1492) A335

Christmas: a, Entire painting. b, Detail of faces. c, Detail of dome.

1992, Nov. 16 Litho. ***Perf. 14½***

1270 Triptych 4.00 4.00
a.-c. A335 750 l any single 1.00 1.00

Contemporary Art — A336

Paintings: 750 l, Stars, by Nicola de Maria. 850 l, Abstract face, by Mimmo Paladino.

1993, Jan. 29 Litho. ***Perf. 11½***

1271 A336 750 l multicolored *.95 .95*
1272 A336 850 l multicolored *1.10 1.10*

Europa.

1993 Sporting Events — A337

300 l, Tennis. 400 l, Cross-country skiing. 550 l, Women running. 600 l, Fisherman. 700 l, Men running. 1300 l, Sailboat, runners.

1993, Jan. 29 ***Perf. 13½x14***

1273 A337 300 l multicolored .40 .40
1274 A337 400 l multicolored .50 .50
1275 A337 550 l multicolored .70 .70
1276 A337 600 l multicolored .75 .75
1277 A337 700 l multicolored .80 .80
1278 A337 1300 l multicolored 1.75 1.75
Nos. 1273-1278 (6) 4.90 4.90

No. 1273, Youth Games. No. 1274-1275, European Youth Olympic Days. No. 1276, World Championships for Freshwater Angling Clubs, Ostellato, Italy. No. 1277, Games of Small European Countries, Malta. No. 1278, Mediterranean Games, Roussillon, France.

Physicists Type of 1991

Design: 750 l, Edouard Branly (1844-1940).

1993, Mar. 26 Photo. ***Perf. 14x13½***

1279 A326 750 l multicolored 1.00 1.00

Radio, cent. (in 1995).

Souvenir Sheet

Inauguration of State Television — A338

Designs: a, 100-meter finals, World Track Championships, Tokyo, 1991. b, San Marino. c, Neil Armstrong on moon, 1969.

1993, Mar. 26 Litho. ***Perf. 13½***

1280 A338 Sheet of 3 7.75 7.75
a.-c. 2000 l any single 2.25 2.25

Soaking may affect the hologram on No. 1280b.

World Wildlife Fund — A339

Butterflies — No. 1281, Iphiclides podalirius. No. 1282, Colias crocea. No. 1283, Nymphalis antiopa. No. 1284, Melitaea cinxia.

1993, May 26 Litho. ***Perf. 14x15***

1281 A339 250 l multicolored .75 .75
1282 A339 250 l multicolored .75 .75
1283 A339 250 l multicolored .75 .75
1284 A339 250 l multicolored .75 .75
a. Block or strip of 4, #1281-1284 3.75 3.75

Miniature Sheet

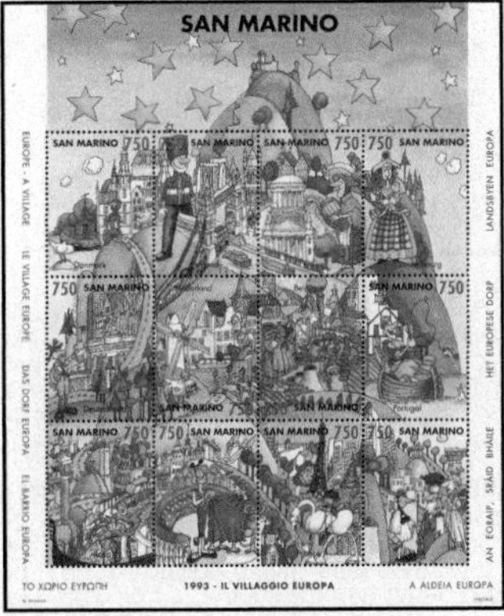

United Europe — A340

Village of Europe: No. 1285a, Denmark. b, England. c, Ireland. d, Luxembourg. e, Germany. f, Netherlands. g, Belgium. h, Portugal. i, Italy. j, Spain. k, France. l, Greece.

1993, May 26 ***Perf. 13½x14***

1285 A340 750 l Sheet of 12 11.50 11.50
a. Any single, #a.-l. .80 .80

Famous Men A341

Designs: 550 l, Carlo Goldoni (1707-93), playwright, vert. 650 l, Horace (65-8 BC), poet and satrist, vert. 850 l, Claudio Monteverdi (1567-1643), composer. 1850 l, Guy de Maupassant (1850-93), writer.

1993, Sept. 17 Litho. ***Perf. 13½x14***

1286 A341 550 l multicolored .70 .70
1287 A341 650 l multicolored .80 .80
1288 A341 850 l multicolored .90 .90
1289 A341 1850 l multicolored 2.25 2.25
Nos. 1286-1289 (4) 4.65 4.65

Christmas A342

Designs: 600 l, San Marino in winter, vert.
Paintings by Gerard van Honthorst: 750 l, Adoration of the Child. 850 l, Adoration of the Shepherds, vert.

1993, Nov. 12 Litho. ***Perf. 14½***

1290 A342 600 l multicolored .70 .70
1291 A342 750 l multicolored .90 .90
1292 A342 850 l multicolored 1.10 1.10
Nos. 1290-1292 (3) 2.70 2.70

10th Intl. Dog Show A343

Designs: 350 l, Dachshund. 400 l, Afghan hound. 450 l, Belgian tervueren shepherd dog. 500 l, Boston terrier. 550 l, Mastiff. 600 l, Alaskan malamute.

1994, Jan. 31 Litho. ***Perf. 15x14***

1293 A343 350 l multicolored .45 .45
1294 A343 400 l multicolored .50 .50
1295 A343 450 l multicolored .55 .55
1296 A343 500 l multicolored .60 .60
1297 A343 550 l multicolored .65 .65
1298 A343 600 l multicolored .70 .70
Nos. 1293-1298 (6) 3.45 3.45

Souvenir Sheet

1994 Winter Olympics, Lillehammer — A344

a, 90-meter ski jump. b, Downhill skiing. c, Giant slalom skiing. d, Pairs figure skating.

1994, Jan. 31 ***Perf. 13½***

1299 A344 750 l 2 each #a.-d. 7.00 7.00

Physicists Type of 1991

Aleksandr Stepanovich Popov (1859-1905).

1994, Mar. 11 Photo. ***Perf. 14x13½***

1300 A326 750 l multicolored 1.00 1.00

Radio cent. (in 1995).

Gardens — A345

1994, Mar. 11 Litho. *Perf. 13*

1301 A345 100 l Gate .25 .25
1302 A345 200 l Grape arbor .25 .25
1303 A345 300 l Well .40 .40
1304 A345 450 l Gazebo .60 .60
1305 A345 1850 l Pond 2.00 2.00
Nos. 1301-1305 (5) 3.50 3.50

Intl. Olympic Committee, Cent. A346

1994, Mar. 11 Photo. *Perf. 14x13½*

1306 A346 600 l multicolored 1.10 1.10

A347

Various soccer plays: a, Two players, one with #8 on shirt. b, Player in blue shirt kicking ball upward. c, Player heading ball. d, Players, one with #6 on shirt. e, Goal keeper.

1994, May 23 Litho. *Perf. 14*

1307 A347 600 l Strip of 5, #a.-e. 3.50 3.50

1994 World Cup Soccer Championships, US.
No. 1307 has a continuous design.

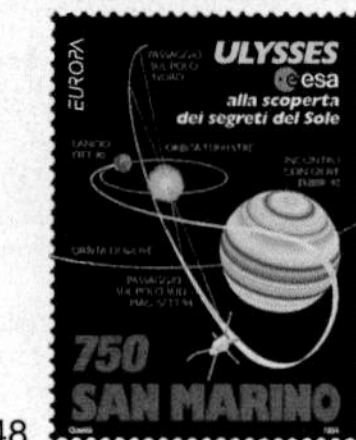

A348

Europa (Ulysses spacecraft and: 750 l, Flight path around Sun and Jupiter. 850 l, Sun.

1994, May 23

1308 A348 750 l multicolored *.95 .95*
1309 A348 850 l multicolored *1.10 1.10*

Inauguration of Government Building, Cent. — A349

Designs: 150 l, Exterior in shade, vert. 600 l, Exterior in sunshine, vert. 650 l, Clock tower. 1000 l, Interior.

Perf. 13½x13, 13x13½

1994, Sept. 30 Litho.

1310 A349 150 l multicolored .25 .25
1311 A349 600 l multicolored .70 .70
1312 A349 650 l multicolored .80 .80
1313 A349 1000 l multicolored 1.10 1.10
Nos. 1310-1313 (4) 2.85 2.85

Dedication of St. Mark's Basilica, 900th Anniv. A350

1994, Oct. 8 Photo. *Perf. 13½x13*

1314 A350 750 l multicolored 3.50 3.50
a. Souvenir sheet of 2, tete beche 4.50 4.50

No. 1314 printed with se-tenant label. No. 1314a contains No. 1314 and Italy No. 2003. Only No. 1314 was valid for postage in San Marino.

Touring Club of Italy, Cent. — A351

Vehicles traveling on road in middle of flower field: a, Traffic cop, bus. b, Tandem tanker truck. c, Sailboat, volcano. d, Truck loaded with animals, camper, fish in lake.

1994, Nov. 18 Litho. *Perf. 14x13½*

1315 A351 Block of 4 4.75 4.75
a.-d. 1000 l any single 1.00 1.00

No. 1315 is a continuous design.

A352

The Enthroned Madonna and Child with Saints, by Giovanni Santi (1440-1494) (Christmas): 600 l, Drummer, piper. 750 l, Madonna and Child. 850 l, Piper, harpist.

1994, Nov. 18 *Perf. 14x15*

1316 A352 600 l multicolored .70 .70
1317 A352 750 l multicolored .85 .85
1318 A352 850 l multicolored 1.00 1.00
Nos. 1316-1318 (3) 2.55 2.55

A353

Sporting Events of 1995: 1319, Junior World Cycling Championships, Forli, San Marino. 1320, Volleyball, cent. 1321, Men's Speed Skating World Championships, Baselga di Pine, Italy. 1322, World Track & Field Championships, Goteborg, Sweden.

1995, Feb. 10 Photo. *Perf. 13x14*

1319 A353 100 l Cycling .25 .25
1320 A353 500 l Volleyball .60 .60
1321 A353 650 l Speed skater .80 .80
1322 A353 850 l Runner 1.00 1.00
Nos. 1319-1322 (4) 2.65 2.65

European Nature Conservation Year — A354

Nature scenes with flowers, water: a, Snails, dragonfly, fish. b, Frog, snake. c, Ladybugs, butterfly. d, Ducklings, frog. e, Ducks, snail.

1995, Feb. 10

1323 A354 600 l Strip of 5, #a.-e. 3.75 3.75

No. 1323 is a continuous design.

UN, 50th Anniv. — A355

Designs: 550 l, UN emblem surrounded by people. 600 l, Emblem in center of rose. 650 l, Hourglass shaped from halves of globe. 1200 l, "50," Emblem, rainbow.

1995, Mar. 24 Litho. *Perf. 14x15*

1324 A355 550 l multicolored .60 .60
1325 A355 600 l multicolored .75 .75
1326 A355 650 l multicolored .85 .85
1327 A355 1200 l multicolored 1.25 1.25
Nos. 1324-1327 (4) 3.45 3.45

Peace & Freedom A356

1995, Mar. 24 *Perf. 15x14*

1328 A356 750 l shown *.95 .95*
1329 A356 850 l Sheep, meadow *1.00 1.00*

Europa.

World Tourism Organization, 20th Anniv. — A357

Designs: 750 l, Mt. Titano encircled by five colored lines symbolizing continents. 850 l, Airplane over globe. 1200 l, Five lines encircling earth.

1995, May 5 Litho. *Perf. 15x14*

1330 A357 600 l multicolored .80 .80
1331 A357 750 l multicolored .95 .95
1332 A357 850 l multicolored 1.00 1.00
1333 A357 1200 l multicolored 1.25 1.25
Nos. 1330-1333 (4) 4.00 4.00

Santa Croce Basilica, Florence, 700th Anniv. A358

1200 l, Detail from fresco, The Legend of the True Cross, by Agnolo Gaddi, facade of the basilica. 1250 l, Painting, The Madonna and Child with Saints, by Andrea della Robbia, Santa Croce Cloister, Pazzi Chapel.

1995, May 5

1334 A358 1200 l multicolored 1.40 1.40
1335 A358 1250 l multicolored 1.50 1.50

Radio, Cent. — A359

Designs: No. 1336, Stations on radio dial. No. 1337, Guglielmo Marconi (1874-1937), transmitting equipment.

1995, June 8 Litho. *Perf. 14*

1336 850 l multicolored 1.00 1.00
1337 850 l multicolored 1.00 1.00
a. A359 Pair, #1336-1337 2.50 2.50

Printed in sheets of 10 stamps.
See Germany No. 1900, Ireland Nos. 973-974, Italy Nos. 2038-2039, Vatican City Nos. 978-979.

Miniature Sheet

Motion Picture, Cent. — A360

Different frames from films:
The General: a, 1. b, 2. c, 3. d, 4.
Il Gattopardo: e, 1. f, 2. g, 3. h, 4.
Allegro Non Troppo: i, 1. j, 2. k, 3. l, 4.
Braveheart: m, 1. n, 2. o, 3. p, 4.

1995, Sept. 14 Litho. *Perf. 15x14*

1338 A360 Sheet of 16 5.00 5.00
a.-p. 250 l any single .30 .30

Exhibition Type of 1980

Qianmen complex of Zhengyangmen Rostrum, Embrasured Watchtower, Beijing: No. 1339, In 1914. No. 1340, In 1995.

1995, Sept. 14 *Perf. 14*

1339 A222 1500 l multicolored 1.50 1.50
1340 A222 1500 l multicolored 1.50 1.50
a. Pair, #1339-1340 3.75 3.75

Beijing '95.

Neri of Rimini, 14th Cent. Artist — A361

Designs: 650 l, The Annunciation.

1995, Nov. 6 Litho. *Perf. 14x15*

1341 A361 650 l multicolored 1.00 1.00

Christmas — A362

Designs: a, Santa, sleigh, reindeer. b, Children, Christmas tree. c, Nativity, star.

1995, Nov. 6 Litho. *Perf. 14x15*

1342 A362 Strip of 3 3.50 3.50
a.-c. 750 l any single .75 .75

No. 1342 is a continuous design.

Express Mail Service A363

1995, Nov. 6 ***Perf. 15x14***
1343 A363 6000 l multicolored 6.75 6.75

A364

1996, Feb. 12 Litho. ***Perf. 14x15***
1344 A364 100 l Discus .25 .25
1345 A364 500 l Wrestling .70 .70
1346 A364 650 l Athletics .80 .80
1347 A364 1500 l Javelin 1.75 1.75
1348 A364 2500 l Running 3.00 3.00
Nos. 1344-1348 (5) 6.50 6.50

1996 Summer Olympics, Atlanta.

Europa — A365

Portrait of Mother Teresa of Calcutta, by Gina Lollobrigida.

Granite Paper

1996, Mar. 22 Photo. ***Perf. 12***
1349 A365 750 l multicolored *1.75 1.75*

China '96 Philatelic Exhibition, Beijing A366

1996, Mar. 22 ***Perf. 14x13½***
1350 A366 1250 l multicolored 1.90 1.90

Marco Polo's return from China, 700th anniv. (in 1995).
See Italy No. 2070.

Nature World Exhibition A367

Photographs of wildlife: 50 l, Dolphin. 100 l, Frog. 150 l, Penguins. 1000 l, Butterfly. 3000 l, Ducks.

1996, Mar. 22 ***Perf. 12***
Granite Paper
1351 A367 50 l multicolored .25 .25
1352 A367 100 l multicolored .25 .25
1353 A367 150 l multicolored .25 .25
1354 A367 1000 l multicolored 1.00 1.00
1355 A367 3000 l multicolored 3.00 3.00
Nos. 1351-1355 (5) 4.75 4.75

China-San Marino Relations, 25th Anniv. A368

No. 1356, Great Wall of China. No. 1357, Wall surrounding Mount Titano, San Marino.

1996, May 6 Litho. ***Perf. 12***
1356 A368 750 l multicolored .75 .75
1357 A368 750 l multicolored .75 .75
a. Pair, Nos. 1356-1357 2.50 2.50
b. Souvenir sheet, No. 1357a 2.75 2.75

No. 1357a is a continuous design.
See People's Republic of China Nos. 2675-2676.

Medieval Days Celebration A369

Festival activities: No. 1358, Woman weaving yarn, vert. No. 1359, Potter, vert. No. 1360, Woman making brushes, vert. No. 1361, Man playing checkers, vert. No. 1362, Group blowing trumpets. No. 1363, Group holding banners. No. 1364, Men seated with crossbows. No. 1365, Street performers.

Perf. 14 on 2 Sides
1996, May 6 Litho. & Photo.
Booklet Stamps
1358 A369 750 l multicolored .80 .80
1359 A369 750 l multicolored .80 .80
1360 A369 750 l multicolored .80 .80
1361 A369 750 l multicolored .80 .80
1362 A369 750 l multicolored .80 .80
1363 A369 750 l multicolored .80 .80
1364 A369 750 l multicolored .80 .80
1365 A369 750 l multicolored .80 .80
a. Booklet pane, #1358-1365 9.00
Complete booklet, #1365a 11.00

Festival Bar A370

History of Italian Songs — A371

Singer, allegory of song: a, Enrico Caruso, "O Sole Mio." b, Armando Gill, "Come Pioveva." c, Ettore Petrolini, "Gastone." d, Vittorio de Sica, "Parlami D'Amore Mariu." e, Odoardo Spadaro, "La Porti un Bacione a Firenze." f, Alberto Rabagliati, "O Mia Bela Madonina." g, Beniamino Gigli, "Mamma." h, Claudio Villa, "Luna Rossa." i, Secondo Casadei, "Romagna Mia." j, Renato Rascel, "Arrivederci Roma." k, Fred Buscaglione, "Guarda Che Luna." l, Domenico Modugno, "Nel Blu Dipinto di Blu."

1996, May 25 Litho. ***Perf. 14x13½***
1366 A370 2000 l shown 2.50 2.50

Granite Paper
Photo.
Perf. 12x11½
1367 A371 750 l Sheet of 12, #a.-l. 10.00 10.00

Gazzetta Dello Sport, Cent. — A372

1996, May 25 ***Perf. 12***
Granite Paper
1368 A372 1850 l multicolored 2.25 2.25

UNICEF, 50th Anniv. A373

1996, Sept. 20 Photo. ***Perf. 12***
Granite Paper
1369 A373 550 l Hen, chicks .60 .60
1370 A373 1000 l Baby birds 1.40 1.40

UNESCO, 50th Anniv. A374

World Heritage Sites: 450 l, Yellowstone Natl. Park, US. 500 l, Prehistoric caves, Vézère Valley, France. 650 l, Old town center, San Gimignano, Italy. 1450 l, Church of the Wies Pilgrimage, Germany.

1996, Sept. 20 Granite Paper
1371 A374 450 l multicolored .60 .60
1372 A374 500 l multicolored .65 .65
1373 A374 650 l multicolored .80 .80
1374 A374 1450 l multicolored 1.75 1.75
Nos. 1371-1374 (4) 3.80 3.80

Christmas — A375

Scenes looking through windows of a home: a, Playing game underneath Christmas tree. b, Tags draped from holly branch. c, Girl reading book, Santa in sleigh. d, Christmas tree. e, Fruits, candles, nuts. f, Streaking star, snowflakes. g, Toys. h, Presents. i, Santa Claus puppet. j, Nativity. k, Mistletoe. l, Stocking hung by fireplace. m, Family eating, drinking. n, Christmas tree, silhouettes of mother, father, wreath. o, Wreath, silhouettes of children & grandmother, snowman. p, Calendar, champaigne bottle popping cork.

1996, Nov. 8 Photo. ***Perf. 14½***
1375 A375 750 l Sheet of 16, #a.-p. 14.00 14.00

Souvenir Sheet

Hong Kong — A376

View from harbor: a, 1897. b, 1997.

1997, Feb. 12 Litho. ***Perf. 12½***
1376 A376 750 l Sheet of 2, #a.-b. 1.90 1.90

World Alpine Skiing Championships, Sestrière, Italy — A377

Scene of people skiing on mountain: a, Skier jumping left, birds. b, Ski lift, bird in sky. c, Coming down mountain, sleigh. d, Coming down mountain, Sestrière sign.

1997, Feb. 12 ***Perf. 12***
Granite Paper
1377 A377 1000 l Block of 4, #a.-d. 5.00 5.00

No. 1377 is a continuous design.

San Marino Townships (Castelli) A378

100 l, Acquaviva. 200 l, Borgomaggiore. 250 l, Chiesanuova. 400 l, Domagnano. 500 l, Faetano. 550 l, Fiorentino. 650 l, Montegiardino. 750 l, Serravalle. 5000 l, San Marino.

1997, Mar. 21 Photo. ***Perf. 12***
Granite Paper
1378 A378 100 l multi .25 .25
1379 A378 200 l multi .25 .25
1380 A378 250 l multi .35 .35
1381 A378 400 l multi .50 .50
1382 A378 500 l multi .60 .60
1383 A378 550 l multi .70 .70
1384 A378 650 l multi .80 .80
1385 A378 750 l multi .90 .90
1386 A378 5000 l multi 5.50 5.50
Nos. 1378-1386 (9) 9.85 9.85

Stories and Legends — A379

St. Marinus, Mt. Titano: 650 l, St. Marinus talking to bear that killed the mule. 750 l, Mother begging St. Marinus to forgive her son for trying to kill him.

1997, Mar. 21 Granite Paper
1387 A379 650 l multicolored *.85 .85*
1388 A379 750 l multicolored *.95 .95*

Europa.

Sporting Events A380

500 l, Giro d'Italia cycling event. 550 l, 10th Tennis Intl. 750 l, Formula 1 San Marino Grand Prix. 850 l, Republic of San Marino (Soccer) Trophy. 1000 l, Bowls (pétanque) World Championship. 1250 l, Motorcross 250cc World Championship. 1500 l, Mille Miglia classic car spectacle.

1997, May 19 Photo. ***Perf. 12***
Granite Paper
1389 A380 500 l multicolored .50 .50
1390 A380 550 l multicolored .60 .60
1391 A380 750 l multicolored .85 .85

1392 A380 850 l multicolored .95 .95
1393 A380 1000 l multicolored 1.10 1.10
1394 A380 1250 l multicolored 1.50 1.50
1395 A380 1500 l multicolored 1.75 1.75
Nos. 1389-1395 (7) 7.25 7.25

5th Intl. Symposium on UFO's and Associated Phenomena A381

1997, May 19 **Granite Paper**
1396 A381 750 l multicolored 1.00 1.00

Trees — A382

50 l, Pinus pinea. 800 l, Quercus pubescens. 1800 l, Juglans regia. 2000 l, Pirus communis.

1997, June 27 **Photo.** ***Perf. 12***
Granite Paper
1397 A382 50 l multicolored .25 .25
1398 A382 800 l multicolored .90 .90
1399 A382 1800 l multicolored 2.00 2.00
1400 A382 2000 l multicolored 2.50 2.50
Nos. 1397-1400 (4) 5.65 5.65

First Stamps of San Marino, 120th Anniv. — A383

Designs: No. 1401, G. Battista Barbavara di Gravellona, director general of Sardinian Post Office. No. 1402, Enrico Repettati, chief engraver for Officina Carte Valori, Turin. No. 1403, Otto Bickel, German stamp dealer, promoter of San Marino-Philatelist. No. 1404, Alfredo Reffi, San Marino stamp dealer, publisher of post cards, stamp catalogue.

1997, June 27 ***Perf. 11½***
Granite Paper
1401 A383 800 l multicolored .75 .75
1402 A383 800 l multicolored .75 .75
1403 A383 800 l multicolored .75 .75
1404 A383 800 l multicolored .75 .75
a. Strip of 4, #1401-1404 4.00 4.00

Beatification of Bartolomeo Maria Dal Monte (1726-78) A384

1997, Sept. 18 **Photo.** ***Perf. 12***
Granite Paper
1405 A384 800 l multicolored 1.00 1.00

Italian Comic Book Characters A385

Designs: a, "Quadratino," by Antonio Rubino. b, "Signor Bonaventura," by Sergio Tofano. c, "Kit Carson," by Rino Albertarelli. d, "Cocco Bill," by Benito Jacovitti. e, "Tex Willer," by Gian Luigi Bonelli and Arelio Galleppini. f, "Diabolik," by Angela and Luciana Giussani and Franco Paludetti. g, "Valentina," by Guido Crepax. h, "Corto Maltese," by Hugo Pratt. i, "Sturmtruppen," by Franco Bonvicini. j, "Alan Ford," by Max Bunker. k, "Lupo Alberto," by Guido Silvestri. l, "Pimpa," by Francesco Tullio Altan. m, "Bobo," by Sergio Staino. n, "Zanardi," by Andrea Pazienza. o, "Martin Mystère," by Alfredo Castelli and Giancarlo Alessandrini. p, "Dylan Dog," by Tiziano Sclavi and Angelo Stano.

1997, Sept. 18 **Granite Paper**
Sheet of 16
1406 A385 800 l #a.-p. 15.00 15.00

Adoration of the Magi, by Georgio Vasari (1511-74) — A386

1997, Nov. 14 **Photo.** ***Perf. 12***
Granite Paper
1407 A386 800 l multicolored 1.10 1.10

Volunteer Service, Solidarity A387

Designs: 550 l, St. Francis of Assisi, doves. 650 l, Mariele Ventre, children. 800 l, Children circling hands around world, Zecchino d'Oro song festival.

1997, Nov. 14 **Granite Paper**
1408 A387 550 l multicolored .70 .70
1409 A387 650 l multicolored .85 .85
1410 A387 800 l multicolored 1.00 1.00
Nos. 1408-1410 (3) 2.55 2.55

Volkswagen Beetle A388

Designs: a, Maggiolino (old Beetle). b, Golf I. c, New Beetle. d, Golf IV.

1997, Nov. 14 **Granite Paper**
1411 A388 800 l Sheet of 4, #a.-d. 4.50 4.50

No. 1411 was issued with attached entry form for drawing to win a new Beetle car. Entry form is rouletted at top to separate from bottom of sheet. Values are for sheets with entry form attached.

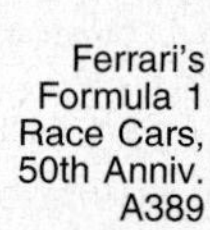

Ferrari's Formula 1 Race Cars, 50th Anniv. A389

Model number, year: a, 125S, 1947. b, 500F2, 1952. c, 801, 1956. d, 246 Dino, 1958. e, 156, 1961. f, 158, 1964. g, 312T, 1975. h, 312T4, 1979. i, 126C, 1981. j, 156/85, 1985. k, 639, 1989. l, F310, 1996.

1998, Feb. 11 **Litho.** ***Perf. 13***
1412 A389 800 l Sheet of 12, #a.-l. 12.00 12.00

A390

6th World Day of the Sick: 1500 l, Rainbow pulled over earth by dove.

1998, Feb. 11 ***Perf. 14x14½***
1413 A390 650 l shown .75 .75
1414 A390 1500 l multicolored 1.75 1.75

A391

Europa (Natl. Feasts and Festivals): 650 l, Installation of the Captains Regent. 1200 l, Feast Day of the Republic's Patron Saint.

1998, Mar. 31 **Litho.** ***Perf. 14x15***
1415 A391 650 l multicolored *.85 .85*
1416 A391 1200 l multicolored *1.60 1.60*

Giacomo Leopardi (1798-1837), Poet — A392

Words from poem, illustration: 550 l, "The Infinite," 1819, hedges, hill. 650 l, "A Village Saturday," 1829, woman walking. 900 l, "Nocturne of a Wandering Asian Shepherd," 1822-30, man looking at moon. 2000 l, "To Sylvia," woman's face.

1998, Mar. 31 ***Perf. 15x14***
1417 A392 550 l multicolored .75 .75
1418 A392 650 l multicolored .85 .85
1419 A392 900 l multicolored 1.00 1.00
1420 A392 2000 l multicolored 2.50 2.50
Nos. 1417-1420 (4) 5.10 5.10

1998 World Cup Soccer Championships, France — A393

Soccer players: 650 l, At goal. 800 l, In black & yellow, in blue. 900 l, In red, in black & blue.

1998, May 28 **Photo.** ***Perf. 11½x12***
Granite Paper
1421 A393 650 l multicolored 1.00 1.00
a. Booklet pane of 4 4.00
1422 A393 800 l multicolored 1.25 1.25
a. Booklet pane of 4 5.00
1423 A393 900 l multicolored 1.75 1.75
a. Booklet pane of 4 7.00
Complete booklet, #1421a, 1422a, 1423a 19.00
Nos. 1421-1423 (3) 4.00 4.00

Emigration A394

Designs: 800 l, People on ship's deck, group photograph in front of Mt. Titano, 3rd class ticket to New York, passport. 1500 l, People at work, work permit, residency permit, pay slip, US dollar.

1998, May 28 **Granite Paper**
1424 A394 800 l multicolored .80 .80
1425 A394 1500 l multicolored 1.75 1.75

Souvenir Sheet

San Marino Natl. Flag in Space — A395

Designs: a, Launch of US space shuttle. b, Shuttle in orbit, flag of San Marino. c, Earth, space shuttle.

1998, May 28 **Granite Paper**
1426 A395 2000 l Sheet of 3, #a.-c. 7.50 7.50

A396

Riccione 1998, Intl. Stamp Fair: 800 l, Sun, sail on boat as canceled stamp. 1500 l, Dolphin diving through canceled stamp.

1998, Aug. 28 **Photo.** ***Perf. 12x11½***
Granite Paper
1427 A396 800 l multicolored .90 .90
1428 A396 1500 l multicolored 1.75 1.75

A397

Science Fiction: a, Twenty Thousand Leagues Under the Sea, by Jules Verne (1828-1905). b, War of the Worlds, by H.G. Wells (1866-1946). c, Brave New World, by Aldous Huxley (1894-1963). d, 1984, by George Orwell (1903-50). e, Chronicles of the Galaxy, by Isaac Asimov (1920-92). f, City without End, by Clifford D. Simak (1904-88). g, Fahrenheit 451, by Ray Bradbury (b. 1920). h, The Seventh Victim, by Robert Sheckley (b. 1928). i, The Space Merchants, by Frederik Pohl (b. 1919) and C.M. Kornbluth (1923-58). j, Neighbors from the Middle Ages and the Future, by Roberto Vacca (b. 1927). k, Stranger in a Strange Land, by Robert Heinlein (1907-88). l, A Clockwork Orange, by Anthony Burgess (1917-93). m, Drowned World, by James G. Ballard (b. 1930). n, Dune, by Frank Herbert (1920-86). o, 2001, A Space Odessy, by Arthur Clarke (b. 1917). p, Blade Runner (Do Androids Dream of Electric Sheep), by Phillip K. Dick (1928-82).

Granite Paper

1998, Aug. 28 ***Perf. 14½***
1429 A397 800 l Sheet of 16, #a.-p. 15.00 15.00

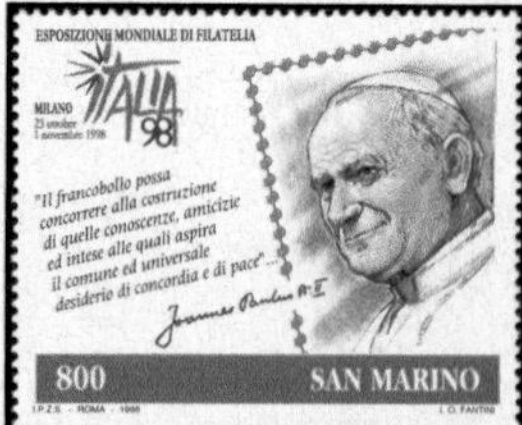

Italia '98 A398

800 l, Pope John Paul II.

1998, Oct. 23 **Photo.** ***Perf. 14***
1430 A398 800 l multicolored 1.40 1.40

See Italy No. 2265, Vatican City No. 1085.

A399

Christmas (Children of different races, Christmas tree made up of Santa Clauses, gifts): a, Boy running left, star on tree. b, Child from tropical region, star on tree. c, Child, rabbit, bottom of tree. d, Dog, girl, bottom of tree.

1998, Oct. 23 ***Perf. 12x11½***
Granite Paper

1431 A399 800 l Block of 4, #a.-d. 4.25 4.25

No. 1431 is a continuous design.

A400

1998, Oct. 23 **Granite Paper**

1432 A400 900 l Woman 1.00 1.00
1433 A400 900 l Man 1.00 1.00
a. Pair, #1432-1433 2.25 2.25

Universal Declaration of Human Rights, 50th Anniv. No. 1433a is a continuous design.

A401

Italia '98: Statue, "Girl," by Emilio Greco.

1998, Oct. 23 **Granite Paper**

1434 A401 1800 l multicolored 2.25 2.25

For Nos. 1435-1521, denominations are shown in euros and lira. For listing purposes, face values in lira are shown.

A402

1999 World Hang Gliding Championships, Italy: 800 l, Hand using feather to write in sky. 1800 l, Man on glider, holding balloon.

1999, Feb. 12 **Litho.** ***Perf. 13½x13***

1435 A402 800 l multicolored 1.00 1.00
1436 A402 1800 l multicolored 2.25 2.25

Operas in San Marino, 400th Anniv. — A403

Opera, composer: a, "L'incoronazione di Poppea," by Monteverdi. b, "Dido and Aeneas," by Purcell. c, "Orpheus and Euridice," by Gluck. d, "Don Giovanni," by Mozart. e, "The Barber of Seville," by Rossini. f, "Norma," by Bellini. g, "Lucia di Lammermour," by Donizetti. h, "Aida," by Verdi. i, "Faust," by Gounod. j, "Carmen," by Bizet. k, "The Ring of the Nibelungen," by Wagner. l, "Boris Godonov," by Mussorgski. m, "Tosca," by Puccini. n, "Love for Three Oranges," by Prokofiev. o, "Porgy and Bess," by Gershwin. p, "West Side Story," by Bernstein.

1999, Feb. 12 ***Perf. 13x13½***
Sheet of 16

1437 A403 800 l #a.-p. 16.00 16.00

Bonsai '99, San Marino Bonsai Exhibition A404

50 l, Pinus mugo. 300 l, Olea europaea. 350 l, Pinus silvestris. 500 l, Quercus robar.

1999, Mar. 27 **Litho.** ***Perf. 13x13½***

1438 A404 50 l multicolored .25 .25
1439 A404 300 l multicolored .35 .35
1440 A404 350 l multicolored .40 .40
1441 A404 500 l multicolored .60 .60
Nos. 1438-1441 (4) 1.60 1.60

Mount Titano Natl. Park A405

Europa: 650 l, Eastern slopes, fortress tower. 1250 l, Walled enclosure, Cesta tower.

1999, Mar. 27

1442 A405 650 l multicolored *.80 .80*
1443 A405 1250 l multicolored *1.75 1.75*

1999 World Cycling Championships, Veneto, Italy — A406

900 l, Building, emblem. 3000 l, Colosseum, emblem.

1999, Mar. 27

1444 A406 900 l multicolored 1.00 1.00
1445 A406 3000 l multicolored 3.75 3.75

2nd Roman Republic, Garibaldi's Escape to San Marino, 150th Anniv. A407

1999, May 12 **Litho.** ***Perf. 13x13¼***

1446 A407 1250 l multicolored 1.60 1.60

Council of Europe, 50th Anniv. — A408

1999, May 12 ***Perf. 13¼x13***

1447 A408 1300 l multicolored 1.75 1.75

UPU, 125th Anniv. A409

800 l, Text from original UPU Treaty, Swiss Parliament Building, Bern. 3000 l, World map highlighting UPU's 22 founding countries.

1999, May 12 ***Perf. 13x13¼***

1448 A409 800 l multicolored .90 .90
1449 A409 3000 l multicolored 3.75 3.75

Holy Year 2000 A410

650 l, Map of route of 15th cent. European pilgrims, Canterbury Cathedral. 800 l, Fresco of priest blessing pilgrim, 11th cent., Reims Cathedral. 900 l, Fresco of hospice welcoming pilgrims, 15th cent., Duomo de Pavia. 1250 l, Bas-relief of pilgrims on the road, Cathedral of Fidenza, 12th cent. 1500 l, View of Rome from Monte Mario, by Sir Charles Eastlake, St. Peter's Basilica, Rome.

1999, June 5

1450 A410 650 l multicolored .65 .65
1451 A410 800 l multicolored .90 .90
1452 A410 900 l multicolored 1.00 1.00
1453 A410 1250 l multicolored 1.50 1.50
1454 A410 1500 l multicolored 2.00 2.00
Nos. 1450-1454 (5) 6.05 6.05

Fauna of San Marino A411

500 l, Lepus europaeus. 650 l, Sciurus vulgaris. 1100 l, Meles meles. 1250 l, Vulpes vulpes. 1850 l, Hystrix cristata.

1999, June 5

1455 A411 500 l multicolored .60 .60
1456 A411 650 l multicolored .75 .75
1457 A411 1100 l multicolored 1.10 1.10
1458 A411 1250 l multicolored 1.50 1.50
1459 A411 1850 l multicolored 2.50 2.50
Nos. 1455-1459 (5) 6.45 6.45

Architecture — A412

Designs: 50 l, Sant'Agata Feltria, Rocca Fregosa. 250 l, San Leo, Rocca Feltresca. 650 l, Urbino, Ducal Palace. 1300 l, Sassocorvaro, Rocca Ubaldinesca. 6000 l, Montale and Rocca towers, San Marino.

1999, Sept. 20 **Litho.** ***Perf. 13x13¼***

1460 A412 50 l multicolored .25 .25
1461 A412 250 l multicolored .35 .35
1462 A412 650 l multicolored .85 .85
1463 A412 1300 l multicolored 1.60 1.60
1464 A412 6000 l multicolored 7.50 7.50
Nos. 1460-1464 (5) 10.55 10.55

San Marino Red Cross, 50th Anniv. A413

1999, Sept. 20

1465 A413 800 l St. Martin of Tours 1.10 1.10

Souvenir Sheet

Milan Soccer Club, 100th Anniv. — A414

Designs: a, 1901 team, trophy on table. b, Players Gren, Nordahl and Liedholm. c, 1963 team, black and white photograph. d, 1990 team, white shirts. e, 1994 team, hanging banners. f, 1999 team, player holding trophy.

1999, Sept. 20

1466 A414 800 l Sheet of 6, #a.-f. 6.75 6.75

Souvenir Sheet

Audi Automobiles — A415

Designs: a, Horch. b, Audi TT. c, Audi A8. d, Auto Union.

1999, Nov. 5 **Litho.** ***Perf. 13x13¼***

1467 A415 1500 l Sheet of 4, #a.-d. 7.75 7.75

No. 1467 was issued with attached entry form for drawing to win a new Audi A3 car. Entry form is rouletted at top to separate from bottom of sheet. Values are for sheets with entry form attached.

Christmas A416

1999, Nov. 5

1468 A416 800 l multicolored 1.10 1.10

Millennium — A417

Designs: a, Tank, soldiers and refugees of World Wars. b, Syringe and vial, MRI machine, DNA molecule. c, Washing machine, subway, Tiffany lamp. d, Radio, telephone operators, person at computer. e, Airplanes, airship, astronaut on moon. f, Pollution. g, Automobiles and truck. h, Atomic diagram, nuclear submarine, mushroom cloud. i, Charlie Chaplin in "Modern Times," comic strip, chair. j, Crossword puzzle, art gallery visitors, car and trailer, people exercising. k, Advertisements and slogans. l, Cyclist, soccer players, stadium.

2000, Feb. 2 Litho. *Perf. 13x13¼*
1469 A417 650 l Sheet of 12, #a.-l. 11.00 11.00

Souvenir Sheet

Holy Year 2000 — A418

Designs: a, St. John Lateran Basilica, St. Marinus and Mt. Titano. b, Basilica of St. Paul, statue of St. Marinus, the Rocca. c, Basilica of St. Mary Major, Basilica of San Marino. d, St. Peter's Basilica, St. Marinus.

2000, Feb. 2
1470 A418 1000 l Sheet of 4, #a.-d. 5.25 5.25

A419

Designs: 650 l, Rotary emblem and towers. 800 l, Palace, coat of arms, Statue of Liberty, Rotary emblem.

2000, Apr. 27 Litho. *Perf. 13¼x13*
1471 A419 650 l multi .90 .90
1472 A419 800 l multi 1.10 1.10

Rotary Club of San Marino, 40th anniv.

A420

Bologna, European City of Culture: 650 l, Government Palace and Statue of Liberty, San Marino, and Fiera Towers, Bologna. 800 l, Marconi's workbench, radio antenna, Bologna buildings. 1200 l, Microchip, drums, keyboards, Bologna buildings. 1500 l, Still Life, by Giorgio Morandi, antique books, Bologna buildings.

2000, Apr. 27
1473 A420 650 l multi .70 .70
1474 A420 800 l multi .90 .90
1475 A420 1200 l multi 1.50 1.50
1476 A420 1500 l multi 2.00 2.00
Nos. 1473-1476 (4) 5.10 5.10

Community of San Patrignano's Fight Against Drug Abuse — A421

Designs: 650 l, Vincenzo Muccioli, community's founder. 1200 l, Rainbow emblem. 2400 l, Muccioli and community residents.

2000, Apr. 27 *Perf. 13x13¼*
1477 A421 650 l multi .85 .85
1478 A421 1200 l multi 1.50 1.50
1479 A421 2400 l multi 2.75 2.75
Nos. 1477-1479 (3) 5.10 5.10

Europa Issue
Common Design Type

2000, Apr. 27 *Perf. 13¼x13*
1480 CD17 800 l multi *1.00 1.00*

Stampin' the Future Children's Stamp Design Contest Winner A422

2000, May 31 *Perf. 13x13¼*
1481 A422 800 l multi 1.00 1.00

Intl. Cycling Union, Cent. A423

2000, May 31
1482 A423 1200 l multi 1.50 1.50

2000 Summer Olympics, Sydney — A424

Designs: a, Dog, butterfly. b, Hippopotamus, penguin. c, Elephant, ladybug. d, Rabbit, snail.

2000, May 31 *Perf. 13¼x13*
1483 A424 1000 l Block of 4, #a-d 5.50 5.50

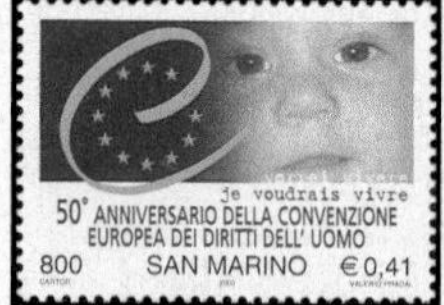

European Convention on Human Rights, 50th Anniv. A425

2000, Sept. 15 Litho. *Perf. 13x13¼*
1484 A425 800 l multi 1.00 1.00

Intl. Rights of the Child Convention, 10th Anniv. A426

Child: 650 l, And army helmet. 800 l, In corner of room. 1200 l, As flower. 1500 l, With book.

2000, Sept. 15
1485-1488 A426 Set of 4 5.50 5.50

Art of the Montefeltro A427

650 l, Basilica of San Marino, Statue of St. Marinus, by Adamo Tadolini. 800 l, Santa Maria d'Antico Church, Madonna and Child statue, by Luca Della Robbia. 1000 l, San Lorenzo Church, church door. 1500 l, Interior and exterior of San Leo Church. 1800 l, Frescoes, Santuario Madonna della Grazie.

2000, Sept. 15
1489-1493 A427 Set of 5 7.25 7.25

Republic of San Marino, 1700th Anniv. — A428

No. 1494: a, Melchiorre Delfico (1744-1835), historian. b, Giuseppe Garibaldi. c, Abraham Lincoln. d, World War II refugees. e, Jewels from Treasure of Domagnano. f, Map after 1643 war. g, Napoleon Bonaparte's offer to extend territory. h, Arengo of 1906. i, Child's head. j, Young man's head. k, Woman's head. l, Old man's head. m, St. Marinus, by Francesco Manzocchi di Forli, left half of arms. n, Right half of arms, St. Marinus, work attributed to Ghirlandaio. o, St. Marinus, by School of Guercino (blue denomination at top). p, St. Marinus in Glory, by anonymous artist. q, Double throne of Regents. r, Republican statutes, 17th cent. s, Palace Guards on parade. t, Flags of San Marino and other countries.

2000, Nov. 14 Photo. *Perf. 11¾*
1494 Souvenir booklet 25.00
a.-l. A428 800 l Any single 1.00 1.00
m.-t. A428 1200 l Any single 1.50 1.50
u. Booklet pane, #1494a-1494d 4.00
v. Booklet pane, #1494e-1494h 4.00
w. Booklet pane, #1494i-1494l 4.00
x. Booklet pane, #1494m-1494p 6.00
y. Booklet pane, #1494q-1494t 6.00

No. 1494 includes an 800 l postal card.

Virgin With the Infant Jesus, by Ludovico Carracci A429

2000, Nov. 14 Litho. *Perf. 13x13½*
1495 A429 800 l multi 2.75 2.75

Christmas.

Souvenir Sheet

Ferrari, 2000 Formula 1 Racing Champion — A430

a, Car on track. b, Car, track wall.

2001, Jan. 10
1496 A430 1500 l #a-b 4.00 4.00

Heritage of the Malatesta Family A431

Sigismondo Malatesta and: 800 l, Malatestian Temple, by Leon Battista Alberti. 1200 l, Pieta by Giovanni Bellini.

2001, Feb. 19 Litho. *Perf. 13x13¼*
1497-1498 A431 Set of 2 4.00 4.00

24 Hours of San Marino Regatta — A432

Hull colors: a, Green. b, Orange. c, Black. d, Brown.

2001, Feb. 19 *Perf. 13¼x13*
1499 A432 1200 l Block or strip of 4, #a-d 7.00 7.00

Giuseppe Verdi (1813-1901), Composer — A433

Verdi and scenes from operas: a, Nabucco. b, Ernani. c, Rigoletto. d, Il Trovatore. e, La Traviata. f, I Vespri Siciliani. g, Un Ballo in Maschera. h, La Forza del Destino. i, Don Carlos. j, Aida. k, Otello. l, Falstaff.

2001, Feb. 19 *Perf. 13x13¼*
1500 A433 Sheet of 12 13.00 13.00
a.-l. 800 l Any single 1.00 1.00

Europa — A434

Designs: 800 l, Safe in forest. 1200 l, Faucet on mountain.

2001, Apr. 17 Litho. *Perf. 13¼x13*
1501-1502 A434 Set of 2 *2.60 2.60*

Emigration to the US — A435

Immigrants viewing Statue of Liberty and: 1200 l, Ellis Island Immigration Museum, New York. 2400 l, San Marino Social Club, Detroit.

2001, Apr. 17 *Perf. 13x13¼*
1503-1504 A435 Set of 2 4.50 4.50

Euroflora 2001, Genoa — A436

Designs: 800 l, Dahlia variabilis, ship. 1200 l, Zantedeschia aethiopica, ship. 1500 l, Helen Troubel rose, ship. 2400 l, Amaryllis hippeastrum, Lanterna.

2001, Apr. 17 ***Perf. 13¼x13***
1505-1508 A436 Set of 4 7.75 7.75

9th Games of the Small European States — A437

No. 1509: a, Bocce, running. b, Swimming. c, Cycling. d, Shooting. e, Judo. f, Tennis, table tennis. g, Basketball and volleyball. h, Mascot carrying torch.

2001, Apr. 17
1509 A437 800 l Sheet of 8, #a-h 8.25 8.25

Opening of New State Museum A438

Various holdings: 550 l, 800 l, 1500 l, 2000 l.

2001, June 23 ***Perf. 13x13¼***
1510-1513 A438 Set of 4 6.50 6.50

UN High Commisioner for Refugees, 50th Anniv. — A439

No. 1514: a, Emblem at bottom. b, Emblem at top.

2001, June 23 ***Perf. 13¼x13***
1514 A439 1200 l Horiz. pair, #a-b 3.50 3.50

Foundation of the Republic, 1700th Anniv. — A440

No. 1515: a, Uninhabited land. b, People on horses. c, Small community. d, Town with highway.

2001, June 23 ***Perf. 13x13¼***
1515 A440 1200 l Block of 4, #a-d 6.25 6.25

Homage to Artist Joseph Beuys A441

2001, Sept. 10
1516 A441 2400 l multi 3.25 3.25

Year of Dialogue Among Civilizations A442

2001, Sept. 10 ***Perf. 13¼x13***
1517 A442 2400 l multi 3.25 3.25

United Mutual Aid Society, 125th Anniv. — A443

Allegory of assistance and: a, Old building. b, Modern building.

2001, Sept. 10 ***Perf. 13x13¼***
1518 A443 1200 l Horiz. pair, #a-b 3.00 3.00

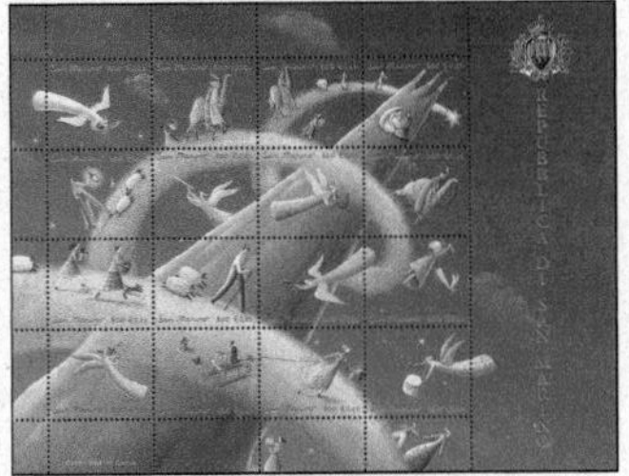
Christmas — A444

No. 1519: a, Angel with lute. b, Woman with basket, Magus on camel. c, Magus on camel, shepherd with sheep, woman with gift. d, Man with gift, castles, star, Holy Family. e, Man with lantern, goose, chicken, sheep. f, Angel with long, thin-mouthed, horn. g, Angel with harp. h, Magus on camel. i, Two women with baskets, dog. j, Shepherd with two sheep. k, Angel with short, wide-mouthed horn. l, Woman with gift, angel with horn. m, Angel with violin. n, Man, sleigh, gifts. o, Woman with gift, pulling sleigh. p, Angel with drum.

2001, Oct. 18 **Litho.** ***Perf. 13***
1519 A444 800 l Sheet of 16, #a-p 17.50 17.50

Introduction of the Euro (in 2002) A445

Map of Europe and: 1200 l, Coins of various countries, 1-euro coin. 2400 l, Banknotes of various countries, 100-euro banknote.

2001, Oct. 18 ***Perf. 13x13¼***
1520-1521 A445 Set of 2 4.50 4.50

100 Cents = 1 Euro (€)

A446

Designs: 1c, Rabbits. 2c, Sunset over San Marino. 5c, Cactus. 10c, Field of grain. 25c, Aerial view of alpine landscape. 50c, Wet olive branches. €1, Sparrows. €5, Baby.

2002, Jan. 16 **Litho.** ***Perf. 13¼x13***

1522	A446 1c multi	.25	.25
1523	A446 2c multi	.25	.25
1524	A446 5c multi	.25	.25
1525	A446 10c multi	.30	.30
1526	A446 25c multi	.65	.65
1527	A446 50c multi	1.50	1.50
1528	A446 €1 multi	2.00	2.00
1529	A446 €5 multi	13.00	13.00
	Nos. 1522-1529 (8)	18.20	18.20

Manuel Poggiali, 2001 World 125cc Class Motorcycling Champion — A447

No. 1530: a, "2001" at UR. b, "2001" at UL.

2002, Jan. 16 ***Perf. 13x13¼***
1530 A447 62c Horiz. pair, #a-b 4.00 4.00

2002 Winter Olympics, Salt Lake City — A448

No. 1531: a, Dog skiing. b, Hippopotamus skating. c, Rabbit skiing. d, Elephant playing ice hockey.

2002, Jan. 16 ***Perf. 13¼x13***
1531 A448 41c Block of 4, #a-d 5.00 5.00

Europa — A449

Designs: 36c, Lion tamer, clown, trapeze artist, tightrope walker. 62c, Trapeze artist, horse act, clown, acrobat.

2002, Mar. 22 **Litho.** ***Perf. 13¼x13***
1532-1533 A449 Set of 2 *10.00 10.00*

Priority Mail A450

Designs: 62c, Cyclist. €1.24, Hurlder.

2002, Mar. 22 ***Perf. 13x13¼***
Stamp + Etiquette
1534-1535 A450 Set of 2 4.75 4.75

2002 World Cup Soccer Championships, Japan and Korea — A451

Scenes from Italian team's victorious matches in: a, 1934. b, 1938. c, 1970. d, 1982. e, 1990. f, 1994.

2002, Mar. 22
1536 A451 41c Sheet of 6, #a-f 6.00 6.00

Maastricht Treaty, 10th Anniv. A452

2002, June 3 **Litho.** ***Perf. 13x13¼***
1537 A452 €1.24 multi 3.00 3.00

Intl. Year of Mountains — A453

No. 1538: a, Clouds at and above level of Mt. Titano. b, Clouds below Mt. Titano. c, Mt. Titano with no clouds.

2002, June 3 ***Perf. 13¼x13***
1538 A453 41c Horiz. strip of 3, #a-c 3.50 3.50

Souvenir Sheet

San Marino Postage Stamps, 125th Anniv. — A454

No. 1539: a, Parts of #1, 7. b, Parts of #7, 11. c, Parts of #11, 15. d, Parts of #15, 17.

2002, June 3 ***Perf. 13¼***
1539 A454 €1.24 Sheet of 4, #a-d 12.00 12.00

Intl. Amateur Radio Conference A455

Emblems of San Marino and International Amateur Radio Associations, Morse code and map in: 36c, Green. 62c, Orange.

2002, Sept. 19 ***Perf. 13¼x13***
1540-1541 A455 Set of 2 2.25 2.25

Craftsmen — A456

Designs: 26c, Blacksmith. 36c, Broom maker. 41c, Chair mender. 77c, Scribe. €1.24, Knife grinder. €1.55, Charcoal maker.

2002, Sept. 19
1542-1547 A456 Set of 6 11.00 11.00

Souvenir Sheet

Tourist Attractions — A457

No. 1548: a, Public Palace (30x52mm). b, Guaita (First Tower), buildings at bottom (45x30mm). c, Cesta and Montale (Second and Third Towers) (45x30mm). d, Basilica del Santo (building with steps at left (45x30mm). e, Cappucini Church (building with steps at center) (45x30mm). f, Gate of San Francesco (40x40mm).

2002, Sept. 19 ***Perf. 12½***
1548 A457 62c Sheet of 6, #a-f 9.50 9.50

Greetings — A458

Designs: No. 1549, 41c, "Da mi basia mille. . . " No. 1550, 41c, "Hello." No. 1551, 41c, "Best Wishes." No. 1552, 41c, "Ehi! Ci sono anch'io." No. 1553, 41c, "?????!!!!!" No. 1554, 41c, "Sorry."

2002, Oct. 31 ***Perf. 13¼x13***
1549-1554 A458 Set of 6 6.00 6.00

Christmas — A459

No. 1555: a, Baby's hands grasping adult's hands. b, Baby looking up towards mother. c, Baby breastfeeding. d, Mother and baby asleep. e, Hands cradling baby. f, Baby and mother in blanket. g, Mother kissing baby. h, Mother showing open mouth to baby. i, Baby on mother's shoulder. j, Mother smiling at baby. k, Mother nuzzling baby's hand. l, Two babies.

2002, Oct. 31 ***Perf. 12½***
1555 A459 41c Sheet of 12, #a-l 12.00 12.00

Paintings — A460

Designs: 52c, Woman with Mango, by Paul Gauguin (1848-1903). 62c, Wheatfield with Flight of Crows, by Vincent Van Gogh (1853-90). €1.55, Portrait of a Young Woman, by Il Parmigianino (1503-40).

2003, Jan. 24 **Litho.** ***Perf. 13¼x13***
1556-1558 A460 Set of 3 6.50 6.50

2003 World Nordic Skiing Championships, Val di Fiemme, Italy — A461

No. 1559: a, Skiers #4, 13. b, Skier #37. c, Skiers #6, 7.

2003, Jan. 24
1559 A461 77c Sheet of 3, #a-c 6.00 6.00

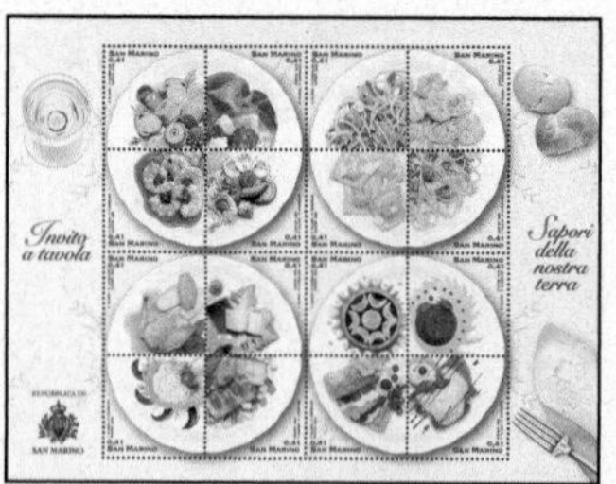

Cuisine — A462

No. 1560: a, Artichoke and mushroom salad. b, Prosciutto, sausage and cheese. c, Spaghetti with chopped tomatoes. d, Tortellini with ham. e, Shrimp. f, Octopus. g, Ravioli. h, Fettucini with tomato sauce. i, Breast of fowl. j, Fish, shrimp and salad greens. k, Dessert with red sauce in starburst design. l, Dessert with yellow sauce. m, Salad with cherry tomato garnish. n, Meat on bed of vegetables. o, Dessert with raspberry, grape and whipped cream garnishes. p, Custard in shell with lines of chocolate sauce.

2003, Jan. 24 ***Perf. 12½***
1560 A462 41c Sheet of 16, #a-p 20.00 17.50

Girolamo Fracastoro (1478-1553), Physician and Verona, Italy — A463

2003, Mar. 18 **Litho.** ***Perf. 13x13¼***
1561 A463 77c multi 2.00 2.00

100th Veronafil Philatelic Exhibition, Verona, Italy.

Europa — A464

Poster art by: 28c, Armando Testa. 77c, Henri de Toulouse-Lautrec.

2003, Mar. 18 ***Perf. 13¼x13***
1562-1563 A464 Set of 2 *10.00 10.00*

Race Horses — A465

Designs: 11c, Molvedo. 15c, Tornese. 26c, Ribot. €1.55, Varenne.

2003, Mar. 18
1564-1567 A465 Set of 4 5.50 5.50

Start of Stagecoach Mail Service, 120th Anniv. A466

Designs: 41c, Stagecoach going to Rimini. 77c, Stagecoach drawn by four horses.

2003, June 7 ***Perf. 13x13¼***
1568-1569 A466 Set of 2 3.00 3.00

Powered Flight, Cent. A467

Designs: 36c, Wright Flyer. 41c, Bleriot XI. 62c, Aermacchi MB339. 77c, Italian 313th Acrobatic Training Group (Frecce Tricolori).

2003, June 7
1570-1573 A467 Set of 4 5.00 5.00

St. Petersburg, Russia, 300th Anniv. A468

Designs: 15c, Bridge across Winter Canal, Fortress, Cathedral of Sts. Peter and Paul. 26c, Architect Bartolomeo Francesco Rastrelli, Opera House. 36c, View of city from Trinity Bridge. 41c, Aleksandr Pushkin. 77c, Empress Catherine II (the Great). €1.55, Czar Peter I (the Great).

2003, June 7
1574-1579 A468 Set of 6 9.00 9.00

Souvenir Sheet

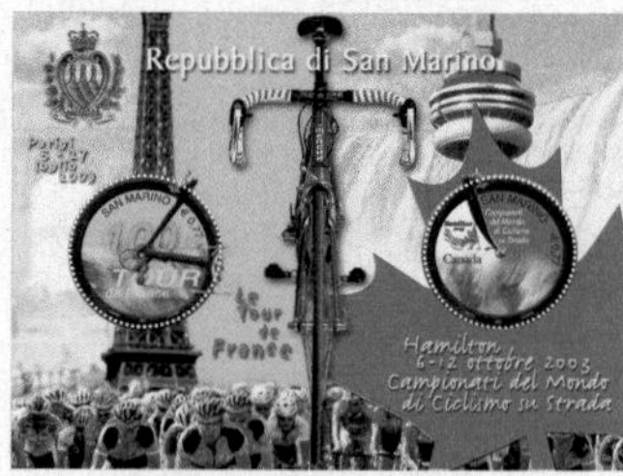

Bicycle Races — A469

No. 1580: a, Tour de France, cent. b, 2003 Road Cycling World Championships, Hamilton, Ont., Canada.

2003, June 7 ***Perf.***
1580 A469 77c Sheet of 2, #a-b 4.00 4.00

No. 1580 contains two 38mm diameter stamps.

2003 Rugby World Cup, Australia — A470

Various rugby players: 41c, 62c, 77c, €1.55.

2003, Sept. 15 **Litho.** ***Perf. 13¼x13***
1581-1584 A470 Set of 4 8.00 8.00

Children's Games A471

Designs: 36c, Cart racing. 41c, Blind man's buff. 62c, Hoop rolling. 77c, Marbles. €1.24, Handkerchief game. €1.55, Tug-of-war.

2003, Sept. 15 ***Perf. 13x13¼***
1585-1590 A471 Set of 6 12.00 12.00

Puppetry — A472

No. 1591: a, Puppets with drum and cymbals. b, Puppet with horn. c, Audience, puppet with flower. d, Audience, puppets with sticks.

2003, Sept. 15
1591 A472 41c Block of 4, #a-d 4.00 4.00

Reconstruction of La Fenice Theater, Venice — A473

Litho. & Embossed

2003, Oct. 24 ***Perf. 13¼x13***

1592 A473 €3.72 multi *15.00 15.00*

Christmas — A474

No. 1593: a, Christmas cards. b, Holy Family c, Shepherds and Magi. d, Angel. e, Christmas tree, vert. f, Girl and games. g, Children, fruit and cake. h, Carolers. i, Stocking on Christmas tree, vert. j, Cornucopia. k, Arms of San Marino. l, Girl, toys and gift, vert. m, Wreath. n, Boy, sled and snowman. o, Santa Claus. p, Children, toys and Christmas tree.

2003, Oct. 24 **Litho.** ***Perf. 13½***

1593 A474 41c Sheet of 16, #a-p 16.00 16.00

Manuel Poggiali, 2003 250cc Motorcycle World Champion A475

2004, Feb. 6 **Litho.** ***Perf. 13x13¼***

1594 A475 €1.55 multi 3.50 3.50

Venice Carnival A476

Designs: 77c, Doges' Palace. €1.55, Costumed carnival participant, canal and bridge.

2004, Feb. 6

1595-1596 A476 Set of 2 5.50 5.50

Latin Union, 50th Anniv. A477

Designs: 41c, Ballerina, by Edgar Degas, tango dancers. 77c, Illustration from *Don Quixote,* scene from *Dona Flor and Her Two Husbands.* €1.55, Susanna and the Elders, by Tintoretto, and Sunday Afternoon, by Fernando Botero.

2004, Feb. 6

1597-1599 A477 Set of 3 6.50 6.50

FIFA (Fédération Internationale de Football Association), Cent. — A478

2004, Apr. 16 **Litho.** ***Perf. 13¼x13***

1600 A478 €2.80 multi 6.50 6.50

European Bonsai Association, 20th Convention A479

Trees and: 45c, Black Japanese pine bonsai, by Kunjo Kobayashi. 60c, Dwarf pine bonsai, by Pius Notter.

2004, Apr. 16

1601-1602 A479 Set of 2 3.00 3.00

Souvenir Sheet

People's Republic of China, 55th Anniv. — A480

No. 1603: a, Tien-an-men Palace, Beijing, and Government Palace, San Marino. b, Mount San Marino, Great Wall of China. c, Tower of San Marino, Pagoda of the Temple of Heaven, Peace Statue, vert.

Perf. 13x13¼, 13¼x13 (#1603c)

2004, Apr. 16

1603 A480 80c Sheet of 3, #a-c 6.00 6.00

Europa — A481

Fantasy vacation vehicles made up of: 45c, Automobile, airplane and boat. 80c, Boat, camper, train and bus.

Perf. 13¼x13, 13x13¼

2004, May 21 **Litho.**

1604-1605 A481 Set of 2 *3.25 3.25*

2004 Summer Olympics, Athens — A482

No. 1606: a, Chariot, boxers, javelin thrower. b, Discus thrower, wrestlers, torch bearer. c, Relay race runner, cyclist, golfer. d, Tennis player, weight lifter, gymnasts.

2004, May 21 ***Perf. 13x13¼***

1606 A482 Horiz. strip of 4 9.50 9.50

a.-d. 90c Any single 2.00 2.00

Volkswagen Automobiles in Italy, 50th Anniv. — A483

No. 1607: a, Blue Volkswagen Golf. b, Old and new Volkswagen Beetles, blue denomination. c, Old and new Volkswagen Beetles, green denomination. d, Silver Volkswagen Golf.

2004, May 21 ***Perf. 13x13¼***

1607 A483 Booklet pane of 4 14.00 14.00

a.-d. €1.50 Any single 3.00 3.00

Complete booklet, #1607 15.00

Sao Paolo, Brazil, 450th Anniv. A484

Designs: 60c, Founding of city by Jesuits Manuel de Nobrega and José Anchieta. 80c, Mario de Andrade, artist, Antonio Alcantara Machado, writer, and Municipal Theater. €1.40, City skyline, monastery building.

2004, Aug. 20

1608-1610 A484 Set of 3 7.00 7.00

Writers — A485

Designs: 45c, Petrarch (1304-74). €1.50, Oscar Wilde (1854-1900). €2.20, Anton Chekhov (1860-1904).

2004, Aug. 20 ***Perf. 13¼x13***

1611-1613 A485 Set of 3 10.00 10.00

Fairy Tales — A486

Designs: 45c, Hansel and Gretel. 60c, Little Red Riding Hood. 80c, Pinocchio. €1, Puss in Boots.

2004, Aug. 20

1614-1617 A486 Set of 4 7.00 7.00

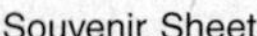

Souvenir Sheet

Meeting of Rimini, 25th Anniv. — A487

No. 1618: a, Man with tie, two men with construction helmets. b, Woman wearing glasses, child, woman. c, Child, woman and man. d, Priest, rabbi and man.

2004, Aug. 20 ***Perf. 13½***

1618 A487 €1 Sheet of 4, #a-d 9.00 9.00

Christmas — A488

No. 1619 — Angels and: a, Musical instruments. b, Bag of toys. c, Christmas tree. d, Cornucopia and "2005."

2004, Nov. 12 ***Perf. 13¼x13***

1619 A488 60c Block of 4, #a-d 6.00 6.00

Paintings A489

Designs: 45c, Rebecca at the Well, by Giovanni Battista Piazzetta (1682-1754). €1.40, Piazza Navona, by Scipione Gino Bonichi (1904-33). €1.70, The Persistence of Memory, by Salvador Dali (1904-89).

2004, Nov. 12 ***Perf. 14¾x14¼***

1620-1622 A489 Set of 3 8.50 8.50

Souvenir Sheet

Reopening of La Scala Theater, Milan — A490

No. 1623: a, Composer Antonio Salieri, theater's stage. b, Theater's facade. c, Conductor Riccardo Muti, audience.

2004, Nov. 12 ***Perf. 13¼***
1623 A490 €1.50 Sheet of 3, #a-c 11.00 11.00

Dec. 26, 2004 Tsunami Relief A491

2005, Feb. 28 Litho. ***Perf. 13x13¼***
1624 A491 €1.50 multi 4.00 4.00

Profits from the sale of this stamp went to charities involved with tsunami relief.

Intl. Weight Lifting Federation, Cent. — A492

2005, Feb. 28 ***Perf. 13¼x13***
1625 A492 €2.20 multi 5.25 5.25

2004 Beatification of Alberto Marvelli — A493

Designs: 90c, Marvelli assisting injured man. €1.80, Marvelli, Pope John Paul II, Loreto Basilica.

2005, Feb. 28
1626-1627 A493 Set of 2 6.50 6.50

Ferrari Race Cars — A494

Race cars and: 1c, Juan Manuel Fangio. 4c, Niki Lauda. 5c, John Surtees. 45c, Michael Schumacher. 62c, Ferrari emblem. €1.50, Alberto Ascari.

2005, Feb. 28
1628-1633 A494 Set of 6 6.50 6.50

Europa — A495

Designs: 62c, Bread. €1.20, Wine.

2005, Apr. 25 Litho. ***Perf. 13¼x13***
1634-1635 A495 Set of 2 *5.00 5.00*

78th Annual Reunion of Italian Alpine Troops — A496

Soldier: 36c, Climbing mountain. 45c, Picking flower. 62c, Assisting mother and child. €1, With other soldiers at reunion.

2005, Apr. 25
1636-1639 A496 Set of 4 6.00 6.00

Uniformed Militia — A497

Designs: 36c, Officer with saber, Third Tower. 45c, Soldier with musket, Second Tower. 62c, Standard bearer, Palazzo Pubblico. €1.50, Officer with saber, member of Military Band, First Tower.

2005, Apr. 25 ***Perf. 13¼x14***
1640-1643 A497 Set of 4 7.00 7.00

History of Mail Service A498

Designs: 36c, Courier, ship, train. 45c, Man reading letter. 60c, Men reading letter. 62c, Man and woman.

2005, June 4 ***Perf. 13x13¼***
1644-1647 A498 Set of 4 5.00 5.00

Coins A499

Designs: 36c, 1864 copper 5-centisimi coin. 45c, 1898 silver 5-lire coin. €1, Gold 10 and 20-lire coins, euro coins. €2.20, Euro coins.

2005, June 4
1648-1651 A499 Set of 4 9.50 9.50

Miniature Sheet

Musical Theater — A500

No. 1652: a, Erminio Macario in *Made in Italy.* b, Wanda Osiris in *Gran Baraonda.* c, Toto in *A Prescindere.* d, Anna Magnani in *Volumeide.* e, Aldo Fabrizzi in *Rugantino.* f, Renato Rascel in *Rascelinaria.* g, Nino Taranto in *Napoli che Ride.* h, Delia Scala in *Il Delia Scala Show.* i, Tino Scotti in *Ghe Pensi Mi.* j, Carlo Dapporto in *Giove in Doppiopetto.*

2005, June 4 ***Perf. 13¼x13***
1652 A500 45c Sheet of 10, #a-j 11.00 11.00

Giovanni Pascoli (1855-1912), Poet — A501

Poetry and: 36c, Kite and child. 45c, Mt. Titano. €1, Tower and horse. €2, Pascoli and church bell tower.

2005, Aug. 26 ***Perf. 13x13¼***
1653-1656 A501 Set of 4 9.00 9.00

Venice Gondola Regatta A502

Designs: €1.40, Statues of angel and devil as racing gondoliers. €2, Gondolier, vert.

Perf. 13x13¼, 13¼x13
2005, Aug. 26 Litho.
1657-1658 A502 Set of 2 8.50 8.50

Miniature Sheet

Italian Wine Bottle Labels — A503

No. 1659: a, Ferrari Brut. b, Amarone della Valpolicella. c, Canevel. d, Biondi-Santi. e, Vecchioflorio. f, Fazi Battaglia. g, Sassicaia, vert. h, Piano di Monte Vergine dei Feudi di San Gregorio, vert. i, Schiopetto, vert. j, Barolo, vert.

Perf. 13x13¼, 13¼x13 (vert. stamps)
2005, Aug. 26
1659 A503 45c Sheet of 10, #a-j 12.00 12.00

Dahlia — A504

Serpentine Die Cut 6¾ Vert.
2005, Nov. 17 Photo.
Self-Adhesive
Coil Stamp
1660 A504 (45c) multi 1.25 1.25

Pope Clement XIV (1705-74) A505

Designs: 80c, Wearing monk's habit and cardinal's biretta. €1, Giving blessing.

2005, Nov. 17 Litho. ***Perf. 13x13¼***
1661-1662 A505 Set of 2 4.50 4.50

Artists and Writers — A506

Designs: 36c, Baptistry door panel by Lorenzo Ghiberti (1378-1455), sculptor. 62c, The Annunciation, by Fra Angelico (c. 1400-1455). €1, Jules Verne (1828-1905), writer. €1.30, Hans Christian Andersen (1805-75), writer.

2005, Nov. 17 ***Perf. 13¼x13***
1663-1666 A506 Set of 4 8.50 8.50

Christmas A507

Designs: 62c, Annunciation. €1.55, Holy Family. €2.20, Adoration of the Magi.

2005, Nov. 17 ***Perf. 13x13¼***
1667-1669 A507 Set of 3 11.00 11.00

2004 Winter Olympics, Turin — A508

No. 1670 — Ski slope with: a, American flag at left. b, Eagle and airplane at right. c, Finish line. d, Skaters at right.

2006, Feb. 1 ***Perf. 12½x12¾***
1670 A508 45c Block of 4, #a-d 5.00 5.00

Christopher Columbus (1451-1506), Explorer — A509

Columbus and: 90c, Native American. €1.80, Ship and globe.

2006, Feb. 1 ***Perf. 13x13¼***
1671-1672 A509 Set of 2 6.75 6.75

Assembly of the Patriarchs, Cent. — A510

Assembled patriarchs and: 45c, Government Palace. 62c, Statue of Liberty. €1.50, Basilica.

2006, Feb. 1 ***Perf. 13¼x13***
1673-1675 A510 Set of 3 6.50 6.50

Souvenir Sheet

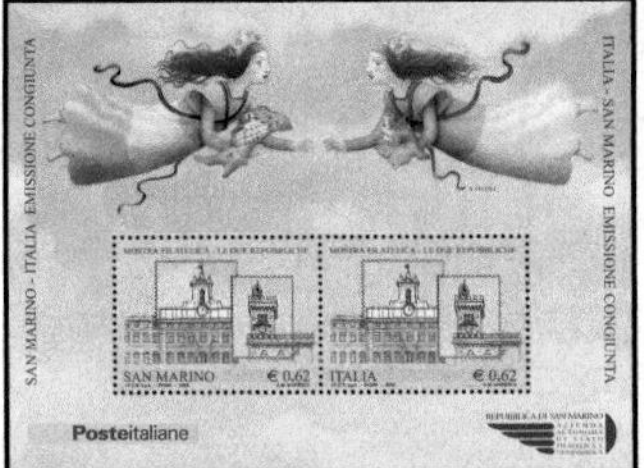

"Two Republics" Philatelic Exhibition — A511

2006, Apr. 5 Photo. ***Perf. 13x13¼***

1676 A511 Sheet, #1676a, Italy #2740 4.00 4.00
a. 62c multi 2.00 2.00

See Italy No. 2740. On No. 1676, the San Marino stamp is on the left. On Italy No. 2740a, the San Marino stamp is on the right. Both stamps in No. 1676 have text printed on reverse.

2006 World Cup Soccer Championships, Germany — A512

2006, Apr. 5 Litho. ***Perf. 13¼x13***

1677 A512 €2.20 multi 5.50 5.50

Art — A513

Designs: 36c, Bathers, by Paul Cézanne (1839-1906). 45c, Bathsheba With King David's Letter, by Rembrandt (1606-69). 60c, Coronation of the Virgin, by Gentile da Fabriano (c. 1370-1427). €1.80, The Bridal Chamber, fresco by Andrea Mantegna (1431-c. 1506).

2006, Apr. 5 ***Perf. 13x13¼***

1678-1681 A513 Set of 4 8.00 8.00

Children's Health — A514

2006, June 19 ***Perf. 13¼***

1682 A514 €2.20 multi + label 6.50 6.50

Europa A515

Designs: 45c, Butterfly with children's faces. 62c, Leonardo da Vinci's Vitruvian Man as jigsaw puzzle.

2006, June 19 ***Perf. 13x13¼***

1683-1684 A515 Set of 2 *2.75 2.75*

Crossbow Federation, 50th Anniv. — A516

Designs: 36c, Flag bearers, drummer. 45c, Flag bearers carrying flags of the nine San Marino castles. 62c, Crossbowman preparing to shoot, flag of Federation. €1, Two crossbowmen positioning weapons. € 1.50, Flag-throwers and drummers. €2.80, Flags of Federation and San Marino, man holding target with shot arrows.

2006, June 19 ***Perf. 13¼x13***

1685-1690 A516 Set of 6 16.50 16.50

Italy's Victory in 2006 World Cup Soccer Championships A517

2006, Aug. 21

1691 A517 €1 multi 3.00 3.00

Intl. Gymnastics Federation, 125th Anniv. — A518

Emblem and: 15c, Rings. €2.80, Female gymnast.

2006, Aug. 21

1692-1693 A518 Set of 2 7.00 7.00

Italian Philatelic Press Union, 40th Anniv. — A519

Emblem and: 90c, Castle turrets. €2.20, Arch and statues.

2006, Aug. 21

1694-1695 A519 Set of 2 7.50 7.50

Duke Guidubaldo, Carlo Bo and University of Urbino — A520

2006, Nov. 13 Litho. ***Perf. 13***

1696 A520 €2.20 multi 5.50 5.50

University of Urbino, 500th anniv.

Famous Men — A521

Artist's interpretations of famous works by: 5c, Roberto Rossellini (1906-77), film director. 65c, Luchino Visconti (1906-76), film director. 85c, Jacopone da Todi (c. 1236-1306), poet. €1.40, Wolfgang Amadeus Mozart (1756-91), composer.

2006, Nov. 13 ***Perf. 13¼x13***

1697-1700 A521 Set of 4 7.25 7.25

A522

Christmas — A523

The Nativity, by Tiepolo: No. 1701, Joseph (detail). No. 1702, Angel (detail). No. 1703, Infant Jesus (detail). No. 1704, Virgin Mary (detail). €2.80, Entire painting.

2006, Nov. 13 Litho. ***Perf. 13¼***

1701 A522 60c multi + label 1.75 1.75
1702 A522 60c multi + label 1.75 1.75
1703 A522 65c multi + label 1.90 1.90
1704 A522 65c multi + label 1.90 1.90
1705 A523 €2.80 multi 8.50 8.50
a. Booklet pane, #1701-1705, + label, perf. 13¼ on 3 sides 16.00 —
Complete booklet, #1705a 16.00
Nos. 1701-1705 (5) 15.80 15.80

No. 1705a lacks the small labels attached to Nos. 1701-1704.

San Marino's Presidency of the Council of Europe Committee of Ministers — A524

2007, Jan. 23 Litho. ***Perf. 13¼***

1706 A524 65c multi 1.75 1.75

Printed in sheets of 4.

Alessandro Glaray, San Marino Philatelic Expert A525

2007, Jan. 23 ***Perf. 13x13¼***

1707 A525 €1.80 multi 4.50 4.50

Gina Lollobrigida, Actress and Artist — A526

Designs: 65c, Self-portrait. 85c, "Potato Seller," photograph by Lollobrigida. €1, "Esmerelda," sculpture by Lollobrigida. €3.20, Lollobrigida and Mother Teresa.

2007, Jan. 23 ***Perf. 13¼x13***

1708-1711 A526 Set of 4 14.00 14.00

25th San Gabriel Intl. Philatelic Art Award — A527

2007, Apr. 20

1712 A527 €1.50 multi 3.75 3.75

Items Designed by Bruno Munari (1907-98) A528

Designs: 36c, Window-dresser's tool. 65c, Milk carton. €1.40, Shutter lock. €2, Hangable shop light.

2007, Apr. 20 ***Perf. 12½x12¾***

1713-1716 A528 Set of 4 11.00 11.00

Giuseppe Garibaldi (1807-82), Italian Nationalist Leader — A529

Designs: 65c, Garibaldi, San Marino flag, men on horseback. €1.40, Garibaldi landing at Marsala, battle scene. €2, Garibaldi on horseback, Garibaldi shaking hands with King Victor Emmanuel II of Italy.

2007, Apr. 20 Litho. ***Perf. 13¼x13***

1717-1719 A529 Set of 3 10.00 10.00

Europa — A530

Designs: 60c, Scouts, stylized globe, compass. 65c, Scouts, stylized globe, map of San Marino.

2007, June 2

1720-1721 A530 Set of 2 3.25 3.25

Scouting, cent.

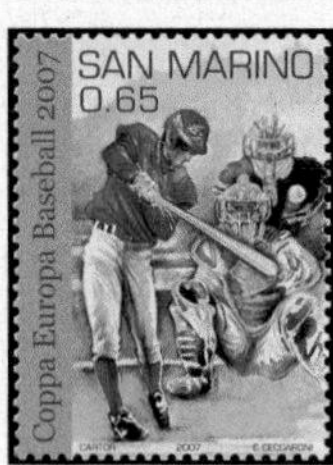

2007 European Baseball Cup, San Marino — A531

Designs: 65c, Batter, catcher and umpire. €1, Pitcher.

2007, June 2
1722-1723 A531 Set of 2 4.25 4.25

2007 World Track and Field Championships, Osaka, Japan — A532

Designs: 60c, High jump. 85c, Long jump, horiz. €1.50, Runners, horiz.

2007, June 2 ***Perf. 13***
1724-1726 A532 Set of 3 6.50 6.50

Souvenir Sheet

Postilions, 400th Anniv. — A533

Litho. & Engr.

2007, June 2 ***Perf. 13¼***
1727 A533 €4.50 multi 11.00 11.00

Intl. Assoc. of Editors of Stamp Catalogues, Albums and Philatelic Publications (ASCAT), 30th Anniv. — A534

2007, Aug. 24 Litho. ***Perf. 13¼x13***
1728 A534 65c multi 1.75 1.75

Castles — A535

No. 1729: a, Rocca, San Marino. b, Orava Castle, Slovakia.

Litho. & Engr.

2007, Aug. 24 ***Perf. 13***
1729 A535 65c Horiz. pair, #a-b 3.25 3.25

No. 1729 was printed in sheets containing four pairs. See Slovakia No. 525.

Miniature Sheet

European Wine Labels — A536

No. 1730: a, 1996 Porto Quinta do Estanho. b, Tarlant Cuvée Louis Brut Champagne, horiz. c, Bauget-Jouette Champagne, horiz. d, 2006 Zlahtina. e, 2006 Petri Riesling. f, 1999 Tokaji, horiz. g, Carmelo Rodero Ribera de Duero, horiz. h, Teodor Belo Simcic.

Perf. 13¼x13, 13x13¼ (horiz. stamps)

2007, Aug. 24 **Litho.**
1730 A536 65c Sheet of 8, #a-h, + 2 labels 12.50 12.50

Equal Opportunity To All — A537

2007, Dec. 3 Litho. ***Perf. 13¼x13***
1731 A537 €1 multi 6.50 6.50

Famous People — A538

Designs: 60c, Arturo Toscanini (1867-1957), conductor. 65c, Sculpture of Paolina Borghese, by Antonio Canova (1757-1822). €1, Carlo Goldoni (1707-93), playwright. €1.80, Via Toscanella, painting by Ottone Rosai (1895-1957).

2007, Dec. 3
1732-1735 A538 Set of 4 10.00 10.00

Christmas — A539

Designs: 60c, Government Palace, Christmas tree, and Star of Bethlehem. 65c, Santa Claus. 85c, Holy Family.

2007, Dec. 3
1736-1738 A539 Set of 3 5.25 5.25

Milan International Soccer Team, Cent. — A540

2008, Feb. 26 Litho. ***Perf. 13¼x13***
1739 A540 €1 multi *2.50 2.50*

San Marino Post Office, 175th Anniv. A541

2008, Feb. 26 ***Perf. 13x13¼***
1740 A541 €1.80 multi 4.50 4.50

Paintings — A542

Designs: 36c, The Crucifixion, by Giovanni Bellini. 60c, Madonna and Child with St. John, by Jacopo Bassano. 65c, Venus and Love, by Gian Antonio Pellegrini. 85c, Old Man's Face, by Giandomenico Tiepolo.

2008, Feb. 26 ***Perf. 13¼x13***
1741-1744 A542 Set of 4 6.00 6.00

Intl. Year of Planet Earth A543

Designs: 60c, Stylized skeleton and car emitting exhaust. 85c, Stylized sun and person. €1.40, Drop of water and tipped glass. €2, Earth on fire.

2008, Feb. 26 ***Perf. 13x13¼***
1745-1748 A543 Set of 4 12.00 12.00

European Year of Intercultural Dialogue — A544

2008, Apr. 8 Litho. ***Perf. 14¼x14½***
1749 A544 65c multi 1.75 1.75

Printed in sheets of 3.

Concetto Marchesi (1878-1957), Historian of Italian and Latin Literature — A545

2008, Apr. 8 ***Perf. 13x13¼***
1750 A545 €1 multi 2.50 2.50

Apparition at Lourdes, 150th Anniv. — A546

Designs: 36c, Bernadette Soubirous, first miracle healing. 60c, Procession of faithful at Lourdes. €2, Apparition of Virgin Mary before Soubirous.

2008, Apr. 8 ***Perf. 13¼x13***
1751-1753 A546 Set of 3 7.25 7.25

Our Lady of Mercy, Bas-relief by Leonardo Blanco — A547

Litho. & Embossed

2008, June 13 ***Perf. 13¼x13***
1754 A547 €1 multi 2.75 2.75

San Marino-America Friendship Association, 30th Anniv. — A548

2008, June 13 **Litho.**
1755 A548 €1.50 multi 3.75 3.75

Europa A549

Boy and girl: 60c, On ships. 65c, On globe releasing doves.

2008, June 13 ***Perf. 13x13¼***
1756-1757 A549 Set of 2 3.25 3.25

Souvenir Sheet

2008 Summer Olympics, Beijing — A550

No. 1758: a, 36c, Table tennis. b, 65c, Fencing. c, 85c, Swimming.

2008, June 13
1758 A550 Sheet of 3, #a-c 4.75 4.75

Andrea Palladio (1508-80), Architect A551

2008, Aug. 22 Litho. ***Perf. 13x13¼***
1759 A551 €1 multi 2.75 2.75

A552

Road Cycling World Championships, Varese, Italy — A553

2008, Aug. 22 ***Perf. 13¼x13***
1760 A552 85c multi 2.25 2.25
1761 A553 €3.25 multi 8.75 8.75

Famous People — A554

Designs: 60c (No. 1762), Posters for operas by Giacomo Puccini (1858-1924). 60c (No. 1763), Scenes from *Cuore,* by Edmondo De Amicis (1846-1908). €1, Rotonda di Palmieri and Vita Militare, paintings by Giovanni Fattori (1825-1908). €1.40, Book cover designs and actors in movie based on works by Giovannino Guareschi (1908-68), writer. €1.70, Piece of pottery and painting, The Print Collectors, by Honoré Daumier (1808-79), artist. €2.20, Scene from *La Luna e i Falò,* by Cesare Pavese (1908-50).

2008
1762-1767 A554 Set of 6 12.00 12.00

Issued: No. 1762, €1, €1.40, €1.70, 8/22; No. 1763, €2.20, 11/18.

International Polar Year — A555

Designs: 60c, Mountain. €1, Penguins. €1.20, Helicopter over ice sheet.

2008, Nov. 18 ***Perf. 13x13¼***
1768-1770 A555 Set of 3 7.25 7.25

Miniature Sheet

Addition of San Marino Historic Center and Mt. Titano to UNESCO World Heritage List — A556

No. 1771: a, Cesta Tower. b, Basilica. c, Statue of Liberty, Government Palace. d, Omerelli neighborhood. e, Buildings near wall. f, Guaita Tower.

2008, Nov. 18 ***Perf. 13¼x13***
1771 A556 €1 Sheet of 6, #a-f 13.50 13.50

Christmas A557

Designs: 36c, Angel playing trumpet. 60c, Holy Family. €1, Angel with gift.

2008, Nov. 18
1772-1774 A557 Set of 3 5.00 5.00

San Marino Olympic Committee, 50th Anniv. — A558

2009, Feb. 20 Litho. ***Perf. 13¼x14***
1775 A558 €1.80 multi 4.25 4.25

Ceramics A559

Designs: 36c, Amphora, by Libero Cellarosi. 60c, Amphora, by Umberto Masi. 85c, Vase, by Giorgio Monti.

2009, Feb. 20 ***Perf. 13x13¼***
1776-1778 A559 Set of 3 4.25 4.25

Miniature Sheet

Futurist Manifesto, by Filippo Tomasso Marinetti, Cent. — A560

No. 1779: a, Dog on a Leash, painting by Giacomo Balla (40x30mm). b, Armored Train, painting by Giono Severini (30x40mm). c, Electric Power Plant, painting by Antonio Sant'Elia (30x45mm). d, Zang Tumb Tumb, by Marinetti (45x30mm). e, Red Horseman, painting by Carlo Carra (40x30mm). f, Noise machine, by Luigi Russolo (53x30mm). g, Cyclist, painting by Umberto Boccioni (40x30mm). h, Still Life with Red Egg, by Ardeng Soffici (30x38mm). i, Unique Forms of Continuity in Space, sculpture by Boccioni (30x38mm). j, Futurist Evening, drawing by Boccioni (45x30mm).

2009, Feb. 20 ***Perf. 12½ to 13¼***
1779 A560 60c Sheet of 10, #a-j, + label 14.50 14.50

38th Intl. Criminal Police Organization and Interpol European Regional Conference, San Marino — A561

2009, May 8 Litho. ***Perf. 14x13¼***
1780 A561 €2 multi 5.00 5.00

San Marino Expo 2010 Pavilion and Shanghai Skyline — A562

2009, May 8 Litho. ***Perf. 13***
1781 A562 €2.20 multi 5.50 5.50

Europa — A563

Designs: 60c, Earth, Saturn, Neptune, astronomical instruments. 65c, Solar System, star ring of European Union flag, Mount Titano.

2009, May 8 Litho. ***Perf. 13½x14***
1782-1783 A563 Set of 2 3.25 3.25

Intl. Year of Astronomy.

World Air Games, Turin — A564

Doves and: 60c, Hot-air balloon. 85c, Glider. €1.50, Helicopter. €1.80, Airplane.

2009, May 8 Litho. ***Perf. 13¼***
1784-1787 A564 Set of 4 11.00 11.00

Louis Braille (1809-52), Educator of the Blind — A565

Litho. & Embossed

2009, June 16 ***Perf. 13¼x13***
1788 A565 €1.50 multi 3.75 3.75

Writers of Detective Stories A566

Designs relating to and names of characters from stories by: 36c, Edgar Allan Poe (1809-49). 85c, Arthur Conan Doyle (1859-1930). €1.40, Raymond Chandler (1888-1959).

2009, June 16 Litho. ***Perf. 14x13¼***
1789-1791 A566 Set of 3 6.00 6.00

16th Mediterranean Games, Pescara, Italy — A567

Designs: 60c, Running. €1.40, Cycling. €1.70, Wrestling.

2009, June 16
1792-1794 A567 Set of 3 9.75 9.75

Miniature Sheet

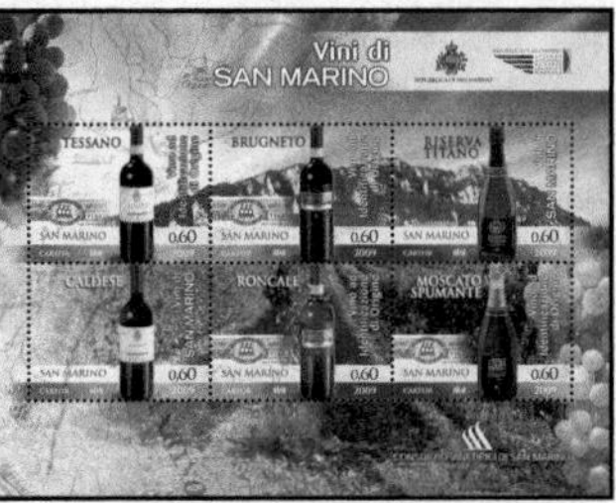

Wines of San Marino — A568

No. 1795: a, Tessano. b, Brugneto. c, Riserva Titano. d, Caldese. e, Roncale. f, Moscato Spumante.

2009, June 16 ***Perf. 13x13¼***
1795 A568 60c Sheet of 6, #a-f 8.00 8.00

Bologna Soccer Club, Cent. A569

2009, Aug. 25
1796 A569 €1 multi 2.50 2.50

30th Rimini Meeting — A570

2009, Aug. 25 Litho. ***Perf. 13½x14***
1797 A570 €1.80 multi 4.50 4.50

Souvenir Sheets

Attractions of San Marino — A571

No. 1798, €1 — Interior of Palazzo Pubblico with: a, Entire denomination on vignette. b,

Part of final "0" of denomination on black frame.

No. 1799, €1 — Statue of St. Marinus with: a, Entire denomination on vignette. b, Part of final "0" of denomination on black frame.

No. 1800, €1 — Statue of Liberty and Piazza della Libertà with: a, "1" of denomination below "a" of "San." b, "1" of denomination below "S."

2009, Aug. 25 Litho. ***Perf. 13¾x14***
1798-1800 A571 Set of 3 15.00 15.00

European Year of Creativity and Innovation. Nos. 1798-1800 were sold as a set with a €1.40 postal card that opened up to serve as a stereoscope for the stamp sheets. The set included a pair of plastic lenses for the stereoscope, an instruction card for assembling the stereoscope, a self-adhesive seal for the postal card, and an imperforate sample stereoscope card depicting the vignette shown on the postal card that was not valid for postage. Values are for the set of 3 sheets only.

Italian Language Day — A572

2009, Oct. 21 Photo. ***Perf. 13¼x13***
1801 A572 60c multi + label 2.50 2.50

Issued in sheets of 5 + 5 labels. See Italy No. 2966; Vatican City No. 1426.

Pets A573

Winning photographs in pet photography contest: 36c, Cat, by Natascia Stefanelli. 60c, Poodle, by Tina Woodcock. 65c, Duck, by Ettore Zonzini. 75c, Kid, foal and dog, by Anna Rosa Francioni. 85c, Turtle, by Maria Eleonora Vaglio. €1.20, Dog and butterfly, by Lorenzo Zamagni.

2009, Oct. 21 Litho. ***Perf. 14x13¼***
1802-1807 A573 Set of 6 11.50 11.50

Souvenir Sheet

Christmas — A574

No. 1808 — Rest on the Flight Into Egypt, by Caravaggio: a, €1.50, Joseph and angel. b, €2, Madonna and Child, horiz.

2009, Oct. 21 ***Perf. 13¾***
1808 A574 Sheet of 2, #a-b 8.75 8.75

San Marino Association of Blood and Organ Donors, 50th Anniv. — A575

2010, Feb. 9 Litho. ***Perf. 13¾***
1809 A575 €1.80 multi 4.50 4.50

Flowers — A576

No. 1810: a, 10c, Daffodils. b, 85c, Hyacinths. c, €1, Grape hyacinths. d, €1.50, Tulips.

2010, Feb. 9 ***Perf. 13¼x13***
1810 A576 Block or strip of 4, #a-d 8.75 8.75

Souvenir Sheet

2010 Winter Olympics, Vancouver — A577

No. 1811: a, 65c, Ski jumping, snowboarding, ice hockey, speed skating. b, 85c, Downhill skiing, cross-country skiing, curling, bobsledding. c, €1, Speed skating, figure skating, downhill skiing.

2010, Feb. 9 ***Perf. 13x13¼***
1811 A577 Sheet of 3, #a-c 6.25 6.25

Miniature Sheet

Expo 2010, Shanghai — A578

No. 1812: a, 65c, San Marino flag, Third Tower on Mt. Titano (30x40mm). b, €1, Second Tower, Great Wall of China (30x40mm). c, €1.50, First Tower, spear of Statue of Liberty (30x40mm). d, €1.80, San Marino Government Building, Statue of Liberty (36x51mm).

Perf. 13¼x13, 13¼ (#1812d)

2010, Feb. 9
1812 A578 Sheet of 4, #a-d 12.00 12.00

Men's Volleyball World Championships, Italy — A579

2010, Mar. 17 ***Perf. 13¼x14***
1813 A579 €1 multi 2.50 2.50

2010 World Cup Soccer Championships, South Africa — A580

2010, Mar. 17 ***Perf. 14x13¼***
1814 A580 €1.50 multi 3.50 3.50

Italian Cyclists — A581

No. 1815: a, €1.40, Gino Bartali (1914-2000). b, €1.50, Fausto Coppi (1919-60).

2010, Mar. 17
1815 A581 Horiz. pair, #a-b 7.25 7.25

Europa A582

Designs: 60c, Girl with wings of book pages. 65c, Girl asleep on a book in space.

2010, Mar. 17 ***Perf. 14¾x14***
1816-1817 A582 Set of 2 3.00 3.00

Miniature Sheet

Friendship Between San Marino and Japan — A583

No. 1818: a, Statue of La Repubblica, by Vittorio Pochini, La Rocca tower, San Marino. b, Himeji Castle, Japan. c, Apparition of Saint Marinus to His People, mural by Emilio Retrosi. d, Nihonbashi Bridge in the Morning, painting by Hiroshige.

2010, Mar. 17 ***Perf. 13x13¼***
1818 A583 €1.50 Sheet of 4, #a-d 14.00 14.00

See Japan No. 3217.

San Marino Lions Club, 50th Anniv. A584

Various photos of San Marino with country name in: 36c, Red violet. 60c, Orange brown.

2010, July 26 Litho. ***Perf. 14x13¼***
1819-1820 A584 Set of 2 2.25 2.25

F.C. Internazionale, 2009-10 Italian Soccer Champions — A585

No. 1821: a, Italian flag, soccer ball, F.C. Internazionale emblem. b, Shield inscribed "18," part of soccer ball. c, Part of soccer ball, European Union flag.

2010, July 26
1821 Horiz. strip of 3 7.50 7.50
a.-c. A585 €1 Any single 2.40 2.40

Miniature Sheet

Sites in San Marino and Gibraltar — A586

No. 1822: a, Second Tower, San Marino. b, Moorish Castle, Gibraltar. c, Mt. Titano, San Marino. d, Rock of Gibraltar.

2010, July 26
1822 A586 €1.50 Sheet of 4, #a-d 15.00 15.00

See Gibraltar No. 1237.

Famous People A587

Designs: 60c, Moon, hands of Frédéric Chopin (1810-49), composer. 65c, Scenes from movies, *The Seven Samurai, Ran,* and *Dersu Uzala,* directed by Akira Kurosawa (1910-98). 85c, Symphony orchestra and conductor Gustav Mahler (1860-1911), composer. €1, *The Birth of Venus,* by Sandro Botticelli (1445-1510), vert. €1.40, *The Tempest,* by Giorgione da Castelfranco (c. 1477-1510), vert. €1.45, *The Supper at Emmaus,* by Caravaggio (1571-1610), vert. €1.50, *The Football Players,* by Henri Rousseau (1844-1910), vert. €4.95, Characters from "The Adventures of Huckleberry Finn," and Mark Twain (1835-1910), author.

2010 ***Perf. 14x13¼, 13¼x14***
1823-1830 A587 Set of 8 30.00 30.00

Issued: 60c, 65c, 85c, €4.95, 10/5; others, 7/26.

Luciano Pavarotti (1935-2007), Opera Singer — A588

2010, Oct. 5 ***Perf. 14x13¼***
1831 A588 €2.20 multi 5.25 5.25

Christmas A589

Christmas tree with background color of: 60c, Blue. 65c, Green. 85c, Red.

Litho. With Foil Application
2010, Oct. 5 ***Perf. 13x13¼***
1832-1834 A589 Set of 3 5.00 5.00

Sport in the Philately of San Marino Exhibition A590

2011, Feb. 8 Litho. ***Perf. 14¼x13¾***
1835 A590 €1.50 multi 3.50 3.50

San Marino Choir, 50th Anniv. — A591

2011, Feb. 8
1836 A591 €2.20 multi 5.25 5.25

Luigi Einaudi (1874-1961), President of Italy — A592

2011, Feb. 8 ***Perf. 14¾x14¼***
1837 A592 €3.30 multi 7.75 7.75

Paintings A593

Designs: 10c, Self-portrait with a Beret, by Paul Cézanne. 50c, Horse Racing at Longchamp, by Edgar Degas. 85c, View from the Artist's Window, by Camille Pissarro. €1, Flower Beds at Vétheuil, by Claude Monet. €2.50, Jacques Bergeret as a Child, by Pierre-Auguste Renoir.

2011, Feb. 8 ***Perf. 13¾***
1838-1842 A593 Set of 5 11.00 11.00

Europa A594

Designs: 60c, Forest. 65c, Stacked logs.

2011, Apr. 5 Litho. ***Perf. 14¾x14¼***
1843-1844 A594 Set of 2 3.00 3.00

Intl. Year of Forests.

First Men in Space, 50th Anniv. A595

Designs: 50c, Yuri Gagarin (1934-68), Soviet cosmonaut. €2.40, Alan B. Shepard, Jr. (1923-98), American astronaut.

2011, Apr. 5
1845-1846 A595 Set of 2 6.75 6.75

Souvenir Sheet

Flowers — A596

No. 1847: a, Delphinium "Verissimo del Titano." b, Dianthus "Sant'Agata." c, Rosa "Repubblica di San Marino."

2011, Apr. 5
1847 A596 €1.50 Sheet of 3, #a-c 11.00 11.00

Miniature Sheet

Tourism — A597

No. 1848 — Sites in San Marino: a, Prima Torre (First Tower). b, Basilica del Santo, horiz. c, Chiesa dei Cappuccini (Church of the Capuchin), horiz. d, Palazzo del Governo (Government Building). e, Chiesa di San Francesco (San Francesco Church). f, Porta San Francesco (San Francesco Gate).

2011, Apr. 5 ***Perf. 14¾***
1848 A597 65c Sheet of 6, #a-f 9.50 9.50

Brescia Soccer Team, Cent. — A598

2011, June 4 ***Perf. 14x14¾***
1849 A598 €1 multi 2.75 2.75

Visit of Pope Benedict XVI to San Marino A599

2011, June 4 ***Perf. 14¾x14***
1850 A599 €1 multi 2.75 2.75

Souvenir Sheet

Anita and Giuseppe Garibaldi, First Tower of San Marino — A600

2011, June 4 ***Perf. 14x13¼***
1851 A600 €1.50 multi 3.75 3.75

Granting of San Marino citizenship to Garibaldis. See Italy No. 3070.

Miniature Sheet

World Theater Day — A601

No. 1852: a, Statue of Liberty, San Marino, buildings. b, Mask with tassels, buildings. c, Character with arms extended. d, Face, three towers of San Marino. e, Face, dancers in ring. f, Dancers in ring.

2011, June 4 ***Perf. 13¾x13¼***
1852 A601 85c Sheet of 6, #a-f 12.00 12.00

A.C. Milan, 2010-11 Italian Soccer Champions A602

2011, Oct. 11 ***Perf. 14***
1853 A602 €1 multi 2.50 2.50

Alcide De Gasperi (1881-1954), Italian Prime Minister — A603

No. 1854 — De Gasperi and: a, 50c, Family, scales, war damage. b, €2.64, Torch, map of Europe.

2011, Oct. 11 ***Perf. 14x13½***
1854 A603 Horiz. pair, #a-b 7.50 7.50

Souvenir Sheet

European Year of Volunteering — A604

2011, Oct. 11 ***Perf. 14¾x14¼***
1855 A604 €4.95 multi 12.00 12.00

Souvenir Sheet

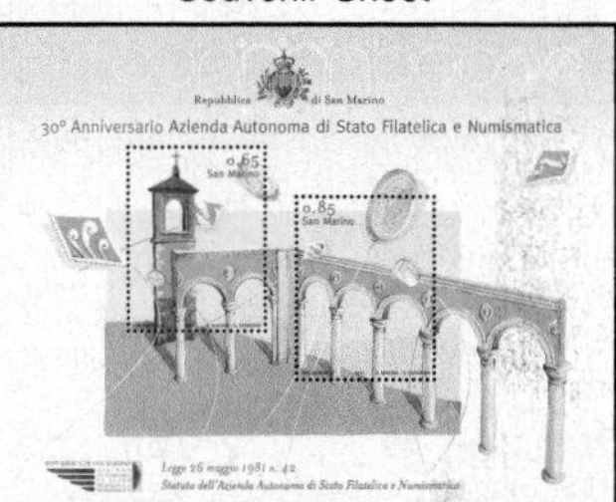

Philatelic and Numismatic Bureau of San Marino, 30th Anniv. — A605

No. 1856: a, 65c, Tower, arches, stamp and coins. b, 85c, Arches, stamp and coins.

2011, Oct. 11 ***Perf. 13½x14***
1856 A605 Sheet of 2, #a-b 3.50 3.50

Miniature Sheet

Christmas — A606

No. 1857: a, 85c, Angels. b, €1, Magi. c, €1.50, Shepherd and Mary. d, €2.50, Mary and infant Jesus.

2011, Oct. 11
1857 A606 Sheet of 4, #a-d 14.00 14.00

Milano Marittima, Italy, Cent. — A607

2012, Feb. 29
1858 A607 €1 multi 2.75 2.75

Miniature Sheet

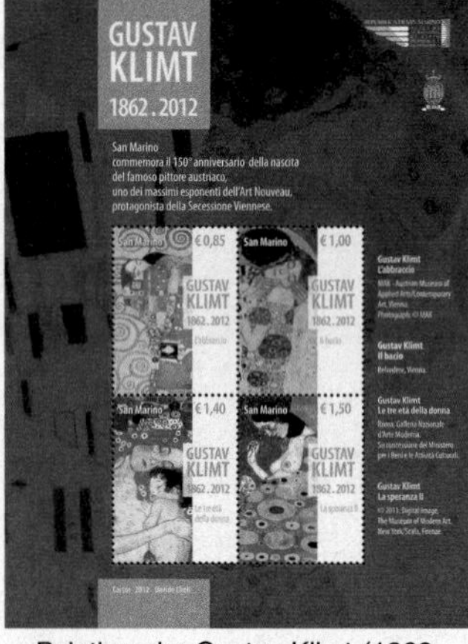

Paintings by Gustav Klimt (1862-1918) — A608

No. 1859: a, 85c, The Embrace (L'abbraccio). b, €1, The Kiss (Il bacio). c, €1.40, The Three Ages of Woman (Le tre età della donna). d, €1.50, Hope II (La speranza II).

2012, Feb. 29 ***Perf. 13¼x13***
1859 A608 Sheet of 4, #a-d 12.50 12.50

Souvenir Sheet

New San Marino Coat of Arms — A609

No. 1860: a, 60c, Crown, arms in blue. b, 85c, Berry on branch, arms in silver. c, €4.95, Old arms in circle, new arms in gold.

Litho. With Foil Application
2012, Feb. 29 ***Perf. 13x13¼***
1860 A609 Sheet of 3, #a-c 17.00 17.00

Faetano Ceramics, 50th Anniv. A610

2012, May 9 **Litho.** ***Perf. 14***
1861 A610 65c multi 1.75 1.75

Santos Soccer Team, Cent. — A611

2012, May 9 ***Perf. 14x14¾***
1862 A611 €1 multi 2.50 2.50

Intl. Year of Sustainable Energy For All — A612

No. 1863: a, Biomass energy. b, Geothermic energy. c, Hydroelectric and marine energy. d, Wind and solar energy.

2012, May 9 ***Perf. 13x13¼***
1863 A612 50c Block of 4, #a-d 5.00 5.00

Miniature Sheet

United Nations Convention on Preservation of World Heritage, 40th Anniv. — A613

No. 1864: a, Mt. Titano, construction workers, rose, painter holding brush, woman looking through binoculars. b, Painter, Pyramid, Egyptian statues, volcano. c, Charles Darwin, man and woman in water, pteranosaur, Galapagos sea tortoise. d, Scroll, rainbow, sailboat, man on ladder, cyclist, Eiffel Tower, building, sculpture.

2012, May 9 ***Perf. 13***
1864 A613 €1.50 Sheet of 4, #a-d 15.00 15.00

Juvenus, 2011-12 Italian Soccer Champions A614

2012, May 29 ***Perf. 13¼x13***
1865 A614 €1 multi 2.50 2.50

25th San Marino CEPU Open Tennis Championships — A615

2012, June 13 ***Perf. 13x13¼***
1866 A615 60c multi 1.50 1.50

Europa — A616

2012, June 13 ***Perf. 13¼x13***
1867 A616 65c multi 1.60 1.60

2012 Summer Olympics, London — A617

No. 1868: a, Olympic flame, woman wearing laurel garland. b, Swimmer wearing goggles and swim cap. c, Male athlete. d, Shooter wearing cap and ear protection.

2012, June 13 ***Perf. 13¼x13¾***
1868 A617 Horiz. strip of 4 5.00 5.00
a.-d. 50c Any single 1.25 1.25

Souvenir Sheet

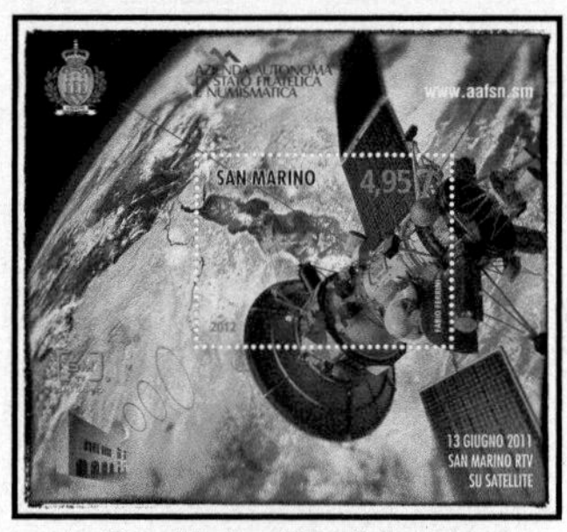

San Marino Television on Satellite — A618

2012, June 13 ***Perf. 13¾x14***
1869 A618 €4.95 multi 12.50 12.50

Italian Earthquake Relief — A619

2012, Aug. 30 ***Perf. 14***
1870 A619 €1 multi 2.60 2.60

San Marino-Rimini Electric Railway, 80th Anniv. — A620

2012, Oct. 16
1871 A620 €2.64 multi 6.75 6.75

Italian Socialist Politicians — A621

No. 1872: a, Filippo Turati (1857-1932). b, Giacomo Matteotti (1885-1924).

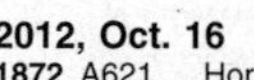

2012, Oct. 16 ***Perf. 13¼***
1872 A621 Horiz. pair + central label 11.50 11.50
a. €1.74 multi 4.50 4.50
b. €2.64 multi 6.75 6.75

Miniature Sheet

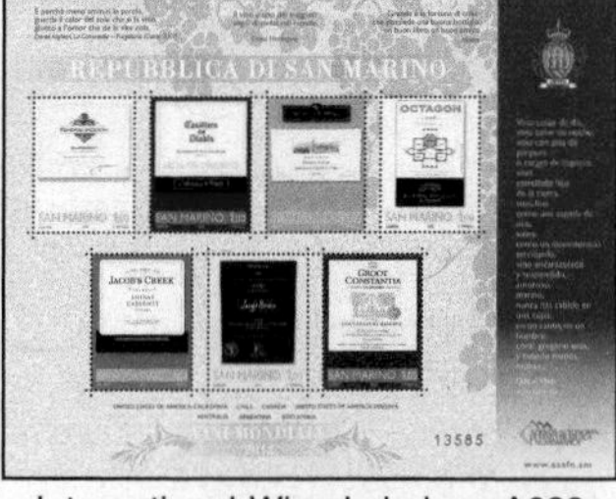

International Wine Labels — A622

No. 1873: a, Kendall-Jackson Chardonnay, United States. b, Casillero del Diablo Cabernet Sauvignon, Chile. c, Mission Hill Family Estate Pinot Noir, Canada. d, Octagon Red Table Wine, United States. e, Jacob's Creek Shiraz Cabernet, Australia. f, Luigi Bosca Malbec, Argentina. g, Groot Constantia Landgoed, South Africa.

2012, Oct. 16 ***Perf. 13¼x13***
1873 A622 €1 Sheet of 7, #a-g 18.00 18.00

Souvenir Sheet

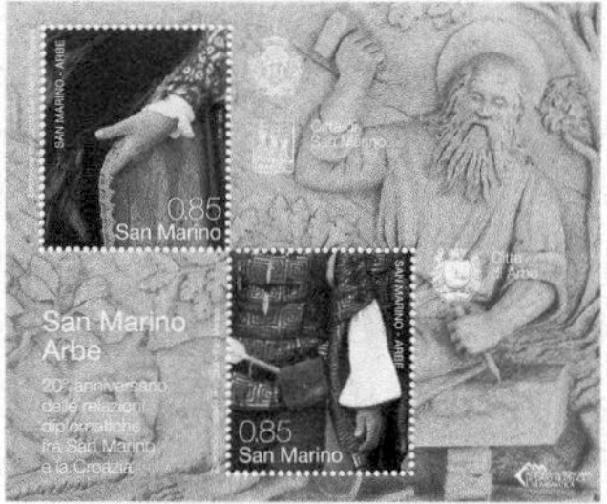

Diplomatic Relations Between San Marino and Croatia, 20th Anniv. — A623

No. 1874 — Traditional costumes with denomination at: a, LR. b, LL.

2012, Oct. 16 ***Perf. 14***
1874 A623 85c Sheet of 2, #a-b 4.50 4.50

See Croatia No. 851.

Madonna and Child, by Marco Ventura — A624

2012, Oct. 16
1875 A624 85c multi 2.25 2.25

Christmas.

A625

2013, Feb. 13 ***Perf. 13x13¼***
1876 A625 85c multi 2.25 2.25

San Marino World Symposium on Unidentified Flying Objects, 20th Anniv.

Souvenir Sheet

Edict of Milan, 1700th Anniv. — A626

No. 1877: a, Men and women, bas-reliefs of Roman Emperors Constantine and Licinius. b, Map of Europe, chrismon, medal.

2013, Feb. 13
1877 A626 €2.50 Sheet of 2, #a-b 13.00 13.00

Souvenir Sheet

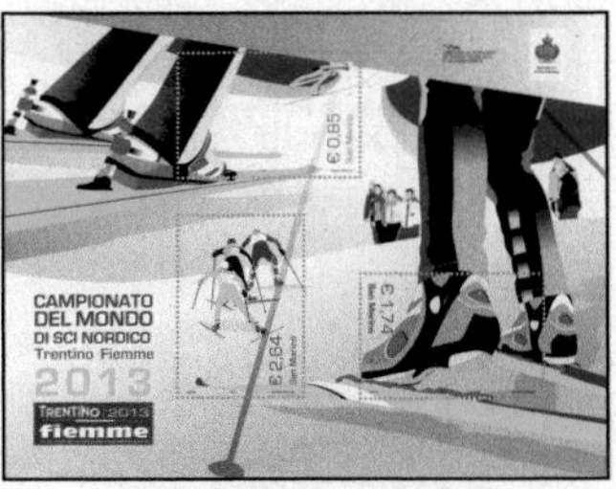

2013 World Nordic Skiing Championships, Val di Fiemme, Italy — A627

No. 1878: a, 85c, Ski jumper. b, €1.74, Boots of Nordic combined skier. c, €2.64, Cross-country skiers, vert.

2013, Feb. 13 ***Perf. 13***
1878 A627 Sheet of 3, #a-c 13.50 13.50

Tre Monti Cake and Emblem of La Serenissima Cake Company A628

2013, Apr. 3 ***Perf. 13x13$\frac{1}{4}$***
1879 A628 70c multi 1.90 1.90

Rimini to San Marino Flight of Gianni Widmer, Cent. — A629

2013, Apr. 3 ***Perf. 14***
1880 A629 €1.90 multi 5.00 5.00

Campaign to Prevent Cardiovascular Disease — A630

2013, Apr. 3
1881 A630 €2 multi 5.25 5.25

Europa A631

Designs: 70c, Porta San Francesco, automobile from early 20th cent., envelope. 85c, Parva Domus, Volkswagen van, 1950s, stamped cover.

2013, Apr. 3 ***Perf. 13x13$\frac{1}{4}$***
1882-1883 A631 Set of 2 4.00 4.00

Souvenir Sheet

Donation of Mount La Verna to St. Francis of Assisi, 800th Anniv. — A632

2013, Apr. 3 ***Perf. 13$\frac{1}{4}$x13$\frac{1}{2}$***
1884 A632 €3.50 multi 9.00 9.00

Genoa Cricket and Soccer Team, 120th Anniv. — A633

2013, Apr. 13 ***Perf. 14x14$\frac{3}{4}$***
1885 A633 €1 multi 2.60 2.60

European Patent Convention, 40th Anniv. — A634

2013, June 7 ***Perf. 13$\frac{1}{4}$x13***
1886 A634 85c multi 2.25 2.25

Juventus, 2012-13 Italian Soccer Champions A635

2013, June 7 ***Perf. 14***
1887 A635 €1 multi 2.75 2.75

Assistance of San Marino in Building of Nursery School in Matola, Malawi — A636

Rainbow and: 10c, Children, map of Africa. 70c, School building, horiz.

2013, June 7
1888-1889 A636 Set of 2 2.25 2.25

Souvenir Sheet

Church of St. John the Baptist, San Marino — A637

No. 1890: a, €1.90, Church exterior. b, €3.20, Church altar.

2013, June 7 ***Perf. 13$\frac{1}{4}$x13***
1890 A637 Sheet of 2, #a-b 14.00 14.00

Miniature Sheet

Determination of San Marino Borders, 550th Anniv. — A638

No. 1891 — Map of various border areas of San Marino, and: a, 70c, Insect. b, 85c, Bird. c, €1.90, Bird and flowers. d, €2, Bird, flowers, wax seal.

2013, June 7 ***Perf. 14x13$\frac{1}{4}$***
1891 A638 Sheet of 4, #a-d 15.00 15.00

See Italy No. 3191.

Italian Thematic Philately Center, 50th Anniv. — A639

2013, Oct. 9 Litho. ***Perf. 13$\frac{1}{2}$x14***
1892 A639 €1 multi 2.75 2.75

Scenes From Operas A640

Scene from: 70c, Aida, by Giuseppe Verdi (1813-1901). 85c, The Ring of the Nibelung, by Richard Wagner (1813-83).

2013, Oct. 9 Litho. ***Perf. 13x13$\frac{1}{4}$***
1893-1894 A640 Set of 2 4.25 4.25

Rally Legend, 10th Anniv. — A641

No. 1895: a, Lancia Delta, emblem at UL. b, Volkswagen Golf, emblem at UR.

2013, Oct. 9 Litho. ***Perf. 13x13$\frac{1}{4}$***
1895 A641 €1 Horiz. pair, #a-b 5.50 5.50

Miniature Sheet

UNESCO World Heritage Sites in Italy — A642

No. 1896: a, Basilica of St. Francis, Assisi (990). b, Ducal Palace, Urbino (828). c, Mausoleum of Theodoric, Ravenna (788). d, Estense Castle, Ferrara (733bis).

2013, Oct. 9 Litho. ***Perf. 13x13$\frac{1}{4}$***
1896 A642 €1.40 Sheet of 4, #a-d 15.50 15.50

Souvenir Sheet

Admission of San Marino to Council of Europe, 25th Anniv. — A643

No. 1897 — Arms of San Marino, ring of stars and "25" with: a, Dark blue background at left. b, White background at right.

2013, Oct. 9 Litho. ***Perf. 13x13$\frac{1}{4}$***
1897 A643 85c Sheet of 2, #a-b 4.75 4.75

Souvenir Sheet

Christmas — A644

No. 1898 — Various creche figures made by children with denominations in: a, Black, at LL. b, Brown, at LL. c, Black, at UL.

2013, Oct. 9 Litho. ***Perf. 13x13$\frac{1}{4}$***
1898 A644 70c Sheet of 3, #a-c 5.75 5.75

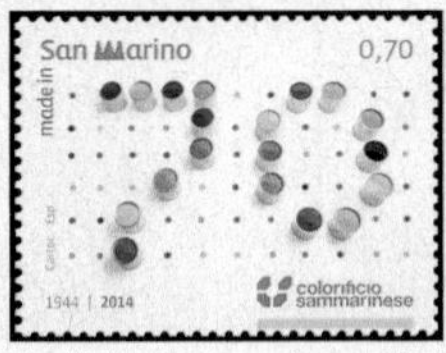

Colorificio Sammarinese Paint Manufacturer, 70th Anniv. — A645

2014, Mar. 17 Litho. ***Perf. 13x13$\frac{1}{4}$***
1899 A645 70c multi 2.00 2.00

Special Olympics Federation of San Marino, 30th Anniv. A646

2014, Mar. 17 Litho. ***Perf. 13x13$\frac{1}{4}$***
1900 A646 70c multi 2.00 2.00

A647

2014, Mar. 17 Litho. *Perf. 13x13¼*
1901 A647 85c multi 2.40 2.40

35th World Convention of the Intl. Confederation of Sport Fishing, San Marino.

Soroptimist International Single Club San Marino, 25th Anniv. — A648

2014, Mar. 17 Litho. *Perf. 13¼x13*
1902 A648 85c multi 2.40 2.40

Europa A649

Designs: 70c, Trumpet. 85c, French horn.

2014, Mar. 17 Litho. *Perf. 13¼*
1903-1904 A649 Set of 2 4.25 4.25

Campaign Against Gender-Based Violence — A650

Designs: 5c, Girl covering her eyes. 85c, Boy breaking stones (child labor). €1.90, Boy carrying military rifle, vert. €3.60, Frightened woman, vert.

Perf. 13x13¼, 13¼x13
2014, Mar. 17 Litho.
1905-1908 A650 Set of 4 17.50 17.50

Souvenir Sheet

Declaration of Rights Law, 40th Anniv. — A651

No. 1909 — Extended arms with denomination at: a, Center. b, Right.

2014, Mar. 17 Litho. *Perf. 13*
1909 A651 €2.50 Sheet of 2, #a-b 14.00 14.00

Convention of Friendship Between San Marino and Italy, 75th Anniv. A652

2014, June 5 Litho. *Perf. 13x13¼*
1910 A652 70c multi 1.90 1.90

See Italy No. 3243.

58th Plenary Assembly of PostEurop, San Marino A653

2014, June 5 Litho. *Perf. 13x13¼*
1911 A653 85c multi 2.40 2.40

Juventus, 2013-14 Italian Soccer Champions A654

2014, June 5 Litho. *Perf. 13x13¼*
1912 A654 €1 multi 2.75 2.75

Ayrton Senna (1960-94), Formula 1 Race Car Driver A655

2014, June 5 Litho. *Perf. 13x13¼*
1913 A655 €2.50 multi 7.00 7.00

Renata Tebaldi (1922-2004), Opera Singer — A656

No. 1914 — Tebaldi and: a, La Scala Theater, Milan. b, Titano Theater, Titano. c, San Carlo Theater, Naples.

2014, June 5 Litho. *Perf. 13x13¼*
1914 Horiz. strip of 3 19.00 19.00
a. A656 70c multi 1.90 1.90
b. A656 €2.50 multi 7.00 7.00
c. A656 €3.60 multi 10.00 10.00

Miniature Sheet

Municipalities in San Marino — A657

No. 1915 — Municipal arms and: a, Bell tower and cable car, Borgo Maggiore, b, Fountain, Acquaviva. c, Church, Faetano. d, Castellaccio of Mount Seghizzo, Fiorentino. e, Government Building, Città. f, Town Hall, Chiesanuova. g, Church, Domagnano. h, Church of St. Laurence, Montegiardino. i, Clock tower, Serravalle.

2014, June 5 Litho. *Perf. 14x14¼*
1915 A657 70c Sheet of 9, #a-i 17.50 17.50

Pitti Tondo, by Michelangelo (1475-1564) A658

2014, Oct. 22 Litho. *Perf. 13¼x13*
1916 A658 €5.35 multi 13.50 13.50

Galileo Galilei (1564-1642), Astronomer — A659

Designs: No. 1917, 70c, Globe, orrery, trial of Galileo. No. 1918, 70c, Telescope and compass.

2014, Oct. 22 Litho. *Perf. 13x13¼*
1917-1918 A659 Set of 2 3.50 3.50

Miniature Sheet

UNESCO World Heritage Sites in Italy — A660

No. 1919: a, €1, Verona Arena, Verona (797rev). b, €1.40, Piazza Ducale, Sabbioneta (1287). c, €2, Cathedral of Modena (827). d, €2.50, Palazzo Comunale and tower, San Gimignano (550).

2014, Oct. 22 Litho. *Perf. 13x13¼*
1919 A660 Sheet of 4, #a-d 17.50 17.50

Christmas — A661

Designs: 50c, Angel, Government Building, San Marino. 70c, Holy Family, Three Towers. 85c, Magi, Basilica of San Marino.

2014, Oct. 22 Litho. *Perf. 13¼x13*
1920-1922 A661 Set of 3 5.25 5.25

Europa A662

Designs: 80c, Rocking horse. 95c, Toy car.

2015, Mar. 10 Litho. *Perf. 13x13¼*
1923-1924 A662 Set of 2 4.00 4.00

Intl. Day of Happiness — A663

Happy children on: 95c, Globe. €2.30, Bird.

2015, Mar. 10 Litho. *Perf. 13¼x13*
1925-1926 A663 Set of 2 7.25 7.25

Revolution in Three-Dimensional Printing — A664

Designs: 10c, Apple in printer. 80c, Sphere in printer. €2.15, Woman's head in printer.

2015, Mar. 10 Litho. *Perf. 13¼x13*
1927-1929 A664 Set of 3 6.75 6.75

Buildings Designed by Gino Zani (1883-1964) — A665

Designs: 20c, Puntone della Murata Nuova. 30c, Portici del Mercato. €4, Portici e Cripta di Sant'Agata.

2015, Mar. 10 Litho. *Perf. 13x13¼*
1930-1932 A665 Set of 3 10.00 10.00

Souvenir Sheet

Expo 2015, Milan — A666

No. 1933: a, Man, grapes. b, Woman, jar of olive oil. c, Man, wheat.

Litho. With Foil Application
2015, Mar. 10 *Perf. 13¼x13*
1933 A666 €1 Sheet of 3, #a-c 6.75 6.75

Abolition of the Death Penalty in San Marino, 150th Anniv. — A667

2015, June 16 Litho. *Perf. 13¼x13*
1934 A667 €1.20 red & black 2.75 2.75

World Kiss Day — A668

No. 1935 — Stylized face of man or woman with background color: a, 5c, Green. b, 15c, Purple, c, 95c, Blue. d, €2.50, Yellow orange.

2015, June 16 Litho. *Perf. 13*
1935 A668 Block of 4, #a-d 8.25 8.25

World Teachers Day A669

Designs: 80c, Students standing on books, teacher. 95c, Teacher with flashlight leading students.

2015, June 16 Litho. *Perf. 13x13¼*
1936-1937 A669 Set of 2 4.00 4.00

World Toilet Day — A670

Stylized figures on toilet with background color of: 5c, Yellow orange. 15c, Red orange. €3, Blue.

2015, June 16 Litho. *Perf. 13¼x13*
1938-1940 A670 Set of 3 7.25 7.25

St. John Paul II (1920-2005) — A671

St. John Paul II: 70c, Praying. €2, Wearing miter. €2.15, Wearing zucchetto.

2015, June 16 Litho. *Perf. 13x13¼*
1941-1943 A671 Set of 3 11.00 11.00

Juventus, 2014-15 Italian Soccer Champions A672

2015, June 23 Litho. *Perf. 13¼x13*
1944 A672 €2 multi 4.50 4.50

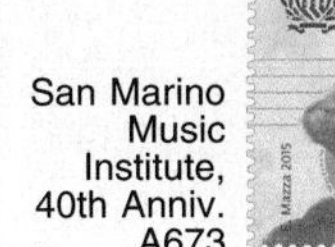

San Marino Music Institute, 40th Anniv. A673

2015, Oct. 23 Litho. *Perf. 14¾x14*
1945 A673 €3.30 multi 7.25 7.25

San Marino-Italy Techno Science Park — A674

Designs: €1.60, Balloon, flags of San Marino and Italy, stylized lightbulb, drone. €2.50, Lightbulb in head.

2015, Oct. 23 Litho. *Perf. 14¾x14*
1946-1947 A674 Set of 2 9.00 9.00

See Italy Nos. 3340-3341.

Design Degree Course of Study at University of San Marino, 10th Anniv. A675

Designs: €2, Stylized "10." €2.30, Man and woman in costumes of digits "1" and "0."

2015, Oct. 23 Litho. *Perf. 13¼*
Booklet Stamps
1948 A675 €2 gray & black 4.50 4.50
1949 A675 €2.30 multi 5.25 5.25
a. Booklet pane of 2, #1948-1949 9.75 —
Complete booklet, #1949a 9.75

St. John Bosco (1815-88) — A676

St. John Bosco: €1.20, Wearing biretta. €2.40, Without biretta.

Litho. With Foil Application
2015, Oct. 23 *Perf. 14x14¾*
1950-1951 A676 Set of 2 8.00 8.00

Bicent. of birth of St. John Bosco.

Christmas A677

Designs: 70c, Dove with olive branch. 80c, Two snowmen. 95c, San Marino buildings, Christmas tree, rainbow.

Litho. With Foil Application
2015, Oct. 23 *Perf. 14¾x14*
1952-1954 A677 Set of 3 5.50 5.50

Europa A678

2016, Mar. 10 Litho. *Perf. 13x13¼*
1955 A678 €1 multi 2.25 2.25

Think Green Issue.

Maria Lea Pedini, First Female Captain Regent — A679

2016, Mar. 10 Litho. *Perf. 13¼x13*
1956 A679 €2.55 multi 5.75 5.75

World Poetry Day — A680

Human head on: 95c, Tree. €1.20, Bird. €2.20, Flower.

2016, Mar. 10 Litho. *Perf. 13¼*
1957-1959 A680 Set of 3 10.00 10.00

Souvenir Sheet

Little Tony (1941-2013), Singer — A681

No. 1960 — Text comprising: a, Head of Little Tony. b, Heart. c, Mouth.

2016, Mar. 10 Litho. *Perf. 13¼x13*
1960 A681 €1.20 Sheet of 3, #a-c 8.25 8.25

Souvenir Sheet

International Jazz Day — A682

No. 1961: a, Drummer. b, Trumpet player. c, Guitarist.

2016, Mar. 10 Litho. *Perf. 13¼x13*
1961 A682 €1.60 Sheet of 3, #a-c 11.00 11.00

Juventus, 2015-16 Italian Soccer Champions A683

2016, June 7 Litho. *Perf. 13¼x13*
1962 A683 €2 multi 4.50 4.50

Italian Fertility Day — A684

No. 1963: a, Father (brt blue background). b, Mother (cerise background). c, Baby (white background).

2016, June 7 Litho. *Perf. 13¼*
1963 Horiz. strip of 3 6.00 6.00
a. A684 5c multi .25 .25
b. A684 10c multi .25 .25
c. A684 €2.50 multi 5.50 5.50

A gummed plastic circle with petunia seeds underneath is affixed to the face of No. 1963c.

Transfer of Body of St. Leo, 1000th Anniv. — A685

Designs: 20c, Fort of St. Leo. €2.70, St. Leo and church.

2016, June 7 Litho. *Perf. 13¼x13*
1964-1965 A685 Set of 2 6.50 6.50

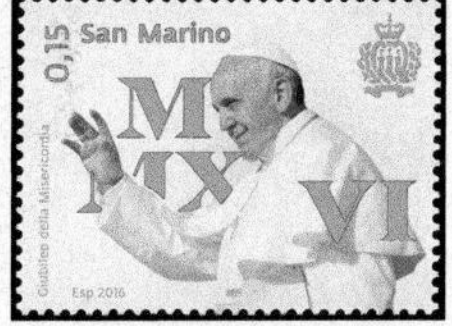

Jubilee of Mercy A686

Pope Francis: 15c, Giving blessing. 95c, Opening Holy Gate of St. Peter's Basilica. €1.60, Kissing sick child. €2, Touching hands of refugees.

Litho. With Foil Application
2016, June 7 *Perf. 13x13¼*
1966-1969 A686 Set of 4 10.50 10.50

Souvenir Sheet

Technological Love — A687

No. 1970: a, Couple taking selfie. b, Couple communicating over computer. c, Couple communicating on smartphones.

Serpentine Die Cut 12¼

2016, June 7 Litho.

Self-Adhesive

1970 A687 €1.60 Sheet of 3, #a-c, + 6 labels 11.00 11.00

Artificial Intelligence A688

Designs: 10c, Lightbulb with "Eureka" and "Startup" written as filament. €1, Woman's head, musical staff. €1.20, Stylized brain and electrical cords. €1.60, Stylized brain and lightbulbs.

2016, Oct. 18 Litho. ***Perf. 13***
1971-1974 A688 Set of 4 8.75 8.75

Souvenir Sheet

Fortifications of San Marino and Malta — A689

No. 1975: a, First Tower, San Marino. b, Citadella, Gozo, Malta.

2016, Oct. 18 Litho. ***Perf. 13x13¼***
1975 A689 €1.60 Sheet of 2, #a-b 7.25 7.25

See Malta No. 1578.

Souvenir Sheet

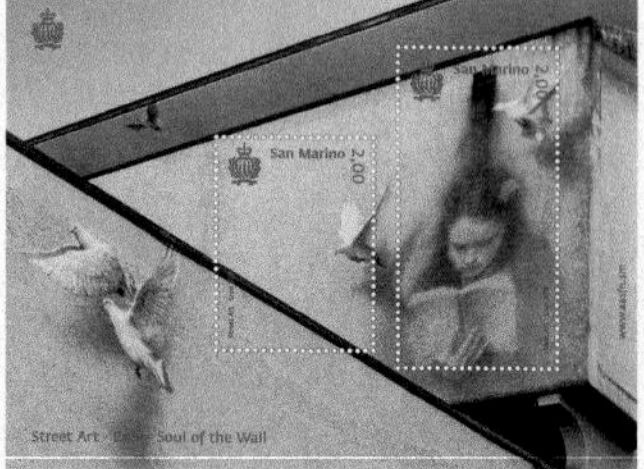

Soul of the Wall, by Eron — A690

No. 1976: a, Bird and edge of wall (30x40mm). b, Bird and girl reading book (30x60mm).

Perf. 13¼x13, 13 (#1976b)

2016, Oct. 18 Litho.
1976 A690 €2 Shet of 2, #a-b 9.00 9.00

Miniature Sheet

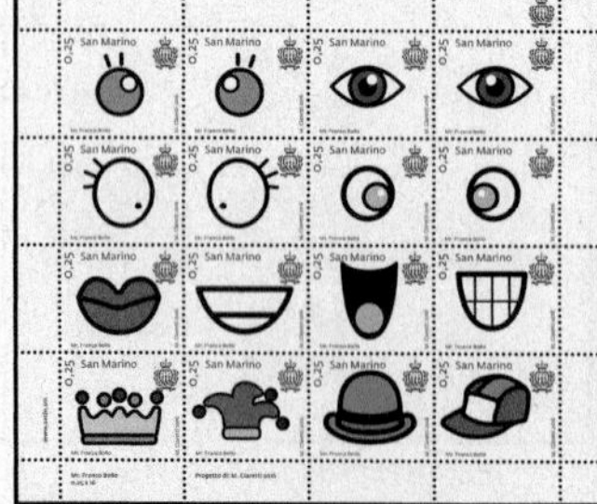

Body Parts and Head Coverings for Mr. Stamp — A691

No. 1977: a, Eye with two lashes, pupil at UR. b, Eye with two lashes, pupil at UL. c, Eye with brown iris, reflection circle at UR. d, Eye with brown iris, reflection circle at UL. e, Eye with three lashes, pupil at LR. f, Eye with three lashes, pupil at LL. g, Eye with blue iris at right. h, Eye with blue iris at left. i, Lips. j, Smile with one horizontal line. k, Open mouth and tongue. l, Smile with teeth. m, Crown. n, Jester's cap. o, Bowler hat. p, Cap.

2016, Oct. 18 Litho. ***Perf. 13¼***
1977 A691 25c Sheet of 16, #a-p 9.00 9.00

No. 1977 was sold with two unfranked postal cards with a line drawing that could be colored in and upon which stamps could be affixed.

Christmas A692

Designs: 70c, Girl embracing First Tower. 95c, Girl embracing Second Tower. €1, Family climbing toward Third Tower.

2016, Oct. 18 Litho. ***Perf. 13¼***
1978-1980 A692 Set of 3 6.00 6.00

Mario Simoncelli (1987-2011), Motorcycle Racer — A693

2017, Mar. 7 Litho. ***Perf. 13¼x13***
1981 A693 €2 multi 4.25 4.25

Europa — A694

Castles of San Marino: 95c, Cesta (second tower). €1, Guaita (first tower).

2017, Mar. 7 Litho. ***Perf. 13¼x13***
1982-1983 A694 Set of 2 4.25 4.25

Apparition of the Virgin Mary at Fatima, Portugal, Cent. — A695

Designs: €1, Fatima Basilica. €2.90, Apparition of Virgin Mary to children.

2017, Mar. 7 Litho. ***Perf. 13¼x13***
1984-1985 A695 Set of 2 8.50 8.50

2017 Games of the Small States of Europe, San Marino — A696

Designs: €2, San Marino tower and shooting target. €2.50, San Marino stylized wall and track lanes.

2017, Mar. 7 Litho. ***Perf. 13¼x13***
1986-1987 A696 Set of 2 9.75 9.75

Souvenir Sheet

David Bowie (1947-2016), Rock Musician — A697

No. 1988: a, Bowie as astronaut Major Tom. b, Lightning bolt. c, Bowie and crown.

2017, Mar. 7 Litho. ***Perf. 13¼x13***
1988 A697 €1.60 Sheet of 3, #a-c 10.50 10.50

A.S. Roma Soccer Team, 90th Anniv. — A698

2017, June 13 Litho. ***Perf. 13¼x13***
1989 A698 €2 multi 4.75 4.75

Juventus, 2016-17 Italian Soccer Champions A699

2017, June 13 Litho. ***Perf. 13¼x13***
1990 A699 €2 multi 4.75 4.75

First San Marino Postage Stamp, 140th Anniv. A700

Embroidered

2017, June 13 ***Imperf.***

Self-Adhesive

1991 A700 €4.70 white, *blue* 11.00 11.00

Campaign Against the Mafia A701

Designs: 95c, Murdered man. €1, Hand holding pistol. €2.20, Hand holding pistol in eye of skull.

2017, June 13 Litho. ***Perf. 13x13¼***
1992-1994 A701 Set of 3 9.50 9.50

Souvenir Sheet

Lorenzo Milani (1923-67), Catholic Priest — A702

No. 1995 — Milani: a, With head resting on hand. b, With speech balloon.

2017, June 13 Litho. ***Perf. 13¼x13***
1995 A702 €2 Sheet of 2, #a-b 9.25 9.25

Biometric Password Technology A703

Designs: 70c, Fingerprint. €1, Retina. €2.20, Voice scan.

Litho. With Foil Application

2017, Sept. 26 ***Perf. 13***
1996-1998 A703 Set of 3 9.25 9.25

Ban on Animal Testing in San Marino, 10th Anniv. — A704

Microscope and: 95c, Mouse. €1.20, Monkey. €2, Cat.

2017, Sept. 26 Litho. ***Perf. 13¼x13***
1999-2001 A704 Set of 3 9.75 9.75

World Refugee Day — A705

No. 2002 — Color of face: a, Dull mauve. b, Brown. c, Beige.

2017, Sept. 26 Litho. ***Perf. 13***
2002 Strip of 3 14.50 14.50
a.-c. A705 €2 Any single 4.75 4.75

Souvenir Sheet

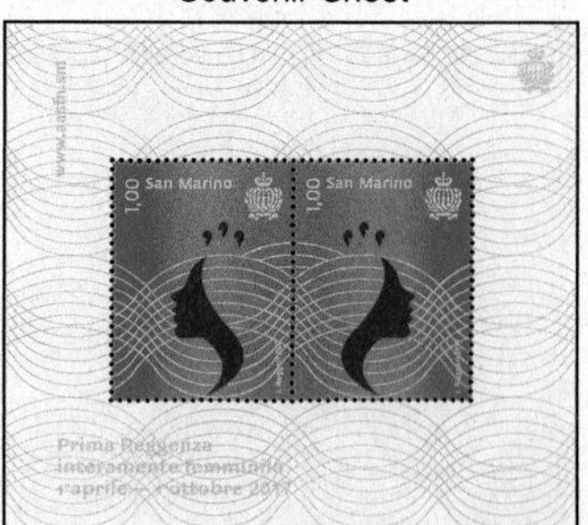

First Election of Two Female Captains Regent — A706

No. 2003 — Woman facing: a, Left. b, Right.

2017, Sept. 26 Litho. ***Perf. 13¼x13***
2003 A706 €1 Sheet of 2, #a-b 4.75 4.75

Christmas A707

Litho. With Foil Application

2017, Sept. 26 ***Perf. 13¼x13***
2004 A707 95c multi 2.25 2.25

Inter Milan Soccer Team, 110th Anniv. — A708

2018, Mar. 13 Litho. ***Perf. 13¼x13***
2005 A708 €2 sil & multi 5.00 5.00

Europa A709

Designs: 95c, Valdragone Railway Bridge and Three Towers. €1, Valdragone Railway Bridge.

2018, Mar. 13 Litho. ***Perf. 13x13¼***
2006-2007 A709 Set of 2 5.00 5.00

International Day of Families — A710

Designs: 70c, Child holding hugging parents (family as shelter). €1.20, Family, dog and stars (family structure). €2.50, Family on bicycle (family as a journey).

2018, Mar. 13 Litho. ***Perf. 13¼x13***
2008-2010 A710 Set of 3 11.00 11.00

Greetings — A711

Designs: 15c, Mother and child, "felicitazioni." €1, Birthday cake, balloon, gift, "buon compleanno." €1.60, Family, dog in car with luggage, "buone vacanze." €2.20, Couple drinking, Palazzo Pubblico, "buone feste."

2018, Mar. 13 Litho. ***Perf. 13¼x13***
2011-2014 A711 Set of 4 12.50 12.50

San Marino and Rab, Croatia as Sister Cities, 50th Anniv. A712

No. 2015: a, Tower on Mt. Titano, San Marino. b, St. Marinus. c, Bell Tower and seaside buildings, Rab.

2018, Mar. 13 Litho. ***Perf. 13x13¼***
2015 Horiz. strip of 3 9.00 9.00
a.-c. A712 €1.20 Any single 3.00 3.00

Metal Packaging by ASA Group — A713

2018, June 5 Litho. ***Perf. 13¼x13***
2016 A713 €1 yel & silver 2.40 2.40

Postal Services A714

Designs: 50c, Deer mailing letter. €1.60, Frog delivering letter to fish. €2, Elephants examining stamp collection.

2018, June 5 Litho. ***Perf. 13x13¼***
2017-2019 A714 Set of 3 9.50 9.50

Europe-China Tourism Year — A715

Combined European and Chinese buildings and: 70c, Cloud. 95c, Sun. €2.50, Rainbow.

2018, June 5 Litho. ***Perf. 13x13¼***
2020-2022 A715 Set of 3 9.75 9.75

Souvenir Sheet

San Marino Jinja — A716

No. 2023: a, Cherry blossoms and Three Towers of San Marino. b, Torii.

2018, June 5 Litho. ***Perf. 13½***
2023 A716 €2 Sheet of 2, #a-b 9.25 9.25

Souvenir Sheet

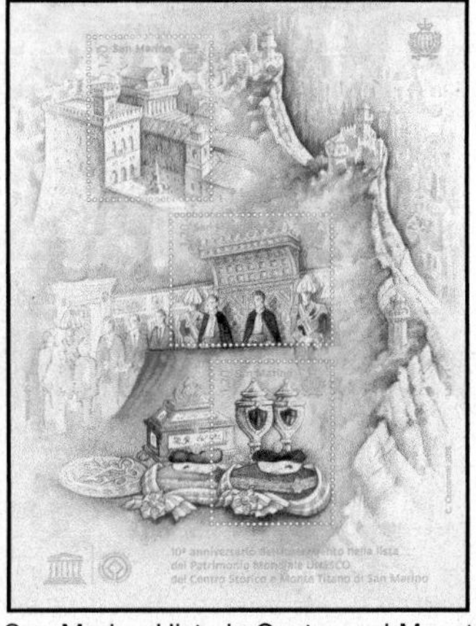

San Marino Historic Center and Mount Titano UNESCO World Heritage Sites — A717

No. 2024: a, Government Building and Parva Domus (30x40mm). b, Investiture ceremony of Captains Regent (40x32mm). c, Symbols of the Captains Regent (30x40mm).

Perf. 13¼x13 (#2024a, 2024c), 13½x13¾ (#2024b)

2018, June 5 Litho.
2024 A717 €1.20 Sheet of 3, #a-c 8.50 8.50

San Marino, First Nation in Europe With 5G Network A718

2018, Oct. 16 Litho. ***Perf. 13x13¼***
2025 A718 70c multi 1.60 1.60

Seventh Consecutive Italian Series A Championship of Juventus Soccer Team — A719

2018, Oct. 16 Litho. ***Perf. 13x13¼***
2026 A719 €2 multi 4.50 4.50

Paintings by Tintoretto (1518-94) A720

Designs: 5c, Annunciation. 40c, Visitation. €1.10, Adoration of the Magi. €2.60, Flight into Egypt.

2018, Oct. 16 Litho. ***Perf. 13x13¼***
2027-2030 A720 Set of 4 9.50 9.50

Souvenir Sheet

End of World War I, Cent. — A721

No. 2031: a, Reproduction of #B8 with text, "La pace è un processo, non un evento." b, Reproduction of #B7 with text, "I principe di pace sono ancora e saranno sempre immortali." c, Reproduction of #B6 with text, "La pace è un inizio, non una fine."

2018, Oct. 16 Litho. ***Perf. 13***
2031 A721 €1.20 Sheet of 3, #a-c 8.25 8.25

Souvenir Sheet

Christmas — A722

No. 2032 — Details from Pala Oliva altarpiece by Giovanni Santi (c. 1434-95): a, Saints George, Francis, Anthony the Great, and Jerome. b, Madonna and Child. c, Count Carlo Oliva and angel musicians.

Litho. With Foil Application

2018, Oct. 16 ***Perf. 13½***
2032 A722 €1.60 Sheet of 3, #a-c 11.00 11.00

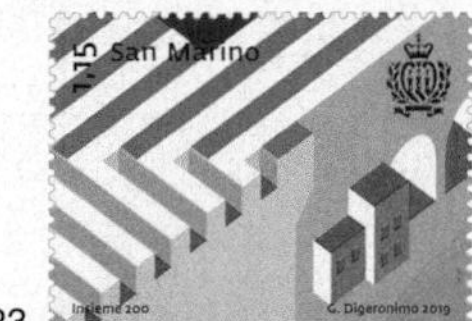

A723

2019, Feb. 26 Litho. ***Perf. 13x13¼***
2033 A723 €1.15 multi 2.60 2.60

Consular relations between San Marino and the United States, 200th anniv.

Europa A724

First Tower and: €1.10, Two peregrine falcons. €1.15, Peregrine falcon and chicks.

2019, Feb. 26 Litho. ***Perf. 13x13¼***
2034-2035 A724 Set of 2 5.25 5.25

National Alpini Association, Cent. — A725

Designs: 5c, Alpine soldier on side of mountain. €1.30, Alpine soldier on mountain peak. €2, Two Alpine soldiers at Mozza Column Memorial, Mount Ortigara, Italy.

2019, Feb. 26 Litho. ***Perf. 13¼x13***
2036-2038 A725 Set of 3 7.25 7.25

Paintings
A726

Designs: 10c, Annunciation, by Leonardo da Vinci (1452-1519). 50d, Madonna with Child and Two Angels, by Fra Filippo Lippi (c. 1406-69). €2.60, Self-portrait as a Young Man, by Rembrandt (1606-69).

2019, Feb. 26 Litho. *Perf. 13¼*
2039-2041 A726 Set of 3 7.25 7.25

International Day of Sport for Development and Peace — A727

Designs: 70c, Cycling. €1.10, Weight lifting. €1.30, Swimming. €1.60, Horse racing.

2019, Feb. 26 Litho. *Perf. 13x13¼*
2042-2045 A727 Set of 4 10.50 10.50

Souvenir Sheet

International Women's Day — A728

No. 2046 — Female: a, Ice skater. b, Gymnast. c, Runner.

2019, Feb. 26 Litho. *Perf. 13¼x13*
2046 A728 €1.20 Sheet of 3, #a-c 8.25 8.25

2019 European Men's Under-21 Soccer Championships, Italy and San Marino — A729

2019, May 7 Litho. *Perf. 13x13¼*
2047 A729 €2 multi 4.50 4.50

Italian Words A730

Designs: 25c, Scusa (sorry). 40c, Per favore (please). €1.10, Permesso (excuse me). €2.90, Grazie (thank you).

2019, May 7 Litho. *Perf. 13x13¼*
2048-2051 A730 Set of 4 10.50 10.50

Souvenir Sheet

San Marino Comics Festival — A731

No. 2052: a, First Tower, San Marino. b, Diabolik and Eva Kant kissing.

2019, May 7 Litho. *Perf. 13½*
2052 A731 €2 Sheet of 2, #a-b 9.00 9.00

Souvenir Sheet

Anniversaries of European Organizations — A732

No. 2053: a, Council of Europe, 70th anniv. (dove flying left). b, European Court of Human Rights, 60th anniv. (dove flying right).

2019, May 7 Litho. *Perf. 13¼x13*
2053 A732 €2.20 Sheet of 2, #a-b 10.00 10.00

Abarth Automobiles, 70th Anniv. — A733

2019, Oct. 2 Litho. *Perf. 13¼*
2054 A733 €1.60 multi 3.75 3.75

Juventus, 2018-19 Italian Soccer Champion A734

2019, Oct. 2 Litho. *Perf. 13¼x13*
2055 A734 €2 multi 4.50 4.50

A. C. Milan Soccer Team, 120th Anniv. A735

2019, Oct. 2 Litho. *Perf. 13x13¼*
2056 A735 €2.20 gold & multi 5.00 5.00

Souvenir Sheet

First Man on the Moon, 50th Anniv. — A736

No. 2057: a, Astronaut's foot touching Moon. b, Command and Service Module in space. c, Astronaut and Earth.

Litho. With Lenticular Lens Affixed
2019, Oct. 2 *Perf. 14½x14¾*
2057 A736 €2 Sheet of 3, #a-c 13.50 13.50

If you tilt No. 2057 one way it shows in left margin date of 1969 and foot above moon. If you tilt it the other way the date changes to 2019 and the foot touches the moon.

Souvenir Sheet

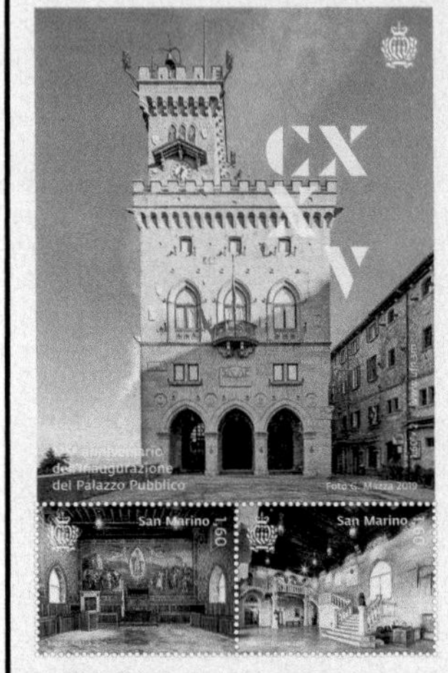

Palazzo Publico, 125th Anniv. — A737

No. 2058: a, Council Hall. b, Foyer and staircase.

2019, Oct. 2 Litho. *Perf. 13x13¼*
2058 A737 €1.60 Sheet of 2, #a-b 7.25 7.25

Souvenir Sheet

Christmas — A738

No. 2059: a, Annunciation (40x26mm). b, Nativity (40x40mm).

Perf. 13x13¼ (#2059a), 14 (#2059b)
2019, Oct. 2 Litho.
2059 A738 €2 Sheet of 2, #a-b 9.00 9.00

SEMI-POSTAL STAMPS

Regular Issue of 1903 Surcharged

a

b

1917, Dec. 15 Wmk. 140 *Perf. 14*

B1	A10(a)	25c on 2c violet	15.00	15.00
B2	A11(b)	50c on 2 l violet	60.00	60.00

Statue of Liberty — SP1

View of San Marino SP2

1918, June 1 Typo.

B3	SP1	2c dl vio & blk	3.75	3.75
B4	SP1	5c bl grn & blk	3.75	3.75
B5	SP1	10c lake & blk	3.75	3.75
B6	SP1	20c brn org & blk	3.75	3.75
B7	SP1	25c ultra & blk	3.75	3.75
B8	SP1	45c yel brn & blk	3.75	3.75
B9	SP2	1 l bl grn & blk	20.00	*24.00*
B10	SP2	2 l vio & blk	17.00	*21.00*
B11	SP2	3 l claret & blk	17.00	*21.00*
		Nos. B3-B11 (9)	76.50	88.50

These stamps were sold at an advance of 5c each over face value, the receipts from that source being devoted to the support of a hospital for Italian soldiers.

For surcharges see Nos. 89-92. See No. 2031 for surcharges on reproduced stamps.

Nos. B6-B8 Overprinted

1918, Dec. 12

B12	SP1	20c brn org & blk	6.00	6.00
B13	SP1	25c ultra & blk	6.00	6.00
B14	SP1	45c yel brn & blk	6.00	6.00

Nos. B9-B11 Ovptd.

B15	SP2	1 l blue grn & blk	10.50	10.50
B16	SP2	2 l violet & blk	19.00	20.00
B17	SP2	3 l claret & blk	19.00	20.00
		Nos. B12-B17 (6)	66.50	68.50

Celebration of Italian Victory over Austria. Inverted overprints were privately produced.

Coat of Arms
SP3

Liberty
SP4

1923, Sept. 20 **Engr.**

B18 SP3 5c + 5c olive grn .80 .80
B19 SP3 10c + 5c orange .80 .80
B20 SP3 15c + 5c dk green .80 .80
B21 SP3 25c + 5c brn lake .80 .80
B22 SP3 40c + 5c vio brn 4.00 4.00
B23 SP3 50c + 5c gray 2.40 .80
B24 SP4 1 l + 5c blk & bl 8.00 8.00
Nos. B18-B24 (7) 17.60 16.00

St. Marinus
SP5

Wmk. 140

1944, Apr. 25 **Photo.** ***Perf. 14***

B25 SP5 20 l + 10 l gldn brn 2.40 2.40
Never hinged 5.00 5.00
Sheet of 8 110.00 110.00
Never hinged 225.00

The surtax was used for workers' houses. See No. CB1.

No. 256 Surcharged in Red "L. 10"

1946, Aug. 24 **Unwmk.**

B26 A46 50 l + 10 l 20.00 20.00
Never hinged 40.00
Sheet of 10 *800.00* *800.00*
Never hinged 1,500.

Third Philatelic Day, Rimini. The surtax was for the exhibition.

Air Post Types of 1946 Surcharged "CONVEGNO FILATELICO / 30 NOVEMBRE 1946 / + LIRE 25" (or "LIRE 50") in Red or Violet

1946, Nov. 30 **Wmk. 277**

B26A AP7 3 l + 25 l dk brn (R) .95 .95
B26B AP8 5 l + 25 l red org (V) .95 .95
B26C AP6 10 l + 50 l ultra (R) 7.25 6.75
Nos. B26A-B26C (3) 9.15 8.65
Set, never hinged 20.00

Inscription "Posta Aerea" does not appear on these stamps.

No. 260 Surcharged in Black

1947, Nov. 13 **Wmk. 217** ***Perf. 12***

B27 A53 1 l + 1 l brt grn & vio .30 .30
B28 A53 1 l + 2 l brt grn & vio .30 .30
B29 A53 1 l + 3 l brt grn & vio .30 .30
B30 A53 1 l + 4 l brt grn & vio .30 .30
B31 A53 1 l + 5 l brt grn & vio .30 .30
a. Strip of 5, #B27-B31 2.00 2.00

Surcharged on No. 261

B32 A53 2 l + 1 l pur & olive .30 .30
B33 A53 2 l + 2 l pur & olive .30 .30
B34 A53 2 l + 3 l pur & olive .30 .30
B35 A53 2 l + 4 l pur & olive .30 .30
B36 A53 2 l + 5 l pur & olive .30 .30
a. Strip of 5, #B32-B36 2.00 2.00

Surcharged on No. 262

B37 A53 4 l + 1 l 2.10 2.10
B38 A53 4 l + 2 l 2.10 2.10
a. Pair, #B37-B38 14.50 14.50
Nos. B27-B38 (12) 7.20 7.20
Set, never hinged 18.00

Surcharges on Nos. B27-B38 are arranged consecutively, changing from ascending to descending order of denomination on alternate rows in the sheet.

Catalogue values for unused stamps in this section, from this point to the end of the section, are for Never Hinged items.

Refugee Boy — SP6

1982, Dec. 15 **Photo.** ***Perf. 11½***

B39 SP6 300 l + 100 l multi .40 .40

Surcharge was for refugee support.

AIR POST STAMPS

View of San Marino
AP1

Wmk. 217

1931, June 11 **Engr.** ***Perf. 12***

C1 AP1 50c blue grn 32.50 22.50
C2 AP1 80c red 32.50 22.50
C3 AP1 1 l bister brn 9.50 11.00
C4 AP1 2 l brt violet 9.50 11.00
C5 AP1 2.60 l Prus bl 65.00 *80.00*
C6 AP1 3 l dk gray 55.00 62.50
C7 AP1 5 l olive grn 9.50 11.00
C8 AP1 7.70 l dk brown 19.00 22.50
C9 AP1 9 l dp orange 19.00 22.50
C10 AP1 10 l dk blue 325.00 *500.00*
Nos. C1-C10 (10) 576.50 765.50
Set, never hinged 1,400.

Exist imperf. Value, set $15,000.
For surhcarges see Nos. C11-C20.

Graf Zeppelin Issue

Stamps of Type AP1 Surcharged in Blue or Black

1933, Apr. 28

C11 AP1 3 l on 50c org 8.50 *155.00*
C12 AP1 5 l on 80c ol grn 42.50 *155.00*
C13 AP1 10 l on 1 l dk bl (Bk) 42.50 *200.00*
C14 AP1 12 l on 2 l yel brn 42.50 *250.00*
C15 AP1 15 l on 2.60 l dl red (Bk) 42.50 *260.00*
C16 AP1 20 l on 3 l bl grn (Bk) 42.50 *425.00*
Nos. C11-C16 (6) 221.00 *1,445.*
Set, never hinged 440.00

Exist imperf.

Nos. C1 and C2 Surcharged

1936, Apr. 14

C17 AP1 75c on 50c blue grn 2.10 2.10
C18 AP1 75c on 80c red 12.50 12.50
Set, never hinged 37.50

Nos. C5 and C6 Surcharged with New Value and Bars

1941, Jan. 12

C19 AP1 10 l on 2.60 l 85.00 85.00
C20 AP1 10 l on 3 l 27.50 27.50
Set, never hinged 225.00

View of Arbe — AP2

Wmk. 140

1942, Mar. 16 **Photo.** ***Perf. 14***

C21 AP2 25c brn & gray blk .30 .30
C22 AP2 50c grn & brn .30 .30
C23 AP2 75c gray bl & red brn .30 .30
C24 AP2 1 l ocher & brn .70 .70
C25 AP2 5 l bis brn & bl 6.25 6.25
Nos. C21-C25 (5) 7.85 7.85
Set, never hinged 14.00

Return of the Italian flag to Arbe.

AP3

Overprinted in Black

1943, Aug. 27

C26 AP3 25c yellow org .30 .30
C27 AP3 50c car rose .30 .30
C28 AP3 75c dark brown .30 .30
C29 AP3 1 l dk rose vio .30 .30
C30 AP3 2 l sapphire .30 .30
C31 AP3 5 l orange red 1.40 1.40
C32 AP3 10 l deep green 2.10 2.10
C33 AP3 20 l black 7.00 7.00
Nos. C26-C33 (8) 12.00 12.00
Set, never hinged 21.00

See footnote after No. 227. Nos. C26-C33 exist without overprint (not regularly issued). Value $1,500.

San Marino Map, Fasces and Wing — AP4

Overprinted in Black

1943, Aug. 27

C34 AP4 25c yellow org .30 .30
C35 AP4 50c car rose .30 .30
C36 AP4 75c dark brown .30 .30
C37 AP4 1 l dk rose vio .30 .30
C38 AP4 5 l orange red 1.10 1.10
C39 AP4 20 l black 2.75 2.75
Nos. C34-C39 (6) 5.05 5.05
Set, never hinged 8.50

Government Palace — AP5

1945, Mar. 15 **Photo.**

C40 AP5 25 l bister brn 5.75 5.75

See note after No. 239.

Gulls and San Marino Skyline
AP6

Plane and View of San Marino
AP7

Planes over Mt. Titano — AP8

Plane over Globe
AP9

Photo., Engr. (20 l, 50 l)

1946-47 **Unwmk.** ***Perf. 14***

C41 AP6 25c blue blk .25 .25
C42 AP7 75c red org .25 .25
C43 AP6 1 l brown .25 .25
C44 AP7 2 l dull green .25 .25
C45 AP7 3 l violet .25 .25
C46 AP8 5 l violet blue .25 .25
C47 AP6 10 l crimson .25 .25
C48 AP8 20 l brown lake 1.60 1.60
C49 AP8 35 l orange red 4.75 *6.00*
C50 AP8 50 l dk yellow grn 8.00 *9.00*
C51 AP9 100 l sepia ('47) 1.25 1.25
Nos. C41-C51 (11) 17.35 19.60
Set, never hinged 30.00

Some values exist imperforate.
Issue dates: 35 l, Nov. 3, 1946; 100 l, Mar. 27, 1947; others, Aug. 8, 1946.
For surcharges and overprint see Nos. B26A-B26C, C54.

Roosevelt Type of Regular Issue, 1947

F. D. Roosevelt and: 1 l, 31 l, 50 l, Eagle. 2 l, 20 l, 100 l, San Marino arms. 5 l, 200 l, Flags of San Marino and US, vert.

Wmk. 277

1947, May 3 **Photo.** ***Perf. 14***

C51A A52a 1 l dp ultra & sep .25 .25
C51B A52a 2 l org red & sep .25 .25
C51C A52a 5 l multicolored .25 .25
C51D A52a 20 l choc & sep .25 .25
C51E A52a 31 l org & sep .50 .50
C51F A52a 50 l dk car & sep .90 .90
C51G A52a 100 l bl & sepia 3.00 1.75
C51H A52a 200 l multicolored 18.50 15.00
Nos. C51A-C51H (8) 23.90 19.15
Set, never hinged 50.00

Nos. C51A-C51E, C51H exist imperf. Value, set $150.

Nos. C51A-C51C Surcharged

1947, June 16

C51I A52a 3 l on 1 l dp ultra & sep .40 .40
C51J A52a 4 l on 2 l org red & sep .40 .40
C51K A52a 6 l on 5 l multicolored .40 .40
Nos. C51I-C51K (3) 1.20 1.20
Set, never hinged 2.50

St. Marinus Type of Regular Issue, 1947

Wmk. 217

1947, July 18 Engr. *Perf. 12*

Center in Bright Blue

C52 A53 25 l deep orange 1.25 1.25
C53 A53 50 l red brown 2.75 2.50
Set, never hinged 8.00

No. C51 Overprinted in Red

1947, July 18 Unwmk. *Perf. 14*

C54 AP9 100 l sepia 1.25 1.25
Never hinged 2.00
a. Double overprint 160.00
Never hinged 260.00
b. Inverted overprint 160.00
Never hinged 260.00

Rimini Phil. Exhib., July 18-20.

US No. 1 and Mt. Titano AP11

Wmk. 277

1947, Dec. 24 Engr. *Perf. 14*

C55 AP11 100 l dk pur & dk brn 10.00 10.00
Never hinged 20.00
Sheet of 10 *2,500.*
a. Imperf. 160.00
Never hinged 300.00
As "a," sheet of 10 *8,000.*

1st US postage stamps, cent.

No. 264 Surcharged in Black

1948, Oct. 9 Wmk. 217 *Perf. 12*

C56 A53 200 l on 25 l 30.00 30.00
Never hinged 60.00

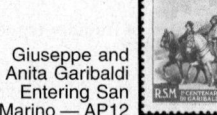

Giuseppe and Anita Garibaldi Entering San Marino — AP12

Wmk. 277

1949, June 28 Photo. *Perf. 14*

Size: 27½x22mm

C57 AP12 2 l brn red & ultra .30 .30
C58 AP12 3 l dk grn & sep .30 .30
C59 AP12 5 l dk bl grn & ultra .30 .30

Size: 37x22mm

C60 AP12 25 l dk green & vio 2.75 1.75
C61 AP12 65 l grnsh blk & gray blk 12.00 9.00
Nos. C57-C61 (5) 15.65 11.65
Set, never hinged 30.00

Garibaldi's escape to San Marino, cent.

Stagecoach on Road from San Marino AP13

1950, Feb. 9 Engr. *Perf. 14*

C62 AP13 200 l deep blue 1.50 1.50
Never hinged 2.50
a. Perf. 13½x14 ('51) 3.50 3.50
Never hinged 5.00
As "a," sheet of 6 40.00 40.00
Never hinged 70.00
b. Imperf ('51) 22.50 20.00
As "b," sheet of 6 275.00 275.00
Never hinged 450.00

UPU, 75th anniv. No. C62 was issued in sheets of 25; Nos. C62a & C62b in sheets of 6. See No. C75.

AP14

AP15

AP16

Various Views of San Marino.

1950, Apr. 12 Photo. *Perf. 14*

Size: 27½x21½mm, 21½x27½mm

C63 AP14 2 l vio & dp grn .35 .25
C64 AP14 3 l blue & brn .35 .25
C65 AP15 5 l brn blk & rose red .35 .25
C66 AP14 10 l grnsh blk & bl 1.40 .60
C67 AP14 15 l grnsh blk & vio 1.60 .75

Size: 36x26½mm, 26½x36mm

C68 AP15 55 l dp bl & dp grn 24.00 18.00
C69 AP14 100 l car & gray 18.00 15.00
C70 AP15 250 l violet & brn 77.50 40.00

Engr.

C71 AP16 500 l bl, dk grn & vio brn 65.00 *85.00*
Nos. C63-C71 (9) 188.55 160.10
Set, never hinged 425.00

See No. C78. For overprints and surcharges see Nos. C72-C74, C76, C79.

Types of 1950 Overprinted in Black, Blue or Brown

1950, Apr. 12 Photo.

New Colors; Sizes as Before

C72 AP15 5 l dp bl & dp grn .25 .25
C73 AP14 15 l car & gray (Bl) .55 .55
C74 AP15 55 l vio & brn (Br) 4.00 4.00
Nos. C72-C74 (3) 4.80 4.80
Set, never hinged 7.50

San Marino's participation in the 28th Intl. Fair of Milan, Apr., 1950.
Overprint on Nos. C73-C74 is on four lines.

Stagecoach Type of 1950

1951, Jan. 31 Engr. *Perf. 13½x14*

C75 AP13 300 l rose brn & brn 19.00 19.00
Never hinged 30.00
Sheet of 6 200.00 225.00
Never hinged 400.00
a. Imperf. *800.00*
Never hinged *1,400.*
Sheet of 6 *4,500.* 5,000.
Never hinged *8,000.*

No. C71 Surcharged in Black "Giornata Filatelica San Marino-Riccione 20-8-1951," New Value and Bars

1951, Aug. 20 *Perf. 14*

C76 AP16 300 l on 500 l 35.00 35.00
Never hinged 80.00

Flag and Plane AP17

Perf. 13½x14

1951, Nov. 22 Engr. Wmk. 277

C77 AP17 1000 l multi 500.00 500.00
Never hinged 700.00
Sheet of 6 *7,000.* *7,000.*
Never hinged *9,000.*

Type of 1950

1951, Apr. 28 Photo. *Perf. 14*

Size: 36x26½mm

C78 AP16 500 l dk grn & brn 110.00 110.00
Never hinged 250.00
Sheet of 6 2,250. 2,250.
Never hinged 3,000.

No. C78 exists imperf.

No. C70 Surcharged in Black

1951, Dec. 6

C79 AP15 100 l on 250 l 4.00 4.00
Never hinged 6.50

Issued to raise funds for flood victims in northern Italy.

Columbus, Globe, Statue of Liberty and Buildings AP18

1952, Jan. 28 Engr.

C80 AP18 200 l dk bl & blk 27.50 27.50
Never hinged 55.00

Issued to honor Christopher Columbus.

No. C80 Overprinted in Red

1952, June 29

C81 AP18 200 l blk brn & choc 35.00 35.00
Never hinged 70.00

4th Intl. Sample Fair of Trieste.

Cyclamen — AP19

Flowers and Seacoast — AP20

2 l, As Nos. C85-C87 with flowers omitted. 3 l, Rose.

1952, Aug. 25 Photo. *Perf. 10x14*

C82 AP19 1 l pur & lil rose .25 .25
C83 AP19 2 l blue & bl grn .25 .25
C84 AP19 3 l dk brn & red .25 .25

Perf. 14

C85 AP20 5 l rose lil & brn .25 .25
C86 AP20 25 l vio & bl grn .25 .25

Perf. 13

Engr.

C87 AP20 200 l multi 40.00 40.00
Sheet of 6, #C87 800.00 800.00
Never hinged 1,000.
Nos. C82-C87 (6) 41.25 41.25
Set, never hinged 80.00

Riccione Phil. Exhib., Aug. 25, 1952.

Plane Making Photographic Survey — AP21

75 l, Aerial survey, seen through window.

1952, Nov. 17 Photo. *Perf. 14*

C88 AP21 25 l olive green 1.25 1.25
C89 AP21 75 l red brn & pur 4.25 4.25
Set, never hinged 8.00

Aerial photographic survey of San Marino, 1952.

Skier AP22

1953, Apr. 20 Engr.

C90 AP22 200 l bl grn & dk grn 45.00 45.00
Never hinged 90.00
Sheet of 6 1,000. 800.00
Never hinged 1,250.

Plane and Arms of San Marino AP23

1954, Apr. 5

C91 AP23 1000 l dk blue & brn 100.00 100.00
Never hinged 150.00
Sheet of 6 1,000. 1,000.
Never hinged 1,250.

Type of Regular Issue, 1954

1954, Dec. 16 Photo. *Perf. 13*

C92 A71 120 l dp bl & red brn 1.10 1.10
Never hinged 2.25

Hurdler AP25

1955, June 26 Wmk. 303 *Perf. 14*
C93 AP25 80 l shown 1.00 1.00
C94 AP25 120 l Relay 1.50 1.25
Set, never hinged 4.75

San Marino's first Intl. Exhib. of Olympic Stamps, June.

Ski Jumper
AP26

1955, Dec. 15
C95 AP26 200 l blk & red org 17.50 17.50
Never hinged 35.00

7th Winter Olympic Games at Cortina d'Ampezzo, Jan. 26-Feb. 5, 1956.

No. 372 Overprinted in Upper Right Corner with Plane and "Posta Aerea"

1956, Dec. 10
C96 A76 100 l blk & Prus grn 1.40 *2.00*
Never hinged 2.75

Catalogue values for unused stamps in this section, from this point to the end of the section, are for Never Hinged items.

Helicopter, Plane and Modernistic Building — AP27

Wmk. 303
1958, Apr. 12 Photo. *Perf. 14*
C97 AP27 125 l lt blue & brn 3.25 3.25

10th participation in Milan Fair.
See Nos. 414-415.

View of San Marino — AP28

Design: 300 l, Road from Mt. Titano.

Wmk. 303
1958, June 23 Engr. *Perf. 13*
C98 200 l brn & dk blue 4.75 4.75
C99 300 l magenta & vio 4.75 4.75
a. AP28 Strip, Nos. C98, C99 + label 10.00 10.00

Printed in sheets containing 20 each of Nos. C98 and C99 flanking a center label with San Marino coat of arms. Nos. C98 and C99 also come se-tenant in sheet.

Naples Stamps Type of Regular Issue

Design: Bay of Naples and 50g stamp of Naples.

1958, Oct. 8 Photo. *Perf. 14*
C100 A85 125 l brn & red brn 2.75 2.75

Sea Gull
AP29

Birds: 10 l, Falcon. 15 l, Mallard. 120 l, Stock dove. 250 l, Barn swallow.

1959, Feb. 12 *Perf. 14*
C101 AP29 5 l green & gray .25 .25
C102 AP29 10 l blue & org brn .25 .25
C103 AP29 15 l red & multi .25 .25
C104 AP29 120 l rose red, yel & gray blk 1.25 .60
C105 AP29 250 l dp grn, yel & blk 4.00 2.25
Nos. C101-C105 (5) 6.00 3.60

Pierre de Coubertin
AP30

Wmk. 303
1959, May 19 Engr. *Perf. 13*
C106 AP30 120 l sepia 4.50 3.25

Pierre de Coubertin; 1960 Olympic Games in Rome.

Alitalia Viscount Over San Marino
AP31

1959, June 3 Photo. *Perf. 14*
C107 AP31 120 l bright violet 2.00 2.00

First flight San Marino-Rimini-London.

Lincoln Type of Regular Issue, 1959

Design: Abraham Lincoln and San Marino peaks.

1959, July 1 Engr. *Perf. 14x13*
C108 A87 200 l dark blue 5.75 5.00

Romagna Stamps Type

Design: Bologna view, 3b Romagna stamp.

Wmk. 303
1959, Aug. 29 Photo. *Perf. 14*
C109 A88 120 l blk & blue grn 2.00 1.75

Sicily Stamps Type

Design: Fishing boats, Monte Pellegrino and 50g stamp of Sicily, horiz.

1959, Oct. 16
C110 A89 200 l multicolored 2.50 2.25

Olympic Games Type

Sports: 20 l, Basketball. 40 l, Sprint race. 80 l, Swimming, horiz. 125 l, Target shooting, horiz.

1960, May 23 Wmk. 303 *Perf. 14*
C111 A92 20 l lilac .25 .25
C112 A92 40 l bis brn & dk red .25 .25
C113 A92 80 l ultra & buff .25 .25
C114 A92 125 l ver & dk brn .35 .25
Nos. C111-C114 (4) 1.10 1.00

Souvenir sheets are valued and described below No. 465.

Lions Intl. Type

Design: 200 l, Globe and Lions emblem.

1960, July 1 Photo.
C115 A94 200 l ol grn, brn & ultra 7.50 7.50

12th Stamp Fair Type

1960, Aug. 27 Wmk. 303 *Perf. 14*
C116 A95 125 l multicolored 1.30 1.30

Helicopter and Mt. Titano
AP32

1961, July 6 Engr. *Perf. 14*
C117 AP32 1000 l rose car 52.50 35.00
Sheet of 6 350.00 250.00

Tupolev TU-104A
AP33

Planes: 10 l, Boeing 707, vert. 15 l, Douglas DC-8. 25 l, Boeing 707. 50 l, Vickers Viscount 837. 75 l, Caravelle, vert. 120 l, Vickers VC10. 200 l, D. H. Comet 4C. 300 l, Boeing 727. 500 l, Rolls Royce Dart turbo-prop. 1000 l, Boeing 707.

1963-65 Wmk. 339 Photo. *Perf. 14*
C118 AP33 5 l bl & vio brn .30 .30
C119 AP33 10 l org & dk bl .30 .30
C120 AP33 15 l violet & red .30 .30
C121 AP33 25 l violet & car .30 .30
C122 AP33 50 l grnsh bl & red .30 .30
C123 AP33 75 l emer & dp org .30 .30
C124 AP33 120 l vio bl & red .30 .30
C125 AP33 200 l brt yel & blk .50 .50
C126 AP33 300 l org & blk .50 .50

Perf. 13
C127 AP33 500 l multicolored 5.75 5.75
Sheet of 4 22.50 22.50
C128 AP33 1000 l lil rose, ultra & yel 2.75 2.75
Sheet of 4 25.00 25.00
Nos. C118-C128 (11) 11.60 11.60

Issued: Nos. C118-C126, Dec. 5, 1963. No. C127, Mar. 4, 1965. No. C128, Mar. 12, 1964.
No. C128 exists imperf.

Mt. Titano and Flight Symbolized
AP34

1972, Oct. 25 Unwmk. *Perf. 11½*
Granite Paper
C129 AP34 1000 l multi 1.75 1.75

Glider
AP35

Designs: Each stamp shows a different type of air current in background.

1974, Oct. 9 Photo. *Perf. 11½*
Granite Paper
C130 AP35 40 l multicolored .25 .25
C131 AP35 120 l multicolored .25 .25
C132 AP35 500 l multicolored .55 .55
Nos. C130-C132 (3) 1.05 1.05

50th anniversary of gliding in Italy.

San Marino 77 Type of 1977

1977, Jan. 28 Photo. *Perf. 11½*
C133 A193 200 l grn, blue & yel .30 .30

See Nos. 897-899.

Wright Brothers' Flyer A — AP36

1978, Sept. 28 Photo. *Perf. 11½*
C134 AP36 10 l multicolored .25 .25
C135 AP36 50 l multicolored .25 .25
C136 AP36 200 l multicolored .25 .25
Nos. C134-C136 (3) .75 .75

75th anniversary of first powered flight.

AIR POST SEMI-POSTAL STAMP

View of San Marino
APSP1

Wmk. 140
1944, Apr. 25 Photo. *Perf. 14*
CB1 APSP1 20 l + 10 l ol grn 2.40 2.40
Never hinged 4.75
Sheet of 8 100.00 100.00
Never hinged 175.00

The surtax was used for workers' houses.
No. CB1 exists imperf.

SPECIAL DELIVERY STAMPS

SD1

Unwmk.
1907, Apr. 25 Engr. *Perf. 12*
E1 SD1 25c carmine 35.00 17.50

For surcharges see Nos. E3, E5.

Type of Regular Issue of 1903 Overprinted

Perf. 14½x14
1923, May 30 Wmk. 140
E2 A11 60c violet 1.75 1.25

For surcharge see No. 103.

Type of 1907 Issue Surcharged

1923, July 26 *Perf. 14*
E3 SD1 60c on 25c carmine 1.50 1.25
a. Vert. pair, imperf. between 275.00

No. E2 Surcharged

1926, Nov. 25 *Perf. 14½x14*
E4 A11 1.25 l on 60c violet 1.90 1.90

No. E3 Surcharged

1927, Sept. 15

E5	SD1 1.25 l on 60c on 25c	1.50	1.25
a.	Inverted surcharge	175.00	
b.	Vert. pair, imperf. between	800.00	
c.	Double surcharge	190.00	

Statue of Liberty and View of San Marino — SD2

Wmk. 217

1929, Aug. 29 Engr. *Perf. 12*

E6	SD2 1.25 l green	.65	.50

Overprinted in Red

E7	SD2 2.50 l deep blue	1.00	1.00

Arms of San Marino SD3

Wmk. 140

1943, Sept. Photo. *Perf. 14*

E8	SD3 1.25 l green	.25	.25
E9	SD3 2.50 l reddish orange	.25	.25

View of San Marino SD4

Pegasus SD5

1945-46 Photo. Wmk. 140

E12	SD4 2.50 l deep green	.25	.25
E13	SD4 5 l deep orange	.25	.25

Unwmk.

E14	SD4 5 l carmine rose	1.00	.50

Wmk. 277

E15	SD4 10 l sapphire ('46)	2.00	2.00

Engr. Unwmk.

E16	SD5 30 l deep ultra ('46)	3.50	4.00
	Nos. E12-E16 (5)	7.00	7.00

See Nos. E22-E23. For surcharges see Nos. E17-E21, E24-E25.

No. E16 exists imperf.

Nos. E14 and E15 Srchd. in Black

1947 Unwmk. *Perf. 14*

E17	SD4 15 l on 5 l car rose	.25	.25

Wmk. 277

E18	SD4 15 l on 10 l saph	.25	.25

No. E16 Surcharged in Carmine

No E19

No. E20

No. E21

1947-48 Unwmk.

E19	SD5 35 l on 30 l ('48)	35.00	30.00
E20	SD5 60 l on 30 l	2.00	3.50
E21	SD5 80 l on 30 l ('48)	17.50	17.50
	Nos. E19-E21 (3)	54.50	51.00
	Set, never hinged	100.00	

Types of 1945-46

1950, Dec. 11 Photo. Wmk. 277

E22	SD4 60 l rose brown	7.50	7.50
E23	SD5 80 l deep blue	7.50	7.50
	Set, never hinged	30.00	

Nos. E22-E23 Surcharged with New Value and Three Bars

1957, Dec. 12 *Perf. 14*

E24	SD4 75 l on 60 l rose brn	1.75	*2.75*
E25	SD5 100 l on 80 l dp blue	1.75	*2.75*
	Set, never hinged	7.00	

Catalogue values for unused stamps in this section, from this point to the end of the section, are for Never Hinged items.

Crossbow and Mount Titan SD6

Design: No. E27, "Espresso" at left; crossbow casts two shadows.

1965, Aug. 28 Photo. Wmk. 339

E26	SD6 120 l on 75 l blk, gray & yel	.25	.25
E27	SD6 135 l on 100 l blk & org	.25	.25

SD6a

Design: 75 l, As No. E26 without surcharge. 80 l, 100 l, Without surcharge and "Espresso" at left; crossbow casts two shadows.

1966, Mar. 29

E28	SD6 75 l blk, gray & yel	.25	.25
E29	SD6a 80 l blk & lilac	.25	.25
E30	SD6a 100 l blk & orange	.25	.25
	Nos. E28-E30 (3)	.75	.75

SEMI-POSTAL SPECIAL DELIVERY STAMP

SPSD1

Wmk. 140

1923, Sept. 20 Engr. *Perf. 14*

EB1	SPSD1 60c + 5c brown red	1.75	1.75

POSTAGE DUE STAMPS

D1

D2

D3

D4

Wmk. 140

1897-1920 Typo. *Perf. 14*

J1	D1 5c bl grn & dk brn	1.25	1.25
J2	D2 10c bl grn & dk brn	1.25	1.25
a.	Numerals inverted	375.00	—
J3	D2 30c bl grn & dk brn	3.25	3.00
J4	D2 50c bl grn & dk brn	3.50	3.50
a.	Numerals inverted	375.00	—
J5	D2 60c bl grn & dk brn	40.00	20.00
J6	D3 1 l claret & dk brn	7.50	7.50
J7	D4 3 l claret & brn ('20)	20.00	25.00
J8	D4 5 l claret & dk brn	80.00	55.00
J9	D2 10 l claret & dk brn	40.00	35.00
	Nos. J1-J9 (9)	196.75	151.50

See Nos. J10-J36, J61. For surcharges see Nos. J37-J60, J64.

1924

J10	D1 5c rose & brown	1.75	1.75
J11	D2 10c rose & brown	1.75	1.75
J12	D2 30c rose & brown	3.00	3.00
J13	D2 50c rose & brown	3.25	3.25
J14	D2 60c rose & brown	12.00	12.00
J15	D3 1 l green & brown	20.00	20.00
J16	D4 3 l green & brown	55.00	55.00
J17	D4 5 l green & brown	70.00	70.00
J18	D2 10 l green & brown	325.00	325.00
	Nos. J10-J18 (9)	491.75	491.75

Postage Due Types of 1897 and

D5

1925-39 *Perf. 14*

J19	D1 5c blue & brn	1.50	.75
a.	Numerals inverted	300.00	—
J20	D2 10c blue & brn	1.50	.75
a.	Numerals inverted	300.00	—
J21	D2 15c blue & brn ('39)	1.00	.80
J22	D2 20c blue & brn ('39)	1.00	.80
J23	D2 25c blue & brn ('39)	1.50	1.25
J24	D2 30c blue & brn	1.50	.80
J25	D2 40c blue & brn ('39)	7.50	9.00
J26	D2 50c blue & brn	2.50	1.25
a.	Numerals inverted	300.00	—
J27	D2 60c blue & brn	6.50	1.60
J28	D3 1 l buff & brn	9.50	1.60
J29	D4 2 l buff & brn ('39)	4.00	3.00
J30	D4 3 l buff & brn	125.00	50.00
J31	D4 5 l buff & brn	35.00	7.50
J32	D2 10 l buff & brn	47.50	20.00
J33	D5 15 l buff & brn ('28)	5.50	2.00
J34	D5 25 l buff & brn ('28)	67.50	40.00
J35	D5 30 l buff & brn ('28)	11.50	18.00
J36	D5 50 l buff & brn ('28)	13.50	18.00
	Nos. J19-J36 (18)	343.50	177.10

Postage Due Stamps of 1925 Surcharged in Black and Silver

1931, May 18

J37	D1 15c on 5c bl & brn	1.50	1.50
J38	D2 15c on 10c bl & brn	1.50	1.50
J39	D2 15c on 30c bl & brn	1.50	1.50
J40	D1 20c on 5c bl & brn	1.50	1.50
J41	D2 20c on 10c bl & brn	1.50	1.50
J42	D2 20c on 30c bl & brn	1.50	1.50
J43	D1 25c on 5c bl & brn	4.50	3.00
J44	D2 25c on 10c bl & brn	4.50	3.00
J45	D2 25c on 30c bl & brn	25.00	20.00
J46	D1 40c on 5c bl & brn	4.50	1.50
J47	D2 40c on 10c bl & brn	5.50	1.50
J48	D2 40c on 30c bl & brn	5.50	1.50
J49	D1 2 l on 5c bl & brn	55.00	55.00
J50	D2 2 l on 10c bl & brn	140.00	100.00
J51	D2 2 l on 30c bl & brn	90.00	75.00
	Nos. J37-J51 (15)	343.50	269.50

Nos. J19, J24-J25, J30, J34, J33, J22 Surcharged in Black

Perf. 14, 14½x14

1936-40 Wmk. 140

J52	D1 10c on 5c ('38)	5.50	3.00
J53	D2 25c on 30c ('38)	17.50	16.00
J54	D1 50c on 5c ('37)	17.50	16.00
J55	D2 1 l on 30c	67.50	11.00
J56	D2 1 l on 40c ('40)	11.50	12.00
J57	D4 1 l on 3 l ('37)	67.50	4.75
J58	D5 1 l on 25 l ('39)	110.00	30.00
J59	D5 2 l on 15 l ('38)	55.00	35.00
J60	D2 3 l on 20c ('40)	35.00	35.00
	Nos. J52-J60 (9)	387.00	162.75

Postage Due Type of 1897

1939 Typo. *Perf. 14*

J61	D2 5c blue & brown	1.25	.50

Nos. J61 and J36 Surcharged

1940-43

J62	D2 10c on 5c	.80	.40
J63	D2 50c on 5c	4.00	1.50
J64	D5 25 l on 50 l ('43)	3.50	3.50
	Nos. J62-J64 (3)	8.30	5.40

Coat of Arms — D6

Unwmk.

1945, June 7 Photo. *Perf. 14*

J65	D6 5c dk green	.25	.25
J66	D6 10c orange brn	.25	.25
J67	D6 15c rose red	.25	.25
J68	D6 20c dp ultra	.25	.25
J69	D6 25c dk purple	.25	.25
J70	D6 30c rose lake	.25	.25
J71	D6 40c bister	.25	.25
J72	D6 50c slate blk	.25	.25
J73	D6 60c chestnut	.25	.25
J74	D6 1 l dp orange	.25	.25
J75	D6 2 l carmine	.25	.25
J76	D6 5 l dull violet	.25	.25
J77	D6 10 l dark blue	.50	.35
J78	D6 20 l dark green	7.00	*8.00*
J79	D6 25 l red orange	7.00	*8.00*
J80	D6 50 l dark brown	7.00	*8.00*
	Nos. J65-J80 (16)	24.50	27.35

PARCEL POST STAMPS

These stamps were used by affixing them to the way bill so that one half remained on it following the parcel, the other half staying on the receipt given the sender. Most used halves are right halves. Complete stamps were and are obtainable canceled, probably to order. Both unused and used values are for complete stamps. Most exist imperf and are scarce to rare thus.

PP1

Engraved, Typographed

1928, Nov. 22 Unwmk. *Perf. 12*

Pairs are imperforate between

No.	Type	Description	Unused	Used
Q1	PP1	5c blk brn & bl	.60	.60
a.		Imperf.	75.00	
Q2	PP1	10c dk bl & bl	.60	.60
Q3	PP1	20c gray blk & bl	.60	.60
a.		Imperf.	75.00	
Q4	PP1	25c car & blue	.60	.60
Q5	PP1	30c ultra & blue	.60	.60
Q6	PP1	50c orange & bl	.60	.60
Q7	PP1	60c rose & blue	.60	.60
Q8	PP1	1 l violet & brn	.60	.60
a.		Imperf.	75.00	
Q9	PP1	2 l green & brn	1.50	1.00
Q10	PP1	3 l bister & brn	1.75	1.25
Q11	PP1	4 l gray & brn	2.25	1.50
Q12	PP1	10 l rose lilac & brn	4.75	3.00
Q13	PP1	12 l red brn & brn	18.00	18.00
Q14	PP1	15 l olive grn & brn	27.50	27.50
a.		Imperf.	75.00	
Q15	PP1	20 l brn vio & brn	45.00	45.00
		Nos. Q1-Q15 (15)	105.55	102.05

Halves Used

Q1-Q8	.25
Q9-Q10	.25
Q11	.25
Q12	.35
Q13	.65
Q14	2.75
Q15	3.00

1945-46 Wmk. 140 *Perf. 14*

Pairs are perforated between

No.	Type	Description	Unused	Used
Q16	PP1	5c rose vio & red org	.25	.25
Q17	PP1	10c red org & blk	.25	.25
Q18	PP1	20c dark red & grn	.25	.25
Q19	PP1	25c yel & blk	.25	.25
Q20	PP1	30c red vio & org red	.25	.25
Q21	PP1	50c dull pur & blk	.25	.25
Q22	PP1	60c rose lake & blk	.25	.25
Q23	PP1	1 l brown & dp bl	.25	.25
Q24	PP1	2 l dk brn & dk bl	.25	.25
Q25	PP1	3 l olive brn & brn	.25	.25
Q26	PP1	4 l blue grn & brn	.25	.25
Q27	PP1	10 l bl blk & brt pur	.25	.25
Q28	PP1	12 l myr grn & dl bl	3.00	2.00
Q29	PP1	15 l green & purple	2.00	1.75
Q30	PP1	20 l rose lil & brn	1.50	1.75
Q31	PP1	25 l dp car & ultra ('46)	27.50	27.50
Q32	PP1	50 l yel & dp org ('46)	42.50	55.00
		Nos. Q16-Q32 (17)	79.50	91.00

Halves Used

Q16-Q27	.25
Q28	.25
Q29	.25
Q30	.25
Q31	.30
Q32	.60

Nos. Q32 and Q31 Surcharged with New Value and Wavy Lines in Black

1948-50

No.	Type	Description	Unused	Used
Q33	PP1	100 l on 50 l	42.50	42.50
		Half, used		1.00
Q34	PP1	200 l on 25 l ('50)	140.00	125.00
		Half, used		1.00

1953, Mar. 5 Wmk. 277 *Perf. 13½*

Pairs Perforated Between

No.	Type	Description	Unused	Used
Q35	PP1	10 l dk grn & rose lil	32.50	19.00
		Half, used		1.40
Q36	PP1	300 l pur & lake	110.00	110.00
		Half, used		1.40

1956 Wmk. 303 *Perf. 13½*

No.	Type	Description	Unused	Used
Q37	PP1	10 l gray & brt pur	.25	.25
		Half, used		.25
Q38	PP1	50 l yel & dp org	.60	.80
		Half, used		.25

No. Q38 Surcharged with New Value and Wavy Lines In Black

No.	Type	Description	Unused	Used
Q39	PP1	100 l on 50 l	.50	.70
		Half, used		.25

Catalogue values for unused stamps in this section, from this point to the end of the section, are for Never Hinged items.

1960-61

No.	Type	Description	Unused	Used
Q40	PP1	300 l violet & brn	52.50	37.50
		Half, used		.75
Q41	PP1	500 l dk brn & car ('61)	2.40	2.40
		Half, used		.30

1965-72 Wmk. 339 *Perf. 13½*

Pairs Perforated Between

No.	Type	Description	Unused	Used
Q42	PP1	10 l gray & brt pur	.25	.25
Q43	PP1	50 l yel & red org	.25	.25
Q44	PP1	100 l on 50 l yel & red org	.80	.80
Q45	PP1	300 l violet & brown	.30	.30
Q46	PP1	500 l brn & red ('72)	6.00	6.00
Q47	PP1	1000 l bl grn & lt red brn ('67)	.80	.80
		Nos. Q42-Q47 (6)	8.40	8.40

Halves Used

Q42-Q43	.25
Q44-Q45	.25
Q46	.50
Q47	.25

SARAWAK

sə-'rä-ˌwäˌk

LOCATION — Northwestern part of the island of Borneo, bordering on the South China Sea
GOVT. — Former British Crown Colony
AREA — 48,250 sq. mi. (approx.)
POP. — 1,954,300 (1997 est.)
CAPITAL — Kuching

The last ruling Raja, who retired in 1946 when he ceded Sarawak to the British Crown, was Sir Charles Vyner Brooke, an Englishman. He inherited the title from his father, Sir Charles Johnson Brooke, who in turn received it from his uncle, Sir James Brooke. The title of Raja was conferred on Sir James by Raja Muda Hassim after Sir James had aided him in subduing a rebellion. The title and right of succession were duly recognized by the Sultan of Brunei and by Great Britain.

Sarawak joined the Federation of Malaysia in 1963.

100 Cents = 1 Dollar

Catalogue values for unused stamps in this country are for Never Hinged items, beginning with Scott 155.

Watermarks

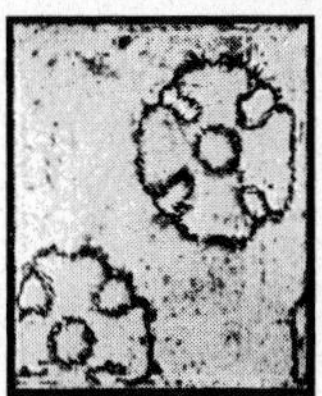

Wmk. 47 — Multiple Rosettes

Wmk. 71 — Rosette

Wmk. 231 — Oriental Crown

Unused examples of Nos. 1-7, 25 and 32-35 are valued without gum. Stamps with original gum are worth more.

Sir James Brooke — A1

Unwmk.

1869, Mar. 1 Litho. *Perf. 11*

No.	Type	Description	Unused	Used
1	A1	3c brown, *yellow*	60.00	240.00

Sir Charles Johnson Brooke — A2

1871, Jan.

No.	Type	Description	Unused	Used
2	A2	3c brown, *yellow*	3.50	4.00
a.		Vertical pair, imperf between	600.00	
b.		Horizontal pair, imperf between	1,000.	
c.		Period after "THREE"	70.00	85.00

No. 2 surcharged "TWO CENTS" is believed to be bogus.

There are a number of lithographic flaws, including narrow A, "period" after THREE, etc.

Imperfs. of Nos. 1, 2 are proofs.

A papermaker's watermark, "LNL," usually appears once or twice in each pane.

For surcharges see Nos. 25, 32.

1875, Jan. 1 *Perf. 12*

No.	Type	Description	Unused	Used
3	A2	2c gray lilac, *lilac*	27.50	22.00
4	A2	4c brown, *yellow*	7.50	4.00
b.		Vertical pair, imperf between	925.00	975.00
5	A2	6c green, *green*	6.00	6.00
6	A2	8c blue, *blue*	6.25	8.50
7	A2	12c red, *rose*	14.00	8.00
		Nos. 3-7 (5)	61.25	48.50

Nos. 3-7 have each five varieties of the words of value.

Imperfs are proofs.

A papermaker's watermark usually appears once or twice in each pane of Nos. 3-7, "LNT" on No. 5, "LNL" on others.

Some examples of No. 7 have the appearance of being on laid paper, but the lines are accidental and not constant within the sheets.

For surcharges see Nos. 33-35.

Sir Charles Johnson Brooke — A4

1888-97 Typo. *Perf. 14*

No.	Type	Description	Unused	Used
8	A4	1c lilac & blk ('92)	6.50	1.60
9	A4	2c lilac & carmine	7.50	5.00
10	A4	3c lilac & blue	12.50	5.75
11	A4	4c lilac & yellow	45.00	70.00
12	A4	5c lilac & grn ('91)	42.50	5.50
13	A4	6c lilac & brown	32.50	70.00
14	A4	8c green & car	24.00	6.00
a.		8c green & rose ('97)	40.00	19.00
15	A4	10c grn & vio ('91)	62.50	16.50
16	A4	12c green & blue	20.00	16.00
17	A4	16c gray grn & org ('97)	72.50	95.00
18	A4	25c green & brown	82.50	52.50
19	A4	32c gray grn & blk ('97)	62.50	77.50
20	A4	50c gray green ('97)	87.50	130.00
21	A4	$1 gray grn & blk ('97)	125.00	135.00
		Nos. 8-21 (14)	683.00	686.35

No. 21 shows the numeral on white tablet.

Three higher values — $2, $5, $10 — were prepared but not issued. Value $1,250 each.

For surcharges see Nos. 22-24, 26-27.

Nos. 14 and 16 Surcharged in Black

No. 22 No. 23

5c.

No. 24

1889-91

No.	Type	Description	Unused	Used
22	A4	2c on 8c	4.50	12.00
a.		Double surcharge	525.00	
b.		Pair, one without surcharge	8,500.	
c.		Inverted surcharge	4,500.	
23	A4	5c on 12c ('91)	40.00	62.50
a.		Double surcharge	1,400.	1,400.
b.		Pair, one without surcharge	13,000.	
c.		No period after "C"	45.00	75.00
d.		Without "C"	925.00	1,100.
e.		Double surch., one vert.	4,250.	
24	A4	5c on 12c ('91)	350.00	375.00
a.		No period after "C"	190.00	200.00
b.		Double surcharge	1,500.	
c.		"C" omitted	1,400.	1,500.

No. 2 Surcharged in Black

1892, May 23 *Perf. 11*

No.	Type	Description	Unused	Used
25	A2	1c on 3c brown, *yel*	2.50	3.00
b.		Without bar	275.00	275.00
c.		Period after "THREE"	57.50	70.00
d.		Double surcharge	475.00	550.00
e.		Vertical pair, imperf between	800.00	
f.		Vertical pair, imperf horiz.	800.00	

Examples of No. 25b must be from the first printing, wherein the bar was applied after the surcharge. Examples of No. 25 with parts of the surcharge and/or bar omitted are stamps that had gum on the face prior to the surcharging operation. The ink was removed when the gum was washed off.

No. 10 Surcharged in Black

e

f

1892 *Perf. 14*

No.	Type	Description	Unused	Used
26	A4(e)	1c on 3c lil & bl	3.75	3.75
a.		No period after "cent"	275.00	300.00
27	A4(f)	1c on 3c lil & bl	80.00	50.00
b.		Double surcharge	800.00	850.00

Issued: #26, Feb.; #27, Jan. 12.

Sir Charles Johnson Brooke
A11 A12

A13

A14

1895, Jan. 1 Engr. *Perf. 11½, 12*

No.	Type	Description	Unused	Used
28	A11	2c red brn	17.50	9.75
a.		Perf. 12½	27.00	6.00
b.		Vertical pair, imperf between	650.00	
c.		Horizontal pair, imperf between	500.00	
d.		As "a," horiz. pair, imperf between	750.00	

29 A12 4c black 17.50 3.75
a. Horizontal pair, imperf between 875.00
30 A13 6c violet 20.00 *9.75*
31 A14 8c deep green 45.00 6.00
Nos. 28-31 (4) 100.00 29.25

The 2c and 8c imperf are proofs. Perforated stamps of these designs in other colors are color trials, which exist surcharged with new values in pence. These surcharged varieties were used in trial printings of a British South African issue.

Stamps of 1871-75 Surcharged in Black or Red

1899 ***Perf. 11***
32 A2 2c on 3c brown, *yel* 4.25 2.00
a. Period after "THREE" 90.00 *90.00*
b. Vertical pair, imperf between 1,000.

Perf. 12
33 A2 2c on 12c red, *rose* 4.00 *6.00*
a. Inverted surcharge 1,000. *1,400.*
34 A2 4c on 6c grn, *grn* (R) 62.50 *125.00*
35 A2 4c on 8c blue, *bl* (R) 10.00 *16.00*
Nos. 32-35 (4) 80.75 *149.00*

Sir Charles J. Brooke — A16

1899-1908 **Typo.** ***Perf. 14***
36 A16 1c blue & car ('01) 1.75 *1.75*
37 A16 2c gray green 2.25 1.00
38 A16 3c dull violet ('08) 26.00 .75
39 A16 4c aniline car 3.00 .25
40 A16 8c yellow & black 2.75 .90
41 A16 10c ultra 7.75 1.10
42 A16 12c light violet ('99) 7.00 6.00
43 A16 16c org brn & grn 8.50 1.90
44 A16 20c brn ol & vio ('00) 8.50 7.50
45 A16 25c brown & ultra 11.00 *7.00*
46 A16 50c ol grn & rose 35.00 *40.00*
47 A16 $1 rose & green 100.00 *130.00*
Nos. 36-47 (12) 213.50 *198.15*

A 5c was prepared but not issued. Value $16.

See the *Scott Classic Catalogue* for listings of shades.

1901 **Wmk. 71**
48 A16 2c gray green 62.50 23.00

Sir Charles Vyner Brooke — A17

1918-23 **Unwmk.**
50 A17 1c slate bl & rose 2.60 *3.25*
51 A17 2c deep green 3.00 1.75
52 A17 2c violet ('23) 2.25 *3.00*
53 A17 3c violet brown 3.75 3.00
54 A17 3c dp grn ('22) 5.00 1.40
55 A17 4c carmine rose 9.00 4.25
56 A17 4c purple brn ('23) 2.50 *2.75*
57 A17 5c orange ('23) 3.00 2.75
58 A17 6c lake brn ('22) 2.25 *1.60*
59 A17 8c yellow & blk 17.50 *75.00*
60 A17 8c car rose ('22) 5.25 *35.00*
61 A17 10c ultra 7.00 6.50
a. 10c blue 7.00 6.50
62 A17 10c black ('23) 4.50 *5.00*
63 A17 12c violet 22.50 *57.50*
64 A17 12c ultra ('22) 12.50 *21.00*
65 A17 16c brn & blue grn 7.00 *8.50*
66 A17 20c olive bis & vio 9.50 *7.50*
a. 20c olive green & violet 9.50 *7.50*
67 A17 25c brown & blue 4.75 *25.00*
68 A17 30c bis & gray ('22) 4.25 *4.75*
69 A17 50c ol grn & rose 11.50 *17.00*
70 A17 $1 car rose & grn 42.50 *32.50*
Nos. 50-70 (21) 182.10 *319.00*

In 1918 a supply of the 1c (No. 50) had the value tablet printed, by error, in slate blue instead of rose. It is officially stated that this stamp was never issued and had no franking power. Value $22.

The $1 denomination shows numeral of value in color on white tablet.

Nos. 61 and 63 Surcharged

1st Printing — Bars 1¼mm apart.
2nd Printing — Bars ¾mm apart.

1923, Jan.
77 A17 1c on 10c ultra 16.50 *62.50*
a. "cnet" 25,000.
b. Bars ¾mm apart 180.00 *500.00*
78 A17 2c on 12c violet 11.00 *55.00*
a. Bars ¾mm apart 92.50 *350.00*

No. 77b was created with "cnet" by the post office to sell additional error sheets to dealers after No. 77a had been corrected.Sale of these items was quickly discontinued.

Type of 1918 Issue

1928-29 **Typo.** **Wmk. 47**
79 A17 1c slate blue & rose 1.75 .80
80 A17 2c dull violet 2.75 1.80
81 A17 3c deep green 4.50 *5.75*
82 A17 4c purple brown 2.10 .25
83 A17 5c orange ('29) 14.00 5.75
84 A17 6c brown lake 1.50 .35
85 A17 8c carmine 4.00 *35.00*
86 A17 10c black 2.00 1.40
87 A17 12c ultra 4.00 *45.00*
88 A17 16c dp brn & bl grn 4.00 *4.50*
89 A17 20c dp olive & vio 4.00 *10.00*
90 A17 25c dk brown & ultra 7.00 *9.75*
91 A17 30c olive bis & gray 5.50 *11.50*
92 A17 50c olive grn & rose 15.00 *26.00*
93 A17 $1 car rose & grn 22.50 *27.50*
Nos. 79-93 (15) 94.60 *185.35*
Set, never hinged 170.00

Sir Charles Vyner Brooke — A18

Wmk. 231

1932, Jan. 1 **Engr.** ***Perf. 12½***
94 A18 1c indigo 1.00 1.10
95 A18 2c dark green 1.25 *2.25*
96 A18 3c deep violet 5.00 1.10
97 A18 4c deep orange 12.00 .85
98 A18 5c brown lake 8.50 1.40
99 A18 6c deep red 9.75 *11.00*
100 A18 8c orange yel 11.00 *9.75*
101 A18 10c black 2.75 *3.75*
102 A18 12c violet blue 5.00 *11.00*
103 A18 15c orange brown 8.25 *11.00*
104 A18 20c violet & org 8.00 *9.00*
105 A18 25c org brn & yel 15.00 *25.00*
106 A18 30c org red & ol brn 12.50 *42.50*
107 A18 50c olive grn & red 17.50 *15.00*
108 A18 $1 car & green 25.00 *40.00*
Nos. 94-108 (15) 142.50 *184.70*

Sir Charles Vyner Brooke — A19

1934-41 **Unwmk.** ***Perf. 12***
109 A19 1c brown violet 1.50 .25
110 A19 2c blue green 1.75 .25
111 A19 2c black ('41) 4.75 *1.75*
112 A19 3c black 1.40 .25
113 A19 3c blue grn ('41) 8.00 *5.00*
114 A19 4c magenta 2.25 .25
115 A19 5c violet 2.25 .25
116 A19 6c deep rose 3.00 .70
117 A19 6c red brn ('41) 8.75 *9.00*
118 A19 8c red brown 2.50 .25
119 A19 8c dp rose ('41) 9.25 .25
120 A19 10c red 5.00 .45
121 A19 12c deep ultra 3.50 .30
122 A19 12c orange ('41) 7.50 *6.25*
123 A19 15c orange 8.00 *12.00*
124 A19 15c deep blue ('41) 9.75 *20.00*
125 A19 20c dp rose & olive 8.50 1.50
126 A19 25c orange & vio 8.50 *2.00*
127 A19 30c vio & red brn 8.50 *3.25*
128 A19 50c red & violet 12.50 1.00
129 A19 $1 dk brn & red 7.00 1.00
130 A19 $2 violet & mag 30.00 34.00
131 A19 $3 bl grn & rose 50.00 *55.00*
132 A19 $4 red & ultra 50.00 *80.00*
133 A19 $5 red brn & red 80.00 *85.00*
134 A19 $10 orange & blk 35.00 *85.00*
Nos. 109-134 (26) 369.15 *404.95*

Issue dates: May 1, 1934, Mar. 1, 1941.

For overprints see #135-154, 159-173, N1-N22.

Stamps of 1934-41 Overprinted in Black or Red

1945, Dec. 17
135 A19 1c brown violet .85 *.70*
136 A19 2c black (R) 3.00 *1.50*
137 A19 3c blue green .85 *2.00*
138 A19 4c magenta 2.25 .35
139 A19 5c violet (R) 3.00 1.50
140 A19 6c red brown 3.50 .90
141 A19 8c deep rose 9.50 *23.00*
142 A19 10c red 1.50 .80
143 A19 12c orange 4.00 *4.25*
144 A19 15c deep blue 6.00 .45
145 A19 20c dp rose & ol 4.00 *5.50*
146 A19 25c org & vio (R) 4.50 *3.50*
147 A19 30c vio & red brn 4.75 *4.25*
148 A19 50c red & violet 1.50 .40
149 A19 $1 dk brn & red 2.00 *5.00*
150 A19 $2 violet & mag 6.75 *21.00*
151 A19 $3 bl grn & rose 19.00 *92.50*
152 A19 $4 red & ultra 24.00 *65.00*
153 A19 $5 red brn & red 125.00 *275.00*
154 A19 $10 org & blk (R) 110.00 *250.00*
Nos. 135-154 (20) 335.95 *757.60*
Set, never hinged 500.00

Catalogue values for unused stamps in this section, from this point to the end of the section, are for Never Hinged items.

A20

Designs: Sir James Brooke, Sir Charles V. Brooke and Sir Charles J. Brooke.

1946, May 18
155 A20 8c dark carmine 4.75 1.75
156 A20 15c dark blue 5.00 2.50
157 A20 50c red & black 5.00 3.00
158 A20 $1 sepia & black 5.00 *42.50*
Nos. 155-158 (4) 19.75 *49.75*

Type of 1934-41 Overprinted in Blue or Red

1947, Apr. 16 **Wmk. 4** ***Perf. 12***
159 A19 1c brown violet .25 *.30*
160 A19 2c black (R) .25 .25
161 A19 3c blue green (R) .25 .25
162 A19 4c magenta .30 .25
163 A19 6c red brown .50 *.90*
164 A19 8c deep rose 1.00 .25
165 A19 10c red .50 .25
166 A19 12c orange .70 *1.00*
167 A19 15c deep blue (R) .50 *.55*
168 A19 20c dp rose & ol (R) 2.00 .65
169 A19 25c orange & vio (R) .65 .55
170 A19 50c red & violet (R) 1.25 .80
171 A19 $1 dk brown & red 1.50 *1.00*
172 A19 $2 violet & magenta 3.75 *6.50*
173 A19 $5 red brown & red 9.00 3.25
Nos. 159-173 (15) 22.40 16.75

Common Design Types pictured following the introduction.

Silver Wedding Issue
Common Design Types

1948, Oct. 25 **Photo.** ***Perf. 14x14½***
174 CD304 8c scarlet .40 .40

Perf. 11½x11

Engraved; Name Typographed
175 CD305 $5 light brown 50.00 *52.50*

UPU Issue
Common Design Types
Engr.; Name Typo. on 15c, 25c
Perf. 13½, 11x11½

1949, Oct. 10 **Wmk. 4**
176 CD306 8c rose carmine 1.40 .60
177 CD307 15c indigo 3.25 2.25
178 CD308 25c green 1.75 1.50
179 CD309 50c violet 1.75 *6.50*
Nos. 176-179 (4) 8.15 10.85

Troides Brookiana A21

Western Tarsier — A22

Designs: 3c, Kayan tomb. 4c, Kayan girl and boy. 6c, Bead work. 8c, Dyak dancer. 10c, Scaly anteater. 12c, Kenyah boys. 15c, Fire making. 20c, Kelemantan rice barn. 25c, Pepper vines. 50c, Iban woman. $1, Kelabit smithy. $2, Map of Sarawak. $5, Arms of Sarawak.

Perf. 11½x11, 11x11½

1950, Jan. 3 **Engr.**
180 A21 1c black .75 .30
181 A22 2c orange red .45 *.50*
182 A22 3c green .60 *1.00*
183 A22 4c brown 1.00 .25
184 A22 6c aquamarine .75 .25
185 A21 8c red 1.00 .30
186 A21 10c orange 3.00 *5.50*
187 A21 12c purple 3.25 1.40
188 A21 15c deep blue 4.25 .25
189 A21 20c red org & brn 2.50 .50
190 A21 25c carmine & grn 3.75 .60
191 A22 50c purple & brn 8.00 .45
192 A21 $1 dk brn & bl grn 25.00 4.25
193 A21 $2 rose car & blue 40.00 16.00

Engr. and Typo.
194 A21 $5 dp vio, blk, red & yel 30.00 18.00
Nos. 180-194 (15) 124.30 49.55

1952, Feb. 1
195 A21 10c orange *(Map)* 2.00 .65

Coronation Issue
Common Design Type

1953, June 3 **Engr.** ***Perf. 13½x13***
196 CD312 10c ultra & black 2.00 *1.75*

Logging — A23

Hornbill A24

Elizabeth II — A25

Designs: 2c, Young Orangutan. 4c, Kayan Dancing. 8c, Shield with spears. 10c, Kenyah ceremonial carving. 12c, Barong Panau (sailboat). 15c, Turtles. 20c, Melanau basket making. 25c, Astana, Kuching (Governor's Residence). $1, $2, Queen Elizabeth II (Portrait like Fiji A39). $5, Arms.

Perf. 11x11½, 11½x11, 12x12½ (A25)

1955-57 Wmk. 4 Engr.

No.	Type	Denomination	Unused	Used
197	A23	1c green	.25	*.30*
198	A23	2c red orange	.35	*.55*
199	A23	4c brown carmine	1.50	.60
200	A24	6c greenish blue	3.75	3.25
201	A24	8c rose red	.40	.30
202	A24	10c dark green	.30	.25
203	A24	12c purple	3.75	.55
204	A24	15c ultra	2.25	.30
205	A24	20c brown & olive	1.00	.25
206	A24	25c brt green & brn	6.50	.25
207	A25	30c violet & red brn	8.50	.30
208	A25	50c car rose & blk	2.50	.40
209	A25	$1 org brn & grn	15.00	2.25
210	A25	$2 green & violet	26.00	3.50

Engr. and Typo.

No.	Type	Denomination	Unused	Used
211	A24	$5 dp vio, blk, red & yel	40.00	21.00
		Nos. 197-211 (15)	112.05	34.05

Issued: 30c, 6/1/55; others, 10/1/57.

See Nos. 215-222.

Freedom from Hunger Issue

Common Design Type

Perf. 14x14½

1963, June 4 Photo. Wmk. 314

No.	Type	Denomination	Unused	Used
212	CD314	12c sepia	1.60	*1.75*

OCCUPATION STAMPS

Issued under Japanese Occupation

Stamps of 1934-41 Handstamped in Violet

1942 Unwmk. *Perf. 12*

No.	Type	Denomination	Unused	Used
N1	A19	1c brown vio	45.00	*85.00*
N2	A19	2c blue green	125.00	*200.00*
N3	A19	2c black	170.00	*200.00*
N3A	A19	3c black	*500.00*	*500.00*
N4	A19	3c blue green	100.00	*110.00*
N5	A19	4c magenta	130.00	*140.00*
N6	A19	5c violet	160.00	*170.00*
N7	A19	6c deep rose	225.00	180.00
N8	A19	6c red brown	120.00	*160.00*
N8A	A19	8c red brown	*500.00*	*500.00*
N9	A19	8c deep rose	100.00	*120.00*
N10	A19	10c red	130.00	*150.00*
N11	A19	12c deep ultra	250.00	*250.00*
N12	A19	12c orange	200.00	*200.00*
N12A	A19	15c orange	*600.00*	*600.00*
N13	A19	15c deep blue	180.00	*190.00*
N14	A19	20c dp rose & ol	95.00	*120.00*
N15	A19	25c org & vio	130.00	*150.00*
N16	A19	30c vio & red brn	100.00	*120.00*
N17	A19	50c red & vio	100.00	*120.00*
N18	A19	$1 dk brn & red	150.00	*170.00*
N19	A19	$2 vio & mag	375.00	*475.00*
N19A	A19	$3 blue grn & rose	*3,750.*	*3,750.*
N20	A19	$4 red & ultra	325.00	*475.00*
N21	A19	$5 red brn & red	325.00	*475.00*
N22	A19	$10 org & blk	325.00	*475.00*
		Nos. N1-N22 (26)	*9,210.*	*10,085.*

Stamps overprinted with Japanese characters in oval frame or between 2 vertical black lines were not for paying postage.

SASENO

ˈsə-ˈzä-ˌnō

LOCATION — An island in the Adriatic Sea, lying at the entrance of Valona Bay, Albania.
GOVT. — Italian possession
AREA — 2 sq. mi.

Italy occupied this Albanian islet in 1914, and returned it to Albania in 1947.

100 Centesimi = 1 Lira

Used values in italics are for postally used stamps. CTO's or stamps with fake cancels sell for about the same as unused, hinged stamps.

Italian Stamps of 1901-22 Overprinted

1923 Wmk. 140 *Perf. 14*

No.	Type	Denomination	Unused	Used
1	A48	10c claret	32.50	*82.50*
a.		Double overprint	—	
2	A48	15c slate	32.50	*82.50*
3	A50	20c brown orange	32.50	*82.50*
4	A49	25c blue	32.50	*82.50*
5	A49	30c yellow brown	32.50	*82.50*
6	A49	50c violet	32.50	*82.50*
7	A49	60c carmine	32.50	*82.50*
8	A46	1 l brown & green	32.50	*82.50*
a.		Double overprint	475.00	
b.		Vertical overprint	190.00	
		Nos. 1-8 (8)	260.00	*660.00*
		Set, never hinged	600.00	

Superseded by postage stamps of Italy.

SAUDI ARABIA

ˈsau-dē ə-ˈrā-bē-ə

LOCATION — Southwestern Asia, on the Arabian Peninsula between the Red Sea and the Persian Gulf
GOVT. — Kingdom
AREA — 849,400 sq. mi.
POP. — 17,880,000 (1995 est.)
CAPITAL — Riyadh

In 1916 the Grand Sherif of Mecca declared the Sanjak of Hejaz independent of Turkish rule. In 1925, Ibn Saud, then Sultan of the Nejd, captured the Hejaz after a prolonged siege of Jedda, the last Hejaz stronghold.

The resulting Kingdom of the Hejaz and Nejd was renamed Saudi Arabia in 1932.

40 Paras = 1 Piaster = 1 Guerche (Garch, Qirsh)
11 Guerche = 1 Riyal (1928)
110 Guerche = 1 Sovereign (1931)
440 Guerche = 1 Sovereign (1952)
20 Piasters (Guerche) = 1 Riyal (1960)
100 Halalas = 1 Riyal (1976)

Catalogue values for unused stamps in this country are for Never Hinged items, beginning with Scott 178 in the regular postage section, Scott C1 in the airpost section, Scott J28 in the postage due section, Scott O7 in official section, and Scott RA6 in the postal tax section.

Watermarks

Wmk. 337 — Crossed Swords and Palm Tree

Watermark lines are thicker than the paper.

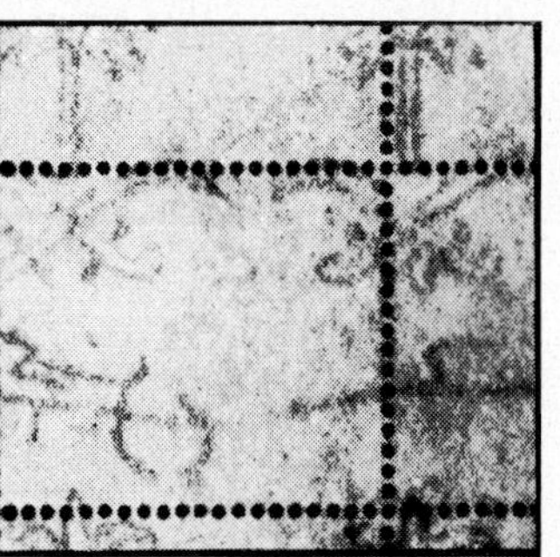

Wmk. 361 — Crossed Swords, Palm Tree and Arabic Inscription

HEJAZ

Sherifate of Mecca

Adapted from Carved Door Panels of Mosque El Salih Talay, Cairo — A1

Taken from Page of Koran in Mosque of El Sultan Barquq, Cairo — A2

Taken from Details of an Ancient Prayer Niche in the Mosque of El Amri at Qus in Upper Egypt — A3

Perf. 10, 12

1916, Oct. Unwmk. Typo.

No.	Type	Denomination	Unused	Used
L1	A1	¼pi green	60.00	50.00
L2	A2	½pi red	60.00	45.00
a.		Perf. 10	225.00	90.00
L3	A3	1pi blue	20.00	18.00
a.		Perf. 12	250.00	200.00
b.		Perf. 10x12	1,450.	2,000.
		Nos. L1-L3 (3)	140.00	113.00

Exist imperf. Forged perf. exist.

See Nos. L5-L7, L10-L12. For overprints see Nos. L16-L18, L26-L28, L52-L54, L57-L59, L61-L66, L67, L70-L72, L77-L81, 37.

A4

Designs: Central Design Adapted from a Koran Design for a Tomb. Background is from Stone Carving on Entrance Arch to the Ministry of Wakfs.

1916-17 *Roulette 20*

No.	Type	Denomination	Unused	Used
L4	A4	⅛pi orange ('17)	5.50	2.00
L5	A1	¼pi green	8.00	2.00
L6	A2	½pi red	9.75	2.00
L7	A3	1pi blue	10.50	2.00
		Nos. L4-L7 (4)	33.75	8.00

See No. L9. For overprints & surcharge see Nos. L15c, L16c, L17b, L18d, L25, L51, L56, L69, 33.

Adapted from Stucco Work above Entrance to Cairo R. R. Station A5

Adapted from First Page of the Koran of Sultan Farag — A6

1917 *Serrate Roulette 13*

No.	Type	Denomination	Unused	Used
L8	A5	1pa lilac brown	5.75	2.00
L9	A4	⅛pi orange	6.25	3.00
L10	A1	¼pi green	6.25	3.00
L11	A2	½pi red	7.00	4.40
L12	A3	1pi blue	7.25	4.40
L13	A6	2pi magenta	32.50	14.50
		Nos. L8-L13 (6)	65.00	31.30

Designs A1-A6 are inscribed "Hejaz Postage."

For overprints and surcharge see Nos. L14-L31, L55-60, L62, L65--L75, L79a-81.

Kingdom of the Hejaz

Stamps of 1917-18 Overprinted in Black, Red or Brown

1921, Dec. 21 *Serrate Roulette 13*

No.	Type	Denomination	Unused	Used
L14	A5	1pa lilac brown	65.00	24.00
a.		Date omitted at right	200.00	
b.		Date omitted at left	250.00	
L15	A4	⅛pi orange	35.00	27.50
a.		Inverted overprint	175.00	
b.		Double overprint	265.00	
c.		Roulette 20	1,000.	1,000.
d.		As "c," invtd. overprint	1,825.	*1,825.*
e.		Double overprint, one inverted	900.00	
f.		Double overprint, both inverted	900.00	
g.		Date omitted at right	185.00	
h.		Date omitted at left	500.00	
L16	A1	¼pi green	20.00	9.00
a.		Inverted overprint	110.00	
b.		Double overprint	225.00	
c.		Roulette 20	1,100.	1,100.
d.		As "c," invtd. overprint	2,050.	2,050.
e.		Double overprint, one inverted	825.00	
f.		Double overprint, both inverted	225.00	
g.		Date omitted at right	60.00	
h.		Date omitted at left	200.00	
L17	A2	½pi red	21.00	6.75
a.		Inverted overprint	200.00	77.50
b.		Roulette 20	1,000.	1,000.
c.		Double overprint	600.00	
d.		Double overprint, both inverted	600.00	
e.		Date omitted at right	100.00	
L18	A3	1pi blue (R)	20.00	10.00
a.		Brown overprint	85.00	37.50
b.		Black overprint	155.00	82.50
c.		As "b," invtd. overprint	500.00	
d.		Roulette 20	1,000.	1,000.
e.		Date omitted at right	400.00	
L19	A6	2pi magenta	25.00	15.00
a.		Double overprint	*4,500.*	
b.		Date omitted at right	150.00	
c.		As "a," date omitted at right	15,000.	
		Nos. L14-L19 (6)	186.00	92.25

Nos. L15-L17, L18b and L19 exist with date (1340) omitted at left or right side.

All values except No. L15 exist with gold overprint.

No. L19c is unique.

For errors and varieties in never hinged condition add 50%.

No. L14 With Additional Surcharge

a

b

L22 A5(a) ½pi on 1pa 500.00 225.00
L23 A5(b) 1pi on 1pa 500.00 225.00

Forgeries of Nos. L14-L23 abound.

Stamps of 1917-18 Overprinted in Black

1922, Jan. 7

L24 A5 1pa lilac brown 12.50 4.50
a. Inverted overprint 150.00
b. Double overprint 150.00
c. Double ovpt., one inverted 250.00
L25 A4 ⅛pi orange 20.00 12.50
a. Inverted overprint 175.00
b. Double ovpt., one inverted 250.00
L26 A1 ¼pi green 5.75 4.50
a. Inverted overprint 175.00
b. Double ovpt., one inverted 250.00
L27 A2 ½pi red 10.00 3.25
a. Inverted overprint 135.00
b. Double ovpt., one inverted 275.00
L28 A3 1pi blue 5.00 1.40
a. Double overprint 275.00
b. Inverted overprint 165.00
L29 A6 2pi magenta 10.00 10.00
a. Double overprint 275.00

With Additional Surcharge of New Value

L30 A5(a) ½pi on 1pa lil brn 40.00 21.00
L31 A5(b) 1pi on 1pa lil brn 4.00 1.50
a. Inverted surcharge 145.00
b. Double surcharge 165.00
c. Dbl. surch., one invtd., ovpt. invtd. 300.00
d. Inverted overprint 145.00
e. Inverted overprint and surcharge 300.00
f. Inverted overprint, double surcharge 300.00
g. Words of surcharge transposed 300.00
h. Overprint and surcharge inverted, words of surcharge transposed 500.00
i. Right hand character of surcharge inverted 110.00
Nos. L24-L31 (8) 107.25 58.65

The 1921 and 1922 overprints read: "The Arab Hashemite Government, 1340."

The overprint on No. L28 in red is bogus.

Forgeries abound.

For errors and varieties in never hinged condition add 50%.

Types A7 and A8

Very fine examples will be somewhat off center but perforations will be clear of the framelines.

Arms of Sherif of Mecca — A7

1922, Feb. Typo. *Perf. 11½*

L32 A7 ⅛pi red brown 3.00 .85
L34 A7 ½pi red 3.25 .60
a. Horiz. pair, imperf. btwn. 87.50 *35.00*
b. Vert. pair, imperf. btwn. — —
L35 A7 1pi dark blue 3.50 .60
a. Vert. pair, imperf. btwn. 87.50
L36 A7 1½pi violet 4.00 .85
L37 A7 2pi orange 4.00 .90
L38 A7 3pi olive brown 4.00 .85
L39 A7 5pi olive green 4.25 .85
Nos. L32-L39 (7) 26.00 5.50

Numerous shades exist. Some values were printed in other colors in 1925 for handstamping by the Nejdi authorities in Mecca. These exist without handstamps.

Exist imperf.

Forgeries exist, usually perf. 11.

Reprints of Nos. L32, L35 exist; paper and shades differ.

See Nos. L48A-L49. For surcharges and overprints see Nos. L40-L48, L76, L82-L159, 7-20, 38A-48, 55A-58A, LJ11-LJ16, LJ26-LJ39, J1-J8, J10-J11, P1-P3, Jordan 64-72, 91, 103-120, J1-J17, O1.

Stamps of 1922 Surcharged with New Values in Arabic

c

d

1923

L40 A7(c) ¼pi on ⅛pi org brn 55.00 50.00
Never hinged 82.50
a. Double surcharge 375.00
b. Double inverted surcharge 8.00
c. Double surch., one invtd. 475.00
d. Inverted surcharge — —
L41 A7(d) 10pi on 5pi ol grn 82.50 42.50
Never hinged 125.00
a. Double surch., one invtd. 375.00
b. Inverted surcharge 800.00

Forgeries exist.

Caliphate Issue

Stamps of 1922 Overprinted in Gold

1924

L42 A7 ⅛pi orange brown 7.00 *15.00*
L43 A7 ½pi red 4.50 *15.00*
L44 A7 1pi dark blue 7.00 *12.50*
a. Inverted overprint 375.00
L45 A7 1½pi violet 7.00 *12.50*
L46 A7 2pi orange 7.00 *10.00*
a. Inverted overprint 375.00
L47 A7 3pi olive brown 9.50 *15.00*
L48 A7 5pi olive green 8.25 *15.00*
a. Inverted overprint 400.00
Nos. L42-L48 (7) 50.25 95.00

Assumption of the Caliphate by King Hussein in Mar., 1924. The overprint reads "In commemoration of the Caliphate, Shaaban, 1342."

The overprint was typographed in black and dusted with "gold" powder while wet. Inverted overprints on other values are forgeries. So-called black overprints are either forgeries or gold overprints with the gold rubbed off. No genuine black overprints are known.

The overprint is 18-20mm wide. The 1st setting of the ½p is 16mm.

Forgeries exist.

Nos. L43-L44, L46 exist with postage due overprint as on Nos. LJ11-LJ13.

Type of 1922 and

Arms of Sherif of Mecca — A8

1924 *Perf. 11½*

L48A A7 ¼pi yellow green 9.00 *9.00*
b. Tête bêche pair *155.00* 125.00
c. Cracked plate *50.00*
d. Cracked plate in tête-bêche pair *350.00*
L49 A7 3pi brown red 30.00 *14.50*
a. 3pi dull red 5.00 *7.50*
L50 A8 10pi vio & dk brn 7.00 *7.00*
a. Center inverted *100.00* 90.00
c. 10pi purple & sepia 7.00 *7.50*
Nos. L48A-L50 (3) 46.00 30.50

Nos. L48A, L50, L50a exist imperf.

Several printings of Nos. L48A-L50 exist; paper and shades differ.

A plate flaw in position 13 of No. L48A, which appears as a large white gash in the upper left portion of the stamp, exists. Values: unused single, $50; unused tête-bêche pair, $250.

Forgeries exist, usually perf. 11.

For overprints see Nos. L76A, Jordan 121.

Used values for #L51-L186 and LJ17-LJ39 are for genuine cancels. Privately applied cancels exist for "Mekke" (Mecca, bilingual or all Arabic), Khartoum, Cairo, as well as for Jeddah. Many private cancels have wrong dates, some as early as 1916. These are worth half the used values.

Jedda Issues

Stamps of 1916-17 Overprinted

The Jedda overprints on Nos. L51-L159 read: "Al-hukuma al Hejaziyeh, 5 Rabi al'awwal 1343"

(The Hejaz Government, October 4, 1924). This is the date of the accession of King Ali.

Counterfeits exist of all Jedda overprints.

Jedda issues were also used in Medina and Yambo.

Red Overprint

1925, Jan. *Roulette 20*

L51 A4 ⅛pi orange 27.50 *27.50*
a. Inverted overprint 135.00
b. Ovptd. on face and back 250.00
c. Normal ovpt. on face, double ovpt. on back — —
d. As "b," both inverted 350.00
e. Dbl. ovpt., both inverted 500.00
L52 A1 ¼pi green 27.50 *22.00*
a. Inverted overprint 82.50
b. Double overprint 82.50
c. Double overprint, one invtd. 210.00
L53 A2 ½pi red 100.00 *100.00*
a. Inverted overprint 185.00
L54 A3 1pi blue 55.00 *55.00*
a. Inverted overprint *185.00*
b. Double ovpt., one invtd. 185.00
Nos. L51-L53 (3) 155.00 *149.50*

Serrate Roulette 13

L55 A5 1pa lilac brown 30.00 *20.00*
a. Inverted overprint 82.50
b. Double overprint 87.50
c. Ovptd. on face and back *200.00*
d. Normal ovpt. on face, double ovpt. on back 210.00
L56 A4 ⅛pi orange 72.50 *55.00*
L57 A1 ¼pi green 37.50 *30.00*
a. Pair, one without overprint *2,250.*
b. Inverted overprint 120.00
c. Double ovpt., one inverted 325.00
L58 A2 ½pi red 55.00 *45.00*
a. Inverted overprint *175.00*
L59 A3 1pi blue 60.00 *50.00*
a. Inverted overprint *150.00*
L60 A6 2pi magenta 55.00 *50.00*
a. Inverted overprint *155.00*
Nos. L55-L60 (6) 310.00 *250.00*

Gold Overprint

Roulette 20

L61 A1 ¼pi grn, gold on red ovpt. *2,750.*
Never hinged 4,000.
No gum 1,000.
a. Gold on blue ovpt. 4,750. *7,000.*

Serrate Roulette 13

L62 A1 ¼pi grn, gold on red ovpt. 45.00 *35.00*
a. Inverted overprint *300.00*

The overprint on No. L61 was typographed in red or blue (No. L62 only in red) and dusted with "gold" powder while wet.

For errors and varieties in never hinged condition add 50%.

Blue Overprint

Roulette 20

L63 A1 ¼pi green 150.00 *35.00*
a. Inverted overprint 185.00
b. Ovptd. on face and back 250.00 *550.00*
L64 A2 ½pi red, invtd. ovpt. 225.00 *80.00*
a. Upright overprint 200.00

Serrate Roulette 13

L65 A1 ¼pi green 35.00 *25.00*
a. Inverted overprint 77.50
b. Vert. ovpt. reading down 1,100.
c. Vert. ovpt. reading up 4,000.
L66 A2 ½pi red 55.00 *45.00*
a. Inverted overprint *135.00*
L66B A6 2pi mag, invtd. ovpt. *2,275.*

Blue overprint on Nos. L4, L8, L9 are bogus.

Same Overprint in Blue on Provisional Stamps of 1922

Overprinted on No. L17

L67 A2 ½pi red *4,250.*

Overprinted on Nos. L24-L29

L68 A5 1pa lilac brn 250.00 *250.00*
L69 A4 ⅛pi orange *3,750.* *3,000.*
a. Inverted overprint 7,250.
L70 A1 ¼pi green 100.00 *100.00*
a. Inverted overprint 1,550.
L71 A2 ½pi red 145.00 *135.00*
a. Inverted overprint 1,675.
L72 A3 1pi blue 145.00 *145.00*
L73 A6 2pi magenta 250.00 *250.00*
a. Inverted overprint 1,825.

Same Overprint on Nos. L30 and L31

L74 A5(a) ½pi on 1pa 145.00 *145.00*
L75 A5(b) 1pi on 1pa 110.00 *110.00*
a. Inverted overprint 2,100.

Same Overprint in Blue Vertically, Reading Up or Down, on Stamps of 1922-24

Perf. 11½

L76 A7 ½pi red *1,600.* *1,600.*
L76A A8 10pi vio & dk brn *3,250.* *3,000.*

Nos. L5, L10 Overprinted Reading Up in Blue or Red

(Overprint reads up in illustration.)

Roulette 20

L77a A1 ¼pi green (Bl) *775.00* *775.00*
L78 A1 ¼pi green (R) *725.00* *725.00*

Serrate Roulette 13

L79a A1 ¼pi green (Bl) 450.00 *450.00*
L80 A1 ¼pi green (R) 100.00 *100.00*

Overprint Reading Down

Roulette 20

L77 A1 ¼pi green (Bl) *1,550.* —

Serrate Roulette 13

L79 A1 ¼pi green (Bl) 725.00 —
L80a A1 ¼pi green (R) 385.00 —
L80b A1 ¼pi grn (R), double ovpt. 725.00
L80c A1 ¼pi grn (R), double ovpt., 1 reading up and 1 reading down 1,625.

L80d	A1	¼pi grn (R), triple ovpt., all reading up	—	—

Nos. L10, L32-L39, L48A, L49a, L50 Overprinted

Serrate Roulette 13

Red Overprint (vertical, reading down)

No.	Type	Description	Unused	Used
L81	A1	¼pi green	*1,850.*	
a.		Overprint reading up	1,500.	
b.		Overprint horizontal	2,000.	
c.		As "b," overprint inverted	2,250.	

Perf. 11½

Blue Overprint

No.	Type	Description	Unused	Used
L82	A7	⅛pi red brown	7.75	*7.00*
a.		Inverted overprint	75.00	
L83	A7	½pi red	15.00	*7.25*
a.		Double overprint	90.00	
b.		Inverted overprint	75.00	*45.00*
c.		Double ovpt., one invtd.	135.00	
d.		Overprint reading up	190.00	
L84	A7	1pi dark blue	*900.00*	
a.		Inverted overprint	*1,100.*	
L85	A7	1½pi violet	22.50	*20.00*
a.		Inverted overprint	140.00	*45.00*
b.		Horiz. pair, imperf. vert.	*175.00*	
c.		Pair, one with invert. ovpt., one without ovpt.	*1,825.*	
L86	A7	2pi orange	12.50	*12.50*
a.		Double ovpt., one invtd.	145.00	
b.		Inverted overprint	125.00	
c.		Double overprint	135.00	
d.		Pair, one without overprint	1,375.	
L87	A7	3pi olive brown	12.00	*10.00*
a.		Inverted overprint	80.00	
b.		Double ovpt., one invtd.	135.00	
c.		Overprint reading up	275.00	
d.		Dbl. ovpt., both invtd.	175.00	
L88	A7	3pi dull red	12.50	*12.50*
a.		Inverted overprint	80.00	
b.		Double ovpt., one invtd.	135.00	
c.		Pair, one without ovpt.	*550.00*	
L89	A7	5pi olive green	16.00	*15.00*
a.		Inverted overprint	145.00	

For errors and varieties in never hinged condition add 50%.

Black Overprint

No.	Type	Description	Unused	Used
L90	A7	⅛pi red brown	*75.00*	
a.		Inverted overprint	*275.00*	
L91	A7	½pi red	7.50	7.25
a.		Inverted overprint	85.00	
L92	A7	1pi dark blue	*900.00*	
a.		Inverted overprint	*1,100.*	
L93	A7	1½pi violet	20.00	*20.00*
a.		Inverted overprint	135.00	
L94	A7	2pi orange	11.50	*11.50*
a.		Inverted overprint	55.00	
b.		Horiz. pair, imperf. btwn.	155.00	
L95	A7	3pi olive brown	12.00	*9.25*
a.		Inverted overprint	87.50	*87.50*
L96	A7	3pi dull red	15.00	*12.00*
a.		Inverted overprint	90.00	
L97	A7	5pi olive green	16.00	*15.00*
		Never hinged	27.50	
a.		Inverted overprint	67.50	
b.		Double ovpt., one invert.	350.00	

Red Overprint

No.	Type	Description	Unused	Used
L98	A7	⅛pi red brn, invtd.	*1,600.*	
L99	A7	¼pi yellow grn	26.00	*26.00*
a.		Tête bêche pair	100.00	
b.		Inverted overprint	55.00	
c.		Tête bêche pair, one with inverted overprint	125.00	
d.		Double overprint	155.00	
L100	A7	½pi red	*1,750.*	*800.00*
a.		Inverted overprint	*2,250.*	—
L101	A7	1pi dark blue	13.50	*13.50*
a.		Inverted overprint	55.00	
b.		Double ovpt., one invtd.	80.00	
c.		Vert. pair, imperf. horiz.	155.00	
L102	A7	1½pi violet	7.25	*7.25*
a.		Inverted overprint	90.00	
b.		Horiz. pair, imperf. vert.	60.00	
L103	A7	2pi orange	20.00	*20.00*
a.		Inverted overprint	90.00	
b.		Overprint reading up	350.00	
L104	A7	3pi olive brown	20.00	*20.00*
a.		Inverted overprint	40.00	
b.		Vert. pair, imperf. btwn.	155.00	
L105	A7	3pi dull red, invtd.	*1,700.*	
L106	A7	5pi olive green	20.00	*11.50*
a.		Inverted overprint	90.00	
b.		Overprint reading up	365.00	
c.		Overprint reading down	365.00	
d.		Pair, one without ovpt.	400.00	
L107	A8	10pi vio & dk brn	26.00	*27.50*
a.		Inverted overprint	155.00	
b.		Center inverted	155.00	
c.		As "b," invtd. ovpt.	*250.00*	
d.		Ovpt. reading up	190.00	
e.		Ovpt. reading down	300.00	

Nos. L98, L105 with normal overprint are fakes.

Gold Overprint

No.	Type	Description	Unused	Used
L108	A7	⅛pi red brown	45.00	*42.50*
L109	A7	½pi red	45.00	*42.50*
L110	A7	1pi dark blue	45.00	*42.50*
L111	A7	1½pi violet	185.00	*180.00*
L112	A7	2pi orange	145.00	*150.00*
L113	A7	3pi olive brown	55.00	*55.00*
L114	A7	3pi dull red	165.00	*160.00*
L115	A7	5pi olive green	155.00	*140.00*
		Nos. L108-L115 (8)	840.00	*812.50*

Inverted overprints are forgeries.

Same Overprint on Nos. L42-L48

Blue Overprint

No.	Type	Description	Unused	Used
L116	A7	⅛pi red brown	60.00	*60.00*
a.		Double ovpt., one invtd.	*350.00*	
L117	A7	½pi red	135.00	*135.00*
L118	A7	1pi dark blue	92.50	*85.00*
L119	A7	1½pi violet	110.00	*100.00*
L120	A7	2pi orange	460.00	*440.00*
a.		Inverted overprint	*500.00*	
L121	A7	3pi olive brown	165.00	*165.00*
a.		Inverted overprint	*230.00*	
L122	A7	5pi olive green	60.00	*60.00*
a.		Inverted overprint	*250.00*	
		Nos. L116-L122 (7)	1,083.	*1,045.*

Black Overprint

No.	Type	Description	Unused	Used
L123	A7	⅛pi red brown	75.00	*65.00*
a.		Inverted overprint	*275.00*	
L125	A7	1½pi violet	250.00	*210.00*
a.		Inverted overprint	*300.00*	
L127	A7	3pi olive brown	165.00	*175.00*
a.		Inverted overprint	*300.00*	
L128	A7	5pi olive green	250.00	*210.00*
a.		Inverted overprint	*300.00*	
		Nos. L123-L128 (4)	740.00	*660.00*

Red Overprint

No.	Type	Description	Unused	Used
L129	A7	1pi dark blue	165.00	*145.00*
L130	A7	1½pi violet	165.00	*165.00*
L131	A7	2pi orange	165.00	*150.00*
		Nos. L129-L131 (3)	495.00	*460.00*

Overprints on stamps or in colors other than those listed are forgeries.

For errors and varieties in never hinged condition add 50%.

Stamps of 1922-24 Surcharged

a

and Handstamp Surcharged

b — 1/4pi

b — 1pi

b — 10pi

1925 **Litho.** ***Perf. 11½***

No.	Type	Description	Unused	Used
L135	A7	¼pi on ¼pi on ⅛pi red brn	77.50	*77.50*
c.		Pair, one without handstamp	*275.00*	
d.		Overprint inverted	155.00	
e.		Double overprint	185.00	
f.		Violet handstamp overprint	190.00	
g.		As "f," dbl. ovpt., both invtd.	190.00	
h.		As "g," overprinted on both sides inverted on back	190.00	
L136	A7	¼pi on ¼pi on ½pi red	45.00	*45.00*
c.		1pi on ¼pi on ½pi	160.00	*65.00*
d.		As "c," handstamped in violet	*750.00*	
e.		Pair, one without handstamp	250.00	
f.		Overprint inverted	150.00	
g.		Double overprint	175.00	
h.		Dbl. ovpt., one inverted	325.00	
i.		Ovpt. on both sides	350.00	
L138	A7	1pi on 1pi on 2pi orange	45.00	*45.00*
a.		¼pi on ¼pi on 2pi org	125.00	
b.		10pi on 1pi on 2pi org	125.00	
c.		¼pi on 1pi on 2pi org	75.00	
d.		1pi on ¼pi on 2pi org	*125.00*	
f.		Pair, one without handstamp	350.00	
g.		Overprint inverted	145.00	
h.		Double overprint	175.00	
i.		Violet handstamp	190.00	
j.		As "i," inverted overprint	190.00	
L139	A7	1pi on 1pi on 3pi ol brn	40.00	*40.00*
b.		Pair, one without handstamp	210.00	
c.		Overprint inverted	125.00	
d.		Dbl. ovpt., one inverted	275.00	
e.		Violet handstamp	150.00	
L140	A7	1pi on 1pi on 3pi dl red	55.00	*55.00*
b.		¼pi on 1pi on 3pi dl red	350.00	
c.		Pair, one without handstamp	*275.00*	
d.		Overprint inverted	150.00	
e.		Double overprint	175.00	
f.		Violet handstamp	275.00	
g.		As"f," inverted overprint	275.00	
L141	A7	10pi on 10pi on 5pi ol grn	27.50	*27.50*
		Nos. L135-L141 (6)	290.00	*290.00*

The printed surcharge (a) reads "The Hejaz Government. October 4, 1924." with new denomination in third line. This surcharge alone was used for the first issue (Nos. L135a-L141a). The new denomination was so small and indistinct that its equivalent in larger characters was soon added by handstamp (b) at bottom of each stamp for the second issue (Nos. L135-L141).

The handstamped surcharge (b) is found double, inverted, etc. It is also known in dark violet.

Without Handstamp "b"

No.	Type	Description	Unused
L135a	A7	¼pi on ⅛pi red brn	155.00
L136b	A7	¼pi on ½pi red	155.00
L138e	A7	1pi on 2pi orange	155.00
L139a	A7	1pi on 3pi olive brn	155.00
L140a	A7	1pi on 3pi dull red	155.00
L141a	A7	10pi on 5pi olive grn	155.00
		Nos. L135a-L141a (6)	930.00

Stamps of 1922-24 Surcharged

Black Surcharge

No.	Type	Description	Unused	Used
L142	A7	⅛pi on ½pi red	13.50	13.50
a.		Inverted surcharge	60.00	
L143	A7	¼pi on ½pi red	13.50	13.50
a.		Inverted surcharge	60.00	
L144	A7	1pi on ½pi red	13.50	13.50
a.		Inverted surcharge	60.00	
L145	A7	1pi on 1½pi vio	13.50	13.50
a.		Inverted surcharge	60.00	
L146	A7	1pi on 2pi org	13.50	13.50
a.		"10pi"	100.00	
b.		Inverted surcharge	70.00	
c.		As "a," inverted surcharge	185.00	
L147	A7	1pi on 3pi ol brn	13.50	13.50
a.		"10pi"	100.00	
b.		Inverted surcharge	70.00	
c.		As "a," inverted surcharge	185.00	
d.		Horiz. pair, imperf. vert.	150.00	
L148	A7	10pi on 5pi ol grn	22.00	24.00
a.		Inverted surcharge	90.00	
		Nos. L142-L148 (7)	103.00	*105.00*

Blue Surcharge

No.	Type	Description	Unused	Used
L149	A7	⅛pi on ½pi red	22.50	*17.00*
a.		Inverted surcharge	90.00	
b.		Double surcharge	350.00	
L150	A7	¼pi on ½pi red	22.50	*17.00*
a.		Inverted surcharge	90.00	
L151	A7	1pi on ½pi red	22.50	*17.00*
a.		Inverted surcharge	90.00	
b.		Double surcharge	125.00	275.00
L152	A7	1pi on 1½pi vio	22.50	*20.00*
a.		Inverted surcharge	290.00	
L153	A7	1pi on 2pi org	27.50	*27.50*
a.		"10pi"	100.00	
b.		Inverted surcharge	90.00	
c.		As "a," inverted surcharge	290.00	
L154	A7	1pi on 3pi ol brn	37.50	*37.50*
a.		"10pi"	110.00	
b.		Inverted surcharge	140.00	
L155	A7	10pi on 5pi ol grn	40.00	*40.00*
a.		Inverted surcharge	110.00	
		Nos. L149-L155 (7)	195.00	*176.00*

Red Surcharge

No.	Type	Description	Unused	Used
L156	A7	1pi on 1½pi vio	30.00	*30.00*
a.		Inverted surcharge	110.00	
L157	A7	1pi on 2pi org	30.00	*30.00*
a.		"10pi"	110.00	
b.		Inverted surcharge	120.00	
L158	A7	1pi on 3pi ol brn	30.00	*30.00*
a.		"10pi"	140.00	
b.		Inverted surcharge	110.00	
L159	A7	10pi on 5pi ol grn	32.50	*22.50*
a.		Inverted surcharge	110.00	
		Nos. L156-L159 (4)	122.50	*112.50*
		Nos. L142-L159 (18)	420.50	*393.50*

The "10pi" surcharge is found inverted on Nos. L146a, L147a. The existence of genuine inverted "10pi" surcharges on Nos. L153a, L154a, L157a and L158a is in doubt.

The 10pi on 1½pi is bogus.

Forr errors and varieties in never hinged condition add 50%.

King Ali Issue

A9

A10

A11

A12

1925, May-June ***Perf. 11½***

Black Overprint

No.	Type	Description	Unused	Used
L160	A9	⅛pi chocolate	2.25	*1.50*
L161	A9	¼pi ultra	2.25	*1.50*
L162	A9	½pi car rose	2.25	*1.50*
L163	A10	1pi yellow green	3.00	*1.75*
L164	A10	1½pi orange	3.00	*1.75*
L165	A10	2pi blue	3.50	*2.25*
L166	A11	3pi dark green	3.50	*2.25*
L167	A11	5pi orange brn	3.50	*2.25*
L168	A12	10pi red & green	6.00	*4.50*
a.		Center inverted	90.00	
		Nos. L160-L168 (9)	29.25	*19.25*

Red Overprint

No.	Type	Description	Unused	Used
L169	A9	⅛pi chocolate	4.00	*2.75*
L170	A9	¼pi ultra	2.50	*1.60*
L171	A10	1pi yellow green	3.00	*2.00*
L172	A10	1½pi orange	3.00	*2.00*
L173	A10	2pi deep blue	3.50	*2.50*
L174	A11	3pi dark green	3.25	*2.75*
a.		Horiz. pair, imperf. vert.	75.00	
L175	A11	5pi org brn	4.00	*2.75*
L176	A12	10pi red & green	6.50	*5.50*
		Nos. L169-L176 (8)	29.75	*21.85*

Blue Overprint

No.	Type	Description	Unused	Used
L177	A9	⅛pi chocolate	2.75	*1.75*
L179	A9	½pi car rose	2.75	*1.75*
L180	A10	1pi yellow green	2.75	*1.75*
L181	A10	1½pi orange	2.75	*1.75*
L182	A11	3pi dark green	2.75	*1.75*
L183	A11	5pi orange brn	6.75	*5.50*
L184	A12	10pi red & green	9.00	*7.25*
L185	A12	10pi red & org	275.00	
		Nos. L177-L184 (7)	29.50	*21.50*

Without Overprint

No.	Type	Description	Unused	Used
L186	A12	10pi red & green	8.00	*6.75*
a.		Dbl. impression of center	*90.00*	

The overprint in the tablets on Nos. L160-L185 reads: "5 Rabi al'awwal, 1343" (Oct. 4, 1924), the date of the accession of King Ali.

The tablet overprints vary slightly in size. Each is found reading upward or downward and at either side of the stamp. These control overprints were first applied in Jedda by the government press.

They were later made from new plates by the stamp printer in Cairo. In the Jedda overprint, the bar over the "0" figure extends to the left.

Some values exist with 13m or 15mm instead of 18mm between tablets. They sell for more. The lines of the Cairo overprinting are generally wider, but more lightly printed, usually appearing slightly grayish and the bar is at center right. The Cairo overprints are believed not to have been placed in use.

Imperforates exist.

Nos. L160-L168 are known with the overprints spaced as on type D3 and aligned horizontally.

Examples of these stamps (perforated or imperforate) without the overprint, except No. L186 were not regularly issued and not available for postage.

No. L185 exists only with Cairo overprint. Imperfs of No. L185 sell for much less than No. L185. Fake perfs have been added to the imperfs.

The ¼pi with blue overprint is bogus.

No. L186 in other colors are color trials.

For overprints see #58B-58D, Jordan 122-129.

For more detailed listings see the *Scott Classic Specialized Catalogue of Stamps and Covers.*

NEJDI ADMINISTRATION OF HEJAZ

Handstamped in Blue, Red, Black or Violet

The overprint reads: "1343. Barid al Sultanat an Nejdia" (1925. Post of the Sultanate of Nejd).

The overprints on this and succeeding issues are handstamped and, as usual, are found double, inverted, etc. These variations are scarce.

On Stamp of Turkey, 1915, With Crescent and Star in Red

1925, Mar.-Apr. Unwmk. *Perf. 12*

1 A22 5pa ocher (Bl) 30.00 27.50
2 A22 5pa ocher (R) 30.00 20.00
3 A22 5pa ocher (Bk) 30.00 22.50
4 A22 5pa ocher (V) 30.00 18.00

On Stamp of Turkey, 1913

5 A28 10pa green (Bl) 40.00 16.00
a. Inverted overprint 500.00
6 A28 10pa green (R) 40.00 12.50

On Stamps of Hejaz, 1922-24
Perf. 11½

7 A7 ⅛pi red brn (R) 70.00 24.00
8 A7 ⅛pi red brn (Bk) 70.00 35.00
9 A7 ⅛pi red brn (V) 50.00 24.00
10 A7 ¼pi car (R) 70.00 30.00
11 A7 ¼pi car (Bk) 70.00 35.00
12 A7 ¼pi car (V) *50.00 27.50*
13 A7 ½pi red (Bl) 40.00 22.50
14 A7 ½pi red (V) 40.00 18.00
15 A7 1½pi vio (R) 60.00 24.00
16 A7 2pi yel buff (R) 85.00 57.50
a. 2pi orange (R) 110.00
17 A7 2pi yel buff (V) 85.00 57.50
a. 2pi orange (V) 100.00 32.50
18 A7 3pi brn red (Bl) 70.00 30.00
19 A7 3pi brn red (R) 70.00 22.50
20 A7 3pi brn red (V) 70.00 25.00

Many Hejaz stamps of the 1922 type were especially printed for this and following issues. The re-impressions are usually more clearly printed, in lighter shades than the 1922 stamps, and some are in new colors.

Counterfeits exist.

Arabic Inscriptions
R1 R2

On Hejaz Bill Stamp

22 R1 1pi violet (R) 40.00 15.00

On Hejaz Notarial Stamps

23 R2 1pi violet (R) 50.00 20.00
24 R2 2pi blue (R) 50.00 30.00
25 R2 2pi blue (V) 50.00 27.50

For overprint see No. 49.

On Hejaz Railway Tax Stamps

Locomotive — R3

Type I

Type II

Two design types appear on the basic revenue stamps. Type 1 depicts the cab's window and the band at the center of the boiler as a series of horizontal lines, the top of the cab does not touch the frame line above it, and the coupler at rear of car appears as a fine hook that does not touch the right frame. Type 2 depicts the cab's window and band on boiler as open vertical spaces, the top of the cab touches the frame line above it, and the coupler appears as a blob connected to the right frame line. Type 2 appears in position 12 in the sheet of 18 (6x3) of the 500pi value, and in position 30 in the 36-stamp (6x6) sheets in which the other values were printed.

Type 1

26 R3 1pi blue (R) 40.00 9.00
a. Type 2 60.00
27 R3 2pi ocher (R) 60.00 14.00
a. Type 2 90.00
28 R3 2pi ocher (V) 60.00 14.00
a. Type 2 90.00
29 R3 3pi lilac (R) 60.00 20.00
a. Type 2 90.00
Nos. 1-20,22-29 (28) 1,510. 698.50

For overprints and surcharges see Nos. 34, 50-54, 55, 59-68, J12-J15.

Pilgrimage Issue

Various Stamps Handstamp Surcharged in Blue and Red in Types "a" and "b" and with Tablets with New Values

a

b

Surcharge "a" reads: "Tezkar al Hajj al Awwal Fi 'ahd al Sultanat al Nejdia, 1343" (Commemorating the first pilgrimage under the Nejdi Sultanate, 1925).

"b" reads: "Al Arba" (Wednesday.)

On Stamps of Turkey, 1913

1925, July 1 *Perf. 12*

30 A28 1pi on 10pa grn (Bl & R) 100.00 55.00
31 A30 5pi on 1pi bl (Bl & R) 100.00 55.00

On Stamps of Hejaz, 1917-18
Serrate Roulette 13

32 A5 2pi on 1pa lil brn (R & Bl) 125.00 67.50
33 A4 4pi on ⅛pi org (R & Bl) 400.00 350.00

On Hejaz Railway Tax Stamp
Perf. 11½

34 R3 3pi lilac, type 1 (Bl & R) 200.00 40.00
a. Type 2 300.00
Nos. 30-34 (5) 925.00 567.50

No. 30 with handstamp "a" in black was a favor item. Nos. 30 and 33 with both handstamps in red are forgeries.

The below handstamp is said to be in private hands at this time. Extreme caution is advised before buying rare items.

Handstamped in Blue, Red, Black or Violet

This overprint has practically the same meaning as that described over No. 1. The Mohammedan year (1343) is omitted.

On Stamp of Turkey, 1915, with Crescent and Star in Red

1925, July-Aug. *Perf. 12*

35 A22 5pa ocher (Bl) 50.00 24.00

On Stamps of Turkey, 1913

36 A28 10pa green (Bl) 60.00 20.00
a. Black overprint 120.00
b. As "a," overprint inverted 650.00

On Stamps of Hejaz, 1922 (Nos. L28-L29)
Serrate Roulette 13

37 A3 1pi blue (R) 120.00 *67.50*
38 A6 2pi magenta (Bl) 120.00 *67.50*

On Stamps of Hejaz, 1922-24
Perf. 11½

38A A7 ⅛pi red brn (Bk) *4,500.*
38B A7 ⅛pi red brn (Bl) *3,750.*
39 A7 ½pi red (Bl) 12.50 10.00
a. Imperf., pair 25.00 22.50
39B A7 ½pi red (Bk) 20.00 18.00
c. Imperf., pair 50.00 37.50
40 A7 1pi gray vio (R) 50.00 29.00
a. 1pi black violet (R) *50.00*
41 A7 1½pi dk red (Bk) 50.00 30.00
a. 1½pi brick red (Bk) 50.00
42 A7 2pi yel buff (Bl) 80.00 47.50
a. 2pi orange (Bl) 110.00 55.00
43 A7 2pi deep vio (Bl) 85.00 52.50
44 A7 3pi brown red (Bl) 50.00 30.00
45 A7 5pi scarlet (Bl) 70.00 37.50
Never hinged 110.00
Nos. 35-38,39-45 (12) 767.50 *433.50*

Overprint on Nos. 38A, 39B, 39C is blue-black.

See note above No. 35.

With Additional Surcharge of New Value Typo. in Black

c

d

e

Color in parenthesis is that of overprint on basic stamp.

46 A7(c) 1pi on ½pi (Bl) 12.50 1.75
a. Imperf, pair 40.00
b. Ovpt. & surch. inverted 90.00
47 A7(d) 1½pi on ½pi (Bl) 17.50 7.25
a. Imperf., pair 30.00
48 A7(e) 2pi on 3pi (Bl) 17.50 16.00
Nos. 46-48 (3) 47.50 25.00

Several variations in type settings of "c," "d" and "e" exist, including inverted letters and values.

On Hejaz Notarial Stamp

49 R2 2pi blue (Bk) 50.00 20.00

On Hejaz Railway Tax Stamps

50 R3 1pi blue, type 1 (R) 40.00 25.00
a. Type 2 60.00
51 R3 1pi blue, type 1 (Bk) 60.00 9.00
a. Type 2 90.00
52 R3 2pi ocher, type 1 (Bl) 60.00 9.00
a. Type 2 90.00
53 R3 3pi lilac, type 1 (Bl) 70.00 22.50
a. Type 2 100.00
54 R3 5pi grn, type 1 (Bl) 60.00 20.00
a. Type 2 90.00
Nos. 49-54 (6) 340.00 105.50

Hejaz Railway Tax Stamp Handstamped in Black

This overprint reads: "Al Saudia. — Al Sultanat al Nejdia." (The Saudi Sultanate of Nejd.)

1925-26 Small Handstamp

55 R3 1pi blue, type 1 — *250.00*
b. Type 2 500.00

On Nos. L34, L36-L37, L41

56 A7 1½pi violet — *425.00*
57 A7 2pi orange — *450.00*
57A A7 10pi on 5pi ol grn — *450.00*

On Nos. L95 and L97

58 A7 3pi olive brown — *450.00*
58A A7 5pi olive green — *450.00*

On Nos. L162-L163, L173
Perf. 11½

58B A9 ½pi car rose 400.00 —
58C A10 1pi yel grn — *300.00*
58D A10 2pi blue — *400.00*

Large Handstamp

58K R3 1pi blue *12,000.*
58L A7 3pi brn (#L95b) reading up *1,500.*
a. Overprint reading down 1,500.
58M A10 1pi yel grn (#L163) 1,750. *1,250.*

Nos. 55-58M were provisionally issued at Medina after its capitulation.

Only one example of No. 58K, a single stamp used on piece, is known.

This overprint exists on Nos. L160-L161, L164-L172, L174-L175, L180-L183. These 17 are known as bogus items, but may exist genuine.

Lithographed overprints are forgeries.

Medina Issue

Hejaz Railway Tax Stamps Handstamped

and Handstamp Surcharged in Various Colors

The large overprint reads: "The Nejdi Posts — 1344 — Commemorating Medina, the Illustrious." The tablet shows the new value.

1925

59 R3 1pi on 10pi vio, type 1 (Bk & V) 70.00 70.00
a. Type 2 100.00
60 R3 2pi on 50pi lt bl, type 1 (R & Bl) 70.00 70.00
a. Type 2 100.00
61 R3 3pi on 100pi red brn, type 1 (Bl & Bk) 70.00 70.00
a. Type 2 100.00
62 R3 4pi on 500pi dull red, type 1 (Bl & Bk) 70.00 70.00
a. Type 2 100.00

63 R3 5pi on 1000pi dp red, type 1 (Bl & Bk)	70.00	70.00
a. Type 2	100.00	
Nos. 59-63 (5)	350.00	350.00

JEDDA ISSUE

Hejaz Railway Tax Stamps Handstamped and Tablet with New Value in Various Colors

This handstamp reads: "Commemorating Jedda — 1344 — The Nejdi Posts."

1925

64 R3 1pi on 10pi vio, type 1 (Bk & Bl)	70.00	70.00
b. Type 2	100.00	
65 R3 2pi on 50pi lt bl, type 1 (R & Bk)	70.00	70.00
a. Type 2	100.00	
66 R3 3pi on 100pi red brn, type 1 (R & Bl)	70.00	70.00
a. Type 2	100.00	
67 R3 4pi on 500pi dl red, type 1 (Bk & Bl)	70.00	70.00
a. Type 2	100.00	
68 R3 5pi on 1000pi dp red, type 1 (Bk & Bl)	70.00	70.00
a. Type 2	100.00	
Nos. 64-68 (5)	350.00	350.00

Nos. 59-63 and 64-68 were prepared in anticipation of the surrender of Medina and Jedda.

Kingdom of Hejaz-Nejd

Arabic Inscriptions and Value — A1

A2

Inscriptions in upper tablets: "Barid al Hejaz wa Nejd" (Posts of the Hejaz and Nejd)

1926, Feb. Typo. Unwmk. *Perf. 11*

69 A1 ¼pi violet	45.00	18.00
70 A1 ½pi gray	45.00	18.00
71 A1 1pi deep blue	45.00	22.00
72 A2 2pi blue green	45.00	18.00
73 A2 3pi carmine	45.00	19.00
74 A2 5pi maroon	45.00	20.00
Nos. 69-74 (6)	270.00	115.00

Nos. 69-72, 74 exist imperf. Value, each $40.
Used values are for favor cancels.

1926, Mar. *Perf. 11*

75 A1 ¼pi orange	12.00	10.00
a. Horiz. pair, imperf between	100.00	
76 A1 ½pi blue green	5.25	*15.00*
a. Horiz. pair, imperf between	100.00	
b. Vertz. pair, imperf between	100.00	
77 A1 1pi carmine	4.25	*7.50*
a. Horiz. pair, imperf between	100.00	
b. Vert. pair, imperf between	100.00	
78 A2 2pi violet	5.25	*12.50*
a. Horiz. pair, imperf between	100.00	
b. Vert. pair, imperf between	100.00	
79 A2 3pi dark blue	5.25	*7.50*
a. Horiz. pair, imperf between	100.00	
b. Vert. pair, imperf between	100.00	
80 A2 5pi lt brown	10.00	*20.00*
a. 5pi olive brown		
b. Horiz. pair, imperf between	100.00	
c. Vert. pair, imperf between	100.00	
Nos. 75-80 (6)	42.00	72.50

Nos. 75-80 also exist imperf. Value, twice the values shown above. Examples that are perforated 14, 14x11 and 11x14 were privately produced.

Counterfeits of types A1 and A2 are perf. 11½. They exist with and without overprints.

Types A1 and A2 in colors other than listed are proofs.

Pan-Islamic Congress Issue

Stamps of 1926 Hstmpd.

1926 *Perf. 11*

92 A1 ¼pi orange	12.00	5.00
93 A1 ½pi blue green	12.00	5.00
94 A1 1pi carmine	12.00	5.00
95 A2 2pi violet	12.00	5.00
96 A2 3pi dark blue	12.00	5.00
97 A2 5pi light brown	12.00	5.00
Nos. 92-97 (6)	72.00	30.00

The overprint reads: "al Mootamar al Islami 20 Zilkada, Sanat 1344." (The Islamic Congress, June 1, 1926.)

See counterfeit note after No. 80.

Tughra of King Abdul Aziz — A3

1926-27 Typo. *Perf. 11½*

98 A3 ⅛pi ocher	5.00	.60
99 A3 ¼pi gray green	6.00	1.50
100 A3 ½pi dull red	6.00	1.50
On paper wrapper		75.00
On cover		100.00
On cover, single franking		200.00
b. Horiz. pair, imperf between	400.00	
101 A3 1pi deep violet	6.50	1.50
102 A3 1½pi gray blue	18.00	2.25
103 A3 3pi olive green	14.00	4.75
104 A3 5pi brown orange	27.50	5.00
105 A3 10pi dark brown	70.00	7.00
Nos. 98-105 (8)	153.00	24.10

Inscription at top reads: "Al Hukumat al Arabia" (The Arabian Government). Inscription below tughra reads: "Barid al Hejaz wa Nejd" (Post of the Hejaz and Nejd).

Stamps of 1926-27 Handstamped in Black or Red

1927

107 A3 ⅛pi ocher	13.00	4.75
108 A3 ¼pi gray grn	13.00	4.75
109 A3 ½pi dull red	13.00	4.75
110 A3 1pi deep violet	13.00	4.75
111 A3 1½pi gray bl (R)	13.00	4.75
112 A3 3pi olive green	13.00	4.75
113 A3 5pi brown orange	14.50	4.75
114 A3 10pi dark brown	16.00	4.75
Nos. 107-114 (8)	108.50	38.00
Set, never hinged	175.00	

The overprint reads: "In commemoration of the Kingdom of Nejd and Dependencies, 25th Rajab 1345."

Inverted varieties have not been authenticated.

Turkey No. 258 Surcharged in Violet

1925 *Perf. 12*

115 A28 1g on 10pa green	175.00	

Similar surcharges of 6g and 20g were made in red, but were not known to have been issued. Values: 6g, $350; 20g, $500.

A4

1929-30 Typo. *Perf. 11½*

117 A4 1¾g gray blue	40.00	4.50
119 A4 20g violet	50.00	12.50
120 A4 30g green	80.00	25.00

A5

1930 *Perf. 11, 11½*

125 A5 ½g rose	19.00	3.25
126 A5 1½g violet	19.00	2.10
127 A5 1¾g ultra	19.00	2.75
128 A5 3½g emerald	19.00	4.25
Perf. 11		
129 A5 5g black brown	30.00	6.50
Nos. 125-129 (5)	106.00	18.85

Anniversary of King Ibn Saud's accession to the throne of the Hejaz, January 8, 1926.

A6

1931-32 *Perf. 11½*

130 A6 ⅛g ocher ('32)	22.50	3.25
131 A6 ¼g blue green	22.50	2.50
133 A6 1¾g ultra	37.50	3.25
Nos. 130-133 (3)	82.50	9.00

A7

1932 *Perf. 11½*

135 A7 ¼g blue green	16.00	32.50
a. Perf 11		
136 A7 ½g scarlet	47.50	5.25
a. Perf 11		
137 A7 2¼g ultra	90.00	8.50
a. Perf 11		
Nos. 135-137 (3)	153.50	46.25

Kingdom of Saudi Arabia

A8

1934, Jan. *Perf. 11½, Imperf.*

138 A8 ¼g yellow green	11.00	10.00
Never hinged	15.00	
139 A8 ½g red	11.00	10.00
Never hinged	15.00	
140 A8 1½g light blue	21.00	19.00
Never hinged	27.50	
141 A8 3g blue green	21.00	19.00
Never hinged	27.50	
142 A8 3½g ultra	37.50	7.75
Never hinged	47.50	
143 A8 5g yellow	50.00	37.50
Never hinged	65.00	
144 A8 10g red orange	90.00	
Never hinged	120.00	
145 A8 20g bright violet	110.00	
Never hinged	150.00	
146 A8 ¼s claret	225.00	
Never hinged	300.00	
147 A8 30g dull violet	140.00	
Never hinged	180.00	
148 A8 ½s chocolate	475.00	
Never hinged	700.00	
149 A8 1s violet brown	1,075.	
Never hinged	1,750.	
Nos. 138-149 (12)	2,267.	

Proclamation of Emir Saud as Heir Apparent of Arabia. Perf. and imperf. stamps were issued in equal quantities.

Favor cancels exist on Nos. 144-149.

Tughra of King Abdul Aziz — A9

1934-57 *Perf. 11, 11½*

159 A9 ⅛g yellow	5.25	.45
160 A9 ¼g yellow grn	5.25	.45
161 A9 ½g rose red ('43)	3.75	.25
a. ½g dark carmine	12.00	1.40
162 A9 ⅞g lt blue ('56)	6.50	.55
163 A9 1g blue green	5.25	.45
164 A9 2g olive grn ('57)	9.00	2.25
a. 2g olive bister ('57)	25.00	7.25
165 A9 2⅞g violet ('57)	6.50	.55
166 A9 3g ultra ('38)	6.50	.25
a. 3g light blue	20.00	1.75
167 A9 3½g lt ultra	35.00	2.25
168 A9 5g orange	6.50	.55
169 A9 10g violet	19.00	1.75
170 A9 20g purple brn	32.50	1.10
a. 20g purple black	25.00	2.25
171 A9 100g red vio ('42)	90.00	5.25
172 A9 200g vio brn ('42)	115.00	7.00
Nos. 159-172 (14)	346.00	23.10
Set, never hinged	450.00	

The ½g has two types differing in position of the tughra.

No. 162 measures 31x22mm. No. 164 30½x21½mm. No. 165, 30½x22mm. No. 166 30x21mm. No. 171, 31x22mm. No. 172, 30½x21½mm. Rest of set, 29x20½mm. Grayish paper was used in 1946-49 printings.

No. 168 exists with pin-perf 6.

For overprint see No. J24.

Yanbu Harbor near Radwa — A10

1945 Typo. *Perf. 11½*

173 A10 ½g brt carmine	7.75	.50
174 A10 3g lt ultra	10.00	1.75
175 A10 5g purple	27.50	2.75
176 A10 10g dk brown vio	60.00	5.00
Nos. 173-176 (4)	105.25	10.00
Set, never hinged	145.00	

Meeting of King Abdul Aziz and King Farouk of Egypt at Jebal Radwa, Saudi Arabia, Jan. 24, 1945.

Catalogue values for unused stamps in this section, from this point to the end of the section, are for Never Hinged items.

Arms of Saudi Arabia and Afghanistan A12

1950, Mar. *Perf. 11*

178 A12 ½g carmine	8.00	1.10
179 A12 3g violet blue	13.50	1.10

Visit of Zahir Shah of Afghanistan, March 1950. One 3g in each sheet inscribed POSTFS, value $45.

Old City Walls, Riyadh A13

1950 Center in Red Brown

180 A13 ½g magenta	55.00	1.50
181 A13 1g lt blue	12.00	2.25
182 A13 3g violet	19.00	4.00
183 A13 5g vermilion	40.00	7.00
184 A13 10g green	70.00	14.50
a. Singular "guerche" in Arabic	525.00	180.00
Nos. 180-184 (5)	196.00	29.25

50th lunar anniversary of King Ibn Saud's capture of Riyadh, Jan. 16, 1902.

No. 184a: On the 3g, 5g and 10g the currency is expressed in the plural in both French (grouche) and Arabic. One stamp in each sheet of 20 (4x5), position 11, of the 10g shows the Arabic characters in the singular form of "guerche," as on the ½g and 1g.

Arms of Saudi Arabia and Jordan — A14

1951, Nov. *Perf. 11*

185 A14 ½g carmine 12.00 1.40
a. "BOYAUME" *275.00* 100.00
186 A14 3g violet blue 20.00 2.25
a. "BOYAUME" *275.00* 100.00

Visit of King Tallal of Jordan, Nov. 1951.

Bedouins and Train — A15

1952, June **Engr.** *Perf. 12*

187 A15 ½q redsh brown 9.00 2.75
188 A15 1q deep green 9.75 3.25
189 A15 3q violet 18.00 2.75
190 A15 10q rose pink 35.00 11.50
191 A15 20q blue 72.50 27.00
Nos. 187-191 (5) 144.25 47.25

Inaugural trip over the Saudi Government Railroad between Riyadh and Dammam.

Saudi Arabia Arms and Lebanon Emblem — A16

1953, Feb. **Typo.** *Perf. 11*

192 A16 ½g carmine 7.25 1.40
193 A16 3g violet blue 14.00 3.25

Visit of President Camille Chamoun of Lebanon.

Arms of Saudi Arabia and Emblem of Pakistan A17

1953, Mar.

194 A17 ½g dark carmine 8.00 1.40
195 A17 3g violet blue 17.00 3.25

Visit of Gov.-Gen. Ghulam Mohammed of Pakistan.

Arms of Saudi Arabia and Jordan — A18

1953, July **Unwmk.**

196 A18 ½g carmine 8.00 1.40
a. "GOERCHE" *75.00*
197 A18 3g violet blue 17.00 3.25

Visit of King Hussein of Jordan, July, 1953.

Globe — A18a

1955, July **Litho.**

198 A18a ½g emerald 4.00 .80
199 A18a 3g violet 10.00 1.50
200 A18a 4g orange 14.00 4.25
Nos. 198-200 (3) 28.00 6.55

Founding of the Arab Postal Union, July 1, 1954.

Ministry of Communications Building, Riyadh — A19

1960, Apr. 12 **Photo.** *Perf. 13*

201 A19 2p bright blue 1.30 .80
202 A19 5p deep claret 3.00 1.15
203 A19 10p dark green 6.50 1.50
Nos. 201-203 (3) 10.80 3.45

Arab Postal Union Conference, at Riyadh, Apr. 11. Imperfs. exist.

Arab League Center, Cairo A20

1960, Mar. 22 *Perf. 13x13½*

204 A20 2p dull grn & blk 2.25 1.15

Opening of the Arab League Center and the Arab Postal Museum in Cairo. Exists imperf.

Radio Tower and Waves A21

1960, June 4

205 A21 2p red & black 2.00 1.00
206 A21 5p brown blk & mar 3.75 1.50
207 A21 10p bluish blk & ultra 6.75 3.00
Nos. 205-207 (3) 12.50 5.50

1st international radio station in Saudi Arabia. Imperfs. exist.

Map of Palestine, Refugee Camp and WRY Emblem — A22

1960, Oct. 30 **Litho.** *Perf. 13*

208 A22 2p dark blue .40 .25
209 A22 8p lilac .40 .25
210 A22 10p green 1.50 .80
Nos. 208-210 (3) 2.30 1.30

World Refugee Year, July 1, 1959-June 30, 1960. Imperfs. exist.

Wadi Hanifa Dam, near Riyadh — A23

Type I (Saud Cartouche) (Illustrated over No. 286)

1960-62 **Unwmk.** **Photo.** *Perf. 14*

Size: 27½x22mm

211 A23 ½p bis brn & org 1.50 .25
212 A23 1p ol bis & pur 1.50 .25
213 A23 2p blue & sepia 1.50 .25
214 A23 3p sepia & blue 1.50 .25
215 A23 4p sepia & ocher 1.50 .25
216 A23 5p blk & dk violet 1.50 .25
217 A23 6p brn blk & car rose ('62) 1.50 .40
a. 6p black & carmine rose 1.50 .35
218 A23 7p red & gray ol 1.50 .25
219 A23 8p dk bl & brn blk 1.50 .30
220 A23 9p org brn & scar 1.60 .40
c. 9p yel brn & metallic red 1.60 .45
221 A23 10p emer grn & mar ('62) 1.75 .40
a. 10p blue green & maroon 2.10 .70
222 A23 20p brown & green 4.00 .55
223 A23 50p black & brown 24.00 2.50
224 A23 75p brown & gray 70.00 4.00
225 A23 100p dk bl & grn bl 65.00 3.00
226 A23 200p lilac & green 110.00 8.00
Nos. 211-226 (16) 289.85 21.30

Gas-Oil Separating Plant, Buqqa — A24

1960-61

227 A24 ½p maroon & org 1.40 1.25
228 A24 1p blue & red org 1.40 1.25
229 A24 2p ver & blue 1.40 1.25
230 A24 3p lilac & brt grn 1.40 1.25
231 A24 4p yel grn & lilac 1.40 1.25
232 A24 5p dk gray & brn red 1.40 1.25
233 A24 6p brn org & dk vio 1.40 1.25
234 A24 7p vio & dull grn 1.40 1.25
235 A24 8p blue grn & gray 2.25 1.25
236 A24 9p ultra & sepia 4.00 1.25
237 A24 10p dk blue & rose 2.00 .40
238 A24 20p org brn & blk 7.25 .60
239 A24 50p red & brn grn 20.00 1.60
240 A24 75p red & blk brn 34.00 3.25
241 A24 100p dk bl & red brn 52.50 3.25
242 A24 200p dk gray & ol grn 100.00 7.00
Nos. 227-242 (16) 233.20 28.60

Nearly all of Nos. 211-242 exist imperf; probably not regularly issued.

See Nos. 258-273, 286-341, 393-450, 461-483.

Dammam Port — A25

Wmk. 337

1961, Aug. 16 **Litho.** *Perf. 13*

243 A25 3p lilac 1.50 .25
244 A25 6p light blue 2.50 .55
245 A25 8p dark green 4.00 .70
Nos. 243-245 (3) 8.00 1.50

Expansion of the port of Dammam. Imperf min. sheets of 4 were for presentation purposes and have wmk. sideways. Value, set $425. Imperforate pairs or margined imperfs with upright watermark come from full sheets not perforated by the print shop.

Globe, Radio and Telegraph A26

Perf. 13x13½

1961, Aug. 7 **Photo.** **Unwmk.**

246 A26 3p dull purple 1.50 .25
247 A26 6p gray black 2.25 .70
248 A26 8p brown 4.00 .55
Nos. 246-248 (3) 7.75 1.50

Arab Union of Telecommunications. Imperfs. exist.

Arab League Building, Cairo — A27

1962, Apr. 22 **Wmk. 337** *Perf. 13*

249 A27 3p olive green 1.40 .25
250 A27 6p carmine rose 3.00 .35
251 A27 8p slate blue 4.00 .45
Nos. 249-251 (3) 8.40 1.05

Arab League Week, Mar. 22-28.

Imperforate or missing-color varieties of Nos. 249-285 and 344-353 were not regularly issued.

Malaria Eradication Emblem — A28

1962, May 7 **Litho.** **Wmk. 337**

252 A28 3p red org & blue 1.25 .25
253 A28 6p emerald & Prus bl 1.60 .35
254 A28 8p black & lil rose 2.40 .50
a. Souv. sheet of 3, #252-254, imperf. 26.00 26.00
Nos. 252-254 (3) 5.25 1.10

WHO drive to eradicate malaria.

Nos. 252-254 are known unofficially overprinted with new dates only or with "AIR MAIL" and two plane silhouettes.

A 4p exists as an essay.

Koran A29

1963, Mar. 12 **Wmk. 337** *Perf. 11*

255 A29 2½p lilac rose & pink 1.00 .50
256 A29 7½p blue & pale grn 1.75 .40
257 A29 9½p green & gray 3.00 .50
Nos. 255-257 (3) 5.75 1.40

First anniversary of the Islamic Institute, Medina. A 3p exists as an essay. Copies of the 2½p exist with virtually all the pink background omitted. No copies are known with the pink completely omitted.

Dam Type of 1960 Redrawn
Type I (Saud Cartouche)

Perf. 13½x13

1963-65 **Wmk. 337** **Litho.**

Size: 28½x23mm

258 A23 ½p bis brn & org 14.00 1.30

Nos. 258, 264-265 are widely spaced in the sheet, producing large margins.

Perf. 14

Photo.

Size: 27½x22mm

259 A23 ½p bis brn & org ('65) 22.50 1.50
260 A23 3p sepia & blue 9.00 .65
261 A23 4p sepia & ocher ('64) 12.50 .80
262 A23 5p black & dk vio 12.50 .80
263 A23 20p dk car & grn 22.50 1.60
Nos. 258-263 (6) 93.00 6.65

A 1p was prepared but not issued. It is known only imperf.

Gas-Oil Plant Type of 1960 Redrawn
Type I (Saud Cartouche)

Perf. 13½x13

1963-65 **Wmk. 337** **Litho.**

Size: 28½x23mm

264 A24 ½p mar & org 12.00 1.25
265 A24 1p bl & red org ('64) 6.50 .65

Photo.

Perf. 14

Size: 27½x22mm

266 A24 ½p mar & org ('64) 10.50 .50
267 A24 1p blue & red org 9.00 .40
268 A24 3p lilac & brt grn 21.00 1.00
269 A24 4p yel grn & lilac 14.00 .50
270 A24 5p dk gray & brn red 12.00 .50
271 A24 6p brn org & dk vio ('65) 17.00 .75

272 A24 8p dull grn & blk 40.00 1.15
273 A24 9p blue & sepia 30.00 1.50
Nos. 264-273 (10) 172.00 8.20

The 3p, 4p and 6p exist imperf.

Hands Holding Wheat Emblem A30

1963, Mar. 21 Litho. *Perf. 11*

274 A30 2½p lilac rose & rose 1.10 .25
275 A30 7½p brt lilac & pink 1.10 .35
276 A30 9p red brn & lt blue 2.25 .55
Nos. 274-276 (3) 4.45 1.15

FAO "Freedom from Hunger" campaign. The 3p imperf in various colors are essays.

Jet over Dhahran Airport — A31

1963, July 27 Litho. *Perf. 13*

277 A31 1p blue gray & ocher 1.30 .30
278 A31 3½p ultra & emer 3.25 .35
279 A31 6p emerald & rose 5.25 .55
a. "Thahran" for "Dharan" in Arabic 8.75 *27.50*
280 A31 7½p lilac rose & lt bl 5.25 .65
281 A31 9½p ver & dull vio 7.25 .70
Nos. 277-281 (5) 22.30 2.55

Opening of the US-financed terminal of the Dhahran Airport and inauguration of international jet service.

On No. 279a the misspelling consists of an omitted dot over character near top left in one horiz. row of five.

Nos. 277-281 with a second impression of the frame are forgeries.

Flame — A32

1964, Apr. Wmk. 337 *Perf. 13x13½*

282 A32 3p lil, pink & Prus bl 3.50 .30
283 A32 6p yel grn, lt bl & Prus bl 4.00 .70
284 A32 9p brn, buff & Prus bl 8.00 1.00
Nos. 282-284 (3) 15.50 2.00

15th anniv. of the signing of the Universal Declaration of Human Rights.

The 3p in other colors is an essay.

King Faisal and Arms of Saudi Arabia A33

1964, Nov. Litho. *Perf. 13*

285 A33 4p dk blue & emerald 6.00 .50

Installation of Prince Faisal ibn Abdul Aziz as King, Nov. 2, 1964.

Dam Type of 1960 Redrawn

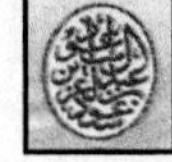

King Saud's Cartouche — Type I

King Faisal's Cartouche — Type II

Type I (Saud Cartouche)

1965-70 Litho. Unwmk. *Perf. 14*
Size: 27x22mm

286 A23 1p ol bis & pur 26.00 1.30
287 A23 2p dk blue & sep 5.00 .40
288 A23 3p sepia & blue 4.00 .40
289 A23 4p sepia & ocher 7.25 .40
290 A23 5p blk & dk vio 6.50 .40
291 A23 6p blk & car rose 15.50 .75
292 A23 7p brn & gray 15.50 .40
293 A23 8p dk bl & gray *100.00* 6.50
294 A23 9p org brn & scar *80.00* 6.50
295 A23 10p bl grn & mar *75.00* 4.00
296 A23 11p red & yel grn 7.00 2.60
297 A23 12p org & dk bl 7.00 .40
298 A23 13p dk ol & rose 7.00 .50
299 A23 14p org brn & yel grn 7.00 .50
300 A23 15p sepia & gray grn 7.00 2.60
301 A23 16p dk red & dl vio 8.50 .60
302 A23 17p rose lil & dk bl 8.50 3.00
303 A23 18p grn & brt bl 8.50 .60
304 A23 19p blk & bis 12.00 .70
305 A23 20p brn & grn 11.00 1.30
306 A23 23p mar & lilac 9.25 2.60
307 A23 24p ver & blue 12.00 .80
308 A23 26p olive & yel 14.50 .90
309 A23 27p ultra & red brn 14.50 .90
310 A23 31p gray & dull bl 14.50 1.00
311 A23 33p ol grn & lilac 14.50 1.00
312 A23 100p dk bl & grnsh bl *525.00* *65.00*
313 A23 200p dull lil & grn *525.00* *65.00*
Nos. 286-313 (28) *1,548.* *171.05*

A 50p exists but was never placed in use.

Issue years: 1966, 2p, 4p, 10p-20p, 1968, 6p-9p. 1970, 100p-200p.

Gas-Oil Plant Type of 1960 Redrawn
Type I (Saud Cartouche)

1964-70 Litho. Unwmk.
Size: 27x22mm

314 A24 1p bl & red org 7.75 .35
315 A24 2p vermilion & bl 12.50 .35
316 A24 3p lilac & brt grn 5.00 .35
317 A24 4p yel grn & lilac 7.75 .35
318 A24 5p dl gray vio & dk red brn 27.50 1.90
319 A24 6p brn org & dk vio 57.50 5.00
320 A24 7p vio & dull grn 30.00 1.90
321 A24 8p bl grn & gray 7.00 .30
322 A24 9p ultra & sepia 14.00 .80
323 A24 10p dk blue & rose *525.00* 37.50
324 A24 11p olive & org 4.25 .30
325 A24 12p bister & grn 4.25 .30
326 A24 13p rose red & dk bl 4.25 .40
327 A24 14p vio & lt brown 6.25 .40
328 A24 15p rose red & sep 7.00 .55
329 A24 16p grn & rose red 8.50 .55
330 A24 17p car rose & red brn 14.00 1.50
331 A24 18p gray & ultra 8.50 .55
332 A24 19p brown & yel 8.50 .55
333 A24 20p dull org & dk gray 30.00 1.90
334 A24 23p orange & car 8.50 .70
335 A24 24p emer & org yel 8.50 .80
336 A24 26p lil & red brn 12.50 .80
337 A24 27p ver & dk gray 12.50 .80
338 A24 31p dull grn & car 21.00 1.50
339 A24 33p red brn & gray 19.00 1.50
340 A24 50p red brn & dull grn *525.00* *52.50*
341 A24 200p dk gray & ol gray *525.00* *52.50*
Nos. 314-341 (28) *1,922.* *166.90*

A 100p exists but was never placed in use.

Issue years: 1965, 4p, 8p, 9p, 23p-33p. 1966, 1p, 2p, 5p, 11p-14p, 16p-20p. 1967, 15p. 1968, 6p, 7p. 1969, 50p. 1970, 200p. Others, 1964.

Holy Ka'aba, Mecca — A34

1965, Apr. 17 Wmk. 337 *Perf. 13*

344 A34 4p salmon & blk 4.00 .40
345 A34 6p brt pink & blk 5.75 .70
346 A34 10p yel grn & blk 8.00 1.00
Nos. 344-346 (3) 17.75 2.10

Mecca Conf. of the Moslem World League.

Arms of Saudi Arabia and Tunisia A35

1965, Apr. Litho.

347 A35 4p car rose & silver 3.00 .80
348 A35 8p red lilac & silver 4.50 1.50
349 A35 10p ultra & silver 6.50 2.00
Nos. 347-349 (3) 14.00 4.30

Visit of Pres. Habib Bourguiba of Tunisia, Feb. 22-26.

Highway, Hejaz Mountains — A36

1965, June 2 Wmk. 337 *Perf. 13*

350 A36 2p red & blk 1.60 .30
351 A36 4p blue & blk 3.25 .40
352 A36 6p lilac & blk 4.75 .70
353 A36 8p brt green & blk 6.00 .80
Nos. 350-353 (4) 15.60 2.20

Opening of highway from Mecca to Tayif.

ICY Emblem A37

1965, Nov. 13 Unwmk. *Perf. 13*

354 A37 1p yellow & dk brn 1.40 .25
355 A37 2p orange & ol grn 1.40 .35
356 A37 3p lt blue & gray 1.50 .50
357 A37 4p yel grn & dk sl grn 2.00 .65
358 A37 10p orange & magenta 4.50 1.50
Nos. 354-358 (5) 10.80 3.25

International Cooperation Year, 1965.

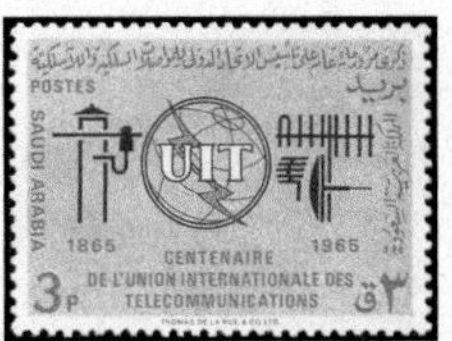

ITU Emblem, Old and New Communication Equipment — A38

1965, Dec. 22 Litho. *Perf. 13*

359 A38 3p blue & blk 1.75 .25
360 A38 4p lilac & dk grn 1.75 .35
361 A38 8p emerald & dk brn 2.40 .65
362 A38 10p dull org & dk grn 3.25 .80
Nos. 359-362 (4) 9.15 2.05

Centenary of the ITU.

Library Aflame and Lamp A39

1966, Jan. Litho. *Perf. 12x12½*

363 A39 1p orange 1.50 .40
364 A39 2p dark red 1.90 .40
365 A39 3p red violet 2.75 .40
366 A39 4p violet 4.00 .40
367 A39 5p lilac rose 4.50 .60
368 A39 6p vermilion 7.75 .80
Nos. 363-368 (6) 22.40 3.00

Burning of the Library of Algiers, June 7, 1962. Nos. 363-368 were withdrawn from sale Jan. 26, 1966, due to incorrect Arabic inscriptions. Later some values were inadvertently again placed in use.

Arab Postal Union Emblem — A40

1966, Mar. 15 Litho. *Perf. 14*

369 A40 3p dull pur & olive 1.25 .30
370 A40 4p deep blue & olive 1.25 .30
371 A40 6p maroon & olive 4.00 .70
372 A40 7p deep green & olive 4.00 .70
Nos. 369-372 (4) 10.50 2.00

10th anniv. (in 1964) of the APU. Printed in sheets of two panes, so horizontal gutter pairs exist.

Dagger in Map of Palestine — A41

1966, Mar. 19 Litho. *Perf. 13*

373 A41 2p yel grn & blk 1.75 .40
374 A41 4p lt brown & blk 3.25 .80
375 A41 6p dull blue & blk 4.00 1.00
376 A41 8p ocher & blk 6.50 1.30
Nos. 373-376 (4) 15.50 3.50

Deir Yassin massacre, Apr. 9, 1948.

Emblems of World Boy Scout Conference and Saudi Arabian Scout Association A42

1966, Mar. 23 Unwmk.

377 A42 4p yel, blk, grn & gray 4.50 1.50
378 A42 8p yel, blk, org & lt bl 4.50 1.50
379 A42 10p yel, blk, sal & bl 9.00 2.10
Nos. 377-379 (3) 18.00 5.10

Arab League Rover Moot (Boy Scout Jamboree).

WHO Headquarters, Geneva, and Flag — A43

1966, May Litho. *Perf. 13*

380 A43 4p aqua & multi 1.40 .55
381 A43 6p yel brn & multi 3.00 .80
382 A43 10p pink & multi 5.50 1.25
Nos. 380-382 (3) 9.90 2.60

Opening of the WHO Headquarters, Geneva.

UNESCO Emblem — A44

1966, Sept. Unwmk. *Perf. 12*
383 A44 1p apple grn & multi 1.40 .25
384 A44 2p dull org & multi 1.40 .25
385 A44 3p lilac rose & multi 2.00 .35
386 A44 4p pale green & multi 2.00 .40
387 A44 10p gray & multi 3.00 1.00
Nos. 383-387 (5) 9.80 2.25

20th anniv. of UNESCO.

Radio Tower, Telephone and Map of Arab Countries — A45

1966, Nov. 7 Litho. *Perf. 12½*
Design in Black, Carmine & Yellow
388 A45 1p vio blue 1.50 .25
389 A45 2p bluish lilac 1.50 .35
390 A45 4p rose lilac 3.00 .55
391 A45 6p lt olive grn 4.25 .95
392 A45 7p gray green 5.00 1.10
Nos. 388-392 (5) 15.25 3.20

Issued to publicize the 8th Congress of the Arab Telecommunications Union, Riyadh.

Dam Type of 1960 Redrawn Type II (Faisal Cartouche) (Illustrated over No. 286)

1966-76 Litho. Unwmk. *Perf. 14*
Size: 27x22mm
393 A23 1p ol bis & pur *180.00 24.00*
394 A23 2p dk blue & sep 21.00 1.60
395 A23 3p blk & dk bl 12.50 .85
396 A23 4p sepia & ocher 17.00 .40
397 A23 5p blk & dk vio 42.50 8.50
398 A23 6p blk & car rose 40.00 7.75
399 A23 7p sepia & gray 20.00 1.90
400 A23 8p dk bl & gray 12.50 .55
401 A23 9p org brn & scar 8.50 .85
402 A23 10p bl grn & mar 17.00 1.50
403 A23 11p red & yel grn 12.50 1.50
404 A23 12p org & dk bl 7.25 1.50
405 A23 13p blk & rose 24.00 1.50
406 A23 14p org brn & yel grn 21.00 1.50
407 A23 15p sep & gray grn 21.00 1.90
408 A23 16p dk red & dl vio 29.00 3.50
409 A23 17p rose lil & dk bl 34.00 1.90
410 A23 18p grn & brt bl 24.00 2.60
411 A23 19p blk & bis 8.50 .85
412 A23 20p brown & grn 85.00 *2.40*
413 A23 23p maroon & lil *300.00 5.00*
414 A23 24p ver & blue 62.50 6.25
415 A23 26p olive & yel 7.75 .80
416 A23 27p ultra & red brn 8.50 .85
417 A23 33p ol grn & lilac 47.50 2.40
419 A23 50p blk & brn *240.00 40.00*
420 A23 100p dk bl & grnsh bl *500.00 45.00*
421 A23 200p dl lil & grn *400.00 85.00*
Nos. 393-421 (28) 2,204. 252.35

A 31p has been reported.

Issue years: 1966, 1p. 1967, 2p, 10p. 1968, 3p, 4p, 6p, 7p, 20p; 1969, 5p, 8p. 1970, 9p, 23p; 1972, 12p, 15p, 16p. 1973, 11p; 1974, 17p, 50p-200p; 1975, 13p, 14p, 19p, 24p-33p; 1976, 18p.

Gas-Oil Plant Type of 1960 Redrawn Type II (Faisal Cartouche) (Illustrated over No. 286)

1966-78 Unwmk.
Size: 27x22mm
422 A24 1p bl & red org 37.50 *3.00*
423 A24 2p ver & dull bl 7.75 .35
424 A24 3p lilac & brt grn 15.00 .60
425 A24 4p grn & dull lil 9.00 .35
426 A24 5p dl gray vio & dk red brn 40.00 1.90
427 A24 6p brn org & dull pur 25.00 3.75
428 A24 7p vio & dull grn 35.00 1.90
429 A24 8p bl grn & grnsh gray 6.00 .35
430 A24 9p ultra & sep 4.25 .35
431 A24 10p dk bl & rose 5.00 .60
432 A24 11p olive & org 85.00 8.50
433 A24 12p bister & grn 5.00 .75
434 A24 13p rose red & dk bl 47.50 .35
435 A24 14p vio & lt brn 45.00 2.50
436 A24 15p car & sepia 12.50 .70
437 A24 16p grn & rose red 15.50 .75
438 A24 17p car rose & red brn 11.00 .60
439 A24 18p gray & ultra 15.50 1.60
440 A24 19p brown & yel 17.50 1.60
441 A24 20p brn org & gray 14.00 1.60
442 A24 23p orange & car 22.50 1.90
443 A24 24p emer & org yel 10.00 .75
444 A24 26p lilac & red brn *225.00*
445 A24 27p ver & dk gray 37.50 3.75
446 A24 31p grn & rose car 12.00 .75
447 A24 33p brown & gray 22.50 1.25
448 A24 50p red brn & dl grn 425.00 *160.00*
449 A24 100p dk bl & red brn 400.00 *45.00*
450 A24 200p dk gray & ol gray 425.00 *62.50*
Nos. 422-450 (29) 2,033. 308.00

Issue years: 1967, 20p; 1968, 3p, 5p-9p, 15p, 16p; 1969, 100p; 1970, 11p, 14p, 200p; 1973, 13p, 18p, 24p; 1974, 19p, 50p; 1975, 12p, 17p, 27p-33p; 1978, 26p; others, 1966.

No. 442 with a double impression of the frame is a forgery.

Emblem of Saudi Arabian Scout Association A46

1967, Mar. 28 Litho. *Perf. 13½*
Emblem in Green, Red, Yellow & Black
451 A46 1p dk blue & blk 2.10 .60
452 A46 2p blue grn & blk 2.25 .60
453 A46 3p lt blue & blk 3.50 .60
454 A46 4p rose brn & blk 4.25 .60
455 A46 10p brown & blk 10.00 1.60
Nos. 451-455 (5) 22.10 4.00

2nd Arabic League Rover Moot, Mecca, March 13-28.

Meteorological Instruments and WMO Emblem — A47

1967, July Unwmk. *Perf. 13*
456 A47 1p brt magenta 1.00 .25
457 A47 2p violet 2.00 .25
458 A47 3p olive 2.00 .30
459 A47 4p blue green 7.25 .30
460 A47 10p blue 10.50 .60
Nos. 456-460 (5) 22.75 1.70

Issued for World Meteorological Day.

Dam Type of 1960 Redrawn Type II (Faisal Cartouche)

1968-76 Wmk. 361 Litho. *Perf. 14*
461 A23 1p ol bis & pur ('68) *1,400. 300.00*
462 A23 2p dk blue & sep 90.00 *5.25*
463 A23 3p blk & dk bl 57.50 *3.00*
464 A23 4p sepia & ocher 500.00 *90.00*
465 A23 5p blk & dk vio 75.00 *5.25*
466 A23 6p blk & car rose 70.00 *4.00*
467 A23 7p sepia & gray 100.00 *8.00*
468 A23 8p dk bl & gray 52.50 2.60
469 A23 9p org brn & ver 190.00 *18.00*
470 A23 10p bl grn & mar 130.00 *10.50*
471 A23 11p red & yel grn 160.00 *16.00*
472 A23 12p org & sl bl 140.00 *13.00*
473 A23 13p black & rose 190.00 *20.00*
Nos. 462-473 (12) 1,755. *195.60*

Issue years: 1968, 2p, 10p; 1969, 3p; 1970, 8p; 1971, 1p, 5p; 1972, 6p, 9p, 11p, 12p; 1973, 4p; 1974, 13p; 1976, 9p.

Gas-Oil Plant Type of 1960 Redrawn Type II (Faisal Cartouche)

1968-76 *Perf. 14*
474 A24 1p bl & red org 9.50 1.00
475 A24 2p ver & dl bl 6.25 .55
476 A24 4p grn & dl lil 90.00 *9.00*
477 A24 5p dk brn & red brn ('73) 22.50 1.60
478 A24 6p brn org & dk vio ('73) 28.00 2.00
479 A24 9p dk bl & sep ('76) 45.00 4.00
480 A24 10p dk bl & rose 9.25 .70
481 A24 11p ol & org ('72) 34.00 2.00
482 A24 12p bis & grn ('72) 35.00 3.25
483 A24 23p org & car ('74) 60.00 3.25
Nos. 474-483 (10) 339.50 27.35

Map Showing Dammam to Jedda Road, and Dates — A48

Wmk. 361
1968, Aug. Litho. *Perf. 14*
484 A48 1p yellow & multi 1.60 .25
485 A48 2p orange & multi 1.60 .25
486 A48 3p lilac & multi 3.25 .25
487 A48 4p mauve & multi 3.25 .50
488 A48 10p turq grn & multi 9.00 .80
Nos. 484-488 (5) 18.70 2.05

Issued to commemorate the completion of the trans-Saudi Arabia highway in 1967.

Several positions in the sheet have the dots representing Dammam and Riyadh omitted. Most had the dots added by pen before issuance.

Prophet's Mosque, Medina — A49

Wmk. 361, 337 (#489, 493)
1968-76 Litho. *Perf. 13½x14*
Design A49
489 A49 1p org & grn ('70) 2.40 .30
490 A49 2p red brn & grn, redrawn ('72) 4.00 .40
a. 2p red brn & grn, wmk. 337 7.00 .30
b. As "a," redrawn *250.00* 25.00
491 A49 3p vio & grn ('72) 3.50 .40
a. 3p vio & grn, wmk. 337 ('70) 3.00 .30
492 A49 4p ocher & grn 4.00 .40
a. Redrawn ('71) 5.50 .45
b. 4p ocher & green, redrawn, wmk. 337 7.00 .35
493 A49 5p dp lil rose & grn ('71) 14.00 1.00
494 A49 6p blk & grn ('73) 11.00 1.00
a. 6p gray & green ('76) 18.00 .90
495 A49 10p brown & grn 14.00 1.00
a. Redrawn 9.00
496 A49 20p dk brn & grn ('70) 17.00 1.90
a. Redrawn 18.00
497 A49 50p sepia & grn ('75) 21.00 6.25
498 A49 100p dk bl & grn ('75) 17.00 5.00
499 A49 200p red & grn ('75) 21.00 7.00
Nos. 489-499 (11) 128.90 24.65

See redrawn note following design A55. No. 494 exists imperf.

Warning: Stamps of design A49 in other colors, double frames, inverted centers or centers omitted are forgeries. They are printed on sheet selvage.

New Arcade, Mecca Mosque — A50

1968-69 Wmk. 361
500 A50 3p dp org & gray ('69) 400.00 100.00
501 A50 4p green & gray 6.25 .55
502 A50 10p mag & gray 9.25 .90
Nos. 500-502 (3) 415.50 101.45

Expansion of Prophet's Mosque — A51

1968-76 Wmk. 361
503 A51 1p org & grn ('72) 5.00 .25
504 A51 2p brn & grn ('72) 8.50 .25
c. As No. 504, redrawn
505 A51 3p blk & grn ('69) 7.00 .40
b. 3p gray & green ('76) 20.00 1.90
c. As No. 505, redrawn 4.50
506 A51 4p org & grn ('70) 7.00 .55
a. Redrawn 4.50 .45
507 A51 5p red & grn, redrawn ('74) 7.75 .85
508 A51 6p Prus bl & grn ('72) 10.00 1.00
509 A51 8p rose red & grn ('76) 24.00 1.90
510 A51 10p brn red & grn ('70) 9.25 .55
b. 10p org & grn, redrawn ('76) 20.00 1.00
511 A51 20p vio & grn ('74) 20.00 2.40
Nos. 503-511 (9) 98.50 8.15

Wmk. 337
503a A51 1p 5.75 .40
504a A51 2p ('70) 7.25 .40
b. As "a," redrawn 35.00
505a A51 3p ('71) 8.50 .80
d. As "a," redrawn —
506b A51 4p Redrawn ('72) 9.00 .60
507a A51 5p ('70) 5.00 .55
508a A51 6p ('72) 7.00 .55
510a A51 10p ('70) 12.50 .70
c. As "a," redrawn 18.00
511a A51 20p ('72) 20.00 .80
Nos. 503a-511a (8) 75.00 4.80

See redrawn note following design A55.

Madayin Saleh — A52

1968-75
512 A52 2p ultra & bis brn ('70) 22.50 4.00
513 A52 4p dk & lt brown 6.00 .80
514 A52 7p org & lt brn ('75) 45.00 *10.00*
515 A52 10p sl grn & lt brn 14.50 2.00
516 A52 20p lil rose & brn ('71) 16.00 1.60
Nos. 512-516 (5) 104.00 *18.40*

Arabian Stallion — A53

517 A53 4p mag & org brn 6.50 .80
518 A53 10p blk & org brn 16.00 3.25
519 A53 14p bl & ocher ('71) 26.00 6.50
520 A53 20p ol grn & ocher ('71) 9.00 2.00
Nos. 517-520 (4) 57.50 12.55

Camels and Oil Derrick — A54

1969-71
521 A54 4p dk pur & redsh brn ('71) 26.00 4.00
522 A54 10p ultra & hn brn 23.00 3.25

Holy Ka'aba, Mecca — A55

Original

Redrawn

On the original stamps the knob-shaped Arabic letter, located under the two square dots in the middle of the top panel, has a small central dot. The dot often is missing.

On the redrawn stamps the dot has been enlarged into a conspicuous irregular oval. The 3p also has a period added after the value and the 4p has the "4" under the "T" instead of the "S." There are other small differences.

Numeral & "Postage" on Gray Background, 8p on White

1969-75

523 A55 4p dp grn & blk ('70) 8.50 .80
a. Redrawn, value corner white ('74) 17.00 1.90
b. Redrawn ('75) 14.00
524 A55 6p dp lil rose & blk ('71) 5.00 .40
a. Value corner white ('74) 24.00 3.00
525 A55 8p red & blk ('75) 29.00 3.00
526 A55 10p org & blk ('69) 18.50 1.50
a. Redrawn, value corner white ('74) 20.00 1.90
b. Redrawn ('75) 18.00
Nos. 523-526 (4) 61.00 5.70

Rover Moot Badge — A56

Perf. 13½x14

1969, Feb. 19 Litho. Wmk. 337

607 A56 1p orange & multi 1.60 4.00
608 A56 4p dull purple & multi 5.75 3.00
609 A56 10p orange brn & multi 14.00 6.50
Nos. 607-609 (3) 21.35 13.50

3rd Arab League Rover Moot, Mecca, Feb. 19-Mar. 3.

Traffic Light and Intersection — A57

1969, Feb. Wmk. 361 *Perf. 13½*

610 A57 3p dl bl, red & brt bl grn 2.25 .25
a. 3p dull blue, red & gray green 32.50 2.00
611 A57 4p org brn, red & gray grn 2.25 .25
612 A57 10p dl pur, red & gray grn 4.50 .85
Nos. 610-612 (3) 9.00 1.35

Issued for Traffic Day.

WHO Emblem — A58

1969, Oct. 20 Wmk. 337 *Perf. 14*

613 A58 4p lt bl, vio bl & yel 10.50 .55

20th anniv. (in 1968) of WHO.

Islamic Conference Emblem A59

1970, Mar. 23 Litho. Wmk. 361

614 A59 4p blue & black 3.00 .25
615 A59 10p yellow bis & blk 4.25 .45

Islamic Conference of Foreign Ministers, Jedda, March 1970.

Open Book and Satellite Earth Receiving Station — A60

Perf. 14x13½

1970, Aug. 1 Litho. Wmk. 337

616 A60 4p violet bl & multi 5.00 .40
617 A60 10p green & multi 9.75 1.40

World Telecommunications Day.

Steel Rolling Mill, Jedda A61

1970, Oct. 26 Wmk. 337 *Perf. 13½*

618 A61 3p yellow org & multi 4.25 .25
619 A61 4p violet & multi 6.50 .35
620 A61 10p brt green & multi 11.50 .80
Nos. 618-620 (3) 22.25 1.40

Inauguration of 1st steel mill in Saudi Arabia.

Rover Moot Emblem — A62

1971, Feb. Litho. *Perf. 14*

621 A62 10p brt blue & multi 9.00 .85

4th Arab League Rover Moot, 1971.

Telecommunications Symbol — A63

1971, May 17 Wmk. 337 *Perf. 14*

622 A63 4p blue & blk 2.40 .25
623 A63 10p lilac & blk 5.00 .55

World Telecommunications Day.

University Emblem — A64

Wmk. 337; Wmk. 361 (4p)

1971, Aug. Litho. *Perf. 14*

624 A64 3p brt green & black 1.75 .25
625 A64 4p brown & black 3.75 .55
626 A64 10p blue & black 6.50 1.00
Nos. 624-626 (3) 12.00 1.80

King Abdul Aziz National University.

Arab League Emblem — A65

1971, Nov. Wmk. 337 *Perf. 13½*

627 A65 10p multicolored 6.50 .85

Arab League Week.

Education Year Emblem — A66

1971, Nov. Litho.

628 A66 4p apple grn & brn red 6.00 .25

International Education Year 1970.

OPEC Emblem — A67

1971, Dec. *Perf. 14*

629 A67 4p light blue 6.50 .25

10th anniversary of OPEC (Organization of Petroleum Exporting Countries).

Globe A68

1972, Aug. Wmk. 361 *Perf. 14*

630 A68 4p multicolored 6.50 .25

4th World Telecommunications Day.

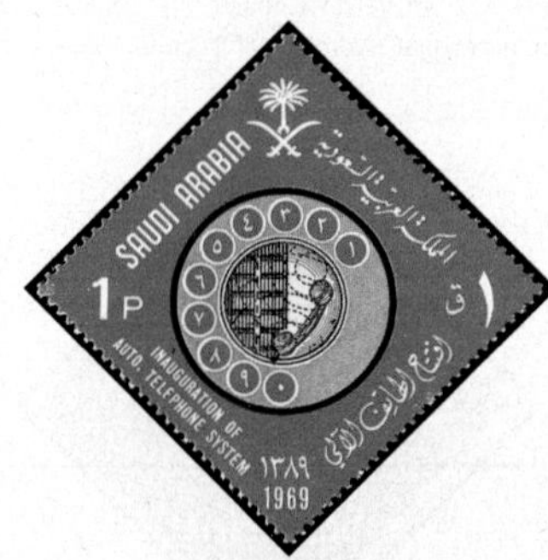
Telephone — A69

1972, Oct. Wmk. 337, 361 (5p)

631 A69 1p red, blk & grn 2.40 .25
632 A69 4p dk grn, blk & grn 2.40 .25
633 A69 5p lil, blk & grn 4.00 .35
634 A69 10p tan, blk & grn 8.50 .80
Nos. 631-634 (4) 17.30 1.65

Inauguration of automatic telephone system (1969).

Writing Hand — A70

1972, Sept. 8 Litho. Wmk. 361

635 A70 10p multicolored 9.00 .65

World Literacy Day, Sept. 8.

Holy Ka'aba and Grand Mosque, Mecca A71

Rover Moot Emblem and: 4p, Prophet's Mosque, Medina. 10p, Plains of Arafat.

1973

636 A71 4p lt blue & multi 3.75 .70
637 A71 6p lilac & multi 7.25 1.00
638 A71 10p salmon & multi 11.50 2.50
Nos. 636-638 (3) 22.50 4.20

5th Arab League Rover Moot.

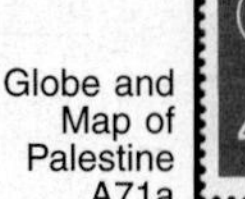
Globe and Map of Palestine A71a

1973 Litho. Wmk. 361 *Perf. 14*

639 A71a 4p black, yel & red 4.00 .25
640 A71a 10p blue, yel & red 7.50 .85

Palestine Week.

Leaf and Emblem — A72

1973

641 A72 4p yellow & multi 6.50 .30

International Hydrological Decade 1965-74.

Arab Postal Union Emblem — A73

1973, Dec. Litho. *Perf. 14*

642 A73 4p sepia & multi 5.00 .35
643 A73 10p purple & multi 11.50 1.30

25th anniversary (in 1971) of the Conference of Sofar, Lebanon, establishing the Arab Postal Union.

Balloons and Pacifier — A74

1973, Dec.

644 A74 4p lt blue & multi 8.00 .40

Universal Children's Day (stamp dated 1971).

Arab Postal and UPU Emblems A75

1974, July 7 Wmk. 361 *Perf. 14*

645 A75 3p yellow & multi *50.00* 4.25
646 A75 4p rose & multi *52.50* 7.75
647 A75 10p lt green & multi *62.50* 9.00
Nos. 645-647 (3) *165.00* 21.00

Centenary of the Universal Postal Union.

Handshake and UNESCO Emblem — A76

1974, May 21 *Perf. 13½*

648 A76 4p orange & multi 3.00 .25
649 A76 10p green & multi 11.50 .95

International Book Year, 1972.

Desalination Plant — A77

1974, Sept. 3 Wmk. 361 *Perf. 14*

650 A77 4p dp orange & bl 2.25 .25
651 A77 6p emerald & vio 4.75 .30
652 A77 10p rose red & blk 7.25 .80
Nos. 650-652 (3) 14.25 1.35

Opening (in 1971) of sea water desalination plant, Jedda.

A78

Design: INTERPOL emblem.

1974, Nov. 1

653 A78 4p venetian red & ultra 7.75 .35
654 A78 10p emerald & ultra 14.50 1.60

50th anniversary (in 1973) of International Criminal Police Organization.

A79

APU emblem, tower and letter.

1974, Oct. 26 Litho. Wmk. 361

655 A79 4p multicolored 7.25 .25

Arab Consultative Council for Postal Studies, 3rd session.

UPU Headquarters, Bern — A80

1974, Nov. 15 *Perf. 13½*

656 A80 3p orange & multi 3.75 .30
657 A80 4p lilac & multi 7.00 .60
658 A80 10p blue & multi 9.00 1.60
Nos. 656-658 (3) 19.75 2.50

Opening of new Universal Postal Union Headquarters, Bern, May 1970.

Tank, Planes, Rockets and Flame A81

1974, Dec. 15 *Perf. 14*

659 A81 3p slate & multi 2.25 .25
660 A81 4p brown & multi 4.50 .30
661 A81 10p lilac & multi 11.50 1.60
Nos. 659-661 (3) 18.25 2.15

King Faisal Military Cantonment, 1971.

A82

Red Crescent flower.

1974, Dec. 17 *Perf. 14x14½*

662 A82 4p gray & multi 1.75 .30
663 A82 6p lt green & multi 5.00 .85
664 A82 10p lt blue & multi 9.75 1.60
Nos. 662-664 (3) 16.50 2.75

Saudi Arabian Red Crescent Society, 10th anniversary (in 1973).

A83

Saudi Arabian scout emblem and minarets.

1974, Dec. 23 Wmk. 361 *Perf. 14*

665 A83 4p brown & multi 5.00 .35
666 A83 6p blue blk & multi 9.75 .65
667 A83 10p purple & multi 14.50 1.60
Nos. 665-667 (3) 29.25 2.60

6th Arab League Rover Moot, Mecca.

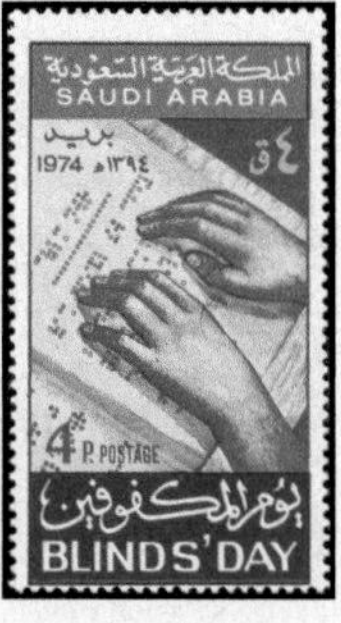

A84

Design: Reading braille.

1975, Mar. 31 *Perf. 14x13½*

668 A84 4p multicolored 11.50 .30
669 A84 10p multicolored 8.00 .70

Day of the Blind.

Anemometer and Weather Balloon with WMO Emblem — A85

Perf. 13½x14

1975, May 8 Litho. Wmk. 361

670 A85 4p multicolored 9.00 .40

Centenary (in 1973) of International Meteorological Cooperation.

King Faisal — A86

1975, July 6 Unwmk. *Perf. 14*

671 A86 4p green & rose brn 3.00 .35
672 A86 16p violet & green 4.00 .75
673 A86 23p dk green & vio 8.00 1.25
Nos. 671-673 (3) 15.00 2.35

Imperf

674 A86 40p Prus bl & ocher *350.00 350.00*

King Faisal ibn Abdul-Aziz Al Saud (1906-1975). Size of No. 674: 71x80mm.

Conference Emblem — A87

1975, July 11 *Perf. 14*

675 A87 10p rose brn & blk 5.25 .55

6th Islamic Conference of Foreign Ministers, Jedda, July 12.

Wheat and Sun — A88

1975, Sept. 17 Litho. Wmk. 361

676 A88 4p lilac & multi 3.50 .25
677 A88 10p blue & multi 9.00 .40

Charity Society, 20th anniversary.

Holy Ka'aba, Globe, Clasped Hands — A89

1975, Sept. 17 *Perf. 14*

678	A89	4p olive bis & multi		*7.75*	.25
679	A89	10p orange & multi		*16.00*	.45

Conference of Moslem Organizations, Mecca, Apr. 6-10, 1974.

Saudia Tri-Star and DC-3 — A90

1975, Sept. **Litho.** **Unwmk.**

680	A90	4p buff & multi	*9.00*	.35
681	A90	10p lt blue & multi	*15.50*	.60

Saudia, Saudi Arabian Airline, 30th anniversary.

Conference Centers in Mecca and Riyadh A91

1975, Sept. *Perf. 14*

682	A91	10p multicolored	*12.00*	.60

Friday Mosque, Medina, and Juwatha Mosque, al-Hasa — A92

1975, Oct. 26 **Litho.** **Unwmk.**

683	A92	4p green & multi	*6.50*	.35
684	A92	10p vermilion & multi	*9.00*	.60

Ancient Islamic holy places.

FAO Emblem — A93

1975, Oct. 26

685	A93	4p gray & multi	5.00	.25
686	A93	10p buff & multi	14.00	.60

World Food Program, 10th anniversary (in 1973). Stamps are dated 1973.

Conference Emblem — A94

1976, Mar. 20 **Unwmk.** *Perf. 14*

687	A94	4p multicolored	16.00	.40

Islamic Solidarity Conference of Science and Technology.

Saudi Arabia Map, Transmission Tower, TV Screen — A95

1976, May 26 **Litho.** *Perf. 14*

688	A95	4p multicolored	21.00	.40

Saudi Arabian television, 10th anniversary.

Grain, Atom Symbol, Graph A96

1976, June 28 **Litho.** *Perf. 14*

689	A96	20h yellow & multi	4.50	.35
690	A96	50h yellow & multi	7.75	.65

Second Five-year Plan.

Holy Ka'aba A97

Type I

Type II

Two types:
I — "White" minarets. Gray vignette.
II — Black minarets and vignette. Design redrawn, strengthened, darkened, clarified.

1976-79 **Litho.** **Wmk. 361** *Perf. 14*
Type II

691	A97	5h lilac & blk	.40	.25
692	A97	10h lt violet & blk	.40	.25
693	A97	15h salmon & blk	.40	.25
a.		Type I	4.75	.40
694	A97	20h lt bl & blk, II	4.50	.25
a.		Type I	5.50	.40
695	A97	25h yellow & blk	1.25	.25
696	A97	30h gray grn & blk	1.75	.25
697	A97	35h bister & blk	1.00	.25
698	A97	40h lt green & blk	4.00	.25
a.		Type I ('77)	7.00	.40
699	A97	45h dull rose & blk	1.30	.25
700	A97	50h pink & blk	1.25	.25
703	A97	65h gray blue & blk	1.50	.25
710	A97	1r lt yel grn & blk	2.00	.35
711	A97	2r green & black	9.00	.55
		Nos. 691-711 (13)	28.75	3.65

No. 698 imperf exists as an issued error. Value, $110. Nos. 691-711 also exist as imperfs not regularly issued.

Issue years: 20h, 1977; 5h-15h, 25h-50h, 1r, 1978; 65h, 2r, 1979.

See Nos. 872-882, 961-968.

Quba Mosque, Medina, built 622 — A98

1976-77

719	A98	20h orange & blk	2.25	.25
720	A98	50h emer & lilac ('77)	3.25	.25

Reissued in 1978 in different shades. No. 720 exists imperf as an issued error.

Globe, Telephones 1876 and 1976 A100

1976, July 17 **Unwmk.** *Perf. 13½*

721	A100	50h multicolored	*7.25*	.40

Centenary of first telephone call by Alexander Graham Bell, Mar. 10, 1876.

Arab Leaders A101

1976, Oct. 30 **Litho.** *Perf. 14*

722	A101	20h ultra & emerald	*4.50*	.25

Arab Summit Conference, Riyadh, October. Leaders pictured: Pres. Elias Sarkis, Lebanon; Pres. Anwar Sadat, Egypt; Pres. Hafez al Assad, Syria; King Khalid, Saudi Arabia; Amir Sabah, Kuwait; Yasir Arafat, Palestine Liberation Organization chairman.

WHO Emblem and Eye A102

1976, Nov. 28 **Litho.** *Perf. 14*

723	A102	20h multicolored	*12.00*	.40

World Health Day; Prevention of Blindness.

Holy Ka'aba — A103

1976, Nov. 28 **Unwmk.**

724	A103	20h multicolored	*8.00*	.40

50th anniversary of installation of new covering of Holy Ka'aba, Mecca.

Conference Emblem A104

Unwmk.

1977, Feb. 18 **Litho.** *Perf. 14*

725	A104	20h multicolored	*8.00*	.40

Islamic Jurisprudence Conference, Riyadh, Oct. 24-Nov. 2, 1976.

A105

Design: Sharia College emblem.

1977, Feb. 25 *Perf. 14*

726	A105	4p multicolored	*7.25*	.40

25th anniversary (in 1974) of the founding of Sharia (Islamic Law) College, Mecca.

A106

1977

727	A106	20h dk brn & brt grn	2.00	.25
a.		Incorrect date	20.00	18.00
728	A106	80h bl blk & brt grn	4.00	.55
a.		Incorrect date	20.00	18.00

2nd anniversary of installation of King Khalid ibn Abdul-Aziz. Nos. 727a-728a, issued Mar. 3, have incorrect Arabic date in bottom panel, last characters of 2nd and 3rd rows identical "ir." Stamps withdrawn after a few days and replaced Aug. 14 with corrected date, last characters in 3rd row changed to "ro."

Diesel Train and Map of Route A107

1977, May 23 **Litho.** *Perf. 14*

729	A107	20h multicolored	*24.00*	1.90

Dammam-Riyadh railroad, 25th anniversary.

Arabic Ornament and Names — A108

Designs (Names from Left to Right): UL, Malik Ben Anas (715-795). UR, Mohammad Ben Idris Al-Shafi'i (767-820). LL, Abu Hanifa an-Nu'man (699-767). LR, Ahmed Ben Hanbal (780-855).

1977, Aug. 15 Litho. *Perf. 14*

730	A108	Block of 4	*52.50*	3.25
a.-d.		20h, single stamp	*7.25*	.80

Famous Imams (7th-9th centuries), founders of traditional schools of Islamic jurisprudence. Sheets of 60 stamps (15 blocks).

No. 730 exists with a double impression of the blue color. Stamps with double impressions of the black color are forgeries.

Al Khafji Oil Rig — A109

1976-80 Wmk. 361

731	A109	5h vio blue & org	.40	.25
732	A109	10h yel grn & org	.40	.25
733	A109	15h brown & org	.40	.25
734	A109	20h green & org	.40	.25
735	A109	25h dk pur & org	.40	.25
736	A109	30h blue & orange	.40	.25
737	A109	35h sepia & org	.40	.25
738	A109	40h mag & org	.40	.25
a.		40h dull purple & org	*175.00*	
739	A109	45h violet & orange	.40	.25
740	A109	50h rose & orange	.65	.35
a.		50h dull org & org (error)	*75.00*	*8.50*
741	A109	55h grnsh bl & org	22.50	4.00
743	A109	65h sepia & org	1.50	.50
750	A109	1r gray & orange	1.90	.80
751	A109	2r dk vio & org ('80)	4.25	1.25
		Nos. 731-751 (14)	34.40	9.15

All values exist with extra dot in Arabic "Al Khafji." The 20h, 25h, 50h, 65h and 1r were retouched to remove the dot.

Color of flame varies from light orange to vermilion.

No. 737 imperf exists as an issued error. Value, $275. Nos. 731-751 also exist as imperfs not regularly issued.

See Nos. 885-892, 1300A.

Mohenjo-Daro Ruins — A110

1977, Oct. 23 Litho. Unwmk.

761	A110	50h multicolored	10.00	.40

UNESCO campaign to save Mohenjo-Daro excavations in Pakistan.

Idrisi's World Map, 1154 — A111

1977, Nov. 1 Litho. *Perf. 14*

762	A111	20h multicolored	3.00	.35
763	A111	50h multicolored	5.75	.60

First International Symposium on Studies in the History of Arabia at the University of Riyadh, Apr. 23-26, 1977.

King Faisal Specialist Hospital, Riyadh — A112

1977, Nov. 13 Litho. Unwmk.

764	A112	20h multicolored	3.50	.25
765	A112	50h multicolored	5.50	.40

Conference Emblem — A113

1978, Jan. 24 Litho. *Perf. 14*

766	A113	20h vio blue & yel	4.50	.40

1st World Conf. on Moslem Education.

APU Emblem, Members' Flags A114

1978, Jan. 21

767	A114	20h multicolored	2.00	.25
768	A114	80h multicolored	4.00	.60

25th anniversary of Arab Postal Union.

Taif-Abha-Jizan Highway — A115

1978, Oct. 15 Litho. *Perf. 14*

769	A115	20h multicolored	2.00	.25
770	A115	80h multicolored	4.00	.40

Inauguration of Taif-Abha-Gizan highway.

No. 770 exists with black (road) missing and with black double.

Pilgrims, Mt. Arafat and Holy Ka'aba — A116

Unwmk.

1978, Nov. 6 Litho. *Perf. 14*

771	A116	20h multicolored	2.00	.25
772	A116	80h multicolored	4.00	.40

Pilgrimage to Mecca.

No. 772 exists with inscriptions (black and blue colors) omitted.

Gulf Postal Organization Emblem — A117

1979, Feb. 6 Litho. *Perf. 14*

773	A117	20h multicolored	1.50	.25
774	A117	50h multicolored	3.00	.35

1st Conf. of Gulf Postal Organization, Baghdad.

Saudi Arabia No. 129, King Abdul Aziz ibn Saud A118

Unwmk.

1979, June 4 Litho. *Perf. 14*

775	A118	20h multicolored	1.60	.25
776	A118	50h multicolored	3.75	.30
777	A118	115h multicolored	5.50	.85
		Nos. 775-777 (3)	10.85	1.40

Imperf

778	A118	100h multicolored	*90.00*	90.00

1st commemorative stamp, 50th anniv. No. 778 contains one stamp with simulated perforations. Size: 101x76mm.

Crown Prince Fahd A119

1979, June 25 *Perf. 14*

779	A119	20h multicolored	2.00	.25
780	A119	50h multicolored	4.00	.35

Crown Prince Fahd ibn Abdul Aziz.

Dome of the Rock, Jerusalem A120

1979, July 2 Wmk. 361

781	A120	20h multi (shades)	2.75	.50

No. 781 exists with inscriptions (green and mauve colors) omitted.

Imperfs. exist. See No. 866.

Gold Door, Holy Ka'aba — A121

1979, Oct. 13 Litho. *Perf. 14*

782	A121	20h multicolored	1.75	.25
783	A121	80h multicolored	3.75	.40

Installation of new gold doors. Imperfs. exist.

Pilgrims at Holy Ka'aba, Mecca Mosque — A122

1979, Oct. 27

784	A122	20h multicolored	1.25	.25
785	A122	50h multicolored	3.25	.50

Pilgrimage to Mecca. Imperfs. exist.

Birds in Trees, IYC Emblem — A123

IYC Emblem and: 50h, Child's drawing.

1980, Feb. 17 Litho. *Perf. 14*

786	A123	20h multicolored	*10.00*	.25
787	A123	50h multicolored	*16.00*	.85

Intl. Year of the Child (1979). Imperfs. exist.

King Abdul Aziz ibn Saud on Horseback, Saudi Flag A124

1980, Apr. 5 Litho. *Perf. 14*

788	A124	20h multicolored	1.50	.25
789	A124	80h multicolored	3.75	.55

Saudi Arabian Army, 80th anniv. (1979). Imperfs. exist.

Arab League, 35th Anniversary A125

1980, Apr. 27 Litho. *Perf. 14*

790	A125	20h multicolored	1.75	.25

Imperfs. exist.

International Bureau of Education, 50th Anniversary — A126

1980, May 4

791	A126 50h multicolored		2.25	.30

Imperfs. exist.

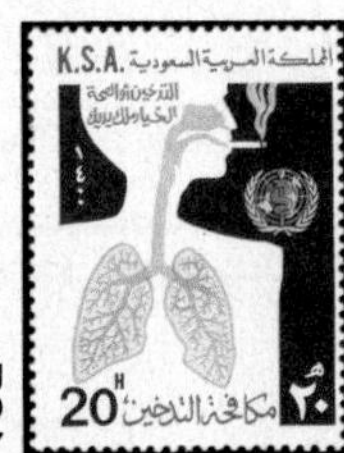

Smoke Entering Lungs, WHO Emblem — A127

1980, May 20

792	A127 20h shown	1.40	.25
793	A127 50h Cigarette, horiz.	3.50	.25

Anti-smoking campaign. Imperfs. exist.

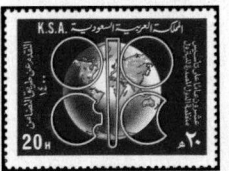

20th Anniversary of OPEC A128

Design: 50h, Workers holding OPEC emblem (Organization of Petroleum Exporting Countries).

1980, Sept. 1 **Litho.** ***Perf. 14***

794	A128 20h multicolored	1.60	.25
795	A128 50h multi, vert.	2.75	.40

Pilgrims Arriving at Jedda Airport A129

1980, Oct. 18

796	A129 20h multicolored	1.10	.25
797	A129 50h multicolored	2.00	.50

Pilgrimage to Mecca.

Conference Emblem A130

Holy Ka'aba, Mecca Mosque — A131

No. 800, Prophet's Mosque, Medina. No. 801, Dome of the Rock, Jerusalem.

1981, Jan. 25 **Litho.** ***Perf. 14***

798	A130 20h shown	1.00	.25
799	A131 20h shown	1.00	.25
800	A131 20h multicolored	1.00	.25
801	A131 20h multicolored	1.00	.25
	Nos. 798-801 (4)	4.00	1.00

Third Islamic Summit Conference, Mecca.

Hegira, 1500th Anniv. A132

1981, Jan. 26

802	A132 20h multicolored	.90	.25
803	A132 50h multicolored	1.75	.35
804	A132 80h multicolored	3.25	.50
	Nos. 802-804 (3)	5.90	1.10

Souvenir Sheet

805	A132 300h multicolored	115.00	115.00

Industry Week A133

1981, Feb. 21

806	A133 20h multicolored	.80	.25
807	A133 80h multicolored	2.60	.45

Line Graph and Telephone A134

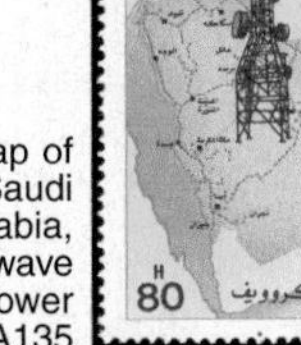

Map of Saudi Arabia, Microwave Tower A135

115h, Earth satellite station.

1981, Feb. 28

808	A134 20h shown	.60	.25
809	A135 80h shown	2.60	.45
810	A134 115h multicolored	3.25	.70
	Nos. 808-810 (3)	6.45	1.40

Imperf

811	A134 100h like #808	52.50	50.00
812	A135 100h like #809	52.50	50.00
813	A134 100h like #810	52.50	50.00

Ministry of Posts and Telecommunications achievements.

Arab City Day — A135a

1981, Apr. 2 **Litho.** ***Perf. 14***

814	A135a 20h multicolored	.40	.25
815	A135a 65h multicolored	1.25	.40
816	A135a 80h multicolored	1.75	.40
817	A135a 115d multicolored	2.40	.75
	Nos. 814-817 (4)	5.80	1.80

King Abdulaziz International Airport, Jeddah — A136

80h, Plane over airport, facing right.

1981, Apr. 12

818	A136 20h shown	.65	.25
819	A136 80h multicolored	3.00	.55

1982 World Cup Soccer Preliminary Games — A137

1981, July 26 **Litho.** ***Perf. 14***

820	A137 20h multicolored	2.25	.30
821	A137 80h multicolored	4.50	.45

Intl. Year of the Disabled — A138

1981, Aug. 5

822	A138 20h Reading braille	1.75	.25
823	A138 50h Man weaving rug	3.25	.35

3rd Five-year Plan (1981-1985) — A139

1981, Sept. 5

824	A139 20h multicolored	1.50	.25

King Abdul Aziz, Map of Saudi Arabia A140

1981, Sept. 23 **Litho.** ***Perf. 14***

825	A140 5h multicolored	.25	.25
826	A140 10h multicolored	.25	.25
827	A140 15h multicolored	.25	.25
828	A140 20h multicolored	.40	.25
829	A140 50h multicolored	.75	.35
830	A140 65h multicolored	1.00	.40
831	A140 80h multicolored	2.75	.40
832	A140 115h multicolored	3.50	.60
	Nos. 825-832 (8)	9.15	2.75

Imperf

833	A140 10r multicolored	*90.00*	90.00

50th anniv. of kingdom. No. 833 shows king, map, document. Size: 100x75mm.

Pilgrimage to Mecca A141

1981, Oct. 7

834	A141 20h multicolored	1.75	.25
835	A141 65h multicolored	3.00	.50

World Food Day A142

1981, Oct. 16

836	A142 20h multicolored	2.60	.40

2nd Session of the Gulf Cooperative Council Summit Conference, Riyadh, Nov. 10 — A143

1981, Nov. 10 **Litho.** ***Perf. 14***

837	A143 20h multicolored	1.00	.30
838	A143 80h multicolored	3.00	.60

King Saud University, 25th Anniv. A144

1982, Mar. 10 **Litho.** ***Perf. 14***

839	A144 20h multicolored	.90	.25
840	A144 50h multicolored	2.00	.40

New Regional Postal Centers A145

20h, Riyadh P.O. 65h, Jedda. 80h, Dammam. 115h, Automated sorting.

1982, July 14 **Litho.** ***Perf. 14***

841	A145 20h multi	.40	.25
842	A145 65h multi	1.25	.40
843	A145 80h multi	1.50	.40
844	A145 115h multi	2.00	.65
	Nos. 841-844 (4)	5.15	1.70

Four 300h souvenir sheets exist in same designs as Nos. 841-844 respectively. Value, $22.50 each.

Riyadh Television Center — A146

1982, Sept. 4

845	A146 20h multicolored	1.25	.25

25th Anniv. of King's Soccer Cup A147

1982, Sept. 8
846 A147 20h multicolored .90 .25
847 A147 65h multicolored 1.75 .40

30th Anniv. of Arab Postal Union A148

1982, Sept. 8
848 A148 20h Emblem .80 .25
849 A148 65h Map, vert. 2.00 .40

Pilgrimage to Mecca A149

1982, Sept. 26
850 A149 20h multicolored .80 .25
851 A149 50h multicolored 2.00 .40

World Standards Day A150

1982, Oct. 14
852 A150 20h multicolored 1.50 .35

World Food Day A151

1982, Oct. 16
853 A151 20h multicolored 1.50 .35

Coronation of King Fahd, June 14, 1982 A152

Installation of Crown Prince Abdullah, June 14, 1982 A153

1983, Feb. 12 Litho. *Perf. 14*
854 A152 20h multicolored .40 .25
855 A153 20h multicolored .40 .25
856 A152 50h multicolored .75 .35
857 A153 50h multicolored .75 .35
858 A152 65h multicolored 1.15 .40
859 A153 65h multicolored 1.15 .40
860 A152 80h multicolored 1.30 .55
861 A153 80h multicolored 1.30 .55
862 A152 115h multicolored 2.00 .75
863 A153 115h multicolored 2.00 .75
Nos. 854-863 (10) 11.20 4.60

Two one-stamp souvenir sheets contain Nos. 862-863, perf. 12½. Value $300.

6th Anniv. of United Arab Shipping Co. — A154

Various freighters.

1983, Aug. 9 Litho. *Perf. 14*
864 A154 20h multicolored .65 .35
865 A154 65h multicolored 2.25 .80

Dome of the Rock, Jerusalem A155

1983, Sept. Wmk. 361 *Perf. 12*
866 A155 20h multicolored .90 .40

See No. 781.

Pilgrimage to Mecca A156

1983, Sept. 16 Litho. *Perf. 14*
867 A156 20h brt blue & multi .40 .25
868 A156 65h black & multi 1.50 .25

World Communications Year — A157

20h, Post and UPU emblems. 80h, Telephone and ITU emblems.

1983, Oct. 8 Litho. *Perf. 14*
869 A157 20h multicolored .35 .25
870 A157 80h multicolored 1.50 .35

Holy Ka'aba Type of 1976
Type II

Perf. 14x13½

1982-86 Litho. Wmk. 361

Size: 26x21mm

872 A97 10h lt vio & blk ('83) .40 .25
874 A97 20h lt blue & blk .40 .25
880 A97 50h pink & blk ('83) .65 .25
881 A97 65h gray bl & blk .70 .25
882 A97 1r lt yel grn & blk 2.10 .35

Perf. 13½

874c A97 20h lt blue & blk .40 .25
880a A97 50h pink & blk ('83) .65 .25
881a A97 65h gray bl & blk .70 .25
882a A97 1r lt yel grn & blk 5.75 .35

Perf. 12

872b A97 10h lt vio & blk .40 .25
873 A97 15h sal & blk ('85) .40 .25
874a A97 20h lt blue & blk ('84) .40 .25
880b A97 50h pink & blk ('86) .40 .25
881b A97 65h gray bl & blk ('84) .70 .25
882b A97 1r lt yel grn & blk ('83) 2.25 .35

Perf. 12

Unwmk.

872a A97 10h lt vio & blk ('87) .40 .25
874b A97 20h lt blue & blk .40 .25
881c A97 65h gray bl & blk ('84) .70 .25
882c A97 1r lt yel grn & blk ('85) 1.60 .35
Nos. 872-882c (7) 10.40 1.95

Counterfeits of the 1r are perf. 11.

Al Khafji Oil Rig Type of 1976

Perf. 14x13½

1982-84 Litho. Wmk. 361

Size: 26x21mm

885 A109 5h vio bl & org .40 .25
886 A109 10h yel grn & org .40 .25
887 A109 15h bis brn & org .40 .25
888 A109 20h green & org .40 .25
890 A109 50h rose & org .30 .25
891a A109 65h sepia & orange 3.25 1.50
892 A109 1r gray & org .70 .30

Perf. 13½

885a A109 5h .40 .25
886a A109 10h .40 .25
887a A109 15h .40 .25
888a A109 20h .40 .25
890a A109 50h .30 .25
891 A109 65h sepia & org ('84) .95 .25
892a A109 1r .95 .30

1983 *Perf. 12*
886b A109 10h .40 .25
887b A109 15h .40 .25
888b A109 20h .40 .25
889 A109 25h dk pur & org .65 .25
890b A109 50h .30 .25
891b A109 65h .65 .25
892b A109 1r .95 .30
Nos. 885-892b (8) 4.20 2.05

Opening of King Khalid International Airport — A158

1983, Nov. 16 Litho. *Perf. 13½x14*
893 A158 20h shown .60 .25
894 A158 65h blue & multi 1.75 .65

World Food Day — A159

20h, Wheat, Irrigation, Silos.

1983, Nov. 29 Litho. *Perf. 14*
895 A159 20h multicolored 1.50 .25

Aqsa Mosque, Jerusalem A160

1983, Dec. 13 Litho. *Perf. 14*
896 A160 20h multicolored .80 .30

Old and Modern Riyadh — A161

Shobra Palace, Taif — A162

Old and New Jedda (Waterfront) — A163

Damman — A164

1984-95 Litho. Wmk. 361 *Perf. 12*
897 A161 20h lilac rose & multi .40 .25
898 A162 20h Prus grn & multi .25 .25
899 A161 50h black & multi .40 .25
900 A162 50h brn & multi .80 .45

Unwmk.

901 A161 50h multicolored .95 .40
902 A162 50h multicolored .80 .45
903 A163 50h multicolored 1.15 .60
904 A164 50h grn & multi .60 .35
905 A161 75h grn & multi .80 .45
906 A162 75h multicolored .80 .45
907 A163 75h pink & multi 1.15 .60
908 A164 75h blue & multi .80 .45
909 A161 150h pink & multi 1.90 .90
910 A162 150h grn & multi 1.90 .90
911 A163 150h grn & multi 2.00 .90
911A A164 150h red lilac & multi 2.60 1.40
Nos. 897-911A (16) 17.30 9.05

Issued: #897, 6/27/84; #898, 10/13/84; #899, 8/29/84; #900, 3/10/87; #910, 9/3/87; #902, 11/3/87; #909, 5/4/88; #903, 911, 1/31/89; #906, 1990; #901, 907, 1991; #905, 1992; #904, 908, 911A, 1995.

For similar design see Nos. 1320-1321.

Estate Development Fund, 10th Anniv. — A165

1984, July 28 Unwmk.
912 A165 20h multicolored .65 .25

Opening of Solar Village, near Al-Eyenah A166

80h, Stylized sun, solar panels.

1984, Aug. 14 Litho. *Perf. 12*
913 A166 20h multicolored .50 .25
914 A166 80h multicolored 1.50 .35

Imperf

Size: 81x81mm

915 A166 100h like 20h *30.00*
916 A166 100h like 80h *30.00*

Pilgrimage to Mecca — A167

Al-Kheef Mosque: 65h, Aerial view.

1984, Sept. 4 **Litho.** ***Perf. 14***

917 A167 20h brown & multi .60 .25

Perf. 12

918 A167 65h olive gray & multi 1.75 .35

Participation of Saudi Arabian Soccer Team in 1984 Olympics — A168

1984, Sept. 25 **Litho.** ***Perf. 12***

919 A168 20h blue & multi 1.60 1.00

920 A168 115h green & multi 5.75 1.60

"Games" and "Olympiad" are misspelled on both stamps.

World Food Day A169

1984, Oct. 16 **Litho.** ***Perf. 12***

921 A169 20h multicolored .65 .30

Beginning with Nos. 922-923 some issues are printed in sheets that have labels inscribed in Arabic. Generally there are from 2 to 6 labels per sheet. Stamps with label attached command a premium.

90th Anniv. International Olympic Committee — A170

1984, Dec. 23 **Litho.** ***Perf. 12***

922 A170 20h multicolored 1.00 .40

923 A170 50h multicolored 3.00 .55

Launch of ARABSAT — A171

20h, ARABSAT, view of Earth.

1985, Feb. 9 **Litho.** ***Perf. 12***

924 A171 20h multicolored 2.00 .25

7th Holy Koran Competition — A172

1985, Feb. 10 **Litho.** ***Perf. 12***

925 A172 20h multicolored .50 .25

926 A172 65h multicolored 1.25 .40

4th Five-Year Development Plan, 1985-1990 — A173

Portrait of King Fahd, industry emblems and: 20h, Dhahran Harbor, Jubail. 50h, Television tower, earth receiver, microwave tower. 65h, Agriculture. 80h, Harbor, Yanbu.

1985, Mar. 23 **Litho.** ***Perf. 13x12***

927 20h multicolored .40 .25

928 50h multicolored 1.00 .25

929 65h multicolored 1.25 .25

930 80h multicolored 1.75 .35

a. A173 Block of 4, #927-930 5.75 1.90

Intl. Youth Year A174

1985, May 4 ***Perf. 12***

931 A174 20h multicolored .45 .35

932 A174 80h multicolored 1.25 .40

Self-sufficiency in Wheat Production A175

1985, May 4

933 A175 20h multicolored .65 .30

East-West Pipeline — A176

20h, Tanker loading berth, Yanbu. 65h, Pipeline, map.

1985, June 9

934 A176 20h multicolored .60 .25

935 A176 65h multicolored 1.50 .40

Shuttle Launch — A177

Shuttle, Missions Emblem — A178

1985, July 7

936 A177 20h multicolored 1.00 .45

937 A178 115h multicolored 5.75 2.10

Prince Sultan Ibn Salman Al-Saud, 1st Arab-Moslem astronaut, on Discovery 51-G.

UN, 40th Anniv. A179

1985, July 15

938 A179 20h multicolored .75 .30

Highway, Map, Holy Ka'aba in Mecca to Prophet's Mosque in Medina — A180

1985, July 22

939 A180 20h multicolored .50 .25

940 A180 65h multicolored 1.25 .30

Mecca-Medina Highway opening, 10/11/84.

Post Code Inauguration — A181

1985, July 24

941 A181 20h Covers .60 .25

1984 Asian Soccer Cup Victory A182

1985, July 30

942 A182 20h multicolored .40 .35

943 A182 65h multicolored 1.25 .40

944 A182 115h multicolored 2.60 .80

Nos. 942-944 (3) 4.25 1.55

Pilgrimage to Mecca — A183

1985, Aug. 25 **Litho.** ***Perf. 12***

945 A183 10h multicolored .30 .25

946 A183 15h multicolored .30 .25

947 A183 20h multicolored .45 .25

948 A183 65h multicolored 1.25 .40

Nos. 945-948 (4) 2.30 1.15

1st Gulf Olympics Day, Riyadh, May 2 A184

1985, Sept. 8

949 A184 20h multicolored .40 .25

950 A184 115h multicolored 2.00 .40

World Food Day A185

1985, Oct. 16

951 A185 20h multicolored .90 .40

952 A185 65h multicolored 3.00 .85

King Abdul Aziz, Masmak Fort and Horsemen — A186

1985, Dec. 1

953 A186 15h multicolored .25 .25

954 A186 20h multicolored .25 .25

955 A186 65h multicolored .80 .40

956 A186 80h multicolored 1.00 .55

Nos. 953-956 (4) 2.30 1.45

Intl. Conference on the History of King Abdul Aziz Al-Sa'ud, Riyadh. An imperf. souvenir sheet showing smaller versions of Nos. 953-956 and the conference emblem exists. Sold for 10r. Value $26.50.

King Fahd Koran Publishing Center, Medina — A187

1985, Dec. 18

957 A187 20h multicolored .25 .25

958 A187 65h multicolored 1.25 .30

OPEC, 25th Anniv. A188

1985, Dec. 24

959 A188 20h multicolored .35 .25

960 A188 65h multicolored 1.75 .30

Holy Ka'aba Type of 1976
Booklet Stamps
Size: 29x19mm
Type II

1986, Feb. 17 Litho. *Perf. 12*

961	A97 10h lt vio & blk		6.50	6.50
a.	Booklet pane of 4		*30.00*	
965	A97 20h bluish grn & blk		11.00	10.50
968	A97 50h pink & black		22.00	18.00
a.	Bklt. pane of 4, #961, 2 #965, #968		*60.00*	
	Nos. 961-968 (3)		39.50	35.00

Due to vending machine breakdowns, distribution of this set has been very limited. The government does have stocks of these stamps but they are not currently being sold.

Intl. Peace Year — A189

1986, Jan. 8 Litho. *Perf. 12*

971	A189 20h multicolored	1.25	.40

A190

1986, Mar. 24 *Perf. 14, 12 (65h)*

972	A190 20h multicolored	.50	.35
a.	Perf. 12	.50	.35
973	A190 65h multicolored	1.25	.40

Riyadh Municipality, 50th aAnniv.

A191

1986, Apr. 21 *Perf. 12*

974	A191 20h multicolored	.60	.35
975	A191 50h multicolored	1.25	.40

UN child survival campaign.

General Establishment for Electric Power, 10th Anniv. — A192

1986, Apr. 26

976	A192 20h multicolored	.40	.30
977	A192 65h multicolored	1.30	.40

Continental Maritime Cable Inauguration — A193

1986, June 1 Litho. *Perf. 12*

978	A193 20h multicolored	.65	.35
979	A193 50h multicolored	1.25	.40

Natl. Guard Housing Project, Riyadh, Inauguration — A194

1986, July 19

980	A194 20h multicolored	.40	.35
981	A194 65h multicolored	1.25	.40

Islamic Arch, Holy Ka'aba — A195

1986-2015 Litho. *Perf. 12*

984	A195	30h blk & bluish grn	.35	.35
985	A195	40h blk & lil rose	.40	.35
986	A195	50h blk & brt grn	1.10	.60
987	A195	75h blk & Prus bl	1.40	.70
a.		Perf. 13½x14	1.10	.60
987B	A195	100h black & red		
988	A195	100h blk & bl green	1.60	.80
989	A195	150h blk & rose lil	2.75	1.40
a.		Perf. 13½x14	2.50	1.25
990	A195	2r blk & vio blue	3.00	1.60
a.		Perf. 13½x14	—	—
990B	A195	2r blk & bl green	—	—
		Nos. 984-990B (9)	10.60	5.80

Issued: 30h, 40h, 8/5; 75h, 150h, 7/30/90; 50h, 10/9/90; #987a, 6/13/92; #989a, 6/6/92; 2r, 4/99; #987B, 988, 9/21/96; No. 990a, 1999 ? No. 990B, 2015.

Pilgrimage to Mecca — A196

Designs of: a, A116. b, A129. c, A156. d, A149. e, A141. f, A122. g, A183. h, A167.

1986, Aug. 13 Litho. *Perf. 12*

1002	A196 Block of 8	*18.00*	*18.00*
a.-h.	20h, any single	1.90	1.50

Discovery of Oil, 50th Anniv. — A197

1986, Sept. 16

1003	A197 20h Well, refinery	.50	.35
1004	A197 65h Well, map	1.75	.40

Because of difficulty in separation most stamps have damaged perfs.

World Food Day — A198

1986, Oct. 18

1005	A198 20h shown	.35	.35
1006	A198 115h Stylized plant	1.50	.70

Massacre of Palestinian Refugees, Sept. 17, 1982 — A199

1986, Nov. 1 Litho. *Perf. 12*

1007	A199 80h multicolored	1.00	.50
1008	A199 115h multicolored	1.60	.80

Definitive stamps generally do not have an official date of issue. Any dates shown probably reflect sales at the Riyadh or Dammam post offices only.

Saudi Universities

Imam Mohammed ibn Saud — A200

Umm al-Qura — A201

King Saud — A202

King Fahd Petroleum and Minerals — A203

King Faisal — A204

King Abdul Aziz — A205

Medina Islamic — A206

1986-91

1009	A200	15h sage grn & blk	.35	.35
1010	A200	20h ultra & black	.35	.35
1011	A200	50h ultra & black	.60	.40
1012	A200	65h brt bl & blk	.75	.70
1013	A200	75h brt bl & blk	.80	.50
1014	A200	100h rose & black	1.00	.95
1015	A200	150h rose cl & blk	1.60	.80
1016	A201	50h ultra & black	.75	.40
1017	A201	65h brt bl & blk	.80	.40
1018	A201	75h brt bl & blk	.80	.50
1019	A201	100h dull rose & blk	1.50	.75
1020	A201	150h rose cl & blk	1.90	.90
1021	A202	50h ultra & black	.70	.40
1022	A202	75h brt bl & blk	.80	.50
1023	A202	100h dull rose & blk	1.60	.75
1024	A202	150h rose cl & blk	1.75	.80
1025	A203	50h ultra & black	.60	.40
1026	A203	75h brt bl & blk	.80	.50
1027	A203	150h rose cl & blk	2.00	.80
1028	A204	50h ultra & black	.55	.40
1029	A204	75h brt bl & blk	.80	.50
1030	A204	150h rose cl & blk	1.90	.80
1031	A205	50h ultra & black	.70	.40
1032	A205	75h brt bl & blk	.80	.55
1033	A205	150h rose cl & blk	1.90	.80
1034	A206	50h ultra & black	.65	.35
1035	A206	75h brt bl & blk	.80	.50
1036	A206	150h rose cl & blk	2.00	.80
		Nos. 1009-1036 (28)	29.55	16.25

Issued: #1009-1010, 1012, 1014, 11/26; #1019, 3/29; #1023, 7/22; #1016, 1020, 8/8; #1015, 1027, 1036, 1/31/89; #1011, 1025, 1028, 1031, 2/25/89; #1017, 3/89; #1024, 1030, 1033, 4/29/89; #1034, 7/4/89; #1021, 1989; #1013, 1018, 1026, 1990; #1022, 1029, 1032, 1035, 1991.

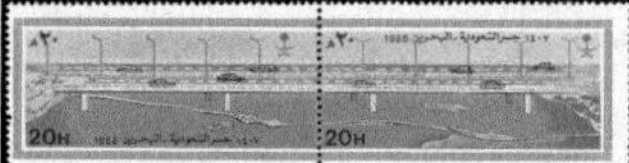

Saudi-Bahrain Highway Inauguration — A207

1986, Nov. 26 *Perf. 14*

1039	A207 Strip of 2	2.60	.80
a.-b.	20h any single	1.15	.40

Printed se-tenant in a continuous design.

1st Modern Olympic Games, Athens, 90th Anniv. A208

1986, Dec. 27

1040	A208 20h multicolored	1.25	.60
1041	A208 100h multicolored	6.50	1.60

General Petroleum and Minerals Organization (Petromin), 25th Anniv. — A209

Unwmk.

1987, Feb. 23 Litho. *Perf. 12*

1042	A209 50h multicolored	.80	.40
1043	A209 100h multicolored	1.60	.75

Restoration and Expansion of Quba Mosque, Medina — A210

Design: View of mosque and model of expanded mosque.

1987, Mar. 21

1044 A210 50h multicolored .80 .40
1045 A210 75h multicolored 1.25 .50

Vocational Training — A211

Designs: a, Welding. b, Drill press operation. c, Lathe operation. d, Electrician.

Unwmk.

1987, Apr. 8 Litho. *Perf. 12*

1046 A211 Block of 4 7.00 7.00
a.-d. 50h any single 1.60 1.40

Cairo Exhibition A212

Design: Desert fortifications in silhouette, Riyadh television tower, King Khalid Intl. Airport hangars and pyramid of Giza.

Unwmk.

1987, June 17 Litho. *Perf. 12*

1047 A212 50h multicolored .80 .40
1048 A212 75h multicolored 1.60 .65

A213

Inauguration of King Fahd Telecommunications Center, Jedda — A214

1987, July 21

1049 A213 50h multicolored .80 .40
1050 A214 75h multicolored 1.60 .65

Afghan Resistance Movement A215

1987, July 25

1051 A215 50h multicolored .80 .40
1052 A215 100h multicolored 1.60 .75

Pilgrimage to Mecca — A216

Design: View of Ihram and Meqat Wadi Muhrim Mosque from Wadi Muhrim Meqat.

1987, Aug. 3

1053 A216 50h multicolored .80 .40
1054 A216 75h multicolored 1.25 .50
1055 A216 100h multicolored 1.50 .75
Nos. 1053-1055 (3) 3.55 1.65

Home for Disabled Children, 1st Anniv. — A217

1987, Oct. 3

1056 A217 50h multicolored .90 .45
1057 A217 75h multicolored 1.40 .60

World Post Day — A218

1987, Oct. 10

1058 A218 50h multicolored .80 .35
1059 A218 150h multicolored 2.00 .80

World Food Day A219

1987, Oct. 17

1060 A219 50h multicolored .80 .35
1061 A219 75h multicolored 1.50 .40

Social Welfare Society, 25th Anniv. — A220

1987, Oct. 26

1062 A220 50h multicolored .80 .40
1063 A220 100h multicolored 1.60 .65

Dome of the Rock — A221

1987, Dec. 5

1064 A221 75h multicolored 1.90 .50
1065 A221 150h multicolored 4.00 1.10

Restoration and Expansion of the Prophet's Mosque, Medina — A222

1987, Dec. 15 *Perf. 14*

1066 A222 50h multicolored .75 .40
1067 A222 75h multicolored 1.00 .85
1068 A222 150h multicolored 2.00 1.25
Nos. 1066-1068 (3) 3.75 2.50

An imperf. 300h souvenir sheet exists. Value $52.50.

Battle of Hattin, 800th Anniv. A223

Warriors in silhouette and Dome of the Rock.

1987, Dec. 21 *Perf. 12*

1069 A223 75h multicolored 1.75 .40
1070 A223 150h multicolored 3.75 .90

Saladin's conquest of Jerusalem.

A224

1987, Dec. 26

1071 A224 50h multicolored .80 .40
1072 A224 75h multicolored 1.25 .50

8th session of the Supreme Council of the Gulf Cooperation Council.

A225

1988, Feb. 13 Litho. *Perf. 12*

1073 A225 50h multicolored 1.50 .75
1074 A225 75h multicolored 1.75 .85

3rd Regional Highways Conf. of the Middle East.

A226

Inauguration of King Fahd Intl. Stadium — A227

1988, Mar. 2

1075 A226 50h multicolored .80 .40
1076 A227 150h multicolored 2.40 1.00

Blood Donation — A228

1988, Apr. 13 Litho. *Perf. 12*

1077 A228 50h multicolored .80 .40
1078 A228 75h multicolored 1.00 .50

WHO, 40th Anniv. — A229

1988, Apr. 7

1079 A229 50h multicolored .90 .40
1080 A229 75h multicolored 1.15 .50

King Fahd, Custodian of the Holy Mosques — A230

King Fahd and mosques at Medina and Mecca.

1988, Apr. 23 Litho. *Perf. 12*

1081 A230 50h multicolored .60 .35
1082 A230 75h multicolored .80 .40
1083 A230 150h multicolored 1.75 .80
Nos. 1081-1083 (3) 3.15 1.55

A 75h souvenir sheet exists containing an enlarged version of No. 1082. Sold for 3r. Value $67.50.

Environmental Protection A231

1988, June 5

1084 A231 50h multicolored .80 .40
1085 A231 75h multicolored 1.25 .85

Palestinian Uprising, Gaza and the West Bank A232

1988, July 10

1086 A232 75h multicolored 1.25 .50
1087 A232 150h multicolored 2.40 .90

Pilgrimage to Mecca — A233

1988, July 23 Litho. *Perf. 12*

1088 A233 50h multicolored .90 .35
1089 A233 75h multicolored 1.50 .55

World Food Day A234

1988, Oct. 16 Litho. *Perf. 12*

1090 A234 50h multicolored 1.00 .55
1091 A234 75h multicolored 1.60 .80

Qiblatain Mosque Expansion — A235

1988, Nov. 9

1092 A235 50h multicolored .80 .35
1093 A235 75h multicolored 1.25 .45

5th World Youth Soccer Championships, Riyadh, Dammam, Jedda and Taif — A250

1989, Feb. 16 Litho. *Perf. 12*

1094 A250 75h multicolored 1.40 .65
1095 A250 150h multicolored 2.75 1.25

World Health Day — A251

1989, Apr. 8 Litho. *Perf. 12*

1096 A251 50h multicolored .90 .35
1097 A251 75h multicolored 1.50 .45

Sea Water Desalination Plant — A252

1989, May 30 Litho. *Perf. 12*

1098 A252 50h multicolored .65 .35
1099 A252 75h multicolored .90 .60

Proclamation of the State of Palestine, Nov. 15, 1988 — A253

1989, June 6 Litho. *Perf. 12*

1100 A253 50h multicolored .80 .25
1101 A253 75h multicolored 1.25 .35

Pilgrimage to Mecca — A254

Design: Al-Tan'eem Mosque, Mecca.

1989, July 12 Litho. *Perf. 12*

1102 A254 50h multicolored .75 .25
1103 A254 75h multicolored 1.15 .40

World Food Day A255

1989, Oct. 16 Litho. *Perf. 12*

1104 A255 75h multicolored .65 .40
1105 A255 150h multicolored 1.25 .90

Holy Mosque Expansion — A256

1989, Dec. 30 Litho. *Perf. 12*

1106 A256 50h multicolored .65 .35
1107 A256 75h multicolored .90 .55
1108 A256 150h multicolored 1.75 .90
Nos. 1106-1108 (3) 3.30 1.80

A souvenir sheet containing an enlarged version of design A256 exists. Sold for 5r. Value, perf or imperf, each $35.00.

Youth Soccer Cup Championships A257

1989, Dec. 20

1109 A257 75h multicolored 1.00 .40
1110 A257 150h multicolored 1.90 .90

UNESCO World Literacy Year — A258

1990, Jan. 9

1111 A258 50h multicolored .80 .35
1112 A258 75h multicolored 1.25 .45

World Health Day — A259

Unwmk.

1990, Apr. 7 Litho. *Perf. 12*

1113 A259 75h multicolored .90 .40
1114 A259 150h multicolored 1.75 .80

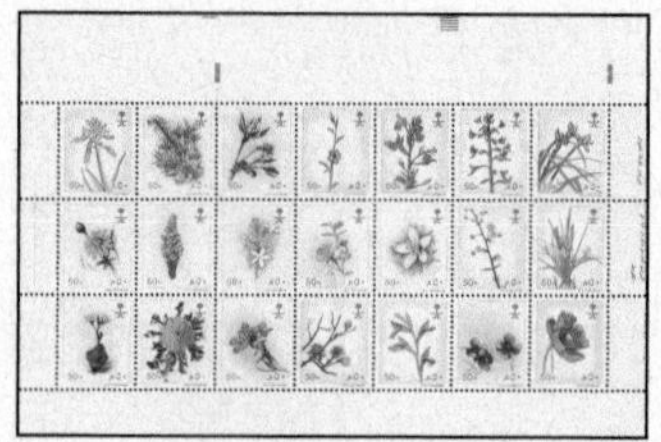

Flowers — A262

1990

1115 A262 Sheet of 21 9.75
a.-u. 50h any single .50 .25
1116 A262 Sheet of 21 15.50
a.-u. 75h any single .65 .35
1117 A262 Sheet of 21 30.00
a.-u. 150h any single 1.30 .75
Nos. 1115-1117 (3) 55.25

21 Different species pictured on the sheets. Issued: 50h, 75h, Feb. 6; 150h, Jan. 17.
See No. 1292A.

Islamic Conference, 20th Anniv. — A263

1990, Feb. 7 Litho. *Perf. 12*

1118 A263 75h blue & multi .65 .35
1119 A263 150h gray & multi 1.25 .65

Islamic Heritage — A264

Designs: b, Arabic script in rectangle. c, Circular design. d, Mosque and minaret.

1990, July 29

1120 A264 Block of 4 3.75 2.25
a.-d. 75h any single .90 .60

Horses — A265

1990, Apr. 14 Color of Horse

1121 A265 Block of 4 3.25 1.15
a. 50h white, red tassels on bridle .90 .35
b. 50h black .90 .35
c. 50h white, brown bridle .90 .35
d. 50h chestnut .90 .35
1122 A265 50h like #1121d .70 .35
1123 A265 75h like #1121b 1.00 .55
1124 A265 100h like #1121a 1.40 .70
1125 A265 150h like #1121c 2.00 1.00
Nos. 1121-1125 (5) 8.35 3.75

No. 1121 has white border on two sides. Nos. 1122-1125 have white border on four sides.

Pilgrimage to Mecca — A266

1990, June 28

1126 A266 75h multicolored 1.00 .40
1127 A266 150h multicolored 1.90 .90

Television Tower — A267

1990, July 21

1128 A267 75h multicolored .90 .40
1129 A267 150h multicolored 1.75 .90

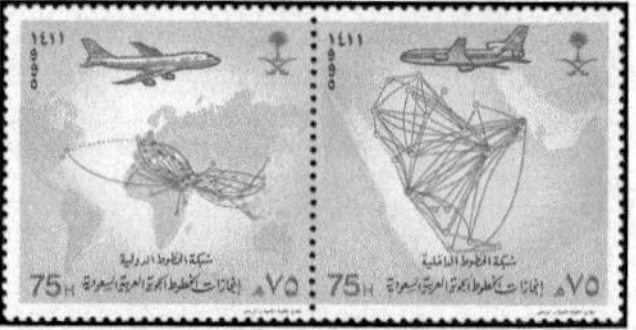

Saudi Arabian Airlines Route Map — A268

1990, Sept. 3

1130 75h Global routes .65 .40
1131 75h Domestic routes .65 .40
a. A268 Pair, #1130-1131 1.40 .80
1132 150h like #1130 1.30 .80
1133 150h like #1131 1.30 .80
a. A268 Pair, #1132-1133 2.60 1.75
Nos. 1130-1133 (4) 3.90 2.40

World Food Day A269

1990, Oct. 16 Litho. *Perf. 12*

1134 A269 75h multicolored .90 .55
1135 A269 150h multicolored 2.00 1.00

Organization of Petroleum Exporting Countries (OPEC), 30th Anniv. — A270

1990, Sept. 26

1136 A270 75h multicolored 1.40 .50
1137 A270 150h multicolored 2.40 1.30

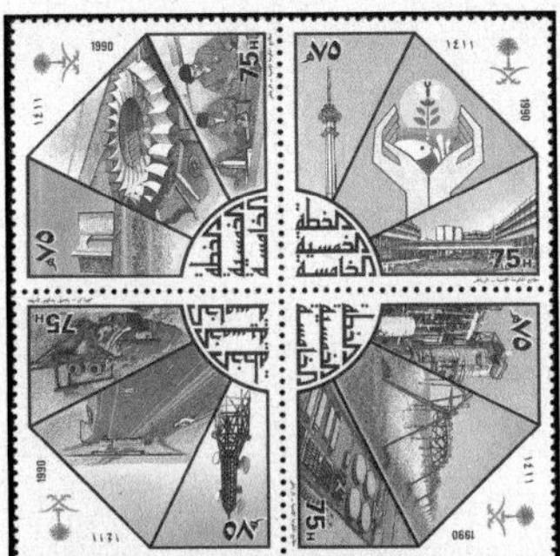

Fifth Five Year Development Plan — A271

Designs: a, Oil refinery, irrigation, and oil storage tanks. b, Radio tower, highway, and mine. c, Monument, sports stadium, and vocational training. d, Television tower, environmental protection, and modern architecture.

1990, Oct. 30

1138 A271 75h Block of 4, #a.-d. 4.50 2.25

Battle of Badr, 624 — A272

1991, Apr. 3 **Litho.** ***Perf. 12***

1139 A272 75h org, dk grn & grn .90 .40
1140 A272 150h lt bl, dk bl & grn 1.75 .80

World Health Day — A273

1991, Apr. 9

1141 A273 75h multicolored .90 .40
1142 A273 150h multicolored 1.75 .80

Animals — A274

Designs: a, k, Impala. b, l, Ibex. c, m, Oryx. d, n, Fox. e, o, Bat. f, p, Hyena. g, q, Cat. h, r, Dugong. i, s, Leopard.

Blocks of 9

1991 **Litho.** ***Perf. 12***

1143 A274 25h Block, #a.-i. 3.00 1.50
1144 A274 50h Block, #a.-i. 6.50 3.75
1145 A274 75h Block, #a.-i. 9.50 6.25
1146 A274 100h Block, #a.-i. 13.00 7.75
1146J A274 150h Block, #k.-s. 19.00 14.50
t. Perf 14x13½ 23.00 15.50
Nos. 1143-1146J (5) 51.00 33.75

Issued: #1143-1146, May 1; #1146J, Dec. 1. No. 1146J exists imperf.

Pilgrimage to Mecca — A275

1991, June 20 **Litho.** ***Perf. 14***

1147 A275 75h blue & multi .90 .40
1148 A275 150h green & multi 1.60 .80

World Telecommunications Day — A276

1991, June 3 ***Perf. 12***

1149 A276 75h multicolored .90 .40
1150 A276 150h multicolored 1.60 .80

Liberation of Kuwait — A277

1991, May 11

1151 A277 75h multicolored .90 .65
1152 A277 150h multicolored 2.00 1.25

Literacy Day — A278

1991, Sept. 8 **Litho.** ***Perf. 12***

1153 A278 75h blue & multi 1.25 .65
1154 A278 150h buff & multi 2.40 1.25

World Food Day — A279

1991, Oct. 16 **Litho.** ***Perf. 12***

1155 A279 75h green & multi .90 .40
1156 A279 150h orange & multi 1.60 .90

Childrens' Day A280

1991, Dec. 7

1157 A280 75h green & multi 1.40 .75
1158 A280 150h dk blue & multi 2.40 1.50

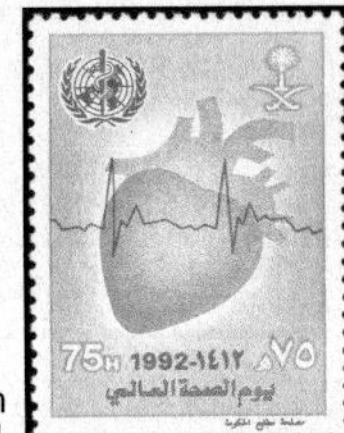

World Health Day — A281

1992, Apr. 8 **Litho.** ***Perf. 12***

1159 A281 75h lt blue & multi .90 .50
1160 A281 150h lt org & multi 1.75 .90

War Between the Arabs of Medina and Mecca, 624-630 A282

1992, Apr. 18

1161 A282 75h lt org & grn .80 .45
1162 A282 150h lt bl, dk bl & grn 1.60 .90

Pilgrimage to Mecca A283

Unwmk.

1992, June 9 **Litho.** ***Perf. 12***

1163 A283 75h lt blue & multi .90 .50
1164 A283 150h lt orange & multi 1.75 .90

Population and Housing Census — A284

1992, Sept. 26 **Litho.** ***Perf. 14***

1165 A284 75h blue & multi .65 .40
1166 A284 150h org yel & multi 1.25 .80

World Food Day A285

1992, Oct. 17 ***Perf. 12***

1167 A285 75h Vegetables 1.00 .55
1168 A285 150h Fruits 2.00 1.00

Consultative Council — A286

Document: d, g, 12 lines. e, h, 13 lines. f, i, 11 lines. 5r, Scrolls of 12, 11, & 13 lines.

1992, Dec. 12 **Litho.** ***Perf. 12***

1168A A286 75h Strip of 3, #d.-f. 1.90 1.15
1168B A286 150h Strip of 3, #g.-i. 4.75 2.40

Imperf

Size: 120x79mm

1168C A286 5r multicolored 22.50 21.00

Birds — A287

a, k, Woodpecker. b, l, Arabian bustard. c, m, Lark. d, n, Turtle dove. e, o, Heron. f, p, Partridge. g, q, Hoopoe. h, r, Falcon. i, s, Houbara bustard.

1992-97 **Blocks of 9** ***Perf. 14x13½***

1169 A287 25h #a.-i. 4.50 4.25
j. Perf. 12, #k.-s. 22.00 14.50
1170 A287 50h #a.-i. 8.00 5.25
j. Perf. 12, #k.-s.
1171 A287 75h #a.-i. 9.25 5.50
j. Perf. 12, #k.-s. 9.25 5.75
1172 A287 100h #a.-i. 20.00 12.00
j. Perf. 12, #k.-s. 20.00 12.00
1173 A287 150h #a.-i. 32.00 18.00
j. Perf. 12, #k.-s. 32.00 18.00
Nos. 1169-1173 (5) 73.75 45.00

Issued: 150h, 3/18/92; 75h, 7/14/92; 100h, 3/1/93; 25h, 50h, 11/6/94; #1171j, 1173j, 8/94; 1169j, 1996; 1170j, 1997(?).

World Health Day A288

1993, Apr. 7 **Litho.** ***Perf. 12***

1175 A288 75h red & multi .80 .40
1175A A288 150h blue & multi 1.60 .80

King Fahd Championship Soccer Cup — A289

1993, Mar. 15

1176 A289 75h green & multi 1.40 .60
1176A A289 150h rose red & multi 2.40 1.40

Pilgrimage to Mecca — A290

1993, May 30 **Litho.** ***Perf. 12***

1177 A290 75h green & multi .80 .40
1178 A290 150h blue & multi 1.40 .80

Intl. Telecommunications Day — A291

1993, May 17 **Inscription Color**
1179 A291 75h dark blue .80 .40
1180 A291 150h red lilac 1.40 .80

Battle of Alkandk A292

1993, May 15
1181 A292 75h lt org & grn .80 .40
1182 A292 150h lt bl, dk bl & grn 1.40 .80

World Food Day — A293

1993, Dec. 14 **Litho.** ***Perf. 12***
1183 A293 75h black & multi .90 .45
1184 A293 150h red & multi 2.00 .90

World Dental Health Day A294

1994, Apr. 9 **Litho.** ***Perf. 12***
1185 A294 75h multicolored .90 .40
1186 A294 150h multicolored 1.75 .80

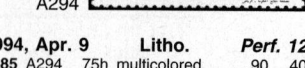

Intl. Olympic Committee, Cent. A295

1994, Apr. 23 **Litho.** ***Perf. 12***
1187 A295 75h blue & multi .90 .55
1188 A295 150h red & multi 2.00 .90

Battle of Khaybar A296

1994, June 14 **Litho.** ***Perf. 12***
1189 A296 75h bister & green .90 .40
1190 A296 150h sil, bl & grn 1.75 .80

Pilgrimage to Mecca — A297

1994, May 14
1191 A297 75h green & multi .75 .40
1192 A297 150h red & multi 1.30 .90

Consultative Council — A298

Design: 150h, Different view of building, inscription tablet at right.

1994, July 12 **Litho.** ***Perf. 12***
1193 A298 75h multicolored .80 .40
1194 A298 150h multicolored 1.60 .80
a. Souv. sheet of 2, #1193-1194, imperf. *28.00*

No. 1194a sold for 5r.

A299

1994 World Soccer Cup Championships, U.S. — A300

1994, June 18
1195 A299 75h multicolored .80 .40
1196 A300 150h multicolored 1.60 .80

King Abdul Aziz Port, Dammam — A301

1994-95 **Litho.** ***Perf. 12***
1198 A301 25h multicolored .65 .40
1199 A301 50h multicolored .65 .40
1200 A301 75h multicolored .80 .55
1201 A301 100h multicolored 1.15 .60
1202 A301 150h multicolored 1.75 .80
Nos. 1198-1202 (5) 5.00 2.75

Issued: 75h, 8/22/94; 150h, 11/5/94; 100h, 3/11/95; 50h, 11/28/95; 25h, 12/27/95.

A304

World Food Day A305

1994, Oct. 16 **Litho.** ***Perf. 12***
1212 A304 75h Green house 1.40 .60
1213 A305 150h Foods 2.60 1.40

A306

Arab League, 50th Anniv. A307

1995, Mar. 25 **Litho.** ***Perf. 12***
1214 A306 75h multicolored .80 .40
1215 A307 150h multicolored 1.50 .80

A308

UN, 50th Anniv. — A309

1995, Feb. 19
1216 A308 75h multicolored .80 .40
1217 A309 150h multicolored 1.60 .80

Refugee Care A310

1995, Apr. 9 **Litho.** ***Perf. 12***
1218 A310 75h green & multi .80 .40
1219 A310 150h tan & multi 1.50 .80

Pilgrimage to Mecca A311

1995, May 3 **Litho.** ***Perf. 12***
1220 A311 75h blue & multi .80 .40
1221 A311 150h tan & multi 1.50 .80

Deaf Week — A312

1995, May 3 **Litho.** ***Perf. 12***
1222 A312 75h shown .80 .40
1223 A312 150h Hand sign, ear 1.60 .80

Saudi Arabian Airlines, 50th Anniv. A313

75h, Anniv. emblem, vert.

1995, Aug. 21
1224 A313 75h multicolored .80 .40
1225 A313 150h shown 1.60 .80

FAO, 50th Anniv. — A314

1995, Oct. 16 **Litho.** ***Perf. 12***
1226 A314 75h shown 1.40 .60
1227 A314 150h Emblem over globe 2.40 1.40

Jeddah Port — A315

1996 **Litho.** ***Perf. 12***
1228 A315 25h multicolored .40 .30
1229 A315 50h multicolored .90 .55
1230 A315 75h multicolored 1.30 .80
1230A A315 100h multicolored 1.75 1.75
1230B A315 150h multicolored 2.60 1.60
Nos. 1228-1230B (5) 6.95 5.00

Issued: 25h and 50h, 1/27/96; 75h, 2/7/96; 100h, 11/25/96; 150h, 3/30/96.

1996 Summer Olympics, Atlanta A316

1996, June 23
1231 A316 150h orange & multi 1.75 .90
1232 A316 2r blue & multi 2.75 1.25

Pilgrimage to Mecca — A317

Al Khafji Oil Rig Type of 1976-80 Redrawn With Palm Trees and Swords at Upper Right

Perf. 14x13½

2000, Sept. 13 Litho. Unwmk.

Size: 26x21mm

1300A A109 25h dk pur & org .65 .65

King Abdul Aziz City for Science and Technology A363

2000, Oct. 28

1301 A363 1r multi 1.10 .55

King Khalid University A364

2000, Dec. 5 ***Perf. 14***

1302 A364 1r multi 1.10 .55

Buraydah — A365

2000 ***Perf. 13¾x14***

1303 A365 50h blue & multi .40 .40
1304 A365 1r grn & multi .80 .80
1305 A365 2r blk & multi 1.60 1.60
Nos. 1303-1305 (3) 2.80 2.80

Buraydah — A366

2000-01 ***Perf. 13¾x14***

1306 A366 50h blue & multi .40 .40
1307 A366 1r grn & multi .80 .80
1308 A366 2r blk & multi 1.60 1.60
Nos. 1306-1308 (3) 2.80 2.80

No. 1308 issued 2/2/01.

King Fahd Printing Press A367

Denomination color: 50h, Pink. 1r, Blue. 2r, Black.

2001, Apr. 25 Litho. ***Perf. 14***

1309-1311 A367 Set of 3 3.00 3.00

King Abdul Aziz Center for Gifted Care — A368

2001, May 13

1312 A368 1r multi 1.10 .55

Pilgrimage to Mecca — A369

No. 1313: a, Mosque, tower at center, b, Holy Ka'aba. c, Mosque, tower at left and center. d, Mosque, tower and two men at left. e, Mosque, tower at right, mountain in background. f, Mosque, tower and five pilgrims at left. g, Mosque, tower at right. h, Mosque, orange background.

2001, Feb. 28 ***Perf. 13¾x14***

1313 A369 1r Block of 8, #a-h 6.50 6.50

Palestinian Intifada A370

Designs: 1r, Map of Israel, Palestinian boy and father. 2r, Barbed wire, boy and father, vert.

2001, May 30 Litho. ***Perf. 14***

1314-1315 A370 Set of 2 2.75 2.75

A souvenir sheet containing an imperforate 49x36mm example of No. 1314 sold for 5r. Value $35.

King Abdul Aziz Historical Center — A371

No. 1316: a, Building with curved, pointed wall. b, Building with one tree in front. c, Building with towers. d, Aerial view of building.

2001, June 25

1316 A371 1r Block of 4, #a-d 3.25 3.25

World Teacher's Day — A372

2001, Oct. 6

1317 A372 1r multi 1.00 .80

Paintings A373

No. 1318: a, Abstract cityscape in green and yellow. b, Horse and geometric designs. c, Building windows. d, Landscape in yellow, orange and brown. e, Building with blue sky.

2001, Oct. 15

1318 Horiz. strip of 5 4.00 4.00
a.-e. A373 1r Any single .80 .80

7th Five-Year Plan A374

2002, Jan. 19 Litho. ***Perf. 14***

1319 A374 1r multi .80 .80

A375

Abha — A376

2002, Jan. 19

1320 A375 1r blue & multi .80 .80
1321 A376 2r green & multi 1.60 1.60

Islamic Educational, Scientific and Cultural Organization — A377

2002, Jan. 29

1322 A377 1r multi 1.15 .80

Pilgrimage to Mecca A378

2002, Feb. 13

1323 A378 1r multi .80 .80

20 Years of Achievements Under King Fahd — A379

Litho. with Foil Application

2002, Apr. 13

1324 A379 1r multi .80 .80

An imperforate 3r souvenir sheet overprinted in gold and depicting an example of No. 1324 and various other stamps, in whole or in part, exists. Value $3.

King Fahd Port, Yanbu A380

2002, May 26 Litho. ***Perf. 14***

1325 A380 1r yel & multi .80 .80
1326 A380 2r gray & multi 1.60 1.60

King Fahd Port, Al Jubail A381

2002, May 26

1327 A381 1r black & multi .80 .80
1328 A381 2r multi 1.60 1.60

Issued: 1r, 7/13.

Pilgrimage to Mecca A382

2003, Feb. 7 Litho. ***Perf. 14***

1329 A382 1r multi .80 .80

Water Conservation — A383

Designs: No. 1330, 1r, Two water drops. No. 1331, 1r, One water drop, vert.

2003, Mar. 30 Litho. ***Perf. 14***

1330-1331 A383 Set of 2 1.60 1.60

Civil Defense A384

2003, Apr. 29
1332 A384 1r multi .80 .80

Saudi Arabian Red Cresecent Society A385

2003, May 20
1333 A385 1r multi .95 .80

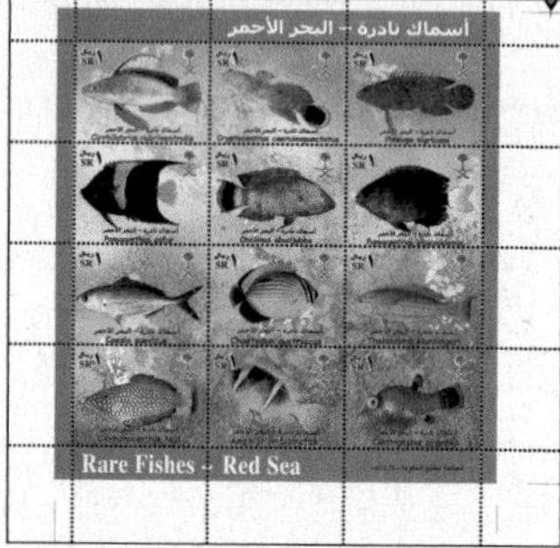

Fish — A386

Designs: Nos. 1334a, 1335a, Cirrhilabrus rubriventralis. Nos. 1334b, 1335b, Cryptocentrus caeruleopunctatus. Nos. 1334c, 1335c, Plesiops nigricans. Nos. 1334d, 1335d, Pomacanthus asfur. Nos. 1334e, 1335e, Cheilinus abudjubbe. Nos. 1334f, 1335f, Pomacentrus albicaudatus. Nos. 1334g, 1335g, Caesio suevicus. Nos. 1334h, 1335h, Chaetodon austriacus. Nos. 1334i, 1335i, Thalassoma klunzingeri. Nos. 1334j, 1335j, Oxymonacanthus halli. Nos. 1334k, 1335k, Amphiprion bicinctus. Nos. 1334l, 1335l, Canthigaster pygmaea.

2003
1334 A386 1r Sheet of 12, #a-l 11.00 11.00
1335 A386 2r Sheet of 12, #a-l 19.50 18.00

Issued: No. 1334, 5/26; No. 1335, 6/21.

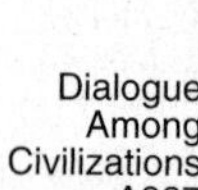

Dialogue Among Civilizations A387

2003, July 1
1336 A387 1r multi .80 .80

Electricity Conservation — A388

2003, Sept. 27
1337 A388 1r multi .80 .80

World Post Day — A389

2003, Oct. 9
1338 A389 1r multi .95 .80

Ninth Gulf Cooperation Council Stamp Exhibition — A390

2003, Oct. 18
1339 A390 1r multi .80 .80

First Saudi Commemorative Stamp, 75th Islamic Year Anniv. — A391

2003, Oct. 20
1340 A391 1r No. 129 .80 .80

Supreme Council for Handicapped Affairs — A392

2003, Nov. 11
1341 A392 1r multi .80 .80

King Abdul Aziz Equestrian Race Course, Janadriyah A393

2003, Dec. 17
1342 A393 1r multi .80 .80

Pilgrimage to Mecca A394

2003, Dec. 24
1343 A394 1r multi .80 .80
  a. Arabian "1" missing in denomination 20.00 —

Mosque, Buraydah A395

Mosque, Medina A396

Mosque, Riyadh A397

Mosque, Dammam A398

Mosque, Baha A399

Mosque, Khobar A400

Mosque, Taif — A401

Mosque, Najran A402

2003, Dec. 24
1344 Sheet of 8 6.25 6.25
  a. A395 1r bl & multi .80 .80
  b. A396 1r bl & multi .80 .80
  c. A397 1r bl & multi .80 .80
  d. A398 1r bl & multi .80 .80
  e. A399 1r bl & multi .80 .80
  f. A400 1r bl & multi .80 .80
  g. A401 1r bl & multi .80 .80
  h. A402 1r bl & multi .80 .80
1345 Sheet of 8 13.50 13.50
  a. A395 2r red & multi 1.60 1.60
  b. A396 2r red & multi 1.60 1.60
  c. A397 2r red & multi 1.60 1.60
  d. A398 2r red & multi 1.60 1.60
  e. A399 2r red & multi 1.60 1.60
  f. A400 2r red & multi 1.60 1.60
  g. A401 2r red & multi 1.60 1.60
  h. A402 2r red & multi 1.60 1.60

Mosques built in reign of King Fahd.

Tabouk — A403

2004, Jan. 19
1346 A403 1r blk & multi .80 .80
1347 A403 2r red & multi 1.60 1.60

MD-11 A404

Boeing 747 — A405

Boeing 777 — A406

MD-90 A407

2004, Jan. 19
1348 Block of 4 3.25 3.25
  a. A404 1r multi .80 .80
  b. A405 1r multi .80 .80
  c. A406 1r multi .80 .80
  d. A407 1r multi .80 .80

New airplanes of Saudi Arabian Airlines.

Judicial Systems A408

2004, Apr. 5 **Litho.** ***Perf. 14***
1349 A408 1r multi .80 .80

Hail — A409

2004, Oct. 16 **Litho.** ***Perf. 13¾x14***
1350 A409 1r blk & multi .80 .80
1351 A409 2r red & multi 1.60 1.60

World Summit on the Information Society A410

2004, Nov. 1 ***Perf. 14***
1352 A410 1r multi .80 .80

Tourism — A411

No. 1353: a, Sand dune. b, Funicular cars. c, Sea coast. d, Rock climbers.

2004, Nov. 1
1353 A411 2r Block of 4, #a-d 6.50 6.50

"Islam is Peace" A412

2004, Dec. 27
1354 A412 2r multi 1.60 1.60

Pilgrimage to Mecca A413

2005, Jan. 4
1355 A413 1r multi .80 .80

Municipal Elections — A414

2005, Jan. 8 **Litho.** ***Perf. 14***
1356 A414 1r multi .80 .80

Islamic Solidarity Games — A415

2005, Apr. 2
1357 A415 1r multi .80 .80

Anti-Terrorism Campaign A416

2005, July 9 **Litho.** ***Perf. 14***
1358 A416 1r multi .95 .80

An imperf. souvenir sheet with simulated perfs sold for 3r. Value $9.

Arar A417

2005, July 16 **Litho.** ***Perf. 14***
1359 A417 1r multi .80 .80
a. Missing Arabian "1" at right — —

No. 1359a appears in position 10 on some sheets.

Ancient Artifacts — A418

Ruins — A419

No. 1360: a, Bowl. b, Head of animal. c, Head of human. d, Inscribed tablet.

No. 1361: a, Ruin with two towers, walls in foreground, year in black. b, Building with one tower, year in white. c, Fort with towers at corners, year in white. d, Ruins on hilltop, year in black.

2005, Aug. 20
1360 A418 1r Block of 4, #a-d 3.50 3.50
1361 A419 2r Block of 4, #a-d 6.50 6.50

Mecca, Capital of Islamic Culture — A420

2005, July 16 **Litho.** ***Perf. 14***
1362 A420 3r multi 2.00 2.00

A souvenir sheet of one exists. Value, $20.

King Fahd (1921-2005) A421

Denominations: 2r, 3r.

2005, Dec. 21
1363-1364 A421 Set of 2 3.25 3.25

An imperf 105x80mm stamp with picture reversed sold for 5r. Value $18.

Pilgrimage to Mecca A422

2005, Dec. 28
1365 A422 2r multi 2.75 1.50

An imperf 80x105mm stamp depicting pilgrims to Mecca sold for 5r.

King Abdullah — A423

Crown Prince Sultan — A424

Litho. with Foil Application

2006, Jan. 18
1366 A423 2r multi 1.30 1.30
1367 A424 2r multi 1.30 1.30
1368 A423 3r multi 2.00 2.00
1369 A424 3r multi 2.00 2.00
Nos. 1366-1369 (4) 6.60 6.60

Installation of new king and crown prince. An imperf 106x80mm stamp depicting the new king and crown prince sold for 5r. Value $22.50.

National Society for Human Rights A425

2006, Jan. 30 **Litho.** ***Perf. 14***
1370 A425 2r multi 1.30 1.30

An 80x105mm imperforate stamp depicting a stylized person sold for 5r. Value $22.50.

OPEC Intl. Development Fund, 30th Anniv. — A426

2006, Mar. 13
1371 A426 2r multi 1.50 1.50

King Faisal International Prize — A427

Color of denomination: 2r, Blue. 3r, Green.

2006, Apr. 3
1372-1373 A427 Set of 2 3.25 3.25

Saudi Post Mailboxes A428

2006, Apr. 22
1374 A428 2r multi 1.50 1.50

King Saud University A429

2006, May 14
1375 A429 2r multi 1.30 1.30

2006 World Cup Soccer Championships, Germany A430

Emblem and: 2r, Players. 3r, World map.

2006, May 20
1376-1377 A430 Set of 2 4.75 4.75

Gulf Cooperation Council, 25th Anniv. — A431

Litho. With Foil Application

2006, May 25
1378 A431 2r multi 1.60 1.60

An imperf. 165x105mm stamp depicting flags of Gulf Cooperation council members sold for 5r. Value $52.50.

See Bahrain Nos. 628-629, Kuwait Nos. 1646-1647, Oman Nos. 477-478, and Qatar Nos. 1007-1008.

Saudi Center for Organ Transplantation A432

2006, June 17 **Litho.**
1379 A432 2r multi 1.60 1.60

Al Medina Al Munawara A433

2006, Sept. 5
1380 A433 2r multi 1.50 1.50

An imperf. 105x80mm stamp depicting a smaller version of No. 1380 and the doorway shown at the lower left of No. 1380 sold for 5r. Value $19.50.

Riyadh Intl. Book Fair A434

2006, Sept. 9
1381 A434 2r multi 1.50 1.50

National Day A435

2006, Sept. 23
1382 A435 2r multi 1.50 1.50

Arabian Horses A436

No. 1383: a, Brown horse facing right, no shadow. b, Brown horse facing left, no shadow. c, Brown horse facing right, with shadow. d, Brown horse facing left, with shadow. e, White horse. f, Horse and colt.

2006, Nov. 13
1383 Block of 6 9.00 9.00
a.-f. A436 2r Any single 1.30 1.30

Pilgrimage to Mecca A437

2006, Dec. 11
1384 A437 2r multi 1.60 1.60

Kingdom of Humanity A438

2007, Apr. 23
1385 A438 2r multi 1.60 1.60

An imperf. 105x80mm stamp depicting flag and King Abdullah sold for 5r.

2006 World Cup Soccer Championships, Germany A439

2007, May 14
1386 A439 2r multi 1.60 1.60

Elimination of Poliomyelitis From Saudi Arabia — A440

2007, June 9
1387 A440 2r multi 1.60 1.60

Butterflies A441

Nos. 1388 and 1389: a, Junonia hierta. b, Melitaea deserticola. c, Junonia orithya cheesmani. d, Eurema hecabe. e, Papilio demoleus. f, Colotis calais. g, Colotis phisadia. h, Vanessa cardui. Backgrounds differ on Nos. 1388 and 1389.

2007, Aug. 20
1388 Sheet of 8 13.00 13.00
a.-h. A441 2r Any single 1.30 1.30
1389 Sheet of 8 19.00 19.00
a.-h. A441 3r Any single 1.90 1.90

The Latin names of the butterflies on Nos. 1388c, 1388d, 1388f, 1389c, 1389d and 1389f are incorrect on the stamps.

Direct Mail Conference, Riyadh — A442

No. 1390: a, PosTech 2007 emblem. b, Flags and emblems of postal services of Gulf Cooperation Council countries. c, Emblem of 13th Gulf Cooperation Council Postage Stamp Exhibition. d, Emblem for UPU Regional Roundtable and map.

2007, Nov. 11
1390 A442 2r Block of 4, #a-d 6.00 6.00

Women in Science and Education — A443

No. 1391: a, Woman teaching children. b, Woman at microscope. c, Women in classroom. d, Woman at computer in laboratory.

2007, Nov. 11
1391 A443 2r Block of 4, #a-d 6.00 6.00

Third OPEC Summit, Riyadh A444

2007, Nov. 17
1392 A444 2r multi 1.60 1.60

National Day A445

2007, Dec. 1
1393 A445 2r multi 1.60 1.60

Pilgrimage to Mecca A446

2007, Dec. 9 **Litho.** ***Perf. 14***
1394 A446 2r multi 1.60 1.60

Harmony Through Intellectual Dialogue — A447

2007, Dec. 29
1395 A447 2r multi 1.60 1.60

Camels — A448

No. 1396: a, Al majaheem. b, Al wad'h. c, Al shog'h. d, Al shoe'l.

2008, Apr. 21
1396 A448 2r Block of 4, #a-d 6.00 6.00

An imperf. 105x75mm stamp depicting smaller versions of Nos. 1396a-1396d sold for 5r.

Aramco, 75th Anniv. — A449

No. 1397: a, Workmen on oil drilling platform. b, Scuba diver and fish. c, Child's drawing of oil drilling. d, Child's drawing of Saudi people.

2008, May 20 ***Perf. 13¾x14***
1397 A449 2r Block of 4, #a-d 6.00 6.00

Development of Riyadh, 50th Anniv. — A450

2008, June 21 ***Perf. 14***
1398 A450 2r multi 1.60 1.60

An imperf. 105x80mm stamp depicting Riyadh and King Abdullah sold for 5r.

Intl. Electrotechnical Commission, Cent. — A451

2008, July 19
1399 A451 2r multi 1.60 1.60

A souvenir sheet containing two perf. 13¾x13¼ stamps for Arab Postal Day sold for 10r.

Pilgrimage to Mecca A452

2008, Dec. 1 **Litho.** ***Perf. 14***
1400 A452 2r multi 1.60 1.60

Compare with types A437 and A446.

King Abdullah University of Science and Technology — A453

2009, Sept. 23 ***Perf. 13¾x14***
1401 A453 2r multi 1.50 1.50

An imperf. 105x75mm stamp depicting King Abdullah and the university sold for 5r.

Jerusalem, Capital of Arab Culture — A454

2009, Oct. 25 ***Perf. 14***
1402 A454 2r multi 1.90 1.90

National Day A455

2009, Nov. 18
1403 A455 2r multi 1.50 1.50

Pilgrimage to Mecca — A456

2009, Nov. 18 ***Perf. 13¾x14***
1404 A456 2r multi 1.50 1.50

Organization of Petroleum Exporting Countries, 50th Anniv. — A457

2010, Jan. 9 ***Perf. 14***
1405 A457 2r multi 1.50 1.50

Janandriyah Festival, 25th Anniv. — A458

2010, Nov. 9 ***Perf. 14***
1406 A458 2r multi 1.50 1.50

National Day — A459

2010, Nov. 10 ***Perf. 13¾x14***
1407 A459 2r multi 1.50 1.50

Souvenir Sheet

Pilgrimage to Mecca — A460

No. 1408: a, Pilgrims and train. b, Pilgrims, train, King Abdullah, Mecca Royal Clock Hotel Tower, Holy Ka'aba. c, Mecca Royal Clock Hotel Tower, Holy Ka'aba, clock.

2010, Nov. 10 ***Perf. 14***
1408 A460 2r Sheet of 3, #a-c, + 3 labels 11.50 11.50
d. As #1408, missing black inscriptions in sheet margin and below "2r" denomination —

Miniature Sheets

Jewelry — A461

No. 1409: a, Bracelet with ruby. b, Gold bracelet. c, Three horseshoe bracelets. d, Silver armlets. e, Silver bangles. f, Two bracelets.

No. 1410 — Stamps with gray brown background: a, Headdress ornament. b, Earrings. c, Earrings with hooks visible at top. d, Head ornament. e, Rings. f, Forehead ornament.

No. 1411 — Stamps with pink background: a, Gold, cornelian and ruby necklace. b, Silver necklace. c, Necklace with red stone. d, Waist belt. e, Necklace. f, Silver necklace with large square pendants.

2010-11 ***Perf. 14***
1409 A461 2r Sheet of 6, #a-f 9.00 9.00
1410 A461 2r Sheet of 6, #a-f 9.00 9.00
1411 A461 2r Sheet of 6, #a-f 9.00 9.00
Nos. 1409-1411 (3) 27.00 27.00

Issued: No. 1409, 12/29. No. 1410, 4/4/11; No. 1411, 9/12/11.

World Map, Dove and Scouting Emblem — A462

2011 ***Perf. 13¾x14***
1412 A462 2r multi 1.50 1.50

King Abdullah Haram Expansion Project — A463

2011
1413 A463 2r multi 1.50 1.50

Prince Sultan (1928-2011) A464

2012, Sept. 15 ***Perf. 14***
1414 A464 2r multi 1.50 1.50

An imperforate 105x75mm stamp depicting Prince Sultan sold for 5r.

Installation of Crown Prince Nayef A465

2012, Sept. 15
1415 A465 2r multi 1.50 1.50

An imperforate 105x75mm stamp depicting Crown Prince Nayef sold for 5r.

Crown Prince Nayef (1934-2012) A466

2012, Sept. 15
1416 A466 2r multi 1.50 1.50

An imperforate 106x75mm stamp depicting Crown Prince Nayaf sold for 5r.

Installation of Crown Prince Suleiman A467

2012, Sept. 23
1417 A467 2r multi 1.50 1.50

An imperforate 105x75mm stamp depicting Crown Prince Suleiman sold for 5r.

National Day — A468

2012, Sept. 23
1418 A468 2r multi 1.50 1.50

Arab Postal Day — A469

2012, Oct. 17 ***Perf. 13¾x14***
1419 A469 2r multi 1.50 1.50

18th Gulf Cooperation Council Stamp Exhibition, Jeddah — A470

2012, Oct. 17 ***Perf. 14***
1420 A470 2r multi 1.50 1.50

Souvenir Sheet

Pilgrimage to Mecca — A471

No. 1421: a, Aerial view of mosque and surrounding plaza. b, Aerial view of Grand Mosque and Holy Ka'aba, Mecca.

2012, Oct. 22 ***Perf. 13¾x14***
1421 A471 2r Sheet of 2, #a-b 3.00 3.00

A472

Princess Nora Bint Abdul Rahman University, Riyadh A473

2013, Feb. 16 ***Perf. 14***

1422 A472 2r multi 1.50 1.50
1423 A473 3r multi 2.25 2.25

A474

King Abdullah Prize for Translation — A475

2013, Mar. 3 ***Perf. 14***

1424 A474 2r multi 1.50 1.50

Perf. 13¾x14

1425 A475 3r multi 2.25 2.25

Arabian Fatherhood Symbol A476

2013, Apr. 6 ***Perf. 14***

1426 A476 2r multi 1.50 1.50

Pilgrimage to Mecca A477

2013, Aug. 3

1427 A477 2r multi 1.50 1.50

Souvenir Sheet

Medina, 2013 Capital of Islamic Culture — A478

No. 1428: a, Emblem for Third Arab Stamps Exhibition. b, Emblem for Medina as Capital of Islamic Culture

2013, Sept. 1 **Litho.** ***Perf. 14***

1428 A478 2r Sheet of 2, #a-b 3.00 3.00

National Day A479

2013, Sept. 23 **Litho.** ***Perf. 14***

1429 A479 2r multi 1.50 1.50

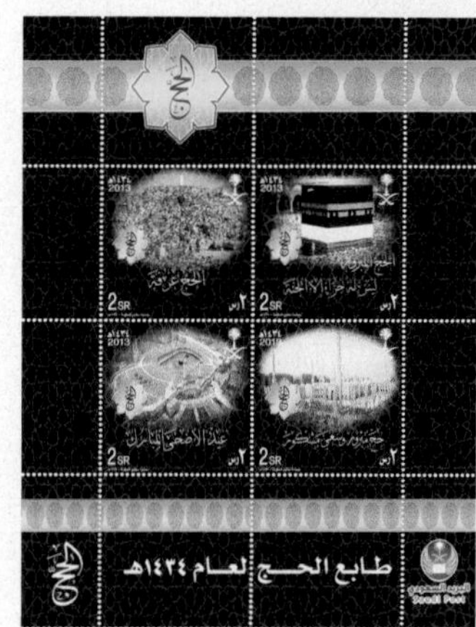

Pilgrimage to Mecca — A480

No. 1430: a, Worshipers on pilgrimage. b, Worshipers and Holy Ka'aba. c, Aerial view of Grand Mosque. d, Worshipers outside of mosque.

2013, Oct. 9 **Litho.** ***Perf. 14***

1430 A480 2r Sheet of 4, #a-d, + 2 labels 6.00 6.00

Charity Committee for Orphans Care A481

2014, Jan. 13 **Litho.** ***Perf. 14***

1431 A481 2r multi 1.50 1.50

Souvenir Sheet

King Abdullah Sports City — A482

No. 1432: a, Interior of stadium. b, Emblem. c, Aerial view of stadium.

2014, May 1 **Litho.** ***Perf. 13¾x14***

1432 A482 2r Sheet of 3, #a-c, + 6 labels 4.50 4.50

Miniature Sheet

Handicrafts — A483

No. 1433: a, Clothing. b, Baskets. c, Woman cooking. d, Decorations and storage bags. e, Decorations and baskets with lids. f, Handbags.

2014, Aug. 19 **Litho.** ***Perf. 14***

1433 A483 2r Sheet of 6, #a-f 9.00 9.00

Emblem of Okaz Souk A484

2014, Sept. 1 **Litho.** ***Perf. 14***

1434 A484 2r multi 1.50 1.50

Installation of Deputy Crown Prince Muqrin A485

2014, Sept. 14 **Litho.** ***Perf. 14***

1435 A485 2r multi 1.50 1.50

An imperforate 106x76mm stamp depicting Deputy Crown Prince Muqrin sold for 5r.

National Day A486

2014, Sept. 23 **Litho.** ***Perf. 14***

1436 A486 2r multi 1.50 1.50

Souvenir Sheet

Pilgrimage to Mecca — A487

No. 1437: a, Aerial view of Kaaba and the Great Mosque. b, Mosque interior. c, King Abdullah Gate and minarets.

2014, Sept. 28 **Litho.** ***Perf. 14***

1437 A487 2r Sheet of 3, #a-c 4.50 4.50

Emblem of Saudi Standards, Metrology, and Quality Organization — A488

2014, Oct. 16 **Litho.** ***Perf. 14***

1438 A488 2r multi 1.50 1.50

Miniature Sheet

King Abdullah (1924-2015) — A489

No. 1439 — King Abdullah: a, With microphones recording speech. b, Walking with cane. c, Greeting man. d, Giving baby bottle to child.

2015, Apr. 27 **Litho.** ***Perf. 14***

1439 A489 2r Sheet of 4, #a-d 6.00 6.00

An imperforate 105x78mm stamp depicting King Abdullah sold for 5r.

Installation of King Salman A490

Deposed Crown Prince Muqrin A491

Installation of Crown Prince Muhammad A492

2015, Apr. 27 **Litho.** ***Perf. 14***

1440 A490 2r multi 1.50 1.50
1441 A491 2r multi 1.50 1.50
1442 A492 2r multi 1.50 1.50
Nos. 1440-1442 (3) 4.50 4.50

An imperforate 105x78mm stamp depicting King Salman, deposed Crown Prince Muqrin and Crown Prince Muhammad sold for 5r.

22nd Arabian Gulf Cup Soccer Tournament, Riyadh — A493

2015, June 11 **Litho.** ***Perf. 14***

1443 A493 2r multi 1.50 1.50

No. 1443 was printed in sheets of 4, with each stamp on the sheet having a different pattern of triangles in the background.

Souvenir Sheet

Pilgrimage to Mecca — A494

No. 1444: a, Holy Ka'aba. b, Aerial view of Grand Mosque and Holy Ka'aba. c, Hand of pilgrim.

2015, Sept. 17 **Litho.** ***Perf. 14***

1444 A494 2r Sheet of 3, #a-c 4.50 4.50

Crown Prince Muhammad bin Nayef — A495

2015, Oct. 13 **Litho.** ***Perf. 14***
1445 A495 2r multi 1.50 1.50

An imperforate 105x75mm stamp depicting Crown Prince Muhammad bin Nayef and Deputy Crown Prince Mohammad bin Salman Al Saud sold for 5r.

Installation of Deputy Crown Prince Mohammad bin Salman Al Saud — A496

2015, Oct. 13 **Litho.** ***Perf. 14***
1446 A496 2r multi 1.50 1.50

Deputy Crown Prince Mohammad bin Salman Al Saud, King Salman, and Crown Prince Muhammad bin Nayef A497

2015, Nov. 2 **Litho.** ***Perf. 14***
1447 A497 2r multi 1.50 1.50

National Day. No. 1447 was printed in sheets of 3.

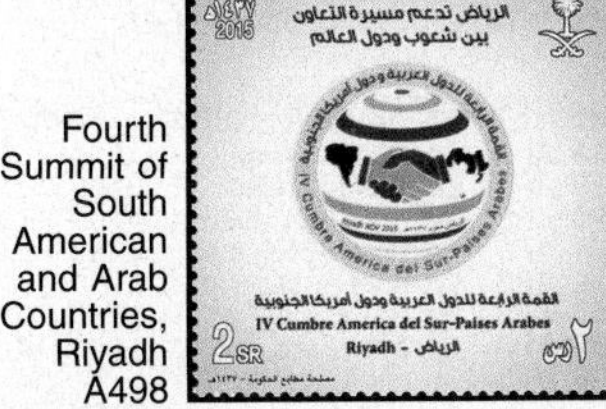

Fourth Summit of South American and Arab Countries, Riyadh A498

2015, Dec. 31 **Litho.** ***Perf. 14***
1448 A498 2r multi 1.50 1.50

World's Tallest Flagpole, Jeddah A499

2016, Mar. 9 **Litho.** ***Perf. 14***
1449 A499 2r multi 1.50 1.50

Saudi Arabian Philatelic Society, 50th Anniv. (in 2015) A500

2016, May 15 **Litho.** ***Perf. 14***
1450 A500 2r multi 1.50 1.50

Souvenir Sheet

Vision 2030 — A501

No. 1451: a, Emblem. b, Deputy Crown Prince Mohammad bin Salman Al Saud, King Salman, and Crown Prince Muhammad bin Nayef.

2016, Oct. 23 **Litho.** ***Perf. 14***
1451 A501 2r Sheet of 2, #a-b 3.00 3.00

An imperforate 105x75mm stamp depicting Crown Prince Muhammad bin Nayef, King Salman, and Deputy Crown Prince Mohammad bin Salman Al Saud sold for 5r.

National Day A502

2016, Sept. 25 **Litho.** ***Perf. 14***
1452 A502 2r multi 1.50 1.50

Souvenir Sheet

Pilgrimage to Mecca — A503

No. 1453: a, Corner of Holy Ka'aba. b, Grand Mosque and Holy Ka'aba. c, Black Stone of Holy Ka'aba. d, Holy Ka'aba doors and Kiswah.

2016, Sept. 6 **Litho.** ***Perf. 14***
1453 A503 2r Sheet of 4, #a-d 6.00 6.00

King Faisal Air Academy, 50th Anniv. A504

2017, May 21 **Litho.** ***Perf. 14***
1454 A504 2r multi 1.50 1.50

Souvenir Sheet

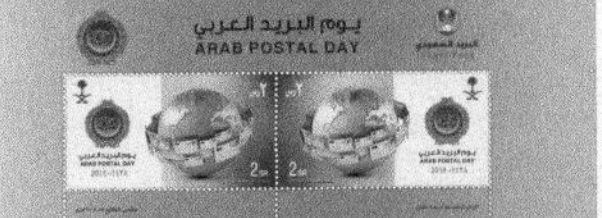

Arab Postal Day — A505

No. 1455 — Globe and letters at: a, Right. b, Left.

2017, May 21 **Litho.** ***Perf. 14***
1455 A505 2r Sheet of 2, #a-b 3.00 3.00

Pilgrimage to Mecca — A506

2017, Aug. 23 **Litho.** ***Perf. 14***
1456 A506 2r multi 1.50 1.50

Crown Prince Mohammad bin Salman Al Saud A507

2017, Aug. 23 **Litho.** ***Perf. 14***
1457 A507 2r multi 1.50 1.50

An imperforate 76x105mm stamp depicting the Crown Prince sold for 5r.

National Day — A508

2017, Sept. 25 **Litho.** ***Perf. 14***
1458 A508 2r multi 1.50 1.50

Abha, Capital of Arab Tourism A509

2017, Nov. 11 **Litho.** ***Perf. 14***
1459 A509 2r multi 1.50 1.50

Arab Islamic American Summit — A510

2017, Nov. 11 **Litho.** ***Perf. 14***
1460 A510 2r multi 1.50 1.50

Souvenir Sheet

Medina, Capital of Islamic Tourism — A511

No. 1461: a, Nighttime view of Quba Mosque. b, Daytime view of the Prophet's Mosque.

2017, Nov. 13 **Litho.** ***Perf. 14***
1461 A511 2r Sheet of 2, #a-b 3.00 3.00

Souvenir Sheet

Riyadh Metro — A512

No. 1462: a, Orange and white train at station. b, Green and white train.

2017, Nov. 13 **Litho.** ***Perf. 14***
1462 A512 2r Sheet of 2, #a-b 3.00 3.00

King Abdulaziz Complex for Manufacturing Cover for Holy Ka'aba — A513

2017, Dec. 12 **Litho.** ***Perf. 14***
1463 A513 2r multi 1.50 1.50

Souvenir Sheet

King Abdulaziz Camel Festival — A514

No. 1464 — Festival emblem, and in background: a, Camel and driver at head of line. b, Camels following leader.

2018, Apr. 8 **Litho.** ***Perf. 13¾x14***
1464 A514 2r Sheet of 2, #a-b 3.00 3.00

Arab League Summit on Palestine A515

2018, July 8 **Litho.** ***Perf. 14***
1465 A515 2r multi 1.50 1.50

An imperforate 75x106mm stamp depicting the Crown Prince and emblem sold for 5r.

Souvenir Sheet

2018 World Cup Soccer Championships, Russia — A516

No. 1466 — Mascot of Saudi Arabia team, buildings, Saudi Arabian flag and: a, White sky. b, Green sky.

2018, July 11 **Litho.** ***Perf. 14***
1466 A516 2r Sheet of 2, #a-b 3.00 3.00

An imperforate 106x75mm stamp depicting the Saudi Arabian soccer team and mascot and emblems of the 2018 World Cup and the

Saudi Arabian General Sports Authority sold for 5r.

Pilgrimage to Mecca — A517

2018, Aug. 15 Litho. *Perf. 14*

1467 A517 3r multi	2.25	2.25

No. 1467 was printed in sheets of 2. An imperforate 106x75mm stamp depicting the map of the world sold for 5r.

National Day — A518

2018, Sept. 23 Litho. *Perf. 14*

1468 A518 3r multi	2.25	2.25

No. 1468 was printed in sheets of 2. An imperforate 105x74mm stamp depicting various emblems sold for 5r.

Remembrance of Martyrs — A519

2018, Dec. 26 Litho. *Perf. 14*

1469 A519 3r multi	2.25	2.25

No. 1469 was printed in sheets of 2.

Express Mail Service, 20th Anniv. A520

2019, Apr. 21 Litho. *Perf. 14*

1470 A520 3r multi	2.25	2.25

No. 1470 was printed in sheets of 2.

Souvenir Sheet

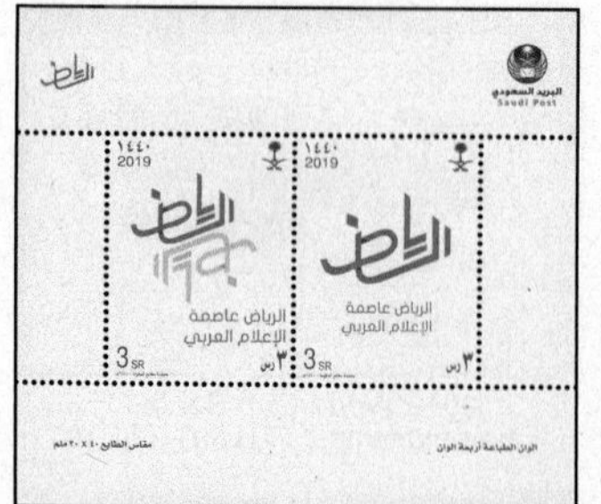
Riyadh, Arab Media Capital — A521

No. 1471: a, "Riyadh" in Arabic script above reversed and mirrored image of "Riyadh" in Arabic script. b, "Riyadh" in Arabic script.

2019, May 1 Litho. *Perf. 14*

1471 A521 3r Sheet of 2, #a-b	4.50	4.50

Pilgrimage to Mecca — A522

2019, Aug. 4 Litho. *Perf. 14*

1472 A522 3r multi	2.25	2.25

No. 1472 was printed in sheets of 3. An imperforate 105x75mm stamp depicting the Holy Ka'aba and a dove sold for 5r.

Miniature Sheet

Caves — A523

No. 1473: a, Mouth of cave. b, Mouth of cave as seen from inside. c, Cave passage. d, Mouth of cave as seen from inside, diff. e, Narrow cave passage. f, Stalactites.

2019, Sept. 11 Litho. *Perf. 14*

1473 A523 3r Sheet of 6, #a-f	13.50	13.50

National Day — A524

2019, Sept. 22 Litho. *Perf. 14*

1474 A524 3r multi	2.25	2.25

No. 1474 was printed in sheets of 2. An imperforate 105x75mm stamp depicting the national flag and a stalk of grain sold for 5r.

AIR POST STAMPS

Catalogue values for unused stamps in this section are for Never Hinged items.

Airspeed Ambassador Airliner — AP1

1949-58 Unwmk. Typo. *Perf. 11*

C1 AP1	1g blue green	4.00	.40
C2 AP1	3g ultra	5.25	.40
a.	3g blue ('58)	20.00	1.75
C3 AP1	4g orange	5.25	.40
C4 AP1	10g purple	14.50	.90
C5 AP1	20g brn vio ('58+)	12.00	2.00
a.	20g chocolate ('49)	25.00	2.40
C6 AP1	100g violet rose	140.00	20.00
	Nos. C1-C6 (6)	181.00	24.10

Imperfs. exist, not regularly issued.

The 1st printings are on grayish paper and sell for more.

No. C3 exists with pin-perf 6.

+ The date for No. C5 is not definite.

Saudi Airlines Convair 440 — AP2

Type I (Saud Cartouche) (Illustrated over No. 286)

1960-61 Photo. *Perf. 14*

C7 AP2	1p dull pur & grn	.65	.25
C8 AP2	2p grn & dull pur	.65	.25
C9 AP2	3p brn red & bl	.65	.25
C10 AP2	4p bl & dull pur	.65	.25
C11 AP2	5p grn & rose red	.65	.25
C12 AP2	6p ocher & slate	1.15	.30
C13 AP2	8p rose & gray ol	1.30	.30
C14 AP2	9p pur & red brn	2.00	.30
C15 AP2	10p blk & dl red brn	5.75	.60
C16 AP2	15p bl & bis brn	5.75	.50
C17 AP2	20p bis brn & emer	5.75	.55
C18 AP2	30p sep & Prus grn	13.00	1.55
C19 AP2	50p green & indigo	28.00	1.10
C20 AP2	100p gray & dk brn	57.50	3.25
C21 AP2	200p dk vio & black	92.50	4.75
	Nos. C7-C21 (15)	215.95	14.45

Nos. C7-C18 exist imperf., probably not regularly issued.

1963-64 Photo. Wmk. 337
Size: 27½x22mm

C24 AP2	1p lilac & green	2.60	.30
C25 AP2	2p green & dull pur	9.75	.30
C26 AP2	4p blue & dull pur	4.00	.30
C27 AP2	6p ocher & slate	9.75	.95
C28 AP2	8p rose & gray olive	20.00	1.60
C29 AP2	9p pur & red brn ('64)	14.00	1.05
	Nos. C24-C29 (6)	60.10	4.50

Redrawn
Perf. 13½x13
1964 Wmk. 337 Litho.
Size: 28½x23mm

C30 AP2	3p brn red & dull bl	8.00	.80
C31 AP2	10p blk & dk red brn	14.50	1.20
C32 AP2	20p bis brn & emer	30.00	3.00
	Nos. C30-C32 (3)	52.50	5.00

Nos. C30-C32 are widely spaced in the sheet, producing large margins.

Saudi Airline Boeing 720-B Jet — AP3

Type I (Saud Cartouche) (Illustrated over No. 286)

1965-70 Unwmk. Litho. *Perf. 14*

C33 AP3	1p lilac & green	*100.00*	3.25
C34 AP3	2p grn & dull pur	*3,100.*	*120.00*
C35 AP3	3p rose lil & dull bl	10.50	.25
C36 AP3	4p blue & dull pur	6.50	.25
C37 AP3	5p ol & rose red	*2,000.*	*450.00*
C38 AP3	6p ocher & slate	*120.00*	*2.00*
C39 AP3	7p rose & ol gray	7.25	.40
C40 AP3	8p rose & gray ol	*100.00*	*2.00*
C41 AP3	9p purple & red brn	6.50	.35
C42 AP3	10p blk & dk red brn	*90.00*	*6.50*
C43 AP3	11p grn & bis	*90.00*	*21.00*
C44 AP3	12p org & gray	6.50	.35
C45 AP3	13p dk grn & yel grn	5.00	.35
C46 AP3	14p dk blue & org	5.00	.40
C47 AP3	15p blue & bis brn	*90.00*	*6.50*
C48 AP3	16p black & ultra	7.25	.60
C49 AP3	17p bis & sep	6.00	.40
C50 AP3	18p dk bl & yel grn	6.00	.40
C51 AP3	19p car & dp org	6.50	.60
C52 AP3	20p bis brn & emer	*170.00*	7.25
C53 AP3	23p olive & bister	*175.00*	*13.00*
C54 AP3	24p dk bl & sep	6.00	.60
C55 AP3	26p ver & bl grn	6.00	.60
C56 AP3	27p ol brn & ap grn	6.50	.60
C57 AP3	31p car rose & rose red	9.00	.60
C58 AP3	33p red & dull pur	10.50	.60

The 50p, 100p and 200p exist but were not placed in use.

Issue years: 1966, 1p, 3p, 7p, 10p, 12p-14p, 16p-19p; 1969, 5p, 11p; 1970, 2p, 6p, 8p, 15p, 20p; others, 1965.

Type II (Faisal Cartouche)

1966-78 Unwmk. Litho. *Perf. 14*

C59 AP3	1p dull pur & grn	*22.50*	*1.10*
C60 AP3	2p grn & dl pur	*22.50*	*1.60*
C61 AP3	3p brn red & dull bl	*22.50*	.55
C62 AP3	4p blue & dull pur	11.50	.25
C63 AP3	5p ol & rose red	*2,000.*	*500.00*
C64 AP3	6p ocher & slate	150.00	*11.00*
C65 AP3	7p rose & ol gray	65.00	*7.25*
C66 AP3	8p rose & gray ol	90.00	*13.50*
C67 AP3	9p purple & red brn	6.25	.60
C68 AP3	10p blk & dull red brn	18.00	1.10
C69 AP3	11p grn & bis	15.00	.55
C70 AP3	12p org & gray	*55.00*	*4.00*
C71 AP3	13p dk grn & yel grn	16.00	1.10
C72 AP3	14p dk blue & org	16.00	1.75
C73 AP3	15p blue & bis brn	13.50	.80
C74 AP3	16p blk & ultra	*18.00*	3.25
C75 AP3	17p bis & sep	*16.00*	1.60
C76 AP3	18p dk bl & yel grn	*16.00*	2.60
C77 AP3	19p car & org	*21.00*	1.10
C78 AP3	20p brn & brt grn	*190.00*	*15.00*
C79 AP3	23p ol & bis	26.00	3.25
C80 AP3	24p dk blue & blk	*30.00*	3.25
C83 AP3	31p car rose & rose red	—	
C84 AP3	33p red & dull pur	13.50	.55
C85 AP3	50p emer & ind	*800.00*	*210.00*
C86 AP3	100p gray & dk brn	*900.00*	*325.00*
C87 AP3	200p dk vio & blk	*1,125.*	*210.00*

The existence of 26p and 27p denominations has been reported.

The status of the 31p has been questioned. If it exists it may not have been issued.

Issue years: 1968, 4p, 33p; 1969, 7p; 1970, 8p, 9p, 20p; 1971, 13p, 16p; 1974, 50p, 200p; 1975, 12p, 14p, 15p, 17p, 19p, 24p; 1976, 18p; 1978, 31p, 100p; others, 1966.

1968-71 Wmk. 361 Litho. *Perf. 14*

C88 AP3	1p lilac & green	7.25	.25
C89 AP3	2p green & lilac	9.00	.25
C90 AP3	3p rose lil & dull bl	40.00	*2.00*
C91 AP3	4p blue & dull pur	10.50	1.20
C92 AP3	7p rose & gray	10.50	1.75
C93 AP3	8p red & gray ol	*45.00*	*7.25*
C94 AP3	9p pur & red brn	*65.00*	*9.00*
C95 AP3	10p blk & dull red brn	*35.00*	4.00
	Nos. C88-C95 (8)	*222.25*	*25.70*

Issue years: 1969, 3p, 10p; 1970, 4p; 1971, 7p-9p; others, 1968.

Falcon — AP4

Perf. 13½x14
1968-71 Litho. Wmk. 361

C96 AP4	1p green & red brn	15.00	.30
C97 AP4	4p dk red & red brn	*240.00*	*16.00*
C98 AP4	10p blue & red brn	40.00	4.00
C99 AP4	20p green & red brn ('71)	72.50	8.00
	Nos. C96-C99 (4)	*367.50*	*28.30*

Nine other denominations were printed but are not known to have been issued.

HEJAZ POSTAGE DUE STAMPS

From Old Door at El Ashraf Barsbai in Shari el Ashrafiya, Cairo — D1

Serrate Roulette 13

1917, June 27 Typo. Unwmk.

LJ1 D1 20pa red 4.25 *4.00*
LJ2 D1 1pi blue 4.25 *4.00*
LJ3 D1 2pi magenta 4.25 *4.00*
Nos. LJ1-LJ3 (3) 12.75 *12.00*

For overprints see Nos. LJ4-LJ10, LJ17-LJ25, J9.

Nos. LJ1-LJ3 Overprinted in Black or Red — a

1921, Dec. Type a

LJ4 D1 20pa red 27.50 4.25
Never hinged 40.00
a. Double overprint, one at left 225.00
b. Overprint at left 55.00 32.50
Never hinged 86.00
LJ5 D1 1pi blue (R) 9.00 5.50
Never hinged 15.00
a. Date at top omitted 15.00
LJ6 D1 1pi bl, ovpt. at left 42.50 50.00
Never hinged 65.00
a. Overprint at right 30.00 32.50
Never hinged 47.50
LJ7 D1 2pi magenta 15.00 11.00
Never hinged 24.00
a. Double overprint, one at left 225.00
b. Overprint at left 72.50
Never hinged 100.00
c. Date at top omitted 72.50
Nos. LJ4-LJ7 (4) 94.00 70.75

Nos. LJ1-LJ3 Overprinted in Black — b

1922, Jan. Type b

LJ8 D1 20pa red 35.00 40.00
Never hinged 55.00
a. Overprint at left 60.00
LJ9 D1 1pi blue 5.00 5.00
Never hinged 8.00
a. Overprint at left 85.00
LJ10 D1 2pi magenta 5.00 5.00
Never hinged 8.00
a. Overprint at left 55.00
Nos. LJ8-LJ10 (3) 45.00 50.00

Regular issue of 1922 Overprinted

1923 Black Overprint *Perf. 11½*

LJ11 A7 ½pi red 5.50 2.00
a. Inverted overprint 67.50
LJ12 A7 1pi dark blue 10.00 2.25
a. Inverted overprint 100.00
b. Double overprint 165.00
LJ13 A7 2pi orange 5.50 3.00
a. Inverted overprint 60.00
Nos. LJ11-LJ13 (3) 21.00 7.25

1924 Blue Overprint

LJ14 A7 ½pi red 25.00 4.25
a. Inverted overprint 110.00
LJ15 A7 1pi dark blue 55.00 4.25
a. Inverted overprint 145.00
LJ16 A7 2pi orange 42.50 7.00
a. Inverted overprint 110.00
Nos. LJ14-LJ16 (3) 122.50 15.50

This overprint reads "Mustahaq" (Due).

Used values for #L51-L186 and LJ17-LJ39 are for genuine cancels. Privately applied cancels exist for "Mekke" (Mecca, bilingual or all Arabic), Khartoum, Cairo, as well as for Jeddah. Many private cancels have wrong dates, some as early as 1916. These are worth half the used values.

Jedda Issues

Nos. LJ1-LJ3 Overprinted in Red or Blue (Overprint reads up in illustration)

Jedda issues were also used in Medina and Yambo.

1925, Jan. *Serrate Roulette 13*

LJ17 D1 20pa red (R) 550.00 *550.00*
LJ18 D1 20pa red (Bl) *725.00* 725.00
LJ19 D1 1pi blue (R) 27.50 *27.50*
LJ20 D1 1pi blue (Bl) 45.00 *45.00*
LJ21 D1 2pi mag (Bl) 21.00 *21.00*

Overprint Reading Down

LJ17a D1 20pa *550.00* *550.00*
LJ18a D1 20pa 825.00
LJ19a D1 1pi 25.00 *25.00*
LJ20a D1 1pi 155.00 *80.00*
LJ21a D1 2pi 125.00 *60.00*

Nos. LJ1-LJ3 Overprinted in Blue or Red

1925

LJ22 D1 20pa red (Bl) 725.00 *725.00*
a. Inverted overprint 350.00 *325.00*
LJ24 D1 1pi blue (R) 35.00 *35.00*
a. Inverted overprint 40.00 *32.50*
LJ25 D1 2pi magenta (Bl) 40.00 *40.00*
a. Inverted overprint 27.50 *45.00*
b. Double overprint 375.00

No. LJ2 with this overprint in blue is bogus.

Regular Issues of 1922-24 Overprinted

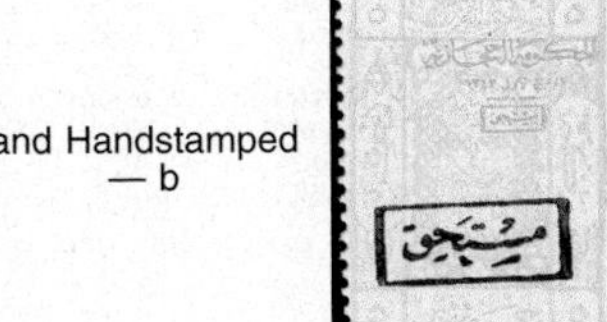

and Handstamped — b

1925 *Perf. 11½*

LJ26 A7 ⅛pi red brown 30.00 *30.00*
Never hinged 45.00
b. Pair, one without handstamp *250.00* —
c. Overprint inverted 100.00 —
d. Violet handstamp 150.00 —
e. Double overprint 150.00
LJ27 A7 ½pi red 37.50 *37.50*
Never hinged 42.50
b. Pair, one without handstamp *250.00* —
c. Overprint inverted 100.00 —
d. Double overprint 125.00 —
LJ28 A7 1pi dark blue 27.50 *30.00*
Never hinged 42.50
b. Pair, one without handstamp *250.00* —
c. Overprint inverted 120.00 —
d. Double overprint 120.00 —
LJ29 A7 1½pi violet 30.00 *18.00*
Never hinged 45.00
b. Pair, one without handstamp *200.00* —
c. Overprint inverted 100.00 —
d. Violet handstamp 110.00 —
e. Horiz. pair, imperf. vert. *175.00*
f. Double ovpt., one invert. 225.00
g. Double ovpt., one vert. up 325.00
h. Double ovpt., one vert. down 325.00
i. Ovpt. on both sides, invert. on back 300.00
LJ30 A7 2pi orange 30.00 *30.00*
Never hinged 45.00
b. Pair, one without handstamp 200.00 —
c. Overprint inverted 110.00 —
d. Violet handstamp 125.00 —
LJ31 A7 3pi olive brown 30.00 *30.00*
Never hinged 45.00
b. Pair, one without handstamp *250.00* —
c. Overprint inverted 110.00 —
LJ32 A7 3pi dull red 72.50 *72.50*
Never hinged 115.00
b. Pair, one without handstamp *250.00* —
c. Overprint inverted 110.00 —
d. Violet handstamp 120.00 —
e. Double ovpt., one invert. 275.00
LJ33 A7 5pi olive green 30.00 *30.00*
Never hinged 45.00
b. Pair, one without handstamp *250.00* —
c. Overprint inverted 90.00 —
LJ34 A7 10pi vio & dk brn 45.00 *40.00*
Never hinged 67.50
b. Pair, one without handstamp *250.00* —
c. Overprint inverted 110.00 —
d. Violet handstamp 110.00 —
Nos. LJ26-LJ34 (9) 332.50 *318.00*

The printed overprint *(a)*, consisting of the three top lines of Arabic, was used alone for the first issue (Nos. LJ26a-LJ34a). The "postage due" box was so small and indistinct that its equivalent in larger characters was added by boxed handstamp *(b)* at bottom of each stamp for the second issue (Nos. LJ26-LJ34).

The handstamped overprint *(b)* is found double, inverted, etc. It is also known in dark violet.

Counterfeits exist of both overprint and handstamp.

Without Boxed Handstamp "b"

LJ26a A7 ⅛pi red brown 55.00
f. Triple ovpt., one vert. up, one vert. down 275.00
g. Double ovpt., one vert. up 400.00
LJ27a A7 ½pi red 60.00
e. Inverted overprint 90.00
f. Double ovpt., one vert. up 175.00
g. Triple ovpt., one vert. up, one vert. down 250.00
LJ28a A7 1pi dark blue 60.00
e. Inverted overprint 90.00
LJ29a A7 1½pi violet 60.00
j. Inverted overprint 100.00
LJ30a A7 2pi orange 60.00
e. Inverted overprint 100.00
f. Double ovpt., one invert. 250.00
g. Double ovpt., one vert. up 225.00
h. Triple ovpt., one vert. up, one vert. down 300.00
LJ31a A7 3pi olive brown 60.00
LJ32a A7 3pi dull red 60.00
f. Inverted overprint 135.00
g. Double ovpt., one vert. up 240.00
h. Double ovpt., one vert. down 240.00
i. Triple ovpt., one vert. up, one vert. down 300.00
LJ33a A7 5pi olive green 87.50
d. Inverted overprint 150.00
LJ34a A7 10pi vio & dk brn 87.50
e. Double overprint 300.00
Nos. LJ26a-LJ34a (9) 590.00

Regular Issue of 1922 Overprinted

and Handstamped

LJ35 A7 ½pi red *150.00* *140.00*
LJ36 A7 1½pi violet *150.00* *140.00*
a. Overprint in red, boxed handstamp violet *3,500.* *1,400.*
LJ37 A7 2pi orange *200.00* *175.00*
LJ38 A7 3pi olive brown *150.00* *140.00*
a. Violet handstamp *300.00*
LJ39 A7 5pi olive green *125.00* *140.00*
Nos. LJ35-LJ39 (5) *775.00* *735.00*
Set, never hinged 1,000.

Counterfeits exist of Nos. LJ4-LJ39.

Arabic Numeral of Value — D2

1925, May-June *Perf. 11½*

LJ40 D2 ½pi light blue 3.00
LJ41 D2 1pi orange 3.00
LJ42 D2 2pi lt brown 3.00
LJ43 D2 3pi pink 3.00
Nos. LJ40-LJ43 (4) 12.00

Nos. LJ40-LJ43 have no overprint and were not officially issued. Examples offered as used bear fake cancellations.

Nos. LJ40-LJ43 exist imperforate. Impressions in colors other than issued are trial color proofs.

Arabic Numeral of Value — D3

1925 Black Overprint

LJ44 D3 ½pi light blue 4.50
Never hinged 6.75
LJ45 D3 1pi orange 4.50
Never hinged 6.75
LJ46 D3 2pi light brown 4.50
Never hinged 6.75
LJ47 D3 3pi pink 4.50
Never hinged 6.75
Nos. LJ44-LJ47 (4) 18.00

Nos. LJ44-LJ47 exist with either Jedda or Cairo overprints and the tablets normally read upward. Values are for Cairo overprints; Jedda overprints sell for more.

Red Overprint

LJ48 D3 ½pi light blue 3.75
Never hinged 6.00
LJ49 D3 1pi orange 3.75
Never hinged 6.00
LJ50 D3 2pi light brown 3.75
Never hinged 6.00
LJ51 D3 3pi pink 3.75
Never hinged 6.00

Blue Overprint

LJ52 D3 ½pi light blue 3.75
Never hinged 6.00
LJ53 D3 1pi orange 3.75
Never hinged 6.00
LJ54 D3 2pi light brown 3.75
Never hinged 6.00
LJ55 D3 3pi pink 3.75
Never hinged 6.00
Nos. LJ40-LJ55 (16) 60.00

Red and blue overprints are from Cairo. Nos. LJ44-LJ55 exist imperf.

NEJDI ADMINISTRATION OF HEJAZ POSTAGE DUE STAMPS

Nos. LJ11-LJ16 Handstamped in Blue, Red or Black

1925, Apr.-June Unwmk. *Perf. 11½*
J1 A7 ½pi red (Bl) 27.50 27.50
J2 A7 1pi lt blue (R) 55.00 55.00
a. 1pi dark blue (R) 35.00 35.00
J3 A7 2pi yel buff (Bl) 55.00 55.00
a. 2pi orange (Bl) 47.50 47.50
Nos. J1-J3 (3) 137.50 137.50

The original boxed overprint is printed on Nos. J1, J2a and J3a. Nos. J2-J3 are overprinted on a new printing of the basic stamps with handstamped boxed overprints.

Same, with Postage Due Overprint in Blue

J4 A7 ½pi red (Bl) *140.00*
J5 A7 1pi dk blue (R) *650.00*
J6 A7 2pi orange (Bl) *175.00*

On Hejaz Stamps of 1922-24 Handstamped in Blue

J7 A7 ½pi red (Bl & Bl) 16.00 16.00
J8 A7 3pi brn red (Bl & Bl) 19.00 19.00

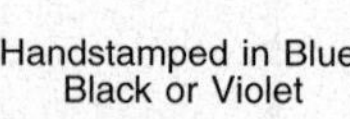

Handstamped in Blue, Black or Violet

On Hejaz No. LJ9
Serrate Roulette 13½

J9 D1 1pi blue (V) 60.00 27.50

Same Overprint on Hejaz Stamps of 1924 with additional Handstamp in Black, Blue or Red

Perf. 11½

J10 A7 3pi brn red (Bl & Bk) 11.00 11.00
J11 A7 3pi brn red (Bk & Bl) 11.00 11.00

Same Handstamps on Hejaz Railway Tax Stamps

J12 R3 1pi blue, type 1 (Bk & R) 12.00 12.00
a. Type 2 40.00
Never hinged 60.00
J13 R3 2pi ocher, type 1 (Bl & Bk) 12.00 12.00
a. Type 2 40.00
Never hinged 60.00
J14 R3 5pi green, type 1 (Bk & R) 20.00 20.00
a. Type 2 60.00
Never hinged 90.00
J15 R3 5pi green, type 1 (V & BK) 20.00 9.00
a. Type 2 60.00
Never hinged 90.00
Nos. J10-J15 (6) 86.00 75.00

The second handstamp, which is struck on the lower part of the Postage Due Stamps, is the word Mustahaq (Due) in various forms.
#J13 exists with 2nd handstamp in blue.

Hejaz-Nejd

D1

1926 Typo. *Perf. 11*
J16 D1 ½pi carmine 4.00 *10.00*
J17 D1 2pi orange 4.00 *10.00*
J18 D1 6pi light brown 4.00 *10.00*
Nos. J16-J18 (3) 12.00 *30.00*

Nos. J16-J18 exist with perf. 14, 14x11 and 11x14, and imperf. These sell for six times the values quoted.
Nos. J16-J18 in colors other than listed (both perf. and imperf.) are proofs.
Counterfeit note after No. 80 also applies to Nos. J16-J21.

Pan-Islamic Congress Issue
Postage Due Stamps of 1926 Handstamped like Regular Issue

J19 D1 ½pi carmine 5.50 4.50
Never hinged 8.00
J20 D1 2pi orange 5.50 4.50
Never hinged 8.00
J21 D1 6pi light brown 5.50 4.50
Never hinged 8.00
Nos. J19-J21 (3) 16.50 13.50

D2

1927 *Perf. 11½*
J22 D2 1pi slate 18.00 .45
a. Inscription reads "2 piastres" in upper right circle 200.00 100.00
J23 D2 2pi dark violet 5.75 .45

Saudi Arabia

Saudi Arabia No. 161 Handstamped in Black

1935
J24 A9 ⅛g dark carmine 450.00

Two types of overprint.

D3

1937-39 Unwmk.
J25 D3 ½g org brn ('39) 20.00 20.00
Never hinged 40.00
J26 D3 1g light blue 20.00 20.00
Never hinged 40.00
J27 D3 2g rose vio ('39) 29.00 13.50
Never hinged 57.50
Nos. J25-J27 (3) 69.00 53.50

Catalogue values for unused stamps in this section, from this point to the end of the section, are for Never Hinged items.

D4

1961 Litho. *Perf. 13x13½*
J28 D4 1p purple 5.00 5.00
J29 D4 2p green 8.50 4.00
J30 D4 4p rose red 10.00 10.00
Nos. J28-J30 (3) 23.50 19.00

The use of Postage Due stamps ceased in 1963.

OFFICIAL STAMPS

Official stamps were normally used only on external correspondence.

O1

1939 Unwmk. Typo. *Perf. 11½*
O1 O1 3g deep ultra 5.25 2.40

Perf. 11, 11½
O2 O1 5g red violet 6.75 3.00

Perf. 11
O3 O1 20g brown 14.00 6.25
O4 O1 50g blue green 27.50 13.00
O5 O1 100g olive grn 110.00 60.00
O6 O1 200g purple 90.00 40.00
Nos. O1-O6 (6) 253.50 124.65

Catalogue values for unused stamps in this section, from this point to the end of the section, are for Never Hinged items.

O2

1961 Litho. *Perf. 13x13½*
Size: 18x22-22½mm
O7 O2 1p black 1.60 .30
O8 O2 2p dark green 2.40 .50
O9 O2 3p bister 3.00 .80
O10 O2 4p dark blue 4.50 .95
O11 O2 5p rose red 5.25 1.25
O12 O2 10p maroon 8.00 2.60
O13 O2 20p violet blue 14.00 5.00
O14 O2 50p dull brown 32.00 13.00
O15 O2 100p dull green 70.00 25.00
Nos. O7-O15 (9) 140.75 49.40

Nos. O8, O10-O15 exist imperf., probably not regularly issued.

1964-65 Wmk. 337 *Perf. 13½x13*
Size: 21x26mm
O16 O2 1p black 2.40 .50
O17 O2 2p green ('65) 4.00 .90
O18 O2 3p bister 12.00 3.00
O19 O2 4p dark blue 9.00 2.25
O20 O2 5p rose red 11.50 2.10
Nos. O16-O20 (5) 38.90 8.75

1965-70 Wmk. 337 Typo. *Perf. 11*
O21 O2 1p dark brn 6.50 1.90
O22 O2 2p green 6.50 1.90
O23 O2 3p bister 6.50 1.90
O24 O2 4p dark blue 6.50 1.90
O25 O2 5p deep org 11.50 2.40
O26 O2 6p red lilac 11.50 2.40
O27 O2 7p emerald 11.50 2.40
O28 O2 8p car rose 11.50 2.40
O29 O2 9p red *210.00* *50.00*
O30 O2 10p red brown 45.00 2.40
O31 O2 11p pale green *85.00*
O32 O2 12p violet *400.00*
O33 O2 13p blue 20.00 3.75
O34 O2 14p purple 24.00 3.75
O35 O2 15p orange *300.00*
O36 O2 16p black *300.00*
a. "19" instead of "16" *750.00*
O37 O2 17p gray green *300.00*
O38 O2 18p yellow *300.00*
O39 O2 19p dp red lil *300.00*
O39A O2 20p lt bl grn 2,750.
O40 O2 23p ultra *320.00*
O41 O2 24p yel grn *300.00*
O42 O2 26p bister *320.00*
O43 O2 27p pale lilac *320.00*
O44 O2 31p pale sal *400.00*
O45 O2 33p yel grn *320.00*
O46 O2 50p olive bister *725.00* *300.00*
O47 O2 100p ol gray ('70) *1,200.* 500.00
Nos. O21-O39,O40-O47 (27) *6,261.*

Nos. O21-O28, O30 and O33-O34 were released to the philatelic trade in 1964. Nos. O21-O47 were printed from new plates; lines of the design are heavier. The numerals have been enlarged and the P's are smaller. Head of "P" 2mm wide on 1964-65 issue, 1mm wide on 1965-70 issue.
No. O39A is only known used. All known examples are faulty.

O3

Wmk. 361, 337 (7p, 8p, 9p, 11p, 12p, 23p)
1970-72 Litho. *Perf. 13½x14*
O48 O3 1p red brown 4.50 1.20
O49 O3 2p deep green 5.00 1.20
O50 O3 3p rose red 6.50 1.90
O51 O3 4p bright blue 7.75 2.40
O52 O3 5p brick red 7.75 2.40
O53 O3 6p orange 7.75 2.40
a. Wmk. 337 *375.00* *45.00*
O54 O3 7p deep salmon *325.00*
O55 O3 8p violet 425.00
O56 O3 9p dk blue grn 425.00
O57 O3 10p blue 9.00 7.75
a. Wmk. 337 275.00
O58 O3 11p olive green 425.00
O58A O3 12p black brown 650.00
O59 O3 20p gray violet 22.00 6.25
a. Wmk. 337 *300.00* *90.00*
O59B O3 23p ocher ('72) *600.00*
O60 O3 31p deep plum *65.00* *26.00*
O61 O3 50p light brown *975.00* 200.00
O62 O3 100p green *1,100.* 325.00

Use of official stamps ceased in 1974.

NEWSPAPER STAMPS

Nos. 8, 9 and 14 with Additional Overprint in Black

1925 Unwmk. *Perf. 11½*
P1 A7 ⅛pi red brown (Bk) *1,800.* *1,800.*
P2 A7 ⅛pi red brown (V) *1,400.* *900.*
P3 A7 ½pi red (V) *2,750.* *1,800.*

Overprint reads: "Matbu'a" (Newspaper), but these stamps were normally used for regular postage. Counterfeits exist.
The status of this set in question. The government may have declared it to be unauthorized.

POSTAL TAX STAMPS

PT1

1934, May 15 Unwmk. *Perf. 11½*
RA1 PT1 ½g scarlet *100.00* 4.50

No. RA1 collected a "war tax" to aid wounded of the 1934 Saudi-Yemen war.

Nos. RA2-RA8 raised funds for the Medical Aid Society.

General Hospital, Mecca PT2

PT2a

1936, Oct. Size: 37x20mm
RA2 PT2 ⅛g scarlet *400.00* 9.00

Type of 1936, Redrawn

1937-42 Size: 30½x18mm
RA3 PT2a ⅛g scarlet 35.00 .90
a. ⅛g rose ('39) *60.00* 1.75
b. ⅛g rose car, perf. 11 ('42) *125.00* 6.75

General Hospital, Mecca — PT3

1943 Typo. *Perf. 11½, 11*
Grayish Paper
RA4 PT3 ⅛g car rose *35.00* .25
a. ⅛g scarlet *35.00* .25

The 1g green and 5g indigo were not for postal use.
See Nos. RA5-RA8.

Map of Saudi Arabia Type I — (Flag inscriptions intact) — PT4

Type II — (Flag inscriptions scratched out)

1946 Unwmk. *Perf. 11½*
RA4B PT4 ½g magenta (II) 16.00 1.00
c. Type I 55.00 1.00
d. Type I, perf. 11 45.00 9.00
e. Type II, perf. 11 67.50 —

Return of King Ibn Saud from Egypt.
This stamp was required on all mail during Jan.-July.

Type of 1943, Redrawn

1948-53 Litho. *Perf. 10*
RA5 PT3 ⅛g rose brn ('53) *20.00* .30
c. Perf. 11x10 *27.50* 3.00

Catalogue values for unused stamps in this section, from this point to the end of the section, are for Never Hinged items.

1950 *Rouletted*
RA6 PT3 ⅛g red brown 5.50 .30
a. ⅛g rose 7.25 .30
b. ⅛g carmine 9.00 .30

All lines in lithographed design considerably finer; some shading in center eliminated.

Type of 1943

1955-56 Photo. *Perf. 11*
RA7 PT3 ⅛g rose car 8.00 .30
RA8 PT3 ¼g car rose ('56) 4.75 .30

The tax on postal matter was discontinued in May, 1964.

Coat of Arms, Waves and View — PT5

Wmk. 361
1974, Oct. Litho. *Perf. 14*
RA9 PT5 1r blue & multi *200.00*

Obligatory on all mailed entries in a government television contest during month of Ramadan in 1974 and 1975. The tax aided a benevolent society.

SCHLESWIG

'shles-ˌwig

LOCATION — In the northern part of the former Schleswig-Holstein Province, in northern Germany.

Schleswig was divided into North and South Schleswig after the Versailles Treaty, and plebiscites were held in 1920. North Schleswig (Zone 1) voted to join Denmark, South Schleswig to stay German.

100 Pfennig = 1 Mark
100 Ore = 1 Krone

Watermark

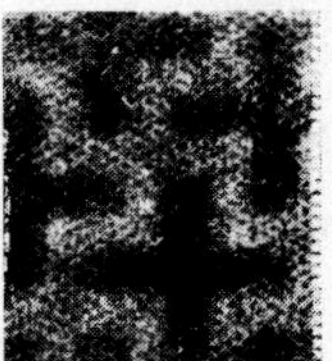

Wmk. 114 — Multiple Crosses

Plebiscite Issue

Arms — A11

View of Schleswig A12

Perf. 14x15
1920, Jan. 25 Typo. Wmk. 114
1 A11 2½pf gray .25 *.25*
2 A11 5pf green .25 *.30*
3 A11 7½pf yellow brown .25 *.60*
4 A11 10pf deep rose .25 *.60*
5 A11 15pf red violet .25 *.60*
6 A11 20pf deep blue .25 *.70*
7 A11 25pf orange .35 .80
8 A11 35pf brown .45 *1.50*
9 A11 40pf violet .30 *.85*
10 A11 75pf greenish blue .90 *1.50*
11 A12 1m dark brown .90 *1.50*
12 A12 2m deep blue 2.10 *3.25*
13 A12 5m green 3.00 4.50
14 A12 10m red 6.00 *6.75*
Nos. 1-14 (14) 15.50 *23.70*
Set, never hinged 55.00

The colored areas of type A11 are white, and the white areas are colored, on Nos. 7-10.

Types of 1920 Overprinted in Blue

1920, May 20
15 A11 1o dark gray .25 *2.40*
16 A11 5o green .25 *1.75*
17 A11 7o yellow brn .25 *1.60*
18 A11 10o rose red .25 *1.60*
19 A11 15o lilac rose .25 *2.50*
20 A11 20o dark blue .25 *2.75*
21 A11 25o orange .25 *8.00*
22 A11 35o brown .85 *14.50*
23 A11 40o violet .25 *4.75*
24 A11 75o greenish blue .45 *8.00*
25 A12 1k dark brown .65 *13.00*
a. Double overprint —
26 A12 2k deep blue 7.00 *47.50*
27 A12 5k green 3.50 *47.50*
28 A12 10k red 8.00 *87.50*
Nos. 15-28 (14) 22.45 *243.35*
Set, never hinged 165.00

OFFICIAL STAMPS

Nos. 1-14 Overprinted

1920 Wmk. 114 *Perf. 14x15*
O1 A11 2½pf gray 65.00 *92.50*
O2 A11 5pf green 65.00 *110.00*
O3 A11 7½pf yellow brn 65.00 *92.50*
O4 A11 10pf deep rose 65.00 *120.00*
O5 A11 15pf red violet 42.50 *60.00*
O6 A11 20pf dp blue 65.00 *67.50*
a. Double overprint 1,500.
O7 A11 25pf orange 125.00 *175.00*
a. Inverted overprint *1,050.*
O8 A11 35pf brown 125.00 *175.00*
O9 A11 40pf violet 110.00 100.00
O10 A11 75pf grnsh blue 125.00 *250.00*
O11 A12 1m dark brown 125.00 *250.00*
O12 A12 2m deep blue 185.00 *275.00*
O13 A12 5m green 275.00 *425.00*
O14 A12 10m red 500.00 *625.00*
Nos. O1-O14 (14) 1,938. *2,818.*
Set, never hinged 3,800.

The letters "C.I.S." are the initials of "Commission Interalliée Slesvig," under whose auspices the plebiscites took place.
Counterfeit overprints exist.

SENEGAL

ˌse-ni-'gäl

LOCATION — West coast of Africa, bordering on the Atlantic Ocean
GOVT. — Republic
AREA — 76,000 sq. mi.
POP. — 10,051,930 (1999 est.)
CAPITAL — Dakar

The former French colony of Senegal became part of French West Africa in 1943. The Republic of Senegal was established Nov. 25, 1958. From Apr. 4, 1959, to June 20, 1960, the Republic of Senegal and the Sudanese Republic together formed the Mali Federation. After its breakup, Senegal resumed issuing its own stamps in 1960.

100 Centimes = 1 Franc

Catalogue values for unused stamps in this country are for Never Hinged items, beginning with Scott 193 in the regular postage section, Scott B16 in the in the semi-postal section, Scott C26 in the airpost section, Scott CB2 in the airpost semi-postal section, Scott J32 in the postage due section, and Scott O1 in the official section.

French Colonies Nos. 48, 49, 51, 52, 55, Type A9, Surcharged

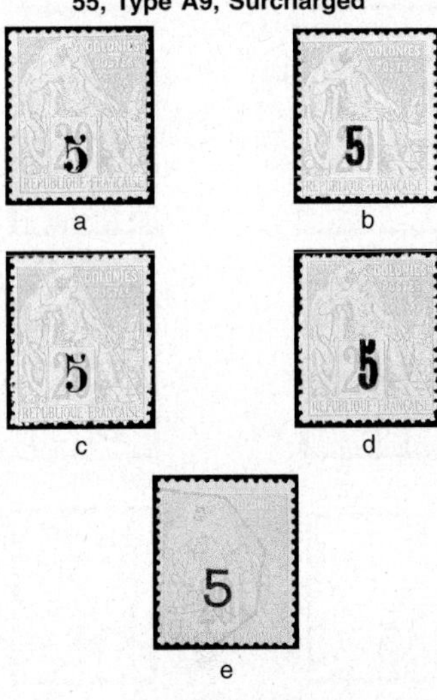

1887 Unwmk. *Perf. 14x13½*
Black Surcharge
1 (a) 5c on 20c red, *grn* 210.00 210.00
a. Double surcharge 550.00
2 (b) 5c on 20c red, *grn* 375.00 375.00
3 (c) 5c on 20c red, *grn* 1,250. 1,250.
4 (d) 5c on 20c red, *grn* 260.00 260.00
5 (e) 5c on 20c red, *grn* 475.00 475.00
6 (a) 5c on 30c brn, *bis* 325.00 325.00
7 (b) 5c on 30c brn, *bis* 1,500. 1,500.
8 (d) 5c on 30c brn, *bis* 475.00 475.00
Nos. 1-8 (8) 4,870. 4,870.

See Madagascar #6-7 for stamps with surcharge like "d" on 10c and 25c stamps.

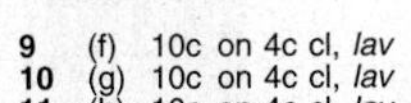

9 (f) 10c on 4c cl, *lav* 160.00 160.00
10 (g) 10c on 4c cl, *lav* 240.00 240.00
11 (h) 10c on 4c cl, *lav* 120.00 120.00

12 (i) 10c on 4c cl, *lav* 120.00 120.00
a. "1" without top stroke
13 (f) 10c on 20c red, *grn* 725.00 725.00
14 (g) 10c on 20c red, *grn* 750.00 750.00
15 (h) 10c on 20c red, *grn* 650.00 650.00
16 (i) 10c on 20c red, *grn* *4,250.* *4,250.*
17 (j) 10c on 20c red, *grn* 750.00 750.00
18 (k) 10c on 20c red, *grn* 3,000. 3,000.
19 (l) 10c on 20c red, *grn* 750.00 750.00
20 (m) 10c on 20c red, *grn* 750.00 750.00

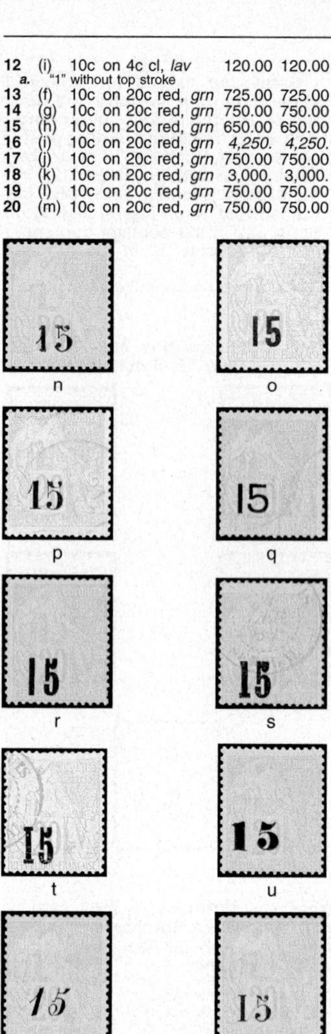

n o p q r s t u v w

21 (n) 15c on 20c red, *grn* 130.00 130.00
22 (o) 15c on 20c red, *grn* 110.00 110.00
23 (p) 15c on 20c red, *grn* 87.50 87.50
24 (q) 15c on 20c red, *grn* 160.00 160.00
25 (r) 15c on 20c red, *grn* 100.00 100.00
26 (s) 15c on 20c red, *grn* 100.00 100.00
27 (t) 15c on 20c red, *grn* 260.00 260.00
28 (u) 15c on 20c red, *grn* 87.50 87.50
29 (v) 15c on 20c red, *grn* 120.00 120.00
30 (w) 15c on 20c red, *grn* 425.00 425.00
Nos. 21-30 (10) 1,580. 1,580.

Counterfeits exist of Nos. 1-34.

French Colonies Stamps of 1881-86 Surcharged

1892 **Black Surcharge**
31 A9 75c on 15c blue 450.00 200.00
a. "SENEGAL" double 950.00
32 A9 1fr on 5c grn, *grnsh* 450.00 200.00
a. "SENEGAL" double 14,750.
b. "SENEGAL" omitted 2,800.
c. "1F" double 325.00

"SENEGAL" in Red

33 A9 75c on 15c blue *16,500.* *5,750.*
34 A9 1fr on 5c grn, *grnsh* *7,500.* *1,600.*

Navigation and Commerce — A24

Name of Colony in Blue or Carmine

1892-1900 **Typo.** ***Perf. 14x13½***
35 A24 1c blk, *lil bl* 1.60 1.20
36 A24 2c brn, *buff* 2.25 2.25
37 A24 4c claret, *lav* 3.50 1.75
38 A24 5c grn, *grnsh* 3.50 2.25
39 A24 5c yel grn ('00) 3.50 1.40
40 A24 10c blk, *lav* 10.00 5.50
41 A24 10c red ('00) 7.00 1.40
42 A24 15c bl, quadrille paper 15.00 2.25
43 A24 15c gray ('00) 7.25 2.50
44 A24 20c red, *grn* 10.50 7.00
45 A24 25c blk, *rose* 17.50 7.25
46 A24 25c blue ('00) 40.00 35.00
47 A24 30c brn, *bis* 17.50 10.00
48 A24 40c red, *straw* 25.00 21.00
49 A24 50c car, *rose* 45.00 30.00
50 A24 50c brn, *az* ('00) 50.00 45.00
51 A24 75c vio, *org* 22.50 17.50
52 A24 1fr brnz grn, *straw* 25.00 21.00
Nos. 35-52 (18) 306.60 214.25

Perf. 13½x14 stamps are counterfeits.
For surcharges see Nos. 53-56, 73-78.

Stamps of 1892 Surcharged

1903
53 A24 5c on 40c red, *straw* 17.50 17.50
54 A24 10c on 50c car, *rose* 25.00 25.00
55 A24 10c on 75c vio, *org* 25.00 25.00
56 A24 10c on 1fr brnz grn, *straw* 80.00 80.00
Nos. 53-56 (4) 147.50 147.50

General Louis Faidherbe A25

Oil Palms — A26

Dr. Noel Eugène Ballay A27

1906 **Typo.**

"SÉNÉGAL" in Red or Blue

57 A25 1c slate 1.40 1.40
a. "SENEGAL" omitted 140.00 140.00
58 A25 2c choc (R) 1.40 1.40
58A A25 2c choc (Bl) 2.75 2.10
59 A25 4c choc, *gray bl* 2.75 2.10
60 A25 5c green 2.75 1.20
a. "SENEGAL" omitted 130.00
61 A25 10c car (Bl) 14.00 1.20
a. "SENEGAL" omitted 450.00 450.00
62 A25 15c violet 7.00 3.50
63 A26 20c blk, *az* 10.50 4.25
64 A26 25c bl, *pnksh* 3.50 2.75
65 A26 30c choc, *pnksh* 10.50 5.50
66 A26 35c blk, *yellow* 27.50 2.75
a. "SENEGAL" double 210.00 *225.00*
67 A26 40c car, *az* (Bl) 14.00 6.25
67A A26 45c choc, *grnsh* 25.00 15.00
68 A26 50c dp violet 14.00 6.25
69 A26 75c bl, *org* 10.50 7.75
70 A27 1fr blk, *azure* 27.50 27.50
71 A27 2fr blue, *pink* 35.00 35.00
72 A27 5fr car, *straw* (Bl) 72.50 62.50
Nos. 57-72 (18) 282.55 188.40

Stamps of 1892-1900 Surcharged in Carmine or Black

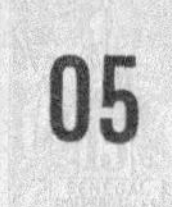

1912
73 A24 5c on 15c gray (C) 1.10 1.10
74 A24 5c on 20c red, *grn* 2.10 *2.10*
75 A24 5c on 30c brn, *bis* (C) 1.40 1.40
76 A24 10c on 40c red, *straw* 1.75 1.75
77 A24 10c on 50c car, *rose* 4.25 *5.00*
78 A24 10c on 75c vio, *org* 7.00 *7.75*
Nos. 73-78 (6) 17.60 19.10

Two spacings between the surcharged numerals found on Nos. 73 to 78. For detailed listings, see the *Scott Classic Specialized Catalogue of Stamps and Covers.*

Senegalese Preparing Food A28

1914-33 **Typo.**
79 A28 1c ol brn & vio .25 .25
80 A28 2c black & blue .25 .25
81 A28 4c gray & brn .25 .25
82 A28 5c yel grn & bl grn .35 .25
83 A28 5c blk & rose ('22) .25 .25
a. Center double 300.00
84 A28 10c org red & rose 1.45 .25
85 A28 10c yel grn & bl grn ('22) .35 .30
86 A28 10c red brn & bl ('25) .35 .35
87 A28 15c red org & brn vio ('17) .35 .35
88 A28 20c choc & blk .35 .30
89 A28 20c grn & bl grn ('26) .35 .35
90 A28 20c db & lt bl ('27) .70 .70
91 A28 25c ultra & bl 1.10 .45
92 A28 25c red & blk ('22) .70 .30
93 A28 30c black & rose .75 .35
94 A28 30c red org & rose ('22) .70 .30
95 A28 30c gray & bl ('26) .35 .35
96 A28 30c dl grn & dp grn ('28) .70 .70
97 A28 35c orange & vio .70 .45
98 A28 40c violet & grn 1.10 .45
99 A28 45c bl & ol brn 1.75 1.40
100 A28 45c rose & bl ('22) 1.10 .45
101 A28 45c rose & ver ('25) .70 .70
102 A28 45c ol brn & org ('28) 3.50 2.75
103 A28 50c vio brn & bl 1.75 1.10
104 A28 50c ultra & bl ('22) 2.75 1.75
105 A28 50c red org & grn ('26) .70 .35
106 A28 60c vio, *pnksh* ('26) .70 .35
107 A28 65c rose red & dp grn ('28) 2.10 1.40
108 A28 75c gray & rose 1.40 .70
109 A28 75c dk bl & lt bl ('25) 1.10 1.10
110 A28 75c rose & gray bl ('26) 2.10 1.05
111 A28 90c brn red & rose ('30) 5.00 5.00
112 A28 1fr violet & blk 1.40 .70
113 A28 1fr blue ('26) 1.05 1.05
114 A28 1fr blk & gray bl ('26) 1.75 1.05
115 A28 1.10fr bl grn & blk ('28) 4.25 *4.50*
116 A28 1.25fr dp grn & dp org ('33) 1.40 1.40
117 A28 1.50fr dk bl & bl ('30) 3.25 3.25
118 A28 1.75fr dk brn & Prus bl ('33) 7.25 1.40
119 A28 2fr carmine & bl 3.50 2.50
120 A28 2fr lt bl & brn ('22) 2.75 .90
121 A28 3fr red vio ('30) 3.50 2.10
122 A28 5fr green & vio 5.00 1.75
Nos. 79-122 (44) 71.10 45.90

Nos. 79, 82, 84 and 97 are on both ordinary and chalky paper.
For surcharges see Nos. 123-137, B1-B2.

No. 108 and Type of 1914 Srchd.

1922-25
123 A28 60c on 75c vio, *pnksh* 1.40 .90
a. Double surcharge 125.00
124 A28 65c on 15c red org & dl vio ('25) 1.40 1.40
125 A28 85c on 15c red org & dl vio ('25) 1.40 1.40
126 A28 85c on 75c ('25) 1.40 1.40

No. 87 Srchd. in Various Colors

1922
127 A28 1c on 15c (Bk) .70 .70
128 A28 2c on 15c (Bl) .70 .70
129 A28 4c on 15c (G) .70 .70
130 A28 5c on 15c (R) .70 .70
Nos. 123-130 (8) 8.40 7.90

Stamps and Type of 1914 Surcharged with New Value and Bars in Black or Red

1924-27
131 A28 25c on 5fr grn & vio .85 .85
132 A28 90c on 75c brn red & cer ('27) 1.40 1.10
a. Double surcharge 125.00
133 A28 1.25fr on 1fr bl & lt bl (R) ('26) 1.40 1.10
134 A28 1.50fr on 1fr dk bl & ultra ('27) 1.40 1.10
135 A28 3fr on 5fr mag & ol brn ('27) 3.50 2.25
136 A28 10fr on 5fr dk bl & red org ('27) 7.75 3.50
137 A28 20fr on 5fr vio & ol bis ('27) 7.00 7.00
Nos. 131-137 (7) 23.30 16.90

Common Design Types pictured following the introduction

Colonial Exposition Issue
Common Design Types
Name of Country Typographed in Black

1931 **Engr.** ***Perf. 12½***
138 CD70 40c deep green 5.00 5.00
139 CD71 50c violet 5.00 5.00
140 CD72 90c red orange 5.00 5.00
a. "SENEGAL" double 175.00
141 CD73 1.50fr dull blue 5.00 5.00
Nos. 138-141 (4) 20.00 20.00

Faidherbe Bridge, St. Louis A29

Diourbel Mosque A30

1935-40 ***Perf. 12½x12***
142 A29 1c violet blue .25 .25
143 A29 2c brown .25 .25
144 A29 3c violet ('40) .25 .25
145 A29 4c gray blue .25 .25
146 A29 5c orange red .25 .25
147 A29 10c violet .25 .25
148 A29 15c black .25 .25
149 A29 20c dk carmine .30 .25
150 A29 25c black brn .30 .25
151 A29 30c green .30 .30
152 A29 40c rose lake .35 .30
153 A29 45c dk blue grn .35 .30
154 A30 50c red orange .35 .25
155 A30 60c violet ('40) .25 .30
156 A30 65c dk violet .35 .30
157 A30 70c red brn ('40) .70 .70

158 A30 75c brown .70 .55
159 A30 90c rose car 2.10 1.40
160 A30 1fr violet 10.50 2.50
161 A30 1.25fr redsh brn 1.40 1.10
162 A30 1.25fr rose car ('39) .85 .85
163 A30 1.40fr dk bl grn ('40) .70 .85
164 A30 1.50fr dk blue .35 .35
165 A30 1.60fr pck bl ('40) .70 .85
166 A30 1.75fr dk blue grn .35 .35
167 A30 2fr blue .70 .35
168 A30 3fr green .70 .45
169 A30 5fr black brn .70 .70
170 A30 10fr rose lake 1.75 1.10
171 A30 20fr grnsh slate 1.75 1.10
Nos. 142-171 (30) 28.25 17.20

Nos. 143, 148 and 156 surcharged with new values are listed under French West Africa.
For surcharges see Nos. B9, B11-B12.

Paris International Exposition Issue
Common Design Types

1937 ***Perf. 13***
172 CD74 20c deep violet 1.75 1.75
a. Sénégal omitted 90.00 *100.00*
173 CD75 30c dark green 1.75 1.75
174 CD76 40c car rose 1.75 1.75
175 CD77 50c dark brown 1.75 1.40
176 CD78 90c red 1.75 1.40
177 CD79 1.50fr ultra 1.75 1.75
Nos. 172-177 (6) 10.50 9.80

Colonial Arts Exhibition Issue
Souvenir Sheet
Common Design Type

1937 **Unwmk.** ***Imperf.***
178 CD76 3fr rose violet 10.50 14.00
a. Inscriptions inverted 1,400.

Senegalese Woman — A31

1938-40 ***Perf. 12x12½, 12½x12***
179 A31 35c green .35 .55
180 A31 55c chocolate .70 .55
181 A31 80c violet 1.10 .65
182 A31 90c lt rose vio ('39) .70 .70
183 A31 1fr car lake 1.75 1.10
184 A31 1fr cop brn ('40) .35 .65
185 A31 1.75fr ultra 1.10 .70
186 A31 2.25fr ultra ('39) .90 .90
187 A31 2.50fr black ('40) 1.40 1.40
Nos. 179-187 (9) 8.35 7.20

For surcharge see No. B10.

Caillié Issue
Common Design Type

1939 **Engr.** ***Perf. 12½x12***
188 CD81 90c org brn & org .35 .70
189 CD81 2fr brt vio .35 1.10
190 CD81 2.25fr ultra & dk bl .35 1.10
Nos. 188-190 (3) 1.05 2.90
Set, never hinged 2.40

For No. 188 surcharged 20fr and 50fr, see French West Africa.

New York World's Fair Issue
Common Design Type

1939 ***Perf. 12½x12***
191 CD82 1.25fr car lake .70 1.40
192 CD82 2.25fr ultra .70 1.40
Set, never hinged 2.10

Catalogue values for unused stamps in this section, from this point to the end of the section, are for Never Hinged items.

Diourbel Mosque and Marshal Pétain A32

1941 **Engr.**
193 A32 1fr green .70
194 A32 2.50fr blue .70

Nos. 193-194 were issued by the Vichy government in France, but were not placed on sale in Senegal.

For surcharges, see Nos. B15A-B15B.

Types of 1935-38 Without "RF"

1943-44 ***Perf. 12½***
194A A29 40c rose lake 1.00
194B A31 1fr red brn & dk blue 1.40
194C A30 1.50fr bl grn & blk .70
194D A30 2fr Prus blue & red 1.10
194E A30 3fr grn & red vio 1.40
194F A30 5fr dp ol brn & lake 1.40
194G A30 10fr rose lake & blue 1.40
194H A30 20fr gray bl & red 3.50
Nos. 194A-194H (8) 11.90

Nos. 194A-194H were issued by the Vichy government in France, but were not placed on sale in Senegal.

See French West Africa No. 69 for additional stamp inscribed "Senegal" and "Afrique Occidentale Francaise."

Republic

Roan Antelope — A33

Animals: 10fr, Savannah buffalo, horiz. 15fr, Wart hog. 20fr, Giant eland. 25fr, Bushbuck, horiz. 85fr, Defassa waterbuck.

1960 **Unwmk.** **Engr.** ***Perf. 13***
195 A33 5fr brn, grn & claret .30 .25
196 A33 10fr grn & brn .55 .25
197 A33 15fr blk, claret & org brn .65 .30
198 A33 20fr brn, grn, ocher & sal .85 .40
199 A33 25fr brn, lt grn & org 1.40 .60
200 A33 85fr brn, grn, olive & bis 3.25 1.40
Nos. 195-200 (6) 7.00 3.20

Imperforates
Most Senegal stamps from 1960 onward exist imperforate in issued and trial colors, and also in small presentation sheets in issued colors.

Allegory of Independent State — A34

1961, Apr. 4
201 A34 25fr bl, choc & grn .80 .25

Independence Day, Apr. 4.

Wrestling A35

1fr, Pirogues racing. 2fr, Horse race. 30fr, Male tribal dance. 45fr, Lion game.

1961, Sept. 30 ***Perf. 13***
202 A35 50c ol, bl & choc .25 .25
203 A35 1fr grn, bl & maroon .25 .25
204 A35 2fr ultra, bis & sepia .70 .25
205 A35 30fr carmine & claret 1.10 .55
206 A35 45fr indigo & brn org 1.75 .65
Nos. 202-206 (5) 4.05 1.95

UN Headquarters, New York and Flag — A36

1962, Jan. 6 **Engr.** ***Perf. 13***
207 A36 10fr grn, ocher & car .35 .25
208 A36 30fr car, ocher & grn .65 .40
209 A36 85fr grn, ocher & car 2.00 .65
Nos. 207-209 (3) 3.00 1.30

1st anniv. of Senegal's admission to the United Nations, Sept. 28, 1960.

Map of Africa, ITU Emblem and Man with Telephone A37

1962, Jan. 22 **Photo.** ***Perf. 12½x12***
210 A37 25fr blk, grn, red & ocher .85 .35

Meeting of the Commission for the Africa Plan of the ITU, Dakar.

African and Malgache Union Issue
Common Design Type

1962, Sept. 8 **Unwmk.**
211 CD110 30fr grn, bluish grn, red & gold .80 .50

Boxing — A38

15fr, Diving, horiz. 20fr, High jump, horiz. 25fr, Soccer. 30fr, Basketball. 85fr, Running.

1963, Apr. 11 **Engr.** ***Perf. 13***
Athletes in Dark Brown
212 A38 10fr ver & emer .30 .25
213 A38 15fr dk bl & bis .40 .25
214 A38 20fr ver & dk bl .45 .25
215 A38 25fr grn & dk bl .65 .25
216 A38 30fr ver & grn 1.25 .50
217 A38 85fr vio bl 2.75 1.10
Nos. 212-217 (6) 5.80 2.60

Friendship Games, Dakar, Apr. 11-21.

UPU Monument, Bern A39

1963, June 14 **Unwmk.** ***Perf. 13***
218 A39 10fr grn & ver .45 .25
219 A39 15fr dk bl & red brn .45 .25
220 A39 30fr red brn & dk bl 1.00 .40
Nos. 218-220 (3) 1.90 .90

2nd anniv. of Senegal's admission to the UPU.

Charaxes Varanes — A40

Butterflies: 45fr, Papilio nireus. 50fr, Colotis danae. 85fr, Epiphora bauhiniae. 100fr, Junonia hierta. 500fr, Danaus chrysippus.

Butterflies in Natural Colors

1963, July 20 **Photo.** ***Perf. 12½x13***
221 A40 30fr bl gray & blk .90 .50
222 A40 45fr org & blk 1.40 .70
223 A40 50fr brt yel & blk 1.50 .90
224 A40 85fr red & blk 4.00 1.25
225 A40 100fr bl & blk 4.75 2.00
226 A40 500fr emer & blk 16.00 6.50
Nos. 221-226 (6) 28.55 11.85

Prof. Gaston Berger (1896-1960), Philosopher, and Owl — A41

1963, Nov. 13 ***Perf. 12½x12***
227 A41 25fr multi .75 .30

Scales, Globe, Flag and UNESCO Emblem A42

1963, Dec. 10
228 A42 60fr multi 1.10 .50

15th anniv. of the Universal Declaration of Human Rights.

Flag, Mother and Child — A43

1963, Dec. 21 ***Perf. 12x12½***
229 A43 25fr multi .80 .30

Issued for the Senegalese Red Cross.

Dredging of Titanium-bearing Sand — A44

Designs: 10fr, Titanium extraction works. 15fr, Cement works at Rufisque. 20fr, Phosphate quarry at Pallo. 25fr, Extraction of phosphate ore at Taiba. 85fr, Mineral dock, Dakar.

1964, July 4 **Engr.** ***Perf. 13***
230 A44 5fr grnsh bl, car & dk brn .25 .25
231 A44 10fr ocher, grn & ind .25 .25
232 A44 15fr dk bl, brt grn & dk brn .35 .25
233 A44 20fr ultra, ol & pur .55 .25

234 A44 25fr dk bl, yel & blk .70 .25
235 A44 85fr bl, red & brn 2.00 .85
Nos. 230-235 (6) 4.10 2.10

Cooperation Issue

Common Design Type

1964, Nov. 7 Engr. *Perf. 13*

236 CD119 100fr dk grn, dk brn & car 1.60 .85

St. Theresa's Church, Dakar A45

10fr, Mosque, Touba. 15fr, Mosque, Dakar, vert.

1964, Nov. 28 Unwmk. *Perf. 13*

237 A45 5fr bl, grn & red brn .25 .25
238 A45 10fr dk bl, ocher & blk .25 .25
239 A45 15fr brn, bl & sl grn .90 .25
Nos. 237-239 (3) 1.40 .75

Leprosy Examination — A46

Leprosarium, Peycouk Village — A47

1965, Jan. 30 Engr. *Perf. 13*

240 A46 20fr brn red, grn & blk .50 .30
241 A47 65fr org, dk bl & grn 1.50 .55

Issued to publicize the fight against leprosy.

Upper Casamance Region — A48

Views: 30fr, Sangalkam. 45fr, Forest along Senegal River.

1965, Feb. 27 Unwmk. *Perf. 13*

242 A48 25fr red brn, sl bl & grn .55 .25
243 A48 30fr indigo & lt brn .65 .30
244 A48 45fr yel grn, red brn & dk brn 1.40 .50
Nos. 242-244,C41 (4) 5.10 2.05

Abdoulaye Seck — A49

General Post Office, Dakar A50

1965, Apr. 24 Unwmk. *Perf. 13*

245 A49 10fr dk brn & blk .35 .25
246 A50 15fr brn & dk sl grn .45 .25

Berthon-Ader Telephone — A51

Designs: 60fr, Cable laying ship "Alsace." 85fr, Picard's cable relay for submarine telegraph.

1965, May 17 Engr.

247 A51 50fr bl grn & org brn .65 .30
248 A51 60fr mag & dk bl 1.25 .45
249 A51 85fr ver, bl & red brn 1.40 .50
Nos. 247-249 (3) 3.30 1.25

ITU, centenary.

Plowing with Ox Team A52

Designs: 60fr, Harvesting millet, vert. 85fr, Men working in rice field.

1965, July 3 Unwmk. *Perf. 13*

250 A52 25fr dk ol grn, brn & pur .55 .30
251 A52 60fr ind, sl grn & dk brn 1.25 .50
252 A52 85fr dp car, sl grn & brt grn 1.75 .55
Nos. 250-252 (3) 3.55 1.35

Gorée Sailboat A53

Designs: 20fr, Large Seumbediou canoe. 30fr, Fadiouth one-man canoe. 45fr, One-man canoe on Senegal River.

1965, Aug. 7 Photo. *Perf. 12½x13*

253 A53 10fr multi .25 .25
254 A53 20fr multi .55 .25
255 A53 30fr multi 1.00 .30
256 A53 45fr multi 1.75 .60
Nos. 253-256 (4) 3.55 1.40

Cashew — A54

1965 Photo. *Perf. 12½*

257 A54 10fr shown .25 .25
258 A54 15fr Papaya .45 .25
259 A54 20fr Mango .65 .30
260 A54 30fr Peanuts 1.25 .30
Nos. 257-260 (4) 2.60 1.10

Issued: 10fr, 15fr, 20fr, Nov. 6. 30fr, Dec. 18.

"Elegant Man" — A55

Dolls of Gorée: 2fr, "Elegant Woman." 3fr, Woman peddling fruit. 4fr, Woman pounding grain.

1966, Jan. 22 Engr. *Perf. 13*

261 A55 1fr brn, rose car & ultra .25 .25
262 A55 2fr brn, bl & org .25 .25
263 A55 3fr brn, red & bl .25 .25
264 A55 4fr brn, lil & emer .25 .25
Nos. 261-264 (4) 1.00 1.00

Drummer and Map of Africa — A56

15fr, Sculpture; mother & child. #267, Music; stringed instrument. 75fr, Dance; carved antelope headpiece (Bambara). 90fr, Ideogram.

1966

265 A56 15fr dk red brn, bl & ocher .35 .25
266 A56 30fr brn, red & grn .70 .25
267 A56 30fr dk red brn, bl & yel 1.10 .60
268 A56 75fr dk red brn, bl & blk 1.75 .60
269 A56 90fr dk red brn, org & sl grn 2.10 .65
a. Souv. sheet of 4, #265, 267-269 6.25 6.25
Nos. 265-269 (5) 6.00 2.35

Intl. Negro Arts Festival, Dakar, Apr. 1-24. Issued: #266, 2/5; others, 4/2. See #364.

Fish — A57

1966, Feb. 26 Photo. *Perf. 12½x13*

270 A57 20fr Tuna .50 .25
271 A57 30fr Merou .60 .30
272 A57 50fr Girella 1.25 .65
273 A57 100fr Parrot fish 2.75 .85
Nos. 270-273 (4) 5.10 2.05

Arms of Senegal — A58

1966, July 2 Litho. *Perf. 13x12½*

274 A58 30fr multi .80 .25

Flowers — A59

1966, Nov. 19 Photo. *Perf. 11½*

275 A59 45fr Mexican poppy 1.25 .25
276 A59 55fr Mimosa 1.25 .35
277 A59 60fr Haemanthus 1.60 .45
278 A59 90fr Baobab 2.10 .65
Nos. 275-278 (4) 6.20 1.70

Harbor, Gorée Island A60

Designs: 25fr, S.S. France in roadstead, Dakar and seagulls. 30fr, Hotel and tourist village, N'Gor. 50fr, Hotel and bay, N'Gor.

1966, Dec. 25 Engr. *Perf. 13*

279 A60 20fr mar & vio bl .25 .25
280 A60 25fr red, grn & blk 2.00 .30
281 A60 30fr dk red & dp bl .40 .25
282 A60 50fr brn, sl grn & emer .65 .30
Nos. 279-282 (4) 3.30 1.10

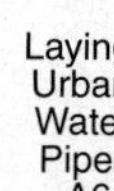

Laying Urban Water Pipes A61

Symbolic Water Cycle — A62

20fr, Cattle at water trough. 50fr, Village well.

1967, Mar. 25 Engr. *Perf. 13*

283 A61 10fr org brn, grn & dk bl .25 .25
284 A61 20fr grn, brt bl & org brn .65 .25

Typo.

Perf. 13x14

285 A62 30fr sky bl, blk & org .70 .25

Engr.

Perf. 13

286 A62 50fr brn red, brt bl & bis 1.50 .35
Nos. 283-286 (4) 3.10 1.10

Intl. Hydrological Decade (UNESCO), 1965-74.

Lions Emblem A63

1967, May 27 Photo. *Perf. 12½x13*

287 A63 30fr lt ultra & multi 1.00 .40

50th anniversary of Lions International.

Blaise Diagne A64

1967, June 10 Engr. *Perf. 13*

288 A64 30fr ocher, sl grn & dk red brn .80 .30

Blaise Diagne (1872-1934), member of French Chamber of Deputies and Colonial Minister.

For surcharge see No. 380.

City Hall and Arms, Dakar A65

1967, June 10

289 A65 90fr bl, dk grn & blk 1.75 .50

Eagle and Antelope Carvings — A66

150fr, Flags, maple leaf and EXPO '67 emblem.

1967, Sept. 2 Photo. *Perf. 13x12½*

290 A66 90fr red & blk 2.00 .50
291 A66 150fr red & multi 2.50 .80

EXPO '67 Intl. Exhib., Montreal, 4/28-10/27.

International Tourist Year Emblem — A67

Tourist Photographing Hippopotamus and Siminti Hotel — A68

1967, Oct. 7 Typo. *Perf. 14x13*

292 A67 50fr blk & bl .90 .40

Perf. 13

Engr.

293 A68 100fr blk, sl grn & ocher 3.50 1.10

International Tourist Year.

Monetary Union Issue

Common Design Type

1967, Nov. 4 Engr. *Perf. 13*

294 CD125 30fr multi .60 .25

West African Monetary Union, 5th anniv.

Lyre-shaped Megalith, Kaffrine — A69

70fr, Ancient covered bowl, Bandiala.

1967, Dec. 2 Engr. *Perf. 13*

295 A69 30fr grn, grnsh bl & red brn 1.25 .35
296 A69 70fr red brn, ocher & brt bl 2.10 .85

Nurse Feeding Child — A70

1967, Dec. 23

297 A70 50fr bl grn, red & red brn 1.00 .40

Issued for the Senegalese Red Cross.

Human Rights Flame — A71

1968, Jan. 20 Photo. *Perf. 13x12½*

298 A71 30fr brt grn & gold .80 .30

International Human Rights Year.

Parliament, Dakar A72

1968, Apr. 16 Photo. *Perf. 12½x13*

299 A72 30fr car rose .80 .25

Inter-Parliamentary Union Meeting, Dakar.

Pied Kingfisher — A73

Goose Barnacles A74

10fr, Green lobster. 15fr, African jacana. 20fr, Sea cicada. 35fr, Shrimp. 70fr, African anhinga.

1968-69 Photo. *Perf. 11½*

Dated "1968" or (70fr) "1969"

Granite Paper

300 A73 5fr brn & multi .35 .25
301 A74 10fr red & multi .50 .25
302 A73 15fr yel & multi .75 .35
303 A74 20fr ultra & multi .90 .35
304 A74 35fr car rose & ol grn 2.25 .40
305 A73 70fr Prus bl & multi 2.75 1.00
306 A74 100fr yel grn & multi 6.50 1.75
Nos. 300-306 (7) 14.00 4.35

Issued: 5fr, 7/13/68; 15fr, 12/21/68; 70fr, 4/26/69; others 5/18/68. Nos. 300-306 exist as tete-beche pairs. Value, set of pairs $30.

See Nos. C53-C57.

Steer and Hypodermic Syringe — A75

1968, Aug. 17 Engr. *Perf. 13*

307 A75 30fr dk grn, dp bl & brn red 1.00 .40

Campaign against cattle plague.

Boy and WHO Emblem — A76

1968, Nov. 16 Engr. *Perf. 13*

308 A76 30fr blk, grn & car .55 .30
309 A76 45fr red brn, grn & blk 1.10 .30

WHO, 20th anniversary.

Bambara Antelope Symbol — A77

Design: 30fr, School of Medicine and Pharmacology, Dakar, horiz.

1969, Jan. 13 Engr. *Perf. 13*

310 A77 30fr emer, brt bl & ind .80 .30
311 A77 50fr red, gray ol & bl grn .90 .30

6th Medical Meeting, Dakar, Jan. 13-18.

Panet, Camels and Mogador-St. Louis Route — A78

1969, Feb. 15 Engr. *Perf. 13*

312 A78 75fr ultra, Prus bl & brn 2.50 .80

Leopold Panet (1819-1859), first explorer of the Mauritanian Sahara.

ILO Emblem A79

1969, May 3 Photo. *Perf. 12½x13*

313 A79 30fr blk & grnsh bl .55 .25
314 A79 45fr blk & dp car .80 .25

ILO, 50th anniversary.

Arms of Casamance — A80

Design: 20fr, Arms of Gorée Island.

1969, July 26 Litho. *Perf. 13½*

315 A80 15fr rose & multi .25 .25
316 A80 20fr bl & multi .75 .25

Development Bank Issue

Common Design Type

1969, Sept. 10 Engr. *Perf. 13*

317 CD130 30fr gray, grn & ocher .65 .25
318 CD130 45fr brn, grn & ocher .90 .25

Mahatma Gandhi — A81

1969, Oct. 2 Engr. *Perf. 13*

319 A81 50fr multi 1.50 .35
a. Miniature sheet of 4 6.00 3.00

Mohandas K. Gandhi (1869-1948), leader in India's fight for independence.

Rotary Emblem and Symbolic Ship — A82

1969, Nov. 29 Photo. *Perf. 12½x13*

320 A82 30fr ultra, yel & blk .80 .30

Dakar Rotary Club, 30th anniversary.

ASECNA Issue

Common Design Type

1969, Dec. 12 Engr. *Perf. 13*

321 CD132 100fr dark gray 1.60 .50

Niokolo-Koba Campsite — A83

Tourism: 20fr, Cape Skiring, Casamance. 35fr, Elephants at Niokolo-Koba National Park. 45fr, Millet granaries, pigs and boats, Fadiouth Island.

1969, Dec. 27

322 A83 20fr bl, red brn & ol .75 .25
323 A83 30fr bl, red brn & ocher 1.00 .25
324 A83 35fr grnsh bl, blk & ocher 4.00 .65
325 A83 45fr vio bl & hn brn 2.00 .55
Nos. 322-325 (4) 7.75 1.70

Bottle-nosed Dolphins — A84

1970, Feb. 21 Photo. *Perf. 12x12½*

326 A84 50fr dl bl, blk & red 7.50 1.50

Lenin (1870-1924) — A85

1970, Apr. 22 Photo. *Perf. 11½*

327 A85 30fr brn, buff & ver 2.50 .65

Souvenir Sheet

Perf. 12x11½

327A A85 50fr brn, buff & ver 4.00 1.75

No. 327A contains one 32x48mm stamp.

UPU Headquarters Issue

Common Design Type

1970, May 20 Engr. *Perf. 13*

328 CD133 30fr dk red, ind & dp cl .55 .25
329 CD133 45fr dl brn, dk car & bl grn 1.00 .30

Textile Plant, Thies — A86

Design: 45fr, Fertilizer plant, Dakar.

1970, Nov. 21 Engr. *Perf. 13*

330 A86 30fr grn, brt bl & brn red .65 .25
331 A86 45fr brn red & brt bl 1.00 .30

Industrialization of Senegal.

Boy Scouts — A87

Design: 100fr, Lord Baden-Powell, map of Africa with Dakar, and fleur-de-lis.

1970, Dec. 11 Photo. ***Perf. 11½***

332 A87 30fr multi .55 .25
333 A87 100fr multi 2.25 .60

1st African Boy Scout Conf., Dakar, Dec. 11-14.

Three Heads and Sun — A88

Design: 40fr, African man and woman, globe with map of Africa.

1970, Dec. 19 Engr. ***Perf. 13***

334 A88 25fr ultra, org & vio brn .65 .25
335 A88 40fr brn ol, dk brn & org 1.00 .40

International Education Year.

Senegal Arms — A89

1970-76 Photo. ***Perf. 12***

336 A89 30fr yel grn & multi .50 .25
336A A89 35fr brt pink & multi ('71) .50 .25
b. Bklt. pane of 10 ('72) 5.00
336C A89 50fr bl & multi ('75) .50 .25
336D A89 65fr lil rose & multi ('76) .50 .25
Nos. 336-336D (4) 2.00 1.00

The booklet pane has a control number in the margin.
See No. 654.

Refugees and UN Emblem A90

1971, Jan. 16 ***Perf. 12½x12***

337 A90 40fr ver, blk, yel & grn 1.00 .30

High Commissioner for Refugees, 20th anniversary. See No. C94.

Mare "Mbayang" A91

Horses: 25fr, Mare Madjiguene. 100fr, Stallion Pass. 125fr, Stallion Pepe.

Granite Paper

1971 Photo. ***Perf. 11½***

338 A91 25fr multi 1.00 .50
339 A91 40fr multi 1.50 .65
340 A91 100fr multi 4.00 2.25
341 A91 125fr multi 5.25 1.90
Nos. 338-341 (4) 11.75 5.30

Improvements in horse breeding.
For surcharge see No. 392.

UN Emblem, Black and White Children — A92

UN Emblem, Four Races A93

Perf. 13x12½, 12½x11

1971, Mar. 21 Litho.

342 A92 30fr multi .85 .35
343 A93 50fr multi 1.40 .60

Intl. Year against Racial Discrimination.

Globe and Telephone — A94

Design: 40fr, Radar, satellite, orbits.

1971, May 17 Engr. ***Perf. 13***

344 A94 30fr pur, grn & brn .45 .25
345 A94 40fr Prus bl, dk brn & red brn 1.10 .30

3rd World Telecommunications Day.

Drummer (Hayashida) — A95

50fr, Dwarf Japanese quince and grape hyacinth. 65fr, Judo. 75fr, Mt. Fuji.

1971, Aug. 7 Photo. ***Perf. 13½***

346 A95 35fr lt ultra & multi 1.25 .30
347 A95 50fr yel & multi 1.50 .45
348 A95 65fr dp org & multi 2.25 .60
349 A95 75fr grn & multi 2.75 .95
Nos. 346-349 (4) 7.75 2.30

13th Boy Scout World Jamboree, Asagiri Plain, Japan, Aug. 2-10.

Map of West Africa with Senegal, UNICEF Emblem A97

100fr, Nurse, children, UNICEF emblem.

1971, Oct. 30 ***Perf. 12½***

352 A97 35fr dl bl, org & blk .90 .35
353 A97 100fr multi 3.00 .65

UNICEF, 25th anniv.

Basketball and Games' Emblem — A98

40fr, Basketball. 75fr, Emblem.

1971, Dec. 24 Photo. ***Perf. 13½x13***

354 A98 35fr lt vio & multi .70 .25
355 A98 40fr emer & multi 1.00 .30
356 A98 75fr ocher & multi 1.60 .65
Nos. 354-356 (3) 3.30 1.20

6th African Basketball Championships, Dakar, Dec. 25, 1971-Jan. 2, 1972.

"The Exile of Albouri" — A99

Design: 40fr, "The Merchant of Venice."

1972, Mar. 25 ***Perf. 13x12½***

357 A99 35fr dk red & multi .55 .30
358 A99 40fr dk red & multi .90 .30

Intl. Theater Day. See No. C112.

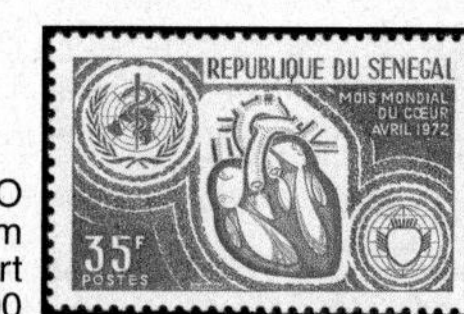

WHO Emblem and Heart A100

Design: 40fr, Physician with patient, WHO emblem and electrocardiogram.

1972, Apr. 7 Engr. ***Perf. 13***

359 A100 35fr brt bl & red brn .50 .25
360 A100 40fr slate grn & brn 1.00 .25

"Your heart is your health," World Health Month.

Containment of the Desert, Environment Emblem — A101

1972, June 3 Photo. ***Perf. 13x12½***

361 A101 35fr multi 1.60 .60

UN Conference on Human Environment, Stockholm, June 5-16. See No. C113.

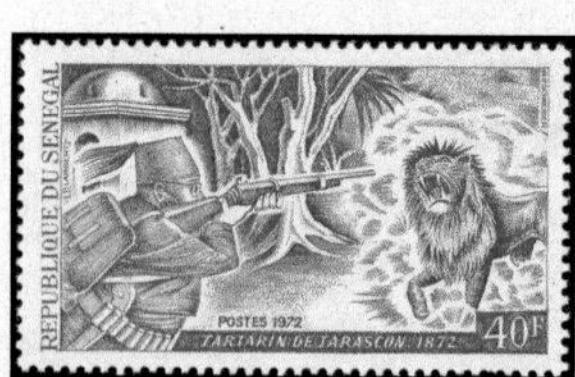

Tartarin Shooting the Lion — A102

Design: 100fr, Alphonse Daudet.

1972, June 24 Engr. ***Perf. 13***

362 A102 40fr brt grn, rose car & brn 2.00 1.10
363 A102 100fr Prus bl, bl & brn 3.00 1.10

Alphonse Daudet (1840-1897), French novelist, and centenary of the publication of his "Tartarin de Tarascon."

Souvenir Sheet

Stringed Instrument — A103

1972, July 1 Engr. ***Perf. 11½***

364 A103 150fr rose red 4.00 3.00

Belgica 72, Intl. Phil. Exhib., Brussels, June 24-July 9. No. 364 contains one stamp in design similar to No. 267.

Wrestling, Olympic Rings — A104

20fr, 100-meter dash. 100fr, Basketball. 125fr, Judo.
240fr, Torchbearer and Munich.

1972, July 22 Photo. ***Perf. 14x13½***

365 A104 15fr shown .35 .25
366 A104 20fr multi .80 .25
367 A104 100fr multi 2.50 .50
368 A104 125fr multi 3.00 .65
Nos. 365-368 (4) 6.65 1.65

Souvenir Sheet

Perf. 13½x14½

369 A104 240fr multi 6.25 3.25

20th Olympic Games, Munich, 8/26-9/11.

Book Year Emblem, Children Reading A105

1972, Sept. 16 Photo. ***Perf. 13***

370 A105 50fr gray & multi .90 .35

International Book Year.

Senegalese Fashion — A106

1972-76 Engr.

371 A106 25fr black .35 .25
a. Booklet pane of 5 2.00
b. Booklet pane of 10 5.00
372 A106 40fr brt ultra .50 .25
a. Booklet pane of 5 3.00
b. Booklet pane of 10 7.50
372C A106 60fr brt grn ('76) .50 .25
372D A106 75fr lil rose .50 .25
Nos. 371-372D (4) 1.85 1.00

See Nos. 563-573, 1153-1164, 1249-1257D, 1345A-1345C.

Aleksander Pushkin — A107

1972, Oct. 28 Photo. *Perf. 11½*

373 A107 100fr salmon & purple 3.00 .65

Aleksander Pushkin (1799-1837), Russian writer.

West African Monetary Union Issue
Common Design Type

Design: 40fr, African couple, city, village and commemorative coin.

1972, Nov. 2 Engr. *Perf. 13*

374 CD136 40fr ol brn, bl & gray .50 .30

Amphicra-sphedum Murrayanum A108

Marine Life: 10fr, Pterocanium tricolpum. 15fr, Ceratospyris polygona. 20fr, Cortiniscus typicus. 30fr, Theopera cortina.

1972-73 Photo. *Perf. 11½*

375	A108	5fr multi	1.00	.35
376	A108	10fr multi	1.25	.40
377	A108	15fr multi	2.50	.40
378	A108	20fr multi	1.50	.40
379	A108	30fr multi	4.00	.50
		Nos. 375-379,C115-C118 (9)	34.75	7.30

Issued: #375-377, 11/25/72; #378-379, 7/28/73.

No. 288 Surcharged in Vermilion

1972, Dec. 9 Engr. *Perf. 13*

380 A64 100fr on 30fr multi 2.25 .60

Blaise Diagne (1872-1934).

Melchior — A109

1972, Dec. 23 Photo. *Perf. 13x13½*

381	A109	10fr shown	.25	.25
382	A109	15fr Caspar	.25	.25
383	A109	40fr Balthasar	.80	.35
384	A109	60fr Joseph	.85	.40
385	A109	100fr Virgin and Child	1.50	.65
a.		Strip of 5, #381-385	5.25	2.00

Christmas. No. 385a has continuous design, showing traditional Gorée dolls.

Black and White Men Carrying Emblem — A110

Europafrica Issue

1973, Jan. 20 Engr. *Perf. 13*

386 A110 65fr blk & grn 1.40 .40

Earth Station, Gandoul A111

1973, May 17 Engr. *Perf. 13*

387 A111 40fr multi .80 .30

Phases of Solar Eclipse A112

Designs: 65fr, Moon between earth and sun casting shadow on earth. 150fr, Diagram of areas of partial and total eclipse, satellite in space.

1973, June 30 Photo. *Perf. 13x14*

388	A112	35fr dk bl & multi	.75	.30
389	A112	65fr dk bl & multi	1.25	.45
390	A112	150fr dk bl & multi	2.75	1.00
		Nos. 388-390 (3)	4.75	1.75

Total solar eclipse over Africa, June 30.

Men Holding Torch over Africa — A113

1973, July 7 *Perf. 12½x13*

391 A113 75fr multi 1.00 .40

Org. for African Unity, 10th anniv.

No. 338 Srchd. with New Value, 2 Bars, and Ovptd. in Ultramarine "SECHERESSE / SOLIDARITE AFRICAINE"
Granite Paper

1973, July 21 Photo. *Perf. 11½*

392 A91 100fr on 25fr multi 2.25 .85

African solidarity in drought emergency.

African Postal Union Issue
Common Design Type

1973, Sept. 12 Engr. *Perf. 13*

393 CD137 100fr dk grn, vio & dk red 1.60 .50

Child, Map of Senegal, WMO Emblem A114

1973, Sept. 22

394 A114 50fr multi .80 .35

Intl. meteorological cooperation, cent.

INTERPOL Headquarters, Paris — A115

1973, Oct. 6 Engr. *Perf. 13*

395 A115 75fr ultra, bis & slate grn 1.60 .50

50th anniv. of Intl. Criminal Police Org.

Souvenir Sheet

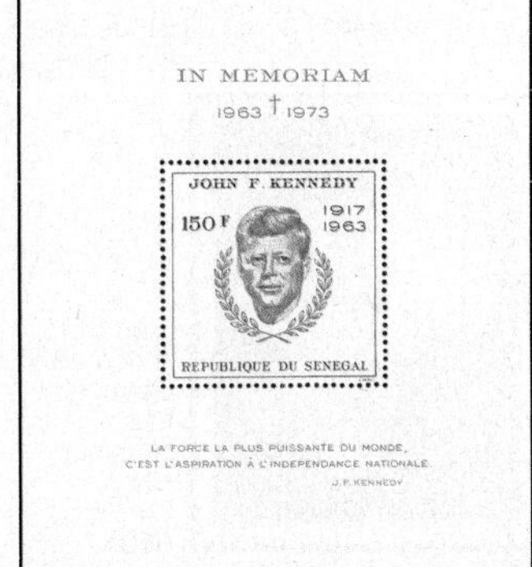

John F. Kennedy (1917-1963) — A116

1973, Nov. 22 Engr. *Perf. 13*

396 A116 150fr ultra 2.75 2.75

Amilcar Cabral — A117

1973, Dec. 15 Photo. *Perf. 12½x13*

397 A117 75fr multi 1.25 .40

Cabral (1924-1973), leader of anti-Portuguese guerrilla movement in Portuguese Guinea.

Victorious Athletes and Flag — A118

1974, Apr. 6 Photo. *Perf. 12½x13*

398	A118	35fr shown	.80	.25
399	A118	40fr Folk theater	.80	.25

National Youth Week.

Soccer Cup, Yugoslavia-Brazil Game, Our Lady's Church, Munich — A119

Soccer Cup and Games: 40fr, Australia-Germany (Fed. Rep.) and Belltower, Hamburg. 65fr, Netherlands-Uruguay and Tower, Hanover. 70fr, Zaire-Italy and Church, Stuttgart.

1974, June 29 Photo. *Perf. 13x14*

400	A119	25fr car & multi	.35	.25
401	A119	40fr car & multi	.65	.25
402	A119	65fr car & multi	.90	.30
403	A119	70fr car & multi	1.50	.40
		Nos. 400-403 (4)	3.40	1.20

World Cup Soccer Championship, Munich, June 13-July 7.

For surcharge see No. 406.

UPU Emblem, Envelopes and Means of Transportation — A120

1974, Oct. 9 Engr. *Perf. 13*

404 A120 100fr multi 3.00 .85

Centenary of Universal Postal Union.

Fair Emblem — A121

1974, Nov. 28 Engr. *Perf. 12½x13*

405 A121 100fr bl, org & dk brn 1.75 .50

Dakar International Fair.

No. 401 Surcharged in Black on Gold

1975, Feb. 1 Photo. *Perf. 13x14*

406 A119 200fr on 40fr multi 3.25 1.25

World Cup Soccer Championships, 1974, victory of German Federal Republic.

Pres. Senghor and King Baudouin — A122

1975, Feb. 28 Photo. *Perf. 13x13½*

407	A122	65fr lilac & blue	.80	.35
408	A122	100fr org & dk grn	2.00	.50

Visit of King Baudouin of Belgium.

ILO Emblem A123

1975, Apr. 30 Photo. *Perf. 13½x13*

409 A123 125fr multi 1.75 .50

International Labor Festival.

Globe, Stamp, Letters, España 75 Emblem — A124

1975, June 6 Engr. *Perf. 13*

410 A124 55fr indigo, grn & red 1.25 .40

Espana 75 Intl. Phil. Exhib., Madrid, 4/4-13.

Apollo of Belvedere, Arphila 75 Emblem, Stamps — A125

1975, June 6

411 A125 95fr dk brn, brn & bis 2.25 .80

Arphila 75 International Philatelic Exhibition, Paris, June 6-16.

Professional Instruction — A126

1975, June 28 Engr. *Perf. 13*

412 A126 85fr multi 1.25 .40

Dr. Albert Schweitzer (1875-1965), Medical Missionary, Lambarene Hospital — A127

1975, July 5

413 A127 85fr grn & vio brn 1.75 .65

Senegalese Soldier, Batallion Flag, Map of Sinai — A128

1975, July 10 Litho. *Perf. 12½*

414 A128 100fr multi 1.75 .50

Senegalese Battalion of the UN' Sinai Service, 1973-74.

Women and Child — A129

55fr, Women pounding grain, vert.

1975, Oct. 18 Photo. *Perf. 13½*

415	A129	55fr silver & multi	1.75	.35
416	A129	75fr silver & multi	2.25	.50

International Women's Year.

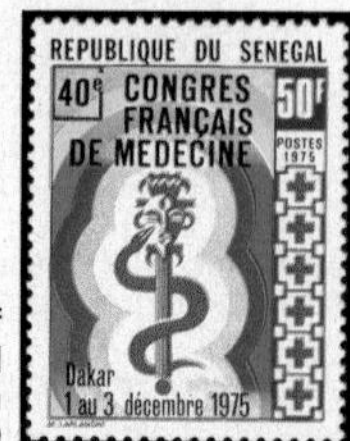

Staff of Aesculapius and African Mask — A130

1975, Dec. 1 Photo. *Perf. 12½x13*

417 A130 50fr multi .80 .30

40th French Medical Cong., Dakar, Dec. 1-3.

Map of Africa with Senegal and Namibia, UN Emblem A131

1976, Jan. 5 Photo. *Perf. 13*

418 A131 125fr vio bl & multi 1.00 .35

International Human Rights and Namibia Conference, Dakar, Jan. 5-8.

Sailfish Fishing A132

200fr, Racing yachts & Oceanexpo 75 emblem.

1976, Jan. 28 Photo. *Perf. 13½x13*

419	A132	140fr multi	5.25	1.50
420	A132	200fr multi	3.50	1.60

Oceanexpo 75, 1st Intl. Oceanographic Exhib., Okinawa, July 20, 1975-Jan. 1976.

Servals — A133

Designs: 3fr, Black-tailed godwits. 4fr, River hogs. 5fr, African fish eagles. No. 425, Okapis. No. 426, Sitatungas.

1976, Feb. 26 Photo. *Perf. 13*

421	A133	2fr gold & multi	.30	.25
422	A133	3fr gold & multi	.65	.25
423	A133	4fr gold & multi	.30	.25
424	A133	5fr gold & multi	1.00	.50
425	A133	250fr gold & multi	6.25	1.75
426	A133	250fr gold & multi	6.25	1.75
a.		Strip of 2, #425-426 + label	14.50	
		Nos. 421-426 (6)	14.75	4.75

Basse Casamance National Park.

See Nos. 473-478.

A. G. Bell, Telephone, ITU Emblem — A134

1976, Mar. 31 Litho. *Perf. 12½x13*

427 A134 175fr multi 2.50 .80

Centenary of first telephone call by Alexander Graham Bell, Mar. 10, 1876.

Map of African French-speaking Countries — A135

1976, Apr. 12 Litho. *Perf. 13½*

428 A135 60fr yel grn & multi .80 .30

Scientific and Cultural Meeting of the African Dental Association, Dakar, Apr. 12-17.

Family and Graph A136

1976, Apr. 26

429 A136 65fr multi 1.00 .40

1st population census in Senegal, Apr. 1976.

Thomas Jefferson and 13-star Flag — A137

1976, June 19 Engr. *Perf. 13*

430 A137 50fr bl, red & blk 1.00 .30

American Bicentennial.

Planting Seedlings — A138

1976, Aug. 21 Litho. *Perf. 12*

431 A138 60fr yel & multi 1.00 .25

Reclamation of Sahel region.

Campfire A139

Jamboree Emblem, Map of Africa — A140

1976, Aug. 30 Litho. *Perf. 12½*

432	A139	80fr multi	.90	.40
433	A140	100fr multi	1.75	.55

1st All Africa Scout Jamboree, Sherehills, Jos, Nigeria, Apr. 2-8, 1977.

A140a

1976 Summer Olympics, Montreal — A140b

5fr, Swimming. 10fr, Weightlifting. 15fr, Hurdles, horiz. 20fr, Equestrian, horiz. 25fr, Steeplechase, horiz. 50fr, Wrestling, horiz. 60fr, Field hockey. 65fr, Track. 70fr, Women's gymnastics. 100fr, Cycling, horiz. 400fr, Boxing. 500fr, Judo.

No. 433M, Basketball. No. 433Q, Boxers, city skyline.

1976, Sept. 11 Litho. *Perf. 13½*

433A	A140a	5fr multi	.25	.25
433B	A140a	10fr multi	.25	.25
433C	A140a	15fr multi	.25	.25
433D	A140a	20fr multi	.25	.25
433E	A140a	25fr multi	.35	.25
433F	A140a	50fr multi	.55	.25
433G	A140a	60fr multi	.70	.25
433H	A140a	65fr multi	.80	.25
433I	A140a	70fr multi	1.00	.40
433J	A140a	100fr multi	1.25	.50
433K	A140a	400fr multi	4.50	.95
433L	A140a	500fr multi	5.75	1.10
		Nos. 433A-433L (12)	15.90	4.95

Litho. & Embossed

433M A140b 1000fr multi 9.00 3.75

Souvenir Sheet

433Q A140b 1000fr multi 9.00 3.75

Nos. 433K-433Q are airmail.

Mechanized Tomato Harvest — A141

1976, Oct. 23 Photo. *Perf. 13*

434 A141 180fr multi 3.00 1.25

Map of Dakar and Gorée A142

Designs: 60fr, Star over Africa. 70fr, Students in laboratory and library. 200fr, Handshake over world map, Pres. Senghor.

1976, Oct. 9 Litho. *Perf. 13½x14*

435 A142 40fr multi .35 .25
436 A142 60fr multi .50 .25
437 A142 70fr multi 1.00 .25
438 A142 200fr multi 2.75 .85
Nos. 435-438 (4) 4.60 1.60

70th birthday of Pres. Leopold Sedar Senghor.

Scroll with Map of Africa, Senegalese People — A143

1977, Jan. 8 *Perf. 12½*

439 A143 60fr multi .80 .30

Day of the Black People.

Joe Frazier and Muhammad Ali — A144

Design: 60fr, Ali and Frazier in ring, vert.

1977, Jan. 7 Photo. *Perf. 13x13½*

440 A144 60fr blue & blk .65 .25
441 A144 150fr emerald & blk 2.25 .60

World boxing champion Muhammad Ali.

Dancer and Musician A145

Festival Emblem and: 75fr, Wood carving and masks. 100fr, Dancers and ancestor statuette.

1977, Feb. 10 Litho. *Perf. 12½*

442 A145 50fr yellow & multi .55 .25
443 A145 75fr green & multi 1.25 .30
444 A145 100fr rose & multi 1.40 .50
Nos. 442-444 (3) 3.20 1.05

2nd World Black and African Festival, Lagos, Nigeria, Jan. 15-Feb. 12.

Cogwheels and Symbols of Industry — A146

1977, Mar. 28 Engr. *Perf. 13*

445 A146 70fr yel grn & ocher .80 .30

Dakar Industrial Zone, 1st anniversary.

Burning Match and Burnt Trees — A147

60fr, Burnt trees and house, fire-truck, horiz.

1977, Apr. 30 Litho. *Perf. 12½*

446 A147 40fr green & multi 1.00 .35
447 A147 60fr slate & multi 1.75 .55

Prevention of forest fires.

Drummer, Telephone, Agriculture and Industry — A148

Electronic Tree and ITU Emblem — A149

1977, May 17 Litho. *Perf. 13*

448 A148 80fr multi .80 .40
449 A149 100fr multi 1.25 .60

World Telecommunications Day.

Symbol of Language Studies — A150

Sassenage Castle, Grenoble — A151

Perf. 12x12½, 12½

1977, May 21 Litho.

450 A150 65fr multi .65 .25
451 A151 250fr multi 2.75 1.00

10th anniv. of Intl. French Language Council.

Woman in Boat, Wooden Shoe A152

Design: 125fr, Senegalese woman, symbolic tulip and stamp, vert.

1977, June 4 *Perf. 13½x14, 14x13½*

452 A152 50fr blue grn & multi .50 .25
453 A152 125fr ocher & multi 1.50 .45

Amphilex '77 International Philatelic Exhibition, Amsterdam, May 26-June 5.

Adult Reading Class A153

Design: 65fr, Man learning to read.

1977, Sept. 10 Litho. *Perf. 12½*

454 A153 60fr multi .70 .25
455 A153 65fr multi .70 .25

National Literacy Week, Sept. 8-14.

Paintings A154

20fr, Mercury, by Rubens. 25fr, Daniel in the Lions' Den, by Peter Paul Rubens (1577-1640). 40fr, The Empress, by Titian (1477-1576). 60fr, Flora, by Titian. 65fr, Jo, the Beautiful Irish Woman, by Gustave Courbet (1819-1877). 100fr, The Painter's Studio, by Courbet.

1977, Nov. Photo. *Perf. 13x13½*

456 A154 20fr multi .55 .25
457 A154 25fr multi .55 .25
458 A154 40fr multi .55 .25
459 A154 60fr multi 1.00 .25
460 A154 65fr multi 1.40 .55
461 A154 100fr multi 3.00 1.00
Nos. 456-461 (6) 7.05 2.55

Christmas A155

20fr, Adoration by People of Various Races. 25fr, Decorated arch and procession. 40fr, Christmas tree, mother and child. 100fr, Adoration of the Kings, horiz.

1977, Dec. 22 Litho. *Perf. 12½*

462 A155 20fr multi .25 .25
463 A155 25fr multi .40 .25
464 A155 40fr multi .65 .25
465 A155 100fr multi 1.25 .65
Nos. 462-465 (4) 2.55 1.40

Fisherman Holding Net — A155a

1977 Litho. *Perf. 12¾*

465A A155a 25fr shown — —

See Nos. C145A-C145D.

Regatta at Soumbedioun A156

Tourism: 10fr, Senegalese wrestlers. 65fr, Regatta at Soumbedioun. 100fr, Dancers.

1978, Jan. 7 Litho. *Perf. 12½*

466 A156 10fr multi .25 .25
467 A156 30fr multi .35 .25
468 A156 65fr multi, horiz. .80 .40
469 A156 100fr multi, horiz. 1.75 .50
Nos. 466-469 (4) 3.15 1.40

Acropolis, Athens, and African Buildings A157

1978, Jan. 30

470 A157 75fr multi .80 .30

UNESCO campaign to save world's cultural heritage.

Solar-powered Pump, Field and Sheep — A158

Energy in Senegal: 95fr, Pylon bringing electricity to villages and factories.

1978, Feb. 25

471 A158 50fr multi .55 .25
472 A158 95fr multi 1.25 .40

Park Type of 1976

5fr, Caspian terns in flight, royal terns on ground. 10fr, Pink-backed pelicans. 15fr, Wart hog & gray heron. 20fr, Greater flamingoes, nests, eggs & young. #477, Gray heron & royal terns. #478, Abyssinian ground hornbill & wart hog.

1978, Apr. 22 Photo. *Perf. 13*

473 A133 5fr gold & multi .25 .25
474 A133 10fr gold & multi .55 .25
475 A133 15fr gold & multi 1.10 .25
476 A133 20fr gold & multi 1.25 .40
477 A133 150fr gold & multi 5.25 1.00
478 A133 150fr gold & multi 5.25 1.00
a. Strip of 2, #477-478 + label 11.50
Nos. 473-478 (6) 13.65 3.15

Salum Delta National Park.

Dome of the Rock, Jerusalem A159

1978, May 15 Litho. *Perf. 12½*

479 A159 60fr multi .80 .25

Palestinian fighters and their families.

Vaccination, Dr. Jenner, WHO Emblem — A160

1978, June 3
480 A160 60fr multi .80 .35

Eradication of smallpox.

Soccer, Flags: Argentina, Hungary, France, Italy — A161

Soccer, Cup, Argentina '78 Emblem and Flags of: 40fr, No. 486a, Poland, German Democratic Rep., Tunisia, Mexico. 65fr, 125fr, Austria, Spain, Sweden, Brazil. 75fr, No. 484, Netherlands, Iran, Peru, Scotland. 150fr, like 25fr.

1978, June 24 Photo. *Perf. 13*
481 A161 25fr multi .25 .25
482 A161 40fr multi .55 .25
483 A161 65fr multi .80 .30
484 A161 100fr multi 1.50 .30
Nos. 481-484 (4) 3.10 1.10

Souvenir Sheets

485 Sheet of 2 2.75
a. A161 75fr multi .60
b. A161 125fr multi 1.10
486 Sheet of 2 2.75
a. A161 100fr multi .85
b. A161 150fr multi 1.10

11th World Cup Soccer Championship, Argentina, June 1-25.

Mahatma Gandhi — A162

Design: 150fr, No. 489a, Martin Luther King. No. 489b, like 125fr.

1978, June 27 *Perf. 12*
487 A162 125fr multi 1.75 .35
488 A162 150fr multi 2.25 .60

Souvenir Sheet

489 Sheet of 2 4.00
a. A162 200fr multi 1.60
b. A162 200fr multi 1.60

Mahatma Gandhi and Martin Luther King, advocates of non-violence.

Homes and Industry — A163

1978, Aug. 5 Litho. *Perf. 12½*
490 A163 110fr multi 1.25 .40

3rd Intl. Fair, Dakar, Nov. 28-Dec. 10.

Wright Brothers and Flyer — A164

Designs: 150fr, like 75fr. 100fr, 250fr, Yuri Gagarin and spacecraft. 200fr, 300fr, US astronauts Frank Borman, William Anders, James Lovell Jr. and spacecraft.

1978, Sept. 25 Litho. *Perf. 13½x14*
491 A164 75fr multi .90 .25
492 A164 100fr multi 1.25 .40
493 A164 200fr multi 2.25 .85
Nos. 491-493 (3) 4.40 1.50

Souvenir Sheet

494 Sheet of 3 6.25
a. A164 150fr multi .60
b. A164 250fr multi 1.40
c. A164 300fr multi 2.00

75th anniv. of 1st powered flight; 10th anniv. of the death of Yuri Gagarin, first man in space; 10th anniv. of Apollo 8 flight around moon.

Henri Dunant (1828-1910), Founder of Red Cross, and Patients — A165

Design: 20fr, Henri Dunant, First Aid station, Red Cross flag.

1978, Oct. 28 Photo. *Perf. 11½*
495 A165 5fr brt blue & red .25 .25
496 A165 20fr multi .45 .25

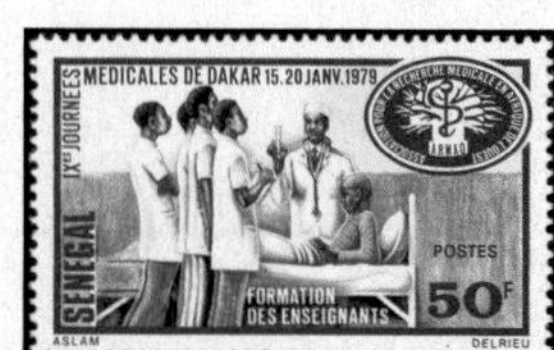

Bedside Lecture and Emblem — A166

100fr, Pollution, fish and mercury bottles.

1979, Jan. 15 Litho. *Perf. 13½x13*
497 A166 50fr multi .45 .25
498 A166 100fr multi 1.10 .30

9th Medical Days, Dakar, Jan. 15-20.

Map of Senegal with Shortwave Stations A167

60fr, Children on vacation, ambulance, soccer player. 65fr, Rural mobile post office.

1978, Dec. 27 Litho. *Perf. 13½x13*
499 A167 50fr multi .55 .25
500 A167 60fr multi .55 .25
501 A167 65fr multi .70 .25
Nos. 499-501 (3) 1.80 .75

Achievements of postal service.

Farmer A168

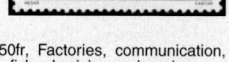

Design: 150fr, Factories, communication, transportation, fish, physician and worker.

1979, Feb. 17 Litho. *Perf. 12½*
502 A168 30fr multi .35 .25
503 A168 150fr multi 1.40 .50

Pride in workmanship.

Children's Village and Children — A169

Design: 60fr, Different view of village.

1979, Mar. 30 *Perf. 12x12½*
504 A169 40fr multi .45 .25
505 A169 60fr multi .70 .25

Children's SOS villages.

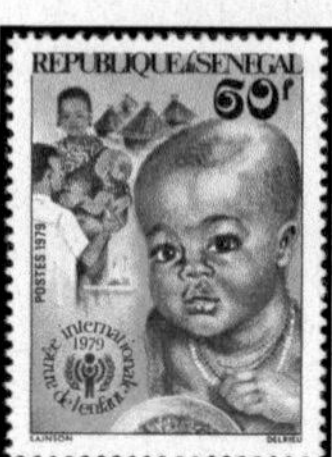

Infant, Physician Vaccinating Child, IYC Emblem — A170

65fr, Boys with book, globe, IYC emblem.

1979, Apr. 21 Litho. *Perf. 13½x13*
506 A170 60fr multi .65 .25
507 A170 65fr multi .65 .25

International Year of the Child.

Drum, Carrier Pigeon, Satellite — A171

Design: 60fr, Baobab tree and flower, Independence monument with lion, vert.

1979, June 8 *Perf. 12½x13*
Size: 36x48mm
508 A171 60fr multi 1.75 .85
Perf. 12½
Size: 36x36mm
509 A171 150fr multi 3.50 1.50

Philexafrique II, Libreville, Gabon, June 8-17. Nos. 508, 509 each printed with labels showing UAPT '79 emblem.

People Walking through Open Book A172

1979, Sept. 15 Photo. *Perf. 11½x12*
510 A172 250fr multi 2.50 .80

Intl. Bureau of Education, Geneva, 50th anniv.

Sir Rowland Hill (1795-1879), Originator of Penny Postage, Type AP3 with Exhibition Cancel — A173

1979, Oct. 9 *Perf. 11½*
511 A173 500fr multi 5.25 2.00

Black Trees, by Hundertwasser A174

100fr, Head of a man. 200fr, Rainbow windows.

Litho. & Engr.

1979, Dec. 10 *Perf. 13½x14*
512 A174 60fr shown *45.00* 11.00
a. Souvenir sheet of 4 175.00 175.00
513 A174 100fr multi *45.00* 13.00
a. Souvenir sheet of 4 175.00 175.00
514 A174 200fr multi *45.00* 15.00
a. Souvenir sheet of 4 175.00 175.00
Nos. 512-514 (3) 135.00 39.00

Paintings by Friedensreich Hundertwasser, pseudonym of Friedrich Stowasser (b. 1928).

Running, Championship Emblem A175

1980, Jan. 14 Litho. *Perf. 13*
515 A175 20fr shown .25 .25
516 A175 25fr Javelin .25 .25
517 A175 50fr Relay race .55 .25
518 A175 100fr Discus 1.25 .45
Nos. 515-518 (4) 2.30 1.20

1st African Athletic Championships.

Mudra Afrique Arts Festival A176

50fr, Musicians. 100fr, Dancers, festival building. 200fr, Drummer, dancers.

1980, Mar. 22 Photo. *Perf. 14*
519 A176 50fr multi .45 .25
520 A176 100fr multi 1.00 .45
521 A176 200fr multi 1.75 .85
Nos. 519-521 (3) 3.20 1.55

Lions Emblem, Map of Dakar Harbor A177

1980, May 17 Litho. *Perf. 13*
522 A177 100fr multi 1.10 .40

22nd Cong., Lions Intl. District 403, Dakar.

Chimpanzees — A178

1980, June 2 Photo. *Perf. 13½*

No.	Type	Value	Description	Unused	Used
523	A178	40fr	shown	.85	.25
524	A178	60fr	Elephants	1.25	.40
525	A178	65fr	Derby's elands	1.50	.45
526	A178	100fr	Hyenas	2.25	.50
527			Pair	9.00	5.00
a.	A178	200fr	Herd	4.25	1.00
b.	A178	200fr	Guest house	4.25	1.00
			Nos. 523-527 (5)	14.85	6.60

Souvenir Sheet

No.	Description	Unused	Used
528	Sheet of 4	8.00	8.00
a.	A178 125fr like #523	1.50	1.50
b.	A178 125fr like #524	1.50	1.50
c.	A178 125fr like #525	1.50	1.50
d.	A178 125fr like #526	1.50	1.50

Niokolo Koba National Park. No. 527 printed in continuous design with label showing location of park.

Tree Planting Year — A179

1980, June 27 Litho. *Perf. 13*

No.	Type	Value	Description	Unused	Used
529	A179	60fr	multi	.90	.40
530	A179	65fr	multi	1.00	.40

Rural Women Workers A180

Rural women workers. 50fr, 200fr, horiz.

1980, July 19

No.	Type	Value	Description	Unused	Used
531	A180	50fr	multi	.35	.25
532	A180	100fr	multi	1.25	.35
533	A180	200fr	multi	2.00	.80
			Nos. 531-533 (3)	3.60	1.40

Wrestling, Moscow '80 Emblem — A181

60fr, Wrestling. 65fr, Running. 70fr, Sports, map showing Moscow. 100fr, Judo. 200fr, Basketball.

1980, Aug. 21 *Perf. 14½*

No.	Type	Value	Description	Unused	Used
534	A181	60fr	multicolored	.45	.25
535	A181	65fr	multicolored	.55	.30
536	A181	70fr	multicolored	.55	.30
537	A181	100fr	multicolored	.80	.40
538	A181	200fr	multicolored	1.75	.80
			Nos. 534-538 (5)	4.10	2.05

Souvenir Sheet

No.	Description	Unused	Used
539	Sheet of 2	2.00	
a.	A181 75fr like #534	.65	.25
b.	A181 125fr like #535	1.00	.35
540	Sheet of 2	2.00	
a.	A181 75fr like #527	.65	.25
b.	A181 125fr like #538	1.00	.35

22nd Summer Olympic Games, Moscow, July 19-Aug. 3.

Caspian Tern and Sea Gulls, Kalissaye Bird Sanctuary A182

National Park Wildlife: 70fr, Laughing gulls and Hansel's tern, Barbarie Spit. 85fr, Turtle and crab, Madeleine Islands. 150fr, Cormorant, Madeleine Islands.

1981, Jan. 31 Litho. *Perf. 14½x14*

No.	Type	Value	Description	Unused	Used
541	A182	50fr	multi	3.50	.50
542	A182	70fr	multi	3.50	.70
543	A182	85fr	multi	1.75	.70
544	A182	150fr	multi	7.00	1.75
			Nos. 541-544 (4)	15.75	3.65

Souvenir Sheet

No.	Description	Unused	Used
545	Sheet of 4	22.50	22.50
a.	A182 125fr like #541	3.50	2.75
b.	A182 125fr like #542	3.50	2.75
c.	A182 125fr like #543	3.50	2.75
d.	A182 125fr like #544	3.50	2.75

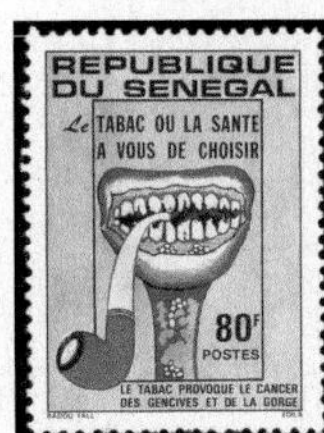

Anti-Tobacco Campaign — A183

1981, June 20 Litho. *Perf. 13*

No.	Type	Value	Description	Unused	Used
546	A183	75fr	Healthy people	.70	.30
547	A183	80fr	shown	.90	.30

4th Intl. Dakar Fair, Nov. 25-Dec. 7 A184

1981, Sept. 19 Litho. *Perf. 12½*

No.	Type	Value	Description	Unused	Used
548	A184	80fr	multi	.80	.30

Natl. Hero Lat Dior A185

1982, Jan. 11 Photo. *Perf. 14*

No.	Type	Value	Description	Unused	Used
549	A185	80fr	Portrait, vert.	.55	.35
550	A185	500fr	Battle	4.50	1.40

Local Flora — A186

50fr, Nymphaea lotus. 75fr, Strophanthus sarmentosus. 200fr, Crinum moorei. 225fr, Cochlospermum tinctorium.

1982, Feb. 1 *Perf. 11½*

No.	Type	Value	Description	Unused	Used
551	A186	50fr	multicolored	.55	.25
552	A186	75fr	multicolored	.90	.30
553	A186	200fr	multicolored	2.25	.65
554	A186	225fr	multicolored	2.25	.85
			Nos. 551-554 (4)	5.95	2.05

Inscribed 1981.

Euryphrene Senegalensis — A187

55fr, Hypolimnas salmacis. 75fr, Cymothoe caenis. 80fr, Precis cebrene.

1982, Feb. 27 Litho. *Perf. 14*

No.	Type	Value	Description	Unused	Used
555	A187	45fr	multicolored	2.25	.50
556	A187	55fr	multicolored	3.00	.60
557	A187	75fr	multicolored	3.25	.75
558	A187	80fr	multicolored	4.00	.90
			Nos. 555-558 (4)	12.50	2.75

Souvenir Sheet

Perf. 14½

No.	Description	Unused	Used
559	Sheet of 4	20.00	20.00
a.	A187 100fr like 45fr	2.00	1.50
b.	A187 150fr like 55fr	3.00	2.50
c.	A187 200fr like 75fr	4.00	3.50
d.	A187 250fr like 80fr	5.00	4.00

Destructive Insects — A188

Various insects. 80fr, 100fr horiz.

1982, Apr. 7 Litho. *Perf. 14*

No.	Type	Value	Description	Unused	Used
560	A188	75fr	multi	1.75	.40
561	A188	80fr	multi	3.25	.70
562	A188	100fr	multi	2.50	.90
			Nos. 560-562 (3)	7.50	2.00

Fashion Type of 1972

1982-93 Engr. *Perf. 13*

No.	Type	Value	Description	Unused	Used
563	A106	5fr	Prus blue	.25	.25
564	A106	10fr	dull red	.25	.25
565	A106	15fr	orange	.25	.25
566	A106	20fr	dk purple	.25	.25
567	A106	30fr	henna brn	.25	.25
568	A106	45fr	orange yellow	.35	.25
569	A106	50fr	bright magenta	.40	.25
570	A106	90fr	brt carmine	.50	.30
571	A106	125fr	ultramarine	.95	.50
572	A106	145fr	orange	.85	.35
573	A106	180fr	gray blue	1.40	.70
			Nos. 563-573 (11)	5.70	3.60

Issued: 5, 10, 15, 20, 30fr, Apr. 30; 90fr, Dec., 1984; 180fr, 1991; 45, 50, 125fr, 1993; 145fr, 1995.

Banner and Stamp — A189

1982, Dec. 30 Photo. *Perf. 13*

No.	Type	Value	Description	Unused	Used
575	A189	100fr	shown	.70	.35
576	A189	500fr	Stamp, arrows	4.50	1.50

PHILEXFRANCE Intl. Stamp Exhibition, Paris, June 11-21.

Senegambia Confederation, Feb. 1 — A190

1982, Nov. 15 Litho. *Perf. 12½*

No.	Type	Value	Description	Unused	Used
577	A190	225fr	Map, flags	2.00	.65
578	A190	350fr	Arms	2.75	1.00

Local Birds — A191

1982, Dec. 1 Photo. *Perf. 11½*

Granite Paper

No.	Type	Value	Description	Unused	Used
579	A191	45fr	Godwit	.65	.25
580	A191	75fr	Jabiru	1.10	.35
581	A191	80fr	Francolin	1.25	.55
582	A191	500fr	Eagle	6.25	2.25
			Nos. 579-582 (4)	9.25	3.40

1982 World Cup — A192

1982, Dec. 11 Litho. *Perf. 12½x13*

No.	Type	Value	Description	Unused	Used
583	A192	30fr	Player	.25	.25
584	A192	50fr	Player, diff.	.35	.25
585	A192	75fr	Ball	.80	.25
586	A192	80fr	Cup	.90	.35
			Nos. 583-586 (4)	2.30	1.10

Souvenir Sheets

Perf. 12½

No.	Type	Value	Description	Unused	Used
587	A192	75fr	like 30fr	.80	.80
588	A192	100fr	like 50fr	1.10	1.10
589	A192	150fr	like 75fr	1.50	1.50
590	A192	200fr	like 80fr	2.25	2.25
			Nos. 587-590 (4)	5.65	5.65

A193

A193a

Designs: 60fr, Exhibition poster, viewers, horiz. 70fr, Simulated butterfly stamps. 90fr, Simulated stamps under magnifying glass. 95fr, Coat of Arms over Exhibition Building.

1983, Aug. 6 Litho. *Perf. 12½*

No.	Type	Value	Description	Unused	Used
591	A193	60fr	multi	.55	.25
592	A193a	70fr	multi	1.40	.30
593	A193a	90fr	multi	1.75	.30
594	A193a	95fr	multi	1.75	.40
			Nos. 591-594 (4)	5.45	1.25

Dakar '82 Stamp Exhibition.

A194

1983, Oct. 25 Litho. *Perf. 12½x13*

No.	Type	Value	Description	Unused	Used
595	A194	90fr	Electricity	.85	.40
596	A194	95fr	Gasoline	1.00	.45
597	A194	260fr	Coal, wood	2.25	.65
			Nos. 595-597 (3)	4.10	1.50

Energy conservation.

Namibia Day — A195

Designs: 90fr, Torch. 95fr, Chain, fist. 260fr, Woman bearing torch.

1983, Nov. 14 Litho. *Perf. 13½x13*

598 A195 90fr multi .80 .35
599 A195 95fr multi .90 .35
600 A195 260fr multi 2.75 .65
Nos. 598-600 (3) 4.45 1.35

West African Monetary Union, 20th Anniv. — A196

Designs: 60fr, Mask emblem, Ziguinchor Agency building, Dakar, horiz. 65fr, Monetary Union headquarters, emblem.

Perf. 13½x13, 13x13½

1983, Nov. 28

601 A196 60fr multi .65 .25
602 A196 65fr multi .65 .25

Dakar Alizes Rotary Club, First Anniv. — A197

1983, Dec. 5 *Perf. 13x13½*

603 A197 70fr green & multi .90 .35
604 A197 500fr blue & multi 4.50 1.75

Customs Cooperation Council, 30th Anniv. — A198

1983, Dec. 23 *Perf. 12½x13*

605 A198 90fr multi .65 .25
606 A198 300fr multi 3.00 .80

Economic Comm. for Africa, 25th Anniv. — A199

1984, Jan. 10 *Perf. 12½*

607 A199 90fr multi .70 .35
608 A199 95fr multi .90 .35

SOS Children's Village A200

90fr, Village. 95fr, Mother & child, vert. 115fr, Brothers & sisters. 260fr, House, vert.

1984, Mar. 29 *Perf. 13½x13, 13x13½*

609 A200 90fr multicolored .80 .25
610 A200 95fr multicolored 1.00 .40
611 A200 115fr multicolored 1.10 .40
612 A200 260fr multicolored 2.50 .85
Nos. 609-612 (4) 5.40 1.90

Scouting Year A201

1984, May 28 Litho. *Perf. 13*

613 A201 60fr Sign .55 .25
614 A201 70fr Emblem .55 .25
615 A201 90fr Scouts .70 .30
616 A201 95fr Baden-Powell .90 .30
Nos. 613-616 (4) 2.70 1.10

1984 Olympic Games — A202

1984, July 28 Litho. *Perf. 13*

617 A202 90fr Javelin .70 .25
618 A202 95fr Hurdles .90 .35
619 A202 165fr Soccer 1.50 .50
Nos. 617-619 (3) 3.10 1.10

Souvenir Sheet

Perf. 13x12½

620 Sheet of 3 4.50 4.50
a. A202 125fr like 90fr .95 .95
b. A202 175fr like 95fr 1.50 1.50
c. A202 250fr like 165fr 1.75 1.75

World Food Day A203

Perf. 13x12½, 12½x13

1984, Dec. 16 Litho.

621 A203 65fr Food production .55 .30
622 A203 70fr Cooking, vert. .70 .30
623 A203 225fr Dining 2.25 .85
Nos. 621-623 (3) 3.50 1.45

No. 612 Overprinted "AIDE AU SAHEL 84"

1984, Dec. *Perf. 13x13½*

624 A200 260fr multi 2.25 1.25

Drought relief.

UNESCO World Heritage Campaign A204

90fr, William Ponty School. 95fr, Island map, horiz. 250fr, History Museum. 500fr, Slave Prison, horiz.

1984, Dec. 6 Litho. *Perf. 13½*

625 A204 90fr multi 1.10 .40
626 A204 95fr multi 1.10 .40
627 A204 250fr multi 3.25 1.00
628 A204 500fr multi 6.00 2.25
Nos. 625-628 (4) 11.45 4.05

Souvenir Sheet

Perf. 13x12½, 12½x13

629 Sheet of 4 11.00 11.00
a. A204 125fr like No. 625 1.00 .75
b. A204 150fr like No. 626 1.25 1.00
c. A204 325fr like No. 627 2.25 2.00
d. A204 675fr like No. 628 5.25 5.00

Restoration of historic sites, Goree Island.

Water Emergency Plan — A205

40fr, Well and pump. 50fr, Spigot and crops. 90fr, Water tanks, livestock. 250fr, Women at well.

1985, Mar. 28 *Perf. 13x12½, 12½x13*

630 A205 40fr multi .60 .25
631 A205 50fr multi .70 .35
632 A205 90fr multi 1.40 .55
633 A205 250fr multi 3.00 1.10
Nos. 630-633 (4) 5.70 2.25

Nos. 631-633 horiz.

World Communications Year — A206

Designs: 95fr, Maps of Africa and Senegal, transmission tower. 350fr, Globe, pigeon with letter.

1985, Apr. 13 Litho. *Perf. 13*

634 A206 90fr multi .70 .35
635 A206 95fr multi .90 .35
636 A206 350fr multi 3.25 1.25
Nos. 634-636 (3) 4.85 1.95

Traditional Musical Instruments — A207

50fr, Gourd fiddle, bamboo flute. 85fr, Drums, stringed instrument. 125fr, Musician playing balaphone, drums. 250fr, Rabab, shawm & single-string fiddles.

1985, May 4 *Perf. 12½x13, 13x12½*

637 A207 50fr multi .75 .25
638 A207 85fr multi 1.10 .45
639 A207 125fr multi 1.60 .60
640 A207 250fr multi 3.25 1.00
Nos. 637-640 (4) 6.70 2.30

Nos. 638-640 vert. For surcharge see No. 676.

PHILEXAFRICA '85, Lome, Togo, Nov. 16-24 — A208

100fr, Political and civic education. 125fr, Vocational training. 150fr, Culture, space exploration. 175fr, Self-sufficiency in food production.

1985, Oct. 21 *Perf. 13*

641 A208 100fr multi .70 .25
642 A208 125fr multi 1.00 .40
643 A208 150fr multi 1.25 .50
644 A208 175fr multi 2.25 .85
Nos. 641-644 (4) 5.20 2.00

Intl. Youth Year A209

40fr, Vocational training. 50fr, Communications. 90fr, World peace. 125fr, Cultural exchange.

1985, Nov. 30 *Perf. 14*

645 A209 40fr multicolored .35 .25
646 A209 50fr multicolored .45 .25
647 A209 90fr multicolored .80 .30
648 A209 125fr multicolored 1.25 .35
Nos. 645-648 (4) 2.85 1.15

Senegal Arms Type of 1970

1985, Dec. Litho. *Perf. 13*

Background Color

654 A89 95fr bright orange .80 .25

Fishing at Kayar A210

40fr, Hauling boat. 50fr, Women on beach. 100fr, Fisherman, catch. 125fr, Women buying fish. 150fr, Unloading fish.

1986, Jan. 28 Litho. *Perf. 14*

659 A210 40fr multi .35 .25
660 A210 50fr multi .55 .25
661 A210 100fr multi 1.00 .35
662 A210 125fr multi 1.40 .50
663 A210 150fr multi 1.60 .60
Nos. 659-663 (5) 4.90 1.95

Nos. 661-662 vert.

Folk Costumes — A211

1985, Dec. 28 Litho. *Perf. 13½*

664 A211 40fr multi .25 .25
665 A211 95fr multi, vert., diff. .80 .30
666 A211 100fr multi, vert., diff. .90 .30
667 A211 150fr multi, vert., diff. 1.25 .50
Nos. 664-667 (4) 3.20 1.35

Coiffures — A212

90fr, Perruque, Ceeli. 125fr, Ndungu, Kearly, Rasta. 250fr, Jamono Kura, Kooraa. 300fr, Mbaram, Jeere.

1986, Mar. 3 *Perf. 13*

668 A212 90fr multicolored .70 .35
669 A212 125fr multicolored 1.00 .40
670 A212 250fr multicolored 2.25 .75
671 A212 300fr multicolored 2.75 .90
Nos. 668-671 (4) 6.70 2.40

1986 Africa Soccer Cup, Cairo — A213

115fr, Soccer ball, flags. 125fr, Athlete, map. 135fr, Pyramid, heraldic lion. 165fr, Flag, lions, map.

1986, Mar. 7 *Perf. 13½*

672 A213 115fr multi 1.00 .30
673 A213 125fr multi 1.00 .35
674 A213 135fr multi 1.10 .40
675 A213 165fr multi 1.40 .50
Nos. 672-675 (4) 4.50 1.55

No. 638 Surcharged with Lions Intl. Emblem, Two Bars, and "Ve CONVENTION / MULTI-DISTRICT / 403 / 8-10 / MAI / 1986" in Dark Ultramarine

1986, May 8 Litho. *Perf. 13x12½*
676 A207 165fr on 85fr multi 1.40 .50

World Wildlife Fund — A214

Ndama gazelles.

1986, June 30 *Perf. 13*
677 A214 15fr multi 1.00 .40
678 A214 45fr multi 1.75 .60
679 A214 85fr multi 3.00 1.25
680 A214 125fr multi 5.00 2.00
Nos. 677-680 (4) 10.75 4.25

UN Child Survival Campaign — A215

1986, Sept. 5 Litho. *Perf. 14*
681 A215 50fr Immunization .45 .25
682 A215 85fr Nutrition .70 .30

1986 World Cup Soccer Championships, Mexico — A216

Various plays, world cup and artifacts: 125fr, Ceremonial vase. 135fr, Mayan mask, Palenque. 165fr, Gold breastplate. 340fr, Porcelain mask, Teofihuacan, 7th cent. B.C.

1986, Nov. 17 *Perf. 12½x12*
683 A216 125fr multi 1.00 .40
684 A216 135fr multi 1.10 .40
685 A216 165fr multi 1.40 .55
686 A216 340fr multi 2.75 1.10
Nos. 683-686 (4) 6.25 2.45

Nos. 683-686 Overprinted "ARGENTINE 3 / R.F.A. 2" in Scarlet

1986, Nov. 17
687 A216 125fr multi 1.00 .40
688 A216 135fr multi 1.10 .45
689 A216 165fr multi 1.40 .55
690 A216 340fr multi 2.75 1.10
Nos. 687-690 (4) 6.25 2.50

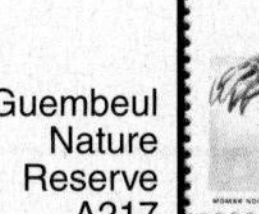

Guembeul Nature Reserve A217

Designs: 50fr, Ostriches. 65fr, Kob antelopes. 85fr, Giraffes. 100fr, Ostrich, buffalo, kob, giraffe. 150fr, Buffaloes.

1986, Dec. 4 Litho. *Perf. 13½*
691 A217 50fr multi 1.25 .25
692 A217 65fr multi .45 .25
693 A217 85fr multi .60 .40
694 A217 100fr multi 2.00 .50
695 A217 150fr multi 1.25 .60
Nos. 691-695 (5) 5.55 2.00

Inscribed 1985.

Christmas A218

70fr, Puppet, vert. 85fr, Folk musicians. 150fr, Outdoor celebration, vert. 250fr, Boy praying, creche.

1986, Dec. 22 Litho. *Perf. 14*
696 A218 70fr multicolored .55 .25
697 A218 85fr multicolored .80 .25
698 A218 150fr multicolored 1.25 .50
699 A218 250fr multicolored 2.25 .85
Nos. 696-699 (4) 4.85 1.85

Inscribed 1985.

Statue of Liberty, Cent. — A219

1986, Dec. 30 Litho. *Perf. 12½*
700 A219 225fr multi 2.00 .65

Marine Life A220

Designs: 50fr, Jellyfish, coral. 85fr, Sea urchin, starfish. 100fr, Spiny lobster. 150fr, Dolphin. 200fr, Octopus.

1987, Jan. 2 *Perf. 14*
701 A220 50fr multi .55 .25
702 A220 85fr multi 1.00 .25
703 A220 100fr multi 1.60 .50
704 A220 150fr multi 2.10 .65
705 A220 200fr multi 3.25 .90
Nos. 701-705 (5) 8.50 2.55

Inscribed 1985.

Senegal Stamp Cent. — A221

1987, Apr. 8 *Perf. 13*
706 A221 100fr Intl. express mail 1.40 .30
707 A221 130fr #37 1.60 .40
708 A221 140fr Similar to #201 1.75 .40
709 A221 145fr #151, similar to #154 1.75 .50
710 A221 320fr #27 5.00 1.10
Nos. 706-710 (5) 11.50 2.70

Designs of Nos. 37, 151 and 27 same as originally released but perfs simulated.
For overprint see No. 784.

Paris-Dakar Rally — A222

Designs: 115fr, Motorcycle, truck, vert. 125fr, Official, race. 135fr, Sabine, truck. 340fr, Eiffel Tower, Dakar huts, vert.

1987, Jan. 22 *Perf. 14*
711 A222 115fr multi 1.25 .40
712 A222 125fr multi 1.75 .40
713 A222 135fr multi 1.75 .55
714 A222 340fr multi 3.25 1.25
Nos. 711-714 (4) 8.00 2.60

Homage to Thierry Sabine. Inscribed 1986.

Ferlo Nature Reserve — A223

1987, Feb. 5 *Perf. 13½*
715 A223 55fr Antelope .80 .30
716 A223 70fr Ostrich 1.10 .45
717 A223 85fr Warthog 1.10 .45
718 A223 90fr Elephant 1.25 .50
Nos. 715-718 (4) 4.25 1.70

Inscribed 1985.

Agena-Gemini 8 Link-up in Outer Space, 20th Anniv. — A224

1987, Feb. 27 Litho. *Perf. 13*
719 A224 320fr multi 2.75 1.25

Souvenir Sheet

Perf. 12½
720 A224 500fr multi 6.25 6.25

Nos. 719-720 inscribed 1986 and have erroneous "10e Anniversaire" inscription.

Solidarity Against South African Apartheid — A225

140fr, Mandela, hand, broken chain, vert. 145fr, Mandela, dove, death.

1987, July 31 Litho. *Perf. 13*
721 A225 130fr multicolored 1.00 .40
722 A225 140fr multicolored 1.10 .45
723 A225 145fr multicolored 1.10 .50
Nos. 721-723 (3) 3.20 1.35

Inscribed 1986.

Intelsat, 20th Anniv. A226

Designs: 50fr, Emblem. 125fr, Satellite. 150fr, Emblem, globe. 200fr, Earth, satellite in space.

1987, Aug. 31 *Perf. 14*
724 A226 50fr multi .45 .25
725 A226 125fr multi 1.00 .40
726 A226 150fr multi 1.10 .50
727 A226 200fr multi 2.00 .70
Nos. 724-727 (4) 4.55 1.85

Inscribed 1985. Nos. 726-727 vert.

West African Union, 10th Anniv. — A227

Design: 125fr, Emblem, handshake.

1987, Sept. 7
728 A227 40fr shown .35 .25
729 A227 125fr multi 1.00 .45

Inscribed 1985.

Dakar Rotary Club, 45th Anniv. — A228

1987, Sept. 29 *Perf. 13*
730 A228 500fr multi 4.50 1.75

Inscribed 1985.

United Nations, 40th Anniv. — A229

Designs: 85fr, Emblem, NYC office. 95fr, Emblem. 150fr, Hands, emblem.

1987, Oct. 8 *Perf. 14*
731 A229 85fr multi .90 .30
732 A229 95fr multi .90 .30
733 A229 150fr multi 1.25 .55
Nos. 731-733 (3) 3.05 1.15

Inscribed 1985.

Cathedral of African Memory, 50th Anniv. A230

130fr, Statue of saint, Fr. Daniel Brottier, vert.

1987, Oct. 16 *Perf. 12½x13, 13x12½*
734 A230 130fr multi 1.25 .65
735 A230 140fr multi 1.25 .65

Inscribed 1986.

Lat Dior, King of Cayor (d. 1887) A231

1987, Oct. 27 Litho. *Perf. 14*
736 A231 130fr Battle of Dekhele 1.25 .50
737 A231 160fr Lat Dior 1.25 .50

World Food Day A232

Designs: 130fr, Earth storing grain, vert. 145fr, Emblem, vert.

1987, Oct. 30 Litho. *Perf. 12½*

738 A232 130fr multi 1.00 .60
739 A232 140fr shown 1.25 .60
740 A232 145fr multi 1.50 .60
Nos. 738-740 (3) 3.75 1.80

Inscribed 1986.

A233

Fauna, Bassa Casamance Natl. Park — A234

No. 741, Felis servaline. No. 742, Galagoides demi-dovii. No. 743, Potamochoerus porcus. No. 744, Panthera pardus. No. 745, Aigrette. No. 746, Guepier.

1987, Nov. 9 *Perf. 13*

741 A233 115fr multi 1.00 .55
742 A233 135fr multi 1.40 .60
743 A233 150fr multi 1.50 .65
744 A233 250fr multi 2.75 1.25
745 300fr multi 12.50 3.75
746 300fr multi 12.50 3.75
a. A234 Pair, #745-746 + label 27.50 8.00
Nos. 741-746 (6) 31.65 10.55

Inscribed 1986. No. 745-746 has continuous design with corner label picturing map of Senegal with park highlighted.

Traditional Wrestling — A235

Various moves.

1987, Nov. 30 Litho. *Perf. 14*

747 A235 115fr multi, horiz. 1.10 .45
748 A235 125fr multi, diff., horiz. 1.10 .50
749 A235 135fr multi, diff. 1.25 .55
750 A235 165fr multi, diff. 1.60 .75
Nos. 747-750 (4) 5.05 2.25

Birds in Djoudj Natl. Park — A236

115fr, Stork. 125fr, Pink flamingos, horiz. 135fr, White pelicans, horiz. 300fr, Pelicans in water. No. 755, like 125fr, horiz. No. 756, like 135fr, horiz.

1987, Dec. 4

751 A236 115fr multi 1.75 .40
752 A236 125fr multi 2.00 .40
753 A236 135fr multi 2.50 .65
754 A236 300fr multi 5.00 1.25
755 A236 350fr multi 5.25 1.75
756 A236 350fr multi 5.25 1.75
a. Pair, #755-756 + label 11.50 11.50
Nos. 751-756 (6) 21.75 6.20

Inscribed 1986.

Christmas A237

Designs: 145fr, Youth dreaming of presents. 150fr, Madonna and child. 180fr, Holy Family, congregation praying. 200fr, Holy Family, candle and Christmas tree.

1987, Dec. 24 *Perf. 12½x13*

757 A237 145fr multi 1.25 .40
758 A237 150fr multi 1.25 .40
759 A237 180fr multi 1.75 .65
760 A237 200fr multi 2.00 .65
Nos. 757-760 (4) 6.25 2.10

Dakar Intl. Fair, 10th Anniv. (in 1985) — A238

1988, Feb. 27 Litho. *Perf. 13*

761 A238 125fr multi .90 .45

Inscribed 1985.

Fish — A239

5fr, Amelurus nebulosus. 100fr, Heniochus acuminatus. 145fr, Anthias anthias. 180fr, Cyprinus carpio.

1988, Feb. 29 Litho. *Perf. 13*

762 A239 5fr multicolored .30 .30
763 A239 100fr multicolored 1.25 .60
764 A239 145fr multicolored 2.25 .90
765 A239 180fr multicolored 4.00 1.50
Nos. 762-765 (4) 7.80 3.30

World Meteorology Day — A240

1988, Mar. 15 *Perf. 13½*

766 A240 145fr multi 1.25 .55

Paris-Dakar Rally, 10th Anniv. (in 1987) — A241

Various motorcycle and automobile entries in desert settings.

1988 *Perf. 13*

767 A241 145fr Motorcycle 1.60 .55
768 A241 180fr Race car 2.00 .60
769 A241 200fr Race car, truck 2.10 .90
770 A241 410fr Thierry Sabine 4.50 1.75
Nos. 767-770 (4) 10.20 3.80

Inscribed 1987. For surcharges, see Nos. 1051, 1194A.

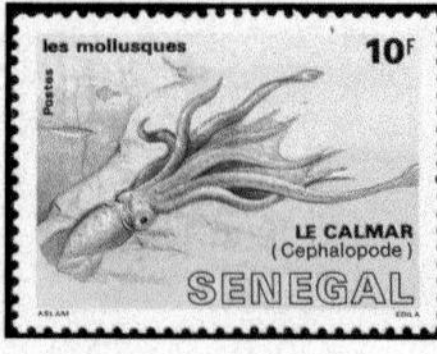

Mollusks A242

Designs: 10fr, Squid. 20fr, Donax trunculus. 145fr, Achatina fulica, vert. 165fr, Helix nemoralis.

1988, Apr. 20 *Perf. 12½*

771 A242 10fr multi .25 .25
772 A242 20fr multi .25 .25
773 A242 145fr multi 1.75 .65
774 A242 165fr multi 2.25 .85
Nos. 771-774 (4) 4.50 2.00

1988 African Soccer Cup Championships, Rabat — A243

80fr, Cameroun (winner). 100fr, Kick, CAF emblem. 145fr, Map, players, final score. 180fr, Trophy.

1988, May 10 Litho. *Perf. 13*

775 A243 80fr multi .70 .30
776 A243 100fr multi .90 .35
777 A243 145fr multi 1.25 .40
778 A243 180fr multi 1.75 .60
Nos. 775-778 (4) 4.60 1.65

Nos. 776-778 vert.

US Peace Corps in Senegal, 25th Anniv. — A244

1988, May 11 Litho. *Perf. 13*

779 A244 190fr multi 1.50 .65

Marine Flora — A245

10fr, Dictyota atomaria. 65fr, Agarum gmelini. 145fr, Saccorrhiza bulbosa. 180fr, Rhodymenia palmetta.

1988, June 13 Litho. *Perf. 12½*

780 A245 10fr multicolored .25 .25
781 A245 65fr multicolored .65 .25
782 A245 145fr multicolored 1.40 .50
783 A245 180fr multicolored 1.75 .65
Nos. 780-783 (4) 4.05 1.65

Inscribed 1987.

No. 710 Overprinted

1988, Aug. 27 Litho. *Perf. 13*

784 A221 320fr multi 2.75 1.25

Stamp Fair, Riccione, Aug. 27-29, 1988. Stamp incorrectly overprinted "89," instead of "88."

ENDA — A246

125fr, Thierno Saidou Nourou Tall Center.

1988 Litho. *Perf. 13*

785 A246 125fr multi 1.00 .50

For surcharge, see No. 824.

1988 Summer Olympics, Seoul — A247

75fr, Running, swimming, soccer. 300fr, Character trademark, torch. 410fr, Emblems, running.

1988, Sept. 17 Litho. *Perf. 13*

786 A247 5fr multi .25 .25
787 A247 75fr multi .70 .35
788 A247 300fr multi 2.75 1.00
789 A247 410fr multi 3.50 1.40
Nos. 786-789 (4) 7.20 3.00

Industries A248

5fr, Phosphate, Thies. 20fr, I.C.S. 145fr, Seib Mill, Diourbel. 410fr, Mbao refinery.

1988, Nov. 7 Litho. *Perf. 13*

790 A248 5fr multi .25 .25
791 A248 20fr multi .25 .25
792 A248 145fr multi 1.25 .45
793 A248 410fr multi 3.75 1.60
Nos. 790-793 (4) 5.50 2.55

Postcards, c. 1900 — A249

20fr, Boys, Government Palace. 145fr, Wrestlers, St. Louis Great Mosque. 180fr,

Dakar Depot, young woman in folk costume. 200fr, Governor's Residence, housewife using mortar & pestle.

1988, Nov. 26

794 A249 20fr red brn & blk .25 .25
795 A249 145fr red brn & blk 1.25 .55
796 A249 180fr red brn & blk 1.60 .75
797 A249 200fr red brn & blk 1.90 1.00
Nos. 794-797 (4) 5.00 2.55

Indigenous Flowers — A250

20fr, Packia biglobosa. 60fr, Eurphorbia pulcherrima. 65fr, Cyrtosperma senegalense. 410fr, Bombax costatum.

1988, Dec. 4 ***Perf. 13x12½***

798 A250 20fr multi .25 .25
799 A250 60fr multi .55 .25
800 A250 65fr multi .65 .25
801 A250 410fr multi 3.75 1.50
Nos. 798-801 (4) 5.20 2.25

11th Paris-Dakar Rally A251

10fr, Mask, vehicle, Eiffel Tower. 145fr, Helmet, desert scene. 180fr, Turban, rallyist in desert. 220fr, Thierry Sabine.

1989, Jan. 13 Litho. ***Perf. 13½***

802 A251 10fr multi .25 .25
803 A251 145fr multi 1.50 .50
804 A251 180fr multi 1.75 .65
805 A251 220fr multi 2.25 .85
Nos. 802-805 (4) 5.75 2.25

For surcharge see No. 1050.

Tourism A252

1989, Feb. 15 ***Perf. 13***

806 A252 10fr Teranga .25 .25
807 A252 80fr Campement .70 .30
808 A252 100fr Saly .90 .40
809 A252 350fr Dior 2.75 1.10
Nos. 806-809 (4) 4.60 2.05

Inscribed 1988.

Tourism — A253

130fr, Natl. tourism emblem, vert. 140fr, Visiting rural community. 145fr, Sport fishing. 180fr, Water skiing, polo.

1989, Mar. 11

810 A253 130fr multi 1.00 .40
811 A253 140fr multi 1.10 .45
812 A253 145fr multi 1.40 .65
813 A253 180fr multi 1.40 .80
Nos. 810-813 (4) 4.90 2.30

Inscribed 1987.

French Revolution, Bicent. — A254

Designs: 180fr, Governor's Palace, St. Louis. 220fr, Declaration of Human Rights and Citizenship, vert. 300fr, Flag, revolutionaries.

1989, May 24 Litho. ***Perf. 13***

814 A254 180fr shown 1.75 1.00
815 A254 220fr multi 2.00 1.00
816 A254 300fr multi 3.00 1.60
Nos. 814-816 (3) 6.75 3.60

PHILEXFRANCE '89 — A255

Designs: 25fr, Simulated stamp, map of France. 75fr, Exhibit. 145fr, Affixing stamp.

1989, July 7 Litho. ***Perf. 13x12½***

817 A255 10fr shown .25 .25
818 A255 25fr multi .25 .25
819 A255 75fr multi .65 .30
820 A255 145fr multi 1.25 .50
Nos. 817-820 (4) 2.40 1.30

Antoine de Saint-Exupery (1900-1944), French Aviator and Writer — A256

Scenes from novels: 180fr, *Southern Courier,* 1929. 220fr, *Night flier,* 1931. 410fr, *Bomber pilot,* 1942.

1989, Aug. 30 Litho. ***Perf. 13***

821 A256 180fr multi 1.50 .50
822 A256 220fr multi 1.75 .85
823 A256 410fr multi 4.00 1.40
Nos. 821-823 (3) 7.25 2.75

No. 785 Surcharged in Bright Green

1989 Litho. ***Perf. 13***

824 A246 555fr on 125fr multi 4.25 2.00

3rd Francophone Summit on the Arts and Culture — A257

Designs: 5fr, Palette, quill pen in ink pot, dancer, vert. 30fr, Children reading. 100fr, Architecture, women, Earth. 200fr, Artist sketching, easel, gear wheels, chemist, computer operator.

1989 ***Perf. 13x13½, 13½x13***

825 A257 5fr multicolored .25 .25
826 A257 30fr multicolored .25 .25
827 A257 100fr multicolored .80 .45
828 A257 200fr multicolored 1.75 .95
Nos. 825-828 (4) 3.05 1.90

Pottery A258

30fr, Potter, three-handled urn. 75fr, Vases. 145fr, Woman carrying pottery.

1989, Nov. 1 ***Perf. 13***

829 A258 15fr shown .25 .25
830 A258 30fr multicolored .35 .25
831 A258 75fr multicolored .65 .35
832 A258 145fr multicolored 1.25 .45
Nos. 829-832 (4) 2.50 1.30

"30," Dakar Cancel — A259

30fr, Telephone handset, map. 180fr, Map, simulated stamp, phone handset. 220fr, Telecommunications satellite, globe, map.

1989, Oct. 9 ***Perf. 13½***

833 A259 25fr multicolored .25 .25
834 A259 30fr multicolored .25 .25
835 A259 180fr multicolored 1.50 .50
836 A259 220fr multicolored 1.75 .65
Nos. 833-836 (4) 3.75 1.65

Conference of Postal and Telecommunication Administrations of West African Nations (CAPTEAO), 30th anniv.

Natl. Archives, 75th Anniv. — A260

Designs: 15fr, Stacks, postal card of 1922. 40fr, Document, 1825. 145fr, Document, Archives building. 180fr, Tome.

1989, Oct. 23 ***Perf. 11½***

837 A260 15fr multicolored .25 .25
838 A260 40fr multicolored .35 .25
839 A260 145fr multicolored 1.25 .55
840 A260 180fr multicolored 1.40 .65
Nos. 837-840 (4) 3.25 1.70

Jawarharlal Nehru, 1st Prime Minister of Independent India — A261

1989, Nov. 14 ***Perf. 13***

841 A261 220fr Portrait, vert. 1.75 .65
842 A261 410fr shown 3.75 1.40

Marine Life A262

10fr, Grapsus grapsus. 60fr, Hippocampus guttulatus. 145fr, Lepas anatifera. 220fr, Beach flea.

1989, Nov. 27

843 A262 10fr multicolored .25 .25
844 A262 60fr multicolored .85 .30
845 A262 145fr multicolored 1.75 .55
846 A262 220fr multicolored 1.90 .95
Nos. 843-846 (4) 4.75 2.05

Children's March to the Sanctuary A263

1989, Dec. 9 Litho. ***Perf. 13½***

847 A263 145fr shown 1.10 .40
848 A263 180fr Church 1.50 .60

Pilgrimage to Notre Dame de Popenguine, cent.

Birds A263a

Designs: 10fr, Phalacrocovax carbolucidus, Anhinga rufa. 45fr, Lavius cirrocephalus. 100fr, Dwarf bee-eater, Lophogetus occipitalis. 180fr, Egretta gularis.

1989, Dec. 11 ***Perf. 13***

849 A263a 10fr multicolored .35 .30
850 A263a 45fr multicolored 1.00 .40
851 A263a 100fr multicolored 2.00 .60
852 A263a 180fr multicolored 6.00 1.00
Nos. 849-852 (4) 9.35 2.30

Natl. parks: Djoudj (10fr), Langue de Barbarie (45fr), Basse Casamance (100fr) and Saloum (180fr).

Christmas — A264

1989, Dec. 22 Litho. ***Perf. 13***

853 A264 10fr shown .25 .25
854 A264 25fr Teddy bear .25 .25
855 A264 30fr Manger .25 .25
856 A264 200fr Mother and child 1.75 .80
Nos. 853-856 (4) 2.50 1.55

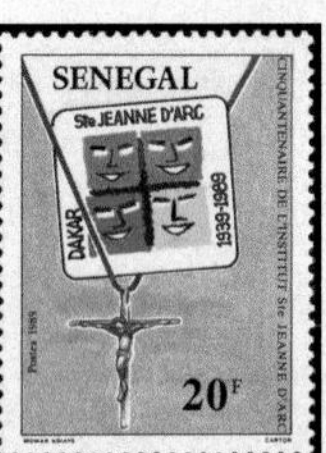

Joan of Arc Institute, 50th Anniv. — A265

1989, Dec. 26 ***Perf. 13½***

857 A265 20fr shown .25 .25
858 A265 500fr Institute 4.25 1.40

Flight of the 1st Seaplane, Mar. 28, 1910 — A266

Designs: 130fr, Seaplane, Fabre. 475fr, Fabre, schematic of aircraft, vert.

Perf. 13x12½, 12½x13

1989, Dec. 30 **Litho.**

859 A266 125fr shown 1.00 .30
860 A266 130fr multi 1.10 .40
861 A266 475fr multi 4.25 1.00
Nos. 859-861 (3) 6.35 1.70

Souvneir Sheet

862 A266 700fr like 475fr, vert. 6.00 5.00

Henri Fabre (1882-1984), aviator.

1992 Summer Olympics, Barcelona — A267

Various athletes and monuments or architecture.

1990, Jan. 8 ***Perf. 12½***

863 A267 10fr Basketball .25 .25
864 A267 130fr High jump .90 .25
865 A267 180fr Discus 1.25 .30
866 A267 190fr Running 1.50 .40
867 A267 315fr Tennis 2.25 .50
868 A267 475fr Equestrian 3.75 .60
Nos. 863-868 (6) 9.90 2.30

Souvenir Sheet

869 A267 600fr Soccer 4.50 1.00

Fight AIDS Worldwide A268

100fr, Umbrella. 145fr, Fist crushing virus. 180fr, Hammering away at virus.

1989, Dec. 1 **Litho.** ***Perf. 13½***

870 A268 5fr shown .25 .25
871 A268 100fr multicolored .90 .35
872 A268 145fr multicolored 1.10 .50
873 A268 180fr multicolored 1.50 .65
Nos. 870-873 (4) 3.75 1.75

12th Paris-Dakar Rally — A269

25fr, Motorcycle. 180fr, Trophy winner, crowd. 200fr, Thierry Sabine.

1990, Jan. 16 ***Perf. 13***

874 A269 20fr shown .25 .25
875 A269 25fr multi .25 .25
876 A269 180fr multi 1.60 .65
877 A269 200fr multi 1.60 .80
Nos. 874-877 (4) 3.70 1.95

1990 World Cup Soccer Championships, Italy — A270

Various athletes and: 45fr, Trophy, the Piazza Della Signoria, Florence. 140fr, Piazza Navona, Rome. 180fr, *The Virgin with St. Anne and the Infant Jesus,* by Leonardo da Vinci. 220fr, Portrait of Giuseppe Garibaldi (1807-1882), Risorgimento Museum, Turin. 300fr, *The Sistine Madonna,* by Raphael. 415fr, *The Virgin and Child,* by Daniele da Volterra. 700fr, Columbus Monument, Milan.

1990, Jan. 31 **Litho.** ***Perf. 13x12½***

878 A270 45fr multicolored .35 .25
879 A270 140fr multicolored 1.00 .40
880 A270 180fr multicolored 1.40 .45
881 A270 220fr multicolored 1.50 .55
882 A270 300fr multicolored 2.50 .75
883 A270 415fr multicolored 3.50 1.25
Nos. 878-883 (6) 10.25 3.65

Nos. 878-883 exist in souvenir sheets of 1.

Souvenir Sheet

884 A270 700fr multicolored 6.00 3.00

1990 African Soccer Cup Championships, Algeria — A271

Designs: 60fr, Goalie. 100fr, Exchange of flags. 500fr, Ball, trophy.

1990, Mar. 2 **Litho.** ***Perf. 13***

885 A271 20fr shown .25 .25
886 A271 60fr multi .55 .25
887 A271 100fr multi .90 .40
888 A271 500fr multi 4.50 1.75
Nos. 885-888 (4) 6.20 2.65

Postal Services A272

5fr, Facsimile transmission. 15fr, Express mail. 100fr, Postal money orders. 180fr, CNE.

1990, Apr. 30 **Litho.** ***Perf. 13***

889 A272 5fr multicolored .25 .25
890 A272 15fr multicolored .25 .25
891 A272 100fr multicolored .75 .30
892 A272 180fr multicolored 1.25 .50
Nos. 889-892 (4) 2.50 1.30

Multinational Postal School, 20th Anniv. — A273

180fr, Hand, wreath, envelope.

1990, May 31 ***Perf. 13½***

893 A273 145fr shown 1.25 .45
894 A273 180fr multicolored 1.50 .75

A274

1990, May 31

895 A274 5fr shown .25 .25
896 A274 500fr Family 3.75 1.25

S.O.S. Children's Village appeal for aid.

Boy Scouts A275

Scouting emblems and: 30fr, Camping. 100fr, Hiking at lakeshore. 145fr, Following trail. 200fr, Scout, vert.

1990, Nov. 5 **Litho.** ***Perf. 11½***

897 A275 30fr multicolored .25 .25
898 A275 100fr multicolored .70 .30
899 A275 145fr multicolored 1.00 .50
900 A275 200fr multicolored 1.60 .60
Nos. 897-900 (4) 3.55 1.65

Medicinal Plants — A276

95fr, Cassia tora. 105fr, Tamarindus indica. 125fr, Cassia occidentalis. 175fr, Leptadenia hastata.

1990, Nov. 30 ***Perf. 13x13½***

901 A276 95fr multi 1.00 .40
902 A276 105fr multi 1.10 .45
903 A276 125fr multi 1.40 .55
904 A276 175fr multi 1.75 .65
Nos. 901-904 (4) 5.25 2.05

Christmas A277

145fr, Angel, stars, people. 180fr, Adoration of the Magi. 200fr, Animals, baby in manger.

1990, Dec. 24 **Litho.** ***Perf. 13½***

905 A277 25fr multi .25 .25
906 A277 145fr multi 1.25 .65
907 A277 180fr multi 1.60 .65
908 A277 200fr multi 1.75 .65
Nos. 905-908 (4) 4.85 2.20

A278

1991, Jan. 2 **Litho.** ***Perf. 13x12½***

909 A278 180fr multicolored 1.50 .65

Intl. Red Cross, 125th Anniv., Senegalese Red Cross, 25th anniv. No. 909 inscribed 1988.

Paris-Dakar Rally — A279

125fr, Car, motorcycle. 180fr, Car racing in water. 220fr, Two motorcycles, beach.

1991, Jan. 17

910 A279 15fr shown .25 .25
911 A279 125fr multicolored .90 .40
912 A279 180fr multicolored 1.50 .65
913 A279 220fr multicolored 2.00 .85
Nos. 910-913 (4) 4.65 2.15

Reptiles A280

15fr, Python sebae. 60fr, Chelonia mydas. 100fr, Crocolylus niloticus. 180fr, Chameleo senegalensis.

1991, Jan. 31 ***Perf. 13½x13***

914 A280 15fr multicolored .25 .25
915 A280 60fr multicolored .90 .25
916 A280 100fr multicolored 1.50 .50
917 A280 180fr multicolored 2.50 .85
Nos. 914-917 (4) 5.15 1.85

Inscribed 1990.

African Film Festival A281

Designs: 30fr, Sphinx, slave house, cave paintings, tomb of Mohammed. 60fr, Dogon mask, mosque of Dioulasso, drawing of Osiris, man on camel. 100fr, Ruins, drum, statue of scribe, camels. 180fr, mask, mosque of Djenne, pyramids, Moroccan architecture.

1991, Feb. 23 ***Perf. 11½***

918 A281 30fr org & multi .25 .25
919 A281 60fr org & multi .50 .25
920 A281 100fr org & multi 1.00 .45
921 A281 180fr org & multi 1.75 .65
Nos. 918-921 (4) 3.50 1.60

Alfred Nobel (1833-1896), Industrialist — A282

Designs: 145fr, Drawing of Nobel.

1991, Mar. 29 Litho. *Die Cut*
Self-adhesive
922 A282 145fr multi, vert. 2.00 .65
923 A282 180fr shown 2.50 .85

Antelope — A283

Designs: 5fr, Ouerbia ourebi. 10fr, Gazella dorcas. 180fr, Kobos kob kob. 555fr, Alcelaphus bucelaphus major.

1991, Apr. 24 Litho. *Perf. 13½x13*
924 A283 5fr multi .25 .25
925 A283 10fr multi .25 .25
926 A283 180fr multi 1.40 .60
927 A283 555fr multi 5.00 2.00
Nos. 924-927 (4) 6.90 3.10

Trees A284

90fr, Ancardium occidentalus. 100fr, Mangifera indica. 125fr, Borassus flabellifer, vert. 145fr, Elaeis guineensis, vert.

1991, May 30 *Perf. 13½x13, 13x13½*
928 A284 90fr multicolored .75 .40
929 A284 100fr multicolored 1.00 .50
930 A284 125fr multicolored 1.00 .50
931 A284 145fr multicolored 1.25 .60
Nos. 928-931 (4) 4.00 2.00

Christopher Columbus — A285

100fr, Meeting Haitian natives. 145fr, Columbus' personal coat of arms, vert. 180fr, Santa Maria, Columbus. 200fr, 220fr, Columbus, ships. 500fr, Details of voyages. 625fr, Columbus at chart table.

1991, July 8 Litho. *Perf. 13*
932 A285 100fr multicolored .90 .40
a. Sheet of 1, perf. 12½ .90 .40
933 A285 145fr multicolored 1.25 .55
a. Sheet of 1, perf. 12½ 1.25 .60
934 A285 180fr multicolored 1.60 .65
a. Sheet of 1, perf. 12½ 1.75 .75
935 A285 200fr multicolored 1.75 .75
a. Sheet of 1, perf. 12½ 1.75 .75
936 A285 220fr multicolored 2.00 .80
a. Sheet of 1, perf. 12½ 2.00 .80
937 A285 500fr multicolored 4.50 1.90
a. Sheet of 1, perf. 12½ 4.50 2.00
938 A285 625fr multicolored 5.75 2.25
a. Sheet of 1, perf. 12½ 5.75 2.50
Nos. 932-938 (7) 17.75 7.30

Tourism A286

Designs: 10fr, Canoe excursion, Basse-Casamance. 25fr, Shore at Boufflers Hotel, Goree Island. 30fr, Huts built on stilts, Fadiouth Island. 40fr, Salt collecting on lake.

1991, July 30 Litho. *Perf. 13*
939 A286 10fr multicolored .25 .25
940 A286 25fr multicolored .25 .25
941 A286 30fr multicolored .35 .25
942 A286 40fr multicolored .35 .25
Nos. 939-942 (4) 1.20 1.00

Dated 1989.

Louis Armstrong, Jazz Musician, 20th Death Anniv. — A287

1991, Oct. 7 *Perf. 13½*
943 A287 10fr shown .25 .25
944 A287 145fr Singing 1.25 .60
945 A287 180fr With trumpets 1.50 .75
946 A287 220fr Playing trumpet 1.75 .90
Nos. 943-946 (4) 4.75 2.50

Yuri Gagarin, First Man in Space, 30th Anniv. — A288

Various portraits of Gagarin with Vostok I in Earth orbit.

1991, Nov. 25 Litho. *Perf. 13½*
947 A288 15fr multicolored .25 .25
948 A288 145fr multicolored 1.25 .60
949 A288 180fr multicolored 1.50 .75
950 A288 220fr multicolored 1.75 .90
Nos. 947-950 (4) 4.75 2.50

Rural Water Supply Project — A289

30fr, Bowl of water. 145fr, Water faucet, huts. 180fr, Dripping faucet, flags. 220fr, Water tower, huts.

1991, Dec. 2 Litho. *Perf. 13½*
951 A289 30fr multicolored .25 .25
952 A289 145fr multicolored 1.25 .65
953 A289 180fr multicolored 1.60 .80
954 A289 220fr multicolored 1.90 .95
Nos. 951-954 (4) 5.00 2.65

6th Islamic Summit — A290

145fr, Upraised hands. 180fr, Congress Center, Dakar. 220fr, Grand Mosque, Dakar.

1991, Dec. 9
955 A290 15fr shown .25 .25
956 A290 145fr multicolored 1.25 .65
957 A290 180fr multicolored 1.60 .80
958 A290 220fr multicolored 1.90 .95
Nos. 955-958 (4) 5.00 2.65

Basketball, Cent. — A291

145fr, Player dribbling ball. 180fr, Couple holding trophy. 220fr, Lion, basketball, trophies.

1991, Dec. 21 Litho. *Perf. 13½*
959 A291 125fr multicolored 1.00 .50
960 A291 145fr multicolored 1.25 .60
961 A291 180fr multicolored 1.50 .75
962 A291 220fr multicolored 1.75 .90
Nos. 959-962 (4) 5.50 2.75

Christmas A292

5fr, Jesus. 145fr, Madonna and Child. 160fr, Angels. 220fr, Christ Child, animals.

1991, Dec. 24 Litho. *Perf. 13½*
963 A292 5fr multicolored .25 .25
964 A292 145fr multicolored 1.25 .60
965 A292 160fr multicolored 1.40 .70
966 A292 220fr multicolored 1.90 .95
Nos. 963-966 (4) 4.80 2.50

For surcharge see No. 975.

A293

Musical score and: 5fr, Bust of Mozart. 150fr, Mozart conducting. 180fr, Mozart at piano. 220fr, Portrait.

1991, Dec. 31
967 A293 5fr multicolored .25 .25
968 A293 150fr multicolored 1.25 .65
969 A293 180fr multicolored 1.60 .80
970 A293 220fr multicolored 1.90 .95
Nos. 967-970 (4) 5.00 2.65

Wolfgang Amadeus Mozart, death bicent.

A293a

Mermoz and: 145fr, Outline maps of South America, Africa. 180fr, Airplane. 200fr, Aiplane in flight.

1991? Litho. *Perf. 13½*
970A A293a 15fr multicolored .25 .25
970B A293a 145fr multicolored 1.00 .35
970C A293a 180fr multicolored 1.50 .35
970D A293a 200fr multicolored 2.00 .65
Nos. 970A-970D (4) 4.75 1.60

Jean Mermoz (1901-36), pilot.
Nos. 970A-970D exist in imperf. souvenir sheets of 1.

A294

1992, Jan. 12 Litho. *Perf. 13½*
971 A294 10fr shown .25 .25
972 A294 145fr Map, soccer balls 1.25 .60
973 A294 200fr Lion, trophy 1.60 .85
974 A294 220fr Players 1.75 .90
Nos. 971-974 (4) 4.85 2.60

18th African Soccer Cup Championships.

No. 965 Surcharged

1992, Feb. 19 Litho. *Perf. 13½*
975 A292 180fr on 160fr 2.00 1.00

Natl. Parks A295

10fr, Delta Du Saloum. 125fr, Djoudj. 145fr, Niokolo-Koba. 220fr, Basse Casamance.

1992, Mar. 20 *Perf. 13½x13*
976 A295 10fr multi .45 .25
977 A295 125fr multi 1.60 .50
978 A295 145fr multi 2.25 .60
979 A295 220fr multi 2.75 .90
Nos. 976-979 (4) 7.05 2.25

Senegal's Participation in Gulf War — A296

Designs: 30fr, Oil wells, flag and missiles. 145fr, Oil wells, soldier. 180fr, Holy Ka'aba, soldier with gun. 220fr, Peace dove with flag, map.

1992, Apr. 4 *Perf. 13½*
980 A296 30fr multicolored .25 .25
981 A296 145fr multicolored 1.25 .60
982 A296 180fr multicolored 1.50 .75
983 A296 220fr multicolored 1.75 .90
Nos. 980-983 (4) 4.75 2.50

Fish Industry A297

Stylized designs: 5fr, Catching fish. 60fr, Retail outlets. 100fr, Processing plant. 150fr, Packaging.

1992, Apr. 6 Litho. *Perf. 13½*
984 A297 5fr multicolored .25 .25
985 A297 60fr multicolored .55 .30
986 A297 100fr multicolored .90 .45
987 A297 150fr multicolored 1.25 .65
Nos. 984-987 (4) 2.95 1.65

Tourism — A298

Designs: 5fr, Niokolo complex. 10fr, Casamance River. 150fr, Dakar region. 200fr, Saint-Louis excursion.

1992, May 5 *Perf. 13½x13*

988	A298	5fr multi	.25	.25
989	A298	10fr multi	.25	.25
990	A298	150fr multi	1.25	.65
991	A298	200fr multi	1.75	.95
		Nos. 988-991 (4)	3.50	2.10

Planting Trees A299

Various designs showing children planting trees.

1992, May 29 *Perf. 13½x13, 13x13½*

992	A299	145fr multi	1.25	.65
993	A299	180fr multi	1.60	.80
994	A299	200fr multi	1.75	.90
995	A299	220fr multi, vert.	1.90	.95
		Nos. 992-995 (4)	6.50	3.30

Public Works Projects A300

Various scenes of people cleaning and repairing public walkways.

Perf. 13½x13, 13x13½

1992, June 1 **Litho.**

996	A300	25fr multi	.25	.25
997	A300	145fr multi	1.25	.65
998	A300	180fr multi, vert.	1.60	.80
999	A300	220fr multi, vert.	2.00	1.00
		Nos. 996-999 (4)	5.10	2.70

Children's Rights — A301

1992, June 12 *Perf. 13*

1000	A301	20fr Education	.25	.25
1001	A301	45fr Guidance	.40	.25
1002	A301	165fr Instruction	1.40	.70
1003	A301	180fr Health care	1.60	.80
		Nos. 1000-1003 (4)	3.65	2.00

African Integration A302

Designs: 10fr, Free trade. 30fr, Youth activities. 145fr, Communications. 220fr, Women's movements.

1992, June 29 **Litho.** *Perf. 13*

1004	A302	10fr multi	.25	.25
1005	A302	30fr multi	.25	.25
1006	A302	145fr multi	1.25	.60
1007	A302	220fr multi	2.00	1.00
		Nos. 1004-1007 (4)	3.75	2.10

1992 Summer Olympics, Barcelona A303

1992, July 25 **Litho.** *Perf. 13½*

1008	A303	145fr Map, horiz.	1.10	.55
1009	A303	180fr Runner	1.50	.70
1010	A303	200fr Sprinter, horiz.	2.00	.75
1011	A303	300fr Torch bearer	2.75	1.10
		Nos. 1008-1011 (4)	7.35	3.10

Blue Train — A304

Designs: 145fr, Train yard. 200fr, Train, passengers. 220fr, Station.

1992, Aug. 3

1012	A304	70fr shown	.70	.30
1013	A304	145fr multi	1.40	.55
1014	A304	200fr multi	2.00	.75
1015	A304	220fr multi	2.10	.85
		Nos. 1012-1015 (4)	6.20	2.45

Intl. Maritime Heritage Year — A305

25fr, Map of Antarctica. 100fr, Ocean, sea life. 180fr, Man addressing UN. 220fr, Hands holding globe, flags, ship, fish.

1992, Sept. 4

1016	A305	25fr multi, horiz.	.25	.25
1017	A305	100fr multi	1.00	.40
1018	A305	180fr multi	2.00	.70
1019	A305	220fr multi	2.25	.85
		Nos. 1016-1019 (4)	5.50	2.20

Corals A306

Various coral formations.

Perf. 13½x13, 13x13½

1992, Sept. 18 **Litho.**

1020	A306	50fr multicolored	.40	.25
1021	A306	100fr multicolored	1.10	.40
1022	A306	145fr multi, vert.	1.50	1.10
1023	A306	220fr multicolored	2.25	.90
		Nos. 1020-1023 (4)	5.25	2.65

Konrad Adenauer (1876-1967) — A307

Designs: 5fr, Portrait, vert. 145fr, Schaumburg Palace, Bonn. 180fr, Hands clasped. 220fr, Map of West Germany.

Perf. 13x13½, 13½x13

1992, Sept. 30 **Litho.**

1024	A307	5fr multicolored	.25	.25
1025	A307	145fr multicolored	1.25	.60
1026	A307	180fr multicolored	1.50	.75
1027	A307	220fr multicolored	1.75	.90
		Nos. 1024-1027 (4)	4.75	2.50

Shellfish — A308

1992, Oct. 1 **Litho.** *Perf. 13½*

1028	A308	20fr Crab	.25	.25
1029	A308	30fr Spider crab	.35	.25
1030	A308	180fr Lobster	1.75	.70
1031	A308	200fr Shrimp	2.10	.75
		Nos. 1028-1031 (4)	4.45	1.95

Fruit-bearing Plants — A309

10fr, Parkia biglobosa. 50fr, Balanites aegyptiaca. 200fr, Parinari macrophylla. 220fr, Opuntiatuna.

1992, Oct. 16 **Litho.** *Perf. 13x13½*

1032	A309	10fr multicolored	.25	.25
1033	A309	50fr multicolored	.45	.25
1034	A309	200fr multicolored	1.60	.70
1035	A309	220fr multicolored	1.75	.90
		Nos. 1032-1035 (4)	4.05	2.10

John Glenn's Orbital Flight, 30th Anniv. — A310

15fr, Astronaut in spacesuit, flag, map, spacecraft, horiz. 145fr, American flag, Glenn, horiz. 180fr, Flag, lift-off of rocket, Glenn in spacesuit, horiz. 200fr, Astronaut in spacesuit, spacecraft.

1992, Nov. 30 **Litho.** *Perf. 13½*

1036	A310	15fr multicolored	.25	.25
1037	A310	145fr multicolored	1.25	.60
1038	A310	180fr multicolored	1.60	.70
1039	A310	200fr multicolored	1.75	.80
		Nos. 1036-1039 (4)	4.85	2.35

Maps Featuring Bakari II — A311

100fr, Map from Spanish Atlas, 1375. 145fr, Stone head, Vera Cruz, Mexico, world map, 1413.

1992, Dec. 2 *Perf. 13*

1040	A311	100fr multicolored	1.50	.40
1041	A311	145fr multicolored	2.25	.60

No. 1041 issued only with black bar obliterating "Mecades."

Biennial of Dakar — A312

20fr, Picture frame. 50fr, Puppet head, stage. 145fr, Open book. 220fr, Musical instrument.

1992, Dec. 14 *Perf. 13½*

1042	A312	20fr multicolored	.25	.25
1043	A312	50fr multicolored	.45	.25
1044	A312	145fr multicolored	1.25	.60
1045	A312	220fr multicolored	2.10	.90
		Nos. 1042-1045 (4)	4.05	2.00

Christmas A313

Designs: 15fr, Children dancing around large ornament, horiz. 145fr, Christmas tree. 180fr, Jesus Christ. 200fr, Santa Claus.

1992, Dec. 24 *Perf. 13½*

1046	A313	15fr multicolored	.25	.25
1047	A313	145fr multicolored	2.00	.60
1048	A313	180fr multicolored	2.50	.70
1049	A313	200fr multicolored	2.75	.90
		Nos. 1046-1049 (4)	7.50	2.45

Nos. 770, 804 Srchd. in Red

1993, Jan. 17 **Litho.** *Perf. 13½*

1050	A251	145fr on 180fr #804	1.75	1.00

Perf. 13

1051	A241	220fr on 410fr #770	2.75	1.25

Size and location of surcharge varies.

Environmental Protection — A314

Accident Prevention A315

Designs: 20fr, Medical clinic. 25fr, Preventing industrial accidents. 145fr, Preventing chemical spills. 200fr, Red Cross helicopter, airline crash.

Perf. 13 (#1052, 1055), 13½

1993, Mar. 22 **Litho.**

1052	A314	20fr multicolored	.25	.25
1053	A315	25fr multicolored	.25	.25
1054	A315	145fr multicolored	1.10	.60
1055	A314	200fr multicolored	1.60	.80
		Nos. 1052-1055 (4)	3.20	1.90

Abdoulaye Seck Marie Parsine (1873-1931), PTT Director — A316

1993, Apr. 21 **Litho.** ***Perf. 13½***
1056 A316 220fr multicolored 2.10 .90

Wild Animals A317

30fr, Crocuta crocuta. 50fr, Panthera leo. 70fr, Panthera pardus. 150fr, Giraffa camelopardalis peratta, vert. 180fr, Cervus.

1993, Nov. 26 **Litho.** ***Perf. 13½***
1057 A317 30fr multicolored .25 .25
1058 A317 50fr multicolored .25 .25
1059 A317 70fr multicolored .55 .25
1060 A317 150fr multicolored 1.00 .30
1061 A317 180fr multicolored 1.60 .35
Nos. 1057-1061 (5) 3.65 1.40

Christmas A318

Designs: 80fr, Two children seated by Christmas tree. 145fr, Santa holding presents, three children. 150fr, Girl, Santa with present.

1993, Dec. 24 **Litho.** ***Perf. 13x13½***
1062 A318 5fr multicolored .25 .25
1063 A318 80fr multicolored .30 .25
1064 A318 145fr multicolored .55 .30
1065 A318 150fr multicolored .60 .30
Nos. 1062-1065 (4) 1.70 1.10

Paris-Dakar Rally, 16th Anniv. — A319

Designs: 145fr, Truck, car, motorcycle racing by tree. 180fr, Racing through desert, men with camel. 220fr, Car, truck, village.

1994, Jan. 5 ***Perf. 13½***
1066 A319 145fr multicolored .70 .30
1067 A319 180fr multicolored .90 .35
1068 A319 220fr multicolored 1.00 .45
Nos. 1066-1068 (3) 2.60 1.10

Assassination of John F. Kennedy, 30th Anniv. — A320

555fr, Kennedy, White House.

1993, Dec. 31 **Litho.** ***Perf. 13***
1069 A320 80fr shown .30 .25
1070 A320 555fr multi 2.25 1.10

Fishing Industry A321

5fr, Drying eels. 90fr, Sifting for shellfish. 100fr, Salting fish. 200fr, Cooking fish.

1994, Feb. 28
1071 A321 5fr multicolored .25 .25
1072 A321 90fr multicolored .35 .25
1073 A321 100fr multicolored .40 .25
1074 A321 200fr multicolored .80 .40
Nos. 1071-1074 (4) 1.80 1.15

Flowers — A321a

Design: 80fr, Gloriosa superba. 100fr, Erythrina senegalensis. 145fr, Spathodea campanulata. 220fr, Hibiscus rosa-sinensis. 250fr, Satanocrater berhautii.

Perf. 13¼x13½
1994, Feb. 28 **Litho.**
1074A A321a 80fr multi *4.00* —
1074B A321a 100fr multi *5.00* —
1074C A321a 145fr multi *7.25* —
1074D A321a 220fr multi — —
1074E A321a 250fr multi *11.00* —

Dated 1993.

Conservation of the Seashore — A322

Stylized designs: 5fr, Halting removal of sand. 75fr, Fight against drifting sand dunes. 100fr, Dams, dikes against beach erosion. 200fr, Healthy, aesthetic environment.

1994, Mar. 7
1075 A322 5fr multicolored .25 .25
1076 A322 75fr multicolored .30 .25
1077 A322 100fr multicolored .55 .40
1078 A322 200fr multicolored .80 .60
Nos. 1075-1078 (4) 1.90 1.50

Save the Elephant A323

60fr, Elephant in "SOS". 90fr, Elephants forming "SOS". 145fr, Elephant, tusks.

1994, Apr. 18
1079 A323 30fr shown .25 .25
1080 A323 60fr multicolored .65 .25
1081 A323 90fr multicolored 1.25 .45
1082 A323 145fr multicolored 1.60 .50
Nos. 1079-1082 (4) 3.75 1.45

Arrival of Portuguese in Senegal, 550th Anniv. A324

1994, Nov. 17 **Litho.** ***Perf. 12***
1083 A324 175fr multicolored .80 .40

See Portugal No. 2036.

Shells — A325

20fr, Murex saxatilis, horiz. 45fr, Nerita senegalensis. 75fr, Polymita picea, horiz. 175fr, Scalaria pretiosa. 215fr, Conus gloria maris.

1994, Oct. 3 **Litho.** ***Perf. 13½***
1084 A325 20fr multicolored .25 .25
1085 A325 45fr multicolored .25 .25
1086 A325 75fr multicolored .30 .25
1087 A325 175fr multicolored .75 .40
1088 A325 215fr multicolored .95 .50
Nos. 1084-1088 (5) 2.50 1.65

Intl. Olympic Committee, Cent. — A326

1994, Nov. 4
1089 A326 175fr multi, horiz. .75 .40
1090 A326 215fr multi, horiz. .95 .50
1091 A326 275fr multicolored 1.25 .60
1092 A326 290fr multi, diff. 1.25 .65
Nos. 1089-1092 (4) 4.20 2.15

Wild Animals A327

60fr, Canis aureus. 70fr, Aonyx capensis. 100fr, Herpestes ichneumon. 175fr, Manis gigantea. 215fr, Varanus niloticus.

1994, Oct. 28 **Litho.** ***Perf. 13½***
1093 A327 60fr multicolored .30 .25
1094 A327 70fr multicolored .30 .25
1095 A327 100fr multicolored .45 .25
1096 A327 175fr multicolored .75 .40
1097 A327 215fr multicolored .95 .45
Nos. 1093-1097 (5) 2.75 1.60

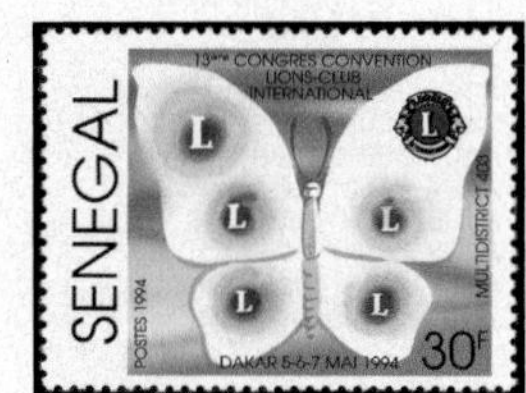

Lions Club Intl., 13th Multidistrict Convention, Dakar — A328

60fr, Emblem, butterfly. 175fr, Emblem, "L's". 215fr, Colors, emblem.

1994, May 5 **Litho.** ***Perf. 13½x13***
1098 A328 30fr shown .25 .25
1099 A328 60fr multi .30 .25
1100 A328 175fr multi .85 .40
1101 A328 215fr multi 1.00 .50
Nos. 1098-1101 (4) 2.40 1.40

African Children's Day A329

UNICEF emblem and: 175fr, Children playing. 215fr, Family, huts.

1994, June 16 **Litho.** ***Perf. 13½***
1102 A329 175fr multicolored 2.00 .40
1103 A329 215fr multicolored 2.25 .50

1994 World Cup Soccer Championships, US — A330

Designs: 45fr, Flags of participants, soccer ball, vert. 175fr, Top of globe, bottom of soccer ball, vert. 215fr, Player. 665fr, Two players.

1994, June 17
1104 A330 45fr multicolored .25 .25
1105 A330 175fr multicolored .80 .40
1106 A330 215fr multicolored 1.00 .50
1107 A330 665fr multicolored 3.00 1.50
Nos. 1104-1107 (4) 5.05 2.65

UPU Congress, Seoul — A331

Designs: 10fr, Rainbow. 175fr, Dove with wings like postage stamp. 300fr, 260fr, Stylized stamp. Stylized globe, air mail envelope, hands.

1994, Aug. 16 **Litho.** ***Perf. 13½x13***
1108 A331 10fr multicolored .30 .25
1109 A331 175fr multicolored 1.50 1.00
1110 A331 260fr multicolored 2.00 1.10
1111 A331 300fr multicolored 2.25 1.25

Intl. Year of the Family A333

UN emblem and: 5fr, People of different races, national flags, peace dove, globe, sun. 175fr, Globe, flags, people. 215fr, Globe, mother & child. 290fr, Buildings, family, dove, sun, globe.

1994, Aug. 19 ***Perf. 13½x13***
1113 A333 5fr multicolored .25 .25
1114 A333 175fr multicolored .80 .40
1115 A333 215fr multicolored 1.00 .50
1116 A333 290fr multicolored 1.40 .70
Nos. 1113-1116 (4) 3.45 1.85

10th Toulouse to Saint-Louis Air Rally — A334

1994, Apr. 10 ***Perf. 13½***

1117 A334 100fr Breguet 14 .50 .25
1118 A334 145fr Guillaumet .65 .35
1119 A334 180fr Jean Mermoz .85 .40
1120 A334 220fr Saint-Exupery 1.00 .50
Nos. 1117-1120 (4) 3.00 1.50

Dated 1993.

Christmas — A335

175fr, Santa Claus, Christ, children, presents. 215fr, Christmas trees, religious scenes. 275fr, Magi, Christ Child. 290fr, Madonna & Child.

Perf. 13x13½, 13½x13
1994, Nov. 24

1121 A335 175fr multi, vert. .80 .40
1122 A335 215fr multi, vert. 1.00 .50
1123 A335 275fr multi 1.25 .65
1124 A335 290fr multi, vert. 1.40 .70
Nos. 1121-1124 (4) 4.45 2.25

Historical Sites — A336

Designs: 100fr, Goree Chateau. 175fr, Soudan Mansion. 215fr, Goree Island. 275fr, Pinet Laprade fort, Sedhiou.

1994, Mar. 20 **Litho.** ***Perf. 13½x13***

1125 A336 100fr multicolored .45 .25
1126 A336 175fr multicolored .80 .40
1127 A336 215fr multicolored 1.00 .50
1128 A336 275fr multicolored 1.25 .65
Nos. 1125-1128 (4) 3.50 1.80

Kallisaye Natl. Park A337

Water birds: 100fr, Ardea melanocephala, vert. 275fr, Sterna caspia, vert. 290fr, Egretta gularis, vert. 380fr, Pelecanus rufescens.

1995, Feb. 2 ***Perf. 13½***

1129 A337 100fr multicolored .50 .25
1130 A337 275fr multicolored 1.40 .70
1131 A337 290fr multicolored 1.60 .75
1132 A337 380fr multicolored 2.00 .95
Nos. 1129-1132 (4) 5.50 2.65

Dinosaurs A338

1995, Jan. 27

1133 A338 100fr Diplodocus .45 .25
1134 A338 175fr Brontosaurus .75 .40
1135 A338 215fr Triceratops 1.00 .50
1136 A338 290fr Stegosaurus 1.75 .70
1137 A338 300fr Tyrannosaurus 2.50 1.00
Nos. 1133-1137 (5) 6.45 2.85

Flowers — A340

Designs: 30fr, Bombax costatum. 75fr, Allamanda cathartica. 100fr, Catharantus roseus. 1000fr, Clerodendron speciossimum.

1995, Apr. 9

1139 A340 30fr multicolored .25 .25
1140 A340 75fr multicolored .40 .25
1141 A340 100fr multicolored .50 .25
1142 A340 1000fr multicolored 5.00 2.50
Nos. 1139-1142 (4) 6.15 3.25

A341

1995, May 11 **Litho.** ***Perf. 11½***

1143 A341 260fr shown 1.25 .65
1144 A341 275fr Emblem, dove 1.40 .70

District 9100 Conference of Rotary, Intl.

A342

Map of Africa with countries highlighted, native item or animal: 10fr, Sudan, musical instrument. 15fr, Dahomey (Benin), huts, canoes. 30fr, Ivory Coast, elephant. 70fr, Mauritania, camel. 175fr, Guinea, string instrument, bananas. 180fr, Upper Volta (Burkina Faso), ox, vegetables, drum. 215fr, Niger, Cross of Agadès. 225fr, Senegal, lions.

1995, June 17

1145 A342 10fr multicolored .25 .25
1146 A342 15fr multicolored .25 .25
1147 A342 30fr multicolored .25 .25
1148 A342 70fr multicolored .35 .25
1149 A342 175fr multicolored .90 .45
1150 A342 180fr multicolored .95 .45
1151 A342 215fr multicolored 1.10 .55
1152 A342 225fr multicolored 1.25 .60
Nos. 1145-1152 (8) 5.30 3.05

Fashion Type of 1972

1995, June 30 ***Perf. 13½x13***

Size: 21x26mm

1153 A106 5fr yel brown .25 .25
1154 A106 10fr bright green .25 .25
1155 A106 20fr henna brown .25 .25
1156 A106 25fr olive .25 .25
1157 A106 30fr light olive .25 .25
1158 A106 40fr yellow green .25 .25
1159 A106 100fr slate blue .50 .25
1160 A106 150fr deep blue .75 .35
1161 A106 175fr dull brown .90 .45
1162 A106 200fr black 1.00 .50
1163 A106 250fr red 1.25 .60
1164 A106 275fr rose carmine 1.40 .80
Nos. 1153-1164 (12) 7.30 4.45

Economic Community of West African States (ECOWAS), 20th Anniv. — A343

Designs: 175fr, Satellite dish, telephone, computer, map, dam, vert. 215fr, Flags of member nations, fruits, vegetables.

1995, Sept. 11 **Litho.** ***Perf. 13½***

1165 A343 175fr multicolored .90 .45
1166 A343 215fr multicolored 1.10 .55

Louis Pasteur (1822-95) — A345

275fr, Holding vial. 500fr, In laboratory.

1995, Sept. 28 **Litho.** ***Perf. 11½***

1168 A345 275fr multicolored 1.25 .60
1169 A345 500fr multicolored 2.25 1.25

Motion Pictures, Cent. A346

Early developments by Lumiere Brothers: 100fr, Scene from "The Water Sprinkler." 200fr, First pulbic showing of motion picture. 250fr, Auguste, Louis Lumiere watching picture of train arriving at station. 275fr, Demonstrating cinematography.

1995, Oct. 2 ***Perf. 13½***

1170 A346 100fr multicolored .45 .25
1171 A346 200fr multicolored 1.00 .45
1172 A346 250fr multicolored 1.25 .55
1173 A346 275fr multicolored 1.75 .70
Nos. 1170-1173 (4) 4.45 1.95

FAO, 50th Anniv. A347

Designs: 175fr, Farmer, oxen. 215fr, Technician, bringing water to arid regions. 260fr, Gathering fish. 275fr, Nutrition of infants.

1995, Oct. 16

1174 A347 175fr multicolored .80 .40
1175 A347 215fr multicolored .95 .50
1176 A347 260fr multicolored 1.10 .55
1177 A347 275fr multicolored 1.25 .60
Nos. 1174-1177 (4) 4.10 2.05

UN, 50th Anniv. — A348

1995, Oct. 24 ***Perf. 11½***

1178 A348 275fr shown 1.25 .60
1179 A348 1000fr Building 4.25 2.00

A349

1995, Nov. 2

1180 A349 150fr shown .70 .35
1181 A349 500fr Contestants 2.25 1.10

La Francophonie, 25th anniv.

Wild Animals — A350

Designs: a, 90fr, Syncerus nanus savanensis. b, 150fr, Phacochoerus aethiopicus. c, 175fr, Tragelaphus scriptus. d, 275fr, Goechelone sulcata. e, 300fr, Hystrix cristata.

1995, Nov. 13 ***Perf. 13½***

1182 A350 Strip of 5, #a.-e. 5.75 5.75

Endangered Birds — A351

90fr, Hydroprogne caspia. 145fr, Gelochelidon nilotica. 150fr, Sterna maxima. 180fr, Sterna hirunda.

1995, Nov. 30 ***Perf. 13½x13***

1183 A351 90fr multicolored .45 .25
1184 A351 145fr multicolored .80 .30
1185 A351 150fr multicolored 1.40 .35
1186 A351 180fr multicolored 1.75 .55
Nos. 1183-1186 (4) 4.40 1.45

Butterflies A352

Designs: 45fr, Meganostoma eurydice. 100fr, Luehdorfia japonica. 200fr, Hebomoia glaucippe. 220fr, Aglais urticae.

1995, Dec. 4 ***Perf. 13***

1187 A352 45fr multicolored .40 .25
1188 A352 100fr multicolored .80 .30
1189 A352 200fr multicolored 1.90 .50
1190 A352 220fr multicolored 2.25 .80
Nos. 1187-1190 (4) 5.35 1.85

Tourism A353

1995, Dec. 28 ***Perf. 13½***

1191 A353 100fr Bassari Festival .45 .25
1192 A353 175fr Baawnaan, vert. .80 .40
1193 A353 220fr Traditional huts 1.00 .50
1194 A353 500fr Turu 2.25 1.10
Nos. 1191-1194 (4) 4.50 2.25

No. 770 Surcharged

1995 ? Litho. *Perf. 13*

1194A	A241	275fr on 410fr #770		—

A354

Paris-Granada-Dakar Rally, 17th Anniv.: 215fr, Car, silhouettes of three people. 275fr, Man racing on motorcycle, vert. 290fr, Car under Eiffel Tower, car racing toward finish line. 665fr, Two cars going over hill.

1996, Jan. 16 Litho. *Perf. 11½*

1195 A354	215fr multicolored	1.10	.60
1196 A354	275fr multicolored	1.50	.75
1197 A354	290fr multicolored	1.60	.80
1198 A354	665fr multicolored	3.50	1.75
	Nos. 1195-1198 (4)	7.70	3.90

A355

Flowers: 175fr, Gossypium barbadense. 275fr, Hibiscus sabdariffa. 290fr, Hibiscus asper. 500fr, Nymphaea lotus.

1996, Feb.2

1199 A355	175fr multicolored	.95	.45
1200 A355	275fr multicolored	1.50	.75
1201 A355	290fr multicolored	1.60	.80
1202 A355	500fr multicolored	2.75	1.40
	Nos. 1199-1202 (4)	6.80	3.40

Sports A356

1996, Mar. 29 Litho. *Perf. 11½*

1203 A356	125fr Boxing	.65	.35
1204 A356	215fr Judo	1.10	.60
1205 A356	275fr Javelin	1.50	.75
1206 A356	320fr Discus	1.75	.90
	Nos. 1203-1206 (4)	5.00	2.60

Art by Serge Correa, Hall of Pearls A357

1996,Apr. 18

1207 A357	260fr Corridor 1	1.25	.70
1208 A357	320fr Symphony 1	1.75	.85

National Parks A358

Designs: 175fr, Dolphin, flamingo, heron, Saloum Delta. 200fr, Chimpanzee, giraffe, elephant, Niokolo-Koba. 220fr, Crustaceans, bird in cave, Madeleine Island. 275fr, Abyssinia hornbill, crocodile, hippopotamus, Basse Casamance.

1996, Mar. 4

1209 A358	175fr multicolored	.95	.50
1210 A358	200fr multicolored	1.10	.55
1211 A358	220fr multicolored	1.25	.60
1212 A358	275fr multicolored	1.50	.75
	Nos. 1209-1212 (4)	4.80	2.40

Intl. Olympic Committee, Cent. A359

1996, July 1 Litho. *Perf. 12½*

1213 A359	215fr multicolored	1.25	.60

1996 Summer Olympic Games, Atlanta A360

1996, July 15 *Perf. 13*

1214 A360	10fr Swimming	.25	.25
1215 A360	80fr Gymnastics	.40	.25
1216 A360	175fr Running	1.00	.50
1217 A360	260fr Hurdles	1.40	.70
	Nos. 1214-1217 (4)	3.05	1.70

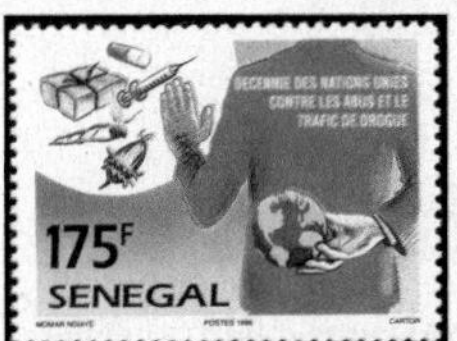

Decade of UN Against Illegal Drug Abuse and Trafficking A361

215fr, UN emblem, hand holding red stop sign, drug paraphernalia.

1996, June 21 *Perf. 13½*

1218 A361	175fr multicolored	.95	.50
1219 A361	215fr multicolored	1.10	.60

Red Cross of Senegal — A362

1996, Oct. 21 *Perf. 12½*

1220 A362	275fr multicolored	1.50	.75

Primates A363

Designs: 10fr, Cercopithecus aethiops. 30fr, Erthrocebus patas. 90fr, Cercopithecus campbelli. 215fr, Pantroglodytes verus. 260fr, Papio papio.

1996, Nov. 29 Litho. *Perf. 13x13½*

1221 A363	10fr multicolored	.30	.25
1222 A363	30fr multicolored	.30	.25
1223 A363	90fr multicolored	.50	.25
1224 A363	215fr multicolored	.90	.50
1225 A363	260fr multicolored	1.00	.60
a.	Strip of 5, #1221-1225	4.00	3.00

UNICEF, 50th Anniv. A364

1996, Dec. 11 *Perf. 13½x13*

1226 A364	75fr shown	.30	.25
1227 A364	275fr Child, diff.	1.25	.60

19th Dakar-Agades-Dakar Rally — A365

25fr, Semi-truck. 75fr, Man pushing car, figure of man. 215fr, Race car. 300fr, Man on motorcycle.

1997, Jan. 19 Litho. *Perf. 13x13½*

1228 A365	25fr multicolored	.25	.25
1229 A365	75fr multicolored	.30	.25
1230 A365	215fr multicolored	.90	.45
1231 A365	300fr multicolored	1.25	.65
	Nos. 1228-1231 (4)	2.70	1.60

Trees — A366

Designs: 80fr, Faidherbia albida. 175fr, Eucalyptus. 220fr, Khaya senegalensis. 260fr, Casuarina equisetifolia.

1997, Mar. 31

1232 A366	80fr multicolored	.35	.25
1233 A366	175fr multicolored	.75	.35
1234 A366	220fr multicolored	.90	.45
1235 A366	260fr multicolored	1.00	.50
	Nos. 1232-1235 (4)	3.00	1.55

Birds — A367

25fr, Platalea leucorodia. 70fr, Leptilos crumeniferus. 175fr, Balcarica pavonina. 215fr, Ephippiarhychus senegalensis. 220fr, Numenius arquata.

1997, Feb. 28

1236 A367	25fr multicolored	.25	.25
1237 A367	70fr multicolored	.30	.25
1238 A367	175fr multicolored	.75	.35
1239 A367	215fr multicolored	.90	.45
1240 A367	220fr multicolored	.95	.50
a.	Strip of 5, #1236-1240	5.00	5.00

Insects A368

Designs: 10fr, Mantis religiosa. 50fr, Forficula auricularia. 75fr, Schistocerca gregaria. 215fr, Cicindela lunulata. 220fr, Gryllus campestris.

1997, Jan. 31 *Perf. 13½x13*

1241 A368	10fr multicolored	.25	.25
1243 A368	50fr multicolored	.25	.25
1244 A368	75fr multicolored	.30	.25
1245 A368	215fr multicolored	.90	.45
1246 A368	220fr multicolored	.95	.45
a.	Strip of 5, #1241-1246	4.00	4.00

Postal officials in Senegal have declared Greenpeace sheets of nine with values of 250fr and 425fr "fake" and "illegal".

Cheikh Anta Diop (1923-86), Historian — A369

Diop: 175fr, And Egyptian hieroglyphs, Sphinx. 215fr, Performing carbon 14 test.

1996, Feb. 26 Litho. *Perf. 13¼*

1247-1248 A369	Set of 2	3.50	1.50

Fashion Type of 1972

1996-97 Engr. *Perf. 13½x13*

Size: 21x26mm

1249	A106	15fr green		
1250	A106	50fr green	.25	.25
1251	A106	60fr olive grn	*.40*	
1251A	A108	70fr olive green	*.40*	
1252	A106	80fr green	*.60*	—
1253	A106	190fr olive green	*.75*	
1254	A106	215fr dark blue	*.80*	.40
1254A	A106	225fr dark blue	*1.00*	—
1255	A106	240fr brown	*1.40*	
1256	A106	260fr red brown	*1.00*	.50
1256A	A106	300fr red lilac	*1.40*	
1256B	A106	320fr rose lilac	*1.50*	
1257	A106	350fr henna brown	*1.60*	
1257B	A106	410fr lake	*1.75*	
1257C	A106	500fr brn violet	*2.25*	
1257D	A106	1000fr carmine	*4.50*	

Issued: 80fr, 225fr, 4/13/96. 50fr, 70fr, 215fr, 260fr, 4/13; 190fr, 240fr, 300fr, 350fr, 1000fr, 6/97.

Additional stamps were released in this set. The editors would like to examine them. Numbers will change if necessary.

Third World A370

Design: 500fr, Hot air balloon in flight.

1996, Apr. 13 Litho. *Perf. 13½*

1258 A370	215fr shown	.75	.40
1259 A370	500fr multicolored	1.75	.90

See Mali Nos. 812-813.

Pres. Leopold Senghor, 90th Birthday A371

Pictures of Senghor and: 175fr, Map of Senegal. 275fr, Quotation, vert.

1996, Oct. 9 Litho. *Perf. 13¼*

1260-1261 A371	Set of 2	1.75	1.75

Niokolo-Badiar Natl. Park — A372

Designs: 30fr, Haliaetus vacifer. 90fr, Hippopotamus amphibius. 240fr, Loxindonta africana oxyotis. 300fr, Taurotragus derbianus.

1997, July 21 Litho. *Perf. 13½x13*

1262 A372 30fr multicolored .65 .25
1263 A372 90fr multicolored .65 .25
1264 A372 240fr multicolored 1.00 .50
1265 A372 300fr multicolored 1.25 .65
Nos. 1262-1265 (4) 3.55 1.65

Shells — A373

Designs: a, 15fr, Cassis tesselata. b, 40fr, Pugilina meria. c, 190fr, Cyprea mappa. d, 200fr, Natica adansoni. e, 300fr, Bullia miran.

1997, Aug. 19 *Perf. 13x13½*

1266 A373 Strip of 5, #a.-e. 4.00 4.00

Wild Animals — A374

a, 25fr, African buffaloes. b, 90fr, Gazelles. c, 100fr, Gnu. d, 200fr, Wild dogs. e, 240fr, Cheetah.

1997, June 27

1267 A374 Strip of 5, #a.-e. 4.00 4.00

Goree Island A375

1997, May 30 *Perf. 13½*

1268 A375 180fr multicolored .75 .40

No. 1268 is dated 1992 and has word "almadies" obliterated.

Dakar-Dakar Rally, 20th Anniv. — A376

Designs: 20fr, Truck traveling across Sahel. 45fr, Motorcycle arriving at Lake Rose. 190fr, Sports utility vehicle crossing Mauritanian Desert. 240fr, Car at Senegal River.

1998, Jan. 1 Litho. *Perf. 13½x13*

1269 A376 20fr multicolored .25 .25
1270 A376 45fr multicolored .25 .25
1271 A376 190fr multicolored .80 .40
1272 A376 240fr multicolored 1.00 .50
Nos. 1269-1272 (4) 2.30 1.40

Food Day A377

190fr, Receiving grain through cereal bank. 200fr, Proper nutrition for women.

1997, Oct. 16

1273 A377 190fr multicolored .80 .40
1274 A377 200fr multicolored .85 .45

A378

Masks: 45fr, Planche, Burkina Faso. 90fr, Kpeliyehe, Ivory Coast. 200fr, Nimba, Guinea Bissau. 240fr, Walu, Mali. 300fr, Dogon, Mali.

1997, Nov. 28

1275 A378 45fr multicolored .25 .25
1276 A378 90fr multicolored .45 .25
1277 A378 200fr multicolored .85 .40
1278 A378 240fr multicolored 1.00 .50
1279 A378 300fr multicolored 1.25 .65
a. Strip of 5, #1275-1279 4.00 2.50

Heinrich von Stephan (1831-97) — A379

1997 *Perf. 11½*

1280 A379 310fr multicolored 1.25 .65

A380

De Gama and: 40fr, Route of spices. 75fr, Port of Zanzibar. 190fr, Caravel revolution. 200fr, Maps being printed.

1997, Nov. 22

1281 A380 40fr multicolored .35 .25
1282 A380 75fr multicolored .35 .25
1283 A380 190fr multicolored 1.40 .40
1284 A380 200fr multicolored 1.40 .40
Nos. 1281-1284 (4) 3.50 1.30

Vasco de Gama (1460-1524), Expedition Around Cape of Good Hope, 500th Anniv.

Trains A381

Designs: 15fr, CC2400. 90fr, Loco-tractor. 100fr, Mountain train. 240fr, Maquinista. 310fr, Freight train, series 151-A.

1997, Dec. 16 *Perf. 13x13½*

1285 A381 15fr multicolored .25 .25
1286 A381 90fr multicolored .50 .25
1287 A381 100fr multicolored .55 .30
1288 A381 240fr multicolored 1.00 .55
1289 A381 310fr multicolored 1.25 .70
a. Strip of 5, #1285-1289 3.50 2.75

Musical Instruments A382

1997, Nov. 22 *Perf. 13x13½*

1290 A382 125fr Riiti *.75* .25
1291 A382 190fr Kora *1.00* .40
1292 A382 200fr Fama *1.25* .45
1293 A382 240fr Dioung dioung *1.50* .50
Nos. 1290-1293 (4) 4.50 1.60

World Wildlife Fund A383

Profelis aurata: 100fr, Climbing on tree limb. 240fr, Lying on tree limb. 300fr, Two cubs.

1997, Dec. 24 Litho. *Perf. 11½*

1294 A383 45fr multicolored .50 .30
1295 A383 100fr multicolored .75 .40
1296 A383 240fr multicolored 1.25 .95
1297 A383 300fr multicolored 1.75 1.25
a. Souvenir sheet of 4, #1294-1297 — —
Nos. 1294-1297 (4) 4.25 2.90

SOS Children's Village, Ziguinchor A384

1998, Jan. 14 Litho. *Perf. 11½*

1298 A384 190fr shown .80 .40
1299 A384 240fr Child, buildings 1.00 .50

Club Aldiana, 25th Anniv. — A385

Designs: 290fr, Hut, people at market, mother and baby. 320fr, People on boats, woman in traditional dress, fish in basket.

1998, Jan. 12 *Perf. 13½*

1300 A385 290fr multicolored 2.25 .60
1301 A385 320fr multicolored 2.50 .65

Diana, Princess of Wales (1967-97) A386

Various portraits.

1998

1302 A386 240fr like #1304g 1.00 .50

Sheets of 9

1303 A386 200fr #a.-i. 7.50 3.75
1304 A386 250fr #a.-i. 9.50 4.75

Nos. 1303-1304 are continuous designs.

Souvenir Sheets

1305 A386 1000fr Portrait 4.25 2.10
1306 A386 1500fr With her sons 6.25 3.25
1307 A386 2000fr Wearing tiara 8.25 4.25

1998 World Cup Soccer Cup Championships, France — A387

Designs: 25fr, Soccer players. 50fr, Player's legs kicking ball. 150fr, Mascot, ball in air. 300fr, Country flags in shape of soccer players.

1998, June 10 Litho. *Perf. 13x13½*

1308 A387 25fr multicolored .25 .25
1309 A387 50fr multicolored .25 .25
1310 A387 150fr multicolored .60 .25
1311 A387 300fr multicolored 1.00 .50
Nos. 1308-1311 (4) 2.10 1.25

Henriette Bathily Women's Museum A388

1998, May 16 Litho. *Perf. 13*

1312 A388 190fr shown 1.25 .60
1313 A388 270fr Emblem at right 1.90 .90

Abolition of Slavery, 150th Anniv. — A389

Designs: 20fr, Slavery Museum, Goree. 40fr, Frederick Douglass. 190fr, Mother, child. 290fr, Victor Schoelcher.

1998, Apr. 27

1314 A389 20fr multicolored .25 .25
1315 A389 40fr multicolored .25 .25
1316 A389 190fr multicolored 1.40 .65
1317 A389 290fr multicolored 2.00 1.00
Nos. 1314-1317 (4) 3.90 2.15

SOS Children's Village — A390

Children's drawings: 30fr, House, car. 50fr, shown. 180fr, Sun, flowers. 300fr, Lakes, trees.

1998, June 16

1318 A390 30fr multicolored .25 .25
1319 A390 50fr multicolored .25 .25
1320 A390 180fr multicolored .70 .35
1321 A390 300fr multicolored 1.10 .55
Nos. 1318-1321 (4) 2.30 1.40

Navigational Aids — A391

Designs: 50fr, Red buoy. 100fr, Mamelles Lighthouse. 190fr, Lighted buoy. 240fr, Port entrance lighthouse.

1998, July 3 *Perf. 12*

1322 A391 50fr multicolored .25 .25
1323 A391 100fr multicolored .40 .25
1324 A391 190fr multicolored .70 .35
1325 A391 240fr multicolored .90 .45
Nos. 1322-1325 (4) 2.25 1.30

21st Paris-Dakar Rally — A392

Designs: 150fr, Race car broken down, hood up, helicopter, rescue van. 175fr, Man with shovels, vehicle stuck in sand, helicopter. 240fr, Motorcycles racing, one down, camel. 290fr, Motorcycle racing, man walking, vehicle broken down.

1999, Jan. 17 Litho. *Perf. 11½*

1326 A392 150fr multicolored .55 .30
1327 A392 175fr multicolored .65 .35
1328 A392 240fr multicolored .90 .45
1329 A392 290fr multicolored 1.00 .50
Nos. 1326-1329 (4) 3.10 1.60

Women's Hair Styles, Headdresses A393

Designs: 100fr, Long hair over shoulders. 240fr, Shorter hair. 300fr, Head wrapped.

1998, Nov. 30

1330 A393 40fr red brn & blk .25 .25
1331 A393 100fr brt grn & blk .35 .25
1332 A393 240fr violet & black .90 .45
1333 A393 300fr blue & black 1.10 .55
Nos. 1330-1333 (4) 2.60 1.50

Endangering Marine Fauna A394

Designs: 50fr, Intensive net fishing. 100fr, Sewage and pollutants in sea. 310fr, Use of dynamite for fishing. 365fr, Oil slicks released from tanker ships.

1998, Dec. 29

1334 A394 50fr multicolored .25 .25
1335 A394 100fr multicolored .40 .25
1336 A394 310fr multicolored 1.25 .65
1337 A394 365fr multicolored 1.50 .75
Nos. 1334-1337 (4) 3.40 1.90

Intl. Year of the Ocean A395

1998, Oct. 30 *Perf. 13x13½*

1338 A395 190fr shown .70 .35
1339 A395 790fr Sea life, diff. 2.75 1.50

Universal Declaration of Human Rights, 50th Anniv. A396

1998, Dec. 9

1340 A396 200fr Prisoner 1.25 .70
1341 A396 350fr Free people 2.25 1.10

Hotel Palm Beach, Voyages of Fram, 50th Anniv. A397

Designs: 240fr, Huts, trees, aerial view of hotel grounds. 300fr, Woman braiding another's hair, beach at hotel.

1998, Nov. 6 Litho. *Perf. 13½x13*

1342 A397 240fr multicolored 1.60 .80
1343 A397 300fr multicolored 2.00 1.00

Italia '98 Intl. Philatelic Exhibition — A398

Design: Leaning Tower of Pisa.

1998, Oct. 23

1344 A398 290fr multicolored 1.00 .50

Italia '98 Intl Philatelic Exhibition A398a

No. 1344A — Race drivers and automobiles: b, Alberto Ascari. c, Giuseppe Farina. d, Ricardo Patrese. e, Michele Alboreto. f, Elio de Angelis. g, Andrea de Cesaris.

1998, Oct. 23 Litho. *Perf. 13¼*

1344A A398a 100fr Sheet of 6, #b-g *8.00 8.00*

Souvenir Sheet

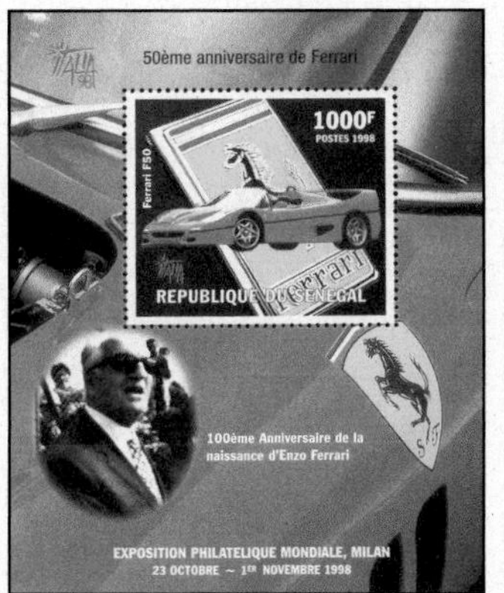

Ferrari Automobiles, 50th Anniv. — A399

1998, Oct. 23 Litho. *Perf. 13½*

1345 A399 1000fr multicolored *4.75 4.75*

Italia '98.

Fashion Type of 1972

1998 Engr. *Perf. 13½x13*

Size: 21x26mm

1345A A106 125fr dark olive *.50 .40*
1345B A106 290fr violet *1.25 1.00*
1345C A106 310fr purple brown *1.40 1.10*

Souvenir Sheet

De Tomaso Automobiles, 40th Anniv. — A400

Automobile colors: a, black, shown. b, silver. c, black, diff. d, red.

1999, Feb. 28 Litho. *Perf. 12¼*

1346 A400 250fr Sheet of 4, #a.-d. *9.50 9.50*

Italia '98. Dated 1998.

Actors & Actresses — A401

No. 1347: a, Romy Schneider. b, Yves Montand. c, Catherine Deneuve. d, Gina Lollobrigida. e, Marcello Mastroianni. f, Sophia Loren. g, Frank Sinatra. h, Dean Martin. i, Marilyn Monroe.

1500fr, Monroe, diff. 2000fr, Mastroianni, diff.

1999, Feb. 28 Litho. *Perf. 12x12¼*

1347 A401 200fr Sheet of 9, #a.-i. *7.00 7.00*

Souvenir Sheets

Perf. 13½

1348 A401 1500fr multicolored *6.00 6.00*
1349 A401 2000fr multicolored *9.50 9.50*

Italia '98. Dated 1998.

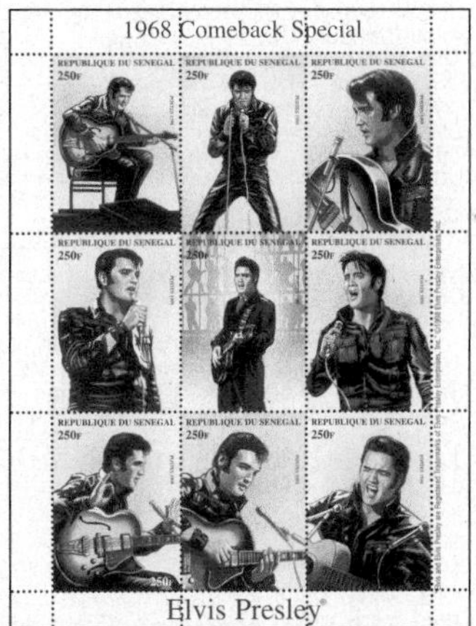

Elvis Presley — A402

Various portraits.

1999, Feb. 28 Litho. *Perf. 12x12¼*

1350 A402 250fr Sheet of 9, #a.-i. *9.50 9.50*

Dated 1998.

A sheet similar to No. 1350 exists. Stamps are perf 13¼ and have Italia '98 logo. The top margins of the sheet are not inscribed.

PhilexFrance 99 — A403

1999, July 2 Litho. *Perf. 13*

1351 A403 240fr multicolored *1.25 1.10*

No. 1351 has a holographic image. Soaking in water may affect hologram.

Chess Pieces and Scenes of the Crusades A404

Designs: No. 1353, Pope Urban II, 1053.

No. 1354: a, Muslim army. b, Bishopric of St. George. c, Army of Karbuqha. d, Muslim troops attacking Christians. e, Baldwin I, King of Jerusalem. f, Christian Army. g, Third crusade, Richard the Lion-Hearted. h, Capture of Acre, 1191. i, Crusaders leave for Jaffa, 1191.

No. 1355: a, Pope Urban II, diff. b, Peter the Hermit. c, Byzantine Emperor Alexius. d, People's Crusade, 1096. e, Godfrey of Bouillon. f, Crusaders at Constantinople, 1097. g, Knights of St. John. h, Crusaders cross Alps. i, Capture of Jerusalem.

No. 1356: a, Chateau-gaillard of Richard the Lion-Hearted. b, Capture of Arsuf, 1191. c, Truce between Richard the Lion-Hearted and Saladin, 1192. d, Arrival of Louis IX at Damietta, 1248. e, Children's Crusade. f, Capture of Louis IX. g, Flood at El Mansurah. h, Treaty between Sultan al-Kamil and Frederick II. i, Monks record history of Crusades.

1999, July 16 Litho. *Perf. 13½*

1353 A404 250fr multicolored *1.25 1.25*

Sheets of 9

1354 A404 200fr #a.-i. 7.50 7.50
1355 A404 250fr #a.-i. 9.25 9.25
1356 A404 400fr #a.-i. 15.00 15.00

Athletes — A405

No. 1357, Jackie Robinson with bat behind back. No. 1358, Muhammad Ali, arm raised by referee.

No. 1359: a-h, various portraits of Jackie Robinson.

No. 1360: a-h, various portraits of Muhammad Ali.

1000fr, Muhammad Ali in robe. 1500fr, Close-up of Jackie Robinson like No. 1359g. No. 1363, Robinson at bat. No. 1364, Ali with both fists clenched.

1999, July 16 Litho. *Perf. 13½*

1357 A405 250fr multicolored 1.00 1.00
1358 A405 300fr multicolored 1.25 1.25

Sheets of 9

1359 A405 250fr #1357, 1359a.-h. 9.25 9.25
1360 A405 300fr #1358, 1360a.-h. 11.50 11.50

Souvenir Sheets

1361 A405 1000fr multicolored 4.25 4.25
1362 A405 1500fr multicolored 6.25 6.25
1363 A405 2000fr multicolored 8.25 8.25
1364 A405 2000fr multicolored 8.25 8.25

Nos. 1361-1364 each contain one 36x42mm stamp.

Sports A405a

Designs: 200fr, Ayrton Senna, Formula 1 racing champion. 300fr, Ludger Beerbaum, equestrian competitor, vert. 400fr, Pete Sampras, tennis player, vert.

No. 1366 — Formula 1 racing champions: a, Juan Manuel Fangio. b, Alberto Ascari. c, Graham Hill. d, Jim Clark. e, Jack Brabham. f, Jackie Stewart. g, Niki Lauda. h, Like No. 1365, no white margin. i, Alain Prost.

No. 1367 — Equestrian competitors, vert.: a, Martin Schaudt. b, Klaus Balkenhol. c, Nadine Capellman-Biffar. d, Willi Melliger. e, Like No. 1365A, without printer's name at LL. f, Ulrich Kirchhoff. g, Sally Clark. h, Bettina Overesch-Boker. i, Karen O'Conner.

No. 1368 — Tennis and table tennis players, vert.: a, Liu Guoliang. b, Martina Hingis. c, Deng Yaping. d, Andre Agassi. e, Jean-Philippe Gatien. f, Anna Kournikova. g, Mikael Appelgren. h, Like No. 1365B, no white margin. i, Jan-Ove Waldner.

1500fr, German Equestrian jumping team. No. 1370, Ayrton Senna. No. 1370A, Table tennis players Vladimir Samsonov, Deng Yaping, Jörg Rosskopf.

1999, July 16 Litho. *Perf. 13½*

1365-1365B A405a Set of 3 3.75 3.75

Sheets of 9, #a-i

1366 A405a 200fr multi 7.50 7.50
1367 A405a 300fr multi 11.00 11.00
1368 A405a 400fr multi 15.00 15.00

Souvenir Sheets

1369 A405a 1500fr multi 6.25 6.25
1370 A405a 2000fr multi 8.00 8.00
1370A A405a 2000fr multi 8.00 8.00

Transportation — A406

Designs: 250fr, Sailboat of Sir Thomas Lipton. 300fr, Sinking of Titanic. 325fr, Bentley coupe. 350fr, Prussian locomotive. 375fr, Ducati Motorcycle. 500fr, Concorde.

1999, July 23 Litho. *Perf. 13½*

1371 A406 250fr multicolored 1.00 1.00
1372 A406 300fr multicolored 1.25 1.25
1373 A406 325fr multicolored 1.40 1.40
1374 A406 350fr multicolored 1.40 1.40
1375 A406 375fr multicolored 1.50 1.50
1376 A406 500fr multicolored 2.00 2.00
Nos. 1371-1376 (6) 8.55 8.55

See Nos. 1385-1399.

Intl. Year of Older Persons A407

30fr, Picture in book. 150fr, Man with mallet. 290fr, Musicians. 300fr, Scientists, vert.

Perf. 13¼x13, 13x13¼

1999, Aug. 10 Litho.

1377 A407 30fr multicolored .25 .25
1378 A407 150fr multicolored .60 .60
1379 A407 290fr multicolored 1.10 1.10
1380 A407 300fr multicolored 1.25 1.25
Nos. 1377-1380 (4) 3.20 3.20

Mushrooms A408

Scouting emblem and: 60fr, "Amanite phalloide." 175fr, Coprinus atramantarius. 220fr, "Amanite vireuse." 250fr, Agaricus campester.

Perf. 13¼x13½

1999, Aug. 27 Litho.

1381 A408 60fr multicolored .30 .30
1382 A408 175fr multicolored .75 .75
1383 A408 220fr multicolored 1.00 1.00
1384 A408 250fr multicolored 1.10 1.10
Nos. 1381-1384 (4) 3.15 3.15

Transportation Type of 1999

No. 1385 — Boats and ships: a, France. b, United States. c, Finnjet. d, Chusan. e, Sheers. f, Vendredi 13. g, Like No. 1371 without white margin. h, Pen Duick 11. i, Jester.

No. 1386 — Titanic: a, Construction. b, Launching. c, Departing. d, At start of voyage. e, Collision with iceberg. f, Like No. 1372 without white margin. g, Exploration of wreckage. h, Bow, passengers. i, Captain Edward John Smith.

No. 1387 — Automobiles: a, Duryea. b, Menon. c, Petite Renault. d, Zero Fiat. e, Spa. f, Packard. g, Like No. 1373 without white margin. h, Mercedes-Benz. i, Morris Minor.

No. 1388 — Trains: a, Mikado. b, 241P. c, Ten-wheeler. d, The Milwaukee. e, Class 1.S. f, Prussian locomotive G12. g, Like No. 1374 without white margin. h, KK-SEB Series 310. i, Outrance.

No. 1389 — Motorcycles and bicycles: a, Brooklands. b, Moto Brough Superior. c, 1903 race. d, Like No. 1375 without inscription at LL. e, Dave Thorpe Moto-cross Yamaha. f, Kevin Schwantz Moto Suzuki. g, Michaux bicycle. h, Racing bicycle with helmeted rider. i, Women on bicycles.

No. 1390 — Rockets, vert.: a, R.D. 107, USSR. b, Soyuz, USSR. c, Proton, USSR. d, Atlas-Centaur, US. e, Atlas-Agena, US. f, Atlas-Mercury, US. g, Titan 2, US. h, Juno 2, US. i, Saturn 1, US.

No. 1391 — Express trains: a, Acela, US. b, Class 332, Great Britain. c, ICE, Germany. d, TEE, Luembourg. e, Nevada Super Speed, US. f, Inter City 250, Great Britain. g, Korean High Speed. h, Eurostar, France & Great Britain. i, Thalys PBA, France.

No. 1392 — Supersonic aircraft or prototypes: a, SR-71. b, Maglifter. c, S.M. d, Super Concorde. e, TU-144. f, Boeing X. g, X-33. h, Like No. 1376 without white margin. i, X-34.

1000fr, Eric Tabarly and Pen Duick IV. No. 1394, Marc Seguin, arrival of train at Mont-Saint-Michel, vert. No. 1395, Walter P. Chrysler, 1924 Chrysler. No. 1396, Etienne Chambron, TGV trains, vert. No. 1397, Bobby Julich on racing bicycle. No. 1398, Concorde, diff. 2500fr, Neil Armstrong.

Sheets of 9

1999, July 23 Litho. *Perf. 13½*

1385 A406 250fr #a.-i. 9.25 9.25
1386 A406 300fr #a.-i. 11.00 11.00
1387 A406 325fr #a.-i. 12.00 12.00
1388 A406 350fr #a.-i. 13.00 13.00
1389 A406 375fr #a.-i. 14.00 14.00
1390 A406 400fr #a.-i. 15.00 15.00
1391 A406 450fr #a.-i. 17.00 17.00
1392 A406 500fr #a.-i. 18.00 18.00

Souvenir Sheets

1393 A406 1000fr multicolored 4.25 4.25
1394 A406 1500fr multicolored 5.50 5.50
1395 A406 1500fr multicolored 6.00 6.00
1396 A406 2000fr multicolored 8.25 8.25
1397 A406 2000fr multicolored 8.25 8.25
1398 A406 2000fr multicolored 8.25 8.25
1399 A406 2500fr multicolored 10.50 10.50

No. 1390 contains nine 35x50mm stamps. Nos. 1393, 1395, 1397-1399 each contain one 50x35 stamp. Nos. 1394 and 1396 each contain one 35x50mm stamp.

UPU, 125th Anniv. — A409

UPU emblem and: 270fr, Rainbows, envelope. 350fr, "125."

1999, Oct. 9 Litho. *Perf. 11½x11¾*

1400 A409 270fr multi 1.10 1.10
1401 A409 350fr multi 1.40 1.40

First Manned Moon Landing, 30th Anniv. — A410

Designs: 25fr, Two astronauts on moon, flag. 145fr, Neil Armstrong, flag, astronaut on moon, vert. 180fr, Astronaut, flag, rocket, vert. 500fr, Astronaut on moon, space shuttle, vert.

1999, Oct. 9 *Perf. 13½x13, 13x13½*

1402 A410 25fr multi .25 .25
1403 A410 145fr multi .60 .60
1404 A410 180fr multi .70 .70
1405 A410 500fr multi 2.00 2.00
Nos. 1402-1405 (4) 3.55 3.55

Mother Teresa — A411

Mother Teresa and: 75fr, Child, facing away. 100fr, Three children. 290fr, Priest. 300fr, Child.

1999, Oct. 9 *Perf. 11½x11¾*

1406 A411 75fr multi .25 .25
1407 A411 100fr multi .40 .40
1408 A411 290fr multi 1.10 1.10
1409 A411 300fr multi 1.25 1.25
Nos. 1406-1409 (4) 3.00 3.00

Awarding of Nobel Peace Prize to Mother Teresa, 20th anniv.

Fauna A412

Designs: 60fr, Hippotragus equinus. 90fr, Haematopus ostralegus. 300fr, Dendrocygna viduada. 320fr, Demochelys coriacea.

1999, Oct. 9 *Perf. 13½x13*

1410 A412 60fr multi .25 .25
1411 A412 90fr multi .35 .35
1412 A412 300fr multi 1.25 1.25
1413 A412 320fr multi 1.25 1.25
Nos. 1410-1413 (4) 3.10 3.10

Paintings by Paul Cézanne — A413

Various paintings.

1999 *Perf. 13¼*

1414 A413 200fr Sheet of 9, #a.-i. 8.00 8.00

Betty Boop — A414

Designs: No. 1415, 250fr, With red guitar. No. 1416, 250fr, With microphone. No. 1417, 400fr, On chair.

No. 1418, 250fr: a, With saxophone. b, With tambourine. c, Like #1415 (continuous design). d, With pink guitar. e, On piano keys. f, With drumsticks. g, With earphones. h, Like #1416 (continuous design). i, With purple jacket.

No. 1419, 400fr: a, With red dress. b, With flowers. c, With blue pants. d, With purple dress. e, Like #1417 (continuous design). f, With black pants. g, With ankh earrings. h, With black dress. i, With purple shirt and pants.

No. 1420, 1000fr, With saxophone. No. 1421, 1500fr, With red dress. No. 1422, 2000fr, With purple shirt.

1999 Litho. *Perf. 13¼*

1415-1417 A414 Set of 3 3.75 3.75

Sheets of 9, #a-i

1418-1419 A414 Set of 2 24.00 24.00

Souvenir Sheets

1420-1422 A414 Set of 3 12.00 12.00

Actors and Actresses — A415

No. 1423, 250fr: a, Clark Gable. b, Rudolph Valentino. c, Errol Flynn. d, Cary Grant. e, Robert Taylor. f, Gary Cooper. g, James Dean. h, Humphrey Bogart. i, Marlon Brando.

No. 1424, 425fr: a, Grace Kelly. b, Marilyn Monroe. c, Audrey Hepburn. d, Greta Garbo. e, Jean Harlow. f, Loretta Young. g, Jane Russell. h, Dorothy Lamour. i, Veronica Lake.

No. 1425, 450fr: a, Ginger Rogers, Fred Astaire. b, Cary Grant, Katharine Hepburn, James Stewart. c, Melvyn Douglas, Greta Garbo. d, Vivien Leigh, Clark Gable. e, Burt Lancaster, Deborah Kerr. f, Humphrey Bogart, Lauren Bacall. g, Steve McQueen, Jacqueline Bisset. h, Gene Kelly, Rita Hayworth. i, Ingrid Bergman, Cary Grant.

1999 Sheets of 9, #a-i

1423-1425 A415 Set of 3 32.50 32.50

I Love Lucy — A416

Designs: No. 1426, 300fr, Fred, Ethel and Lucy with chick boxes. No. 1427, 300fr, Lucy reading murder mystery, vert.

No. 1428: a, Ethel, Lucy holding box. b, Ricky, Lucy, Fred and Ethel. c, Fred, Ethel and Lucy standing. d, Lucy with chicks. e, Fred, Ethel, Lucy and Ricky at table. f, Ethel and Lucy bending over. g, Lucy. h, Lucy, Ethel and Fred at table.

No. 1429, vert. — Lucy with: a, Telephone. b, Green dress. c, Black vest. d, Black hair bow. e, Spoon and bottle. f, Salad. g, Lilac jacket. h, Tan coat.

No. 1430, 1000fr, Lucy holding box, vert. No. 1431, 2000fr, Lucy holding bag, vert.

1999

1426-1427 A416 Set of 2 2.40 2.40
1428 A416 300fr Sheet of 9, #1426, 1428a-1428h 11.00 11.00
1429 A416 300fr Sheet of 9, #1427, 1429a-1429h 11.00 11.00

Souvenir Sheets

1430-1431 A416 Set of 2 12.00 12.00

The Three Stooges — A417

Designs: No. 1432, Larry with scissors, Curly, Moe with drill.

No. 1433: a, Larry and Moe on bed. b, Larry, Moe, Curly in police uniforms. c, Moe, Larry on telephone. d, Larry and Moe with scissors, Curly. e, Larry, Curly, Moe behind operating room equipment. f, Moe on floor, Larry, Curly. g, Moe, Curly, Larry with ladder. h, Moe with plank, Larry, Curly.

No. 1434, 1000fr, Moe with feathers in hair, Curly, vert. No. 1435, 1500fr, Curly with hat, vert.

1999

1432 A417 400fr multi 1.60 1.60
1433 A417 400fr Sheet of 9, #1432, 1433a-1433h 14.50 14.50

Souvenir Sheets

1434-1435 A417 Set of 2 10.00 10.00

Picasso Paintings — A418

No. 1436: a, Country name in yellow, denomination at UL. b, Country name in white. c, Country name in yellow, denomination at UR. d, Country name in red.

1999

1436 A418 375fr Sheet of 4, #a-d 5.50 5.50

22nd Paris-Cairo-Dakar Rally — A419

Designs: 75fr, Motorcycles, car, truck, helicopter, Pyramids. 100fr, Cars, truck, Sphinx, Pyramid, camel and driver. 220fr, Motorcycle, truck, helicopter. 320fr, Camel and driver, motorcycle, car, Pyramids.

2000 Litho. ***Perf. 11¾x11½***

1437-1440 A419 Set of 4 3.50 3.50

World Meteorological Organization, 50th Anniv. A420

Designs: 100fr, Satellite dish, map, weather station. 790fr, Weather measuring equipment, vert.

2000 ***Perf. 11¾x11½, 11½x11¾***

1441-1442 A420 Set of 2 3.25 3.25

23rd Paris-Cairo-Dakar Rally — A421

Stylized head and: 190fr, Motorcyclist. 220fr, Facial features with text, vert. 240fr, Camel, vert. 790fr, Car.

Perf. 13½x13¼, 13¼x13½

2001, Jan. 6

1443-1446 A421 Set of 4 6.50 6.50

Advent of New Millennium A422

Millennium emblem and: 20fr, National Festival of Arts and Culture. 100fr, Pan-African Plastic Arts. 150fr, National Heritage Day. 300fr, Goree Memorial, horiz.

2001, Feb. 13 ***Perf. 13½x13, 13x13½***

1447-1450 A422 Set of 4 2.50 2.50

Dated 2000.

2000 Summer Olympics, Sydney — A423

Designs: 40fr, Swimming, weight lifting. 80fr, Taekwondo. 240fr, 200-meter race. 290fr, Handball.

2001, Feb. 28 ***Perf. 13¼x13½***

1451-1454 A423 Set of 4 3.25 3.25

Dated 2000.

Kermel Artisan Market — A424

Building and: 50fr, Woman, flowers. 90fr, Mask, drum. 250fr, Masks, bowls, horiz. 350fr, Woman, carvings.

Perf. 13¼x13½, 13½x13¼

2001, Mar. 15

1455-1458 A424 Set of 4 3.25 3.25

Medicinal Plants — A425

Designs: 240fr, Maytenus senegalensis. 320fr, Boscia senegalensis. 350fr, Euphorbia hirta. 500fr, Guierra senegalensis.

2001, Apr. 16 Litho. ***Perf. 13¼x13***

1459-1462 A425 Set of 4 6.00 6.00

19th Lions Intl. Convention, Dakar A426

Lions Intl. emblem and: 190fr, People in canoe, map of Senegal. 300fr, Lion, vert.

Perf. 13½x13¼, 13¼x13½

2001, May 21

1463-1464 A426 Set of 2 2.40 2.40

UN High Commissioner for Refugees, 50th Anniv. — A427

Emblem and: 240fr, Tank, refugees. 320fr, Refugee, globe, vert.

Perf. 13½x13¼, 13¼x13½

2001, June 20

1465-1466 A427 Set of 2 2.00 2.00

Intl. Teacher's Day — A428

UNESCO emblem and: 225fr, Book, teacher, vert. 290fr, Teacher, world map.

Perf. 13¼x13, 13x13¼

2001, Oct. 5 Litho.

1467-1468 A428 Set of 2 1.75 1.75

Dated 2000.

National Parks A429

Designs: 75fr, Antelope, lion. 125fr, Heron and marabou stork. 275fr, Cranes and elephant. 300fr, Zebras, vert.

Perf. 13¾x13½

2001, Nov. 12 Litho.

1469 A429 75fr multicolored .50 .25
1470 A429 125fr multicolored .90 .25
1471 A429 275fr multicolored 1.75 1.00
1472 A429 300fr multicolored 1.90 1.00
Nos. 1469-1472 (4) 5.05 2.50

Dated 2000.

Tourism A430

Tourism emblem and: 145fr, Drummer and dancer. 290fr, Tree, windsurfer, person on air mattress, vert.

Perf. 13x13¼, 13¼x13

2001, Dec. 3 Litho.

1473-1474 A430 Set of 2 1.60 1.60

Dated 2000.

2002 African Cup Soccer Tournament, Mali A431

Tournament emblem and: 250fr, Flags, player holding cup, players and soccer ball. 380fr, Players near goal. 425fr, Players kicking ball at goal. 440fr, Player, cup, vert.

2002, Jan. 9

1475-1478 A431 Set of 4 5.25 5.25

24th Paris-Dakar Rally A432

Designs: 250fr, Two motorcyclists. 360fr, Two cars in rally. 370fr, Motorcyclist, Eiffel Tower, map of Africa, vert. 425fr, Motorcyclist, vert.

Perf. 13x13¼, 13¼x13

2002, Jan. 13 Litho.

1479-1482 A432 Set of 4 — —

Peulh Woman — A433a
A433

Linguère — A434a
A434

On types A433a and A434a, the numerals in the denominations have thin serifs and zeroes that are thin at top and bottom. On types A433 and A434 the lines of these numerals are the same thickness.

2002 Litho. *Perf. 13½x13*

No.	Type	Denom.	Color	Unused	Used
1483	A433	5fr	lilac rose	—	—
1483A	A433a	5fr	lilac rose		—
1484	A433	10fr	brt orange	—	—
1484A	A433a	10fr	orange	—	—
1485	A433	20fr	orange	—	—
1485A	A433a	20fr	orange		—
1486	A433	25fr	rose red	—	—
1486A	A433a	25fr	rose red		—
1487	A433	40fr	bright pink	—	—
1488	A433	50fr	light blue	—	—
1488A	A433a	50fr	light blue	—	—
1489	A433	60fr	lt bl grn	—	—
1490	A433	70fr	lt yel grn	—	—
1490A	A433	75fr	dark green	—	—
1490B	A433	80fr	dark blue		—
1490C	A433	90fr	brown		—
1491	A433	100fr	brt yel grn	—	—
1491A	A433	125fr	silver	—	—
1491B	A433a	125fr	silver		—
1492	A433	150fr	olive green	—	—
1493	A433	175fr	yel brn	—	—
1494	A434	200fr	olive green	—	—
1494A	A434	225fr	lilac	—	—
1495	A434	250fr	ocher	—	—
1496	A434	290fr	red brown	—	—
1497	A434	300fr	brt rose lil	—	—
1497A	A434a	350fr	brt rose lil	—	—
1498	A434	360fr	violet	—	—
1499	A434	370fr	blue		—
1499A	A434	380fr	brt green		—
1500	A434	390fr	Prus blue	—	—
1500A	A434	400fr	light brown	—	—
1501	A434	425fr	bright green	—	—
1501A	A434	450fr	green		—
1502	A434	500fr	olive brown	—	—
1502A	A434a	600fr	gray	—	—
1502B	A434a	700fr	bright lilac	—	—
1503	A434	800fr	black	—	—
1504	A434	1000fr	brt blue	—	—
1504A	A434a	1000fr	brt blue		—

Issued: 10fr (#1484), 10fr (#1484A), 50fr (#1488A), 75fr, 100fr, 300fr, 500fr, 1000fr, 2002; 5fr, 20fr, 25fr, 40fr, 50fr (#1488), 60fr, 150fr, 175fr, 200fr, 250fr, 290fr, 360fr, 370fr, 390fr, 425fr, 800fr, 3/12/02; 225fr, 400fr, 2003; 125fr, 350fr, 600fr, 700fr, 4/5/04; No. 1501A, 2007. Issue dates for Nos. 1483A, 1485A, 1486A, 1490B, 1490C, 1491B, 1499, 1499A and 1504A are uncertain, because examples seen used are from 2005 and 2006. Nos. 1490B, 1490C, 1491B, and 1499A have "2003" year dates, while others have "2002" year dates. No. 1501A has "2007" year date.

Proclamation of the Act of African Union — A435

Map of Africa and: 330fr, Handshake, vert. 390fr, Hands, flags.

2002 Litho. *Perf. 13¼x13, 13x13¼*
1505-1506 A435 Set of 2 2.50 2.50

Door of the Third Millennium A436

Various depictions with frame colors of: 200fr, Orange. 290fr, Blue. 390fr, Olive green. 725fr, Rose pink.

2002 *Perf. 13¼x13*
1507-1510 A436 Set of 4 4.50 4.50

Dak'Art 2002 A437

Art by: 200fr, Zehirum Yetmgeta. 380fr, Moustapha Dime, vert. 400fr, Abdoulaye Konate. 425fr, Gora Mbengue.

2002, Apr. 30 *Perf. 13x13¼, 13¼x13*
1511-1514 A437 Set of 4 5.00 5.00

Star and Map of Senegal — A438

Denomination color: 200fr, Green. 380fr, Red.

2002, May 15 *Perf. 13¼x13*
1515-1516 A438 Set of 2 2.00 2.00

Year of Dialogue Among Civilizations A439

UPU and United Nations emblems and: 290fr, Globe, building, native shelters. 380fr, Stylized people and methods of communications.

2002, June 26 Litho. *Perf. 13¼x13*
1517-1518 A439 Set of 2 — —

Horses A440

Designs: 30fr, Mbayar du Baol. 200fr, Mpar du Cayor. 250fr, Narougor. 300fr, Foutanke.

2002, Dec. 20 Litho. *Perf. 13x13¼*
1519-1522 A440 Set of 4 2.50 2.50

Ecotourism A441

Designs: 90fr, Sacred baobab tree. 250fr, Birds, Djoudj National Park. 300fr, Mangroves. 380fr, Wood and vine bridge.

2002, Dec. 20 Litho. *Perf. 13x13¼*
1523-1526 A441 Set of 4 7.75 7.75

Fauna A442

Designs: 75fr, Gorilla gorilla. 290fr, Ceratotherium simum. 360fr, Geochelone sulcata, ostrich and snake. 380fr, Giraffa camelopardalis, vert.

2002, Dec. 26 *Perf. 13x13¼, 13¼x13*
1527-1530 A442 Set of 4 5.75 5.75

25th Paris-Dakar Rally A443

Designs: 360fr, Automobiles, man with camel. 425fr, Motorcyclists.

2003, Jan. 19 Litho. *Perf. 13x13¼*
1531-1532 A443 Set of 2 4.25 4.25

Dated 2002.

A444

A445

New Partnership for African Development — A446

Designs: 250fr, Map of Africa, symbols of industry. 290fr, Map of Africa, bird, model of atom.

Perf. 13¼x13, 13x13¼
2003, June 22 Litho.

No.	Type	Denom.	Description	Unused	Used
1533	A444	200fr	shown	.70	.70
1534	A444	250fr	multi	.85	.85
1535	A445	250fr	shown	.85	.85
1536	A444	290fr	multi	1.00	1.00
1537	A446	360fr	shown	1.25	1.25
			Nos. 1533-1537 (5)	4.65	4.65

Traditional Costumes — A447

Designs: 250fr, Goumbé Lébou. 360fr, Badiaranké. 390fr, Grand Boubou. 500fr, Bowede.

2003, July 16 *Perf. 13¼x13*
1538-1541 A447 Set of 4 5.25 5.25

Marine Life A448

Designs: 290fr, Cymbium cymbium. 370fr, Herring. 380fr, Catfish. 400fr, Chelonia mydas.

2003, July 16 Litho. *Perf. 13x13¼*
1542-1545 A448 Set of 4 5.00 5.00

Sculptures A449

Designs: 200fr, Le Cailcédrat Mort. 300fr, Tete d'un Sorcier. 380fr, Le Laard. 440fr, Le Thioury.

2003, July 16 Litho. *Perf. 13¼x13*
1546-1549 A449 Set of 4 *11.50 11.50*

Léopold Sédar Senghor (1906-2001), First President of Senegal — A450

Senghor: 200fr, Seated in front of flag of Senegal. 300fr, Holding book of poetry and diploma. 1000fr, Standing in front of fireworks.

2003, Dec. 17 Litho. *Perf. 13¼x13*

Booklet Stamps

1550 A450 200fr multi — —
1551 A450 300fr multi — —
a. Booklet pane of 2, #1550-1551 — —

Size: 40x52mm

Perf. 13

1552 A450 1000fr multi — —
a. Booklet pane of 1 —
Complete booklet, #1551a, 1552a —

26th Paris-Dakar Rally — A451

Designs: 390fr, Motorcyclists. 500fr, Motorcyclist and car.

2004, Jan. 14 Litho. *Perf. 13x13¼*
1553-1554 A451 Set of 2 3.50 3.50

Dated 2003.

Intl. Cycling Union, Cent. (in 2000) A452

Designs: 45fr, Stylized cyclists facing left. 275fr, Two cyclists, vert. 290fr, Two cyclists on road. 310fr, Victorious cyclist celebrating, vert.

2004? Litho. *Perf. 13¼x13, 13x13¼*

1555 A452 45fr multi — —
1556 A452 275fr multi — —
1557 A452 290fr multi — —
1558 A452 310fr multi — —

Dated 2000.

Historic Sites A453

Designs: 240fr, Dakar Railroad Station. 370fr, Fort Podor. 390fr, Dakar City Hall. 500fr, Notre Dame des Victoires Cathedral.

2004, Apr. 29 Litho. ***Perf. 13x13¼***
1559-1562 A453 Set of 4 5.50 5.50

Dated 2003.

A453a

Land Transportation — A453b

Design: 200fr, Small bus (Car rapide). 250fr, Horse-drawn wagon (Charrette). 290fr, Dakar Dem Dikk bus. 380fr, Automobile, buses, truck, motorcycle and train.

2004 Litho. ***Perf. 13x13¼***
1562A A453a 200fr multi — —
1562B A453a 250fr multi — —
1562C A453a 290fr multi — —
1562D A453b 380fr multi — —

African Cup of Nations Soccer Tournament A454

Designs: 200fr, Cup, emblem. 300fr, Cup, soccer ball, stadium, television, horiz. 400fr, Emblems, players shaking hands, horiz. 425fr, Players in action, horiz.

2004 ***Perf. 13¼x13, 13x13¼***
1563-1566 A454 Set of 4 5.50 5.50

Art — A454a

Designs: 300fr, Dak'art, by Amadou Sow. 400fr, Chaise, by Vincent Amian Niamen. 450fr, Prototype I, by Issa Diabaté. 525fr, Choses au Mur, by Viyé Diba.

2004 Litho. ***Perf. 13¼x13***
1566A-1566D A454a Set of 4 — —

Houses of Worship A455

Designs: 200fr, Omarienne de Guédé Mosque. 225fr, Popenguine Basilica, vert. 250fr, Grand Mosque, Touba. 300fr, Grand Mosque, Tivaouane.

Perf. 13x13¼, 13¼x13
2004, Oct. 9 Litho.
1567-1570 A455 Set of 4 3.75 3.75

Locally Produced Crops — A456

Designs: 100fr, Millet. 150fr, Cowpeas, millet and corn, horiz. 200fr, Corn. 300fr, Rice.

2004, Dec. 6 ***Perf. 13¼x13, 13x13¼***
1571-1574 A456 Set of 4 3.00 3.00

27th Paris-Dakar Rally — A457

Designs: 450fr, Automobile, motorcycle and truck. 550fr, Motorcycle, vert.

Perf. 13x13¼, 13¼x13
2005, Jan. 16 Litho.
1575-1576 A457 Set of 2 4.00 4.00

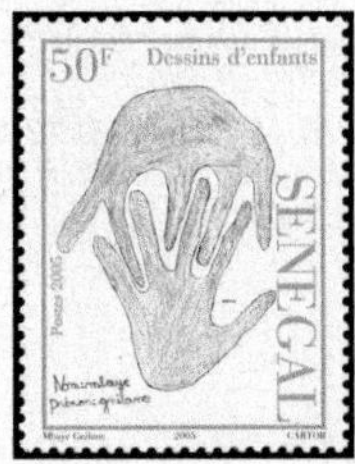

Children's Art — A458

Various drawings by: 50fr, Mbaye Gnilane. 75fr, Pape Cheick Diack, horiz. 100fr, Aly Gueye, horiz. 425fr, Abdourahim Diallo, horiz.

Perf. 13¼x13, 13x13¼
2005, Feb. 28 Litho.
1577-1580 A458 Set of 4 2.75 2.75

28th Paris-Dakar Rally A459

Design: 500fr, Rally emblem, camels, tents, automobile. 1000fr, Rally emblem, helicopter, man repairing car, men carrying car doors.

2006, Jan. 14 Litho. ***Perf. 13x13¼***
1581 A459 500fr multi — —
1582 A459 1000fr multi — —

Dolls — A460

Designs: 200fr, Tooiodo Peulh. 250fr, La Reine Siguare. 375fr, Zulu doll. 425fr, Woloff stuffed dolls.

Litho., Litho & Engr. (375fr)
2006, Apr. 5 ***Perf. 13¼x13***
1583-1586 A460 Set of 4 7.25 7.25

Campaign Against HIV A461

Designs: 200fr, Family discussing HIV and AIDS, map of Senegal. 250fr, Woman, molecular model, drop of water, vert. 290fr, Couples with thought balloons. 425fr, Group of seated men, huts.

Perf. 13x13¼, 13¼x13
2006, Apr. 5 Litho.
1587-1590 A461 Set of 4 4.50 4.50

Dated 2004.

World Numerical Solidarity Day — A462

Designs: 200fr, Satellite, computer screen, Earth's hemispheres. 250fr, Earth, people using telephones, clasped arms. 370fr, Satellite, map of Senegal, city skyline, horiz. 380fr, Satellite, computer screen, hand with computer disk, horiz.

Perf. 13½x13, 13x13½
2006, May 3 Litho.
1591-1594 A462 Set of 4 4.75 4.75

Flowers A463

Designs: 100fr, Malva silvestris. 150fr, Moringa olifera, vert. 300fr, Cichorum intybus, vert. 450fr, Dandelion.

Perf. 13x13¼, 13¼x13
2006, July 10 Litho.
1595-1598 A463 Set of 4 9.00 9.00

Dated 2005.

Wrestling A464

Designs: 100fr, Two wrestlers standing. 200fr, Two wrestlers in ring. 250fr, Wrestler, vert. 500fr, Wrestler pouring water on himself, vert.

Perf. 13x13¼, 13¼x13
2007, July 10 Litho.
1599-1602 A464 Set of 4 9.50 9.50

Demba and Dupont Memorial, Dakar — A465

Various views of statue: 200fr, 450fr.

2006, Aug. 23 Litho. ***Perf. 13¼x13***
1603-1604 A465 Set of 2 3.75 3.75

Pres. Léopold Sedar Senghor (1906-2001) A466

Denomination color: 200fr, Red. 450fr, Green.

2006, Oct. 9 Litho. ***Perf. 13¼x13***
1605-1606 A466 Set of 2 5.75 5.75

Campaign Against Mutilation of Female Genitalia — A467

Designs: 50fr, Woman grabbing another woman, man holding sign. 200fr, Two women, two children, razor blade. 350fr, Woman, health workers, razor blade. 370fr, Women, girl with raised hand.

2006, Dec. 8 Litho. ***Perf. 13¼x13***
1607-1610 A467 Set of 4 4.00 4.00

Air Transport A468

Design: 100fr, Earth, Map of Africa, jet, Concorde in flight. 250fr, Airship and airplane. 370fr, Airplane on runway, control tower. 500fr, Airplane and passengers.

2006 Litho. ***Perf. 13x13¼***
1611 A468 100fr multi — —
1612 A468 250fr multi — —
1613 A468 370fr multi — —
1614 A468 500fr multi — —

Birds A469

Designs: 30fr, Luscinia phoenicurus. 75fr, Rouge-gorge bleu (robin), vert. 200fr, Pica pica, vert. 400fr, Corneille (crow), vert.

2006 Litho. ***Perf. 13x13¼, 13¼x13***
1615-1618 A469 Set of 4 12.50 12.50

Fishing — A469a

Design: 15fr, Fishermen removing catch from boat. 50fr, Fishermen in boat pulling in net. 150fr, Fisherman in boat casting net. 300fr, Fishermen in boat and in water drawing in net.

2006 ***Perf. 13x13¼***
1618A A469a 15fr multi — —
1618B A469a 50fr multi — —
1618C A469a 150fr multi — —
1618D A469a 300fr multi — —

29th Paris-Dakar Rally
A470

Designs: 450fr, Two automobiles, two motorcycles. 550fr, Motorcyclist passing rally watchers.

2007, Jan. 20 Litho. *Perf. 13x13¼*
1619-1620 A470 Set of 2 — —

National Solidarity Day
A471

Designs: 50fr, Exchange of books and corn. 100fr, Shell, hands, star, map of Senegal. 200fr, Map of Senegal, hands, bowl. 500fr, Map of Senegal, items produced in Senegal.

2007, Sept. 11 Litho. *Perf. 13x13¼*
1621-1624 A471 Set of 4 3.75 3.75

Dated 2006.

Gorée Diaspora Festival — A472

Designs: 50fr, Emblem. 200fr, Emblem, pendant and prism, horiz. 450fr, Hands with quill pen, building. 525fr, Ship, emblem, Gorée Island.

Perf. 13¼x13, 13x13¼
2007, Sept. 11
1625-1628 A472 Set of 4 5.50 5.50

Tourism
A473

Designs: 75fr, Patas monkey, flamingos, Sine Saloum Park. 125fr, Wildlife, Niokolo-koba Park. 200fr, Lion, elephant and giraffes, Niokolo-koba Park. 450fr, Pelicans, Faidherbe Bridge, Saint-Louis.

2008, Feb. 27 Litho. *Perf. 13x13¼*
1629 A473 75fr multi — —
1630 A473 125fr multi — —
1631 A473 200fr multi — —
1632 A473 450fr multi — —

Dated 2007.

Environmental Protection — A474

Designs: 100fr, Do not cut down trees. 200fr, Fire is dangerous, vert. 300fr, Man picking up litter. 450fr, Protect the vegetation.

Perf. 13x13¼, 13¼x13
2008, June 5 Litho.
1633-1636 A474 Set of 4 5.00 5.00

Dated 2007.

Flora
A475

Designs: 200fr, Strichnos nux vomica. 290fr, Conium maculatum, vert. 300fr, Tree bud, vert. 450fr, Pitcher plant, vert.

Perf. 13x13¼, 13¼x13
2008, Sept. 5 Litho.
1637-1640 A475 Set of 4 5.50 5.50

Dated 2007.

Miniature Sheet

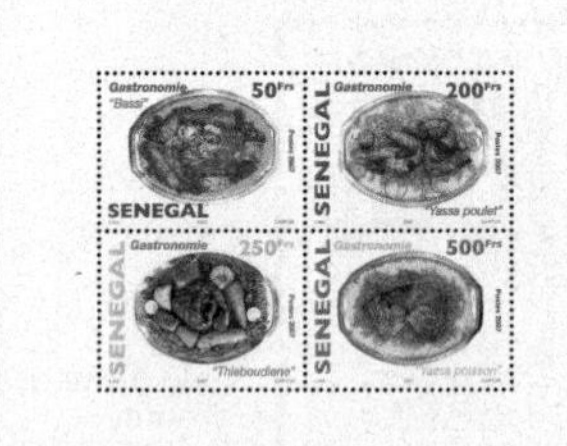

Native Dishes — A476

No. 1641: a, 50fr, Bassi (seasoned meat and vegetables). b, 200fr, Yassa poulet (marinated chicken and vegetables). c, 250fr, Thieboudiene (marinated fish. d, 500fr, Yassa poisson (marinated fish and vegetables).

2008, Sept. 5 Litho. *Perf. 13x13¼*
1641 A476 Sheet of 4, #a-d 4.50 4.50

30th Paris-Dakar Rally — A476a

Designs: 450fr, Motorcyclist, van, camel. 550fr, Motorcyclist, car, horiz.

Perf. 13¼x13, 13x13¼
2009, Jan. 29 Litho.
1643-1644 A476a Set of 2 4.00 4.00

Dated 2008.

Mother's Day
A477

Mothers receiving flowers from daughters, with background color of: 200fr, Lilac. 450fr, Yellow, vert.

Perf. 13x13¼, 13¼x13
2009, June 3 Litho.
1645-1646 A477 Set of 2 2.75 2.75

Blind Boy Reading Braille Book — A478

Designs: 200fr, Shown. 450fr, "9" in Braille text.

Litho. & Embossed
2009, May 20 *Perf. 13¼x13*
1647-1648 A478 Set of 2 2.75 2.75

Louis Braille (1809-52), educator of the blind.

Independence, 50th Anniv. — A479

Denomination color: 300fr, Green. 500fr, Red.

2010, Apr. 4 Litho. *Perf. 13x13¼*
1649-1650 A479 Set of 2 3.50 3.50

West African Economic and Monetary Union, 11th Anniv. (in 2005) — A480

Designs: 500fr, Coin, balls and emblem. 790fr, Map of member countries, emblems, building, birthday cake with candle, horiz.

2010, Apr. 5 *Perf. 13¼x13, 13x13¼*
1651-1652 A480 Set of 2 5.50 5.50

Dated 2006.

Democracy and Liberty — A481

Designs: 150fr, Peaceful protest. 250fr, Woman holding election card. 400fr, Woman casting ballot. 450fr, Newspapers, radio, television.

2010, Apr. 5 Litho. *Perf. 13¼x13*
1653-1656 A481 Set of 4 5.25 5.25

Dated 2006.

Dances — A482

Designs: 100fr, Ndaw rabine. 200fr, Niary gorom, horiz. 250fr, Daganthe. 450fr, Ndaa daly.

2010, Apr. 21 *Perf. 13¼x13, 13x13¼*
Granite Paper
1657-1660 A482 Set of 4 4.25 4.25

Insects
A483

Designs: 150fr, Praying mantis. 200fr, Wasp. 250fr, Grasshopper. 500fr, Ant.

2010, Apr. 21 Litho. *Perf. 13x13¼*
1661-1664 A483 Set of 4 4.50 4.50

Grand Agricultural Offensive for Food Security — A484

Designs: 100fr, Map of Africa, farmers with team of oxen, fruits and vegetables. 200fr, Map of Senegal, farmers with plow and crops, horiz. 250fr, Maps of Africa and Senegal, crops, people with grain sacks. 500fr, People and vegetables.

Perf. 13¼x13, 13x13¼
2010, Aug. 5 Litho.
1665-1668 A484 Set of 4 — —

Dated 2009.

SOS Children's Village
A485

Denomination in: 300fr, Orange. 400fr, Yellow.

2010, Sept. 15 Litho. *Perf. 13x13¼*
1669-1670 A485 Set of 2 3.00 3.00

Fifth Gorée Diaspora Festival
A486

Festival emblem and: 190fr, Men and buildings. 200fr, Dancers, Gorée Island, Aimé Césaire (1913-2008), poet. 250fr, Girls dancing. 450fr, Gorée Island and statue of freed slaves.

2010, Nov. 4 Litho. *Perf. 13x13¼*
1671 A486 190fr multi — —
1672 A486 200fr multi — —
1673 A486 250fr multi — —
1674 A486 450fr multi — —

Dated 2009.

World Festival of Negro Arts — A487

Designs: 200fr, Woman with arms raised, vert. 300fr, Map of Africa. 450fr, Sphere, stylized people with arms raised, vert. 500fr, Carving of woman smoking pipe, table, vert.

Perf. 13x13¼, 13¼x13
2010, Dec. 21 Litho.
1675 A487 200fr multi — —
1676 A487 300fr multi — —
1677 A487 450fr multi — —
1678 A487 500fr multi — —

Dated 2007.

Birds — A488

Designs: 10fr, Ibis religionas, horiz. 200fr, Ardea pavonia. 450fr, Spoonbill (spatule). 500fr, Himantopus himantopus.

2011, Apr. 6 Litho. *Perf. 13x13¼*
1679 A488 10fr multi — —

Perf. 13¼x13
1680 A488 200fr multi — —
1681 A488 450fr multi —
1682 A488 500fr multi —

Dated 2009.

Pottery — A489

Design: 150fr, Water container and lid (canari réservoir d'eau). 200fr, Drinking cup (canari de libation). 225fr, Clay stove (fourneau athé). 425fr, Censer (encensoir).

2011, Apr. 6 Litho. *Perf. 13¼x13*
1683 A489 150fr multi —
1684 A489 200fr multi —
1685 A489 225fr multi — —
1686 A489 425fr multi — —

Dated 2007.

Islands A490

Design: 50fr, Ile du Sine Saloume. 100fr, Ile aux Oiseaux (Bird Island). 450fr, Ilot Sarpant. 500fr, Ile de Carabane.

2011 Litho. *Perf. 13x13¼*
1687 A490 50fr multi — —
1688 A490 100fr multi —
1689 A490 450fr multi — —
1690 A490 500fr multi — —

Dated 2009.

Horses in Sports A491

Designs: 10fr, Steeplechase. 50fr, Dressage. 250fr, Horse and jockey. 500fr, Horse race.

2012, June 5 Litho. *Perf. 13x13¼*
1691-1694 A491 Set of 4 — —

Diplomatic Relations Between Senegal and Vatican City, 50th Anniv. A492

Designs: 50fr, Flags of Senegal and Vatican City. 200fr, Christ Giving the Keys to St. Peter, by Pietro Perugino, vert.

2012 Litho. *Perf. 13x13¼, 13¼x13*
1695-1696 A492 Set of 2 1.40 1.40

Weaving — A493

Designs: 50fr, Weaver winding yarn on bobbin. 150fr, Yarn on swift and shuttles, horiz. 300fr, Weaver at loom. 500fr, Weaver with finished fabric, horiz.

Perf. 13¼x13, 13x13¼
2012, Sept. 18 Litho.
1697-1700 A493 Set of 4 4.00 4.00

Dated 2009.

2002 Sinking of the Joola Ferry A494

Joola Ferry: 75fr, Afloat near Ziguinchor, and sinking (in inset). 100fr, At sea. 200fr, At dock with door open. 250fr, Next to small boat near Ile de Carabane.

2012 ? Litho. *Perf. 13x13¼*
1701 A494 75fr multi — —
1702 A494 100fr multi —
1703 A494 200fr multi —
1704 A494 250fr multi — —

Dated 2003.

Fruits — A495

Designs: 25fr, Balanites aegyptiaca. 200fr, Citrullus vulgaris, horiz. 450fr, Cashew. 500fr, Saba senegalensis.

2013 Litho. *Perf. 13¼x13, 13x13¼*
1705-1708 A495 Set of 4 — —

Keur Moussa Benedictine Abbey, 50th Anniv. — A496

Designs: 200fr, Cross, heart, monk praying. 450fr, Fiftieth anniversary emblem.

2013 Litho. *Perf. 13¼x13*
1709-1710 A496 Set of 2 — —

Gueumbeul Reserve A497

Designs: 25fr, Reptiles, mushrooms, birds and flowers near pond. 50fr, Antelopes at pond. 200fr, Mammals, birds and fruit. 450fr, Birds on Senegal River.

2013, Dec. 18 Litho. *Perf. 13x13¼*
1711-1714 A497 Set of 4 3.00 3.00

Blaise Diagne (1872-1934), Mayor of Dakar — A498

2014 Litho. *Perf. 13¼x13*
1715 A498 25fr multi — —

World War I, Cent. A499

Designs: 200fr, Assassination of Archduke Franz Ferdinand. 450fr, Soldiers in trenches, vert. 500fr, Senegalese soldiers.

2014 Litho. *Perf. 13x13¼, 13¼x13*
1716-1718 A499 Set of 3 — —

A souvenir sheet containing one 2000fr air post stamp depicting Senegalese soldiers was produced in limited quantities.

Bodies of Water A500

Designs: 100fr, Lake Rétba. 1000fr, Dindefelo Falls, vert.

2014 Litho. *Perf. 13x13¼*
1719 A500 100fr multi — —

Perf. 13¼x13
1720 A500 1000fr multi — —

Admission of Senegal to United Nations, 55th Anniv. — A502

2015, Nov. 16 Litho. *Perf. 13¼x13*
1723 A502 450fr multi —

An additional stamp was issued in this set. The editors would like to examine any examples of it.

Economic Community of West African States, 40th Anniv. A503

Perf. 13¼x13½
2015, Dec. 17 Litho.
1725 A503 200fr multi — —

A504

Nelson Mandela (1918-2013), President of South Africa — A505

2016, Jan. 8 Litho. *Perf. 13¼x13*
1726 A504 200fr multi —
1727 A505 500fr multi —

Dated 2014.

African Philatelic Hub — A511

2016, Oct. 4 Litho. *Perf. 13¼x13*
1729 A511 200fr multi —

An additional stamp was issued in this set. The editors would like to examine any examples of it.

Dakar Train Station A512

Faidherbe Bridge and Monument, Place Faidherbe, Saint-Louis A514

House of Slaves, Gorée Island — A515

2016, Dec. 7 Litho. *Perf. 13x13¼*
1731 A512 100fr multi —

Perf. 13¼x13
1733 A514 450fr multi —
1734 A515 500fr multi —

An additional stamp was issued in this set. The editors would like to examine any examples of it.

African Cup of Nations, 60th Anniv. A517

Designs: 200fr, Golden soccer ball, map of Africa, fans at final.

2017, Jan. 21 Litho. *Perf. 13x13¼*

1736 A517 200fr multi —

An additional stamp was issued in this set. The editors would like to examine any examples of it.

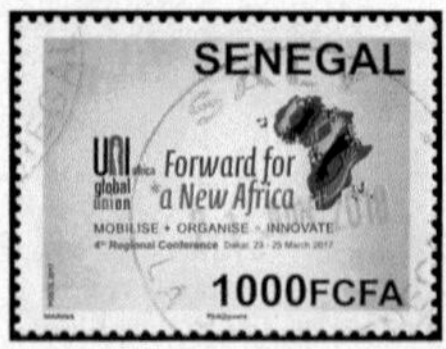

UNI Global Union Fourth Regional Conference, Dakar — A519

2017, Mar. 25 Litho. *Perf. 13x13¼*

Text in English

1741 A519 1000fr multi —

Two additional stamps were issued in this set. The editors would like to examine any examples.

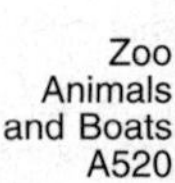

Zoo Animals and Boats A520

2017, June 5 Litho. *Perf. 13x13¼*

1742 A520 300fr multi —

Environmental protection. An additional stamp was issued in this set. The editors would like to examine any examples of it.

Fort of Podor A522

Promenade, Thiès — A523

Niokolo-Koba National Park — A525

2017, Dec. 7 Litho. *Perf. 13x13¼*

1744 A522 250fr multi —
1745 A523 300fr multi —
1747 A525 500fr multi —

An additional stamp was issued in this set. The editors would like to examine any examples of it.

SEMI-POSTAL STAMPS

No. 84 Surcharged in Red

1915 Unwmk. *Perf. 14x13½*

B1 A28 10c + 5c org red & rose 1.75 1.75
a. Chalky paper 1.75 1.75

No. B1 is on both ordinary and chalky paper.

Same Surcharge on No. 87

1918

B2 A28 15c + 5c red org & brn vio 1.75 1.75

Curie Issue

Common Design Type

1938 Engr. *Perf. 13*

B3 CD80 1.75fr + 50c brt ultra 10.50 10.50

French Revolution Issue

Common Design Type

Photo., Name & Value Typo. in Black

1939

B4 CD83 45c + 25c green 8.50 8.50
B5 CD83 70c + 30c brown 8.50 8.50
B6 CD83 90c + 35c red org 8.50 8.50
B7 CD83 1.25fr + 1fr rose pink 8.50 8.50
B8 CD83 2.25fr + 2fr blue 8.50 8.50
Nos. B4-B8 (5) 42.50 42.50

Stamps of 1935-38 Surcharged in Red or Black

1941 *Perf. 12x12½, 12*

B9 A30 50c + 1fr red org 3.50
B10 A31 80c + 2fr vio (R) 7.25
B11 A30 1.50fr + 2fr dk bl 7.25
B12 A30 2fr + 3fr blue 7.25
Nos. B9-B12 (4) 25.25

Common Design Type and

Bambara Sharpshooter SP1

Colonial Soldier SP2

1941 Photo. *Perf. 13½*

B13 SP1 1fr + 1fr red 1.25
B14 CD86 1.50fr + 3fr maroon 1.25
B15 SP2 2.50fr + 1fr blue 1.25
Nos. B13-B15 (3) 3.75

The surtax was for the defense of the colonies.

Nos. B13-B15 were issued by the Vichy government, but it is doubtful whether they were placed in use in Senegal.

Nos. 193-194 Srchd. in Black or Red

1944 Engr. *Perf. 12½x12*

B15A 50c + 1.50fr on 2.50fr dp bl (R) .80
B15B + 2.50fr on 1fr green .80

Colonial Development Fund.

Nos. B15A-B15B were issued by the Vichy government in France, but were not placed on sale in Senegal.

Catalogue values for unused stamps in this section, from this point to the end of the section, are for Never Hinged items.

Republic

Anti-Malaria Issue

Common Design Type

Perf. 12½x12

1962, Apr. 7 Engr. Unwmk.

B16 CD108 25fr + 5fr brt grn 1.10 .65

Freedom from Hunger Issue

Common Design Type

1963, Mar. 21 *Perf. 13*

B17 CD112 25fr + 5fr dp vio, grn & brn .80 .50

SP3

2002 World Cup Soccer Championships, Japan and Korea — SP4

World Cup: 290fr+50fr, Soccer ball and stadium. 360fr+50fr, Soccer field and crowd.

2002 Litho. *Perf. 13½*

B18 SP3 75fr +100fr shown .75 .75

Perf. 13x13¼

B19 SP4 200fr +100fr shown 1.25 1.25
B20 SP4 290fr +50fr multi 1.40 1.40
B21 SP4 360fr +50fr multi 1.60 1.60
Nos. B18-B21 (4) 5.00 5.00

Value for No. B18 is for example with surrounding selvage.

AIR POST STAMPS

Landscape AP1

Caravan AP2

Perf. 12½x12, 12x12½

1935 Engr. Unwmk.

C1 AP1 25c dk brown .30 .30
C2 AP1 50c red orange .35 .45
C3 AP1 1fr rose lilac .30 .30
C4 AP1 1.25fr yellow grn .30 .30
C5 AP1 2fr blue .30 .30
C6 AP1 3fr olive grn .30 .30
C7 AP2 3.50fr violet .35 .30
C8 AP2 4.75fr orange .35 .45
C9 AP2 6.50fr dk blue 1.10 1.10
C10 AP2 8fr black 1.10 1.75
C11 AP2 15fr rose lake 1.40 1.40
Nos. C1-C11 (11) 6.15 6.95

No. C8 surcharged "ENTR' AIDE FRANCAIS + 95f 25" in green, red violet or blue, was never issued in this colony.

Common Design Type

1940 Engr. *Perf. 12½x12*

C12 CD85 1.90fr ultra .50 .50
C13 CD85 2.90fr dk red .50 .50
C14 CD85 4.50fr dk gray grn .55 .55
C15 CD85 4.90fr yellow bis .85 .85
C16 CD85 6.90fr dp orange 1.10 1.10
Nos. C12-C16 (5) 3.50 3.50

Common Design Types

1942

C17 CD88 50c car & bl .30
C18 CD88 1fr brn & blk .50
C19 CD88 2fr dk grn & red brn .50
C20 CD88 3fr dk bl & scar 1.05
C21 CD88 5fr vio & brn red .70

Frame Engr., Center Typo.

C22 CD89 10fr ultra, ind & hn .70
C23 CD89 20fr rose car, mag & choc 1.10
C24 CD89 50fr yel grn, dl grn & yel 2.10 *2.75*

Engr. & Photo.

Size: 47x26mm

C25 CD88 100fr dk red & bl 2.50 *3.75*
Nos. C17-C25 (9) 9.45

There is doubt whether Nos. C17 to C23 were officially placed in use.

Catalogue values for unused stamps in this section, from this point to the end of the section, are for Never Hinged items.

Republic

Abyssinian Roller — AP3

Designs: 50fr, Carmine bee-eater, vert. 200fr, Violet touraco, vert. 250fr, Red bishop, vert. 500fr, Fish eagle, vert.

Perf. 12½x13, 13x12½

1960-63 Photo. Unwmk.

Birds in Natural Colors

C26 AP3 50fr blk & gray bl ('61) 2.25 .50
C27 AP3 100fr blk, yel & lil 4.00 1.00
C28 AP3 200fr blk, grn & bl ('61) 9.00 2.50
C29 AP3 250fr blk & pale grn ('63) 9.00 3.00
C30 AP3 500fr blk & bl 25.00 5.25
Nos. C26-C30 (5) 49.25 12.25

Air Afrique Issue

Common Design Type

1962, Feb. 17 Engr. *Perf. 13*

C31 CD107 25fr vio brn, sl grn & ocher .80 .30

African Postal Union Issue

Common Design Type

1963, Sept. 8 Photo. *Perf. 12½*

C32 CD114 85fr choc, ocher & red 1.75 .50

Air Afrique Issue

Common Design Type

1963, Nov. 19 Unwmk. *Perf. 13x12*

C33 CD115 50fr multicolored 2.00 .65

Independence Monument — AP4

1964, Apr. 4 Photo. *Perf. 12x13*
C34 AP4 300fr ultra, tan, ocher & grn 5.00 1.75

Symbolic European and African Cities — AP5

1964, Apr. 18 Engr. *Perf. 13*
C35 AP5 150fr grn, brn red & blk 4.00 1.40

Congress of the Intl. Federation of Twin Cities, Dakar.

Europafrica Issue

Peanuts, Globe, Factory, Figures of "Africa," and "Europe" — AP6

1964, July 20 Photo. *Perf. 13x12*
C36 AP6 50fr multicolored 2.00 .60

See note after Madagascar No. 357.

Basketball AP7

1964, Aug. 22 Engr. *Perf. 13*
C37 AP7 85fr shown 2.50 .65
C38 AP7 100fr Pole vault 2.75 1.00

18th Olympic Games, Tokyo, Oct. 10-25.

Launching of Syncom 2 — AP8

1964, Oct. 24 Unwmk. *Perf. 13*
C39 AP8 150fr grn, red brn & ultra 3.00 1.00

Communication through space.

Pres. John F. Kennedy (1917-1963) AP9

1964, Dec. 5 Photo. *Perf. 13*
C40 AP9 100fr brt yel, dk grn & brn red 2.75 1.00
a. Souvenir sheet of 4 12.00 12.00

Scenic Type of Regular Issue

View: 100fr, Shore of Gambia River in Eastern Senegal.

1965, Feb. 27 Engr. *Perf. 13*
Size: 48x27mm
C41 A48 100fr brn blk, grn & bis 2.50 1.00

Mother and Child, Globe and Emblems AP10

1965, Sept. 25 Unwmk. *Perf. 13*
C42 AP10 50fr choc, brt bl & grn 1.25 .40

International Cooperation Year.

A-1 Satellite and Earth — AP11

Designs: No. C44, Diamant rocket. 90fr, Scout rocket and FR-1 satellite.

1966, Feb. 19 Engr. *Perf. 13*
C43 AP11 50fr yel brn, dk grn & blk 1.00 .40
C44 AP11 50fr Prus bl, lt red brn & car rose 1.00 .40
C45 AP11 90fr dk red brn, dk gray & Prus bl 2.50 .85
Nos. C43-C45 (3) 4.50 1.65

French achievements in space.

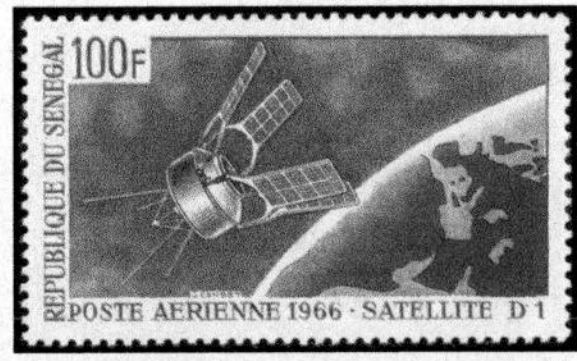

D-1 Satellite over Globe — AP12

1966, June 11 Engr. *Perf. 13*
C46 AP12 100fr dk car, sl & vio 2.50 .80

Launching of the D-1 satellite at Hammaguir, Algeria, Feb. 17, 1966.

Air Afrique Issue
Common Design Type

1966, Aug. 31 Photo. *Perf. 13*
C47 CD123 30fr red brn, blk & lem .80 .30

Mermoz Plane "Arc-en-Ciel" — AP13

Jean Mermoz — AP14

Designs: 35fr, Latecoére 300 "Croix du Sud." 100fr, Map showing last flight from Dakar to Brazil.

1966, Dec. 7 Engr. *Perf. 13*
C48 AP13 20fr bl, rose lil & indigo .80 .25
C49 AP13 35fr slate, brn & grn 1.00 .30
C50 AP13 100fr grn, lt grn & mar 1.75 .50
C51 AP14 150fr blk, ultra & mar 3.50 1.00
Nos. C48-C51 (4) 7.05 2.05

Jean Mermoz (1901-36), French aviator, on the 30th anniv. of his last flight.

Dakar-Yoff Airport — AP15

1967, Apr. 22 Engr. *Perf. 13*
C52 AP15 200fr red brn, ind & brt bl 3.50 1.00

Knob-billed Goose — AP16

Flowers and Birds: 100fr, Mimosa. 150fr, Flowering cactus. 250fr, Village weaver. 500fr, Bateleur.

1967-69 Photo. *Perf. 11½*
Granite Paper
Dated "1967"
C53 AP16 100fr gray, yel & grn 3.00 1.00
C54 AP16 150fr multicolored 5.00 1.50

Dated "1969"
C55 AP16 250fr gray & multi 8.00 1.75

Dated "1968"
C56 AP16 300fr brt bl & multi 12.50 3.00
C57 AP16 500fr orange & multi 17.50 4.25
Nos. C53-C57 (5) 46.00 11.50

Issued: 100fr, 150fr, 6/24/67; 500fr, 7/13/68; 300fr, 12/21/68; 250fr, 4/26/69.

The Girls from Avignon, by Picasso AP17

1967, July 22 *Perf. 12x13*
C59 AP17 100fr multicolored 3.50 1.00

African Postal Union Issue
Common Design Type

1967, Sept. 9 Engr. *Perf. 13*
C60 CD124 100fr brt grn, vio & car lake 1.75 .50

Konrad Adenauer AP18

1968, Feb. 17 Photo. *Perf. 12½*
C61 AP18 100fr dk red, ol & blk 2.25 .60
a. Souvenir sheet of 4 10.00 10.00

Konrad Adenauer (1876-1967), chancellor of West Germany (1949-63).

Weather Balloon, Vegetation and WMO Emblem — AP19

1968, Mar. 23 Engr. *Perf. 13*
C62 AP19 50fr blk, ultra & bl grn 1.25 .40

8th World Meteorological Day, Mar. 23.

19th Olympic Games, Mexico City, Oct. 12-27 — AP20

1968, Oct. 12 Engr. *Perf. 13*
C63 AP20 20fr Hurdling .55 .25
C64 AP20 30fr Javelin .70 .30
C65 AP20 50fr Judo 1.40 .35
C66 AP20 75fr Basketball 2.25 .65
Nos. C63-C66 (4) 4.90 1.55

PHILEXAFRIQUE Issue

Young Woman Reading Letter, by Jean Raoux AP21

1968, Oct. 26 Photo. *Perf. 12½*

C67 AP21 100fr buff & multi 3.50 2.00

PHILEXAFRIQUE, Phil. Exhib. in Abidjan, Feb. 14-23, 1969. Printed with alternating buff label.

2nd PHILEXAFRIQUE Issue

Common Design Type

Senegal #160 and Boulevard, Dakar.

1969, Feb. 14 Engr. *Perf. 13*

C68 CD128 50fr grn, gray & pur 2.00 1.40

Tourist Emblem with Map of Africa and Dove — AP22

1969 Photo. *Perf. 13*

C69 AP22 100fr red, lt grn & lt bl 1.75 .50

Year of African Tourism, 1969.

Pres. Lamine Gueye (1891-1968) AP23

Design: 45fr, Pres. Gueye wearing fez.

1969, June 10 Photo. *Perf. 12½*

C70 AP23 30fr brn, org & blk .45 .25

C71 AP23 45fr brn, lt grnsh bl & blk 1.25 .30

a. Min. sheet, 2 ea #C70-C71 3.50 3.50

"Transmission of Thought" Tapestry by Ousmane Faye — AP24

Fari, Tapestry by Allaye N'Diaye — AP25

1969, Oct. 25 Photo. *Perf. 12½*

C72 AP24 25fr multicolored .90 .35

Perf. 12x12½

C73 AP25 50fr multicolored 2.00 .65

Europafrica Issue

Baila Bridge — AP26

1969, Nov. 15 Photo. *Perf. 13x12*

C74 AP26 100fr multicolored 2.00 .50

Emile Lécrivain, Plane and Toulouse-Dakar Route — AP27

1970, Jan. 31 Engr. *Perf. 13*

C75 AP27 50fr grn, slate & rose brn 1.25 .40

40th anniv. of the disappearance of the aviator Emile Lécrivain (1897-1929).

René Maran, Martinique AP28

Portraits: 45fr, Marcus Garvey, Jamaica. 50fr, Dr. Price Mars, Haiti.

1970, Mar. 21 Photo. *Perf. 12½*

C76 AP28 30fr red brn, lt grn & blk .35 .25

C77 AP28 45fr blue, pink & blk 1.00 .25

C78 AP28 50fr grn, buff & blk 1.10 .40

Nos. C76-C78 (3) 2.45 .90

Issued to honor prominent Negro leaders.

"One People, One Purpose, One Faith" AP29

1970, Apr. 3 Photo. *Perf. 11½*

C79 AP29 500fr gold & multi 7.50 3.00

a. Souvenir sheet 10.00 10.00

10th anniv. of independence. No. C79 sold for 600fr.

Bay of Naples and Dakar Post Office — AP30

1970, May 2 Photo. *Perf. 13x12½*

C80 AP30 100fr multicolored 2.00 .60

10th Europa Phil. Exhib., Naples, May 2-10.

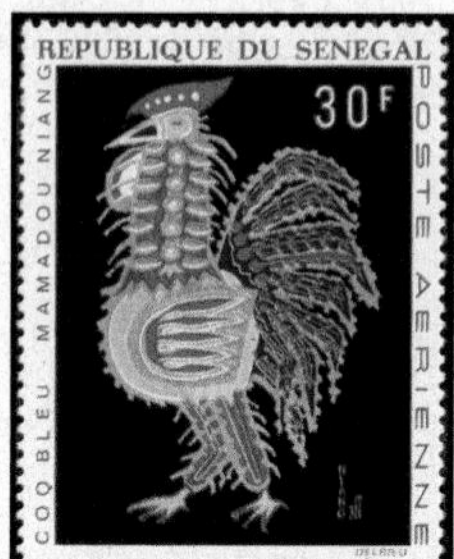

Blue Cock, by Mamadou Niang AP31

Tapestries: 45fr, Fairy. 75fr, "Lunaris," by Jean Lurçat.

1970, June 20 Photo. *Perf. 12½x12*

C81 AP31 30fr black & multi .55 .35

C82 AP31 45fr dk red brn & multi 2.00 .50

C83 AP31 75fr yellow & multi 3.00 .65

Nos. C81-C83 (3) 5.55 1.50

Head of the Courtesan Nagakawa, by Chobunsai Yeishi, and Mt. Fuji, by Hokusai — AP32

EXPO Emblem and: 25fr, Woman Playing Guitar, by Hokusai, and Sun Tower, vert. 150fr, "One of the Present-day Beauties of Nanboku" by Katsukawa Shuncho, vert.

1970, July 18 Engr. *Perf. 13*

C84 AP32 25fr red & green .65 .25

C85 AP32 75fr yel grn, dk bl & red brn 1.75 .35

C86 AP32 150fr bl, red brn & ocher 2.75 .80

Nos. C84-C86 (3) 5.15 1.40

EXPO '70 Intl. Exhib., Osaka, Japan, Mar. 15-Sept. 13.

Tuna, Processing Plant and Ship — AP33

Urban Development in Dakar — AP34

1970, Aug. 22 Engr. *Perf. 13*

C87 AP33 30fr dl red, blk & brt bl 1.00 .25

C88 AP34 100fr chocolate & grn 1.75 .60

Progress in industrialization and urbanization in Dakar.

Beethoven; Napoleon and Allegory of Eroica Symphony AP35

Design: 100fr, Beethoven holding quill.

1970, Sept. 26 Engr. *Perf. 13*

C89 AP35 50fr ol, brn & ocher 2.25 .50

C90 AP35 100fr Prus grn & dp claret 4.50 1.10

Ludwig van Beethoven (1770-1827), composer.

Globe, Scales and Women of Four Races — AP36

1970, Oct. 24 Engr. *Perf. 13*

C91 AP36 100fr grn, ocher & red 2.25 .80

25th anniversary of United Nations.

De Gaulle, Map of Africa, Symbols — AP37

100fr, Charles de Gaulle & map of Senegal.

1970, Dec. 31 Photo. *Perf. 12½*

C92 AP37 50fr multicolored 1.75 .85

C93 AP37 100fr blue & multi 3.50 1.60

Honoring Pres. Charles de Gaulle as liberator of the colonies.

"A Roof for Every Refugee" — AP38

1971, Jan. 16

C94 AP38 100fr multicolored 1.75 .65

High Commissioner for Refugees, 20th anniv.

Phillis Wheatley, American Poet — AP39

Prominent Blacks: 40fr, James E. K. Aggrey, Methodist missionary, Ghana. 60fr, Alain Le Roy Locke, American educator. 100fr, Booker T. Washington, American educator.

1971, Apr. 10 Photo. *Perf. 12½*

C95	AP39	25fr multicolored	.25	.25
C96	AP39	40fr blk, bl & bis	.45	.30
C97	AP39	60fr blk, bl & emer	1.00	.40
C98	AP39	100fr blk, bl & red	1.50	.60
		Nos. C95-C98 (4)	3.20	1.55

Napoleon as First Consul, by Ingres AP40

Designs: 25fr, Napoleon in 1809, by Robert Lefevre. 35fr, Napoleon on his death bed, by Georges Rouget. 50fr, Awakening into Immortality, sculpture by Francois Rude.

1971, June 19 Photo. *Perf. 13*

C99	AP40	15fr gold & multi	.70	.40
C100	AP40	25fr gold & multi	1.00	.50
C101	AP40	35fr gold & multi	1.40	.60
C102	AP40	50fr gold & multi	2.75	1.00
		Nos. C99-C102 (4)	5.85	2.50

Napoleon Bonaparte (1769-1821).

Gamal Abdel Nasser — AP41

1971, July 17 *Perf. 12½*

C103	AP41	50fr multicolored	1.00	.30

Nasser (1918-1970), President of Egypt.

Alfred Nobel — AP41a

1971, Sept. 25 Photo. *Perf. 13½x13*

C103A	AP41a	100fr multicolored	2.25	.60

Alfred Nobel (1833-1896), inventor of dynamite who established the Nobel Prizes.

Iranian Flag and Senegal Coat of Arms — AP42

1971, Oct. 15 *Perf. 13x12½*

C104	AP42	200fr multicolored	3.00	1.00

2500th anniversary of the founding of the Persian empire by Cyrus the Great.

African Postal Union Issue
Common Design Type

Design: 100fr, Arms of Senegal and UAMPT Building, Brazzaville, Congo.

1971, Nov. 13 *Perf. 13x13½*

C105	CD135	100fr blue & multi	1.60	.50

Louis Armstrong (1900-1971), American Jazz Musician — AP43

1971, Nov. 27 Photo. *Perf. 12½*

C106	AP43	150fr gold & dk brn	6.75	1.60

Sapporo Olympic Emblem and Speed Skating — AP44

Sapporo '72 Emblem and: 10fr, Bobsledding. 125fr, Skiing.

1972, Jan. 22 *Perf. 13*

C107	AP44	5fr multicolored	.25	.25
C108	AP44	10fr multicolored	.25	.25
C109	AP44	125fr multicolored	3.00	.60
		Nos. C107-C109 (3)	3.50	1.10

11th Winter Olympic Games, Sapporo, Japan, Feb. 3-13.

Fonteghetto della Farina, by Canaletto — AP45

Design: 100fr, San Giorgio Maggiore, by Giovanni Antonio Guardi, vert.

1972, Feb. 26

C110	AP45	50fr gold & multi	1.25	.65
C111	AP45	100fr gold & multi	2.50	1.25

UNESCO campaign to save Venice.

Theater Type of Regular Issue

150fr, Daniel Sorano as Shylock, vert.

1972, Mar. 25 Photo. *Perf. 12½x13*

C112	A99	150fr multicolored	4.00	1.50

Environment Type of Regular Issue

100fr, Protection of the ocean (oil slick).

1972, June 3 Photo. *Perf. 13x12½*

C113	A101	100fr multicolored	2.25	.60

Emperor Haile Selassie, Ethiopian and Senegalese Flags — AP46

1972, July 23 Photo. *Perf. 13½x13*

C114	AP46	100fr gold & multi	1.75	.60

80th birthday of Emperor Haile Selassie of Ethiopia.

Swordfish — AP47

Designs: 65fr, Killer whale. 75fr, Rhincodon. 125fr, Common rorqual (whale).

1972-73 Photo. *Perf. 11½*

C115	AP47	50fr multi	3.75	.75
C116	AP47	65fr multi	5.00	1.25
C117	AP47	75fr multi	7.25	1.50
C118	AP47	125fr multi	8.50	1.75
		Nos. c115-c118 (4)	24.50	5.25

Issued: #C115, C118, 11/25/72; #C116-C117, 7/28/73.

Palace of the Republic — AP48

1973, Apr. 3 Photo. *Perf. 13*

C119	AP48	100fr multi	1.75	.60

Hotel Teranga, Dakar — AP49

1973, May 26 Photo. *Perf. 13*

C120	AP49	100fr multi	1.75	.60

Emblem of African Lions Club — AP50

1973, June 2

C121	AP50	150fr multi	2.50	.80

15th Congress of Lions Intl., District 403, Dakar, June 1-2.

"Couple with Mimosa," by Marc Chagall AP51

1973, Aug. 11 Photo. *Perf. 13*

C122	AP51	200fr multi	7.00	2.75

Map of Italy with Riccione — AP52

1973, Aug. 25 Engr.

C123	AP52	100fr dk grn, red & pur	2.25	.60

Intl. Phil. Exhib., Riccione 1973.

Raoul Follereau and World Map — AP53

100fr, Dr. Armauer G. Hansen & leprosy bacilli.

1973, Dec. 22 Engr. *Perf. 13*

C124	AP53	40fr sl grn, pur & red brn	1.10	.25
C125	AP53	100fr sl grn, mag & plum	2.40	.75

Centenary of the discovery of the Hansen bacillus, the cause of leprosy.

Human Rights Flame and People — AP54

65fr, Human Rights flame and drummer.

1973, Dec. 15 Photo. *Perf. 13½*

C126	AP54	35fr grn & multi	.70	.25
C127	AP54	65fr org & multi	1.00	.40

25th anniv. of the Universal Declaration of Human Rights.

Men of Four Races, Arms of Dakar, Congress Emblem — AP55

50fr, Key joining twin cities & emblem, vert.

1973, Dec. 26 **Photo.**
C128 AP55 50fr org & multi .90 .35
C129 AP55 125fr red & multi 1.75 .50

8th Congress of the World Federation of Twin Cities, Dakar, Dec. 26-29.

Finfoots — AP56

2fr, Spoonbills. 3fr, Crown cranes. 4fr, Egrets. No. C134, Flamingos, sun UR corner. No. C135, Flamingos, sun UL corner.

1974, Feb. 9 **Photo.** ***Perf. 13***
C130 AP56 1fr shown .25 .25
C131 AP56 2fr multi .25 .25
C132 AP56 3fr multi .30 .25
C133 AP56 4fr multi .30 .25
C134 AP56 250fr multi 7.00 1.60
C135 AP56 250fr multi 7.00 1.60
a. Strip of 2 + label 12.50
Nos. C130-C135 (6) 15.10 4.20

Djoudj Park bird sanctuary. Denomination in gold on No. C134, in black on No. C135.

Tiger Attacking Wild Horse, by Delacroix — AP57

Design: 200fr, Tiger Hunt, by Eugéne Delacroix (1798-1863).

1974, Mar. 23 **Photo.** ***Perf. 13***
C136 AP57 150fr gold & multi 3.00 .80
C137 AP57 200fr gold & multi 3.75 1.25

Intl. Fair, Dakar — AP57a

1974, Nov. 28 **Embossed** ***Perf. 10½***
C137A AP57a 350fr silver 5.75 4.50
C137B AP57a 1500fr gold 27.50 18.00

Soyuz and Apollo, Space Docking Emblem — AP58

1975, May 23 **Engr.** ***Perf. 13***
C138 AP58 125fr multi 2.00 .60

US-USSR space cooperation.
For overprint see No. C140.

Senegal Type D6, Tuscany Type A1, Map of Italy AP59

1975, Aug. 23 **Engr.** ***Perf. 13***
C139 AP59 125fr org, vio & dk red 2.00 .65

Intl. Phil. Exhib., Riccione 1975.

No. C138 Overprinted "JONCTION / 17 Juil. 1975"

1975, Oct. 21 **Engr.** ***Perf. 13***
C140 AP58 125fr multi 2.00 .60

Apollo-Soyuz link-up in space, July 17, 1975.

Boston Massacre — AP60

Design: 500fr, Lafayette, Washington, Rochambeau and Battle of Yorktown.

1975, Dec. 20 **Engr.** ***Perf. 13***
C141 AP60 250fr ultra, red & brn 3.00 1.10
C142 AP60 500fr bl & ver 6.75 2.50

American Bicentennial.

Concorde and Map — AP61

1976, Jan. 21 **Litho.** ***Perf. 13***
C143 AP61 300fr multi 4.00 2.00

First commercial flight of supersonic jet Concorde, Paris to Rio de Janeiro, Jan. 21.
For overprint see No. C145.

2nd Intl. Fair, Dakar — AP61a

1976, Dec. 3 **Embossed** ***Perf. 10½***
C143A AP61a 500fr silver 6.50 6.50
C143B AP61a 1500fr gold 27.50 27.50

Spaceship and Control Room — AP62

1977, June 25 **Litho.** ***Perf. 12½***
C144 AP62 300fr multi 3.25 1.25

Viking space mission to Mars.

No. C143 Overprinted in Red "22.11.77 / PARIS NEW-YORK"

1977, Nov. 22 ***Perf. 13***
C145 AP61 300fr multi 4.00 2.00

Concorde, 1st commercial flight, Paris-New York.

Evolution of Fishing — AP62a

Designs: 10fr, Fishermen hauling in netted catch. 15fr, Two fishermen in canoe. 20fr, Ship, man holding fish.

1977 **Litho.** ***Perf. 12¾***
C145A AP62a 5fr shown — —
C145B AP62a 10fr multi — —
C145C AP62a 15fr multi — —
C145D AP62a 20fr multi — —

Philexafrique II-Essen Issue
Common Design Types

Designs: No. C146, Lion & Senegal #C28. No. C147, Capercaillie & Schleswig-Holstein #1.

1978, Nov. 1 **Litho.** ***Perf. 12½***
C146 CD138 100fr multi 2.00 1.50
C147 CD139 100fr multi 2.00 1.50
a. Pair, #C146-C147 10.00 4.00

J. Dabry, L. Gimie, and J. Mermoz, Airplane, Map of Route (St. Louis-Natal) — AP63

1980, Dec. **Photo.** ***Perf. 13***
C148 AP63 300fr multi 3.25 1.00

1st airmail crossing of So. Atlantic, 50th anniv.

1st Transatlantic Commercial Airmail Flight, 55th Anniv. — AP64

1985, May 12 **Litho.** ***Perf. 13***
C149 AP64 250fr multi 2.75 1.00

Clement Ader (1841-1926), Engineer and Aviation Pioneer — AP65

Ader and: 145fr, Automobile, microphone. 180fr, 615fr, 940fr, Bat-winged steam powered airplane.

1991, June 7 **Litho.** ***Perf. 13***
C150 AP65 145fr multicolored 2.00 .40
C151 AP65 180fr multicolored 2.25 .65
C152 AP65 615fr multi, vert. 7.50 2.25
Nos. C150-C152 (3) 11.75 3.30

Souvenir Sheet

C153 AP65 940fr multi, vert. 7.00 3.50

AIR POST SEMI-POSTAL STAMPS

French Revolution Issue
Common Design Type

1939 **Unwmk.** **Photo.** ***Perf. 13***
Name and Value Typo. in Orange
CB1 CD83 4.75 + 4fr brn blk 14.00 14.00

Surtax used for the defense of the colonies.

Dahomey Types SPAP1-SPAP3 Inscribed Senegal
Perf. 13½x12½, 13 (#CB4)
Photo, Engr. (#CB4)

1942, June 22
CB2 SPAP1 1.50fr + 3.50fr grn .80 *6.50*
CB3 SPAP2 2fr + 6fr brown .80 *6.50*
CB4 SPAP3 3fr + 9fr car red .80 *6.50*
Nos. CB2-CB4 (3) 2.40 *19.50*

Native children's welfare fund.

Colonial Education Fund
Common Design Type
Perf. 12½x13½

1942, June 22 **Engr.**
CB5 CD86a 1.20fr + 1.80fr blue & red .80 *6.50*

Catalogue values for unused stamps in this section, from this point to the end of the section, are for Never Hinged items.

Republic

Nile Gods Uniting Upper and Lower Egypt (Abu Simbel) — SPAP1

1964, Mar. 7 **Engr.** ***Perf. 13***
CB6 SPAP1 25fr + 5fr Prus bl, red brn & sl grn 1.60 .65

UNESCO campaign to save historic monuments in Nubia.

POSTAGE DUE STAMPS

Postage Due Stamps of French Colonies Surcharged

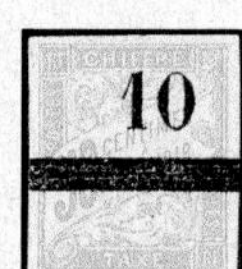

1903 **Unwmk.** ***Imperf.***
J1 D1 10c on 50c lilac 105.00 105.00
J2 D1 10c on 60c brown, *buff* 105.00 105.00
J3 D1 10c on 1fr rose, *buff* 425.00 425.00
Nos. J1-J3 (3) 635.00 635.00

D2

1906 **Typo.** ***Perf. 14x13½***
J4 D2 5c green, *grnsh* 7.00 4.25
J5 D2 10c red brown 7.00 5.00
J6 D2 15c dark blue 7.00 6.25
J7 D2 20c black, *yellow* 10.50 6.25
J8 D2 30c red, *straw* 10.50 10.00
J9 D2 50c violet 10.50 7.50
J10 D2 60c black, *buff* 17.00 15.00
J11 D2 1fr black, *pinkish* 27.50 22.50
Nos. J4-J11 (8) 97.00 76.75

D3

1914

No.	Type	Denomination	Unused	Used
J12	D3	5c green	.70	.45
J13	D3	10c rose	.70	.45
J14	D3	15c gray	1.10	.70
J15	D3	20c brown	1.10	1.10
J16	D3	30c blue	1.40	1.10
J17	D3	50c black	1.75	1.40
J18	D3	60c orange	2.10	1.40
J19	D3	1fr violet	2.10	1.75
		Nos. J12-J19 (8)	10.95	8.35

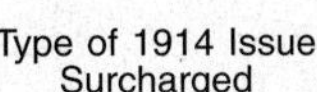
Type of 1914 Issue Surcharged

1927

No.	Type	Denomination	Unused	Used
J20	D3	2fr on 1fr lilac rose	10.50	7.00
J21	D3	3fr on 1fr org brn	10.50	7.00

D4

1935 **Engr.** ***Perf. 12½x12***

No.	Type	Denomination	Unused	Used
J22	D4	5c yellow green	.25	.25
J23	D4	10c red orange	.25	.25
J24	D4	15c violet	.25	.25
J25	D4	20c olive green	.25	.25
J26	D4	30c reddish brown	.25	.25
J27	D4	50c rose lilac	1.40	1.40
J28	D4	60c orange	1.40	1.40
J29	D4	1fr black	1.10	1.10
J30	D4	2fr dark blue	1.10	1.10
J31	D4	3fr dark carmine	1.40	1.40
		Nos. J22-J31 (10)	7.65	7.65

Catalogue values for unused stamps in this section, from this point to the end of the section, are for Never Hinged items.

Republic

D5

1961, Feb. 20 **Typo.** ***Perf. 14x13½***

No.	Type	Denomination	Unused	Used
J32	D5	1fr orange & red	.25	.25
J33	D5	2fr ultra & red	.25	.25
J34	D5	5fr brown & red	.25	.25
J35	D5	20fr green & red	.60	.60
J36	D5	25fr red lilac & red	1.25	1.25
		Nos. J32-J36 (5)	2.60	2.60

Lion — D6

1966-83 **Typo.** ***Perf. 14x13***
Lion in Gold

No.	Type	Denomination	Unused	Used
J37	D6	1fr red & black	.25	.25
J38	D6	2fr yel brn & black	.25	.25
J39	D6	5fr red lilac & black	.25	.25
J40	D6	10fr brt blue & black	.25	.25
J41	D6	20fr emerald & black	.40	.40
J42	D6	30fr gray & black	.80	.80
J43	D6	60fr blue & black	.40	.40
J44	D6	90fr rose & black	.60	.40
		Nos. J37-J44 (8)	3.20	3.00

Issued: 1fr-30fr, 12/1/66; others, 10/1983.

OFFICIAL STAMPS

Catalogue values for unused stamps in this section are for Never Hinged items.

Arms — O1

Perf. 14x13½
1961, Sept. 18 **Typo.** **Unwmk.**
Denominations in Black

No.	Type	Denomination	Unused	Used
O1	O1	1fr sepia & bl	.25	.25
O2	O1	2fr dk bl & org	.25	.25
O3	O1	5fr maroon & grn	.25	.25
O4	O1	10fr ver & bl	.25	.25
O5	O1	25fr vio bl & ver	.65	.25
O6	O1	50fr ver & gray	1.00	.45
O7	O1	85fr lilac & org	2.00	.60
O8	O1	100fr ver & yel grn	2.75	1.10
		Nos. O1-O8 (8)	7.40	3.40

Baobab Tree — O2

1966-77 **Typo.** ***Perf. 14x13***

No.	Type	Denomination	Unused	Used
O9	O2	1fr yel & blk	.25	.25
O10	O2	5fr org & blk	.25	.25
O11	O2	10fr red & blk	.25	.25
O12	O2	20fr dp red lil & blk	.25	.25
O13	O2	25fr dp lil & blk ('75)	.45	.25
O14	O2	30fr bl & blk	.45	.25
O15	O2	35fr bl & blk ('73)	.55	.25
O16	O2	40fr grnsh bl & blk ('75)	.55	.25
O17	O2	55fr emer & blk	1.00	.45
O18	O2	60fr emer & blk ('77)	.55	.25
O19	O2	90fr dk bl grn & blk	1.40	.25
O20	O2	100fr brn & blk	1.75	.25
		Nos. O9-O20 (12)	7.70	3.20

See Nos. O22-O25.

No. O17 Surcharged with New Value and Two Bars

1969

No.	Type	Denomination	Unused	Used
O21	O2	60fr on 55fr emer & blk	1.75	.25

1983, Oct. **Typo.** ***Perf. 14x13***

No.	Type	Denomination	Unused	Used
O22	O2	90fr dk grn & blk	.60	.25

"90F" is shorter and wider than on No. O19.

Types of 1966-77 Official Stamps

1991 **Litho.** ***Perf. 13x13¼***

No.	Type	Denomination	Unused	Used
O22B	O2	45fr blue & black	—	—
O23	O2	50fr red & blk	1.00	1.00
O24	O2	145fr brt grn & blk	2.75	2.75
O25	O2	180fr org yel & blk	3.25	3.25
		Nos. O23-O25 (3)	7.00	7.00

An additional stamp was issued in this set. The editors would like to examine any example.

No. O22B Surcharged

2010 ? **Litho.** ***Perf. 13x13¼***

No.	Type	Denomination	Unused	Used
O26	O2	100fr on 45fr #O22B		—

SENEGAMBIA & NIGER

ˌse-nə-ˈgam-bē-ə and ˈnī-jər

A French Administrative unit for the Senegal and Niger possessions in Africa during the period when the French possessions in Africa were being definitively divided into colonies and protectorates. The name was dropped in 1904 when this territory was consolidated with part of French Sudan, under the name Upper Senegal and Niger.

100 Centimes = 1 Franc

Navigation and Commerce — A1

1903 **Unwmk.** **Typo.** ***Perf. 14x13½***
Name of Colony in Blue or Carmine

No.	Type	Denomination	Unused	Used
1	A1	1c black, *lil bl*	2.10	*2.75*
2	A1	2c brown, *buff*	2.10	*2.75*
3	A1	4c claret, *lav*	5.75	*6.25*
4	A1	5c yel grn	7.00	*7.50*
5	A1	10c red	7.00	*7.25*
6	A1	15c gray	14.50	14.50
7	A1	20c red, *green*	12.50	*12.50*
8	A1	25c blue	21.00	17.50
9	A1	30c brn, *bister*	17.50	*19.00*
10	A1	40c red, *straw*	21.00	*25.00*
11	A1	50c brn, *azure*	45.00	*50.00*
12	A1	75c deep vio, *org*	52.50	*52.50*
13	A1	1fr brnz grn, *straw*	70.00	*70.00*
		Nos. 1-13 (13)	277.95	287.50

Perf. 13½x14 stamps are counterfeits.

SERBIA

'sər-bē-ə

LOCATION — In southeastern Europe, bounded by Romania and Bulgaria on the east, the former Austro-Hungarian Empire on the north, Greece on the south, and Albania and Montenegro on the west
GOVT. — Kingdom
AREA — 18,650 sq. mi.
POP. — 2,911,701 (1910)
CAPITAL — Belgrade

A powerful kingdom during the Middle Ages, Serbia was conquered by the Ottoman Turks in 1389 and remained under Turkish rule until 1829, when it became an autonomous region. In 1878 it became fully independent and led the movement to unite the southern Slavs into a single state under Serbian rule. Occupied by Germany, Austria-Hungary and Bulgaria during World War I, the collapse of Austria-Hungary in the autumn of 1918 made it possible for Serbia to realize its national ambitions.

On December 1, 1918, Serbia absorbed Montenegro, Bosnia and Herzegovina, Croatia, Dalmatia and Slovenia, to form the Kingdom of the Serbs, Croats and Slovenes, which became the Kingdom of Yugoslavia in 1929.

During World War II, Yugoslavia was broken up by its Axis occupiers, and a German satellite regime was established in Serbia. After the war, it became one of the constituent republics of the Socialist Federal Republic of Yugoslavia.

In 1992, with the dissolution of the greater Yugoslav republic, only Montenegro remained associated with Serbia, first in the Federal Republic of Yugoslavia and, after 2002, in the looser federation of Serbia & Montenego.

After a referendum on independence on May 21, 2006, Montenegro seceded from Serbia and Montenegro, declaring independence on June 3, 2006. Serbia formally accepted this secession on June 7. While some stamps issued after June 7 bear the "Serbia and Montengro" inscription, they were sold only in Serbia.

100 Paras = 1 Dinar

Catalogue values for unused stamps in this country are for Never Hinged items, beginning with Scott 180 in the regular postage section and Scott RA2 in the postal tax section.

Coat of Arms — A1

Prince Michael (Obrenovich III) — A2

1866 Unwmk. Typo. *Imperf.*

Paper colored Through

1 A1 1p dk green, *dk vio rose* 72.50

Surface Colored Paper, Thin or Thick

2 A1 1p dk green, *lil rose* 72.50
a. 1p olive green, *rose* 72.50
b. 1p deep grn, *pale rose* (thick paper) 2,750.
c. 1p lt olive grn, *pale rose* 72.50
3 A1 2p red brown, *lilac* 72.50
a. 2p red brn, *lil gray* (thick paper) 450.00
b. 2p dl grn, *lil gray* (thick paper) 2,750.
Nos. 1-3 (3) 217.50

Vienna Printing
Perf. 12

4 A2 10p orange 1,600. 1,050.
5 A2 20p rose 1,350. 375.00
6 A2 40p blue 1,200. 160.00
a. Half used as 20p on cover
Nos. 4-6 (3) 4,150. 1,585.

Belgrade Printing
Perf. 9½

7 A2 1p green 24.00 *725.00*
8 A2 2p bister brn 37.50 *725.00*
9 A2 20p rose 19.00 *29.00*
a. Vert. pair, imperf. between
10 A2 40p ultra 300.00 *325.00*
a. Half used as 20p on cover 17,000.
Nos. 7-10 (4) 380.50

Pelure Paper

11 A2 10p orange 110.00 *140.00*
12 A2 20p rose 95.00 19.00
a. Pair, imperf. between
13 A2 40p ultra 75.00 50.00
a. Horiz. pair, imperf. between 5,500. 6,250.
b. Half used as 20p on cover 12,000.
Nos. 11-13 (3) 280.00 209.00

Nos. 1-3, 7-8, 14-16, 25-26 were used only as newspaper tax stamps.

1868-69 Ordinary Paper *Imperf.*

14 A2 1p green 67.50
a. 1p olive green ('69) *4,000.*
15 A2 2p brown 95.00
a. 2p bister brown ('69) 425.00

Counterfeits of type A2 are common.

Prince Milan (Obrenovich IV) — A3

Perf. 9½, 12 and Compound

1869-78

16 A3 1p yellow 6.00 *120.00*
17 A3 10p red brown 9.50 5.25
a. 10p yellow brown *475.00* 75.00
18 A3 10p orange ('78) 2.40 *8.00*
19 A3 15p orange 85.00 32.50
20 A3 20p gray blue 1.50 2.50
a. 20p ultramarine 4.75 2.40
b. Half used as 10p on cover
21 A3 25p rose 2.40 *8.00*
22 A3 35p lt green 4.75 4.75
23 A3 40p violet 2.40 *3.25*
a. Half used as 20p on cover
24 A3 50p blue green 12.00 8.00
Nos. 16-24 (9) 125.95 *192.25*

The first setting, which included all values except No. 18, had the stamps 2-2½mm apart.

A new setting, introduced in 1878, had the stamps 3-4mm apart, providing wider margins. Only Nos. 17, 18, 20 and 21 exist in this new setting, which differs also in shades from the earlier setting.

The narrow-spaced Nos. 17, 20 and 21 are rarer, especially unused, as are the early shades of Nos. 23 and 24.

All values except Nos. 19 and 24 are known in various partly perforated varieties.

Counterfeits exist.

See No. 25.

Prince Milan (Obrenovich IV) — A4

1872-79 *Imperf.*

25 A3 1p yellow 8.50 *32.50*
a. Tête bêche pair
26 A4 2p blk, thin paper ('79) 1.90 .85
a. Thick paper ('73) 4.50 *32.50*

Used value of No. 26 is for canceled-to-order.

King Milan I — A5

1880 *Perf. 13x13½*

27 A5 5p pale green 2.00 .45
28 A5 10p carmine 2.75 .45
29 A5 20p orange 1.40 .95
a. 20p yellow 4.75 2.00
30 A5 25p ultra 1.90 1.40
a. 25p blue 2.25 1.40
31 A5 50p brown 1.90 *6.00*
a. 50p brown violet 275.00 5.75
32 A5 1d violet 13.50 14.50
Nos. 27-32 (6) 23.45 23.75

King Alexander (Obrenovich V) — A6

1890

33 A6 5p green .45 .25
34 A6 10p rose red 1.60 .25
35 A6 15p red violet 1.40 .25
36 A6 20p orange .95 .25
37 A6 25p blue 1.90 .45
38 A6 50p brown 3.75 3.75
39 A6 1d dull lilac 14.50 14.50
Nos. 33-39 (7) 24.55 19.70

King Alexander — A7

1894-96 *Perf. 13x13½*

Granite Paper

40 A7 5p green 5.25 .25
a. Perf. 11½ 16.00 .80
41 A7 10p car rose 8.00 .25
b. Perf. 11½ 160.00 1.90
42 A7 15p violet 13.00 .30
43 A7 20p orange 120.00 .95
a. Half used as 10p on cover *450.00*
44 A7 25p blue 24.00 .45
45 A7 50p brown 29.00 .95
46 A7 1d dk green 2.40 3.75
47 A7 1d red brn, *bl* ('96) 28.00 8.00
Nos. 40-47 (8) 229.65 14.90

1896-1900 *Perf. 13x13½*

Ordinary Paper

48 A7 1p dull red .40 .25
49 A7 5p green ('98) 4.50 .25
a. Compound perf., with 11½ 32.50 1.50
50 A7 10p rose ('98) 127.50 .30
a. Compound perf., with 11½ 475.00 16.00
51 A7 15p violet ('00) 175.00 1.90
a. Compound perf., with 11½ 400.00 16.00
53 A7 25p deep blue ('00) 80.00 1.60
a. Compound perf., with 11½ 325.00 47.50
Nos. 48-53 (5) 387.40 4.30

1898-1906 *Perf. 11½*

48b A7 1p dull red ('06) .40 .25
49b A7 5p green 4.50 .25
50b A7 10p rose 80.00 .25
51b A7 15p violet ('00) 9.25 .30
52 A7 20p orange ('00) 7.25 .30
53b A7 25p deep blue ('00) 2.25 .45
c. 25p ultramarine ('02) 7.25 .45
54 A7 50p brown ('00) 29.00 2.25
c. 50p red brown ('02) 24.00 4.50
Nos. 48b-54 (7) 103.94 4.05

Nos. 49-54 exist imperf.

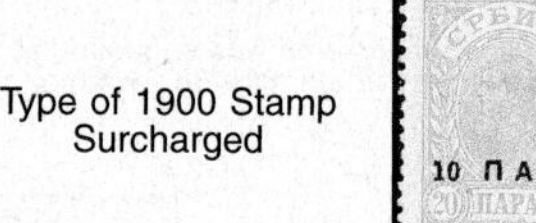
Type of 1900 Stamp Surcharged

1900

56 A7 10p on 20p rose 7.25 .95

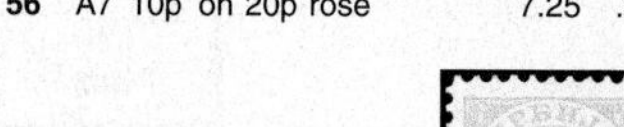
Same, Surcharged

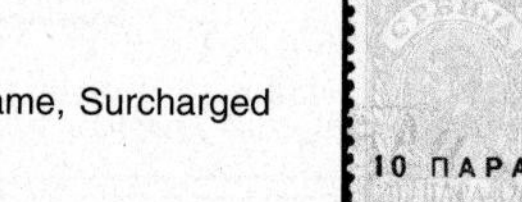

1901

57 A7 10p on 20p rose 7.50 .95
58 A7 15p on 1d red brn, *bl* 13.00 1.90
a. Inverted surcharge *100.00* *110.00*

King Alexander (Obrenovich V)
A8 A9

1901-03 Typo. *Perf. 11½*

59 A8 5p green ('01) .80 .40
60 A8 10p rose ('02) .40 .40
61 A8 15p red violet ('03) .40 .40
62 A8 20p orange ('03) .40 .40
63 A8 25p ultra ('(03) .40 .40
64 A8 50p bister ('03) .80 .80
65 A9 1d brown ('03) 1.20 2.00
66 A9 3d brt rose 24.00 10.00
67 A9 5d deep violet 20.00 10.00
a. 5d violet ('02) 12.00 *16.00*
Nos. 59-67 (9) 48.40 24.80

Counterfeits of Nos. 66-67 exist. Nos. 59-67 imperf. value of set of pairs, $100.

Arms of Serbia on Head of King Alexander — A10

Type I Type II

Two Types of the Overprint

Type I — Overprint 12mm wide. Bottom of mantle defined by a single line. Wide crown above shield.

Type II — Overprint 10mm wide. Double line at bottom of mantle. Smaller crown above shield.

Arms Overprinted in Blue, Black, Red and Red Brown

1903-04 Type I *Perf. 13½*

68 A10 1p red lil & blk (Bl) 1.10 1.40
a. Inverted overprint 24.00
69 A10 5p yel grn & blk (Bl) .95 .45
70 A10 10p car & blk (Bk) .70 .45
a. Double overprint 24.00
71 A10 15p ol gray & blk (Bk) .70 .45
a. Double overprint 24.00
72 A10 20p org & blk (Bk) .95 .45
73 A10 25p bl & blk (Bk) .95 .45
a. Double overprint 24.00
74 A10 50p gray & blk (R) 5.75 1.40

There were two printings of the type I overprint on Nos. 68-74, one typographed and one lithographed.

Type II

75 A10 1d bl grn & blk (Bk) 14.50 5.75

Nos. 68-75 with overprint omitted are from the remainders. Value, set *$575.*

Perf. 11½

Type I

75A A10 5p (Bl) .95 1.90
75B A10 50p (R) 1.90 9.25
75C A10 1d (Bk) 2.75 19.00

Type II

76 A10 3d vio & blk (R Br) 4.00 4.25
a. Perf. 13½ *175.00*
77 A10 5d lt brn & blk (Bl) 4.00 4.50

Type I With Additional Surcharge

78 A10 1p on 5d (R) 2.75 *14.50*
a. Perf. 13½ *1,200.*
Nos. 68-78 (14) 41.95 64.20

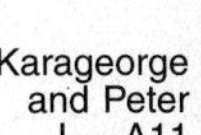

Karageorge and Peter I — A11

Insurgents, 1804 — A12

1904 **Typo.**

79 A11 5p yellow green 1.60 .80
80 A11 10p rose red .95 .80
81 A11 15p red violet .95 .80
82 A11 25p blue 1.75 1.60
83 A11 50p gray brown 1.90 1.90
84 A12 1d bister 2.75 *6.50*
85 A12 3d blue green 3.75 *9.25*
86 A12 5d violet 4.50 *11.50*
Nos. 79-86 (8) 18.15 33.15

Centenary of the Karageorgevich dynasty and the coronation of King Peter. Counterfeits of Nos. 79-86 exist.

King Peter I Karageorgevich — A13

1905 **Thin Wove Paper** ***Perf. 11½***

87 A13 1p gray & blk .30 .25
88 A13 5p yel grn & blk 1.40 .25
89 A13 10p red & blk 3.25 .25
90 A13 15p red lil & blk 3.75 .25
91 A13 20p yellow & blk 6.50 .30
92 A13 25p ultra & blk 9.25 .30
93 A13 30p sl grn & blk 5.75 .30
94 A13 50p dk brown & blk 7.25 .65
95 A13 1d bister & blk 24.00 2.25
96 A13 3d blue grn & blk 2.25 2.25
97 A13 5d violet & blk 16.00 5.75
Nos. 87-97 (11) 79.70 12.80

Counterfeits of Nos. 87-97 abound.

Perf. 12x11½

Thick Wove Paper

87a A13 1p gray & black .30 .25
88a A13 5p yel grn & blk 1.10 .25
89a A13 10p red & blk 3.25 .25
90a A13 15p red lilac & blk 4.50 .30
91a A13 20p yellow & blk 8.50 .30
92a A13 25p ultra & blk 8.00 .30
93a A13 30p sl green & blk 8.00 .30
94a A13 50p dk brown & blk 8.00 .45
95a A13 1d bister & blk 1.00 .45
96a A13 3d blue grn & blk 1.00 1.10
97a A13 3d violet & blk 4.50 3.25

1907-11 **Horiz. Laid Paper**

87b A13 1p gray & black ('08) .45 .25
88b A13 5p yel grn & blk 2.75 .30
89b A13 10p red & blk 8.00 .25
90b A13 15p red lilac & blk ('08) 11.50 .30
91b A13 20p yellow & blk ('08) 8.00 .30
92b A13 25p ultra & blk ('08) 8.00 .30
93b A13 30p sl green & blk ('08) 10.50 .45
94b A13 50p dk brown & blk ('11) 15.00 .95

1911 **Vert. Laid Paper**

87c A13 1p gray & black 3.75 1.10
88c A13 5p yel grn & blk 5.75 .95
89c A13 10p red & blk 45.00 1.90
93c A13 30p sl green & blk 72.50 7.25

1908 **Laid Paper**

98 A13 1p gray & blk .35 .25
99 A13 5p yel grn & blk 2.25 .25
100 A13 10p red & blk 6.75 .25
101 A13 15p red lilac & blk 9.00 .25
102 A13 20p yellow & blk 9.00 .35
103 A13 25p ultra & blk 6.75 .35
104 A13 30p gray grn & blk 10.00 .35
105 A13 50p dk brn & blk 13.00 .75
Nos. 98-105 (8) 57.10 2.80

Nos. 90, 98-100, 102-104 are known imperforate but are not believed to have been issued in this condition.

Values of Nos. 98-105 are for horizontally laid paper. Four values also exist on vertically laid paper (1p, 5p, 10p, 30p).

King Peter I Karageorgevich A14

1911-14 **Thick Wove Paper**

108 A14 1p slate green .25 .25
109 A14 2p dark violet .25 .25
110 A14 5p green .25 .25
111 A14 5p pale yel grn ('14) .40 .25
112 A14 10p carmine .25 .25
113 A14 10p red ('14) .25 .25
114 A14 15p red violet .40 .25
115 A14 15p slate blk ('14) .25 .25
a. 15p red (error) *1,600.* —
116 A14 20p yellow .40 .25
117 A14 20p brown ('14) .65 .40
118 A14 25p deep blue .55 .25
119 A14 25p indigo ('14) .25 .40
120 A14 30p blue green .40 .30
121 A14 30p olive grn ('14) .25 .40
122 A14 50p dk brown .65 .45
123 A14 50p brn red ('14) .55 .45
124 A14 1d orange 29.00 *160.00*
125 A14 1d slate ('14) 4.50 *9.25*
126 A14 3d lake 37.50 *240.00*
127 A14 3d olive yel ('14) 190.00 *1,750.*
128 A14 5d violet 29.00 *200.00*
129 A14 5d dk violet ('14) 7.50 *24.00*
Nos. 108-129 (22) 303.50 *2,388.*

Counterfeits exist.

King Peter and Military Staff — A15

1915 ***Perf. 11½***

132 A15 5p yellow green .45 —
133 A15 10p scarlet .45 —
134 A15 15p slate 7.25
135 A15 20p brown 1.90
136 A15 25p blue 14.50
137 A15 30p olive green 14.50
138 A15 50p orange brown 37.50
Nos. 132-138 (7) 76.55

Nos. 134-138 were prepared but not issued for postal use. Instead they were permitted to be used as wartime emergency currency. Some are known imperf. The 15p also exists in blue from an erroneous cliche in the 25p plate; value $425.

Stamps of France, 1900-1907, with this handstamped control were used in 1916-1918 by the Serbian Postal Bureau on the Island of Corfu. On the 1c to 35c, the handstamp covers 2 or 3 stamps. It was applied after the stamps were on the cover.

King Peter and Prince Alexander — A16

Paris Printing

Clear Impression, Medium White Paper

1918, Jan. 10 **Typo.** ***Perf. 11***

155 A16 1p black .25 .25
a. Horiz. pair, imperf. between 11.00
156 A16 2p olive brown .25 .25
a. Horiz. pair, imperf. between 11.00
157 A16 5p apple green .25 .25
158 A16 10p red .25 .25
a. Horiz. pair, imperf. between 14.00
159 A16 15p black brown .25 .25
160 A16 20p red brown .25 .25
162 A16 25p deep blue .25 .25
163 A16 30p olive green .25 .25
164 A16 50p violet .25 .25
a. Horiz. pair, imperf. between 14.00
165 A16 1d violet brown .95 .55
166 A16 3d slate green 1.40 1.10
167 A16 5d red brown 2.25 1.40
Nos. 155-167 (13) 11.35 6.40

Nos. 157-160, 164 exist imperf. Value each $12.

First Belgrade Printing

1919, Sept. ***Rough Perf. 11½***

Coarse Impression, Thick White Paper

155b A16 1p black .95 .30
159b A16 15p pale red brown 4.50 2.25
161 A16 20p violet 4.50 1.10
165b A16 1d pale red brown 7.50 2.25

Second Belgrade Printing

1920 ***Perf. 11½***

Poor Impression, Rough Perf, Small Holes

Pelure Paper

155c A16 1p black .25 .25
156c A16 2p olive brown .25 .25

Medium to Thick Paper

157c A16 5p yellow green .25 .25
d. Perf. 9 *200.00* *675.00*
158c A16 10p red .25 .25
159c A16 15p black brown .25 .25
160c A16 20p red brown .25 .25
d. 20p chestnut .25 .25
162c A16 25p dull blue .25 .25
163c A16 30p pale olive gray .25 .25
164c A16 50p pale violet .25 .25
165c A16 1d deep brown .45 .30
166c A16 3d dp blue green 2.00 1.40
167c A16 5d red brown 3.50 2.25

Medium to Thin Oily Paper

159e A16 15d black brown .95 .95
160e A16 20d pale red brown — .95
162e A16 25d dull blue — 1.90

Clean-Cut Perfs, Large Hole

155f A16 1p black .25 .25
156f A16 2p olive brown .25 .25

Medium to Thick Paper

157f A16 5p yellow green .25 .25
158f A16 10p red .25 .25
159f A16 15p black brown .25 .25
160f A16 20p red brown .25 .25
g. 20p chestnut .25 .25
162f A16 25p dull blue .25 .25
163f A16 30p pale olive gray .25 .25
164f A16 50p pale violet .25 .25
165f A16 1d deep brown .45 .30
166f A16 3d dp blue green 2.25 1.25

Medium to Thin Oily Paper

159h A16 15p black brown 1.75 .90
160h A16 20p red brown .90 .90
i. 20p chestnut 1.75 1.40
162h A16 25p dull blue — 1.40

Paris Printing

Clear Impression, Clean-Cut Perfs

1920 ***Perf. 11½***

Pelure Paper

169 A16 1p black .25 .25
170 A16 2p olive brown .25 .25

Catalogue values for unused stamps in this section, from this point to the end of the section, are for Never Hinged items.

SERBIA & MONTENEGRO

100 Paras = 1 Dinar

Yugoslavia became Serbia & Montenegro Feb. 4, 2003, with each section of the country maintaining and operating their own postal service, and each having their own currency. After a referendum on independence on May 21, 2006, Montenegro seceded from Serbia and Montenegro, declaring independence on June 3. On June 7, Serbia recognized the dissolution of the union.

The listings below contain stamps bearing the dinar currency, for use in Serbia, or those bearing both the dinar and euro currencies, which were issued for use in either Serbia or Montenegro. Stamps inscribed in euro currency only were used in Montenegro and may be found in listings for that country.

Council of Europe — A20

Map color: 16d, Red violet. 28.70d, Blue.

2003, Apr. 3 **Litho.** ***Perf. 13¾***

180-181 A20 Set of 2 2.75 2.75

Easter — A21

Religious paintings: 12d, From 16th cent. 16d, By D. Bacevic. 26.20d, From 1616. 28.70d, By Giovanni Bellini.

2003, Apr. 18

182-185 A21 Set of 4 4.25 4.25

Belgrade Choral Society, 150th Anniv. A22

2003, Apr. 22 ***Perf. 13¼ Syncopated***

186 A22 16d multi 1.75 1.75

Europa — A23

Man pasting poster on: 28.70d, Pillar. 50d, Wall.

2003, May 9 ***Perf. 13¾***

187-188 A23 Set of 2 *4.50 4.50*

Flowers — A24

2003, May 13

189 Horiz. strip of 4 + central label 4.75 4.75
a. A24 16d Galanthus nivalis .75 .75
b. A24 24d Erythronium dens-canis 1.00 1.00
c. A24 26.20d Hepatica nobilis 1.10 1.10
d. A24 28.70d Anemone ramunculoides 1.25 1.25

Actors and Actresses — A25

No. 190: a, Ilija Stanojevic (1859-1930). b, Dobrivoje Dobrica Milutinovic (1880-1956). c, Zivana Zanka Stokic (1887-1947). d, Ljubinka Bobic (1897-1978). e, Radomir-Rasa Plaovic (1899-1977). f, Milivoje Zivanovic (1900-76). g, Miloslav Mija Aleksic (1923-95). h, Zoran Radmilovic (1933-85).

2003, May 20

190 A25 16d Sheet of 8, #a-h, + 8 labels 6.50 6.50

First Automobile in Belgrade, Cent. — A26

2003, June 3 ***Perf. 13¼ Syncopated***
191 A26 16d multi 6.50 6.50

Nature Protection A27

Views of Zasavicz Nature Reserve: 28.70d, River. 50d, Swamp, vert.

2003, June 12
192-193 A27 Set of 2 4.50 4.50

Yugoslavia No. F1 and Type of Yugoslavia No. 2258 Surcharged

2003, July 3 **Litho.** ***Perf. 12½***
194 RL1 1d on (R) ultra *4.25 4.25*
195 A751 12d on 20p lil rose & pale vio *7.75 7.75*

No. 189b Under Magnifying Glass — A28

Postal Van and Parcels — A29

Woman With Headset A30

Postal Van A31

Cable Television System — A32

2003 **Litho.** ***Perf. 12½***
196 A28 1d multi .60 .60
197 A29 8d multi .80 .80
198 A30 12d multi 1.20 1.20
199 A31 16d multi 1.60 1.60
200 A32 32d multi 3.75 3.75
Nos. 196-200 (5) 7.95 7.95

Issued: 16d, 8/4; others 8/7.

Military Museum, Belgrade, 125th Anniv. — A33

2003, Aug. 27 ***Perf. 13x13¾***
201 A33 16d (25c) multi 1.00 1.00

Serbian Women's Circle, Cent. — A34

Perf. 13¼ Syncopated
2003, Aug. 28
202 A34 16d (25c) multi 1.00 1.00

Serbian and Montenegrin States, 125th Anniv. — A35

Designs: No. 203, 16d (25c), Serbian arms, denomination at UR. No. 204, 16d (25c), Montenegrin arms, denomination at UL.

2003, Sept. 10
203-204 A35 Set of 2 1.75 1.75

Ninth European Model Rocketry Championship, Sremska Mitrovica A36

2003, Sept. 12 ***Perf. 13x13¾***
205 A36 16d (25c) multi 1.00 1.00

Second Danube Countries Conference on Art and Culture — A37

Carved rocks with: No. 206, 16d (25c), Denomination at UL. No. 207, 16d (25c), Denomination at UR.

2003, Sept. 17
206-207 A37 Set of 2 1.60 1.60

Nos. 206-207 were each printed in sheets of 8 + label.

Souvenir Sheet

Serbiafila XIII Philatelic Exhibition — A38

No. 208: a, Belgrade in the 17th century. b, Sculpture.

2003, Sept. 22 ***Perf. 13½***
208 A38 32d (50c) Sheet of 2, #a-b 4.25 4.25

Joy of Europe — A39

Children's drawings: 28.70d (50c), Man, woman, bird and flower. 50d (80c), Rabbit, flowers, horiz.

2003, Oct. 14 ***Perf. 13¼***
209-210 A39 Set of 2 4.25 4.25

Vecernje Novosti Newspaper, 50th Anniv. — A40

2003, Oct. 16
211 A40 32d (50c) multi 1.75 1.75

Stamp Day — A41

2003, Oct. 24
212 A41 16d (25c) multi 3.50 3.50

Association of Applied Artists and Designers, 50th Anniv. — A42

2003, Oct. 29
213 A42 16d (25c) multi 1.10 1.10

National Theater of Montenegro, 50th Anniv. — A43

2003, Nov. 1 ***Perf. 13¾x13***
214 A43 32d (50c) multi 1.60 1.60

City of Pancevo, 850th Anniv. — A44

2003, Nov. 12 ***Perf. 13x13¾***
215 A44 32d (50c) multi 1.75 1.75

Christmas — A45

Designs: 10d, Santa Claus and reindeer. 13.50d, Ornaments. 26.20d, Snowflakes.

2003, Nov. 24 ***Perf. 13¼***
216-218 A45 Set of 3 3.50 3.50
Complete booklet, 10 #216 8.25
Complete booklet, 10 #217 9.25

Serbian Orthodox Church Museum Exhibits — A46

No. 219: a, Painting of St. John the Baptist, 1645. b, Cross, 1602. c, Miter, 15th cent. d, Tabernacle, 1550-51.

2003, Nov. 26 ***Perf. 13¾x13***
219 Horiz. strip of 4 + central label 4.75 4.75
a. A46 16d (25c) multi .80 .80
b. A46 24d (35c) multi 1.10 1.10
c. A46 26.20d (40c) multi 1.25 1.25
d. A46 28.70d (50c) multi 1.35 1.35

Christmas A47

Religious paintings: 12d (20c), Nativity, 1983. 16d (25c), Nativity, 18th cent. 26.20d (40c), Madonna and Child, 2000. 28.70d (50c), Adoration of the Magi, by Albrecht Durer.

2003, Dec. 2 ***Perf. 13x13¼***
220-223 A47 Set of 4 4.00 4.00

Submarine Units, 75th Anniv. — A48

2003, Dec. 10 ***Perf. 13¼***
224 A48 32d (50c) multi 3.00 3.00

Printed in sheets of 8 + label.

Powered Flight, Cent. — A49

Designs: 16d (25c), Wright Brothers and airplane. 28.70d (50c), Airplane in flight, horse-drawn carriages.

2003, Dec. 17
225-226 A49 Set of 2 9.50 9.50

Politika Newspaper, Cent. — A50

Centenary emblem and: No. 227, 16d (25c), Typewriter. No. 228, 16d, (25c), Office building, vert.

2004, Jan. 21
227-228 A50 Set of 2 2.00 2.00

Worldwide Fund for Nature (WWF) A51

No. 229 — Insects: a, Parnassius apollo. b, Rosalia alpina. c, Aeshna viridis. d, Saga pedo.

2004, Jan. 30 ***Perf. 13¼***
229 Horiz. strip of 4 + central label 5.00 5.00
a. A51 12d (20c) multi .60 .60
b. A51 16d (25c) multi .75 .75
c. A51 26.20d (40c) multi 1.25 1.25
d. A51 28.70d (50c) multi 1.50 1.50

First Serbian Rebellion, Bicent. — A52

Bicentennial emblem and: No. 230, 16d (25c), Flag, Karageorge (George Petrovic). No. 231, 16d (25c), Children and map of Europe.

2004, Feb. 13 ***Perf. 13x13¾***
230-231 A52 Set of 2 1.75 1.75

Flora and Butterflies — A53

No. 232: a, Ramonda serbica. b, Ramonda nathaliae. c, Heodes virgaureae. d, Lysandra bellargus.

2004, Feb. 16 ***Perf. 13¾x13***
232 Horiz. strip of 4 + central label 5.50 5.50
a. A53 16d (25c) multi .85 .85
b. A53 24d (35c) multi 1.15 1.15
c. A53 26.20d (40c) multi 1.30 1.30
d. A53 28.70d (50c) multi 1.75 1.75

2004 Summer Olympics, Athens — A54

Serbia and Montenegro Olympic Committee emblem and: 32d (50c), Runner. 56d (80c), Wrestlers.

2004, Feb. 27 ***Perf. 13x13¾***
233-234 A54 Set of 2 4.00 4.00

First Serbian Rebellion, Bicent. A55

Designs: 12d, Rebels. 16d, Flag, gun, vert. 28.70d, Karageorge (George Petrovic), vert. 32d, Children, globe, vert.

2004, Mar. 1 Litho. ***Perf. 13¼***
235-238 A55 Set of 4 4.50 4.50

Campaign Against Terrorism — A56

2004, Mar. 12 ***Perf. 13¾x13***
239 A56 16d (25c) multi 1.25 1.25

Easter — A57

Designs: 16d (25c), The Crucifixion, by Vlasios Coconis. 28.70d (50c), The Resurrection, by Klemens Katounakis.

2004, Mar. 15 ***Perf. 13x13¾***
240-241 A57 Set of 2 2.50 2.50

Milutin Milankovic (1879-1958), Climatologist A58

2004, Mar. 22
242 A58 16d (25c) multi 1.10 1.10

Albert Einstein (1879-1955), Physicist — A59

2004, Mar. 31 ***Perf. 13¾x13***
243 A59 16d (25c) multi *7.75 7.75*

Printed in sheets of 8 + label.

Selection of Kotor as World Heritage Site, 25th Anniv. — A60

2004, Apr. 7 ***Perf. 13x13¾***
244 A60 16d (25c) multi .95 .95

Printing of First History of Montenegro, by Vasilije Petrovic, 250th Anniv. — A61

2004, Apr. 29
245 A61 16d (25c) multi 1.50 1.50

Europa — A62

Designs: 16d (25c), Paragliders. No. 247, 56d (80c), Sailboat, swimmer, horiz.

No. 248: a, 32d (50c), Sailboats, paraglider, horiz. b, 56d (80c), Rowboats, horiz.

2004, May 5 ***Perf. 13¾x13, 13x13¾***
246-247 A62 Set of 2 *4.00 4.00*

Souvenir Sheet

248 A62 Sheet of 2, #a-b *8.00 8.00*

Church of St. Sava, Belgrade — A63

Designs: 16d (25c), Church, St. Sava. 28.70d (50c), Church, statue of St. Sava, horiz.

2004, May 10 ***Perf. 13¾x13, 13x13¼***
249-250 A63 Set of 2 2.75 2.75

Michael Pupin (1854-1935), Inventor — A64

2004, May 13 Engr. ***Perf. 13¼***
251 A64 16d (25c) violet .95 .95

FIFA (Fédération Internationale de Football Association), Cent. — A65

2004, May 21 Litho. ***Perf. 13x13¾***
252 A65 28.70d (50c) multi 2.00 2.00

Nature Protection A66

Designs: 32d (50c), Ravnjak River. 56d (80c), Sara National Park.

2004, June 10
253-254 A66 Set of 2 4.75 4.75

Each stamp printed in sheet of 8 + label.

Souvenir Sheet

JUFIZ XII Philatelic Exhibition, Belgrade — A67

No. 255: a, Lion from Terazije Fountain. b, Entire fountain.

2004, June 21 ***Perf. 13¼***
255 A67 32d (50c) Sheet of 2, #a-b 4.50 4.50

2004 Summer Olympics, Athens — A68

Athens Olympics emblem, ancient Greek ruins and: 16d (25c), Runners. 28.70d (50c), Runners, diff. 32d (50c), Long jumper. 57.40d (80c), Hurdlers.

2004, June 24 ***Perf. 13x13¾***
256-259 A68 Set of 4 7.75 7.75

Each stamp printed in sheets of 8 + label.

Yugoslavia Nos. 2255-2256 Surcharged

Methods as Before

2004, June 25 ***Perf. 12½***
260 A751 12d on 1p #2255a 3.00 3.00
a. on #2255, perf. 13¼ *150.00 150.00*
261 A751 32d on 5p #2256a 5.50 5.50
a. on #2256, perf. 13¼ *450.00 450.00*

See Yugoslavia No. 2577 for stamp similar to No. 260, but with violet surcharge.

Volujica Telegraph Station, Cent. — A69

2004, Aug. 3 Litho. ***Perf. 13x13¾***
262 A69 16d (25c) multi 1.50 1.50

Joy of Europe — A70

Children's drawings: 32d (50c) Bridge and city skyline. 56d (80c), City buildings, vert.

2004, Oct. 2 ***Perf. 13¾***
263-264 A70 Set of 2 4.75 4.75

Each stamp printed in sheets of 8 + label.

Port of Bar, 125th Anniv. — A71

2004, Oct. 12

265 A71 32d (50c) multi 1.75 1.75

Stamp Day — A72

2004, Oct. 22 ***Perf. 13¾x13***

266 A72 16d (25c) multi 2.40 2.40

National Bank of Serbia, 120th Anniv. — A73

Designs: 16d (25c), Bank building. 32d (50c), Bank building, George Vajfert.

Perf. 13¼ Syncopated

2004, Oct. 28 **Engr.**

267-268 A73 Set of 2 2.50 2.50

Each stamp printed in sheet of 8 + label.

Silver Objects From 1899 — A74

2004, Nov. 2 **Litho.** ***Perf. 13¾x13***

269 Horiz. strip of 4 + central label 5.00 5.00

a. A74 16d (25c) Plate on pedestal .75 .75
b. A74 24d (35c) Box 1.10 1.10
c. A74 26.20d (40c) Bowl 1.25 1.25
d. A74 28.70d (50c) Bowl with lid 1.50 1.50

Buildings A75

2004, Nov. 15 ***Perf. 13x13¾***

270 Horiz. strip of 4 + central label 5.00 5.00

a. A75 16d (25c) Lombardic Palace .75 .75
b. A75 24d (35c) Pima Palace 1.10 1.10
c. A75 26.20d (40c) Grgurina Palace 1.25 1.25
d. A75 28.70d (50c) Bizanti Palace 1.50 1.50

Christmas A76

Designs: 16d (25c), Nativity, by Vasilis Leurac. 28.70d (50c), Nativity, by Ememija Profeta.

2004, Dec. 1

271-272 A76 Set of 2 2.50 2.50

Endangered Birds — A77

2005, Jan. 31 **Litho.** ***Perf. 13¼***

273 Horiz. strip of 4 + central label 6.00 6.00

a. A77 16.50d (25c) Egretta alba .70 .70
b. A77 33d (40c) Podiceps nigricollis 1.25 1.25
c. A77 41.50d (50c) Aythya nyroca 1.75 1.75
d. A77 49.50d (60c) Ciconia nigra 2.00 2.00

Yugoslavia No. F1 Surcharged in Blue

No. 199 Surcharged in Black

No. 200 Surcharged in Black

2005, Feb. 3 **Litho.** ***Perf. 12½***

274 RL1 50p on R #F1 (Bl) *52.50 15.00*
275 A31 16.50d on 16d #199 *25.00 15.00*
276 A32 33d on 32d #200 *40.00 15.00*
Nos. 274-276 (3) 117.50 45.00

Stamp Collecting — A78

2005, Feb. 3 **Litho.** ***Perf. 12½***

277 A78 50p multi *1.40 1.40*

Flora and Fauna — A79

Designs: a, Capparis spinosa. b, Mustela erminea. c, Trollius europaeus. d, Rupicapra rupicapra.

2005, Feb. 16 ***Perf. 13x13¾***

278 Horiz. strip of 4 + central label 6.00 6.00

a. A79 16.50d (25c) multi .70 .70
b. A79 33d (40c) multi 1.25 1.25
c. A79 41.50d (50c) multi 1.75 1.75
d. A79 49.50d (60c) multi 2.00 2.00

Montenegrin Table Tennis Assoc., 50th Anniv. — A80

2005, Feb. 28

279 A80 16.50d (25c) multi *12.50 12.50*

Easter — A81

Designs: 16.50d (25c), Fresco, 18th cent. 28.70d (50c), Crucifixion, 1602.

2005, Mar. 1

280-281 A81 Set of 2 2.50 2.50

Mountain Scenes — A82

2005, Mar. 7 **Litho.** ***Perf. 12½***

282 A82 16.50d Zlatibor 1.00 1.00
283 A82 33d Kopaonik 3.00 3.00

See Nos. 295A-295B.

Serbian Law University, Cent. — A83

2005, Mar. 12 ***Perf. 13x13¾***

284 A83 16.50d (25c) multi 1.00 1.00

Miniature Sheet

Theater Celebrities — A84

No. 285: a, Jovan Djordjevic (1826-1900). b, Milan Predic (1881-1972). c, Milan Grol (1876-1952). d, Mira Trailovic (1924-89). e, Soja Jovanovich (1922-2002). f, Hugo Klajn (1894-1981). g, Mata Milosevic (1901-97). h, Bojan Stupica (1910-70).

2005, Mar. 25 ***Perf. 13¾x13***

285 A84 16.50d (25c) Sheet of 8, #a-h, + central label 6.50 6.50

European Philatelic Cooperation, 50th Anniv. (in 2006) — A85

Elements of Europa common design types (CD) or Yugoslavian stamps: No. 286, CD12. No. 287, CD13, No. 288, CD14. No. 289, CD15. No. 290, CD16. No. 291, Yugoslavia #1206. No. 292, Yugoslavia #1678. No. 293, CD13, CD15 and Yugoslavia #1678.

2005, Mar. 31 ***Perf. 13x13¾***

Background Color

286 A85 16.50d (25c) green *.70 .70*
287 A85 16.50d (25c) claret *.70 .70*
288 A85 16.50d (25c) claret *.70 .70*
289 A85 16.50d (25c) blue *.70 .70*
a. Souvenir sheet, #286-289 *7.50 7.50*
290 A85 41.50d (50c) claret *1.75 1.75*
291 A85 41.50d (50c) olive gray *1.75 1.75*
292 A85 41.50d (50c) blue *1.75 1.75*
293 A85 41.50d (50c) orange *1.75 1.75*
a. Souvenir sheet, #290-293 *11.00 11.00*
Nos. 286-293 (8) 9.80 9.80

Europa stamps, 50th anniv. (in 2006).

Hans Christian Andersen (1805-75), Author — A86

Silhouette of Andersen and: 41.50d (50c), The Little Mermaid. 58d (70c), The Snow Queen.

2005, Apr. 1 ***Perf. 13¾x13***

294-295 A86 Set of 2 3.75 3.75

Mountain Scenes Type of 2005

Design: 5d, Goc, 13d, Jastrebac.

2005, Apr. 1 **Litho.** ***Perf. 12¾x12¼***

295A A82 5d multi 1.00 .25
295B A82 13d multi 2.00 .45

Europa — A87

Designs: No. 296, 41.50d (50c), Dumplings and rolls. No. 297, 73d (90c), Fish dish, tomato, lettuce, garlic, oil cruet, pepper mill.

No. 298: a, 41.50d (50c), Cake, flower, cup of coffee. b, 73d (90c), Slice of pie, apples.

2005, May 5 ***Perf. 13x13¾***

296-297 A87 Set of 2 *4.25 4.25*

Souvenir Sheet

298 A87 Sheet of 2, #a-b *4.25 4.25*

Captains and Their Ships A88

2005, May 13 ***Perf. 13¼***

299 Horiz. strip of 4 + central label 5.00 5.00

a. A88 16.50d (25c) Marko Ivanovic .60 .60
b. A88 33d (40c) Petar Zelalic 1.15 1.15
c. A88 41.50d (50c) Matija Balovic 1.50 1.50
d. A88 49.50d (60c) Ivan Bronza 1.60 1.60

Emblem of Red Star Sports Club — A89

Emblem of Partisan Sports Club — A90

No. 302 — Knight with shield with emblem of: a, Red Star. b, Partisan.

2005, May 23 ***Perf. 13x13¾***

300 A89 16.50d (25c) multi .90 .90
301 A90 16.50d (25c) multi .90 .90

Souvenir Sheet

302 Sheet of 2 2.00 2.00
a. A89 16.50d (25c) multi .90 .90
b. A90 16.50d (25c) multi .90 .90

Souvenir Sheet

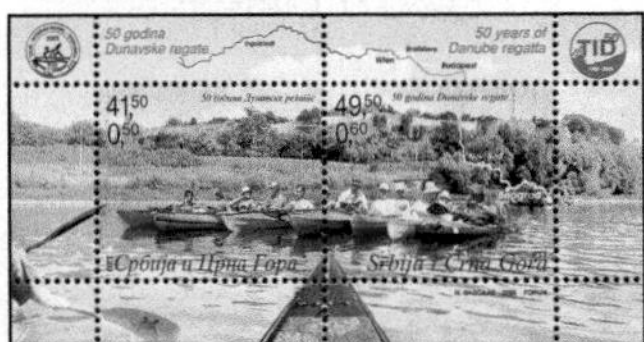

Danube Regatta, 50th Anniv. — A91

No. 303: a, 41.50d (50c), Rowers in boats. b, 49.50d (60c), Rowers in boats, map.

2005, June 6

303 A91 Sheet of 2, #a-b 3.75 3.75

Intl. Year of Physics A92

Theory of Relativity, Cent. — A93

2005, June 10

304 A92 41.50d (50c) multi 1.60 1.60
305 A93 58d (70c) multi 2.25 2.25

European Nature Protection A94

Various views of Koviljsko-Petrovaradinski Rit Special Nature Reserve: 41.50d (50c), 58d (70c).

2005, June 20

306-307 A94 Set of 2 4.00 4.00

European Volleyball Championships, Belgrade and Rome — A95

2005, Sept. 2 **Litho.** ***Perf. 13x13¾***

310 A95 16.50d (25c) multi 3.00 3.00

Printed in sheets of 8 + label.

European Basketball Championships, Serbia & Montenegro — A96

2005, Sept. 16

311 A96 16.50d (25c) multi 3.00 3.00

Printed in sheets of 8 + label.

A97

Joy of Europe — A98

Perf. 13¾x13, 13x13¾

2005, Sept. 21

312 A97 41.50d (50c) multi 1.40 1.40
313 A98 58d (70c) multi 2.10 2.10

Each stamp printed in sheets of 8 + label.

World Youth Day — A99

2005, Sept. 30 ***Perf. 13x13¾***

314 A99 41.50d (50c) multi 1.50 1.50

Printed in sheets of 8 + label.

Start of European Union Accession Negotiations — A100

2005, Oct. 10 ***Perf. 13¾x13***

315 A100 16.50d (25c) multi .90 .90

World Air Sports Federation, Cent. — A101

Emblem and: 49.50d (60c), Alberto Santos-Dumont's 14-bis airplane. 58d (70c), Parachute, glider, ultra-light aircraft.

2005, Oct. 14 ***Perf. 13x13¾***

316-317 A101 Set of 2 4.25 4.25

Each stamp printed in sheets of 8 + label.

Stamp Day — A102

2005, Oct. 24

318 A102 16.50d (25c) multi .90 .90

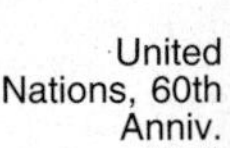

United Nations, 60th Anniv. A103

2005, Oct. 24

319 A103 16.50d (25c) multi .90 .90

St. Petar of Cetinje (1782-1830), Montenegrin Leader A104

2005, Oct. 28

320 A104 16.50d (25c) multi .90 .90

First Montenegrin Constitution, Cent. — A105

2005, Nov. 14

321 A105 16.50d (25c) multi .90 .90

Stevan Sremac (1855-1906), Humorist — A106

2005, Nov. 23 ***Perf. 13¼***

322 A106 16.50d (25c) multi .90 .90

Paintings of Monasteries A107

No. 323: a, Studenica Monastery, by Djordje Krstic. b, Sopocani Monastery, by Paja Jovanovic. c, Zica Monastery, by Krstic. d, Gracanica Monastery, by Milan Milanovic.

2005, Nov. 28

323 Horiz. strip of 4 + central label 5.50 5.50
a. A107 16.50d (25c) multi .65 .65
b. A107 33d (40c) multi 1.15 1.15
c. A107 41.50d (50c) multi 1.60 1.60
d. A107 49.50d (60c) multi 1.75 1.75

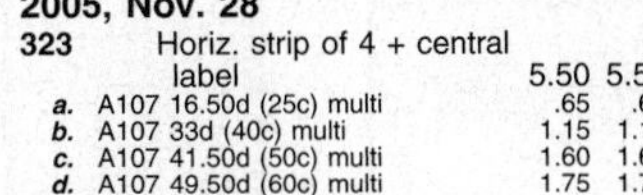

Paintings in Museums A108

No. 324: a, Girl with a Blue Ribbon, by F. X. Winterhalter. b, Adoration of the Child, by Andrea Alovidi. c, Madonna and Child with Saints, by Biagio d'Antonio. d, Remorse, by Vlaho Bukovac.

2005, Dec. 9

324 Horiz. strip of 4 + central label 5.50 5.50
a. A108 16.50d (25c) multi .65 .65
b. A108 33d (40c) multi 1.15 1.15
c. A108 41.50d (50c) multi 1.60 1.60
d. A108 49.50d (60c) multi 1.75 1.75

Christmas A109

Designs: 16.50d (25c), Nativity. 46d (50c), Nativity, diff.

2005, Dec. 12 ***Perf. 13x13¾***

325-326 A109 Set of 2 2.50 2.50

Stevan Stojanovic Mokranjac (1856-1914), Composer A110

2006, Jan. 9 ***Perf. 13¾x13***

327 A110 46d (50c) multi 1.75 1.75

Jovan Sterija Popovic (1806-56), Writer — A111

2006, Jan. 13

328 A111 33d (40c) multi 1.25 1.25

2006 Winter Olympics, Turin — A112

Designs: 53d (60c), Ski jumping. 73d (80c), Downhill skiing.

2006, Feb. 10 ***Perf. 13x13¾***

329-330 A112 Set of 2 4.75 4.75

Each stamp printed in sheets of 8 + label.

National Theater, Belgrade — A113

2006, Feb. 1 **Litho.** ***Perf. 13¼***

331 A113 46d multi 2.00 2.00

Easter — A114

Designs: 16.50d (20c), Easter egg with Cyrillic inscription. 46d (50c), Basket of Easter eggs.

2006, Mar. 1 *Perf. 13¾x13¼*
332-333 A114 Set of 2 2.25 2.25

Danube Commission, 150th Anniv. A115

No. 334: a, Novi Sad (shown). b, Smederevo. c, Belgrade. d, Tabula Traiana.

2006, Mar. 6 *Perf. 13¼x13¾*
334 Horiz. strip of 4 + central label 5.25 5.25
a.-b. A115 16.50d (20c) Either single .70 .70
c.-d. A115 46d (50c) Either single 1.90 1.90

Fauna A116

No. 335: a, Canis lupus. b, Otis tarda. c, Vormela peregusna. d, Ursus arctos.

2006, Apr. 3
335 Horiz. strip of 4 + central label 5.00 5.00
a.-b. A116 16.50d (20c) Either single .65 .65
c.-d. A116 46d (50c) Either single 1.75 1.75

2006 World Cup Soccer Championships, Germany — A117

2006 World Cup emblem and: 33d (40c), Soccer players. 46d (50c), Soccer player and stadium.

No. 338, horiz.: a, Stadium, text in Cyrillic letters. b, Stadium, text in Latin letters.

2006, Apr. 12 *Perf. 13¾x13¼*
336-337 A117 Set of 2 *20.00 20.00*

Souvenir Sheet

Perf. 13¼x13¾

338 A117 46d (50c) Sheet of 2, #a-b *25.00 25.00*

Europa A118

Children's drawings: No. 339, 46d (50c), Beach umbrella, person in winter jacket on beach towel, penguin. No. 340, 73d (80c), Lion and lamb.

No. 341: a, 46d (50c), Girls talking. b, 73d (80c), Children at open door, rainbow.

2006, May 4 *Perf. 13¼x13¾*
339-340 A118 Set of 2 5.00 5.00

Souvenir Sheet

341 A118 Sheet of 2, #a-b 6.00 6.00

Nikola Tesla (1856-1943), Electrical Engineer — A119

Designs: 16.50d (20c), Tesla, lightning. No. 343, 46d (50c), Tesla, electrical generator.

No. 344, horiz.: a, 46d (50c), Tesla. b, 112d (€1.30), Turbine.

2006, May 26 *Perf. 13¾x13¼*
342-343 A119 Set of 2 4.00 4.00

Souvenir Sheet

Perf. 13¾

344 A119 Sheet of 2, #a-b 7.50 7.50

Rose Varieties A120

No. 345: a, Aqua. b, Vendela. c, Sphinx. d, Red Berlin.

Perf. 13¼x13¾

2006, June 20 **Litho.**
345 Horiz. strip of 4 + central label 5.25 5.25
a.-b. A120 16.50d Either single .70 .70
c.-d. A120 46d Either single 1.90 1.90

As these stamps were released after the breakup of Serbia and Montenegro, they were sold only in Serbia.

Nature Protection A121

Designs: 46d, Fusoski Park, Novi Sad. 58d, Gradski Park, Vrsac.

2006, June 20
346-347 A121 Set of 2 4.50 4.50

As these stamps were released after the breakup of Serbia and Montenegro, they were sold only in Serbia. Each stamp was printed in a sheet of 8 + label.

Battle of Mishar, by Paja Jovanovic A122

2006, June 30
348 A122 46d multi 2.40 2.40

Battle of Mishar, 200th anniv.

Flag — A123

Coat of Arms — A124

2006, June 30 *Perf. 12½*
349 A123 16.50d multi 1.75 1.00
350 A124 20d multi 1.75 1.00

European Water Polo Championships, Belgrade — A125

2006, Sept. 1 *Perf. 13¼x13¾*
351 A125 46d multi 2.00 2.00

Serbian Victory at European Water Polo Championships — A126

2006, Sept. 13
352 A126 46d mult 2.25 2.25

Joy of Europe A127

Children's drawings: 46d, Buildings. 73d, Girl touching bird.

2006, Sept. 29
353-354 A127 Set of 2 5.25 5.25

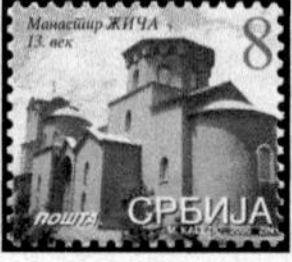

Zhica Monastery — A128

2006, Oct. 7 *Perf. 12½*
355 A128 8d multi 1.00 1.00
a. Perf. 13¼ 2.50 2.50

Stamp Day — A129

2006, Oct. 24 *Perf. 13¾x13¼*
356 A129 46d Serbia #1 2.00 2.00

First Serbian postage stamps, 140th anniv.

Bridal Jewelry A130

No. 357: a, Bracelet, 19th cent. b, Ring, 17th-19th cent. c, Earrings, 20th cent. d, Necklace, 19th cent.

2006, Oct. 30 *Perf. 13¼x13¾*
357 Horiz strip of 4 + central label 5.50 5.50
a.-b. A130 16.50d Either single .70 .70
c.-d. A130 46d Either single 1.90 1.90

Atelje 212 Theater, 50th Anniv. — A131

2006, Nov. 10 *Perf. 13¾x13¼*
358 A131 46d multi 1.75 1.75

Wolfgang Amadeus Mozart (1756-91), Composer A132

Rembrandt (1606-69), Painter — A133

2006, Nov. 16
359 A132 46d multi 4.00 4.00
360 A133 46d multi 4.00 4.00

A134

Christmas A135

2006, Nov. 20 *Perf. 13¼x13¾*
361 A134 16.50d multi .85 .85
362 A135 46d multi 2.25 2.25

New Year 2007 — A136

2006, Dec. 1
363 A136 46d multi 1.90 1.90

UNICEF, 60th Anniv. A137

2006, Dec. 11
364 A137 16.50d multi .80 .80

Liberation of Belgrade, 200th Anniv. A138

2006, Dec. 13
365 A138 16.50d multi .80 .80

Flower — A139

Flowers A140

Apple Orchard A141

River — A142

Goc A143

Zlatibor A144

Kopaonik A145

Belgrade — A146

2007, Jan. 1 Litho. *Perf. 13¾x13¼*
366 A139 50p multi .35 .35

Perf. 13¼x13¾
367 A140 1d multi .35 .35
368 A141 5d multi .35 .35
369 A142 10d multi .50 .50

Perf. 13¼
370 A143 13d multi .65 .65
371 A144 33d multi 1.60 1.60
372 A145 50d multi 2.60 2.60
373 A146 100d multi 5.25 5.25
Nos. 366-373 (8) 11.65 11.65

Intl. Polar Year — A147

2007, Jan. 30 *Perf. 13¼x13¾*
374 A147 46d multi 2.00 2.00

Miniature Sheet

Actors and Actresses — A148

No. 375: a, Petar Dobrinovic (1853-1923). b, Milka Grgurova Aleksic (1840-1924). c, Ljubisa Jovanovic (1908-71). d, Rahela Ferari (1911-94). e, Miodrag Petrovic Ckalja (1924-2003). f, Branko Plesa (1926-2001). g, Ljuba Tadic (1929-2005). h, Danila Bata Stojkovic (1934-2002).

2007, Feb. 16
375 A148 16.50d Sheet of 8, #a-h, + central label 5.50 5.50

Easter — A149

Designs: 20d, Crucifixion. 46d, Crucifixion in silhouette.

2007, Mar. 1 *Perf. 13¾x13¼*
376-377 A149 Set of 2 3.00 3.00

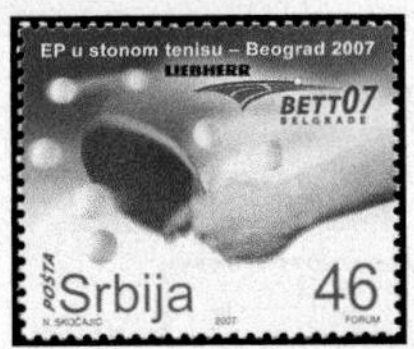
2007 European Table Tennis Championships, Belgrade — A150

2007, Mar. 23 *Perf. 13¼x13¾*
378 A150 46d multi 2.25 2.25

Souvenir Sheet
Perf. 13¾
379 A150 112d Player, net 5.00 5.00

No. 378 printed in sheets of 8 + label.

Art From St. Sava Church — A150a

2007, Apr. 1 Litho. *Perf. 13¼*
379A A150a 10d multi 1.00 1.00

Rose — A151

2007, Apr. 4 *Perf. 13¼*
380 A151 40d multi 2.00 2.00

Worldwide Fund for Nature (WWF) — A152

No. 381 — Dryocopus martius: a, Facing right. b, Facing right, feeding chicks. c, Facing left, feeding chicks. d, Facing left.

2007, Apr. 6 *Perf. 13¾x13¼*
381 Horiz. strip of 4 + central label 5.25 5.25
a.-b. A152 20d Either single .75 .75
c.-d. A152 40d Either single 1.60 1.60

Parks — A153

Designs: 40d, Vrnacka Banja Park. 46d, Pionirski Park, Belgrade.

2007, Apr. 20 *Perf. 13¼x13¾*
382-383 A153 Set of 2 3.75 3.75

Europa A154

International and Serbian Scouting emblems and: No. 384, 20d, Scouts, tents and compass. 46d, Scouts in canoe, Scout hat, neckerchief and backpack.

No. 386: a, c, e, Milos Popovic and compass. b, d, f, Lord Robert Baden-Powell, Scout hat, neckerchief and backpack.

2007, May 3 Litho. *Perf. 13¼x13¾*
384-385 A154 Set of 2 3.00 3.00

Miniature Sheet
386 Sheet of 6 5.25 5.25
a. A154 20d multi, perf. 13¼x13¾, imperf. at top .85 .85
b. A154 20d multi, perf. 13¼x13¾, imperf. at top .85 .85
c. A154 20d multi, perf. 13¼x13¾, imperf. at top and right .85 .85
d. A154 20d multi, perf. 13¼x13¾, imperf. at bottom .85 .85
e. A154 20d multi, perf. 13¼x13¾, imperf. at bottom .85 .85
f. A154 20d multi, perf. 13¼x13¾, imperf. at bottom and right .85 .85

Scouting, cent. Nos. 384-385 each printed in sheets of 8 + label. No. 386 was sold with but not attached to a booklet cover.

Serbian Chairmanship of Council of Europe A155

2007, May 10 *Perf. 13¼x13¾*
387 A155 20d multi 1.40 1.40

First Air Crossing of Atlantic by Amelia Earhart, 75th Anniv. A156

2007, May 21 Litho.
388 A156 50d multi 2.25 2.25

Printed in sheets of 8 + label.

Dositej Obradovic's Arrival in Serbia, Bicent. — A157

2007, May 28 *Perf. 13¾x13¼*
389 A157 20d multi .90 .90

Jovan Zmaj's Children's Games, 50th Anniv. A158

2007, June 1 *Perf. 13¼x13¾*
390 A158 20d multi 1.00 1.00

Souvenir Sheet

Srbijafila XIV, Belgrade — A159

No. 391: a, 20d, Stefan Lazarevic. b, 46d, Castle.

2007, June 11 *Perf. 13¾*
391 A159 Sheet of 2, #a-b 2.75 2.75

Souvenir Sheet

European Olympic Youth Festival, Belgrade — A160

No. 392: a, Swimmer. b, Runner.

2007, June 20
392 A160 46d Sheet of 2, #a-d 3.75 3.75

Equestrian Events A161

No. 393: a, Endurance jumping. b, Carriage pull. c, Dressage. d, Show jumping.

2007, June 28 *Perf. 13¼x13¾*
393 Horiz. strip of 4 + central label 5.50 5.50
a.-b. A161 20d Either single .85 .85
c.-d. A161 40d Either single 1.75 1.75

Scientists — A162

Designs: 40d, William Thomson, Lord Kelvin (1824-1907), physicist. No. 395, 46d, Giuseppe Occhialini (1907-93), physicist. No. 396, 46d, Dmitri Mendeleev (1834-1907), chemist.

2007, July 10 ***Perf. 13¾x13¼***
394-396 A162 Set of 3 5.50 5.50

Petar Lubarda (1907-74), Painter A163

2007, July 27 ***Perf. 13¼***
397 A163 20d multi 1.00 1.00

Kalenic Monastery, 600th Anniv. — A164

2007, Aug. 28 ***Perf. 13¾x13¼***
398 A164 20d multi 1.00 1.00

Haliaeetus Albicilla A165

2007, Sept. 7 **Photo.** ***Perf. 13¾***
399 A165 46d multi 2.10 2.10

See Austria No. 2116.

Ozone Layer Protection A166

Perf. 13¾x13¼
2007, Sept. 17 **Litho.**
400 A166 20d multi 1.00 1.00

Printed in sheets of 8 + label.

Archaeological Sites — A167

Gamzigrad-Romulijana site: 46d, No. 401, Cyrillic inscriptions, denomination at UL. No. 402, Latin inscriptions, denomination at UR.

2007, Sept. 21 ***Perf. 13¼x13¾***
401-402 A167 Set of 2 5.00 5.00

Nos. 401-402 each were printed in sheets of 9 + label.

Joy of Europe A168

2007, Sept. 28
403 A168 46d multi 1.75 1.75

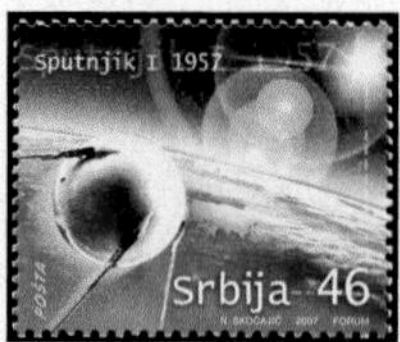
Launch of Sputnik 1, 50th Anniv. A169

2007, Oct. 4
404 A169 46d multi 2.00 2.00

Belgrade Observatory, 120th Anniv. — A170

2007, Oct. 15
405 A170 20d multi 1.00 1.00

Printed in sheets of 24 + label.

Evzhen Deroko (1860-1944) and Serbia No. 24 — A171

2007, Oct. 24
406 A171 46d multi 2.00 2.00

Stamp Day.

Paintings — A172

Paintings by: 20d, Dura Jaksic (1832-78). No. 408, 46d, Uros Predic (1857-1953). No. 409, 46d, Frida Kahlo (1907-54).

2007, Nov. 1 ***Perf. 13¾x13¼***
407-409 A172 Set of 3 4.25 4.25

Christmas A173

Nativity paintings: 20d, 46d.

2007, Nov. 9 ***Perf. 13¼x13¾***
410-411 A173 Set of 2 3.00 3.00

Danube River Harbors and Ships — A174

Ships and: 20d, Novi Sad, Serbia. 46d, Orsova, Romania.
No. 414 — Ships: a, 40d, Sirona. b, 50d, Orsova.

2007, Nov. 14 ***Perf. 13¼x13¾***
412-413 A174 Set of 2 3.25 3.25

Souvenir Sheet

Perf. 13¾

414 A174 Sheet of 2, #a-d 4.25 4.25

See Romania Nos. 5003-5005.

Diplomatic Relations Between Serbia and Japan, 125th Anniv. A175

Perf. 13¼x13¾
2007, Dec. 23 **Litho.**
415 A175 46d multi 2.00 2.00

Printed in sheets of 8 + label.

Vinca Archaeological Excavations, Cent. — A176

2008, Jan. 28
416 A176 20d multi 1.75 1.75

Paintings of Predrag-Peda Milosavljevic (1908-87) A177

Designs: 20d, Cluny Museum, Paris. 46d, Notre Dame Cathedral, Paris.

2008, Feb. 4
417-418 A177 Set of 2 2.60 2.60

Intl. Swimming Federation (FINA), Cent. — A178

2008, Feb. 18
419 A178 50d multi 2.00 2.00

Printed in sheets of 8 + label.

2008 Summer Olympics, Beijing A179

Designs: 46d, Tennis. 50d, Hurdlers.

2008, Mar. 7
420-421 A179 Set of 2 3.50 3.50

Nos. 420-421 each were printed in sheets of 8 + label.

Easter — A180

Designs: 20d, Shown. 46d, Jesus, cross, diff.

2008, Mar. 21 ***Perf. 13¾x13¼***
422-423 A180 Set of 2 2.75 2.75

2008 Serbian Olympic Tennis Team — A181

Designs: 20d, Janko Tipsarevic. No. 425, 30d, Nenad Zimonjic. No. 426, 30d, Jelena Jankovic. 40d, Ana Ivanovic. 46d, Novak Djokovic.

2008, Apr. 8 ***Perf. 13¼x13¾***
424-428 A181 Set of 5 9.00 9.00

Endangered Animals — A182

No. 429: a, Cervus elaphus. b, Meles meles. c, Felis silvestris. d, Sus scrofa.

2008, Apr. 7 ***Perf. 13¾x13¼***
429 Horiz. strip of 4 + central label 5.50 5.50
a.-b. A182 20d Either single .80 .80
c.-d. A182 46d Either single 1.75 1.75

Souvenir Sheet

2008 Eurovision Song Contest, Belgrade — A183

2008, Apr. 11 ***Perf. 13¾***
430 A183 177d multi 8.00 8.00

Europa A184

Stamped cover, letter and: 46d, Quill pen. 50d, Letter opener.

2008, May 5 ***Perf. 13¼x13¾***
431-432 A184 Set of 2 3.50 3.50

Nos. 431-432 each were printed in sheets of 8 + label.

European Nature Protection A185

Designs: 20d, Vlasina Lake. 46d, Djavolja Varos rock formations.

2008, May 23
433-434 A185 Set of 2 3.00 3.00

Nos. 433-434 each were printed in sheets of 8 + label.

Oriental Express, 125th Anniv. — A186

Train and: 20d, Eiffel Tower and Arc de Triomphe. 50d, Hagia Sophia, Istanbul.

2008, June 9
435-436 A186 Set of 2 3.00 3.00

Nos. 435-436 each were printed in sheets of 8 + label.

Television Belgrade, 50th Anniv. — A187

2008, June 16 **Litho.**
437 A187 46d multi 1.75 1.75

Printed in sheets of 8 + label.

University of Belgrade, Bicent. A188

2008, July 10 ***Perf. 13¼x13¾***
438 A188 20d multi .90 .90

Grapes and Vineyards A189

No. 439: a, Riesling grapes, vineyard in Fruska Gora (grapes at left). b, Sauvignon Blanc grapes, vineyard in Oplenac (grapes at right). c, Prokupac grapes, vineyard in Zupa. d, Frankovka grapes, vineyard in Vrsac.

2008, Sept. 25

439	Horiz. strip of 4 + central label	6.00 6.00
a.-b.	A189 20d Either single	.90 .90
c.-d.	A189 46d Either single	1.90 1.90

Joy of Europe A190

2008, Sept. 26
440 A190 46d multi 2.00 2.00

Printed in sheets of 8 + label.

First Telephone Station in Belgrade, 125th Anniv. — A191

2008, Oct. 24
441 A191 46d multi 2.00 2.00

Stamp Day.

Traditional Children's Costumes A192

Girl from: 46d, Sumadija. 50d, Kumodraz.

2008, Nov. 10 ***Perf. 13¾x13¼***
442-443 A192 Set of 2 3.75 3.75

Nos. 442-443 each were printed in sheets of 9 + label.

Danube Navigation Convention, 60th Anniv. — A193

2008, Nov. 20 ***Perf. 13¼x13¾***
444 A193 46d multi 2.00 2.00

Printed in sheets of 8 + label.

Christmas A194

Designs: 20d, Nativity, by unknown artist. 46d, Nativity, by Dimitrije Bacevic.

2008, Nov. 28 ***Perf. 13¾x13¼***
445-446 A194 Set of 2 2.60 2.60

Dadov Theater, Belgrade, 50th Anniv. — A195

2008, Dec. 5
447 A195 20d multi .90 .90

Osisani Jez Magazine, 75th Anniv. — A196

2009, Jan. 5 **Litho.** ***Perf. 13¾x13¼***
448 A196 20d multi .90 .90

Printed in sheets of 8 + central label.

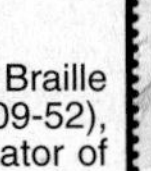

Louis Braille (1809-52), Educator of the Blind — A197

2009, Jan. 5 ***Perf. 13¼x13¾***
449 A197 46d multi 1.90 1.90

Coat of Arms Type of 2006 Surcharged

2009, Jan. 28 **Litho.** ***Perf. 13¼***
450 A124 22d on 20d multi .90 .90

Belt and Buckle — A198

Ring — A199

Embroidery A200

Kalemegdan, Belgrade A201

2009, Jan. 28 ***Perf. 13¾***

451	A198 11d multi	.45 .45
a.	Dated 2012	.25 .25
b.	Dated "2013"	.25 .25
c.	Perf. 13¼, dated "2010"	—
d.	Dated "2015," perf. 13¼	.25 .25
e.	Dated "2017," perf. 13¾	.25 .25
f.	Dated "2018," perf. 13¾	.25 .25
452	A199 22d multi	.90 .90
a.	Perf. 13¼, dated "2010"	—
453	A200 44d multi	1.90 1.90
454	A201 55d multi	2.25 2.25
454a	Dated "2013"	1.75 1.75
	Nos. 451-454 (4)	5.50 5.50

Issued: No. 451a, 2012; No. 451b, 4/18/13; No. 451f, 3/20/18. No. 454a, 4/12/13.

Protected Mammals — A202

No. 455: a, Mustela ermina. b, Micromys minutus. c, Sicista subtilis. d, Spermophilus citellus.

2009, Feb. 16 ***Perf. 13¾x13¼***

455	Horiz. strip of 4 + central label	4.75 4.75
a.-b.	A202 22d Either single	.75 .75
c.-d.	A202 46d Either single	1.60 1.60

Politikin Zabavnik Magazine, 70th Anniv. — A203

2009, Feb. 28 ***Perf. 13¼x13¾***
456 A203 22d multi 1.25 1.25

Printed in sheets of 8 + central label.

Birds A204

Designs: 22d, Scolopax rusticola. 46d, Monticola saxatilis.

2009, Mar. 2 ***Perf. 13¾x13¼***
457-458 A204 Set of 2 2.50 2.50
458a Souvenir sheet, #457-458 2.50 2.50

See Bulgaria Nos. 4498-4499.

Easter A205

Icons from church in Topola: 22d, Last Supper. 46d, Entombment of Jesus.

2009, Mar. 9 ***Perf. 13¼***
459-460 A205 Set of 2 2.25 2.25

Miniature Sheet

Actors and Actresses — A206

No. 461: a, Vela Nigrinova (1862-1908). b, Milan Ajvaz (1897-1980). c, Nevenka Urbanova (1909-2007). d, Stevo Zigon (1926-2005). e, Slobodan Perovic (1926-78). f, Stevan Salajic (1929-2002). g, Neda Spasojevic (1941-81). h, Milos Zutic (1939-93).

2009, Mar. 27 ***Perf. 13¼x13¾***
461 A206 22d Sheet of 8, #a-h, + central label 6.00 6.00

25th Summer Universiade, Belgrade A207

Belgrade skyline, emblem, and birds in sports: 22d, Diving, fencing, basketball, soccer, swimming. 46d, Handball, gymnastics, tennis, judo, hurdling.

2009, Mar. 31 **Litho.**
462-463 A207 Set of 2 2.25 2.25

Paintings — A208

Designs: 22d, Self-portrait with a Veil, by Milena Pavlovic Barili (1909-45). No. 465, 46d, Young Woman in a Pink Dress, by Paja Jovanovic (1859-1957). No. 466, 46d, Still Life with Parrot, by Jovan Bijelic (1884-1964).

2009, Apr. 6 ***Perf. 13¾x13¼***
464-466 A208 Set of 3 3.75 3.75

Europa A209

Designs: 46d, Goddess Urania, Galileo's telescope, Milky Way. 50d, Radio telescope, Horsehead Nebula.

2009, May 5 ***Perf. 13¼x13¾***
467-468 A209 Set of 2 3.25 3.25

Intl. Year of Astronomy. Nos. 467-468 were each printed in sheets of 8 + central label.

Laying of Cornerstone of St. Sava Cathedral, 70th Anniv. A210

2009, May 9 ***Perf. 13¼***
469 A210 22d multi .80 .80

European Nature Protection A211

Designs: 22d, Gyps fulvus over Uvac River. 46d, Pcinja Valley.

2009, May 20 ***Perf. 13¾x13¼***
470-471 A211 Set of 2 2.75 2.75

Nos. 470-471 were each printed in sheets of 8 + central label.

Miniature Sheet

Composers — A212

No. 472: a, Kornelije Stankovic (1831-65). b, Josif Marinkovic (1851-1931). c, Petar Konjovic (1883-1970). d, Stevan Hristic (1885-1958). e, Miloje Milojevic (1884-1946). f, Mihovil Logar (1902-98). g, Lyubica Maric (1909-2003). h, Vasilije Mokranjac (1923-84).

2009, May 29
472 A212 22d Sheet of 8, #a-h, + central label 5.75 5.75

Battle of Cegar, 200th Anniv. A213

Designs: 22d, Battle of Cegar, painting by Boza Ilic. 46d, Stevan Sindelic, soldiers at Skull Tower.

2009, May 29 ***Perf. 13¼x13¾***
473-474 A213 Set of 2 2.25 2.25

Painting of Frescoes in Church of the Virgin Mary, Studenica, 800th Anniv. — A214

2009, June 8 ***Perf. 13¼***
475 A214 22d multi .80 .80

Famous Men — A215

Designs: No. 476, 22d, Pavle Savic (1909-94), physicist. No. 477, 22d, Dimitrije Putnikovic (1859-1910), educator. No. 478, 46d, Pierre Curie (1859-1906), physicist. No. 479, 46d, Charles Darwin (1809-82), naturalist.

2009, June 22 ***Perf. 13¾x13¼***
476-479 A215 Set of 4 4.50 4.50

Railroads in Serbia, 125th Anniv. — A216

Designs: 22d, CS No. 1 steam locomotive, Belgrade Station. 46d, JZ 441 electric locomotive, Nis Station.

2009, Sept. 8 **Litho.** ***Perf. 13¼***
480-481 A216 Set of 2 2.40 2.40

Golden Pen International Biennale of Illustrations, 50th Anniv. — A217

2009, Sept. 21 ***Perf. 13¾x13¼***
482 A217 22d gold & black .85 .85

Joy of Europe A218

2009, Sept. 30 ***Perf. 13¼x13¾***
483 A218 46d multi 1.25 1.25

Printed in sheets of 8 + label.

Gold Medalists at 2009 FINA World Swimming Championships, Rome — A219

Designs: No. 484, 46d, Nadja Higl (shown). No. 485, 46d, Milorad Cavic. 50d, Serbian Water Polo team.

2009, Oct. 9
484-486 A219 Set of 3 5.25 5.25

Nos. 484-486 each were printed in sheets of 8 + label.

Stamp Day — A220

2009, Oct. 23 ***Perf. 13¾x13¼***
487 A220 46d multi 1.75 1.75

Michel Stamp Catalogs, Cent.

Exhibition of Dinosaurs From Argentina, Belgrade A221

Designs: 22d, Herrerrasaurus ischigualastensis. 46d, Giganotosaurus carolinii.

2009, Nov. 9 ***Perf. 13¼x13¾***
488-489 A221 Set of 2 2.50 2.50

Nos. 488-489 each were printed in sheets of 9 + label.

Christmas A222

Frescoes from Krusedol Monastery by Jov Vasilijevic: 22d, Christ's Birth. 46d, Epiphany.

2009, Nov. 23 **Litho.** ***Perf. 13¼***
490-491 A222 Set of 2 2.25 2.25

NIN Magazine, 75th Anniv. — A223

2010, Jan. 26 ***Perf. 13¾x13¼***
492 A223 22d multi .65 .65

New Year 2010 (Year of the Tiger) — A224

Tiger at: 22d, Right. 50d, Left.

2010, Jan. 27 ***Perf. 13¼x13¾***
493-494 A224 Set of 2 2.00 2.00

European Nature Protection A225

Paeonia officinalis and: 22d, Deliblato Sands. 46d, Vrsac Mountains.

2010, Feb. 10 ***Perf. 13¼x13¾***
495-496 A225 Set of 2 2.00 2.00
496a Souvenir sheet, #495-496, perf. 13¾ 2.00 2.00

2010 Winter Olympics, Vancouver A226

Designs: 22d, Cross-country skiing. 50d, Downhill skier.

2010, Feb. 12 ***Perf. 13¾***
497-498 A226 Set of 2 2.25 2.25

Nos. 497-498 each were printed in sheets of 8 + central label.

Serbian Olympic Committee, Cent. — A227

2010, Feb. 23 **Litho.** ***Perf. 13¾***
499 A227 22d multi .70 .70

Expo 2010, Shanghai A228

Serbian Pavilion and: 22d, People, birds. 50d, Shanghai buildings.

2010, Feb. 26 ***Perf. 13¾x13¼***
500-501 A228 Set of 2 2.25 2.25

Frédéric Chopin (1810-49), Composer A229

2010, Mar. 1

502 A229 50d multi 1.75 1.75

Printed in sheets of 8 + central label.

Easter — A230

Red Easter egg and: 22d, Crucifixion painting. 46d, Egg depicting resurrected Jesus.

2010, Mar. 2 ***Perf. 13¼x13¾***

503-504 A230 Set of 2 2.25 2.25

Military Academy, Belgrade, 160th Anniv. A231

Perf. 13¼x13¾

2010, Mar. 18 **Litho.**

505 A231 22d multi .70 .70

Zastava 750, 55th Anniv. — A232

2010, Apr. 8

506 A232 22d multi .80 .80

Birds A233

No. 507: a, Passer domesticus. b, Phoenicurus ochruros. c, Columba livia. d, Parus major.

2010, Apr. 12 ***Perf. 13¾***

507 Horiz. strip of 4 + central label 5.25 5.25
- ***a.*** A233 22d multi .70 .70
- ***b.*** A233 33d multi 1.00 1.00
- ***c.*** A233 46d multi 1.40 1.40
- ***d.*** A233 50d multi 1.60 1.60

Industrialization of Serbia, 140th Anniv. — A234

2010, Apr. 19 ***Perf. 13¾***

508 A234 22d multi .85 .85

Europa — A235

Designs: 66d, Girl reading on stack of books, vine, house, rabbit, giraffe, chicks. 77d, Girl standing on stack of books, boy in sling under moon, pumpkins, fairies.

2010, May 5

509-510 A235 Set of 2 4.25 4.25

Nos. 509-510 each were printed in sheets of 8 + central label.

2010 World Cup Soccer Championships, South Africa — A236

Emblem of 2010 World Cup and: 22d, Map of Africa, two players. 50d, Map of Africa, two players, flags of South Africa and Serbia.

177d, Feet of soccer player, soccer balls, horiz.

2010, May 6 ***Perf. 13¾***

511-512 A236 Set of 2 3.00 3.00

Souvenir Sheet

Perf. 13¾x¼

513 A236 177d multi 5.50 5.50

No. 513 contains one 43x35mm stamp. Nos. 511-512 each were printed in sheets of 8 + label.

50th Tour de Serbie Bicycle Race — A237

2010, June 1 ***Perf. 13¾x13¼***

514 A237 50d multi 1.60 1.60

Printed in sheets of 8 + label.

Icons — A238

No. 515: a, Archangel Michael, by Andrei Rublev, 15th cent., Russia. b, Odigitria Virgin, Belgrade, 14th cent.

2010, June 28 ***Perf. 13¼x13¾***

515 A238 50d Pair, #a-b 2.75 2.75

No. 515 was printed in sheets of 8, containing 4 of each stamp, + central label. See Russia No. 7221.

50th Trumpet Festival, Guca A239

2010, Aug. 13 ***Perf. 13¾***

516 A239 44d multi 1.60 1.60

Printed in sheets of 8 + label. See Bosnia & Herzegovina (Serb Administration) No. 402.

2010 Youth Olympics, Singapore A240

2010, Aug. 14

517 A240 51d multi 1.60 1.60

Printed in sheets of 8 + label.

Mother Teresa (1910-97), Humanitarian A241

2010, Aug. 26 ***Perf. 13¾x13¼***

518 A241 50d multi 1.60 1.60

Miniature Sheet

Writers — A242

No. 519: a, Laza Kostic (1841-1910). b, Branislav Nusic (1864-1938). c, Borisav Stankovic (1876-1927). d, Ivo Andric (1892-1975). e, Milos Crnjanski (1893-1977). f, Mesa Selimovic (1910-82). g, Borislav Pekic (1930-92). h, Danilo Kis (1935-89).

2010, Nov. 26 ***Perf. 13¼***

519 A242 22d Sheet of 8, #a-h, + central label 5.25 5.25

Plate, 16th Cent. — A243

Figurine, 19th Cent. — A244

2010, Nov. 26

520 A243 22d multi .75 .75

521 A244 44d multi 1.50 1.50

Belgrade Art Museum, 60th anniv.

Serbian Postal Service, 170th Anniv. A245

2010, Nov. 26 ***Perf. 13¼***

522 A245 46d multi 1.50 1.50

Stamp Day.

Joy of Europe A246

2010, Nov. 26

523 A246 46d multi 1.50 1.50

Printed in sheets of 8 + central label.

Christmas A247

Nativity paintings from church in Zemun by: 22d, Arsenija Teodorovic. 46d, Unknown artist.

2010, Nov. 30

524-525 A247 Set of 2 2.25 2.25

Ivan Saric (1876-1966), Aviation Pioneer, and Saric No. 1 Airplane A248

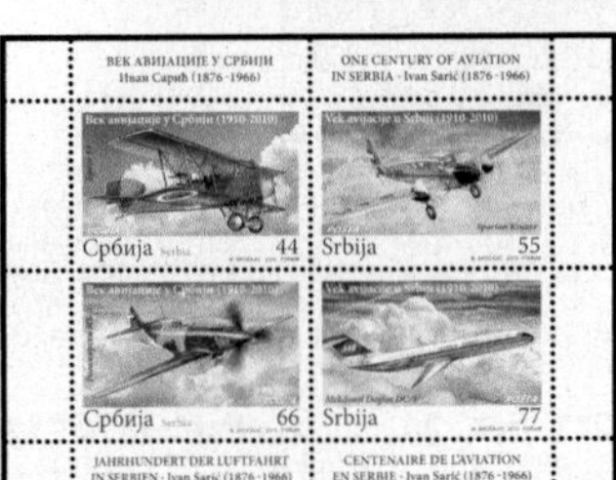

Airplanes — A249

No. 527: a, 44d, Breguet 14. b, 55d, Spartan Cruiser. c, 66d, Rogozarski IK-3. d, 77d, McDonnell Douglas DC-9.

2010, Dec. 9 ***Perf. 13¼***

526 A248 22d multi .75 .75

Perf. 13¾

527 A249 Sheet of 4, #a-d 7.50 7.50

Souvenir Sheet

Preservation of Polar Regions and Glaciers — A250

No. 528: a, 46d, Iceberg. b, 66d, Glacier.

2011, Jan. 31 **Litho.** ***Perf. 13¼***
528 A250 Sheet of 2, #a-b 3.00 3.00

New Year 2011 (Year of the Rabbit) A251

Rabbit, ring of Chinese Zodiac animals and: 22d, Geometric design. 55d, Chinese character for "rabbit."

2011, Feb. 7
529-530 A251 Set of 2 2.25 2.25

Serbian Membership in Intl. Telecommunications Union, 145th Anniv. — A252

2011, Feb. 9 ***Perf. 13¼x13¾***
531 A252 46d multi 1.25 1.25

Printed in sheets of 8 + label.

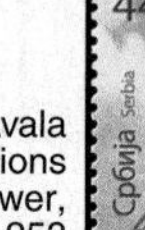

Rebuilding of Avala Telecommunications Tower, Belgrade — A253

2011, Feb. 14 ***Perf. 13¼***
532 A253 44d multi 1.40 1.40
532a Dated "2013" 1.40 1.40

Issued: No. 532a, 4/11/13.

Art — A254

Designs: 22p, Self-portrait of Katarina Ivanovic (1811-82). 33d, Woman in Traditional Dress, by Uros Knezevic (1811-76). 44d, Self-portrait, sculpture, by Djordje Jovanovic (1861-1953). 66d, Self-portrait with Wife and Son, by Bora Baruh (1911-42).

2011, Feb. 25 ***Perf. 13¾x13¼***
533-536 A254 Set of 4 4.50 4.50

Kornelije Stankovic (1831-65), Composer A255

2011, Mar. 15 ***Perf. 13¼x13¾***
537 A255 22d multi .70 .70

Stankovic Music School, cent.

Easter — A256

Religious paintings by Arsenije Teodorovic (1767-1826): 22d, Christ's Arrival in Jerusalem. 112d, Resurrection.

2011, Mar. 25 ***Perf. 13¾***
538-539 A256 Set of 2 4.00 4.00

Serbian National Theater, Novi Sad, 150th Anniv. A257

2011, Mar. 28
540 A257 22d multi .70 .70

Printed in sheets of 24 + central label.

Rotary International Polio Plus Program A258

2011, Mar. 31 ***Perf. 13¾x13¼***
541 A258 50d multi 1.25 1.25

Worldwide Fund for Nature (WWF) A259

No. 542 — Phalacrocorax pygmaeus: a, Two birds, one on branch. b, Bird on rock. c, Two birds in flight. d, Two birds in water.

2011, Apr. 11 ***Perf. 13¼x13¾***
542 Horiz. strip of 4 + central label 4.50 4.50
a. A259 22d multi .65 .65
b. A259 33d multi .95 .95
c. A259 44d multi 1.15 1.15
d. A259 66d multi 1.75 1.75

Intl. Year of Biodiversity — A260

2011, Apr. 15 ***Perf. 13¾***
543 A260 50d multi 1.40 1.40

Europa A261

Forest and: 33d, Logs. 66d, Tree leaves.

2011, May 5 **Litho.**
544-545 A261 Set of 2 2.75 2.75

Intl. Year of Forests. Nos. 544-545 each were printed in sheets of 8 + central label.

Scouting in Serbia, Cent. — A262

2011, May 6 ***Perf. 13¼x13¾***
546 A262 22d multi .60 .60

Bora Stankovic Gymnasium, Vranje, 130th Anniv. — A263

2011, May 10 ***Perf. 13¾x13¼***
547 A263 22d multi .70 .70

Dr. Laza Lazarevic (1851-91), Writer and Psychiatrist A264

2011, May 13
548 A264 22d multi .70 .70

Berries A265

No. 549: a, Rubus idaeus. b, Fragaria vesca. c, Ribes rubrum. d, Vaccinium macrocarpon.

2011, May 27 ***Perf. 13¼x13¾***
549 Horiz. strip of 4 + central label 4.50 4.50
a. A265 22d multi .60 .60
b. A265 33d multi .85 .85
c. A265 44d multi 1.25 1.25
d. A265 66d multi 1.75 1.75

Campaign Against AIDS, 30th Anniv. — A266

2011, June 1 ***Perf. 13¾x13¼***
550 A266 50d multi 1.40 1.40

Digital Serbia — A267

Designs: 22d, Keyhole on Earth, key. 44d, Stylized eye, "@" and "www."

2011, June 3 ***Perf. 13¼***
551-552 A267 Set of 2 1.75 1.75

European Nature Protection A268

Waterfalls: 22d, Mokranjska Stena. 46d, Beli Izvorac.

2011, June 13 ***Perf. 13¾x13¼***
553-554 A268 Set of 2 2.00 2.00

Franz Liszt (1811-86), Composer A269

2011, June 14 ***Perf. 13¾***
555 A269 50d multi 1.40 1.40

Bridges A270

Designs: 22d, Danube River Bridge, near Beska. 44d, Sava River Railway Bridge, Belgrade. 46d, Danube River Bridge, Novi Sad.

2011, June 20 **Litho.**
556-558 A270 Set of 3 3.00 3.00

Duzijanca Harvest Festival, Cent. — A271

Designs: 22d, Model of cathedral in Subotica. 55d, Centenary wheat crown.

2011, July 1
559-560 A271 Set of 2 2.00 2.00

Nos. 559-560 each were printed in sheets of 9 + label.

Belgrade Zoo, 75th Anniv. A272

Designs: 22d, Lion, white lion and cubs. No. 562, vert. — White or albino animals: a, 33d, Panthera tigris tigris. b, 44d, Neophron percnopterus. c, 46d, Macropus rufogriseus. d, 50d, Panthera leo.

2011, July 12 ***Perf. 13¾***

561 A272 22d multi .75 .75
562 A272 Sheet of 4, #a-d 5.75 5.75

No. 562 was sold with, but unattached to, a booklet cover.

Computer Mouse Flower — A273

2011, July 13

563 A273 22d multi 1.10 1.10
563a Dated 2013 1.10 1.10

Issued: No. 563a, 2/19/13.

Soko Galeb Jet, 50th Anniv. A274

2011, July 20 ***Perf. 13¼x13¾***

564 A274 50d multi 1.40 1.40

Printed in sheets of 8 + central label.

First Conference of Non-Aligned Countries, 50th Anniv. — A275

2011, Sept. 1 ***Perf. 13¾x13¼***

565 A275 22d multi .75 .75

European Women's Volleyball Championships, Italy and Serbia — A276

2011, Sept. 20 ***Perf. 13¾***

566 A276 46d multi 1.25 1.25

Printed in sheets of 8 + central label.

Joy of Europe A277

2011, Sept. 30 ***Perf. 13¼x13¾***

567 A277 46d multi 1.25 1.25

Printed in sheets of 8 + central label.

First Serbian Motion Picture, Cent. A278

2011, Oct. 3 ***Perf. 13¾***

568 A278 22d multi .80 .80

Stamp Day — A279

2011, Oct. 25 ***Perf. 13¾x13¼***

569 A279 46d multi 1.40 1.40

Beogradfila Stamp Exhibition, Belgrade.

Writers A280

Designs: 22d, Rachel de Queiroz (1910-2003), Brazilian writer. 46d, Ivo Andric (1892-1975), Yugoslvian writer, and Nobel medal.

2011, Oct. 26 ***Perf. 13¾***

570-571 A280 Set of 2 2.25 2.25

See Brazil No. 3198.

Christmas A281

Designs: 22d, Birth of Christ, icon, c. 1780. 112d, Birth of Christ, by Arsenije Teodorovic.

2011, Nov. 15

572-573 A281 Set of 2 4.00 4.00

Journalist's Association of Serbia, 130th Anniv. — A282

2011, Nov. 25

574 A282 22d multi .70 .70

Moravica Hydroelectric Plant, Cent. — A283

2011, Dec. 19 ***Perf. 13¼x13¾***

575 A283 22d multi .65 .65

Serbian Victories at 2011 Men's and Women's European Volleyball Championships A284

Designs: No. 576, 22d, Two male players. No. 577, 22d, Three female players.

2011, Dec. 20 ***Perf. 13¾x13¼***

576-577 A284 Set of 2 1.50 1.50

African National Congress, Cent. — A285

2012, Jan. 6 **Litho.**

578 A285 46d multi 1.40 1.40

New Year 2012 (Year of the Dragon) A286

Designs: 22d, Dragon. 55d, Dragon, diff.

2012, Feb. 6 ***Perf. 13¼x13¾***

579-580 A286 Set of 2 4.00 4.00

Architecture A287

Designs: 22d, Department store, Belgrade. 33d, Telephone Exchange Building, Belgrade, horiz. 46d, Hotel Moskva, Belgrade, horiz. 55d, City Hall, Subotica, horiz.

Perf. 13¾x13¼, 13¼x13¾

2012, Mar. 2

581-584 A287 Set of 4 4.00 4.00

National Theater, Nis, 125th Anniv. A288

2012, Mar. 9 ***Perf. 13¼***

585 A288 22d multi .65 .65

Easter — A289

Designs: 22d, Ceremonial cross. 46d, Resurrection of Christ.

2012, Mar. 15 ***Perf. 13¾***

586-587 A289 Set of 2 1.75 1.75

Academy Anniversaries — A290

Woman and building: 22d, Music Academy, Belgrade, 75th anniv. 33d, Art Academy, Belgrade, 75th anniv. 44d, Science Academy, Pozarevac, 150th anniv.

2012, Mar. 30

588-590 A290 Set of 3 2.50 2.50

Ján Koniarek (1878-1952), Sculptor — A291

2012, Apr. 13

591 A291 50d multi 1.60 1.60

Printed in sheets of 8 + central label. See Slovakia No. 636.

25th Belgrade Marathon A292

2012, Apr. 21

592 A292 22d multi .70 .70

Europa A293

Designs: 44d, Church and angel. 77d, Snowboarder, mountainside forest in winter, cottage, lakefront building.

2012, May 4

593-594 A293 Set of 2 3.00 3.00

Nos. 593-594 each were printed in sheets of 8 + central label

Reptiles A294

No. 595: a, Coronella austriaca. b, Podarcis taurica. c, Lacerta viridis. d, Emys orbicularis.

2012, May 21 ***Perf. 13¼x13¾***

595 Horiz. strip of 4 + central label 4.00 4.00
a. A294 22d multi .55 .55
b. A294 33d multi .80 .80
c. A294 44d multi 1.00 1.00
d. A294 66d multi 1.60 1.60

European Nature Protection A295

Forest and: 22d, Pinus nigra. 46d, Acer heldreichii.

2012, June 1 ***Perf. 13¾***
596-597 A295 Set of 2 1.75 1.75

Nos. 596-597 each were printed in sheets of 8 + central label.

Archangel Michael Cathedral, Belgrade, 175th Anniv. — A296

2012, July 13 ***Perf. 13¾x13¼***
598 A296 22d multi .70 .70

No. 598 was printed in sheets of 8 + central label.

2012 Summer Olympics, London — A297

Emblem of 2012 Summer Olympics and: 44d, Torch and stadium. 77d, London landmarks.

2012, July 27
599-600 A297 Set of 2 2.75 2.75

Nos. 599-600 each were printed in sheets of 8 + central label.

Writers A298

Designs: 22d, Vojislav Ilic (1860-94), poet. 33d, Janko Veselinovic (1862-1905), novelist. 44d, Vuk Stefanovic Karadzic (1787-1864), linguist.

2012, Sept. 3 ***Perf. 13x13¾***
601-603 A298 Set of 3 2.40 2.40

Items in National Museum A299

Designs: 22d, Statue, 4th cent. 55d, Sword, 20th cent.

2012, Sept. 27
604-605 A299 Set of 2 1.75 1.75

Nos. 604-605 each were printed in sheets of 9 + label.

Joy of Europe A300

2012, Oct. 1
606 A300 46d multi 1.10 1.10

No. 606 was printed in sheets of 8 + central label.

Digital Television — A301

2012, Oct. 4 ***Perf. 13¾***
607 A301 50d multi 1.10 1.10

Battle of Kumanovo, Cent. — A302

Designs: 22d, Gen. Radomir Putnik, Gen. Stepa Stepanovic, Col. Zivojin Misic, and Prince Regent Alexander Karageorgevich. 50d, Revenge of Kosovo, painting by Paja Jovanovic.

2012, Oct. 24
608-609 A302 Set of 2 1.75 1.75

Nos. 608-609 each were printed in sheets of 8 + central label.

Stamp Day A303

2012, Oct. 25
610 A303 22d multi .70 .70

First Serbian stamp exhibition, 75th anniv.

Christmas A304

Nativity icons by, 22d, Dimitrije Bacevic. 46d, Dimitrije Bratoglic.

2012, Nov. 1
611-612 A304 Set of 2 1.60 1.60

Miniature Sheet

Serbian Air Force, Cent. — A305

No. 613: a, 22d, Military balloon. b, 22d, Rogozarski IK-3 propeller airplane. c, 22d, Soko Jastreb jet fighter. d, 55d, Fizir FN biplane. e, 55d, Ikarus S-49. f, 55d, Lasta 95.

2012, Dec. 24 ***Perf. 13¼x13¾***
613 A305 Sheet of 6, #a-f 5.75 5.75

New Year 2013 (Year of the Snake) — A306

Designs: 22d, Snake and lotus flower. 46d, Snake.

2013, Feb. 8 ***Perf. 13¾***
614-615 A306 Set of 2 1.75 1.75

Serbian Historical Museum, 50th Anniv. A307

Museum exhibits: 22d, Gospel of King Alexander Obrenovich. 50d, Crown of King Peter I Karageorgevich.

2013, Feb. 20 **Litho.**
616-617 A307 Set of 2 1.75 1.75

Nos. 616-617 each were printed in sheets of 9 + label.

Easter — A308

Frescos from Most Holy Theotokos Monastery Church: 22d, Crucifixion. 46d, Descent to Hell.

2013, Mar. 1
618-619 A308 Set of 2 1.60 1.60

Composers — A309

Designs: 22d, Oskar Danon (1913-2009). 46d, Richard Wagner (1813-83). 50d, Giuseppe Verdi (1813-1901).

2013, Mar. 4 ***Perf. 13¾***
620-622 A309 Set of 3 3.00 3.00

Edict of Milan, 1700th Anniv. — A310

Bust of Emperor Constantine and: 50d, Chrismon. 112d, Ship, map of Adriatic area, horiz.

2013, Apr. 5 ***Perf. 13¾x13¼***
623 A310 50d multi 1.25 1.25

Souvenir Sheet

Perf. 13¾

624 A310 112d multi 2.75 2.75

No. 623 was printed in sheets of 8 + central label.

Intl. Red Cross, 150th Anniv. — A311

2013, May 8 ***Perf. 13¾***
625 A311 50d black & red 1.25 1.25

No. 625 was printed in sheets of 9 + label.

Europa A312

Postal vehicles: 44d, Old postal truck. 112d, Modern postal van.

2013, May 9 ***Perf. 13¼x13¾***
626-627 A312 Set of 2 3.75 3.75

Nos. 626-627 each were printed in sheets of 8 + central label.

European Nature Protection A313

Designs: 46d, Man with scythe in meadow near Mt. Rajac. 50d, Resava Cave.

2013, May 13
628-629 A313 Set of 2 2.25 2.25

Nos. 628-629 each were printed in sheets of 8 + central label.

Miniature Sheet

Actors and Actresses — A314

No. 630: a, Zivojin Zika Milenkovic (1927-2008). b, Radmila Rada Savicevic (1926-2001). c, Petar Kralj (1941-2011). d, Radomir Rade Markovic (1921-2010). e, Ksenija Jovanovic (1928-2012). f, Predrag Tasovac (1922-2010). g, Pavle Paja Vujisic (1926-88). h, Dragan Lakovic (1929-90).

2013, May 24 ***Perf. 13¾x13¼***
630 A314 22d Sheet of 8, #a-h, + central label 4.25 4.25

Diplomatic Relations Between Serbia and Cuba, 70th Anniv. — A315

2013, May 29 ***Perf. 13¼x13¾***
631 A315 46d multi 1.10 1.10

Orchids A316

No. 632: a, Cymbidium Burgundium. b, Masdevallia kimballiana. c, Angraecum leonis. d, Cymbidium Fort George.

2013, June 14
632 Horiz. strip of 4 + central label 4.00 4.00
a. A316 22d multi .55 .55
b. A316 33d multi .75 .75
c. A316 46d multi 1.10 1.10
d. A316 66d multi 1.60 1.60

50th Ljubicevo Equestrian Games — A317

No. 633: a, Joceky with helmet on horse facing right. b, Rider with crop on horse, bullseye target. c, Rider with crop on horse, watermelon on stand. d, Rider on horse facing left.

2013, Aug. 30 **Litho.** ***Perf. 13¾***
633 Horiz. strip of 4 + central label 2.00 2.00
a.-d. A317 22d Any single .50 .50

Joy of Europe — A318

Children's drawings of: 22d, Children and bicycle. 46d, Boy and girl playing musical instruments, vert.

Perf. 13¼x13¾, 13¾x13¼
2013, Sept. 2 **Litho.**
634-635 A318 Set of 2 1.60 1.60

Nos. 634-635 are each printed in sheets of 8 + central label.

Constitutional Court, 50th Anniv. — A319

2013, Oct. 14 **Litho.** ***Perf. 13¼x13¾***
636 A319 22d multi .50 .50

Stamp Day — A320

No. 637a, With "NS" in oval handstamp in green area of stamp near top left corner of yellow envelope.

2013, Oct. 25 **Litho.** ***Perf. 13¼x13¾***
637 A320 22d multi .50 .50
a. multi *.50* *.50*

First postal law in Serbia, 170th anniv. No. 637a is the 7th stamp in the sheet of 25.

Christmas — A321

Icons depicting the Nativity from: 22d, 1866-67. 46d, 1868.

2013, Oct. 28 **Litho.** ***Perf. 13¾***
638-639 A321 Set of 2 1.60 1.60

Petar II Petrovic-Njegos (1813-51), Prince of Montenegro A322

2013, Nov. 13 **Litho.** ***Perf. 13¼***
640 A322 46d multi 1.10 1.10

No. 640 was printed in sheets of 8 + central label.

Mitrovica High School, 175th Anniv. — A323

Pancevo High School, 150th Anniv. A324

Novi Pazar High School, Cent. A325

Prijepolje High School, Cent. A326

2013, Nov. 20 **Litho.** ***Perf. 13¼***
641 A323 22d multi .55 .55
642 A324 22d multi .55 .55
643 A325 22d multi .55 .55
644 A326 22d multi .55 .55
Nos. 641-644 (4) 2.20 2.20

King Alexander of Yugoslavia (1888-1934) A327

2013, Nov. 25 **Litho.** ***Perf. 13¼***
645 A327 50d multi 1.25 1.25

No. 645 was printed in sheets of 8 + central label.

Zastava Arms Factory, Kragujevac, 160th Anniv. A328

2013, Nov. 28 **Litho.** ***Perf. 13¼***
646 A328 22d multi .55 .55

Souvenir Sheet

Rugs — A329

No. 647 — Rugs with inscriptions in: a, Latin letters. b, Cyrillic letters.

2013, Dec. 2 **Litho.** ***Perf. 13¾***
647 A329 46d Sheet of 2, #a-b 2.25 2.25

See Algeria No. 1632.

Grand Prince Stefan Namanja (c. 1113-99) — A330

2013, Dec. 6 **Litho.** ***Perf. 13¼***
648 A330 22d multi .55 .55

Start of Negotiations for Serbian Admittance to European Union A331

2014, Jan. 21 **Litho.** ***Perf. 13¼***
649 A331 22d multi .50 .50

New Year 2014 (Year of the Horse) A332

Ring of Chinese Zodiac animals and: 22d, Horse. 46d, Pegasus.

2014, Jan. 31 **Litho.** ***Perf. 13¼***
650-651 A332 Set of 2 1.60 1.60

2014 Winter Olympics, Sochi, Russia — A333

Designs: 22d, Figure skating. 46d, Ski jumping.

2014, Feb. 7 **Litho.** ***Perf. 13¼***
652-653 A333 Set of 2 1.60 1.60

Nos. 652-653 are each printed in sheets of 8 + central label.

Easter A334

Icons depicting: 22d, The Last Supper. 46d, Entombment of Christ.

2014, Feb. 17 **Litho.** ***Perf. 13¼***
654-655 A334 Set of 2 1.60 1.60

Writers — A335

Designs: 22d, Branislav Nusic (1864-1938). 46d, Mikhail Lermontov (1814-41). 50d, William Shakespeare (1564-1616).

2014, Mar. 28 **Litho.** ***Perf. 13¼***
656-658 A335 Set of 3 3.00 3.00

Electronic Communications A336

2014, Apr. 1 **Litho.** ***Perf. 13½***
659 A336 1d multi .25 .25

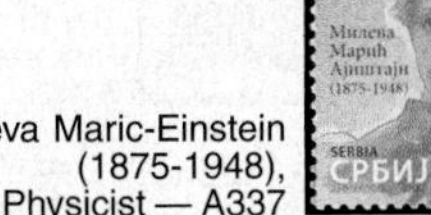

Mileva Maric-Einstein (1875-1948), Physicist — A337

2014, Apr. 1 **Litho.** ***Perf. 13½***
660 A337 23d multi .55 .55
a. Dated "2015" .45 .45
b. Dated "2016," perf. 13¾ .40 .40
c. Dated "2016," perf. 13¼ .40 .40
d. Dated "2017," perf. 13¾ .45 .45
e. Dated "2018," perf. 13¾ .50 .50

Issued: No. 660e, 3/20/18.

Europa A338

Musician playing: 69d, Fife. 74d, Bagpipes.

2014, Apr. 26 Litho. *Perf. 13¼*
661-662 A338 Set of 2 3.50 3.50

Nos. 661-662 were each printed in sheets of 8 + central label.

European Nature Protection A339

Animals at: 35d, Stara Planina Nature Park. 70d, Zaovine Lake.

2014, May 22 Litho. *Perf. 13¼*
663-664 A339 Set of 2 2.50 2.50

Nos. 663-664 were each printed in sheets of 8 + central label.

World War I, Cent. A340

Paintings and objects: 23d, Serbian Army Crossing Albania, by Milos Golubovic, 1915, and regiment flag. 35d, Another View, by Golubovic, 1915-16, swords and war medal. 46d, Serbian Army Arriving at the Sea, bu Vasa Eskicevic, 1916, army helmet and regiment flag. 70d, Goodbye, My Children, by Golubovic, 1915-16, Order of the Star with Swords.

2014, June 24 Litho. *Perf. 13¼*
665-668 A340 Set of 4 4.25 4.25

Nos. 665-668 were each printed in sheets of 9 + label.

Wild Animals A341

2014, June 30 Litho. *Perf. 13¼*
669 Horiz. strip + central label 4.25 4.25
a. A341 23d Felis silvestris .55 .55
b. A341 35d Vulpes vulpes .85 .85
c. A341 46d Canis lupus 1.10 1.10
d. A341 70d Lynx lynx 1.75 1.75

Joy of Europe A342

2014, Sept. 2 Litho. *Perf. 13¼*
670 A342 70d multi 1.60 1.60

No. 670 was printed in sheets of 8 + central label.

Patriarch Pavle (1914-2009) A343

2014, Sept. 11 Litho. *Perf. 13¼*
671 A343 23d multi .50 .50

No. 671 was printed in sheets of 8 + central label.

Stamp Day — A344

2014, Sept. 23 Litho. *Perf. 13¼*
672 A344 23d multi .50 .50

Museum Exhibits — A345

Coats of Arms in Museum of Applied Arts, Belgrade: 23d, Arms of the Nemajic Dynasty. 69d, Arms of the Brankovic Dynasty.

2014, Oct. 1 Litho. *Perf. 13¼*
673-674 A345 Set of 2 2.00 2.00

Nos. 673-674 were each printed in sheets of 9 + label.

Scientists A346

Designs: 23d, Petar Stevanovic (1914-99), geologist and paleontologist. 74d, Josef Pancic (1814-88), botanist.

2014, Oct. 8 Litho. *Perf. 13¼*
675-676 A346 Set of 2 2.00 2.00

Christmas A347

Designs: 23d, Fresco from Zica Monastery, 1309-16. 70d, Fresco from Zica Monastery, music for hymn *Slava Vo Visnjih Bogu.*

2014, Oct. 17 Litho. *Perf. 13¼*
677-678 A347 Set of 2 2.00 2.00

Souvenir Sheet

Liberation of Belgrade, 70th Anniv. — A348

No. 679: a, 50d, Belgrade war damage. b, 170d. Rebuilt buildings in Belgrade.

2014, Oct. 20 Litho. *Perf. 14x13¾*
679 A348 Sheet of 2, #a-b 4.75 4.75

Fables A349

Designs: 23d, The Dog and His Shadow. 35d, The Fox and the Crow. 46d, The Rooster and the Precious Stone. 70d, The Turtle and the Eagle.

2014, Nov. 17 Litho. *Perf. 13¼*
680-683 A349 Set of 4 3.75 3.75

Nos. 680-683 were each printed in sheets of 8 + central label.

Miniature Sheet

Architecture of Nikolai Krasnov (1864-1939) — A350

No. 684: a, 23d, Krasnov and dome of Ministry of Forests and Mines Building (now Ministry of Foreign Affairs Building), Belgrade (35x29mm). b, 23d, Ministry of Finance Building (now Serbian Government Building), Belgrade (dome visible, 35x29mm). c, 23d, Ministry of Finance Building, different view (no dome visible, 35x29mm). d, 35d, Watercolor of Old General Staff Building in Belgrade, by Krasnov (trolley in street, 35x29mm). e, 35d, State Archives Building, Belgrade (35x29mm). f, 35d, King Alexander I Bridge, Belgrade (35x29mm). g, 70d, Church of the Haraks Palace and Hunting Lodge of Prince Felix Yusupov, Yalta (denomination in white, 35x58mm). h, 70d, Palace of Grand Duke Peter Nikolaevich (denomination in brown, 35x58mm).

Perf. 13¼x13¾ (#684a-684f), 13¾ (#684g-684h)

2014, Nov. 27 Litho.
684 A350 Sheet of 8, #a-h 6.50 6.50

No. 684 has a fold between the horizontal and vertical stamps and was sold with, but unattached to, a booklet cover.

Souvenir Sheet

Diplomatic Relations Between Serbia and South Korea, 25th Anniv. — A351

No. 685: a, 50d, Buildings in Belgrade, flag of Serbia. b, 170d, Seoul skyline, flag of South Korea.

2014, Dec. 3 Litho. *Perf. 14x13¾*
685 A351 Sheet of 2, #a-b 4.50 4.50

Ljubica Cuca Sokic (1914-2009), Painter A352

2014, Dec. 9 Litho. *Perf. 13¼*
686 A352 23d multi .45 .45

No. 686 was printed in sheets of 8 + central label.

Branko Copic (1915-84), Writer — A353

2015, Jan. 27 Litho. *Perf. 13¼*
687 A353 35d multi .65 .65

No. 687 was printed in sheets of 8 + central label.

New Year 2015 (Year of the Goat) A354

Ring of Zodiac animals and: 23d, Goat's head. 74d, Goat.

2015, Feb. 19 Litho. *Perf. 13¼*
688-689 A354 Set of 2 1.75 1.75

Easter A355

Easter eggs decorated with depiction of: 23d, Resurrection of Christ. 74d, Christ's entry into Jerusalem.

2015, Feb. 25 Litho. *Perf. 13¼*
690-691 A355 Set of 2 1.75 1.75

Miniature Sheet

Theatrical and Film Directors — A356

No. 692: a, Radivoje Lola Dukic (1923-95). b, Ognjenka Milicevic (1927-2008). c, Aleksandar Dordevic (1924-2005). d, Slavojub Stefanovic (1927-96). e, Miroslav Belovic (1927-2013). f, Ljubomir Muci Draskic (1937-2004). g, Sava Mrmak (1929-2002). h, Jovan Ristic Rica (1939-2013).

2015, Mar. 26 Litho. *Perf. 13¼*
692 A356 23d Sheet of 8, #a-h, + central label 3.50 3.50

Europa — A357

Old toys with wheels: 69d, Xylophone and telephone. 100d, Rabbit and baby carriage.

2015, Apr. 16 Litho. *Perf. 13¼*
693-694 A357 Set of 2 3.25 3.25

Nos. 693-694 were each printed in sheets of 8 + central label.

Souvenir Sheet

Second Serbian Uprising, 200th Anniv. — A358

No. 695: a, 50d, Detail of *The Takovo Uprising,* by Paja Jovanovic, swordsman from Takovo Uprising Monument, by Petar Ubavkic. b, 170d, Priest from Takovo Uprising Monument, Prince Milos Obrenovich, monument in Takovo, roof of church.

2015, Apr. 23 Litho. *Perf. 14x13¾*
695 A358 Sheet of 2, #a-b 4.25 4.25

Famous Men — A359

Designs: 23d, Jovan Cvijic (1865-1927), founder of Serbian Geographic Society, map and books. 74d, Dr. Joakim Medovic (1815-93), physician, cadeuceus and books.

2015, May 8 Litho. *Perf. 13¼*
696-697 A359 Set of 2 1.75 1.75

Nos. 696-697 were each printed in sheets of 8 + central label.

International Telecommunication Union, 150th Anniv. — A360

2015, May 15 Litho. *Perf. 13¼*
698 A360 74d multi 1.40 1.40

No. 698 was printed in sheets of 8 + central label.

European Nature Protection A361

Designs: 35d, Sargan-Mokra Gora Nature Park. 70d, Goc-Gvozdac Nature Preserve.

2015, May 20 Litho. *Perf. 13¼*
699-700 A361 Set of 2 1.90 1.90

Nos. 699-700 were each printed in sheets of 8 + central label.

Fruit — A362

No. 701: a, Cydonia oblonga. b, Malus sylvestris. c, Prunus domestica. d, Pyrus communis.

2015, May 27 Litho. *Perf. 13¼*
701 Horiz. strip of 4 + central label 3.25 3.25
a. A362 23d multi .45 .45
b. A362 35d multi .65 .65
c. A362 46d multi .85 .85
d. A362 70d multi 1.25 1.25

Dusko Radovic (1922-84) and Mica Tatic (1923-91), Radio Hosts, Bird and Microphone A363

2015, June 1 Litho. *Perf. 13¼*
702 A363 23d multi .45

Good Morning, Children radio show, 60th anniv.

Serbia Post, 175th Anniv. A364

Designs: 23d, Postal coach, post riders, Serbia #1, 4, post office. 74d, Modern post offices.

2015, June 5 Litho. *Perf. 13¼*
703-704 A364 Set of 2 1.75 1.75

Nos. 703-704 were each printed in sheets of 8 + central label.

Paintings A365

Designs: 23d, Amsterdam Street, by Petar Dobrovic (1890-1942). 70d, Manasija Monastery, by Dimitrije Avramovic (1815-55).

2015, June 10 Litho. *Perf. 13¼*
705-706 A365 Set of 2 1.75 1.75

Nos. 705-706 were each printed in sheets of 8 + central label.

Prince Milos Obrenovich (1780-1860) — A366

2015, Aug. 3 Litho. *Perf. 13¼*
707 A366 35d multi .65 .65
a. Dated "2016," perf. 13¾ .60 .60
b. Dated "2017," perf. 13¾ .65 .65
c. Dated "2018," perf. 13¾ .75 .75

Issued: No. 707c, 3/20/18.

International Year of Light — A367

Designs: 23d, Light bulb over Earth. 74d, Angel with torch and flashlight.

2015, Aug. 26 Litho. *Perf. 13¼*
708-709 A367 Set of 2 1.90 1.90

Souvenir Sheet

Serbian Men's Under-20 Soccer Team, 2015 World Champions — A368

2015, Sept. 24 Litho. *Perf. 13¼*
710 A368 184d multi 3.50 3.50

Joy of Europe A369

2015, Oct. 2 Litho. *Perf. 13¼*
711 A369 70d multi 1.40 1.40

World War I Defense of Belgrade, Cent. A370

2015, Oct. 6 Litho. *Perf. 13¼*
712 A370 23d multi .45 .45

Michael I. Pupin (1854-1935), Physicist and Inventor — A371

2015, Oct. 9 Litho. *Perf. 13¼*
713 A371 23d multi .45 .45

No. 713 was printed in sheets of 8 + central label.

Christmas A372

Icons: 23d, Annunciation, by D. Bacevic. 70d, Adoration of the Magi, by N. Neskovic.

2015, Oct. 15 Litho. *Perf. 13¼*
714-715 A372 Set of 2 1.75 1.75

Serbian Chairmanship of Organization for Security and Cooperation in Europe — A373

2015, Oct. 20 Litho. *Perf. 13¼*
716 A373 74d multi 1.40 1.40

Fairy Tales — A374

No. 717: a, *The Princess and the Frog,* by the Brothers Grimm. b, *Snow White and the Seven Dwarves,* by the Brothers Grimm. c, *Beauty and the Beast,* by Charles Perrault. d, *Sleeping Beauty,* by the Brothers Grimm.

2015, Nov. 4 Litho. *Perf. 13¼*
717 A374 23d Block of 4, #a-d 1.60 1.60

Davorin Jenko (1835-1914), Composer A375

2015, Nov. 9 Litho. *Perf. 13¼*
718 A375 70d multi 1.25 1.25

No. 718 was printed in sheets of 8 + central label. See Slovenia No. 1145.

A376

Anniversaries of Museum Exhibits — A376a

Designs: 23d, Copperplate engraving of Saints Peter and Paul, 200th anniv. 35d, Copperplate engvaving of Studenica Monastery, 275th anniv. 70d, Icon of St. Demetrius, 275th anniv.

2015, Nov. 18 Litho. *Perf. 13¼*
719 A376 23d multicolored .75 .75
720 A376a 35d multicolored .75 .75
721 A376 70d multicolored .75 .75
Nos. 719-721 (3) 2.25 2.25

Serbian Men's Water Polo Team, 2015 World Champions A377

2015, Nov. 24 Litho. *Perf. 13¼*
722 A377 23d multi .40 .40

Serbian Women's Basketball Team, 2015 European Champions
A378

2015, Nov. 27 Litho. *Perf. 13¼*
723 A378 23d multi .40 .40

Portrait of Milos Obrenovich, by Vsevolod Guljevic, and Order of Milos the Great — A379

2015, Dec. 2 Litho. *Perf. 13¼*
724 A379 23d multi .45 .45

Army Day, 200th anniv.

Krusevac Gymnasium, 150th Anniv.
A380

2015, Dec. 3 Litho. *Perf. 13¼*
725 A380 23d multi .45 .45

Miniature Sheet

British Heroines of World War I in Serbia — A381

No. 726: a, Flora Sandes (1876-1956) (35x47mm). b, Dr. Katherine Stewart MacPhail (1887-1974) (35x47mm). c, Elsie Maud Inglis (1864-1917) (48x47mm). d, Dr. Isabel Emslie Galloway Hutton (1887-1960) (35x47mm). e, Evelina Haverfield (1867-1920) (35x47mm). f, Dr. Elizabeth Ness MacBean Ross (1878-1915) (48x47mm).

Perf. 13¼x13¾ on 2 or 3 Sides
2015, Dec. 8 Litho.
726 A381 74d Sheet of 6, #a-f 8.00 8.00

No. 726 was sold with, but unattached to, a booklet cover.

Stamp Day — A382

2015, Dec. 10 Litho. *Perf. 13¼*
727 A382 23d multi .45 .45

Centenary of the "King Peter in the Battlefield in 1914."

UNESCO World Heritage Sites in Kosovo
A383

Designs: 23d, Mother of God Ljeviska Church, Prizren. 46d, Gracanica Monastery, Gracanica. 69d, Visoki Decani Monastery, Decani. 70d, Patriarchate of Pec Monastery, Pec.

2016, Jan. 28 Litho. *Perf. 13¼*
728-731 A383 Set of 4 3.75 3.75

New Year 2016 (Year of the Monkey)
A384

Ring of Chinese Zodiac animals and: 23d, Monkey. 74d, Head of monkey.

2016, Feb. 8 Litho. *Perf. 13¼*
732-733 A384 Set of 2 1.75 1.75

Jovan Zujovic (1856-1936), Anthropologist, and Serbian Geological Society — A385

2016, Feb. 23 Litho. *Perf. 13¼*
734 A385 23d multi .40 .40

Serbian Geological Society, 125th anniv. No. 734 was printed in sheets of 8 + central label.

Easter — A386

Icons of Resurrection of Christ from: 23d, 18th cent. 74d, 19th cent.

2016, Feb. 25 Litho. *Perf. 13¼*
735-736 A386 Set of 2 1.75 1.75

Worldwide Fund for Nature (WWF)
A387

Various depictions of Zerynthia polyxena.

2016, Mar. 16 Litho. *Perf. 13¼*
737 Horiz. strip of 4 + central label 3.75 3.75
a. A387 23d multi .45 .45
b. A387 46d multi .85 .85
c. A387 50d multi .95 .95
d. A387 70d multi 1.40 1.40

Schools — A388

Designs: 23d, Mathematical Grammar School, Belgrade, 50th anniv. 46d, Sremski Karlovci Gymnasium, 225th anniv.

2016, Apr. 13 Litho. *Perf. 13¼*
738-739 A388 Set of 2 1.25 1.25

Fauna
A389

No. 740: a, Castor fiber. b, Aquila heliaca. c, Gyps fulvus. d, Lutra lutra.

2016, Apr. 27 Litho. *Perf. 13¼*
740 Horiz. strip of 4 + central label 3.75 3.75
a. A389 23d multi .45 .45
b. A389 46d multi .90 .90
c. A389 50d multi .95 .95
d. A389 70d multi 1.40 1.40

A390

Europa
A391

2016, May 9 Litho. *Perf. 13¼*
741 A390 69d multi 1.25 1.25
742 A391 100d multi 1.90 1.90

Think Green Issue.
Nos. 741-742 were each printed in sheets of 8 + central label.

European Nature Protection
A392

Designs: 50d, Flowers and forest, Kucaj-Beljanica Mountain Massif. 74d, Pestersko Polje Special Nature Reserve.

2016, May 26 Litho. *Perf. 13¼*
743-744 A392 Set of 2 2.25 2.25

Nos. 743-744 were each printed in sheets of 8 + central label.

First Serbian Postage Stamps, 150th Anniv. — A393

No. 745: a, Serbia #4, 5 and 6. b, Serbia #1.

2016, June 7 Litho. *Perf. 13¼*
745 A393 23d Pair, #a-b .85 .85

2016 Summer Olympics, Rio de Janeiro
A394

Designs: 23d, Taekwondo. 70d, Tennis.
No. 748 — Long jumper: a, Running and jumping. b, Jumping and landing.

2016, June 7 Litho. *Perf. 13¼*
746-747 A394 Set of 2 1.75 1.75

Souvenir Sheet
Perf. 13¾
748 Sheet of 2 4.00 4.00
a. A394 50d multi 1.00 1.00
b. A394 170d multi 3.00 3.00

Nos. 746-747 were each printed in sheets of 8 + central label. No. 748 contains two 35x35mm stamps.

Patenting of Resonant Transformer of Nikola Tesla, 125th Anniv. — A395

2016, June 21 Litho. *Perf. 13¼*
749 A395 70d multi 1.25 1.25

No. 749 was printed in sheets of 8 + central label.

Miniature Sheet

23rd International Congress of Byzantine Studies, Belgrade — A396

No. 750: a, 23d, Painting of Sava, First Serbian Archbishop, from Mileseva Monastery, c. 1227. b, 23d, "V" in illuminated manuscript, 14th cent. c, 23d, Gracanica Monastery, c. 1315. d, 23d, Painting of Emperor Uros and King Vukasin from Pasca Monastery, 1366-71. e, 70d, Sculpture of Mother of God and Infant Jesus from Sokolica Monastery, c. 1315. f, 70d, Painting of Mother of God from the Annunciation, Mileseva Monastery, c. 1227. g, 70d, Decoration from sarcophagus of St. Stefan Decanski, 1343. h, 70d, Kalenic Monastery, c. 1420.

Perf. 13¼x13¾
2016, Aug. 22 Litho.
750 A396 Sheet of 8, #a-h 6.75 6.75

Belgrade International Theater Festival, 50th Anniv. — A397

Designs: 23d, Mila Trailovic (1924-89), director. 70d, Jovan Cirilov (1930-2014), playwright.

2016, Sept. 1 Litho. *Perf. 13¼*
751-752 A397 Set of 2 1.75 1.75

Battle of Kajmakcalan, Cent.
A398

2016, Sept. 12 Litho. *Perf. 13¼*
753 A398 23d multi .45 .45

Combatants From Kadinjaca, by Dragoljub Vuksanovic, and Kadinjaca Monument
A399

2016, Sept. 23 Litho. *Perf. 13¼*
754 A399 23d multi .45 .45

Republic of Uzice, 75th anniv.

Dog, by Katarina Kovacevic
A400

2016, Sept. 29 Litho. *Perf. 13¼*
755 A400 70d multi 1.25 1.25

Joy of Europe Children's Art Competition.
No. 755 was printed in sheets of 8 + central label.

Stamp Day — A401

Designs: 23d, Yugoslavia #1004. 70d, Yugoslavia #1371.

2016, Oct. 11 Litho. *Perf. 13¼*
756-757 A401 Set of 2 1.75 1.75

Europa stamps, 60th anniv.

Christmas
A402

Details from Nativity fresco, Gradac Monastery: 23d, Bathing of Newborn Christ. 100d, Flight into Egypt.

2016, Oct. 18 Litho. *Perf. 13¼*
758-759 A402 Set of 2 2.25 2.25

Kragujevac Massacre, 75th Anniv.
A403

2016, Oct. 21 Litho. *Perf. 13¼*
760 A403 23d multi .45 .45

No. 760 was printed in sheets of 8 + central label.

Medieval Tombstones
A404

Tombstone from: 23d, Burdica Rast, 14th cent. 46d, Mramorje, 14th cent. 50d, Hrta Village, 14th-15th cent.

2016, Nov. 3 Litho. *Perf. 13¼*
761-763 A404 Set of 3 2.10 2.10

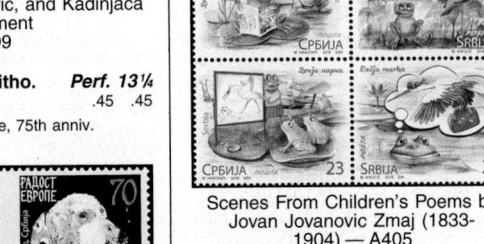

Scenes From Children's Poems by Jovan Jovanovic Zmaj (1833-1904) — A405

No. 764: a, Frog reading newspaper under umbrella. b, Stork flying over snorkeling frog. c, Frogs in school. d, Frog dreaming about stork leaving.

2016, Nov. 9 Litho. *Perf. 13¼*
764 A405 23d Block of 4, #a-d 1.60 1.60

Miniature Sheet

Famous Men — A406

No. 765: a, 23d, Sima Milutinovic Sarajlija (1791-1847), poet, books, quill pen and inkwell. b, 23d, Stanislav Vinaver (1891-1955), poet, stack of books. c, 23d, Mikhail Bulgakov (1891-1940), writer and playwright, books, cat wearing top hat. d, 23d, Wassily Kandinsky (1866-1944), painter, artist's palette and paint brushes. e, 70d, Laza Kostic (1841-1910), writer, domed building and woman. f, 70d, Tin Ujevic (1891-1955), poet, books on shelf, open book. g, 70d, Lajos Zilahy (1891-1974), writer, stack of books. h, 70d, Antonín Dvorák (1841-1904), composer, musical scores.

Perf. 13¼x13¾
2016, Nov. 23 Litho.
765 A406 Sheet of 8, #a-h 6.50 6.50

Dr. Vojislav M. Subotic (1866-1922), Psychiatrist, Red Cross Official — A407

2016, Dec. 9 Litho. *Perf. 13¼*
766 A407 23d multi .45 .45

New Year 2017 (Year of the Rooster)
A408

Designs: 23d, Rooster. 74d, Head of rooster.

2017, Jan. 27 Litho. *Perf. 13¼*
767-768 A408 Set of 2 1.75 1.75

Easter
A409

Frescoes from Church of the Virgin, Studenica Monastery: 23d, Last Supper. 74d, Crucifixion of Christ.

2017, Feb. 7 Litho. *Perf. 13¼*
769-770 A409 Set of 2 1.75 1.75

Toplica Uprising, Cent.
A410

2017, Feb. 21 Litho. *Perf. 13¼*
771 A410 23d multi .40 .40

Black Sea Economic Cooperation Organization, 25th Anniv.
A411

2017, Mar. 14 Litho. *Perf. 13¼*
772 A411 74d multi 1.25 1.25

Owls — A412

No. 773: a, Athene noctua. b, Tyto alba. c, Asio otus. d, Otus scops.

2017, Mar. 16 Litho. *Perf. 13¼*
773 Horiz. strip of 4 + central label 3.50 3.50
a. A412 23d multi .40 .40
b. A412 46d multi .80 .80
c. A412 50d multi .90 .90
d. A412 70d multi 1.25 1.25

Miniature Sheet

Actors and Actresses — A413

No. 774: a, Marija Crnobori (1918-2014). b, Vlastimir-Duza Stojiljkovic (1929-2015). c, Borivoje Bora Todorovic (1929-2014). d, Dragoslav Dragan Nikolic (1943-2016). e, Ruzica Sokic (1934-2013). f, Olivera Markovic (1925-2011). g, Bekim Fehmiu (1936-2010). h, Nikola Simic (1934-2014).

2017, Mar. 27 Litho. *Perf. 13¼*
774 A413 23d Sheet of 8, #a-h, + central label 3.25 3.25

Scientists — A414

Designs: 23d, Kosta Stojanovic (1867-1921), mathematician and governmental minister. 46d, Marie Curie (1867-1934), physicist and chemist.

2017, Apr. 10 Litho. *Perf. 13¼*
775-776 A414 Set of 2 1.25 1.25

Belgrade
A415

Novi Sad — A416

Nis — A417

2017, Apr. 13 Litho. *Perf. 13¼*
777 A415 70d multi 1.25 1.25
778 A416 70d multi 1.25 1.25
779 A417 70d multi 1.25 1.25
Nos. 777-779 (3) 3.75 3.75

Nos. 777-779 were each printed in sheets of 8 + central label.

Souvenir Sheet

Prince Mihailo Obrenovic Receiving Keys to City of Belgrade, 150th Anniv. — A418

2017, Apr. 19 Litho. *Perf. 13¾*
780 A418 100d multi 1.75 1.75

30th Belgrade Marathon
A419

2017, Apr. 21 Litho. *Perf. 13¼*
781 A419 23d multi .40 .40

Fruits and Nuts — A420

No. 782: a, Pyris communis. b, Prunus domestica. c, Malus sylvestris. d, Juglans regia.

2017, Apr. 27 Litho. *Perf. 13¼*

782 Horiz. strip of 4 + central label 3.50 3.50
a. A420 23d multi .40 .40
b. A420 46d multi .85 .85
c. A420 50d multi .90 .90
d. A420 70d multi 1.25 1.25

Stojan Novakovic (1842-1915), Original Member of Serbian Literary Cooperative
A421

2017, Apr. 28 Litho. *Perf. 13¼*

783 A421 23d multi .40 .40

Serbian Literary Cooperative, 125th anniv. No. 783 was printed in sheets of 24 + central label.

Europa
A422

Designs: 69d, Maglic Castle. 100d, Smederevo Castle.

2017, May 9 Litho. *Perf. 13¼*

784-785 A422 Set of 2 3.25 3.25

Nos. 784-785 were each printed in sheets of 8 + central label.

Paintings in Jevrem Grujic House — A423

No. 786: a, Jevrem Grujic, by Steva Todorovic, 1888. b, Mileva Naumovic, by Uros Knezevic, 1854. c, Jelena Milojevic with Daughters Milica and Milena, by V. Volkov, 1925. d, Queen Natalia Obrenovich, by Todorovic, 1884.

2017, May 19 Litho. *Perf. 13¼*

786 Horiz. strip of 4 + central label 3.50 3.50
a. A423 23d multi .45 .45
b. A423 46d multi .85 .85
c. A423 50d multi .95 .95
d. A423 70d multi 1.25 1.25

European Nature Protection
A424

Designs: 50d, Aldrovanda vesiculosa. 74d, Aythya nyroca.

2017, June 1 Litho. *Perf. 13¼*

787-788 A424 Set of 2 2.25 2.25

Nos. 787-788 were each printed in sheets of 8 + central label.

Serbian Newspaper and Prince Milos Obrenovich of Serbia (1780-1860) and Sir George Lloyd Hodges (1790-1862)
A425

2017, June 5 Litho. *Perf. 13¼*

789 A425 74d multi 1.40 1.40

Diplomatic relations between Serbia and Great Britain, 180th anniv. No. 789 was printed in sheets of 8 + central label.

Air Serbia, 90th Anniv.
A426

2017, Aug. 21 Litho. *Perf. 13¼*

790 A426 23d multi .45 .45

Ljubicevo Equestrian Games
A427

2017, Sept. 1 Litho. *Perf. 13¼*

791 A427 70d multi 1.40 1.40

Joy of Europe
A428

2017, Sept. 29 Litho. *Perf. 13¼*

792 A428 70d multi 1.40 1.40

No. 792 was printed in sheets of 8 + 7 labels.

A429

Christmas
A430

2017, Oct. 2 Litho. *Perf. 13¼*

793 A429 23d multi .45 .45
794 A430 74d multi 1.50 1.50

Coronation of King Stefan, the First-Crowned (c. 1165-1228), 800th Anniv. — A431

2017, Oct. 6 Litho. *Perf. 13¼*

795 A431 23d multi .45 .45

No. 795 was printed in sheets of 23 + 2 labels.

Serbian International Reply Coupon
A432

2017, Oct. 9 Litho. *Perf. 13¼x13¾*

796 A432 23d multi .45 .45

Stamp Day.

Miniature Sheet

Famous Men — A433

No. 797: a, Dositej Obradovic (1742-1811), Minister of Education, and globe. b, Haji Nikola Zivkovic (1792-1870), Supervisor of Official Establishments, and building. c, Anastas Jovanovic (1817-99), lithographer and photographer, and photographic equipment. d, Vasa Eskicevic (1867-1933), painter, brushes and palette. e, Milutin Bojic (1892-1917), writer, and lyre. f, Ivo Andric (1892-1975), 1961 Nobel Laureate in Literature, books and quill pen.

2017, Nov. 1 Litho. *Perf. 13¼x13¾*

797 A433 23d Sheet of 6, #a-f 2.75 2.75

Juvenile Animals at Belgrade Zoo — A434

No. 798: a, Rhea. b, Dorcas gazelle. c, Serval. d, Hippopotami.

2017, Nov. 9 Litho. *Perf. 13¼*

798 A434 23d Block of 4, #a-d 1.90 1.90

Serbian Technicians Society, 150th Anniv. — A435

2018, Feb. 2 Litho. *Perf. 13¼x13¾*

799 A435 23d multi .50 .50

2018 Winter Olympics, PyeongChang, South Korea — A436

Emblem of Serbian Olympic Committee and: 23d, Snowboarding. 74d, Speed skating.

2018, Feb. 9 Litho. *Perf. 13¾*

800-801 A436 Set of 2 2.00 2.00

Nos. 800-801 were each printed in sheets of 8 + central label.

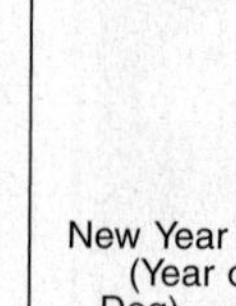

New Year 2018 (Year of the Dog) — A437

Designs: 23d, Dog. 74d, Head of dog.

Perf. 13¼x13¾

2018, Feb. 14 Litho.

802-803 A437 Set of 2 2.00 2.00

A438

Easter — A439

2018, Mar. 1 Litho. *Perf. 13¾*

804 A438 23d multi .50 .50
805 A439 74d multi 1.50 1.50

National Theater, Belgrade, 150th Anniv. — A440

Perf. 13¼x13¾

2018, Mar. 12 Litho.

806 A440 23d multi .50 .50

No. 806 was printed in sheets of 8 + central label.

Zivojin Misic (1855-1921), Field Marshal
A441

Radomir Putnik (1847-1917), Field Marshal
A442

Milunka Savic (c. 1892-1973), War Heroine A443

Nadezda Petrovic (1873-1915), Painter and World War I Nurse A444

Mihajlo Pupin (1858-1935), Physicist — A445

2018, Mar. 23 Litho. *Perf. 13¾*

807	A441	8d multi	.25	.25
808	A442	10d multi	.25	.25
809	A443	46d multi	.95	.95
810	A444	50d multi	1.10	1.10
811	A445	100d multi	2.10	2.10
	Nos. 807-811 (5)		4.65	4.65

Fish — A446

No. 812: a, Acipenser rytenus. b, Huso huso. c, Esox lucius. d, Polyodon spathula.

Perf. 13¼x13¾

2018, Mar. 30 Litho.

812	Horiz. strip of 4	4.25	4.25
a.	A446 23d multi	.50	.50
b.	A446 46d multi	.95	.95
c.	A446 50d multi	1.10	1.10
d.	A446 70d multi	1.50	1.50

No. 812 was printed in sheets of 16 (four strips) + 4 labels.

Kragujevac A447

Subotica A448

2018, Apr. 11 Litho. *Perf. 13x13¾*

813	A447	70d multi	1.50	1.50
814	A448	70d multi	1.50	1.50

Nos. 813-814 were each printed in sheets of 8 + central label.

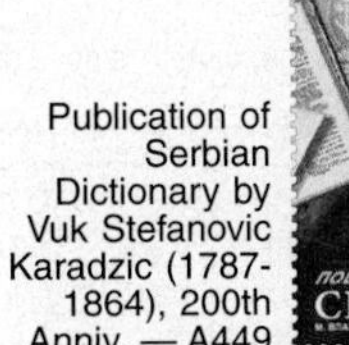

Publication of Serbian Dictionary by Vuk Stefanovic Karadzic (1787-1864), 200th Anniv. — A449

2018, Apr. 24 Litho. *Perf. 13¾*

815	A449	23d multi	.50	.50

No. 815 was printed in sheets of 9 + label.

Europa A450

Designs: 69d, Gazelle Bridge, Belgrade. 100d, Zezelj Bridge, Novi Sad.

2018, May 9 Litho. *Perf. 13¾*

816-817	A450	Set of 2	3.50 3.50

Nos. 816-817 were each printed in sheets of 8 + central label.

Items From Post, Telegraph and Telephone Museum, Belgrade A451

No. 818: a, Carraige, 19th cent. b, Telephone of King Peter I Karageorgevich. c, Telephone switchboard. d, Hughes telegraph machine.

2018, May 18 Litho. *Perf. 13¾x13¼*

818	Horiz. strip of 4 + central label	3.75	3.75
a.	A451 23d multi	.45	.45
b.	A451 46d multi	.90	.90
c.	A451 50d multi	1.00	1.00
d.	A451 70d multi	1.40	1.40

Miniature Sheet

Writers — A452

No. 819: a, Ivan S. Turgenev (1818-83), books at right. b, Kosta Trifkovic (1843-75). c, Maxim Gorky (1868-1936), books at left. d, Aleksa Santic (1868-1924). e, Milos Crnjanski (1893-1977), books at left and right. f, Aleksandr Solzhenitsyn (1918-2008).

2018, May 31 Litho. *Perf. 13¼x13¾*

819	A452	23d Sheet of 6, #a-f	2.75 2.75

European Nature Protection A453

Designs: 50d, Cerje Cave. 74d, Sopotnica Waterfall.

2018, June 5 Litho. *Perf. 13¼x13¾*

820-821	A453	Set of 2	2.50 2.50

Nos. 820-821 were each printed in sheets of 8 + central label.

2018 World Cup Soccer Championships, Russia — A454

Designs: 23d, Soccer player and circle. 74d, Two soccer players, soccer field lines. 170d, Soccer ball as Sputnik satellite, horiz.

Perf. 13¾x13¼

2018, June 14 Litho.

822-823	A454	Set of 2	1.90 1.90

Souvenir Sheet

824	A454	170d multi	3.50 3.50

Nos. 822-823 were each printed in sheets of 8 + central label. No. 824 contains one 44x35mm stamp.

Juvenile Animals at Belgrade Zoo — A455

No. 825: a, Patagonian mara. b, Black swan. c, Arctic wolf. d, Miniature goat.

2018, June 19 Litho. *Perf. 13¾*

825	A455	23d Block of 4, #a-d	1.90 1.90

Miniature Sheet

Scientists — A456

No. 826: a, Antal Koch (1843-1927), geologist and paleontologist. b, Vladimir D. Laskarev (1868-1954), geologist. c, Stevan Boskovic (1868-1957), geographer. d, Mihailo P. Alas (1868-1943), mathematician and inventor.

2018, July 10 Litho. *Perf. 13¾*

826	A456	23d Sheet of 4, 3a-d	1.90 1.90

No. 826 was sold with, but unattached to, a booklet cover.

Tourism in Zlatibor, 125th Anniv. A457

2018, Aug. 20 Litho. *Perf. 13¾*

827	A457	23d multi	.45 .45

Ljubicevo Equestrian Games — A458

2018, Aug. 31 Litho. *Perf. 13¾*

828	A458	70d multi	1.40 1.40

Manasija Monastery, 600th Anniv. — A459

Perf. 13¼x13¾

2018, Sept. 14 Litho.

829	A459	23d multi	.45 .45

Printed in sheets of 20 + 5 labels.

Diplomatic Relations Between Serbia and India, 70th Anniv. — A460

No. 830: a, Nikola Tesla (1856-1943), inventor. b, Swami Vivekananda (1863-1902), lecturer on Indian philosophies in Western world.

Perf. 13¼x13¾

2018, Sept. 15 Litho.

830	A460	70d Horiz. pair, #a-b	2.75 2.75

Printed in sheets containing 4 pairs + 4 central labels. See India Nos. 3056-3057.

Joy of Europe A461

Perf. 13¼x13¾

2018, Sept. 28 Litho.

831	A461	70d multi	1.40 1.40

Printed in sheets of 8 + 7 labels.

Radiograms A462

2018, Oct. 2 Litho. *Perf. 13¼x13¾*

832	A462	23d multi	.45 .45

Stamp Day.

Birth of Jesus From Nativity Fresco, Sopocani Monastery A463

Bathing of Jesus From Nativity Fresco, Sopocani Monastery A464

2018, Oct. 16 Litho. *Perf. 13¼x13¾*

833	A463	23d multi	.45	.45
834	A464	100d multi	2.00	2.00

Christmas.

Synagogue, Belgrade A465

Synagogue, Subotica A466

Synagogue, Novi Sad — A467

2018, Oct. 19 Litho. *Perf. 13¼x13¾*

835	Horiz. strip of 3	1.40 1.40
a.	A465 23d multi	.45 .45
b.	A466 23d multi	.45 .45
c.	A467 23d multi	.45 .45

Miniature Sheet

Liberation of Serbia, Cent. — A468

No. 836: a, Voivode Stepa Stepanovic (1856-1929), with soldiers at the Salonika front. b, General Louis Franchet d'Espèry (1856-1942), riding horses at the Salonika front with Prince Regent Alexander Karageorgevic (1888-1934) and Field Marshal Zivojin Misic (1855-1921). c, Misic and Danube Division soldiers marching. d, General Auguste-Charles Tranié (1862-1931) entering liberated Prokuplje on horseback. e, Voivode Petar Bojovic (1858-1945) with Prince Regent Alexander Karageorgevic and Serbian officers at the Salonika front. f, General Paul Prosper Henrys (1862-1943), receiving Order of the White Eagle from Field Marshal Misic.

2018, Nov. 1 Litho. *Perf. 13¾*

836 A468 23d Sheet of 6, #a-f 2.75 2.75

No. 836 was sold with, but unattached to, a booklet cover.

Miniature Sheet

Doctors of World War I — A469

No. 837: a, Dr. Vojislav J. Subbotic (1859-1923), surgeon, and other surgeons. b, Dr. William Hunter (1861-1937) and ambulance train. c, Dr. Milos D. Popovic (1876-1954), military dentist, and dental clinic. d, Dr. Edward Ryan (1883-1923), chief of American Red Cross mission in Serbia, and medical staff. e, Dr. Mihailo Mika Petrovic (1863-1934), surgeon, and hospital. f, Dr. Ludwik Hirszfeld (1884-1954), microbiologist, and medical staff.

2018, Nov. 9 Litho. *Perf. 13¾x13¼*

837 A469 23d Sheet of 6, #a-f 2.75 2.75

End of World War I, cent. No. 837 was sold with, but unattached to, a booklet cover.

Souvenir Sheet

Great National Assembly in Novi Sad, November 25, 1918, by Anastas Bocaric — A470

2018, Nov. 23 Litho. *Perf. 13¾*

838 A470 100d multi 2.00 2.00

Unification of Vojvodina and the Kingdom of Serbia, cent.

Church of the Holy Emperor Constantine and Empress Helen, Crvena Jabuka, 150th Anniv. — A471

Perf. 13¼x13¾

2018, Nov. 27 Litho.

839 A471 23d multi .45 .45

International Day of Persons with Disabilities A472

2018, Dec. 3 Litho. *Perf. 13¾x13¼*

840 A472 23d multi .45 .45

A473

A474

Design: Icon of St. Stephen, Cresset, St. Stephen's Day Cake and Cake Mold. No. 841, Early 20th cent. No. 842, Late19th cent.

2018, Dec. 4 Litho. *Perf. 13¾*

841	A473 23d multi	.45 .45
842	A474 23d multi	.45 .45

Miniature Sheet

Photographs of Soldiers and Citizens of World War I Era — A475

No. 843 — Photograph of: a, Radenko Krivokuca (soldier in oval photograph). b, Sparic and Katarina Pantelija on wedding day. c, Marko Ivkovic (soldier with uniform with aiguillettes and cross-shaped medal). d, Two soldiers and table. e, Dragoljub Z. Jankovic. f, Milan Spasojevic, his wife, Kostadin, his mother, Savet, and his daughter, Smiljan.

2018, Dec. 5 Litho. *Perf. 13¾*

843 A475 23d Sheet of 6, #a-f, + 3 central labels 2.75 2.75

New Year 2019 (Year of the Pig) — A476

Designs: 23d, Pig. 74d, Head of pig.

2019, Feb. 5 Litho. *Perf. 13¼x13¾*

844-845 A476 Set of 2 1.90 1.90

A477

Easter — A478

Perf. 13¾x13¼

2019, Feb. 21 Litho.

846	A477 23d multi	.45 .45
847	A478 74d multi	1.40 1.40

Mohandas K. Gandhi (1869-1948), Indian Nationalist Leader — A479

2019, Feb. 28 Litho. *Perf. 13¾*

848 A479 75d multi 1.50 1.50

No. 848 was printed in sheets of 8 + central label.

Mushrooms — A480

No. 849: a, Psilocybe serbica. b, Tuber petrophilum. c, Coprinopsis picacea. d, Octospora pannosa.

2019, Mar. 7 Litho. *Perf. 13¾x13¼*

849 A480 50d Block of 4, #a-d 4.00 4.00

Radio Belgrade, 50th Anniv. — A481

2019, Mar. 12 Litho. *Perf. 13¾*

850 A481 23d multi .45 .45

Association of Drama Artists of Serbia, Cent. — A482

Perf. 13¼x13¾

2019, Mar. 27 Litho.

851 A482 23d multi .45 .45

Miniature Sheet

Actors and Actresses — A483

No. 852: a, Velimir Zivojnovic (1933-2016). b, Ljubisa Samardzic (1936-2017). c, Mira Stupica (1923-2016). d, Slobodan Aligrudic (1934-85). e, Predrag Lakovic (1929-97). f, Sonja Savic (1961-2008). g, Milorad Mandic (1961-2016). h, Nebojsa Glogovac (1969-2018).

Perf. 13¼x13¾

2019, Mar. 27 Litho.

852 A483 23d Sheet of 8, #a-h 3.50 3.50

City Hall, Zrenjanin A484

Street Scene, Pancevo A485

2019, Apr. 11 Litho. *Perf. 13¾*

853 A484 70d multi 1.40 1.40
854 A485 70d multi 1.40 1.40

Protected Animals A486

No. 855: a, Plecotus macrobullaris. b, Mustela eversmanii. c, Rupicapra balcanica. d, Ursus arctos.

2019, Apr. 18 Litho. *Perf. 13¼x13¾*

855 Horiz. strip of 4 + central label 3.75 3.75
a. A486 23d multi .45 .45
b. A486 46d multi .90 .90
c. A486 50d multi .95 .95
d. A486 70d multi 1.40 1.40

Miniature Sheet

Dancers — A487

No. 856: a, Maga Magazinovic (1882-1968). b, Smiljana Mandukic (1907-92). c, Jovanka Bjegojevic (1931-2015). d, Dusanka Sifnios (1933-2016).

2019, Apr. 23 Litho. *Perf. 13¾*

856 A487 50d Sheet of 4, #a-d 4.00 4.00

No. 856 was sold with, but unattached to, a booklet cover.

Europa A488

Birds: 69d, Tichodroma muraria. 100d, Ardeola ralloides.

2019, May 9 Litho. *Perf. 13¾*

857-858 A488 Set of 2 3.25 3.25

Nos. 857-858 were each printed in sheets of 8 + central label.

National Museum, Belgrade, 175th Anniv. — A489

Designs: 23d, Boy Plucking a Thorn, sculpture by Simeon Roksandic. 74d, Nude, by Pierre-Auguste Renoir.

2019, May 17 Litho. *Perf. 13¾*

859-860 A489 Set of 2 1.90 1.90

Nos. 859-860 were each printed in sheets of 8 + central label.

Nikola Tesla (1856-1943), Inventor A490

Milutin Milankovic (1879-1958), Climatologist A491

2019, May 23 Litho. *Perf. 13¾*

861 A490 23d multi .45 .45
862 A491 35d multi .70 .70

Souvenir Sheet

St. Sava and Zica Monastery — A492

2019, June 13 Litho. *Perf. 13¾*

863 A492 100d multi 2.00 2.00

Autocephaly of the Serbian Orthodox Church, 800th anniv.

Scientists — A493

Designs: 23d, Svetolik Stevanovic (1869-1953), mineralogist, and crystal. 74d, Jelenko Mihailovic (1869-1956), seismologist, and seismograph.

2019, July 10 Litho. *Perf. 13¾x13¼*

864-865 A493 Set of 2 1.90 1.90

Children's Internet Safety — A494

2019, Aug. 1 Litho. *Perf. 13¾*

866 A494 4d multi .25 .25

Ljubicevo Equestrian Games A495

Perf. 13¼x13¾

2019, Aug. 15 Litho.

867 A495 27d multi .50 .50

European Nature Protection A496

Designs: 50d, Rtanj Special Nature Reserve. 74d, Borac Karst rock formation.

2019, Aug. 20 Litho. *Perf. 13¾*

868-869 A496 Set of 2 2.40 2.40

Nos. 868-869 were each printed in sheets of 8 + central label.

Sokobanja A497

2019, Aug. 21 Litho. *Perf. 13¾*

870 A497 27d multi .50 .50

Diplomatic Relations Between Serbia and Turkey, 140th Anniv. A498

2019, Aug. 27 Litho. *Perf. 13¾*

871 A498 74d multi 1.40 1.40

Children's Day, Cent. — A499

No. 872 — Art of school children: a, Ornaments (yellow background). b, Dinosaur figurines (pink background). c, Figurines depicting people (blue background). d, Drawing of dog, cat and butterfly (green background).

2019, Sept. 5 Litho. *Perf. 13¾*

872 A499 27d Block of 4, #a-d 2.00 2.00

Mileseva Monastery, 800th Anniv. — A500

Perf. 13¼x13¾

2019, Sept. 25 Litho.

873 A500 27d multi .50 .50

No. 873 was printed in sheets of 20 + 5 labels.

Joy of Europe A501

Perf. 13¼x13¾

2019, Sept. 27 Litho.

874 A501 70d multi 1.40 1.40

No. 874 was printed in sheets of 8 + 7 labels.

Jan Kolar Grammar School, Backi Petrovac, Cent. A502

2019, Oct. 1 Litho. *Perf. 13¾*

875 A502 27d multi .50 .50

Stamp Day — A503

2019, Oct. 8 Litho. *Perf. 13¼x13¾*

876 A503 27d multi .55 .55

Postal cards, 150th anniv.

A504

Christmas A505

2019, Oct. 16 Litho. *Perf. 13¾x13¼*

877 A504 27d multi .55 .55
878 A505 100d multi 1.90 1.90

Filmske Novosti Newsreels, 75th Anniv. — A506

2019, Oct. 21 Litho. *Perf. 13x13¾*

879 A506 27d multi .55 .55

No. 879 was printed in sheets of 8 + 7 labels.

Miniature Sheet

Art — A507

No. 880: a, Girl from Skopska, Crna Gora, 1952, by Zora Petrovic (1894-1962). b, Torso of a Girl, 1971, sculpture by Risto Stijovic (1894-1974). c, Paris, 1926, by Dusan Jankovic (1894-1950). d, Landscape with Round Tree Tops, 1922, by Ivan Radovic (1894-1973). e, By the Window, 1918, by Henri Matisse (1869-1954).

2019, Nov. 1 Litho. *Perf. 14*

880 A507 27d Sheet of 5, #a-e, + label 2.60 2.60

No. 880 was sold with, but unattached to, a booklet cover.

Zica Monastery A508

Hylotelephium Spectabile A509

2019, Nov. 7 Litho. *Perf. 13¾*

881 A508 27d multi .50 .50
882 A509 40d multi .75 .75

Aleksandar Deroko (1894-1988), Architect — A510

Slobodan Jovanovic (1869-1959), Writer and Educator — A511

Miloje Vasic (1869-1956), Archaeologist A512

2019, Nov. 14 Litho. *Perf. 13¾x13*

883 A510 27d multi .50 .50
884 A511 27d multi .50 .50
885 A512 27d multi .50 .50
Nos. 883-885 (3) 1.50 1.50

Jedinstvo Newspaper, 75th Anniv. — A513

Perf. 13¼x13¾

2019, Nov. 26 Litho.

886 A513 27d multi .50 .50

Icon of St. Sava (1174-1236) A514

2019, Dec. 3 Litho. *Perf. 13¾*

887 A514 27d multi .55 .55

Serbian Women's Volleyball Team, 2019 European Champions — A515

Serbian Men's Volleyball Team, 2019 European Champions — A516

2019, Dec. 6 Litho. *Perf. 13¾*

888 A515 74d multi 1.40 1.40
889 A516 74d multi 1.40 1.40

Nos. 888-889 were each printed in sheets of 8 + central label.

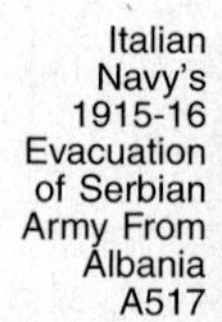

Italian Navy's 1915-16 Evacuation of Serbian Army From Albania A517

No. 890: a, Evacuation of troops in boats. b, Evacuation of Prince Alexander. c, Evacuation of Field Marshal Radomir Putnik. d, Evacuation of Serbian officers.

2020, Jan. 21 Litho. *Perf. 13¾*

890	Horiz. strip of 4	3.75	3.75
a.	A517 27d multi	.50	.50
b.	A517 40d multi	.75	.75
c.	A517 54d multi	1.00	1.00
d.	A517 70d multi	1.40	1.40

Printed in sheets of two strips + a central strip of 4 labels.

New Year 2020 (Year of the Rat) — A518

Rat facing: 27d, Right. 70d, Left.

2020, Jan. 24 Litho. *Perf. 13¼x13¾*

891-892 A518 Set of 2 1.90 1.90

A524

Serbian Postal Service, 180th Anniv. — A525

2020, Feb. 27 Litho. *Perf. 13¾*

898 A524 27d multi .55 .55

Souvenir Sheet

899 A525 108d multi 2.10 2.10

No. 898 was printed in sheets of 8 + central label.

Self-portrait, by Momcilo Momo Kapor (1937-2010), Illustrator and Writer — A526

2020, Mar. 3 Litho. *Perf. 13¾*

900 A526 27d multi .55 .55

No. 900 was printed in sheets of 8 + central label.

POSTAGE DUE STAMPS

Coat of Arms — D1

1895 Unwmk. Typo. *Perf. 13x13½*

Granite Paper

J1	D1 5p red lilac		6.00	1.00
J2	D1 10p blue		6.00	.45
J3	D1 20p orange brown		50.00	9.25
J4	D1 30p green		.40	.95
J5	D1 50p rose		.40	1.25
a.	Cliché of 5p in plate of 50p		120.00	*190.00*
	Nos. J1-J5 (5)		62.80	12.90

No. J1 exists imperf. Value $75.

1898-1904 Ordinary Paper

J6	D1 5p magenta ('04)	.60	.45
J7	D1 20p brown	9.50	1.10
a.	Tête bêche pair	150.00	*160.00*
J8	D1 20p dp brn ('04)	6.25	1.00
	Nos. J6-J8 (3)	16.35	2.55

1906 Granite Paper *Perf. 11½*

J9 D1 5p magenta 13.00 3.75

1909 Laid Paper

J10	D1 5p magenta	.95	.65
J11	D1 10p pale blue	5.00	9.25
J12	D1 20p pale brown	.45	.95
	Nos. J10-J12 (3)	6.40	10.85

1914 White Wove Paper

J13	D1 5p rose	.80	3.25
J14	D1 10p deep blue	8.00	16.00

Coat of Arms — D2

1918-20 *Perf. 11*

Paris Printing

Clear Impression, Clean-Cut Perfs

J15	D2 5p red	.45	.90
J16	D2 10p yellow green	.45	.90
J17	D2 20p olive brown	.45	.90
J18	D2 30p slate green	.45	.90
J19	D2 50p chocolate	.95	1.60
	Nos. J15-J19 (5)	2.75	5.20

Belgrade Printing

Coarse Impression, Rough Perfs

J15a	D2 5p red brown	.45	.90
J18a	D2 30p olive black	.95	1.35
J19a	D2 50p yellow brown	1.35	2.00

NEWSPAPER STAMPS

N1

Overprinted with Crown-topped Shield in Black

1911 Unwmk. Typo. *Perf. 11½*

P1	N1 1p gray	.95	.95
P2	N1 5p green	.95	.95
P3	N1 10p orange	.95	.95
a.	Cliché of 1p in plate of 10p	*1,500.*	
P4	N1 15p violet	.95	.95
P5	N1 20p yellow	.95	.95
a.	Cliché of 50p in plate of 20p	160.00	*160.00*
P6	N1 25p blue	.95	.95
P7	N1 30p slate	9.25	9.25
P8	N1 50p brown	7.50	7.50
P9	N1 1d bister	7.50	7.50
P10	N1 3d rose red	7.50	7.50
P11	N1 5d gray vio	7.50	7.50
	Nos. P1-P11 (11)	44.95	44.95

POSTAL TAX STAMPS

Catalogue values for unused stamps in this section, from this point to the end of the section, are for Never Hinged items.

Ksenofon Sahovic (1898-1956), Pathologist — PT1

2006, July 10 Litho. *Perf. 12½*

RA1 PT1 8d multi 1.75 .30

Campaign against cancer. Obligatory on mail July 10-Aug. 5.

Red Cross and Disabled People — PT2

2006, Sept. 14 *Perf. 13¾*

RA2 PT2 8d multi .60 .30

Obligatory on mail Sept. 14-21.

Red Cross and Children — PT3

2006, Sept. 22

RA3 PT3 8d multi .60 .30

Obligatory on mail Sept. 22-29.

Children's Week — PT4

2006, Oct. 2 **Litho.** ***Perf. 12½***

RA4 PT4 8d multi 1.75 .80

Obligatory on mail Oct. 2-8.

AIDS Prevention — PT5

2006, Oct. 9 ***Perf. 13¾***

RA5 PT5 8d multi .75 .30

Obligatory on mail Oct. 9-31.

European Olympic Youth Festival, Belgrade — PT6

2006, Dec. 1 **Litho.** ***Perf. 13¾***

RA6 PT6 8d multi .75 .30

Obligatory on mail Dec. 1-31.

2007 European Judo Championships, Belgrade — PT7

2007, Jan. 22

RA7 PT7 8d multi .80 .30

Obligatory on mail Jan. 22-27.

Dr. Blagoje Neskovic (1907-86), Politician — PT8

2007, Mar. 5 ***Perf. 12½***

RA8 PT8 8d multi 1.10 .30

Campaign against cancer. Obligatory on mail Mar. 5-31.

Red Cross Week — PT9

2007, May 8 ***Perf. 13¾***

RA9 PT9 10d multi .80 .35

Obligatory on mail May 8-15.

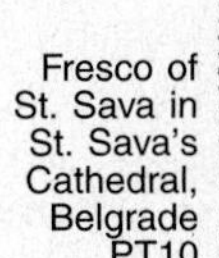

Fresco of St. Sava in St. Sava's Cathedral, Belgrade PT10

2007, May 16 ***Perf. 13¼***

RA10 PT10 10d multi .80 .35

Restoration of St. Sava Cathedral. Obligatory on mail May 16-Sept. 13.

Red Cross Solidarity Week — PT11

2007, Sept. 14 ***Perf. 13¾***

RA11 PT11 10d multi .80 .40

Obligatory on mail Sept. 14-21.

Children's Week — PT12

2007, Oct. 1 ***Perf. 13¼***

RA12 PT12 10d multi 1.25 .40

Obligatory on mail Oct. 1-7.

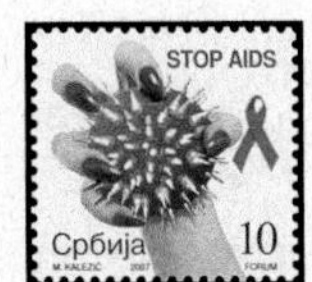

Campaign Against AIDS — PT13

2007, Nov. 1 ***Perf. 13¾***

RA13 PT13 10d multi 1.10 .40

Obligatory on mail Nov. 1-30.

Ana and Vlade Divac Foundation — PT14

2007, Dec. 24

RA14 PT14 10d multi .80 .40

Obligatory on mail Dec. 24-29.

Campaign Against Sex Slavery PT15

2008, Jan. 21 ***Perf. 13¼***

RA15 PT15 10d multi .60 .35

Obligatory on mail Jan. 21-26.

Zivojin Misic Statue, Mionica, 90th Anniv. — PT16

2008, Apr. 21 ***Perf. 13¾***

RA16 PT16 10d multi .80 .40

Obligatory on mail Apr. 21-May 7.

Red Cross Week — PT17

2008, May 8 ***Perf. 13¾***

Dated "2008"

RA17 PT17 10d multi .80 .40

Obligatory on mail May 8-15. See Nos. RA25, RA35, RA40, RA58.

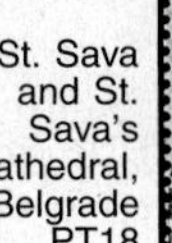

St. Sava and St. Sava's Cathedral, Belgrade PT18

St. Sava's Cathedral PT19

2008, May 16 ***Perf. 13¼***

RA18 PT18 10d multi .80 .40

RA19 PT19 10d multi .80 .40

Obligatory on mail May 16-Sept. 13.

Red Cross Solidarity Week — PT20

2008, Sept. 14 ***Perf. 13¾***

RA20 PT20 10d multi .80 .35

Obligatory on mail Sept. 14-21.

Children's Week — PT21

2008, Oct. 6 ***Perf. 13¼***

RA21 PT21 10d multi .80 .35

Obligatory on mail Oct. 6-12.

Avram Josif Vinaver (1862-1915, Physician — PT22

2008, Oct. 13

RA22 PT22 10d multi .80 .30

Campaign against cancer. Obligatory on mail Oct. 13-31.

Avala Telecommunications Tower, Belgrade — PT23

2008, Nov. 3 ***Perf. 13¾***

RA23 PT23 10d multi .80 .30

Obligatory on mail Nov. 3-29.

Dr. Aleksandar Simic (1899-1966) — PT24

2009, Apr. 6 ***Perf. 13¼***

RA24 PT24 10d multi .80 .30

Campaign against cancer. Obligatory on mail Apr. 6-25.

Red Cross Week Type of 2008

2009, May 8 ***Perf. 13¾***

Dated "2009"

RA25 PT17 10d multi .80 .30

Obligatory on mail May 8-15.

King Alexander I (1888-1934) — PT26

2009, June 8

RA26 PT26 10d multi .80 .30

Obligatory on mail June 8-13.

St. Sava Cathedral, Belgrade — PT27

2009, June 29

RA27 PT27 10d multi .80 .30

Obligatory on mail June 29-Aug. 29.

Red Cross Solidarity Week — PT28

2009, Sept. 14

RA28 PT28 10d multi .80 .35

Obligatory on mail Sept. 14-21.

Children's Week — PT29

2009, Oct. 5 ***Perf. 13¼***

RA29 PT29 10d multi .80 .35

Obligatory on mail Oct. 5-11.

Monument PT30

2009, Nov. 9 ***Perf. 13¼x13¾***

RA30 PT30 10d multi .80 .35

Cultural preservation. Obligatory on mail Nov. 9-14.

Homeless Children — PT31

2009, Dec. 23 ***Perf. 13¾***

RA31 PT31 10d multi .80 .30

Obligatory on mail Dec. 23-31.

Refugees — PT32

2010, Feb. 1

RA32 PT32 10d multi .60 .30

Obligatory on mail Feb. 1-6.

Dragoljub Jovanovic (1895-1977), Politician — PT33

2010, Mar. 8 Litho. *Perf. 13½*

RA33 PT33 10d multi 1.25 .30

Obligatory on mail Mar. 8-31.

European Water Polo Championships, Zagreb — PT34

2010, Apr. 16 Litho. *Perf. 13¼x13¾*

RA34 PT34 10d multi .75 .30

Obligatory on mail Apr. 16-24.

Red Cross Week Type of 2009 Dated "2010"

2010, May 8 *Perf. 13¾*

RA35 PT17 10d multi 1.00 .30

Obligatory on mail May 8-15.

Bells and St. Sava's Cathedral, Belgrade PT36

2010, Aug. 2 *Perf. 13x13¾*

RA36 PT36 10d multi 1.00 .30

Restoration of St. Sava's Catahedral. Obligatory on mail Aug. 2-Sept. 13.

Red Cross Solidarity Week — PT37

Dated "2010"

2010, Sept. 14 *Perf. 13¾*

RA37 PT37 10d multi 1.00 .30

Obligatory on mail Sept. 14-21. See Nos. RA42, RA52, RA61, RA72, RA78, RA84.

Children's Week — PT38

2010, Oct. 4 *Perf. 13¼*

RA38 PT38 10d multi 1.00 .30

Obligatory on mail Oct. 4-10.

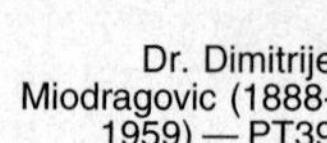

Dr. Dimitrije Miodragovic (1888-1959) — PT39

2011, Apr. 4

RA39 PT39 10d multi 1.00 .30

Campaign against cancer. Obligatory on mail Apr. 4-30.

Red Cross Week Type of 2008 Dated "2011"

2011, May 8 Litho. *Perf. 13¼*

RA40 PT17 10d multi 1.00 .30

Obligatory on mail May 8-15.

Bells and St. Sava's Cathedral, Belgrade — PT40

2011, June 6 *Perf. 13¾*

RA41 PT40 10d multi 1.00 .30

Restoration of St. Sava's Cathedral. Obligatory on mail, June 6-Aug. 20.

Red Cross Solidarity Week Type of 2010 Dated "2011"

2011, Sept. 14 *Perf. 13¼*

RA42 PT37 10d multi 1.00 .30

Obligatory on mail Sept. 14-21.

Children's Week — PT41

2011, Oct. 3

RA43 PT41 10d multi 1.00 .30

Obligatory on mail Oct. 3-9.

UNICEF — PT42

2011, Nov. 21

RA44 PT42 10d blue & black 1.00 .30

Obligatory on mail Nov. 21-27.

Refugee Assistance — PT43

2011, Dec. 19

RA45 PT43 10d multi 1.00 .30

Obligatory on mail Dec. 19-25.

European Wrestling Championships, Belgrade — PT45

2012, Feb. 27 Litho. *Perf. 13¼*

RA47 PT45 10d multi 1.00 .30

Obligatory on mail Feb. 27.

Aleksije Milosavljevic (1919-2002), Physician — PT46

2012, Mar. 26 Litho. *Perf. 13½*

RA48 PT46 10d multi 1.00 .30

Obligatory on mail Mar. 26-Apr. 14.

St. Sava's Cathedral, Belgrade — PT48

2012, June 11 Litho. *Perf. 13¾*

RA51 PT48 10d multi 1.00 .30

Obligatory on mail June 11-Aug. 31.

Red Cross Solidarity Week Type of 2010

2012, Sept. 14 Litho. *Perf. 13¼*

Dated "2012"

RA52 PT37 10d multi 1.00 .30

Obligatory on mail Sept. 14-21.

Children's Week — PT49

2012, Oct. 1 Litho. *Perf. 13¼*

RA53 PT49 10d multi 1.00 .30

Obligatory on mail Oct. 1-7.

National Library, 180th Anniv. — PT50

2012, Oct. 29 Litho. *Perf. 13¾*

RA54 PT50 10d multi 1.00 .30

Obligatory on mail Oct. 29-Nov. 17.

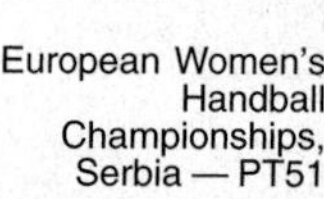

European Women's Handball Championships, Serbia — PT51

2012, Dec. 4 Litho. *Perf. 13¾*

RA55 PT51 10d multi 1.00 .30

Obligatory on mail Dec. 4-16.

Refugee Assistance — PT52

2013, Jan. 30 Litho. *Perf. 13¼*

RA56 PT52 10d multi 1.00 .30

Obligatory on mail Jan. 30-Feb. 14.

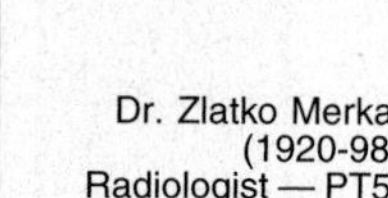

Dr. Zlatko Merkas (1920-98), Radiologist — PT53

2013, Apr. 10 Litho. *Perf. 13¼*

RA57 PT53 10d multi 1.00 .30

Campaign against cancer. Obligatory on mail Apr. 10-30.

Red Cross Week Type of 2008

2013, May 8 Litho. *Perf. 13¾*

Dated "2012"

RA58 PT17 10d multi 1.00 .30

Obligatory on mail May 6-15.

2013 World Cadet Wrestling Championships, Zrenjanin — PT54

2013, May 20 Litho. *Perf. 13¾*

RA59 PT54 10d multi 1.00 .30

Obligatory on mail May 20-26.

St. Sava's Cathedral, Belgrade — PT55

2013, June 18 Litho. *Perf. 13¾*

RA60 PT55 10d multi 1.00 .30

Obligatory on mail June 18-Aug. 31.

Red Cross Solidarity Week Type of 2010

2013, Sept. 14 Litho. *Perf. 13¼*

Dated "2013"

RA61 PT37 10d multi 1.00 .30

Obligatory on mail Sept. 14-21.

Children's Week — PT56

2013, Oct. 7 Litho. *Perf. 13¼*

RA62 PT56 10d multi 1.00 .30

Obligatory on mail Oct. 7-14.

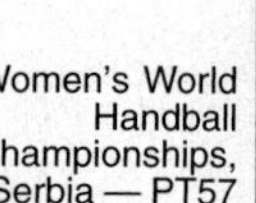

2013 Women's World Handball Championships, Serbia — PT57

2013, Nov. 4 Litho. *Perf. 13¼*

RA63 PT57 10d multi 1.00 .30

Obligatory on mail Nov. 4-10.

Renovation of National Library, 40th Anniv. — PT58

2013, Nov. 18 Litho. *Perf. 13¾*

RA64 PT58 10d multi 1.00 .30

Obligatory on mail Nov. 18-Dec. 12.

Environmental Protection — PT59

2014, Feb. 10 **Litho.** ***Perf. 13¼***

RA65 PT59 10d multi .80 .30

Obligatory on mail Feb. 10-23.

2014 European Men's Rowing Championships, Belgrade — PT60

2014, Mar. 10 **Litho.** ***Perf. 13¾***

RA66 PT60 10d multi .80 .30

Obligatory on mail Mar. 10-16.

Dr. Mladomir Pantelic (1921-2009), Oncologist — PT61

2014, Apr. 9 **Litho.** ***Perf. 13¼***

RA67 PT61 10d multi .80 .30

Campaign against cancer. Obligatory on mail Apr. 9-30.

Tour de Serbie Bicycle Race — PT62

2014, June 9 **Litho.** ***Perf. 13¾***

RA68 PT62 10d multi .80 .30

Obligatory on mail June 9-16.

St. Sava's Cathedral, Belgrade — PT63

2014, June 16 **Litho.** ***Perf. 13¾***

RA69 PT63 10d multi .80 .30

Obligatory on mail June 16- Aug. 31.

Children's Week — PT64

2014, Oct. 6 **Litho.** ***Perf. 13¼***

RA70 PT64 10d multi .80 .30

Obligatory on mail Oct. 6-12.

Housing Assistance — PT65

2015, Feb. 23 **Litho.** ***Perf. 13¼***

RA71 PT65 10d multi .80 .30

Obligatory on mail Feb. 23-Mar. 7.

Red Cross Solidarity Week Type of 2010

2015, May 8 **Litho.** ***Perf. 13¾***

Dated "2015"

RA72 PT37 10d multi .80 .30

Obligatory on mail May 8-15.

St. Sava's Cathedral, Belgrade — PT66

2015, June 15 **Litho.** ***Perf. 13¾***

RA73 PT66 10d multi .80 .30

Obligatory on mail June 15- Aug. 31.

2016 European Water Polo Championships, Belgrade — PT68

2015, Oct. 26 **Litho.** ***Perf. 13¼***

RA75 PT68 10d multi .80 .30

Obligatory on mail Oct. 26-Nov. 1.

Environmental Protection — PT69

2016, Feb. 22 **Litho.** ***Perf. 13¼***

RA76 PT69 10d multi .70 .30

Obligatory on mail Feb. 22-Mar. 6.

2016 Paralympics, Rio de Janeiro — PT70

2016, Apr. 21 **Litho.** ***Perf. 13¼***

RA77 PT70 10d multi .70 .30

Obligatory on mail Apr. 21-28.

Red Cross Solidarity Week Type of 2010

2016, May 8 **Litho.** ***Perf. 13¾***

Dated "2016"

RA78 PT37 10d multi .70 .30

Obligatory on mail May 8-15.

Cross From St. Sava's Cathedral, Belgrade — PT71

2016, June 15 **Litho.** ***Perf. 13¾***

RA79 PT71 10d multi .70 .30

Obligatory on mail June 15- Aug. 31.

Children's Week — PT72

2016, Oct. 3 **Litho.** ***Perf. 13¼***

RA80 PT72 10d multi .70 .30

Obligatory on mail Oct. 3-9.

European Indoor Track and Field Championships, Belgrade — PT73

2017, Feb. 27 **Litho.** ***Perf. 13¾***

RA81 PT73 10d multi .55 .30

Obligatory on mail Feb. 27-Mar. 5.

Housing Assistance — PT74

2017, Apr. 10 **Litho.** ***Perf. 13¼***

RA82 PT74 10d multi .55 .30

Obligatory on mail Apr. 10-26.

European Wrestling Championships, Novi Sad — PT75

2017, Apr. 27 **Litho.** ***Perf. 13¾***

RA83 PT75 10d multi .55 .30

Obligatory on mail Apr. 27-May 6.

Red Cross Solidarity Week Type of 2010

2017, May 8 **Litho.** ***Perf. 13¾***

Dated "2017"

RA84 PT37 10d multi .55 .30

Obligatory on mail May 8-15.

Children's Week — PT76

2017, Oct. 2 **Litho.** ***Perf. 13¼***

RA85 PT76 10d multi .25 .25

Obligatory on mail Oct. 2-8.

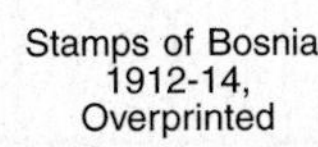

Cross and Interior of St. Sava's Cathedral, Belgrade — PT77

2017, Oct. 9 **Litho.** ***Perf. 13¾***

RA86 PT77 10d multi .25 .25

Obligatory on mail Oct. 9-Dec. 3.

ISSUED UNDER AUSTRIAN OCCUPATION

100 Heller = 1 Krone

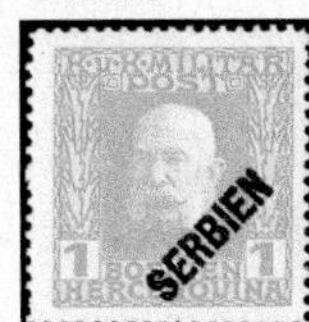

Stamps of Bosnia, 1912-14, Overprinted

1916 **Unwmk.** ***Perf. 12½***

1N1	A23	1h	olive green	2.40	6.25
1N2	A23	2h	brt blue	2.40	6.25
1N3	A23	3h	claret	2.40	6.25
1N4	A23	5h	green	.40	.80
1N5	A23	6h	dk gray	1.60	5.50
1N6	A23	10h	rose carmine	.40	.80
1N7	A23	12h	dp olive grn	1.60	4.00
1N8	A23	20h	orange brown	.80	2.40
1N9	A23	25h	ultra	.80	2.40
1N10	A23	30h	orange red	.80	2.40
1N11	A24	35h	myrtle grn	.80	2.40
1N12	A24	40h	dk violet	.80	2.40
1N13	A24	45h	olive brown	.80	2.40
1N14	A24	50h	slate blue	.80	2.40
1N15	A24	60h	brown violet	.80	2.40
1N16	A24	72h	dark blue	.80	2.40
1N17	A25	1k	brn vio, *straw*	2.40	6.25
1N18	A25	2k	dk gray, *bl*	2.40	6.25
1N19	A26	3k	carmine, *grn*	2.40	6.25
1N20	A26	5k	dk vio, *gray*	2.40	6.25
1N21	A25	10k	dk ultra, *gray*	16.00	50.00
			Nos. 1N1-1N21 (21)	44.00	126.45

Stamps of Bosnia, 1912-14, Overprinted "SERBIEN" Horizontally at Bottom

1916

1N22	A23	1h	olive green	8.00	20.00
1N23	A23	2h	bright blue	8.00	20.00
1N24	A23	3h	claret	8.00	20.00
1N25	A23	5h	green	1.60	3.25
1N26	A23	6h	dark gray	8.00	20.00
1N27	A23	10h	rose carmine	1.60	3.25
1N28	A23	12h	dp olive grn	8.00	20.00
1N29	A23	20h	orange brn	8.00	20.00
1N30	A23	25h	ultra	8.00	20.00
1N31	A23	30h	orange red	8.00	20.00
1N32	A24	35h	myrtle green	8.00	20.00
1N33	A24	40h	dark violet	8.00	20.00
1N34	A24	45h	olive brown	8.00	20.00
1N35	A24	50h	slate blue	8.00	20.00
1N36	A24	60h	brown violet	8.00	20.00
1N37	A24	72h	dark blue	8.00	20.00
1N38	A25	1k	brn vio, *straw*	20.00	45.00
1N39	A25	2k	dk gray, *bl*	20.00	45.00
1N40	A26	3k	carmine, *grn*	24.00	52.50
1N41	A26	5k	dk vio, *gray*	27.50	65.00
1N42	A25	10k	dk ultra, *gray*	55.00	110.00
			Nos. 1N22-1N42 (21)	261.70	604.00

Nos. 1N22-1N42 were prepared in 1914, at the time of the 1st Austrian occupation of Serbia. They were not issued at that time because of the retreat. The stamps were put on sale in 1916, at the same time as Nos. 1N1-1N21.

ISSUED UNDER GERMAN OCCUPATION

In occupied Serbia, authority was ostensibly in the hands of a government created by the former Yugoslav General, Milan Nedich, supported by the Chetniks, a nationalist organization which turned fascist. Actually the German military ran the country.

Types of Yugoslavia, 1939-40, Overprinted in Black

1941 **Unwmk.** **Typo.** ***Perf. 12½***

Paper with colored network

2N1	A16	25p	blk *(lt grn)*	.55	*8.00*
2N2	A16	50p	org *(pink)*	.55	4.00
2N3	A16	1d	yel grn *(lt grn)*	.55	4.00
2N4	A16	1.50d	red *(pink)*	.55	4.00
2N5	A16	2d	dp mag *(pink)*	.55	4.00
2N6	A16	3d	dl red brn *(pink)*	1.60	*32.50*
2N7	A16	4d	ultra *(lt grn)*	1.20	*6.50*
2N8	A16	5d	dk bl *(lt grn)*	1.60	*16.00*
2N9	A16	5.50d	dk vio brn *(pink)*	1.60	*16.00*
2N10	A16	6d	sl bl *(pink)*	1.60	*16.00*
2N11	A16	8d	sep *(lt grn)*	3.25	*24.00*
2N12	A16	12d	brt vio *(lt grn)*	3.25	*24.00*
2N13	A16	16d	dl vio *(pink)*	4.00	*80.00*
2N14	A16	20d	bl *(lt grn)*	17.50	*280.00*
2N15	A16	30d	brt pink *(lt grn)*	32.50	*1,100.*
			Nos. 2N1-2N15 (15)	70.85	*1,619.*
			Set, never hinged	135.00	

Double overprints exist on 50p, 1d, 5d, 5.50d and 12d. Value, $250.

Stamps of Yugoslavia, 1939-40, Overprinted in Black

Paper with colored network

2N16	A16	25p	blk *(lt grn)*	.55	*24.00*
2N17	A16	50p	org *(pink)*	.55	*5.50*
2N18	A16	1d	yel grn *(lt grn)*	.55	*5.50*
2N19	A16	1.50d	red *(pink)*	.55	*5.50*
2N20	A16	2d	dp mag *(pink)*	.65	*5.50*
2N21	A16	3d	dl red brn *(pink)*	.90	*21.00*
2N22	A16	4d	ultra *(lt grn)*	.90	*5.50*

2N23 A16 5d dk bl *(lt grn)* .90 *10.50*
2N24 A16 5.50d dk vio brn *(pink)* 1.75 *21.00*
2N25 A16 6d sl bl *(pink)* 1.75 *21.00*
2N26 A16 8d sep *(lt grn)* 2.00 *32.50*
2N27 A16 12d brt vio *(lt grn)* 2.25 *32.50*
2N28 A16 16d dl vio *(pink)* 2.50 *100.00*
2N29 A16 20d bl *(lt grn)* 2.50 *325.00*
2N30 A16 30d brt pink *(lt grn)* 22.50 *1,000.*
Nos. 2N16-2N30 (15) 40.80 *1,615.*
Set, never hinged 80.00

Lazaritza Monastery — OS1

Ruins of Manassia Monastery OS4

Designs: 1d, Kalenica Monastery. 1.50d, Ravanica Monastery. 3d, Ljubostinja Monastery. 4d, Sopocane Monastery. 7d, Tsitsa Monastery. 12d, Goriak Monastery. 16d, Studenica Monastery.

1942-43 **Typo.** ***Perf. 11½***
2N31 OS1 50p brt violet .25 *.50*
2N32 OS1 1d red .25 *.50*
2N33 OS1 1.50d red brn 1.75 *6.50*
2N34 OS1 1.50d green ('43) .25 *.50*
2N35 OS4 2d dl rose violet .25 *.50*
2N36 OS4 3d brt blue 1.75 *6.50*
2N37 OS4 3d rose pink ('43) .25 *.50*
2N38 OS4 4d ultra .25 *.50*
2N39 OS4 7d dk slate grn .25 *.50*
2N40 OS1 12d lake .25 *3.25*
2N41 OS1 16d grnsh blk 2.75 *3.50*
Nos. 2N31-2N41 (11) 8.25 *23.25*
Set, never hinged 18.00

For surcharges see Nos. 2NB29-2NB37.

Post Rider — OS10

Post Wagon — OS11

9d, Mail train. 30d, Mail truck. 50d, Mail plane.

1943, Oct. 15 **Photo.** ***Perf. 12½***
2N42 OS10 3d copper red & gray lilac 1.20 *5.50*
2N43 OS11 8d vio rose & gray 1.20 *5.50*
2N44 OS10 9d dk bl grn & sep 1.20 *5.50*
2N45 OS10 30d chnt & sl grn 1.20 *5.50*
2N46 OS10 50d dp bl & red brn 1.20 *5.50*
Nos. 2N42-2N46 (5) 6.00 *27.50*
Set, never hinged 14.00

Centenary of postal service in Serbia. Printed in sheets of 24 containing 4 of each stamp and 4 labels.

OCCUPATION SEMI-POSTAL STAMPS

Smederevo Fortress on the Danube OSP1

Refugees OSP2

Perf. 11½x12½

1941, Sept. 22 **Typo.** **Unwmk.**
2NB1 OSP1 50p + 1d dk brn 1.20 *2.00*
2NB2 OSP2 1d + 2d dk gray grn .30 *2.40*
2NB3 OSP2 1.50d + 3d dp cl 2.40 *3.75*
a. Perf. 12½ 4.50 *16.00*
Never hinged 9.50
2NB4 OSP1 2d + 4d dk bl 2.40 *13.50*
Nos. 2NB1-2NB4 (4) 6.30 *21.65*
Set, never hinged 16.50

Souvenir Sheets

2NB5 Sheet of 2 120.00 *725.00*
Never hinged 275.00
a. OSP2 1d + 49d rose lake 40.00 *72.50*
b. OSP1 2d + 48d gray 40.00 *72.50*

Imperf

2NB6 Sheet of 2 120.00 *725.00*
Never hinged 275.00
a. OSP2 1d + 49d gray 40.00 *72.50*
b. OSP1 2d + 48d rose lake 40.00 *72.50*

The surtax aided the victims of an explosion at Smederevo and was used for the reconstruction of the town.

Christ and Virgin Mary — OSP4

a

b

With Rose Burelage

1941, Dec. 5 **Photo.** ***Perf. 11½***
2NB7 OSP4 50p + 1.50d brn red .65 *6.50*
2NB8 OSP4 1d + 3d sl grn .65 *6.50*
2NB9 OSP4 2d + 6d dp red .65 *6.50*
2NB10 OSP4 4d + 12d dp bl .65 *6.50*
Nos. 2NB7-2NB10 (4) 2.60 *26.00*
Set, never hinged 6.50

With Symbol "a" Outlined in Cerise

2NB7a OSP4 50p 24.00 *72.50*
2NB8a OSP4 1d 24.00 *72.50*
2NB9a OSP4 2d 24.00 *72.50*
2NB10a OSP4 4d 24.00 *72.50*
Nos. 2NB7a-2NB10a (4) 96.00 *290.00*
Set, never hinged 240.00

With Symbol "b" Outlined in Cerise

2NB7b OSP4 50p 24.00 *72.50*
2NB8b OSP4 1d 24.00 *72.50*
2NB9b OSP4 2d 24.00 *72.50*
2NB10b OSP4 4d 24.00 *72.50*
Nos. 2NB7b-2NB10b (4) 96.00 *290.00*
Set, never hinged 240.00

Without Burelage

2NB7c OSP4 50p 1.80 *20.00*
2NB8c OSP4 1d 1.80 *20.00*
2NB9c OSP4 2d 1.80 *20.00*
2NB10c OSP4 4d 1.80 *20.00*
Nos. 2NB7c-2NB10c (4) 7.20 *80.00*
Set, never hinged 16.00

These stamps were printed in sheets of 50, in 2 panes of 25. In the panes, #8, 12, 13, 14, 18, forming a cross, are without burelage. #7, 17 are type "a," #9, 19 type "b." 16 of the 25 stamps have overall burelage.

Surtax aided prisoners of war.

Thicker Paper, Without Burelage

1942, Mar. 26
2NB11 OSP4 50p + 1.50d brn 1.60 *4.00*
2NB12 OSP4 1d + 3d bl grn 1.60 *4.00*
2NB13 OSP4 2d + 6d mag 1.60 *4.00*
2NB14 OSP4 4d + 12d ultra 1.60 *4.00*
Nos. 2NB11-2NB14 (4) 6.40 *16.00*
Set, never hinged 22.50

OSP5

OSP6

OSP7

OSP8

Designs: Anti-Masonic symbolisms.

1942, Jan. 1
2NB15 OSP5 50p + 50p yel brn 2.00 *3.75*
2NB16 OSP6 1d + 1d dk grn 2.00 *3.75*
2NB17 OSP7 2d + 2d rose car 2.00 *6.50*
2NB18 OSP8 4d + 4d indigo 2.00 *6.50*
Nos. 2NB15-2NB18 (4) 8.00 *20.50*
Set, never hinged 16.00

Anti-Masonic Exposition of Oct. 22, 1941. The surtax was used for anti-Masonic propaganda.

Mother and Children — OSP9

1942
2NB19 OSP9 2d + 6d brt pur 8.00 *16.00*
2NB20 OSP9 4d + 8d dp bl 8.00 *16.00*
2NB21 OSP9 7d + 13d dk bl grn 8.00 *16.00*
2NB22 OSP9 20d + 40d dp rose lake 8.00 *16.00*
Nos. 2NB19-2NB22 (4) 32.00 *64.00*
Set, never hinged 80.00

Nos. 2NB19-2NB22 were issued in sheets of 16 consisting of a block of four of each denomination. The surtax aided war orphans.

Broken Sword — OSP10

Wounded Flag-bearer OSP11

Designs: 1.50d+48.50d, Broken sword. 3d+5d, 2d+48d, Wounded soldier. 3d+47d, Wounded flag-bearer. 4d+10d, 4d+46d, Tending casualty.

1943
2NB23 OSP10 1.50d + 1.50d dk brn 3.25 *4.00*
2NB24 OSP11 2d + 3d dk bl grn 3.25 *4.00*
2NB25 OSP11 3d + 5d dp rose vio 4.75 *5.50*
2NB26 OSP10 4d + 10d dp bl 4.75 *6.50*
Nos. 2NB23-2NB26 (4) 16.00 *20.00*
Set, never hinged 35.00

Souvenir Sheets

Thick Paper

2NB27 Sheet of 2 110.00 *6,500.*
Never hinged 240.00
a. OSP10 1.50d + 48.50d dk brn 32.50 *2,900.*
b. OSP10 4d + 46d dp bl 32.50 *2,900.*
2NB28 Sheet of 2 110.00 *6,500.*
Never hinged 240.00
a. OSP11 2d + 48d dk bl grn 32.50 *2,900.*
b. OSP11 3d + 47d dp rose vio 32.50 *2,900.*

The sheets measure 150x110mm. The surtax aided war victims.

Stamps of 1942-43 Surcharged in Black

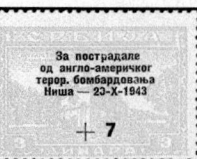

Pale Green Burelage

1943, Dec. 11
2NB29 OS1 50p + 2d brt vio .65 *47.50*
2NB30 OS1 1d + 3d red .65 *47.50*
2NB31 OS1 1.50d + 4d dp grn .65 *47.50*
2NB32 OS4 2d + 5d dl rose vio .65 *47.50*
2NB33 OS4 3d + 7d rose pink .65 *47.50*
2NB34 OS4 4d + 9d ultra .65 *47.50*
2NB35 OS4 7d + 15d dk sl grn 1.20 *47.50*
2NB36 OS1 12d + 25d lake 1.20 *225.00*

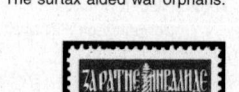

2NB37 OS1 16d + 33d grnsh blk 1.75 *360.00*
Nos. 2NB29-2NB37 (9) 8.05 *917.50*
Set, never hinged 20.00

The surtax aided victims of the bombing of Nisch.

OCCUPATION AIR POST STAMPS

Types of Yugoslavia, 1937-40, Overprinted in Carmine or Maroon

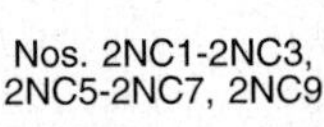
Nos. 2NC1-2NC3, 2NC5-2NC7, 2NC9

Nos. 2NC4, 2NC8, 2NC10

Paper with colored network

1941 Unwmk. *Perf. 12½*
2NC1 AP6 50p brown 8.00 *175.00*
2NC2 AP7 1d yel grn 8.00 *175.00*
2NC3 AP8 2d bl gray 8.00 *175.00*
2NC4 AP9 2.50d rose red (M) 8.00 *175.00*
2NC5 AP6 5d brn vio 8.00 *175.00*
2NC6 AP7 10d brn lake (M) 8.00 *175.00*
2NC7 AP8 20d dk green 12.50 *175.00*
2NC8 AP9 30d ultra 12.50 *175.00*
2NC9 AP10 40d Prus grn & pale grn (C) 16.00 *650.00*
2NC10 AP11 50d sl bl & gray bl (C) 24.00 *1,100.*
Nos. 2NC1-2NC10 (10) 113.00 *3,150.*
Set, never hinged 240.00

Nos. 2NC1-2NC2 exist without network.

Same Surcharged in Maroon or Carmine

No. 2NC13

No. 2NC14

Without colored network
2NC11 AP7 1d on 10d 6.50 *200.00*
2NC12 AP8 3d on 20d 6.50 *200.00*
2NC13 AP9 6d on 30d 6.50 *200.00*
2NC14 AP10 8d on 40d 12.50 *400.00*
2NC15 AP11 12d on 50d 16.00 *875.00*
Nos. 2NC11-2NC15 (5) 48.00 *1,875.*
Set, never hinged 95.00

Regular Issue of Yugoslavia, 1939-40, Surcharged in Black

1942 Green Network
2NC16 A16 2d on 2d dp mag .40 *2.00*
2NC17 A16 4d on 4d ultra .40 *2.00*
2NC18 A16 10d on 12d brt vio .40 *4.00*
2NC19 A16 14d on 20d blue .40 *4.00*
2NC20 A16 20d on 30d brt pink .80 *16.00*
Nos. 2NC16-2NC20 (5) 2.40 *28.00*
Set, never hinged 6.75

OCCUPATION POSTAGE DUE STAMPS

Types of Yugoslavia Similar to OD3-OD4 Overprinted

1941 Unwmk. Typo. *Perf. 12½*
2NJ1 OD3 50p violet 1.00 *40.00*
2NJ2 OD3 1d lake 1.00 *40.00*
2NJ3 OD3 2d dark blue 1.00 *40.00*
2NJ4 OD3 3d red 1.00 *60.00*
2NJ5 OD4 4d lt blue 2.00 *140.00*
2NJ6 OD4 5d orange 2.00 *140.00*
2NJ7 OD4 10d violet 3.50 *360.00*
2NJ8 OD4 20d green 12.50 *950.00*
Nos. 2NJ1-2NJ8 (8) 24.00 *1,770.*
Set, never hinged 45.00

OD3

OD4

1942 *Perf. 12½*
2NJ9 OD3 1d mar & grn 1.10 *8.00*
2NJ10 OD3 2d dk bl & red 1.10 *8.00*
2NJ11 OD3 3d ver & bl 1.10 *12.00*
2NJ12 OD4 4d blue & red 1.10 *12.00*
2NJ13 OD4 5d orange & bl 1.75 *32.50*
2NJ14 OD4 10d violet & red 1.75 *32.50*
2NJ15 OD4 20d green & red 12.00 *140.00*
Nos. 2NJ9-2NJ15 (7) 19.90 *245.00*
Set, never hinged 40.00

OD5

2NJ16 OD5 50p black 1.60 *8.00*
2NJ17 OD5 3d violet 1.60 *8.00*
2NJ18 OD5 4d blue 1.60 *8.00*
2NJ19 OD5 5d dk slate grn 1.60 *8.00*
2NJ20 OD5 6d orange 1.60 *32.50*
2NJ21 OD5 10d red 4.00 *32.50*
2NJ22 OD5 20d ultra 12.00 *65.00*
Nos. 2NJ16-2NJ22 (7) 24.00 *162.00*
Set, never hinged 45.00

OCCUPATION OFFICIAL STAMP

OOS1

1943 Unwmk. Typo. *Perf. 12½*
2NO1 OOS1 3d red lilac .80 *2.40*
Never hinged 2.40

SEYCHELLES

sā-ˈshelz

LOCATION — A group of islands in the Indian Ocean, off the coast of Africa north of Madagascar.
GOVT. — Republic
AREA — 175 sq. mi.
POP. — 79,164 (1999 est.)
CAPITAL — Victoria

The islands were attached to the British colony of Mauritius from 1810 to 1903, when they became a separate colony. Seychelles achieved internal self-government in October 1975 and independence on June 29, 1976.

100 Cents = 1 Rupee

Catalogue values for unused stamps in this country are for Never Hinged items, beginning with Scott 149 in the regular postage section and Scott J1 in the postage due section.

Watermark

Wmk. 380 — "POST OFFICE"

Queen Victoria — A1

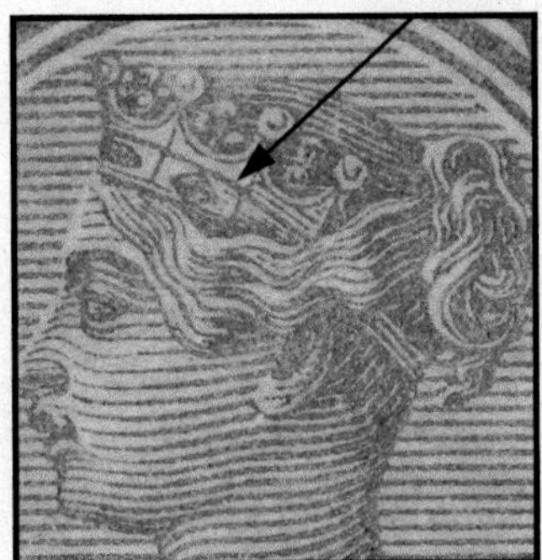
Die I

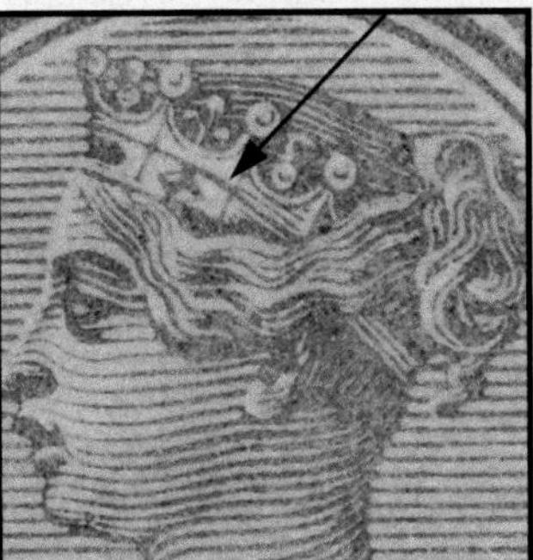
Die II

Two dies of 2c, 4c, 8c, 10c, 13c, 16c:
Die I — Shading lines at right of diamond in tiara band.
Die II — No shading lines in this rectangle.

1890-1900 Typo. Wmk. 2 *Perf. 14*
1 A1 2c grn & rose (II) 3.50 1.25
a. Die I 8.50 *21.00*
2 A1 2c org brn & grn ('00) 2.50 *3.25*
3 A1 3c dk vio & org ('93) 2.00 .75
4 A1 4c car rose & grn (II) 3.50 1.75
a. Die I 50.00 *21.00*
5 A1 6c car rose ('00) 4.50 .75
6 A1 8c brn vio & ultra (II) 17.50 2.50
a. 8c brn vio & bl (I) 18.50 *4.50*
7 A1 10c ultra & brn (II) 17.50 4.25
a. 10c bl & brn (I) 18.50 *42.50*
8 A1 12c ol gray & grn ('93) 3.50 1.25
9 A1 13c slate & blk (II) 8.50 2.50
a. Die I 8.00 *21.00*
10 A1 15c ol grn & vio ('93) 9.50 2.75
11 A1 15c ultra ('00) 11.00 8.50
12 A1 16c org brn & bl (I) 16.00 5.50
a. 16c org brn & ultra (II) 52.50 14.50
13 A1 18c ultra ('97) 14.00 1.75
14 A1 36c brn & rose ('97) 50.00 8.00
15 A1 45c brn & rose ('93) 30.00 *45.00*
16 A1 48c ocher & green 27.50 15.00
17 A1 75c yel & pur ('00) 60.00 *87.50*
18 A1 96c violet & car 72.50 60.00
19 A1 1r vio & red ('97) 16.00 8.50
20 A1 1.50r blk & rose ('00) 90.00 *100.00*
21 A1 2.25r vio & grn ('00) 115.00 *100.00*
Nos. 1-21 (21) 574.50 460.75

Numerals of 75c, 1r, 1.50r and 2.25r of type A1 are in color on plain tablet.
For surcharges see Nos. 22-37.

Surcharged in Black

1893
22 A1 3c on 4c car rose & grn (II) 1.50 2.00
a. Inverted surcharge 375.00 *450.00*
b. Double surcharge 600.00
d. Pair, one without surcharge *14,000.*
23 A1 12c on 16c org brn & ultra (II) 21.00 3.50
a. 12c on 16c org brn & bl (I) 7.50 *8.50*
b. Inverted surcharge (I) 575.00
d. Double surcharge (I) *15,750.* *11,000.*
e. Double surcharge (II) 5,500. 5,500.
24 A1 15c on 16c org brn & ultra (II) 27.50 4.00
a. 15c on 16c org brn & bl (I) 16.00 17.50
b. Inverted surcharge (I) 400.00 375.00
c. Inverted surcharge (II) 1,100. 1,250.
d. Double surcharge (I) 1,500. 1,500.
e. Double surcharge (II) 825.00 875.00
f. Triple surcharge (II) *5,000.*
25 A1 45c on 48c ocher & grn 37.50 8.00
26 A1 90c on 96c vio & car 70.00 52.50
Nos. 22-26 (5) 157.50 70.00

No. 15 Surcharged in Black

1896
27 A1 18c on 45c brn & rose 11.50 4.25
a. Double surcharge 1,850. 1,850.
b. Triple surcharge *2,750.*
28 A1 36c on 45c brn & rose 12.00 *70.00*
a. Double surcharge 1,850.

Surcharged in Black

1901
29 A1 3c on 10c bl & brn (II) 3.50 .90
a. Double surcharge 950.00
b. Triple surcharge 3,250.
30 A1 3c on 16c org brn & ultra (II) 7.00 *9.50*
a. "3 cents" omitted (II) 675.00 675.00
b. Inverted surcharge (II) 800.00 800.00
c. Double surcharge (II) 625.00 650.00
31 A1 3c on 36c brn & rose 2.10 1.10
a. Without bars — —
b. Double surcharge 950.00 *1,100.*
c. "3 cents" omitted 800.00 850.00
32 A1 6c on 8c brn vio & ultra (II) 7.00 4.00
a. Inverted surcharge 800.00 *925.00*
Nos. 29-32 (4) 19.60 *15.50*

Stamps of 1890-1900 Surcharged

1902, June
33 A1 2c on 4c car rose & grn (II) 5.00 3.50
34 A1 30c on 75c yel & pur 3.00 *7.50*
a. Narrow "0" in "30" 10.00 *50.00*
35 A1 30c on 1r vio & red 20.00 *52.50*
a. Narrow "0" in "30" 40.00 *120.00*
b. Double surcharge 1,750.
36 A1 45c on 1r vio & red 9.50 *60.00*
37 A1 45c on 2.25r vio & grn 52.50 *160.00*
a. Narrow "5" in "45" 250.00 450.00
Nos. 33-37 (5) 90.00 *283.50*

King Edward VII — A6

Numerals of 75c, 1.50r and 2.25r of type A6 are in color on plain tablet.

1903, May 26 Typo. Wmk. 2
38 A6 2c red brn & grn 2.25 2.50
39 A6 3c green 1.25 *1.60*
40 A6 6c carmine rose 3.50 1.60
41 A6 12c ol gray & grn 5.25 3.25
42 A6 15c ultra 7.00 3.25
43 A6 18c pale yel grn & rose 5.25 *8.25*
44 A6 30c purple & grn 10.00 *19.00*
45 A6 45c brown & rose 8.75 *19.00*
46 A6 75c yel & pur 12.50 *35.00*
47 A6 1.50r black & rose 55.00 *87.50*
48 A6 2.25r red vio & grn 50.00 *110.00*
Nos. 38-48 (11) 160.75 *290.95*

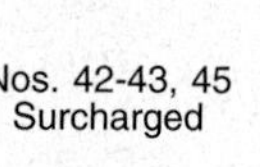
Nos. 42-43, 45 Surcharged

1903
49 A6 3c on 15c 1.40 *4.25*
50 A6 3c on 18c 4.00 *52.50*
51 A6 3c on 45c 4.25 *4.25*
Nos. 49-51 (3) 9.65 *61.00*

Type of 1903

1906 Wmk. 3
52 A6 2c red brn & grn 1.90 *5.50*
53 A6 3c green 1.90 1.90
54 A6 6c car rose 2.50 1.00
55 A6 12c ol gray & grn 4.00 4.00
56 A6 15c ultra 4.00 *2.50*
57 A6 18c pale yel grn & rose 4.00 *8.00*
58 A6 30c purple & grn 7.75 *10.00*
59 A6 45c brown & rose 4.00 *14.00*
60 A6 75c yellow & pur 11.00 *67.50*
61 A6 1.50r black & rose 65.00 *72.50*
62 A6 2.25r red vio & grn 55.00 *72.50*
Nos. 52-62 (11) 161.05 *259.40*

King George V — A7

Numerals of 75c, 1.50r and 2.25r of type A7 are in color on plain tablet.

1912 *Perf. 14*
63 A7 2c org brn & grn 1.00 *7.50*
64 A7 3c green 6.25 .70
65 A7 6c car rose 4.75 3.00
66 A7 12c ol gray & grn 1.50 *6.75*
67 A7 15c ultra 5.00 1.75
68 A7 18c pl yel grn & rose 3.50 *12.50*
69 A7 30c pur & grn 14.00 3.00
70 A7 45c brn & rose 3.00 *50.00*
71 A7 75c yell & pur 3.25 *7.00*
72 A7 1.50r blk & rose 13.00 1.10
73 A7 2.25r vio & grn 75.00 3.25
Nos. 63-73 (11) 130.25 96.55

King George V — A8

For description of dies I and II see Dies of British Colonial Stamps in the Table of Contents.

The 5c of type A8 has a colorless numeral on solid-color tablet. Numerals of 9c, 20c, 25c, 50c, 75c, and 1r to 5r of type A8 are in color on plain tablet.

1917-20 Die I
74 A8 2c org brn & grn .55 *3.00*
75 A8 3c green 2.25 1.40
76 A8 5c brown ('20) 4.50 *14.00*
77 A8 6c carmine rose 4.75 1.60
78 A8 12c gray 2.60 1.75
79 A8 15c ultra 1.90 1.60
80 A8 18c violet, *yel* 4.75 *60.00*
a. Die II ('20) 4.25 *27.50*
81 A8 25c blk & red, *yel* ('20) 4.25 *52.50*
a. Die II ('20) 5.25 *19.00*
82 A8 30c dull vio & ol grn 1.60 *16.00*
83 A8 45c dull vio & org 3.75 *50.00*
84 A8 50c dull vio & blk ('20) 13.00 *62.50*
85 A8 75c blk, *bl grn*, ol back 2.25 *27.50*
a. 75c blk, *emer* (Die II) ('20) 1.50 *25.00*
86 A8 1r dl vio & red ('20) 23.00 *70.00*
87 A8 1.50r vio & bl, *bl* 10.00 *57.50*
a. Die II ('20) 22.00 *35.00*
88 A8 2.25r gray grn & dp vio 55.00 *160.00*
89 A8 5r gray grn & ultra ('20) 140.00 *275.00*
Nos. 74-89 (16) 274.15 *854.35*

Die II

1921-32 Ordinary Paper Wmk. 4
91 A8 2c org brn & grn .30 .25
92 A8 3c green 1.90 .25
93 A8 3c black ('22) 1.10 .35
94 A8 4c green ('22) 1.10 *2.75*
95 A8 4c ol grn & rose red ('28) 7.25 *21.00*
96 A8 5c dk brown 1.25 *6.00*
97 A8 6c car rose 4.75 *10.00*
98 A8 6c violet ('22) 1.60 .25
99 A8 9c rose red ('27) 4.00 *4.75*
100 A8 12c gray 3.00 .25
a. Die I ('32) 32.50 .70
101 A8 12c carmine ('22) 2.25 .35
102 A8 15c ultra 2.25 *65.00*
103 A8 15c yellow ('22) 1.10 *3.00*
104 A8 18c violet, *yel* 2.75 *17.00*
105 A8 20c ultra ('22) 1.60 .40

Chalky Paper
106 A8 25c blk & red, *yel* ('25) 3.00 *28.00*
107 A8 30c dull vio & ol grn 1.60 *17.00*
108 A8 45c dull vio & org 1.40 *5.75*
109 A8 50c dull vio & blk 2.75 2.50
110 A8 75c blk, *emer* ('24) 9.00 *24.00*
111 A8 1r dull vio & red 29.00 *20.00*
a. Die I ('32) 12.50 *37.50*
112 A8 1.50r vio & bl, *bl* ('24) 17.50 *25.00*
113 A8 2.25r green & vio 21.00 *16.00*
114 A8 5r green & ultra 120.00 *175.00*
Nos. 91-114 (24) 241.45 *444.85*

Common Design Types pictured following the introduction.

Silver Jubilee Issue
Common Design Type

1935, May 6 Engr. *Perf. 11x12*
118 CD301 6c black & ultra 1.00 *2.75*
119 CD301 12c indigo & grn 4.50 1.75
120 CD301 20c ultra & brown 3.25 5.50
121 CD301 1r brn vio & indigo 7.00 *30.00*
Nos. 118-121 (4) 15.75 *40.00*
Set, never hinged 27.00

Coronation Issue
Common Design Type

1937, May 12 *Perf. 11x11½*
122 CD302 6c olive green .30 .25
123 CD302 12c deep orange .45 *.55*
124 CD302 20c deep ultra .45 *1.10*
Nos. 122-124 (3) 1.20 *1.90*
Set, never hinged 2.00

Coco-de-mer Palm — A9

Seychelles Giant Tortoise — A10

Fishing Canoe — A11

Ordinary or Chalky Paper

Perf. 13½x14½, 14½x13½

1938-41 Photo. Wmk. 4

Ordinary Paper
125 A9 2c violet brown .25 *1.75*
126 A10 3c green 7.25 3.00
127 A10 3c orange ('41) .75 *1.50*
128 A11 6c orange 10.00 3.75
129b A11 6c green ('41) 1.50 *2.00*
130 A9 9c rose red 11.00 4.25
131 A9 9c peacock blue ('45) 4.75 3.25
132 A10 12c violet 30.00 1.75
133 A10 15c copper red 5.75 *4.75*
134 A9 18c rose lake 5.50 3.75
135 A11 20c brt bl ('41) 27.50 6.25
136 A11 20c ocher 2.00 *3.25*
137 A9 25c ocher 30.00 15.00
138 A10 30c rose lake 30.00 12.00
139 A10 30c bright blue 1.90 *6.50*
140 A11 45c brown 3.00 3.00
141 A9 50c dl lil ('49) 3.50 4.00
142 A10 75c gray blue 52.50 52.50
143 A10 75c dull violet 2.50 *9.00*
144 A11 1r yel grn 90.00 *90.00*
145 A11 1r gray 3.50 *6.50*
146 A9 1.50r ultra 5.75 *18.00*
147 A10 2.25r olive bister 19.50 *40.00*
148 A11 5r copper red 19.50 *16.00*
Nos. 125-148 (24) 367.90 311.75
Set, never hinged 600.00

Issued: Nos. 126, 128, 132, 135, 137, 1/1; Nos. 125, 130, 138, 140-142, 144, 146-148, 2/10; others, 8/8/41.

See Nos. 158-169, 174-188.

For detailed listings, see the Scott Classic Specialized catalogue.

Catalogue values for unused stamps in this section, from this point to the end of the section, are for Never Hinged items.

Peace Issue
Common Design Type
Perf. 13½x14

1946, Sept. 23 Engr. Wmk. 4
149 CD303 9c light blue .25 .25
150 CD303 30c dark blue .30 .25

Silver Wedding Issue
Common Design Types

1948, Nov. 11 Photo. *Perf. 14x14½*
151 CD304 9c bright ultra .25 *.75*

Engraved; Name Typographed
Perf. 11½x11
152 CD305 5r rose carmine 16.00 *47.50*

UPU Issue
Common Design Types
Perf. 13½, 11x11½

1949, Oct. 10 Engr.
153 CD306 18c red violet .25 .25
154 CD307 50c dp rose violet 1.75 *3.25*
155 CD308 1r gray .55 .40
156 CD309 2.25r olive .45 *1.25*
Nos. 153-156 (4) 3.00 5.15

Types of 1938-41 Redrawn and

Sailfish — A12

Map — A13

Perf. 14½x13½, 13½x14½

1952, Mar. 3 Photo. Wmk. 4
157 A12 2c violet .75 .75
158 A10 3c orange .75 .30
159 A9 9c chalky blue .70 *1.75*
160 A11 15c yellow green .60 *1.00*
161 A13 18c rose lake 1.75 .25
162 A11 20c ocher 2.00 1.50
163 A10 25c bright red .80 3.25
164 A12 40c ultra 1.25 2.50
165 A11 45c violet brown 1.50 .35
166 A9 50c brt violet 1.40 1.75
167 A13 1r gray 4.75 4.25
168 A9 1.50r brt blue 11.00 *17.50*
169 A10 2.25r olive bister 17.50 *20.00*
170 A13 5r copper red 18.00 *21.00*
171 A12 10r green 25.00 *47.50*
Nos. 157-171 (15) 87.75 *123.65*

The redrawn design shows a new portrait of King George VI surmounted by crown, as on type A12.

Nos. 157-170 exist with watermark 4a (error). See the *Scott Classic Specialized Catalogue of Stamps and Covers* for listings.

Coronation Issue
Common Design Type

1953, June 2 Engr. *Perf. 13½x13*
172 CD312 9c dark blue & blk .80 .80

Types of 1938-52 with Portrait of Queen Elizabeth II

Perf. 14½x13½, 13½x14½

1954-56 Photo.
173 A12 2c violet .25 .25
174 A10 3c orange .25 .25
175 A9 9c peacock blue .25 .25
176 A9 10c blue ('56) .70 *2.25*
177 A11 15c yellow grn 2.50 .30
178 A13 18c rose lake .25 .25
179 A11 20c ocher 1.50 .50
180 A10 25c bright red 2.50 1.25
181 A13 35c mag ('56) 6.50 1.75
182 A12 40c ultra 1.00 .25
183 A11 45c violet brn .25 .25
184 A9 50c brt violet .35 .80
185 A11 70c vio brn ('56) 7.50 2.25
186 A13 1r gray 1.75 .60
187 A9 1.50r brt blue 11.00 *14.00*
188 A10 2.25r olive bister 9.50 *9.50*
189 A13 5r copper red 18.00 10.00
190 A12 10r green 28.00 18.00
Nos. 173-190 (18) 92.05 62.70

Issued: 10c, 35c, 70c, 9/15/56; others, 2/1/54.

For surcharge see No. 193.

"Stone of Possession" — A14

Perf. 14½x14

1956, Nov. 15 Wmk. 4
191 A14 40c ultra .25 .25
192 A14 1r gray black .30 .30

Bicentenary of French colonization.

No. 183 Surcharged "5 cents" and Bars

1957, Sept. 16 *Perf. 13½x14½*
193 A11 5c on 45c violet brn .50 .50
a. Double surcharge 550.00
b. Thick bars omitted 1,100.

The "c," "e" or "s" of surcharge may be found in italic.

Flying Fox — A15

1957, Oct. 25 ***Perf. 14½x13½***
194 A15 5c light violet 2.75 .30

Mauritius Stamp of 1859 with Seychelles "B64" Cancellation A16

Engr. & Typo.
Perf. 11½x11
1961, Dec. 11 **Wmk. 314**
Stamp in Dull Blue & Black
195 A16 10c lilac .30 .25
196 A16 35c dull green .40 .25
197 A16 2.25r orange brown 1.10 1.10
Nos. 195-197 (3) 1.80 1.60

1st post office in Victoria, Seychelles, cent.

Black Parrot — A17

Anse Royal Bay — A18

Designs: 10c, Vanilla. 15c, Fisherman. 20c, Denis Island Lighthouse. 25c, Clock Tower, Victoria. 30c, 35c, Anse Royal Bay. 40c, Government House. 45c, Fishing boat. 50c, Cascade Church. 60c, Flying fox. 70c, 85c, Sailfish. 75c, Coco-de-mer palm. 1r, Cinnamon. 1.50r, Copra. 2.25r, Map of Indian Ocean. 3.50r, Settlers' homes. 5r, Regina Mundi Convent. 10r, Badge of Seychelles.

Perf. 14½x13½, 13½x14½
1962-69 **Photo.** **Wmk. 314**
Size: 24x31mm, 31x24mm
198 A17 5c multicolored 3.25 .25
a. Wmkd. sideways ('67) .35 *2.25*
199 A17 10c multicolore 1.50 .25
a. Wmkd. sideways ('68) .30 .25
200 A17 15c multicolored .35 .25
201 A17 20c multicolored .40 .25
202 A17 25c multicolored .50 .25
202A A18 30c multicolored 8.50 *6.00*
203 A18 35c multicolored 2.00 2.25
204 A18 40c multicolored .25 *1.00*
204A A18 45c multicolored 3.75 *5.50*
205 A17 50c multicolored .45 .30
b. Wmkd. sideways ('69) 1.75 3.75
205A A17 60c multicolored 2.00 .50
206 A17 70c multicolored 7.00 3.25
206A A17 75c multicolored 2.75 *4.25*
206B A17 85c multicolored 1.10 .45
207 A18 1r multicolored 1.00 .25
208 A18 1.50r multicolored 5.50 *7.00*
209 A18 2.25r multicolored 5.50 8.00
210 A18 3.50r multicolored 2.50 *7.00*
211 A18 5r multicolored 8.00 2.75

Perf. 13x14
Size: 22½x39mm
212 A17 10r multicolored 16.00 4.00
Nos. 198-212 (20) 72.30 53.75

Issued: 45c, 75c, 8/1/66; No. 198a, 2/7/67; 30c, 60c, 85c, 7/15/68; others 2/21/62.
The 60c and 85c have watermark sideways.
For surcharges and overprints see Nos. 216-217, 233-236, 241-243.
For overprints see British Indian Ocean Territory Nos. 1-15.

Freedom from Hunger Issue
Common Design Type
1963, June 4 ***Perf. 14x14½***
213 CD314 70c lilac .85 .35

Red Cross Centenary Issue
Common Design Type
1963, Sept. 2 **Litho.** ***Perf. 13***
214 CD315 10c black & red .25 .25
215 CD315 75c ultra & red .75 *1.25*

Nos. 203 and 206 Surcharged with New Value and Bars
Perf. 14x14½, 14½x14
1965, Apr. **Photo.** **Wmk. 314**
216 A18 45c on 35c .25 .25
217 A17 75c on 70c .50 .40

ITU Issue
Common Design Type
Perf. 11x11½
1965, June 1 **Litho.** **Wmk. 314**
218 CD317 5c orange & vio bl .25 .25
219 CD317 1.50r red lil & apple grn .50 .35

Intl. Cooperation Year Issue
Common Design Type
1965, Oct. 25 ***Perf. 14½***
220 CD318 5c blue grn & claret .25 .25
221 CD318 40c lt violet & green .55 .35

Churchill Memorial Issue
Common Design Type
1966, Jan. 24 **Photo.** ***Perf. 14***
Design in Black, Gold and Carmine Rose
222 CD319 5c bright blue .25 .40
223 CD319 15c green .35 .30
224 CD319 75c brown 1.00 .40
225 CD319 1.50r violet 1.60 *3.25*
Nos. 222-225 (4) 3.20 4.35

World Cup Soccer Issue
Common Design Type
1966, July 1 **Litho.** ***Perf. 14***
226 CD321 15c multicolored .25 .25
227 CD321 1r multicolored .60 .50

WHO Headquarters Issue
Common Design Type
1966, Sept. 20 **Litho.** ***Perf. 14***
228 CD322 20c multicolored .45 .30
229 CD322 50c multicolored .80 .35

UNESCO Anniversary Issue
Common Design Type
1966, Dec. 1 **Litho.** ***Perf. 14***
230 CD323 15c "Education" .25 .25
231 CD323 1r "Science" .55 .55
232 CD323 5r "Culture" 1.60 1.60
Nos. 230-232 (3) 2.40 2.40

Nos. 200, 204A, 206A and 210 Overprinted "UNIVERSAL / ADULT / SUFFRAGE / 1967"
Perf. 14½x14, 14x14½
1967, Sept. 18 **Photo.** **Wmk. 314**
233 A17 15c multicolored .25 .25
234 A18 45c brt bl & multi .25 .25
235 A17 75c multicolored .25 .25
236 A18 3.50r multicolored .25 *.50*
Nos. 233-236 (4) 1.00 1.25

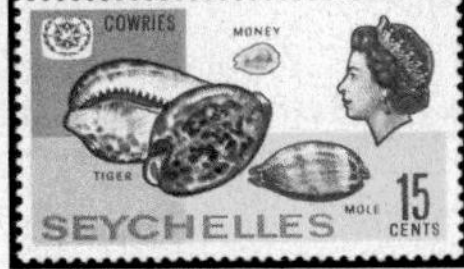

Cowries: Tiger, Mole, Money A19

Sea Shells (ITY Emblem and): 40c, Textile, betulinus and virgin cones. 1r, Arthritic spider conch. 2.25r, Triton and subulate auger.

Perf. 14x13½
1967, Dec. 4 **Photo.** **Wmk. 314**
237 A19 15c multicolored .30 .25
238 A19 40c multicolored .40 .25
239 A19 1r multicolored .55 .40
240 A19 2.25r multicolored .90 *1.10*
Nos. 237-240 (4) 2.15 2.00

Issued for International Tourist Year, 1967.

Nos. 204, 204A and 206A Surcharged
Perf. 14x14½, 14½x14
1968, Apr. 16 **Photo.** **Wmk. 314**
241 A18 30c on 40c multicolored .25 *.50*
242 A18 60c on 45c blue & yel .25 .25
243 A17 85c on 75c multicolored .30 .30
Nos. 241-243 (3) .80 1.05

The surcharge on No. 241 includes 2 bars; on Nos. 242-243 it includes 3 bars and "CENTS."

Family, Rising Sun and Human Rights Flame A20

Perf. 14½x14
1968, Sept. 2 **Litho.** **Wmk. 314**
244 A20 20c chocolate & multi .25 .25
245 A20 50c vio blue & multi .25 .25
246 A20 85c black & multi .25 .25
247 A20 2.25r brown & multi .25 *1.40*
Nos. 244-247 (4) 1.00 2.15

International Human Rights Year.

First Landing on Praslin Island — A21

Designs: 50c, La Digue and La Curieuse at anchor, vert. 85c, Coco-de-mer and black parrot, vert. 2.25r, La Digue and La Curieuse under sail.

Litho.; Head Embossed in Gold
Perf. 14x14½
1968, Dec. 30 **Wmk. 314**
248 A21 20c multicolored .30 .25
249 A21 50c dk blue, blk & red .40 .35
250 A21 85c rose red & multi 1.00 .40
251 A21 2.25r ultra & multi 1.50 *3.00*
Nos. 248-251 (4) 3.20 4.00

Landing on Praslin Island of the Chevalier Marion Dufresne expedition, 200th anniv.

Separation of Rocket and Spacecraft — A22

5c, Launching of Apollo XI, vert. 50c, Landing module & men on the moon. 85c, Seychelles tracking station. 2.25r, Moonscape & earth.

1969, Sept. 9 **Litho.** ***Perf. 13½***
252 A22 5c multicolored .25 .25
253 A22 20c multicolored .25 .25
254 A22 50c multicolored .30 .25
255 A22 85c multicolored .40 .35
256 A22 2.25r multicolored .65 *1.50*
Nos. 252-256 (5) 1.85 2.60

See note after US No. C76.

Lazare Picault Landing in 1741 — A23

History of Seychelles: 10c, US satellite tracking station. 15c, German cruiser Königsberg at Aldabra, 1915. 20c, British fleet refueling, St. Anne, 1939-45. 25c, Ashanti King Prempeh in exile, 1896. 30c, 40c, Stone of Possession placed, 1756. 50c, 65c, Pirates. 60c, Corsairs. 85c, 95c, Jet and airport. 1r, First capitulation of the French to the British, 1794. 1.50r, Battle between the sailing vessels Sybille and Chiffone, 1801. 3.50r, Visit of Duke of Edinburgh, 1956. 5r, Chevalier Queau de Quincy. 10r, Map of Indian Ocean, 1574. 15r, Seychelles coat of arms.

Perf. 13x12½
1969-72 **Litho.** **Wmk. 314**
257 A23 5c multicolored .25 .25
258 A23 10c multicolored .25 .25
259 A23 15c multicolored 3.00 2.25
260 A23 20c multicolored 2.00 .25
261 A23 25c multicolored .25 .25
262 A23 30c multicolored 1.25 *4.00*
262A A23 40c multicolored 3.00 1.25
263 A23 50c multicolored .40 .25
264 A23 60c multicolored 1.25 *1.50*
264A A23 65c multicolored 6.00 *8.00*
265 A23 85c multicolored 3.50 2.00
265A A23 95c multicolored 6.50 4.25
266 A23 1r multicolored .40 .25
267 A23 1.50r multicolored 2.00 *2.25*
268 A23 3.50r multicolored 1.25 *2.25*
269 A23 5r multicolored 1.25 *3.00*
270 A23 10r multicolored 2.75 *8.00*
271 A23 15r multicolored 4.50 *14.00*
Nos. 257-271 (18) 39.80 54.25

Issued: 40, 65, 95c, 12/11/72; others, 11/3/69.
For overprints & surcharges see Nos. 294-298, 323-330, 361-369.

St. Anne Island, Ship and Gulls A24

Designs: 50c, Flying fish, island and ship. 85c, Map of Seychelles and compass rose. 3.50r, Anchor, chain on sea bottom.

1970, Apr. 27 ***Perf. 14***
272 A24 20c multicolored 1.00 .60
273 A24 50c multicolored .55 .45
274 A24 85c multicolored .55 .45
275 A24 3.50r multicolored .80 *1.25*
Nos. 272-275 (4) 2.90 2.75

Bicentenary of first settlement on St. Anne.

Girl and Eye Chart A25

Designs: 50c, Infant on scales and milk bottles. 85c, Mother and child, vert. 3.50r, Red Cross branch headquarters.

1970, Aug. 4 **Litho.** **Wmk. 314**
276 A25 20c lt blue & multi .35 .25
277 A25 50c multicolored .50 .50
278 A25 85c multicolored .70 .70
279 A25 3.50r multicolored 1.50 2.60
Nos. 276-279 (4) 3.05 4.05

Centenary of British Red Cross Society.

Pitcher Plant — A26

Flowers: 50c, Wild vanilla. 85c, Tropic-bird flower. 3.50r, Vare hibiscus.

1970, Dec. 29 ***Perf. 14½***
280 A26 20c multicolored .35 .25
281 A26 50c multicolored .45 .45
282 A26 85c multicolored 1.00 1.00
283 A26 3.50r multicolored 3.50 2.25
a. Souvenir sheet of 4, #280-283 7.75 *13.00*
Nos. 280-283 (4) 5.30 3.95

Souvenir Sheet

Map Showing Location of Seychelles — A27

Perf. 13½x14

1971, Apr. 20 Litho. Wmk. 314

284 A27 5r yellow grn & multi 4.00 *9.00*

Issued to publicize Seychelles' location.

Consolidated Catalina Amphibian — A28

Designs: 5c, Piper Navajo, vert. 20c, Westland Wessex, vert. 60c, Grumman Albatross amphibian, vert. 85c, "G" class Short Brothers flying boat. 3.50r, Vickers supermarine "Walrus" amphibian.

Perf. 14x14½, 14½x14

1971, June 28 Litho. Wmk. 314

285 A28 5c orange & multi .25 .25
286 A28 20c purple & multi .25 .25
287 A28 50c olive & multi .65 .25
288 A28 60c sepia & multi .80 .30
289 A28 85c brown & multi 1.10 .40
290 A28 3.50r blue & multi 7.00 3.00
Nos. 285-290 (6) 10.05 4.45

Completion of Seychelles Airport.

Santa Claus, by Jean-Claude Waye Hive — A29

Christmas (Children's Drawings): 15c, Santa Claus riding a tortoise, by Edison Thérésine. 3.50r, Santa Claus on the seashore, by Isabelle Tirant.

1971, Oct. 12 ***Perf. 13½***

291 A29 10c dark blue & multi .25 .25
292 A29 15c dark green & multi .25 .25
293 A29 3.50r violet & multi .50 *2.00*
Nos. 291-293 (3) 1.00 2.50

Nos. 262, 264-265 Surcharged with New Value and 5 Bars

1971, Dec. 21 ***Perf. 13x12½***

294 A23 40c on 30c multicolored .55 *.65*
295 A23 65c on 60c multicolored .65 *.80*
296 A23 95c on 85c multicolored .80 *1.10*
Nos. 294-296 (3) 2.00 2.55

Nos. 260, 269 Overprinted in Black or Gold "ROYAL VISIT 1972"

1972, Mar. 21 Litho. Wmk. 314

297 A23 20c multicolored .25 .25
298 A23 5r multicolored (G) 1.40 *2.75*

Visit of Elizabeth II and Prince Philip.

Brush Warbler — A30

20c, Scops owl. 50c, Blue pigeons. 65c, Magpie robin. 95c, Paradise flycatchers. 3.50r, Kestrel.

1972, July 15 ***Perf. 14x13½***

299 A30 5c shown 1.00 .50
300 A30 20c multi 2.50 .50
301 A30 50c multi 2.75 .60
302 A30 65c multi 3.00 .65
303 A30 95c multi 3.00 2.75
304 A30 3.50r multi 8.00 *12.00*
a. Souvenir sheet of 6, #299-304 37.50 *40.00*
Nos. 299-304 (6) 20.25 17.00

Fireworks — A31

15c, Canoe race, horiz. 25c, Women in local costumes. 5r, Water-skiing, horiz.

1972, Sept. 18 Litho. ***Perf. 14***

305 A31 10c shown .30 .25
306 A31 15c multi .30 .25
307 A31 25c multi .30 .25
308 A31 5r multi .70 1.00
Nos. 305-308 (4) 1.60 1.75

Seychelles Festival 1972.

Silver Wedding Issue, 1972

Common Design Type

Design: Queen Elizabeth II, Prince Philip, giant tortoise and leaping sailfish.

1972, Nov. 20 Photo. ***Perf. 14x14½***

309 CD324 95c multicolored .25 .25
310 CD324 1.50r multicolored .65 .65

Princess Anne's Wedding Issue

Common Design Type

1973, Nov. 14 Litho. ***Perf. 14***

311 CD325 95c ocher & multi .30 .30
312 CD325 1.50r slate & multi .35 .35

Soldierfish — A32

Wmk. 314

1974, Mar. 5 Litho. ***Perf. 14***

313 A32 20c shown .30 .25
314 A32 50c Filefish .50 .25
315 A32 95c Butterflyfish 1.00 .60
316 A32 1.50r Gaterin 2.40 2.40
Nos. 313-316 (4) 4.20 3.50

Envelope and Globe — A33

UPU, cent.: 50c, Globe with location of Seychelles and radio tower. 95c, Cancellation and globe. 1.50r, "UPU" with emblems.

Perf. 12½x12

1974, Oct. 9 Wmk. 314

317 A33 20c multicolored .25 .25
318 A33 50c multicolored .25 .25
319 A33 95c multicolored .30 .30
320 A33 1.50r multicolored .50 .50
Nos. 317-320 (4) 1.30 1.30

Winston Churchill A34

Design: 1.50r, Churchill, different portrait.

1974, Nov. 30 Litho. ***Perf. 14½***

321 A34 95c lt blue & multi .25 .25
322 A34 1.50r lt green & multi .55 .55
a. Souvenir sheet of 2, #321-322 .90 *1.60*

Sir Winston Churchill (1874-1965).

Nos. 260, 263, 265A and 267 Overprinted in Black or Silver

Perf. 13x12½

1975, Feb. 8 Wmk. 314

323 A23 20c multi (B) .30 .25
324 A23 50c multi (B) .30 .25
325 A23 95c multi (S) .35 *.40*
326 A23 1.50r multi (B) .50 *1.50*
Nos. 323-326 (4) 1.45 2.40

Visit of cruise ship Queen Elizabeth II, Mahe, Seychelles.

Nos. 260, 264A, 266, 268 Overprinted in Gold

1975, Oct. 1 Litho. Wmk. 314

327 A23 20c multicolored .25 .25
328 A23 65c multicolored .35 .35
329 A23 1r multicolored .60 .55
330 A23 3.50r multicolored 1.60 2.00
Nos. 327-330 (4) 2.80 3.15

Queen Elizabeth I A35

Portraits: 15c, Gladys Aylward. 20c, Elizabeth Fry. 25c, Emmeline Pankhurst. 65c, Florence Nightingale. 1r, Amy Johnson. 1.50r, Joan of Arc. 3.50r, Eleanor Roosevelt.

Wmk. 314

1975, Dec. 15 Litho. ***Perf. 13½***

331 A35 10c dp brown & multi .25 .25
332 A35 15c dk brown & multi .25 .25
333 A35 20c dk green & multi .25 .25
334 A35 25c purple & multi .25 .25
335 A35 65c dk blue & multi .45 .40
336 A35 1r Prus blue & multi .70 .65
337 A35 1.50r dp violet & multi .75 *1.25*
338 A35 3.50r dk olive & multi 1.75 *3.00*
Nos. 331-338 (8) 4.65 6.30

International Women's Year.

Praslin Map and Grand Anse Postmark, 1907 — A36

Designs: 65c, La Digue map and postmark, 1916. 1r, Partial map of Mahé and Victoria postmark, 1917. 1.50r, Southern part of Mahé and Anse Royale postmark, 1938.

1976, Mar. 30 Wmk. 373 ***Perf. 14***

339 A36 20c lt blue & multi .25 .25
340 A36 65c lt blue & multi .35 .35
341 A36 1r lt blue & multi .50 .50
342 A36 1.50r lt blue & multi .70 .70
a. Souvenir sheet of 4, #339-342 3.00 *3.25*
Nos. 339-342 (4) 1.80 1.80

Rural posts of Seychelles.

First Landing, 1609, and James Mancham — A37

Designs: 25c, Stone of Possession. 40c, Arrival of 1st settlers, 1770 (ship). 75c, Le Chevalier Quéau de Quincy. 1r, Sir Bickham Sweet-Escott. 1.25r, Government House. 1.50r, Coat of arms of Internal Self-government. 3.50r, Seychelles flag.

1976, June 29 ***Perf. 14***

343 A37 20c rose & multi .25 .25
344 A37 25c yellow & multi .25 .25
345 A37 40c lilac & multi .25 .25
346 A37 75c green & multi .35 .50
347 A37 1r salmon & multi .55 .55
348 A37 1.25r multicolored .65 .90
349 A37 1.50r ocher & multi .75 .90
350 A37 3.50r blue & multi 1.60 2.00
Nos. 343-350 (8) 4.65 5.60

Seychelles' independence, June 29, 1976.

Flags of Seychelles and US — A38

US bicent.: 10r, State House, Seychelles, and Independence Hall, Philadelphia.

1976, July 12 Litho.

351 A38 1r blue & multi .30 .30
352 A38 10r red & multi 1.40 *3.00*

Swimming — A39

Designs (Olympic Rings and): 65c, Hockey. 1r, Basketball. 3.50r, Soccer.

1976, July 26 ***Perf. 14½***

353 A39 20c vio blue & blk .30 .25
354 A39 65c dk grn, yel grn & blk .45 .25
355 A39 1r brown, grn & blk .45 .25
356 A39 3.50r car rose & blk .70 *2.40*
Nos. 353-356 (4) 1.90 3.15

21st Olympic Games, Montreal, Canada, July 17-Aug. 1.

Seychelles Sunbird — A40

Seychelles Birds (James R. Mancham, Congress Emblem and): 20c, Paradise flycatcher, vert. 1.50r, Gray white-eye. 5r, Black parrot, vert.

Wmk. 373

1976, Nov. 8 Litho. *Perf. 14½*

357 A40 20c multicolored .25 .25
358 A40 1.25r multicolored 1.25 .80
359 A40 1.50r multicolored 1.50 1.10
360 A40 5r multicolored 2.50 *4.00*
a. Souvenir sheet of 4, #357-360 7.50 *10.50*
Nos. 357-360 (4) 5.50 6.15

4th Pan-African Ornithological Cong., Mahe Beach Hotel, Nov. 6-13.

Nos. 260, 263, 265A-266, 268-271, 264A Ovptd. or Srchd. "Independence / 1976"

Perf. 13x12½

1976, Nov. 22 Litho. Wmk. 314

361 A23 20c multicolored 1.00 *2.25*
362 A23 50c multicolored .90 *2.25*
363 A23 95c multicolored 2.50 2.25
364 A23 1r multicolored .90 *2.25*
365 A23 3.50r multicolored 4.00 4.75
366 A23 5r multicolored 3.50 *7.00*
367 A23 10r multicolored 4.75 *12.00*
368 A23 15r multicolored 5.25 *12.00*
369 A23 25r on 65c multi 6.50 *16.00*
Nos. 361-369 (9) 29.30 60.75

Washington's Inauguration — A41

American Bicentennial: 2c, Jefferson and map of Louisiana Purchase. 3c, Seward and map of Alaska Purchase. 4c, Pony Express, 1860. 5c, Lincoln's Emancipation Proclamation, 1863. 1.50r, Completion of Transcontinental Railroad, 1869. 3.50r, Wright Brothers' 1st flight, 1903. 5r, Ford assembly line, 1913. 10r, Kennedy and Apollo 11 moon landing, 1969. 25r, Declaration of Independence, 1776.

Perf. 14x13½

1976, Dec. 21 Wmk. 373

370 A41 1c rose & plum .25 .25
371 A41 2c lilac & vio .25 .25
372 A41 3c blue & vio bl .25 .25
373 A41 4c yellow & brn .25 .25
374 A41 5c brt yel & grn .25 .25
375 A41 1.50r yel brn & brn .55 .55
376 A41 3.50r brt grn & bl grn .80 .80
377 A41 5r yellow & brn 1.10 1.10
378 A41 10r dull bl & dk bl 1.75 1.75
Nos. 370-378 (9) 5.45 5.45

Souvenir Sheet

379 A41 25r lilac rose & pur 5.50 5.50

Seychelles Islands and Arms — A42

The Orb — A43

Designs: 40c, 5r, 10r, similar to 20c. 1r, St. Edward's Crown. 1.25r, Ampulla and Spoon. 1.50r, Scepter with Cross.

1977, Sept. 5 Litho. *Perf. 14*

380 A42 20c multicolored .25 .25
381 A42 40c multicolored .25 .25
382 A43 50c multicolored .25 .25
383 A43 1r multicolored .25 .25
384 A43 1.25r multicolored .25 .25
385 A43 1.50r multicolored .25 .25
386 A42 5r multicolored .30 .30
387 A42 10r multicolored .55 .55
a. Souv. sheet of 4, #380, 382, 383, 387 1.75 2.00
Nos. 380-387 (8) 2.35 2.35

25th anniv. of reign of Elizabeth II.

Coral Reef — A44

5c, Reef fish. 10c, Hawksbill turtle. 15c, Coco de mer. 20c, Wild vanilla. 25c, Butterfly. 40c, Coral reef. 50c, Giant tortoise. 75c, Crayfish. 1r, Madagascar cardinal. 1.25r, Fairy tern. 1.50r, Flying fox. 3.50r, Green gecko. 5r, Octopus, vert. 10r, Tiger cowrie, vert. 15r, Pitcher plant, vert. 20r, Arms, vert.

Sizes: 40c, 1, 1.25, 1.50r, 30x25mm, Others 28x23mm

Without Date Imprint

Perf. 14, 14x14½ (40c, 1, 1.25, 1.50r)

1977-91 Litho. Wmk. 373

388 A44 5c multi .25 1.50
389 A44 10c multi .25 .25
a. Inscribed "1979" .30 .25
c. Inscribed "1982" .30 .25
d. Inscribed "1988" .35 .35
390 A44 15c multi .25 1.25
a. Inscribed "1979" .30 .25
391 A44 20c multi 1.25 .25
c. Inscribed "1982" 4.00 3.25
392 A44 25c multi 1.25 1.50
a. Inscribed "1979" 3.25 3.25
d. Inscribed "1988" 1.50 1.50
393 A44 40c multi .25 .25
a. Inscribed "1979" .30 .25
b. Inscribed "1981" .30 .25
c. Inscribed "1982" .30 .25
394 A44 50c multi .25 .25
a. Inscribed "1979" .60 .25
d. Inscribed "1988" .60 .25
e. Inscribed "1991" .60 .25
f. Wmk. 384, perf. 14x14½, inscr. "1991" .30 .30
395 A44 75c multi .25 .25
a. Inscribed "1979" .75 .45
396 A44 1r multi .35 .30
a. Inscribed "1979" 12.00 1.10
d. Inscribed "1988" 1.50 1.10
397 A44 1.25r multi 1.00 .40
398 A44 1.50r multi 1.00 .45
b. Inscribed "1979" 3.00 .75
398A A44 3r like #399, wmk. 384 2.00 1.75
399 A44 3.50r multi 1.25 2.75

Perf. 13

Size: 27x35mm

400 A44 5r multi 1.90 1.25
401 A44 10r multi 3.75 2.75
402 A44 15r multi 5.00 2.75
403 A44 20r multi 5.50 .275
Nos. 388-403 (17) 25.75 18.18

Issued: 40c, 1r, 1.25r, 1.50r, 10/31/77; Nos. 394a, 398A, 11/1991; others, 1978.
For surcharge see No. 446.

Denomination "R" Instead of "Re." or "Rs."

"1980" Imprint Beneath Design

Sizes: 1.10r, 28x23mm, Others, 30x25mm

Perf. 14x14½, 14 (1.10r)

1981, Jan. 6 Litho.

403A A44 1r like No. 396 .55 .55
b. Inscribed "1982" .55 .55
d. Inscribed "1986" .55 .55
e. Inscribed "1988" .55 .55
f. Inscribed "1990" .55 .55
g. Inscribed "1991" 1.75 1.25
403B A44 1.10r like No. 399 1.00 1.00
a. Inscribed "1981" 2.10 1.75
403C A44 1.25r like No. 397 .75 .75
i. Wmk. 384 ('89) .80 .80
403D A44 1.50r like No. 398 .80 .80
b. Inscribed "1982" .90 1.25
g. Inscribed "1991" .90 1.25

Perf. 13

k. Inscribed "1981" — —
403E A44 5r like No. 400 3.00 3.00
c. Inscribed "1985" 2.25 2.25
j. Perf. 14x14½, Wmk 384 ('90) 4.00 4.00
403F A44 10r like No. 401 6.25 6.25
403G A44 15r like No. 402 9.00 9.00
403H A44 20r like No. 403 12.50 12.50
Nos. 403A-403H (8) 33.85 33.85

See No. 576 for No. 403C with commemorative inscription. For overprint see No. 605.

Cruiser Aurora, Star and Flag — A45

1977, Nov. 7 Unwmk. *Perf. 12*

404 A45 1.50r red, black & gold .80 .65
a. Souvenir sheet 1.75 1.75

60th anniv. of Russian Oct. Revolution.

St. Roch Roman Catholic Church, Bel Ombre — A46

Christmas: 1r, Anglican Cathedral, Victoria. 1.50r, R. C. Cathedral, Victoria. 5r, St. Mark's Anglican Church, Praslin.

Perf. 13½x14

1977, Dec. 5 Wmk. 373

405 A46 20c multicolored .25 .25
406 A46 1r multicolored .25 .25
407 A46 1.50r multicolored .25 .25
408 A46 5r multicolored .25 .40
Nos. 405-408 (4) 1.00 1.15

Calendar Page, June 5, 1977 — A47

1.25r, Hands holding rifle, torch & Seychelles flag. 1.50r, Fisherman & farmer holding hands. 5r, Soldiers & waving children.

Perf. 14x13½

1978, June 5 Litho. Wmk. 373

409 A47 40c multicolored .25 .25
410 A47 1.25r multicolored .25 .25
411 A47 1.50r multicolored .25 .25
412 A47 5r multicolored .40 .40
Nos. 409-412 (4) 1.15 1.15

First anniversary of Liberation Day.

Edward VII, George V, George VI — A48

Designs: 1.50r, Queens Victoria and Elizabeth II. 3r, Queen Victoria Monument, Seychelles. 5r, Queen's Building, Victoria, Seychelles.

1978, Aug. 21 Litho. *Perf. 14*

413 A48 40c multicolored .25 .25
414 A48 1.50r multicolored .25 .25
415 A48 3r multicolored .25 .25
416 A48 5r multicolored .30 .30
a. Souvenir sheet of 4, #413-416 1.25 1.25
Nos. 413-416 (4) 1.05 1.05

25th anniv. of coronation of Elizabeth II.

Gardenia from Aride Island — A49

Designs (Coat of Arms and): 1.25r, Magpie robin of Fregate Island. 1.50r, Seychelles paradise flycatchers. 5r, Green turtle.

Perf. 13½x14

1978, Oct. 16 Litho. Wmk. 373

417 A49 40c multicolored .25 .25
418 A49 1.25r multicolored 2.00 .75
419 A49 1.50r multicolored 2.00 .75
420 A49 5r multicolored 1.75 1.75
Nos. 417-420 (4) 6.00 3.50

"Stone of Possession" — A50

1978, Dec. 15 Litho. *Perf. 13½*

421 A50 20c shown .25 .25
422 A50 1.25r Map, 1782 .25 .25
423 A50 1.50r Clock tower .25 .25
424 A50 5r Pierre Poivre .25 .60
Nos. 421-424 (4) 1.00 1.35

Bicentennary of the founding of Victoria.

Seychelles Fody — A51

Birds: No. 426, Green-backed heron. No. 427, Seychelles bulbul. No. 428, Seychelles cave swiftlets. No. 429, Grayheaded lovebirds.

1979, Feb. 27 Litho. *Perf. 14*

425 A51 2r multicolored .85 .85
426 A51 2r multicolored .85 .85
427 A51 2r multicolored .85 .85
428 A51 2r multicolored .85 .85
429 A51 2r multicolored .85 .85
a. Strip of 5, #425-429 4.50 4.50
Nos. 425-429 (5) 4.25 4.25

Patrice Lumumba — A52

African Liberation Heroes: 2r, Kwame Nkrumah. 2.25r, Dr. Eduardo Mondlane. 5r, Amilcar Cabral.

1979, June 5 Litho. *Perf. 14½*

430 A52 40c violet & blk .25 .25
431 A52 2r dark blue & blk .25 .25
432 A52 2.25r orange brn & blk .25 .25
433 A52 5r olive grn & blk .25 1.00
Nos. 430-433 (4) 1.00 1.75

Coat of Arms, Rowland Hill, Seychelles No. 412 — A53

Coat of Arms, Hill, Seychelles stamps: 2.25r, No. 301. 3r, No. 205. 5r, No. 4.

1979, Aug. 27 Litho. *Perf. 14x14½*

434 A53 40c multicolored .25 .25
435 A53 2.25r multicolored .30 .50
436 A53 3r multicolored .35 .75
Nos. 434-436 (3) .90 1.50

Souvenir Sheet

437 A53 5r multicolored .80 1.10

Sir Rowland Hill (1795-1879), originator of penny postage.

Schoolboy, IYC Emblem — A54

IYC Emblem and: 2.25r, Children. 3r, Boy with ball, vert. 5r, Girl with puppet, vert.

Perf. 14½x14, 14x14½

1979, Oct. 25 Litho.

438 A54 40c multicolored .25 .25
439 A54 2.25r multicolored .25 .25
440 A54 3r multicolored .25 .25
441 A54 5r multicolored .25 .60
Nos. 438-441 (4) 1.00 1.35

International Year of the Child.

Three Kings Bearing Gifts A55

Christmas (Stained Glass Windows): 20c, Angel, vert. 2.25r, Virgin and Child, vert. 5r, Flight into Egypt.

1979, Dec. 3 Litho. *Perf. 14½*

442 A55 20c multicolored .25 .25
443 A55 2.25r multicolored .30 .30
444 A55 3r multicolored .35 .35
Nos. 442-444 (3) .90 .90

Souvenir Sheet

445 A55 5r multicolored .80 .80

No. 399 Surcharged

Wmk. 373

1979, Dec. 7 Litho. *Perf. 14*

446 A44 1.10r on 3.50r multicolored .50 .50

Seychelles Kestrel — A56

Seychelles Kestrel: a, shown. b, Pair. c, Female, eggs. d, Mother and chick. e, Chicks nesting.

1980, Feb. 29 Litho. *Perf. 14*

447 Strip of 5 5.75 5.75
a.-e. A56 2r any single 1.10 1.10

See Nos. 468, 483.

50-Rupee Bank Note, London 1980 Emblem — A57

New Currency: 40c, 1.50r, horiz.

1980, Apr. 18 Litho. *Perf. 14*

448 A57 40c multicolored .25 .25
449 A57 1.50r multicolored .40 .40
450 A57 2.25r multicolored .50 .50
451 A57 5r multicolored .85 .85
a. Souvenir sheet of 4, #448-451 2.25 2.25
Nos. 448-451 (4) 2.00 2.00

London 1980 Intl. Stamp Exhib., May 6-14.

Sprinting, Moscow '80 Emblem — A58

1980, June 13 *Perf. 14½*

452 A58 40c shown .25 .25
453 A58 2.25r Weight lifting .25 .25
454 A58 3r Boxing .35 .35
455 A58 5r Yachting .85 .85
a. Souvenir sheet of 4, #452-455 2.75 2.75
Nos. 452-455 (4) 1.70 1.70

22nd Summer Olympic Games, Moscow, July 19-Aug. 3.

Boeing 747 A59

2.25r, Tour bus. 3r, Ocean liner, pirogue. 5r, Tour motor boat.

1980, Aug. 22 Litho. *Perf. 14*

456 A59 40c shown .25 .25
457 A59 2.25r multicolored .30 .30
458 A59 3r multicolored .50 .50
459 A59 5r multicolored .85 .85
Nos. 456-459 (4) 1.90 1.90

World Tourism Conf., Manila, Sept. 27.

Female Coco-de-Mer Palm Tree — A60

1980, Oct. 31 Litho. *Perf. 14*

460 A60 40c shown .25 .25
461 A60 2.25r Male tree .35 .35
462 A60 3r Bowls .50 .50
463 A60 5r Gourds, canoes .80 .80
a. Souvenir sheet of 4, #460-463 3.00 3.00
Nos. 460-463 (4) 1.90 1.90

Vasco da Gama's San Gabriel, 1497 A61

2.25r, Mascarenhas' Caravel, 1505. 3.50r, Darwin's Beagle, 1831. 5r, Queen Elizabeth 2, 1968.

Wmk. 373

1981, Feb. Litho. *Perf. 14½*

464 A61 40c multi .25 .25
465 A61 2.25r multi .55 .55
466 A61 3.50r multi .75 .75
467 A61 5r multi .95 .95
a. Souvenir sheet of 4, #464-467 3.50 3.50
Nos. 464-467 (4) 2.50 2.50

Bird Type of 1980

1981, Apr. 10 Litho. *Perf. 14*

468 Strip of 5, multi 6.50 6.50
a. A56 2r Male fairy tern 1.25 1.25
b. A56 2r Pair 1.25 1.25
c. A56 2r Female on nest 1.25 1.25
d. A56 2r Female on nest, egg 1.25 1.25
e. A56 2r Adult bird, chick 1.25 1.25

Prince Charles, Lady Diana, Royal Yacht Charlotte A61a

Prince Charles and Lady Diana — A61b

Wmk. 380

1981, June 23 Litho. *Perf. 14*

469 A61a 1.50r Couple, Victoria & Albert I .25 .25
a. Bklt. pane of 4, perf. 12 1.10
470 A61b 1.50r Couple .45 .45
471 A61a 5r Cleveland .55 .55
472 A61b 5r like #470 1.50 1.50
a. Bklt. pane of 2, perf. 12 1.75
473 A61a 10r Britannia 1.25 1.25
474 A61b 10r like #470 3.25 3.25
Nos. 469-474 (6) 7.25 7.25

Each denomination issued in sheets of 7 (6 type A61a, 1 type A61b).
For surcharges see Nos. 528-533.

Souvenir Sheet

1981 Litho. *Perf. 12*

474A A61b 7.50r Couple 2.25 2.25

Seychelles Intl. Airport, 10th Anniv. — A62

40c, Britten-Norman Islander. 2.25r, Britten-Norman Trislander. 3.50r, Vickers VC-10. 5r, Boeing 747.

Wmk. 373

1981, July 27 Litho. *Perf. 14½*

475 A62 40c multicolored .25 .25
476 A62 2.25r multicolored .65 .65
477 A62 3.50r multicolored .90 .90
478 A62 5r multicolored 1.25 1.25
Nos. 475-478 (4) 3.05 3.05

Flying Foxes — A63

Designs: 40c, Four in flight. 2.25r, Eating upside down. 3r, On branch. 5r, Hanging upside down.

1981, Oct. 9 Litho. *Perf. 14*

479 A63 40c multicolored .25 .25
480 A63 2.25r multicolored .35 .35
481 A63 3r multicolored .50 .50
482 A63 5r multicolored .90 .90
a. Souvenir sheet, #479-482 3.50 3.50
Nos. 479-482 (4) 2.00 2.00

Bird Type of 1980

a, Male Chinese bittern. b, Female. c, Hen on nest. d, Nest, eggs. e, Hen, chicks.

Wmk. 373

1982, Feb. 4 Litho. *Perf. 14*

483 Strip of 5 16.00 16.00
a.-e. A56 3r any single 3.00 3.00

A65

40c, Map of Silhouette Island and La Digue. 1.50r, Denis & Bird Islands. 2.75r, Curieuse Island, Praslin. 7r, Mahe.

1982, Apr. 22 Litho. *Perf. 14½*

487 A65 40c multicolored .25 .25
488 A65 1.50r multicolored .35 .35
489 A65 2.75r multicolored .60 .60
490 A65 7r multicolored 1.50 1.50
a. Souvenir sheet of 4, #487-490 4.00 4.00
Nos. 487-490 (4) 2.70 2.70

5th Anniv. of Liberation A66

40c, Bookmobile. 1.75r, Mobile dental clinic. 2.75r, Farming. 7r, Construction site.

1982, June 5 *Perf. 14*

491 A66 40c multicolored .25 .25
492 A66 1.75r multicolored .25 .25
493 A66 2.75r multicolored .40 .40
494 A66 7r multicolored 1.25 1.25
a. Souvenir sheet of 4, #491-494 4.75 4.75
Nos. 491-494 (4) 2.15 2.15

Tourism A67

Hotels.

1982, Sept. 1

495 A67 1.75r Northolme .35 .35
496 A67 1.75r Reef .35 .35
497 A67 1.75r Barbarons Beach .35 .35
498 A67 1.75r Coral Strand .35 .35
499 A67 1.75r Beau Vallon Bay .35 .35
500 A67 1.75r Fisherman's Cove .35 .35
501 A67 1.75r Mahe Beach .35 .35
502 A67 1.75r Island scene .35 .35
Nos. 495-502 (8) 2.80 2.80

Tata Bus
A68

Wmk. 373

1982, Nov. 18 Litho. *Perf. 14*
503 A68 20c shown .25 .25
504 A68 1.75r Mini moke .35 .35
505 A68 2.75r Ox cart .55 .55
506 A68 7r Truck 1.25 1.25
Nos. 503-506 (4) 2.40 2.40

World Communications Year — A69

40c, Radio control room. 2.75r, Satellite earth station. 3.50fr, TV control room. 5r, Postal services.

1983, Feb. 25
507 A69 40c multicolored .25 .25
508 A69 2.75r multicolored .45 .45
509 A69 3.50r multicolored .60 .60
510 A69 5r multicolored .85 .85
Nos. 507-510 (4) 2.15 2.15

Commonwealth Day — A70

40c, Agricultural research. 2.75r, Food processing plant. 3.50r, Fishing industry. 7r, Flag.

1983, Mar. 14
511 A70 40c multicolored .25 .25
512 A70 2.75r multicolored .25 .25
513 A70 3.50r multicolored .35 .35
514 A70 7r multicolored 1.00 1.00
Nos. 511-514 (4) 1.85 1.85

Denis Isld. Lighthouse, 1910 — A71

2.75r, Seychelles Hospital, 1924. 3.50r, Supreme Court, 1894. 7r, State House, 1911.

1983, July 14 *Perf. 14x13½*
515 A71 40c shown .25 .25
516 A71 2.75r multicolored .25 .25
517 A71 3.50r multicolored .45 .45
518 A71 7r multicolored .90 .90
a. Souvenir sheet of 4, #515-518 5.00 5.00
Nos. 515-518 (4) 1.85 1.85

Manned Flight Bicentenary — A72

40c, Royal Vauxhall balloon, 1836. 1.75r, DeHavilland D.H.-50j. 2.75r, Grumman Albatross. 7r, Swearingen Merlin.

1983, Sept. 15 *Perf. 14*
519 A72 40c multicolored .25 .25
520 A72 1.75r multicolored .55 .55
521 A72 2.75r multicolored .80 .80
522 A72 7r multicolored 1.25 1.25
Nos. 519-522 (4) 2.85 2.85

First Intl. Air Seychelles Flight — A73

1983, Oct. 26 Litho.
523 A73 2r DC10 aircraft 2.50 2.50

Paintings, Marianne North — A74

40c, Swamp Plant and Moorhen. 1.75r, Wormia flagellaria. 2.75r, Asiatic Pancratium. 7r, Pitcher Plant.

1983, Nov. 17 Litho. *Perf. 14*
524 A74 40c multicolored .25 .25
525 A74 1.75r multicolored .45 .45
526 A74 2.75r multicolored .70 .70
527 A74 7r multicolored 1.60 1.60
a. Souvenir sheet of 4, #524-527 6.00 6.00
Nos. 524-527 (4) 3.00 3.00

Nos. 469-474 Surcharged

Wmk. 380

1983, Dec. 28 Litho. *Perf. 14*
528 A61a 50c on 1.50r multi .25 .25
529 A61b 50c on 1.50r multi .25 .25
530 A61a 2.25r on 5r multi 1.40 1.40
531 A61b 2.25r on 5r multi 1.40 1.40
532 A61a 3.75r on 10r multi 2.25 2.25
533 A61b 3.75r on 10r multi 2.25 2.25
Nos. 528-533 (6) 7.80 7.80

Handicrafts — A75

50c, Coconut kettle. 2r, Scarf, doll. 3r, Coconut-fiber roses. 10r, Carved fishing boat, doll.

Wmk. 373

1984, Feb. 29 Litho. *Perf. 14*
534 A75 50c multi .25 .25
535 A75 2r multi .50 .70
536 A75 3r multi .65 1.00
537 A75 10r multi 2.00 3.75
Nos. 534-537 (4) 3.40 5.70

Lloyd's List Issue

Common Design Type

50c, Port Victoria. 2r, Steamship, 1930s. 3r, Cruise liner. 10r, Ennerdale.

1984, May 21 Litho. *Perf. 14½x14*
538 CD335 50c multi .25 .25
539 CD335 2r multi .75 .75
540 CD335 3r multi 1.00 1.00
541 CD335 10r multi 3.00 3.00
Nos. 538-541 (4) 5.00 5.00

People's United Party, 20th Anniv. A76

50c, Original headquarters. 2r, Liberation statue, vert. 3r, New headquarters. 10r, Pres. Rene, vert.

1984, June 2 Litho. *Perf. 14*
542 A76 50c multicolored .25 .25
543 A76 2r multicolored .40 .40
544 A76 3r multicolored .60 .60
545 A76 10r multicolored 1.25 1.25
Nos. 542-545 (4) 2.50 2.50

Souvenir Sheet

UPU Congress — A77

1984, June 18 *Perf. 14½*
546 A77 5r No. 156 3.00 3.00

1984 Summer Olympics A78

1984, July 28 *Perf. 14*
547 A78 50c Long jump .25 .25
548 A78 2r Boxing .45 .45
549 A78 3r Diving .60 .60
550 A78 10r Weight lifting 2.25 2.25
a. Souvenir sheet of 4, #547-550 4.25 4.25
Nos. 547-550 (4) 3.55 3.55

Scuba Diving A79

1984, Sept. 24
551 A79 50c shown .25 .25
552 A79 2r Paragliding .90 .90
553 A79 3r Sailing 1.25 1.25
554 A79 10r Water skiing 4.50 4.50
Nos. 551-554 (4) 6.90 6.90

Whale Conservation — A80

1984, Nov. Litho.
555 A80 50c Humpback whale 2.75 2.75
556 A80 2r Sperm whale 4.75 4.75
557 A80 3r Right whale 5.75 5.75
558 A80 10r Blue whale 9.75 9.75
Nos. 555-558 (4) 23.00 23.00

Audubon Birth Bicent. — A81

Bare-legged scops owls.

1985, Mar. 11 Litho. *Perf. 14*
559 A81 50c multicolored 2.50 2.50
560 A81 2r multicolored 4.25 4.25
561 A81 3r multicolored 4.50 4.50
562 A81 10r multicolored 7.75 7.75
Nos. 559-562 (4) 19.00 19.00

EXPO '85, Tsukuba — A82

Wmk. 373

1985, Mar. 15 Litho. *Perf. 14*
563 A82 50c Giant tortoise .30 .30
564 A82 2r Fairy tern 1.60 1.60
565 A82 3r Wind surfing 2.25 2.25
566 A82 5r Coco de mer 3.75 3.75
a. Souvenir sheet of 4, #563-566 9.50 9.50
Nos. 563-566 (4) 7.90 7.90

See No. 604.

Queen Mother 85th Birthday

Common Design Type

50c, Queen Elizabeth, 1930. 2r, With grandchildren, 1970. 3r, 75th birthday celebration. 5r, Holding Prince Henry.
10r, Exiting from helicopter.

Perf. 14½x14

1985, June 7 Litho. Wmk. 384
567 CD336 50c multi .25 .25
568 CD336 2r multi .75 .75
569 CD336 3r multi 1.10 1.10
570 CD336 5r multi 1.60 1.60
Nos. 567-570 (4) 3.70 3.70

Souvenir Sheet

571 CD336 10r multi 5.00 5.00

2nd Indian Ocean Islands Games A83

1985, Aug. 24
572 A83 50c Boxing .25 .25
573 A83 2r Soccer .80 .80
574 A83 3r Swimming 1.25 1.25
575 A83 10r Wind surfing 4.25 4.25
Nos. 572-575 (4) 6.55 6.55

Air Seychelles 1st Airbus — A83a

1985, Nov. 1 Wmk. 384
576 A83a 1.25r Fairy tern 3.25 3.25

Intl. Youth Year — A84

1985, Nov. 28
577 A84 50c Agriculture .25 .25
578 A84 2r Construction .70 .70
579 A84 3r Carpentry 1.00 1.00
580 A84 10r Science education 3.25 3.25
Nos. 577-580 (4) 5.20 5.20

Vintage Cars A85

50c, 1919 Ford Model T. 2r, 1922 Austin Seven. 3r, 1924 Morris Bullnose Oxford. 10r, 1929 Humber Coupe.

1985, Dec. 18

581	A85	50c multicolored	.25	.25
582	A85	2r multicolored	1.40	1.40
583	A85	3r multicolored	1.60	1.60
584	A85	10r multicolored	5.50	5.50
		Nos. 581-584 (4)	8.75	8.75

Halley's Comet — A86

Perf. 14x14½

1986, Feb. 28 **Wmk. 384**

585	A86	50c Transit instrument	.25	.25
586	A86	2r Quadrant	.75	.75
587	A86	3r Trajectory diagram	1.25	1.25
588	A86	10r Edmond Halley	3.50	3.50
		Nos. 585-588 (4)	5.75	5.75

Giselle, Performed by the Ballet Louvre, Apr. 4-8 — A87

Wmk. 384

1986, Apr. 4 **Litho.** ***Perf. 14***

589	A87	2r Heroine	.80	.80
590	A87	3r Hero	1.10	1.10

Souvenir Sheet

591	A87	10r United	3.75	3.75

First ballet performed in the Seychelles.

Queen Elizabeth II 60th Birthday

Common Design Type

Designs: 50c, Marrying the Duke of Edinburgh, 1947. 1.25r, State opening of Parliament, 1982. 2r, Greeting child aboard the Britannia, Qatar Harbor. 3r, Silver Jubilee celebration. 5r, Visiting Crown Agents' offices, 1983.

1986, Apr. 21 ***Perf. 14½***

592	CD337	50c scarlet, blk & sil	.25	.25
593	CD337	1.25r ultra & multi	.25	.25
594	CD337	2r green & multi	.45	.45
595	CD337	3r violet & multi	.65	.65
596	CD337	5r rose vio & multi	1.10	1.10
		Nos. 592-596 (5)	2.70	2.70

For overprints see Nos. 625-629.

AMERIPEX '86, Inter-island Communications — A88

50c, La Digue Ferry. 2r, Phone booth, vert. 3r, Victoria P.O., vert. 7r, Air Seychelles trislander.

Wmk. 384

1986, May 22 **Litho.** ***Perf. 14***

597	A88	50c multicolored	.35	.35
598	A88	2r multicolored	1.40	1.40
599	A88	3r multicolored	2.40	2.40
600	A88	7r multicolored	5.50	5.50
		Nos. 597-600 (4)	9.65	9.65

Coptic Catholic Knights of Malta Celebration Day — A89

5r, Natl. arms, assoc. emblem.

Perf. 14½x14

1986, June 7 **Litho.** **Wmk. 384**

601	A89	5r multicolored	2.00	2.00
a.		Souvenir sheet of 1	4.25	4.25

Royal Wedding Issue, 1986

Common Design Type

2r, Informal portrait. 10r, Andrew, helicopter.

1986, July 23 **Litho.** ***Perf. 14***

602	CD338	2r multicolored	.50	.50
603	CD338	10r multicolored	2.00	2.00

Tsukuba Expo Type of 1985

Souvenir Sheet

Wmk. 384

1986, July 12 **Litho.** ***Perf. 14***

604		Sheet of 4	6.25	6.25
a.	A82	50c multicolored	.25	.25
b.	A82	2r multicolored	1.25	1.25
c.	A82	3r multicolored	1.75	1.75
d.	A82	5r multicolored	2.75	2.75

No. 604 inscribed "Seychelles Philatelic Exhibition-Tokyo-1986" and printed without EXPO '85 emblem on margin or on individual stamps. Nos. 604a-604d inscribed "1986."

No. 403Ad Overprinted

Perf. 14½x14

1986, Oct. 28 **Wmk. 373**

605	A44	1r multicolored	6.25	6.25

Intl. Creole Day.

State Visit of Pope John Paul II — A90

Pope and: 50c, Seychelles Airport. 2r, Cathedral. 3r, Baie Lazare parish church. 10r, People's Stadium.

1986, Dec. 1 **Wmk. 384** ***Perf. 14½***

606	A90	50c multicolored	.25	.25
607	A90	2r multicolored	1.50	1.50
608	A90	3r multicolored	2.25	2.25
609	A90	10r multicolored	8.00	8.00
a.		Souvenir sheet of 4, #606-609	18.00	18.00
		Nos. 606-609 (4)	12.00	12.00

Butterflies — A91

1r, Melanitis leda. 2r, Phalanta philiberti. 3r, Danaus chrysippus. 10r, Euploea mitra.

Wmk. 384

1987, Feb. 18 **Litho.** ***Perf. 14½***

610	A91	1r multi	.90	.90
611	A91	2r multi	1.75	1.75
612	A91	3r multi	2.50	2.50
613	A91	10r multi	8.75	8.75
		Nos. 610-613 (4)	13.90	13.90

Seashells — A92

1r, Gloripallium pallium. 2r, Spondylus aurantius. 3r, Harpa ventricosa, Lioconcha ornata. 10r, Strombus lentiginosus.

1987, May 7 **Wmk. 373**

614	A92	1r multi	1.10	1.10
615	A92	2r multi	2.25	2.25
616	A92	3r multi	3.25	3.25
617	A92	10r multi	10.00	10.00
		Nos. 614-617 (4)	16.60	16.60

Liberation, 10th Anniv. — A93

1r, Liberation monument. 2r, Hospital, horiz. 3r, Orphanage, horiz. 10r, Fish monument.

Perf. 14x14½, 14½x14

1987, June 5 **Wmk. 384**

618	A93	1r multi	.25	.25
619	A93	2r multi	.45	.45
620	A93	3r multi	.75	.75
621	A93	10r multi	1.75	1.75
		Nos. 618-621 (4)	3.20	3.20

Natl. Banking Cent. — A94

1r, Savings Bank, Praslin. 2r, Development Bank. 10r, Central Bank.

1987, June 25 ***Perf. 14½x14***

622	A94	1r sage grn & dp ol	.25	.25
623	A94	2r sal & reddish brn	.40	.40
624	A94	10r lt blue & blue	1.50	1.50
		Nos. 622-624 (3)	2.15	2.15

Nos. 592-596 Ovptd. in Silver

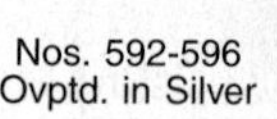

Wmk. 384

1987, Dec. 9 **Litho.** ***Perf. 14½***

625	CD337	50c scar, blk & sil	.25	.25
626	CD337	1.25r ultra & multi	.25	.25
627	CD337	2r green & multi	.50	.50
628	CD337	3r violet & multi	.75	.75
629	CD337	5r rose vio & multi	1.25	1.25
		Nos. 625-629 (5)	3.00	3.00

Fishing Industry A95

50c, Tuna cannery. 2r, Fishing trawler. 3r, Weighing fish. 10r, Hauling catch from net.

Wmk. 384

1987, Dec. 11 **Litho.** ***Perf. 14***

630	A95	50c multi	.25	.25
631	A95	2r multi	.75	.75
632	A95	3r multi	1.10	1.10
633	A95	10r multi	4.25	4.25
		Nos. 630-633 (4)	6.35	6.35

Beach Scenes A96

1r, Para-sailing, windsurfing, kayaks. 2r, Boating. 3r, Yacht at anchor. 10r, Hotel, cabanas.

Wmk. 384

1988, Feb. 9 **Litho.** ***Perf. 14½***

634	A96	1r multi	.45	.45
635	A96	2r multi	1.10	1.10
636	A96	3r multi	1.60	1.60
637	A96	10r multi	5.25	5.25
		Nos. 634-637 (4)	8.40	8.40

Green Turtles — A97

No. 638, Newly hatched turtles headed toward ocean. No. 639, Offspring hatching. No. 640, Female emerging from ocean. No. 641, Female laying eggs in sand. Stamps of same denomination printed se-tenant in a continuous design.

1988, Apr. 22 **Wmk. 373**

638	A97	2r multicolored	2.75	2.75
639	A97	2r multicolored	2.75	2.75
640	A97	3r multicolored	3.50	3.50
641	A97	3r multicolored	3.50	3.50
		Nos. 638-641 (4)	12.50	12.50

A98

Designs: 1r, No. 647a, Shot put. Nos. 643, 647b, High jump. 3r, No. 647c, Medal winner, grandstand and flags. 4r, No. 647d, Running. 5r, No. 647e, Javelin. 10r, Tennis.

1988, July 29 **Wmk. 384** ***Perf. 14½***

642	A98	1r multicolored	.30	.30
643	A98	2r multicolored	.70	.70
644	A98	3r multicolored	1.00	1.00
645	A98	4r multicolored	1.40	1.40
646	A98	5r multicolored	1.60	1.60
647		Strip of 5	3.25	3.25
a.-e.	A98	2r any single	.65	.65
		Nos. 642-647 (6)	8.25	8.25

Souvenir Sheet

Wmk. 373

648	A98	10r multicolored	7.50	7.50

No. 647 has a continuous design.

1988 Summer Olympics, Seoul, (1r-5r). Intl. Tennis Fed., 75th anniv. (10r). No. 648 contains one stamp, size: 28x39mm.

Lloyds of London, 300th Anniv.

Common Design Type

Designs: 1r, Leadenhall Street, London, 1928. 2r, Cinq Juin, horiz. 3r, Queen Elizabeth II, horiz. 10r, Explosion of the Hindenburg, Lakehurst, New Jersey, 1937.

Wmk. 384

1988, Sept. 30 **Litho.** ***Perf. 14***

649	CD341	1r multicolored	1.00	1.00
650	CD341	2r multicolored	1.10	1.10
651	CD341	3r multicolored	2.25	2.25
652	CD341	10r multicolored	8.50	8.50
		Nos. 649-652 (4)	12.85	12.85

Defense Forces Day, 1st Anniv. A99

1r, Motorcycle police. 2r, Air force helicopter. 3r, Navy patrol boat. 10r, Tank.

1988, Nov. 25 Litho. Wmk. 373

653	A99	1r multi	1.20	1.20
654	A99	2r multi	2.40	2.40
655	A99	3r multi	3.75	3.75
656	A99	10r multi	12.50	12.50
		Nos. 653-656 (4)	19.85	19.85

Christmas A100

Illustrations by local artists.

1988, Dec. 1 Litho. Wmk. 373

657	A100	50c Selwyn Hoareau	.25	.25
658	A100	2r Robin Leste	.75	.75
659	A100	3r France Anacoura	1.25	1.25
660	A100	10r Andre McGaw	4.25	4.25
		Nos. 657-660 (4)	6.50	6.50

Orchids A101

1r, Dendrobium, vert. 2r, Arachnis hybrid. 3r, Vanda caerulea, vert. 10r, Dendrobium phalaenopsis.

Wmk. 384

1988, Dec. 21 Litho. *Perf. 14*

661	A101	1r multi	.70	.70
662	A101	2r multi	1.40	1.40
663	A101	3r multi	2.00	2.00
664	A101	10r multi	6.75	6.75
		Nos. 661-664 (4)	10.85	10.85

Jawaharlal Nehru (1889-1964), 1st Prime Minister of Independent India A102

1989, Mar. 30 *Perf. 13½*

665	A102	2r India Type A409	1.25	1.25
666	A102	10r Portrait	6.75	6.75

People's United Party (SPUP), 25th Anniv. — A103

1r, Rally, old office. 2r, Maison Du Peuple. 3r, Pres. Rene, banner, torch. 10r, Torch, flag, Rene.

1989, June 5 *Perf. 14*

667	A103	1r multi	.35	.35
668	A103	2r multi	.65	.65
669	A103	3r multi	1.00	1.00
670	A103	10r multi	3.25	3.25
		Nos. 667-670 (4)	5.25	5.25

Moon Landing, 20th Anniv.

Common Design Type

Apollo 15: 1r, Saturn 5 lift-off. 2r, David R. Scott, Alfred M. Worden and James B. Irwin. 3r, Mission emblem. 5r, Irwin salutes flag in front of the Hadley Delta. 10r, Buzz Aldrin about to step onto the Moon, Apollo 11 mission.

Size of Nos. 677-678: 29x29mm

1989, July 20

676	CD342	1r multicolored	.45	.45
677	CD342	2r multicolored	1.10	1.10
678	CD342	3r multicolored	1.75	1.75
679	CD342	5r multicolored	2.75	2.75
		Nos. 676-679 (4)	6.05	6.05

Souvenir Sheet

680	CD342	10r multicolored	10.00	10.00

Intl. Red Cross and Red Crescent Organizations, 125th Annivs. — A104

1r, Ambulance, 1870. 2r, H.M. Hospital Ship Liberty, 1914-18. 3r, Sunbeam Standard Army Ambulance, 1914-18. 10r, The White Train, 1899-1902.

1989, Sept. 12 *Perf. 14½*

681	A104	1r multi	1.40	1.40
682	A104	2r multi	3.00	3.00
683	A104	3r multi	5.00	5.00
684	A104	10r multi	15.00	15.00
		Nos. 681-684 (4)	24.40	24.40

Island Birds — A105

1989, Oct. 16 *Perf. 14½x14*

685	A105	50c Black parrot	.35	.35
686	A105	2r Sooty tern	3.75	3.75
687	A105	3r Magpie robin	5.00	5.00
688	A105	5r Roseate tern	8.50	8.50
a.		Souvenir sheet of 4, #685-688	20.00	20.00
		Nos. 685-688 (4)	17.60	17.60

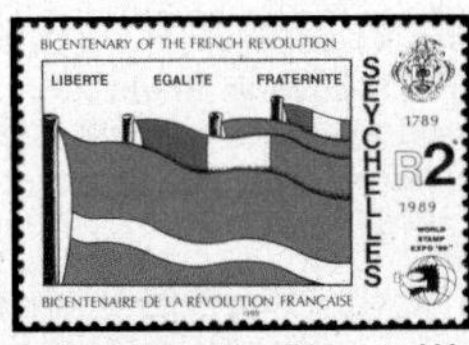

French Revolution Bicent., World Stamp Expo '89 — A106

2r, Flags. 5r, Storming of the Bastille. 10r, Raising French flag, Seychelles, 1791.

1989, Nov. 17 *Perf. 14*

689	A106	2r multicolored	2.10	2.10
690	A106	5r multicolored	5.25	5.25

Souvenir Sheet

691	A106	10r multicolored	10.00	10.00

African Development Bank, 25th Anniv. — A107

1r, Beau Vallon School, horiz. 2r, Fishing Authority headquarters, horiz. 3r, Variola. 10r, Deneb.

1989, Dec. 29 Wmk. 384

692	A107	1r multicolored	1.00	1.00
693	A107	2r multicolored	1.90	1.90
694	A107	3r multicolored	3.00	3.00
695	A107	10r multicolored	11.00	11.00
		Nos. 692-695 (4)	16.90	16.90

Orchids — A108

1r, Disperis tripetaloides. 2r, Vanilla phalaenopsis. 3r, Angraecum eburneum superbum. 10r, Polystachya concreta.

1990, Jan. 26

696	A108	1r multi	1.40	1.40
697	A108	2r multi	3.00	3.00
698	A108	3r multi	4.25	4.25
699	A108	10r multi	14.00	14.00
		Nos. 696-699 (4)	22.65	22.65

Expo '90 (International Garden & Greenery Exposition), Japan — A109

Designs: 2r, Fumiyo Sako. 3r, Coco-de-mer, male and female plants. 5r, Pitcher plant, Aldabra lily. 7r, Gardenia, Arms of Seychelles.

1990, June 8 Litho. Wmk. 373

700	A109	2r multicolored	1.60	1.60
701	A109	3r multicolored	2.25	2.25
702	A109	5r multicolored	4.00	4.00
703	A109	7r multicolored	5.50	5.50
a.		Souvenir sheet of 4, #700-703	13.50	13.50
		Nos. 700-703 (4)	13.35	13.35

Penny Black 150th Anniv., Stamp World London '90 A110

Exhibition emblem and stamps on stamps: 1r, Seychelles #38, Great Britain #80 canceled. 2r, Seychelles #81, Great Britain #64 canceled. 3r, Seychelles #74, Great Britain #62 canceled. 5r, Seychelles #2, Great Britain #3 canceled. 10r, Seychelles #197, Great Britain #1 canceled.

1990, May 3 *Perf. 12½*

704	A110	1r multicolored	1.00	1.00
705	A110	2r multicolored	2.10	2.10
706	A110	3r multicolored	2.75	2.75
707	A110	5r multicolored	5.00	5.00
		Nos. 704-707 (4)	10.85	10.85

Souvenir Sheet

708	A110	10r multicolored	13.50	13.50

Boeing 767-200ER A111

Wmk. 384

1990, July 27 Litho. *Perf. 14½*

709	A111	3r multicolored	5.00	5.00

Printed in panes of 10 (2 strips of 5 separated by pictorial gutter).

Queen Mother, 90th Birthday

Common Design Types

2r, Queen Elizabeth in coronation robes, 1937. 10r, Visiting workshops, 1947.

1990, Aug. 4 Wmk. 384 *Perf. 14x15*

710	CD343	2r multicolored	1.10	1.10

Perf. 14½

711	CD344	10r multicolored	5.50	5.50

Intl. Literacy Year — A112

1r, Blackboard. 2r, Reading mail. 3r, Reading directions. 10r, Crossword puzzle.

1990, Sept. 8 Wmk. 373 *Perf. 14*

712	A112	1r multicolored	.90	.90
713	A112	2r multicolored	1.90	1.90
714	A112	3r multicolored	2.75	2.75
715	A112	10r multicolored	9.00	9.00
		Nos. 712-715 (4)	14.55	14.55

Festival Kreol — A113

Various Sega Dancers: a, Pink and white skirt, white blouse. b, Yellow dress. c, Blue, sky blue and pink dress. d, Yellow, green and pink dress. e, White and pink skirt, green blouse.

1990, Oct. 27 *Perf. 13½x14*

716		Strip of 5	14.50	14.50
a.-e.	A113	2r any single	2.75	2.75

First Regional Seminar, Indian Ocean Petroleum Exploration A114

1990, Dec. 10 Wmk. 384 *Perf. 14½*

717	A114	3r Beach	3.00	3.00
718	A114	10r Geological map	10.50	10.50

Orchids — A115

1r, Bulbophyllum intertextum. 2r, Agrostophyllum occidentale. 3r, Vanilla planifolia. 10r, Malaxis seychellarum.

1991, Feb. 1 *Perf. 14*

719	A115	1r multi	1.10	1.10
720	A115	2r multi	2.25	2.25
721	A115	3r multi	3.50	3.50
722	A115	10r multi	10.00	10.00
		Nos. 719-722 (4)	16.85	16.85

Elizabeth & Philip, Birthdays

Common Design Types

1991, June 17 *Perf. 14½*

723	CD345	4r multicolored	2.00	2.00
724	CD346	4r multicolored	2.00	2.00
a.		Pair, #723-724 + label	5.00	5.00

Butterflies A116

1.50r, Precis rhadama. 3r, Lampides boeticus. 3.50r, Zizeeria knysna. 10r, Phalanta phalanta aethiopica.
No. 729, Eagris sabadius.

Perf. 14½x14

1991, Nov. 15 Litho. Wmk. 373

725 A116 1.50r multi 1.75 1.75
726 A116 3r multi 3.75 3.75
727 A116 3.50r multi 4.75 4.75
728 A116 10r multi 12.50 12.50
Nos. 725-728 (4) 22.75 22.75

Souvenir Sheet

729 A116 10r multi 14.00 14.00

Phila Nippon '91.

Christmas A117

Woodcuts: 50c, The Holy Virgin, Joseph, the Holy Child and St. John by Raphael, engraved by S. Vouillemont. 1r, The Holy Virgin, the Child and an Angel by Van Dyck, engraved by A. Blooting. 2r, The Holy Family, St. John and St. Anna by Rubens, engraved by Lucas Vorsterman. 7r, The Holy Family, an Angel and St. Catherine, painting and engraving by Cornelius Bloemaert.

1991, Dec. 2 Wmk. 384 *Perf. 14*

730 A117 50c multicolored .25 .25
731 A117 1r multicolored 1.25 1.25
732 A117 2r multicolored 2.75 2.75
733 A117 7r multicolored 9.00 9.00
Nos. 730-733 (4) 13.25 13.25

Queen Elizabeth II's Accession to the Throne, 40th Anniv.

Common Design Type

1992, Feb. 6 Wmk. 373

734 CD349 1r multicolored .80 .80
735 CD349 1.50r multicolored 1.10 1.10
736 CD349 3r multicolored 2.40 2.40
737 CD349 3.50r multicolored 2.50 2.50
738 CD349 5r multicolored 3.75 3.75
Nos. 734-738 (5) 10.55 10.55

Flora and Fauna A118

Designs: 10c, Brush warbler. 25c, Bronze gecko, vert. 50c, Seychelles tree frog. 1r, Seychelles splendid palm, vert. 1.50r, Seychelles skink, vert. 2r, Giant tenebrionid beetle. 3r, Seychelles sunbird. 3.50r, Seychelles killifish. 4r, Magpie robin. 5r, Seychelles vanilla, vert. 10r, Tiger chameleon. 15r, Coco-de-mer, vert. 25r, Paradise flycatcher, vert. 50r, Giant tortoise.

Wmk. 373

1993, Mar. 1 Litho. *Perf. 13½*

"1993" Date Imprint Beneath Design

739 A118 10c multicolored .30 .30
b. Inscribed "1996" .50 .30
d. Inscribed "2000" — —
740 A118 25c multicolored .30 .30
b. Inscribed "1996" .50 .30
741 A118 50c multicolored .30 .30
b. Inscribed "1996" .50 .30
d. Inscribed "2000" — —
742 A118 1r multicolored .40 .40
a. Inscribed "1994" 1.20 1.20
d. Inscribed "2000" — —
743 A118 1.50r multicolored .65 .65
744 A118 2r multicolored .90 .90
b. Inscribed "1996" 1.75 1.75
745 A118 3r multicolored 1.35 1.35
c. Inscribed "1998" 3.50 3.50
d. Inscribed "2000" — —
746 A118 3.50r multicolored 1.75 1.75
d. Inscribed "2000" — —
e. Perf. 14x13¾ — 18.00
747 A118 4r multicolored 1.75 1.75
748 A118 5r multicolored 2.25 2.25
a. Inscribed "1994" 7.25 7.25
749 A118 10r multicolored 4.50 4.50
a. Inscribed "1994" 13.00 13.00
750 A118 15r multicolored 6.50 6.50
b. Inscribed "1996" 13.00 13.00
d. Inscribed "2000" — —
751 A118 25r multicolored 11.00 11.00
a. Inscribed "1994" 32.50 32.50
752 A118 50r multicolored 22.50 22.50
Nos. 739-752 (14) 54.45 54.45

No. 746e is dated 2000.
For surcharges see Nos. 844-850.

First Visit to Seychelles by Archbishop of Canterbury — A119

Archbishop and: 3r, Anglican Cathedral, Victoria. 10r, Air France, Air Seychelles airplanes.

1993, June 8 *Perf. 13½*

753 A119 3r multicolored 2.50 1.25
754 A119 10r multicolored 8.75 4.50

4th Indian Ocean Island Games — A120

1993, Aug. 21 *Perf. 14½*

755 A120 1.50r Running 1.10 1.10
756 A120 3r Soccer 2.00 2.00
757 A120 3.50r Cycling 2.40 2.40
758 A120 10r Sailing 6.00 6.00
Nos. 755-758 (4) 11.50 11.50

Telecommunications, Cent. — A121

Designs: 1r, Cable ship Scotia, Victoria, 1893. 3r, Eastern Telegraph Company's Office, Victoria, 1904. 4r, HF Transmitting Station, operational 1971. 10r, New Telecoms House, Victoria, 1993.

1993, Nov. 12 *Perf. 13*

759 A121 1r multicolored .85 .85
760 A121 3r multicolored 2.50 2.50
761 A121 4r multicolored 3.75 3.75
762 A121 10r multicolored 9.50 9.50
Nos. 759-762 (4) 16.60 16.60

Zil Elwannyen Sesel Nos. 59, 61, 63, 64 Srchd.

1994, Feb. 18 *Perf. 14x14½*

763 A9 1r on 2.10r #59 .70 .70
764 A9 1.50r on 2.75r #61 1.10 1.10
765 A9 3.50r on 7r #63 2.10 2.10
766 A9 10r on 15r #64 6.75 6.75
Nos. 763-766 (4) 10.65 10.65

Hong Kong '94. Size and location of surcharge varies.

Butterflies A122

1.50r, Eurema floricola. 3r, Coeliades forestan. 3.50r, Borbo borbonica. 10r, Zizula hylax.

1994, Aug. 16 Wmk. 384 *Perf. 14*

767 A122 1.50r multi 1.50 1.50
768 A122 3r multi 3.25 3.25
769 A122 3.50r multi 3.50 3.50
770 A122 10r multi 10.00 10.00
Nos. 767-770 (4) 18.25 18.25

Queen Mother, 95th Birthday — A123

1.50r, Age 9. 3r, Wedding day. 3.50r, 1936 Portrait. 10r, 1975 Photograph.

1995, Sept. 26 Wmk. 373

771 A123 1.50r multi .95 .95
772 A123 3r multi 1.75 1.75
773 A123 3.50r multi 2.00 2.00
774 A123 10r multi 5.75 5.75
Nos. 771-774 (4) 10.45 10.45

World Wildlife Fund — A124

Black Paradise Flycatcher.

Wmk. 384

1996, July 12 Litho. *Perf. 14*

775 A124 1r Female on branch 1.00 1.00
776 A124 1r Male in flight 1.00 1.00
777 A124 1r Male on branch 1.00 1.00
778 A124 1r Female, young 1.00 1.00
a. Strip of 4, #775-778 4.75 4.75

Souvenir Sheet

779 A124 10r Female, male birds 8.50 8.50

Stamps in No. 778a may be out of Scott number sequence.

Modern Olympic Games, Cent. — A125

1996, July 15

780 A125 50c Swimming .25 .25
781 A125 1.50r Running .95 .95
782 A125 3r Sailing 2.10 2.10
783 A125 5r Boxing 3.50 3.50
Nos. 780-783 (4) 6.80 6.80

A126

Wmk. 373

1996, Aug. 19 Litho. *Perf. 14*

784 A126 3r shown 2.00 2.00
785 A126 10r Portrait up close 6.25 6.25

Archbishop Makarios of Cyprus, Exiled in Seychelles, 40th anniv.

Birds — A127

No. 786, Aldabra souimanga sunbird. No. 787, Seychelles sunbird. No. 788, Aldabra blue pigeon. No. 789, Seychelles blue pigeon. No. 790, Aldabra red headed fody. No. 791, Seychelles fody. No. 792, Aldabra white-eye. No. 793, Seychelles white-eye.

Wmk. 373

1996, Nov. 11 Litho. *Perf. 14½*

786 3r multicolored 2.50 2.50
787 3r multicolored 2.50 2.50
a. A127 Pair, #786-787 5.00 5.00
788 3r multicolored 2.50 2.50
789 3r multicolored 2.50 2.50
a. A127 Pair, #788-789 5.00 5.00
790 3r multicolored 2.50 2.50
791 3r multicolored 2.50 2.50
a. A127 Pair, #790-791 5.00 5.00
792 3r multicolored 2.50 2.50
793 3r multicolored 2.50 2.50
a. A127 Pair, #792-793 5.00 5.00
Nos. 786-793 (8) 20.00 20.00

Zil Elwannyen Sesel No. 58 Srchd.

1997, Feb. 12 *Perf. 14x14½*

794 A9 1.50r on 2r 3.25 3.25

Hong Kong '97.

Queen Elizabeth II and Prince Philip, 50th Wedding Anniv. — A128

Designs: No. 795, Queen in red & white dress. No. 796, Prince driving four-in-hand team. No. 797, Prince in business suit. No. 798, Queen, horse. No. 799, Prince Charles, Princess Anne. No. 800, Prince, Queen.
10r, Queen and Prince in open carriage, horiz.

Wmk. 373

1997, Nov. 20 Litho. *Perf. 13*

795 1r multicolored .85 .85
796 1r multicolored .85 .85
a. A128 Pair, #795-796 1.75 1.75
797 1.50r multicolored 1.10 1.10
798 1.50r multicolored 1.10 1.10
a. A128 Pair, #797-798 2.25 2.25

799 3r multicolored 2.25 2.25
800 3r multicolored 2.25 2.25
a. A128 Pair, #799-800 4.50 4.50
Nos. 795-800 (6) 8.40 8.40

Souvenir Sheet

801 A128 10r multicolored 7.50 7.50

Diana, Princess of Wales (1961-97)
Common Design Type

Designs: a, In red dress. b, Wearing white blouse, printed vest. c, In blue dress, flowers. d, Wearing white dress.

Perf. 14½x14
1998, Mar. 31 Litho. Wmk. 373
802 CD355 3r Sheet of 4, #a.-d. 6.25 6.25

No. 802 sold for 12r + 3r, with surtax from international sales being donated to the Princess Diana Memorial Fund and surtax from national sales being donated to designated local charity.

Intl. Year of the Ocean — A129

Designs: a, Blue and yellow fish. b, School of gold-colored fish. c, Lionfish. d, Various small fish. e, Anemones. f, Turtle.

1998 Litho. *Perf. 14*
803 A129 3r Strip of 6, #a.-f. 9.50 9.50
Complete booklet, 2 #803 20.00

Australia '99, World Stamp Expo A130

18th Cent. ships: 1.50r, Vierge du Cap, 1721. 3r, Elizabeth, 1741. 3.50r, Curieuse, 1768. 10r, Le Flèche, 1801.
20r, The Cheval Marin, 1774, vert.

1999 Litho. Wmk. 384 *Perf. 14*
804 A130 1.50r multicolored .75 .75
805 A130 3r multicolored 1.50 1.50
806 A130 3.50r multicolored 1.75 1.75
807 A130 10r multicolored 5.25 5.25
Nos. 804-807 (4) 9.25 9.25

Souvenir Sheet

808 A130 20r multicolored 12.00 12.00

Nos. 804-807 each issued with se-tenant label.

Wedding of Prince Edward and Sophie Rhys-Jones A131

Wmk. 373
1999, Sept. 1 Litho. *Perf. 13¼*
809 A131 3r shown 2.25 2.25
810 A131 15r In carriage 7.25 7.25

Christmas and Millennium A132

1r, Cathedral of the Immaculate Conception. 1.50r, Fairy tern. 2.50r, Dolphin. 10r, Comet.

Perf. 14x14½
1999, Dec. 14 Litho. Wmk. 373
811 A132 1r multi .75 .75
812 A132 1.50r multi 1.10 1.10
813 A132 2.50r multi 1.60 1.60
814 A132 10r multi 6.50 6.50
Nos. 811-814 (4) 9.95 9.95

Queen Mother, 100th Birthday — A133

Designs: 3r, As child. 5r, As young woman. 7r, With King George VI. 10r, As old woman.

Wmk. 373
2000, Aug. 4 Litho. *Perf. 14¼*
815 A133 3r multi 1.50 1.50
816 A133 5r multi 2.50 2.50
817 A133 7r multi 3.50 3.50
818 A133 10r multi 4.50 4.50
Nos. 815-818 (4) 12.00 12.00

Anniversaries — A134

Designs: 1r, Arrival of the Jacobin deportees, 200th anniv. 1.50r, Victoria as capital of Seychelles, 160th anniv. 3r, Arrival of Father Leon Des Avanchers, 150th anniv. 3.50r, Victoria Fountain, cent., vert. 5r, Botanical Gardens, cent. 10r, Independence, 25th anniv., vert.

Wmk. 373
2001, July 25 Litho. *Perf. 14*
819-824 A134 Set of 6 8.50 8.50

Nos. 819 and 824 lack Age of Victoria emblem.

Ducks A135

Designs: No. 825, 3r, Garganey. No. 826, 3r, Northern shoveler. No. 827, 3r, Ruddy shelduck. No. 828, 3r, White-faced whistling duck.

Wmk. 384
2001, Oct. 4 Litho. *Perf. 14*
825-828 A135 Set of 4 8.75 8.75

Birdlife International World Bird Festival — A136

Seychelles Scops owl: a, In flight. b, In tree. c, Standing on branch, vert. d, Standing on tip of broken branch, vert. e, Standing on branch.

Perf. 14¼x14½, 14½x14¼
2001, Oct. 4
829 A136 3r Sheet of 5, #a-e 13.50 13.50

Queen Mother Elizabeth (1900-2002)
Common Design Type
Souvenir Sheet

No. 830: a, 5r, As young woman, without hat. b, 10r, As old woman, wearing hat.

Perf. 14½x14¼
2002, Aug. 5 Litho. Wmk. 373
Without Purple Frames
830 CD361 Sheet of 2, #a-b 6.50 6.50

Worldwide Fund for Nature (WWF) A137

Frogs: No. 831, 1r, Seychelles frog. No. 832, 1r, Palm frog. No. 833, 1r, Thomasset's frog. No. 834, 1r, Gardiner's frog.
20r, Seychelles tree frog.

Wmk. 373
2003, Feb. 3 Litho. *Perf. 14*
831-834 A137 Set of 4 3.75 3.75

Souvenir Sheet

835 A137 20r multi 11.00 11.00

Fish A138

Designs: 10c, Seychelles blenny. 50c, Seychelles anemonefish. 1r, Indian butterflyfish. 1.50r, Goldbar wrasse. 3r, Seychelles squirrelfish. 5r, Greenthroat parrotfish. 50r, Whale shark.

Wmk. 373
2003, Nov. 3 Litho. *Perf. 14*
836 A138 10c multi .30 .30
837 A138 50c multi .30 .30
838 A138 1r multi .55 .55
839 A138 1.50r multi .80 .80
840 A138 3r multi 1.30 1.30
841 A138 5r multi 2.10 2.10
a. Wmk. 406, dated "2010" .95 .95
842 A138 50r multi 21.00 21.00
a. Wmk. 406, dated "2010" 9.50 9.50
Nos. 836-842 (7) 26.35 26.35

See Nos. 852-858, 893-896.
Issued: Nos. 841a, 842a, 7/5/10.

Indian Ocean Commission, 20th Anniv. — A139

Wmk. 373
2004, Feb. 16 Litho. *Perf. 13¼*
843 A139 15r multi 5.25 5.25

Nos. 743, 745, 748-752 Surcharged

Methods and Perfs As Before
2004, July 1 Wmk. 373
844 A118 1r on 1.50r #743 .80 .80
845 A118 2r on 3r #745 1.40 1.40
846 A118 3.50r on 5r #748 2.60 2.60
847 A118 3.50r on 10r #749 2.60 2.60
848 A118 3.50r on 15r #750 2.60 2.60
849 A118 4r on 25r #751 3.00 3.00
850 A118 4r on 50r #752 3.00 3.00
Nos. 844-850 (7) 16.00 16.00

Pope John Paul II (1920-2005) A140

Wmk. 373
2005, Aug. 18 Litho. *Perf. 14*
851 A140 5r multi 3.50 3.50

Fish Type of 2003

Designs: 25c, African pygmy angelfish. 2r, Picasso triggerfish. 3.50r, Palette surgeonfish. 4r, Longfin batfish. 10r, Masked moray eel. 15r, Lyretail grouper. 25r, Emperor snapper.

2005, Oct. 3 Wmk. 373 *Perf. 14*
852 A138 25c multi .30 .30
853 A138 2r multi 1.00 1.00
a. Wmk. 406, dated "2012" .55 .55
854 A138 3.50r multi 1.90 1.90
a. Wmk. 406, dated "2010" .65 .65
855 A138 4r multi 2.10 2.10
a. Wmk. 406, dated "2010" .80 .80
b. Wmk. 406, dated "2012" .65 .65
856 A138 10r multi 4.25 4.25
a. Wmk. 406, dated "2010" 1.90 1.90
857 A138 15r multi 5.75 5.75
a. Wmk. 406, dated "2010" 2.75 2.75
858 A138 25r multi 9.50 9.50
a. Wmk. 406, dated "2010" 4.75 4.75
Nos. 852-858 (7) 24.80 24.80

Issued: Nos. 854a, 855a, 856a, 857a, 858a, 7/5/10. Nos. 853a, 855b, 12/1/12.

Exile of Archbishop Makarios in Seychelles, 50th Anniv. — A141

Designs: 3.50r, Archbishop Makarios and Seychelles natives. 15r, Archbishop Makarios.

Wmk. 373
2006, June 28 Litho. *Perf. 14*
859-860 A141 Set of 2 11.00 11.00

Independence, 30th Anniv. — A142

Designs: 50c, Possesion Stone. 1r, Seychelles flag. 1.50r, Valee de Mai World Heritage Site. 2r, School children. 3.50r, Jacob Marie holding bonm. 4r, Ship "Seychelles Progress." 15r, Independence anniversary emblem.

Wmk. 373
2006, June 28 Litho. *Perf. 14*
861-867 A142 Set of 7 18.50 18.50

Selection of Aldabra as UNESCO World Heritage Site, 25th Anniv. — A143

Designs: 2r, Zangiv flowers. 3.50r, Dugongs. 10r, Giant tortoises.

Perf. 12½x13
2007, Nov. 19 Litho. Wmk. 373
868-870 A143 Set of 3 6.00 6.00

2008 Summer Olympics, Beijing A144

Designs: 1r, Bamboo, kayaking. 1.50r, Dragon, swimming. 2r, Lantern, sailing. 3.50r, Fish, javelin.

Wmk. 373

2008, Apr. 30 Litho. *Perf. 13¼*
871-874 A144 Set of 4 3.00 3.00

Aldabra Drongos A145

Aldabra Red-headed Fodies — A146

Wmk. 373

2008, Oct. 1 Litho. *Perf. 14*
875 A145 1r shown .55 .55
876 A145 1r Drongos, diff. .55 .55
877 A146 1r shown .55 .55
878 A146 1r Fodies, diff. .55 .55
Nos. 875-878 (4) 2.20 2.20

Souvenir Sheet

879 A146 20r Fody and drongo 7.00 7.00

Worldwide Fund for Nature (WWF).

Explorers and Ships — A147

Designs: 1.50r, Ferdinand Magellan. 3.50r, Sir Martin Frobisher. 6.50r, Sir Francis Drake. 8r, Henry Hudson. 15r, Abel Tasman. 27r, Sir John Franklin.
7r, The Ascension.

Wmk. 406

2009, May 25 Litho. *Perf. 14*
880-885 A147 Set of 6 10.00 10.00

Souvenir Sheet

886 A147 7r multi 2.25 2.25

Space Exploration A148

Designs: 3.50r, X-1 jet being loaded under Superfortress, 1951. 7r, Lunar landing research vehicle, 1964. 8r, Apollo 11 launch site, 1969. 13r, Space Shuttle flight STS-86 on launch pad, 1997. 20r, Soyuz TMA-13 rolls out to launch pad, 2008.
24r, Astronaut on Moon, painting by Capt. Alan Bean, vert.

Wmk. 406

2009, July 20 Litho. *Perf. 13¼*
887-891 A148 Set of 5 9.50 9.50

Souvenir Sheet

Perf. 13x13¼

892 A148 24r multi 5.00 5.00

No. 892 contains one 40x60mm stamp. Nos. 887-891 each were printed in sheets of 6.

Fish Type of 2003

Designs: 6.50r, Queen coris. 7r, White-lined goatfish. 8r, Three-spot angelfish. 100r, Coral grouper.

Wmk. 406

2010, July 5 Litho. *Perf. 14*
893 A138 6.50r multi 1.10 1.10
894 A138 7r multi 1.25 1.25
895 A138 8r multi 1.40 1.40
a. Dated "2012" 1.40 1.40
896 A138 100r multi 17.50 17.50
Nos. 893-896 (4) 21.25 21.25

Issued: No. 895a, 12/1/12.

Wedding of Prince William and Catherine Middleton — A149

Couple: 3.50r, Waving in coach. 4r, Kissing, vert. 7r, Standing and waving, vert. 25r, Holding hands, vert.

2011, Aug. 1
897-900 A149 Set of 4 7.00 7.00

State House, Cent. A150

2011, Nov. 11
901 A150 3.50r multi 1.00 1.00

Seychelles Post Office, 150th Anniv. — A151

Designs: 3.50r, Post Office, Victoria, 2011. 7r, Old Post Office, Victoria, 1900s.

2011, Dec. 12
902-903 A151 Set of 2 2.00 2.00

Green Turtle A152

2014, Oct. 9 Litho. *Perf. 13x13¼*
904 A152 50r multi 8.00 8.00

See Comoro Islands No. , France No. 4695, French Southern & Antarctic Territories No. 511, Malagasy Republic No. 1637, Mauritius No. 1144.

Hindu Temple, Victoria, and Flags of India and Seychelles — A153

Wmk. 406

2016, Oct. 14 Litho. *Perf. 14*
905 A153 10r multi 1.60 1.60

Seychelles India Day.

Lions Clubs International, Cent. — A154

Wmk. 406

2017, May 30 Litho. *Perf. 13*
906 A154 5r multi 1.10 1.10

POSTAGE DUE STAMPS

Catalogue values for unused stamps in this section are for Never Hinged items.

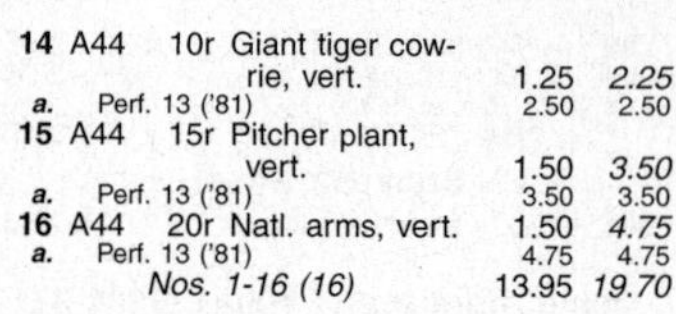

D1

Engr.; Denomination Typo. in Carmine

1951, Mar. 1 Wmk. 4 *Perf. 11½*
J1 D1 2c carmine 1.50 *3.00*
J2 D1 3c blue green 2.25 *3.00*
J3 D1 6c ocher 2.25 *2.25*
J4 D1 9c brown orange 2.25 *4.00*
J5 D1 15c purple 2.10 *12.50*
J6 D1 18c deep blue 2.75 *13.00*
J7 D1 20c black brown 2.75 *13.00*
J8 D1 30c red brown 2.75 *9.00*
Nos. J1-J8 (8) 18.60 *59.75*

Engr.; Denomination Typo.

1964-65 Wmk. 314
J9 D1 2c carmine 2.25 *15.50*
J10 D1 3c green & red 2.25 *18.00*

Issue dates: July 7, 1964, Sept. 14, 1965.

Dated "1980"

1980 Litho. *Perf. 14*
J11 D1 5c lilac rose & red .25 *1.50*
J12 D1 10c dk green & red .25 *1.50*
J13 D1 15c bister & red .25 *1.50*
J14 D1 20c brown org & red .25 *1.50*
J15 D1 25c violet & red .25 *1.50*
J16 D1 75c dk red brown & red .30 *1.50*
J17 D1 80c dk blue & red .35 *1.60*
J18 D1 1r claret & red .35 *1.60*
Nos. J11-J18 (8) 2.25 12.20

ZIL ELWANNYEN SESEL

LOCATION — South of Seychelles

The islands of Aldabra, Farquhar and Des Roches. Formerly part of the British Indian Ocean Territory.

Catalogue values for unused stamps in this country are for Never Hinged items.

Type of Seychelles, 1977-78

Imprinted "1980" Beneath Design

Size: 30x26mm (40c, 1r, 1.25r, 1.50r)

Perf. 14, 14½x14 (40c, 1r, 1.25r, 1.50r)

1980-81 Litho. Wmk. 373
1 A44 5c Reef fish .25 *.60*
2 A44 10c Hawksbill turtle .25 *.60*
3 A44 15c Coco-de-mer .25 *.60*
4 A44 20c Wild vanilla .30 *.60*
5 A44 25c Butterfly 1.25 *.60*
6 A44 40c Coral reef .45 *.60*
7 A44 50c Giant tortoise .45 *.50*
8 A44 75c Crayfish .55 .50
9 A44 1r Madagascar fody 1.50 *.90*
10 A44 1.10r Green gecko .60 *.90*
11 A44 1.25r Fairy tern 2.00 .80
12 A44 1.50r Flying fox .75 .60

Size: 27x35mm

13 A44 5r Octopus, vert. 1.10 *1.40*
a. Perf. 13 ('81) 1.50 1.50
14 A44 10r Giant tiger cowrie, vert. 1.25 *2.25*
a. Perf. 13 ('81) 2.50 2.50
15 A44 15r Pitcher plant, vert. 1.50 *3.50*
a. Perf. 13 ('81) 3.50 3.50
16 A44 20r Natl. arms, vert. 1.50 *4.75*
a. Perf. 13 ('81) 4.75 4.75
Nos. 1-16 (16) 13.95 *19.70*

Nos. 13a-16a have "1981" date imprint beneath design.

1981 Inscribed "1981"
1a A44 5c multicolored .25 *.60*
2a A44 10c multicolored .25 *.60*
3a A44 15c multicolored .25 *.60*
4a A44 20c multicolored .30 *.60*
5a A44 25c multicolored 1.50 *.60*
6a A44 40c multicolored .60 *.60*
7a A44 50c multicolored .60 .50
8a A44 75c multicolored .60 .50
9a A44 1r multicolored 1.50 .90
10a A44 1.10r multicolored .90 .90
11a A44 1.25r multicolored 2.00 .80
12a A44 1.50r multicolored .90 .60
Nos. 1a-12a (12) 9.65 7.80

Traveling Post Office A1

1980, Oct. 24 *Perf. 14*
17 A1 1.50r Cinq Juin .25 .25
18 A1 2.10r Canceling letters .30 .30
19 A1 5r Map .60 .60
Nos. 17-19 (3) 1.15 1.15

The 5r showing Agalega as part of the Seychelles was not issued.

Marine Life — A2

1980, Nov. 28
20 A2 1.50r Yellowfin Tuna .50 .50
21 A2 2.10r Blue marlin .55 .55
22 A2 5r Sperm whale 1.05 1.05
Nos. 20-22 (3) 2.10 2.10

Royal Wedding Types of Seychelles

1981, June 23 Wmk. 380 *Perf. 14*
23 A61a 40c Royal Escape .25 .25
a. Bklt. pane of 4, perf. 12½x12, unwmkd. 1.10 1.10
24 A61b 40c Couple .40 .40
25 A61a 5r Victoria & Albert II .80 .80
26 A61b 5r like #24 1.25 1.25
a. Bklt pane of 2, perf. 12½x12, unwmkd. 3.00 3.00
27 A61a 10r Britannia 1.50 1.50
28 A61b 10r like #24 2.50 2.50
Nos. 23-28 (6) 6.70 6.70

Souvenir Sheet

Perf. 12½x12

29 A61b 7.50r like #24 2.40 2.40

Each denomination issued in sheets of 7 (6 type A61a, 1 type A61b).
For surcharges see Nos. 70-75.

Wildlife A3

1981, Dec. 11 Wmk. 373 *Perf. 14*
30 A3 1.40r Wright's skink .35 .35
31 A3 2.25r Tree frog .45 .45
32 A3 5r Robber crab .70 .70
Nos. 30-32 (3) 1.50 1.50

Workboats — A4

1982, Mar. 11 ***Perf. 14x14½***

33 A4 1.75r Cinq Juin .50 .45
34 A4 2.10r Junon .60 .55
35 A4 5r Diamond M. Dragon .75 .70
Nos. 33-35 (3) 1.85 1.70

Mailboats A5

1982, July 22 **Wmk. 373** ***Perf. 14***

36 A5 40c Paulette .40 .30
37 A5 1.75r Janette .55 .70
38 A5 2.75r Lady Esme .70 .85
39 A5 3.50r Cinq Juin .75 .90
Nos. 36-39 (4) 2.40 2.75

Aldabra, World Heritage Site — A6

40c, Birds flying over island. 2.75r, Map. 7r, Giant tortoises.

1982, Nov. 19

40 A6 40c multi .30 .30
41 A6 2.75r multi .65 .65
42 A6 7r multi 1.40 1.40
Nos. 40-42 (3) 2.35 2.35

Wildlife A7

1.75r, Red land crab. 2.75r, Black terrapin. 7r, Madagascar green gecko.

1983, Feb. 25 ***Perf. 14x14½***

43 A7 1.75r multi .45 .45
44 A7 2.75r multi .80 .80
45 A7 7r multi 2.00 2.00
Nos. 43-45 (3) 3.25 3.25

Maps — A8

40c, Poivre Island, Ile du Sud. 1.50r, Ile des Roches. 2.75r, Astove Island. 7r, Coetivy Island.

1983, Apr. 27 ***Perf. 14½***

46 A8 40c multi .30 .30
47 A8 1.50r multi .30 .30
48 A8 2.75r multi .55 .55
49 A8 7r multi 1.40 1.40
a. Souvenir sheet of 4, #46-49 4.25 4.25
Nos. 46-49 (4) 2.55 2.55

Birds — A9

5c, Aldabra brush warbler. 10c, Barred ground dove. 15c, Aldabra nightjar. 20c, Malagasy grass warbler. 25c, Aldabra white-eye. 40c, Aldabra fody. 50c, Aldabra rail. 75c, Aldabra bulbul. 2r, Dimorphic little egret. 2.10r, Aldabra sunbird. 2.50r, Aldabra turtle dove. 2.75r, Aldabra sacred ibis. 3.50r, Aldabra coucal. 7r, Aldabra kestrel. 15r, Aldabra blue pigeon. 20r, Greater flamingo.

Perf. 14x14½

1983, July 13 **Wmk. 373**

50 A9 5c multicolored .25 .25
51 A9 10c multicolored .25 .25
52 A9 15c multicolored .25 .25
53 A9 20c multicolored .25 .25
54 A9 25c multicolored .25 .25
55 A9 40c multicolored .25 .25
56 A9 50c multicolored .25 .25
57 A9 75c multicolored .30 .30
58 A9 2r multicolored 1.10 1.10
59 A9 2.10r multicolored 1.25 1.40
60 A9 2.50r multicolored 1.50 1.50
61 A9 2.75r multicolored 1.60 1.75

Perf. 14½x14

62 A9 3.50r multicolored 2.00 2.10
63 A9 7r multicolored 4.25 4.50
64 A9 15r multicolored 8.50 9.00
65 A9 20r multicolored 10.50 11.00
Nos. 50-65 (16) 32.75 34.40

Nos. 62-65 vert. See Nos. 96-100. For surcharges see Seychelles Nos. 763-766.

World Tourism Day A10

1983, Sept. 27 ***Perf. 14***

66 A10 50c Windsurfing .30 .30
67 A10 2r Hotel .30 .30
68 A10 3r Beach .50 .50
69 A10 10r Sunset 1.40 1.40
Nos. 66-69 (4) 2.50 2.50

Nos. 23-28 Surcharged

1983 **Wmk. 380** ***Perf. 14***

70 A61a 30c on 40c multi .35 .35
71 A61b 30c on 40c multi .35 .35
72 A61a 2r on 5r multi 1.40 1.40
73 A61b 2r on 5r multi 1.40 1.40
74 A61a 3r on 10r multi 2.00 2.00
75 A61b 3r on 10r multi 2.00 2.00
Nos. 70-75 (6) 7.50 7.50

Each denomination issued in sheets of 7 (6 type A61a, 1 type A61b).

Aldabra Post Office, Reopening — A11

1984, Mar. 30 **Wmk. 373** ***Perf. 14***

76 A11 50c Map, postmark .25 .25
77 A11 2.75r Aldabra rail .80 .80
78 A11 3r Giant tortoise .90 .90
79 A11 10r Red-footed booby 3.25 3.25
Nos. 76-79 (4) 5.20 5.20

Game Fishing A12

50c, Fishing boat. 2r, Hooked fish, vert. 3r, Weighing catch, vert. 10r, Fishing boat, stern view.

1984, May 31

80 A12 50c multicolored .25 .25
81 A12 2r multicolored .60 .60
82 A12 3r multicolored .80 .80
83 A12 10r multicolored 2.50 2.50
Nos. 80-83 (4) 4.15 4.15

Crabs A13

1984, Aug. 24 ***Perf. 14½***

84 A13 50c Giant hermit crab .25 .25
85 A13 2r Fiddler crabs .75 .75
86 A13 3r Ghost crab 1.00 1.00
87 A13 10r Spotted pebble crab 3.50 3.50
Nos. 84-87 (4) 5.50 5.50

Constellations A14

1984, Oct. 16 ***Perf. 14***

88 A14 50c Orion .25 .25
89 A14 2r Cygnus .65 .65
90 A14 3r Virgo .90 .90
91 A14 10r Scorpio 2.40 2.40
Nos. 88-91 (4) 4.20 4.20

Mushrooms — A15

50c, Lenzites elegans. 2r, Xylaria telfairei. 3r, Lentinus sajor-caju. 10r, Hexagonia tenuis.

Wmk. 373

1985, Jan. 31 **Litho.** ***Perf. 14***

92 A15 50c multi .25 .25
93 A15 2r multi 1.60 1.60
94 A15 3r multi 2.25 2.25
95 A15 10r multi 7.75 7.75
Nos. 92-95 (4) 11.85 11.85

Bird Type of 1983

Year Imprint ( ) Beneath Design

Inscribed "Zil Elwannyen Sesel"

Wmk. 373, 384 (5c)

1985-88 ***Perf. 14x14½***

96 A9 5c Like #50 ('88) *5.50 5.50*
97 A9 10c Like #51 *5.50 5.50*
a. Inscribed "1987" *5.50 5.50*
b. Wmk. 384 ('88) *5.50 5.50*
98 A9 25c Like #54 *5.50 5.50*
99 A9 50c Like #56 ('87) *5.50 5.50*
a. Wmk. 384 ('88) *5.50 5.50*
100 A9 2r Like #58 *7.50 7.50*
a. Wmk. 384 ('88) *7.50 7.50*
b. As "a," inscribed "1990" *7.50 7.50*
Nos. 96-100 (5) *29.50 29.50*

Common Design Types pictured following the introduction.

Queen Mother 85th Birthday

Common Design Type

1r, Coronation portrait. 2r, With Princess Anne. 3r, Wearing tiara. 5r, Holding Prince Henry. 10r, In river taxi, Venice.

Perf. 14½x14

1985, June 1 **Wmk. 384**

101 CD336 1r multicolored .25 .25
102 CD336 2r multicolored .60 .60
103 CD336 3r multicolored .90 .90
104 CD336 5r multicolored 1.60 1.60
Nos. 101-104 (4) 3.35 3.35

Souvenir Sheet

105 CD336 10r multicolored 3.25 3.25

World Wildlife Fund A16

50c, Giant tortoise. 75c, Tortoises crossing stream. 1r, Three tortoises. 2r, Tortoise facing right.
10r, Two tortoises.

1985, Sept. 27 ***Perf. 14***

106 A16 50c multicolored 8.25 3.00
107 A16 75c multicolored 9.00 1.00
108 A16 1r multicolored 9.75 4.00
109 A16 2r multicolored 13.00 5.50
Nos. 106-109 (4) 40.00 13.50

Souvenir Sheet

Perf. 13x13½

110 A16 10r multicolored 29.00 29.00

See Nos. 131-134.

Famous Visitors A17

Visitors and their ships: 50c, Phoenician trader, 600 B.C. 2r, Sir Hugh Scott, HMS Sealark, 1908. 10r, Vasco de Gama, Sao Gabriel, 1502.

1985, Oct. 25 **Wmk. 373** ***Perf. 14***

111 A17 50c multicolored .30 .30
112 A17 2r multicolored 1.25 1.25
113 A17 10r multicolored 6.00 6.00
Nos. 111-113 (3) 7.55 7.55

Queen Elizabeth II, 60th Birthday

Common Design Type

Designs: 75c, As princess. 1r, With Prince Philip. 1.50r, Wearing blue cape. 3.75r, Portrait. 5r, Wearing red hat.

Perf. 14½x14

1986, Apr. 21 **Wmk. 384**

114 CD337 75c scar, blk & sil .25 .25
115 CD337 1r blue & multi .25 .25
116 CD337 1.50r grn & multi .25 .25
117 CD337 3.75r vio & multi .55 .55
118 CD337 5r rose vio & multi .85 .85
Nos. 114-118 (5) 2.15 2.15

For overprints see Nos. 135-139.

Royal Wedding

Common Design Type

3r, Sarah Ferguson, Prince Andrew. 7r, Andrew.

1986, July 23 ***Perf. 14***

119 CD338 3r multicolored .70 .70
120 CD338 7r multicolored 1.60 1.60

Coral — A18

Continuous design: a, Acropora palifera, Tubastraea coccinea. b, Echinopora lamellosa, Favia pallida. c, Sarcophyton sp, Porites lutea. d, Goniopora sp, Goniastrea retiformis. e, Tubipora musica, Fungia fungites.

1986, Sept. 17

121 A18 2r Strip of 5, #a.-e. 12.50 12.50

Flowers — A19

50c, Hibiscus tiliaceus. 2r, Crinum angustum. 3r, Phaius tetragonus. 10r, Rothmannia annae.

1986, Nov. 12

122 A19 50c multicolored .30 .30
123 A19 2r multicolored 1.50 1.50
124 A19 3r multicolored 2.25 2.25
125 A19 10r multicolored 7.50 7.50
Nos. 122-125 (4) 11.55 11.55

Fish — A20

Continuous design: a, Chaetodon unimaculatus. b, Ostorhincus fleurieu. c, Platax orbicularis. d, abudefduf annulatus. e, Chaetodon lineolatus.

1987, Mar. 26

126 A20 2r Strip of 5, #a-e. 9.25 9.25

Trees — A21

1987, Aug. 26 *Perf. 14½*

127 A21 1r Coconut .80 .80
128 A21 2r Mangrove 1.75 1.75
129 A21 3r Pandanus palm 3.00 3.00
130 A21 5r Indian almond 5.00 5.00
Nos. 127-130 (4) 10.55 10.55

Nos. 106-109 Redrawn World Wildlife Fund Emblem without Circle

1987, Sept. 9 Wmk. 384 *Perf. 14*

131 A16 50c multicolored 9.75 5.50
132 A16 75c multicolored 12.50 7.00
133 A16 1r multicolored 15.00 8.50
134 A16 2r multicolored 20.00 11.50
Nos. 131-134 (4) 57.25 32.50

Nos. 114-118 Ovptd. in Silver "40TH WEDDING ANNIVERSARY"

1987, Dec. 9 *Perf. 14½x14*

135 CD337 75c scar, blk & sil .25 .25
136 CD337 1r blue & multi .30 .30
137 CD337 1.50r grn & multi .50 .50
138 CD337 3.75r vio & multi 1.25 1.25
139 CD337 5r rose vio & multi 1.75 1.75
Nos. 135-139 (5) 4.05 4.05

Mai Valley Tropical Forest — A22

Continuous design: b, Trunk of palm tree at right. c, Bamboo.

1987, Dec. 16 *Perf. 14*

140 A22 3r Strip of 3, #a.-c. 11.00 11.00

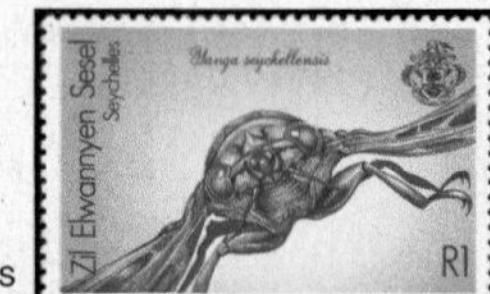

Insects A23

1r, Yanga seychellensis. 2r, Belenois aldabraensis. 3r, Polyspilota seychelliana. 5r, Polposipus herculeanus.

1988, July 28 **Wmk. 373**

141 A23 1r multi 2.10 2.10
142 A23 2r multi 3.25 3.25
143 A23 3r multi 4.00 4.00
144 A23 5r multi 4.75 4.75
Nos. 141-144 (4) 14.10 14.10

Souvenir Sheet

1988 Summer Olympics, Seoul — A24

1988, Aug. 31 **Wmk. 384**

145 A24 10r multicolored 7.50 7.50

Lloyds' of London, 300th Anniv.
Common Design Type

Designs: 1r, Lloyd's building, 1988. 2r, Cable ship Retriever, horiz. 3r, Chantel, horiz. 5r, Torrey Canyon aground off Cornwall, 1967.

1988, Oct. 28 **Wmk. 373**

146 CD341 1r multicolored 1.10 1.10
147 CD341 2r multicolored 1.90 1.90
148 CD341 3r multicolored 3.00 3.00
149 CD341 5r multicolored 5.25 5.25
Nos. 146-149 (4) 11.25 11.25

Christmas — A25

1r, Santa, toys in canoe. 2r, Church, vert. 3r, Santa riding bird, vert. 5r, Sleigh over island.

Perf. 13½x14, 14x13½

1988, Nov. 18 **Wmk. 384**

150 A25 1r multicolored .45 .45
151 A25 2r multicolored .75 .75
152 A25 3r multicolored 1.15 1.15
153 A25 5r multicolored 1.90 1.90
Nos. 150-153 (4) 4.25 4.25

Moon Landing, 20th Anniv.
Common Design Type

Apollo 18: 1r, Firing room, Launch Control Center. 2r, Astronauts Slayton, Stafford, Brand and cosmonauts Leonov and Kubasov. 3r, Mission emblem. 5r, Apollo and Soyuz docking in space. 10r, Apollo 11 lifted aboard USS Hornet.

Size of Nos. 155-156: 29x29mm

Perf. 14x13½, 14 (#155-156)

1989, July 20

154 CD342 1r multicolored 1.25 1.25
155 CD342 2r multicolored 2.10 2.10
156 CD342 3r multicolored 3.25 3.25
157 CD342 5r multicolored 5.25 5.25
Nos. 154-157 (4) 11.85 11.85

Souvenir Sheet

158 CD342 10r multicolored 15.00 15.00

Poisonous Plants — A26

1989, Oct. 9 *Perf. 14*

159 A26 1r Dumb cane 1.40 1.40
160 A26 2r Star of Bethlehem 3.00 3.00
161 A26 3r Indian licorice 4.50 4.50
162 A26 5r Black nightshade 6.75 6.75
Nos. 159-162 (4) 15.65 15.65

See Nos. 173-176.

Creole Cooking — A27

1r, Tec-tec broth. 2r, Pilaf a la Seychelloise. 3r, Mullet grilled in banana leaves. 5r, Daube.

1989, Dec. 18

163 A27 1r multi 1.40 1.40
164 A27 2r multi 2.75 2.75
165 A27 3r multi 4.00 4.00
166 A27 5r multi 6.50 6.50
a. Souvenir sheet of 4, #163-166 16.00 16.00
Nos. 163-166 (4) 14.65 14.65

No. 166a has continuous design.

Stamp World London '90 A28

Designs: 1r, #22. 2r, #13. 3r, #61. 5r, #32.

Wmk. 373

1990, May 3 Litho. *Perf. 12½*

167 A28 1r multicolored 1.40 1.40
168 A28 2r multicolored 3.00 3.00
169 A28 3r multicolored 4.25 4.25
170 A28 5r multicolored 7.25 7.25
a. Souvenir sheet of 4, #167-170 14.50 14.50
Nos. 167-170 (4) 15.90 15.90

Queen Mother 90th Birthday
Common Design Types

Designs: 2r, As Duchess of York with infant Elizabeth. 10r, With King George VI viewing bomb-damaged London, 1940.

1990, Aug. 4 Wmk. 384 *Perf. 14x15*

171 CD343 2r multi 1.25 1.25

Perf. 14½

172 CD344 10r yel brn & blk 7.00 7.00

Poisonous Plants Type of 1989

Wmk. 373

1990, Nov. 5 Litho. *Perf. 12½*

173 A26 1r Ordeal plant 1.40 1.40
174 A26 2r Thorn apple 2.50 2.50
175 A26 3r Strychnine tree 3.75 3.75
176 A26 5r Bwa zasmen 6.75 6.75
Nos. 173-176 (4) 14.40 14.40

Elizabeth & Philip, Birthdays
Common Design Types

Wmk. 384

1991, June 17 Litho. *Perf. 14½*

177 CD345 4r multicolored 3.00 3.00
178 CD346 4r multicolored 3.00 3.00
a. Pair, #177-178 + label 6.25 6.25

Shipwrecks — A29

1.50r, St. Abbs, 1860. 3r, Norden, 1862. 3.50r, Clan Mackay, 1894. 10r, Glenlyon, 1905.

Wmk. 373

1991, Oct. 28 Litho. *Perf. 14*

179 A29 1.50r multi 2.25 2.25
180 A29 3r multi 3.75 3.75
181 A29 3.50r multi 4.25 4.25
182 A29 10r multi 11.00 11.00
Nos. 179-182 (4) 21.25 21.25

Queen Elizabeth II's Accession to the Throne, 40th Anniv.
Common Design Type

1992, Feb. 6

183 CD349 1r multicolored .75 .75
184 CD349 1.50r multicolored 1.00 1.00
185 CD349 3r multicolored 1.90 1.90
186 CD349 3.50r multicolored 2.25 2.25
187 CD349 5r multicolored 3.50 3.50
Nos. 183-187 (5) 9.40 9.40

Aldabra World Heritage Site, 10th Anniv. — A30

Designs: 1.50r, Lomatopyllum aldabrense. 3r, Dryolimnas cuvieri aldabranus. 3.50r, Birgus latro. 10r, Dicrurus aldabranus.

1992, Nov. 19 *Perf. 14½*

188 A30 1.50r multicolored 2.10 2.10
189 A30 3r multicolored 4.25 4.25
190 A30 3.50r multicolored 5.00 5.00
191 A30 10r multicolored 13.00 13.00
Nos. 188-191 (4) 24.35 24.35

SHANGHAI

shaŋ-'hī

LOCATION — A city on the Whangpoo River, Kiangsu Province, China
POP. — 3,489,998

A British settlement was founded there in 1843 and by agreement with China settlements were established by France and the United States. Special areas were set aside for the foreign settlements and a postal system independent of China was organized which was continued until 1898.

16 Cash = 1 Candareen
100 Candareens = 1 Tael
100 Cents = 1 Dollar (1890)

Watermark

Wmk. 175 — Kung Pu (Municipal Council)

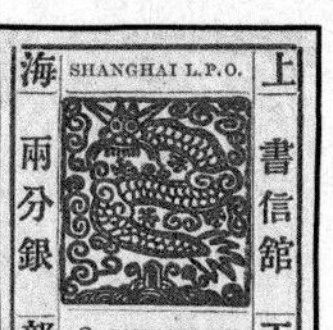

Dragon — A1

Antique Numerals
Roman "I" in "I6"
"Candareens" Plural

1865-66 Unwmk. Typo. *Imperf.*

Wove Paper

1 A1 2ca black 775.00 *7,500.*
a. Pelure paper 900.00
2 A1 4ca yellow 1,000. *5,250.*
a. Pelure paper 1,000. —
b. Double impression —
3 A1 8ca green 700.00 *6,000.*
a. 8ca yellow green 825.00 —
4 A1 16ca scarlet 2,250. *6,000.*
a. 16ca vermilion 2,250.
b. Pelure paper 2,250.
Nos. 1-4 (4) 4,725. 24,750.

No. 1: top character of three in left panel as illustrated. No. 5: top character is two horiz. lines.

Nos. 2, 3: center character of three in left panel as illustrated. Nos. 6, 7: center character much more complex.

Antique Numerals
"Candareens" Plural
Pelure Paper

5 A1 2ca black 650.00
a. Wove paper 650.00 6,250.
6 A1 4ca yellow 825.00 3,750.
7 A1 8ca dp grn 875.00 —
Nos. 5-7 (3) 2,350.

Antique Numerals
"Candareen" Singular
Laid Paper

8 A1 1ca blue 800.00 *6,000.*
9 A1 2ca black 11,000.
10 A1 4ca yellow 3,000.
Nos. 8-10 (3) 14,800.

Wove Paper

11 A1 1ca blue 500.00 *7,750.*
12 A1 2ca black 650.00 *7,750.*
13 A1 4ca yellow 775.00 8,000.
14 A1 8ca ol grn 700.00 —
15 A1 16ca vermilion 700.00 —
a. "1" of "16" omitted 26,000.
Nos. 11-15 (5) 3,325.

Roman "I," Antique "2"
"Candareens" Plural Except on 1ca
Wove Paper

16 A1 1ca blue 1,100. *3,800.*
17 A1 12ca fawn 375.00
18 A1 12ca choc 600.00
Nos. 16-18 (3) 2,075.

Antique Numerals
"Candareens" Plural Except on 1ca
Wove Paper

19 A1 1ca indigo, pelure paper 450.00 *5,500.*
a. 1ca blue, wove paper 425.00 *5,750.*
20 A1 3ca org brn 500.00 *4,250.*
a. Pelure paper 525.00 *3,750.*
21 A1 6ca red brn 350.00
22 A1 6ca fawn 875.00 —
23 A1 6ca vermilion 500.00
24 A1 12ca org brn 325.00
25 A1 16ca vermilion 325.00 *1,500.*
a. "1" of "16" omitted *500.00*
Nos. 19-25 (7) 3,325.

Examples of No. 22 usually have the straight lines cutting through the paper.

Antique Numerals
Roman "I"
"Candareens" Plural Except on 1ca
Laid Paper

26 A1 1ca blue *35,000.*
27 A1 2ca black *10,000.*
28 A1 3ca red brn *30,000.* —

Examples of No. 28 usually have the straight lines cutting through the paper.

Modern Numerals
"Candareen" Singular

29 A1 1ca sl bl 250.00 *4,500.*
a. 1ca dark blue 250.00 *4,250.*
30 A1 3ca red brn 250.00 *5,000.*

"Candareens" Plural Except the 1c

31 A1 2ca gray 225.00
32 A1 3ca red brn 225.00 *3,400.*

Coarse Porous Wove Paper

33a A1 1ca blue 160.00
34a A1 2ca black 210.00
b. Grayish paper 275.00
35a A1 3ca red brown 150.00
36a A1 4ca yellow 350.00
37a A1 6ca olive green 190.00
38a A1 8ca emerald 225.00
39a A1 12ca org ver 160.00
40a A1 16ca red 250.00 *875.00*
41a A1 16ca red brown 225.00 *875.00*
Nos. 33a-41a (9) 1,920.

Chinese characters change on same denomination stamps.

Nos. 1, 2, 11 and 32 exist on thicker paper, usually toned. Most authorities consider these four stamps and Nos. 33a-41a to be official reprints made to present sample sets to other post offices. The tone in this paper is an acquired characteristic, due to various causes. Many shades and minor varieties exist of Nos. 1-41a.

A2

A3

A4

A5

1866 Litho. *Perf. 12*

42 A2 2c rose 27.50 *35.00*
43 A3 4c lilac 47.50 *60.00*
44 A4 8c gray blue 52.50 *55.00*
45 A5 16c green 82.50 *110.00*
Nos. 42-45 (4) 210.00 260.00

Nos. 42-45 imperf. are proofs. See No. 50. For surcharges see Nos. 51-61, 67.

A6

A7

A8

A9

1866 *Perf. 15*

46 A6 1ca brown 11.00 17.50
a. "CANDS" 200.00 200.00
47 A7 3ca orange 45.00 *60.00*
48 A8 6ca slate 47.50 *55.00*
49 A9 12ca olive gray 72.50 *110.00*
Nos. 46-49 (4) 176.00 242.50

See Nos. 69-77. For surcharges see Nos. 62-66, 68, 78-83.

1872

50 A2 2c rose 170.00 *200.00*

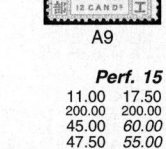

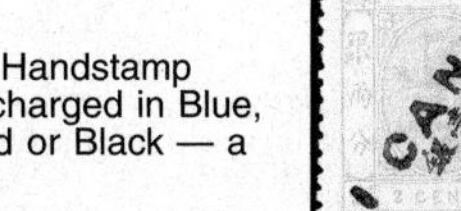

Handstamp Surcharged in Blue, Red or Black — a

1873 *Perf. 12*

51 A2 1ca on 2c rose 60.00 *65.00*
52 A3 1ca on 4c lilac 25.00 *37.50*
a. Inverted surcharge 625.00
b. Double surcharge 725.00
53 A3 1ca on 4c lilac (R) *9,000.* *3,750.*
54 A3 1ca on 4c lil (Bk) 25.00 *37.50*
a. Inverted surcharge 300.00
55 A4 1ca on 8c gray bl 52.50 *55.00*
a. Double surcharge 625.00
56 A4 1ca on 8c gray bl (R) *22,000.* *16,000.*
57 A5 1ca on 16c green *4,250.* *3,250.*
a. Double surcharge *15,000.*
58 A5 1ca on 16c green (R) *35,000.* *13,500.*

Perf. 15

59 A2 1ca on 2c rose 72.50 *75.00*

1875 *Perf. 12*

60 A2 3ca on 2c rose 300.00 250.00
61 A5 3ca on 16c green *4,250.* *3,250.*

Perf. 15

62 A7 1ca on 3ca org *38,000.* *18,000.*
63 A8 1ca on 6ca slate 875.00 650.00
64 A8 1ca on 6ca slate (R) *12,000.* *4,500.*
65 A9 1ca on 12ca ol gray 1,100. 900.00
66 A9 1ca on 12ca ol gray (R) *8,000.* *4,000.*
67 A2 3ca on 2c rose 875.00 750.00
68 A9 3ca on 12ca olive gray *6,000.* *6,000.*

Counterfeits exist of Nos. 51-68.

Types of 1866

1875 *Perf. 15*

69 A6 1ca yel, *yel* 45.00 37.50
70 A7 3ca rose, *rose* 45.00 37.50

Perf. 11½

71 A6 1ca yel, *yel* 900.00 650.00

1876 *Perf. 15*

72 A6 1ca yellow 25.00 *30.00*
73 A7 3ca rose 95.00 *95.00*
74 A8 6ca green 140.00 *160.00*
75 A9 9ca blue 250.00 300.00
76 A9 12ca light brown 275.00 325.00
Nos. 72-76 (5) 785.00 910.00

1877 Engr. *Perf. 12½*

77 A6 1ca rose 2,250. *3,000.*

Stamps of 1875-76 Surcharged type "a" in Blue or Red

1877 Litho. *Perf. 15*

78 A7 1ca on 3ca rose, *rose* 550.00 475.00
79 A7 1ca on 3ca rose 170.00 150.00
a. Double surcharge 2,250.
80 A8 1ca on 6ca green 300.00 250.00
81 A9 1ca on 9ca blue 550.00 550.00
82 A9 1ca on 12ca lt brn 3,250. 2,000.
83 A9 1ca on 12ca lt brn (R) *8,500.* *5,500.*

Counterfeits exist of Nos. 78-83.

A11

A12

A13

A14

1877 *Perf. 15*

84 A11 20 cash blue vio 16.50 *15.00*
a. 20 cash violet 13.00 10.00
85 A12 40 cash rose 22.50 20.00
86 A13 60 cash green 25.00 23.00
87 A13 80 cash blue 32.50 35.00
88 A14 100 cash brown 30.00 *32.50*
Nos. 84-88 (5) 126.50 125.50

Handstamp Surcharged in Blue — b

1879 *Perf. 15*

89 A12 20 cash on 40c rose 45.00 37.50
a. Inverted surcharge 550.00
90 A14 60 cash on 80c blue 55.00 *70.00*
91 A14 60 cash on 100c brn 65.00 *65.00*
Nos. 89-91 (3) 165.00 172.50

Types of 1877

1880 *Perf. 11½*

92 A11 20 cash violet 11.00 *11.00*
a. Horiz. pair, imperf. btwn. 800.00
b. Vert. pair, imperf. horiz. 850.00
93 A12 40 cash rose 17.50 15.00
a. Horiz. pair, imperf. btwn. 900.00
94 A13 60 cash green 20.00 *20.00*
95 A14 80 cash blue 21.00 *20.00*
96 A14 100 cash brown 24.00 *22.50*

Perf. 15x11½

97 A11 20 cash lilac 170.00 *150.00*
Nos. 92-97 (6) 263.50 238.50

Surcharged type "b" in Blue

1884 *Perf. 11½*

98 A12 20 cash on 40c rose 24.00 22.00
a. Double surcharge 700.00
99 A14 60 cash on 80c blue 35.00 *36.00*
100 A14 60 cash on 100c brn 42.50 42.50
Nos. 98-100 (3) 101.50 100.50

Types of 1877

1884

101 A11 20 cash green 10.50 10.00

1885 *Perf. 15*

102 A11 20 cash green 8.25 5.00
103 A12 40 cash brown 10.00 9.00
104 A13 60 cash violet 17.50 17.00
a. 60 cash red violet 22.50 *25.00*
b. Vert. pair, imperf. btwn. 1,000.
105 A14 80 cash buff 16.50 15.00
a. Horiz. pair, imperf. btwn. 800.00
106 A14 100 cash yellow 20.00 *20.00*

Perf. 11½x15

107 A11 20 cash green 16.50 15.00
108 A13 60 cash red vio 17.50 15.00
Nos. 102-108 (7) 106.25 96.00

Surcharged type "b" in Blue or Red

1886 *Perf. 15*

109 A14 40 cash on 80c buff 13.50 12.00
a. Inverted surcharge 20.00 18.00
b. Red surcharge 550.00
110 A14 60 cash on 100c yellow 20.00 18.00
a. Inverted surcharge 100.00 100.00
b. Double surcharge 225.00
c. Red surcharge 600.00

Types of 1877

1888 *Perf. 15*

111 A11 20 cash gray 9.50 5.50
112 A12 40 cash black 13.00 *9.50*
113 A13 60 cash rose 20.00 12.00
a. Third character at left lacks dot at top 27.50 *20.00*
114 A14 80 cash green 14.00 10.00
115 A14 100 cash lt blue 20.00 *17.50*
Nos. 111-115 (5) 76.50 54.50

Nos. 106, 103, 105 Handstamp Surcharged in Blue or Red Type "b" or

c

d

1888 *Perf. 15*

116 A14(b) 40 cash on 100c yel 16.50 16.00
a. Inverted surcharge 125.00
b. Double surcharge 140.00
c. Red surcharge 32.50 30.00
118 A12(c) 20 cash on 40c brn 27.50 25.00
a. Inverted surcharge 200.00 175.00
b. Double surcharge 350.00
c. Red surcharge 400.00 —
119 A14(c) 20 cash on 80c buff 14.50 12.00
a. Inverted surcharge 250.00 140.00
b. Double surcharge 650.00 550.00
c. Red surcharge 425.00
120 A12(d) 20 cash on 40c brn 27.50 *26.00*
a. Inverted surcharge 300.00 275.00
Nos. 116-120 (4) 86.00 79.00

Omitted surcharges paired with normal stamp exist on Nos. 116, 119.

Handstamp Surcharged in Black and Red (100 cash) or Red (20 cash) — e

1889 **Unwmk.**

121 A14(e) 100 cash on 20c on 100c yel 200.00 *225.00*
a. Without the surcharge "100 cash" 500.00
b. Blue & red surcharge 1,800. —
122 A14(c) 20 cash on 80c grn 16.50 15.00
a. Inverted surcharge 140.00
123 A14(c) 20 cash on 100c bl 16.50 15.00
a. Double surcharge 350.00
Nos. 121-123 (3) 233.00 255.00

Counterfeits exist of Nos. 116-123.

1889 **Wmk. 175** *Perf. 15*

124 A11 20 cash gray 5.75 4.25
125 A12 40 cash black 8.50 7.00
126 A13 60 cash rose 27.50 *27.50*
a. Third character at left lacks dot at top 30.00 *30.00*

Perf. 12

127 A14 80 cash green 11.00 *22.00*
a. Horiz. pair, imperf. btwn. 2,000.
128 A14 100 cash dk bl 17.50 22.00
Nos. 124-128 (5) 70.25 82.75

Nos. 124-126 are sometimes found without watermark. This is caused by the sheet being misplaced in the printing press, so that the stamps are printed on the unwatermarked margin of the sheet.

Shield with Dragon Supporters — A20

1890 **Unwmk.** **Litho.** *Perf. 15*

129 A20 2c brown 4.25 *4.75*
130 A20 5c rose 12.00 8.00
131 A20 15c blue 27.50 15.00

Nos. 129-131 imperforate are proofs.

Wmk. 175

132 A20 10c black 17.50 12.00
a. Perf. 12 1,000. 550.00
133 A20 15c blue 25.00 18.00
134 A20 20c violet 17.50 14.00
Nos. 129-134 (6) 103.75 71.75

See Nos. 135-141. For surcharges and overprints see Nos. 142-152, J1-J13.

1891 *Perf. 12*

135 A20 2c brown 3.00 2.00
136 A20 5c rose 13.00 7.00

1892

137 A20 2c green 3.50 2.50
138 A20 5c red 8.25 7.25
139 A20 10c orange 22.00 *22.00*
140 A20 15c violet 13.50 10.00
141 A20 20c brown 14.50 13.00
Nos. 137-141 (5) 61.75 54.75

No. 130 Handstamp Surcharged in Blue — f

1892 **Unwmk.** *Perf. 15*

142 A20 2c on 5c rose 175.00 80.00
a. Inverted surcharge 1,000. 850.00

Counterfeits exist of Nos. 142-152.

Stamps of 1892 Handstamp Surcharged in Blue

g

h

1893 **Wmk. 175** *Perf. 12*

143 A20 ½c on 15c violet 20.00 13.00
a. Double surcharge 375.00
b. Vert. pair, imperf. btwn. 350.00 325.00
144 A20 1c on 20c brown 20.00 13.00
a. ½c on 20c brown (error) *26,000.*

Nos. 144 and 144a exist in se-tenant pairs. Example pairs with black surcharge come from a trial printing.

Surcharged in Blue or Red (#152) on Halves of #136 (#145-147), #138 (#148-150), #135 (#151), #137 (#152)

½ Ct. ½ Ct. ½ Ct. 1 Ct.
i j k m

145 A20(i) ½c on half of 5c 13.50 10.00
146 A20(j) ½c on half of 5c 13.50 10.00
147 A20(k) ½c on half of 5c 275.00 200.00
148 A20(i) ½c on half of 5c 13.50 10.00
149 A20(j) ½c on half of 5c 13.50 10.00
150 A20(k) ½c on half of 5c 225.00 160.00
151 A20(m) 1c on half of 2c 3.50 3.00
c. Dbl. surch., one in green 1,600. *350.00*
d. Dbl. surch., one in black 1,700. *350.00*
152 A20(m) 1c on half of 2c 16.50 12.00
Nos. 145-152 (8) 574.00 415.00

The ½c surcharge setting of 20 (2x10) covers a vertical strip of 10 unsevered stamps, with horizontal gutter midway. This setting has 11 of type "i," 8 of type "j" and 1 of type "k." Nos. 145-152 are perforated vertically down the middle.

Inverted surcharges exist on Nos. 145-151. Double surcharges, one inverted, are also found in this issue.

Handstamped provisionals somewhat similar to Nos. 145-152 were issued in Foochow by the Shanghai Agency.

Coat of Arms — A24

Typo. (Dot)

Litho. (No Dot)

Frame Inscriptions in Black

1893 **Litho.** *Perf. 13½x14*

153 A24 ½c orange 7.25 3.00
b. Horiz. pair, imperf vert. 225.00
154 A24 1c brown 7.25 1.75
155 A24 2c vermilion 8.00 2.50
a. Imperf, pair 225.00
156 A24 5c blue 1.10 .65
a. Black inscriptions inverted 1,800.
b. Black inscriptions double 900.00
157 A24 10c green 10.00 *11.00*
158 A24 15c yellow 1.10 .90
159 A24 20c lilac 11.00 9.00
Nos. 153-159 (7) 45.70 28.80

Typographed

153a A24 ½c orange .55 .50
154a A24 1c brown .55 .50

Typo & Litho

157a A24 10c green 2.75 *3.00*
159a A24 20c lilac 3.00 *5.00*

On Nos. 157 and 159, frame inscriptions are lithographed, rest of design typographed.

See Nos. 170-172. For overprints and surcharges see Nos. 160-166, 168-169.

Stamps of 1893 Overprinted in Black

1893, Dec. 14

160 A24 ½c (On #153a) .50 .50
a. Inverted overprint 165.00 150.00
161 A24 1c (On #154a) .65 .65
a. Double overprint 67.50 50.00
162 A24 2c (On #155) .90 .90
a. Inverted overprint 165.00 120.00
163 A24 5c (On #156) 3.50 *5.00*
a. Inverted overprint 325.00
164 A24 10c (On #157a) 11.00 *12.00*
165 A24 15c (On #158) 7.25 6.50
166 A24 20c (On #159) 9.50 *10.00*
Nos. 160-166 (7) 33.30 35.55

50th anniv. of the first foreign settlement in Shanghai.

Mercury — A26

1893, Nov. 11 **Litho.** *Perf. 13½*

167 A26 2c vermilion & black 1.10 1.00

Nos. 158 and 159 Handstamp Surcharged in Black

1896 *Perf. 13½x14*

168 A24 4c on 15c yel & blk 11.00 8.00
169 A24 6c on 20c lil & blk (#159) 11.00 8.00
a. On #159a 55.00 25.00

Surcharge occurs inverted or double on Nos. 168-169.

Arms Type of 1893

1896

170 A24 2c scarlet & blk .30 *1.60*
a. Black inscriptions inverted 2,000. 1,800.
b. Black inscriptions double 1,400. 1,200.
171 A24 4c org & blk, *yel* 7.25 *5.50*
172 A24 6c car & blk, *rose* 8.25 *8.50*
Nos. 170-172 (3) 15.80 *15.60*

POSTAGE DUE STAMPS

Postage Stamps of 1890-92 Handstamped in Black, Red or Blue

1892 **Unwmk.** *Perf. 15*

J1 A20 2c brown (Bk) 900.00 *900.00*
a. Inverted overprint 2,500.
J2 A20 5c rose (Bk) 25.00 *14.00*
a. Inverted overprint 425.00
J3 A20 15c blue (Bk) 52.50 47.50
a. Inverted overprint 400.00
b. Blue overprint 425.00

Wmk. 175

J4 A20 10c black (R) 35.00 32.50
J5 A20 15c blue (Bk) 30.00 27.50
a. Inverted overprint 600.00
b. Double overprint 300.00
c. Pair, one without ovpt. 1,300.
J6 A20 20c violet (Bk) 22.50 20.00
Nos. J1-J6 (6) 1,065. 1,042.

1892-93 *Perf. 12*

J7 A20 2c brown (Bk) 3.75 3.75
a. Inverted overprint 175.00 160.00
b. Double overprint 400.00
c. Pair, one without ovpt. 1,000.
J8 A20 2c brown (Bl) 3.50 *3.00*
J9 A20 5c rose (Bl) 15.50 9.00
a. Inverted overprint 225.00
J10 A20 10c orange (Bk) 250.00 225.00
J11 A20 10c orange (Bl) 20.00 15.00
a. Inverted overprint 325.00
J12 A20 15c violet (R) 32.50 30.00
J13 A20 20c brown (R) 32.50 30.00
Nos. J7-J13 (7) 357.75 *315.75*

D2

1893 **Litho.** *Perf. 13½*

J14 D2 ½c orange & blk .55 .55

Perf. 14x13½

J15 D2 1c brown & black .65 .55
a. Horiz. pair, imperf. vert. 350.00
J16 D2 2c ver & blk .65 .55
a. Horiz. pair, imperf. vert. 350.00
J17 D2 5c blue & black 1.00 .90
J18 D2 10c green & black 6.00 2.00
J19 D2 15c yellow & black 4.75 4.00
J20 D2 20c violet & black 1.75 1.50
Nos. J14-J20 (7) 15.35 10.05

Stamps of Shanghai were discontinued in 1898.

SHARJAH & DEPENDENCIES

'shär-jə

LOCATION — Oman Peninsula, Arabia, on Persian Gulf
GOVT. — Sheikdom under British protection
POP. — 5,000 (estimated)
CAPITAL — Sharjah

The dependencies on the Gulf of Oman are Dhiba, Khor Fakkan, and Kalba.

Sharjah is one of six Persian Gulf sheikdoms to join the United Arab Emirates which proclaimed independence Dec. 2, 1971. See United Arab Emirates.

100 Naye Paise = 1 Rupee
20 Piastres = 1 Riyal (1966)
100 Dirhams = 1 Riyal (1966)

Catalogue values for all unused stamps in this country are for Never Hinged items.

Sheik Saqr bin Sultan al Qasimi, Flag and Map — A1

Perf. 14½x14

1963, July 10 Photo. Unwmk.

Black Portrait and Inscriptions; Lilac Rose Flag

1	A1	1np lt bl grn & pink	.25	.75
2	A1	2np grnsh bl & sal	.25	.75
3	A1	3np violet & yel	.25	.75
4	A1	4np emerald & gray	.25	.75
5	A1	5np aqua & lt grn	.25	.75
6	A1	6np dl grn & brt yel	.25	.75
7	A1	8np Prus bl & bis	.25	.75
8	A1	10np aqua & tan	.25	.75
9	A1	16np ultra & bis	.30	1.40
10	A1	20np lt vio & lem	.35	1.40
11	A1	30np rose lil & brt yel grn	.50	1.40
12	A1	40np dk bl & yel grn	.60	2.10
13	A1	50np green & fawn	.80	3.00
14	A1	75np ultra & fawn	1.40	3.50
15	A1	100np ol bis & rose	1.75	10.00
		Nos. 1-15 (15)	7.70	28.80

See Nos. C1-C12, O1-O9.
For overprints and surcharges see Nos. 100-112, 210-216.

Malaria Eradication Emblem — A2

1963, Aug. 8

16	A2	1np grnsh blue	.25	.25
17	A2	2np dull blue	.25	.25
18	A2	3np violet blue	.25	.25
19	A2	4np emerald	.25	.25
20	A2	90np yellow brown	2.25	1.10
		Nos. 16-20 (5)	3.25	2.10

Miniature Sheet

Imperf

21	A2	100np bright blue	3.25	1.40

WHO drive to eradicate malaria.
No. 21 contains one 39x67mm stamp.
For surcharge see No. 35.

Red Crescent and Sheik — A3

1963, Aug. 25 ***Perf. 14x14½***

22	A3	1np purple & red	.25	.25
23	A3	2np brt green & red	.25	.25
24	A3	3np dark blue & red	.25	.25
25	A3	4np dark green & red	.25	.25
26	A3	5np dark brown & red	.25	.25
27	A3	85np green & red	1.40	.75
		Nos. 22-27 (6)	2.65	2.00

Miniature Sheet

Imperf

28	A3	100np plum & red	3.25	1.75

Cent. of the Intl. Red Cross.
Imperfs. exist. Value, set $11.
No. 28 contains one 67mm x 39mm stamp.

Nos. 36-40 and No. 20 Surcharged

Nos. 29-34

No. 35

1963, Oct. 6 Photo. ***Perf. 14½x14***

29	A4	10np on 1np brt grn	.25	.25
30	A4	20np on 2np red brn	.45	.35
31	A4	30np on 3np ol grn	.70	.60
32	A4	40np on 4np dp ultra	.95	.85
33	A4	75np on 90np carmine	1.75	1.40
34	A4	80np on 90np carmine	2.10	1.50
35	A2	1r on 90np yel brn	3.00	2.25
		Nos. 29-35 (7)	9.20	7.20

Due to a stamp shortage the surcharged set appeared before the commemorative issue. Some first day covers are dated Oct. 5.

Wheat Emblem and Hands with Broken Chains — A4

1963, Oct. 15 ***Perf. 14½x14***

36	A4	1np brt green	.25	.25
37	A4	2np red brown	.25	.25
38	A4	3np olive green	.25	.25
39	A4	4np deep ultra	.25	.25
40	A4	90np carmine	1.50	.75
		Nos. 36-40 (5)	2.50	1.75

Miniature Sheet

Imperf

41	A4	100np purple	3.25	1.40

"Freedom from Hunger" campaign of the FAO.
Imperfs. exist. Value, set $10.
No. 41 contains one 39x67mm stamp.
For surcharges see Nos. 29-34, 136-144.

A5

Orbiting Astronomical Observatory — A5a

Satellites: 2np, Nimbus weather satellite. 3np, Pioneer V space probe. 4np, Explorer XIII. 5np, Explorer XII. 35np, Relay satellite. 50np, Orbiting Solar Observatory.

1964, Feb. 5 Photo. ***Perf. 14***

42	A5	1np blue	.25	.25
43	A5	2np red brn & yel grn	.25	.25
44	A5	3np blk & grnsh bl	.25	.25
45	A5	4np lemon & blk	.25	.25
46	A5	5np brt pur & lem	.25	.25
47	A5	35np grnsh bl & pur	.75	.60
48	A5	50np ol grn & redsh brn	1.40	.85
		Nos. 42-48 (7)	3.40	2.70

Miniature Sheet

Imperf

48A	A5a	100np dk blue & gold	6.50	1.40

Space research.
Nos. 42-48 exist imperf. Value, set $8.
No. 48A contains one 112x80mm stamp.

Runner — A6

1964, Mar. 3 **Unwmk.**

49	A6	1np shown	.25	.25
50	A6	2np Discus	.25	.25
51	A6	3np Hurdler	.25	.25
52	A6	4np Shot put	.25	.25
53	A6	20np High jump	.35	.25
54	A6	30np Weight lifting	.60	.30
55	A6	40np Javelin	.70	.35
56	A6	1r Diving	1.75	1.00
		Nos. 49-56 (8)	4.40	2.90

Miniature Sheet

Imperf

56A	A6	1r Diving	7.00	5.75

18th Olympic Games, Tokyo, Oct. 10-25, 1964.
Nos. 49-56 exist imperf. Value, set $10.
First day covers are dated Feb. 29, 1964.
No. 56A is the same design as No. 56. Size of stamp: 67x67mm, size of sheet: 102x102mm.

Girl Scouts A7

1964, June 30 ***Perf. 14x14½***

57	A7	1np grnsh gray	.25	.25
58	A7	2np emerald	.25	.25
59	A7	3np brt blue	.25	.25
60	A7	4np brt violet	.25	.25
61	A7	5np carmine rose	.25	.25
62	A7	2r dark red brown	2.25	1.50
		Nos. 57-62 (6)	3.50	2.75

Miniature Sheet

Imperf

62A	A7	2r red org	3.50	2.50

Nos. 57-62 exist imperf. Value, set $9.
No. 62A contains one 67x40mm stamp. Size of sheet: 102½x76mm.

Sharjah Boy Scout — A8

Marching Scouts With Drummers — A9

Designs: 3np, 2r, Boy Scout portrait.

Perf. 14½x14, 14x14½

1964, June 30 Photo. Unwmk.

63	A8	1np gray green	.25	.25
64	A9	2np emerald	.25	.25
65	A8	3np brt blue	.25	.25
66	A8	4np brt violet	.35	.30
67	A9	5np brt carmine rose	.45	.35
68	A8	2r dk red brown	1.50	1.00
		Nos. 63-68 (6)	3.05	2.40

Miniature Sheet

Imperf

68A	A8	2r red org	3.50	2.50

Issued to honor the Sharjah Boy Scouts.
Nos. 63-68 exist imperf. Value, set $4.10.
No. 68A contains a single 39½x67mm stamp in the design of No. 68. Size of sheet: 77x103mm.

Olympic Torch and Rings — A10

1964, Oct. 15 Litho. ***Perf. 14***

69	A10	1np olive green	.25	.25
70	A10	2np ultra	.25	.25
71	A10	3np orange brown	.25	.25
72	A10	4np blue green	.25	.25
73	A10	5np dark violet	.25	.25
74	A10	40np brt blue	.30	.25
75	A10	50np dark red brown	.50	.25
76	A10	2r bister	2.50	1.25
		Nos. 69-76 (8)	4.55	3.00

Miniature Sheet

Imperf

76A	A10	2r olive green	7.00	5.75

18th Olympic Games, Tokyo, Oct. 10-25.
Nos. 69-76 exist imperf. Value, set $12.
No. 76A contain one stamp measuring 82mm at base. Size of sheet: 107x76mm.
For surcharges see Nos. 217-224.

Early Telephone — A11

Designs: No. 78, Modern telewriter. No. 79, 1895 car. No. 80, American automobile, 1964. No. 81, Early X-ray. No. 82, Modern X-ray. No. 83, Mail coach. No. 84, Telstar and Delta rocket. No. 85, Sailing vessel. No. 86, Nuclear ship "Savannah." No. 87, Early astronomers. No. 88, Jodrell Bank telescope. No. 89, Greek messengers. No. 90, Relay satellite, Delta rocket and globe. No. 91, Early flying machine. No. 92, Caravelle plane. No. 93, Persian water wheel. No. 94, Hydroelectric dam. No. 95, Old steam locomotive. No. 96, Diesel locomotive.

Unwmk.

1965, Apr. 26 Litho. *Perf. 14*

No.	Type	Denomination / Color	Unused	Used
77	A11	1np rose red & blk	.25	.25
78	A11	1np rose red & blk	.25	.25
79	A11	2np orange & indigo	.25	.25
80	A11	2np orange & indigo	.25	.25
81	A11	3np dk brn & emer	.25	.25
82	A11	3np emer & dk brn	.25	.25
83	A11	4np yel grn & dk vio	.25	.25
84	A11	4np dk vio & yel grn	.25	.25
85	A11	5np bl grn & brn	.25	.25
86	A11	5np bl grn & brn	.25	.25
87	A11	30np gray & bl	.25	.25
88	A11	30np blue & gray	.25	.25
89	A11	40np vio bl & yel	.30	.25
90	A11	40np vio bl & yel	.30	.25
a.		Imperf souvenir sheet of 2, #89-90	4.25	1.10
91	A11	50np blue & sepia	.35	.25
92	A11	50np blue & sepia	.35	.25
93	A11	75np brt grn & dk brn	.35	.25
94	A11	75np brt grn & dk brn	.35	.25
95	A11	1r yellow & vio bl	1.75	.75
96	A11	1r yellow & vio bl	1.75	.75
a.		Imperf souvenir sheet of 2, #95-96	5.75	1.75
		Nos. 77-96 (20)	8.50	6.00

Issued to show progress in science, transport and communications. Each two stamps of same denomination are printed se tenant.

Nos. 77-96 exist imperf. Value, set $30.

Stamps of Sharjah & Dependencies were replaced in 1972 by those of United Arab Emirates.

AIR POST STAMPS

Type of Regular Issue, 1963

Black Portrait and Inscriptions; Lilac Rose Flag

Perf. 14½x14

1963, July 10 Photo. Unwmk.

No.	Type	Denomination / Color	Unused	Used
C1	A1	1r ultra & fawn	.85	.45
C2	A1	2r lt violet & lemon	1.50	.70
C3	A1	3r dl grn & brt yel	1.75	1.25
C4	A1	4r grnsh bl & sal	3.00	1.50
C5	A1	5r emerald & gray	4.00	2.10
C6	A1	10r olive bis & rose	7.00	4.25
		Nos. C1-C6 (6)	18.10	10.25

For overprints or surcharges see Nos. C7-C12.

Nos. C1-C6 Overprinted

Black Portrait and Inscriptions; Lilac Rose Flag

1964, Apr. 7

No.	Type	Denomination / Color	Unused	Used
C7	A1	1r ultra & fawn	2.10	2.10
C8	A1	2r lt violet & lem	4.25	4.25
C9	A1	3r dull grn & brt yel	7.00	7.00
C10	A1	4r grnsh blue & sal	8.50	8.50
C11	A1	5r emerald & gray	13.00	13.00
C12	A1	10r olive bis & rose	18.50	18.50
		Nos. C7-C12 (6)	53.35	53.35

Pres. John F. Kennedy (1917-63).

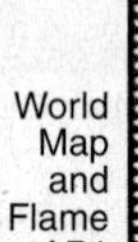

World Map and Flame AP1

1964, Apr. 15 *Perf. 14x14½*

No.	Type	Denomination / Color	Unused	Used
C13	AP1	50np red brown	.45	.25
C14	AP1	1r purple	.85	.50
C15	AP1	150np Prus green	1.50	.85
		Nos. C13-C15 (3)	2.80	1.60

Miniature Sheet

Imperf

No.	Type	Denomination / Color	Unused	Used
C15A	AP1	3r red	3.00	1.75

Issued for Human Rights Day.

Nos. C13-C15 exist imperf. Value, set $7.

No. C15A contain one 67x40mm stamp. Size of sheet: 89x64mm.

View of Khor Fakkan — AP2

Designs: 20np, Beni Qatab Bedouin camp near Dhaid. 30np, Oasis of Dhaid. 40np, Kalba Castle. 75np, Sharjah street with wind tower. 100np, Sharjah Fortress.

1964, Aug. 13 Photo. Unwmk.

No.	Type	Denomination / Color	Unused	Used
C16	AP2	10np multi	.25	.25
C17	AP2	20np multi	.25	.25
C18	AP2	30np multi	.30	.25
C19	AP2	40np multi	.35	.25
C20	AP2	75np multi	.80	.30
C21	AP2	100np multi	1.40	.35
		Nos. C16-C21 (6)	3.35	1.65

Nos. C16-C21 may exist imperf. The editors would like to examine any examples.

Unisphere and Sheik Saqr — AP3

20np, Offshore oil rig. 1r, New York skyline.

Perf. 14½x14

1964, Sept. 5 Photo. Unwmk.

Size: 26x45mm

No.	Type	Denomination / Color	Unused	Used
C22	AP3	20np multi	.45	.25
C23	AP3	40np multi	.70	.25

Size: 86x45mm

No.	Type	Denomination / Color	Unused	Used
C24	AP3	1r multi, horiz.	1.75	.50
a.		Strip of 3, Nos. C22-C24	3.00	.85

Miniature Sheet

Imperf

No.	Type	Denomination / Color	Unused	Used
C24B	AP3	40np multi	4.25	1.40
		Nos. C22-C24B (4)	7.15	2.40

New York World's Fair, 1964-65.

No. C24a exists imperf. Value, strip $6.

No. C24B contains one 40x68mm stamp in the design of No. C23. Size of sheet: 76x108mm.

J. F. Kennedy, Statue of Liberty — AP4

1964, Nov. 22 *Perf. 14x13½*

No.	Type	Denomination / Color	Unused	Used
C25	AP4	40np multicolored	1.40	.70
C26	AP4	60np multicolored	1.40	.70
C27	AP4	100np multicolored	1.40	.70
a.		Imperf souvenir sheet of 3, #C25-C27	7.00	5.75
		Nos. C25-C27 (3)	4.20	2.10

Pres. John F. Kennedy.

Nos. C25-C27 exist imperf. from sheets. Value, set $17.50.

Rock Dove AP5

Birds: 40np, 2r, Red jungle fowl. 75np, 3r, Hoopoe.

Perf. 14x14½

1965, Feb. 20 Photo. Unwmk.

No.	Type	Denomination / Color	Unused	Used
C28	AP5	30np gray & multi	.60	.25
C29	AP5	40np multicolored	.75	.25
C30	AP5	75np brt blue & multi	1.00	.35
C31	AP5	150np blue & multi	2.10	.70
C32	AP5	2r multicolored	3.00	.85
C33	AP5	3r red & multi	3.50	1.40
		Nos. C28-C33 (6)	10.95	3.80

Exist imperf. Value, set $15.

OFFICIAL STAMPS

Nos. 7-15 Overprinted

Perf. 14½x14

1965, Jan. 13 Photo. Unwmk.

No.	Type	Denomination / Color	Unused	Used
O1	A1	8np multi	.25	.25
O2	A1	10np multi	.25	.25
O3	A1	16np multi	.25	.25
O4	A1	20np multi	.25	.25
O5	A1	30np multi	.25	.25
O6	A1	40np multi	.35	.35
O7	A1	50np multi	1.00	1.00
O8	A1	75np multi	2.25	2.25
O9	A1	100np multi	4.25	4.25
		Nos. O1-O9 (9)	9.10	9.10

SIBERIA

sī-ˈbir-ē-ə

LOCATION — A vast territory of Russia lying between the Ural Mountains and the Pacific Ocean.

The anti-Bolshevist provisional government set up at Omsk by Adm. Aleksandr V. Kolchak issued Nos. 1-10 in 1919. The monarchist, anti-Soviet government in Priamur province issued Nos. 51-118 in 1921-22.

(Stamps of the Czechoslovak Legion are listed under Czechoslovakia.)

100 Kopecks = 1 Ruble

Russian Stamps of 1909-17 Surcharged

a

b

On Stamps of 1909-12

1919 Unwmk. *Perf. 14x14½*

Wove Paper

Lozenges of Varnish on Face

No.	Type	Denomination / Color	Unused	Used
1	A14(a)	35k on 2k dull grn	.60	*2.00*
a.		Inverted surcharge	75.00	
b.		"5" omitted	*150.00*	
c.		Double surcharge	—	
2	A14(a)	50k on 3k car	.60	*2.00*
a.		Inverted surcharge	75.00	
3	A14(a)	70k on 1k dl org yel	1.00	*4.25*
a.		Inverted surcharge	75.00	
4	A15(b)	1r on 4k car	1.25	*2.00*
a.		Dbl. surch., one inverted	150.00	*110.00*
b.		Inverted surcharge	75.00	
c.		Double surcharge	200.00	
5	A14(b)	3r on 7k blue	7.00	*9.00*
a.		Double surcharge	75.00	*30.00*
b.		Inverted surcharge	75.00	*100.00*
c.		Pair, one without surcharge	400.00	
d.		"3" omitted	—	
6	A11(b)	5r on 14k dk bl & car	9.50	*17.50*
a.		Double surcharge	75.00	*40.00*
b.		Inverted surcharge	100.00	*40.00*

On Stamps of 1917

Imperf

No.	Type	Denomination / Color	Unused	Used
7	A14(a)	35k on 2k gray grn	1.25	*4.25*
a.		Inverted surcharge	*100.00*	
8	A14(a)	50k on 3k red	1.00	*4.25*
a.		Inverted surcharge	150.00	
b.		Double surcharge	*100.00*	
9	A14(a)	70k on 1k orange	.75	*4.25*
a.		Inverted surcharge	100.00	
b.		Dbl. surch., one inverted	—	
10	A15(b)	1r on 4k car	9.50	*14.00*
		Nos. 1-10 (10)	32.45	*63.50*

Nos. 1-10 were first issued in Omsk during the regime of Admiral Kolchak. Later they were used along the line of the Trans-Siberian railway to Vladivostok.

Some experts question the postal use of most off-cover canceled examples of Nos. 1-10.

25

Similar surcharges, handstamped as above are bogus.

Priamur Government Issues

Nikolaevsk Issue

A5

A6

A7

1909-17 Russian Stamps Handstamp Surcharged or Overprinted

1921 Unwmk. *Perf. 14x14½, 13½*

51 A5 10k on 4k carmine *250.00 250.00*
52 A5 10k on 10k dark blue *1,500.*
53 A6 15k on 14k dk blue & car *200.00 200.00*
a. Inverted surcharge *750.00*
54 A6 15k on 15k red brn & dp blue *75.00 100.00*
55 A6 15k on 35k red brn & grn *75.00* 100.00
56 A6 15k on 50k brn vio & grn *75.00*
57 A6 15k on 70k brn & red org *150.00 200.00*
58 A7 15k on 1r brn & org *200.00*
59 A5 on 20k dl bl & dk car *300.00 350.00*
60 A5 on 20k on 14k dk bl & car (#118) *200.00*
a. 15k on 20k on 14k dk bl & car (error) *1,100.*
61 A7 20k on 3½r mar & lt grn *250.00 300.00*
62 A7 20k on 5r indigo, grn & lt bl *950.00 950.00*
63 A7 20k on 7r dk grn & pink *900.00 950.00*
a. Inverted surcharge 1,500.
b. Double surcharge 2,500.

Nos. 59-60 are overprinted with initials but original denominations remain.

A 10k on 5k claret (Russia No. 77) and a 15k on 20k blue & carmine (Russia No. 82a) were not officially issued. Some authorities consider them bogus.

Reprints exist.

On Russian Semi-Postal Stamp No. B6

64 SP5 20k on 3k mar & gray grn, *pink 750.00*

On Stamps of 1917
Imperf

65 A5 10k on 1k orange *100.00*
66 A5 10k on 2k gray green *75.00 100.00*
67 A5 10k on 3k red *100.00 100.00*
68 A5 10k on 5k claret — *700.00*
69 A6 15k on 1r pale brn, brn & red org *150.00 150.00*
70 A7 20k on 1r pale brn, brn & red org *200.00 200.00*
71 A7 20k on 3½r mar & lt grn *325.00 400.00*
72 A7 20k on 7r dk grn & pink *950.00 950.00*

The letters of the overprint are the initials of the Russian words for "Nikolaevsk on Amur Priamur Provisional Government."

As the surcharges on Nos. 51-72 are handstamped, a number exist inverted or double.

A 20k blue & carmine (Russia No. 126) with Priamur overprint and a 15k on 20k (Russia No. 126) were not officially issued. Some authorities consider them bogus.

No evidence found of genuine usage of Nos. 51-72.

Stamps of Far Eastern Republic Overprinted

1922

78 A2 2k gray green 25.00 25.00
a. Inverted overprint 200.00
79 A2a 4k rose 25.00 25.00
a. Inverted overprint *250.00*
80 A2 5k claret 25.00 25.00
81 A2a 10k blue 25.00 25.00
Nos. 78-81 (4) 100.00 100.00

Anniv. of the overthrow of the Bolshevik power in the Priamur district.

The letters of the overprint are the initials of "Vremeno Priamurski Pravitel'stvo" i.e. Provisional Priamur Government, 26th May.

Russian Stamps of 1909-21 Overprinted in Dark Blue or Vermilion

On Stamps of 1909-18

1922 *Perf. 14x14½*

85 A14 1k dull org yel 75.00 100.00
86 A14 2k dull green 125.00 110.00
87 A14 3k carmine 30.00 50.00
88 A15 4k carmine 25.00 35.00
89 A14 5k dk claret 35.00 40.00
90 A14 7k blue (V) 100.00 45.00
91 A15 10k dark blue (V) 60.00 70.00
92 A11 14k dk bl & car 75.00 85.00
93 A11 15k red brn & dp bl 10.00 15.00
94 A8 20k dl bl & dk car 50.00 25.00
95 A11 20k on 14k dk bl & car 125.00 150.00
96 A11 25k dl grn & dk vio (V) 50.00 50.00
97 A11 35k red brn & grn 20.00 15.00
a. Inverted overprint 200.00
98 A8 50k brn vio & grn 20.00 50.00
99 A11 70k brn & red org 50.00 55.00
Nos. 85-99 (15) 850.00 895.00

On Stamps of 1917
Imperf

100 A14 1k orange 15.00 *25.00*
a. Inverted overprint 200.00 100.00
101 A14 2k gray green 15.00 25.00
102 A14 3k red 20.00 25.00
103 A15 4k carmine 100.00 100.00
104 A14 5k claret 35.00 25.00
105 A11 15k red brn & dp bl *100.00* 125.00
106 A8 20k blue & car 125.00 75.00
107 A9 1r pale brn, brn & red org 40.00 *60.00*
Nos. 100-107 (8) 450.00 460.00

On Stamps of Siberia, 1919
Perf. 14½x15

108 A14 35k on 2k green 100.00 100.00

Imperf

109 A14 70k on 1k orange 250.00 120.00

On Stamps of Far Eastern Republic, 1921

110 A2 2k gray green 20.00 *25.00*
111 A2a 4k rose 20.00 *25.00*
112 A2 5k claret 20.00 *25.00*
a. Inverted overprint 100.00
113 A2a 10k blue (R) 20.00 *25.00*
Nos. 109-113 (5) 330.00 220.00

Same, Surcharged with New Values

114 A2 1k on 2k gray grn 20.00 *25.00*
115 A2a 3k on 4k rose 20.00 *25.00*

The overprint is in a rectangular frame on stamps of 1k to 10k and 1r; on the other values the frame is omitted. It is larger on the 1 ruble than on the smaller stamps.

The overprint reads "Priamurski Zemski Krai," Priamur Rural Province.

Far Eastern Republic Nos. 30-32 Overprinted in Blue

Perf. 14½x15

116 A14 35k on 2k green 20.00 *25.00*

Imperf

117 A14 35k on 2k green 60.00 *120.00*
118 A14 70k on 1k orange 30.00 15.00
Nos. 116-118 (3) 110.00 160.00

Counterfeits of Nos. 51-118 abound.

SIERRA LEONE

sē-ˌer-ə lē-ˈōn

LOCATION — West coast of Africa, between Guinea and Liberia
GOVT. — Republic in British Commonwealth
AREA — 27,925 sq. mi.
POP. — 5,296,651 (1999 est.)
CAPITAL — Freetown

Sierra Leone was a British colony and protectorate. In 1961 it became fully independent, remaining within the Commonwealth. It became a republic April 19, 1971.

12 Pence = 1 Shilling
20 Shillings = 1 Pound
100 Cents = 1 Leone (1964)

Catalogue values for unused stamps in this country are for Never Hinged items, beginning with Scott 186 in the regular postage section and Scott C1 in the air post section.

Watermark

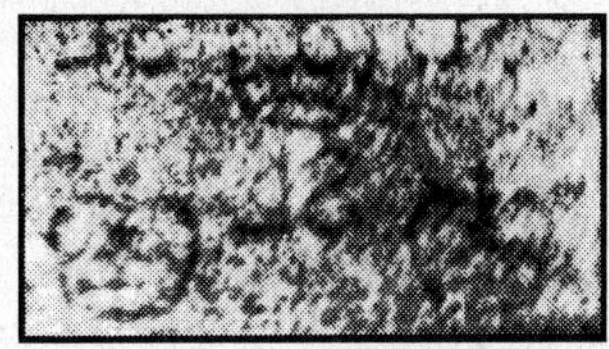
Wmk. 336 — St. Edwards Crown & SL, Multiple

Queen Victoria — A1

1859-74 Unwmk. Typo. *Perf. 14*

1 A1 6p reddsh lilac ('74) 77.50 30.00
a. 6p dull purple ('59) 275.00 55.00
b. 6p gray lilac ('65) 300.00 45.00

1872 *Perf. 12½*

5 A1 6p violet 425.00 70.00

Queen Victoria — A2

1872 Wmk. 1 Sideways *Perf. 12½*

6 A2 1p rose 85.00 50.00
8 A2 3p yellow buff 160.00 50.00
9 A2 4p blue 200.00 45.00
10 A2 1sh yellow green 525.00 62.50

1873 Wmk. 1 Upright

6a A2 1p 140.00 35.00
7 A2 2p magenta 150.00 55.00
8a A2 3p 550.00 95.00
9a A2 4p 375.00 57.50
10a A2 1sh 675.00 110.00

1876-96 Wmk. 1 Upright *Perf. 14*

11 A2 ½p bister 7.75 18.50
12 A2 1p rose 60.00 16.00
13 A2 1½p violet ('77) 55.00 10.00
14 A2 2p magenta 75.00 4.50
15 A2 3p yellow buff 65.00 8.75
16 A2 4p blue 225.00 7.25
17 A1 6p brt violet ('85) 72.50 27.50
a. Half used as 3p on cover 2,750.
18 A1 6p violet brn ('90) 28.00 16.00
19 A1 6p brown vio ('96) 3.00 *11.00*
20 A2 1sh green 92.50 7.25
Nos. 11-20 (10) 683.75 126.75

For surcharge see No. 32.

1883-93 Wmk. Crown and C A (2)

21 A2 ½p bister 50.00 65.00
22 A2 ½p dull green ('84) 3.50 3.50
23 A2 1p carmine ('84) 17.50 1.90
a. 1p rose carmine 32.50 9.50
b. 1p rose 225.00 40.00
24 A2 1½p violet ('93) 3.50 9.75
25 A2 2p magenta 77.50 9.50
26 A2 2p slate ('84) 62.50 4.50
27 A2 2½p ultra ('91) 19.00 2.00
28 A2 3p org yel ('92) 4.00 *16.00*
29 A2 4p blue 1,150. 32.50
30 A2 4p bister ('84) 2.75 4.00
31 A2 1sh org brn ('88) 27.50 22.00
Nos. 21-28,30-31 (10) 267.75 138.15

For surcharge see No. 33.

Nos. 13 and 24 Surcharged in Black

1893 Wmk. 1

32 A2 ½p on 1½p violet 575.00 *800.00*
a. "PFNNY" 3,750. *4,500.*

Wmk. 2

33 A2 ½p on 1½p violet 9.75 4.75
a. "PFNNY" 85.00 *82.50*
b. Inverted surcharge 125.00 125.00
c. Same as "a," inverted 4,000. *5,500.*
d. Double surcharge *1,200.*

A4

1896-97

34 A4 ½p lilac & grn ('97) 2.75 3.50
35 A4 1p lilac & car 5.00 2.00
36 A4 1½p lilac & blk ('97) 4.50 24.00
37 A4 2p lilac & org 2.75 5.50
38 A4 2½p lilac & ultra 2.75 1.40
39 A4 3p lilac & sl ('97) 9.50 7.75
40 A4 4p lilac & car ('97) 10.50 14.50
41 A4 5p lilac & blk 14.50 16.00
42 A4 6p lilac ('97) 9.00 27.50
43 A4 1sh green & blk 6.75 22.50
44 A4 2sh green & ultra 34.00 *80.00*
45 A4 5sh green & car 90.00 *250.00*
46 A4 £1 violet, *red* 325.00 *600.00*
Nos. 34-46 (13) 517.00 1,055.

Numerals of Nos. 39-46 of type A4 are in color on plain tablet.

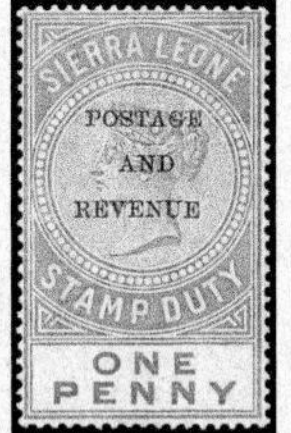
A5

A6

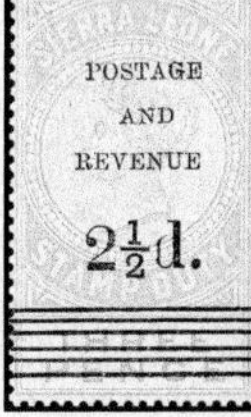
a

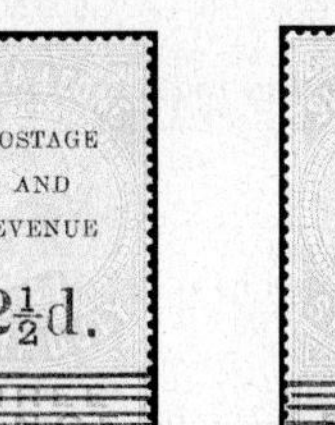
b

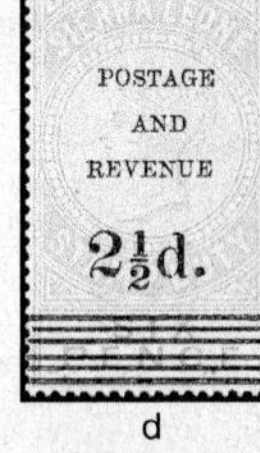
c

d

e

f

1897 Wmk. C A over Crown (46)

47 A5 1p lilac & grn 9.75 4.25
a. Double overprint *2,000. 2,000.*

48 A6(a) 2½p on 3p lil & grn 13.50 *22.50*
a. Double surcharge *40,000.*
b. Double surcharge, types "a" and "b" *32,000.*
c. Double surcharge, types "a" and "c" *55,000.*
49 A6(b) 2½p on 3p 70.00 *95.00*
50 A6(c) 2½p on 3p 200.00 *250.00*
51 A6(d) 2½p on 3p 400.00 *525.00*
52 A6(a) 2½p on 6p lil & grn 10.00 *22.50*
53 A6(b) 2½p on 6p 55.00 *85.00*
54 A6(c) 2½p on 6p 150.00 190.00
55 A6(d) 2½p on 6p 325.00 *400.00*
56 A6(a) 2½p on 1sh lilac 110.00 80.00
57 A6(b) 2½p on 1sh lilac 1,100. 1,100.
58 A6(c) 2½p on 1sh lilac 550.00 500.00
59 A6(e) 2½p on 1sh lilac 1,750. 2,000.
59A A6(f) 2½p on 1sh lilac 1,800. 1,500.
60 A6(a) 2½p on 2sh lilac 2,250. *3,000.*
61 A6(b) 2½p on 2sh lilac *20,000. 25,000.*
62 A6(c) 2½p on 2sh lilac *12,000. 17,000.*
a. Italic "N" in "REVENUE" 50,000. 55,000.
63 A6(e) 2½p on 2sh lilac *47,500.*
63A A6(f) 2½p on 2sh lilac *50,000. 55,000.*

The words "POSTAGE AND REVENUE" on Nos. 56-63A are set in two lines and overprinted below instead of above "2½d."

The "d" in type "f" is 3½mm wide; that in type "a" is 3mm.

Very fine examples of Nos. 47-63A will have perforations touching the frameline on one or more sides.

Nos. 56-59A are often found discolored. Such stamps sell for about half the values quoted.

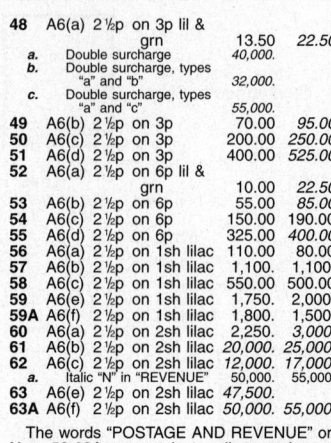

King Edward VII — A7

Numerals of 3p to £1 of type A7 are in color on plain tablet.

1903 Wmk. Crown and C A (2)

64 A7 ½p violet & grn 3.25 *6.50*
65 A7 1p violet & car 2.25 1.10
66 A7 1½p violet & blk 1.50 *19.00*
67 A7 2p violet & brn org 4.50 *17.50*
68 A7 2½p violet & ultra 5.00 *9.00*
69 A7 3p violet & gray 17.50 *23.50*
70 A7 4p violet & car 8.00 *22.00*
71 A7 5p violet & blk 16.00 *50.00*
72 A7 6p violet & dull vio 12.50 *42.50*
73 A7 1sh green & blk 26.00 *80.00*
74 A7 2sh green & ultra 55.00 *80.00*
75 A7 5sh green & car 80.00 *140.00*
76 A7 £1 violet, *red* 275.00 350.00
Nos. 64-76 (12) 505.00 822.10

1904-05 Wmk. 3 Chalky Paper

77 A7 ½p violet & grn 5.75 5.25
78 A7 1p violet & car 7.25 1.75
79 A7 1½p violet & blk 3.50 *20.00*
80 A7 2p violet & brn org 4.75 4.50
81 A7 2½p violet & ultra 8.25 2.25
82 A7 3p violet & gray 45.00 4.00
83 A7 4p violet & car 14.00 8.00
84 A7 5p violet & blk 16.00 *40.00*
85 A7 6p violet & dl vio 9.00 *3.75*
86 A7 1sh green & blk 8.50 *10.00*
87 A7 2sh green & ultra 37.50 *40.00*
88 A7 5sh green & car 50.00 65.00
89 A7 £1 violet, *red* 300.00 350.00
Nos. 77-89 (13) 509.50 554.50

For watermarks see the *British Colonial and Crown Agents Watermarks* section in the introduction in the front of the catalog.

1907-10 Ordinary Paper

90 A7 ½p green 1.25 .60
91 A7 1p carmine 18.50 .80
92 A7 1½p orange ('10) 3.50 2.25
93 A7 2p gray 3.50 1.75
94 A7 2½p ultra 4.00 3.25

Chalky Paper

95 A7 3p violet, *yel* 14.00 *3.25*
96 A7 4p blk & red, *yel* 2.60 1.75
97 A7 5p vio & ol grn 27.00 8.50
98 A7 6p vio & red vio 22.50 9.00
99 A7 1sh black, *green* 6.25 5.75
100 A7 2sh vio & bl, *bl* 26.00 22.50
101 A7 5sh grn & red, *yel* 50.00 70.00
102 A7 £1 vio & blk, *red* 300.00 250.00
Nos. 90-102 (13) 479.10 379.40

The 3p also exists on ordinary paper. Value, unused $26, used $15.

King George V and Seal of the Colony
A8 A9

Die I

For description of dies I and II see "Dies of British Colonial Stamps" in Table of Contents.

Numerals of 3p, 4p, 5p, 6p and 10p of type A8 are in color on plain tablet. Numerals of 7p and 9p are on solid-color tablet.

1912-24 Ordinary Paper Wmk. 3

103 A8 ½p green 5.00 3.50
104 A8 1p scarlet 10.00 1.00
a. 1p carmine 2.25 .45
105 A8 1½p orange 2.25 *2.75*
106 A8 2p gray 1.50 .25
107 A8 2½p ultra 1.25 1.00

Chalky Paper

108 A9 3p violet, *yel* 6.25 3.75
109 A8 4p blk & red, *yel* 3.25 *17.50*
a. Die II ('24) 7.25 *6.00*
110 A8 5p violet & ol grn 2.10 *7.00*
111 A8 6p vio & red vio 5.00 *6.75*
112 A8 7p violet & org 3.50 *14.00*
113 A8 9p violet & blk 5.75 *14.00*
114 A8 10p violet & red 3.50 *22.00*
115 A9 1sh black, *green* 10.00 *5.25*
a. 1sh black, *emerald* *190.00*
116 A9 2sh vio & ultra, *bl* 31.00 7.00
117 A9 5sh grn & red, *yel* 29.00 *42.50*
118 A9 10sh grn & red, *grn* 110.00 *160.00*
119 A9 £1 vio & blk, *red* 250.00 *325.00*
120 A9 £2 violet & ultra 950.00 *1,400.*
121 A9 £5 gray grn & org *3,750. 5,000.*
Nos. 103-119 (17) 479.35 633.25

The status of #115a has been questioned.

Die II

1921-27 Ordinary Paper Wmk. 4

122 A8 ½p green 2.90 1.10
123 A8 1p violet ('26) 9.00 .25
a. Die I ('24) 7.00 *2.50*
124 A8 1½p scarlet 2.00 1.50
125 A8 2p gray ('22) 1.90 .25
126 A8 2½p ultra 3.50 *21.00*
127 A8 3p ultra ('22) 1.75 1.40
128 A8 4p blk & red, *yel* 6.75 3.75
129 A8 5p vio & ol grn 1.50 1.40

Chalky Paper

130 A8 6p dp vio & red vio 1.50 *3.25*
131 A8 7p vio & org ('27) 5.75 *30.00*
132 A8 9p dl vio & blk ('22) 6.75 *26.00*
133 A8 10p violet & red 6.75 *37.50*
134 A9 1sh blk, *emerald* 17.50 8.50
135 A9 2sh vio & ultra, *bl* 12.50 11.50
136 A9 5sh grn & red, *yel* 12.50 *62.50*
137 A9 10sh grn & red, *grn* 175.00 *350.00*
138 A9 £2 violet & ultra 900.00 *1,300.*
139 A9 £5 gray grn & org *3,500. 4,750.*
Nos. 122-137 (16) 267.55 559.90

Rice Field — A10

Palms and Kola Tree — A11

1932, Mar. 1 Engr. Perf. 12½

140 A10 ½p green .25 1.10
141 A10 1p dk violet .40 .30
142 A10 1½p rose car .80 *3.00*
143 A10 2p yellow brn .75 .30
144 A10 3p ultra 2.25 *3.25*
145 A10 4p orange 1.90 *16.00*
146 A10 5p olive green 3.00 *8.25*
147 A10 6p light blue 1.50 *5.25*
148 A10 1sh red brown 7.50 *16.00*

Perf. 12

149 A11 2sh dk brown 7.75 *9.75*
150 A11 5sh indigo 21.00 *28.00*
151 A11 10sh deep green 90.00 *145.00*
152 A11 £1 deep violet 180.00 *275.00*
Nos. 140-152 (13) 317.10 511.20

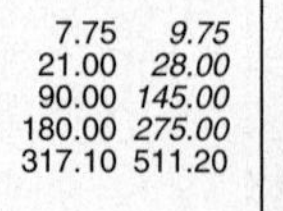

Wilberforce Issue

Arms of Sierra Leone — A12

Slave Throwing Off Shackles — A13

Map of Sierra Leone — A14

Old Slave Market, Freetown A15

Fruit Seller — A16

Government Sanatorium — A17

Bullom Canoe — A18

Punting near Banana Islands — A19

Government Buildings, Freetown A20

Old Slavers' Resort, Bunce Island — A21

African Elephant — A22

George V A23

Freetown Harbor — A24

1933, Oct. 2

153 A12 ½p dp grn 1.00 *1.25*
154 A13 1p brn & blk .85 .25
155 A14 1½p org brn 8.50 4.75
156 A15 2p violet 3.50 .25
157 A16 3p ultra 6.50 1.75
158 A17 4p dk brn 7.00 *10.00*
159 A18 5p red brn & sl grn 7.50 *11.00*
160 A19 6p dp org & blk 14.00 7.00
161 A20 1sh dk vio 7.50 *20.00*
162 A21 2sh bl & dk brn 42.50 *50.00*
163 A22 5sh red vio & blk 160.00 *200.00*
164 A23 10sh grn & blk 300.00 *525.00*
165 A24 £1 yel & dk vio 650.00 *850.00*
Nos. 153-165 (13) 1,209. *1,681.*

Abolition of slavery in the British colonies and cent. of the death of William Wilberforce, English philanthropist and agitator against the slave trade.

Common Design Types pictured following the introduction.

Silver Jubilee Issue

Common Design Type

1935, May 6 Perf. 11x12

166 CD301 1p black & ultra 1.60 *2.10*
167 CD301 3p ultra & brown 2.50 *7.25*
168 CD301 5p indigo & green 3.50 *21.00*
169 CD301 1sh brn vio & ind 16.00 *20.00*
Nos. 166-169 (4) 23.60 *50.35*
Set, never hinged 42.50

Coronation Issue

Common Design Type

1937, May 12 Perf. 11x11½

170 CD302 1p deep orange .40 .90
171 CD302 2p dark violet .65 1.00
172 CD302 3p deep ultra .90 3.75
Nos. 170-172 (3) 1.95 5.65
Set, never hinged 3.75

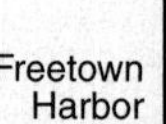
Freetown Harbor A25

Rice Harvesting A26

1938-44 Perf. 12½

173 A25 ½p grn & blk .25 .35
174 A25 1p dp cl & blk .25 .50
175 A26 1½p rose red 9.75 .85
175A A26 1½p red vio ('41) .25 *.50*
176 A26 2p red violet 24.00 2.50
176A A26 2p dk red ('41) .25 *1.60*
177 A25 3p ultra & blk .35 *.45*
178 A25 4p red brn & blk 1.25 *3.50*
179 A26 5p olive green 1.35 3.75
180 A26 6p gray .75 .45
181 A25 1sh ol grn & blk 1.75 .60
181A A26 1sh3p org yel ('44) .40 .50
182 A25 2sh sepia & blk 2.25 2.25
183 A26 5sh red brown 7.25 *14.50*

184 A26 10sh emerald 18.50 16.00
185 A25 £1 dk blue 10.50 *29.00*
Nos. 173-185 (16) 79.10 77.30
Set, never hinged 150.00

Catalogue values for unused stamps in this section, from this point to the end of the section, are for Never Hinged items.

Peace Issue
Common Design Type
Perf. 13½x14
1946, Oct. 1 Engr. Wmk. 4
186 CD303 1½p lilac .25 .25
187 CD303 3p bright ultra .25 .25

Silver Wedding Issue
Common Design Types
1948, Dec. 1 Photo. *Perf. 14x14½*
188 CD304 1½p brt red violet .25 .25

Engraved; Name Typographed
Perf. 11½x11
189 CD305 £1 dark blue 25.00 *29.50*

UPU Issue
Common Design Types
Engr.; Name Typo. on 3p, 6p
1949, Oct. 10 *Perf. 13½, 11x11½*
190 CD306 1½p rose violet .25 *.30*
191 CD307 3p indigo 1.60 *3.50*
192 CD308 6p gray .70 *4.75*
193 CD309 1sh olive .35 *.60*
Nos. 190-193 (4) 2.90 *9.15*

Coronation Issue
Common Design Type
1953, June 2 Engr. *Perf. 13½x13*
194 CD312 1½p purple & black .40 .40

Cape Lighthouse A27

Cotton Tree, Freetown — A28

1p, Queen Elizabeth II Quay. 1½d, Piassava workers. 3p, Rice harvesting. 4p, Iron ore production, Marampa. 6p, Whale Bay, York Village. 1sh, Bullom boat. 1sh3p, Map of Sierra Leone & plane. 2sh6p, Orugu Bridge. 5sh, Kuranko chief. 10sh, Law Courts, Freetown. £1, Government House.

Perf. 13 (A27), 13½ (A28)
1956, Jan. 2 Engr. Wmk. 4
Center in Black
195 A27 ½p lt violet .80 *2.00*
196 A27 1p reseda .70 .30
197 A27 1½p ultra 1.25 *4.75*
198 A28 2p lt brown .55 .30
199 A28 3p ultra 1.00 .25
a. Perf 13x13½ 2.25 *14.00*
200 A27 4p gray blue 2.00 1.60
201 A27 6p violet .80 .25
202 A28 1sh carmine 1.00 .40
203 A27 1sh3p gray brown 8.75 .25
204 A28 2sh6p brown org 15.00 9.50
205 A28 5sh green 7.00 *2.75*
206 A27 10sh red violet 3.50 2.10
207 A27 £1 orange 23.00 *32.50*
Nos. 195-207 (13) 65.35 56.95

For surcharges and overprints see Nos. 242-247, 251-253, 255-256, 319, 322, C1-C7, C13.

Independent State

Carrying Oil Palm Fruit — A29

Diamond Miner and Badge A30

Badge and: 1½p, 5sh, Bundu mask. 2p, 10sh, Bishop Crowther and Old Fourah Bay College. 3p, 6p, Sir Milton Margai. 4p, 1sh3p, Lumley Beach, Freetown. £1, Bugler.

Perf. 13x13½, 13½x13
1961, Apr. 27 Engr. Wmk. 336
208 A29 ½p bl grn & dk brn .25 .25
209 A30 1p gray grn & brn org 1.50 .25
210 A29 1½p green & blk .25 .25
211 A29 2p vio blue & blk .25 .25
212 A30 3p brn org & ultra .25 .25
213 A30 4p rose red & grnsh bl .25 .25
214 A30 6p lilac & gray .25 .25
215 A29 1sh org & dk brn .35 .25
216 A30 1sh3p vio & grnsh bl .35 .25
217 A30 2sh6p black & grn 2.75 .40
218 A29 5sh rose red & blk 1.00 *1.50*
219 A29 10sh emerald & blk 1.25 *1.50*
220 A29 £1 carmine & yel 8.50 *13.00*
Nos. 208-220 (13) 17.20 18.65

Sierra Leone's Independence.
For surcharges see Nos. 254, 274, 279-280, 285-286, 290-291, 294, 296, 299, C10, C29-C31, C132-C133.

Royal Charter, 1799 — A31

House of Representatives, Freetown, 1924 — A32

Designs: 4p, King's Yard Gate, Freetown, 1817. 1sh3p, Yacht "Britannia."

1961, Nov. 25 Engr. Wmk. 336
221 A31 3p vermilion & blk .25 .25
222 A31 4p violet & blk .75 .75
223 A32 6p orange & blk .90 .90
224 A32 1sh3p blue & blk 1.75 1.75
Nos. 221-224 (4) 3.65 3.65

Visit of Elizabeth II to Sierra Leone, Nov., 1961.
For overprints and surcharges see Nos. 272, 278, C8-C9, C11-C12.

Malaria Eradication Emblem — A33

1962, Apr. 7 *Perf. 11x11½*
225 A33 3p crimson .25 .25
226 A33 1sh3p green .25 .25

WHO drive to eradicate malaria.

Fireball Lily — A34

Jina Gbo — A35

Plants: 1½p, Stereospermum. 2p, Black-eyed Susan. 3p, Beniseed. 4p, Blushing hibiscus. 6p, Climbing lily. 1sh, Beautiful crinum. 1sh3p, Bluebells. 2sh6p, Broken hearts. 5sh, Ra-ponthi. 12sh, Blue plumbago. £1, African tulip tree.

1963, Jan. 1 Photo. *Perf. 14*
Flowers in Natural Colors
227 A34 ½p olive brown .25 .25
228 A35 1p org ver & dk red .25 .25
229 A34 1½p green .25 .25
230 A35 2p olive bister .25 .25
231 A34 3p dark green .25 .25
232 A34 4p lt violet blue .25 .25
233 A35 6p indigo .25 .25
234 A34 1sh brt yel grn & red .50 .25
235 A35 1sh3p dk yellow grn 1.20 .25
236 A34 2sh6p dk gray 1.50 .60
237 A34 5sh deep violet 1.75 .80
238 A34 10sh red lilac 3.75 1.25
239 A35 £1 bright blue 10.00 5.50
Nos. 227-239 (13) 20.45 10.40

For surcharges see Nos. 271, 273, 276-277, 283-284, 289, 295, 300-305, 317-318, 320-321, 329-332, C37-C41, C57-C60, C134.

Wheat Emblem, Grain Bin and Threshing Machine A36

1sh3p, Bullom woman examining onion crop.

Perf. 11½x11
1963, Mar. 21 Engr. Wmk. 336
240 A36 3p orange yel & blk .30 .25
241 A36 1sh3p green & brown .45 .25

FAO "Freedom from Hunger" campaign.
For surcharges see Nos. 275, C28.

Nos. 195, 197 and 199 Surcharged in Red, Brown, Orange, Violet or Blue

On A27

On A28

Perf. 13, 13½
1963, Apr. 27 Wmk. 4
Center in Black
242 A27 3p on ½p lt vio (R) .40 .25
243 A27 4p on 1½p ultra (Br) .25 .25
244 A27 6p on ½p lt vio (O) .30 .25
245 A28 10p on 3p ultra (R) .50 .25
246 A28 1sh6p on 3p ultra (V) .30 .25
247 A28 3sh6p on 3p ultra (Bl) .40 .25
Nos. 242-247 (12) 8.55 4.40

Type "a" exists in two settings, varying in the width of the line "19 Progress 63." In each sheet of 60, this line measures 19½-21mm on 55 stamps, and 17½-18mm on 5 stamps.
See Nos. C1-C7.

Centenary Emblem — A37

Design: 6p, Red Cross. 1sh3p, Centenary Emblem with curved-lines background.

Perf. 11x11½
1963, Nov. 1 Engr. Wmk. 336
248 A37 3p purple & red .40 .25
249 A37 6p black & red .40 .25
250 A37 1sh3p dark green & red .70 .45
Nos. 248-250 (3) 1.50 .95

Centenary of International Red Cross.
For surcharge see No. C56.

Nos. 199, 197, 216 and 195 Ovptd. or Srchd. in Pink, Red, Violet or Brown

Perf. 13, 13½, 13½x13
1963, Nov. 4 Engr. Wmk. 4
Center in Black except No. 254
251 A28 3p (P) .25 .25
252 A27 4p on 1½p (R) .25 .25
253 A27 9p on 1½p (V) .25 .25
254 A30 1sh on 1sh3p (R) .25 .25
255 A27 1sh6p on ½p (P) .25 .25
256 A28 2sh on 3p (Br) .25 .25
Nos. 251-256,C8-C13 (12) 35.95 35.65

Oldest postal service (1st stamps in 1859) and the newest GPO in West Africa. Overprint in 5 lines on Nos. 251 and 256. A number of surcharge varieties and errors exist.

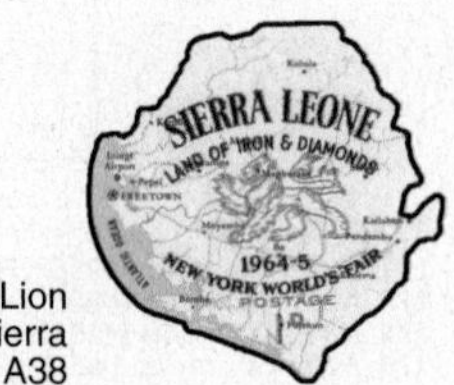

Map and Lion of Sierra Leone — A38

Engraved and Lithographed
1964, Feb. 10 Unwmk. *Die Cut*
Self-adhesive
257 A38 1p multicolored .25 .25
258 A38 3p multicolored .25 .25
259 A38 4p multicolored .25 .25
260 A38 6p multicolored .25 .25
261 A38 1sh multicolored .25 .25
262 A38 2sh multicolored .30 .30
263 A38 5sh multicolored .60 .60
Nos. 257-263,C14-C20 (14) 5.30 5.80

New York World's Fair, 1964-65.
For surcharges see Nos. 288, 297, 335 and note under No. 299.

"John F. Kennedy, American Patriot, World Humanitarian" A39

1964, May 11 **Self-adhesive**

264	A39	1p multicolored	.25	.25
265	A39	3p multicolored	.25	.25
266	A39	4p multicolored	.25	.25
267	A39	6p multicolored	.25	.25
268	A39	1sh multicolored	.25	.25
269	A39	2sh multicolored	.35	.35
270	A39	5sh multicolored	.60	*1.25*
		Nos. 264-270,C21-C27 (14)	5.15	8.00

For surcharges see Nos. 281-282, 287, 292-293, 298, 333, 336, and note under No. 299.

Issues of 1961-63 Srchd. in Red, Black, Dark Blue, Violet or Orange

Nos. 271, 278

No. 272

No. 273

No. 274

Nos. 275-276, 279

No. 277

1964, Aug. 4

271	A35	1c on 6p (#233) (R)	.25	.25
272	A31	2c on 3p (#221)	.25	.25
273	A34	3c on 3p (#231)	.25	.25
274	A29	5c on ½p (#208) (DB)	.25	.25
275	A36	8c on 3p (#240) (R)	.25	.25
276	A35	10c on 1sh3p (#235) (R)	.30	.25
277	A34	15c on 1sh (#234)	.40	.40
278	A32	25c on 6p (#223) (V)	.60	.60
279	A30	50c on 2sh6p (#217) (O)	1.20	1.20
		Nos. 271-279,C28-C31 (13)	5.70	5.65

No. 212 Srchd. in Black

No. 257 Srchd. in Black

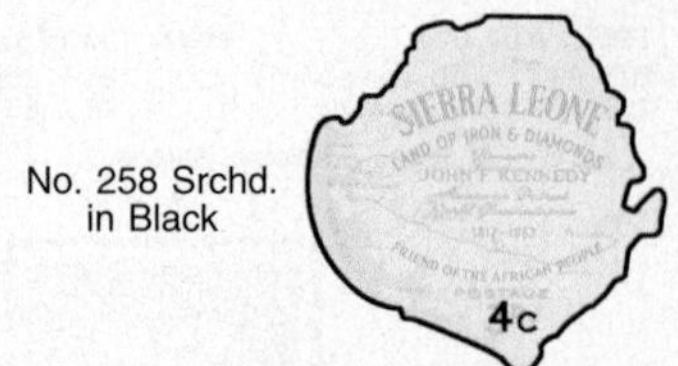

No. 258 Srchd. in Black

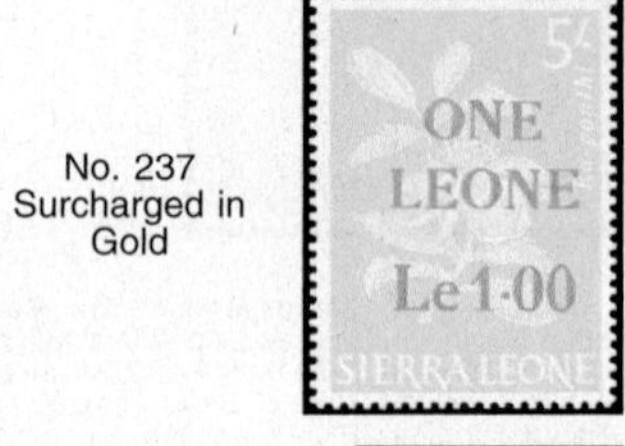

No. 230 Srchd. in Black

No. 237 Surcharged in Gold

No. 220 Surcharged in Black

1965, Jan. 20

280	A30	1c on 3p (#212)	.25	.25
281	A39	2c on 1p (#264)	.25	.25
282	A39	4c on 3p (#265)	.25	.25
283	A35	5c on 2p (#230)	.25	.25
284	A34	1 le on 5sh (#237) (G)	2.50	2.50
285	A29	2 le on £1 (#220)	5.25	5.25
		Nos. 280-285 (6)	8.75	8.75

The surcharges on Nos. 284-285 are given in numerals and spelled out in two lines; numeral on Nos. 280-283.

Issues of 1961-64 Srchd. in Red, Black, Orange, Blue or Pink

No. 286

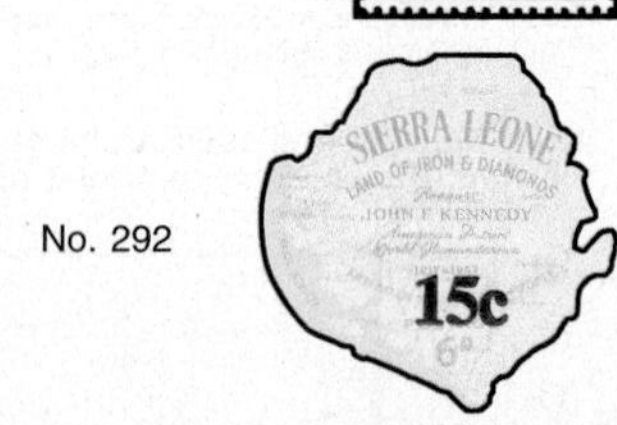

No. 292

No. 299

1965, Apr.

286	A29	1c on 1½p (#210) (R)	.25	.25
287	A39	2c on 3p (#265)	.25	.25
288	A38	2c on 4p (#259)	.25	.25
289	A35	3c on 1p (#228)	.25	.25
290	A29	3c on 2p (#211) (O)	.25	.25
291	A30	5c on 1sh3p (#216) (O)	.25	.25
292	A39	15c on 6p (#267)	2.75	2.75
293	A39	15c on 1sh (#268) (O)	5.00	5.00
294	A30	20c on 6p (#214) (O)	1.25	1.25
295	A35	25c on 6p (#233) (R)	1.60	1.60
296	A30	50c on 3p (#212) (R)	3.25	3.25
297	A38	60c on 5sh(#263) (Bl)	7.50	7.50
298	A39	1 le on 4p (#266) (P)	9.75	9.75
299	A29	2 le on £1 (#220) (Bl)	18.00	18.00
		Nos. 286-299 (14)	50.60	50.60

Additional surcharges exist: "1c" on Nos. 260, 262, 269-270. See note after No. C41 for airmails. Value $4 each.

For surcharges see Nos. 333, 335-336.

Nos. 228, 231, 234, 235, 232, 237 Srchd.

Designs of Surcharge: Nos. 301, 304, Sir Milton Margai. Nos. 302, 305, Sir Winston Churchill.

Wmk. 336

1965, May 19 **Photo.** ***Perf. 14***

300	A35	2c on 1p multi	.40	.25
301	A34	3c on 3p multi	.25	.25
302	A34	10c on 1sh multi	.60	.30
303	A35	20c on 1sh3p multi	1.10	.30
304	A34	50c on 4p multi	1.00	.50
305	A34	75c on 5sh multi	4.00	2.00
		Nos. 300-305,C37-C41 (11)	27.35	12.35

For surcharges see Nos. 329-332.

Cola Nut and Plant — A40

Coat of Arms A41

Typographed; Embossed on Silver Foil

1965 **Unwmk.** ***Die Cut***

Self-adhesive

310	A40	1c multicolored	.25	.25
311	A40	2c multicolored	.25	.25
312	A40	3c multicolored	.25	.25
313	A40	4c multicolored	.50	.40
314	A40	5c multicolored	.50	.40

Engr.; Embossed on Paper

315	A41	20c multi, *cream*	2.00	.75
316	A41	50c multi, *cream*	4.00	4.00
		Nos. 310-316,C53-C55 (10)	14.30	11.80

Various advertisements printed on peelable paper backing. Nos. 310-316 have side tabs for handling and come packed in boxes of 100. Nos. 310-312 and 314 were released during November due to a stamp shortage; official release date for set, Dec. 17, 1965. See #338-356, C67, C97. For surcharges see #334, 337, 364-368.

Nos. 197-198, and 232-234, 236 Surcharged & Overprinted in Black or Ultramarine

No. 318

No. 319

1966, Apr. 27 **Wmk. 4, 336**

317	A35	1c on 6p multi	.25	.25
318	A34	2c on 4p multi	.25	.25
319	A27	3c on 1½p ultra & blk (U)	.25	.25
320	A34	8c on 1sh multi (U)	1.00	.50
321	A34	10c on 2sh6p multi (U)	.25	.25
322	A28	20c on 2p lt brown (U)	.50	.25
		Nos. 317-322,C56-C60 (11)	7.65	7.55

5th anniv. of independence. The surcharge on No. 317 includes an "X" over old denomination.

Lion's Head Coin — A42

Designs: 2c, 3c, ¼ Golde coin. 5c, 8c, ½ Golde coin. 25c, 1 le, 1 Golde coin. (3c, 8c, 1 le, Map of Sierra Leone.)

Diameter: 2c, 3c, 38mm; 5c, 8c, 54mm; 25c, 1 le, 82mm

Self-adhesive

Litho.; Embossed on Gilt Foil

1966, Nov. 12 **Unwmk.** ***Die Cut***

323	A42	2c org & dp plum	.25	.25
324	A42	3c red lil & emer	.25	.25
325	A42	5c vio bl & red org	.25	.25
326	A42	8c black & Prus blue	.25	.25
327	A42	25c emerald & violet	.50	.50
328	A42	1 le red & orange	2.75	2.75
		Nos. 323-328,C61-C66 (12)	11.05	11.15

1st gold coinage of Sierra Leone. Advertising printed on paper backing.

Nos. 297-298, 303-305 and 316 Surcharged in Red, Silver, Violet, Green, Blue or Black

on A34, A35

on A38, A39

on A41

1967, Dec. 2

329 A34 6½c on 75c on 5sh (R) .30 .30
330 A34 7½c on 75c on 5sh (S) .30 .30
331 A34 9½c on 50c on 4p (G) .40 .40
332 A35 12½c on 20c on 1sh3p (V) .50 .50
333 A39 17½c on 1 le on 4p (Bl) 3.50 3.50
334 A41 17½c on 50c 3.50 3.50
335 A38 18½c on 60c on 5sh 10.00 10.00
336 A39 18½c on 1 le on 4p 3.50 3.50
337 A41 25c on 50c 1.00 1.00
Nos. 329-337,C67-C69 (12) 24.90 24.90

Self-adhesive & Die Cut

Nos. 338-421 are self-adhesive and die cut.

Cola Nut Type of 1965
White Numeral Tablet
Typographed; Embossed on White Paper

1967-68 **Unwmk.**

338 A40 ½c brt car, grn & yel .25 .45
339 A40 1c brt car, grn & yel .25 .25
340 A40 1½c orange, grn & yel .30 .30
341 A40 2c brt car, grn & yel .50 .25
342 A40 2½c emer, bl grn & yel .75 .65
343 A40 3c brt car, grn & yel .50 .25
344 A40 3½c olive, rose & ultra 3.25 1.60
345 A40 4½c gray ol, grn & yel .75 .65
346 A40 5c brt car, grn & yel .75 .25
347 A40 5½c red brn, grn & yel .75 .75
Nos. 338-347 (10) 8.05 5.40

Advertisements printed on peelable backing except on the 2c, 3c, 3½c and 5c.

Colored Numeral Tablet

348 A40 ½c brt car, grn & yel .25 .25
349 A40 1c brt car, grn & yel .25 .25
350 A40 2c pink, brn & car 2.75 2.75
351 A40 2c brt car, grn & yel 6.25 *7.50*
352 A40 2½c bl grn, vio & org 7.00 *8.25*
353 A40 2½c emer, bl grn & yel 3.00 *3.25*
354 A40 3c brt car, grn & yel 3.00 1.00
355 A40 3½c lilac rose, grn & yel .75 .70
356 A40 4c brt car, grn & yel .75 .25
Nos. 348-356 (9) 24.00 24.20

Nos. 344, 348-354 issued in 1968.

Advertisements printed on peelable backing on the 3½c and 4c.

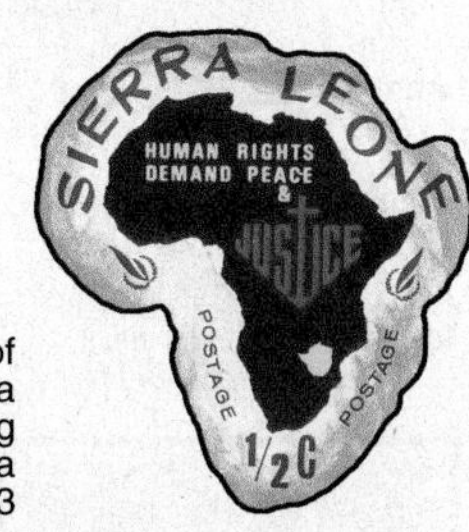

Map of Africa Showing Rhodesia A43

Each denomination shows map of Africa with map of one of the following countries — Portuguese Guinea, South Africa, Mozambique, Rhodesia, South West Africa or Angola.

1968, Sept. 25 **Unwmk.** **Litho.**

357 A43 ½c multicolored .25 .25
358 A43 2c multicolored .25 .25
359 A43 2½c multicolored .25 .25
360 A43 3½c multicolored .25 .25
361 A43 10c multicolored .30 .30
362 A43 11½c multicolored .35 .35
363 A43 15c multicolored .40 .40
Nos. 357-363 (7) 2.05 2.05
7 Strips of 6 (1 of each design) (42) 17.50

Intl. Human Rights Year. Sheets of 30 have 5 horizontal rows containing one stamp of each design. Advertisements printed on peelable backing.

See #C72-C78. For surcharges see #C106-C111.

No. 316 Surcharged or Overprinted

Engraved; Embossed on Paper

1968, Nov. 30

364 A41 6½c on 50c multi .25 .25
365 A41 17½c on 50c multi .30 .30
366 A41 22½c on 50c multi .60 .60
367 A41 28½c on 50c multi .75 .75
368 A41 50c multi 1.10 1.10
Nos. 364-368,C79-C83 (10) 6.20 6.20

19th Olympic Games, Mexico City, 10/12-27. No. 368 does not have a new denomination or obliterator.

Sierra Leone Type A1, 1859 A44

2c, Design A40, 2c, 1965. 3½c, #220. 5c, #315. 12½c, #189. 1 le, Design A9, #2, 1912.

1969, Mar. 1 **Litho.**

369 A44 1c multicolored .25 .25
370 A44 2c multicolored .25 .25
371 A44 3½c multicolored .25 .25
372 A44 5c multicolored .25 .25
373 A44 12½c multicolored .40 .40
374 A44 1 le multicolored 3.50 2.75
Nos. 369-374,C84-C89 (12) 20.75 19.40

5th anniv. of free-form self-adhesive postage stamps. Various advertisements printed on peelable paper backing. No. 369 has side tab for handling and comes packed in boxes of 50. Nos. 370-374 are without side tabs and come 20 stamps attached to one sheet.

Globe, Freighter, Flags of Sierra Leone and Japan — A45

Map of Europe and Africa, Freighter, Flags of Sierra Leone and Netherlands — A46

Anvil Shape with Flags of Sierra Leone and: 3½c, Union Jack. 10c, 50c, West Germany. 18½c, Netherlands.

1969, July 10

375 A45 1c multicolored .25 .25
376 A46 2c multicolored .25 .25
377 A46 3½c multicolored .25 .25
378 A46 10c multicolored .25 .25
379 A46 18½c multicolored .45 .45
380 A46 50c multicolored 1.00 1.00
Nos. 375-380,C90-C95 (12) 8.20 8.20

Completion of the Pepel Port iron ore carrier terminal. Various advertisements printed on peelable paper backing. No. 375 has side tab for handling and comes packed in boxes of 50. Nos. 376-380 are without side tabs and come 20 stamps attached to one sheet.

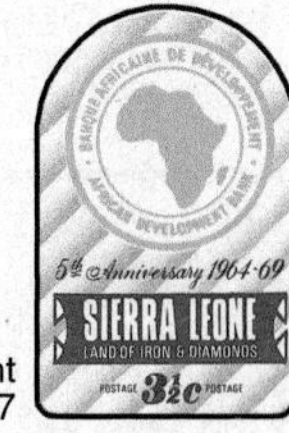

African Development Bank Emblem — A47

Lithographed; Gold Impressed

1969, Sept. 10

381 A47 3½c lt blue, grn & gold .40 *1.00*

5th anniv. of the African Development Bank. Advertising printed on peelable paper backing, 20 imperf. stamps to a sheet of backing, roulette 10. See No. C96.

Diamond and Boy Scout Emblem A48

1969, Dec. 6 **Litho.**

382 A48 1c multicolored .25 .25
383 A48 2c multicolored .25 .25
384 A48 3½c multicolored .25 .25
385 A48 4½c multicolored .25 .25
386 A48 5c multicolored .30 .30
387 A48 75c multicolored 9.50 9.50
Nos. 382-387,C100-C105 (12) 92.80 71.35

60th anniv. of the Sierra Leone Boy Scouts. Various advertising printed on peelable paper backing. No. 382 has side tab for handling and comes packed in boxes of 100. Nos. 383-387 are without side tabs and come 20 stamps attached to one sheet.

EXPO '70 Emblems, Torii, Maps of Sierra Leone and Japan — A49

1970, June 22

388 A49 2c multicolored .25 .25
389 A49 3½c multicolored .25 .25
390 A49 10c multicolored .25 .25
391 A49 12½c multicolored .30 .30
392 A49 20c multicolored .35 .35
393 A49 45c multicolored .60 .60
Nos. 388-393,C112-C117 (12) 8.35 8.35

EXPO '70 Intl. Exhib., Osaka, Japan, Mar. 15-Sept. 13. Various advertising printed on peelable paper backing.

Diamond A50

Palm Kernel — A51

Lithographed and Embossed

1970, Oct. 3 **Unwmk.**

Light Blue Background

394 A50 1c carmine & blk .25 .25
395 A50 1½c brt green & car .25 .25
396 A50 2c lilac & yel grn .25 .25
397 A50 2½c ocher & dk bl .25 .25
398 A50 3c vio bl & org red .45 .25
399 A50 3½c dk blue & grn .50 .25
400 A50 4c olive & ultra .50 .25
401 A50 5c black & lilac .50 .25

Orange Brown Background

402 A51 6c bright green .60 .25
403 A51 7c rose lilac .65 .30
404 A51 8½c orange .70 .30
405 A51 9c lilac .70 .30
406 A51 10c dark blue .75 .30
407 A51 11½c blue 1.00 .50
408 A51 18½c yellow green 2.00 .75
Nos. 394-408,C118-C124 (22) 51.05 44.90

Advertisements printed on peelable paper backing. Packed in boxes of 500.

Sewa Diadem in Jewelry Box — A52

1970, Dec. 30

409 A52 2c multicolored .50 .25
410 A52 3½c multicolored .50 .25
411 A52 10c multicolored .90 .35
412 A52 12½c multicolored 1.00 .45
413 A52 40c multicolored 2.75 1.50
414 A52 1 le multicolored 13.00 11.00
Nos. 409-414,C125-C130 (12) 58.30 51.60

Diamond industry. Advertisement printed on peelable paper backing. Sheets of 20.

Traffic Pattern — A53

1971, Mar. 1 **Litho.**

415 A53 3½c orange & vio blue 3.00 3.00

Right hand traffic change-over. See No. C131. Advertisements printed on peelable paper backing.

Flag and Lion's Head — A54

Litho.; Embossed in Silver

1971, Apr. 27

416 A54 2c multicolored .25 .25
417 A54 3½c multicolored .25 .25
418 A54 10c multicolored .25 .25
419 A54 12½c multicolored .25 .25
420 A54 40c multicolored .80 .80
421 A54 1 le multicolored 1.75 1.75
Nos. 416-421,C137-C142 (12) 10.50 10.50

10th anniversary of independence. Advertisements printed on peelable paper backing. Stamps are in shape of Sierra Leone map.

Pres. Siaka Stevens — A55

1972 Litho. *Perf. 13*

422 A55 1c pink & multi .25 .25
423 A55 2c violet & multi .25 .25
424 A55 4c lt ultra & multi .25 .25
425 A55 5c buff & multi .25 .25
426 A55 7c rose & multi .25 .25
427 A55 10c olive & multi .25 .25
428 A55 15c emerald & multi .25 .25
429 A55 18c yellow & multi .30 .30
430 A55 20c lt blue & multi .35 .35
431 A55 25c orange & multi .40 .40
432 A55 50c brt green & multi 1.00 .60
433 A55 1 le multicolored 1.60 1.25
434 A55 2 le red org & multi 3.00 3.00
435 A55 5 le multicolored 5.00 8.50
Nos. 422-435 (14) 13.40 16.15

Shades from later printings are found on several denominations including 1c, 2c, 7c, 10c, 1 le, 2 le.

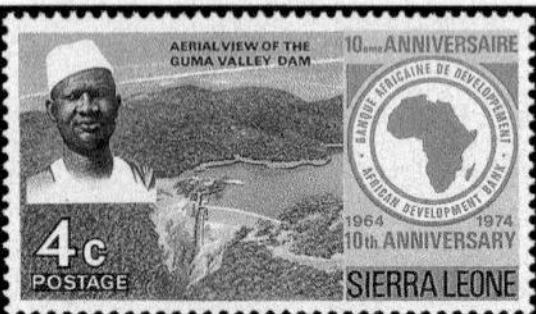

Guma Valley Dam and Bank Emblem — A56

1975, Jan. 14 Litho. *Perf. 13½*

436 A56 4c multicolored *125.00* *50.00*

African Development Bank, 10th anniversary. See No. C143.

Pres. Siaka Stevens and Opening of Congo Bridge — A57

1975, Aug. 24 Litho. *Perf. 13x13½*

437 A57 5c multicolored *15.00* *15.00*

Congo Bridge opening and Pres. Siaka Stevens' 70th birthday. See No. C144.

Pres. Tolbert and Stevens, Hands across Mano River — A58

1975, Oct. 3 Litho. *Perf. 13x13½*

438 A58 4c multicolored 1.50 1.50

Mano River Union Agreement between Liberia and Sierra Leone, signed Oct. 3, 1973. See No. C145.

Mohammed Ali Jinnah, Flags of Sierra Leone and Pakistan — A59

1977, Jan. 28 Litho. *Perf. 13 rough*

439 A59 30c multicolored 1.10 1.10

Mohammed Ali Jinnah (1876-1948), First Governor General of Pakistan.

Elizabeth II — A60

1977, Nov. 28 Litho. *Perf. 12½x12*

440 A60 5c multicolored .25 .25
441 A60 1 le multicolored 1.20 1.20

25th anniv. of the reign of Elizabeth II.

Fourah Bay College — A61

Design: 20c, Old College, vert.

Perf. 12x12½, 12½x12

1977, Dec. 19 Litho.

442 A61 5c multicolored .25 .25
443 A61 20c multicolored .35 .35

Fourah Bay College, Mt. Aureol, Freetown, founded 1827.

St. Edward's Crown and Scepters — A62

Designs: 50c, Elizabeth II in coronation coach. 1 le, Elizabeth II and Prince Philip on coronation day.

1978, Sept. 14 Litho. *Perf. 14½x14*

444 A62 5c multicolored .25 .25
445 A62 50c multicolored .45 .45
446 A62 1 le multicolored .60 .60
Nos. 444-446 (3) 1.30 1.30

25th anniv. of coronation of Elizabeth II.

Fig Tree Blue A63

Butterflies: 15c, Narrow blue-banded swallowtail. 25c, Pirate. 1 le, African giant swallowtail.

1979, Apr. 9 Litho. *Perf. 14½*

447 A63 5c multicolored .30 .30
448 A63 15c multicolored .65 .65
449 A63 25c multicolored 1.05 1.05
450 A63 1 le multicolored 4.00 4.00
Nos. 447-450 (4) 6.00 6.00

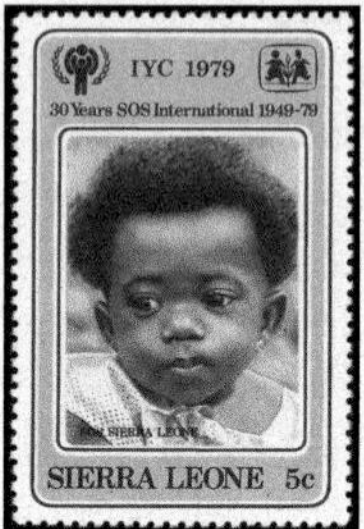

Child, IYC and SOS Emblems — A64

Designs (Emblems and): 27c, Girl and infant. 1 le, Mother and infant.

Perf. 14x13½

1979, Aug. 13 Litho. Wmk. 373

451 A64 5c multicolored .25 .25
452 A64 27c multicolored .45 .45
453 A64 1 le multicolored .80 .80
a. Souvenir sheet of 1 2.25 2.25
Nos. 451-453 (3) 1.50 1.50

Intl. Year of the Child and 30th anniv. of SOS villages (villages for homeless children).

Presidents Stevens and Tolbert, Pigeon Post, Mano River — A65

1979, Oct. 3 *Perf. 13½*

454 A65 5c multicolored .25 .25
455 A65 22c multicolored .25 .25
456 A65 27c multicolored .30 .30
457 A65 35c multicolored .35 .35
458 A65 1 le multicolored 1.05 1.05
a. Souvenir sheet of 1 1.25 1.25
Nos. 454-458 (5) 2.20 2.20

Mano River Union, 5th anniv.; Postal Union, 1st anniv.

Sierra Leone No. 9, Hill — A66

1979, Dec. 19 Litho. *Perf. 14½x14*

459 A66 10c Grt. Britain #6 .25 .25
460 A66 15c shown .25 .25
461 A66 50c Sierra Leone #220 .50 .50
Nos. 459-461 (3) 1.00 1.00

Souvenir Sheet

462 A66 1 le Sierra Leone #119 .80 .80

Sir Rowland Hill (1795-1879), originator.

Touraco A67

2c, Olive-bellied sunbird. 3c, Black-headed oriole. 5c, Spur-winged goose. 7c, White-bellied didric cuckoo. 10c, Gray parrot, vert. 15c, African blue quail, vert. 20c, West African wood owl, vert. 30c, Blue plantain eater, vert. 40c, Nigerian blue-breasted kingfisher, vert. 50c, Black crake, vert. 1 le, Hartlaub's duck. 2 le, Black bee-eater. 5 le, Denham's bustard.

1980, Jan. 29 *Perf. 14*

No Date Inscription Below Design

463 A67 1c multicolored .80 .80
464 A67 2c multicolored .80 .80
465 A67 3c multicolored .95 .95
466 A67 5c multicolored .75 .75
467 A67 7c multicolored .65 .65
468 A67 10c multicolored .90 .90
469 A67 15c multicolored 1.75 1.75
470 A67 20c multicolored 2.00 2.00
471 A67 30c multicolored 2.00 2.00
472 A67 40c multicolored 2.40 2.40
473 A67 50c multicolored 2.10 2.10
474 A67 1 le multicolored 2.50 2.50
475 A67 2 le multicolored 4.50 4.50
476 A67 5 le multicolored 10.50 10.50
Nos. 463-476 (14) 32.60 32.60

For surcharges see Nos. 632-636. For overprints see Nos. 637-638.

1981 Inscribed "1981"

463a A67 1c multicolored 1.00 1.00
464a A67 2c multicolored 1.00 1.00
465a A67 3c multicolored 1.00 1.00
466a A67 5c multicolored .80 .80
468a A67 10c multicolored .80 .80
469a A67 15c multicolored 1.50 1.50
470a A67 20c multicolored 1.60 1.60
471a A67 30c multicolored 1.90 1.90
472a A67 40c multicolored 1.90 1.90
473a A67 50c multicolored 1.90 1.90
474a A67 1 le multicolored 3.00 3.00
475a A67 2 le multicolored 5.75 5.75
476a A67 5 le multicolored 11.50 11.50
Nos. 463a-476a (13) 33.65 33.65

For surcharges see Nos. 632a-636a. For overprints see Nos. 637a, 638a.

1982 Inscribed "1982"

463b A67 1c multicolored 1.00 1.00
464b A67 2c multicolored 1.00 1.00
465b A67 3c multicolored 1.10 1.10
466b A67 5c multicolored .85 .85
467b A67 7c multicolored 9.25 9.25
468b A67 10c multicolored 1.00 1.00
469b A67 15c multicolored 2.00 2.00
470b A67 20c multicolored 2.25 2.25
471b A67 30c multicolored 2.25 2.25
472b A67 40c multicolored 2.75 2.75
473b A67 50c multicolored 2.40 2.40
474b A67 1 le multicolored 3.00 3.00
475b A67 2 le multicolored 5.00 5.00
476b A67 5 le multicolored 12.00 12.00
Nos. 463b-476b (14) 45.85 45.85

For surcharges see Nos. 632b-636b. For overprints see Nos. 637b, 638b.

For this design dated 1983, without watermark, see Nos. 600A-600K.

Rotary Intl., 75th Anniv. A68

1980, Feb. 23 *Perf. 14*

477 A68 5c orange & multi .25 .25
478 A68 27c red & multi .30 .30
479 A68 50c green & multi .50 .50
480 A68 1 le blue & multi 1.00 1.00
Nos. 477-480 (4) 2.05 2.05

Mail Ship "Maria," 1884, London '80 Emblem A69

1980, May 6 Litho. *Perf. 14*

481 A69 6c shown .25 .25
482 A69 31c "Tarquah," 1902 .45 .45
483 A69 50c "Aureol," 1951 1.00 1.00
484 A69 1 le "Africa Palm," 1974 1.60 1.60
Nos. 481-484 (4) 3.30 3.30

London 80 Intl. Stamp Exhib., May 6-14.

Conf. Emblem — A70

1980, July 1 Litho. *Perf. 14½*

485 A70 20c multicolored .25 .25
486 A70 1 le multicolored 1.00 1.00

17th African Summit Conf., Freetown, July 1-4.

Small Striped Swordtail — A71

27c, Pearl charaxes. 35c, White barred charaxes. 1 le, Zaddach's forester.

1980, Oct. 6 Litho. *Perf. 14*

487 A71 5c shown .25 .25
488 A71 27c multi .90 .90
489 A71 35c multi 1.10 1.10
490 A71 1 le multi 3.25 3.25
Nos. 487-490 (4) 5.50 5.50

Freetown Airport — A72

26c, Mammy Yoko Hotel. 31c, Freetown Cotton Tree. 40c, Beindomgo Falls. 50c, Water skiing. 1 le, Elephant.

1980, Dec. 5 Litho. *Perf. 13½*

491 A72 6c shown .25 .25
492 A72 26c multi .30 .30
493 A72 31c multi .35 .35
494 A72 40c multi .50 .50
495 A72 50c multi .60 .60
496 A72 1 le multi 1.25 1.25
Nos. 491-496 (6) 3.25 3.25

Servals — A73

Cats and Kittens: No. 498, Serval kittens. No. 500a, African golden cats. No. 502a, Leopards. No. 504a, Lions. Pairs have continuous design.

1981, Feb. 23 Litho. *Perf. 14*

497 6c multicolored .25 .25
498 6c multicolored .25 .25
a. A73 Pair, #497-498 .25 .25
499 31c multicolored .65 .65
500 31c multicolored .65 .65
a. A73 Pair, #499-500 1.60 1.60
501 50c multicolored 1.25 1.25
502 50c multicolored 1.25 1.25
a. A73 Pair, #501-502 3.00 3.00
503 1 le multicolored 3.00 3.00
504 1 le multicolored 3.00 3.00
a. A73 Pair, #503-504 6.00 6.00
Nos. 497-504 (8) 10.30 10.30

Ambulance Clinic — A74

6c, Soldiers, vert. 40c, Traffic policeman, vert. 1 le, Coast Guard ship.

Wmk. 373

1981, Apr. 18 Litho. *Perf. 14½*

505 A74 6c multi .30 .30
506 A74 31c shown 1.60 1.60
507 A74 40c multi 2.10 2.10
508 A74 1 le multi 5.00 5.00
Nos. 505-508 (4) 9.00 9.00

Anniv.: independence, 20th; republic, 10th.

Royal Wedding Issue
Common Design Type

31c, Bouquet. 35c, Sandringham. 45c, Charles. 60c, Charles. 1 le, Couple. 1.30 le, Charles. 1.50 le, Couple. 2 le, Couple. 3 le, Royal landau.

1981 Litho. *Perf. 12, 14*

509 CD331 31c multi .40 .40
510 CD331a 35c multi .60 .60
511 CD331 45c multi .75 .75
512 CD331a 60c multi .75 .75
513 CD331a 70c like 35c 2.00 2.00
514 CD331 1 le multi 1.00 1.00
515 CD331a 1.30 le multi 2.00 2.00
516 CD331a 1.50 le multi 1.00 1.00
517 CD331a 2 le multi 4.00 4.00
Nos. 509-517 (9) 12.50 12.50

Souvenir Sheet

518 CD331 3 le multi 3.00 3.00

31c, 45c, 1 le, 3 le issued July 22, perf. 14. 35c, 60c, 1.50 le issued in sheets of 5 plus label; perf. 12, Sept. 9. 70c, 1.30 le, 2 le issued in booklets only, perf. 14.

For surcharges see #540-546, 714, 716, 721.

Soccer Player — A75

Wmk. 373

1981, Sept. 30 Litho. *Perf. 14*

519 A75 6c shown .25 .25
520 A75 31c Boys planting trees .40 .40
521 A75 1 le Duke of Edinburgh .90 .90
522 A75 1 le Pres. Stevens .90 .90
Nos. 519-522 (4) 2.45 2.45

Duke of Edinburgh's Awards and Pres. Steven's Awards, 25th anniv.

Pineapples — A76

Woman Tending Rice Plants — A77

No. 524, Peanuts for export. No. 525, Peanuts. No. 526, Crushing, eating cassava. No. 527, Cassava fruits. No. 529, Rice plants. No. 530, Men tending pineapple plants.

Perf. 14, 14½ (A77)

1981 Litho. Wmk. 373

523 A76 6c shown .25 .25
524 A77 6c multi .25 .25
525 A76 31c multi .50 .50
526 A77 31c multi .50 .50
527 A76 50c multi .85 .85
528 A77 50c shown .85 .85
529 A76 1 le multi 1.75 1.75
530 A77 1 le multi 1.75 1.75
Nos. 523-530 (8) 6.70 6.70

World Food Day. Issue dates: Nos. 523, 525, 527, 529, Oct. 16; others, Nov. 2.

Princess Diana Issue
Common Design Type

31c, Caernarvon Castle. 50c, Honeymoon. 2 le, Wedding.
3 le, Diana.

1982, July Litho. *Perf. 14½*

531 CD332 31c multi .45 .45
532 CD332 50c multi .75 .75
533 CD332 2 le multi 2.25 2.25
Nos. 531-533 (3) 3.45 3.45

Souvenir Sheet

534 CD332 3 le multi 3.75 3.75

Also issued in sheetlets of 5 + label.

For overprints and surcharges see Nos. 552-555, 713, 715, 717-720, 722-723.

Scouting Year A78

20c, Studying animal husbandry. 50c, Botanical study. 1 le, Baden-Powell. 2 le, Fishing at campsite.
3 le, Raising flag.

1982, Aug. 23 *Perf. 14*

535 A78 20c multi .30 .30
536 A78 50c multi .90 .90
537 A78 1 le multi 1.75 1.75
538 A78 2 le multi 3.25 3.25
Nos. 535-538 (4) 6.20 6.20

Souvenir Sheet

539 A78 3 le multi 5.50 5.50

For surcharges see Nos. 694-698.

Nos. 509-512, 514, 516, 518 Surcharged

1982, Aug. 30 Wmk. 373

540 CD331 50c on 31c 1.60 1.60
541 CD331 50c on 35c 1.60 1.60
542 CD331 50c on 45c 1.60 1.60
543 CD331 50c on 60c 1.60 1.60
544 CD331 90c on 1 le 2.75 2.75
545 CD331 2 le on 1.50 le 6.00 6.00
Nos. 540-545 (6) 15.15 15.15

Souvenir Sheet

546 CD331 3.50 le on 3 le 2.50 2.50

1982 World Cup — A79

Designs: Various soccer players.

1982, Sept. 7

547 A79 20c multicolored .50 .50
548 A79 30c multicolored .70 .70
549 A79 1 le multicolored 2.50 2.50
550 A79 2 le multicolored 4.50 4.50
Nos. 547-550 (4) 8.20 8.20

Souvenir Sheet

551 A79 3 le multicolored 6.75 6.75

For overprints see Nos. 561-565.

Nos. 531-534 Overprinted: "ROYAL BABY/ 21.6.82"

1982, Oct. 15 Litho. *Perf. 14½*

552 CD332 31c multicolored .30 .30
553 CD332 50c multicolored .50 .50
554 CD332 2 le multicolored 1.75 1.75
Nos. 552-554 (3) 2.55 2.55

Souvenir Sheet

555 CD332 3 le multicolored 2.75 2.75

Birth of Prince William of Wales, June 21.
Also issued in sheetlets of 5 + label.
For surcharges see #715, 719-720, 723.

George Washington — A80

Various paintings of Washington. 31c, 1 le, vert.

1982, Oct. 30 Litho. *Perf. 14*

556 A80 6c multicolored .25 .25
557 A80 31c multicolored .40 .40
558 A80 50c multicolored .65 .65
559 A80 1 le multicolored 1.00 1.00
Nos. 556-559 (4) 2.30 2.30

Souvenir Sheet

560 A80 2 le multicolored 2.25 2.25

Nos. 547-551 Overprinted with Finalists and Score

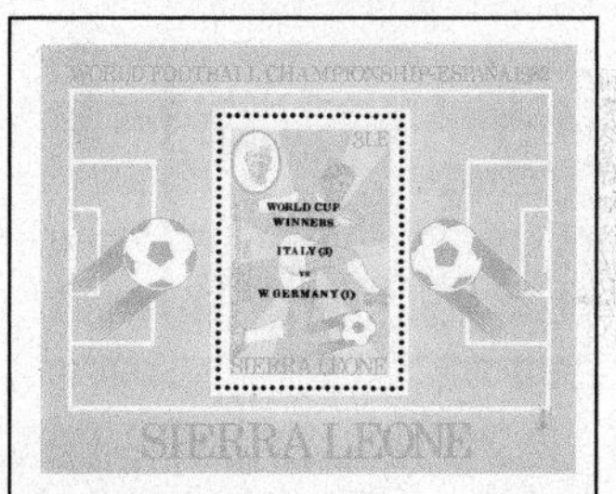

1982, Nov. 9 *Perf. 14*

561 A79 20c multicolored .40 .40
562 A79 30c multicolored .55 .55
563 A79 1 le multicolored 1.50 1.50
564 A79 2 le multicolored 2.10 2.10
Nos. 561-564 (4) 4.55 4.55

Souvenir Sheet

565 A79 3 le multicolored 2.50 2.50

Italy's victory in 1982 World Cup.

Christmas — A81

Stained-glass Windows, St. George's Cathedral, Freetown.

1982, Nov. 18 *Perf. 14*

566 A81 6c Temptation of Christ .35 .35
567 A81 31c Baptism of Christ .50 .50
568 A81 50c Annunciation .65 .65
569 A81 1 le Nativity 1.00 1.00
Nos. 566-569 (4) 2.50 2.50

Souvenir Sheet

570 A81 2 le Mary and Joseph 2.50 2.50

Charles Darwin (1809-82) A82

6c, Long-snouted crocodile. 31c, Rainbow lizard. 50c, River turtle. 1 le, Chameleon.
2 le, Royal python, vert.

1982, Dec. 10

No.	Type	Description	Unused	Used
571	A82	6c multicolored	1.75	1.75
572	A82	31c multicolored	2.25	2.25
573	A82	50c multicolored	3.25	3.25
574	A82	1 le multicolored	4.75	4.75
		Nos. 571-574 (4)	12.00	12.00

Souvenir Sheet

No.	Type	Description	Unused	Used
575	A82	2 le multicolored	4.50	4.50

500th Birth Anniv. of Raphael — A83

School of Athens, Fresco, Vatican: 6c, Diogenes. 31c, Euclid, Ptolemy. 50c, Euclid and his Students. 2 le, Pythagoras, Heraclitus.
3 le, Entire painting.
Nos. 576-579 show details.

1983, Jan. 28 Litho. *Perf. 14*

No.	Type	Description	Unused	Used
576	A83	6c multicolored	.25	.25
577	A83	31c multicolored	.45	.45
578	A83	50c multicolored	.75	.75
579	A83	2 le multicolored	2.25	2.25
		Nos. 576-579 (4)	3.70	3.70

Souvenir Sheet

No.	Type	Description	Unused	Used
580	A83	3 le multicolored	2.75	2.75

A83a

6c, Agricultural training. 10c, Tourism development. 50c, Broadcast training. 1 le, Airport services.

1983, Mar. 14 Litho. *Perf. 14*

No.	Type	Description	Unused	Used
581	A83a	6c multicolored	.25	.25
582	A83a	10c multicolored	.25	.25
583	A83a	50c multicolored	.65	.65
584	A83a	1 le multicolored	1.40	1.40
		Nos. 581-584 (4)	2.55	2.55

Commonwealth Day.

25th Anniv. of Economic Commission for Africa — A84

1983, Apr. 29 Litho. *Perf. 13½x13*

No.	Type	Description	Unused	Used
585	A84	1 le multicolored	1.10	1.10

Endangered Chimpanzees, World Wildlife Fund Emblem — A85

Various chimpanzees from Outamba-Kilimi Natl. Park. 10c, 31c, vert.

1983, May Litho. *Perf. 14*

No.	Type	Description	Unused	Used
586	A85	6c multicolored	*1.75*	*1.75*
587	A85	10c multicolored	*2.10*	*2.10*
588	A85	31c multicolored	*4.00*	*4.00*
589	A85	60c multicolored	*6.25*	*6.25*
		Nos. 586-589 (4)	*14.10*	*14.10*

Souvenir Sheet

No.	Type	Description	Unused	Used
590	A85	3 le Elephants	*6.50*	*6.50*

For surcharges see No. 2906-2909.

World Communications Year — A86

6c, Traditional communications. 10c, Mano River mail. 20c, Satellite ground station. 1 le, English packet, 1805.
2 le, Map, phone, envelope.

1983, July 14 *Perf. 14*

No.	Type	Description	Unused	Used
591	A86	6c multicolored	.25	.25
592	A86	10c multicolored	.25	.25
593	A86	20c multicolored	.30	.30
594	A86	1 le multicolored	1.25	1.25
		Nos. 591-594 (4)	2.05	2.05

Souvenir Sheet

No.	Type	Description	Unused	Used
595	A86	2 le multicolored	2.00	2.00

Manned Flight Bicentenary — A87

6c, Montgolfiere, 1783, vert. 20c, Deutschland blimp, 1897. 50c, Norge I blimp, North Pole, 1926. 1 le, Cape Sierra sport balloon, Freetown, 1983, vert.
2 le, Futuristic airship.

1983, Aug. 31 Litho. *Perf. 14*

No.	Type	Description	Unused	Used
596	A87	6c multicolored	.30	.30
597	A87	20c multicolored	.80	.80
598	A87	50c multicolored	1.90	1.90
599	A87	1 le multicolored	3.75	3.75
		Nos. 596-599 (4)	6.75	6.75

Souvenir Sheet

No.	Type	Description	Unused	Used
600	A87	2 le multicolored	3.00	3.00

Birds Type of 1980

1c, Touraco. 2c, Olive-bellied sunbird. 5c, Spur-winged goose. 10c, Gray parrot, vert. 15c, African blue quail, vert. 20c, West African wood owl, vert. 30c, Blue plantain eater, vert. 40c, Nigerian blue-breasted kingfisher, vert. 50c, Black crake, vert. 2 le, Black bee-eater. 5 le, Denham's bustard.

1983, Oct. 1 Unwmk. *Perf. 14*

Inscribed "1983"

No.	Type	Description	Unused	Used
600A	A67	1c multi	1.50	1.50
600B	A67	2c multi	1.50	1.50
600C	A67	5c multi	1.00	1.00
600D	A67	10c multi	1.25	1.25
600E	A67	15c multi	1.75	1.75
600F	A67	20c multi	2.75	2.75
600G	A67	30c multi	2.50	2.50
600H	A67	40c multi	3.50	3.50
600I	A67	50c multi	3.50	3.50
600J	A67	2 le multi	10.00	10.00
600K	A67	5 le multi	15.00	15.00
		Nos. 600A-600K (11)	44.25	44.25

For surcharges see Nos. 632-636E. For overprints see Nos. 637-638D.

Walt Disney, Space Ark Fantasy — A88

No. 601, Hippopotamus, Huey, Dewey and Louie. No. 602, Mickey Mouse and Snake. No. 603, Elephant and Donald Duck. No. 604, Zebra and Goofy. No. 605, Lion and Ludwig von Drake. No. 606, Rhinoceros and Goofy. No. 607, Giraffe and Mickey Mouse. No. 608, Monkey and Donald Duck.
No. 609, Mickey Mouse and animals.

1983, Nov.

No.	Type	Description	Unused	Used
601	A88	1c multicolored	.25	.25
602	A88	1c multicolored	.25	.25
603	A88	3c multicolored	.25	.25
604	A88	3c multicolored	.25	.25
605	A88	10c multicolored	.25	.25
606	A88	10c multicolored	.25	.25
607	A88	2 le multicolored	1.90	1.90
608	A88	3 le multicolored	2.75	2.75
		Nos. 601-608 (8)	6.15	6.15

Souvenir Sheet

No.	Type	Description	Unused	Used
609	A88	5 le multicolored	5.50	5.50

10th Anniv. of Mano River Union A89

6c, Teaching Program graduates. 25c, Emblem. 31c, Map, presidents. 41c, Guinea Accession signing.

1984, Feb. 8 Litho. *Perf. 15*

No.	Type	Description	Unused	Used
610	A89	6c multicolored	.25	.25
611	A89	25c multicolored	.25	.25
612	A89	31c multicolored	.25	.25
613	A89	41c multicolored	.35	.35
a.		Souvenir sheet of 1	.70	.70
		Nos. 610-613 (4)	1.10	1.10

23rd Olympic Games, Los Angeles, July 28-Aug. 12 — A90

1984, Mar. 15 *Perf. 14*

No.	Type	Description	Unused	Used
614	A90	90c Gymnastics	.50	.50
615	A90	1 le Hurdles	.70	.70
616	A90	3 le Javelin	1.40	1.40
		Nos. 614-616 (3)	2.60	2.60

Souvenir Sheet

No.	Type	Description	Unused	Used
617	A90	7 le Boxing	3.75	3.75

For surcharges see Nos. 699-702.

Apollo 11, 15th Anniv. — A91

50c, Lift off. 75c, Lunar landing. 1.25 le, 1st step on moon. 2.50 le, Walking on moon.
5 le, TV transmission, horiz.

1984, May 14 Litho. *Perf. 14*

No.	Type	Description	Unused	Used
618	A91	50c multicolored	.40	.40
619	A91	75c multicolored	.60	.60
620	A91	1.25 le multicolored	1.00	1.00
621	A91	2.50 le multicolored	2.00	2.00
		Nos. 618-621 (4)	4.00	4.00

Souvenir Sheet

No.	Type	Description	Unused	Used
622	A91	5 le multicolored	3.50	3.50

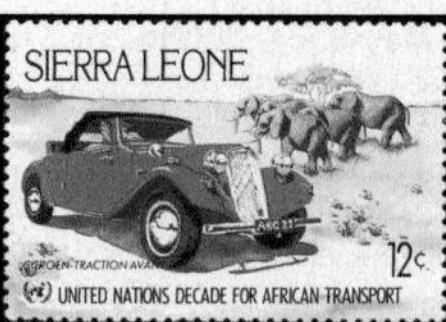

UPU Congress A92

No. 623, Concorde.
No. 624, UPU emblem, von Stephan.

1984, June 19

No.	Type	Description	Unused	Used
623	A92	4 le multicolored	5.00	5.00

Souvenir Sheet

No.	Type	Description	Unused	Used
624	A92	4 le multicolored	3.75	3.75

UN Decade for African Transportation — A93

Various cars: 12c, Citroen. 60c, Locomobile. 90c, AC Ace. 1 le, Vauxhall Prince Henry. 1.50 le, Delahaye-185. 2 le, Mazda.
6 le, Volkswagon Beetle.

1984, July 16 *Perf. 14½x15*

No.	Type	Description	Unused	Used
625	A93	12c multicolored	.25	.25
626	A93	60c multicolored	.65	.65
627	A93	90c multicolored	.85	.85
628	A93	1 le multicolored	1.10	1.10
629	A93	1.50 le multicolored	1.60	1.60
630	A93	2 le multicolored	2.00	2.00
		Nos. 625-630 (6)	6.45	6.45

Souvenir Sheet

Perf. 15

No.	Type	Description	Unused	Used
631	A93	6 le multicolored	6.00	6.00

Nos. 466, 468, 475 Surcharged

Wmk. 373

1984, Aug. 3 Litho. *Perf. 14*

No.	Type	Description	Unused	Used
632	A67	25c on 10c multi	*7.50*	*7.50*
633	A67	40c on 10c multi	*7.50*	*7.50*
634	A67	50c on 2 le multi	*7.50*	*7.50*
635	A67	70c on 5c multi	*7.50*	*7.50*
636	A67	10 le on 5c multi	*7.50*	*7.50*
		Nos. 632-636 (5)	*37.50*	*37.50*

Nos. 466a, 468a, 475a Surcharged

No.	Type	Description	Unused	Used
632a	A67	25c on 10c multi	*7.50*	*7.50*
633a	A67	40c on 10c multi	*7.50*	*7.50*
634a	A67	50c on 2 le	*7.50*	*7.50*
635a	A67	70c on 5c	*7.50*	*7.50*
636a	A67	10 le on 5c	*7.50*	*7.50*
		Nos. 632a-636a (5)	*37.50*	*37.50*

Nos. 466b, 468b, 475b Surcharged

No.	Type	Description	Unused	Used
632b	A67	25c on 10c multi	*7.50*	*7.50*
633b	A67	40c on 10c multi	*7.50*	*7.50*
634b	A67	50c on 2 le	*7.50*	*7.50*
635b	A67	70c on 5c	*7.50*	*7.50*
636b	A67	10 le on 5c	*7.50*	*7.50*
		Nos. 632b-636b (5)	*37.50*	*37.50*

Nos. 600C, 600D, 600J Surcharged

1984, Aug. 3 Unwmk. *Perf.*

No.	Type	Description	Unused	Used
636A	A67	25c on 10c multi	1.40	1.40
636B	A67	40c on 10c multi	1.00	1.00
636C	A67	50c on 2 le multi	1.00	1.00
636D	A67	70c on 5c multi	1.00	1.00
636E	A67	10 le on 5c multi	4.50	4.50
		Nos. 636A-636E (5)	8.90	8.90

Nos. 473, 476 Overprinted

Wmk. 373

1984, Aug. 22 Litho. *Perf. 14*

No.	Type	Description	Unused	Used
637	A67	50c multi (#473)	8.00	8.00
a.		On #473a	8.00	8.00
b.		On #473b	8.00	8.00

638 A67 5 le multi (#476) 22.00 22.00
a. On #476a 22.00 22.00
b. On #476b 22.00 22.00

Nos. 600I, 600K Overprinted in Black

638C A67 50c multicolored 2.50 2.50
638D A67 5 le multicolored 8.00 8.00

Portuguese Caravel Da Sintra — A94

5c, Merlin of Bristol. 10c, Golden Hind. 15c, Interloper Morduant. 20c, Navy Board Transport Atlantic. 25c, Navy Vessel Lapwing. 30c, Brig Traveller. 40c, Schooner Amistad. 50c, Teazer. 70c, Cable Ship Scotia. 1 le, Alecto. 2 le, Blonde. 5 le, Fox. 10 le, Mail ship Accra.

1984
639 A94 2c multi .95 1.75
640 A94 5c multi .95 .95
641 A94 10c multi 1.50 .70
642 A94 15c multi 2.40 .70
643 A94 20c multi 1.75 .70
644 A94 25c multi 1.75 .70
645 A94 30c multi 1.75 .70
646 A94 40c multi 1.90 1.05
647 A94 50c multi 2.10 1.30
648 A94 70c multi 2.40 1.90
649 A94 1 le multi 3.00 2.75
650 A94 2 le multi 6.00 5.50
651 A94 5 le multi 16.00 14.00
652 A94 10 le multi 28.00 28.00
Nos. 639-652 (14) 70.45 60.70

Issued: Nos. 639-649, 9/5; Nos. 650-651, 10/9; 10 le, 11/7.

See Nos. 739-740. For surcharges see Nos. 809-812.

1985 ***Perf. 12½x12***
639a A94 2c .30 .30
640a A94 5c .30 .30
641a A94 10c .30 .30
643a A94 20c .30 .30
644a A94 25c .30 .30
645a A94 30c .30 .30
646a A94 40c .30 .30
647a A94 50c .30 .30
648a A94 70c .30 .30
649a A94 1 le 1.75 1.75
650a A94 2 le 3.50 3.50
651a A94 5 le 8.50 8.50
652a A94 10 le 16.00 16.00
Nos. 639a-652a (13) 32.45 32.45

125th Anniv. of Sierra Leone Postage Stamps A95

50c, Mail messenger, No. 2. 2 le, Post Master receiving letters, No. 2. 3 le, Cover. 5 le, Penny Black, No. 2.

1984, Oct. 9
653 A95 50c multicolored .45 .45
654 A95 2 le multicolored 2.00 2.00
655 A95 3 le multicolored 3.00 3.00
Nos. 653-655 (3) 5.45 5.45

Souvenir Sheet
656 A95 5 le multicolored 2.40 2.40

50th Anniv. of Donald Duck — A95a

1c, Wise Little Hen. 2c, Boat Builders. 3c, Three Caballeros. 4c, Mathmagic Land. 5c, Mickey Mouse Club. 10c, On Parade. 1 le, Don Donald. 2 le, Donald gets drafted, p. 12½x12. 4 le, Tokyo Disneyland.
5 le, Sketches.

1984, Nov. **Litho.** ***Perf. 14x13½***
657 A95a 1c multi .25 .25
658 A95a 2c multi .25 .25
659 A95a 3c multi .25 .25
660 A95a 4c multi .25 .25
661 A95a 5c multi .25 .25
662 A95a 10c multi .25 .25
663 A95a 1 le multi 1.25 1.25
663A A95a 2 le multi 2.50 2.50
664 A95a 4 le multi 4.75 4.75
Nos. 657-664 (9) 10.00 10.00

Souvenir Sheet
665 A95a 5 le multi 10.00 10.00

Christmas — A96

Mother and Child paintings.

1984, Nov. 28 ***Perf. 14***
666 A96 20c Pisanello .40 .40
667 A96 1 le Memling .75 .75
668 A96 2 le Raphael 1.30 1.30
669 A96 3 le van der Werff 1.60 1.60
Nos. 666-669 (4) 4.05 4.05

Souvenir Sheet
670 A96 6 le Picasso 4.50 4.50

Songbirds A97

40c, Straw-tailed whydah. 90c, Spotted flycatcher. 1.30 le, Garden warbler. 3 le, Speke's weaver.
5 le, Great gray shrike.

1985, Jan. 31 **Litho.**
671 A97 40c multi .95 .95
672 A97 90c multi 2.10 2.10
673 A97 1.30 le multi 3.25 3.25
674 A97 3 le multi 5.75 5.75
Nos. 671-674 (4) 12.05 12.05

Souvenir Sheet
675 A97 5 le multi 6.75 6.75

International Youth Year — A98

1.15 le, Fishing. 1.50 le, Timber. 2.15 le, Rice farming.
5 le, Diamond Polishing.

1985, Feb. 14 **Litho.**
676 A98 1.15 le multi .80 .80
677 A98 1.50 le multi .90 .90
678 A98 2.15 le multi 1.40 1.40
Nos. 676-678 (3) 3.10 3.10

Souvenir Sheet
679 A98 5 le multi 4.75 4.75

Intl. Civil Aviation Org., 40th Anniv. A100

Early aviators and their aircraft: 70c, Eddie Rickenbacker, Spad XIII (1918). 1.25 le, Samuel P. Langley, Aerodrome No. 5. 1.30 le, Orville and Wilbur Wright, Flyer 1. 2 le, Charles Lindbergh, Spirit of St. Louis.
5 le, Jet over Freetown.

1985, Feb. 28 **Litho.** ***Perf. 14***
680 A100 70c multicolored 1.40 1.40
681 A100 1.25 le multicolored 2.50 2.50
682 A100 1.30 le multicolored 2.50 2.50
683 A100 2 le multicolored 4.75 4.75
Nos. 680-683 (4) 11.15 11.15

Souvenir Sheet
684 A100 5 le multi 4.00 4.00

Easter A101

Religious paintings — 45c, The Temptation of Christ. 70c, Christ at the Column. 1.55 le, Pieta. 10 le, Christ on the Cross. 12 le, Man of Sorrows
Nos. 685, 687, 689 by Botticelli (1445-1510). Nos. 686, 688 by Velazquez (1599-1660).

1985, Apr. 29
685 A101 45c multicolored .25 .25
686 A101 70c multicolored .30 .30
687 A101 1.55 le multicolored .85 .85
688 A101 10 le multicolored 6.50 6.50
Nos. 685-688 (4) 7.90 7.90

Souvenir Sheet
689 A101 12 le multicolored 6.25 6.25

Queen Mother, 85th Birthday — A102

Designs: 1 le, Queen Mother at St. Peter's Cathedral, London, vert. 1.70 le, With Double Star at Sandown Racetrack. 10 le, Attending the gala ballet at Covent Garden, 1971, vert. 12 le, With Princess Anne at Ascot, vert.

1985, July 8 **Litho.** ***Perf. 14***
690 A102 1 le multicolored .25 .25
691 A102 1.70 le multicolored .50 .50
692 A102 10 le multicolored 3.00 3.00
Nos. 690-692 (3) 3.75 3.75

Souvenir Sheet
693 A102 12 le multicolored 3.50 3.50

Nos. 535-539 Surcharged in Black

1985, July 25
694 A78 70c on 20c multi 1.00 1.00
695 A78 1.30 le on 50c multi 2.25 2.25
696 A78 5 le on 1 le multi 1.50 1.50
697 A78 7 le on 2 le multi 2.75 2.75
Nos. 694-697 (4) 7.50 7.50

Souvenir Sheet
698 A78 15 le on 3 le multi 5.75 5.75

Nos. 614-617 Surcharged in Black

No. 699, Ma Yanhonjg, China. No. 700, E. Moses, USA. No. 701, A. Haerkoenen, Finland.
No. 702, M. Taylor, USA.

1985, July 25
699 A90 2 le on 90c multi .90 .90
700 A90 4 le on 1 le multi 1.60 1.60
701 A90 8 le on 3 le multi 3.25 3.25
Nos. 699-701 (3) 5.75 5.75

Souvenir Sheet
702 A90 15 le on 7 le multi 6.00 6.00

1905 Chater-Lea, Hill Station House — A103

Designs: 2 le, Honda XR 350 R, QE II Quay. 4 le, Kawasaki Vulcan, Bo Clock Tower. 5 le, Harley-Davidson Electra-Glide, Makeni. 12 le, 1893 Millet.

1985, Aug. 15
703 A103 1.40 le multicolored 1.10 1.10
704 A103 2 le multicolored 1.50 1.50
705 A103 4 le multicolored 3.00 3.00
706 A103 5 le multicolored 3.75 3.75
Nos. 703-706 (4) 9.35 9.35

Souvenir Sheet
707 A103 12 le multicolored 8.00 8.00

Motorcycle cent., Decade for African Transport.

A104

1985, Sept. 3
708 A104 70c Viola pomposa .50 .50
709 A104 3 le Spinet 2.25 2.25
710 A104 4 le Lute 3.00 3.00
711 A104 5 le Oboe 3.25 3.25
Nos. 708-711 (4) 9.00 9.00

Souvenir Sheet
712 A104 12 le Portrait 7.50 7.50

Johann Sebastian Bach (1685-1750), composer. Nos. 708-712 show music from "Clavier Ubang."

Nos. 510, 512, 516, 531-534, 552-555 Surcharged

1985, Sept. 30 ***Perfs. as Before***
Designs CD331-CD332
713 70c on 31c #531 .65 .65
714 1.30 le on 60c #512 4.50 4.50
715 1.30 le on 31c #552 1.60 1.60
716 2 le on 35c #510 5.75 5.75
717 4 le on 50c #532 3.75 3.75
718 5 le on 2 le #533 3.75 3.75
719 5 le on 50c #553 4.75 4.75
720 7 le on 2 le #554 4.75 4.75
721 8 le on 1.50 le #516 18.00 18.00
Nos. 713-721 (9) 47.50 47.50

Souvenir Sheets
722 15 le on 3 le #534 12.00 12.00
723 15 le on 3 le #555 12.00 12.00

Christmas — A105

Madonna and child paintings by: 70c, Carlo Crivelli (c. 1430-1494). 3 le, Dirk Bouts (c. 1400-1475). 4 le, Antonello de Messina (c. 1430-1479). 5 le, Stefan Lochner (c. 1400-1451). 12 le, Miniature from the Book of Kells, 9th cent., Ireland.

1985, Oct. 18 Litho. *Perf. 14*

724	A105	70c multicolored	.25	.25
725	A105	3 le multicolored	1.10	1.10
726	A105	4 le multicolored	1.25	1.25
727	A105	5 le multicolored	1.75	1.75
		Nos. 724-727 (4)	4.35	4.35

Miniature Sheet

728	A105	12 le multicolored	3.50	3.50

Jacob and Wilhelm Grimm, Fabulists — A106

Mark Twain, American Humorist A107

Walt Disney characters acting out Twain quotes (A107) or in Rumpelstiltskin (A106).

1985, Oct. 30 Litho. *Perf. 14*

729	A106	70c multicolored	.30	.30
730	A106	1.30 le multicolored	.45	.45
731	A107	1.50 le multicolored	1.15	1.15
732	A106	2 le multicolored	.65	.65
733	A107	3 le multicolored	1.35	1.35
734	A107	4 le multicolored	1.45	1.45
735	A107	5 le multicolored	1.60	1.60
736	A106	10 le multicolored	3.00	3.00
		Nos. 729-736 (8)	9.95	9.95

Souvenir Sheets

737	A106	15 le multicolored	4.75	4.75
738	A107	15 le multicolored	6.00	6.00

Nos. 731, 733-735 bear the Intl. Youth Year emblem.

Ship Type of 1984

1985, Nov. 15

739	A94	15 le Favourite	6.00	6.00
740	A94	25 le Euryalus	9.75	9.75

UN, 40th Anniv. A108

Stamps of UN and famous men: 2 le, No. 30, Kennedy. 4 le, No. 59, Einstein. 7 le, No. 44, Maimonides (1135-1204), medieval Judaic scholar. 12 le, Martin Luther King, Jr. (1929-1968), civil rights leader, vert.

1985, Nov. 28 Litho. *Perf. 14½*

741	A108	2 le multicolored	1.35	1.35
742	A108	4 le multicolored	2.40	2.40
743	A108	7 le multicolored	5.00	5.00
		Nos. 741-743 (3)	8.75	8.75

Souvenir Sheet

744	A108	12 le multicolored	3.50	3.50

1986 World Cup Soccer Championships A109

Various soccer plays.

1986, Mar. 3 *Perf. 14*

745	A109	70c multicolored	.40	.40
746	A109	3 le multicolored	1.50	1.50
747	A109	4 le multicolored	2.10	2.10
748	A109	5 le multicolored	2.75	2.75
		Nos. 745-748 (4)	6.75	6.75

Souvenir Sheet

749	A109	12 le multicolored	3.50	3.50

For overprints and surcharges see Nos. 788-792.

Statue of Liberty, Cent. — A110

New York City: 40c, Times Square, 1905. 70c, Times Square, 1986. 1 le, Tally Ho Coach, c. 1880, horiz. 10 le, Liberty Lines express bus, 1986. 12 le, Statue of Liberty.

1986, Mar. 11

750	A110	40c multicolored	.25	.25
751	A110	70c multicolored	.25	.25
752	A110	1 le multicolored	.55	.55
753	A110	10 le multicolored	3.00	3.00
		Nos. 750-753 (4)	4.05	4.05

Souvenir Sheet

754	A110	12 le multicolored	4.25	4.25

A111

Halley's Comet — A112

15c, Johannes Kepler (1571-1630), German astronomer, & Paris Observatory. 50c, US space shuttle landing, 1985. 70c, Bayeux Tapestry (detail), 1066 sighting. 10 le, Arthurian magician, Merlin, sights comet, 530. 12 le, Comet over Sierra Leone.

1986, Apr. 1

755	A111	15c multicolored	.25	.25
756	A111	50c multicolored	.25	.25
757	A111	70c multicolored	.35	.35
758	A111	10 le multicolored	4.75	4.75
		Nos. 755-758 (4)	5.60	5.60

Souvenir Sheet

759	A112	12 le multicolored	2.75	2.75

For overprints and surcharges see Nos. 813-817.

Queen Elizabeth II, 60th Birthday

Common Design Type

10c, Cranwell, 1951. 1.70 le, Garter Ceremony. 10 le, Braemar Games, 1970.
12 le, Windsor Castle, 1943.

1986, Apr. 21

760	CD339	10c multi	.25	.25
761	CD339	1.70 le multi	.50	.50
762	CD339	10 le multi	2.00	2.00
		Nos. 760-762 (3)	2.75	2.75

Souvenir Sheet

763	CD339	12 le multi	2.50	2.50

For surcharges see Nos. 793-795.

AMERIPEX '86 — A113

Locomotives — 50c, Hiawatha, Milwaukee. 2 le, The Rocket, Rock Is. 4 le, Prospector, Rio Grande. 7 le, Daylight, So. Pacific.
12 le, Broadway, Pennsylvania.

1986, May 22

764	A113	50c multi	1.10	1.10
765	A113	2 le multi	1.90	1.90
766	A113	4 le multi	3.25	3.25
767	A113	7 le multi	4.00	4.00
		Nos. 764-767 (4)	10.25	10.25

Souvenir Sheet

768	A113	12 le multi	5.00	5.00

Royal Wedding Issue, 1986

Common Design Type

Designs: 10c, Prince Andrew and Sarah Ferguson. 1.70 le, Andrew with shotgun. 10 le, Andrew saluting.
12 le, Couple, diff.

1986, July 23

769	CD340	10c multi	.25	.25
770	CD340	1.70 le multi	.35	.35
771	CD340	10 le multi	1.75	1.75
		Nos. 769-771 (3)	2.35	2.35

Souvenir Sheet

772	CD340	12 le multi	3.00	3.00

For surcharges see Nos. 796-798.

Indigenous Flowers — A114

70c, Monodora myristica. 1.50 le, Gloriosa simplex. 4 le, Mussaenda erythrophylla. 6 le, Crinum ornatum. 8 le, Bauhinia purpurea. 10 le, Bombax costatum. 20 le, Hibiscus rosa-sinensis. 30 le, Cassia fistula.
No. 781, Clitoria ternatea. No. 782, Plumbago auriculata.

1986, Aug. 25 Litho. *Perf. 15*

773	A114	70c multi	.25	.25
774	A114	1.50 le multi	1.00	1.00
775	A114	4 le multi	.45	.45
776	A114	6 le multi	.70	.70
777	A114	8 le multi	.80	.80
778	A114	10 le multi	1.00	1.00
779	A114	20 le multi	1.75	1.75
780	A114	30 le multi	2.10	2.10
		Nos. 773-780 (8)	8.05	8.05

Souvenir Sheets

781	A114	40 le multi	3.75	3.75
782	A114	40 le multi	3.75	3.75

US Peace Corps in Sierra Leone, 25th Anniv. A115

1986, Aug. 26 Litho. *Perf. 14*

783	A115	10 le multi	1.40	1.40

Intl. Peace Year A116

1986, Sept. 1

784	A116	1 le Transportation	.40	.40
785	A116	2 le Education	.55	.55
786	A116	5 le Communications	1.15	1.15
787	A116	10 le Fishing	1.75	1.75
		Nos. 784-787 (4)	3.85	3.85

Nos. 745-749 Ovptd. or Surcharged "WINNERS / Argentina 3 / West Germany 2" in Gold

1986, Sept. 15 *Perf. 14*

788	A109	70c multi	.35	.35
789	A109	3 le multi	.80	.80
790	A109	4 le multi	.85	.85
791	A109	40 le on 5 le multi	7.50	7.50
		Nos. 788-791 (4)	9.50	9.50

Souvenir Sheet

792	A109	40 le on 12 le multi	4.75	4.75

Nos. 760, 762-763 Surcharged in Silver or Black

1986, Sept. 15

793	CD339	70c on 10c multi	.50	.25
794	CD339	45 le on 10 le multi	3.50	3.50

Souvenir Sheet

795	CD339	50 le on 12 le (B)	4.00	4.00

Nos. 769, 771-772 Surcharged in Silver

No. 796

No. 797

1986, Sept. 15

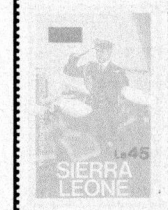

796	CD340	70c on 10c multi	.25	.25
797	CD340	45 le on 10 le multi	3.50	3.50

Souvenir Sheet

798	CD340	50 le on 12 le multi	4.00	4.00

STOCKHOLMIA '86 — A117

Disney characters in Mother Goose fairy tales — 70c, Jack and Jill. 1 le, Wee Willie

Winkie. 2 le, Little Miss Muffet. 4 le, Old King Cole. 5 le, Mary Quite Contrary. 10 le, Little Bo Peep. 25 le, Polly Put the Kettle On. 35 le, Rub-a-Dub-Dub.
No. 807, Old Woman in the Shoe. No. 808, Simple Simon.

1986, Sept. 22 *Perf. 11*
799 A117 70c multi .25 .25
800 A117 1 le multi .25 .25
801 A117 2 le multi .25 .25
802 A117 4 le multi .55 .55
803 A117 5 le multi .85 .85
804 A117 10 le multi 1.25 1.25
805 A117 25 le multi 3.25 3.25
806 A117 35 le multi 4.50 4.50
Nos. 799-806 (8) 11.15 11.15

Souvenir Sheets

807 A117 40 le multi 5.25 5.25
808 A117 40 le multi 5.25 5.25

Nos. 639, 645-646 and 648 Surcharged

1986, Oct. 15
809 A94 30 le on 2c multi 3.50 3.50
810 A94 40 le on 30c multi 3.50 *4.00*
811 A94 45 le on 40c multi 3.00 3.00
812 A94 50 le on 70c multi 7.00 4.75
Nos. 809-812 (4) 17.00 15.25

Nos. 755-759 Ovptd. or Srchd. with Halley's Comet Emblem in Black or Silver

Nos. 813-814

Nos. 815-817

1986, Oct. 15
813 A111 50c multi .35 .35
814 A111 70c multi .35 .35
815 A111 1.50 le on 15c multi .35 .35
816 A111 45 le on 10 le multi 7.00 7.00
Nos. 813-816 (4) 8.05 8.05

Souvenir Sheet

817 A112 50 le on 12 le multi (S) 5.75 5.75

Christmas A118

Paintings by Titian: 70c, Virgin and Child with St. Dorothy. $1.50 le, The Gypsy Madonna, vert. 20 le, The Holy Family. 30 le, Virgin and Child in an Evening Landscape, vert. 40 le, Madonna with the Pesaro Family.

1986, Nov. 17 **Litho.** *Perf. 14*
818 A118 70c multi .25 .25
819 A118 1.50 le multi .25 .25
820 A118 20 le multi 3.00 3.00
821 A118 30 le multi 4.00 4.00
Nos. 818-821 (4) 7.50 7.50

Souvenir Sheet

822 A118 40 le multi 11.00 11.00

Statue of Liberty, Cent. A119

Pictures of the statue by Peter B. Kaplan before and after renovation — 70c, Torch assembly. 1.50 le, Liberty holding torch. 2 le, Torch assembly, diff. 3 le, Man, torch. 4 le, Crown. 5 le, Lighting of the statue. 10 le, Lighting, diff. 25 le, Liberty Island. 30 le, Face.
Nos. 823, 825-826, 828-829, 831, vert.

1987, Jan. 2 *Perf. 14*
823 A119 70c multicolored .25 .25
824 A119 1.50 le multicolored .25 .25
825 A119 2 le multicolored .25 .25
826 A119 3 le multicolored .25 .25
827 A119 4 le multicolored .25 .25
828 A119 5 le multicolored .30 .30
829 A119 10 le multicolored .60 .60
830 A119 25 le multicolored 1.50 1.50
831 A119 30 le multicolored 1.75 1.75
Nos. 823-831 (9) 5.40 5.40

UNICEF, 40th Anniv. A120

1987, Mar. 18 **Litho.** *Perf. 14*
832 A120 10 le multi .70 .70

Nomoli Soapstone Sculpture — A121

Tall Ship in Harbor, Freetown — A122

1987, Jan. 2 *Perf. 15*
833 A121 2 le shown .25 .25
834 A121 5 le King's Yard Gate, 1817 .30 .30

Souvenir Sheet

835 A122 60 le shown 4.00 4.00

First settlement of liberated slaves returned to the African continent by the British, Freetown, bicent.

America's Cup — A123

Constellation, 1964 — A124

No. 836, USA, 1987. No. 837, New Zealand, 1987. No. 838, French Kiss, 1987. No. 839, Stars & Stripes, 1987. No. 840, Australia II, 1983. No. 841, Freedom, 1980. No. 842, Kookaburra III, 1987.

1987, June 15 **Litho.** *Perf. 14*
836 A123 1 le multi .25 .25
837 A123 1.50 le multi .25 .25
838 A123 2.50 le multi .25 .25
839 A123 10 le multi 1.10 1.10
840 A123 15 le multi 1.40 1.40
841 A123 25 le multi 2.25 2.25
842 A123 30 le multi 2.25 2.25
Nos. 836-842 (7) 7.75 7.75

Souvenir Sheet

843 A124 50 le multi 4.50 4.50

Nos. 837, 839 and 842 horiz.
For overprint see No. 964.

CAPEX '87 — A125

Disney characters, Canadian sights — 2 le, Parliament. 5 le, Totem poles. 10 le, Perce Rock. 20 le, Canadian Rockies. 25 le, Old Quebec City. 45 le, Aurora Borealis. 50 le, Yukon P.O. 75 le, Niagara Falls.
No. 857, Exploring Newfoundland. No. 858, Calgary Exhibition and Stampede.

1987, June 15 *Perf. 11*
849 A125 2 le multi .25 .25
850 A125 5 le multi .35 .35
851 A125 10 le multi .60 .60
852 A125 20 le multi 1.05 1.05
853 A125 25 le multi 1.40 1.40
854 A125 45 le multi 2.10 2.10
855 A125 50 le multi 2.40 2.40
856 A125 75 le multi 4.25 4.25
Nos. 849-856 (8) 12.40 12.40

Souvenir Sheets

857 A125 100 le multi 6.00 6.00
858 A125 100 le multi 6.00 6.00

Butterflies — A126

10c, Blue salamis. 20c, Pale-tailed blue. 40c, Acraea swallowtail. 1 le, Broad blue-banded swallowtail. 2 le, Giant blue swallowtail. 3 le, Blood-red cymothoe. 5 le, Green-spotted swallowtail. 10 le, Small-striped swordtail. 20 le, Congo long-tailed blue. 25 le, Blue monarch. 30 le, Black and yellow swallowtail. 45 le, Western blue charaxes. 60 le, Violet-washed charaxes. 75 le, Orange admiral. 100 le, Blue-patched judy.

1987, Aug. 4 *Perf. 14*
859 A126 10c multi 1.60 .50
b. Inscribed "1989" 1.75 1.00
860 A126 20c multi 1.60 .50
b. Inscribed "1989" 1.75 1.00
861 A126 40c multi 1.60 .50
b. Inscribed "1989" 1.75 .75
862 A126 1 le multi 1.60 .50
b. Inscribed "1989" 2.50 1.10
863 A126 2 le multi 1.60 .50
b. Inscribed "1989" 3.00 1.00
864 A126 3 le multi 2.10 .90
b. Inscribed "1989" 4.00 1.00
865 A126 5 le multi 2.10 .50
866 A126 10 le multi 3.50 1.00
867 A126 20 le multi 6.00 3.00
868 A126 25 le multi 6.50 3.25
869 A126 30 le multi 6.50 4.00
870 A126 45 le multi 11.00 5.00
871 A126 60 le multi 2.75 *4.50*
872 A126 75 le multi 3.75 *4.75*
873 A126 100 le multi 4.50 *6.50*
Nos. 859-873 (15) 56.70 35.90

See Nos. 1257-1260, 1332A-1332M.

1988-89 *Perf. 12x12½*
859a A126 10c .60 .25
859c A126 10c Inscribed "1989" 8.00 —
860a A126 20c .90 .25
860c A126 20c Inscribed "1989" 8.00 —
861a A126 40c .90 .25
861c A126 40c Inscribed "1989" 8.00 —
862a A126 1 le .90 .25
862c A126 1 le Inscribed "1989" 8.00 —
863a A126 2 le 1.00 .25
863c A126 2 le Inscribed "1989" 8.00 —
864a A126 3 le 1.00 .25
865a A126 5 le 1.00 .25
866a A126 10 le 1.00 .40
867a A126 20 le 1.25 .80
868a A126 25 le 1.25 1.00
869a A126 30 le 1.40 1.25
870a A126 45 le 1.60 1.60
871a A126 60 le 2.75 2.75
872a A126 75 le 3.00 3.00
873a A126 100 le 5.75 5.00
Nos. 859a-873a (15) 24.30 17.55

Inscribed "1989"

1989 *Perf. 12½x11½*
859d A126 10c 1.75
860d A126 20c 2.25
861d A126 40c 2.25
862d A126 1 le 2.25
863d A126 2 le 3.75
864d A126 3 le 4.50
Nos. 859d-864d (6) 16.75

No. 864 has been reported inscribed "1989" in perf. 12x12½. The editors would like to examine any examples.

1988 Summer Olympics, Seoul — A127

5 le, Cycling. 10 le, Equestrian. 45 le, Running. 50 le, Tennis.
100 le, Gold medal, map.

1987, Aug. 10
874 A127 5 le multi .25 .25
875 A127 10 le multi .60 .60
876 A127 45 le multi 2.75 2.75
877 A127 50 le multi 3.00 3.00
Nos. 874-877 (4) 6.60 6.60

Souvenir Sheet

878 A127 100 le multi 6.75 6.75

Works of Art by Marc Chagall, (1887-1985) A128

3 le, The Quarrel, 1911-1912. 5 le, Rebecca Giving Abraham's Servant a Drink. 10 le, The Village. 20 le, Ida at the Window, 1924. 25 le, Promenade, 1913. 45 le, Peasants. 50 le, Turquoise Plate. 75 le, Cemetery Gate, 1917.
No. 887, Wedding Feast, Stravinsky's Ballet, 1945. No. 888, The Falling Angel.

1987, Aug. 17 *Perf. 14*
879 A128 3 le multi .25 .25
880 A128 5 le multi .25 .25
881 A128 10 le multi .50 .50
882 A128 20 le multi .85 .85
883 A128 25 le multi 1.50 1.50
884 A128 45 le multi 3.25 3.25
885 A128 50 le multi 4.00 4.00
886 A128 75 le multi 5.50 5.50
Nos. 879-886 (8) 16.10 16.10

Size: 111x95mm
Imperf

887 A128 100 le multi 8.00 8.00
888 A128 100 le multi 8.00 8.00

Nos. 879-886 printed in sheets of 10 (5x2). Stamp selvage inscribed with name of painting.

A129

Transportation Innovations — A129a

3 le, Apollo 8, 1968, vert. 5 le, Blanchard's Balloon, 1793. 10 le, Lockheed Vega, 1932. 15 le, Vicker's Vimy, 1919. 20 le, Tank Mk1, c. 1918. 25 le, Sikorsky VS-300, 1939. 30 le, Flyer 1, 1903. 35 le, Bleriot XI, 1909. 40 le, Paraplane, 1983, vert. 50 le, Daimler's motorcycle, 1885.

1987, Aug. 28 ***Perf. 15***

889	A129	3 le multi	.25	.25
890	A129a	5 le multi	.25	.25
891	A129a	10 le multi	.50	.50
892	A129a	15 le multi	.90	.90
893	A129	20 le multi	1.55	1.55
894	A129a	25 le multi	1.75	1.75
895	A129	30 le multi	2.25	2.25
896	A129a	35 le multi	2.50	2.50
897	A129	40 le multi	3.00	3.00
898	A129	50 le multi	3.75	3.75
		Nos. 889-898 (10)	16.70	16.70

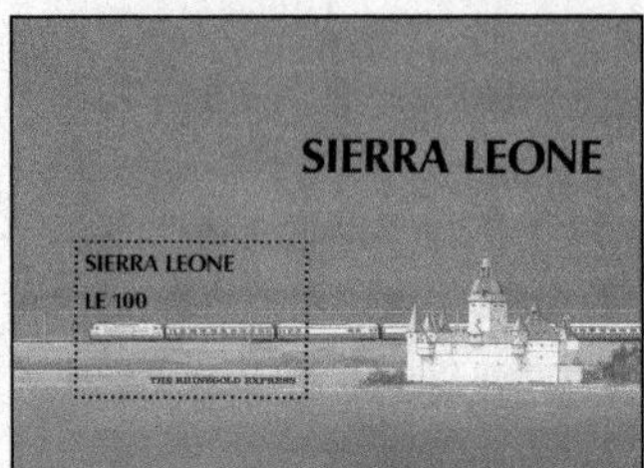

Rhinegold Express, Ireland (1st Electric Railroad, 1884) — A129a

1987, Aug. 28 Litho. ***Perf. 15***

898A	A129a	100 le multi	6.75	6.75

Wimbledon Tennis Champions — A130

2 le, Evonne Goolagong, Australia. 5 le, Martina Navratilova, US-Czechoslovakia. 10 le, Jimmy Connors, US. 15 le, Bjorn Borg, Sweden. 30 le, Boris Becker, West Germany. 40 le, John McEnroe, US. 50 le, Chris Evert Lloyd, US. 75 le, Virgina Wade, Great Britain. #907, Steffi Graf, German Open 1986. #908, Boris Becker.

1987, Sept. 4 ***Perf. 14***

899	A130	2 le multicolored	.30	.30
900	A130	5 le multicolored	.75	.75
901	A130	10 le multicolored	1.10	1.10
902	A130	15 le multicolored	1.50	1.50
903	A130	30 le multicolored	2.75	2.75
904	A130	40 le multicolored	3.00	3.00
905	A130	50 le multicolored	3.25	3.25
906	A130	75 le multicolored	4.50	4.50
		Nos. 899-906 (8)	17.15	17.15

Souvenir Sheets

907	A130	100 le multicolored	8.00	8.00
908	A130	100 le multicolored	8.00	8.00

For overprints see Nos. 965, 1023-1024.

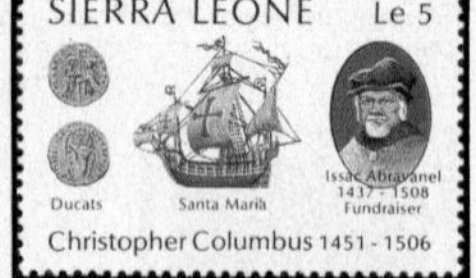

Discovery of America, 500th Anniv. (in 1992) A131

5 le, Ducats, Santa Maria, Issac Abravanel (1437-1508), fund raiser. 10 le, Astrolabe, Pinta, Abraham Zacuto (1452-1515), astronomer. 45 le, Maravedis (coins), Nina, Luis de Santangel (1448-1498), fund raiser. 50 le, Tobacco leaves, plant, Luis de Torres (1453-1522), translator.

1987, Sept. 11

909	A131	5 le multicolored	1.00	1.00
910	A131	10 le multicolored	1.25	1.25
911	A131	45 le multicolored	3.50	3.50
912	A131	50 le multicolored	4.25	4.25
		Nos. 909-912 (4)	10.00	10.00

Souvenir Sheet

913	A131	100 le Columbus, map	6.00	6.00

For overprint see No. 966.

Fauna and Flora A132

3 le, Cotton tree. 5 le, Dwarf crocodile. 10 le, Kudu. 20 le, Yellowbells. 25 le, Hippopotamus. 45 le, Comet orchid. 50 le, Baobab tree. 75 le, Elephant.

No. 922, Banana, papaya, coconut, pineapple. No. 923, Leopard.

1987, Sept. 15

914	A132	3 le multi	.25	.25
915	A132	5 le multi	.25	.25
916	A132	10 le multi	.65	.65
917	A132	20 le multi	1.50	1.50
918	A132	25 le multi	2.00	2.00
919	A132	45 le multi	3.25	3.25
920	A132	50 le multi	3.75	3.75
921	A132	75 le multi	6.00	6.00
		Nos. 914-921 (8)	17.65	17.65

Souvenir Sheets

922	A132	100 le multi	4.50	4.50
923	A132	100 le multi	4.50	4.50

16th World Scout Jamboree, Australia, 1987-88 A133

Scouts, jamboree emblem, map of Australia and: 5 le, Ayers Rock. 15 le, Sailing. 40 le, Sydney skyline. 50 le, Sydney Harbour Bridge, Opera House. 100 le, Flags of Sierra Leone, Australia and Scouts.

1987, Oct. 5 Litho. ***Perf. 15***

924	A133	5 le multicolored	.45	.45
925	A133	15 le multicolored	1.10	1.10
926	A133	40 le multicolored	2.40	2.40
927	A133	50 le multicolored	3.75	3.75
		Nos. 924-927 (4)	7.70	7.70

Souvenir Sheet

928	A133	100 le multicolored	8.75	8.75

1.50 le stamps like the 50 le were printed but not issued.

US Constitution Bicentennial — A134

Designs: 5 le, White House. 10 le, George Washington. 30 le, Patrick Henry. 65 le, New Hampshire state flag. 100 le, John Jay.

1987, Nov. 9 ***Perf. 14***

929	A134	5 le multi	.25	.25
930	A134	10 le multi, vert.	.85	.85
931	A134	30 le multi, vert.	1.25	1.25
932	A134	65 le multi	2.60	2.60
		Nos. 929-932 (4)	4.95	4.95

Souvenir Sheet

933	A134	100 le multi, vert.	4.75	4.75

Tokyo Disneyland, 5th Anniv. — A135

Disney animated characters and attractions at Tokyo Disneyland — 20c, Space Mountain. 40c, Country Bear Jamboree. 80c, Mickey Mouse Review. 1 le, Mark Twain's River Boat. 2 le, Western River Railroad. 3 le, Pirates of the Caribbean. 10 le, Big Thunder Mountain train. 20 le, It's a Small World. 30 le, Park entrance.

65 le, Cinderella's Castle.

1987, Dec. 9 Litho. ***Perf. 14***

934	A135	20c multicolored	.25	.25
935	A135	40c multicolored	.25	.25
936	A135	80c multicolored	.25	.25
937	A135	1 le multicolored	.25	.25
938	A135	2 le multicolored	.25	.25
939	A135	3 le multicolored	.25	.25
940	A135	10 le multicolored	.75	.75
941	A135	20 le multicolored	1.60	1.60
942	A135	30 le multicolored	2.25	2.25
		Nos. 934-942 (9)	6.10	6.10

Souvenir Sheet

943	A135	65 le multicolored	9.50	9.50

Mickey Mouse, 60th anniv.

Christmas — A136

Paintings by Titian: 2 le, The Annunciation. 10 le, Madonna and Child with Saints. 20 le, Madonna and Child with Saints Ulfus and Brigid. 35 le, Madonna of the Cherries. 65 le, Pesaro Altarpiece, vert.

1987, Dec. 21

944	A136	2 le multicolored	.30	.30
945	A136	10 le multicolored	1.00	1.00
946	A136	20 le multicolored	1.75	1.75
947	A136	35 le multicolored	2.60	2.60
		Nos. 944-947 (4)	5.65	5.65

Souvenir Sheet

948	A136	65 le multicolored	5.75	5.75

40th Wedding Anniv. of Queen Elizabeth II and Prince Philip — A137

2 le, Ceremony, 1947. 3 le, Elizabeth, Charles, 1948. 10 le, Elizabeth, Anne, Charles, c. 1950. 50 le, Elizabeth, c. 1970.

65 le, Wedding portrait.

1988, Feb. 15 Litho. ***Perf. 14***

949	A137	2 le multicolored	.25	.25
950	A137	3 le multicolored	.25	.25
951	A137	10 le multicolored	.75	.75
952	A137	50 le multicolored	3.50	3.50
		Nos. 949-952 (4)	4.75	4.75

Souvenir Sheet

953	A137	65 le multicolored	4.50	4.50

Mushrooms A138

3 le, Russula cyanoxantha. 10 le, Lycoperdon perlatum. 20 le, Lactarius deliciosus. 30 le, Boletus edulis.

65 le, Amanita muscaria.

1988, Feb. 29

954	A138	3 le multicolored	.25	.25
955	A138	10 le multicolored	1.50	1.50
956	A138	20 le multicolored	3.00	3.00
957	A138	30 le multicolored	4.50	4.50
		Nos. 954-957 (4)	9.25	9.25

Miniature Sheet

958	A138	65 le multicolored	7.50	7.50

Fish A139

1988, Apr. 13 ***Perf. 15***

959	A139	3 le Golden pheasant	.25	.25
960	A139	10 le Banded toothcarp	.50	.50
961	A139	20 le Jewel fish	.80	.80
962	A139	35 le Butterfly fish	1.25	1.25
		Nos. 959-962 (4)	2.80	2.80

Miniature Sheet

963	A139	65 le African longfin	4.00	4.00

Nos. 841, 903 and 911 Ovptd. for Philatelic Exhibitions in Black

a

b

c

1988, Apr. 19 Litho. ***Perf. 14***

964	A123(a)	25 le multicolored	2.10	2.10
965	A130(b)	30 le multicolored	2.50	2.50
966	A131(c)	45 le multicolored	3.50	3.50
		Nos. 964-966 (3)	8.10	8.10

Intl. Fund for Agricultural Development (IFAD), 10th Anniv. — A140

1988, May 3 Litho. ***Perf. 14***

967	A140	3 le Cocoa, coffee	.25	.25
968	A140	15 le Tropical fruit	.85	.85
969	A140	25 le Rice harvest	1.40	1.40
		Nos. 967-969 (3)	2.50	2.50

1988 Summer Olympics, Seoul — A141

3 le, Basketball. 10 le, Judo. 15 le, Gymnastics. 40 le, Synchronized swimming.
65 le, Torch-bearer.

1988, June 15

970 A141 3 le multicolored .25 .25
971 A141 10 le multicolored .50 .50
972 A141 15 le multicolored .60 .60
973 A141 40 le multicolored 1.90 1.90
Nos. 970-973 (4) 3.25 3.25

Souvenir Sheet

974 A141 65 le multicolored 3.00 3.00

Birds — A142

3 le, Swallow-tailed bee-eater. 5 le, Tooth-billed barbet. 8 le, African golden oriole. 10 le, Red bishop. 12 le, Red-billed shrike. 20 le, European bee-eater. 35 le, Barbary shrike. 40 le, Black-headed oriole.
No. 983, Saddlebill stork. No. 984, Purple heron.

1988, June 25

975 A142 3 le multicolored 1.00 1.00
976 A142 5 le multicolored 1.25 1.25
977 A142 8 le multicolored 1.60 1.60
978 A142 10 le multicolored 1.60 1.60
979 A142 12 le multicolored 1.60 1.60
980 A142 20 le multicolored 1.75 1.75
981 A142 35 le multicolored 2.50 2.50
982 A142 40 le multicolored 3.00 3.00
Nos. 975-982 (8) 14.30 14.30

Souvenir Sheets

983 A142 65 le multicolored 4.00 4.00
984 A142 65 le multicolored 4.00 4.00

For surcharges see Nos. 2892-2896.

Merchant Marine A143

3 le, Aureol. 10 le, Dunkwa. 15 le, Melampus. 30 le, Dumbaia.
65 le, Loading containers.

1988, July 1

985 A143 3 le multicolored .75 .75
986 A143 10 le multicolored 1.90 1.90
987 A143 15 le multicolored 2.60 2.60
988 A143 30 le multicolored 3.25 3.25
Nos. 985-988 (4) 8.50 8.50

Souvenir Sheet

989 A143 65 le multicolored 3.75 3.75

Paintings by Titian A144

1 le, The Concert, 1512. 2 le, Philip II of Spain, c. 1550-51. 3 le, St. Sebastian, c. 1520-22. 5 le, Martyrdom of St. Peter Martyr, c. 1528-30. 15 le, St. Jerome, 1560. 20 le, St. Mark Enthroned with Saints Cosmas and Damian, Roch & Sebastian, c. 1508-09. 25 le, Portrait of a Young Man, 1506. 30 le, St. Jerome in Penitence, 1555. #998, Self-portrait, 1567. #999, Orpheus and Eurydice, 1508.

1988, Aug. 22 Litho. *Perf. 13½x14*

990 A144 1 le multicolored .25 .25
991 A144 2 le multicolored .25 .25
992 A144 3 le multicolored .25 .25
993 A144 5 le multicolored .50 .50
994 A144 15 le multicolored 1.30 1.30
995 A144 20 le multicolored 1.45 1.45
996 A144 25 le multicolored 1.75 1.75
997 A144 30 le multicolored 2.00 2.00
Nos. 990-997 (8) 7.75 7.75

Souvenir Sheets

998 A144 50 le multicolored 3.25 3.25
999 A144 50 le multicolored 3.25 3.25

John F. Kennedy A145

Kennedy half-dollar and space achievements: 3 le, Recovery of a Mercury capsule by the US Navy. 5 le, Splashdown and recovery of Liberty Bell 7, July 21, 1961, piloted by Virgil "Gus" Grissom, vert. 15 le, Launch of Freedom 7, piloted by Alan B. Shepard, May 5, 1961, vert. 40 le, Friendship 7 in orbit, piloted by John Glenn, Feb. 20, 1962. 65 le, Kennedy, speech excerpt.

1988, Sept. 26 Litho. *Perf. 14*

1000 A145 3 le multicolored .30 .30
1001 A145 5 le multicolored .70 .70
1002 A145 15 le multicolored 2.10 2.10
1003 A145 40 le multicolored 2.75 2.75
Nos. 1000-1003 (4) 5.85 5.85

Souvenir Sheet

1004 A145 65 le multicolored 3.75 3.75

Intl. Red Cross and Red Crescent Organizations, 125th Annivs. — A146

3 le, Africa food relief. 10 le, Battle of Solferino. 20 le, WWII Pacific. 40 le, WWI Europe.
65 le, Alfred Nobel, Dunant, horiz.

1988, Nov. 1

1005 A146 3 le multicolored .85 .85
1006 A146 10 le multicolored 2.75 2.75
1007 A146 20 le multicolored 3.75 3.75
1008 A146 40 le multicolored 4.75 4.75
Nos. 1005-1008 (4) 12.10 12.10

Souvenir Sheet

Size: 41x28mm

1009 A146 65 le multicolored 4.50 4.50

Miniature Sheet

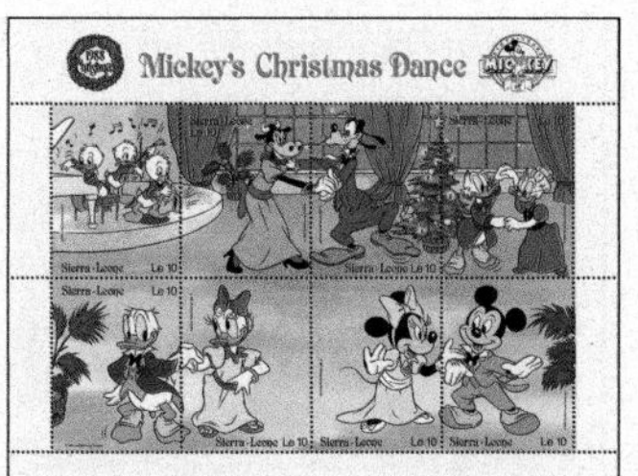

Christmas, Mickey Mouse 60th Anniv. — A147

Walt Disney characters dancing: No. 1010a, Huey, Dewey and Louie. No. 1010b, Clarabelle Cow. No. 1010c, Goofy. No. 1010d, Scrooge McDuck and Grandma Duck. No. 1010e, Donald Duck. No. 1010f, Daisy Duck. No. 1010g, Minnie Mouse. No. 1010h, Mickey Mouse. No. 1011, Dance, c. 1920. No. 1012, Dance, c. 1950.

1988, Dec. 1 *Perf. 13½x14*

1010 A147 Sheet of 8 7.25 7.25
a.-h. 10 le any single .65 .65

Souvenir Sheets

1011 A147 70 le multicolored 4.75 4.75
1012 A147 70 le multicolored 4.75 4.75

Christmas A148

Paintings by Rubens (details): 3 le, Adoration of the Magi (Virgin and Child). 3.60 le, Adoration of the Shepherds (shepherds and child). 5 le, Adoration of the Magi (Magi). 10 le, Adoration of the Shepherds (Virgin and Child). 20 le, Virgin and Child Surrounded by Flowers. 40 le, St. Gregory the Great and Other Saints (Virgin and Child). 60 le, Adoration of the Magi, (Virgin, Child and Magi), diff. 80 le, Madonna and Child with Saints. No. 1021, St. Gregory the Great and Other Saints. No. 1022, Virgin and Child Enthroned with Saints.

1988, Dec. 15 Litho. *Perf. 13½x14*

1013 A148 3 le multicolored .25 .25
1014 A148 3.60 le multicolored .25 .25
1015 A148 5 le multicolored .35 .35
1016 A148 10 le multicolored .55 .55
1017 A148 20 le multicolored 1.00 1.00
1018 A148 40 le multicolored 2.00 2.00
1019 A148 60 le multicolored 2.75 2.75
1020 A148 80 le multicolored 3.75 3.75
Nos. 1013-1020 (8) 10.90 10.90

Souvenir Sheets

1021 A148 100 le multicolored 5.00 5.00
1022 A148 100 le multicolored 5.00 5.00

No. 907 Ovptd. "GRAND SLAM WINNER" in Gold

Souvenir Sheets

1989, Jan. 16 Set of 4 *Perf. 14*

1023A-1023D A130 100 le 22.50 22.50

Gold marginal overprints: No. 1023A, "AUSTRALIAN OPEN / JANUARY 11-24, 1988 / GRAF v EVERET / 6-1 / 7-6." 1023B, "FRENCH OPEN / MAY 23-JUNE 5, 1988 / GRAF v ZVEREVA / 6-0 / 6-0." 1023C, "WIMBLEDON / JUNE 20-JULY 4, 1988 / GRAF v NAVRATILOVA / 5-7 / 6-2 / 6-1." 1023D, "U.S. OPEN / AUGUST 29-SEPTEMBER 11, 1988 / GRAF v SABATINI / 6-3 / 3-6 / 6-1."

No. 907 Ovptd. "GOLD MEDALIST" in Gold

1989, Jan. 16 Litho. *Perf. 14*

1024 A130 100 le multi 6.00 6.00

Marginal overprint: "SEOUL OLYMPICS 1988 / GRAF v SABATINI / 6-3 / 6-3."

Medalists of the 1988 Summer Olympics, Seoul A149

Designs: 3 le, Christian Schenk, German Democratic Republic, decathlon. 6 le, Hitoshi Saito, Japan, heavyweight judo. 10 le, Jutta Niehaus, Federal Republic of Germany, women's road race. 15 le, Tomas Lange, German Democratic Republic, single sculls. 20 le, Matthew Biondi, US, 50m and 100m freestyle. 30 le, Carl Lewis, US, 100m sprint. 40 le, Nicole Uphoff, Federal Republic of Germany, individual dressage. 50 le, Andras Sike, Hungary, 126-pound Greco-Roman wrestling. No. 1033, Gold medal, five-ring emblem. No. 1034, Torch, five-ring emblem.

1989, Apr. 28 Litho. *Perf. 14*

1025 A149 3 le multicolored .95 .95
1026 A149 6 le multicolored 1.25 1.25
1027 A149 10 le multicolored 1.75 1.75
1028 A149 15 le multicolored 1.90 1.90
1029 A149 20 le multicolored 1.90 1.90
1030 A149 30 le multicolored 2.25 2.25
1031 A149 40 le multicolored 3.00 3.00
1032 A149 50 le multicolored 3.00 3.00
Nos. 1025-1032 (8) 16.00 16.00

Souvenir Sheets

1033 A149 100 le multicolored 5.50 5.50
1034 A149 100 le multicolored 5.50 5.50

Name of athlete not inscribed on No. 1031.

1990 World Cup Soccer Championships, Italy — A150

3 le, Brazil vs. Sweden. 6 le, Germany vs. Hungary. 8 le, England vs. Germany. 10 le, Argentina vs. The Netherlands. 12 le, Brazil vs. Czechoslovakia. 20 le, Germany vs. The Netherlands. 30 le, Italy vs. Germany. 40 le, Brazil vs. Italy.
No. 1043, Uruguay vs. Brazil. No. 1044, Argentina vs. Germany.

1989, May 8

1035 A150 3 le multi .25 .25
1036 A150 6 le multi .55 .55
1037 A150 8 le multi .70 .70
1038 A150 10 le multi .90 .90
1039 A150 12 le multi 1.10 1.10
1040 A150 20 le multi 1.75 1.75
1041 A150 30 le multi 2.75 2.75
1042 A150 40 le multi 3.50 3.50
Nos. 1035-1042 (8) 11.50 11.50

Souvenir Sheets

1043 A150 100 le multi 4.50 4.50
1044 A150 100 le multi 4.50 4.50

Mano River Union, 15th Anniv. A151

Designs: 1 le, Sierra Leone-Guinea postal service. 3 le, Presidents Momoh, Conte of Guinea and Doe of Liberia. 10 le, Freetown-Monrovia Highway under construction. 15 le, Presidents signing the Communique at a 1988 summit.

1989, May 19 *Perf. 14*

1045 A151 1 le multicolored .80 .80
1046 A151 3 le multicolored 1.40 1.40
1047 A151 10 le multicolored 2.25 2.25
Nos. 1045-1047 (3) 4.45 4.45

Souvenir Sheet

1048 A151 15 le multicolored 3.50 3.50

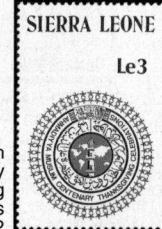

Ahmadiyya Muslim Centenary Thanksgiving Celebrations A152

1989, June 8

1049 A152 3 le black & brt blue .60 .60

Miniature Sheets

Shakespeare's 425th Birth Anniv. — A153

Scenes from the playwright's works.

No. 1050: a, Richard III. b, Othello (Desdemona and two men). c, The Two Gentlemen of Verona. d, Macbeth (chamber). e, Hamlet. f, Taming of the Shrew (scene with dog). g, The Merry Wives of Windsor. h, Henry IV (assembly room).

No. 1051: a, Macbeth (horsemen). b, Romeo and Juliet. c, Merchant of Venice. d, As You Like It. e, Taming of the Shrew (ruined meal). f, King Lear. g, Othello (death scene). h, Henry IV (street scene).

1989, May 30 ***Perf. 13***

1050 A153 Sheet of 8 + label 7.00 7.00
a.-h. 15 le any single .50 .50
1051 A153 Sheet of 8 + label 7.00 7.00
a.-h. 15 le any single .50 .50

Souvenir Sheets

1052 A153 100 le Portrait 6.75 6.75
1053 A153 100 le Portrait, coat of arms 6.75 6.75

Nos. 1050-1051 contain center label picturing Shakespeare's portrait (No. 1050) or his birthplace in Stratford (No. 1051).

Paintings by Takeuchi Seiho (1864-1942) — A154

Designs: 3 le, Lapping Waves. 6 le, Hazy Moon, vert. 8 le, Passing Spring, vert. 10 le, Mackerels. 12 le, Calico Cat. 30 le, The First Time To Be a Model, vert. 40 le, Kingly Lion. 75 le, After a Shower, vert. No. 1062, Domesticated Monkeys and Rabbits. No. 1063, Dozing in the Midst of All the Chirping, vert.

Perf. 14x13½, 13½x14

1989, July 3 **Litho.**

1054 A154 3 le multicolored .25 .25
1055 A154 6 le multicolored .30 .30
1056 A154 8 le multicolored .45 .45
1057 A154 10 le multicolored .55 .55
1058 A154 12 le multicolored .60 .60
1059 A154 30 le multicolored 1.60 1.60
1060 A154 40 le multicolored 2.25 2.25
1061 A154 75 le multicolored 4.25 4.25
Nos. 1054-1061 (8) 10.25 10.25

Souvenir Sheets

1062 A154 150 le multicolored 7.25 7.25
1063 A154 150 le multicolored 7.25 7.25

Hirohito (1901-89) and enthronement of Akihito as emperor of Japan.

See Nos. 1098-1129.

PHILEXFRANCE '89, French Revolution Bicent. — A155

Famous people, sites, exhibition and anniv. emblems: 6 le, Robespierre (1758-94), the Bastille. 20 le, Georges Jacques Danton (1759-94), the Louvre. 45 le, Marie Antoinette (1755-93), Notre Dame Cathedral interior. 80 le, Louis XVI (1754-93), Palace of Versailles. 150 le, Revolutionaries in Paris, vert.

1989, July 14 **Litho.** ***Perf. 14***

1064 A155 6 le multicolored .65 .65
1065 A155 20 le multicolored 1.25 1.25
1066 A155 45 le multicolored 2.25 2.25
1067 A155 80 le multicolored 3.75 3.75
Nos. 1064-1067 (4) 7.90 7.90

Souvenir Sheet

1068 A155 150 le multicolored 7.00 7.00

Miniature Sheets

Space Exploration — A156

Satellites, probes and spacecraft.

No. 1069: a, Sputnik, 1957. b, Telstar, 1962. c, Rendezvous of Gemini 6 and 7, 1965. d, Yuri Gagarin, 1st man in space, 1961. e, Mariner, 1964. f, Surveyor on Mars, 1966. g, US-Canadian Alouette satellite, 1962. h, Edward White, 1st American to walk in space, 1965. i, OGO-4 satellite, 1967.

No. 1070: a, Buzz Aldrin on the Moon, Apollo 11 mission, 1969. b, Apollo 15 mission lunar rover. c, Apollo 15 crew member. d, Conducting experiments on the lunar surface. e, Splitrock, Valley of Taurus-Littrow. f, Saluting the flag, Apollo 15 lunar module. g, Solar wind experiment. h, Lunar rover, diff. i, Apollo command module.

No. 1071: a, Module separation. b, Docking maneuvers. c, Lunar module in space. d, Second stage separation. e, Module transposition. f, Lunar module controlled descent, Moon's surface. g, Apollo 11 liftoff, 1969. h, Lunar module separates from command module. i, Neil Armstrong's first step on the Moon.

No. 1072: a, Mariner-Mars, 1971. b, Mariner 10, 1973. c, Viking, 1975. d, Skylab, 1974. e, Soyuz-Salyut, 1974. f, Viking robot craft, 1974. g, Pioneer 2, 1973. h, Apollo-Soyuz, 1975. i, Pioneer-Venus, 1978.

No. 1073: a, Apollo 17 lunar module, 1972. b, Command module jettison of service module before reentry. c, Soyuz 11, 1971. d, Lunar module liftoff. e, U.S. Navy recovery operation. f, Mars 2, 1971. g, Command module in docking position. h, Luna 17, 1970. i, Mars 3, 1971.

No. 1074: a, Voyager 1 and 2, 1977. b, Columbia space shuttle, 1981. c, Mir space station, 1986. d, IUE-Ultraviolet Explorer, US, U.K. and the European Space Agency, 1978. e, Astronaut operating out of shuttle cargo bay, 1983. f, Magellan, 1989. g, Soyuz-Salyut, 1978. h, STS-10, 1984. i, Shuttle, space telescope, 1989.

No. 1075, Spacelab. No. 1076, Future space station. No. 1077, Voyager.

1989, July 20 **Litho.** ***Perf. 14***

1069 A156 Sheet of 9 5.00 5.00
a.-i. 10 le any single .55 .55
1070 A156 Sheet of 9 5.00 5.00
a.-i. 10 le any single .55 .55
1071 A156 Sheet of 9 5.00 5.00
a.-i. 10 le any single .55 .55
1072 A156 Sheet of 9 8.00 8.00
a.-i. 15 le any single .85 .85
1073 A156 Sheet of 9 8.00 8.00
a.-i. 15 le any single .85 .85
1074 A156 Sheet of 9 8.00 8.00
a.-i. 15 le any single .85 .85
Nos. 1069-1074 (6) 39.00 39.00

Souvenir Sheets

1075 A156 100 le multicolored 7.50 7.50
1076 A156 100 le multicolored 7.50 7.50
1077 A156 100 le multicolored 7.50 7.50

Nos. 1069f is incorrectly inscribed "Mars" instead of "Moon."

Orchids — A157

3 le, Bulbophyllum barbigerum. 6 le, Bulbophyllum falcatum. 12 le, Habenaria macrara. 20 le, Eurychone rothchildiana. 50 le, Calyptrochilum christyanum. 60 le, Bulbophyllum distans. 70 le, Eulophia guineensis. 80 le, Diapha-nanthe pellu-cida.

No. 1086, Cyrtorchis arcuata. No. 1087, Butterflies, Eulophia cucullata.

1989, Sept. 8 **Litho.** ***Perf. 14***

1078 A157 3 le multi .80 .80
1079 A157 6 le multi 1.20 1.20
1080 A157 12 le multi 1.60 1.60
1081 A157 20 le multi 2.10 2.10
1082 A157 50 le multi 3.25 3.25
1083 A157 60 le multi 3.75 3.75
1084 A157 70 le multi 3.75 3.75
1085 A157 80 le multi 4.25 4.25
Nos. 1078-1085 (8) 20.70 20.70

Souvenir Sheets

1086 A157 100 le multi 10.00 10.00
1087 A157 100 le multi 10.00 10.00

Butterflies — A158

6 le, Salamis temora. 12 le, Pseudacraea lucretia. 18 le, Charaxes boueti. 30 le, Graphium antheus. 40 le, Colotis protomedia. 60 le, Asterope pechueli. 72 le, Coenura aurantiaca. 80 le, Precis octavia.

No. 1096, Charaxes cithaeron. No. 1097, Euphaedra themis.

1989, Sept. 11

1088 A158 6 le multi 1.00 1.00
1089 A158 12 le multi 1.25 1.25
1090 A158 18 le multi 1.60 1.60
1091 A158 30 le multi 2.75 2.75
1092 A158 40 le multi 3.75 3.75
1093 A158 60 le multi 4.00 4.00
1094 A158 72 le multi 4.50 4.50
1095 A158 80 le multi 4.50 4.50
Nos. 1088-1095 (8) 23.35 23.35

Souvenir Sheets

1096 A158 100 le multi 12.00 12.00
1097 A158 100 le multi 12.00 12.00

Nos. 1088-1090, 1095 and 1097 horiz.

Art Type of 1989

Paintings by Hiroshige in the series Fifty-three Stations on the Tokaido: No. 1098, Coolies Warming Themselves at Hamamatsu. No. 1099, Imakiri Ford at Maisaka. No. 1100, Pacific Ocean Seen from Shirasuka. No. 1101, Futakawa Street Singers. No. 1102, Repairing Yoshida Castle. No. 1103, The Inn at Akasaka. No. 1104, The Bridge to Okazaki. No. 1105, Samurai's Wife Entering Narumi. No. 1106, Harbour at Kuwana. No. 1107, Autumn in Ishiyakushi. No. 1108, Snowfall at Kameyama. No. 1109, The Frontier Station of Seki. No. 1110, Teahouse at Sakanoshita. No. 1111, Kansai Houses at Minakushi. No. 1112, Kusatsu Station. No. 1113, Ferry to Kawasaki. No. 1114, The Hilly Town of Hodogaya. No. 1115, Lute Players at Fujisawa. No. 1116, Mild Rainstorm at Oiso. No. 1117, Lake Ashi and Mountains of Hakone. No. 1118, Twilight at Numazu. No. 1119, Mount Fuji From Hara. No. 1120, Samurai's Children Riding Through Yoshiwara. No. 1121, Mountain Pass at Yui. No. 1122, Harbour at Ejiri. No. 1123, Stopping at Fujieda. No. 1124, Misty Kanaya on the Oi River. No. 1125, The Bridge to Kakegawa. No. 1126, Teahouse at Fukuroi. No. 1127, The Ford at Mistuke. No. 1128, Sanjo Bridge in Kyoto. No. 1129, Nibonbashi Bridge in Edo.

1989, Nov. 13 **Litho.** ***Perf. 14x13½***

1098-1127 A154 25 le Set of 30 35.00 35.00

Souvenir sheets

1128-1129 A154 120 le each 14.00 14.00

Hirohito (1901-1989) and enthronement of Akihito as emperor of Japan.

Souvenir Sheet

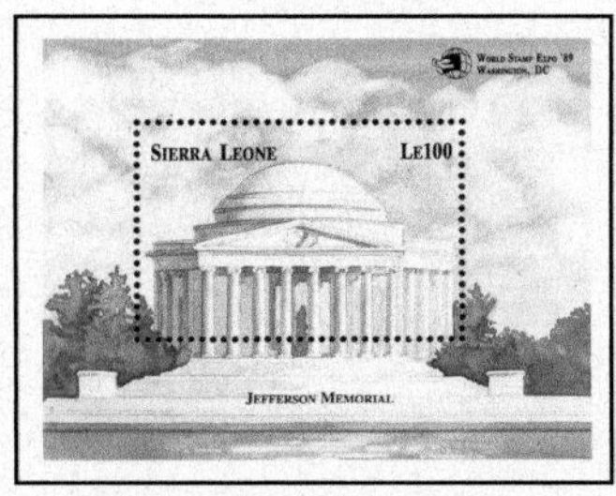

Jefferson Memorial, Washington, DC — A159

1989, Nov. 17 **Litho.** ***Perf. 14***

1136 A159 100 le multicolored 2.25 2.25

World Stamp Expo '89.

Endangered Species — A160

6 le, Humpback whale. 9 le, Formosan sika deer. 16 le, Spanish lynx. 20 le, Goitered gazelle. 30 le, Japanese sea lion. 50 le, Long-eared owl. 70 le, Chinese copper pheasant. 100 le, Siberian tiger.

No. 1145, Mauritius kestrel falcon. No. 1146, Crested ibis.

1989, Nov. 29 ***Perf. 14***

1137 A160 6 le multi .30 .30
1138 A160 9 le multi .35 .35
1139 A160 16 le multi .60 .60
1140 A160 20 le multi .85 .85
1141 A160 30 le multi 1.25 1.25
1142 A160 50 le multi 2.00 2.00
1143 A160 70 le multi 3.00 3.00
1144 A160 100 le multi 4.00 4.00
Nos. 1137-1144 (8) 12.35 12.35

Souvenir Sheets

1145 A160 150 le multi 7.25 7.25
1146 A160 150 le multi 7.25 7.25

World Stamp Expo '89.

Christmas — A161

Disney characters and classic automobiles: 3 le, 1934 Phantom II Rolls-Royce Roadstar. 6 le, 1935 Mercedes-Benz 500K. 10 le, 1938 Jaguar SS-100. 12 le, 1941 Jeep. 20 le, 1937 Buick Roadmaster Sedan Model 91. 30 le, 1948 Tucker. 40 le, 1933 Alfa Romeo. 50 le, 1937 Cord. No. 1155, 1938 Fiat Topolino. No. 1156, 1931 Pontiac Model 401, 1929 Pontiac Landau.

1989, Dec. 18 ***Perf. 14x13½***

1147 A161 3 le multicolored .80 .80
1148 A161 6 le multicolored 1.00 1.00
1149 A161 10 le multicolored 1.40 1.40
1150 A161 12 le multicolored 1.50 1.50
1151 A161 20 le multicolored 2.10 2.10
1152 A161 30 le multicolored 2.40 2.40
1153 A161 40 le multicolored 2.60 2.60
1154 A161 50 le multicolored 3.00 3.00
Nos. 1147-1154 (8) 14.80 14.80

Souvenir Sheets

1155 A161 100 le multicolored 6.00 6.00
1156 A161 100 le multicolored 6.00 6.00

Christmas — A162

Religious paintings by Rembrandt: 3 le, Adoration of the Magi. 6 le, The Holy Family with a Cat. 10 le, The Holy Family with Angels. 15 le, Simeon in the Temple. 30 le, The Circumcision. 90 le, The Holy Family. 100 le, The Visitation. 120 le, The Flight into Egypt. No. 1165, The Adoration of the Shepherds. No. 1166, The Presentation of Jesus in the Temple.

1989, Dec. 22 ***Perf. 14***

1157 A162 3 le multicolored .60 .60
1158 A162 6 le multicolored .75 .75
1159 A162 10 le multicolored 1.10 1.10
1160 A162 15 le multicolored 1.25 1.25
1161 A162 30 le multicolored 1.90 1.90
1162 A162 90 le multicolored 3.50 3.50
1163 A162 100 le multicolored 3.50 3.50
1164 A162 120 le multicolored 3.50 3.50
Nos. 1157-1164 (8) 16.10 16.10

Souvenir Sheets

1165 A162 150 le multicolored 4.75 4.75
1166 A162 150 le multicolored 4.75 4.75

Miniature Sheets

Exploration of Mars — A163

No. 1167: a, Kepler. b, Galileo. c, Drawings by Huygens in 1672 and Schiaparelli in 1886. d, Sir W. Herschel. e, Percival Lowell in Arizona, 1896-1907. f, Mars. g, Mariner 4, 1965. h, Mars 2, 1971. i, Mars 3, 1971.

No. 1168: a, Mariner 9, 1971. b, Mariner 9, Phobos. c, Cydonia Region. d, South polar cap. e, Profile of Mars. f, Polar cap, diff. g, Nix Olympica. h, Grand Canyon of Mars. i, North Pole.

No. 1169: a, Olympus Mons. b, Viking 1, July 1976. c, Viking 2 releases Lander, Sept. 1976. d, Lander entering Mars's atmosphere. e, Parachute deployed. f, Terminal descent. g, Viking Lander on Mars. h, Soil sampler (robotic arm). i, Soil Sampler (US flag, machine).

No. 1170: a, Martian dusk. b, Project Deimos. c, Exploration of Mars (astronauts surveying land). d, Return to Rombus. e, US rocket bound for Mars. f, Spacecraft bound for Mars. g, Spacecraft in Martian orbit. h, Mission to Mars (astronauts weightless in spacecraft cabin). i, Space station.

No. 1171, "The Face," Mars.

1990 Litho. *Perf. 14*

1167 Sheet of 9 20.00 20.00
a.-i. A163 175 le any single 2.00 2.00
1168 Sheet of 9 20.00 20.00
a.-i. A163 175 le any single 2.00 2.00
1169 Sheet of 9 20.00 20.00
a.-i. A163 175 le any single 2.00 2.00
1170 Sheet of 9 20.00 20.00
a.-i. A163 175 le any single 2.00 2.00
Nos. 1167-1170 (4) 80.00 80.00

Souvenir Sheet

1171 A163 150 le multicolored 6.00 6.00
1171A A163 150 le Space station 6.00 6.00

Issued: No. 1171A, Dec. 24; others, Jan. 15.

Extreme speculation has occured with this issue, centered around No. 1171, the face on Mars stamp.

World War II — A164

USAF aircraft — No. 1172, Doolittle Raid B-25. No. 1173, B-24 Liberator. No. 1174, A-20 Boston. No. 1175, P-38 Lightning. No. 1176, B-26. No. 1177, B-17 F. No. 1178, B-25 D Mitchell. No. 1179, Boeing B-29. No. 1180, B-17 G. No. 1181, The Enola Gay.

No. 1182, B-25, USS Hornet. No. 1183, B-17 G.

1990, Feb. 5 Litho. *Perf. 14*

1172 A164 1 le multi .25 .25
1173 A164 2 le multi .25 .25
1174 A164 3 le multi .25 .25
1175 A164 9 le multi .50 .50
1176 A164 12 le multi .55 .55
1177 A164 16 le multi .80 .80
1178 A164 50 le multi 2.25 2.25
1179 A164 80 le multi 3.50 3.50
1180 A164 90 le multi 4.25 4.25
1181 A164 100 le multi 4.50 4.50
Nos. 1172-1181 (10) 17.10 17.10

Souvenir Sheets

1182 A164 150 le multi 6.75 6.75
1183 A164 150 le multi 6.75 6.75

Stage and Screen Roles Played by Sir Laurence Olivier (1907-1989) A165

3 le, Antony & Cleopatra, 1951. 9 le, Henry V, 1943. 16 le, Oedipus, 1945. 20 le, Wuthering Heights, 1939. 30 le, Marathon Man, 1976. 70 le, Othello, 1964. 175 le, Beau Geste, 1929. 200 le, Richard III, 1956.

No. 1192, The Battle of Britain, 1969. No. 1193, Hamlet, 1947.

1990, Apr. 27

1184 A165 3 le multi .25 .25
1185 A165 9 le multi .25 .25
1186 A165 16 le multi .40 .40
1187 A165 20 le multi .60 .60
1188 A165 30 le multi .80 .80
1189 A165 70 le multi 1.75 1.75
1190 A165 175 le multi 5.00 5.00
1191 A165 200 le multi 5.50 5.50
Nos. 1184-1191 (8) 14.55 14.55

Souvenir Sheets

1192 A165 250 le multi 6.00 6.00
1193 A165 250 le multi 6.00 6.00

Walt Disney Characters, Settings in Sierra Leone — A166

3 le, Bauxite mine. 6 le, Panning for gold. 10 le, Lungi Intl. Airport. 12 le, Old Fourah Bay College. 16 le, Mining bauxite. 20 le, Rice harvest. 30 le, The Cotton Tree. 100 le, Rutile Mine. 200 le, Fishing at Goderich. 225 le, Bintumani Hotel.

No. 1204, Market Place, King Jimmy. No. 1205, Diamond mining.

1990, Apr. 23

1194 A166 3 le multi .25 .25
1195 A166 6 le multi .25 .25
1196 A166 10 le multi .25 .25
1197 A166 12 le multi .25 .25
1198 A166 16 le multi .30 .30
1199 A166 20 le multi .40 .40
1200 A166 30 le multi .75 .75
1201 A166 100 le multi 2.60 2.60
1202 A166 200 le multi 5.25 5.25
1203 A166 225 le multi 5.50 5.50
Nos. 1194-1203 (10) 15.80 15.80

Souvenir Sheets

1204 A166 250 le multi 6.00 6.00
1205 A166 250 le multi 6.00 6.00

Penny Black, 150th Anniv. — A167

1990, May 3 *Perf. 14*

1206 A167 50 le deep ultra 2.25 2.25
1207 A167 100 le violet brown 5.00 5.00

Souvenir Sheet

1208 A167 250 le black 6.75 6.75

World Cup Soccer Championships, Italy — A168

Team photographs: No. 1209, Colombia. No. 1210, United Arab Emirates. No. 1211, South Korea. No. 1212, Cameroun. No. 1213, Costa Rica. No. 1214, Romania. No. 1215, Yugoslavia. No. 1216, Egypt. No. 1217, Netherlands. No. 1218, Uruguay. No. 1219, USSR. No. 1220, Czechoslovakia. No. 1221, Scotland. No. 1222, Belgium. No. 1223, Austria. No. 1224, Sweden. No. 1225, W. Germany. No. 1226, England. No. 1227, United States. No. 1228, Ireland. No. 1229, Spain. No. 1230, Brazil. No. 1231, Italy. No. 1232, Argentina.

1990, May 11 Litho. *Perf. 14*

1209 A168 15 le multicolored .90 .90
1210 A168 15 le multicolored .90 .90
1211 A168 15 le multicolored .90 .90
1212 A168 15 le multicolored .90 .90
1213 A168 15 le multicolored .90 .90
1214 A168 15 le multicolored .90 .90
1215 A168 15 le multicolored .90 .90
1216 A168 15 le multicolored .90 .90
1217 A168 30 le multicolored .90 .90
1218 A168 30 le multicolored .90 .90
1219 A168 30 le multicolored .90 .90
1220 A168 30 le multicolored .90 .90
1221 A168 30 le multicolored .90 .90
1222 A168 30 le multicolored .90 .90
1223 A168 30 le multicolored .90 .90
1224 A168 30 le multicolored .90 .90
1225 A168 45 le multicolored .90 .90
1226 A168 45 le multicolored .90 .90
1227 A168 45 le multicolored .90 .90
1228 A168 45 le multicolored .90 .90
1229 A168 45 le multicolored .90 .90
1230 A168 45 le multicolored .90 .90
1231 A168 45 le multicolored .90 .90
1232 A168 45 le multicolored .90 .90
Nos. 1209-1232 (24) 21.60 21.60

No. 1209 spelled "Columbia," No. 1218 "Uraguay," No. 1220 "Czecheslovakia" on stamps.

Great Crested Grebe A169

6 le, Green woodhoopoe. 10 le, African jacana. 12 le, Avocet. 20 le, African finfoot. 80 le, Glossy ibis. 150 le, Hamerkop. 200 le, Greater honey guide.

No. 1241, Painted snipe. No. 1242, Palm swift.

1990, June 4

1233 A169 3 le multi .30 .30
1234 A169 6 le multi .30 .30
1235 A169 10 le multi .35 .35
1236 A169 12 le multi .35 .35
1237 A169 20 le multi .45 .45
1238 A169 80 le multi 1.75 1.75
1239 A169 150 le multi 3.25 3.25
1240 A169 200 le multi 4.25 4.25
Nos. 1233-1240 (8) 11.00 11.00

Souvenir Sheets

1241 A169 250 le multi 5.50 5.50
1242 A169 250 le multi 5.50 5.50

Mickey as Yeoman Warder A170

Disney characters: 6 le, Scrooge as lamplighter. 12 le, Knight Goofy. 15 le, Clarabell as Anne Boleyn. 75 le, Minnie Mouse as Queen Elizabeth I. 100 le, Donald Duck as chimmey sweep. 125 le, Pete as King Henry VIII. 150 le, May dancers in Salisbury. No. 1251, Boadicea, Queen of the Iceni. No. 1252, Lawyers at Parliament House.

1990, June 6 *Perf. 13½x14*

1243 A170 3 le multicolored .25 .25
1244 A170 6 le multicolored .25 .25
1245 A170 12 le multicolored .25 .25
1246 A170 15 le multicolored .30 .30
1247 A170 75 le multicolored 2.00 2.00
1248 A170 100 le multicolored 2.60 2.60
1249 A170 125 le multicolored 3.25 3.25
1250 A170 150 le multicolored 4.00 4.00
Nos. 1243-1250 (8) 12.90 12.90

Souvenir Sheets

1251 A170 250 le multicolored 5.50 5.50
1252 A170 250 le multicolored 5.50 5.50

Queen Mother, 90th Birthday — A171

No. 1254, Wearing black hat. No. 1255, Wearing yellow hat.

1990, July 5 *Perf. 14*

1253 A171 75 le shown 1.50 1.50
1254 A171 75 le multicolored 1.50 1.50
1255 A171 75 le multicolored 1.50 1.50
a. Strip of 3, #1253-1255 5.00 5.00
Nos. 1253-1255 (3) 4.50 4.50

Souvenir Sheet

1256 A171 250 le Like No. 1253 5.00 5.00

Butterfly Type of 1987

1990 *Perf. 12½x11½*

1257 A126 3 le like No. 861 7.00 7.00
1258 A126 9 le like No. 864 4.25 4.25
1259 A126 12 le like No. 859 4.25 4.25
a. Perf. 14 — 8.00
1260 A126 16 le like No. 860 *5.00* 5.00
Nos. 1257-1260 (4) 20.50 20.50

Inscribed 1989. Nos. 1257-1258 have been reported in perf. 12x12½. Nos. 1257-1258 and 1260 have been reported in perf. 14. The editors would like to examine any examples.

Miniature Sheet

Wildlife — A172

Designs: No. 1261a, Golden cat. b, White-backed night heron. c, Bateleur eagle. d, Marabou stork. e, White-faced whistling duck. f, Aardvark. g, Royal antelope. h, Pygmy hippopotamus. i, Leopard. j, Sacred ibis. k, Mona monkey. l, Darter. m, Chimpanzee. n, African elephant. o, Potto. p, African manatee. q, African fish eagle. r, African spoonbill.

150 le, Crowned eagle, vert.

1990, Sept. 24 Litho. *Perf. 14*

1261 A172 Sheet of 18 18.00 18.00
a.-r. 25 le any single .80 .80

Souvenir Sheet

1262 A172 150 le multi 10.00 10.00

No. 1261 printed in continuous design showing map of Sierra Leone in background.

Carousel Animals — A173

5 le, Rabbit. 10 le, Horse with panther saddle. 20 le, Ostrich. 30 le, Zebra. 50 le, White horse. 80 le, Sea monster. 100 le, Giraffe. 150 le, Armored horse. 200 le, Camel.
No. 1272, Centaur, Lord Baden-Powell. No. 1273, Horse head.

1990, Oct. 22 Litho. *Perf. 14*

No.	Type	Denom.	Description	Unused	Used
1263	A173	5 le	multi	.25	.25
1264	A173	10 le	multi	.25	.25
1265	A173	20 le	multi	.35	.35
1266	A173	30 le	multi	.55	.55
1267	A173	50 le	multi	.90	.90
1268	A173	80 le	multi	1.25	1.25
1269	A173	100 le	multi	1.60	1.60
1270	A173	150 le	multi	2.50	2.50
1271	A173	200 le	multi	3.25	3.25
			Nos. 1263-1271 (9)	10.90	10.90

Souvenir Sheets

No.	Type	Denom.	Description	Unused	Used
1272	A173	300 le	multi	7.00	7.00
1273	A173	300 le	multi	7.00	7.00

1992 Summer Olympics, Barcelona — A174

5 le, Men's 100-meter race. 10 le, Men's 4x400-meter relay. 20 le, Men's 100-meter race, diff. 30 le, Weight lifting. 40 le, Freestyle wrestling. 80 le, Water polo. 150 le, Women's gymnastics. 200 le, Cycling.
No. 1282, Boxing. No. 1283, Olympic flag.

1990, Nov. 12 Litho. *Perf. 14*

No.	Type	Denom.	Description	Unused	Used
1274	A174	5 le	multi	.25	.25
1275	A174	10 le	multi	.25	.25
1276	A174	20 le	multi	.30	.30
1277	A174	30 le	multi	.55	.55
1278	A174	40 le	multi	.75	.75
1279	A174	80 le	multi	1.50	1.50
1280	A174	150 le	multi	2.60	2.60
1281	A174	200 le	multi	3.75	3.75
			Nos. 1274-1281 (8)	9.95	9.95

Souvenir Sheets

No.	Type	Denom.	Description	Unused	Used
1282	A174	400 le	multi	6.75	6.75
1283	A174	400 le	multi	6.75	6.75

Christmas A175

Paintings: 10 le, The Holy Family Resting by Rembrandt. 20 le, The Holy Family with St. Elizabeth by Andrea Mantegna. 30 le, Virgin and Child with an Angel by Correggio. 50 le, The Annunciation by Bernardo Strozzi. 100 le, Madonna and Child Appearing to St. Anthony by Filippino Lippi. 175 le, Virgin and Child by Giovanni Boltraffio. 200 le, The Esterhazy Madonna by Raphael. 300 le, Coronation of Mary by Orcagna. No. 1292, Adoration of the Shepherds by Bronzino. No. 1293, Adoration of the Shepherds by Gerard David.

1990, Dec. 17 *Perf. 13*

No.	Type	Denom.	Description	Unused	Used
1284	A175	10 le	multicolored	.25	.25
1285	A175	20 le	multicolored	.30	.30
1286	A175	30 le	multicolored	.45	.45
1287	A175	50 le	multicolored	.70	.70
1288	A175	100 le	multicolored	1.75	1.75
1289	A175	175 le	multicolored	3.50	3.50
1290	A175	200 le	multicolored	3.75	3.75
1291	A175	300 le	multicolored	5.25	5.25
			Nos. 1284-1291 (8)	15.95	15.95

Souvenir Sheets

No.	Type	Denom.	Description	Unused	Used
1292	A175	400 le	multicolored	7.00	7.00
1293	A175	400 le	multicolored	7.00	7.00

Christmas A176

Walt Disney characters in "The Night Before Christmas."

No. 1294a, 'Twas the night. . . b, Not a creature. . . c, The stockings were hung. . . d, And Mama in her kerchief. . . e, When out on the lawn. . . f, I sprang from my bed. . . g, Away to the window. . . h, Tore open the shutter. . .

No. 1295a, The moon on the breast. . . b, When what to my wondering. . . c, With a little old driver. . . d, More rapid than eagles. . . e, To the top of the porch. . . f, And then in a twinkling. . . g, As I drew in my head. . . h, He was dressed. . .

No. 1296a, A bundle of toys. . . b, The stump of a pipe. . . c, He had a broad face. . . d, He was chubby and plump. . . e, A wink of his eye. . . f, Then turned with a jerk. . . g, And giving a nod. . . h, He sprang to his sleigh. . .

No. 1297, The children were nestled. . . No. 1298, His eyes, how they twinkled. . . No. 1299, He spoke not a word. . . No. 1300, And he whistled. . . No. 1301, As dry leaves. . . No. 1302, But I heard him exclaim. . .

1990, Dec. 17 Litho. *Perf. 13*

Miniature Sheets of 8

No.	Type	Denom.	Description	Unused	Used
1294	A176	50 le	#a.-h.	5.25	5.25
1295	A176	75 le	#a.-h.	15.00	15.00
1296	A176	100 le	#a.-h.	7.75	7.75

Souvenir Sheets

No.	Type	Denom.	Description	Unused	Used
1297	A176	400 le	multi	4.50	4.50
1298	A176	400 le	multi, horiz.	4.50	4.50
1299	A176	400 le	multi	4.50	4.50
1300	A176	400 le	multi, horiz.	4.50	4.50
1301	A176	400 le	multi, horiz.	4.50	4.50
1302	A176	400 le	multi	4.50	4.50

Peter Paul Rubens (1577-1640), Painter A177

Entire paintings or different details from: 5 le, Helena Fourment as Hagar in the Wilderness. 10 le, Isabella Brant. 20 le, 60 le, Countess of Arundel and Her Party. 80 le, Nicolaas Rockox. 100 le, Adriana Perez. 150 le, George Villiers, Duke of Buckingham. 300 le, Countess of Buckingham. No. 1311, Veronica Spinola Doria. No. 1312, Giovanni Carlo Dorio.

1990, Dec. 24 *Perf. 14*

No.	Type	Denom.	Description	Unused	Used
1303	A177	5 le	multicolored	.30	.30
1304	A177	10 le	multicolored	.40	.40
1305	A177	20 le	multicolored	.60	.60
1306	A177	60 le	multicolored	.85	.85
1307	A177	80 le	multicolored	1.25	1.25
1308	A177	100 le	multicolored	1.50	1.50
1309	A177	150 le	multicolored	2.50	2.50
1310	A177	300 le	multicolored	4.50	4.50
			Nos. 1303-1310 (8)	11.90	11.90

Souvenir Sheets

No.	Type	Denom.	Description	Unused	Used
1311	A177	350 le	multicolored	6.25	6.25
1312	A177	350 le	multicolored	6.25	6.25

Mushrooms A178

Designs: 3 le, Chlorophyllum molybdites. 5 le, Lepista nuda. 10 le, Clitocybe nebularis. 15 le, Cyathus striatus. 20 le, Bolbitius vitellinus. 25 le, Leucoagaricus naucinus. 30 le, Suillus luteus. 40 le, Podaxis pistillaris. 50 le, Oudemansiella radicata. 60 le, Phallus indusiatus. 80 le, Macrolepiota rhacodes. 100 le, Mycena pura. 150 le, Volvariella volvacea. 175 le, Omphalotus olearius. 200 le, Sphaerobolus stellatus. 250 le, Schizophyllum commune.

Each 350 le: No. 1329, Agaricus campestris. No. 1330, Hypholama fasciculare. No. 1331, Suillus granulatus. No. 1332, Psilocybe coprophila.

1990, Dec. 31 *Perf. 14*

No.	Type	Denom.	Description	Unused	Used
1313	A178	3 le	multicolored	.25	.25
1314	A178	5 le	multicolored	.25	.25
1315	A178	10 le	multicolored	.25	.25
1316	A178	15 le	multicolored	.25	.25
1317	A178	20 le	multicolored	.30	.30
1318	A178	25 le	multicolored	.45	.45
1319	A178	30 le	multicolored	.55	.55
1320	A178	40 le	multicolored	.70	.70
1321	A178	50 le	multicolored	.85	.85
1322	A178	60 le	multicolored	.95	.95
1323	A178	80 le	multicolored	1.40	1.40
1324	A178	100 le	multicolored	2.25	2.25
1325	A178	150 le	multicolored	2.75	2.75
1326	A178	175 le	multicolored	3.50	3.50
1327	A178	200 le	multicolored	4.25	4.25
1328	A178	250 le	multicolored	5.00	5.00
			Nos. 1313-1328 (16)	23.95	23.95

Souvenir Sheets

No.	Type	Description	Unused	Used
1329-1332	A178	Set of 4	24.00	24.00

Butterfly Type of 1987 With "Sierra Leone" in Blue

1991 Litho. *Perf. 14*

No.	Type	Denom.	Description	Unused	Used
1332A	A126	10c	Like #868	6.50	2.00
1332B	A126	50c	Like #861	5.00	2.00
n.			Perf. 12½x11½	3.50	
o.			Perf. 12x12½	3.00	
1332C	A126	1 le	Like #862	8.00	1.75
1332D	A126	2 le	Like #863	5.00	1.75
1332E	A126	5 le	Like #865	27.50	3.00
1332F	A126	10 le	Like #866	15.00	1.25
1332G	A126	20 le	Like #867	27.50	3.00
1332H	A126	30 le	Like #864	27.50	3.00
1332I	A126	50 le	Like #859	15.00	1.25
p.			Perf. 12½x11½	4.00	
q.			Perf. 12x12½	3.00	
1332J	A126	60 le	Like #871	15.00	2.00
1332K	A126	80 le	Like #860	10.00	3.00
r.			Perf. 12½x11½	5.50	
s.			Perf. 12x12½	3.00	
1332L	A126	100 le	Like #873	27.50	5.00
1332M	A126	300 le	Like #869	10.00	6.00
t.			Perf. 12½x11½	7.50	
u.			Perf. 12x12½	3.00	
			Nos. 1332A-1332M (13)	199.50	35.00

Every sixth perforation hole is larger on Perf. 12½x11½ stamps. These stamps are not known used. All stamps are dated "1990."

Easter A179

Entire works or details from paintings by Rubens: 10 le, Flight of St. Barbara. 20 le, No. 1341, The Last Judgement. 30 le, St. Gregory of Nazianzus. 50 le, Doubting Thomas. 80 le, No. 1342, The Way to Calvary. 100 le, St. Gregory with Sts. Domitilla, Maurus and Papianus. 175 le, Sts. Gregory, Maurus and Papianus. 300 le, Christ and the Penitent Sinners.

1991, Apr. 8 Litho. *Perf. 13½x14*

No.	Type	Denom.	Description	Unused	Used
1333	A179	10 le	multicolored	.30	.30
1334	A179	20 le	multicolored	.45	.45
1335	A179	30 le	multicolored	.70	.70
1336	A179	50 le	multicolored	1.15	1.15
1337	A179	80 le	multicolored	1.60	1.60
1338	A179	100 le	multicolored	2.10	2.10
1339	A179	175 le	multicolored	3.75	3.75
1340	A179	300 le	multicolored	6.25	6.25
			Nos. 1333-1340 (8)	16.30	16.30

Souvenir Sheets

No.	Type	Denom.	Description	Unused	Used
1341-1342	A179	400 le	Set of 2	14.00	14.00

Phila Nippon '91 A180

Japanese locomotives: 10 le, Class 1400 steam. 20 le, Streamlined C55 steam. 30 le, ED17 electric. 60 le, EF13 electric. 100 le, Baldwin Mikado steam. 150 le, C62 steam. 200 le, KiHa 81 class diesel. 300 le, Class 8550 steam.

Each 400 le: No. 1351, Hikari bullet train. No. 1352, Class 7000 electric. No. 1353, D51 steam. No. 1354, Class 9600 steam.

1991, May 13 Litho. *Perf. 14*

No.	Type	Denom.	Description	Unused	Used
1343	A180	10 le	multicolored	.25	.25
1344	A180	20 le	multicolored	.35	.35
1345	A180	30 le	multicolored	.55	.55
1346	A180	60 le	multicolored	1.00	1.00
1347	A180	100 le	multicolored	1.75	1.75
1348	A180	150 le	multicolored	2.50	2.50
1349	A180	200 le	multicolored	3.50	3.50
1350	A180	300 le	multicolored	5.25	5.25
			Nos. 1343-1350 (8)	15.15	15.15

Souvenir Sheets

No.	Type	Description	Unused	Used
1351-1354	A180	Set of 4	24.00	24.00

Fish A181

10 le, Aphyosemion ghana. 20 le, Black-lipped panchax. 30 le, Peter's killie. 60 le, Micro-walkeri killie. 100 le, Butterfly fish. 150 le, Green panchax. 200 le, Six-barred panchax. 300 le, Banded puffer.

No. 1363, Spotfin synodontis. No. 1364, Two-striped panchax.

1991, June 3 Litho. *Perf. 14*

No.	Type	Denom.	Description	Unused	Used
1355	A181	10 le	multi	.50	.50
1356	A181	20 le	multi	.75	.75
1357	A181	30 le	multi	.90	.90
1358	A181	60 le	multi	1.60	1.60
1359	A181	100 le	multi	1.75	1.75
1360	A181	150 le	multi	2.10	2.10
1361	A181	200 le	multi	2.50	2.50
1362	A181	300 le	multi	2.50	2.50
			Nos. 1355-1362 (8)	12.60	12.60

Souvenir Sheets

No.	Type	Denom.	Description	Unused	Used
1363	A181	400 le	multi	6.25	6.25
1364	A181	400 le	multi	6.25	6.25

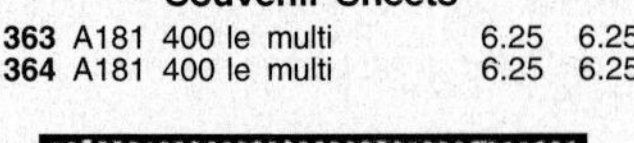

Paintings by Vincent Van Gogh — A182

Designs: 10c, The Langlois Bridge at Arles. 50c, Trees in the Garden of Saint-Paul Hospital, vert. 1 le, Wild Flowers and Thistles in a Vase, vert. 2 le, Still Life: Vase with Oleanders and Books. 5 le, Farmhouses in a Wheat Field Near Arles. 10 le, Self-Portrait, Sept. 1889, vert. 20 le, Portrait of Patience Escalier, vert. 30 le, Portrait of Doctor Felix Rey, vert. 50 le,

The Iris, vert. 60 le, The Shepherdess, vert. 80 le, Vincent's House in Arles (The Yellow House). 100 le, The Road Menders. 150 le, The Garden of Saint-Paul Hospital, vert. 200 le, View of the Church of Saint-Paul-De-Mausole. 250 le, Seascape at Saintes-Maries. 300 le, Pieta, vert.

Each 400 le: No. 1381, Church at Auvers Sur Dise, vert. No. 1382, Vineyards with a View of Auvers. No. 1383, The Trinquetaille Bridge. No. 1384, Two Poplars on a Road Through the Hills, vert. No. 1385, Haystacks in Provence. No. 1386, The Garden of Saint-Paul Hospital, diff.

1991, June 28 Litho. *Perf. 13½*

1365	A182	10c	multicolored	.30	.30
1366	A182	50c	multicolored	.30	.30
1367	A182	1 le	multicolored	.30	.30
1368	A182	2 le	multicolored	.30	.30
1369	A182	5 le	multicolored	.30	.30
1370	A182	10 le	multicolored	.30	.30
1371	A182	20 le	multicolored	.30	.30
1372	A182	30 le	multicolored	.45	.45
1373	A182	50 le	multicolored	.80	.80
1374	A182	60 le	multicolored	.95	.95
1375	A182	80 le	multicolored	1.30	1.30
1376	A182	100 le	multicolored	1.60	1.60
1377	A182	150 le	multicolored	2.40	2.40
1378	A182	200 le	multicolored	3.50	3.50
1379	A182	250 le	multicolored	4.50	4.50
1380	A182	300 le	multicolored	5.00	5.00
			Nos. 1365-1380 (16)	22.60	22.60

Size: 102x76mm

Imperf

1381-1386 A182	Set of 6	29.00	29.00

Royal Family Birthday, Anniversary

Common Design Type

1991, July 5 Litho. *Perf. 14*

1387	CD347	10 le	multi	.25	.25
1388	CD347	20 le	multi	.25	.25
1389	CD347	30 le	multi	.45	.45
1390	CD347	80 le	multi	1.00	1.00
1391	CD347	100 le	multi	1.40	1.40
1392	CD347	200 le	multi	3.00	3.00
1393	CD347	250 le	multi	3.50	3.50
1394	CD347	300 le	multi	4.00	4.00
			Nos. 1387-1394 (8)	13.85	13.85

Souvenir Sheets

1395	CD347	400 le	Elizabeth, Philip	6.25	6.25
1396	CD347	400 le	Charles, Diana, sons	6.25	6.25

10 le, 30 le, 200 le, 250 le, No. 1395, Queen Elizabeth II, 65th birthday. Others, Charles and Diana, 10th wedding anniversary.

Butterflies A183

10 le, Coppery swallowtail. 30 le, Orange forester. 50 le, Large striped swordtail. 60 le, Lilac beauty. 80 le, African leaf. 100 le, Blue diadem. 200 le, Beautiful monarch. 300 le, Veined swallowtail.

No. 1405, Blue banded nymph. No. 1406, Western red charaxes. No. 1407, Broad-bordered grass yellow. No. 1408, African clouded yellow.

1991, Aug. 5 Litho. *Perf. 14x13½*

1397	A183	10 le	multi	.25	.25
1398	A183	30 le	multi	.75	.75
1399	A183	50 le	multi	1.25	1.25
1400	A183	60 le	multi	1.50	1.50
1401	A183	80 le	multi	1.75	1.75
1402	A183	100 le	multi	2.50	2.50
1403	A183	200 le	multi	5.00	5.00
1404	A183	300 le	multi	7.25	7.25
			Nos. 1397-1404 (8)	20.25	20.25

Souvenir Sheets

Perf. 13x12

1405	A183	400 le	multi	7.50	7.50
1406	A183	400 le	multi	5.00	5.00
1407	A183	400 le	multi	5.00	5.00
1408	A183	400 le	multi	5.00	5.00

While numbers 1406-1407 have the same issue date as Nos. 1397-1405, the dollar value of Nos. 1406-1407 was lower when they were released. While No. 1408 has the same issue date as Nos. 1397-1407, the value of No. 1408 was different when released.

World War II Motion Pictures A184

Designs: 2 le, To Hell and Back, Audie Murphy. 5 le, Attack, Jack Palance. 10 le, Mrs. Miniver, Greer Garson and Walter Pidgeon. 20 le, The Guns of Navarone. 30 le, The Great Dictator, Paulette Goddard and Charlie Chaplin. 50 le, The Train. 60 le, The Diary of Anne Frank. 80 le, The Bridge on the River Kwai, William Holden. 100 le, Lifeboat, Alfred Hitchcock, Tallulah Bankhead. 200 le, Sands of Iwo Jima, John Wayne. 300 le, Thirty Seconds Over Tokyo, Van Johnson and Spencer Tracy. 350 le, Casablanca, Humphrey Bogart and Ingrid Bergman. No. 1421, Twelve O'Clock High, Gregory Peck. No. 1422, Tora! Tora! Tora!. No. 1423, Patton, George C. Scott.

1991, Oct. 14 Litho. *Perf. 14*

1409	A184	2 le	multicolored	.25	.25
1410	A184	5 le	multicolored	.25	.25
1411	A184	10 le	multicolored	.25	.25
1412	A184	20 le	multicolored	.25	.25
1413	A184	30 le	multicolored	.35	.35
1414	A184	50 le	multicolored	.75	.75
1415	A184	60 le	multicolored	.85	.85
1416	A184	80 le	multicolored	1.15	1.15
1417	A184	100 le	multicolored	1.60	1.60
1418	A184	200 le	multicolored	3.00	3.00
1419	A184	300 le	multicolored	4.50	4.50
1420	A184	350 le	multicolored	5.00	5.00
			Nos. 1409-1420 (12)	18.20	18.20

Souvenir Sheets

1421	A184	450 le	multicolored	6.25	6.25
1422	A184	450 le	multicolored	6.25	6.25
1423	A184	450 le	multicolored	6.25	6.25

Miniature Sheets

Botanic Gardens — A185

Munich Botanic Garden: No. 1424a, Meissen China ornament. b, Masdevallia. c, White Egyptian lotus. d, French marigold. e, Pitcher plant. f, The Palm House. g, Dog's tooth violet. h, Passion flower. i, Hedge rose. j, Sensitive plant. k, Pitcher plant, diff. l, Trillium. m, Wild plantain. n, German primrose. o, Tulip. p, Spring walk.

Kyoto Botanic Garden: No. 1425a, Flowering cherry. b, Gardenia. c, The Domed Conservatory. d, Chrysanthemums. e, Bleeding heart. f, Hibiscus. g, Hiryu azalea. h, Sweet honeysuckle. i, Goldband lily. j, Non-traditional garden art. k, Viburnum. l, Japanese iris. m, Orchid. n, Hydrangea. o, View of Kyoto Botanic Garden. p, Camelia.

Brooklyn Botanic Garden: No. 1426a, The Palm House. b, Kurume azalea. c, Southern magnolia. d, Oleander. e, Chinese wisteria. f, Sourwood tree. g, Cattleya orchid. h, Gingko tree. i, Japanese Hill and Pond Garden. j, Rose. k, German iris. l, East Indian lotus. m, Speciosum lily. n, Lilac. o, Rose bay. p, Cranford Rose Garden.

Each 600 le: No. 1427, Rhododendron, Munich, horiz. No. 1428, Chrysanthemum, Kyoto, horiz. No. 1429, Magnolia soulangeana, Brooklyn, horiz.

1991, Oct. 28 Sheets of 16

1424	A185	60 le	#a.-p.	12.50	12.50
1425	A185	60 le	#a.-p.	12.50	12.50
1426	A185	60 le	#a.-p.	12.50	12.50

Souvenir Sheets

1427-1429 A185	Set of 3	21.50	21.50

Christmas A186

Details from paintings or engravings by Albrecht Durer: 6 le, Mary being Crowned by Two Angels. 60 le, St. Christopher. 80 le, Virgin and Child. 100 le, Madonna and Child (Virgin with the Pear). 200 le, Madonna and Child. 300 le, The Virgin in Half-Length. 700 le, The Madonna with the Siskin.

Each 600 le: No. 1437, The Feast of the Rose Garlands. No. 1438, Virgin and Child with St. Anne.

1991, Dec. 9 Litho. *Perf. 12*

1430	A186	6 le	pink & black	.25	.25
1431	A186	60 le	blue & black	.65	.65
1432	A186	80 le	multicolored	.80	.80
1433	A186	100 le	multicolored	1.00	1.00
1434	A186	200 le	multicolored	2.00	2.00
1435	A186	300 le	multicolored	3.00	3.00
1436	A186	700 le	multicolored	7.00	7.00
			Nos. 1430-1436 (7)	14.70	14.70

Souvenir Sheets

Perf. 14½

1437-1438 A186	Set of 2	12.50	12.50

Wolfgang Amadeus Mozart, Death Bicent. A187

Mozart and: 50 le, National Theatre, Prague. 100 le, St. Peter's Abbey, Salzburg. 500 le, Scene from opera, "Idomeneo."

1991, Dec. 20 *Perf. 14*

1439	A187	50 le	multicolored	.60	.60
1440	A187	100 le	multicolored	1.15	1.15
1441	A187	500 le	multicolored	5.75	5.75
			Nos. 1439-1441 (3)	7.50	7.50

Souvenir Sheet

1442	A187	600 le	Bust, vert.	7.50	7.50

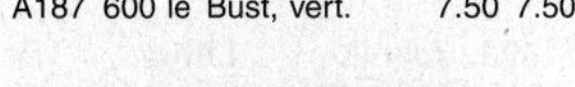

17th World Scout Jamboree, Korea — A188

Designs: 250 le, Scouts learning to sail. 300 le, Lord Robert Baden-Powell, founder. 400 le, Scouts playing baseball. 750 le, Jamboree emblem, vert.

1991, Dec. 20

1443	A188	250 le	multicolored	1.75	1.75
1444	A188	300 le	multicolored	2.25	2.25
1445	A188	400 le	multicolored	3.25	3.25
			Nos. 1443-1445 (3)	7.25	7.25

Souvenir Sheet

1446	A188	750 le	multicolored	7.25	7.25

Miniature Sheet

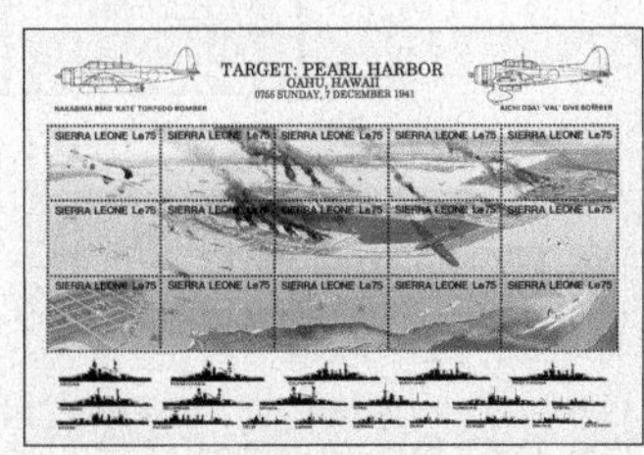

Attack on Pearl Harbor, 50th Anniv. — A189

Designs: a, Japanese D3A1 Val dive bomber. b, Plane amid rising smoke over Ford Island. c, Battleships ablaze. d, Naval station, three planes. e, Drydock ablaze, tank farm. f, Two Vals over water, ships. g, USS Utah and Ford Island installations ablaze, ship underway. h, Installations on Ford Island ablaze. i, US P-40 Warhawk fighter plane. j, Two Japanese torpedo bombers, plane on fire falling from sky. k, Three Japanese bombers over Pearl City. l, Two Japanese bombers diving on four ships, one burning ship. m, Japanese plane on fire. n, Two Japanese planes. o, One Japanese plane over Waipio Peninsula.

1991, Dec. 20 *Perf. 14½x15*

1447	A189	75 le Sheet of 15, #a.-o.	16.00	16.00

Walt Disney Christmas Cards — A190

Designs and year of issue: 12 le, Mickey and Donald decorating tree, 1952. 30 le, Characters surrounding book with "Alice in Wonderland", 1950. 60 le, Dwarf asleep with hare and tortoise, 1938. 75 le, Minnie, Donald, Mickey and Pluto mailing Christmas card, 1936. 100 le, Costumed characters in front of Magic Kingdom, 1984. 125 le, Mickey singing, Donald's nephews and Pluto reading 20,000 Leagues Under the Sea, 1954. 150 le, 101 Dalmations with season's greetings, 1960. 200 le, Donald and Mickey among gifts, 1948. 300 le, Mickey, Minnie at home for Christmas, 1983. 400 le, Donald and ducks preparing for Christmas watching Mickey Mouse Club, 1956. Characters on parade with Christmas cheer. 500 le, Disney characters, 50th birthday of Walt Disney Productions, 1972.

Each 900 le: No. 1460, Map of Magic Kingdom, 1955, vert. No. 1461, Seven dwarfs in bobsled, 1959, vert. No. 1462, Alice in Wonderland at tea party, 1950, vert.

1991, Dec. 24 Litho. *Perf. 14x13½*

1448	A190	12 le	multicolored	.35	.35
1449	A190	30 le	multicolored	.50	.50
1450	A190	60 le	multicolored	.70	.70
1451	A190	75 le	multicolored	.80	.80
1452	A190	100 le	multicolored	1.00	1.00
1453	A190	125 le	multicolored	1.30	1.30
1454	A190	150 le	multicolored	1.60	1.60
1455	A190	200 le	multicolored	2.00	2.00
1456	A190	300 le	multicolored	2.60	2.60
1457	A190	400 le	multicolored	3.00	3.00
1458	A190	500 le	multicolored	3.00	3.00
1459	A190	600 le	multicolored	3.00	3.00
			Nos. 1448-1459 (12)	19.85	19.85

Souvenir Sheets

Perf. 13½x14

1460-1462 A190	Set of 3	18.00	18.00

Disney Characters on World Tour A192

Designs: 6 le, Chiquita Minnie in Central America. 10 le, Gold Medal Goofy in Ancient Greece. 20 le, Donald, Daisy having Flamenco Fun in Spain. 30 le, Goofy guarding Donald at London's Buckingham Palace. 50 le, Mickey and Minnie dressed in Paris originals. 100 le, Goofy with mountain goat in Switzerland. 200 le, Daisy, Minnie as luau ladies in Hawaii. 350 le, Mickey, Donald and Goofy as ancient Egyptian comic strips, horiz. 500 le, Daisy and Minnie as can-can dancers in Paris, horiz.

Each 700 le: No. 1479, Mickey playing bagpipes in Scotland. No. 1480, Goofy fishes from Donald's gondola in Venice, Italy. No. 1481, Mickey and Goofy taking crash course in Greek.

Perf. 13x13½, 13½x13

1992, Feb. Litho.

1470 A192 6 le multicolored .35 .35
1471 A192 10 le multicolored .35 .35
1472 A192 20 le multicolored .55 .55
1473 A192 30 le multicolored .75 .75
1474 A192 50 le multicolored .90 .90
1475 A192 100 le multicolored 1.35 1.35
1476 A192 200 le multicolored 2.50 2.50
1477 A192 350 le multicolored 3.50 3.50
1478 A192 500 le multicolored 3.75 3.75
Nos. 1470-1478 (9) 14.00 14.00

Souvenir Sheets

1479-1481 A192 Set of 3 19.00 19.00

Queen Elizabeth II's Accession to the Throne, 40th Anniv.

Common Design Type

1992, Feb. 6 Litho. *Perf. 14*

1482 CD348 60 le multi .65 .65
1483 CD348 100 le multi 1.10 1.10
1484 CD348 300 le multi 3.00 3.00
1485 CD348 400 le multi 4.25 4.25
Nos. 1482-1485 (4) 9.00 9.00

Souvenir Sheets

1486 CD348 700 le Queen, hillside 6.75 6.75
1487 CD348 700 le Queen, houses 6.75 6.75

Spanish Art — A193

Paintings by Francisco de Zurbaran: 1 le, The Visit of St. Thomas Aquinas to St. Bonaventure. 10 le, St. Gregory. 30 le, St. Andrew. 50 le, St. Gabriel the Archangel. 60 le, The Blessed Henry Suso. 100 le, St. Lucy. 300 le, St. Casilda. 400 le, St. Margaret of Antioch. 500 le, St. Apollonia. 600 le, St. Bonaventure at the Council of Lyons. 700 le, St. Bonaventure on His Bier. 800 le, The Martyrdom of St. James (detail). No. 1496, St. Hugh in the Refectory, horiz. No. 1497, The Martyrdom of St. James. No. 1497A, The Young Virgin.

1992, May 25 Litho. *Perf. 13*

1487A A193 1 le multi .50 .50
1488 A193 10 le multi .50 .50
1489 A193 30 le multi .50 .50
1490 A193 50 le multi .50 .50
1491 A193 60 le multi .50 .50
1491A A193 100 le multi .55 .55
1491B A193 300 le multi 1.55 1.55
1492 A193 400 le multi 3.00 3.00
1493 A193 500 le multi 4.25 4.25
1494 A193 600 le multi 4.75 4.75
1495 A193 700 le multi 3.50 3.50
1495A A193 800 le multi 4.25 4.25

Size: 120x95mm

Imperf

1496 A193 900 le multi 5.25 5.25
1497 A193 900 le multi 5.25 5.25
1497A A193 900 le multi 5.25 5.25
Nos. 1487A-1497A (15) 40.10 40.10

Granada '92.

While Nos. 1487A-1497A all have the same issue date, the dollar value of Nos. 1487A, 1489-1490, 1491A-1491B, 1492, 1495, 1497-1497A was lower when they were released.

Prehistoric Animals — A194

Designs: No. 1498a, Rhamphorhynchus. b, Pteranodon. c, Dimorphodon. d, Pterodactyl. e, Archaeopteryx. f, Iguanodon. g, Hypsilophodon. h, Nothosaurus. i, Brachiosaurus. j, Kentrosaurus. k, Plesiosaurus. l, Trachodon. m, Hesperornis. n, Henodus. o, Steneosaurus. p, Stenopterygius. q, Eurhinosaurus r, Placodus. s, Mosasaurus. t, Mixosaurus. No. 1499, Herperornis, diff.

1992, June 8 *Perf. 14*

1498 A194 50 le Sheet of 20, #a.-t. 19.00 19.00

Souvenir Sheet

1499 A194 50 le multicolored 2.40 2.40

"Sierra Leone" is 22mm wide on No. 1499.

A195

Tropical Birds: 30 le, Greater flamingo. 50 le, White-crested hornbill. 100 le, Verreaux's touraco. 170 le, Yellow-spotted barbet. 200 le, African spoonbill. 250 le, Saddlebill stork. 300 le, Red-headed lovebird. 600 le, Yellow-billed barbet. No. 1508, Fire-bellied woodpecker. No. 1509, Swallow-tailed bee-eater.

1992, July 20 Litho. *Perf. 14*

1500 A195 30 le multi .40 .40
1501 A195 50 le multi .65 .65
1502 A195 100 le multi .80 .80
1503 A195 170 le multi 1.50 1.50
1504 A195 200 le multi 2.40 2.40
1505 A195 250 le multi 2.00 2.00
1506 A195 300 le multi 2.50 2.50
1507 A195 600 le multi 7.50 7.50
Nos. 1500-1507 (8) 17.75 17.75

Souvenir Sheets

1508 A195 1000 le multi 8.50 8.50
1509 A195 1000 le multi 7.00 7.00

While Nos. 1500-1509 all have the same release date, the value of Nos. 1502-1503, 1505-1506, 1509 was lower when they were released.

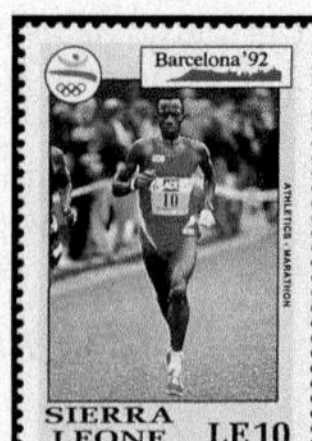

A196

1992 Summer Olympics, Barcelona: 10 le, Marathon. 20 le, Gymnastics, parallel bars. 30 le, Discus. 50 le, 110-meter hurdles, horiz. 60 le, Women's long jump. 100 le, Gymnastics, floor exercise, horiz. 200 le, Windsurfing. 300 le, Road race cycling. 400 le, Weight lifting. 900 le, Soccer, horiz.

1992 Litho. *Perf. 14*

1510 A196 10 le multicolored .25 .25
1511 A196 20 le multicolored .25 .25
1512 A196 30 le multicolored .40 .40
1513 A196 50 le multicolored .55 .55
1514 A196 60 le multicolored .75 .75
1515 A196 100 le multicolored 1.25 1.25
1516 A196 200 le multicolored 2.40 2.40
1517 A196 300 le multicolored 3.50 3.50
1518 A196 400 le multicolored 4.75 4.75
Nos. 1510-1518 (9) 14.10 14.10

Souvenir Sheet

1519 A196 900 le multicolored 8.00 8.00

1992 Winter Olympics, Albertville — A197

Designs: 250 le, Women's biathlon, vert. 500 le, Speed skating, vert. 600 le, Men's downhill skiing.

Each 900 le: No. 1523, Men's single luge. No. 1524, Ice dancing, vert.

1992, Sept. 8 Litho. *Perf. 14*

1520 A197 250 le multicolored 2.00 2.00
1521 A197 500 le multicolored 4.00 4.00
1522 A197 600 le multicolored 4.75 4.75
Nos. 1520-1522 (3) 10.75 10.75

Souvenir Sheets

1523-1524 A197 Set of 2 12.00 12.00

Discovery of America, 500th Anniv. A198

Designs: 300 le, Ferdinand, Isabella, Columbus. 500 le, Landing in New World. 900 le, Columbus, vert.

1992, Oct. Litho. *Perf. 14*

1525 A198 300 le multicolored 2.75 2.75
1526 A198 500 le multicolored 4.25 4.25

Souvenir Sheet

1527 A198 900 le multicolored 7.00 7.00

Birds — A199

Designs: 50c, Pygmy goose. 1 le, Spotted eagle owl. 2 le, Verreaux's touraco. 5 le, Saddlebill stork. 10 le, African golden oriole. 20 le, Malachite kingfisher. 30 le, Fire-crowned bishop. 40 le, Fire-bellied woodpecker. 50 le, Red-billed fire-finch. 80 le, Blue fairy flycatcher. 100 le, Crested malimbe. 150 le, Vitelline masked weaver. 170 le, Blue plantain-eater. 200 le, Superb sunbird. 250 le, Swallow-tailed bee-eater. 300 le, Cabani's yellow bunting. 500 le, Crocodile bird. 750 le, White-faced owl. 1000 le, Blue cuckoo-shrike. 2000 le, Bare-headed rock-fowl. 3000 le, Red-tailed buzzard.

No Date Imprint

1992-93 Litho. *Perf. 14x15*

1528 A199 50c multi .25 .25
1529 A199 1 le multi .25 .25
1530 A199 2 le multi .25 .25
1531 A199 5 le multi .25 .25
1532 A199 10 le multi .25 .25
1533 A199 20 le multi .25 .25
1534 A199 30 le multi .25 .25
1535 A199 40 le multi .25 .25
1536 A199 50 le multi .25 .25
a. Inscribed "1994" — —
c. Inscribed "1997" — —
1537 A199 80 le multi .40 .40
1538 A199 100 le multi .50 .50
a. Inscribed "1994" — —
b. Inscribed "1996" *3.50 3.50*
c. Inscribed "1997" — —
d. Inscribed "1999" — —
e. Inscribed "2000" — —
1539 A199 150 le multi .80 .80
a. Inscribed "1994" — —
1540 A199 170 le multi .90 .90
1541 A199 200 le multi 1.00 1.00
a. Inscribed "1994" — —
b. Inscribed "1996" *5.00 5.00*
c. Inscribed "1997" — —
d. Inscribed "1999" — —
e. Inscribed "2000" — —
g. Inscribed "2006" *5.00 5.00*
1542 A199 250 le multi 1.25 1.25
c. Inscribed "1997" — —
e. Inscribed "2000" — —
f. Inscribed "2002" — —
g. Inscribed "2006" *5.00 5.00*
1543 A199 300 le multi 1.90 1.90
a. Inscribed "1994" — —
b. Inscribed "1996" *5.00 5.00*
c. Inscribed "1997" — —
d. Inscribed "1999" — —
e. Inscribed "2000" — —
g. Inscribed "2006" 5.00 5.00
1544 A199 500 le multi 3.25 3.25
b. Inscribed "1996" *5.00 5.00*
c. Inscribed "1997" — —
e. Inscribed "2000" — —
f. Inscribed "2002" — —
g. Inscribed "2006" *6.00 6.00*
1545 A199 750 le multi 4.75 4.75
e. Inscribed "2000" — —
g. Inscribed "2006" *7.50 7.50*
1546 A199 1000 le multi 6.25 6.25
c. Inscribed "1996" *7.50 7.50*
d. Inscribed "1999" — —
e. Inscribed "2000" — —
f. Inscribed "2002" — —
g. Inscribed "2006" *7.50 7.50*
1546A A199 2000 le multi 11.00 11.00
i. Inscribed "2000" — —
j. Inscribed "2002" — —
k. Inscribed "2006" *12.00 12.00*
1546B A199 3000 le multi 11.00 11.00
l. Inscribed "1996" *12.00 12.00*
m. Inscribed "2000" — —
n. Inscribed "2002" — —
o. Inscribed "2006" *12.00 12.00*
Nos. 1528-1546B (21) 45.25 45.25

Issued: Nos. 1528-1546, 9/92; Nos. 1546A-1546B, 1993.

No. 1546A was issued inscribed "1999." The editors would like to examine an example.

See Nos. 2152-2155.

Model Trains — A200

Lionel models: No. 1547a, Pennsylvannia RR GG-1 electric #6-18306, O gauge, 1992. b, Wabash RR Hudson #8610, O gauge, 1985. c, Locomotive #1911, standard gauge, 1911. d, Chesapeake & Ohio 4-4-2 #6-18627, O gauge, 1992. e, Gang car #50, O gauge, 1954. f, #8004, 1980 model of Rock Island & Peoria RR engine built for Columbian Exposition of 1893, O gauge. g, Western Maryland RR Shay #6-18023, O gauge, 1992. h, (Kenner-Parker) Boston & Albany Hudson #784, O gauge, 1986. i, Locomotive #6, standard gauge, 1906.

No. 1548a, Pennsylvania RR Torpedo #238EW, O gauge, 1936. b, Denver & Rio Grande Western Alco Pa No. 6-18107, O gauge, 1992. c, #408E Locomotive, standard gauge, 1930. d, Mickey Mouse 60th birthday boxcar No. 19241, O gauge, 1991. e, Polished brass locomotive, No. 54, standard gauge, 1913. f, Broadway limited #392E, standard gauge, 1936. g, Great Northern RR EP-5 #18302, O gauge, 1988. h, 4-4-0 Locomotive #6, standard gauge, 1918. i, 4-4-4 Locomotive No. 400E, standard gauge, 1933.

No. 1549a, Special F-3 diesel engine, O gauge, 1947. b, Pennsylvania RR GE 44-ton switcher #6-18905, O gauge, 1992. c, #1 trolley, standard gauge, 1913. d, Seaboard RR freight diesel, O gauge, 1958. e, Pennsylvania S-2 turbine, O gauge, 1991. f, Western Pacific RR GP-9 diesel #6-18822, O gauge, 1992. g, #10 with Ives plates transition model, standrad gauge, 1929. h, 4-4-4 locomotive #400E, standard gauge, 1931. i, #384E, standard gauge, 1928.

Each 1000 le: No. 1550, Hudson No. 8210 Special, O gauge. No. 1551, #381E, standard gauge, 1928. No. 1552, 2-Rail electric model #300 trolley with converse body, 2⅞-inch gauge.

Sheets of 9

1992, Nov. 23 Litho. *Perf. 14*

1547 A200 150 le #a.-i. 11.50 11.50
1548 A200 170 le #a.-i. 13.00 13.00
1549 A200 170 le #a.-i. 13.00 13.00

Souvenir Sheets

Perf. 13

1550-1552 A200 Set of 3 20.00 20.00

Genoa '92 (#1547-1549). Nos. 1550-1552 contains one 51x39mm stamp.

Walt Disney Characters in Christmas Scenes
A201

10 le, Minnie & Chip. 20 le, Goofy as Santa. 30 le, Daisy, Minnie. 50 le, Mickey, Goofy. 80 le, Pete. 100 le, Donald Duck. 150 le, Morty & Ferdie. 200 le, Mickey. 300 le, Goofy with ornament. 500 le, Chip & Dale. 600 le, Donald & Dale. 800 le, Huey, Dewey & Louie.

No. 1565, Mickey Mouse. No. 1566, Angel with Chip, horiz. No. 1567, Mickey & Minnie, horiz.

1992, Nov. 16 ***Perf. 13½x14***

1553	A201	10 le multi	.35	.35
1554	A201	20 le multi	.50	.50
1555	A201	30 le multi	.50	.50
1556	A201	50 le multi	.70	.70
1557	A201	80 le multi	.85	.85
1558	A201	100 le multi	.85	.85
1559	A201	150 le multi	1.90	1.90
1560	A201	200 le multi	2.00	2.00
1561	A201	300 le multi	2.25	2.25
1562	A201	500 le multi	3.25	3.25
1563	A201	600 le multi	3.25	3.25
1564	A201	800 le multi	4.00	4.00
		Nos. 1553-1564 (12)	20.40	20.40

Souvenir Sheets

1565	A201	900 le multi	6.75	6.75

Perf. 14x13½

1566	A201	900 le multi	6.75	6.75
1567	A201	900 le multi	6.75	6.75

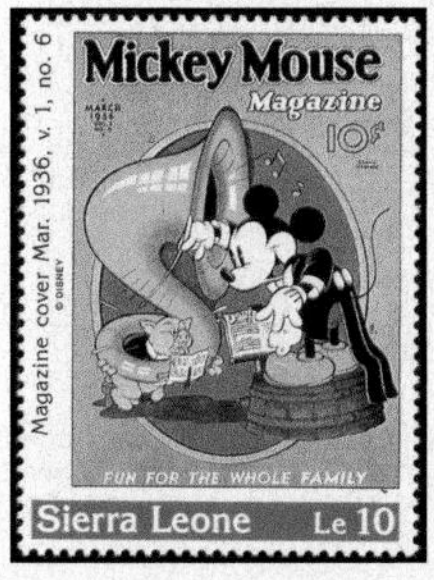

Mickey Mouse Magazines and Books
A202

10 le, Magazine cover, Mar. 1936, v. 1, #6. 20 le, Magazine cover, June 1936, v. 1, #9. 30 le, Magazine cover, Nov. 1936, v. 2, #2. 40 le, Magazine cover, Aug. 1937, v. 2, #11. 50 le, Magazine cover, Oct. 1937, v. 2, #13. 60 le, Magazine cover, Dec. 1937, v. 3, #3. 70 le, Magazine cover, Jan. 1938, v. 3, #4. 150 le, Cover, Big Book #4062, 1935. 170 le, Story book cover, 1936. 200 le, Comic book cover, unnumbered. 300 le, Comic book cover, No. 181. 400 le, Comic book cover #194. 500 le, Story book cover, Book 1, 1931. No. 1581, Boys' and Girls' March of Comics cover, 1948. No. 1582, First Mickey Mouse Magazine cover for June-Aug. 1935, v. 1, #1, horiz. No. 1583, Cover of early Mickey Mouse story book published in England, 1933, horiz.

1992 ***Perf. 13½x14***

1568	A202	10 le multicolored	.25	.25
1569	A202	20 le multicolored	.25	.25
1570	A202	30 le multicolored	.25	.25
1571	A202	40 le multicolored	.25	.25
1572	A202	50 le multicolored	.30	.30
1573	A202	60 le multicolored	.35	.35
1574	A202	70 le multicolored	.40	.40
1575	A202	150 le multicolored	.80	.80
1576	A202	170 le multicolored	1.10	1.10
1577	A202	200 le multicolored	1.25	1.25
1578	A202	300 le multicolored	1.90	1.90
1579	A202	400 le multicolored	2.40	2.40
1580	A202	500 le multicolored	3.25	3.25
		Nos. 1568-1580 (13)	12.75	12.75

Souvenir Sheets

1581	A202	900 le multicolored	5.50	5.50

Perf. 14x13½

1582	A202	900 le multicolored	5.50	5.50
1583	A202	900 le multicolored	5.50	5.50

Christmas
A203

Details or entire paintings: 1 le, Virgin and Child, by Fiorenzo di Lorenzo. 10 le, Madonna and Child on a Wall, by Circle of Dirk Bouts. 20 le, Virgin and Child with the Flight into Egypt, by Master of Hoogstraeten. 30 le, Madonna and Child before Firescreen, by Master of Flemalle. 50 le, Mary in a Rose Garden, by Hans Memling. 100 le, Virgin Mary and Child, by Lucas Cranach the Elder. 170 le, Virgin and Child, by Rogier van der Weyden. 200 le, Madonna and Saints, by Perugino. 250 le, Madonna Enthroned with Saints Catherine and Barbara, by Master of Hoogstraeten. 300 le, The Virgin in a Rose Arbor, by Stefan Lochner. 500 le, Madonna and Child with Angels, by Sandro Botticelli. 1000 le, Madonna and Child with Young St. John the Baptist, by Fra Bartolemmeo.

Each 900 le: No. 1596, The Virgin with the Green Cushion, by Andrea Solario. No. 1597, The Virgin and Child, by Jan Gossaert. No. 1598, The Virgin and Child, by Lucas Cranach the Younger.

1992, Dec. 7 Litho. ***Perf. 13½x14***

1584	A203	1 le multi	.25	.25
1585	A203	10 le multi	.25	.25
1586	A203	20 le multi	.25	.25
1587	A203	30 le multi	.25	.25
1588	A203	50 le multi	.40	.40
1589	A203	100 le multi	.70	.70
1590	A203	170 le multi	1.25	1.25
1591	A203	200 le multi	1.40	1.40
1592	A203	250 le multi	1.75	1.75
1593	A203	300 le multi	2.25	2.25
1594	A203	500 le multi	3.75	3.75
1595	A203	1000 le multi	6.75	6.75
		Nos. 1584-1595 (12)	19.25	19.25

Souvenir Sheets

1596-1598	A203	Set of 3	20.00	20.00

Anniversaries and Events — A204

150 le, Emblems of FAO, ICN, WHO. No. 1600, Graf Zeppelin. No. 1601, Cow, emblems, grain stalk. 200 le, Starving child. No. 1603, Lions Intl. emblem, map. No. 1604, Cottonwood tree. 300 le, African elephant. 600 le, Space Shuttle. 700 le, Graf Zeppelin LZ 127, specifications.

Each 900 le: No. 1608, Astronaut. No. 1609, Count Zeppelin.

1992, Dec. Litho. ***Perf. 14***

1599	A204	150 le multicolored	1.10	1.10
1600	A204	170 le multicolored	1.10	1.10
1601	A204	170 le multicolored	1.40	1.40
1602	A204	200 le multicolored	1.40	1.40
1603	A204	250 le multicolored	1.75	1.75
1604	A204	250 le multicolored	2.00	2.00
1605	A204	300 le multicolored	2.10	2.10
1606	A204	600 le multicolored	4.00	4.00
1607	A204	700 le multicolored	5.00	5.00
		Nos. 1599-1607 (9)	19.85	19.85

Souvenir Sheets

1608-1609	A204	Set of 2	10.00	10.00

Intl. Conference on Nutrition, Rome (#1599, 1601). Count Zeppelin, 75th anniv. of death (#1600, 1607, 1609). World Health Organization (#1602). Lions Intl., 75th anniv. (#1603). Earth Summit, Rio de Janeiro (#1604-1605). Intl. Space Year (#1606, 1608).

Miniature Sheet

Boxing — A205

Boxing movies, stars, each 200 le: No. 1610a, The Champ, Wallace Beery. b, Golden Boy, William Holden. c, Body and Soul, John Garfield. d, Champion, Kirk Douglas. e, The Set-Up, Robert Ryan. f. Requiem for a Heavyweight, Anthony Quinn. g, Kid Galahad, Elvis Presley. h, Fat City, Jeff Bridges.

Boxing champions, each 200 le: No. 1611a, Joe Louis. b, Archie Moore. c, Muhammad Ali. d, George Foreman. e, Joe Frazier. f, Marvin Hagler. g, Sugar Ray Leonard. h, Evander Holyfield.

Each 1000 le: No. 1612, Gentlemen Jim, Errol Flynn. No. 1613, Muhammad Ali, diff. No. 1614, Rocky III, Sylvester Stallone.

1993, Feb. 8 Litho. ***Perf. 13½x14***

1610	A205	Sheet of 8, #a.-h.	12.00	12.00
1611	A205	Sheet of 8, #a.-h.	12.00	12.00

Souvenir Sheets

1612-1614	A205	Set of 3	17.00	17.00

Miniature Sheets

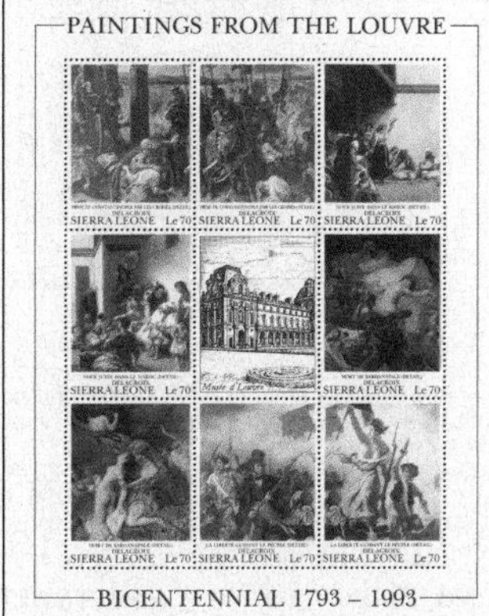

Louvre Museum, Bicent. — A206

Details or entire paintings by Eugene Delacroix (1798-1863): Nos. 1615a-1615b, Entry of the Crusaders into Constantinople (left, right). c-d, Jews Purchasing Brides in Morocco (left, right). e-f, The Death of Sardanapalus (left, right). g-h, Liberty Guiding the People (left, right).

No. 1616a, An Orphan at the Cemetery. b-c, Women of Algiers in their Apartment (left, right). d, Dante and Virgil in the Infernal Regions. e, Self-Portrait. f-g, Massacre at Chios (left, right). h, Frederic Chopin.

No. 1617, Rape of the Sabine Women, by Jacques-Louis David (1748-1825).

1993, Mar. 8 Litho. ***Perf. 12x12½***

1615	A206	70 le Sheet of 8, #a.-h. + label	5.50	5.50
1616	A206	70 le Sheet of 8, #a.-h. + label	5.50	5.50

Souvenir Sheet

Perf. 14½

1617	A206	900 le multicolored	6.50	6.50

Mushrooms
A207

Designs: 30 le, Amanita flammeola. 50 le, Cantharellus pseudocbarius. 100 le, Volvariella volvacea. 200 le, Termitomyces microcarpus. 300 le, Auricularia auricula. 400 le, Pleurotus tuberregium. 500 le, Schizophyllum commune. 600 le, Termitomyces robustus.

Each 1000 le: No. 1626, Phallus rubicundus. No. 1627, Daldina concentrica.

1993, May 5 ***Perf. 14***

1618	A207	30 le multi	.45	.45
1619	A207	50 le multi	.60	.60
1620	A207	100 le multi	.85	.85
1621	A207	200 le multi	1.30	1.30
1622	A207	300 le multi	1.90	1.90
1623	A207	400 le multi	2.10	2.10
1624	A207	500 le multi	2.40	2.40
1625	A207	600 le multi	2.50	2.50
		Nos. 1618-1625 (8)	12.10	12.10

Souvenir Sheets

1626-1627	A207	Set of 2	13.00	13.00

Butterflies — A208

20 le, False acraea. 30 le, Blue temora. 50 le, Foxy charaxes. 100 le, Leaf blue. 150 le, Blue-banded swallowtail. 170 le, African monarch. 200 le, Mountain beauty. 250 le, Gaudy commodore. 300 le, Palla butterfly. 500 le, Pirate butterfly. 600 le, Painted lady. 700 le, Gold-banded forester.

Each 1000 le: #1640, Blue diadem. #1641, Blue swallowtail. #1642, African leaf butterfly.

1993, May 5

1628-1639	A208	Set of 12	15.00	15.00

Souvenir Sheets

1640-1642	A208	Set of 3	14.50	14.50

Miniature Sheets

Cats — A209

Designs, each 150 le: No. 1643a, Somali. b, Egyptian Mau smoke. c, Chocolate-point Siamese. d, Mi-Ke Japanese bobtail. e, Chinchilla. f, Red Burmese. g, British shorthair brown tabby. h, Blue Persian. i, British silver classic tabby. j, Oriental ebony. k, Red Persian. l, British calico shorthair.

Each 150 le: No. 1644a, Black Persian. b, Blue-point Siamese. c, American wirehair. d, Birman. e, Scottish fold (silver tabby). f, American shorthair red tabby. g, Blue & white Persian bicolor. h, Havana brown. i, Norwegian forest cat. j, Brown tortie Burmese. k. Angora. l, Exotic shorthair.

Each 1000 le: No. 1645, American shorthair blue tabby, horiz. No. 1646, Seal-point colorpoint, horiz.

1993, May 17 Litho. ***Perf. 14***

1643	A209	Sheet of 12, #a.-l.	13.00	13.00
1644	A209	Sheet of 12, #a.-l.	13.00	13.00

Souvenir Sheets

1645-1646	A209	Set of 2	15.00	15.00

Nos. 1643-1646 Ovptd. with Hong Kong '94 Emblem

1994 Litho. ***Perf. 14***

1643m	On #1643b & in sheet margin	9.50	9.50
1644m	On #1644b & in sheet margin	9.50	9.50
1645a	Ovptd. in sheet margin	5.25	5.25
1646a	Ovptd. in sheet margin	5.25	5.25

Wild Animals A210

30 le, Gorilla. 100 le, Bongo. 150 le, Potto. 170 le, Chimpanzee. 200 le, Dwarf galago. 300 le, African linsang. 500 le, Banded duiker. 750 le, Diana monkey.
No. 1655, Leopard. No. 1656, Elephant.

1993, June 17

1647 A210 30 le multi .60 .60
1648 A210 100 le multi .70 .70
1649 A210 150 le multi .80 .80
1650 A210 170 le multi 1.00 1.00
1651 A210 200 le multi 1.10 1.10
1652 A210 300 le multi 1.50 1.50
1653 A210 500 le multi 2.75 2.75
1654 A210 750 le multi 4.00 4.00
Nos. 1647-1654 (8) 12.45 12.45

Souvenir Sheets

1655 A210 1200 le multi 7.00 7.00
1656 A210 1200 le multi 7.00 7.00

Flowers A211

30 le, Bleeding-heart vine. 40 le, Passion vine. 50 le, Hydrangea. 60 le, Wax begonia. 100 le, Hibiscus. 150 le, Crape-myrtle. 170 le, Bougainvillea. 200 le, Leadwort. 250 le, Gerbera daisy. 300 le, Black-eyed susan. 500 le, Gloriosa lily. 900 le, Sweet violet.
Each 1200 le: #1669, Gloriosa lily, diff. #1670, Passion vine, diff. #1671, Hibiscus, diff.

1993, July 15 Litho. *Perf. 14*

1657 A211 30 le multi .40 .40
1658 A211 40 le multi .50 .50
1659 A211 50 le multi .50 .50
1660 A211 60 le multi .50 .50
1661 A211 100 le multi .65 .65
1662 A211 150 le multi 1.00 1.00
1663 A211 170 le multi 1.10 1.10
1664 A211 200 le multi 1.25 1.25
1665 A211 250 le multi 1.60 1.60
1666 A211 300 le multi 1.75 1.75
1667 A211 500 le multi 2.10 2.10
1668 A211 900 le multi 3.75 3.75
Nos. 1657-1668 (12) 15.10 15.10

Souvenir Sheets

1669-1671 A211 Set of 3 18.00 18.00

Coronation of Queen Elizabeth II, 40th Anniv. — A212

100 le, Queen, Princess Anne. 200 le, Coronation procession. 600 le, Official coronation photograph. 1500 le, Portrait, by Pietro Annigoni, 1954-55.

1993, Oct. Litho. *Perf. 14*

1672 A212 100 le multi .80 .80
1673 A212 200 le black 1.50 1.50
1674 A212 600 le multi 3.25 3.25
Nos. 1672-1674 (3) 5.55 5.55

Souvenir Sheet

1675 A212 1500 le multi 10.00 10.00

Copernicus (1473-1543) A213

250 le, Early telescope. 800 le, Moon's surface.

1993, Oct.

1676 A213 250 le multicolored 1.50 1.50
1677 A213 800 le multicolored 5.00 5.00

Picasso (1881-1973) A214

Sculpture: 170 le, Woman with Hat, 1961.
Paintings: 200 le, Buste de Femme, 1958. 800 le, Maya with a Doll, 1938. 1000 le, Women of Algiers (after Delacroix), 1955.

1993, Oct.

1678 A214 170 le multicolored 1.10 1.10
1679 A214 200 le multicolored 1.50 1.50
1680 A214 800 le multicolored 4.00 4.00
Nos. 1678-1680 (3) 6.60 6.60

Souvenir Sheet

1681 A214 1000 le multicolored 6.50 6.50

Christmas A215

Details or entire paintings, by Raphael: 50 le, 100 le, 1200 le (No. 1690), Madonna of the Fish. 150 le, Madonna & Child Enthroned with Five Saints. 800 le, The Holy Family with the Lamb.
Details or entire woodcuts, by Durer: 200 le, 250 le, 300 le, The Circumcision. 500 le, 1200 le (No. 1691), Holy Clan with Saints and Two Angels Playing Music.

1993, Dec. *Perf. 13½x14*

1682 A215 50 le multi .25 .25
1683 A215 100 le multi .45 .45
1684 A215 150 le multi .70 .70
1685 A215 200 le multi 1.00 1.00
1686 A215 250 le multi 1.25 1.25
1687 A215 300 le multi 1.40 1.40
1688 A215 500 le multi 2.50 2.50
1689 A215 800 le multi 4.25 4.25
Nos. 1682-1689 (8) 11.80 11.80

Souvenir Sheets

1690-1691 A215 Set of 2 12.00 12.00

Christmas A216

Disney characters celebrate Christmas: different.
Each 1200 le: #1700, Santa. #1701, Elves, horiz. #1702, Santa, horiz. #1703, Mickey, Minnie, horiz.

1993, Dec. 17 *Perf. 13½x14*

1692 A216 50 le multi .25 .25
1693 A216 100 le multi .50 .50
1694 A216 170 le multi .90 .90
1695 A216 200 le multi 1.00 1.00
1696 A216 250 le multi 1.40 1.40
1697 A216 500 le multi 2.75 2.75
1698 A216 600 le multi 3.25 3.25
1699 A216 800 le multi 4.50 4.50
Nos. 1692-1699 (8) 14.55 14.55

Souvenir Sheets

Perf. 13½x14, 14x13½

1700-1703 A216 Set of 4 24.00 24.00

1994 World Cup Soccer Championships, US — A217

Players, country: 30 le, Jose Luis Brown (R), Argentina. 50 le, Gary Lineker, England. 100 le, Carlos Valderrama, Colombia. 250 le, Skuhravy, Czechoslovakia; Marchena, Costa Rica. 300 le, Butragueno, Spain. 400 le, Roger Milla, Cameroun. 500 le, Roberto Donadoni, Italy. 700 le, Enzo Scifo, Belgium.
Each 1200 le: No. 1712, 1200 le, Socrates, Brazil. No. 1713, 1200 le, Wright, England; Demol, Belgium.

1993 *Perf. 13½x14*

1704-1711 A217 Set of 8 13.00 13.00

Souvenir Sheets

1712-1713 A217 Set of 2 17.50 17.50

A218

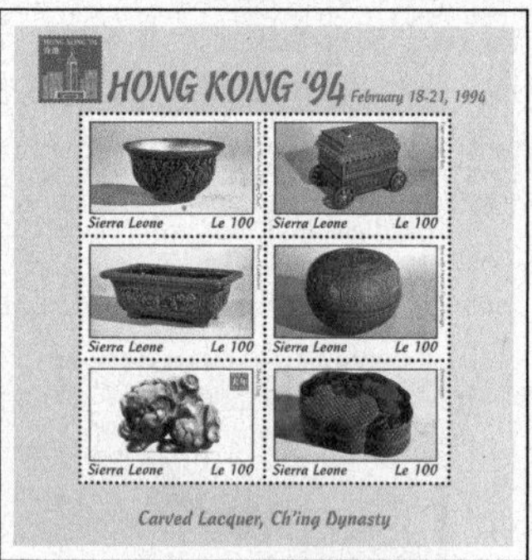

Hong Kong '94 — A219

Stamps and: No. 1714, Hong Kong #455, pagoda, Tiger Baum Garden. No. 1715, Ai Par Garden, #1084.
Carved lacquer, Qing Dynasty: No. 1716a, Bowl with "Wan-Sui-Ch'ang-Chun." b, Four-wheeled box. c, Flower container. d, Box with human figure design. e, Shishi dog (not lacquer). f, Persimmon.

1994, Feb. 18 Litho. *Perf. 14*

1714 200 le multicolored 1.00 1.00
1715 200 le multicolored 1.00 1.00
a. A218 Pair, #1714-1715 2.00 2.00

Miniature Sheet

1716 A219 100 le Sheet of 6, #a.-f. 5.75 5.75

Nos. 1714-1715 issued in sheets of 5 pairs. No. 1715a is a continuous design.
New Year 1994 (Year of the Dog) (#1716e).

Miniature Sheet

New Year 1994 (Year of the Dog) — A220

a, 100 le, Pekingese. b, 150 le, Doberman pinscher. c, 200 le, Tibetan terrier. d, 250 le, Weimaraner. e, 400 le, Rottweiler. f, 500 le, Akita. g, 600 le, Schnauzer. h, 1000 le, Tibetan spaniel.
Each 1200 le: No. 1718, Wire-haired pointing Griffon. No. 1719, Shih Tzu.

1994, June 20 Litho. *Perf. 14*

1717 A220 Sheet of 8, #a.-h. 14.00 14.00

Souvenir Sheets

1718-1719 A220 Set of 2 11.00 11.00

D-Day, 50th Anniv. A221

Designs: 500 le, British paratroops drop behind enemy lines. 750 le, US paratrooper jumps from C47 transport.
1000 le, C47 Douglas Dakota, paratroops.

1994, July 11 Litho. *Perf. 14*

1720 A221 500 le multicolored 2.25 2.25
1721 A221 750 le multicolored 3.25 3.25

Souvenir Sheet

1722 A221 1000 le multicolored 6.00 6.00

A222

PHILAKOREA '94 — A223

100 le, Traditional wedding, Korea House, Seoul. 400 le, Royal tombs, Koryo Dynasty, Kaesong. 600 le, Terraced farm land, near Chungmu.
Tiger paintings, Choson Dynasty: No. 1726: a, Tiger, cubs, 19th cent. b, Munsa-pasal seated on lion. c, Extinct Korean tiger. d, Tiger, bamboo. e, Tiger guarding 3 cubs, 4 magpies. f, Tiger, 19th cent. g, Mountain Spirit. h, Tiger, bird in tree.
No. 1727, Wall painting of mounted hunters from Tomb of the Dancers of Kungnaesong, Koguryo period.

Perf. 14, 13½ (#1726)

1994, July 11 Litho.

1723-1725 A222 Set of 3 5.00 5.00

Miniature Sheet of 8

1726 A223 200 le #a.-h. 8.00 8.00

Souvenir Sheet

1727 A222 1200 le multi 8.00 8.00

Miniature Sheets of 6

First Manned Moon Landing, 25th Anniv. — A224

No. 1728, each 200 le: a, Edwin E. Aldrin, Jr. b, Michael Collins. c, Neil A. Armstrong. d, Apollo 11 liftoff. e, Aldrin descending to lunar surface. f, Armstrong, lunar module Eagle reflected in Aldrin's face shield.
No. 1729, each 200 le: a, Aldrin gathering soil samples. b, Eagle with Aldrin deploying solar wind experiment. c, Aldrin, ALSEP & Eagle at Tranquility Base. d, US flag, Aldrin, Tranquility Base. e, Plaque on moon. f, Apollo 11 crew, stamp ceremony.
1000 le, First footprint on moon.

Sheets of 6, #a-f

1994, July 11 *Perf. 14*
1728-1729 A224 Set of 2 9.00 9.00

Souvenir Sheet

1730 A224 1000 le multicolored 5.00 5.00

Miniature Sheet of 6

A225

1994 World Cup Soccer Championships, U.S. — A226

Players: No. 1731a, Kim Ho, South Korea. b, Cobi Jones, U.S. c, Claudio Suarez, Mexico. d, Tomas Brolin, Sweden. e, Ruud Gullit, Netherlands. f, Andreas Herzog, Austria.
Each 1500 le: No. 1732, Sierra Leone team. No. 1733, Giants Stadium, New Jersey.

1994, July 15
1731 A225 250 le #a.-f. 7.00 7.00

Souvenir Sheets

1732-1733 A226 Set of 2 13.00 13.00

Birds A227

250 le, Black kite. 300 le, Superb sunbird. 500 le, Martial eagle. 800 le, Red bishop.
No. 1738 - White-necked picathartes: a, 50 le, Feeding young. b, 100 le, On brown tree limb. c, 150 le, Two at nest. d, 200 le, On gray limb, green leaves.
No. 1739, 1200 le, Greater flamingo, vert. No. 1740, 1200 le, White-necked picathartes up close, vert.

1994, Aug. 10
1734-1737 A227 Set of 4 12.00 12.00
1738 A227 Vert. Strip of 4, #a.-d. 4.50 4.50

Souvenir Sheets

1739-1740 A227 Set of 2 15.00 15.00

World Wildlife Fund (#1738).
For surcharge see No. 2903.

Orchids — A228

Designs: 50 le, Aerangis kotschyana. 100 le, Brachycorythis kalbreyeri. 150 le, Diaphananthe pellucida. 200 le, Eulophia guineensis. 300 le, Eurychone rothschildana. 500 le, Tridactyle tridactylites. 750 le, Cyrtorchis arcuata. 900 le, Ancistrochilus rothschildianus.
Each 1500 le: No. 1749, Plectrelminthus caudatus. No. 1750, Polystachaya affinis.

1994, Sept. 1
1741-1748 A228 Set of 8 15.00 15.00

Souvenir Sheets

1749-1750 A228 Set of 2 12.00 12.00

Christmas A229

Details or entire paintings: 50 le, The Birth of the Virgin, by Murillo. 100 le, Education of the Virgin, by Murillo. 150 le, Annunciation, by Filippino Lippi. 200 le, Marriage of the Virgin, by Bernard van Orley. 250 le, The Visitation, by Nicolas Vleughels. 300 le, Holy Infant from Castelfranco altarpiece, by Giorgione. 400 le, Adoration of the Magi, Workshop of Bartholome Zeitblom. 600 le, Presentation of Infant Jesus in the Temple, by Memling.
Each 1500 le: No. 1759, Nativity Altarpiece, by Lorenzo Monado. No. 1760, Allendale Nativity, by Giorgione.

1994, Dec. 1 Litho. *Perf. 13½x14*
1751-1758 A229 Set of 8 10.50 10.50

Souvenir Sheets

1759-1760 A229 Set of 2 10.00 10.00

Intl. Year of the Family A230

300 le, Working in field. 350 le, At beach.

1994, Dec. 20 Litho. *Perf. 14*
1761 A230 300 le multi 1.00 1.00
1762 A230 350 le multi 1.25 1.25

Disney Christmas — A231

Designs: 50 le, Mickey's Christmas cat. 100 le, Goofy's Christmas tree, vert. 150 le, Daisy's Christmas gift. 200 le, Donald's Christmas surprise, vert. 250 le, Minnie's Christmas flight. 300 le, Goofy's Christmas snowball, vert. 400 le, Goofy's Christmas letters. 500 le, Christmas sled ride, vert. 600 le, Mickey's Christmas snowman. 800 le, Pluto's Christmas treat, vert.
Each 1500 le: No. 1773, Goofy hanging outdoor lights. No. 1774, Mickey asleep in chair, vert.

Perf. 14x13½, 13½x14

1995, Jan. 23 Litho.
1763-1772 A231 Set of 10 13.50 13.50

Souvenir Sheets

1773-1774 A231 Set of 2 12.00 12.00

Donald Duck's Gallery of Old Masters A232

Name of painting, inspiration: 50 le, Madonna Duck, Leonardo da Vinci. 100 le, Portrait of a Venetian Duck, Tintoretto. 150 le, Duck with a Glove, Frans Hals. 200 le, Donald with a Pink, Quentin Massys. 250 le, Pinkie Daisy, Sir Thomas Lawrence. 300 le, Donald's Whistling Mother, Whistler. 400 le, El Quacko, El Greco. 500 le, The Noble Snob, Rembrandt. 600 le, The Blue Duck, by Gainsborough. 800 le, Modern Quack, Picasso.
Each 1500 le: No. 1785, Soup's On, Brueghel. No. 1786, Duck Dancers, Degas, horiz.

1995, Jan. 23 *Perf. 13½x14, 14x13½*
1775-1784 A232 Set of 10 11.00 11.00

Souvenir Sheets

1785-1786 A232 Set of 2 11.00 11.00

Miniature Sheets of 12

Olympic Medal Winners — A233

Summer Olympics: No. 1787a, Ragnar Lundberg, 1952 men's pole vault. b, Karin Janz, 1972 all-round gymnastics. c, Matthias Volz, 1936 gymnastics. d, Carl Lewis, 1988 long jump. e, Sara Simeoni, 1976 high jump. f, Daley Thompson, 1980 decathlon. g, Japan vs. Britain, 1964 soccer. h, Gabriella Dorio, 1984 1500-meters run. i, Daniela Hunger, 1988 200-meters individual medley swimming. j, Kyoko Iwasaki, 1992 200-meters breast stroke. k, Italian team member, 1960 water polo. l, David Wilkie, 1976 200-meters breast stroke.
1994 Winter Olympics, Lillehammer: No. 1788a, Katja Seizinger, downhill skiing. b, Hot air balloon (no medalist). c, Elvis Stojko, figure skating. d, Jens Weissflog, individual large hill ski jump. e, Bjorn Daehlie, 10k cross-country skiing. f, Germany, four-man bobsled. g, Markus Wasmeier, men's super giant slalom. h, Georg Hackl, luge. i, Trovill & Dean, ice dancing. j, Bonnie Blair, speed skating. k, Nancy Kerrigan, figure skating. l, Team Sweden, hockey.
Each 1000 le: No. 1789, torchbearer, horiz. No. 1790, Oksana Baiul, Nancy Kerrigan, Chen Lu, 1994 figure skating, horiz.

1995, Feb. 6 Litho. *Perf. 14*
1787 A233 75 le #a.-l. 3.25 3.25
1788 A233 200 le #a.-l. 8.50 8.50

Souvenir Sheets

1789-1790 A233 Set of 2 9.25 9.25

Miniature Sheets

Dinosaurs — A234

No. 1791, each 200 le: a, Ceratosaurus (d). b, Brachiosaurus. c, Pteranodon (b). d, Stegoceras. e, Saurolophus (h). f, Ornithomumus. g, Compsognathus (j). h, Deinonychus (i). i, Ornitholestes. j, Archaeopteryx. k, Heterodontosaurus (l). l, Lesothosaurus.
No. 1792: a, 100 le, Triceratops. b, 250 le, Protoceratops (c). c, 400 le, Monoclonius (b). d, 800 le, Styracosaurus (c).
Each 2500 le: No. 1793, Deinonychus. No. 1794, Rhamphorynchus.

1995, May 4 Litho. *Perf. 14*
1791 A234 Sheet of 12, #a.-l. 8.00 8.00
1792 A234 Sheet of 4, #a.-d. 5.25 5.25

Souvenir Sheets

1793-1794 A234 Set of 2 12.00 12.00

Sierra Club, Cent. A235

No. 1795, vert, each 150 le: a, L'Hoest's guenon. b, Black-footed cat. c, Colobus monkey up close. d, Colobus monkey in tree. e, Mandrill facing forward. f, Bonobo with young. g, Bonobo lying down. h, Mandrill facing right. i, Colobus monkey standing.
No. 1796, each 150 le: a, Black-faced impala facing forward. b, Herd of black-faced impala. c, Black-faced impala drinking. d, Bonobo. e, Black-footed cat. f, Black-footed cat up close. g, L'Hoest's guenon. h, L'Hoest's guenon, seated. i, Mandrills.

1995, May 10 Sheets of 9, #a-i
1795-1796 A235 Set of 2 13.00 13.00

Nos. 1795-1796 exist imperf. Value, set of 2, $25.

New Year 1995 (Year of the Boar) — A236

Stylized boars, each 100 le: No. 1797a, red & multi, facing left. b, green & multi, facing right. c, green & multi, facing left. d, red & multi, facing right.
500 le, Two boars, vert.

1995, May 8 Litho. *Perf. 14*
1797 A236 Block of 4, #a.-d. 3.00 3.00

Souvenir Sheet

1798 A236 500 le multicolored 3.75 3.75

Singapore '95 — A237

Marine life, each 300 le: No. 1799a, Pufferfish. b, Coral grouper. c, Hawksbill turtle. d, Hogfish. e, Emperor angelfish. f, Butterflyfish. g, Lemon butterflyfish. h, Parrotfish. i, Moray eel.
Water birds, marine life, each 300 le: No. 1800a, Cape pigeons. b, Pelican. c, Puffin. d, Humpback whale. e, Greater shearwater. f, Bottlenose dolphin. g, Gurnard. h, Salmon. i, John dory.
Each 1500 le: #1801, Surgeonfish. #1802, Angelfish, vert.

1995 Sheets of 9, #a-i
1799-1800 A237 Set of 2 19.50 19.50

Souvenir Sheets

1801-1802 A237 Set of 2 10.50 10.50

Miniature Sheets of 6 or 8

A238

End of World War II, 50th Anniv. — A239

No. 1803: a, USS Idaho. b, HMS Ark Royal. c, Admiral Graf Spee. d, Destroyer. e, HMS Nelson. f, PT 109. g, USS Iowa. h, Bismark.
No. 1804: a, B-17. b, B-25. c, B-24 Liberator. d, USS Missouri. e, A-20 Boston. f, Pennsylvania, Colorado, Louisville, Portland, Columbia enter Lingayen Gulf.
No. 1805, HMS Indomitable launching aircraft. No. 1806, B-29 bomber.

1995, July 10

1803 A238 250 le #a.-h. + label 7.25 7.25
1804 A239 300 le #a.-f. + label 7.25 7.25

Souvenir Sheet

1805 A238 1500 le multi 7.25 7.25
1806 A239 1500 le multi 4.50 4.50

No. 1805 contains one 57x42mm stamp.

UN, 50th Anniv. — A240

No. 1807: a, 300 le, Dais, UN General Assembly. 400 le, Sec. Gen. U. Thant. 500 le, UN building, dove.
1500 le, Sec. Gen. Dag Hammarskjold.

1995, July 10 Litho. *Perf. 14*

1807 A240 Strip of 3, #a.-c. 3.50 3.50

Souvenir Sheet

1808 A240 1500 le multicolored 4.25 4.25

No. 1807 is a continuous design.

1995 Boy Scout Jamboree, Holland A241

No. 1809: a, 400 le, Natl. flag. b, 500 le, Lord Baden-Powell. c, 600 le, Scout sign.
1500 le, Scout salute.

1995, July 10

1809 A241 Strip of 3, #a.-c. 4.50 4.50

Souvenir Sheet

1810 A241 1500 le multicolored 4.75 4.75

Queen Mother, 95th Birthday A242

No. 1811: a, Drawing. b, Holding bouquet of flowers. c, Formal portrait. d, Without hat.
1500 le, Blue hat, dress.

1995, July 10 *Perf. 13½x14*

1811 A242 400 le Block or strip of 4, #a.-d. 5.00 5.00

Souvenir Sheet

1812 A242 1500 le multicolored 4.75 4.75

No. 1811 was issued in sheets of 8 stamps.
For surcharges see Nos. 2544-2545.

FAO, 50th Anniv. A243

No. 1813: a, 300 le, Man working with sack of food. b, 400 le, Boy carrying bundle of sticks on head. c, 500 le, Woman holding bowl of fruit.
1500 le, Woman holding baby, vert.

1995, July 10 *Perf. 14*

1813 A243 Strip of 3, #a.-c. 3.75 3.75

Souvenir Sheet

1814 A243 1500 le multicolored 4.25 4.25

Rotary Intl., 90th Anniv. A244

Designs: 500 le, Natl. flag, Rotary emblem. 1000 le, Paul Harris, Rotary emblem.

1995, July 10

1815 A244 500 le multicolored 2.00 2.00

Souvenir Sheet

1816 A244 1000 le multicolored 3.75 3.75

Singapore '95 — A245

Flora & fauna, each 300 le: No. 1817a, African tulip tree. b, Senegal bush locust. c, Killifish. d, Bird of paradise. e, Mandrill. f, Painted reed frog. g, Large spotted acraea. h, Carmine bee-eater.
No. 1818, each 300 le: a, Flame lily. b, Grants gazelle. c, Dogbane. d, Gold-banded forester. e, Horned chameleon. f, Malachite kingfisher. g, Leaf beetle. h, Acanthus.
Each 1500 le: No. 1819, Lion. No. 1820, African elephant.

1995, Sept. 5 Litho. *Perf. 14*

Sheets of 8, #a-h

1817-1818 A245 Set of 2 20.00 20.00

Souvenir Sheets

1819-1820 A245 Set of 2 10.00 10.00

Third UN Decade for Advancement of Women — A246

Designs: 300 le, Development. 500 le, Peace. 700 le, Equality.

1995 Litho. *Perf. 14*

1821-1823 A246 Set of 3 5.25 5.25

Sierra Leone Grammar School, 150th Anniv. A247

1995, Sept. 27 Litho. *Perf. 14*

1824 A247 300 le multicolored 1.00 1.00

Christmas A248

Details or entire paintings: 50 le, Holy Family, by Beccafumi. 100 le, Rest on Flight into Egypt, by Barocci. 150 le, La Vierge, by Bellini. 200 le, The Flight, by d'Arpino. 600 le, Adoration of the Magi, by Francken. 800 le, The Annunciation, by da Conegliano.
Each 1500 le: No. 1831, Virgin and child, by Cranach. No. 1832, Madonna and Child, by Berlinghiero.

1995, Dec. 1 Litho. *Perf. 13½x14*

1825-1830 A248 Set of 6 5.75 5.75

Souvenir Sheets

1831-1832 A248 Set of 2 8.75 8.75

Disney Christmas A249

Antique Disney toys: 5 le, Mickey Mouse doll. 10 le, Donald rag drum major. 15 le, Donald wind up. 20 le, Toothbrush holder. 25 le, Mickey telephone. 30 le, Walking wind-up. 800 le, Movie projector. 1000 le, Goofy tricycle.
Each 1500 le: No. 1841, Black Mickey Mouse. No. 1842, First Mickey book.

1995, Dec. 4 *Perf. 13½x14*

1833-1840 A249 Set of 8 7.75 7.75

Souvenir Sheets

1841-1842 A249 Set of 2 10.00 10.00

Nobel Prize Fund Established, Cent. — A250

Recipients, each 250 le: No. 1843a, Andrew Huxley, medicine, 1963. b, Nelson Mandela, peace, 1993. c, Gabriela Mistral, literature, 1945. d, Otto Diels, chemistry, 1950. e, Hannes Alfven, physics, 1970. f, Wole Soyinka, literature, 1986. g, Hans G. Dehmelt, physics, 1989. h, Desmond Tutu, peace, 1984. i, Leo Esaki, physics, 1973.
No. 1844, each 250 le: a, Maria Goeppert Mayer, physics, 1963. b, Irène Joliot-Curie, chemistry, 1935. c, Mother Teresa, peace, 1979. d, Selma Lagerlöf, literature, 1909. e, Rosalyn Yalow, medicine, 1977. f, Dorothy Hodgkin, chemistry, 1964. g, Rita Levi-Montalcini, medicine, 1986. h, Mairead Corrigan, peace, 1976. i, Betty Williams, peace, 1976.
No. 1845, each 250 le: a, Tobias Asser, peace, 1911. b, Andrei Sakharov, peace, 1975. c, Frederic Passy, peace, 1901. d, Dag Hammarskjöld, peace, 1961. e, Aung San Suu Kyi, peace, 1991. f, Ludwig Quidde, peace, 1927. g, Elie Wiesel, peace, 1986. h, Bertha von Suttner, peace, 1905. i, Dalai Lama, peace, 1989.
No. 1846, each 250 le: a, Richard Zsigmondy, chemistry, 1925. b, Robert Huber, chemistry, 1988. c, Wilhelm Ostwald, chemistry, 1909. d, Johann Deisenhofer, chemistry, 1988. e, Heinrich Wieland, chemistry, 1927. f, Gerhard Herzberg, chemistry, 1971. g, Hans von Euler-Chelpin, chemistry, 1929. h, Richard Willstätter, chemistry, 1915. i, Fritz Haber, chemistry, 1918.
Each 1500 le: No. 1847, Albert Einstein, physics, 1921. No. 1848, Wilhelm Röentgen, physics, 1901. No. 1849, Sin-Itiro Tomonaga, physics, 1965.

Sheets of 9, #a-i

1995, Dec. 29 Litho. *Perf. 14*

1843-1846 A250 Set of 4 40.00 40.00

Souvenir Sheets

1847-1849 A250 Set of 3 13.00 13.00

Railways of the World A251

No. 1850, each 200 le: a, Denver and Rio Grande Western. b, Central of Georgia. c, Seaboard Air Line. d, Missouri Pacific Lines. e, Atchison, Topeka and Santa Fe. f, Chicago, Milwaukee, St. Paul and Pacific. g, Texas and Pacific. h, Minneapolis, St. Paul & Sault Saint Marie. (Soo Line). i, Western Pacific. j, Great Northern. k, Baltimore & Ohio. l, Chicago, Rock Island and Pacific.
No. 1851, each 200 le: a, Southern Pacific 4-8-4 "Daylight" express, US. b, Belgian National 4-4-2 express. c, Indian Railways 4-6-2 "WP" express. d, South Australian 4-8-4 express. e, Union Pacific 4-8-8-4 "Big Boy," US. f, UK 4-6-2 "Royal Scot" streamlined. g, German Federal, class 052 2-10-0. h, Japanese National, 4-6-4 express. i, Pennsylvania, 4-4-4-4 streamlined, US. j, East African 4-8-2+2-8-4 Beyer-Garratt. k, Milwaukee Road 4-6-4 "Hiawatha" express, US. l, Paris-Orleans, 4-6-2 Pacific, France.
No. 1852, each 250 le: a, "Eurostar" express. b, ETR 401 Pendolino four-car tilting train, Italy. c, HST 125 inter-city high speed train, UK. d, "Virgin" B-B class high speed diesel-hydraulic express, Spain. e, French Natl. Railways TGV. f, Amtrak "Southwest Chief," US. g, TGV "Atlantique," France. h, "Peloponnese Express," Greece. i, "Shin-Kansen" high-speed electric train, Japan. j, Canadian Natl. turbo train. k, XPT high-speed diesel-electric train, Australia. l, SS1 Co-Co electric locomotive, China.
No. 1853, each 300 le: a, Canadian Natl. U1-F. b, Central Pacific No. 119 at Promontory, US. c, LNER "A4" class streamlined 4-6-2, UK. d, New York Central J32 "Empire State Express," US. e, Canadian Natl. 4-8-4. f, Class 38 Pacific 4-6-2 express, Australia. g, Canadian Pacific 4-6-2 express. h, Southern "West Country" class 4-6-2, UK.i, Norfolk & Western Class J 4-8-4, US. j, RM Class 4-6-0 Pacific, China. k, P-36 class 4-8-4 express, USSR. l, Great Western "King" class 4-6-0, UK.
Each 1500 le: No. 1853M, British Railways Jubilee class 4-6-0, No. 45627 named "Sierra Leone." No. 1853N, Denver & Rio Grande Western "California Zephyr," US. No. 1853O, 1st train to cross newly opened bridge over Yangtze River, 1968, China. No. 1853P, Beijing-Shanghai Express, China. No. 1853Q, China Railways, "QJ" class 2-10-2.

Sheets of 12, #a-l

1995, May 23 Litho. *Perf. 14*

1850-1851 A251 Set of 2 15.00 15.00
1852 A251 250 le multi 9.00 9.00
1853 A251 300 le multi 11.00 11.00

Souvenir Sheets

1853M-1853Q A251 Set of 5 22.00 22.00

Nos. 1853M-1853Q each contain one 56x43mm stamp. No. 1850 exists with two different top margin inscriptions, "THE COLOURFUL RAILROADS OF NORTH AMERICA" and "THE COLOURFUL RAILROADS OF THE WORLD."

New Year 1996 (Year of the Rat) — A252

Different stylized rats: No. 1854a, Facing left, purple & multi. b, Facing right, blue green & multi. c, Facing left, blue green & multi. d, Facing right, blue & multi.
No. 1856, Rat, vert.

1996, Jan. 6

1854 A252 200 le Block of 4, #a.-d. 2.75 2.75

Miniature Sheet of 4

1855 A252 200 le #1854a-1854d 2.75 2.75

Souvenir Sheet

1856 A252 500 le multicolored 2.75 2.75

No. 1854 was issued in sheets of 16 stamps.

Disney Characters as Circus Performers A253

Designs: 100 le, Mickey, the magician. 200 le, Clarabelle Cow, the tightrope walker. 250 le, The clowns, Donald and Huey, Dewey and Louie. 300 le, Donald, the lion tamer. 800 le, Minnie, the bareback rider. 1000 le, Goofy and Minnie, the trapeze artists.
Each 1500 le: #1863, Mickey, horiz. #1864, Pluto, horiz.

1996, Jan. 29 Litho. *Perf. 14x13½*

1857-1862 A253 Set of 6 9.75 9.75

Souvenir Sheets

Perf. 13½x14½

1863-1864 A253 Set of 2 9.75 9.75

Motion Pictures, Cent. A254

No. 1865, each 250 le: a, Film projector. b, Pete. c, Silver. d, Rin-Tin-Tin. e, King Kong. f, Flipper. g, Jaws. h, Elsa. i, Moby Dick.
No. 1866, Directors or stars, scene from movie, each 250 le: a, Lumière Brothers. b, George Méliès. c, Toshiro Mifune d, Clark Gable, Vivian Leigh, David O. Selznick. e, Fritz Lang, Metropolis. f, Akira Kurosawa, Ran. g, Charlie Chaplin. h, Marlène Dietrich. i, Steven Spielberg, ET.
Each 1500 le: #1867, Lassie. #1868, Cecil B. de Mille.

Sheets of 9, #a-i

1996, Feb. 26 Litho. *Perf. 14*

1865-1866 A254 Set of 2 16.00 16.00

Souvenir Sheets

1867-1868 A254 Set of 2 9.50 9.50

Paintings from Metropolitan Museum of Art — A255

Entire paintings or details: No. 1869, each 200 le: a, Honfleur, by Jongkind. b, A Boat on the Shore, by Courbet. c, Barges at Pontoise, by Pissarro. d, The Dead Christ with Angels, by Manet. e, Salisbury Cathedral, by Constable. f, A Lady with a Setter Dog, by Eakins. g, Tahitian Women Bathing, by Gaugin. h, Majas on a Balcony, by Goya.
By Renoir: No. 1870, each 200 le: a, In the Meadow. b, By the Seashore. c, Still Life with Peaches and Grapes. d, Marguerite (Margot) Bérard. e, Young Girl in Pink and Black Hat. f, A Waitrress at Duval's Restaurant. g, A Road in Louveciennes. h, Two Young Girls at the Piano.
No. 1871, each 200 le: a, Morning, an Overcast Day, Rouen, by Pissarro. b, The Horse Fair, by Bonheur. c, High Tide: the Bathers, by Homer. d, The Dance Class, by Degas. e, The Brioche, by Manet. f, The Grand Canal, Venice, by Turner. g, St. Thecla Interceding for Plague-stricken Este, by G. B. Tiepolo. h, Bridge at Villeneuve, by Sisley.
No. 1872, each 200 le: a, Madame Charpentier, by Renoir. b, Head of Christ, by Rembrandt. c, The Standard-Bearer, by Rembrandt. d, Girl Asleep, by Vermeer. e, Lady with a Lute, by Vermeer. f, Portrait of a Woman, by Rembrandt. g, La Grenouillère, by Monet. h, Woman with Chrysanthemums, by Degas.
Each 1500 le: No. 1873, The Death of Socrates, by J.L. David. No. 1874, Battle of Constantine and Maxentius, by Rubens. No. 1875, Samson and Delilah, by Rubens. No. 1876, The Emblem of Christ Appearing to Constantine, by Rubens.

Sheets of 8, #a-h, + label

1996 Litho. *Perf. 13½x14*

1869-1872 A255 Set of 4 21.00 21.00

Souvenir Sheets

Perf. 14

1873-1876 A255 Set of 4 12.00 12.00

Nos. 1873-1876 each contain one 85x57mm.
Nos. 1874-1876 are not in the Metropolitan.

1996 Summer Olympic Games, Atlanta A256

100 le, 1932 Olympic Stadium, Los Angeles. 150 le, Archery. 500 le, Rings (gymnastics). 600 le, Pole vault.
No. 1881: a, Field hockey. b, Swimming. c, Equestrian. d, Boxing. e, Pommel horse. f, 100-meter dash.

1996, June 11 Litho. *Perf. 14*

1877-1880 A256 Set of 4 4.75 4.75

1881 A256 300 le Sheet of 6, #a.-f. 6.00 6.00

Souvenir Sheet

1882 A256 1500 le Runner 5.00 5.00

Queen Elizabeth II, 70th Birthday A257

Designs: a, Portrait. b, Receiving flowers. c, Holding flowers, wearing black hat, coat.
1500 le, Waving from balcony.

1996, July 15 Litho. *Perf. 13½x14*

1886 A257 600 le Strip of 3, #a.-c. 4.75 4.75

Souvenir Sheet

1887 A257 1500 le multicolored 4.75 4.75

No. 1886 was issued in sheets of 9 stamps.

UNICEF, 50th Anniv. A258

Designs: 300 le, Children reading. 400 le, Young man, woman reading. 500 le, Children in class.
1500 le, Children's faces.

1996, July 15 *Perf. 14*

1888-1890 A258 Set of 3 3.50 3.50

Souvenir Sheet

1891 A258 1500 le multicolored 5.00 5.00

Cats — A259

No. 1892, each 200 le a, Abyssinian. b, British tabby. c, Norwegian forest. d, Maine coon. e, Bengal. f, Asian. g, American curl. h, Devon rex. i, Tonkinese. j, Egyptian mau. k, Burmese. l, Siamese.
No. 1893, each 200 le: a, British shorthair. b, Tiffany. c, Birman. d, Somali. e, Malayan. f, Japanese bobtail. g, Himalayan. h, Tortoiseshell. i, Oriental. j, Ocicat. k, Chartreux. l, Ragdoll.
Each 2000 le: No. 1894, Persian. No. 1895, Burmilla.

1996, June 17 Sheets of 12, #a-l

1892-1893 A259 Set of 2 23.00 23.00

Souvenir Sheets

1894-1895 A259 Set of 2 12.00 12.00

Mushrooms — A260

50 le, Cinnabar-red chanterelle. 300 le, Larch suillus. 400 le, Yellow more. 500 le, Variable cort.
No. 1900, each 250 le: a, African driver ant, Indigo milky, Marshall's false monarch (e). b, Scally inky cap. c, Pyxie cup (b). d, Barometer earthstar (c), rainbow grasshopper (h). e, Feltringed agaricus, long-horned longhorn. f, Spotted mycena. g, Orange latex milky. h, Tawny grissett amanita fulva, lamellicorn larva.
No. 1901, each 250 le: a, Millar tiger, little nest polymore. b, Coral slime. c, Red-gilled cort. d, Parasitic volvamella, veined tiger. e, Onion-stalked lepiota. f, Blusher. g. Orange mock oyster. h, Lizard claw, red and yellow barbet.
Each 1500 le: No. 1902, Netted rhodotus. No. 1903, Parasitic psathyrella.

1996, June 17

1896-1899 A260 Set of 4 4.00 4.00

Sheets of 8, #a.-h.

1900-1901 A260 Set of 2 12.00 12.00

Souvenir Sheets

1902-1903 A260 Set of 2 10.00 10.00

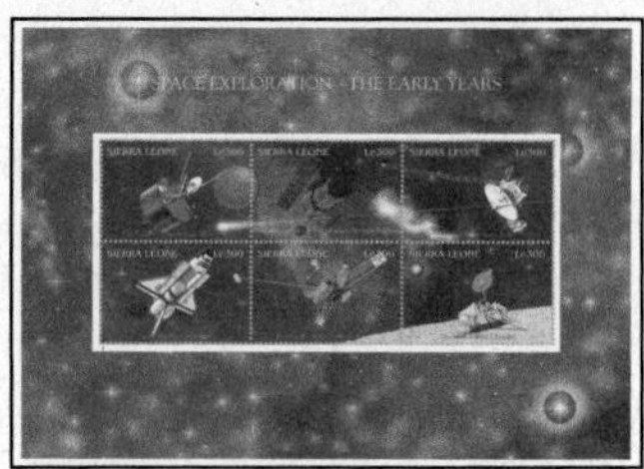

Space Exploration — A261

Designs: a, Pioneer-Venus orbiter, 1986-92. b, Hubble space telescope. c, Voyager probe. d, Space Shuttle Challenger in orbit. e, Pioneer II. f, Mars-Viking 1 lander.
1500 le, Shuttle Challenger landing.

1996

1904 A261 300 le Sheet of 6, #a.-f. 6.00 6.00

Souvenir Sheet

1905 A261 1500 le multicolored 5.25 5.25

Butterflies A262

Designs: 150 le, Charaxes pleione. 200 le, Eurema brigitta. 300 le, Charaxes ameliae. 500 le, Kallimoides rumia.
No. 1910, each 250 le: a, Precis orithya. b, Palla ussheri. c, Junonia orithya. d, Cymothoe sangaris. e, Cyrestis camillus. f, Precis rhadama. g, Precis cebrene. h, Hypolimnas misippus. i, Colotis danae.
Each 1500 le: No. 1911, Charaxes bohemani. No. 1912, Papilio antimachus.

1996, Aug. 15 Litho. *Perf. 14*

1906-1909 A262 Set of 4 5.00 5.00

1910 A262 Sheet of 9, #a.-i. 8.25 8.25

Souvenir Sheets

1911-1912 A262 Set of 2 10.00 10.00

Flowers — A263

Designs: 150 le, Tulipa. 200 le, Helichrysum bracteatum. 400 le, Viola. 500 le, Phalaenopsis.
No. 1917, each 200 le: a, Fountain. b, Begonia multiflora. c, Narcissus. d, Crocus speciosus. e, Chrysanthemum frutescens. Petunia. f, Cosmos pipinnatus. g, Anemone coronaria. h, Convolvulus minor.
No. 1918, each 300 le: a, Paphiopedilum. b, Cymbidium "Peach bloom." c, Sailboat. d, Miltonia. e, Parides gundalachianus. f, Laeliocatt leya. g, Lycaste aromatica. h, Brassolaeliocatt leya. i, Cymbidium "Southern Lace," Catastica teutila.
Each 1500 le: No. 1919, Helianthus annuus. No. 1920, Cymbidium "Lucifer."

1996, Aug. 19

1913-1916 A263 Set of 4 5.00 5.00

1917 A263 Sheet of 9, #a.-i. 5.50 5.50

1918 A263 Sheet of 9, #a.-i. 8.00 8.00

Souvenir Sheets

1919-1920 A263 Set of 2 8.75 8.75

Chinese Lunar Calendar A264

Year of the: a, Rat. b, Ox. c, Tiger. d, Hare. e, Dragon. f, Snake. g, Horse. h, Sheep. i, Monkey. j, Rooster. k, Dog. l, Pig.

1996, July 15 Litho. *Perf. 13½x14*
1921 A264 150 le Sheet of 12, #a.-l. 8.00 8.00

Ships — A265

No. 1922, each 300 le: a, Clipper ship, "Cutty Sark," 19th cent. b, SS Great Britain, 1846. c, "Dreadnaught," 1906. d, RMS Queen Elizabeth, 1940-72. e, Ocean-going racing yacht, 1962. f, SS United States, 1952. g, Nuclear powered submarine, 1950's. h, Super tanker, 1960's. i, USS Enterprise, 1980s.
No. 1923, each 300 le: a, Greek war galley, 4th cent. BC. b, Roman war galley, 50AD. c, Viking ship, 9th cent. d, Flemish carrack, 15th cent. e, Merchant man, 16th cent. f, Tudor warship, 16th cent. g, Elizabethan galleon, 17th cent. h, Dutch Man of War, 17th cent. i, "Maestrale," Maltese galley, 18th cent.
Each 1500 le: No. 1924, Cruise ship "Legend of the Seas," 1996 Panama Canal. No. 1925, Egyptian ocean-going ship, 1480BC.

Sheets of 9, #a-i

1996, Oct. 29 Litho. *Perf. 14*
1922-1923 A265 Set of 2 19.00 19.00

Souvenir Sheets

1924-1925 A265 Set of 2 11.00 11.00

Nos. 1924-1925 each contain one 56x43mm stamp.

Christmas A266

Details or entire paintings, by Filippo Lippi: 200 le, Madonna of Humility. 250 le, Coronation of the Virgin. 400 le, 500 le, Annunciation. 600 le, Barbadori Altarpiece. 800 le, Coronation of the Virgin, diff.
Each 2000 le: Paintings by Rubens: No. 1932, Adoration of the Magi. No. 1933, Holy Family with St. Anne.

1996, Dec. 12 Litho. *Perf. 13½x14*
1926-1931 A266 Set of 6 8.75 8.75

Souvenir Sheets

1932-1933 A266 Set of 2 9.25 9.25

Souvenir Sheets

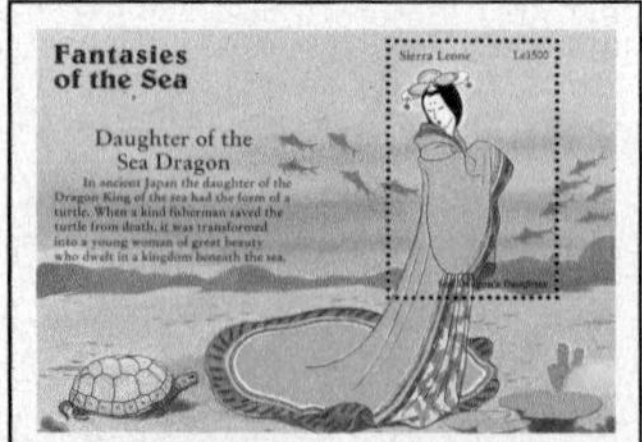

Fantasies of the Sea — A267

Each 1500 le: #1934, Sea Dragon's Daughter. #1935, Homo Aquaticus. #1936, Chinese Sea Fairy. #1937, Sea Totem. #1938, The Turtle, horiz. #1939, Mermaid, horiz. #1940, How the Whale Got its Throat, horiz. #1941, Killer Whale Crest. #1942, Aphrodite. #1943, Ship Figurehead. #1944, Lilith. #1945, Queen of the Orkney Islands. #1946, Haida Eagle. #1947, Captain Ahab. #1948, Waskos. #1949, Jonah. #1950, Odysseus. #1951, The Little Mermaid. #1952, Squamish Indians. #1953, Boy on a Dolphin. $1954, Airship to Atlantis. #1955, Sea Bishop. #1956, 20,000 Leagues Under the Sea. #1957, Whale Song. #1958, Arion. #1959, Dragonrider of Pern. #1960, Kelpie. #1961, Natsihlane. #1962, Merman. #1963, Albatross. #1964, City under polar ice melt. #1965, Tom Swift. #1966, The Flying Dutchman, horiz. #1967, Sea Centaur. #1968, Lang (dragon), horiz. #1969, Triton. #1970, Sea Serpent. #1971, Arthropod sea monster. #1972, The Ancient Mariner. #1973, Poseidon.

1996, Dec. 19 Litho. *Perf. 14*
1934-1973 A267 Set of 40 175.00 175.00

New Year 1997 (Year of the Ox) — A268

Various stylized oxen, background color: Nos. 1975-1976: a, purple. b, green. c, blue. d, claret.
800 le, like #1975d, vert.

1997, Jan. 8 Litho. *Perf. 14*
1975 A268 150 le Block of 4, #a.-d. 1.60 1.60
1976 A268 250 le Sheet of 4, #a.-d. 5.00 5.00

Souvenir Sheet

1977 A268 800 le multicolored 2.40 2.40

No. 1975 was issued in sheets of 16 stamps.

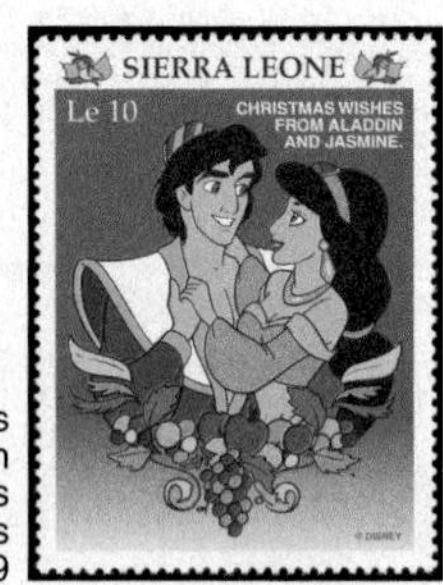

Disney's Aladdin in Christmas Scenes A269

Designs: 10 le, Aladdin, Jasmine. 15 le, Santa, Genie. 20 le, Aladdin, Jasmine on magic carpet. 25 le, Genie as Christmas tree. 30 le, Aladdin, Genie "Santa." 100 le, Jasmine, Aladdin, Genie. 800 le, Genie's letter to Santa. 1000 le, Genie's Christmas carol.
Each 2000 le: No. 1986, Aladdin, Abu. No. 1987, Jasmine, Aladdin, horiz.

1997, Jan. 27 *Perf. 14x13½*
1978-1985 A269 Set of 8 9.50 9.50

Souvenir Sheets

Perf. 14x13½, 13½x14

1986-1987 A269 Set of 2 10.00 10.00

Hong Kong — A270

Panoramic view of Hong Kong, each 500 le: No. 1988, in daytime. No. 1989, at night.

1997, Feb. 12 Litho. *Perf. 14*

Sheets of 4, #a-d

1988-1989 A270 Set of 2 10.50 10.50

UNESCO, 50th Anniv. A271

World Heritage Sites: 60 le, Town of Kizhi Pogost, Russia. 200 le, Durmitor Natl. Park, Yugoslavia. 250 le, City of Nessebar, Bulgaria. 400 le, City of Bukhara, Uzbekistan. 500 le, Monastery of Kiev-Pechersk, Ukraine. 700 le, Mountain Walks, Vlkolinec, Slovakia.
No. 1996, each 300 le: a, Town of Roros, Norway. b, City of Warsaw, Poland. c, Cathedral of Notre Dame, Luxembourg. d, City of Vilnius, Lithuania. e, Jelling, Denmark. f, Old Church of Petäjävesi, Finland. g, Sweden. h, Cathedral City of Bern, Switzerland.
No. 1997, each 300 le: a, Area surrounding Mt. Kilimanjaro, Tanzania. b, Monument, Fasil Ghebbi, Ethiopia. c, Natl. Park, Mt. Ruwenzori, Uganda. d, Abu Simbel, Egypt. e, Tsingy Bemaraha Strict Nature Reserve, Madagascar. f, House, Djenne, Mali. g, Traditional house construction, Ghana. h, Large house, Aromey.
Various views of Himeji-Jo, Japan, vert: No. 1998: a, b, c, d, e.
Each 2000 le: No. 1999, Natl. Bird Sanctuary, Djudj, Senegal, horiz. No. 2000, Acropolis, Athens, Greece, horiz.

1997, Mar. 24 Litho. *Perf. 13½x14*
1990-1995 A271 Set of 6 8.00 8.00

Sheets of 8, #a-h, + Label

1996-1997 A271 Set of 2 13.50 13.50

Sheet of 5 + Label

1998 A271 500 le #a.-e. 7.25 7.25

Souvenir Sheets

1999-2000 A271 Set of 2 10.50 10.50

Paintings by Hiroshige (1797-1858) — A272

No. 2001, each 400 le: a, Hatsune Riding Grounds, Bakuro-cho. b, Mannen Bridge, Fukagawa. c, Ryogoku Bridge and the Great Riverbank. d, Asakusa River, Great Riverbank, Miyato River. e, Silk-goods Lane, Odenmacho. f, Mokuboji Temple, Uchigawa Inlet, Gozensaihata.
Each 1500 le: No. 2002, Tsukudajima from Eitai Bridge. No. 2003, Nihonbashi Bridge and Edobashi Bridge.

1997 Litho. *Perf. 13½x14*
2001 A272 Sheet of 6, #a.-f. 6.75 6.75

Souvenir Sheets

2002-2003 A272 Set of 2 7.25 7.25

Chernobyl Disaster, 10th Anniv. A273

Designs: 1000 le, UNESCO. 1500 le, Chabad's Children of Chernobyl.

1997, June 23
2004 A273 1000 le multicolored 2.75 2.75
2005 A273 1500 le multicolored 4.00 4.00

Queen Elizabeth II and Prince Philip, 50th Wedding Anniv. — A274

No. 2006: a, Queen. b, Royal arms. c, Black & white photograph, Prince in dress uniform. d, Black & white photograph, Prince in tuxedo, bow tie. e, Palace of Holyroodhouse. f, Prince in hat guiding horses.
1500 le, Queen, Prince in colored photograph.

1997, June 23 *Perf. 14*
2006 A274 400 le Sheet of 6, #a.-f. 11.50 11.50

Souvenir Sheet

2007 A274 1500 le multi 4.00 4.00

Return of Hong Kong to China — A275

Designs: 400 le, Flag of China, map of China, Hong Kong, Victoria at night. 500 le, 650 le, Flag of China, July 1, 1997, city scene inside letters spelling "Hong Kong." 550 le, 600 le, Flag of China, Victoria harbor inside letters spelling "Hong Kong '97." 800 le, Victoria harbor, Deng Xiaoping (1904-97).

1997, June 23
2008-2013 A275 Set of 6 8.75 8.75

Nos. 2008-2013 were each issued in sheets of 3.

Souvenir Sheets

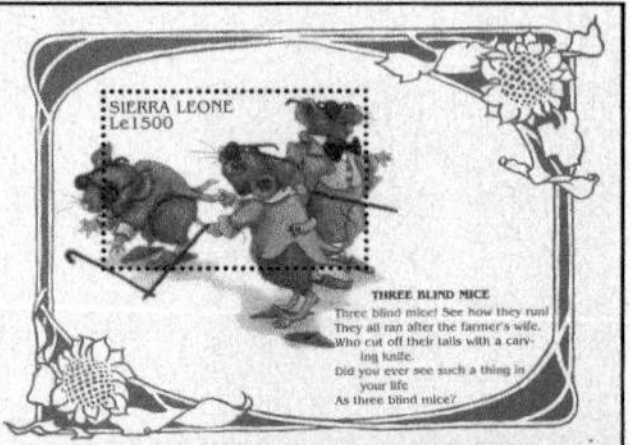

Mother Goose — A276

Designs, each 1500 le: No. 2014, Three Blind Mice. No. 2015, Woman holding out full skirt as "Myself."

1997, June 23 Litho. *Perf. 14*
2014-2015 A276 Set of 2 8.00 8.00

1998 Winter Olympic Games, Nagano A277

Designs: 250 le, Stadium, Calgary, 1988, American Indian. 300 le, Freestyle aerial skiing, vert. 500 le, Ice hockey, vert. 800 le, Dan Jansen, 1000-meter speed skater, vert.
No. 2022, vert, each 300 le: a, Peggy Fleming, figure skating. b, Japanese ski jumper, Nordic combined. c, 2-man luge, Germany. d, Frank-Peter Roetsch, biathlon, E. Germany.
Each 1500 le: No. 2023, Jamaican bobsled team, vert. No. 2024, Johann Olav Koss, Norway, vert.

1997, July 16 Litho. *Perf. 14*
2018-2021 A277 Set of 4 5.50 5.50

2022 A277 Strip of 4, #a.-d. 3.75 3.75

Souvenir Sheets

2023-2024 A277 Set of 2 8.00 8.00

No. 2022 was issued in sheets of 8 stamps.

1998 World Cup Soccer Championships, France — A278

Players: 100 le, Stabile, Uruguay. 150 le, Schiavio, Italy. 200 le, Kocsis, Hungary. 250 le, Nejedly, Czechoslovakia. 500 le, Leonidas, Brazil. 600 le, Ademir, Brazil.

No. 2031, each 300 le: a, Dwight Yorke, Trinidad & Tobago. b, Dennis Bergkamp, Holland. c, Steve McManaman, England. d, Ryan Giggs, Wales. e, Romario, Brazil, f, Faustino Asprilla, Colombia. g, Roy Keane, Ireland. h, Peter Schmeichel, Denmark.

Each 1500 le: No. 2032, Pele, Brazil, horiz. No. 2033, Lato, Poland, horiz.

1997, July 23 ***Perf. 13½x14, 14x13½***

2025-2030 A278 Set of 6 5.00 5.00

Sheet of 8

2031 A278 #a.-h. + 2 labels 7.00 7.00

Souvenir Sheets

2032-2033 A278 Set of 2 11.00 11.00

Classic Horror Movies — A279

Lead character, movie: No. 2034, each 300 le: a, Lon Chaney, "Phantom of the Opera," 1934. b, Boris Karloff, "The Mummy," 1932. c, Fredric March, "Dr. Jekyll & Mr. Hyde," 1932. d, Lon Chaney, Jr., "The Wolf Man," 1941. e, Charles Laughton, "Island of Lost Souls," 1933. f, Lionel Atwill, "Mystery of the Wax Museum," 1933. g, Bela Lugosi, "Dracula," 1931. h, Vincent Price, "The Haunted Palace," 1963. i, Elsa Lanchester, "Bride of Frankenstein," 1935.

3000 le, Bela Lugosi, Boris Karloff, "Son of Frankenstein," 1939.

1997, Aug. 15 ***Perf. 14***

2034 A279 Sheet of 9, #a.-i. 10.00 10.00

Souvenir Sheet

2035 A279 3000 le multi 8.00 8.00

Domestic Cats — A280

Designs: 150 le, American short hair tabby. 200 le, British short hair. 500 le, Turkish angora.

No. 2039, each 400 le: a, Chartreux. b, Abyssinian. c, Burmese. d, White angora. e, Japanese bobtail. f, Cymric.

1500 le, Egyptian mau.

1997, Aug. 29

2036-2038 A280 Set of 3 3.00 3.00

2039 A280 Sheet of 6, #a.-f. 6.50 6.50

Souvenir Sheet

2040 A280 1500 le multicolored 5.25 5.25

No. 2040 contains one 64x32mm stamp.

Butterflies — A281

Designs: 150 le, Vindula erota. 200 le, Pereutel leucodrosime. 250 le, Dynstor napolean. 300 le, Thauria aliris. 600 le, Papilio aegeus. 800 le, Amblypodia anita. 1500 le, Kallimoides rumia. 2000 le, Papilio dardanas.

No. 2049: a, Lycaena dispar. b, Graphium sarpedon. c, Euploe core. d, Papilio cresphontes. e, Colotis danae. f, Battus philenor.

No. 2050: a, Mylothris chloris. b, Argynnis lathonia. c, Elymnias agondas. d, Palla ussheri. e, Papilio glaucus. f, Cercyonis pegala.

Each 3000 le: No. 2051, Hebomoia glaucippe, horiz. No. 2052, Colias eurytheme, horiz.

1997, Aug. 1 **Litho.** ***Perf. 14***

2041-2048 A281 Set of 8 24.50 24.50

Sheets of 6

2049 A281 500 le #a.-f. 8.00 8.00

2050 A281 600 le #a.-f. 9.50 9.50

Souvenir Sheets

2051-2052 A281 Set of 2 16.00 16.00

For surcharges see Nos. 2897-2898.

Orchids — A282

Designs: 150 le, Ansellia africana. 200 le, Maxillaria praestans. 250 le, Cymbidium mimi. 300 le, Dendrobium bigibbum. 500 le, Encyclia vitellina. 800 le, Epidendrum prismatocarpum.

No. 2059, each 400 le: a, Laelia anceps. b, Paphiopedilum fairrieanum. c, Restrepia lansbergii. d, Yamadara cattleya. e, Cleistes divaricata. f, Calypso bulbosa.

Each 1500 le: No. 2060, Odontoglossum schlieperianum. No. 2061, Paphiopedilum tonsum.

1997, Sept. 1

2053-2058 A282 Set of 6 6.00 6.00

2059 A282 Sheet of 6, #a.-f. 6.50 6.50

Souvenir Sheets

2060-2061 A282 Set of 2 8.00 8.00

Motion Pictures Directed by Alfred Hitchcock — A283

No. 2062, each 350 le: a, Ray Milland in "Dial M for Murder." b, James Stewart, Kim Novak in "Vertigo." c, Cary Grant, Ingrid Bergman in "Notorious." d, John Dall, James Stewart in "Rope." e, Cary Grant in "North by Northwest." f, Grace Kelly, James Stewart in "Rear Window." g, Joan Fontaine, Laurence Olivier in "Rebecca." h, Tippi Hedren in "The Birds." i, Janet Leigh in "Psycho."

1500 le, Alfred Hitchcock.

1997, Aug. 15 **Litho.** ***Perf. 14***

2062 A283 Sheet of 9, #a.-i. 10.00 10.00

Souvenir Sheet

2063 A283 1500 le multi 5.50 5.50

Dogs — A284

Designs: 100 le, Shetland sheep dog. 250 le, Alaskan husky. 600 le, Jack Russell terrier.

No. 2067, each 400 le: a, Basset hound. b, Irish setter. c, St. Bernard. d, German shepherd. e, Dalmatian. f, Cocker spaniel.

1500 le, Boxer.

1997, Aug. 29

2064-2066 A284 Set of 3 2.75 2.75

2067 A284 Sheet of 6, #a.-f. 6.25 6.25

Souvenir Sheet

2068 A284 1500 le multicolored 5.00 5.00

No. 2068 contains one 31x63mm stamp.

Disney Christmas Stamps A285

Designs: 150 le, Huey, Dewey, & Louie. 200 le, Mickey's kids. 250 le, Daisy Duck. 300 le, Minnie. 400 le, Mickey. 500 le, Donald Duck. 600 le, Pluto. 800 le, Goofy.

No. 2077, each 50 le: a, like #2071. b, like #2069. c, like #2074. d, like #2072. e, like #2070. f, like #2073.

Each 2000 le: No. 2078, Mickey in sleigh. No. 2079, Mickey, Donald, Daisy in Santa suits, horiz.

1997, Oct. 1 ***Perf. 13½x14, 14x13½***

2069-2076 A285 Set of 8 12.00 12.00

2077 A285 Sheet of 6, #a.-f. 1.75 1.75

Souvenir Sheets

2078-2079 A285 Set of 2 13.00 13.00

For overprints see Nos. 2117-2119.

Civilian Airliners — A286

No. 2080, each 600 le: a, SUD Caravelle 6. b, DeHavilland comet. c, Boeing 707. d, Airbus industrie A-300.

No. 2080E, each 600 le: f, Benoist Type XIV. g, Junkers JU52/3m. h, Douglas DC-3. i, Sikorsky S-42.

Each 2000 le: #2081, Concorde. #2081A, Lockheed L-1649A Starliner.

1997, Oct. 6 ***Perf. 14***

2080 A286 Sheet of 4, #a.-d. + label 6.50 6.50

2080E A286 Sheet of 4, #f.-i. + label 6.50 6.50

Souvenir Sheets

2081-2081A A286 Set of 2 10.50 10.50

Nos. 2081-2081A contain one 91x34mm stamp.

Christmas A287

Entire paintings or details: 100 le, 150 le, The Annunciation, by Titian (diff. details). 200 le, Madonna of Foligno, by Raphael. 250 le, The Annunciation, by Michelino. 500 le, The Prophet Isaiah, by Michelangelo. 600 le, Three Angels, by Master of the Rhenish Housebook.

Each 2000 le: No. 2088, The Fall of the Rebel Angels, by Peter Bruegel the Elder, horiz. No. 2089, Unidentified painting of Angel pointing hand in air, man with book, horiz.

1997, Dec. 24

2082-2087 A287 Set of 6 5.25 5.25

Souvenir Sheets

2088-2089 A287 Set of 2 9.75 9.75

Diana, Princess of Wales (1961-97) — A288

Various portraits, each 400 le, color of sheet margin: No. 2090, Pale pink. No. 2091, Pale blue. No. 2092, Pale yellow.

Each 1500 le: No. 2093, Wearing wide-brimmed hat. No. 2094, With Prince Harry (in margin). No. 2095, Helping to feed needy.

1998, Jan. 12 **Litho.** ***Perf. 14***

Sheets of 6, #a.-f.

2090-2092 A288 Set of 3 17.50 17.50

Souvenir Sheets

2093-2095 A288 Set of 3 11.00 11.00

New Year 1998 (Year of the Tiger) — A289

Various stylized tigers in: No. 2096: a, purple. b, maroon. c, bright lilac rose. d, orange. 800 le, maroon, vert.

1998, Jan. 26 Litho. *Perf. 14*

2096 A289 250 le Sheet of 4, #a.-d. 2.75 2.75

Souvenir Sheet

2097 A289 800 le red org & multi 2.25 2.25

Flora and Fauna A290

Designs: 200 le, Metagyrphus nitens, vert. 250 le, Lord Derby's parakeet, vert. 300 le, Narcissus, vert. 400 le, Barbus tetrazona. 500 le, Agalychnis callidryas. 600 le, Wolverine.

No. 2104, each 450 le: a, Japanese white-eyes. b, Rhododendron. c, Slow loris. d, Violet flowers. e, Orthetrum albistylum. f, Coluber jugularis.

No. 2105, each 450 le: a, Cheetah. b, Ornithogalum thyrsoides. c, Ostrich. d, Common chameleon. e, Fennec fox. f, Junonia hierta cebrene.

Each 2000 le: No. 2106, Tricolored heron, vert. No. 2107, Atheris squamiger.

1998, Aug. 4 Litho. *Perf. 14*

2098-2103 A290 Set of 6 4.50 4.50

Sheets of 6, #a.-f.

2104-2105 A290 Set of 2 13.50 13.50

Souvenir Sheets

2106-2107 A290 Set of 2 8.50 8.50

Dinosaurs A291

Designs: 200 le, Hypsilophodon, vert. 400 le, Lambeosaurus, vert. 500 le, Corythosaurus, vert. 600 le, Stegosaurus, vert. 800 le, Antrodemus.

No. 2113, each 500 le, vert: a, Plateosaurus. b, Tyrannosaurus. c, Brachiosaurus. d, Iguanodon. e, Styracosaurus. f, Hadrosaurus.

No. 2114, each 500 le: a, Tyrannosaurus. b, Tenontosaurus. c, Deinonychus. d, Triceratops. e, Maiasaura. f, Struthiomimus.

Each 2000 le: No. 2115, Tyrannosaurus. No. 2116, Triceratops.

1998, Aug. 18 Litho. *Perf. 14*

2108-2112 A291 Set of 5 5.00 5.00

Sheets of 6, #a.-f.

2113-2114 A291 Set of 2 12.50 12.50

Souvenir Sheets

2115-2116 A291 Set of 2 8.75 8.75

Nos. 2077-2079 Ovptd.

Perf. 13½x14, 14x13½

1998, Aug. 31

2117 A285 50 le Sheet of 6, #a.-f. 6.00 6.00

Souvenir Sheets

2118-2119 A285 Set of 2 12.00 12.00

Emblem and "MICKEY & MINNIE — 70TH ANNIVERSARY" appear in sheet margin on Nos. 2118-2119.

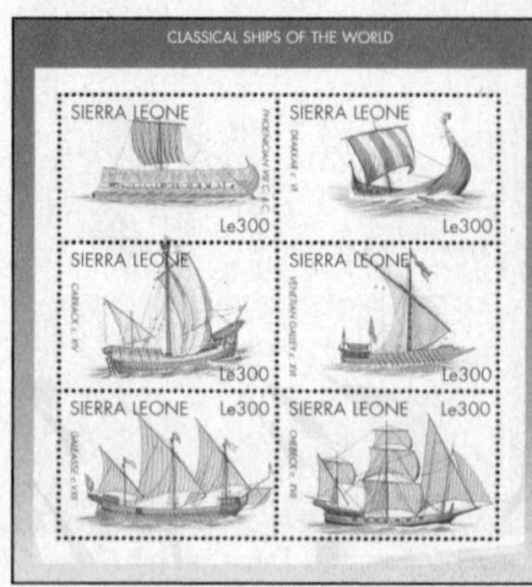

Ships of the World — A292

No. 2120, each 300 le: a, Phoenician, 8th cent. BC. b, Drakkar, 6th cent. c, Carrack, 14th cent. d, Venetian Galley, 16th cent. e, Galeasse, 17th cent. f, Chebeck, 17th cent.

No. 2121, each 300 le: a, Junk, 19th cent. b, HMS Victory, 19th cent. c, Savanna, 19th cent. d, Gaissa, 19th cent. e, Warrior, 19th cent. f, Preussen, 20th cent.

Each 2000 le: No. 2122, Santa Maria, 1492. No. 2123, Titanic, 1912.

Sheets of 6, #a.-f.

1998, Sept. 1 *Perf. 14*

2120-2121 A292 Set of 2 16.00 16.00

Souvenir Sheets

2122-2123 A292 Set of 2 9.00 9.00

Nos. 2122-2123 each contain one 57x43mm stamp.

For surcharges see Nos. 2899-2900.

Disney's The Lion King, Simba's Pride — A293

No. 2124, each 500 le: a, Kiara (with bird). b, Pumbaa. c, Kiara & Kovu. d, Kovu. e, Kiara & Kovu (red background). f, Timon (orange background).

No. 2125, each 500 le: a, Kiara (with butterfly). b, Timon & Pumbaa. c, Kiara. d, Kiara & Kovu (green background). e, Kovu (with bird). f, Kiara & Kovu (pink background).

Each 2500 le: No. 2126, Pumbaa & Timon. No. 2127, Kiara & Kovu, horiz.

Perf. 13½x14, 14x13½

1998, Sept. 15 Sheets of 6, #a.-f.

2124-2125 A293 Set of 2 16.00 16.00

Souvenir Sheets

2126-2127 A293 Set of 2 13.50 13.50

Paintings by Picasso — A294

Paintings: 400 le, Man with Straw Hat and Ice Cream Cone, 1938. 600 le, Woman in Red Armchair, 1932. 800 le, Nude in a Garden, 1934.

2000 le, Child Holding a Dove, 1901.

1998, Dec. 15 Litho. *Perf. 14½*

2128-2130 A294 Set of 3 6.50 6.50

Souvenir Sheet

2131 A294 2000 le multicolored 3.75 3.75

Gandhi — A295

1998, Dec. 15 *Perf. 14*

2132 A295 600 le Portrait 5.00 5.00

Souvenir Sheet

2133 A295 2000 le Close-up 5.50 5.50

No. 2132 printed in sheets of 4.

For surcharge see No. 2904.

Royal Air Force, 80th Anniv. — A296

No. 2134, each 800 le: a, McDonnell Douglas Phantom FRG2. b, Two Panavia Tornado GR1. c, Jaguar GR1A. d, Hercules C-130.

Each 2000 le: No. 2135, Eagle, biplane. No. 2136, Lysander, Eurofighter.

1998, Dec. 15

2134 A296 Sheet of 4, #a.-d. 11.50 11.50

Souvenir Sheets

2135-2136 A296 Set of 2 13.00 13.00

19th World Scouting Jamboree, Chile — A297

No. 2137, each 1500 le: a, Dan Beard, Robert Baden-Powell, 1937. b, Kuwaiti Scouts. c, Scout leader bottle feeding bear cub.

No. 2138, each 1500 le, vert.: a, William D. Boyce, Lone Scouts founder. b, Guion S. Bluford. c, Ellison S. Onizuka.

Each 3000 le: No. 2139, Lord, Lady Robert Baden-Powell. No. 2140, Bear cub drinking from bottle.

1998, Dec. 15 Sheets of 3, #a.-c.

2137-2138 A297 Set of 2 16.00 16.00

Souvenir Sheets

2139-2140 A297 Set of 2 12.00 12.00

For surcharge see No. 2901.

Christmas A298

Entire paintings or details: 200 le, Penitent of Mary Magdalen, by Titian. 500 le, Lamentation of Christ, by Veronese. 1500 le, The Building of Noah's Ark, by Guido Reni. 2000 le, Abraham and Isaac, by Rembrandt.

Each 3000 le: No. 2145, Adoration of the Shepherds, by Bartolomé Estéban Murillo. No. 2146, The Assumption of the Virgin, by Murillo.

1998, Dec. 14 Litho. *Perf. 14*

2141-2144 A298 Set of 4 6.75 6.75

Souvenir Sheets

2145-2146 A298 Set of 2 10.50 10.50

Ferrari Automobiles — A298a

No. 2146A, each 800 le: c, 400 Superamerica. d, 250 GT Lusso. e, 342 America.

2000 le, 330 GTC.

1998, Dec. 15 Litho. *Perf. 14*

2146A A298a Sheet of 3, #c-e 2.75 2.75

Souvenir Sheet

2146B A298a multi 2.40 2.40

No. 2146A contains three 39x25mm stamps.

Diana, Princess of Wales (1961-97) — A299

No. 2147: a, Inscription panel at left. b, Panel at right.

1998, Dec. 15 *Perf. 14½x14*

2147 A299 600 le Horiz. pair, #a-b 3.50 3.50

No. 2147 was issued in sheets of 3 pairs.

New Year 1999 (Year of the Rabbit) — A300

Color of stylized rabbits — #2148: a, red. b, red violet. c, blue. d, light violet.

1500 le, Rabbit, vert.

1998, Dec. 24 *Perf. 14*

2148 A300 700 le Sheet of 4, #a.-d. 6.50 6.50

Souvenir Sheet

2149 A300 1500 le multicolored 5.50 5.50

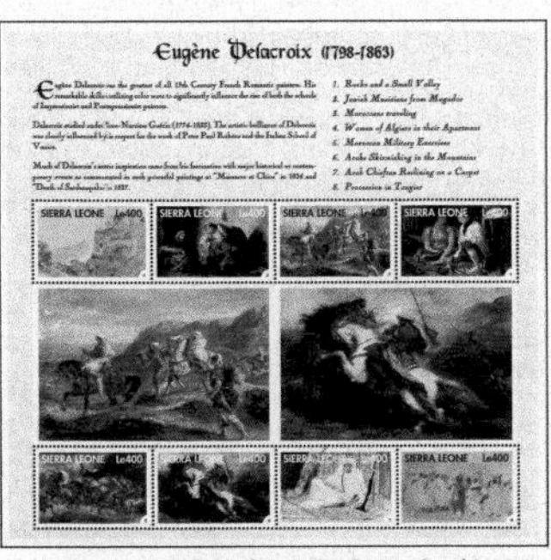

Paintings by Eugène Delacroix (1798-1863) — A301

Designs: a, Rocks and a Small Valley. b, Jewish Musicians from Magador. c, Moroccans Traveling. d, Women of Algiers in their Apartment. e, Moroccan Military Exercises. f, Arabs Skirmishing in the Mountains. g, Arab Chieftan Reclining on a Carpet. h, Procession in Tangier.

No. 2151, Chopin, vert.

1998

2150 A301 400 le Sheet of 8, #a.-h. 11.00 11.00

Souvenir Sheet

2151 A301 400 le multicolored 5.50 5.50

Bird Type of 1992

Designs: 4000 le, Gray-headed bush-shrike. 5000 le, Black-backed puffback. 6000 le, Crimson-breasted shrike. 10,000 le, Northern shrike.

1999 Litho. *Perf. 14x15*

No Date Imprint

2152	A199	4000 le multi	12.00	12.00
2153	A199	5000 le multi	14.00	14.00
a.		Inscribed "2002"	14.00	14.00
b.		Inscribed "2006"	14.00	14.00
2154	A199	6000 le multi	18.00	18.00
2155	A199	10,000 le multi	22.50	22.50
b.		Inscribed "2006"	22.50	22.50
		Nos. 2152-2155 (4)	66.50	66.50

Issued: 4000 le, 5000 le, 2/18/99.

Birds, Marine Life — A302

150 le, Powder blue surgeon. 250 le, Frilled anemone. 600 le, Red beard sponge. 800 le, Red-finned batfish.

No. 2160, each 400 le: a, Eastern reef egret. b, Dolphins. c, Sailing ship, Humpback whale. d, Red and green macaw. e, Blue tangs. f, Guitarfish. g, Manatees. h, Hammerhead shark. i, Blue shark. j, Lemon goby, moorish idol. k, Ribbon eels. l, Loggerhead turtle.

Sharks — #2161, each 500 le: a, Blue shark. b, Tiger shark. c, Bull shark. d, Great white. e, Scalloped hammerhead. f, Oceanic whitetip. g, Zebra shark. h, Leopard shark. i, Horn shark.

Dolphins, whales — #2162, each 500 le: a, Hector's dolphin. b, Tucuxi. c, Hourglass dolphin. d, Bottlenose dolphin. e, Gray's beaked whale. f, Bowhead whale. g, Fin whale. h, Gray whale. i, Blue whale.

Each 3000 le: No. 2163, Purple firefish. No. 2164, Spotted eagle ray. No. 2165, Leatherback turtle.

1999, Feb. 22 *Perf. 14*

2156-2159 A302 Set of 4 3.75 3.75
2160 A302 Sheet of 12, #a.-l. 9.50 9.50

Sheets of 9, #a.-i.

2161-2162 A302 Set of 2 18.00 18.00

Souvenir Sheets

2163-2165 A302 Set of 3 24.00 24.00

Intl. Year of the Ocean (#2160-2162, #2164-2165).

Airplanes A303

200 le, Grumman X-29. 300 le, Rocket-powered Bell X-1. 400 le, MiG-21 Fishbed, 1956, USSR. 600 le, Blériot X1 Monoplane, 1909. 800 le, Southern Cross, Fokker F.VII, 1928. 1500 le, Supermarine S.6B.

No. 2172, each 600 le: a, Grumman F3F-1, 1940. b, North American F-86A Sabre Jet, 1949. c, Cessna 377 Super Skymaster. d, F-16 Fighting Falcon, 1973. e, Voyager, Experimental Aircraft, Dick Rutan, Jeana Yeager. f, Fairchild A10A Thunderbolt II, 1975. g, Lockheed Vega, 1933. h, Lockheed Vega, 1930.

No. 2173, each 600 le: a, Sopwith Tabloid, 1914, UK. b, Vickers F.B.5 Gun Bus, 1915. c, Savoia Marchetti S.M. 79-II Sparviero, 1940. d, Mitsubishi A6M3 Zero Sen, 1942. e, Morane-Saulnier L, 1915. f, Shorts 360. g, Tupolev TU-160, 1988. h, Mikoyan-Gurevich MiG-15, 1948.

No. 2174, each 600 le: a, Nieuport 11C. 1, 1915. b, D.H. Vampire N.F. 10, 1951. c, Aerospatiale-Aeritalia ATR 72. d, Fiat CR.32, 1933. e, Curtiss P-6E Hawk, 1932. f, Saab JA 37 Viggen, 1977. g, Piper Pa-46 Malibu. h, F-14 Tomcat.

Each 3000 le: No. 2175, Spirit of St. Louis. No. 2176, Canadair CL-215.

1999, Mar. 22 Litho. *Perf. 14*

2166-2171 A303 Set of 6 6.00 6.00

Sheets of 8, #a.-h.

2172-2174 A303 Set of 3 26.00 26.00

Souvenir Sheets

2175-2176 A303 Set of 2 13.00 13.00

Australia '99 World Stamp Expo A304

Flowers: 150 le, Geranium wallchianum. 200 le, Osmanthus x burkwoodu. 250 le, Iris pallida, vert. 500 le, Rhododendron, vert. 600 le, Rose, vert. 800 le, Papoose, vert. 1500 le, Viola labradorica, vert. 2000 le, Rosa banksiae, vert.

No. 2185, each 600 le: a, Jack snipe. b, Alstroemeria ligtu. c, Lilium (yellow). d, Marjorie fair. e, Aemone coranaria. f, Clematis ranncu.

No. 2186, each 600 le: a, Aquilegiaa olympica. b, Lilium (orange). c, Magnolia grandiflora. d, Polygonatum x hybridum. e, Clematis montana. f, Vinca minor.

No. 2187, each 600 le: a, Colchicum speciosum. b, Scandere. c, Helianthus annuus. d, Lady Kerkrade. e, Clematix x durandil. f, Lilium regale.

No. 2188, each 600 le, vert.: a, Clematis hybrida. b, Cardiospermum halicacabum. c, Fritillaria imperialis. d, Iris ibetidiisima. e, Pyracantina. f, Hepatica transsilvanica.

Each 4000 le: No. 2189, Clerodendrum trichotomum. No. 2190, Holboellia. No. 2191, Crocus angustifolius, vert. No. 2192, Rubus fruitcosus, vert.

1999, Apr. 14

2177-2184 A304 Set of 8 9.00 9.00

Sheets of 6, #a-f

2185-2188 A304 Set of 4 23.00 23.00

Souvenir Sheets

2189-2192 A304 Set of 4 27.00 27.00

Birds — A305

No. 2193, each 600 le: a, Cattle egret. b, White-fronted bee-eater. c, African gray parrot. d, Cinnamon-chested bee-eater. e, Malachite kingfisher. f, White-throated bee-eater. g, Yellow-billed stork. h, Hildebrandt's starling.

No. 2194, each 600 le: a, Great white pelican. b, Superb starling. c, Red-throated bee-eater. d, Woodland kingfisher. e, Purple swamphen. f, Pied kingfisher. g, African spoonbill. h, Crocodile bird.

Each 3000 le: No. 2195, African fish-eagle. No. 2196, Richenow's weaver.

1999, May 18 Litho. *Perf. 14*

Sheets of 8, #a.-h.

2193-2194 A305 Set of 2 19.00 19.00

Souvenir Sheets

2195-2196 A305 Set of 2 12.00 12.00

For surcharge see No. 2902.

Fauna — A306

Designs: 300 le, Diana monkey. 400 le, Red-vented malimbe. 500 le, Eurasian kestrel. 600 le, Little owl. 800 le, Bush pig. 1500 le, Lion.

No. 2203, each 900 le: a, Flap-necked chameleon. b, Golden oriole (c). c, Europeon bee-eater. d, Leopard. e, Lion (d). f, Chimpanzee (e).

No. 2204, each 900 le: a, Senagal galago. b, Hoopoe. c, Long-tailed pangolin (f). d, Hippopotamus. e, African elephant (d). f, Red-billed hornbill.

Each 3000 le: No. 2205, West African linsang. No. 2206, Gray parrot.

1999, May 31 Litho.

2197-2202 A306 Set of 6 9.00 9.00

Sheets of 6, #a-f

2203-2204 A306 Set of 2 19.00 19.00

Souvenir Sheets

2205-2206 A306 Set of 2 13.50 13.50

Queen Mother (b. 1900) — A307

No. 2207, each 1300 le: a, With Duke of York and Princess Elizabeth, 1926. b, In 1979. c, In Nairobi, 1959. d, In 1991.

4000 le, With crown, 1937.

1999, Aug. 4 Litho. *Perf. 14*

Gold Frames

2207 A307 Sheet of 4, #a.-d. + label 10.00 10.00

Souvenir Sheet

Perf. 13½

2208 A307 4000 le multi 9.00 9.00

No. 2208 contains one 38x51mm stamp.

See Nos. 2512-2513.

Trains — A308

Designs: 100 le, Rocket. 150 le, Benguela Railway, horiz. 200 le, Sudan Railways 310 2-8-2, horiz. 250 le, Chicago, Burlington & Quincy Railroad, horiz. 300 le, Terrier, horiz. 400 le, Dublin-Cork Express, horiz. 500 le, George Stephenson, horiz. 600 le, Shay, horiz. 1500 le, South Wind, horiz.

No. 2218, each 800 le, horiz.: a, American. b, Flying Scotsman. c, Lord Nelson. d, Mallard. e, Evening Star. f, Britannia.

No. 2219, each 800 le, horiz.: a, Class 19D 4-8-2. b, Double-headed train. c, Egyptian Railways Bo-Bo. d, GMAM Garratt 4-8-2+2-8-4. e, Passenger train, Rabat. f, Rhodesian Railway 14A Class 2-2 Garratt.

Each 3000 le: No. 2220, Mountain Class Garratt. No. 2221, Royal train.

1999, Aug. 4 *Perf. 14*

2209-2217 A308 Set of 9 6.50 6.50

Sheets of 6, #a-f

2218-2219 A308 Set of 2 16.00 16.00

Souvenir Sheets

2220-2221 A308 Set of 2 12.00 12.00

Inscription on No. 2218f is misspelled.

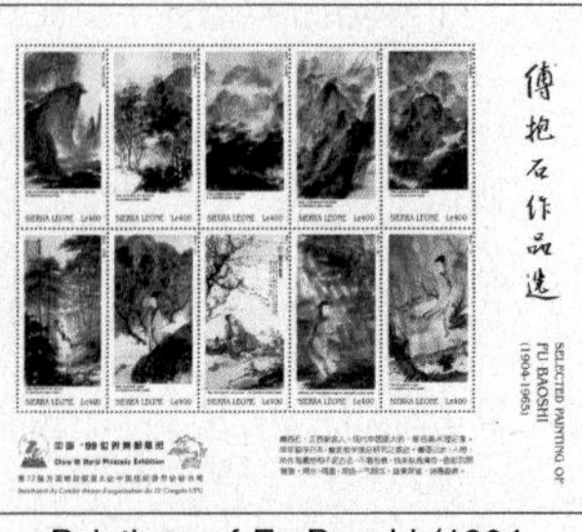

Paintings of Fu Baoshi (1904-65) — A309

No. 2222: a, Interpretation of a Poem of Shi-Tao. b, Autumn of Ho-Pao. c, Landscape in Rain (bridge). d, Landscape in Rain, diff. e, Landscape in Rain (house on mountain). f, Portrait of To-Fu. g, Classic Lady (trees with leaves). h, Portrait of Li-Pai. i, Sprite of the Mountain. j, Classic Lady (bare trees).

No. 2223: a, 800 le, Four Seasons — Winter, horiz. b, 1500 le, Four Seasons — Summer, horiz.

1999, Aug. 4 *Perf. 12¾*

2222 A309 400 le Sheet of 10, #a.-j. 9.00 9.00

Perf. 13

2223 A309 Sheet of 2, #a.-b. 7.25 7.25

China 1999 World Philatelic Exhibition. No. 2223 contains 51x38mm stamps.

1999 Return of Macao to People's Republic of China — A310

1999, Aug. 4 *Perf. 14*

2224 A310 1200 le multi 3.75 3.75

China 1999 World Philatelic Exhibition. Issued in sheets of 3 stamps.

Hokusai Paintings — A311

No. 2225, each 1000 le: a, Hanging Cloud Bridge. b, Timber Yard by the Tate River. c, Bird Drawings (owl). d, As "c," (ducks). e, Travelers Crossing the Oi River. f, Travelers on the Tokaido Road at Hodogaya.

No. 2226, each 1000 le: a, People Admiring Mount Fuji from a Tea House. b, People on a Temple Balcony. c, Sea Life (crustacean). d, Sea Life (clam). e, Pontoon Bridge at Sano in Winter. f, A Shower Below the Summit.

Each 3000 le: No. 2227, A View of Mount Fuji and Travelers by a Bridge, vert. No. 2228, A Sudden Gust of Wind at Eijiri, vert.

1999, Aug. 4 *Perf. 13¾*

Sheets of 6, #a.-f.

2225-2226 A311 Set of 2 17.00 17.00
2227-2228 A311 Set of 2 11.00 11.00

Johann Wolfgang von Goethe (1749-1832), German Poet — A312

No. 2229: a, Witch besieges faust. b, Goethe and Friedrich von Schiller. c, Margaret places flowers before the niche of Mater Dolorosa.

No. 2230: a, Helena with her chorus. b, Faust takes a seat beside Helena.

Each 3000 le: #2231, Angelic spirit. #2232, Ariel, vert.

1999, Aug. 4 Sheets of 3 *Perf. 14*

2229 A312 1600 le #a.-c. 8.00 8.00
2230 A312 1600 le #a.-b, 2229b 8.00 8.00

Souvenir Sheets

2231-2232 A312 Set of 2 12.00 12.00

Souvenir Sheets

PhilexFrance '99 — A313

Designs, each 3000 le: No. 2233, Crampton locomotive. No. 2234, De Glehn compound with Lemaitre front end 4-4-2.

1999, Aug. 4 *Perf. 13¾*

2233-2234 A313 Set of 2 11.00 11.00

IBRA '99 — A314

1999 *Perf. 14x14½*

2235 A314 1500 le Class 4-4-0 3.50 3.50
2236 A314 2000 le Class 05 4.50 4.50

Rights of the Child — A315

No. 2237: a, Girl holding candle. b, Two children. c, Girl, diff.

2000 le, Child, horiz.

1999, Aug. 4 Litho. *Perf. 14*

2237 A315 1600 le Sheet of 3, #a.-c. 9.00 9.00

Souvenir Sheet

2238 A315 3000 le multi 7.50 7.50

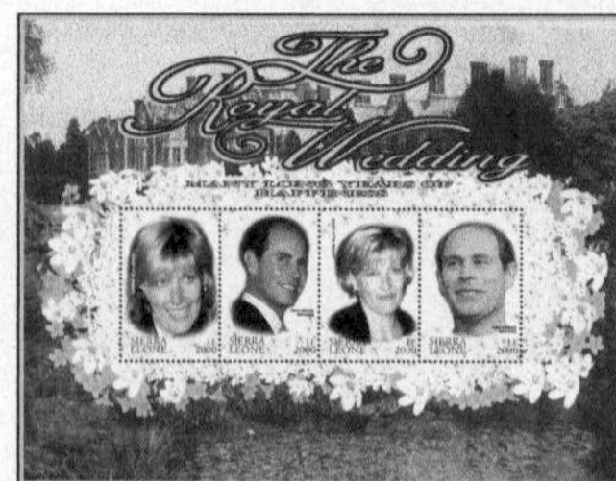

Wedding of Prince Edward and Sophie Rhys-Jones — A316

No. 2239: a, Sophie, close-up. b, Edward (shirt and tie). c, Sophie, diff. d, edward, diff.

4000 le, Couple.

1999, Aug. 4 *Perf. 13¾x13¼*

2239 A316 2000 le Sheet of 4, #a.-d. 10.00 10.00

Souvenir Sheet

Perf. 13¼x13¾

2240 A316 4000 le multi 10.00 10.00

Birds of Africa — A317

No. 2241, each 600 le: a, African paradise monarch. b, Lilac-breasted roller. c, Common Scops owl. d, African emerald cuckoo. e, Blue monarch. f, African golden oriole. g, White-throated bee eater. h, Black-bellied seed-cracker. i, Hoopoe.

No. 2242, each 600 le: a, White-faced whistling duck. b, Black-headed heron. c, Black-headed gonolek. d, Malachite king-fisher. e, Fish eagle. f, African spoonbill. g, African skimmer. h, Black heron. i, Allen's gallinule.

No. 2243, each 600 le: a, Scimitarbill. b, Bateleur. c, Black-headed weaver. d, Variable sunbird. e, Blue swallow. f, Black-winged red bishop. g, Namaqua dove. h, Golden-breasted bunting. i, Hartlaub's bustard.

No. 2244, each 600 le: a, Montagu's harrier. b, Booted eagle. c, Yellow crested helmet-shrike. d, Scarlet-tufted malachite sunbird. e, Pin-tailed whydah. f, Red-headed malimbe. g, Western violet-backed sunbird. h, Yellow white eye. i, Brubru.

Each 4000 le: No. 2245, Rwenzori turaco, vert. No. 2246, African pygmy kingfisher, vert. No. 2247, Gray crowned crane, vert. No. 2248, Shoebill, vert.

1999 Litho. *Perf. 14*

Sheets of 9, #a.-i.

2241-2244 A317 Set of 4 32.50 32.50

Souvenir Sheets

2245-2248 A317 Set of 4 24.00 24.00

For surcharge see No. 2905.

New Year 2000 (Year of the Dragon) — A318

No. 2249 (dragon color): a, Brown red. b, Blue green. c, Bright red. d, Lilac.

4000 le, Red dragon, vert.

2000, Feb. 5 Litho. *Perf. 14*

2249 A318 1500 le Sheet of 4, #a.-d. 8.00 8.00

Souvenir Sheet

2250 A318 4000 le multi 7.50 7.50

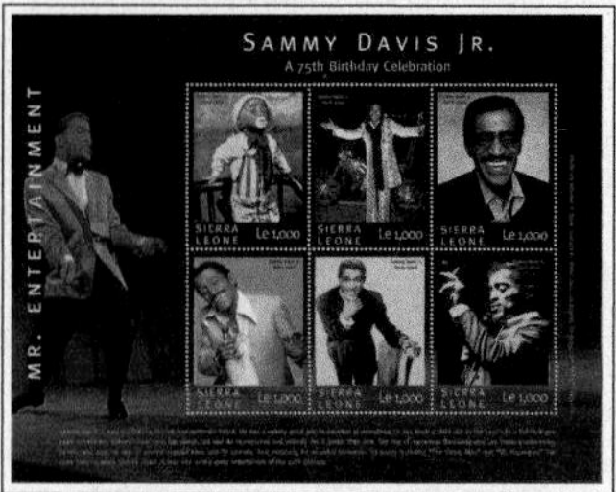

Sammy Davis, Jr. — A319

No. 2251: a, As child. b, With motorcycle. c, With red checked shirt. d, With microphone. e, With leg on chair. f, Holding cigarette.

5000 le, With other people.

2000, Mar. 8 *Perf. 13¾*

2251 A319 1000 le Sheet of 6, #a.-f. 5.75 5.75

Souvenir Sheet

2252 A319 5000 le multi 4.75 4.75

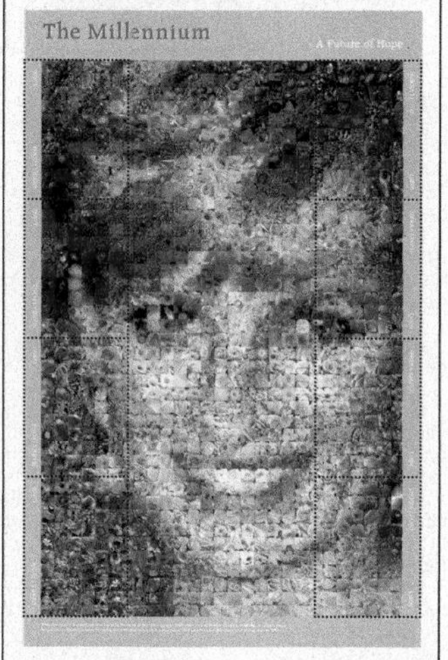

Flowers — A320

Various flowers making up a photomosaic of Princess Diana.

2000, Mar. 28

2253 A320 800 le Sheet of 8, #a.-h. 6.50 6.50

See Nos. 2359-2360.

Millennium — A321

Highlights of 1600-1650: a, Election of Michael Romanov as Russian tsar. b, William Shakespeare publishes "Hamlet." c, Kung Hsien paints "Thousand Peaks and Myriad Ravines." d, Francis Bacon publishes his works. e, Founding of Jamestown, Virginia. f, Reign of Louis XIV of France. g, Founding of Quebec. h, Birth of Isaac Newton. i, Nicholas Poussin paints "Rape of the Sabine Women." j, Johannes Kepler publishes "The New Astronomy." k, The Mayflower arrives in America. l, King James Bible is published. m, Dutch East India Company introduces tea to Europe. n, René Descartes develops his philosophy. o, Galileo defends Copernican system. p, Queen Elizabeth I dies (60x40mm). q, Miguel de Cervantes publishes "Don Quixote."

2000, Mar. 28 *Perf. 12¾x12½*

2254 A321 400 le Sheet of 17, #a.-q., + label 6.50 6.50

Paintings of Anthony Van Dyck — A322

No. 2255, each 1000 le: a, Portrait of a Man. b, Anna Wake, Wife of Peter Stevens. c, Peter Stevens. d, Adriaen Stevens. e, Maria Bosschaerts, Wife of Adriaen Stevens. f, Portrait of a Woman.

No. 2256, each 1000 le: a, Self-portrait, 1617-18. b, Self-portrait, 1620-21. c, Self-portrait, 1622-23. d, Andromeda Chained to the Rock. e, Self-portrait, late 1620s-early 1630s. f, Mary Ruthven.

No. 2257, each 1000 le: a, The Betrayal of Judas (detail of The Taking of Christ.) b, Ecce Homo, 1625-26. c, Christ Carrying the Cross (showing woman with blue garment). d, The Raising of Christ on the Cross. e, The Crucifixion, c. 1627 f, The Lamentation, c. 1616 (actually the "Mocking of Christ").

No. 2258, each 1000 le: a, The Taking of Christ. b, The Mocking of Christ. c, Ecce Homo, 1628-32. d, Christ Carrying the Cross (showing poleax). e, The Crucifixion, c. 1629-30. f, The Lamentation 1618-20.

No. 2258G, each 1000 le: h, The Duchess of Crow With Her Son. i, Susanna Fourment and Her Daughter. j, Geronima Brignole-Sale With Her Daughter Maria Aurelia. k, A Woman With Her Daughter. l, A Genoese Noblewoman With Her Child. m, A Genoese Noblewoman (Paola Adorno) and Her Son.

Each 5000 le: No. 2259, Self-portrait With a Sunflower. No. 2260, Self-portrait with Endymion Porter. No. 2261, Young Woman With a Child. No. 2262, Porzia Imperiale With Her Daughter Maria Francesca. No. 2263, Portrait of a Mother and Her Daughter. No. 2264, A Woman and a Child, horiz.

2000, Apr. 10 *Perf. 13¾*

Sheets of 6, #a.-f.

2255-2258G A322 Set of 5 29.00 29.00

Souvenir Sheets

2259-2264 A322 Set of 6 29.00 29.00

Easter (Nos. 2257-2258).

Mario Andretti — A323

No. 2265: a, Behind wheel. b, With helmet, facing left. c, In pits. d, In crash. e, Inspecting tire. f, With white shirt. g, Without shirt. h, In car #50.

5000 le, With others in front of old car.

2000, Mar. 28 Litho. *Perf. 13¾*

2265 A323 600 le Sheet of 8, #a-h 5.00 5.00

Souvenir Sheet

2266 A323 5000 le multi 5.00 5.00

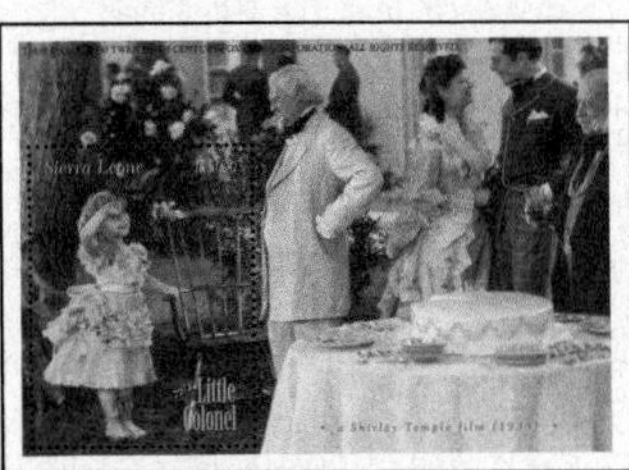

Scenes from "The Little Colonel" with Shirley Temple — A324

Temple — No. 2267: a, With Colonel Lloyd (Lionel Barrymore), standing. b, With Walker (Bill Robinson). c, With two children. d, With soldiers. e, With mother (Evelyn Venable), Becky (Hattie McDaniel). f, Hugging Colonel Lloyd.

No. 2268: a, With Becky and Walker. b, With Walker, diff. c, Alone. d, Tugging Colonel Lloyd's coat.

No. 2269, Holding chair.

2000, Mar. 28 Sheets of 6 and 4

2267 A324 1200 le #a-f 7.50 7.50

2268 A324 1500 le #a-d 6.25 6.25

Souvenir Sheet

2269 A324 5000 le multi 5.00 5.00

See also Nos. 2550-2552.

Parrots — A325

Designs: 200 le, African gray parrot. 1500 le, Sulfur-crested cockatoo, horiz.

No. 2272, each 800 le: a, Monk parakeet. b, Citron-crested cockatoo. c, Queen-of-Bavaria conure. d, Budgerigar. e, Yellow-chevroned parakeet. f, Cockatiel. g, Amazon parrot. h, Sun conure. i, Malabar parakeet.

No. 2273, each 800 le: a, Grand eclectus parrot. b, Sun parakeet. c, Red fan parakeet. d, Fischer's lovebird. e, Blue masked lovebird. f, White belly rosella. g, Plum-headed parakeet. h, Striated lorikeet. i, Gold-mantled rosella.

4000 le, Blue and gold macaw.

2000, May 16 *Perf. 13¾x14, 14x13¾*

2270-2271 A325 Set of 2 1.90 1.90

Sheets of 9, #a-i

2272-2273 A325 Set of 2 16.00 16.00

Souvenir Sheet

2274 A325 multi 4.50 4.50

The Stamp Show 2000, London (Nos. 2272-2274). Size of stamps: Nos. 2272-2273, 28x42mm; No. 2274, 38x50mm.

Orchids A326

Designs: 300 le, Aeranthes henrici. 500 le, Ophrys apifera. 600 le, Disa crassicornis. 2000 le, Aeranthes grandiflora.

No. 2279, each 1100 le: a, Oeleoclades maculata. b, Polystachya campyloglossa. c, Polystachya pubescens. d, Tridactyle bicaudata. e, Angraecum veitcii. f, Sobennikoffia robusta.

No. 2280, each 1100 le: a, Aerangis curnowiana. b, Aerangis fastudsa. c, Angraecum magdalenae. d, Angraecum sororium. e, Eulophia speciosa. f, Ansellia africana.

Each 4000 le: No. 2281, Angraecum compactum. No. 2282, Angraecum eburneum.

2000, May 16 *Perf. 14*

2275-2278 A326 Set of 4 3.75 3.75

Sheets of 6, #a-f

2279-2280 A326 Set of 2 15.00 15.00

Souvenir Sheets

2281-2282 A326 Set of 2 9.00 9.00

Prince William, 18th Birthday — A327

Various photos.

2000, May 29 *Perf. 14*

2283 A327 1100 le Sheet of 4, #a-d 5.00 5.00

Souvenir Sheet

Perf. 13¾

2284 A327 5000 le multi 5.50 5.50

No. 2284 contains one 38x50mm stamp.

Souvenir Sheet

2000 Summer Olympics, Sydney — A328

Designs: a, Hurdler. b, Soccer player. c, Finnish flag, Helsinki Stadium. d, Ancient Greek wrestlers.

2000, May 29 *Perf. 14*

2285 A328 1500 le Sheet of 4, #a-d 6.25 6.25

First Zeppelin Flight, Cent. — A329

No. 2286: a, LZ-129. b, LZ-4. c, LZ-6. 4000 le, LZ-127.

2000, May 29 *Perf. 14*

2286 A329 2000 le Sheet of 3, #a-c 6.25 6.25

Souvenir Sheet

Perf. 14¼

2287 A329 4000 le multi 4.25 4.25

Size of stamps: No. 2286, 38x24mm.

Betty Boop — A330

No. 2288: a, Wearing flowered dress. b, Carrying shopping bags. c, Wearing baseball cap. d, Holding shoes. e, Sitting in chair. f, Wearing jacket. g, Playing guitar. h, Holding lasso. i, Holding flower.

Each 5000 le: No. 2289, Pointing at dog. No. 2290, Riding bicycle.

2000, Mar. 8 Litho. *Perf. 13¾*

2288 A330 800 le Sheet of 9, #a-i 8.25 8.25

Souvenir Sheets

2289-2290 A330 Set of 2 11.50 11.50

I Love Lucy — A331

No. 2291, each 800 le — Lucy: a, Wearing blue cap. b, With arms in front, with Vitameatavegamin bottle. c, Wearing pink nightgown. d, Wearing pink nightgown, sticking out tongue. e, Wearing blue cap on television screen. f, Holding bottle near table. g, With arms at side, with bottle. h, Holding bottle near cheek. i, Pouring out liquid in bottle.

Each 5000 le: No. 2292, Wearing blue cap on television, Ricky touching television. No. 2293, Lucy and Fred Mertz.

2000, Mar. 8

2291 A331 Sheet of 9, #a-i 8.25 8.25

Souvenir Sheets

2292-2293 A331 Set of 2 11.50 11.50

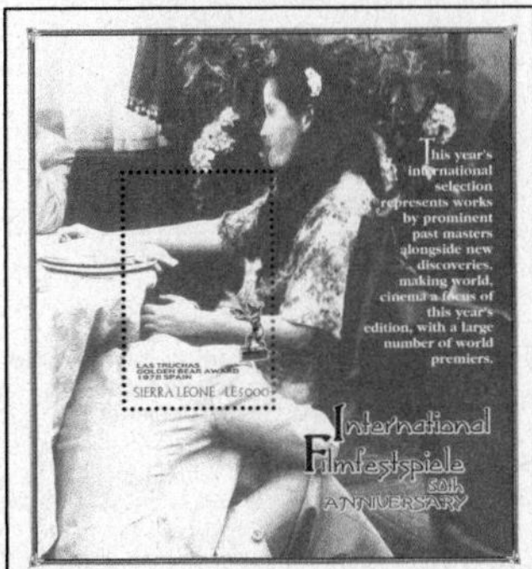

Berlin Film Festival, 50th Anniv. — A332

No. 2294, each 1100 le: a, Las Palabras de Max. b, Ascendancy. c, Deprisa, Deprisa. d, Die Sehnsucht der Veronika Voss. e, Heartland. f, La Colmena.

5000 le, Las Truchas.

2000, May 29 *Perf. 14*

2294 A332 Sheet of 6, #a-f 7.50 7.50

Souvenir Sheet

2295 A332 5000 le multi 5.75 5.75

Souvenir Sheet

Public Railways, 175th Anniv. — A333

No. 2296, each 3000 le: a, Locomotion No. 1, George Stephenson. b, James Watt's original design for a separate condenser engine.

2000, May 29

2296 A333 Sheet of 2, #a-b 7.00 7.00

Souvenir Sheet

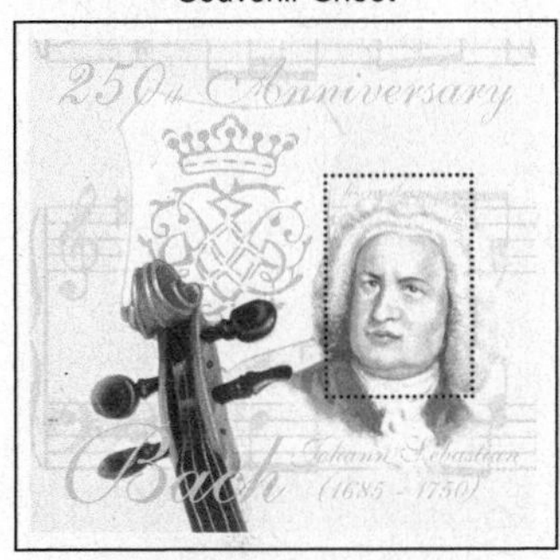

Johann Sebastian Bach (1685-1750) — A334

2000, May 29

2297 A334 5000 le multi 5.75 5.75

Sea Birds A335

Designs: 400 le, Herring gull. 600 le, Caspian tern. 800 le, Red phalarope. 2000 le, Magnificent frigatebird.

No. 2302, each 1000 le: a, Caspian tern, diff. b, Glaucous gull. c, Northern gannet. d, Long-tailed jaeger. e, Brown pelican. f, Great skua.

No. 2303, each 1000 le: a, Wandering albatross. b, Fork-tailed storm petrel. c, Great shearwater. d, Blue-footed booby. e, Great cormorant. f, Atlantic puffin.

Each 5000 le: No. 2304, Brown booby, vert. No. 2305, Red-tailed tropicbird, vert.

2000, May 16 Litho. *Perf. 14*

2298-2301 A335 Set of 4 3.75 3.75

Sheets of 6, #a-f

2302-2303 A335 Set of 2 12.00 12.00

Souvenir Sheets

2304-2305 A335 Set of 2 10.00 10.00

Richard Petty, Stock Car Racer — A336

No. 2306, each 800 le: a, Car in pits. b, With family. c, Wearing red jacket. d, Wearing Pontiac cap. e, Wearing white hat, uniform with two STP logos. f, Wearing STP cap. g, Standing in car. h, Profile, wearing STP logos on shoulder. i, Wearing headphones.

No. 2307, each 800 le: a, Holding trophy. b, Wearing Winston cap. c, Wearing black hat. d, Hatless, blue background. e, Wearing shirt with red collar. f, Holding helmet. g, Leaning on blue and red car. h, With arm in car. i, Leaning head out of car.

No. 2308, each 800 le: a, Wearing red shirt, white hat. b, Hatless, orange background. c, Wearing Pontiac cap. d, Strapped in car, without helmet. e, Holding timer. f, Wearing red and blue helmet. g, Wearing white hat, blue uniform. h, With trophy, wearing STP cap. i, With white hat, reclining.

Each 5000 le: No. 2309, Standing in car, diff. No, 2310, In race, horiz.

2000, Aug. 15 ***Perf. 13¾***

Sheets of 9, #a-i

2306-2308 A336 Set of 3 21.00 21.00

Souvenir Sheets

2309-2310 A336 Set of 2 10.00 10.00

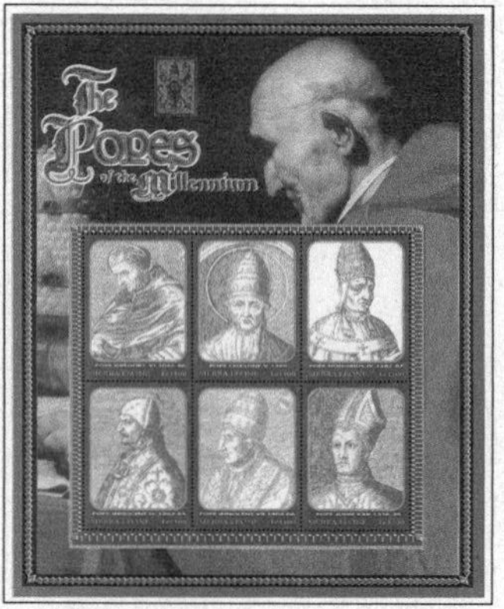

Popes — A337

No. 2311, each 1100 le: a, Gregory VI (1045-46). b, Celestine V (1294). c, Honorius IV (1285-87). d, Innocent IV (1243-54). e, Innocent VII (1404-06). f, John XXII (1316-34).

No. 2312, each 1100 le: a, Martin IV (1281-85). b, Nicholas II (1059-61). c, Nicholas IV (1288-92). d, Urban IV (1261-64). e, Urban V (1362-70). f, Urban VI (1378-89).

Each 5000 le: No. 2313, Nicholas IV (1288-92), diff. No. 2314, Clement XI (1700-21).

2000, Aug. 21 **Sheets of 6, #a-f**

2311-2312 A337 Set of 2 13.00 13.00

Souvenir Sheets

2313-2314 A337 Set of 2 10.00 10.00

Monarchs — A338

No. 2315, each 1100 le: a, Emperor Hung Wu of China. b, Emperor Hsuan Te of China. c, King Sejong of Korea. d, Emperor T'ung Chih of China. e, Emperor T'ai Tsu (Chao K'uang-yin) of Chin. f, Empress Yung Ching of China.

No. 2316, Kublai Khan of China.

2000, Aug. 21

2315 A338 Sheet of 6, #a-f 6.50 6.50

Souvenir Sheet

2316 A338 5000 le multi 5.00 5.00

European Soccer Championships — A339

No. 2317, each 1300 le — Germany: a, Worns. b, Team photo. c, Babbel. d, Franz Beckenbauer. e, Selessin Stadium, Liege, Belgium. f, Stefan Kuntz.

No. 2318, each 1300 le — Italy: a, Walter Zenga. b, Team photo. c, Roberto Bettega. d, Totti. e, Philips Stadium, Eindhoven, Netherlands. f, Vieri.

No. 2319, each 1300 le — Portugal: a, Dimas. b, Team photo. c, Pinto. d, Santos. e, Gelredome Stadium, Arnhem, Netherlands. f, Sousa.

No. 2320, each 1300 le — Romania: a, Munteanu. b, Team photo. c, Petre. d, Petrescu. e, Popescu.

Each 5000 le: No. 2321, German coach Erich Ribbeck, vert. No. 2322, Italian coach Dino Zoff, vert. No. 2323, Portuguese coach Humberto Coelho, vert. No. 2324, Romanian coach Emerich Jenei, vert.

Sheets of 6, #a-f (#2317-2319); Sheet of 6 #a-e, #2319e (#2320)

2000, Aug. 21

2317-2320 A339 Set of 4 30.00 30.00

Souvenir Sheets

2321-2324 A339 Set of 4 20.00 20.00

Souvenir Sheet

Albert Einstein (1879-1955) — A340

2000, May 29 **Litho.** ***Perf. 14***

2325 A340 5000 le multi 5.00 5.00

Apollo-Soyuz Mission, 25th Anniv. — A341

No. 2326, each 1200 le, vert.: a, Apollo 18. b, Soyuz 19. c, Apollo and Soyuz docked.

5000 le, Apollo and Soyuz docking.

2000, May 29

2326 A341 Sheet of 3, #a-c 3.50 3.50

Souvenir Sheet

2327 A341 5000 le multi 5.00 5.00

Queen Mother, 100th Birthday — A342

Litho. & Embossed

2000, Aug. 4 ***Die Cut Perf. 8¾***

Without Gum

2328 A342 18,000 le gold & multi

Dogs and Cats A343

500 le, Bulldog. 800 le, Brown tabby. 1500 le, Burmese. 2000 le, Dachshund.

No. 2333, 1000 le: a, Beagle. b, Scottish terrier. c, Bloodhound. d, Greyhound. e, German shepherd. f, Cocker spaniel.

No. 2334, 1000 le: a, Red tabby stumpy Manx. b, Red self. c, Maine Coon cat. d, Black smoke. e, Chinchilla. f, Russian Blue.

No. 2335, 1100 le: a, Pointer. b, Doberman pinscher. c, Collie. d, Chihuahua. e, Afghan hound. f, Boxer.

No. 2336, 1100 le: a, Singapura. b, Himalayan. c, Abyssinian. d, Black cat. e, Siamese. f, North African wild cat.

No. 2337, 5000 le, Fox terrier, vert. No. 2338, 5000 le, Calico, vert.

2000, Oct. 2 **Litho.** ***Perf. 14***

2329-2332 A343 Set of 4 5.00 5.00

Sheets of 6, #a-f

2333-2336 A343 Set of 4 26.00 26.00

Souvenir Sheets

2337-2338 A343 Set of 2 10.50 10.50

Paintings from the Prado — A344

No. 2339, 1000 le: a, The Transport of Mary Magdalen, by José Antolinez. b, The Holy Family, by Francisco de Goya. c, Our Lady of the Immaculate Conception, by Antolinez. d, Charles IV as Prince, by Anton Raphael Mengs. e, Louis XIII of France, by Philippe de Champaigne. f, Prince Ferdinand VI by Jean Ranc.

No. 2340, 1000 le: a, Adam, by Albrecht Dürer. b, Moor, by Manuel Benedito Vives. c, Eve, by Dürer. d, A Gypsy, by Raimundo Madrazo y Garreta. e, Maria Guerrero, by Joaquin Sorolla y Bastida. f, The Model Aline Masson with a White Mantilla, by Madrazo y Garreta.

No. 2341, 1000 le: a, Figure in yellow robe from Madonna and Child Between Saints Catherine and Ursula, by Giovanni Bellini. b, Madonna and Child from Madonna and Child Between Saints Catherine and Ursula. c, Figure in red robe from Madonna and Child Between Saints Catherine and Ursula. d, Giovanni Mateo Ghiberti, by Bernardino India. e, The Marchioness of Santa Cruz, by Agustín Esteve. f, Self-portrait, by Orazio Borgianni.

No. 2342, 1000 le: a, Mary from The Holy Family with a Bird, by Bartolomé Esteban Murillo. b, Jesus from The Holy Family with a Bird. c, Joseph, from The Holy Family with a Bird. d, Cardinal Carlos de Borja, by Andrea Procaccini. e, St. Dominic de Guzmán, by Claudio Coello. f, Christ Supported by an Angel, by Alonso Cano.

No. 2343, 1000 le: a, Woman from The Seller of Fans, by José del Castillo. b, Allegory of Summer, by Mariano Salvador Maella. c, Man with basket from The Seller of Fans. d, Portrait of a Girl, by Carlos Luis de Ribera y Fieve. e, The Poultry Keeper, by Pensionante del Saraceni. f, The Death of Cleopatra, by Guido Reni.

No. 2344, 1000 le; a, Feliciana Bayeu, by Francisco Bayeu y Subias. b, Tomás de Iriarte by Joaquin Inza. c, St. Elizabeth of Portugal, by Francisco de Zurbarán. d, Christ from The Vision of St. Francis at Porziuncola, by Murillo. e, Monk from The Vision of St. Francis at Porziuncola. f, Woman from The Vision of St. Francis at Porziuncola.

No. 2345, 5000 le, Lot and His Daughters, by Francesco Furini. No. 2346, 5000 le, The Execution of Torrijos and His Companions, by Antonio Gisbert Pérez. No. 2347, 5000 le, the Concert, by Vicente Palmaroli y González. No. 2348, 5000 le, The Finding of Joseph's Cup in Benjamin's Bag, by Jacopo Amigoni. No. 2349, 5000 le, Vulcan's Forge, by Diego Velázquez. No. 2350, 5000 le, The Two Friends, by Joaquin Agrasot y Juan, horiz.

2000, Oct. 6 ***Perf. 12x12¼, 12¼x12***

Sheets of 6, #a-f

2339-2344 A344 Set of 6 37.50 37.50

Souvenir Sheets

2345-2350 A344 Set of 6 32.50 32.50

Espana 2000 Intl. Philatelic Exhibition.

Mushrooms — A345

Designs: 600 le, Tuberous polyphore. 900 le, Cultivated agaricus. 1200 le, Scarlet wax cap. 2500 le, Blue-green psilocybe.

No. 2355, 1000 le, vert.: a, Armed stinkhorn. b, Red-staining inocybe. c, Amanitopsis vaginata. d, Inocybe jurana. e, Xerula longipes. f, Tricholoma matsutake.

No. 2356, 1000 le, vert.: a, Orange-staining mycena. b, Russula amoema. c, Cinnabar chanterelle. d, Calodon aurantiacum. e, Lentinus lepidus. f, Gomphidius roseus.

No. 2357, 5000 le, Orange latex lactarius. No. 2358, 5000 le, Common morel, vert.

2000, Oct. 30 **Litho.** ***Perf. 14***

2351-2354 A345 Set of 4 5.50 5.50

Sheets of 6, #a-f

2355-2356 A345 Set of 2 12.50 12.50

Souvenir Sheets

2357-2358 A345 Set of 2 10.50 10.50

Flower Photomosaic Type of 2000

No. 2359, 800 le: Various flowers making up a photomosaic of the Queen Mother.

No. 2360, 900 le: Various photographs of religious scenes making up a photomosaic of Pope John Paul II.

2000, Oct. 30 ***Perf. 13¾***

Sheets of 8, #a-h

2359-2360 A320 Set of 2 14.50 14.50

Massacre of Israeli Olympic Athletes, 1972 — A346

No. 2361, horiz.: a, Kahat Shor. b, Andrei Schpitzer. c, Joseph Romano. d, Yaakov Springer. e, Eliazer Halffin. f, Amitsur Shapira. g, Moshe Weinberg. h, Mark Slavin. i, Torchbearer, Israeli flag. j, Joseph Gottfreund. k, Ze'ev Friedman. l, David Berger.

2000, Nov. 9 ***Perf. 14***

2361 A346 500 le Sheet of 12, #a-l 6.25 6.25

Souvenir Sheet

2362 A346 5000 le Torchbearer 5.25 5.25

Circus A347

Designs: 800 le, Tightrope rider. 1000 le, Bear and ball. 1500 le, Tiger on ball. 2000 le, Camels.

No. 2367, 1100 le: a, Polar bear on roller. b, Ape. c, Clown, green background. d, Tightrope walker. e, Seals. f, Camel.

No. 2368, 1100 le: a, Clown, brown background. b, Tiger on wires. c, Monkey. d, Dogs. e, Bear on skates. f, Trapeze artists.

No. 2369, 1100 le, vert.: a, Acrobat. b, Giraffe. c, Bear on poles. d, Elephant. e, Horse. f, Fire eater.

No. 2370, 5000 le, Trainer on elephant's trunk, vert. No. 2371, 5000 le, Tiger jumping through flaming hoop, vert. No. 2372, 5000 le, Cannon flyer, vert.

2000, Dec. 1 **Litho.**

2363-2366 A347 Set of 4 5.75 5.75

Sheets of 6, #a-f

2367-2369 A347 Set of 3 21.00 21.00

Souvenir Sheets

2370-2372 A347 Set of 3 16.00 16.00

Queen Mother, 100th Birthday — A348

2000, Dec. 18

2373 A348 1100 le multi 1.10 1.10

Issued in sheets of 6.

New Year 2001 (Year of the Snake) — A349

No. 2374, horiz.: a, Blue snake. b, Red snake. c, Purple snake. d, Green snake.

2001, Jan. 2

2374 A349 800 le Sheet of 4, #a-d 3.50 3.50

Souvenir Sheet

2375 A349 2500 le Green snake 2.60 2.60

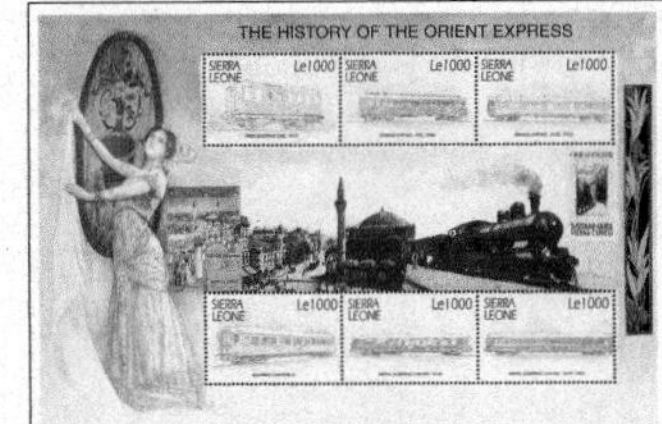

History of the Orient Express — A350

No. 2376, 1000 le: a, First sleeping car, 1872. b, Dining car #193, 1886. c, Dining car #2422, 1913. d, Sleeping car Type S1. e, Metal sleeping car #2645. f, Metal sleeping car #2644, 1922.

No. 2377, 1000 le: a, Dining car, Series #8341. b, Dining car, Series #3342. c, Sleeping car, Series #3312 Type Z. d, Sleeping car, Series #3879, 1950. e, Sleeping car, Series #3311 Type Z. f, Dining car, Series #3785, 1932.

No. 2378, 1100 le: a, Ostend-Vienna. b, Engine East 230, #3175. c, Dual cylinder locomotive. d, Simplon Orient Express, 1919. e, Engine East 220, #2405. f, Caboose of Simplon Express, c. 1906.

No. 2379, 1100 le: a, Sleeping car #507, 1897. b, Sleeping car #438, 1894. c, Sleeping car #313, 1880. d, Sleeping car #190, 1886. e, Sleeping car #102, 1882. f, Sleeping car #77, 1881.

No. 2380, 5000 le, Locomotive. No. 2381, 5000 le, Georges Nagelmackers, vert. No. 2382, 5000 le, Mata Hari, vert. No. 2383, 5000 le, Agatha Christie, vert.

2001, Jan. 15 ***Perf. 14***

Sheets of 6, #a-f

2376-2379 A350 Set of 4 26.00 26.00

Souvenir Sheets

2380-2383 A350 Set of 4 21.00 21.00

Reptiles A351

Designs: 250 le, Natal Mixands dwarf chameleon. 400 le, Cape cobra. 500 le, Western sand lizard. 600 le, Pan-hinged terrapin. 800 le, Many-horned adder. 1500 le, Hawequa flat gecko.

No. 2390, 1200 le: a, Reticulated desert lizard. b, Ball python. c, Gaboon viper. d, Dumeril's boa. e, Common egg-eater. f, Helmet turtle.

No. 2391, 1200 le: a, Asian saw-scaled viper. b, Namibian sand snake. c, Angolan garter snake. d, Striped skaapsteker. e, Brown house snake. f, Shield-nosed cobra.

No. 2392, 5000 le, Green water snake. No. 2393, 5000 le, Flap-necked chameleon.

2001, Jan. 15

2384-2389 A351 Set of 6 4.25 4.25

Sheets of 6, #a-f

2390-2391 A351 Set of 2 15.00 15.00

Souvenir Sheets

2392-2393 A351 Set of 2 10.50 10.50

Rijksmuseum, Amsterdam, Bicent. (in 2000) — A352

No. 2394, 1100 le, vert.: a, Gentleman Writing a Letter, by Gabriel Metsu. b, Self-portrait, by Carel Fabritius. c, The Windmill at Wijk bij Duurstede, by Jacob van Ruisdael. d, Bentheim Castle, by van Ruisdael. e, Ships on a Stormy Sea, by Willem van de Velde, the Younger. f, David from David Playing the Harp, by Jan de Bray.

No. 2395, 1100 le, vert.: a, St. Paul from St. Paul Healing the Cripple at Lystra, by Karel Dujardin. b, Two hatless men from The Meagre Company, by Frans Hals and Pieter Codde. c, Man from Elegant Couple in an Interior, by Eglon van der Neer. d, Laid Table With Cheese and Fruit, by Floris van Dijck. e, Bacchanal, by Moses van Uyttenbroeck. f, Kneeling woman from St. Paul Healing the Cripple at Lystra.

No. 2396, 1100 le, vert.: a, Lady Reading a Letter, by Metsu. b, Portrait of Titus, by Rembrandt. c, Portrait of Gerard de Lairesse, by Rembrandt. d, Portrait of a Family in an Interior, by Emanuel de Witte. e, The Letter, by Gerard Terborch. f, Three Women and a Man in a Courtyard Behind a House, by Pieter de Hooch.

No. 2397, 1100 le, vert.: a, Candlebearers from David Playing the Harp. b, Hand of St. Paul from St. Paul Healing the Cripple at Lystra. c, Two men, one with hat, from The Meagre Company. d, The Gray, by Ohilips Wouwerman. e, Couple from Elegant Couple in an Interior. f, The Hut, by Adriaen van de Velde.

No. 2398, 5000 le, Road in the Dunes With a Passenger Coach, by Salomon van Ruysdael. No. 2399, 5000 le, Cows in the Meadow, by Albert Gerard Bilders. No. 2400, 5000 le, Lot and His Daughters, by Hendrick Goltzius. No. 2401, 5000 le, Arrival of Queen Wilhelmina at the Frederiksplein in Amsterdam, by Otto Eerelman.

2001, Jan. 15 ***Perf. 13¾***

Sheets of 6, #a-f

2394-2397 A352 Set of 4 27.50 27.50

Souvenir Sheets

2398-2401 A352 Set of 4 21.00 21.00

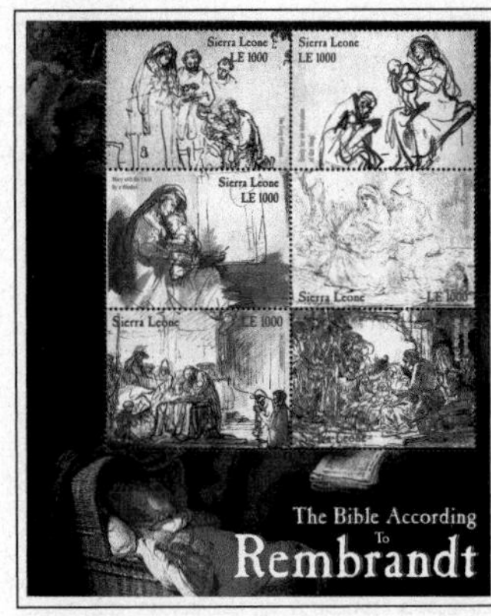

Battle of Britain, 60th Anniv. — A353

No. 2402, 1000 le: a, Bombed village near London. b, The Underground as a bomb shelter. c, Firemen. d, Home Guard. e, Setting lights out time. f, Pilots resting between flights. g, Brendan "Paddy" Finucane, ace pilot. h, Hawk 75.

No. 2403, 1000 le: a, St. Paul's Cathedral. b, Eastenders leaving London. c, Winston Churchill being cheered by British crew. d, Rescue pilot. e, Boy Scouts helping children. f, Big gunners, 1940. g, Plane spotter lights. h, Survey watchers.

No. 2404, 1000 le: a, Post Office Engineer, WAFF. b, Women munitions workers. c, Churchill as prime minister and defense minister. d, German Dornier DO17. e, Church fires from Nazi bombs, London, 1940. f, All-night raid on London, 1940. g, Lunchtime in the Underground. h, People in the Underground, 1940.

No. 2405, 1000 le: a, London Bridge. b, Surrey Home Guard. c, British Cruiser tank MK III. d, Newfoundland men at the guns, 1940. e, Lady Astor's Constituency hit, 1940. f, Churchill worried with war, 1940. g, Bomb blast at Parliament. h, Development of radar, 1940.

No. 2406, 6000 le, Churchill and wife inspecting harbor damage. No. 2407, 6000 le, London, 1940. No. 2408, 6000 le, British Supermarine Spitfire. No. 2409, 6000 le, Bombing crew preparing for flight, 1940, vert.

2001, Jan. 30 ***Perf. 14***

Sheets of 8, #a-h

2402-2405 A353 Set of 4 35.00 35.00

Souvenir Sheets

2406-2409 A353 Set of 4 25.00 25.00

Biblical Scenes by Rembrandt — A354

No. 2410, 1000 le: a, The Song of Simeon. b, Study for Adoration of the Magi. c, Mary With the Child by a Window. d, The Rest on the Flight Into Egypt. e, The Circumcision. f, The Shepherds Worship the Child.

No. 2411, 1000 le: a, The Angel Rises Up in the Flame of Manoah's Sacrifice. b, Tobias Frighterned by the Fish. c, The Angel of the Lord Stands in Balaam's Path. d, The Angel Appears to Hagar in the Desert. e, Jacob's Dream. f, The Healing of Tobit.

No. 2412, 5000 le, Simeon's Prophecy to Mary. No. 2413, 5000 le, The Angel Prevents the Sacrifice of Isaac. No. 2414, 5000 le, The Angel Leaves Tobit and His Family, vert. No. 2415, 5000 le, The Adoration of the Magi, vert.

2001, Feb. 13 ***Perf. 13¾***

Sheets of 6, #a-f

2410-2411 A354 Set of 2 12.50 12.50

Souvenir Sheets

2412-2415 A354 Set of 4 21.00 21.00

Racehorses A355

Designs: 200 le, Native Dancer. 500 le, Citation. 1500 le, Spectre. 2000 le, Carbine.

No. 2420, 1200 le: a, Arkle. b, Golden Miller. c, Phar Lap. d, Battleship. e, Kelso. f, Nijinsky.

No. 2421, 1200 le: a, Red Rum. b, Sir Ken. c, War Admiral. d, Troytown. e, Shergar. f, Allez France.

No. 2422, 5000 le, Cigar. No. 2423, 5000 le, Desert Orchid. No. 2424, 5000 le, Trophy. No. 2425, 5000 le, Horses on turf track, horiz.

2001, Feb. 27 ***Perf. 14***

2416-2419 A355 Set of 4 4.50 4.50

Sheets of 6, #a-f

2420-2421 A355 Set of 2 15.00 15.00

Souvenir Sheets

2422-2425 A355 Set of 4 21.00 21.00

Automobiles — A356

No. 2426, 1000 le: a, 1898 Benz Velo. b, 1909 Rolls-Royce Silver Ghost. c, 1912 Ford Model T. d, 1937 Duesenberg SJ. e, 1938-40 Grosser Mercedes. f, 1938 Citroen Light 15.

No. 2427, 1000 le: a, 1939 Lincoln Zephyr. b, 1947 Volkswagen Beetle. c, 1959 Jaguar Mark II. d, 1968 Ford Shelby Mustang GT500. e, 1987-94 Opel/Vauxhall Senator. f, 2002 Mercedes Maybach.

No. 2428, 5000 le, 1928 Bentley 3-liter short chassis Tourer. No. 2429, 5000 le, 1999 Ferrari 360 Modena.

2001, Apr. 30 ***Perf. 13¾***

Sheets of 6, #a-f, + 6 labels

2426-2427 A356 Set of 2 12.50 12.50

Souvenir Sheets

2428-2429 A356 Set of 2 10.50 10.50

Butterflies A357

Designs: 250 le, Eurema floricola. 400 le, Papilio dardanus. 800 le, Amauris nossima. 1500 le, Gideona lucasi.

No. 2434, 1100 le: a, Papilio dardanus. b, Cymothoe sangaris. c, Epiphora albida. d, African giant swallowtail. e, Papilio nobilis nobilis. f, Charaxes hadnanus.

No. 2435, 1100 le: a, Charaxes lucretia. b, Euxanthe closslex. c, Charaxes phenix. d, Charaxes acraeades. e, Charaxes protoclea azota. f, Charaxes lydiae.

No. 2436, 5000 le, Clotis zoe. No. 2437, 5000 le, Acraea ranaualona, vert.

Perf. 13¼x13½, 13½x13¼

2001, Apr. 30 **Litho.**

2430-2433 A357 Set of 4 3.25 3.25

Sheets of 6, #a-f

2434-2435 A357 Set of 2 14.50 14.50

Souvenir Sheets

2436-2437 A357 Set of 2 11.00 11.00

Queen Elizabeth II, 75th Birthday — A358

No. 2438: a, Wearing hat. b, With infant. c, Wearing crown. d, Wearing black blouse.

2001, June 18 **Litho.** ***Perf. 14***

2438 A358 2000 le Sheet of 4, #a-d 8.25 8.25

Souvenir Sheet

Perf. 13¾

2439 A358 5000 le As older woman 5.25 5.25

No. 2438 contains four 28x42mm stamps.

Japanese Art — A359

Designs: 50 le, Iziu Chinuki No Hi, by Hokkei, horiz. 100 le, A Visit to Enoshima, by Kiyonaga Torii, horiz. 150 le, Inn on a Harbor, by Sadahide, horiz. 200 le, Entrance to Foreigner's Establishment, by Sadahide, horiz. 250 le, Courtesans at Cherry Blossom Time, by Kiyonaga, horiz. 300 le, Cherry Blossom Viewing at Ueno, by Toyohara Chikanobu, horiz. 400 le, A Summer Evening at a Restaurant by the Sumida River, by Torii, horiz. 500 le, Ichikana Yaozo I As Samurai, by Buncho. 600 le, The Actor Nakamura Noshoi II as a Street Walker, by Shunzan Katsukawa. 800 le, Arashi Sangoro II, by Shokosai. 1500 le, bando Mitsugoro I by Shunko. No. 2451, 2000 le, Matsumoto Koshiro II, by Masanobu.

No. 2452, 2000 le: a, Nakamura Shikan II and Nakamura Baiko, by Shigeharu. b, Women Making Rice Cakes, by Shunsho. c, Youth Sending Letter by Arrow, by Harushige. d, Woman with green sash from Six Girls, by Eisho.

No. 2453, 2000 le: a, Woman with checked kimono, from Six Girls. b, Courtesan on a Bench, by Eiri. c, Courtesan and Her Two Kamuro, by Suzuki Harunobu. d, Clearing Weather at Awazu, by Shigemasa.

No. 2454, 2000 le — Paintings by Harunobu: a, Promenade. b, Wine Tasters. c, Rain in May. d, Lovers by the Wall.

No. 2455, 2000 le — Paintings by Harunobu: a, Young Woman Attended by Maid. b, Lovers by Lespedeza Bush. c, Girl Contemplating a Landscape. d, Young Man Unrolling a Hanging Scroll.

No. 2456, 5000 le, Searching for the Hermit, by Harunobu. No. 2457, 5000 le, Courtesan and Two Kamuro, by Harunobu. No. 2458, 5000 le, Drying Clothes, by Harunobu. No. 2459, 5000 le, Komachi Praying For Rain, by Harunobu. No. 2460, 5000 le, Girl Contemplating Landscape, by Harunobu.

2001, July 2 ***Perf. 13½***

2440-2451 A359 Set of 12 7.25 7.25

Sheets of 4, #a-d

2452-2455 A359 Set of 4 32.50 32.50

Souvenir Sheets

2456-2460 A359 Set of 5 26.00 26.00

Phila Nippon '01, Japan (#2452-2460).

Marlene Dietrich — A360

No. 2461: a, Looking over shoulder. b, Wearing necklace. c, Wearing coat with flower. d, Holding cigarette.

2001, June 18 **Litho.** ***Perf. 13¾***

2461 A360 2000 le Sheet of 4, #a-d 8.25 8.25

Toulouse-Lautrec Paintings — A361

No. 2462, horiz.: a, A La Mie. b, A Corner of the Moulin de la Gallete. c, The Start of the Quadrille.

5000 le, La Goulue.

2001, June 18

2462 A361 2200 le Sheet of 3, #a-c 7.00 7.00

Souvenir Sheet

2463 A361 5000 le multi 5.25 5.25

Monet Paintings — A362

No. 2464, horiz.: a, The Road to Vétheuil, Winter. b, The Church at Vétheuil, Snow. c, Breakup of the Ice Near Vétheuil. d, The Boulevard de Pontoise at Argenteuil, Snow.

5000 le, Irises by the Pond.

2001, June 18

2464 A362 1500 le Sheet of 4, #a-d 6.25 6.25

Souvenir Sheet

2465 A362 5000 le multi 5.25 5.25

Giuseppe Verdi (1813-1901), Opera Composer — A363

No. 2466: a, Vladimir Popov. b, Enrico Caruso. c, Rudolf Bockelmann. d, Stage.

5000 le, Aprile Millo and Barseg Tumanyan.

2001, June 18 ***Perf. 14***

2466 A363 1700 le Sheet of 4, #a-d 7.00 7.00

Souvenir Sheet

2467 A363 5000 le multi 5.25 5.25

Royal Navy Submarines, Cent. — A364

No. 2468: a, C Class submarine. b, HMS Spartan. c, HMS Exeter. d, HMS Chatham. e, HMS Verdun. f, HMS Marlborough.

5000 le, HMS Vanguard.

2001, June 18

2468 A364 1100 le Sheet of 6, #a-f 7.00 7.00

Souvenir Sheet

2469 A364 5000 le multi 5.25 5.25

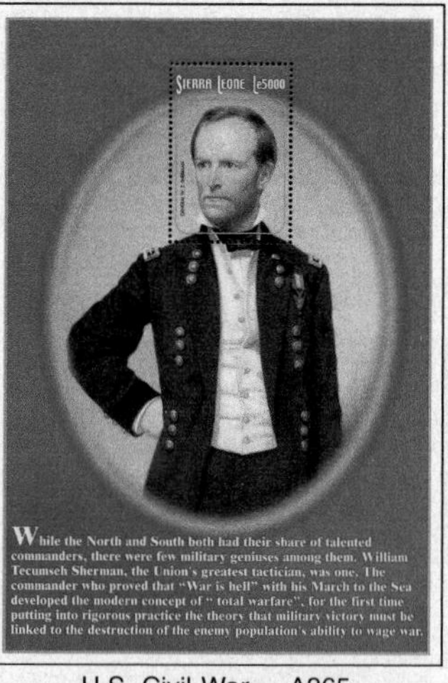

U.S. Civil War — A365

No. 2470, 2000 le — Generals: a, Ulysses S. Grant. b, John Bell Hood. c, Jeb Stuart. d, Robert E. Lee.

No. 2471, 2000 le: a, Gen. Joshua Chamberlain. b, Gen. Stonewall Jackson. c, Gen. George McClellan. d, Adm. David Farragut.

No. 2472, 2000 le — Battle scenes: a, Shiloh. b, Bull Run. c, Fair Oaks. d, Chattanooga.

No. 2473, 2000 le — Battle scenes: a, Fredericksburg. b, Gettysburg. c, Mobile Bay. d, Fort Sumter.

No. 2474, 5000 le, Gen. William Tecumseh Sherman. No. 2475, 5000 le, Gen. George A. Custer. No. 2476, 5000 le, Battle of Vicksburg. No. 2477, 5000 le, Battle of Antietam.

2001, Aug. 27

Sheets of 4, #a-d

2470-2473 A365 Set of 4 32.50 32.50

Souvenir Sheets

2474-2477 A365 Set of 4 21.00 21.00

Horses in Literature and Mythology — A366

No. 2478, 1100 le: a, Piebald, from National Velvet, by Enid Bagnold. b, Strider, by Leo Tolstoy. c, Black Beauty, by Anna Sewell. d, Red Pony, by John Steinbeck. e, Black Stallion, by Walter Farley. f, Misty of Chincoteague, by Marguerite Henry.

No. 2479, 1100 le: a, Arvak Alsvid. b, Pegasus. c, Sleipnir. d, Veillanfif. e, Grani. f, Galathe, from Troilus and Cressida, by William Shakespeare.

No. 2480, 5000 le, Rosinante, from Don Quixote, by Miguel de Cervantes. No. 2481, 5000 le, Xanthus and Balius.

2001, Feb. 27 **Litho.** ***Perf. 14***

Sheets of 6, #a-f

2478-2479 A366 Set of 2 14.00 14.00

Souvenir Sheets

2480-2481 A366 Set of 2 10.50 10.50

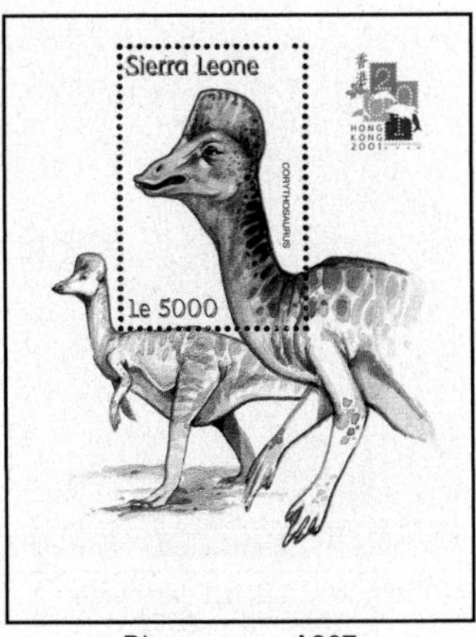

Dinosaurs — A367

No. 2482, 1000 le: a, Acrocanthosaurus. b, Edmontosaurus. c, Archaeopteryx. d, Hadrosaurus. e, Mongolian avimimus. f, Pachyrhinosaurus. g, Iguanodons (with tree trunk). h, Iguanodons, diff.
No. 2483, 1000 le, horiz.: a, Albertosaurus. b, Pteranodon ingens. c, Asiatic iguanodon. d, Sordes. e, Coelophysis. f, Saichania. g, Bactrosaurus. h, Triceratops.
No. 2484, 5000 le, Corythosaurus. No. 2485, 5000 le, Stenonychosaurus.

2001, Mar. 1 ***Perf. 13½***

Sheets of 8, #a-h

2482-2483 A367 Set of 2 17.00 17.00

Souvenir Sheets

2484-2485 A367 Set of 2 10.50 10.50

Hong Kong 2001 Stamp Exhibition.

Souvenir Sheets

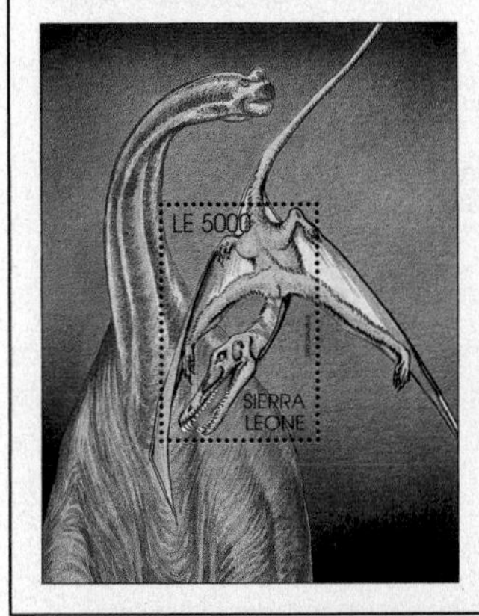

Dinosaurs — A367a

Designs: No. 2485A, 5000 le, Dryosaurus. No. 2485B, 5000 le, Diplodocids. No. 2485C, 5000 le, Allosaurus.

2001, Mar. 1 **Litho.** ***Perf. 13½***

2485A-2485C A367a Set of 3 15.00 15.00

Nos. 2485A-2485C were not available in the marketplace until 2002.

Butterflies — A368

No. 2486, 1100 le: a, Teinopalpus imperialis. b, Swallowtail. c, Doris. d, Northern Jezebel. e, Beautiful monarch. f, Gaudy commodore.
No. 2487, 1100 le: a, Plain tiger. b, Tiger. c, Morpho cypris. d, Castnia litus. e, Dismorphia nemesis. f, Blue and yellow butterfly (inscribed African violets).
No. 2488, 5000 le, Scarce swallowtail. No. 2489, 5000 le, Clouded yellow, vert.

2001, Apr. 30 **Sheets of 6, #a-f**

2486-2487 A368 Set of 2 14.50 14.50

Souvenir Sheets

2488-2489 A368 Set of 2 11.00 11.00

Photomosaic of Queen Elizabeth II — A369

2001, June 18 ***Perf. 14***

2490 A369 1000 le multi 1.10 1.10

Printed in sheets of 8.

Mao Zedong (1893-1976) — A370

No. 2492, 1100 le — Map of China and Mao: a, Without hat. b, With green cap. c, With blue cap.
No. 2493, 1100 le — Red frame and Mao with: a, Uniform. b, Shirt with open collar. d, Cap.
No. 2493, 5000 le, Mao wearing black suit. No. 2494, 5000 le, Mao in white.

2001, June 18 **Sheets of 3, #a-c**

2491-2492 A370 Set of 2 7.00 7.00

Souvenir Sheets

2493-2494 A370 Set of 2 10.50 10.50

Ferrari Automobiles — A371

Designs: 100 le, 2001 360 Challenge. 500 le, 1971 712 Can Am. 600 le, 1970 512M. 1000 le, 1988 F40. 1500 le, 1982 365 GT4/BB. 2000 le, 1972 365 GTB/4.

2001, Oct. 8 ***Perf. 13¾***

2495-2500 A371 Set of 6 6.00 6.00

Souvenir Sheets

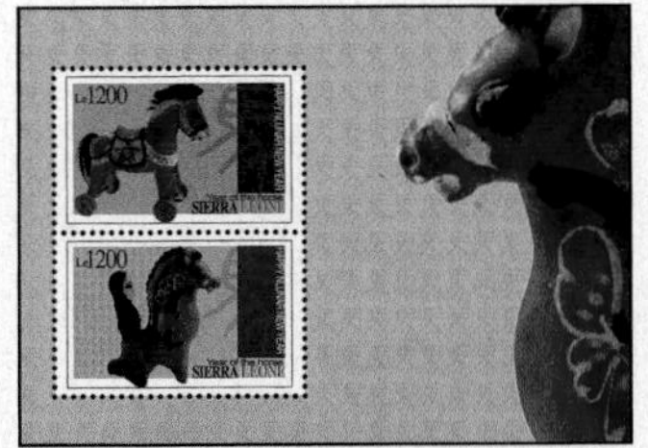

Horses — A372

Chinese Character for Horse — A373

No. 2501: a, Green background. b, Blue background.
No. 2502 — "2002" in: a, Green. b, Red. c, Orange. d, Purple.

2001, Nov. 29 ***Perf. 13***

2501 A372 1200 le Sheet of 2, #a-b 2.50 2.50

Perf. 13x13¼

2502 A373 1200 le Sheet of 4, #a-d 5.00 5.00

New Year 2002 (Year of the Horse).

2002 World Cup Soccer Championships, Japan and Korea — A374

No. 2503, 1400 le: a, Newspaper article, 1950. b, Jules Rimet, 1954. c, Pele and teammates, 1958. d, Vava and Schroiff, 1962. e, Bobby Charlton, 1966. f, Pele, 1970.
No. 2504, 1400 le: a, Daniel Passarella, 1978. b, Karl-Heinz Rummenigge, 1982. c, Diego Maradona, 1986. d, Roger Milla, 1990. e, Romario, 1994. f, Zinedine Zidane, 1998.
No. 2505, 5000 le, Head from Jules Rimet trophy, 1930. No. 2506, 5000 le, Head and globe from World Cup trophy, 2002.

2001, Dec. 7 ***Perf. 13¾x14¼***

Sheets of 6, #a-f

2503-2504 A374 Set of 2 17.00 17.00

Souvenir Sheets

Perf. 14½x14¼

2505-2506 A374 Set of 2 10.00 10.00

Christmas A375

Paintings by Filippo Lippi: 300 le, Madonna of Humility. 600 le, Annunciation. 1500 le, Annunciation, vert. 2000 le, Adoration of the Child and Saints, vert.
5000 le, Barbadori Altarpeice, vert.

2001, Dec. 26 ***Perf. 14***

2507-2510 A375 Set of 4 4.50 4.50

Souvenir Sheet

2511 A375 5000 le multi 5.00 5.00

Queen Mother Type of 1999 Redrawn

No. 2512: a, With Duke of York and Princess Elizabeth, 1926. b, In 1979. c, In Nairobi, 1959. d, In 1991.
4000 le, With crown, 1937.

2001, Dec. ***Perf. 14***

Yellow Orange Frames

2512 A307 1300 le Sheet of 4, #a-d, + label 5.25 5.25

Souvenir Sheet

Perf. 13¾

2513 A307 4000 le multi 4.00 4.00

Queen Mother's 101st birthday. No. 2513 contains one 38x51mm stamp with a slightly darker backdrop than that found on No. 2208. Sheet margins of Nos. 2512-2513 lack embossing and gold arms and frames found on Nos. 2207-2208.

SOS Children's Village — A376

2002, Jan. 24 ***Perf. 14***

2514 A376 2000 le multi 2.00 2.00

Steam and Electric Inventions and Their Inventors — A377

No. 2515, 1100 le: a, The Rocket steam locomotive, 1829. b, High-speed electric passenger train. c, 1863 Steam pumper. d, Early electric trolley. e, 1893 Steam automobile. f, Electric monorail.
No. 2516, 1100 le: a, Early steam pumper. b, Telephone. c, Steam liner. d, Battery and light bulb. e, 1770 Steam carriage. f, Electric passenger train.
No. 2517, 1100 le: a, Robert Fulton and steamboat. b, Thomas Edison and light bulb. c, 1899 T9 steam locomotive. d, Radio and antennae. e, James Watt, and steam engine diagram. f, Alexander Graham Bell and telephone.
No. 2518, 5000 le, 1899 Steam locomotive. No. 2519, 5000 le, Telephone, radio and light bulb. No. 2520, 5000 le, Benjamin Franklin, vert.

Perf. 13¼x13½, 13½x13¼

2002, Jan. 24 **Sheets of 6, #a-f**

2515-2517 A377 Set of 3 20.00 20.00

Souvenir Sheets

2518-2520 A377 Set of 3 15.00 15.00

United We Stand — A378

2002, Feb. 6 ***Perf. 13½x13¼***

2521 A378 2000 le multi 2.25 2.25

Reign of Queen Elizabeth II, 50th Anniv. — A379

No. 2522: a, With young Prince Charles and Princess Anne. b, Wearing tiara and stole, looking forward. c, Wearing tiara and stole, looking right. d, Wearing hat.
5000 le, Wearing hat and gloves.

2002, Feb. 6 ***Perf. 14¼***

2522 A379 2000 le Sheet of 4, #a-d 9.00 9.00

Souvenir Sheet

2523 A379 5000 le multi 5.50 5.50

2002 Winter Olympics, Salt Lake City A380

Designs: Nos. 2524, 2525, 2000 le, Curling. Nos. 2524A, 2525A, 2000 le, Ice hockey.

2002, Apr. 22 Litho. ***Perf. 14***

Olympic Rings in Color

2524-2524A A380 Set of 2 4.00 4.00
2524Ab Souvenir sheet, #2524-2524A 4.00 4.00

Olympic Rings in White on Black Background

Perf. 13¼x13½

2525-2525A A380 Set of 2 4.00 4.00
2525Ab Souvenir sheet, #2525-2525A 4.00 4.00

Flowers — A381

Designs: 400 le, Jerusalem artichoke. 500 le, Painted trillium. 600 le, Bluebells. 1000 le, Rough-fruited cinquefoil. 1500 le, Wake robin. 2000 le, Seashore mallow.
No. 2532, 1300 le, horiz.: a, Hepatica. b, Star of Bethlehem. c, Wood lily. d, Wild geranium. e, Hedge bindweed. f, Gloxinias.
No. 2533, 1300 le, horiz.: a, Laevigata iris. b, Dietes. c, Day lily. d, Cardinal flower. e, Mountain pink. f, Seaside gentian.
No. 2534, 5000 le, Dame's rocket. No. 2535, 5000 le, Pinxter flower.

2002, Apr. 29 Litho. ***Perf. 14x14½***

2526-2531 A381 Set of 6 6.00 6.00

Perf. 14

Sheets of 6, #a-f

2532-2533 A381 Set of 2 15.00 15.00

Souvenir Sheets

2534-2535 A381 Set of 2 10.00 10.00

Nos. 2532-2533 contain six 42x38mm stamps; Nos. 2534-2535 contain one 38x42mm stamp.

Wildlife — A382

Designs: 200 le, Giraffe. 400 le, L'Host's guenon. 1500 le, Jentik's duiker.
No. 2539, 1100 le, horiz.: a, Kudu. b, Caracal. c, Oribi. d, Aardwolf. e, Bushpig. f, Suricates.
No. 2540, 1100 le, horiz.: a, African buffalo. b, Wild dog. c, Black-backed jackal. d, Aardvark. e, Impala. f, Waterbuck.
No. 2541, 8000 le, Vervet monkey. No. 2542, 8000 le, Springbok.

2002, Apr. 29 ***Perf. 14***

2536-2538 A382 Set of 3 2.10 2.10

Sheets of 6, #a-f

2539-2540 A382 Set of 2 13.00 13.00

Souvenir Sheets

2541-2542 A382 Set of 2 16.00 16.00

Chiune Sugihara, Japanese Diplomat Who Saved Jews in World War II — A383

2002, July 1 Litho. ***Perf. 14***

2543 A383 2000 le multi 2.00 2.00

Printed in sheets of 4.

Nos. 1811-1812 Surcharged

Methods & Perfs. As Before

2002, July 1

2544 A242 800 le on 400 le Block or strip of 4, #a-d 3.25 3.25

Souvenir Sheet

2545 A242 5000 le on 1500 le multi 5.00 5.00

Queen Mother Elizabeth (1900-2002). No. 2544 was issued in sheets of eight stamps. Sheet margins of 2544-2544 were overprinted with black border and "In Memoriam / 1900-2002."

Intl Year of Ecotourism — A384

No. 2546: a, Bullom boats. b, Dinkongor Falls. c, Rokel River. d, Pygmy hippopotamus. e, Hills of Soa Chiefdom. f, Long Beach.
5000 le, Photo safari.

2002, July 1 Litho. ***Perf. 14***

2546 A384 1300 le Sheet of 6, #a-f 7.75 7.75

Souvenir Sheet

2547 A384 5000 le multi 5.00 5.00

First Non-stop Solo Transatlantic Flight, 75th Anniv. — A385

No. 2548, horiz. — The Spirit of St. Louis: a, Being towed from Ryan Airlines factory. b, Being towed May 20, 1927. c, Taking off, May 20, 1927.
No. 2549, Charles Lindbergh.

2002, July 1

2548 A385 2500 le Sheet of 3, #a-c 7.50 7.50

Souvenir Sheet

2549 A385 2500 le multi 2.50 2.50

Shirley Temple Movie Type of 2000

Temple in scenes from "Wee Willie Winkie" — No. 2550: a, With woman, man in army uniform, two men wearing turbans. b, Resting head near mirror. c, With boy wearing army uniform and kilt. d, With man wearing turban. e, With man in army uniform. f, Giving note to man in prison.
No. 2551, vert: a, With woman. b, With man wearing turban. c, With woman and man. d, With man in army uniform.
5000 le, With man in army uniform, vert.

2002, July 1 ***Perf. 12¼***

2550 A324 1100 le Sheet of 6, #a-f 6.50 6.50
2551 A324 1300 le Sheet of 4, #a-d 5.25 5.25

Souvenir Sheet

2552 A324 5000 le multi 5.00 5.00

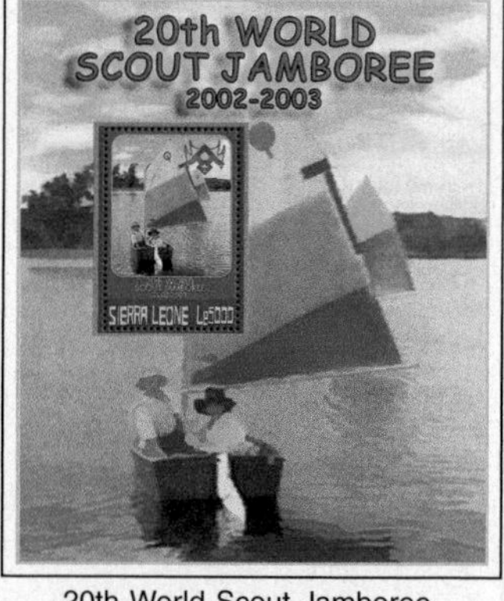

20th World Scout Jamboree, Thailand — A386

No. 2553: a, Boys on rocks fishing. b, Scouts without caps. c, Scouts in water holding fish. d, Scouts with caps.
5000 le, Scouts in sailboat.

2002, July 1 ***Perf. 14***

2553 A386 2000 le Sheet of 4, #a-d 8.00 8.00

Souvenir Sheet

2554 A386 5000 le multi 5.00 5.00

Intl. Year of Mountains — A387

No. 2555: a, Mt. Etna, Italy. b, Cotopaxi, Ecuador. c, Mt. Everest, Nepal. d, Mt. Popocatepetl, Mexico.
5000 le, Mt. Machhapuchare, Nepal.

2002, July 1

2555 A387 2000 le Sheet of 4, #a-d 8.00 8.00

Souvenir Sheet

2556 A387 5000 le multi 5.00 5.00

Pokémon — A388

No. 2557, vert.: a, Sudowoodo. b, Aipom. c, Shuckle. d, Miltank. e, Hitmontop. f, Ledian.
5000 le, Lugia.

2002, Aug. 26 ***Perf. 13¾***

2557 A388 1500 le Sheet of 6, #a-f 9.25 9.25

Souvenir Sheet

2558 A388 5000 le multi 5.25 5.25

Popeye in New York — A389

No. 2559, vert. — Popeye and: a, And Olive Oyl on river tour. b, And Olive Oyl in Central Park. c, And Olive Oyl near Brooklyn Bridge. d, Statue of Liberty. e, Flatiron Building. f, Empire State Building.
5000 le, Popeye and Olive Oyl skating at Rockefeller Center.

2002, Aug. 26 *Perf. 12¼*
2559 A389 1300 le Sheet of 6, #a-f 8.00 8.00

Souvenir Sheet

2560 A389 5000 le multi 5.25 5.25

No. 2559 contains six 38x50mm stamps.

A390

Teddy Bears, Cent. — A391

No. 2561: a, Bear with green bow. b, Bears with harlequin costumes. c, Bear with red headdress. d, Bear with black and gold neckband.
No. 2562: a, Baby girl bear. b, School girl bear. c, Bear in overalls. d, Bear in pajamas.

2002, Sept. 23 *Perf. 14*
2561 A390 1700 le Sheet of 4, #a-d 6.50 6.50
2562 A391 2000 le Sheet of 4, #a-d 7.75 7.75

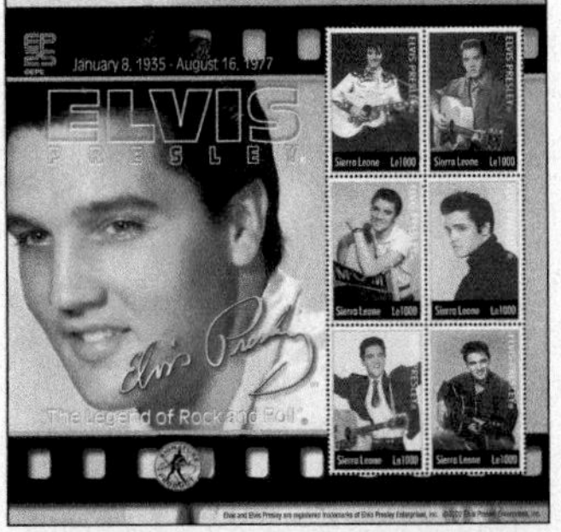
Elvis Presley (1935-77) — A392

No. 2563: a, Wearing flowered shirt. b, Wearing jacket, holding light-colored guitar. c, Seated in chair. d, Wearing sweater. e, With arms raised. f, With black guitar.

2002, Oct. 7 **Litho.**
2563 A392 1000 le Sheet of 6, #a-f 5.75 5.75

2002 World Cup Soccer Championships, Japan and Korea — A393

No. 2564, 1400 le — Germany vs. Paraguay: a, Michael Ballack. b, Oliver Kahn. c, Miroslav Klose. d, Diego Gacilan. e, Jose Luis Chilavert. f, Guido Alvarenga.
No. 2565, 1400 le — Denmark vs. England: a, Jesper Gronkjaer. b, Thomas Helveg. c, Dennis Rommedahl. d, Michael Owen. e, David Seaman. f, Rio Ferdinand.
No. 2566, 1400 le — Mexico vs. U.S.: a, Rafael Marquez. b, Oscar Perez. c, Jared Borgetti. d, Landon Donovan. e, Brad Friedel. f, DaMarcus Beasley.
No. 2567, 1400 le — Japan vs. Turkey: a, Ryuzo Morioka. b, Kazuyuki Toda. c, Atsushi Yanagisawa. d, Fatih Akyel. e, Yildiray Basturk. f, Umit Davala.
No. 2568, 2500 le — Germany: a, Coach Rudi Voeller. b, Dietmar Hamann.
No. 2569, 2500 le — Paraguay: a, Julio Cesar Caceres. b, Coach Cesare Maldini.
No. 2570, 2500 le — Denmark: a, Coach Morten Olsen. b, Jon Dahl Tomasson.
No. 2571, 2500 le — England: a, David Beckham. b, Coach Sven Goran Eriksson.
No. 2572, 2500 le — Mexico: a, Coach Javier Aguirre. b, Jesus Arellano.
No. 2573, 2500 le — United States: a, Brian McBride. b, Coach Bruce Arena.
No. 2574, 2500 le — Japan: a, Coach Philippe Troussier. b, Junichi Inamoto.
No. 2575, 2500 le — Turkey: a, Vildiray Basturk. b, Coach Senol Gunes.

2002, Nov. 18 *Perf. 13¼*

Sheets of 6, #a-f

2564-2567 A393 Set of 4 40.00 40.00

Souvenir Sheets of 2, #a-b

2568-2575 A393 Set of 8 47.50 47.50

Christmas — A394

Designs: 50 le, Madonna and Child Between Saints John the Baptist and Catherine of Alexandria, by Perugino. 100 le, Madonna and Child Enthroned Between Angels and Saints, by Domenico Ghirlandaio. 150 le, The Virgin, by Giovanni Bellini. 500 le, Stories of the Virgin Birth of Mary, by Ghirlandaio. 5000 le, Adoration of the Magi, by Ghirlandaio.
6000 le, Madonna Enthroned with Saints, by Ghirlandaio.

2002, Nov. 18 *Perf. 14*
2576-2580 A394 Set of 5 6.75 6.75

Souvenir Sheet

2581 A394 6000 le multi 7.00 7.00

Pres. Ronald Reagan — A395

No. 2582, 1700 le — Country name in black: a, Wearing brown tie. b, Wearing red tie.
No. 2583, 1700 le — Country name in white: a, Wearing spotted tie. b, Wearing striped tie.

2002, Dec. 30 **Pairs, #a-b** **Litho.**
2582-2583 A395 Set of 2 6.75 6.75

Nos. 2582-2583 each were printed in sheets containing two pairs.

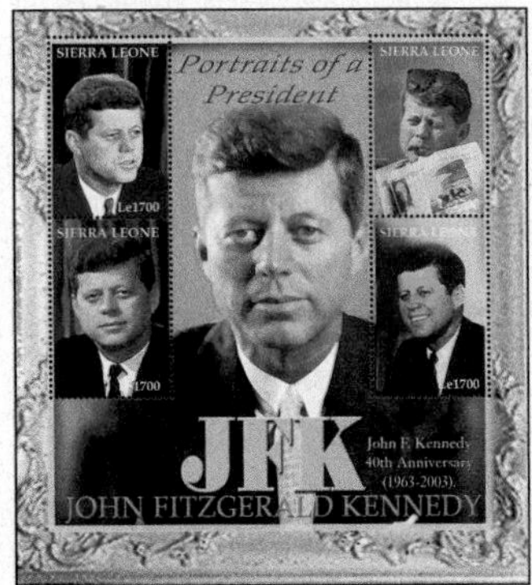
Pres. John F. Kennedy (1917-63) — A396

No. 2584, 1700 le: a, Wearing red tie. b, With newspaper. c, In front on brown curtain. d, In front of brown and tan background.
No. 2585, 1700 le — John and Jacqueline: a, In formal wear greeting man. b, With purple background. c, Playing with child. d, At Love Field, Nov. 22, 1963.

2002, Dec. 30 *Perf. 14*

Sheets of 4, #a-d

2584-2585 A396 Set of 2 13.50 13.50

Princess Diana (1961-97) — A397

Designs: No. 2586, 1700 le, Wearing black dress. No. 2587, 1700 le, Wearing blue dress and tiara.

2002, Dec. 30
2586-2587 A397 Set of 2 3.50 3.50

Nos. 2586-2587 each were printed in sheets of 4.

Birds, Flowers and Insects of Africa — A398

No. 2588, 1300 le — Birds: a, Great blue turaco. b, Helmet vanga. c, Scarlet-tufted malachite sunbird. d, African pitta. e, African jacana. f, Southern carmine bee-eater.
No. 2589, 1300 le — Flowers: a, Ancistrochilus rothschildianus. b, Oeceoclades maculata. c, Eulophia guineensis. d, Angraecum distichum. e, Disa uniflora. f, Vanilla imperialis.
No. 2590, 1300 le — Insects: a, Panther-spotted grasshopper. b, Basker moth. c, Charaxes samagdalis. d, Carpenter ant. e, Worker bee. f, Ten-spot dragonfly.
No. 2591, 5000 le, European robin. No. 2592, 5000 le, Bulbophyllum lepidum. No. 2593, 5000 le, Common dotted border butterfly, horiz.

2003, Jan. 13 **Sheets of 6, #a-f**
2588-2590 A398 Set of 3 25.00 25.00

Souvenir Sheets

2591-2593 A398 Set of 3 16.00 16.00

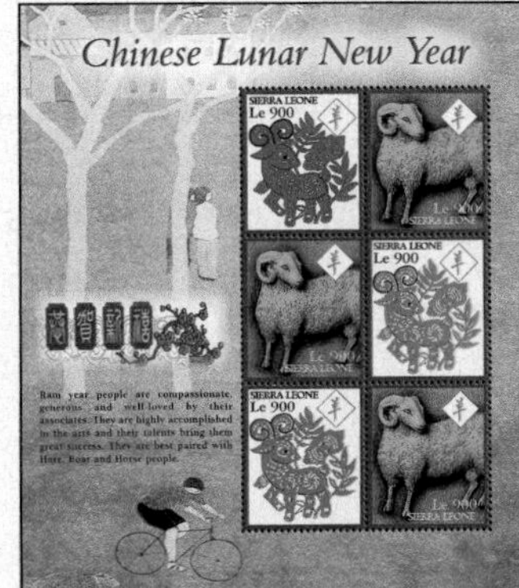
New Year 2003 (Year of the Ram) — A399

No. 2594 — Color of ram: a, Green. b, Orange. c, Red violet. d, Orange brown.

2003, Feb. 10
2594 A399 900 le Sheet of 6, #a-c, 3 #d 5.75 5.75

Astronauts Killed in Space Shuttle Columbia Accident — A400

No. 2595: a, Mission Specialist 1 David M. Brown. b, Commander Rick D. Husband. c, Mission Specialist 4 Laurel Blair Salton Clark. d, Mission Specialist 4 Kalpana Chawla. e, Payload Commander Michael P. Anderson. f, Pilot William C. McCool. g, Payload Specialist 4 Ilan Ramon.

2003, Apr. 7 *Perf. 13½x13¼*
2595 A400 1000 le Sheet of 7, #a-g 6.25 6.25

A401

Teddy Bears, Cent. — A402

No. 2596, vert.: a, Bear with umbrella. b, Bear with belt. c, Bear with pink dress. d, Bear with horn.
5000 le, Bear in automobile.
12,000 le, Bear with flower.

2003 **Litho.** *Perf. 14¼*
2596 A401 1500 le Sheet of 4, #a-d 5.25 5.25

Souvenir Sheet

2597 A401 5000 le multi 4.25 4.25

Embroidered

Imperf

2598 A402 12,000 le multi 10.50 10.50

Issued: Nos. 2596, 2597, 7/1, No. 2598, Apr. No. 2598 issued in sheets of 4.

A403

Coronation of Queen Elizabeth II, 50th Anniv. — A404

Designs: No. 2599, 1500 le, Crowning of the Queen. No. 2600, 1500 le, Queen signs the oath. No. 2601, 1500 le, Sovereign's sword. No. 2602, 1500 le, Anointing of the Queen. No. 2603, 1500 le, Queen presented with Holy Bible. No. 2604, 1500 le, Royal onlookers. No. 2605, 1500 le, Ampulla and spoon. No. 2606, 1500 le, Orb and scepter.
5000 le, Queen with crown. 15,000 le, Queen with hat.

2003 **Litho.** *Perf. 13¼*
2599-2606 A403 Set of 8 10.50 10.50

Souvenir Sheet

Perf. 14¼

2607 A403 5000 le multi 4.25 4.25

Miniature Sheet

Litho. & Embossed

Perf. 13¼x13

2608 A404 15,000 le multi 13.00 13.00

Issued: Nos. 2599-2607, 7/1; No. 2608, 4/7. No. 2607 contains one 37x50mm stamp.

Rembrandt Paintings A405

Designs: 800 le, Young Man with Pointed Beard. 1000 le, Old Man with Book. 1200 le, The Shipbuilder Jan Rijcksen and His Wife, Griet Jans, horiz. 2000 le, Portrait of a Young Jew.
No. 2613: a, Juno. b, Bellona, Goddess of War. c, Artemesia. d, Esther Preparing to Intercede with Ahasuerus.
5000 le, Two Scholars Disputing.

Perf. 14¼, 13¼ (#2613)

2003, May 13 **Litho.**
2609-2612 A405 Set of 4 4.50 4.50
2613 A405 1700 le Sheet of 4, #a-d 6.00 6.00

Souvenir Sheet

2614 A405 5000 le multi 4.50 4.50

Japanese Art — A406

Designs: 800 le, Priest Raigo Transformed Into a Rat, by Yoshitoshi Tsukioka. 1000 le, The Spirit of Tamichi as a Great Snake, by Yoshitoshi Tsukioka. 1500 le, The Gathering and Gossiping of Various Tools, by Kuniyoshi Utagawa. 2500 le, Caricatures of Actors as Three Animals Playing Ken, by Kuniyoshi Utagawa.
No. 2619 — Paintings by Yoshitoshi Tsukioka: a, The Fox Woman Leaving Her Child. b, Fox Cry. c, The Lucky Teakettle of Morin Temple. d, The Ghost of Okiku.
5000 le, Fox in a Thunderstorm, by Kunisada Utagawa.

2003, May 13 *Perf. 14¼*
2615-2618 A406 Set of 4 5.25 5.25
2619 A406 2000 le Sheet of 4, #a-d 7.25 7.25

Souvenir Sheet

2620 A406 5000 le multi 4.50 4.50

Paintings by Pablo Picasso A407

Designs: 400 le, Glass, Pipe and Playing Card. 500 le, Still-Life on a Pedestal in front of a Window. 600 le, Woman in a Feathered Hat. 700 le, Pedestal and Guitar. 1000 le, The Bread Carrier. 3000 le, Female Acrobat.
No. 2627: a, Portrait of a Woman. b, Woman in a Red Armchair. c, Seated Woman with Small Round Hat (Dora Maar). d, Woman with Crossed Hands.
No. 2628, Boy in Black Shorts. No. 2629, Bathers, horiz.

2003, May 13 *Perf. 14¼*
2621-2626 A407 Set of 6 5.50 5.50
2627 A407 2000 le Sheet of 4, #a-d 7.25 7.25

Imperf

Size: 82x105mm

2628 A407 5000 le multi 4.50 4.50

Size: 103x82mm

2629 A407 5000 le multi 4.50 4.50

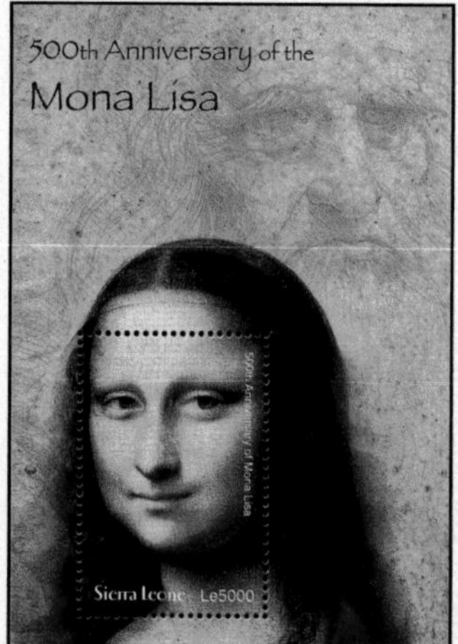

Painting of Mona Lisa, 500th Anniv. — A408

No. 2629A, 500th Anniversary of Mona Lisa (complete painting).
No. 2630 — Inscribed: a, Chartier: Mona Lisa — Mistress of Francis I. b, Copy of Mona Lisa, Cheramy Collection.
5000 le, 500th Anniversary of Mona Lisa (face).

2003, July 1 *Perf. 14*
2629A A408 2000 le multi 1.75 1.75
2630 A408 2000 le Sheet of 3, #a-b, No. 2629A 5.25 5.25

Souvenir Sheet

2631 A408 5000 le multi 4.25 4.25

No. 2629A was issued in two sheets of six with different selvage in 2004.

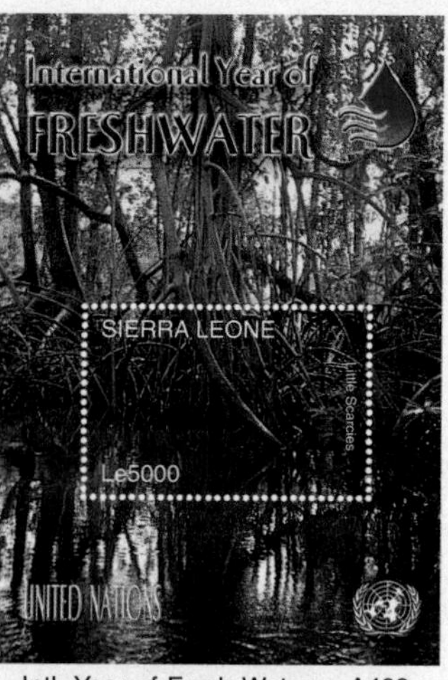

Intl. Year of Fresh Water — A409

No. 2632 a, Waterfalls of Mount Tonkoui. b, Tagbaladougou Falls. c, Cascades d'Ouzoud.
5000 le, Little Scarcies.

2003, July 1
2632 A409 2000 le Sheet of 3, #a-c 5.25 5.25

Souvenir Sheet

2633 A409 5000 le multi 4.25 4.25

Rotary Club of Sierra Leone, 40th Anniv. — A410

No. 2634 — Rotarians and: a, People in canoe. b, Cacheted first day cover envelope, Sierra Leone natives. c, Girl with flowers.
6000 le, Bhichal Rattakul, Rotary President.

2003, July 1
2634 A410 2500 le Sheet of 3, #a-c 6.50 6.50

Souvenir Sheet

2635 A410 6000 le multi 5.25 5.25

Prince William, 21st Birthday — A411

No. 2636: a, Wearing solid shirt. b, Wearing striped shirt. c, Wearing sweater.
5000 le, Wearing plaid shirt.

2003, July 1
2636 A411 2500 le Sheet of 3, #a-c 6.50 6.50

Souvenir Sheet

2637 A411 5000 le multi 4.25 4.25

Circus Performers — A412

No. 2638, 2000 le: a, Peggy Williams. b, Nico. c, Steve T. J. Tatter Smith. d, Uncle Dippy.
No. 2639, 2000 le: a, Caracal. b, Chairs. c, Elena Panova. d, Chinese Circus.

Sheets of 4, #a-d

2003, July 1 **Litho.**
2638-2639 A412 Set of 2 13.50 13.50

Powered Flight, Cent. — A413

No. 2640, 1500 le: a, Wright Brothers first plane (gray background). b, Voisin-Farmin (blue background). c, Levavasseur Antoinette (pink background). d, Nieuport (numbered 345).
No. 2641, 1500 le: a, Wright Brothers first plane (blue background). b, Voisin-Farmin (gray background). c, Levavasseur Antoinette (blue background). d, Nieuport (no number on plane).
No. 2642, 5000 le, Henri Farmin Crossing Finish Line in Voisin-Farmin plane. No. 2643, 5000 le, Roland Garros and others around airplane.

2003, July 14 **Sheets of 4, #a-d**
2640-2641 A413 Set of 2 10.50 10.50

Souvenir Sheets
2642-2643 A413 Set of 2 8.50 8.50

Inscriptions on No. 2640 are incorrect.
See also No. 2751.

Tour de France Bicycle Race, Cent. — A414

No. 2644, 1500 le: a, Ferdinand Kubler, 1950. b, Hugo Koblet, 1951. c, Fausto Coppi, 1952. d, Louison Bobet, 1953.
No. 2645, 1500 le: a, Bobet, 1954. b, Bobet, 1955. c, Roger Walkowiak, 1956. d, Jacques Anquetil, 1957.
No. 2646, 1500 le: a, Eddy Merckx, 1970. b, Merckx, 1971. c, Merckx, 1972. d, Luis Ocana, 1973.
No. 2647, 5000 le, Bobet, 1953-55. No. 2648, 5000 le, Anquetil, 1957, diff. No. 2649, 5000 le, Bernard Hinault, 1978.

Sheets of 4, #a-d

2003, July 14 ***Perf. 13¼***
2644-2646 A414 Set of 3 15.50 15.50

Souvenir Sheets
2647-2649 A414 Set of 3 13.00 13.00

Olympic Medalists A415

Designs: 300 le, Forrest Smithson, 1908. 400 le, Hannes Kolehmainen, 1912. 500 le, Larissa Latynina, 1964. 800 le, Klaus Dibiasi, 1976. 1000 le, Archie Hahn, 1904. 1500 le, M. Hurley. 2000 le, Ray Ewry, 1900. 3000 le, Henry Taylor, 1908.

2003, Nov. 17 ***Perf. 13¼***
2650-2657 A415 Set of 8 7.75 7.75

Christmas A416

Paintings by Pontormo Rosso Fiorentino: 100 le, Madonna and Child with St. Anne and Four Saints. 150 le, Madonna and Child with Two Saints. 500 le, Madonna and Child Enthroned with Four Saints (Ognissanti Altarpiece). 4000 le, Madonna Enthroned Between Two Saints.
5000 le, Madonna with Saints.

2003, Nov. 17 ***Perf. 14¼***
2658-2661 A416 Set of 4 4.00 4.00

Souvenir Sheet
2662 A416 5000 le multi 4.25 4.25

New Year 2004 (Year of the Monkey) — A417

No. 2663 — Background color: a, Yellow orange. b, Blue. c, Rose pink. d, Dark orange
2500 le, Pink.

2004, Jan. 15 ***Perf. 13¾***
2663 A417 1200 le Sheet of 4, #a-d 4.00 4.00

Souvenir Sheet
Perf. 14
2664 A417 2500 le multi 2.10 2.10

No. 2664 contains one 42x28mm stamp.

Paintings of Chiao Ping-chen (1689-1726) — A418

No. 2665: a, Untitled painting depicting courtyard. b, Untitled landscape. c, Court Ladies (woman with purple robe at LR). d, Court Ladies (woman with purple robe at center)
5000 le, The Beauty of Traditional Chinese Architecture in Painting.

2004, Jan. 21 ***Perf. 13¼***
2665 A418 2000 le Sheet of 4, #a-d 6.50 6.50

Imperf
2666 A418 5000 le shown 4.25 4.25

No. 2665 contains four 38x50mm stamps.

British Council, 60th Anniv. A419

Frame colors: 500 le, Gray green. 1000 le, Dull green. 2000 le, Purple. 3000 le, Red.

2004, Jan. 29 ***Perf. 14***
2667-2670 A419 Set of 4 5.50 5.50

Map & Lion Type of 1964 Redrawn

2004, Feb. 4 **Self-Adhesive** ***Die Cut***
2671 A38 1000 le multi .85 .85

Printed in sheets of 10.

Paintings by Norman Rockwell — A420

No. 2672: a, Ice Cream Carrier. b, The Voyeur. c, Teacher's Birthday. d, Fisk Tires Advertisement.
5000 le, Cousin Reginald Plays Pirate.

2004, Feb. 24 **Litho.** ***Perf. 13½***
2672 A420 2000 le Sheet of 4, #a-d 6.50 6.50

Souvenir Sheet
2673 A420 5000 le multi 4.25 4.25

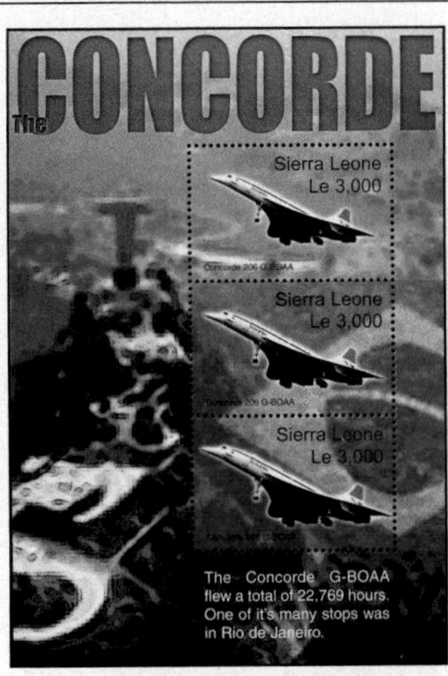

Cessation of Concorde Flights in 2003 — A421

No. 2674, 3000 le — Concorde 206-G BOAA and: a, Blue background. b, Top half of Brazilian flag. b, Bottom half of Brazilian flag.
No. 2675, 3000 le — Concorde G-AXDN and: a, Pink background. b, Top half of Egyptian flag (red stripe). c, Bottom half of Egyptian flag.
No. 2676, 3000 le — Concorde G-ADXN Aircraft 101 and: a, City skyline. b, Top half of Kenyan flag (black stripe). c, Bottom half of Kenyan flag.

2004, Feb. 24 ***Perf. 13¼x13½***

Sheets of 3, #a-c
2674-2676 A421 Set of 3 22.50 22.50

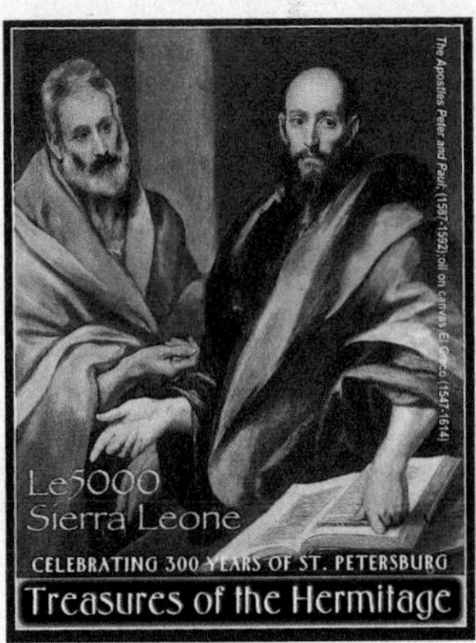

Paintings from the Hermitage, St. Petersburg, Russia — A422

No. 2677: a, The Birth of St. John the Baptist, by Jacopo Tintoretto. b, Penitent Mary Magdalene, by Titian. c, The Death of St. Petronilla, by Simone Pignoni. d, The Assumption of the Virgin, by Bartolomé Esteban Murillo. e, St. Jerome Hears the Trumpet, by Jusepe de Ribera. f, St. George and the Dragon, by Tintoretto.
No. 2678 — Paintings by Elisabeth Vigée-Lebrun: a, Countess A. S. Stroganova and Her Son. b, Count G. I. Chernyshev Holding a Mask. c, Self-portrait. d, Baron G. A. Stroganov.
No. 2679, The Apostles Peter and Paul, by El Greco. No. 2680, A Visit to the Priest, by Jean-Baptiste Greuze, horiz.

2004, Feb. 24 **Litho.** ***Perf. 13¼***
2677 A422 1400 le Sheet of 6, #a-f 7.00 7.00
2678 A422 2000 le Sheet of 4, #a-d 6.50 6.50

Imperf
2679 A422 5000 le shown 4.25 4.25

Size: 100x69mm
2680 A422 5000 le multi 4.25 4.25

Marilyn Monroe (Larger Final Zero) — A423

Marilyn Monroe (Zeroes Same Size) — A424

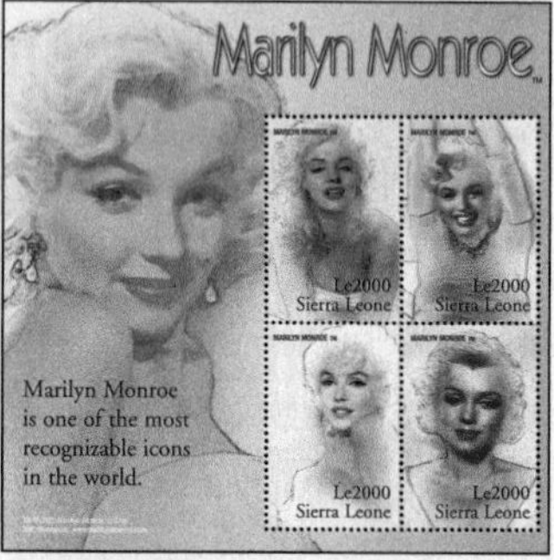

Marilyn Monroe — A425

2004, May 3 *Perf. 14*

2681 A423 1000 le Pair, #a-b 1.60 1.60

Perf. 13½x13¼

2682 A424 1000 le Pair, #a-b 1.60 1.60
2683 A425 2000 le Sheet of 4, #a-d 6.50 6.50

First Orbiting Astronauts of China, US and Russia — A426

No. 2684, horiz. — Yang Lewei: a, Wearing flight jumpsuit. b, Wearing uniform. c, Wearing space suit. d, Wearing space suit, giving hand gesture.

No. 2685: a, Vostok 1. b, John Glenn. c, Friendship 7. d, Yuri Gagarin. e, Shenzhou 5. f, Yang Lewei, diff.

No. 2686, 5000 le, Yang Lewei, diff. No. 2687, 5000 le, Glenn, diff.

2004, May 10 *Perf. 13¼x13½*

2684 A426 900 le Horiz. strip of 4, #a-d 2.75 2.75

Perf. 13½x13¼

2685 A426 1200 le Sheet of 6, #a-f 5.50 5.50

Souvenir Sheets

2686-2687 A426 Set of 2 7.75 7.75

No. 2684 printed in sheets containing two strips.

Cats A427

Designs: 100 le, Ruddy Somali. 800 le, Bombay. 1200 le, Burmese. 3000 le, Blue British Shorthair.

No. 2692, vert.: a, Persian. b, Colorpoint Shorthair. c, Cornish Rex. d, Blue Point Balinese.

5000 le, Devon Rex.

Perf. 13¼x13½, 13½x13¼

2004, May 17

2688-2691 A427 Set of 4 4.25 4.25
2692 A427 1700 le Sheet of 4, #a-d 5.50 5.50

Souvenir Sheet

2693 A427 5000 le multi 4.00 4.00

Moths and Butterflies A428

Designs: 200 le, Io moth. 300 le, Hackberry butterfly. 400 le, Red admiral butterfly. 4000 le, Spangled fritillary butterfly.

No. 2698: a, Pearl crescent butterfly. b, Pipevine swallowtail butterfly. c, Alfalfa looper moth. d, Tiger swallowtail butterfly.

5000 le, Cecropia moth.

2004, May 17 *Perf. 13¼x13½*

2694-2697 A428 Set of 4 4.00 4.00
2698 A428 1700 le Sheet of 4, #a-d 5.50 5.50

Souvenir Sheet

2699 A428 5000 le multi 4.00 4.00

Birds — A429

Designs: 500 le, Belted kingfisher. 1000 le, Burrowing owl. 1500 le, Crested caracara. 2000 le, Red-headed finch.

No. 2704, horiz.: a, Snail kite. b, Avocet. c, Greater flamingo. d, Bald eagle.

5000 le, Ring-necked pheasant, horiz.

Perf. 13½x13¼, 13¼x13½

2004, May 17

2700-2703 A429 Set of 4 4.00 4.00
2704 A429 1700 le Sheet of 4, #a-d 5.50 5.50

Souvenir Sheet

2705 A429 5000 le multi 4.00 4.00

Fish A430

Designs: 800 le, Banded sculpin. 1100 le, Black durgon. No. 2708, 1400 le, Atlantic spadefish. No. 2709, 1400 le, Queen triggerfish.

No. 2710: a, Peacock flounder. b, Northern puffer. c, Sea raven. d, Tiger shark.

5000 le, Sea lamprey, vert.

Perf. 13¼x13½, 13½x13¼

2004, May 17

2706-2709 A430 Set of 4 4.00 4.00
2710 A430 1700 le Sheet of 4, #a-d 5.50 5.50

Souvenir Sheet

2711 A430 5000 le multi 4.00 4.00

Election of Pope John Paul II, 25th Anniv. (in 2003) — A431

No. 2712 — Pope John Paul II: a, Visiting Australia, 1986. b, With John Bonica, 1987. c, Visiting Croatia, 2003. d, Celebrating 25th anniversary mass, 2003.

2004, May 24 *Perf. 13¼x13½*

2712 A431 2000 le Sheet of 4, #a-d 6.50 6.50

Souvenir Sheet

Deng Xiaoping (1904-97), Chinese Leader — A432

2004, June 1 *Perf. 14*

2713 A432 5000 le multi 4.00 4.00

2004 Summer Olympics, Athens A433

Designs: 250 le, Marathon, 1908. 300 le, Dimitrios Vikelas, first president of Intl. Olympic Committee. 1500 le, 1896 Olympic medal. 2000 le, Discus thrower.

2004, June 6 *Perf. 14¼*

2714-2717 A433 Set of 4 3.25 3.25

A434

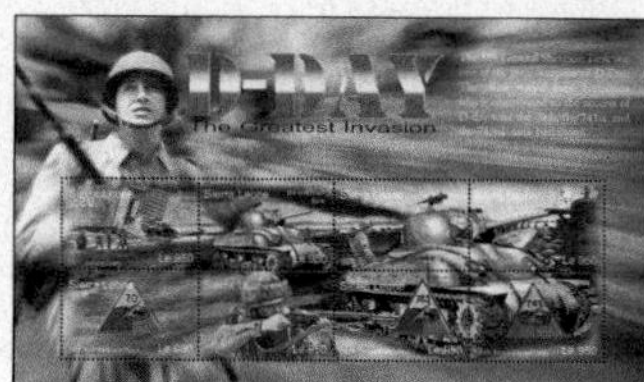

D-Day, 60th Anniv. — A435

No. 2718: a, Gen. Dwight D. Eisenhower. b, Rear Adm. Don P. Moon. c, Lt. Gen. Omar N. Bradley. d, Rear Adm. Alan G. Kirk. e, Maj. Gen. Clarence R. Huebner. f, Maj. Gen. Maxwell D. Taylor.

No. 2719, 950 le: a, LST landing craft. b, M4 Sherman tank. c, M4 Sherman tank and soldier. d, Tank cannon. e, 70th Tank Battalion patch. f, Soldier with rifle. g, 743rd Tank Battalion patch. h, 741st Tank Battalion patch.

No. 2720, 1000 le: a, P-51 Mustang over battle. b, Paratroopers, map. c, Map. d, P-38 Lightning. e, M4 Sherman tank, diff. f, Soldiers. g, LCM landing craft, map. h, US light cruiser, map with numbers.

No. 2721, 1000 le: a, P-47 Thunderbolt. b, Paratroopers, airplanes, map. c, Tank, map. d, Soldier with rifle, map. e, US heavy cruiser. f, US light cruiser, map. g, Ships. h, US destroyer escorts.

No. 2722, 1000 le: a, Spitfire. b, Typhoon. c, Tail of Typhoon, wing of P-38 Lightning, other airplane. d, P-51 Mustang. e, C-47 Skytrain. f, Wing of Typhoon, fuselage of C-47 Skytrain, other airplane. g, P-38 Lightning. h, US Air Force patch.

No. 2723, 1100 le: a, US light cruiser, blimps. b, LST landing craft, blimps. c, Landing craft with door open. d, LST landing craft. e, US armored car. f, Soldiers, tank. g, US medical transport vehicle. h, US armored car leaving landing craft.

No. 2724, 1100 le: a, Soldier with rifle, map, diff. b, Paratrooper, 101st Airborne Division patch. c, Paratrooper, tail of plane. d, Nose of airplane. e, Gen. Eisenhower. f, Gen. Bernard Montgomery. g, Paratrooper, 82nd Airborne Division patch. h, Two paratroopers, C-47 Skytrain.

2004, June 1 *Perf. 14*

2718 A434 1400 le Sheet of 6, #a-f 7.00 7.00

Sheets of 8, #a-h

2719-2724 A435 Set of 6 40.00 40.00

British Lighthouses A436

Designs: 1800 le, Smalls Lighthouse. 2000 le, Needles Rocks Lighthouse. 2500 le, St. John's Point Lighthouse. 3500 le, Bell Rock Lighthouse. 4000 le, Eddystone Lighthouse.

2004, June 17 *Perf. 14¾x14*

2725-2729 A436 Set of 5 11.50 11.50

American Indian Artifacts — A437

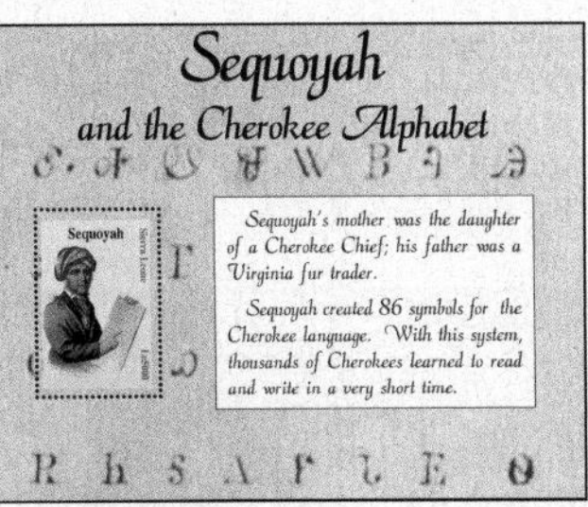

American Indians — A438

No. 2730: a, Arapaho pipe bag. b, Apache basket. c, Blackfoot parfleche. d, Crow elkhide robe. e, Iroquois moccasins. f, Hopi canteen. g, Sioux parfleche. h, Navajo rug. i, Nez Perce cradle.

No. 2731 — Ioway chiefs and warriors: a, Ne-O-Mon-Ne. b, Ma-Has-Kah. c, Moa-Na-Hon-Ga. d, Tah-Ro-Hon. e, Not-Chi-Mi-Ne. f, Shau-Hau-Napo-Tinia.

No. 2732, horiz. — Paintings by Charles Russell: a, Medicine Man. b, War Party. c, Signal Smoke.

5000 le, Sequoyah.

2004, July 5 ***Perf. 14***

2730 A437 1000 le Sheet of 9, #a-i 7.50 7.50
2731 A438 1500 le Sheet of 6, #a-f 7.50 7.50
2732 A438 3000 le Sheet of 3, #a-c 7.50 7.50
Nos. 2730-2732 (3) 22.50 22.50

Souvenir Sheet

2733 A438 5000 le multi 4.00 4.00

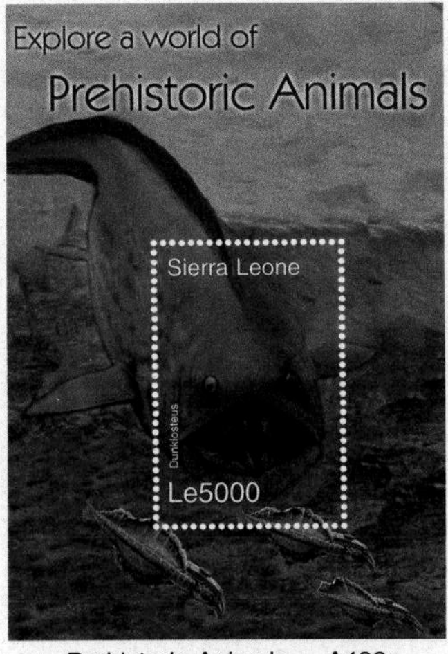

Prehistoric Animals — A439

No. 2734, 2000 le: a, Apatosaurus. b, Styracosaurus. c, Plateosaurus. d, Pachyrhinosaurus.

No. 2735, 2000 le, horiz.: a, Camarasaurus. b, Iystrosaurus. c, Ankylosaurus. d, Herrerasaurus.

No. 2736, 5000 le, Dunklosteus. No. 2737, 5000 le, Archaeopteryx, horiz.

2004 **Sheets of 4, #a-d** ***Perf. 14***

2734-2735 A439 Set of 2 13.00 13.00

Souvenir Sheets

2736-2737 A439 Set of 2 8.25 8.25

No. 2734 has two labels.

Orchids — A440

Designs: 150 le, Catasetum pileatum. No. 2739, 400 le, Cattleya araguainsis. No. 2740, 400 le, Barkeria spectabilis. 3500 le, Catasetum fimbriatum.

No. 2742: a, Odontonia vesta. b, Ancistro rothschildianus. c, Ansellia africana. d, Aspasia epidendroides.

5000 le, Bulbophyllum lobbii.

2004, May 17 **Litho.** ***Perf. 12½***

2738-2741 A440 Set of 4 3.75 3.75
2742 A440 1700 le Sheet of 4, #a-d 5.50 5.50

Souvenir Sheet

2743 A440 5000 le multi 4.25 4.25

Dogs — A441

Designs: 250 le, Great Pyrenees. 600 le, Kerry Blue terrier. 1300 le, Mastiff. 1800 le, English sheepdog.

No. 2748: a, Sealyham terrier. b, Norwich terrier. c, Wheaton terrier. d, Bull terrier.

5000 le, Greyhound.

2004, May 17

2744-2747 A441 Set of 4 3.25 3.25
2748 A441 1700 le Sheet of 4, #a-d 5.50 5.50

Souvenir Sheet

2749 A441 5000 le multi 4.25 4.25

Souvenir Sheet

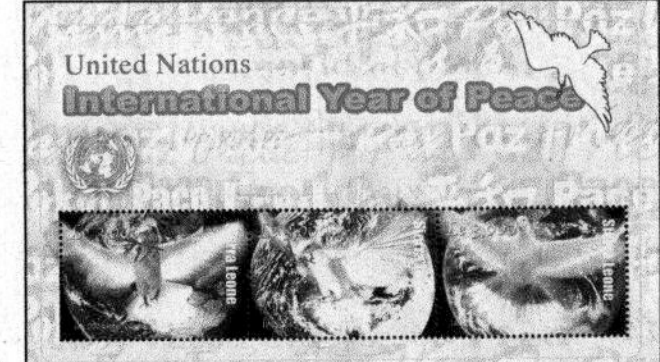

Intl. Year of Peace — A442

No. 2750 — Position of olive branch carried by dove: a, Below last two zeros of denomination. b, Below three and first two zeros of denomination. c, Covered by last two zeros of denomination.

2004, June 1 ***Perf. 14***

2750 A442 3000 le Sheet of 3, #a-c 7.50 7.50

Powered Flight Type of 2003

No. 2751: a, Curtiss Triad. b, Avro Biplane. c, Curtiss America. d, Farnborought Be-2.

2004, July 17

2751 A413 1500 le Sheet of 4, #a-d 5.00 5.00

Worldwide Fund for Nature (WWF) — A443

No. 2752 — Patas monkey: a, Monkey grooming another. b, Monkeys and flower. c, Adult and juvenile. d, Head of monkey.

2004, Oct. 11 ***Perf. 13¼x13½***

2752 A443 1000 le Block of 4, #a-d 3.75 3.75
e. Miniature sheet, 2 each #2752a-2752d 8.00 8.00

for surcharge see No. 2910.

National Basketball Association Players — A444

Designs: No. 2753, 700 le, Kobe Bryant, Los Angeles Lakers. No. 2754, 700 le, Carmelo Anthony, Denver Nuggets. No. 2755, 700 le, Yao Ming, Houston Rockets. No. 2756, 700 le, Jermaine O'Neal, Indiana Pacers. No. 2757, 700 le, Leandro Barbosa, Phoenix Suns. 2000 le, Vlade Divac, Sacramento Kings.

2004 ***Perf. 14***

2753-2758 A444 Set of 6 4.50 4.50

Issued: Nos. 2753, 2758, 11/2; No. 2754, 11/4; Nos. 2755-2756, 11/6; No. 2757, 12/13. Each stamp printed in a sheet of 12.

George Herman "Babe" Ruth (1895-1948), Baseball Player — A445

2004, Dec. 13

2759 A445 500 le multi .40 .40

Printed in sheet of 16.

National Soccer Team — A446

2004, Dec. 13 ***Perf. 12***

2760 A446 2000 le multi 1.75 1.75

Pres. Ronald Reagan and Queen Elizabeth II — A447

No. 2761, Reagan and Queen: a, With spouses. b, Making a toast.

2004, Dec. 13 ***Perf. 13½***

2761 A447 2000 le Horiz. pair, #a-b 3.25 3.25

Printed in sheets containing three each of Nos. 2761a and 2761b.

Ocean Liners A448

Designs: 600 le, Paris. 800 le, Statendam. 1000 le, Stavengerfjord. 1500 le, Campania. 2000 le, Drottningholm. 3000 le, Lusitania.

5000 le, United States, horiz.

2004, Dec. 13 ***Perf. 14¼***

2762-2767 A448 Set of 6 7.25 7.25

Souvenir Sheet

2768 A448 5000 le multi 4.25 4.25

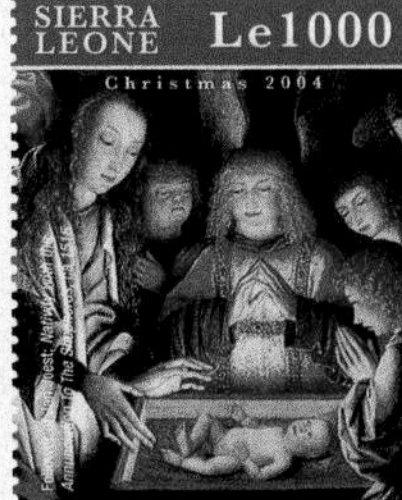

Christmas A449

Designs: 1000 le, Nativity with the Annunciation to the Shepherds, by Follower of Jan Joest. 1500 le, Christmas Snow, by Norman Rockwell. 2000 le, The Christmas Tree, by E. Osborn. 5000 le, The Spirit of Christmas, by Rockwell.

8000 le, Madonna and Child Enthroned with Two Angels, by Fra Filippo Lippi.

2004, Dec. 13 ***Perf. 12¼x12***

2769-2772 A449 Set of 4 7.75 7.75

Souvenir Sheet

2773 A449 8000 le multi 6.50 6.50

Miniature Sheet

Yasujiro Ozu (1903-63), Film Director — A450

No. 2774 — Posters or scenes from: a, Tokyo Story. b, Late Spring. c, Early Summer. d, Equinox Flower. e, Good Morning. f, An Autumn Afternoon.

2004, Dec. 13 ***Perf. 13¼***

2774 A450 1400 le Sheet of 6, #a-f 7.00 7.00

Miniature Sheets

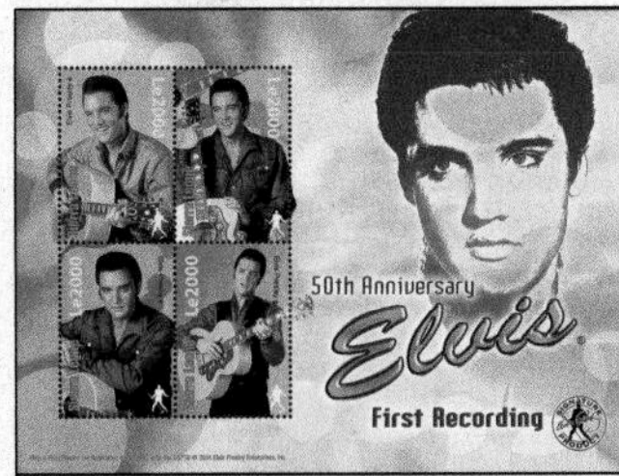

A451

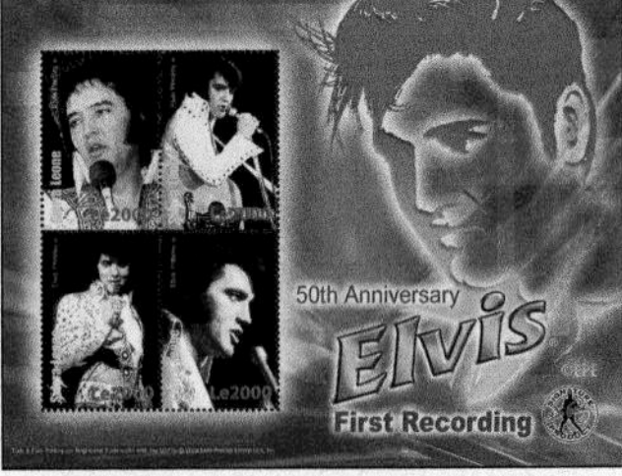

Elvis Presley (1935-77) — A452

Various depictions of Presley.

2004, Dec. 13 ***Perf. 13½***

2775 A451 2000 le Sheet of 4, #a-d 6.50 6.50
2776 A452 2000 le Sheet of 4, #a-d 6.50 6.50

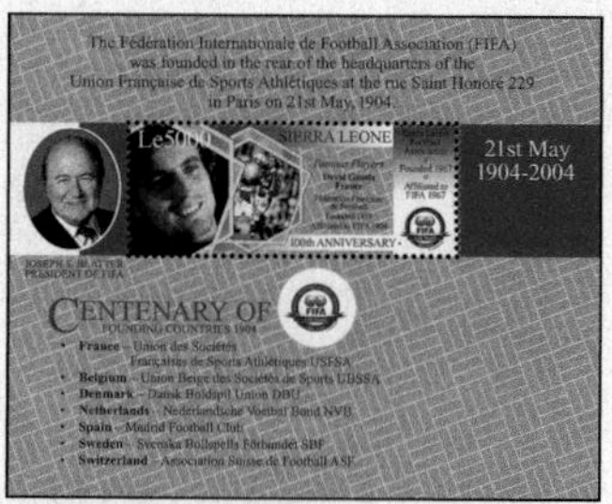

FIFA (Fédération Internationale de Football Association), Cent. — A453

No. 2777: a, Diego Simeone. b, Careca. c, Oliver Bierhoff. d, Kevin Keegan.
5000 le, David Ginola.

2004, Dec. 13 *Perf. 12¾x12½*
2777 A453 2000 le Sheet of 4, #a-d 6.50 6.50

Souvenir Sheet

2778 A453 5000 le multi 4.25 4.25

Locomotives, 200th Anniv. — A454

No. 2779, 1000 le: a, Stephenson's Rocket. b, Indonesian State Railway B50 class 2-4-0. c, Eurostar Paris-London train. d, China Railways SY Class 2-8-2. e, Baldwin 0-6-0. f, Hunsle 0-4-2T. g, Bagnall 0-6-0 ST Progress. h, North British-built 4-8-2T. i, Baldwin 0-6-2l.

No. 2780, 1000 le, vert.: a, GWR Mogul, Severn Valley Railway. b, Kitson Meyer 0-6-6-0. c, China Railways SL7 Class Pacific. d, Fireman fueling Yugoslav Class 20 2-6-0. e, Lookout man with flag. f, Workers filling sandboxes. g, Indian Railways locomotive taking water. h, Man on Indian Railways ZP Pacific Pulgeon. i, Worker cleaning smokebox.

No. 2781, 1000 le, vert.: a, LMS 8F 2-8-0, Great Central Railway. b, Rhodesia Railways 12 Class 4-8-2. c, DR German Railways 01 Class Pacific. d, Indian Railways McArthur 2-8-2. e, USATC 0-6-0T. f, China Railways KD6 2-8-0. g, Polish Feldbahn 0-8-0T, h, Indian Railways Mawd 2-8-2. i, North British 2-10-0.

No. 2782, 1000 le, vert.: a, B12 Class 4-6-0. b, Uruguay Railways Beyer Peacock Mogul 2-6-0. c, Ghana Railways Diesel-electric locomotive. d, Bagnall 0-4-0. e, Ledo Brickworks, Upper Assam. f, Train at Indian sugar mill. g, Carbon converter, Tangshan Locomotive Works, China. h, Crane loading timber on train car, Lanxiang, China. i, Worker carrying clay to train at Ledo Brickworks.

No. 2783, 5000 le, Ghan. No. 2784, 5000 le, Hudson Line. No. 2785, 5000 le, Blue Train. No. 2786, 5000 le, Bullet Train.

Perf. 13¼x13½, 13½x13¼

2004, Dec. 13 **Sheets of 9, #a-i**
2779-2782 A454 Set of 4 30.00 30.00

Souvenir Sheets

2783-2786 A454 Set of 4 16.50 16.50

New Year 2005 (Year of the Rooster) — A455

No. 2787: a, Country name in blue. b, Country name in red.

2005, Feb. 23 *Perf. 12*
2787 A455 600 le Pair, #a-b 1.00 1.00

Printed in sheets containing two pairs.

Pope John Paul II (1920-2005) and French President Jacques Chirac — A456

2005, May 24 Litho. *Perf. 13½x13¼*
2788 A456 1800 le multi 1.60 1.60

Printed in sheet of 6.

Maimonides (1135-1204), Philosopher A457

2005, May 24 *Perf. 12*
2789 A457 2000 le multi 1.75 1.75

Printed in sheets of 4.

Rotary International, Cent. — A458

No. 2790: a, Map, handshake. b, Map, people, "Service Above Self." c, Emblem. d, Founder Paul P. Harris.

2005, May 24 *Perf. 12¾*
2790 A458 1800 le Sheet of 4, #a-d 6.25 6.25

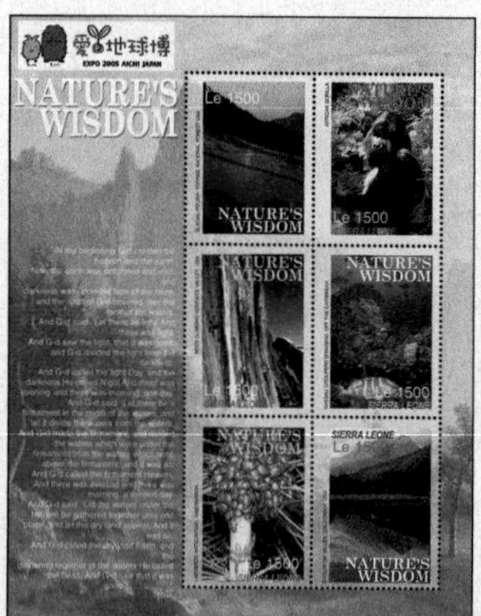

Expo 2005, Aichi, Japan — A459

No. 2791: a, Glacial polish, Toiyabe National Forest, Nevada. b, African gorilla. c, Rock climber, Yosemite Valley, California. d, Nassau grouper spawning, Caribbean Sea. e, Ladybug swarm. f, Evolution Valley, California.

2005, May 24 *Perf. 12*
2791 A459 1500 le Sheet of 6, #a-f 7.75 7.75

Hans Christian Andersen (1805-75), Author — A460

No. 2792: a, Little Claus and Big Claus. b, Little Ida's Flowers. c, The Tinderbox.
5000 le, The Princess and the Pea.

2005, May 24 *Perf. 12¾*
2792 A460 3000 le Sheet of 3, #a-c 7.75 7.75

Souvenir Sheet

Perf. 12

2793 A460 5000 le multi 4.25 4.25

No. 2792 contains three 42x28mm stamps.

Friedrich von Schiller (1759-1805), Writer — A461

No. 2794: a, Statue of Schiller, Berlin. b, Statue of Schiller, Munich. c, Statue of Schiller and Johann Wolfgang von Goethe.
5000 le, Schiller.

2005, May 24 *Perf. 12¾*
2794 A461 3000 le Sheet of 3, #a-c 7.75 7.75

Souvenir Sheet

2795 A461 5000 le multi 4.25 4.25

Jules Verne (1828-1905), Writer — A462

No. 2796: a, Verne's tomb, Amiens, France. b, Michael Arden, From the Earth to the Moon. c, Verne, Moon.
5000 le, Verne, hot air balloon.

2005, May 24
2796 A462 3000 le Sheet of 3, #a-c 7.75 7.75

Souvenir Sheet

2797 A462 5000 le multi 4.25 4.25

Battle of Trafalgar, Bicent. — A463

Paintings of various battle scenes: 500 le, 1000 le, 2000 le, 5000 le.
8000 le, Battle scene, diff.

2005, May 24 *Perf. 12¾*
2798-2801 A463 Set of 4 7.25 7.25

Souvenir Sheet

Perf. 12

2802 A463 8000 le multi 7.00 7.00

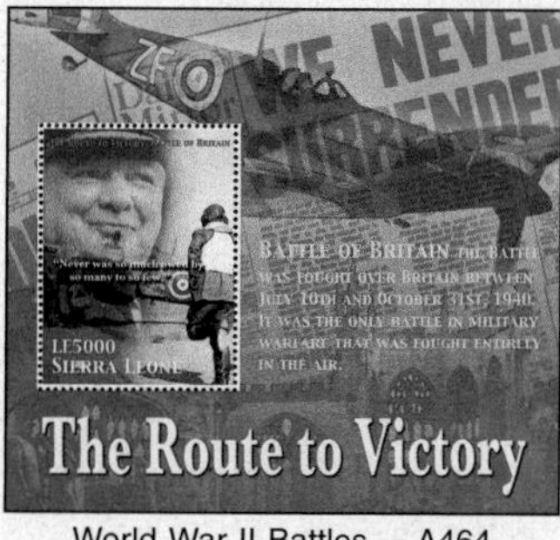

World War II Battles — A464

No. 2803, 2000 le, horiz. — Battle of Britain: a, Luftwaffe launches air strikes on Britain. b, Civilians take cover on underground station platform. c, Pilots race to planes. d, War in the sky.

No. 2804, 2000 le, horiz. — Battle of Stalingrad: a, Russians counterattack. b, Destroyed German tank. c, End of the German 6th Army. d, German prisoners of war.

No. 2805, 5000 le, Winston Churchill. No. 2806, 5000 le, Russian victory at Stalingrad, horiz.

2005, May 24 *Perf. 13¼*

Sheets of 4, #a-d

2803-2804 A464 Set of 2 14.00 14.00

Souvenir Sheets

2805-2806 A464 Set of 2 8.50 8.50

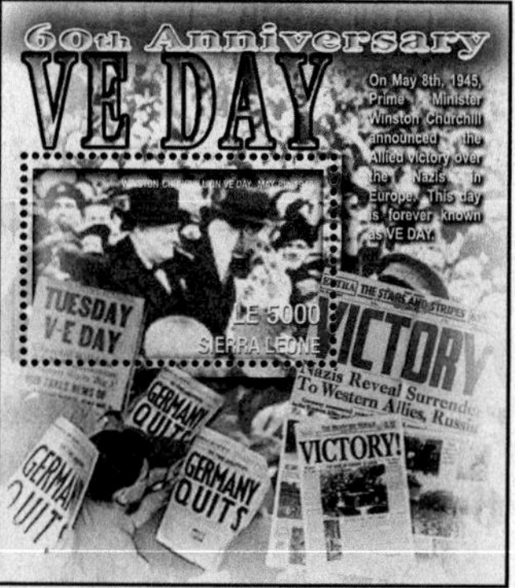

End of World War II, 60th Anniv. — A465

No. 2807, 2000 le: a, Franklin D. Roosevelt, Winston Churchill. b, Secretary of Defense Louis Johnson, Generals Douglas MacArthur and Omar Bradley. c, Meeting of Allied Expeditionary Force commanders. d, Winston Churchill.

No. 2808, 2000 le: a, Roosevelt's address to Congress after Pearl Harbor attack. b, "Little Boy" atomic bomb. c, "Fat Man" atomic bomb. d, Japanese surrender ceremony.

No. 2809, 5000 le, Winston Churchill on V-E Day. No. 2810, 5000 le, Women reading newspapers.

2005, May 24 *Perf. 12¾*

Sheets of 4, #a-d

2807-2808 A465 Set of 2 14.00 14.00

Souvenir Sheets

2809-2810 A465 Set of 2 8.50 8.50

The picture used for No. 2807b is not from the World War II era as Johnson was not Secretary of Defense until 1949.

Fire Fighting Apparatus A466

Designs: 900 le, Boss Hoss Limited Edition fire motorcycle, German flag. 1200 le, Pumper

8 by 10, Austrian flag. 1500 le, Hydraulic platform truck, Germany, Ireland flag. 1800 le, Scania fire appliance, Australian flag.

No. 2815, 2000 le — Trucks from: a, Japan. b, Germany. c, Canada. d, Ireland.

No. 2816, 2000 le: a, Mercedes-Benz 2635 Thoma, Germany. b, 1997 Dennis Sabre water tender, Ireland. c, Microscopic fire truck, Japan. d, Scania fire appliance, Australia, diff.

No. 2817, 2000 le: a, 1935 Chevrolet fire truck. b, 1914 International fire truck. c, 1885 Chemical fire engine. d, 1963 Mason FD1.

No. 2818, 5000 le, Fire engine, US flag. No. 2819, 5000 le, 1890 horse-driven fire wagon, British flag.

2005, May 24 ***Perf. 12¾***

2811-2814 A466 Set of 4 4.75 4.75

Sheets of 4, #a-d

2815-2817 A466 Set of 3 21.00 21.00

Souvenir Sheets

2818-2819 A466 Set of 2 8.50 8.50

Quesnard Lighthouse, Alderney — A467

2005, June 17

2820 A467 4500 le multi 4.00 4.00

Wedding of Prince Charles and Camilla Parker Bowles A468

Designs: No. 2821, 2000 le, Families of bride and groom. No. 2822, 2000 le, Charles and Camilla, vert. No. 2823, 2000 le, Charles, Camilla and bookstand, vert.

Perf. 13¼x13½, 13½x13¼

2005, Sept. 22 **Litho.**

2821-2823 A468 Set of 3 5.25 5.25

A469

Elvis Presley (1935-70) — A470

No. 2824, 2000 le — Elvis with microphone with background colors of: a, Blue. b, Dark green. c, Yellow green. d, Red and violet.

No. 2825, 2000 le — Elvis: a, Playing guitar, blue denomination. b, Holding guitar, pale olive denomination. c, Holding guitar, pink denomination. d, Playing guitar, lilac denomination.

2005, Dec. 1 **Litho.** ***Perf. 13¼***

Sheets of 4, #a-d

2824-2825 A469 Set of 2 13.50 13.50

Litho. & Embossed

Serpentine Die Cut 8¾

2826 A470 18,000 le gold & multi 15.50 15.50

Christmas — A471

Paintings: 500 le, The Virgin with Grapes, by Pierre Mignard. 1500 le, Adoration of the Shepherds, by Bartolomé Esteban Murillo. 2000 le, Madonna with the Child, by Murillo. 3000 le, Fountain of Life, by Hans Holbein, the Elder.

6000 le, Adoration of the Shepherds, by Murillo, diff.

2005, Dec. 13 **Litho.** ***Perf. 12½***

2827-2830 A471 Set of 4 6.00 6.00

Souvenir Sheet

2831 A471 6000 le multi 5.25 5.25

Souvenir Sheet

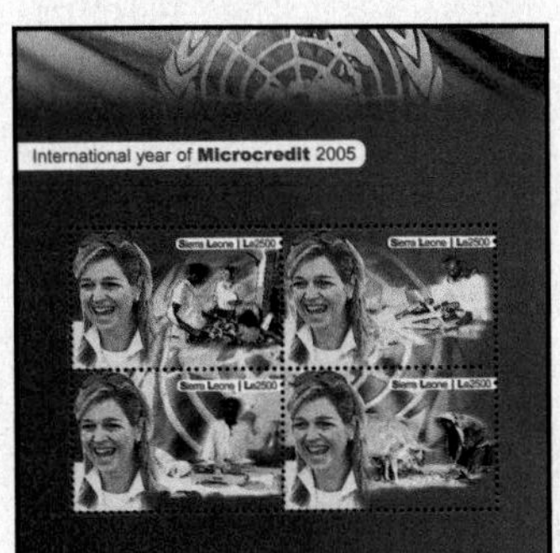

Intl. Year of Microcredit — A472

No. 2832 — Woman at left and: a, Man and woman. b, Man holding stick. c, Man with scales. d, Woman and cow.

2005

2832 A472 2500 le Sheet of 4, #a-d 8.50 8.50

New Year 2006 (Year of the Dog) — A473

In its Position, by Xu Beihong: 600 le, Detail. 2000 le, Entire painting.

2006 ***Perf. 13¼***

2833 A473 600 le multi .50 .50

Souvenir Sheet

Perf. 11¼x11½

2834 A473 2000 le multi 1.75 1.75

No. 2833 printed in sheets of 4. No. 2834 contains one 26x60mm stamp.

Pope Benedict XVI — A474

2006, Jan. 24 ***Perf. 13¼***

2835 A474 10,000 le multi 8.50 8.50

Printed in sheets of 4.

Miniature Sheet

Indian Chiefs — A475

No. 2836 — Chief and tribe: a, Medicine Crow, Crow. b, Quanah Parker, Comanche. c, Garfield, Jicarilla. d, Pretty Eagle, Crow. e, Plenty Coups, Crow. f, He Dog, Oglala. g, Crow King, Hunkpapa. h, Pontiac, Ottawa. i, Naiche, Chiricahua. j, Gall, Hunkpapa.

2006, Jan. 31

2836 A475 1250 le Sheet of 10, #a-j 11.00 11.00

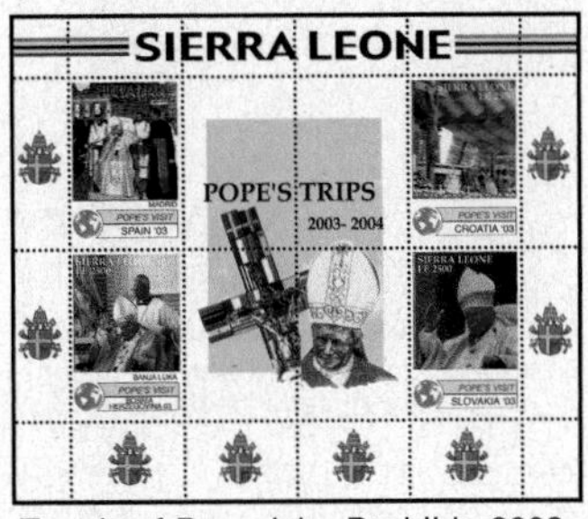

Travels of Pope John Paul II in 2003-04 — A476

No. 2837, 2500 le: a, Madrid, Spain. b, Croatia. c, Banja Luka, Bosnia & Herzegovina. d, Slovakia.

No. 2838, 2500 le: a, Pompeii, Italy. b, Bern Switzerland. c, Lourdes, France. d, Loreto, Italy.

2006, Feb. 27 ***Perf. 13½***

Sheets of 4, #a-d, + 4 Labels

2837-2838 A476 Set of 2 17.00 17.00

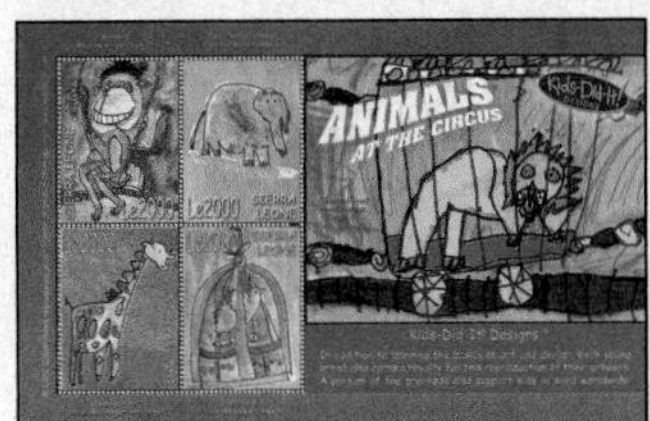

Children's Art — A477

No. 2839, 2000 le — Circus animals: a, Monkey. b, Red-toed elephant. c, Colored giraffe. d, Colored bird.

No. 2840, 2000 le — Reptiles: a, Green gecko. b, Frog. c, Spotted lizard. d, Orange lizard.

No. 2841, 2000 le — Flowers: a, Yellow flowers. b, Poppies. c, Orange flowers. d, Lilies.

2006 **Sheets of 4, #a-d** ***Perf. 13¼***

2839-2841 A477 Set of 3 21.00 21.00

2006 Winter Olympics, Turin A478

Designs: 1000 le, US #1146. 1300 le, Canada #1152. 2000 le, Poster for 1988 Calgary Winter Olympics. 3000 le, Poster for 1960 Squaw Valley Winter Olympics.

2006, Apr. 7 **Litho.** ***Perf. 13¼***

2842-2845 A478 Set of 4 6.25 6.25

Messengers of Peace — A479

No. 2846: a, Michael Douglas, actor. b, United Nations Building, New York.

2006, May 29

2846 A479 2000 le Pair, #a-b 3.50 3.50

Printed in sheets containing 3 each #2846a-2846b.

Souvenir Sheet

US #300, Benjamin Franklin — A480

2006, May 29

2847 A480 6000 le multi 5.25 5.25

Washington 2006 World Stamp Exhibition.

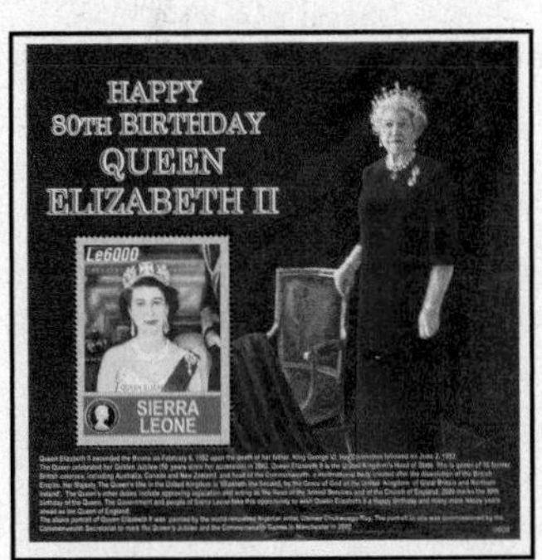

Queen Elizabeth II, 80th Birthday — A481

No. 2848 — Queen wearing: a, Green hat. b, Blue hat. c, No hat. d, Yellow hat.

6000 le, Wearing tiara.

2006, June 13 ***Perf. 14¼***

2848 A481 3000 le Sheet of 4, #a-d 10.50 10.50

Souvenir Sheet

2849 A481 6000 le multi 5.25 5.25

Souvenir Sheet

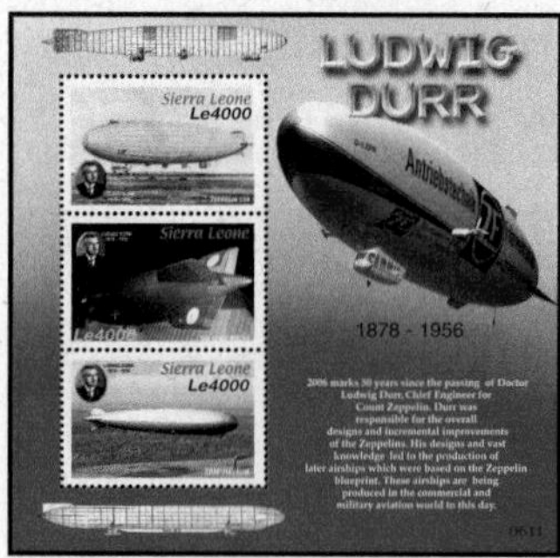

Ludwig Durr (1878-1956), Engineer, and Zeppelins — A482

No. 2850 — Durr and: a, Zeppelin L30. b, The Hindenburg. c, Graf Zeppelin.

2006, July 26 ***Perf. 12¾***
2850 A482 4000 le Sheet of 3, #a-c 10.50 10.50

Rembrandt (1606-69), Painter A483

Designs: 800 le, Abraham Frans. 1000 le, The Rat Catcher. 2000 le, Young Man with Velvet Cap. 8000 le, The Flute Player.
No. 2855, 3000 le: a, Abraham and Isaac. b, Abraham Entertaining the Angels. c, Return of the Prodigal Son. d, Adam and Eve.
No. 2856, 3000 le — Details from The Night Watch: a, Man with black hat, neck ruffle and sash. b, Man holding gun below chin. c, Man with white hat. d, Man with red hat holdiing gun.
No. 2857, 6000 le, Portrait of an Amsterdam Citizen as a Militiaman. No. 2858, 6000 le, Maria Trip, Daughter of Alotte Adriaenson. No. 2859, 6000 le, Homer Dictating to a Scribe.

2006, July 26 ***Perf. 12, 13¼ (#2855)***
2851-2854 A483 Set of 4 10.00 10.00

Sheets of 4, #a-d

2855-2856 A483 Set of 2 21.00 21.00

Imperf
Size: 70x100mm

2857-2859 A483 Set of 3 15.50 15.50

Souvenir Sheet

Elvis Presley (1935-77) — A484

No. 2860 — Presley in: a, White costume. b, Black and white cape. c, Army uniform. d, Blue jacket.

2006, Dec. 21 ***Perf. 13¼***
2860 A484 2000 le Sheet of 4, #a-d 6.75 6.75

Christmas — A485

Details from Main Altar of the Jesuit Church, Antwerp, by Peter Paul Rubens: 1000 le, Angel. 1500 le, Madonna and Child. No. 2863, 2000 le, Angel, diff., with denomination in white at UL. 3000 le, Angel, diff.
No. 2865, 2000 le: a, Like 1000 le. b, Like 1500 le. c, Like No. 2863, with denomination in black at LR. d, Like 3000 le.

2006, Dec. 21 ***Perf. 14***
2861-2864 A485 Set of 4 6.50 6.50

Souvenir Sheet

2865 A485 2000 le Sheet of 4, #a-d 6.75 6.75

Souvenir Sheet

Wolfgang Amadeus Mozart (1756-91), Composer — A486

2006, Dec. 21 **Litho.** ***Perf. 13¼***
2866 A486 7000 le multi 6.00 6.00

Miniature Sheets

Pres. John F. Kennedy (1917-63) — A487

No. 2867, 2000 le — Kennedy: a, At microphones on inauguration day. b, Portrait and cover of inaugural program. c, Taking oath, medal depicting Kennedy. d, And Robert Frost and poem.
No. 2868, 2000 le: a, Kennedy and map of Cuba. b, Map of US, Soviet Premier Nikita Khrushchev, and Soviet R-12 missile. c, Map of Cuba, Kennedy meeting with Soviet Foreign Minister Andrei Gromyko. d, Cuban President Fidel Castro, John and Robert Kennedy.

2006, Dec. 21 ***Perf. 13¼***
Sheets of 4, #a-d

2867-2868 A487 Set of 2 14.00 14.00

Miniature Sheet

Marilyn Monroe (1926-62), Actress — A488

No. 2869: a, With hand on shoulder. b, With straps of brown dress showing. c, With hand behind head. d, Leaning to left.

2006, Dec. 21
2869 A488 2000 le Sheet of 4, #a-d 7.00 7.00

Space Achievements — A489

No. 2870: a, Mir Space Station. b, Space Shuttle Challenger. c, Giotto Comet Probe. d, Luna 9. e, Viking 1. f, International Space Station.
No. 2871, 3000 le: a, Launch of Boeing Delta II rocket. b, Calipso. c, CloudSat. d, Aura, Parasol, Calipso, CloudSat, Aqua and OCO satellites in orbit.
No. 2872, 3000 le, vert. — Artist's conceptions of: a, NASA's crew launch. b, New spacecraft to rendezvous with International Space Station. c, New lunar lander. d, Parachutes deploying after reentry.
No. 2873, 3000 le, vert. — Photos of International Space Station from: a, June 3, 1999. b, Dec. 2, 2000. c, June 15, 2002. d, Aug. 6, 2005.
No. 2874, 6000 le, Apollo 11 Lunar Module. No. 2875, 6000 le, Impactor with Deep Impact Probe. No. 2876, 6000 le, Mars Reconnaissance Orbiter. No. 2877, 6000 le, Space Shuttle Columbia, vert.

2006, Dec. 21
2870 A489 2000 le Sheet of 6, #a-f 10.50 10.50

Sheets of 4, #a-d

2871-2873 A489 Set of 3 32.50 32.50

Souvenir Sheets

2874-2877 A489 Set of 4 21.00 21.00

New Year 2007 (Year of the Pig) A490

2007, Jan. 3 ***Perf. 13¼***
2878 A490 2000 le multi 1.75 1.75

Printed in sheets of 4.

Scouting, Cent. — A491

Designs: 3000 le, Dove, inscriptions in various languages. 6000 le, Dove, inscriptions in various languages, symbols.

2007, Feb. 15
2879 A491 3000 le multi 2.60 2.60

Souvenir Sheet

2880 A491 6000 le multi 5.25 5.25

No. 2867 was printed in sheets of 4 with stamps having slightly different gradations of background color.

Princess Diana (1961-97) — A492

No. 2881, vert. — Diana wearing: a, Yellow dress, country name in red. b, Blue dress, country name in red. c, White dress, country name in green at bottom. d, Yellow dress, country name in green. e, No dress shown, country name in red. f, White dress, country name in green at top.
7000 le, Diana with blue hat.

2007, Mar. 15 **Litho.** ***Perf. 13¼***
2881 A492 1500 le Sheet of 6, #a-f 7.75 7.75

Souvenir Sheet

2882 A492 7000 le multi 6.00 6.00

Concorde — A493

No. 2883, 2000 le: a, Air speed indicator showng speed record. b, Concorde in flight.
No. 2884, 2000 le, horiz.: a, Concorde, Royal Air Force Red Arrows and British flag. b, Concorde over Buckingham Palace.

2007, Mar. 15 **Litho.**
Pairs, #a-b

2883-2884 A493 Set of 2 7.00 7.00

Nos. 2883-2884 each printed in sheets containing three of each stamp.

Pope Benedict XVI — A494

2007, July 12
2885 A494 1500 le multi 1.00 1.00

Printed in sheets of 8.

Miniature Sheet

Ferrari Automobiles, 60th Anniv. — A495

No. 2886: a, 1948 166 Inter. b, 2004 612 Scaguetti. c, 1995 F50. d, 2000 550 Barchetta Pininfarina. e, 1957 250 GT Cabriolet. f, 1963 250 P. g, 1961 246 SP. h, 1981 126 CK.

2007, July 12
2886 A495 1400 le Sheet of 8, #a-h 7.75 7.75

Christmas A496

Painting details: 1000 le, The Annunciation, by Raphael. 1500 le, The Adoration of the Magi, by Raphael. 2000 le, The Presentation of the Christ Child in the Temple, by Raphael. 3000 le, The Nativity and the Arrival of the Magi, by Giovanni di Pietro.

2007, Nov. 28 ***Perf. 14¾x14***
2887-2890 A496 Set of 4 5.00 5.00

Miniature Sheet

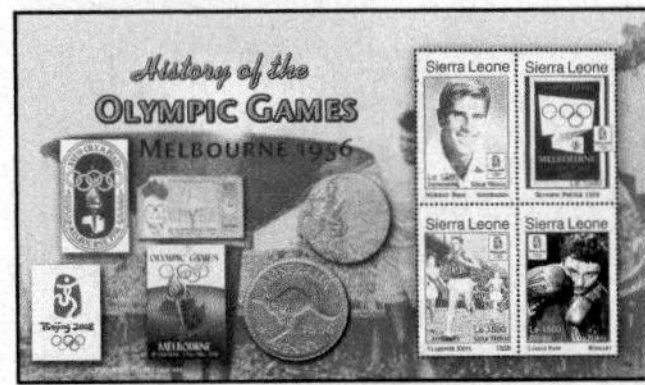

2008 Summer Olympics, Beijing — A497

No. 2891 — 1956 Melbourne Summer Olympics: a, Murray Rose, swimming gold medalist. b, Poster for 1956 Summer Olympics. c, Vladimir Kuts, track gold medalist. d, Laszlo Papp, boxing gold medalist.

2008, Jan. 8 **Litho.** ***Perf. 14***
2891 A497 1500 le Sheet of 4, #a-d 4.00 4.00

Nos. 975-977, 980-981 Surcharged

Methods and Perfs. As Before
2008, Mar. 10

2892 A142 800 le on 3 le #975	*.55*	*.55*
2893 A142 800 le on 5 le #976	*.55*	*.55*
2894 A142 800 le on 8 le #977	*.55*	*.55*
2895 A142 800 le on 20 le #980	*.55*	*.55*
2896 A142 800 le on 35 le #981	*.55*	*.55*
Nos. 2892-2896 (5)	*2.75*	*2.75*

Nos. 2049-2050 Surcharged

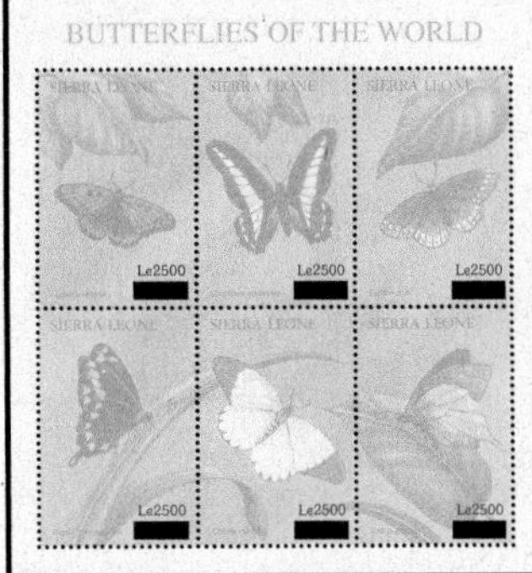

Methods and Perfs. As Before
2008, Mar. 10
2897 A281 2500 le on 500 le Sheet of 6, #a-f, #2049 *10.00 10.00*
2898 A281 2500 le on 600 le Sheet of 6, #a-f, #2050 *10.00 10.00*

Nos. 2120-2121 Surcharged

Methods and Perfs. As Before
2008, Mar. 10
2899 A292 2800 le on 300 le Sheet of 6, #a-f, #2120 *11.50 11.50*
2900 A292 4000 le on 300 le Sheet of 6, #a-f, #2121 *16.00 16.00*

No. 2138 Surcharged

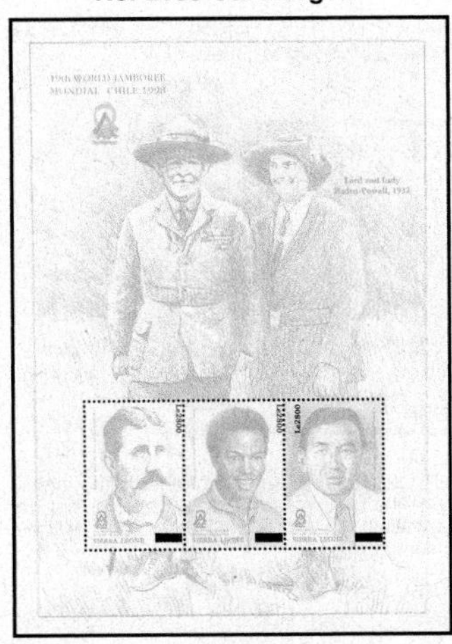

Methods and Perfs As Before
2008, Mar. 10
2901 A297 2800 le on 1500 le Sheet of 3, #a-c *5.75 5.75*

No. 2193 Surcharged

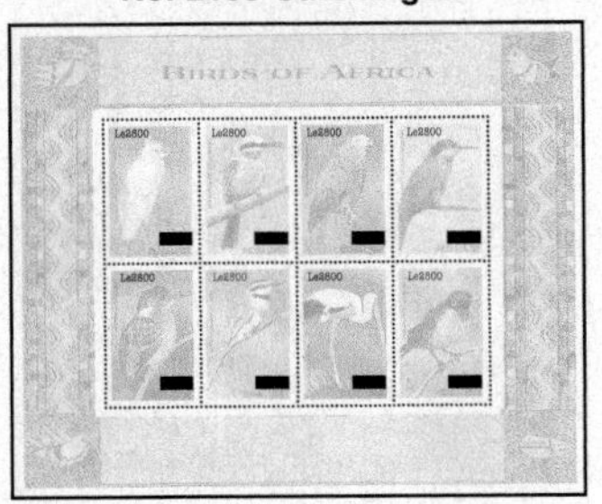

Methods and Perfs As Before
2008, Mar. 10
2902 A305 2800 le on 600 le Sheet of 8, #a-h, #2193 *15.00 15.00*

Nos. 1738a-1738d Surcharged

Methods and Perfs. As Before
2008, Mar. 10

2903 Vert. strip of 4	*9.75*	*9.75*
a. A227 3500 le on 50 le #1738a	*2.40*	*2.40*
b. A227 3500 le on 100 le #1738b	*2.40*	*2.40*
c. A227 3500 le on 150 le #1738c	*2.40*	*2.40*
d. A227 3500 le on 200 le #1738d	*2.40*	

No. 2903 amd a miniature sheet of 3 vertical strips of 4 exist imperf.

No. 2132 Surcharged

Methods and Perfs. As Before
2008, Mar. 10
2904 A295 3500 le on 600 le #2132 2.40 2.40

No. 2241 Surcharged

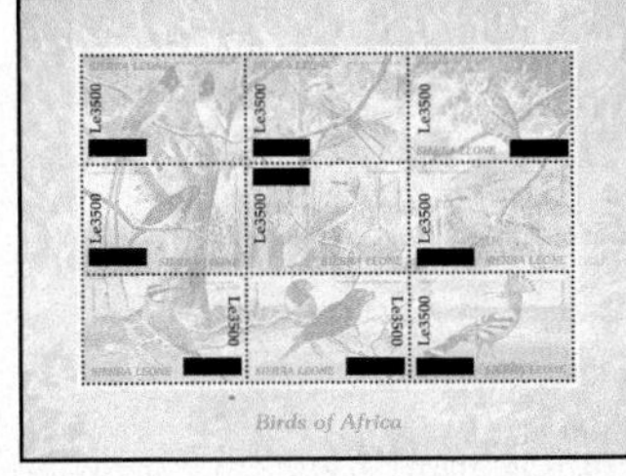

Methods and Perfs. As Before
2008, Mar. 10
2905 A317 3500 le on 600 le Sheet of 9, #a-i, #2241 *21.00 21.00*

Nos. 586-589 Surcharged

Methods and Perfs. As Before
2008, Mar. 10

2906 A85 4000 le on 6c #586	*2.75*	*2.75*
2907 A85 4000 le on 10c #587	*2.75*	*2.75*
2908 A85 4000 le on 31c #588	*2.75*	*2.75*
2909 A85 4000 le on 60c #589	*2.75*	*2.75*
Nos. 2906-2909 (4)	*11.00*	*11.00*

No. 2752 Surcharged in Black and Red

Methods and Perfs. As Before
2008, Mar. 10
2910 A443 4000 le on 1000 le Block of 4, #a-d, #2752 *11.00*

No. 2910 exists imperf. in a souvenir sheet of 8 and miniature sheet of 16.

2008 World Stamp Championship, Israel — A498

2008, May 14 **Litho.** ***Imperf.***
2911 A498 7500 le multi 5.25 5.25

Miniature Sheet

Discovery and Exploration of Oregon — A499

No. 2912: a, Joel Palmer locates pass through the Cascades (30x50mm). b, Sir Francis Drake, first European to view Oregon coast, horiz. (40x25mm). c, Capt. Robert Gray, discoverer of the Columbia River, horiz. (40x25mm), d, Meriwether Lewis, William Clark and Multnomah Falls (30x50mm).

2008, June 13 ***Perf. 13¼***
2912 A499 1500 le Sheet of 4, #a-d 4.25 4.25

2008 National Topical Stamp Show, Portland, Oregon.

Wedding of Queen Elizabeth II and Prince Philip, 60th Anniv. — A500

No. 2913: a, Couple. b, Queen.

2008, June 19
2913 A500 1500 le Pair, #a-b 2.10 2.10

Printed in sheets containing three of each stamp.

32nd America's Cup Yacht Races — A501

Various yachts with large panel in: a, Blue. b, Orange. c, Red. d, Olive brown.

2008, June 19

2914 Strip of 4	8.00	8.00
a. A501 200 le multi	.25	.25
b. A501 500 le multi	.35	.35
c. A501 1000 le multi	.70	.70
d. A501 10,000 le multi	6.75	6.75

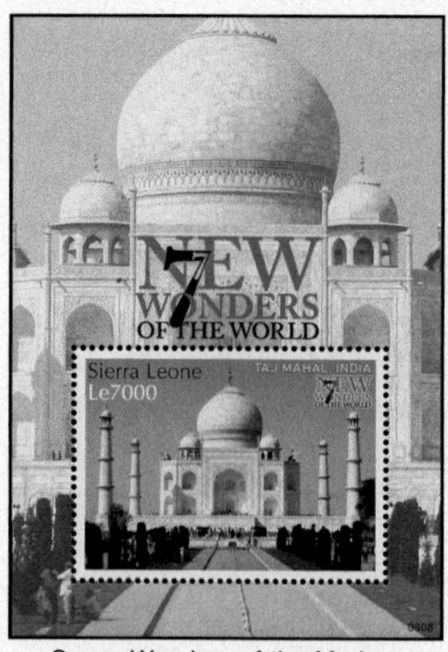

Seven Wonders of the Modern World — A502

No. 2915, vert.: a, Statue of Christ the Redeemer, Brazil. b, Roman Colosseum, Italy. c, Great Wall of China. d, Machu Picchu, Peru. e, Petra, Jordan. f, Chichén Itzá, Mexico.
7000 le, Taj Mahal, India.

2008, June 19
2915 A502 1500 le Sheet of 6, #a-f 6.25 6.25

Souvenir Sheet

2916 A502 7000 le multi 4.75 4.75

Khilafat Ahmadiyya, Cent. — A503

Denominations: 800 le, 1000 le, 2000 le, 3000 le.

2008, June 20 ***Perf. 12¾***
2917-2920 A503 Set of 4 4.75 4.75

A504

Elvis Presley (1935-77) — A505

No. 2921 — Presley: a, Both shoulders showing. b, Right shoulder showing. c, Left shoulder showing.
No. 2922: a, Denomination in yellow green, country name in blue. b, Denomination in red, country name in yellow green. c, Denomination in blue, country name in red. d, Denomination in blue, country name in yellow green. e, Denomination in yellow green, country name in red. f, Denomination in red, country name in blue.

2008, Oct. 28 ***Perf. 11½***
2921 Horiz. strip of 3 3.00 3.00
a.-c. A504 1500 le Any single 1.00 1.00

Perf. 13¼

2922 A505 1500 le Sheet of 6, #a-f 6.00 6.00

No. 2921 was printed in sheets containing two of each stamp.

Intl. Polar Year — A506

No. 2923 — Penguins with background color of: a, Red. b, Purple. c, Blue green. d, Orange.
7000 le, Penguins on ice.

2008, Oct. 28 ***Perf. 13¼***
2923 A506 3000 le Sheet of 4, #a-d 8.00 8.00

Souvenir Sheet

2924 A506 7000 le multi 4.75 4.75

Christmas A507

Designs: 1000 le, Nativity. 1500 le, Virgin Mary and Jesus. 2000 le, Joseph and Jesus. 3000 le, Angels and Jesus.

2008, Dec. 11 ***Perf. 14¼x14¾***
2925-2928 A507 Set of 4 5.00 5.00

Inauguration of Barack Obama as US President — A508

2009, Jan. 20 ***Perf. 12¼x11¾***
2929 A508 3000 le multi 2.00 2.00

Printed in sheets of 4.

Miniature Sheets

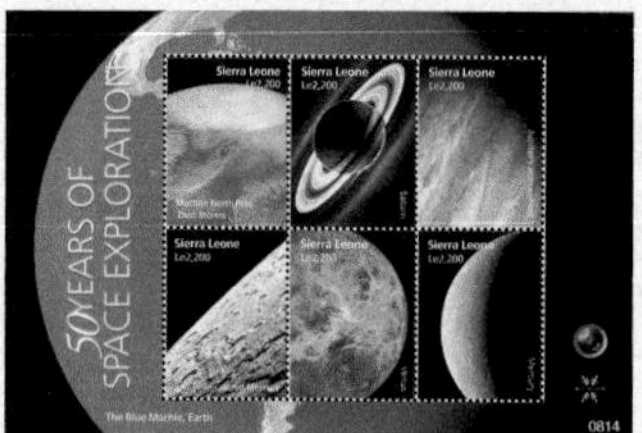

Space Exploration, 50th Anniv. (in 2007) — A509

No. 2930, 2200 le: a, Martian North Pole dust storms. b, Saturn. c, Jupiter's atmosphere. d, Craters on Mercury. e, Venus. f, Mercury.
No. 2931, 2200 le, horiz.: a, Spitzer Space Telescope. b, Galaxy M81. c, Hubble Space Telescope. d, Evil Eye Galaxy (M64). e, Cat's Eye Nebula. f, Hoag's Object.
No. 2932, 3000 le: a, Apollo 11 Lunar Module. b, Mercury Redstone rocket. c, Space Shuttle Atlantis on launch pad. d, Space Shuttle Endeavour.
No. 2933, 3000 le, horiz.: a, Sun shining, astronaut. b, South Pole of the Sun. c, Solar eruption. d, Solar eclipse.

2009, Jan. 27 ***Perf. 12***

Sheets of 6, #a-f

2930-2931 A509 Set of 2 17.00 17.00

Sheets of 4, #a-d

2932-2933 A509 Set of 2 15.50 15.50

Miniature Sheet

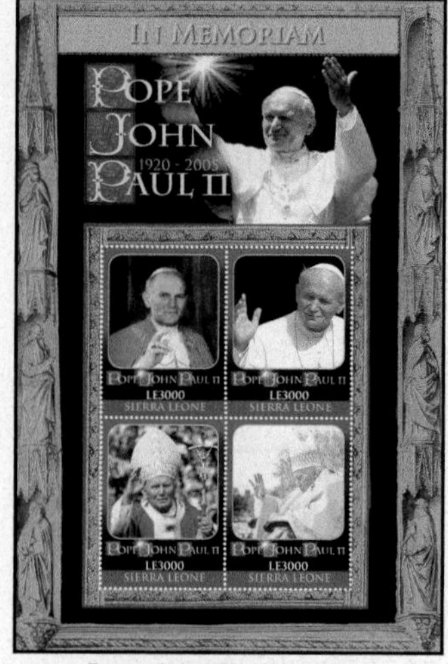

Pope John Paul II (1920-2005) — A510

No. 2934 — Color of vestments: a, Red. b, White. c, Green. d, Yellow.

2009, Feb. 4 **Litho.** ***Perf. 13¼***
2934 A510 3000 le Sheet of 4, #a-d 7.75 7.75

Yi Jianlian, National Basketball Association Player — A511

No. 2935: a, Wearing white uniform, holding basketball. b, Wearing dark uniform, holding basketball. c, Wearing white uniform, without basketball.

2009, Feb. 20
2935 Vert. strip of 3 3.00 3.00
a.-c. A511 1500 le Any single 1.00 1.00

Printed in sheets of 6, containing two each Nos. 2935a-2935c.

Miniature Sheets

A512

A513

China 2009 World Stamp Exhibition, Luoyang — A514

No. 2936 — Art of Chang Dai-chien (1899-1983): a, Landscape of Yangshuo. b, Scholar Admiring Plum Blossoms. c, The Golden Summit of Mount Emei. d, Lotuses After the Rain.
No. 2937 — Chinese landmarks: a, Temple of Heaven, Beijing. b, Dalian Exhibition Center, Dalian. c, Xian South Gate, Shaanxi Province. d, National Grand Theater, Beijing.
No. 2938 — Sports: a, Javelin. b, Fencing. c, Soccer. d, Weight lifting.

2009 **Litho.** ***Perf. 12¾***
2936 A512 1500 le Sheet of 4, #a-d 4.00 4.00

Perf. 12½

2937 A513 1500 le Sheet of 4, #a-d 4.00 4.00

Perf. 11½

2938 A514 2000 le Sheet of 4, #a-d 5.25 5.25

Issued: No. 2938, 2/16; Nos. 2936-2937, 4/10.

Peonies A515

2009, Apr. 10 ***Perf. 13¼***
2939 A515 1500 le multi .95 .95

Printed in sheets of 6.

Miniature Sheet

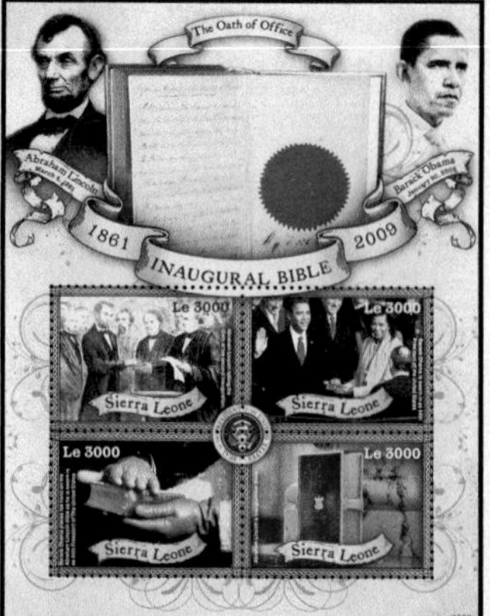

U.S. Inaugural Bibles of 1861 and 2009 — A516

No. 2940: a, Abraham Lincoln taking oath of office, 1861. b, Barack Obama taking oath of office, 2009. c, Obama's hand on Bible. d, Lincoln's inaugural Bible.

2009, May 14 ***Perf. 11½***

2940 A516 3000 le Sheet of 4, #a-d 7.50 7.50

Miniature Sheet

Elvis Presley (1935-77) — A517

No. 2941 — Presley and: a, Light blue denomination, purple background. b, Yellow denomination, brown background. c, Light blue denomination, green and black background. d, Yellow denomination, dull purple background.

2009, May 14 ***Perf. 13¼***

2941 A517 3000 le Sheet of 4, #a-d 7.50 7.50

Miniature Sheet

George Frideric Handel (1685-1759), Composer — A518

No. 2942: a, Handel's birthplace, Halle, Germany. b, Foundling Hospital where Handel directed concerts. c, Portrait of Handel, by Thomas Hudson. d, Ranelagh Gardens. e, Statue of Handel, by Louis-François Roubiliac. f, Farinelli and Senesino from opera, "Flavio."

2009, May 14 ***Perf. 11½***

2942 A518 2500 le Sheet of 6, #a-f 9.50 9.50

Miniature Sheets

2009 National Basketball Association All-Star Teams — A519

No. 2943, 1250 le — Eastern Division All-Stars: a, Ray Allen. b, Kevin Garnett. c, Danny Granger. d, Devin Harris. e, Dwight Howard. f, Allen Iverson. g, LeBron James. h, Joe Johnson. i, Rashard Lewis. j, Paul Pierce. k, Dwayne Wade. l, Mo Williams.

No. 2944, 1250 le — Western Division All-Stars: a, Chauncey Billups. b, Kobe Bryant. c, Tim Duncan. d. Pau Gasol. e, Yao Ming. f, Dirk Nowitzki. g, Shaquille O'Neal. h, Tony Parker. i, Chris Paul. j, Brandon Ray. k, Amare Stoudemire. l, David West.

2009, May 14 ***Perf. 14¼x14¾***

Sheets of 12, #a-l

2943-2944 A519 Set of 2 19.00 19.00

Miniature Sheet

Ferrari Race Cars — A520

No. 2945: a, 1977 312 T2. b, 1982 126 C2. c, 1983 126 C3. d, 2007 F2007.

2009, July 6 ***Perf. 14¼***

2945 A520 3000 le Sheet of 4, #a-d 7.50 7.50

Miniature Sheet

First Man on the Moon, 40th Anniv. — A521

No. 2946: a, Apollo 11 Command and Lunar Modules. b, Astronaut Neil Armstrong. c, Apollo 11 plaque. d, Apollo 11 Command Module. e, Apollo 11 Lunar Module. f, Apollo 11 crew in quarantine.

2009, July 20 **Litho.** ***Perf. 13¼***

2946 A521 2500 le Sheet of 6, #a-f 8.75 8.75

Souvenir Sheet

35th G8 Summit, L'Aquila, Italy — A522

2009, Sept. 30

2947 A522 8000 le multi 4.25 4.25

Miniature Sheet

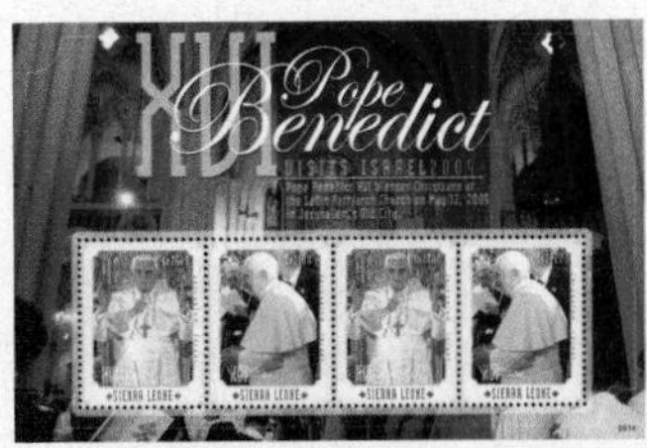

Pope Benedict XVI — A523

No. 2948 — Pope Benedict XVI: a, 2600 le, Facing forward. b, 2600 le, Facing left. c, 2800 le, As "a." d, 2800 le, As "b."

2009, Sept. 30 ***Perf. 11½***

2948 A523 Sheet of 4, #a-d 5.75 5.75

Miniature Sheets

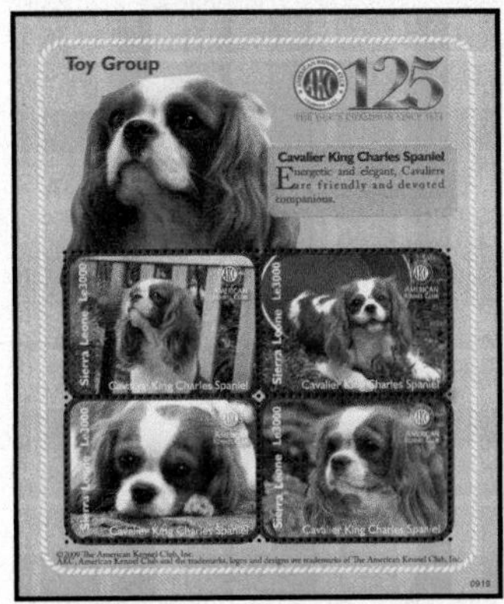

Dogs — A524

No. 2949, 3000 le — Cavalier King Charles spaniel: a, In front of fence. b, In bucket. c, With head on ground. d, With flowers at left.

No. 2950, 3000 le — English Springer spaniel: a, On wooden planks. b, Head. c, Standing. d, In front of overturned bucket.

2009, Sept. 30 ***Perf. 11½x12***

Sheets of 4, #a-d

2949-2950 A524 Set of 2 13.00 13.00

Cats A525

Designs: 1000 le, Birman lilac point. 1500 le, Singapura sepia agouti. No. 2953, 2000 le, Scottish Fold blue tortie tabby and white. 3000 le, Asian Shaded lilac shaded silver.

No. 2955, 2000 le: a, Somali lilac. b, British Angora red shaded silver. c, Maine coon Maine wave. d, Turkish Van tortie and white.

2009, Sept. 30 ***Perf. 14¾x14¼***

2951-2954 A525 Set of 4 4.00 4.00

2955 A525 2000 le Sheet of 4, #a-d 4.25 4.25

A526

Wildlife — A527

Designs: 1000 le, Giraffe. 1500 le, Bonobo. No. 2958, 2000 le, African bush elephant. 3000 le, Zebra.

No. 2960, 2000 le: a, Cheetah. b, Red colobus monkey. c, Hippopotamus. d, Lion.

2009, Sept. 30 ***Perf. 14***

2956-2959 A526 Set of 4 4.00 4.00

2960 A527 2000 le Sheet of 4, #a-d 4.25 4.25

A528

Birds — A529

Designs: 1000 le, Pied kingfisher. 1500 le, House sparrow. No. 2963, 2000 le, Skylark. 3000 le, Black-chested snake-eagle.

No. 2965, 2000 le: a, Greenfinch. b, Pangani longclaw. c, Barn swallow. d, Namaqua sandgrouse.

2009, Sept. 30 ***Perf. 14¾x14¼***

2961-2964 A528 Set of 4 4.00 4.00

2965 A529 2000 le Sheet of 4, #a-d 4.25 4.25

A530

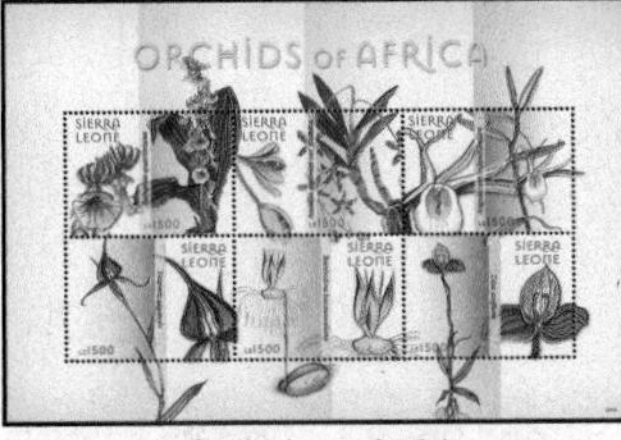

Orchids — A531

Designs: 1000 le, Penthea filicornis. No. 2967, 1500 le, Herschelia graminifolia. 2000 le, Satyrium princeps. 3000 le, Herschelia charpentieriana.

No. 2970, 1500 le: a, Eulophia quartiniana. b, Ansellia gigantea. c, Angraecum infundibulare. d, Disperis capensis. e, Bartholina burmanniana. f, Disa uniflora.

2009, Sept. 30 ***Perf. 14¼x14¾***

2966-2969 A530 Set of 4 4.00 4.00

Perf. 14¾x14¼

2970 A531 1500 le Sheet of 6, #a-f 5.00 5.00

A532

Mushrooms — A533

Designs: 1000 le, Fringed panaeolus. 1500 le, Orange latex lactarius. 2000 le, Purple laccaria. 3000 le, Liver lactarius.

No. 2975: a, Death cap. b, Cinnabar polypore. c, King bolete. d, Panther amanita. e, Fly amanita. f, Mica inky cap.

2009, Sept. 30 *Perf. 14*

2971-2974 A532 Set of 4 4.00 4.00

Perf. 14¾x14¼

2975 A533 1700 le Sheet of 6, #a-f 5.50 5.50

Chinese Aviation, Cent. — A534

No. 2976 — Feng Ru (1884-1912), pilot: a, And newspaper story. b, With airplane in Auckland. c, With airplane in 1912. d, And Feng Ru II airplane.

7500 le, Feng Ru and airplane.

2009, Nov. 12 *Perf. 14¼*

2976 A534 2700 le Sheet of 4, #a-d 5.75 5.75

Souvenir Sheet

2977 A534 7500 le multi 4.00 4.00

Aeropex 2009, Beijing. No. 2976 contains four 42x28mm stamps.

Miniature Sheet

The Three Stooges — A535

No. 2978 — Moe, Larry and Curly: a, Looking over the back of a sofa. b, Holding bottles. c, With wringer washer. d, Holding glasses.

2009, Dec. 9 *Perf. 11½x11¼*

2978 A535 2700 le Sheet of 4, #a-d 5.50 5.50

Bridges — A536

No. 2979: a, Tower Bridge, London. b, Hangzhou Bay Bridge, Zhejiang, China. c, Juscelino Kubitschek Bridge, Brasilia, Brazil. d, Sydney Harbour Bridge, Sydney. e, Ponte Vecchio, Florence, Italy. f, Bosporus Bridge, Istanbul.

7000 le, Golden Gate Bridge, San Francisco.

2009, Dec. 9

2979 A536 2000 le Sheet of 6, #a-f 6.25 6.25

Souvenir Sheet

2980 A536 7000 le multi 3.75 3.75

Miniature Sheet

Chinese Zodiac Animals — A537

No. 2981: a, Rat. b, Ox. c, Tiger. d, Rabbit. e, Dragon. f, Snake. g, Horse. h, Ram. i, Monkey. j, Rooster. k, Dog. l, Pig.

2010, Jan. 4 **Litho.** *Perf. 12*

2981 A537 800 le Sheet of 12, #a-l 5.00 5.00

Souvenir Sheet

New Year 2010 (Year of the Tiger) — A538

No. 2982 — Tiger with denomination at: a, Right. b, Left.

2010, Jan. 4 *Perf. 11½x12*

2982 A538 8000 le Sheet of 2, #a-b 8.25 8.25

Flag, Coat of Arms and Title of National Anthem of Sierra Leone A539

2010, Mar. 1 *Perf. 13½*

2983 A539 2000 le multi 1.10 1.10

Pres. Abraham Lincoln (1809-65) A540

2010, Mar. 1 *Perf. 12x11½*

2984 A540 2700 le multi 1.40 1.40

Printed in sheets of 4.

Miniature Sheet

Election of Pres. John F. Kennedy, 50th Anniv. — A541

No. 2985 — Kennedy: a, Standing in limousine. b, Pointing. c, Sitting in chair. d, On campaign button.

2010, Mar. 1 *Perf. 12x11½*

2985 A541 4000 le Sheet of 4, #a-d 8.50 8.50

Miniature Sheet

Charles Darwin (1809-82), Naturalist — A542

No. 2986: a, Darwin's frog. b, Darwin's fox. c, Galapagos tortoise. d, Galapagos marine iguana.

2010, Mar. 1 *Perf. 13¼*

2986 A542 2500 le Sheet of 4, #a-d 5.25 5.25

A543

A544

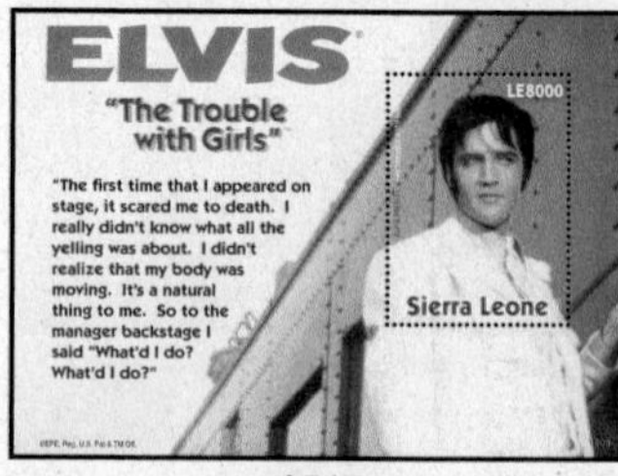

A545

A546

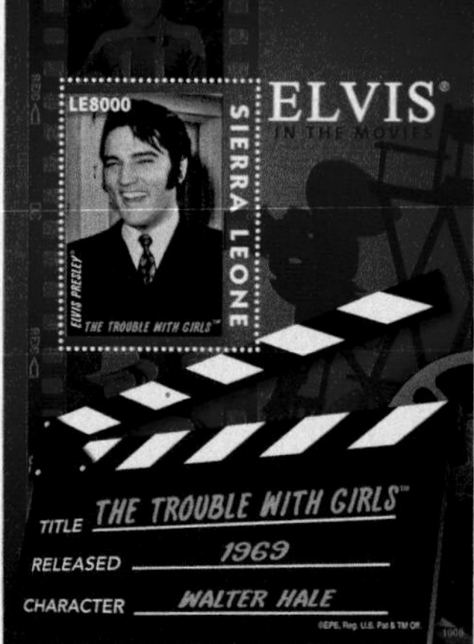

Elvis Presley (1935-77) — A547

No. 2987 — Presley: a, Holding microphone on stand. b, With arm raised and other on neck of guitar. c, With hand resting on guitar. d, Singing, not holding microphone.

2010, Mar. 1 *Perf. 11½x12*

2987 A543 2700 le Sheet of 4, #a-d 5.75 5.75

Souvenir Sheets

Perf. 13¼

2988 A544 8000 le multi 4.25 4.25
2989 A545 8000 le multi 4.25 4.25
2990 A546 8000 le multi 4.25 4.25
2991 A547 8000 le multi 4.25 4.25
Nos. 2988-2991 (4) 17.00 17.00

Teams Participating in 2010 World Cup Soccer Championships, South Africa — A548

Team and flag of: No. 2992, 1900 le, Algeria. No. 2993, 1900 le, Argentina. No. 2994, 1900 le, Australia. No. 2995, 1900 le, Brazil. No. 2996, 1900 le, Cameroun. No. 2997, 1900 le, Chile. No. 2998, 1900 le, Denmark. No. 2999, 1900 le, England. No. 3000, 1900 le, France. No. 3001, 1900 le, Germany. No. 3002, 1900 le, Ghana. No. 3003, 1900 le, Greece. No. 3004, 1900 le, Honduras. No. 3005, 1900 le, Italy. No. 3006, 1900 le, Ivory Coast. No. 3007, 1900 le, Japan. No. 3008, 1900 le, North Korea. No. 3009, 1900 le, South Korea. No. 3010, 1900 le, Mexico. No. 3011, 1900 le, Netherlands. No. 3012, 1900 le, New Zealand. No. 3013, 1900 le, Nigeria. No. 3014, 1900 le, Paraguay. No. 3015, 1900 le, Portugal. No. 3016, 1900 le, Serbia. No. 3017, 1900 le, Slovakia. No. 3018, 1900 le, Slovenia. No. 3019, 1900 le, South Africa. No. 3020, 1900 le, Spain. No. 3021, 1900 le, Switzerland. No. 3022, 1900 le, United States. No. 3023, 1900 le, Uruguay.

2010, Mar. 1 ***Perf. 14¼***

2992-3023 A548 Set of 32 32.00 32.00

Nos. 2992-3023 each were printed in sheets of 6.

An imperf. set 32 exists. Value, $400.

Miniature Sheets

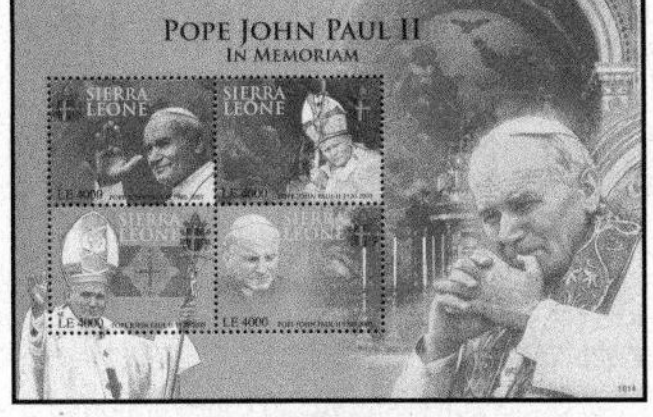

A549

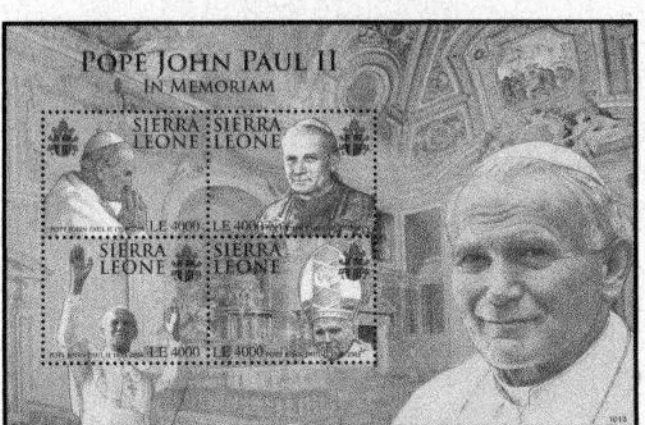

Pope John Paul II (1920-2005) — A550

No. 3024 — Country name in yellow with Pope John Paul II: a, Waving. b, Wearing miter with large cross. c, Wearing miter with central panel of hexagons and triangles. d, With candlestick at right.

No. 3025 — Country name in black with Pope John Paul II: a, Praying. b, Wearing red vestments. c, With both arms raised. d, Wearing miter.

2010, Apr. 26 ***Perf. 11½x12***

3024 A549 4000 le Sheet of 4, #a-d 8.25 8.25

3025 A550 4000 le Sheet of 4, #a-d 8.25 8.25

Miniature Sheets

A551

Michael Jackson (1958-2009), Singer — A552

No. 3026 — Blue background with Jackson: a, Looking right. b, Holding microphone with silver head. c, Holding microphone with black head. d, Wearing red shirt.

No. 3027 — Purple background with Jackson: a, Facing left, wearing shiny costume. b, Wearing white jacket. c, With head raised. d, Holding microphone.

2010, Apr. 26 ***Perf. 12***

3026 A551 4000 le Sheet of 4, #a-d 8.25 8.25

3027 A552 4000 le Sheet of 4, #a-d 8.25 8.25

Miniature Sheets

A553

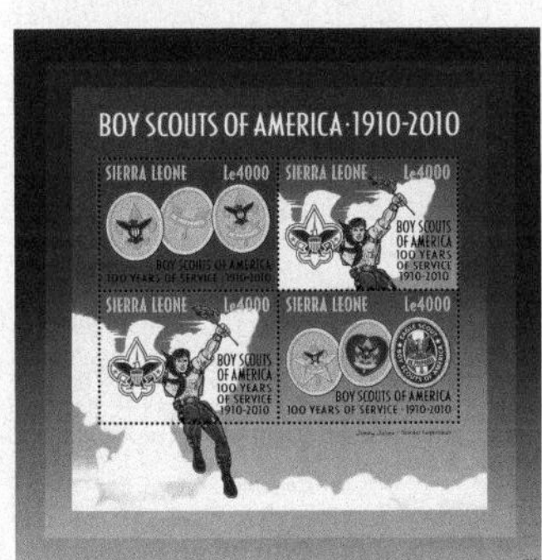

Boy Scouts of America, Cent. — A554

No. 3028 — Eagle-shaped cloud and: a, Eagle Scout badge, Dog Care, Small Boat Sailing, Law and Botany merit badges. b, Eagle Scout badge, Astronomy, Energy, Theater and Home Repairs merit badges. c, Boy Scouts of America emblem, Scout holding branch.

No. 3029: a, Badges for Tenderfoot, Second Class and First Class Scout ranks. b, Badges for Star, Life and Eagle Scout ranks. c, Boy Scouts of America emblem, Scout holding branch, eagle-shaped cloud.

2010, Apr. 26 ***Perf. 13¼***

3028 A553 4000 le Sheet of 4, #3028a-3028b, 2 #3028c 8.25 8.25

3029 A554 4000 le Sheet of 4, #3029a-3029b, 2 #3029c 8.25 8.25

Butterflies — A555

No. 3030: a, Protogoniomorpha parhassus. b, Kallimoides rumia rumia. c, Precis pelarga. d, Salamis cacta cacta.

No. 3031, 6000 le: a, Hypolimnas misippus. b, Hypolimnas salmacis salmacis.

No. 3032, 6000 le: a, Junonia sophia sophia. b, Junonia oenone.

2010, Apr. 26 ***Perf. 12***

3030 A555 4000 le Sheet of 4, #a-d 8.25 8.25

Souvenir Sheets of 2, #a-b

3031-3032 A555 Set of 2 12.50 12.50

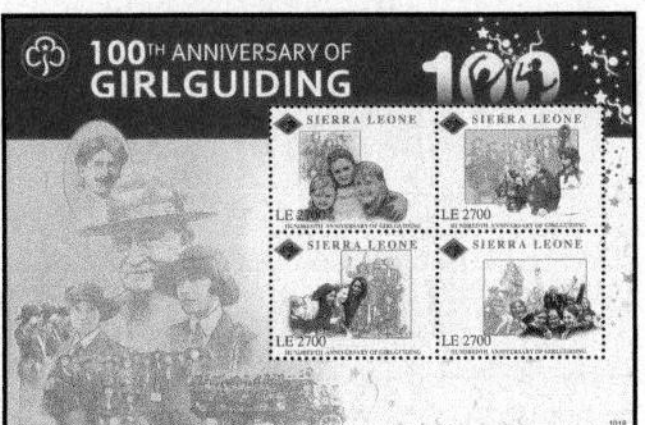

Girl Guides, Cent. — A556

No. 3033 — Pictures of Girl Guides of the past in frames and: a, Three Girl Guides. b, Two Girl Guides blowing bubbles, Girl Guide wearing balloon sculpture. c, Four Girl Guides. d, Eight Girl Guides.

8000 le, Brownie saluting, vert.

2010, June 17 ***Perf. 11½x12***

3033 A556 2700 le Sheet of 4, #a-d 5.50 5.50

Souvenir Sheet

Perf. 11½

3034 A556 8000 le multi 4.25 4.25

Henri Dunant (1828-1910), Founder of the Red Cross — A557

No. 3035 — Dunant, Red Cross and: a, Harriet Beecher Stowe (1811-96), writer. b, Charles Dickens (1812-70), writer. c, Bertha von Suttner (1843-1914), writer. d, Victor Hugo (1802-85), writer.

10,000 le, Dunant and Frédéric Passy (1822-1912), co-winner of 1901 Nobel Peace Prize.

2010, Oct. 14 ***Perf. 11½x12***

3035 A557 4000 le Sheet of 4, #a-d 7.75 7.75

Souvenir Sheet

Perf. 11½

3036 A557 10,000 le multi 5.00 5.00

Miniature Sheets

A558

Mother Teresa (1910-97), Humanitarian — A559

No. 3037 — Mother Teresa at left with: a, Five children, child at left in red. b, Three children. c, Five children, all with head coverings. d, With four children.

No. 3025 — Mother Teresa: a, Holding child and wrapping hand around another child. b, Speaking to woman. c, Holding child. d, Holding baby, children near hut.

2010, Oct. 14 ***Perf. 13x13¼***

3037 A558 4000 le Sheet of 4, #a-d 7.75 7.75

3038 A559 4000 le Sheet of 4, #a-d 7.75 7.75

Princess Diana (1961-97) — A560

No. 3039 — Background color: a, Red violet. b, Green. c, Blue violet. d, Orange.

No. 3040, 10,000 le, Red violet background. No. 3041, 10,000 le, Blue violet background.

2010, Oct. 14 ***Perf. 12***

3039 A560 4000 le Sheet of 4, #a-d 7.75 7.75

Souvenir Sheets

3040-3041 A560 Set of 2 9.75 9.75

Souvenir Sheet

New Year 2011 (Year of the Rabbit) — A561

No. 3042 — Rabbit with: a, Head lowered. b, Head raised.

2010, Nov. 7

3042 A561 6000 le Sheet of 2, #a-b 5.75 5.75

Miniature Sheets

Chinese Emperors — A562

No. 3043: a, Text "Emperor / Gaozu / Han Dynasty" and Chinese characters. b, Portrait of Emperor Gaozu (c. 256-195 B.C).

No. 3044: a, Text "Emperor / Hongwu / Ming Dynasty" and Chinese characters. b, Color portrait of Emperor Hongwu (1328-98). c, Ink drawing of Emperor Hongwu. d, Empress Ma (1333-82).

No. 3045: a, Text "Emperor / Kangxi / Qing Dynasty" and Chinese characters. b, Emperor Kangxi (1654-1722), wearing purple robe. c, Emperor Kangxi on throne. d, Emperor Kangxi holding calligrapher's brush.

2010, Nov. 7 ***Perf. 12***

3043 A562 3000 le Sheet of 4, #3043a, 3 #3043b 5.75 5.75
3044 A562 3000 le Sheet of 4, #a-d 5.75 5.75
3045 A562 3000 le Sheet of 4, #a-d 5.75 5.75
Nos. 3043-3045 (3) 17.25 17.25

China 2010 World Philatelic Exhibition, Beijing.

Miniature Sheets

A563

Pope John Paul II (1920-2005) — A564

No. 3046 — Denominations at left with Pope John Paul II: a, Wearing miter with large cross. b, Wearing zucchetto and red vestments, denomination in black. c, Wearing zucchetto and red vestments, denomination in orange. d, Wearing miter with central panel of hexagons and triangles.

No. 3047 — Denominations at right with Pope John Paul II: a, Holding cross. b, Waving. c, Wearing red vestments. d, Praying.

2010, Dec. 30 ***Perf. 12***

3046 A563 2700 le Sheet of 4, #a-d 5.25 5.25
3047 A564 2700 le Sheet of 4, #a-d 5.25 5.25

Miniature Sheets

A565

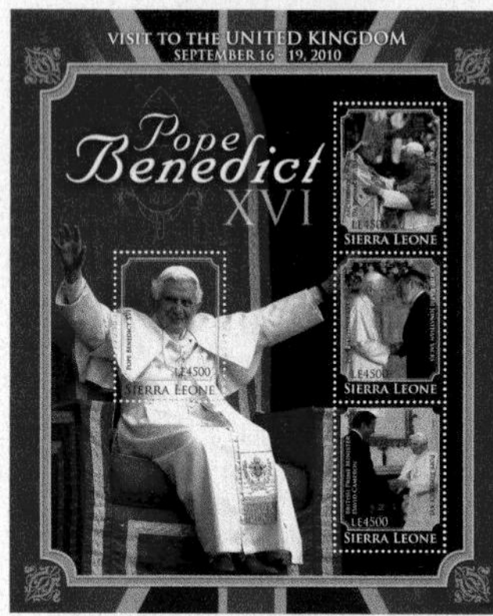

Visit of Pope Benedict XVI to United Kingdom — A566

No. 3048 — Pope Benedict XVI: a, At Cotton Park, Birmingham. b, At Hyde Park, London. c, Celebrating mass at Westminster Cathedral, London. d, Waving at Westminster Abbey, London.

No. 3049 — Pope Benedict XVI: a, Meeting Archbishop of Canterbury Rowan Williams. b, Seated. c, Meeting Chief Rabbi Jonathan Sacks. d, Meeting British Prime Minister David Cameron.

2010, Dec. 30 ***Perf. 12x12½***

3048 A565 4500 le Sheet of 4, #a-d 8.75 8.75

Perf. 12x11½

3049 A566 4500 le Sheet of 4, #a-d 8.75 8.75

Souvenir Sheets

Popes and Their Coats of Arms — A567

No. 3050, 14,000 le: a, Pope Paul VI. b, Arms of Pope Paul VI.

No. 3051, 14,000 le: a, Pope John Paul I. b, Arms of Pope John Paul I.

2010, Dec. 30 **Litho.** ***Imperf.***

Without Gum

Sheets of 2, #a-b

3050-3051 A567 Set of 2 27.00 27.00

A568

Whales — A569

No. 3052: a, Southern minke whale. b, Common minke whale. c, Blue whale. d, Sei whale.

No. 3053, Bryde's whale. No. 3054, Fin whale.

2011, Jan. 12 ***Perf. 12***

3052 A568 4000 le Sheet of 4, #a-d 7.75 7.75

Souvenir Sheets

Perf. 13 Syncopated

3053 A568 8000 le multi 4.00 4.00
3054 A569 8000 le multi 4.00 4.00

Lotus Flowers — A570

No. 3055: a, Country name at LL, denomination at top right, Latin name at right reading down. b, Country name at LL, denomination at top right, Latin name at top. c, Country name at UL, denomination at LR. Latin name at right reading down. d, Country name at LR. denomination at UL, Latin name at top right.

10,000 le, Lotus flower, vert.

2011, Feb. 1 ***Perf. 14¾x14¼***

3055 A570 4000 le Sheet of 4, #a-d 7.50 7.50

Souvenir Sheet

Perf. 14¼x14¾

3056 A570 10,000 le multi 4.75 4.75

Indipex Intl. Philatelic Exhibition, New Delhi.

Miniature Sheet

Jewish Anti-apratheid Activists — A571

No. 3057: a, Ray Alexander (1914-2004). b, Baruch Hirson (1921-99). c, Norma Kitson (1933-2002). d, Yetta Barenblatt (1913-99).

2011, Mar. 1 ***Perf. 12***

3057 A571 4500 le Sheet of 4, #a-d 8.50 8.50

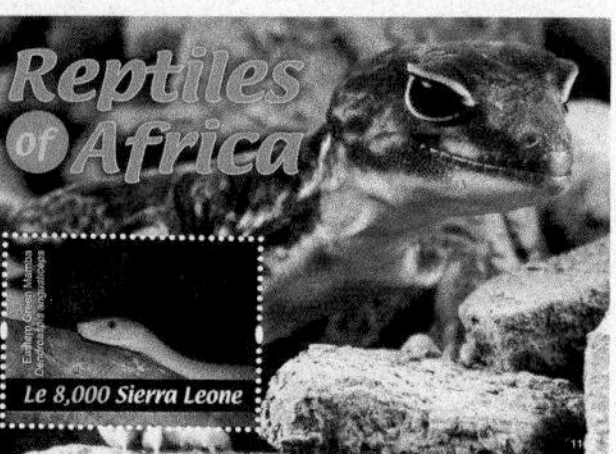

Reptiles and Amphibians — A572

No. 3058, 4000 le — Reptiles: a, Nile crocodile. b, African clawed gecko. c, African spurred tortoise. d, Rainbow agama.

No. 3059, 4000 le — Frogs and toads: a, Big-eyed tree frog. b, Marbled reed frog. c, African red toad. d, African clawed frog.

No. 3060, 8000 le, Eastern green mamba. No. 3061, 8000 le, African bullfrog.

2011, Mar. 25 ***Perf. 13 Syncopated***

Sheets of 4, #a-d

3058-3059 A572 Set of 2 15.00 15.00

Souvenir Sheets

3060-3061 A572 Set of 2 7.50 7.50

Paintings by Sandro Botticelli (c. 1445-1510) — A573

No. 3062: a, Portrait of a Young Man. b, Flight into Egypt. c, Crucified Christ. d, Three Miracles of Saint Zenobius.

8000 le, The Annunciation, horiz.

2011, Mar. 25 ***Perf. 12***

3062 A573 4000 le Sheet of 4, #a-d 7.50 7.50

Souvenir Sheet

Perf. 12¾

3063 A573 8000 le multi 3.75 3.75

No. 3063 contains one 51x38mm stamp.

Miniature Sheets

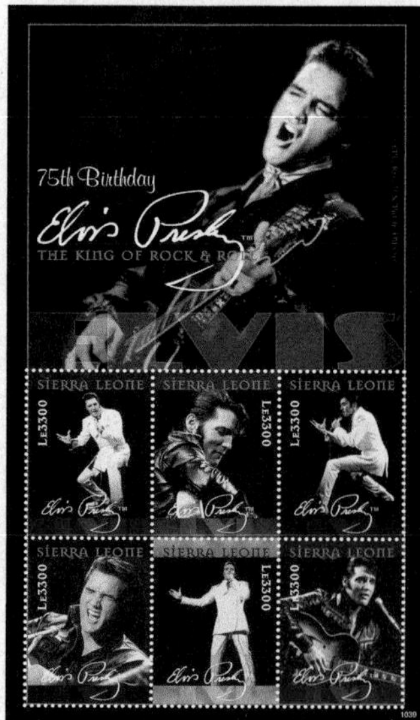

A574

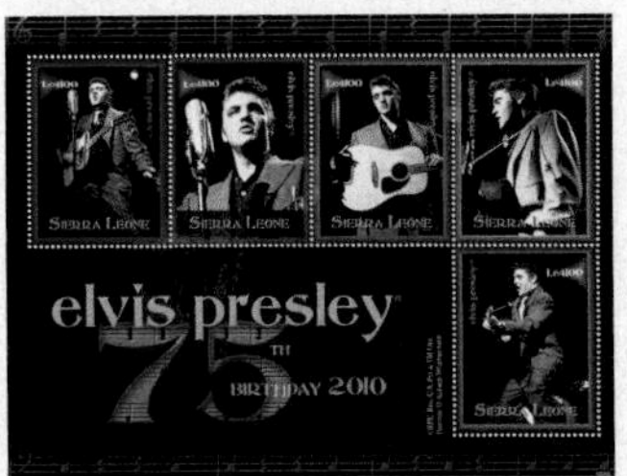

Elvis Presley (1935-77) — A575

No. 3064 — Presley wearing: a, White suit, with knees bent, facing forward. b, Leather jacket, no microphone visible. c, White suit with knees bent, facing left. d, Leather jacket, with microphone at left. e, White suit, legs straight. f, Leather jacket, microphone at right.
No. 3065 — Presley with frame in: a, Bright blue. b, Dark brown. c, Green. d, Yellow brown. e, Blue.

2011, Mar. 25 ***Perf. 12***

3064 A574 3300 le Sheet of 6, #a-f 9.25 9.25

Perf. 12½

3065 A575 4100 le Sheet of 5, #a-e 9.50 9.50

Miniature Sheets

President Barack Obama — A576

No. 3066, 4000 le: a, Afghanistan Pres. Hamid Karzai. b, Presidents Karzai and Obama seated. c, Presidents Karzai and Obama shaking hands. d, Pres. Obama.
No. 3067, 4000 le: a, Pres. Obama at left, flag at right. b, Pres Obama and Representative Nancy Pelosi. c, Pres. Obama and Senator Harry Reid. d, Pres. Obama in center, unidentified people in background, flag at right.

2011, Mar. 25 ***Perf. 13 Syncopated***

Sheets of 4, #a-d

3066-3067 A576 Set of 2 15.00 15.00

Miniature Sheets

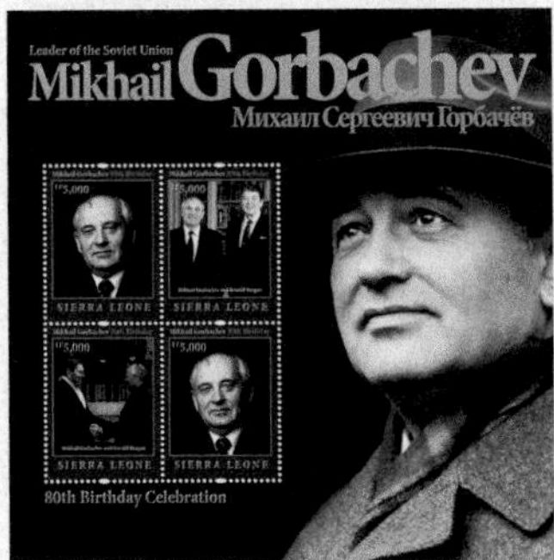

Soviet Union General Secretary Mikhail Gorbachev — A577

No. 3068: a, Gorbachev standing next to Pres. Ronald Reagan. b, Gorbachev and Reagan shaking hands. c, Gorbachev looking forward.
No. 3069: a, Gorbachev wearing hat. b, Gorbachev looking left. c, Gorbachev and Reagan seated. d, Gorbachev and Pres. George H. W. Bush.

2011, Mar. 25 **Litho.**

3068 A577 5000 le Sheet of 4, #3068a-3068b, 2 #3068c 9.25 9.25

3069 A577 5000 le Sheet of 4, #a-d 9.25 9.25

Engagement of Prince William and Catherine Middleton — A578

Designs: No. 3070, 4000 le, Couple.
No. 3071, vert.: a, Prince William. b, Middleton. c, Couple, hands visible. d, Couple, hands not visible.
No. 3072, 5000 le: a, Middleton. b, Prince William.
No. 3073, 5000 le, vert: a, Middleton. b, Prince William.

2011, Mar. 25 ***Perf. 12***

3070 A578 4000 le multi 1.90 1.90

3071 A578 4000 le Sheet of 4, #a-d 7.50 7.50

Souvenir Sheets of 2, #a-b

Perf. 13 Syncopated

3072-3073 A578 Set of 2 9.25 9.25

No. 3070 was printed in sheets of 4.

Wedding of Prince William and Catherine Middleton — A579

No. 3074: a, Prince William. b, Catherine Middleton. c, Prince Charles. d, Princess Diana. e, Prince Philip. f, Queen Elizabeth II.
No. 3075, 5500 le: a, Prince William. b, Couple in coach.
No. 3076, 5500 le: a, Middleton. b, Couple kissing.

2011 ***Perf. 13 Syncopated***

3074 A579 3500 le Sheet of 6, #a-f, + 5 labels 9.75 9.75

Souvenir Sheets of 2, #a-b, + Central Label

3075-3076 A579 Set of 2 10.50 10.50

The stated day of issue of Apr. 29 for this issue is incorrect as the stamps show photographs from the wedding held that day.

Dr. Sun Yat-sen (1866-1925), President of China — A580

No. 3077A: b, Sun Yat-sen, diff. c, Flag of People's Republic of China.

2011, Oct. 3 ***Perf. 12***

3077 A580 4000 le multi 1.90 1.90

Without Gum

Imperf

3077A A580 8000 le Sheet of 2, #a-b 7.25 7.25

Printed in sheets of 4.

Miniature Sheet

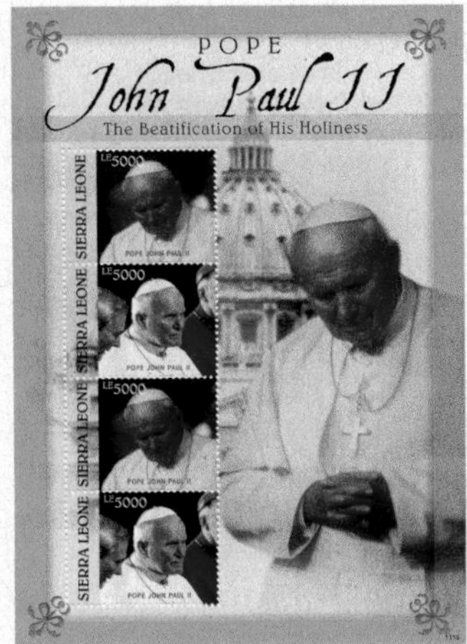

Beatification of Pope John Paul II — A581

No. 3078: a, Pope John Paul II looking down, beige under country name. b, Pope John Paul II, cardinal at right, beige area under "Leone" only. c, As "a," dark areas under country name. d, As "b," beige area under "Sierra" only.

2011, Oct. 3 **Litho.**

3078 A581 5000 le Sheet of 4, #a-d 9.00 9.00

Worldwide Fund for Nature (WWF) — A582

No. 3079 — Forest puff adder with country name and denomination in: a, Red. b, Purple. c, Yellow. d, Blue.

2011, Oct. 3 ***Perf. 13¼***

3079	Strip of 4	5.75	5.75
a.-d.	A582 3100 le Any single	1.40	1.40
e.	Souvenir sheet of 8, 2 each #a-d	11.50	11.50

Miniature Sheets

Chinese Civil Engineering Projects — A583

No. 3080 — Qingdao Cross-sea Bridge: a, Bridge, both shores visible. b, Bridge span.
No. 3081 — Qingdao-Jiaozhouwan Undersea Tunnel: a, Tunnel entrance. b, Tunnel cross-section.

2011, Oct. 3 ***Perf. 13 Syncopated***

3080 A583 1500 le Sheet of 6, 3 each #a-b 4.25 4.25

3081 A583 2500 le Sheet of 4, 2 each #a-b 4.50 4.50

Intl. Year of Forests — A584

No. 3082: a, Forest. b, Boy in forest. c, Red-eyed tree frog. d, Red-crested turaco. e, Logger with chain saw. f, U.N. Secretary-General Ban Ki-moon.
No. 3083: a, Intl. Year of Forests emblem. b, Forest, diff.

2011, Oct. 3 ***Perf. 12x11½***

3082 A584 2500 le Sheet of 6, #a-f, + 3 labels 6.75 6.75

Souvenir Sheet

Perf. 11½

3083 A584 5000 le Sheet of 2, #a-b 4.50 4.50

Miniature Sheets

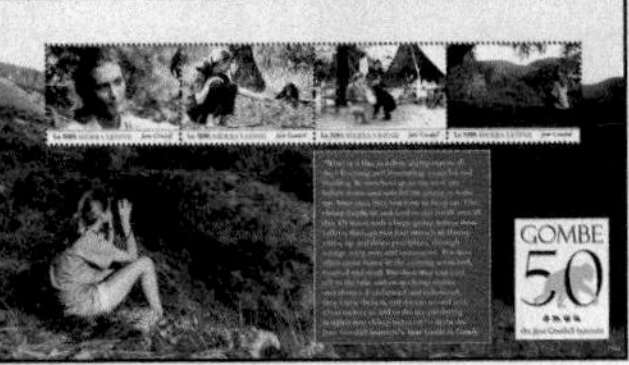

Jane Goodall Institute, 50th Anniv. — A585

No. 3084, 5000 le: a, Black-and-white photograph of Goodall. b, Color photograph of Goodall extending arm towards chimpanzee. c, Black-and-white photograph of Goodall and chimpanzee. d, Color photograph of Goodall.
No. 3085, 5000 le: a, Goodall writing in journal. b, Goodall, holding camera, observing chimpanzee. c, Goodall extending arm toward three chimpanzees. d, Goodall holding cup with sun on horizon.

2011, Oct. 3 ***Perf. 13 Syncopated***

Sheets of 4, #a-d

3084-3085 A585 Set of 2 18.00 18.00

Princess Diana (1961-97) — A586

No. 3086 — Various photographs of Princess Diana with upper and lower panels in: a, Black. b, Pale pink. c, Red. d, Orange red.
11,000 le, Princess Diana, diff.

2011, Oct. 3 ***Perf. 12***

3086 A586 5000 le Sheet of 4, #a-d 9.00 9.00

Souvenir Sheet

3087 A586 11,000 le multi 5.00 5.00

Sept. 11, 2001 Terrorist Attacks, 10th Anniv. — A587

No. 3088: a, Memorial wall dedicated to firefighters. b, Tribute in light, Brooklyn Bridge in foreground. c, Pentagon memorial. d, Commemorative flag. e, Field with American flags. f, Cross of steel beams at Ground Zero.

11,000 le, Tribute in light, vert.

2011, Oct. 3 ***Perf. 12***
3088 A587 3400 le Sheet of 6, #a-f 9.25 9.25

Souvenir Sheet
Perf. 12½

3089 A587 11,000 le multi 5.00 5.00

No. 3089 contains one 38x51mm stamp.

Pres. Abraham Lincoln (1809-65) — A588

No. 3090: a, US flag, bust of Lincoln. b, Painting of Lincoln.

No. 3091 — Photograph of Lincoln and: a, Union soldier's cap. b, Lincoln's stovepipe hat. c, Confederate soldier's cap.

2011, Oct. 3 ***Perf. 11½***
3090 A588 4000 le Sheet of 4, 2 each #a-b 7.25 7.25

Perf. 11½x12
3091 A588 6000 le Sheet of 3, #a-c 8.25 8.25

American Civil War, 150th anniv.

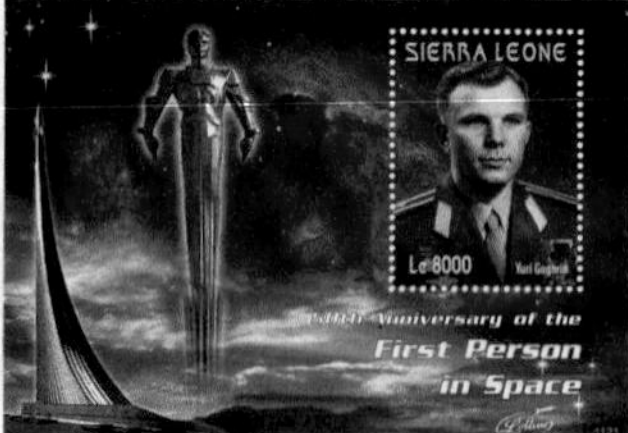

First Man in Space, 50th Anniv. — A589

No. 3092, 4000 le, horiz.: a, Vostok rocket on pedestal. b, MiG 15. c, Yuri Gagarin, first man in space. d, Alan Shepard, Jr., first American in Space.

No. 3093, 4000 le, horiz.: a, Vostok rocket in space. b, Vostok capsule. c, Vostok mission patch for Gagarin's space flight. d, L. Gordon Cooper, American astronaut.

No. 3094, 8000 le, Gagarin. No. 3095, 8000 le, Vostok capsule.

2011, Oct. 3 ***Perf. 12½x12***
Sheets of 4, #a-d
3092-3093 A589 Set of 2 14.50 14.50

Souvenir Sheets
Perf. 12x12½
3094-3095 A589 Set of 2 7.25 7.25

Orchids — A590

No. 3096: a, Bolusiella imbricata. b, Bulbophyllum scaberulum. c, Oeceoclades maculata. d, Ancistrochilus rothschildianus. e, Sarracenia flava. f, Phaius.

No. 3097: a, Ancistrochilus rothschildianus, diff. b, Angraecum subulatum. c, Eulophia guineensis. d, Eurychone rothschildiana.

No. 3098, 11,000 le, Monodora myristica. No. 3099, 11,000 le, Polystachya galeata.

Perf. 11½, 12x12½ (#3097)
2011, Oct. 3
3096 A590 3400 le Sheet of 6, #a-f 9.25 9.25
3097 A590 4800 le Sheet of 4, #a-d 8.75 8.75

Souvenir Sheets
3098-3099 A590 Set of 2 10.00 10.00

Intl. Year of Forests.

Marine Life — A591

No. 3100, 5000 le: a, Comb jellyfish. b, Benthocodon pedunculata. c, Glowing sucker octopus. d, Hatchetfish.

No. 3101, 5000 le, vert.: a, Dumbo octopus. b, Vampire squid. c, Gulper eel. d, Ping pong tree sponge.

No. 3102, 11,000 le, Dana octopus squid. No. 3103, 11,000 le, Anglerfish.

2011, Oct. 3 ***Perf. 12***
Sheets of 4, #a-d
3100-3101 A591 Set of 2 18.00 18.00

Souvenir Sheets
Perf. 12½
3102-3103 A591 Set of 2 10.00 10.00

Nos. 3102-3103 each contain one 51x38mm stamp.

Miniature Sheet

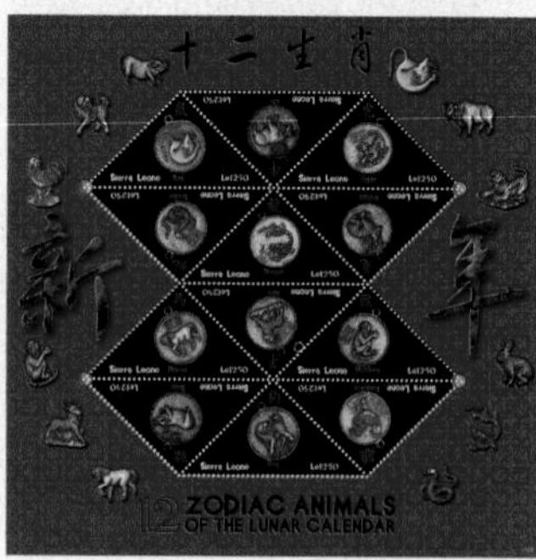

Chinese Zodiac Animals — A592

No. 3104: a, Rat. b, Ox. c, Tiger. d, Snake. e, Dragon. f, Rabbit. g, Horse. h, Ram. i, Monkey. j, Boar. k, Dog. l, Rooster.

2011, Oct. 3
3104 A592 1250 le Sheet of 12, #a-l 6.75 6.75

Miniature Sheet

Chinese Art by Lu Lujun — A593

No. 3105: a, Calligraphy with two red chops below left column of characters (30x40mm). b, Two birds on tree branch (30x40mm). c, Forest (60x40mm). d, Flowers, calligraphy at top red chop at left (30x40mm). e, Two birds on ground below tree (30x40mm). f, Calligraphy with two red chops to left of left column of characters (30x40mm). g, 18mm wide abstract work (30x40mm). h, Trees with red chop at lower right (30x40mm). i, Calligraphy and cat (60x40mm). j, Calligraphy and Chinese person (30x40mm). k, Flowers, calligraphy at top, two red chops at left (30x40mm). l, Flowers, calligraphy at right (30x40mm).

2011, Oct. 22 ***Perf. 14***
3105 A593 1300 le Sheet of 12, #a-l 7.25 7.25

Miniature Sheet

Freddy Will, Musician — A594

No. 3106 — Will wearing: a, T-shirt, black background. b, Suit, with hands clasped. c, Suit, brick wall in background. d, T-shirt, chain link fence in background.

2011, Oct. 22 ***Perf. 13 Syncopated***
3106 A594 4000 le Sheet of 4, #a-d 7.50 7.50

Birds — A595

No. 3107, 4000 le: a, Greater flamingo. b, Fulvous whistling duck. c, Cory's shearwater. d, Purple heron.

No. 3108, 4000 le: a, Pink-backed pelican. b, Abdim's stork. c, Western reef heron. d, African spoonbill.

No. 3109, 10,000 le, African sacred ibis, horiz. No. 3110, 10,000 le, Squacco heron, horiz.

2011, Sept. 26 **Sheets of 4, #a-d**
3107-3108 A595 Set of 2 14.50 14.50

Souvenir Sheets
3109-3110 A595 Set of 2 9.00 9.00

Miniature Sheet

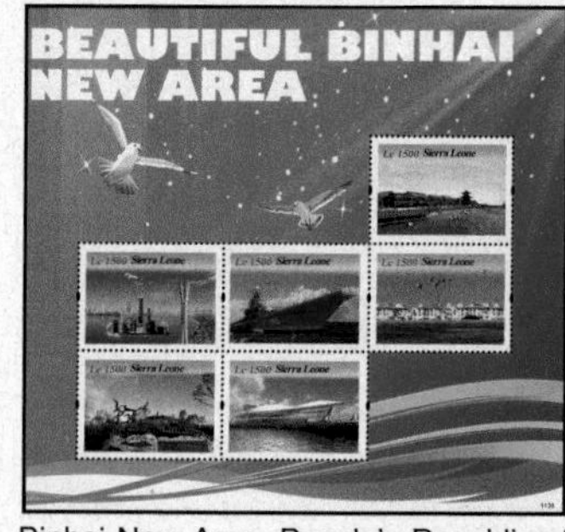

Binhai New Area, People's Republic of China — A596

No. 3111: a, Waterfront buildings and pagoda. b, Skyscrapers, shoreline, airplanes. c, Aircraft carrier. d, Birds over buildings. e, Windmill, trees, plaque. f, Building with curved roof.

2011, Oct. 26 ***Perf. 13 Syncopated***
3111 A596 1500 le Sheet of 6, #a-f 4.25 4.25

Christmas A597

Paintings: 1000 le, The Adoration of the Magi, by Stefano da Verona. 2000 le, Madonna and Child, by Taddeo di Bartolo. 3000 le, Madonna, by Lorenzo Monaco. 3500 le, Virgin and Child, by Gentile da Fabriano.

2011, Dec. 20 ***Perf. 14***
3112-3115 A597 Set of 4 4.50 4.50

Mao Zedong (1893-1976), Chinese Leader — A598

Mao Zedong: No. 3116, 1100 le, On beach. No. 3117, 1100 le, As young man, wearing cap. No. 3118, 1100 le, Seated. No. 3119, 1100 le, In airplane door, waving hat (35x35mm).

No. 3120: a, Like No. 3116. b, Like No. 3117. c, Like No. 3118.

10,000 le, Like No. 3119.

Perf. 14, 13¾ (#3119, 3121)
2012, Feb. 22
3116-3119 A598 Set of 4 2.10 2.10
3120 A598 5200 le Sheet of 3, #a-c 7.25 7.25

Souvenir Sheet
3121 A598 10,000 le multi 4.75 4.75

Miniature Sheet

2012 Summer Olympics, London — A599

No. 3122: a, Runners in blue, emblem at UL. b, Runners in blue, emblem at LR. c, Runners in red, emblem at UL. d, Runners in red, emblem at LR.

2012, May 30 *Perf. 14*

3122 A599 3600 le Sheet of 4, #a-d 6.75

No. 3122 exists imperf. Value, $12.50.

A600

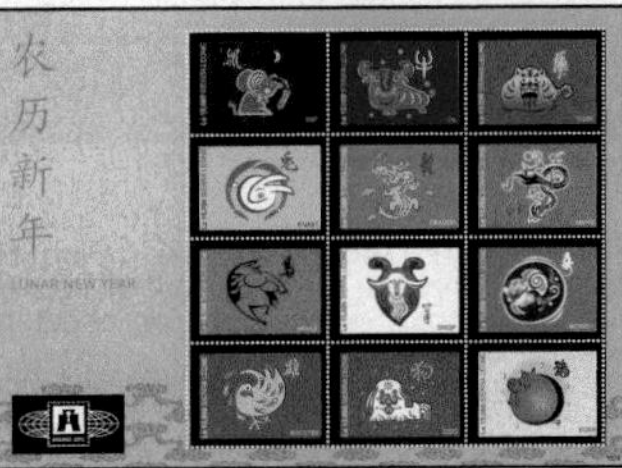

Chinese Zodiac Animals — A601

Designs: No. 3123, 1000 le, Dog. No. 3124, 1000 le, Boar.

No. 3125: a, Rat. b, Ox. c, Tiger. d, Rabbit. e, Dragon. f, Snake. g, Horse. h, Sheep. i, Monkey. j, Rooster. k, Dog. l, Boar.

2012, July 25 *Perf. 13¼x13*

3123-3124 A600 Set of 2 .95 .95

Perf. 14

3125 A601 15,000 le Sheet of 12, #a-l 82.50 82.50

Beijing 2012 Intl. Stamp Exhibition (#3125).

Sinking of the Titanic, Cent. — A602

No. 3126: a, John J. Astor IV, passenger who died. b, Sidney Goodwin, passenger who died. c, William T. Stead, passenger who died. d, Stern of Titanic. e, Bow of Titanic. f, Capt. Edward J. Smith.

3127, horiz.: a, J. P. Morgan, financier of Titanic. b, Titanic under construction. c, Titanic sets sail.

2012, July 25 *Perf. 14*

3126 A602 3000 le Sheet of 6, #a-f 8.25 8.25

Souvenir Sheet

3127 A602 7000 le Sheet of 3, #a-c 9.75 9.75

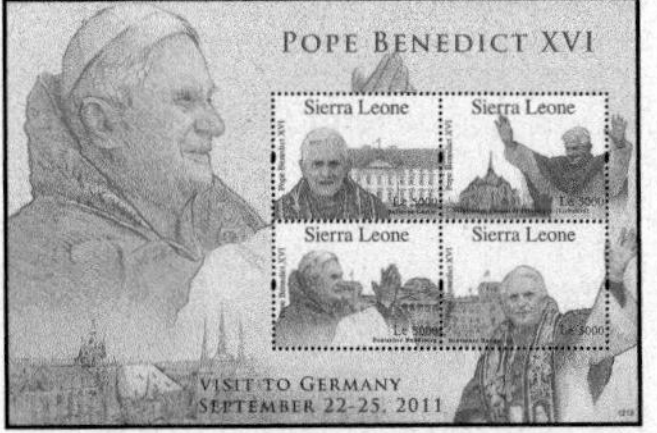

2011 Visit of Pope Benedict XVI to Germany — A603

No. 3128 — Pope Benedict XVI and: a, Bellevue Castle. b, Pilgrimage Church of Etzelsbach. c, Bundestag (Pope facing right with hands together). d, Bundestag (Pope facing forward, arm raised).

15,000 le, Pope Benedict XVI, vert.

2012, Sept. 25 *Perf. 13 Syncopated*

3128 A603 5000 le Sheet of 4, #a-d 9.25 9.25

Souvenir Sheet

3129 A603 15,000 le multi 7.00 7.00

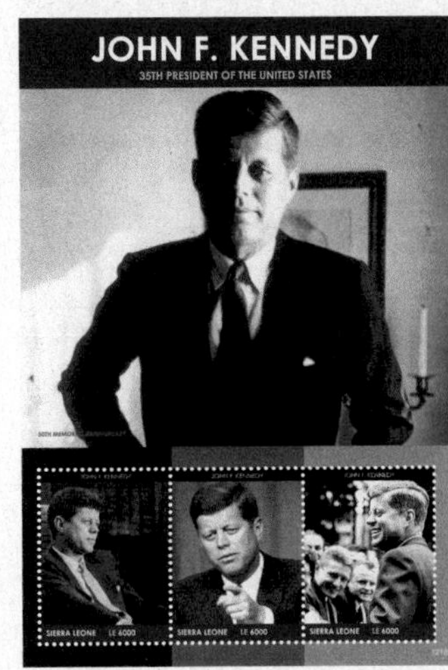

Pres. John F. Kennedy (1917-63) — A604

No. 3130 — Pres. Kennedy: a, Seated. b, Pointing. c, With group of people.

15,000 le, Pres. Kennedy at desk, horiz.

2012, July 25 *Perf. 12*

3130 A604 6000 le Sheet of 3, #a-c 8.25 8.25

Souvenir Sheet

3131 A604 15,000 le multi 7.00 7.00

No. 3131 contains one 50x30mm stamp.

Dedication of the Lincoln Memorial, 90th Anniv. — A605

No. 3132: Lincoln Memorial and various depictions of Pres. Lincoln, as shown.

No. 3133, 15,000 le, Photograph of Pres. Lincoln, arms visible. No. 3134, 15,000 le, Photograph of Pres. Lincoln, arms not visible.

2012, July 25 *Perf. 14*

3132 A605 5000 le Sheet of 4, #a-d 9.25 9.25

Souvenir Sheets

3133-3134 A605 Set of 2 14.00 14.00

Christmas — A606

Paintings: 1000 le, Nativity, by Hans Memling. 1500 le, Nativity, by unattributed artist. 2000 le, The Presentation of Christ, by Melchior Broederlam. 3000 le, Madonna and Child, by Fra Angelico. 3900 le, Adoration of the Shepherds, by Correggio. 6000 le, Holy Family on the Steps, by Nicolas Poussin.

2012, July 25 **Litho.**

3135-3140 A606 Set of 6 8.00 8.00

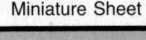

2012 UEFA European Soccer Championships, Poland and Ukraine — A607

No. 3141: a, Poland team. b, Greece team. c, Russia team. d, Netherlands team. e, Czech Republic team. f, Denmark team. g, Germany team. h, Portugal team. i, Soccer ball and upper deck of stadium.

No. 3142: a, Spain team. b, Italy team. c, Ireland team. d, Ukraine team. e, Croatia team. f, Sweden team. g, France team. h, England team.

No. 3143a, National Stadium, Poland. No. 3143b, Municipal Stadium, Poland (field visible at bottom). No. 3144a, PGE Arena, Poland. No. 3145a, Metalist Stadium, Ukraine. No. 3146a, Arena Lviv, Ukraine. No. 3147a, Donbass Arena, Ukraine. No. 3148a, Municipal Stadium, Poland (field not visible at bottom). No. 3148b, Olympic Stadium, Ukraine.

2012, July 26 *Perf. 14*

3141 A607 Sheet of 9 11.50 11.50
a.-i. 2500 le Any single 1.25 1.25
3142 A607 Sheet of 9, #3141i, 3142a-3142h 11.50 11.50
a.-h. 2500 le Any single 1.25 1.25
3143 A607 Sheet of 6, #3143a-3143b, 4 #3141a (Poland) 7.50 7.50
a.-b. 2500 le Either single 1.25 1.25
c. Sheet of 6, #3143a, 3143b, 4 #3141b (Greece) 7.50 7.50
d. Sheet of 6, #3143a, 3143b, 4 #3141e (Czech Republic) 7.50 7.50
3144 A607 Sheet of 6, #3143a, 3144a, 4 #3141c (Russia) 7.50 7.50
a. 2500 le multi 1.25 1.25
3145 A607 Sheet of 6, #3144a, 3145a, 4 #3141d (Netherlands) 7.50 7.50
a. 2500 le multi 1.25 1.25
3146 A607 Sheet of 6, #3143a, 3146a, 4 #3141f (Denmark) 7.50 7.50
a. 2500 le multi 1.25 1.25
b. Sheet of 6, #3145a, 3146a, 4 #3141g (Germany) 7.50 7.50
c. Sheet of 6, #3145a, 3146a, 4 #3141h (Portugal) 7.50 7.50
3147 A607 Sheet of 6, #3144a, 3147a, 4 #3142a (Spain) 7.50 7.50
a. 2500 le multi 1.25 1.25
3148 A607 Sheet of 6, #3148a-3148b, 4 #3142b (Italy) 7.50 7.50
a.-b. 2500 le Either single 1.25 1.25
c. Sheet of 6, #3144a, 3148a, 4 #3142c (Ireland) 7.50 7.50
d. Sheet of 6, #3147a, 3148b, 4 #3142d (Ukraine) 7.50 7.50
e. Sheet of 6, #3143a, 3148a, 4 #3142e (Croatia) 7.50 7.50
f. Sheet of 6, #3143a, 3148b, 4 #3142f (Sweden) 7.50 7.50
g. Sheet of 6, #3147a, 3148b, 4 #3142g (France) 7.50 7.50
h. Sheet of 6, #3147a, 3148b, 4 #3142h (England) 7.50 7.50
Nos. 3141-3148 (8) 68.00 68.00

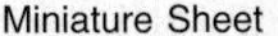

Miniature Sheet

Bees A608

No. 3149: a, African honey bee. b, Honey bee. c, Leafcutter bee. d, Maranga bee. e, Stingless bee.

2012, Aug. 7 **Litho.**

3149 A608 5000 le Sheet of 5, #a-e 12.00 12.00

Souvenir Sheets

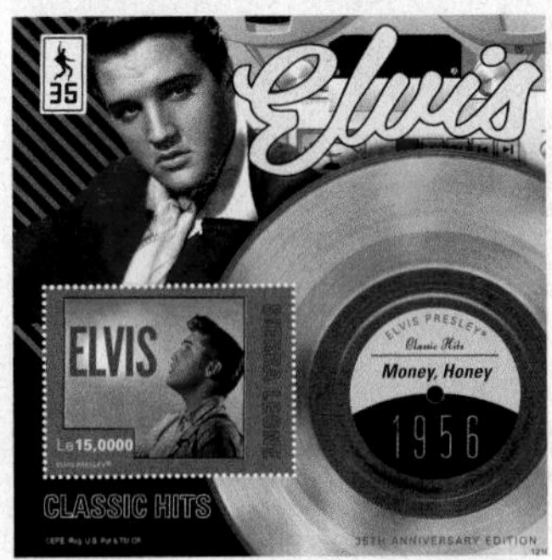

Elvis Presley (1935-77) — A609

Presley: No. 3150, 15,000 le, Facing left, red frame. No. 3151, 15,000 le, On *One Night* and *I Got Stung* record cover, black frame. No. 3152, 15,000 le, Holding microphone, purple frame. No. 3153, 15,000 le, Holding microphone, diff., gray frame. No. 3154, 15,000 le, Holding microphone, spotlight in background, red frame.

2012, Sept. 27 *Perf. 12¾*

3150-3154 A609 Set of 5 35.00 35.00

Miniature Sheet

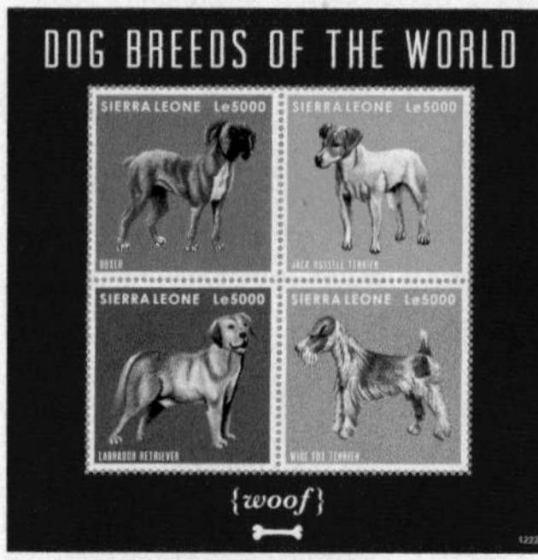

Dogs — A610

No. 3155: a, Boxer. b, Jack Russell terrier. c, Labrador retriever. d, Wire fox terrier.

2012, Nov. 28 ***Perf. 13¾***
3155 A610 5000 le Sheet of 4, #a-d 9.25 9.25

Carnivorous Plants — A611

No. 3156: a, Dewy pine. b, Nepenthes pitcher. c, Waterwheel plant. d, Pitcher plant.
16,000 le, African sundew, vert.

2012, Nov. 28 ***Perf. 13¾***
3156 A611 5000 le Sheet of 4, #a-d 9.25 9.25

Souvenir Sheet
Perf. 12¾

3157 A611 16,000 le multi 7.50 7.50

No. 3157 contains one 38x51mm stamp.

Primates — A612

No. 3158: a, Eastern chimpanzee. b, Nigeria-Cameroon chimpanzee. c, Western lowland gorilla. d, Western chimpanzee.
15,000 le, Sumatran orangutan, horiz.

2012, Nov. 28 ***Perf. 12***
3158 A612 5500 le Sheet of 4, #a-d 10.50 10.50

Souvenir Sheet
Perf. 12¾

3159 A612 15,000 le multi 7.00 7.00

No. 3159 contains one 51x38mm stamp.

Miniature Sheets

Completion of Painting of Sistine Chapel Ceiling by Michelangelo, 500th Anniv. — A613

No. 3160, 5000 le: a, The Prophet Jonah. b, The Creation of Eve. c, The Downfall of Adam and Eve. d, The Sacrifice of Noah.
No. 3161, 5000 le, vert.: a, Deluge. b, Detail from the Eleazar lunette. c, The Ezechias spandrel. d, First Day of Creation.

2012, Nov. 28 ***Perf. 12¾***
Sheets of 4, #a-d
3160-3161 A613 Set of 2 18.50 18.50

Souvenir Sheet

Elvis Presley (1935-77) — A614

Litho., Sheet Margin Embossed With Foil Application
2013, July 23 ***Imperf.***
3162 A614 42,500 le multi 20.00 20.00

Shells — A615

No. 3163: a, Conus algoensis scitulus. b, Columbarium radiale. c, Fusivoluta clarkei. d, Burnupena cincta.
16,000 le, Melapium lineatum.

2013, Sept. 9 **Litho.** ***Perf. 14***
3163 A615 5000 le Sheet of 4, #a-d 9.25 9.25

Souvenir Sheet
Perf. 12

3164 A615 16,000 le multi 7.50 7.50

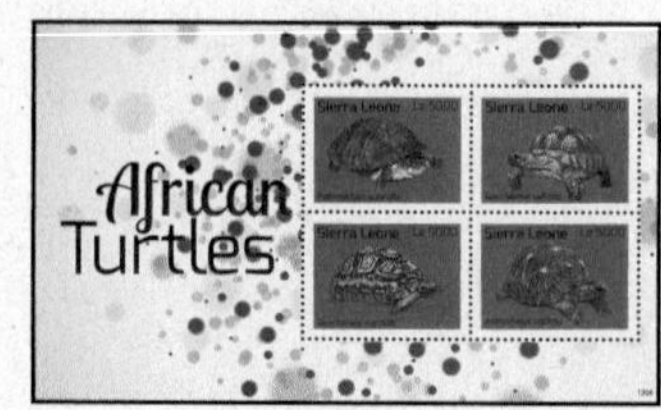

Turtles — A616

No. 3165: a, Pelomedusa subrufa. b, Geochelone sulcata. c, Geochelone pardalis. d, Astrochelys radiata.
16,000 le, Pelusios castanoides.

2013, Sept. 9 **Litho.** ***Perf. 12***
3165 A616 5000 le Sheet of 4, #a-d 9.25 9.25

Souvenir Sheet

3166 A616 16,000 le multi 7.50 7.50

Insects — A617

No. 3167: a, Analeptes trifasciata. b, Eotithoes palinii. c, Hecphora latefasciata. d, Gnathoenia flavovariegata.
16,000 le, Goliathus regius.

2013, Sept. 9 **Litho.** ***Perf. 12***
3167 A617 5000 le Sheet of 4, #a-d 9.25 9.25

Souvenir Sheet
Perf. 14

3168 A617 16,000 le multi 7.50 7.50

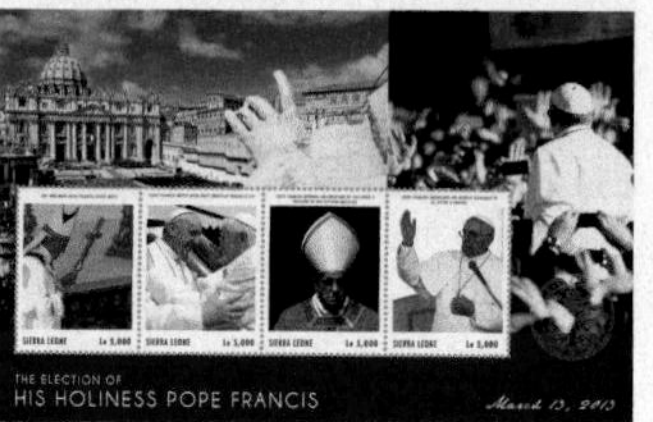

Election of Pope Francis — A618

No. 3169: a, Pope Francis celebrating mass. b, Pope Francis with Pope Emeritus Benedict XVI. c, Pope Francis attending celebration of the Lord's Passionin the Vatican Basilica. d, Pope Francis addressing weekly audience.
16,000 le, Pope Francis at Inauguration Mass.

2013, Sept. 9 **Litho.** ***Perf. 14***
3169 A618 5000 le Sheet of 4, #a-d 9.25 9.25

Souvenir Sheet
Perf. 12½

3170 A618 16,000 le multi 7.50 7.50

No. 3170 contains one 38x51mm stamp.

Pres. John F. Kennedy (1917-63) — A619

No. 3171 — Pres. Kennedy: a, On telephone. b, Behind microphones. c, Holding daughter, Caroline. d, Holding microphone, waving.
16,000 le, Pres. Kennedy reading, horiz.

2013, Sept. 9 **Litho.** ***Perf. 13¾***
3171 A619 5000 le Sheet of 4, #a-d 9.25 9.25

Souvenir Sheet
Perf. 12½

3172 A619 16,000 le multi 7.50 7.50

No. 3172 contains one 51x38mm stamp.

World Environment Day — A620

No. 3173 — Inscriptions: a, Buy local to cut back on emissions. b, Save water. c, Limit food waste.
16,000 le, Think before you eat and help save the environment!

2013, Sept. 9 **Litho.** ***Perf. 13¾***
3173 A620 6000 le Sheet of 3, #a-c 8.50 8.50

Souvenir Sheet

3174 A620 16,000 le multi 7.50 7.50

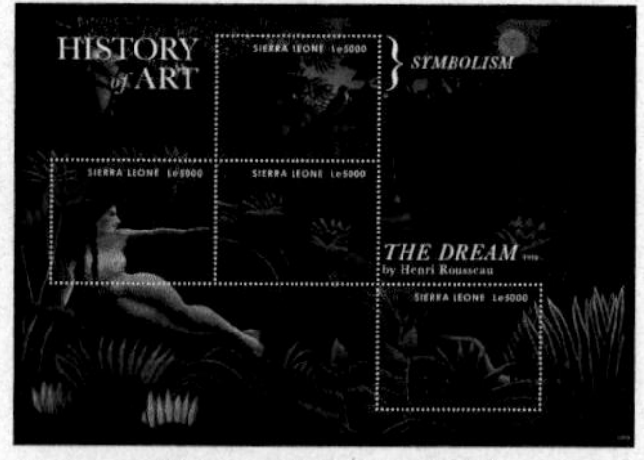

History of Art — A621

No. 3175 — Details from *The Dream*, by Henri Rousseau: a, Bird and fruit in tree. b, Nude woman. c, Flowers and head of cat. d, Head of cat, foliage, tail.
No. 3176, vert.: a, *The Yellow Tree*, by Emile Bernard. b, *Woman Holding a Fruit*, by Paul Gauguin. c, *Vase with Oleanders and Books*, by Vincent van Gogh.
No. 3177, vert. — Paintings by Henri de Toulouse-Lautrec: a, *Aristide Bruant*. b, *Moulin Rouge*. c, *Jane Avril*.
16,000 le, *Arrangement in Gray and Black, No. 1*, by James Abbott McNeill Whistler.

2013, Sept. 9 **Litho.** ***Perf. 12½***
3175 A621 5000 le Sheet of 4, #a-d 9.25 9.25
3176 A621 6000 le Sheet of 3, #a-c 8.50 8.50
3177 A621 6000 le Sheet of 3, #a-c 8.50 8.50
Nos. 3175-3177 (3) 26.25 26.25

Souvenir Sheet

3178 A621 16,000 le multi 7.50 7.50

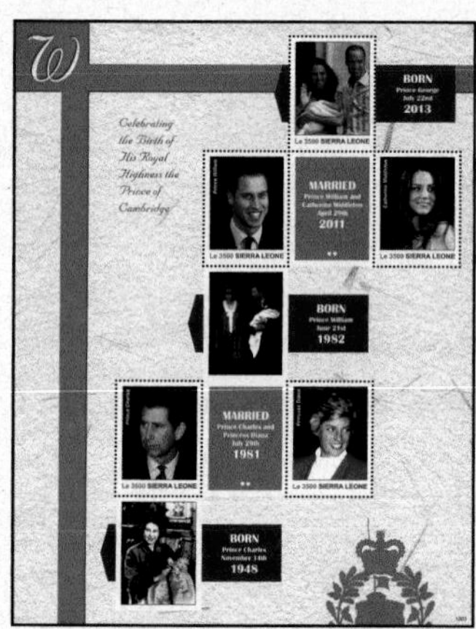

Birth of Prince George of Cambridge — A622

No. 3179: a, Duke and Duchess of Cambridge with Prince George. b, Prince William (Duke of Cambridge). c, Catherine Middleton (Duchess of Cambridge). d, Prince Charles. e, Princess Diana.
16,000 le, Duke and Duchess of Cambridge with Prince George, diff.

2013, Sept. 10 **Litho.** ***Perf. 14***
3179 A622 3500 le Sheet of 5, #a-e 8.25 8.25

Souvenir Sheet
Perf. 12

3180 A622 16,000 le multi 7.50 7.50

A623

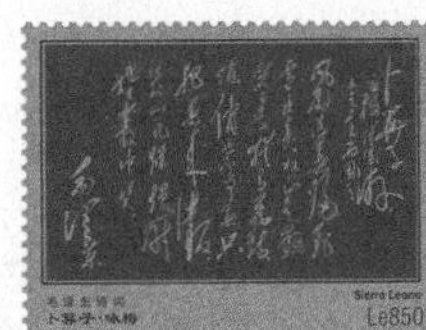
A624

Poetry of Mao Zedong A625

A626

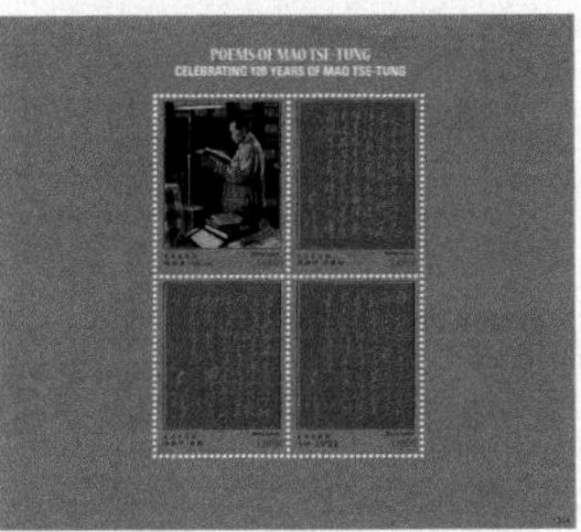
Mao Zedong (1893-1976), Chinese Communist Leader — A627

No. 3182 — Paintings depicting Mao Zedong: a, Standing behind tree, extending hand to old man. b, At table, with scribe at side. c, With child in lap. d, Standing with old man.

No. 3183: a, Painting of Mao Zedong in library. b, Poem by Mao Zedong, half line of Chinese text at right. c, Poem by Mao Zedong, half line of Chinese text in second vertical column, with bottom character in that line being two curved lines that do not touch. d, As "c," with bottom character in second line having crossed lines.

2013, Sept. 10 Litho. *Perf. 14*

3181 Horiz. strip of 3 1.20 1.20
a. A623 850 le multi .40 .40
b. A624 850 le multi .40 .40
c. A625 850 le multi .40 .40

Miniature Sheets

3182 A626 850 le Sheet of 4, #a-d 1.60 1.60
3183 A627 850 le Sheet of 4, #a-d 1.60 1.60

No. 3181 was printed in sheets of 6 containing two of each stamp.

Parrots — A628

No. 3184, 5000 le: a, African gray parrot. b, Senegal parrot. c, Meyer's parrot. d, Cape parrot.

No. 3185, 5000 le: a, Madagascar lovebird. b, Rosy-faced lovebird. c, Masked lovebird. d, Fischer's lovebird.

No. 3186, 16,000 le, Jardine's parrot. No. 3187, 16,000 le, Lilian's lovebird.

2013, Sept. 17 Litho. *Perf. 12½*
Sheets of 4, #a-d

3184-3185 A628 Set of 2 18.50 18.50

Souvenir Sheets

3186-3187 A628 Set of 2 15.00 15.00

Miniature Sheet

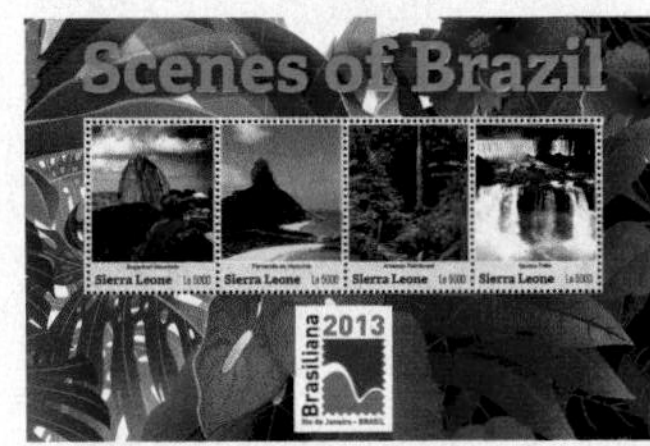

Brasiliana 2013 World Stamp Exhibition, Rio de Janeiro — A629

No. 3188 — Brazilan landscapes: a, Sugarloaf Mountain. b, Fernando de Noronha. c, Amazon rainforest. d, Iguaçu Falls.

Perf. 13½x12½

2013, Nov. 18 Litho.

3188 A629 5000 le Sheet of 4, #a-d 9.25 9.25

New Year 2014 (Year of the Horse) A630

2013, Nov. 25 Embroidered *Imperf.*
Self-Adhesive

3189 A630 34,000 le multi 16.00 16.00

Christmas A631

Paintings: 1000 le, *Toppling of the Pagan Idols*, by Bedford Master. 2000 le, *The Flight into Egypt*, by Vittore Carpaccio. 3000 le, *The Annunciation*, by Melchior Broederlam. 6000 le, *The Virgin*, by Carlo Dolci.

16,000 le, *The Adoration of the Shepherds*, by Giorgione.

2013, Dec. 2 Litho. *Perf. 12½*

3190-3193 A631 Set of 4 5.50 5.50

Souvenir Sheet

3194 A631 16,000 le multi 7.50 7.50

A632

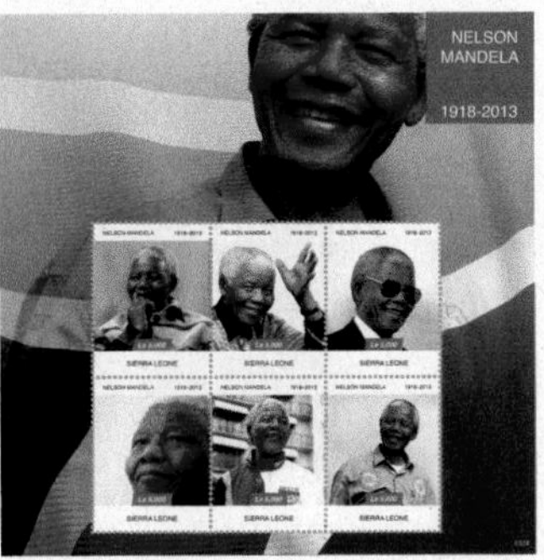

Nelson Mandela (1918-2013), President of South Africa — A633

Nos. 3195, 3196: Various photographs of Mandela, as shown.
16,000 le, Mandela, diff.
43,000 le, Mandela, diff.

2013, Dec. 15 Litho. *Perf. 14*

3195 A632 5000 le Sheet of 6, #a-f 14.00 14.00
3196 A633 5000 le Sheet of 6, #a-f 14.00 14.00

Souvenir Sheets

3197 A633 16,000 le multi 7.50 7.50

Litho., Margin Embossed With Foil Application
Imperf

3198 A633 43,000 le multi 20.00 20.00

No. 3198 contains one 40x40mm stamp.

Games — A634

No. 3199: a, Backgammon. b, Go. c, Mah Jongg. d, Mancala.
16,000 le, Chess.

2013, Dec. 18 Litho. *Perf. 13¾*

3199 A634 5000 le Sheet of 4, #a-d 9.25 9.25

Souvenir Sheet

3200 A634 16,000 le multi 7.50 7.50

Birds — A635

No. 3201: a, Crested barbet. b, White-fronted bee-eater. c, Starling. d, Crimson-breasted shrike.
16,000 le, Lilac-breasted roller.

2013, Dec. 23 Litho. *Perf. 14*

3201 A635 5000 le Sheet of 4, #a-d 9.25 9.25

Souvenir Sheet
Perf. 12

3202 A635 16,000 le multi 7.50 7.50

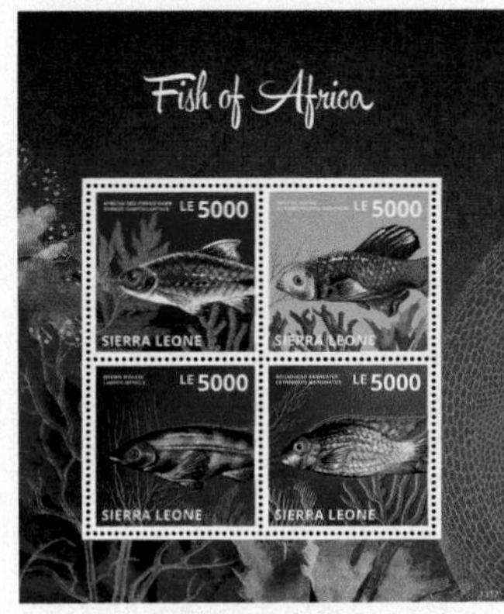

Fish — A636

No. 3203: a, African red-finned barb. b, Redtail notho. c, Brown wrasse. d, Roundhead sandeater.
16,000 le, Broadhead sleeper, African butter catfish, horiz.

2013, Dec. 23 Litho. *Perf. 13¾*

3203 A636 5000 le Sheet of 4, #a-d 9.25 9.25

Souvenir Sheet
Perf. 12½

3204 A636 16,000 le multi 7.50 7.50

No. 3204 contains one 51x38mm stamp.

Miniature Sheet

Mushrooms — A637

No. 3205: a, Delicious milk cap. b, Amethyst deceiver. c, Penny bun. d, Japanese umbrella. e, Glistening ink cap. f, Panther cap.

2013, Dec. 23 Litho. *Perf. 13¾*

3205 A637 4000 le Sheet of 6, #a-f 11.00 11.00

Worldwide Fund for Nature (WWF) — A638

Nos. 3206 and 3207: Various photographs of Western Bongo, as shown.

2014, Apr. 2 Litho. *Perf. 14*

3206 A638 3900 le Block or vert. strip of 4, #a-d 7.25 7.25
3207 A638 4300 le Block or vert. strip of 4, #a-d 8.00 8.00

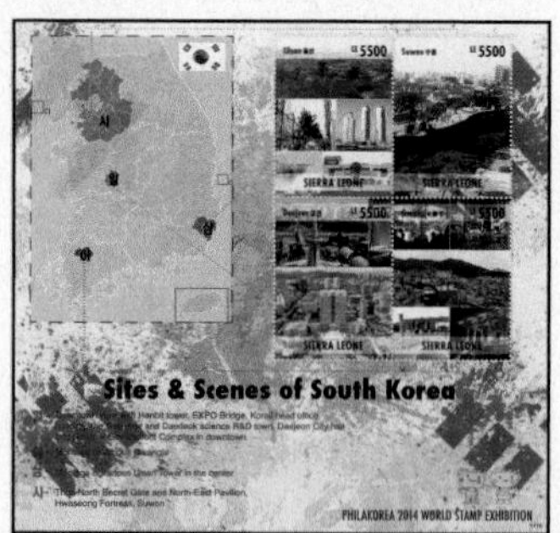
Cities of South Korea — A639

No. 3208, 5500 le: a, Ulsan. b, Suwon. c, Daejeon. d, Gwangju.
No. 3209, 5500 le: a, Seoul. b, Incheon. c, Busan. d, Daegu.
No. 3210, 9000 le: a, Seongnam. b, Yongin.
No. 3211, 9000 le: a, Changwon. b, Goyang.

2014, June 17 Litho. *Perf. 13¼*
Sheets of 4, #a-d

3208-3209 A639 Set of 2 20.50 20.50

Souvenir Sheets of 2, #a-b

3210-3211 A639 Set of 2 17.00 17.00

Philakorea 2014 World Stamp Exhibition, Seoul.

Farm Animals — A640

No. 3212, 6000 le: a, Dog. b, Cat. c, Duck.
No. 3213, 6000 le: a, Cow. b, Donkey. c, Horse.
No. 3214, 9000 le: a, Pig. b, Sheep.
No. 3215, 9000 le: a, Goose. b, Pigeon.

Perf. 14, 12½ (#3213, 3215)
2014, June 23 Litho.
Sheets of 3, #a-c

3212-3213 A640 Set of 2 17.00 17.00

Souvenir Sheets of 2, #a-b

3214-3215 A640 Set of 2 17.00 17.00

No. 3213 contains three 51x38mm stamps. No. 3215 contains two 51x38mm stamps.

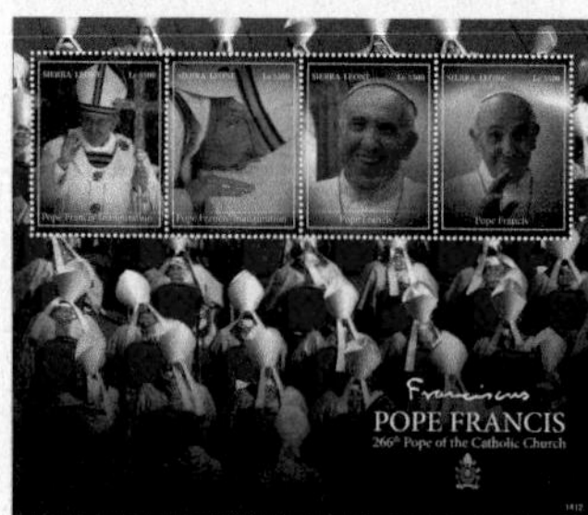
Pope Francis — A641

No. 3216 — Pope Francis: a, Holding cross. b, Kissing Bible. c, Laughing. c, Smiling, hand visible.
18,000 le, Pope Francis, horiz.

2014, June 23 Litho. *Perf. 14*

3216 A641 5500 le Sheet of 4, #a-d 10.50 10.50

Souvenir Sheet
Perf. 12½

3217 A641 18,000 le multi 8.50 8.50

No. 3217 contains one 51x38mm stamp.

Christmas A642

Paintings by Raphael (1483-1520): 3000 le, Solly Madonna. 5500 le, Sistine Madonna. 6000 le, Madonna and Child, 1508. 9000 le, Madonna and Child, 1508, diff.

2014, June 23 Litho. *Perf. 12½*

3218-3221 A642 Set of 4 11.00 11.00

World War I, Cent. — A643

No. 3222, 5500 le — Military aircraft: a, Nieuport 17C. b, De Havilland DH4. c, Fokker E III. d, Sopwith Camel.
No. 3223, 5500 le: a, Airplane of Capt. Brown of Royal Canadian Flying Corps. b, Airplanes in battle. c, Observation balloons. d, Airplane of Baron Manfred von Richtofen on fire.
No. 3224, 9000 le, vert.: a, Nieuport 10. b, Fokker DR1.
No. 3225, 9000 le — Airplane and Baron Manfred von Richtofen (1892-1918), military pilot, wearing uniform with: a Open collar. b, Closed collar.

2014, July 7 Litho. *Perf. 12*
Sheets of 4, #a-d

3222-3223 A643 Set of 2 20.00 20.00

Souvenir Sheets of 2, #a-b
Perf. 12½

3224-3225 A643 Set of 2 16.50 16.50

No. 3224 contains two 38x51mm stamps. No. 3225 contains two 51x38mm stamps.

Chinese Trains — A644

No. 3226 — Chinese Railways CRH1: a, Emblem and side windows. b, Passenger car interior. c, Two locomotives. d, Locomotive in motion.
No. 3227 — Chinese Railways CRH380CL: a, Instrument panel in locomotive. b, Locomotive exterior.

2014, July 7 Litho. *Perf. 14*

3226 A644 5500 le Sheet of 4, #a-d 10.00 10.00

Souvenir Sheet
Perf. 12½

3227 A644 9000 le Sheet of 2, #a-b 8.25 8.25

No. 3227 contains two 51x38mm stamps.

A645

Wild Cats — A646

No. 3228: a, Lion. b, Cheetah. c, Caracal. d, African leopard.
No. 3229: a, Lion, diff. b, Cheetah, diff. c, Serval. d, African leopard, diff.
No. 3230, 9000 le: a, Cheetah, diff. b, Lion, diff.
No. 3231, 9000 le: a, Caracal, diff. b, Serval, diff.

2014, Dec. 31 Litho. *Perf. 14*

3228 A645 5500 le Sheet of 4, #a-d 10.50 10.50
3229 A646 5500 le Sheet of 4, #a-d 10.50 10.50

Souvenir Sheets of 2, #a-b

3230-3231 A646 Set of 2 17.00 17.00

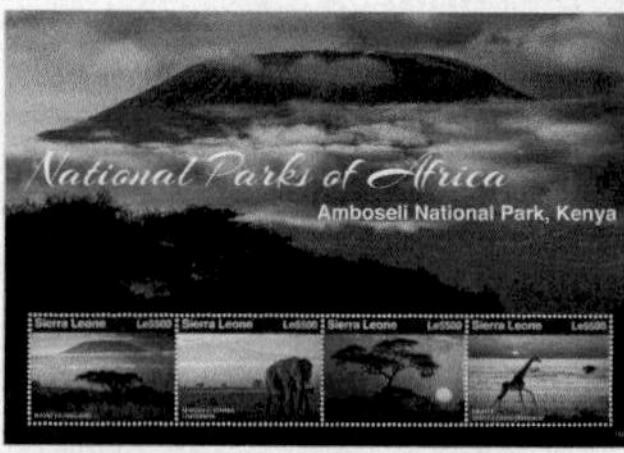
National Parks of Africa — A647

No. 3232 — Amboseli National Park, Kenya: a, Mount Kilimanjaro. b, African elephant. c, Tree and Sun. d, Giraffe.
No. 3233 — Kruger National Park, South Africa: a, Greater kudu, b, Trees in fog. c, Tree and Sun. d, Leopard. e, Burchell's zebra. f, Watering hole.
No. 3234, 18,000 le, River, Ranomafana National Park, Madagascar. No. 3235, 18,000 le, Tree and Sun, Serengeti National Park, Tanzania.

2014, Dec. 31 Litho. *Perf. 14*

3232 A647 5500 le Sheet of 4, #a-d 10.50 10.50

Perf. 12

3233 A647 5500 le Sheet of 6, #a-f 15.50 15.50

Souvenir Sheets
Perf. 12½

3234-3235 A647 Set of 2 17.00 17.00

No. 3233 contains six 50x30mm stamps. Nos. 3234 and 3235 each contain one 51x38mm stamp.

International Year of Light — A648

No. 3236: Various astronomical objects, as shown.
18,000, Stars and gas clouds, horiz.

2014, Dec. 31 Litho. *Perf. 13¾*

3236 A648 5500 le Sheet of 6, #a-f 15.50 15.50

Souvenir Sheet
Perf. 12

3237 A648 18,000 le multi 8.50 8.50

No. 3237 contains one 40x30mm stamp.

Mei Lanfang (1894-1961), Chinese Opera Performer — A649

No. 3238 — Various photographs of Mei Lanfang, as shown.
18,000 le, Mei Lanfang in costume.

2014, Dec. 31 Litho. *Perf. 12½*

3238 A649 5500 le Sheet of 4, #a-d 10.50 10.50

Souvenir Sheet

3239 A649 18,000 le multi 8.50 8.50

A650

New Year 2015 (Year of the Ram) A651

No. 3241: a, Boy and ram. b, Ram with shoes and mirror.

2014, Dec. 31 Litho. *Perf. 14*

3240 A650 5500 le multi 2.60 2.60

Perf. 12½

3241 A651 5500 le Vert. pair, #a-b 5.25 5.25

No. 3240 was printed in sheets of 6. No. 3241 was printed in sheets containing two pairs.

Birth of Princess Charlotte of Cambridge — A652

No. 3242: a, Princess Charlotte in arms of Duchess of Cambridge, face not shown. b, Princess Charlotte and Duchess of Cambridge, face shown. c, Prince George and Duke of Cambridge. d, Head of Princess Charlotte.
24,000 le, Head of Princess Charlotte, diff.

2015, May 22 Litho. *Perf. 13¼*

3242 A652 6500 le Sheet of 4, #a-d 12.00 12.00

Souvenir Sheet

3243 A652 24,000 le multi 11.00 11.00

African Wildlife and Dinosaurs — A653

No. 3244, 4300 le — African buffalo (Syncerus caffer): a, Head, with horn touching left frame. b, Entire animal. c, Head, both horns within frame. d, Buffalo and calf. e, Head, with horn touching right frame. f, Two adults.

No. 3245, 4300 le — Common chimpanzee (Pan troglodytes): a, Sitting with arms crossed. b, Hanging, with feet grasping vine. c, Mother holding juvenile. d, Juvenile on mother's back. e, Adult and juvenile sitting. f, With hand at mouth.

No. 3246, 4300 le — Western gorilla (Gorilla gorilla gorilla): a, Walking, with one hand just above ground. b, On tree. c, Juvenile on mother's back. d, Sitting. e, With hand at mouth. f, Standing on all fours.

No. 3247, 4300 le — Bats: a, Rhinolophus guineensis. b, Hipposideros cyclops. c, Myonycteris torquata. d, Eidolon helvum. e, Taphozous mauritianus. f, Lavia frons.

No. 3248, 4300 le — Leopards (Panthera pardus pardus): a, Standing, looking right. b, With head on paws. c, Standing looking left. d, With paw dangling off tree branch. e, Walking right. f, Seated on tree branch.

No. 3249, 4300 le — Lions (Panthera leo): a, Male facing right, roaring. b, Female and cub. c, Male resting, Latin name at UL. d, Male resting, Latin name at R. e, Female resting. f, Male facing left, roaring.

No. 3250, 4300 le — African wild dogs (Lycaon pictus): a, Standing, facing forward. b, Standing with head at left. c, Walking. d, Standing with head at left, baring teeth. e, Two dogs fighting. f, With tail at front, turning head.

No. 3251, 4300 le — Elephants: a, Loxodonta cyclotis facing right. b, Adult Loxodonta africana and juvenile. c, Loxodonta africana with raised trunk. d, Head of Loxodonta africana. e, Herd of Loxodonta africana. f, Loxodonta cyclotis facing left.

No. 3252, 4300 le — Dolphins: a, Stenella attenuata. b, Dephinus capensis. c, Grampus griseus. d, One Lagenorhynchus cruciger. e, Tursiops truncatus. f, Two Lagenorhynchus cruciger.

No. 3253, 4300 le — African manatees (Trichechus senegalensis): a, Two manatees, Latin name at bottom. b, One manatee. c, Adult and juvenile manatees, Latin name at top. d, Two manatees, tail of one hidden behind other manatee, Latin name at UL. e, Two manatees, both tails visible, Latin name at UL. f, Two manatees, Latin name at right.

No. 3254, 4300 le — Birds of prey: a, Terathopius ecaudatus. b, Kaupifalco monogrammicus. c, Aviceda jerdoni. d, Falco cuvierii. e, Stephanoaetus coronatus. f, Circaetus beaudouini.

No. 3255, 4300 le — African fish eagles (Haliaeetus vocifer): a, One bird perched on tree branch. b, Two birds perched on tree branches. c, Bird in flight. d, Bird in flight with fish in talons. e, Bird flying near tree. f, Head of bird.

No. 3256, 4300 le — Owls: a, Scotopelia peli. b, Strix woodfordii. c, Otus scops. d, Bubo poensis. e, Bubo ascalaphus. f, Ptilopsis leucotis.

No. 3257, 4300 le — Cuckoos: a, Two Chrysococcyx klaas. b, Cuculus solitarius. c, Clamator glandarius. d, Chrysococcyx caprius. e, Cuculus canorus. f, One Chrysococcyx klaas.

No. 3258, 4300 le — Butterflies: a, Aterica galene. b, Acraea serena. c, Acraea eponina. d, Spialia mafa. e, Antanartia delius. f, Papilio zalmoxis.

No. 3259, 4300 le — Pythons: a, Python sebae and tree branch, Latin name at L. b, Python regius wrapped around vertical tree branch, Latin name at UL. c, Python sebae, Latin name at R. d, Python sebae, Latin name at UR. e, Python regius, Latin name at R. f, Python regius wrapped around horizontal tree branch, Latin name at L.

No. 3260, 4300 le — Turtles: a, Cyclanorbis elegans. b, Lepidochelys olivacea. c, Caretta caretta. d, Dermochelys coriacea. e, Centrochelys sulcata. f, Pelusios castaneus.

No. 3261, 4300 le — Nile crocodiles (Crocodylus niloticus): a, Two crocodiles, one eating buffalo. b, Crocodile with open mouth, tail of crocodile. c, Crocodile, tail touching left frame. d, One crocodile, Latin name at UL. e, One crocodile, Latin name at bottom. f, Crocodile chasing zebra.

No. 3262, 4300 le — Dinosaurs: a, Carcharodontosaurus saharicus. b, Coelurus bauri. c, Massospondylus carinatus. d, Paralititan stromeri. e, Baryonyx walkeri. f, Nigersaurus taqueti.

No. 3263, 10,000 le, Two Syncerus caffer, diff. No. 3264, 10,000 le, Adult Pan troglodytes and two juveniles. No. 3265, 10,000 le, Adult Gorilla gorilla gorilla and juvenile, diff. No. 3266, 10,000 le, Rousettus aegyptiacus. No. 3267, 10,000 le, Adult Panthera pardus pardus and juvenile. No. 3268, 10,000 le, Male Panthera leo, diff. No. 3269, 10,000 le, Lycaon pictus with pup in mouth. No. 3270, 10,000 le, Adult Loxodonta africana and two juveniles. No. 3271, 10,000 le, Two Grampus griseus, diff. No. 3272, 10,000 le, Adult Tricherus senegalensis and juvenile, diff. No. 3273, 10,000 le, Falco alopex. No. 3274, 10,000 le, Haliaeetus vocifer at nest. No. 3275, 10,000 le, Bubo lacteus. No. 3276, 10,000 le, Clamator levaillantii. No. 3277, 10,000 le, Papilio machaon. No. 3278, 10,000 le, Python regius, diff. No. 3279, 10,000 le, Pelusios niger. No. 3280, 10,000 le, Two Crocodylus niloticus. No. 3281, 10,000 le, Rugops primus.

No. 3282, 14,000 le, Two Syncerus caffer, diff. No. 3283, 14,000 le, Jane Goodall and two Pan troglodytes. No. 3284, 14,000 le, Two adult Gorilla gorilla gorilla and juvenile. No. 3285, 14,000 le, Nycteris thebaica. No. 3286, 14,000 le, Panthera pardus pardus, diff. No. 3287, 14,000 le, Male Panthera leo, diff. No. 3288, 14,000 le, Lycaon pictus, diff. No. 3289, 14,000 le, Loxodonta africana, diff. No. 3290, 14,000 le, Sousa teuszii. No. 3291, 14,000 le, Two Trichechus senegalensis, diff. No. 3292, 14,000 le, Polyboroides typus. No. 3293, 14,000 le, Haliaeetus vocifer with fish in talons, diff. No. 3294, 14,000 le, Bubo leucostictus. No. 3295, 14,000 le, Centropus senegalensis. No. 3296, 14,000 le, Hypolimnas salmacis. No. 3297, 14,000 le, Python sebae, diff. No. 3298, 14,000 le, Chelonia mydas. No. 3299, 14,000 le, Crocodylus niloticus, diff. No. 3300, 14,000 le, Ouranosaurus nigeriensis.

2015, May 22 Litho. *Perf. 13¼*

Sheets of 6, #a-f

3244-3262 A653 Set of 19 225.00 225.00

Souvenir Sheets

3263-3281 A653 Set of 19 87.50 87.50
3282-3300 A653 Set of 19 120.00 120.00

Nos. 3263-3300 each contain one 45x45mm stamp.

Personalized Stamp A654

Perf. 12¾x13¼

2015, June 26 Litho.

3301 A654 11,000 le multi 5.25 5.25

No. 3301 was printed in sheets of 20 and could be personalized. Two generic images found on No. 3301 include the Sierra Leone coat of arms and flag.

A655

No. 3302, 3500 le — Jacques-Yves Cousteau (1910-97), conservationist and filmmaker: a, Cousteau and SP-350 Denise submarine. b, Oceanographic Museum of Monaco and shark. c, RV Calypso. d, Cousteau and Oceanographic Museum of Monaco.

No. 3303, 6000 le — Battle of Waterloo, 200th anniv.: a, Napoleon Bonaparte (1769-1821), Emperor of France, and map of battle. b, Michel Ney (1769-1815), French marshal, and mounted soldier. c, Arthur Wellesley, First Duke of Wellington (1769-1852), and mounted soldier. d, Gebhard Leberecht von Blücher (1742-1819), German field marshal, and battle scene.

No. 3304, 6000 le — End of American Civil War, 150th anniv.: a, Jefferson Davis (1808-89), President of Confederate States, and Confederate flag. b, Abraham Lincoln (1809-65), U.S. President, and U.S. flag. c, George Armstrong Custer (1839-76), Union cavalry commander, and Union soldiers. d, James Longstreet (1821-1904), Confederate general, and Confederate soldiers.

No. 3305, 6000 le — End of World War II, 70th anniv.: a, Russian soldiers at Battle of Berlin. b, Russian and American soldiers shaking hands. c, Surrender of German soldiers at Battle of Cisterna, 1944. d, General Douglas MacArthur (1880-1964), signs Japanese surrender documents.

No. 3306, 6000 le — United Nations, 70th anniv.: a, United Nations troop transporters. b, United Nations boat. c, United Nations airplane. d, United Nations trucks.

No. 3307, 6000 le — L0 Series, fastest train in world: a, Mountain in background. b, Bridge in background. c, Blurred background. d, Interior of train car.

No. 3308, 6000 le — Formula 1 cars and drivers, 65th anniv.: a, Alberto Ascari (1916-55). b, Niki Lauda. c, Ayrton Senna (1960-94). d, Jackie Stewart.

No. 3309, 6000 le — National Advisory Committee for Aeronautics, 100th anniv.: a, George P. Scriven (1854-1940), first chairman, airplane and aviators. b, Neil Armstrong (1930-2012), first man on Moon, and Lunar Module. c, Hubble Space Telescope. d, Charles F. Bolden, Jr., astronaut and administrator of National Aeronautics and Space Administration, and Pioneer 10.

No. 3310, 6000 le — First spacewalk, 50th anniv.: a, Alexey Leonov on space walk, "Voskhod 2" at UL. b, Head of Leonov, Leonov on space walk. c, Leonov in space suit, saluting. d, Leonov on space walk, "Voskhod 2" at bottom.

No. 3311, 6000 le — Endurance Expedtion of the Antarctic, 100th anniv.: a, Tom Crean (1877-1938), expedition member, and ship. b, Frank Wild (1873-1939), expedition member, and ship. c, Frank Worsley (1872-1943), expedition member, and ship. d, Ernest Shackleton (1874-1922), expedition leader, and ship.

No. 3312, 6000 le — Penny Black, 175th anniv.: a, Royal Mail coach. b, Queen Victoria (1819-1901), writing, and Penny Black. c, Queen Victoria and Penny Black, diff. d, Jacob Perkins press and Penny Black.

No. 3313, 6500 le — Louis Pasteur (1822-95), microbiologist: a, With microscope. b, Examining sheep. c, Administering vaccine to man. d, Holding bottle for sample of saliva from rabid dog.

No. 3314, 6500 le — Return to India of Mahatma Gandhi (1869-1948): a, Gandhi and Gateway of India, Mumbai. b, Gandhi and Indian flag. c, Gandhi and map of Eastern hemisphere. d, Gandhi and Sabarmati Ashram.

No. 3315, 6500 le — 25th anniv. of prison release of South African President Nelson Mandela (1918-2013): a, Mandela and dove. b, Mandela and hands. c, Mandela, hands and globe. d, Mandela, microphone and map of Africa.

No. 3316, 6500 le — Sir Winston Churchill (1874-1965), with: a, Gen. Charles de Gaulle (1890-1970) and airplanes. b, Military equipment. c, Ship. d, Airplanes.

No. 3317, 6500 le — Queen Elizabeth II, world's longest-reigning monarch, with: a, Prince William and his family. b, Pope John

Paul II (1920-2005). c, Mother Teresa (1910-97). d, Princess Diana (1961-97) and Prince William.

No. 3318, 6500 le — Pope John Paul II (1920-2005): a, Raising Bible. b, Wearing miter. c, Wearing red stole. d, Holding crucifix.

No. 3319, 6500 le — Elvis Presley (1935-77): a, Scene from *Girls! Girls! Girls!*. b, Scene from *Charro!*. c, With Ann-Margret. d, Scene from *Clambake*.

No. 3320, 6500 le — 2016 European Soccer Championships: a, Stade de France. b, Flags of 1996-2012 champions. c, Map of France with host cities. d, Flag of France on country map.

No. 3321, 14,000 le, Cousteau and Oceanographic Museum of Monaco, diff. No. 3322, 24,000 le, Napoleon Bonaparte and Waterloo battle scene. No. 3323, 24,000 le, Pres. Ulysses S. Grant (1822-85) in military uniform. No. 3324, 24,000 le, Pres. Harry S. Truman (1884-1972), announcing end of World War II. No. 3325, 24,000 le, United Nations helicopter and flag. No. 3326, 24,000 le, L0 Series train, diff. No. 3327, 24,000 le, Michael Schumacher, Formula 1 driver, and race car. No. 3328, Howard Clifton Lilly (1916-48), test pilot, and Space Shuttle Challenger. No. 3329, 24,000 le, Leonov and Earth. No. 3330, 24,000 le, Shackleton, ship and Aptenodytes forsteri. No. 3331, 24,000 le, Penny Black and Sir Rowland Hill (1795-1879), postal reformer. No. 3332, 26,000 le, Pasteur at examination of sheep. No. 3333, 26,000 le, Gandhi, ship and Taj Mahal. No. 3334, 26,000 le, Mandela and soccer players. No. 3335, 26,000 le, Churchill and Parliament Building. No. 3336, 26,000 le, Queen Elizabeth II and Prince Philip. No. 3337, 26,000 le, Pope John Paul II holding baby. No. 3338, 26,000 le, Presley and Juliet Prowse (1936-96), actress. No. 3339, 26,000 le, Foot of soccer player, ball, flag of France.

2015, June 26 Litho. *Perf. 13¼*

Sheets of 4, #a-d

3302-3320 A655 Set of 19 220.00 220.00

Souvenir Sheets

3321-3339 A655 Set of 19 220.00 220.00

MonacoPhil 2015 Philatelic Exhibition (Nos. 3302, 3321).

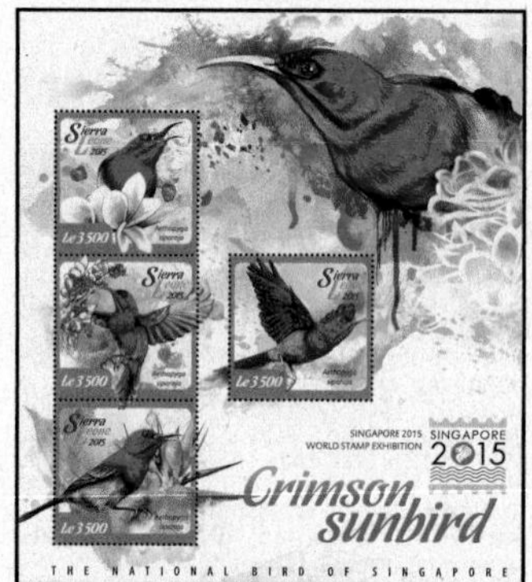

Aethopyga Siparaja — A656

No. 3340 — Crimson sunbird: a, Behind flower with beak open. b, Flying near flower, facing left. c, Flying, facing right. d, In front of flower with beak open.

14,000 le, Crimson sunbird and flower, diff.

2015, June 26 Litho. *Perf. 13¼*

3340 A656 3500 le Sheet of 4, #a-d 6.75 6.75

Souvenir Sheet

3341 A656 14,500 le multi 6.75 6.75

Singapore 2015 World Stamp Exhibition.

A657

No. 3342, 5500 le — Sled dogs: a, Three dogs, sled and driver. b, Two dogs and sled. c, Four dogs leading sled. d, Ten dogs, sled and driver.

No. 3343, 6000 le — Pony Express, 155th anniv.: a, Jack Keetley (1841-1912), rider. b, Alexander Majors (1814-1900), founder. c, "Broncho" Charlie Miller (1850-1955), rider. d, Johnny Fry (1840-63), rider, and station at Simpson Springs, Utah.

No. 3344, 6000 le — Tall ships: a, Amphitrite. b, Terra Nova. c, Niagara. d, Pamir.

No. 3345, 6000 le — Submarines: a, SMX-25, France. b, Necker Nymph, Virgin Islands. c, DeepFlight Super Falcon, Virgin Islands. d, HMS Ambush, United Kingdom.

No. 3346, 6000 le — Locomotion No. 1, 190th anniv.: a, Locomotion No. 1 on tracks. b, Locomotion No. 1 and inventor George Stephenson (1781-1848). c, Locomotion No. 1 on Skerne Bridge. d, Locomotion No. 1 going under Skew Bridge.

No. 3347, 6000 le — Moscow Metro, 80th anniv.: a, Railway crane KMP-65M. b, Train and Chekhovskay Station mosaic. c, Train and Dinamo Station decoration. d, Maintenance car AS1-19.

No. 3348, 6000 le — High-speed trains: a, Yamanashi MLX01. b, THSR 700T. c, L0 Series. d, E5 Series Shinkansen.

No. 3349, 6000 le — Automobiles: a, 1967 Ford Mustang. b, 1938 Bugatti 57 SC Atlantic. c, 1961 Porsche 356B. d, 1965 Shelby Superformance Cobra Redux.

No. 3350, 6000 le — Motorcycles: a, Harley-Davidson V-Rod Cafe Racer. b, BMW R69S. c, 1964 BMW R27. d, 1910 Indian.

No. 3351, 6000 le — Fire engines: a, 1956 Seagrave Anniversary Series 1000300 pumper. b, 1951 Dennis. c, 1979 American LaFrance Century Type 1000. d, 1952 GMC 1500-gallon tanker.

No. 3352, 6000 le — Special transport: a, DAF YP-408. b, DeHavilland Canada CS2F. c, Rosenbauer Panther CA5. d, Ford F-150 police vehicle.

No. 3353, 6000 le — Zeppelins and dirigibles: a, Zeppelin LZ-1. b, Airship Patrie. c, L-9 airship. d, Airship Roma.

No. 3354, 6000 le — Concorde: a, Concorde 101 facing right. b, Concorde 101 facing left. c, Concorde 102 facing right. d, Concorde 102 facing left.

No. 3355, 6000 le — Military transport: a, B-2 Stealth bomber. b, Leopard 2 tank. c, M1126 Stryker ICV. d, USS Independence.

No. 3356, 6000 le — Exploration of Mars: a, 2001 Mars Odyssey. b, Mars Express. c, Mars Orbiter Mission. d, Mars Reconnaissance Orbiter.

No. 3357, 6000 le — New Horizons Mission to Pluto: a, New Horizons, Charon and Pluto, Charon at top. b, New Horizons and Pluto, spacecraft at right. c, New Horizons and Pluto, spacecraft at left. d, New Horizons, Pluto and Charon, Charon at right.

No. 3358, 6000 le — International Year of Light: a, Laser beam optical technologies for measuring distances. b, NASA spacecraft lasers. c, Light painting. d, Laser eye surgery.

No. 3359, 6500 le — Albert Einstein (1879-1955), physicist, and: a, Diagram with circles and arrows. b, Diagram of bending of space-time. c, Model of atomic structure. d, Exploding star.

No. 3360, 6500 le — Nobel Prize Winners: a, Wilhelm C. Röntgen (1845-1923), 1901 Physics laureate. b, Marie Sklodowska-Curie (1867-1934), 1903 Physics and 1911 Chemistry laureate. c, Ernest Hemingway (1899-1961), 1954 Literature laureate. d, Mother Teresa (1910-97), 1979 Peace laureate.

No. 3361, 6500 le — Fight against malaria: a, Anopheles mosquito. b, Smear of blood on microscope slide. c, Doctor treating child. d, Anti-mosquito netting.

No. 3362, 22,000 le, Four Siberian huskies and dog sled. No. 3363, 24,000 le, William F. "Buffalo Bill" Cody (1846-1917), Pony Express rider and showman. No. 3364, 24,000 le, Glenlee at Riverside Museum, Glasgow. No. 3365, 24,000 le, Pisces V submarine, Canada. No. 3366, 24,000 le, Locomotion No. 1, diff. No. 3367, 24,000 le, Guitarist and Moscow Metro train. No. 3368, 24,000 le, NTV Alstom AGV 575. No. 3369, 24,000 le, 1930 Duesenberg Model J Convertible Sedan. No. 3370, 24,000 le, Bald Terrier Harley-Davidson Sportster 1200. No. 3371, 24,000 le, 1966 Dodge Polara Fire Chief car. No. 3372, 24,000 le, Citroen DS ambulance. No. 3373, 24,000 le, USS Los Angeles airship. No. 3374, 24,000 le, Concorde 102, diff. No. 3375, 24,000 le, High Mobility Multipurpose Wheeled Vehicle. No. 3376, 24,000 le, Curiosity Rover on Mars. No. 3377, 24,000 le, Launch of Atlas V rocket, New Horizons, Pluto and Charon. No. 3378, 24,000 le, Prince Andrew and Sydney, Australia light show. No. 3379, 26,000 le, Einstein and model of atom. No. 3380, 26,000 le, Einstein, 1921 Nobel Physics laureate. No. 3381, 26,000 le, Child, Anopheles mosquito, Red Cross flag.

2015, July 24 Litho. *Perf. 13¼*

Sheets of 4, #a-d

3342-3361 A657 Set of 20 235.00 235.00

Souvenir Sheets

3362-3381 A657 Set of 20 235.00 235.00

Miniature Sheet

Doctors Killed by Ebola Virus — A658

No. 3382: a, Dr. Olivette Buck. b, Dr. Martin Maada Salia. c, Dr. Godfrey Alexandra Jonathan George. d, Dr. Modupe Cole. e, Dr. Sahr Jimmy Rogers. f, Dr. Sheik Umar Khan. g, Dr. Thomas Tivo Rogers. h, Dr. Victor Willoughby.

2015, Aug. 21 Litho. *Perf. 13¼*

3382 A658 3500 le Sheet of 8, #a-h 14.00 14.00

See Nos. 3583, 3585.

A659

No. 3383, 5500 le — Pandas (Ailuropoda melanoleuca): a, Adult on tree, head at UL. b, Adult and juvenile. c, Adult on tree, head at center. d, Adult with head between tree branches.

No. 3384, 5500 le — Seals: a, Phoca largha. b, Arctocephalus pusillus. c, Arctocephalus tropicalis. d, Lobodon carcinophaga.

No. 3385, 5500 le — Tigers (Panthera tigris): a, Facing right with front paw raised. b, Resting, with mouth open. c, Running left. d, Walking to right, looking left.

No. 3386, 5500 le — Cats: a, Chartreux. b, Kurlian Bobtail cats. c, Devon Rex cats. d, Toyger.

No. 3387, 5500 le — Dogs: a, British bulldog. b, Afghan hound. c, Yorkshire terriers. d, Basset hounds.

No. 3388, 5500 le — Horses: a, Mustangs. b, Arabian horses, dark blue sky. c, Arabian horses, clouds in sky. d, Cleveland Bay horses.

No. 3389, 5500 le — Whales: a, Megaptera novaeangliae. b, Eschrichtius robustus. c, Physeter macrocephalus. d, Balaenoptera musculus.

No. 3390, 5500 le — Eagles: a, Haliaeetus leucocephalus. b, Polemaetus bellicosus. c, Aquila audax. d, Haliaeetus albicilla.

No. 3391, 5500 le — Kingfishers: a, Megaceryle maxima. b, Halcyon leucocephala. c, Megaceryle alcyon facing right. d, Megaceryle alcyon facing left.

No. 3392, 5500 le — Water birds: a, Aix galericulata. b, Gavia pacifica. c, Ardea herodias. d, Mycteria leucocephala.

No. 3393, 5500 le — Bees: a, Apis cerana. b, Thyreus nitidulus. c, Dasypoda hirtipes. d, Apis mellifera.

No. 3394, 5500 le — Butterflies: a, Anartia jatrophae. b, Siproeta stelenes. c, Vanessa kershawi. d, Myscelia ethusa.

No. 3395, 5500 le — Tropical fish: a, Pomacanthus imperator. b, Amphiprion ocellaris. c, Paracanthurus hepatus. d, Chaetodon semilarvatus.

No. 3396, 5500 le — Shells: a, Scapharca inaequivalvis. b, Rapa rapa. c, Ranella olearium. d, Rapana rapiformis.

No. 3397, 5500 le — Snakes: a, Hydrophis platurus. b, Epicrates cenchria. c, Lampropeltis elapsoides. d, Thamnophis sirtalis infernalis.

No. 3398, 5500 le — Prehistoric water animals: a, Dinichthys terrelli. b, Basilosaurus cetoides. c, Prognathodon saturator. d, Helicoprion bessonovi.

No. 3399, 5500 le — Extinct animals: a, Smilodon populator. b, Elasmotherium sibiricum. c, Raphus cucullatus. d, Mammuthus primigenius.

No. 3400, 5500 le — Endangered species: a, Panthera uncia. b, Zalophus wollebaeki. c, Dermochelys coriacea. d, Pongo abelii.

No. 3401, 5500 le — Orchids: a, Paphiopedilum lowii. b, Laelia anceps var. barkeriana. c, Paphiopedilum hybrid. d, Phalaenopsis stuartiana var. nobilis.

No. 3402, 5500 le — Mushrooms: a, Cantharellus cibarius. b, Hydnum repandum. c, Xerocomus subtomentosus. d, Morchella esculenta.

No. 3403, 22,000 le, Ailuropoda melanoleuca, diff. No. 3404, 22,000 le, Phoca vitulina. No. 3405, 22,000 le, Panthera tigris altaica. No. 3406, 22,000 le, Manx cat. No. 3407, 22,000 le, German shepherd. No. 3408, 22,000 le, Akhal-Teke horses. No. 3409, 22,000 le, Balaenoptera brydei. No. 3410, 22,000 le, Aquila chrysaetos. No. 3411, 22,000 le, Halcyon pileata. No. 3412, 22,000 le, Pelecanus onocrotalus. No. 3413, 22,000 le, Halictus scabiosae. No. 3414, 22,000 le, Protographium marcellus. No. 3415, 22,000 le, Synchiropus splendidus. No. 3416, 22,000 le, Spondylus americanus. No. 3417, 22,000 le, Diadophis punctatus regalis. No. 3418, 22,000 le, Plesiosaurus brachypterygius. No. 3419, 22,000 le, Glyptodon clavipes. No. 3420, 22,000 le, Diceros bicornis. No. 3421, 22,000 le, Cattleya hybrid. No. 3422, 22,000 le, Boletus pinophilus.

2015, Aug. 21 Litho. *Perf. 13¼*

Sheets of 4, #a-d

3383-3402 A659 Set of 20 220.00 220.00

Souvenir Sheets

3403-3422 A659 Set of 20 220.00 220.00

Paintings — A660

No. 3423, 6000 le — Paintings by Fredéric Bazille (1841-70): a, Portrait of Paul Verlaine. b, Landscape of Aigues-Mortes. c, Bazille's Studio. d, African Woman with Peonies.

No. 3424, 6000 le — Paintings by Emile Bernard (1868-1941): a, The Harbor at Saint-Briac. b, Pont-Aven. c, Breton Women Attending a Pardon. d, Still Life with Flowers.

No. 3425, 6000 le — Paintings by Pierre Bonnard (1867-1947): a, The Port of Cannes. b, The French Window. c, Siesta. d, In Summer.

No. 3426, 6000 le — Paintings by Gustave Caillebotte (1848-94): a, Close of the Abbesses. b, Europe Bridge. c, The Floor Scrapers. d, Laundry Drying, Petit Gennevilliers.

No. 3427, 6000 le — Paintings by Mary Cassatt (1844-1926): a, Portrait of a Young Woman. b, The Boating Party. c, Tea. d, A Kiss for Baby Anne.

No. 3428, 6000 le — Paintings by Paul Cézanne (1839-1906): a, The Three Skulls. b, Mont Sainte-Victoire. c, Still Life with Apples and Oranges. d, The Card Players.

No. 3429, 6000 le — Paintings by Edgar Degas (1834-1917): a, Women Ironing. b, Blue Dancers. c, At the Races. d, The Millinery Shop.

No. 3430, 6000 le — Paintings by Paul Gauguin (1848-1903): a, Self-portrait. b, Tahitian Mountains. c, Still Life with Teapot and Fruits. d, Portrait of Vincent van Gogh.

No. 3431, 6000 le — Paintings by Edouard Manet (1832-83): a, Portrait of Stéphane Mallarmé. b, Boating. c, The Grand Canal of Venice (Blue Venice). d, A Bar at the Folies-Bergère.

No. 3432, 6000 le — Paintings by Henri Matisse (1869-1954): a, Landscape Near Collioure. b, The Lute. c, Music. d, Dishes and Fruit.

No. 3433, 6000 le — Paintings by Claude Monet (1840-1926): a, Haystacks, Sun in the Mist. b, The Seine at Vétheuil. c, Water Lilies. d, Springtime.

No. 3434, 6000 le — Paintings by Berthe Morisot (1841-95): a, Young Girl and the Budgie. b, Grain Field. c, The Harbor at Lorient. d, Lucie Leon at the Piano.

No. 3435, 6000 le — Paintings by Camille Pissarro (1830-1903): a, The Harvest, Pontoise. b, Autumn Morning at Eragny. c, Jalais Hill, Pontoise. d, Washerwomen, Eragny.

No. 3436, 6000 le — Paintings by Pierre-Auguste Renoir (1841-1919): a, Luncheon of the Boating Party. b, View at Guernsey. c, Armful of Roses. d, Dance at Le Moulin de la Galette.

No. 3437, 6000 le — Paintings by Théo van Rysselberghe (1862-1926): a, Summer Afternoon. b, A Reading in the Garden. c, Three Children in Blue. d, Canal in Flanders.

No. 3438, 6000 le — Paintings by Paul Sérusier (1864-1927): a, Still Life with Apples and Violets. b, The Embroideress. c, The Snake Eaters. d, The Aqueduct.

No. 3439, 6000 le — Paintings by Georges Seurat (1859-91): a, Riverman. b, Gray Weather, Grande Jatte. c, Bathers at Asnières. d, A Sunday Afternoon on the Island of the Grande Jatte.

No. 3440, 6000 le — Paintings by Alfred Sisley (1839-99): a, The Bridge of Moret-sur-Loing. b, Louveciennes, Sentier de la Mi Cote. c, Avenue of Chestnut Trees. d, Seaside, Langland.

No. 3441, 6000 le — Paintings by Henri de Toulouse-Lautrec (1864-1901): a, Equestrienne (At the Circus Fernando). b, At the Races. c, Marcelle Lender Dancing the Bolero in "Chilpéric". d, Hangover.

No. 3442, 6000 le — Paintings by American Impressionists: a, Roses in a Silver Bowl on a Mahogany Table, by J. Alden Weir (1852-1919). b, Happy Days, by Edward Henry Potthast (1857-1927). c, Mother and Child in a Boat, by Edmund C. Tarbell (1862-1938). d, The Water Garden, by Childe Hassam (1859-1935).

No. 3443, 24,000 le, Family Reunion, by Bazille. No. 3444, 24,000 le, Breton Women at a Wall, by Bernard. No. 3445, 24,000 le, Girl in a Straw Hat (Femme au Chapeau Rouge), by Bonnard. No. 3446, 24,000 le, Paris Street, Rainy Day, by Caillebotte. No. 3447, 24,000 le, Little Girl in a Blue Armchair, by Cassatt. No. 3448, 24,000 le, Still Life with Onions, by Cézanne. No. 3449, 24,000 le, Dance Class at the Opera, by Degas. No. 3450, 24,000 le, Tahitian Women on the Beach, by Gauguin. No. 3451, 24,000 le, The Railway, by Manet. No. 3452, 24,000 le, The Red Room, by Matisse. No. 3453, 24,000 le, Camille Monet on a Garden Bench, by Monet. No. 3454, 24,000 le, Reading, by Morisot. No. 3455, 24,000 le, The Boulevard Montmartre on a Winter Morning, by Pissarro. No. 3456, 24,000 le, Landscape, by Renoir. No. 3457, 24,000 le, Madame Théo van Rysselberghe and Her Daughter, by Rysselberghe. No. 3458, 24,000 le, Boys on a Riverbank, by Sérusier. No. 3459, 24,000 le, Fishing in the Seine, by Seurat. No. 3460, 24,000 le, Grande Jatte, by Sisley. No. 3461, 24,000 le, In the Salon at the Rue des Moulins, by Toulouse-Lautrec. No. 3462, 24,000 le, Dolce Far Niente, by John Singer Sargent (1856-1925).

2015, Sept. 25 Litho. *Perf. 13¼*

Sheets of 4, #a-d

3423-3442 A660 Set of 20 230.00 230.00

Souvenir Sheets

3443-3462 A660 Set of 20 230.00 230.00

Nos. 3443-3462 each contain one 51x36mm stamp.

Birds — A661

No. 3463, 6000 le — African penguins (Spheniscus demersus): a, Three penguins. b, Two penguins. c, Two penguins and fish. d, Two penguins swimming.

No. 3464, 6000 le — Bee-eaters: a, Merops apiaster facing right. b, Four Merops pusillus. c, Merops apiaster facing left. d, Two Merops viridis.

No. 3465, 6000 le — Birds-of-paradise: a, Paradisaea decora. b, Paradisaea raggiana, head facing left. c, Paradisaea minor. d, Paradisaea raggiana, head facing right.

No. 3466, 6000 le — Birds of prey: a, Haliaeetus albicilla. b, Haliaeetus leucocephalus with wings spread. c, Haliaeetus pelagicus. d, Pithecophaga jeffreyi with wings spread.

No. 3467, 6000 le — Ducks: a, Histrionicus histrionicus. b, Somateria spectabilis. c, Anas platyrhynchos. d, Aix sponsa.

No. 3468, 6000 le — Eagles: a, Aquila audax. b, Pandion haliaetus. c, Pithecophaga jeffreyi on rock. d, Haliaeetus leucocephalus and chick.

No. 3469, 6000 le — Flamingos: a, Phoenicopterus roseus. b, Two Phoenicopterus ruber. c, Phoenicopterus chilensis. d, Two Phoenicopterus ruber and flower.

No. 3470, 6000 le — Hummingbirds: a, Calothorax lucifer, Hylocharis xantusii. b, Calothorax lucifer, Selasphorus rufus. c, Lampornis clemenciae. d, Selasphorus calliope.

No. 3471, 6000 le — Ibises: a, Geronticus calvus. b, Threskiornis molucca. c, Geronticus eremita. d, Lophotibis cristata.

No. 3472, 6000 le — Kingfishers: a, One Ceyx erithaca. b, Halcyon smyrnensis, Halcyon leucocephala. c, Megaceryle alcyon. d, Ceyx azureus.

No. 3473, 6000 le — Owls: a, Bubo africanus. b, Otus ireneae. c, Ptilopsis granti. d, Jubula lettii.

No. 3474, 6000 le — Parrots: a, Psittacus erithacus. b, Polytelis anthopeplus. c, Ara macao. d, Ara ararauna.

No. 3475, 6000 le — Peacocks: a, Pavo cristatus, Latin name in white. b, Pavo muticus. c, Pavo cristatus mut. alba. d, Pavo cristatus, Latin name in black.

No. 3476, 6000 le — Pigeons and doves: a, Otidiphaps nobilis. b, Ptilinopus porphyreus. c, Ptilinopus regina. d, Ducula pinon.

No. 3477, 6000 le — Protected birds: a, Lamprotornis hildebrandti. b, Callipepla californica. c, Loxia scotica. d, Clangula hyemalis.

No. 3478, 6000 le — Sea birds: a, Morus bassanus. b, Sula nebouxii. c, Phalacrocorax atriceps. d, Pygoscelis papua.

No. 3479, 6000 le — Tropical birds: a, Two Ceyx erithaca. b, Cyanerpes cyaneus. c, Sicalis flaveola. d, Paroaria coronata.

No. 3480, 6000 le — Warblers: a, Dendroica tigrina. b, Dendroica dominica, Dendroica angelae. c, Dendroica angelae. d, Sylvia mystacea.

No. 3481, 6000 le — Water birds: a, Egretta tricolor. b, Platalea ajaja. c, Ephippiorhynchus senegalensis. d, Grus canadensis (incorrect identification).

No. 3482, 6000 le — White-breasted guinea fowl (Agelastes meleagrides): a, Two birds, one with lifted leg. b, One bird facing right. c, One bird facing left. d, Heads of two birds.

No. 3483, 24,000 le, Two Spheniscus demersus, diff. No. 3484, 24,000 le, Merops ornatus. No. 3485, 24,000 le, Paradisaea apoda. No. 3486, 24,000 le, Milvus milvus. No. 3487, 24,000 le, Tadorna tadorna. No. 3488, 24,000 le, Haliaeetus vocifer. No. 3489, 24,000 le, Two Phoenicopterus ruber, diff. No. 3490, 24,000 le, Cynanthus latirostris, Selasphorus calliope, Hylocharis leucotis. No. 3491, 24,000 le, Eudocimus ruber. No. 3492, 24,000 le, Halcyon senegalensis. No. 3493, 24,000 le, Glaucidium tephronotum. No. 3494, 24,000 le, Trichoglossus haematodus. No. 3495, 24,000 le, Pavo cristatus, mut. pied. No. 3496, 24,000 le, Geophaps plumifera, Macropygia ruficeps. No. 3497, 24,000 le, Calyptura cristata. No. 3498, 24,000 le, Phalacrocorax punctatus. No. 3499, 24,000 le, Buceros bicornis. No. 3500, 24,000 le, Setophaga petechia. No. 3501, 24,000 le, Anhinga anhinga. No. 3502, 24,000 le, Agelastes meleagrides, diff.

2015, Oct. 23 Litho. *Perf. 13¼*

Sheets of 4, #a-d

3463-3482 A661 Set of 20 215.00 215.00

Souvenir Sheets

3483-3502 A661 Set of 20 215.00 215.00

A662

No. 3503, 6000 le — End of Viet Nam War, 40th anniv.: a, U.S. helicopter, soldier aiming bazooka. b, U.S. helicopter, infantryman. c, U.S. soldiers assisting wounded soldier. d, Vietnamese combatants shooting and hiding underground.

No. 3504, 6000 le — Apollo 13, 45th anniv.: a, Commander James Lovell. b, Lunar Module Pilot Fred Haise. c, Command Module Pilot Jack Swigert (1931-82). d, Ken Mattingly, astronaut replaced due to illness.

No. 3505, 6000 le — 2015 Nobel Prize Winners: a, Physiology or Medicine laureates Satoshi Omura, Tu Youyou, and William C. Campbell. b, Economic Sciences laureate Angus Deaton. c, Chemistry laureates Paul L. Modrich, Aziz Sancar, and Tomas Lindahl. d, Literature laureate Svetlana Alexievich.

No. 3506, 6000 le — First stadium concert of the Beatles, 50th anniv.: a, George Harrison (1943-2001). b, Paul McCartney. c, John Lennon (1940-80). d, Ringo Starr.

No. 3507, 6000 le — 2015 World Track and Field Championships, Beijing: a, Pole vaulter Shawnacy Barber. b, Sprinter Usain Bolt. c, Race walkers Liu Hong and Lü Xiuzhi. d, Discus thrower Piotr Malachowski.

No. 3508, 6000 le — 2015 Chess Championships: a, Hou Yifan. b, Peter Svidler. c, Sergey Karjakin. d, Dmitry Jakovenko.

No. 3509, 6000 le — South African lighthouses: a, St. Helena Bay Lighthouse. b, Roman Rock Lighthouse. c, Cape Point Lighthouse. d, Kalk Bay Lighthouse.

No. 3510, 6000 le — Pilgrimage to Mecca: a, Pilgrim resting in Mina. b, Pilgrims at the Jamrah. c, Pilgrims praying at Mount Arafat. d, Pilgrim head shaving after stoning the Jamarat.

No. 3511, 6000 le — Paintings by Peter Paul Rubens (1577-1640): a, Night Scene. b, Helena Fourment with Her Children. c, The Fall of Phaeton. d, Ruben's Son, Nikolas.

No. 3512, 6000 le — Paintings by Vincent van Gogh (1853-90): a, La Mousmé. b, The Night Café. c, The Church at Auvers. d, Self-portrait with Bandaged Ear and Pipe.

No. 3513, 6000 le — Christmas paintings: a, The Virgin of the Veil, by Ambrogio Borgognone (c. 1470-c. 1523). b, The Nativity with Donors and Saints Jerome and Leonard, by Gerard David (1460-1523). c, The Nativity, by Conrad von Soest (1370-1422). d, Adoration of the Magi, by Gentile da Fabriano (1370-1427).

No. 3514, 24,000 le, Plant growing through bullet hole in Viet Nam War Army helmet. No. 3515, 24,000 le, Damaged Apollo 13 in space. No. 3516, 24,000 le, Nobel Physics laureates Takaaki Kajita and Arthur B. McDonald. No. 3517, 24,000 le, Lennon playing guitar. No. 3518, 24,000 le, Hammer thrower Anita Wlodarczyk. No. 3519, 24,000 le, Alexander Grischuk at chess board. No. 3520, 24,000 le, Mouille Point Lighthouse, South Africa, and sculpture by Marieke Prinsloo-Rowe. No. 3521, 24,000 le, Pilgrim kissing black stone in Holy Ka'aba. No. 3522, 24,000 le, Two Satyrs, by Rubens. No. 3523, 24,000 le, Portrait of Postman Joseph Roulin, by van Gogh. No. 3524, 24,000 le, The Adoration of the Kings, by Pieter Bruegel the Elder (1525-69).

2015, Nov. 27 Litho. *Perf. 13¼*

Sheets of 4, #a-d

3503-3513 A662 Set of 11 125.00 125.00

Souvenir Sheets

3514-3524 A662 Set of 11 125.00 125.00

A663

No. 3525, 6000 le — Sierra Leone Red Cross Society: a, Woman wearing Red Cross jacket. b, Worker in protective suit holding hand of girl. c, Worker wearing mask and hair net. d, Worker in protective suit holding arm of patient in bed.

No. 3526, 6000 le — Alfred Hitchcock (1899-1980), movie director: a, Hitchcock holding clapboard. b, James Stewart (1908-97), and Janet Leigh (1927-2004), movie actors. c, Tippi Hedren, movie actress. d, Hitchcock and bird's head.

No. 3527, 6000 le — George Frideric Handel (1685-1759), composer: a, Handel and harpsichord. b, Alessandro, from production of Goethe Theater, Bad Lauchstädt, Louise Kemény, operatic actress in *Ottone*. c, Bust of Handel, and Teatro Niccolini, Florence, Italy. d, Handel and column from Teatro Niccolini.

No. 3528, 6000 le — Georges Bizet (1838-75), composer: a, Bizet. b, Carmen from opera *Carmen*. c, Escamillo and Don José from opera *Carmen*. d, Henri Meilhac (1830-97) and Ludovic Halévy (1834-1908), librettists for *Carmen*.

No. 3529, 6000 le — Pope Francis: a, On visit to Brazil. b, On visit to Israel, Jordan and Palestine. c, On visit to the Philippines. d, Facing left.

No. 3530, 6000 le — Pope Benedict XVI, 10th anniv. of inauguration: a, Waving in 2013. b, Facing backwards, Pope Francis facing left. c, Wearing crucifix around neck. d, Wearing miter.

No. 3531, 6000 le — Mother Teresa (1910-97), humanitarian: a, Facing right. b, With Pope John Paul II. c, Holding child. d, With dove.

No. 3532, 6000 le — World War I aircraft: a, German Zeppelin, British bombadier holding bomb. b, German airplanes. c, German pilot. d, Russian and British airplanes.

No. 3533, 6000 le — New Year 2016 (Year of the Monkey): a, Head of monkey, Chinese character for "monkey" at LR. b, Chinese character for "monkey", "2016" at LR. c, Monkeys, Chinese character for "monkey" at UR. d, Monkey, Chinese character for "monkey" at LR.

No. 3534, 24,000 le, Red Cross workers, loudspeaker. No. 3535, 24,000 le, Hitchcock, diff. No. 3536, 24,000 le, Handel, diff. No. 3537, 24,000 le, Bizet, diff. No. 3538, 24,000 le, Pope Francis, diff. No. 3539, 24,000 le, Pope Benedict XVI, diff. No. 3540, 24,000 le, Mother Teresa, diff. No. 3541, 24,000 le, German fighter airplane and gunner. No. 3542, 24,000 le, Monkey and Chinese character for "monkey" at UR, diff.

2015, Nov. 27 Litho. *Perf. 13¼*

Sheets of 4, #a-d

3525-3533 A663 Set of 9 100.00 100.00

Souvenir Sheets

3534-3542 A663 Set of 9 100.00 100.00

A664

No. 3543, 6000 le — Judo: a, Judokas in white robes, judoka's head near denomination. b, Judokas in white and blue robes, judoka's head above denomination. c, Female judokas in white and blue robes. d, Judokas in white robes, judoka's hand above denomination.

No. 3544, 6000 le — Rugby: a, Players wearing red and blue shirts chasing ball. b, Player with yellow shirt making tackle. c, Player holding ball extending arm while being tackled. d, Player wearing scrum cap holding ball being tackled.

No. 3545, 6000 le — Horse racing: a, Jockey wearing red and blue silks. b, Jockeys wearing red and green and green and white checked silks. c, Jockey wearing light blue and yellow silks. d, Jockey wearing blue and orange silks.

No. 3546, 6000 le — Cricket: a, Batsman in blue uniform and wicket-keeper at wicket. b, Batsman in blue uniform. c, Batsman in white uniform. d, Batsman in white uniform and wicket-keeper at wicket.

No. 3547, 6000 le — 2015 Africa Cup of Nations Soccer Championships: a, Stadium and hands holding trophy. b, One player. c, Two players. d, Soccer ball hitting goal netting.

No. 3548, 6000 le — Scuba diving and sport fishing: a, Scuba divers, one with camera, and fish. b, Fisherman with Coryphaena hippurus. c, Fishermen with Thunnus albacares near boat. d, Scuba diver and Makaira nigricans.

No. 3549, 6000 le — Rowing: a, Women's double scull. b, Men's coxless four. c, Women's eight. d, Men's single scull.

No. 3550, 6000 le — Tour de France bicycle race champions: a, Vincenzo Nibali, 2014. b, Christopher Froome, 2015. c, Froome, 2013. d, Cadel Evans, 2011.

No. 3551, 6000 le — Tennis players: a, Novak Djokovic. b, Serena Williams. c, Maria Sharapova. d, Andy Murray.

No. 3552, 6000 le — Table tennis players: a, Kasumi Ishikawa. b, Ma Long. c, Zhang Jike. d, Koki Niwa.

No. 3553, 6000 le — Golfers: a, Rory McIlroy. b, Michelle Wie. c, Choi Na-yeon. d, Tiger Woods.

No. 3554, 6000 le — Chess players: a, Levon Aronian. b, Judit Polgár. c, Viswanathan Anand. d, Magnus Carlsen.

No. 3555, 6000 le — André Gustave Citroen (1878-1935), automobile manufacturer, and: a, Citroen 11 CV. b, Citroen B14. c, Citroen H Van and Ami 6. d, Citroen 7 CV.

No. 3556, 6000 le — Charles Darwin (1809-82), naturalist: a, Stegosaurus stenops. b, Darwin and ship. c, Darwin and Allosaurus fragilis. d, Pterodactylus macronyx.

No. 3557, 6500 le — Ludwig van Beethoven (1770-1827), composer: a, Writing. b, Conducting. c, At harpsichord. d, As young man, buildings in background.

No. 3558, 6500 le — Sir Alexander Fleming (1881-1955), biologist: a, Fleming and Penicillium mold. b, Fleming's Nobel medal and tree mushroom. c, Polyporus umbelattus, soldier's helmet, and drug boxes and vials. d, Fleming and Ganoderma lucidum.

No. 3559, 6500 le — Marilyn Monroe (1926-62), actress, and Joe DiMaggio (1914-99), baseball player: a, Couple, hands not showing. b, Couple, holding hands. c, DiMaggio in baseball uniform to left of Monroe. d, DiMaggio in baseball uniform to right of Monroe.

No. 3560, 6500 le — Nelson Mandela (1918-2013), President of South Africa, and minerals: a, Amethyst. b, Rutile. c, Gold. d, Zirconium.

No. 3561, 6500 le — Early members of Rotary International and orchids: a, Silvester Schele (1870-1945), and Calypso bulbosa. b, Harry L. Ruggles (1868-1959), and Anacamptis coriophora. c, Hiram E. Shorey (1862-1944), and Miltonia spectabilis. d, Paul Harris (1868-1947), founder, and Cattleya cultivar.

No. 3562, 6500 le — 2015 World Scout Jamboree, Kirarahama, Japan: a, Boy Scout saluting and butterfly. b, Boy Scout, tent, Lord Robert Baden-Powell. c, Boy Scout, Japanese high-speed train. d, Boy Scouts building campfire.

No. 3563, 24,000 le, Judokas, diff. No. 3564, 24,000 le, Two rugby players, diff. No. 3565, 24,000 le, Steeplechase horse race. No. 3566, 24,000 le, Cricket player on knees. No. 3567, 24,000 le, Two soccer players, emblem of 2015 Africa Cup of Nations. No. 3568, 24,000 le, Fisherman and Lutjanus campechanus. No. 3569, 24,000 le, Men's double scull. No. 3570, 24,000 le, Bradley Wiggins, 2012 Tour de France champion. No. 3571, 24,000 le, Djokovic, diff. No. 3572, 24,000 le, Zhou Yu playing table tennis. No. 3573, 24,000 le, Jordan Spieth, golfer. No. 3574, 24,000 le, Wilhelm Steinitz (1836-1900), chess player. No. 3575, 24,000 le, Citroen, automobile and Eiffel Tower. No. 3576, 24,000 le, Darwin and Tyrannosaurus rex. No. 3577, 26,000 le, Beethoven, diff. No. 3578, 26,000 le, Fleming and Hericium erinaceus. No. 3579, 26,000 le, Monroe and DiMaggio, diff. No. 3580, 26,000 le, Mandela and diamond. No. 3581, 26,000 le, Harris and Phalaenopsis amboinensis. No. 3582, 26,000 le, Boy Scout and Japanese high-speed train, diff.

2015, Dec. 21 Litho. *Perf. 13¼*

Sheets of 4, #a-d

3543-3562 A664 Set of 20 240.00 240.00

Souvenir Sheets

3563-3582 A664 Set of 20 240.00 240.00

Doctors Killed by Ebola Virus Type of 2015 and

Medical Workers Killed by Ebola Virus — A665

Nos. 3583 and 3585: a, Dr. Olivette Buck. b, Dr. Martin Maada Salia. c, Dr. Godfrey Alexandra Jonathan George. d, Dr. Modupe Cole. e, Dr. Sahr Jimmy Rogers. f, Dr. Sheik Umar Khan. g, Dr. Thomas Tivo Rogers. h, Dr. Victor Willoughby.

Nos. 3584 and 3586: a, Fatmata Turay. b, Fiema Bockarie. c, Hajara Serry. d, Jane Turay. e, Mbalu Fonnie. f, Mohamed Thulla. g, Prince Vandi Koroma. h, Princess Iye Gborie.

2016, Jan. 25 Litho. *Perf. 13¼*

3583	A658	2000 le	Sheet of 8, #a-h	8.00	8.00
3584	A665	2000 le	Sheet of 8, #a-h	8.00	8.00
3585	A658	5000 le	Sheet of 8, #a-h	20.00	20.00
3586	A665	5000 le	Sheet of 8, #a-h	20.00	20.00
	Nos. 3583-3586 (4)			56.00	56.00

Dated 2015.

Wildlife — A666

No. 3587, 6000 le — Hippopotamus (Hippopotamus amphibius): a, Animal in front facing forward. b, Facing right. c, Facing left. d, Adult and juvenile.

No. 3588, 6000 le — Red river hog (Potamochoerus porcus): a, Facing right, Latin name in black. b, Two hogs, Latin name in white. c, Two hogs, Latin name in black. d, Facing left, Latin name in white.

No. 3589, 6000 le — Primates: a, Papio ursinus. b, Pan troglodytes. c, Saimiri sciureus. d, Macaca arctoides.

No. 3590, 6000 le — Hyenas: a, Hyaena hyaena. b, Crocuta crocuta with closed mouth. c, Hyaena brunnea. d, Crocuta crocuta with open mouth.

No. 3591, 6000 le — African leopard (Panthera pardus pardus) with Latin name in: a, White at UR. b, Black at LL. c, White at LR in 3 lines. d, White at LR in 2 lines.

No. 3592, 6000 le — Lions (Panthera leo): a, Male and female lions. b, Male lion. c, Female lion. d, Two female lions.

No. 3593, 6000 le — African bush elephant (Loxodonta africana): a, Adult walking. b, Adult and juvenile at watering hole. c, Adult and juvenile in grass. d, Adult in grass facing right.

No. 3594, 6000 le — Manatees: a, Trichechus manatus latirostris, Latin name in black in 3 lines. b, Trichechus manatus latirostris, Latin name in black on 2 lines. c, Trichechus manatus. d, Trichechus manatus latirostris, Latin name in white in 3 lines.

No. 3595, 6000 le — Dolphins: a, Tursiops truncatus at surface, Latin name at bottom. b, Delphinus delphis. c, Delphinus capensis. d, Tursiops truncatus leaping above water, Latin name at LR.

No. 3596, 6000 le — Orcas (Orcinus orca): a, Leaping right, Latin name in white at LR. b, Leaping, Latin name in black. c, Leaping right with underside showing, Latin name in white at LR . d, Leaping left, Latin name in white at bottom.

No. 3597, 6000 le — Whales: a, Two Megaptera novaeangliae underwater. b, One Megaptera novaeangliae, Latin name in black. c, One Megaptera novaeangliae, Latin name in white. d, Delphinapterus leucas.

No. 3598, 6000 le — Doves: a, Streptopelia decaocto. b, Geopelia striata. c, Gallicolumba tristigmata. d, Ducula badia.

No. 3599, 6000 le — Hawks: a, Accipiter gentilis. b, Buteo jamaicensis. c, Melierax canorus. d, Accipiter striatus.

No. 3600, 6000 le — Cuckoos: a, Chrysococcyx cupreus. b, Chrysococcyx klaas. c, Coccyzus americanus. d, Cacomantis merulinus.

No. 3601, 6000 le — Owls: a, Ptilopsis granti. b, Athene noctua. c, Strix varia. d, Strix nebulosa.

No. 3602, 6000 le — Butterflies: a, Heliconius melpomene. b, Papilio demoleus. c, Zerynthia polyxena. d, Limenitis archippus.

No. 3603, 6000 le — Fish: a, Chelmon rostratus. b, Scatophagus argus. c, Acanthurus leucosternon. d, Symphorichthys spilurus.

No. 3604, 6000 le — Lizards: a, Agama agama. b, Varanus komodoensis. c, Varanus niloticus. d, Chamaeleo dilepis.

No. 3605, 6000 le — Crocodiles (Crocodylus niloticus) with Latin name in: a, Black at right. b, White at left. c, White at bottom. d, White at top.

No. 3606, 6000 le — Turtles: a, Eretmochelys imbricata. b, Trachemys scripta elegans. c, Emys orbicularis. d, Stigmochelys pardalis.

No. 3607, 24,000 le, Hippopotamus amphibius, diff. No. 3608, 24,000 le, Potamochoerus porcus, diff. No. 3609, 24,000 le, Pongo pygmaeus. No. 3610, 24,000 le, Hyaena hyaena, diff. No. 3611, 24,000 le, Panthera pardus pardus, diff. No. 3612, 24,000 le, Female Panthera leo, diff. No. 3613, 24,000 le, Loxodonta africana, diff. No. 3614, 24,000 le, Trichechus manatus latirostris, diff. No. 3615, 24,000 le, Delphinus capensis, diff. No. 3616, 24,000 le, Orcinus orca, diff. No. 3617, 24,000 le, Megaptera novaeangliae, diff. No. 3618, 24,000 le, Goura victoria. No. 3619, 24,000 le, Accipiter nisus. No. 3620, 24,000 le, Cuculus canorus. No. 3621, 24,000 le, Asio flammeus. No. 3622, 24,000 le, Zerynthia polyxena, diff. No. 3623, 24,000 le, Pomacanthus annularis. No. 3624, 24,000 le, Cordylus cataphractus. No. 3625, 24,000 le, Crocodylus niloticus, diff. No. 3626, 24,000 le, Dermochelys coriacea.

2016, Jan. 28 Litho. *Perf. 13¼*

Sheets of 4, #a-d

3587-3606 A666 Set of 20 235.00 235.00

Souvenir Sheets

3607-3626 A666 Set of 20 235.00 235.00

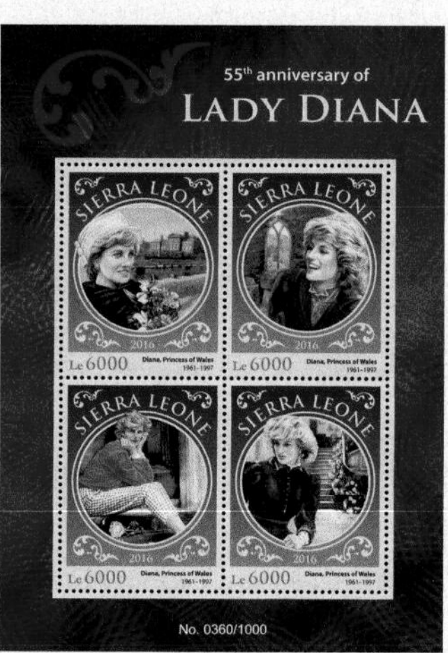

A667

No. 3627, 6000 le — Princess Diana (1961-97): a, Holding flowers. b, With window in background. c, Wearing red and white checked pants. d, With stairway in background.

No. 3628, 6000 le — Queen Elizabeth II, 90th birthday: a, Waving. b, With Prince Philip. c, With young Prince Charles and Princess Anne. d, With coat of arms.

No. 3629, 6000 le — Pope Francis: a, Holding eucharist. b, With St. Peter's Basilica in background. c, Holding personalized Argentina soccer jersey. d, Blessing boy.

No. 3630, 6000 le — Rabindranath Tagore (1861-1941), 1913 Nobel laureate in Literature, with: a, Wife, Mrinalini Devi. b, Albert Einstein. c, Romain Rolland. d, Mahatma Gandhi.

No. 3631, 6000 le — Thomas Edison (1847-1931), inventor: a, Edison and phonograph. b, 1916 Detroit electric car. c, Edison and light bulb. d, Edison and Vitascope projector.

No. 3632, 6000 le — Lord Robert Baden-Powell (1857-1941), founder of Scouting movement: a, With emblem of Boy Scouts of America. b, Boy Scout at campfire. c, With two Boy Scouts. d, Facing right.

No. 3633, 6000 le — Otto Lilienthal (1848-96), developer of gliders: a, Flying glider above restored Lilienthal glider. b, Holding glider wing. c, Portrait, with glider in flight. d, Flying glider above field.

No. 3634, 6000 le — Edgar Mitchell (1930-2016), astronaut: a, In spacesuit. b, With U.S. flag and lunar globe. c, With Apollo 14 capsule. d, Portrait, with Mitchell on Moon in background.

No. 3635, 6000 le — Elizabeth Taylor (1932-2011), actress: a, Facing right. b, Holding bed post. c, Seated. d, Wearing flowered headdress.

No. 3636, 6000 le — Marilyn Monroe (1926-62), actress: a, Seated. b, Wearing blue blouse. c, Holding flower. d, In swimsuit.

No. 3637, 6000 le — Wolfgang Amadeus Mozart (1756-91), composer: a, At harpsichord. b, Scene from opera, *The Marriage of Figaro*. c, With Masonic symbol. d, Scene from opera *Don Giovanni*.

No. 3638, 6000 le — Paintings by Claude Monet (1840-1926): a, Impression, Sunrise. b, Haystacks (Midday). c, A Field of Tulips in Holland. d, The Cliff, Etretat, Sunset.

No. 3639, 6000 le — Art by Pablo Picasso (1881-1973): a, Self-portrait. b, Large Vase with Veiled Women. c, Bust of a Woman. d, Breakfast of a Blind Man.

No. 3640, 6000 le — Ice hockey: a, Players and referee at face-off. b, Skates, stick and puck. c, Goaltender and puck . d, Two players.

No. 3641, 6000 le — Athletes at 2014 Winter Olympics, Sochi, Russia: a, Martin Fourcade, biathlon. b, Vic Wild, snowboarding. c, Michael Mulder, speed skating. d, Dario Cologna, cross-country skiing.

No. 3642, 6000 le — Sports of 2016 Summer Olympics, Rio de Janeiro: a, Badminton. b, Track. c, Taekwondo. d, Field hockey.

No. 3643, 6000 le — Attack on Pearl Harbor, 75th anniv.: a, Boeing P-26 Peashooter and Japanese airplane. b, Mitsubishi A6M Rei-sen (Zero) attacking ship. c, Aichi E13A (Jake) floatplane. d, Curtiss P-36 Hawk.

No. 3644, 6000 le — Dogs and Tanks in World War II: a, M24 Chaffee tank, U.S. soldier and German shepherd. b, Tiger I tank, German soldier and German shepherd. c, SU-122 tank, Russian soldier and Black Russian terrier. d, Tiger I tank, German soldiers and German shepherd attacking.

No. 3645, 6000 le — Campaign against Zika virus: a, Health worker at microscope, Zika virus. b, Health worker measuring head of infant. c, Infant and men spraying insecticide. d, Aedes aegypti.

No. 3646, 24,000 le, Princess Diana, diff. No. 3647, 24,000 le, Monogram of Queen Elizabeth II. No. 3648, 24,000 le, Pope Francis washing person's feet. No. 3649, 24,000 le, Tagore. No. 3650, 24,000 le, Edison, motion picture camera and U.S. flag. No. 3651, 24,000 le, Baden-Powell, diff. No. 3652, 24,000 le, Lilienthal and glider, diff. No. 3653, 24,000 le, Mitchell and rocket on launch pad. No. 3654, 24,000 le, Taylor, diff. No. 3655, 24,000 le, Monroe and dog. No. 3656, 24,000 le, Mozart and violin. No. 3657, 24,000 le, Woman with a Parasol, by Monet. No. 3658, 24,000 le, The Old Guitarist, by Picasso. No. 3659, 24,000 le, Ice hockey players, diff. No. 3660, 24,000 le, Matthias Mayer, Alpine skiing. No. 3661, 24,000 le, Swimming. No. 3662, 24,000 le, Aichi D3A bomber. No. 3663, 24,000 le, Medium tank, U.S. soldier and German shepherd. No. 3664, 24,000 le, Infant, mosquito and map showing countries with outbreak of Zika virus.

2016, Feb. 26 Litho. *Perf. 13¼*

Sheets of 4, #a-d

3627-3645 A667 Set of 19 225.00 225.00

Souvenir Sheets

3646-3664 A667 Set of 19 225.00 225.00

Visit of Pope Francis to New York — A668

No. 3665 — Pope Francis: a, At September 11 Memorial. b, Speaking at United Nations Headquarters. c, In Central Park. d, Leading Mass at Madison Square Garden.

14,000 le, Pope Francis.

Litho., Sheet Margin Litho. With Foil Application

2016, Feb. 26 *Perf. 13¼*

3665 A668 3500 le Sheet of 4, #a-d 7.00 7.00

Souvenir Sheet

Perf.

3666 A668 14,000 le multi 7.00 7.00

2016 World Stamp Show, New York. No. 3666 contains one 40mm diameter stamp.

A669

No. 3667, 6000 le — Polar bear (Ursus maritimus): a, Walking left. b, Facing right with open mouth. c, Climbing ice, facing left. d, Facing forward with open mouth.

No. 3668, 6000 le — Hippopotamus (Hippopotamus amphibius): a, Two with mouths open. b, Head of hippopotamus. c, Hippopotamus and crocodile. d, Two with mouths closed.

No. 3669, 6000 le — Sea lions: a, Zalophus californianus. b, Eumetopias jubatus. c, Otaria flavescens. d, Phocarctos hookeri.

No. 3670, 6000 le — Dolphins: a, Lagenorhynchus obscurus. b, Cephalorhynchus commersonii. c, Grampus griseus. d, Tursiops truncatus.

No. 3671, 6000 le — Whales: a, Balaenoptera physalus. b, Physeter macrocephalus. c, Megaptera novaeangliae. d, Delphinapterus leucas.

No. 3672, 6000 le — Penguins: a, Eudyptes pachyrhynchus. b, Aptenodytes patagonicus. c, Pygoscelis adeliae. d, Spheniscus demersus.

No. 3673, 6000 le — Kingfishers: a, Alcedo atthis. b, Halcyon leucocephala. c, Halcyon smyrnensis. d, Ceyx rufidorsa.

No. 3674, 6000 le — Terns: a, Chlidonias hybrida. b, Chlidonias niger. c, Onychoprion fuscatus. d, Sterna hirundo.

No. 3675, 6000 le — Water birds: a, Podiceps cristatus. b, Anser cygnoides. c, Gavia pacifica. d, Rollandia rolland, Podiceps auritus.

No. 3676, 6000 le — Sharks: a, Isurus oxyrinchus. b, Chlamydoselachus anguineus. c, Sphyrna lewini. d, Alopias pelagicus.

No. 3677, 6000 le — Piranhas: a, Pygocentrus cariba. b, Pygocentrus nattereri. c, Pygocentrus piraya. d, Serrasalmus sanchezi.

No. 3678, 6000 le — Goldfish (Carassius auratus) varieties: a, Butterfly tail. b, Veiltail. c, Red cap oranda. d, Ryukin.

No. 3679, 6000 le — Fish: a, Aulonocara Dragon's Blood, Aulonocara Fire Fish OB Blueberry. b, Siamese fighting fish. c, Leopard skin discus. d, Angelfish.

No. 3680, 6000 le — Frogs: a, Atelopus zeteki. b, Heterixalus alboguttatus. c, Dendropsophus microcephalus. d, Silverstoneia flotator.

No. 3681, 6000 le — Crocodiles: a, Crocodylus porosus. b, Eye of Crocodylus porosus. c, Gavialis gangeticus. d, Crocodylus rhombifer.

No. 3682, 6000 le — Water snakes: a, Enhydris plumbea. b, Nerodia fasciata. c, Helicops angulatus. d, Homalopsis buccata.

No. 3683, 6000 le — Turtles: a, Eretmochelys imbricata. b, Chelonia mydas, facing forward. c, Chelonia mydas, facing left. d, Head of Chelonia mydas.

No. 3684, 6000 le — Prehistoric water animals: a, Dunkleosteus. b, Tylosaurus. c, Nothosaurus. d, Henodus.

No. 3685, 6000 le — Lighthouses: a, Fanad Head Lighthouse, Ireland (incorrect identification). b, Lindau Lighthouse, Germany. c, Bass Harbor Head Lighthouse, Maine. d, Middle Bay Lighthouse, Alabama.

No. 3686, 6000 le — Ships: a, Concordia. b, Elissa. c, Kaiwo Maru. d, Khersones.

No. 3687, 24,000 le, Ursus maritimus, diff. No. 3688, 24,000 le, Hippopotamus amphibius, diff. No. 3689, 24,000 le, Eumetopias jubatus. No. 3690, 24,000 le, Cephalorhynchus heavisidii. No. 3691, 24,000 le, Balaena mysticetus. No. 3692, 24,000 le, Eudyptes pachyrhynchus, Pygoscelis adeliae. No. 3693, 24,000 le, Syma torotoro with fish. No. 3694, 24,000 le, Thalasseus bergii, Onychoprion fuscatus. No. 3695, 24,000 le, Anas formosa. No. 3696, 24,000 le, Carcharodon carcharias. No. 3697, 24,000 le, Pygocentrus cariba, diff. No. 3698, 24,000 le, Carassius auratus Bubble eye. No. 3699, 24,000 le, Orange head. No. 3700, 24,000 le, Pelophylax lessonae. No. 3701, 24,000 le, Crocodylus rhombifer, diff. No. 3702, 24,000 le, Cerberus rynchops. No. 3703, 24,000 le, Chelonia mydas, diff. No. 3704, 24,000 le, Megalodon, Diplocaulus. No. 3705, 24,000 le, Fanad Head Lighthouse, Ireland, diff. No. 3706, 24,000 le, Santa Maria Manuela.

2016, Mar. 25 Litho. *Perf. 13¼*

Sheets of 4, #a-d

3667-3686 A669 Set of 20 240.00 240.00

Souvenir Sheets

3687-3706 A669 Set of 20 240.00 240.00

A670

No. 3707, 6000 le — Sea Hunter unmanned ship: a, View of bow of ship. b, Aerial view of aft of ship. c, Aerial view of bow of ship, flag on mast. d, Deck-level view of bow of ship.

No. 3708, 6000 le — Steam locomotives: a, The Countess of Dufferin. b, Rocket of China. c, Baroneza. d, Mogul.

No. 3709, 6000 le — High-speed trains: a, Thalys PBKA. b, AVE S-102. c, CRH380A. d, HEMU-430X.

No. 3710, 6000 le — Military aircraft of World War II: a, Messerschmitt Bf 109E. b, P-47G Thunderbolt. c, Mitsubishi A6M3 Zero. d, MiG-3 Fighter.

No. 3711, 6000 le — Military transport: a, Freedom class combat ship. b, Alenia C-27J Spartan. c, M1128 Mobile Gun System armored car. d, M997 military ambulance.

No. 3712, 6000 le — Public transport: a, CRH series prototype train. b, Checker A11/A12 taxi cab. c, MV Britannia. d, RTM Caillols tram.

No. 3713, 6000 le — Special transport: a, Canadair CL-600-2B16. b, Mercedes-Benz Sprinter 324 emergency car. c, Royal National Lifeboat Institution George & Mary Webb lifeboat. d, Ferrari FF police car.

No. 3714, 6000 le — Fire engines: a, 1924 Stutz. b, 1952 Ford F6 F1. c, 1983 American LaFrance. d, 2013 Ford F554.

No. 3715, 6000 le — Motorcycles: a, Metalback concept. b, Harley-Davidson Sportster custom. c, IZH 2012 Hybrid concept. d, Ferrari V4 concept.

No. 3716, 6000 le — Louis Blériot (1872-1936), aviator and aircraft manufacturer: a, Blériot holding propeller, airplane in foreground. b, Blériot wearing helmet, airplane in background. c, Airplane and signature. d, Blériot, mechanical drawings in background.

No. 3717, 6000 le — William Boeing (1881-1956), aircraft manufacturer: a, Boeing, Space Launch System. b, Boeing and Eddie Hubbard (1889-1928), test pilot. c, Boeing 747-8 and 737 MAX airplanes. d, Boeing and F/A-18E/F Super Hornet.

No. 3718, 6000 le — First space flight of Yuri Gagarin (1934-68), 55th anniv.: a, Gagarin and newspapers. b, Gagarin in space suit. c, Gagarin and Soviet premier Nikita Khrushchev (1894-1971). d, Gagarin and Klushino, Russia birthplace.

No. 3719, 6000 le — Exploration of Mars: a, Mars Orbiter Mission. b, Mars Reconnaissance Orbiter. c, Nozomi probe. d, MAVEN Mars orbiter.

No. 3720, 6000 le — Juno spacecraft: a, Technician working on Juno. b, Juno with panels opening. c, Juno with panels extended. d, Technicians examining Juno.

No. 3721, 6000 le — Nobel Prize Winners: a, Marie Curie (1867-1934), 1903 Physics laureate. b, Svetlana Alexievich, 2015 Literature laureate. c, Jean-Paul Sartre (1905-80), 1964 Literature laureate. d, 14th Dalai Lama, 1989 Peace laureate.

No. 3722, 6000 le — Explorers: a, Sir Edmund Hillary (1918-2008), mountaineer. b, Roald Amundsen (1872-1928), Antarctic explorer. c, Robert Peary (1856-1920), Arctic explorer. d, Charles Lindbergh (1902-74), aviator, and Spirit of St. Louis.

No. 3723, 6000 le — Invention of the stethoscope, 200th anniv.: a, René Laennec (1781-1826), and his stethoscope. b, Red Cross doctor using stethoscope in child's examination. c, Red Cross doctor in protective gear in Ebola crisis. d, Hands holding stethoscope.

No. 3724, 6000 le — Publication of the Theory of Relativity by Albert Einstein (1879-1955), cent.: a, Einstein and paper on relativity. b, Einstein and mass-energy equivalence equation. c, Einstein and Nobel medal. d, Einstein and planet.

No. 3725, 6000 le — Conrad Gessner (1516-65), naturalist: a, Gessner and Fragaria vesca. b, Ostrich and Ramonda pyrenaica. c, Owl and Achimena erecta. d, Panther and Tulipa suaveolens.

No. 3726, 6000 le — Sled dogs: a, Alaskan huskies. b, Chinooks. c, Canadian Eskimo dogs. d, Alaskan malamutes.

No. 3727, 24,000 le, Sea Hunter, diff. No. 3728, 24,000 le, Rocket locomotive. No. 3729, 24,000 le, UB2X 2501 train. No. 3730, 24,000 le, P-40 Warhawk. No. 3731, 24,000 le, International MaxxPro fighting vehicle. No. 3732, 24,000 le, British Airways Concorde G-BOAA. No. 3733, 24,000 le, Christoph 1 D-HLIR helicopter. No. 3734, 24,000 le, 1937 Leyland Cub FK6 fire engine. No. 3735, 24,000 le, Magpul Ronin motorcycle. No. 3736, 24,000 le, Blériot in cockpit. No. 3737, 24,000 le, Boeing and Boeing B&W seaplane. No. 3738, 24,000 le, Gagarin, diff. No. 3739, 24,000 le, Mars Science Laboratory. No. 3740, 24,000 le, Juno spacecraft, diff. No. 3741, 24,000 le, Aung San Suu Kyi, 1991 Nobel Peace laureate. No. 3742, 24,000 le, Sir Ernest Shackleton (1874-1922), Antarctic explorer. No. 3743, 24,000 le, Red Cross doctor using stethoscope in child's examination, diff. No. 3744, 24,000 le, Einstein and diagram showing bending of space-time. No. 3745, 24,000 le, Horse. No. 3746, 24,000 le, Siberian huskies.

2016, Apr. 29 Litho. *Perf. 13¼*

Sheets of 4, #a-d

3707-3726 A670 Set of 20 245.00 245.00

Souvenir Sheets

3727-3746 A670 Set of 20 245.00 245.00

A671

Designs: No. 3747, Ploceus nigerimus. No. 3748, Tauraco persa buffoni. No. 3749, Panthera leo, denomination in dull green. No. 3750, Panthera leo, diff., denomination in dark red. 1000 le, Iron ore. 2000 le, Rutile sand. No. 3753, Cut diamond. No. 3754, Ribbon for campaign against breast cancer. No. 3755, Girl and baby, "Stop child marriage." No. 3756, Girl and baby, diff., "Girls not brides." No. 3757, Young family, "Early and forced marriage is wrong!" 7000 le, Child Labor, child breaking rocks with hammer. 8000 le, Man, child with AIDS virus. 9000 le, Doctor treating child with malaria. 10,000 le, Three street children. No. 3762, Two street children. No. 3763, Street child.

2016, May 9 Litho. *Perf. 13¼x13*

3747	A671	300 le multi	.25	.25
3748	A671	300 le multi	.25	.25
3749	A671	500 le multi	.25	.25
3750	A671	500 le multi	.25	.25
3751	A671	1000 le multi	.50	.50
3752	A671	2000 le multi	1.00	1.00
3753	A671	3000 le multi	1.60	1.60
3754	A671	3000 le multi	1.60	1.60
3755	A671	5000 le multi	2.60	2.60
3756	A671	5000 le multi	2.60	2.60
3757	A671	5000 le multi	2.60	2.60
3758	A671	7000 le multi	3.75	3.75
3759	A671	8000 le multi	4.25	4.25
3760	A671	9000 le multi	4.75	4.75
3761	A671	10,000 le multi	5.25	5.25
3762	A671	20,000 le multi	10.00	10.00
3763	A671	20,000 le multi	10.00	10.00
	Nos. 3747-3763 (17)		51.50	51.50

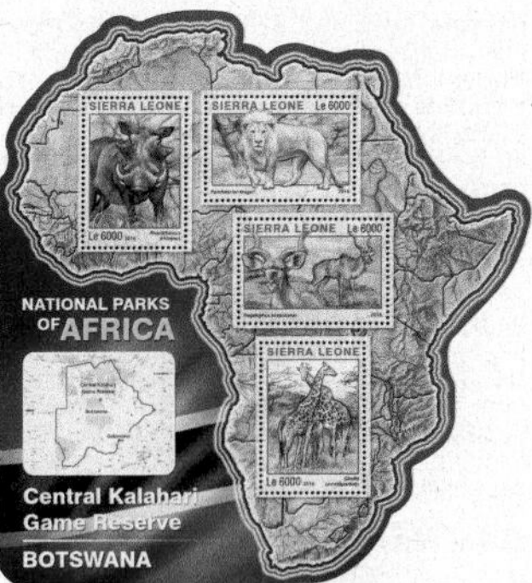

Wildlife of African National Parks and Reserves — A672

No. 3764, 6000 le — Central Kalahari Game Reserve, Botswana: a, One Phacochoerus africanus. b, Panthera leo krugeri, horiz. c, Tragelaphus strepsiceros, four horns above frame line, horiz. d, Giraffa camelopardalis.

No. 3765, 6000 le — Chobe National Park, Botswana: a, Two Loxodonta africana. b, Tragelaphus strepsiceros, two horns above frame line, horiz. c, Phacochoerus aethiopicus, horiz. d, Leptoptilos crumeniferus, Ceryle rudis.

No. 3766, 6000 le — Moremi Game Reserve, Botswana: a, Orycteropus afer. b, Panthera leo bleyenberghi, horiz. c, Gyps coprotheres, horiz. d, Two Aepyceros melampus.

No. 3767, 6000 le — Amboseli National Park, Kenya: a, One Acinonyx jubatus jubatus. b, Ceratotherium simum, horiz. c, Mycteria ibis, horiz. d, Giraffa camelopardalis tippelskirchi.

No. 3768, 6000 le — Maasai Mara National Reserve, Kenya: a, One Otocyon megalotis. b, Acinonyx jubatus, horiz. c, One Diceros bicornis, horiz. d, Damaliscus lunatus jimela.

No. 3769, 6000 le — Etosha National Park, Namibia: a, Struthio camelus australis. b, Canis mesomelas, horiz. c, Ceratotherium simum simum, horiz. d, Antidorcas marsupialis.

No. 3770, 6000 le — Mudumu National Park, Namibia: a, Suricata suricatta. b, Rynchops flavirostris, horiz. c, Taurotragus oryx, horiz. d, Hydrocynus vittatus.

No. 3771, 6000 le — Gola Rainforest National Park, Sierra Leone: a, Malimbus ballmanni. b, Cephalophus jentinki, horiz. c, Scotopelia ussheri, horiz. d, Cercocebus atys.

No. 3772, 6000 le — Outamba-Kilimi National Park, Sierra Leone: a, Coracias cyanogaster. b, Pan troglodytes, horiz. c, Tragelaphus eurycerus, horiz. d, Two Phacochoerus africanus.

No. 3773, 6000 le — Western Area Peninsula National Park, Sierra Leone: a, Pan troglodytes verus. b, Cephalophus zebra, horiz. c, Trichechus senegalensis, horiz. d, One Procolobus badius.

No. 3774, 6000 le — Kruger National Park, South Africa: a, Two Acinonyx jubatus jubatus. b, Equus quagga burchellii running left, horiz. c, Two Diceros bicornis, horiz. d, One Loxodonta africana.

No. 3775, 6000 le — Ruaha National Park, Tanzania: a, Lepus capensis. b, Agama lionotus elgonis, horiz. c, Otolemur garnettii, horiz. d, Two Otocyon megalotis.

No. 3776, 6000 le — Selous Game Reserve, Tanzania: a, Crocodylus niloticus. b, Haliaeetus vocifer, horiz. c, Panther leo nubica, horiz. d, Two Hippopotamus amphibius.

No. 3777, 6000 le — Serengeti National Park, Tanzania: a, One Aepyceros melampus. b, Genetta tigrina, horiz. c, Agama agama, horiz. d, Chamaeleo dilepis.

No. 3778, 6000 le — Bwindi Impenetrable National Park, Uganda: a, Pternistis nobilis. b, Gorilla beringei beringei, horiz. c, Balaeniceps rex, horiz. d, Colobus guereza.

No. 3779, 6000 le — Kidepo Valley National Park, Uganda: a, One Tragelaphus sylvaticus. b, Equus quagga burchellii walking right, horiz. c, Syncerus caffer, horiz. d, Kobus ellipsiprymnus.

No. 3780, 6000 le — Kafue National Park, Zambia: a, Two Taurotragus oryx. b, Kobus vardonii, horiz. c, Lycaon pictuss, horiz. d, Kobus leche.

No. 3781, 6000 le — South Luangwa National Park, Zambia: a, Giraffa camelopardalis thornicrofti. b, Equus quagga crawshayi, horiz. c, One Hippopotamus amphibius, horiz. d, Necrosyrtes monachus.

No. 3782, 6000 le — Mana Pools National Park, Zimbabwe: a, Manis temminckii. b, Aonyx capensis, horiz. c, Dendropicos fuscescens, horiz. d, Hystrix cristata.

No. 3783, 24,000 le, Hyaena brunnea, horiz. No. 3784, 24,000 le, Merops nubicoides, Mungos mungo, horiz. No. 3785, 24,000 le, Suricata suricatta, Lycaon pictus, horiz. No. 3786, 24,000 le, Two Loxodonta africana, horiz. No. 3787, 24,000 le, Crocodylus niloticus, horiz. No. 3788, 24,000 le, Phoeniconaias minor, horiz. No. 3789, 24,000 le, Head of Syncerus caffer, horiz. No. 3790, 24,000 le, Odontobatrachus natator, horiz. No. 3791, 24,000 le, Two Procolobus badius, horiz. No. 3792, 24,000 le, Picathartes gymnocephalus, horiz. No. 3793, 24,000 le, Panthera leo, horiz. No. 3794, 24,000 le, Sagittarius serpentarius, horiz. No. 3795, 24,000 le, Platalea alba, horiz. No. 3796, 24,000 le, Panthera pardus pardus, horiz. No. 3797, 24,000 le, Chrysococcyx cupreus, horiz. No. 3798, 24,000 le, Potamochoerus larvatus, horiz. No. 3799, 24,000 le, Two Tragelaphus sylvaticus, horiz. No. 3800, 24,000 le, Lepus microtis, horiz. No. 3801, 24,000 le, Mellivora capensis, horiz.

2016, May 27 Litho. *Perf. 13¼*

Sheets of 4, #a-d

3764-3782 A672 Set of 19 235.00 235.00

Souvenir Sheets

3783-3801 A672 Set of 19 235.00 235.00

Nos. 3783-3801 each contain one 45x33mm stamp.

World Youth Day — A673

No. 3802: a, St. John Paul II (1920-2005). b, St. Maria Faustina Kowalska (1905-38). c, Pope Francis. d, Stanislaw Cardinal Dziwisz, Archbishop of Cracow, Poland.
24,000 le, The Divine Mercy, by Eugeniusz Kazimirowski.

2016, May 27 Litho. *Perf. 13¼*

3802 A673 6000 le Sheet of 4, #a-d 12.50 12.50

Souvenir Sheet

3803 A673 24,000 le multi 12.50 12.50

No. 3803 contains one 51x90mm stamp.

Paintings — A674

No. 3804, 6000 le — Russian religious art: a, The Lord Almighty (21x30mm). b, Triptych of Holy Mother Vladimirskaya (39x30mm). c, The Annunciation of Holy Archangel Gabriel to Most Holy Mary Mother of God (39x30mm). d, The Last Judgement (21x30mm).
No. 3805, 6000 le — Renaissance paintings: a, Exorcism of the Demons of Arezzo, by Giotto (21x30mm). b, The Wedding at Cana, by Paolo Veronese (39x30mm). c, Christ at the Sea of Galilee, by Tintoretto (39x30mm). d, Salome with the Head of John the Baptist, by Titian (21x30mm).
No. 3806, 6000 le — Baroque paintings: a, Self-portrait with Two Circles, by Rembrandt van Rijn (21x30mm). b, The Taking of Christ, by Caravaggio (39x30mm). c, Autumn, or The Spies with the Bunch of Grapes of the Promised Land, by Nicolas Poussin (39x30mm). d, Portrait of Pope Innocent X, by Diego Velázquez (21x30mm).
No. 3807, 6000 le — Dutch Golden Age paintings: a, Two Boys Singing, by Frans Hals (21x30mm). b, Great Garden Palace, by Dirck van Delen (39x30mm). c, The Maas at Dordrecht, by Aelbert Cuyp (39x30mm). d, Woman Holding a Balance, by Johannes Vermeer (21x30mm).
No. 3808, 6000 le — Romantic paintings: a, Ave Maria, by Adrian Ludwig Richter (21x30mm). b, The Grand Canal, Venice, by William Turner (39x30mm). c, A Horse Frightened by Lightning, by Théodore Géricault (39x30mm). d, Wanderer Above the Sea of Fog, by Caspar David Friedrich (21x30mm).
No. 3809, 6000 le — Impressionist paintings: a, La Débâcle, by Theodore Robinson (21x30mm). b, A Holiday at Mentone, by Charles Conder (39x30mm). c, A Sunday Afternoon on the Island of La Grande Jatte, by Georges Seurat (39x30mm). d, The Dance Class, by Edgar Degas (21x30mm).
No. 3810, 6000 le — American Impressionist paintings: a, Portrait of Miss Dora Wheeler, by William Merritt Chase (21x30mm). b, In the Orchard, by Edmund C. Tarbell (39x30mm). c, World's Columbian Exposition, by Robinson (39x30mm). d, Young Woman in a Black and Green Bonnet, by Mary Cassatt (21x30mm).
No. 3811, 6000 le — Post-Impressionist paintings: a, Bouquet of Flowers, by Henri Rousseau (21x30mm). b, Maison Maria on the Way to Château Noir, by Paul Cézanne (39x30mm). c, Portrait of Félix Fénéon, by Paul Signac (39x30mm). d, The Café Terrace on the Place du Forum, by Vincent van Gogh (21x30mm).
No. 3812, 6000 le — Symbolist paintings: a, Mystery, by Odilon Redon (21x30mm). b, Separation, by Edvard Munch (39x30mm). c, Ruins in the Moonlit Landscape, by Arnold Böcklin (39x30mm). d, Dream, by Hugo Simberg (21x30mm).
No. 3813, 6000 le — Realist paintings: a, The Song of the Lark, by Jules Breton (21x30mm). b, Rue Transnonain, Arpil 15, 1834, by Honoré Daumier (39x30mm). c, The Gleaners, by Jean-François Millet (39x30mm). d, The Gross Clinic, by Thomas Eakins (21x30mm).
No. 3814, 6000 le — Surrealist paintings: a, I and the Village, by Marc Chagall (21x30mm). b, Gare Montparnasse, by Giorgio de Chirico (39x30mm). c, Metamorphosis of Narcissus, by Salvador Dalí (39x30mm). d, Aquis Submersus, by Max Ernst (21x30mm).
No. 3815, 6000 le — Cubist paintings: a, Three Musicians, by Pablo Picasso (21x30mm). b, The Conquest of the Air, by Roger de La Fresnaye (39x30mm). c, The Coffee Grinder, by Juan Gris (39x30mm). d, Still Life with Clarinet, by Georges Braque (21x30mm).
No. 3816, 6000 le — Paintings by Raphael (1483-1520): a, Portrait of Maddalena Doni (21x30mm). b, The School of Athens (39x30mm). c, Areopagus Sermon (39x30mm). d, Saint George and the Dragon (21x30mm).
No. 3817, 6000 le — Paintings by Leonardo da Vinci (1452-1519): a, Lady with an Ermine (21x30mm). b, Annunciation (39x30mm). c, The Baptism of Christ (39x30mm). d, Ginevra de Benci (21x30mm).
No. 3818, 6000 le — Paintings by Peter Paul Rubens (1577-1640): a, Raising of the Cross (21x30mm). b, Landscape with Milkmaids and Cattle (39x30mm). c, Tiger Hunt (39x30mm). d, Portrait of Ludovicus Nonnius (21x30mm).
No. 3819, 6000 le — Paintings by Pierre-Auguste Renoir (1841-1919): a, Portrait of Berthe Morisot and Daughter, Julie Manet (21x30mm). b, Portrait of Charles and Georges Durand-Ruel (39x30mm). c, The Return of the Boating Party (39x30mm). d, Spring Bouquet (21x30mm).
No. 3820, 6000 le — Paintings by Vincent van Gogh (1853-90): a, Sunflowers (21x30mm). b, The Starry Night Over the Rhône (39x30mm). c, Red Vineyards Near Arles (39x30mm). d, Self-portrait with Bandaged Ear (21x30mm).
No. 3821, 6000 le — Paintings by Joan Miró (1893-1983): a, Dutch Interior I (21x30mm). b, Untitled, 1972 (39x30mm). c, Untitled, 1933 (39x30mm). d, The Gold of the Azure (21x30mm).
No. 3822, 6000 le — Paintings by Qi Baishi (1864-1957): a, Butterfly and Flowering Plum (21x30mm). b, Birds of Paradise (39x30mm). c, A Lone Traveler on a Moonlit Night (39x30mm). d, Likvidambra Taiwan and the Cicada (21x30mm).
No. 3823, 6000 le — Japanese paintings: a, Eagles in a Ravine, by Hogai Kano (21x30mm). b, The Great Wave off Kanagawa, by Hokusai Katsushika (39x30mm). c, Chinese Guardian Lions, by Eitoku Kano (39x30mm). d, Woman Wiping Sweat, by Utamaro Kitagawa (21x30mm).
No. 3824, 24,000 le, Enthroned Christ as "King of Kings and Lord of Lords," vert. No. 3825, 24,000 le, The Disrobing of Christ, by El Greco, vert. No. 3826, 24,000 le, William Feilding, 1st Earl of Denbigh, by Anthony van Dyck, vert. No. 3827, 24,000 le, Woman with Basket of Beans in the Kitchen Garden, by Pieter de Hooch, vert. No. 3828, 24,000 le, Greece on the Ruins of Missolonghi, by Eugène Delacroix, vert. No. 3829, 24,000 le, The Umbrellas, by Renoir, vert. No. 3830, 24,000 le, The Avenue in the Rain, by Childe Hassam, vert. No. 3831, 24,000 le, Marthe at Her Easel, by Henri Lebasque, vert. No. 3832, 24,000 le, The Woman in Gold, by Gustav Klimt, vert. No. 3833, 24,000 le, Symphony in White, No. 1: The White Girl, by James Whistler, vert. No. 3834, 24,000 le, The Son of Man, by René Magritte, vert. No. 3835, 24,000 le, Deux Nus, by Jean Metzinger, vert. No. 3836, 24,000 le, St. Michael Vanquishing Satan, by Raphael, vert. No. 3837, 24,000 le, Mona Lisa, by Leonardo, vert. No. 3838, 24,000 le, Rubens with Hélène Fourment and Their Son, Peter Paul, by Rubens, vert. No. 3839, 24,000 le, Dance at Bougival, by Renoir, vert. No. 3840, 24,000 le, Road with Cypresses, by van Gogh, vert. No. 3841, 24,000 le, The Beautiful Bird Revealing the Unknown to a Pair of Lovers, by Miró, vert. No. 3842, 24,000 le, Sparrow on a Branch, by Baishi, vert. No. 3843, 24,000 le, Winter Landscape, by Toyo Sesshu, vert.

Litho. & Silk-Screened

2016, June 30 *Perf. 13¼*

Sheets of 4, #a-d

3804-3823 A674 Set of 20 175.00 175.00

Souvenir Sheets

3824-3843 A674 Set of 20 175.00 175.00

Nos. 3824-3843 each contain one 39x66mm stamp.

A675

No. 3844, 6000 le — European migrant crisis: a, Flag of European Union, man lifting child. b, Woman holding baby, silhouettes of refugees. c, Red Cross workers assisting refugees on beach. d, Pope Francis greeeting people.
No. 3845, 6000 le — Wilhelm Carl Grimm (1786-1859), writer of fairy tales: a, Scene from *The Magic Pipe.* b, Scene from *The Turnip.* c, Scene from *Cat and Mouse in Partnership.* d, Scene from *The Frog Prince.*
No. 3846, 6000 le — Walt Disney (1901-66), creator of animated films: a, Disney drawing, Neuschwanstein Castle. b, Disney and model of cartoon character. c, Disney writing and smoking. d, Disney in striped shirt.
No. 3847, 6000 le — Sergei Prokofiev (1891-1953), composer, and scene from: a, Opera *The Love of Three Oranges.* b, Ballet *Romeo and Juliet.* c, Ballet *Cinderella.* d, Opera *War and Peace.*
No. 3848, 6000 le — Great Fire of London, 350th anniv.: a, Painting of fire at night by unknown artist. b, Account of fire by Samuel Pepys (1633-1703). c, Coin and Jan Griffier painting in background. d, Painting of fire with boats in foreground by unknown artist.
No. 3849, 6000 le — Battle of Gallipoli, cent.: a, British Field Marshal Herbert Kitchener (1850-1916). b, Transport of heavy artillery. c, British soldiers in trench. d, German General Otto Liman von Sanders (1855-1929).
No. 3850, 6000 le — Battle of Moscow, 75th anniv.: a, Soviet General Georgy Zhukov (1896-1974), and aides. b, Soviet soldiers. c, German soldiers and Panzer IV tank. d, German General Heinz Guderian (1888-1954) and airplanes.
No. 3851, 6000 le — Sergei Korolev (1907-66), Soviet rocket engineer, and: a, Soyuz spacecraft. b, Sputnik 2 and dog. c, Sputnik model. d, Luna 2 spacecraft.
No. 3852, 6000 le — Paintings by Berthe Morisot (1841-95): a, The Fable. b, Children with a Bowl. c, Eugène Manet and His Daughter at Bougival. d, Woman and Child Seated in a Meadow.
No. 3853, 6000 le — Paintings by Paul Cézanne (1839-1906): a, Compotier Glass and Apples (Still Life). b, The Card Players. c, Still Life Flowers in a Vase. d, Mont Sainte-Victoire Seen from Bibémus Quarry.
No. 3854, 6000 le — Paintings in Musée d'Orsay, Paris: a, Billiard Room at Ménil-Hubert, by Edgar Degas. b, In the Black Country, by Constantin Meunier. c, Procession at Penmarc'h, by Lucien Simon. d, Christ with the Peasants, by Fritz von Uhde.
No. 3855, 6500 le — James Dean (1931-55), actor, and scene from: a, *East of Eden.* b, *Rebel Without a Cause* (automobile). c, *Rebel Without a Cause* (actress). d, *Giant.*
No. 3856, 6500 le — Film director Steven Spielberg, 70th birthday, and scenes from: a, *Jaws.* b, *Jurassic Park.* c, *Indiana Jones and the Last Crusade.* d, *The BFG.*
No. 3857, 6500 le — Nancy Reagan (1921-2016), First Lady and actress: a, With husband, son Ron Reagan and daughter, Patti Davis. b, As actress. c, With Princess Diana. d, With husband and Pope John Paul II.
No. 3858, 6500 le — Paintings by Wassily Kandinsky (1866-1944): a, Two Movements. b, Sketch for Composition II. c, Sketch for picture XVI The Great Tower of Kiev. d, Small Pleasures.
No. 3859, 6500 le — Queen Victoria (1819-1901): a, With dog and statue. b, With Prince Consort Albert (1819-61). c, With Prince Consort Albert and children. d, Statue of Queen Victoria.
No. 3860, 6500 le — Princess Charlotte of Cambridge, 1st birthday, with: a, Stuffed animal. b, Parents, Duke and Duchess of Cambridge, and brother, Prince George. c, Mother. d, Parents.
No. 3861, 6500 le — Holy Year of Mercy: a, Pope Francis embracing man. b, Pope Francis kneeling. c, Popes Francis and Benedict XVI. d, Receiving crucifix from man.
No. 3862, 24,000 le, German Chancellor Angel Merkel and refugees. No. 3863, 24,000 le, Wilhelm Grimm, and brother Jacob Ludwig Carl Grimm (1785-1863). No. 3864, 24,000 le, Disney and drawing of artist's studio. No. 3865, 24,000 le, Prokofiev conducting orchestra. No. 3866, 24,000 le, The Great Fire of London, painting by Philippe Jacques de Loutherbourg. No. 3867, 24,000 le, Mustafa Kemal Atatürk (1881-1938), Ottoman commander. No. 3868, 24,000 le, Zhukov and statue of soldier. No. 3869, 24,000 le, Korolev and Yuri Gagarin (1934-68), first man in space. No. 3870, 24,000 le, Girl Playing the Mandolin, by Morisot. No. 3871, 24,000 le, Still Life with a Ginger Jar and Eggplants, by Cézanne. No. 3872, 24,000 le, Poplars, by Cézanne. No. 3873, 26,000 le, Dean and actress, diff. No. 3874, 26,000 le, Speilberg and scene from *The Adventures of Tintin.* No. 3875, 26,000 le, Mrs. Reagan wearing jacket and swimsuit. No. 3876, 26,000 le, Black Accompaniment, by Kandinsky. No. 3877, 26,000 le, Young and old depictions of Queen Victoria. No. 3878, 26,000 le, Prince George and Princess Charlotte. No. 3879, 26,000 le, Popes Benedict XVI and Francis, diff.

2016, July 29 Litho. *Perf. 13¼*

Sheets of 4, #a-d

3844-3861 A675 Set of 18 160.00 160.00

Souvenir Sheets

3862-3879 A675 Set of 18 160.00 160.00

2018 World Cup Soccer Championships, Russia — A676

No. 3880 — Flag of Russia and: a, Two players, orange ball. b, Two players, white ball on foot. c, One player, orange ball. d, Player and goal, yellow ball.
26,000 le, Two players, white ball, and flag of Russia.

2016, July 29 Litho. *Perf. 13¼*

3880 A676 6500 le Sheet of 4, #a-d 9.50 9.50

Souvenir Sheet

3881 A676 26,000 le multi 9.50 9.50

No. 3881 contains one 48x36mm stamp.

PhilaTaipei 2016 World Philatelic Exhibition — A677

No. 3882 — Original inhabitants of Taiwan: a, Amis man. b, Rukai man. c, Bunun man. d, Saisiyat man.
20,000 le, Map of Taiwan.

Litho. With Foil Application

2016, July 29 *Perf. 13¼*

3882 A677 5000 le Sheet of 4, #a-d 7.25 7.25

Souvenir Sheet
Perf. 13¼x9¼

3883 A677 20,000 le multi 7.25 7.25

No. 3883 contains one 50x50mm octagonal stamp.

A678

No. 3884, 6000 le — Pandas (Ailuropoda melanoleuca): a, Near rocks in foreground. b, Head of panda eating. c, Seated panda eating. d, Panda walking.

No. 3885, 6000 le — Seals: a, Pagophilus groenlandicus. b, Mirounga leonina. c, Leptonychotes weddellii. d, Hydrurga leptonyx.

No. 3886, 6000 le — Bats: a, Pteropus giganteus. b, Nyctalus noctula. c, Epomorphorus gambianus. d, Pipistrellus pipistrellus.

No. 3887, 6000 le — Tigers: a, Panthera tigris jacksoni. b, Panthera tigris altaica. c, Panthera tigris tigris facing right. d, Panthera tigris tigris facing left at water hole.

No. 3888, 6000 le — Snow leopard (Panthera uncia): a, On snowy rock ledge facing right. b, Running left in snow. c, On rocks ready to leap. d, Two leopards.

No. 3889, 6000 le — Big cats: a, Puma concolor. b, Neofelis nebulosa. c, Acinonyx jubatus. d, Panthera leo.

No. 3890, 6000 le — Dolphins: a, Stenella longirostris. b, Namius latinicus prolongicus (incorrect Latin name). c, Inia geoffrensis. d, Delphinus delphis.

No. 3891, 6000 le — Birds of prey: a, Milvago chimachima. b, Haliaeetus leucocephalus. c, Pandion haliaetus. d, Gyps fulvus.

No. 3892, 6000 le — Owls: a, Strix nebulosa. b, Bubo scandiacus. c, Bubo bubo. d, Asio flammeus.

No. 3893, 6000 le — Hummingbirds: a, Amazilia tzacatl. b, Calypte anna. c, Archilochus colubris. d, Ocreatus underwoodii.

No. 3894, 6000 le — Parrots: a, Aratinga solstitialis. b, Melopsittacus undulatus. c, Nestor notabilis. d, Ara ararauna.

No. 3895, 6000 le — Sunbirds: a, Leptocoma brasiliana. b, Nectarinia venusta. c, Cinnyris lotenius. d, Cinnyris afer.

No. 3896, 6000 le — Bees: a, Anthidium florentinum. b, Apis mellifera on flower. c, Apis mellifera on honeycomb. d, Amegilla cingulata.

No. 3897, 6000 le — Butterflies: a, Anartia amathea. b, Cethosia cyane. c, Fabriciana adippe. d, Papilio polyxenes.

No. 3898, 6000 le — Shells: a, Murex aduncospinosus. b, Mauritia arabica arabica. c, Namius latinicus prolongicus. d, Cassis cornuta.

No. 3899, 6000 le — Extinct animals: a, Thylacinus cyanocephalus. b, Smilodon fatalis. c, Elasmotherium. d, Raphus cucullatus.

No. 3900, 6000 le — Dinosaurs and minerals: a, Prenocephale. b, Quartz. c, Tourmaline. d, Gasosaurus.

No. 3901, 6000 le — Orchids: a, Epidendrum radicans. b, Neotinea tridentata. c, Zygopetalum maculatum. d, Oncidium papilio.

No. 3902, 6000 le — Mushrooms: a, Cantharellus cibarius. b, Laccaria amethystina. c, Entoloma hochstetteri. d, Pleurotus ostreatus.

No. 3903, 6000 le — Christmas: a, Santa Claus reading list. b, Children with gifts under Christmas tree. c, Reindeer. d, Santa Claus reading book, girl in background.

No. 3904, 24,000 le, Ailuropoda melanoleuca in tree. No. 3905, 24,000 le, Phoca vitulina. No. 3906, 24,000 le, Rhinolophus ferrumequinum. No. 3907, 24,000 le, Panthera tigris sumatrae. No. 3908, 24,000 le, Panthera uncia, diff. No. 3909, 24,000 le, Panthera onca. No. 3910, 24,000 le, Tursiops truncatus. No. 3911, 24,000 le, Accipiter tachiro. No. 3912, 24,000 le, Tyto alba. No. 3913, 24,000 le, Ocreatus underwoodii, diff. No. 3914, 24,000 le, Cacatua alba. No. 3915, 24,000 le, Leptocoma brasiliana, diff. No. 3916, 24,000 le, Xylocopa virginica. No. 3917, 24,000 le, Polyommatus bellargus. No. 3918, 24,000 le, Chicoreus brunneus. No. 3919, 24,000 le, Mammuthus primigenius. No. 3920, 24,000 le, Mandschurosaurus and Malachite. No. 3921, 24,000 le, Dendrobium christyanum. No. 3922, 24,000 le, Phallus indusiatus. No. 3923, 24,000 le, Santa Claus reading letter.

2016, Aug. 29 Litho. *Perf. 13¼*
Sheets of 4, #a-d

3884-3903 A678 Set of 20 170.00 170.00

Souvenir Sheets

3904-3923 A678 Set of 20 170.00 170.00

A679

No. 3924, 6000 le — Polo: a, Player with light blue shirt. b, Player with white shirt holding mallet near ground. c, Player in white shirt holding mallet above head. d, Two players.

No. 3925, 6000 le — Cricket batsmen with: a, Blue shirt with knee on ground. b, Yellow shirt with knees off ground. c, Yellow shirt with knee on ground. d, Blue shirt with knees off ground.

No. 3926, 6000 le — Table tennis champions: a, Zhang Jike (2011, 2013). b, Xu Xin and Yang Ha-eun, 2015. c, Liu Shiwen and Zhu Yuling, 2015. d, Werner Schlager, 2003.

No. 3927, 6000 le — Olympic Judo champions: a, Hitoshi Saito (1961-2015) and opponent Angelo Parisi, 1984. b, David Douillet and opponent Shinichi Shinohara, 2000. c, Kayla Harrison and opponent Gemma Gibbons, 2012. d, Teddy Riner and opponent Hisayoshi Harasawa, 2016.

No. 3928, 6000 le — Rugby players: a, Bryan Habana, South Africa. b, Dan Carter, New Zealand. c, Jonah Lomu (1975-2015), New Zealand. d, Jonny Wilkinson, England.

No. 3929, 6000 le — Cybathlon 2016 events: a, Powered leg prosthesis race. b, Powered wheelchair race. c, Powered exoskeleton race. d, Powered arm prosthesis race.

No. 3930, 6000 le — Golfers: a, Yang Yong-eun. b, Lydia Ko. c, Tiger Woods. d, Jack Nicklaus.

No. 3931, 6000 le — Soccer players in 2016 European Soccer Championships: a, Gareth Bale, Wales. b, Emre Can, Germany. c, Dimitri Payet, France. d, Cristiano Ronaldo, Portugal.

No. 3932, 6000 le — Formula 1 racing champions: a, Sebastian Vettel, 2010-13. b, Michael Schumacher, 1994-95, 2000-04. c, Kimi Räikkönen, 2007. d, Jenson Button, 2009.

No. 3933, 6000 le — Chess champions: a, Sergey Karjakin. b, Garry Kasparov. c, Anatoly Karpov. d, Fabiano Caruana.

No. 3934, 6500 le — Lionel Messi, soccer player, wearing: a, Light blue shirt. b, Light blue and white striped shirt, player in background. c, Light blue and white striped shirt, chasing ball. d, Red and blue striped shirt.

No. 3935, 6500 le — Jean-Henri Dunant (1828-1910), founder of Red Cross, and: a, Red Cross, Headquarters Building, Geneva. b, Red Cross workers. c, Red Cross nurse administering to injured person. d, Red Cross flag, Nobel medal.

No. 3936, 6500 le — Mother Teresa (1910-97), humanitarian: a, With Pope Francis. b, Embracing Pope John Paul II (1920-2005). c, With Pope John Paul II. d, Alone.

No. 3937, 6500 le — Sir Winston Churchill (1874-1965), British Prime Minister, and: a, Gen. Charles de Gaulle (1890-1970). b, Pres. Franklin D. Roosevelt (1882-1945) and Gen. Bernard Montgomery (1887-1976). c, Holding lit cigar. d, Wearing glasses.

No. 3938, 6500 le — Nelson Mandela (1918-2013), President of South Africa: a, In native costume and in boxing trunks. b, Alone. c, With Princess Diana (1961-97). d, With Pope John Paul II.

No. 3939, 6500 le — Mahatma Gandhi (1869-1948), Indian nationalist: a, Sitting with legs crossed. b, With hands together. c, Greeting crowd. d, With flowers.

No. 3940, 6500 le — Paul P. Harris (1868-1947), founder of Rotary International: a, Portrait of Harris by John Doctoroff. b, People with water buckets, Paul Harris Fellow pin. c, Child receiving vaccine. d, Harris and Rotary International emblem.

No. 3941, 6500 le — Elvis Presley (1935-77): a, Holding microphone. b, At Graceland. c, In movie scene with actress. d, Playing guitar.

No. 3942, 6500 le — World Youth Day: a, Pope Francis. b, Pope John Paul II with hand raised. c, Pope Francis kissing child. d, Pope John Paul II.

No. 3943, 24,000 le, Polo player on rearing horse. No. 3944, 24,000 le, Cricket batsman, diff. No. 3945, 24,000 le, Ma Long playing table tennis. No. 3946, 24,000 le, Naidangiin Tüvshinbayar, 2008 Olympic judo gold medalist. No. 3947, 24,000 le, Brian O'Driscoll, Irish rugby player. No. 3948, 24,000 le, FES bike race. No. 3949, 24,000 le, Jimmy Walker, golfer. No. 3950, 24,000 le, Antoine Griezmann, French soccer player and William Carvalho, Portuguese soccer player. No. 3951, 24,000 le, Formula 1 car of Lewis Hamilton, 2008, 2014-15 champion. No. 3952, 24,000 le, Karpov and Kasparov. No. 3953, 26,000 le, Messi, diff. No. 3954, 26,000 le, Dunant and Red Cross flag. No. 3955, 26,000 le, Mother Teresa and Pope Francis, diff. No. 3956, 26,000 le, Churchill smoking cigar. No. 3957, 26,000 le, Mandela, diff. No. 3958, 26,000 le, Gandhi and Raj Ghat Memorial. No. 3959, 26,000 le, Paul Harris Fellow pin. No. 3960, 26,000 le, Presley holding microphone, diff. No. 3961, 26,000 le, Pope John Paul II, diff.

2016, Sept. 29 Litho. *Perf. 13¼*
Sheets of 4, #a-d

3924-3942 A679 Set of 19 170.00 170.00

Souvenir Sheets

3943-3961 A679 Set of 19 170.00 170.00

China 2016 International Stamp Exhibition, Nanning — A680

No. 3962 — Panda: a, On all fours, facing right. b, On all fours, facing forward. c, Reclining. d, Sitting.
24,000 le, Panda, diff.

Litho. With Foil Application
2016, Sept. 29 ***Perf.***

3962 A680 6000 le Sheet of 4, #a-d 8.50 8.50

Souvenir Sheet

3963 A680 24,000 le multi 8.50 8.50

A681

No. 3964, 6000 le — Betty Grable (1916-73), actress, with image in foreground wearing: a, Blue swimsuit. b, Blue and white dress. c, Black dress. d, Checked scarf and shorts.

No. 3965, 6000 le — Rudolph Valentino (1895-1926), actor: a, With wife, Natacha Rambova (1897-1966). b, In scene from *Monsieur Beaucaire*. c, In scene from *The Son of the Sheik*. d, Holding pipe.

No. 3966, 6000 le — Erasmus of Rotterdam (1466-1536), theologian: a, Turning pages of book. b, Sitting at desk. c, Pointing. d, In library.

No. 3967, 6000 le — Fyodor Dostoyevsky (1821-81), writer: a, Building in background. b, Scene from *Crime and Punishment*. c, In Siberian exile. d, Seated in foreground.

No. 3968, 6000 le — Barcelona structures designed by Antoni Gaudí (1852-1926), architect: a, Casa Batlló. b, Casa del Guarda. c, Casa Milà. d, Artigas Gardens.

No. 3969, 6000 le — Paintings by Francisco Goya (1746-1828): a, Saturn Devouring One of His Sons. b, Manuel Osorio Manrique de Zuñiga. c, Witches' Sabbath. d, The Clothed Maja.

No. 3970, 6000 le — Max Ernst (1891-1976), painter and sculptor: a, Painting. b, With sculptures. c, With wife, Dorothea Tanning (1910-2012). d, Holding sculpture.

No. 3971, 6000 le — 14th Dalai Lama, 1989 Nobel Peace laureate: a, With Pope John Paul II (1920-2005). b, With Potala Palace in background. c, Holding Nobel medal and diploma. d, With Nelson Mandela (1918-2013).

No. 3972, 6000 le — Battle of Verdun, cent.: a, Map of France, Gen. Philippe Pétain (1856-1951), Marshal Joseph Joffre (1852-1931). b, German General Erich von Falkenhayn (1861-1922). c, Cannons. d, Recapture of Fort Douaumont, painting by Henri Georges Jacques Chartier.

No. 3973, 6000 le — Battle of the Somme, cent.: a, German Gen. Fritz von Below (1853-1918). b, French Gen. Ferdinand Foch (1851-1929). c, German Gen. Max von Gallwitz (1852-1937). d, British Field Marshal Douglas Haig (1861-1928).

No. 3974, 6000 le — Clipper ships in the Great Tea Race, 150th anniv.: a, Ariel. b, Fiery Cross. c, Taitsing. d, Taeping.

No. 3975, 6000 le — Royal Mail, 500th anniv.: a, Packet boat, 1660. b, Royal Mail Ship Britannia, 1840. c, Airco DH4A de Havilland biplane, 1919. d, British Airways Airbus A380-800, 2010.

No. 3976, 6000 le — BMW automobiles, cent.: a, 1951 BMW 501. b, 1961 BMW 700 RS. c, 1962-63 Martini BMW 700. d, 1968 BMW 2800CS.

No. 3977, 6000 le — Dream Chaser spacecraft: a, Front, top and profile drawings. b, Landing. c, Take-off. d, With Space Shuttle Endeavour.

No. 3978, 6000 le — Butterflies: a, Urbanus proteus. b, Danaus plexippus. c, Battus philenor. d, Junonia coenia.

No. 3979, 6000 le — International Year of Pulses: a, Kidney beans. b, Green peas. c, Red lentils. d, Chickpeas.

No. 3980, 6000 le — Volcanic eruptions: a, Mount Vesuvius, Italy. b, Mount Sinabung, Indonesia. c, Mount Merapi, Indonesia. d, Calbuco, Chile.

No. 3981, 6000 le — Global warming: a, Earth. b, Thermometer and factory. c, Polar bears on shrinking ice. d, Automobile tail pipe and tire.

No. 3982, 24,000 le, Grable and U.S. flag. No. 3983, 24,000 le, Valentino and actress. No. 3984, 24,000 le, Books by Erasmus of Rotterdam. No. 3985, 24,000 le, Dostoyevsky in prison. No. 3986, 24,000 le, Gaudí and interior of Casa Batlló. No. 3987, 24,000 le, The Parasol, by Goya. No. 3988, 24,000 le, Ernst and sculpture. No. 3989, 24,000 le, 14th Dalai Lama seated. No. 3990, 24,000 le, Airplane and soldier at Battle of Verdun. No. 3991,

24,000 le, Soldiers at Battle of the Somme. No. 3992, 24,000 le, Clipper ships Ariel and Taeping. No. 3993, 24,000 le, Royal Mail messenger delivering King's letter. No. 3994, 24,000 le, 1959 BMW 507 Roadster. No. 3995, 24,000 le, Dream Chaser, diff. No. 3996, 24,000 le, Polygonia interrogationis. No. 3997, 24,000 le, Fava beans. No. 3998, 24,000 le, Krakatoa, Indonesia. No. 3999, 24,000 le, Diagram of iceberg calving.

2016, Oct. 28 Litho. *Perf. 13¼*

Sheets of 4, #a-d

3964-3981 A681 Set of 18 155.00 155.00

Souvenir Sheets

3982-3999 A681 Set of 18 155.00 155.00

New Year 2016 (Year of the Monkey) — A682

No. 4000 — Rhinopithecus roxellana: a, On branch. b, Head. c, Two monkeys. d, Three monkeys.
24,000 le, Two monkeys, diff.

Litho. With Foil Application

2016, Oct. 28 *Perf. 13¼*

4000 A682 6000 le Sheet of 4, #a-d 8.75 8.75

Souvenir Sheet

4001 A682 24,000 le multi 8.75 8.75

China 2016 International Stamp Exhibition, Nanning.

New Year 2017 (Year of the Rooster) — A683

No. 4002 — Rooster: a, Facing right. b, Facing left, head near ground. c, Head at right, looking left. d, Facing left, head up.
24,000 le, Rooster, diff.

2016, Oct. 28 Litho. *Perf. 13¼*

4002 A683 6000 le Sheet of 4, #a-d 8.75 8.75

Souvenir Sheet

4003 A683 24,000 le multi 8.75 8.75

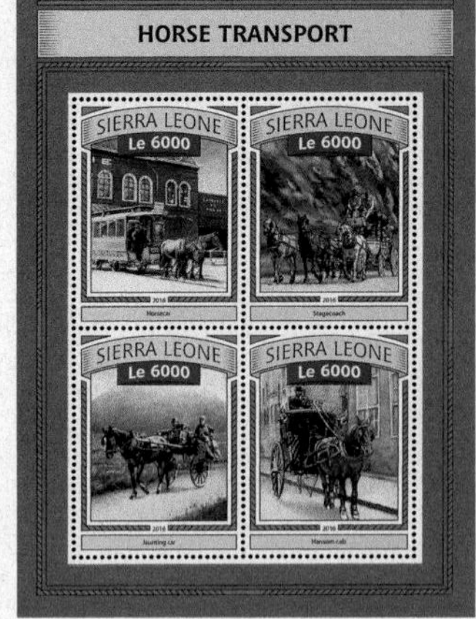

A684

No. 4004, 6000 le — Horse transport: a, Horsecar. b, Stagecoach. c, Jaunting car. d, Hansom cab.

No. 4005, 6000 le — Christopher Columbus (1451-1506), explorer: a, Ships Santa Maria and Pinta. b, The Landing of Columbus on San Salvador, by John Vanderlyn. c, Columbus Before the Queen, by Emanuel Leutze. d, Ship Niña.

No. 4006, 6000 le — Icebreakers: a, Fram. b, Yermak. c, Oden. d, NS Yamal.

No. 4007, 6000 le — Steamboats: a, Queen of Seattle. b, Natchez. c, Delta Queen. d, Stadt Rapperswil.

No. 4008, 6000 le — Steam trains: a, 2-4-0, Great Britain. b, S160 2-8-0, China. c, 4-4-0, Colorado. d, 2-6-2, Russia.

No. 4009, 6000 le — European high-speed trains: a, Eurostar e320, Great Britain. b, Alfa Pendular 4000 series, Portugal. c, TGV, France. d, RENFE Class 130, Spain.

No. 4010, 6000 le — Ferruccio Lamborghini (1916-93), vehicle manufacturer, and: a, Lamborghini Nitro tractor. b, Lamborghini Avendator. c, Lamborghini Murcielago. d, Lamborghini Espada.

No. 4011, 6000 le — Toyota Corolla, 50th anniv.: a, E10/11. b, E30. c, E170. d, E110.

No. 4012, 6000 le — GAZ-M20 Pobeda automobile, 70th anniv.: a, Yellow car. b, Two red cars. c, Red and black car. d, Gray car.

No. 4013, 6000 le — Fire trucks: a, Titan field truck, Australia. b, Land Rover Defender, United Kingdom. c, Hummer brush fire truck, U.S. d, SISU-E11, Finland.

No. 4014, 6000 le — Max Immelmann (1890-1916), fighter pilot: a, Fokker E.11. b, Immelmann, decorations and airplane. c, Immelmann standing near propeller. d, Immelmann in cockpit.

No. 4015, 6000 le — Concorde: a, Air France Concorde. b, Aerospatiale/BAC. c, BA Concorde. d, BA Concorde G-BOAB.

No. 4016, 6000 le — Future planes: a, Dassault Systèmes Air Cruiseship. b, APH hybrid electric commercial aircraft. c, Northrop Grumman long-range strike bomber. d, Northrop Grumman B-21 Stealth bomber.

No. 4017, 6000 le — Valentina Tereshkova, first woman in space: a, In helmet, facing left. b, Seated, stars in background. c, Seated with electric probes attached, Earth in background. d, Two images of Tereshkova.

No. 4018, 6000 le — Luna 10, 50th anniv.: a, Molniya-M. b, Above Moon, Earth in background. c, Moon in background. d, Orbit around Moon.

No. 4019, 6000 le — Space tourism: a, Anousheh Ansari, fourth space tourist. b, Virgin Galactic SpaceShipTwo flight plan. c, Concept of Excalibur Almaz cislunar spaceflight. d, Charlie Simonyi, fifth space tourist.

No. 4020, 6000 le — 2016 Nobel laureates: a, Bob Dylan, Literature. b, Juan Manuel Santos, Peace. c, Jean-Pierre Sauvage, Sir James Fraser Stoddart, Bernard Lucas Feringa, Chemistry. d, Oliver Hart, Bengt Robert Holmström, Economic Sciences.

No. 4021, 6000 le — Charles Darwin (1809-82), naturalist: a, Darwin and fossils. b, Ship the Beagle, and map of its voyage, drawings of birds and insects. c, Microscope and drawings of evolving creatures. d, Darwin and primate.

No. 4022, 6000 le — Davy lamp, 200th anniv., and minerals: a, Crocidolite. b, Lepidolite. c, Ametrine. d, Enargite.

No. 4023, 6000 le — Election of Donald Trump as U.S. President: a, Trump, and opponent, Hillary Clinton. b, Trump at podium. c, Trump and electoral map. d, Trump with raised fist.

No. 4024, 24,000 le, Horse drawing Blue Cross wagon. No. 4025, 24,000 le, Columbus and ship. No. 4026, 24,000 le, U.S. Coast Guard Cutter Healy. No. 4027, 24,000 le, Spirit of Peoria. No. 4028, 24,000 le, 82 008 steam locomotive, Germany. No. 4029, 24,000 le, ICE train, Germany. No. 4030, 24,000 le, Lamborghini and Lamborghini Reventon. No. 4031, 24,000 le, Toyota Corolla E160. No. 4032, 24,000 le, Gray GAZ-M20 Pobeda automobile, diff. No. 4033, 24,000 le, Foremost Nodwell 240 tracked fire vehicle, Canada. No. 4034, 24,000 le, Immelmann in cockpit, diff. No. 4035, 24,000 le, Aerospatiale/BAC Concorde, diff. No. 4036, 24,000 le, Tohoku University supersonic biplane concept. No. 4037, 24,000 le, Tereshkova, diff. No. 4038, 24,000 le, Luna 10, diff. No. 4039, 24,000 le, Talgat Musabayev, Yuri Baturin and Dennis Tito, first space tourist, on Soyuz TM-32 flight. No. 4040, 24,000 le, Yoshinori Ohsumi, 2016 Nobel Physiology or Medicine laureate. No. 4041, 24,000 le, Darwin and evolutionary tree. No. 4042, 24,000 le, Milerite, statue of coal miner and family, Rhondda, Wales. No. 4043, 24,000 le, Trump and Hillary Clinton, diff.

2016, Nov. 28 Litho. *Perf. 13¼*

Sheets of 4, #a-d

4004-4023 A684 Set of 20 175.00 175.00

Souvenir Sheets

4024-4043 A684 Set of 20 175.00 175.00

Primates A685

Designs: No. 4044, 6000 le, One Western lowland gorilla. No. 4045, 6000 le, Two Western lowland gorillas. No. 4046, 6000 le, Baby chimpanzee. No. 4047, 6000 le, Muller's gray gibbon.
24,000 le, Sumatran orangutan.

Perf. 12¾x13¼

2016, Dec. 29 Litho.

4044-4047 A685 Set of 4 8.75 8.75

Souvenir Sheet

Perf. 13¼

4048 A685 24,000 le multi 8.75 8.75

No. 4048 contains one 48x39mm stamp.

A686

No. 4049, 6000 le — Polar bears (Ursus maritimus): a, One adult facing forward. b, One adult and two cubs. c, Two adults walking. d, One adult facing left.

No. 4050, 6000 le — Gorillas: a, Adult, at left, and juvenile Gorilla beringei beringei. b, Gorilla gorilla. c, Juvenile Gorilla beringei beringei on tree. d, Adult, at right, and juvenile Gorilla beringei beringei.

No. 4051, 6000 le — Cats: a, Norwegian Forest cat. b, Scottish Fold cats. c, Ocicats. d, Russian Blue cat.

No. 4052, 6000 le — Dogs: a, German shepherd. b, Catahoula leopard dog. c, Gordon setters. d, Bavarian mountain hound.

No. 4053, 6000 le — Dugongs (Dugong dugon): a, Two dugongs, foreground dugong facing left. b, Two dugongs, forward dugong facing forward. c, Two dugongs, foreground dugong facing right. d, Dugong and fish.

No. 4054, 6000 le — Whales: a, Balaenoptera musculus brevicauda. b, Eschrichtius robustus. c, Physeter macrocephalus. d, Balaenoptera physalus.

No. 4055, 6000 le — Hornbills: a, Buceros rhinoceros, Buceros hydrocorax. b, Aceros cassidix. c, Buceros bicornis. d, Buceros bicornis, Rhyticeros narcondami.

No. 4056, 6000 le — Water birds: a, Diomedea amsterdamensis. b, Sterna albostriata. c, Oceanites maorianus. d, Papasula abbotti.

No. 4057, 6000 le — Indigo birds: a, Female Passerina cyanea, eggs in nest. b, Male Passerina cyanea. c, Female Passerina cyanea. d, Male and female Passerina cyanea.

No. 4058, 6000 le — Bee-eaters: a, Merops pusillus cyanostictus. b, Nyctyornis amictus. c, Merops apiaster. d, Merops oreobates.

No. 4059, 6000 le — Butterflies: a, Aricia agestis. b, Cupido argiades. c, Junonia orithya. d, Polygonia c-album.

No. 4060, 6000 le — Reef fish: a, Stegastes planifrons. b, Bodianus rufus. c, Ctenochaetus binotatus. d, Paracanthurus hepatus.

No. 4061, 6000 le — Corals: a, Dendronephthya. b, Plerogyra sinuosa. c, Acropora cervicornis. d, Sarcophyton.

No. 4062, 6000 le — Turtles: a, Stemotherus odoratus. b, Testudo graeca. c, Chelonoidis nigra. d, Centrochelys sulcata.

No. 4063, 6000 le — Flying dinosaurs: a, Peteinosaurus zambellii. b, Pterodactylus antiquus. c, Pterodactylus. d, Zhenyuanopterus longirostris.

No. 4064, 6000 le — Endangered species: a, Atelopus zeteki. b, Ara glaucogularis. c, Rhinopithecus roxellana. d, Elephas maximus.

No. 4065, 6000 le — Cacti: a, Lophophora williamsii. b, Myrtillocactus geometrizans. c, Ferocactus pilosus. d, Echinopsis silvestrii.

No. 4066, 6000 le — Orchids: a, Pink Phalaenopsis. b, White Phalaenopsis. c, Blue Phalaenopsis. d, Phalaenopsis amabilis.

No. 4067, 6000 le — Scouts and mushrooms: a, Xerocomus badius. b, Cortinarius caperatus. c, Pleurotus ostreatus. d, Cantharellus cibarius.

No. 4068, 24,000 le, Ursus maritimus, diff. No. 4069, 24,000 le, Gorilla beringei graueri. No. 4070, 24,000 le, Ragdoll cat. No. 4071, 24,000 le, Saluki. No. 4072, 24,000 le, Two Dugong dugon, diff. No. 4073, 24,000 le, Balaenoptera musculus. No. 4074, 24,000 le, Aceros nipalensis. No. 4075, 24,000 le, Spheniscus mendiculus. No. 4076, 24,000 le, Male Passerina cyanea, diff. No. 4077, 24,000 le, Merops ornatus. No. 4078, 24,000 le, Chlosyne rosita. No. 4079, 24,000 le, Acanthurus japonicus. No. 4080, 24,000 le, Alcyonacea. No. 4081, 24,000 le, Caretta caretta. No. 4082, 24,000 le, Dimorphodon macronyx. No. 4083, 24,000 le, Manis pentadactyla. No. 4084, 24,000 le, Cylindropuntia imbricata. No. 4085, 24,000 le, Pink Phalaenopsis, diff. No. 4086, 24,000 le, Scouts and Lepista nuda.

2016, Dec. 29 Litho. *Perf. 13¼*

Sheets of 4, #a-d

4049-4067 A686 Set of 19 165.00 165.00

Souvenir Sheets

4068-4086 A686 Set of 19 165.00 165.00

A687

No. 4087, 6000 le — Zsa Zsa Gabor (1917-2016), actress: a, With Ezio Pinza (1892-1957), opera singer. b, Wearing light blue dress and pearl necklace. c, In automobile. d, Holding glass.

No. 4088, 6000 le — Transportation of Pres. Donald Trump: a, Mercedes-Benz SLR McLaren. b, Rolls-Royce Phantom. c, Sikorsky S-76 helicopter. d, Rolls-Royce Silver Cloud.

No. 4089, 6000 le — Renaissance paintings: a, Gates of Paradise, by Lorenzo Ghiberti. b, The Tower of Babel, by Pieter Bruegel, the Elder. c, The Birth of Venus, by Sandro Botticelli. d, The School of Athens, by Raphael.

No. 4090, 6000 le — Baroque paintings: a, The Conversion on the Way to Damascus, by Caravaggio. b, Charles I with M. de St. Antoine, by Antony van Dyck. c, A Table of Desserts, by Jan Davidsz. de Heem. d, Girl with a Pearl Earring, by Johannes Vermeer.

No. 4091, 6000 le — Romantic era paintings: a, Falstaff in the Laundry Basket, by Henry Fuseli. b, Orphan Girl at the Cemetery, by Eugène Delacroix. c, The Cornfield, by John Constable. d, The Meeting of Orestes and Hermione, by Anne-Louis Girodet de Roussy-Trioson.

No. 4092, 6000 le — Realist paintings: a, Iron and Coal, by William Bell Scott. b, A Shy Peasant, by Ilya Repin. c, Street Scene (Hester Street), by George Luks. d, Portrait of Jo, by Gustave Courbet.

No. 4093, 6000 le — Impressionist paintings: a, The Cafe Concert, by Edouard Manet. b, Apples and Oranges, by Paul Cézanne. c,

The Promenade, by Pierre-Auguste Renoir. d, The Dance Class, by Edgar Degas.

No. 4094, 6000 le — Post-impressionist paintings: a, Boy in a Red Waistcoat, by Cézanne. b, When Will You Marry?, by Paul Gauguin. c, Sorrowing Old Man (At Eternity's Gate), by Vincent van Gogh. d, At the Moulin Rouge: Two Women Waltzing, by Henri de Toulouse-Lautrec.

No. 4095, 6000 le — Cubist paintings: a, Nature Morte (Fruit Dish, Ace of Clubs), by Georges Braque. b, Jar, Bottle and Glass, by Juan Gris. c, Girl with Mandolin, by Pablo Picasso. d, The Glass of Absinthe, by Braque.

No. 4096, 6000 le — Surrealist paintings: a, Indefinite Divisibility, by Yves Tanguy. b, The Son of Man, by René Magritte. c, The Human Condition, by Magritte. d, The Song of Love, by Giorgio de Chirico.

No. 4097, 6000 le — Art of Ancient Egypt: a, Breastplate in the form of a scarab. b, Anubis guarding treasure chest. c, Wedjat eye, pendant from tomb of Tutankhamun. d, Statue of Akhenaten, relief of Akhenaten, Nerfertiti and their children.

No. 4098, 6000 le — Dutch Golden Age paintings: a, The Anatomy Lesson of Dr. Nicolaes Tulp, by Rembrandt. b, Portrait of Pieter van der Broecke, by Frans Hals. c, The Mill at Wijk-bij-Duurstede, by Jacob van Ruysdael. d, Woman in Blue Reading a Letter, by Vermeer.

No. 4099, 6000 le — American impressionist paintings: a, For the Little One (Hall at Shinnecock), by William Merritt Chase. b, Calm Morning, by Frank Weston Benson. c, Descending the Steps, by Childe Hassam. d, The Fountain, Villa Torlonia, Fraascati, Italy, by John Singer Sargent.

No. 4100, 6000 le — Russian paintings: a, Vasilisa the Beautiful, by Ivan Bilibini. b, Self-Portrait at the Dressing Table, by Zinaida Serebriakova. c, On the Balcony, by Konstantin Korovin. d, Pan, by Mikhail Vrubel.

No. 4101, 6000 le — Paintings by Ivan Aivazovsky (1817-1900): a, Boat Ride by Kumkapi in Constantinople. b, Battle of Cesme at Night. c, View of Constantinople and the Bosporus. d, A Tower, Shipwreck.

No. 4102, 6000 le — Paintings by Gustav Klimt (1862-1918): a, Danae. b, Portrait of Adele Bloch-Bauer I. c, The Three Ages of Women. d, Hygieia.

No. 4103, 6000 le — Paintings by Degas (1834-1917): a, At the Stables, Horse and Dog. b, Mary Cassatt at the Louvre. c, Dancer Tilting. d, A Roman Beggar Woman.

No. 4104, 6000 le — Paintings by Frida Kahlo (1907-54): a, Flower of Life. b, Self-portrait with Loose Hair. c, Portrait of Luther Burbank. d, Tree of Hope, Remain Strong.

No. 4105, 6000 le — Art by Auguste Rodin (1840-1917): a, The Hand of God (sculpture). b, In the S. . . (painting) c, Damend Women (sculpture). d, Cambodian Dancer (painting).

No. 4106, 6000 le — Art of the Pompidou Center, Paris: a, The Blue Circus, painting by Marc Chagall. b, Light Sentence, sculpture by Mona Hatoum. c, Le Rhinoceros, sculpture by Xavier Veilhan. d, La Muse, by Picasso.

No. 4107, 24,000 le, Gabor, diff. No. 4108, 24,000 le, 1997 Lamborghini Diablo Roadster VT. No. 4109, 24,000 le, Lady with an Ermine, by Leonardo da Vinci. No. 4110, 24,000 le, An Old Man in Military Costume, by Rembrandt. No. 4111, 24,000 le, This is Our Corner (Laurence and Anna Alma-Tadema), by Lawrence Alma-Tadema. No. 4112, 24,000 le, October, by Jules Bastien-Lepage. No. 4113, 24,000 le, Woman with a Parasol - Madame Monet and Her Son, by Claude Monet. No. 4114, 24,000 le, Tiger in a Tropical Storm, by Henri Rousseau. No. 4115, 24,000 le, Woman in an Armchair (Eva), by Picasso. No. 4116, 24,000 le, The Temptation of St. Anthony, by Max Ernst. No. 4117, 24,000 le, Funerary mask of Tutankhamun. No. 4118, 24,000 le, Self-portrait in a Flat Cap, by Rembrandt. No. 4119, 24,000 le, Girl in Blue Arranging Flowers, by Frederick Carl Frieseke. No. 4120, 24,000 le, Merry Structure, by Wassily Kandinsky. No. 4121, 24,000 le, Coffee-house by the Ortaköy Mosque in Constantinople, by Aivazovsky. No. 4122, 24,000 le, Farmhouse with Birch Trees, by Klimt. No. 4123, 24,000 le, Four Dancers, by Degas. No. 4124, 24,000 le, Self-portrait Along the Borderline Between Mexico and the United States, by Kahlo. No. 4125, 24,000 le, Orpheus and Eurydice, sculpture by Rodin. No. 4126, 24,000 le, Model of Tatlin's Tower, sculpture by Vladimir Tatlin.

2017, Jan. 30 Litho. *Perf. 13¼*

Sheets of 4, #a-d

4087-4106 A687 Set of 20 130.00 130.00

Souvenir Sheets

4107-4126 A687 Set of 20 130.00 130.00

Nos. 4107-4126 each contain one 45x64mm stamp.

New Year 2017 (Year of the Rooster) — A688

No. 4127: a, Rooster with wings extended. b, Head of rooster facing left. c, Rooster facing forward. d, Rooster facing left.

40,000 le, Rooster facing right.

2017, Feb. 27 Litho. *Perf. 13¼*

4127 A688 9800 le Sheet of 4, #a-d 10.50 10.50

Souvenir Sheet

4128 A688 40,000 le multi 11.00 11.00

A689

No. 4129, 9800 le — Mata Hari (1876-1917), exotic dancer and executed World War I spy: a, With arms extended. b, Facing left. c, With one hand visible. d, With arms close to torso.

No. 4130, 9800 le — First Battle of Gaza, cent.: a, Cavalry approaching machine gun emplacement. b, Airplane dropping bomb. c, Soldiers and cannon. d, Archibald James Murray (1860-1945), British general.

No. 4131, 9800 le — Protestant Reformation, 500th anniv.: a, Martin Luther (1483-1586), theologian, and his 95 Theses. b, Execution of Jan Hus (c. 1369-1415), religious reformer. c, Luther burning papal bull. d, Religious battle between Protestants and Roman Catholics.

No. 4132, 9800 le — Franz Schubert (1797-1828), composer: a, With musical score. b, With piano. c, Sculpture of Schubert and 1928 Austrian coin depicting him. d, Writing.

No. 4133, 9800 le — Pres. John F. Kennedy (1917-63): a, With wife, Jacqueline (1929-94). b, Reading papers. c, With Marilyn Monroe (1926-62), actress. d, With wife and daughter, Caroline.

No. 4134, 9800 le — Rotary International emblem and: a, People involved in Rotary education projects. b, Paul P. Harris (1868-1947), founder. c, Rotary water access project. d, Rotary water sanitation project.

No. 4135, 9800 le — Shackleton Antarctic expedition: a, Frank Worsley (1872-1943), captain of the Endurance. b, Man on bridge of the Endurance. c, Ernest Shackleton (1874-1922), expedition leader, and Frank Hurley (1885-1962), photographer. d, Frank Wild (1873-1939), expedition member, and wreck of the Endurance.

No. 4136, 9800 le — Mother Teresa (1910-97), humanitarian, with: a, Crucifix. b, Angel. c, Pope Francis. d, Cross and religious medal depicting her.

No. 4137, 9800 le — Princess Diana (1961-97), and: a, Queen Elizabeth II. b, Her children, Princes William and Harry in school uniforms. c, Elton John. d, Princes William and Harry as teenagers, in suits.

No. 4138, 9800 le — Indian Rebellion, 160th anniv.: a, Canna indica and soldier. b, Mangal Pandey (1827-57), soldier. c, Queen Victoria (1819-1901). d, Soldiers holding Enfield rifles.

No. 4139, 9800 le — Russian October Revoluiton, cent.: a, Lenin (1870-1924), Russian head of government. b, Cruiser Aurora and Winter Palace. c, Lenin and wife, Nadezhda Krupskaya (1869-1939). d, Tsar Nicholas II (1868-1918).

No. 4140, 9800 le — Russian Railways, 180th anniv.: a, Three locomotives and anniversary emblem. b, TEM14-0001 locomotive. c, Class P36 locomotive. d, ES1-027 Lastochka and EVS1/EV2 Sapsan locomotives.

No. 4141, 9801 le — Alexander Pushkin (1799-1837), writer: a, Pushkin, quill pen in ink bottle. b, Wife, Natalia (1812-63). c, Pushkin's Farewell to the Sea, painting by Ivan Aivazovsky (1817-1900) and Ilya Repin (1844-1930). d, Pushkin and Queen of Spades.

No. 4142, 9800 le — Battle of Stalingrad, 75th anniv.: a, Russian tank. b, Statues. c, Barbed wire, German and Soviet Union flags. d, Soldier with Molotov cocktail.

No. 4143, 9800 le — Beginning of Cold War, 70th anniv.: a, Boeing B-29 Superfortresses in flight. b, Forrest Sherman class destroyer and Foxtrot class submarine. c, 2K11 Krug (SA 4 Ganef) on maneuvers. d, RB-47E reconnaisance airplane and Mikoyan-Gurevich MiG-17.

No. 4144, 9800 le — Cuban Missile Crisis, 55th anniv.: a, Fidel Castro (1926-2016), President of Cuba. b, American airplane over tank-mounted missiles. c, USS Enterprise, airplane and helicopter. d, Nikita Khrushchev (1894-1971), Russian premier, and Pres. John F. Kennedy (1917-63).

No. 4145, 9800 le — 80th birthday of Valentina Tereshkova, cosmonaut: a, With Yuri Gagarin (1934-68), cosmonaut. b, Tershkova reading book. c, Tereshkova wearing space helmet, and with Gagarin. d, Tereshkova in space suit, rocket launch.

No. 4146, 9800 le — Launch of dog, Laika, into orbit, 60th anniv.: a, Laika in space capsule. b, Laika wearing monitors. c, Laika and Sputnik 2 on launch pad. d, Laika sitting in capsule seat.

No. 4147, 9800 le — Outer Space Treaty, 50th anniv.: a, United Nations delegates discussing peaceful uses of outer space, 1962. b, No weapons of mass destruction in space. c, No sovereignty or occupation of outer space. d, World map and outer space.

No. 4148, 40,000 le, Mata Hari, diff. No. 4149, 40,000 le, Gen. Friedrich Freiherr Kress von Kressenstein (1870-1948). No. 4150, 40,000 le, Offering of indulgences. No. 4151, 40,000 le, Schubert and violin. No. 4152, 40,000 le, Pres. Kennedy, diff. No. 4153, 40,000 le, Rotary International emblem, map of Sri Lanka and Alphonsea sclerocarpa. No. 4154, 40,000 le, Shackleton, the Endurance and sea birds. No. 4155, 40,000 le, Mother Teresa, diff. No. 4156, 40,000 le, Princess Diana, diff. No. 4157, 40,000 le, Rani Lakshmibai of Jhansi (1828-58), leader of Indian Rebellion. No. 4158, 40,000 le, Austin-Putilov armored car. No. 4159, 40,000 le, 2TE10U Diesel locomotive. No. 4160, 40,000 le, Self-portrait of Pushkin. No. 4161, 40,000 le, Airplane and soldiers at the Battle of Stalingrad. No. 4162, 40,000 le, Sir Winston Churchill (1874-1965) delivering Iron Curtain speech. No. 4163, 40,000 le, Cuban flag and 1950s Chevrolet. No. 4164, 40,000 le, Tereshkova and spacecraft. No. 4165, 40,000 le, Laika and Sputnik 2 rocket in space. No. 4166, 40,000 le, Balance and balls depicting flags of United States, Soviet Union and Great Britain.

2017, Feb. 27 Litho. *Perf. 13¼*

Sheets of 4, #a-d

4129-4147 A689 Set of 19 200.00 200.00

Souvenir Sheets

4148-4166 A689 Set of 19 205.00 205.00

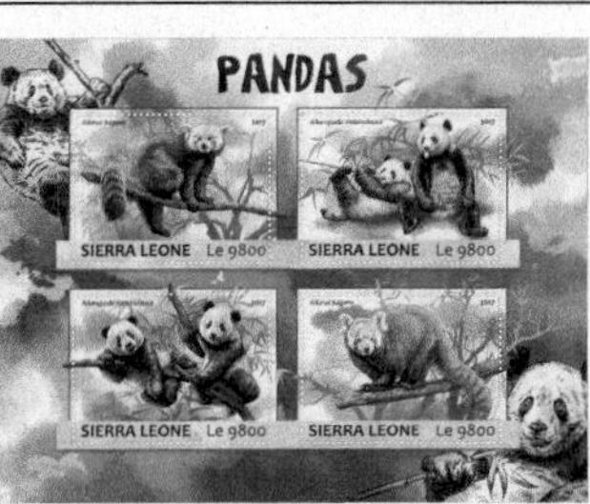

A690

No. 4167, 9800 le — Pandas: a, Ailurus fulgens, tail at left. b, Two Ailuropoda melanoleuca on ground. c, Two Ailuropoda melanoleuca in tree. d, Ailurus fulgens, tail at right.

No. 4168, 9800 le — Panthera leo: a, Lioness on rock. b, Lion attacking prey. c, Lion and lioness. d, Lion facing left.

No. 4169, 9800 le — Tigers: a, Panthera tigris corbetti. b, Panthera tigris tigris. c, Panthera tigris jacksoni. d, Panthera tigris altaica.

No. 4170, 9800 le — Cat breeds: a, Russian Blue. b, Bengal. c, Sokoke. d, Sphynx.

No. 4171, 9800 le — Dog breeds: a, Neapolitan mastiff. b, Leonberger. c, Bloodhounds. d, Appenzeller sennenhund.

No. 4172, 9800 le — Horse breeds: a, Appaloosa. b, Haflinger. c, Rocky Mountain horse. d, Gypsy Vanner.

No. 4173, 9800 le — Birds of prey: a, Gypohierax angolensis. b, Polyboroides typus. c, Circus macrourus. d, Buteo auguralis.

No. 4174, 9800 le — Seabirds: a, Larus ridibundus. b, Ardenna grisea. c, Thalasseus bengalensis. d, Phalacrocorax aristotelis.

No. 4175, 9800 le — Owls: a, Ptilopsis leucotis. b, Tyto alba. c, Bubo poensis. d, Strix woodfordii.

No. 4176, 9800 le — Butterflies: a, Papilio zalmoxis. b, Danaus chrysippus. c, Charaxes varanes. d, Graphium antheus.

No. 4177, 9800 le — Fish: a, Callopanchax occidentalis. b, Sargocentron hastatum. c, Balistes punctatus. d, Coris julis.

No. 4178, 9800 le — Crocodiles: a, Crocodylus palustris. b, Osteolaemus tetraspis. c, Crocodylus niloticus, head at right. d, Crocodylus niloticus, head at left.

No. 4179, 9800 le — Turtles: a, Eretmochelys imbricata. b, Pelusios castaneus. c, Dermochelys coriacea. d, Chelonia mydas.

No. 4180, 9800 le — Dinosaurs: a, Parasaurolophus cyrtocristatus. b, Eousdryosaurus nanohallucis. c, Dilophosaurus wetherilli. d, Suchomimus tenerensis.

No. 4181, 9800 le — Animals affected by global warming: a, Aptenodytes patagonicus. b, Ovibos moschatus. c, Odobenus rosmarus. d, Fratercula arctica.

No. 4182, 9800 le — Orchids: a, Disa uniflora. b, Cymbidium hybrid. c, Pleione limprichtii. d, Vandopsis lissochiloides.

No. 4183, 9800 le — Mushrooms: a, Sarcoscypha coccinea. b, Boletus aereus. c, Myriostoma coliforme. d, Cantharellus lateritius.

No. 4184, 9800 le — Minerals: a, Dioptase. b, Copper. c, Wulfenite. d, Fluorite.

No. 4185, 9800 le — Aung San Suu Kyi, First State Counsellor of Myanmar: a, Sitting in tree. b, With Nobel Peace Prize medal and Archbishop Desmond Tutu. c, With Pope Francis. d, With flag of European Union.

No. 4186, 40,000 le, One Ailuropoda melanoleuca. No. 4187, 40,000 le, Two male Panthera leo. No. 4188, 40,000 le, Panthera tigris tigris, diff. No. 4189, 40,000 le, Maine Coon cat. No. 4190, 40,000 le, Salukis. No. 4191, 40,000 le, Arabian horses. No. 4192, 40,000 le, Terathopius ecaudatus. No. 4193, 40,000 le, Sula leucogaster. No. 4194, 40,000 le, Bubo lacteus. No. 4195, 40,000 le, Papilio antimachus. No. 4196, 40,000 le, Balistes vetula. No. 4197, 40,000 le, Crocodylus niloticus, diff. No. 4198, 40,000 le, Chelonia mydas, diff. No. 4199, 40,000 le, Spinosaurus maroccanus. No. 4200, 40,000 le, Ursus maritimus. No. 4201, 40,000 le, Thelymitra pulcherrima. No. 4202, 40,000 le, Rhodotus palmatus. No. 4203, 40,000 le, Gold. No. 4204, 40,000 le, Aung San Suu Kyi and 1991 Nobel Peace Prize medal.

2017, Mar. 30 Litho. *Perf. 13¼*

Sheets of 4, #a-d

4167-4185 A690 Set of 19 200.00 200.00

Souvenir Sheets

4186-4204 A690 Set of 19 205.00 205.00

Nos. 4186-4204 each contain one 61x41mm stamp. Compare Nos. 4184 and 4203 with Nos. 4207-4208.

Indonesian Animals — A691

No. 4205: a, Pavo muticus. b, Rhinoceros sondaicus. c, Panthera tigris sumatrae. d, Muntiacus montanus.

No. 4206: a, Varanus komodoensis. b, Bubalus quarlesi.

Litho., Sheet Margin Litho. With Foil Application

2017, Mar. 30 ***Perf.***

4205 A691 9800 le Sheet of 4, #a-d 10.50 10.50

Souvenir Sheet

4206 A691 20,000 le Sheet of 2, #a-b 11.00 11.00

Bandung 2017 International Stamp Exhibition.

Minerals — A692

No. 4207: a, 6.48-carat rough diamond. b, Chromite. c, Corundum. d, Pastor Emmanuel Momoh and 706-carat diamond he discovered.

40,000 le, Hands holding 706-carat diamond.

2017, Apr. 28 Litho. ***Perf. 13¼***

4207 A692 9800 le Sheet of 4, #a-d 10.50 10.50

Souvenir Sheet

4208 A692 40,000 le multi 11.00 11.00

No. 4208 contains one 61x41mm stamp. Compare Nos. 4207-4208 with Nos. 4184, 4203.

A693

No. 4209, 9800 le — Wilbur Wright (1867-1912), aviation pioneer: a, At left, Wright Flyer at right. b, With mechanical drawing of Wright Flyer. c, At right, Wright Flyer at left. d, With brother, Orville (1871-1948).

No. 4210, 9800 le — Disappearance of Amelia Earhart (1898-1937), 80th anniv.: a, Earhart and Merrill CIT-9 safety plane. b, Lockheed Electra 10E. c, Lockheed Vega 5C. d, Earhart and Lockheed Vega 5C.

No. 4211, 9800 le — Military airplanes: a, Lockheed F-117 Nighthawk. b, Panavia Tornado. c, Northrup Grumman E-2 Hawkeye. d, Northrup Grumman B-2 Spirit.

No. 4212, 9800 le — Concorde: a, Air France Concorde in flight. b, British Airways Concorde taking off. c, British Airways Concorde in Flight. d, British Airways Concorde on runway.

No. 4213, 9800 le — Zeppelins and airships: a, Concept design of Sky Tug. b, LZ-129 Hindenburg. c, Airship Norge. d, Aeroscraft Dragon Dream airship.

No. 4214, 9800 le — Tall ships: a, Schooner Juan Sebastian Elcano, flag of Spain. b, Royal Clipper, flag of Malta. c, Barque STS Sedov, flag of Russia. d, Barque NRP Sagres, flag of Portugal.

No. 4215, 9800 le — Submarines: a, HMS Ambush. b, U-boat Biber. c, U-2540. d, USS Scamp SSN-588.

No. 4216, 9800 le — Sinking of the Titanic, 105th anniv.: a, Titanic at sea. b, Lifeboats near sinking Titanic. c, Titanic sinking, no lifeboats visible. d, Titanic on ocean floor.

No. 4217, 9800 le — 50th anniv. of fatal crash of Donald Campbell (1921-67): a, Bluebird K7 and splash from crash at left. b, Bluebird K7 at left, Campbell at right. c, Campbell at left, crashing Bluebird K7 at right. d, Bluebird K7.

No. 4218, 9800 le — First Ferrari automobile, 70th anniv.: a, Ferrari 250 GT. b, Enzo Ferrari (1898-1988), manufacturer, in Ferrari 125 S. c, Ferrari 166 MM/212. d, Ferrari 250 GT Lusso.

No. 4219, 9800 le — Fire engines: a, 1979 E8439 Seagrave pumper. b, 1974 International. c, 36 Restored Crown Firecoach. d, 1975 International.

No. 4220, 9800 le — Special transport: a, ZIL-29061 amphibious screw vehicle. b, ZIL-4906 space capsule recovery vehicle. c, CCGS Mamilossa hovercraft. d, HB-XKE Kamov KA-32 A12 helicopter.

No. 4221, 9800 le — Steam trains: a, London and North Eastern Railway A4 4498 Sir Nigel Gresley. b, Connecticut Valley Railroad 3025. c, Chesapeake & Ohio No. 490 "Hudson." d, Norfolk & Western Railway J Class 611.

No. 4222, 9800 le — High-speed trains: a, NTV Alstom AGV 575, Italy. b, AVE Class 103, Spain. c, Shinkansen 500 Type EVA, Japan. d, HEMU-430X, South Korea.

No. 4223, 9800 le — Marie Curie (1867-1934), chemist and physicist: a, With husband, Pierre (1859-1906). b, With Nobel Prize medals. c, On stained-glass medallion by Josef Mazur, and roses. d, With atomic diagram of polonium.

No. 4224, 9800 le — 75th birthday of Stephen Hawking (1942-2018), physicist: a, Hawking and Virgin Galactic SpaceShipTwo. b, Hawking and Pres. Barack Obama. c, Kepler 452-b. d, Hawking and black hole.

No. 4225, 9800 le — Service dogs: a, Cardigan Welsh corgi as seizure alert dog. b, Poodle as autism service dog. c, Labrador retriever as wheelchair assistance dog. d, Welsh Springer spaniel as guide dog.

No. 4226, 9800 le — Red Cross: a, Red Cross worker in Ebola virus protective gear, map of Africa. b, Red Cross service dog. c, Red Cross volunteers providing first aid after earthquake. d, Three Red Cross workers near hospital bed.

No. 4227, 40,000 le, Wilbur Wright and Wright Flyer, diff. No. 4228, 40,000 le, Lockheed Vega 5B flown by Earhart. No. 4229, 40,000 le, Lockheed-Martin F-35 Lightning II. No. 4230, 40,000 le, British Airways Concorde, diff. No. 4231, 40,000 le, Ferdinand von Zeppelin (1838-1917), manufacturer of Zeppelins. No. 4232, 40,000 le, Barque Kaiwo Maru, flag of Japan. No. 4233, 40,000 le, C.B. 20 midget submarine. No. 4234, 40,000 le, Edward John Smith (1850-1912), captain of the Titanic. No. 4235, 40,000 le, Bluebird K7, diff. No. 4236, 40,000 le, Enzo Ferrari and Ferrari 212 Inter Vignale Cabriolet. No. 4237, 40,000 le, SOC vehicle. No. 4238, 40,000 le, Lockheed C-130 Hercules. No. 4239, 40,000 le, Southern Pacific Class GS-4. No. 4240, 40,000 le, THSR 700T, Taiwan. No. 4241, 40,000 le, Marie Curie and Albert Einstein (1879-1955), physicist. No. 4242, 40,000 le, Hawking and exoplanet Proxima Centauri b. No. 4243, 40,000 le, Labrador retriever service dog. No. 4244, 40,000 le, Red Cross volunteer providing drinking water.

2017, Apr. 28 Litho. ***Perf. 13¼***

Sheets of 4, #a-d

4209-4226 A693 Set of 18 190.00 190.00

Souvenir Sheets

4227-4244 A693 Set of 18 195.00 195.00

Genghis Khan (c. 1162-1227), Founder of Mongol Empire — A694

No. 4245: a, Genghis Khan in armor on horse. b, Mausoleum of Genghis Khan, flag of Mongolia. c, Statue of Genghis Khan. d, Genghis Khan with sword.

40,000 le, Statue of Genghis Khan, flag of Mongolia, warriors on horseback.

Litho. With Foil Application

2017, Apr. 28 ***Perf. 13¼***

4245 A694 9800 le Sheet of 4, #a-d 10.50 10.50

Souvenir Sheet

4246 A694 40,000 le multi 11.00 11.00

Models of Billy Karam — A695

No. 4247: a, Car No. 1 on curve facing right. b, Tank and troop transport vehicle. c, Car No. 1 facing left. d, Tank. e, Car No. 1 facing right with front wheels turned. f, Tank with Lebanese flag. g, Car No. 12. h, Biplane.

40,000 le, Karam holding Guinness World Record certificates.

Litho. with Foil Application

2017, May 30 ***Perf. 13¼***

4247 A695 4900 le Sheet of 8, #a-h 10.50 10.50

Souvenir Sheet

4248 A695 40,000 le multi 11.00 11.00

No. 4248 contains one 45x33mm stamp.

Worldwide Fund for Nature (WWF) — A696

No. 4249 — Phoeniconaias minor: a, Two flamingos touching beaks. b, Three flamingos in flight. c, Two flamingos feeding. d, Flamingo in water, flamingo grooming itself

40,000 le, Mother feeding chicks.

2017, May 30 Litho. ***Perf. 13¼***

4249 A696 9800 le Sheet of 4, #a-d 10.50 10.50

Souvenir Sheet

4250 A696 40,000 le multi 11.00 11.00

A697

A698

A699

David Bowie (1947-2016), Rock Musician A700

2017, May 30 Litho. ***Perf. 13¼***

4251 A697 6600 le multi 1.75 1.75
4252 A698 6600 le multi 1.75 1.75
4253 A699 6600 le multi 1.75 1.75
4254 A700 6600 le multi 1.75 1.75
Nos. 4251-4254 (4) 7.00 7.00

Souvenir Sheet

4255 A700 40,000 le Bowie, diff. 11.00 11.00

Ludwig van Beethoven (1770-1827), Composer A701

Designs: No. 4256, 6600 le, Beethoven, painting and harpsichord. No. 4257, 6600 le, Beethoven, violin and harpsichord. No. 4258, 6600 le, Beethoven writing score, violin. No. 4259, 6600 le, Bust of Beethoven by Hugo Hagen, Beethoven House, Bonn.

40,000 le, Beethoven conducting.

2017, May 30 Litho. ***Perf. 13¼***

4256-4259 A701 Set of 4 7.00 7.00

Souvenir Sheet

4260 A701 40,000 le multi 11.00 11.00

Pope Francis
A702

Arms of Pope Francis and Pope Francis: No. 4261, 6600 le, Kissing man's feet. No. 4262, 6600 le, Touching crucifix. No. 4263, 6600 le, Riding in Popemobile. No. 4264, 6600 le, In green vestments.
40,000 le, Consecrating host.

2017, May 30 Litho. *Perf. 13¼*
4261-4264 A702 Set of 4 7.00 7.00

Souvenir Sheet

4265 A702 40,000 le multi 11.00 11.00

Prince William, 35th Birthday
A703

Prince William: No. 4266, 6600 le, Wearing military uniform. No. 4267, 6600 le, With grandmother, Queen Elizabeth II. No. 4268, 6600 le, As child, with mother, Princess Diana. No. 4269, 6600 le, With son, Prince George of Cambridge.
40,000 le, Wearing military uniform, diff.

2017, May 30 Litho. *Perf. 13¼*
4266-4269 A703 Set of 4 7.00 7.00

Souvenir Sheet

4270 A703 40,000 le multi 11.00 11.00

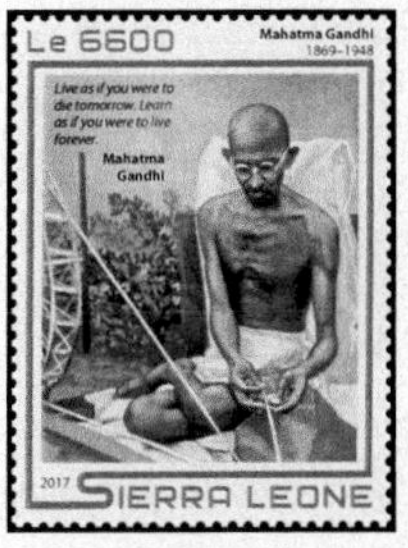

Mahatma Gandhi (1869-1948), Indian Nationalist Leader
A704

Gandhi: No. 4271, 6600 le, Spinning thread. No. 4272, 6600 le, With lotus flower. No. 4273, 6600 le, With dove. No. 4274, 6600 le, With map and flag of India.
40,000 le, Gandhi and Taj Mahal.

2017, May 30 Litho. *Perf. 13¼*
4271-4274 A704 Set of 4 7.00 7.00

Souvenir Sheet

4275 A704 40,000 le multi 11.00 11.00

Nelson Mandela (1918-2013), President of South Africa — A705

Mandela: No. 4276, 6600 le, Behind barbed wire. No. 4277, 6600 le, Holding 1993 Nobel Peace Prize medal and diploma. No. 4278, 6600 le, Holding World Cup. No. 4279, 6600 le, With Pope John Paul II (1920-2005).
40,000 le, Mandela, barbed wire, flag of South Africa.

2017, May 30 Litho. *Perf. 13¼*
4276-4279 A705 Set of 4 7.00 7.00

Souvenir Sheet

4280 A705 40,000 le multi 11.00 11.00

Scouting Movement, 110th Anniv.
A706

Scouting emblem and: No. 4281, 6600 le, Lord Robert Baden-Powell (1857-1941), founder. No. 4282, 6600 le, Scout with Scouting flag. No. 4283, 6600 le, Scout making knot. No. 4284, 6600 le, Scout at campfire.
40,000 le, Lady Olave Baden-Powell (1889-1977), wife of founder.

2017, May 30 Litho. *Perf. 13¼*
4281-4284 A706 Set of 4 7.00 7.00

Souvenir Sheet

4285 A706 40,000 le multi 11.00 11.00

Passage of United States Espionage Act, Cent. — A707

Designs: No. 4286, 6600 le, Eugene V. Debs (1855-1926), Socialist candidate for U.S. President. No. 4287, 6600 le, Thomas Watt Gregory (1861-1933), U.S. Atttorney General. No. 4288, 6600 le, Albert Sidney Burleson (1863-1937), U.S. Postmaster General. No. 4289, 6600 le, Ship, soldier and policeman.
40,000 le, Pres. Woodrow Wilson (1856-1924).

2017, May 30 Litho. *Perf. 13¼*
4286-4289 A707 Set of 4 7.00 7.00

Souvenir Sheet

4290 A707 40,000 le multi 11.00 11.00

Alexander Graham Bell (1847-1922), Inventor of Telephone
A708

Designs: No. 4291, 6600 le, Bell writing, old desk telephone. No. 4292, 6600 le, Bell, old wall telephone, patent diagram, emblem of American Telephone and Telegraph Company. No. 4293, 6600 le, Bell, his signature, Bell speaking on telephone, emblem of American Telephone and Telegraph Company. No. 4294, 6600 le, Statue of Bell, his signature, early telephone, smartphone.
40,000 le, Bell talking into first telephone.

2017, May 30 Litho. *Perf. 13¼*
4291-4294 A708 Set of 4 7.00 7.00

Souvenir Sheet

4295 A708 40,000 le multi 11.00 11.00

Henry Ford (1863-1947), Automobile Manufacturer
A709

Designs: No. 4296, 6600 le, Ford and 1902 Ford 999. No. 4297, 6600 le, Ford and 1920 Ford Model T. No. 4298, 6600 le, Ford's signature and 1919 Ford Model T Coupes. No. 4299, 6600 le, Front and side views of 1928 Ford Model A Business Coupe.
40,000 le, 1924 Ford Model T.

2017, May 30 Litho. *Perf. 13¼*
4296-4299 A709 Set of 4 7.00 7.00

Souvenir Sheet

4300 A709 40,000 le multi 11.00 11.00

Physicists
A710

Designs: No. 4301, 6600 le, J. Robert Oppenheimer (1904-67). No. 4302, 6600 le, Oppenheimer and Albert Einstein (1879-1955). No. 4303, 6600 le, Paul Dirac (1902-84), duality wave-corpuscle. No. 4304, 6600 le, Percy Williams Bridgman (1882-1961), Nobel Physics Prize medal and Rumford Prize medal.
40,000 le, Oppenheimer wearing hat.

2017, May 30 Litho. *Perf. 13¼*
4301-4304 A710 Set of 4 7.00 7.00

Souvenir Sheet

4305 A710 40,000 le multi 11.00 11.00

Apollo 1 Fire, 50th Anniv.
A711

Designs: No. 4306, 6600 le, Apollo 1 rocket and capsule. No. 4307, 6600 le, Crew members killed in fire, Ed White II (1930-67), Gus Grissom (1926-67), Roger Chaffee (1935-67). No. 4308, 6600 le, Grissom. No. 4309, 6600 le, Front pages of newspaper, wreath.
40,000 le, Saturn IB rocket, U.S. flag.

2017, May 30 Litho. *Perf. 13¼*
4306-4309 A711 Set of 4 7.00 7.00

Souvenir Sheet

4310 A711 40,000 le multi 11.00 11.00

Louis Braille (1809-52), Developer of Writing for the Blind — A712

Statue of Braille and: No. 4311, 6600 le, His alphabet. No. 4312, 6600 le, Woman reading Braille book. No. 4313, 6600 le, Rainbow, hands reading Braille book. No. 4304, 6600 le, Boy reading Braille book, rocket.
40,000 le, Statue of Braille, Bermuda.

2017, May 30 Litho. *Perf. 13¼*
4311-4314 A712 Set of 4 7.00 7.00

Souvenir Sheet

4315 A712 40,000 le multi 11.00 11.00

50th Anniv. of Publication of *The Master and Margarita*, by Mikhail Bulgakov (1891-1940)
A713

Book and: No. 4316, 6600 le, Bulgakov and Margarita. No. 4317, 6600 le, Azazello. No. 4318, 6600 le, Pontius Pilate. No. 4319, 6600 le, Behemoth.
40,000 le, Book, Bulgakov and man holding candle.

2017, May 30 Litho. *Perf. 13¼*
4316-4319 A713 Set of 4 7.00 7.00

Souvenir Sheet

4320 A713 40,000 le multi 11.00 11.00

Awarding of Pulitzer Prizes, Cent. — A714

Designs: No. 4321, 6600 le, Joseph Pulitzer (1847-1911), newspaper publisher and namesake of prize, Pulitzer Prize medal. No. 4322, 6600 le, Charles Lindbergh (1902-74), aviation and 1954 prize winner. No. 4323, 6600 le, Ray Bradbury (1920-2012), writer and winner of 2007 special citation. No. 4324, 6600 le, Ernest Hemingway (1899-1961), writer and 1953 prize winner.
40,000 le, Herbert Bayard Swope (1882-1958), journalist and 1917 prize winner.

2017, May 30 Litho. *Perf. 13¼*
4321-4324 A714 Set of 4 7.00 7.00

Souvenir Sheet

4325 A714 40,000 le multi 11.00 11.00

Jacques-Yves Cousteau (1910-97), Conservationist and Filmmaker — A715

Cousteau and: No. 4326, 6600 le, Carcharodon carcharias, Betta splendens. No. 4327, 6600 le, Enteroctopus dofleini. No. 4328, 6600 le, Amphiprion ocellaris, submarine. No. 4329, 6600 le, Tursiops truncatus.
40,000 le, Cousteau and Stenella frontalis.

2017, May 30 Litho. *Perf. 13¼*
4326-4329 A715 Set of 4 7.00 7.00

Souvenir Sheet

4330 A715 40,000 le multi 11.00 11.00

Steve Irwin (1962-2006), Conservationist and Wildlife Documentarian — A716

Irwin and: No. 4331, 6600 le, His daughter, Bindi, and Alligator mississippiensis. No. 4332, 6600 le, Globe and Alligator mississippiensis. No. 4333, 6600 le, Macropus agilis. No. 4334, 6600 le, Snake.

40,000 le, Irwin, his wife, Terri, and Chelonoidis nigra abingdonii.

2017, May 30 Litho. *Perf. 13¼*

4331-4334 A716 Set of 4 7.00 7.00

Souvenir Sheet

4335 A716 40,000 le multi 11.00 11.00

A717

A718

A719

Arthur C. Clarke (1917-2008), Writer A720

2017, May 30 Litho. *Perf. 13¼*

4336 A717 6600 le multi 1.75 1.75
4337 A718 6600 le multi 1.75 1.75
4338 A719 6600 le multi 1.75 1.75
4339 A720 6600 le multi 1.75 1.75
Nos. 4336-4339 (4) 7.00 7.00

Souvenir Sheet

4340 A720 40,000 le Clarke, diff. 11.00 11.00

A721

No. 4341, 9800 le — Dugong dugon: a, One dugong, facing right. b, Adult and juvenile dugong facing left. c, Two dugongs facing forward. d, Two adult dugongs facing left.

No. 4342, 9800 le — Dolphins: a, Cephalorhynchus heavisidii. b, Cephalorhynchus commersonii. c, Tursiops aduncus. d, Lagenorhynchus albirostris.

No. 4343, 9800 le — Whales: a, Physeter macrocephalus. b, Eschrichtius robustus. c, Balaenoptera acutorostrata. d, Balaena mysticetus.

No. 4344, 9800 le — Big cats: a, Panthera pardus. b, Panthera tigris. c, Acinonyx jubatus. d, Panthera onca.

No. 4345, 9800 le — Hornbills: a, Bycanistes brevis. b, Anthracoceros coronatus. c, Aceros cassidix. d, Buceros hydrocorax.

No. 4346, 9800 le — Sunbirds: a, Cinnyris venustus. b, Anthobaphes violacea. c, Cinnyris asiaticus. d, Aethopyga siparaja.

No. 4347, 9800 le — Owls, country name in orange: a, Strix seloputo. b, Aegolius acadicus. c, Glaucidium gnoma. d, Phodilus badius.

No. 4348, 9800 le — Parrots, country name in green, each stamp with incorrect inscriptions of: a, Strix seloputo. b, Aegolius acadicus. c, Glaucidium gnoma. d, Phodilus badius.

No. 4349, 9800 le — Bee-eaters: a, Merops muelleri. b, Merops ornatus. c, Merops nubicoides. d, Merops bullockoides.

No. 4350, 9800 le — Rare birds: a, Prodotiscus insignis. b, Gymnobucco peli. c, Tockus hartlaubi. d, Telacanthura melanopygia.

No. 4351, 9800 le — Butterflies: a, Limenitis arthemis. b, Euphydryas aurinia. c, Heliconius ismenius. d, Agalis io.

No. 4352, 9800 le — Shells: a, Melongena corona. b, Trochus niloticus. c, Sinistrofulgur perversum. d, Neptunea polycostata.

No. 4353, 9800 le — Crocodiles: a, Osteolaemus tetraspis. b, Crocodylus niloticus. c, Crocodylus intermedius. d, Crocodylus acutus.

No. 4354, 9800 le — Snakes: a, Ahaetulla prasina. b, Trimeresurus sumatranus. c, Lampropeltis triangulum hondurensis. d, Calliophis bivirgata.

No. 4355, 9800 le — Turtles: a, Chelonia mydas. b, Dermochelys coriacea. c, Malaclemys terrapin. d, Caretta caretta.

No. 4356, 9800 le — Extinct animals: a, Tyrannosaurus rex. b, Mammuthus trogontherii, Mammuthus columbi. c, Thylacinus cynocephalus. d, Equus quagga quagga.

No. 4357, 9800 le — Stamps depicting animals: a, Poland #3050. b, State of Oman sticker depicting cat. c, Moldova #386. d, Cuba #2768.

No. 4358, 9800 le — Orchids: a, Laelia dayana coerulea. b, Angraecum leonis. c, Bifrenaria inodora. d, Epidendrum hybrid.

No. 4359, 9800 le — Mushrooms: a, Panaeolus papilionaceus. b, Amanita pantherina. c, Cortinarius archeri. d, Psilocybe aztecorum.

No. 4360, 9800 le — Minerals: a, Wulfenite with Mimetite. b, Proustite. c, Metatorberanite. d, Hauyne.

No. 4361, 40,000 le, One Dugong dugon, diff. No. 4362, 40,000 le, Stenella frontalis. No. 4363, 40,000 le, Megaptera novaeangliae. No. 4364, 40,000 le, Puma concolor. No. 4365, 40,000 le, Bucorvus leadbeateri. No. 4366, 40,000 le, Cinnyris regius. No. 4367, 40,000 le, Pulsatrix perspicillata. No. 4368, 40,000 le, Pseudeos fuscata. No. 4369, 40,000 le, Nyctyornis amictus. No. 4370, 40,000 le, Himantornis haematopus. No. 4371, 40,000 le, Protogoniomorpha cytora. No. 4372, 40,000 le, Nassarius reticulatus. No. 4373, 40,000 le, Crocodylus porosus. No. 4374, 40,000 le, Morelia viridis. No. 4375, 40,000 le, Lepidochelys olivacea. No. 4376, 40,000 le, Beipiaosaurus inexpectus. No. 4377, 40,000 le, Hungary #C427A. No. 4378, 40,000 le, Bulbophyllum monanthum. No. 4379, 40,000 le, Amanita phalloides. No. 4380, 40,000 le, Graphite.

2017, June 30 Litho. *Perf. 13¼*

Sheets of 4, #a-d

4341-4360 A721 Set of 20 210.00 210.00

Souvenir Sheets

4361-4380 A721 Set of 20 215.00 215.00

Birdpex 2018 International Philatelic Exhibition, Mondorf-les-Bains, Luxembourg (Nos. 4351, 4371).

A722

No. 4381, 9800 le — Sled dogs: a, Team of six Alaskan malamutes pulling sled. b, Three Chinook dogs. c, Canadian Eskimo dog and sled. d, Team of four Siberian huskies pulling sled.

No. 4382, 9800 le — Horse transport: a, Hanoverian horse and phaeton. b, Barouche. c, Stagecoach. d, Cleveland Bay horse and governess cart.

No. 4383, 9800 le — African trains: a, E1397 Transnet Freight Rail Class 6E1. b, Transnet Freight Rail Class 20E Electric. c, South African Class Afro 4000. d, Gautrain.

No. 4384, 9800 le — European high-speed trains: a, Railjet. b, British Rail Class 222. c, British Rail Class 390. d, Eurostar e320.

No. 4385, 9800 le — Icebreakers: a, MV Arctic Sunrise. b, Shirase. c, MV Xue Long. d, Otso.

No. 4386, 9800 le — Military ships: a, USS San Antonio. b, Russian cruiser Moskva. c, USS Enterprise. d, FNS Hanko 82.

No. 4387, 9800 le — Cruise ships: a, Carnival Sunshine. b, Norwegian Escape. c, Norwegian Breakaway. d, MV Britannia.

No. 4388, 9800 le — Dirigibles: a, Esperia. b, R34. c, U.S. Navy M class. d, U.S. Navy ZMC-2.

No. 4389, 9800 le — Russian aircraft: a, Beriev Be-12 Chaika. b, Ilyushin Il-96. c, Beriev Be-200 Altair. d, Antonov An-148-100E.

No. 4390, 9800 le — Unmanned aircraft: a, Schiebel Camcopter S-100. b, MQ-9 Reaper. c, RQ-4 Global Hawk. d, Skeldar V-200.

No. 4391, 9800 le — Public transport: a, Airbus A380. b, Urbos 3 tram. c, Chicago Water Taxi. d, 1971 Fiat 1100D taxi, Mumbai, India.

No. 4392, 9800 le — Adam Opel (1837-95), automobile manufacturer: a, Opel and cover of bicycle brochure. b, 2015 Opel Adam Rocks S. c, 2015 Opel Adam S. d, Opel and cover of sewing machine brochure.

No. 4393, 9800 le — Fire engines: a, 1924 American LaFrance. b, Pierce Arrow XT. c, Janus 4000. d, 1935 Mack.

No. 4394, 9800 le — Mail transport: a, 1963 Studebaker Zip Van. b, DXP NZ. c, Toyota COMS. d, USPS Grumman LLV mail truck.

No. 4395, 9800 le — Motorcycles: a, 2016 Harley-Davidson Electra Glide Ultra Classic. b, 2014 Honda Valkyrie GL 1800CA ABS. c, 2017 Kawasaki Ninja H2R. d, 2017 KTM 1290 Super Duke GT.

No. 4396, 9800 le — Launch of Sputnik 1, 60th anniv.: a, Sputnik 1 and Kremlin, Moscow. b, Sputnik 1 and mechanical drawings. c, Sputnik 1 and Soviet Union flag. d, Sputnik 1 and Kremlin clock tower, Moscow.

No. 4397, 9800 le — Invention of dynamite by Alfred Nobel (1833-96), 150th anniv.: a, Sculpture of Nobel, dynamite sticks, newspaper advertisement for dynamite. b, Nobel, laboratory, and Nobel Prize medal. c, Nobel, building, and Nobel Prize medal. d, Statue of Novle, box of Extradynamit sticks.

No. 4398, 9800 le — Invention of induction motor by Nikola Tesla (1856-1943): a, Tesla Roadster Sport 2.5. b, Induction motor at left, Tesla at right. c, Tesla at left, induction motor at right. d, Tesla Roadster.

No. 4399, 40,000 le, Team of five Alaskan malamutes pulling sled. No. 4400, 40,000 le, Phaeton. No. 4401, 40,000 le, Class 18E electric locomotive. No. 4402, 40,000 le, CD Class 680 Pendolino. No. 4403, 40,000 le, CCGS Louis S. St. Laurent. No. 4404, 40,000 le, Russian battlecruiser Pyotr Velikiy. No. 4405, 40,000 le, Disney Dream. No. 4406, 40,000 le, USS Macon. No. 4407, 40,000 le, Sukhoi SU-30. No. 4408, 40,000 le, Piaggio P.1HH Hammerhead. No. 4409, 40,000 le, Tuk tuk taxi, Thailand. No. 4410, 40,000 le, Opel and poster for Opel factory. No. 4411, 40,000 le, 1935 Ford-Bufallo fire truck. No. 4412, 40,000 le, Royal Mail Boeing 737-3Y0 (SF). No. 4413, 40,000 le, 2017 Yamaha YZF-R1. No. 4414, 40,000 le, Sputnik 1, diff. No. 4415, 40,000 le, Nobel and dynamite sticks, diff. No. 4416, 40,000 le, Induction motor at left, Tesla at right, diff.

2017, July 28 Litho. *Perf. 13¼*

Sheets of 4, #a-d

4381-4398 A722 Set of 18 185.00 185.00

Souvenir Sheets

4399-4416 A722 Set of 18 190.00 190.00

Nos. 4399-4416 each contain one 61x41mm stamp.

Lighthouses — A723

No. 4417: a, Thomas Point Shoal Light, Maryland. b, Little Sable Point Light, Michigan. c, Europa Point Lighthouse, Gibraltar. d, St. Joseph North Pier Lighthouses, Michigan.

40,000 le, Peggys Point Lighthouse, Nova Scotia, Canada.

Litho. With Foil Application

2017, July 28 *Perf. 13¼*

4417 A723 9800 le Sheet of 4, #a-d 10.50 10.50

Souvenir Sheet

4418 A723 40,000 le multi 11.00 11.00

Dinosaurs — A724

No. 4418: a, Parksosaurus warreni. b, Herrerasarus ischigualastensis. c, Cryolophosaurus ellioti. d, Plateosaurus engelhardti.

40,000 le, Ankylosaurus magniventris.

2017, July 28 Litho. *Perf. 13¼*

4419 A724 9800 le Sheet of 4, #a-d 10.50 10.50

Souvenir Sheet

4420 A724 40,000 le multi 11.00 11.00

No. 4420 contains one 61x41mm stamp.

A725

No. 4421, 9800 le — Various depictions of Jimi Hendrix (1942-70), rock musician, with central curved panel in: a, Red violet. b, Purple. c, Dark red. d, Green.

No. 4422, 9800 le — Various depictions of Igor Stravinsky (1882-1971), composer, with central curved panel in: a, Brown ochre. b, Red violet. c, Dark blue. d, Deep green.

No. 4423, 9800 le — Eva Perón (1919-52), First lady of Argentina: a, Wearing flower. b, With arms raised. c, With husband, Juan. d, Wearing hat.

No. 4424, 9800 le — Pres. Franklin D. Roosevelt (1882-1945): a, With Sir Winston Churchill (1874-1965), British Prime Minister, at Atlantic Conference, 1941. b, Giving address on the attack on Pearl Harbor, 1941. c, With stamp collection. d, Addressing Congress on the Yalta Conference, 1945.

No. 4425, 9800 le — Muhammad Ali (1942-2016), boxer: a, Standing over knocked-out Sonny Liston (1932-70). b, With arms on boxing ring ropes. c, With towel over head. d, Boxing Joe Frazier (1944-2011).

No. 4426, 9800 le — Fourth birthday of Prince George of Cambridge: a, Prince George with parents, Duke and Duchess of Cambridge. b, Prince George at play with mother. c, Prince George being held by father. d, Prince George with dog, Lupo.

No. 4427, 9800 le — Louis Blériot (1872-1936), aviation pioneer: a, Blériot XI flying left. b, Blériot, blue green central curved panel. c, Blériot, deep olive central panel. d, Blériot XI flying right.

No. 4428, 9800 le — Renault automobiles: a, Renault Caravelle, 1958-68. b, 2020 Renault Trezor. c, 2012 Renault Twizy. d, Renault 4L, 1961-92.

No. 4429, 9800 le — Thomas Edison (1847-1931), inventor: a, With cylinder phonograph, c. 1899. b, With second phonograph, 1878. c, With his movie camera and George Eastman (1854-1932), industrialist. d, With light bulb and 1869 stock ticker.

No. 4430, 9800 le — Charles Darwin (1809-82), naturalist: a, Darwin and Galapagos Islands. b, Drawings of finches. c, HMS Beagle. d, Darwin and Chelonoidis nigra.

No. 4431, 9800 le — Volcanic eruptions: a, 1943 Parícutin eruption, Mexico. b, 1982 Mount Galunggung eruption, Indonesia. c, 1902 Mt. Pelée eruption, Martinique. d, 1992 Mount Spurr eruption, Alaska.

No. 4432, 9800 le — Melting of Antarctica: a, Aptenodytes forsteri. b, Leptonychotes weddellii. c, Orcinus orca. d, Eubalaena australis.

No. 4433, 9800 le — International Year of Sustainable Tourism for Development: a, Gorilla beringei. b, Pongo pygmaeus. c, Cercopithecus kandti. d, Cercopithecus aethiops.

No. 4434, 9800 le — Birds of prey: a, Buteogallus meridionalis. b, Aegypius monachus. c, Aviceda jerdoni. d, Geranoaetus polyosoma.

No. 4435, 9800 le — Paintings by Bartolomé Esteban Murillo (1617-82): a, The Holy Family with Dog. b, St. John the Baptist as a Child. c, Two Women at a Window. d, The Flight into Egypt.

No. 4436, 9800 le — Metropolitan Museum of Art, 145th anniv.: a, Head of Tutankhamun, c. 1336-1327 B.C. b, View of Toledo, by El Greco (1541-1614). c, Museum exterior. d, Jeanne Hébuterne, by Amedeo Modigliani (1884-1920).

No. 4437, 9800 le — Space tourism: a, Space Shuttle Atlantis. b, Space plane, blue central curved panel. c, Starship concept craft. d, XCOR Aerospace vehicles.

No. 4438, 9800 le — Pope Benedict XVI, 90th birthday: a, Waving. b, With Pope Francis. c, In prayer, wearing miter. d, With statue.

No. 4439, 9800 le — Christmas: a, Ded Moroz and Snegurochka. b, Joulupukki. c, Saint Nicholas. d, Santa Claus.

No. 4440, 40,000 le, Hendrix, diff. No. 4441, 40,000 le, Stravinsky, diff. No. 4442, 40,000 le, Eva Perón, diff. No. 4443, 40,000 le, Roosevelt, diff. No. 4444, 40,000 le, Ali boxing Ernie Terrell (1939-2014). No. 4445, 40,000 le, Prince George with great-grandmother, Queen Elizabeth II. No. 4446, 40,000 le, Blériot, diff. No. 4447, 40,000 le, 1898 Renault Type A Voiturette. No. 4448. 40,000 le, Edison and 1880 spear point lamp. No. 4449, 40,000 le, Darwin and his notes. No. 4450, 40,000 le, 1977 Mount Nyiragongo eruption, Congo Democratic Republic. No. 4451, 40,000 le, Leptonychotes weddellii and Aptenodytes forsteri. No. 4452, 40,000 le, Pan troglodytes. No. 4453, 40,000 le, Gyps himalayensis. No. 4454, 40,000 le, Self-portrait, by Murillo. No. 4455, 40,000 le, U.S. flag outside of Metropolitan Museum of Art. No. 4456, 40,000 le, Training of space tourists. No. 4457, 40,000 le, Pope Benedict XVI with children. No. 4458, 40,000 le, Grandfather Frost.

2017, Aug. 30 Litho. *Perf. 13¼*

Sheets of 4, #a-d

4421-4439 A725 Set of 19 195.00 195.00

Souvenir Sheets

4440-4458 A725 Set of 19 200.00 200.00

Nos. 4440-4458 each contain one 51x45mm stamp.

Endangered Species of China — A726

No. 4459: a, Grus nigricollis. b, Panthera tigris amoyensis. c, Lipotes vexillifer. d, Rhinopithecus roxellana.

40,000 le, Ailuropoda melanoleuca.

Litho. With Foil Application

2017, Aug. 30 *Perf. 13¼*

4459 A726 9800 le Sheet of 4, #a-d 10.50 10.50

Souvenir Sheet

4460 A726 40,000 le multi 11.00 11.00

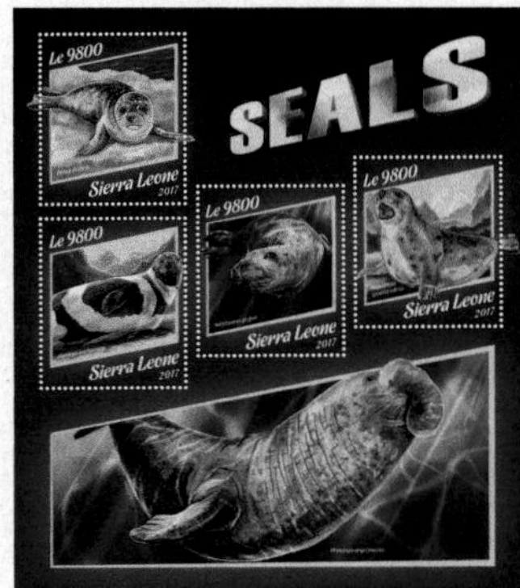

A727

No. 4461, 9800 le — Seals: a, Phoca vitulina. b, Histriophoca fasciata. c, Halichoerus grypus. d, Pagophilus groenlandicus.

No. 4462, 9800 le — Sea lions: a, Eumetopias jubatus. b, Neophoca cinerea. c, Zalophus californianus. d, Arctocephalus forsteri.

No. 4463, 9800 le — Dolphins: a, Stenella coeruleoalba. b, Tursiops truncatus. c, Cephalorhynchus commersonii. d, Tursiops aduncus.

No. 4464, 9800 le — Penguins: a, Eudyptes chrysocome. b, Pygoscelis papua. c, Pygoscelis adeliae. d, Spheniscus magellanicus.

No. 4465, 9800 le — Water birds: a, Anhinga rufa. b, Marus bassanus. c, Podica senegalensis. d, Sula leucogaster.

No. 4466, 9800 le — Bees: a, Tetragonula carbonaria. b, Apis cerana. c, Melipona beecheii. d, Melipona scutellaris.

No. 4467, 9800 le — Butterflies: a, Hypolycaena antifaunus. b, Myrina silenus. c, Graphium policenes. d, Colotis euippe.

No. 4468, 9800 le — Fish: a, Carassius auratus. b, Makaira nigricans. c, Amphiprion ocellaris. d, Astronotus ocellatus.

No. 4469, 9800 le — Sharks: a, Isurus oxyrinchus. b, Sphyrna mokarran. c, Negaprion acutidens. d, Galeocerdo cuvier.

No. 4470, 9800 le — Piranhas: a, Serrasalmus rhombeus. b, Pristobrycon careospinus. c, Pygocentrus nattereri. d, Serrasalmus manueli.

No. 4471, 9800 le — Turtles: a, Gopherus berlandieri. b, Chelonoidis carbonaria. c, Testudo kleinmanni. d, Indotestudo forstenii.

No. 4472, 9800 le — Prehistoric water animals: a, Liopleurodon pachydeirus. b, Carcharocles megalodon. c, Plesiosaurus dolichodeirus. d, Kronosaurus queenslandicus.

No. 4473, 9800 le — Dinosaurs: a, Herrerasaurus ischigualastensis. b, Parasaurolophus walkeri. c, Archaeopteryx lithographica. d, Gallimimus bullatus.

No. 4474, 9800 le — Endangered species: a, Pan paniscus. b, Ailurus fulgens. c, Nasalis larvatus. d, Ara glaucogularis.

No. 4475, 9800 le — Animals in Sierra Leone national parks: a, Lamprotornis splendidus. b, Choeropsis liberiensis. c, Tragelaphus eurycerus. d, Cercocebus atys.

No. 4476, 9800 le — Orchids: a, Helcia brevis. b, Lycaste aromatica. c, Goodyera pubescens. d, Bartholina burmanniana.

No. 4477, 9800 le — Mushrooms: a, Cantharellus cibarius. b, Morchella elata. c, Amanita phalloides. d, Boletus badius.

No. 4478, 9800 le — Minerals: a, Sulphur and ruby. b, Chalcopyrite. c, Zircon. d, Malachite.

No. 4479, 9800 le — Lighthouses: a, Arisaig Lighthouse, Nova Scotia, Canada. b, North Tower, Schiermonnikoog, Netherlands. c, Split Rock Lighthouse, Minnesota. d, Le Four Light, Chenal du Four, France.

No. 4480, 9800 le — Red Cross: a, Red Cross workers lowering coffin into grave. b, Red Cross workers carrying coffin. c, People wearing surgical masks. d, Red Cross workers in vehicle.

No. 4481, 40,000 le, Mirounga angustirostris. No. 4482, 40,000 le, Zalophus wollebaeki. No. 4483, 40,000 le, Orcaella brevirostris. No. 4484, 40,000 le, Spheniscus magellanicus, diff. No. 4485, 40,000 le, Pelecanus rufescens. No. 4486, 40,000 le, Apis dorsata. No. 4487, 40,000 le, Axiocerses harpax. No. 4488, 40,000 le, Arothron manilensis. No. 4489, 40,000 le, Carcharodon carcharias. No. 4490, 40,000 le, Catoprion mento. No. 4491, 40,000 le, Testudo hermanni. No. 4492, 40,000 le, Temnodontosaurus eurycephalus. No. 4493, 40,000 le, Deinonychus antirrhopus. No. 4494, 40,000 le, Tapirus indicus. No. 4495, 40,000 le, Megaceryle maxima. No. 4496, 40,000 le, Cymbidiella rhodochila. No. 4497, 40,000 le, Tricholomopsis rutilans. No. 4498, 40,000 le, Vanadinite. No. 4499, 40,000 le, Holland Harbor Light, Michigan. No. 4500, 40,000 le, Red Cross workers carrying corpse in body bag.

2017, Sept. 29 Litho. *Perf. 13¼*

Sheets of 4, #a-d

4461-4480 A727 Set of 20 205.00 205.00

Souvenir Sheets

4481-4500 A727 Set of 20 210.00 210.00

A728

No. 4501, 9800 le — 30th birthday of Andy Murray, tennis player, with denomination in: a, Orange brown. b, Green. c, Dark blue. d, Violet.

No. 4502, 9800 le — 65th birthday of Sir Vivian Richards, cricket player, with denomination in: a, Orange brown (no wickets or ball). b, Dark blue. c, Dark green. d, Orange brown (wickets and ball visible).

No. 4503, 9800 le — Rugby players: a, Israel Folau. b, Maro Itoje. c, Dane Coles. d, Jamie Heaslip.

No. 4504, 9800 le — 2017 Ice Hockey World Championships: a, William Nylander, flag of Sweden. b, Flag and players from Russia and Finland. c, Flag and players from Sweden and Canada. d, Andrei Vasilevskiy, flag of Russia.

No. 4505, 9800 le — Table tennis players: a, Fan Zhendong. b, Ding Ning. c, Zhang Jike. d, Xu Xin.

No. 4506, 9800 le — Boston Marathon, 120th anniv.: a, Edna Kiplagat, flag of Kenya. b, Katherine Switzer, flag of United States. c, Tom Longboat, old flag of Canada. d, Geoffrey Kirui, flag of Kenya.

No. 4507, 9800 le — 2017 World Track and Field Championships: a, Women's pole vault. b, Shot put. c, Discus. d, 100-meter hurdles.

No. 4508, 9800 le — Formula 1 race car drivers and race cars: a, Valtteri Bottas. b, Lewis Hamilton. c, Daniel Ricciardo. d, Kimi Räikkönen.

No. 4509, 9800 le — Polo players: a, Juan Martín Nero. b, Gonzalo Pieres, Jr. c, Facundo Pieres. d, Pablo Mac Donough.

No. 4510, 9800 le — Golfers: a, Hideki Matsuyama. b, Jordan Spieth. c, Jason Day. d, Rory McIlroy.

No. 4511, 9800 le — 30th birthday of Lionel Messi, soccer player, with denomination in: a, Dark blue (ball on ground). b, Deep mauve. c, Violet. d, Dark blue (ball in air).

No. 4512, 9800 le — 2014 Winter Olympics, Sochi, Russia: a, Ole Einar Bjorndalen, biathlon. b, Jamie Anderson, snowboarding. c, Michael Mulder, speed skating. d, Matthias Mayer, Alpine skiing.

No. 4513, 9800 le — Chess players and chess piece: a, Paul Morphy (1837-84). b, Viswanathan Anand. c, Robert James Fischer (1943-2008). d, Vladimir Kramnik.

No. 4514, 9800 le — Ella Fitzgerald (1917-96), singer: a, Standing behind microphone. b, With Frank Sinatra (1915-98). c, With Louis Armstrong (1901-71). d, Holding microphone.

No. 4515, 9800 le — Marilyn Monroe (1926-62), actress: a, With hand visible. b, With Clark Gable (1901-60). c, With husband, Joe DiMaggio (1914-99). d, With hands behind back.

No. 4516, 9800 le — Charlie Chaplin (1889-1977), actor: a, Seated with dog. b, With wife, Oona O'Neill (1925-91). c, Two images of Chaplin. d, Wearing prisoner's uniform.

No. 4517, 9800 le — John Glenn (1921-2016), astronaut: a, With Friendship 7 space capsule. b, With Space Shuttle Discovery. c, With Mercury capsule and escape tower. d, Wearing space helmet.

No. 4518, 9800 le — 4th birthday of Princess Charlotte of Cambridge: a, With mother, Catherine, Duchess of Cambridge. b, Waving. c, Holding flowers. d, With father, Prince William.

No. 4519, 40,000 le, Murray, diff. No. 4520, 40,000 le, Richards, diff. No. 4521, 40,000 le, Beauden Barrett. No. 4522, 40,000 le, Henrik Lundkvist, flag of Sweden. No. 4523, 40,000 le, Ma Long. No. 4524, 40,000 le, John J. McDermott, winner of 1897 Boston Marathon, flag of United States. No. 4525, 40,000 le, Javelin. No. 4526, 40,000 le, Sebastian Vettel and race car. No. 4527, 40,000 le, Adolfo Cambiaso. No. 4528, 40,000 le, Dustin Johnson. No. 4529, 40,000 le, Messi, diff. No. 4530, 40,000 le, Vic Wild, snowboarding. No. 4531, 40,000 le, Magnus Carlsen, chess piece. No. 4532, 40,000 le, Fitzgerald, diff. No. 4533, 40,000 le, Monroe, diff. No. 4534, 40,000 le, Chaplin, diff. No. 4535, 40,000 le, Glenn, diff. No. 4536, Princess Charlotte, diff.

2017, Oct. 30 Litho. *Perf. 13x13¼*

Sheets of 4, #a-d

4501-4518 A728 Set of 18 185.00 185.00

Souvenir Sheets

Perf. 13¼

4519-4536 A728 Set of 18 190.00 190.00

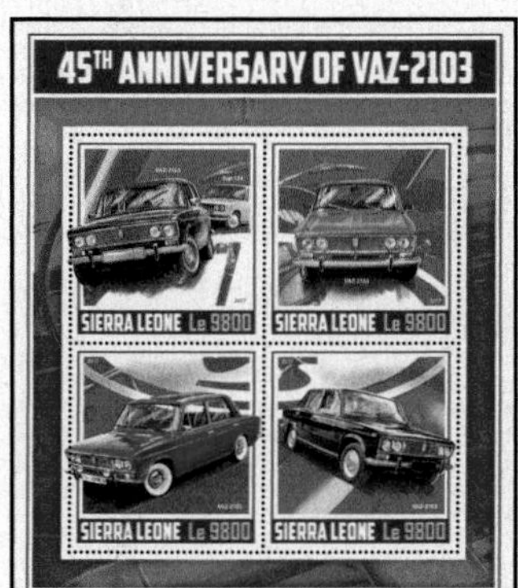

VAZ-2103 Automobile, 45th Anniv. — A729

No. 4537: a, Black VAZ-2103, Fiat 124. b, Red VAZ-2103. c, Blue VAZ-2103. d, Black VAZ-2103.

40,000 le, Brown VAZ-2103.

2017, Oct. 30 Litho. *Perf. 13¼*

4537 A729 9800 le Sheet of 4, #a-d 10.50 10.50

Souvenir Sheet

4538 A729 40,000 le multi 10.50 10.50

Salvation Army — A730

No. 4539 — Salvation Army member: a, Giving bowl of food to mudslide survivor in

Sierra Leone. b, Assisting in earthquake rescue, Mexico c, Serving soldiers in World War I. d, Rescuing flood victims, India.

40,000 le, Salvation Army member holding flag.

2017, Oct. 30 Litho. *Perf. 13¼*

4539 A730 9800 le Sheet of 4, #a-d 10.50 10.50

Souvenir Sheet

4540 A730 40,000 le multi 10.50 10.50

A731

No. 4541, 9800 le — 75th birthday of Paul McCartney, rock musician: a, Playing guitar, denomination at UL. b, Singing into microphone at left, denomination at UR. c, Head of McCartney at left, denomination at UL. d, Playing guitar, denomination at UR.

No. 4542, 9800 le — Johnny Cash (1932-2003), musician: a, Seated, playing guitar. b, Holding cat. c, Standing, train and horse in background. d, Playing guitar, crowd in background.

No. 4543, 9800 le — Isadora Duncan (1877-1927), dancer: a, With column at right. b, Facing backwards at left. c, Dancing, with arms raised. d, With husband, Sergei Yesenin (1895-1925), poet.

No. 4544, 9800 le — Grace Kelly (1929-82), actress and Princess of Monaco, with: a, Frank Sinatra (1915-98), singer. b, Pres. John F. Kennedy (1917-63). c, Husband, Prince Rainier III (1923-2005). d, Cary Grant (1904-86), actor.

No. 4545, 9800 le — Elizabeth Taylor (1932-2011), actress: a, Wearing pearl necklace. b, Wearing necklace with gemstones. c, Wearing lavender dress. d, With Paul Newman (1925-2008), actor.

No. 4546, 9800 le — St. John Paul II (1920-2005): a, Blessing man. b, Embracing child. c, With arms raised. d, With koala.

No. 4547, 9800 le — 70th wedding anniversary of Queen Elizabeth II and Prince Philip: a, Queen Elizabeth II, Prince Philip and Bristish flags. b, Queen Elizabeth II, Princes Philip and Charles, Princess Diana. c, Prince Philip and family of Prince William. d, Queen Elizabeth II, Princess Diana and Prince William.

No. 4548, 9800 le — Alexander Alekhine (1892-1946), world chess champion: a, With black knight and rook at right. b, With white queen and pawn at left. c, Playing chess, clock at LL. d, With hand touching side of his face.

No. 4549, 9800 le — Pierre de Coubertin (1863-1937), founder of International Olympic Committee, with: a, High jumper. b, Rhythmic gymnast with hoop. c, Gymnast in handstand. d, Hurdler.

No. 4550, 9800 le — Polar explorers: a, Richard Evelyn Byrd (1888-1957), and Aptenodytes forsteri. b, Sir Edgeworth David (1858-1934). c, Shirase Nobu (1861-1946). d, Sir Ernest Henry Shackleton (1874-1922), and ship, Endurance.

No. 4551, 9800 le — Inventors: a, Alexander Graham Bell (1847-1922). b, Thomas Edison (1847-1931). c, Alexander Fleming (1881-1955). d, Nikola Tesla (1856-1943).

No. 4552, 9800 le — Paintings and their painters: a, Vision of a Knight, by Raphael (1483-1520). b, The Doni Tondo, by Michelangelo (1475-1564). c, Boys with Mastiff, by Francisco Goya (1746-1828). d, Christ in the Storm on the Sea of Galilee, by Rembrandt (1606-69).

No. 4553, 9800 le — Scouting emblem and: a, Scouts with canoe near tent. b, Scout and Lord Robert Baden-Powell (1857-1941). c, Baden-Powell and flag of Great Britain. d, Scouts pulling rope.

No. 4554, 9800 le — 2017 Nobel Prize winners: a, Economic Sciences laureate Richard Thaler. b, Physics laureates Barry Barish, Rainer Weiss, and Kip Thorne. c, Physiology or Medicine laureates Michael Young, Michael Rosbash, and Jeffrey Hall. d, Chemistry laureates Joachim Frank, Richard Henderson, and Jacques Dubochet.

No. 4555, 9800 le — Sergei Korolev (1907-66), spacecraft designer: a, R7 rocket. b, Korelev and R7 rocket. c, Sputnik 1 and Sputnik 2. d, Luna 3.

No. 4556, 9800 le — Dmitri Mendeleev (1834-1907), formulator of periodic table of elements: a, Writing. b, Standing in laboratory. c, Seated near lab apparatus. d, Holding book.

No. 4557, 9800 le — Caritas Internationalis, 120th anniv.: a, Lorenz Werthmann (1858-1921), founder. b, Children and water bottle. c, Two children with open hands. d, Werthmann holding book.

No. 4558, 9800 le — Red Cross-Red Crescent campaign against malaria: a, World map and mosquito. b, Red Cross worker treating infant. c, Child and mosquito. d, Red Cross worker spraying insecticide.

No. 4559, 40,000 le, McCartney, vert. No. 4560, 40,000 le, Cash, vert. No. 4561, 40,000 le, Portrait of Isadora Duncan, Wearing a Blue Dress and Colored Bead Necklace, by Paul Swan (1883-1972), vert. No. 4562, 40,000 le, Kelly, vert. No. 4563, 40,000 le, Taylor, vert. No. 4564, 40,000 le, St. John Paul II, vert. No. 4565, 40,000 le, Queen Elizabeth II and Prince Philip, vert. No. 4566, 40,000 le, Alekhine and white king, vert. No. 4567, 40,000 le, Coubertin and runner, vert. No. 4568, 40,000 le, Roald Amundsen (1872-1928), polar explorer, vert. No. 4569, 40,000 le, Albert Einstein (1879-1955), physicist, vert. No. 4570, 40,000 le, Mona Lisa, by Leonardo da Vinci (1452-1519), vert. No. 4571, 40,000 le, Baden-Powell, tents and Scouting emblem, vert. No. 4572, 40,000 le, Kazuo Ishiguro, 2017 Nobel laureate in Literature, vert. No. 4573, 40,000 le, Korolev and mechanical drawings, vert. No. 4574, 40,000 le, Mendeleev, vert. No. 4575, 40,000 le, Werthmann, vert. No. 4576, 40,000 le, Child holding sign, mosquito, Red Cross-Red Crescent emblem.

2017, Nov. 30 Litho. *Perf. 13¼*

Sheets of 4, #a-d

4541-4558 A731 Set of 18 185.00 185.00

Souvenir Sheets

4559-4576 A731 Set of 18 190.00 190.00

Nos. 4559-4576 each contain one 41x61mm stamp.

Protestant Reformation, 500th Anniv. — A732

No. 4577 — Religious reformers: a, John Calvin (1509-64). b, William Farel (1489-1565). c, Ulrich Zwingli (1484-1531). d, Martin Bucer (1491-1551).

40,000 le, Martin Luther (1483-1546).

2017, Nov. 30 Litho. *Perf. 13¼*

4577 A732 9800 le Sheet of 4, #a-d 10.50 10.50

Souvenir Sheet

4578 A732 40,000 le Sheet of 4, #a-d 10.50 10.50

No. 4578 contains one 61x41mm stamp.

New Year 2018 (Year of the Dog) — A733

No. 4579: a, Two dogs. b, One dog, Chinese characters and foliage at bottom. c, One dog, Chinese characters at LL, foliage at UR. d, One dog, Chinese characters at UL.

40,000 le, Two dogs, diff.

2017, Nov. 30 Litho. *Perf. 13¼*

4579 A733 9800 le Sheet of 4, #a-d 10.50 10.50

Souvenir Sheet

4580 A733 40,000 le Sheet of 4, #a-d 10.50 10.50

A734

No. 4581, 9800 le — Potamochoerus porcus: a, Hog with nose to ground, Latin name to right of denomination. b, Hog facing forward, Latin name above denomination. c, Hog facing left, Latin name above denomination. d, Hog with head above ground, Latin name to right of denomination.

No. 4582, 9800 le — Hyenas: a, Hyaena hyaena, head at right. b, Crocuta crocuta, head raised above shoulders. c, Crocuta crocuta, head even with shoulders. d, Hyaena hyaena, head at left.

No. 4583, 9800 le — Hippopotamus amphibius: a, Latin name at LR. b, Latin name at UL. c, Mouth closed, Latin name at UR. d, Mouth open, Latin name at UR.

No. 4584, 9800 le — Primates: a, Cercopithecus diana. b, Papio anubis. c, Pan troglodytes verus. d, Procolobus badius.

No. 4585, 9800 le — Bats: a, Epomophorus gambianus. b, Pteropus seychellensis. c, Lavia frons. d, Rousettus aegyptiacus.

No. 4586, 9800 le — Panthera pardus pardus: a, Latin name at UL. b, Head at right, Latin name at UR. c, Latin name at LR. d, Head at left, Latin name at UR.

No. 4587, 9800 le — Loxodonta africana: a, Facing right. b, Facing forward. c, Four elephants. d, Facing left.

No. 4588, 9800 le — Trichechus senegalensis, head pointing to: a, LL. b, UR. c, Right. d, UL.

No. 4589, 9800 le — Dolphins: a, Stenella frontalis. b, Sousa teuszii. c, Lagenodelphis hosei. d, Feresa attenuata.

No. 4590, 9800 le — Orcinus orca: a, Head at LR. b, Two killer whales. c, Head at right. d, Head at top.

No. 4591, 9800 le — Owls: a, Glaucidium tephronotum. b, Strix woodfordii. c, Tyto alba. d, Glaucidium perlatum.

No. 4592, 9800 le — Doves: a, Oena capensis. b, Streptopelia turtur. c, Spilopelia senegalensis. d, Turtur tympanistria.

No. 4593, 9800 le — Hawks: a, Macheiramphus alcinus. b, Melierax metabates. c, Aviceda cuculoides. d, Polyboroides typus.

No. 4594, 9800 le — Cuckoos: a, Chrysococcyx cupreus. b, Clamator glandarius. c, Clamator levaillantii. d, Chrysococcyx caprius.

No. 4595, 9800 le — Kingfishers: a, Halcyon badia. b, Ceryle rudis. c, Megaceryle maxima. d, Alcedo quadribrachys.

No. 4596, 9800 le — Indigo birds: a, Vidua camerunensis. b, Vidua wilsoni. c, Vidua funerea. d, Vidua larvaticola.

No. 4597, 9800 le — Butterflies: a, Belenois aurota. b, Hypolimnas salmacis. c, Euphaedra medon. d, Abisara gerontes.

No. 4598, 9800 le — Lizards: a, Varanus niloticus. b, Chamaeleo gracilis. c, Agama agama. d, Hemidactylus angulatus.

No. 4599, 9800 le — Richard F. Gordon, Jr. (1929-2017), astronaut, and: a, Saturn V rocket. b, Gemini space capsule. c, Apollo 12 patch. d, Apollo 12 crewmates, Pete Conrad (1930-99) and Alan Bean (1932-2018).

No. 4600, 9800 le — First solar-powered train: a, Train and red ribbon. b, Aerial view of train in station at Byron Bay, New South Wales, Australia. c, Train, map of Australia and solar panel. d, Trainside view of train in Byron Bay station.

No. 4601, 40,000 le, Potamochoerus porcus adult and juvenile. No. 4602, 40,000 le, Crocuta crocuta, diff. No. 4603, 40,000 le, Hippopotamus amphibius, diff. No. 4604, 40,000 le, Chlorocebus sabaeus. No. 4605, 40,000 le, Pteropus vampyrus. No. 4606, 40,000 le, Panthera pardus pardus, diff. No. 4607, 40,000 le, Loxodonta africana, diff. No. 4608, 40,000 le, Trichechus senegalensis, diff. No. 4609, 40,000 le, Stenella frontalis, diff. No. 4610, 40,000 le, Orcinus orca, diff. No. 4611, 40,000 le, Ptilopsis leucotis. No. 4612, 40,000 le, Streptopelia semitorquata. No. 4613, 40,000 le, Melierax metabates. No. 4614, 40,000 le, Cuculus canorus. No. 4615, 40,000 le, Ispidina picta. No. 4616, 40,000 le, Vidua chalybeata. No. 4617, 40,000 le, Acraea alciope. No. 4618, 40,000 le, Agama agama, diff. No. 4619, 40,000 le, Gordon holding model of space capsule. No. 4620, 40,000 le, Solar-powered train, Myzomela sanguinolenta.

2017, Dec. 29 Litho. *Perf. 13¼*

Sheets of 4, #a-d

4581-4600 A734 Set of 20 205.00 205.00

Souvenir Sheets

4601-4620 A734 Set of 20 210.00 210.00

A735

No. 4621, 9800 le — Pandas: a, Ailurus fulgens looking forward. b, Ailuropoda melanoleuca adult. c, Ailuropoda melanoleuca adult and cub. d, Ailurus fulgens looking right.

No. 4622, 9800 le — Cats: a, Singapura. b, Turkish Angora. c, Siberian. d, Exotic shorthair.

No. 4623, 9800 le — Fish: a, Phractocephalus hemioliopterus. b, Tetraodon mbu. c, Nemateleotris decora. d, Oxycirrhites typus.

No. 4624, 9800 le — Turtles: a, Elusor macrurus. b, Carettochelys insculpta. c, Chelodina mccordi. d, Pelusios castaneus.

No. 4625, 9800 le — Mushrooms: a, Rubroboletus satanas. b, Cortinarius caperatus. c, Suillus grevillei. d, Boletus edulis.

No. 4626, 9800 le — Minerals: a, Celestine. b, Chiastolite. c, Brazilianite. d, Benitoite and neptunite.

No. 4627, 9800 le — Lighthouses and birds: a, Cape Blanco Lighthouse, Oregon, and Larus pacificus. b, Gay Head Lighthouse, Massachusetts, and Larus fuscus. c, White Shoal Lighthouse, Michigan, and Chroicocephalus philadelphia. d, Point Vicente Lighthouse, California, and Ichthyaetus melanocephalus.

No. 4628, 9800 le — Rotary International: a, Toyota Land Cruiser of Rotary International in Africa. b, Head of Rotary founder Paul P. Harris (1868-1947). c, Harris holding shovel. d, Brazil #1079 and Paul Harris fellow pin and society hanger.

No. 4629, 9800 le — Paintings by Pablo Picasso (1881-1973): a, Girl with a Mandolin (Fanny Tellier). b, The Dream. c, Asleep. d, Three Musicians.

No. 4630, 9800 le — Giuseppe Verdi (1813-1901), composer: a, Seated. b, With jester in red costume. c, With three opera characters. d, With clown.

No. 4631, 9800 le — David Livingstone (1813-73), African explorer: a, Bust of Livingstone, David Livingstone Center, Blantyre, Scotland. b, Seated, holding map. c, With Africans. d, Livingstone and the Lion, statue at David Livingstone Center.

No. 4632, 9800 le — Mohandas K. "Mahatma" Gandhi (1869-1948), Indian nationalist leader: a, Waving. b, With building and lotus flower. c, Head of Gandhi, woman and man. d, Gandhi, woman, lotus flower and flag of India.

No. 4633, 9800 le — Mustafa Kemal Atatürk (1881-1938), President of Turkey: a, Holding top hat. b, On horse. c, With soldiers, wearing top hat. d, Battle of Gallipoli.

No. 4634, 9800 le — 50th birthday of King Felipe VI of Spain: a, With Queen Letizia, Princess Leonor and Infanta Sofia. b, In suit and tie, waving. c, In military uniform, waving. d, With King Juan Carlos, Princess Leonor and Infanta Sofia.

No. 4635, 9800 le — Papcy of Pope Francis, 5th anniv: a, Seated behind microphone. b, Dome ceiling in background. c, Crucifix in background. d, With child and flag of Argentina.

No. 4636, 9800 le — 55th birthday of Garry Kasparov, chess champion: a, With chessboard and clock. b, With signature. c, With knight at left. d, With pawn at left.

No. 4637, 9800 le — Henry Ford (1863-1947), automobile manufacturer, and: a, 1916 Model T Red Cross ambulance. b, 1965 Ford Mustang. c, 1941 Soybean car prototype. d, 1929 Ford Model AA fire truck.

No. 4638, 9800 le — Special transportation: a, Kamov KA-32 helicopter, MV Xue Long. b, BAS Twin Otter airplane, Bandvagn 206. c,

UNICAT TerraCross 59 truck, Iveco Daily 4x4 van. d, Mercedes-Benz road-rail Unimog truck.

No. 4639, 9800 le — Fire vehicles: a, Royal Air Force Whirlwind HAR.10 helicopter. b, Alvis Salamander Mk 6 crash tender. c, Royal Air Force Scammell/Carmichael MkX crash tender. d, Sikorsky S-64 firefighting air-crane.

No. 4640, 9800 le — High-speed trains: a, ETR 1000, France. b, CR400AF, People's Republic of China. c, NSB BM 74, Norway. d, TCDD HT80000, Turkey.

No. 4641, 40,000 le, Ailurus fulgens, diff. No. 4642, 40,000 le, British shorthair cat. No. 4643, 40,000 le, Pomacanthus paru. No. 4644, 40,000 le, Geochelone nigra. No. 4645, 40,000 le, Agaricus silvicola. No. 4646, 40,000 le, Spessartine garnet. No. 4647, 40,000 le, Duxbury Pier Lighthouse, Massachusetts. No. 4648, 40,000 le, Harris and Rotary International emblem.No. 4649, 40,000 le, Violin, by Picasso. No. 4650, 40,000 le, Verdi and clown, diff. No. 4651, 40,000 le, Livingstone. No. 4652, 40,000 le, Lotus flowers, and Gandhi in crowd. No. 4653, 40,000 le, Atatürk and flag of Turkey. No. 4654, 40,000 le, Wedding of King Felipe VI of Spain and Queen Letizia. No. 4655, 40,000 le, Pope Francis and dove. No. 4656, 40,000 le, Kasparov, diff. No. 4657, 40,000 le, Ford and 1908 Ford Model T and 1964 Ford GT40. No. 4658, 40,000 le, ZIL-2906 truck. No. 4659, 40,000 le, Carmichael MFV crash tender. No. 4660, 40,000 le, W7 Series Shinkansen train, Japan.

2018, Jan. 30 Litho. *Perf. 13¼*

Sheets of 4, #a-d

4621-4640 A735 Set of 20 205.00 205.00

Souvenir Sheets

4641-4660 A735 Set of 20 210.00 210.00

Nos. 4641-4660 each contain one 43x66mm stamp.

2018 World Cup Soccer Championships, Russia — A736

2018 World Cup mascot, Zabivaka: No. 4661, 7750 le, With soccer ball on back. No. 4662, 7750 le, Dribbling soccer ball. No. 4663, 7750 le, Running without ball. No. 4664, 7750 le, On knees.

Perf. 13¼x12¾

2018, Feb. 27 Litho.

4661-4664 A736 Set of 4 8.25 8.25

A737

No. 4665, 9800 le — Ursus maritimus: a, Walking to right. b, Adult and cub. c, Walking forward. d, In water.

No. 4666, 9800 le — Service dogs: a, Belgian Malinois special services dogs. b, Labrador retriever guide dog. c, St. Bernard mountain rescue dog. d, Rottweiler police dog.

No. 4667, 9800 le — Whales: a, Physeter macrocephalus. b, Orcinus orca. c, Monodon monoceros. d, Delphinapterus leucas.

No. 4668, 9800 le — Bee-eaters: a, Merops oreobates. b, Merops apiaster. c, Merops nubicoides. d, Merops persicus chrysocercus.

No. 4669, 9800 le — Parrots: a, Ara macao. b, Guaruba guarouba. c, Amazona aestiva. d, Aratinga solstitialis.

No. 4670, 9800 le — Extinct animals: a, Coelodonta antiquitatis. b, Aphanapteryx bonasia. c, Mammuthus primigenius. d, Smilodon gracilis.

No. 4671, 9800 le — Stamps on stamps: a, Laos #42 and others. b, Cayman Islands #87 and others. c, South Africa #1022 and others. d, Poland #1309 and others.

No. 4672, 9800 le — Reichstag Fire, 85th anniv.: a, Ground level view of Reichstag burning. b, Paul von Hindenburg (1847-1934), President of German Reich, and truck. c, Aerial view of Reichstag burning. d, Marinus van der Lubbe (1909-34), convicted arsonist, and soldiers.

No. 4673, 9800 le — Red Cross: a, Red Cross horse-drawn carriage. b, Red Cross workers in World War I. c, Red Cross Mutt Jeep. d, Red Cross Airbus helicopter.

No. 4674, 9800 le — International Committee of the Red Cross, 155th anniv.: a, Child and dog sleeping under Red Cross blankets. b, Female Red Cross worker holding child. c, Red Cross workers and crowd of people. d, Red Cross worker assisting injured man.

No. 4675, 9800 le — Roald Amundsen (1872-1928), polar explorer: a, Amundsen, flag of Norway, map of Arctic. b, Dornier Wal N-24 used in polar expedition. c, Sled dogs and the Fram. d, Amundsen wearing parka.

No. 4676, 9800 le — Camille Pissarro (1830-1903), and his paintings: a, Farm at Montfoucault. b, The Bazincourt Steeple. c, The Roofs of Old Rouen, Gray Weather. d, Pont Boieldieu, Rouen, Damp Weather.

No. 4677, 9800 le — Pyotr Ilyich Tchaikovsky (1840-93), composer: a, Playing piano. b, With ballet dancers. c, Conducting. d, Portrait of Tchaikovsky, by Vasily Svarog (1883-1946).

No. 4678, 9800 le — George Michael (1963-2016), rock musician: a, Dancing at left, singing at right. b, Wearing red jacket at left. c, Wearing jacket, no shirt at left. d, Holding guitar at left.

No. 4679, 9800 le — George Stephenson (1781-1848), inventor and railroad pioneer: a, 1835 Adler locomotive. b, 1825 Locomotion No. 1. c, 1838 LMR 57 Lion. d, 1830 Planet locomotive.

No. 4680, 9800 le — Ferrari automobiles: a, Ferrari 348. b, Ferrari F50. c, Ferrari LaFerrari. d, Ferrari 488 GTB.

No. 4681, 9800 le — Submarines: a, K-152 Nerpa, Russia. b,Type 212, Germany. c, USS Jimmy Carter, U.S. d, HMS Astute, Great Britain.

No. 4682, 9800 le — Flight of Vostok 6, 55th anniv.: a, Valentina Tereshkova waving. b, Vostok 6. c, Tereshkova, diff. d, Sergei Korolev (1907-66), rocket engineer.

No. 4683, 9800 le — Aircraft piloted by John Young (1930-2018), astronaut: a, McDonnell F4H-1 Phantom II. b, XF8U-3 Crusader III. c, Space Shuttle Columbia (launch). d, Space Shuttle Columbia in orbit.

No. 4684, 40,000 le, Ursus maritimus in water, diff. No. 4685, 40,000 le, East European shepherd anti-tank dog. No. 4686, 40,000 le, Megaptera novaeangliae. No. 4687, 40,000 le, Merops philippinus. No. 4688, 40,000 le, Ara macao and Ara ararauna. No. 4689, 40,000 le, Deinotherium giganteum. No. 4690, 40,000 le, Russia #7735b and other stamps. No. 4691, 40,000 le, 1926 Mercedes L1 LKw near Reichstag fire. No. 4692, 40,000 le, Henry Dunant (1828-1910), founder of International Red Cross, Nobel medal, Red Cross worker holding child. No. 4693, 40,000 le, Red Cross flag, child getting water from faucet. No. 4694, 40,000 le, Amundsen's airship, Norge. No. 4695, 40,000 le, Pissarro and The Artist's Garden at Eragny. No. 4696, 40,000 le, Tchaikovsky, score, piano keys, and signature. No. 4697, 40,000 le, Michael, diff. No. 4698, 40,000 le, Stephenson, British flag, railroad tracks. No. 4699, 40,000 le, Ferrari Enzo. No. 4700, 40,000 le, A26 submarine, Sweden. No. 4701, 40,000 le, Tereshkova and Vostok 6. No. 4702, 40,000 le, Young, space helmet, U.S. flag.

2018, Feb. 27 Litho. *Perf. 13¼*

Sheets of 4, #a-d

4665-4683 A737 Set of 19 195.00 195.00

Souvenir Sheets

4684-4702 A737 Set of 19 200.00 200.00

A738

No. 4703, 9800 le — Princess Diana (1961-97): a, Holding child. b, Wearing red sweater. c, Wearing tiara. d, Feeding children.

No. 4704, 9800 le — Dr. Martin Luther King, Jr. (1929-68), civil rights leader: a, With his family, at piano. b, With Nobel Medal. c, With U.S. flag. d, With U.S. flag and doves.

No. 4705, 9800 le — Nelson Mandela (1918-2013), President of South Africa: a, With Pope John Paul II (1920-2005). b, With crowd, placard and joined hands. c, With his first wife, Evelyn Mase (1922-2004), child and dove. d, With Princess Diana.

No. 4706, 9800 le — Yuri Gagarin (1934-68), first man in space: a, Monument to Gagarin in Kyrgyzstan. b, Lifting dumbbells. c, Wearing space helmet. d, With Vostok 1.

No. 4707, 9800 le — Paintings by Ivan Shishkin (1832-98): a, Twilight. b, Wood in the Evening. c, Morning in a Pine Forest. d, Little House in Dusseldorf.

No. 4708, 9800 le — Richard Wagner (1813-83), composer: a, Facing forward. b, At piano. c, Richard Wagner in Venice, painting by Vicente Garcia de Paredes (1845-1903). d, Facing left.

No. 4709, 9800 le — James Bond character, 65th anniv.: a, Bond as portrayed by Roger Moore (1927-2017). b, Bond's Aston Martin DB5. c, Bond's Lotus Esprit S1. d, Bond as portrayed by Pierce Brosnan.

No. 4710, 9800 le — 1941-42 Battle of Moscow: a, Soviet soldier and clock tower. b, German soldiers and tanks. c, German soldiers, tank and signpost. d, Soviet soldiers and barricades.

No. 4711, 9800 le — Oragnization of African Unity, 55th anniv.: a, Child playing with tire, child waving. b, African woman. c, Bob Marley (1945-81), Reggae musician, and instruments. d, Eliud Kipchoge, marathon runner.

No. 4712, 9800 le — Table tennis players: a, Hou Yingchao. b, Xu Xin. c, Koki Niwa. d, Omar Assar.

No. 4713, 9800 le — Lamborghini vehicles, 55th anniv.: a, Lamborghini 350 GT. b, Lamborghini Miura and Lamborghini Huracan. c, Lamborghini Estoque and Lamborghini Aventador. d, Lamborghini Diablo and Lamborghini 1R tractor.

No. 4714, 9800 le — Harley-Davidson motorcycles, 115th anniv.: a, Harley-Davidson Electra Glide Ultra Classic. b, Harley-Davidson XL1200C. c, Harley-Davidson Dyna. d, Harley-Davidson WL.

No. 4715, 9800 le — Dogs: a, Chihuahua. b, Poodle. c, Dalmatian. d, Jack Russell terrier.

No. 4716, 9800 le — Dugong dugon: a, With Remora remora. b, With three Gnathanodon speciosus. c, With two Gnathanodon speciosus. d, Alone.

No. 4717, 9800 le — Water birds: a, Lophodytes cucullatus. b, Mergus merganser. c, Bucephala islandica. d, Fulmarus glacialis.

No. 4718, 9800 le — Butterflies: a, Eurytides serville. b, Morpho deidamia. c, Stichophthalma louisa. d, Charaxes jasius.

No. 4719, 9800 le — Shells: a, Pomacea bridgesii. b, Liguus fasciatus. c, Papustyla pulcherrima. d, Oreohelix idahoensis.

No. 4720, 9800 le — Dinosaurs: a, Protoceratops andrewsi. b, Stegosaurus stenops. c, Therizinosaurus cheloniformis. d, Dilophosaurus wetherilli.

No. 4721, 9800 le — Orchids: a, Masdevallia ignea. b, Coelogyne fimbriata. c, Coelogyne nitida. d, Arundina graminifolia.

No. 4722, 40,000 le, Princess Diana holding child, diff. No. 4723, 40,000 le, Dr. King behind microphones. No. 4724, 40,000 le, Mandela, dove and South Africans. No. 4725, 40,000 le, Gagarin near airplane. No. 4726, 40,000 le, Walk in the Forest, by Shishkin. No. 4727, 40,000 le, Wagner facing right. No. 4728, 40,000 le, Bond as portrayed by Timothy Dalton. No. 4729, 40,000 le, Gen. Georgy Zhukov (1896-1974). No. 4730, 40,000 le, Mandela, diff. No. 4731, 40,000 le, Chen Meng, table tennis player. No. 4732, 40,000 le, Lamborghini Urus and Lamborghini LM002. No. 4733, 40,000 le, Harley-Davidson VRSC. No. 4734, 40,000 le, German shepherd. No. 4735, 40,000 le, Dugong dugon, diff. No. 4736, 40,000 le, Fratercula arctica. No. 4737, 40,000 le, Panacea prola. No. 4738, 40,000 le, Tropidophora cuvieriana. No. 4739, 40,000 le, Brasilotitan nemophagus. No. 4740, 40,000 le, Stanheopea wardii.

2018, Mar. 30 Litho. *Perf. 13¼*

Sheets of 4, #a-d

4703-4721 A738 Set of 19 190.00 190.00

Souvenir Sheets

4722-4740 A738 Set of 19 195.00 195.00

2018 Winter Olympics, Pyeong Chang, South Korea — A739

No. 4741 — Events, names of gold medalists and flags of their country: a, Alpine skiing, Frida Hansdottir, Sweden. b, Figure skating, Aljona Savchenko, Bruno Massot, Germany. c, Speed skating, Carlijn Achtereekte, Netherlands. d, Biathon, Johannes Thingnes Bo, Norway.

40,000 le, Cross-country skiing, Simen Hegstad Krüger, Norway.

2018, Mar. 30 Litho. *Perf. 13¼*

4741 A739 9800 le Sheet of 4, #a-d 10.00 10.00

Souvenir Sheet

4742 A739 40,000 le multi 10.50 10.50

A740

No. 4743, 9800 le — Adult Panthera leo and: a, Children and Rotary International emblem. b, Women and Lions Club International emblem. c, Man, woman, Lions Club International emblem. d, Lion cub and Rotary International emblem.

No. 4744, 9800 le — Tigers: a, Panthera tigris tigris, blue green panel at top. b, Panthera tigris sondaica, blue green panel at top. c, Panthera tigris sondaica, blue green panel at bottom. d, Panthera tigris tigris, blue green panel at bottom.

No. 4745, 9800 le — Siberian husky sled dogs with: a, Dark blue panel at top, denomination at LL. b, Dark blue panel at top, denomination at LR. c, Dark blue panel at bottom, denomination at UL. d, Dark blue panel at bottom, denomination at UR.

No. 4746, 9800 le — Dolphins: a, Lagenorhynchus obliquidens. b, Cephalorhynchus commersonii. c, Lagenorhynchus albirostris. d, Sousa chinensis.

No. 4747, 9800 le — Owls: a, Bubo ascalaphus. b, Bubo capensis. c, Strix woodfordii. d, Bubo africanus.

No. 4748, 9800 le — Kingfishers: a, Halcyon coromanda. b, Todiramphus macleayii. c, Ceryle rudis. d, Actenoides concretus.

No. 4749, 9800 le — Bees: a, Apis mellifera, denomination at LL. b, Apis mellifera, denomination at LR. c, Bombus jonellus. d, Bombus terrestris.

No. 4750, 9800 le — Endangered species: a, Gorilla gorilla. b, Eretmochelys imbricata. c, Neophocaena asiaeorientalis. d, Eudorcas tilonura.

No. 4751, 9800 le — Alexander Wilson (1766-1813), ornithologist: a, Wilson and Setophaga pinus. b, Ardea cinerea. c, Icterus galbula. d, Sialia currocoides.

No. 4752, 9800 le — Paintings by Edouard Manet (1832-83): a, Self-portrait with Palette. b, The Railway. c, The Balcony. d, The Luncheon on the Grass.

No. 4753, 9800 le — Louvre Museum, Paris, 225th anniv: a, Louvre Palace and Pyramid, flag of France. b, Louis XIV on Horseback, sculpture by François Girardon (1628-1715). c, Armchair made by Jean-Baptiste-Claude Séné (1748-1803) and agate ewer. d, Imaginary View of Grande Galerie in the Louvre, by Hubert Robert (1733-1808).

No. 4754, 9800 le — Princess Charlotte of Cambridge, 3rd birthday: a, With mother, Duchess of Cambridge. b, Wearing scarf. c, Holding flowers. d, With parents and brother, Prince George.

No. 4755, 9800 le — Birth of Prince Louis of Cambridge: a, With parents. b, Wearing hospital cap. c, Princes Willliam and George, Princess Charlotte. d, With mother, Duchess of Cambridge.

No. 4756, 9800 le — Baroness Margaret Thatcher (1925-2013), Prime Minister of Great Britain: a, With her family in 1959. b, Standing near mine field. c, Shaking hands with Nelson Mandela (1918-2013), President of South Africa. d, With Indira Gandhi (1917-84), Prime Minister of India.

No. 4757, 9800 le — Walt Disney Company, 95th anniv.: a, Walt Disney (1901-66), founder, and Neuschwanstein Castle. b, Disney and film strip. c, Disney and cartoon sketch pad. d, Disney and movie camera.

No. 4758, 9800 le — Bobby Fischer (1943-2008), World Chess Champion: a, Denomination at LL. b, Denomination at LR. c, Denomination at UL. d, Denomination at UR.

No. 4759, 9800 le — Volkswagen Beetle, 80th anniv.: a, 1973 Super Beetle. b, 2017 Volkswagen Beetle Dune. c, 1957 Volkswagen Type 1 Beetle Cabriolet. d, 2011 Volkswagen Beetle RSI 3200cc.

No. 4760, 9800 le — Chinese high-speed trains: a, CRH380A. b, CRH2. c, Transrapid SMT. d, CRH5.

No. 4761, 9800 le — National Aeronautics and Space Administration, 60th anniv: a, Ed White (1930-67), astronaut and Gemini 4. b, John Glenn (1921-2016), astronaut and senator, and Friendship 7. c, Pres. John F. Kennedy (1917-63), Kennedy Space Center and U.S. flag. d, John Young (1930-2018), astronaut, and Apollo 16 Moon Rover.

No. 4762, 40,000 le, Panthera leo and Lions Club International emblem. No. 4763, 40,000 le, Panthera tigris tigris, diff. No. 4764, 40,000 le, Greenland dogs. No. 4765, 40,000 le, Delphinus delphis. No. 4766, 40,000 le, Bubo lacteus. No. 4767, 40,000 le, Dacelo novaeguineae. No. 4768, 40,000 le, Apis mellifera, diff. No. 4769, 40,000 le, Dendrolagus matschiei. No. 4770, 40,000 le, Wilson and Dryocopus pileatus, No. 4771, 40,000 le, A Bar at the Folies-Bergère, by Manet. No. 4772, 40,000 le, Bust of Marie Antoinette (1755-93), by Louis-Simon Boizot (1743-1809), and bust of Guillaume-Chrétien de Lamoignon de Malesherbes (1721-94), by Antoine-Denis Chaudet (1763-1810). No. 4773, 40,000 le, Princess Charlotte and Duchess of Cambridge, diff. No. 4774, 40,000 le, Prince Louis of Cambridge, diff. No. 4775, 40,000 le, Thatcher and Queen Elizabeth II. No. 4776, 40,000 le, Disney drawing at easel. No. 4777. 40,000 le, Fischer, diff. No. 4778, 40,000 le, 1938 Volkswagen Beetle. No. 4779, 40,000 le, CRH6. No. 4780, 40,000 le, Neil Armstrong (1930-2012), astronaut, and Apollo 11.

2018, Apr. 27 Litho. *Perf. 13¼*

Sheets of 4, #a-d

4743-4761	A740	Set of 19	190.00	190.00

Souvenir Sheets

4762-4780	A740	Set of 19	195.00	195.00

Independence of the Baltic States, Cent. — A741

No. 4781: a, Jonas Basanavicius (1851-1927), leader of Lithuanian independence movement, House of the Signatories, Vilnius, and flag of Lithuania. b, Karlis Ulmanis (1877-1942), Prime Minister of Latvia, Latvian National Theater, Riga, and flag of Latvia. c, Konstantin Päts (1874-1956), first President of Estonia, Endla Theate, Pärnu, flag of Estonia. d, Statues of Liberty in Kaunas, Lithuania, Riga, Latvia and Tallinn, Estonia, map of Lithuania, Latvia and Estonia.

40,000 le, Map of Sierra Leone.

2018, Apr. 27 Litho. *Perf. 13¼*

4781	A741	9800 le Sheet of 4, #a-d	10.00	10.00

Souvenir Sheet

4782	A741	40,000 le multi	10.50	10.50

2018 Estonian Philatelic Exhibition, Tallinn.

AIR POST STAMPS

Catalogue values for unused stamps in this section are for Never Hinged items.

Independence — Progress Issue

Nos. 197, 199, 204 and 206 Surcharged in Carmine, Red, Violet, Blue or Orange

No. C3

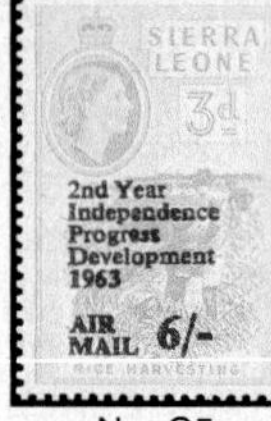

No. C5

Perf. 13, 13½

1963, Apr. 27 Wmk. 4 Engr.

Center in Black

C1	A27	7p on 1½p (C)	.25	.25
C2	A27	1sh3p on 1½p (R)	.25	.25
C3	A28	2sh6p brn org (V)	2.50	.50
C4	A28	3sh on 3p (Bl)	.40	.25
C5	A28	6sh on 3p (O)	1.00	.25
C6	A27	11sh on 10sh (C)	2.00	1.40
C7	A27	11sh on £1 (C)	800.00	300.00
		Nos. C1-C6 (6)	6.40	2.90

Nos. 221, 224, 213, 223 and 207 Srchd. or Ovptd. in Brown, Red, Black, Violet, Ultra or Orange

Perf. 13x13½, 13½x13, 13

1963, Nov. 4 Wmk. 4, 336

C8	A31	7p on 3p (Br)	.25	.25
C9	A32	1sh3p blue & blk (R)	1.50	1.20
C10	A30	2sh6p on 4p (Bk)	1.00	1.00
C11	A31	3sh on 3p (V)	1.90	1.90
C12	A32	6sh on 6p (U)	.80	.80
C13	A27	£1 org & blk (O)	29.00	29.00
		Nos. C8-C13 (6)	34.45	34.15

Overprint is in 6 lines on Nos. C8, C11 and C12. A number of surcharge varieties and errors exist.

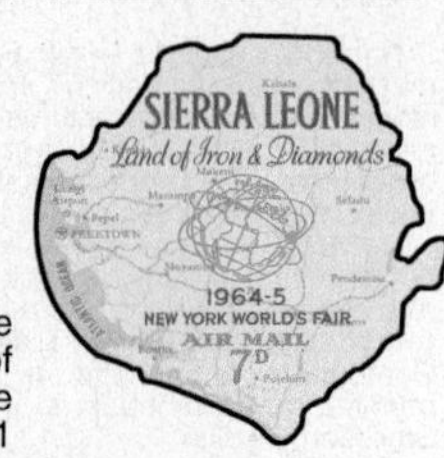

Unisphere and Map of Sierra Leone AP1

Engraved and Lithographed

1964, Feb. 10 Unwmk. *Die Cut*

Self-adhesive

C14	AP1	7p	multicolored	.25	.25
C15	AP1	9p	multicolored	.25	.25
C16	AP1	1sh3p	multicolored	.25	.25
C17	AP1	2sh6p	multicolored	.35	.35
C18	AP1	3sh6p	multicolored	.50	.50
C19	AP1	6sh	multicolored	.65	.65
C20	AP1	11sh	multicolored	.90	1.40
			Nos. C14-C20 (7)	3.15	3.65

New York World's Fair, 1964-65.

For surcharge see No. C33.

John F. Kennedy AP2

1964, May 11 Self-adhesive

C21	AP2	7p	multicolored	.25	.25
C22	AP2	9p	multicolored	.25	.25
C23	AP2	1sh3p	multicolored	.25	.25
C24	AP2	2sh6p	multicolored	.35	.30
C25	AP2	3sh6p	multicolored	.40	.60
C26	AP2	6sh	multicolored	.65	1.25
C27	AP2	11sh	multicolored	.80	2.25
			Nos. C21-C27 (7)	2.95	5.15

For surcharges see Nos. C32, C34-C36.

Nos. 241, 213, 219 and 218 Srchd. in Dark Blue, Black, Red or Violet Blue

Perf. 11½x11, 13½x13, 13x13½

1964, Aug. 4 Engr. Wmk. 336

C28	A36	7c on 1sh3p (#241) (DB)	.25	.25
C29	A30	20c on 4p (#213)	.40	.40
C30	A29	30c on 10sh (#219) (R)	.60	.60
C31	A29	40c on 5sh (#218) (VB)	.70	.70
		Nos. C28-C31 (4)	1.95	1.95

Map-shaped Issues of 1964 Surcharged in Red or Black

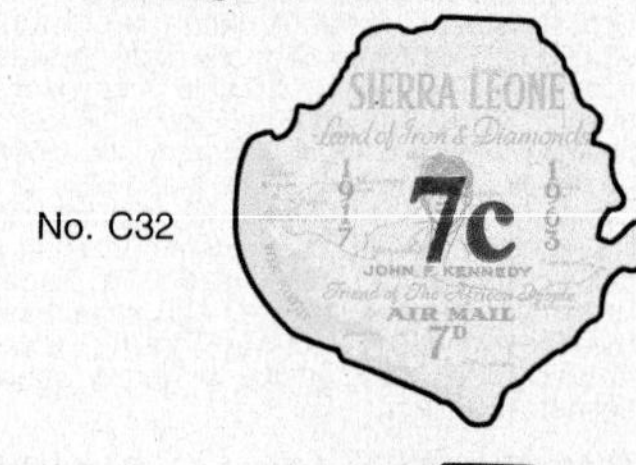

No. C32

No. C33

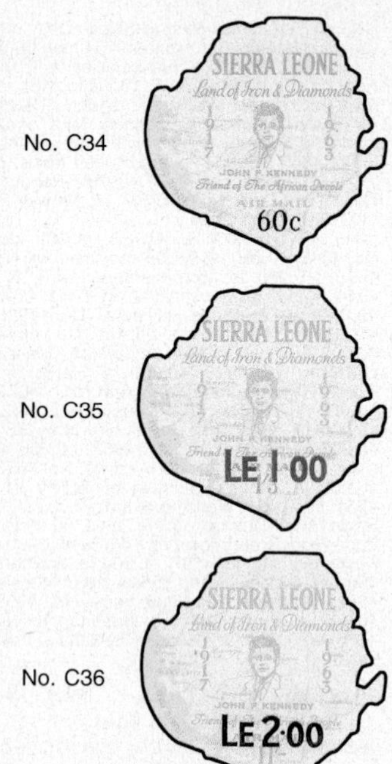

No. C34

No. C35

No. C36

Engraved and Lithographed

1964-65 Unwmk. *Die Cut*

C32	AP2	7c on 7p (#C21) (R)	.25	.25
C33	AP1	7c on 9p (#C15)	.85	.85
C34	AP2	60c on 9p (#C22)	1.25	1.25
C35	AP2	1 le on 1sh3p (#C23) (R)	1.00	2.00
C36	AP2	2 le on 11sh (#C27)	2.00	3.75
		Nos. C32-C36 (5)	5.35	8.10

Issue dates: Aug. 4, 1964, Nos. C35-C36. Jan. 20, 1965, Nos. C32, C34. April, 1965, No. C33.

Regular Issue of 1963 Surcharged with "AIRMAIL" added

Designs of Surcharge: No. C37, C39-C40, Sir Milton Margai and Sir Winston Churchill. No. C38, Margai. No. C41, Churchill.

Wmk. 336

Photo. *Perf. 14*

C37	A35	7c on 2p (#230)	.65	.25
C38	A34	15c on ½p (#227)	.45	.75
C39	A35	30c on 6p (#233)	1.90	.50
C40	A35	1 le on £1 (#239)	5.50	1.75
C41	A34	2 le on 10sh (#238)	11.50	5.50
		Nos. C37-C41 (5)	20.00	8.75

The portraits and inscription on No. C39 are white, the denomination and "AIRMAIL" are orange.

Ten more surcharges were issued Nov. 9, 1965: "2c" on Nos. C16, C23 and C25. "3c" on Nos. C14 and C22. "5c" on Nos. C17-C19, C24, and C26. Value $4 each.

One further surcharge was issued Jan. 28, 1966: "TWO/Leones" on No. C39. Value $10.

Type of Regular Issue and

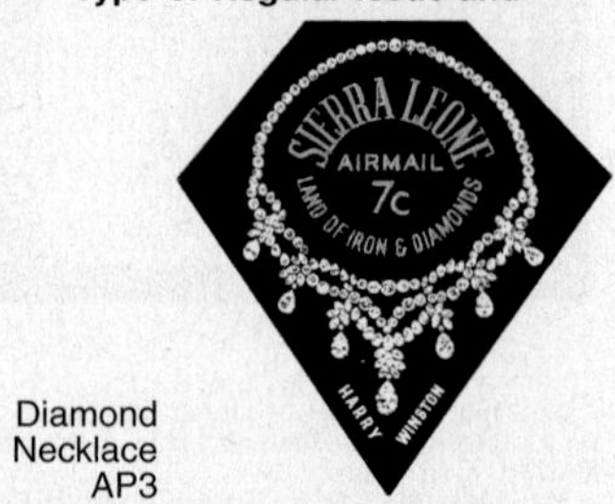

Diamond Necklace AP3

Litho.; Reversed Embossing
1965, Dec. 17 Unwmk. *Die Cut*
Self-adhesive

C53 AP3 7c blk, grn, gold & bl .80 .25
C54 AP3 15c blk, brnz, car & bl 1.75 1.25

Engr. and Embossed on Paper

C55 A41 40c multi, *cream* 4.00 4.00
Nos. C53-C55 (3) 6.55 5.50

Various advertisements printed on peelable paper backing. Nos. C54-C55 have side tabs for handling and come packed in boxes of 100. No. C53 is without side tab and comes 25 stamps attached to one sheet.

For overprints and surcharges see Nos. C68-C69, C79-C83.

Nos. 248, 229, 234 and 236 Surcharged and Overprinted

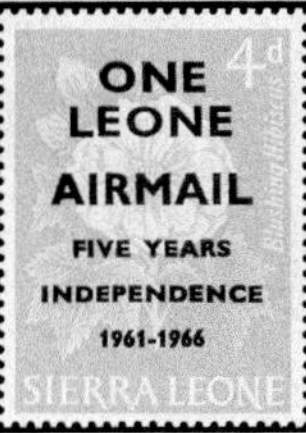

Nos. 232 Surcharged and Overprinted

1966, Apr. 27 Wmk. 336

C56 A37 7c on 3p pur & red .25 .25
C57 A34 15c on 1sh multi 1.00 .40
C58 A34 25c on 2sh6p multi .65 .65
C59 A34 50c on 1½p multi 1.25 1.25
C60 A34 1 le on 4p multi 2.00 *3.25*
Nos. C56-C60 (5) 5.15 5.80

The denomination on No. C60 is spelled out "One Leone."

Self-adhesive & Die Cut
Nos. C61-C131, C135-C142 are self-adhesive and die cut.

Gold Coin Type of Regular Issue

Designs: 7c, 10c, ¼ Golde coin. 15c, 30c, ½ Golde coin. 50c, 2 le, 1 Golde coin. (7c, 15c, 50c, Map of Sierra Leone. 10c, 30c, 2 le, Lion's head.)

Diameter: 7c, 10c, 38mm; 15c, 30c, 54mm; 50c, 2 le, 82mm.

Lithographed; Embossed on Gilt Foil
1966, Nov. 12 Unwmk.

C61 A42 7c red & orange .25 .25
C62 A42 10c dull blue & red .25 .25
C63 A42 15c red & orange .30 .30
C64 A42 30c black & rose lilac .50 .60
C65 A42 50c rose lilac & emer 1.00 1.00
C66 A42 2 le green & black 4.50 4.50
Nos. C61-C66 (6) 6.80 6.90

Advertising printed on paper backing.

Type of Regular Issue, 1965 and No. C55 Surcharged

1967, Dec. 2 Engr. & Embossed

C67 A41 10c multi (red frame), *cream* .50 .50
a. Black frame .50 .50
C68 A41 11½c on 40c multi, *cr* .40 .40
C69 A41 25c on 40c multi, *cr* 1.00 1.00
Nos. C67-C69 (3) 1.90 1.90

Eagle — AP4

Embossed Foil on Black Paper
1967, Dec. 2 Unwmk.

C70 AP4 9½c black, gold & red .90 .90
C71 AP4 15c black, gold & grn 1.40 1.40

Various advertisements printed on peelable paper backing. See Nos. C98-C99, C118-C124.

Map Type of Regular Issue

Designs: Each denomination shows map of Africa with map of one of the following countries — Portuguese Guinea, South Africa, Mozambique, Rhodesia, South West Africa or Angola. Sheets of 30 (6x5) have 5 horizontal rows containing one stamp of each design.

1968, Sept. 25 Litho.

C72 A43 7½c multicolored .25 .25
C73 A43 9½c multicolored .30 .30
C74 A43 14½c multicolored .35 .35
C75 A43 18½c multicolored .35 .35
C76 A43 25c multicolored .45 .45
C77 A43 1 le multicolored 3.25 4.50
C78 A43 2 le multicolored 9.00 10.50
Nos. C72-C78 (7) 13.95 16.70
7 Strips of 6, 1 of each design 122.50

No. C55 Ovptd. and Srchd. in Red Similar to Nos. 364-368
Engraved and Embossed on Paper
1968, Nov. 30

C79 A41 6½c on 40c multi .25 .25
C80 A41 17½c on 40c multi .55 .55
C81 A41 22½c on 40c multi .55 .55
C82 A41 28½c on 40c multi .75 .75
C83 A41 40c multicolored 1.10 1.10
Nos. C79-C83 (5) 3.20 3.20

Scroll Type of Regular Issue

7½c, #C54. 9½c, #C70. 20c, #C16. 30c, #C26. 50c, #165. 2 le, #207 with "2nd Year of Independence" overprint. All are horiz.

1969, Mar. 1 Litho.

C84 A44 7½c multicolored .30 .25
C85 A44 9½c multicolored .30 .30
C86 A44 20c multicolored .50 .50
C87 A44 30c multicolored .75 .70
C88 A44 50c multicolored 2.00 1.50
C89 A44 2 le multicolored 12.00 12.00
Nos. C84-C89 (6) 15.85 15.25

Various advertisements printed on peelable paper backing. No. C84 has side tab for handling and comes packed in boxes of 50. Nos. C85-C89 are without side tabs and come 20 stamps attached to one sheet.

For surcharges see Nos. C135-C136.

Pepel Port Types of Regular Issue

Designs: 7½c, 15c, Globe, tanker, flags of Sierra Leone and Japan. Anvil Shape with Flags of Sierra Leone and: 9½c, 2 le, Union Jack. 25c, Netherlands. 1 le, West Germany.

1969, July 10

C90 A45 7½c multicolored .25 .25
C91 A46 9½c multicolored .25 .25
C92 A45 15c multicolored .40 .40
C93 A46 25c multicolored .60 .60
C94 A46 1 le multicolored 1.75 1.75
C95 A46 2 le multicolored 2.50 2.50
Nos. C90-C95 (6) 5.75 5.75

Various advertisements printed on peelable paper backing. No. C90 has side tab for handling and comes packed in boxes of 50. Nos. C91-C95 are without side tabs and come 20 stamps attached to one sheet.

Bank Type of Regular Issue
Lithographed; Gold Impressed
1969, Sept. 10

C96 A47 9½c yel grn, vio & gold .90 .90

Advertising printed on peelable paper backing; 20 imperf. stamps to a sheet of backing, roulette 10.

Cola Nut Type of Regular Issue and Type of 1967
Typo.; Embossed on White Paper
1969, Sept. 10

C97 A40 7c yel, mar & car 10.00 5.00

Embossed Foil on Black Paper

C98 AP4 9½c blk, gold & bl 7.00 7.00
C99 AP4 15c blk, gold & red 9.00 9.00
Nos. C97-C99 (3) 26.00 21.00

No. C97 has side tab for handling and comes packed in boxes of 100. Nos. C98-C99 have advertisements printed on peelable paper backing, side tabs and come packed in boxes of 50.

Boy Scout, Lord Baden-Powell and Scout Emblem — AP5

1969, Dec. 6 Litho.

C100 AP5 7½c multicolored .50 .40
C101 AP5 9½c multicolored .60 .50
C102 AP5 15c multicolored .90 .90
C103 AP5 22c multicolored 2.00 1.50
C104 AP5 55c multicolored 8.00 7.25
C105 AP5 3 le multicolored 70.00 50.00
Nos. C100-C105 (6) 82.00 60.55

60th anniv. of the Sierra Leone Boy Scouts. Various advertising printed on peelable paper backing. No. C100 has side tab for handling and comes packed in boxes of 100. Nos. C101-C105 are without side tabs and come 20 stamps attached to one sheet.

No. 357 Srchd. "AIRMAIL" and New Denomination in Metallic Emerald, Lilac, Blue, Green, Bronze or Silver
1970, Mar 28

C106 A43 7½c on ½c (E) .30 .30
C107 A43 9½c on ½c (L) .40 .40
C108 A43 15c on ½c (Bl) .55 .55
C109 A43 28c on ½c (G) 1.00 1.00
C110 A43 40c on ½c (Br) 1.75 1.75
C111 A43 2 le on ½c (S) 9.00 9.00
Nos. C106-C111 (6) 13.00 13.00
6 Strips of 6 (1 of each design) (36) 80.00

See design paragraph over No. 357.

EXPO Type of Regular Issue

Maps of Sierra Leone and Japan.

1970, June 22 Litho.

C112 A49 7½c multicolored .25 .25
C113 A49 9½c multicolored .25 .25
C114 A49 15c multicolored .35 .35
C115 A49 25c multicolored .60 .60
C116 A49 50c multicolored .90 .90
C117 A49 3 le multicolored 4.00 4.00
Nos. C112-C117 (6) 6.35 6.35

Various advertising printed on peelable paper backing.

Eagle Type of 1967
1970, Oct. 3 Embossed Foil

C118 AP4 7½c crim & gold .55 .55
C119 AP4 9½c emer & cop .65 .65
C120 AP4 15c grnsh bl & sil 1.25 1.25
C121 AP4 25c brt red lil & gold 2.75 2.25
C122 AP4 50c gold & emer 5.50 4.50
C123 AP4 1 le silver & dk bl 12.00 12.00
C124 AP4 2 le gold & brt bl 19.00 19.00
Nos. C118-C124 (7) 41.70 40.20

Advertisements printed on peelable paper backing. Issued in sheets of 10.

"Treasure of Sierra Leone" Diamond — AP6

Lithographed and Embossed
1970, Dec. 30

C125 AP6 7½c multicolored .75 .25
C126 AP6 9½c multicolored .90 .30
C127 AP6 15c multicolored 1.25 .50
C128 AP6 25c multicolored 1.75 1.75
C129 AP6 75c multicolored 7.50 7.50
C130 AP6 2 le multicolored 27.50 27.50
Nos. C125-C130 (6) 39.65 37.80

Diamond industry. Advertisement printed on peelable paper backing. Sheets of 20.

Traffic Type of Regular Issue
1971, Mar. 1 Litho.

C131 A53 9½c vio blue & org 3.00 3.00

Advertisements printed on peelable paper backing.

Nos. 211, 215, 228 and C87 Surcharged in Dark Red, Dark Blue or Black

a

b

1971, Mar. 1 Engr. Wmk. 336

C132 A29(a) 10c on 2p (DR) .75 .50
C133 A29(a) 20c on 1sh (DB) 1.25 1.00

Photo. *Perf. 14*

C134 A35(a) 50c on 1p (Bk) 2.40 2.00

Unwmk.
Litho. *Imperf.*

C135 A44(b) 70c on 30c (DB) 3.50 3.50
C136 A44(b) 1 le on 30c (Bk) 4.25 4.25
Nos. C132-C136 (5) 12.15 11.25

Lion's Head and Bugles AP7

Lithographed and Embossed (Gold)
1971, Apr. 27

C137 AP7 7½c multicolored .25 .25
C138 AP7 9½c multicolored .25 .25
C139 AP7 15c multicolored .25 .25
C140 AP7 25c multicolored .45 .45

C141	AP7	75c multicolored	1.75	1.75
C142	AP7	2 le multicolored	4.00	4.00
		Nos. C137-C142 (6)	6.95	6.95

10th anniversary of independence. Advertisements printed on peelable paper backing. Stamps are in shape of Sierra Leone map and in flag colors.

Guma Valley Dam and Bank Emblem — AP8

1975, Jan. 14 Litho. *Perf. 13½*

C143 AP8 15c multicolored 1.00 1.00

African Development Bank, 10th anniv.

Congo River Type of 1975

1975, Aug. 24 Litho. *Perf. 13x13½*

C144 A57 20c multicolored .50 .50

Mano River Type of 1975

1975, Oct. 3 *Perf. 13x13½*

C145 A58 15c multicolored .30 .30

SINGAPORE

ˈsiŋ-ə-ˌpor

LOCATION — An island just off the southern tip of the Malay Peninsula, south of Johore

GOVT. — Republic in British Commonwealth

AREA — 250 sq. mi.

POP. — 3,531,600 (1999 est.)

CAPITAL — Singapore

Singapore, Malacca and Penang were the British settlements which, together with the Federated Malay States, composed the former colony of Straits Settlements. On April 1, 1946, Singapore became a separate colony when the Straits Settlements colony was dissolved. Malacca and Penang joined the Malayan Union, which was renamed the Federation of Malaya in 1948. In 1959 Singapore became a state with internal self-government.

Singapore joined the Federation of Malaysia in 1963 and withdrew in 1965.

100 Cents = 1 Dollar

Catalogue values for all unused stamps in this country are for Never Hinged items.

Watermark

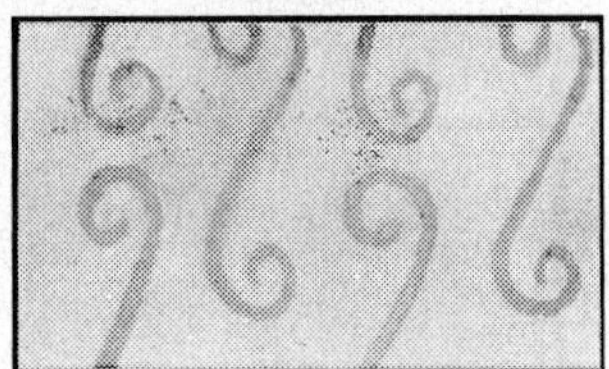

Wmk. 366 — S multiple

King George VI — A1

1948 Wmk. 4 Typo. *Perf. 14*

1	A1	1c	black	.25	*.50*
2	A1	2c	orange	.25	*.50*
3	A1	3c	green	.75	*.80*
4	A1	4c	chocolate	.50	*.50*
6	A1	6c	gray	.60	*.65*
7	A1	8c	rose red	1.10	*.95*
9	A1	10c	plum	.50	.25
11	A1	15c	ultra	8.50	.40
12	A1	20c	dk green & blk	5.00	.55
14	A1	25c	org & rose lilac	6.00	.60
16	A1	40c	dk vio & rose red	10.00	8.00
17	A1	50c	ultra & black	5.50	.40
18	A1	$1	vio brn & ultra	14.00	4.50
19	A1	$2	rose red & emer	55.00	8.00
20	A1	$5	chocolate & emer	135.00	9.00
			Nos. 1-20 (15)	242.95	35.60
			Set, hinged	130.00	

1949-52 *Perf. 18*

1a	A1	1c	black ('52)	.75	1.75
2a	A1	2c	orange	1.50	1.50
4a	A1	4c	chocolate	2.00	.25
5	A1	5c	rose violet ('52)	4.75	1.00
6a	A1	6c	gray ('52)	2.00	2.00
8	A1	8c	green ('52)	9.00	3.00
9a	A1	10c	plum ('50)	.70	.25
10	A1	12c	rose red ('52)	14.00	12.50
11a	A1	15c	ultra ('50)	22.50	.50
12a	A1	20c	dark green & black	12.00	4.00
13	A1	20c	ultra ('52)	10.00	.75
14a	A1	25c	org & rose lil ('50)	4.00	.25
15	A1	35c	dk vio & rose red ('52)	10.00	2.50
16a	A1	40c	dk vio & rose red ('51)	42.50	18.00
17a	A1	50c	ultra & black ('50)	7.50	.30
18a	A1	$1	violet brown & ultra	16.50	.90
b.			Wmk. 4a (error)	*16,500.*	*6,500.*
19a	A1	$2	rose red & emer ('51)	95.00	3.25
b.			Wmk. 4a (error)	*21,000.*	
20a	A1	$5	choc & emerald ('51)	225.00	7.00
			Nos. 1a-20a (18)	479.70	59.70
			Set, hinged	225.00	

Common Design Types pictured following the introduction.

Silver Wedding Issue

Common Design Types

Inscribed: "Singapore"

1948, Oct. 25 Photo. *Perf. 14x14½*

21	CD304	10c	purple	1.00	.40

Perf. 11½x11

Engraved; Name Typographed

22	CD305	$5	light brown	115.00	45.00
			Nos. 21-22 (2)	116.00	45.40

UPU Issue

Common Design Types

Inscribed: "Malaya-Singapore"

Engr.; Name Typo. on 15c, 25c

Perf. 13½, 11x11½

1949, Oct. 10 Wmk. 4

23	CD306	10c	rose violet	1.00	.70
24	CD307	15c	indigo	5.00	3.00
25	CD308	25c	orange	6.00	5.00
26	CD309	50c	slate	7.00	5.00
			Nos. 23-26 (4)	19.00	13.70

Coronation Issue

Common Design Type

1953, June 2 Engr. *Perf. 13½x13*

27	CD312	10c	mag & blk	2.50	.40

Chinese Sampans — A2

Sir Stamford Raffles Statue — A3

Singapore River — A4

Designs: 2c, Malay kolek. 4c, Twa-kow. 5c, Lombok sloop. 6c, Trengganu pinas. 8c, Palari. 10c, Timber tongkong. 12c, Hylam trader. 20c, Cocos-Keeling schooner. 25c, Argonaut plane. 30c, Oil tanker. 50c, Liner (M.S. Chusan). $5, Arms of Singapore.

Perf. 13½x14½

1955, Sept. 4 Photo. Wmk. 4

28	A2	1c	sepia	.25	*.80*
29	A2	2c	orange yellow	2.00	1.25
30	A2	4c	orange brown	1.50	.25
31	A2	5c	magenta	.90	.30
32	A2	6c	gray blue	1.00	.40
33	A2	8c	aqua	1.25	1.25
34	A2	10c	dark purple	2.75	.25
35	A2	12c	rose red	4.00	3.00
36	A2	20c	violet blue	2.75	.30
37	A2	25c	orange & purple	4.00	.50
38	A2	30c	purple & plum	3.75	.25
39	A2	50c	brt blue & black	2.25	.35

Perf. 13½x14, 14x13½

Engr.

40	A3	$1	blue & purple	37.50	.90
a.			Purple (Queen's head) omitted	26,000.	
41	A4	$2	blue green & red	45.00	3.50

Engr.; Arms Typo.

42	A3	$5	multicolored	47.50	9.00
			Nos. 28-42 (15)	156.40	22.30

For a later printing of the 10c and 50c, plates with finer screen (250) than normal (200) were used.

Singapore Lion and Administrative Center — A5

Perf. 11½x12

1959, June 1 Photo. Wmk. 314

Lion in Gold

43	A5	4c	deep rose red	.75	.75
44	A5	10c	magenta	1.10	.50
45	A5	20c	ultra	2.50	*2.75*
46	A5	25c	yellow green	2.50	2.75
47	A5	30c	bright violet	3.00	*3.25*
48	A5	50c	bluish gray	3.75	3.75
			Nos. 43-48 (6)	13.60	13.75

New Constitution of Singapore.

State Flag of Singapore A6

1960, June 3 Litho. *Perf. 13½*

49	A6	4c	blue, red & yellow	1.75	.75
50	A6	10c	gray, red & yellow	3.25	1.10

Issued for National Day, June 3, 1960.

Hands and Map of Singapore A7

1961, June 3 Photo.

51	A7	4c	brown, yellow & gray	1.25	1.10
52	A7	10c	green, yellow & gray	1.75	.25

Issued for National Day, June 3, 1961.

Sea Horse — A8

Malayan Fish: 4c, Tiger barb, horiz. 5c, Anemone fish, horiz. 6c, Archerfish. 10c, Harlequin fish, horiz. 20c, Butterflyfish. 25c, Two-spot gournami, horiz.

Perf. 14½x13½, 13½x14½

1962, Mar. 31 Wmk. 314

53	A8	2c	lt grn & red brn	.40	*.60*
54	A8	4c	red orange & blk	.40	*.60*
a.			Black omitted	1,400.	
55	A8	5c	gray & red org	.30	.25
a.			Red orange omitted	900.00	
b.			Wmkd. sideways ('67)	3.25	1.00
56	A8	6c	yellow & blk	.55	.55
57	A8	10c	dk gray & red org	.75	.25
a.			Red orange omitted	450.00	400.00
b.			Wmkd. sideways ('67)	1.60	.50
c.			Black omitted	7,500.	
58	A8	20c	blue & orange	1.50	.25
a.			Orange omitted	1,100.	
59	A8	25c	orange & black	1.25	.25
a.			Black omitted	1,300.	
b.			Wmkd. sideways ('67)	2.50	.25
			Nos. 53-59 (7)	5.15	2.75

For surcharge see No. 370.

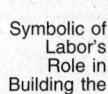

Symbolic of Labor's Role in Building the Nation — A9

1962, June 3 Unwmk. *Perf. 11½*

60	A9	4c	brt rose, blk & yel	1.40	1.40
61	A9	10c	brt blue, blk & yel	1.75	.75

Issued for National Day, June 3, 1962.

Vanda Tan Chay Yan — A10

Yellow-Breasted Sunbird — A11

Designs: 1c, Arachnis Maggie Oei, horiz. 12c, Grammatophyllum speciosum. 30c, Vanda Miss Joaquim. 50c, Shama, horiz. $1, White-breasted kingfisher, horiz. $5, White-tailed sea eagle.

Perf. 12½, 13½x13 (50c, $1), 13x13½ ($2, $5)

1963, Mar. 10 Photo. Wmk. 314

Flowers and Birds in Natural Colors

Size: 37x26mm, 26x37mm

62	A10	1c	brt pink & ultra	.30	.25
a.			Wmkd. sideways ('67)	1.50	.50
63	A10	8c	lt blue & mag	1.25	*2.00*
64	A10	12c	salmon & brown	1.25	*2.00*
65	A10	30c	tan & ol green	1.50	.40
a.			Tan omitted	150.00	

Size: 35½x25½mm, 25½x35½mm

66	A11	50c	yel green & blk	1.60	.40
a.			Wmkd. sideways ('66)	5.00	4.50
67	A11	$1	yellow & blk	20.00	.80
a.			Wmkd. sideways ('67)	16.00	14.00
68	A11	$2	dull blue & blk	13.00	1.90
69	A11	$5	pale blue & blk	35.00	8.50
			Nos. 62-69 (8)	73.90	16.25

See No. 76.

Government Housing Project — A12

1963, June 3 *Perf. 12½*

70	A12	4c	multicolored	1.00	.70
71	A12	10c	multicolored	2.00	.40

Issued for National Day, June 3, 1963.

Folk Dancers — A13

1963, Aug. 8 Photo. *Perf. 14x14½*

72	A13	5c	multicolored	.85	.50

Southeast Asia Cultural Festival.

1st ANNIVERSARY 15¢

REPUBLIC OF SINGAPORE

Workers, Factory and Apartment House A14

Wmk. 314 (30c), Unwmd. (15, 20c)

1966, Aug. 9 Photo. ***Perf. 12½x13***

73 A14 15c ultra & multi .75 .30
74 A14 20c red & multi 1.25 .25
75 A14 30c yellow & multi 2.25 1.50
Nos. 73-75 (3) 4.25 2.05

First anniversary of the Republic.

Bird Type of 1963

Design: 15c, Black-naped tern (sterna).

1966, Nov. 9 Wmk. 314 ***Perf. 12½***
Bird in Natural Colors
Size: 26x37mm

76 A11 15c blue & black 3.50 .25
a. Orange (eye) omitted 80.00

Marching Women, Chinese Inscription — A15

15c, Malay inscription. 50c, Tamil inscription.

Perf. 14x14½

1967, Aug. 9 Photo. Unwmk.

77 A15 6c lt brn, gray & red .70 .75
78 A15 15c multicolored 1.00 .25
79 A15 50c multicolored 2.25 1.75
Nos. 77-79 (3) 3.95 2.75

"Build a Vigorous Singapore" campaign.

Buildings and Map of Africa and Southeast Asia — A16

1967, Oct. 7 ***Perf. 14x13½***
Black Overprint

80 A16 10c multicolored .55 .30
81 A16 25c multicolored 1.00 1.10
82 A16 50c multicolored 1.75 1.50
Nos. 80-82 (3) 3.30 2.90

2nd Afro-Asian Housing Cong., Oct. 7-15.

No. 80 exists without overprint. Value, $1,500.

Map of Singapore and Symbolic Worker — A17

Stamps are inscribed "Work for Prosperity" in English and: 6c, Chinese. 15c, Malay. 50c, Tamil.

Perf. 13½x14½

1968, Aug. 9 Photo. Unwmk.

83 A17 6c red, black & gold .35 .25
84 A17 15c brt yel grn, blk & gold .50 .40
85 A17 50c brt blue, blk & gold 1.50 1.50
Nos. 83-85 (3) 2.35 2.15

Issued for National Day, 1968.

Sword Dance — A18

Designs: 6c, Lion dance. 10c, Bharatha Natyam, Indian dance. 15c, Tari Payong, Sumatran dance. 20c, Kathak Kali, Indian dance mask. 25c, Lu Chih Shen and Lin Chung, Chinese opera masks. 30c, Dragon dance, horiz. 50c, Tari Lilin, Malayan candle dance. 75c, Tarian Kuda Kepang, Javanese dance. $1, Yao Chi, Chinese opera mask.

Wmk. Rectangles (334)

1968 Photo. ***Perf. 14***

86 A18 5c yellow & multi .50 *.75*
87 A18 6c orange & multi 1.00 1.00
88 A18 10c bl grn & multi .40 .25
89 A18 15c lt brown & multi .60 .25
a. Booklet pane of 4 ('69) 55.00
90 A18 20c brown & multi .90 .30
91 A18 25c dp car & multi 1.10 .50
92 A18 30c pink & multi .50 .50
93 A18 50c brown org & multi .75 .75
94 A18 75c brt rose & multi 3.00 *1.25*
95 A18 $1 olive grn & multi 3.75 *1.25*
Nos. 86-95 (10) 12.50 6.80

Issue dates: 6c, 20c, 30c, 50c, 75c, Dec. 1; 5c, 10c, 15c, 25c, $1, Dec. 29.

1973 ***Perf. 13***

86a A18 5c yellow & multi 7.00 6.00
88a A18 10c blue green & multi 10.00 7.00
90a A18 20c brown & multi 14.00 8.00
91a A18 25c deep car & multi 12.00 10.00
92a A18 30c pink & multi 14.00 10.00
93a A18 50c brown org & multi 15.00 11.00
95a A18 $1 olive green & multi 25.00 22.50
Nos. 86a-95a (7) 97.00 74.50

Cogwheel and Emblem A19

1969, Apr. 15 Unwmk. ***Perf. 13***

96 A19 15c blue, black & silver .50 .25
97 A19 30c red, black & silver 1.00 1.00
98 A19 75c violet, black & silver 4.00 *2.00*
Nos. 96-98 (3) 5.50 3.25

25th Plenary Session of the Economic Commission for Asia and the Far East (ECAFE), Singapore, Apr. 15-28.

"Homes for the People" — A20

Perf. 13x13½

1969, July 20 Litho. Unwmk.

99 A20 25c emerald & black 1.40 .50
100 A20 50c dark blue & black 2.00 1.50

1960-69 building program of the Housing and Development Board.

Plane over Docks of Singapore — A21

30c, UN emblem and map of Singapore. 75c, Flags and map of Malaya and Borneo. $1, Uplifted hands and Singapore flag. $5, Tail of Japanese plane and searchlights. $10, Statue of Sir Thomas Stamford Raffles.

1969, Aug. 9 ***Perf. 14x14½***

101 A21 15c yel, blk & org 2.50 1.50
102 A21 30c brt blue & blk 2.50 2.00
103 A21 75c orange & multi *4.50* 3.00
104 A21 $1 red & black *10.00* *10.00*
105 A21 $5 gray, blk & red *30.00* *30.00*
106 A21 $10 emerald & blk *45.00* *45.00*
a. Souv. sheet of 6, #101-106 *600.00* *500.00*
Nos. 101-106 (6) *94.50* *91.50*

Sesquicent. of the founding of Singapore.

Mirudhangam, South Indian Drum — A22

Musical Instruments: 4c, Pi Pa, Chinese, 4 strings, vert. $2, Rebab, Malay violin, 3 strings, vert. $5, Vina, Indian, 7 strings. $10, Ta Ku, Chinese drum, vert.

1969 Photo. Wmk. 366 ***Perf. 13***

107 A22 1c multicolored .25 *1.25*
108 A22 4c multicolored .60 *1.25*
109 A22 $2 multicolored 5.25 1.25
110 A22 $5 multicolored 15.00 2.40
111 A22 $10 multicolored 45.00 16.00
Nos. 107-111 (5) 66.10 22.15

Issued: 1c, 4c, $2, $5, Nov. 10; $10, Dec. 6.

Sea Shells — A23

Designs: 30c, Tropical fish. 75c, Greater flamingo and helmeted hornbill. $1, Orchids.

Perf. 13½

1970, Mar. 15 Unwmk. Litho.

112 A23 15c pale vio & multi 1.00 .25
113 A23 30c lt blue & multi 2.50 1.25
114 A23 75c yellow & multi 7.50 4.25
115 A23 $1 lt green & multi 9.50 6.00
a. Souvenir sheet of 4, #112-115 35.00 35.00
Nos. 112-115 (4) 20.50 11.75

EXPO '70 International Exposition, Osaka, Japan, Mar. 15-Sept. 13. Compare with type A396.

Child Playing (Kindergarten) — A24

50c, Sports activities. 75c, Cultural activities.

1970, July 1 Unwmk. ***Perf. 13½***

116 A24 15c dp org & blk 1.00 .25
117 A24 50c org, blk & vio bl 2.50 2.50
118 A24 75c blk & dp lilac rose 4.25 4.25
Nos. 116-118 (3) 7.75 7.00

People's Association, 10th anniversary.

Soldier and Map of Singapore — A25

Map and soldiers in various positions.

1970, Aug. 9 Litho. Unwmk.

119 A25 15c emer, blk & org 1.50 .25
120 A25 50c org, blk & brt mag 4.25 3.75
121 A25 $1 brt mag, blk & emer 5.75 *5.75*
Nos. 119-121 (3) 11.50 9.75

National military service.

Runners A26

1970, Aug. 23 Photo. ***Perf. 13***

122 A26 10c shown 1.25 1.25
123 A26 15c Swimmers 2.50 2.50
124 A26 25c Badminton 2.75 2.75
125 A26 50c Automobile race 3.50 3.50
a. Strip of 4, #122-125 14.00 14.00

1970 Festival of Sports.

Ship and Emblem of National Line (Neptune Oriental Lines) — A27

Designs: 30c, Ship in first container berth. 75c, Ship repairing and ship building.

1970, Nov. 1 Litho. ***Perf. 12***

126 A27 15c vio bl, lem & red 3.00 .75
127 A27 30c dp ultra & lemon 6.00 6.00
128 A27 75c red & lemon 12.00 12.00
Nos. 126-128 (3) 21.00 18.75

Singapore shipping industry.

Flags of Commonwealth Nations — A28

Designs: 15c, Circular arrangement of names of Commonwealth members. 30c, Flags arranged in circle. $1, Flags (different arrangement).

1971, Jan. 14 ***Perf. 15x14½***
Size: 46½x31mm

129 A28 15c gold & multi 1.25 .50
130 A28 30c gold & multi 2.00 1.00
131 A28 75c gold & multi 3.00 3.00

Size: 67x31mm
Perf. 14

132 A28 $1 gold & multi 4.00 4.00
Nos. 129-132 (4) 10.25 8.50

Commonwealth Heads of Government Meeting, Singapore, Jan. 12-14.

Cycle Rickshaws A29

Houses of Worship in Singapore — A30

Perf. 11½

1971, Apr. 4 Unwmk. Litho.

133 A29 15c shown 1.00 .25
134 A29 20c Sampans 1.50 .60
135 A29 30c Market place 2.00 1.40

Perf. 13x13½

136 A30 50c Waterfront 4.50 *5.50*
137 A30 75c shown 6.75 6.75
Nos. 133-137 (5) 15.75 14.50

Tourist publicity.

Chinese New Year — A31

Singapore Festivals: 30c, Hari Raya Puasa (Moslem). 50c, Deepavali (Hindu). 75c, Christmas.

1971, Aug. 9 Litho. *Perf. 14*

138 A31 15c multicolored 1.75 1.50
139 A31 30c multicolored 2.75 3.75
140 A31 50c multicolored 4.25 4.25
141 A31 75c multicolored 6.25 6.25
a. Souvenir sheet of 4, #138-141 140.00 110.00
Nos. 138-141 (4) 15.00 15.75

Satellite Earth Station, Sentosa Island — A32

No. 143 as 15c, enlarged to cover 4 stamps.

1971, Oct. 23 Unwmk. *Perf. 13½*

142 A32 15c red & multi 3.00 3.00
143 A32 Block of 4 50.00 50.00
a. 30c (yellow numeral) 11.00 10.00
b. 30c (green numeral) 11.00 10.00
c. 30c (rose numeral) 11.00 10.00
d. 30c (orange numeral) 11.00 10.00

Establishment of Singapore's satellite earth station, Sentosa Island.

Singapore River and Fort Canning, 1843-1847 — A33

Views of Singapore, from 19th century art works: 15c, The Padang, 1851. 20c, Waterfront, 1848-1849. 35c, View from Fort Canning, 1846. 50c, View from Mount Wallich, 1857. $1, Waterfront with ships, from the sea, 1861.

1971, Dec. 5 Unwmk. *Perf. 13x12½*

Size: 52x45mm

144 A33 10c gold & multi 4.00 3.00
145 A33 15c gold & multi 5.00 2.00
146 A33 20c gold & multi 5.50 5.00
147 A33 35c gold & multi 10.50 9.50

Perf. 12½x13

Size: 68x47mm

148 A33 50c gold & multi 12.50 11.00
149 A33 $1 gold & multi 22.50 20.00
Nos. 144-149 (6) 60.00 50.50

George V 1c Copper Coin, 1920 A34

Singapore Coins: 35c, Silver dollar, 1969. $1, Gold $150, 1969 commemorative coin for sesquicentennial of founding of Singapore.

1972, June 4 Litho. *Perf. 13½*

150 A34 15c dk grn, dp org & blk 1.50 1.50
151 A34 35c red & black 3.00 3.00
152 A34 $1 ultra, yellow & blk 5.00 5.00
Nos. 150-152 (3) 9.50 9.50

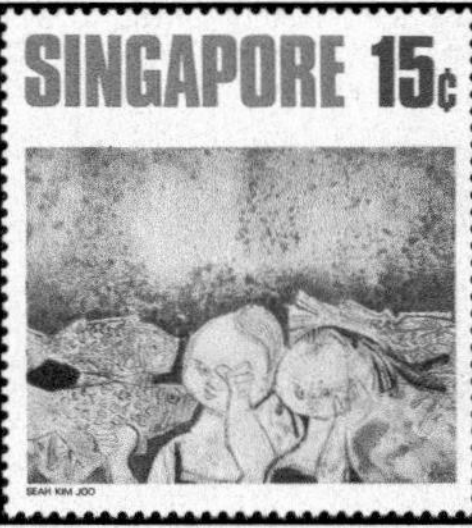

"Moon Festival," by Seah Kim Joo — A35

Paintings by Singapore Artists: 35c, "Complimentary Force," by Thomas Yeo. 50c, "Rhythm in Blue," by Yusman Aman. $1, "Gibbons," by Chen Wen Hsi.

1972, July 9 Litho. *Perf. 12½*

Size: 40x43½mm

153 A35 15c brown org & multi 1.00 .50

Size: 35½x53½mm

154 A35 35c bl grn & multi 2.00 2.00
155 A35 50c dull violet & multi 2.50 2.50

Size: 40x43½mm

156 A35 $1 bister & multi 7.00 7.00
Nos. 153-156 (4) 12.50 12.00

Chinese New Year — A36

Festivals: 35c, Hari Raya Puasa (candles and ornament). 50c, Deepavali (incense and teapot). 75c, Christmas (candle and stained glass window).

1972, Aug. 9 Litho. *Perf. 13x12½*

157 A36 15c deep rose & multi 1.00 .25
158 A36 35c violet & multi 1.25 1.25
159 A36 50c green & multi 2.50 2.50
160 A36 75c blue & multi 3.50 3.50
Nos. 157-160 (4) 8.25 7.50

Technical and Scientific Training — A37

Designs: 35c, Sport. $1, Art and culture.

1972, Oct. 1 Photo. *Perf. 12*

161 A37 15c orange & multi 1.25 .75
162 A37 35c blue & multi 3.50 2.25
163 A37 $1 orange & multi 4.50 3.75
Nos. 161-163 (3) 9.25 6.75

Youth of Singapore.

Neptune Ruby A38

1972, Dec. 17 Litho. *Perf. 14x14½*

Size: 42x28½mm

164 A38 15c shown 2.50 .80

Size: 29½x28½mm

165 A38 75c Maria Rickmers 6.00 6.00
166 A38 $1 Chinese junk 9.00 9.00
a. Souvenir sheet of 3, #164-166 47.50 47.50
Nos. 164-166 (3) 17.50 15.80

Singapore shipping industry.

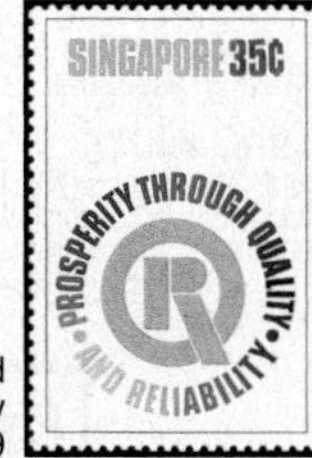

Quality and Reliability Emblem — A39

15c, Emblem & initials of participating organizations: Singapore Institute of Standards & Industrial Research, Singapore Manufacturers' Association, Natl. Trades Union Congress. 75c, Emblem & "Prosperity through Quality & Reliability" in multiple rows. $1, Quality & Reliability emblem.

1973, Feb. 25 Litho. *Perf. 14½x14*

167 A39 15c gold & multi .75 .40
168 A39 35c gold & multi 1.75 1.75
169 A39 75c gold & multi 2.00 2.00
170 A39 $1 gold & multi 2.50 2.25
Nos. 167-170 (4) 7.00 6.40

Prosperity through Quality and Reliability campaign.

Birds, Jurong Bird Park — A40

Landmarks: 35c, Dancers, National Theater. 50c, City Hall and ballplayers. $1, Singapore River with boats and buildings.

1973, Apr. 29 *Perf. 12½*

171 A40 15c vermilion & blk 1.10 .50
172 A40 35c dull green & blk 2.00 2.00
173 A40 50c brown & blk 3.50 3.50
174 A40 $1 dark violet & blk 4.50 4.50
Nos. 171-174 (4) 11.10 10.50

Airline Emblems A41

35c, Emblem of Singapore Airlines and intl. destinations. 75c, SIA emblem on stylized tail of Boeing jet. $1, SIA emblems circling globe.

1973, June 24 Litho. *Perf. 13½*

175 A41 10c multicolored .80 .30
176 A41 35c multicolored 2.00 2.00
177 A41 75c multicolored 2.00 2.00
178 A41 $1 multicolored 3.00 3.00
Nos. 175-178 (4) 7.80 7.30

Singapore Intl. Airport at Paya Lebar.

Entertainers A42

Composite of various forms of entertainment.

1973, Aug. 9 Litho. *Perf. 13½x14*

179 A42 10c blk & org red 1.50 1.50
180 A42 35c blk & org red 1.75 1.75
181 A42 50c blk & org red 2.00 2.00
182 A42 75c blk & org red 2.25 2.25
a. Block of 4, #179-182 10.00 10.00

National Day 1973.

Running, Judo, Boxing — A43

Designs: 15c, Bicycling, weight lifting, pistol shoot, yachting. 25c, Various balls. 35c, Tennis racket, ball, hockey stick. 50c, Swimming. $1, Singapore National Stadium.

Size: 25x25mm

1973, Sept. 1 Photo. *Perf. 14*

183 A43 10c gold, silver & ind .75 .75
184 A43 15c gold & dk brown 2.00 2.00
185 A43 25c silver, gold & blk 1.75 1.75
186 A43 35c gold, silver & dk pur 2.75 2.75

Perf. 13x14

Size: 40½x25mm

187 A43 50c gold & multi 3.00 3.00
188 A43 $1 sil, vio bl & emer 5.00 5.00
a. Souvenir sheet of 6, #183-188 47.50 47.50
Nos. 183-188 (6) 15.25 15.25

7th South East Asia (SEAP) Games, Singapore.

Agave A44

Mangosteen A45

Designs: Stylized flowers and fruit: 5c, Coleus blumei. 10c, Madagascar periwinkle. 15c, Sunflower. 20c, Dwarf palm. 25c, Yellow daisy. 35c, Chrysanthemum. 50c, Costus. 75c, Transvaal daisy. $2, Jackfruit. $5, Coconuts. $10, Pineapple.

1973, Sept. 30 Photo. *Perf. 13*

189 A44 1c shown .25 .70
190 A44 5c multi .25 .25
a. Booklet pane of 10 (4 #190, 4 #191 + 2 #193) 20.00
191 A44 10c multi .25 .25
192 A44 15c multi 1.00 .25
193 A44 20c multi .60 .50
194 A44 25c multi 1.75 .45
195 A44 35c multi .95 .65
196 A44 50c multi 1.25 .25
197 A44 75c multi 2.50 .75
198 A45 $1 shown 3.00 .75
199 A45 $2 multi 3.75 1.25
200 A45 $5 multi 9.00 9.00
201 A45 $10 multi 17.50 17.50
Nos. 189-201 (13) 42.05 32.55

Nos. 189-201 have fluorescent underprint "Singapore" in multiple rows.

Nos. 189-201 exist imperf. Value, set of pairs $200.

Tiger and Orangutans — A46

10c, Leopard and deer. 35c, Panther and stag. 75c, White horse & lion.

1973, Dec. 16 Litho. *Perf. 13*

202 A46 5c shown 1.25 1.25
203 A46 10c multi 1.60 .85
204 A46 35c multi 4.75 4.75
205 A46 75c multi 6.50 6.50
Nos. 202-205 (4) 14.10 13.35

Opening of Singapore Zoo.

Tropical Fish — A47

Designs: Various poecilia reticulata fish.

1974, Apr. 21 ***Perf. 13½x14***

206 A47 5c apple grn & multi 1.00 1.00
207 A47 10c pink & multi 1.25 .40
208 A47 35c brt blue & multi 3.25 3.25
209 A47 $1 brt green & multi 5.50 5.50
Nos. 206-209 (4) 11.00 10.15

Scout Conference Emblem A48

1974, June 9 ***Perf. 13½x14½***

210 A48 10c multicolored .65 .65
211 A48 75c multicolored 2.00 2.00

9th Asia-Pacific Boy Scout Conf., Singapore.

UPU Emblem, Circle and "Centenary" Multiple — A49

UPU, cent.: 35c, Circle and UN emblems, multiple. 75c, Circle and pigeons, multiple.

1974, July 7 **Litho.** ***Perf. 14½x13½***

212 A49 10c orange brn & multi .50 .50
213 A49 35c blue & multi 1.50 1.50
214 A49 75c emerald & multi 2.00 *2.00*
Nos. 212-214 (3) 4.00 4.00

Family — A50

35c, Symbols for male & female. 75c, World map and WPY emblem.

1974, Aug. 9 **Litho.** ***Perf. 13x13½***

215 A50 10c shown .50 .50
216 A50 35c multicolored 1.25 1.25
217 A50 75c multicolored 1.75 *1.75*
Nos. 215-217 (3) 3.50 3.50

Natl. Day and World Population Year 1974.

"Sun and Tree" — A51

Children's Drawings: 10c, "My Daddy and Mommy." 35c, "A Dump Truck." 50c, "My Aunt."

1974, Oct. 1 **Photo.** ***Perf. 14x13½***

218 A51 5c multicolored .50 .50
219 A51 10c multicolored .60 .40
220 A51 35c multicolored 2.25 2.25
221 A51 50c multicolored 2.75 2.75
a. Souv. sheet, #218-221, perf 13 27.50 27.50
Nos. 218-221 (4) 6.10 5.90

Children's drawings for Children's Day (UNICEF).

Alfresco Dining A52

Tourist publicity: 20c, Singapore River. $1, "Kelong" fish traps.

1975, Jan. 26 **Litho.** ***Perf. 14***

222 A52 15c multicolored .85 .50
223 A52 20c multicolored 1.60 1.50
224 A52 $1 multicolored 4.50 4.00
Nos. 222-224 (3) 6.95 6.00

Prows of Barges and Wave Design A53

25c, Cargo ships & ship's wheel. 50c, Tanker & signal flags. $1, Container ship & propellers.

1975, Mar. 10 **Litho.** ***Perf. 13½***

225 A53 5c multicolored .50 .25
226 A53 25c multicolored 1.75 1.75
227 A53 50c multicolored 2.50 2.50
228 A53 $1 multicolored 3.75 3.75
Nos. 225-228 (4) 8.50 8.25

9th Biennial Conf. of the Intl. Assoc. of Ports and Harbors, Singapore, Mar. 8-15.

Satellite Earth Stations, Sentosa Island — A54

Oil Refinery — A55

Science and Industry: 75c, Brain surgery, Medical Center, Jurong.

1975, June 29 **Photo.** ***Perf. 13½***

229 A54 10c multicolored .50 .25
230 A55 35c multicolored 2.50 2.50
231 A54 75c multicolored 2.75 2.75
Nos. 229-231 (3) 5.75 5.50

"10" and "Homes and Gardens for the People" — A56

Tenth Natl. Day ("10" and): 35c, "Shipping and ship building." 75c, "Communications and technology." $1, "Trade, commerce and industry."

1975, Aug. 9 **Litho.** ***Perf. 13½***

232 A56 10c multicolored .50 .45
233 A56 35c multicolored 1.25 1.25
234 A56 75c multicolored 2.50 2.50
235 A56 $1 multicolored 2.75 2.75
Nos. 232-235 (4) 7.00 6.95

Crowned Cranes — A57

Birds: 10c, Great hornbill. 35c, White-breasted and white-collared kingfishers. $1, Sulphur-crested cockatoo and blue and yellow macaw.

1975, Oct. 5 **Litho.** ***Perf. 14½x13½***

236 A57 5c emerald & multi 2.25 2.25
237 A57 10c emerald & multi 2.50 2.50
238 A57 35c emerald & multi 9.00 9.00
239 A57 $1 emerald & multi 12.00 12.00
Nos. 236-239 (4) 25.75 25.75

IWY Emblem, Peace Dove as "Equality" — A58

IWY Emblem: 35c, Peace dove with eggs in basket, symbolizing "Development." 75c, Peace dove & young, symbolizing "Peace."

1975, Dec. 7 **Litho.** ***Perf. 13½***

240 A58 10c blk, blue & pink .30 .30
241 A58 35c orange & multi 2.00 2.00
242 A58 75c dp violet & multi 2.75 2.75
a. Souvenir sheet of 3, #240-242 20.00 20.00
Nos. 240-242 (3) 5.05 5.05

International Women's Year 1975.

Yellow Flame — A59

Wayside Trees: 35c, Cabbage tree. 50c, Rose of India. 75c, Variegated coral tree.

1976, Apr. 18 **Litho.** ***Perf. 14***

243 A59 10c multicolored .75 .25
244 A59 35c multicolored 2.00 2.00
245 A59 50c multicolored 2.75 2.75
246 A59 75c multicolored 3.75 3.75
Nos. 243-246 (4) 9.25 8.75

Aranda Hybrid — A60

Designs: Varieties of aranda orchids.

1976, June 20 **Litho.** ***Perf. 14***

247 A60 10c black & multi 1.25 .50
248 A60 35c black & multi 3.25 3.25
249 A60 50c black & multi 3.75 3.75
250 A60 75c black & multi 5.50 5.50
Nos. 247-250 (4) 13.75 13.00

"10" and Children's Band A61

35c, Running boys. 75c, Dancing children.

1976, Aug. 9 **Litho.** ***Perf. 12½***

251 A61 10c multicolored .40 .30
252 A61 35c multicolored 1.50 1.50
253 A61 75c multicolored 1.75 1.75
Nos. 251-253 (3) 3.65 3.55

Singapore Youth Festival, 10th anniversary.

Queen Elizabeth Walk — A62

Paintings of Old Singapore, c. 1905-10: 50c, The Padang. $1, Raffles Place.

1976, Nov. 14 **Litho.** ***Perf. 14***

254 A62 10c multicolored 1.00 1.00
255 A62 50c multicolored 2.25 2.25
256 A62 $1 multicolored 5.00 5.00
a. Souvenir sheet of 3, #254-256, perf. 13½ 22.50 22.50
Nos. 254-256 (3) 8.25 8.25

Chinese Bridal Costume — A63

Designs: 35c, Indian bridal costume. 75c, Malay bridal costume.

1976, Dec. 19 **Litho.** ***Perf. 14½***

257 A63 10c lt green & multi .75 .55
258 A63 35c lilac & multi 1.75 1.75
259 A63 75c yellow & multi 3.00 3.00
Nos. 257-259 (3) 5.50 5.30

Radar, Surface to Air Missile, Soldiers — A64

50c, Infantry soldiers and tank. 75c, Jet fighter, pilot, telecommunications center.

1977, Mar. 12 **Litho.** ***Perf. 14½***

260 A64 10c multicolored .75 .50
261 A64 50c multicolored 2.75 2.50
262 A64 75c multicolored 4.00 4.00
Nos. 260-262 (3) 7.50 7.00

National Service, 10th anniversary.

Lyrate Cockle A65

Spotted Hermit Crab A66

Sea Shells: 5c, Folded scallop. 10c, Marble cone. 15c, Scorpion conch. 20c, Amplustre bubble. 25c, Spiral Babylon. 35c, Regal thorny oyster. 50c, Winged frog shell. 75c, Troschel's murex.

Marine Life: $2, Stingray. $5, Cuttlefish. $10, Lionfish.

1977 ***Perf. 13½***

263 A65 1c orange & multi 1.10 *1.60*
264 A65 5c orange & multi .25 .25
a. Bklt. pane, 4 #264, 8 #265 9.00 *12.00*
265 A65 10c orange & multi .25 .25
a. Imperf., pair 500.00
266 A65 15c orange & multi 1.00 .40
267 A65 20c orange & multi 1.00 .25
268 A65 25c orange & multi 1.25 *2.25*
269 A65 35c orange & multi 1.50 1.40
270 A65 50c orange & multi 2.00 .25
271 A65 75c orange & multi 2.75 .25

Perf. 14

272 A66 $1 multicolored 2.50 .25
273 A66 $2 multicolored 2.50 .75
274 A66 $5 multicolored 4.00 4.00
275 A66 $10 multicolored 7.50 6.00
Nos. 263-275 (13) 27.60 17.90

No. 264a has a large inscribed selvage, the size of 6 stamps.
Issued: #263-271, Apr. 9; others, June 4.

Singapore Harbor Improvements A67

Labor Day: 50c, Construction workers. 75c, Road workers.

1977, May 1 Litho. *Perf. 13x12½*

276 A67 10c multicolored .60 .50
277 A67 50c multicolored 1.50 1.50
278 A67 75c multicolored 2.00 2.00
Nos. 276-278 (3) 4.10 4.00

"Key to Savings" — A68

Designs: 35c, "On-line Banking Service." 75c, "GIRO Service."

1977, July 16 Litho. *Perf. 13, 14*

279 A68 10c multicolored .30 .25
a. Perf 14 *29.00 29.00*
280 A68 35c multicolored 1.00 1.00
a. Perf 14 *105.00 105.00*
281 A68 75c multicolored 2.10 2.10
a. Perf 14 *130.00 130.00*
Nos. 279-281 (3) 3.40 3.35

Centenary of Post Office Savings Bank.

Grain and Cattle — A69

10c, Flags of founding members: Thailand, Indonesia, Singapore, Malaysia, Philippines. 75c, Steel, oil & chemical industries.

1977, Aug. 8 Litho. *Perf. 14*

282 A69 10c multicolored .35 .25
283 A69 35c multicolored 1.00 1.00
284 A69 75c multicolored 2.10 2.10
Nos. 282-284 (3) 3.45 3.35

Association of South East Asian Nations (ASEAN), 10th anniversary.

Bus Stop — A70

Children's Drawings: 10c, Chingay procession, vert. 75c, Playground.

1977, Oct. 1 *Perf. 12½*

285 A70 10c multicolored .35 .25
286 A70 35c multicolored 1.00 .65
287 A70 75c multicolored 2.50 2.00
a. Souvenir sheet of 3, #285-287 14.50 14.50
Nos. 285-287 (3) 3.85 2.90

Symbols of Life Sciences — A71

Singapore Science Center: 35c, "Physical sciences." 75c, "Science and technology." $1, Science Center.

1977, Dec. 10 Litho. *Perf. 14½x14*

288 A71 10c multicolored .45 .40
289 A71 35c multicolored .50 .45
290 A71 75c multicolored 1.25 1.40
291 A71 $1 multicolored 2.00 2.00
Nos. 288-291 (4) 4.20 4.25

Botanical Gardens — A72

Singapore Parks and Gardens: 10c, Jurong Bird Park, horiz. 35c, East Coast Lagoon and Park.

1978, Apr. 22 Litho. *Perf. 14½*

292 A72 10c multicolored .25 .25
293 A72 35c multicolored .85 .85
294 A72 75c multicolored 1.75 1.75
Nos. 292-294 (3) 2.85 2.85

Red-whiskered Bulbul — A73

Songbirds: 35c, White eyes. 50c, White-rumped shama. 75c, White-crested laughing thrush.

1978, July 1 Litho. *Perf. 13½*

295 A73 10c multicolored .75 .75
296 A73 35c multicolored 2.00 2.00
297 A73 50c multicolored 2.25 2.25
298 A73 75c multicolored 3.00 3.00
Nos. 295-298 (4) 8.00 8.00

Thian Hock Keng Temple — A74

National Monuments: No. 303a, like No. 299. Nos. 300, 303b, Hajjah Fatimah Mosque. Nos. 301, 303c, Armenian Church. Nos. 302, 303d, Sri Mariamman Temple.

1978, Aug. 9

299 A74 10c tan & multi .70 .70
300 A74 10c green & multi .70 .70
301 A74 10c blue & multi .70 .70
302 A74 10c lilac & multi .70 .70
Nos. 299-302 (4) 2.80 2.80

Souvenir Sheet

303 Sheet of 4 7.50 7.50
a. A74 35c tan & multi 1.00
b. A74 35c green & multi 1.00
c. A74 35c blue & multi 1.00
d. A74 35c lilac & multi 1.00

Map of Proposed Cable Network A75

1978, Oct. 30 Litho. *Perf. 14*

304 A75 10c multicolored .25 .25
305 A75 35c multicolored 1.00 1.00
306 A75 50c multicolored 1.00 1.10
307 A75 75c multicolored 1.25 1.25
Nos. 304-307 (4) 3.50 3.60

ASEAN Submarine Cable Network. Nos. 304-307 printed in sheets of 100. Stamps have perforations around design and around edges. See No. 429a.

Neptune Spinel — A76

Ships: 35c, Neptune Aries. 50c, Arno Temasek. 75c, Neptune Pearl.

1978, Nov. 18 Litho. *Perf. 13½x14*

308 A76 10c multicolored 1.00 .65
309 A76 35c multicolored 1.75 1.75
310 A76 50c multicolored 2.00 2.00
311 A76 75c multicolored 2.75 2.75
Nos. 308-311 (4) 7.50 7.15

Neptune Oriental Shipping Lines, 10th anniv.

Concorde A77

Aviation Development: 35c, Boeing 747B. 50c, Vickers-Vimy, 1st aircraft to land in Singapore. 75c, Wright Brothers' Flyer I.

1978, Dec. 16 *Perf. 13½*

312 A77 10c yellow green & blk .60 .40
313 A77 35c blue & black 1.40 1.25
314 A77 50c carmine & black 1.60 1.60
315 A77 75c brown & black 2.50 2.50
Nos. 312-315 (4) 6.10 5.75

75th anniversary of 1st powered flight.

Distance Marker in Kilometers — A78

Designs: 35c, Tape measure in centimeters. 75c, Scales in grams and kilograms.

1979, Jan. 24 Litho. *Perf. 13x13½*

316 A78 10c multicolored .25 .25
317 A78 35c multicolored .50 .50
318 A78 75c multicolored 1.25 1.25
Nos. 316-318 (3) 2.00 2.00

Introduction of metric system.

Vanda Orchids — A79

Varieties of vanda hybrids. 10c, 35c, horiz.

Perf. 14½x14, 14x14½

1979, Apr. 14 Litho.

319 A79 10c multicolored .30 .30
320 A79 35c multicolored .75 .75
321 A79 50c multicolored 1.25 1.25
322 A79 75c multicolored 1.50 1.50
Nos. 319-322 (4) 3.80 3.80

Envelope Addressed to Postmaster A80

50c, Envelope addressed to Philatelic Bureau.

1979, July 1 Litho. *Perf. 12½x13*

323 A80 10c orange & multi .25 .25
324 A80 50c dark blue & multi 1.00 1.00

Singapore's postal code system.

Old Phone, Telephone Lines — A81

Designs: 35c, Dial, world map. 50c, Push-button phone, skyline. 75c, Line network.

1979, Oct. 5 Litho. *Perf. 13½*

325 A81 10c multicolored .25 .25
326 A81 35c multicolored .60 .60
327 A81 50c multicolored .75 .75
328 A81 75c multicolored 1.25 1.25
Nos. 325-328 (4) 2.85 2.85

Telephone service centenary.

IYC Emblem, Lanterns Festival A82

IYC Emblem, Children's Drawings: 35c, Singapore Harbor. 50c, "Use Your Hands." 75c, Soccer.

1979, Nov. 10 Litho. *Perf. 13*

329 A82 10c multicolored .25 .25
330 A82 35c multicolored .60 .60
331 A82 50c multicolored .75 .75
332 A82 75c multicolored 1.25 1.25
a. Souvenir sheet of 4, #329-332 6.00 6.00
Nos. 329-332 (4) 2.85 2.85

International Year of the Child.

Botanic Gardens, 120th Anniversary — A83

1979, Dec. 15 *Perf. 13½*

333 A83 10c shown .25 .25
334 A83 50c Gazebo 1.25 1.25
335 A83 $1 Greenhouse 2.00 2.00
Nos. 333-335 (3) 3.50 3.50

Hainan Junk — A84

5c, Clipper. 10c, Fujian junk. 15c, Golekkan. 20c, Palari. 25c, East Indiaman. 35c, Galleon. 50c, Caravel. 75c, Jiangsu trader. $1, Coaster. $2, Oil tanker. $5, Screw steamer. $10, Paddle wheel steamer.

1980 Litho. *Perf. 14*

336 A84 1c shown .30 .30
337 A84 5c multi .25 .25
338 A84 10c multi .25 .25
a. Booklet pane of 10 4.00
339 A84 15c multi .25 .25
340 A84 20c multi .25 .25
341 A84 25c multi .30 .25
342 A84 35c multi .50 .25
343 A84 50c multi .60 .25
344 A84 75c multi 1.00 .30

Size: 41½x24½mm

Perf. 13½

345 A84 $1 multi 1.25 .35
a. Imperf., pair 350.00
346 A84 $2 multi 2.50 .60
347 A84 $5 multi 5.00 1.75
348 A84 $10 multi 11.00 6.00
Nos. 336-348 (13) 23.45 11.05

Issued: #336-344, Apr. 26; others, Apr. 5.

Straits Settlements No. 1, Old Singapore Map, London 1980 Emblem — A85

London 1980 Emblem and: 35c, Straits Settlements No. 146, letter. $1, Singapore No. 19, map of Straits. $2, Singapore No. 106, letter, 1819.

1980, May 6 Litho. *Perf. 13*

349 A85 10c multicolored .30 .30
350 A85 35c multicolored .60 .35
351 A85 $1 multicolored 1.10 1.10
352 A85 $2 multicolored 1.50 1.50
a. Souvenir sheet of 4, #349-352 5.00 5.00
Nos. 349-352 (4) 3.50 3.25

London 1980 Intl. Stamp Exhib., May 6-14.

Fund Board Emblem, Keys to Retirement — A86

50c, Home ownership savings. $1, Old age savings.

1980, July 1 Litho. *Perf. 13*

353 A86 10c shown .25 .25
354 A86 50c multicolored .50 .50
355 A86 $1 multicolored 1.25 1.25
Nos. 353-355 (3) 2.00 2.00

Central Provident Fund Board, 25th anniv.

Map Showing Singapore-Indonesia Cable Route — A87

1980, Aug. 8 Litho. *Perf. 14*

356 A87 10c multicolored .25 .25
357 A87 35c multicolored .80 .80
358 A87 50c multicolored 1.10 1.10
359 A87 75c multicolored 1.50 1.50
Nos. 356-359 (4) 3.65 3.65

ASEAN Submarine Cable Network extension. Stamps perforated around design and around edges. See No. 429a.

Fair Emblem A88

1980, Oct. 3 Litho. *Perf. 13*

360 A88 10c multicolored .25 .25
361 A88 35c multicolored .40 .40
362 A88 75c multicolored .85 .85
Nos. 360-362 (3) 1.50 1.50

Asean Trade Fair, Oct. 3-12.

A89

1980, Nov. 2 Litho. *Perf. 13½*

363 A89 10c Flame of the wood .25 .25
364 A89 35c Golden trumpet .55 .55
365 A89 50c Sky vine .65 .65
366 A89 75c Bougainvillea 1.25 1.25
Nos. 363-366 (4) 2.70 2.70

A90

1981, Jan. 24 Litho. *Perf. 14x14½*

367 A90 10c multicolored .30 .30
368 A90 35c multicolored .40 .40
369 A90 75c multicolored .75 .75
Nos. 367-369 (3) 1.45 1.45

Monetary Authority of Singapore, 10th anniv.

No. 54 Surcharged

Perf. 13½x14½

1981, Mar. 5 Photo. Wmk. 314

370 A8 10c on 4c red org & blk .45 .45

A91

10c, Technical Training (Woodworking). 35c, Building construction. 50c, Electronics. 75c, Precision machinery.

Unwmk.

1981, Apr. 11 Litho. *Perf. 13*

371 A91 10c multicolored .30 .30
372 A91 35c multicolored .55 .55
373 A91 50c multicolored .65 .65
374 A91 75c multicolored .85 .85
Nos. 371-374 (4) 2.35 2.35

A92

Sports For All: Various sports.

1981, Aug. 25 Litho. *Perf. 14*

375 A92 10c multicolored .60 .25
376 A92 75c multicolored 2.25 2.25
377 A92 $1 multicolored 2.75 2.75
Nos. 375-377 (3) 5.60 5.25

Intl. Year of the Disabled — A93

10c, Man in wheelchair. 35c, Group. 50c, Teacher, student. 75c, Blind communications worker.

1981, Nov. 24 Litho. *Perf. 14½*

378 A93 10c multicolored .25 .25
379 A93 35c multicolored .60 .60
380 A93 50c multicolored .70 .70
381 A93 75c multicolored .80 .80
Nos. 378-381 (4) 2.35 2.35

Changi Airport Opening — A94

1981, Dec. 29 Litho. *Perf. 14x13½*

382 A94 10c multicolored .30 .30
383 A94 35c multicolored .40 .40
384 A94 50c multicolored .50 .50
385 A94 75c multicolored .70 .70
386 A94 $1 multicolored .90 .90
a. Souvenir sheet of 5, #382-386 4.50 4.50
Nos. 382-386 (5) 2.80 2.80

A95

10c, Clipper. 50c, Blue grassy tiger. $1, Raja Brooke's birdwing.

1982, Mar. 3 Litho. *Perf. 14x14½*

387 A95 10c multicolored .50 .50
388 A95 50c multicolored 1.50 1.50
389 A95 $1 multicolored 2.00 2.00
Nos. 387-389 (3) 4.00 4.00

15th ASEAN Ministerial Meeting — A96

1982, June 14 Litho. *Perf. 14*

390 A96 10c multicolored .25 .25
391 A96 35c multicolored .55 .55
392 A96 50c multicolored .65 .65
393 A96 75c multicolored .85 .85
Nos. 390-393 (4) 2.30 2.30

1982 World Cup — A97

1982, July 9 Litho. *Perf. 12*

394 A97 10c multicolored .25 .25
395 A97 75c multicolored .95 .95
396 A97 $1 multicolored 1.50 1.50
Nos. 394-396 (3) 2.70 2.70

Sultan Shoal Lighthouse, 1896 — A98

1982, Aug. 7

397 A98 10c shown .65 .65
398 A98 75c Horsburgh, 1851 1.40 1.40
399 A98 $1 Raffles, 1855 1.75 1.75
a. Souvenir sheet of 3, #397-399 5.50 5.50
Nos. 397-399 (3) 3.80 3.80

10th Anniv. of PSA Container Terminal A99

1982, Sept. 15 Litho. *Perf. 13½*

400 A99 10c Yard gantry cranes .25 .25
401 A99 35c Computer .50 .50
402 A99 50c Freightlifter .65 .65
403 A99 75c Straddle carrier 1.00 1.00
Nos. 400-403 (4) 2.40 2.40

Scouting Year — A100

1982, Oct. 15 Litho. *Perf. 14x13½*

404 A100 10c Color guard .25 .25
405 A100 35c Hiking .55 .55
406 A100 50c Building tower .65 .65
407 A100 75c Kayaking 1.10 1.10
Nos. 404-407 (4) 2.55 2.55

Productivity Movement A101

10c, Text. 35c, Housing. 50c, Quality control meeting. 75c, Participation.

1982, Nov. 17 *Perf. 13½*

408 A101 10c multicolored .25 .25
409 A101 35c multicolored .45 .45
410 A101 50c multicolored .55 .55
411 A101 75c multicolored .90 .90
Nos. 408-411 (4) 2.15 2.15

Commonwealth Day — A102

1983, May 14 Litho. *Perf. 13½x13*

412 A102 10c multicolored .25 .25
413 A102 35c multicolored .45 .45
414 A102 75c multicolored .50 .50
415 A102 $1 multicolored .85 .85
Nos. 412-415 (4) 2.05 2.05

12th Southeast Asia Games — A103

1983, May 28 Litho. *Perf. 14x13½*

416	A103	10c Soccer	.25	.25
417	A103	35c Racket games	.45	.45
418	A103	75c Athletics	.90	.90
419	A103	$1 Swimming	1.10	1.10
		Nos. 416-419 (4)	2.70	2.70

Neighborhood Watch Safety Campaign A104

1983, June 24 Litho. *Perf. 14*

420	A104	10c Family	.40	.25
421	A104	35c Children	.70	.70
422	A104	75c Community	1.10	1.10
		Nos. 420-422 (3)	2.20	2.05

BANGKOK '83 Intl. Stamp Show, Aug. 4-13 — A105

10c, #282-284, statue of King Chulalongkorn (1868-1910). 35c, #304-307, map of southeast Asia. $1, #390-393, Declaration of ASEAN (Assoc. of South East Asian Nations) signatures, 1976.

1983, Aug. 4 Litho. *Perf. 14x14½*

423	A105	10c multicolored	.35	.25
424	A105	35c multicolored	.65	.65
425	A105	$1 multicolored	1.40	1.40
a.		Souvenir sheet of 3, #423-425	4.75	4.75
		Nos. 423-425 (3)	2.40	2.30

ASEAN Submarine Cable Network A106

1983, Sept. 27 Litho. *Perf. 14*

426	A106	10c multicolored	.30	.25
427	A106	35c multicolored	.90	.90
428	A106	50c multicolored	1.10	1.10
429	A106	75c multicolored	1.75	1.75
a.		Souv. sheet of 6, #304, 359, 426-429	7.00	7.00
		Nos. 426-429 (4)	4.05	4.00

World Communications Year — A107

10c, Telex service. 35c, Telephone numbering plan. 75c, Satellite transmission. $1, Sea communications.

1983, Nov. 10 Litho. *Perf. 13*

430	A107	10c multicolored	.35	.25
431	A107	35c multicolored	.70	.70
432	A107	75c multicolored	1.25	1.25
433	A107	$1 multicolored	1.75	1.75
		Nos. 430-433 (4)	4.05	3.95

Coastal Birds — A108

10c, Slaty-breasted rail. 35c, Black bittern. 50c, Brahminy kite. 75c, Common moorhens.

Perf. 14½x13½

1984, Mar. 15 Litho.

434	A108	10c multicolored	.50	.25
435	A108	35c multicolored	1.25	1.25
436	A108	50c multicolored	1.75	1.75
437	A108	75c multicolored	2.75	2.75
		Nos. 434-437 (4)	6.25	6.00

Natl. Monuments A109

10c, House of Tan Yeok Nee (merchant), 1885. 35c, Thong Chai Building (former hospital), 1892. 50c, Telok Ayer Market, 1894. $1, Nagore Durgha Muslim Shrine, 1828.

1984, June 7 Litho. *Perf. 12*

438	A109	10c multicolored	.25	.25
439	A109	35c multicolored	.50	.50
440	A109	50c multicolored	.75	.75
441	A109	$1 multicolored	1.75	1.75
		Nos. 438-441 (4)	3.25	3.25

A110

1984, Aug. 9 Litho. *Perf. 14*

442	A110	10c No. 121	.25	.25
443	A110	35c No. 377	.45	.45
444	A110	50c No. 99	.65	.65
445	A110	75c No. 243	1.00	1.00
446	A110	$1 No. 386	1.40	1.40
447	A110	$2 No. 367	2.50	2.50
a.		Souvenir sheet of 6, #442-447	9.00	9.00
		Nos. 442-447 (6)	6.25	6.25

25th anniv. of self-government.

A111

Total Defense: a, This is our country. b, We are one. c, We work together. d, We are prepared. e, We are ready.

1984, Oct. 26 Litho. *Perf. 12*

448		Strip of 5	1.00	1.00
a.-e.		A111 10c any single	.25	.25

Bridges A112

1985, Mar. 15 Engr. *Perf. 14½x14*

449	A112	10c Coleman	.25	.25
450	A112	35c Cavenagh	.40	.40
451	A112	75c Elgin	1.00	1.00
452	A112	$1 Benjamin Sheares	1.50	1.50
		Nos. 449-452 (4)	3.15	3.15

Insects — A113

5c, Ceriagrion cerinorubellum. 10c, Apis javana. 15c, Delta arcuata. 20c, Xylocopa caerulea. 25c, Donacia javana. 35c, Heteroneda reticulata. 50c, Catacanthus nigripes. 75c, Chremistica pontianaka. $1, Homoeoxipha lycoides. $2, Traulia azureipennis. $5, Trithemis aurora. $10, Scambophyllum sangiunolentum.

1985 Litho. *Perf. 13x13½*

453	A113	5c multicolored	.25	.25
454	A113	10c multicolored	.25	.25
455	A113	15c multicolored	.25	.25
456	A113	20c multicolored	.25	.25
457	A113	25c multicolored	.30	.30
458	A113	35c multicolored	.50	.50
459	A113	50c multicolored	.65	.65
460	A113	75c multicolored	1.25	1.25

Litho. & Engr.

Size: 35x30mm

461	A113	$1 multicolored	2.25	.60
462	A113	$2 multicolored	3.00	2.00
463	A113	$5 multicolored	7.25	5.00
464	A113	$10 multicolored	14.00	8.00
		Nos. 453-464 (12)	30.20	19.30

Issued: #453-460, 4/24; #461-464, 6/5.

Redrawn

1988 *Perf. 13x13½*

453a	A113	5c	1.00	.30
454a	A113	10c	1.00	.30
455a	A113	15c	1.00	.30
456a	A113	20c	5.00	.30
457a	A113	25c	9.00	.80
458a	A113	35c	15.00	1.00
459a	A113	50c	30.00	1.50
460a	A113	75c	50.00	2.00
		Nos. 453a-460a (8)	112.00	6.50

Singapore is 20½mm long on Nos. 453a-454a; 21mm long on Nos. 453-454. Rock is 1½mm from bottom right on No. 455; 2½mm on No. 455a. Pink flower touches frame on No. 456; is clear of the frame on No. 456a. Feelers indistinct and left one touches frame on No. 457; feelers sharp and left one ends just below frame on No. 457a.

Vein of leaf at lower left stops short of frame on No. 458; vein touches frame on No. 458a. Leaf at top touches frame on No. 459; leaf is below frame on No. 459a. Wing ends 1½mm above frame on No. 460; wing touches frame at bottom on No. 460a.

Other differences exist in the position and sharpness of the design and colors.

People's Assoc., 25th Anniv. — A114

Montage of public services.

1985, July 1 *Perf. 13½x14*

465	A114	10c multicolored	.25	.25
466	A114	35c multicolored	.40	.40
467	A114	50c multicolored	.70	.75
468	A114	75c multicolored	1.00	1.00
		Nos. 465-468 (4)	2.35	2.40

Public Housing, 25th Anniv. — A115

Modern housing developments.

1985, Aug. 9

469	A115	10c multicolored	.25	.25
470	A115	35c multicolored	.45	.45
471	A115	50c multicolored	.60	.60
472	A115	75c multicolored	.90	.90
a.		Souv. sheet of 4, #469-472	4.50	4.50
		Nos. 469-472 (4)	2.20	2.20

Girl Guides, 75th Anniv. — A116

Activities.

1985, Nov 6 *Perf. 14½x14*

473	A116	10c Brownies	.25	.25
474	A116	35c Guides	.50	.50
475	A116	50c Seniors	.65	.65
476	A116	75c Guide leaders	1.10	1.10
		Nos. 473-476 (4)	2.50	2.50

Intl. Youth Year — A117

10c, Youth assoc. emblems. 75c, Hand, sapling. $1, Dove, stick figures.

1985, Dec. 18 *Perf. 13*

477	A117	10c multicolored	.25	.25
478	A117	75c multicolored	.90	.75
479	A117	$1 multicolored	1.10	1.10
		Nos. 477-479 (3)	2.25	2.10

Indigenous Fruit — A118

10c, Psidium guajava. 35c, Eugenia aquea. 50c, Nephelium lappaceum. 75c, Manilkara zapota.

1986, Feb. 26 Litho. *Perf. 14½x14*

480	A118	10c multicolored	.40	.25
481	A118	35c multicolored	.95	.75
482	A118	50c multicolored	1.25	1.25
483	A118	75c multicolored	1.75	1.75
		Nos. 480-483 (4)	4.35	4.00

Natl. Trade Unions Cong., 25th Anniv. — A119

Progress: a, Science and technology. b, Communications. c, Industry. d, Education.

1986, May 1 *Perf. 13½*

484		A119 Strip of 4	1.75	1.75
a.-d.		10c any single	.25	.25

Souvenir Sheet

485		Sheet of 4	4.75	4.75
a.-d.		A119 35c any single	.50	.50

EXPO '86, Vancouver A120

1986, May 2 *Perf. 14½x14*

486		Strip of 3	3.50	3.50
a.		A120 50c Calligraphy	.60	.60
b.		A120 75c Garland making	1.10	1.10
c.		A120 $1 Batik printing	1.25	1.25

Economic Development Board, 25th Anniv. — A121

10c, Automation. 35c, Precision engineering. 50c, Electronics. 75c, Biotechnology.

1986, Aug. 1 ***Perf. 15***

487	A121	10c multicolored	.25	.25
488	A121	35c multicolored	.40	.40
489	A121	50c multicolored	.60	.60
490	A121	75c multicolored	.70	.70
		Nos. 487-490 (4)	1.95	1.95

Submarine Cable — A122

1986, Sept. 8 ***Perf. 13½***

491	A122	10c multicolored	.45	.25
492	A122	35c multicolored	.90	.60
493	A122	50c multicolored	1.25	1.00
494	A122	75c multicolored	1.50	1.50
		Nos. 491-494 (4)	4.10	3.35

Citizens' Consultative Committees, 21st Anniv. — A123

1986, Oct 15 ***Perf. 12***

495	A123	Block of 4	2.75	2.75
a.		10c multicolored	.25	.25
b.		35c multicolored	.50	.50
c.		50c multicolored	.75	.75
d.		75c multicolored	1.10	1.10

Intl. Peace Year — A124

10c, People. 35c, Southeast Asia map. $1, Globe.

1986, Dec. 17 Litho. ***Perf. 14x13½***

496	A124	10c multicolored	.30	.25
497	A124	35c multicolored	.70	.70
498	A124	$1 multicolored	1.40	1.40
		Nos. 496-498 (3)	2.40	2.35

Views of Singapore A125

10c, Orchard Road. 50c, Central business district. 75c, Marina Center, Raffles City.

1987, Feb. 25 ***Perf. 12x12½***

499	A125	10c multicolored	.25	.25
500	A125	50c multicolored	.75	.75
501	A125	75c multicolored	1.00	1.00
		Nos. 499-501 (3)	2.00	2.00

Assoc. of Southeast Asian Nations (ASEAN), 20th Anniv. — A126

1987, June 15 ***Perf. 12***

502	A126	10c multicolored	.25	.25
503	A126	35c multicolored	.45	.45
504	A126	50c multicolored	.70	.70
505	A126	75c multicolored	1.00	1.00
		Nos. 502-505 (4)	2.40	2.40

National Service, 20th Anniv. — A127

Designs: a, Army. b, Navy. c, Air Force. d, Pledge of Allegiance. e, Singapore Lion.

1987, July 1 ***Perf. 15x14***

506	A127	Strip of 4	2.25	2.25
a.-d.		10c any single	.25	.25
507	A127	Sheet of 5	5.00	5.00
a.-e.		35c any single	.45	.45

River Life — A128

1987, Sept. 2 ***Perf. 14***

508	A128	10c Singapore River	.30	.25
509	A128	50c Kallang Basin	.90	.90
510	A128	$1 Kranji Reservoir	2.75	2.75
		Nos. 508-510 (3)	3.95	3.90

Natl. Museum Cent. A129

Views of the museum and artifacts: 10c, Majapahis gold bracelet, 14th-15th cent. 75c, Ming fluted kendi (water jar). $1, Seventeen-wave kris (sword with silver hilt, sheath), property of Sultan Abdul Jalil Sabat, 1699.

1987, Oct. 12 Litho. ***Perf. 13½x14***

511	A129	10c multicolored	.45	.25
512	A129	75c multicolored	1.50	1.50
513	A129	$1 multicolored	1.75	1.75
		Nos. 511-513 (3)	3.70	3.50

Singapore Science Center, 10th Anniv. A130

Attractions.

1987, Dec. 10 ***Perf. 14½***

514	A130	10c Omni Theater	.35	.25
515	A130	35c Omni Planetarium	1.00	1.00
516	A130	75c Cellular model	2.00	2.00
517	A130	$1 Science exhibits	2.60	2.60
		Nos. 514-517 (4)	5.95	5.85

Artillery, Cent. A131

Designs: 10c, 155-Gun Howitzer and Khatib Camp, headquarters of the Singapore Gunners. 35c, 25-Pound gun salute and Singapore City Hall. 50c, 4.5-inch Howitzer and Singapore Cricket Club, c. 1928. $1, Ft. Fullerton Drill Hall, c. 1893, and .405 Maxim gun.

1988, Feb. 22 Litho. ***Perf. 13½x14***

518	A131	10c multicolored	.60	.25
519	A131	35c multicolored	1.75	1.25
520	A131	50c multicolored	2.00	2.00
521	A131	$1 multicolored	2.75	2.40
		Nos. 518-521 (4)	7.10	5.90

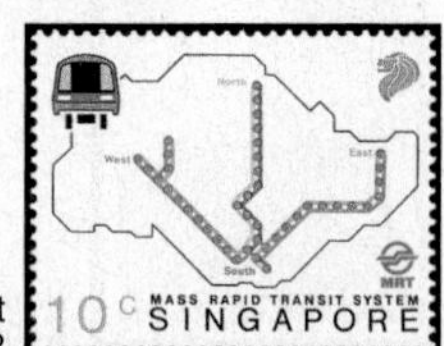

Mass Transit A132

1988, Mar. 12 ***Perf. 14***

522	A132	10c Rail car, map	1.20	.25
523	A132	50c Elevated train	2.75	2.50
524	A132	$1 Urban subway	4.50	4.00
		Nos. 522-524 (3)	8.45	6.75

See No. 1064.

Natl. Television Broadcast System, 25th Anniv. A133

35c, Studio. 75c, Television, transmission tower. $1, Screen, satellite dish.

1988, Apr. 4 Litho. ***Perf. 13½x14***

525	A133	10c shown	.40	.25
526	A133	35c multicolored	.85	.85
527	A133	75c multicolored	1.25	1.25
528	A133	$1 multicolored	2.25	2.25
		Nos. 525-528 (4)	4.75	4.60

Public Utilities Board, 25th Anniv. — A134

1988, May 4 Litho. ***Perf. 13½***

529	A134	10c Water works	.35	.25
530	A134	50c Electric company	1.20	1.20
531	A134	$1 Fossil fuels	2.10	2.00
a.		Souvenir sheet of 3, #529-531	6.00	6.00
		Nos. 529-531 (3)	3.65	3.45

Courtesy Campaign, 10th Anniv. — A135

Singa the lion (character trademark) and: 10c, Neighbors. 30c, Store service counter. $1, Helping the elderly.

1988, July 6 Litho. ***Perf. 14½***

532	A135	10c multicolored	.35	.25
533	A135	30c multicolored	.70	.70
534	A135	$1 multicolored	1.90	1.90
		Nos. 532-534 (3)	2.95	2.85

Fire Service, Cent. A136

10c, Turntable ladder truck. $1, 1890s Steam pump.

1988, Nov. 1 Litho. ***Perf. 13½***

535	A136	10c multicolored	1.00	.25
536	A136	$1 multicolored	4.75	4.75

Port Authority, 25th Anniv. — A137

Various facilities.

1989, Apr. 3 Litho. ***Perf. 14x13½***

537	A137	10c multicolored	.80	.25
538	A137	30c multi, diff.	1.20	.60
539	A137	75c multi, diff.	1.75	1.75
540	A137	$1 multi, diff.	2.00	2.00
		Nos. 537-540 (4)	5.75	4.60

Old Chinatown A138

1989, May 17 Litho. ***Perf. 14½***

541	A138	10c Sago St.	.55	.30
542	A138	35c Pagoda St.	1.40	1.00
543	A138	75c Trengganu St.	2.50	2.50
544	A138	$1 Temple St.	2.75	2.75
		Nos. 541-544 (4)	7.20	6.55

Maps of Singapore — A139

Early 19th cent. map Singapore Showing Principal Residences and Places of Interest: No. 545a, Upper left. No. 545b, Upper right. No. 545c, Lower left. No. 545d, Lower right.

No. 546, Singapore and Dependencies. No. 547, Plan of the British Settlement.

1989, July 26 Litho. ***Perf. 14½***

545	A139	Block of 4	7.00	7.00
a.-d.		15c any single	1.75	1.60

Size: 33x31mm

Perf. 12½x13

546	A139	50c multi	3.00	2.50
547	A139	$1 multi	3.50	3.50
		Nos. 545-547 (3)	13.50	13.00

Fish — A140

15c, Clown triggerfish. 30c, Majestic angelfish. 75c, Emperor angelfish. $1, Royal empress angelfish.

1989, Sept. 6 *Perf. 14*

548 A140 15c multicolored 2.00 2.00
549 A140 30c multicolored 2.10 2.50
550 A140 75c multicolored 4.00 4.00
551 A140 $1 multicolored 4.50 4.25
Nos. 548-551 (4) 12.60 12.75

Festivals — A141

Children's drawings: 15c, *Hari Raya Puasa,* by Loke Yoke Yen. 35c, *Chinese New Year,* by Simon Koh. 75c, *Thaipusam,* by Henry Setiono. $1, *Christmas,* by Wendy Ang Lin.

1989, Oct. 25 Litho. *Perf. 14½*

552 A141 15c multicolored .30 .25
553 A141 35c multicolored 1.75 1.75
554 A141 75c multicolored 2.50 2.50
555 A141 $1 multicolored 2.00 2.00
a. Souv. sheet of 4, #552-555, perf. 14 5.50 5.50
Nos. 552-555 (4) 6.55 6.50

Singapore Indoor Stadium — A142

1989, Dec. 27 Litho. *Perf. 14½*

556 A142 30c North entrance 1.00 .35
557 A142 75c Interior 2.00 1.50
558 A142 $1 East entrance 2.50 1.75
a. Souvenir sheet of 3, #556-558 6.50 6.50
Nos. 556-558 (3) 5.50 3.60

Sports issue.

Lithographs of 19th Cent. Singapore A143

15c, Singapore River, 1839. 30c, Chinatown, 1837. 75c, Waterfront, 1837. $1, View from Ft. Canning, 1824.

1990, Feb. 21 Litho. *Perf. 13*

559 A143 15c multicolored .90 .25
Complete booklet, 10 #559 12.00
560 A143 30c multicolored 1.25 .75
561 A143 75c multicolored 2.25 2.25
562 A143 $1 multicolored 2.75 2.75
Nos. 559-562 (4) 7.15 6.00

First Postage Stamps, 150th Anniv. — A144

Maps and: 50c, Nos. 101-106. 75c, Cover to Scotland. $1, Cover to Ireland $2, Great Britain Nos. 1, 2.

1990, May 3 Litho. *Perf. 13½*

563 A144 50c multicolored .75 .70
564 A144 75c multicolored 1.10 1.25
565 A144 $1 multicolored 2.25 2.00
566 A144 $2 multicolored 3.75 3.00
a. Souvenir sheet of 4, #563-566 10.50 10.50
Nos. 563-566 (4) 7.85 6.95

Tourism A145

1990, July 4 *Perf. 14½*

567 A145 5c Zoo .25 .25
568 A145 15c Resort .25 .25
a. Booklet pane of 10 12.00
569 A145 20c City .25 .25
a. Booklet pane of 10 — —
Complete booklet, #569a —
570 A145 25c Dragon boat race .25 .25
571 A145 30c Hotel .35 .35
572 A145 35c Caged birds .45 .40
573 A145 40c Park .50 .45
574 A145 50c Festival .60 .50
575 A145 75c Building, diff. .90 .60
Nos. 567-575 (9) 3.80 3.30

Issued: No. 569a, 3/6/91.

Independence, 25th Anniv. — A146

1990, Aug. 16 Litho. *Perf. 14x14½*

576 A146 15c shown 1.25 .40
a. Booklet pane of 10 17.50
577 A146 35c One Singapore 1.40 1.00
578 A146 75c One hope 2.25 2.25
579 A146 $1 One people 2.75 2.75
Nos. 576-579 (4) 7.65 6.40

Tourism A147

$1, Chinese opera singer, Siong Lim Temple. $2, Malay dancer, Sultan Mosque. $5, Indian dancer, Sri Mariamman Temple. $10, Ballet dancer, Victoria Memorial Hall.

Photo. & Engr.

1990, Oct. 10 *Perf. 15x14*

580 A147 $1 multicolored 1.75 1.60
581 A147 $2 multicolored 3.25 2.50
582 A147 $5 multicolored 7.50 6.50
583 A147 $10 multicolored 14.00 14.00
Nos. 580-583 (4) 26.50 24.60

Ferns A148

1990, Nov. 14 Litho. *Perf. 14*

584 A148 15c Stag's horn .35 .25
585 A148 35c Maiden hair .75 .75
586 A148 75c Bird's nest 1.50 1.50
587 A148 $1 Rabbit's foot 1.90 1.90
Nos. 584-587 (4) 4.50 4.40

Houses of Worship A149

Designs: 20c, Hong San See Temple, 1912. 50c, Abdul Gattoor Mosque, 1910. 75c, Sri Perumal Temple, 1961. $1, St. Andrew's Cathedral, 1863.

1991, Jan. 23 Litho. *Perf. 14½*

588 20c multicolored .35 .35
589 20c multicolored .35 .35
a. A149 Pair, #588-589 .90 .90
590 50c multicolored .85 .85
591 50c multicolored .85 .85
a. A149 Pair, #590-591 2.00 2.00
592 75c multicolored 1.25 1.25
593 75c multicolored 1.25 1.25
a. A149 Pair, #592-593 3.00 3.00
594 $1 multicolored 1.50 1.50
595 $1 multicolored 1.50 1.50
a. A149 Pair, #594-595 4.50 4.50
Nos. 588-595 (8) 7.90 7.90

Singapore '95 Intl. Philatelic Exhibition — A151

No. 596, Vanda Miss Joaquim. No. 597, Dendrobium Anocha.

1991, Apr. 24 Litho. *Perf. 14*

596 $2 multicolored 3.00 1.50
597 $2 multicolored 3.00 1.50
a. A151 Pair, #596-597 + label 8.00 8.00
b. Souvenir sheet, #596-597 12.00 12.00

See Nos. 615-616, 664-665, 685-686, 716-717.

Civilian Airports A152

Designs: 20c, Boeing 747, Changi Terminal II, 1991. 75c, Boeing 747, Changi Terminal I, 1981. $1, Concorde, Paya Lebar, 1955-1981. $2, DC-3, Kallang, 1937-1955.

Perf. 13½x14½

1991, July 1 **Litho. & Engr.**

598 A152 20c multicolored .50 .40
599 A152 75c multicolored 1.75 1.50
600 A152 $1 multicolored 2.25 2.25
601 A152 $2 multicolored 6.00 6.00
Nos. 598-601 (4) 10.50 10.15

Arachnopsis Eric Holttum A153

Orchids: 30c, Cattleya Meadii. $1, Calanthe vestita.

1991, Aug. 8 Litho. *Perf. 14½x13½*

602 A153 20c multicolored 1.00 .50
603 A153 30c multicolored 1.40 1.40
604 A153 $1 multicolored 3.50 3.50
Nos. 602-604 (3) 5.90 5.40

Birds — A154

Designs: 20c, Common tailorbird. 35c, Scarlet-backed flowerpecker. 75c, Black-naped oriole. $1, Common tora.

1991, Sept. 19 *Perf. 14*

605 A154 20c multicolored .45 .25
a. Booklet pane of 10 22.50 *22.50*
606 A154 35c multicolored 1.50 1.50
607 A154 75c multicolored 2.50 2.00
608 A154 $1 multicolored 3.75 3.00
Nos. 605-608 (4) 8.20 6.75

10 Years of Productivity A155

$1, Construction engineers.

1991, Nov. 1 Litho. *Perf. 14x14½*

609 A155 20c shown .25 .25
610 A155 $1 multicolored 1.60 1.60

Phila Nippon '91 — A156

Flowers: 30c, Railway creeper. 75c, Asystasia. $1, Singapore rhododendron. $2, Coat buttons.

1991, Nov. 16 *Perf. 14½x14*

611 A156 30c multicolored .90 .45
612 A156 75c multicolored 1.40 1.40
613 A156 $1 multicolored 1.75 1.75
614 A156 $2 multicolored 3.25 3.25
a. Souvenir sheet of 4, #611-614 10.00 10.00
Nos. 611-614 (4) 7.30 6.85

Flower Type of 1991

Designs: No. 615, Dendrobium Sharifah Fatimah. No. 616, Phalaenopsis Shim Beauty.

1992, Jan. 22 Litho. *Perf. 14*

615 A151 $2 multicolored 3.50 3.00
616 A151 $2 multicolored 3.50 3.00
a. Pair, #615-616 + label 7.25 7.25
b. Souvenir sheet of 2, #615-616 13.00 13.00

Singapore '95 Intl. Philatelic Exhibition.

Paintings A157

20c, Singapore Waterfront, 1958. 75c, Kampung Hut, 1973. $1, Bridge, 1983. $2,

1992, Mar. 11 Litho. *Perf. 14*

617 A157 20c multicolored .50 .30
618 A157 75c multicolored 1.00 1.00
619 A157 $1 multicolored 2.00 1.00
620 A157 $2 multicolored 3.50 2.50
Nos. 617-620 (4) 7.00 4.80

1992 Summer Olympics, Barcelona
A158

1992, Apr. 24 ***Perf. 14***

621 A158 20c Soccer .35 .30
622 A158 35c Relay races .45 .35
623 A158 50c Swimming .70 .70
624 A158 75c Basketball 1.25 1.25
625 A158 $1 Tennis 1.75 1.75
626 A158 $2 Sailing 2.40 2.40
a. Souvenir sheet of 6, #621-626 11.00 11.00
Nos. 621-626 (6) 6.90 6.75

No. 626a exists with two different inscriptions in the bottom selvage: "XXVth Olympic Games 1992 Barcelona" and "Games of the XXVth Olympiad."

Costumes, 1910 — A159

20c, Chinese family. 35c, Malay family. 75c, Indian family. $2, Straits Chinese family.

1992, Apr. 24 **Litho.** ***Perf. 14½***

627 A159 20c multi .45 .30
628 A159 35c multi .70 .55
629 A159 75c multi 1.50 1.50
630 A159 $2 multi 2.25 2.25
Nos. 627-630 (4) 4.90 4.60

Natl. Military Forces, 25th Anniv. — A160

Designs: 35c, Frogman with gun, fighter plane, artillery. $1, Fighter, tank, ship.

1992, July 1

631 A160 20c multicolored .40 .25
632 A160 35c multicolored 1.00 .75
633 A160 $1 multicolored 3.00 3.00
Nos. 631-633 (3) 4.40 4.00

Visit ASEAN Year, 25th Anniv. A161

Designs: 20c, Mask, bird, sea life. 35c, Costumed women. $1, Outdoor scenery.

1992, Aug. 8

634 A161 20c multicolored .45 .30
635 A161 35c multicolored 1.25 1.25
636 A161 $1 multicolored 2.40 2.40
Nos. 634-636 (3) 4.10 3.95

Crabs
A162

Designs: 20c, Mosaic crab. 50c, Johnson's freshwater crab. 75c, Singapore freshwater crab. $1, Swamp forest crab.

1992, Aug. 21 ***Perf. 14½x15***

637 A162 20c multicolored .45 .30
a. Booklet pane of 10 13.00
638 A162 50c multicolored 1.00 1.00
639 A162 75c multicolored 1.75 1.75
640 A162 $1 multicolored 2.25 2.25
Nos. 637-640 (4) 5.45 5.30

Currency, Notes and Coins — A163

1992, Oct. 2 **Litho.** ***Perf. 14½***

641 20c Coins .75 .40
642 75c Coin, flowers on note 1.50 1.50
643 $1 Boat on note, coins 2.00 2.00
644 $2 Bird on note 3.00 3.00
a. A163 Block of 4, #641-644 8.25 *8.25*
Nos. 641-644 (4) 7.25 6.90

Wild Animals A164

1993, Jan. 13 **Litho.** ***Perf. 14½x15***

645 A164 20c Sun bear .30 .30
646 A164 30c Orangutan .60 .60
647 A164 75c Slow loris 1.40 1.40
648 A164 $2 Large mouse deer 4.00 4.00
Nos. 645-648 (4) 6.30 6.30

Greetings Stamps — A165

a, Thank you. b, Congratulations. c, Best wishes. d, Happy birthday. e, Get well soon.

Perf. 14½x14 on 3 Sides

1993, Feb. 10 **Booklet Stamps**

649 A165 20c Strip of 5, #a.-e. 3.50 *3.50*
f. Booklet pane of 2 #649 7.25 *7.25*

Preservation of Tanjong Pagar — A166

30c, Building facade, tower. $2, Aerial view.

1993, Mar. 10 **Litho.** ***Perf. 14***

650 A166 20c shown .40 .30
651 A166 30c multi 1.50 1.50
652 A166 $2 multi 4.50 4.50
Nos. 650-652 (3) 6.40 6.30

Cranes, by Chen Wen Hsi — A167

1993, May 29 ***Perf. 12x11½***

653 A167 $2 multicolored 3.25 2.00

Indopex '93.

A168

1993, June 12 **Litho.** ***Perf. 14***

654 A168 20c Soccer .40 .30
655 A168 35c Basketball .70 .60
656 A168 50c Badminton .90 .90
657 A168 75c Running 1.00 1.00
658 A168 $1 Water polo 1.40 1.40
659 A168 $2 Yachting 2.25 2.00
Nos. 654-659 (6) 6.65 6.20

17th Southeast Asian (SEA) Games, Singapore.

Butterflies A169

20c, Plain tiger. 50c, Malay lacewing. 75c, Palm king. $1, Banded swallowtail.

1993, Aug. 21 **Litho.** ***Perf. 14½***

660 A169 20c multi .30 .30
a. Booklet pane of 10 11.50
661 A169 50c multi .80 .80
662 A169 75c multi 1.50 1.50
663 A169 $1 multi 2.00 2.00
Nos. 660-663 (4) 4.60 4.60

Flower Type of 1991

No. 664, Phalaenopsis amabilis. No. 665, Vanda sumatrana.

1993, Aug. 13 **Size: 26x34mm**

664 A151 $2 multicolored 3.00 3.00
665 A151 $2 multicolored 3.00 3.00
a. Pair, #664-665 + label 7.50 *7.50*
b. Souvenir sheet of 2, #664-665, perf. 15x14½ 8.00 8.00

Singapore '95 World Stamp Exhibition and Taipei '93, Asian Intl. Invitation Stamp Exhibition (#665b).

Fruits — A170

1993, Oct. 1 **Litho.** ***Perf. 14½x14***

666 A170 20c Papaya .50 .30
667 A170 35c Pomegranate .75 .60
668 A170 75c Starfruit 1.50 1.50
669 A170 $2 Durian 2.25 2.25
a. Souvenir sheet of 4, #666-669 6.00 6.00
Nos. 666-669 (4) 5.00 4.65

Bangkok '93 (#669a).

Chinese Egrets — A171

Designs: 20c, Two, one with bill in water. 25c, Two, one with fish in mouth. 30c, Two facing opposite directions. 35c, In flight.

1993, Nov. 10 **Litho.** ***Perf. 13½x14***

670 A171 20c multicolored *.75* *.40*
671 A171 25c multicolored *.80* *.80*
672 A171 30c multicolored *1.25* *1.25*
673 A171 35c multicolored *1.50* *1.50*
a. Strip of 4, #670-673 *5.25* *5.25*

World Wildlife Fund.

Palm Tree — A171a

1993, Nov. 24 **Photo.** ***Die Cut***

Self-Adhesive

Booklet Stamp

673B A171a (20c) multicolored .75 .75
c. Booklet pane of 15 13.50 13.50

By its nature, No. 673c is a complete booklet. The peelable backing serves as a booklet cover.

Marine Life — A172

5c, Tiger cowrie. 20c, Sea fan. (20c), Blue-spotted stingray. 25c, Tunicate. 30c, Clownfish. 35c, Nudibranch. 40c, Sea urchin. 50c, Soft coral. 75c, Pin cushion star. $1, Knob coral. $2, Mushroom coral. $5, Bubble coral. $10, Octopus coral. No. 684B, Blue-spotted stingray.

Perf. 13x13½, 13½x14 (#675B)

1994 **Litho.**

674 A172 5c multi .25 .25
675 A172 20c multi .35 .25
a. Booklet pane of 10 4.00
675B A172 (20c) multi .40 .25
676 A172 25c multi .50 .30
677 A172 30c multi .55 .30
678 A172 35c multi .65 .50
679 A172 40c multi .70 .30
680 A172 50c multi .90 .30
681 A172 75c multi 1.40 1.00

Litho. & Engraved

Perf. 14 Syncopated

682 A172 $1 sil & multi 2.00 1.00
683 A172 $2 sil & multi 5.00 3.00
684 A172 $5 sil & multi 9.00 6.00
684A A172 $10 sil & multi 15.00 6.00
Nos. 674-684A (13) 36.70 19.45

Self-Adhesive

Die Cut Perf. 8½

684B A172 (20c) multi .75 .75
c. Booklet pane of 10 13.00

Nos. 675B, 684B inscribed "FOR LOCAL ADDRESSES ONLY." By its nature, No. 684Bc is a complete booklet. The peelable paper backing serves as a booklet cover.

Issued: 5c-75c, 1/12/94; $1-$10, 3/23/94; #675B, 684B, 11/16/94.

See Nos. 816-824.

Flower Type of 1991

Designs: No. 685, Paphiopedilum victoriaregina. No. 686, Dendrobium smillieae.

1994, Feb. 18 **Litho.** ***Perf. 14½***

Size: 26x35mm

685 A151 $2 multicolored 3.50 3.50
686 A151 $2 multicolored 3.50 3.50
a. Pair, #685-686 + label 8.50 *8.50*
b. Souvenir sheet of 2, #685-686 9.00 9.00

Singapore '95 and Hong Kong '94 (#686b).

Spring Festival — A173

1994, May 18 **Litho.** ***Perf. 13½***

687 A173 20c Ballet .40 .25
688 A173 30c Mime, puppets .80 .80
689 A173 50c Musicians 1.00 1.00
690 A173 $1 Crafts 2.00 2.00
Nos. 687-690 (4) 4.20 4.05

Operationally Ready Natl. Servicemen, 25th Anniv. — A174

Civilian-soldiers: 20c, Saluting flag, aiming anti-tank missile. 30c, With family, on jungle patrol with automatic rifle. 35c, Reading newspaper, aiming machine gun. 75c, Working with computer, and as commander, looking through binoculars.

1994, July 1 Litho. *Perf. 13½*

691	A174	20c multicolored	.75	.40
692	A174	30c multicolored	1.00	1.00
693	A174	35c multicolored	1.25	1.25
694	A174	75c multicolored	2.00	2.00
		Nos. 691-694 (4)	5.00	4.65

Herons — A175

20c, Black-crowned night heron. 50c, Little heron. 75c, Purple heron. $1, Gray heron.

1994, Aug. 16 Litho. *Perf. 14*

695		20c multicolored	.65	.65
a.		Booklet pane of 10	11.50	
696		50c multicolored	.95	.95
697		75c multicolored	1.00	1.00
698		$1 multicolored	1.40	1.40
a.	A175	Block of 4, #695-698	5.50	*5.50*
		Nos. 695-698 (4)	4.00	4.00

Greetings Stamps — A175a

#698B, Birthday cake. #698C, Bouquet of flowers. #698D, Gift-wrapped present. #698E, Fireworks. #698F, Balloons.

Die Cut Perf. 11½

1994, Sept. 14 Litho.

Self-Adhesive

Booklet Stamps

698B	A175a	(20c) multicolored	.75	*.85*
698C	A175a	(20c) multicolored	.75	*.85*
698D	A175a	(20c) multicolored	.75	*.85*
698E	A175a	(20c) multicolored	.75	*.85*
698F	A175a	(20c) multicolored	.75	*.85*
g.		Bklt. pane, 2 ea #698B-698F	7.50	*8.50*
		Nos. 698B-698F (5)	3.75	*4.25*

Nos. 698B-693F inscribed "For Local Addresses Only." By its nature, No. 698Fg is a complete booklet. The peelable paper backing serves as a booklet cover. The outside of the cover contains 10 peelable labels.

Modern Singapore, 175th Anniv. — A176

Early, modern scenes: 20c, Schoolchildren reading, graduating seniors. 50c, Horse-drawn carriages, high-speed train. 75c, Small boats, container ship dock. $1, Skyline.

1994, Sept. 30 *Perf. 13½x14*

699	A176	20c multicolored	.55	.55
700	A176	50c multicolored	.90	.90
701	A176	75c multicolored	1.10	1.10
702	A176	$1 multicolored	1.50	1.50
a.		Souvenir sheet of 4, #699-702	5.00	5.00
		Nos. 699-702 (4)	4.05	4.05

No. 702a exists with Singpex '94 overprint. Value $25.

ICAO, 50th Anniv. A177

Designs: 35c, Control tower, passenger jet. 75c, Terminal, Concord jet. $2, Control tower, communication satellite, passenger jet.

1994, Oct. 5 Litho. *Perf. 14*

703	A177	20c multicolored	.35	.35
704	A177	35c multicolored	.65	.65
705	A177	75c multicolored	1.00	1.00
706	A177	$2 multicolored	2.75	2.75
		Nos. 703-706 (4)	4.75	4.75

Love Stamps — A178

#707, "Love" in three different inscriptions. #708, Spiral of "Love." #709, "Love" on two lines. #710, "Love" in different languages. #711, Geometrical "Love."

Die Cut Perf. 11½

1995, Feb. 8 Litho.

Self-Adhesive

Booklet Stamps

707	A178	(20c) multicolored	1.10	1.10
708	A178	(20c) multicolored	1.10	1.10
709	A178	(20c) multicolored	1.10	1.10
710	A178	(20c) multicolored	1.10	1.10
711	A178	(20c) multicolored	1.10	1.10
a.		Booklet pane, 2 each #707-711	12.50	
		Nos. 707-711 (5)	5.50	5.50

Nos. 707-711 inscribed "FOR LOCAL ADDRESSES ONLY." By its nature, No. 711a is a complete booklet. The peelable paper backing serves as a booklet cover. The outside of the cover contains 10 peelable labels.

Meet in Singapore — A179

Scenes in Suntec City: (20c), Intl. Convention & Exhibition Center. 75c, High rise buildings. $1, Temasek Boulevard. $2, Fountain Terrace.

1995, Jan. 11 *Perf. 13½x14*

712	A179	(20c) multicolored	.40	.30
713	A179	75c multicolored	1.00	1.00
714	A179	$1 multicolored	1.50	1.50
715	A179	$2 multicolored	3.00	3.00
		Nos. 712-715 (4)	5.90	5.80

Singapore '95. No. 712 inscribed "FOR LOCAL ADDRESSES ONLY."

Souvenir Sheets of 2, #712, 715 Inscribed:

715a	FIP DAY	8.50	8.50
715b	OLYMPIC DAY-YOUTH	8.50	8.50
715c	FIAP DAY	8.50	8.50
715d	LETTER WRITING DAY	8.50	8.50
715e	STAMP COLLECTING DAY	8.50	8.50
715f	SINGAPORE '95 DAY	8.50	8.50
715g	PHILATELIC MUSEUM DAY	8.50	8.50
715h	SINGAPORE POST DAY	8.50	8.50
715i	AWARDS DAY	8.50	8.50
715j	THEMATIC PHILATELY DAY	8.50	8.50

Flower Type of 1991

Designs: No. 716, Vanda Marlie Dolera, No. 717, Vanda limbata.

1995, Mar. 15 Litho. *Perf. 14*

716	A151	$2 multicolored	2.50	2.50
717	A151	$2 multicolored	2.50	2.50
a.		Pair, #716-717 + label	6.00	*6.00*
b.		Souvenir sheet, #716-717	11.50	11.50
c.		Souvenir sheet, #716-717	10.00	10.00

Singapore '95 (#717a-717c).

The margin of No. 717b pictures a chimpanzee in the jungle and No. 717c pictures a fish. No. 717b exists imperf. Value, $50.

Three limited edition sheets were issued 9/1/95 at the show. They sold for 50, 12.5 and 2.9 times face. Values, $550, $220, $350.

Independence, 30th Anniv. — A180

"My Singapore, My Country, Happy Birthday" in various languages and: 20c, "30" formed in ribbon, vert. 50c, #471, flower. 75c, #598, Music sheet. $1, Natl. flag, #489, music sheets, vert.

Perf. 14x13½, 13½x14

1995, Apr. 19 Litho.

718	A180	(20c) multicolored	.40	.30
719	A180	50c multicolored	.80	.80
720	A180	75c multicolored	1.25	1.25
721	A180	$1 multicolored	1.50	1.50
a.		Souvenir sheet of 4, #718-721	6.00	6.00
		Nos. 718-721 (4)	3.95	3.85

No. 718 inscribed "For Local Addresses Only." No. 721a is a continuous design.

End of World War II, 50th Anniv. A181

Designs: (20c), Crowd celebrating, Straits Settlements #271, vert. 60c, Lord Mountbatten receiving Japanese surrender of Singapore, Straits Settlements #265, vert. 70c, Food kitchen. $2, Police road block.

Perf. 14x13½, 13½x14

1995, June 21 Litho.

723	A181	(20c) multicolored	.30	.30
724	A181	60c multicolored	.90	.90
725	A181	70c multicolored	1.05	1.05
726	A181	$2 multicolored	2.75	2.75
		Nos. 723-726 (4)	5.00	5.00

No. 723 inscribed "For Local Addresses Only" and sold for 20c on day of issue.

New Six Digit Postal Code A182

$2, Six boxes, numbers.

1995, Sept. 1 Litho. *Perf. 14x14½*

727	A182	(20c) shown	.40	.30
728	A182	$2 multicolored	2.75	2.75

No. 728 inscribed "For Local Addresses Only."

Philatelic Museum, Singapore A183

Museum building, various stamps, featuring: 20c, #12. 50c, #157. 60c, #661. $2, Displays of stamps.

1995, Aug. 19 *Perf. 13x13½*

729	A183	(20c) multicolored	1.00	1.00
730	A183	50c multicolored	1.10	1.10
731	A183	60c multicolored	1.25	1.25
732	A183	$2 multicolored	3.25	3.25
		Nos. 729-732 (4)	6.60	6.60

No. 729 inscribed "For Local Addresses Only."

Fish A184

(20c), Yellow-faced angelfish. 60c, Harlequin sweetlips. 70c, Lionfish. $1, Longfin bannerfish.

1995, July 19 Litho. *Perf. 13½x14*

733	A184	(20c) multi	.40	.40
		Complete booklet, 10 #733	5.00	
734	A184	60c multi	1.00	1.00
735	A184	70c multi	1.25	1.25
736	A184	$1 multi	1.75	1.75
		Nos. 733-736 (4)	4.40	4.40

No. 733 inscribed "For Local Addresses Only."

Paintings in Singapore Art Museum A185

Designs: (20c), Tropical Fruits, by Georgette Chen. 30c, Bali Beach, by Cheong Soo Pieng. 70c, Gibbons, by Chen Wen Hsi. $2, Shi (Lion), by Pan Shou (calligraphy).

1995, Oct. 20 Litho. *Perf. 12½*

737	A185	(20c) multicolored	.40	.40
738	A185	30c multicolored	.60	.60
739	A185	70c multicolored	1.25	1.25

Perf. 13½x13

740	A185	$2 multicolored	3.75	3.75
		Nos. 737-740 (4)	6.00	6.00

No. 737 inscribed "For Local Addresses Only." No. 740 is 22½x39mm.

New Year 1996 (Year of the Rat) — A186

1996, Feb. 9 Litho. *Perf. 12*

741	A186	(20c) shown	.40	.30
742	A186	$2 Rat with orange	3.50	3.50

Souvenir Sheet

742A	A186	Sheet of 2, #742, 742Ab	40.00	40.00
b.		22c like #741	.25	.25
c.		As #742A, diff. sheet margin	22.50	22.50
d.		As #742A, diff. sheet margin	25.00	25.00

No. 741 inscribed "For Local Addresses Only."

Sheet margins contain exhibition emblems for: #742A: Indonesia '96; #742Ac, China '96; #742Ad, CAPEX '96.

Issued: #742A, 3/21; #742Ac, 5/18; #742Ad, 6/8.

Architectural Styles — A187

Designs: (20c), Bukit Pasoh, Chinatown. 35c, Jalan Sultan, Kampong Glam. 70c, Dalhousie Lane, Little India. $1, Supreme Court, Civic District.

1996, Jan. 17 ***Perf. 13½x14***

743 A187 (20c) multicolored .45 .30
744 A187 35c multicolored .65 .65
745 A187 70c multicolored 1.25 1.25
746 A187 $1 multicolored 1.75 1.75
Nos. 743-746 (4) 4.10 3.95

No. 743 inscribed "For Local Addresses Only."

Old Maps of Singapore A188

Designs: (20c), Old Straits. 60c, Detail of town. $1, Part of Malay Penisula, Singapore. $2, Town and entrance.

1996, Mar. 13 **Litho.** ***Perf. 12***

747 A188 (20c) multicolored .50 .25
748 A188 60c multicolored 1.00 1.00
749 A188 $1 multicolored 1.50 1.50
750 A188 $2 multicolored 2.75 2.75
Nos. 747-750 (4) 5.75 5.50

No. 747 inscribed "For Local Addresses Only."

Greetings Stamps — A189

Children's drawings about courtesy: (22c), #755Bc, Child telling another to be quiet in library. 35c, Children helping elderly during outdoor activities. 50c, Giving seat at bus stop to expectant mother. 60c, Sharing umbrella. $1, Giving up seat on bus to senior citizen.

Booklet Stamps

Die Cut Perf. 11

1996, July 10 **Litho.**

Self-Adhesive

751 A189 (22c) multicolored .40 .30
a. Booklet pane of 10 4.50
752 A189 35c multicolored .75 .75
753 A189 50c multicolored 1.00 1.00
754 A189 60c multicolored 1.25 1.25
755 A189 $1 multicolored 1.75 1.75
a. Booklet pane of 10, 5 #751, 2 #752, 1 each #753-755 9.50
Nos. 751-755 (5) 5.15 5.05

Souvenir Sheet

755B A189 Sheet of 5, #752-755, 755Bc 6.50 6.50
c. 22c multicolored *1.25 1.25*

No. 751 inscribed "For Local Addresses Only." By their nature Nos. 751a and 755a are complete booklets. The peelable paper backing serves as a booklet cover. The outside of the cover contains 10 peelable labels.

1996 Summer Olympic Games, Atlanta — A190

Designs: (22c), #759Ab, Board, dinghy sailing. 60c, Soccer, tennis. 70c, Pole vault, hurdles. $2, Diving, swimming.

1996, July 19 **Litho.** ***Perf. 14½***

756 A190 (22c) multicolored .50 .30
757 A190 60c multicolored 1.00 1.00
758 A190 70c multicolored 1.25 1.25
759 A190 $2 multicolored 2.50 2.50
Nos. 756-759 (4) 5.25 5.05

Souvenir Sheet

759A A190 Sheet of 4, #757-759, 759Ab 5.75 5.75
b. 22c multicolored 1.00 1.00

No. 756 inscribed "For Local Addresses Only."

Asian Civilizations Museum — A191

(22c), Calligraphy in Caoshu, Ming Dynasty, 17th cent. 60c, Javanese Divination manuscript, Surkarta (Solo), Indonesia, 1842. 70c, Temple hanging, Tamilnadu. South India, 19th cent. $2, Calligraphic implements, Persia and Turkey, 17th-19th cent.

1996, June 5 **Litho.** ***Perf. 13½x14***

760 A191 (22c) multicolored .50 .50
761 A191 60c multicolored 1.00 1.00
762 A191 70c multicolored 1.25 1.25
763 A191 $2 multicolored 2.75 2.75
Nos. 760-763 (4) 5.50 5.50

No. 760 inscribed "For Local Addresses Only."

Care for Nature — A192

Native trees: (22c), Cinnamomum iners. 60c, Hibiscus tiliaceus. 70c, Parkia speciosa. $1, Terminalia catappa.

1996, Sept. 11 **Litho.** ***Perf. 13½***

764 A192 (22c) multicolored .35 .30
a. Booklet pane of 10 7.00
Complete booklet, #764a 7.50
765 A192 60c multicolored .90 .90
766 A192 70c multicolored 1.00 1.00
767 A192 $1 multicolored 1.50 1.50
Nos. 764-767 (4) 3.75 3.70

No. 764 inscribed "For Local Addresses Only."

Panmen, Suzhou, China — A193

Design: 60c, Singapore waterfront.

1996, Oct. 9 **Litho.** ***Perf. 13x13½***

768 A193 (22c) multicolored .35 .30
769 A193 60c multicolored 1.60 1.60

Souvenir Sheet

769A A193 Sheet of 2, #769, 769Ab 4.00 4.00
b. 22c like #768 .75 .75
c. As #769A, ovptd. in sheet margin 30.00 30.00

No. 768 inscribed "For Local Addresses Only."

No. 769Ac is ovptd. in sheet margin with violet on gold Singapore-China Stamp Exhibition emblem.

See People's Republic of China Nos. 2733-2734.

First World Trade Organization Ministerial Conference — A194

1996, Nov. 20 **Litho.** ***Perf. 14***

770 A194 (22c) pink, vio & multi .50 .40
771 A194 60c ver, grn & multi 1.00 1.00
772 A194 $1 bl, yel org & multi 1.50 1.50
773 A194 $2 grn, car & multi 2.50 2.50
Nos. 770-773 (4) 5.50 5.40

No. 770 inscribed "For Local Addresses Only."

New Year 1997 (Year of the Ox) A195

Nos. 774, 775, Different stylized oxen.

1997, Jan. 10 ***Perf. 13½x14***

774 A195 (22c) multicolored .65 .65
775 A195 $2 multicolored 3.00 3.00
a. Sheet, 9 each #774-775 45.00
b. Souvenir sheet, #775, #775d 12.50 12.50
c. As "b," diff. sheet margin 12.00 12.00
d. 22c like #774 *4.50 5.00*
e. As "b," diff. sheet margin 10.00 10.00

No. 774 inscribed "For Local Addresses Only."

Sheet margin contains exhibition emblem: #775b Hong Kong '97; #775c Pacific '97; #775e Shanghai 1997.

Issued: #775b, 2/12/97; #775c, 5/29/97; #775e, 11/19/97.

Traditional Games — A196

1997, Feb. 21 **Litho.** ***Perf. 14½***

776 A196 (22c) Shuttlecock .30 .30
777 A196 35c Marbles .50 .50
778 A196 60c Tops .80 .80
779 A196 $1 Fivestones 1.40 1.40
Nos. 776-779 (4) 3.00 3.00

Souvenir Sheet

779A Sheet of 4, #777-779, 779Ab 4.00 4.00
b. A196 22c Like #776 .40 .40

No. 776 inscribed "For Local Addresses Only." Singpex '97 (#779a).

Ground Transportation — A197

1997, Mar. 19 ***Perf. 13½***

780 A197 5c Bullock cart .25 .25
781 A197 20c Bicycle .30 .25
782 A197 (22c) Rickshaw .30 .25
783 A197 30c Electric tram .40 .40
784 A197 35c Trolley bus .50 .50
785 A197 40c Trishaw .55 .55
786 A197 50c Vintage car .70 .70
787 A197 60c Horse-drawn carriage .85 .85
788 A197 70c Fire engine .95 .95
Nos. 780-788 (9) 4.80 4.70

Souvenir Sheet

788A A197 Sheet, #780-781, 783-788, 788Ab 6.50 6.50
b. 22c like #782 .90 .90

Self-Adhesive

Serpentine Die Cut Perf. 11½

Booklet Stamp

789 A197 (22c) like #782 .40 .40
a. Booklet pane of 10 7.00

Nos. 782, 789 are inscribed "For Local Addresses Only." Nos. 780, 783-784, 787-788 are horiz.

By its nature No. 789a is a complete booklet. The peelable paper backing serves as a booklet cover.

Size: 28x35mm (#790, 792), 43x24mm (#791, 793)

$1, Taxi. $2, Bus, horiz. $5, Mass rapid transit system. $10, Light rapid transit system, horiz.

Litho. & Engr.

1997, Apr. 23 ***Perf. 13x13¼***

790 A197 $1 multicolored 1.25 1.00
791 A197 $2 multicolored 3.00 2.00
792 A197 $5 multicolored 6.00 5.00
793 A197 $10 multicolored 12.00 12.00
a. Souvenir sheet, #790-793 25.00 25.00
Nos. 790-793 (4) 22.25 20.00

In the souvenir sheet the $2 and the $10 are perforated 13 on the top and bottom. The vertical perforations are 13¾ in the center and widen to about 13 on the last four perforations on the top and bottom. In the souvenir sheet the $1 is perforated 13¾ on the top, bottom and right and perforated 13¼ on the left. In the souvenir sheet the $5 is perforated 13¾ on the top, bottom and left and perforated 13¼ on the right.

Greetings Stamps — A198

Word "Friends" used in making designs: #794, Man's head. #795, Sharing umbrella. #796, Penguins. #797, Butterflies, hand. #798, Coffee cup. #799, Flower. #800, Candle. #801, Tree. #802, Jar holding stars. #803, Two cans connected by string.

Serpentine Die Cut 14½

1997, May 14 **Litho.**

Self-Adhesive

Booklet Stamps

794 A198 (22c) multicolored .55 .55
795 A198 (22c) multicolored .55 .55
796 A198 (22c) multicolored .55 .55
797 A198 (22c) multicolored .55 .55
798 A198 (22c) multicolored .55 .55
a. Booklet pane, 2 each #794-798 5.50 *5.50*
Nos. 794-798 (5) 2.75 2.75
799 A198 (22c) multicolored .55 .55
800 A198 (22c) multicolored .55 .55
801 A198 (22c) multicolored .55 .55
802 A198 (22c) multicolored .55 .55
803 A198 (22c) multicolored .55 .55
a. Booklet pane, 2 each #799-803 5.50 *5.50*
Nos. 799-803 (5) 2.75 2.75

Nos. 794-803 are inscribed "For Local Addresses Only." By their nature Nos. 798a and 803a are complete booklets. The peelable paper backing serves as a booklet cover. The outside cover contains 10 peelable labels.

Upgrading of Public Housing — A199

Designs: (22c) New look for the precinct. 30c, Outdoor facilities. 70c, Landscaped gardens. $1, Additional space, balcony.

1997, July 16 Litho. *Perf. 14*

No.	Type	Description	Unused	Used
804	A199	(22c) multicolored	.35	.25
805	A199	30c multicolored	.45	.45
806	A199	70c multicolored	1.00	1.00
807	A199	$1 multicolored	1.25	1.25
		Nos. 804-807 (4)	3.05	2.95

No. 804 is inscribed "For Local Addresses Only."

ASEAN, 30th Anniv. — A200

Designs: (22c), 30 years of "dates," globe, hands clasped, sky. 35c, Southeast Asian cultures. 60c, Satellite dish, circuit board, map of Southeast Asia, sky. $1, Tourist attractions in ASEAN countries.

1997, Aug. 8 Litho. *Perf. 14*

No.	Type	Description	Unused	Used
808	A200	(22c) multicolored	.40	.25
809	A200	35c multicolored	.55	.55
810	A200	60c multicolored	.90	.90
811	A200	$1 multicolored	1.40	1.40
		Nos. 808-811 (4)	3.25	3.10

No. 808 is inscribed "For Local Addresses Only."

Value is for stamp with surrounding selvage.

Protection of the Environment — A201

(22c), Clean Environment. 60c, Clean waters. 70c, Clean air. $1, Clean homes.

1997, Sept. 13 Litho. *Perf. 14x13½*

No.	Type	Description	Unused	Used
812	A201	(22c) multicolored	.30	.25
a.		Booklet pane of 10	3.75	
		Complete booklet, #812a	3.75	
813	A201	60c multicolored	.70	.70
814	A201	70c multicolored	.80	.80
815	A201	$1 multicolored	1.00	1.00
		Nos. 812-815 (4)	2.80	2.75

No. 812 is inscribed "For Local Addresses Only."

Marine Life Type of 1994

1997 Photo. *Perf. 13x13½*

No.	Type	Description	Unused	Used
816	A172	5c like #674	2.00	.50
816A	A172	(20c) like #675B	1.00	.30
817	A172	25c like #676	15.00	3.50
818	A172	30c like #677	1.00	.30
819	A172	35c like #678	2.00	1.00
820	A172	40c like #679	2.00	1.00
821	A172	50c like #680	3.00	.50

Photo. & Embossed

Perf. 14 Syncopated Type A (2 Sides)

No.	Type	Description	Unused	Used
822	A172	$1 like #682	10.00	3.50
822A	A172	$2 like #683	11.00	6.00
823	A172	$5 like #684	40.00	20.00
824	A172	$10 like #684A	55.00	25.00
		Nos. 816-824 (11)	142.00	61.60

No. 816A is inscribed "For Local Addresses Only."

Nos. 822-824 have embossed logo in center of stamp and denomination and country are white. Nos. 682, 684, 684A have embossed lettering for country name and denomination.

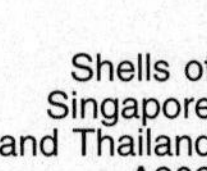

Shells of Singapore and Thailand A202

Designs: (22c), Drupa morum. 35c, Nerita chamaeleon. 60c, Littoraria melanostoma. $1, Cryptospira elegans.

1997, Oct. 9 Litho. *Perf. 13x14*

No.	Type	Description	Unused	Used
825	A202	(22c) multicolored	.40	.25
826	A202	35c multicolored	.45	.45
827	A202	60c multicolored	.80	.80
828	A202	$1 multicolored	1.50	1.50
		Nos. 825-828 (4)	3.15	3.00

Souvenir Sheet

No.	Type	Description	Unused	Used
828A	A202	Sheet of 4, #826-828, #828Ab	3.50	3.50
b.		22c like #825	.85	*.85*

No. 825 inscribed "For Local Addresses Only."

See Thailand Nos. 1771-1774.

New Year 1998 (Year of the Tiger) A203

Different stylized tigers.

1998, Jan. 9 Litho. *Perf. 13x14*

No.	Type	Description	Unused	Used
829	A203	(22c) multicolored	.35	.30
830	A203	$2 multicolored	2.25	2.25
a.		Horiz. or vert. pair, #829-830	3.00	*3.00*
b.		Sheet of 9 each, #829-830	30.00	*30.00*

Souvenir Sheet

No.	Type	Description	Unused	Used
830C	A203	Sheet of 2, #830, #830Cd	5.00	5.00
d.		22c like #829	.90	*.90*
e.		As #830C, diff. inscription	5.25	5.25

Israel '98 (#830C). Italia '98 (#830Ce).

No. 829 inscribed "For Local Addresses Only."

Stamps in No. 830b are arranged in a checkerboard fashion.

Issued: #830Ce, 10/23/98.

Dinosaurs — A204

Self-Adhesive

1998, Apr. 22 Photo. *Die Cut*

No.	Type	Description	Unused	Used
831	A204	(22c) Pentaceratops	.35	.35
832	A204	(22c) Apatosaurus	.35	.35
833	A204	(22c) Albertosaurus	.35	.35
a.		Pane, 5 each #831-833	*12.00*	
		Nos. 831-833 (3)	1.05	1.05

Nos. 831-833 are inscribed "For Local Addresses Only."

A205

Songbirds: (22c), Lesser green leafbird. 60c, Magpie robin. 70c, Straw-headed bulbul. $2, Yellow-bellied prinia.

Granite Paper

1998, May 6 Photo. *Perf. 11½*

No.	Type	Description	Unused	Used
834	A205	(22c) multicolored	.50	.30
835	A205	60c multicolored	1.00	1.00
836	A205	70c multicolored	1.10	1.10
837	A205	$2 multicolored	2.00	2.00
		Nos. 834-837 (4)	4.60	4.40

No. 834 is inscribed "For Local Addresses Only."

A206

"Hello" stamps.

Self-Adhesive
Booklet Stamps

Serpentine Die Cut 11

1998, May 20 Litho.

No.	Type	Description	Unused	Used
838	A206	(22c) yellow & multi	.65	.65
839	A206	(22c) orange & multi	.65	.65
840	A206	(22c) green & multi	.65	.65
841	A206	(22c) blue & multi	.65	.65
842	A206	(22c) black & multi	.65	.65
a.		Booklet pane, 2 each #838-842	6.50	

Nos. 838-842 are inscribed "For Local Addresses Only."

By its nature No. 842a is a complete booklet. The peelable paper backing serves as a booklet cover. The outside cover contains 10 peelable labels.

Fauna from "Fragile Forest," Singapore Zoological Gardens — A207

No. 843, Rhino beetle. No. 844, Surinam horned frog. No. 845, Atlas moth. No. 846, Green iguana. No. 847, Giant scorpion. No. 848, Hissing cockroach. No. 849, Two-toed sloth. No. 850, Archer fish. No. 851, Cobalt blue tarantula. No. 852, Greater mousedeer.

Self-Adhesive
Booklet Stamps

Serpentine Die Cut 11½

1998, June 5 Litho.

No.	Type	Description	Unused	Used
843	A207	(22c) multicolored	.65	.50
844	A207	(22c) multicolored	.65	.50
845	A207	(22c) multicolored	.65	.50
846	A207	(22c) multicolored	.65	.50
847	A207	(22c) multicolored	.65	.50
a.		Booklet, 2 each #843-847	6.50	
848	A207	(22c) multicolored	.65	.50
849	A207	(22c) multicolored	.65	.50
850	A207	(22c) multicolored	.65	.50
851	A207	(22c) multicolored	.65	.50
852	A207	(22c) multicolored	.65	.50
a.		Booklet, 2 each #848-852	6.50	

Nos. 843-852 are inscribed "For Local Addresses Only."

The peelable paper backing of Nos. 847a & 852a serves as a booklet cover. In the margins of Nos. 847a & 852a there is a leaf-shaped scratch-off that reveals an animal.

The Singapore Story (Moments in History) — A208

(22c), 22c, "Turbulent years," 1955-59. 60c, "Self-government," 1959-63. $1, "Towards merger and independence," 1961-65. $2, "A nation is born," 1965.

1998, July 7 *Perf. 13x13½*

No.	Type	Description	Unused	Used
853	A208	(22c) multicolored	.35	.30
854	A208	60c multicolored	.65	.65
855	A208	$1 multicolored	1.10	1.10
856	A208	$2 multicolored	2.40	2.40
		Nos. 853-856 (4)	4.50	4.45

Souvenir Sheet

No.	Type	Description	Unused	Used
857		Souvenir sheet of 4	12.50	12.50
a.		22c multicolored	1.50	1.50
b.		60c multicolored	1.75	1.75
c.		$1 multicolored	2.50	2.50
d.		$2 multicolored	4.75	4.75

Issued: #853-856, 7/7/98; #857, 7/23/98.

No. 853 is inscribed "For Local Addresses Only." No. 857 has a UV varnish producing a shiny effect on portions of the design. No. 857 sold for $7.

Singpex '98 (#857).

Orchids of Singapore and Australia — A209

1998, Aug. 6 Photo. *Perf. 11½*

No.	Type	Description	Unused	Used
858	A209	(22c) Moth orchid	.45	.35
859	A209	70c Bamboo orchid	1.40	1.40
860	A209	$1 Tiger orchid	1.50	1.50
861	A209	$2 Cooktown orchid	2.75	2.00
		Nos. 858-861 (4)	6.10	5.25

Souvenir Sheet

No.	Type	Description	Unused	Used
861A	A209	Sheet of 4, #859-861, #861Ab	8.25	8.25
b.		22c like #858	2.00	*2.00*

No. 858 is inscribed "For Local Addresses Only."

See Australia Nos. 1681-1684.

Flowers A210

Designs: No. 862, Wedilia trilobata. No. 863, Dillenia suffruticosa. No. 864, Canna hybrid. No. 865, Caesalpinia pulcherrima.

No. 866, Zephyranthes rosea. No. 867, Cassia alata. No. 868, Heliconia rostrata. No. 869, Allamanda cathartica.

1998, Sept. 9 Litho. *Perf. 14*

No.	Type	Description	Unused	Used
862	A210	(22c) multicolored	.45	.35
863	A210	(22c) multicolored	.45	.35
864	A210	(22c) multicolored	.45	.35
865	A210	(22c) multicolored	.45	.35
a.		Strip of 4, #862-865	2.00	2.00
b.		Booklet pane, 3 each #864-865, 2 each #862-863	5.00	
		Complete booklet, #865b	5.00	
866	A210	35c multicolored	.60	.60
867	A210	35c multicolored	.60	.60
868	A210	60c multicolored	.85	.85
869	A210	60c multicolored	.85	.85
a.		Strip of 4, #866-869	3.00	3.00
b.		Souvenir sheet of 8, #862-869	4.75	4.75

Stamps in #869b are in pairs, #864-863, 862/865 horiz., #866-867, 868, 869 vert.

A211

Festivals — A212

#870, 874 Eid al-Fitr. #871, 875, Christmas. #872, 876, Chinese New Year. #873, 877, Deepavali.

1998, Oct. 7 Litho. *Perf. 13x14*

No.	Type	Description	Unused	Used
870	A211	(22c) multicolored	.30	.30
871	A211	(22c) multicolored	.30	.30
872	A211	(22c) multicolored	.30	.30
873	A211	(22c) multicolored	.30	.30
a.		Block of 4, #870-873	1.75	1.75
874	A212	30c multicolored	.45	.45
875	A212	30c multicolored	.45	.45
876	A212	30c multicolored	.45	.45
877	A212	30c multicolored	.45	.45
		Nos. 870-877 (8)	3.00	3.00

Nos. 870-873 are inscribed "For Local Addresses Only."

Serpentine Die Cut 8

No.	Type	Description	Unused	Used
878	A211	(22c) like #870	.80	.80
879	A211	(22c) like #871	.80	.80
880	A211	(22c) like #872	.80	.80
881	A211	(22c) like #873	.80	.80
		Nos. 878-881 (4)	3.20	3.20

Historical Buildings — A213

(22c), Parliament House. 70c, Former Convent of the Holy Infant Jesus Chapel. $1, Hill Street Building. $2, Sun Yat Sen Nanyang Memorial Hall.

1998, Nov. 4 *Perf. 13½*
882 A213 (22c) multicolored .35 .35
883 A213 70c multicolored .90 .90
884 A213 $1 multicolored 1.40 1.40
885 A213 $2 multicolored 3.00 3.00
Nos. 882-885 (4) 5.65 5.65

No. 882 inscribed "For Local Addresses Only."

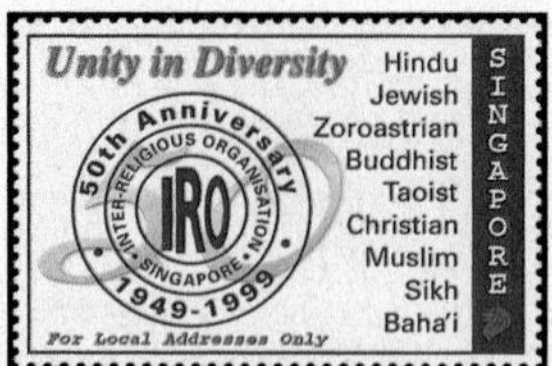

Inter-Religious Organization, 50th Anniv. — A214

1999, Jan. 15 Litho. *Perf. 13x13½*
886 A214 (22c) cream & multi .35 .25
887 A214 60c pink & multi .85 .85
888 A214 $1 blue & multi 1.40 1.40
Nos. 886-888 (3) 2.60 2.50

No. 886 is inscribed "For Local Addresses Only."

New Year 1999 (Year of the Rabbit) A215

Various stylized rabbits.

1999, Jan. 15 *Perf. 14*
889 A215 (22c) multicolored .50 .50
890 A215 $2 multicolored 2.00 2.00
a. Horiz. or vert. pair, #889-890 3.50 2.50
b. Sheet, 9 each #829-830 30.00 30.00

Souvenir Sheet

890C Sheet of 2, #890 & 890Cd 4.00 4.00
d. A215 22c like #889 1.25 *1.25*
e. As #890C, with PhilexFrance 99 margin 4.25 4.25
f. As #890C, with China 1999 World Phil. Exhib. margin 4.25 4.25

No. 889 is inscribed "For Local Addresses Only."
No. 890C was issued 4/27 for IBRA '99, World Philatelic Exhibition, Nuremberg.
Issued: #890Ce, 7/2/99; #890Cf, 8/21/99.

19th Century Sailing Ships — A216

1999, Mar. 19 Litho. *Perf. 14½*
891 A216 (22c) Clipper .60 .35
892 A216 70c Twakow, vert. 1.00 1.00
893 A216 $1 Fujian junk, vert. 1.50 1.50
894 A216 $2 Golekkan 2.50 2.50
Nos. 891-894 (4) 5.60 5.35

Souvenir Sheet

894A A216 Sheet of 4, #892-894, #894Ab 5.75 5.75
b. 22c like #891 1.50 *1.50*

Australia '99 World Stamp Expo (#894A).
No. 891 is inscribed "For Local Address Only."

Greetings Stamps — A217

Expressions of kindness: a, "Think of others." b, "Do not litter." c, "Be kind to animals." d, "Be considerate." e, "Be generous."

Serpentine Die Cut 9½

1999, May 12 Litho.

Self-Adhesive

Booklet Stamps

895 A217 (22c) Booklet pane, 2 each #a.-e. 4.25 4.25

Nos. 895a-895e are inscribed "For Local Addresses Only."
No. 895 is a complete booklet. The peelable paper backing serves as a booklet cover. Stamps are printed 2 each #895a-895c on one side, 2 each #895d-895e on the other with 3 labels on each side.

Hong Kong and Singapore Tourism — A218

(22c), Hong Kong Harbor. 35c, Skyline of Singapore. 50c, Giant Buddha, Hong Kong. 60c, Merlion Sentosa Island, Singapore. 70c, Hong Kong Street scene. $1, Bugis Junction, Singapore.

1999, July 1 Litho. *Perf. 13½x13¼*
896 A218 (22c) multicolored .40 .40
897 A218 35c multicolored .50 .50
898 A218 50c multicolored .80 .80
899 A218 60c multicolored 1.00 1.00
900 A218 70c multicolored 1.10 1.10
901 A218 $1 multicolored 1.60 1.60
Nos. 896-901 (6) 5.40 5.40

Souvenir Sheet

902 Sheet of 6, #897-901, #902a 5.50 5.50
a. A218 22c like #896 .90 *.90*

No. 896 is inscribed for "For Local Addresses Only."
See Hong Kong Nos. 849-854.

Butterflies A219

Perf. 12½x12¾

1999, Aug. 12 Litho. & Engr.
903 A219 (22c) Peacock .60 .40
904 A219 70c Blue pansy 1.00 1.00
905 A219 $1 Great egg-fly 1.75 1.75
906 A219 $2 Red admiral 3.00 3.00
Nos. 903-906 (4) 6.35 6.15

Souvenir Sheet

907 A219 Sheet of 4, #904-906, #907a 6.75 6.75
a. A219 22c like #903 1.75 *1.75*

No. 903 is inscribed "For Local Addresses Only."
See Sweden No. 2356.

Yusof bin Ishak (1910-70), First President of Singapore A220

Perf. 13¼x13¾

1999, Sept. 9 Litho. & Engr.
908 A220 $2 multicolored 2.75 2.75

Issued in sheets of 4.

Amphibians & Reptiles — A221

(22c), Green turtle. 60c, Green crested lizard. 70c, Copper-cheeked frog. $1, Water monitor.

1999, Oct. 13 Litho. *Perf. 14*
909 A221 (22c) multi .30 .30
Complete booklet, 10 #909 3.50
910 A221 60c multi .90 .90
911 A221 70c multi 1.00 1.00
912 A221 $1 multi 1.40 1.40
Nos. 909-912 (4) 3.60 3.60

No. 909 inscribed "For Local Addresses Only."

New Parliament House — A222

Perf. 13¼x13¾

1999, Nov. 17 Litho.
913 A222 (22c) North view .45 .35
914 A222 60c Northeast view .75 .75
915 A222 $1 Southeast view 1.25 1.25
916 A222 $2 West view 2.75 2.75
Nos. 913-916 (4) 5.20 5.10

#913 inscribed "For Local Address Only."

Singapore in the 20th Century A223

No. 917: a, Colonialism. b, Education. c, Immigration. d, Government. e, Japanese occupation. f, National service. g, Transportation. h, Tourism. i, Housing. j, Economic progress.

Perf. 13¼x12½

1999, Dec. 31 Litho.
917 Sheet of 10 + 5 labels 8.50 8.50
a.-b. A223 (22c) Any single .35 .35
c.-d. A223 35c Any single .45 .45
e.-f. A223 60c Any single .85 .85
g.-h. A223 70c Any single 1.00 1.00
i.-j. A223 $1 Any single 1.50 1.50

Nos. 917a-917b inscribed "For Local Addresses Only."

Millennium — A224

No. 918: a, (22c), Information technology. b, 60c, Arts and culture. c, $1, Heritage. d, $2, Globalization.

2000, Jan. 1 Photo. *Perf. 14¼x14¾*

Granite Paper

918 A224 Horiz. strip of 4, #a-d *5.00 5.00*

Souvenir Sheet

918E A224 Sheet of 4, #918b-918d, 918Ef 6.00 6.00
f. 22c Like #918a .35 .35

No. 918a inscribed "For Local Addresses Only."

New Year 2000 (Year of the Dragon) A225

Dragon: (22c), 22c, Facing left. $2, $10, Facing right.

2000 Litho. *Perf. 13x13¼*
919 A225 (22c) multi .50 .50
920 A225 $2 multi 2.75 2.75
a. Horiz. pair, #919-920 3.50 3.50
b. Souvenir sheet, #920a 3.50 3.50

Souvenir Sheets

921 Sheet of 2, #920, 922a, with Bangkok 2000 margin 4.00 4.00
a. A225 22c multi 1.00 *1.00*
b. As No. 921, with The Stamp Show 2000 margin 4.00 4.00
c. As No. 921, with Naba 2000 margin 5.50 5.50

Litho. & Embossed

922 A225 $10 gold & multi 14.00 14.00

Issued: No. 920b, 10/30; No. 921, 3/25; No. 921b, 5/22; No. 921c, 6/21; others, 1/1. No. 919 inscribed "For Local Addresses Only."

Millennium Personalized Stamp — A225a

2000, Mar. 8 Litho. *Perf. 14x14¼*
923 A225a (22c) multi + label 1.25 1.25

No. 923 printed in sheets of 20 stamps + labels that could be personalized. Sheets sold for $20 for the first sheet with additional sheets available for $10. The design on No. 923 is similar to that on No. 918a, but is 19x46mm and lacks frame.

Post Offices and Cancels A226

Designs: (22c), Original post office, B172 cancel. 60c, General Post Office, Fullerton Building, c. 1873, 1875 cancel. $1, General Post Office, 1928, 1935 cancel. $2, Singapore Post Center, 1998 cancel.

2000, Mar. 8 Litho. *Perf. 13½*
935 A226 (22c) multi .40 .40
936 A226 60c multi .85 .85
a. Booklet pane, 4 #935, 2 #936 3.25
937 A226 $1 multi 1.25 1.25
938 A226 $2 multi 3.00 3.00
a. Booklet pane, 4 #937, 2 #938 12.00
Complete bklt., #936a, 938a 15.25
Nos. 935-938 (4) 5.50 5.50

Souvenir Sheet

939 A226 Sheet of 4, #936-938, 939a 4.50 4.50
a. A226 22c like No. 935 1.00 *1.00*

No. 935 is inscribed "For Local Addresses Only."

Celebrations A227

Designs: No. 940, (22c), Yipee. No. 940A, (22c), Yeah. No. 940B, (22c), Hurray. No. 940C, (22c), Yes. No. 941, (22c), Happy.

Serpentine Die Cut 9½

2000, May 10 **Litho.**

Self-Adhesive

940-941 A227 Set of 5 2.75 2.75
941a Booklet, 2 each #940-941 5.50

Nos. 940-941 are inscribed "For Local Addresses Only." Eight self-adhesive die cut labels are affixed to the opposite side of the peelable backing paper.

Singapore River — A228

No. 942: a, River community, 1920s. b, South Boat Quay, 1930s. c, Social gathering, 1950s. d, Changing skyline, 1980s. e, River Regatta, 1990s. f, the river mouth, 1990s. g, Stevedores, 1910s. h, Lighters, 1940s. i, Men at work, 1960s. j, Working with cranes, 1970s.

2000, June 21 ***Perf. 14***

942 A228 Sheet of 10 6.00 6.00
a.-e. (22c) Any single .35 .35
f.-j. 60c Any single .80 .80

Nos. 942a-942e are inscribed "For Local Addresses Only."

Stampin' the Future A229

Children's Stamp Design Contest Winners: (22c), Future lifestyle, art by Liu Jiang Wen. 60c, Future homes, art by Shaun Yew Chuan Bin. $1, Home automation, art by Gwendolyn Soh Shihui. $2, Floating city, art by Dawn Koh.

2000, July 7 **Litho.** ***Perf. 14x12¾***

943-946 A229 Set of 4 5.00 5.00
946a Souvenir sheet, #943-946 5.25 5.25

World Stamp Expo 2000, Anaheim (No. 946a). No. 943 is inscribed "For Local Addresses Only."

Care for Nature, Wetlands Wildlife — A230

No. 947: a, Archer fish. b, Smooth otter. c, Collared kingfisher. d, Orange fiddler crab.

2000, Aug. 11 **Photo.** ***Perf. 14½***

Granite Paper

947 A230 Block of 4 4.50 4.50
a.-b. (22c) Any single .40 .40
c.-d. $1 Any single 1.80 1.80
e. Booklet pane, 5 each #947a, 947b 7.00
Booklet, #947e 7.00
f. Souv. sheet, #947, 947 imperf 8.00 8.00

Nos. 947a-947b are inscribed "For Local Addresses Only."

No. 947f sold for $5.

2000 Summer Olympics, Sydney — A231

Designs: (22c), Swimming and high jump. 60c, Badminton and discus. $1, Soccer and hurdles. $2, Table tennis and gymnastics.

2000, Sept. 15 **Litho.** ***Perf. 13½***

948-951 A231 Set of 4 5.50 5.50

No. 948 is inscribed "For Local Addresses Only."

A232

Festivals and Holidays A233

Designs: Nos. 952, 960, (22c), 956, 30c, Christmas. Nos. 953, 961, (22c), 957, 30c, Eid ul-Fitr. Nos. 954, 962, (22c), 958, 30c, Chinese New Year. Nos. 955, 963, (22c), 959, 30c, Deepavali.

2000, Oct. 11 **Litho.** ***Perf. 13***

952-955 A232 Set of 4 2.75 2.75
956-959 A233 Set of 4 2.75 2.75

Serpentine Die Cut 12¾x13¼

Self-Adhesive

960-963 A232 Set of 4 3.75 3.75

Nos. 952-955, 960-963 are inscribed "For Local Addresses Only."

New Year 2001 (Year of the Snake) A234

Designs: (22c), Snake and branch. $2, Two snakes.

2001, Jan. 12 ***Perf. 14½x14***

964 A234 (22c) multi .50 .50
965 A234 $2 multi 2.50 2.50
a. Horiz. pair, #964-965 3.50 3.50
b. Souvenir sheet, #964-965, with Hong Kong 2001 margin 5.00 5.00
c. Souvenir sheet, #964-965, with Belgica 2001 margin 5.00 5.00
d. Souvenir sheet, #964-965, with Phila Nippon '01 margin 5.00 5.00

Issued: No. 965c, 6/9; No. 965d, 7/1.

Early Singaporeans A235

Designs: No. 966, $1, Tan Tock Seng (1798-1850), philanthropist. No. 967, $1, Eunos bin Abdullah (1876-1933), politician. No. 968, $1, P. Govindasamy Pillai (1887-1980), businessman. No. 969, $1, Edwin John Tessensohn (1855-1926), politician.

2001, Feb. 28 **Photo.** ***Perf. 11¾***

Granite Paper

966-969 A235 Set of 4 5.50 5.50

Commonwealth Day, 25th Anniv. — A236

Designs: (22c), Co-operation. 60c, Education. $1, Sports. $2, Arts and culture.

2001, Mar. 12 **Litho.** ***Perf. 14x14¼***

970-973 A236 Set of 4 5.75 5.75

No. 970 inscribed "For Local Addresses Only."

Greetings A237

Serpentine Die Cut 10

2001, Apr. 25 **Litho.**

Self-Adhesive

974 A237 (22c) Balloons .45 .45
975 A237 (22c) Fireworks .45 .45
976 A237 (22c) Roses .45 .45
977 A237 (22c) Gifts .45 .45
978 A237 (22c) Musical instruments .45 .45
a. Booklet, 2 each #974-978 + 10 labels 4.50
Nos. 974-978 (5) 2.25 2.25

Nos. 974-978 inscribed "For Local Addresses Only."

Perf. 14

Water-Activated Gum

978B A237 (22c) Fireworks 1.00 1.00
978C A237 (22c) Musical instruments 1.00 1.00
978D A237 (22c) Roses 1.00 1.00
978E A237 (22c) Balloons 1.00 1.00
978F A237 (22c) Gifts 1.00 1.00
g. Vert. strip, #978B-978F + 5 labels 5.00 5.00

Nos. 978B-978F were printed in sheets containing four of each stamp and 20 labels that could be personalized. Sheets sold for $11 for the first sheet with additional sheets available for $10. At least three different sheets of 6 of No. 978B and 6 non-personalizable labels exist. These sheets sold as part of a set of 8 sheets with various face values that sold for $8.50 per sheet, and later as part of another set of 8 sheets, for $9 per sheet..

Singapore Arts Festival — A238

No. 979: a, (22c), "a." b, 60c, "r." c, $1, "t." d, $2, "s."

2001, May 16 ***Perf. 14***

979 A238 Block of 4, #a-d 4.75 4.75

No. 979a inscribed "For Local Addresses Only."

Pets — A239

No. 980: a, Fish. b, Cockatoos. c, Ducklings. d, Turtle. e, Dog and fish. f, Cat and mice. g, Bird and dog. h, Dog and cat. i, Parrots. j, Cat and rabbit.

2001, July 26 ***Perf. 13½***

980 A239 Sheet of 10 7.00 7.00
a.-d. (22c) Any single, 25x25mm .40 .40
e.-f. (22c) Any single, 25x35mm .40 .40
g.-h. 50c Any single, 25x42mm .90 .90
i.-j. $1 Any single, 25x42mm 1.60 1.60

Nos. 980a-980f are inscribed "For Local Addresses Only." Singpex '01.

Frame — A240

Serpentine Die Cut 15x14½

2001, July 26 **Self-Adhesive**

981 A240 (22c) multi .80 .80

Size: 24x34mm

982 A240 (22c) multi .80 .80
a. Pane, 6 #981, 4 #982 +16 labels 8.00

Nos. 981-982 inscribed "For Local Addresses Only." No. 982a contains three examples of No. 982 with differing white paw prints, and one example without paw print. Singpex '01.

Care for Nature — A241

Orangutans: (22c), Adult hanging on tree. 60c, Two adults. No. 983c, Adult and child. No. 983d, Two adults and child.

2001, Sept. 5 ***Perf. 13½x13***

983 A241 Horiz. strip of 4 3.75 3.75
a. (22c) multi .30 .30
b. 60c multi .75 .75
c.-d. $1 Any single 1.25 1.25
e. Souvenir sheet, #983 6.00 6.00
f. Sheet, 2 each #983c-983d, + 8 labels, perf. 12¾('05) 8.75 8.75

Self-Adhesive

Booklet Stamp

Serpentine Die Cut 12½

984 A241 (22c) multi .50 .50
a. Booklet of 10 5.00

Nos. 983a, 984 inscribed "For Local Addresses Only."

No. 983e sold for $3.90, with 50c of that donated to the Care for Nature Trust Fund.

No. 983f issued 5/1/05. No. 983f sold for $6.

Flowers A242

Designs: (22c), Melastoma malabathricum. 60c, Leontopodium alpinum. $1, Saraca cauliflora. $2, Gentiana clusii.

2001, Sept. 20 ***Perf. 13¼x12¾***

985-988 A242 Set of 4 5.50 5.50
988a Souvenir sheet, #985-988 5.50 5.50

No. 985 inscribed "For Local Addresses Only."

See Switzerland No. 1107.

Tropical Fish — A243

Designs: 5c, Moorish idol. 20c, Threadfin butterflyfish. (22c), Copperband butterflyfish. (23c), Copperband butterflyfish. 30c, Pearl-scale butterflyfish. 31c, Eight-banded butterflyfish. 40c, Rainbow butterflyfish. 50c, Yellow-faced angelfish. 60c, Emperor angelfish. 70c, Striped sailfin tang. 80c, Palette tang.

2001-05 ***Perf. 13x13¼***

989	A243	5c multi	.25	.35
990	A243	20c multi	.30	.25
991	A243	(22c) multi	.35	.25
992	A243	30c multi	.50	.45
992A	A243	31c multi	.50	.25
992B	A243	(31c) multi	.50	.25
993	A243	40c multi	.75	.40
994	A243	50c multi	1.00	1.00
995	A243	60c multi	1.10	1.10
996	A243	70c multi	1.40	1.40
997	A243	80c multi	1.50	1.50
a.		Sheet of 9, #989-997	8.25	8.25
		Nos. 989-997 (11)	8.15	7.20

Self-Adhesive

Serpentine Die Cut 12½

998	A243	(22c) multi	.40	.40
a.		Booklet of 10	4.00	
998B	A243	(23c) multi	.50	.50
c.		Booklet pane of 10	5.00	

Issued: Nos. 989-992, 993-998 issued 10/24/01. 31c, 2/3/04; (23c), 7/7/04; No. 992B, 3/18/05.

Nos. 991, 998 inscribed "For Local Addresses Only." No. 998B is inscribed "1st Local." No. 992B is inscribed "2nd Local."

See Nos. 1018-1021.

New Year 2002 (Year of the Horse) A244

Designs: Nos. 999, 1001a, (22c), One horse. Nos. 1000, 1001b, $2, Two horses.

Litho., Litho & Embossed with Foil Application (#1001a, 1001b)

2002, Jan. 10 ***Perf. 13½x13¼***

999-1000	A244	Set of 2	4.00	4.00
1000a		Souvenir sheet, #999-1000, perf. 13x13¼	4.00	4.00
1001		Sheet, #1001a-1001b, 8 each #999-1000	26.00	26.00
a.		A244 (22c) silver & multi	.30	.30
b.		A244 $2 gold & multi	2.50	2.50

A souvenir sheet containing one each of Nos. 1001a and 1001b exists. It was sold only in year sets.

No. 1000a issued 8/2/02, for Philakorea.

William Farquhar Collection of Natural History Drawings — A245

No. 1002, (22c) — Animals and Reptiles: a, Landak raya. b, Cipan, Badak murai. c, Landak kelubu. d, Kongkang. e, Biawak tanah. f, Tupai terbang merah. g, Memerang kecil. h, Biawak pasir. i, Tupai kerawak, vert. j, Napuh, vert.

No. 1003, (22c) — Fruits and Plants: a, Buah rumenia. b, Manggis hutan. c, Cempedak. d, Bunga dedap. e, Jeringau, vert. f, Rotang, vert. g, Tuba, vert. h, Tebu gagak, vert. i, Temu kunci, vert. j, Rambutan, vert.

No. 1004, (22c) — Birds: a, Burung gaji-gaji. b, Kuau cermin. c, Ayam kolam. d, Kelengking. e, Burung kuang. f, Puhung. g, Burung kunyit, vert. h, Burung pacat sayap biru, vert. i, Burung mural, vert. j, Burung berek-berek, vert.

No. 1005, (22c) — Fish: a, Ikan tenggiri papan. b, Ikan kertang. c, Ikan kakatua. d, Ikan bambangan. e, Ikan parang. f, Ikan buntai pisang. g, Ikan ketang. h, Pari hitam. i, Telinga gajah. j, Ikan babi.

Designs: No. 1006, Like No. 1002. No. 1007, Like No. 1003. No. 1008, Like No. 1004. No. 1009, Like No. 1005.

Perf. 13¼x13¾, 13¾x13¼

2002 **Sheets of 10, #a-j** **Litho.**

1002-1005	A245	Set of 4	14.00	14.00

Serpentine Die Cut 12½

Sheets of 10, #a-j

Self-Adhesive

1006-1009	A245	Set of 4	16.50	16.50

Issued: Nos. 1002-1003, 2/20; Nos. 1004-1005, 3/20. Nos. 1006-1007, 2/20; Nos. 1008-1009, 3/20. Nos. 1002-1009 inscribed "For Local Addresses Only."

Toys A246

Designs: (22c), Lego blocks. 60c, Cowboys and Indians, robot. 70c, Dolls. $1, Racing cars.

2002, May 22 ***Perf. 14½x14***

1010-1013	A246	Set of 4	3.50	3.50

No. 1010 inscribed "For local addresses only."

Tropical Birds — A247

Designs: (22c), Red-throated sunbird. 40c, Asian fairy bluebird. $1, Black-naped oriole. $2, White-bellied woodpecker.

2002, June 27 ***Perf. 13¼x14***

1014-1017	A247	Set of 4	5.00	5.00
1017a		Souvenir sheet, #1014-1017	6.00	6.00

No. 1014 inscribed "For local addresses only."

See Malaysia Nos. 886-888.

Fish Type of 2001

Discus fish: $1, Blue turquoise. $2, Brown discus. $5, Red alenquer. $10, Red turquoise.

2002, July 24 ***Perf. 13½x13¼***

Size: 29x25mm

1018	A243	$1 multi	1.75	1.75
1019	A243	$2 multi	3.50	3.00
1020	A243	$5 multi	8.00	5.00
1021	A243	$10 multi	14.00	7.00
a.		Souvenir sheet, #1018-1021	27.50	27.50
		Nos. 1018-1021 (4)	27.25	16.75

A248

Festivals and Holidays A249

Designs: Nos. 1022, 50c; 1026, 1030, (22c), Christmas. Nos. 1023, 50c; 1027, 1031, (22c), Chinese New Year. Nos. 1024, 50c; 1028, 1032, (22c), Deepavali. Nos. 1025, 50c; 1029, 1033, (22c), Eid ul-Fitr.

Litho. with Hologram Affixed

2002, Aug. 21 ***Perf. 13¼x13¾***

1022-1025	A248	Set of 4	3.00	3.00
1026-1029	A249	Set of 4	1.75	1.75

Self-Adhesive

Serpentine Die Cut 13¼x13¾

1030-1033	A249	Set of 4	3.75	3.75

Nos. 1026-1033 are inscribed "For Local Addresses Only."

Heritage Trees — A250

Designs: Nos. 1034, 1038, (22c), Flame of the Forest. 60c, Rain Tree. No. 1036, $1, Tembusu. No. 1037, $1, Kapok Tree.

2002, Sept. 25 **Litho.** ***Perf. 13½x13***

1034-1037	A250	Set of 4	3.50	3.50

Self-Adhesive

Booklet Stamp

Serpentine Die Cut 12½

1038	A250	(22c) multi	.50	.50
a.		Booklet of 10	5.00	

Nos. 1034, 1038 are inscribed "For Local Addresses Only."

A sheet containing 2 each Nos. 1035-1036 and 2 stamps similar to No. 1034 but inscribed "1st Local" + 6 non-personalizable labels sold for $9.90.

Opening of Esplanade Performing Arts Center A251

Various views of complex with background colors of: (22c), Orange. 60c, Brown. $1, Blue green. $2, Dark blue.

2002, Oct. 12 **Litho.** ***Perf. 13¼x13¾***

1039-1042	A251	Set of 4	5.00	5.00
1042a		Souvenir sheet, #1039-1042	5.00	5.00

No. 1039 is inscribed "For local addresses only."

Singapore, A Global City — A252

No. 1043: a, Sailboats. b, Conductor's hands.

2002-04 ***Perf. 14¼x14***

1043	A252	$2 Horiz. pair, #a-b + central label	5.25	5.25
1043c		Souvenir sheet, #1043a-1043b, + American Express label	6.25	6.25
d.		As "c," with Coca-Cola label	6.25	6.25
e.		As "c," with McDonald's label	6.25	6.25
f.		As "c," with Reader's Digest label	6.25	6.25
g.		As "c," with Swatch label	6.25	6.25
h.		As "c," ovptd. in margin with World Stamp Championship emblem in silver	6.25	6.25
i.		As "d," ovptd. in margin with World Stamp Championship emblem in silver	6.25	6.25
j.		As "e," ovptd. in margin with World Stamp Championship emblem in silver	6.25	6.25
k.		As "f," ovptd. in margin with World Stamp Championship emblem in silver	6.25	6.25
l.		As "g," ovptd. in margin with World Stamp Championship emblem in silver	6.25	6.25

Issued: Nos. 1043-1043g, 11/20/02. Nos. 1043h-1043l, 6/23/04. Nos. 1043h-1043l sold for $4.53 each.

New Year 2003 (Year of the Ram) A253

Designs: (22c) Red violet ram. $2, Tree and yellow green ram.

2003, Jan. 10 **Litho.** ***Perf. 13x13½***

1044-1045	A253	Set of 2	2.75	2.25
1045a		Sheet, 9 each #1044-1045	23.00	23.00
1045b		Souvenir sheet, #1044-1045, with Bangkok 2003 margin	4.25	4.25
1045c		Souvenir sheet, #1044-1045, with China 2003 margin	4.25	4.25

No. 1044 inscribed "For Local Addresses Only."

Issued: No. 1045b, 10/4; No. 1045c, 11/20.

History of Empress Place Building A254

Designs: (22c), Government offices. 60c, Government offices, diff. $1, Empress Place Museum. $2, Asian Civilizations Museum.

2003, Feb. 26 ***Perf. 14½***

1046-1049	A254	Set of 4	5.25	5.25

No. 1046 inscribed "For local addresses only."

Nocturnal Animals A255

Designs: (22c), Tarsier. 40c, Barn owl. $1, Babirusa. $2, Clouded leopard.

2003, Mar. 20 **Litho.** ***Perf. 13¼***

1050-1053	A255	Set of 4	5.00	5.00
1053a		Souvenir sheet, #1050-1053	6.00	6.00

No. 1050 inscribed "For Local Addresses Only." Glow-in-the-dark ink was applied to portions of No. 1053a by silk-screening.

Singapore Police Force — A256

Designs: (22c), Community policing. 40c, Traffic policing. $1, Maritime policing. $2, International peacekeeping.

2003, Apr. 23 **Litho.** ***Perf. 13¼x13***

1054-1057	A256	Set of 4	5.75	5.75

No. 1054 inscribed "For Local Addresses Only."

Singapore, A Global City — A257

No. 1058: a, Spacecraft. b, Robot.

2003, May 21 Litho. *Perf. 14¼x14*

1058 A257 $2 Horiz. pair, #a-b + central label 5.50 5.50
c. Souvenir sheet, #1058a-1058b + CNN label 6.00 6.00
d. As "c," with Creative Technology label 6.00 6.00
e. As "c," with Microsoft label 6.00 6.00
f. As "c," with Siemens label 6.00 6.00
g. As "c," with Singapore Airlines label 6.00 6.00
h. As "c," ovptd. in margin with World Stamp Championship emblem in silver 6.00 6.00
i. As "d," ovptd. in margin with World Stamp Championship emblem in silver 6.00 6.00
j. As "e," ovptd. in margin with World Stamp Championship emblem in silver 6.00 6.00
k. As "f," ovptd. in margin with World Stamp Championship emblem in silver 6.00 6.00
l. As "g," ovptd. in margin with World Stamp Championship emblem in silver 6.00 6.00

Issued: Nos. 1058-1058g, 5/21/03. Nos. 1058h-1058l, 6/23/04. Nos. 1058h-1058l sold for $4.53 each.

Joy and Caring — A258

Designs and inscriptions: Nos. 1059a, 1060a, Cat (Joy). Nos. 1059b, 1060b, Running heart (Joy). Nos. 1059c, 1060c, Teddy bear (Joy). Nos. 1059d, 1060d, Laughing man (Joy). Nos. 1059e, 1060e, Ostrich head (Joy). Nos. 1059f, 1060f, Apple (Caring). Nos. 1059g, 1060g, Hand and heart (A helping hand). Nos. 1059h, 1060h, Hearts (Togetherness). Nos. 1059i, 1060i, Flower (Beauty of a caring heart). Nos. 1059j, 1060j, Stars (Keeping in touch keeps us going).

2003, June 25 *Perf. 14½*

1059 A258 Sheet of 10 + 2 labels 4.75 4.75
a.-j. (22c) Any single .45 .45
k. Sheet, 10 each #1059c, 1059h + 20 labels 12.00 12.00
l. Sheet of 20 #1059i + 20 labels 12.50 12.50
m. Sheet, 10 each #1059c, 1059h + 20 labels 14.00 14.00

Self-Adhesive

Serpentine Die Cut 10x9¾

1060 Booklet of 10 + 6 labels 5.00 5.00
a.-j. A258 (22c) Any single .50 .50

Inscribed "For Local Addresses Only." Labels on No. 1059k could be personalized for an additional fee.

Issued: No. 1059l, 8/8; No. 1059m, 11/25/04. Nos. 1059l and 1059m each sold for $8. A sheet of 5 #1059j and 5 non-personalizable labels sold for $9.90.

See Nos. 1119-1121.

Opening of North East Line of Rapid Transit System A259

Designs: (22c), Map of Rapid Transit System, train. 60c, Entrance gates, station cross-section, train. $2, System control room, train.

No. 1064: a, (22c), Like No. 522. b, 60c, Like No. 523. c, $2, Like No. 524.

2003, July 18 *Perf. 13¾*

1061-1063 A259 Set of 3 4.00 4.00

Souvenir Sheet

1064 A259 Sheet of 6, #1061-1063, 1064a-1064c 7.00 7.00

Nos. 1061, 1064a are inscribed "For Local Addresses Only."

National Day — A260

Designs: (22c), Flag. 60c, National flower, Vanda Miss Joaquim orchid. $1, Merlion and buildings. $2, People of Singapore.

2003, Aug. 9 *Perf. 13¼x13½*

1065-1068 A260 Set of 4 4.75 4.75
1065a Sheet of 20 + 20 labels 12.50 12.50
1068a Souvenir sheet, #1065-1068 5.00 5.00

1068B Sheet, 3 #1068Bc, 2#1068Bd + 10 labels 10.00 10.00
c. A260 60c Like #1066, 35x28mm 1.50 1.50
d. A260 $1 Like #1067, 35x28mm 2.50 2.50

No. 1065 is inscribed "For local addresses only."

No. 1065a sold for $8. Labels could be personalized.

Numerous different sheets containing 5 stamps similar to No. 1065 but inscribed "1st Local" + 10 non-personalizable labels (sheets having various labels and margins) exist. Sheets sold for $6. A sheet containing 3 stamps similar to No. 1068Bc exists, sold as part of a series of sheets sold with a book for $39.90.

Size of Nos. 1066-1067: 33x28mm. No. 1068B sold for $6.

Aircraft — A261

No. 1069 — Military aircraft: a, Alouette III helicopter. b, E-2C Hawkeye. c, Hawker Hunter. d, Super Puma AS-332M helicopter. e, Hercules C-130H. f, F-16 C/D Fighting Falcon. g, AH-64D Apache helicopter. h, KC-135R Stratotanker. i, Cessna 172. j, F-5E Tiger II.

No. 1070 — Civil aircraft: a, Airbus 340-500. b, Boeing 747-400. c, Boeing 777-200. d, Boeing 747-400 Freighter. e, Airbus 320. f, Concorde. g, Boeing 737-100. h, Comet IV. i, Viscount. j, Airspeed Consul.

2003, Sept. 3 *Perf. 13¼x13½*

1069 A261 Sheet of 10 3.75 3.75
a.-j. (22c) Any single .35 .35
1070 A261 Sheet of 10 3.75 3.75
a.-j. (22c) Any single .35 .35
k. Sheet of 20, #1069a-1069j, 1070a-1070j 8.00 8.00

Self-Adhesive

Serpentine Die Cut 12½

1071 A261 Sheet of 10 5.00
a.-j. (22c) Any single .50 .50
1072 A261 Sheet of 10 5.00
a.-j. (22c) Any single .50 .50

Inscribed "For local addresses only." Powered flight, cent.; Singapore Air Force, 35th anniv.

Singapore, A Garden City — A262

Designs: Nos. 1073, 1077, (22c), Singapore Botanic Gardens. 60c, Fort Canning Park. No. 1075, $1, Marina City Park. No. 1076, $1, Sungei Buloh Wetland Reserve.

2003, Oct. 22 Litho. *Perf. 13½*

1073-1076 A262 Set of 4 4.00 4.00

Booklet Stamp

Self-Adhesive

Serpentine Die Cut 10x9½

1077 A262 (22c) multi .55 .55
a. Booklet pane of 10 5.50 *5.50*

Nos. 1073, 1077 are inscribed "For Local Addresses Only."

A sheet containing Nos. 1075, 1076, 2 No. 1074 and 2 stamps similar to No. 1073 inscribed "1st Local" + 6 non-personalizable labels sold for $9.90.

New Year 2004 (Year of the Monkey) A263

Designs: (22c), Monkey and heart. $2, Two monkeys.

2004, Jan. 9 *Perf. 14x13¼*

1078-1079 A263 Set of 2 3.00 2.00
1079a Sheet, 9 each #1078-1079 32.50 32.50
1079b Souvenir sheet, #1078-1079, with Hong Kong 2004 Stamp Expo margin 3.50 3.50

No. 1078 is inscribed "For Local Addresses Only." No. 1079a is reserved.

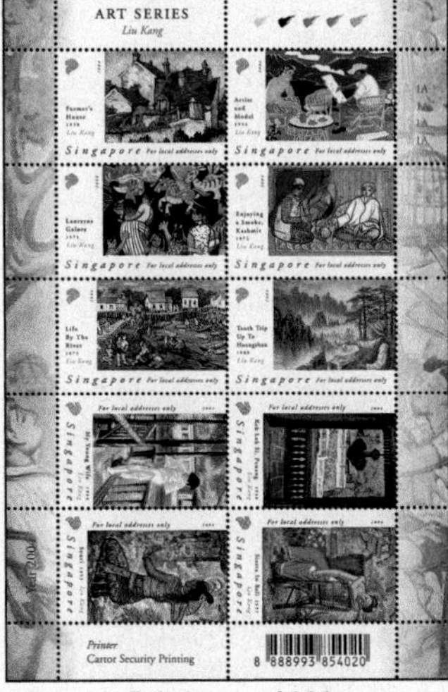

Paintings — A264

Nos. 1080, 1082 — Paintings of Liu Kang: a, Farmer's House. b, Artist and Model. c, Lanterns Galore. d, Enjoying a Smoke, Kashmir. e, Life by the River. f, Tenth Trip Up to Huangshan. g, My Young Wife, vert. h, Kek Lok Si, Penang, vert. i, Souri, vert. j, Siesta in Bali, vert.

Nos. 1081, 1083 — Paintings of Ong Kim Seng: a, Kampong Tengah, Singapore. b, Gyantse Market. c, Sebatu Spring, Bali. d, Jetty, Bangkok. e, Resort, Bali. f, Dance Studio, Bali. g, Telok Ayer Market. h, Kathmandu, Nepal. i, Portofino, Italy, vert. j, Boats at Rest, vert.

Perf. 13¼x13½, 13½x13¼ (Vert. stamps)

2004, Feb. 18

1080 A264 Sheet of 10 3.75 3.75
a.-j. (23c) Any single .35 .35
1081 A264 Sheet of 10 3.75 3.75
a.-j. (23c) Any single .35 .35

Self-Adhesive

Serpentine Die Cut 12½x12¼, 12¼x12½ (Vert. stamps)

1082 A264 Sheet of 10 4.50 4.50
a.-j. (23c) Any single .45 .45
1083 A264 Sheet of 10 4.50 4.50
a.-j. (23c) Any single .45 .45
Nos. 1080-1083 (4) 16.50 16.50

Inscribed "For local addresses only."

Suzhou, China Industrial Park, 10th Anniv. A265

2004, Mar. 1 Litho. *Perf. 13x13½*

1084 A265 60c multi 1.25 1.25
a. Sheet of 8 10.00 10.00

Singapore Skyline A266

Designs: (23c), Buildings as seen from street level. 60c, Fountain. 70c, Buildings as seen from distance.

$1, Singapore, circa 1900. $5, Singapore, 2004.

Perf. 14¼x14½

2004, Mar. 24 Litho.

1085-1087 A266 Set of 3 2.50 2.50
1087a Sheet, 3 #1086, 2 #1087, + 10 labels, perf. 12¾x13 ('05) 8.75 8.75

Souvenir Sheets

Perf. 14¼x14

1088 A266 $1 multi 1.75 1.75

Litho. & Engr.

1089 A266 $5 multi 8.00 8.00

No. 1085 is inscribed "1st Local." Nos. 1088 and 1089 each contain one 95x35mm stamp

No. 1087a issued 5/1/05. No. 1087a sold for $6.

Singapore, A Global City — A267

No. 1090: a, Cargo containers. b, Gas tanks.

2004 Litho. *Perf. 14½x14¼*

1090 A267 Horiz. pair with central label 6.00 6.00
a.-b. $2 Either single 2.75 2.75
c. Souvenir sheet, #1090a-1090b + AIA label 6.00 6.00
d. As "c," with GlaxoSmithKline label 6.00 6.00
e. As "c," with HSBC label 6.00 6.00
f. As "c," with Shell Oil label 6.00 6.00
g. As "c," with Sony label 6.00 6.00
h. As "c," ovptd. in margin with World Stamp Championship emblem in silver 6.00 6.00
i. As "d," ovptd. in margin with World Stamp Championship emblem in silver 6.00 6.00
j. As "e," ovptd. in margin with World Stamp Championship emblem in silver 6.00 6.00
k. As "f," ovptd. in margin with World Stamp Championship emblem in silver 6.00 6.00
l. As "g," ovptd. in margin with World Stamp Championship emblem in silver 6.00 6.00
m. Souvenir sheet, #1043a, 1043b, 1058a, 1058b, 1090a, 1090b 22.50 22.50

Issued: Nos. 1090, 1090c-1090g, 4/21; 1090h-1090l, 6/23; No. 1090m, 8/28. Nos. 1090h-1090l sold for $4.53 each. No. 1090m sold for $12.60 and exists imperf.

FIFA (Fédération Internationale de Football Association), Cent. — A268

FIFA emblem and: 30c, Soccer field. 60c, Soccer ball. $1, Player's shirt. $2, World map.

Litho. & Embossed

2004, May 21 *Perf. 13*

Flocked Paper

1091-1094 A268 Set of 4 6.00 6.00

Festivals and Holidays — A269

Designs: Nos. 1095, 1103, (23c), Santa Claus, reindeer (Christmas). Nos. 1096, 1104, (23c), Flowers, fruit (Chinese New Year). Nos.

1097, 1105, (23c), Candles (Deepavali). Nos. 1098, 1106, Candle (Eid ul-Fitr). No. 1099, 50c, Carolers (Christmas). No. 1100, 50c, Woman (Chinese New Year). No. 1101, 50c, Woman and candle (Deepavali). No. 1102, 50c, Child with sparkler (Eid ul-Fitr).

2004, July 7 Litho. *Perf. 13*

1095-1102 A269 Set of 8 4.25 4.25
1095a Perf. 12¾x13 + label .35 .35
1099a Perf. 12¾x13 + label .80 .80
1102a Sheet, #1099-1102, + 8 labels, perf. 12¾x13 8.00 8.00

Self-Adhesive

Serpentine Die Cut 12½

1103-1106 A269 Set of 4 2.75 2.75

Nos. 1103-1106 were each printed in sheets of 10. Nos. 1095-1098, 1103-1106 are inscribed "1st Local."

Nos. 1095a, 1099a issued 11/7/05. Nos. 1095a, 1099a issued in sheets of 8 + 8 labels.

No. 1102a issued 5/1/05. No. 1102a sold for $6.

National Monuments — A270

No. 1107, (23c): a, Column, City Hall. b, City Hall.

No. 1108, 30c: a, Tower, Victoria Theater and Concert Hall. b, Victoria Theater and Concert Hall.

No. 1109, 60c: a, Dome, Supreme Court. b, Supreme Court.

No. 1110, $1: a, Decoration, Istana (President's residence). b, Istana.

Sizes: Nos. 1107a-1110a, 41x46mm. Nos. 1107b-1110b, 41x27mm.

2004, Aug. 9 *Perf. 13¼x13¾*

Vert. Pairs, #a-b

1107-1110 A270 Set of 4 6.25 6.25
1110c Souvenir sheet, #1107b, 1108b, 1109b, 1110b 3.50 3.50

No. 1107 is inscribed "1st Local."

2004 Summer Olympics, Athens A271

Carved rocks with stylized: (23c), Runners. 30c, Swimmers. $1, Weight lifter. $2, Sailor.

2004, Aug. 13 *Perf. 13¾*

1111-1114 A271 Set of 4 5.25 5.25

No. 1111 is inscribed "1st Local."

Nos. 1111-1114 exist imperf. Value, set $250.

Use of Postage Stamps in Singapore, 150th Anniv. — A272

Cancels, buildings, stamp vignettes and: (23c), Singapore #27, 49, 1067. 60c, Straits Settlements #N27, 271, Singapore #11. $1, Straits Settlements #124, 167, 251. $2, India #6, Straits Settlements #1, 18.

2004, Aug. 28 *Perf. 12¼x11¾*

1115-1118 A272 Set of 4 5.25 5.25
1115a Sheet of 15 + 15 labels 9.50 9.50
1118a Souvenir sheet, #1115-1118 6.00 6.00

No. 1115a sold for $6 and labels could be personalized for an additional fee.

Joy and Caring Type of 2003 Inscribed "1st Local"

Designs: No. 1119, Flower (Beauty of a Caring Heart). No. 1120, Hearts (Togetherness). No. 1121, Teddy bear (Joy).

2004 Litho. *Perf. 14½*

1119 A258 (23c) multi + label 1.75 1.75
1120 A258 (23c) multi + label .50 .50
a. Pair, #1119-1120 + 2 labels 3.50 3.50
1121 A258 (23c) multi + label .50 .50
a. Pair, #1120-1121 + 2 labels 1.00 1.00
Nos. 1119-1121 (3) 2.75 2.75

Issued: Nos. 1119, 1120, 8/28; No. 1121, 8/30. Nos. 1119 and 1120 were printed in a sheet containing five of each stamp and ten labels that sold for $15. Nos. 1120 and 1121 were printed in a sheet containing ten of each stamp and 20 labels that sold for $8, and a sheet containing 8 No. 1120 and 6 No. 1121 and 18 labels that sold for $20.

Three sheets containing 4 smaller-sized versions of No. 1120 + 4 labels (each sheet with different label and margin) sold for $5 per sheet.

A sheet with 6 No. 1120 with smaller "1st Local" inscriptions and 6 non-personalizable labels sold for $9.90. A similar sheet later sold as part of a set of 8 sheets with various face values for $8.50 per sheet. A similar set of sheets with various face values containing similar sheets containing 6 No. 1120 and 6 non-personalizable labels later sold for $9 per sheet.

Care For Nature, Chek Jawa — A273

Designs: Nos. 1122a, 1123 Seashore nutmeg. Nos. 1122b, 1124, Oriental pied hornbill. No. 1122c, Knobby sea star. No. 1122d, Common seahorse.

2004, Oct. 20 *Perf. 14*

1122 A273 Horiz. strip of 4 4.00 4.00
a.-b. (23c) Either single .35 .35
c.-d. $1 Either single 1.60 1.60

Booklet Stamps

Self-Adhesive

Serpentine Die Cut 10¼x9½

1123 A273 (23c) multi .45 .45
1124 A273 (23c) multi .45 .45
a. Booklet pane, 5 each #1123-1124 4.50

Nos. 1122a-1122b, 1123-1124 are inscribed "1st Local."

New Year 2005 (Year of the Rooster) A274

Designs: (23c), Rooster. $2, Rooster and hen.

2005, Jan. 14 *Perf. 13¼x13½*

1125-1126 A274 Set of 2 3.50 3.50
1126a Sheet, 9 each #1125-1126 32.50 32.50
1126b Souvenir sheet, #1125-1126, perf. 12¾, with Pacific Explorer emblem in margin 3.75 3.75
1126c Souvenir sheet, #1125-1126, perf. 12¾, with Taipei 2005 emblem in margin 3.75 3.75

No. 1125 is inscribed "1st Local."
No. 1126b issued 4/21; No. 1126c, 8/19.

Greetings A275

Designs: Nos. 1127a, 1132, Balloon animal. Nos. 1127a, 1131, Orchid. Nos. 1127c, 1130, Gift. Nos. 1127d, 1129, Flowers and teddy bears. Nos. 1127e, 1128, Candle and goblets.

2005, Feb. 23 *Perf. 13½x13¾*

1127 Vert. strip of 5 1.80 1.80
a.-e. A275 (23c) Any single .35 .35

Booklet Stamps

Self-Adhesive

Serpentine Die Cut 11¼

1128 A275 (23c) multi .35 .35
1129 A275 (23c) multi .35 .35
1130 A275 (23c) multi .35 .35
1131 A275 (23c) multi .35 .35
1132 A275 (23c) multi .35 .35
a. Booklet pane, 2 each #1128-1132 3.50

Inscribed "1st Local." Two sheets, each containing 4 each of Nos. 1127c and 1127d and 5 non-personalizable labels sold for $10. The labels on these sheets could be personalized for an additional fee.

Hans Christian Andersen (1805-75), Author A276

Stories: (23c), Thumbelina. 60c, The Ugly Duckling. $1, The Emperor's New Clothes. $2, The Little Mermaid.

2005, Mar. 30 Litho. *Perf. 13x12¾*

1133-1136 A276 Set of 4 5.50 5.50
1136a Souvenir sheet, #1133-1136 5.50 5.50

No. 1133 is inscribed "1st Local."

University Education in Singapore, Cent. — A277

Designs: (23c), Global knowledge enterprise. 60c, Quality education. 70c, Artistic and cultural hub. $1, Research excellence.

2005, Apr. 20 *Perf. 12¼*

1137-1140 A277 Set of 4 3.75 3.75

No. 1137 is inscribed "1st Local."

A278 A279

A280 A281

"Uniquely Singapore" — A282

2005, May 1 *Perf. 12¾*

1141 Miniature sheet of 5 + 10 labels 8.00 8.00
a. A278 $1 multi 1.60 1.60
b. A279 $1 multi 1.60 1.60
c. A280 $1 multi 1.60 1.60
d. A281 $1 multi 1.60 1.60
e. A282 $1 multi 1.60 1.60

No. 1141 sold for $6. Labels could be personalized.

Sheets containing one each of stamps similar to Nos. 1141a-1141e, lacking "Uniquely" and containing 5 or 10 non-personalizable labels sold for a variety of prices. A sheet of three stamps similar to No. 1141a, lacking "Uniquely" and containing three non-personalizable labels sold for $8.50.

Numerous sheets containing $1.10 stamps of types A278-A282 and two similar types showing other geometric designs, all lacking "Uniquely," and with different colors, exist. Various combinations and quantities of stamps exist on such sheets and all such sheets have non-personalizable labels in various quantities. All of these sheets sold for prices well above face value. Some sheets were sold only together with a variety of other non-philatelic products.

Malay Heritage Center A283

Designs: (31c), Building, drummers. 60c, Fountain pen, seal, manuscript. $1, Stringed instrument, man and woman. $2, Sailor, boat.

2005, May 31 *Perf. 13¾*

1142-1145 A283 Set of 4 5.75 5.75

No. 1142 is inscribed "2nd Local."

Admiral Zheng He's Voyages, 600th Anniv. A284

Map and: No. 1146, (23c), Admiral Zheng He, ship. No. 1147 (23c), Ships. 60c, Ships, diff. $1, Ships, diff.

2005, June 28 *Perf. 13¼x13½*

1146-1149 A284 Set of 4 3.25 3.25
1147a Sheet, 5 each #1146-1147, perf. 12¾ 3.75 3.75

Nos. 1146 and 1147 are inscribed "1st Local."

117th International Olympic Committee Session, Singapore — A285

Emblem, world map showing Singapore and candidates for hosting 2012 Olympics and: (23c), Cycling, running, table tennis. 50c, Running, basketball, tennis. 60c, Soccer, tennis, javelin. $1, Gymnastics, weight lifting.

2005, July 5 *Perf. 14¼*

Size: 44x25mm

1150-1153 A285 Set of 4 3.25 3.25

Perf. 12¼

1154 Miniature sheet, #1154a-1154b, 2 each #1154c-1154d, + 6 labels 7.25 7.25
a. A285 (23c) multi, 44x28mm .45 .45
b. A285 50c multi, 44x28mm .95 .95
c. A285 60c multi, 44x28mm 1.10 1.10
d. A285 $1 multi, 44x28mm 1.75 1.75

Nos. 1150, 1154a are inscribed "1st Local." No. 1154 sold for $6, and labels could be personalized.

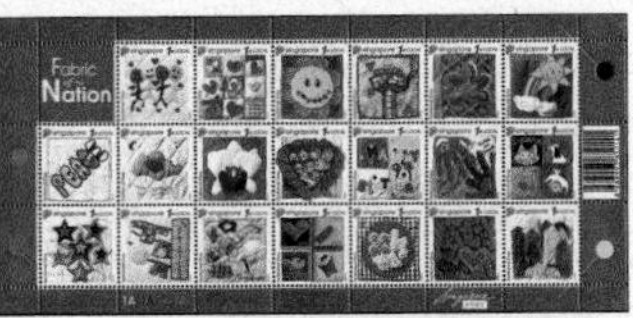

A286

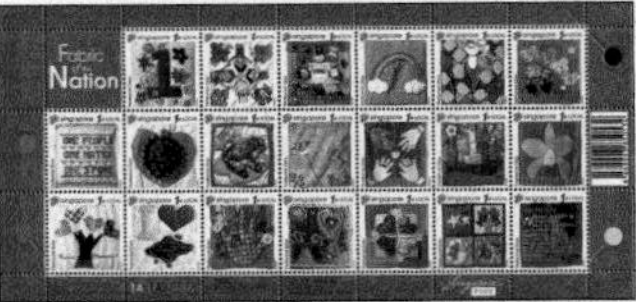

A287

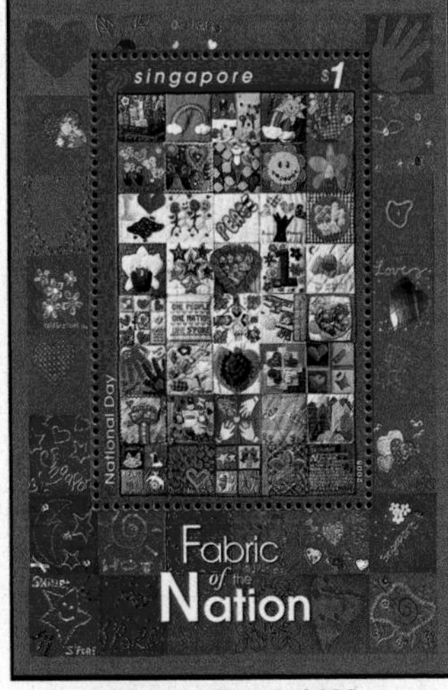

National Day — A288

Nos. 1155 and 1157 — Patchwork quilt blocks depicting: a, Stylized people, nine hearts. b, Hearts in a block of nine. c, Flower with face. d, Tower and hearts. e, Red orchid on green patterned background. f, Sun and rainbow. g, "Peace." h, Crescent and heart on Singapore map. i, White and purple orchid. j, Heart with red lace border. k, "Happy Birthday." l, Hands, "One Singapore," and "United We Stand." m, Cats and dog, "Singapore Is Our Home Too." n, Five stars around large star. o, Clothes on line, "One Nation Many Colors." p, Airplane, clouds. q, Love, star, dove, smiling face, "Love, Hope, Peace, Joy." r, Plate of food. s, Hearts and "Many Hearts One Nation." t, Stylized buildings and trees.

Nos. 1156 and 1158 — Patchwork quilt blocks depicting: a, "1" and flowers. b, Children with arms raised, "Home. . . Everyone Fits In!" c, Heads around flag. d, Rainbow and clouds. e, Person looking up, butterflies. f, Sun, butterflies, flowers, "Love Singapore." g, "One People, One Nation, One S'pore." h, Heart and durian. i, Frog on lily pad. j, Bird kites and flowers, "Flying High, My Singapore." k, Hands and heart. l, Singapore skyline, "Singapore My Home." m, Yellow, purple and green orchid on red background. n, Tree, hearts, "Racial Harmony." o, "I", heart, map of Singapore. p, Hand with buttons, child. q, Heart, stars, "Singapore." r, Four hearts in squares. s, Stars, hearts, stylized people in block of four. t, The Pledge.

$1, Entire quilt.

2005, Aug. 9 ***Perf. 14¼x14½***

1155 A286 (23c) Sheet of 20, #a-t, + label 6.50 6.50
1156 A287 (23c) Sheet of 20, #a-t, + label 6.50 6.50

Self-Adhesive (#1157-1158)

Serpentine Die Cut 10x9½

1157 A286 (23c) Sheet of 20, #a-t, + label 7.50 7.50
1158 A287 (23c) Sheet of 20, #a-t, + label 7.50 7.50

Souvenir Sheet

Perf. 14

1159 A288 $1 multi 1.75 1.75
a. Sheet of 4 #1159 9.25 9.25

Each stamp on Nos. 1155-1158 inscribed "1st Local." No. 1159a sold for $5.50.

A sheet containing 2 each Nos. 1155b, 1155c, 1155j, 1155n, 1156d, 1156r, and 12 labels that could not be personalized sold for $6. This sheet was available with personalized labels for an additional fee. Three different sheets of 6 Nos. 1155n, 1156d or 1156r, and 6 non-personalizable labels each sold as part of a set of 8 sheets with various face values for $8.50 per sheet. A sheet containing 3 each of Nos. 1156d and 1156r and 5 non-personalizable labels sold for $10.50.

Buildings in Belgium and Singapore
A289

Designs: (23c), Belgian Center for Comic Strip Art, Brussels. 60c, Shop on Kandahar Street, Singapore. $1, Shops on Bukit Pasoh Road, Singapore. $2, Museum of Musical Instruments, Brussels.

2005, Sept. 9 ***Perf. 12¾***

1160-1163 A289 Set of 4 5.50 5.50
1160a Perf. 13½x13¼ + label .70 .70
1161a Perf. 13½x13¼ + label 1.00 1.00
1162a Perf. 13½x13¼ + label 1.75 1.75
1163a Souvenir sheet, #1160-1163 5.25 5.25

No. 1160 is inscribed "1st Local."

See Belgium Nos. 2104-2107.

Nos. 1160a, 1161a, 1162a issued 11/7/05. Nos. 1160a issued in sheets of 8 + 8 labels that sold for $5. Nos. 1161a and 1162a were issued in sheets containing four of each stamp + eight labels that sold for $9.

HSBC Tree Top Walk — A290

No. 1164: a, (23c), Colugo. b, 60c, Adenia. c, $1, Red-crowned barbet. d, $1, Common tree nymph butterfly.

2005, Oct. 19 ***Perf. 14***

1164 A290 Horiz. strip of 4, #a-d 4.50 4.50

Booklet Stamp

Self-Adhesive

Serpentine Die Cut 10x9½

1165 A290 (23c) Like #1164a .60 .60
a. Booklet pane of 10 5.00 5.00

New Year 2006 (Year of the Dog)
A291

Designs: (23c), Dog. $2, Two dogs.

2006, Jan. 6 **Litho.** ***Perf. 13x13¼***

1167-1168 A291 Set of 2 3.25 3.25
1167a Perf. 13x12¾, + label .50 .50
1168a Sheet, 9 each #1167-1168 30.00 30.00
1168b Souvenir sheet, #1167-1168, with Washington 2006 World Philatelic Exhibition emblem in sheet margin 4.00 4.00
1168c Souvenir sheet, #1167-1168, with Belgica '06 emblem in sheet margin 4.00 4.00

Issued: Nos. 1167-1168, 1167a, 1168a, 1/6; No. 1168b, 5/27; No. 1168c, 11/16. No. 1167a printed in sheets of 10 + 10 labels.

No. 1167 is inscribed "1st Local."

Art by Tan Swie Hian
A292

No. 1169: a, White Cloud. b, Ganges. c, Soaring over the Flower Field. d, Kuta is a Song. e, The Winged Steed.

No. 1170, vert.: a, Black Panther (Pine). b, Ginkgo (Male). c, White Elephant. d, Summer Lotus. e, Water Dhyana.

$2, Calligraphy, vert.

2006, Feb. 22 ***Perf. 12***

1169 Horiz. strip of 5 1.75 1.75
a.-e. A292 (23c) Any single .35 .35

Perf. 12¾

Size: 27x57mm

1170 Horiz. strip of 5 4.25 4.25
a.-e. A292 50c Any single .85 .85

Souvenir Sheet

1171 A292 $2 multi 3.50 3.50

Nos. 1169a-1169e are inscribed "1st Local." No. 1171 contains one 40x60mm stamp.

Marine Mammals — A293

Designs: (23c), Indo-Pacific bottlenose dolphin. (31c), Indo-Pacific humpbacked dolphin. $1, Finless porpoise. $2, Dugong.

2006, Mar. 22 ***Perf. 13¼***

1172-1175 A293 Set of 4 5.50 5.50
1175a Souvenir sheet, #1172-1175 5.50 5.50

Self-Adhesive

1175B A293 (23c) Like #1172 .35 .35

Nos. 1172 and 1175B are inscribed "1st Local;" No. 1173, "2nd Local."

A294

Festivals and Holidays — A295

Designs: Nos. 1176, 1184, (23c), Dove (Christmas). Nos. 1177, 1185, (23c), Fruit (Chinese New Year). Nos. 1178, 1186, (23c), Candle (Deepavali). Nos. 1179, 1187 (23c), Crescent and star (Eid ul-Fitr).

No. 1180, 50c, Dove (Christmas), diff. No. 1181, 50c, Fruit (Chinese New Year), diff. No. 1182, 50c, Candle (Deepavali), diff. No. 1183, 50c, Crescent and star (Eid ul-Fitr), diff.

2006, Apr. 19 ***Perf. 14½x14***

1176-1179 A294 Set of 4 1.25 1.25
1180-1183 A295 Set of 4 3.00 3.00

Self-Adhesive

Die Cut Perf. 14½x14

1184-1187 A294 Set of 4 1.60 1.60

Nos. 1176-1179, 1184-1187 are inscribed "1st Local." Nos. 1184-1187 were each issued in sheets of 10.

Traveler's Palm — A296

2006, May 2 **Litho.** ***Perf. 12¾***

1188 Vert. strip of 5 + 5 labels 2.40 2.40
a. A296 (23c) beige & multi + label .40 .40
b. A296 (23c) light green & multi + label .40 .40
c. A296 (23c) yellow & multi + label .40 .40
d. A296 (23c) lt blue & multi + label .40 .40
e. A296 (23c) pale rose & multi + label .40 .40

No. 1188 was printed in sheets containing 2 strips of stamps and labels. The sheet sold for $3. Nos. 1188a-1188e are inscribed "1st Local." Two sheets containing 4 examples of Nos. 1188c and 1188d, each with four non-personalizable labels sold as part of a set of eight sheets with various face values that sold for $9 each.

Orchid — A297

2006, May 2

1189 Vert. strip of 4 + 4 labels 3.25 3.25
a. A297 50c black, red & pink + label .80 .80
b. A297 50c lilac, black & purple + label .80 .80
c. A297 50c org yel, black & brown + label .80 .80
d. A297 50c lt grn, black & dark grn + label .80 .80

No. 1189 was printed in sheets containing 2 strips of stamps and labels. Two sheets, differing in label and marginal image, were created. Each sheet sold for $5.

Sheets containing five No. 1189a or five No. 1189c, and five non-personalizable labels sold for $8.50 per sheet. A sheet containing 2 each of Nos. 1189b, 1189c, and 1189d and 6 non-personalizable labels sold as part of a set of 8 sheets with various face values for $8.50 per sheet. A sheet containing two each of Nos. 1189c and 1189d and 4 non-personalizable labels sold as part of a set of 8 sheets with various face values that sold for $9 per sheet.

Vanishing Occupations
A298

Designs: Nos. 1190, 1200, (23c), Clog maker. Nos. 1191, 1201, (23c), Wooden bucket maker. Nos. 1192, 1202, (23c), Spice grinder. Nos. 1193, 1203, (23c), Snake charmer. Nos. 1194, 1204, (23c), Satay man. No. 1195, 80c, Mama store worker. No. 1196, 80c, Roti man. No. 1197, 80c, Backlane barber. No. 1198, 80c, Chinese medicinal tea shop worker. No. 1199, 80c, Tin bucket maker.

2006, May 24 ***Perf. 13***

1190-1199 A298 Set of 10 7.50 7.50

Self-Adhesive

Serpentine Die Cut 10

1200-1204 A298 Set of 5 1.75 1.75

Nos. 1190-1194, 1200-1204 are inscribed "1st Local."

Infocomm, National Computerization Program, 25th Anniv. — A299

Use of computer technology in: (23c), Government. 60c, Trade. 80c, Education. $1, Telecommunications.

2006, June 20 ***Perf. 12¾***

1205-1208 A299 Set of 4 4.00 4.00

No. 1205 is inscribed "1st Local."

Singapore Chinese Chamber of Commerce and Industry, Cent. — A300

Map, centenary emblem, Chinese characters and: (23c), Chamber building. (31c),

Orchids. 80c, Emblem of World Chinese Entrepreneurs Convention. $1, Nanyang University Administration Building. $2, War Memorial and Sun Yat-sen Nanyang Memorial Hall.

2006, July 19 ***Perf. 12¾x12***

1209-1213 A300 Set of 5 6.75 6.75
1213a Souvenir sheet, #1209-1213 6.75 6.75

No. 1209 is inscribed "1st Local;" No. 1210 is inscribed "2nd Local."

National Day — A301

Globe and: (23c), Buildings (partial globe). 60c, People. 80c, Shipping containers. $1, Entertainers and fireworks.

$2, Buildings (full globe).

2006, Aug. 9 ***Perf. 12¾***

1214-1217 A301 Set of 4 3.75 3.75

Souvenir Sheet

Perf. 12¾x13

1218 A301 $2 multi 3.50 3.50

No. 1214 is inscribed "1st Local." No. 1218 contains one 49x49mm stamp. A sheet containing 3 #1214 exists, sold as part of a series of sheets sold with a book for $39.90.

Singapore Biennale 2006 — A302

2006, Sept. 13 ***Perf. 14¼x14***

1219 A302 $2 multi 3.00 3.00

A303

Intl. Monetary Fund World Bank Group Board of Governors Annual Meeting A304

Designs: 50c, Orchids. 80c, Esplanade Performing Arts Center. No. 1222, Buildings. No. 1223, Coin depicting orchid. $5, Coin depicting traveler's palm.

Perf. 13½x13¾

2006, Sept. 13 **Litho.**

1220 A303 50c multi .80 .80
1221 A303 80c multi 1.25 1.25
1222 A303 $1 multi 1.75 1.75
a. Miniature sheet, 4 each #1220, 1222, perf. 13½x13¼, + 4 labels *18.00 18.00*

Litho. With Foil Application

Perf. 13¼

1223 A304 $1 gold & blk 1.75 1.75
1224 A304 $5 silver & blk 8.50 8.50
Nos. 1220-1224 (5) 14.05 14.05

Orchids and Paintings — A305

Designs: Nos. 1225, 1231a, (23c), Vanda Mimi Palmer orchid. Nos. 1226, 1231b, (23c), Renanthera Singaporean orchid. Nos. 1227, 1231c, 70c, Vanda Miss Joaquim orchid. Nos. 1228, 1231d, 70c, Mokara Lion's Gold orchid. $1, Hollyhocks and Egret, by Hoitsu Sakai, horiz. (49x34mm). Nos. 1230, 1231e, $2, Irises and Moorhens, by Sakai, horiz. (49x34mm).

2006, Oct. 3 **Litho.** ***Perf. 14¼***

1225-1230 A305 Set of 6 7.25 7.25
1230a Miniature sheet, #1229-1230, 3 each #1227-1228, perf. 13½x13¼, + 6 labels *16.00 16.00*

Litho. With Foil Application (#1231a-1231e)

Perf. 14¼

1231 A305 Miniature sheet, #1229, 1231a-1231e 7.75 7.75

Nos. 1225-1226, 1231a-1231e are inscribed "1st Local." No. 1230a sold for $8; No. 1231 sold for $5.10.

See Japan No. 2966.

A sheet containing 3 perf. 13¼ examples of No. 1230 and three labels that could not be personalized sold for $8.50.

Diplomatic Relations Between Singapore and Vatican City, 25th Anniv. — A306

Designs: 50c, Merlion and St. Peter's Basilica. $2, Flags of Singapore and Vatican City.

2006, Oct. 12 **Litho.** ***Perf. 13½x13¼***

1232-1233 A306 Set of 2 4.25 4.25
1233a Souvenir sheet, #1232-1233, perf. 12¾ 4.25 4.25

See Vatican City Nos. 1336-1337.

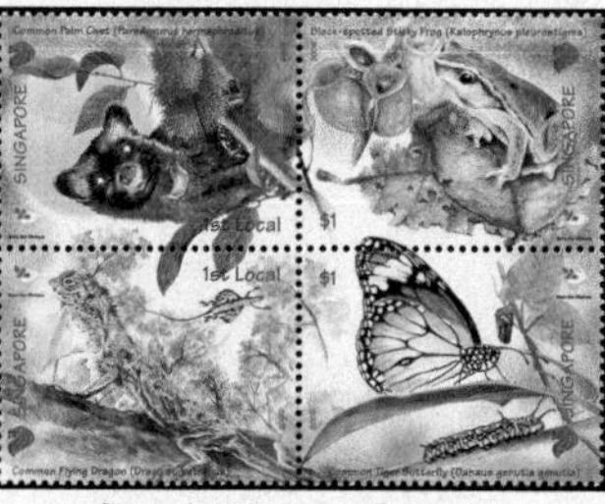

Care for Nature, Fun with Nature — A307

Designs: Nos. 1234a, 1235, Common palm civet. Nos. 1234b, 1236, Common flying dragon. No. 1234c, Black-spotted sticky frog. No. 1234d, Common tiger butterfly.

2006, Oct. 31 ***Perf. 13x13¼***

1234 A307 Block of 4 3.75 3.75
a.-b. (23c) Either single .35 .35
c.-d. $1 Either single 1.50 1.50

Booklet Stamps

Self-Adhesive

Serpentine Die Cut 11x11¼

1235 A307 (23c) multi .50 .50
1236 A307 (23c) multi .50 .50
a. Booklet pane, 5 each #1235-1236 5.00

Nos. 1234a, 1234b, 1235 and 1236 are inscribed "1st Local."

New Year 2007 (Year of the Pig) — A308

Designs: (25c), One pig. $2, Two pigs.

2007, Jan. 19 ***Perf. 13½x13¼***

1237-1238 A308 Set of 2 3.25 3.25
1238a Miniature sheet, 9 each #1237-1238, perf. 12¾ 32.50 32.50
1238b Souvenir sheet, #1237-1238, perf. 12¾ 4.00 4.00

No. 1237 is inscribed "1st Local."

Bangkok 2007 World Stamp Exhibition (#1238b).

A collector's souvenir sheet exists with No. 1237-1238 including previous 12 sets of Chinese Zodiac stamps. Value, $60.

Kindness Movement, 10th Anniv. — A309

Children's drawings: Nos. 1239a, 1240a, Boy in wheelchair, children with joined hands. Nos. 1239b, 1240b, Child opening elevator door. Nos. 1239c, 1240c, Girl assisting fallen girl, horiz. Nos. 1239d, 1240h, Red Cross volunteers helping people, horiz. Nos. 1239e, 1240g, Four people under open umbrella, horiz. Nos. 1239f, 1240f, Children visiting people at hospital, horiz. Nos. 1239g, 1240j, People in subway car, horiz. Nos. 1239h, 1240e, Boy assisting person slipping in rain, horiz. Nos. 1239i, 1240i, Boy helping blind man, horiz. Nos. 1239j, 1240d, People in crosswalk, horiz.

Perf. 13¼x13, 13x13¼ (horiz. stamps)

2007, Feb. 8

1239 A309 Sheet of 10 3.50 3.50
a.-j. (25c) Any single .35 .30

Booklet Stamps

Self-Adhesive

Serpentine Die Cut 10x10½, 10½x10 (horiz. stamps)

1240 A309 Booklet pane of 10 3.50 3.50
a.-j. (25c) Any single .35 .30

Each stamp is inscribed "1st Local."

Traditional Wedding Costumes — A310

No. 1241: a, Korean (mountains in background). b, Korean (flowers in background). c, Chinese. d, Indian. e, Malay. f, Eurasian. g, Korean (flowers in background). h, Korean (ducks in background).

Perf. 13½x13¼

2007, Mar. 30 **Litho.**

1241 A310 Block of 8 8.50 8.50
a.-b. (25c) Either single .40 .40
c.-f. 65c Any single 1.05 1.05
g.-h. $1.10 Either single 1.75 1.75
i. Souvenir sheet, #1241 8.50 8.50

Nos. 1241a-1241b are inscribed "1st Local." See South Korea No. 2250.

Cultural Dances — A311

Dancers from: (25c), Chinese culture. (31c), Indian culture. $1.10, Eurasian and Western cultures. $2, Malay culture.

2007, May 16 ***Perf. 15x14¾***

1242-1245 A311 Set of 4 5.75 5.75

No. 1242 is inscribed "1st Local;" No. 1243, "2nd Local."

Birds A312

Flowers — A313

Mammals — A314

Designs: 5c, Crimson sunbird. 20c, Yellow-rumped flycatcher. (25c), Frangipani. 30c, Blue-throated bee-eater. (31c), Torch ginger. 45c, Yellow wagtail. 50c, Stork-billed kingfisher. 55c, Blue-crowned hanging parrot. 65c, Common goldenback. 80c, Jambu fruit dove. $1.10, Large Indian civet. $2, Banded leaf monkey. $5, Malayan pangolin. $10, Cream-colored giant squirrel.

2007, June 6 **Litho.** ***Perf. 14***

1246 A312 5c multi .25 .25
a. Dated "2007B" .25 .25
b. Dated "2007C" .25 .25
1247 A312 20c multi .30 .30
a. Dated "2007B" .30 .30
b. Dated "2007C" .30 .30
c. Dated "2007D" .30 .30
d. Dated "2007E" .25 .25
e. Dated "2007F" .25 .25
f. Dated "2007G" .25 .25
1248 A313 (25c) multi .40 .40
1249 A312 30c multi .45 .45
a. Dated "2007B" .45 .45
b. Dated "2007C" .35 .35
c. Dated "2007D" .35 .35
d. Dated "2007E" .35 .35
1250 A313 (31c) multi .50 .50
a. Dated "2007B" .50 .50
b. Dated "2007C" .50 .50
c. Dated "2007D" .50 .50
d. Dated "2007E" .40 .40
1251 A312 45c multi .70 .70
a. Dated "2007B" .70 .70
b. Dated "2007C" .70 .70
c. Dated "2007D" .70 .70
d. Dated "2007E" .60 .60
e. Dated "2007F" .60 .60
f. Dated "2007G" .60 .60
1252 A312 50c multi .80 .80
a. Dated "2007B" .80 .80
b. Dated "2007C" .80 .80
c. Dated "2007D" .65 .65
d. Dated "2007E" .65 .65
e. Dated "2007F" .65 .65
f. Dated "2007G" .65 .65
1253 A312 55c multi .90 .90
a. Dated "2007B" .90 .90
b. Dated "2007C" .70 .70
c. Dated "2007D" .70 .70
1254 A312 65c multi 1.05 1.05
a. Dated "2007B" 1.05 1.05
b. Dated "2007C" 1.05 1.05
c. Dated "2007D" 1.05 1.05
d. Dated "2007E" .85 .85
e. Dated "2007F" .85 .85
1255 A312 80c multi 1.25 1.25
a. Dated "2007B" 1.25 1.25
b. Dated "2007C" 1.25 1.25
c. Dated "2007D" 1.00 1.00
d. Dated "2007E" 1.00 1.00
e. Dated "2007F" 1.00 1.00

f.	Dated "2007G"	1.00	1.00

Perf. 15x14¾

1256	A314 $1.10 multi	1.75	1.75
a.	Dated "2007B"	1.75	1.75
b.	Dated "2007C"	1.75	1.75
c.	Dated "2007D"	1.40	1.40
d.	Dated "2007E"	1.40	1.40
1257	A314 $2 multi	3.25	3.25
1258	A314 $5 multi	8.00	8.00
a.	Dated "2007B"	8.00	8.00
b.	Dated "2007C"	8.00	8.00
c.	Dated "2007D"	6.50	6.50
1259	A314 $10 multi	16.00	16.00
a.	Miniature sheet, #1246-1259	40.00	40.00
b.	Dated "2007B"	16.00	16.00
c.	Dated "2007C"	16.00	16.00
d.	Dated "2007D"	13.00	13.00
	Nos. 1246-1259 (14)	35.60	35.60

Serpentine Die Cut 9½x10

Self-Adhesive

1260	A313 (25c) multi	.40	.40
a.	Booklet pane of 10	4.00	
b.	Dated "2007B"	.40	.40
c.	Dated "2007C"	.40	.40
d.	Dated "2007D"	.40	.40
e.	Dated "2007E"	.30	.30
f.	Booklet pane of 10 #1260e	3.00	

Nos. 1248 and 1260 are inscribed "1st Local;" No. 1250, "2nd Local." No. 1260a sold for $2.55. No. 1259a sold for $28.

See Nos. 1370-1374, 1439-1441.

National Service Act, 40th Anniv. — A315

Designs: (26c), Enlistees taking oath of allegiance. (32c), Soldiers in basic training. $1.10, Soldiers in drill. $2, Soldiers in action.

2007, July 2 ***Perf. 14½x14***

1261-1264 A315 Set of 4 5.25 5.25

No. 1261 is inscribed "1st Local;" No. 1262, "2nd Local."

Miniature Sheet

Association of South East Asian Nations (ASEAN), 40th Anniv. — A316

No. 1265: a, Secretariat Building, Bandar Seri Begawan, Brunei. b, National Museum of Cambodia. c, Fatahillah Museum, Jakarta, Indonesia. d, Typical house, Laos. e, Malayan Railway Headquarters Building, Kuala Lumpur, Malaysia. f, Yangon Post Office, Myanmar (Burma). g, Malacañang Palace, Philippines. h, National Museum of Singapore. i, Vimanmek Mansion, Bangkok, Thailand. j, Presidential Palace, Hanoi, Viet Nam.

2007, Aug. 8 ***Perf. 13¼***

1265 A316 (26c) Sheet of 10, #a-j 4.00 4.00

Each stamp on No. 1265 is inscribed "1st Local." No. 1265 sold for $2.55.

See Brunei No. 607, Burma No. 370, Cambodia No. 2339, Indonesia Nos. 2120-2121, Laos Nos. 1717-1718, Malaysia No. 1170, Philippines Nos. 3103-3105, Thailand No. 2315, and Viet Nam Nos. 3302-3311.

Tourist Attractions — A317

Designs: (26c), Chinatown. 65c, Kampong Glam. 80c, Little India. $1.10, Orchard Road. $5, Merlion, vert.

2007, Aug. 9 **Litho.** ***Perf. 12¼***

1266-1269 A317 Set of 4 4.25 4.25

Souvenir Sheet

Litho. & Embossed

1270 A317 $5 multi 7.25 7.25

No. 1266 is inscribed "1st Local."

Uniforms of Youth Organizations A318

Organization: No. 1271, (32c), National Cadet Corps. No. 1272, (32c), Singapore Scout Association. No. 1273, (32c), Girl Guides Singapore. No. 1274, (32c), Girls' Brigade Singapore. No. 1275, (32c), Boys' Brigade in Singapore. No. 1276, (32c), St. John Ambulance Brigade Singapore. No. 1277, (32c), Red Cross Youth. No. 1278, (32c), National Police Cadet Corps. No. 1279, (32c), National Civil Defense Cadet Corps.

2007, Sept. 19 **Litho.** ***Perf. 13¼x13***

1271-1279 A318 Set of 9 4.25 4.25

Nos. 1271-1279 are each inscribed "2nd Local."

Coral Reef Inhabitants — A319

Designs: Nos. 1280a, 1281, False clown anemonefish, Sea anemone. Nos. 1280b, 1282, Singapore goby, Blind shrimp. No. 1280c, Hawksbill turtle, Remora. No. 1280d, Razorfish, Sea urchin.

2007, Oct. 17 ***Perf. 13x13¼***

1280	A319 Block of 4	4.50	4.50
a.-b.	(26c) Either single	.40	.40
c.-d.	$1.10 Either single	1.75	1.75

Booklet Stamps

Self-Adhesive

1281	A319 (26c) multi	.40	.40
1282	A319 (26c) multi	.40	.40
a.	Booklet pane of 10, 5 each #1281-1282	4.25	

Nos. 1280a, 1280b, 1281, 1282 are each inscribed "1st Local."

National Library Board A320

Slogans: (26c), Libraries Spark Imagination. 80c, Libraries Bring Knowledge Alive. $1.10, Libraries Create Possibilities. $2, Libraries for Life, Knowledge for Success.

2007, Nov. 12

1283-1286 A320 Set of 4 5.75 5.75

No. 1283 is inscribed "1st Local."

Opening of Changi Airport Terminal 3 — A321

Designs: (26c), Clouds, Interior of Terminal 3. 65c, Exterior of Terminal 3, Airbus A380. $1.10, Plant leaves, Terminal 3 Vertical Garden. $2, Airplane in flight, Airport control tower, baggage handlers outside Terminal 3.

2008, Jan. 9 ***Perf. 14¼x14***

1287-1290 A321 Set of 4 6.00 6.00

No. 1287 is inscribed "1st Local."

New Year 2008 (Year of the Rat) A322

Designs: (26c), Rat. 65c, Rat and tangerine. $1.10, Two rats, vert.

No. 1294: a, Rat (pig hologram). b, Rat and tangerine (ox hologram).

2008, Jan. 18 **Litho.** ***Perf. 14***

1291	A322 (26c) multi	.40	.40
a.	Perf. 13½x13¼	.40	.40
1292	A322 65c multi	1.05	1.05
a.	Perf. 13½x13¼	1.05	1.05

Size: 35x45mm

Perf. 14¼x14½

1293	A322 $1.10 multi	1.75	1.75
a.	Souvenir sheet, #1291a, 1292a, 1293, with Taiwan 2008 emblem in sheet margin	3.25	3.25
b.	As "a," with Olympex 2008 sheet margin	3.25	3.25
c.	As "a," with Jakarta 2008 emblem in sheet margin	3.25	3.25
	Nos. 1291-1293 (3)	3.20	3.20

Souvenir Sheet

Litho. With Transparent Holographic Film

Perf. 13x13¼

1294	Sheet of 2	22.50	22.50
a.	A322 $5 multi	7.00	7.00
b.	A322 $10 multi	14.00	14.00

Litho.

Self-Adhesive

Serpentine Die Cut 10

1295 A322 (26c) multi .40 .40

Nos. 1291 and 1295 are inscribed "1st Local."

Issued: Nos. 1291a, 1292a, 1293a, 3/7; No. 1293b, 8/18; No. 1293c, 10/23.

Festivals — A323

Designs: Nos. 1296, 1308, (26c), Christmas. Nos. 1297, 1309, (26c), Chinese New Year. Nos. 1298, 1310, (26c), Deepavali. Nos. 1299, 1311, (26c), Eid ul-Fitr. No. 1300, (32c), Easter. No. 1301, (32c), Mid-autumn festival. No. 1302, (32c), Pongal. No. 1303, (32c), Hari Raya Haji. No. 1304, 55c, Christmas, diff. No. 1305, 55c, Chinese New Year, diff. No. 1306, 55c, Deepavali, diff. No. 1307, 55c, Eid ul-Fitr, diff.

2008, Feb. 29 **Litho.** ***Perf. 14x14½***

1296-1307 A323 Set of 12 6.25 6.25

Self-Adhesive

Die Cut Perf. 14x14½

1308-1311 A323 Set of 4 1.50 1.50

Nos. 1296-1299, 1308-1311 are inscribed "1st Local;" Nos. 1300-1303, "2nd Local."

Embroidery, Beadwork and Porcelain Designs of Peranakan Culture — A324

No. 1312, (26c) — Various designs with bottom panel color of: a, Orange. b, Red.

No. 1313, (32c) — Various designs with bottom panel color of: a, Red violet. b, Green.

No. 1314, 65c — Various designs with bottom panel color of: a, Green. b, Blue.

No. 1315, $1.10 — Various designs with bottom panel color of: a, Olive green. b, Dark red.

$5, Deer with red violet top panel.

2008, Apr. 8 **Litho.** ***Perf. 13x13½***

Horiz. Pairs, #a-b

1312-1315 A324 Set of 4 6.25 6.25

Souvenir Sheet

Litho. With Beads Applied

Perf. 13¾

1316 A324 $5 multi *55.00 55.00*

Nos. 1312a-1312b each inscribed "1st Local;" Nos. 1313a-1313b each inscribed "2nd Local." No. 1316 sold for $8 and contains one 44x44mm stamp.

Selection of Singapore as Host of 2010 Youth Olympic Games — A325

No. 1317: a, (26c), People celebrating. b, $2, People, flag, building.

2008, June 25 **Litho.** ***Perf. 12¾***

1317 A325 Horiz. pair, #a-b 3.50 3.50

No. 1317a is inscribed "1st Local."

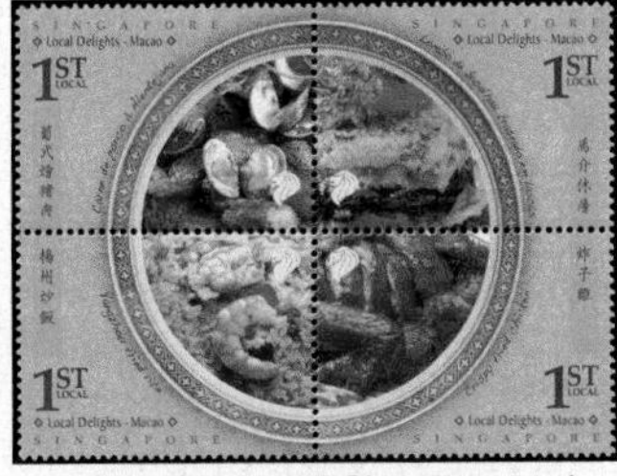

Native Cuisine of Singapore and Macao — A326

No. 1318, (26c) — Macao dishes: a, Carne de porco à Alentejana. b, Lombo de bacalhau braseado em lascas. c, Yangzhou fried rice. d, Crispy fried chicken.

No. 1319, 65c — Singapore dishes: a, Roti Prata. b, Hainanese chicken rice. c, Laksa. d, Satay.

No. 1320, vert.: a, Clay pot rice, Macao. b, Chili crab, Singapore.

2008, July 4 ***Perf. 14x13¼***

Blocks of 4, #a-d

1318-1319 A326 Set of 2 5.50 5.50

Souvenir Sheet

Perf. 13¼x14

1320 A326 $2 Sheet of 2, #a-b 5.50 5.50

Nos. 1318a-1318d are each inscribed "1st Local." See Macao Nos. 1248-1249.

2008 Summer Olympics, Beijing — A327

Designs: (26c), Table tennis. (32c), Sailing. No. 1323, $1.10, Shooting. No. 1324, $1.10, Badminton.

2008, Aug. 8 ***Perf. 13***
1321-1324 A327 Set of 4 4.00 4.00

No. 1321 is inscribed "1st Local;" No. 1322, "2nd Local."

National Day — A328

Various photographs of buildings and Singapore daily life by: No. 1325, (26c), No. 1330, 50c, David Tay Poey Cher. No. 1326, (26c), No. 1331, 50c, Tan Lip Seng. No. 1327, (26c), No. 1332, 50c, Chua Soo Bin. No. 1328, (26c), No. 1333, 50c, Foo Tee Jun. No. 1329, (26c), No. 1334, 50c, Teo Bee Yen.
$2, Photographs by the various photographers.

2008, Aug. 9 ***Perf. 14¼***
1325-1334 A328 Set of 10 5.50 5.50

Souvenir Sheet

Perf. 14½

1335 A328 $2 multi 2.75 2.75

Nos. 1325-1329 each are inscribed "1st Local." No. 1335 contains one 61x61mm stamp.

Singapore Air Force, 40th Anniv. A329

Designs: (26c), Pilots, airplane, helicopter. (32c), Weapon systems officers, plane. 65c, Unmanned aerial vehicle pilot, drone. 80c, Air engineering officer, Senior technician, helicopter. $1.10, Weapons system officers, missiles.

2008, Aug. 28 ***Perf. 14***
1336-1340 A329 Set of 5 4.25 4.25

No. 1336 is inscribed "1st Local;" No. 1337, "2nd Local."

2008 Formula 1 Singapore Grand Prix — A330

No. 1341 — Formula 1 race car and: a, Singapore skyline. b, Checkered flag.

2008, Sept. 26 ***Perf. 13½***
1341 A330 $2 Horiz. pair, #a-b 6.00 6.00

No. 1341 exists imperf.

Singapore Post Office, 150th Anniv. — A331

Postman: (26c), On scooter, 2008. (32c), And scooter, c. 1980. 50c, And bicycle, c. 1970. 80c, And mailbox, c. 1950. $1.10, And post office, c. 1910.

2008, Oct. 29 ***Perf. 12¾x13¼***
1342-1346 A331 Set of 5 4.00 4.00

No. 1342 is inscribed "1st Local;" No. 1343, "2nd Local."

Cash Crops — A332

Designs: (26c), Pepper. 65c, Tapioca. $1.10, Rubber. $2, Nutmeg.

2008, Nov. 12 ***Perf. 13½***
1347-1350 A332 Set of 4 6.00 6.00

Booklet Stamp

Self-Adhesive

Serpentine Die Cut 10x9½

1351 A332 (26c) multi .40 .40
a. Booklet pane of 10 4.00

Nos. 1347 and 1351 are inscribed "1st Local."

Fruit — A333

Designs: 65c, Dragon fruit. $1.10, Durian.

2008, Nov. 18 ***Perf. 13¾***
1352-1353 A333 Set of 2 2.25 2.25
1353a Souvenir sheet, #1352-1353 2.25 2.25

See Viet Nam Nos. 3345-3346.

New Year 2009 (Year of the Ox) A334

Designs: Nos. 1354, 1357a, 1358, Ox facing right. Nos. 1355, 1357b, Ox facing left. $1.10, Two oxen, vert. (35x45mm).

2009, Jan. 9 Litho. ***Perf. 13x13¼***
1354 A334 (26c) multi .40 .40
1355 A334 65c multi 1.05 1.05

Perf. 13

1356 A334 $1.10 multi 1.75 1.75
a. Souvenir sheet, #1354-1356, with China 2009 emblem in sheet margin 3.25 3.25
b. As "a," with Hong Kong 2009 emblem in sheet margin 3.25 3.25
Nos. 1354-1356 (3) 3.20 3.20

Souvenir Sheet

Litho. With Hologram

Perf. 13x13¼

1357 Sheet of 2 22.50 22.50
a. A334 $5 multi 7.00 7.00
b. A334 $10 multi 14.00 14.00

Self-Adhesive

Litho.

Serpentine Die Cut 12

1358 A334 (26c) multi .40 .40

Nos. 1354 and 1358 are inscribed "1st Local."
Issued: No. 1356a, 4/10; No. 1356b, 5/14.

Greetings A335

Designs: Nos. 1359a, 1364, Man and woman kissing, bowl and umbrella. Nos. 1359b, 1360, Girl blowing out candles. Nos. 1359c, 1361, Boy and girl in frame. Nos. 1359d, 1362, Girl, teddy bear, gift boxes. Nos. 1359e, 1363, Boy with balloons.

2009, Feb. 11 Litho. ***Perf. 14x14½***
1359 Horiz. strip of 5 2.10 2.10
a.-e. A335 (26c) Any single .40 .40

Booklet Stamps

Self-Adhesive

Serpentine Die Cut 11¼x10½

1360 A335 (26c) multi .40 .40
1361 A335 (26c) multi .40 .40
1362 A335 (26c) multi .40 .40
1363 A335 (26c) multi .40 .40
1364 A335 (26c) multi .40 .40
a. Booklet pane of 10, 2 each #1360-1364 4.00
Nos. 1360-1364 (5) 2.00 2.00

Nos. 1359a-1359e, 1360-1364 are each inscribed "1st Local."

Old Movie Theaters A336

Designs: (26c), Cathay Theater, 1939. 50c, Majestic Theater, 1928. 80c, Capitol Theater, 1933. No. 1368, $1.10, Queens Theater, c. 1920. No. 1369, $1.10, Rex Theater, 1946.

2009, Mar. 20 Litho. ***Perf. 14¼***
1365-1369 A336 Set of 5 5.50 5.50

No. 1365 is inscribed "1st Local."

Flower Type of 2007

Designs: Nos. 1370, 1373, Blue pea vine. Nos. 1371, 1372, 1374, Pigeon orchid.

2009, May 6 Litho. ***Perf. 14***
1370 A313 (26c) multi .40 .40
1371 A313 (26c) multi .40 .40

Souvenir Sheet

Litho. With Embroidered Flower Affixed

1372 A313 $5 multi 11.00 11.00

Self-Adhesive

Litho.

Serpentine Die Cut 9¾x10

1373 A313 (26c) multi .40 .40
a. Booklet pane of 10 4.00
b. Dated "2009B" .40 .40
c. Booklet pane of 10 #1373b 4.00
d. Dated "2009C" .40 .40
e. Booklet pane of 10 #1373d 3.50
1374 A313 (26c) multi .40 .40
a. Booklet pane of 10 4.00
b. Dated "2009B" .40 .40
c. Booklet pane of 10 #1374b 3.50
d. Dated "2009C" .40 .40
e. Booklet pane of 10 #1374d 3.50

Nos. 1370-1371, 1373-1374 are inscribed "1st Local." No. 1372 sold for $8.

Opening of First Stations on Singapore Mass Rapid Transit Circle Line — A337

Designs: (26c), Map of Singapore and Circle Line. 80c, People in station. $1.10, Circle Line train. $2, People in operation control center.

2009, May 28 Litho. ***Perf. 13¾***
1375-1378 A337 Set of 4 6.00 6.00

No. 1375 is inscribed "1st Local." Values are for stamps with surrounding selvage.

Singapore Botanic Gardens, 150th Anniv. A338

No. 1379: a, Visitor Center. b, Bandstand. c, Burkill Hall, Girl on a Swing sculpture. d, Swans in flight, bridge.
$2, Swans on lake, bridge

2009, June 19 ***Perf. 14***
1379 Horiz. strip of 4 3.75 3.75
a.-b. A338 (26c) Either single .35 .35
c.-d. A338 $1.10 Either single 1.50 1.50

Souvenir Sheet

Perf. 15x14½

1380 A338 $2 multi 3.25 3.25

Nos. 1379a-1379b are inscribed "1st Local." No. 1380 contains one 48x48mm stamp.

Desserts — A339

Designs: (26c), Ice kacang. (32c), Ondeh-ondeh. 65c, Ang ku kueh. 80c, Lapis sagu. $1.10, Mithai.

2009, July 17 ***Perf. 12¾***
1381-1385 A339 Set of 5 4.25 4.25

No. 1381 is inscribed "1st Local;" No. 1382, "2nd Local."

Sculpture — A340

Works by: No. 1386, 50c, Teo Eng Seng. No. 1387, 50c, Anthony Poon. No. 1388, 50c, Han Sai Por. No. 1389, 50c, Wee Beng Chong. No. 1390, 50c, Ng Eng Teng, horiz. No. 1391, 50c, Brother Joseph McNally, horiz. No. 1392, 50c, Tay Chee Toh.
$2, All 7 sculptures, horiz.

Perf. 13¼x13¾, 13¾x13¼

2009, Aug. 9
1386-1392 A340 Set of 7 4.75 4.75

Souvenir Sheet

Perf. 14¾x14

1393 A340 $2 multi 3.00 3.00

No. 1393 contains one 96x37mm stamp.

2010 Youth Olympic Games, Singapore — A341

Designs: (26c), Diver. 65c, Two women athletes. $1.10, Four men. $2, Hurdler.

2009, Aug. 14 *Perf. 13¼*
1394-1397 A341 Set of 4 5.50 5.50

No. 1394 is inscribed "1st Local."

Diplomatic Relations Between Singapore and the Philippines, 40th Anniv. — A342

Bridges: (26c), Bamban Bridge, Philippines. 65c, Cavenagh Bridge, Singapore. 80c, Henderson Waves and Alexandra Arch Bridges, Singapore. $1.10, Marcelo B. Fernan Bridge, Philippines.

2009, Aug. 28 *Perf. 12¾*
1398-1401 A342 Set of 4 3.75 3.75
1401a Souvenir sheet, #1398-1401 3.75 3.75

No. 1398 is inscribed "1st Local." See Philippines No. 3231.

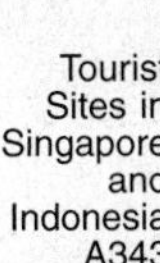

Tourist Sites in Singapore and Indonesia A343

Designs: (26c), Singaraja Statue, Indonesia. 65c, Merlion, Singapore. 80c, Taman Mini Indonesia Indah (Beautiful Indonesia Miniature Park). $1.10, Sentosa, Singapore.

2009, Oct. 28 *Perf. 14x13½*
1402-1405 A343 Set of 4 3.75 3.75
1405a Souvenir sheet, #1402-1405 3.75 3.75

No. 1402 is inscribed "1st Local." See Indonesia Nos. 2213-2216.

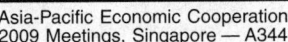

Asia-Pacific Economic Cooperation 2009 Meetings, Singapore — A344

No. 1406: a, Singapore skyline. b, Port of Singapore.
No. 1407: a, Singapore at night. b, Singapore Airport.

2009, Nov. 9 *Perf. 14x14½*
1406 A344 Horiz. pair, #a-b, + central label 3.00 3.00
a. (26c) multi .40 .40
b. $2 multi 2.50 2.50
1407 A344 Horiz. pair, #a-b, + central label 2.75 2.75
a. 80c multi 1.00 1.00
b. $1.10 multi 1.50 1.50

No. 1406a is inscribed "1st Local."

New Year 2010 (Year of the Tiger) A345

Designs: (26c), $5, Tiger, yellow green and yellow background. 65c, $10, Tiger, pink and rose background. $1.10, Two tigers, vert. (35x40mm).

2010, Jan. 8 **Litho.** *Perf. 13½*
1408 A345 (26c) multi .40 .40
1409 A345 65c multi 1.05 1.05

Perf. 13x13¼

1410 A345 $1.10 multi 1.75 1.75
a. Souvenir sheet of 3, #1408-1410, with London 2010 emblem in sheet margin 3.00 3.00
b. Souvenir sheet of 3, #1408-1410, with Bangkok 2010 emblem in sheet margin 3.00 3.00
Nos. 1408-1410 (3) 3.20 3.20

Souvenir Sheet

Litho. With Transparent Holographic Film

1411 Sheet of 2 25.00 25.00
a. A345 $5 multi 7.00 7.00
b. A345 $10 multi 14.00 14.00

Self-Adhesive

Litho.

Serpentine Die Cut 9¾x10½

1412 A345 (26c) multi .40 .40

Nos. 1408 and 1412 are inscribed "1st Local."
Issued: No. 1410a, 5/8; No. 1410b, 8/4.

Anniversaries A346

Designs: No. 1413, 50c, Housing and Development Board, 50th anniv. No. 1414, 50c, People's Association, 50th anniv. No. 1415, $1, Customs Department, cent., horiz. No. 1416, $1, Singapore Scout Association, cent., horiz.

2010, Jan. 26 **Litho.** *Perf. 13*
1413-1416 A346 Set of 4 4.25 4.25

Playgrounds — A347

Designs: No. 1417 (26c) West Coast Park. No. 1418, 50c Toa Payoh. No. 1419, 65c Bukit Timah Peak. No. 1420, 80c Sengkang Sculptural Park. No. 1421, $1.10 Vivo City. No. 1422, $2 Pasir Ris Park.

2010, Mar. 9 *Perf. 13½*
1417-1422 A347 Set of 6 8.50 8.50

No. 1417 is inscribed "1st Local."

Butterflies A348

Designs: Nos. 1423, 1427, (26c), Common birdwing. 80c, Tailed jay. $1.10, Common posy. $2, Blue glassy tiger.

2010, Apr. 21 **Litho.** *Perf. 14*
1423-1426 A348 Set of 4 6.00 6.00

Booklet Stamp

Self-Adhesive

Serpentine Die Cut 9½x10

1427 A348 (26c) multi .40 .40
a. Booklet pane of 10 4.00

Trees A349

Designs: Nos. 1428, 1438a, (26c), Saga tree. Nos. 1429, 1438b, (26c), Rain tree. Nos. 1430, 1438c, (26c), Yellow flame tree. Nos. 1431, 1438d, (26c), Tembusu tree. Nos. 1432, 1438e, (26c), Angsana tree, vert. Nos. 1433, 1438f, (26c), Sea almond tree, vert. Nos. 1434, 1438g, (26c), Broad-leafed mahogany tree, vert. Nos. 1435, 1438h, (26c), Sea apple tree, vert. Nos. 1436, 1438i, (26c), Senegal mahogany tree, vert. Nos. 1437, 1438j, (26c), Trumpet tree, vert.

Perf. 14x14¼, 14¼x14

2010, May 26 **Litho.**
1428-1437 A349 Set of 10 3.50 3.50

Booklet Stamps

Self-Adhesive

Serpentine Die Cut 9½x10, 10x9½

1438 Booklet pane of 10 3.75
a.-j. A349 (26c) Any single .35 .35

Nos. 1428-1437, 1438a-1438j are inscribed "1st Local."

Flower Type of 2007

Designs: (26c), Simpoh air. (32c), Singapore rhododendron.

2010, June 23 *Perf. 14*
1439 A313 (26c) multi .40 .40
1440 A313 (32c) multi .50 .50
a. Dated "2010B" .50 .50
b. Dated "2010C" .50 .50

Self-Adhesive

Serpentine Die Cut 9¾x10

1441 A313 (26c) multi .40 .40
a. Booklet pane of 10 4.00
b. Dated "2010B" .40 .40
c. Booklet pane of 10 #1441b 4.00

Nos. 1439, 1441 are inscribed "1st Local." No. 1440 is inscribed "2nd Local."

National Monuments — A350

Buildings and their architectural features: (26c), Bowyer Block. (32c), College of Medicine Building. 55c, Command House. 65c, Hwa-Chong Institution Clock Tower. 80c, Former Raffles College. $1.10, Tan Teck Guan Building.
$2, Architectural features of the aforementioned buildings.

2010, Aug. 4 *Perf. 13½x13¾*
1442-1447 A350 Set of 6 5.00 5.00

Souvenir Sheet

Perf. 14x13¼

1448 A350 $2 multi 2.75 2.75

No. 1442 is inscribed "1st Local." No. 1443 is inscribed "2nd Local."

2010 Youth Olympics, Singapore — A351

Lyo and Merly, Youth Olympics Mascots: (26c) Sitting on globe. 65c, Sitting under palm tree. $1.10, Merly swimming. $2, Lyo playing basketball.

2010, Aug. 14 *Perf. 13½x13¾*
1449-1452 A351 Set of 4 5.50 5.50
1452a Sheet of 4, #1449-1452, + 2 labels, perf. 13½x13¼ 22.00 22.00

No. 1449 is inscribed "1st Local." No. 1452a with personalized labels sold for $15.50, and for $19.90 with generic labels depicting the 2010 Youth Olympics emblem and mascots.

Heritage Trail and Kent Ridge Park Trail A352

No. 1453: a, Flowers, Bukit Chandu War Museum, sculpture of soldiers. b, Bird, flowers, elevated walkway. c, Flowers, sheltered walkway, eagle. d, Flowers, gazebo.

2010, Sept. 22 *Perf. 12¾*
1453 Horiz. strip of 4 4.00 4.00
a. A352 (32c) multi .45 .45
b. A352 65c multi .80 .80
c. A352 80c multi 1.25 1.25
d. A352 $1.10 multi 1.50 1.50

No. 1453a is inscribed "2nd Local."

Festivals — A353

Designs: Nos. 1454, 1463, (26c), Lion and fish (Chinese New Year). Nos. 1455, 1464, (26c), Candles (Christmas). Nos. 1456, 1465, (26c), Oil lamps (Eid ul-Fitr). Nos. 1457, 1466 (26c), Peacocks (Deepavali). Nos. 1458, 1462a, 55c, Chinese characters, fruit (Chinese New Year). Nos. 1459, 1462b, 55c, Ornaments (Christmas). Nos. 1460, 1462c, 55c, Crescent moon and star, diamonds (Eid ul-Fitr). Nos. 1461, 1462d, 55c, Oil lamp (Deepavali). No. 1462e, Lion, fish, Chinese character, flowers (Chinese New Year). No. 1462f, Ornaments and stars (Christmas). No. 1462g, Oil lamps (Eid ul-Fitr). No. 1462h, Peacocks (Deepavali).

2010, Oct. 20 **Litho.** *Perf. 14½*

Stamps With White Frames

1454-1461 A353 Set of 8 4.50 4.50

Litho. With Foil Application

Stamps Without White Frames

1462 Sheet of 8 17.00 17.00
a.-d. A353 55c Any single 1.40 1.40
e.-h. A353 $1.10 Any single 2.75 2.75

Litho.

Booklet Stamps

Self-Adhesive

Stamps With White Frames

Serpentine Die Cut 10x9¾

1463 A353 (26c) multi .40 .40
a. Booklet pane of 10 4.00
1464 A353 (26c) multi .40 .40
a. Booklet pane of 10 4.00
1465 A353 (26c) multi .40 .40
a. Booklet pane of 10 4.00
1466 A353 (26c) multi .40 .40
a. Booklet pane of 10 4.00
Nos. 1463-1466 (4) 1.60 1.60

Nos. 1454-1457, 1463-1466 are inscribed "1st Local." No. 1462 sold for $10.80.

New Year 2011 (Year of the Rabbit) A354

Designs: (26c), $5, Rabbit facing right. 65c, $10, Rabbit facing left. $1.10, Two rabbits, vert. (35x40mm).

2011 **Litho.** *Perf. 13½*
1467 A354 (26c) multi .40 .40
1468 A354 65c multi 1.00 1.00

Perf. 13x13¼

1469 A354 $1.10 multi 1.75 1.75
a. Souvenir sheet of 3, #1467-1469, with Indipex 2011 emblem in sheet margin 3.25 3.25
b. As "a," with PhilaNippon '11 emblem in sheet margin 3.50 3.50
c. As "a," with China 2011 exhibition emblem in sheet margin 3.25 3.25
Nos. 1467-1469 (3) 3.15 3.15

Souvenir Sheet

Litho. With Transparent Holographic Film

1470 Sheet of 2 25.00 25.00
a. A354 $5 multi 7.00 7.00
b. A354 $10 multi 14.00 14.00

Self-Adhesive

Litho.

Serpentine Die Cut 9¾x10½

1471 A354 (26c) multi .40 .40

Nos. 1467 and 1471 are inscribed "1st Local." Issued: No. 1469a, 2/12; No. 1469b, 7/28; No. 1469c, 11/11; others, 1/7.

Spirit of Giving — A355

Children's art with panel at bottom in: $1.10, Blue. $2, Purple.

2011, Jan. 24 Litho. *Perf. 12¾x13¼*
1472-1473 A355 Set of 2 4.25 4.25

Intl. Association of Volunteer Efforts World Volunteer Conference, Singapore.

Pond Life A356

Flora and fauna: 5c, White-collared kingfisher. 20c, Diving beetle. (26c), Water lily (30x27mm). 30c, Common redbolt. (32c), Water hyacinth (30x27mm). 45c, Ornate coraltail. 50c, Black marsh terrapin. 55c, White-breasted waterhen. 65c, Common greenback. 80c, Common toad. $1.10, Common tilapia (50x30mm). $2, Pond wolf spider (50x30mm). $5, Water strider (50x30mm). $10, Water scorpion (50x30mm).

Perf. 13x13¼ Syncopated, 13¼ Syncopated (#1476, 1478, 1484-1487)

2011 Photo.

1474	A356	5c multi	.25	.25
a.		Dated "2011B"	—	—
1475	A356	20c multi	.35	.35
a.		Dated "2011B"	—	—
1476	A356	(26c) multi	.30	.30
1477	A356	30c multi	.40	.40
a.		Dated "2011B"	—	—
1478	A356	(32c) multi	.60	.40
a.		Dated "2011B"	—	—
1479	A356	45c multi	.60	.40
a.		Dated "2011B"	—	—
1480	A356	50c multi	.75	.40
a.		Dated "2012B"	—	—
1481	A356	55c multi	1.00	1.00
1482	A356	65c multi	1.00	1.00
1483	A356	80c multi	1.50	.75
1484	A356	$1.10 multi	1.75	1.25
1485	A356	$2 multi	3.00	1.25
1486	A356	$5 multi	8.00	4.00
1487	A356	$10 multi	16.00	6.00
a.		Miniature sheet of 14, #1474-1487	37.50	37.50
		Nos. 1474-1487 (14)	35.50	17.75

Booklet Stamp
Self-Adhesive

Die Cut Perf. 13¼ Syncopated

1488	A356	(26c) multi	.45	.45
a.		Booklet pane of 10	4.50	
b.		Dated "2011B"	—	
c.		Booklet pane of 10 #1488b	—	

Nos. 1476 and 1488 are inscribed "1st Local." No. 1478 is inscribed "2nd Local." Issued: Nos. 1484-1487, 2/16; others, 4/13.

See Nos. 1532-1534, 1597-1599.

Aviation in Singapore, Cent. A357

Silhouettes of people with airplanes and airports: (26c), Bristol Box Kite airplane, Old Racecourse. 45c, Fokker F7-A, Seletar Airport. 65c, Airspeed Consul, Kallang Airport. 80c, F-15SG, Paya Lebar Air Base. $1.10, Airbus A380, Singapore Changi Airport.

2011, Mar. 16 Litho. *Perf. 13¼*
1489-1493 A357 Set of 5 5.25 5.25

No. 1489 is inscribed "1st Local."

Hawker Centers A358

Hawker centers: No. 1494, 80c, Lau Pa Sat. No. 1495, 80c, East Coast. No. 1496, 80c, Maxwell. No. 1497, 80c, Newton.

2011, May 18 Litho. *Perf. 13x13¼*
1494-1497 A358 Set of 4 5.00 5.00

Oriental Small-clawed Otter — A359

No. 1498 — Otter: a, Underwater. b, On log with crab. c, Pair looking at dragonfly. d, Head.

2011, June 3 Litho. *Perf. 12¾*

1498	A359	Horiz. strip of 4	5.00	5.00
a.-b.		50c Either single	.80	.80
c.-d.		$1.10 Either single	1.75	1.75
e.		Souvenir sheet #1498, imperf	175.00	

Spices and Dishes They Are In — A360

Designs: (26c), Cinnamon, Masala teh. (32c), Coriander, Satay. 65c, Star anise, Braised duck. 80c, Tamarind, Assam prawns. $1.10, Turmeric, Fish head curry.

2011, July 15 *Perf. 14*
1499-1503 A360 Set of 5 5.00 5.00

No. 1499 is inscribed "1st Local." No. 1500 is inscribed "2nd Local."

Economic Development in Singapore, 50th Anniv — A361

Designs: (26c), "HOME." $2, Stylized tree.

2011, Aug. 1 *Perf. 12¾x13*
1504-1505 A361 Set of 2 3.50 3.50

No. 1504 is inscribed "1st Local."

Historic Areas of Singapore — A362

Designs: No. 1506, 50c, Joo Chiat. No. 1507, 50c, Taman Jurong. No. 1508, $1.10, Old Joo Chiat. No. 1509, $1.10, Old Taman Jurong.

$2, Old and new Joo Chiat and Taman Jurong.

2011, Aug. 8 *Perf. 13¼*
1506-1509 A362 Set of 4 4.50 4.50

Souvenir Sheet

1510 A362 $2 multi 3.25 3.25

No. 1510 contains one 72x51mm stamp.

A363

A364

A365

A366

A367

A368

A369

A370

A371

Your Singapore A372

2011, Sept. 14 *Perf. 12¾*

1511		Sheet of 10	4.50	4.50
a.	A363	(26c) multi	.45	.45
b.	A364	(26c) multi	.45	.45
c.	A365	(26c) multi	.45	.45
d.	A366	(26c) multi	.45	.45
e.	A367	(26c) multi	.45	.45
f.	A368	(26c) multi	.45	.45
g.	A369	(26c) multi	.45	.45
h.	A370	(26c) multi	.45	.45
i.	A371	(26c) multi	.45	.45
j.	A372	(26c) multi	.45	.45

Self-Adhesive

Serpentine Die Cut 13½x13¼

1512		Booklet pane of 10	4.50	4.50
a.	A363	(26c) multi	.45	.45
b.	A364	(26c) multi	.45	.45
c.	A365	(26c) multi	.45	.45
d.	A366	(26c) multi	.45	.45
e.	A367	(26c) multi	.45	.45
f.	A368	(26c) multi	.45	.45
g.	A369	(26c) multi	.45	.45
h.	A370	(26c) multi	.45	.45
i.	A371	(26c) multi	.45	.45
j.	A372	(26c) multi	.45	.45

Nos. 1511a-1511j, 1512a-1512j each are inscribed "1st Local."

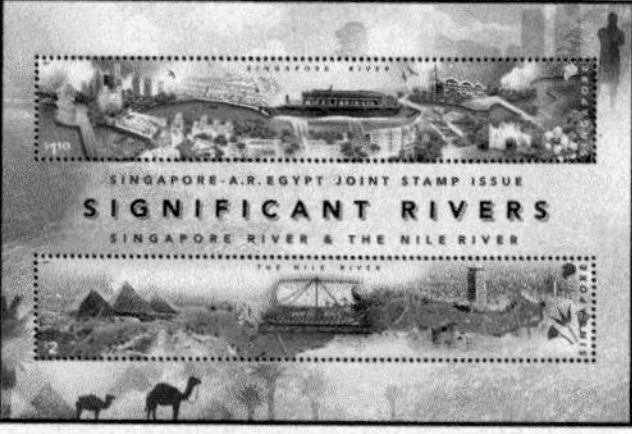

Rivers — A373

Designs: $1.10, Singapore River. $2, Nile River.

2011, Oct. 17 *Perf. 13¼*

Size: 163x30mm

1513 A373 $1.10 multi 1.50 1.50
1514 A373 $2 multi 3.00 3.00

Souvenir Sheet

Perf. 12¾

1515	A373	Sheet of 2	4.25	4.25
a.		$1.10 multi, 120x22mm	1.50	1.50
b.		$2 multi, 120x22mm	2.75	2.75

See Egypt No. 2080.

20th World Orchid Conference, Singapore A374

Orchid varieties: (26c), Vanda Miss Joaquim. 45c, Renanthera 20th WOC Singapore 2011. 65c, Dendrobium World Peace. 80c, Cyrtocidium goldiana. $2, Grammatophyllum speciosum.

$5, Grammatophyllum speciosum, Renanthera 20th WOC Singapore, 2011, Dendrobium World Peace, Vanda Miss Joaquim, Cyrtocidiuim goldiana, horiz.

2011, Nov. 12 Litho. *Perf. 14*
1516-1520 A374 Set of 5 6.00 6.00

Souvenir Sheet

Perf. 14½

1521 A374 $5 multi 10.00 10.00

No. 1516 is inscribed "1st Local." No. 1521 contains one 78x40mm stamp.

New Year 2012 (Year of the Dragon)
A375

Designs: (26c), $5, Dragon facing right. 65c, $10, Dragon facing left. $1.10, Two dragons, vert. (35x45mm).

2012, Jan. 5 ***Perf. 13½***
1522 A375 (26c) multi .45 .45
1523 A375 65c multi 1.10 1.10

Perf. 13x13¼

1524 A375 $1.10 multi 1.75 1.75
a. Souvenir sheet of 3, #1522-1524 3.25 3.25
b. As "a," with Beijing Intl. Stamp and Coin Expo emblem in sheet margin 3.25 3.25
Nos. 1522-1524 (3) 3.30 3.30

Souvenir Sheet

1525 Sheet of 2 25.00 25.00
a. A375 $5 multi 7.50 7.50
b. A375 $10 multi 14.00 14.00

Self-Adhesive

Serpentine Die Cut 9¾x10½

1526 A375 (26c) multi .45 .45

Nos. 1522 and 1526 are inscribed "1st Local." No. 1525 sold for $15.70.
Issued: No. 1524a, 6/18. Indonesia 2012 World Stamp Exhibition, Jakarta (#1524a.) No. 1524b, 11/2.

Local Tea Time Snacks — A376

Designs: Nos. 1527, 1531, (26c), Lapis Sagu (nine-layered kueh). 50c, Kueh Dadar (coconut pancake). 80c, Bao (Chinee buns). $1.10, Kueh Tutu.

2012, Feb. 8 ***Perf. 13¼x13½***
1527-1530 A376 Set of 4 3.75 3.75

Booklet Stamp
Self-Adhesive

Serpentine Die Cut 10x9½

1531 A376 (26c) multi .45 .45
a. Booklet pane of 10 4.50

Nos. 1527 and 1531 each are inscribed "1st Local."

Pond Life Type of 2011

Designs: (26c), Yellow burhead flower (30x27mm). (32c), Water lettuce (30x27mm).

Perf. 13¼ Syncopated

2012, Mar. 12 **Photo.**
1532 A356 (26c) multi .45 .45
1533 A356 (32c) multi .50 .50

Booklet Stamp
Self-Adhesive

Die Cut Perf. 13¼ Syncopated

1534 A356 (26c) multi .45 .45
a. Booklet pane of 10 4.50
b. Dated "2012B" — —
c. Booklet pane of 10 #1534b —

Nos. 1532 and 1534 are inscribed "1st Local." No. 1533 is inscribed "2nd Local."

Reservoirs — A377

Designs: No. 1535, (26c), Serangoon Reservoir. No. 1536, (26c), Marina Reservoir. No. 1537, (26c), Lower Selatar Reservoir. No. 1538, (26c), Punggol Reservoir. No. 1539, (26c), Jurong Lake. No. 1540, 50c, Upper Selatar Reservoir. No. 1541, 50c, Pandan Reservoir. No. 1542, 50c, Bedok Reservoir. No. 1543, 50c, MacRitchie Reservoir. No. 1544, 50c, Lower Peirce Reservoir.

2012, Mar. 22 **Litho.** ***Perf. 14¼x14***
1535-1544 A377 Set of 10 5.50 5.50

Nos. 1535-1539 are each inscribed "1st Local."

A378

A379

A380

Local Markets
A381

Designs: No. 1545, fruit stall. No. 1546, vegetable stall. No. 1547, fish stall. No. 1548, poultry stall.

2012, Apr. 18 ***Perf. 14x13¼***
1545 A378 80c multi 1.10 1.10
1546 A379 80c multi 1.10 1.10
1547 A380 80c multi 1.10 1.10
1548 A381 80c multi 1.10 1.10
Nos. 1545-1548 (4) 5.60 5.60

Intl. Year of Cooperatives — A382

Designs: No. 1549, (26c), Singapore skyline, 2012. No. 1550, (26c), Birth of Singapore National Cooperative Federation, 1980. 50c, Birth of National Trade Unions Congress Cooperatives, 1969. No. 1552, $1.10, Birth of Singapore's first cooperative, the Singapore Government Staff Credit Cooperative Society, 1925. No. 1553, $1.10, Founders of the Cooperative Principles, 1844.

2012, May 31 **Litho.** ***Perf. 14½***
1549-1553 A382 Set of 5 4.25 4.25

Nos. 1549-1550 are inscribed "1st Local."

Gardens by the Bay — A383

Designs: No. 1554, $1.10, Conservatory, flowers and trees. No. 1555, $1.10, Tree, kingfisher and dragonfly.

2012, June 28 ***Perf. 12¾***
1554-1555 A383 Set of 2 3.50 3.50

2012 Summer Olympics, London — A384

Designs: (26c), Table tennis. 65c, Swimming. $1.10, Sailing. $2, Badminton.

2012, July 27 ***Perf. 13¼***
1556-1559 A384 Set of 4 6.00 6.00

No. 1556 is inscribed "1st Local."

Historical Places in Singapore — A385

Designs: (32c), Tiong Bahru in 2012. 50c, Balestier in 2012. 80c, Tiong Bahru in the past. $1.10, Balestier in the past.
$2, Tiong Bahru and Balestier.

2012, Aug. 2 ***Perf. 14x13¼***
1560-1563 A385 Set of 4 4.00 4.00

Souvenir Sheet

1564 A385 $2 multi 2.75 2.75

No. 1560 is inscribed "2nd Local." No. 1564 contains one 100x41mm stamp.

Birds — A386

Designs: Nos. 1565a, 1566a, Haliaeetus leucogaster. Nos. 1565b, 1566b, Leptocoma jugularis.

2012, Aug. 31 **Photo.** ***Perf. 13***
1565 A386 Horiz. pair + central label 5.75 5.75
a.-b. $2 Either single 2.75 2.75

Souvenir Sheet
Litho. & Embossed

Perf. 13¼x13

1566 A386 Sheet of 2 16.50 16.50
a.-b. $5 Either single 8.25 8.25

Singapore 2015 World Philatelic Exhibition.

Giant Pandas — A387

Designs: Nos. 1567, 1571, 50c, Head of Giant panda. 65c, Giant panda in tree. $2, Two Giant pandas (39x74mm).
$10, Like $2, with different colors in background.

Perf. 12¾, 12x12¼ ($2)

2012, Sept. 6 **Litho.**
1567-1569 A387 Set of 3 4.50 4.50

Souvenir Sheet

Perf. 12¾x13

1570 A387 $10 multi 18.00 18.00

Booklet Stamp
Self-Adhesive

Serpentine Die Cut 10x9½

1571 A387 50c multi .75 .75
a. Booklet pane of 10 7.50

Diplomatic relations between Singapore and People's Republic of China, 22nd anniv. No. 1570 contains one 39x74mm stamp.

Festivals — A388

Designs: Nos. 1572, 1581, (26c), Christmas. No. 1573, 1582, (26c), Deepavali. Nos. 1574, 1583, (26c), Chinese New Year. Nos. 1575, 1584, (26c), Eid ul-Fitr. No. 1576, 55c, Christmas, diff. No. 1577, 55c, Deepavali, diff. No. 1578, 55c, Chinese New Year, diff. No. 1579, 55c, Eid ul-Fitr, diff.
$5, Celebrants of the various festivals.

2012, Oct. 17 **Litho.** ***Perf. 13¼x12¾***
1572-1579 A388 Set of 8 4.50 4.50

Souvenir Sheet

Perf. 12¾x13¼

1580 A388 $5 multi 9.00 9.00

Booklet Stamps
Self-Adhesive

Serpentine Die Cut 13¾x14

1581 A388 (26c) multi .40 .40
a. Booklet pane of 10 4.50
1582 A388 (26c) multi .40 .40
a. Booklet pane of 10 4.50
1583 A388 (26c) multi .40 .40
a. Booklet pane of 10 4.50
1584 A388 (26c) multi .40 .40
a. Booklet pane of 10 4.50
Nos. 1581-1584 (4) 1.60 1.60

Nos. 1572-1575, 1581-1584 each are inscribed "1st Local." No. 1580 contains one 100x36mm stamp.

Currency Interchangeability Agreement Between Singapore and Brunei, 45th Anniv. — A389

Designs: No. 1585, $1, Images from Singapore banknotes issued in 1967, 1976, 1984 and 1999. $2, Singapore Skyline, and Mosque, Brunei.
No. 1587a, $1, Images from Brunei banknotes issued in 1967, 1989, 1996 and 2007.

2012, Nov. 27 ***Perf. 12¾***
1585-1586 A389 Set of 2 4.25 4.25

Souvenir Sheet

1587 A389 Sheet of 3, #1585-1586, 1587a 5.50 5.50
a. $1 multi 1.40 1.40

See Brunei Nos. 633-634.

New Year 2013 (Year of the Snake)
A390

Designs: Nos. 1588, 1591a, 1592, Snake facing right. Nos. 1589, 1591b, Snake facing left. $1.10, Two snakes, vert. (35x45mm).

2013, Jan. 4 ***Perf. 12¾***
1588 A390 (26c) multi .45 .45
1589 A390 65c multi 1.10 1.10

Perf. 13

1590 A390 $1.10 multi 1.75 1.75
a. Souvenir sheet of 3, #1588-1590, with Australia 2013 Stamp Exhibition emblem in sheet margin 3.25 3.25
b. Souvenir sheet of 3, #1588-1590, with Thailand 2013 Stamp Exhibition emblem in sheet margin 3.25 3.25
Nos. 1588-1590 (3) 3.30 3.30

Souvenir Sheet

Perf. 13x13¼

1591 Sheet of 2 25.00 25.00
a. A390 $5 multi 8.00 8.00
b. A390 $10 multi 16.00 16.00

Self-Adhesive

Serpentine Die Cut 13¾x13½

1592 A390 (26c) multi .45 .45

Nos. 1588 and 1592 are each inscribed "1st Local."

A sheet containing perf. 13 examples of Nos. 1293, 1356, 1410, 1469, 1524 and 1590 sold for $15.70.

Issued: No. 1590a, 5/10; No. 1590b, 8/2.

History of Singapore Railroads — A391

Designs: (26c), Tanjong Pagar Station exterior. 65c, Bukit Timah Station. $1.10, Tanjong Pagar Station interior. $2, Bukit Timah Railway track and bridge.

2013, Feb. 28 *Perf. 13½*

1593-1596 A391 Set of 4 6.50 6.50

No. 1593 is inscribed "1st Local."

Pond Life Type of 2011

Designs: (26c), Geli geli (30x27mm). (32c), Water gentian (30x27mm).

Perf. 13¼ Syncopated

2013, Mar. 20 **Photo.**

1597 A356 (26c) multi .45 .45
1598 A356 (32c) multi .50 .50

Booklet Stamp
Self-Adhesive

Die Cut Perf. 13¼ Syncopated

1599 A356 (26c) multi .45 .45
a. Booklet pane of 10 4.50

Nos. 1597 and 1599 are inscribed "1st Local." No. 1598 is inscribed "2nd Local."

Marina Bay Skyline — A392

No. 1600: a, Fullerton Hotel. b, Singapore Flyer (Ferris wheel). c, Esplanade —Theaters on the Bay. d, Marina Bay Sands Resort.

$5, Marina Bay skyline.

2013, May 28 **Litho.** *Perf. 14¼*

1600 A392 Block of 4 5.25 5.25
a. (26c) multi .40 .40
b. (32c) multi .50 .50
c. 65c multi 1.10 1.10
d. $2 multi 3.25 3.25

Souvenir Sheet

Litho. With Foil Application

Perf. 14¼x14

1601 A392 $5 multi 12.00 12.00

No. 1600a is inscribed "1st Local"; No. 1600b, "2nd Local." No. 1601 contains one 50x50mm stamp and sold for $7.48.

Sign Language — A393

Frequently-used signs: Nos. 1602a, 1603, Hi. Nos. 1602b, 1604, Welcome. Nos. 1602c, 1605, I love you. Nos. 1602d, 1606, Thanks. Nos. 1602e, 1607, Goodbye.

2013, June 17 **Litho.** *Perf. 12¾*

1602 A393 Horiz. strip of 5 2.00 2.00
a.-e. (26c) Any single .40 .40

Booklet Stamps
Self-Adhesive

Serpentine Die Cut 13¼x13½

1603 A393 (26c) multi .40 .40
1604 A393 (26c) multi .40 .40
1605 A393 (26c) multi .40 .40
1606 A393 (26c) multi .40 .40
1607 A393 (26c) multi .40 .40
a. Booklet pane of 10, 2 each #1603-1607 4.00
Nos. 1603-1607 (5) 2.00 2.00

Nos. 1602a-1602e and 1603-1607 are each inscribed "1st Local."

"Our City in a Garden" A394

City buildings and: Nos. 1608, 1613a, (26c), Sunda pangolin, Green-crested lizard, Collared kingfisher, Dendrobium leonis, Moss rose. Nos. 1609, 1613b, 50c, Oriental pied hornbill, Pink mempat, Cymbidium bicolor, Tree-climbing crab, Crimson sunbird. 80c, Crepe myrtle, Dragon scales, Blue-spotted crow caterpillar, Blue pansy butterfly, Torch ginger, Magpie robin, Ferns, Heliconias, Tiger orchid. $1.10, Crimson dropwing, Baya weaver, Ridley's staghorn fern, Smooth otter, Cannonball tree flower and fruits, Yellow flame, Knobbly sea star, Angsana tree, Rain trees.

$5, Composite of Nos. 1608-1611.

2013, July 13 **Litho.** *Perf. 13¼*

1608-1611 A394 Set of 4 4.25 4.25

Souvenir Sheet

Litho., Sheet Margin Litho. & Embossed

1612 A394 $5 multi 13.00 13.00

Self-Adhesive

Serpentine Die Cut 12½

1613 Sheet of 4, 2 each #1613a-1613b *9.00*
a. A394 (26c) multi .75 .50
b. A394 50c multi 1.25 .95

Nos. 1608 and 1613a are inscribed "1st Local." No. 1612 contains one 140x35mm stamp, and sold for $8. No. 1613 sold for $1.55. Portulaca grandiflora seeds are found under gummed plastic circles affixed to Nos, 1612 and 1613a.

Independence, 48th Anniv. — A395

Inscriptions: (26c), Beating SARS together. 50c, Cleaning and greening our city. 65c, Conquering our water challenges. 80c, Living together in harmony. $1.10, Forging a vibrant economy.

$2, 48 years of independence.

2013, Aug. 5 **Litho.** *Perf. 13¾*

1614-1618 A395 Set of 5 5.25 5.25

Souvenir Sheet

Litho. With Foil Application

Perf. 13¼

1619 A395 $2 multi 3.25 3.25

No. 1614 is inscribed "1st Local." No. 1619 contains one 48x48mm stamp.

Singapore 2015 World Stamp Exhibition — A396

Nos. 1620 and 1621: a, Sea shells. b, Tropical fish.

2013, Aug. 23 **Litho.** *Perf. 14x14½*

1620 A396 $2 Horiz. pair, #a-b, + central label 6.50 6.50

Souvenir Sheet

Litho. & Embossed With Transparent Holographic Film

1621 A396 $5 Sheet of 2, #a-b 19.00 19.00

Compare types A396 and A23. No. 1621 sold for $12. Imperforate examples of No. 1621 were offered in a folder that sold for $46.73.

Singapore's Globalization Journey — A397

Designs: (26c), Truck and agricultural products. 65c, Ship, cranes and containers. 80c, Airplane and Singapore skyline. $1.10, Train, people, and flags.

2013, Sept. 10 **Litho.** *Perf. 13x13¼*

1622-1625 A397 Set of 4 4.50 4.50

No. 1622 is inscribed "1st Local."

Birds A398

Designs: (26c), Gray peacock pheasants. $2, Red juunglefowl.

2013, Sept. 12 **Litho.** *Perf. 12¾*

1626-1627 A398 Set of 2 3.25 3.25
1627a Souvenir sheet of 2, #1626-1627 3.25 3.25

Diplomatic relations between Singapore and Viet Nam, 40th anniv. No. 1626 is inscribed "1st Local."

See Viet Nam Nos. 3485-3486.

Vanishing Trades — A399

Designs: (26c), Dairy man. (32c), Maker of beaded slippers.

5c, Kachung puteh (nuts and legumes) seller. 20c, Lantern maker. 30c, Songkok (religious head covering) maker. 45c, Goldsmith. 50c, Cobbler. 55c, Knife sharpener. 65c, Ice ball seller. 80c, Parrot astrologer.

2013, Oct. 16 **Litho.** *Perf. 14*

1628 A399 (26c) multi .40 .40
1629 A399 (32c) multi .50 .50
a. Dated "2013B" — —
b. Dated "2014C" — —
c. Dated "2014D" — —
d. Dated "2015E" — —
e. Dated "2016F" — —
f. Dated "2017G" — —
g. Dated "2017H" — —

Size: 32x28mm

Perf. 13¼x13½

1630 A399 5c multi .25 .25
a. Dated "2013B" — —
b. Dated "2013C" — —
c. Dated "2014D" — —
d. Dated "2014E" — —
e. Dated "2015F" — —
f. Dated "2015G" — —
g. Dated "2016H" — —
h. Dated "2017I" — —
i. Dated "2018J" — —
j. Dated "2018K" — —
1631 A399 20c multi .35 .35
a. Dated "2013B" — —
b. Dated "2013C" — —
c. Dated "2014D" — —
d. Dated "2014E" — —
e. Dated "2015F" — —
f. Dated "2015G" — —
g. Dated "2016H" — —
h. Dated "2017I" — —
i. Dated "2019G" — —
j. Dated "2019J" — —
1632 A399 30c multi .50 .50
a. Dated "2013B" — —
b. Dated "2014C" — —
1633 A399 45c multi .75 .75
a. Dated "2013B" — —
b. Dated "2013C" — —
c. Dated "2014D" — —
1634 A399 50c multi .80 .80
a. Dated "2014B" — —
b. Dated "2014C" — —
c. Dated "2018D" — —
1635 A399 55c multi .90 .90
1636 A399 65c multi 1.10 1.10
a. Dated "2014B" — —
1637 A399 80c multi 1.25 1.25
a. Dated "2014B" — —
Nos. 1628-1637 (10) 6.80 6.80

Booklet Stamps
Self-Adhesive
Size: 30x27mm

Serpentine Die Cut 9¼x9½

1638 A399 (26c) multi .40 .40
a. Booklet pane of 10 4.00
b. Dated "2013B" — —
c. Booklet pane of 10 #1638b —
d. Dated "2014C" — —
e. Booklet pane of 10 #1638d —
f. Dated "2014D" — —
g. Booklet pane of 10 #1638f —
h. Dated "2014E" — —
i. Booklet pane of 10 #1638h —
j. Dated "2014F" — —
k. Booklet pane of 10 #1638j —
l. Dated "2015G" — —
m. Booklet pane of 10 #1638l —
n. Dated "2015H" — —
o. Booklet pane of 10 #1638n —
p. Dated "2016I" — —
q. Booklet pane of 10 #1638p —
r. Dated "2017J" — —
s. Booklet pane of 10 #1638r —
t. Dated "2017K" — —
u. Booklet pane of 10 #1638t —
v. Dated "2017L" — —
w. Booklet pane of 10 #1638v —
x. Dated "2018M" — —
y. Booklet pane of 10 #1638x —
z. Dated "2018N" — —
aa. Booklet pane of 10 #1638z —
ab. Dated "2018O" — —
ac. Booklet pane of 10 #1638ab —
ad. Dated "2018P" — —
ae. Booklet pane of 10 #1638ad —

Size: 32x28mm

1639 A399 50c multi .80 .80
a. Booklet pane of 10 8.00
b. Dated "2013B" — —
c. Booklet pane of 10 #1639b —
d. Dated "2014C" — —
e. Booklet pane of 10 #1639d —
f. Dated "2014D" — —
g. Booklet pane of 10 #1639f —
h. Dated "2013C" — —
i. Booklet pane of 10 #1639h —

Nos. 1628 and 1638 are inscribed "1st Local." No. 1629 is inscribed "2nd Local." See Nos. 1708-1711.

Fashion A400

Designs: (26c), Three women wearing white dresses. 65c, Three dress forms. $1.10, Flower, three women wearing white dresses. $2, Finished dresses on three dress forms.

2013, Nov. 8 **Litho.** *Perf. 13x13¼*

1640-1643 A400 Set of 4 5.50 5.50
1643a Souvenir sheet of 4, #1640-1643 5.50 5.50

No. 1640 is inscribed "1st Local." See France Nos. 4528-4531.

Television Broadcasting in Singapore, 50th Anniv — A401

Designs: (26c), People with high definition and tablet televisions. 50c, People looking at on-screen programming guide. 65c, Cameraman and television performers. 80c, People watching soccer game on color television. $1.10, People watching black-and-white television.

2013, Nov. 22 Litho. *Perf. 14x13¼*
1644-1648 A401 Set of 5 5.25 5.25

No. 1644 is inscribed "1st Local."

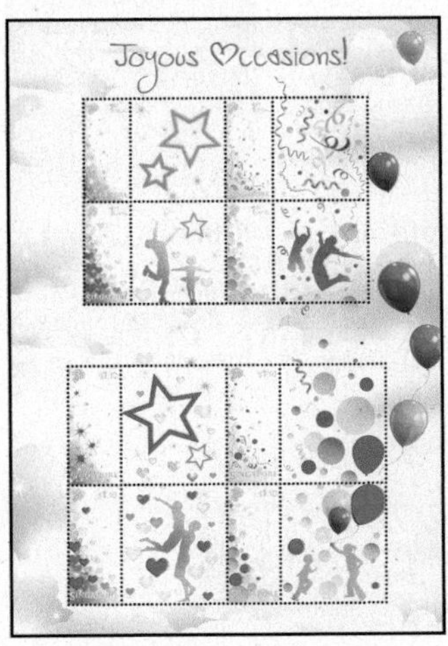

This sheet, released Dec. 7, 2013, containing four "1st Local" stamps with a franking value of 26c each, and four $1.10 stamps, plus eight non-personalizable labels sold for $11.22.

New Year 2014 (Year of the Horse) A402

Designs: Nos. 1649, 1652a, 1653, Horse facing left. Nos. 1650, 1652b, Horse facing right. $1.10, Two horses, vert. (35x45mm).

2014, Jan. 3 Litho. *Perf. 13½*
1649 A402 (26c) multi .40 .40
1650 A402 65c multi 1.00 1.00

Perf. 13

1651 A402 $1.10 multi 1.75 1.75
a. Souvenir sheet of 3, #1649-1651, with Philakorea 2014 emblem in sheet margin 5.00 5.00
a. Souvenir sheet of 3, #1649-1651, with World Youth Stamp Exhibition emblem in sheet margin 5.00 5.00
Nos. 1649-1651 (3) 3.15 3.15

Souvenir Sheet

Litho. With Transparent Holographic Film

Perf. 13x13¼

1652 Sheet of 2 25.00 25.00
a. A402 $5 multi 8.50 8.50
b. A402 $10 multi 16.50 16.50

Litho.

Self-Adhesive

Serpentine Die Cut 9¾x10½

1653 A402 (26c) multi .40 .40

Issued: No. 1651a, 8/7; No. 1651b, 12/1. Nos. 1649 and 1653 are inscribed "1st Local." No. 1652 sold for $15.70.

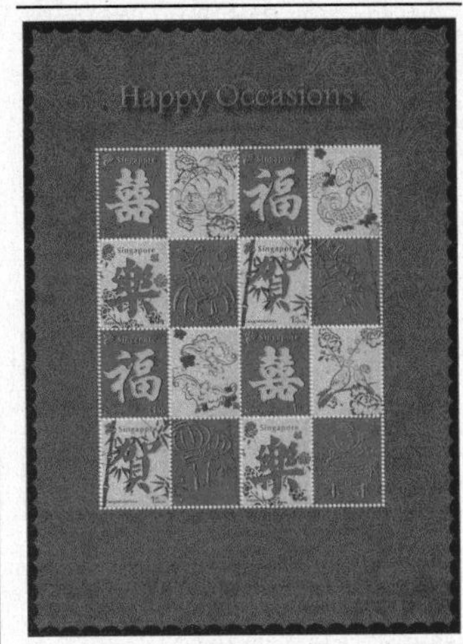

This sheet, released Jan. 3, 2014, containing four "1st Local" stamps in two different designs, each with a franking value of 26c each, two 50c stamps, two $1.10 stamps, and eight non-personalizable labels sold for $11.22. A sheet containing three examples of the $1.10 stamp and three examples of one of the "1st Local" stamps and six non-personalizable labels, also was released on that day, and also sold for $11.22. A sheet containing two "1st Local" stamps with bamboo backgroundm two $1.10 stamps, + label, and another sheet containing six "1st Local" stamps with bamboo background and eight $1.10 stamps + 12 labels, were released on Jan. 8, 2016, and sold as a set for $21.80.

Ferns — A403

Designs: (26c), Angiopteris evecta. 50c, Angiopteris evecta, diff. 80c, Cibotium barometz. Nos. 1657, 1658, $1, Cibotium barometz, diff.

2014, Feb. 26 Litho. *Perf. 12¾*
1654-1657 A403 Set of 4 4.00 4.00

Booklet Stamp
Self-Adhesive

Serpentine Die Cut 13¼x13½

1658 A403 $1 multi 1.60 1.60
a. Booklet pane of 10 16.00

No. 1654 is inscribed "1st Local."

Greetings — A404

Designs: Nos. 1659, 1666, Cupcake and candle. Nos. 1660, 1667, Heart and "love." Nos. 1661, 1668, Wedding rings. 50c, Champagne flutes. $1, Pinwheel.

2014, Mar. 26 Litho. *Perf. 12¾*
1659 A404 (26c) multi .40 .40
1660 A404 (26c) multi .40 .40
1661 A404 (26c) multi .40 .40
1662 A404 50c multi .80 .80
1663 A404 $1 multi 1.60 1.60
Nos. 1659-1663 (5) 3.60 3.60

Size: 28x33mm
Self-Adhesive

Serpentine Die Cut 13¼x13

1664 A404 50c multi .80 .80
1665 A404 $1 multi 1.60 1.60

Booklet Stamps

1666 A404 (26c) multi .40 .40
1667 A404 (26c) multi .40 .40
1668 A404 (26c) multi .40 .40
a. Booklet pane of 10, 3 each #1666, 1668, 4 #1667 4.00
Nos. 1664-1668 (5) 3.60 3.60

Nos. 1659-1661, 1666-1668 are inscribed "1st Local." Nos. 1664 and 1665 are each printed in sheets of 4.

Street Scenes — A405

Designs: $1.10, Woman carrying baby, street stalls. $1.15, Bicyclist, children walking near harbor. $1.30, Street stalls. $2, Cyclist, trolley, pedicab. $5, Ice cream vendor, street performance. $10, Crowded street, building with advertisement sign on roof.

2014 Litho. *Perf. 14x13¼*
1669 A405 $1.10 multi 1.75 1.75
a. Dated "2014B" — —
1670 A405 $1.15 multi 1.75 1.75
a. Dated "2015B" — —
b. Dated "2017C" — —
1671 A405 $1.30 multi 2.00 2.00
1672 A405 $2 multi 3.25 3.25
1673 A405 $5 multi 8.00 8.00
1674 A405 $10 multi 16.00 16.00
a. Souvenir sheet of 6, #1669-1674 33.00 33.00
Nos. 1669-1674 (6) 32.75 32.75

Issued: $1.10, $2, $5, $10, 5/28; $1.15, $1.30, 11/26.

Festivals — A406

Designs: Nos. 1675, 1683, (26c), Christmas. Nos. 1676, 1684, (26c), Chinese New Year. No. 1677, (26c), Eid ul-Fitr. No. 1678, (26c), Deepavali. No. 1679, 55c, Christmas, diff. No. 1680, 55c, Chinese New Year, diff. No. 1681, 55c, Eid ul-Fitr, diff. No. 1682, 55c, Deepavali, diff.

2014, June 25 Litho. *Perf. 12½*
1675-1682 A406 Set of 8 5.25 5.25

Booklet Stamps
Self-Adhesive

Die Cut

1683 A406 (26c) multi .45 .45
a. Booklet pane of 10 4.50
1684 A406 (26c) multi .45 .45
a. Booklet pane of 10 4.50

Nos. 1675-1678, 1683-1684 are inscribed "1st Local."

Pulau Ubin A407

Designs: (32c), Jetty. 65c, Chek Jawa. 80c, Wayang Stage. $1.10, Quarry.

2014, July 18 Litho. *Perf. 13x13¼*
1685-1688 A407 Set of 4 4.75 4.75

No. 1685 is inscribed "2nd Local."

A408

Independence, 49th Anniv. — A409

No. 1689: a, I (candle and "49" on cake shaped like Singapore). b, Speech bubble with "I am Singaporean!" c, A (leaves, flowers and geometric shapes). d, M (fish and crabs). e, S (interlocking hands). f, I (tree with hearts as leaves). g, N (soldier). h, G (woman, shopping bags, sale tags). i, A (Airport control tower, runways and airplanes). j, P (people in parks). k, O (orchids). l, R (people with joined hands). m, E (Esplanade Theaters, boat, guitarist). n, A (letters from Singaporean acronyms). o, N (people in National Day Parade).

2014, Aug. 4 Litho. *Perf. 12¾x13*
1689 A408 (26c) Sheet of 15, #a-o 6.25 6.25

Litho. & Embossed With Foil Application
Souvenir Sheet

Perf. 13¼

1690 A409 $2 gray & silver 3.25 3.25

No.s 1689a-1689o are each inscribed "1st Local."

Singapore 2015 World Stamp Exhibition A410

No. 1691 — Map of Singpore, joined hands, with background color of: a, Brown. b, Green.

2014, Aug. 28 Litho. *Perf. 12¾*
1691 Horiz. pair + central label 6.50 6.50
a.-b. A410 $2 Either single 3.25 3.25

A souvenir sheet containing litho. and embossed stamps like Nos. 1691a and 1691b sold for $12.

Singapore Sports Hub — A411

No. 1692: a, Aerial view of National Stadium, denomination at right. b, Interior of National Stadium, denomination at left. c, Aquatic Center, denomination at right. d, Aerial view of National Stadium, denomination at left.

2014, Sept. 5 Litho. *Perf. 13x13¼*
1692 A411 Block of 4 5.25 5.25
a.-b. 50c Either single .80 .80
c.-d. $1.10 Either single 1.75 1.75

Myths and Legends A412

Scenes from legends: No. 1693, (26c), People on shore, school of swordfish off shore (Attack of the Swordfish). No. 1694, (26c), Boat in storm (Sang Nila Utama). No. 1695, (32c), Swordfish attacking person (Attack of the Swordfish). No. 1696, (32c), Men and crab on beach (Sang Nila Utama). No. 1697, 50c, People watching swordfish getting trapped on barricade of tree trunks (Attack of the Swordfish). No. 1698, 50c, Men watching lion (Sang Nila Utama). No. 1699, $2, King with bloody knife (Attack of the Swordfish). No. 1700, $2, Map of island of Singapura (Sang Nila Utama).

2014, Oct. 3 Litho. *Perf. 13*

1693-1700 A412 Set of 8 9.75 9.75
1700a Souvenir sheet of 8, #1693-1700 15.00 15.00

Nos. 1693-1694 are inscribed "1st Local"; Nos. 1695-1696, "2nd Local."

Issued: No. 1700a, 5/26/16. No. 1700a was sold as a set with No. 1779a for $20.80.

Tourism in Singapore — A413

Designs: (30c), Food and drink. (37c), Cyclists and walkers on elevated path near tall buildings. 60c, Aerial cable cars, gate, signs, building. 90c, Merlion statue, statue of Sir Stamford Raffles, tourists. $1.30, Wildlife, Gardens by the Bay, Henderson Wave Bridge.

2014, Oct. 31 Litho. *Perf. 14*

1701-1705 A413 Set of 5 5.50 5.50

No. 1701 is inscribed "1st Local"; No. 1702, "2nd Local."

Painting by Jens W. Beyrich A414

Painting by Hong Sek Chern A415

2014, Nov. 10 Litho. *Perf. 13x13¼*

1706 A414 $1.30 multi 2.00 2.00
1707 A415 $1.30 multi 2.00 2.00
a. Souvenir sheet of 2, #1706-1707 4.00 4.00

See Liechtenstein Nos. 1625-1626.

Vanishing Trades Type of 2013

Designs: 40c, Cage maker. 60c, Garland maker. 70c, Kite maker. 90c, Chinese calligrapher.

Perf. 13¼x13½

2014, Nov. 26 Litho.

Size: 32x28mm

1708 A399 40c multi .60 .60
1709 A399 60c multi .95 .95
a. Dated "2017B" — —
b. Dated "2018C" — —
c. Dated "2018D" — —
1710 A399 70c multi 1.10 1.10
a. Dated "2015B" — —
b. Dated "2016C" — —
c. Dated "2017D" — —
d. Dated "2018E" — —
1711 A399 90c multi 1.40 1.40
a. Souvenir sheet of 14, #1628-1637, 1708-1711 18.50 18.50
b. Dated "2017B" — —
c. Dated "2018C" — —
Nos. 1708-1711 (4) 4.05 4.05

No. 1711a sold for $12.

New Year 2015 (Year of the Goat) A416

Designs: Nos. 1712, 1715a, 1716, Goat facing right. Nos. 1713, 1715b, Goat facing left. $1.30, Two goats (35x45mm), vert.

2015 Litho. *Perf. 13½*

1712 A416 (30c) multi .45 .45
a. Perf. 14 .45 .45
1713 A416 70c multi 1.10 1.10
a. Perf. 14 1.10 1.10

Perf. 13

1714 A416 $1.30 multi 1.90 1.90
a. Perf. 14¼x14 1.90 1.90
b. Souvenir sheet of 3, #1712a, 1713a, 1714a 3.50 3.50
Nos. 1712-1714 (3) 3.45 3.45

Souvenir Sheet

Perf. 13x13¼

1715 Sheet of 2 25.00 25.00
a. A416 $5 multi 8.00 8.00
b. A416 $10 multi 15.50 15.50

Self-Adhesive

Serpentine Die Cut 9¾x10½

1716 A416 (30c) multi .45 .45

Issued: Nos. 1712-1716, 1/9; Nos. 1712a, 1713a, 1714a, 1714b, 4/24. Taipei 2015 International Stamp Exhibition (No. 1714b). Nos. 1712 and 1716 are inscribed "1st Local." No. 1715 sold for $15.70.

Biscuits — A417

Designs: (30c), Almond biscuit. (37c), Kueh bangkit. 50c, Murukku. 70c, Kueh makmur. 90c, Gem biscuit. $1.30, Cream cracker.

Litho. & Embossed

2015, Mar. 25 *Perf. 13x12¾*

1717-1722 A417 Set of 6 6.00 6.00

No. 1717 is inscribed "1st Local"; No. 1718, "2nd Local."

Lee Kong Chian Natural History Museum — A418

Items in zoological collection: (30c), Sauropod skeleton. 70c, Giant hawkers, vert. 90c, Black-and-yellow broadbill, vert. $1.30, Leathery turtle.

2015, Apr. 18 Litho. *Perf. 12¾*

1723-1726 A418 Set of 4 5.00 5.00

No. 1723 is inscribed "1st Local."

Street Art — A419

Designs: (30c), Eiffel Tower, Paris graffiti. $2, Merlion, aerial cable cars, Singapore graffiti.

2015, May 18 Litho. *Perf. 13¼x13*

1727-1728 A419 Set of 2 3.50 3.50
1728a Souvenir sheet of 2, #1727-1728 3.50

No. 1727 is inscribed "1st Local." The French contribution to this joint issue was produced on personalizable sheets.

28th Southeast Asian Games, Singapore A420

Lion mascot, Nila, and inscription: (30c), "Courage." 70c, "Friendship." 90c, "Passion." $1.30, "Celebrate."

2015, June 5 Litho. *Perf. 14*

1729-1732 A420 Set of 4 4.75 4.75

No. 1729 is inscribed "1st Local."

Flag of Singapore A421

No. 1733 — Background color: a, Olive green. b, Gray blue.

2015, July 1 Litho. *Perf. 13½*

1733 Horiz. pair + central label 6.00 6.00
a.-b. A421 $2 Either single 3.00 3.00

2015 Singapore World Stamp Exhibition. A souvenir sheet on silk-face paper containing two stamps similar to Nos. 1733a-1733b sold for $12.

Independence, 50th Anniv. — A422

Designs: (30c), Singaporeans, soldiers and airplanes. (37c), Singaporeans, buildings, robot and automobile. 60c, Singaporeans doing physical activities. 70c, Professional Singaporeans, buildings, children and globe. 90c, Singaporean dancers and musicians. $1.30, Singaporeans and buildings.
$5, "50 Years of Independence."

Litho. & Embossed With Foil Application

2015, Aug. 5 *Perf. 13*

1734-1739 A422 Set of 6 6.75 6.75

Souvenir Sheet

Embossed With Foil Application, Sheet Margin Litho.

Perf. 13¼

1740 A422 $5 gold 8.00 8.00

No. 1734 is inscribed "1st Local;" No. 1735, "2nd Local." No. 1740 contains one 45x45mm stamp.

Singapore Botanic Garden UNESCO World Heritage Site — A423

No. 1741: a, Birds and buildings. b, Bird, otters, pond, building and gate.

2015, Aug. 7 Litho. *Perf. 12¾*

1741 A423 $1.30 Vert. pair, #a-b 4.25 4.25

Flags and Emblem of Association of Southeast Asian Nations A424

2015, Aug. 8 Litho. *Perf. 13¾*

1742 A424 60c multi .95 .95

See Brunei No. 656, Burma Nos. 417-418, Cambodia No. 2428, Indonesia No. 2428, Laos No. , Malaysia No. 1562, Philippines No. 3619, Thailand No. 2875, and Viet Nam No. 3529.

Houses of Parliament A425

Houses of Parliament in: No. 1743, $1.30, Singapore. No. 1744, $1.30, Australia. No. 1745, $1.30, New Zealand.

2015, Aug. 14 Litho. *Perf. 14¼*

1743-1745 A425 Set of 3 6.25 6.25
1745a Souvenir sheet of 3, #1743-1745 6.25 6.25

See Australia Nos. 4331-4333, New Zealand No. 2600.

Diplomatic Relations Between Singapore and Thailand, 50th Anniv. A426

Designs: (30c), Khao Niew Manuang (mango sticky rice). $2, Ice cream sandwiches.

Perf. 13½x13¼

2015, Sept. 18 Litho.

1746-1747 A426 Set of 2 3.75 3.75
1747a Souvenir sheet of 2, #1746-1747 3.75 3.75

No. 1746 is inscribed "1st Local." See Thailand No. 2876.

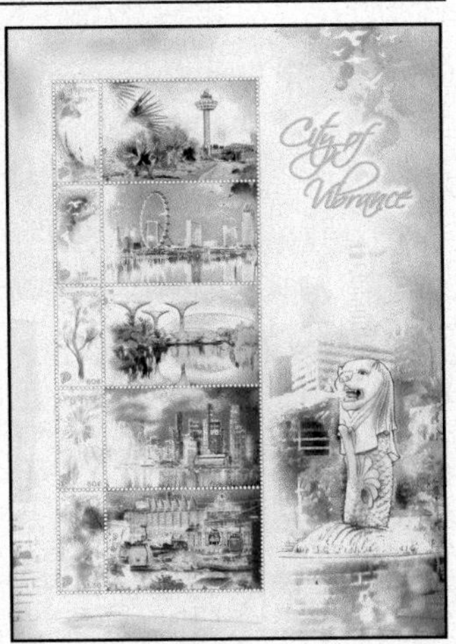

This sheet, released Aug. 16, 2015, containing two "1st Local" stamps in two different designs, each with a franking value of 30c each, two 60c stamps, one $1.30 stamps, and five non-personalizable labels sold for $7.48.

Citizens Consultative Committees, 50th Anniv. — A427

Singapore flag, various people and background color of: (30c), Blue. $2, Red lilac.

2015, Oct. 24 Litho. *Perf. 13¼*

1748-1749 A427 Set of 2 3.25 3.25

No. 1748 is inscribed "1st Local."

Indian Heritage Center — A428

Designs: (30c), Night view of Indian Heritage Center. 70c, Ganesha and Patolu. 90c, Chettinad doorway. $1.30, Kasumalai and Pheta.

Perf. 13¾x13¼

2015, Nov. 16 Litho.

1750-1753 A428 Set of 4 4.25 4.25

No. 1750 is inscribed "1st Local."

Paintings in National Gallery — A429

Designs: No. 1754, $1.30, National Language Class, by Chua Mia Tee. No. 1755, $1.30, Pagodas II, Pago-Pago Series, by Latiff Mohidin. No. 1756, $1.30, Wounded Lion, by Raden Saleh. No. 1757, $1.30, Drying Salted Fish, by Cheong Soo Pieng (74x32mm).

2015, Nov. 24 Litho. *Perf. 13¾*

1754-1757 A429 Set of 4 7.50 7.50

Diplomatic Relations Between Singapore and India, 50th Anniv. A430

Presidential residences: (30c), Istana, Singapore. $2, Rashtrapati Bhavan, India.

2015, Nov. 24 Litho. *Perf. 12¾*

1758-1759 A430 Set of 2 3.25 3.25

No. 1758 is inscribed "1st Local." A souvenir sheet containing No. 1758 and a perf. 12¾ version of India No. 2770 was sold only in Singapore for $8. See India Nos. 2769-2770.

8th ASEAN Para Games, Singapore A431

Designs: (30c), Mascot. $2, Athletes.

2015, Dec. 3 Litho. *Perf. 13¼x13*

1760-1761 A431 Set of 2 3.25 3.25

No. 1760 is inscribed "1st Local."

New Year 2016 (Year of the Monkey) A432

Designs: Nos. 1762, 1765a, 1766, Monkey facing right. Nos. 1763, 1765b, Monkey facing left. $1.30, Two monkeys (35x45mm).

2016 Litho. *Perf. 13½X13¼*

1762	A432	(30c) multi	.45	.45
1763	A432	70c multi	1.00	1.00

Perf. 14¼

1764	A432 $1.30 multi	1.90	1.90
a.	Souvenir sheet of 3, #1762-1764, with Thailand 2016 emblem in sheet margin	3.50	3.50
b.	As "a," with Philataipei 2016 emblem in sheet margin	3.50	3.50
	Nos. 1762-1764 (3)	3.35	3.35

Souvenir Sheet

Perf. 13x13¼

1765	Sheet of 2	22.00	22.00
a.	A432 $5 multi	7.50	7.50
b.	A432 $10 multi	14.50	14.50

Self-Adhesive

Serpentine Die Cut 9¾x10½

1766 A432 (30c) multi .45 .45

Issued: Nos. 1762-1766, 1/8; No. 1764a, 8/10; No. 1764b, 10/21. Nos. 1762 and 1766 are inscribed "1st Local." No. 1765 sold for $15.70.

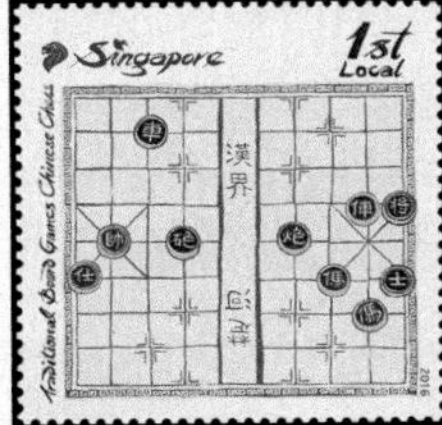

Traditional Board Games A433

Designs: (30c), Chinese chess. (37c), Diamond game. 50c, Aeroplane chess. 70c, Snakes and Ladders. $1.30, Checkers.

2016, Apr. 27 Litho. *Perf. 13*

1767-1771 A433 Set of 5 4.75 4.75

No. 1767 is inscribed "1st Local"; No. 1768, "2nd Local."

Myths and Legends A434

Designs: No. 1772, (30c), Minah and Lina, mortar and pestle (Sisters' Islands). No. 1773, (30c), Fishermen in boats in storm (Kusu Island). No. 1774, (37c), Minah and Lina, Chief and boat (Sisters' Islands). No. 1775, (37c), Sea turtle (Kusu Island). No. 1776, 50c, Lina and Chief watching wave engulf Minah (Sisters' Islands). No. 1777, 50c, Men and sea turtle (Kusu Island). No. 1778, $2, Pulau Subar Darat and Pulau Subar Laut (Sisters' Islands). No, 1779, $2, House on Kusu Island (Kusu Island).

2016, May 25 Litho. *Perf. 13*

1772-1779	A434	Set of 8	9.25	9.25
1779a		Souvenir sheet of 8, #1772-1779	15.00	15.00

Nos. 1772 and 1773 are inscribed "1st Local." No. 1779a was sold as a set with No. 1700a for $20.80.

Singapore Youth Festival, 50th Anniv. — A435

Designs: (30c), Art. (37c), Dance. 50c, Drama. 70c, Music. $1.30, Festival emblem.

2016, July 1 Litho. *Perf. 14*

1780-1784 A435 Set of 5 4.75 4.75

No. 1780 is inscribed "1st Local"; No. 1781, "2nd Local."

2016 Summer Olympics, Rio de Janeiro A436

Designs: (30c), Swimming. 70c, Shooting. 90c, Table tennis. $1.30, Sailing.

2016, Aug. 5 Litho. *Perf. 13x13¼*

1785-1788 A436 Set of 4 4.75 4.75

No. 1785 is inscribed "1st Local."

National Day Parade, 50th Anniv. A437

Designs: (30c), Flag of Singapore carried by row of men. (37c), Marchers holding ribbons. 60c, Motorcycle policemen. 70c, Singapore flag in stadium. 90c, Helicopters flying flag. $1.30, Celebrations in stadium with retractable roof.

$2, Soldiers carrying various flags.

Litho. With Foil Application

2016, Aug. 8 *Perf. 12¾*

1789-1794 A437 Set of 6 6.25 6.25

Souvenir Sheet

Litho.

Perf. 13

1795 A437 $2 multi 3.00 3.00

No. 1789 is inscribed "1st Local"; No. 1790, "2nd Local." No. 1795 contains one 45x45mm stamp with laser-cut country name.

Birds of Prey A438

Designs: (30c), Changeable hawk eagle. 70c, White-bellied sea eagle. 90c, Brahminy kite. $1.30, Black-winged kite.

2016, Sept. 21 Litho. *Perf. 12¾*

1796-1799 A438 Set of 4 4.75 4.75

No. 1796 is inscribed "1st Local."

Diplomatic Relations Between Singapore and Pakistan, 50th Anniv. A439

National Flowers: No. 1800, $1.30, Vanda Miss Joaquim orchid (Singapore). No. 1801, $1.30, Jasmine (Pakistan).

2016, Oct. 18 Litho. *Perf. 12¾x13*

1800-1801 A439 Set of 2 3.75 3.75

A souvenir sheet containing Nos. 1800-1801 sold fof $7.48. See Pakistan No. 1239.

Festival — A440

Designs: Nos. 1802, 1810, (30c), Chinese New Year, fish. Nos. 1803, 1811, (30c), Christmas, trees, snowflakes. No. 1804, (30c), Deepavali. No. 1805, (30c), Hari Raya Aidilfitri (Eid ul-Fitr). No. 1806, 70c, Chinese New Year, rooster. No. 1807, 70c, Christmas, boy, house. No. 1808, 70c, Deepavali. No. 1809, 70c, Hari Raya Aidalfitri, temples.

2016, Oct. 19 Litho. *Perf. 14¼*

1802-1809 A440 Set of 8 5.75 5.75

Booklet Stamps

Self-Adhesive

Serpentine Die Cut 9¾

1810	A440 (30c) multi	.45	.45
a.	Booklet pane of 10	4.50	
1811	A440 (30c) multi	.45	.45
a.	Booklet pane of 10	4.50	

Nos. 1802-1805, 1810-1811 are inscribed "1st Local."

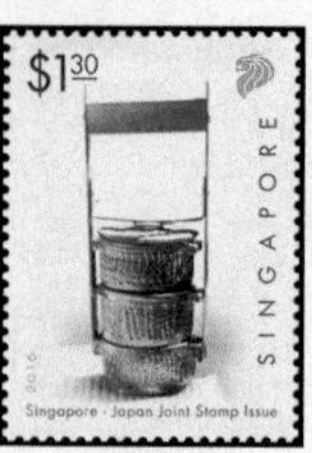
Three Singaporean Pots with Handles — A441

Two Japanese Bowls — A442

2016, Nov. 29 Litho. *Perf. 13½*

1812 A441 $1.30 multi 1.90 1.90
1813 A442 $1.30 multi 1.90 1.90
a. Souvenir sheet of 6, 3 each #1812-1813, + 4 labels 19.50 19.50

Diplomatic relations between Singapore and Japan, 50th anniv. No. 1813a sold for $13.80. See Japan No. 4065.

New Year 2017 (Year of the Rooster) A443

Designs: Nos. 1814, 1817a, 1818, Rooster facing right. Nos. 1815, 1817b, Rooster facing left. $1.30, Two roosters (35x45mm).

2017 Litho. *Perf. 13½X13¼*

1814 A443 (30c) multi .45 .45
1815 A443 70c multi 1.00 1.00

Perf. 14¼

1816 A443 $1.30 multi 1.90 1.90
a. Souvenir sheet of 3, #1814-1816, with 2017 Melbourne Stamp and Coin Show emblem in sheet margin 3.25 3.25
b. As No. 1816a, with Bandung 2017 emblem in sheet margin, perf. 14 3.50 3.50
Nos. 1814-1816 (3) 3.35 3.35

Souvenir Sheet

Perf. 13x13¼

1817 Sheet of 2 22.50 22.50
a. A443 $5 multi 7.50 7.50
b. A443 $10 multi 15.00 15.00

Self-Adhesive

Serpentine Die Cut 9¾x10½

1818 A443 (30c) multi .45 .45

Issued: Nos. 1814-1818, 1/8; No. 1816a, 3/30. No. 1816b, 8/3. Nos. 1814 and 1818 are inscribed "1st Local." No. 1817 sold for $15.70.

Anniversaries of Organizations — A444

Designs: (30c), Singapore Girl Guides, cent. 70c, Outward Bound Singapore, 50th anniv. $1.30, Lions Clubs International, cent.

Perf. 13¼x13¾

2017, Feb. 17 Litho.

1819-1821 A444 Set of 3 3.25 3.25

No. 1819 is inscribed "1st Local."

National Service, 50th Anniv. — A445

Inscriptions: Nos. 1822, 1829, (30c), Passing of the National Service (Amendment) Bill, 1967. No. 1823, 1830, (30c), First batch of NSFs (full-time national servicemen) enlisted into SAF (Singapore Armed Forces), 1967. 70c, First batch of NSFs enlisted into SPF (Singapore Police Force), 1975. 90c, First batch of NSFs enlisted into SCDF (Singapore Civil Defense Force), 1981. $1.30, Introduction of Open Mobilization System, 1985.

No. 1827, National Servicemen in uniform and children, horiz.

No. 1828: a, Like #1822. b, Like #1823.

2017, Mar. 14 Litho. *Perf. 12¾*

1822-1826 A445 Set of 5 5.00 5.00

Souvenir Sheet

Perf. 12¼

1827 A445 $2 multi 3.00 3.00

Litho. & Embossed

Perf. 12¾

1828 A445 $2 Sheet of 2, #a-b — —

Self-Adhesive

Litho.

Serpentine Die Cut 13¼x13½

1829 A445 (30c) multi — —
1830 A445 (30c) multi — —

No. 1822 is inscribed "1st Local." No. 1827 contains one 84x44mm stamp.

Kingfishers — A446

Designs: (30c), Black-capped kingfisher. 70c, Blue-eared kingfisher. 90c, Black-backed kingfisher. $1.30, White-throated kingfisher.

2017, Apr. 26 Litho. *Perf. 13*

1831-1834 A446 Set of 4 4.75 4.75

No. 1831 is inscribed "1st Local."

Baby Animals A447

Designs: (30c), Kitten and puppy. 70c, Two rabbit kits. 90c, Two bear cubs. $1.30, Two ducklings.

2017, June 28 Litho. *Perf. 13¾*

1835-1838 A447 Set of 4 4.75 4.75

No. 1835 is inscribed "1st Local."

A448

A449

A450

Wedding Jewelry — A451

2017, July 12 Litho. *Perf. 13¼*

1839 A448 90c gold & multi 1.40 1.40
1840 A449 90c gold & multi 1.40 1.40
1841 A450 90c gold & multi 1.40 1.40
1842 A451 90c gold & multi 1.40 1.40
Nos. 1839-1842 (4) 5.60 5.60

A souvenir sheet of four $10 stamps with the same designs as Nos. 1839-1842 was printed in limited quantities and sold for $68.

Morning in Singapore — A452

Designs: (30c), Children in school zone. (37c), Bus picking up passengers at bus stop. 60c, People at Hawker Center. 70c, Cyclists and runners on path. 90c, People on exercize equipment in park. $1.30, People shopping at Wet Market.

$2, School children in school zone, bus, people exercizing in park, woman walking dog.

2017, Aug. 4 Litho. *Perf. 13¼*

1843-1848 A452 Set of 6 6.25 6.25

Souvenir Sheet

Perf. 12¾

1849 A452 $2 multi 3.00 3.00

No. 1843 is inscribed "1st Local." No. 1844 is inscribed "2nd Local." No. 1849 contains one 45x45mm stamp with laser-cut country name.

Papilionanthe "Miss Joaquim," National Flower of Singapore A453

2017, Aug. 6 Litho. *Perf. 13½*

1850 A453 (30c) multi .45 .45

Souvenir Sheet

1851 A453 $5 multi 7.25 7.25

Association of Southeast Asian Nations, 50th anniv. No. 1850 is inscribed "1st Local."

First Stamps of Straits Settlements, 150th Anniv. — A454

Designs: (30c), Straits Settlements #1. (37c), Block of four of Straits Settlements #3. 60c, Cover to Switzerland bearing Straits Settlements #6 and 7. 70c, Cover to England bearing four Straits Settlements #6. $1.30, $1.30, Cover to Scotland bearing #9.

2017, Sept. 1 Litho. *Perf. 13x13¼*

1852-1856 A454 Set of 5 5.00 5.00

No. 1852 is inscribed "1st Local." No. 1853 is inscribed "2nd Local."

A455

Corals and Fish — A456

2017, Sept. 7 Litho. *Perf. 12¾*

1857 A455 $1.30 multi 1.90 1.90
1858 A456 $1.30 multi 1.90 1.90
a. Souvenir sheet of 2, #1857-1858 3.80 3.80

See Indonesia No. 2470.

Opening of New General Post Office — A457

Designs: (30c), Old and new post office counters, cover to Switzerland bearing British Military Administration overprints. 60c, Old and new post office counters, clock, horiz. 90c, Old and new buildings, cancels, horiz. $1.30, Mobile post office, philatelic store and mail box.

Litho. With Foil Application

2017, Oct. 9 *Perf. 13*

1859-1862 A457 Set of 4 4.50 4.50

No. 1859 is inscribed "1st Local."

Greetings A458

Merlion and slogan: Nos. 1863a, 1870, Congrats. Nos. 1863b, 1871, Selfie. Nos. 1863c, 1872, High five. Nos. 1863d, 1873, Well done. Nos. 1863e, 1874, All the best. Nos. 1864a, 1865, Miss you. Nos. 1864b, 1866, Good luck. Nos. 1864c, 1867, Cool. Nos. 1864d, 1868, Love. Nos. 1864e, 1869, Hello.

2017, Nov. 15 Litho. *Perf. 13¾*

1863 Horiz. strip of 5 2.25 2.25
a.-e. A458 (30c) Any single .45 .45
1864 Horiz. strip of 5 2.75 2.75
a.-e. A458 (37c) Any single .55 .55

Self-Adhesive

Serpentine Die Cut 11¼

1865 A458 (37c) sil & multi .55 .55
1866 A458 (37c) sil & multi .55 .55
1867 A458 (37c) sil & multi .55 .55
1868 A458 (37c) sil & multi .55 .55
1869 A458 (37c) sil & multi .55 .55
a. Horiz. strip of 5 2.75
Nos. 1865-1869 (5) 2.75 2.75

Booklet Stamps

1870 A458 (30c) sil & multi .45 .45
1871 A458 (30c) sil & multi .45 .45
1872 A458 (30c) sil & multi .45 .45
1873 A458 (30c) sil & multi .45 .45
1874 A458 (30c) sil & multi .45 .45
a. Booklet pane of 10, 2 each #1870-1874 4.50 4.50
Nos. 1870-1874 (5) 2.25 2.25

Nos. 1863a-1863e, 1870-1874 are inscribed "1st Local." Nos. 1864a-1864e, 1865-1869 are inscribed "2nd Local."

New Year 2018 (Year of the Dog) A459

Designs: Nos. 1875, 1878a, 1879, Dog, light green background. Nos. 1876, 1878b, Dog, yellow background. $1.30. Two dogs (35x45mm).

2018, Jan. 5 Litho. *Perf. 13½x13¼*
1875 A459 (30c) multi .45 .45
1876 A459 70c multi 1.10 1.10

Perf. 14¼
1877 A459 $1.30 multi 2.00 2.00
a. Souvenir sheet of 3, #1875-1877, with Macao 2018 emblem in sheet margin, perf. 14 3.75 3.75
Nos. 1875-1877 (3) 3.55 3.55

Souvenir Sheet
Perf. 13x13¼
1878 Sheet of 2 25.50 25.50
a. A459 $5 multi 8.50 8.50
b. A459 $10 multi 17.00 17.00

Self-Adhesive
Serpentine Die Cut 9¾x10½
1879 A459 (30c) multi .45 .45

Issued: No. 1877a, 9/21. Nos. 1875 and 1879 are inscribed "1st Local." No. 1877a sold for $2.45. No. 1878 sold for $16.80.

Historical Areas A460

Designs: No. 1880, (30c), Present-day Arab Street. No. 1881, (30c), Present-day Kampong Glam. No. 1882, $1.30, Arab Street of the past. No. 1883, $1.30, Kampong Glam of the past.

2018, Mar. 21 Litho. *Perf. 13*
1880-1883 A460 Set of 4 5.00 5.00

Nos. 1880 and 1881 are inscribed "1st Local."

Trades of Old Singapore A461

Designs: (30c), Samsui woman. 60c, Sikh guard. 90c, Boatman. $1.30, Coolie.
$5, Boatman, coolie, Samsui woman, Sikh guard.

2018, Apr. 18 Litho. *Perf. 13¼*
1884-1887 A461 Set of 4 4.75 4.75

Souvenir Sheet
Perf. 13
1888 A461 $5 multi 7.50 7.50

No. 1884 is inscribed "1st Local." No. 1888 contains one 50x50mm stamp and sold for $80.

50th Anniversaries of Organizations — A462

Organizational headquarters of: No. 1889, $1.30, Institute of Southeast Asian Studies (ISEAS). No. 1890, $1.30, Jurong Town Corporation (JTC). No. 1891, $1.30, Islamic Religious Council of Singapore (MUIS).

2018, May 16 Litho. *Perf. 13x12¾*
1889-1891 A462 Set of 3 6.00 6.00

Singapore and Russia Joint Issue — A463

Designs: No. 1892, $1.30, Gardens by the Bay, Singapore. No. 1893, $1.30, Covered amphitheater. Zaryadye Park, Moscow.

2018, June 1 Litho. *Perf. 12x12¼*
1892-1893 A463 Set of 2 4.00 4.00
1893a Souvenir sheet of 2, #1892-1893 4.00 4.00

See Russia No. 7933.

A464

Cultivation of Vanda Miss Joaquim Orchid, 125th Anniv. A465

Various depictions of Vanda Miss Joaquim orchids.

Perf. 14¼x14 (A464), 14 (A465)
Litho. With Foil Application
2018, June 22
1894 A464 (30c) multi .45 .45
1895 A465 70c multi 1.10 1.10
1896 A465 90c multi 1.40 1.40
1897 A464 $1.30 multi 1.90 1.90
Nos. 1894-1897 (4) 4.85 4.85

Souvenir Sheet
Litho., Litho & Embossed Sheet Margin
1898 A464 $5 multi 7.50 7.50

No. 1894 is inscribed "1st Local." No. 1898 contains one 50x50mm stamp.

Souvenir Sheet

First Summit Meeting of U.S. Pres. Donald Trump and North Korean Supreme Leader Kim Jong-un, Singapore — A466

2018, July 20 Litho. *Perf. 13*
1899 A466 $10 multi 16.00 16.00

No. 1899 was sold with a folder for $10.70.

Native Ginger Plants A467

Designs: (30c), Zingiber singapurense. 70c, Cheilocostus globosus. 90c, Phrynium hirtum. $1.30, Conamomum xanthophlebium.

2018, July 24 Litho. *Perf. 13*
1900-1903 A467 Set of 4 4.75 4.75

No. 1900 is inscribed "1st Local."

Evening in Singapore A468

Designs: (30c), Family at dinner table. (37c), People exercizing outdoors. 60c, People on bridge fishing. 70c, Joggers. 90c, People at outdoor market. $1.30, People dining at outdoor café.
$2, People at outdoor market, vehicles on street.

2018, Aug. 3 Litho. *Perf. 12¾*
1904-1909 A468 Set of 6 6.00 6.00

Souvenir Sheet
Perf. 13
1910 A468 $2 multi 3.00 3.00

National Day. No. 1904 is inscribed "1st Local." No. 1905 is inscribed "2nd Local." No. 1910 contains one 45x45mm stamp that has laser-cut country name.

A469

A470

Singapore, 2018 Chair of Association of Southeast Asian Nations — A471

2018, Aug. 4 Litho. *Perf. 12¼*
1911 A469 $1.30 multi 1.90 1.90
1912 A470 $1.30 multi 1.90 1.90
1913 A471 $1.30 multi 1.90 1.90
Nos. 1911-1913 (3) 5.70 5.70

Republic of Singapore Air Force, 50th Anniv. — A472

Designs: (30c), Airman and jets. (37c), Helicopters, airman on rescue mission. 60c, Aircraft spotters and monitors, mid-air jet refueling. 70c, Drones and drone pilots. 90c, Technicians and mechanics. $1.30, Airman, missile launchers. $2, Airport control tower, airman with binoculars, airman with headphones.

Litho. With Foil Application
2018, Sept. 1 *Perf. 13*
1914-1920 A472 Set of 7 9.00 9.00

No. 1914 is inscribed "1st Local." No. 1915 is inscribed "2nd Local."

Early Education for Girls — A473

Designs: (30c), Girls learning to cook and clean. 70c, Girl learning to sew. 90c, Girls reading. $1.30, Girls sitting at school desks.

2018, Oct. 11 Litho. *Perf. 13¼*
1921-1924 A473 Set of 4 4.75 4.75

No. 1921 is inscribed "1st Local."

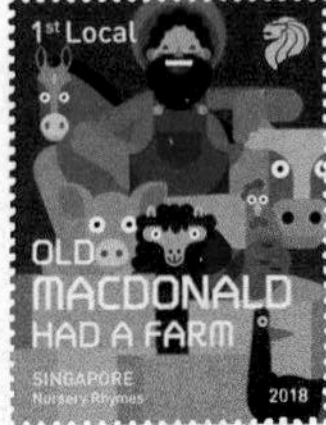
Nursery Rhymes — A474

Designs: Nos. 1925, 1933, (30c), Old MacDonald Had a Farm. Nos. 1926, 1934, (30c), Kokarako Crowing Rooster! Nos. 1927, 1935, (30c), Stork, Oh Stork. Nos. 1928, 1936, (30c), Donkey. No. 1929, 70c, Baa, Baa, Black Sheep. No. 1930, 70c, Elephant, Where Do You Want to Go? No. 1931, 70c, Jump, Frog, Jump. No. 1932, 70c, Tigers.

2018, Oct. 17 Litho. *Perf. 14*
1925-1932 A474 Set of 8 6.00 6.00

Self-Adhesive
Serpentine Die Cut 10½x9¾
1933-1936 A474 Set of 4 1.75 1.75

Nos. 1925-1928, 1933-1936 were each inscribed "1st Local."

Festival Foods A475

Festival Symbols A476

Foods for: Nos. 1937, 1945 (30c), Christmas. No. 1938, (30c), Deepavali. No. 1939, (30c), Hari Raya Aidilfitri. Nos. 1940, 1946, (30c), Chinese New Year.
Symbols for: No. 1941, 60c, Christmas. No. 1942, 60c, Deepavali. No. 1943, 60c, Hari Raya Aidilfitri. No. 1944, 60c, Chinese New Year.

2018, Nov. 21 Litho. *Perf. 13½*
1937-1940 A475 Set of 4 1.75 1.75

Litho. With Foil Application

1941-1944 A476 Set of 4 3.50 3.50

Booklet Stamps
Self-Adhesive
Litho.

Serpentine Die Cut 9½x10

1945 A475 (30c) multi .45 .45
a. Booklet pane of 10 4.50
1946 A475 (30c) multi .45 .45
a. Booklet pane of 10 4.50

Nos. 1937-1940, 1945-1946 are each inscribed "1st Local."

New Year 2019 (Year of the Pig) A477

Designs: Nos. 1947, 1950a, 1951, Pig facing left. Nos. 1948, 1950b, Pig facing right. $1.30, Two pigs (35x46mm).

2019 Litho. *Perf. 13½x13¼*

1947 A477 (30c) multi .45 .45
a. Perf. 14x13¾ .50 .50
1948 A477 70c multi 1.00 1.00
a. Perf. 14x13¾ 1.10 1.10

Perf. 14¼x14

1949 A477 $1.30 multi 2.00 2.00
a. Souvenir sheet of 3, #1947a, 1948a, 1949 3.75 3.75
Nos. 1947-1949 (3) 3.45 3.45

Souvenir Sheet
Perf. 13x13¼

1950 Sheet of 2 25.00 25.00
a. A477 $5 multi 8.50 8.50
b. A477 $10 multi 16.50 16.50

Self-Adhesive
Serpentine Die Cut 9¾x10½

1951 A477 (30c) gold & multi .45 .45

Singpex 2019 International Stamp Exhibition (No. 1949a). Issued: Nos. 1947a, 1948a, 1949a, 7/31; others 1/4. No. 1949a sold for $2.45 and No. 1950 sold for $16.80. Nos. 1947 and 1951 are inscribed "1st Local."

Souvenir Sheet

Yusheng (Raw Fish Salad) — A478

Litho. With Foil Application

2019, Feb. 4 *Perf. 13*

1952 A478 $8 multi 13.00 13.00

No. 1952 sold for $8.55.

Hotels A479

Designs: Nos. 1953, 1958, 60c, Goodwood Park Hotel. Nos. 1954, 1959, 60c, Raffles Hotel. Nos. 1955, 1960, 60c, Hotel Fort Canning (61x30mm). Nos. 1956, 1961, 60c, Capella Hotel (61x30mm). Nos. 1957, 1962, 60c, Fullerton Hotel (61x30mm).

Litho. & Engr.

2019, Mar. 22 *Perf. 14x13¼*

1953-1957 A479 Set of 5 4.50 4.50

Self-Adhesive
Die Cut Perf. 14x13¼

1958-1962 A479 Set of 5 4.50 4.50

Confections A480

Designs: (30c), Kaya bread. 70c, Kuh semperit. 90c, Jilebi. $1.30, Sugee cake.

Litho. & Embossed

2019, Apr. 17 *Perf. 13*

1963-1966 A480 Set of 4 4.75 4.75

No. 1963 is inscribed "1st Local." A souvenir sheet containing Nos. 1963-1966 sold for $8.

A481

Diplomatic Relations Between Singapore and Israel, 50th Anniv. — A482

2019, May 8 Litho. *Perf. 13¼x13½*

1967 A481 $1.30 multi 1.90 1.90
1968 A482 $1.30 multi 1.90 1.90
a. Souvenir sheet of 2, #1967-1968 3.80 3.80

See Israel Nos. 2222-2223.

Diplomatic Relations Between Singapore and Philippines, 50th Anniv. A483

Designs: No. 1969, Common rose butterfly. No. 1970, Luzon lacewing butterfly.

2019, May 16 Litho. *Perf. 13½x13¼*

1969 A483 $1.30 multi 1.90 1.90
a. Perf. 14 2.00 2.00
1970 A483 $1.30 multi 1.90 1.90
a. Perf. 14 2.00 2.00
b. Souvenir sheet of 2, #1969a, 1970a 4.00 4.00

No. 1970b sold for $2.75. See Philippines No. 3812.

Founding of Singapore, 200th Anniv. — A484

Inscriptions: No. 1971, (30c), Prequel, Before 1400. No. 1972, (30c), Prequel, 1400s-1600s. (37c), Colonial, 1819. 40c, Colonial, Free Port. 50c, Colonial, Immigrants. 60c, World War II. 70c, Pre-independence. 90c, Independence. $1.15, 2019. $1.30, Future.

Litho., Litho. With Foil Application (#1980)

2019, June 22 *Perf. 14¾x14¼*

1971-1980 A484 Set of 10 9.75 9.75

Nos. 1971 and 1972 are inscribed "1st Local;" No. 1973, "2nd Local." A souvenir sheet containing 10 stamps similar to Nos. 1971-1980, but with gold text, sold for $16.80. No. 1979 was done by hot stamping.

Early Forms of Public Entertainment A485

Designs: (30c), Street story-telling. 70c, Puppet show. 90c, Cinema on wheels. $1.30, Bangsawan.

2019, July 17 Litho. *Perf. 13½*

1981-1984 A485 Set of 4 4.75 4.75

No. 1981 is inscribed "1st Local."

First London-Sydney Air Mail Flight Via Singapore, Cent. — A486

Designs: 60c, Cover bound for Australia, pilots and airplane. $2, Cover bearing stamps of ten countries bound for Australia, map of route, airplane and pilot.

2019, July 31 Litho. *Perf. 12¾*

1985-1986 A486 Set of 2 3.75 3.75
1986a Souvenir sheet of 2, #1985-1986 4.00 4.00

No. 1986a sold for $2.75. Imperforate examples of Nos. 1985-1986 and 1986a were produced in limited quantities and sold in press sheets that were available only at the 2019 Singpex International Stamp Exhibition. A limited number of imperforate examples of No. 1986a with serial numbers were also sold singly at the exhibition.

Traditional Clothing of Chinese, Malay, Indian and Eurasian Singaporeans — A487

2019, Aug. 1 Litho. *Perf. 12¾*

1987 A487 $1.30 gold & multi 1.90 1.90

ASEAN Issue.

Parks — A488

Designs: (30c), Admiralty Park. 70c, Bishan-Ang Mo Kio Park. 90c, East Coast Park. $1.30, Labrador Park.

$2, Parks and signpost pointing to named parks, vert.

2019, Aug. 9 Litho. *Perf. 12*

1988-1991 A488 Set of 4 4.75 4.75

Souvenir Sheet

1992 A488 $2 multi 3.00 3.00

No. 1988 is inscribed "1st Local." No. 1992 contains one 50x60mm stamp.

Istana (President's Residence), 150th Anniv. — A489

Designs: (30c), People near gate. 70c, Artillery emplacement. 90c, People near builidng. $1.30, Istana (76x35mm).

Litho. With Foil Application

2019, Oct. 8 *Perf. 13¾*

1993-1996 A489 Set of 4 4.75 4.75

No. 1993 is inscribed "1st Local."

Diplomatic Relations Between Singapore and Poland, 50th Anniv. — A490

Designs: No. 1997, $1.30, Oriental pied hornbill. No. 1998, $1.30, Peregrine falcon.

2019, Oct. 30 Litho. *Perf. 12¾*

1997-1998 A490 Set of 2 3.75 3.75
1998a Souvenir sheet of 2, #1997-1998 4.00 4.00

No. 1998a sold for $2.75. See Poland No. 4461.

Goldfish — A491

Designs: 5c, Tosakin. 20c, Black oranda. Nos. 2001, 2008, Ranchu. Nos. 2002, 2009, Telescope eye pearlscale. (37c), Red cap oranda. 60c, Short tail ryukin. 70c, Red oranda. 80c, Butterfly tail. 90c, Bubble eye.

2019, Nov. 22 Litho. *Perf. 13x13¼*

1999 A491 5c multi .25 .25
2000 A491 20c multi .30 .30
2001 A491 (30c) multi .45 .45
2002 A491 (30c) multi .45 .45
2003 A491 (37c) multi .55 .55
2004 A491 60c multi .90 .90
2005 A491 70c multi 1.00 1.00
2006 A491 80c multi 1.25 1.25
2007 A491 90c multi 1.40 1.40
Nos. 1999-2007 (9) 6.55 6.55

Booklet Stamps
Self-Adhesive
Serpentine Die Cut 9½x9¼

2008 A491 (30c) multi .45 .45
a. Booklet pane of 10 4.50
2009 A491 (30c) multi .45 .45
a. Booklet pane of 10 4.50

Nos. 2001-2002, 2008-2009 are inscribed "1st Local;" No. 2002, "2nd Local."

POSTAGE DUE STAMPS

D1

Wmk. 314

1968, Feb. 1 Litho. *Perf. 9*

J1 D1 1c emerald .50 .50
J2 D1 2c red org .80 .80
J3 D1 4c yel org 2.00 2.00
J4 D1 8c brown 1.25 1.25
J5 D1 10c rose mag 2.00 2.00
J6 D1 12c dl vio 3.00 3.00
J7 D1 20c brt bl 3.75 3.75
J8 D1 50c gray grn 11.50 11.50
Nos. J1-J8 (8) 24.80 24.80

1973-77 *Perf. 13x13½*

J1a D1 1c Unwmkd. ('77) *55.00 35.00*
J3a D1 4c Unwmkd. ('77) *70.00 35.00*
J5a D1 10c 2.00 *2.00*
b. Unwmkd. ('77) *90.00 35.00*
J7a D1 20c Unwmkd. ('77) *125.00 55.00*
J8a D1 50c *16.00 15.00*
b. Unwmkd. ('77) *135.00 70.00*

D2

1981 Unwmk. *Perf. 12x11½*

J9 D2 1c emerald .35 1.00
J10 D2 4c orange .35 1.00
J11 D2 10c carmine 1.10 3.00
J12 D2 20c light blue 2.25 3.00
J13 D2 50c light yellow green 3.25 4.00
Nos. J9-J13 (5) 7.30 12.00

1978, Sept. 25 *Perf. 13x13½*

J9a D2 1c 1.25 1.50
J10a D2 4c 1.25 1.50
J11a D2 10c 1.60 1.60
J12a D2 20c 1.90 1.90
J13a D2 50c 2.75 2.75
Nos. J9a-J13a (5) 8.75 9.25

D3

1989, July 12 Litho. *Perf. 13x13½*

J14 D3 5c red lilac .25 .25
J15 D3 10c red .35 .25
J16 D3 20c light blue .55 .55
J17 D3 50c yellow green 1.10 1.10
J18 D3 $1 brown 1.00 1.00
Nos. J14-J18 (5) 3.25 3.15

Issued: $1, 4/30/93; others, 7/12/89.

1997, Nov. 7 Litho. *Perf. 13x13½*

J19 D3 1c green *60.00* —
J20 D3 4c brown orange *90.00* —

A small quantity of Nos. J19-J20 were produced, which was sold locally only, in late 1997. Postage due stamps were replaced by machine-generated labels on Dec. 31, 1997.

SLOVAKIA

slō-ˈvä-kē-ə

LOCATION — Central Europe
GOVT. — Republic
AREA — 18,932 sq. mi.
POP. — 5,396,193 (1999 est.)
CAPITAL — Bratislava

Formerly a province of Czechoslovakia, Slovakia declared its independence in Mar., 1939. A treaty was immediately concluded with Germany guaranteeing Slovakian independence but providing for German "protection" for 25 years.

In 1945 the republic ended and Slovakia again became a part of Czechoslovakia.

On January 1, 1993, Czechoslovakia split into the Czech Republic and Slovakia.

100 Halierov = 1 Koruna

Catalogue values for unused stamps in this country are for never hinged items, beginning with Scott 26 in the regular postage section, Scott B1 in the semi-postal section, Scott C1 in the airmail section, Scott EX1 in the personal delivery section, Scott J1 in the postage due section, and Scott P10 in the newspaper section.

Watermark

Wmk. 263 — Double-Barred Cross Multiple

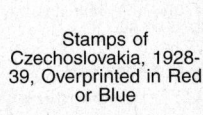

Stamps of Czechoslovakia, 1928-39, Overprinted in Red or Blue

1939 *Perf. 10, 12½, 12x12½*

2 A29 5h dk ultra .60 *1.25*
3 A29 10h brown .25 .25
4 A29 20h red (Bl) .25 .25
5 A29 25h green 2.00 2.00
6 A29 30h red vio (Bl) .25 .25
7 A61a 40h dark blue .25 .25
8 A73 50h deep green .25 .25
9 A63 50h deep green .25 .25
10 A63 60h dull violet .25 .25
11 A63 60h dull blue 10.00 *20.00*
12 A60 1k rose lake (Bl) (On No. 212) .25 .25

Overprinted Diagonally

13 A64 1.20k rose lil (Bl) 1.25 1.25
14 A65 1.50k carmine (Bl) 1.25 1.25
15 A79 1.60k ol grn (Bl) 2.00 *2.75*
16 A66 2k dk bl grn 2.00 *2.75*
17 A67 2.50k dark blue 1.25 1.25
18 A68 3k brown 1.25 1.25
19 A69 3.50k dk violet 16.00 *32.50*
20 A69 3.50k dk vio (Bl) 30.00 *40.00*
21 A70 4k dk violet 12.00 *20.00*
22 A71 5k green 16.00 *27.50*
23 A72 10k blue 180.00 *225.00*
Nos. 2-23 (22) 277.60 *380.75*
Set, never hinged 550.00

Excellent counterfeit overprints exist.

Stefánik Type of Czechoslovakia

Gen. Milan Stefánik

1939, Mar. 30 Engr. *Perf. 12½*

23A A63 60h dark blue 22.50 *37.50*

Prepared by Czechoslovakia prior to the German occupation March 15, 1939. Subsequently issued for use in Slovakia.

Andrej Hlinka — A1

Overprinted in Red or Blue

Perf. 12½

1939, Apr. Unwmk. Photo.

24 A1 50h dk grn (R) .40 .40
a. Perf. 10½ 2.00 1.25
b. Perf. 10½x12½ 8.00 3.75
25 A1 1k dk car rose (Bl) .40 .40
a. Perf. 10½ 1,000. 1,000.
Never hinged 2,100.
b. Perf. 10½x12½ 16.00 8.00

Catalogue values for unused stamps in this section, from this point to the end of the section, are for Never Hinged items.

Andrej Hlinka — A2

1939 Unwmk. *Perf. 12½*

26 A2 5h brt ultra .55 .50
27 A2 10h olive green .95 .80
a. Perf. 10½x12½ 160.00 120.00
b. Perf. 10½ 400.00 100.00
28 A2 20h orange red .95 .80
a. Imperf. .85 .80
29 A2 30h dp violet .95 .80
a. Imperf. 1.00 *1.25*
b. Perf. 10½x12½ 25.00 20.00
c. Perf. 10½ 42.50 20.00
30 A2 50h dk green .95 .80
31 A2 1k dk carmine rose 1.40 .80
32 A2 2.50k brt blue 1.40 .30
a. Perf. 10½x12½ 260.00 130.00
33 A2 3k black brown 3.25 .55
a. Perf. 10½x12½ 13.00 7.00
b. Perf. 10½ 10.00 7.00
Nos. 26-33 (8) 10.40 *5.35*

On Nos. 32 and 33 a pearl frame surrounds the medallion. See Nos. 55-57, 69.

General Stefánik and Memorial Tomb — A3

1939, May *Perf. 12½*

Size: 25x20mm

34 A3 40h dark blue 1.25
35 A3 60h slate green 1.25
36 A3 1k gray violet 1.25

Size: 30x23¾mm

37 A3 2k bl vio & sepia 1.25
Nos. 34-37 (4) 5.00

20th anniv. of the death of Gen. Milan Stefánik, but not issued. Exists favor-canceled. Values, same as mint stamps.

Rev. Josef Murgas and Radio Towers — A4

1939 Unwmk.

38 A4 60h purple .40 .30
39 A4 1.20k slate black .80 .25
a. Imperf. 160.00

10th anniv. of the death of Rev. Josef Murgas. See No. 65.

Girl Embroidering A5

Woodcutter A6

Girl at Spring — A7

1939-44 Wmk. 263 *Perf. 12½*

40 A5 2k dk blue green 5.75 .50
41 A6 4k copper brown 1.40 1.00
42 A7 5k orange red 1.00 .50
a. Perf. 10 ('44) 1.25 1.00
Nos. 40-42 (3) 8.15 2.00

Dr. Josef Tiso — A8

1939-44 Wmk. 263 *Perf. 12½*

43 A8 50h slate green .45 .45
c. Imperf. 120.00
43A A8 70h dk red brn ('42) .40 .25
b. Perf. 10½ ('44) .40 .25

See No. 88.

Presidential Residence — A9

1940, Mar. 14

44 A9 10k deep blue 1.00 .80
a. Imperf. 160.00

Tatra Mountains A10

Krivan Peak A11

Edelweiss in the Tatra Mountains A12

Chamois A13

Church at Javorina — A14

1940-43 Wmk. 263 *Perf. 12½*

Size: 17x21mm

45 A10 5h dk olive grn .30 .25
46 A11 10h deep brown .25 .25
a. Imperf. 240.00
47 A12 20h dark blue gray .25 .25
48 A13 25h olive brown .55 .25
a. Imperf. 32.50
49 A14 30h chestnut brown .35 .25
a. Perf. 10½ ('43) 2.50 1.00
Nos. 45-49 (5) 1.70 1.25

See Nos. 84-87, 103-107.

Hlinka Type of 1939

1940-42 Wmk. 263 *Perf. 12½*

No.	Type	Value	Color	Unused	Used
55	A2	1k	dk car rose	.95	.60
56	A2	2.50k	brt blue ('42)	1.40	.75
a.			Perf. 10½	.65	.66
57	A2	3k	black brn ('41)	2.40	1.00
a.			Perf. 10½	2.00	.90

On Nos. 56 and 57 a pearl frame surrounds the medallion.

Stiavnica A15

Lietava A16

Spissky Hrad — A17

Bojnice — A18

1941 *Perf. 12½*

No.	Type	Value	Color	Unused	Used
58	A15	1.20k	rose lake	.25	.25
59	A16	1.50k	rose pink	.25	.25
60	A17	1.60k	royal blue	.25	.25
61	A18	2k	dk gray green	.25	.25
			Nos. 58-61 (4)	1.00	1.00

Slovakian Castles.

S. M. Daxner and Stefan Moyses A19

1941, May 26 Photo. Wmk. 263

No.	Type	Value	Color	Unused	Used
62	A19	50h	olive green	2.00	1.60
63	A19	1k	slate blue	8.00	7.25
64	A19	2k	black	6.50	5.50
			Nos. 62-64 (3)	16.50	14.35

80th anniv. of the Memorandum of the Slovak Nation.

Murgas Type of 1939

1941 Wmk. 263

No.	Type	Value	Color	Unused	Used
65	A4	60h	purple	.40	.25

Andrej Hlinka — A20

1942, Mar. 20

No.	Type	Value	Color	Unused	Used
69	A20	1.30k	dark purple	.50	.25

Post Horn and Miniature Stamp — A21

Philatelist — A22

Philatelist — A23

1942, May 23

No.	Type	Value	Color	Unused	Used
70	A21	30h	dark green	1.20	1.10
71	A22	70h	dk car rose	1.20	1.10
72	A23	80h	purple	1.20	1.10
73	A21	1.30k	dark brown	1.20	1.10
			Nos. 70-73 (4)	4.80	4.40

Natl. Philatelic Exhibition at Bratislava.

On No. 70 the miniature stamp bears the coat-of-arms of Bratislava; on No. 73 it shows the National arms of Slovakia.

St. Stephen's Cathedral, Vienna — A24

1942, Oct. 12 *Perf. 14*

No.	Type	Value	Color	Unused	Used
74	A24	70h	blue green	.80	.80
75	A24	1.30k	olive green	1.60	1.60
76	A24	2k	sapphire	2.50	2.50
			Nos. 74-76 (3)	4.90	4.90

European Postal Congress held in Vienna.

Slovakian Educational Society — A25

1942, Dec. 14

No.	Type	Value	Color	Unused	Used
77	A25	70h	black	.25	.25
78	A25	1k	rose red	.30	.25
79	A25	1.30k	sapphire	.30	.25
80	A25	2k	chestnut brown	.40	.25
81	A25	3k	dark green	.55	.30
82	A25	4k	dull purple	.55	.30
			Nos. 77-82 (6)	2.35	1.60

Slovakian Educational Soc., 150th anniv.

Andrej Hlinka — A26

1943 Wmk. 263

No.	Type	Value	Color	Unused	Used
83	A26	1.30k	brt ultra	.40	.40
a.			Imperf.	160.00	

See Nos. 93-94A.

Types of 1939-40

1943 Unwmk. *Perf. 12½*

No.	Type	Value	Color	Unused	Used
84	A11	10h	deep brown	.25	.25
85	A12	20h	blue black	.70	.50
86	A13	25h	olive brown	.70	.50
87	A14	30h	chestnut brown	.50	.35
88	A8	70h	dk red brown	.85	.95
			Nos. 84-88 (5)	3.00	2.55

Presov Church — A27

Locomotive A28

Railway Tunnel A29

Viaduct — A30

1943, Sept. 5 *Perf. 14*

No.	Type	Value	Color	Unused	Used
89	A27	70h	dk rose violet	.65	.55
90	A28	80h	sapphire	.65	.55
91	A29	1.30k	black	.65	.55
92	A30	2k	dk violet brn	.65	.55
			Nos. 89-92 (4)	2.60	2.20

Inauguration of the new railroad line between Presov and Strazske.

Hlinka Type of 1943 and

Ludovit Stur — A31

Martin Razus — A32

1944 Unwmk.

No.	Type	Value	Color	Unused	Used
93	A31	80h	slate green	.35	.25
94	A32	1k	brown red	.35	.25
94A	A26	1.30k	brt ultra	1.00	.80
			Nos. 93-94A (3)	1.70	1.30

Prince Pribina — A33

Designs: 70h, Prince Mojmir. 80h, Prince Ratislav. 1.30k, King Svatopluk. 2k, Prince Kocel. 3k, Prince Mojmir II. 5k, Prince Svatopluk II. 10k, Prince Braslav.

1944, Mar. 14

No.	Type	Value	Color	Unused	Used
95	A33	50h	dark green	.25	.25
96	A33	70h	lilac rose	.25	.25
97	A33	80h	red brown	.25	.25
98	A33	1.30k	brt ultra	.30	.25
99	A33	2k	Prus blue	.30	.25
100	A33	3k	dark brown	.40	.25
101	A33	5k	violet	.80	.40
102	A33	10k	black	2.50	1.40
			Nos. 95-102 (8)	5.05	3.30

Scenic Types of 1940

1944, Apr. 1 *Perf. 14*

Size: 18x23mm

No.	Type	Value	Color	Unused	Used
103	A11	10h	bright carmine	.25	*.30*
104	A12	20h	bright blue	.25	*.30*
105	A13	25h	brown red	.25	*.30*
106	A14	30h	red violet	.25	*.30*
107	A10	50h	deep green	.25	*.30*
			Nos. 103-107 (5)	1.25	*1.50*

5th anniv. of Slovakia's independence.

See Nos. B25-B26.

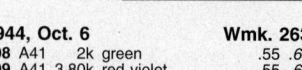

Symbolic of National Protection A41

1944, Oct. 6 Wmk. 263

No.	Type	Value	Color	Unused	Used
108	A41	2k	green	.55	*.65*
109	A41	3.80k	red violet	.55	*.65*

President Josef Tiso — A42

1945 Unwmk.

No.	Type	Value	Color	Unused	Used
110	A42	1k	orange	.55	.40
111	A42	1.50k	brown	.30	.25
112	A42	2k	green	.30	*.40*
113	A42	4k	rose red	.95	.55
114	A42	5k	sapphire	.80	.40

Wmk. 263

No.	Type	Value	Color	Unused	Used
115	A42	10k	red violet	.75	.40
			Nos. 110-115 (6)	3.65	2.40

6th anniv. of the Republic of Slovakia's declaration of independence, Mar. 14, 1939.

Natl. Arms — A50

1993 Photo. & Engr. *Perf. 11½*

No.	Type	Value	Color	Unused	Used
150	A50	3k	multicolored	.50	.30

Engr.

Perf. 12

Size: 30x44mm

No.	Type	Value	Color	Unused	Used
151	A50	8k	multicolored	4.00	3.00

Issued: 3k, Jan. 2; 8k, Jan. 1. No. 151 does not have black frameline.

No. 151 was issued in sheets of 6.

Castles & Churches — A51

2k, Nitra church. 3k, Banska Bystrica church. 5k, Ruzomberok church, horiz. 10k, Kosice church. 30k, Zvolen castle, horiz. 50k, Bratislava castle.

Perf. 11½x12, 12x11½

1993-95 Photo. & Engr.

No.	Type	Value	Color	Unused	Used
152	A51	2k	multi	.25	.25
153	A51	3k	multi	.30	.25
154	A51	5k	multi	.40	.25
155	A51	10k	multi	.90	.45
156	A51	30k	multi	2.50	1.20
157	A51	50k	multi	4.25	2.40
			Nos. 152-157 (6)	8.60	4.80

Issued: 5k, 10k, 1993; 30k, 9/12/93; 50k, 12/31/93; 3k, 11/15/94; 2k, 3/15/95.

See Nos. 218-227.

St. John Nepomuk, 600th Death Anniv. A57

Photo. & Engr.

1993, Mar. 11 *Perf. 12x11½*

No.	Type	Value	Color	Unused	Used
158	A57	8k	multicolored	1.10	.50

See Czech Republic No. 2880; Germany No. 1776.

President Michal Kovac — A58

1993 Engr. *Perf. 12x11½*

159 A58 2k dark gray blue .30 .25
159A A58 3k red brown & red .35 .25

Issued: 2k, 3/2/93; 3k, 11/3/93.

Trees — A59

3k, Quercus robur. 4k, Carpinus betulus. 10k, Pinus silvestris.

Photo. & Engr.

1993, May 14 *Perf. 11½*

160 A59 3k multi .60 .25
161 A59 4k multi .60 .30
162 A59 10k multi .80 .50
Nos. 160-162 (3) 2.00 1.05

A60

Famous Men: 5k, Jan Levoslav Bella (1843-1936), composer. 8k, Alexander Dubcek (1921-92), politician. 20k, Jan Kollar (1793-1852), writer.

Photo. & Engr.

1993, May 20 *Perf. 12x11½*

163 A60 5k red brown & blue .45 .35
164 A60 8k brown & lilac red .90 .45
165 A60 20k gray blue & orange 1.75 1.00
Nos. 163-165 (3) 3.10 1.80

A61

Woman with Pitcher, by Marian Cunderlik.

1993, May 31 Engr. *Perf. 12*

166 A61 14k multicolored 5.00 4.00

Europa. Issued in sheets of 4.

Literary Slovak Language, 150th Anniv. A62

Design: 8k, Arrival of St. Cyril and St. Methodius, 1130th Anniv.

Photo. & Engr.

1993, June 22 *Perf. 12x11½*

167 A62 2k multicolored .30 .25
168 A62 8k multicolored 1.00 .50

See Czech Republic No. 2886.

A63

Arms of Dubnica nad Vahom.

Photo. & Engr.

1993, July 8 *Perf. 12x11½*

169 A63 1k multicolored .50 .25

A64

The Big Pets, by Lane Smith.

Photo. & Engr.

1993, Sept. 2 *Perf. 11½*

170 A64 5k multicolored .65 .30

Bratislava Biennial of Illustrators.

Gabcikovo Dam — A65

Photo. & Engr.

1993, Nov. 12 *Perf. 11½*

172 A65 10k multicolored .90 .60

No. 172 issued se-tenant with label.

Madonna and Child, by J. B. Klemens (1817-83) — A66

Photo. & Engr.

1993, Dec. 1 *Perf. 11½*

173 A66 2k multicolored .40 .25

Christmas.

Souvenir Sheet

Monument to Gen. Milan Stefanik — A67

1993, Dec. 17 Engr. *Perf. 11½x12*

174 A67 16k multicolored 2.00 2.00

Art from Bratislava Natl. Gallery — A68

Sculpture: 9k, Plough of Springtime, by Josef Kostka.

1993, Dec. 31

175 A68 9k multicolored 2.25 2.00

Issued in sheets of 4.
See Nos. 199-200, 237-238, 255.

A69

Photo. & Engr.

1994, Jan. 26 *Perf. 11x11½*

176 A69 2k multicolored .50 .25
Complete booklet, 10 #176 6.00

1994 Winter Olympics, Lillehammer.

Intl. Year of the Family — A70

Photo. & Engr.

1994, Apr. 29 *Perf. 11x11½*

177 A70 3k multicolored .45 .25
Complete booklet, 5 #177 3.50

Jan Andrej Segner (1704-77), Physicist — A71

Design: 9k, Antoine de Saint-Exupery (1900-44), aviator, author.

Photo. & Engr.

1994, May 25 *Perf. 11½x11*

178 A71 8k red brown & blue .85 .45
179 A71 9k black, blue & pink .85 .45

See Nos. 196-198.

Josef Murgas (1864-1929), Inventor of Radio Transmitters — A72

1994, May 27 Engr. *Perf. 11½*

180 A72 28k multicolored 3.25 2.50

Europa. Issued in sheets of 4

A73

Photo. & Engr.

1994, May 31 *Perf. 11½x11*

181 A73 3k multicolored .40 .25

Intl. Stop Smoking Day.

A74

Photo. & Engr.

1994, June 10 *Perf. 11½*

182 A74 2k blue, black & green .40 .25

1994 World Cup Soccer Championships, US.

Intl. Olympic Committee, Cent. — A75

Photo. & Engr.

1994, June 23 *Perf. 12x11½*

183 A75 3k multicolored .40 .25

No. 183 issued with se-tenant label.

Raptors — A76

Photo. & Engr.

1994, July 4 *Perf. 11½x12*

184 A76 4k Aquila chrysaetos .90 .25
185 A76 5k Falco peregrinus .90 .25
186 A76 7k Bubo bubo 1.40 .30
Nos. 184-186 (3) 3.20 .80

Prince Svatopluk of Moravia (870-894) — A77

1994, July 20 Engr. *Perf. 12*

187 A77 12k red brn, buff & blk 1.60 1.50

Issued in sheets of 4.

UPU, 120th Anniv. — A78

Photo. & Engr.

1994, Aug. 1 *Perf. 11½x12*

188 A78 8k multicolored .90 .45

Slovak Uprising, 50th Anniv. — A79

Design: 6k, Gen. Rudolf Viest, Gen. Jan. Golian. 8k, French Volunteers' Memorial, Strecno hill.

Photo. & Engr.

1994, Aug. 27 *Perf. 12x11½*

189 A79 6k multicolored .65 .40
190 A79 8k multicolored .65 .40

Nos. 189-190 printed with se-tenant label.

Souvenir Sheet

Janko Matuska, Lyricist, 150th Death Anniv. — A80

Design: 34k, Matuska, woman with pitcher, verse of "A Well She Dug."

Photo. & Engr.

1994, Sept. 1 ***Perf. 12x11½***

191 A80 34k multicolored 3.25 3.25

Comenius University, 75th Anniv. — A81

Photo. & Engr.

1994, Oct. 18 ***Perf. 11½x12***

192 A81 12k multicolored 1.25 .60

Mojmirovce Horse Race, 180th Anniv. A82

1994, Oct. 25 ***Perf. 12x11½***

193 A82 2k multicolored .40 .25

St. George's Church, Kostotany pod Tribecom — A83

1994, Nov. 8 ***Perf. 11***

194 A83 20k multicolored 2.00 1.00

Christmas — A84

1994, Nov. 29 ***Perf. 11½***

195 A84 2k multicolored .35 .25

Personalities Type of 1994

Designs: 5k, Chatam Sofer (1762-1839), rabbi. 6k, Wolfgang Kempelen (1734-1804), polytechnician. 10k, Stefan Banic (1870-1941), inventor of aviation parachute.

1994, Dec. 12 ***Perf. 11½x11***

196 A71 5k multicolored .55 .30
Complete booklet, 5 #196 8.00
197 A71 6k multicolored .60 .35
198 A71 10k multicolored 1.00 .50
Nos. 196-198 (3) 2.15 1.15

Bratislava Art Type of 1993

Designs: 7k, Girls, by Janko Alexy, horiz. 14k, The Bulls, by Vincent Hloznik.

Perf. 12x11½, 11½x12

1994, Dec. 15 **Engr.**

199 A68 7k multicolored .75 .75
200 A68 14k multicolored 1.50 1.50

Ships — A85

5k, Cargo ship, NL EMS. 8k, Cargo ship, Ryn. 10k, 400-passenger cruise ship.

Photo. & Engr.

1994, Dec. 30 ***Perf. 12x11½***

201 A85 5k multicolored .50 .35
202 A85 8k multicolored .90 .70
203 A85 10k multicolored .90 .70
Nos. 201-203 (3) 2.30 1.75

Samuel Jurkovic, Founder of the Landlords Assoc., 1845 — A86

Photo. & Engr.

1995, Feb. 8 ***Perf. 11½***

204 A86 9k multicolored .90 .45

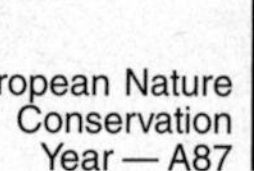

European Nature Conservation Year — A87

Protected plants: 2k, Ciminalis clusii. 3k, Pulsatilla slavica. 8k, Onosma tornense.

1995, Feb. 28

205 A87 2k multicolored .50 .25
Complete booklet, 10 #205 18.00
206 A87 3k multicolored .50 .25
Complete booklet, 5 #206 18.00
207 A87 8k multicolored .90 .40
Nos. 205-207 (3) 1.90 .90

Slovak Natl. Theatre, 75th Anniv. A88

1995, Feb. 28 ***Perf. 12x11½***

208 A88 10k multicolored 1.00 .45

1995 Group B World Cup Ice Hockey Championships, Bratislava — A89

1995, Mar. 29 ***Perf. 11½***

209 A89 5k blue & yellow .50 .25

Bela Bartok (1881-1945), Composer A90

6k, Jan Bahyl (1856-1916), inventor.

Photo. & Engr.

1995, Apr. 20 ***Perf. 12x11½***

210 A90 3k multicolored .30 .25
211 A90 6k multicolored .65 .30

Souvenir Sheet

Ludovit Stur (1815-56), Writer — A91

1995, Apr. 20 ***Perf. 11½***

212 A91 16k multicolored 1.60 1.60

Europa A92

1995, May 5 **Engr.** ***Perf. 12***

213 A92 8k multicolored 1.40 1.40

Liberation of the Concentration Camps, 50th Anniv. — A93

Photo. & Engr.

1995, May 5 ***Perf. 11***

214 A93 12k multicolored 1.25 .90

Slovak Scouting — A94

1995, May 18 ***Perf. 11½x11***

215 A94 5k multicolored .80 .30

Visit of Pope John Paul II — A95

1995, May 29 **Engr.**

216 A95 3k red .80 .40
Complete booklet, 10 #216 18.00

Organized Philately in Slovakia, Cent. — A96

Photo. & Engr.

1995, June 1 ***Perf. 11½x12***

217 A96 3k blue, black & gray .55 .35
a. Souv. sheet of 2 1.25 1.25

Dunafila '95.

Castles & Churches — A100

Perf. 11¾x11¼, 11¼x11¾ (#218, 225-226)

1995-2001 **Photo. & Engr.**

218 A100 50h Bardejov, horiz. .25 .25
219 A100 4k Nova Bana .50 .25
220 A100 4k Presov .40 .25
221 A100 5k Trnava .50 .25
222 A100 7k Martin .65 .30
223 A100 8k Trencin Castle 1.25 .60
224 A100 9k Zilina .85 .40
225 A100 20k Roznava, horiz. 1.90 .95
226 A100 40k Piestany, horiz. 4.00 2.00
227 A100 50k Komarno 5.00 2.50
Nos. 218-227 (10) 15.30 7.75

Issued: 4k (No. 219), 6/15/95; 8k, 9/12/95. 9k, 4/15/97. 7k, 7/17/97. 5k. 9/12/98. 4k (No. 220), 11/3/98. 50h, 2/1/00. 20k, 7/26/00. 40k, 5/25/01. 50k, 4/26/01.

See Nos. 401-402, 424-425, 447.

UNESCO World Heritage Sites A107

7k, Banska Stiavnica, vert. 10k, Spissky Hrad. 15k, Vlkolinec.

Perf. 11½x12, 12x11½

1995, July 19 **Photo. & Engr.**

228 A107 7k multi .65 .35
229 A107 10k multi 1.25 .55
230 A107 15k multi 1.50 .75
Nos. 228-230 (3) 3.40 1.65

Volleyball, Cent. — A108

1995, Aug. 16 ***Perf. 11½***

231 A108 9k multicolored 1.00 .50

A109

Bratislava Biennial of Illustrators: 2k, Clown, by Lorenzo Mattotti, Italy. 3k, Two characters, by Dusan Kallay, Slovakia.

Photo. & Engr.

1995, Sept. 5 ***Perf. 11½***

232 A109 2k multicolored .25 .25
Complete booklet, 10 #232 3.25
233 A109 3k multicolored .30 .25
Complete booklet, 10 #233 4.25

St. Adalbert Assoc. — A110

1995, Sept. 14

234 A110 4k multicolored .55 .30

The Cleveland Agreement, 80th Anniv. A111

Photo. & Engr.

1995, Oct. 20 ***Perf. 12x11½***
235 A111 5k multicolored .55 .30

UN, 50th Anniv. A112

1995, Oct. 24 **Engr.** ***Perf. 11½x12***
235A A112 8k multicolored 1.10 .55

Issued in sheets of 8 + 2 labels.

Christmas A113

Photo. & Engr.

1995, Oct. 27 ***Perf. 11½***
236 A113 2k multicolored .50 .30

Bratislava Art Type of 1993

Designs: 8k, The Hlohovec Nativity. 16k, Two Women, by Mikulás Galanda.

Photo. & Engr.

1995, Nov. 30 ***Perf. 11½x12***
237 A68 8k multicolored .85 .45
238 A68 16k multicolored 1.90 .95

Issued in sheets of 4 + 2 labels.

Jozef Cíger-Hronsky (1896-1960) A114

4k, Jozef L'udovít Holuby (1836-1923).

Photo. & Engr.

1996, Feb. 15 ***Perf. 11½***
239 A114 3k multicolored .40 .25
240 A114 4k multicolored .60 .35

See Nos. 293-295, 320-322.

Olympic Games, Cent. — A115

1996, Feb. 15
241 A115 9k multicolored 1.10 .55

Folk Traditions — A116

Easter tradition of dousing women with water

Photo. & Engr.

1996, Mar. 15 ***Perf. 11½***
242 A116 2k multicolored .50 .25
Complete booklet, 10 #242 5.00

Souvenir Sheet

Year for the Eradication of Poverty — A117

1996, Apr. 15 **Engr.** ***Perf. 12***
243 A117 7k multicolored 1.10 1.10

A118

Europa: a, Holding thistle, carduus textorianus marg. b, Portrait, daphne cneorum.

1996, May 3 **Engr.** ***Perf. 11½***
244 A118 8k Pair, #a.-b. 1.75 1.75

Izabela Textorisová (1866-1949), Slovakia's 1st female botanist. Issued in sheets of 4.

Souvenir Sheet

A119

Motion Pictures, Cent.: Two frames from 1936 film, Jánosík.

1996, May 15 ***Perf. 11½x12***
245 A119 16k multicolored 2.00 2.00

Printed se-tenant with label.

Round Slovakia Cycle Race — A120

1996, May 30 **Engr.** ***Perf. 11½***
246 A120 3k multicolored .60 .25
Complete booklet, 10 #246 7.50

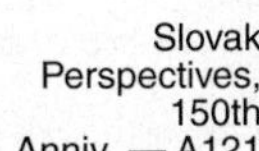

Slovak Perspectives, 150th Anniv. — A121

1996, May 30
247 A121 18k multicolored 2.00 1.10

A122

Photo. & Engr.

1996, June 14 ***Perf. 12x11½***
248 A122 6k Coat of arms .65 .35

Town of Senica.

A123

Nature protection: No. 249, Ovis musimon. No. 250, Bison bonasus. No. 251, Rupicapra rupicapra.

1996, July 16 ***Perf. 11½x12***
249 A123 4k multicolored .50 .25
Complete booklet, 10 #249 6.00
250 A123 4k multicolored .50 .25
Complete booklet, 10 #250 6.00
251 A123 4k multicolored .50 .25
Complete booklet, 10 #251 6.00
Nos. 249-251 (3) 1.50 .75

Splendors of Homeland — A124

Photo. & Engr.

1996, Sept. 25 ***Perf. 11½x12***
252 A124 4k Popradské Lake .40 .25
253 A124 8k Skalnaté Lake .75 .35
254 A124 12k Strbské Lake 1.10 .55
Nos. 252-254 (3) 2.25 1.15

Bratislava Art Type of 1993

The Baroque Chair, by Endre Nemes (1909-85).

1996, Oct. 5 **Engr.** ***Perf. 11½x12***
255 A68 14k multicolored 2.25 2.25

See Czech Republic No. 2995, Sweden No. 2199. Issued in sheets of 4 + label.

Technological Advances A125

4k, Bratislava-Trnava horse-drawn railway. 6k, Andrej Kvasz's (1883-1974) airplane.

Photo. & Engr.

1996, Oct. 15 ***Perf. 11***
256 A125 4k multicolored .50 .25
Complete booklet, 10 #256 6.50
257 A125 6k multicolored .75 .30
Complete booklet, 10 #257 8.50

Queen Ntombi Twala, by Andy Warhol (1928-87) — A126

Design: 10k, Suppressed Laughter, by Franz Xaver Messerschmidt (1736-83).

1996 **Engr.** ***Perf. 11½***
258 A126 7k multicolored .85 .85
259 A126 10k multicolored 1.25 1.25

Each issued in sheets of 4.

Issued: 7k, 11/13/96; 10k, 10/5/96.

See Nos. 284-286, 311, 314-315, 340-341, 366-367, 389-391, 417-418, 430, 443-445, 465-466, 488-489, 508-509, 530-531, 555-556, 584-585, 605-606, 628, 650, 676-677, 703-704, 729-730.

Christmas, Kysuce Village — A127

Photo. & Engr.

1996, Nov. 5 ***Perf. 11½***
260 A127 2k multicolored .50 .25

A128

3k, Michael Martikén, Olympic Gold Medalist, Canoeing.

Photo. & Engr.

1996, Dec. 18 ***Perf. 12x11½***
261 A128 3k brown & yellow .50 .25

Stamp Day — A129

Designs: Unexecuted 1938 stamp design of a woman with patriarchal cross, dove, Martin Benka, stamp designer.

1996, Dec. 18
262 A129 3k violet & buff .70 .70
Complete booklet, 9 #262 14.00

No. 262 was printed se-tenant with label.

Bishop Stefan Moyses (1797-1869) — A130

Design: 4k, Svetozar Hurban Vajansky (1847-1916), politician.

Photo. & Engr.

1997, Jan. 16 ***Perf. 11½***
263 A130 3k multicolored .30 .25
264 A130 4k multicolored .35 .25

A131

Photo. & Engr.

1997, Jan. 31 ***Perf. 11½***
265 A131 6k multicolored .55 .25

1997 World Biathlon Championships, Osrblie.

A132

Photo. & Engr.

1997, Feb. 15 ***Perf. 11½***
266 A132 3k multicolored .45 .25
Complete booklet, 10 #266 5.00

Folk Tradition of collecting dew.

Franciscan Church, Bratislava, 700th Anniv. — A133

Photo. & Engr.

1997, Mar. 25 ***Perf. 11½x12***
267 A133 16k multicolored 1.50 1.10

Radio, Cent. A135

1997, Apr. 15 ***Perf. 12x11½***
269 A135 10k multicolored 1.00 .50

A136

Europa (Stories and Legends): Miraculous rain near Hron.

1997, May 5 **Engr.** ***Perf. 12x11½***
270 A136 9k multicolored 1.10 .55

Issued in sheets of 7 + 3 labels.

A137

Limestone Formations: 6k, Domica Cavern, Silická. 8k, Aragonit Cavern, Octiná.

1997, June 12 **Engr.** ***Perf. 12x11½***
271 A137 6k multicolored .55 .30
272 A137 8k multicolored .75 .45

Nos. 271-272 issued in sheets of 8 + label.

Souvenir Sheet

Folklore Festival, Východná — A138

1997, June 12 **Photo. & Engr.**
273 A138 11k multicolored 1.10 1.10

Triennale of Naive Art, Bratislava A139

Photo. & Engr.

1997, June 26 ***Perf. 12x11½***
274 A139 3k multicolored .60 .30
Complete booklet, 10 #274 6.00

World Year of Slovaks — A140

1997, July 17 ***Perf. 11½***
276 A140 9k multicolored .80 .40

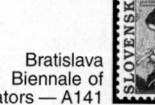

Bratislava Biennale of Illustrators — A141

Photo. & Engr.

1997, Aug. 5 ***Perf. 11½***
277 A141 3k multicolored .60 .30
Complete booklet, 10 #277 6.00

Water Mill, Jelka — A142

1997, Aug. 5
278 A142 4k multicolored .60 .30
Complete booklet, 10 #278 6.00

Constitution, 5th Anniv. — A143

Photo. & Engr.

1997, Sept. 1 ***Perf. 11½***
279 A143 4k multicolored .50 .25

A144

1997, Sept. 17
280 A144 9k multicolored .85 .40

6th Half Marathon World Championships, Kosice.

Mushrooms — A145

Designs: No. 283: a, 9k, Boletus aereus. b, 9k, Morchella esculenta. c, 9k, Catathelasma imperiale.

1997, Sept. 17 ***Perf. 12***
283 A145 Sheet of 3, #a-c 3.75 3.75

Art Type of 1996

Designs: 9k, Self-portrait, by Ján Kupecky (1667-1740). 10k, Bojnice Altar, St. Peter and St. Lucia, by Nardo Di Cione, 14th cent., horiz. 12k, Towards the Goal (The Miners), by Koloman Sokol (b. 1902).

1997, Oct. 15 **Engr.** ***Perf. 11½***
284 A126 9k multicolored .90 .55
285 A126 10k multicolored 1.10 .65
286 A126 12k multicolored 1.40 .80
Nos. 284-286 (3) 3.40 2.00

Cernova 1907 — A146

4k, Lamenting woman, church.

Photo. & Engr.

1997, Oct. 24 ***Perf. 11½x12***
287 A146 4k multi .50 .25

Christmas — A147

1997, Nov. 3 ***Perf. 11½***
288 A147 3k Nativity .50 .25

Ondrej Nepala, Figure Skater — A148

1997, Nov. 3
289 A148 5k multicolored .60 .30

Resurrection of Christ — A149

Photo. & Engr.

1997, Dec. 1 ***Perf. 11½***
290 A149 4k multi .60 .25
Complete booklet, 10 #290 6.00

Spiritual renewal. See #301, 327.

Stamp Day — A150

1997, Dec. 18
291 A150 4k dark brown & blue .60 .30
Complete booklet, 9 #291 + 12 labels 7.75

No. 291 was printed se-tenant with label.

Slovak Republic, 5th Anniv. — A151

Photo. & Engr.

1998, Jan. 1 ***Perf. 11½***
292 A151 4k multicolored .50 .25
Complete booklet, 10 #292 7.50

Personality Type of 1996

Writers: No. 293, Martin Rázus (1888-1937), politician. No. 294, Ján Smrek (1898-1982), poet. No. 295, Jozef Skultéty (1853-1948), linquist, editor.

1998, Jan. 19
293 A114 4k multicolored .35 .25
294 A114 4k multicolored .35 .25
295 A114 4k multicolored .35 .25
Nos. 293-295 (3) 1.05 .75

1998 Winter Olympic Games, Nagano A152

1998, Jan. 19 ***Perf. 12x11½***
296 A152 19k Hockey player 1.75 .90

Folk Tradition, Banishing of Winter — A153

Photo. & Engr.

1998, Mar. 3 ***Perf. 11½***
297 A153 3k multicolored .40 .25
Complete booklet, 10 #297 5.25

Castles A154

1998, Mar. 3
298 A154 6k Budatin .50 .35
299 A154 11k Krásna Horka 1.10 .55

Souvenir Sheet

300 A154 18k Nitra 2.00 2.00

Spiritual Renewal Type of 1997

Design: Descent of the Holy Spirit, flames above peoples' heads.

Photo. & Engr.

1998, May 5 ***Perf. 11½***
301 A149 4k multicolored .50 .25
Complete booklet, 10 #301 5.00

Folklore Festivals — A155

1998, May 5
302 A155 12k Tekov wedding 1.50 .75

Europa. Issued in sheet of 8 + label.

Child's Drawing — A156

Photo. & Engr.

1998, June 1 ***Perf. 11½***
303 A156 3k multicolored 1.00 .50
Complete booklet, 10 #303 10.00

The Children's Center, Ruzomberok.

A157

Design: Viktor Kolibik (1890-1918), wireworker, leader of revolt.

1998, June 1
304 A157 3k multicolored .50 .25

Mutiny at Kragujevac, 80th anniv.

Slovak Uprising of 1848-49 A158

1998, June 1
305 A158 4k multi, with 1 or 2 labels 2.00 1.00

Railways in Slovakia, Cent. — A159

Designs: 4k, Bihar steam locomotive. 10k, Lubochna-Mocidla electrified narrow-gauge trolley. 15k, Diesel locomotive.

Photo. & Engr.

1998, Aug. 20 ***Perf. 11½***
306 A159 4k multicolored .45 .25
307 A159 10k multicolored .85 .45
308 A159 15k multicolored 1.25 .70
Nos. 306-308 (3) 2.55 1.40

Fish A160

Designs: a, 4k, Umbra krameri. b, 11k, Zingel zingel. c, 16k, Cyprinus carpio.

1998, Sept. 7 **Sheet of 3**
309 A160 #a.-c. + label 4.00 4.00

Art Type of 1996

1564 Wooden "Pieta" statue, by unknown artist, Sastín.

1998, Sept. 14 ***Perf. 11½x12***
311 A126 18k multicolored 2.25 2.00

Issued in sheets of 4.

"No" to Drugs — A161

Photo. & Engr.

1998, Oct. 5 ***Perf. 11x11½***
312 A161 3k multicolored .50 .25

Ektopfilm, Ecology-Related Film Festival, 25th Anniv. — A162

1998, Oct. 5 ***Perf. 11***
313 A162 4k multicolored .70 .30
Complete booklet, 10 #313 8.75

Art Type of 1996

Designs: 10k, Terchova Landscape, by Martin Benka (1888-1971). 12k, Fishermen, by L'udovít Fulla (1902-80).

1998, Oct. 15 **Engr.** ***Perf. 11½x12***
314 A126 10k multicolored .80 .80
315 A126 12k multicolored 1.15 1.15

Adoration of the Magi — A163

1998, Nov. 3 ***Perf. 11x11½***
317 A163 3k Christmas .50 .25
Complete booklet, 10 #317 5.00

Stamp Day — A164

Photo. & Engr.

1998, Dec. 18 ***Perf. 12x11½***
318 A164 4k multi, with 1 or 2 labels 1.00 1.00
Complete booklet, 9 #318 + 12 labels 10.00

Values are for stamp with one attached label. Value with two labels, as shown, $3.

19th World Winter Universiad Games, 4th European Youth Olympic Days — A165

Photo. & Engr.

1999, Jan. 12 ***Perf. 12x11½***
319 A165 12k multicolored 2.50 1.25

No. 319 is printed se-tenant with 2 labels.

Personality Type of 1996

Designs: 3k, Matej Bel (1684-1749), teacher, pastor. 4k, Juraj Haulik (1788-1869), 1st cardinal of Croatia. 11k, Pavol Országh-Hviezdoslav (1849-1921), poet, dramatist.

1999, Jan. 28 ***Perf. 11½***
320 A114 3k multicolored .30 .25
321 A114 4k multicolored .40 .25
322 A114 11k multicolored 1.00 .40
Nos. 320-322 (3) 1.70 .90

See Croatia 388.

UPU, 125th Anniv. — A166

Photo. & Engr.

1999, Mar. 12 ***Perf. 11½***
323 A166 4k multicolored .50 .25
Complete booklet, 10 #323 5.00

Traditional Bonnets — A167

Litho. & Engr.

1999, Mar. 12 ***Perf. 11½x12***
324 A167 4k Cajkov .35 .30
325 A167 15k Helpa 1.10 1.00
326 A167 18k Madunice 1.25 1.10
Nos. 324-326 (3) 2.70 2.40

Nos. 324-326 were each issued in sheets of 10.

Spiritual Renewal Type of 1997

Design: "Transfiguration," by Vincent Hloznik, depicting ascension of Christ.

Photo. & Engr.

1999, May 5 ***Perf. 11½***
327 A149 5k multicolored .60 .30
Complete booklet, 10 #327 6.00

Tatra National Park A168

1999, May 5 **Engr.** ***Perf. 11½***
328 A168 9k shown .90 .60
329 A168 11k Mountains, diff. 1.10 .80
a. Pair, #328-329 2.25 2.25

Europa. No. 329a is a continuous design. Issued in sheets of 8 + label.

Council of Europe, 50th Anniv. A169

1999, May 5 **Engr.** ***Perf. 12x11½***
330 A169 16k multicolored 1.60 1.60
a. Souvenir sheet of 1 2.25 2.25

A170

Photo. & Engr.

1999, June 15 ***Perf. 11½x11¾***
331 A170 4k multicolored .50 .25

Slovak Philharmonic Orchestra, 50th anniv.

Intl. Year of Older Persons — A171

1999, June 15 ***Perf. 11½***
332 A171 5k multicolored .60 .30

Souvenir Sheet

Astronaut Ivan Bella, First Slovak in Space — A172

1999, June 15 ***Perf. 11¾x11½***
333 A172 12k multicolored 2.00 2.00

UPU, 125th Anniv. — A173

Photo. & Engr.

1999, July 15 ***Perf. 11½***
334 A173 12k Zilina University 1.00 .50
335 A173 16k Globe 1.25 .60

A174

Photo. & Engr.

1999, Sept. 3 ***Perf. 11¼x11¾***
336 A174 4k multicolored .50 .25

Bratislava Univ. of Fine Arts, 50th anniv.

A175

1999, Sept. 3 *Perf. 11¼x11½*
337 A175 5k multicolored .70 .30
Complete booklet, 10 #337 7.00

Bratislava Biennale of Illustrators.

Mine Water Pump Invented By Jozef Hell (1713-89) A176

1999, Sept. 21 *Perf. 11x11¼*
338 A176 7k sepia & yellow .95 .30

Souvenir Sheet

Birds — A177

a, 14k, Panurus biarmicus. b, 15k, Lanius collurio. c, 16k, Phoenicurus phoenicurus.

Litho. & Engr.

1999, Sept. 21 *Perf. 11¾*
339 A177 Sheet of 3, #a.-c. 4.75 4.75

Art Type of 1996

Designs: 13k, Malatiná, by Milos Alexander Bazovsky (1899-1968), horiz. 14k, Study of the Blacksmith, by Dominik Skutecky.

1999, Oct. 5 **Engr.** *Perf. 11¾*
340 A126 13k multicolored 1.25 1.25
341 A126 14k multicolored 1.25 1.25

Each issued in sheets of 4.

Christmas — A178

Photo. & Engr.

1999, Nov. 3 *Perf. 11¾x11¼*
342 A178 4k multicolored .60 .30
Complete booklet, 10 #342 6.00

Czechoslovakia's "Velvet Revolution," 10th Anniv. — A179

1999, Nov. 17 *Perf. 12x11¼*
343 A179 5k multicolored .80 .30

Ceramic Urns, Museum of Jewish Culture — A180

Litho. & Engr.

1999, Nov. 23 *Perf. 11¾*
344 12k 1776 urn 1.00 .65
345 18k 1734 urn 1.60 1.00
a. A180 Pair, #344-345 2.75 2.75

Issued in sheets of 8.
See Israel Nos. 1380-1381.

Albín Brunovsky (1935-97), Stamp Designer A181

Photo. & Engr.

1999, Dec. 18 *Perf. 12x11¼*
346 A181 5k multi .75 .30
Complete booklet, 9 #346 10.00

Stamp Day.
Issued se-tenant with label. Value with labels at left and right, $2.

Rivers and Gaps — A182

Designs: a, 10k, Dunajec. b, 12k, Váh.

Litho. & Engr.

2000, Jan. 1 *Perf. 11¾*
347 A182 Pair, #a.-b. 2.50 2.50

Issued in sheets of 8.

Famous People — A183

4k, Hana Melickova (1900-78), actress. 5k, Stefan Anián Jedlik (1800-95), inventor.

Photo. & Engr.

2000, Jan. 11 *Perf. 11½x11¼*
348 A183 4k multi .60 .30
349 A183 5k multi .80 .30

Basketball — A184

Photo. & Engr.

2000, Feb. 15 *Perf. 11¼x11½*
351 A184 4k multi .65 .30

Ruzomberok team, 1999 European Women's Basketball League champions.

World Mathematics Year — A185

2000, Feb. 15 *Perf. 11¾x11¼*
352 A185 5k multi .60 .30

Juraj Hronec (1881-1959), Stefan Schwarz (1914-96), mathematicians.

Easter — A186

2000, Feb. 15 **Engr.** *Perf. 11¼x11½*
353 A186 4k brown .60 .30
Complete booklet, 10 #353 6.00

Ján Holly (1785-1849), Poet — A187

Photo. & Engr.

2000, Mar. 24 *Perf. 11½x11¼*
354 A187 5.50k multi .70 .30

Europa, 2000

Common Design Type

Litho. & Engr.

2000, May 9 *Perf. 11¾*
355 CD17 12k multi 1.60 .80

UNICEF A188

Photo. & Engr.

2000, June 1 *Perf. 11½x11¼*
356 A188 5.50k multi .65 .30

A189

Postman and Austria design A1.

Photo. & Engr.

2000, June 1 *Perf. 11¼x11¾*
357 A189 10k multi 1.25 .55

First postage stamp used in Slovakia, 150th anniv.

Pres. Rudolf Schuster — A190

Perf. 11¾x11¼

2000, June 15 **Engr.**
358 A190 5.50k brown .50 .30

See also No. 421.

2000 Summer Olympics, Sydney — A191

Photo. & Engr.

2000, June 27 *Perf. 11¼x11½*
359 A191 18k multi + label 2.75 1.50

Organization for Security and Cooperation in Europe, 25th Anniv. — A192

2000, Aug. 18 *Perf. 11½x11¼*
361 A192 4k black & blue .70 .30

Wooden Bridge, Kluknava A193

2000, Sept. 14 *Perf. 11¼*
362 A193 6k multi .70 .30

Souvenir Sheet

Berries — A194

No. 363: a, 11k, Rubus idaeus. b, 13k, Fragaria vesca. c, 15k, Vaccinium myrtillus.

Litho. & Engr.

2000, Sept. 14 *Perf. 11¾*
363 A194 Sheet of 3, #a-c 4.00 4.00

Holy Year 2000 — A195

Photo. & Engr.

2000, Oct. 5 *Perf. 11¼x11½*
364 A195 4k multi .70 .30
Booklet, 10 #364 7.00

Postal Agreement with Sovereign Military Order of Malta — A196

2000, Oct. 13 *Perf. 11¼x11¾*
365 A196 10k multi 1.10 .55

Art Type of 1996

Designs: 18k, Nativity, from church in Spisska Stara Ves. 20k, Crucifixion, from church in Kocelovce, horiz.

Perf. 11½x11¾, 11¾x11½

2000, Oct. 17 **Engr.**
366-367 A126 Set of 2 3.75 2.75

Stamp Day — A197

Photo. & Engr.

2000, Dec. 18 *Perf. 11¾x11½*
368 A197 5.50k multi + label 1.10 .55
Booklet, 9 #368 11.00

POFIS, 50th Anniv.

History of Postal Law A198

2000, Dec. 18 **Engr.** ***Perf. 11¾***
369 A198 20k multi 2.75 2.25

Issued in sheets of 4.

Mantel Clock, c. 1780 — A199

Photo. & Engr.

2001, Jan. 1 ***Perf. 11¼x11½***
370 A199 13k multi 1.25 .60

Janko Blaho (1901-81), Singer — A200

2001, Jan. 15
371 A200 5.50k multi .65 .30

2001 European Figure Skating Championships, Bratislava — A201

2001, Jan. 16
372 A201 16k multi 1.40 .70

Agricultural Control Institute, 50th Anniv. — A202

2001, Feb. 22 ***Perf. 11¾x11¼***
373 A202 12k multi 1.25 .60

Traditional Costumes — A203

Designs: 5.50k, Man from Detva. 6k, Woman and child from Detva.

2001, Feb. 22 ***Perf. 11¼x11½***
374 A203 5.50k multi .50 .30
Booklet, 10 #374 5.00
375 A203 6k multi .60 .30
Booklet, 10 #375 6.50

Archaeological Sites — A204

No. 376: a, 12k. Havránok. b, 15k, Ducové.

2001, Apr. 10 **Engr.** ***Perf. 11¾***
376 A204 Horiz. pair, #a-b 2.00 2.00

Issued in sheets of 4 pairs + 1 label.

Europa A205

2001, May 5 **Engr.** ***Perf. 11¾***
379 A205 18k multi 1.60 .85

Issued in sheets of 10.

Souvenir Sheet

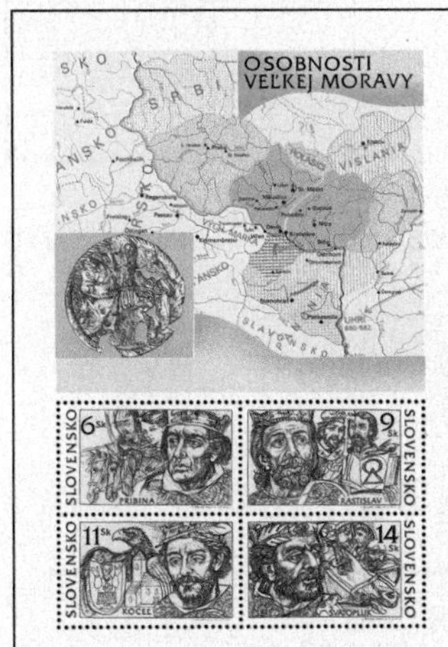

Princes of Great Moravia — A206

No. 380: a, 6k, Pribina. b, 9k, Rastislav. c, 11k, Kocel. d, 14k, Svatopluk.

Litho. & Engr.

2001, July 4 ***Perf. 11¾***
380 A206 Sheet of 4, #a-d 3.25 3.25

Souvenir Sheet

Wild Animals — A207

No. 381: a, 14k, Ursus arctos. b, 15k, Canis lupus. c, 16k, Lynx lynx.

2001, July 10 ***Perf. 11¾x11½***
381 A207 Sheet of 3, #a-c 4.25 4.25

Dobro Resonator Guitar and US Map — A208

Photo. & Engr.

2001, Aug. 1 ***Perf. 11¾x11¼***
382 A208 19k multi 1.75 .85

Bratislava Biennale of Illustrators A209

2001, Aug. 15 ***Perf. 11½x11¼***
383 A209 7k multi .75 .30
Booklet, 10 #383 7.50

The Righteous Among Nations — A210

2001, Sept. 9 ***Perf. 11¾x11¼***
384 A210 14k multi 1.25 .60

Souvenir Sheet

Alexander Dubcek (1921-92), Czechoslovakian Communist Leader — A211

Litho. & Engr.

2001, Sept. 18 ***Perf. 11¾***
385 A211 18k multi 2.00 2.00

Banská Bystrica Postal Museum — A212

Photo. & Engr.

2001, Oct. 9 ***Perf. 11¼x11½***
386 A212 6k multi .70 .30

Remembrance of Political Trial Victims — A213

2001, Oct. 9
387 A213 10k multi 1.10 .55

Maria Valeria Bridge Reconstruction — A214

2001, Oct. 11 ***Perf. 11¾x11¼***
388 A214 10k multi 1.25 .60

See Hungary No. 3776.

Art Type of 1996

Designs: 16k, Raftsman's Dream, by Imrich Weiner-Král'. 18k, Light of the Soul, by Albín Brunovsky. 20k, St. Michael the Archangel with Saints, by unknown artist.

2001, Oct. 15 **Engr.** ***Perf. 11¾***
389-391 A126 Set of 3 4.25 3.50

Christmas A215

Photo. & Engr.

2001, Oct. 15 ***Perf. 11½x11¼***
392 A215 5.50k multi .70 .30
Booklet, 10 #392 7.00

Famous Men — A216

Designs: 10k, Juraj Papánek (1738-1802), historian. 14k, Bjornsterne Bjornson (1832-1910), 1903 Nobel laureate for Literature.

2002, Jan. 15
393-394 A216 Set of 2 2.75 1.40

SLOVENSKO ZOH SALT LAKE CITY 2002 18 Sk

2002 Winter Olympics, Salt Lake City — A217

2002, Jan. 25 ***Perf. 11¾x11¼***
395 A217 18k multi 1.60 .80

SLOVENSKO Sk 6

European Dog Sled Championships A218

2002, Feb. 8 ***Perf. 11¼x11½***
396 A218 6k multi .80 .30

Easter — A219

2002, Feb. 15

397 A219 5.50k multi .70 .30
Booklet, 10 #397 7.00

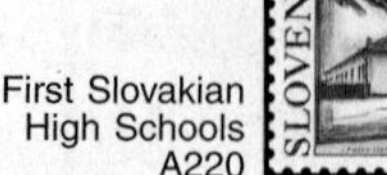

First Slovakian High Schools A220

Designs: 12k, Martin, 1866. 13k, Revuca, 1862. 15k, Klástor pod Znievom, 1869.

2002, Mar. 20 ***Perf. 11½x11¼***

398-400 A220 Set of 3 3.25 1.60

Castles and Churches Type of 1995

Perf. 11¾x11¼, 11¼x11¾

2002 **Photo. & Engr.**

401 A100 10k Kezmarok 1.40 .70
402 A100 16k Levoca, horiz. 1.60 .80

Issued: 10k, 5/6; 16k, 4/18.

Europa — A221

2002, May 6 **Engr.** ***Perf. 11¾***

403 A221 18k multi 2.00 2.00

Issued in sheets of 8.

Wine Production — A222

Designs: 7k, Barrels. 9k, Wine press.

Photo. & Engr.

2002, June 24 ***Perf. 11¾x11¼***

Stamps + labels

404-405 A222 Set of 2 1.75 1.25

Souvenir Sheet

Butterflies — A223

No. 406: a, 10k, Zerynthia polyxena. b, 16k, Inachis io. c, 25k, Papilio machaon.

Litho. & Engr.

2002, June 26 ***Perf. 11¾***

406 A223 Sheet of 3, #a-c, + 4 labels 6.50 4.50

Souvenir Sheet

Alexander Cardinal Rudnay (1760-1831) — A224

2002, July 4 **Engr.**

407 A224 17k multi *3.00 3.00*

Doves and Roses — A225

Photo. & Engr.

2002, July 4 ***Perf. 11¾x11¼***

408 A225 6k multi + label 1.40 .70

Issued in sheets of 12 stamps + 12 labels which could be personalized.

Victory at 2002 World Ice Hockey Championships — A226

2002, July 4

409 A226 10k multi 1.10 .60

Architecture in Slovakia and China — A227

No. 410: a, 6k, Handan Congtai Pavilion, People's Republic of China. b, 12k, Bojnice Castle, Slovakia.

2002, Oct. 12 ***Perf. 11¾x11½***

410 A227 Horiz. pair, #a-b 1.75 1.75

Issued in sheets of 4 pairs.
See People's Republic of China No. 3239.

Kosice Technological University, 50th Anniv. — A228

Photo. & Engr.

2002, Oct. 17 ***Perf. 11¼x11½***

411 A228 6k multi .65 .30

Christmas — A229

2002, Nov. 8

412 A229 5.50k multi .65 .30
Complete booklet, 10 #412 7.00

Churches — A230

Designs: 7k, St. Michael's Church, Klizske Hradiste. 14k, St. George's Rotunda, Skalica. 22k, St. Martin's Cathedral, Spisska Kapitula.

2002, Nov. 15 **Engr.** ***Perf. 11¾x11½***

413-415 A230 Set of 3 3.00 3.00

Issued in sheets of 10.

Miniature Sheet

Astronaut Eugene Cernan and Lunar Rover — A231

Photo. & Engr.

2002, Dec. 6 ***Perf. 11¾x11¼***

416 A231 20k multi + label 2.00 2.00

Apollo 17 mission, 30th anniv.

Art Type of 1996

Designs: 20k, The Beheading of St. John the Baptist, by Master Pavol of Levoca. 23k, In the Studio, by Koloman Sokol.

2002 **Engr.** ***Perf. 11¾***

417-418 A126 Set of 2 3.75 3.75

Nos. 417-418 issued in sheets of 4.
Issued: 20k, 12/18; 23k, 12/12.

Stamp Day — A232

Photo. & Engr.

2002, Dec. 18 ***Perf. 11¾x11¼***

419 A232 10k multi + 2 labels 1.40 .50

Nitrafila Stamp Exhibition, Nitra.

Independent Slovakia, 10th Anniv. — A233

Perf. 11¾x11½

2003, Jan. 1 **Litho. & Engr.**

420 A233 20k multi 1.50 .85

Issued in sheets of 6.

Pres. Schuster Type of 2000

2003, Feb. 5 **Engr.** ***Perf. 11¾x11¼***

421 A190 7k blue .70 .40

Roses — A234

Photo. & Engr.

2003, Feb. 14 ***Perf. 11½x11¼***

422 A234 7k multi .75 .40
a. Sheet of 8 + 8 labels 14.00 14.00

No. 422a issued 4/30. Labels on No. 422a could be personalized.

Easter — A235

2003, Mar. 10 *Perf. 11¼x11½*
423 A235 7k multi .75 .40
Booklet, 10 #423 7.50

Churches and Castles Type of 1995-2001

Photo. & Engr.

2003 *Perf. 11¾x11¼*
424 A100 18k Kremnica 1.25 .65
425 A100 100k Pezinok 6.75 2.75

Issued: 18k, 3/20, 100k, 9/18.

Souvenir Sheet

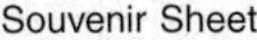

Saints Cyril and Methodius — A236

No. 426: a, 17k, St. Cyril. b, 22k, St. Methodius.

Litho. & Engr.

2003, Apr. 6 *Perf. 11¾*
426 A236 Sheet of 2, #a-b, + 2 labels 3.50 3.50

Ludwig van Beethoven (1770-1827), Composer A237

Photo. & Engr.

2003, Apr. 24 *Perf. 11½x11¼*
427 A237 15k multi 1.25 1.00

Milan Stefánik (1880-1919), Czechoslovakian General — A238

Litho. & Engr.

2003, May 3 *Perf. 11¾*
428 A238 14k multi 1.40 1.00

Issued in sheets of 8.
See France No. 2942.

Europa — A239

2003, May 9
429 A239 14k multi 1.40 .75

Issued in sheets of 10.

Art Type of 1996

Design: The Brook, by Ladislav Mednansky, horiz.

2003, May 9 **Engr.** *Perf. 11¾*
430 A126 18k multi 1.50 .80

Issued in sheets of 4.

Sts. Benedict and Andrej Svorad — A240

Photo. & Engr.

2003, May 16 *Perf. 11½x11¼*
431 A240 13k multi 1.25 .60

Third Place Finish of Slovakian Ice Hockey Team at World Championships, Finland — A241

2003, May 30 **Litho.** *Perf. 13½*
432 A241 20k multi 2.10 1.10

Issued in sheets of 4.

Matko and Kubko — A242

Photo. & Engr.

2003, June 1 *Perf. 11¼x11½*
433 A242 7k multi .75 .35
Complete booklet, 10 #433 7.50

Intl. Children's Day.

Worldwide Fund for Nature (WWF) — A243

Various views of Felis silvestris silvestris: a, 13k. b, 14k. c, 16k. d, 18k.

Litho. & Engr.

2003, June 25 *Perf. 11¾*
434 A243 Sheet of 4, #a-d 6.00 6.00

World Swimming Championships, Barcelona A244

Photo. & Engr.

2003, July 7 *Perf. 11½x11¼*
435 A244 11k multi 1.10 .55

Banska Stiavnica Reservoirs — A245

No. 436: a, 9k, Lake Klinger. b, 12k, Rozgrund Reservoir.

2003, July 15 **Engr.** *Perf. 11¾*
436 A245 Pair, #a-b 2.25 2.00

Issued in sheets of 4 pairs + 1 label.

Bratislava Biennale of Illustrators — A246

Photo. & Engr.

2003, Aug. 15 *Perf. 11¼x11½*
437 A246 12k multi 1.20 .70
Complete booklet, 10 # 437 12.00

Visit of Pope John Paul II — A247

Die Cut Perf. 14¾x14½

2003, Sept. 7 **Litho.**

Self-Adhesive

438 A247 12k violet 1.25 .60

Issued in sheets of 4.

Father Ján Baltazár Magin (1681-1734), Poet — A248

Photo. & Engr.

2003, Sept. 17 *Perf. 11½x11¼*
439 A248 8k multi .75 .50

Christmas A249

2003, Oct. 30
440 A249 7k multi .75 .40
Complete booklet, 10 #440 7.50

Bronze Buttons, Sword Hilt and Cross A250

2003, Nov. 17 *Perf. 11¾x11¼*
441 A250 18k multi 1.60 1.00

"Travel of History" exhibit of archaeological treasures.

Powered Flight, Cent. — A251

2003, Nov. 17 *Perf. 11½x11¼*
442 A251 18k multi 1.60 1.00

Art Type of 1996

Designs: 14k, St. Catherine, by Simon Vouet. 16k, Bagpipes, by Rudolf Krivos, horiz. 21k, The Annunciation, by Master Jan.

2003, Nov. 28 **Engr.** *Perf. 11¾*
443-445 A126 Set of 3 4.00 2.25

Nos. 443-445 issued in sheets of 4.

Marginal Design from Czechoslovakia No. 2517 Sheet, by Josef Baláz — A252

Photo. & Engr.

2003, Nov. 28 *Perf. 11¾x11¼*
446 A252 12k multi + label 1.10 .55

Stamp Day.

Castles and Churches Type of 1995-2001

9k, Liptovsky Mikulás, horiz.

2004, Jan. 30 **Litho.** *Perf. 14¼x14*
447 A100 9k multicolored .85 .40

St. Valentine's Day — A253

Litho. & Embossed

2004, Jan. 30 *Perf. 11¾*
448 A253 8k multi .75 .35

Lilium Royal Parade — A254

Perf. 14¾x14½ Syncopated

2004, Feb. 12 **Litho.**
449 A254 8k multi .75 .35

Tulip Kaufmanniana — A255

2004, Feb. 12 *Perf. 13¼*
450 A255 9k multi + label .85 .40

Printed in sheets of 8 + 8 labels which could be personalized. Value (any label picture), mint $12.50, used $10.

Easter Egg — A256

2004, Mar. 10 *Die Cut Perf. 14½*

Self-Adhesive

451 A256 8k multi 1.25 .80
a. Booklet pane of 10 12.50

Wedding Clothing From Pata — A257

Designs: 15k, Groom. 28k, Bride.

2004, Apr. 16 ***Perf. 13¼***
452-453 A257 Set of 2 3.50 2.00

Europa — A258

Perf. 14x14¼ Syncopated
2004, Apr. 23
454 A258 20k multi 1.75 .80
Issued in sheets of 10.

Admission Into European Union A259

2004, May 1 ***Perf. 13½***
455 A259 18k multi 1.75 .85
Issued in sheets of 10.

Admission Into NATO — A260

2004, May 1 ***Perf. 14***
456 A260 60k multi 6.25 4.00

Grandfather, From Evening Tales Television Program — A261

2004, May 21 ***Perf. 13¼***
Granite Paper
457 A261 8k multi .85 .35

2004 Paralympics, Athens — A262

2004, May 31 ***Perf. 13¼x13½***
458 A262 34k multi 2.75 1.25

Pres. Ivan Gasparovic — A263

2004, June 15 ***Perf. 13***
Granite Paper
459 A263 8k multi .85 .35

Dobroc Forest A264

2004, June 17 ***Perf. 14***
Granite Paper
460 A264 12k multi 1.10 .55

Tatra Omnibus, 1904-06 A265

2004, June 30 ***Perf. 13¼x13½***
Granite Paper
461 A265 14k multi 1.25 .60
Issued in sheets of 8.

Spania Valley Mining Water System A266

2004, June 30 **Granite Paper**
462 A266 24k multi 2.00 .90
Issued in sheets of 8.

Dunajec River Raftsmen — A267

2004, Sept. 3 ***Perf. 13¼x13***
463 A267 21k multi 1.75 1.00
See Poland No. 3752.

Roman Legions in Trencin — A268

2004, Oct. 15 ***Perf. 13***
464 A268 26k multi 2.10 .90

Art Type of 1996

Designs: 33k, Cock Fight, by Jakub Bogdan, horiz. 35k, Don Quixote, by Július Jakoby.

Litho. & Engr.
2004, Oct. 20 ***Perf. 11¾***
465-466 A126 Set of 2 6.00 5.50
Nos. 465-466 issued in sheets of 4.

Christmas A269

2004, Nov. 5 **Litho.** ***Perf. 13***
467 A269 8k multi .85 .35
Complete booklet, 10 #467 8.50

Medalists at 2004 Summer Olympics — A270

No. 468: a, Jozef Gonci, air rifle bronze medalist. b, Kayak 1000-meter fours team, bronze medalists. c, Jozef Krnac, 66-kilogram judo silver medalist. d, Michal Martikán, men's canoe slalom silver medalist. e, Elena Kaliská, women's canoe slalom gold medalist. f, Pavol and Peter Hochschornerovci, canoe slalom doubles gold medalists.

Serpentine Die Cut 12½
2004, Nov. 5 **Self-Adhesive** **Litho.**
468 Booklet of 6 10.00 8.00
a.-b. A270 8k Either single .85 .55
c.-d. A270 14k Either single 1.00 .65
e.-f. A270 20k Either single 1.75 .85

Stamp Day — A271

2004, Dec. 18 ***Perf. 13***
469 A271 9k multi .85 .40

St. Valentine's Day — A272

2005, Jan. 31 **Litho.** ***Perf. 13½***
470 A272 9k multi .85 .40

Family — A273

2005, Feb. 14 ***Perf. 13½x13***
471 A273 9k multi 1.00 .40

Banska Bystrica, 750th Anniv. — A274

2005, Feb. 14 ***Perf. 13½***
472 A274 16k multi 1.50 .75

A275

25k, Summit Meeting of Presidents George W. Bush and Vladimir Putin.

2005, Feb. 24 ***Perf. 13***
473 A275 25k multi 2.25 1.50

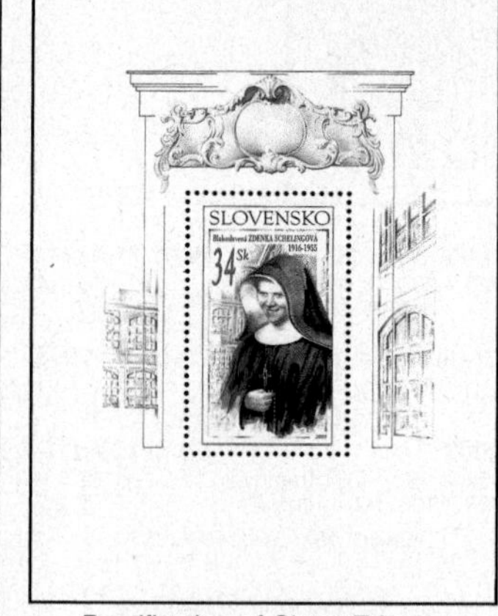
Easter — A276

2005, Mar. 10 **Litho.** ***Perf. 13½***
474 A276 9k multi .85 .40
Complete booklet, 10 #474 8.50

Souvenir Sheet

Beatification of Sister Zdenka Schelingová — A277

2005, Mar. 10 ***Perf. 13x13¼***
475 A277 34k multi 3.00 3.00

Cycling for the Handicapped A278

2005, Mar. 30 ***Perf. 13½***
476 A278 22k multi 1.75 .85

Poor Mother, by Frantisek Studeny — A279

Perf. 11¾x11½
2005, Mar. 30 **Litho. & Engr.**
477 A279 25k blk & lt grn 2.25 1.50
Issued in sheets of 8.
An unstated portion of the receipts were donated to UNICEF for relief works for the Dec. 26, 2004 tsunami.

Europa A280

2005, Apr. 22 **Litho.** ***Perf. 13¾***
478 A280 19k multi 1.75 1.00
Issued in sheets of 8.

Peace of Bratislava (Pressburg), Bicent. — A281

2005, Apr. 29 ***Perf. 13½***
479 A281 23k multi 2.00 1.00

Intl. Year of Physics A282

2005, May 16 Litho. *Perf. 13½*
480 A282 18k multi 1.75 .85

Fish — A283

2005, May 23 Litho. *Perf. 13½*
481 A283 9k multi .85 .40
Complete booklet, 10 #481 8.50

Biennale of Children's Book Illustrations, Bratislava — A284

2005, May 23
482 A284 30k multi 2.50 1.25

Holic and Town Arms — A285

2005, June 3 Litho. *Perf. 13¼x13*
483 A285 22k multi 2.10 1.00

Pres. Ivan Gasparovic — A286

Perf. 11¾x11¼
2005, June 15 Litho. & Engr.
484 A286 9k brn & buff .85 .40

Souvenir Sheet

Horses — A287

No. 485: a, 29k, Lippizaners, carriage. b, 31k, Slovak warm-bloods, rider.

2005, June 30 *Perf. 11¾*
485 A287 Sheet of 2, #a.-b. 10.00 6.00

Locomotives — A288

Designs: 24k, Ciernohronska Railroad. 33k, Vychylovka.

Litho. & Engr.

2005, Sept. 22 *Perf. 11¾*
486-487 A288 Set of 2 6.00 4.50

Nos. 486-487 issued in sheets of 8 + 1 label.

Art Type of 1996

Designs: 28k, Supper at Emmaus, by Rembrandt. 35k, Magic of Still Life Paintings V, by Karol Baron, horiz.

2005, Oct. 20 Engr.
488-489 A126 Set of 2 5.50 2.75

Nos. 488-489 issued in sheets of 4.

Christmas — A289

2005, Nov. 16 Litho. *Perf. 13¼*
490 A289 9k multi .85 .50
Complete booklet, 10 #490 8.50

Stamp Day — A290

2005, Nov. 25 *Perf. 13¼x13½*
491 A290 15k multi + label 1.25 .80

Karol Kuzmány (1806-66), Writer — A291

2006, Feb. 3 *Perf. 13½*
492 A291 16k multi 1.25 1.00

2006 Winter Olympics, Turin — A292

2006, Feb. 3 *Perf. 13¼x13½*
493 A292 21k multi + label 3.00 2.00

Poprad and Town Arms — A293

2006, Feb. 3 *Perf. 13¼*
494 A293 23k multi 1.60 1.10

Narcissus — A294

2006, Mar. 24 Litho. *Perf. 13¼*
495 A294 10k multi .95 .60

Easter — A295

2006, Mar. 31 *Perf. 13½*
496 A295 10k multi .75 .60
Complete booklet, 10 #496 8.00

Souvenir Sheet

Geological Formations — A296

No. 497: a, 32k, Sandberg. b, 35k, Somoska.

Litho. & Engr.

2006, Apr. 21 *Perf. 11¾*
497 A296 Sheet of 2, #a-b 7.50 5.50

Europa A297

Litho. & Embossed

2006, May 5 *Perf. 13¼x13*
498 A297 18k multi 1.50 .85

Issued in sheets of 10.

Belfries — A298

Designs: 27k, Kezmarok. 29k, Podolinec.

Photo. & Engr.

2006, May 19 *Perf. 11½x11¾*
499-500 A298 Set of 2 4.50 3.75

Children's Art — A299

2006, May 31 Litho. *Perf. 11¼*
501 A299 10k multi 1.00 .60
Complete booklet, 10 #501 10.00

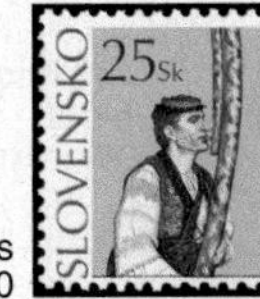

Shepherd's Pipe — A300

2006, June 9 *Perf. 11¼x12¼*
502 A300 25k multi 2.00 1.60

Devín Castle — A301

2006, June 9 Litho. *Perf. 12¾x12¼*
503 A301 10k multi + label 2.50 2.00

Printed in sheets of 8 + 8 labels which could be personalized.

Objects in Museums — A302

Designs: 28k, Blue cobalt glass goblet, 16th cent. 31k, Copper measuring cup, 1576.

Litho. & Engr.

2006, June 23 *Perf. 11¾*
504-505 A302 Set of 2 5.00 4.00

Nos. 504-505 issued in sheets of 8 containing 4 of each stamp.

Puppets — A303

Designs: 22k, Indonesian puppet. 25k, Slovakian marionette.

2006, July 27 Litho. *Perf. 13¼x13*
506-507 A303 Set of 2 4.00 3.00

Nos. 506-507 issued in sheets of 6 containing 3 of each stamp.
See Indonesia No. 2092.

Art Type of 1996

Designs: 37k, Krivy Jarok, by Dezider Milly, horiz. 38k, Moravian Venus sculpture fragment.

2006, Oct. 20 Engr. *Perf. 11¾*
508-509 A126 Set of 2 6.00 4.25

Nos. 508-509 issued in sheets of 4.

Christmas A304

2006, Nov. 10 Litho. *Perf. 11*
510 A304 10k multi 1.00 .60
Complete booklet, 10 #510 10.00

Jozef Cincík (1909-92), Stamp Designer — A305

2006, Nov. 24 *Perf. 13¼x12½*
511 A305 19k multi 1.50 .85

Stamp Day.

Modra and Town Arms — A306

2007, Feb. 7 Litho. ***Perf. 12¼x11½***
512 A306 14k multi 1.25 .85

Terézia Vansová (1857-1942), Writer — A307

2007, Feb. 7 ***Perf. 11***
513 A307 19k multi 1.40 .80

Flowers — A308

2007, Feb. 14 ***Perf. 12x11½***
514 A308 (10k) multi 1.00 .55

Easter — A309

2007, Mar. 15 ***Perf. 11x11¼***
515 A309 10k multi .90 .50
Complete booklet, 10 #515 10.00

Women's Tennis — A310

2007, Mar. 21 ***Perf. 11***
516 A310 16k multi 1.30 .90

Souvenir Sheet

Dogs — A311

No. 517: a, Slovakian cuvac. b, Slovakian kopov.

Litho. & Engr.

2007, Apr. 18 ***Perf. 11¾***
517 A311 31k Sheet of 2, #a-b 9.00 5.00

Slovak League of America, Cent. — A312

2007, May 15 Litho. ***Perf. 11¾x11½***
518 A312 22k multi 1.60 1.10

Janko Hrasko, by Stefan Cpin — A313

2007, May 30 ***Perf. 13½***
519 A313 10k multi 1.00 .55
Complete booklet, 10 #519 10.00

Europa A314

2007, May 30 ***Perf. 13¾***
520 A314 18k multi 1.60 1.00

Issued in sheets of 10.

Monasteries A315

Designs: 30k, Jasov Monastery. 34k, Hronsky Benadik Monastery.

Photo. & Engr.

2007, June 6 ***Perf. 11¼x11¾***
521-522 A315 Set of 2 6.00 4.75

Biennale of Children's Book Illustrations, Bratislava — A316

2007, June 27 Litho. ***Perf. 13½***
523 A316 25k multi 2.00 1.50

Souvenir Sheet

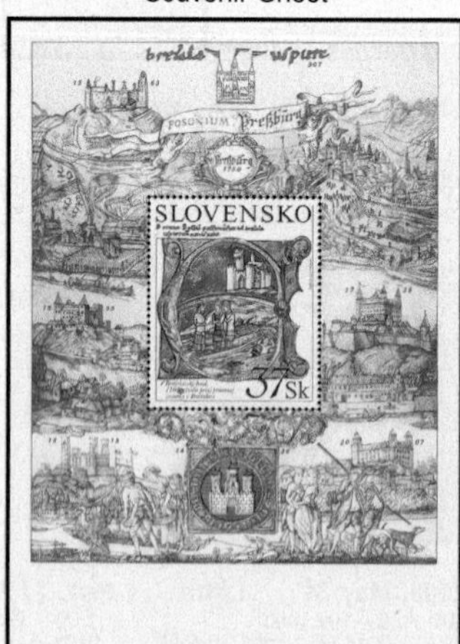

Bratislava Castle — A317

Litho. & Engr.

2007, June 27 ***Perf. 11¾x12***
524 A317 37k multi 8.00 4.00

Castles — A318

No. 525: a, Rocca, San Marino. b, Orava Castle, Slovakia.

2007, Aug. 24 ***Perf. 11¾***
525 A318 21k Horiz. pair, #a-b 5.00 3.50

No. 525 was printed in sheets containing four pairs. See San Marino No. 1729.

Jozef Miloslav Hurban (1817-88), Nationalist Leader — A319

2007, Sept. 1 Litho. ***Perf. 11¼x11¾***
526 A319 31k multi 2.25 1.75

Král'ova Bridge, Senec A320

Photo. & Engr.

2007, Sept. 5 ***Perf. 11¼***
527 A320 29k multi 2.50 2.00

Gospel Book of Nitra — A321

2007, Sept. 22 ***Perf. 11¼x11¾***
528 A321 15k multi 1.10 .85

Robert William Seton-Watson (1879-1951), Historian A322

2007, Oct. 26 Litho. ***Perf. 11¾x11¼***
529 A322 24k multi 1.90 1.50

Art Type of 1996

Designs: No. 530, 33k, St. Elizabeth of Hungary, by Frantisek X. K. Palko. No. 531, 33k, Bouquet of Chrysanthemums, by Ján Zelibsky, horiz.

2007, Nov. 14 Engr. ***Perf. 11¾***
530-531 A126 Set of 2 6.00 4.75

Each stamp printed in sheets of 4.

Christmas — A323

Perf. 11¼x11¾

2007, Nov. 14 Litho.
532 A323 10k multi 1.00 .60
Complete booklet, 10 #532 10.00

Field Post — A324

2007, Nov. 28 ***Perf. 11¾x11¼***
533 A324 28k multi + label 2.75 2.00

Stamp Day.

Independence, 15th Anniv. — A325

2008, Jan. 1 Litho. ***Perf. 11¾x11¼***
534 A325 (16k) multi 1.25 .80

Easter — A326

2008, Feb. 28 ***Perf. 11¼x11¾***
535 A326 (10k) multi .80 .55
Complete booklet, 10 #535 9.00

Krupina Arms and Church — A327

2008, Mar. 6 ***Perf. 11¾x11¼***
536 A327 (14k) multi 1.25 .90

Dahlias — A328

2008, Mar. 20
537 A328 (10k) multi + label 1.00 1.00

Printed in sheets of 8 stamps + 8 labels that could be personalized.

Constitutional Court, 15th Anniv. — A329

2008, Apr. 3 ***Perf. 11¼x11¾***
538 A329 25k multi 2.00 1.60

Eugen Suchon (1908-93), Composer — A330

2008, Apr. 17

539 A330 (15k) multi 1.25 1.00

Masa Hal'amová (1908-86), Poet — A331

2008, Apr. 17 ***Perf. 11¾x11¼***

540 A331 (18k) multi 1.75 1.40

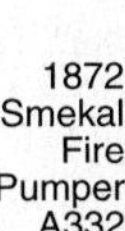

1872 Smekal Fire Pumper A332

1880 Seltenhofer Fire Pumper — A333

2008, Apr. 30 **Litho. & Engr.**

541 A332 (19k) multi 2.00 1.25

542 A333 (31k) multi 3.00 2.25

Europa — A334

2008, May 5 **Litho.** ***Perf. 11¼x11¾***

543 A334 21k multi 2.25 2.00

Multi-headed Dragon from Stories by Pavol Dobsinsky — A335

2008, May 29 ***Perf. 11¼x11½***

544 A335 (10k) multi .85 .60

Complete booklet, 10 #544 8.50

2008 Summer Olympics, Beijing — A336

2008, June 4 ***Perf. 11¾x11¼***

545 A336 25k multi 2.60 1.75

2008 Paralympics, Beijing — A337

2008, June 6

546 A337 30k multi 2.75 2.00

9th Cent. Copper Plaque Found at Bojná — A338

Litho. & Engr.

2008, June 30 ***Perf. 11¾***

547 A338 33k multi + label 4.25 3.00

Printed in sheets of 3 stamps + 3 labels.

Souvenir Sheet

Karol Plicka (1894-1987), Photographer — A339

2008, Sept. 12

548 A339 40k multi + 2 labels 4.50 3.00

See Czech Republic No. 3397.

Coronation of King Matthias Corvinus, 550th Anniv. A340

2008, Sept. 25 **Litho.** ***Perf. 11¼***

549 A340 (16k) multi 1.50 1.00

Wooden Churches — A341

No. 550 — Church in: a, Hervartov. b, Dobroslava.

Litho. & Engr.

2008, Oct. 9 ***Perf. 11¾***

550 A341 (18k) Horiz. pair, #a-b, + central label 5.00 3.50

Printed in sheets containing two of each stamp + 2 labels.

Orchids A342

Designs: (14k), Cypripedium calceolus. (15k), Ophrys apifera.

Photo. & Engr.

2008, Oct. 23 ***Perf. 12x11¼***

551-552 A342 Set of 2 4.00 2.25

No. 551 is inscribed "T2 100g;" No. 552, "T2 500g."

Christmas — A343

Perf. 11¼x11¾

2008, Nov. 13 **Litho.**

553 A343 (10k) multi 1.00 .45

Complete booklet, 10 #553 10.00

Post Rider For Bratislava-Ruzomberok-Kosice Mail Route — A344

2008, Nov. 27 ***Perf. 11¾x11¼***

554 A344 (16k) multi + label 1.60 1.60

Stamp Day.

Art Type of 1996

Designs: (31k), Illustration by Josef Baláz, from book *The Seven-colored Flower.* (37k), A Girl in White with Factory Chimneys and Flowers, by Zoltán Palugyay.

2008, Nov. 27 **Engr.** ***Perf. 11¾***

555-556 A126 Set of 2 6.25 4.50

Nos. 555-556 each were printed in sheets of 4. No. 555 is inscribed "T2 1000g"; No. 556, "T1 1000g."

100 Cents = 1 Euro

Euro Symbol and Map of Slovakia — A345

Perf. 11¾x11½

2009, Jan. 1 **Litho. & Engr.**

557 A345 €1 multi 2.50 1.75

Introduction of Euro currency.

Issued in sheets of 6.

A346

Architecture and Architectural Decorations — A347

Designs: 1c, Chapel of St. Margaret, Kopcany. 2c, Sculpture from Church of the Virgin Mary, Boldog. 5c, Rotunda of Church of St. Margaret, Sivetice. 10c, Altar from Church of St. John the Baptist, Pominovce. 20c, Church, Svätuse. 33c, Church, Cierny Brod. 50c, Sculpture of lion from Church of St. Martin, Spisská Kapitula, horiz. 66c, Columns, Church of St. Egidius, Ilija, vert. 83c, Mural from Church of St. Stephen the King, Zilina-Zavodie, vert. €1, Capital from Church of the Virgin Mary, Bina. €2, Church of St. Michael the Archangel, Drazovce.

€1.33, Church of the Holy Cross, Hamuliakovo.

Photo. & Engr., Litho. (33c, 66c, 83c)

Perf. 11¾x11¼, 11¼x11¾

2009, Jan. 2

558	A346	1c multi	.25	.25
559	A346	2c multi	.25	.25
560	A346	5c multi	.25	.25
561	A346	10c multi	.30	.25
562	A346	20c multi	.55	.25
563	A347	33c multi	.95	.45
564	A346	50c multi	1.10	.50
565	A347	66c multi	1.40	1.00
566	A347	83c multi	1.90	1.25
567	A346	€1 multi	2.25	1.60
568	A346	€2 multi	4.50	3.00
	Nos. 558-568 (11)		13.70	9.05

Souvenir Sheet

Perf. 11¾

569 A346 €1.33 multi 3.00 2.25

See Nos. 587, 610, 631, 654, 679, 706, 734, 757, 785.

Easter — A348

Perf. 11¾x11¼

2009, Feb. 27 **Litho.**

570 A348 33c multi 1.50 .40

Serpentine Die Cut 16½x15

Booklet Stamp

Self-Adhesive

570A A348 33c multi 3.25 .40

b. Booklet pane of 10 32.50

Karate — A349

2009, Mar. 13 ***Perf. 11¼x11¾***

571 A349 60c multi 1.40 .80

Aurel Stodola (1859-1942), Engineer A350

2009, Apr. 17 ***Perf. 11¾x11¼***

572 A350 33c multi .90 .55

Union of Slovak Philatelists, 40th Anniv. — A351

Perf. 11½x11¼

2009, Apr. 29 Litho. & Engr.

573 A351 (33c) multi + label .90 .65

Supreme Audit Office, 40th Anniv. — A352

Photo. & Engr.

2009, May 7 ***Perf. 11½x11¼***

574 A352 80c multi 1.75 1.25

Europa A353

2009, May 28 Litho. ***Perf. 11¾x11¼***

575 A353 90c multi 2.25 1.25

Intl. Year of Astronomy.
Issued in sheets of 8.

Souvenir Sheet

Zofia Bosniaková (1609-44), Founder of Poorhouse — A354

Litho. & Engr.

2009, June 2 ***Perf. 11¾***

576 A354 80c multi 1.90 1.10

Souvenir Sheet

Pres. Ivan Gasparovic — A355

Litho. With Foil Application

2009, June 15 ***Perf. 11¾x12***

577 A355 €1 gold + 2 labels 2.50 1.50

2009 Biennale of Illustrations, Bratislava — A356

2009, Aug. 14 Engr. ***Perf. 11¼x11¾***

578 A356 (33c) brown .95 .45

Souvenir Sheet

Archaeological Excavations of Roman Military Camps — A357

No. 579: a, Carnuntum. b, Gerulata.

Perf. 11½x11¾

2009, Sept. 11 Litho. & Engr.

579 A357 60c Sheet of 2, #a-b 2.75 1.75

See Austria No. 2220.

Nature Preservation A358

Designs: No. 580, €1.10, Salamandra salamandra. No. 581, €1.10, Emys orbicularis.

2009, Oct. 23 ***Perf. 11¾x11½***

580-581 A358 Set of 2 5.00 3.50

Nos. 580-581 were printed in sheets of 6 containing 3 of each stamp.

Christmas — A359

Perf. 11¼x11¾

2009, Nov. 11 Litho.

582 A359 40c multi .90 .60

Booklet Stamp
Self-Adhesive

Serpentine Die Cut 15x16½

583 A359 40c multi 1.10 .60
a. Booklet pane of 10 11.00

Art Type of 1996

Designs: No. 584, €1.20, Madonna with Black Nimbus, by Ján Mudroch. No. 585, €1.20, Don Quixote, by Cyprián Majerník.

2009, Nov. 27 Engr. ***Perf. 11¾***

584-585 A126 Set of 2 5.75 3.75

Nos. 584-585 were each printed in sheets of 4 + 2 labels.

Louis Braille (1809-52), Educator of the Blind — A360

2009, Dec. 4 Litho. ***Perf. 11¾x11¼***

586 A360 70c multi + label 1.60 1.25

Stamp Day.

Architecture and Architectural Decorations Type of 2009

Design: Cross, Church of the Assumption of the Virgin Mary, Spisská Nová Ves.

Photo. & Engr.

2010, Jan. 4 ***Perf. 11¾x11¼***

587 A346 60c multi 1.40 1.00

2010 Winter Olympics, Vancouver — A361

2010, Jan. 15 Litho.

588 A361 €1 multi 2.25 1.40

Pres. Ivan Gasparovic — A362

2010, Jan. 29 Photo. & Engr.

589 A362 40c multi 1.10 .55

Easter — A363

Perf. 11¼x11¾

2010, Feb. 26 Litho.

590 A363 40c multi .90 .55

Serpentine Die Cut 15x16½

Booklet Stamp
Self-Adhesive

591 A363 40c multi .90 .55
a. Booklet pane of 10 9.00

Count Matthew Csák of Trencin (c. 1260-1321), Palatine A364

2010, Mar. 12 Litho. ***Perf. 11¼***

592 A364 70c multi 1.60 1.10

Souvenir Sheet

Zilina Synod, 400th Anniv. — A365

Litho. & Engr.

2010, Mar. 30 ***Perf. 11¾***

593 A365 €1.10 multi 2.75 1.50

Milan Hodza (1878-1944), Journalist A366

2010, Apr. 16 Litho. ***Perf. 11¾x11¼***

594 A366 40c multi 1.10 .55

Europa — A367

2010, May 4 ***Perf. 11¼x11¾***

595 A367 90c multi 2.00 1.25

Issued in sheets of 8.

Souvenir Sheet

2010 World Cup Soccer Championships, South Africa — A368

Litho. With Three-Dimensional Plastic Affixed

2010, June 8 ***Die Cut***

Self-Adhesive

596 A368 Sheet of 2 12.00 12.00
a. €2.30 Single stamp 6.00 6.00

Topol'cianky Castle — A369

Betliar Castle A370

Photo. & Engr.

2010, June 18 ***Perf. 11¾x11¼***
597 A369 40c multi 1.00 .50
598 A370 40c multi 1.00 .50

Miniature Sheet

Saints — A371

No. 599: a, St. Gorazd. b. St. Clement.

2010, July 16 ***Perf. 11¾***
599 A371 Sheet of 5, 3 #599a, 2 #599b, + 5 labels 8.00 5.00
a.-b. 60c Either single 1.60 1.00

Topol'cany Castle — A372

Perf. 11¾x11¼

2010, Sept. 17 **Litho.**
600 A372 40c multi + label 1.00 .55

Printed in sheets of 8 stamps + 8 labels that could be personalized.

Egyptian Alabaster Canopic Jar — A373

2010, Oct. 8 **Litho. & Engr.**
601 A373 €1 multi 2.25 1.40

See Egypt No. 2069.

Miniature Sheet

Protected Flowers of the Muránska Plain — A374

No. 602: a, Primula auricula. b, Daphne arbuscula.

2010, Oct. 15 ***Perf. 11½x11¾***
602 A374 Sheet of 4, 2 each #a-b, + 2 labels 8.00 4.50
a.-b. 80c Either single 2.00 1.10

Christmas — A375

Perf. 11¼x11¾

2010, Nov. 12 **Litho.**
603 A375 40c multi 1.00 .55

Self-Adhesive Booklet Stamp

Serpentine Die Cut 15x16½

604 A375 40c multi 1.00 .55
a. Booklet pane of 10 10.00

Art Type of 1996

Designs: No. 605, €1.20, Coronation of Charles I of Hungary (Charles Robert), by unknown artist, St. Martin Cathedral, Spisská Kapitula (denomination in black). No. 606, €1.20, Madonna and Child, statue by Master Paul of Levoca, Assumption of the Virgin Mary Church, L'ubica (denomination in blue).

2010, Nov. 26 **Engr.** ***Perf. 11¾***
605-606 A126 Set of 2 6.25 3.25

Nos. 605-606 each were printed in sheets of 4 + 2 labels

Campaign Against AIDS — A376

2010, Dec. 1 **Litho.** ***Perf. 11¼***
607 A376 40c multi 1.00 .55

No. 607 has a die cut cross-shaped hole at lower left.

Karol Ondreicka (1944-2003), Stamp Designer — A377

Perf. 11¾x11¼

2010, Dec. 3 **Litho. & Engr.**
608 A377 70c multi + label 1.60 .95

Stamp Day.

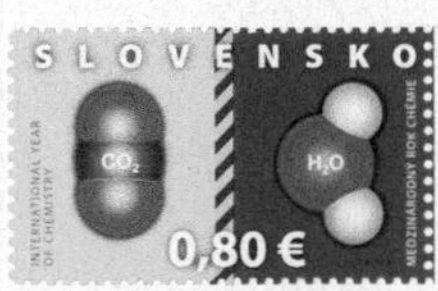

Intl. Year of Chemistry — A378

2011, Jan. 17 **Litho.** ***Perf. 11¾x11¼***
609 A378 80c multi + label 1.75 1.10

Architecture and Architectural Decorations Type of 2009

Design: Sculpture of St. George Killing Dragon, Church of St. George, Svaty Jur.

2011, Jan. 28 **Photo. & Engr.**
610 A346 70c multi 1.60 .95

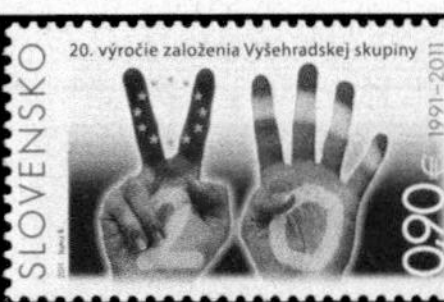

Visegrád Group, 20th Anniv. A379

2011, Feb. 11 **Litho.**
611 A379 90c multi 2.25 1.25

Issued in sheets of 8.

See Czech Republic No. 3490, Hungary No. 4183, Poland No. 4001.

Meringue Lamb — A380

2011, Mar. 4 ***Perf. 11¾x11¼***
612 A380 40c multi 1.00 .55

Booklet Stamp Self-Adhesive

Serpentine Die Cut 16½x15

613 A380 40c multi 1.00 .55
a. Booklet pane of 10 10.00

Easter.

2011 World Ice Hockey Championships, Slovakia — A381

No. 614: a, 40c, Slovakian player Pavol Demitra (1974-2011). b, 50c, Russian goaltender.

Perf. 11¼x11¾

2011, Mar. 25 **Litho.**
614 A381 Horiz. pair, #a-b 2.00 1.25

Dobsinská Ice Cave UNESCO World Heritage Site — A382

Perf. 11¾x11½

2011, Apr. 15 **Litho. & Engr.**
615 A382 €1.10 multi 2.50 1.60

Issued in sheets of 6.

Beatification of Pope John Paul II — A383

2011, Apr. 29 ***Perf. 11¾***
616 A383 40c multi 1.25 .60

Pritned in sheets of 4 + label.

Europa — A384

2011, May 6
617 A384 90c multi 2.25 1.25

Intl. Year of Forests.
Issued in sheets of 8.

Flower — A385

2011, June 3 **Litho.** ***Perf. 11¼x11¾***
618 A385 (40c) multi + label 1.10 .60

Printed in sheets of 8 stamps + 8 labels that could be personalized.

Souvenir Sheet

Memorandum of the Slovak Nation, 150th Anniv. — A386

Litho. & Engr.

2011, June 6 ***Perf. 11¾***
619 A386 €1.20 multi 3.00 2.25

Old Automobiles — A387

Designs: 40c, Aero 30. 80c, Tatra 87.

Photo. & Engr.

2011, July 1 ***Perf. 11¾x11¼***
620-621 A387 Set of 2 3.00 2.00

Ján Cikker (1911-89), Composer A388

2011, July 29 **Litho.**
622 A388 50c multi 1.25 .90

2011 Biennale of Illustrations, Bratislava — A389

2011, Sept. 2 ***Perf. 11¼x11¾***
623 A389 40c multi 1.00 .65

Michal Miloslav Hodza (1811-70), Nationalist Leader and Poet — A390

Photo. & Engr.

2011, Sept. 22 ***Perf. 11½x11¼***
624 A390 40c multi 1.00 .65

Otis Tarda — A391

Litho. & Engr.

2011, Oct. 14 ***Perf. 11¾***
625 A391 €1.10 multi 2.60 1.75

Printed in sheets of 4 + 2 labels.

Fish-shaped Honey Cake — A392

Perf. 11¾x11¼

2011, Nov. 11 **Litho.**
626 A392 40c multi 1.00 .65

Booklet Stamp
Self-Adhesive

Serpentine Die Cut 16½x15

627 A392 40c multi 1.00 .65
a. Booklet pane of 10 10.00

Christmas. No. 626 is impregnated with a cinnamon scent.

Art Type of 1996

Design: Woodcut of Historian Ján Sambucus (1534-81), by Tobias Stimmer.

Litho. & Engr.

2011, Nov. 25 ***Perf. 11¾***
628 A126 €1.20 blk & beige 2.75 1.75

Mailbox and Postrider — A393

2011, Dec. 2 **Litho.** ***Perf. 11¾x11¼***
629 A393 50c multi + label 1.25 .80

Stamp Day.

Souvenir Sheet

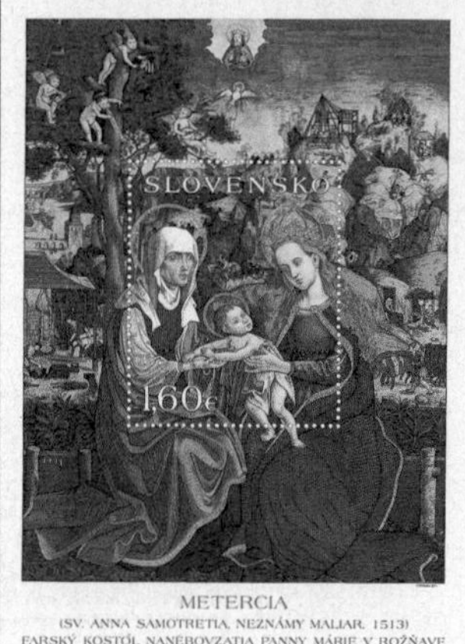
Virgin and Child with St. Anne (Roznava Metercia), by Unknown Artist — A394

Litho. & Engr.

2011, Dec. 13 ***Perf. 11¾***
630 A394 €1.60 multi 3.75 3.00

Architecture and Architectural Decorations Type of 2009

Design: Angel, Piarist Church, Prievidza.

Photo. & Engr.

2012, Jan. 27 ***Perf. 11¾x11¼***
631 A346 80c multi 1.90 1.25

Jonás Záborsky (1812-76), Writer — A395

2012, Feb. 3 **Litho.**
632 A395 40c multi 1.00 .65

Samo Chalupka (1812-83), Poet — A396

2012, Feb. 27
633 A396 50c multi 1.25 .80

Christ Carrying the Cross, by Hans von Aachen A397

2012, Mar. 9 ***Perf. 11¾x11¼***
634 A397 40c multi 1.00 .65

Booklet Stamp
Self-Adhesive

Serpentine Die Cut 16½x15

635 A397 40c multi 1.00 .65
a. Booklet pane of 10 10.00

Souvenir Sheet

Ján Koniarek (1878-1952), Sculptor — A398

Perf. 11¾x11½

2012, Apr. 13 **Litho. & Engr.**
636 A398 Sheet of 2, #636a + central label 5.00 3.50
a. €1.20 Single stamp 2.50 1.75

See Serbia No. 591.

Europa A399

2012, May 4 **Litho.** ***Perf. 11¾x11¼***
637 A399 90c multi 2.00 1.25

Printed in sheets of 8 + 4 labels.

Slovakian Men's Ice Hockey Team's Second-Place Finish in 2012 World Championships A400

2012, May 25 ***Perf. 11¼x11¾***
638 A400 40c multi 1.00 .60

Intl. Children's Day — A401

2012, June 1 ***Perf. 11¼x11¾***
639 A401 (40c) multi + label 1.00 .60

Booklet Stamp
Self-Adhesive

Serpentine Die Cut 15x16½

640 A401 (40c) multi 1.00 .60
a. Booklet pane of 10 10.00

No. 639 was printed in sheets of 8 stamps + 8 labels that could be personalized.

Souvenir Sheet

Battle of Rozhanovce, 700th Anniv. — A402

Litho. & Engr.

2012, June 15 ***Perf. 11¾***
641 A402 €1.20 multi 2.75 1.75

2012 Summer Olympics and Paralympics, London — A403

No. 642: a, Runners, Nike with sword, Greek bronze statue. b, London Eye, wheelchair racer, Slovakian Paralympics emblem.

Perf. 11¾x11¼

2012, June 28 **Litho.**
642 A403 90c Pair, #a-b 4.00 2.75

Church, Skalka A404

2012, July 13 **Photo. & Engr.**
643 A404 40c multi 1.00 .60

Basilica of Our Lady of Sorrows, Sastín — A405

2012, Sept. 14 ***Perf. 11½x11¾***
644 A405 40c lt blue & blue 1.00 .60

Souvenir Sheet

Anton Bernolák (1762-1813). Linguist — A406

2012, Oct. 3 **Litho. & Engr.**
645 A406 €1.10 multi 2.50 1.75

Souvenir Sheet

Flowers of the Low Tatras National Park — A407

No. 646: a, Loiseleuria procumbens. b, Saxifraga mutata.

2012, Oct. 12 ***Perf. 11¾***
646 A407 70c Sheet of 2, #a-b, + 3 labels 3.25 2.10

L'ubovna Castle
A408

2012, Nov. 8
647 A408 90c multi 2.00 1.25

Christmas
A409

Perf. 11¾x11¼

2012, Nov. 16 Litho.
648 A409 40c multi 1.00 .60

Booklet Stamp
Self-Adhesive

Serpentine Die Cut 16½x15

649 A409 40c multi 1.00 .60
a. Booklet pane of 10 10.00

Art Type of 1996

Design: Untitled painting by Viera Zilincanová, horiz.

2012, Nov. 23 Engr. *Perf. 11¾*
650 A126 €1.20 multi 2.75 1.75

No. 650 was printed in sheets of 4 + central label.

Souvenir Sheet

Sala Terrena Fresco, Cerveny Kamen Castle — A410

2012, Nov. 23 Litho. & Engr.
651 A410 €1.60 multi 3.50 2.50

Pavol Sochán (1862-1941), Photographer — A411

2012, Dec. 3 Litho. *Perf. 11¾x11¼*
652 A411 50c multi + label 1.25 .80

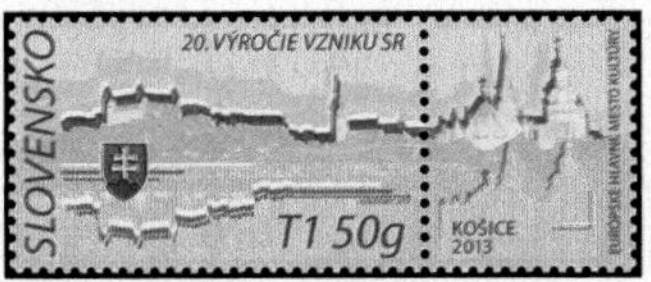

Slovak Republic, 20th Anniv. — A412

2013, Jan. 1
653 A412 (65c) multi + label 1.50 1.00

Architecture and Architectural Decorations Type of 2009

Design: Putti with theater mask, Empire Theater, Hlohovec.

2013, Jan. 25 Photo. & Engr.
654 A346 90c multi 2.00 1.40

Ján Popluhár (1935-2011), Soccer Player — A413

2013, Feb. 14 Litho.
655 A413 65c multi 1.50 .85

Easter — A414

2013, Mar. 1 *Perf. 11¼x11¾*
656 A414 45c multi 1.00 .60

Booklet Stamp
Self-Adhesive

Serpentine Die Cut 15x16½

657 A414 45c multi 1.00 .60
a. Booklet pane of 10 10.00

Dominik Tatarka (1913-89), Writer — A415

2013, Mar. 14 *Perf. 11¾x11¼*
658 A415 65c multi 1.40 .85

Breast Cancer Awareness — A416

2013, Apr. 12 *Perf. 11¼x11¾*
659 A416 €1.10 multi 2.50 1.50

Windmill, Holic — A417

2013, Apr. 26 Photo. & Engr.
660 A417 (45c) multi 1.25 .60

Europa
A418

2013, May 9 Litho. *Perf. 11¾x11¼*
661 A418 90c multi 2.25 1.25

Booklet Stamp
Self-Adhesive

Serpentine Die Cut 16½x15

662 A418 90c multi 2.25 1.25
a. Booklet pane of 6 14.00

Lúcnica Art Ensemble Dancers, Slovakia — A419

Pansori Performers, South Korea — A420

Perf. 11½x11¾

2013, May 31 Litho. & Engr.
663 A419 €1 multi 2.50 1.50
664 A420 €1 multi 2.50 1.50

Nos. 663-664 were printed in sheets of 6 containing 3 of each stamp. See South Korea No. 2405.

Sun and Zodiac Symbols — A421

2013, June 7 Litho. *Perf. 11¼x11¾*
665 A421 (45c) multi + label 1.10 .70

No. 665 was printed in sheets of 8 + 8 labels that could be personalized.

Souvenir Sheet

Mission of Sts. Cyril and Methodius to Slavic Lands, 1150th Anniv. — A422

Litho. & Engr.

2013, June 12 *Perf. 11¾*
666 A422 €1.60 multi 4.00 2.50

See Bulgaria No. 4647, Czech Republic No. 3573, Vatican City No. 1536.

Gorazd Zvonicky (1913-95), Missionary and Poet — A423

Perf. 11¾x11¼

2013, June 28 Litho.
667 A423 65c multi 1.50 .85

Matica Slovenská Foundation, 150th Anniv. — A424

2013, Aug. 2 Litho. *Perf. 11¾*
668 A424 80c multi 1.75 1.10

Printed in sheets of 8 + 1 label

2013 Biennale of Illustrations, Bratislava — A425

2013, Sept. 2 Litho. *Perf. 11¼x11¾*
669 A425 (45c) multi 1.10 .70

Tatra Mountains — A426

Designs: €1.25, Small Cold Valley. €1.45, Chalet at Zelene Pleso.

Photo. & Engr.

2013, Sept. 20 *Perf. 11¼x11¾*
670-671 A426 Set of 2 6.00 4.25

Minerals — A427

No. 672: a, Scepter quartz crystal from Sobova (denomination at UL). b, Opal from Dubnik (denomination at LR).

Perf. 11¾x11½

2013, Oct. 11 Litho. & Engr.
672 A427 60c Horiz. pair, #a-b 3.00 1.60

Printed in sheets of 6, containing 3 each No. 672a and No. 672b.

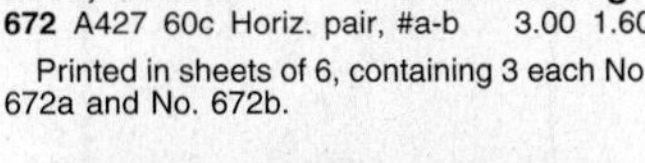

A428

Christmas — A429

2013 Litho. *Perf. 11¼x11¾*

673 A428 45c multi + label 1.10 .60
674 A429 45c multi 1.00 .60

**Booklet Stamp
Self-Adhesive**

Serpentine Die Cut 15x16½

675 A428 45c multi 1.00 .60
a. Booklet pane of 10 10.00

Issued: Nos. 673, 675, 11/4; No. 674, 11/13. No. 673 was printed in sheets of 8 + 8 labels that could be personalized.

No. 675 is impregnated with a baked apple scent.

Art Type of 1996

Designs: €1.20, Po Dojeni (After Milking), photograph by Martin Martincek. €1.25, Portrait of Count Jan Joseph Hadik de Futak, by Ján Jakub Stunder.

2013, Nov. 29 Engr. *Perf. 11¾*
676-677 A126 Set of 2 6.00 3.75

Drawing by Igor Rumansky (1946-2006), Stamp Designer — A430

Photo. & Engr.

2013, Dec. 6 *Perf. 11¾x11¼*
678 A430 65c multi + label 1.50 1.00

Stamp Day.

Architecture and Architectural Decorations Type of 2009

Design: Synagogue, Levice, horiz.

Photo. & Engr.

2014, Jan. 2 *Perf. 11¼x11¾*
679 A346 65c multi 1.50 1.00

2014 Winter Olympics, Sochi, Russia — A431

2014, Jan. 15 Litho. *Perf. 11¾x11¼*
680 A431 90c multi 2.50 1.25

2014 Winter Paralympics, Sochi, Russia — A432

2014, Jan. 15 Litho. *Perf. 11¾x11¼*
681 A432 90c multi 2.25 1.25

International Year of Crystallography — A433

Perf. 11¾x11¼

2014, Feb. 14 Litho.
682 A433 €1 multi + label 2.50 1.40

Easter — A434

Perf. 11¼x11¾

2014, Mar. 10 Litho.
683 A434 45c multi 1.10 .60

**Booklet Stamp
Self-Adhesive**

***Serpentine Die Cut 11½x11¼
Syncopated***

684 A434 45c multi 1.10 .60
a. Booklet pane of 10 11.00

Stefan Osusky (1889-1973), Diplomat A435

Photo. & Engr.

2014, Mar. 31 *Perf. 11¾x11¼*
685 A435 45c multi 1.10 .60

Motorcycles — A436

Designs: €1.10, Manet M90. €1.25, Jawa 50/550 Pionier.

Photo. & Engr.

2014, Apr. 17 *Perf. 11¾x11¼*
686-687 A436 Set of 2 6.00 3.25

Bagpipes — A437

2014, May 5 Litho. *Perf. 11¼x11¾*
688 A437 90c multi 2.25 1.25

**Booklet Stamp
Self-Adhesive**

Serpentine Die Cut 16½x15

689 A437 90c multi 2.25 1.25
a. Booklet pane of 6 14.00

Europa.

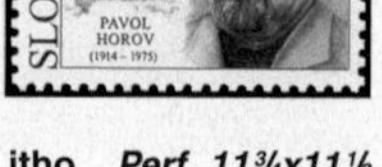

Pavol Horov (1914-75), Poet — A438

2014, May 23 Litho. *Perf. 11¾x11½*
690 A438 45c multi 1.25 .60

Regietów, Poland World War I Cemetery Memorials Designed by Dusan Jurkovic — A439

2014, June 2 Litho. *Perf. 11¾x11½*
691 A439 65c multi 1.75 .90

Dandelion and Ladybug — A440

2014, June 6 Litho. *Perf. 11¼x11¾*
692 A440 (45c) multi + label 1.25 .60

No. 692 was printed in sheets of 8 + 8 labels that could be personalized.

Pres. Andrej Kiska — A441

Photo. & Engr.

2014, June 13 *Perf. 11¾x11¼*
693 A441 45c multi 1.25 .60

Slovak National Uprising Monument, Banská Bystrica A442

2014, Aug. 29 Litho. *Perf. 11¼*
694 A442 65c multi 1.75 .85

Slovak National Uprising, 70th anniv.

Wedding Palace, Bytca A443

Litho. & Engr.

2014, Sept. 19 *Perf. 11¾*
695 A443 €1.30 blk & gray 3.25 1.60

No. 695 was printed in sheets of 8 + label.

Father Andrej Hlinka (1864-1938), Politician — A444

2014, Sept. 26 Litho. *Perf. 11¾*
696 A444 80c multi 2.10 1.10

No. 696 was printed in sheets of 4 + label.

International Peace Marathon, Kosice, 90th Anniv. — A445

2014, Oct. 5 Litho. *Perf. 12*
697 A445 45c multi 1.10 .55

Souvenir Sheet

Insects in Sitno National Nature Reserve — A446

No. 698: a, Oryctes nasicornis. b, Lucanus cervus.

Litho. & Engr.

2014, Oct. 10 *Perf. 11¾*
698 A446 80c Sheet of 2, #a-b, + 2 labels 4.00 2.00

Obverse and Reverse of Silver Half Denarius of King Charles II of Western Francia — A447

Litho. & Engr.

2014, Nov. 6 *Perf. 11¾*
699 A447 €1 multi + 2 labels 2.50 1.25

History of customs in central Europe.

Christmas

A448 A449

2014 Litho. *Perf. 11¼x11¾*
700 A448 45c multi 1.10 .55
701 A449 (45c) multi 1.10 .55

**Booklet Stamp
Self-Adhesive**

Serpentine Die Cut 15x16½

702 A449 (45c) multi 1.10 .55
a. Booklet pane of 10 11.00

Issued: No. 700, 11/14; Nos. 701-702, 11/13.

Art Type of 1996

Designs: €1.30, Portrait of the Artist's Wife, by Peter Michal Bohún. €1.65, Dying Deer, sculpture by Alojz Stróbl, horiz.

Litho. & Engr.

2014, Nov. 25 *Perf. 11¾*
703 A126 €1.30 multi 3.25 1.60

Souvenir Sheet

704 A126 €1.65 multi 4.25 2.10

Severín Zrubec (1921-2011), Philatelist — A450

Photo. & Engr.

2014, Dec. 5 ***Perf. 11¼x11½***
705 A450 60c multi + 2 labels 1.50 .75

Stamp Day.

Architecture and Architectural Decorations Type of 2009

Design: Andrassy Mausoleum, Krásnohorské Podhradie.

Photo. & Engr.

2015, Jan. 2 ***Perf. 11¾x11¼***
706 A346 €1.15 multi 2.75 .40

Heart and QR Code — A451

2015, Jan. 30 Litho. ***Perf. 11¼x11¾***
707 A451 (45c) red & blue + label 1.10 .55

No. 707 was printed in sheets of 8 + 8 labels that could be personalized.

Stefan Pilárik (1615-93), Poet and Priest A452

2015, Feb. 6 Litho. ***Perf. 12***
708 A452 60c multi 1.40 .70

Head of Christ, by Karol Ondreicka (1898-1961) A453

2015, Mar. 6 Litho. ***Perf. 11¼x11¾***
709 A453 45c multi 1.00 .50

Booklet Stamp Self-Adhesive

Serpentine Die Cut 15x16½
710 A453 45c multi 1.00 .50
a. Booklet pane of 10 10.00

Easter.

Bone Marrow Transplant Unit of University Children's Hospital and Clinic, Bratislava, 20th Anniv. — A454

2015, Mar. 16 Litho. ***Perf. 12***
711 A454 €1.15 multi 2.60 1.25

Vladimír Dzurilla (1942-95), Ice Hockey Goaltender — A455

Perf. 11¾x11¼

2015, Mar. 31 Litho.
712 A455 80c multi + label 3.00 1.50

Locomotives — A456

Designs: No. 713, 45c, 4.98.104 Albatros. No. 714, 45c, 464.001 steam locomotive.

Photo. & Engr.

2015, Apr. 17 ***Perf. 11¾x11¼***
713-714 A456 Set of 2 2.10 1.10

Europa A457

2015, May 5 Litho. ***Perf. 11¾x11¼***
715 A457 90c multi 2.10 1.10

Booklet Stamp Self-Adhesive

Die Cut Perf. 16½x15
716 A457 90c multi 2.10 1.10
a. Booklet pane of 6 13.00

End of World War II, 70th Anniv. — A458

2015, May 8 Litho. ***Perf. 11¼x11¾***
717 A458 €1 multi 2.25 1.10

Souvenir Sheet

Academia Istropolitana, Bratislava, 550th Anniv. — A459

Litho. & Engr.

2015, June 26 ***Perf. 11¾***
718 A459 €1.40 multi 3.25 1.60

St. John Bosco (1815-88) — A460

Litho. & Engr.

2015, Aug. 14 ***Perf. 11¾***
719 A460 €1.20 multi 2.75 1.40

2015 Biennal of Illustrations, Bratislava A461

2015, Sept. 2 Litho. ***Perf. 12***
720 A461 45c multi 2.00 1.00

Landscapes — A462

Designs: 80c, Súl'ov Rocks. 90c, Manín Gorge, vert.

Perf. 11¾x11¼, 11¼x11¾

2015, Sept. 18 Photo. & Engr.
721-722 A462 Set of 2 4.00 2.00

Souvenir Sheet

Nature Protection — A463

No. 723: a, Lutra lutra (54x22mm). b, Ciconia nigra (27x45mm).

Litho. & Engr.

2015, Oct. 9 ***Perf. 11¾***
723 A463 65c Sheet of 2, #a-b, + 5 labels 3.00 1.50

L'udovit Stúr (1815-56), Slovak Nationalist and Writer — A464

Photo. & Engr.

2015, Oct. 23 ***Perf. 11¼x11¾***
724 A464 €1 multi 2.25 1.10

National Cancer Institute, Bratislava, 25th Anniv. A465

2015, Nov. 5 Litho. ***Perf. 12½x12¾***
725 A465 €1.10 multi 2.40 1.25

Children's Drawing of Fish — A466

Madonna of the Mountains, by Karol Ondreicka — A467

Perf. 11¾x11¼

2015, Nov. 13 Litho.
726 A466 (45c) multi .95 .50

Perf. 11¼x11¾
727 A467 45c multi .95 .50

Booklet Stamp Self-Adhesive

Serpentine Die Cut 15x16½
728 A467 45c multi .95 .50
a. Booklet pane of 10 9.50

Christmas.

Art Type of 1996

Designs: €1.20, Hail to You, Blessed Source of Health, by Alfons Mucha. €1.50, House of Culture, Skalica, designed by Dusan Samuel Jurkovic, horiz.

2015, Nov. 25 Litho. ***Perf. 11¾***
729 A126 €1.20 multi 2.60 1.40

Litho. & Engr.

Souvenir Sheet
730 A126 €1.50 multi 3.25 1.60

Bratislava Main Post Office — A468

Photo. & Engr.

2015, Dec. 4 ***Perf. 11¾x11¼***
731 A468 65c multi + label 1.40 .70

Slovak Police Force, 25th Anniv. — A469

2016, Jan. 25 Litho. ***Perf. 12***
732 A469 (65c) multi 1.40 .70

2016 European Figure Skating Championships, Bratislava — A470

2016, Jan. 27 Litho. ***Perf. 11¾x11¼***
733 A470 90c multi 2.00 1.00

Architecture and Architectural Decorations Type of 2009

Design: Green Frog Swimming Pool, Trencianske Teplice, horiz.

Photo. & Engr.
2016, Feb. 10 ***Perf. 11¼x11¾***
734 A346 €1.60 multi 3.50 1.75

Easter — A471

Perf. 11¼x11¾
2016, Feb. 26 Litho.
735 A471 45c multi 1.00 .50

Booklet Stamp Self-Adhesive

Sawtooth Die Cut 10¼
736 A471 45c multi 1.00 .50
a. Booklet pane of 10 10.00

Matej Hrebenda (1796-1880), Writer and Book Seller A472

Photo. & Engr.
2016, Mar. 10 ***Perf. 11¼***
737 A472 65c pur brn & red 1.50 .75

1894 Umrath Traction Engine A473

Photo. & Engr.
2016, Apr. 15 ***Perf. 11¼***
738 A473 €1.15 multi 2.75 1.40

Peter Sagan, Winner of 2015 World Road Cycling Championships — A474

2016, Apr. 21 Litho. ***Perf. 11¾x11¼***
739 A474 €1 multi 3.50 1.75

Europa A475

2016, May 5 Litho. ***Perf. 11¾x11¼***
740 A475 90c multi 2.00 1.00

Booklet Stamp Self-Adhesive

Serpentine Die Cut 16½x15
741 A475 90c multi 2.00 1.00
a. Booklet pane of 6 12.00

Think Green Issue.

Flying Bird with Mail Bag — A476

2016, June 3 Litho. ***Perf. 11¾x11¼***
742 A476 (45c) multi + label 1.00 .50

No. 742 was printed in sheets of 8 + 8 labels that could be personalized.

Jan Jessenius (1566-1621), Physician and Professor of Anatomy — A477

Photo. & Engr.
2016, June 22 ***Perf. 11¼x11¾***
743 A477 90c multi + label 2.00 1.00

See Czech Republic No. 3677, Hungary No. 4393, Poland No. 4232.

A478

Design: Slovakian Presidency of the Council of the European Union.

Sawtooth Die Cut 11
2016, July 1 Litho.
Self-Adhesive
744 A478 €1.40 multi 3.25 1.60

2016 Summer Olympics, Rio de Janeiro — A479

2016, July 8 Litho. ***Perf. 11¾x11¼***
745 A479 €1 multi 2.25 1.10

No. 745 was printed in sheets of 30 + 20 labels.

2016 Summer Paralympics, Rio de Janeiro — A480

2016, July 8 Litho. ***Perf. 11¼x11¾***
746 A480 €1 multi 2.25 1.10

101st World Esperanto Congress — A481

2016, July 23 Litho. ***Perf. 11¾x11¼***
747 A481 €1.20 multi 2.75 1.40

Herl'any Geyser — A482

Litho. & Engr.
2016, Sept. 19 ***Perf. 11¾***
748 A482 80c multi 1.90 .95

Souvenir Sheet

Flora of Súr National Nature Reserve — A483

No. 749: a, Frangula alnus. b, Alnus glutinosa. c, Dryopteris carthusiana.

Litho. & Engr.
2016, Oct. 7 ***Perf. 11¾***
749 A483 65c Sheet of 3, #a-c 4.50 2.25

Art of the Slovak National Gallery, Bratislava — A484

Designs: No. 750, €1.40, Chess Composition, painting by Ester Simerová-Martinceková. No. 751, €1.40, Untitled sculpture by Maria Bartuszová.

Litho. & Engr.
2016, Oct. 24 ***Perf. 11¾***
750-751 A484 Set of 2 6.25 3.25

Three Magi, by Vaneska Peceková A485

Bobbin Lace Angel A486

Perf. 11¼x11¾
2016, Nov. 11 Litho.
752 A485 (50c) multi 1.10 .55
753 A486 50c multi 1.10 .55

Booklet Stamp Self-Adhesive

Sawtooth Die Cut 10x10¼
754 A486 50c multi 1.10 .55
a. Booklet pane of 10 11.00

Christmas.

Frantisek Dibarbora (1916-87), Actor A487

2016, Nov. 18 Litho. ***Perf. 12***
755 A487 85c black 1.90 .95

Piest'any Post Office — A488

Photo. & Engr.
2016, Dec. 2 ***Perf. 11¾x11¼***
756 A488 95c multi + label 2.10 1.10

Stamp Day.

Architecture and Architectural Decorations Type of 2009

Design: Slovak University of Agriculture, Nitra, horiz.

Photo. & Engr.
2017, Jan. 9 ***Perf. 11¼x11¾***
757 A346 €1.25 multi 2.75 1.40

International Physics Olympiad, Yogyakarta, Indonesia — A489

Perf. 11¼x11¾
2017, Feb. 10 Litho.
758 A489 €1.45 multi 3.25 1.60

Souvenir Sheet

Apparition of the Virgin Mary at Fatima, Portugal, Cent. — A490

2017, Mar. 13 Litho. ***Perf. 12***
759 A490 €1.60 gold & multi 3.50 1.75

See Luxembourg No. 1461, Poland No. 4277, Portugal No. 3888.

Jozef Miloslav Hurban (1817-88), Writer and Leader of Slovak National Council — A491

Photo. & Engr.

2017, Mar. 17 ***Perf. 11¼x11¾***
760 A491 50c multi 1.10 .55

Uniform of Jewish Concentration Camp Internee — A492

Perf. 11¼x11¾

2017, Mar. 24 **Litho.**
761 A492 85c multi 1.90 .95

First deportation of Slovakian Jews to concentration camps, 75th anniv.

Easter — A493

Perf. 11¼x11¾

2017, Mar. 24 **Litho.**
762 A493 50c multi 1.10 .55

Booklet Stamp
Self-Adhesive

Sawtooth Die Cut 10x10¼

763 A493 50c multi 1.10 .55
a. Booklet pane of 10 11.00

Orava Dam A494

Photo. & Engr.

2017, Apr. 21 ***Perf. 11¾x11¼***
764 A494 95c multi 2.10 1.10

Lietava Castle A495

2017, May 5 **Litho.** ***Perf. 11¾x11¼***
765 A495 90c multi 2.00 1.00

Booklet Stamp
Self-Adhesive

Serpentine Die Cut 16½x15

766 A495 90c multi 2.00 1.00
a. Booklet pane of 6 12.00

Europa.

Buildings in Bratislava and Kosice in Slovakian Coat of Arms — A496

2017, June 2 **Litho.** ***Perf. 11¼x11¾***
767 A496 (50c) multi + label 1.25 .60

No. 767 was printed in sheets of 8 + 8 labels that could be personalized.

Andrej Radlinsky (1817-79), Priest and Language Researcher A497

Litho. & Engr.

2017, July 7 ***Perf. 11¾***
768 A497 €1.30 multi 3.25 1.60

2017 Biennal of Illustrations, Bratislava A498

2017, Sept. 4 **Litho.** ***Perf. 12***
769 A498 50c multi 1.25 .60

Andrej Kvasnák (1936-2007), Soccer Player, Václav Nedomansky, Ice Hockey Player, and Július Torma (1922-91), Boxer — A499

2017, Sept. 7 **Litho.** ***Perf. 11¼x11¾***
770 A499 €1 multi + label 2.40 1.25

Radvan Fair, 360th Anniv. — A500

2017, Sept. 8 **Litho.** ***Die Cut***
Self-Adhesive
771 A500 €1.65 multi 4.00 2.00

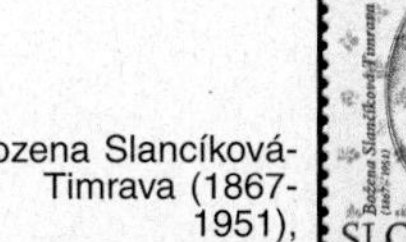

Bozena Slancíková-Timrava (1867-1951), Writer — A501

Photo. & Engr.

2017, Oct. 2 ***Perf. 11¼x11½***
772 A501 85c multi 2.00 1.00

Mushrooms — A502

No. 773: a, Caloscypha fulgens. b, Clavaria zollingeri.

Perf. 11½x11¾

2017, Oct. 12 **Litho. & Engr.**
773 Vert. pair 3.00 1.50
a.-b. A502 65c Either single 1.50 .75

No. 773 was printed in sheets containing three each Nos. 773a and 773b.

Portrait of Ms. Juppová, by Jozef Bozetech Klemens — A503

Altar, Church of St. James, Levoca — A504

Litho. & Engr.

2017, Oct. 23 ***Perf. 11¾***
774 A503 €1.20 multi 2.75 1.40

Souvenir Sheet

775 A504 €2.60 multi + 2 labels 6.00 3.00

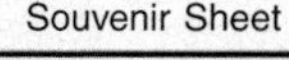

Souvenir Sheet

Organ From Wooden Articular Church, Kezmarok — A505

Litho. & Engr.

2017, Oct. 31 ***Perf. 11¾***
776 A505 €1.15 multi + label 2.75 1.40

Protestant Reformation, 500th anniv.

Snowman A506

Folk Painting From Church of Our Lady of Seven Sorrows, Vajnory — A507

2017 **Litho.** ***Perf. 13½***
777 A506 (50c) multi 1.25 .60
778 A507 50c multi 1.25 .60

Booklet Stamp
Self-Adhesive

Die Cut Perf. 9¾x9½

779 A507 50c multi 1.25 .60
a. Booklet pane of 10 12.50

Christmas. Issued: No. 777, 11/10; Nos. 778-779, 11/16.

BECEP Traffic Safety — A508

Perf. 13¾x13½

2017, Nov. 24 **Litho.**
780 A508 50c multi 1.25 .60

Jozef Vlcek (1902-71), Stamp Designer — A509

2017, Dec. 4 **Litho.** ***Perf. 13½x13¾***
781 A509 95c multi + label 2.40 1.25

Stamp Day.

Bratislava Castle and Slovakian Coat of Arms — A510

Photo. & Engr.

2018, Jan. 2 ***Perf. 11¾x11½***
782 A510 €1.60 multi 4.00 2.00

Independent Slovakia, 25th anniv.

Monument, Central Military Cemetery of the Royal Romanian Army, Zvolen — A511

2018, Jan. 5 **Litho.** ***Perf. 13½x13¾***
783 A511 €1.30 multi 3.25 1.60

See Romania No. 6048.

2018 Winter Olympics, PyeongChang, South Korea — A512

2018, Jan. 19 **Litho.** ***Perf. 13½x13¾***
784 A512 €1 multi 2.50 1.25

Architecture and Architectural Decoration Type of 2009

Design: Vseobecná Uverová Bank, Bratislava.

Photo. & Engr.

2018, Feb. 16 ***Perf. 11¾x11¼***
785 A346 €1.45 multi 3.50 1.75

2018 Winter Paralympics, PyeongChang, South Korea — A513

Perf. 13½x13¾

2018, Feb. 23 **Litho.**
786 A513 €1 multi 2.50 1.25

Embroidered Parament A514

Die Cut Perf. 9½x9¾

2018, Feb. 27 **Litho.**

Self-Adhesive

787 A514 (50c) multi 1.25 .60
a. Booklet pane of 10 12.50

Easter. No. 787 was printed in sheets of 40 and booklet panes of 10.

Adam Frantisek Kollár (1718-83), Historian and Library Director — A515

2018, Mar. 1 **Litho.** ***Perf. 13¾x13½***
788 A515 50c multi 1.25 .60

Karol L. Zachar (1918-2003), Stage Actor and Director — A516

2018, Mar. 14 **Litho.** ***Perf. 13½***
789 A516 70c multi 1.75 .85

Prince's Bier, Poprad-Matejovice Archaelogical Site — A517

2018, Apr. 27 **Litho.** ***Perf. 13½***
790 A517 95c multi 2.25 1.10

Souvenir Sheet

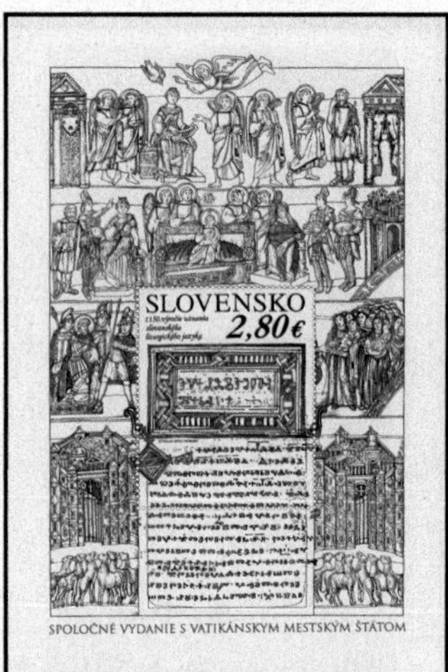

Old Church Slavonic Liturgical Language, 1150th Anniv. — A518

Litho. & Engr.

2018, May 3 ***Perf. 13½x14***
791 A518 €2.80 multi 6.50 3.25

Slovakia and Vatican City Joint Issue. See Vatican City No. 1686.

Slovak National Uprising Bridge, Bratislava — A519

2018, May 4 **Litho.** ***Perf. 13½***
792 A519 €1.10 multi 2.60 1.40

Booklet Stamp Self-Adhesive

Die Cut Perf. 9¾x9½

793 A519 €1.10 multi 2.60 1.40
a. Booklet pane of 6 16.00

Europa.

Power Plant, Piest'any A520

2018, May 18 **Litho.** ***Perf. 13½***
794 A520 50c multi 1.25 .60

Peonies — A521

2018, June 1 **Litho.** ***Perf. 13½***
795 A521 (50c) multi + label 1.25 .60

No. 795 was printed in sheets of 8 + 8 labels that could be personalized.

International Chemistry Olympiad, 50th Anniv. — A522

2018, June 15 **Litho.** ***Perf. 13½***
796 A522 €1.25 multi 3.00 1.50

Coronation of King Ferdinand II of Hungary, 400th Anniv. — A523

2018, June 22 **Litho.** ***Perf. 14x13½***
797 A523 €1.70 multi 4.00 2.00

Slovakia in European Council, 25th Anniv. A524

Sawtooth Die Cut 2¾

2018, June 27 **Litho.**

Self-Adhesive

798 A524 €1.25 multi 3.00 1.50

Bratislava City Museum, 150th Anniv. — A525

2018, June 30 **Litho.** ***Perf. 13½***
799 A525 €1.30 multi 3.00 1.50

Souvenir Sheet

The Man with Bared Chest in Front of the Occupying Tank, Photograph by Ladislav Bielik (1939-84) — A526

Litho. & Engr.

2018, Aug. 21 ***Perf. 14x13½***
800 A526 €1.80 multi 4.25 2.10

Czechoslovakian Uprising, 50th anniv.

Minerals — A527

No. 801: a, Libethenite. b, Euchroite.

Perf. 11¾x11½

2018, Oct. 12 **Litho. & Engr.**
801 Horiz. pair 7.50 3.75
a.-b. A527 €1.65 Either single 3.75 1.75

No. 801 was printed in sheets containing three each Nos. 801a and 801b.

Madonna and Child Icon, Krásny Brod A528

Litho. & Engr.

2018, Oct. 19 ***Perf. 13½x14***
802 A528 €1.40 multi 3.25 1.60

Printed in sheets of 4 + label.

Slovak Girl in Costume — A529

Litho. & Engr.

2018, Oct. 26 ***Perf. 14x13½***
803 A529 €1.90 multi 4.50 2.25

Independence of Czechoslovakia, cent.

A530

Christmas A531

2018, Nov. 9 **Litho.** ***Perf. 13½***
804 A530 (50c) multi 1.25 .60
805 A531 (50c) multi 1.25 .60

Booklet Stamp
Self-Adhesive
Die Cut Perf. 9½x9¾

806 A531 (50c) multi 1.25 .60
a. Booklet pane of 10 12.50

No. 805 was issued with and without an attached label.

Map From Science Book by Ibrahim Hakki (1705-72) — A532

2018, Nov. 27 **Litho.** ***Perf. 14x13½***
807 A532 €1.30 multi 3.00 1.50

Joint Issue between Slovakia and Turkey. See Turkey No. 3630.

Czechoslovakia Type A1, Designed by Alfons Mucha (1860-1939) — A533

2018, Dec. 3 **Litho.** ***Perf. 13½***
808 A533 95c multi + label 2.25 1.10

Stamp Day.

Slovakian Chairmanship of Organization for Security and Cooperation in Europe — A534

2019, Jan. 2 **Litho.** ***Perf. 13½***
809 A534 (50c) multi 1.25 .60

Michael Strank (1919-45), U.S. Soldier Who Helped Raise Flag at Iwo Jima — A535

2019, Mar. 1 **Litho.** ***Perf. 13¾x13½***
810 A535 €1 mulkti 2.25 1.10

Bird Made of Wire — A536

Perf. 13½x13¾

2019, Mar. 15 **Litho.**
811 A536 (50c) multi 1.10 .55

Booklet Stamp
Self-Adhesive
Die Cut Perf. 9½x9¾

812 A536 (50c) multi 1.10 .55
a. Booklet pane of 10 11.00

Traditional Slovak Tinker.

Timekeeping Devices — A537

No. 813: a, Pleterje Charterhouse sundial, Drca, Slovenia. b, Astronomical clock, Stará Bystrica, Slovakia.

2019, Mar. 22 **Litho.** ***Perf. 13½***
813 A537 €1.20 Horiz. pair, #a.-b. 5.50 2.75

See Slovenia No. 1326.

International Civil Aviation Organization, 75th Anniv. — A538

2019, Apr. 4 **Litho.** ***Perf. 13½***
814 A538 (70c) multi 1.60 .80

Coracias Garrulus A539

2019, May 3 **Litho.** ***Perf. 13½***
815 A539 €1.70 multi 4.00 2.00

Booklet Stamp
Self-Adhesive
Die Cut Perf. 9½x9¾

816 A539 €1.70 multi 4.00 2.00
a. Booklet pane of 6 24.00

Europa.

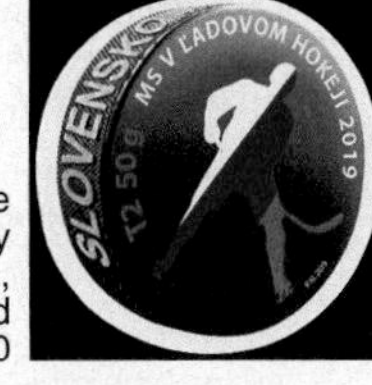

2019 World Ice Hockey Championships, Bratislava and Kosice — A540

2019, May 3 **Litho.** ***Die Cut***
Self-Adhesive
817 A540 (50c) multi 1.10 .55

Souvenir Sheet

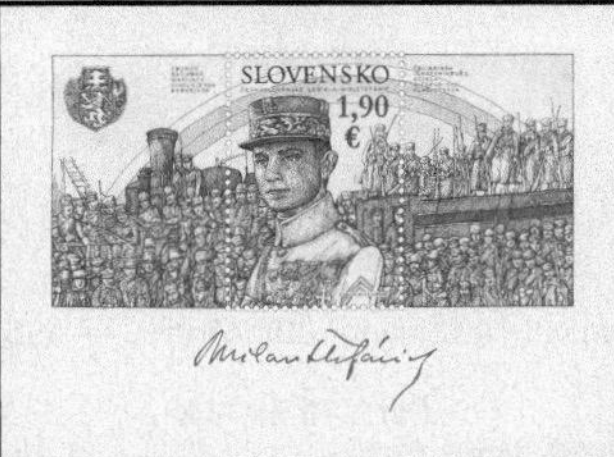

General Milan R. Stefanik (1880-1919), Diplomat — A541

Litho. & Engr.

2019, May 3 ***Perf. 11¾***
818 A541 €1.90 multi 4.25 2.10

Association of Slovak Philatelists, 50th Anniv. — A542

2019, May 17 **Litho.** ***Perf. 13½***
819 A542 (70c) multi + label 1.60 .80

International Mathematical Olympiad — A543

2019, June 7 **Litho.** ***Perf. 13½***
820 A543 €1.25 multi 3.00 1.50

Pres. Zuzana Caputová A544

2019, June 15 **Litho.** ***Perf. 13½***
821 A544 (50c) multi 1.10 .55

Demänovská Ice Cave — A545

Perf. 11½x11¾

2019, June 21 **Litho. & Engr.**
822 A545 €1.20 multi 2.75 1.40

John Amos Comenius (1592-1670), Philosopher, and Comenius University Building — A546

Litho. & Engr.

2019, June 27 ***Perf. 13½x14***
823 A546 €1.90 multi 4.50 2.25

Comenius University, cent.

Slovak National Uprising, 75th Anniv. A547

2019, Aug. 28 **Litho.** ***Perf. 13½***
824 A547 €1.55 multi 3.50 1.75

2019 Biennial of Illustrations, Bratislava A548

Sawtooth Die Cut 5½

2019, Sept. 3 **Litho.**
Self-Adhesive
825 A548 75c multi 1.75 .85

Martyrdom of St. Marko Krizin (1589-1619), St. Stephen Pongrácz (1584-1619), and St. Melchior Grodziecki (c. 1582-1619), 400th Anniv. — A549

2019, Sept. 6 **Litho.** ***Perf. 13½***
826 A549 €1.85 multi 4.00 2.00

Paris Peace Conference, Cent. — A550

2019, Sept. 10 **Litho.** ***Perf. 13½***
827 A550 €1.70 multi 3.75 1.90

Diplomatic Relations Between Slovakia and People's Republic of China, 70th Anniv. — A551

No. 828 — Archaeological discoveries: a, Bronze horse harness fitting, c. 795, Slovakia. b, Incense burner on hook, c. 880, People's Republic of China.

2019, Oct. 7 Litho. *Perf. 13½*
828 A551 €1.30 Horiz. pair. #a-b 5.75 3.00

See People's Republic of China No.

Pyrus Communis Tree and Fruit — A552

Litho. & Engr.
2019, Oct. 11 *Perf. 14x13½*
829 A552 €1.70 multi 3.75 1.90

House of D. V. Woo, Shanghai, Designed by Ladislav Hudec (1893-1958) — A553

Self-portrait with a Paper Cap, by Ernest Zmeták (1919-2004) — A554

Litho. & Engr.
2019, Oct. 18 *Perf. 14x13½*
830 A553 €2.10 multi 4.75 2.40

Perf. 13½x14
831 A554 €2.20 multi 5.00 2.50

Christmas Tree — A555

Wire Heart With Hooks — A556

2019, Nov. 8 Litho. *Perf. 13½*
832 A555 (65c) multi + label 1.50 .75
833 A556 (65c) multi 1.50 .75

Booklet Stamp
Self-Adhesive
Die Cut Perf. 9¾x9½
834 A556 (65c) multi 1.50 .75
a. Booklet pane of 10 15.00

Christmas. Labels on No. 832 could be personalized for an additional fee.

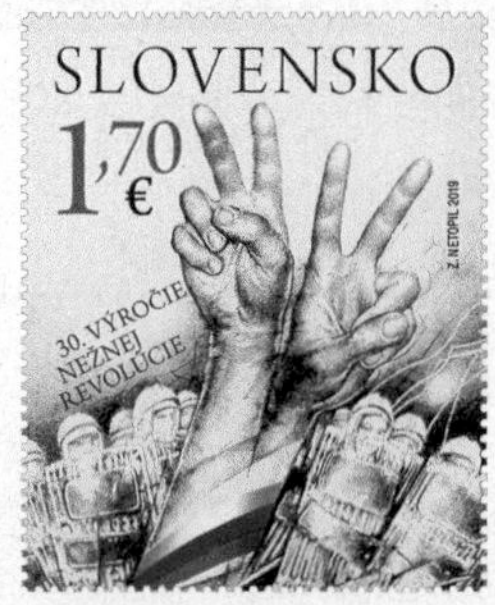

Velvet Revolution, 30th Anniv. — A557

Perf. 13½x13¾
2019, Nov. 13 Litho.
835 A557 €1.70 multi 3.75 1.90

Joint Issue between Slovakia and Czech Republic.
See Czech Republic No. 3809.

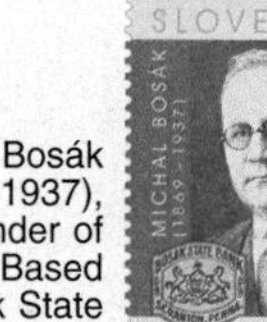

Michal Bosák (1869-1937), Founder of Pennsylvania-Based Bosak State Bank — A558

2019, Nov. 22 Litho. *Perf. 13½*
836 A558 €2 multi 4.50 2.25

Vincent Hloznik (1919-97), Stamp Designer — A559

2019, Dec. 3 Litho. *Perf. 13½*
837 A559 80c multi + label 1.75 .90

Stamp Day.

Nazi Massacres at Ostrom Grún and Kl'ak, 75th Anniv. — A560

Litho. & Engr.
2020, Jan. 17 *Perf. 14x13½*
838 A560 €1.90 multi 4.25 2.10

United Nations, 75th Anniv. A561

Sawtooth Die Cut 5½
2020, Feb. 14 Litho.
Self-Adhesive
839 A561 75c multi 1.75 .85

SEMI-POSTAL STAMPS

Catalogue values for unused stamps in this section are for Never Hinged items.

Josef Tiso — SP1

Wmk. 263
1939, Nov. 6 Photo. *Perf. 12½*
B1 SP1 2.50k + 2.50k royal blue 3.50 *4.00*

The surtax was used for Child Welfare.

Medical Corpsman and Wounded Soldier — SP2

1941, Nov. 10
B2 SP2 50h + 50h dull green .65 .65
B3 SP2 1k + 1k rose lake .65 .65
B4 SP2 2k + 1k brt blue 2.00 1.60
Nos. B2-B4 (3) 3.30 2.90

Mother and Child — SP3

1941, Dec. 10
B5 SP3 50h + 50h dull green 1.00 .90
B6 SP3 1k + 1k brown 1.00 .90
B7 SP3 2k + 1k violet 1.00 .90
Nos. B5-B7 (3) 3.00 2.70

Surtax for the benefit of child welfare.

Soldier and Hlinka Youth — SP4

1942, Mar. 14
B8 SP4 70h + 1k brown org .50 .40
B9 SP4 1.30k + 1k brt blue .50 .40
B10 SP4 2k + 1k rose red 1.60 1.20
Nos. B8-B10 (3) 2.60 2.00

The surtax aided the Hlinka Youth Society "Hlinkova Mladez."

SP5

SP6

National Costumes — SP7

1943 *Perf. 14*
B11 SP5 50h + 50h dk slate grn .30 .25
B12 SP6 70h + 1k dp carmine .30 .25
B13 SP7 80h + 2k dark blue .40 .40
Nos. B11-B13 (3) 1.00 .90

The surtax was for the benefit of children, the Red Cross and winter relief of the Slovakian popular party.

Infantrymen — SP8

Aviator — SP9

Tank and Gun Crew SP10

1943, July 28
B14 SP8 70h + 2k rose brown .80 *.95*
B15 SP9 1.30k + 2k sapphire .80 *.95*
B16 SP10 2k + 2k olive green .80 *.95*
Nos. B14-B16 (3) 2.40 2.85

The surtax was for soldiers' welfare.

"The Slovak Language Is Our Life" — L. Stur — SP11

Slovakian National Museum SP12

Slovakian Foundation SP13

Slovakian Peasant — SP14

1943, Oct. 16
B17 SP11 30h + 1k brown red .55 .40
B18 SP12 70h + 1k slate green .55 .40
B19 SP13 80h + 2k slate blue .55 .40
B20 SP14 1.30k + 2k dull brown .55 .40
Nos. B17-B20 (4) 2.20 1.60

The surtax was for the benefit of Slovakian cultural institutions.

Soccer Player — SP15

Skier — SP16

Diver — SP17

Relay Race — SP18

1944, Apr. 30 **Unwmk.**

B21	SP15	70h + 70h slate grn	.80	*1.00*
B22	SP16	1k + 1k violet	.80	*1.00*
B23	SP17	1.30k + 1.30k Prus bl	.80	*1.00*
B24	SP18	2k + 2k chnt brn	.80	*1.00*
		Nos. B21-B24 (4)	3.20	*4.00*

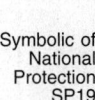

Symbolic of National Protection SP19

1944, Oct. 6 **Wmk. 263**

B25	SP19	70h + 4h sapphire	1.00	*1.20*
B26	SP19	1.30k + 4k red brown	1.00	*1.20*

The surtax was for the benefit of social institutions.

Children — SP20

1944, Dec. 18

B27	SP20	2k + 4k light blue	3.00	*4.00*
a.		Sheet of 8 + Label	50.00	*70.00*

The surtax was to aid social work for Slovak youth.

Red Cross — SP21

Photo. & Engr.

1993, Nov. 15 ***Perf. 11x11½***

B28	SP21	3k +1k red & gray blue	.55	.40

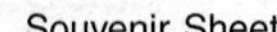
Souvenir Sheet

1996 Summer Olympics, Atlanta — SP22

Photo. & Engr.

1996, May 15 ***Perf. 12x11½***

B29	SP22	12k +2k multi	1.40	1.40

Surcharge for Slovak Olympic Committee.

AIR POST STAMPS

Catalogue values for unused stamps in this section are for Never Hinged items.

Planes over Tatra Mountains
AP1 AP2

Perf. 12½

1939, Nov. 20 **Photo.** **Unwmk.**

C1	AP1	30h violet	.40	.40
C2	AP1	50h dark green	.40	.40
C3	AP1	1k vermilion	.40	.40
C4	AP2	2k grnsh black	.65	.65
C5	AP2	3k dark brown	1.00	1.00
C6	AP2	4k slate blue	2.00	2.00
		Nos. C1-C6 (6)	4.85	4.85

See No. C10.

Plane in Flight — AP3

1940, Nov. 30 **Wmk. 263** ***Perf. 12½***

C7	AP3	5k dk violet brn	1.50	1.50
C8	AP3	10k gray black	1.75	1.75
C9	AP3	20k myrtle green	2.25	2.25
		Nos. C7-C9 (3)	5.50	5.50

Type of 1939

1944, Sept. 15 **Wmk. 263**

C10	AP1	1k vermilion	1.50	1.50

PERSONAL DELIVERY STAMPS

Catalogue values for unused stamps in this section are for Never Hinged items.

PD1

1940 **Wmk. 263** **Photo.** ***Imperf.***

EX1	PD1	50h indigo & blue	1.00	*1.75*
EX2	PD1	50h carmine & rose	1.00	*1.75*

POSTAGE DUE STAMPS

Catalogue values for unused stamps in this section are for Never Hinged items.

D1

1939 **Unwmk.** **Photo.** ***Perf. 12½***

J1	D1	5h bright blue	1.00	.75
J2	D1	10h bright blue	.50	.55
J3	D1	20h bright blue	.50	.55
J4	D1	30h bright blue	3.00	1.50
J5	D1	40h bright blue	.70	.75
J6	D1	50h bright blue	2.50	.90
J7	D1	60h bright blue	2.00	1.10
J8	D1	1k dark carmine	14.00	8.25
J9	D1	2k dark carmine	14.00	5.50
J10	D1	5k dark carmine	8.00	2.50
J11	D1	10k dark carmine	55.00	11.00
J12	D1	20k dark carmine	18.00	8.00
		Nos. J1-J12 (12)	119.20	41.35

1940-41 **Wmk. 263**

J13	D1	5h bright blue ('41)	.75	.55
J14	D1	10h bright blue ('41)	.30	.30
J15	D1	20h bright blue ('41)	.50	.30
J16	D1	30h bright blue ('41)	4.00	2.00
J17	D1	40h bright blue ('41)	.60	.55
J18	D1	50h bright blue ('41)	.75	.95
J19	D1	60h bright blue	.90	.95
J20	D1	1k dk car ('41)	.90	1.10
J21	D1	2k dk car ('41)	20.00	7.00
J22	D1	5k dk car ('41)	4.00	2.50
J23	D1	10k dk car ('41)	3.00	3.00
		Nos. J13-J23 (11)	35.70	19.20

Letter, Post Horn — D2

1942 **Unwmk.** ***Perf. 14***

J24	D2	10h deep brown	.25	.25
J25	D2	20h deep brown	.25	.25
J26	D2	40h deep brown	.25	.25
J27	D2	50h deep brown	1.00	.75
J28	D2	60h deep brown	.25	.25
J29	D2	80h deep brown	.30	.25
J30	D2	1k rose red	.35	.25
J31	D2	1.10k rose red	.70	.60
J32	D2	1.30k rose red	.50	.25
J33	D2	1.60k rose red	.50	.25
J34	D2	2k rose red	1.00	.25
J35	D2	2.60k rose red	1.50	1.25
J36	D2	3.50k rose red	11.00	9.00
J37	D2	5k rose red	3.75	2.25
J38	D2	10k rose red	4.50	3.25
		Nos. J24-J38 (15)	26.10	19.35

NEWSPAPER STAMPS

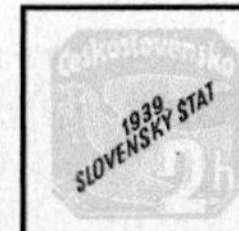

Newspaper Stamps of Czechoslovakia, 1937, Overprinted in Red or Blue

1939, Apr. **Unwmk.** ***Imperf.***

P1	N2	2h bister brn (Bl)	.50	.40
P2	N2	5h dull blue (R)	.50	.40
P3	N2	7h red org (Bl)	.50	.40
P4	N2	9h emerald (R)	.50	.40
P5	N2	10h henna brn (Bl)	.50	.40
P6	N2	12h ultra (R)	.50	.40
P7	N2	20h dk green (R)	1.10	.95
P8	N2	50h dk brown (Bl)	3.00	2.50
P9	N2	1k grnsh gray (R)	11.00	10.00
		Nos. P1-P9 (9)	18.10	15.85

Excellent counterfeits exist of Nos. P1-P9.

Catalogue values for unused stamps in this section, from this point to the end of the section, are for Never Hinged items.

Arms of Slovakia — N1

1939 **Typo.**

P10	N1	2h ocher	.30	.25
P11	N1	5h ultra	.45	.40
P12	N1	7h red orange	.35	.30
P13	N1	9h emerald	.35	.30
P14	N1	10h henna brown	1.60	1.10
P15	N1	12h dk ultra	.40	.35
P16	N1	20h dark green	1.60	1.10
P17	N1	50h red brown	1.90	1.25
P18	N1	1k grnsh gray	1.60	1.10
		Nos. P10-P18 (9)	8.55	6.15

1940-41 **Wmk. 263**

P20	N1	5h ultra	.25	.25
P23	N1	10h henna brown	.25	.25
P24	N1	15h brt purple ('41)	.30	.25
P25	N1	20h dark green	.60	.50
P26	N1	25h lt blue ('41)	.60	.50
P27	N1	40h red org ('41)	.60	.50
P28	N1	50h chocolate	1.10	.75
P29	N1	1k grnsh gray ('41)	1.10	.75
P30	N1	2k emerald ('41)	2.25	1.60
		Nos. P20-P30 (9)	7.05	5.35

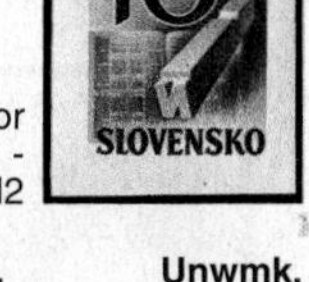

Type Block "N" (for "Noviny" - Newspaper) — N2

1943 **Photo.** **Unwmk.**

P31	N2	10h green	.25	.25
P32	N2	15h dark brown	.25	.25
P33	N2	20h ultra	.35	.35
P34	N2	50h rose red	.35	.35
P35	N2	1k slate green	.45	.45
P36	N2	2k intense blue	.65	.65
		Nos. P31-P36 (6)	2.30	2.30

SLOVENIA

slō-'vē-nē-ə

LOCATION — Southeastern Europe
GOVT. — Independent state
AREA — 7,819 sq. mi.
POP. — 1,970,570 (1999 est.)
CAPITAL — Ljubljana

A constituent republic of Yugoslavia since 1945, Slovenia declared its independence on June 25, 1991.

100 Paras = 1 Dinar
100 Stotin = 1 Tolar
100 Cents = 1 Euro (2007)

Catalogue values for unused stamps in this country are for Never Hinged items, beginning with Scott 100 in the regular postage section and Scott RA1 in the postal tax section.

Declaration of Independence A18

1991, June 26 Litho. *Perf. 10½*
100 A18 5d Parliament building 1.10 1.10

National Arms
A19 A20

1991-92 *Perf. 14*

Background Color

101	A19	1t brown	.35	.35
102	A20	1t brown	.35	.35
103	A20	2t lilac rose	.35	.35
104	A19	4t green	.35	.35
105	A20	4t green	.35	.35
106	A19	5t salmon	.35	.35
107	A20	5t salmon	.35	.35
108	A20	6t yellow	.50	.50
109	A19	11t orange	.70	.70
110	A20	11t orange	.50	.50
111	A20	15t blue	.50	.50
112	A20	20t purple	1.10	1.10
113	A20	50t dark green	1.60	1.60
114	A20	100t gray	2.60	2.60
		Nos. 101-114 (14)	9.95	9.95

Issued: No. 107, 3/6/91; No. 101, 104, 106, 109, 12/26/91; No. 102, 6t, 20t, 50t, 100t, 2/12/92; 2t, 15t, No. 105, 110, 3/16/92.

1992 Winter Olympics, Albertville — A21

a, 30t, Ski jumper. b, 50t, Alpine skier.

1992, Feb. 8
134 A21 Pair, #a.-b., + 1 or 2 labels 8.00 8.00

Rhomboid stamps issued in sheets of 3 No. 134 plus 4 labels. See No. 143.

Ljubljana Opera House, Cent. A22

1992, Mar. 31
135 A22 20t multicolored 1.10 1.10

Giuseppe Tartini (1692-1770), Italian Violinist and Composer A23

1992, Apr. 8
136 A23 27t multicolored 1.10 1.10

Discovery of America, 500th Anniv. — A24

Designs: a, 27t, Map of northwestern Mexico and Gulf of California, Marko Anton Kappus preaching to natives. b, 47t, Map of parts of North and South America, sailing ship.

1992, Apr. 21
137 A24 Pair, #a.-b. 7.25 7.25

Issued in sheets containing 6 No. 137.

Intl. Conference of Interior Designers, Ljubljana — A25

1992, May 17
138 A25 41t multicolored 1.50 1.50

A. M. Slomsek (1800-1862), Bishop of Maribor — A26

1992, May 29
139 A26 6t multicolored .65 .65

Mountain Rescue Service, 80th Anniv. — A27

1992, June 12
140 A27 41t multicolored 1.50 1.50

A28

1992, June 20
141 A28 6t multicolored .40 .40

Ljubljana Boatmen's Competition, 900th anniv.

A29

1992, June 25
142 A29 41t multicolored 1.50 1.50

Independence, 1st anniv.

Olympic Type of 1992

a, 40t, Leon Stukelj, triple medalist in 1924, 1928. b, 46t, Olympic rings, three heads of Apollo.

1992, July 25
143 A21 Pair, #a.-b. +1 or 2 labels 3.25 3.25

1992 Summer Olympics, Barcelona. Rhomboid stamps issued in sheets of 3 No. 143 plus 4 labels.

World Championship of Registered Dogs, Ljubljana — A30

1992, Sept. 4
144 A30 40t Slovenian sheep dog 1.50 1.50

Marij Kogoj (1892-1956), Composer A31

1992, Sept. 30
145 A31 40t multicolored 1.25 1.25

Self-Portrait, by Matevz Langus (1792-1855), Painter — A32

1992, Oct. 30
146 A32 40t multicolored 1.25 1.25

Christmas A33

Designs: 6t, 7t, Nativity Scene, Ljubljana. 41t, Stained glass window of Madonna and Child, St. Mary's Church, Bovec, vert.

1992

147	A33	6t multicolored	.25	.25
147A	A33	7t multicolored	.45	.45
148	A33	41t multicolored	1.10	1.10
		Nos. 147-148 (3)	1.80	1.80

Issued: 6t, 41t, Nov. 20. 7t, Dec. 15.

Herman Potocnik, Theoretician of Geosynchronous Satellite Orbit, Birth Cent. — A34

1992, Nov. 27 Litho. *Perf. 14*
149 A34 46t multicolored 1.25 1.25

Prezihov Voranc (1893-1950), Writer — A35

1993, Jan. 22 Litho. *Perf. 14*
150 A35 7t multicolored .60 .60

Rihard Jakopic (1869-1943), Painter — A36

1993, Jan. 22
151 A36 44t multicolored 1.00 1.00

Jozef Stefan (1835-93), Physicist A37

1993, Jan. 22
152 A37 51t multicolored 1.00 1.00

A38

Designs: 1t, Early cake. 2t, Pan pipes. 5t, Kozolec. 6t, Early building. 7t, Zither. 8t, Water mill. 9t, Sled. 10t, Lonceni bajs. 11t, Kraski kos. 12t, Statue of boy on horseback, Ribnica. 20t, Cross-section of house. 44t, Stone building. 50t, Wind-powered pump. 100t, Potica.

1993-94

153	A38	1t multicolored	.35	.35
154	A38	2t multicolored	.35	.35
155	A38	5t multicolored	.35	.35
156	A38	6t multicolored	.35	.35
157	A38	7t multicolored	.35	.35
158	A38	8t multicolored	.35	.35
159	A38	9t multicolored	.35	.35
160	A38	10t multicolored	.35	.35
160A	A38	11t multicolored	.35	.35
160B	A38	12t multicolored	.35	.35
161	A38	20t multicolored	.40	.40
162	A38	44t multicolored	.60	.60
163	A38	50t multicolored	.85	.85
164	A38	100t multicolored	1.50	1.50
		Nos. 153-164 (14)	6.85	6.85

Issued: 1t, 6t, 7t, 44t, 2/18/93; 2t, 5t, 10t, 20t, 50t, 5/14/93; 8t, 9t, 8/25/93; 11t, 12t, 7/8/94.

See Nos. 208A-220, 370, 373-379, 616-623. For surcharge see No. 371.

Mountain Climbers A39

44t, Route map, mountain.

1993, Feb. 27

165	A39	7t shown	.30	.30
166	A39	44t multicolored	1.00	1.00

Slovenian Alpine Club, centennial (#165). Joza Cop (1893-1975), mountain climber (#166).

Slovenian Post Office, 75th Anniv. — A40

1993, Mar. 19

167	A40	7t multicolored	.40	.40

A41

7t, Altarpiece, by Tintoretto. 44t, Coat of arms.

1993, Apr. 9 Litho. *Perf. 14*

168	A41	7t multicolored	.30	.30
169	A41	44t multicolored	1.00	1.00

Collegiate Church of Novo Mesto, 500th anniv.

Contemporary Art — A42

Europa: 44t, Round Table of Pompeii, by Marij Pregelj (1913-1967). 159t, Little Girl at Play, by Gabrijel Stupica (1913-1990).

1993, Apr. 29 Litho. *Perf. 14*

170		44t multicolored	*1.50*	*1.50*
171		159t multicolored	*3.75*	*3.75*
a.		A42 Pair, #170-171	*6.00*	*6.00*

Schwagerina Carniolica — A43

1993, May 7

172	A43	44t multicolored	1.00	1.00

Admission of Slovenia to UN, 1st Anniv. A44

1993, May 21 Litho. *Perf. 14*

173	A44	62t multicolored	1.40	1.40

Mediterranean Youth Games, Agde, France — A45

1993, June 8

174	A45	36t multicolored	.90	.90

Battle of Sisak, 400th Anniv. A46

1993, June 22 Litho. *Perf. 14*

175	A46	49t multicolored	1.25	1.25

Aphaenopidius Kamnikensis — A47

Designs: 7t, Monolistra spinosissima. 55t, Proteus anguinus. 65t, Zospeum spelaeum.

1993, July 12 Litho. *Perf. 14*

176	A47	7t multicolored	.30	.30
177	A47	40t multicolored	.75	.75
178	A47	55t multicolored	1.20	1.20
179	A47	65t multicolored	1.50	1.50
		Nos. 176-179 (4)	3.75	3.75

World Dressage Competition A48

1993, July 30

180	A48	65t multicolored	1.40	1.40

Coats of Arms — A49

9t, Janez Vajkard Valvasor. 65t, Citizen's Academy of Ljubljana.

1993, Oct. 29 Litho. *Perf. 14*

181	A49	9t multicolored	.30	.30
182	A49	65t multicolored	1.25	1.25

Christmas A50

Designs: 9t, Slovenian Family Viewing Nativity, by Maxim Gaspari (1883-1980). 65t, Archbishop Joze Pogacnik (1902-80), writer.

1993, Nov. 15

183	A50	9t multicolored	.30	.30
184	A50	65t multicolored	1.20	1.20

Famous People — A51

Works by: 8t, Josip Jurcic (1844-81), writer. 9t, Simon Gregorcic (1844-1906), poet. 55t, Stanislav Skrabec (1844-1918), linguist. 65t, Jernej Kopitar (1780-1844), linguist.

1994, Jan. 14 Litho. *Perf. 14*

185	A51	8t multicolored	.25	.25
186	A51	9t multicolored	.25	.25
187	A51	55t multicolored	1.05	1.05
188	A51	65t multicolored	1.20	1.20
		Nos. 185-188 (4)	2.75	2.75

Love — A52

1994, Jan. 25

189	A52	9t multicolored	.50	.50

1994 Winter Olympics, Lillehammer — A53

1994, Feb. 4

190		9t Cross-country skiing	.25	.25
191		65t Slalom skiing	1.35	1.35
a.		A53 Pair, #190-191	1.60	1.60

World Ski Jumping Championships, Planica — A54

1994, Mar. 11 Litho. *Perf. 14*

192	A54	70t multicolored	1.60	1.60

City of Ljubljana, 850th Anniv. A55

1994, Mar. 25 Litho. *Perf. 14*

193	A55	9t multicolored	.50	.50

Europa — A56

70t, Janez Puhar, camera. 215t, Moon, Jurij Vega.

1994, Apr. 22

194		70t multicolored	*1.10*	*1.10*
195		215t multicolored	*3.75*	*3.75*
a.		A56 Pair, #194-195	*5.00*	*5.00*

Miniature Sheet

Flowers of Slovenia — A57

Designs: a, 9t, Primula carniolica. b, 44t, Hladnikia pastinacifolia. c, 60t, Daphne blagayana. d, 70t, Campanula zoysii.

1994, May 20 Litho. *Perf. 14*

196	A57	Sheet of 4 + 2 labels	3.75	3.75

1994 World Cup Soccer Championships, U.S. — A58

1994, June 10

197	A58	44t multicolored	.80	.80

Intl. Olympic Committee, Cent. A59

1994, June 10

198	A59	100t multicolored	2.00	2.00

Mt. Ojstrica — A60

1994, July 1 **Litho.** ***Perf. 14***
199 A60 12t multicolored .50 .50

Max Pletersnik, Professors — A61

1994, July 22
200 A61 70t multicolored 1.40 1.40

First Slovenian-German dictionary published by Max Pletersnik (1840-1932), cent.

Battle of the Frigidus, 1600th Anniv. A62

1994, Sept. 1 **Litho.** ***Perf. 14***
201 A62 60t multicolored 1.40 1.40

Maribor Post Office, Cent. A63

1994, Sept. 23 **Litho.** ***Perf. 14***
202 A63 70t multicolored 1.40 1.40

Ljubljana-Novo Mesto Railway, Cent. — A64

70t, Locomotive 5722, 1893.

1994, Sept. 24 **Litho.** ***Perf. 14***
203 A64 70t multicolored 1.40 1.40

See Nos. 233, 243, 291, 325, 363.

Philharmonic Assoc., Bicent. — A65

Designs: 12t, Building, Ljubljana. 70t, Beethoven, Brahms, Dvorak, Haydn, Paganini.

1994, Oct. 20
204 A65 12t multicolored .30 .30
205 A65 70t multicolored 1.25 1.25

Black Madonna of Loreto, 700th Anniv. — A66

1994, Nov. 18
206 A66 70t multicolored 1.50 1.50

Christmas — A67

1994, Nov. 18
207 A67 12t multicolored .30 .30

Intl. Year of the Family — A68

1994, Nov. 18
208 A68 70t multicolored 1.25 1.25

Type of 1993

13t, Wind rattle, Prlekija. 14t, Sentjernej pottery cock. 15t, Blast furnace, Zelezniki. 16t, Windmill, Stara Gora. 17t, Corn storage building. 55t, Easter eggs, Bela Krajina. 65t, Cobbler's lamp with glass spheres, Trzic. 70t, Snow skis. 75t, 1812 Iron window lattice, Srednja vas, Bohinj. 80t, Palm Sunday bundle. 90t, Beehive. 200t, "Zajec," insect-shaped bootjack, Dvor. 300t, Slamnati doznjek. 400t, Wine press. 500t, Kumer family's table, Koprivna, Carinthia.

1994-99 **Litho.** ***Perf. 14***
Size 25x34mm

208A	A38	13t multicolored	.50	.25
208B	A38	14t multicolored	.25	.25
209	A38	15t multicolored	.25	.25
210	A38	16t multicolored	.25	.25
210A	A38	17t multicolored	.25	.25
211	A38	55t multicolored	.60	.60
212	A38	65t multicolored	.80	.80
213	A38	70t multicolored	1.00	1.00
214	A38	75t multicolored	1.00	1.00
215	A38	80t multicolored	1.25	1.25
216	A38	90t multicolored	1.40	1.40
217	A38	200t multicolored	2.50	2.50
218	A38	300t brown	5.00	5.00
219	A38	400t brown & lake	7.25	7.25
220	A38	500t multicolored	7.00	7.00
		Nos. 208A-220 (15)	29.30	29.05

Issued: 300t, 400t, 11/7/94; 70t, 11/16/95; 55t, 65t, 75t, 3/22/96; 80t, 3/20/97; 13t, 14t, 8/8/97; 90t, 5/30/97; 15t, 6/23/98; 200t, 500t, 11/12/98; 16t, 2/5/99; 17t, 5/7/99.

Ljubljana University, 75th Anniv. A69

Design: 70t, Provincial palace buildings, founders, I. Hribar, M. Rostohar, D. Majaron.

1994, Dec. 3 **Litho.** ***Perf. 14***
221 A69 70t multicolored 1.40 1.40

Postal Service Emblem — A70

1995, Jan. 27
222 A70 13t multicolored .40 .40

Love — A71

1995, Feb. 7
223 A71 20t multicolored .60 .60

Famous People — A72

Works by: 20t, Anton Tomaz Linhart (1756-95), playwright, horiz. No. 225, Ivan Vurnik (1884-1971), architect. No. 226, Lili Novy (1885-1958), poet, horiz.

1995, Feb. 7
224 A72 20t multicolored .50 .50
225 A72 70t multicolored 1.50 1.50
226 A72 70t multicolored 1.50 1.50
Nos. 224-226 (3) 3.50 3.50

A73

1995, Mar. 29 **Litho.** ***Perf. 14***
227 A73 13t multicolored .60 .60

End of World War II, 50th anniv.

Karavankina schellwieni — A74

1995, Mar. 29
228 A74 70t multicolored 1.50 1.50

Liberation of the Concentration Camps, 50th Anniv. — A75

Europa: 60t, Skeleton of Death lying on bride. 70t, Nike going from dark to light.

1995, Mar. 29
229 A75 60t multicolored *1.40 1.40*
230 A75 70t multicolored *1.40 1.40*
a. Pair, #229-230 *3.75 3.75*

No. 230a was issued in sheets of 4.

European Nature Conservation Year — A76

1995, Mar. 29
231 A76 70t Triglav Natl. Park 1.60 1.60

Town of Radovljica, 500th Anniv. A77

1995, June 8 **Litho.** ***Perf. 14***
232 A77 44t multicolored 1.00 1.00

Railways Type of 1994

Design: 70t, Locomotive KRB 37, Podnart.

1995, June 8
233 A64 70t multicolored 1.50 1.50

Ljubljana-Jesenice Line, 125th anniv.

Aljaz Tower, Cent. — A78

1995, June 8 ***Perf. 13½***
234 A78 100t multicolored 2.10 2.10

Portions of the design on No. 234 were applied by a thermogrphic process producing a shiny, raised effect.

Endangered Birds — A79

Designs: a, 13t, Falco naumanni. b, 60t, Coracias garrulus. c, 70t, Lanius minor. d, 215t, Emberiza melanocephala.

1995, June 8 ***Perf. 14***
235 A79 Block of 4, #a.-d. 6.50 6.50

Slovenian Boy Scouts A80

1995, Sept. 26 **Litho.** ***Perf. 14***
236 A80 70t multicolored 1.50 1.50

Comtemporary Art, by France Kralj — A81

No. 237, Death of a Genius, 1921. No. 238, Family of Horses, 1959.

1995, Sept. 26

237 A81 60t multicolored 1.20 1.20
238 A81 70t multicolored 1.40 1.40
a. Pair, #237-238 2.60 2.60

A82

UN, FAO, 50th Anniv.: No. 239, Stylized pictures of food products, faces of people from many nations. No. 240, Black & white figures touching hands, faces of people from many nations.

1995, Sept. 26

239 A82 70t multicolored 1.40 1.40
240 A82 70t multicolored 1.40 1.40
a. Pair, #239-240 3.00 3.00

Issued in miniature sheets of 4 stamps.

A83

Christmas (Paintings): 13t, Winter, by Marlenka Stupica. 70t, St. Mary of Succour, Brezje, by Leopold Layer.

1995, Nov. 16

241 A83 13t multicolored .35 .35
a. Booklet pane of 10 + 2 labels 3.50 3.50
Complete booklet 3.50 3.50
242 A83 70t multicolored 1.40 1.40
a. Booklet pane of 10 + 2 labels 15.50 15.50
Complete booklet 15.50 15.50

Railways Type of 1994

Design: 70t, Locomotive "Aussee."

1996, Jan. 31 **Litho.** ***Perf. 14***

243 A64 70t multicolored 1.25 1.25

The Graz-Celje Line, 150th anniv.

St. Gregory's Day — A84

1996, Jan. 31 **Litho.** ***Perf. 14***

244 A84 13t multicolored .50 .50

Carnival Costumes A85

1996, Jan. 31

245 A85 13t Ptujsko region .30 .30
246 A85 70t Dravsko region 1.20 1.20

See Nos. 281-282, 384-385.

Emys Orbicularis A86

World Wildlife Fund: a, 13t, Peeking head out of water. b, 50t, Laying eggs. c, 60t, Adult crawling though water. d, 70t, Two juveniles.

1996, Jan. 31

247 A86 Strip of 4, #a.-d. 3.75 3.75

No. 247 printed in sheets of 4 vertical or horizontal strips, each having a different order.

Fran Saleski Finzgar (1871-1962), Writer, Priest — A87

1996, Apr. 18 **Litho.** ***Perf. 14***

248 A87 13t multicolored .30 .30

UNICEF, 50th Anniv. — A88

1996, Apr. 18

249 A88 65t multicolored 1.25 1.25

A89

Paintings: 65t, Children on Grass (detail). 75t, Bouquet of Dahlias.

1996, Apr. 18

250 65t multicolored *1.50 1.50*
251 75t multicolored *1.50 1.50*
a. A89 Pair, Nos. 250-251 *3.00 3.00*

Ivana Kobilca (1861-1926), painter. Issued in sheets of 8 stamps. Europa.

Ita Rina (1907-79), Film Actress A90

1996, Apr. 18

252 A90 100t multicolored 1.60 1.60

Visit of Pope John Paul II, May 17-19 — A91

1996, Apr. 18

253 A91 75t multicolored 1.40 1.40

Souvenir Sheet

254 A91 200t multicolored 3.50 3.50

City of Zagorje ob Savi, 700th Anniv. A92

1996, June 6 **Litho.** ***Perf. 14***

255 A92 24t Gallenberg Castle .50 .50

World Junior Cycling Championships, Novo Mesto — A93

1996, June 6

256 A93 55t multicolored 1.00 1.00

Independence, 5th Anniv. — A94

1996, June 6

257 A94 75t multicolored 1.40 1.40

Mushrooms — A95

Designs: a, 65t, Cantharellus cibarius. b, 75t, Boletus aestivalis.

1996, June 6

258 A95 Sheet of 2, #a.-b. 2.75 2.75

Modern Olympic Games, Cent., 1996 Summer Olympics, Atlanta — A96

Designs: 75t, Iztok Cop, rower; Fredja Marsic, kayaker. 100t, Britta Bilac, high jumper; Brigita Bukovec, hurdler.

1996, June 6

259 A96 75t multicolored 1.30 1.30
260 A96 100t multicolored 1.75 1.75
a. Pair, #259-260 + label 3.25 3.25

No. 260a issued in sheets of 6 stamps + 3 labels.

Two versions of the sheet exist. One with white, red & blue flag, the other with white, blue & red flag.

A97

A98

A99

A100

Idrijan Lace

A101 A102

1996, June 21 **Litho.** ***Perf. 14***

261 A97 1t shown .30 .30
262 A97 1t olive gray, diff. .30 .30
a. Pair, #261-262 .60 .60
263 A98 2t shown .30 .30
264 A98 2t carmine, diff. .30 .30
a. Pair, #263-264 .60 .60
265 A99 5t shown .30 .30
266 A99 5t square .30 .30
a. Pair, #265-266 .60 .60
267 A100 12t shown .30 .30
268 A100 12t diamond .30 .30
a. Pair, #267-268 .60 .60
269 A101 13t shown .30 .30
270 A101 13t red, diff. .30 .30
a. Pair, #269-270 .60 .60
271 A102 50t shown .75 .75
272 A102 50t lilac, diff. .75 .75
a. Pair, #272-272 1.50 1.50
Nos. 261-272 (12) 4.50 4.50

Nos. 261-272 were originally issued with a background containing "1996," posthorn, and security lettering that appear under UV light, values as shown above. In 1997 Nos. 261-270 were reissued, with date within fluorescent inscription changed to "1997." Value, set $150.

In their final form, Nos. 261-272 were issued later in 1997 without fluorescent inscription. Value same as for 1996 issue.

See Nos. 297-304.

Modern Cardiology, Cent. — A103

1996, Sept. 6 **Litho.** ***Perf. 14***
273 A103 12t multicolored .40 .40

Grammar School, Novo Mesto, 250th Anniv. A104

1996, Sept. 6
274 A104 55t multicolored 1.00 1.00

A105

Design: 55t, Skocjan Caves, Karst Region, UNESCO World Heritage Site.

1996, Sept. 6
275 A105 55t multicolored 1.00 1.00

Moscon Family Portrait, by Jozef Tominc (1790-1866) — A106

1996, Sept. 6
276 A106 65t multicolored 1.25 1.25

Post Office, Ljubljana, Cent. — A107

1996, Oct. 18 **Litho.** ***Perf. 14***
277 A107 100t multicolored 1.60 1.60

A108

1996, Oct. 20
278 A108 12t multicolored .40 .40

Introduction of automatic letter sorting machines, Maribor.

Children Sledding A109

Nativity A110

1996, Nov. 20 **Litho.** ***Perf. 14***
279 A109 12t multicolored .25 .25
a. Booklet pane of 10 3.00 3.00
Complete booklet, #279a 3.00
280 A110 65t multicolored 1.25 1.25
a. Booklet pane of 10 15.00 15.00
Complete booklet, #280a 15.00

Christmas.

Carnival Costumes Type of 1996

From Cerkno region: 20t, "Ta terjast." 80t, "Pust."

1997, Jan. 21 **Litho.** ***Perf. 14***
281 A85 20t multicolored .25 .25
282 A85 80t multicolored 1.25 1.25

Love A111

1997, Jan. 21 **Litho.** ***Perf. 14***
283 A111 15t multicolored .30 .30

Sneznik Mountain A112

1997, Jan. 21
284 A112 20t multicolored .70 .70

Legend of the Goldenhorn A113

1997, Mar. 27 **Litho.** ***Perf. 14***
285 A113 80t multicolored *3.50 3.50*

Europa.

Wulfenite — A114

1997, Mar. 27
286 A114 80t multicolored 1.25 1.25

A115

Endangered Fish — A115a

1997, Mar. 27
287 A115 12t Salmo marmoratus .30 .30
288 A115 13t Zingel streber .55 .55
289 A115 80t Vimba vimba 1.25 1.25
290 A115 90t Umbra krameri 1.75 1.75
Nos. 287-290 (4) 3.85 3.85

Miniature Sheet

290A A115a Sheet of 4, #a-d 4.50 4.50
a. 12t Salmo marmoratus .30 .30
b. 13t Zingel streber .55 .55
c. 80t Vimba vimba 1.25 1.25
d. 90t Umbra krameri 1.75 1.75

Railways Type of 1994

Design: 80t, Locomotive SZ 03-002, Ljubljana-Trieste Railway Line, 140th anniv.

1997, May 30 **Litho.** ***Perf. 14***
291 A64 80t multicolored 1.40 1.40

A116

1997, May 30
292 A116 70t multicolored 1.25 1.25

Volunteer fire fighting brigades in Slovenia.

A117

Famous People: 13t, Matija Cop (1797-1835), literary expert. 24t, Sigismundus Zois (1747-1819), economist, natural scientist. 80t, Bishop Frederic Baraga (1797-1868), missionary, linguist.

1997, May 30
293 A117 13t multicolored .25 .25
294 A117 24t multicolored .45 .45
295 A117 80t multicolored 1.00 1.00
Nos. 293-295 (3) 1.70 1.70

Souvenir Sheet

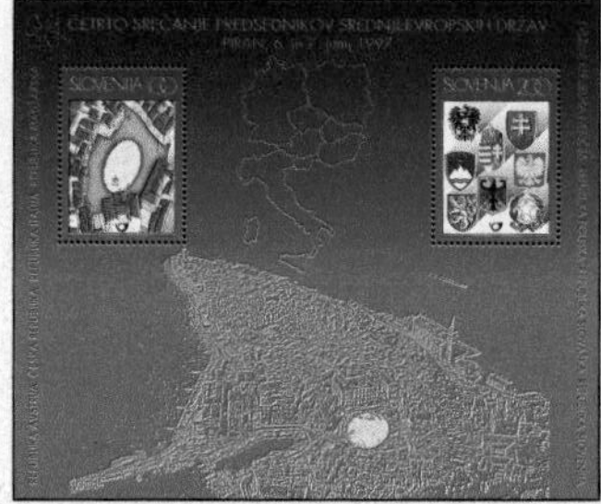

4th Meeting of the Presidents of Central European Countries, Piran — A118

Designs: a, 100t, Tartini Square. b, 200t, Coats of arms from eight countries.

1997, June 6
296 A118 Sheet of 2, #a.-b. 5.00 5.00

Idrijan Lace Type of 1996

Shape of lace: No. 297, Flower in center of oval. No. 298, Circular outside with swirl at bottom. No. 299, Butterfly. No. 300, Diamond. No. 301, Square. No. 302, Circle. No. 303, Leaves. No. 304, Tulip.

1997, June 20 **Litho.** ***Perf. 14***
297 A97 10t magenta .30 .30
298 A97 10t magenta .30 .30
a. Pair, #297-298 .60 .60
299 A97 20t violet .35 .35
300 A97 20t violet .35 .35
a. Pair, #299-300 .70 .70
301 A97 44t bright blue .75 .75
302 A97 44t bright blue .75 .75
a. Pair, #301-302 1.50 1.50
303 A97 100t gray brown 1.60 1.60
304 A97 100t gray brown 1.60 1.60
a. Pair, #303-304 3.25 3.25
Nos. 297-304 (8) 6.00 6.00

Children's Week — A119

1997, Sept. 9
305 A119 14t multicolored .40 .40

Return of Primorska, 50th Anniv. — A120

1997, Sept. 9
306 A120 50t multicolored .85 .85

France Gorse (1897-1986), Sculptor — A121

1997, Sept. 9
307 A121 70t "Bashful Armor" .90 .90
308 A121 80t "Peasant Woman" 1.15 1.15
a. Pair, #307-308 2.25 2.25

A122

1997, Sept. 9
309 A122 90t multicolored 1.50 1.50

MEJP '97, European Youth Judo Championship.

A123

1997, Nov. 18 Litho. *Perf. 14*
310 A123 90t multicolored 1.25 1.25

Golden Fox World Cup Ski Competition for Women, 35th anniv.

Christmas & New Year A124

Designs: 14t, Children watching birds and snow outside window. 90t, Sculptured Nativity scene, by Liza Hribar (1913-96).

1997, Nov. 18
311 A124 14t multicolored .25 .25
312 A124 90t multicolored 1.40 1.40
a. Booklet pane of 8, 5 #311, 3 #312 6.00
Complete booklet, #312a 6.00

New Mail Center, Ljubljana — A125

1997, Nov. 28
313 A125 30t multicolored .50 .50

Borovo Gostüvanje (Pine Wedding) — A126

20t, Participating "players," tree. 80t, Participants, "bride & groom," top of pine tree.

1998, Jan. 22 Litho. *Perf. 14*
314 A126 20t multicolored .35 .35
315 A126 80t multicolored .95 .95
a. Pair, #314-315 1.50 1.50

See Nos. 338-339.

1998 Winter Olympic Games, Nagano A127

1998, Jan. 22
316 A127 70t Woman skater .75 .75
317 A127 90t Biathlete 1.25 1.25
a. Vert. pair, #316-317 + label 3.00 3.00

Issued in sheets of 6 stamps + 3 labels.

EUROCONTROL (European Organization for Safety of Air Navigation), 35th Anniv. — A128

1998, Jan. 22
318 A128 90t multicolored 1.40 1.40

Louis Adamic (1898-1951), Writer — A129

90t, Francesco Robba (1698-1757), sculptor.

1998, Mar. 25 Litho. *Perf. 14*
319 A129 26t multicolored .30 .30
320 A129 90t multicolored 1.40 1.40

Jurjevanje (Green George's Festival) A130

1998, Mar. 25
321 A130 90t multicolored 3.00 3.00

Europa.

Comic Strip Characters, by Miki Muster — A131

1998, Mar. 25
322 A131 14t Fox .40 .40
323 A131 105t Turtle 1.35 1.35
324 A131 118t Wolf 1.75 1.75
a. Sheet, 2 each #322-324 7.00 7.00
Nos. 322-324 (3) 3.50 3.50

Railways Type of 1994

Design: Steam locomotive SZ 06-018.

1998, June 10 Litho. *Perf. 14*
325 A64 80t multicolored 1.25 1.25

Boc Mountain, Pulsatilla Grandis — A132

1998, June 10
326 A132 14t multicolored .50 .50

A133

Conifers: a, 14t, Juniperus communis. b, 15t, Picea abies. c, 80t, Pinus nigra. d, 90t, Larix decidua.

1998, June 10
327 A133 Sheet of 4, #a.-d. 4.00 4.00

A134

1998, June 23 Litho. *Perf. 14*
328 A134 15t multicolored .40 .40

Committee for the Protection of Human Rights, 10th anniv.

United Slovenia, 150th Anniv. A135

1998, June 23
329 A135 80t multicolored 1.25 1.25

Cistercian Order, 900th Anniv. and Sticna Revival, Cent. A136

1998, Sept. 11 Litho. *Perf. 14*
330 A136 14t multicolored .40 .40

Radio Ljubljana, 70th Anniv. A137

1998, Sept. 11
331 A137 50t Cuckoo .80 .80

Avgust Cernigoj (1898-1985), Artist — A138

Designs: 70t, Abstract painting, "Banker." 80t, Sculpture, "El."

1998, Sept. 11
332 A138 70t multicolored .90 .90
333 A138 80t multicolored 1.00 1.00
a. Pair, #332-333 2.25 2.25

Universal Declaration of Human Rights, 50th Anniv. — A139

1998, Sept. 11
334 A139 100t multicolored 1.50 1.50

Christmas A140

Designs: 15t, Children walking through snow, candle. 90t, Fresco of "Bow of the Three Wise Men of the East," Church of St. Nicholas, Mace, 1476.

1998, Nov. 12 Litho. *Perf. 14*
335 A140 15t multicolored .30 .30
a. Booklet pane of 10 3.00 3.00
Complete booklet, #335a 3.00
336 A140 90t multicolored 1.30 1.30
a. Bklt. pane, 6 #335, 4 #336 7.00 7.00
Complete booklet, #336a 7.00

Leon Stukelj, Olympic Gymnastics Champion, 100th Birthday — A141

Designs: a, Portrait. b, As a gymnast. c, With IOC Pres. Juan Antonio Samaranch, horiz. (58x40mm).

1998, Nov. 12
337 A141 100t Sheet of 3, #a.-c. 4.50 4.50

Wedding, Festival Type of 1998

Skoromati carnival mask characters: 20t, Wearing tall hats, Skopit character in black. 80t, Skopit character blowing horn.

1999, Jan. 22 Litho. *Perf. 14*
338 A126 20t multicolored .25 .25
339 A126 80t multicolored 1.00 1.00
a. Pair, #338-339 1.50 1.50

Greetings A142

1999, Jan. 22
340 A142 15t multicolored .50 .50

Famous Men — A143

14t, Peter Kozler (1824-79), geographer. 15t, Bozidar Lavric (1899-1961), surgeon. 70t, Rudolf Maister (1874-1934), general, poet. 80t, France Preseren (1800-49), poet.

1999, Jan. 22

341 A143 14t multicolored .30 .30
342 A143 15t multicolored .30 .30
343 A143 70t multicolored .80 .80
344 A143 80t multicolored 1.10 1.10
Nos. 341-344 (4) 2.50 2.50

Golica Mountain, Narcissus Flowers A144

1999, Mar. 23 Litho. *Perf. 14*
345 A144 15t multicolored .60 .60

Slovenian Philatelic Assoc., 50th Anniv. — A145

1999, Mar. 23
346 A145 16t Yugoslavia #3L5 & #305 .60 .60

Mercury & Cinnabar, Idrija Mine A146

1999, Mar. 23
347 A146 80t multicolored 1.25 1.25

Council of Europe, 50th Anniv. A147

1999, Mar. 23
348 A147 80t multicolored 1.25 1.25

Triglav Natl. Park A148

1999, Mar. 23
349 A148 90t multicolored *2.50 2.50*

Europa.

5th Rescue Dog World Championships — A149

1999, May 21 Litho. *Perf. 14*
350 A149 80t multicolored 1.25 1.25

UPU, 125th Anniv. — A150

Designs: 30t, Early postman with backpack. 90t, Astronaut on moon with backpack.

1999, May 21
351 A150 30t multicolored .60 .60
352 A150 90t multicolored 1.00 1.00
a. Pair, #351-352 1.60 1.60

Horses A151

Designs: 60t, Slovenian cold-blooded horse. 70t, Ljutomer trotter. 120t, Slovenian warm-blooded horse (show jumper). 350t, Lipizzaner.

1999, May 21
353 A151 60t multicolored .85 .85
354 A151 70t multicolored 1.00 1.00
355 A151 120t multicolored 1.60 1.60
356 A151 350t multicolored 5.00 5.00
a. Sheet of 4, #353-356 9.00 9.00
Nos. 353-356 (4) 8.45 8.45

Towards A New Millennium — A152

Designs: 20t, Balanced objects. 70t, Roadway, earth. 80t, Cogwheels. 90t, Tree.

1999, Sept. 16 Litho. *Perf. 13¾*
357 A152 20t multicolored .25 .25
358 A152 70t multicolored .90 .90
359 A152 80t multicolored 1.00 1.00
360 A152 90t multicolored 1.25 1.25
a. Block of 4, #357-360 3.50 3.50

Bozidar Jakac (1899-1989), Painter — A153

Self-portraits and: 70t, Girl drawing curtain. 80t, Landscape.

1999, Sept. 16
361 A153 70t multicolored .85 .85
362 A153 80t multicolored 1.00 1.00
a. Pair, #361-362 2.00 2.00

Railway Type of 1994

1999, Sept. 16
363 A64 80t multicolored 1.25 1.25

Rail Line to Ljubljana, 150th anniv.

Bishop Anton M. Slomsek (1800-62) — A154

1999, Sept. 16
364 A154 90t multicolored 1.40 1.40

Millennium A155

Christmas — A156

1999, Nov. 18 Litho. *Perf. 14*
365 A155 17t multicolored .55 .55
a. Booklet pane of 10 5.50
Complete booklet, #365a 5.50
366 A155 18t multicolored .55 .55
367 A156 80t multicolored 2.25 2.25
a. Booklet pane, 5 #365, 3 #367 + 2 labels 9.50
Complete booklet, #367a 9.50
368 A156 90t multicolored 2.50 2.50
Nos. 365-368 (4) 5.85 5.85

Nos. 365 and 367 were issued only in booklets.

Types of 1993-94 Overprinted & No. 210A Surcharged

Design: 18t, Accordion. 19t on 17t, Corn storage building. A, Post office door, Zgornji Otok. No. 373, Easter eggs. No. 374, Fishing boat. No. 375, Miner's house, Trbovlje. C, Scythe. No. 377, Ljubljana Palm Sunday bundle. No. 378, Horse collar comb. No. 379, Fishing boat and oars.

1999-2004 Litho. *Perf. 14*
Size 25x34mm

370 A38 18t multi .55 .55
371 A38 19t on 17t multi .55 .55
372 A38 A multi 1.15 1.15
373 A38 B multi .70 .70
374 A38 B multi 1.30 1.30
375 A38 B multi 1.50 1.50
376 A38 C multi 3.00 3.00
377 A38 D multi 3.00 3.00
378 A38 D multi 3.50 3.50
379 A38 D multi 3.50 3.50
Nos. 370-379 (10) 18.75 18.75

Issued: 18t, 12/17/99. No. 371, 4/20/2000. Nos. 373, 377, 2/28/02. Nos. 372, 374, 376, 378, 11/19/03. No. 375, 7/3/04. No. 379, 9/22/04.

Nos. 373 and 377 sold for 31t and 107t respectively on day of issue. Nos. 372, 374, 376 and 378 sold for 38t, 44t, 95t and 107t respectively on day of issue. No. 375 sold for 48t on day of issue. No. 379 sold for 107t on day of issue.

Love — A158

2000, Jan. 20 Litho. *Perf. 14*
383 A158 34t multi .70 .70

Carnival Costume Type of 1996

Pustovi masks: 34t, Two masks, horiz. 80t, Four masks, horiz.

2000, Jan. 20
384 A85 34t multi .60 .60
385 A85 80t multi 1.40 1.40

A159

2000, Jan. 20
386 A159 64t multi 1.00 1.00

Tone Seliskar (1900-69), poet.

A160

2000, Jan. 20
387 A160 120t multi 2.00 2.00

Elvira Kralj (1900-78), actress.

Postal Service in Slovenia, 500th Anniv. — A161

2000, Jan. 20
388 A161 500t multi 8.50 8.50

Mt. Storzic A162

2000, Mar. 21 Litho. *Perf. 14*
389 A162 18t multi .80 .80

Return of World War II Exiles A163

2000, Mar. 21
390 A163 25t multi .85 .85

Characters from Children's Books — A164

Nos. 391, 394, Pedenjped. Nos. 392, 395, Mojca Pokrajculja. Nos. 393, 396, Macek Muri.

2000, Mar. 21 ***Perf. 14***

391 A164 20t multi 1.50 1.50
392 A164 20t multi 1.50 1.50
393 A164 20t multi 1.50 1.50

Booklet Stamps
Self-Adhesive
Serpentine Die Cut 7½

394 A164 20t multi 1.25 1.25
395 A164 20t multi 1.25 1.25
396 A164 20t multi 1.25 1.25
a. Booklet pane, 3 each #394-396 + 9 labels 12.00
Nos. 391-396 (6) 8.25 8.25

No. 396a is a complete booklet.

Fossils and Minerals A165

2000, Mar. 21 ***Perf. 14***

397 A165 80t Trilobite 1.50 .80
398 A165 90t Dravite 1.50 .80

See Nos. 453-454, 517.

Souvenir Sheet

Holy Year 2000 — A166

2000, Mar. 21
399 A166 2000t multi 30.00 30.00

Castles — A167

2000-04 **Litho.** ***Perf. 14***
Size 23x32mm

400 A167 1t Predjama .35 .25
401 A167 1t Velenje .35 .25
a. Pair, #400-401 .70 .35
404 A167 A Ptuj .60 .30
405 A167 A Otocec .60 .30
a. Pair, #404-405 1.25 .90
406 A167 B Zuzemberk .60 .30
407 A167 B Turjak .60 .30
a. Pair, #406-407 1.25 .90
410 A167 C Dobrovo 1.50 .75
411 A167 C Breziski 1.50 .75
a. Pair, #410-411 3.00 1.75
411B A167 C Gewerkenegg 1.50 .75
412 A167 100t Podsreda 1.50 .75
413 A167 100t Bled 1.50 .75
a. Pair, #412-413 3.00 1.75
414 A167 D Olimje 1.50 .75
415 A167 D Murska Sobota 1.50 .75
a. Pair, #414-415 3.00 1.75

Size: 38x26mm

415B A167 1000t Kamen 15.00 7.25
Nos. 400-415B (14) 28.60 14.20

Nos. 404-405 each sold for 20t; Nos. 406-407 for 21t; Nos. 410-411 for 95t; No. 411B sold for 95t on day of issue; Nos. 414-415 for 107t on day of issue.

Issued: Nos. 1t, 100t, 4/20; A, B, 6/23; Nos. 410-411, 414-415, 10/4/01. 1000t, 3/24/03. No. 411B, 11/18/04.

See Nos. 624-628.

Fruits, Blossoms and Insects — A168

Designs: No. 416, Apple blossom weevil. No. 417, Apple blossom. No. 418, Apple.

2000, Apr. 20 **Litho.** ***Perf. 13¾***
Vignette Frame Size 20x26½mm

416 A168 10t multi .25 .25
417 A168 10t multi .25 .25
418 A168 10t multi .25 .25
a. Strip, #416-418 .75 .35

Printed in sheets of 15 stamps + 5 labels.

See Nos. 426-428, 464-466, 502-504, 528-530, 568-570, 606-608, 629-646, 676-678.

Amateur Radio A169

2000, May 9 **Litho.** ***Perf. 14***
419 A169 20t multi 1.75 1.75

Slovenian Team Qualification for European Soccer Championships A170

2000, May 9
420 A170 40t multi 1.50 1.50

2000 Summer Olympics, Sydney — A171

2000, May 9
421 80t Sailboats 2.25 2.25
422 90t Sydney Opera House 2.25 2.25
a. A171 Pair, #421-422 4.50 4.50

World Environment Day — A172

2000, May 9
423 A172 90t multi *27.50 27.50*

Issued in sheets of 10 + 5 labels.

Europa, 2000
Common Design Type

2000, May 9 **Litho.** ***Perf. 14***
424 CD17 90t multi *3.25 3.25*

Issued in sheets of 8 + 1 label.

Meteorology A173

2000, May 9 ***Perf. 13¾***
425 A173 150t multi *22.50 22.50*

Issued in sheets of 9 + 1 label.

Fruits, Blossoms and Insects Type of 2000

No. 426, Cherry blossom. No. 427, European cherry fruit fly. No. 428, Cherries.

Vignette Frame Size 20x26½mm

2000, June 23 **Litho.** ***Perf. 13¾***
426 A168 5t multi .25 .25
427 A168 5t multi .25 .25
428 A168 5t multi .25 .25
a. Strip, #426-428 .75 .35

Printed in sheets of 15 stamps + 5 labels.

Paintings by Tone Kralj (1900-75) — A174

2000, Sept. 15 **Litho.** ***Perf. 14***
429 Horiz. pair 2.75 1.25
a. A174 70t multi 1.15 .50
b. A174 80t multi, diff. 1.30 .60

Grape Varieties — A175

Designs: 20t, Zelen. 40t, Ranfol. 80t, Zametovka. 130t, Rumeni Plavec.

2000, Sept. 15
430-433 A175 Set of 4 5.00 5.00
a. Souvenir sheet, #430-433 5.00 5.00

Gold Medalists at 2000 Summer Olympics A176

Winners and events: No. 434, 21t, Iztok Cop, Luka Spik, double sculls. No. 435, 21t, Rajmond Debevec, Men's three-position rifle.

2000, Oct. 16
434-435 A176 Set of 2 1.00 1.00

First Book Printed in Slovenian, 450th Anniv. — A177

2000, Nov. 21
436 A177 50t multi .90 .90

Christmas A178

Designs: B, Children in snow. 90t, Christ in manger.

2000, Nov. 21
437 A178 B multicolored .50 .25
438 A178 90t multicolored 2.00 1.00

Booklet Stamps
Self-Adhesive
Serpentine Die Cut 7¼

439 A178 B multi .60 .30
a. Booklet of 10 + 2 labels 6.00
440 A178 90t multi 2.40 1.25
a. Booklet, 6 #439, 4 #440 + 2 labels 13.50
Nos. 437-440 (4) 5.50 2.80

Nos. 437 and 439 sold for 21t on day of issue.

Advent of New Millennium — A179

2000, Nov. 21 **Litho.** ***Perf. 14***
441 A179 40t multi .90 .90

Wedding Greetings A180

2001, Jan. 19 **Litho.** ***Perf. 14***
442 A180 B multi .90 .45

No. 442 sold for 25t on day of issue.

Carnival Masks, Dobrepolje — A181

Mask wearers including: 50t, Woman with flowers. 95t, Woman in box on cart.

2001, Jan. 19
443-444 A181 Set of 2 2.00 1.00

Writers — A182

Objects symbolic of writer's works: A, Bucket (Dragotin Kette, 1876-99). 95t, Flowers in jar (Ivan Tavcar, 1851-1923). 107t, Coffee cup (Ivan Cankar, 1876-1918).

2001, Jan. 19
445-447 A182 Set of 3 4.00 2.00

No. 445 sold for 24t on day of issue.

Mt. Jalovec and Triglav Flowers — A183

2001, Mar. 21 **Litho.** ***Perf. 14***
448 A183 B multi 1.25 .65

No. 448 sold for 25t on day of issue.

Comic Strip Characters by Bozo Kos — A184

Designs: Nos. 449, 451, Cowboy. Nos. 450, 452, Indian.

2001, Mar. 21
449 A184 B multicolored 1.40 .70
450 A184 B multicolored 1.40 .70

Booklet Stamps
Self-Adhesive
Serpentine Die Cut 7¼

451 A184 B multicolored 1.40 .70
452 A184 B multicolored 1.40 .70
a. Booklet, 4 each #451-452 11.50
Nos. 449-452 (4) 5.60 2.80

Nos. 449-452 each sold for 25t on day of issue.

Fossil and Mineral Type of 2000

No. 453 — Stereoscopic image of fluorite crystal with arrow at: a, Right. b, Left.
107t, Starfish fossil.

2001, Mar. 21 **Litho.** ***Perf. 14***
453 Horiz. pair 3.25 1.60
a.-b. A165 95t Any single 1.60 .80
454 A165 107t Starfish fossil 1.60 .80

Europe Day A185

2001, Mar. 21
455 A185 221t multi 3.50 1.75

Solkan, 1000th Anniv. — A186

2001, Mar. 21
456 A186 261t multi 3.50 2.25

Formation of Liberation Front, 60th Anniv. — A187

2001, Apr. 24 **Litho.** ***Perf. 14***
457 A187 24t multi .95 .45

Independence, 10th Anniv. — A188

2001, May 23
458 A188 100t multi 3.25 2.00

Issued in sheets of 10 + 2 labels.

Europa — A189

2001, May 23
459 A189 107t multi 3.00 1.75

Issued in sheets of 8 + 1 label.

Ljubljana Tram System, Cent. A190

2001, May 23
460 A190 113t multi 1.90 .95

6th World Maxi Basketball Championships, Ljubljana — A191

2001, May 23
461 A191 261t multi 3.75 1.75

Souvenir Sheet

Apiculture — A192

No. 462: a, 24t, Bee on flower. b, 48t, Queen and drones. c, 95t, Worker bees. d, 170t, Hive and apiary.

2001, May 23
462 A192 Sheet of 4, #a-d 5.75 4.00

Flags of US and Russia, Dragon Bridge, Ljubljana — A193

2001, June 14
463 A193 107t multi 1.60 .85
a. Souvenir sheet of 1 2.00 1.10

First meeting of US Pres. George W. Bush and Russian Pres. Vladimir Putin, Brdo Castle, June 16.

Fruit, Blossoms and Insects Type of 2000

Designs: No. 464, Peach blossom. No. 465, Green peach aphid. No. 466, Peach.

2001, July 21 ***Perf. 13¾***
Vignette Frame Size 20x26mm
464 A168 50t multi .90 .45
465 A168 50t multi .90 .45
466 A168 50t multi .90 .45
a. Strip, #464-466 2.75 2.75

Printed in sheets of 15 strips + 5 labels.

Mohorjeve Druzbe Publishing House, 150th Anniv. — A194

2001, Sept. 4 ***Perf. 14***
467 A194 B multi 1.00 .50

No. 467 sold for 27t on day of issue.

Foundation of First Technical High School, Cent. A195

2001, Sept. 21
468 A195 A multi 1.00 .50

No. 468 sold for 26t on day of issue.

World Animal Day — A196

2001, Sept. 21
469 A196 107t multi 1.75 1.00

Year of Dialogue Among Civilizations A197

2001, Sept. 21 **Litho.** ***Perf. 14***
470 A197 107t multi 3.00 1.50

Composers — A198

Designs: 95t, Blaz Arnic (1901-70). 107t, Lucijan Marija Skerjanc (1900-73).

2001, Sept. 21 **Litho.** ***Perf. 14***
471-472 A198 Set of 2 3.00 1.60

New Year's Greetings A199

Christmas A200

2001, Nov. 16 **Litho.** ***Perf. 14***
473 A199 B multi .35 .25
474 A200 D multi 1.90 .95

Self-Adhesive
Booklet Stamps
Serpentine Die Cut 7¼

475 A199 B multi .35 .25
a. Booklet pane of 12 4.25
476 A200 D multi 2.10 1.00
a. Booklet pane, 6 each #475-476 15.00

Nos. 473 and 475 sold for 31t , Nos. 474 and 476 for 107t on day of issue.

Love — A201

2002, Jan. 23 **Litho.** ***Perf. 14***
477 A201 B multi 1.00 .50

No. 477 sold for 31t on day of issue.

Masks — A202

Designs: 56t, Rusa. 95t, Picek.

2002, Jan. 23
478-479 A202 Set of 2 2.00 1.10

Famous Slovenians — A203

Designs: 95t, Joze Plecnik (1872-1957), architect. 107t, Janko Kersnik (1852-97), poet.

2002, Jan. 23
480-481 A203 Set of 2 2.75 1.40

2002 Winter Olympics, Salt Lake City — A204

No. 482: a, 95t, Sledder. b, 107t, Skier.

2002, Jan. 23
482 A204 Horiz. pair, #a-b, + label 3.00 1.60

No. 482 printed in sheets of three pairs. Labels, which have different designs, appear at left and center in other pairs on the sheet.

Insect Fossil A205

2002, Mar. 21
485 A205 C multi 1.75 .85

No. 485 sold for 95t on day of issue.

Kostanjevica on the Krka, 750th Anniv. A206

2002, Mar. 21
486 A206 D multi 1.75 .85

No. 486 sold for 107t on day of issue.

Intl. Year of Mountains A207

Flowers and mountains: A, Clematis alpina and Martuljek Group. D, Lilium carniolicum and Mt. Spik.

2002, Mar. 21
487-488 A207 Set of 2 4.00 2.00

Nos. 487-488 sold for 30t and 107t respectively on day of issue.

Martin Krpan from Vrh, by Fran Levstik — A208

Designs: No. 489, B, Krpan carrying horse. No. 490, B, Krpan at blacksmith's shop. No. 491, B, Krpan in Ljubljana. No. 492, B, Like No. 489. No. 493, B, Like No. 490. No. 494, B, Like No. 491.

2002, Mar. 21 ***Perf. 14***
489-491 A208 Set of 3 3.75 1.90

Self-Adhesive
Booklet Stamps
Serpentine Die Cut 7¼

492-494 A208 Set of 3 3.00 1.50
494a Booklet pane, 3 each #492-494 9.00

Nos. 489-494 each sold for 31t on day of issue.

Europa — A209

2002, May 22 ***Perf. 14***
495 A209 D multi *16.00 8.00*

No. 495 sold for 107t on day of issue.

2002 World Cup Soccer Championships, Japan and Korea — A210

2002, May 22
496 A210 D multi 2.50 1.25

No. 496 sold for 107t on day of issue.

Medicinal Plants — A211

Designs: A, Rosa canina. B, Chamomilla recutita. C, Valeriana officinalis. D, Viola odorata.

2002, May 22
497-499 A211 Set of 3 5.00 2.50

Souvenir Sheet

500 A211 D multi 2.25 1.10

Nos. 497-500 each sold for 30t, 31t, 95t and 107t respectively on day of issue.

Souvenir Sheet

9th Summit of Presidents of Central European States, Bled — A212

No. 501: a, D, Bled Island in map of Europe. b, D, Map of Europe, Brdo Castle.

2002, May 22
501 A212 Sheet of 2, #a-b 3.25 3.25

Nos. 501a and 501b each sold for 107t on day of issue.

Fruit, Blossoms and Insects Type of 2000

Designs: No. 502, Bilberry blossoms. No. 503, Winter moth. No. 504, Bilberries.

2002, July 19 ***Perf. 13¾***
Vignette Frame Size 20x26mm

502 A168 150t multi 3.25 1.50
503 A168 150t multi 3.25 1.50
504 A168 150t multi 3.25 1.50
a. Horiz. strip, #502-504 9.75 4.50

Paintings by Matija Jama (1872-1947) — A213

Designs: 95t, Kolo — A National Dance. 214t, A Village in Winter.

2002, Sept. 19 ***Perf. 14***
505-506 A213 Set of 2 4.00 2.25

Souvenir Sheet

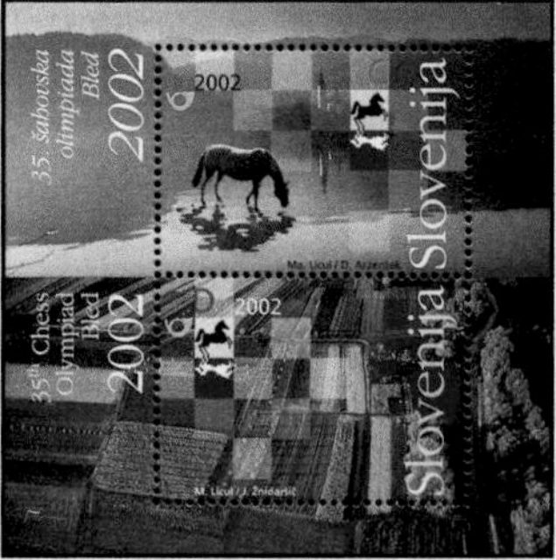

35th Chess Olympiad, Bled — A214

No. 507: a, C, Horse, Bled Castle. b, D, Fields in checkerboard pattern.

2002, Sept. 19
507 A214 Sheet of 2, #a-b 4.00 4.00

Nos. 507a and 507b each sold for 95t and 107t respectively on day of issue.

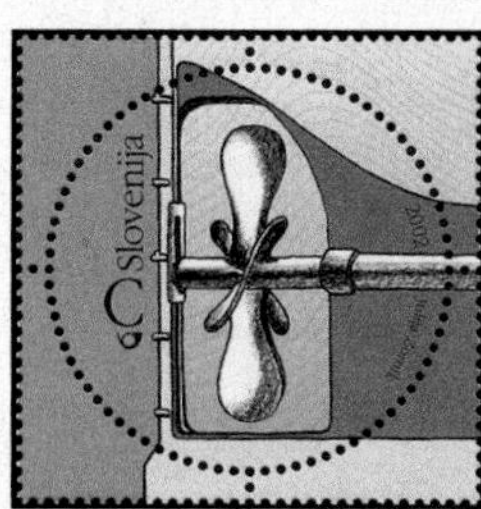

Screw Propeller Invented by Josef Ressel (1793-1857) — A215

2002, Nov. 15 **Litho.** ***Perf. 13¾***
508 A215 C multi 2.40 1.20

No. 508 sold for 95t on day of issue. Values are for stamps with surrounding selvage.

Christmas and New Year's Greetings — A216

Designs: Nos. 509, 511, Snowman. Nos. 510, 512, Girl with evergreen branch.

2002, Nov. 15 **Litho.** ***Perf. 14***
509 A216 B multi .75 .35
510 A216 D multi 2.25 1.10

Booklet Stamps
Self-Adhesive
Serpentine Die Cut 7¼

511 A216 B multi .75 .35
a. Booklet, 12 #511 9.00
512 A216 D multi 2.25 1.10
a. Booklet, 6 each #511-512 18.00
Nos. 509-512 (4) 6.00 2.90

Nos. 509 and 511 each sold for 36t, and Nos. 510 and 512 each sold for 107t on day of issue.

Traditional Istrian Clothing A217

2003, Jan. 21 **Litho.** ***Perf. 14***
513 A217 A multi 1.50 .75

No. 513 sold for 38t on day of issue.

Love A218

2003, Jan. 21 ***Perf. 11***
514 A218 180t multi 3.00 1.50

No. 514 is impregnated with a rose scent. Values are for examples with surrounding selvage.

Famous Men A219

Designs: 107t, Ferdinand Avgustin Hallerstein (1703-74), astronomer and Chinese missionary. 221t, Alfonz Paulin (1853-1942), director of Ljubljana Botanical Gardens.

2003, Jan. 21
515-516 A219 Set of 2 4.50 2.25

Mineral Type of 2000

2003, Mar. 24
517 A165 D Barite 2.00 1.00

No. 517 sold for 107t on day of issue.

Vilenica Cave — A220

2003, Mar. 24
518 A220 D multi 2.00 1.00

No. 518 sold for 107t on day of issue.

Fairy Tales A221

Designs: No. 519, B, The Three Vixens. No. 520, B, The Golden Bird, vert.

2003, Mar. 24 ***Perf. 14***
519-520 A221 Set of 2 2.00 1.00

Serpentine Die Cut 7¼
Booklet Stamps
Self-Adhesive

521 A221 B Like #519 1.50 .75
522 A221 B Like #520 1.50 .75
a. Booklet, 4 each #521-522 13.00

Nos. 519-522 each sold for 44t on day of issue.

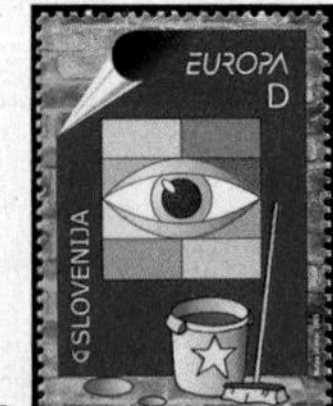

Europa — A222

2003, May 22 **Litho.** ***Perf. 14***
523 A222 D multi 1.90 .95

No. 523 sold for 107t on day of issue. Printed in sheets of 8 + 1 label.

Kresnik, Mythological Character — A223

2003, May 22
524 A223 110t multi 1.60 .80

Souvenir Sheet

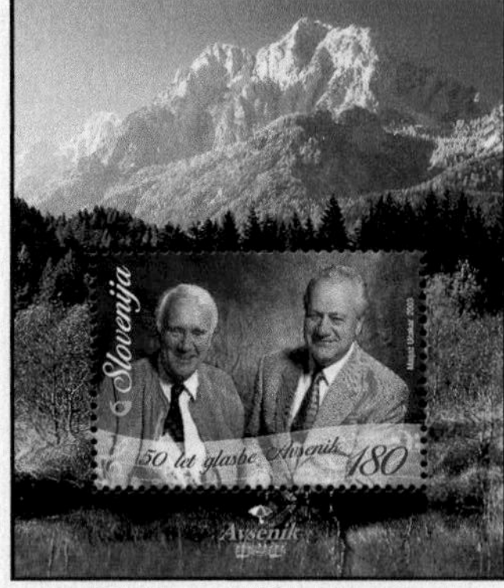

Slavko and Vilko Avsenik, Musicians — A224

2003, May 22
525 A224 180t multi 2.75 2.75

European Water Polo Championships, Kranj and Ljubljana — A225

2003, May 22
526 A225 180t multi 2.50 1.50

Painted Beehive Panel A226

2003, May 22
527 A226 218t multi 3.00 1.60

Fruit, Blossom and Insect Type of 2000

Designs: No. 528, Olive blossom. No. 529, Olive fruit fly. No. 530, Olives on branch.

2003, Sept. 18 ***Perf. 13¾x14***
Vignette Frame Size 20x26½mm

528 A168 B multi .90 .45
529 A168 B multi .90 .45
530 A168 B multi .90 .45
a. Horiz. strip, #528-530 2.75 1.40

Nos. 528-530 each sold for 44t on day of issue.

Stampless Covers, 1830 A227

2003, Sept. 18 ***Perf. 14***
531 A227 A multi 1.00 .50

No. 531 sold for 38t on day of issue.

Illustration from the Tournament Book of Gasper Lamberger — A228

Jousting contest: a, 76t, Riderless horse. b, 570t, Horse with rider.

2003, Sept. 18 ***Perf. 13¾***
532 A228 Horiz. pair, #a-b 8.50 4.75

Farm Animals A229

Designs: 95t, Krsko Polje pig. 107t, Cika cattle. 148t, Jezersko-Solcava sheep. 368t, Styrian hen and rooster, vert.

2003, Sept. 18 ***Perf. 14***
533-535 A229 Set of 3 4.75 2.50

Souvenir Sheet

536 A229 368t multi 4.75 4.75

Opening of Mail Sorting and Logistics Center, Maribor A230

Litho. with Hologram Applied
2003, Nov. 11 ***Perf. 13¾x14¼***
537 A230 221t multi 2.75 1.50

Franja Partisan Hospital, 60th Anniv. A231

2003, Nov. 19 **Litho.** ***Perf. 14***
538 A231 76t brown & bronze 1.10 .60

Wooden Cart A232

2003, Nov. 19
539 A232 221t multi 3.25 1.60

Christmas A233

2003, Nov. 19 ***Perf. 14***
540 A233 D multi 1.50 .75

Serpentine Die Cut 7¼
Booklet Stamp
Self-Adhesive

541 A233 D multi 2.00 1.00
a. Booklet pane of 12 24.00

No. 540 and 541 each sold for 107t on day of issue.

New Year's Greetings A234

2003, Nov. 19 **Litho.** ***Perf. 14***
542 A234 B multi 1.00 .50

Serpentine Die Cut 7¼
Booklet Stamp
Self-Adhesive

543 A234 B multi 1.25 .60
a. Booklet pane of 12 15.00

No. 542 and 543 each sold for 44t on day of issue.

Traditional Clothing from Vipava Valley A235

2004, Jan. 22 **Litho.** ***Perf. 13¾***
544 A235 A multi .75 .35

No. 544 sold for 38t on day of issue.

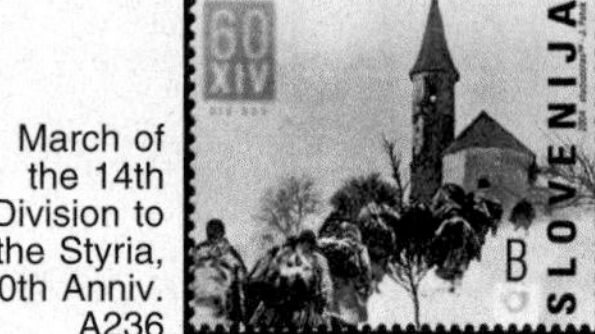

March of the 14th Division to the Styria, 60th Anniv. A236

2004, Jan. 22 ***Perf. 14***
545 A236 B multi .75 .35

Edvard Kocbek (1904-81), Writer A237

2004, Jan. 22
546 A237 D multi 1.50 .75

No. 546 sold for 107t on day of issue.

Love A238

2004, Jan. 22 ***Perf. 11***
547 A238 180t multi 2.50 1.50

Values are for examples with surrounding selvage.

Srecko Kosovel (1904-26), Writer A239

2004, Jan. 22 ***Perf. 14***
548 A239 221t black & red 3.00 1.60

Sixth Men's European Handball Championships A240

2004, Jan. 22
549 A240 221t multi 2.75 1.60

Fossil Type of 2000

2004, Mar. 24 Litho. *Perf. 14*
550 A165 D Fish 1.40 .70

No. 541 sold for 107t on day of issue.

European Men's Gymnastic Championships, Ljubljana — A241

2004, Mar. 24
551 A241 D multi 1.75 .85

No. 551 sold for 107t on day of issue.

Bled, 1000th Anniv. — A242

2004, Mar. 24
552 A242 218t multi 2.75 1.60

Kekec, the Shepherd Boy, by Josip Vandot — A243

Designs: No. 553, B, Kekec. No. 554, B, Pehta. No. 555, B, Kosobrin. No. 556, B, Kekec. No. 557, B, Pehta. No. 558, B, Kosobrin.

2004, Mar. 24 *Perf. 14*
553-555 A243 Set of 3 2.00 1.00

Serpentine Die Cut 7¼

Booklet Stamps

556-558 A243 Set of 3 2.00 1.00
558a Booklet pane, 3 each #556-558 6.00

Nos. 553-558 each sold for 44t on day of issue.

Admission to NATO A244

2004, Apr. 2 Litho. *Perf. 14*
559 A244 D multi 1.50 .75

No. 559 sold for 107t on day of issue.

Admission to the European Union — A245

2004, May 1
560 A245 95t multi 1.25 .60

Laurenz Koschier (1804-79), Proposer of Postage Stamps A246

2004, May 21
561 A246 B multi .80 .40

No. 561 sold for 48t on day of issue.

Posthorns — A247

Booklet Stamp

Serpentine Die Cut 12½

2004, May 21 Self-Adhesive
562 A247 B multi .90 .45
a. Booklet pane of 8 7.25

No. 562 sold for 48t on day of issue. See Nos. 583-583A

Europa — A248

2004, May 21 *Perf. 14*
563 A248 D multi 1.50 .75

No. 563 sold for 107t on day of issue.

Puch Bicycle, Chainwheel and Chain — A249

2004, May 21
564 A249 110t multi 1.25 .60

Painted Beehive Panel and Bee A250

2004, May 21
565 A250 218t multi 3.00 1.50

See also No. 600.

2004 Summer Olympics, Athens — A251

No. 566: a, C, Discus thrower, silhouette of gymnast. b, Long jumper, silhouette of pole vaulter.

2004, May 21
566 A251 Horiz. pair, #a-b 2.75 1.40

No. 566a sold for 95t; No. 566b sold for 107t on day of issue.

Souvenir Sheet

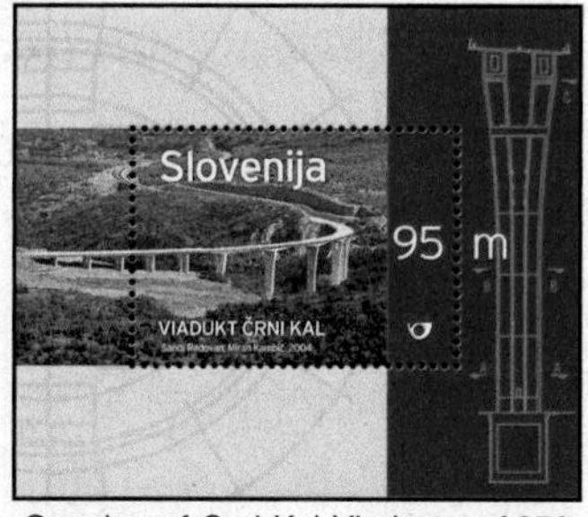

Opening of Crni Kal Viaduct — A252

2004, Sept. 15 Litho. *Perf. 14*
567 A252 95t multi 1.25 1.25

Fruit, Blossoms and Insect Type of 2000

Designs: No. 568, Pear blossom. No. 569, Pear psylla. No. 570, Pear.

Vignette Frame Size 19x26½mm

2004, Sept. 22 *Perf. 13¾*
568 A168 A multi .65 .30
569 A168 A multi .65 .30
570 A168 A multi .65 .30
a. Horiz. strip, #568-570 2.00 1.00

Nos. 568-570 each sold for 45t on day of issue.

First Mention of Town of Maribor in Document, 750th Anniv. A253

2004, Sept. 22 *Perf. 13*
571 A253 C multi 1.50 .75

No. 571 sold for 95t on day of issue.

Orchids A254

Designs: B, Epipactis palustris. D, Ophrys holosericea.

2004, Sept. 22 *Perf. 14*
572 A254 B multi 1.00 .50

Souvenir Sheet

573 A254 D multi 2.00 2.00

Nos. 572 and 573 sold for 52t and 107t respectively on day of issue.
See also Nos. 609-610.

Illuminated Manuscripts — A255

No. 574: a, Illuminated "P." b, Illuminated "Q."

2004, Sept. 22
574 A255 107t Pair, #a-b 2.75 1.40

Souvenir Sheet

Signing of Second London Memorandum, 50th Anniv. — A256

2004, Sept. 22
575 A256 221t multi 3.25 3.25

Christmas A257

2004, Nov. 18 *Perf. 14*
576 A257 C multi 1.50 .75

Booklet Stamp

Self-Adhesive

Serpentine Die Cut 7¼

577 A257 C multi 1.75 .85
a. Booklet pane of 12 21.00

Nos. 576 and 577 each sold for 95t on day of issue.

New Year's Greetings — A258

2004, Nov. 18 *Perf. 14*
578 A258 A multi .70 .35

Booklet Stamp

Self-Adhesive

Serpentine Die Cut 7¼

579 A258 A multi .80 .40
a. Booklet pane of 12 9.50

Nos. 578 and 579 each sold for 45t on day of issue.

Native Dishes — A259

No. 580 — Map and cuisine of the Prekmurje region: a, Prekmurska gibanica (pie). b, Bograc, butja repa (goulash, pickled turnips).

2004, Nov. 18 *Perf. 13¾*
580 A259 52t Pair, #a-b 1.60 .85

Birth Fairies Rojenice and Sojenice — A260

2004, Nov. 18 *Perf. 14*
581 A260 180t multi 2.50 1.40

Traditional Clothing From Pohorje and Kobansko Areas A261

2005, Jan. 21 *Perf. 11¾x11¼*
582 A261 A multi .75 .35

No. 582 sold for 45t on day of issue.

Posthorn Type of 2004

2005 *Perf. 14, 11¼x11¾ (#583A)*
583 A247 83t multi 1.40 .70
583A A247 83t multi 1.40 .70

Issued: No. 583, 1/21; No. 583A, 4/2. Size of No. 583: 25x34mm.

Janez Sigismund Valentin Popovic (1705-74), Linguist, Scientist — A262

2005, Jan. 21 *Perf. 11¼x11¾*
584 A262 107t multi 1.40 .70

Love A263

2005, Jan. 21 *Perf. 11*
585 A263 180t multi 2.50 1.25

Values are for stamps with surrounding selvage.

Janez Trdina (1830-1905), Writer — A264

2005, Jan. 21 *Perf. 11¼x11¾*
586 A264 221t multi 3.50 1.75

Return of Slovenian Exiles, 60th Anniv. A265

2005, Mar. 18 *Perf. 11¾x11¼*
587 A265 A multi 1.00 .50

No. 587 sold for 49t on day of issue.

Victory in World War II, 60th Anniv. A266

2005, Mar. 18
588 A266 B multi 1.10 .60

No. 588 sold for 57t on day of issue.

Souvenir Sheet

National Tourist Association, Cent. — A267

2005, Mar. 18 *Perf. 11¼*
589 A267 100t multi 1.50 1.50

Zoisite A268

2005, Mar. 18 *Perf. 11¾x11¼*
590 A268 D multi 2.00 1.00

No. 590 sold for 107t on day of issue.

Folk Tales — A269

Designs: No. 591, A, The Golden Fish. No. 592, A, The Grateful Bear.

2005, Mar. 18 *Perf. 11¼x11¾*
591-592 A269 Set of 2 1.50 .75

Nos. 591 and 592 each sold for 49t on day of issue.

Folk Tales Type of 2005

Serpentine Die Cut 7¼

2005, Mar. 18 **Litho.**

Booklet Stamps

Self-Adhesive

593 A269 A Like #591 .75 .30
594 A269 A Like #592 .75 .30
a. Booklet pane, 4 each #593, 594 6.00

Nos. 593 and 594 each sold for 49t on day of issue.

Child and Sunflower — A270

Die Cut Perf. 12½x12¼

2005, May 20 **Litho.**

Self-Adhesive

595 A270 A multi .75 .35
a. Serpentine die cut 13¾x14½ .65 .35

No. 595 sold for 49t on day of issue. No. 595a sold for 23c when issued in 2008.

1910 Puch Motorcycle A271

2005, May 20 *Perf. 11¾x11¼*
596 A271 98t multi 1.50 .75

Europa A272

2005, May 20
597 A272 D multi 1.75 .85

No. 597 sold for 107t on day of issue.

Postal Wagon and Mail Box — A273

2005, May 20
598 A273 107t multi 1.50 .75

Vesna, Goddess of Spring — A274

2005, May 20 *Perf. 11¼x11¾*
599 A274 180t multi 2.40 1.25

Painted Beehive Panel Type of 2004

2005, May 20 *Perf. 11¾x11¼*
600 A250 221t Hunter and bird 3.25 1.60

Bishop Anton Jeglic and St. Stanislav's Institute A275

2005, May 20
601 A275 221t multi 3.25 1.60

St. Stanislav's Institute, cent.

European Philatelic Cooperation, 50th Anniv. (in 2006) — A276

Magnifying glass and details from Slovenian stamps: No. 602, 60t, #495 (circus elephant). No. 603, 60t, #285 (ram), and stamp tongs. No. 604, 60t, #349 (river). #605, 60t, #195 (Jurij Vega).

2005, May 20 *Perf. 14x13½*
602-605 A276 Set of 4 3.75 1.90
605a Souvenir sheet, #602-605, perf. 14 3.75 1.90

Fruit, Blossoms and Insects Type of 2000

Designs: No. 606, Apricot blossom. No. 607, Apricots on branch. No. 608, San José scale on branch.

2005, July 5 *Perf. 11¾x11¼*

Size 19x23mm

606 A168 D multi 1.75 .90
607 A168 D multi 1.75 .90
608 A168 D multi 1.75 .90
a. Horiz. strip, #606-608 5.25 2.75

Nos. 606-608 each sold for 107t on day of issue.

Orchids Type of 2004

Designs: B, Dactylorhiza sambucina. D, Platanithera bifolia.

2005, Sept. 23 *Perf. 11¾x11¼*

Size: 37x26mm

609 A254 B multi 1.00 .50

Souvenir Sheet

610 A254 D multi 2.00 2.00

No. 609 sold for 57t and No. 610 sold for 107t on day of issue. No. 610 contains one 41x28mm stamp.

Dance of Death Fresco, by Janez of Kastav — A277

No. 611: a, Denomination in gray. b, Denomination in brown.

Litho. & Embossed

2005, Sept. 23 *Perf. 13½x13¾*
611 A277 107t Horiz. pair, #a-b 3.25 1.60

Dogs A278

Designs: A, Posavec hound. B, Istrian rough-coated hound. C, Slovenian mountain hound.
D, Istrian smooth-coated hound, vert.

2005, Sept. 23 *Perf. 11¾x11¼*
612-614 A278 Set of 3 3.75 2.00

Souvenir Sheet

Perf. 11¼

615 A278 D multi 3.00 2.00

On day of issue, No. 612 sold for 49t, No. 613, 57t, No. 614, 95t, and No. 615, 107t. No. 615 contains one 28x41mm stamp.

Types of 1993 Redrawn

2005 **Litho.** *Perf. 11¼x11¾*

Size: 26x36mm

616 A38 A Like #374 .60 .30
617 A38 B Like #373 .70 .35
618 A38 B Like #375 .70 .35
619 A38 B Like #375A .70 .35
620 A38 90t Like #216 1.25 .60
621 A38 C Like #376 1.25 .60

622 A38 D Like #378 1.50 .75
623 A38 D Like #379 1.50 .75
Nos. 616-623 (8) 8.20 4.05

Issued: Nos. 616-617, 3/18; Nos. 618, 622, 4/2; Nos. 619-621, 623, 5/4. On day of issue No. 616 sold for 49t, Nos. 618-619 each sold for 57t, No. 621 sold for 95t, and Nos. 622-623 each sold for 107t.

Size of Nos. 216, 373-375, 375A, 376, 378-379: 25x34mm.

Castles Type of 2000-04 Redrawn

2005 Litho. *Perf. 11¼x11¾*
Size: 24x34mm

624 A167 1t Predjama .25 .25
625 A167 1t Velenje .25 .25
a. Pair, #624-625 .50 .50
626 A167 C Gewerkenegg 1.25 .60
627 A167 100t Podsreda 1.25 .60
628 A167 100t Bled 1.25 .60
a. Pair, #626-627 2.50 1.25
Nos. 624-628 (5) 4.25 2.30

Issued: Nos. 626, 4/2; others 5/4. No. 626 sold for 95t on day of issue.

Size of Nos. 400-401, 411B, 412-413: 23x32mm.

Fruits, Blossoms and Insects Type of 2000 Redrawn

2005 Litho. *Perf. 11¾x11¼*
Vignette Frame Size: 19x23mm

629 A168 5t Like #426 .25 .25
630 A168 5t Like #427 .25 .25
631 A168 5t Like #428 .25 .25
a. Strip of 3, #629-631 .50 .25
632 A168 10t Like #416 .25 .25
633 A168 10t Like #417 .25 .25
634 A168 10t Like #418 .25 .25
a. Strip of 3, #632-634 .50 .25
635 A168 A Like #568 .60 .30
636 A168 A Like #569 .60 .30
637 A168 A Like #570 .60 .30
a. Strip of 3, #635-637 1.75 .90
638 A168 50t Like #464 .65 .30
639 A168 50t Like #465 .65 .30
640 A168 50t Like #466 .65 .30
a. Strip of 3, #638-640 2.00 .90
641 A168 B Like #528 .80 .40
642 A168 B Like #529 .80 .40
643 A168 B Like #530 .80 .40
a. Strip of 3, #641-643 2.40 1.20
644 A168 150t Like #502 1.75 .85
645 A168 150t Like #503 1.75 .85
646 A168 150t Like #504 1.75 .85
a. Strip of 3, #644-646 5.25 2.50
Nos. 629-646 (18) 12.90 7.05

Issued: Nos. 629-631, 638-640, 5/4; Nos. 632-634, 4/2; Nos. 635-637, 7/22; Nos. 641-643, 6/30; Nos. 644-646, 7/5. On day of issue Nos. 635-637 each sold for 49t; Nos. 641-643 each sold for 57t.

Sizes of vignette frames of Nos. 426-428, 416-418, 568-570, 464-466, 528-530, and 502-504 vary from 19 to 20x26 to 26½mm. Some designs extend beyond vignette frames.

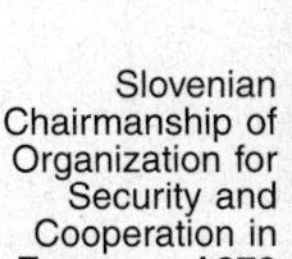

Slovenian Chairmanship of Organization for Security and Cooperation in Europe — A279

2005, Nov. 18 *Perf. 11¼x11¾*
647 A279 107t multi 1.60 .80

Traditional Foods — A280

No. 648: a, Prleska Gibanica and Ajdov Krapec. b, Prleska Tunka (bread, meat, lard and onion on wooden barrel).

2005, Nov. 18
648 A280 107t Pair, #a-b 3.25 1.60

New Year's Day — A281

2005, Nov. 18 *Perf. 11¾x11¼*
649 A281 A multi .85 .40

Size: 40x28mm
Self-Adhesive
Serpentine Die Cut 7¼

650 A281 A multi .85 .40
a. Booklet pane of 12 10.50

Nos. 649-650 each sold for 49t on day of issue.

Christmas A282

2005, Nov. 18 *Perf. 11¾x11¼*
651 A282 C multi 1.40 .70

Size: 40x28mm
Self-Adhesive
Serpentine Die Cut 7¼

652 A282 C multi 1.40 .70
a. Booklet pane of 12 17.00

Nos. 651-652 each sold for 95t on day of issue.

Traditional Carinthian Clothing A283

2006, Jan. 20 *Perf. 14*
653 A283 A multi 1.00 .50

No. 653 sold for 49t on day of issue.

Love A284

2006, Jan. 20 *Perf. 11*
654 A284 B multi 1.00 .50

No. 654 sold for 57t on day of issue. Values are for stamps with surrounding selvage.

Dr. Anton Trstenjak (1906-96), Psychologist — A285

2006, Jan. 20 *Perf. 14*
655 A285 B multi 1.00 .50

No. 655 sold for 57t on day of issue.

Ponikve Carnival — A286

2006, Jan. 20
656 A286 420t multi 4.50 2.25

2006 Winter Olympics, Turin — A287

No. 657: a, 95t, Ski jumper. b, 107t, Snowboarder.

2006, Jan. 20
657 A287 Horiz. pair, #a-b, + label at right 3.00 1.50

Printed in sheets containing 3 pairs and labels.

Pericnik Waterfall — A288

2006, Mar. 24
658 A288 D multi 2.25 1.10

No. 658 sold for 107t on day of issue.

Pereiraea Gervaisi Fossil — A289

2006, Mar. 24
659 A289 D multi 1.75 .90

No. 659 sold for 107t on day of issue.

Butterflies A290

Designs: B, Erannis ankeraria. D, Erebia calcaria.

2006, Mar. 24 *Perf. 14*
660 A290 B multi .80 .50

Souvenir Sheet
Perf. 14x14x13x14

661 A290 D multi 2.00 2.00

On day of issue No. 660 sold for 57t; No. 661 for 107t.

Children's Book Characters — A291

Designs: Nos. 662, 664, A, Zvezdica Zaspanka, by Frane Milicinski Jezek. No. 663, 665, A, Zogica Nogica, by Jan Malik.

2006, Mar. 24 Litho. *Perf. 14*
662-663 A291 Set of 2 1.40 .70

Booklet Stamps
Self-Adhesive
Serpentine Die Cut 7¼

664-665 A291 Set of 2 2.50 1.25
a. Booklet pane, 4 each #664-665 10.00

On day of issue Nos. 662-663, 664-665 each sold for 49t.

World Junior Slalom Kayaking Championships, Solkan — A292

2006, May 19 *Perf. 14*
666 A292 C multi 1.60 .80

No. 666 sold for 95t on day of issue.

Greetings — A293

Serpentine Die Cut 9¼x9
2006, May 19 Self-Adhesive
667 A293 C multi 1.50 .75

No. 667 sold for 95t on day of issue.

Painted Beehive Type of 2004

2006, May 19 *Perf. 14*
668 A250 D Hay rake fighters 2.00 1.00

No. 668 sold for 107t on day of issue.

Europa — A294

2006, May 19
669 A294 D multi 1.60 .80

No. 669 sold for 107t on day of issue. Printed in sheets of 8 + label.

Svarog, Slavic Sun God — A295

2006, May 19

670 A295 D multi 1.50 .85

No. 670 sold for 107t on day of issue.

Souvenir Sheet

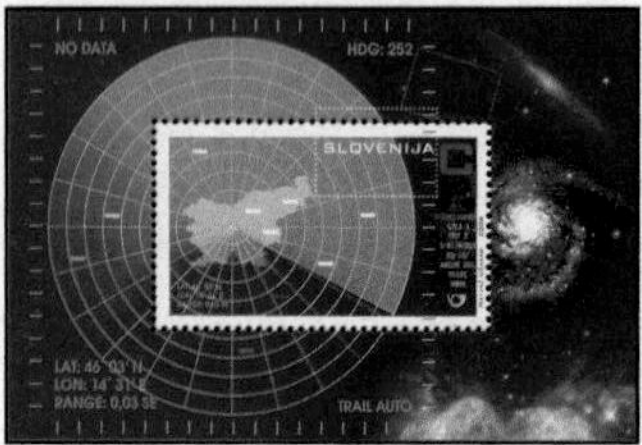
Slovenian Air Traffic Control, 15th Anniv. — A296

2006, June 25 ***Perf. 13¼x14***

671 A296 C multi 2.00 2.00

No. 671 sold for 95t on day of issue.

Ox-drawn Farm Wagon A297

2006, Sept. 22 ***Perf. 14***

672 A297 D multi 1.75 .85

No. 672 sold for 107t on day of issue.

Souvenir Sheet

Ceiling Painting, Celje Mansion — A298

No. 673 — Text "Masa Kozjek, Tomaz Lauko" at: a, LL. b, LR. c, UL. d, UR.

2006, Sept. 22

673 A298 D Sheet of 4, #a-d 5.25 2.50

Nos. 673a-673d each sold for 107t on day of issue.

Aquatic Plants — A299

Designs: A, Salvinia natans and silhouette of frog. D, Marsilea quadrifolia and silhouette of dragonfly.

2006, Sept. 22

674 A299 A multi .85 .40

Souvenir Sheet

675 A299 D multi 1.60 .85

On day of issue No. 674 sold for 49t and No. 675 sold for 107t.

Fruit, Blossoms and Insects Type of 2000

Designs: No. 676, Persimmon blossom (cvet kakija). No. 677, Persimmon (kaki). No. 678, Citrus flatid planthopper (Medeci skrzat).

2006, Nov. 17 ***Perf. 11¾x11¼***

Vignette Size: 19x23mm

676 A168 D multi 1.30 .75
677 A168 D multi 1.30 .75
678 A168 D multi 1.30 .75
a. Horiz. strip of 3, #676-678 4.00 2.25

On day of issue Nos. 676-678 each sold for 107t.

Partisan Couriers of World War II — A300

2006, Nov. 17 ***Perf. 14***

679 A300 C multi 1.40 .75

No. 679 sold for 95t on day of issue.

Traditional Foods — A301

No. 680: a, Roast turkey, bread, corn, apple. b, Yeast cake (kvaseníca).

2006, Nov. 17

680 A301 D Horiz. pair, #a-b 3.00 1.50

On day of issue Nos. 680a-680b each sold for 107t.

Souvenir Sheet

Father Simon Asic (1906-92), Herbalist — A302

2006, Nov. 17

681 A302 D multi 1.75 .85

No. 681 sold for 107t on day of issue.

Christmas — A303

Designs: A, Snowman and bird. C, Carolers.

2006, Nov. 17 ***Perf. 14***

682 A303 A multi .75 .40
683 A303 C multi 1.50 .75

Booklet Stamps
Self-Adhesive
Serpentine Die Cut 7¼

684 A303 A multi .75 .40
a. Booklet pane of 12 9.00
685 A303 C multi 1.50 .75
a. Booklet pane of 12 18.00
Nos. 682-685 (4) 4.50 2.30

On day of issue Nos. 682 and 684 each sold for 49t, and Nos. 683 and 685 each sold for 95t.

100 Cents = 1 Euro

Flora — A304

Designs: 1c, Asplenium adulterinum. 2c, Moehringia tommasinii. 5c, Himantoglossum adriaticum. 10c, Pulsatilla grandis. 20c, Primula carniolica. A, Campanula zoysii. B, Cypripedium calceolus. 25c, Gladiolus palustris. 35c, Cerastium dinaricum. C, Serratula lycopifolia. D, Genisia holopetala. 48c, Adenophora liliifolia. 50c, Aquilegia bertolonii. 75c, Liparis loeselii. 92c, Scilla litardierei. €1, Eryngium alpinum. €2, Rhododendron luteum.

2007, Jan. 1 Litho. ***Perf. 11¼x11¾***

686 A304 1c multi .30 .30
687 A304 2c multi .30 .30
688 A304 5c multi .30 .30
689 A304 10c multi .35 .30
690 A304 20c multi .65 .30
691 A304 A multi .65 .30
692 A304 B multi .75 .35
693 A304 25c multi .80 .40
694 A304 35c multi 1.10 .55
695 A304 C multi 1.40 .70
696 A304 D multi 1.50 .75
697 A304 48c multi 1.50 .75
698 A304 50c multi 1.60 .80
699 A304 75c multi 2.25 1.10
700 A304 92c multi 2.75 1.40
701 A304 €1 multi 3.00 1.50
702 A304 €2 multi 6.00 3.00
Nos. 686-702 (17) 25.20 13.10

On day of issue No. 691 sold for 20c; No. 692 for 24c; No. 695 for 40c; No. 696 for 45c.
See Nos. 787-797, 881-882.

Souvenir Sheet

Introduction of Euro Currency — A305

Perf. 13¼x13 Syncopated

2007, Jan. 1

703 A305 €1 multi 3.25 3.25

Traditional Clothing From Smlednik A306

2007, Jan. 24 ***Perf. 11¾x11¼***

704 A306 20c multi 1.00 .50

Bride and Groom A307

2007, Jan. 24 ***Perf. 11***

705 A307 24c multi .85 .50

Values are for stamps with surrounding selvage.

Vasja Pirc (1907-80), Chess Grandmaster — A308

2007, Jan. 24 ***Perf. 14***

706 A308 48c multi 1.50 .80

A309

A310

A311

Generic Personalized Stamps A312

Serpentine Die Cut 12x11½, 11½x12

2007, Jan. 24 **Self-Adhesive**

707 A309 A multi 1.25 .60
708 A310 A multi 1.25 .60
709 A311 A multi 1.25 .60
710 A312 A multi 1.25 .60
Nos. 707-710 (4) 5.00 2.40

On day of issue Nos. 707-710 each sold for 20c. Images within the frames shown above are generic images and were the only stamps with these frames sold at 20c. Stamps with these frames and other images are personalized stamps, created starting on Mar. 8, which sold in sheets of 20 for €12.51 per sheet.

Aragonite A313

2007, Mar. 23 ***Perf. 11¾x11¼***

711 A313 45c multi 1.40 .80

Mt. Mangart and Geum Reptans A314

2007, Mar. 23 ***Perf. 14***

712 A314 45c multi 1.40 .80

Europa A315

2007, Mar. 23

713 A315 50c multi *4.00 1.75*

Scouting, cent. Printed in sheets of 8 + label.

Worldwide Fund for Nature (WWF) A316

Sciurus vulgaris: Nos. 714, 718a, 48c, Adult. Nos. 715, 718b, 48c, Adult eating acorn. Nos. 716, 718c, 48c, Two adults. Nos. 717, 718d, 48c, Adult and young.

2007, Mar. 23 ***Perf. 11¾x11¼***

Size: 33x24mm

714-717 A316 Set of 4 5.00 2.75

Miniature Sheet

Perf. 13x13¼

Size: 36x26mm

718 A316 48c Sheet, 2 each #a-d 10.50 5.75

Elves — A317

2007, May 25 **Litho.** ***Perf. 14***

719 A317 45c multi 1.40 .80

Treaty of Rome, 50th Anniv. — A318

2007, May 25 ***Perf. 11¼x11¾***

720 A318 45c multi 1.75 .90

Horse-drawn Wagon — A319

2007, May 25 ***Perf. 14***

721 A319 92c multi 2.75 1.40

Butterflies A320

Designs: 24c, Callimorpha quadripunctaria. 45c, Colias myrmidone, vert.

2007, May 25

722 A320 24c multi .85 .45

Souvenir Sheet

723 A320 45c multi 1.75 .90

Souvenir Sheet

Year of the Bible — A321

2007, May 25

724 A321 75c multi 2.25 1.50

Lent Festival, Maribor A322

2007, June 22 ***Perf. 14x13¼***

725 A322 €1 multi 3.25 1.75

Printed in sheets of 6 + 3 labels.

Wall Climbing A323

2007, Sept. 26 ***Perf. 14***

726 A323 48c multi 1.60 .80

Printed in sheets of 6 + 3 labels.

Ceiling Fresco, Church of St. Nicholas, Ljubljana, by Giulio Quaglio A324

2007, Sept. 26 ***Perf. 11¾x11¼***

727 A324 92c multi 2.75 1.40

Aquatic Flowers — A325

Designs: 20c, Nuphar luteum. 24c, Hydrocharis morsus-ranae. 40c, Nymphoides peltata.

45c, Nymphaea alba, horiz.

2007, Sept. 26 ***Perf. 14***

728-730 A325 Set of 3 2.50 1.40

Souvenir Sheet

731 A325 45c multi 1.40 .75

Slovenian Entry Into Schengen Border-Free Zone — A326

2007, Nov. 23 ***Perf. 11¾x11¼***

732 A326 45c multi 1.50 .75

Slovenian Food — A327

No. 733: a, Stajerska sour soup, Pohorski stew. b, Pohorje omelet.

2007, Nov. 23 ***Perf. 11¼x11¾***

733 A327 45c Horiz. pair, #a-b 2.75 1.50

Souvenir Sheet

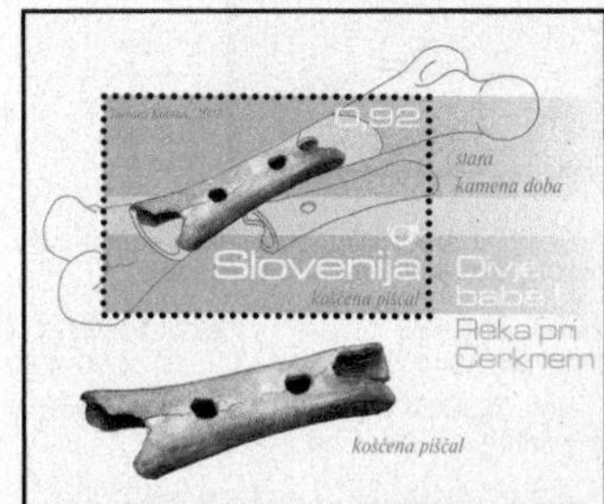

Bear Bone Flute From Divje Babe I Archaeological Site — A328

2007, Nov. 23 ***Perf. 14***

734 A328 92c multi 2.75 1.50

A329

A330

A331

Personalized Stamps A332

Serpentine Die Cut 12x11½, 11½x12

2007, Nov. 23 **Litho.**

735 A329 A green & org .75 .40

736 A330 A green & org .75 .40

737 A331 C gray & org 1.75 .90

738 A332 C gray & org 1.75 .90

Nos. 735-738 (4) 5.00 2.60

On day of issue, Nos. 735-736 each sold for 20c, and Nos. 737-738 each sold for 40c. Images within the frames shown above are generic images and were the only stamps sold at these prices. Stamps with these frames and other images are personalized stamps, which sold for more.

Christmas — A333

Perf. 13½x13¼

2007, Nov. 23 **Litho.**

739 A333 C multi 1.50 .80

No. 739 sold for 40c on day of issue.

New Year 2008 — A334

2007, Nov. 23 ***Perf. 13x13¼***

740 A334 A multi .75 .40

No. 740 sold for 20c on day of issue.

Slovenian postal authorities have declared illegal two sheetlets of six stamps with a denomination of "45" and bearing the name of "Slovenia" in Cyrillic lettering depicting Marilyn Monroe.

Souvenir Sheet

Slovenian Presidency of the European Union Council of Ministers — A335

Litho. With Foil Application

2008, Jan. 1 ***Perf. 14x13½***
741 A335 €2.38 multi 6.50 6.50

Traditional Clothing From Pesnica and Scavnica A336

2008, Jan. 29 Litho. ***Perf. 11¾x11½***
742 A336 20c multi .75 .75

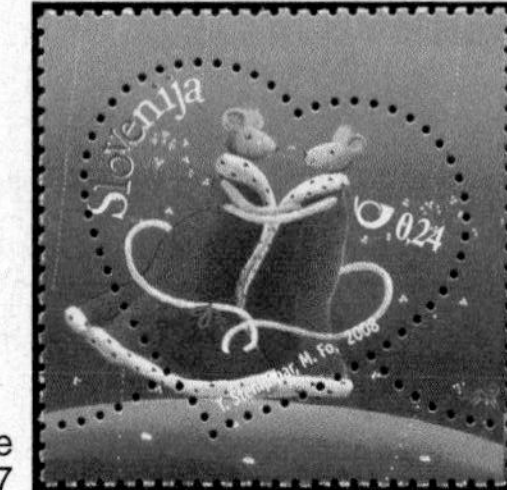

Love A337

2008, Jan. 29 ***Perf. 11***
743 A337 24c multi .75 .75

Values are for stamps with surrounding selvage.

Primoz Trubar (1508-86), Writer A338

2008, Jan. 29 ***Perf. 14***
744 A338 48c multi 1.40 1.40

Vrbica Carnival Masks — A339

2008, Jan. 29 ***Perf. 11¼x11¾***
745 A339 €1.75 multi 4.75 4.75

Dr. Julius Kugy (1858-1944), Botanist, and Scabiosa Trenta — A340

2008, Mar. 28 Litho. ***Perf. 14***
746 A340 45c multi 1.25 1.25

Flowers — A341

Designs: 20c, Paeonia officinalis. 24c, Pulsatilla montana. 40c, Iris illyrica. 45c, Gentiana tergestina.

2008, Mar. 28
747-749 A341 Set of 3 2.75 2.75

Souvenir Sheet

750 A341 45c multi 1.75 1.75

Slovenian Academy of Arts and Sciences, 70th Anniv. A342

2008, May 29 Litho. ***Perf. 14***
751 A342 40c multi 1.25 1.25

Mokos, Slavic Goddess — A343

2008, May 29
752 A343 45c multi 1.50 1.50

Europa A344

Designs: 45c, Winged letters, postal card, parcel. 92c, Letters as townspeople.

2008, May 29 ***Perf. 11¾x11¼***
753-754 A344 Set of 2 4.50 4.50

Nos. 753-754 were each printed in sheets of 8 + label.

2008 Summer Olympics, Beijing — A345

No. 755: a, 40c, Combat sports. b, 45c, Sailing.

2008, May 29
755 A345 Horiz. pair, #a-b 2.50 2.50

Stamp Day — A346

2008, Sept. 29 ***Perf. 11¼x11¾***
756 A346 23c multi .60 .60

Dr. Alojzij Sustar (1920-2007), Archbishop of Ljubljana — A347

2008, Sept. 29 ***Perf. 14***
757 A347 45c multi 1.10 1.10

Rococo Decorations, Gruber Palace — A348

2008, Sept. 29 ***Perf. 11¼x11¾***
758 A348 92c multi 2.50 2.50

Horse-drawn Sledge — A349

2008, Sept. 29 ***Perf. 14***
759 A349 92c multi 2.50 2.50

Souvenir Sheet

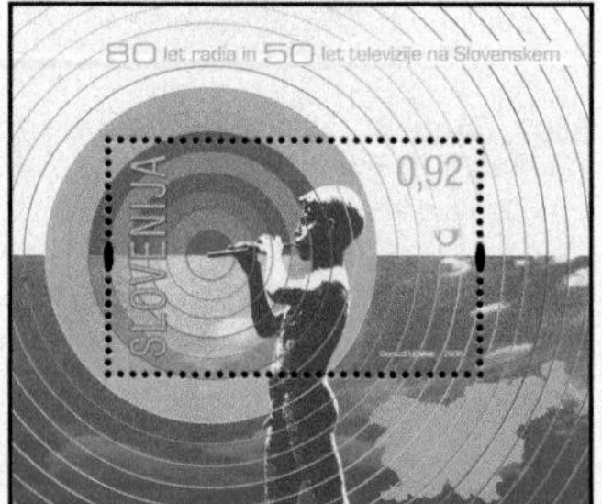

Slovenian Radio, 80th Anniv. and Slovenian Television, 50th Anniv. — A350

Perf. 13¼x14¼ Syncopated

2008, Sept. 29
760 A350 92c multi 2.50 2.50

Amphibians and Reptiles — A351

Designs: 23c, Rana latastei. 27c, Bombina bombina. 40c, Triturus carnifex. 45c, Elaphe quatuorlineata.

2008, Sept. 29 ***Perf. 14***
761-763 A351 Set of 3 2.50 2.50

Souvenir Sheet

764 A351 45c multi 1.40 1.40

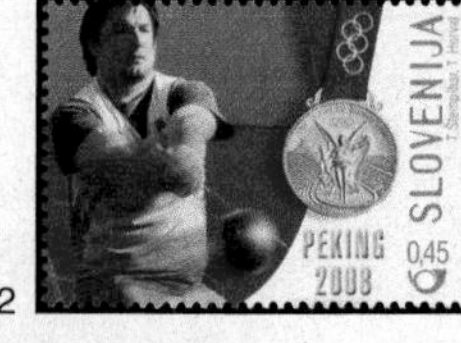

A352

Design: Primoz Kozmus, 2008 Hammer Throw Olympic Gold Medalist.

2008, Oct. 14 **Litho.**
765 A352 45c multi 1.25 1.25

Introduction of the Euro, 10th Anniv. (in 2009) — A353

2008, Nov. 27
766 A353 45c multi 1.25 1.25

End of World War I, 90th Anniv. A354

2008, Nov. 27
767 A354 92c multi 2.25 2.25

Souvenir Sheet

Wheel and Axle, c. 3200 B. C. — A355

2008, Nov. 27
768 A355 92c multi 2.25 2.25

Traditional Foods — A356

No. 769: a, Zgornjesavinjski zelodec (dried sausage), bread. b, Ubrnenik (dumpling), Solcavski sirnek (spiced cheese).

2008, Nov. 27 ***Perf. 11¼x11¾***
769 A356 45c Horiz. pair, #a-b 2.25 2.25

A357

Christmas A358

2008, Nov. 27 ***Perf. 11¼x11¾***

770 A357 A multi .80 .80

Perf. 11¾x11¼

771 A358 C multi 1.25 1.25

On day of issue, Nos. 770 and 771 sold for 23c and 40c, respectively.

Traditional Clothing From Bela Krajina A359

2009, Jan. 30 ***Perf. 11¾x11¼***

772 A359 23c multi .75 .75

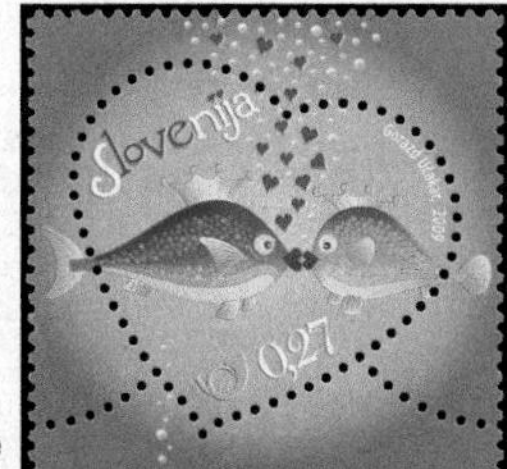

Love A360

2009, Jan. 30 ***Perf. 11***

773 A360 27c multi .75 .75

Values are for stamps with surrounding selvage.

Alojz Knafelc (1859-1937), Mountain Cartographer A361

2009, Jan. 30 ***Perf. 13¼x13***

774 A361 45c multi 1.25 1.25

Jozef Mrak (1709-86), Geodesist A362

2009, Jan. 30 ***Perf. 13x13¼***

775 A362 92c multi 2.50 2.50

Selma Carnival Costumes — A363

2009, Jan. 30 ***Perf. 11¼x11¾***

776 A363 €1.60 multi 4.25 4.25

Souvenir Sheet

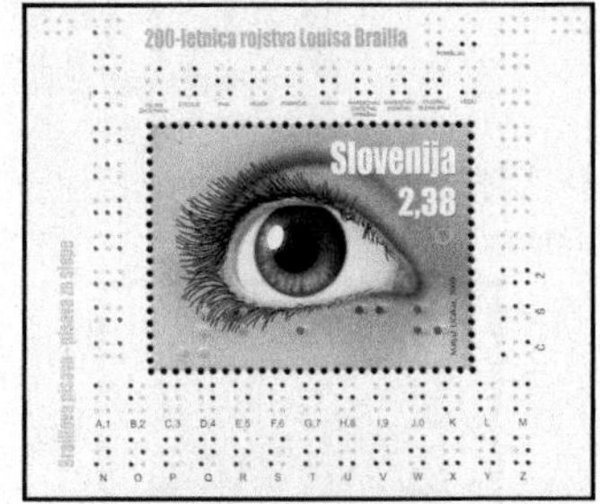

Eye and Braille Letters — A364

Litho. & Embossed

2009, Jan. 30 ***Perf. 13x13¼***

777 A364 €2.38 multi 7.00 7.00

Louis Braille (1809-52), educator of the blind.

Essay for First Stamps of Slovenia A365

Perf. 11¾x11½

2009, Mar. 27 **Litho.**

778 A365 23c multi .75 .75

First Slovenian stamps (Yugoslavia Nos. 3L1-3L8), 90th anniv.

Lovrenc Lakes A366

2009, Mar. 27 ***Perf. 13x13¼***

779 A366 35c multi 1.10 1.10

Zice Charterhouse — A367

2009, Mar. 27

780 A367 92c multi 2.60 2.60

Flowers A368

Designs: 23c, Centaurea cyanus. 27c, Papaver rhoeas. 40c, Agrostemma githago. 45c, Ranunculus arvensis.

2009, Mar. 27 ***Perf. 13x13¼***

781-783 A368 Set of 3 2.50 2.50

Souvenir Sheet

Perf. 14x13½

784 A368 45c multi 1.50 1.50

Souvenir Sheet

Preservation of Polar Regions and Glaciers — A369

No. 785: a, Polar bear and puffins. b, Killer whale and polar bears.

2009, Mar. 27 ***Perf. 13x13¼***

785 A369 45c Sheet of 2, #a-b 3.00 3.00

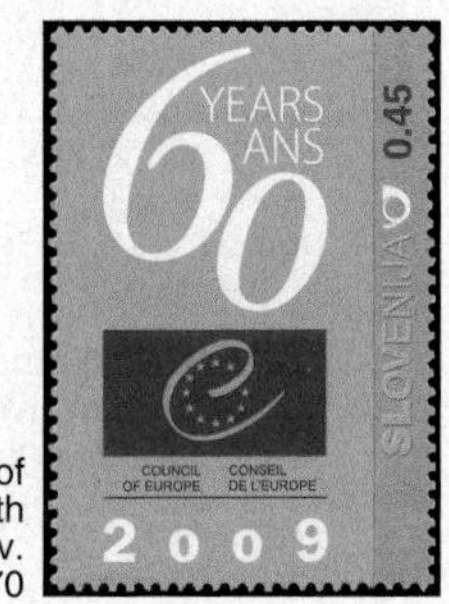

Council of Europe, 60th Anniv. A370

2009, May 8 ***Perf. 11¾x11¼***

786 A370 45c multi 1.25 1.25

Flora Type of 2007

Designs as before.

Self-Adhesive

Size: 23x30mm

Serpentine Die Cut 14x15

2009, May 29 **Litho.**

787	A304	1c multi	.25	.25
788	A304	10c multi	.30	.30
789	A304	20c multi	.55	.55
790	A304	25c multi	.70	.70
791	A304	A multi	.75	.75
a.		Serpentine die cut 11¼x11½		—
792	A304	B multi	.85	.85
a.		Serpentine die cut 11¼x11½		—
793	A304	35c multi	1.00	1.00
794	A304	C multi	1.10	1.10
795	A304	D multi	1.25	1.25
796	A304	75c multi	2.10	2.10
797	A304	€1 multi	2.75	2.75
		Nos. 787-797 (11)	11.60	11.60

On day of issue, No. 791 sold for 26c; No. 792, 30c; No. 794, 40c, No. 795, 45c. Issued: No. 791a, 5/21/13; No. 792a, 11/12/13. Four additional stamps were issued in this set. The editors would like to examine any examples.

Bread in Heart-shaped Loaf — A371

Serpentine Die Cut 14x15

2009, May 29 **Self-Adhesive**

798 A371 C multi 1.50 1.50

No. 798 sold for 40c on day of issue.

World Track and Field Championships, Berlin — A372

2009, May 29 ***Perf. 13¼x13***

799 A372 45c multi 1.25 1.25

Printed in sheets of 6 + 3 labels.

World Plowing Championships, Tesanovci — A373

2009, May 29 ***Perf. 13x13¼***

800 A373 45c multi 1.25 1.25

Werewolf A374

2009, May 29 ***Perf. 13¼x13***

801 A374 70c multi 2.00 2.00

Ljubljana Jazz Festival, 50th Anniv. — A375

2009, May 29 ***Perf. 11½x11¾***

802 A375 92c black & yellow 2.60 2.60

Europa A376

Designs: 45c, Stargazers. 92c, Observatory.

2009, May 29 ***Perf. 13x13¼***

803-804 A376 Set of 2 4.00 4.00

Intl. Year of Astronomy. Nos. 803-804 were each printed in sheets of 8 + label.

Trolleybus, Piran A377

2009, Sept. 25 **Litho.**
805 A377 92c multi 2.75 2.75

Transfer of Seat of the Lavant Diocese, 150th Anniv. — A378

2009, Sept. 25 ***Perf. 11½x11¾***
806 A378 92c multi 2.75 2.75

Bohinj Lake, by Anton Karinger — A379

2009, Sept. 25
807 A379 €1.50 multi 4.25 4.25

Beetles A380

Designs: 26c, Lucanus cervus. 30c, Rosalia alpina. 40c, Osmoderma eremita. 45c, Carabus variolosus.

2009, Sept. 25 ***Perf. 13x13¼***
808-810 A380 Set of 3 3.00 3.00

Souvenir Sheet

811 A380 45c multi 1.40 1.40

Souvenir Sheet

Stone Buildings — A381

No. 812 — Stone buildings in: a, Pazin, Croatia. b, Kopriva na Krasu, Slovenia.

2009, Sept. 25 ***Perf. 13 Syncopated***
812 A381 92c Sheet of 2, #a-b 5.50 5.50

See Croatia No. 743.

Souvenir Sheet

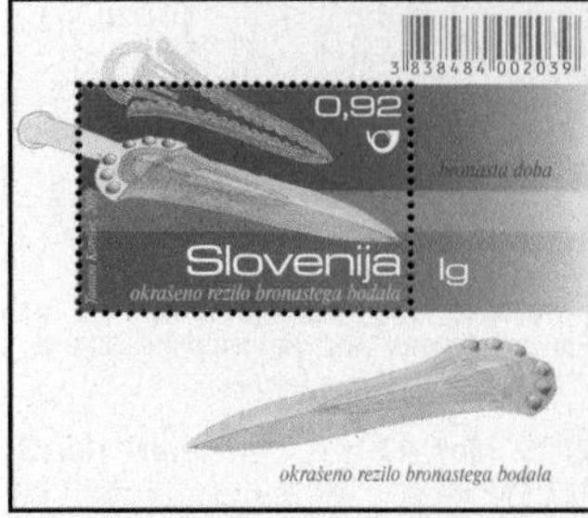

Bronze Age Dagger — A382

2009, Nov. 27 ***Perf. 13x14***
813 A382 92c multi 2.75 2.75

Traditional Foods — A383

No. 814: a, Funsterc ali knapovsko sonce (omelet) and Grenadirmars (potatoes and pasta). b, Zasavska jetrnica (sausage).

2009, Nov. 27 ***Perf. 11½x11¾***
814 A383 45c Horiz. pair, #a-b 2.75 2.75

Christmas
A384 A385

2009, Nov. 27 ***Perf. 11½x11¾***
815 A384 A multi .90 .90
816 A385 C multi 1.50 1.50

Booklet Stamps
Self-Adhesive
Serpentine Die Cut 12¾

817 A384 A multi .90 .90
a. Booklet pane of 12 11.00
818 A385 C multi 1.50 1.50
a. Booklet pane of 12 18.00

On day of issue, Nos. 815 and 817 each sold for 26c, and Nos. 816 and 818 each sold for 40c.

Vertical Orientation, Plain Frame — A386

Vertical Orientation, Candles in Frame — A387

Vertical Orientation, Flower in Frame — A388

Vertical Orientation, Book in Frame — A389

Horizontal Orientation, Plain Frame — A390

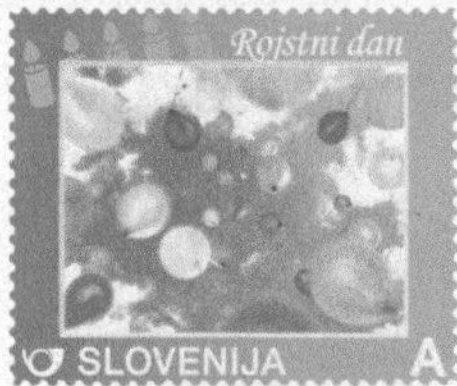

Horizontal Orientation, Candles in Frame — A391

Horizontal Orientation, Flower in Frame — A392

Horizontal Orientation, Book in Frame — A393

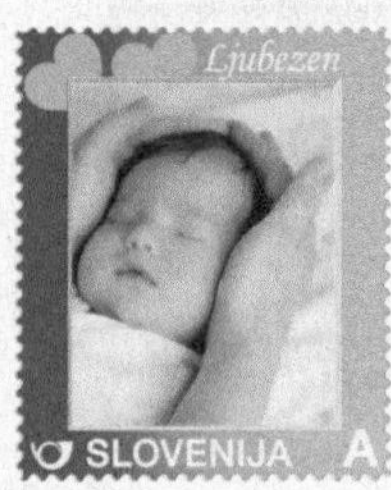

Vertical Orientation, Heart in Frame — A394

Vertical Orientation, Envleopes in Frame — A395

Horizontal Orientation, Heart in Frame — A396

Horizontal Orientation, Envelopes in Frame — A397

Serpentine Die Cut 11½x11¾ (#819, 821), 11¾x11½ (#820, 822)

2009, Nov. 27 **Litho.**

Self-Adhesive

819 Sheet of 20 22.50
a. A386 A red frame .80 .80
b. A387 A green frame .80 .80
c. A386 A white frame .80 .80
d. A388 A purple frame .80 .80
e. A389 A orange frame .80 .80
f. A386 B white frame .90 .90
g. A389 B orange frame .90 .90
h. A386 B red frame .90 .90
i. A388 B purple frame .90 .90
j. A387 B green frame .90 .90
k. A386 C red frame 1.25 1.25
l. A389 C orange frame 1.25 1.25
m. A386 C white frame 1.25 1.25
n. A387 C green frame 1.25 1.25
o. A388 C purple frame 1.25 1.25
p. A389 D orange frame 1.40 1.40
q. A387 D green frame 1.40 1.40
r. A388 D purple frame 1.40 1.40
s. A386 D white frame 1.40 1.40
t. A386 D red frame 1.40 1.40
820 Sheet of 20 22.50
a. A390 A white frame .80 .80
b. A392 A purple frame .80 .80
c. A393 A orange frame .80 .80
d. A391 A green frame .80 .80
e. A390 A red frame .80 .80
f. A390 B white frame .90 .90
g. A390 B red frame .90 .90
h. A391 B green frame .90 .90
i. A392 B purple frame .90 .90
j. A393 B orange frame .90 .90
k. A390 C red frame 1.25 1.25
l. A393 C orange frame 1.25 1.25
m. A392 C purple frame 1.25 1.25
n. A391 C green frame 1.25 1.25
o. A390 C white frame 1.25 1.25
p. A391 D green frame 1.40 1.40
q. A393 D orange frame 1.40 1.40
r. A392 D purple frame 1.40 1.40
s. A390 D white frame 1.40 1.40
t. A390 D red frame 1.40 1.40
821 Sheet of 20 22.50
a. A394 A red frame .80 .80
b. A386 A gray frame .80 .80
c. A395 A blue frame .80 .80
d. A386 B dark blue frame .90 .90
e. A386 B orange frame .90 .90
f. A386 B green frame .90 .90
g. A395 B blue frame .90 .90
h. A386 B gray frame .90 .90
i. A394 B red frame .90 .90
j. A386 C orange frame 1.25 1.25
k. A386 C green frame 1.25 1.25
l. A395 C blue frame 1.25 1.25
m. A386 C dark blue frame 1.25 1.25
n. A394 C red frame 1.25 1.25
o. A394 D red frame 1.40 1.40
p. A386 D green frame 1.40 1.40
q. A386 D dark blue frame 1.40 1.40
r. A386 D orange frame 1.40 1.40
s. A386 D gray frame 1.40 1.40
t. A395 D blue frame 1.40 1.40
822 Sheet of 20 22.50
a. A390 A gray frame .80 .80
b. A397 A blue frame .80 .80
c. A396 A red frame .80 .80
d. A390 B green frame .90 .90
e. A396 B red frame .90 .90
f. A390 B dark blue frame .90 .90
g. A390 B gray frame .90 .90
h. A390 B orange frame .90 .90
i. A397 B blue frame .90 .90
j. A397 C blue frame 1.25 1.25
k. A390 C orange frame 1.25 1.25
l. A390 C green frame 1.25 1.25
m. A396 C red frame 1.25 1.25
n. A390 C dark blue frame 1.25 1.25
o. A396 D red frame 1.40 1.40

p.	A390 D dark blue frame	1.40	1.40
q.	A397 D blue frame	1.40	1.40
r.	A390 D gray frame	1.40	1.40
s.	A390 D green frame	1.40	1.40
t.	A390 D orange frame	1.40	1.40
	Nos. 819-822 (4)	90.00	

On day of issue, stamps inscribed "A" sold for 26c; "B" sold for 30c; "C" sold for 40c; and "D" sold for 45c. Each vignette on Nos. 819-822 is in sepia. All sepia vignettes are different on the four sheets and are generic images found only on those sheets. Stamps can be personalized, printed in sheets of 20 stamps that have one type of frame and frame color and one personalized image in the vignette area.

Traditional Clothing From Prekmurje A398

2010, Jan. 29 **Litho.** ***Perf. 13¾***
823 A398 26c multi .75 .75

Love A399

2010, Jan. 29 ***Perf. 11***
824 A399 30c multi .85 .85

Values are for stamps with surrounding selvage.

Arrows — A400

Serpentine Die Cut 15x14
2010, Jan. 29 **Self-Adhesive**
825 A400 D multi 2.40 2.40

No. 825 sold for 85c on day of issue and is for international priority mail.

New Year 2010 (Year of the Tiger) A401

2010, Jan. 29 ***Perf. 12¾x13***
826 A401 92c multi 3.00 3.00

Stanko Vraz (1810-51), Poet — A402

2010, Jan. 29 ***Perf. 13x12¾***
827 A402 €1.10 multi 3.25 3.25

Pustnaki Procession, Mozirje — A403

2010, Jan. 29 ***Perf. 13½x13¾***
828 A403 €1.60 multi 4.50 4.50

2010 Winter Olympics, Vancouver — A404

2010, Jan. 29 ***Perf. 12¾x13***
829 A404 Horiz. pair + label 2.40 2.40
a. 40c Ski flags 1.10 1.10
b. 45c Hockey puck and stick 1.25 1.25

Braided Palm Branches
A406 A407

Serpentine Die Cut 14x15
2010, Mar. 18 **Self-Adhesive**
830 A406 B multi .80 .80
831 A407 D multi 1.25 1.25

On day of issue, No. 830 sold for 30c and No. 831 sold for 45c.

Souvenir Sheet

World Ski Jumping Championships, Planica — A408

2010, Mar. 18 ***Perf. 13½x13¾***
832 A408 €2.38 multi 6.00 6.00

No. 832 has holes in the sheet margin reading "Planica 2010."

Izola A409

2010, Mar. 26 ***Perf. 12¾x13***
833 A409 92c multi 2.50 2.50

Jurkloster Monastery A410

2010, Mar. 26 **Litho.**
834 A410 92c multi 2.50 2.50

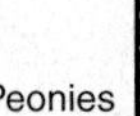

Peonies A411

Designs: 45c, Paeonia officinalis. 92c, Paeonia rockii.

2010, Mar. 26 ***Perf. 12¾x13***
835 A411 45c multi 1.25 1.25
a. Perf. 14¼x13¾ 1.60 1.60
836 A411 92c multi 2.50 2.50
a. Perf. 14¼x13¾ 3.50 3.50
b. Souvenir sheet, #835a-836a 5.00 5.00

Flowers A412

Designs: 26c, Dianthus sanguineus. 30c, Dianthus sternbergii. 40c, Dianthus deltoides. 92c, Dianthus carthusianorum.

2010, Mar. 26 ***Perf. 12¾x13***
837-839 A412 Set of 3 3.00 3.00

Souvenir Sheet
Perf. 14¼x13¾
840 A412 92c multi 2.60 2.60

Carved Wooden Pigeon — A413

Self-Adhesive
Serpentine Die Cut 14x15
2010, May 28 **Litho.**
841 A413 D multi 1.75 1.75

No. 841 sold for 45c on day of issue.

Kurent, Slovenian Deity — A414

2010, May 28 ***Perf. 13x12¾***
842 A414 70c multi 1.75 1.75

Sports World Championships — A415

Designs: No. 843, 92c, Soccer player, 2010 World Cup Soccer Championships, South Africa. No. 844, 92c, Basketball player, 2010 World Basketball Championships, Turkey.

2010, May 28 ***Perf. 13¾***
843-844 A415 Set of 2 4.75 4.75

Values are for stamps with surrounding selvage. Nos. 843-844 were printed in sheets containing four of each stamp and 2 central labels.

Europa A416

Designs: D, Boy reading book. 92c, Girl reading book.

2010, May 28 ***Perf. 13x13¼***
845-846 A416 Set of 2 3.75 3.75

No. 845 sold for 45c on day of issue. Nos. 845-846 each were printed in sheets of 8 + label.

Puppets — A417

Designs: No. 847, 92c, Martin Krpan puppet made by Matjaz Schmidt. No. 848, 92c, Pavilha puppet made by Mara Kralj. No. 849, 92c, Gaspercek puppet made by Milan Klemencic. No. 850, 92c, Desetnica puppet made by Alenka Sotler. No. 851, 92c, Tincek Petelincek puppet made by Matej Vogrincic.

2010, May 28 ***Perf. 13½x13¾***
847-851 A417 Set of 5 12.00 12.00

Souvenir Sheet

Medalists at 2010 Winter Olympics, Vancouver — A418

No. 852: a, Tina Maze, Giant Slalom and Super-G skiing silver medalist. b, Petra Majdic, Individual Sprint Classic cross-country skiing bronze medalist

2010, June 24 ***Perf. 13¾x14¼***
852 A418 70c Sheet of 2, #a-b 3.75 3.75

Design of First UNICEF Greeting Card — A419

Die Cut Perf. 10¼x10
2010, Sept. 24 **Self-Adhesive**
853 A419 A multi .90 .90

No. 853 sold for 29c on day of issue.

Ljubljana Trolleybus A420

2010, Sept. 24 ***Perf. 12¾x13***
854 A420 €1.50 multi 4.00 4.00

The Letter, by Janez Subic — A421

2010, Sept. 24 ***Perf. 13½x13¾***
855 A421 €1.50 multi 4.00 4.00

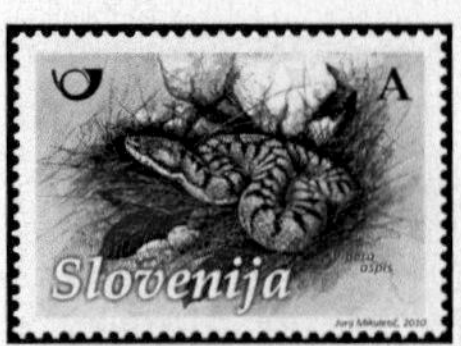

Snakes A422

Designs: A, Vipera aspis. B, Coronella austriaca. C, Natrix natrix.
92c, Vipera ammodytes, vert.

2010, Sept. 24 ***Perf. 12¾x13***
856-858 A422 Set of 3 3.25 3.25

Souvenir Sheet
Perf. 13¾x14¼

859 A422 92c multi 2.60 2.60

On day of issue, Nos. 856-858 sold for 29c, 33c and 44c, respectively.

Souvenir Sheet

Glass Bead Necklace From Early Iron Age — A423

2010, Nov. 26 **Litho.** ***Perf. 13x14***
860 A423 92c multi 2.50 2.50

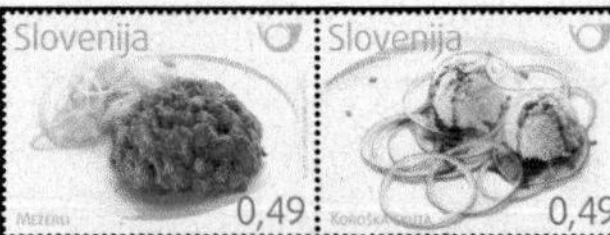

Traditional Foods — A424

No. 861: a, Mezerli (chopped pork ball). b, Koroska skuta (cottage cheese with onions and pumpkin seed oil).

2010, Nov. 26 ***Perf. 13½***
861 A424 49c Horiz. pair, #a-b 2.75 2.75

Christmas
A425 A426

2010, Nov. 26 ***Perf. 11¼x11¾***
862 A425 A multi .80 .80
863 A426 C multi 1.25 1.25

Booklet Stamps
Self-Adhesive
Serpentine Die Cut 12¾

864 A425 A multi .80 .80
a. Booklet pane of 12 9.75
865 A426 C multi 1.25 1.25
a. Booklet pane of 12 15.00

On day of issue, Nos. 862 and 864 each sold for 29c and Nos. 863 and 865 each sold for 44c.

Traditional Clothing From Notranjska A427

2011, Jan. 28 ***Perf. 13½x14***
866 A427 A multi .90 .90

No. 866 sold for 24c on day of issue.

Lips A428

2011, Jan. 28 ***Perf. 13¼***
867 A428 B multi 1.00 1.00

No. 867 sold for 28c on day of issue. Values are for stamp with surrounding selvage.

Dr. Matija Murko (1861-1952), Ethnologist — A429

2011, Jan. 28 ***Perf. 14x13¼***
868 A429 41c multi 1.25 1.25

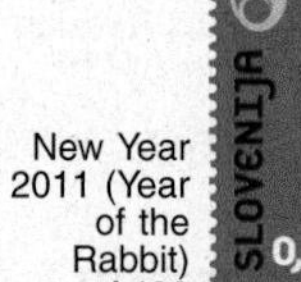

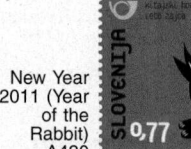

New Year 2011 (Year of the Rabbit) A430

2011, Jan. 28 ***Perf. 14x13¼***
869 A430 77c multi 2.50 2.50

Lieutenant General Franc Rozman (Commander Stane) (1911-43) — A431

2011, Jan. 28 **Litho.**
870 A431 92c multi 2.75 2.75

Godlar Stirring Pot, Sencur A432

2011, Jan. 28 ***Perf. 13¼x14***
871 A432 €1.33 multi 3.75 3.75

Souvenir Sheet

Maribor Post Office Brass Band, 80th Anniv. — A433

2011, Mar. 25 ***Perf. 14***
872 A433 B multi 1.00 1.00

No. 872 sold for 31c on day of issue.

Easter Egg — A434

Serpentine Die Cut 14x15
2011, Mar. 25 **Self-Adhesive**
873 A434 D multi 1.50 1.50

No. 434 sold for 44c on day of issue.

Church of the Holy Spirit, Javorca A435

2011, Mar. 25 ***Perf. 14x13½***
874 A435 44c multi 1.25 1.25

Carthusian Monastery, Bistra A436

2011, Mar. 25 **Litho.**
875 A436 92c multi 2.75 2.75

Treaty of Paris, 60th Anniv. — A437

2011, Mar. 25 ***Perf. 13¼x12¾***
876 A437 92c multi 2.75 2.75

Marsh Plants A438

Designs: A, Drosera rotundifolia. B, Oxycoccus palustris. C, Eriophorum vaginatum.
92c, Andromeda polifolia.

2011, Mar. 25 ***Perf. 14x13½***
877-879 A438 Set of 3 3.00 3.00

Souvenir Sheet
Perf. 13x13¼

880 A438 92c multi 2.75 2.75

On day of issue, Nos. 877-879 sold for 27c, 31c and 40c, respectively.

Flowers Type of 2007

Designs as before.

Size: 23x30mm

Serpentine Die Cut 14x15
2011, Mar. 31 **Litho.**
Self-Adhesive

881 A304 2c multi .35 .35
882 A304 5c multi .35 .35

First Slovenian Motion Picture, 80th Anniv. A439

2011, May 27 ***Perf. 14¼x13¾***
883 A439 44c multi 1.25 1.25

Organization for Economic Cooperation and Development, 50th Anniv. — A440

2011, May 27 ***Perf. 14x13½***
884 A440 D multi 1.25 1.25

No. 884 sold for 44c on day of issue.

Water Man — A441

2011, May 27 ***Perf. 13¼x14***
885 A441 77c multi 2.25 2.25

2011 World Rowing Championships, Bled — A442

2011, May 27 ***Perf. 13¾x14¼***
886 A442 92c multi 2.50 2.50

Printed in sheets of 6 + 3 labels.

Postman Pavli — A443

Postman Pavli: A, Riding bicycle. B, Inserting letter into mailbox.

Serpentine Die Cut 14x15
2011, May 27 **Self-Adhesive**
887 A443 A multi .90 .90
888 A443 B multi 1.00 1.00

On day of issue, No. 887 sold for 27c and No. 888 sold for 31c.
See Nos. 934-935, 971-972.

Europa A444

Designs: D, Fagus sylvatica. 92c, Tallest pine tree in central Europe.

2011, May 27 ***Perf. 13x13¼***
889-890 A444 Set of 2 4.00 4.00

Intl. Year of Forests. No. 889 sold for 44c on day of issue. Nos. 889-890 each were printed in sheets of 8 + label.

Souvenir Sheet

Johann Gerstner (1851-1939), Violinist — A445

Litho. & Engr.
2011, May 27 ***Perf. 13¼***
891 A445 €1.33 multi 4.00 4.00

See Czech Republic No. 3501.

Souvenir Sheet

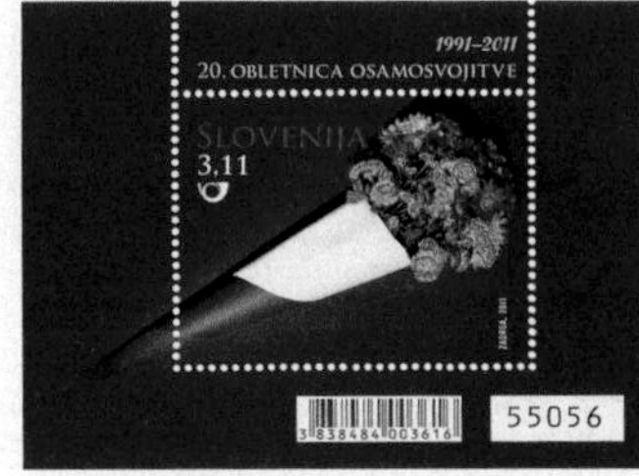

Independence, 20th Anniv. — A446

Litho. & Embossed With Foil Application
2011, June 25 ***Perf. 13¼x13¾***
892 A446 €3.11 multi 8.25 8.25

First University Chair for Slovene Studies, Bicent. A447

2011, Sept. 23 **Litho.** ***Perf. 14x13¼***
893 A447 C multi 1.25 1.25

No. 893 sold for 40c on day of issue.

Tomos Colibri T 12 Moped A448

2011, Sept. 23
894 A448 €1.33 multi 3.50 3.50

The Green Veil, by Rihard Jakopic (1896-1943) A449

2011, Sept. 23 ***Perf. 13¼x14***
895 A449 €1.33 multi 3.50 3.50

Worldwide Fund for Nature (WWF) — A450

No. 896 — Various depictions of Austropotamobius torrentium: a, A. b, B. c, C. d, D.

2011, Sept. 23 ***Perf. 13¼x13***
896 A450 Block of 4, 3a-d 4.00 4.00

On day of issue, Nos. 896a-896d sold for 27c, 31c, 40c and 44c, respectively.

Birds — A451

Designs: A, Numenius arquata. B, Dendrocopos leucotos. C, Emberiza hortulana. 92c, Ciconia ciconia.

2011, Sept. 23 ***Perf. 13¼x14***
897-899 A451 Set of 3 2.75 2.75

Souvenir Sheet
Perf. 13¼x13
900 A451 92c multi 2.50 2.50

On day of issue, Nos. 897-899 sold for 27c, 31c and 40c, respectively.

MKS-Exclusive Microphone, Designed, by Marko Turk (1920-99) — A452

2011, Nov. 25 ***Perf. 14¼x13¾***
901 A452 58c multi 1.60 1.60

Traditional Foods — A453

No. 902: a, Loska smojka (stuffed turnips). b, Blejska kremna rezina (Bled cream slice).

2011, Nov. 25 ***Perf. 14x13¼***
902 A453 D Horiz. pair, #a-b 2.75 2.75

On day of issue Nos. 902a-902b each sold for 44c.

Souvenir Sheet

Secovlje Salina Nature Park — A454

2011, Nov. 25 ***Perf. 13x13¼***
903 A454 77c multi 1.90 1.90

Souvenir Sheet

Bronze Belt Plate With Hunting Motif, 7th-4th Cent. B.C. — A455

2011, Nov. 25 **Litho.** ***Perf. 14***
904 A455 92c multi 2.50 2.50

Personalized Stamps — A456

Frame designs: Nos. 905-912, Christmas gifts, ornaments, bells, crackers and holly. Nos. 913-920, Holly and ribbon.

Country Name in Red
Horizontal Stamps

Serpentine Die Cut 12x11¾, 11¾x12
2011, Nov. 25 **Self-Adhesive**
905 A456 A multi 1.00 1.00
906 A456 B multi 1.10 1.10
907 A456 C multi 1.45 1.45
908 A456 D multi 1.60 1.60
a. Horiz. strip of 4, #905-908 5.25

Vertical Stamps
909 A456 A multi 1.00 1.00
910 A456 B multi 1.10 1.10
911 A456 C multi 1.45 1.45
912 A456 D multi 1.60 1.60
a. Vert. strip of 4, #909-912 5.25

Country Name in Green
Horizontal Stamps
913 A456 A multi 1.00 1.00
914 A456 B multi 1.10 1.10
915 A456 C multi 1.45 1.45
916 A456 D multi 1.60 1.60
a. Horiz. strip of 4, #913-916 5.25

Vertical Stamps
917 A456 A multi 1.00 1.00
918 A456 B multi 1.10 1.10
919 A456 C multi 1.45 1.45
920 A456 D multi 1.60 1.60
a. Vert. strip of 4, #917-920 5.25
Nos. 905-920 (16) 20.60 20.60

On day of issue, stamps inscribed "A" each sold for 27c; stamps inscribed "B" each sold for 31c; stamps inscribed "C" each sold for 40c; and stamps inscribed "D" each sold for 44c. The generic images for each stamp, an example of which is shown, depicts a different work of children's art, with stamps with the same color of country name and orientation issued in sheets of 20 containing five of each stamp. The vignettes of these stamps could be personalized, being printed in sheets of 20 containing the same denomination, frame and orientation.

Christmas Bread — A457

Serpentine Die Cut 14x15
2011, Nov. 25 **Litho.**
Self-Adhesive
921 A457 A multi .75 .75
922 A457 C multi 1.10 1.10

Booklet Stamps
Size: 26x35mm

Serpentine Die Cut 12¾

923 A457 A multi .75 .75
924 A457 C multi 1.10 1.10
a. Booklet pane of 12, 8 #923, 4 #924 10.50

Christmas. On day of issue, Nos. 921 and 923 each sold for 27c, and Nos. 922 and 924 each sold for 40c.

Four-leaf Clover — A458

Serpentine Die Cut 14x15

2011, Nov. 25 **Self-Adhesive**
925 A458 A multi .75 .75
926 A458 C multi 1.10 1.10

Booklet Stamps
Size: 26x35mm

Serpentine Die Cut 12¾

927 A458 A multi .75 .75
928 A458 C multi 1.10 1.10
a. Booklet pane of 12, 8 #927, 4 #928 10.50

New Year 2012. On day of issue, Nos. 925 and 927 each sold for 27c, and Nos. 926 and 928 each sold for 40c.

Traditional Clothing From Bohinj A459

2012, Jan. 27 ***Perf. 11¾x11¼***
929 A459 27c multi .75 .75

Heart Carved in Tree A460

2012, Jan. 27 ***Perf. 13x13¼***
930 A460 31c multi .95 .95

Values are for stamps with surrounding selvage.

New Year 2012 (Year of the Dragon) A461

2012, Jan. 27 ***Perf. 14¼x13¾***
931 A461 92c multi 2.75 2.75

Mira Mihelic (1912-85), Writer — A462

2012, Jan. 27 ***Perf. 13¾x14¼***
932 A462 €1.25 multi 3.25 3.25

Souvenir Sheet

Enclosure of Ljubljana Inside Barbed Wire Fence, 70th Anniv. — A463

2012, Jan. 27 ***Perf. 14¼x13¾***
933 A463 €1.33 multi 3.50 3.50

Postman Pavli Type of 2011

Postman Pavli: C, With children at school. D, With dog and bicycle.

Serpentine Die Cut 14x15

2012, Mar. 30 **Self-Adhesive**
934 A443 C multi 1.25 1.25
935 A443 D multi 1.40 1.40

On day of issue, No. 934 sold for 40c and No. 935 sold for 44c.

Heart-shaped Honey Biscuit — A464

Serpentine Die Cut 14x15

2012, Mar. 30 **Litho.**
Self-Adhesive
936 A464 A multi .75 .75
a. Serpentine die cut 11¼x11½ —

No. 936 sold for 27c on day of issue. Issued: No. 936a, 5/7/13.

Valleys, Solcavsko District A465

2012, Mar. 30 ***Perf. 14¼x13¾***
937 A465 €1.25 multi 2.50 2.50

Sts. Peter and Paul Minorite Monastery, Ptuj — A466

2012, Mar. 30
938 A466 €1.33 multi 3.25 3.25

Europa A467

Abstract design with: 44c, Spiral. 92c, Atomic orbits.

2012, Mar. 30 ***Perf. 11¾x11¼***
939-940 A467 Set of 2 3.75 3.75

Maribor, 2012 European Capital of Culture. Nos. 939-940 each were printed in sheets of 8 + label.

Flowers in Ljubljana Botanical Gardens A468

Designs: 40c, Pastinaca sativa var. fleischmanni. 44c, Primula x venusta. 77c, Scabiosa hladnikiana.
92c, Scopolia carniolica f. hladnikiana.

2012, Mar. 30 ***Perf. 14¼x13¾***
941-943 A468 Set of 3 4.00 4.00

Souvenir Sheet

944 A468 92c multi 2.25 2.25

2012 Summer Olympics, London — A469

No. 945: a, 77c, Judo, sailing. b, 92c, Swimming, handball.

2012, May 25 Litho. ***Perf. 14¼x13¾***
945 A469 Horiz. pair, #a-b 4.25 4.25

Souvenir Sheet

Maribofila 2012 Philatelic Exhibition, Maribor — A470

2012, May 25
946 A470 D multi 1.75 1.75

No. 946 sold for 44c on day of issue.

Souvenir Sheet

Goricko Regional Park — A471

2012, May 25
947 A471 €1.25 multi 2.75 2.75

Souvenir Sheet

Smokehouses and Pottery — A472

No. 948: a, Felsoszölnök, Hungary smokehouse at left, pitcher, two lidded jars. b, Filovci, Slovenia smokehouse at right, jug, colander.

2012, May 25 ***Perf. 14x13¼***
948 A472 92c Sheet of 2, #a-b 4.25 4.25

See Hungary No. 4244.

Urska Zolnir, Judo Gold Medalist in 2012 Summer Olympics, London A473

Perf. 14¼x13¾

2012, Sept. 28 **Litho.**
949 A473 92c multi 2.25 2.25

Lacemaker, by Veno Pilon (1896-1970) A474

2012, Sept. 28 ***Perf. 11¾x11¼***
950 A474 €1.33 multi 3.25 3.25

Bees A475

Designs: 40c, Bombus lapidarius. 44c, Bombus pascuorum. 77c, Bombus humilis. 92c, Bombus lucorum.

2012, Sept. 28 ***Perf. 14¼x13¾***
951-953 A475 Set of 3 4.00 4.00

Souvenir Sheet

954 A475 92c multi 2.25 2.25

Souvenir Sheet

World Youth Chess Championships, Maribor — A476

2012, Sept. 28 ***Perf. 13¾x14¼***
955 A476 €1.33 multi 3.25 3.25

Premiere of Film *The Slopes of Triglav,* 80th Anniv. — A477

2012, Nov. 23
956 A477 58c multi 1.50 1.50

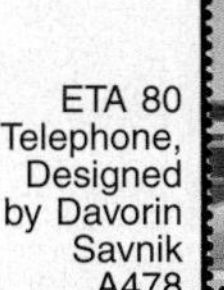

ETA 80 Telephone, Designed by Davorin Savnik A478

2012, Nov. 23 ***Perf. 14¼x13¾***
957 A478 58c multi 1.50 1.50

Traditional Foods — A479

No. 958: a, Carniolan sausage, roll and mustard (Kranjska klobasa). b, Sauteed potatoes (Prazen krompir).

2012, Nov. 23 ***Perf. 11½x11¾***
958 A479 77c Horiz. pair, #a-b 3.75 3.75

Angel A480

Creche Figures A481

Serpentine Die Cut 14x15
2012, Nov. 23 **Litho.**
Self-Adhesive
959 A480 A multi .75 .75
960 A481 C multi 1.25 1.25

Booklet Stamps
Size: 26x35mm
Serpentine Die Cut 12¾
961 A480 A multi .75 .75
a. Booklet pane of 12 9.00
962 A481 C multi 1.25 1.25
a. Booklet pane of 12 15.00

Christmas. On day of issue, Nos. 959 and 961 each sold for 27c, and Nos. 960 and 962 each sold for 40c.

Fairy — A482

Pig — A483

Serpentine Die Cut 14x15
2012, Nov. 23 **Litho.**
Self-Adhesive
963 A482 A multi .75 .75
964 A483 C multi 1.25 1.25

Booklet Stamps
Size: 26x35mm
Serpentine Die Cut 12¾
965 A482 A multi .75 .75
a. Booklet pane of 12 9.00
966 A483 C multi 1.25 1.25
a. Booklet pane of 12 15.00

New Year 2013. On day of issue, Nos. 963 and 965 each sold for 27c, and Nos. 964 and 966 each sold for 40c.

Traditional Clothing From Ljubljana A484

2013, Jan. 25 ***Perf. 11¾x11¼***
967 A484 27c multi .75 .75

Heart-shaped Lock — A485

2013, Jan. 25 ***Perf. 13¼***
968 A485 31c multi .90 .90

Values are for stamps with surrounding selvage.

New Year 2013 (Year of the Snake) A486

2013, Jan. 25 **Litho.**
969 A486 92c multi 2.25 2.25

Fran Miklosic (1813-91), Linguist A487

2013, Jan. 25
970 A487 €1.33 multi 3.50 3.50

Postman Pavli Type of 2011

Postman Pavli and dog with: A, Posthorn, flowers, horiz. B, Watermelon slice, horiz.

Serpentine Die Cut 11½
2013, Mar. 22 **Self-Adhesive**
971 A443 A multi .75 .75
972 A443 B multi .85 .85

On day of issue, No. 971 sold for 27c and No. 972 sold for 31c.

Clay Anthropomorphic Vessel, 3000 B.C. — A488

2013, Mar. 22 **Litho.**
Self-Adhesive
973 A488 D multi 1.75 1.75

No. 973 sold for 64c on day of issue.

Kolpa Valley A489

2013, Mar. 22 ***Perf. 13¼***
974 A489 €1.25 multi 3.00 3.00

Capuchin Monastery, Vipavski Kriz — A490

2013, Mar. 22
975 A490 €1.33 multi 3.25 3.25

Europa A491

Postal vehicles: 64c, Krpan bicycle. 92c, Diligence mail coach, 18th cent.

2013, Mar. 22 ***Perf. 11¾x11½***
976-977 A491 Set of 2 4.00 4.00

Fruit — A492

Designs: 60c, Ziziphus jujuba. 64c, Ficus carica. 92c, Eriobotrya japonica.
97c, Sorbus domestica.

2013, Mar. 22 ***Perf. 13¼***
978-980 A492 Set of 3 5.50 5.50

Souvenir Sheet
981 A492 97c multi 2.50 2.50

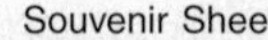

Souvenir Sheet

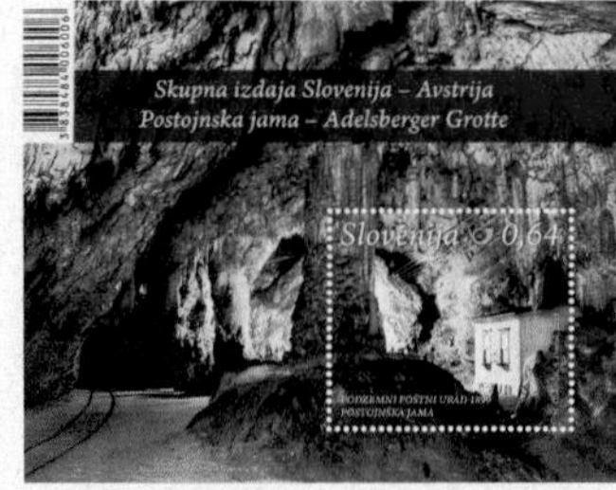

Underground Post Office in Postojna Cave — A493

2013, Mar. 22 ***Perf. 14x13¼***
982 A493 64c multi 1.90 1.90

See Austria No. 2431.

Souvenir Sheet

Tolmin Peasant Rebellion, 300th Anniv. — A494

2013, Mar. 22 ***Perf. 13¼***
983 A494 €2.18 multi 5.50 5.50

2013 European Basketball Championships, Slovenia — A495

2013, May 24 ***Perf. 14¼x13¾***
984 A495 €1.33 multi 3.50 3.50

No. 984 was printed in sheets of 6 + 3 labels.

Bridges — A496

Designs: 27c, Old Bridge, Maribor. 31c, Rail Bridges, Zidani Most. 60c, Triple Bridge, Ljubljana. 64c, Kandija Bridge, Novo Mesto. 97c, Soca River Bridge, Kanal.

2013, May 24 ***Perf. 14¼***
985-989 A496 Set of 5 7.25 7.25

Personalized Stamps — A497

Serpentine Die Cut 12x11¾, 11¾x12
2013, May 24 **Self-Adhesive**
Animal Tracks in Upper Left Corner
Horizontal Stamps
990 A497 A brown .75 .75
991 A497 B brown .85 .85
992 A497 C brown 1.60 1.60

993 A497 D brown 1.75 1.75
a. Horiz. strip of 4, #990-993 5.00

Vertical Stamps

994 A497 A brown .75 .75
995 A497 B brown .85 .85
996 A497 C brown 1.60 1.60
997 A497 D brown 1.75 1.75
a. Vert. strip of 4, #994-997 5.00

Various Pets in Upper Left Corner
Horizontal Stamps

998 A497 A gray .75 .75
999 A497 B gray .85 .85
1000 A497 C gray 1.60 1.60
1001 A497 D gray 1.75 1.75
a. Horiz. strip of 4, #998-1001 5.00

Vertical Stamps

1002 A497 A gray .75 .75
1003 A497 B gray .85 .85
1004 A497 C gray 1.60 1.60
1005 A497 D gray 1.75 1.75
a. Vert. strip of 4, #1002-1005 5.00
Nos. 990-1005 (16) 19.80 19.80

On day of issue, stamps inscribed "A" each sold for 27c; stamps inscribed "B" each sold for 31c; stamps inscribed "C" each sold for 60c; and stamps inscribed "D" each sold for 64c, The generic images for each stamp, an example of which is shown, depicts a different pet, with stamps with the same frame color and orientation issued in sheets of 20 containing five of each stamp. The vignettes of these stamps could be personalized, being printed in sheets of 20 containing the same denomination, frame and orientation.

Marine Life
A498

Designs: 60c, Chromis chromis. 64c, Sepia officinalis. 92c, Caretta caretta. 97c, Liza aurata.

Litho. & Thermography

2013, Sept. 27 ***Perf. 13x13¼***
1006-1008 A498 Set of 3 5.50 5.50

Souvenir Sheet

1009 A498 97c multi 2.50 2.50

Sea salt was added to the thermographic portions on Nos. 1006-1009, producing a rough texture.

Souvenir Sheet

Kozjansko Apple Tree in Kozjansko Regional Park — A499

Perf. 13¼x13½
2013, Sept. 27 **Litho.**
1010 A499 €1.25 multi 3.25 3.25

K67 Kiosks
A500

Perf. 14¼x13¾
2013, Nov. 22 **Litho.**
1011 A500 92c multi 2.40 2.40

Premiere of First Slovene Film *Vesna,* 60th Anniv.
A501

2013, Nov. 22 **Litho.** ***Perf. 14x13¾***
1012 A501 97c multi 2.50 2.50

Traditional Foods — A502

No. 1013: a, Fizolovi struklji s kislim zeljem (bean roll with sauerkraut). b, Pecena gos z mlinci in rdecim zeljem (roast goose with bread and red cabbage).

Perf. 11½x11¾
2013, Nov. 22 **Litho.**
1013 A502 92c Horiz. pair, #a-b 5.25 5.25

Christmas
A503 A504

Serpentine Die Cut 11¼x11½
2013, Nov. 22 **Litho.**

Self-Adhesive

1014 A503 A multi .80 .80
1015 A504 C multi 1.75 1.75

Booklet Stamps
Self-Adhesive
Size: 26x35mm

Serpentine Die Cut 12½x12¾
1016 A503 A multi .80 .80
a. Booklet pane of 12 9.75
1017 A504 C multi 1.75 1.75
a. Booklet pane of 12 21.00

On day of issue, Nos. 1014, 1016 each sold for 29c, Nos. 1015, 1017 each sold for 60c.

New Year's Day 2014
A505 A506

Serpentine Die Cut 11¼x11½
2013, Nov. 22 **Litho.**

Self-Adhesive

1018 A505 A multi .80 .80
1019 A506 C multi 1.75 1.75

Booklet Stamps
Self-Adhesive
Size: 26x35mm

Serpentine Die Cut 12½x12¾
1020 A505 A multi .80 .80
a. Booklet pane of 12 9.75
1021 A506 C multi 1.75 1.75
a. Booklet pane of 12 21.00

On day of issue, Nos. 1018, 1020 each sold for 29c and Nos. 1019, 1021 each sold for 60c.

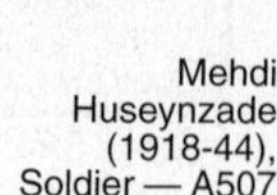

Mehdi Huseynzade (1918-44), Soldier — A507

2013, Dec. 12 **Litho.** ***Perf. 13¼***
1022 A507 97c multi 2.50 2.50

See Azerbaijan No. 1042.

Traditional Clothing From Trieste Area — A508

2014, Jan. 31 **Litho.** ***Perf. 11¾x11¼***
1023 A508 29c multi .70 .70

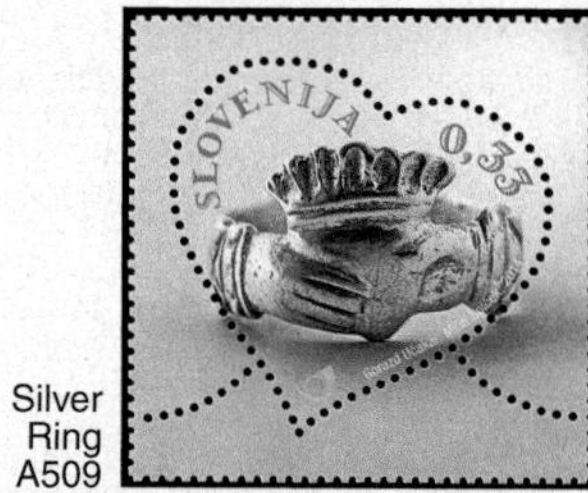

Silver Ring
A509

2014, Jan. 31 **Litho.** ***Perf. 13¼***
1024 A509 33c multi .95 .95

Values are for stamps with surrounding selvage.

New Year 2014 (Year of the Horse) — A510

2014, Jan. 31 **Litho.** ***Perf. 13¼***
1025 A510 92c multi 2.25 2.25

Rado Simoniti (1914-81), Composer
A511

2014, Jan. 31 **Litho.** ***Perf. 13¼***
1026 A511 €1.33 multi 3.50 3.50

2014 Winter Olympics, Sochi, Russia
A512

No. 1027: a, 64c, Ski jumping. b, 97c, Ice hockey.

2014, Jan. 31 **Litho.** ***Perf. 12***
1027 A512 Vert. pair, #a-b, + central label 4.00 4.00

Souvenir Sheet

Enthronement of Duke Ernst the Iron (1377-1422), 600th Anniv. — A513

2014, Jan. 31 **Litho.** ***Perf. 13¼***
1028 A513 €1.25 multi 3.00 3.00

Mortar and Pestle — A514

Serpentine Die Cut 11½
2014, Mar. 28 **Litho.**

Self-Adhesive

1029 A514 B multi .80 .80

No. 1029 sold for 33c on day of issue.

Easter Eggs — A515

The Crucified, Painting by Tone Kralj — A516

Serpentine Die Cut 11½x11
2014, Mar. 28 **Litho.**

Self-Adhesive

1030 A515 A multi .80 .80
1031 A516 C multi 1.75 1.75

Easter. On day of issue, No. 1030 sold for 29c and No. 1031 sold for 60c.

Idrija Tourism — A517

2014, Mar. 28 Litho. *Perf. 13¼*
1032 A517 €1.25 multi 3.25 3.25

Carthusian Monastery, Pleterje A518

2014, Mar. 28 Litho. *Perf. 13¼*
1033 A518 €1.33 multi 3.50 3.50

Old Grapevines A519

Grapevine in: 60c, Sepulje. 64c, Merce. 92c, Brje pri Komnu.
97c, Grapevine in Maribor, horiz.

2014, Mar. 28 Litho. *Perf. 13¼*
1034-1036 A519 Set of 3 5.50 5.50

Souvenir Sheet

1037 A519 97c multi 2.50 2.50

Rescue of Allied Airmen, 70th Anniv. A520

2014, May 30 Litho. *Perf. 13¼*
1038 A520 60c multi 1.60 1.60

Scouting A521

2014, May 30 Litho. *Perf. 12*
1039 A521 77c multi 2.10 2.10

40th World Scout Conference, Ljubljana, 12th World Scout Youth Forum, Ragla. No. 1039 was printed in sheets of 6 + 3 labels.

Tina Maze, Two-time Gold Medalist in Skiing at 2014 Winter Olympics, Sochi, Russia A522

2014, May 30 Litho. *Perf. 13¼*
1040 A522 €1.33 multi 3.50 3.50

Europa A523

Musical instruments: 64c, Haloze flutes. 97c, Rattles.

2014, May 30 Litho. *Perf. 13¼*
1041-1042 A523 Set of 2 4.00 4.00

Birds — A524

Designs: A, Hirundo rupestris. B, Mergus merganser. 36c, Botaurus stellaris. C, Falco naumanni. D, Strix uralensis.

Serpentine Die Cut 11¼x11½
2014-16 Litho.

Self-Adhesive

1043 A524 A multi .80 .80
a. Serpentine die cut 14x14¾ — —
b. Serpentine Die Cut 11½ — —
1044 A524 B multi .90 .90
a. Serpentine die cut 14x14¾ — —
b. Serpentine die cut 11½ — —
1045 A524 36c multi 1.00 1.00
1046 A524 C multi 1.60 1.60
1047 A524 D multi 1.75 1.75
Nos. 1043-1047 (5) 6.05 6.05

Issued: Nos. 1043-1047, 5/30; Nos. 1043a, 1044a, 5/25/15; Nos. 1043b, 044b, 5/27/16. On day of issue, No. 1043 sold for 29c; No. 1043a, 34c; No. 1044, 33c; No. 1044a, 40c; No. 1046, 60c; No. 1047, 64c. No. 1043b sold for 36c on day of issue and has die cutting teeth that are much deeper than those found on No. 1043. No. 1044b sold for 42c on day of issue and has die cutting teeth that are much deeper than those found on No. 1044.

Souvenir Sheet

Kolpa Nature Park — A525

2014, May 30 Litho. *Perf. 13¼*
1048 A525 €1.25 multi 3.25 3.25

Souvenir Sheet

Cargo Ship Martin Krpan — A526

2014, May 30 Litho. *Perf. 13¼*
1049 A526 €1.33 multi 3.50 3.50

Souvenir Sheet

International Year of Crystallography — A527

No. 1050 — Snowflake and molecular diagrams for ice with: a, 10 red atoms. b, 20 red atoms in cube.

2014, May 30 Litho. *Perf. 14x13¼*
1050 A527 64c Sheet of 2, #a-b 3.50 3.50

See Belgium No. 2702.

Euromed Postal Emblem and Mediterranean Area — A528

2014, July 9 Litho. *Perf. 13¼*
1051 A528 64c multi 1.60 1.60

Coat of Arms of the Nobility — A529

Arms of the House of: 34c, Attems. 40c, Lamberg. 46c, Auersperg. 58c, Herberstein. 60c, Thurn-Valsassina.

Perf. 12¾x13¼
2014, Sept. 26 Litho.
1052-1056 A529 Set of 5 6.00 6.00

Bats — A530

Designs: 60c, Myotis bechsteinii. 64c, Rhinolophus hipposideros. 92c, Pipistrellus kuhlii. 97c, Miniopterus schreibersii.

2014, Sept. 26 Litho. *Perf. 13¼*
1057-1059 A530 Set of 3 5.50 5.50

Souvenir Sheet

1060 A530 97c multi 2.50 2.50

Souvenir Sheet

Coronation of Barbara of Cilli, 600th Anniv. — A531

2014, Sept. 26 Litho. *Perf. 13¼*
1061 A531 €2.25 multi 5.75 5.75

Personalized Stamps — A532

Serpentine Die Cut 12x11¾, 11¾x12
2014, Nov. 28 Litho.

Self-Adhesive

Lace in Upper Right and Lower Left Corners

Horizontal Stamps

1062 A532 A multi 1.00 1.00
1063 A532 B multi 1.20 1.20
1064 A532 C multi 1.75 1.75
1065 A532 D multi 1.90 1.90
a. Horiz. strip of 4, #1062-1065 6.00

Vertical Stamps

1066 A532 A multi 1.00 1.00
1067 A532 B multi 1.20 1.20
1068 A532 C multi 1.75 1.75
1069 A532 D multi 1.90 1.90
a. Vert. strip of 4, #1066-1069 6.00

With Green Flowers at Top, Bottom and Right

Horizontal Stamps

1070 A532 A multi 1.00 1.00
1071 A532 B multi 1.20 1.20
1072 A532 C multi 1.75 1.75
1073 A532 D multi 1.90 1.90
a. Horiz. strip of 4, #1070-1073 6.00

Vertical Stamps

1074 A532 A multi 1.00 0.00
1075 A532 B multi 1.20 1.20
1076 A532 C multi 1.75 1.75
1077 A532 D multi 1.90 1.90
a. Vert. strip of 4, #1074-1077 6.00

With Blue Nautilus Shells in Top Left and Bottom Right Corners

Horizontal Stamps

1078 A532 A multi 1.00 1.00
1079 A532 B multi 1.20 1.20
1080 A532 C multi 1.75 1.75
1081 A532 D multi 1.90 1.90
a. Horiz. strip of 4, #1078-1081 6.00

Vertical Stamps

1082 A532 A multi 1.00 1.00
1083 A532 B multi 1.20 1.20
1084 A532 C multi 1.75 1.75
1085 A532 D multi 1.90 1.90
a. Vert. strip of 4, #1082-1085 6.00

With Brown and Yellow Brown Leaves At Top and Sides

Horizontal Stamps

1086 A532 A multi 1.00 1.00
1087 A532 B multi 1.20 1.20
1088 A532 C multi 1.75 1.75
1089 A532 D multi 1.90 1.90
a. Horiz. strip of 4, #1086-1089 6.00

Vertical Stamps

1090 A532 A multi 1.00 1.00
1091 A532 B multi 1.20 1.20
1092 A532 C multi 1.75 1.75

1093 A532 D multi 1.90 1.90
a. Vert. strip of 4, #1090-1093 6.00
Nos. 1062-1093 (32) 46.80 45.80

On day of issue, stamps inscribed "A" each sold for 34c; stamps inscribed "B" each sold for 40c; stamps inscribed "C" each sold for 60c; and stamps inscribed "D" each sold for 64c. Each stamp was printed in sheets of 20 in which vignettes could be personalized. The generic images for each stamp, an example of which is shown, depicts a different picture of winter scenes on Nos. 1062-1069, a different picture of flowers on Nos. 1070-1077, a different picture of seashore scenes on Nos. 1078-1085, and a different picture of autumnal scenes on Nos. 1086-1093.

Monument to Unknown Soldiers, Ljubljana — A533

2014, Nov. 28 Litho. *Perf. 13¼*
1094 A533 40c multi 1.00 1.00

World War I, cent.

Tomos 4 Outboard Motor A534

2014, Nov. 28 Litho. *Perf. 13¼*
1095 A534 58c multi 1.50 1.50

Scene From Film *Don't Cry, Peter* — A535

2014, Nov. 28 Litho. *Perf. 13¼*
1096 A535 92c multi 2.25 2.25

Children's Art — A536

No. 1097: a, 34c, Indian family and house, by Roshan V. Anvekar, India. b, 60c, Dancers, by Sara Zivkovic, Slovenia.

Perf. 11¼x11¾
2014, Nov. 28 Litho.
1097 A536 Horiz. pair, #a-b 2.40 2.40

See India Nos. 2706-2707.

Traditional Foods — A537

No. 1098: a, Fizolova minestra (minestrone soup). b, Vipavski štruklji (sweet dumpling rolls).

Perf. 11¼x11¾
2014, Nov. 28 Litho.
1098 A537 77c Horiz. pair, #a-b 4.00 4.00

Christmas
A538 A539

Serpentine Die Cut 11¼x11½
2014, Nov. 28 Litho.
Self-Adhesive
1099 A538 B multi 1.00 1.00
1100 A539 C multi 1.50 1.50

Booklet Stamps
Self-Adhesive
Size: 26x35mm
Serpentine Die Cut 12½x12¼
1101 A538 B multi 1.00 1.00
a. Booklet pane of 12 12.00
1102 A539 C multi 1.50 1.50
a. Booklet pane of 12 18.00

On day of issue, Nos. 1099 and 1101 each sold for 40c; Nos. 1100 and 1102 each sold for 60c.

New Year's Day 2015
A540 A541

Serpentine Die Cut 11¼x11½
2014, Nov. 28 Litho.
Self-Adhesive
1103 A540 A multi .85 .85
1104 A541 C multi 1.50 1.50

Booklet Stamps
Self-Adhesive
Size: 26x35mm
Serpentine Die Cut 12½x12¼
1105 A540 A multi .85 .85
a. Booklet pane of 12 10.50
1106 A541 C multi 1.50 1.50
a. Booklet pane of 12 18.00

On day of issue, Nos. 1103 and 1105 each sold for 34c; Nos. 1104 and 1106 each sold for 60c.

Traditional Clothing From Prem and the Cicarija Plateau A542

2015, Jan. 30 Litho. *Perf. 11¾x11¼*
1107 A542 34c multi .85 .85

Marriage Spoons on Chain A543

2015, Jan. 30 Litho. *Perf. 13¼*
1108 A543 40c multi 1.00 1.00

Values are for stamps with surrounding selvage.

New Year 2015 (Year of the Goat) A544

2015, Jan. 30 Litho. *Perf. 13¼*
1109 A544 92c multi 2.25 2.25

Max Fabiani (1865-1962), Architect A545

2015, Jan. 30 Litho. *Perf. 13¼*
1110 A545 €1.25 multi 3.25 3.25

Balthazar Hacquet (c. 1739-1815), Scientist — A546

2015, Jan. 30 Litho. *Perf. 13¼*
1111 A546 €1.33 multi 3.25 3.25

Souvenir Sheet

Slovenia Post, 20th Anniv. — A547

2015, Jan. 30 Litho. *Perf. 13¼*
1112 A547 €2.25 multi 5.50 5.50

Lasko A548

2015, Mar. 27 Litho. *Perf. 13¼*
1113 A548 €1.25 multi 3.00 3.00

Cistercian Abbey, Sticna A549

2015, Mar. 27 Litho. *Perf. 13¼*
1114 A549 €1.33 multi 3.25 3.25

Orchids A550

Designs: 60c, Orchis pallens. 64c, Orchis simla. 92c, Orchis ustulata.
97c, Orchis purpurea.

2015, Mar. 27 Litho. *Perf. 13¼*
1115-1117 A550 Set of 3 5.25 5.25

Souvenir Sheet
1118 A550 97c multi 2.40 2.40

Birds and Letters — A551

Designs: 1c, Podiceps cristatus and "P." 2c, Columba oenas and "O." 5c, Ciconia nigra and "S." 10c, Charadrius alexandrinus and "T." 20c, Montifringila nivalis and "A."

Serpentine Die Cut 14¾x14
2015, May 29 Litho.
Self-Adhesive
1119 A551 1c multi .25 .25
1120 A551 2c multi .25 .25
1121 A551 5c multi .25 .25
1122 A551 10c multi .25 .25
1123 A551 20c multi .45 .45
Nos. 1119-1123 (5) 1.45 1.45

Postcrossing A552

2015, May 29 Litho. *Perf. 13¼*
1124 A552 60c multi 1.50 1.50

World Track and Field Championships, Beijing — A553

2015, May 29 Litho. *Perf. 12*
1125 A553 €1.33 multi 3.25 3.25

No. 1125 was printed in sheets of 6 + 3 labels.

Europa — A554

Designs: 64c, Rocking horse. 97c, Wind-up car.

2015, May 29 Litho. *Perf. 13¼*
1126-1127 A554 Set of 2 3.75 3.75

Nos. 1126-1127 each were printed in sheets of 8 + central label.

Mountain Huts — A555

Designs: 34c, Oroznova Koca. 40c, Aljazev Dom. 60c, Presernova Koca. 64c, Ceska Koca. 97c, Ruska Koca.

2015, May 29 Litho. *Perf. 12¾x13¼*
1128-1132 A555 Set of 5 7.00 7.00

Souvenir Sheet

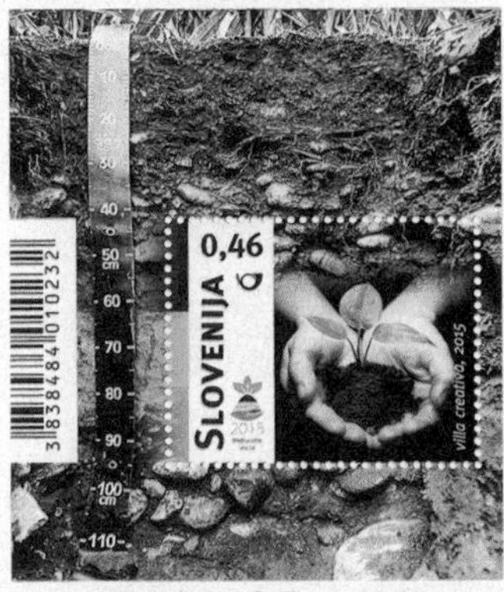
Intl. Year of Soils — A556

2015, May 29 Litho. *Perf. 13¼*
1133 A556 46c multi 1.10 1.10

Souvenir Sheet

Cargo Steamer Rog — A557

2015, May 29 Litho. *Perf. 13¼*
1134 A557 €1.33 multi 3.25 3.25

Tuna Fishermen in Tonera A558

2015, July 9 Litho. *Perf. 13¼*
1135 A558 64c multi 1.50 1.50

Traditional Slovene Breakfast — A559

Perf. 11¼x11¾
2015, Sept. 25 Litho.
1136 A559 77c multi 1.90 1.90

Rodents — A560

Designs: 60c, Muscardinus avellanarius. 64c, Marmota marmota. 92c, Cricetus cricetus.
97c, Castor fiber.

2015, Sept. 25 Litho. *Perf. 13¼*
1137-1139 A560 Set of 3 5.50 5.50

Souvenir Sheet

1140 A560 97c multi 2.40 2.40

Alpine Landscapes — A561

No. 1141: a, Malbuntal, Liechtenstein. b, Herder's dwellings, Velika Planina, Slovenia.

2015, Sept. 25 Litho. *Perf. 12¼*
1141 A561 €1.29 Pair, #a-b 6.25 6.25

See Liechtenstein No. 1654.

Souvenir Sheet

Ljubljansko Barje Nature Park — A562

2015, Sept. 25 Litho. *Perf. 13¼*
1142 A562 €1.33 multi 3.25 3.25

Janez Evangelist Krek (1865-1917), Priest and Politician A563

2015, Nov. 6 Litho. *Perf. 13¼*
1143 A563 47c multi 1.20 1.20

Alpina Elite ESK PRO Cross-Country Ski Boots — A564

2015, Nov. 6 Litho. *Perf. 13¼*
1144 A564 58c multi 1.40 1.40

Davorin Jenko (1835-1914), Composer A565

2015, Nov. 6 Litho. *Perf. 13¼*
1145 A565 60c multi 1.40 1.40

No. 1145 was printed in sheets of 8 + central label. See Serbia No. 718.

Scene of People Leaving Mass in Ljutomer, First Slovenian Film, 1905 — A566

2015, Nov. 6 Litho. *Perf. 13¼*
1146 A566 92c multi 2.25 2.25

Traditional Foods — A567

No. 1147: a, Idrijski zlikrofi z bakalco (stew with dumplings). b, Sebreljski zelodec (salami).

2015, Nov. 6 Litho. *Perf. 11¼x11¾*
1147 A567 77c Horiz. pair, #a-b 3.75 3.75

A568

Christmas — A569

Serpentine Die Cut 15x14
2015, Nov. 6 Litho.
Self-Adhesive
1148 A568 B multi 1.00 1.00

Serpentine Die Cut 14x15
1149 A569 C multi 1.40 1.40

Booklet Stamp
Size: 35x26mm
Serpentine Die Cut 12¼x12½
1150 A568 B multi 1.00 1.00
a. Booklet pane of 12 12.00

Size: 26x35mm
Serpentine Die Cut 12½x12¼
1151 A569 C multi 1.40 1.40
a. Booklet pane of 12 17.00

On day of issue, Nos. 1148 and 1150 each sold for 42c; Nos. 1149 and 1151 each sold for 60c.

A570

New Year's Day 2016 — A571

Serpentine Die Cut 15x14
2015, Nov. 6 Litho.
Self-Adhesive
1152 A570 A multi .85 .85

Serpentine Die Cut 14x15
1153 A571 C multi 1.40 1.40

Booklet Stamp
Size: 35x26mm
Serpentine Die Cut 12¼x12½
1154 A570 A multi .85 .85
a. Booklet pane of 12 10.50

Size: 26x35mm
Serpentine Die Cut 12½x12¼
1155 A571 C multi 1.40 1.40
a. Booklet pane of 12 17.00

On day of issue, Nos. 1152 and 1154 each sold for 36c; Nos. 1153 and 1155 each sold for 60c.

Traditional Clothing of Gottschee Germans in Dolenjska Region A572

2016, Jan. 29 Litho. *Perf. 11¾x11¼*
1156 A572 36c multi .85 .85

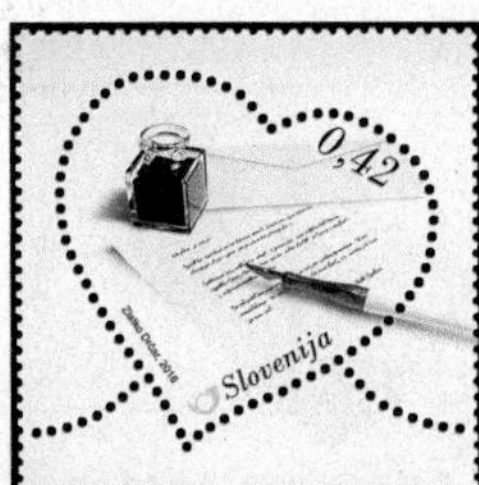
Pen, Ink Bottle and Love Letter A573

2016, Jan. 29 Litho. *Perf. 13¼*
1157 A573 42c multi 1.00 1.00

Values are for stamps with surrounding selvage.

New Year 2016 (Year of the Monkey) — A574

2016, Jan. 29 Litho. *Perf. 14*
1158 A574 92c multi 2.25 2.25

Jakob Handl Gallus (1550-91), Composer — A575

2016, Jan. 29 Litho. *Perf. 14*
1159 A575 €1.33 multi 3.25 3.25

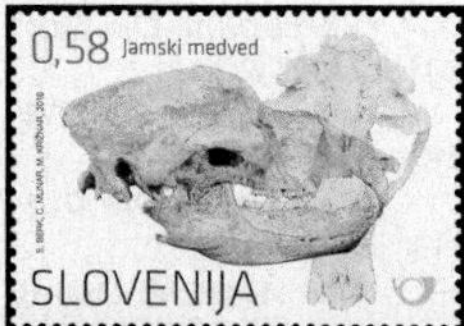
Front and Side Views of Fossilized Cave Bear Skull A576

2016, Mar. 25 Litho. *Perf. 14*
1160 A576 58c multi 1.40 1.40

Art Historians Izidor Cankar (1886-1958), Vojeslav Mole (1886-1973), and France Stele (1886-1972) — A577

2016, Mar. 25 Litho. *Perf. 14*
1161 A577 58c multi 1.40 1.40

Goriska Brda and Local Dishes A578

2016, Mar. 25 Litho. *Perf. 14*
1162 A578 €1.25 multi 3.00 3.00

Flowers A579

Designs: 60c, Leucojum vernum. 64c, Leucojum aestivum. 92c, Galanthus nivalis. 97c, Narcissus radiiflorus.

2016, Mar. 25 Litho. *Perf. 14*
1163-1165 A579 Set of 3 5.25 5.25

Souvenir Sheet

1166 A579 97c multi 2.40 2.40

Souvenir Sheet

2016 Collecta International Collectors' Fair — A580

2016, Mar. 25 Litho. *Perf. 14*
1167 A580 64c multi 1.50 1.50

Souvenir Sheet

Peter Prevc, 2016 World Ski Jumping Champion — A581

2016, May 6 Litho. *Perf. 14*
1168 A581 €2.25 multi 5.50 5.50

Kingdom of Illyria, 200th Anniv. — A582

2016, May 27 Litho. *Perf. 14¼x14*
1169 A582 42c multi 1.00 1.00

17th World Lace Congress, Ljubljana — A583

2016, May 27 Litho. *Perf. 14*
1170 A583 47c multi 1.20 1.20
a. Tete-beche pair 2.40 2.40

Chapel Near Vrsic Built By Russian World War I Prisoners of War, Cent. — A584

2016, May 27 Litho. *Perf. 14x14½*
1171 A584 60c multi 1.50 1.50

No. 1171 was printed in sheets of 7 + label. See Russia No. 7727.

A585

Europa A586

2016, May 27 Litho. *Perf. 14*
1172 A585 64c multi 1.60 1.60
1173 A586 97c multi 2.40 2.40

Think Green Issue.
Nos. 1172-1173 were each printed in sheets of 8 + label.

Water Mills — A587

Designs: 36c, Floating mill on Mura River, Izakovci. 42c, Zager Mill, Podvolovljek Valley. 47c, Sorz Mill, Polze. 58c, Modrijan's Mill near Postojna Cave. 60c, Ferlez Mill, Sibenik.

2016, May 27 Litho. *Perf. 13¼x13*
1174-1178 A587 Set of 5 6.00 6.00

Birds — A588

Designs: 25c, Picus viridis. 30c, Pernis apivorus. 50c, Tetrastes bonasia. 75c, Regulus ignicapilla. €1, Merops apiaster.

Serpentine Die Cut 11½x11¼
2016, May 27 Litho.
Self-Adhesive
1179-1183 A588 Set of 5 6.75 6.75

2016 Summer Olympics, Rio de Janeiro — A589

No. 1184: a, 64c, Cycling. b, 97c, Kayaking.

2016, May 27 Litho. *Perf. 14*
1184 A589 Horiz. pair, #a-b 4.00 4.00

Souvenir Sheet

Independence, 25th Anniv. — A590

2016, May 27 Litho. *Perf. 14*
1185 A590 64c multi 1.60 1.60

Souvenir Sheet

Cargo Ship Piran — A591

2016, May 27 Litho. *Perf. 14*
1186 A591 €1.33 multi 3.25 3.25

Sardina Pilchardus — A592

2016, July 9 Litho. *Perf. 14*
1187 A592 64c multi 1.60 1.60

Souvenir Sheet

Battle of Lissa (Vis), 150th Anniv. — A593

2016, July 18 Litho. *Perf. 14*
1188 A593 60c multi 1.50 1.50

See Croatia No. 1002.

Tina Trstenjak, 2016 Olympic Gold Medalist Judoka A594

2016, Sept. 30 Litho. *Perf. 14*
1189 A594 €1.26 multi 3.00 3.00

Cetaceans A595

Designs: No. 1190, €1, Tursiops truncatus. No. 1191, €1, Balaenoptera physalus. €1.26, Stenella coeruleoalba.
€1.85, Delphinus delphis.

2016, Sept. 30 Litho. *Perf. 14*
1190-1192 A595 Set of 3 8.00 8.00

Souvenir Sheet

1193 A595 €1.85 multi 4.75 4.75

Souvenir Sheet

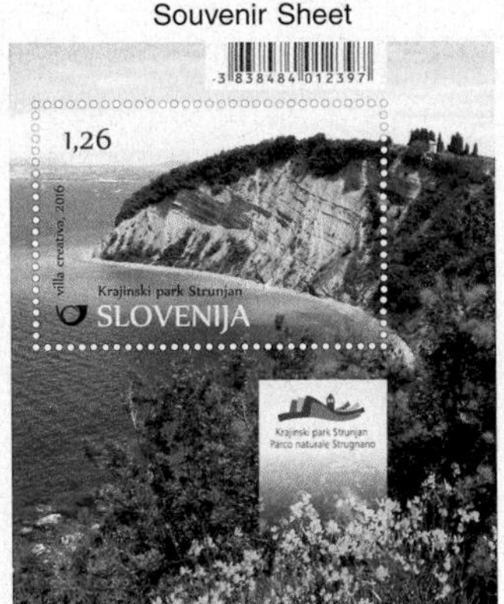

Strunjan Nature Park — A596

2016, Sept. 30 Litho. *Perf. 14*
1194 A596 €1.26 multi 3.00 3.00

Simon Gregorcic (1844-1906), Poet, and Baron Svetozar Boroevic von Bojna (1856-1920), Austro-Hungarian Field Marshal — A597

2016, Nov. 4 Litho. *Perf. 14*
1195 A597 45c multi 1.10 1.10

World War I, cent.

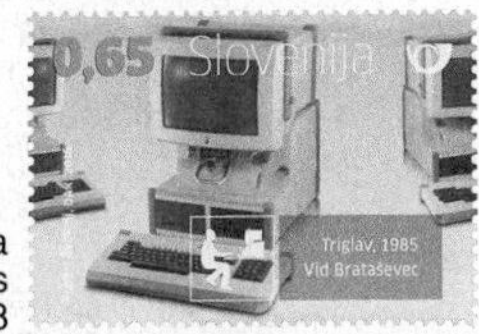

Iskra Delta Computers A598

2016, Nov. 4 Litho. *Perf. 14*
1196 A598 65c multi 1.50 1.50

Scene from *Valley of Peace,* Nominee for Best Picture Award at 1957 Cannes Film Festival A599

2016, Nov. 4 Litho. *Perf. 14*
1197 A599 €1.12 multi 2.60 2.60

Traditional Foods — A600

No. 1198: a, Tolminska frika (fried cheese). b, Kobariski struklji, Bovski krafi (strudel and pastries).

2016, Nov. 4 Litho. *Perf. 11¼x11¾*
1198 A600 97c Horiz. pair, #a-b 4.50 4.50

Souvenir Sheet

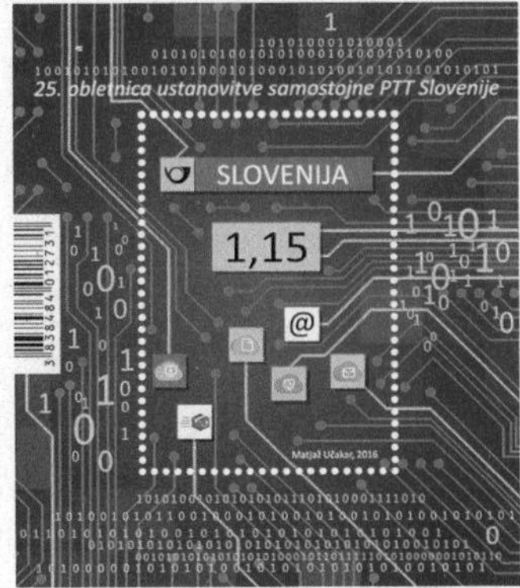

PTT Slovenije (Slovenian Postal Service), 25th Anniv. — A601

2016, Nov. 4 Litho. *Perf. 14*
1199 A601 €1.15 multi 2.75 2.75

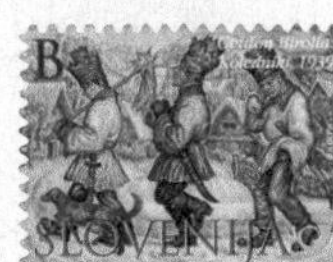

A602

Christmas A603

Serpentine Die Cut 11½
2016, Nov. 4 Litho.
Self-Adhesive

1200 A602 B multi 1.00 1.00
1201 A603 C multi 2.40 2.40

Booklet Stamps
Size: 35x26mm
Serpentine Die Cut 13x12½

1202 A602 B multi 1.00 1.00
a. Booklet pane of 12 12.00
1203 A603 C multi 2.40 2.40
a. Booklet pane of 12 29.00

On day of issue, Nos. 1200 and 1202 each sold for 45c and Nos. 1201 and 1203 each sold for €1.

New Year's Day 2017
A604 A605

Serpentine Die Cut 11½
2016, Nov. 4 Litho.
Self-Adhesive

1204 A604 A multi .85 .85
1205 A605 C multi 2.40 2.40

Booklet Stamps
Size: 26x35mm
Serpentine Die Cut 12½x13

1206 A604 A multi .85 .85
a. Booklet pane of 12 10.50
1207 A605 C multi 2.40 2.40
a. Booklet pane of 12 29.00

On day of issue, Nos. 1204 and 1206 each sold for 37c and Nos. 1205 and 1207 each sold for €1.

Veselka Pevec, Shooting Gold Medalist at 2016 Paralympics — A606

2016, Dec. 7 Litho. *Perf. 14*
1208 A606 €1.26 multi 3.00 3.00

Jewelry Box A607

2017, Jan. 27 Litho. *Perf. 13¼*
1209 A607 45c multi 1.10 1.10

Values are for stamps with surrounding selvage.

New Year 2017 (Year of the Rooster) — A608

2017, Jan. 27 Litho. *Perf. 14*
1210 A608 €1.12 multi 2.60 2.60

Fran Milcinski (1867-1932), Humorist — A609

2017, Jan. 27 Litho. *Perf. 14*
1211 A609 €1.15 multi 2.75 2.75

Souvenir Sheet

Ljubljana Town Hall, Designed by Carlo Martinuzzi (c. 1673-1726) — A610

2017, Jan. 27 Litho. *Perf. 14*
1212 A610 €1.40 multi 3.25 3.25

Map of Slovenia and Fossilized Lower Jaw of Panthera Leo Spelaea A611

2017, Mar. 17 Litho. *Perf. 14*
1213 A611 65c multi 1.60 1.60

Kayakers in Mine Beneath Mount Peca A612

2017, Mar. 17 Litho. *Perf. 14*
1214 A612 €1.40 multi 3.25 3.25

Roses A613

Designs: 97c, Rosa gallica "Officinalis." €1, Rosa x alba "Snezniska." €1.12, Rosa banksiae "Lutea."
€1.26, Rosa "Preseren."

2017, Mar. 17 Litho. *Perf. 14*
1215-1217 A613 Set of 3 7.50 7.50

Souvenir Sheet

1218 A613 €1.26 multi 3.00 3.00

Souvenir Sheet

Holy Roman Empress Maria Theresa (1717-80) — A614

2017, May 13 Litho. *Perf. 14*
1219 A614 €1.77 multi 4.25 4.25

See Austria No. 2677, Croatia No. 1038, Hungary No. 4433, Ukraine No. 1093.

Aljaz Tower on Triglav, Poem by France Preseren — A615

Assumption of Mary Church, Bled Island — A616

Die Cut Perf. 20½

2017, May 26 Coil Stamps Litho.

Self-Adhesive

1220 A615 A multi .85 .85
1221 A616 C multi 2.25 2.25

On day of issue, No. 1220 sold for 37c; No. 1221, €1.

Hammer Throw A617

2017, May 26 Litho. *Perf. 14*
1222 A617 €1.15 multi 2.60 2.60

2017 World Track and Field Championships, London. No. 1222 was printed in sheets of 6 + 3 labels.

Europa A618

Designs: 97c, Reichenburg Castle. €1.26, Sevnica Castle.

2017, May 26 Litho. *Perf. 14*
1223-1224 A618 Set of 2 5.00 5.00

Nos. 1223-1224 were each printed in sheets of 8 + label.

Souvenir Sheet

50th International Trade and Business Fair, Celje — A619

2017, May 26 Litho. *Perf. 14*
1225 A619 €1 gold & multi 2.25 2.25

Souvenir Sheet

Cargo Ship Maribor — A620

2017, May 26 Litho. *Perf. 14*
1226 A620 €1.15 multi 2.60 2.60

Arbutus Unedo A621

2017, July 10 Litho. *Perf. 14*
1227 A621 €1.26 multi 3.00 3.00

Cereal Crops — A622

Designs: 40c, Buckwheat. 48c, Wheat. 58c, Millet. 78c, Barley. €1, Spelt.

2017, Sept. 29 Litho. *Perf. 14*
1228-1232 A622 Set of 5 7.75 7.75

Ladybugs A623

Designs: €1, Psyllobora vigintiduopunctata. €1.15, Anatis ocellata. €1.29, Myzia oblongoguttata.
1.26, Coccinella septempunctata.

2017, Sept. 29 Litho. *Perf. 14*
1233-1235 A623 Set of 3 8.25 8.25

Souvenir Sheet

1236 A623 €1.26 multi 3.00 3.00

Souvenir Sheet

Lake Cerknica, Notranjska Regional Park — A624

2017, Sept. 29 Litho. *Perf. 14*
1237 A624 €1.20 multi 3.00 3.00

Souvenir Sheet

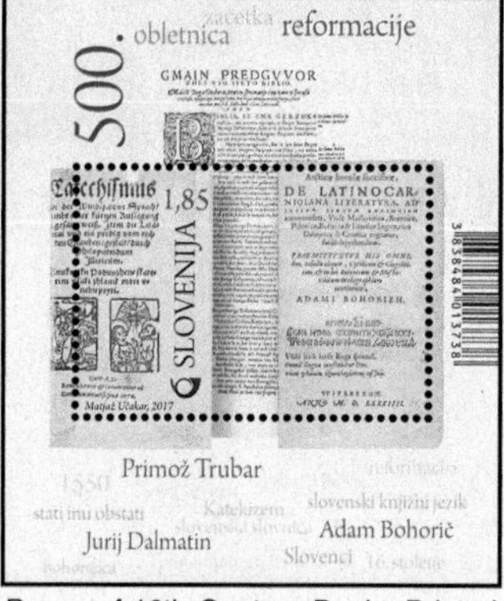

Pages of 16th Century Books Printed in Slovenian Language — A625

2017, Sept. 29 Litho. *Perf. 14*
1238 A625 €1.85 multi 4.50 4.50

Protestant Reformation, 500th anniv.

Souvenir Sheet

Buildings Designed by Joze Plecnik (1872-1957) — A626

No. 1239: a, 40c, National and University Library. b, 48c, Garden of All Saints. c, 58c, Church of St. Michael on the Marsh.

2017, Sept. 29 Litho. *Perf. 14¼x14*
1239 A626 Sheet of 3, #a-c 3.50 3.50

New Emblem of Slovenia Post — A627

Perf. 11¼x11¾

2017, Nov. 10 Litho.
1240 A627 48c multi 1.25 1.25

Janez Evangelist Krek (1865-1917), Politician, Anton Korosec (1872-1940), Politician, and Declaration of May 30, 1917 — A628

2017, Nov. 10 Litho. *Perf. 14*
1241 A628 48c multi 1.25 1.25

Slovenian Walnut Cakes and Argentinian Mate — A629

2017, Nov. 10 Litho. *Perf. 14*
1242 A629 48c multi 1.25 1.25

Slovenian emigration to Argentina.

Gorenje Washing Machines A630

2017, Nov. 10 Litho. *Perf. 14*
1243 A630 78c multi 1.90 1.90

Slovenia Industry.

Scene From 1977 Film, *Hang On, Doggy* — A631

2017, Nov. 10 Litho. *Perf. 14*
1244 A631 €1.29 multi 3.25 3.25

Traditional Foods — A632

No. 1245: a, Belokranjska povitica (cottage cheese cake). b, Pecenon jagnje z rozmarinom (roast lamb with rosemary).

Perf. 11¼x11¾

2017, Nov. 10 Litho.
1245 A632 €1.15 Horiz. pair, #a-b 5.50 5.50

Christmas
A633 A634

Serpentine Die Cut 11¼x11½

2017, Nov. 10 Litho.

Self-Adhesive

1246 A633 B multi 1.25 1.25
1247 A634 C multi 2.40 2.40

Booklet Stamps
Size:26x35mm

Serpentine Die Cut 12¾

1248 A633 B multi 1.25 1.25
 a. Booklet pane of 12 15.00
1249 A634 C multi 2.40 2.40
 a. Booklet pane of 12 29.00

On day of issue, Nos. 1246 and 1248 each sold for 48c, and Nos. 1247 and 1249 each sold for €1.

New Year's Day 2018
A635 A636

Serpentine Die Cut 11¼x11½

2017, Nov. 10 Litho.

Self-Adhesive

1250 A635 A multi .95 .95

Serpentine Die Cut 11½x11¼

1251 A636 C multi 2.40 2.40

Booklet Stamps
Size: 26x35mm

Serpentine Die Cut 12¾

1252 A635 A multi .95 .95
 a. Booklet pane of 12 11.50

Size: 35x26mm

1253 A636 C multi 2.40 2.40
 a. Booklet pane of 12 29.00

On day of issue, Nos. 1250 and 1252 each sold for 40c, and Nos. 1251 and 1253 each sold for €1.

Souvenir Sheet

Victory of Slovenian Men's Basketball Team at 2017 European Championships — A637

2017, Dec. 12 Litho. *Perf. 14*
1254 A637 €1.77 multi 4.25 4.25

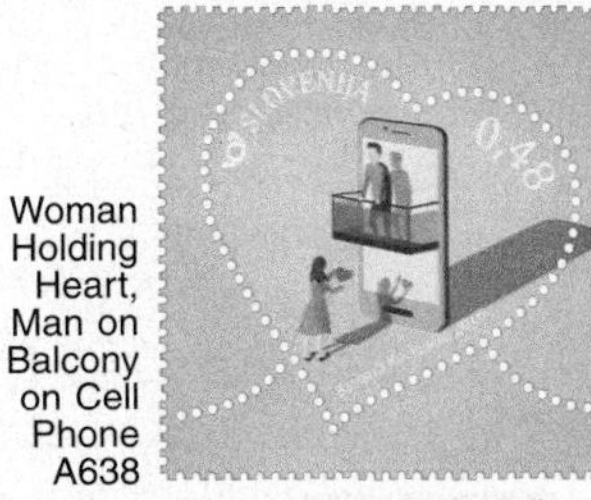
Woman Holding Heart, Man on Balcony on Cell Phone A638

2018, Jan. 26 Litho. *Perf. 13¼*
1255 A638 48c multi 1.25 1.25

Values are for stamps with surrounding selvage.

National Gallery, Cent. A639

2018, Jan. 26 Litho. *Perf. 14*
1256 A639 58c multi 1.50 1.50

Ivan Cankar (1876-1918), Writer — A640

2018, Jan. 26 Litho. *Perf. 14*
1257 A640 78c multi 2.00 2.00

Ivan Vidav (1918-2015), Mathematician A641

2018, Jan. 26 Litho. *Perf. 14*
1258 A641 €1.15 multi 3.00 3.00

New Year 2018 (Year of the Dog) A642

2018, Jan. 26 Litho. *Perf. 14*
1259 A642 €1.29 multi 3.25 3.25

2018 Winter Olympics, PyeongChang, South Korea — A643

No. 1260: a, €1, Ice hockey. b, €1.15, Skiing.

2018, Jan. 26 Litho. *Perf. 14*
1260 A643 Vert. pair, #a-b, + central label 5.50 5.50

Souvenir Sheet

Friedl-Rechar Building, Ljubljana — A644

2018, Jan. 26 Litho. *Perf. 14*
1261 A644 €1.42 multi 3.50 3.50

Fala Hydropwer Plant, Cent. A645

2018, Mar. 23 Litho. *Perf. 14*
1262 A645 48c multi 1.25 1.25

Mastodon and Mastodon Tooth A646

2018, Mar. 23 Litho. *Perf. 14*
1263 A646 78c multi 2.00 2.00

Koper A647

2018, Mar. 23 Litho. *Perf. 14*
1264 A647 €1.42 multi 3.50 3.50

Tourism.

A648

A649

Easter — A650

Serpentine Die Cut 11½
2018, Mar. 23 Litho.
Self-Adhesive

1265 A648 A multi 1.00 1.00
1266 A649 B multi 1.25 1.25
1267 A650 C multi 2.50 2.50
Nos. 1265-1267 (3) 4.75 4.75

On day of issue, No. 1265 sold for 40c; No. 1266, 48c; No. 1267, €1.

Flowers — A651

Designs: €1, Achillea millefolium. €1.15, Salvia officinalis. €1.26, Pulmonaria officinalis.

€1.29, Arnica montana.

2018, Mar. 23 Litho. *Perf. 14*
1268-1270 A651 Set of 3 8.50 8.50

Souvenir Sheet

1271 A651 €1.29 multi 3.25 3.25

Souvenir Sheet

World Design Day — A652

2018, Mar. 23 Litho. *Perf. 14*
1272 A652 €1 multi 2.50 2.50

Donat Mg Mineral Water, 110th Anniv. — A653

2018, May 25 Litho. *Perf. 14*
1273 A653 48c multi 1.25 1.25

Proteus Anguinus A654

2018, May 25 Litho. *Perf. 14*
1274 A654 €1.77 multi 4.25 4.25

Europa A655

Designs: €1.15, Cobblers' Bridge, Ljubljana. €1.26, Puh Bridge, Ptuj.

2018, May 25 Litho. *Perf. 14*
1275-1276 A655 Set of 2 5.75 5.75

Nos. 1275-1276 were each printed in sheets of 8 + label.

Superstitions A656

Designs: 40c, Witch flying on broom. 48c, Black cat. 58c, Necklace of garlic. 78c, Astrological symbols, overturned tea cup and palm of hand. €1, St. John's Day wreath on door.

2018, May 25 Litho. *Perf. 14*
1277-1281 A656 Set of 5 7.75 7.75

Souvenir Sheet

World Bee Day — A657

2018, May 25 Litho. *Perf. 14*
1282 A657 €1 multi 2.40 2.40

Souvenir Sheet

Bulk Carrier Ljubljana — A658

2018, May 25 Litho. *Perf. 14*
1283 A658 €1.15 multi 2.75 2.75

Skratelj House, Divaca — A659

2018, July 9 Litho. *Perf. 14*
1284 A659 €1.26 multi 3.00 3.00

Endangered Animals — A660

Designs: A, Lynx lynx. B, Lepus timidus, vert. €1, Mustela nivalis, vert. C, Neomys anomalus. D, Lutra lutra.

Serpentine Die Cut 11½
2018, Sept. 28 Litho.
Self-Adhesive

1285 A660	A multi		1.00	1.00
1286 A660	B multi		1.25	1.25
1287 A660	€1 multi		2.40	2.40
1288 A660	C multi		2.75	2.75
1289 A660	D multi		3.00	3.00
	Nos. 1285-1289 (5)		10.40	10.40

On day of issue, No. 1285 sold for 43c; No. 1286, 52c; No. 1288, €1.17; No. 1289, €1.31.

Scene From 1948 Film, *On Our Own Land* A661

2018, Sept. 28 Litho. *Perf. 14*
1290 A661 €1.44 multi 3.50 3.50

Farm Animals A662

Designs: €1.17, Bovec sheep. €1.30, Posavina horse. €1.31, Brown cow. €1.44, Dreznica goat.

2018, Sept. 28 Litho. *Perf. 14*
1291-1293 A662 Set of 3 8.75 8.75

Souvenir Sheet
1294 A662 €1.44 multi 3.50 3.50

Souvenir Sheet

Pivka Seasonal Lakes Nature Park — A663

2018, Sept. 28 Litho. *Perf. 14*
1295 A663 €1.30 multi 3.00 3.00

Environmental Protection — A664

Designs: 5c, Wind generators. 10c, Smokestacks. 20c, Faucets. 35c, Garbage in can. 50c, Garbage in sea.

Serpentine Die Cut 11½
2018, Nov. 9 Litho.
Self-Adhesive

1296 A664	5c multi	.25	.25
1297 A664	10c multi	.25	.25
1298 A664	20c multi	.45	.45
1299 A664	35c multi	.80	.80
1300 A664	50c multi	1.10	1.10
	Nos. 1296-1300 (5)	2.85	2.85

A665

Design: Ivan Vavpotic (1877-1943), Designer of First Postage Stamps for Slovenia and Yugoslavia No. 3L6.

2018, Nov. 9 Litho. *Perf. 14*
1301 A665 43c multi 1.00 1.00

First postage stamps for Slovenia, cent.

End of World War I, Cent. — A666

2018, Nov. 9 Litho. *Perf. 14*
1302 A666 52c multi 1.25 1.25

Banjo and Accordion A667

2018, Nov. 9 Litho. *Perf. 14*
1303 A667 52c multi 1.25 1.25

Slovenes in the United States.

General Rudolf Maister (1874-1934) A668

2018, Nov. 9 Litho. *Perf. 14*
1304 A668 78c multi 1.75 1.75

Maister's military campaign to control northern Slovenia, cent.

Traditional Foods — A669

No. 1305: a, Jajcni struklji (boiled egg strudel). b, Forflcova zupa s cesplji (milk soup with pasta and plums).

2018, Nov. 9 Litho. *Perf. 14*
1305 A669 €1.30 Horiz. pair, #a-b 6.00 6.00

Souvenir Sheet

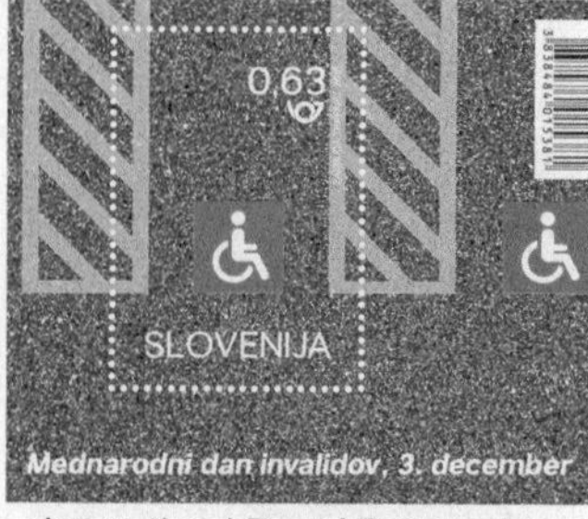

International Day of Persons with Disabilities — A670

2018, Nov. 9 Litho. *Perf. 14*
1306 A670 63c multi 1.50 1.50

Souvenir Sheet

Slovene Ballet, Cent. — A671

2018, Nov. 9 Litho. *Perf. 14*
1307 A671 €1.17 multi 2.75 2.75

Souvenir Sheet

Benko House, Crni Kal — A672

2018, Nov. 9 Litho. *Perf. 14*
1308 A672 €2.15 multi 5.00 5.00

A673

Christmas — A674

Serpentine Die Cut 11½
2018, Nov. 9 Litho.
Self-Adhesive

1309 A673	B multi	1.25	1.25
1310 A674	C multi	2.75	2.75

Booklet Stamps
Size: 26x35mm
Serpentine Die Cut 12¾

1311 A673	B multi	1.25	1.25
a.	Booklet pane of 12	15.00	

Size: 35x26mm

1312 A674	C multi	2.75	2.75
a.	Booklet pane of 12	33.00	

On day of issue, Nos. 1309 and 1311 each sold for 52c and Nos. 1310 and 1312 each sold for €1.17.

New Year's Day 2019
A675 A676

Serpentine Die Cut 11½
2019, Nov. 9 Litho.
Self-Adhesive

1313 A675	A multi	1.00	1.00
1314 A676	C multi	2.75	2.75

Booklet Stamps
Size: 26x35mm
Serpentine Die Cut 12¾

1315 A675	A multi	1.00	1.00
a.	Booklet pane of 12	12.00	
1316 A676	C multi	2.75	2.75
a.	Booklet pane of 12	33.00	

On day of issue, Nos. 1313 and 1315 each sold for 43c and Nos. 1314 and 1316 each sold for €1.17.

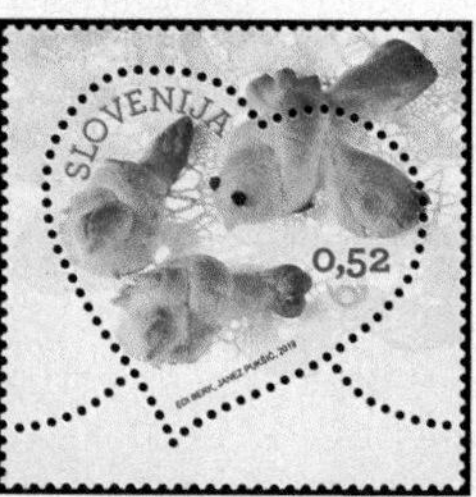

Bread Birds A677

2019, Jan. 25 Litho. *Perf. 13¼*
1317 A677 52c multi 1.25 1.25

St. Valentine's Day and St. Gregory's Day. Values are for stamps with surrounding selvage.

Alma M. Karlin (1889-1950), Traveler and Writer — A678

2019, Jan. 25 Litho. *Perf. 14*
1318 A678 63c multi 1.50 1.50

Ignatius Knoblecher (1819-58), Roman Catholic Missionary in North Africa — A679

2019, Jan. 25 Litho. *Perf. 14*
1319 A679 €1.30 multi 3.00 3.00

Porcelain by Nika Stupica — A680

2019, Jan. 25 Litho. *Perf. 14*
1320 A680 €1.31 multi 3.00 3.00

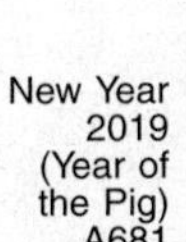

New Year 2019 (Year of the Pig) A681

2019, Jan. 25 Litho. *Perf. 14*
1321 A681 €1.44 multi 3.50 3.50

Souvenir Sheet

Oberrealschule, Ljubljana, Designed by Alexander Bellon — A682

2019, Jan. 25 Litho. *Perf. 14*
1322 A682 €1.57 multi 3.75 3.75

Radio Student, 50th Anniv. — A683

2019, Mar. 22 Litho. *Perf. 14*
1323 A683 52c blk & red 1.25 1.25

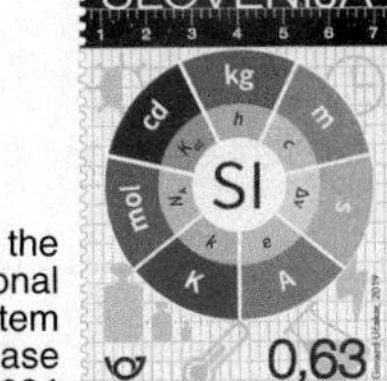

Redefinition of the International Metric System Base Units — A684

2019, Mar. 22 Litho. *Perf. 14*
1324 A684 63c multi 1.40 1.40

Anthracothere and Fossilized Skeleton — A685

2019, Mar. 22 Litho. *Perf. 14*
1325 A685 85c multi 1.90 1.90

Timekeeping Devices — A686

No. 1326: a, Pleterje Charterhouse sundial, Drca, Slovenia. b, Astronomical clock, Stará Bystrica, Slovakia.

Perf. 13½x13¼
2019, Mar. 22 Litho.
1326 A686 €1.17 Horiz. pair, #a.-b. 5.25 5.25

See Slovakia No. 813.

Medals of Franjo Malgai (1894-1919), Military Hero — A687

2019, Mar. 22 Litho. *Perf. 14*
1327 A687 €1.30 multi 3.00 3.00

Stone Building, Stanjel — A688

2019, Mar. 22 Litho. *Perf. 14*
1328 A688 €1.31 multi 3.00 3.00

Hydrangeas A689

Designs: €1.17, Hydrangea paniculata. €1.30, Hydrangea serrata. €1.31, Hydrangea quercifolia. €1.44, Hydrangea macrophylla.

2019, Mar. 22 Litho. *Perf. 14*
1329-1331 A689 multi 8.50 8.50

Souvenir Sheet

1332 A689 €1.44 multi 3.25 3.25

Souvenir Sheet

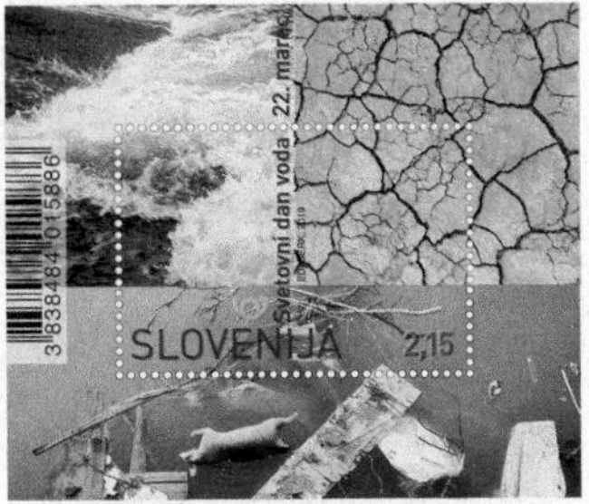

World Water Day — A690

2019, Mar. 22 Litho. *Perf. 14*
1333 A690 €2.15 multi 5.00 5.00

University of Ljubljana, Cent. — A691

2019, May 31 Litho. *Perf. 14*
1334 A691 95c multi 2.25 2.25

Incorporation of Prekmurje Region of Hungary Into Yugoslavia, Cent. — A692

2019, May 31 Litho. *Perf. 14*
1335 A692 €2.01 multi 4.50 4.50

Europa — A693

Birds: €1.31, Panurus biarmicus. €1.45, Ardea purpura.

2019, May 31 Litho. *Perf. 14*
1336-1337 A693 Set of 2 6.25 6.25

Nos. 1336-1337 were each printed in sheets of 8 + central label.

Hay Racks A694

Hay rack from: A, Poljanska Valleys. B, Doljenske. 70c, Bohinj. 95c, Central Slovenia. €1.17, Zasavje.

2019, May 31 Litho. *Perf. 14*
1338-1342 A694 Set of 5 8.75 8.75

On day of issue, Nos. 1338 and 1339 sold for 48c and 58c, respectively.

Souvenir Sheet

Cargo Ship Portoroz — A695

2019, May 31 Litho. *Perf. 14*
1343 A695 €1.51 multi 3.50 3.50

Men's European Volleyball Championships — A696

2019, July 8 Litho. *Perf. 14*
1344 A696 C multi 2.60 2.60

No. 1344 sold for €1.17 on day of issue and was printed in sheets of 6 + 3 central labels.

Man and Woman in Traditional Costumes of Barkovije and Skedenj A697

2019, July 8 Litho. *Perf. 14*
1345 A697 D multi 3.00 3.00

No. 1345 sold for €1.31 on day of issue.

Mohandas K. Gandhi (1869-1948), Indian Nationalist Leader — A698

2019, Sept. 27 Litho. *Perf. 14*
1346 A698 70c multi 1.60 1.60

Slovenian National Theater, Maribor, Cent. A699

2019, Sept. 27 Litho. *Perf. 14*
1347 A699 €1.17 multi 2.60 2.60

Ursus Arctos A700

Designs: €1.17, Brown bear facing left. €1.31, Brown bear rubbing back against tree, vert. €1.45, Two brown bear cubs, vert. €1.67, Adult brown bear and two cubs.

2019, Sept. 27 Litho. *Perf. 14*
1348-1350 A700 Set of 3 8.75 8.75

Souvenir Sheet

1351 A700 €1.67 multi 3.75 3.75

Souvenir Sheet

Logar Valley Nature Park — A701

2019, Sept. 27 Litho. *Perf. 14*
1352 A701 95c multi 2.10 2.10

Dr. Angela Piskernik (1886-1967), Teacher and Conservationist A702

2019, Nov. 8 Litho. *Perf. 14*
1353 A702 58c multi 1.40 1.40

Phascolarctos Cinereus and Rupicapra Rupicapra — A703

2019, Nov. 8 Litho. *Perf. 14*
1354 A703 58c multi 1.40 1.40

Slovenians in Australia.

Traditional Foods — A704

No. 1355: a, Bloska kavla ali trojka (kohlrabi stew). b, Kraska selinka (celery soup).

2019, Nov. 8 Litho. *Perf. 14*
1355 A704 €1.17 Horiz. pair, #a-b 5.25 5.25

Souvenir Sheet

House of Nace Homan, Skofja Loka — A705

2019, Nov. 8 Litho. *Perf. 14*
1356 A705 €2.31 multi 5.25 5.25

A706

Christmas — A707

Serpentine Die Cut 11¼

2019, Nov. 8 Litho.

Self-Adhesive

1357 A706 B multi 1.30 1.30
1358 A707 C multi 2.60 2.60

Booklet Stamps

Serpentine Die Cut 12¾

1359 A706 B multi 1.30 1.30
a. Booklet pane of 12 16.00
1360 A707 C multi 2.60 2.60
a. Booklet pane of 12 31.50

On day of issue, Nos. 1357 and 1359 each sold for 58c, and Nos. 1358 and 1360 each sold for €1.17.

New Year's Day
A708 A709

Serpentine Die Cut 11¼

2019, Nov. 8 Litho.

Self-Adhesive

1361 A708 A multi 1.10 1.10
1362 A709 C multi 2.60 2.60

Booklet Stamps

Serpentine Die Cut 12¾

1363 A708 A multi 1.10 1.10
a. Booklet pane of 12 13.50
1364 A709 C multi 2.60 2.60
a. Booklet pane of 12 31.50

On day of issue, Nos. 1361 and 1363 each sold for 48c, and Nos. 1362 and 1364 each sold for €1.17.

Souvenir Sheet

Mercado de Abasto, Buenos Aires, Designed by Viktor Sulcic (1896-1973) — A710

2019, Dec. 12 Litho. *Perf. 12*
1365 A710 €2.01 multi 4.50 4.50

Joint Issue between Slovenia and Argentina. See Argentina No. 2901.

Man and Woman on Tandem Bicycle A711

2020, Jan. 31 Litho. *Perf. 13¼*
1366 A711 B multi 1.30 1.30

No. 1366 sold for 58c on day of issue. Values are for stamps with surrounding selvage.

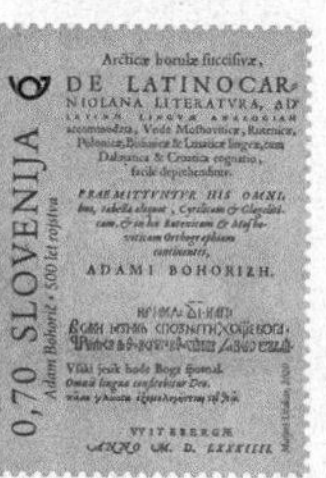

First Slovenian Grammar Book, by Adam Bohoric (c.1520-98) A712

2020, Jan. 31 Litho. *Perf. 14*
1367 A712 70c multi 1.60 1.60

Memorandum on Nature Conservation, Cent. — A713

2020, Jan. 31 Litho. *Perf. 14*
1368 A713 95c multi 2.10 2.10

Damascus Steel Knife Forged by Joze Krmelj — A714

2020, Jan. 31 Litho. *Perf. 14*
1369 A714 €1.31 multi 3.00 3.00

Hugo Wolf (1860-1903), Composer — A715

2020, Jan. 31 Litho. *Perf. 14*
1370 A715 €1.45 multi 3.25 3.25

New Year 2020 (Year of the Rat) — A716

2020, Jan. 31 Litho. *Perf. 14*
1371 A716 €1.51 multi 3.50 3.50

Souvenir Sheet

Municipal Savings Bank, Ljubljana, Designed by Josip Vancas (1859-1932) — A717

2020, Jan. 31 Litho. *Perf. 14*
1372 A717 €1.85 multi 4.25 4.25

2020 Ski Flying World Championships, Planica — A718

2020, Mar. 13 Litho. *Perf. 14*
1373 A718 48c multi 1.10 1.10

No. 1373 was printed in sheets of 6 + 3 central labels.

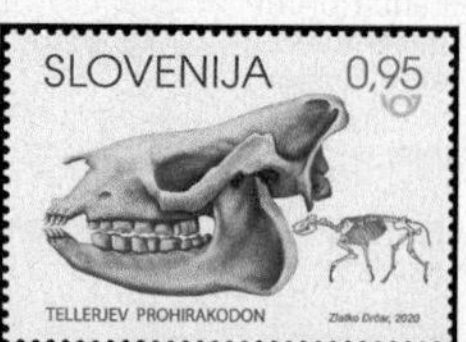

Fossilized Skull of Prohyracodon Telleri — A719

2020, Mar. 13 Litho. *Perf. 14*
1374 A719 95c multi 2.10 2.10

Podcetrtek
A720

2020, Mar. 13 Litho. *Perf. 14*
1375 A720 €1.31 multi 3.00 3.00

A721

A722

Decorated Easter Eggs — A723

Serpentine Die Cut 11¼
2020, Mar. 13 Litho.
Self-Adhesive
1376 A721 A multi 1.10 1.10
1377 A722 B multi 1.25 1.25
1378 A723 C multi 2.60 2.60
Nos. 1376-1378 (3) 4.95 4.95

On day of issue, Nos. 1376-1378 sold for 48c, 58c, and €1.17 respectively.

Tree Flowers
A724

Designs: €1.17, Liriodendron tulipifera. €1.31, Catalpa bignonioides. €1.45, Paulownia tomentosa.
€1.51, Aesculus hippocastanum.

2020, Mar. 13 Litho. *Perf. 14*
1379-1381 A724 Set of 3 8.50 8.50
Souvenir Sheet
1382 A724 €1.51 multi 3.25 3.25

Souvenir Sheet

National Volunteer Week — A725

2020, Mar. 13 Litho. *Perf. 14*
1383 A725 €1.51 multi 3.25 3.25

POSTAL TAX STAMPS

Catalogue values for unused stamps in this section are for Never Hinged items.

Red Cross — PT1

1992, May 8 Litho. *Perf. 14*
RA1 PT1 3t blue, black & red .90 .90

Red Cross, Solidarity — PT2

1992, June 2 *Perf. 14½x14*
RA2 PT2 3t multicolored .60 .60

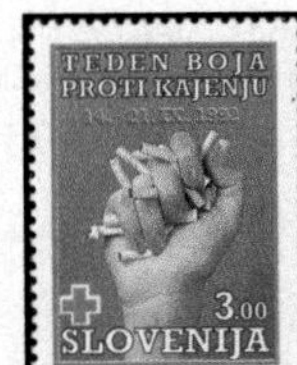

PT3

1992, Sept. 14 Litho. *Perf. 14*
RA3 PT3 3t multicolored .65 .65

Stop Smoking Week, Sept. 14-21.

Red Cross — PT4

1993, May 8 Litho. *Perf. 14*
RA4 PT4 3.50t blue, black & red .60 .60

Rescue Team — PT5

1993, June 1
RA5 PT5 3.50t multicolored .50 .50

Anti-Smoking Campaign PT6

1993, Sept. 14 Litho. *Perf. 14*
RA6 PT6 4.50t multicolored .60 .60

PT7

1994, May 8 Litho. *Perf. 14*
RA7 PT7 4.50t multicolored .45 .45

Obligatory on mail May 8-15.

Red Cross Worker, Child — PT8

1994, June 1
RA8 PT8 4.50t multicolored .45 .45

Obligatory on mail June 1-7.

PT9

1995, May 8 Litho. *Perf. 14*
RA9 PT9 6.50t multicolored .45 .45

Obligatory on mail May 8-15.

Red Cross, Solidarity PT10

1995, June 1 Litho. *Perf. 14*
RA10 PT10 6.50t multicolored .55 .55

Obligatory on mail June 1-7.

Red Cross, Solidarity — PT11

1996, May 8 Litho. *Perf. 14*
RA11 PT11 7t multicolored .45 .45

Obligatory on mail May 8-15.

Red Cross, Solidarity PT12

1996, June 1 Litho. *Perf. 14*
RA12 PT12 7t multicolored .45 .45

Obligatory on mail June 1-7.

Red Cross, Solidarity PT13

1997, May 8 Litho. *Perf. 14*
RA13 PT13 7t multicolored .45 .45

Obligatory on mail May 8-14.

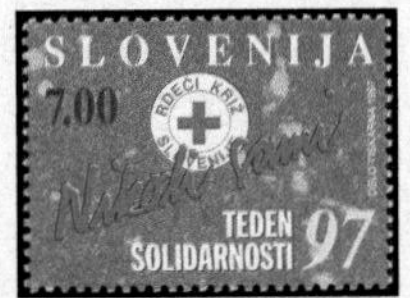

Red Cross, Solidarity PT14

1997, June 1 Litho. *Perf. 14*
RA14 PT14 7t multicolored .45 .45

Obligatory on mail June 1-7.

PT15

1998, May 8 Litho. *Perf. 14*
RA15 PT15 7t black & red .45 .45

Obligatory on mail May 8-14.

Red Cross, Solidarity — PT16

Design: No. RA16a, "7" at lower left. No. RA16b, "7" at upper right.

1998, June 1
RA16 PT16 7t Pair, #a.-b. .75 .75

Obligatory on mail June 1-7.
See also Nos. RA18, RA20.

Red Cross — PT17

1999, May 8 Litho. *Perf. 14*
RA17 PT17 8t black & red .50 .50

Obligatory on mail May 8-15.

Solidarity Type of 1998

a, 9t at LL. b, 9t at UR.

1999, Nov. 1 Litho. *Perf. 14*
RA18 PT16 9t Pair, #a.-b. .70 .70

Obligatory on mail Nov. 1-7.

Red Cross — PT19

2000, May 8 Litho. *Perf. 14*
RA19 PT19 10t blk & red .70 .70

Obligatory on mail May 8-15.

Red Cross Solidarity Type of 1998

No. RA20: a, 10 at LL. b, 10 at UR.

2000, Nov. 1 Litho. *Perf. 14*
RA20 PT16 10t Horiz. pair, #a-b 2.25 2.25

Obligatory on mail Nov. 1-7.

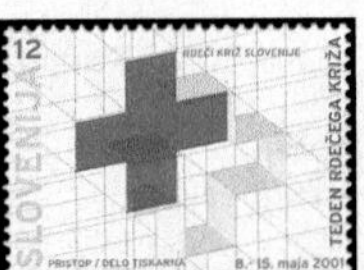

Red Cross — PT20

2001, May 8
RA21 PT20 12t multi .70 .70

Obligatory on mail May 8-15.

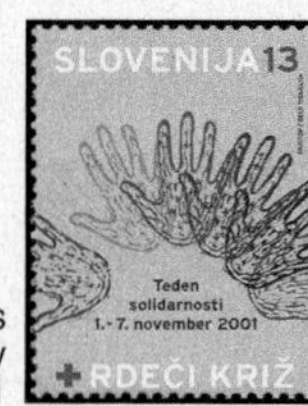
Red Cross Solidarity Week — PT21

2001, Nov. 1 Litho. *Perf. 14*
RA22 PT21 13t multi .65 .65

Obligatory on mail Nov. 1-7.

Red Cross Week — PT22

2002, May 8
RA23 PT22 15t multi 1.25 1.25

Obligatory on mail May 8-15.

Red Cross Solidarity Week — PT23

2002, Nov. 1
RA24 PT23 15t multi 1.00 1.00

Obligatory on mail Nov. 1-7.

Red Cross Week — PT24

2003, May 8 *Perf. 14*
RA25 PT24 19t multi .70 .70

Self-Adhesive
Imperf

RA25A PT24 19t multi 1.00 1.00

Obligatory on mail May 8-15.

Red Cross Solidarity Week — PT25

2003, Nov. 1 Litho. *Perf. 14*
RA26 PT25 19t multi .70 .70

Imperf
Self-Adhesive

RA26A PT25 19t multi 1.00 1.00

Obligatory on mail Nov. 1-7.

Red Cross — PT26

No. RA27: a, Blood droplet. b, Girl. c, Injured boy. d, Old woman.

2004, May 8 Litho. *Perf. 14*
RA27 PT26 19t Block of 4, #a-d 2.00 2.00

Obligatory on mail May 8-15.

Red Cross Solidarity Week — PT27

No. RA28: a, Airplane dropping aid packages. b, House on fire. c, Aid packages landing on ground. d, Damaged building.

2004, Nov. 1 Litho. *Perf. 14*
RA28 PT27 23t Block of 4, #a-d 2.00 2.00

Obligatory on mail Nov. 1-7.

Red Cross Week — PT28

2005, May 8 Litho. *Perf. 14*
RA29 PT28 25t black & red .70 .70

Obligatory on mail May 8-15.

Red Cross Solidarity — PT29

No. RA30: a, House in flood. b, Flood gauge.

2005, Nov. 1 Litho. *Perf. 14*
RA30 PT29 25t Horiz. pair, #a-b 1.25 1.25

Obligatory on mail Nov. 1-7.

Red Cross Week — PT30

2006, May 8 Litho. *Perf. 14*
RA31 PT30 25t multi .75 .75

Obligatory on mail May 8-15.

Fire Protection Week — PT31

2006, Oct. 9
RA32 PT31 25t multi .85 .85

Obligatory on mail Oct. 9-14.

Red Cross Solidarity Week — PT32

2006, Nov. 1
RA33 PT32 25t multi .75 .75

Obligatory on mail Nov. 1-7.

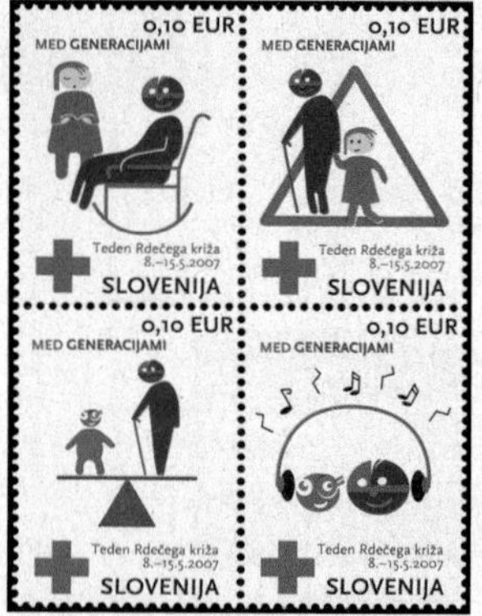
Red Cross Week — PT33

No. RA34: a, Woman, man in rocking chair. b, Man with cane, child, large triangle. c, Child and man with cane on seesaw. d, Man and child with earphones.

2007, May 8 Litho. *Perf. 14*
RA34 PT33 10c Block of 4, #a-d 1.75 1.75

Obligatory on mail May 8-15.

Fire Protection Week — PT34

2007, Oct. 8 Litho. *Perf. 14*
RA35 PT34 11c multi 1.50 1.50

Obligatory on mail Oct. 8-13.

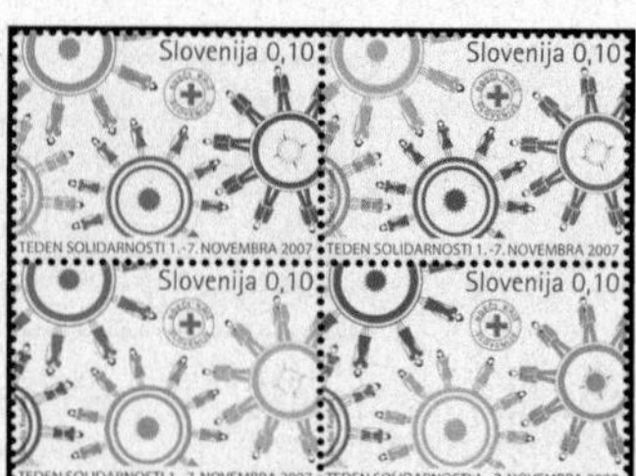
Red Cross Solidarity Week — PT35

No. RA36 — Circle in upper left in: a, Green. b, Yellow orange. c, Pink. d, Blue.

2007, Nov. 1
RA36 PT35 10c Block of 4, #a-d 1.75 1.75

Obligatory on mail Nov. 1-7.

Red Cross Week — PT36

No. RA37: a, Girl in water, fish. b, Boy in water, ship.

2008, May 8 Litho. *Perf. 14*
RA37 PT36 10c Horiz. pair, #a-b 1.40 1.40

Obligatory on mail May 8-15.

Fire Prevention Week — PT37

2008, Oct. 6
RA38 PT37 12c multi .70 .70

Obligatory on mail Oct. 6-11.

Red Cross Solidarity Week — PT38

2008, Nov. 1 Litho. *Perf. 14*
RA39 PT38 12c multi .60 .60

Obligatory on mail Nov. 1-7.

Battle of Solferino, 150th Anniv. — PT39

2009, May 8
RA40 PT39 13c multi .65 .65

Red Cross Week. Obligatory on mail May 8-15.

Fire Prevention Week — PT40

2009, Oct. 5
RA41 PT40 14c multi .70 .70

Obligatory on mail Oct. 5-10.

Red Cross Solidarity Week — PT41

2009, Nov. 1
RA42 PT41 13c multi .65 .65

Obligatory on mail Nov. 1-7.

Red Cross Week — PT42

2010, May 8 ***Perf. 14***
RA43 PT42 13c multi .75 .75

Obligatory on mail May 8-15.

Fire Prevention Week — PT43

2010, Oct. 4
RA44 PT43 14c multi .55 .55

Obligatory on mail Oct. 4-9.

Henri Dunant (1828-1910), Founder of the Red Cross — PT44

2010, Nov. 1
RA45 PT44 13c multi .50 .50

Obligatory on mail Nov. 1-7.

Red Cross Week PT45

2011, May 8
RA46 PT45 15c multi .55 .55

Obligatory on mail May 8-15.

Fire Prevention Week — PT46

2011, Oct. 3 ***Perf. 11¼x12***
RA47 PT46 15c multi .55 .55

Obligatory on mail Oct. 3-8.

Red Cross Solidarity Week PT47

2011, Nov. 1 ***Perf. 14***
RA48 PT47 15c multi .55 .55

Obligatory on mail Nov. 1-7.

Red Cross Week — PT48

2012, May 8 ***Perf. 14¼x14***
RA49 PT48 15c multi .50 .50

Obligatory on mail May 8-15.

Fire Prevention Week — PT49

2012, Oct. 1 Litho. ***Perf. 11¼x11¾***
RA50 PT49 15c multi .50 .50

Obligatory on mail Oct. 1-6.

Red Cross Solidarity Week — PT50

2012, Nov. 1 Litho. ***Perf. 14x14¼***
RA51 PT50 15c multi .50 .50

Obligatory on mail Nov. 1-7.

Red Cross Week — PT51

2013, May 8 Litho. ***Perf. 14¼x14***
RA52 PT51 17c multi .55 .55

Obligatory on mail May 8-15.

Fire Prevention Week — PT52

2013, Oct. 7 Litho. ***Perf. 13¼x13***
RA53 PT52 15c multi .50 .50

Obligatory on mail Oct. 7-12.

Red Cross Solidarity Week — PT53

2013, Nov. 1 Litho. ***Perf. 14***
RA54 PT53 17c multi .55 .55

Obligatory on mail Nov. 1-7.

Red Cross Week — PT54

2014, May 8 Litho. ***Perf. 14***
RA55 PT54 17c multi .55 .55

Obligatory on mail May 8-15.

Fire Prevention Week PT55

2014, Oct. 6 Litho. ***Perf. 13½x12¾***
RA56 PT55 15c multi .50 .50

Obligatory on mail Oct. 6-11.

Red Cross Solidarity Week — PT56

2014, Nov. 1 Litho. ***Perf. 14***
RA57 PT56 17c multi .55 .55

Obligatory on mail Nov. 1-7.

Red Cross Week — PT57

2015, May 8 Litho. ***Perf. 14***
RA58 PT57 17c multi .50 .50

Obligatory on mail May 8-15.

Fire Prevention Week — PT58

2015, Oct. 5 Litho. ***Perf. 14***
RA59 PT58 15c multi .45 .45

Obligatory on mail Oct. 5-10.

Red Cross Solidarity Week — PT59

2015, Nov. 1 Litho. ***Perf. 14***
RA60 PT59 17c multi .50 .50

Obligatory on mail Nov. 1-7.

Red Cross Week — PT60

2016, May 8 Litho. ***Perf. 14***
RA61 PT60 17c multi .50 .50

Obligatory on mail May 8-15.

Fire Prevention Week — PT61

2016, Oct. 3 Litho. ***Perf. 14***
RA62 PT61 15c multi .45 .45

Obligatory on mail Oct. 3-8.

Red Cross Week — PT63

2017, May 8 Litho. ***Perf. 14***
RA64 PT63 17c multi .50 .50

Obligatory on mail May 8-15.

Fire Prevention Week — PT64

2017, Oct. 2 Litho. ***Perf. 11¾x11¼***
RA65 PT64 15c multi .45 .45

Obligatory on mail Oct. 2-7.

Red Cross Solidarity Week — PT65

2017, Nov. 1 Litho. ***Perf. 14***
RA66 PT65 17c multi .40 .40

Obligatory on mail Nov. 1-7.

Red Cross Week — PT66

2018, May 8 Litho. ***Perf. 14***
RA67 PT66 17c multi .40 .40

Obligatory on mail May 8-15.

SOLOMON ISLANDS

'sä-lə-mən 'ī-ləndz

British Solomon Islands

LOCATION — West Pacific Ocean, east of Papua
GOVT. — Independent state in British Commonwealth
AREA — 10,954 sq. mi.
POP. — 455,429 (1999 est.)
CAPITAL — Honiara

The Solomons include 10 large islands and four groups of small islands extending over an area of 375,000 square miles.

The British protectorate of British Solomon Islands changed its name to Solomon Islands in 1975 and achieved independence July 7, 1978.

12 Pence = 1 Shilling
20 Shillings = 1 Pound
100 Cents = 1 Dollar (1966)

Catalogue values for unused stamps in this country are for Never Hinged items, beginning with Scott 80 in the regular postage section and Scott B1 in the semi-postal section.

Watermark

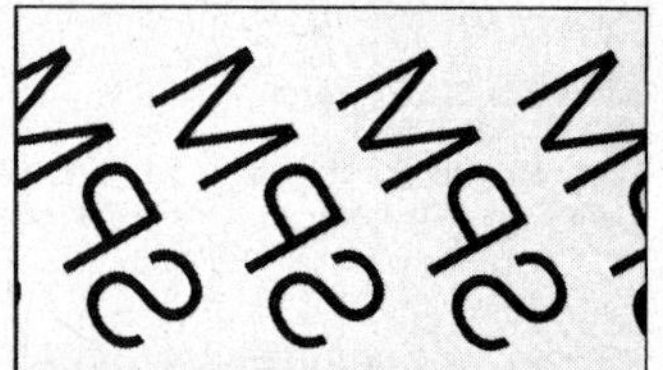

Wmk. 388 — Multiple "SPM"

War Canoe — A1

Unwmk.

1907, Feb. 14 Litho. *Perf. 11*

1	A1	½p ultra	10.00	*15.00*
2	A1	1p red	26.00	*27.50*
3	A1	2p dull blue	50.00	*35.00*
a.		Horiz. pair, imperf. btwn.	*15,000.*	
4	A1	2½p orange	35.00	*50.00*
a.		Vert. pair, imperf. btwn.	*7,500.*	
b.		Horiz. pair, imperf. btwn.	*12,000.*	*7,000.*
5	A1	5p yellow green	65.00	*77.50*
6	A1	6p chocolate	60.00	*77.50*
a.		Vertical pair, imperf. btwn.	*7,000.*	
7	A1	1sh violet	90.00	*95.00*
		Nos. 1-7 (7)	336.00	377.50

Imperf. between varieties should be accompanied by certificates of authenticity issued by competent authorities. Excellent counterfeits are plentiful.

War Canoe — A2

Wmk. Multiple Crown and CA (3)

1908-11 Engr. *Perf. 14*

8	A2	½p green	1.60	1.10
9	A2	1p carmine	1.40	1.25
10	A2	2p gray	1.40	1.10
11	A2	2½p ultra	4.00	2.25
12	A2	4p red, *yel* ('11)	3.75	10.00
13	A2	5p olive green	10.50	7.00
14	A2	6p claret	11.00	7.75
15	A2	1sh black, *green*	9.25	7.00
16	A2	2sh vio, *bl* ('10)	50.00	*60.00*
17	A2	2sh6p red, *bl* ('10)	62.50	*77.50*
18	A2	5sh bl, *yel* ('10)	100.00	*120.00*
		Nos. 8-18 (11)	255.40	*294.95*

George V — A3

Inscribed "POSTAGE - POSTAGE"

1913-24 Typo.

19	A3	½p green	1.10	*3.75*
20	A3	1p carmine	7.00	*17.50*
21	A3	3p violet, *yel*	1.90	*4.25*
a.		3p violet, *orange buff*	12.00	*26.00*
22	A3	11p dull violet & red	3.50	*13.00*

Wmk. 4

23	A3	1½p scarlet ('24)	2.50	.70
		Nos. 19-23 (5)	16.00	*39.20*

Inscribed "POSTAGE - REVENUE"

1914-23 Wmk. 3

28	A3	½p green	2.25	*12.50*
a.		½p yellow green ('17)	6.75	*21.00*
29	A3	1p carmine	1.75	1.40
a.		1p scarlet ('17)	7.50	7.00
30	A3	2p gray	4.75	*10.00*
31	A3	2½p ultra	5.00	4.50

Chalky Paper

32	A3	3p vio, *yel* ('23)	30.00	*140.00*
33	A3	4p blk & red, *yel*	2.25	*2.75*
34	A3	5p dull vio & ol grn	24.00	*32.50*
a.		5p brown purple & olive green	24.00	*32.50*
35	A3	6p dull vio & red vio	6.50	*14.00*
36	A3	1sh blk, *green*	5.00	*7.50*
a.		1sh blk, *bl grn,* ol back	8.00	*24.00*
37	A3	2sh dull vio & ultra, *bl*	9.75	*11.00*
38	A3	2sh6p blk & red, *bl*	10.00	*16.50*
39	A3	5sh grn & red, *yel*	50.00	*55.00*
a.		5sh green & red, *orange buff*	55.00	*75.00*
40	A3	10sh grn & red, *grn*	97.50	75.00
41	A3	£1 vio & blk, *red*	275.00	150.00
		Nos. 28-41 (14)	523.75	532.65

Inscribed "POSTAGE - REVENUE"

1922-31 Wmk. 4

43	A3	½p green	.50	*3.75*
44	A3	1p carmine ('23)	8.50	*12.00*
45	A3	1p violet ('27)	1.10	*8.00*
46	A3	2p gray ('23)	5.50	*16.00*
47	A3	3p ultra ('23)	.75	*4.75*

Chalky Paper

48	A3	4p blk & red, *yel* ('27)	3.75	*26.00*
49	A3	4½p red brn ('31)	3.25	*21.00*
50	A3	5p dull vio & ol grn	3.00	*32.50*
51	A3	6p dull vio & red vio	4.00	*32.50*
52	A3	1sh black, *emer*	3.00	*13.00*
53	A3	2sh dull vio & ultra, *bl* ('27)	25.00	*45.00*
54	A3	2sh6p blk & red, *bl*	9.25	*55.00*
55	A3	5sh grn & red, *yel*	42.50	*65.00*
56	A3	10sh grn & red, *emer* ('25)	150.00	*130.00*
		Nos. 43-56 (14)	260.10	*464.50*

No. 49 is on ordinary paper.

Common Design Types pictured following the introduction.

Silver Jubilee Issue

Common Design Type

1935, May 6 Engr. *Perf. 13½x14*

60	CD301	1½p car & dk bl	1.25	1.50
61	CD301	3p bl & brn	6.00	*7.50*
62	CD301	6p ol grn & lt bl	15.00	12.00
63	CD301	1sh brt vio & ind	6.75	*17.00*
		Nos. 60-63 (4)	29.00	38.00
		Set, never hinged	44.00	

Coronation Issue

Common Design Type

1937, May 13 *Perf. 11x11½*

64	CD302	1p dark purple	.25	*1.00*
65	CD302	1½p dk car	.25	*.55*
66	CD302	3p deep ultra	.40	*.45*
		Nos. 64-66 (3)	.90	2.00
		Set, never hinged	1.40	

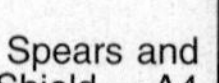

Spears and Shield — A4

Policeman and Chief — A5

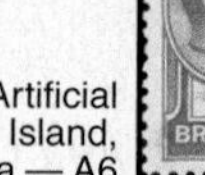

Artificial Island, Malaita — A6

Canoe House, New Georgia A7

Roviana War Canoe — A8

View of Munda Point — A9

Meeting House, Reef Islands A10

Coconut Plantation A11

Breadfruit A12

Tinakula Volcano, Santa Cruz Islands A13

Scrub Fowl — A14

Malaita Canoe — A15

Perf. 12½, 13½ (A7, A13, A14)

1939-51 Wmk. 4

67	A4	½p deep grn & ultra	.25	*1.25*
68	A5	1p dk pur & choc	.25	*1.50*
69	A6	1½p car & sl grn	1.00	*1.75*
70	A7	2p blk & org brn	1.50	*1.75*
a.		2p black & red brown ('43)	.35	*1.75*
b.		Perf. 12 ('51)	.50	*1.50*
71	A8	2½p ol grn & rose vio	2.25	*2.25*
a.		Vert. pair, imperf. horiz.	*31,600.*	
72	A9	3p ultra & blk, perf. 13½	.60	*2.00*
a.		Perf. 12 ('51)	.85	*2.50*
		Never hinged	2.00	
73	A10	4½p dk brn & yel grn	3.25	*13.00*
74	A11	6p rose lil & dk pur	1.50	*1.00*
75	A12	1sh blk & grn	1.50	*1.00*
76	A13	2sh dp org & vio blk ('43)	4.75	*6.50*
77	A14	2sh6p dull vio & blk	18.00	*4.50*
78	A15	5sh red & brt bl grn	18.00	13.00
79	A10	10sh red lil & ol ('42)	2.50	*8.50*
		Nos. 67-79 (13)	55.35	58.00
		Set, never hinged	100.00	

Catalogue values for unused stamps in this section, from this point to the end of the section, are for Never Hinged items.

Peace Issue

Common Design Type

Perf. 13½x14

1946, Oct. 15 Wmk. 4 Engr.

80	CD303	1½p carmine	.25	1.25
81	CD303	3p deep blue	.25	.25

Silver Wedding Issue

Common Design Types

1949, Mar. 14 Photo. *Perf. 14x14½*

82	CD304	2p black	.40	.40

Perf. 11½x11

Engr.; Name Typo.

83	CD305	10sh red violet	13.00	13.00

UPU Issue

Common Design Types

Engr.; Name Typo. on 3p and 5p

Perf. 13½, 11x11½

1949, Oct. 10 Wmk. 4

84	CD306	2p red brown	.60	.85
85	CD307	3p indigo	2.25	1.25
86	CD308	5p green	.60	*1.40*
87	CD309	1sh slate	.60	*1.40*
		Nos. 84-87 (4)	4.05	4.90

Coronation Issue

Common Design Type

1953, June 2 Engr. *Perf. 13½x13*

88	CD312	2p gray & black	1.00	1.00

Ysabel Canoe A16

Prow of Roviana Canoe — A17

Designs: 1p, Roviana canoe. 1½p, Artificial Island, Malaita. 2p, Canoe house. 3p, Malaita canoe. 5p, 1sh3p, Map. 6p, Trading schooner. 8p, 9p, Henderson Field, Guadalcanal. 1sh, Chart of Solomons and H.M.S. Swallow, recalling Capt. Philip Carteret's voyage of 1767. 2sh, Tinakula Volcano. 2sh6p, Meeting house, Reef Islands. 5sh, Alvaro de Mendana de Neyra and Caravel. 10sh, Constable and Chief. £1, Coat of Arms.

Perf. 11½x11, 11x11½, 12, 13

1956-60 Engr. Wmk. 4

89	A16	½p lilac & orange	.25	*.55*
90	A16	1p red brn & ol grn	.25	.25
91	A16	1½p dk car & sl bl	.25	*1.10*
92	A16	2p gray grn & choc	.35	*.30*
93	A17	2½p gray bl & blk	.90	*.90*

94 A16 3p dull red & grn .80 .25
95 A16 5p blue & black .30 *.65*
96 A16 6p bluish grn & blk .65 .30
97 A16 8p black & ultra .45 .25
98 A16 9p black & brt grn 3.50 1.00
99 A16 1sh brn org & sl bl 1.75 .75
100 A16 1sh3p blue & black 6.50 2.00
101 A16 2sh car rose & blk 13.50 3.00
102 A17 2sh6p rose lil & emer 7.50 .55
103 A16 5sh red brown 16.00 5.50
104 A17 10sh black brown 25.00 7.25
105 A16 £1 lt blue & blk 32.50 *35.00*
Nos. 89-105 (17) 110.45 59.60

Issued: £1, 11/5/58; 9p, 1sh3p, 1/28/60; others, 3/1/56.

See Nos. 113-125.

Great Frigate Bird — A18

Perf. 13x12½

1961, Jan. 19 Litho. Wmk. 314

106 A18 2p blue grn & blk .25 *.25*
107 A18 3p rose red & black .25 .25
108 A18 9p lilac & black .25 *.25*
Nos. 106-108 (3) .75 .75

New constitution, brought into operation Oct. 18, 1960. The watermark is sideways and may be found facing both left and right.

Freedom from Hunger Issue
Common Design Type

1963, June 4 Photo. *Perf. 14x14½*

109 CD314 1sh3p ultra 3.00 .85

Red Cross Centenary Issue
Common Design Type

1963, Sept. 2 Litho. *Perf. 13*

110 CD315 2p black & red .25 .25
111 CD315 9p ultra & red 1.00 .90

Types of 1956-60
Perf. 12, 13, 11½x11

1963-64 Engr. Wmk. 314

113 A16 1p red brn & ol grn .40 *.45*
114 A16 1½p dk car & sl bl 1.00 *.80*
115 A16 2p gray grn & choc .30 .25
117 A16 3p dull red & grn .80 .25
119 A16 6p bluish grn & blk 1.00 .65
121 A16 9p black & brt grn 1.10 .55
123 A16 1sh3p blue & blk 1.25 *1.75*
124 A16 2sh car rose & blk 3.00 *6.00*
125 A17 2sh6p rose lil & emer 18.00 16.50
Nos. 113-125 (9) 26.85 27.20

Issued: 3p, 11/16; 6p, 9p, 1sh3p, 7/7/64; 1p, 1½p, 2p, 2sh, 2sh6p, 7/9/64.

ITU Issue
Common Design Type
Perf. 11x11½

1965, June 28 Litho. Wmk. 314

126 CD317 2p ver & grnsh blue .30 .25
127 CD317 3p grnsh bl & ol bis .40 .30

Makira Food Bowl — A19

Designs: 1p, 1sh, 1sh3p, Various orchids. 1½p, Scorpion shell. 2p, Papuan hornbill. 2½p, Ysabel shield. 3p, Rennellese club. 6p, Moorish idol (fish). 9p, Great frigate bird. 2sh, Sanford's sea eagle. 2sh6p, Malaita belt. 5sh, Ornithoptera Victoreae (butterfly). 10sh, White cockatoo. £1, Figurehead, western canoe.

Perf. 13x12½

1965, May 24 Litho. Wmk. 314

Design Subject in Black

128 A19 ½p sl blue & lt bl .25 *1.00*
129 A19 1p orange & yel .35 .50
130 A19 1½p blue & yel grn .25 *.60*
131 A19 2p vio bl & lt bl .25 *1.60*
132 A19 2½p red brn & buff .25 *1.00*
133 A19 3p grn & lt grn .25 .25
134 A19 6p brt car rose & org .25 *.85*
135 A19 9p slate grn & buff 1.00 .50
136 A19 1sh dp cl & rose 1.25 .25
137 A19 1sh3p ver & buff 3.75 2.00
138 A19 2sh dp mag & lil 7.00 3.25
139 A19 2sh6p ol brn & buff .85 .75
140 A19 5sh dk vio bl & lil 10.00 4.00
141 A19 10sh ol grn & yel 11.00 3.75
142 A19 £1 purple & red 7.00 4.75
Nos. 128-142 (15) 43.70 25.05

For surcharges see Nos. 149-166.

Intl. Cooperation Year Issue
Common Design Type

1965, Oct. 25 Litho. *Perf. 14½*

143 CD318 1p bl grn & cl .25 .25
144 CD318 2sh6p lt vio & grn .45 .35

Churchill Memorial Issue
Common Design Type

1966, Jan. 24 Photo. *Perf. 14*

145 CD319 2p multicolored .25 *.25*
146 CD319 9p multicolored .25 .25
147 CD319 1sh3p multicolored .45 .25
148 CD319 2sh6p multicolored .55 *.85*
Nos. 145-148 (4) 1.50 1.60

Nos. 128-142 Srchd. with New Value and Three Bars in Black or Red
Perf. 13x12½

1966-67 Litho. Wmk. 314

149 A19 1c on ½p multi .25 .25
150 A19 2c on 1p multi .25 .25
151 A19 3c on 1½p multi .25 .25
152 A19 4c on 2p multi .25 .25
153 A19 5c on 6p multi .25 .25
154 A19 6c on 2½p multi .25 .25
155 A19 7c on 3p multi .25 .25
156 A19 8c on 9p multi .25 .25
b. "8" inverted 45.00 22.50
157 A19 10c on 1sh .35 .35
158 A19 12c on 1sh3p multi .65 .45
159 A19 13c on 1sh3p multi 2.10 .50
160 A19 14c on 3p multi .55 .50
161 A19 20c on 2sh multi 2.10 .85
162 A19 25c on 2sh6p multi .80 .75
163 A19 35c on 2p multi 2.10 .40
164 A19 50c on 5sh multi (R) 4.00 1.75
165 A19 $1 on 10sh multi 2.00 1.50
166 A19 $2 on £1 multi 1.75 3.00
Nos. 149-166 (18) 18.40 12.05

The 12c, 14c, 35c have watermark sideways.

Issued: 12c, 14c, 35c, 3/1/67; others, 2/14/66.

1966 Wmk. 314 Sideways

149a A19 1c on ½p .25 .25
150a A19 2c on 1p .25 .25
151a A19 3c on 1½p .25 .25
152a A19 4c on 2p .25 .25
153a A19 5c on 6p .30 .30
154a A19 6c on 2½p .35 .35
155a A19 7c on 3p .40 .40
156a A19 8c on 9p .45 .45
157a A19 10c on 1sh .60 .60
159a A19 13c on 1sh3p 4.25 2.75
161a A19 20c on 2sh 3.00 .35
162a A19 25c on 2sh6p 2.25 .35
164a A19 50c on 5sh (R) 9.00 4.75
165a A19 $1 on 10sh 7.00 2.00
166a A19 $2 on £1 6.00 3.00
Nos. 149a-166a (15) 34.60 16.30

World Cup Soccer Issue
Common Design Type

1966, July 1 Litho. *Perf. 14*

167 CD321 8c multicolored .40 .40
168 CD321 35c multicolored .70 .70

WHO Headquarters Issue
Common Design Type

1966, Sept. 20 Litho. *Perf. 14*

169 CD322 3c multicolored .30 .25
170 CD322 50c multicolored .65 .55

UNESCO Anniversary Issue
Common Design Type

1966, Dec. 1 Litho. *Perf. 14*

171 CD323 3c "Education" .25 .25
172 CD323 25c "Science" .50 .25
173 CD323 $1 "Culture" 1.25 1.00
Nos. 171-173 (3) 2.00 1.50

Henderson Field, Guadalcanal — A20

Design: 35c, US Marines landing, Red Beach, Guadalcanal, 1942.

Perf. 14x14½

1967, Aug. 28 Photo. Wmk. 314

174 A20 8c multi & silver .25 .25
175 A20 35c multi & gold .35 .35

Guadalcanal campaign in WW II, 25th anniv.

Mendana's Ship Off Puerta de la Cruz (Honiara), Guadalcanal, 1568 — A21

Designs: 8c, Arrival of Missionaries. 35c, Naval battle during World War II. $1, Honor guard raising Union Jack during proclamation of Protectorate.

1968, Feb. 2 Photo. *Perf. 14½*

176 A21 3c pink & multi .30 .25
177 A21 8c emerald & multi .30 .25
178 A21 35c multicolored .60 .25
179 A21 $1 blue & multi .80 *1.25*
Nos. 176-179 (4) 2.00 2.00

400th anniv. of the discovery of the British Solomon Islands by the Spanish navigator Alvaro de Mendana de Neyra.

Vine Fishing A22

Designs: 2c, Kite fishing. 3c, Platform fishing. 4c, Net fishing. 6c, Gold lip shell diving. 8c, Night fishing. 12c, Boat building. 14c, Cocoa harvest. 15c, Road building. 20c, Geological survey by plane. 24c, Hauling timber. 35c, Copra. 45c, Harvesting rice. $1, Honiara Port. $2, Map of the Islands, plane and route of Internal Air Service.

Wmk. 314

1968, May 20 Photo. *Perf. 14½*

180 A22 1c aqua, brn & blk .25 .25
181 A22 2c lt yel grn, brn & blk .25 .25
182 A22 3c brt grn, dk grn & blk .25 .25
183 A22 4c brt rose lil, brn & blk .25 .25
184 A22 6c multicolored .25 .25
185 A22 8c dp ultra, org & blk .25 .30
186 A22 12c bister, red & blk .55 .35
187 A22 14c red org, brn & blk 1.75 *2.25*
188 A22 15c multicolored .60 .70
189 A22 20c ultra, red & blk 3.00 3.25
190 A22 24c scarlet, yel & blk 1.60 *3.75*
191 A22 35c multicolored 1.60 .45
192 A22 45c yellow, red & blk 1.30 .45
193 A22 $1 vio bl, emer & blk 1.90 1.75
194 A22 $2 multicolored 4.75 4.00
Nos. 180-194 (15) 18.55 18.50

Map of South Pacific and University Degrees — A23

Perf. 12½x12

1969, Feb. 10 Litho. Unwmk.

195 A23 3c multicolored .25 .25
196 A23 12c multicolored .25 .25
197 A23 35c multicolored .25 .25
Nos. 195-197 (3) .75 .75

Inauguration of the University of the South Pacific in 1969, at the Royal New Zealand Air Force Seaplane Station, Laucala Bay, Fiji.

Field Ball and Games' Emblem — A24

Perf. 14½x14

1969, Aug. 13 Photo. Wmk. 314

198 A24 3c shown .25 .25
199 A24 8c Soccer .25 .25
200 A24 14c Running .25 .25
201 A24 45c Rugby .30 .25
a. Souvenir sheet of 4, #198-201 5.50 7.00
Nos. 198-201 (4) 1.05 1.00

3rd S. Pacific Games, Port Moresby, Aug. 13-23.

In No. 201a, shading was added below athlete's foot on 14c, and strengthened on 8c and 45c.

Stained Glass Window with Melanesian Peace Symbol — A25

Christmas: 8c, South Sea Islands scene with palms and Star of Bethlehem.

1969, Nov. 21 Photo. Wmk. 314

202 A25 8c vio, grnsh bl & blk .25 .25
203 A25 35c black & multi .30 .30

C. M. Woodford and Stamp of 1907 — A26

Designs: 7c, British Solomon Islands 1906 handstamp and cancellation, and New South Wales No. 99. 18c, British Solomon Islands No. 18 and 1913 Tulagi cancellation. 23c, New General Post Office, Honiara.

1970, Apr. 15 Litho. *Perf. 13*

204 A26 7c lilac rose & black .25 .25
205 A26 14c lt olive & black .25 .25
206 A26 18c orange, yel & blk .25 .25
207 A26 23c multicolored .25 .25
Nos. 204-207 (4) 1.00 1.00

Issued to publicize the opening of the new General Post Office in Honiara.

Map of Solomon Islands A27

18c, British Solomon Islands coat of arms, vert.

Perf. 14½x14, 14x14½

1970, June 15 Litho. Wmk. 314

208 A27 18c multicolored .30 .30
209 A27 35c multicolored .65 .65

Adoption of the new 1970 Constitution.

Red Cross Headquarters, Honiara — A28

35c, Map of British Solomon Islands showing Red Cross stations, wheelchair.

1970, Aug. 17 *Perf. 14½x14*

210 A28 3c multicolored .25 .25
211 A28 35c multicolored .55 .50

Centenary of British Red Cross Society.

Carved Angel and Southern Cross — A29

Reredos: Symbols of Trinity and Light at St. Luke's Church, Kia — A30

Perf. 14x13½, 13½x14

1970, Oct. 19 **Litho.** **Wmk. 314**

212 A29 8c violet & bister brn .25 .25
213 A30 45c multicolored .55 .50

Christmas 1970.

Count de La Pérouse and "La Boussole" — A31

4c, Astrolabe, Polynesian reed map. 12c, Abel Tasman, sailing ship Heemskerk, 1643. 35c, Te Puki canoe, Santa Cruz.

1971, Jan. 28 *Perf. 14½x14*

214 A31 3c multicolored .90 .50
215 A31 4c multicolored .90 .50
216 A31 12c multicolored 1.10 .75
217 A31 35c multicolored 1.25 1.25
Nos. 214-217 (4) 4.15 3.00

In honor of famous explorers and ships. See Nos. 228-231, 250-253.

Bishop Patteson, J. Atkin and S. Taroniara — A32

Designs: 4c, Last landing of the "Southern Cross" at Nukapu. 14c, Memorial for Bishop Patteson and map of Nukapu, vert. 45c, Ceremonial leaf tag (had been attached to Bishop's body), vert.

Perf. 14½x14, 14x14½

1971, Apr. 5 **Litho.** **Wmk. 314**

218 A32 2c lt green & multi .25 .25
219 A32 4c blue green & multi .25 .25
220 A32 14c brt pink & multi .25 .25
221 A32 45c brown & multi .25 .25
Nos. 218-221 (4) 1.00 1.00

Bishop John Coleridge Patteson (1827-71), head of the Melanesian mission.

Boxing, Games Emblem A33

8c, Soccer. 12c, Running. 35c, Spear fishing.

1971, Aug. 9 *Perf. 14½x14*

222 A33 3c orange & multi .25 .25
223 A33 8c emerald & multi .25 .25
224 A33 12c yellow & multi .25 .25
225 A33 35c blue & multi .25 .25
Nos. 222-225 (4) 1.00 1.00

4th South Pacific Games, Papeete, French Polynesia, Sept. 8-19.

Melanesian Lectern (wood carving) — A34

Christmas: 45c, Stylized birds, painted by school girl Margarita Bara.

1971, Nov. 15 **Litho.** **Wmk. 314**

226 A34 9c orange & multi .25 .25
227 A34 45c blue & multi .55 .55

Explorer Type of 1971

4c, Louis Antoine de Bougainville, La Boudeuse, 1776. 9c, Horizontal planisphere, 1574, ivory backstaff, 1695. 15c, Philip Carteret, H.M.S. Swallow, 1707. 45c, Small canoe of Malaita.

1972, Feb. 1 *Perf. 14½*

228 A31 4c brown & multi .35 .25
229 A31 9c green & multi .55 .25
230 A31 15c lt blue & multi .90 .50
231 A31 45c blue & multi 2.00 2.00
Nos. 228-231 (4) 3.80 3.00

Cupha Woodfordi A35

2c, Ornithoptera priamus. 3c, Vindula sapor. 4c, Papilio orssippus. 5c, Great trevally. 8c, Little bonito. 9c, Sapphire demoiselle. 12c, Costus speciosus. 15c, Orange anemone. 20c, Spathoglottis plicata. 25c, Ephemerantha comata. 35c, Dendrobium cuthbertsonii. 45c, Heliconia salomonica. $1, Blue-finned triggerfish. $2, Ornithoptera allotti. $5, Great frigate bird. Designs: 1c, 2c, 3c, 4c, $2, Butterflies. 5c, 8c, 9c, 15c, $1. Fishes. 12c, 20c, 25c, 35c, 45c, Orchids. $5, Birds.

1972-73 *Perf. 14*

232 A35 1c shown .25 .25
233 A35 2c multicolored .25 .30
234 A35 3c multicolored .25 .30
235 A35 4c multicolored .25 .30
236 A35 5c multicolored .25 .40
237 A35 8c multicolored .40 .50
238 A35 9c multicolored .50 *.70*
239 A35 12c multicolored 1.25 .80
240 A35 15c multicolored 1.25 1.00
241 A35 20c multicolored 3.00 1.25
242 A35 25c multicolored 3.00 1.50
243 A35 35c multicolored 3.00 2.00
244 A35 45c multicolored 2.50 3.00
245 A35 $1 multicolored 3.00 *4.50*
246 A35 $2 multicolored 9.00 *15.00*
247 A35 $5 multicolored 14.00 *16.00*
Nos. 232-247 (16) 42.15 *47.80*

Issued: $5, 7/2/73; others, 7/2/72. For overprints see Nos. 300-311.

Silver Wedding Issue, 1972
Common Design Type

Design: Queen Elizabeth II, Prince Philip, scroll and message drum on woven mat.

1972, Nov. 20 **Photo.** *Perf. 14x14½*

248 CD324 8c car rose & multi .25 .25
249 CD324 45c olive & multi .25 .25

Explorer Type of 1971

Designs: 4c, Antoine R. J. d'Entrecasteaux and "The Recherche," 1791. 9c, Ship's hourglass, 17th century, and chronometer, 1761. 15c, Lieutenant Shortland and "The Alexander," 1788. 35c, Tomoko (war canoe).

Wmk. 314

1973, Mar. 9 **Litho.** *Perf. 14½*

250 A31 4c blue & multi .25 .25
251 A31 9c blue & multi .45 .45
252 A31 15c blue & multi .80 .80
253 A31 35c blue & multi 2.00 2.00
Nos. 250-253 (4) 3.50 3.50

Pan Pipes A36

Musical Instruments: 9c, Castanets. 15c, Bamboo flute. 35c, Bauro gongs. 45c, Bamboo band.

1973, Oct. 1 *Perf. 13½x14*

254 A36 4c brick red & multi .25 .25
255 A36 9c yellow bis & multi .25 .25
256 A36 15c pink & multi .25 .25
257 A36 35c blue green & multi .40 .40
258 A36 45c multicolored .60 .60
Nos. 254-258 (5) 1.75 1.75

Princess Anne's Wedding Issue
Common Design Type

1973, Nov. 14 *Perf. 14*

259 CD325 4c slate & multi .30 .30
260 CD325 35c multicolored .40 .40

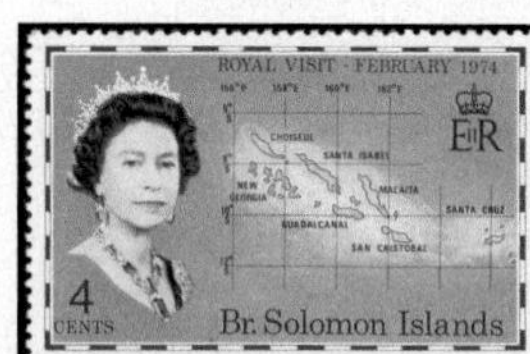

Adoration of the Kings, by Jan Brueghel A37

Adoration of the Kings by: 22c, Peter Brueghel, vert. 45c, Botticelli.

1973, Nov. 26 **Litho.** *Perf. 14*
Size: 39x25mm, 25x39mm

261 A37 8c pink & multi .25 .25
262 A37 22c lilac & multi .25 .25

Perf. 13½
Size: 47x35mm

263 A37 45c gray & multi .50 .50
Nos. 261-263 (3) 1.00 1.00

Christmas 1973.

Map of Solomon Islands — A38

1974, Feb. 18 **Litho.** *Perf. 13½*

264 A38 4c blue & multi .25 .25
265 A38 9c citron & multi .25 .25
266 A38 15c violet gray & multi .40 .40
267 A38 35c emerald & multi .75 .75
Nos. 264-267 (4) 1.65 1.65

Visit of British Royal Family.

First Resident Commissioner Landing at Tulagi — A39

Designs: 9c, Marine radar and scanner unit, map of Islands. 15c, Islanders taken to "Blackbirder" ship. 45c, John F. Kennedy's P.T. 109 off Lumbari Island, 1943.

1974, May 15 **Litho.** *Perf. 14½*

268 A39 4c multicolored .50 .25
269 A39 9c multicolored .50 .35
270 A39 15c multicolored .60 .45
271 A39 45c multicolored 2.00 2.00
Nos. 268-271 (4) 3.60 3.05

Ships and navigators.

Mailman, Map of Islands — A40

9c, Carrier pigeon, horiz. 15c, Angel Gabriel. 45c, Pegasus, horiz. Designs based on origami (folded paper) figures.

1974, Aug. 29 **Wmk. 314** *Perf. 14*

272 A40 4c brt green & multi .25 .25
273 A40 9c lemon & multi .25 .25
274 A40 15c multicolored .30 .30
275 A40 45c blue & multi .60 1.25
Nos. 272-275 (4) 1.40 2.05

Centenary of Universal Postal Union.

Solomon Islands No. 208 A41

1974, Dec. 16 **Litho.** *Perf. 14½*

276 A41 4c shown .25 .25
277 A41 9c No. 107 .25 .25
278 A41 15c same .25 .45
279 A41 35c like 4c .50 .80
a. Souvenir sheet of 4, #276-279 3.80 3.25
Nos. 276-279 (4) 1.25 1.75

New Constitution, inaugurated Oct. 18, 1960.

Golden Whistler A42

Birds: 2c, River kingfisher. 3c, Red-throated fruit dove. 4c, Button quail. $2, Duchess lorikeet.

1975, Apr. 7 **Wmk. 314** *Perf. 14*

280 A42 1c yellow grn & multi .60 *.75*
281 A42 2c lt blue & multi .70 *1.00*
282 A42 3c brt pink & multi .80 *1.00*
283 A42 4c orange & multi .90 *1.00*
284 A42 $2 dp orange & multi 9.00 12.00
Nos. 280-284 (5) 12.00 15.75

See Nos. 316-320, 323, 330-331. For overprints see Nos. 296-299, 310.

BRITISH SOLOMON ISLANDS
4c

Motor Vessel Walande A43

No. 286, M. V. Melanesian. No. 287, Ship Marsina, house flag. No. 288, S. S. Himalaya.

1975, May 29 *Perf. 13½*

285 A43 4c multicolored .40 .25
286 A43 9c multicolored .50 .25
287 A43 15c multicolored .75 .25
288 A43 45c multicolored 1.00 *1.50*
Nos. 285-288 (4) 2.65 2.25

Runner, 800-meters — A44

1975, Aug. 4 **Litho.** *Perf. 13½*

289 A44 4c shown .25 .25
290 A44 9c Long jump .25 .25
291 A44 15c Javelin .25 .25
292 A44 45c Soccer .50 .25
a. Souvenir sheet of 4, #289-292 4.25 4.25
Nos. 289-292 (4) 1.25 1.00

5th South Pacific Games, Guam, Aug. 1-10.

Nativity and Candles A45

Christmas: 35c, Angels, shepherds and candles. 45c, Three Kings approaching Bethlehem, and candles.

1975, Oct. 13 **Wmk. 373** *Perf. 14*

293 A45 15c multicolored .25 .25
294 A45 35c multicolored .35 .35
295 A45 45c multicolored .55 .55
a. Souvenir sheet of 3, #293-295 4.50 4.50
Nos. 293-295 (3) 1.15 1.15

Nos. 236-245, 247, 280-284 Ovptd. with Bar Obliterating "British" in Black or Silver

1975, Nov. 12 **Litho.** **Wmk. 314**

296 A42 1c multicolored 1.00 .70
297 A42 2c multicolored 1.25 .70
298 A42 3c multicolored 1.00 .70
299 A42 4c multicolored 1.25 .70
300 A35 5c multicolored .75 .70
301 A35 8c multicolored .75 .70
302 A35 9c multicolored 1.00 .70
303 A35 12c multicolored 1.75 1.25
304 A35 15c multicolored 1.75 1.75
305 A35 20c multicolored 1.75 2.00
306 A35 25c multicolored 1.75 2.00
307 A35 35c multicolored 1.75 1.75
308 A35 45c multicolored 1.50 1.75
309 A35 $1 multicolored 1.25 *1.60*
310 A42 $2 multicolored 3.50 *5.50*
311 A35 $5 multicolored (S) 3.00 *7.50*
Nos. 296-311 (16) 25.00 *30.00*

Ceremonial Food Bowl — A46

Artifacts: 15c, Barava, chief's money. 35c, Nguzu-nguzu, canoe protector spirit, vert. 45c, Nguzu-nguzu on canoe prow.

Wmk. 314

1976, Jan. 12 **Litho.** *Perf. 14*

312 A46 4c scarlet & black .25 .25
313 A46 15c lt violet & multi .25 .25
314 A46 35c multicolored .40 .40
315 A46 45c multicolored .55 .55
Nos. 312-315 (4) 1.45 1.45

Type of 1975 Inscribed "Solomon Islands" and

Golden Cowries A47

1c, Golden whistler. 2c, River kingfisher. 3c, Red-throated fruit dove. 4c, Button quail. 5c, Willie wagtail. 10c, Glory-of-the-sea cones. 12c, Rainbow lory. 15c, Pearly nautilus. 20c, Venus comb murex. 25c, Commercial trochus. 35c, Melon or baler shell. 45c, Orange spider conch. $1, Pacific triton. $2, Duchess lorikeet. $5, Great frigate bird.

1976 **Wmk. 373** *Perf. 14*

316 A42 1c yel grn & multi .40 .35
317 A42 2c lt blue & multi 1.00 .70
318 A42 3c pink & multi .45 .35
319 A42 4c orange & multi .45 .40
320 A42 5c red brown & multi 1.00 .70
321 A47 6c rose & multi .60 .50
322 A47 10c multicolored .60 .50
323 A42 12c yel grn & multi 1.00 .80
324 A47 15c lilac & multi .55 .35
325 A47 20c ultra & multi 1.00 .75
326 A47 25c dull grn & multi .80 .65
327 A47 35c bister & multi .95 .95
328 A47 45c fawn & multi 1.10 1.10
329 A47 $1 olive & multi 2.50 2.50
330 A42 $2 multicolored 3.00 3.00
331 A42 $5 multicolored 4.00 4.00
Nos. 316-331 (16) 19.40 17.60

Issue dates: $5, Dec. 6; others Mar. 8.

Coast Watchers, World War II A48

American Bicentennial: 20c, "Amagiri" ramming "P.T.109" and Lt. John F. Kennedy. 35c, Plane on Henderson Airfield. 45c, Map showing landing of US forces on Guadalcanal.

1976, May 24 *Perf. 14*

333 A48 6c black & multi .35 .25
334 A48 20c black & multi .90 .55
335 A48 35c black & multi 1.25 .90
336 A48 45c black & multi 1.25 1.10
a. Souvenir sheet of 4, #333-336 6.25 7.75
Nos. 333-336 (4) 3.75 2.80

Alexander Graham Bell — A49

Designs: 20c, Radio-telephone and satellite. 35c, Ericsson's magneto telephone. 45c, Telephone, 1876, and stick telephone.

1976, July 26 **Litho.** *Perf. 14½x14*

337 A49 6c lt ultra & multi .25 .25
338 A49 20c multicolored .30 .30
339 A49 35c orange & multi .45 .45
340 A49 45c bister & multi .60 .60
Nos. 337-340 (4) 1.60 1.60

Centenary of first telephone call by Alexander Graham Bell, Mar. 10, 1876.

One-Eleven BAC — A50

Planes: 20c, Solair Britten Norman Islander. 35c, DC-3 Dakota. 45c, De Havilland DH50A.

1976, Sept. 13 **Wmk. 373** *Perf. 14*

341 A50 6c black & multi .25 .25
342 A50 20c black & multi .65 .40
343 A50 35c black & multi .75 .60
344 A50 45c black & multi .85 1.25
Nos. 341-344 (4) 2.50 2.50

1st flight to Solomon Islands, 50th anniv.

Queen Receiving Lei, 1974 Visit — A51

35c, Communion plate, cup. 45c, Communion.

1977, Feb. 7 **Litho.** *Perf. 14x13½*

345 A51 6c multicolored .25 .25
346 A51 35c multicolored .30 .30
347 A51 45c multicolored .45 .45
Nos. 345-347 (3) 1.00 1.00

25th anniv. of the reign of Elizabeth II.

Carved Wooden Figure — A52

Artifacts: 20c, Sea adaro or spirit. 35c, Shark-headed man. 45c, Seated man.

1977, May 9 *Perf. 14*

348 A52 6c yellow & multi .25 .25
349 A52 20c blue & multi .25 .25
350 A52 35c rose & multi .30 .30
351 A52 45c multicolored .35 .35
Nos. 348-351 (4) 1.15 1.15

Man Spraying House, Anopheles Mosquito — A53

Designs: 20c, Taking blood samples. 35c, Microscope, map of Solomon Islands, Malaria Eradication Program emblem. 45c, Messenger delivering medicine to malaria patient.

1977, July 27 **Litho.** **Wmk. 373**

352 A53 6c multicolored .25 .25
353 A53 20c multicolored .25 .25
354 A53 35c multicolored .25 .25
355 A53 45c multicolored .40 .40
Nos. 352-355 (4) 1.15 1.15

Malaria eradication.

Adoration of the Shepherds — A54

Christmas: 20c, Nativity. 35c, Adoration of the Kings. 45c, Flight into Egypt.

Wmk. 373

1977, Sept. 12 **Litho.** *Perf. 14*

356 A54 6c multicolored .25 .25
357 A54 20c multicolored .25 .25
358 A54 35c multicolored .25 .25
359 A54 45c multicolored .25 .25
Nos. 356-359 (4) 1.00 1.00

Traditional Feather Money — A55

Designs: No. 361, New coins. No. 362, Banknotes. No. 363, Traditional shell money.

1977, Oct. 24 **Litho.** *Perf. 14x14½*

360 6c brt green & multi .25 .25
361 6c brt green & multi .25 .25
a. A55 Pair, #360-361 .50 .50
362 45c buff & multi .50 .50
363 45c buff & multi .50 .50
a. A55 Pair, #362-363 1.50 1.50
Nos. 360-363 (4) 1.50 1.50

New coinage.

Shortland Islands Figure — A56

Artifacts: 20c, Ceremonial shield. 35c, Santa Cruz ritual figure. 45c, Decorative combs.

1978, Jan. 11 *Perf. 14*

364 A56 6c multicolored .25 .25
365 A56 20c multicolored .25 .25
366 A56 35c multicolored .30 .30
367 A56 45c multicolored .45 .45
Nos. 364-367 (4) 1.25 1.25

Elizabeth II Coronation Anniversary Issue

Common Design Types

Souvenir Sheet

Unwmk.

1978, Apr. 21 **Litho.** *Perf. 15*

368 Sheet of 6 2.50 2.50
a. CD326 45c King's dragon .40 .40
b. CD327 45c Elizabeth II .40 .40
c. CD328 45c Sandford eagle .40 .40

No. 368 contains 2 se-tenant strips of Nos. 368a-368c, separated by horizontal gutter with commemorative and descriptive inscriptions and showing central part of coronation procession with coach.

National Flag — A57

Independence: 15c, Governor General's flag. 35c, Cenotaph, Honiara, flags of U.S., Great Britain, New Zealand and Australia. 45c, Coat of Arms.

Wmk. 373

1978, July 7 **Litho.** *Perf. 14*

369 A57 6c multicolored .25 .25
370 A57 15c multicolored .25 .25
371 A57 35c multicolored .60 .60
372 A57 45c multicolored .75 .75
Nos. 369-372 (4) 1.85 1.85

Apostles by Dürer — A58

1978, Oct. 4 Litho. *Perf. 14*

373	A58	6c John	.25	.25
374	A58	20c Peter	.35	.35
375	A58	35c Paul	.60	.60
376	A58	45c Mark	.80	.80
		Nos. 373-376 (4)	2.00	2.00

Albrecht Dürer (1471-1528), German painter, 450th death anniversary.

Scouts Making Fire — A59

Designs: 20c, Camping. 35c, Solomon Islands Scouts. 45c, Canoeing.

1978, Nov. 15 Litho. *Perf. 14*

377	A59	6c multicolored	.25	.25
378	A59	20c multicolored	.35	.35
379	A59	35c multicolored	.60	.60
380	A59	45c multicolored	.80	.80
		Nos. 377-380 (4)	2.00	2.00

50 years of Scouting in Solomon Islands.

Discovery A60

Designs: 18c, Capt. Cook, 1776, painting by Nathaniel Dance. 35c, Sextant. 45c, Capt. Cook after Flaxman / Wedgwood medallion.

Wmk. 373

1979, Jan. 16 Litho. *Perf. 11*

381	A60	8c multicolored	.50	.25
382	A60	18c multicolored	.50	.30
383	A60	35c multicolored	.65	.65

Litho.; Embossed

384	A60	45c multicolored	.80	.80
		Nos. 381-384 (4)	2.45	2.00

Capt. Cook's voyages.

Fish Net Float A61

Artifacts: 20c, Armband made of shell money, vert. 35c, Ceremonial food bowl. 45c, Forehead ornament, vert.

1979, Mar. 21 Litho. *Perf. 14*

385	A61	8c multicolored	.25	.25
386	A61	20c multicolored	.25	.25
387	A61	35c multicolored	.30	.30
388	A61	45c multicolored	.40	.40
		Nos. 385-388 (4)	1.20	1.20

6th South Pacific Games A62

1979, June 4 Litho. Wmk. 373

389	A62	8c Running	.25	.25
390	A62	20c Hurdles	.25	.25
391	A62	35c Soccer	.25	.25
392	A62	45c Swimming	.35	.35
		Nos. 389-392 (4)	1.10	1.10

Solomon Islands No. 14 — A63

Designs (Rowland Hill and): 20c, Great Britain No. 27. 35c, Solomon Islands No. 372. 45c, Solomon Islands No. 40.

1979, Aug. 16 Litho. *Perf. 14*

393	A63	8c multicolored	.25	.25
394	A63	20c multicolored	.30	.30
395	A63	35c multicolored	.45	.45
		Nos. 393-395 (3)	1.00	1.00

Souvenir Sheet

396	A63	45c multicolored	.80	.80

Sir Rowland Hill (1795-1879), originator of penny postage.

Sea Snake — A64

1c, Sea snake. 3c, Red-banded tree snake. 4c, Whip snake. 6c, Pacific boa. 8c, Skink. 10c, Gecko. 12c, Monitor. 15c, Angelhead. 20c, Giant toad. 25c, Marsh frog. 30c, Horned frog. 35c, Tree frog. 40c, Burrowing snake. 45c, Guppy's snake. 50c, Tree gecko. $1, Large skink. $2, Guppy's frog. $5, Estuarine crocodile. $10, Hawksbill turtle.

Perf. 13½x13

1979-83 Litho. Wmk. 373

397	A64	1c multi	.25	1.00
398	A64	3c multi	.25	1.25
399	A64	4c multi	.25	1.25
400	A64	6c multi	.25	1.25
401	A64	8c multi	.25	.80
402	A64	10c multi	.25	1.00
403	A64	12c multi	.50	.70
404	A64	15c multi	.30	1.25
405	A64	20c multi	.30	.60
406	A64	25c multi	.60	.80
407	A64	30c multi	1.50	1.00
408	A64	35c multi	.30	1.00
408A	A64	40c multi	.45	1.75
409	A64	45c multi	.30	1.25
409A	A64	50c multi	.50	1.25
410	A64	$1 multi	1.50	.75
411	A64	$2 multi	.60	1.50
412	A64	$5 multi	1.00	1.75
412A	A64	$10 multi	3.50	*3.50*
		Nos. 397-412A (19)	12.85	23.65

Issued: $10, 9/20/82; 40c, 50c, 1/24/83; others, 9/1979 (undated).

Nos. 403, 406, 410, 412 reissued inscribed "1982." No. 407, "1983."

Madonna and Child, by Morando — A65

IYC Emblem and Madonna and Child: 20c, Bernardino Luini. 35c, Bellini. 50c, Raphael.

1979, Nov. 15 *Perf. 14½*

413	A65	4c multicolored	.25	.25
414	A65	20c multicolored	.25	.25
415	A65	35c multicolored	.25	.25
416	A65	50c multicolored	.50	.50
a.		Souvenir sheet of 4, #413-416	1.75	1.75
		Nos. 413-416 (4)	1.25	1.25

Christmas 1979, Intl. Year of the Child.

Curacoa and Crest A66

Ships and Crests: 20c, Herald, 1854. 35c, Royalist, 1889. 45c, Beagle, 1878.

Wmk. 373

1980, Jan. 23 Litho. *Perf. 14*

417	A66	8c multicolored	.25	.25
418	A66	20c multicolored	.45	.45
419	A66	35c multicolored	.70	.70
420	A66	45c multicolored	.95	*1.40*
		Nos. 417-420 (4)	2.35	2.80

See Nos. 435-438.

Steel Fishery Training Ship — A67

1980, Mar. 27 Litho. *Perf. 13½*

421	A67	8c shown	.25	.25
422	A67	20c Fishery training ship	.25	.25
423	A67	45c Refrigerated carrier	.60	.40
424	A67	80c Research ship	1.00	*1.75*
		Nos. 421-424 (4)	2.10	2.65

"Comliebank," Tulag Cancel — A68

1980, May 6 Litho. *Perf. 14½*

425	Sheet of 4	2.00	2.00
a.	A68 45c shown	.50	.50
b.	A68 45c Douglas C-47	.50	.50
c.	A68 45c BAC 1-11, Honiara cancel	.50	.50
d.	A68 45c "Corabank," Auki cancel	.50	.50

London 1980 Intl. Stamp Exhib., May 6-14.

Queen Mother Elizabeth Birthday Issue

Common Design Type

Wmk. 373

1980, Aug. 4 Litho. *Perf. 14*

426	CD330	45c multicolored	.50	.50

Angel with Trumpet — A69

Christmas: 20c, Angel with violin. 45c, Angel with trumpet. 80c, Angel with lute.

Wmk. 373

1980, Sept. 2 Litho. *Perf. 14½*

427	A69	8c multicolored	.25	.25
428	A69	20c multicolored	.25	.25
429	A69	45c multicolored	.25	.25
430	A69	80c multicolored	.35	.35
		Nos. 427-430 (4)	1.10	1.10

Parthenos Sylvia — A70

No. 432, Delias schoenbergi. No. 433, Jamides cephion. No. 434, Ornithoptera victoriae.

Wmk. 373

1980, Nov. 12 Litho. *Perf. 13½*

431	A70	8c multicolored	.75	.25
432	A70	20c multicolored	.90	.40
433	A70	45c multicolored	1.25	.75
434	A70	80c multicolored	2.00	2.00
		Nos. 431-434 (4)	4.90	3.40

See Nos. 461-464.

Ship & Crest Type of 1980

8c, Mounts Bay, 1959. 20c, Charybdis, 1970. 45c, Hydra, 1972-73. $1, Britannia, 1974.

1981, Jan. 14

435	A66	8c multicolored	.25	.25
436	A66	20c multicolored	.25	.25
437	A66	45c multicolored	.40	.40
438	A66	$1 multicolored	1.10	1.10
		Nos. 435-438 (4)	2.00	2.00

Maurelle's Map, 1742 — A71

No. 439, Francisco Maurelle, vert. No. 441, La Princesa. No. 442, Compass cards, vert.

Wmk. 373

1981, Mar. 23 Litho. *Perf. 14*

439	A71	8c multicolored	.25	.25
440	A71	10c multicolored	.25	.25
441	A71	45c multicolored	.75	.80
442	A71	$1 multicolored	1.00	1.20
		Nos. 439-442 (4)	2.25	2.50

Souvenir Sheet

443	Sheet of 4	1.75	1.75
a.	A71 25c any single	.40	.40

Bicent. of arrival of Francisco Antonio Maurelle and of charts of mapmaker Jean Nicholas Buache (1741-1825). No. 443 contains 4 44x28mm stamps, perf. 14½.

Women's Basketball — A72

Wmk. 373

1981, July 7 Litho. *Perf. 12*

444 A72 8c shown	.25	.25
445 A72 10c Tennis	.25	.25
446 A72 25c Women's running	.30	.30
447 A72 30c Soccer	.30	.30
448 A72 45c Boxing	1.25	1.25
Nos. 444-448 (5)	2.35	2.35

Souvenir Sheet

449 A72 $1 Emblem 1.00 1.00

Mini South Pacific Games, July.

Royal Wedding Issue

Common Design Type

1981, July 22 *Perf. 13½x13*

450 CD331 8c Bouquet	.25	.25
451 CD331 45c Charles	.30	.30
452 CD331 $1 Couple	.70	.70
Nos. 450-452 (3)	1.25	1.25

For surcharge see No. B1.

Duke of Edinburgh's Awards, 25th Anniv. — A73

Wmk. 373

1981, Sept. 28 Litho. *Perf. 14*

453 A73 8c Music	.25	.25
454 A73 25c Handicrafts	.25	.25
455 A73 45c Canoeing	.30	.30
456 A73 $1 Duke of Edinburgh	.70	.70
Nos. 453-456 (4)	1.50	1.50

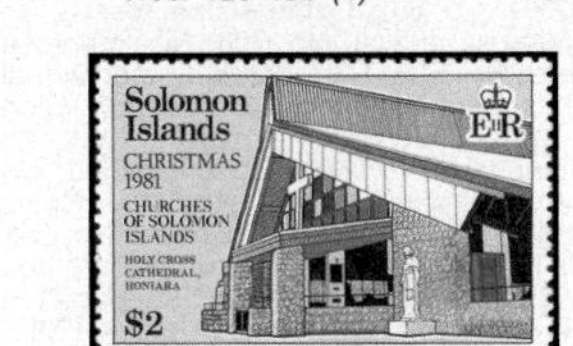

Holy Cross Cathedral, Honiara — A74

Christmas: 8c, 25c, Old churches, diff. 10c, St. Barnabas Anglican Cathedral, Honiara.

1981, Oct. 12

457 A74 8c multicolored	.25	.25
458 A74 10c multicolored	.25	.25
459 A74 25c multicolored	.30	.30
460 A74 $2 multicolored	1.20	1.20
Nos. 457-460 (4)	2.00	2.00

Butterfly Type of 1980

No. 461, Doleschallia bisaltide. No. 462, Papilio bridgei hecataeus. No. 463, Taenaris phorcas. No. 464, Graphium sarpedon.

Wmk. 373

1982, Jan. 5 Litho. *Perf. 13½*

461 A70 10c multicolored	.75	.40
462 A70 25c multicolored	1.00	.75
463 A70 35c multicolored	1.25	1.00
464 A70 $1 multicolored	3.00	3.50
Nos. 461-464 (4)	6.00	5.65

Sanford's Eagle — A75

No. 465, Pair facing left. No. 466, Chick. No. 467, Mother feeding chicks. No. 468, Pair facing right. No. 469, Male flying. No. 470, Pair flying.

1982, May 15 Litho. *Perf. 14*

465 A75 12c multi	.60	.60
466 A75 12c multi	.60	.60
467 A75 12c multi	.60	.60
468 A75 12c multi	.60	.60
469 A75 12c multi	.60	.60
470 A75 12c multi	.60	.60
Nos. 465-470 (6)	3.60	3.60

Se-tenant in sheets of 24. Value of complete sheet, $25. The center horiz. row consists of 4 No. 470 + label. No block of 6 contains all 6 designs.

Princess Diana Issue

Common Design Type

Perf. 14½x14

1982, July 1 Litho. Wmk. 373

471 CD333 12c Arms	.25	.25
472 CD333 40c Diana	.50	.50
473 CD333 50c Wedding	.75	.75
474 CD333 $1 Portrait	1.40	1.40
Nos. 471-474 (4)	2.90	2.90

A76

1982, Oct. 11 Litho. *Perf. 14*

475 A76 25c Running	.35	.35
476 A76 25c Boxing	.35	.35

Souvenir Sheet

477 Sheet of 3, #475-476, 477a	2.75	2.75
a. A76 $1 Britannia facing left	2.75	2.75

12th Commonwealth Games, Brisbane, Australia, Sept. 30-Oct. 9.

1982, Oct. 11

478 A76 12c Royal couple	.25	.25
479 A76 12c Flags	.25	.25

Souvenir Sheet

480 Sheet of 3, #478-479, 480a	4.00	4.00
a. A76 $1 Britannia facing right	3.50	3.50

Visit of Queen Elizabeth II and Prince Philip.

Scouting Year A78

Designs: Nos. 481, 485, Scout patroller. Nos. 482, 486, Brigade bugler. Nos. 483, 487, Baden-Powell. Nos. 484, 488, William Smith.

1982, Nov. 30

481 A78 12c dark blue & multi	.25	.25
482 A78 12c brown & multi	.25	.25
483 A78 25c dark blue & multi	.25	.25
484 A78 25c brown & multi	.25	.25
485 A78 35c green & multi	.25	.25
486 A78 35c red & multi	.25	.25
487 A78 50c green & multi	.40	.40
488 A78 50c red & multi	.40	.40
Nos. 481-488 (8)	2.30	2.30

Turtles A79

1983, Jan. 5 *Perf. 14*

489 A79 18c Leatherback	.75	.75
490 A79 35c Loggerhead	1.00	1.00
491 A79 45c Pacific Ridley	1.00	1.00
492 A79 50c Green	1.00	1.00
Nos. 489-492 (4)	3.75	3.75

Commonwealth Day — A80

No. 493, Oliva vidum, conus generalis, murex tribulus. No. 494, Romu, kurila, kakadu, money belt. No. 495, Shells, bride necklaces. No. 496, Trochus niloticus, natural, polished.

1983, Mar. 14

493 A80 12c multicolored	.25	.25
494 A80 35c multicolored	.50	.50
495 A80 45c multicolored	.60	.60
496 A80 50c multicolored	.65	.65
Nos. 493-496 (4)	2.00	2.00

Manned Flight Bicentenary — A81

No. 497, Montgolfliere, 1783. No. 498, Lockheed Hercules. No. 499, Wright Brothers' Flyer III, 1905. No. 500, Columbia space shuttle. No. 501, Beechcraft Baron-Solair.

Wmk. 373

1983, June 30 Litho. *Perf. 14*

497 A81 30c multicolored	.45	.45
498 A81 35c multicolored	.50	.50
499 A81 40c multicolored	.55	.55
500 A81 45c multicolored	.60	.60
501 A81 50c multicolored	.75	.75
Nos. 497-501 (5)	2.85	2.85

Christmas 1983 — A82

1983, Aug. 25

502 A82 12c Weto dance	.25	.25
503 A82 15c Custom wrestling	.25	.25
504 A82 18c Girl dancers	.25	.25
505 A82 20c Devil dancers	.25	.25
506 A82 25c Bamboo band	.30	.30
507 A82 35c Gilbertese dancers	.40	.40
508 A82 40c Pan pipers	.40	.40
509 A82 45c Afufu girl dancers	.40	.40
510 A82 50c Cross, flowers	.40	.40
a. Souvenir sheet of 9, #502-510	3.00	3.50
Nos. 502-510 (9)	2.90	2.90

Stamps in #510a do not have "Christmas 1983."

For overprints see Nos. 519-520.

World Communications Year — A83

12c, Telephone Exchange building. 18c, Ham radio operator.

Wmk. 373

1983, Dec. 19 Litho. *Perf. 14*

511 A83 12c multi	.25	.25
512 A83 18c multi	.25	.25
513 A83 25c No. 11	.30	.30
514 A83 $1 No. 14	1.10	1.10
a. Souvenir sheet of 1	2.25	2.25
Nos. 511-514 (4)	1.90	1.90

No. 514a is inscribed "1908-1983." See No. 525 for sheet inscribed "1907-1984."

Local Fungi — A84

6c, Calvatia gardneri. 18c, Marasmiellus inoderma. 35c, Pycnoporus sanguineus. $2, Filoboletus manipularis.

1984, Jan. 30 *Perf. 13½*

515 A84 6c multicolored	.30	.30
516 A84 18c multicolored	.50	.50
517 A84 35c multicolored	.75	.75
518 A84 $2 multicolored	3.00	3.00
Nos. 515-518 (4)	4.55	4.55

Type of No. 510 overprinted "VISIT OF POPE JOHN PAUL II May 9th, 1984"

1984, Apr. 16 Wmk. 373

519 A82 12c multicolored	.30	.30
520 A82 50c multicolored	.80	.80

Lloyd's List Issue

Common Design Type

12c, Olivebank, 1892. 15c, Tinhow, 1906. 18c, Oriana, Point Cruz. $1, Point Cruz view.

1984, Apr. 21 Litho. *Perf. 14½x14*

521 CD335 12c multi	.65	.25
522 CD335 15c multi	.85	.65
523 CD335 18c multi	.90	.80
524 CD335 $1 multi	2.25	2.25
Nos. 521-524 (4)	4.65	3.95

WCY Type of 1983

Souvenir Sheet

Wmk. 373

1984, June 18 Litho. *Perf. 14*

525 A83 $1 multicolored 2.25 2.25

UPU Congress. No. 514a is inscribed "1908-1983," No. 525 inscribed "1907-1984."

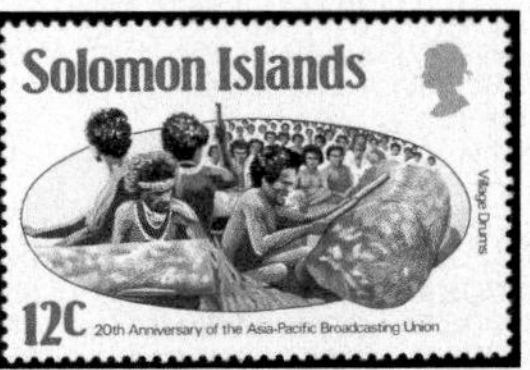

Asia-Pacific Broadcasting Union, 20th Anniv. — A86

12c, Village drums. 45c, Radio City Guadalcanal. 60c, Broadcasting studio. $1, Broadcasting station.

1984, July 2 *Perf. 13½*

526 A86 12c multi	.25	.25
527 A86 45c multi	.50	.50
528 A86 60c multi	.70	.70
529 A86 $1 multi	1.10	1.10
Nos. 526-529 (4)	2.55	2.55

1984 Summer Olympics — A87

12c, Flag, vert. 25c, Lawson Tama Stadium, Honiara. 50c, Honiara Community Center. $1, Olympic Stadium.

95c, Bronte Baths.

Perf. 13½x14

1984, Aug. 4 Litho. Wmk. 373

530 A87 12c multi	.25	.25
531 A87 25c multi	.30	.30
532 A87 50c multi	.65	.65
a. Booklet pane, 2 ea #531-532	3.00	
533 A87 $1 multi	1.30	1.30
Nos. 530-533 (4)	2.50	2.50

Souvenir Sheet

534 A87 95c multi 8.50 8.50

Solomon Islds. first olympic participation. No. 534 available in booklet only. Margin shows swimmer A. Wickham (1886-1976).

Little Pied Cormorant (Ausipex '84) A88

18c, Australian grey duck. 35c, Nankeen night-heron. $1, Dollarbird.

Wmk. 373

1984, Sept. 21 Litho. *Perf. 14½*

535 A88 12c shown .70 .70
536 A88 18c multi .90 .90
537 A88 35c multi 1.15 1.15
538 A88 $1 multi 1.75 1.75
a. Souvenir sheet of 4, #535-538 4.50 4.50
Nos. 535-538 (4) 4.50 4.50

EXPO '85, Tsukuba, Japan A89

Designs: 12c, Japanese Memorial Shrine, Mt. Austen, Guadalcanal. 25c, Digital telephone exchange equipment. 45c, Soltai No. 7 fishing vessel. 85c, Coastal village.

Wmk. 373

1985, June 28 Litho. *Perf. 14*

539 A89 12c multicolored .25 .25
540 A89 25c multicolored .30 .30
541 A89 45c multicolored .55 .55
542 A89 85c multicolored 1.15 1.15
Nos. 539-542 (4) 2.25 2.25

Queen Mother 85th Birthday

Common Design Type

12c, VE Day, 1945. 25c, With Margaret. 35c, St. Patrick's Day celebration. $1, Holding Prince Henry.
$1.50, In a gondola, Venice.

Perf. 14½x14

1985, June 7 Litho. Wmk. 384

543 CD336 12c multicolored .25 .25
544 CD336 25c multicolored .25 .25
545 CD336 35c multicolored .35 .35
546 CD336 $1 multicolored 1.10 1.10
Nos. 543-546 (4) 1.95 1.95

Souvenir Sheet

547 CD336 $1.50 multicolored 2.00 2.00

For surcharge see No. B2.

Christmas — A90

12c, Titiana Village. 25c, Sigana, Santa Isabel. 35c, Artificial Island, Langa Lagoon.

1985, Aug. 30 Wmk. 373 *Perf. 14½*

548 A90 12c multicolored .25 .25
549 A90 25c multicolored .35 .35
550 A90 35c multicolored .45 .45
Nos. 548-550 (3) 1.05 1.05

A $1 stamp is known to exist, but it was not issued by the Solomon Islands Postal Administration.

Intl. Youth Year — A91

12c, Girl Guide activities. 15c, Stop Polio Campaign. 25c, Relay runners, views of the islands. 35c, Relay runners, views of Australia. 45c, Saluting natl. flag, badges.

1985, Sept. 30 *Perf. 14*

551 A91 12c multicolored .90 .25
552 A91 15c multicolored 1.00 .60
553 A91 25c multicolored 1.25 .90
554 A91 35c multicolored 1.40 1.00
a. Souvenir sheet of 2, #553-554 2.25 2.25
555 A91 45c multicolored 2.50 1.50
Nos. 551-555 (5) 7.05 4.25

Girl Guides 75th anniv., 12c, 45c; IYY, others.

Souvenir Sheet

Audubon Birth Bicent. — A92

Bird illustration by Audubon.

1985, Nov. 25 Wmk. 384

556 A92 Sheet of 3, 45c, 2 50c 5.00 5.00
a. Portrait 2.00 2.00
b. Osprey 1.50 1.50

Souvenir Sheet

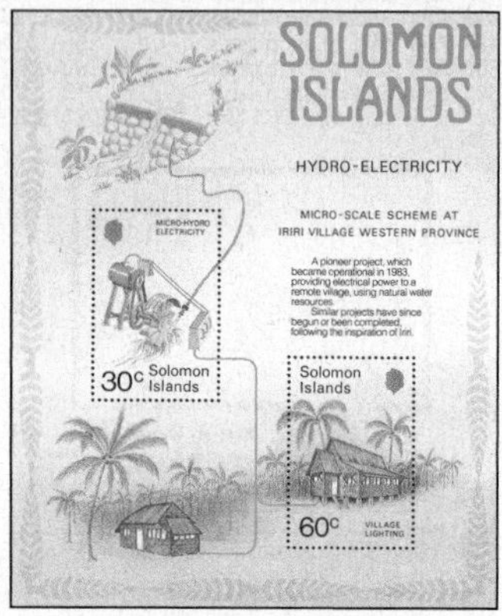

Mini Hydro-Electric Project, Iriri Village — A93

Designs: 30c, Water-driven generator. 60c, Illuminated village house.

1986, Jan. 24 *Perf. 14*

557 A93 Sheet of 2 2.00 2.00
a. 30c multicolored .75 .75
b. 60c multicolored 1.20 1.20

Halley's Comet A94

Operation Raleigh, 1986: 18c, Construction of Red Cross Center, Gizo. 30c, Exploring rain forest. 60c, Observing Halley's Comet. $1, Ships Sir Walter Raleigh and Zebu.

Perf. 14½x14

1986, Mar. 27 Wmk. 373

558 A94 18c multicolored .90 .25
559 A94 30c multicolored 1.50 .50
560 A94 60c multicolored 2.75 1.50
561 A94 $1 multicolored 3.25 2.25
Nos. 558-561 (4) 8.40 4.50

Queen Elizabeth II 60th Birthday

Common Design Type

Designs: 5c, Visiting Clydebank Town Hall with Prince Philip, 1947. 18c, At Queen Mother's 80th birthday, St. Paul's Cathedral, 1980. 22c, Walking among children of the islands, Pacific tour, 1982. 55c, 50th birthday, Windsor Castle, 1976. $2, Visiting Crown Agents' offices, 1983.

1986, Apr. 21 Wmk. 384 *Perf. 14½*

562 CD337 5c scarlet, blk & sil .30 .30
563 CD337 18c ultra & multi .30 .30
564 CD337 22c green & multi .30 .30
565 CD337 55c violet & multi .50 .50
566 CD337 $2 rose vio & multi 1.50 1.50
Nos. 562-566 (5) 2.90 2.90

Royal Wedding Issue, 1986

Common Design Type

Designs: 55c, Informal portrait. 60c, Andrew aboard royal navy vessel.

Wmk. 384

1986, July 23 Litho. *Perf. 14*

567 CD338 55c multicolored .45 .45
568 CD338 60c multicolored .55 .55

Souvenir Sheet

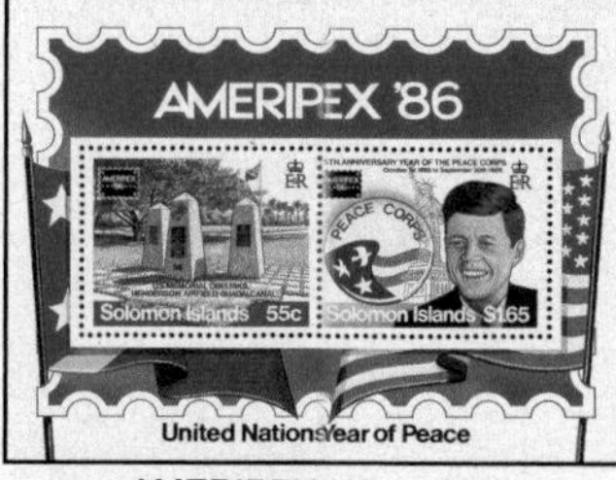

AMERIPEX '86 — A95

55c, U.S. Memorial, Henderson Field, Guadalcanal. $1.65, Peace Corps emblem, Statue of Liberty, Pres. John F. Kennedy.

1986, May 22 Litho. *Perf. 13½*

569 A95 Sheet of 2 2.50 2.50
a. 55c multicolored .60 .60
b. $1.65 multicolored 1.75 1.75

Intl. Peace Year, Peace Corps 25th anniv.
For surcharge see No. B3.

1987 America's Cup — A96

Previous winners, challengers, maps and club emblems: No. 570a, America, US, 1851. b, Magic, US, 1870. c, Madeleine, US, 1876. d, Mischief, US, 1881. e, Columbia, US, 1871. f, British Cup course, 1851. g, America II, US, 1987. h, America's Cup. i, Heart of America, US, 1987. j, French Kiss, France, 1987.

No. 571a, Puritan, US, 1885. b, Mayflower, US, 1886. c, Defender, US, 1895. d, Vigilant, US, 1893. e, Volunteer, US, 1887. f, America Cup course, Newport, 1930-1962. g, South Australia, Australia, 1987. h, KA14, Australia, 1987. i, New Zealand II, New Zealand, 1987. j, St. Francis IX, US, 1987.

No. 572a, Columbia, US, 1899. b, Columbia, US, 1901. c, Enterprise, US, 1930. d, Resolute, US, 1920. e, Reliance, US, 1903. f, America Cup course, 1964-1983. g, Kookaburra, Australia, 1987. h, Eagle, US, 1987. i, True North, Canada, 1987. j, Italia, Italy, 1987.

No. 573a, Rainbow, US, 1934. b, Ranger, US, 1937. c, Constellation, US, 1964. d, Weatherly, US, 1962. e, Columbia, US, 1958. f, Western Australia Cup course, 1987. g, Secret Cove, syndicate, 1987. h, Courageous III, US, 1987. i, France, France, 1987. j, Azzurra, Italy, 1987.

No. 574a, Intrepid, US, 1967. b, Intrepid, US, 1970. c, Freedom, US, 1980. d, Courageous, US, 1977. e, Courageous, US, 1974. f, Australia II, Australia, 1983. g, Crusader, Great Britain, 1987. h, Sail America, US, 1987. i, Australia III, Australia, 1987. j, Royal Perth Yacht Club/America's Cup '87 emblem, 1987.

1986, Aug. 22 Litho. *Perf. 14½*

570 Strip of 10 + label 5.00 5.00
a.-d. A96 18c any single .25 .25
e.-f. A96 30c any single .25 .25
g.-j. A96 $1 any single .60 .60
571 Strip of 10 + label 5.00 5.00
a.-d. A96 18c any single .25 .25
e.-f. A96 30c any single .25 .25
g.-j. A96 $1 any single .60 .60
572 Strip of 10 + label 5.00 5.00
a.-d. A96 18c any single .25 .25
e.-f. A96 30c any single .25 .25
g.-j. A96 $1 any single .60 .60
573 Strip of 10 + label 5.00 5.00
a.-d. A96 18c any single .25 .25
e.-f. A96 30c any single .25 .25
g.-j. A96 $1 any single .60 .60
574 Strip of 10 + label 5.00 5.00
a.-d. A96 18c any single .25 .25
e.-f. A96 30c any single .25 .25
g.-j. A96 $1 any single .60 .60
Nos. 570-574 (5) 25.00 25.00

Nos. 570-574 printed se-tenant with center labels picturing natl. arms, 1987 America's Cup emblem and trophy in sheets of 50.

Souvenir Sheet

$5, Stars and Stripes, U.S., victor.

1987, Feb. 4 Litho. *Perf. 14½*

575 A96 $5 multi 5.50 5.50

Coral — A97

No. 576, Dendrophyllia gracilis. No. 577, Dendronephthya. No. 578, Clavularia. No. 579, Melithaea squamata.

Perf. 14½x14

1987, Feb. 11 Litho. Wmk. 384

576 A97 18c multicolored .40 .25
577 A97 45c multicolored .80 .50
578 A97 60c multicolored 1.00 1.00
579 A97 $1.50 multicolored 2.25 2.25
Nos. 576-579 (4) 4.45 4.00

Flowering Plants — A98

No. 580, Cassia fistula. No. 581, Allamanda cathartica. No. 582, Catharanthus roseus. No. 583, Mimosa pudica. No. 584, Hibiscus rosa-sinensis. No. 585, Clerodendrum thomsonae. No. 586, Bauhinia variegata. No. 587, Gloriosa rothschildiana. No. 588, Heliconia solomonensis. No. 589, Episcia hybrid. No. 590, Bougainvillea hybrid. No. 591, Alpinia purpurata. No. 592, Plumeria rubra. No. 593, Acacia farnesiana. No. 594, Ipomea purpurea. No. 595, Dianella ensifolia. No. 596, Passiflora foetida. No. 596A, Hemigraphis specie ('88).

1987-88

580 A98 1c multicolored .25 .25
581 A98 5c multicolored .30 .25
582 A98 10c multicolored .40 .25
583 A98 18c multicolored .60 .25
584 A98 20c multicolored .60 .25
585 A98 22c multicolored .60 .25
586 A98 25c multicolored .60 .30
587 A98 28c multicolored .65 .30
588 A98 30c multicolored .75 .35
589 A98 40c multicolored .90 .45
590 A98 45c multicolored .90 .50
591 A98 50c multicolored 1.00 .60
592 A98 55c multicolored 1.00 .60
593 A98 60c multicolored 1.00 .70
594 A98 $1 multicolored 2.00 1.10
595 A98 $2 multicolored 2.75 3.50
596 A98 $5 multicolored 3.75 5.75
596A A98 $10 multicolored 6.50 9.00
Nos. 580-596A (18) 24.55 24.65

Issue dates: $10, Mar. 1; others, May 12.

Mangrove Kingfisher — A99

Designs: a, Perched on root. b, Diving. c, Landing in water. d, Emerging with fish.

Perf. 14x14½

1987, July 15 Wmk. 373

597 Strip of 4 12.00 12.00
a.-d. A99 60c any single 3.00 3.00

No. 597 has a continuous design.

Orchids — A100

No. 598, Dendrobium conanthum. No. 599, Spathoglottis plicata. No. 600, Dendrobium gouldii. No. 601, Dendrobium goldfinchii.

Perf. 13½x13

1987, Sept. 23 Wmk. 384

598 A100 18c multi 1.25 .35
599 A100 30c multi 1.75 .40
600 A100 55c multi 2.00 1.00
601 A100 $1.50 multi 3.50 5.50
Nos. 598-601 (4) 8.50 7.25

Christmas 1987.

Transportation and Communications Decade — A101

Designs: 18c, Telecommunications link. 30c, Express mail service. 60c, Guadalcanal Road Improvement Project. $2, Beechcraft Queen Air, Henderson Airfield control tower.

Perf. 14x13½

1987, Oct. 31 Litho. Unwmk.

602 A101 18c multicolored .30 .25
603 A101 30c multicolored .55 .35
604 A101 60c multicolored .70 .70
605 A101 $2 multicolored 3.00 3.00
Nos. 602-605 (4) 4.55 4.30

Queen Victoria's Birdwing Butterfly — A102

Designs: No. 606a, Male. No. 606b, Larva. No. 606c, Pupa. No. 606d, Female.

1987, Nov. 25 Wmk. 384 *Perf. 14½*

606 A102 Strip of 4 18.00 18.00
a.-d. 45c any single 4.25 4.25

Intl. Fund for Agricultural Development (IFAD), 10th Anniv. — A103

Natl. colors and: No. 607, Student, Natl. Agricultural Training Institute (NATI) farm and emblem (left stamp). No. 608, Students in working in NATI field and emblem (right stamp). No. 609, Flatbed truck transporting produce and emblem (left stamp). No. 610, Canoes, seagulls and emblem (right stamp).

Wmk. 384

1988, Feb. 12 Litho. *Perf. 14½*

607 50c multicolored .70 .70
608 50c multicolored .70 .70
a. A103 Pair, #607-608 1.50 1.50
609 $1 multicolored .80 .80
610 $1 multicolored .80 .80
a. A103 Pair, #609-610 1.75 1.75
Nos. 607-610 (4) 3.00 3.00

EXPO '88, Brisbane, Apr. 30-Oct. 30 — A104

Designs: 22c, Yacht in dry dock. 80c, Canoe. $1.50, Huts.

Perf. 13½x14

1988, Apr. 30 Unwmk.

611 A104 22c multicolored .25 .25
612 A104 80c multicolored .75 .75
613 A104 $1.50 multicolored 1.25 1.25
a. Souv. sheet of 3, #611-613 2.50 2.50
b. As "a," surcharged $3.50 in margin ('90) 17.50 17.50
Nos. 611-613 (3) 2.25 2.25

National Independence, 10th Anniv. — A105

22c, Capitana in Estrella Bay. 55c, Flag raising, 1893. 80c, Supreme Court. $1, Traditional celebration.

Perf. 13x13½

1988, July 7 Litho. Wmk. 373

614 A105 22c multicolored 1.10 .25
615 A105 55c multicolored 1.90 .60
616 A105 80c multicolored 1.60 1.40
617 A105 $1 multicolored 1.90 1.90
Nos. 614-617 (4) 6.50 4.15

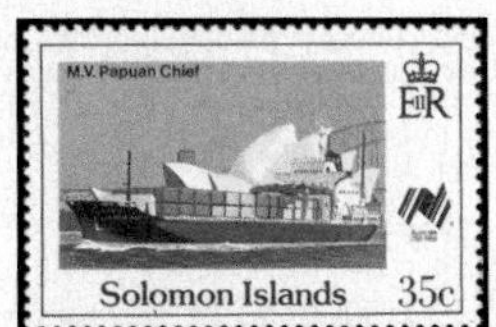

Australia Bicentennial — A106

Ships: 35c, M.V. Papuan Chief. 60c, M.V. Nimos. 70c, S.S. Malaita. $1.30, S.S. Makambo.

1988, July 30 Wmk. 384 *Perf. 14*

618 A106 35c multicolored 1.25 .35
619 A106 60c multicolored 1.60 .55
620 A106 70c multicolored 1.60 .85
621 A106 $1.30 multicolored 2.10 2.10
a. Souvenir sheet of 4, #618-621 4.75 4.75
Nos. 618-621 (4) 6.55 3.85

1988 Summer Olympics, Seoul — A107

22c, Archery. 55c, Weight lifting. 70c, Running. 80c, Boxing.
$2, Olympic Stadium, horiz.

Wmk. 384

1988, Aug. 5 Litho. *Perf. 14½*

622 A107 22c multi .75 .25
623 A107 55c multi 1.00 .65
624 A107 70c multi 1.25 1.25
625 A107 80c multi 1.50 1.50
Nos. 622-625 (4) 4.50 3.65

Souvenir Sheet

Wmk. 373

626 A107 $2 multi 2.50 2.50

Lloyds of London, 300th Anniv.

Common Design Type

Designs: 22c, King George V and Queen Mary at Lloyd's ground-breaking ceremony, 1925. 50c, *Forthbank,* horiz. 65c, Soltel Satellite Ground Station, horiz. $2, *Empress of China.*

1988, Oct. 31 *Perf. 14*

627 CD341 22c multicolored .65 .25
628 CD341 50c multicolored 1.60 .45
629 CD341 65c multicolored 1.75 .75
630 CD341 $2 multicolored 3.00 3.00
Nos. 627-630 (4) 7.00 4.45

Orchids — A108

No. 631, Bulbophyllum dennisii. No. 632, Calanthe langei. No. 633, Bulbophyllum blumei. No. 634, Grammatophyllum speciosum.

Perf. 13½x13

1989, Jan. 20 Litho. Wmk. 373

631 A108 22c multicolored 1.25 .30
632 A108 35c multicolored 1.50 .55
633 A108 55c multicolored 2.00 1.25
634 A108 $2 multicolored 3.25 3.25
Nos. 631-634 (4) 8.00 5.35

Intl. Red Cross, 125th Anniv. — A109

No. 635, Disabled children. No. 636, Children's Center minibus. No. 637, Patient abed. No. 638, Physical therapy.

Perf. 14x14½

1989, May 16 Wmk. 384

635 35c multi 1.00 1.00
636 35c multi 1.00 1.00
a. A109 Pair, #635-636 2.00 2.00
637 $1.50 multi 1.60 1.60
638 $1.50 multi 1.60 1.60
a. A109 Pair, #637-638 3.25 3.25
Nos. 635-638 (4) 5.20 5.20

Sea Slugs A110

No. 639, Phyllidia varicosa. No. 640, Chromodoris bullocki. No. 641, Chromodoris leopardus. No. 642, Phidiana indica.

1989, June 30 Wmk. 373 *Perf. 14½*

639 A110 22c multicolored 1.25 .30
640 A110 70c multicolored 2.50 1.75
641 A110 80c multicolored 2.75 2.50
642 A110 $1.50 multicolored 4.50 4.00
Nos. 639-642 (4) 11.00 8.55

Moon Landing, 20th Anniv.

Common Design Type

Apollo 16: 22c, Splashdown. 35c, Launch. 70c, Mission emblem. 80c, Ultraviolet color enhancement of Earth. $4, The Moon, as photographed during the Apollo 11 mission.

1989, July 20 Wmk. 384 *Perf. 14*

Size of Nos. 644-645: 29x29mm

643 CD342 22c multicolored .65 .25
644 CD342 35c multicolored 1.00 .50
645 CD342 70c multicolored 1.60 1.40
646 CD342 80c multicolored 1.75 1.60
Nos. 643-646 (4) 5.00 3.75

Souvenir Sheet

647 CD342 $4 multicolored 4.00 3.00

Blowing Soap Bubbles A111

Children's games — 5c, Five stones catch, vert. 73c, Coconut shell empire. $1, Seed wind sound, vert.
$3, Baseball, softball, vert.

1989, Nov. 17 Wmk. 384

648 A111 5c multicolored .30 *.55*
649 A111 67c shown 1.50 1.75
650 A111 73c multicolored 1.50 1.75
651 A111 $1 multicolored 2.00 2.50
Nos. 648-651 (4) 5.30 6.55

Souvenir Sheet

Wmk. 373

652 A111 $3 multicolored 8.50 8.50

World Stamp Expo '89.

Christmas — A112

18c, Butterfly, fishermen. 25c, Nativity. 45c, Hospital ward. $1.50, Tug of war.

1989, Nov. 30 Wmk. 384

653 A112 18c multi .70 .30
654 A112 25c multi .80 .35
655 A112 45c multi 1.25 .50
656 A112 $1.50 multi 3.00 3.75
Nos. 653-656 (4) 5.75 4.90

Personal Ornaments A113

1990, Feb. 14 Litho. Wmk. 373

657 A113 5c shown .40 *1.00*
658 A113 12c Necklace .70 .45
659 A113 18c Islander, diff. .75 .60
660 A113 $2 Head ornament 6.75 6.75
Nos. 657-660 (4) 8.60 8.80

Cowrie Shells A114

1990, July 23

666 A114 4c Spindle cowrie .40 *.75*
667 A114 20c Map cowrie 1.10 .40
668 A114 35c Sieve cowrie 1.25 .50
669 A114 50c Egg cowrie 2.00 2.00
670 A114 $1 Prince cowrie 3.00 3.50
Nos. 666-670 (5) 7.75 7.15

Queen Mother, 90th Birthday

Common Design Types

25c, Queen Mother, 1987. $5, Inspecting damage to Buckingham Palace, 1940.

1990, Aug. 4 Wmk. 384 *Perf. 14x15*

671 CD343 25c multicolored 1.00 .30

Perf. 14½

672 CD344 $5 brown & blk 4.00 *5.00*

First Postage Stamp, 150th Anniv. A115

Designs: 35c, Postman, mail van. 45c, Solomon Islands Post Office. 50c, Solomon Islands No. 1. 55c, Young philatelist. 60c, Solomon Islands No. 20, Penny Black.

1990, Oct. 15 Wmk. 373 *Perf. 14*

673 A115 35c multicolored 1.50 .50
674 A115 45c multicolored 1.50 .55
675 A115 50c multicolored 1.75 1.75
676 A115 55c multicolored 1.75 1.75
677 A115 60c multicolored 2.50 2.50
Nos. 673-677 (5) 9.00 7.05

Birds A116

10c, Purple swamphen. 25c, Rufous brown pheasant dove. 30c, Superb fruit dove. 45c, Cardinal honeyeater. $2, Pigmy parrot.

1990, Dec. 5

678	A116	10c	multi	1.00	.80
679	A116	25c	multi	1.75	.70
680	A116	30c	multi	2.00	.75
681	A116	45c	multi	2.25	.90
682	A116	$2	multi	4.00	5.50
	Nos. 678-682 (5)			11.00	8.65

Birdpex '90, 20th Intl. Ornithological Congress, New Zealand.

Crop Pests — A117

7c, Sweet potato weevil. 25c, Melon fly. 40c, Taro beetle. 90c, Cocoa weevil borer. $1.50, Rhinoceros beetle.

Perf. 14x13½

1991, Jan. 16 Litho. Wmk. 373

683	A117	7c	multi	.75	.55
684	A117	25c	multi	1.00	.25
685	A117	40c	multi	1.25	.45
686	A117	90c	multi	2.00	2.50
687	A117	$1.50	multi	2.50	4.00
	Nos. 683-687 (5)			7.50	7.75

For No. 683 overprinted, see No. 884A.

Elizabeth & Philip, Birthdays

Common Design Types

Wmk. 384

1991, June 17 Litho. *Perf. 14½*

688	CD346	90c	multicolored	1.00	1.00
689	CD345	$2	multicolored	2.40	2.40
a.	Pair, #688-689 + label			3.75	3.75

No. 689a exists with two different labels.

Nutritional Foods — A118

1991, June 24 Wmk. 373 *Perf. 14*

690	A118	5c	Coconut water	.25	.50
691	A118	75c	Feed your child	1.50	1.50
692	A118	80c	Mother's milk	1.75	1.75
693	A118	90c	Local food	2.25	2.25
	Nos. 690-693 (4)			5.75	6.00

A 65c value, depicting healthy and unhealthy foods, was prepared but not issued. Value $325.

9th South Pacific Games — A119

Wmk. 384

1991, Aug. 8 Litho. *Perf. 14*

694	A119	25c	Volleyball	1.25	.35
695	A119	40c	Judo	1.50	.75
696	A119	65c	Squash	2.00	2.50
697	A119	90c	Lawn bowling	2.50	2.75
	Nos. 694-697 (4)			7.25	6.35

Souvenir Sheet

698	A119	$2	Games emblem	6.75	6.75

Christmas — A120

10c, Food preparation. 25c, Church service. 65c, Feast. $2, Cricket match.

Wmk. 373

1991, Oct. 28 Litho. *Perf. 14*

699	A120	10c	multi	.45	.25
700	A120	25c	multi	.80	.25
701	A120	65c	multi	2.25	1.00
702	A120	$2	multi	4.50	4.50
a.	Souvenir sheet of 4, #699-702			9.50	9.50
	Nos. 699-702 (4)			8.00	6.00

Phila Nippon '91 — A121

Tuna fishing: 5c, Yellowfin tuna. 30c, Boat for pole and line tuna fishing. 80c, Pole and line tuna fishing. $2, Arabushi processing. No. 707a, Food made from tuna, tori nanban. b, Aka miso soup.

Wmk. 384

1991, Nov. 16 Litho. *Perf. 14*

703	A121	5c	multicolored	.35	.25
704	A121	30c	multicolored	.90	.50
705	A121	80c	multicolored	2.00	2.50
706	A121	$2	multicolored	4.00	4.50
	Nos. 703-706 (4)			7.25	7.75

Souvenir Sheet

707	A121	80c	Sheet of 2, #a.-b.	2.50	2.50

No. 707 contains two 28x45mm stamps.

Queen Elizabeth II's Accession to the Throne, 40th Anniv.

Common Design Type

Wmk. 384 (5c, 60c), 373

1992, Feb. 6 Litho. *Perf. 14*

708	CD349	5c	multicolored	.30	*.60*
709	CD349	20c	multicolored	.50	.25
710	CD349	40c	multicolored	.60	.45
711	CD349	60c	multicolored	.60	1.00
712	CD349	$5	multicolored	3.00	3.00
	Nos. 708-712 (5)			5.00	5.30

Alvaro Mendana de Niera (1541-1595), Discoveries in the Solomon Islands — A122

Granada '92: 10c, Thousand Ships Bay. 65c, Route to the Solomon Islands. 80c, Alvaro Mendana de Niera. $1, Graciosa Bay settlement. $5, Sailing ships.

Perf. 15x14½

1992, Apr. 24 Litho. Wmk. 373

713	A122	10c	multicolored	.85	.45
714	A122	65c	multicolored	1.50	.70
715	A122	80c	multicolored	1.60	1.60
716	A122	$1	multicolored	2.00	2.00
717	A122	$5	multicolored	4.25	4.75
	Nos. 713-717 (5)			10.20	9.50

A123

25c, Early portrait. 70c, Wearing USMC fatigues. 90c, Wearing uniform, cap. $2, Statue.
$4, In dress uniform.

Perf. 14x13½

1992, May 3 Litho. Wmk. 373

718	A123	25c	multi	.70	.40
719	A123	70c	multi	1.40	1.25
720	A123	90c	multi	1.40	1.40
a.	Booklet pane, 2 ea #718, 720			4.00	
721	A123	$2	multi	2.00	2.25
a.	Booklet pane, 2 ea #719, 721			7.00	
	Nos. 718-721 (4)			5.50	5.30

Souvenir Sheet

722	A123	$4	multi	7.25	7.25
a.	Booklet pane of 1			6.50	6.50
	Complete booklet, one each #720a, 721a, 722a			17.00	

Sergeant Major Jacob Vouza (1891-1984). One margin of Nos. 720a, 721a, and 722a is rouletted 8.

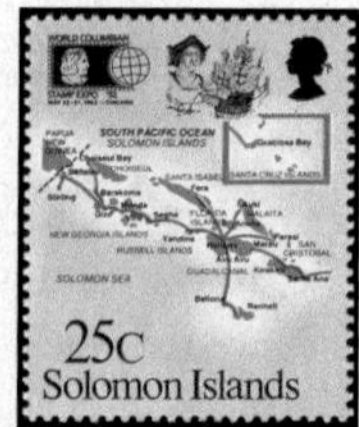

A124

World Columbian Stamp Expo '92, Chicago: 25c, Solomon Airlines domestic routes. 80c, Boeing 737-400 airplanes. $1.50, Solomon Airlines international routes. $5, Columbus and Santa Maria.

1992, May 22

723	A124	25c	multicolored	.75	.25
724	A124	80c	multicolored	2.00	2.00
725	A124	$1.50	multicolored	3.00	3.00
726	A124	$5	multicolored	6.25	6.25
a.	Souvenir sheet of 4, #723-726			12.00	12.00
b.	As "a," ovptd. with Taipei '93 emblem in sheet margin			6.00	6.00
	Nos. 723-726 (4)			12.00	11.50

No. 726b issued Aug. 14, 1993.

Miniature Sheets

Battle of Guadalcanal, 50th Anniv. — A125

Scenes from battle of Guadalcanal: No. 727a, Japanese landing at Esperance. b, US landings. c, Australian Navy cruiser. d, US Navy post office. e, Royal New Zealand Air Force PBY Catalina.

No. 728a, US Marine Wildcat fighters. b, Henderson Field under construction and attack. c, Heavy cruiser USS Quincy. d, Australian Navy heavy cruiser Canberra. e, US Marines land on Guadalcanal. f, Japanese aircraft carrier Ryujo. g, Japanese Zeke fighters attack US positions. h, Japanese bombers attack American beachhead. i, Japanese destroyers of Tokyo Express. j, Japanese heavy cruiser Chokai.

Wmk. 384

1992, Aug. 7 Litho. *Perf. 14*

727	A125	30c	Sheet of 5, #a.-e. + label	4.50	4.50
728	A125	80c	Sheet of 10, #a.-j. + label	17.50	17.50

See No. 889.

Orchids A126

15c, Dendrobium hybrid. 70c, Vanda "Amy Laycock". 95c, Dendrobium mirbelianum. $2.50, Dendrobium macrophyllum.

Perf. 14½x14

1992, Dec. 14 Litho. Wmk. 373

729	A126	15c	multicolored	.90	.25
730	A126	70c	multicolored	1.50	1.25
731	A126	95c	multicolored	2.00	2.25
732	A126	$2.50	multicolored	3.00	3.50
	Nos. 729-732 (4)			7.40	7.25

See Nos. 752-755.

Crabs A127

5c, Stalk-eyed ghost. 10c, Red-spotted. 25c, Flat. 30c, Land hermit. 40c, Grapsid. 45c, Red & white painted. 55c, Swift-footed. 60c, Spanner. 70c, Red hermit. 80c, Red-eyed. 90c, Rathbun red. $1, Coconut. $1.10, Red-spotted white. $4, Ghost. $10, Mangrove fiddler.

Wmk. 373

1993, Jan. 15 Litho. *Perf. 13*

733	A127	5c	multicolored	.25	.55
734	A127	10c	multicolored	.25	.55
735	A127	25c	multicolored	.25	.55
736	A127	30c	multicolored	.25	.25
737	A127	40c	multicolored	.30	.30
738	A127	45c	multicolored	.30	.30
739	A127	55c	multicolored	.35	.35
740	A127	60c	multicolored	.40	.35
741	A127	70c	multicolored	.50	.45
742	A127	80c	multicolored	.55	.50
743	A127	90c	multicolored	.60	.55
744	A127	$1	multicolored	.65	.60
745	A127	$1.10	multicolored	.70	.70
746	A127	$4	multicolored	2.25	*3.00*
a.	Souvenir sheet of 1, perf. 14			4.00	4.00
747	A127	$10	multicolored	3.50	5.50
	Nos. 733-747 (15)			11.10	14.50

No. 746a for Hong Kong '97. Issued: #733-747, 1/15/93; #746a, 2/3/97.

World War II, 50th Anniv. A128

Designs: 30c, US War Memorial, Skyline Ridge. 80c, Country flags, Guadalcanal. 95c, Major General Alexander A. Vandegrift, map. $4, WWII Scouts, Gizo Islands.

Wmk. 373

1993, Apr. 19 Litho. *Perf. 14*

748	A128	30c	multicolored	.25	.25
749	A128	80c	multicolored	1.75	1.40
750	A128	95c	multicolored	2.00	1.75
751	A128	$4	multicolored	6.00	6.00
	Nos. 748-751 (4)			10.00	9.40

Orchid Type of 1992

Perf. 14½x14

1993 Litho. Wmk. 373

752	A126	20c	like #729	.70	.40
753	A126	85c	like #730	1.75	1.50
754	A126	$1.15	like #731	2.10	2.10
755	A126	$3	like #732	3.50	3.50
	Nos. 752-755 (4)			8.05	7.50

Nos. 752, 755 are inscribed "World Orchid Conference." Nos. 753-754 are inscribed "Indopex '93 Exhibition."

Issued: #752, 755, 4/24; #753-754, 4/29.

Sinking of PT 109, 50th Anniv. A129

Designs: 30c, PT 109 about to be rammed. 50c, Native, Lt. John F. Kennedy. 95c, Message for help written on coconut, natives in canoe. $1.10, Kennedy, Navy and Marine Corps Medal. $5, PT 109.

Wmk. 373

1993, July 30 Litho. *Perf. 13*

756 A129	30c multicolored	.75	.50
757 A129	50c multicolored	1.00	.70
758 A129	95c multicolored	1.25	1.25
759 A129	$1.10 multicolored	2.50	2.50
	Nos. 756-759 (4)	5.50	4.95

Souvenir Sheet

Perf. 13x13½

760 A129 $5 multicolored 8.50 8.50

Nicobar Pigeon — A130

50c, One on ground. 65c, Two on branches. 70c, One on branch. $1.10, One on berry branch. $3, Two in flight.

Wmk. 373

1993, Sept. 21 Litho. *Perf. 14*

761 A130	30c multi	.80	.40
762 A130	50c multi	1.00	.70
763 A130	65c multi	1.40	1.00
764 A130	70c multi	2.00	1.25
765 A130	$1.10 multi	.80	.80
766 A130	$3 multi	1.50	1.50
	Nos. 761-766 (6)	7.50	5.65

World Wildlife Fund.

Dogs A131

30c, Dachshund. 80c, German shepherd. 95c, Dobermann pinscher. $1.10, Australian cattle dog.
$4, Boxer.

Wmk. 373

1994, Feb. 18 Litho. *Perf. 14½*

767 A131	30c multi	.50	.50
768 A131	80c multi	.75	.75
769 A131	95c multi	1.25	1.25
770 A131	$1.10 multi	1.75	1.75
	Nos. 767-770 (4)	4.25	4.25

Souvenir Sheet

771 A131 $4 multi 8.50 8.50

Hong Kong '94.

No. 771 overprinted "19-25 Aug. Jakarta '95 Surcharge $2-00." was available only at the exhibition. Value, $14.

Dolphins A132

Wmk. 373

1994, May 9 Litho. *Perf. 14*

772 A132	75c Striped	1.00	.80
773 A132	85c Risso's	1.25	1.25
774 A132	$1.15 Common	1.50	1.50
775 A132	$2.50 Spinner	3.00	3.25
776 A132	$3 Bottlenose	3.25	3.50
	Nos. 772-776 (5)	10.00	10.30

Miniature Sheet

Butterflies — A133

Designs: a, Vindula sapor. b, Papilio aegeus. c, Graphium hicetaon. d, Graphium mendana. e, PHILAKOREA '94 emblem. f, Graphium meeki. g, Danaus schenkii. h, Papilio ptolychus. i, Phaedyma fissizonata.

Wmk. 373

1994, Aug. 16 Litho. *Perf. 13½*

777 A133 70c Sheet of 9, #a.-i. 6.75 6.75

For overprint see No. 842.

Intl. Year of the Family — A134

Designs: a, Girl writing letter in Brisbane, Australia, family reading letter on Santa Isabel, Solomon Islands. b, Boeing 737-400, Brisbane Intl. Airport, Australia. c, Boeing 737-400, Henderson Airfield, Guadalcanal, DHC 6-Twin Otter. d, Fera Airfield, Buala, Santa Isabel. e, Family.

1994, Aug. 18 *Perf. 13*

778 A134 $1.10 Strip of 5, #a.-e. 6.25 6.25
f. Sheet of 1, #778 7.25 7.25

Volcanoes of the Solomon Islands A135

Designs: 30c, Cook Island Volcano erupting under sea, 1967. 70c, Kavachi Volcano erupting from sea, 1977. 80c, Kavachi Volcano forming temporary island, 1978. 90c, Tinakulu Volcano, permanent island.

No. 783: a, Map of Solomon Island volcanoes. b, Diagram illustrating formation of volcanic island archipelago.

Wmk. 373

1994, Oct. 24 Litho. *Perf. 14*

779 A135	30c multicolored	.85	.50
780 A135	70c multicolored	1.00	.75
781 A135	80c multicolored	1.25	1.00
782 A135	90c multicolored	1.40	1.25
	Nos. 779-782 (4)	4.50	3.50

Souvenir Sheet

783 A135 $2 Sheet of 2, #a.-b. 5.50 5.50

La Perouse Expedition, 210th Anniv. A136

Designs: 30c, La Perouse, King Louis XVI. 80c, Map of Ile de La Perouse. 95c, L'Astrolabe. $1.10, La Boussole. $3, L'Astrolabe foundering on reef.

Wmk. 384

1994, Dec. 16 Litho. *Perf. 14*

784 A136	30c multicolored	.50	.25
785 A136	80c multicolored	1.25	.75
786 A136	95c multicolored	1.50	1.00
787 A136	$1.10 multicolored	1.75	1.25
788 A136	$3 multicolored	2.00	3.75
	Nos. 784-788 (5)	7.00	7.00

Visit South Pacific Year A137

30c, Tourists watching traditional dance, land hermit crab. 50c, Dendrobium rennellii, milkweed butterfly. 95c, Diver, moorish idol, fish. $1.15, Boats at shore, grapsid crab.
$4, Flower, yellow-bibbed lorry.

Perf. 15x14½

1995, Feb. 17 Litho. Wmk. 373

789 A137	30c multicolored	.25	.25
790 A137	50c multicolored	.75	.75
791 A137	95c multicolored	.80	.80
792 A137	$1.15 multicolored	1.00	1.00
	Nos. 789-792 (4)	2.80	2.80

Souvenir Sheet

793 A137 $4 multicolored 9.00 9.00

FAO, 50th Anniv. A138

1995, Apr. 5 *Perf. 12*

794 A138	70c Banana	1.00	.90
795 A138	75c Paw paw	1.00	.90
796 A138	95c Pomelo	1.45	1.40
797 A138	$2 Star fruit	2.75	2.75
	Nos. 794-797 (4)	6.20	5.95

Souvenir Sheet

798 A138 $3 Mango 2.50 2.50

End of World War II, 50th Anniv.

Common Design Types

Admirals, aircraft carriers: 95c, Vice Adm. Chuichi Nagumo, Akagi. $1, Rear Adm. Frank J. Fletcher, USS Yorktown. $2, Vice Adm. Robert L. Ghormley, USS Wasp. $3, Vice Adm. William F. Halsey, USS Enterprise.
$5, Reverse of War Medal 1939-45.

1995, May 8 *Perf. 13½*

799 CD351	95c multicolored	1.25	1.25
800 CD351	$1 multicolored	1.25	1.25
801 CD351	$2 multicolored	2.50	2.50
802 CD351	$3 multicolored	3.75	3.75
	Nos. 799-802 (4)	8.75	8.75

Souvenir Sheet

Perf. 14

803 CD352 $5 multicolored 6.00 6.00

Orchids — A139

Designs: 45c, Calanthe triplicata. 75c, Dendrobium mohlianum. 85c, Flickingeria comata. $1.15, Dendrobium spectabile.
$4, Coelogyne asperata.

Wmk. 373

1995, Sept. 1 Litho. *Perf. 14*

804 A139	45c multicolored	1.50	.35
805 A139	75c multicolored	2.00	1.10
806 A139	85c multicolored	2.00	1.50
807 A139	$1.15 multicolored	2.50	2.50
	Nos. 804-807 (4)	8.00	5.45

Souvenir Sheet

808 A139 $4 multicolored 4.00 4.00

Singapore '95 (#808).

Christmas — A140

Designs: 90c, Start of canoe race. $1.05, Pan pipers, Christmas tree. $1.25, Picnic on beach. $1.45, Local church, nativity.

1995, Nov. 6 *Perf. 13x13½*

810 A140	90c multicolored	.80	.60
811 A140	$1.05 multicolored	.80	.80
812 A140	$1.25 multicolored	1.00	1.10
813 A140	$1.45 multicolored	1.40	1.50
	Nos. 810-813 (4)	4.00	4.00

Guglielmo Marconi (1847-1937), Radio, Cent. — A141

Designs: $1.05, Demonstration, Salisbury Plain, 1896. $1.20, Birth of maritime radio, 1900. $1.35, First ground air transmitter, Croydon, 1920. $1.45, Marconi visiting Japan on world tour, 1933-34.

Perf. 14½x14

1996, Feb. 28 Litho. Wmk. 373

814 A141	$1.05 multicolored	1.00	1.00
815 A141	$1.20 multicolored	1.20	1.20
816 A141	$1.35 multicolored	1.40	1.40
817 A141	$1.45 multicolored	1.60	1.60
	Nos. 814-817 (4)	5.20	5.20

Lories A142

75c, Palm lorikeet. $1.05, Duchess lorikeet. $1.20, Yellow-bibbed lory. $1.35, Cardinal lory. $1.45, Meek's lorikeet.
$3, Rainbow lorikeet.

1996, Apr. 10 Litho. *Perf. 14*

818 A142	75c multicolored	.90	.55
819 A142	$1.05 multicolored	1.10	.80
820 A142	$1.20 multicolored	1.25	1.25
821 A142	$1.35 multicolored	1.50	2.00
822 A142	$1.45 multicolored	1.50	2.00
	Nos. 818-822 (5)	6.25	6.60

Souvenir Sheet

823 A142 $3 multicolored 5.00 5.00

CAPEX '96 — A143

Island scenes: 40c, Dug-out canoe. 90c, Man, bicycle. $1.20, Mobile Post Office bus. $1.45, "Tulagi Express."
$4, "Tepuke," traditional canoe from Temotu Province.

Wmk. 384

1996, June 8 Litho. *Perf. 13*

824 A143	40c multicolored	.35	.25
825 A143	90c multicolored	1.25	.80
826 A143	$1.20 multicolored	1.25	1.00
827 A143	$1.45 multicolored	1.75	2.50
	Nos. 824-827 (4)	4.60	4.55

Souvenir Sheet

828 A143 $4 multicolored 4.00 4.00

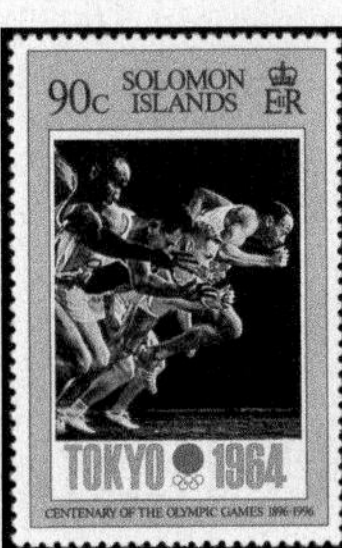

1996 Summer Olympic Games, Atlanta — A144

Olympic posters: 90c, Tokyo, 1964. $1.20, Los Angeles, 1932. $1.35, Paris, 1924. $2.50, London, 1908.

Wmk. 384

1996, June 30 Litho. *Perf. 14*

829 A144	90c multicolored	.60	.55
830 A144	$1.20 multicolored	.75	.75
831 A144	$1.35 multicolored	.80	1.00
832 A144	$2.50 multicolored	1.25	1.60
	Nos. 829-832 (4)	3.40	3.90

First Christian Mission, 150th Anniv. — A145

Designs: 40c, Suiesi, Makira Bay, 1846-47. 65c, Original sketches by Rev. L. Verguet, 1846, Surimahe. $1.35, Bishop Epalle's grave, Isabel, 1845. $1.45, Makira Mission, Jean Claude Colin, Marist founder.

Wmk. 373

1996, Sept. 12 Litho. *Perf. 14*

833 A145 40c multicolored .30 .25
834 A145 65c multicolored .45 .45
835 A145 $1.35 multicolored .60 .75
836 A145 $1.45 multicolored .65 1.00
Nos. 833-836 (4) 2.00 2.45

Souvenir Sheet

Taipei '96 — A146

1996, Oct. 21

837 A146 $1.50 Sandford's eagle 1.60 1.60

UNICEF, 50th Anniv. A147

Wmk. 373

1996, Nov. 21 Litho. *Perf. 14½*

838 A147 40c Food .25 .25
839 A147 $1.05 Recreation .70 .70
840 A147 $1.35 Medicine .80 .80
841 A147 $2.50 Education 1.00 1.50
Nos. 838-841 (4) 2.75 3.25

For surcharge see No. B4.

No. 777 Ovptd. in Red with SINGPEX '97 Emblem

Wmk. 373

1997, Feb. 21 Litho. *Perf. 13½*

842 A133 70c Sheet of 9, #a.-i. 9.00 9.00

Overprint is centered over entire sheet with each stamp containing portion of SINGPEX '97 emblem.

Overprint exists in black from a limited printing.

Northern Common Cuscus A148

15c, In tree. 60c, Eating berries. $2.50, In tree, climbing right. $3, Two in branches.

Wmk. 373

1997, Apr. 21 Litho. *Perf. 12*

843 A148 15c multicolored .25 .25
844 A148 60c multicolored .25 .30
845 A148 $2.50 multicolored .75 1.10
846 A148 $3 multicolored 1.00 1.25
Nos. 843-846 (4) 2.25 2.90

Whales — A149

a, Whale, calf, vert. b, Whale breaching.

Wmk. 373

1997, May 29 Litho. *Perf. 14½*

847 A149 $2 Sheet of 2, #a.-b. 3.50 3.50

PACIFIC 97.

Queen Elizabeth II & Prince Philip, 50th Wedding Anniv. — A150

#848, Queen with two horses. #849, Prince. #850, Prince on polo pony. #851, Queen. #852, Queen, Prince at Royal Ascot.

1997, July 10 *Perf. 13*

848 $3 multicolored 2.25 2.25
849 $3 multicolored 2.25 2.25
a. A150 Pair, #848-849 5.00 5.00
850 $3 multicolored 2.25 2.25
851 $3 multicolored 2.25 2.25
a. A150 Pair, #850-851 5.00 5.00
Nos. 848-851 (4) 9.00 9.00

Souvenir Sheet

852 A150 $3 multicolored 2.50 2.50

South Pacific Commission, 50th Anniv. — A151

Chelonia mydas: 50c, Laying eggs. 90c, Young turtles entering water. $1.50, Group swimming under water. $2, Two adults under water.

Wmk. 384

1997, Sept. 29 Litho. *Perf. 14*

853 A151 50c multicolored .60 .40
854 A151 90c multicolored .80 .75
855 A151 $1.50 multicolored .85 1.25
856 A151 $2 multicolored 1.00 1.40
Nos. 853-856 (4) 3.25 3.80

Christmas A152

Designs: $1.10, Oni mako. $1.40, Ysabel dancing women with bamboo sticks. $1.50, Pan pipers from Small Malaita. $1.70, Western bamboo band.

No. 861, vert.: a, Pachycephala pectoralis. b, Papilio aegeus, graphium meeki.

Wmk. 373

1997, Nov. 24 Litho. *Perf. 13½*

857 A152 $1.10 multicolored .40 .40
858 A152 $1.40 multicolored .60 .60
859 A152 $1.50 multicolored .90 .90
860 A152 $1.70 multicolored 1.10 1.10
Nos. 857-860 (4) 3.00 3.00

Souvenir Sheet of 2

Perf. 14

861 A152 $1.50 #a.-b. 3.25 3.25

China Stamp Exhibition, Bangkok '97 (#861).
Issued: #857-860, 11/24; #861, 12/5.

Game Fish — A153

50c, Black marlin. $1.20, Shortbill swordfish. $1.40, Swordfish. $2, Indo-Pacific sailfish.

Perf. 14½

1998, Feb. 27 Litho. Unwmk.

862 A153 50c multicolored .80 .40
863 A153 $1.20 multicolored 1.25 1.00
864 A153 $1.40 multicolored 1.40 1.40
865 A153 $2 multicolored 1.55 2.00
a. Souv. sheet of 1, wmk. triangles 2.50 2.50
Nos. 862-865 (4) 5.00 4.80

Singpex '98 (#865a). No. 865a issued 7/23 and sold for $3.

Diana, Princess of Wales (1961-97)

Common Design Type

$2, Wearing white dress (without hat).
#867: a, Up close. b, Wearing white hat, dress. c, Wearing evening dress, black background. d, Taking flowers from children.

Perf. 14½x14

1998, Mar. 31 Wmk. 373

866 CD355 $2 multicolored .90 .90
Complete booklet, 10 #866 9.00

Sheet of 4

867 CD355 $2.50 #a.-d. 4.50 4.50

No. 867 sold for $10 + 50c, with surtax from international sales being donated to the Princess Diana Memorial Fund and surtax from national sales being donated to designated local charity.

For overprint see No. 1095; for surcharge see No. B5.

Technical Cooperation Between Solomon Islands and Republic of China A154

Designs: 50c, Harvesting watermelons. $1.50, Harvesting rice.
No. 870: a, 80c, Growing cucumbers. b, $1.20, Growing tomatoes.

Wmk. 373

1998, May 29 Litho. *Perf. 13*

868 A154 50c multicolored .30 .30
869 A154 $1.50 multicolored .95 .95

Souvenir Sheet

870 A154 Sheet of 2, #a.-b. 1.50 1.50

Melanesian Trade and Culture Show — A155

a, Group raising arms during traditional dance. b, Men with bows and arrow. c, Man smiling in front of water. d, Four men with poles in traditional dance. e, Masked man kneeling down with bow and arrow. f, Man in traditional garb, flowers. g, Group carrying poles. h, Man with spear and shield. i, Man in traditional garb, sun over water.

1998, July 3 *Perf. 13½*

871 Sheet of 9 6.00 6.00
a.-c. A155 50c any single .40 .40
d.-f. A155 $1.20 any single .50 .50
g.-i. A155 $1.50 any single .65 .65

Souvenir Sheet

New Natl. Parliament Building — A156

1998, July 7

872 A156 $4 multicolored 3.50 3.50

Independence, 20th anniv.

Souvenir Sheet

Australia '99 World Stamp Expo — A157

Designs: a, HMS Endeavour, 1770. b, Los Reyes being careened at Guadalcanal, 1568.

1999, Mar. 19 *Perf. 13¼x13¾*

873 A157 $10 Sheet of 2, #a.-b. 8.50 8.50

PhilexFrance '99, World Philatelic Exhibition. A158

Marine Life: a, Beach. b, Great frigate bird. c, Coconut crab. d, Green turtle. e, Royal Spanish dancer nudibranch. f, Sun moon and stars butterflyfish. g, Striped Sweetlips. h, Saddle-back butterflyfish. i, Cuttlefish. j, Giant clam. k, Lionfish. l, Spiny lobster.

1999, July 2 *Perf. 13¼*

874 A158 $1 Sheet of 12, #a.-l. 9.00 9.00

1st Manned Moon Landing, 30th Anniv.

Common Design Type

Designs: 50c, Lift-off. $1.50, Lunar module above moon's surface. $2.50, Aldrin beside US flag. $3.40, Splashdown.
$4, Earth as seen from moon.

Perf. 14x13¾

1999, July 20 Litho. Wmk. 384

875 CD357 50c multicolored .25 .25
876 CD357 $1.50 multicolored .75 .75
877 CD357 $2.50 multicolored 1.75 1.75
878 CD357 $3.40 multicolored 2.25 2.25
Nos. 875-878 (4) 5.00 5.00

Souvenir Sheet

Perf. 14

879 CD357 $4 multicolored 2.50 2.50
a Ovptd. in margin in red 3.25 3.25

No. 879 contains one circular stamp 40mm in diameter.

Issued 7/7/2000, overprint on No. 879a reads "WORLD STAMP EXPO - USA VALUE $5.00." Sold for $5.

Queen Mother's Century

Common Design Type

Queen Mother: $1, Inspecting bomb damage at Portsmouth, 1941. $1.50, At the Derby, 1983. $2.30, Receiving birthday wishes. $4.90, As colonel-in-chief of Royal Army Medical Corps.

$3, With King George VI, Winston Churchill, V-E Day, 1945.

1999, Aug. 16 ***Perf. 13½***

880	CD358	$1 multicolored	.65	.30
881	CD358	$1.50 multicolored	.85	.70
882	CD358	$2.30 multicolored	1.25	1.25
883	CD358	$4.90 multicolored	2.25	2.25
		Nos. 880-883 (4)	5.00	4.50

Souvenir Sheet

884	CD358	$5 black	2.50	2.50

No. 683 overprinted "China '99" in red for international stamp exhibition, Beijing

1999, Aug. 21

884A	A117	7c Sweet potato weevil	1.75	1.75

Ferrari Racing Cars
A159

1999, Sept. 27 **Wmk. 373** ***Perf. 14***

885	A159	$1 212E	.65	.40
886	A159	$1.50 250TR	.75	.60
887	A159	$3.30 250LM	1.50	1.75
888	A159	$4.20 612 Can-Am	1.60	2.25
		Nos. 885-888 (4)	4.50	5.00

Guadalcanal Type of 1992

Designs: a, Flags at half staff. b, Cenotaph, Honiara. c, Solomon Peace Memorial Park. d, US War Memorial, Skyline Ridge. e, Reunion ship Ocean Pearl.

1999, Aug. 16 **Wmk. 384**

889	A125	30c Sheet of 5, #a.-e, + label	2.75	2.75
f.		Sheet of 10, #727a-727e, 889a-889e + label	6.75	6.75

Melanesian Mission, 150th Anniv. — A160

Christmas: a, $1, Bishop George Augustus Selwyndd. b, $1, Bishop John Coleridge Patteson. c, $3.30, Text. d, $1.50, Stained glass. e, $1.50, Southern Cross.

1999, Nov. 12 **Unwmk.**

890	A160	Strip of 5, #a.-e.	4.25	4.25

See Norfolk Islands #693.

Millennium
A161

Designs: Nos. 891, 893a, $1 Munda lighthouse, war canoe. Nos. 892, 893b, $4, Tulagi lighthouse, security boat.

2000, Apr. 27 ***Perf. 13½x13¼***

891	A161	$1 multi	1.50	1.00
892	A161	$4 multi	4.25	4.25

Souvenir Sheet

893	A161	Sheet of 2, #a.-b.	7.00	7.00

Nos. 893a, 893b have red violet margins.

Souvenir Sheet

Commonwealth Youth Minister's Meeting — A162

2000, May 22 **Litho.** ***Perf. 13½x13¼***

894	A162	$6 multi	7.75	7.75

Year of the Dragon
A163

Dragon head facing: $1, Front. $3.90, Left.

Perf. 11¾x11½

2000, Nov. 13 **Litho.** **Unwmk.**

895-896	A163	Set of 2	3.00	3.00
896a		Souvenir sheet, #895-896	3.00	3.00

East Rennell Island World Heritage Site
A164

Map and: 50c, Rennell Island. $3.40, Lake Tegano. $4, Rennell shrikebill. $4.90, Endemic orchid.

Perf. 11¾x11½

2000, Nov. 30 **Litho.**

897-900	A164	Set of 4	10.00	10.00

2000 Summer Olympics and Olymphilex, Sydney — A165

Runners in: $1, 100-meter race. $4.50, 1500-meter race.

2000, Dec. 11 ***Perf. 14***

901-902	A165	Set of 2	5.50	5.50
a.		Souvenir sheet, #901-902	5.50	5.50

Birds
A166

Designs: 5c, Yellow-throated white eye. 20c, Purple swamphen. 50c, Blyth's hornbill. 80c, Yellow-faced myna. 90c, Blue-faced parrotfinch. $1, Crested tern. $2, Rainbow lorikeet. $3, Eclectus parrot. $4, Dwarf kingfisher. $10, Beach thick-knee. $20, Brahminy kite. $50, Superb fruit dove.

2001 **Wmk. 373** ***Perf. 14¼x14½***

903	A166	5c multi	.25	.25
904	A166	20c multi	.25	.25
905	A166	50c multi	.30	.30
906	A166	80c multi	.40	.40
907	A166	90c multi	.50	.50
908	A166	$1 multi	.60	.60
909	A166	$2 multi	1.00	1.00
910	A166	$3 multi	1.50	1.50
911	A166	$4 multi	2.00	2.00
912	A166	$10 multi	4.00	4.00

Size: 48x38mm

Perf. 13¾x13½

913	A166	$20 multi	7.50	7.50
913A	A166	$50 multi	20.00	20.00
		Nos. 903-913A (12)	38.30	38.30

Issued: Nos. 5c-$20, 2/1/01; $50, 6/1/01.

East Rennell Island Type of 2000 and

Hong Kong 2001 Stamp Exhibition
A167

Snake color: $1.70, Yellow and brown. $2.30, Green and yellow.

2001, Feb. 1 **Litho.** ***Perf. 11¾x11½***

914-915	A167	Set of 2	3.00	3.00

Souvenir Sheet

916	A164	$5 Like #900	5.50	5.50

UN High Commissioner for Refugees, 50th Anniv. — A168

Designs: 50c, Refugees. $1, Food and medical supplies. $1.90, Shelter. $2.30, Education.

Perf. 14¼

2001, July 28 **Litho.** **Unwmk.**

917-920	A168	Set of 4	4.50	4.50

Souvenir Sheet

New Year 2001 (Year of the Snake) — A168a

No. 920A: b, Red-banded tree snake. c, Whip snake. d, Pacific boa. e, Guppy's snake.

2001, Dec. 13 ***Perf. 14½***

920A	A168a	$1 Sheet of 4, #b-e	3.75	3.75

Reef Fish
A169

Designs: 70c, Amphiprion chrysopterus. 90c, Amphiprion perideraion. $1, Premnas biaculeatus. $1.50, Amphiprion melanopus. $2.10, Amphiprion clarkii. $4.50, Dascyllus trimaculatus.

Wmk. 373

2001, Dec. 27 **Litho.** ***Perf. 14***

921-926	A169	Set of 6	7.25	7.25
926a		Souvenir sheet, #921-926	7.50	7.50

Worldwide Fund for Nature (WWF)
A170

Various depictions of gray cuscus: $1, $1.70, $2.30, $5.

2002, Jan. 31

927-930	A170	Set of 4	5.75	5.75
a.		Horiz. strip of 4	6.25	6.25

Reign Of Queen Elizabeth II, 50th Anniv. Issue

Common Design Type

Designs: Nos. 931, 935a, $1, Princess Elizabeth with baby carriage, 1933. Nos. 932, 935b, $1.90, Wearing sunglasses. Nos. 933, 935c, $2.10, In 1955. Nos. 934, 935d, $2.30, Wearing hat. No. 935e, $10, 1955 portrait by Annigoni (38x50mm).

Perf. 14¼x14½, 13¾ (#935e)

2002, Feb. 6 **Litho.** **Wmk. 373**

With Gold Frames

931	CD360	$1 multicolored	.75	.75
932	CD360	$1.90 multicolored	1.30	1.30
933	CD360	$2.10 multicolored	1.40	1.40
934	CD360	$2.30 multicolored	1.45	1.45
		Nos. 931-934 (4)	4.90	4.90

Souvenir Sheet

Without Gold Frames

935	CD360	Sheet of 5, #a-e	7.50	7.50

Methodist Mission, Cent.
A172

Designs: $1, Typical old school building, Western Solomons. $1.70, Mrs. J. F. Goldie and companions. $2.10, Tandanya, first mission schooner. $2.30, Rev. J. F. Goldie and Solomon Islands chiefs.

$5, Rev. Goldie and Sam Aqarao, vert.

2002, May 23 **Unwmk.** ***Perf. 14¼***

937-940	A172	Set of 4	6.50	6.50

Souvenir Sheet

941	A172	$5 multi	3.25	3.25

United We Stand — A173

Perf. 13½x13¼

2002, June 17 **Unwmk.**

942	A173	$2.10 multi	3.00	3.00

Souvenir Sheet

New Year 2002 (Year of the Horse) — A173a

No. 942A: b, Horse. c, Horse, horiz.

Perf. 13½x13¾, 13¾x13½

2002, July 7 **Litho.**

942A	A173a	$4 Sheet of 2, #a-b	7.50	7.50

No. 942 was printed in sheets of 4.

Cowrie Shells — A174

No. 943: a, $1, Sieve cowrie. b, $1, Kitten cowrie. c, $1, Stolid cowrie, eroded cowrie. d, $1.90, Tapering cowrie. e, $1.90, Tiger cowrie. f, $1.90, Lynx cowrie. g, $2.30, Map cowrie. h, $2.30, Pacific deer cowrie. i, $2.30, Tortoise cowrie.

$10, Golden cowrie.

Perf. 14¼x14½

2002, Aug. 2 Wmk. 373

943 A174 Sheet of 9, #a-i 12.50 12.50

Souvenir Sheet

944 A174 $10 multi 10.00 10.00

Phila Korea 2002 World Stamp Exhibition, Seoul.

Queen Mother Elizabeth (1900-2002)

Common Design Type

Designs: No. 945, $1, Without hat (sepia photograph). No. 946, $2.30, Wearing blue hat.

No. 947: a, $5, Wearing tiara (black and white photograph). b, $5, Wearing green blue hat.

Wmk. 373

2002, Aug. 5 Litho. *Perf. 14¼*

With Purple Frames

945 CD361 $1 multicolored 1.00 1.00
946 CD361 $2.30 multicolored 2.25 2.25

Souvenir Sheet

Without Purple Frames

Perf. 14½x14¼

947 CD361 Sheet of 2, #a-b 6.00 6.00

Battle of Guadalcanal, 60th Anniv. — A175

US servicemen: $1, No. 952d, Coast Guard signalman First Class Douglas Munro. $1.90, No. 952b, Marine Corps Capt. Joe Foss. $2.10, No. 952c, Marine Corps Platoon Sergeant Mitchell Paige. $2.30, No. 952a, Navy Rear Admiral Norman Scott.

2002, Aug. 7 Unwmk. *Perf. 14*

948-951 A175 Set of 4 7.50 7.50

Souvenir Sheet

952 A175 $5 Sheet of 4, #a-d 11.00 11.00

Christmas — A176

Paintings: $1, Christmas Night, by Lucas Cranach, the Elder. $2.10, Madonna and Child, by Giovanni Bellini. $2.30, Nativity, by Perugino, horiz. $5, Madonna and Child, by Simone Martini.

2002, Nov. 25 Litho. *Perf. 14*

953-956 A176 Set of 4 7.75 7.75

New Year 2003 (Year of the Ram) A177

Perf. 14¼x14½

2003, Apr. 15 Litho. Unwmk.

957 A177 $3 multi 3.00 3.00

Issued in sheets of 4.

U. S. Medals of Honor — A178

Designs: $1, Air Force Medal of Honor. $1.90 Navy Medal of Honor. $2.10, Army Medal of Honor. $2.30, Medal of Honor ribbon.

2003, June 6 *Perf. 14*

958-961 A178 Set of 4 7.00 7.00

Prince William, 21st Birthday — A179

No. 962: a, In gray suit. b, In red shirt. c, In black suit.

$15, In blue shirt.

2003, June 21

962 A179 $9 Sheet of 3, #a-c 12.50 12.50

Souvenir Sheet

963 A179 $15 multi 10.00 10.00

Solomon Islands — Republic of China Diplomatic Relations, 20th Anniv. A180

Designs: $1.50, Rice farmers. $2.10, Hospital.

2003, July 8 *Perf. 14¼*

964-965 A180 Set of 2 3.50 3.50

Coronation of Queen Elizabeth II, 50th Anniv. — A181

No. 966: a, Wearing tiara. b, Wearing green hat. c, Wearing blue hat.

$15, Wearing tiara, diff.

2003, June 2 Litho. *Perf. 14*

966 A181 $9 Sheet of 3, #a-c 14.00 14.00

Souvenir Sheet

967 A181 $15 multi 12.50 12.50

Powered Flight, Cent. — A182

No. 968: a, Boeing 747. b, Boeing 707. c, Lockheed Model 649. d, Boeing Model 247D. e, Fokker F.VII. f, Orville and Wilbur Wright.

$15, Concorde.

2003, Dec. 17

968 A182 $4 Sheet of 6, #a-f 14.00 14.00

Souvenir Sheet

969 A182 $15 multi 10.00 10.00

Souvenir Sheet

Visit of Pope John Paul II, 20th Anniv. — A183

No. 970: a, $5, Pope waving. b, $10, Pope with crucifix.

2004, Aug. 6 Litho. *Perf. 14*

970 A183 Sheet of 2, #a-b 7.00 7.00

For No. 970 overprinted, see No. 1025.

2004 Summer Olympics, Athens — A184

Designs: $1.50, Runner at starting blocks. $2, Runner in full stride. $2.20, Runner at finish line. $10, Solomon Islands flag, Olympic rings.

2004, Aug. 13 *Perf. 14*

971-974 A184 Set of 4 5.25 5.25

Orchids A185

No. 975: a, Calanthe triplicata. b, Dendrobium johnsoniae. c, Dendrobium capitulifiorum. d, Spathoglottis plicata. e, Dendrobium mirbelianum. f, Dendrobium polysema. g, Paphiopedilum bougainvilleanum. h, Coelogyne asperata. i, Dendrobium macrophyllum. j, Dendrobium spectabile.

2004, Aug. 28 *Perf. 13½*

975 Block of 10 16.00 16.00
a.-e. A185 $2.60 Any single 1.00 1.00
f.-j. A185 $5 Any single 2.00 2.00

Pres. Ronald Reagan (1911-2004) — A186

2004, Sept. 30 Litho. *Perf. 14*

976 A186 $5 multi 6.25 6.25

Printed in sheets of 4.

Merchant Ships A187

Designs: $1.50, MV Bilikiki. $2.20, MV Spirit of Solomons. $3, SS Oceana. $20, RMS Queen Elizabeth 2.

2004, Oct. 11 *Perf. 13¼*

977-980 A187 Set of 4 12.00 12.00

FIFA (Fédération Internationale de Football Association), Cent. — A188

No. 981, $2.10: a, Player and ball. b, Players.

No. 982, $10: a, Players. b, Player and ball.

2004, Nov. 1 *Perf. 14*

Horiz. Pairs, #a-b

981-982 A188 Set of 2 8.00 8.00

Bird Life International — A189

No. 983, $2.10: a, Rufous-tailed waterhen. b, Buff-banded rail. c, Purple swamphen. d, Woodford's rail e, Roviana rail. f, Makira moorhen.

No. 984, $5: a, Solomon Islands hawk-owl (denomination at LR). b, White-throated eared nightjar (denomination at LR). c, Solomon Islands hawk-owl (denomination at LL). d, White-throated eared nightjar (denomination at UR). e, Marbled frogmouth. f, Fearful owl.

No. 985, $7.50: a, Beach kingfisher. b, Collared kingfisher. c, Ultramarine kingfisher. d, Moustached kingfisher. e, Little kingfisher. f, Variable kingfisher.

2004, Nov. 15 *Perf. 13¾*

Sheets of 6, #a-f

983-985 A189 Set of 3 32.50 32.50

Christmas — A190

Paintings: 10c, Adoration of the Magi, by Peter Paul Rubens. 50c, Madonna della Tenda, by Raphael, vert. $1.50, Madonna and Child, by Titian, vert. $2.60, Madonna by the Arch, by Albrecht Dürer, vert. $3, Holy Family, by Frans Floris. $10, Madonna and Child, by unknown artist.

2004, Dec. 8 *Perf. 14*

986-991 A190 Set of 6 7.00 7.00

Battle of Trafalgar, Bicent. — A191

No. 992, $1.90: a, Vice-Admiral Horatio Lord Nelson. b, HMS Victory. c, Sir Thomas Masterman Hardy. d, The first engagement. e, Breaking the line. f, The death of Nelson.

No. 993, $2.60: a, Lord Cuthbert Collingwood. b, Napoleon Bonaparte. c, Destruction of the Bucentaure. d, Race and chase, 1805. e, The Nelson Touch — Band of Brothers. f, The Nelson Touch.

No. 994, $5: a, Nelson and Hardy on deck. b, Nelson sends the signal "England expects." c, Attempted siege of HMS Victory. d, Neptune tows Victory to Gibraltar. e, Funeral procession on Thames. f, Nelson's Column.

No. 995, $10: a, Nelson's early years. b, The letters of Nelson. c, Siege of Calvi — Nelson loses the sight of his eye. d, Santa Cruz de Tenerife — Nelson loses his arm. e, The Battle of Cape St. Vincent. f, The Battle of the Nile.

2005, Jan. 3 ***Perf. 13¼***

Sheets of 6, #a-f

992-995 A191 Set of 4 42.50 42.50

Baha'is in Solomon Islands, 50th Anniv. — A192

Designs: $1.50, Geometric design. $3, Globe, hands, laurel branches. $5, Alvin and Gertrude Blum, horiz.

2005, Mar. 21 **Litho.** ***Perf. 14¼***

996-998 A192 Set of 3 4.00 4.00

End of World War II, 60th Anniv. — A193

No. 999: a, $2.50, Japanese forces land at Tulagi. b, $2.50, USS Lexington under air attack during Battle of the Coral Sea. c, $2.50, Coastwatcher and Solomon Island scouts. d, $2.50, US forces land at Tulagi and Guadalcanal virtually unopposed. e, $2.50, HMAS Canberra sinking at Iron Bottom Sound. f, $5, Cactus Air Force in action over Henderson Airfield. g, $5, "Tokyo Express" nightly bombardments by Japanese warships. h, $5, P-38 Lightnings shoot down Admiral Yamamoto. i, $5, Lt. John F. Kennedy's PT-109 sank after collision with Japanese warship Amagiri. j, $5, Sgt. Maj. Vouza and medals.

No. 1000, RAN coastwatchers sending enemy intelligence reports by teleradio.

2005, Apr. 21 ***Perf. 13¾***

999 A193 Sheet of 10, #a-j 14.50 14.50

Souvenir Sheet

1000 A193 $5 multi 3.00 3.00

Pacific Explorer 2005 World Stamp Expo, Sydney (#1000).

Europa Stamps, 50th Anniv. (in 2006) A194

No. 1001: a, Spain #1262. b, Netherlands #417.

No. 1002: a, Andorra (French) #174. b, Belgium #573.

No. 1003: a, Belgium #496. b, Spain #1567.

No. 1004: a, Austria #657. b, San Marino #701.

No. 1005: a, Netherlands #494. b, Norway #842.

No. 1006: a, Germany #749. b, Italy #750.

2005, May 16 ***Perf. 13½x13¾***

1001	Horiz. pair	1.25	1.25
a.-b.	A194 $1 Either single	.55	.55
c.	Souvenir sheet, #1001	1.25	1.25
1002	Horiz. pair	2.50	2.50
a.-b.	A194 $2.10 Either single	1.10	1.10
c.	Souvenir sheet, #1002	2.50	2.50
1003	Horiz. pair	2.75	2.75
a.-b.	A194 $2.50 Either single	1.25	1.25
c.	Souvenir sheet, #1003	2.75	2.75
1004	Horiz. pair	4.75	4.75
a.-b.	A194 $5 Either single	2.00	2.00
c.	Souvenir sheet, #1004	4.75	4.75
1005	Horiz. pair	9.00	9.00
a.-b.	A194 $10 Either single	4.25	4.25
c.	Souvenir sheet, #1005	9.00	9.00
1006	Horiz. pair	11.00	11.00
a.-b.	A194 $15 Either single	7.50	7.50
c.	Souvenir sheet, #1006	11.00	11.00
	Nos. 1001-1006 (6)	31.25	31.25

Queen Elizabeth II's Royal Year — A195

No. 1007, $1: a, Order of the Garter. b, Trooping the Color.

No. 1008, $2.10: a, Royal Ascot. b, Garden party.

No. 1009, $2.50: a, Royal visits. b, State visits.

No. 1010, $5: a, State Opening of Parliament. b, Remembrance Day.

No. 1011, $10: a, Investitures. b, Christmas broadcast.

No. 1012, $15: a, Maundy service. b, Chelsea Flower Show.

2005, June 3 ***Perf. 14½***

Horiz. Pairs, #a-b

1007-1012 A195 Set of 6 35.00 35.00

A196

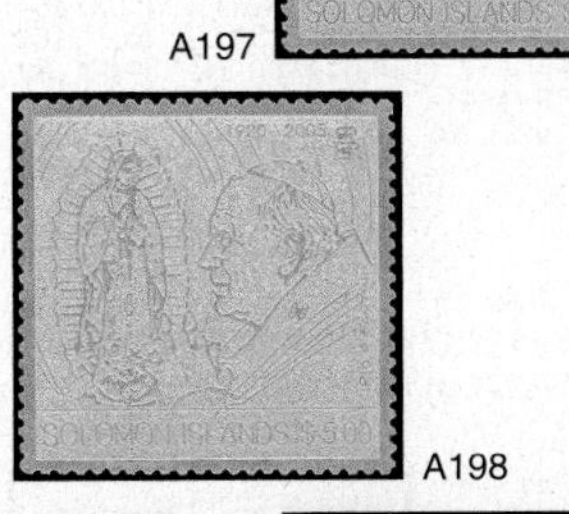

A197

A198

Pope John Paul II (1920-2005) A199

Embossed on Metal

2005, July ***Die Cut Perf. 12½***

Self-Adhesive

1013	A196	$1.20 shown	.70	.70
1014	A196	$1.20 Pope, diff.	.70	.70
1015	A197	$2.60 shown	1.40	1.40
1016	A197	$2.60 Pope, diff.	1.40	1.40
1017	A198	$5 shown	2.75	2.75
1018	A198	$5 Pope, diff.	2.75	2.75
1019	A199	$10 shown	5.75	5.75
1020	A199	$10 Pope, diff.	5.75	5.75
		Nos. 1013-1020 (8)	21.20	21.20

BirdLife International — A200

No. 1021, $2.10: a, Finsch's pygmy parrot. b, Cardinal lory. c, Solomon's cockatoo. d, Eclectus parrot. e, Rainbow lory. f, Song parrot.

No. 1022, $5: a, Red-knobbed imperial pigeon. b, Yellow-bibbed fruit dove. c, Claret-breasted fruit dove. d, Nicobar pigeon. e, Stephan's ground dove. f, Crested cuckoo dove.

No. 1023, $7.50: a, Pied goshawk. b, Imitator sparrowhawk. c, Buff-headed coucal. d, Black-faced pitta. e, Melanesian megapode. f, Blyth's hornbill.

2005, Sept. 1 **Litho.** ***Perf. 14½x14¾***

Sheets of 6, #a-f

1021-1023 A200 Set of 3 32.50 32.50

Rotary International, Cent. — A201

2005, Sept. 12 ***Perf. 14½***

1024 A201 $2.50 multi 1.25 1.25

No. 970 Overprinted

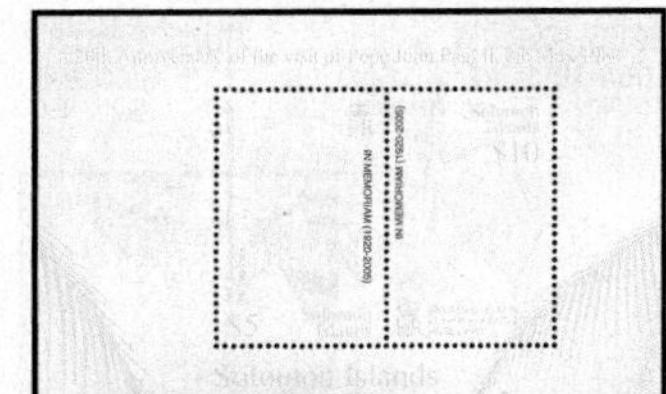

No. 1025: a, $5. b, $10.

2005, Oct. 3 ***Perf. 14***

1025 A183 Sheet of 2, #a-b 5.75 5.75

Christmas — A202

Stories by Hans Christian Andersen (1805-75): $1, The Little Fir Tree. $2.10, The Nightingale. $2.50, The Emperor's New Clothes. $5, The Phoenix. $10, The Tinderbox. $15, The Red Shoes.

2005, Oct. 10

1026-1031 A202 Set of 6 13.00 13.00

Battle of Trafalgar, Bicent. — A203

Designs: $5, HMS Victory. $10, Ship in battle, horiz. $20, Admiral Horatio Nelson.

2005, Oct. 18 ***Perf. 13¼***

1032-1034 A203 Set of 3 17.00 17.00

Worldwide Fund for Nature (WWF) — A204

Various views of prehensile-tailed skink: $1.50, $2.60, $3, $10.

2005, Dec. 7 ***Perf. 14½***

1035-1038 A204 Set of 4 5.25 5.25

1038a Sheet, 2 each # 1035-1038 11.50 11.50

Queen Elizabeth II, 80th Birthday A205

Queen Elizabeth II: $2.10, As young girl. $2.50, As woman. $5, Holding camera. $20, Wearing red hat.

No. 1043: a, $10, Like $2.50. b, $15, Like $5.

2006, Apr. 21 **Litho.** ***Perf. 14***

Stamps With White Frames

1039-1042 A205 Set of 4 10.00 10.00

Souvenir Sheet

Stamps Without Frames

1043 A205 Sheet of 2, #a-b 9.50 9.50

Anniversaries — A206

No. 1044, $2.20: a, Great Eastern. b, Isambard Kingdom Brunel (1806-59), engineer.

No. 1045, $2.50: a, Charles Darwin. b, Green turtle.

No. 1046, $5: a, Diving bell. b, Edmond Halley (1656-1742), astronomer.

No. 1047, $10: a, Locomotive "Rocket." b, George Stephenson (1781-1848), inventor.

2006, Apr. 30 ***Perf. 14¾x14½***

Horiz. Pairs, #a-b

1044-1047 A206 Set of 4 22.50 22.50

Darwin's voyage on the Beagle, 175th anniv. (#1045).

Christopher Columbus (1451-1506), Explorer — A207

Designs: $1.90, Niña. $2.20, Pinta. $2.60, Santa Maria. $10, Arms of Columbus. $20, Columbus.

2006, May 22 ***Perf. 13¼x13***
1048-1051 A207 Set of 4 9.50 9.50

Souvenir Sheet

1051A A207 $20 multi 10.00 10.00

Washington 2006 World Philatelic Exhibition.

2006 World Cup Soccer Championships, Germany — A208

Match scenes from: $4, 1954 West Germany finals victory. $5, 1966 England finals victory. $10, 1998 France finals victory. $20, 2006 Solomon Islands vs. Australia playoff.

2006, June 9 ***Perf. 14***
1052-1055 A208 Set of 4 11.00 11.00

Victoria Cross, 150th Anniv. A209

Victoria Cross and: $1, Captured Russian gun used to cast the Victoria Cross. $2.20, Midshipman Charles Lucas, first recipient of Victoria Cross. $2.50, Queen Victoria awarding first Victoria Crosses. $5, Corporal Sukanaivalu, Fijian infantryman at Bougainville, 1944. $10, Corporal Rattey, Australian infantryman at Bougainville, 1945. $15, Private Partridge, Australian infantryman at Bougainville, 1945.

2006, June 26 ***Perf. 14x14½***
1056-1061 A209 Set of 6 15.00 15.00

Prehistoric Animals — A210

Designs: 5c, Baryonyx. 10c, Diplodocus. $1.50, Pteranodon. $2.15, Argentinosaurus. $2.40, Centrosaurus. $3, Allosaurus. $10, Ankylosaurus. $20, Iguanodon.

2006, Aug. 14 ***Perf. 13¼x13¾***
1062-1069 A210 Set of 8 17.00 17.00

Intl. Coconut Day — A210a

Designs: $1.50, First grade copra drier. $2.40, Standard copra drier. $3, Coconut oil expeller. $5, Coconuts, palm tree, ship, truck on dock, bird.

2006, Sept. 2 **Litho.** ***Perf. 14¼***
1069A-1069D A210a Set of 4 5.00 5.00

Cone Shells — A211

Designs: 5c, Conus marmoreus. 10c, Conus auratinus. 20c, Conus ferrugineus. 50c, Conus consors. 80c, Conus magdalenae. 90c, Conus sulcatus brettinghami. $1, Conus tmetus. $1.50, Conus aureus. $2, Conus corallinus. $3, Conus floccatus. $4, Conus punniculus. $10, Conus pohlianus. $20, Conus proximus. $50, Conus canonicus.

2006, Oct. 31 ***Perf. 13x12½***

1070	A211	5c	multi	.25	*.30*
1071	A211	10c	multi	.25	*.30*
1072	A211	20c	multi	.25	*.30*
1073	A211	50c	multi	.40	.25
1074	A211	80c	multi	.30	.25
1075	A211	90c	multi	.50	.30
1076	A211	$1	multi	.75	.40
1077	A211	$1.50	multi	.90	.60
1078	A211	$2	multi	1.00	.75
1079	A211	$3	multi	1.00	1.25
1080	A211	$4	multi	1.25	1.75
1081	A211	$10	multi	3.50	3.50
1082	A211	$20	multi	6.75	6.75
1083	A211	$50	multi	17.50	17.50
	Nos. 1070-1083 (14)			34.60	34.20

Tales of Beatrix Potter — A212

Designs: $1.50, The Tale of Peter Rabbit. $1.90, The Tale of Squirrel Nutkin. $2.15, The Tailor of Gloucester. $2.40, The Tale of Benjamin Bunny. $2.65, The Tale of Two Bad Mice. $5, The Tale of Mrs. Tiggy-Winkle.

2006, Dec. 4 ***Perf. 13x13½***
1084-1089 A212 Set of 6 8.00 8.00
1089a Miniature sheet, #1084-1089 8.00 8.00

Wedding of Queen Elizabeth II and Prince Philip, 60th Anniv. — A213

Designs: $2.10, Couple looking straight ahead. $2.50, Couple looking at each other. $5, Wedding ceremony. No. 1093, $20, Elizabeth with flowers.
No. 1094, $20, Wedding party.

2007, Jan. 31 ***Perf. 13¾***
1090-1093 A213 Set of 4 11.00 11.00

Souvenir Sheet

Perf. 14

1094 A213 $20 multi 7.00 7.00

No. 1094 contains one 42x56mm stamp.

No. 867 Overprinted "1997-2007" in Metallic Blue

Method, Perf. and Watermark As Before

2007, Aug. 3
1095 CD355 $2.50 Sheet of 4, #a-d 3.00 3.00

No. 1095 sold for $10.50 and is additionally overprinted "10th Anniversary / in Memorium" in sheet margin at upper left and upper right.

Princess Diana (1961-97) A214

Various photographs of Princess Diana: $2.10, $2.50, $5, $20.

Perf. 13x12½

2007, Dec. 8 **Litho.** **Unwmk.**
1096-1099 A214 Set of 4 8.25 8.25

A215

Royal Air Force, 90th Anniv. — A216

Designs: No. 1100, $4, Sir Hugh Trenchard (1873-1956), founder of Royal Air Force. No. 1101, $4, Wing Commander Guy Gibson (1918-44), leader of Dambusters raid. No. 1102, $4, Sir Charles Portal (1893-1971), Marshal. No. 1103, $4, Sir William Sholto Douglas (1893-1969), Marshal. No. 1104, $4, Sir Hugh Dowding (1882-1970), Marshal.
$20, Battle of Britain.

Perf. 14¼x14

2008, Apr. 30 **Wmk. 373**
1100-1104 A215 Set of 5 10.00 10.00

Souvenir Sheet

1105 A216 $20 multi 7.00 7.00

British Monarchs — A217

Designs: No. 1106, $2, William I (1027-87). No. 1107, $2, Henry II (1133-89). No. 1108, $2, Henry IV (1366-1413). No. 1109, $2, Henry VI (1421-71). No. 1110, $2, Richard III (1452-1485). No. 1111, $2, Elizabeth I (1533-1603). No. 1112, $2, James I (1566-1625). No. 1113, $2, Edward VII (1841-1910).

Perf. 13x12½

2008, July 15 **Unwmk.**
1106-1113 A217 Set of 8 7.75 7.75

See Nos. 1122-1129, 1142-1149.

2008 Summer Olympics, Beijing A218

Designs: $2.15, Field hockey, bamboo. $3, Pole vault, dragon. $4, Table tennis, lantern. $5, Runner, fish.

2008, Aug. 8 ***Perf. 13¼***
1114-1117 A218 Set of 4 4.25 4.25

Police A219

Inscriptions: $1.90, Restoration of law and order. $2.15, Freedom of movement. $2.40, Children relaxing. $2.65, Community policing, vert.

2008, Aug. 20 ***Perf. 13¾***
1118-1121 A219 Set of 4 6.00 6.00

British Monarchs Type of 2008

Designs: No. 1122, $2, William II (c. 1056-1100). No. 1123, $2, Richard I (1157-99). No. 1124, $2, Edward III (1312-77). No. 1125, $2, Edward IV (1442-83). No. 1126, $2, Henry VIII (1491-1547). No. 1127, $2, Charles I (1600-49). No. 1128, $2, George I (1660-1727). No. 1129, $2, George V (1865-1936).

Perf. 13x12½

2009, Apr. 21 **Litho.** **Unwmk.**
1122-1129 A217 Set of 8 8.00 8.00

Nos. 1122-1129 each were printed in sheets of 8 + central label.

Ships A220

Alvaro de Mendaña de Neira (1541-95), Discoverer of Solomon Islands — A221

Designs: $3, Discovery. $4, HMS Bounty. $5, Mayflower. $6, USS North Carolina. $10, Boussole and Astrolabe. $20, USS Saratoga.

2009, May 25 **Wmk. 406** ***Perf. 14***
1130-1135 A220 Set of 6 16.00 16.00

Souvenir Sheet

1136 A221 $15 multi 5.25 5.25

Naval Aviation, Cent. A222

Designs: $2, Grumman Hellcat. $2.50, Blackburn Skua. $3.50, Fairey Albacore. $10, Gloster Sea Gladiator.
$20, Short 184 Seaplane.

2009, June 25
1137-1140 A222 Set of 4 10.00 10.00

Souvenir Sheet

1141 A222 $20 multi 7.50 7.50

Nos. 1137-1140 each were printed in sheets of 8 + central label.

British Monarchs Type of 2008

Designs: No. 1142, $2, Henry I (1068-1135). No. 1143, $2, John (1167-1216). No. 1144, $2, Richard II (1367-1400). No. 1145, $2, Edward V (1470-83). No. 1146, $2, Edward VI (1537-53). No. 1147, $2, Charles II (1630-85). No. 1148, $2, George III (1738-1820). No. 1149, $2, George VI (1895-1952).

Perf. 13x12½

2010, Apr. 14 Litho. Unwmk.

1142-1149 A217 Set of 8 10.00 10.00

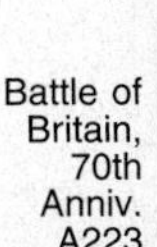

Battle of Britain, 70th Anniv. A223

Various aircraft: $1.50, $1.90, $2.20, $2.65, $10, $15.

$20, Sir Douglas Bader (1910-82) ace fighter pilot, vert.

Perf. 12¾x13

2010, Apr. 14 Litho. Wmk. 406

1150-1155 A223 Set of 6 8.50 8.50

Souvenir Sheet

Perf. 12¾x13

1156 A223 $20 multi 11.50 11.50

Vegetables

Designs: $1.50, Yard beans. $1.90, Tomatoes (35x35mm). $2.20, Eggplant. $3, Pumpkin (35x35mm).

Perf. 13½x13¾, 13¼ (#1158, 1160)

2010, June 30 Litho. Wmk. 388

1157-1160 A224 Set of 4 2.25 2.25

Orchids — A225

No. 1161: a, $2.60, Calanthe triplicata. b, $2.60, Dendrobium johnsoniae. c, $2.60, Dendrobium capituliflorum. d, $2.60, Spathoglottis plicata. e, $2.60, Dendrobium mirbelianum. f, $5, Dendrobium polysema. g, $5, Paphiopedilum bougainvilleanum. h, $5, Coelogyne asperata. i, $5, Dendrobium macrophyllum. j, $5, Dendrobium spectabile.

Perf. 13½

2010, Aug. 4 Litho. Unwmk.

1161 A225 Block of 10, #a-j 9.75 9.75

Miniature Sheet

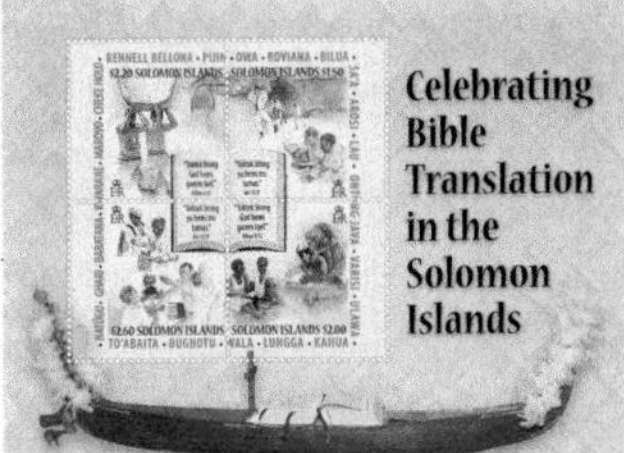

Bible Translation in the Solomon Islands — A226

No. 1162 — Various Solomon Islanders and Bible passage in native language in: a, $1.50, LL. b, $2, UL. c, $2.20, LR. d, $2.60, UR.

Wmk. 388

2010, Sept. 2 Litho. *Perf. 13¼*

1162 A226 Sheet of 4, #a-d 2.25 2.25

Wedding of Prince William and Catherine Middleton — A227

No. 1163: a, Couple, hand visible, "L" in "Islands" over pale yellow background. b, Couple, hand not visible, first "S" in "Islands" over pale yellow background. c, As "a," "L" in "Islands" over gray background. d, As "b," first "S" in "Islands" over gray background.

No. 1164: a, Prince William. b, Catherine Middleton.

Perf. 13 Syncopated

2011, May 15 Litho. Unwmk.

1163 A227 $7.50 Sheet of 4, #a-d 7.75 7.75

Souvenir Sheet

1164 A227 $15 Sheet of 2, #a-b 7.75 7.75

Miniature Sheets

A228

No. 1165 — Two images of Marilyn Monroe (1926-62), actress: a, $9, Wearing fur coat and hat, wearing yellow dress. b, $9, Kneeling on couch, with bare shoulders. c, $9, Wearing gown with thin straps, wearing pink dress and gloves. d, $9, Playing with hair, wearing black dress. e, $27, With hands near mouth, with man.

No. 1166 — 60th anniv. of reign of Queen Elizabeth II, with Queen: a, $9, With Nelson Mandela. b, $9, Trooping the Color. c, $9, In State Coach, 2002. d, $9, With royal family, 1983. e, $27, With Duke and Duchess of Cambridge.

No. 1167 — British royalty: a, $9, Princess Diana. b, $9, Prince Harry. c, $9, Duke and Duchess of Cambridge, child sitting in chair at left. d, $9, Duke and Duchess of Cambridge, with boy standing. e, $27, Princess Diana, diff.

No. 1168 — Bishop Desmond Tutu: a, $9, With South African Truth and Reconciliation Commission. b, $9, With Dalai Lama. c, $9, Embracing 1986 Nobel Peace Prize recipient Wole Soyinka. d, $9, With Mahatma Gandhi. e, $27, Receiving Presidential Medal of Freedom from Pres. Barack Obama.

No. 1169 — Solomon Islands Cathedrals: a, $9, Holy Cross Cathedral, Honaira, Pope John Paul II. b, $9, St. Peter's Cathedral, Gizo, Pope Benedict XVI. c, $9, Anglican St. Barnabas Provincial Cathedral, Honaira. d, $9, Anglican St. Barnabas Provincial Cathedral, Archbishop of Canterbury Rowan Williams and Pope Benedict XVI. e, $27, St. Augustine Cathedral, Auki, Pope John Paul II.

No. 1170 — Maritime history: a, $9, Two Solomon Islands canoes. b, $9, One Solomon Islands canoe. c, $9, Galleon. d, $9, Spanish galleon. e, $27, Alvaro de Mendaña de Neyra (1542-95), discoverer of Solomon Islands.

No. 1171 — Sinking of the Titanic, cent.: a, $9, Titanic hitting iceberg. b, $9, Titanic sinking, lifeboats in water. c, $9, Titanic wreckage underwater. d, $9, Submarine near Titanic wreckage. e, $27, Titanic sinking, lifeboats in water, diff.

No. 1172 — Lighthouses of Oceania and birds: a, $9, Kaipara North Head Lighthouse, New Zealand, Chlidonias albostriatus. b, $9, Cape Liptrap Lighthouse, Australia, Chroicocephalus scopulinus. c, $9, Maatsuyker Island Lighthouse, Australia, Chroicocephalus novaehollandiae. d, $9, Cape Campbell Lighthouse, New Zealand, Sterna anaethetus. e, $27, Cape Reinga Lighthouse, New Zealand, Gelochelidon nilotica.

No. 1173 — Solomon Islands volcanoes and minerals: a, $9, Simbo Island, Cerussite. b, $9, Kavachi, Mimetite with wulfenite. c, $9, Tinakula, Smithsonite. d, $9, Kana Keoki, Tsumcorite. e, $27, Tinakula, Mimetite with smithsonite.

No. 1174 — Lapita pottery and shells: a, $9, Pottery fragment, 1000 B.C., Trochus niloticus. b, $9, 3,000 year-old pottery shard, Conus gloriamus. c, $9, Pottery fragments, 1000 B.C., Lycina aurantium. d, $9, Shard of Lapita pottery with dentate stamping, Nautilus pompilius. e, $27, Lapita pottery ornament, Murex pecten.

No. 1175 — U.S. Medal of Honor and its recipients in Battle of Guadalcanal: a, $9, Lieutenant Colonel Harold William Bauer (1908-42). b, $9, First Lieutenant Jefferson Joseph DeBlanc (1921-2007). c, $9, Colonel Mitchell Paige (1918-2003). d, $9, Gunnery Sergeant John Basilone (1916-45). e, $27, General Alexander Archer Vandegrift (1887-1973).

No. 1176 — 2012 Summer Olympics, London: a, $9, Discus. b, $9, Judo. c, $9, Track cycling. d, $9, Running. e, $27, Rowing.

No. 1177 — Bats: a, $9, Myotis adversus, denomination in black. b, $9, Pipistrellus angulatus. c, $9, Myotis adversus, denomination in white. d, $9, Pteropus admiralitatum. e, $27, Saccolaimus saccolaimus.

No. 1178 — Dolphins: a, $9, Stenella longirostris. b, $9, Tursiops truncatus. c, $9, Stenella coruleoalba. d, $9, Sousa chinensis. e, $27, Stenella attenuata.

No. 1179 — Whales: a, $9, Two Balaenoptera edeni, name of animal at left. b, $9, Megaptera novaeangliae. c, $9, Mesoplodon densirostris. d, $9, Balaenoptera edeni, name of animal at LL. e, $27, Balaenoptera edeni, name of animal at R.

No. 1180 — Birds: a, $9, Rhipidura leucophrys. b, $9, Myzomela cardinalis. c, $9, Cinnyris jugularis. d, $9, Rhipidura rufifrons. e, $27, Pachycephala pectoralis.

No. 1181 — Birds of prey: a, $9, Aviceda subcristata. b, $9, Haliastur indus. c, $9, Haliastur sphenurus. d, $9, Haliaeetus leucogaster. e, $27, Circus approximans.

No. 1182 — Owls: a, $9, Two Tyto alba. b, $9, One Tyto alba. c, $9, Ninox jacquinoti. d, $9, Nesasio solomonensis. e, $27, Two Tyto alba, diff.

No. 1183 — Butterflies: a, $9, Papilio toboroi. b, $9, Ornithoptera victoriae. c, $9, Vindula sapor. d, $9, Graphium hicetaon. e, $27, Papilio aegeus aegeus.

No. 1184 — Reef fish: a, $9, Chaetodon meyeri. b, $9, Chaetodon ephippium. c, $9, Acanthurus lineatus. d, $9, Chaetodon ocellicaudus. e, $27, Heniochus acuminatus.

No. 1185 — Reptiles and amphibians: a, $9, Acrochordus granulatus. b, $9, Crocodylus porosus. c, $9, Corucia zebrata. d, $9, Ceratobatrachus guentheri. e, $27, Cyrtodactylus biordinis.

No. 1186 — Turtles: a, $9, Chelonia mydas. b, $9, Eretmochelys imbricata. c, $9, Caretta caretta. d, $9, Lepidochelys olivacea. e, $27, Dermochelys cariacea.

No. 1187 — Dinosaurs: a, $9, Dimorphodon. b, $9, Kentrosaurus. c, $9, Spinosaurus. d, $9, Liopleurodon. e, $27, Tyrannosaurus rex.

No. 1188 — Orchids: a, $9, Laelia harpophylla. b, $9, Cypripedium parviflorum. c, $9, Chysis bractescens. d, $9, Laelia anceps. e, $27, Cypripedium pubescens.

2012, June 5 Litho. *Perf. 13¼*

Sheets of 5, #a-e

1165-1188 A228 Set of 24 435.00 435.00

A229

A230

A231

Worldwide Fund for Nature (WWF) A232

Perf. 13x13¼

2013, Feb. 15 Litho. Unwmk.

1189	Horiz. strip of 4	8.00	8.00
a.	A229 $7 multi	2.00	2.00
b.	A230 $7 multi	2.00	2.00
c.	A231 $7 multi	2.00	2.00
d.	A232 $7 multi	2.00	2.00
e.	Sheet of 8, 2 each #1189a-1189d, + 2 labels	16.00	16.00

Souvenir Sheet

Perf. 12¾x13¼

1190 A232 $35 Cacatua ducorpsii, diff. 9.75 9.75

No. 1190 contains one 50x39mm stamp lacking the WWF emblem.

A233

No. 1191, $5 — Dogs: a, Australian terrier. b, Australian silky terrier. c, Tenterfield terrier. d, Australian stumpy tail cattle dog.

No. 1192, $5 — Marine life of the Solomon Islands: a, Grampus griseus. b, Stenella attenuata. c, Megaptera novaeangliae. d, Dugong dugon.

No. 1193, $5 — Corals: a, Acanthastrea lordhowensis. b, Platygyra daedalea. c, Alveopora tizardi. d, Acropora florida.

No. 1194, $5 — Corals: a, Dendrophthya sp. b, Sinularia sp. c, Acropora latistella. d, Kalypilidion sp.

No. 1195, $5 — Brids of the Solomon Islands: a, Ptiloris paradiseus. b, Caloenas nicobarica. c, Ptilinopus richardsii. d, Cacomantis variolosus.

No. 1196, $5 — Birds of the Solomon Islands: a, Ardea modesta. b, Ptilinopus superbus. c, Vini australis. d, Cacomantis flabelliformis.

No. 1197, $5 — Second Vatican Council, 50th anniv.: a, Pope John Paul II, *The Immaculate Conception,* by Giovanni Battista Tiepolo. b, Pope Paul VI, statue of St. Dominic, by Pierre Le Gros, the Younger. c, Pope John Paul I, *The Transfiguration,* by Raphael. d, Pope John XXIII and angel with flower.

No. 1198, $5 — Paintings by Edouard Manet (1832-83): a, Suicide. b, Mlle. Victorine in the Costume of a Matador. c, Young Lady. d, Portrait of Julie Manet.

No. 1199, $6 — Paintings by Peter Paul Rubens (1577-1640): a, Deborah Kip and Her Children. b, The Head of Medusa. c, Self-portrait in a Circle of Friends from Mantua. d, Battle of the Amazons.

No. 1200, $6 — History of chess: a, 2008 match between Viswanathan Anand and Vladimir Kramnik. b, Champion players José Raul Capablanca, Emanuel Lasker and Wilhelm Steinitz. c, Champion players Anatoly Karpov and Garry Kasparov. d, Luis Ramírez de Lucena, page from *Repetition of Love and the Art of Playing Chess.*

No. 1201, $6 — Rugby players in the Solomon Islands: a, Dominque Peyroux and another player. b, Gerard Ian Tema and teammates. c, Jardine Bobongie. d, Radike Samo and children.

No. 1202, $6 — Cruise ships: a, Freedom of the Seas. b, Carnival Magic. c, MSC Splendida. d, RMS Queen Mary 2.

No. 1203, $6 — National traditions of the Solomon Islands: a, Canoe prow carving and ornament of male figure with raised arms. b, Breastplate and kap kap. c, Pan pipers. d, Maskmen.

No. 1204, $6 — Spaceflight of Friendship 7, 50th anniv: a, Two images of John Glenn in space helmet. b, Glenn and Friendship 7 in space. c, Glenn near entrance of Friendship 7 capsule. d, Glenn and launch of Friendship 7.

No. 1205, $6, vert. — Mushrooms: a, Trametes versicolor. b, Coprinopsis atramentaria. c, Amanita rubescens. d, Phellodon confluens.

No. 1206, $6, vert. — Princess Diana (1961-97): a, With her children. b, Greeting children of Nepal. c, Visiting Zimbabwe. d, Wearing pink jacket and hat, wearing jacket and tie in background.

No. 1207, $7 — Launch of Sputnik 1, 55th anniv.: a, Antenna behind "$7." b, Antenna above "$7." c, Antennae at left. d, RMS Antenna under final "0" in denomination.

No. 1208, $7 — Cats: a, Manx. b, Bambino. c, Bengal. d, Sphynx.

No. 1209, $7 — Soccer players: a, One player. b, Two players trying to head ball. c, Player dribbling ball near opponent. d, Player attempting kick against sliding tackle.

No. 1210, $7 — Asia-Pacific Scout Region: a, Adult leader showing snake to Scouts. b,

Scouts planting seedling. c, Scouts and tent. d, Scouts carrying injured person on litter.

No. 1211, $7 — Steam locomotives: a, KC Class. b, Cambrian Coast Express. c, Duchess of Hamilton. d, Flying Scotsman.

No. 1212, $7 — Fish: a, Cetoscarus bicolor. b, Sargocentron spiniferum. c, Arothron nigropunctatus. d, Pseudanthias huchtii.

No. 1213, $7, vert. — Rotary International in the Solomon Islands: a, Matching grant projects (children holding banner). b, Malaria control program. c, Devastating tsunami fund support. d, Matching grant projects (child holding pencil).

No. 1214, $24, Australian kelpie. No. 1215, $24, Phyllomedusa sauvagii. No. 1216, $24, Stylaster californicus. No. 1217, $24, Sebae anemone and anemonefish. No. 1218, $24, Pachycephala pectoralis. No. 1219, $24, Caloenas nicobarica, diff. No. 1220, $24, Pope Benedict XVI, statue of St. Peter, vert. No. 1221, $24, At Father Lathuille, by Manet. No. 1222, $28, Night Scene, by Rubens. No. 1223, $28, Louis-Charles Mahé de La Bourdonnais, Marguerite d'Alençon and Brother Francis of Angouleme playing chess. No. 1224, $28, Mai Meninga, rugby player. No. 1225, $28, Norwegian Epic, vert. No. 1226, $28, Bamboo bang. No. 1227, $28, Glenn and cutaway view of Friendship 7. No. 1228, $28, Agaricus dulcidulus, Hydnellum concrescens. No. 1229, $28, Princess Diana, diff., vert. No. 1230, $35, Valentina Tereshkova, first woman in space, and medal. No. 1231, $35, Devon Rex cats. No. 1232, $35, Three soccer players. No. 1233, $35, Scout holding plant, Scouts in canoe. No. 1234, $35, LMS Princess Coronation Class 6229 Duchess of Hamilton. No. 1235, $35, Amphiprion percula. No. 1236, $35, Rotary matching grant projects, diff.

2013, Feb. 15 Litho. *Perf. 13¼*

Sheets of 4, #a-d

1191-1213 A233 Set of 23 150.00 150.00

Souvenir Sheets

1214-1236 A233 Set of 23 185.00 185.00

Dated 2012.

Paintings — A234

No. 1237, $7 — Paintings by Frédéric Bazille (1841-70): a, Queens Gate at Aigues-Mortes. b, The Improvised Field Hospital. c, Still Life with Fish. d, Studio from Rue de la Condamine.

No. 1238, $7 — Paintings by Emile Bernard (1868-1941): a, Buckwheat Harvesters. b, Young Girl on a Hill. c, Portrait of Bernard's Grandmother. d, Still Life with Flowers.

No. 1239, $7 — Paintings by Pierre Bonnard (1867-1947): a, Trouville, the Exit to the Port. b, The Port of Cannes. c, The Luncheon. d, The Terrace at Vernonnet.

No. 1240, $7 — Paintings by Gustave Caillebotte (1848-94): a, The House Painters. b, Roofs Under Snow. c, Boulevard Haussmann Snow. d, Woman at a Dressing Table.

No. 1241, $7 — Paintings by Mary Cassatt (1844-1926): a, Mother Combing Her Child's Hair. b, Portrait of a Yound Woman. c, Children Playing with a Cat. d, Girl with a Banjo.

No. 1242, $7 — Paintings by Paul Cézanne (1839-1906): a, Still Life with Drapery, Pitcher and Fruit Bowl (inscribed Jas de Bouffan). b, Château Noir. c, The Pool (Jas de Bouffan). d, The Card Players.

No. 1243, $7 — Paintings by Henri Edmond Cross (1856-1910): a, Canal de la Guidecca, Venice. b, Cape Layet, Provence. c, Bathers. d, Fishermen.

No. 1244, $7 — Paintings by Edgar Degas (1834-1917): a, Seated Dancer. b, Dance Class at the Opera. c, The Dancing Class. d, Dancer Fastening Her Pump.

No. 1245, $7 — Paintings by Paul Gauguin (1848-1903): a, Parahi Te Marae Aka (There Lies the Temple). b, The Siesta. c, Still Life with Teapot and Fruit. d, Nave Nave Moe Aka (Delightful Drowsiness).

No. 1246, $7 — Paintings by Armand Guillaumin (1841-1927): a, Sunset at Ivry. b, Echo Rock. c, Moret. d, Winter in Saint Sauves.

No. 1247, $7 — Paintings by Georges Lemmen (1865-1916): a, Beach at Heyst. b, Young Woman Sewing. c, Family Gathering at Saint Idesbald. d, River Scene.

No. 1248, $7 — Paintings by Edouard Manet (1832-83): a, Rue Mosnier with Flags. b, The Grand Canal, Venice. c, Boating. d, The Suicide.

No. 1249, $7 — Paintings by Claude Monet (1840-1926): a, The Rose Way in Giverny. b, On the Bank of the Seine, Bennecourt. c, Jean Monet on His Hobby Horse. d, Red Boats at Argenteuil.

No. 1250, $7 — Paintings by Berthe Morisot (1841-95): a, On the Lake in the Bois de Boulogne. b, Paule Gobillard Painting. c, Refuge in Normandy (inscribed Paule Gobillard). d, Children at the Basin.

No. 1251, $7 — Paintings by Camille Pissarro (1830-1903): a, A Street in Pontoise. b, Gelee Blanche (Hoarfrost). c, Little Goose Girl. d, Haymakers Resting.

No. 1252, $7 — Paintings by Pierre-Auguste Renoir (1841-1919): a, Pont Neuf. b, Sailboats at Argenteuil. c, Apples in a Dish. d, The Piazza San Marco, Venice.

No. 1253, $7 — Paintings by Paul Sérusier (1864-1927): a, Breton Women, the Meeting in the Sacred Grove. b, Still Life with Violets. c, Embroiderer in a Landscape of Chateauneuf. d, Daughters of Pelichtim.

No. 1254, $7 — Paintings by Georges Seurat (1859-91): a, Sunday Afternoon on the Island of La Grande Jatte. b, La Maria, Honfleur. c, Bridge at Courbevoie. d, Bathers at Asnieres.

No. 1255, $7 — Paintings by Paul Signac (1863-1935): a, Riverbank, Les Andelys. b, La Corne d'Or, Les Minarets. c, Sunday. d, Women at the Well.

No. 1256, $7 — Paintings by Alfred Sisley (1839-99): a, Provencher's Mill at Moret. b, The Saint-Martin Canal. c, Fete Day at Marly-le-Roi. d, Moret sur Loing: the Porte de Bourgogne.

No. 1257, $7 — Paintings by Henri de Toulouse-Lautrec (1864-1901): a, Seated Dancer in Pink Tights. b, Portrait of Miss Dolly. c, Two Friends. d, In the Restaurant La Mie.

No. 1258, $7 — Paintings by Felix Vallotton (1865-1925): a, Evening on the Loire. b, Woman Doing Her Hair. c, Interior. d, A Vallon Landscape.

No. 1259, $7 — Paintings by Vincent van Gogh (1853-90): a, Sower with the Setting Sun. b, Starry Night Over the Rhone. c, Bedroom in Arles. d, The Night Cafe

No. 1260, $7 — Paintings by Theo van Rysselberghe (1862-1926): a, Madame Theo van Rysselberghe and Her Daughter. b, The Violinist. c, Girl in Green. d, Madame Van de Velde and Her Children.

No. 1261, $35, Two Herrings, by Bazille. No. 1262, $35, Self-portrait, by Bernard. No. 1263, $35, Self-portrait, by Bonnard. No. 1264, $35, Le Pont de l'Europe, by Caillebotte. No. 1265, $35, Breakfast in Bed, by Cassatt. No. 1266, $35, The Bathers, by Cézanne. No. 1267, $35, A Venetian Canal, by Cross, vert. No. 1268, $35, The Star (Dancer on Stage), by Degas, vert. No. 1269, $35, The Wave, by Gauguin. No. 1270, $35, Rocks on the Coast of Agay, by Guillaumin. No. 1271, $35, Beach at Heist, by Lemmen. No. 1272, $35, Young Woman Reclining in Spanish Costume, by Manet. No. 1273, $35, Camille Monet on a Garden Bench, by Monet, vert. No. 1274, $35, At the Ball, by Morisot. No. 1275, $35, The Boulevard Montmartre on a Winter Morning, by Pissarro. No. 1276, $35, Jean Drawing, by Renoir. No. 1277, $35, Portrait of Paul Ranson in Nabi Costume, by Sérusier, vert. No. 1278, $35, The Circus, by Seurat. No. 1279, $35, Place des Lices, Saint-Tropez, by Signac. No. 1280, $35, The Machine at Marly, by Sisley, vert. No. 1281, $35, Yvette Guilbert Singing "Linger, Longer, Loo," by Toulouse-Lautrec, vert. No. 1282, $35, First Rays, by Vallotton. No. 1283, $35, Vase with Twelve Sunflowers, by van Gogh, vert. No. 1284, $35, Berthe Signac, by van Rysselberghe.

2013, Mar. 29 Litho. *Perf. 13¼*

Sheets of 4, #a-d

1237-1260 A234 Set of 24 185.00 185.00

Souvenir Sheets

1261-1284 A234 Set of 24 230.00 230.00

A235

No. 1285, $7 — Chiang Kai-shek (1887-1975), Leader of Republic of China: a, On horseback, waving. b, Wearing military uniform with medals. c, Looking right. d, Looking left.

No. 1286, $7 — Mother Teresa (1910-97), 1979 Nobel Peace Laureate: a, Denomination in black at LR. b, With Pope John Paul II. c, Holding child at left. d, In prayer.

No. 1287, $7 — Tenzin Gyatso, 14th Dalai Lama, 1989 Nobel Peace Laureate: a, Taipei buildings in background. b, Crowd in background. c, At ceremony to comfort typhoon victims. d, Liberty Square Gate, Taipei, in background.

No. 1288, $7 — British monarchs: a, King George III (1738-1820). b, Queen Anne (1665-1714). c, Queen Victoria (1819-1901). d, King George V (1865-1936).

No. 1289, $7 — Minerals: a, Prehnite with epidote, Nelson Mandela (1918-13), President of South Africa. b, Liddicoatite tourmaline, Mandela in suit. c, Liddicoatite and tourmaline. d, Amethyst, Mandela and wife, Graca Machel.

No. 1290, $7 — Golfers: a, Frank Nobilo. b, Richard Green. c, Aaron Baddeley. d, Michael Campbell.

No. 1291, $7 — English castles and country houses: a, Lowther Castle. b, Cholmondeley Castle. c, Haddon Hall. d, Hutton in the Forest.

No. 1292, $7 — Australian fire engines: a, Scania 93M fire engine. b, Isuzu 34CO fire tanker. c, Isuzu BLD light pumper. d, Hino Lexton fire appliance.

No. 1293, $7 — Australian animals and stamps: a, Macrotis lagotis, Australia #3536. b, Macropus rufus, Australia #3534. c, Petaurus breviceps, Australia #3532. d, Canis lupus dingo, Australia #3533.

No. 1294, $7 — Frogs: a, Mixophyes fleayi. b, Mixophyes iteratus. c, Palmatorappia solomonis. d, Phrynosoma.

No. 1295, $7 — New Year 2013 (Year of the Snake): a, Purple snake, denomination in black. b, Green snake. c, Brown snake. d, Brown violet snake, denomination in white.

No. 1296, $7 — Crabs (diamond-shaped stamps): a, Ocypode ceratophthalmus. b, Lissocarcinus orbicularis. c, Dardanus megistos. d, Uca tetragonon.

No. 1297, $20, Chiang Kai-shek wearing cap. No. 1298, $20, Mother Teresa and Pope John Paul II, diff. No. 1299, $20, Dalai Lama, diff. No. 1300, $20, Queen Elizabeth II. No. 1301, $20, Vanadinite and bust of Mandela. No. 1302, $20, Adam Scott, golfer. No. 1303, $20, Mulgrave Castle. No. 1304, $20, Hino Sur Fire tanker. No. 1305, $20, Phascolarctos cinereus, Australia #3535. No. 1306, $20, Ceratophrys stolzmanni. No. 1307, $20, Snake and yin-yang. No. 1308, $20, Percnon planissimum (diamond-shaped).

2013, May 3 Litho. *Perf. 13¼*

Sheets of 4, #a-d

1285-1296 A235 Set of 12 92.50 92.50

Souvenir Sheets

1297-1308 A235 Set of 12 67.50 67.50

Miniature Sheets

A236

Visit of Duke and Duchess of Cambridge to Pacific Islands — A237

A238

Visit of Duke and Duchess of Cambridge to Solomon Islands — A239

No. 1309: a, Duchess of Cambridge wearing flower garland on head in Funafuti, Tuvalu. b, Duchess receiving gift from child in Honiara. c, Duke of Cambridge in Tavanipupu. d, Duke and Duchess drinking from coconuts. e, Duke and Duchess with Solomon Island natives, Honiara. f, Duchess watching Duke holding large knife and coconut. g, Duchess without flower garland in Funafuti. h, Duke and Duchess in Tavanipupu. i, Duke wearing flower garland in Tavanipupu.

No. 1310: a, Duke and Duchess wearing leis, Honiara. b, Duke and Duchess in Honiara, diff. c, Duke and Duchess in Honiara, diff. d, Duchess wearing flower garland on head, Honiara. e, Duke and Duchess dancing, Funafuti. f, Duchess and Solomon Islander, Honiara. g, Duke and Duchess, palanquin chairs. h, Duke wearing flower garland. i, Duchess with Tuvalu native.

No. 1311: a, Duke and Duchess in canoe. b, Duke and Duchess, Solomon Islands building. c, Duke and Duchess at cultural village, Honiara. d, Duchess watching Duke receive flower garland from woman, Marau. e, Duke and Solomon Island children, Honiara. f, Duke and Duchess shaking hands with Solomon Islanders, Marau. g, Duke and Duchess, Duke being carried on palanquin. h, Duke and Duchess watching ceremony, Tavanipupu. i, Duke and Duchess waving.

No. 1312: a, Duke and Duchess in war canoe. b, Duke meeting Solomon Islands Prime Minister Gordon Darcy Lilo. c, Duke and Duchess standing next to woman at cultural village, Honiara. d, Duke and Royal coat of arms. e, Duke, Duchess and Lilo. f, Duchess and Solomon Islands coat of arms. g, Duke inspecting Guard of Honor. h, Duchess walking past line of saluting children. i, Duke and Duchess holding umbrellas, meeting children.

2013, May 3 Litho. *Perf. 13¼*

1309 A236 $7 Sheet of 9, #a-i 17.50 17.50
1310 A237 $7 Sheet of 9, #a-i 17.50 17.50
1311 A238 $7 Sheet of 9, #a-i 17.50 17.50
1312 A239 $7 Sheet of 9, #a-i 17.50 17.50
Nos. 1309-1312 (4) 70.00 70.00

Australian Wildlife — A240

No. 1313, $7 — Tasmanian devil (Sarcophilus harrisii): a, Looking right. b, Facing left. c, Leaping right. d, Looking left.

No. 1314, $7 — Platypus (Ornithorhynchus anatinus): a, Facing right. b, Facing forward, tail at right. c, Facing left, tail at right. d, Facing forward, tail at left.

No. 1315, $7 — Koalas (Phascolarctos cinereus): a, One animal looking down. b, Two animals, Latin name on two lines. c, Two animals, Latin name on one line. d, One animal, with head up.

No. 1316, $7 — Water buffalo (Bubalus bubalis): a, Head at left, Latin name at right. b, Head at left, Latin name at left. c, Animal in water. d, Animal grazing.

No. 1317, $7 — Wombats: a, Vombatus ursinus, head at right. b, Lasiorhinus krefftii, Latin name at right. c, Vombatus ursinus, head at left. d, Lasiorhinus latifrons.

No. 1318, $7 — Brushtail possums: a, Trichosurus cunninghami. b, Trichosurus caninus. c, Trichosurus vulpecula. d, Trichosurus johnstonii.

No. 1319, $7 — Kangaroos: a, Petrogale xanthopus. b, Dendrolagus goodfellowi. c, Macropus robustus. d, Wallabia bicolor.

No. 1320, $7 — Kangaroos: a, Macropus parryi. b, Macropus fuliginosus. c, Macropus giganteus. d, Setonix brachyurus.

No. 1321, $7 — Extinct mammals: a, Thylacinus cynocephalus (incorrect animal shown). b, Lagorchestes leporides. c, Macropus greyi. d, Obdurodon dicksoni.

No. 1322, $7 — Seals: a, Arctocephalus pusillus doriferus. b, Arctocephalus gazella. c, Mirounga leonina. d, Hydrurga leptonyx.

No. 1323, $7 — Sea lions (Neophoca cinerea): a, One animal, head raised. b, One animal, looking down, tail raised. c, Facing left, tail raised. d, Two animals.

No. 1324, $7 — Endangered mammals: a, Lasiorhinus krefftii, Latin name at left. b, Myrmecobius fasciatus. c, Onychogalea fraenata. d, Sarcophilus harrisii, running left.

No. 1325, $7 — Dingos (Canis lupus dingo): a, One animal lying. b, One animal standing. c, Two animals, one standing. d, Two animals lying.

No. 1326, $7 — Dolphins: a, Delphinus delphis, facing forward, tail at left. b, Tursiops aduncus. c, Stenella coeruleoalba. d, Delphinus delphis, facing right, tail at left.

No. 1327, $7 — Whales: a, Mesoplodon grayi. b, Hyperoodon planifrons. c, Mesoplodon densirostris. d, Mesoplodon bowdoini.

No. 1328, $7 — Owls: a, Ninox connivens. b, Ninox strenua. c, Ninox rufa. d, Ninox novaeseelandiae.

No. 1329, $7 — Emu (Dromaius novaehollandiae): a, Head. b, Head at left, raised. c, Head at right. d, Eating.

No. 1330, $7 — Butterflies: a, Graphium aristeus. b, Graphium sarpedon. c, Purple Ornithoptera priamus poseidon. d, Blue and green Ornithoptera priamus poseidon.

No. 1331, $7 — Sharks: a, Sphyrna lewini. b, Galeocerdo cuvier. c, Prionace glauca. d, Carcharodon carcharias.

No. 1332, $7 — Box jellyfish and Blue-ringed octopus: a, Hapalochlaena, all arms above country name. b, Two Cubozoa. c, One Cubozoa. d, Hapalochlaena, arm running through country name.

No. 1333, $7 — Reptiles: a, Chelonia mydas. b, Tiliqua nigrolutea. c, Crocodylus johnstoni. d, Notechis ater serventyi.

No. 1334, $7 — Snakes: a, Pseudonaja textilis, head raised. b, Pseudonaja textilis, head near country name. c, Pseudonaja textilis, head on back. d, Notechus scutatus.

No. 1335, $7 — Saltwater crocodile (Crocodylus porosus): a, Facing forward, tail in center, pointing right. b, Facing right. c, Facing left, tail at right. d, Facing forward, tail at left.

No. 1336, $7 — Huntsman spiders: a, Typostola barbata. b, Neosparassus diana. c, Holconia murrayensis. d, Isopeda villosa.

No. 1337, $35, Sarcophilus harrisii, diff. No. 1338, $35, Ornithrhynchus anatinus, diff. No. 1339, $35, Phascolarctos cinereus, diff. No. 1340, $35, Bubalus bubalis, diff. No. 1341, $35, Vombatus ursinus, diff. No. 1342, $35, Trichosurus johnstonii, diff. No. 1343, $35, Macropus rufus. No. 1344, $35, Procotoptodon goliah. No. 1345, $35, Thylacinus cynocephalus, diff. No. 1346, $35, Arctocephalus forsteri. No. 1347, $35, Neophoca cinerea. No. 1348, $35, Dendrolagus lumholtzi. No. 1349, $35, Canis lupus dingo, diff. No. 1350, $35, Stenella attenuata. No. 1351, $35, Mesoplodon layardii. No. 1352, $35, Tyto tenebricosa. No. 1353, $35, Dromaius novaehollandiae, diff. No. 1354, $35, Belenois java. No. 1355, $35, Carcharodon carcharias, diff. No. 1356, $35, Hapalochlaena, diff. No. 1357, $35, Chlamydosaurus kingii. No. 1358, $35, Notechis scutatus, diff. No. 1359, $35, Crocodylus porosus, diff. No. 1360, $35, Delena cancerides.

2013, May 10 Litho. *Perf. 13¼*

Sheets of 4, #a-d

1313-1336 A240 Set of 24 185.00 185.00

Souvenir Sheets

1337-1360 A240 Set of 24 230.00 230.00

A241

No. 1361, $7 — Various images of Mahatma Gandhi (1869-1948), Indian nationalist leader with denomination at: a, UL. b, UR. c, LL. d, LR.

No. 1362, $7 — Various images of Pope Benedict XVI with denomination at: a, UL. b, UR. c, LL. d, LR.

No. 1363, $7 — Various images of Pope Francis with denomination at: a, UL. b, UR. c, LL. d, LR.

No. 1364, $7 — King Willem-Alexander of the Netherlands and: a, Queen Maxima, denomination at UL. b, Queen Beatrix. c, Windmills. d, Queen Maxima, denomination at LR.

No. 1365, $7 — Margaret Thatcher (1925-2013), British Prime Minister, and: a, Wedding of Prince Charles and Princess Diana. b, Ronald Reagan. c, Pope John Paul II. d, Indira Gandhi.

No. 1366, $7 — Elvis Presley (1935-77): a, With actresses in *King Creole.* b, With Judy Tyler in *Jailhouse Rock.* c, With Ann-Margret. d, In *Girl Happy.*

No. 1367, $7 — Enzo Ferrari (1898-1988), car manufacturer, and: a, Ferrari 375 MM Coupe Scaglietti. b, Ferrari P540 Superfast Aperta. c, Ferrari 575M Maranello. d, Red Enzo Ferrari.

No. 1368, $7 — Various images of Mark Alan Webber, race car driver, with denomination at: a, UL. b, UR. c, LL. d, LR.

No. 1369, $7 — Australian trains: a, Southern Spirit. b, Indian Pacific. c, Tilt Train. d, Gulflander.

No. 1370, $7 — London Underground, 150th anniv.: a, Interior of 1938 car. b, Queen Elizabeth II riding train. c, Modern train in station. d, Train in station, 1863.

No. 1371, $7 — Airbus airplanes: a, A320-212 and Santa Isabel Island. b, A320-211 and Malaita Island. c, A320-211 and Vella Lavella Island. d, A320-212 and Guadalcanal Island.

No. 1372, $7 — Red Cross in the Solomon Islands: a, Worker at tent. b, Worker and child. c, Workers handling packages, Red Cross flag. d, Worker handliing package, Solomon Islands flag.

No. 1373, $7 — Minerals: a, Hematite. b, Sphalerite. c, Chalcocite. d, Epidote.

No. 1374, $7 — East Rennell Island UNESCO World Heritage Site: a, Microcarbo melanoleucos. b, Bruguiera gymnorhiza. c, Seaside cliffs. d, Birgus latro.

No. 1375, $7 — Fruits and nuts: a, Cocos nucifera. b, Durio zibethinus. c, Psidium guajava. d, Pangium edule.

No. 1376, $7 — Dugongs: a, Dugong dugon, denomination at UL. b, Dugong dugon, denomination at UR. c, Dugong dugon, denomination at LL. d, Trichechus manatus, denomination at LR.

No. 1377, $7 — Water birds: a, Accipiter imitator. b, Puffinus pacificus. c, Vanellus miles. d, Circus approximans.

No. 1378, $7 — Solomon Islands skink (Corucia zebrata) with denomination at: a, UL. b, UR. c, LL. d, LR.

No. 1379, $35, Gandhi, diff. No. 1380, $35, Pope Benedict XVI, diff. No. 1381, $35, Pope Francis, diff. No. 1382, $35, King Willem-Alexander and Thalys train. No. 1383, $35, Thatcher and Princess Diana. No. 1384, $35, Presley, diff. No. 1385, $35, Ferrari and Ferrari F12 Berlinetta. No. 1386, $35, Webber, diff. No. 1387, $35, Tilt Train, diff. No. 1388, $35, Lithograph of Baker Street Station, 2013, British London Underground £2 coin. No. 1389, $35, Airbus A320-212, diff. No. 1390, $35, Red Cross worker and child. No. 1391, $35, Chalcocite and Pyrite. No. 1392, $35, Clytorhynchus hamlini. No. 1393, $35, Nypa fruticans. No. 1394, $35, Dugong dugon, diff. No. 1395, $35, Platalea regia. No. 1396, $35, Corucia zebrata, diff.

2013, Aug. 30 Litho. *Perf. 13¼*

Sheets of 4, #a-d

1361-1378 A241 Set of 18 140.00 140.00

Souvenir Sheets

1379-1396 A241 Set of 18 175.00 175.00

Fish A242

Designs: 5c, Broom filefish. 10c, Helfrich's dartfish. 20c, Redfin butterflyfish. 25c, Palenose parrotfish. 30c, Barchin scorpionfish. 40c, Whitecap shrimp goby. 50c, Six-stripe wrasse. 60c, Indo-Pacific sergeant. 70c, Bluespine unicornfish. 80c, Flame angelfish. $1, Clown anemonefish. $2, Palette surgeonfish. $2.50, Bigeye tuna. $3, Indo-Pacific sailfish. $4, White marlin. $4.50, Blue marlin. $5, Yellowfin tuna. $5.50, Bonito. $6, Longtailed red snapper. $7, Short-tail red snapper. $8, Green humphead parrotfish. $10, Great barracuda. $15, Giant trevally. $20, Bluefin tuna. $50, Kingfish.

2013, Oct. 9 Litho. *Perf. 13x13¼*

1397	A242	5c	multi	.25	.25
1398	A242	10c	multi	.25	.25
1399	A242	20c	multi	.25	.25
1400	A242	25c	multi	.25	.25
1401	A242	30c	multi	.25	.25
1402	A242	40c	multi	.25	.25
1403	A242	50c	multi	.25	.25
1404	A242	60c	multi	.25	.25
1405	A242	70c	multi	.25	.25
1406	A242	80c	multi	.25	.25
1407	A242	$1	multi	.30	.30
1408	A242	$2	multi	.55	.55
1409	A242	$2.50	multi	.70	.70
1410	A242	$3	multi	.85	.85
1411	A242	$4	multi	1.10	1.10
1412	A242	$4.50	multi	1.25	1.25
1413	A242	$5	multi	1.40	1.40
1414	A242	$5.50	multi	1.60	1.60
1415	A242	$6	multi	1.75	1.75
1416	A242	$7	multi	2.00	2.00
1417	A242	$8	multi	2.25	2.25
1418	A242	$10	multi	2.75	2.75
1419	A242	$15	multi	4.25	4.25
1420	A242	$20	multi	5.75	5.75
1421	A242	$50	multi	14.00	14.00
	Nos. 1397-1421 (25)			43.00	43.00

A243

No. 1422, $7 — 200th Anniv. of Giuseppe Verdi (1813-1901), composer, with country name at: a, UL. b, UR. c, LL. d, LR.

No. 1423, $7 — Russian royalty of the Romanov Dynasty: a, Tsar Alexis (1629-76). b, Tsar Feodor III (1661-82). c, Emperor Peter I (1672-1725). d, Emperor Alexander II (1818-81).

No. 1424, $7 — Brazilian soccer players: a, Lucas Moura. b, Thiago Silva. c, Kaká. d, Neymar.

No. 1425, $7 — Paintings by American Impressionists: a, Summer, by Frank Weston Benson. b, Connoisseur - The Studio Corner, by William Merritt Chase. c, Mother Jeanne Nursing Her Baby, by Mary Cassatt. d, Two Women, by Colin Campbell Cooper.

No. 1426, $7 — Paintings by Pablo Picasso (1881-1973): a, Self-Portrait. b, Girl on a Pillow. c, Portrait of Marie Therese. d, Jacqueline with Flowers.

No. 1427, $7 — Wild cats: a, Panthera tigris sumatrae. b, Panthera onca. c, Caracal caracal. d, Felis concolor.

No. 1428, $7 — Killer whale (Orcinus orca), with country name at: a, UL. b, UR. c, LL. d, LR.

No. 1429, $7 — Birds of prey: a, Circus approximans. b, Pandion haliaetus. c, Haliastur indus. d, Falco peregrinus.

No. 1430, $7 — Bees and flowers: a, Tetragonula carbonaria, Anigozanthos manglesii. b, Amegilla cingulata, Banksia coccinea. c, Thyreus nitidulus, Wahlenbergia gloriosa. d, Thyreus nitidulus, Gossypium sturtianum.

No. 1431, $7 — Butterflies and orchids: a, Vanessa kershawi, Miltonia binotti. b, Papilio crino, Lepanthes discolor. c, Dryadula phaetusa, Coelogyne usitana. d, Limenitis arthemis astyanax, Lepanthes gargantua.

No. 1432, $7 — Fish: a, Paracanthurus hepatus. b, Amphiprion ocellaris. c, Sparisoma viride. d, Makaira mazara.

No. 1433, $7 — Turtles: a, Eretmochelys imbricata. b, Chelonia mydas. c, Dermochelys coriacea. d, Lepidochelys olivacea.

No. 1434, $7 — Fossils and dinosaurs: a, Ammonoidea and fossil. b, Megapnosaurus. c, Archaeopteryx. d, Parasaurolophus head and fossil.

No. 1435, $7 — Australian mushrooms: a, Microporus xanthopus. b, Cortinarius archeri. c, Cortinarius rotundisporus. d, Trametes versicolor.

No. 1436, $7 — Australian motorcycles: a, 1901 Wearwell-Stevens. b, 1908 Lewis Cycle. c, Australian Harley-Davidson Bobber. d, Ducati Vee Two Alchemy SV-1.

No. 1437, $7 — High-speed trains: a, Acela Express, U.S. b, China Railways CRH2. c, E6 Series Shinkansen, Japan. d, Italo ETR 575, Italy.

No. 1438, $7 — Concorde of: a, Air France, country name at UL. b, British Airways, country name at UR. c, British Airways, country name at LL. d, Air France, country name at LR.

No. 1439, $7 — New Year 2014 (Year of the Horse), with country name at: a, UL. b, UR. c, LL. d, LR.

No. 1440, $35, Verdi, diff. No. 1441, $35, Emperor Nicholas II of Russia (1868-1918). No. 1442, $35, Ronaldinho, soccer player. No. 1443, $35, Calm Morning, by Benson. No. 1444, $35, Picasso and unnamed painting. No. 1445, $35, Panthera leo. No. 1446, $35, Orcinus orca, diff. No. 1447, $35, Haliaeetus leucogaster. No. 1448, $35, Amegilla cingulata, Swainsona formosa. No. 1449, $35, Junonia coenia, Telipogon caulescens. No. 1450, $35, Chaetodon lunulatus. No. 1451, $35, Caretta caretta. No. 1452, $35, Tyrannosaurus rex. No. 1453, $35, Dermocybe austroveneta. No. 1454, $35, 2012 Beyond Transformers road bike. No. 1455, $35, E5 Series Shinkansen, Japan. No. 1456, $35, British Airways Concorde, British flag. No. 1457, $35, Horse, diff.

2013, Nov. 22 Litho. *Perf. 13¼*

Sheets of 4, #a-d

1422-1439 A243 Set of 18 140.00 140.00

Souvenir Sheets

1440-1457 A243 Set of 18 175.00 175.00

Rossica 2013 Intl. Philatelic Exhibition, Moscow (Nos. 1423, 1441); Brasiliana 2013 Intl. Philatelic Exhibition, Rio de Janeiro (Nos. 1424, 1442); Thailand 2013 World Stamp Exhibition, Bangkok (Nos. 1431, 1449).

A244

No. 1458, $7 — Pope John Paul II (1920-2005): a, Holding aspergillum. b, Praying. c, Waving, wearing zucchetto. d, Waving, wearing miter.

No. 1459, $7 — Hector Berlioz (1803-69), composer, with: a, G cleft and sharp sign at left, beamed note at right. b, G clef and sixteenth note at left, thirty-second note at right. c, G clef at right. d, Sixteenth note at left.

No. 1460, $7 — Richard Wagner (1813-83), composer, with: a, Blue jacket, G clef at left, notes and rests at right. b, Notes at left, G clef at right. c, Staff in spiral. d, Maroon jacket. G clef at left, notes and rests at right.

No. 1461, $7 — Nelson Mandela (1918-2013), President of South Africa, with: a, Queen Elizabeth II. b, Pope John Paul II. c, Arnold Schwarzenegger. d, Angela Merkel.

No. 1462, $7 — Birth of Prince George of Cambridge: a, Duke and Duchess of Cambridge, Prince George. b, Duke and Duchess of Cambridge, Prince George, stairs in background. c, Duke of Cambridge holding Prince George, Princess Diana holding baby. d, Duke, waving, and Duchess of Cambridge, Prince George.

No. 1463, $7 — Pierre de Coubertin (1863-1937), founder of International Olympic Committee, with: a, Runner. b, Cyclist. c, Gymnast. d, Volleyball player.

No. 1464, $7 — Cricket players: a, Virat Kohli. b, M. S. Dhoni. c, K. C. Sangakkara. d, A. B. de Villiers.

No. 1465, $7 — Indigenous Australian art: a, Nawarla Gabarnmung rock art. b, Aboriginal rock art, Queensland. c, Kakadu art. d, Wandjina rock art, Kimberley.

No. 1466, $7 — Paintings by Eugène Boudin (1824-98): a, The Honfleur Lighthouse I. b, Figures on the Beach. c, L'entrée du Port, Dieppe. d, Cayeux, Windmill in the Countryside, Morning.

No. 1467, $7 — Paintings by Georges Braque (1882-1963): a, Gray Weather in Cove. b, Landscape at La Ciotat (house on hillside). c, Landscape at La Ciotat (house behind trees). d, Braque and unnamed painting.

No. 1468, $7 — Paintings by Henri Matisse (1869-1954): a, Woman with a Hat. b, Still Life with Blue Tablecloth. c, The Goldfish. d, A Sitting Riffian.

No. 1469, $7 — Japanese Shinkansen high-speed trains: a, N700 Serie. b, E5 Series. c, E6 Series. d, 500 Series.

No. 1470, $7 — Australian lighthouses: a, Macquarie Lighthouse, New South Wales. b, Cape Byron Light, New South Wales. c, Cape Schanck Lighthouse, Victoria. d, Robe Lighthouse, South Australia.

No. 1471, $7 — Shenzhou 10 spaceflight: a, Nie Haisheng. b, Zhang Xiaoguang. c, Wang Yaping. d, Shenzhou 10.

No. 1472, $7 — Solomon white ibis (Threskiornis molucca): a, One bird in flight. b, Bird in flight, bird standing, facing left. c, Bird in flight, bird standing, facing right. d, One bird on branch.

No. 1473, $7 — Shells and birds: a, Cypraea aurantium, Phaeton aethereus. b, Telescopium telescopium, Pelecanus occidentalis californicus. c, Busycon sinistrum, Chloephaga hybrida. d, Tonna selacosa, Fregata minor.

No. 1474, $7 — Fishermen and fish: a, Amphiprion percula. b, Tetrapturus albidu. c, Cetoscarus bicolor. d, Naso unicornis.

No. 1475, $7 — Aquatic dinosaurs: a, Liopleurodon. b, Basilosaurus. c, Tylosaurus. d, Shonisaurus.

No. 1476, $35, Pope John Paul II, diff. No. 1477, $35, Berlioz, diff. No. 1478, $35, Wagner, diff. No. 1479, $35, Mandela and South African flag. No. 1480, $35, Duke and Duchess of Cambridge, Prince George, diff. No. 1481, $35, Coubertin, torch bearer. No. 1482, $35, Hashim Amla, cricket player. No. 1483, $35, Aboriginal rock art, Kakadu National Park. No. 1484, $35, Boudin and his painting, Antibes, the Fortifications. No. 1485, $35, Braque and unnamed painting, diff. No. 1486, $35, Les Toits des Collioure, by Matisse. No. 1487, $35, N700-7000 Series Sakura Shinkansen train. No. 1488, $35, Green Cape Lighthouse, New South Wales. No. 1489, $35, Wang Yaping, diff. No. 1490, $35, Threskiornis molucca, diff. No. 1491, $35, Pleuroploca trapezium, Rynchops niger. No. 1492, $35, Fisherman with fish on spear. No. 1493, $35, Elasmosaurus.

2013, Nov. 29 Litho. *Perf. 13¼*

Sheets of 4, #a-d

1458-1475	A244	Set of 18	140.00	140.00

Souvenir Sheets

1476-1493	A244	Set of 18	175.00	175.00

Golf — A245

No. 1494 — Golfers: a, Vijay Singh. b, Tiger Woods. c, Matt Kuchar. d, Rory McIlroy.

$35, Golf ball.

2014, Mar. 3 Litho. *Perf.*

1494	A245	$7 Sheet of 4, #a-d	7.75	7.75

Souvenir Sheet

1495	A245	$35 multi	9.75	9.75

Dated 2013.

A246

No. 1496, $7 — Princess Diana (1961-97): a, Two photographs, without hat at left. b, One photograph, without hat. c, One photograph, with hat. d, Two photographs, both with hat.

No. 1497, $7 — Nelson Mandela (1918-2013), President of South Africa: a, With South African flag in background. b, Wearing striped suit, with fist raised. c, Wearing dark suit, with fist raised, crowd in background. d, Wearing dark suit, crowd with South African flag in background.

No. 1498, $7 — Australian celebrities: a, Simon Baker, actor. b, Hugh Jackman, actor. c, Nicole Kidman, actress. d, Kylie Minogue, singer.

No. 1499, $7 — Australian astronauts: a, Andrew Thomas. b, Paul Scully-Power. c, Philip K. Chapman. d, Space Shuttle and International Space Station.

No. 1500, $7 — Australian Scouts and leaders with: a, Koala at LR. b, Koala at LL. c, Kangaroo at LR. d, Kangaroo at LL.

No. 1501, $7 — Australian mammals: a, Dasyurus maculatus. b, Pteropus poliocephalus. c, Tachyglossus aculeatus. d, Capra aegragus hircus.

No. 1502, $7 — Domestic cats: a, Cornish Rex. b, Abyssinian. c, Exotic shorthair. d, Cymric.

No. 1503, $7 — Dogs: a, Dalmatians. b, French bulldogs. c, Shar peis. d, Basenjis.

No. 1504, $7 — Dolphins: a, Tursiops truncatus. b, Stenella coeruleoalba. c, Grampus griseus. d, Stenella attenuata.

No. 1505, $7 — Owls: a, Ninox connivens. b, Tyto castanops. c, Ninox boobook. d, Tyto alba.

No. 1506, $7 — Tall ships: a, Christian Radich, Norway. b, NRP Sagres, Portugal, Belem, France. c, Niagara, U.S., Cisne Branco, Brazil. d, Alexander von Humboldt II, Germany.

No. 1507, $7 — Submarines: a, Triton 3300/3. b, USS Seawolf SSN-21. c, Téméraire (S 617), France. d, C-Explorer 5, U-Boat Worx.

No. 1508, $7 — European high-speed trains: a, DB ICE 3. b, TGV TMST. c, Frecciarossa 1000. d, TGV POS.

No. 1509, $7 — Airplanes over Australian airports: a, Qantas Airbus A330-202 over Sydney Airport. b, Alliance Airlines Fokker 100 over Brisbane Airport. c, Australian Air Express Boeing 737-376 (SF) over Melbourne Airport. d, Virgin Australia Boeing 737-8FE over Sydney Airport.

No. 1510, $7 — Fight against malaria: a, Father and son receiving bed net. b, Child, World Health Organization emblem. c, Anopheles stephensi and Rotary International emblem. d, Rotary volunteer working with people.

No. 1511, $7 — Solomon Islands volcanoes and minerals: a, Tinakula, Amethyst. b, Kavachi, Aquamarine. c, Simbo, Golden pyrite, Legrandite. d, Tinakula, Quartz.

No. 1512, $7 — Christmas: a, Adoration of the Child with Saints, by Fra Filippo Lippi. b, Adoration of the Magi, by Gentile da Fabriano. c, Adoration of the Magi, by Pieter Aertsen. d, Adoration of the Shepherds, by Giorgio Barbarelli da Castelfranco.

No. 1513, $35, Princess Diana, diff. No. 1514, $35, Mandela and child. No. 1515, $35, Minogue, diff. No. 1516, $35, Thomas, diff. No. 1517, $35, Australian Scout saluting. No. 1518, $35, Macropus rufus. No. 1519, $35, Korat cat. No. 1520, $35, Shetland sheepdog. No. 1521, $35, Steno bredanensis. No. 1522, $35, Tyto tenebricosa. No. 1523, $35, Kruzenshtern, Germany. No. 1524, $35, Turtle submarine. No. 1525, $35, 390 Pendolino train. No. 1526, $35, Australian Airlines Boeing 767-300ER over Sydney. No. 1527, $35, Tulagi Hospital nurse with people of Solomon Islands. No. 1528, $35, Simbo, Amethyst. No. 1529, $35, Central panel of Bladelin Triptych, by Rogier van der Weyden.

2014, Mar. 3 Litho. *Perf. 13¼*

Sheets of 4, #a-d

1496-1512	A246	Set of 17	130.00	130.00

Souvenir Sheets

1513-1529	A246	Set of 17	165.00	165.00

Dated 2013.

A247

No. 1530, $7 — 70th birthday of Catherine Deneuve, actress, with background color of: a, Lilac. b, Red. c, Blue. d, Brown.

No. 1531, $7 — 70th birthday of Mick Jagger, rock singer: a, Standing in front of mirror. b, Wearing blue jacket, two stage lights at left. c, Wearing blue jacket, stage lights only at top. d, Wearing white t-shirt.

No. 1532, $7 — Yuri Gagarin (1934-68), first man in space: a, With Vostok emblem in background . b, Statue of Gagarin, Moscow. c, In Vostok 1. d, Wearing space helmet.

No. 1533, $7 — Australian Nobel Prize winners in Physiology or Medicine: a, Elizabeth Blackburn, 2009 laureate, telomeres. b, Robin Warren, 2005 laureate, Helicobacter pylori. c, Sir Frank MacFarlane Burnet, 1960 laureate, diagram of clonal selection. d, Sir John Carew Eccles, 1963 laureate, nerve synapse.

No. 1534, $7 — 50th birthday of Garry Kasparov, chess player, with: a, Wearing black suit, large queen at right. b, Wearing red tie, large rook at right. c, Wearing light blue jacket, Large bishop at right. d, Holding chess piece and bag, large knight at left.

No. 1535, $7 — Gold medalists at 2013 World Track and Field Championships, Moscow: a, Aleksandr Menkov, long jump. b, Aleksandr Ivanov, 20-kilometer walk. c, Tatyana Lysenko, hammer throw. d, Elena Lashmanova, 20-kilometer walk.

No. 1536, $7 — Sebastian Vettel, Formula 1 race driver: a, In race car with wheels at left on track apron. b, Race car on track in background. c, Waving, race car on track in background. d, In race car with wheels at right near track apron.

No. 1537, $7 — Porsche 911, 50th anniv.: a, 1986 Porsche 911. b, 1972 Porsche 911T. c, 2013 Porsche 911. d, 2014 Porsche 911 GT3.

No. 1538, $7 — Fire engines: a, 1908 Shand Mason horse-drawn fire engine. b, 1925 REO fire engine with ladders at side. c, 1925 REO fire engine with ladder at top (incorrect inscription). d, 1969 Citroen N350 fire engine.

No. 1539, $7 — Firefighting aircraft: a, Mil Mi-8 helicopter, Russian flag. b, PLZ-Mielic M-18 Dromader airplane, Polish flag. c, Bombardier 415 airplane, Canadian flag. d, Aero Union P-3A Orion airplane, U.S. flag.

No. 1540, $7 — Airplanes: a, 1915 Sikorsky S-16, Russian flag. b, 1917 Hansa Brandenburg W13, German flag. c, 1916 Caproni Ca 36, Italian flag. d, 1909 Blériot XI, French flag.

No. 1541, $7 — Special transport: a, Boeing C-17 Globemaster III. b, Cap Maleas container ship. c, Mercedes-Benz 1524 Atego emergency vehicle. d, Rosenbauer fire truck.

No. 1542, $7 — Chinese trains: a, CRH5. b, CRH2. c, CRH380A. d, Maglev.

No. 1543, $7 — Marine paintings: a, Rocks and Sea, by Paul Gauguin. b, Fishing Boats at Sea, by Vincent van Gogh. c, Struggle for the Catch, by Edward Henry Potthast. d, The Storm on the Sea of Galilee, by Rembrandt.

No. 1544, $7 — Paintings by Eugène Delacroix (1798-1863): a, Lion Mauling a Dead Arab. b, Two Moroccans Seated in the Countryside. c, Arab Saddling His Horse. d, Madame Henri François Riesener.

No. 1545, $7 — Birds of Great Britain: a, Asio flammeus. b, Branta ruficollis. c, Fratercula cirrhata. d, Cygnus olor.

No. 1546, $7 — Insects: a, Polygonia c-album. b, Lucanus cervus. c, Bombus lucorum. d, Crocothemis erythraea.

No. 1547, $7 — Marine life: a, Acanthurus sohal. b, Ranina ranina. c, Fromia monilis. d, Chelonia mydas.

No. 1548, $35, Deneuve, diff. No. 1549, $35, Jagger, diff. No. 1550, $35, Gagarin and medal. No. 1551, $35, Barry Marshall, 2005 Nobel laureate in Physiology or Medicine. No. 1552, $35, Kasparov, diff. No. 1553, $35, Yelena Isinbayeva, pole vault. No. 1554, $35, Vettel, diff. No. 1555, $35, Ferdinand Porsche and 1963 Porsche 911. No. 1556, $35, 1896 Steam-powered fire engine, Sweden. No. 1557, $35, S-64 Erickson Air Crane helicopter, U.S. flag. No. 1558, $35, 1916 Royal Aircraft Factory S.E.5, British flag. No. 1559, $35, Bell 412 RAC rescue helicopter. No. 1560, $35, CRH380A, diff. No. 1561, $35, Sea Study, by Claude Monet. No. 1562, $35, Self-portrait, by Delacroix. No. 1563, $35, Anas carolinensis. No. 1564, $35, Metrioptera roeselii, Melanargia galathea. No. 1565, $35, Chelmon rostratus.

2014, Mar. 10 Litho. *Perf. 13¼*

Sheets of 4, #a-d

1530-1547	A247	Set of 18	140.00	140.00

Souvenir Sheets

1548-1565	A247	Set of 18	175.00	175.00

Dated 2013.

A248

No. 1566, $7 — Extinction of the Passenger pigeon (Ectopistes migratorius), cent.: a, Two birds in tree, beaks touching. b, Two birds in flight. c, Bird in flight, bird on branch. d, Two birds in tree facing in opposite directions.

No. 1567, $7 — Red List of Endangered Animals, 50th anniv.: a, Sarcophilus harrisii. b, Brachionichthys hirsutus. c, Nyctophilus howensis. d, Litoria raniformis.

No. 1568, $7 — Australian Red Cross: a, Workers and medical equipment, worker feeding baby. b, Red Cross flag, worker holding young boy. c, Worker, dog, child at water spigot. d, Red Cross doctor examining patient, horse-drawn carriage with supplies.

No. 1569, $7 — French Empress Josephine de Beauharnais (1763-1814): a, With Napoleon Bonaparte at right. b, With Napoleon Bonaparte at left. c, With roses. d, Portrait by Pierre-paul Prud'hon.

No. 1570, $7 — Jawaharlal Nehru (1889-1964), Prime minister of India: a, With Mahatma Gandhi, archway in background. b, Seated with arm raised. c, Seated in chair. d, With Gandhi, Taj Mahal in background.

No. 1571, $7 — Charles Lindbergh (1902-74), aviator: a, Lindbergh standing in front of airplane. b, Airplane in flight. c, Lindbergh standing in airplane cockpit. d, Lindbergh, airplane in flight.

No. 1572, $7 — Pope Francis: a, With arm extended. b, Holding censer. c, Holding child. d, Carrying lamb on shoulders.

No. 1573, $7 — Renault automobiles: a, 2009 Renault Twizy concept car. b, 1898 Renault Voiturette Type A. c, 1906 Renault Grand Prix. d, 2013 Renault Captur.

No. 1574, $7 — Ayrton Senna (1960-94), race car driver: a, Racing in 1985 Portuguese Grand Prix. b, At 1991 U.S. Grand Prix. c, Racing in 1980 World Karting Championships, Kalmar, Sweden. d, Sitting on wall, McLaren and Mercedes race cars.

No. 1575, $7 — Divers of the Solomon Islands, island maps and marine life: a, Pterapogon kauderni. b, Carcharhinus melanopterus. c, Cetoscarus bicolor. d, Dermochelys coriacea.

No. 1576, $7 — 2014 World Cup Soccer Championships, Brazil: a, One player with pink shirt. b, Two players with yellow and red shirts. c, Two players with red and blue shirts. d, Player with purple shirt.

No. 1577, $7 — Wedding of Joe DiMaggio and Marilyn Monroe, 60th anniv.: a, Monroe, olive green background. b, DiMaggio wearing cap. c, Dimaggio without cap. d, Monroe, red orange background.

No. 1578, $7 — Characters from Charlie Chaplin (1889-1977) films: a, Modern Times (green background). b, The Kid (without hat). c, The Kid (with hat). d, Modern Times (blue background).

No. 1579, $7 — Christoph Willibald Gluck (1714-87), composer: a, With cover of song book. b, Germany #1541. c, With other composers. d, Scene from opera "Paris and Helen."

No. 1580, $7 — Paintings by Paul Cézanne (1839-1906): a, Jas de Bouffan (The Pool). b, The Card Players. c, Still Life with a Curtain. d, Woman in a Green Hat.

No. 1581, $7 — Details from illustrations by Alphonse Mucha (1860-1939): a, Ivy. b, Princess Hyacinth. c, Dance. d, Salomé.

No. 1582, $7 — Paintings by Henri de Toulouse-Lautrec (1864-1901): a, Seated Dancer in Pink Tights. b, At the Moulin Rouge, The Dance. c, Lady Clown Cha-U-Kao. d, Monsieur Louis Pascal.

No. 1583, $7 — Paintings by Salvador Dalí (1904-89): a, Soft Watch at the Moment of First Explosion. b, Premonition of Civil War. c, Atavistic Vestiges After the Rain. d, Geopoliticus Child Watching the Birth of the New Man.

No. 1584, $7 — Famous people of the World War I era: a, King Albert I of Belgium (1875-1934). b, Joseph Joffre (1852-1931), French general. c, Theobald von Bethmann-Hollweg (1856-1921), German chancellor. d, Archduke Franz Ferdinand of Austria (1863-1914).

No. 1585, $7 — Battle of the Bulge, 70th anniv.: a, Panther Ausf. D tank, Germany, British troops. b, Gen. Dwight D. Eisenhower (1890-1969), U.S. troops. c, Field Marshal Bernard Montgomery (1887-1976), M7 Priest tank. d, German soldiers, Nebelwerfer 41.

No. 1586, $35, Two Ectopistes migratorius and nest. No. 1587, $35, Myrmecobius fasciatus. No. 1588, $35, Lady Helen Munro Ferguson (1865-1941), Red Cross official. No. 1589, $35, Empress Josephine and coat of arms. No. 1590, $35, Nehru and Elephas maximus indica. No. 1591, $35, Lindbergh, airplane in flight, diff. No. 1592, $35, Pope Francis, angel. No. 1593, $35, 2010 Renault DeZir. No. 1594, $35, Senna, diff. No. 1595, $35, Diver, map and Arothron hispidus. No. 1596, $35, Soccer player, diff. No. 1597, $35, Monroe and DiMaggio. No. 1598, $35, Chaplin in "The Kid," diff. No. 1599, $35, Gluck and violin. No. 1600, $35, Mont Sainte-Victoire, by Cézanne. No. 1601, $35, Biscuits Lefèvre Utile advertisement, by Mucha. No. 1602, $35, Marcelle Lender Dancing the Bolero in Chilperic, by Toulouse-Lautrec. No. 1603, $35, Soft Self-portrait with Fried Bacon, by Dalí. No. 1604, $35, Marshal Ferdinand Foch (1851-1929), No. 1605, $35, U.S. Soldier, M4A1 Sherman tank, M101A1 105mm howitzer.

2014, July 3 Litho. *Perf. 13¼*

Sheets of 4, #a-d

1566-1585 A248 Set of 20 155.00 155.00

Souvenir Sheets

1586-1605 A248 Set of 20 195.00 195.00

Canonization of Pope John Paul II — A249

No. 1606: a, St. John Paul II waving, two fingers bent. b, St. John Paul II waving, fingers straight. c, St. John Paul II wearing red cloak. d, Pope Francis.

$35, St. John Paul II, diff.

Litho. With Foil Application

2014, Aug. 25 *Perf. 13¼x9½*

1606 A249 $7 Sheet of 4, #a-d 7.75 7.75

Souvenir Sheet

1607 A249 $35 multi 9.75 9.75

2014 Winter Olympics, Sochi, Russia — A250

No. 1608: a, Alpine skiing. b, Snowboarding. c, Figure skating. d, Ice hockey.

$35, Speed skating.

2014, Aug. 25 Litho. *Perf. 13¼x9½*

1608 A250 $7 Sheet of 4, #a-d 7.75 7.75

Souvenir Sheet

1609 A250 $35 multi 9.75 9.75

Wildlife, Mushrooms and Flowers — A251

No. 1610, $7 — Pandas (Ailuropoda melanoleuca): a, One panda walking, head at right. b, One panda walking, head at left. c, One panda sitting. d, Panda and cub.

No. 1611, $7 — Monkeys: a, Alouatta seniculus. b, Nasalis larvatus. c, Mandrillus sphinx. d, Gorilla gorilla.

No. 1612, $7 — Bats: a, Nyctophilus major. b, Leptonycteris yerbabuenae. c, Pteropus scapulatus. d, Chalinolobus gouldii.

No. 1613, $7 — Tiger (Panthera tigris): a, Running. b, On ground (entire animal). c, Head, facing left. d, Head, facing forward.

No. 1614, $7 — Wild cats: a, Lynx canadensis. b, Caracal caracal. c, Prionailurus viverrinus. d, Neofelis nebulosa.

No. 1615, $7 — Dogs: a, Pointer. b, Weimaraner. c, American cocker spaniel. d, Miniature schnauzer.

No. 1616, $7 — Manatees: a, Two Trichechus manatus facing right. b, Two Trichechus manatus facing forward. c, Trichechus manatus latirostris with split tail. d, Trichechus manatus latirostris, tail without split.

No. 1617, $7 — Dolphins: a, Steno bredanensis. b, Peponocephala electra. c, Delphinus capensis. d, Orcaella heinsohni.

No. 1618, $7 — Eagles: a, Aquila audax. b, Aquila chrysaetos. c, Polemaetus bellicosus. d, Pithecophaga jeffreyi.

No. 1619, $7 — Owls: a, Asio otus. b, Otus scops. c, Pulsatrix perspicillata. d, Aegolius funereus.

No. 1620, $7 — Parrots: a, Electus roratus. b, Chalcopsitta cardinalis. c, Cacatua ducorpsii. d, Trichoglossus haematodus.

No. 1621, $7 — Butterflies: a, Celastrina argiolus. b, Callimorpha dominula. c, Callophrys rubi. d, Parnassius apollo.

No. 1622, $7 — Fish: a, Paracheirodon innesi. b, Scleropages formosus. c, Naso lituratus. d, Pseudanthias leucozonus.

No. 1623, $7 — Turtles: a, Chelonoidis nigra. b, Emys orbicularis. c, Gopherus polyphemus. d, Trachemys scripta elegans.

No. 1624, $7 — Dinosaurs: a, Carnotaurus. b, Styracosaurus. c, Quetzalcoatlus. d, Piveteausaurus divesensis.

No. 1625, $7 — Arctic fauna: a, Ovibos moschatus. b, Odobenus rosmarus. c, Balaena mysticetus. d, Vulpes lagopus.

No. 1626, $7 — Mushrooms: a, Armillaria mellea. b, Pycnoporus cinnabarinus. c, Boletus luridus. d, Coprinus comatus.

No. 1627, $7 — Orchids: a, Phalaenopsis sp. b, Tricyrtis hirta. c, Oncidium altissimum. d, Ophrys bombyliflora.

No. 1628, $35, Ailuropoda melanoleuca, diff. No. 1629, $35, Pan troglodytes. No. 1630, $35, Idionycteris phyllotis. No. 1631, $35, Panthera tigris, diff. No. 1632, $35, Panthera uncia. No. 1633, $35, Vizsla. No. 1634, $35, Trichechus manatus latirostris, diff. No. 1635, $35, Cephalorhynchus eutropia. No. 1636, $35, Haliaeetus leucogaster. No. 1637, $35, Surnia ulula. No. 1638, $35, Lorius chlorocercus. No. 1639, $35, Papilio demoleus. No. 1640, $35, Pterois volitans. No. 1641, $35, Geochelone sulcata. No. 1642, $35, Triceratops horridus. No. 1643, $35, Ursus maritimus. No. 1644, $35, Amanita muscaria. No. 1645, $35, Phalaenopsis sp., diff.

2014, Aug. 25 Litho. *Perf. 13¼x9½*

Sheets of 4, #a-d

1610-1627 A251 Set of 18 140.00 140.00

Souvenir Sheets

1628-1645 A251 Set of 18 175.00 175.00

Nos. 1627 and 1645 were impregnated with a floral scent.

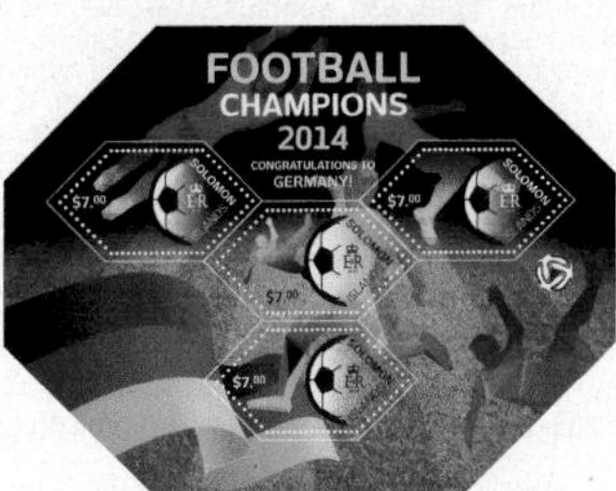

Victory of German Team at 2014 World Cup Soccer Championships, Brazil — A252

No. 1646 — Soccer ball and: a, Two feet of player near denomination. b, One foot of player near denomination. c, Player making bicycle kick. d, Player's foot, German flag.

$35, Player's foot and soccer ball, diff.

2014, Nov. 20 Litho. *Perf. 13¼x9½*

1646 A252 $7 Sheet of 4, #a-d 7.50 7.50

Souvenir Sheet

1647 A252 $35 multi 9.50 9.50

A253

No. 1648, $7 — Barracudas (Sphyraena barracuda): a, Large barracuda in foreground facing LL corner, dark marine life at bottom. b, Large barracuda in foreground facing LR corner, red and yellow marine life at bottom. c, As "a," red and brown marine life at bottom. d, As "b," brown marine life at bottom.

No. 1649, $7 — Fight against malaria in the Solomon Islands: a, Emblem of Against Malaria Foundation, worker inoculating child, child carrying bag. b, Child, workers spraying insecticide. c, Workers in medical laboratory. d, Anopheles mosquito.

No. 1650, $35, Sphyraena barracuda, diff. No. 1651, $35, Child, Anopheles mosquito, worker inoculating child.

2014, Nov. 20 Litho. *Perf. 13¼*

Sheets of 4, #a-d

1648-1649 A253 Set of 2 15.00 15.00

Souvenir Sheets

1650-1651 A253 Set of 2 19.00 19.00

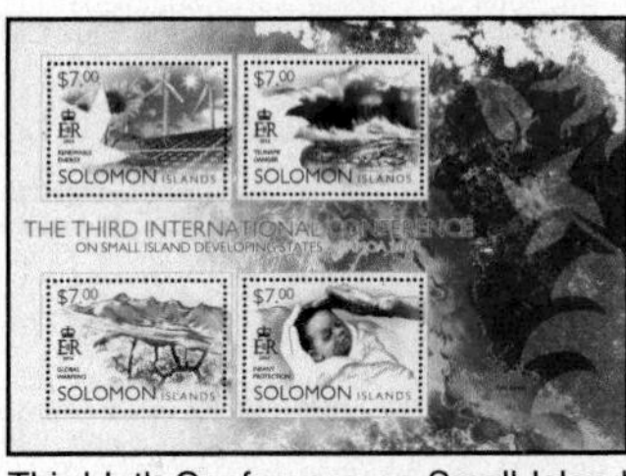

Third Intl. Conference on Small Island Developing States — A254

No. 1652: a, Renewable energy. b, Tsunami danger. c, Global warning. d, Infant protection.

$35, Environmental sustainability.

2014, Nov. 20 Litho. *Perf. 13¼*

Plastic-Faced Paper

1652 A254 $7 Sheet of 4, #a-d 7.50 7.50

Souvenir Sheet

1653 A254 $35 multi 9.50 9.50

A255

No. 1654, $7 — Sailing tepukes: a, With sail at right, two men standing in platform. b, With two sails. c, With sail at right, one man standing in platform. d, With sail at left.

No. 1655, $7 — Traditional dancing in the Solomon Islands: a, Three women dancers in blue skirts standing, face of dancer with painted face. b, Eight dancers. c, Four dancers standing. d, Three dancers in purple skirts dancing, face of dancer with painted face.

No. 1656, $7 — Nobel Peace Prize acceptance speech of Dr. Martin Luther King, Jr., 50th anniv.: a, King, obverse of Nobel medal. b, King, microphone at right. c, King, microphone at left. d, King, reverse of Nobel medal.

No. 1657, $7 — King Felipe VI of Spain: a, With King Juan Carlos, saluting. b, With cap, coat of arms. c, With coat of arms, without cap. d, With King Juan Carlos, without caps.

No. 1658, $7 — Yuri Gagarin (1934-68), first man in space, with silhouette of: a, Cosmonaut waving. b, Rocket lifting off. c, Space capsule and drogue parachute. d, Vostok spacecraft.

No. 1659, $7 — Deng Xiaoping (1904-97), Chinese leader: a, With airplane and train. b, With Mao Zedong. c, With Chinese flag, Gate of Heavenly Peace. d, With Mao Zedong statue.

No. 1660, $7 — Galileo Galilei (1564-1642), astronomer: a, Reading book. b, Holding compass against globe. c, With Moon. d, Pointing.

No. 1661, $7 — Chess players: a, Vladimir Borisovich Kramnik. b, Garry Kasparov. c, Viswanathan Anand. d, Bobby Fischer (1943-2008).

No. 1662, $7 — Round-the-world flight of the Graf Zeppelin, 85th anniv.: a, Ferdinand von Zeppelin (1838-1917), airship manufacturer. b, Underside of Graf Zeppelin. c, Side view of Graf Zeppelin. d, Dr. Hugo Eckener (1868-1954), commander of Graf Zeppelin.

No. 1663, $7 — Concorde: a, British Airways G-BOAB, nose facing UR, landing gear visible. b, British Airways G-BOAB, nose facing LL. c, British Airways G-BOAB, nose facing UR, landing gear not visible. d, Air France Concorde.

No. 1664, $7 — Fire engines: a, Ziegler Z8. b, TFD8-SL. c, Man Cas 24. d, DLK18 12.

No. 1665, $7 — High-speed trains: a, British Rail Class 395. b, W7 Series Shinkansen, Japan. c, KTX-Sancheon, South Korea. d, Afrosiyab, Uzbekistan.

No. 1666, $7 — 2014 Commonwealth Games, Glasgow: a, Boxing. b, Sprinter. c, Cycling. d, Judo.

No. 1667, $7 — Scouting: a, Juliette Gordon Low (1860-1927), founder of Girl Scouts of the U.S.A. b, Three Boy Scouts. c, Low and Girl Scout. d, Robert Baden-Powell (1857-1941), founder of Boy Scouts.

No. 1668, $7 — Lighthouses and birds: a, Coquille River Light, U.S., Onychoprion fuscatus. b, Los Morillos Light, Puerto Rico, Pelecanus conspicillatus. c, Fisgard Lighthouse, Canada, Sula nebouxii. d, North Point Lighthouse, U.S., Morus bassanus.

No. 1669, $7 — Minerals: a, Bumblebee jasper. b, Fluorite on barite. c, Rhodochrosite. d, Aquamarine and muscovite.

No. 1670, $35, Tepuke with one sail, diff. No. 1671, $35, Dancers, diff. No. 1672, $35, King, obverse of Nobel medal, diff. No. 1673, $35, King Felipe VI, coat of arms, diff. No. 1674, $35, Gagarin, shilhouette of Vostok spacecraft, diff. No. 1675, $35, Deng Xiaoping, diff. No. 1676, $35, Galileo and telescope. No. 1677, $35, Magnus Carlsen, chess player. No. 1678, $35, Graf Zeppelin in flight. No. 1679, $35, British Airways G-BOAB Concorde, diff. No. 1680, $35, MAN-29 Airport fire truck. No. 1681, $35, Talgo AVRIL train, Spain. No. 1682, $35, Weight lifting. No. 1683, $35, Scout leader teaching Scouts knot-tying. No. 1684, $35, Spring Point Ledge Lighthouse, U.S., Thalasseus maximus. No. 1685, $35, Andradite and hedenbergite.

2014, Nov. 20 Litho. *Perf. 13¼*

Sheets of 4, #a-d

1654-1669 A255 Set of 16 120.00 120.00

Souvenir Sheets

1670-1685 A255 Set of 16 150.00 150.00

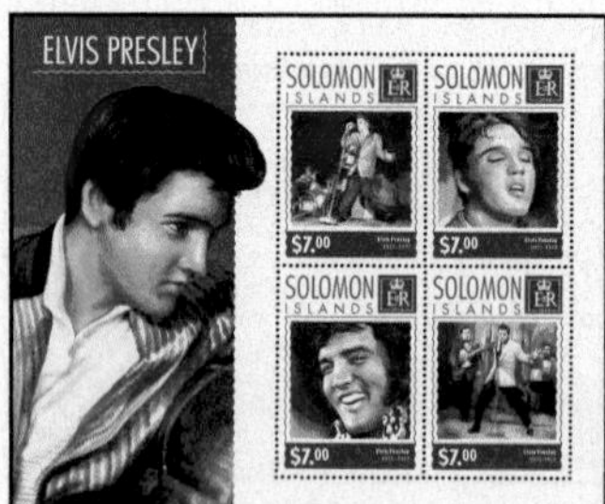

A256

No. 1686, $7 — Elvis Presley (1935-77): a, At microphone, with guitar. b, Head, facing right. c, Head, facing left. d, At microphone, without guitar.

No. 1687, $7 — Concorde: a, Facing left, landing gear visible. b, In flight, nose pointing to UR and bent. c, In flight, nose pointing to UL. d, In flight, nose pointing to UR, not bent.

No. 1688, $7 — European high-speed trains: a, Thalys. b, Alvia. c, ICE. d, Le Frecce.

No. 1689, $7 — Australian naval vessels: a, HMAS Anzac. b, HMAS Kanimbla. c, HMAS Brunei. d, HMAS Balikpapan.

No. 1690, $7 — Fire engines: a, 1938 Seagrave. b, 1971 F108 Dennis. c, 1956 International S-160. d, 1956 Bedford A5 S.

No. 1691, $7 — Lighthouses: a, Fanad Head Lighthouse, Ireland. b, Le Corbière Lighthouse, Jersey. c, Lindau Lighthouse, Germany. d, Les Eclaireurs Lighthouse, Argentina.

No. 1692, $7 — Cricket players: a, William Gilbert (1856-1918). b, Wally Hammond (1903-65). c, Jack Hobbs (1882-1963). d, Eddie Paynter (1901-79).

No. 1693, $7 — Dogs: a, Afghan hound. b, Airedale terrier. c, Chihuahua. d, American cocker spaniel.

No. 1694, $7 — Dolphins: a, One Tursiops truncatus. b, Lagenorhynchus obscurus. c, Stenella frontalis. d, Two Tursiops truncatus.

No. 1695, $7 — Owls: a, Bubo virginianus subarcticus. b, Bubo bubo. c, Tyto alba (brown panel). d, Asio otus.

No. 1696, $7 — Birds of prey: a, Aquila chrysaetos. b, Gyps fulvus. c, Tyto alba (olive green panel). d, Haliaeetus leucocephalus.

No. 1697, $7 — Butterflies: a, Heliconius melpomene. b, Colias cesonia. c, Limenitis archippus. d, Arctia caja.

No. 1698, $7 — Shells: a, Cancellaria reticulata. b, Leptopecten latiauratus. c, Nautilus pompilius. d, Hexaplex radix.

No. 1699, $7 — Turtles: a, Chelonia mydas. b, Lepidochelys kempii. c, Eretmochelys imbricata. d, Caretta caretta.

No. 1700, $7 — Dinosaurs: a, Parasaurolophus. b, Dromiceiomimus. c, Shunosaurus. d, Protoceratosaurus.

No. 1701, $7 — Orchids: a, Phalaenopsis sp. b, Paphiopedilum gratrixianum. c, Zygopetalum crinitum. d, Cattleya hybrid.

No. 1702, $7 — Mushrooms: a, Boletus edulis. b, Leccinum versipelle. c, Russula aurora. d, Leccinum scabrum.

No. 1703, $7 — Minerals: a, Muscovite. b, Fluorite. c, Amethyst. d, Marcasite.

No. 1704, $7 — Christmas: a, The Holy Family with a Shepherd, by Titian. b, Adoration of the Shepherds, by Giacomo Cavedone. c, The Nativity, by Nicolas de Liemaker. d, The Nativity, by Karl von Blaas.

No. 1705, $7 — New Year 2015 (Year of the Goat): a, Goat and Chinese character highlighted on wheel. b, Auriga constellation. c, Goat and flower. d, Goat on wheel.

No. 1706, $35, Presley, diff. No. 1707, $35, Concorde, diff. No. 1708, $35, Eurostar train. No. 1709, $35, HMAS Adelaide. No. 1710, $35, 1948 International KB-5 fire truck. No. 1711, $35, Bodie Island Lighthouse, U.S. No. 1712, $35, Donald Bradman (1908-2001), cricket player. No. 1713, $35, Basenji. No. 1714, $35, Two Tursiops truncatus, diff. No. 1715, $35, Tyto alba, diff. No. 1716, $35, Buteo buteo. No. 1717, $35, Morpho menelaus. No. 1718, $35, Lobatus gigas. No. 1719, $35, Lepidochelys olivacea. No. 1720, $35, Anchiceratops. No. 1721, $35, Miltonia hybrid. No. 1722, $35, Xerocomus chrysenteron. No. 1723, $35, Elbaite. No. 1724, $35, Madonna with Child, by Agostino Ugolini. No. 1725, $35, Goat and flower, diff.

2014, Nov. 28 Litho. *Perf. 13¼*

Sheets of 4, #a-d

1686-1705 A256 Set of 20 150.00 150.00

Souvenir Sheets

1706-1725 A256 Set of 20 190.00 190.00

A257

No. 1726, $5 — Koala (Phascolarctos cinereus): a, Facing right, grasping cut tree branch. b, Sitting, facing forward, front paws down. c, Moving on tree branch. d, Seated with one paw raised.

No. 1727, $5 — Domestic cats: a, Sphynx. b, Maine Coon cat. c, Ragdoll. d, Bengal.

No. 1728, $5 — Whales: a, Balaenoptera musculus. b, Two Megaptera novaeangliae facing right. c, Two Megaptera novaeangliae, facing left and right. d, Physeter macrocephalus.

No. 1729, $5 — Solomon white ibis (Threskiornis molucca pygmaeus): a, In flight. b, At water's edge, facing left. c, In shallow water, facing right. d, On ground, facing left.

No. 1730, $5 — Flamingos: a, Phoenicopterus chilensis. b, Phoenicopterus andinus. c, Phoenicopterus ruber. d, Phoenicopterus minor.

No. 1731, $5 — Kingfishers: a, Dacelo novaeguineae. b, Alcedo atthis. c, Actenoides concretus. d, Alcedo cristata.

No. 1732, $5 — Water birds: a, Haematopus ostralegus. b, Tringa ochropus. c, Egretta thula. d, Jabiru mycteria.

No. 1733, $5 — Fish: a, Chaetodon melannotus. b, Acanthurus leucosternon. c, Pterapogon kauderni. d, Zebrasoma scopas.

No. 1734, $5 — Corals: a, Tubastraea coccinea. b, Lophogorgia vimnalis. c, Tubastraea faulkneri. d, Subergorgia hickson Kashman.

No. 1735, $5 — Reptiles: a, Chamaeleo calyptratus. b, Centrochelys sulcata. c, Trimeresurus popeorum. d, Crocodylus porosus.

No. 1736, $5 — Fossils: a, Shrimp. b, Dinosaur. c, Trilobite. d, Ammonite.

No. 1737, $5 — Antarctic wildlife: a, Phalacrocorax atriceps bransfieldensis. b, Pygoscelis adeliae. c, Arctocephalus gazella. d, Hydrurga leptonyx.

No. 1738, $5 — Endangered animals: a, Gymnogyps californianus. b, Panthera tigris altaica. c, Panthera pardus orientalis. d, Caretta caretta.

No. 1739, $5 — Trains: a, Eritrean Railway Class 440 steam locomotive. b, Baldwin "Iron Horse" steam locomotive No. 486, U.S. c, New Hope & Ivyland Railroad Baldwin steam locomotive No. 40, U.S. d, Valley Railroad Essex steam locomotive, U.S.

No. 1740, $5 — Rescue boats: a, Rescue boat, building in background. b, Cruise ship lifeboat. c, Red rescue boat on hoists. d, Lifeboat on incline.

No. 1741, $5 — Prince George of Cambridge, 1st birthday: a, Duke and Duchess of Cambridge with Prince George. b, Prince George wearing blue overalls. c, Prince George wearng pink overalls. d, Duke and Duchess, Prince George and toy doll.

No. 1742, $5 — Art by Leonardo da Vinci (1452-1519): a, Heads of an Old Man and a Youth. b, Madonna Litta. c, The Baptism of Christ. d, Head of a Girl.

No. 1743, $5 — Paintings by Peter Paul Rubens (1557-1640): a, The Fall of Man. b, Minerva Protects Pax from Mars. c, Mars and Rhea Silvia. d, Descent from the Cross.

No. 1744, $5 — Impressionist paintings: a, Family Reunion, by Frédéric Bazille. b, The Church of St. Jacques in Dieppe, Morning Sun, by Camille Pissarro. c, The Dance Class, by Edgar Degas. d, The Lady with Fans, by Edouard Manet.

No. 1745, $5 — Paintings by Gustav Klimt (1862-1918): a, Mada Primavesi. b, Hygeia. c, Music I. d, Schubert at the Piano II.

No. 1746, $24, Phascolarctos cinereus, diff. No. 1747, $24, European shorthair cat. No. 1748, $24, Megaptera novaeangliae, diff. No. 1749, $24, Threskiornis molucca pygmaeus, diff. No. 1750, $24, Phoenicopterus roseus. No. 1751, $24, Halcyon pileata. No. 1752, $24, Himantopus mexicanus. No. 1753, $24, Betta splendens. No. 1754, $24, Balanophyllia elegans. No. 1755, $24, Eretmochelys imbricata. No. 1756, $24, Ammonite fossils. No. 1757, $24, Pygoscelis papua. No. 1758, $24, Bison bison. No. 1759, $24, C.P. 0166 steam locomotive, Portugal. No. 1760, $24, Italian lifeguard rescue rowboat. No. 1761, $24, Prince George of Cambridge, diff. No. 1762, $24, Mona Lisa, by da Vinci. No. 1763, $24, The Massacre of the Innocents, by Rubens. No. 1764, $24, The Bathers, by Paul Cézanne. No. 1765, $24, Portrait of Adele Bloch-Bauer I, by Klimt.

2014, Dec. 20 Litho. *Perf. 13¼*

Sheets of 4, #a-d

1726-1745 A257 Set of 20 110.00 110.00

Souvenir Sheets

1746-1765 A257 Set of 20 130.00 130.00

Protected Species in Taiwan — A258

No. 1766: a, Owl. b, Monkey. c, Wildcat. d, Turtle.
$20, Deer.

2015, May 24 Litho. *Perf.*

1766 A258 $5 Sheet of 4, #a-d 5.25 5.25

Souvenir Sheet

1767 A258 $20 multi 5.25 5.25

Taipei 2015 Intl. Stamp Exhibition.

Singapore 2015 World Stamp Exhibition — A259

No. 1768: a, Aethopyga siparaja and Kopsia singapurensis. b, Vanda "Miss Joaquim" orchid, ArtScience Museum, Singapore. c, Esplanade — Theaters on the Bay, Singapore, Durio singaporensis. d, Eupoea midamus singapura, Gardens by the Bay, Singapore.
$20, Scleropages formosus, Marina Bay Sands, Singapore.

2015, May 24 Litho. *Perf. 13¼*

1768 A259 $5 Sheet of 4, #a-d 5.25 5.25

Souvenir Sheet

1769 A259 $20 multi 5.25 5.25

A260

No. 1770, $7 — 2015 Europhilex Stamp Exhibition, London: a, Penny Black stamps (Great Britain #1). b, Sir Rowland Hill and Penny Black. c, William Wyon and medals depicting Queen Victoria. d, Penny Black, Two Pence Blue, Penny Red (Great Britain #1, 2, 3).

No. 1771, $12 — Ludwig van Beethoven (1770-1827), composer: a, Herbert von Karajan (1908-89), conductor. b, Statue of Beethoven, Bonn, Germany. c, Bust of Beethoven. d, Beethoven.

No. 1772, $12 — Alessandro Volta (1745-1827), physicist: a, Volta and voltaic pile. b, Volta explaining principle of electric column to Napoleon. c, Statue of Volta, Como, Italy, and Tempio Voltiano, Italy. d, Luigi Galvani (1737-98), physicist.

No. 1773, $12 — Glider flight of the Wright Brothers, 115th anniv: a, Wilbur Wright (1867-1912), inventor, glider and 2001 North Carolina state quarter. b, Orville Wright (1871-1948), inventor, and Wright Brothers National Memorial, North Carolina. c, Glider above lighthouse. d, Glider and Wright Brothers.

No. 1774, $12 — Pres. Abraham Lincoln (1809-65): a, Lincoln and court room. b, Soldiers. c, Lincoln making speech. d, Frederick Douglass (1818-95), abolitionist, and soldiers.

No. 1775, $12 — Nelson Mandela (1918-2013), President of South Africa: a, With crowd. b, With South African flag, facing forward. c, With South African flag, facing left. d, With South African flag, holding World Cup trophy.

No. 1776, $12 — Imperial Trans-Antarctic Expedition (Endurance Expedition), cent.: a, Ship *Endurance*. b, Sir Ernest Shackleton (1874-1922), expedition leader. c, Shackleton and Frank Hurley (1885-1962), expedition member. d, *Endurance* sinking in Weddell Sea.

No. 1777, $12 — Crash of the Concorde, 15th anniv.: a, Concorde and map of Gonesse, France. b, Concorde over Paris. c, Two Concordes in flight. d, Concorde and badge.

No. 1778, $12 — Marilyn Monroe (1926-62), actress: a, Wearing necklace. b, Wearing white dress. c, Wearing white swimsuit. d, Wearing swimsuit in black-and-white and color images.

No. 1779, $12 — Mother Teresa (1910-97), humanitarian: a, With child. b, With Princess Diana. c, With Pope John Paul II. d, Holding infant.

No. 1780, $12 — St. John Paul II (1920-2005): a, Wearing zucchetto, hands not visible. b, Wearing miter, holding crucifix. c, Wearing miter, waving. d, Wearing zucchetto, hands visible.

No. 1781, $12 — Pope Benedict XVI: a, Walking. b, Waving. c, With hands together. d, With arms raised.

No. 1782, $12 — British Women's Institute, Women in World War I, cent.: a, Land girl. b, Munitions worker at Vickers Factory. c, Munitions worker holding wrench. d, Nurse.

No. 1783, $12 — Second Battle of Ypres, cent.: a, Soldier watching comrades in trench. b, Soldiers wearing masks. c, Field Marshal Herbert Plumer (1857-1932) and battle scene. d, Victoria Cross recipient Francis Alexander Caron Scrimger (1880-1937) and battle scene.

No. 1784, $12 — End of World War II, 70th anniv.: a, German prisoners of war in Berlin. b, Gen. Dwight D. Eisenhower (1890-1969) and Sherman tank. c, Field Marshal Bernard Law Montgomery (1887-1976) and other officers. d, Gen. Georgy Zhukov (1896-1974) and damaged buildings.

No. 1785, $12 — End of the Viet Nam War, 40th anniv.: a, Soldier. b, War protest. c, Naval vessel. d, Soldier tending to wounded comrade, helicopter.

No. 1786, $12 — 40th birthday of Eldrick "Tiger" Woods, golfer: a, Woods wearing striped white shirt in background. b, Woods and a tiger. c, Wearing red and blue shirt. d, Wearing red shirt in background.

No. 1787, $12 — 2015 African Cup of Nations soccer championships: a, Ivory Coast and Ghana players, ball in air. b, Ivory Coast players holding trophy. c, Democratic Republic of Congo players. d, Ivory Coast and Ghana players, ball on ground.

No. 1788, $28, Image of Queen Victoria from Penny Black, wax seal. No. 1789, $40, Beethoven and piano. No. 1790, $40, Volta and voltaic pile, diff. No. 1791, $40, Wright Brothers. No. 1792, $40, Lincoln and soldiers. No. 1793, $40, Mandela, diff. No. 1794, $40, Shackleton, diff. No. 1795, $40, Concorde and Capt. Christian Marty (1945-2000), pilot of crashed plane. No. 1796, $40, Monroe, Joe DiMaggio (1914-99) and Pres. John F. Kennedy (1917-63). No. 1797, $40, Mother Teresa and Pope John Paul II, diff. No. 1798, $40, St. John Paul II, diff. No. 1799, $40, Pope Benedict XVI, diff. No. 1800, $40, Women sitting on fence holding farm implements, airplanes. No. 1801, $40, Field Marshal John French (1852-1925) and soldiers. No. 1802, $40, Field Marshal Wilhelm Keitel (1882-1946) singing German surrender papers. No. 1803, $40, Pres. Richard Nixon (1913-94) and soldiers in Viet Nam. No. 1804, $40, Woods, diff. No. 1805, $40, Ivory Coast and Ghana soccer players, diff.

2015, May 24 Litho. *Perf. 13¼*

Sheets of 4, #a-d

1770-1787 A260 Set of 18 225.00 225.00

Souvenir Sheets

1788-1805 A260 Set of 18 190.00 190.00

A261

No. 1806, $12 — Ailuropoda melanoleuca (Panda): a, Eating. b, In field. c, On tree branch. d, With bamboo in background.

No. 1807, $12 — Bats: a, Eidolon helvum. b, Macroderma gigas. c, Rousettus aegyptiacus. d, Artibeus jamaicensis.

No. 1808, $12 — Cats: a, Toyger and Singapura. b, Persian. c, Maine Coon. d, Selkirk Rex.

No. 1809, $12 — Canis lupus dingo (Dingo): a, Two dingos fighting, head of dingo. b, Two dingos, one burying food. c, Three dingos. d, Head of dingo, dingo and suckling pups.

No. 1810, $12 — Horses: a, American Paint. b, Mongol. c, Camarillo. d, Gypsy Cob.

No. 1811, $12 — Dolphins: a, Lagenorhynchus obliquidens. b, Tursiops truncatus. c, Stenella coeruleoalba. d, Tursiops aduncus.

No. 1812, $12 — Seabirds: a, Phoebastria albatrus. b, Fulmarus glacialis. c, Phalacrocorax auritus. d, Pelecanus onocrotalus.

No. 1813, $12 — Australian hawks: a, Circus approximans. b, Accipiter novaehollandiae. c, Aviceda subcristata. d, Circus assimilis.

No. 1814, $12 — Australian owls: a, Ninox strenua. b, Ninox connivens. c, Tyto longimembris. d, Tyto tenebricosa.

No. 1815, $12 — Australian butterflies: a, Ornithoptera euphorion. b, Delias mysis. c, Catopsilia pomona. d, Rapala varuna.

No. 1816, $12 — Coral reef fish: a, Balistapus undulatus. b, Hippocampus sp. c, Balistoides conspicillum. d, Chaetodon capistratus.

No. 1817, $12 — Seashells: a, Tegillarca nodifera. b, Harpa cabriti. c, Gyrineum natator. d, Babylonia spirata.

No. 1818, $12 — Turtles: a, Aldabrachelys gigantea. b, Centrochelys sulcata. c, Chelonia mydas. d, Caretta caretta.

No. 1819, $12 — Extinct animals: a, Macropus greyi. b, Equus quagga quagga. c, Chaeropus ecaudatus. d, Diceros bicornis longipes.

No. 1820, $12 — Mushrooms: a, Kuehneromyces mutabilis. b, Hygrocybe calyptriformis. c, Omphalotus olearius. d, Amanita muscaria.

No. 1821, $12 — Minerals: a, Calcite on sphalerite. b, Tourmaline. c, Chalcanthite. d, Rhodochrosite with quartz.

No. 1822, $12 — Australian lighthouses: a, Cape Banks Lighthouse, South Australia. b, South Solitary Lighthouse, New South Wales. c, Grassy Hill Lighthouse, Queensland. d, Cape du Couedic Lighthouse, Kangaroo Island, South Australia.

No. 1823, $12 — Australian trains: a, Ghan. b, Xplorer. c, Transperth B Series. d, V/Line VLocity.

No. 1824, $12 — High-speed trains: a, TGV, France. b, British InterCity 125, Great Britain. c, ICE 1, Germany. d, CRH3, People's Republic of China.

No. 1825, $12 — Fire engines: a, 2004 Pierce Enforcer. b, 1954 American La France Type 700 pumper. c, Oshkosh Striker. d, Hummer fire truck.

No. 1826, $40, Ailuropoda melanoleuca, diff. No. 1827, $40, Pteropus vampyrus, Pteropus poliocephalus. No. 1828, $40, Manx cat. No. 1829, $40, Four Canis lupus dingos. No. 1830, $40, Arabian horse. No. 1831, $40, Tursiops aduncus, diff. No. 1832, $40, Fregata magnificens. No. 1833, $40, Erythrotriorchis radiatus. No. 1834, $40, Tyto multipunctata, Tyto alba. No. 1835, $40, Belenois java, Delias argenthona. No. 1836, $40, Lutjanus kasmira. No. 1837, $40, Planaxis sulcatus and lighthouse. No. 1838, $40, Eretmochelys imbricata. No. 1839, $40, Capra pyrenaica pyrenaica. No. 1840, $40, Amanita flavoconia. No. 1841, $40, Smoky quartz. No. 1842, $40, Mersey Bluff Lighthouse, Tasmania. No. 1843, $40, Indian Pacific train. No. 1844, $40, Thalys, France. No. 1845, $40, 2005 Rosenbauer Panther 6x6 fire truck.

2015, June 26 Litho. *Perf. 13¼*

Sheets of 4, #a-d

1806-1825 A261 Set of 20 250.00 250.00

Souvenir Sheets

1826-1845 A261 Set of 20 200.00 200.00

MonacoPhil Stamp Exhibition, Monaco (Nos. 1816, 1836).

A262

No. 1846, $12 — Tennis: a, Player without cap. b, Two players with white shirts. c, Player wearing cap. d, Two players with red shirts.

No. 1847, $12 — Rugby players and inscription starting with: a, "Rugby is a free-flowing game. . ." b, "Rugby is named after. . ." c, "Rugby is a game played. . ." d "Rugby is a full-contact sport. . ."

No. 1848, $12 — Chess grandmasters: a, Garry Kasparov. b, Vladimir Kramnik. c, Viswanathan Anand. d, Anand and Magnus Carlsen.

No. 1849, $12 — Scouting: a, Boy Scouts caring for dog. b, Boy Scouts in canoe. c, Girl Scouts selling cookies. d, Boy Scouts at campfire.

No. 1850, $12 — Tall ships: a, Bark James Craig, flag of Australia. b, Brig Roald Amundsen, flag of Germany. c, Full-rigged ship Danmark, flag of Denmark. d, Barquentine Peacemaker, flag of United States.

No. 1851, $12 — Red Cross in Solomon Islands: a, Air ambulance. b, Medical worker and patient. c, Ambulance. d, Worker touching child.

No. 1852, $12 — Journeys of Pope Francis: a, Turkey, 2014. b, Rio de Janeiro, Brazil, 2013. c, South Korea, 2014. d, Colombo, Sri Lanka, 2015.

No. 1853, $12 — Queen Elizabeth II, longest-reigning British monarch, and: a, Duke and Duchess of Cambridge with baby. b, Prince Philip, Pope John Paul II, flag of Great Britain. c, Red Cross ambulance, dog. d, Princess Diana and Princes William and Harry.

No. 1854, $12 — Birth of Princess Charlotte of Cambridge: a, Duke of Cambridge holding Prince George, flag of Great Britain. b, Duke and Duchess of Cambridge with Princess Charlotte, Buckingham Palace. c, Princess Charlotte in arms of Duchess of Cambridge. d, Duke and Duchess of Cambridge with Prince George, flag of Great Britain.

No. 1855, $12 — Agatha Christie (1890-1976), writer, and: a, Double-decker bus. b, Desk and Big Ben. c, Flag of Great Britain and characters from her books. d, Typewriter, Great Pyramid of Giza.

No. 1856, $12 — Elvis Presley (1935-77): a, With dog, Brutus, in beach buggy. b, With arms extended. c, With Tennessee Walking horse. d, Playing guitar.

No. 1857, $12 — Details of paintings by Jean-François Millet (1814-75): a, Noonday Rest. b, Harvesters Resting. c, The Church at Gréville. d, Temptation of St. Anthony.

No. 1858, $12 — Details of paintings by Camille Pissarro (1830-1903): a, Promenade de Bord de l'Eau. b, Outer Harbor of Le Havre. c, Peasant Woman Lying in the Grass. d, The Hill at Jallais, Pontoise.

No. 1859, $12 — Details of paintings by Vincent van Gogh (1853-90): a, Self-portrait, 1889. b, Daubigny's Garden. c, The Red Vineyard. d, Wheatfield Under Thunderclouds.

No. 1860, $12 — Orchids: a, Bipinnula fimbriata. b, Vanda concolor. c, Oncidium excavatum. d, Chloraea bletioides.

No. 1861, $12 — Frigatebirds: a, Two Fregata andrewsi. b, Fregata minor. c, One Fregata andrewsi. d, Fregata ariel.

No. 1862, $12 — Terns: a, Sternula albifrons. b, Anous minutus. c, Sterna hirundo. d, Gygis alba.

No. 1863, $12 — Monarch flycatchers: a, Monarcha frater. b, Myiagra caledonica. c, Clytorhynchus nigrogularis. d, Monarcha cinerascens.

No. 1864, $12 — Honeyeaters: a, Myzomela cardinalis. b, Myzomela tristrami. c, Myzomela eichhorni. d, Manorina melanocephala.

No. 1865, $12 — Dinosaurs: a, Ankylosaurus magniventris. b, Amargasaurus cazaui. c, Archaeopteryx lithographica. d, Avaceratops lammersi.

No. 1866, $40, Tennis player, diff. No. 1867, $40, Rugby players, diff. No. 1868, $40, Anand, diff. No. 1869, $40, Scouts toasting marshmallows over campfire. No. 1870, $40, Bark Kaiwo Maru, flag of Japan. No. 1871, $40, Red Cross worker and infant. No. 1872, $40, Pope Francis in Rio de Janeiro, Brazil, 2013, diff. No. 1873, $40, Queen Elizabeth II, Prince Philip and their children. No. 1874, $40, Princess Charlotte of Cambridge. No. 1875, $40, Christie typing, Greenway Estate. No. 1876, $40, Presley and motorcycle. No. 1877, $40, Diana Resting, by Millet. No. 1878, $40, View of Bazincourt, Sunset, by Pissarro. No. 1879, $40, First Steps, After Millet, by van Gogh. No. 1880, $40, Rhynchostele cordata. No. 1881, $40, Fregata minor, diff. No. 1882, $40, Hydroprogne caspia. No. 1883, $40, Monarcha richardsii. No. 1884, $40, Manorina melanocephala, diff. No. 1885, $40, Allosaurus fragilis.

2015, Sept. 3 Litho. *Perf. 13¼*

Sheets of 4, #a-d

1846-1865 A262 Set of 20 240.00 240.00

Souvenir Sheets

1866-1885 A262 Set of 20 200.00 200.00

A263

No. 1886, $12 — Two Ursus maritimus (Polar bears): a, On ice, denomination at LR. b, On ice, denomination at LL. c, Under water, denomination at LR. d, Under water, denomination at LL.

No. 1887, $12 — Dogs: a, Saint Bernard. b, Dutch shepherd. c, Labrador retriever. d, Dalmatian.

No. 1888, $12 — Dolphins: a, Sousa chinensis. b, Two Tursiops truncatus above water. c, Lagenorhynchus obscurus. d, Tursiops truncatus under water.

No. 1889, $12 — Orcinus orca (killer whales): a, Breaching surface. b, Jumping above water's surface. c, Pod of three whales. d, One whale under water.

No. 1890, $12 — Owls: a, Otus bakkamoena. b, Tyto longimembris. c, Tyto soumagnei and Strix seloputo. d, Phodilus badius and Tyto longimembris.

No. 1891, $12 — Birds of prey: a, Milvus migrans. b, Gyps fulvus. c, Circus pygargus. d, Accipiter gentilis.

No. 1892, $12 — Butterflies: a, Hypochrysops narcissus. b, Rapala varuna. c, Polyura sempronius. d, Danaus affinis malayanus.

No. 1893, $12 — Turtles: a, Chelonia mydas. b, Eretmochelys imbricata. c, Caretta caretta. d, Lepidochelys olivacea.
No. 1894, $12 — Australian mushrooms: a, Aleuria rhenana. b, Anthrocophyllum archeri. c, Austropaxillus infundibuliformis. d, Boletus regius.
No. 1895, $12 — Australian minerals: a, Pyromorphite on malachite. b, Inesite. c, Pyromorphite. d, Red rhodonite.
No. 1896, $12 — Nicoolò Paganini (1782-1840), violinist: a, One image, denomination at LR. b, Two images, denomination at LL. c, Two images, denomination at LR. d, One image, denomination at LL.
No. 1897, $12 — Return to India of Mahatma Gandhi (1869-1948), cent.: a, Gandhi as boy in 1876. b, Gandhi in London, 1888. c, Gandhi in South Africa, 1895. d, Gandhi and his room in Ahmedabad.
No. 1898, $12 — Liberation of Auschwitz, 70th anniv.: a, Prisoners, railroad tracks, camp gate, map of post-war Poland. b, T-34 tank, camp gate. c, Prisoners, fence and barracks, map of post-war Poland. d, T-34 tank, Ilyushin Il-2, fence and barracks.
No. 1899, $12 — United Nations, 70th anniv.: a, Secretary General Ban Ki-moon, airplane and helicopter. b, Secretary General Kofi Annan, meeting room. c, United Nations peacekeeper, children playing soccer. d, United Nations support vehicles in peacekeeping mission.
No. 1900, $12 — First spacewalk, 50th anniv.: a, Astronaut in space and Alexey Leonov wearing helmet. b, Leonov wearing helmet, Soyuz mission medal. c, Leonov spacewalking, Voskhod 2. d, Leonov in military uniform, spacecraft and spacewalker.
No. 1901, $12 — Rotary International in the Solomon Islands: a, Banner of Honiara Rotary Club. b, Two women with crops grown through Food Plant Solutions program. c, Donations being collected in Auki. d, Rotary International District 9600 flag.
No. 1902, $12 — Lighthouses: a, Heceta Head Lighthouse, Oregon. b, Cape Brett Lighthouse, New Zealand. c, Drum Point Lighthouse, Maryland. d, Pigeon Point Lighthouse, California.
No. 1903, $12 — Fastest high-speed trains: a, L0 Series, Japan. b, Shanghai Maglev, People's Republic of China. c, CRH 380A, People's Republic of China. d, NTV Alstom AGV 575, Italy.
No. 1904, $12 — Formula 1 race car drivers: a, Ayrton Senna (1960-94). b, Alberto Ascari (1918-55). c, Niki Lauda. d, Alain Prost.
No. 1905, $12 — 2016 European Soccer Championships, France: a, Goaltender catching ball, map of France. b, Player kicking ball, Eiffel Tower. c, Two players and ball. d, Player kicking ball, map of France.
No. 1906, $40, Polar bears and Battersea Power Station, Great Britain. No. 1907, $40, Siberian husky. No. 1908, $40, Cephalorhynchus heavisidii. No. 1909, $40, Orcinus orca with open mouth. No. 1910, $40, Strix leptogrammica. No. 1911, $40, Pandion haliaetus. No. 1912, $40, Eurema hecabe. No. 1913, $40, Lepidochelys olivacea, diff. No. 1914, $40, Mycena interrupta. No. 1915, $40, Chalcopyrite. No. 1916, $40, Paganini, diff. No. 1917, $40, Gandhi on Salt March, 1930. No. 1918, $40, Oskar Schindler (1908-74), rescuer of Jews, entrance to Auschwitz Concentraion Camp. No. 1919, $40, United Nations transport vehicles. No. 1920, $40, Leonov, Voskhod 2 and Apollo-Soyuz flight emblem. No. 1921, $40, Rotary International emblem, women escaping 2014 Solomon Islands flood. No. 1922, $40, Toledo Harbor Lighthouse, Ohio. No. 1923, $40, L0 Series train, diff. No. 1924, $40, Michael Schumacher and Formula 1 race car. No. 1925, $40, Two soccer players and ball, diff.

2015, Sept. 25 Litho. *Perf. 13¼*

Sheets of 4, #a-d

1886-1905 A263 Set of 20 240.00 240.00

Souvenir Sheets

1906-1925 A263 Set of 20 200.00 200.00

Fish A264

Designs: $5, Pink skunk anemonefish. $10, Orange skunk anemonefish. $15, White-bonnet anemonefish. $20, Clownfish. $25, Saddle-back anemonefish. $30, Clark's anemonefish. $35, Orange-fin anemonefish. $40, Red-and-black anemonefish. $45, Spinecheek anemonefish.

2015, Nov. 1 Litho. *Perf. 13x13¼*

1926-1934 A264 Set of 9 57.50 57.50

A265

A266

A267

Worldwide Fund for Nature (WWF) A268

Design: $40, Cromileptes altivelis, diff.

2015, Nov. 30 Litho. *Perf. 13x13¼*

1935	Horiz. strip of 4	7.00	7.00
a.	A265 $7 multi	1.75	1.75
b.	A266 $7 multi	1.75	1.75
c.	A267 $7 multi	1.75	1.75
d.	A268 $7 multi	1.75	1.75
e.	Souvenir sheet of 4, #1935a-1935d	7.00	7.00
f.	Sheet of 8, 2 each #1935a-1935d, + central label	14.00	14.00

Souvenir Sheet

Perf. 13¼

1936 A268 $40 multi 10.00 10.00

No. 1936 contains one 48x33mm stamp.

A269

No. 1937, $7 — United Nations, 70th anniv.: a, United Nations Headquarters, New York City. b, United Nations Office in Geneva, Switzerland. c, United Nations Office in Vienna, Austria. d, Flag and arms of Solomon Islands.
No. 1938, $7 — Reunification of Germany, 25th anniv.: a, Wolfgang Schäuble and Günther Krause signing Unification Treaty. b, Border-crossing East Germans being greeted. c, Fall of the Berlin Wall. d, Monday evening demonstration in Leipzig.
No. 1939, $7 — Campaign against malaria: a, Fight against mosquitos transmitting malaria. b, Local people keeping safe from malaria infection. c, Doctor treats a malaria-infected child. d, Mother and child awaiting malaria treatment.
No. 1940, $7 — Fire trucks: a, 1927 Dennis Ajax. b, 1967 Land Rover Series IIa HCB Angus LWR. c, 1997 Hummer H1. d, 2010 Lentner Avenger.
No. 1941, $7 — European high-speed trains: a, Railjet, Austria. b, Eurostar e320, Great Britain. c, Alfa Pendular, Portugal. d, Alvia, Spain.
No. 1942, $7 — 2016 Summer Olympics, Rio de Janeiro: a, Canoeing. b, Artistic gymnastics. c, High jump. d, Basketball.
No. 1943, $7 — Apollo space missions: a, Apollo 17 astronaut Ronald E. Evans, Jr. in space. b, Apollo 17 Lunar Rover and astronaut. c, Apollo 17 crew members Eugene Cernan and Evans. d, Astronaut David Scott in Apollo 9 Command Module.
No. 1944, $7 — 2015 Nobel Prize Winners: a, Physics laureates Arthur B. McDonald and Takaaki Kajita. b, Literature laureate Svetlana Alexievich. c, Economics laureate Angus Deaton. d, Physiology or Medicine laureates William C. Campbell, Satoshi Omura, and Youyou Tu.
No. 1945, $7 — Princess Diana (1961-97): a, With Princes William and Harry. b, With young girl. c, With Nelson Mandela. d, With Mother Teresa.
No. 1946, $7 — Paintings by Pierre-Auguste Renoir (1841-1919): a, The Canoeist's Luncheon. b, Beaulieu and Self-portrait. c, The Fisherman and Self-portrait. d, Portrait of Alphonsine Fournaise.
No. 1947, $7 — Salvador Dalí (1904-89), painter: a, Dalí and The Temptation of St. Anthony. b, Swans Reflecting Elephants. c, Melting Watch. d, Dalí and Dreams Caused by the Flight of a Bee Around a Pomegranate a Second Before Awakening.
No. 1948, $7 — Whales: a, Megaptera novaeangliae. b, Physeter macrocephalus. c, Eubalaena australis. d, Balaenoptera acutorostrata.
No. 1949, $7 — Butterflies: a, Precis octavia. b, Graphium policenes. c, Euphaedra janetta. d, Cymothoe mabillei.
No. 1950, $7 — Fish: a, Diodon holocanthus. b, Plectorhinchus lineatus. c, Balistoides conspicillum. d, Amphilophus hybrid.
No. 1951, $7 — Dinosaurs: a, Segnosaurus galbinensis. b, Centrosaurus apertus. c, Ankylosaurus magniventris. d, Scipionyx samniticus.
No. 1952, $7 — Orchids: a, Dendrobium bigibbum. b, Dendrobium loddigesii. c, Flickingeria fimbriata. d, Dendrobium bracteosum.
No. 1953, $7 — Pilgrimage to Mecca: a, Camels and driver, map of pilgrimage. b, Man's head being shaved. c, People in prayer. d, Hands and prayer book.
No. 1954, $7 — Christmas: a, Santa Claus, reindeer and house. b, Nativity scene. c, Adoration of the Magi. d, Santa Claus and sleigh.
No. 1955, $7 — New Year 2016 (Year of the Monkey): a, Monkey walking. b, Adult and juvenile monkeys. c, Monkeys holding each other. d, Monkey swinging from vine.
No. 1956, $40, United Nations Office in Nairobi. No. 1957, $40, Soviet President Mikhail Gorbachev and West German Chancellor Helmut Kohl. No. 1958, $40, Red Cross volunteer giving malaria treatment. No. 1959, $40, 1911 Christie fire truck. No. 1960, $40, Frecciarossa 1000 train, Italy. No. 1961, $40, Discus. No. 1962, $40, Apollo 17 astronauts on Moon. No. 1963, $40, Earth, dove and Tunisian flag (National Dialogue Quartet, 2015 Nobel Peace Prize recipients). No. 1964, $40, Princess Diana, Queen Mother Elizabeth and Prince William. No. 1965, $40, Roses and Jasmine in a Delft Vase and Self-portrait, by Renoir. No. 1966, $40, Rock'n'Roll and self-portrait of Dalí. No. 1967, $40, Pseudorca crassidens. No. 1968, $40, Colotis danae. No. 1969, $40, Oncorhynchus mykiss. No. 1970, $40, Megalosaurus nasicornis. No. 1971, $40, Dendrobium fimbriatum. No. 1972, $40, Pilgrims Going to Mecca, by Léon Belly. No. 1973, $40, Infant Jesus. No. 1974, Face of monkey, mouth open.

2015, Nov. 30 Litho. *Perf. 13¼*

Sheets of 4, #a-d

1937-1955 A269 Set of 19 130.00 130.00

Souvenir Sheets

1956-1974 A269 Set of 19 190.00 190.00

A270

No. 1975, $7 — Phascolarctos cinereus (Koala): a, Sleeping between tree branches. b, On tree branch. c, Two animals sleeping. d, Head.
No. 1976, $7 — Sarcophilus harrisii (Tasmanian devil): a, Facing right with open mouth. b, Facing forward with open mouth. c, Facing right with closed mouth. d, Facing left with closed mouth.
No. 1977, $7 — Vombatus ursinus (Wombat): a, Facing right, head raised. b, Facing left. c, Facing forward, head raised. d, Facing right, head touching ground.
No. 1978, $7 — Kangaroos: a, Macropus rufus. b, Head of Macropus rufus. c, Macropus giganteus. d, Macropus giganteus hopping to right.
No. 1979, $7 — Sea lions: a, Phocarctos hookeri. b, Zalophus wollebaeki. c, Eumetopias jubatus. d, Neophoca cinerea.
No. 1980, $7 — Cats: a, Sphynx. b, British Blue. c, Scottish Fold. d, Persian.
No. 1981, $7 — Tigers: a, Panthera tigris corbetti. b, Panthera tigris jacksoni. c, Panthera tigris tigris. d, White Bengal tiger.
No. 1982, $7 — Dogs: a, Jack Russell terrier. b, Rottweiler. c, Beagle. d, Labrador retriever.
No. 1983, $7 — Canis lupus dingo (dingo): a, With front paws on rock. b, Head. c, Two animals. d, With front paw raised.
No. 1984, $7 — Dromaius novaehollandiae (Emu): a, Head facing left. b, Walking. c, Stretching neck to left. d, Head facing right.
No. 1985, $7 — Owls: a, Strix aluco. b, Asio otus. c, Tyto alba. d, Megascops asio.
No. 1986, $7 — Water birds: a, Alcedo atthis. b, Pelcanus occidentalis. c, Balearica regulorum. d, Larus pacificus.
No. 1987, $7 — Birds of prey: a, Buteo rufofuscus. b, Aquila heliaca. c, Pandion haliaetus. d, Sagittarius serpentarius.
No. 1988, $7 — Butterflies: a, Papilio glaucus. b, Plebeius argus. c, Danaus plexippus. d, Apatura ilia.
No. 1989, $7 — Reef fish: a, Holacanthus ciliaris. b, Pterois volitans. c, Balistoides conspicillum. d, Chelmon rostratus.
No. 1990, $7 — Corals: a, Diploria labyrinthiformis. b, Acropora palmata. c, Dendrogyra cylindrus. d, Diploastrea heliopora.
No. 1991, $7 — Jellyfish: a, Chrysaora fuscescens. b, Phyllorhiza punctata. c, Aurelia labiata. d, Rhizostoma pulmo.
No. 1992, $7 — Shells: a, Cassis tuberosa. b, Melo aethiopica. c, Strombus pugilis. d, Phyllonotus pomum.
No. 1993, $7 — Turtles: a, Chelonia mydas, head at right. b, Eretmochely imbricata. c, Caretta caretta. d, Chelonia mydas, head at left.
No. 1994, $7 — Endangered animals: a, Pongo abelii. b, Astrochelys radiata. c, Lycaon pictus. d, Spheniscus demersus.
No. 1995, $7 — Stamps depicting fauna: a, Romania #3233. b, Laos #1177, Bulgaria #3399. c, Russia #5541, Poland #2679. d, Grenada #854.
No. 1996, $7 — Orchids: a, Cypripedium calceolus. b, Cattleya sp. c, Cattleyas trianae. d, Ophrys apifera.
No. 1997, $7 — Mushrooms: a, Boletus edulis. b, Craterellus cornucopioides. c, Lentinula edodes. d, Amanita caesarea.
No. 1998, $7 — Minerals: a, Smoky quartz with agardite. b, Crystal. c, Citrine. d, Elbaite.
No. 1999, $7 — Lighthouses: a, Urk Lighthouse, Netherlands. b, Start Point Lighthouse, England. c, St. Augustine Lighthouse, Florida. d, Point Cabrillo Lighthouse, California.
No. 2000, $35, Phascolarctos cinereus, diff. No. 2001, $35, Sarcophilus harrisii, diff. No. 2002, $35, Vombatus ursinus, diff. No. 2003, $35, Macropus rufus, diff. No. 2004, $35, Zalophus californianus. No. 2005, $35, Chartreux cat. No. 2006, $35, Panthera tigris altaica. No. 2007, $35, West Highland white terrier. No. 2008, $35, Canis lupus dingo, diff. No. 2009, $35, Dromaius novaehollandiae, diff. No. 2010, $35, Pulsatrix perspicillata. No. 2011, $35, Ephippiorhynchus senegalensis. No. 2012, $35, Aquila chrysaetos. No. 2013, $35, Papilio demoleus. No. 2014, $35, Pomacanthus imperator. No. 2015, $35, Caulastrea furcata. No. 2016, $35, Chrysaora fuscescens, diff. No. 2017, $35, Nautilus pompilius. No. 2018, $35, Caretta caretta, diff. No. 2019, $35, Canis rufus. No. 2020, $35, North Korea #2963, Uzbekistan #65. No. 2021, $35, Paphiopedilum gratixianum. No. 2022, $35, Cantharellus cibarius. No. 2023, $35, Fluorite. No. 2024, $35, White Shoal Lighthouse, Michigan.

2016, May 13 Litho. *Perf. 13¼*

Sheets of 4, #a-d

1975-1999 A270 Set of 25 180.00 180.00

Souvenir Sheets

2000-2024 A270 Set of 25 225.00 225.00

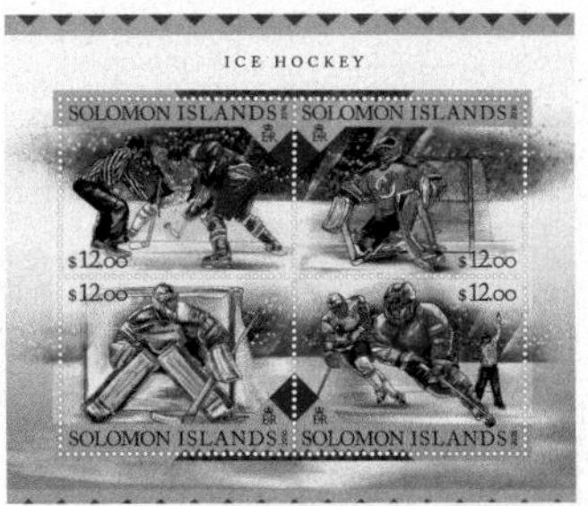

A271

No. 2025, $12 — Ice hockey players: a, Referee dropping puck for face-off. b, Goalie with New Jersey Devils uniform. c, Goalie with green and white uniform. d, Two players chasing puck, referee with arm raised.

No. 2026, $12 — 2018 World Cup Soccer Championships, Russia: a, Russian flag, two eagles, orb and scepter. b, Denis Glushakov, Luzhniki Stadium, Moscow. c, Igor Akinfeev, Spartak Stadium, Moscow. d, Deputy Prime Minister Vitaly Mutko, buildings in Red Square, Moscow.

No. 2027, $12 — 2014 Winter Olympics gold medalists: a, Matthias Mayer, flag of Austria. b, Ted Ligety, flag of United States. c, Adelina Sotnikova, flag of Russia. d, Vic Wild, flag of Russia.

No. 2028, $12 — Royal Mail, 500th anniv.: a, Letter, quill pen, inkwell, woman mailing letter. b, Postman emptying pillar box, Post Office sign. c, Postman on Royal Mail BSA motorbike, Brixton sorting office. d, Postal workers delivering mail.

No. 2029, $12 — Lord Robert Baden-Powell (1857-1941), founder of Scouting movement: a, Wearing Indian headdress, Scouts at campfire. b, Wearing hat, Scouts at flag ceremony. c, Wearing hat, Scouting flag. d, Wearing hat, Scouts giving salute.

No. 2030, $12 — Publication of Albert Einstein's Theory of Relativity, cent.: a, Speed relativity. b, Light relativity. c, Einstein and space curvature. d, Observatory, position of stars according to theory of relativity.

No. 2031, $12 — Zika virus: a, Microcephalic baby infected with Zika virus and Zika virus. b, Red Cross doctors taking care of child. c, Doctor looking for Zika virus. d, Doctor, child, mosquito.

No. 2032, $12 — Prince (1958-2016), rock musician: a, With Madonna. b, Holding guitar. c, Holding guitar and microphone. d, With Apollonia Kotero.

No. 2033, $12 — Walt Disney (1901-66), animated film producer: a, With girl wearing crown. b, Drawing character on easel, lizard. c, Riding miniature train. d, Behind camera.

No. 2034, $12 — Marilyn Monroe (1926-62), actress, and: a, Bus stop sign. b, Playing cards. c, Blowing dress. d, Motion picture film, portraits by Andy Warhol.

No. 2035, $12 — 90th birthday of Queen Elizabeth II, and: a, Royal cypher and St. Edward's crown. b, Prince Philip. c, Grandchildren. d, Royal Cypher as Head of the Commonwealth, horse.

No. 2036, $12 — Princess Diana (1961-97): a, With Prince Charles at wedding. b, With Mother Teresa, child. c, With flowers and houses. d, As infant, with parents Edward Spencer and Frances Ruth Roche.

No. 2037, $12 — First birthday of Princess Charlotte: a, With mother, Duchess of Cambridge. b, With stuffed animal, in baby carriage, with parents and brother. c, With parents and brother. d, With parents, brother, and grandmother, Queen Elizabeth II.

No. 2038, $12 — World Youth Day 2016: a, Youth, flags, Black Madonna, Polish buildings. b, Youths, flags, dove, St. John Paul II (1920-2005) in Poland, 1992. c, St. John Paul II with youth in France, 1997. d, Youth, Brazilian Flags, Pope Francis, 2013.

No. 2039, $12 — Attack on Pearl Harbor, 75th anniv.: a, Aichi D3A, Boeing P-26 Peashooter. b, USS California, Mitsubishi A6M Rei-sen. c, USS Oklahoma, Nakajima B5N. d, Admiral Isoroku Yamamoto (1884-1943), commander of attack.

No. 2040, $12 — Paintings of 1666 Great Fire of London by: a, Jan Griffier, c. 1675. b, Unknown artist, c. 1700. c, Unknown artist, c.1666. d, Philip James de Loutherbourg, 1797.

No. 2041, $12 — Louis Blériot (1872-1936), aviatior and airplane manufacturer: a, Blériot XI and Dover Castle. b, Blériot, flags of Great Britain and France, map of flight crossing English Channel. c, Blériot and Blériot 5190 seaplane. d, Blériot III.

No. 2042, $12 — First flight of the Hindenburg, 80th anniv.: a, Hindenburg above Berlin Cathedral. b, Hindenburg at mooring mast, cameraman and automobile. c, Hindenburg Captain Max Pruss (1891-1960), Hindenburg in flight. d, Hindenburg over Olympic Stadium, Berlin, Mercedes-Benz 770 automobiles.

No. 2043, $12 — First commercial service of the Concorde, 40th anniv.: a, Air France Concorde 205 F-BVFA. b, British Airways Concorde 214 G-BOAG. c, Air France Concorde 203 F-BTSC. d, British Airways Concorde 204, G-BOAC.

No. 2044, $12 — First manned space flight of Yuri Gagarin (1934-68), 55th anniv.: a, Gagarin and Vostok 1. b, Gagarin lifting weights, launch of Vostok 1. c, People watching Gagarin on television. d, Technician checking Gagarin in spacesuit.

No. 2045, $12 — Paintings by American Impressionists: a, April (The Green Gown), by Childe Hassam. b, New York from Brooklyn, by Colin Campbell Cooper. c, Woman Seated in a Garden, by Frederick Carl Frieseke. d, Summer Day, Brighton Beach, by Edward Henry Potthast.

No. 2046, $12 — Paintings by Claude Monet (1840-1926): a, The Red Raod Near Menton. b, Morning on the Seine. c, Plum Trees in Blossom at Vetheuil. d, Argenteuil, Flowers by the Riverbank.

No. 2047, $12 — Paintings by Pablo Picasso (1881-1973): a, The Girls of Avignon. b, Mother and Child (Baladins). c, Reclining Nude. d, Three Musicians.

No. 2048, $12 — Musée d'Orsay, 30th anniv.: a, The Snake Charmer, painting by Henri Rousseau. b, Starry Night Over the Rhone, painting by Vincent van Gogh. c, Sappho, sculpture by James Pradier. d, Apollo's Chariot, painting by Odilon Redon.

No. 2049, $35, Two ice hockey players. No. 2050, $35, Map of Russia made of soccer balls, flag of Russia. No. 2051, $35, Elizabeth Yarnold, 2014 Olympic gold medalist, flag of Great Britain. No. 2052, $35, Royal Mail van, postman watching woman mail letter. No. 2053, $35, Baden-Powell, scouts, Scouting flag. No. 2054, $35, Einstein and clock. No. 2055, $35, Hand holding test tube with blood infected with Zika virus, fetus in womb. No. 2056, $35, Prince and Beyoncé. No. 2057, $35, Disney, bear and deer. No. 2058, $35, Monroe, male actor and motion picture film. No. 2059, $35, Queen Elizabeth II and Princess Diana. No. 2060, $35, Two images of Princess Diana. No. 2061, $35, Princess Charlotte and Prince George of Cambridge. No. 2062, $35, St. Faustina (1905-38), heart and Jesus. No. 2063, $35, Gen. Douglas MacArthur (1880-1964), Vought SB2U airplane, U.S. navy ship. No. 2064, $35, The Great Fire of London, by Griffier. No. 2065, $35, Blériot XI. No. 2066, $35, Hindenburg in flight. No. 2067, $35, Air France Concorde 213 F-BTSD and Air France Concorde 215 F-BVFF. No. 2068, $35, Gagarin wearing space helmet. No. 2069, $35, Summer, by Cooper. No. 2070, $35, Mount Riboudet in Rouen in Spring, by Monet. No. 2071, $35, Houses on the Hill, by Picasso. No. 2072, $35, The Dance Class, by Edgar Degas.

2016, Aug. 1 Litho. *Perf. 13¼*

Sheets of 4, #a-d

2025-2048	A271	Set of 24	295.00	295.00

Souvenir Sheets

2049-2072	A271	Set of 24	215.00	215.00

Nos. 2049-2072 each contain one 50x38mm stamp.

Philataipei 2016 World Stamp Exhibition, Taipei — A272

No. 2073: a, Chiang Kai-shek (1897-1975), President of Republic of China, and wife, Soong Mei-ling (1898-2003). b, Chiang and flag of Republic of China. c, Statue of Chiang. d, Chiang and bird.

$35, Chiang Kai-shek Memorial Hall, Taipei.

Litho. With Foil Application

2016, Aug. 1 *Perf. 13*

2073	A272 $12 Sheet of 4, #a-d		12.50	12.50

Souvenir Sheet

2074	A272 $35 multi		9.00	9.00

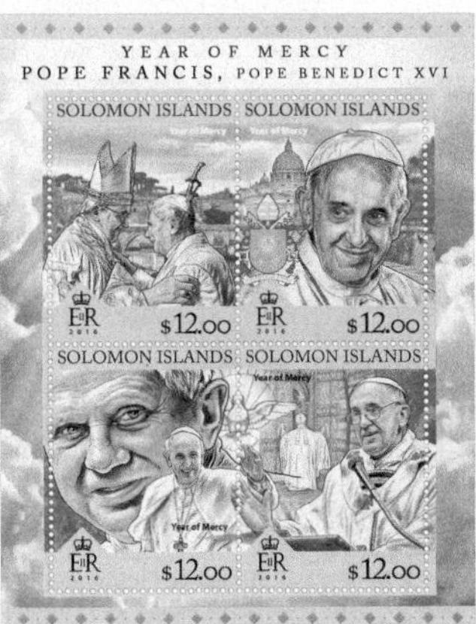

A273

No. 2075, $12 — Year of Mercy: a, Pope Francis embracing Pope Emeritus Benedict XVI. b, Pope Francis and his coat of arms. c, Pope Francis in foreground, Pope Emeritus Benedict XVI in background. d, Pope Francis behind microphone.

No. 2076, $12 — Large airplanes: a, Airbus A380. b, Boeing 747-8. c, Antonov AN-124. d, Tupolev Tu-160.

No. 2077, $12 — High-speed trains: a, Harmony CRH 380A, flag of People's Republic of China. b, AGV Italo, flag of Italy. c, Siemens Velaro E AVE S103, flag of Spain. d, E5 Series Shinkansen hayabusa, Flag of Japan.

No. 2078, $12 — Special transportation: a, Bell CH-146 Griffon helicopter. b, Yamaha WaveRunner jet ski police. c, Response Boat Medium. d, Shannon Class lifeboat FCB2.

No. 2079, $12 — Tall ships: a, Belem. b, Elissa. c, James Craig. d, Europa.

No. 2080, $12 — Submarines: a, Severodvinsk class. b, Dolphin class. c, Seawolf class. d, Astute class.

No. 2081, $12 — Lighthouses: a, Ile Vierge Lighthouse, France. b, Genoa Lighthouse, Italy. c, Baishamen Lighthouse, People's Republic of China. d, Campen Lighthouse, Germany.

No. 2082, $12 — Wolfgang Amadeus Mozart (1756-91), composer: a, Playing harpsichord, building in background. b, With string instrument, rose and score. c, With violin and score. d, With building in background.

No. 2083, $12 — Elvis Presley (1935-77): a, With G clef in background, record at right. b, With musical symbols, record at left. c, With automobile tail fin in background. d, With Graceland in background.

No. 2084, $12 — Bud Spencer (1929-2016), actor, filmmaker and swimmer: a, Spencer in swim trunks, and in suit, waving. b, In scene from *A Fistful of Hell.* c, In scene from *All the Way, Boys.* d, In scene from *God Forgives. . . I Don't!.*

No. 2085, $12 — Nelson Mandela (1918-2013), President of South Africa: a, With South African flag and his book *Long Walk to Freedom.* b, With South African flag. c, Holding World Cup trophy. d, Wearing eyeglasses.

No. 2086, $12 — European royalty: a, Crown Prince Haakon Magnus of Norway and his family. b, King Harald V of Norway. c, King Carl XVI Gustaf and Queen Silvia of Sweden. d, King Willem-Alexander and Queen Máxima of the Netherlands.

No. 2087, $12 — Chess: a, Chess pieces. b, Magnus Carlsen at chess board. c, Garry Kasparov and Anatoly Karpov. d, Fabiano Caruana and chess piece.

No. 2088, $12 — 2016 Summer Olympics, Rio de Janeiro: a, Canoe slalom. b, Fencing. c, Water polo. d, Modern pentathlon.

No. 2089, $12 — Table tennis players: a, Paddle, ball in air, man wearing red shirt. b, Man in green shirt and silhouette of player. c, Woman in magenta and gray shirt. d, Female and male players.

No. 2090, $12 — Paintings by Hieronymus Bosch (c. 1450-1516): a, The Garden of Earthly Delights. b, Adoration of the Magi. c, The Haywain. d, The Wayfarer.

No. 2091, $12 — Paintings by Paul Cézanne (1839-1906): a, Millstone in the Park of the Château Noir. b, Apples and Oranges. c, Boy in a Red Vest. d, The Black Marble Clock.

No. 2092, $12 — Dolphins: a, Grampus griseus, Lagenorhynchus obscurus. b, Cephalorhynchus commersonii and ship. c, Two Tursiops truncatus and sailboat. d, Three Cephalorhynchus heavisidii and ship.

No. 2093, $12 — Owls: a, Micrathene whitneyi. b, Bubo virginianus. c, Pseudoscops grammicus. d, Bubo scandiacus.

No. 2094, $12 — Butterflies and moths: a, Candalides absimilis. b, Anteos maerula. c, Daphnis nerii. d, Nymphalis antiopa.

No. 2095, $12 — Dinosaurs: a, Lambeosaurus. b, Abelisaurus. c, Pachyrhinosaurus. d, Ouranosaurus nigeriensis.

No. 2096, $12 — Mushrooms: a, Tylopilus felleus. b, Gyromitra esculenta. c, Cantharellus cibarius. d, Amanita muscaria.

No. 2097, $35, Pope Francis and Pope Emeritus Benedict XVI embracing. No. 2098, $35, Antonov An-225 Mriya. No. 2099, $35, Shanghai Maglev, flag of People's Republic of China. No. 2100, $35, BMW i3 EV fire vehicle. No. 2101, $35, Khersones. No. 2102, $35, HMAS Rankin. No. 2103, $35, Jeddah Lighthouse, Saudi Arabia. No. 2104, $35, Mozart and statue. No. 2105, $35, Presley with guitar, crown and musical notes. No. 2106, $35, Spencer in scene from *They Call Me Trinity.* No. 2107, $35, Mandela and flag of South Africa, diff. No. 2108, $35, Princesses Victoria and Estelle and Prince Daniel of Sweden. No. 2109, $35, Kasparov, Carlsen and Bobby Fischer, chess board and pieces. No. 2110, $35, Tennis player, flag of Brazil, stadium. No. 2111, $35, Two table tennis players. No. 2112, $35, Christ Crowned With Thorns, by Bosch. No. 2113, $35, Banks of the Marne, by Cézanne. No. 2114, $35, Three Sousa chinensis and junk. No. 2115, $35, Bubo virginianus, diff. No. 2116, $35, Papilio troilus and caterpillar. No. 2117, $35, Stegosaurus and Achelousaurus. No. 2118, $35, Morchella esculenta.

2016, Sept. 1 Litho. *Perf. 13¼*

Sheets of 4, #a-d

2075-2096	A273	Set of 22	270.00	270.00

Souvenir Sheets

2097-2118	A273	Set of 22	200.00	200.00

Nos. 2097-2118 each contain one 38x50mm stamp.

Philataipei 2016 World Stamp Exhibition, Taipei — A274

No. 2119: a, Chiang Kai-shek (1897-1975), President of Republic of China, and Chiang Kai-shek Memorial Hall, Taipei. b, Soong Meiling (1898-2003), wife of Chiang Kai-shek, Taipei 101 Building. c, Urocissa caerulea, Taroko National Park Pagoda, horiz. d, Chiang and Memorial Hall, horiz.

$35, Chiang Kai-shek in military uniform, vert..

Litho. With Foil Application

2016, Sept. 1 *Perf. 13¼*

2119	A274 $7 Sheet of 4, #a-d		7.25	7.25

Souvenir Sheet

2120	A274 $35 multi		9.00	9.00

Philataipei 2016 World Stamp Exhibition, Taipei — A275

No. 2121: a, Dalai Lama with legs crossed. b, Dalai Lama and Ma Ying-jeou, President of Republic of China. c, Dalai Lama and Chen Shui-bian, President of Republic of China. d, Dalai Lama and Annette Lu, Vice-President of Republic of China.

$35, Dalai Lama and Chen Chu, Mayor of Kaohsiung, Republic of China.

2016, Sept. 1 Litho. *Perf.*
2121 A275 $7 Sheet of 4, #a-d 7.25 7.25

Souvenir Sheet

2122 A275 $35 multi 9.00 9.00

Muhammad Ali (1942-2016), Boxer — A276

No. 2123: a, Head of Ali, Ali wearing boxing trunks and red gloves. b, Ali celebrating victory. c, Ali wearing black gloves. d, Ali wearing red gloves.
$35, Ali, diff.

2016, Sept. 1 Litho. *Perf. 13¼*
2123 A276 $12 Sheet of 4, #a-d 12.50 12.50

Souvenir Sheet

2124 A276 $35 multi 9.00 9.00

A277

No. 2125, $12 — Cricket players: a, Batsman with white uniform. b, Batsman with yellow uniform. c, Fielder with green and yellow uniform. d, Fielder with blue and red uniform.
No. 2126, $12 — Sports of 2016 Summer Paralympics, Rio de Janeiro: a, Track and field. b, Tennis. c, Swimming. d, Soccer.
No. 2127, $12 — Battle of Verdun, cent.: a, German soldier and Battle of Verdun Veteran's Cross. b, French Marshal Philippe Pétain, German General Erich von Falkenhayn. c, Helmets on rifles, barbed wire barrier. d, French soldier and Croix de Guerre.
No. 2128, $12 — Battle of Moscow, 75th anniv.: a, German Field Marshal Fedor von Bock (1880-1945). b, German troops attacking Soviet positions. c, Soldiers on parade in Moscow, medal for the defense of Moscow. d, Russian Marshal Aleksandr Vasilevsky (1985-1977).
No. 2129, $12 — Christopher Columbus (1451-1506), explorer: a, Kneeling. b, With ship, Santa Maria. c, With nautical chart and compass. d, Holding staff, ships and map in background.
No. 2130, $12 — Russian cosmonauts: a, Andriyan Nikolayev (1929-2004). b, Pavel Popovich (1930-2009). c, Yuri Gagarin (1934-68). d, Gherman Titov (1935-2000).
No. 2131, $12 — Composers: a, Wolfgang Amadeus Mozart (1756-91). b, Johann Strauss II (1825-99). c, Richard Wagner (1813-83). d, Ludwig van Beethoven (1770-1827).
No. 2132, $12 — Canonization of Mother Teresa: a, Mother Teresa (1910-97). b, Mother Teresa and Pope John Paul II. c, Pope Francis wearing zucchetto, nuns, portrait of Mother Teresa. d, Pope Francis wearing miter, three nuns, portrait of Mother Teresa.
No. 2133, $12 — 2016 Nobel laureates: a, Juan Manuel Santos, Peace. b, Bernard L. Feringa, Sir J. Fraser Stoddart, Jean-Pierre Sauvage, Chemistry. c, J. Michael Kosterlitz, David J. Thouless, Duncan M. Haldane, Physics. d, Yoshinori Ohsumi, Physiology or Medicine.
No. 2134, $12 — Toyota Corolla, 50th anniv.: a, Toyota Corolla (E170). b, Toyota Corolla Levin SR (AE85). c, Toyota Corolla Levin TE27. d, Toyota Corolla (E20).
No. 2135, $12 — Fire fighting equipment: a, 1961American LaFrance truck. b, Erickson S-64 Aircrane helicopter. c, MetalCraft Marine FireStorm 50 boat. d, Rosenbauer Panther 6x6 CA5 airport crash tender.
No. 2136, $12 — Steam trains: a, London and North Eastern Railway Class A4 locomotive 60022 Mallard, 1938. b, American Freedom Train 4449, 1941. c, Norfolk & Western J Class 611, 1950. d, Chesapeake and Ohio No. 490, 1926.
No. 2137, $12 — Sled dogs: a, Samoyeds. b, Chinooks. c, Seppala Siberians. d, Alaskan Malamutes.
No. 2138, $12 — Turtles: a, Graptemys oculifera. b, Geochelone elegans. c, Hydromedusa tectifera. d, Pangshura tecta.
No. 2139, $12 — Orchids: a, Dendrobium hybrid. b, Red Cymbidium sp. c, Oncidium Alliance "Colmanara Wildcat." d, Red and white Cymbidium sp.
No. 2140, $12 — Minerals in jewelry: a, Amethyst. b, Citrine. c, Demantoid garnet. d, Ruby.
No. 2141, $12 — Christmas: a, La Befana, Italy. b, Chysh Khan, Yakutia, Russia. c, Christmas Festival, India. d, Krampus and St. Nikoalus, Austria.
No. 2142, $12 — New Year 2017 (Year of the Rooster), Rooster paintings of roosters by: a, Xu Beihong (1895-1953). b, Gao Jianfu (1879-1951), with tail of rooster extending below country name. c, Gao Jianfu (with tail of rooster within red frame. d, Rèn Yí (1840-96).
No. 2143, $40, Cricket batsman. No. 2144, $40, Paralymics high jumper. No. 2145, $40, French World War I soldiers, military cemetery. No. 2146, $40, Russian General Georgy Zhukov (1896-1974), buildings on Red Square, Moscow. No. 2147, $40, Columbus, compass, map and flag of Castile and Léon. No. 2148, $40, Russian cosmonaut Valentina Tereshkova. No. 2149, $40, Carl Maria von Weber (1786-1826), composer. No. 2150, $40, Painting of Mother Teresa. No. 2151, $40, Bob Dylan, 2016 Nobel Laureate in Literature. No. 2152, $40, Toyota corolla Levin/Sprinter Trueno (AE86) with rally modification. No. 2153, $40, American LaFrance Type 38 fire truck. No. 2154, $40, London Midland and Scottish Railway Coronation Class locomotive, 1938. No. 2155, $40, Siberian husky sled dogs. No. 2156, $40, Dermochelys coriacea. No. 2157, $40, Cymbidium sp. orchid, diff. No. 2158, $40, Turquoise. No. 2159, $40, Christmas dancers, Solomon Islands. No. 2160, $40, Painting of Rooster, by Rèn Yí, diff.

2016, Dec. 1 Litho. *Perf. 13¼*

Sheets of 4, #a-d

2125-2142 A277 Set of 18 220.00 220.00

Souvenir Sheets

2143-2160 A277 Set of 18 185.00 185.00

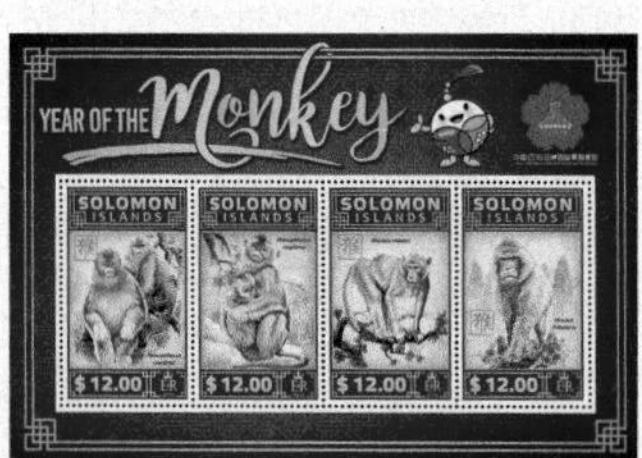

New Year 2016 (Year of the Monkey) — A278

No. 2161: a, Two adult Rhinopithecus roxellana. b, Adult and juvenile Rhinopithecus roxellana. c, Macaca mulatta. d, Macaca thibetana.
$40, People's Republic of China #1586.

2016, Dec. 1 Litho. *Perf. 13¼*
2161 A278 $12 Sheet of 4, #a-d 12.50 12.50

Souvenir Sheet

2162 A278 $40 multi 10.50 10.50

China 2016 International Stamp Exhibition, Nanning.

Chinese Porcelain — A279

No. 2163: a, Kangxi period plate. b, Qing Dynasty eight-sided vase. c, Two Qinglong period vases. d, Ming Dynasty lidded bowl.
$40, Ming Dynasty Qilin lion.

2016, Dec. 1 Litho. *Perf. 13¼*
2163 A279 $12 Sheet of 4, #a-d 12.50 12.50

Souvenir Sheet

2164 A279 $40 multi 10.50 10.50

China 2016 International Stamp Exhibition, Nanning. No. 2164 contains one 36x51mm stamp.

Marilyn Monroe (1926-62), Actress — A280

No. 2165 — Monroe and: a, Clapboard. b, Star of Hollywood Walk of Fame. c, Film reel. d, Motion picture camera.
$40, Monroe and film reel, diff.

Litho. & Embossed With Foil Application

2016, Dec. 1 *Perf.*
2165 A280 $12 Sheet of 4, #a-d 12.50 12.50

Souvenir Sheet

2166 A280 $40 multi 10.50 10.50

No. 2166 contains one 39x41mm heart-shaped stamp.

Cat and Dog Breeds A281

No. 2167 — Cat breeds: a, Ukrainian Levkoy. b, Lykoi. c, Maine Coon cat. d, British Longhair. e, Somali cat. f, Siamese cat. g, Cornish Rex. h, Ragamuffin. i, Brown Oriental Shorthair. j, Manx cat. k, Sphynx cat. l, Scottish Fold. m, Exotic Shorthair/Persian cat. n, Turkish Angora. o, Savannah. p, Burmese cat. q, Singapura. r, Ragdoll. s, Bengal cat. t, White and brown Oriental Shorthair. u, Siberian. v, Russian Blue. w, American Curl. x, Birman. y, Selkirk Rex. z, Arabian Mau. aa, Bambino cat. ab, Japanese Bobtail. ac, Norwegian Forest cat. ad, Abyssinian cat. ae, Burmilla. af, Aegean cat. ag, Exotic Shorthair. ah, Egyptian Mau. ai, Persian cat. aj, German Rex.
No. 2168 — Dog breeds: a, Rough collie. b, Scottish terrier. c, Bernese Mountain dog. d, Irish terrier. e, Old English sheepdog. f, Irish setter. g, Dalmatian. h, Malinois dog. i, Russkiy toy. j, Afghan hound. k, Doberman pinscher. l, Great Dane. m, Viszla. n, Chow chow. o, Dachshund. p, Bordeaux mastiff. q, Husky. r, Poodle. s, Griffon Bruxellois. t, German shorthaired pointer. u, Chinese crested dog. v, Golden retriever. w, White shepherd. x, Welsh corgi. y, Chihuahua. z, Pomeranian. aa, Czechoslovakian wolfdog. ab, French bulldog. ac, Irish wolfhound. ad, St. Bernard. ae, German shepherd. af, Blue-nosed pit bull. ag, Beagle. ah, Australian shepherd. ai, Yorkshire terrier. aj, Pug.

2016, Dec. 1 Litho. *Perf. 13x13¼*
2167 Sheet of 36 65.00 65.00
a.-aj. A281 $7 Any single 1.75 1.75
2168 Sheet of 36 65.00 65.00
a.-aj. A281 $7 Any single 1.75 1.75

Fish A282

No. 2169: a, Chaetodontoplus mesoleucus. b, Amphiprion melanopus. c, Neoglyphidodon thoracotaeniatus. d, Pictichromis paccagnellae. e, Cephalopholis boenak. f, Centropyge bicolor. g, Canthigaster epilampra. h, Parupeneus multifasciatus. i, Dascyllus reticulatus. j, Amphiprion sandaracinos. k, Amblyglyphidodon aureus. l, Hoplolatilus marcosi. m, Chromis retrofasciata. n, Centropyge loriculus. o, Epinephelus fasciatus. p, Cirrhilabrus exquisitus. q, Centropyge fisheri. r, Chrysiptera parasema. s, Acanthurus maculiceps. t, Halichoeres biocellatus. u, Cheilodipterus quinquelineatus. v, Anoplocapros inermis. w, Bodianus mesothorax. x, Chaetodon oxycephalus. y, Betta splendens. z, Lutjanus kasmira. aa, Amphiprion ocellaris. ab, Chrysiptera flavipinnis. ac, Heniochus acuminatus. ad, Centropyge heraldi. ae, Myripristis hexagon. af, Anampses neoguinaicus. ag, Genicanthus lamarck. ah, Coradion altivelis. ai, Abudefduf lorenzi. aj, Chaetodon quadrimaculatus.

2016, Dec. 1 Litho. *Perf. 13x13¼*
2169 Sheet of 36 65.00 65.00
a.-aj. A282 $7 Any single 1.75 1.75

Dinosaurs A283

No. 2170: a, Allosaurus fragilis. b, Alamosaurus sanjuanensis. c, Apatosaurus ajax. d, Baryonyx walkeri. e, Chasmosaurus. f, Cryolophosaurus ellioti. g, Deinonychus antirrhopus. h, Edmontosaurus regalis. i, Euplocephalus tutus. j, Gastonia burgei. k, Hadrosaurus foulkii. l, Herrerasaurus ischiqualastensis. m, Irritator. n, Kentrosaurus aethiopicus. o, Majungasaurus crenatissimus. p, Megaraptor namunhuaiquii. q, Muttaburrasaurus langdoni (name on two lines). r, Muttaburrasaurus langdoni (name on one line). s, Ornithomimus velox. t, Pachycephalosaurus wyomingensis. u, Plateosaurus engelhardti. v, Psittacosaurus mongoliensis. w, Pterodactylus antiquus. x, Rhamphorhynchus muensteri. y, Saurolophus osborni. z, Sauroposeidon proteles. aa, Spinosaurus aegyptiacus. ab, Stegosaurus stenops. ac, Struthiomimus altus. ad, Suchomimus tenerensis. ae, Tenontosaurus. af, Triceratops horridus. ag, Tropeognathus mesembrinus. ah, Tsintaosaurus spinorhinus. ai, Tyrannosaurus rex. aj, Velociraptor mongoliensis.

2016, Dec. 1 Litho. *Perf. 13x13¼*
2170 Sheet of 36 65.00 65.00
a.-aj. A283 $7 Any single 1.75 1.75

A284

No. 2171, $12 — Dugong dugon: a, One dugong eating fish. b, One dugong, head at UL. c, Two dugongs. d, One dugong, head at UR.

No. 2172, $12 — Dolphins: a, Sousa sahulensis. b, Delphinus delphis. c, Grampus griseus. d, Steno bredanensis.

No. 2173, $12 — Kangaroos: a, Macropus giganteus. b, Macropus giganteus, Osphranter rufus. c, Macropus fuliginosus, Osphranter rufus. d, Macropus fuliginosus.

No. 2174, $12 — Pandas: a, Two Ailuropoda melanoleuca. b, Ailurus fulgens. c, Head of Ailurus fulgens. d, Ailuropoda melanoleuca qinlingensis.

No. 2175, $12 — Australian birds of prey: a, Falco cenchroides. b, Falco berigora. c, Pandion haliaetus. d, Haliaeetus leucogaster.

No. 2176, $12 — Australian water birds: a, Nycticorax caledonicus. b, Cygnus olor, Cygnus atratus. c, Dendrocygna arcuata. d, Ardea picata.

No. 2177, $12 — Owls: a, Bubo africanus. b, Bubo sumatranus. c, Bubo lacteus. d, Bubo philippensis.

No. 2178, $12 — Butterflies: a, Colias eurytheme. b, Battus philenor. c, Danaus gilippus. d, Papilio glaucus.

No. 2179, $12 — Australian crocodiles: a, Crocodylus porosus, head at right. b, Crocodylus johnsoni near water. c, Crocodylus johnsoni, no water nearby. d, Crocodylus porosus, head at left.

No. 2180, $12 — Australian endangered species: a, Cacatua tenuirostris. b, Litoria aurea. c, Macrotis lagotis. d, Delma australis.

No. 2181, $12 — COP17 conference emblem, map and endangered species: a, Ceratotherium simum simum. b, Smutsia gigantea. c, Gorilla beringei. d, Loxodonta africana.

No. 2182, $12 — Mushrooms: a, Boletus subcaerulescens. b, Amanita flavoconia. c, Helvella lacunosa. d, Russula emetica.

No. 2183, $12 — Formula 1 race car drivers: a, Michael Schumacher. b, Lewis Hamilton. c, Niki Lauda. d, Ayrton Senna (1960-94).

No. 2184, $12 — Australian ships: a, HMAS Leeuwin. b, HMAS Canberra. c, HMAS Perth. d, HMAS Sirius.

No. 2185, $12 — Australian trains: a, Genesee & Wyoming Australia locomotive GM46. b, Waratah Set A44, Sydney Trains. c, ML2 locomotive B74, Victorian Railways. d, Genesee & Wyoming Australia locomotive CLF5.

No. 2186, $12 — Japanese high-speed trains: a, E2 Series Shinkansen. b, E7 Series Shinkansen. c, E5 Series Shinkansen. d, L0 Series Maglev.

No. 2187, $12 — Shenzhou 11 and Tiangong 2 rendezvous: a, Launch of Shenzhou 11. b, Shenzhou 11 crew member Chen Dong. c, Shenzhou 11 crew member Jing Haipeng. d, Tiangong 2 in orbit.

No. 2188, $12 — Lighthouses: a, Haengdamdo Lighthouse, South Korea, and hot air balloon. b, Niushan Dao Lighthouse, People's Republic of China, and dragon. c, Zeni Shima Lighthouse, Japan, and Haliaeetus pelagicus. d, Môle de l'Est Lighthouse, France, and Rhodostethia rosea.

No. 2189, $12 — Red Cross activities in Solomon Islands: a, Red Cross worker, child in water, Carney Airfield. b, Boy holding stick, building, Red Cross flag. c, Red Cross worker carrying boxes. d, Child drinking water from pipe, Red Cross workers.

No. 2190, $12 — Famous Australians: a, Barry J. Marshall, 2005 Nobel laureate in Physiology or Medicine, and Elizabeth Blackburn, 2009 Nobel laureate in Physiology or Medicine. b, Lleyton Hewitt, tennis player, and Mark Webber, race car driver. c, Russell Crowe, actor, and Cate Blanchett, actress. d, Kylie Minogue and Nick Cave, singers.

No. 2191, $12 — Mohandas K. Gandhi (1869-1948), Indian nationalist leader: a, Statue of Gandhi, and Big Ben, London. b, Gandhi and foliage. c, Gandhi. d, Gandhi and statue of Ganesha.

No. 2192, $12 — Paintings by Paul Gauguin (1848-1903): a, Tahitian Women. b, Breton Girls Dancing, Port-Aven. c, Tahitian Mountains. d, Arearea.

No. 2193, $12 — Paintings by Vincent van Gogh (1853-90): a, Le Moulin de la Galette. b, Van Gogh's Bedroom in Arles. c, Interior of a Restaurant in Arles. d, The Gleize Bridge over the Vigueirat Canal.

No. 2194, $12 — Paintings by Ilya Repin (1844-1930): a, Religious Procession in Kursk Province. b, Ivan the Terrible and His Son, Ivan on November 16, 1581. c, Sadko in the Underwater Kingdom. d, Self-portrait at Work.

No. 2195, $12 — Paintings by Viktor Vasnetsov (1848-1926): a, Maria Magdalene. b, Christ Almighty. c, Bogatyr, the Knight on the Horse. d, Ivan Tsarevich Riding the Gray Wolf.

No. 2196, $40, Dugong dugon and two fish. No. 2197, $40, Lagenorhynchus obscurus. No. 2198, $40, Osphranter rufus. No. 2199, $40, Ailuropoda melanoleuca. No. 2200, $40, Pandion haliaetus, diff. No. 2201, $40, Bubulcus ibis. No. 2202, $40, Asio flammeus. No. 2203, $40, Callophrys gryneus. No. 2204, $40, Crocodylus porosus, diff. No. 2205, $40, Erythrura gouldiae. No. 2206, $40, Psittacus erithacus. No. 2207, $40, Craterellus tubaeformis. No. 2208, $40, Schumacher, diff. No. 2209, $40, HMAS Bundaberg. No. 2210, $40, Duke of Edinbugh 621, South Australian Railways. No. 2211, $40, N700 Series Shinkansen. No. 2212, $40, Shenzhou 11 and Tiangong 2 rendezvous. No. 2213, $40, Joyato Lighthouse, Japan. No. 2214, $40, Red Cross worker carrying boxes, Red Cross flag, child. No. 2215, $40, Zhao Zong-Yuan, chess grandmaster, and Brian Schmidt, 2011 Nobel laureate in Physics. No. 2216, $40, Gandhi and lotus flower. No. 2217, $40, The Day of the God, by Gauguin. No. 2218, $40, Vase with White and Red Carnations, by van Gogh. No. 2219, $40, Barge Haulers on the Volga, by Repin. No. 2220, $40, The Flying Carpet, by Vasnetsov.

2016, Dec. 12 Litho. *Perf. 13¼*
Sheets of 4, #a-d

2171-2195 A284 Set of 25 305.00 305.00

Souvenir Sheet

2196-2220 A284 Set of 25 255.00 255.00

A285

No. 2221, $10 — Disappearance of Amelia Earhart (1897-1937), aviator, 80th anniv.: a, Earhart wearing helmet, airplane in flight. b, Earhart wearig blue blouse near propeller. c, Earhart wearing flight jacket near propeller. d, Earhart wearing helmet and goggles.

No. 2222, $10 — French airplanes: a, First flight of Blériot VII, 1907. b, Blériot XI crossing English Channel, 1909. c, First flight of SPAD S.XIII, 1917. d, First flight of SPAD S.XX, 1918.

No. 2223, $10 — Supersonic aircraft: a, Bell X-1. b, English Electric Lightning. c, SEPECAT Jaguar. d, Saab JAS 39 Gripen.

No. 2224, $10 — Special transportation: a, Self-propelled modular transporter. b, CNH Concept autonomous tractor. c, SBA-60-K2 Bulat 6x6. d, Trailer with modular equipment.

No. 2225, $10 — Military ships: a, USS Independence. b, Zubr Class LCAC. c, Udaloy Class anti-submarine destroyer. d, USS Iwo Jima.

No. 2226, $10 — Opel motor vehicles: a, Adam Opel (1837-95), automobile manufacturer, and 1915 Opel Green Monster. b, 2015 Opel Vivaro. c, 1959 Opel Blitz cattle truck. d, 2000 Opel Speedster.

No. 2227, $10 — Fire engines: a, 1952 Ford. b, 1972 Mercedes-Benz 519. c, Rosenbauer Panther 6x6. d, 1914 Ford Model T.

No. 2228, $10 — Pope Emeritus Benedict XVI, 90th birthday: a, Pope Benedict XVI and Pope Francis praying. b, Pope Benedict XVI with hands together. c, Pope Benedict XVI waving. d, Pope Benedict XVI and Pope Francis embracing.

No. 2229, $10 — Water birds: a, Sterna hirundo. b, Puffinus gavia. c, Fregata minor. d, Sula sula.

No. 2230, $10 — Birds of prey: a, Accipiter fasciatus. b, Circus approximans. c, Pandion haliaetus. d, Haliaeetus leucogaster.

No. 2231, $10 — Butterflies: a, Myscelia cyaniris. b, Abisara neophron. c, Delias eucharis. d, Iphiclides podalirius.

No. 2232, $10 — Dinosaurs: a, Diplodocus carnegii. b, Velociraptor mongoliensis. c, Ankylosaurus magniventris. d, Chasmosaurus russelli.

No. 2233, $10 — Endangered animals: a, Gorilla gorilla diehli. b, Eretmochelys imbricata. c, Panthera pardus orientalis. d, Rhinoceros sondaicus.

No. 2234, $40, Earhart in airplane. No. 2235, $40, Louis Blériot (1872-1936), aviator and aircraft manufacturer. No. 2236, $40, Fairey Delta 2. No. 2237, $40, CAT 797 haul truck. No. 2238, $40, Admiral Kuznetsov aircraft carrier and airplane. No. 2239, $40, 1899 Opel Patent motor car. No. 2240, $40, 1890s Ahrens steam fire engine. No. 2241, $40, Pope Emeritus Benedict XVI. No. 2242, $40, Dendrocygna eytoni. No. 2243, $40, Haliastur indus. No. 2244, $40, Anthocharis cardamines. No. 2245, $40, Triceratops horridus. No. 2246, $40, Elephas maximus sumatranus.

2017, Apr. 12 Litho. *Perf. 13¼*
Sheets of 4, #a-d

2221-2233 A285 Set of 13 135.00 135.00

Souvenir Sheets

2234-2246 A285 Set of 13 135.00 135.00

Works of Renaissance Artists — A286

No. 2247, $10 — Paintings by Hieronymus Bosch (c.1450-1516): a, Adoration of the Child. b, Crucifixion with a Donor. c, The Concert in the Egg. d, Saint Christopher.

No. 2248, $10 — Paintings by Sandro Botticelli (c.1445-1510): a, The Cestello Annunciation. b, The Birth of Venus. c, Primavera. d, Portait of Simonetta Vespucci.

No. 2249, $10 — Paintings by Albrecht Dürer (1471-1528): a, Courtyard of the Former Castle in Innsbruck with Clouds. b, Portrait of Felicitas Tucher. c, The Virgin and Child with Saint Anne. d, Stag Beetle.

No. 2250, $10 — Paintings by Masaccio (1401-28): a, Birth Tray. b, St. Jerome and St. John the Baptist. c, Distribution of Alms and Death of Ananias. d, The Tribute Money.

No. 2251, $10 — Paintings by Michelangelo (1475-1564): a, The Torment of Saint Anthony. b, Satyr's Head. c, Cleopatra. d, The Delphic Sibyl.

No. 2252, $10 — Paintings by Raphael (1483-1520): a, Madonna in the Meadow. b, St. George and the Dragon. c, Vision of a Knight. d, The Holy Family of the Oak Tree.

No. 2253, $10 — Paintings by Paolo Uccello (1397-1475): a, Mary's Presentation in the Temple. b, Stoning of St. Stephen. c, St. George and the Dragon. d, Victory Over Bernardino Della Ciarda.

No. 2254, $10 — Paintings by Giorgio Vasari (1511-74): a, Judith and Holofernes. b, St. Luke Painting the Virgin. c, The Last Supper. d, Holy Family.

No. 2255, $10 — Paintings by Tiziano Vecelli (Titian) (c.1488-1576): a, Empress Isabel of Portugal. b, Equestrian Portrait of Chales V. c, Salome with the Head of John the Baptist. d, Christ Carrying the Cross.

No. 2256, $10 — Paintings by Leonardo da Vinci (1452-1519): a, Ginevra de' Benci. b, Madonna of the Carnation. c, The Virgin and Child with St. Anne. d, Saint John the Baptist.

No. 2257, $40, Christ Mocked (the Crowning with Thorns), by Bosch. No. 2258, $40, Probable Self-portrait in Adoration of the Magi, by Botticelli. No. 2259, $40, Self-portrait, by Dürer. No. 2260, $40, Self-portrait in a Fresco, by Masaccio. No. 2261, $40, Holy Family with St. John the Baptist, by Michelangelo. No. 2262, $40, Self-portrait, approximately age 23, by Raphael. No. 2263, $40, Disputation of St. Stephen, by Uccello. No. 2264, $40, Self-portrait, by Vasari. No. 2265, $40, Portrait of Pope Paul III, by Titian. No. 2266, $40, Portrait of a Bearded Man, Possibly a Self-portrait, by Leonardo.

2017, Apr. 12 Litho. *Perf. 13¼*
Sheets of 4, #a-d

2247-2256 A286 Set of 10 100.00 100.00

Souvenir Sheets

2257-2266 A286 Set of 10 100.00 100.00

Nos. 2257-2266 each contain one 42x51mm stamp.

Bandung 2016 World Stamp Exhibition — A287

No. 2267 — Bandung, Indonesia attractions: a, Palm sculpture, by Nyoman Nuarta. b, Bumi Siliwangi. c, Bandung Institute of Technology. d, Gedung Sate.

$40, Bandung Metro Kapsul.

Litho. With Foil Application

2017, Apr. 12 *Perf. 13¼*

2267 A287 $10 Sheet of 4, #a-d 10.00 10.00

Souvenir Sheet

2268 A287 $40 multi 10.00 10.00

New Year 2017 (Year of the Rooster) A288

2017, Apr. 12 Litho. *Perf. 13¼*

2269 A288 $10 multi 2.50 2.50

No. 2269 was printed in sheets of 4.

A289

No. 2270, $10 — Sled dogs: a, Siberian huskies in race, sled driver wearing number 77. b, Team of Siberian huskies, no sled. c, Alaskan malamutes and sled. d, Siberian huskies and two people.

No. 2271, $10 — Dolphins: a, Lagenorhynchus albirostris, Delphinus capensis. b, Tursiops truncatus, Lagenorhynchus albirostris. c, Inia geoffrensis, Tursiops truncatus. d, Two Tursiops truncatus.

No. 2272, $10 — Owls: a, Bubo virginianus. b, Strix varia. c, Bubo sumatranus. d, Athene cunicularia.

No. 2273, $10 — Mushrooms: a, Hygrocybe psittacina. b, Cantharellus cibarius. c, Russula aurea. d, Boletus satanas.

No. 2274, $10 — Minerals: a, Morganite. b, Beryl. c, Tanzanite. d, Tourmaline.

No. 2275, $10 — Sinking of the Titanic, 105th anniv.: a, Lifeboat near sinking Titanic. b, People on dock watching Titanic depart. c, Titanic, iceberg and ship captain. d, Titanic at sea.

No. 2276, $10 — Wilbur Wright, 150th anniv.: a, Wright Model F, Wilbur Wright (1867-1912). b, Wright Flyer 1, Bodie Island Lighthouse, North Carolina. c, Wright Model A, Wilbur and brother Orville (1871-1948). d, Wright Flyer 1 and Wilbur.

No. 2277, $10 — Ferdinand von Zeppelin (1838-1917), airship builder: a, Zeppelin, without hat, and diagram of airships. b, Zeppelin LZ-5. c, LZ-10 Schwaben. d, Zeppelin, wearing hat, and diagrams of airship.

No. 2278, $10 — European high-speed trains: a, FS Class ETR 500 and flag of Italy. b, V250 and flag of Netherlands. c, CGI of planned HS2 rail line and flag of Great Britain. d, Class 114 train, flag of Spain.

No. 2279, $10 — Ferrari automobiles, 70th anniv., with Ferrari 125 S pointing to: a, Right, wheels straight. b, Left, car covering dots in frame. c, Right, wheels turned. d, Left, car not covering dots in frame.

No. 2280, $40, Siberian huskies pulling sled. No. 2281, $40, Two Lagenorhynchus albirostris. No. 2282, $40, Tyto alba. No. 2283, $40, Gomphidius glutinosus. No. 2284, $40, Moonstone. No. 2285, $40, Iceberg, ship's wheel and captain. No. 2286, $40, Wright Flyer 1 and Wilbur Wright. No. 2287, $40, Zeppelin LZ-4. No. 2288, $40, FS Class ETR 200 and flag of Italy. No. 2289, $40, Enzo Ferrari (1898-1988), automobile manufacturer, and Ferrari 125 S.

2017, May 15 Litho. *Perf. 13¼*

Sheets of 4, #a-d

2270-2279 A289 Set of 10 105.00 105.00

Souvenir Sheets

2280-2289 A289 Set of 10 105.00 105.00

A290

No. 2290, $10 — Ursa maritimus: a, Two polar bears looking right. b, One polar bear looking left. c, One polar bear looking right. d, Two polar bears looking left.

No. 2291, $10 — Pandas: a, Ailurus fulgens, Latin name at UR. b, Ailuropoda melanoleuca. c, Ailuropoda melanoleuca qinlingensis. d, Ailurus fulgens, Latin name at LR.

No. 2292, $10 — Panthera tigris: a, Tiger standing, facing right, front paws above Latin name. b, Tiger standing, facing right, front paw touching Latin name. c, Tiger on rocks. d, Tiger facing left.

No. 2293, $10 — Cats: a, American Curl. b, Cornish Rex. c, Nebelung cat. d, Egyptian Mau.

No. 2294, $10 — Whales: a, Balaenoptera musculus. b, Eubalaena glacialis. c, Eschrichtius robustus. d, Balaenoptera brydei.

No. 2295, $10 — Parrots: a, Lophochroa leadbeateri. b, Eclectus roratus. c, Pseudeos fuscata. d, Cacatua galerita.

No. 2296, $10 — Butterflies: a, Ornithoptera croesus. b, Papilio torquatus. c, Polyommatus bellargus. d, Greta oto.

No. 2297, $10 — Fish: a, Acanthurus achilles. b, Acanthurus olivaceus. c, Gomphosus varius. d, Novaculichthys taeniourus.

No. 2298, $10 — Turtles: a, Dermochelys coriacea. b, Chelonia mydas, swimming downwards. c, Chelonia mydas swimming upwards. d, Eretmochelys imbricata.

No. 2299, $10 — Orchids: a, Ophrys mammosa. b, Cattleya labiata. c, Bulbophyllum lepidum. d, Cyrtochilum macranthum.

No. 2300, $10 — Pres. Frankin D. Roosevelt (1882-1945): a, White House, Roosevelt behind microphones. b, Mitsubishi A6M Zero. c, Roosevelt and ship on fire. d, Roosevelt with Winston Churchill (1874-1965) and Joseph Stalin (1878-1953).

No. 2301, $10 — Apparition of the Virgin Mary at Fatima, Portugal, cent.: a, Lúcia Santos (1907-2005), Jacinta (1910-20), and Francisco Marto (1908-19) praying, lambs in pasture. b, Sister Lúcia and Pope John Paul II (1920-2005). c, Pope Francis praying at Fatima. d, Lúcia Santos, Jacinta and Francisco Marto standing.

No. 2302, $10 — Ships that never sailed: a, HMS Thunder Child from *The War of the Worlds*. b, Pequod from *Moby-Dick*. c, Pirate ship with Jolly Roger flag. d, The Nautilus.

No. 2303, $10 — Steam trains: a, London and North Eastern Railway A4 4468 Mallard. b, Pennsylvania Railroad S1 Big Engine. c, Chesapeake & Ohio Class L 4-6-4 Hudson. d, London and North Eastern Railway A3 4472 Flying Scotsman.

No. 2304, $10 — Lighthouses: a, Castle Hill Lighthouse, Rhode Island. b, Sumiyoshi Lighthouse, Japan. c, South Channel Pile Light, Australia. d, Oswego Harbor West Pierhead Lighthouse, New York.

No. 2305, $40, Ursa maritimus facing right, diff. No. 2306, $40, Ailuropoda melanoleuca, diff. No. 2307, $40, Panthera tigris, diff. No. 2308, $40, Siamese cat. No. 2309, $40, Balaena mysticetus. No. 2310, $40, Amazona autumnalis. No. 2311, $40, Kallima inachis. No. 2312, $40, Pygocentrus nattereri. No. 2313, $40, Eretmochelys imbricata, diff. No. 2314, $40, Cleisocentron merrillianum. No. 2315, $40, Roosevelt, Navy ship, U.S. flag. No. 2316, $40, The Miracle of the Sun, Fatima, Portugal. No. 2317, $40, The Flying Dutchman. No. 2318, $40, South African Railways Class 26 4-8-4. No. 2319, $40, Aniva Lighthouse, Russia.

2017, May 15 Litho. *Perf. 13¼*

Sheets of 4, #a-d

2290-2304 A290 Set of 15 155.00 155.00

Souvenir Sheets

2305-2319 A290 Set of 15 155.00 155.00

A291

No. 2320, $10 — Dromaius novaehollandiae: a, Running left. b, Head, facing left. c, Head, facing right. d, Two emus.

No. 2321, $10 — Rare birds of the Solomon Islands: a, Ptilinopus eugeniae. b, Columba pallidiceps, Gallicolumba beccarii. c, Ducula brenchleyi, Gallicolumba salamonis. d, Micropsitta bruijnii.

No. 2322, $10 — Bees and orchids: a, Bombus terrestris, Cymbidium Clarisse Austin "Best Pink". b, Dasypoda hirtipes, Maxillaria tenuifolia. c, Apis mellifera, Odontoglossum crispum. d, Apis cerana, Oncidium margalefii.

No. 2323, $10 — Dinosaurs: a, Triceratops horridus. b, Ornithomimus velox. c, Ceratosaurus nasicornis. d, Plesiosaurus dolichodeirus.

No. 2324, $10 — Launch of Laika, first dog in space, 60th anniv.: a, Laika in Sputnik 2 capsule. b, Laika in harness. c, Laika, Sputnik 2 capsule. d, Laika in space capsule seat.

No. 2325, $10 — John H. Glenn, Jr. (1921-2016), astronaut and senator: a, In space suit, with space capsule. b, Standing next to military jet. c, Receiving Presidential Medal of Freedom from Pres. Barack Obama. d, In space suit in space capsule.

No. 2326, $10 — Pres. John F. Kennedy (1917-63): a, On boat. b, With Astronaut John Glenn. c, With wife, Jacqueline. d, Campaigning in crowd.

No. 2327, $10 — Nelson Mandela (1918-2013), President of South Africa: a, With Queen Elizabeth II. b, With wife, Graca Machel. c, With Pres. Bill Clinton. d, Alone.

No. 2328, $10 — Pope Francis: a, With Queen Elizabeth II. b, With King Felipe VI and Queen Letizia of Spain. c, With Pres. Donald Trump. d, Alone.

No. 2329, $10 — Princess Diana (1961-97): a, With Mother Teresa and child. b, 1981-96 coat of arms. c, Wearing protective gear. d, With Pope John Paul II.

No. 2330, $10 — Muhammad Ali (1942-2016), boxer: a, Wearing boxing gloves, with title belt. b, With Malcolm X. c, With Nelson Mandela. d, With American flag, WBC championship belt and boxing match posters.

No. 2331, $10 — Charlie Chaplin (1889-1977), actor: a, In spotlight. b, In boat. c, Seated against wall. d, Tipping hat.

No. 2332, $10 — Marilyn Monroe (1926-62), actress, with background color of: a, Blue. b, Green. c, Yellow. d, Red.

No. 2333, $10 — Ludwig van Beethoven (1770-1827), composer: a, Bust on pillar, hands of pianist. b, Head of Beethoven. c, Beethoven and piano. d, Statue of Beethoven, musical score.

No. 2334, $10 — Alexander Pushkin (1799-1837), writer: a, Pushkin House (Institute of Russian Literature), St. Petersburg, Russia, and rose. b, Statue of Pushkin on bench. c, Monument to Pushkin. d, Portrait of Pushkin by Vasily Tropinin.

No. 2335, $10 — Paintings by Edgar Degas (1834-1917): a, Woman Seated Beside a Vase of Flowers. b, Dancer Tilting. c, Café Concert at Les Ambassadeurs. d, Self-portrait and The Millinery Shop.

No. 2336, $10 — Paintings by Ivan Aivazovsky (1817-1900): a, Little Russian Ox Cart in Winter. b, The Rainbow. c, Battle of Chios on June 24, 1770. d, View of the Big Cascade in Petergof and the Great Palace of Petergof.

No. 2337, $10 — Stamps: a, Poland #1403. b, United States #3033, Bermuda #365. c, Russia #6178. d, Brazil #1858.

No. 2338, $10 — Cruise ships: a, Carnival Freedom. b, Viking Star. c, Amsterdam. d, Sirena.

No. 2339, $10 — Australian trains: a, The Ghan FQ01. b, GM29 Rawlinna. c, Genesee & Wyoming Australia GM43. d, Queensland Railways 1620 Class.

No. 2340, $10 — 2017 motorcycles: a, Suzuki VanVan 200. b, Yamaha FZ-09. c, Kawasaki Z1000SX. d, Triumph Street Cup.

No. 2341, $10 — Formula 1 race cars: a, Benetton B192, Mercedes F1 W06 Hybrid. b, Marussia MR03, Benetton B194. c, McLaren MCL32, Force India VJM10. d, Renault R.S. 17, Sauber C-36 Ferrari.

No. 2342, $10 — Table tennis players: a, Zhang Jike. b, Li Xiaoxia. c, Chuan Chih-yuan. d, Fang Bo.

No. 2343, $10 — 2017 Women's World Chess Championships, Tehran: a, Antoaneta Stefanova. b, Zhao Xue. c, Natalia Pogonina. d, Nino Batsiashvili.

No. 2344, $10 — New Year 2018 (Year of the Dog): a, White and black Tibetan mastiff, standing, facing right. b, Brown and black Tibetan mastiff and tower. c, Two Tibetan mastiffs. d, Brown and black Tibetan mastiff standing, facing right.

No. 2345, $40, Two Dromaius novaehollandiae, diff. No. 2346, $40, Puffinus heinrothi. No. 2347, $40, Megachile latimanus, Coelogyne asperata. No. 2348, $40, Stegosaurus stenops. No. 2349, $40, Dog, Laika, and Sputnik 2 capsule, diff. No. 2350, $40, Glenn in space suit, with space capsule, diff. No. 2351, $40, Pres. Kennedy and wife, Jacqueline at White House. No. 2352, $40, Mandela and young woman. No. 2353, $40, Pope Francis, diff. No. 2354, $40, Princess Diana and Prince Charles. No. 2355, $40, Ali and punching bag. No. 2356, $40, Chaplin and ladder. No. 2357, $40, Monroe and husband, Arthur Miller. No. 2358, $40, Beethoven and violin. No. 2359, $40, Portrait of A. S. Pushkin, by Orest Kiprensky. No. 2360, $40, Blue Dancers, by Degas. No. 2361, $40, Self-portrait, by Aivazovsky. No. 2362, $40, Uruguay #751, and philatelist examining stamp. No. 2363, $40, Disney Wonder and Balaenoptera musculus. No. 2364, $40, The Ghan liveried NR75. No. 2365, $40, 2017 Yamaha FJR1300ES motorcycle. No. 2366, $40, Mercedes F1 W04, Ferrari F14T Formula 1 race cars. No. 2367, $40, Miu Hirano playing table tennis. No. 2368, $40, Female chess players, hand moving chess piece. No. 2369, $40, Tibetan mastiff, diff.

2017, Aug. 21 Litho. *Perf. 13¼*

Sheets of 4, #a-d

2320-2344 A291 Set of 25 255.00 255.00

Souvenir Sheets

2345-2369 A291 Set of 25 255.00 255.00

Birdpex 2018, Mondorf-les-Bains, Luxembourg (Nos. 2321, 2346).

A292

No. 2370, $10 — 14th Dalai Lama: a, With St. John Paul II (1920-2005). b, With Tibetan terrier, Senge. c, With drum. d, Waving.

No. 2371, $10 — St. John Paul II: a, Holding infant. b, With hand extended. c, With pillars in background. d, Blessing person.

No. 2372, $10 — St. Teresa of Calcutta (1910-97): a, Serving food. b, With dove. c, With doves. d, With women and infants.

No. 2373, $10 — 35th birthday of Duke of Cambridge (Prince William): a, Duke and Crown of St. Edward. b, Duke and Royal Air Force Sea King helicopter. c, Duke and grandmother, Queen Elizabeth II. d, Duke and Big Ben.

No. 2374, $10 — 300th anniv. of Grand Masonic Lodge of England, and Masons: a, Sir Arthur Conan Doyle (1859-1930), writer. b, Sir Ernest Shackleton (1874-1922), Antarctic explorer. c, Sir Winston Churchill (1874-1965), British Prime Minister. d, Rudyard Kipling (1865-1936), writer.

No. 2375, $10 — Red Cross workers involved in: a, First aid training. b, Blood donation. c, Medical assistance after disasters. d, Medical assistance in conflict zones.

No. 2376, $10 — Submarines: a, USS Gudgeon. b, USS Los Angeles. c, HMS Astute. d, HMS Vanguard.

No. 2377, $10 — Indian trains: a, WDM-3A locomotive, and flag of India. b, B-26 locomotive. c, WDM-3A locomotive. d, WDM-2 locomotive and flag of India.

No. 2378, $10 — Renault automobiles: a, Renault Dauphine Ondine. b, Renault Colorale Prairie. c, Renault Scénic. d, Renault DeZir.

No. 2379, $10 — Henry Ford (1863-1947), automobile manufacturer, and: a, 1896 Ford Quadricycle. b, Thomas Edison (1847-1931), inventor, in automobile. c, 1908 Ford Model T. d, 1928 Ford Model A.

No. 2380, $10 — Fire fighting apparatus: a, Big Wind tank. b, Sikorsky S-64 helicopter. c, 1940 Ford fire truck. d, Pozhtechnika MRU VG-150 bulldozer.

No. 2381, $10 — Concorde: a, Two Concordes in flight. b, Concorde and another airplane on taxiway. c, Nose of Concorde, NASA jet carrying Space Shuttle Endeavour. d, Tail of Concorde and its cockpit.

No. 2382, $10 — Journey to Mars: a, Space tourists on Phobos. b, Astronaut and structures on Mars. c, Space capsule entering Martian atmosphere. d, Terraforming on Mars.

No. 2383, $10 — Bats: a, Two Pteropus lylei. b, Rousettus aegyptiacus. c, Cynopterus sphinx. d, One Pteropus lylei.

No. 2384, $10 — Dogs: a, Golden retriever. b, Shar-pei. c, British bulldog. d, Siberian husky.

No. 2385, $10 — Owls: a, Bubo scandiacus. b, Bubo philippensis. c, Bubo virginianus. d, Asio flammeus.

No. 2386, $10 — Hornbills: a, Bycanistes bucinator. b, Rhyticeros undulatus. c, Tockus erythrorhynchus. d, Anthracoceros albirostris.

No. 2387, $10 — Butterflies: a, Carterocephalus palaemon. b, Eurema hecabe. c, Cymothoe mabillei. d, Gonepteryx rhamni.

No. 2388, $10 — Reef fish: a, Paracanthurus hepatus. b, Zebrasoma flavescens. c, Taeniura lymma. d, Symphysodon discus.

No. 2389, $10 — Shells and lighthouses: a, Fastnet Rock Lighthouse, Ireland, Pigeon Point Lighthouse, California. b, Oliva sayana, Chicoreus ramosus, Architectonica trochlearis, Stellaria solaris. c, Pleuroploca gigantea. d, Race Rock Lighthouse, New York.

No. 2390, $10 — Turtles: a, Chelonoidis denticulata. b, Testudo hermanni. c, Stigmochelys pardalis. d, Astrochelys radiata.

No. 2391, $10 — Prehistoric water animals: a, Dinichthys terrelli. b, Temnodontosaurus burgundiae. c, Bananogmius ellisensis. d, Drepanaspis gemuendenensis.

No. 2392, $10 — Mushrooms and wildlife: a, Laccaria amethystina and Danaus plexippus. b, Boletellus obscurecoccineus and Cepaea hortensis. c, Omphalotus olearius and Vulpes

vulpes. d, Mycena interrupta and Coccinella magnifica.

No. 2393, $10 — Minerals: a, Dioptase. b, Wulfenite. c, Boussingaultite. d, Amazonite.

No. 2394, $10 — Christmas: a, Santa Claus and reindeer in flight, reindeer statue and gifts. b, Reindeer and gifts. c, Child opening Christmas gift. d, Santa Claus holding list.

No. 2395, $40, 14th Dalai Lama and statue of Buddha. No. 2396, $40, St. John Paul II wearing miter. No. 2397, $40, St. Teresa of Calcutta and 1979 medal for Nobel Peace Prize. No. 2398, $40, Duke of Cambridge and Queen Elizabeth II, diff. No. 2399, $40, Anthony Sayer (c. 1672-1741), first Grand Master of Grand Masonic Lodge of England. No. 2400, $40, Red Cross worker holding infant refugee. No. 2401, $40, USS Seawolf. No. 2402, $40, Class YP locomotive, India. No. 2403, $40, Renault Wind. No. 2404, $40, Henry Ford and 1919 Ford Model T. No. 2405, $40, Canadair CL-415 water bomber. No. 2406, $40, Concorde on ground. No. 2407, $40, Orion spacecraft and first humans on Mars. No. 2408, $40, Plecotus auritus and Cynopterus sphinx. No. 2409, $40, Welsh corgi. No. 2410, $40, Bubo scandiacus, diff. No. 2411, $40, Buceros bicornis. No. 2412, $40, Hypolycaena antifaunus. No. 2413, $40, Amphiprion ocellaris and Plocamium coccineum. No. 2414, $40, Strombus listeri, Tangasseri Lighthouse, India. No. 2415, $40, Chelonoidis nigra. No. 2416, $40, Protosphyraena perniciosa. No. 2417, $40, Hygrocybe psittacina. No. 2418, $40, Vanadinite. No. 2419, $40, Reindeer, Christmas tree and gifts.

2017, Sept. 4 Litho. *Perf. 13¼*

Sheets of 4, #a-d

2370-2394 A292 Set of 25 250.00 250.00

Souvenir Sheets

2395-2419 A292 Set of 25 250.00 250.00

SEMI-POSTAL STAMPS

Catalogue values for unused stamps in this section are for Never Hinged items.

No. 452 Ovptd. in Red "+ 50c SURCHARGE / CYCLONE RELIEF FUND / 1982"

Perf. 13½x13

1982, May 3 Litho. Wmk. 373

B1 CD331 $1 + 50c multi 2.25 2.25

Nos. 546 and 569 Srchd. "Cyclone Relief Fund 1986" and New Value in Scarlet

Perf. 14½x14

1986, Sept. 23 Litho. Wmk. 384

B2 CD336 $1 + 50c multi 1.75 1.75

Souvenir Sheet

Perf. 13½

B3 Sheet of 2 7.50 7.50
a. A95 55c + 25c multi 2.25 2.25
b. A95 $1.65 + 75c multi 4.50 4.50

No. 840 Surcharged in Red

Wmk. 373

2003, Feb. 8 Litho. *Perf. 14½*

B4 A147 $1.35 +$3 multi 7.00 7.00

World AIDS Day.

No. 866 Surcharged in Red

Perf. 14½x14

2003, Mar. 17 Wmk. 373

B5 CD355 $2 +$5 multi 7.25 7.25

Surtax for Cyclones Zoe and Beni Relief Fund.

No. 926 Surcharged in Red

Wmk. 373

2008, Oct. 23 Litho. *Perf. 14*

B6 A169 Sheet of 6, #921-925, B6a 3.75 3.75
a. $4.50+$3 multi 2.00 2.00

POSTAGE DUE STAMPS

D1

Perf. 12

1940, Sept. 1 Typo. Wmk. 4

J1	D1	1p emerald	4.50	*8.00*
J2	D1	2p dark red	4.75	*8.00*
J3	D1	3p chocolate	4.75	*13.00*
J4	D1	4p dark blue	7.25	*13.00*
J5	D1	5p deep green	8.00	*27.50*
J6	D1	6p brt red vio	8.00	*20.00*
J7	D1	1sh dull violet	10.00	*32.50*
J8	D1	1sh6p turq green	17.50	*60.00*
		Nos. J1-J8 (8)	64.75	*182.00*
		Set, never hinged	120.00	

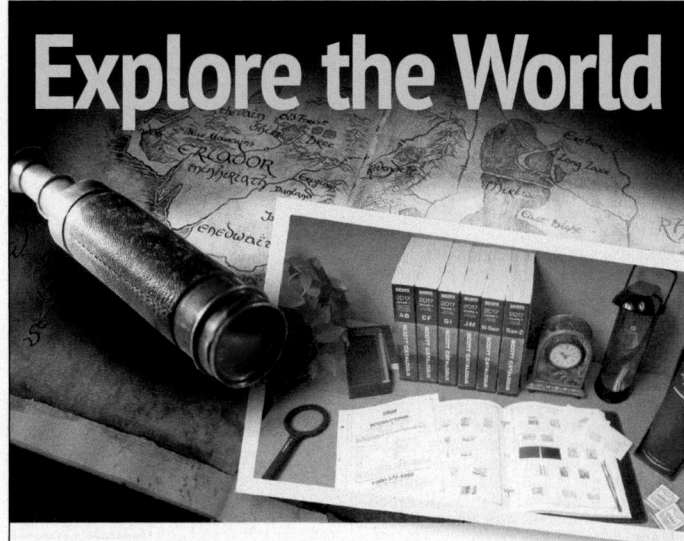

SOMALIA

sō-'mä-lē-ə

(Somali Democratic Republic)

(Italian Somaliland)

(Benadir)

LOCATION — Eastern Africa, bordering on the Indian Ocean and the Gulf of Aden
GOVT. — Probably none
AREA — 246,201 sq. mi.
POP. — 7,140,643 (1999 est.)
CAPITAL — Mogadishu

The former Italian colony which included the territory west of the Juba River became known as Oltre Giuba (Trans-Juba), was absorbed into Italian East Africa in 1936. Somalia stamps continued in use in Italian East Africa for several years. It was under British military administration from 1941-49. Italian trusteeship took effect in 1950, with a UN Advisory Council helping the administrator. On July 1, 1960, the former Italian colony merged with Somaliland Protectorate (British) to form the independent Republic of Somalia.

4 Besas = 1 Anna
16 Annas = 1 Rupee
100 Besas = 1 Rupee (1922)
100 Centesimi = 1 Lira (1905, 1925)
100 Centesimi = 1 Somalo (1950)
100 Centesimi = 1 Somali Shilling (1961)

Catalogue values for unused stamps in this country are for Never Hinged items, beginning with Scott 170 in the regular postage section, Scott B52 in the semi-postal section, Scott C17 in the airpost section, Scott CB11 in the airpost semi-postal section, Scott CE1 in the airpost special delivery section, Scott E8 in the special delivery section, Scott J55 in the postage due section, and Scott Q56 in the parcel post section.

Used values in italics are for postally used Italian Somalia stamps. CTO's or stamps with fake cancels sell for about the same as unused, hinged stamps.

Watermark

Wmk. 140 — Crown

Italian Somaliland

Elephant — A1

Lion — A2

Wmk. 140

1903, Oct. 12 Typo. *Perf. 14*

1 A1 1b brown 127.50 24.00
2 A1 2b blue green 1.40 *13.00*
3 A2 1a claret 1.40 *17.00*
4 A2 2a orange brown 1.90 *34.00*
5 A2 2½a blue 1.50 *34.00*
6 A2 5a orange 1.90 *67.50*
7 A2 10a lilac 1.90 *67.50*
Nos. 1-7 (7) 137.50 *257.00*

For surcharges see Nos. 8-27, 40-50, 70-77.

Surcharged

1905, Dec. 29

8 A2 15c on 5a org *3,000.* 1,000.
9 A2 40c on 10a lilac 950. 400.

Surcharged

1906-07

10 A1 2c on 1b brown 5.00 *15.00*
11 A1 5c on 2b blue grn 5.00 *12.00*
a. Double surcharge 350.00
b. Double surcharge, one invtd. *5,250.*
c. Pair, one without surcharge *5,000.*

Surcharges on No. 11c are virtually on top of each other. Certificates are necessary.

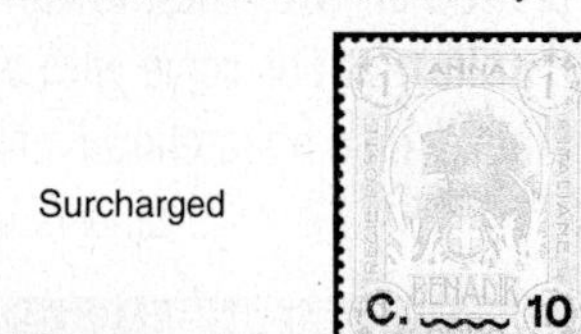

Surcharged

12 A2 10c on 1a claret 5.00 *11.00*
13 A2 15c on 2a brn org ('06) 5.00 *11.50*
14 A2 25c on 2½a blue 12.50 *11.50*
15 A2 50c on 5a yellow *25.00* *29.00*

Surcharged

1 LIRA 1

16 A2 1 l on 10a lilac 25.00 *37.50*
Nos. 10-16 (7) 82.50 *127.50*

Nos. 15 and 16 With Bars Over Former Surcharge and

1916, Apr.

18 A2 5c on 50c on 5a yel 35.00 *40.00*
a. Double surcharge, one invtd. 5,000.
19 A2 20c on 1 l on 10a dl lil 7.50 *30.00*

No. 4 Surcharged

C. 20

20 A2 20c on 2a org brn 15.00 12.00
Nos. 18-20 (3) 57.50 *82.00*

Nos. 11-16 Surcharged

a

b

1922, Feb. 1

22 A1(a) 3b on 5c on 2b 8.50 *16.00*
23 A2(b) 6c on 10c on 1a 16.00 13.00
24 A2(b) 9b on 15c on 2a 16.00 16.00
25 A2(b) 15b on 25c on 2½a 16.00 13.00
a. "15" at left omitted 300.00
26 A2(b) 30b on 50c on 5a 17.00 *36.00*
27 A2(b) 60b on 1 l on 10a 17.00 *60.00*
Nos. 22-27 (6) 90.50 *154.00*

Victory Issue

Italy Nos. 136-139 Surcharged

1922, Apr.

28 A64 3b on 5c olive grn 1.50 *5.25*
29 A64 6b on 10c red 1.50 *5.25*
30 A64 9b on 15c slate grn 1.50 *8.00*
31 A64 15b on 25c ultra 1.50 *8.00*
Nos. 28-31 (4) 6.00 *26.50*

Nos. 10-16 Surcharged with Bars and

c

d

1923, July 1

40 A1 1b brown 6.75 *27.00*
41 A1(c) 2b on 2c on 1b 6.75 *27.00*
42 A1(c) 3b on 2c on 1b 6.75 *13.00*
43 A2(d) 5b on 50c on 5a 6.75 *13.50*
44 A1(c) 6b on 5c on 2b 12.50 13.50
45 A2(d) 18b on 10c on 1a 12.50 13.50
46 A2(d) 20b on 15c on 2a 15.00 13.50
47 A2(d) 25b on 15c on 2a 15.00 13.50
48 A2(d) 30b on 25c on 2½a 17.50 17.50
49 A2(d) 60b on 1 l on 10a 17.50 *37.50*
50 A2(d) 1r on 1 l on 10a 45.00 *45.00*
Nos. 40-50 (11) 162.00 *234.50*

No. 40 is No. 10 with bars over the 1907 surcharge.

Propagation of the Faith Issue

Italy Nos. 143-146 Surcharged

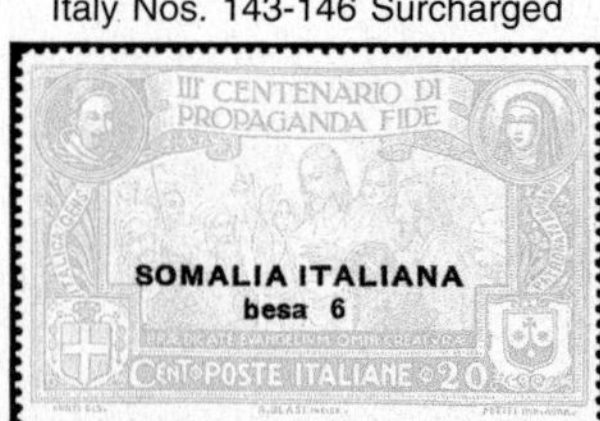

1923, Oct. 24 Wmk. 140

51 A68 6b on 20c ol grn & brn org 9.00 *40.00*
52 A68 13b on 30c cl & brn org 9.00 *40.00*
53 A68 20b on 50c vio & brn org 6.00 *45.00*
54 A68 30b on 1 l bl & brn org 6.00 *70.00*
Nos. 51-54 (4) 30.00 *195.00*

Fascisti Issue

Italy Nos. 159-164 Surcharged in Red or Black

1923, Oct. 29 Unwmk. *Perf. 14*

55 A69 3b on 10c dk grn (R) 12.00 *15.50*
56 A69 13b on 30c dk vio (R) 12.00 *15.50*
57 A69 20b on 50c brn car 12.00 *21.00*

Wmk. 140

58 A70 30b on 1 l blue 12.00 *40.00*
59 A70 1r on 2 l brown 12.00 *47.50*
60 A71 3r on 5 l blk & bl (R) 12.00 *72.50*
Nos. 55-60 (6) 72.00 *212.00*

Manzoni Issue

Italy Nos. 165-170 Surcharged in Red

1924, Apr. 1

61 A72 6b on 10c brn red & blk 8.75 *40.00*
62 A72 9b on 15c bl grn & blk 8.75 *40.00*
63 A72 13b on 30c blk & sl 8.75 *40.00*
64 A72 20b on 50c org brn & blk 8.75 *40.00*

Surcharged in Red

65 A72 30b on 1 l bl & blk 55.00 *300.00*
66 A72 3r on 5 l vio & blk 375.00 *2,300.*
Nos. 61-66 (6) 465.00 *2,760.*

Victor Emmanuel Issue

Italy Nos. 175-177 Overprinted

1925-26 Unwmk. *Perf. 13½, 11*

67 A78 60c brown car 2.00 *12.00*
a. Perf. 11 180.00 *375.00*
68 A78 1 l dk bl, perf. 11 4.50 *19.00*
a. Perf. 13½ 9.50 *50.00*
69 A78 1.25 l dk blue ('26) 2.00 *27.00*
a. Perf. 11 900.00 *1,675.*
Nos. 67-69 (3) 8.50 *58.00*

Stamps of 1907-16 with Bars over Original Values

1926, Mar. 1 Wmk. 140 *Perf. 14*

70 A1 2c on 1b brown 20.00 *42.50*
71 A1 5c on 2b blue grn 14.50 *20.00*
72 A2 10c on 1a rose red 9.50 8.50
73 A2 15c on 2a org brn 9.50 *10.00*
74 A2 20c on 2a org brn 10.00 10.00
75 A2 25c on 2½a blue 10.00 *14.50*
76 A2 50c on 5a yellow 14.50 *28.00*
77 A2 1 l on 10a dull lil 20.00 *36.00*
Nos. 70-77 (8) 108.00 *169.50*

Saint Francis of Assisi Issue

Italy Nos. 178-180 Overprinted

1926, Apr. 12 ***Perf. 14***

78 A79 20c gray green 1.75 *10.00*
79 A80 40c dark violet 1.75 *10.00*
80 A81 60c red brown 1.75 *20.00*

Italy Nos. 182 and Type of 1926 Overprinted in Red

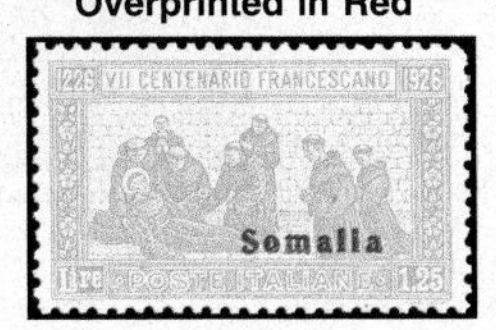

Unwmk. ***Perf. 11***

81 A82 1.25 l dark blue 1.75 *28.00*

Perf. 14

82 A83 5 l + 2.50 l ol grn 5.25 *55.00*
Nos. 78-82 (5) 12.25 *123.00*

Italian Stamps of 1901-26 Overprinted

1926-30 **Wmk. 140**

83 A43 2c org brn 6.00 5.25
84 A48 5c green 6.00 5.25
85 A48 10c claret 6.00 .35
86 A49 20c violet brown 8.75 2.40
87 A46 25c grn & pale grn 6.00 1.25
88 A49 30c gray ('30) 16.00 *40.00*
89 A49 60c brn org 7.25 9.50
a. Double overprint 4,000.
90 A46 75c dk red & rose 125.00 40.00
91 A46 1 l brown & grn 7.25 .65
92 A46 1.25 l blue & ultra 15.00 1.90
93 A46 2 l dk grn & org 34.00 12.50
94 A46 2.50 l dk grn & org 34.00 19.00
95 A46 5 l blue & rose 72.50 45.00
96 A51 10 l gray grn & red 72.50 *77.50*
Nos. 83-96 (14) 416.25 260.55

Volta Issue

Type of Italy, 1927, Overprinted

1927, Oct. 10

97 A84 20c purple 4.50 *28.00*
98 A84 50c deep orange 6.75 *20.00*
a. Double overprint 175.00
Never hinged 375.00
b. As "#98" with "Tripolitania" inverted 525.00
99 A84 1.25 l brt blue 10.00 *45.00*
Nos. 97-99 (3) 21.25 *93.00*

Italian Stamps of 1927-28 Overprinted in Black or Red

1928-30

100 A86 7½c lt brown 25.00 *55.00*
a. Double overprint 550.00
101 A85 50c brn & sl (R) 25.00 4.50
102 A86 50c brt vio ('30) 45.00 *67.50*

Perf. 11

Unwmk.

103 A85 1.75 l deep brown 77.50 14.00
Nos. 100-103 (4) 172.50 *141.00*

Monte Cassino Issue

Monte Cassino Issue of Italy Overprinted in Red or Blue

1929, Oct. 14 **Wmk. 140** ***Perf. 14***

104 A96 20c dk green (R) 4.50 *15.50*
105 A96 25c red org (Bl) 4.50 *15.50*
106 A98 50c + 10c crim (Bl) 4.50 *16.50*
107 A98 75c + 15c ol brn (R) 4.50 *16.50*
108 A96 1.25 l + 25c dk vio (R) 10.00 *32.00*
109 A98 5 l + 1 l saph (R) 10.00 *34.00*

Overprinted in Red

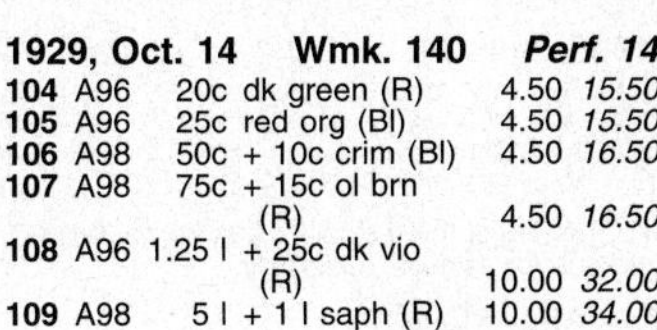

Unwmk.

110 A100 10 l + 2 l gray brn 10.00 *50.00*
Nos. 104-110 (7) 48.00 *180.00*

Royal Wedding Issue

Type of Italian Royal Wedding Stamps of 1930 Overprinted

1930, Mar. 17 **Wmk. 140**

111 A101 20c yellow green 2.25 *6.75*
112 A101 50c + 10c dp org 1.75 *6.75*
113 A101 1.25 l + 25c rose red 1.75 *13.50*
Nos. 111-113 (3) 5.75 *27.00*

Ferrucci Issue

Types of Italian Stamps of 1930 Overprinted in Red or Blue

1930, July 26

114 A102 20c violet (R) 4.50 *4.50*
115 A103 25c dk grn (R) 4.50 *4.50*
116 A103 50c black (R) 4.50 *8.25*
117 A103 1.25 l dp bl (R) 4.50 *16.00*
118 A104 5 l + 2 l dp car (bl) 10.00 *34.00*
Nos. 114-118 (5) 28.00 *67.25*

Virgil Issue

Types of Italian Stamps of 1930 Overprinted in Red or Blue

1930, Dec. 4 **Photo.** **Wmk. 140**

119 A106 15c violet blue .85 *8.25*
120 A106 20c org brn .85 *3.50*
121 A106 25c dark green .85 *3.50*
122 A106 30c lt brown .85 *3.50*
123 A106 50c dull violet .85 *3.50*
124 A106 75c rose red .85 *6.75*
125 A106 1.25 l gray blue .85 *8.25*

Engr.

Unwmk.

126 A106 5 l + 1.50 l dk vio 3.50 *34.00*
127 A106 10 l + 2.50 l ol brn 3.50 *50.00*
Nos. 119-127 (9) 12.95 *121.25*

Saint Anthony of Padua Issue

Types of Italian Stamps of 1931 Overprinted in Blue or Red

1931, May 7 **Photo.** **Wmk. 140**

129 A116 20c brown (Bl) 1.10 *15.50*
130 A116 25c green (R) 1.10 *5.75*
131 A118 30c gray brn (Bl) 1.10 *5.75*
132 A118 50c dull vio (Bl) 1.10 *5.75*
133 A120 1.25 l slate bl (R) 1.10 *28.00*

Overprinted in Red or Black

Engr. **Unwmk.**

134 A121 75c black (R) 1.10 *15.50*
135 A122 5 l + 2.50 l dk brn (Bk) 7.75 *55.00*
Nos. 129-135 (7) 14.35 *131.25*

Italy Nos. 218, 221 Overprinted in Red

1931 **Wmk. 140**

136 A94 25c dk green (R) 11.50 *19.00*
137 A95 50c purple (R) 11.50 3.50

Lighthouse at Cape Guardafui — A3

Tower at Mnara Ciromo — A4

Governor's Palace at Mogadishu — A5

Termite Nest — A6

Ostrich — A7

Hippopotamus — A8

Greater Kudu — A9

Lion — A10

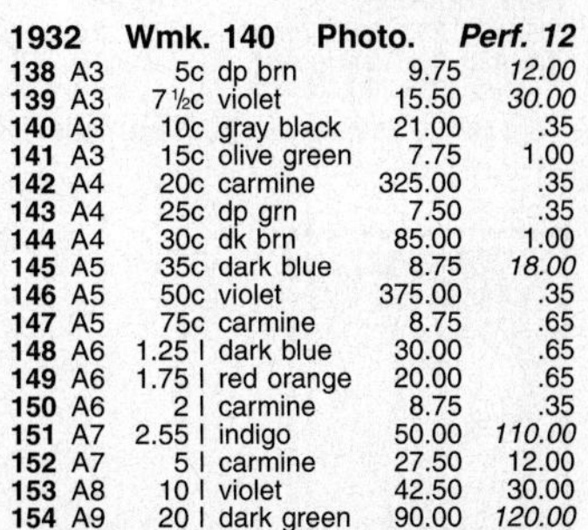

1932 **Wmk. 140** **Photo.** ***Perf. 12***

138 A3 5c dp brn 9.75 *12.00*
139 A3 7½c violet 15.50 *30.00*
140 A3 10c gray black 21.00 .35
141 A3 15c olive green 7.75 1.00
142 A4 20c carmine 325.00 .35
143 A4 25c dp grn 7.50 .35
144 A4 30c dk brn 85.00 1.00
145 A5 35c dark blue 8.75 *18.00*
146 A5 50c violet 375.00 .35
147 A5 75c carmine 8.75 .65
148 A6 1.25 l dark blue 30.00 .65
149 A6 1.75 l red orange 20.00 .65
150 A6 2 l carmine 8.75 .35
151 A7 2.55 l indigo 50.00 *110.00*
152 A7 5 l carmine 27.50 12.00
153 A8 10 l violet 42.50 30.00
154 A9 20 l dark green 90.00 *120.00*
155 A10 25 l dark blue 90.00 *230.00*
Nos. 138-155 (18) 1,223. *567.70*
Set, never hinged 3,000.

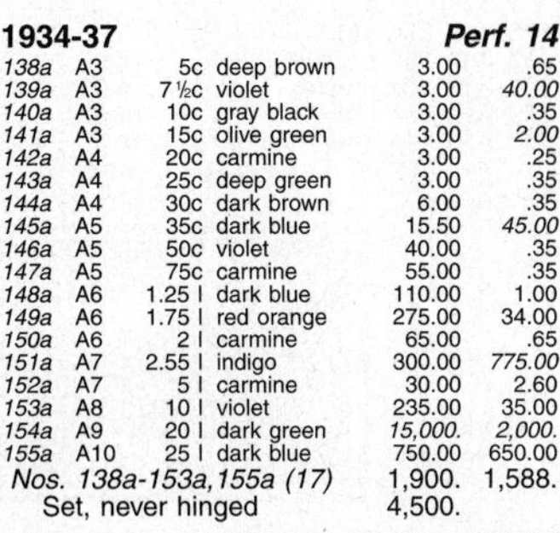

1934-37 ***Perf. 14***

138a A3 5c deep brown 3.00 .65
139a A3 7½c violet 3.00 *40.00*
140a A3 10c gray black 3.00 .35
141a A3 15c olive green 3.00 *2.00*
142a A4 20c carmine 3.00 .25
143a A4 25c deep green 3.00 .35
144a A4 30c dark brown 6.00 .35
145a A5 35c dark blue 15.50 *45.00*
146a A5 50c violet 40.00 .35
147a A5 75c carmine 55.00 .35
148a A6 1.25 l dark blue 110.00 1.00
149a A6 1.75 l red orange 275.00 34.00
150a A6 2 l carmine 65.00 .65
151a A7 2.55 l indigo 300.00 *775.00*
152a A7 5 l carmine 30.00 2.60
153a A8 10 l violet 235.00 35.00
154a A9 20 l dark green *15,000.* *2,000.*
155a A10 25 l dark blue 750.00 650.00
Nos. 138a-153a,155a (17) 1,900. 1,588.
Set, never hinged 4,500.

Nos. 146 and 150 with "POSTA AEREA" overprints were never issued in Somalia.

Eleven denominations in the foregoing series exist perf. 12x14, 14x12 or compound 12 and 14. See the *Scott Classic Specialized Catalogue of Stamps & Covers* for detailed listings.

Types of 1932 Issue Overprinted in Black or Red

1934, May ***Perf. 14***

156 A3 10c brown (Bk) 16.00 *37.50*
157 A4 25c green 16.00 *37.50*
158 A5 50c dull vio (Bk) 16.00 *37.50*
159 A6 1.25 l blue 16.00 *37.50*
160 A7 5 l brown black 16.00 *37.50*
161 A8 10 l car rose (Bk) 16.00 *37.50*
162 A9 20 l dull blue 16.00 *75.00*
163 A10 25 l dark green 16.00 *75.00*
Nos. 156-163 (8) 128.00 *375.00*
Set, never hinged 320.00

Duke of the Abruzzi (Luigi Amadeo, 1873-1933).

Mother and Child A11

1934, Oct.

164 A11 5c ol grn & brn 4.00 *16.00*
165 A11 10c yel brn & blk 4.00 *16.00*
166 A11 20c scarlet & blk 4.00 *14.50*
167 A11 50c dk violet & brn 4.00 *14.50*
168 A11 60c org brn & blk 4.00 *20.00*
169 A11 1.25 l dk blue & grn 4.00 *34.00*
Nos. 164-169,C1-C6 (12) 55.50 *266.00*
Nos. 164-169, never hinged 60.00

Second Colonial Arts Exhibition, Naples.

Catalogue values for unused stamps in this section, from this point to the end of the section, are for Never Hinged items.

Somalia

Tower at Mnara Ciromo — A12

Governor's Palace, Mogadishu — A13

Design: 5c, 20c, 60c, Ostrich.

Wmk. 277

1950, Mar. 24 **Photo.** ***Perf. 14***

170 A12 1c gray black 4.75 *13.50*
171 A12 5c carmine rose .35 .25
172 A13 6c violet 2.40 4.00
173 A12 8c Prus green 2.40 4.00
174 A13 10c dark green .35 .25
175 A12 20c blue green .35 .25

176 A12 35c red 9.00 *13.50*
177 A13 55c brt blue 4.00 .80
178 A12 60c purple 4.00 .80
179 A12 65c brown 12.00 4.75
180 A13 1s deep orange 18.50 4.75
Nos. 170-180,E8-E9 (13) 91.60 81.35

Council in Session A14

1951, Oct. 4
181 A14 20c dk green & brn 3.25 3.25
182 A14 55c brown & violet 8.75 *12.00*
Nos. 181-182,C27A-C27B (4) 24.00 30.25

Meeting of First Territorial Council.

Fair Emblem, Palm Tree and Minaret — A16

1952, Sept. 14 Wmk. 277 *Perf. 14*
185 A16 25c red & dk brown 3.50 *3.50*
186 A16 55c blue & dk brown 3.50 *4.00*
Nos. 185-186,C28 (3) 11.00 11.50

1st Somali Fair, Mogadishu, Sept. 14-28.

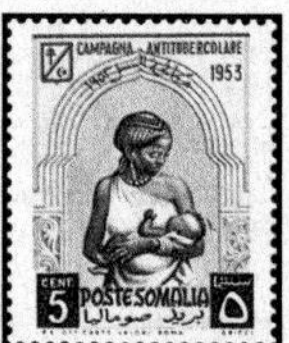

Mother and Child — A17

Center in Dark Brown

1953, May 27
187 A17 5c rose violet .70 *1.75*
188 A17 25c rose .70 *1.75*
189 A17 50c blue 1.25 *1.75*
Nos. 187-189,C29 (4) 5.15 8.25

Anti-tuberculosis campaign.

Laborer at Fair Entrance A18

1953, Sept. 28 Unwmk. *Perf. 11½*
190 A18 25c dk green & gray .50 .75
191 A18 60c blue & gray 1.25 *1.75*
Nos. 190-191,C30-C31 (4) 3.50 4.75

2nd Somali Fair, Mogadishu, 9/28-10/12.

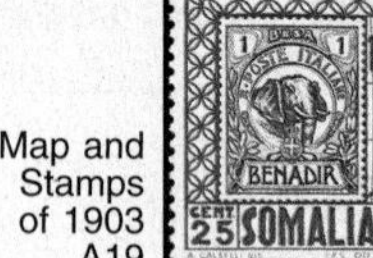

Map and Stamps of 1903 A19

Perf. 13x13½

1953, Dec. 16 Engr. Wmk. 277

"Stamps" in Brown and Rose Carmine

192 A19 25c deep magenta .75 1.00
193 A19 35c dark green .75 1.00
194 A19 60c orange 1.00 1.75
Nos. 192-194,C32-C33 (5) 5.00 8.00

50th anniv. of the 1st Somali postage stamps.

Somalia Brushwood A20

Perf. 12½x13½

1954, June 1 Photo. Unwmk.
195 A20 25c dp blue & dk gray .90 *1.50*
196 A20 60c orange brn & brown .90 *1.50*
Nos. 195-196,C37-C38 (4) 4.50 *6.00*

Convention of Nov. 11, 1953, with the Sovereign Military Order of Malta, providing for the care of lepers.

Somali Flag — A21

Perf. 13½x13

1954, Oct. 12 Litho. Wmk. 277
197 A21 25c blk, grn, bl, red & yel .45 .50

Adoption of a Somali flag. See No. C39.

Adenium Somalense — A22

Flowers: 5c, Haemanthus multiflorus martyn. 10c, Grinum scabrum. 25c, Poinciana elata. 60c, Calatropis procera. 1s, Pancratium. 1.20s, Sesamothamnus bussernus.

1955, Feb. Photo. *Perf. 13*
198 A22 1c bl, dp rose & dk ol brn .30 .30
199 A22 5c bl, rose lil & grn .30 .30
200 A22 10c lilac & green 1.00 .40
201 A22 25c vio brn, yel & grn 1.60 .75
202 A22 60c blk, car & grn .30 .30
203 A22 1s red brn & grn .30 .75
204 A22 1.20s dk brn, yel & grn .65 1.25
Nos. 198-204,E10-E11 (9) 6.75 6.40

See #216-220. For overprint see #242.

Weaver at Loom A23

Design: 30c, Cattle fording stream.

Perf. 13½x14

1955, Sept. 24 Wmk. 303
205 A23 25c dark brown .70 .70
206 A23 30c dark green .70 .70
Nos. 205-206,C46-C47 (4) 3.40 3.90

3rd Somali Fair, Mogadishu, Sept. 1955.

Casting Ballots — A24

1956, Apr. 30 *Perf. 14*
207 A24 5c brown & gray grn .35 .35
208 A24 10c brown & ol bis .35 .35
209 A24 25c brown & brn red .35 .50
Nos. 207-209,C48-C49 (5) 2.55 3.20

Opening of the territory's first democratically elected Legislative Assembly.

Arms of Somalia — A25

Coat of Arms in Dull Yellow, Blue and Black

1957, May 6 Wmk. 303 *Perf. 13½*
210 A25 5c lt red brown .40 .50
211 A25 25c carmine .40 .50
212 A25 60c bluish violet .40 .75
Nos. 210-212,C50-C51 (5) 2.70 3.25

Issued in honor of the new coat of arms.

Dam at Falcheiro A26

10c, Juba River Bridge. 25c, Silos at Margherita.

1957, Sept. 28 Photo. *Perf. 14*
213 A26 5c brown & purple .25 .25
214 A26 10c bister & bl grn .25 .25
215 A26 25c carmine & blue .25 .70
Nos. 213-215,C52-C53 (5) 2.75 3.20

Fourth Somali Fair and Film Festival.

Flower Type of 1955

Flowers: 1c, Adenium Somalense. 10c, Grinum scabrum. 15c, Adansonia digitata. 25c, Poinciana elata. 50c, Gloriosa virescens.

1956-59 Wmk. 303 Photo. *Perf. 13*
216 A22 1c bl, dp rose & dk ol brn .50 .50
217 A22 10c lil, grn & yel ('59) .40 .40
218 A22 15c red, grn & yel ('58) .70 .60
219 A22 25c dull lil, grn & yel ('59) .40 .80
220 A22 50c bl, grn, red & yel ('58) .70 .70
Nos. 216-220 (5) 2.70 3.00

Fencer — A27

Soccer Player A28

Designs: 2c, Runner crossing finish line. 5c, Discus thrower. 6c, Motorcyclist. 10c, Archer. 25c, Boxers.

1958, Apr. 28 Wmk. 303 *Perf. 14*
221 A27 2c violet .25 .25
222 A28 4c green .25 .25
223 A27 5c vermilion .25 .25
224 A28 6c gray .25 .25
225 A27 8c violet blue .25 .25
226 A28 10c orange .25 .25
227 A28 25c dark green .25 .25
Nos. 221-227,C54-C56 (10) 2.50 2.80

Book and Assembly Palace — A29

1959, June 19
228 A29 5c green & ultra .25 .25
229 A29 25c ocher & ultra .25 .25
Nos. 228-229,C59-C60 (4) 2.00 2.50

Opening of Somalia's Constituent Assembly. See No. C60a.

White Stork — A30

Birds: 10c, Saddle-billed stork. 15c, Sacred ibis. 25c, Pink-backed pelican.

1959, Sept. 4 Photo. *Perf. 14*
230 A30 5c yellow, blk & red .35 .25
231 A30 10c brown, red & yel .35 .25
232 A30 15c orange & black .35 .25
233 A30 25c dk car, blk & org .35 .25
Nos. 230-233,C61-C62 (6) 2.90 2.10

Incense Bush — A31

Design: 60c, Girl burning incense.

1959, Sept. 28 Wmk. 303
234 A31 20c orange & black .25 .30
235 A31 60c blk, org & dk red .25 .30
Nos. 234-235,C63-C64 (4) 2.00 2.20

5th Somali Fair, Mogadishu.

Arms of University Institute — A32

Designs: 50c, Map of Africa and arms, horiz. 80c, Arms of University Institute.

1960, Jan. 14 Photo. *Perf. 14*
236 A32 5c brown & salmon .25 .25
237 A32 50c lt vio bl, brn & blk .25 .25
238 A32 80c brt red & blk .35 .35
Nos. 236-238,C65-C66 (5) 1.75 1.85

Opening of the University Institute of Somalia.

Globe and Uprooted Oak Emblem A33

Palm — A34

Design: 60c, Like 10c but with inscription and emblem rearranged.

1960, Apr. 7 *Perf. 14*
239 A33 10c yel brn, grn & blk .25 .25
240 A33 60c dp bister & blk .25 .25
241 A34 80c pink, grn & blk .25 .25
Nos. 239-241,C67 (4) 1.65 2.00

World Refugee Year, 7/1/59-6/30/60.

Republic

No. 217 Overprinted

Wmk. 303
1960, June 26 Photo. *Perf. 13*
242 A22 10c lilac, grn & yel 19.00 *24.00*
Nos. 242,C68-C69 (3) 88.00 96.50

Independence of British Somaliland, which became part of the Republic of Somalia.

Gazelle and Map of Africa — A36

25c, NYC skyline, UN Building and UN flag.

1960, July 1 *Perf. 14*
243 A36 5c lilac & brown .40 .40
244 A36 25c blue .45 .45
Nos. 243-244,C70-C71 (4) 4.90 4.90

Somalia independence.

Boy Drawing Giraffe A37

1960, Nov. 24
245 A37 10c shown .30 .30
246 A37 15c Zebra .40 .40
247 A37 25c Black rhinoceros .45 .45
Nos. 245-247,C72 (4) 4.90 4.90

Olympic Torch, Somalia Flag — A38

10c, Runners, flag and Olympic rings.

1960 Wmk. 303 *Perf. 14*
248 A38 5c green & blue .25 .25
249 A38 10c yellow & blue .25 .25
Nos. 248-249,C73-C74 (4) 3.10 3.10

17th Olympic Games, Rome, 8/25-9/11.

Girl Harvesting Papaya — A39

Girl harvesting: 10c, Durrah (sorghum). 20c, Cotton. 25c, Sesame. 40c, Sugar cane. 50c, Bananas. 75c, Peanuts, horiz. 80c, Grapefruit, horiz.

1961, July 5 **Photo.**
250 A39 5c multicolored .25 .25
251 A39 10c multicolored .25 .25
252 A39 20c multicolored .25 .25
253 A39 25c multicolored .25 .25
254 A39 40c multicolored .30 .25
255 A39 50c multicolored .50 .40
256 A39 75c multicolored .80 .80
257 A39 80c multicolored 2.75 2.75
Nos. 250-257 (8) 5.35 5.20

Shield, Bow and Quiver — A40

Design: 45c, Pottery and incense jug.

1961, Sept. 28
258 A40 25c blk, car & ocher .25 .25
259 A40 45c blk, bl grn & ocher .25 .25
Nos. 258-259,C82-C83 (4) 3.15 3.15

6th Somali Fair, Mogadishu.

Pomacanthus Semicirculatus A41

Fish: 15c, Girl embroidering fish on cloth. 40c, Novaculichthys taeniourus.

1962, Apr. 26 **Photo.**
260 A41 15c brown, blk & pink .35 .35
261 A41 25c orange, blk & ultra .35 .35
262 A41 40c green, blk & rose .65 .65
Nos. 260-262,C84 (4) 4.85 4.85

Mosquito Trapped by Sprays A42

Design: 25c, Man with spray gun and malaria eradication emblem, vert.

1962, Oct. 25 Wmk. 303 *Perf. 14*
263 A42 10c orange red & grn .45 .45
264 A42 25c rose lilac, brn & blk .45 .45
Nos. 263-264,C85-C86 (4) 4.50 4.50

WHO drive to eradicate malaria.

Police Auxiliary Woman A43

10c, Army auxiliary woman. 25c, Radio police car. 75c, First aid army auxiliary, vert.

1963, May 15 Wmk. 303 *Perf. 14*
265 A43 5c multicolored .25 .25
266 A43 10c black & orange .25 .25
267 A43 25c multicolored .25 .25
268 A43 75c multicolored .55 .55
Nos. 265-268,C87-C88 (6) 4.90 4.90

Women's auxiliary forces.

Carved Fork and Spoon and Wheat Emblem A44

1963, June 25 **Photo.**
269 A44 75c green & red brown .65 .65

FAO "Freedom from Hunger" campaign. See No. C89.

Pres. Aden Abdulla Osman — A45

1963, Sept. 15 Wmk. 303 *Perf. 14*
270 A45 25c bl, dk brn, org & lt bl .40 .40
Nos. 270,C90-C91 (3) 2.40 2.40

3rd anniv. of independence.

Dunes Theater A46

55c, African Merchants' and Artisans' Exhibit.

1963, Sept. 28 **Photo.**
271 A46 25c blue green .40 .40
272 A46 55c carmine rose .80 .80
Nos. 271-272,C92 (3) 3.20 3.20

7th Somali Fair, Mogadishu.

Somali Credit Bank Building A47

1964, May 16 Wmk. 303 *Perf. 14*
273 A47 60c indigo, red lil & yel .85 .85
Nos. 273,C93-C94 (3) 5.35 5.35

10th anniv. of the Somali Credit Bank.

Running — A48

1964, Oct. 10 Wmk. 303 *Perf. 14*
274 A48 10c shown .25 .25
275 A48 25c High jump .25 .25
Nos. 274-275,C95-C96 (4) 4.10 4.10

18th Olympic Games, Tokyo, Oct. 10-25. See also Nos. C95-C96.

DC-3 A49

Design: 20c, Passengers leaving DC-3.

1964, Nov. 8 Photo. *Perf. 14*
276 A49 5c dk blue & lil rose .45 .45
277 A49 20c blue & orange .95 .95
Nos. 276-277,C97-C98 (4) 9.55 9.55

Establishment of Somali Air Lines.

ITU Emblem and Map of Africa — A50

1965, May 17 Wmk. 303 *Perf. 14*
278 A50 25c dp blue & dp org .55 .30
Nos. 278,C99-C100 (3) 3.50 2.35

ITU centenary.

Tanning Industry A51

25c, Meat industry; cannery, cattle. 35c, Fishing industry; cannery, fishing boats.

1965, Sept. 28 Photo. *Perf. 14*
279 A51 10c sepia & buff .25 .25
280 A51 25c sepia & pink .25 .25
281 A51 35c sepia & lt blue .35 .25
Nos. 279-281,C101-C102 (5) 4.55 3.40

8th Somali Fair, Mogadishu.

Hottentot Fig and Gazelle A52

Designs: 60c, African tulip and giraffes. 1sh, Ninfea and flamingos. 1.30sh, Pervincia and ostriches. 1.80sh, Bignonia and zebras.

1965, Nov. 1 Wmk. 303 *Perf. 14*
Flowers in Natural Colors
282 A52 20c blk & brt bl .25 .25
283 A52 60c blk & dk gray .25 .25
284 A52 1sh blk, sl grn & ol grn .65 .65
285 A52 1.30sh blk & dp grn 1.50 1.50
286 A52 1.80sh blk & brt bl 3.00 3.00
Nos. 282-286 (5) 5.65 5.65

Narina's Trogon A53

Birds: 35c, Bateleur eagle, vert. 50c, Vulture. 1.30sh, European roller. 2sh, Vulturine guinea fowl, vert.

1966, June 1 Photo. Wmk. 303

287	A53	25c	multicolored	.30	.30
288	A53	35c	brt blue & multi	.30	.30
289	A53	50c	multicolored	.40	.40
290	A53	1.30sh	multicolored	2.00	2.00
291	A53	2sh	multicolored	3.25	3.25
			Nos. 287-291 (5)	6.25	6.25

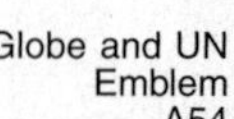
Globe and UN Emblem A54

UN emblem and: 1sh, Map of Africa. 1.50sh, Map of Somalia.

1966, Oct. 24 Litho. *Perf. 13x12½*

292	A54	35c	bl, pur & brt bl	.55	.25
293	A54	1sh	brn, yel & brick red	.55	.25
294	A54	1.50sh	grn, blk, bl & yel	1.00	.60
			Nos. 292-294 (3)	2.10	1.10

21st anniversary of United Nations.

Woman Sitting on Crocodile A55

Paintings: 1sh, Woman and warrior. 1.50sh, Boy leading camel. 2sh, Women pounding grain.

Wmk. 303

1966, Dec. 1 Photo. *Perf. 14*

295	A55	25c	multicolored	.25	.25
296	A55	1sh	multicolored	.35	.25
297	A55	1.50sh	multicolored	.60	.25
298	A55	2sh	multicolored	1.60	.95
			Nos. 295-298 (4)	2.80	1.70

Somali art, exhibited in the Garesa Museum, Mogadishu.

UNESCO Emblem A56

1966, Dec. 20 Wmk. 303 *Perf. 14*

299	A56	35c	blk, dk red & gray	.25	.25
300	A56	1sh	blk, emer & yel	.25	.25
301	A56	1.80sh	blk, ultra & red	1.75	1.75
			Nos. 299-301 (3)	2.25	2.25

UNESCO, 20th anniv.

Haggard's Oribi — A57

Gazelles: 60c, Long-snouted dik-dik. 1sh, Gerenuk. 1.80sh, Soemmering's gazelle.

1967, Feb. 20 Photo. *Perf. 14*

302	A57	35c	blk, ultra & bis	.25	.25
303	A57	60c	blk, org & brn	.25	.25
304	A57	1sh	blk, red & brn	.40	.40
305	A57	1.80sh	blk, yel grn & brn	2.75	2.75
			Nos. 302-305 (4)	3.65	3.65

Dancers — A58

Designs: Various Folk Dances.

Unwmk.

1967, July 15 Litho. *Perf. 13*

306	A58	25c	multicolored	.25	.25
307	A58	50c	multicolored	.25	.25
308	A58	1.30sh	multicolored	.25	.25
309	A58	2sh	multicolored	2.10	2.10
			Nos. 306-309 (4)	2.85	2.85

Boy Scout Giving Scout Sign — A59

Designs: 50c, Boy Scouts with flags. 1sh, Boy Scout cooking and tent. 1.80sh, Jamboree emblem.

1967, Aug. 15

310	A59	35c	multicolored	.25	.25
311	A59	50c	multicolored	.25	.25
312	A59	1sh	multicolored	.55	.55
313	A59	1.80sh	multicolored	2.10	2.10
			Nos. 310-313 (4)	3.15	3.15

12th Boy Scout World Jamboree, Farragut State Park, Idaho, Aug. 1-9.

Pres. Abdirascid Ali Scermarche and King Faisal — A60

Designs: 1sh, Clasped hands, flags of Somalia and Saudi Arabia.

Wmk. 303

1967, Sept. 21 Photo. *Perf. 14*

314	A60	50c	black & lt blue	.25	.25
315	A60	1sh	multicolored	.55	.55
			Nos. 314-315,C103 (3)	2.55	2.55

Visit of King Faisal of Saudi Arabia.

Gaterin Gaterinus A61

Tropical Fish: 50c, Chaetodon semilarvatus. 1sh, Priacanthus hamrur. 1.80sh, Epinephelus summana.

1967, Nov. 15 Litho. *Perf. 14*

316	A61	35c	dk bl, yel & blk	.50	.50
317	A61	50c	brt bl, ocher & blk	.50	.50
318	A61	1sh	emer, org, brn & blk	1.50	1.50
319	A61	1.80sh	pur, yel & blk	2.75	2.75
			Nos. 316-319 (4)	5.25	5.25

Physician Treating Infant — A62

WHO, 20th anniv.: 1sh, Physician examining boy, and nurse. 1.80sh, Physician and nurse treating patient.

Wmk. 303

1968, Mar. 20 Photo. *Perf. 14*

320	A62	35c	blk, scar, bl & brn	.30	.30
321	A62	1sh	blk, grn & brn	.30	.30
322	A62	1.80sh	blk, org & brn	1.60	1.60
			Nos. 320-322 (3)	2.20	2.20

Woman and Basket with Lemons A63

Waterbuck — A64

Designs: 10c, Oranges. 25c, Coconuts. 35c, Papayas. 40c, Limes. 50c, Grapefruit. 1sh, Bananas. 1.30sh, Cotton bolls. 1.80sh, Speke's gazelle. 2sh, Lesser kudu. 5sh, Hunter's hartebeest. 10sh, Clark's gazelle (dibatag).

1968 Litho. *Perf. 11½*

323	A63	5c	lt blue & multi	.25	.25
324	A63	10c	yellow & multi	.25	.25
325	A63	25c	lt lilac & multi	.25	.25
326	A63	35c	salmon & multi	.25	.25
327	A63	40c	buff & multi	.25	.25
328	A63	50c	multicolored	.25	.25
329	A63	1sh	lt blue & multi	.85	.85
330	A63	1.30sh	gray & multi	2.50	2.50
331	A64	1.50sh	lt blue & multi	.45	.45
332	A64	1.80sh	multicolored	.45	.45
333	A64	2sh	pink & multi	1.40	1.40
334	A64	5sh	multicolored	2.75	2.75
335	A64	10sh	multicolored	10.00	10.00
			Nos. 323-335 (13)	19.90	19.90

Issued: #323-330, 4/25; #331-335, 5/10.

Javelin — A65

Wmk. 303

1968, Oct. 12 Photo. *Perf. 14*

336	A65	35c	shown	.25	.25
337	A65	50c	Running	.25	.25
338	A65	80c	High jump	.25	.25
339	A65	1.50sh	Basketball	1.90	1.20
a.			Souvenir sheet of 4, #336-339	6.75	6.75
			Nos. 336-339 (4)	2.65	1.95

19th Olympic Games, Mexico City, Oct. 12-27. No. 339a sold for 3.65sh.

Statuette — A66

Statuettes: 25c, Woman grinding grain. 35c, Woman potter. 2.80sh, Woman mat maker.

Perf. 11½x12

1968, Dec. 1 Litho. Unwmk.

340	A66	25c	rose lil, blk & brn	.25	.25
341	A66	35c	brick red, blk & brn	.25	.25
342	A66	2.80sh	green, blk & brn	1.90	1.20
			Nos. 340-342 (3)	2.40	1.70

Cornflower and Rhinoceros A67

80c, Sunflower & elephant. 1sh, Oleander & antelopes. 1.80sh, Chrysanthemums & storks.

Perf. 13x12½

1969, Mar. 25 Litho. Unwmk.

343	A67	40c	red & multi	.25	.25
344	A67	80c	violet & multi	.25	.25
345	A67	1sh	blue & multi	.65	.65
346	A67	1.80sh	yellow & multi	3.00	3.00
			Nos. 343-346 (4)	4.15	4.15

ILO Emblem and Blacksmiths — A68

Designs: 1sh, Oxdrawn plow. 1.80sh, Drawing water from well.

Wmk. 303

1969, May 10 Photo. *Perf. 14*

347	A68	25c	dk red, dp bis & blk	.25	.25
348	A68	1sh	car rose, brn & blk	.25	.25
349	A68	1.80sh	multicolored	1.75	1.75
			Nos. 347-349 (3)	2.25	2.25

ILO, 50th anniversary.

Mahatma Gandhi — A69

Designs: 1.50sh, Gandhi, globe and hands releasing dove, horiz. 1.80sh, Gandhi seated.

Unwmk.

1969, Oct. 2 Photo. *Perf. 13*

Size: 25x35½mm

350	A69	35c	brown violet	.40	.40

Perf. 14½x14

Size: 37½x20mm

351	A69	1.50sh	bister brn	.60	.60

Perf. 13

Size: 25x35½mm

352	A69	1.80sh	olive gray	4.00	4.00
			Nos. 350-352 (3)	5.00	5.00

Mohandas K. Gandhi (1869-1948), leader in India's fight for independence.

1970

US Space Explorations. Set of seven. 60, 80c, 1, 1.50, 1.80, 2, 2.80sh. Souv. sheet, 14sh, Not officially issued - available Feb. 14. Values: set, $6; souvenir sheet, $32.50.

Nivprale Vevanes
A70

Butterflies: 50c, Leschenault. 1.50sh, Papilio (ornytoptera) aeacus. 2sh, Urania riphaeus.

Perf. 12½x13

1970, Mar. 25 Litho. Unwmk.

353	A70	25c multicolored	.30	.30
354	A70	50c multicolored	.30	.30
355	A70	1.50sh orange & multi	.80	.80
356	A70	2sh yellow & multi	3.00	3.00
		Nos. 353-356 (4)	4.40	4.40

Somali Democratic Republic

Lenin Addressing Crowd — A71

Designs: 25c, Lenin walking with children. 1.80sh, Lenin in his study, horiz.

Perf. 12x12½, 12½x12

1970, Apr. 22 Litho. Unwmk.

357	A71	25c multicolored	.25	.25
358	A71	1sh multicolored	.45	.45
359	A71	1.80sh multicolored	2.10	2.10
		Nos. 357-359 (3)	2.80	2.80

Lenin (1870-1924), Russian communist leader.

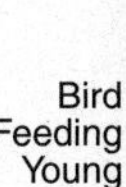

Bird Feeding Young
A72

35c, Monument & Battle of Dagahtur. 1sh, Arms of Somalia, UN emblem, vert. 2.80sh, Boy milking camel, & star, vert.

Perf. 14x13½, 13½x14

1970, July 28 Photo. Wmk. 303

360	A72	25c blue & multi	.25	.25
361	A72	35c slate & multi	.25	.25
362	A72	1sh violet & multi	.55	.55
363	A72	2.80sh blue & multi	2.00	2.00
		Nos. 360-363 (4)	3.05	3.05

10th anniversary of independence.

"Agriculture" — A73

40c, Soldier and flag. 1sh, Hand on open book. 1.80sh, Grain, scales of justice and dove.

Perf. 14x13½

1970, Oct. 21 Photo. Wmk. 303

364	A73	35c green & multi	.25	.25
365	A73	40c ultra & blk	.40	.40
366	A73	1sh red brown & blk	.45	.45
367	A73	1.80sh multicolored	1.25	1.25
		Nos. 364-367 (4)	2.35	2.35

First anniversary of Oct. 21st Revolution.

Snake Strangling Black Man, Map of South Africa
A74

Design: 1.80sh, Concentration camp and symbols of justice holding scales.

Perf. 14x13½

1971, June 20 Photo. Wmk. 303

368	A74	1.30sh multicolored	.55	.55
369	A74	1.80sh gray, red & blk	2.10	2.10

Against racial discrimination in South Africa.

Waves
A75

Design: 2.80sh, Waves and globe.

1971, June 30

370	A75	25c black & blue	.40	.40
371	A75	2.80sh blk, grn & bl	2.10	2.10

3rd World Telecommunications Day, May 17.

Map of Africa and Telecommunications System — A76

Design: 1.50sh, Map of Africa and telecommunications system, diff.

1971, July 25

372	A76	1sh blk, lt bl & grn	.55	.55
373	A76	1.50sh black & yellow	1.50	1.50

Pan-African Telecommunications system.

White Rhinoceros
A77

Wild Animals: 1sh, Cheetahs. 1.30sh, Zebras. 1.80sh, Lion attacking camel.

1971, Aug. 25

374	A77	35c ocher & multi	.40	.40
375	A77	1sh violet & multi	.95	.95
376	A77	1.30sh violet & multi	2.25	2.25
377	A77	1.80sh multicolored	4.50	4.50
		Nos. 374-377 (4)	8.10	8.10

Headquarters, Mogadishu, Flag, Map of Africa — A78

Design: 1.30sh, Desert Fort.

1971, Oct. 18

378	A78	1.30sh blk & red org	.85	.85
379	A78	1.50sh blk, blue & yel	1.75	1.75

East and Central African Summit Conf.

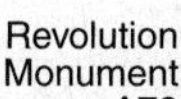

Revolution Monument
A79

1sh, Field workers. 1.35sh, Building workers.

1971, Oct. 21

380	A79	10c black & blue	.25	.25
381	A79	1sh blk, yel brn & grn	.55	.55
382	A79	1.35sh blk, dp brn & yel	1.75	1.75
		Nos. 380-382 (3)	2.55	2.55

2nd anniversary of 1969 revolution.

Vaccination of Cow — A80

1.80sh, Veterinarian vaccinating cow.

Perf. 14x13½

1971, Nov. 28 Photo. Wmk. 303

383	A80	40c blk, red & bl	.40	.25
384	A80	1.80sh lt green & multi	1.75	1.75

Rinderpest campaign.

Postal Union Emblem, Dove and Letter
A81

1972, Jan. 25 Unwmk.

385	A81	1.50sh multicolored	1.75	1.75

10th anniv. of APU. See No. C108.

Children and UNICEF Emblem
A82

Design: 50c, Mother and child, vert.

1972, Mar. 30 *Perf. 13x14, 14x13*

386	A82	50c blk, bis brn & dk brn	.25	.25
387	A82	2.80sh lt blue & multi	2.10	2.10

UNICEF, 25th anniv. (in 1971).

Camel
A83

Designs: 10c, Cattle and cargo ship. 20c, Bull. 40c, Sheep. 1.70sh, Goat.

1972, Apr. 10 *Perf. 14x13*

388	A83	5c green & multi	.25	.25
389	A83	10c multicolored	.30	.30
390	A83	20c multicolored	.30	.30
391	A83	40c orange red & blk	.30	.30
392	A83	1.70sh dull grn & blk	3.75	3.75
		Nos. 388-392 (5)	4.90	4.90

Hands Holding Infant
A84

1sh, Youth Corps emblem, marchers with flags. 1.50sh, Woman, man, tent, tractor.

1972, Oct. 21 Photo. *Perf. 14x13½*

393	A84	70c yellow & multi	.25	.25
394	A84	1sh red & multi	.40	.40
395	A84	1.50sh lt blue & multi	1.60	1.60
		Nos. 393-395 (3)	2.25	2.25

3rd anniversary of October 21 Revolution.

Folk Dance
A85

Folk Dances: 40c, Man and woman, vert. 1sh, Group dance, vert. 2sh, Two men and a woman.

1973 Photo. *Perf. 14x13½, 13½x14*

396	A85	5c dull blue & multi	.25	.25
397	A85	40c brown & multi	.25	.25
398	A85	1sh yellow & multi	.55	.55
399	A85	2sh brick red & multi	1.90	1.90
		Nos. 396-399 (4)	2.95	2.95

Hand Writing Somali Script
A86

40c, Flame and "FAR SOMALI" inscription, vert. 1sh, Woman and sunburst with Somali script.

Perf. 13½x14, 14x13½

1973, Oct. 21 Photo.

400	A86	40c red & multi	.25	.25
401	A86	1sh blue & multi	.35	.35
402	A86	2sh yellow & multi	1.90	1.90
		Nos. 400-402 (3)	2.50	2.50

Publicity for use of Somali script.

Map of Africa and Emblem — A87

Map of Africa with Target on Somalia — A88

1974, June 12 *Perf. 13½x14*

403	A87	40c multicolored	.40	.40
404	A88	2sh multicolored	2.00	2.00

OAU Meeting, Mogadishu.

Hurdler A89

1sh, Runners. 1.40sh, Netball, vert.

1974, Aug. 1 ***Perf. 14x13, 13x14***

405 A89	50c	black & orange	.25	.25
406 A89	1sh	black & green	.40	.40
407 A89	1.40sh	black & olive	2.00	2.00
		Nos. 405-407 (3)	2.65	2.65

Victory Pioneers — A90

Pioneers Helping Woman — A91

1974, Aug. 25 **Photo.** ***Perf. 13x14***

408 A90	40c multicolored	.25	.25
409 A91	2sh multicolored	1.90	1.90

Victory Pioneers, founded Aug. 24, 1972, to defend Socialist Revolution.

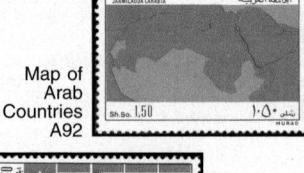

Map of Arab Countries A92

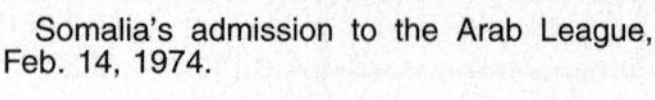
Flags of Arab Countries A93

1974, Sept. 1 ***Perf. 14x13***

410 A92	1.50sh multicolored	.95	.95
411 A93	1.70sh multicolored	3.00	3.00

Somalia's admission to the Arab League, Feb. 14, 1974.

Tank Tracks in Desert A94

Somalis Reading Books — A95

Perf. 14x13½, 13½x14

1974, Oct. 21 **Litho.**

412 A94	40c multicolored	.25	.25
413 A95	2sh multicolored	1.75	1.75

5th anniversary of the Oct. 21st Revolution.

Carrier Pigeons A96

Design: 3sh, Postrider.

1975, Feb. 15 **Litho.** ***Perf. 14x13½***

414 A96	50c blue & multi	.25	.25
415 A96	3sh multicolored	1.75	1.75

UPU centenary (in 1974).

Africa A97

Design: 1.50sh, Carrier pigeons.

1975, Apr. 10

416 A97	1sh	multicolored	.30	.30
417 A97	1.50sh	multicolored	1.60	1.60

African Postal Union.

Somali Warrior — A98

Designs: Traditional costumes of Somali men (1sh, 10sh) and women (40c, 50c, 5sh).

1975, Oct. 27 **Photo.** ***Perf. 13½***

418 A98	10c	yellow & multi	.25	.25
419 A98	40c	lt blue & multi	.25	.25
420 A98	50c	multicolored	.25	.25
421 A98	1sh	green & multi	.25	.25
422 A98	5sh	claret & multi	2.40	.80
423 A98	10sh	rose & multi	6.50	2.40
		Nos. 418-423 (6)	9.90	4.20

Monument — A99

IWY Emblem A100

1975, Dec. 10 **Litho.** ***Perf. 13½x14***

424 A99	50c	blk & red org	.25	.25
425 A100	2.30sh	blk, pink & mag	2.40	2.40

International Women's Year.

Abdulla Hassan Monument A101

Abdulla Hassan with Warriors — A102

1.50sh, Abdulla Hassan speaking to his men. 2.30sh, Attacking horsemen, horiz.

Perf. 14x13½, 13½x14

1976, Nov. 30 **Photo.**

426 A101	50c	multicolored	.25	.25
427 A102	60c	multicolored	.25	.25
428 A102	1.50sh	multicolored	.85	.85
429 A102	2.30sh	multicolored	2.50	2.50
		Nos. 426-429 (4)	3.85	3.85

Sayid Mohammed Abdulla Hassan (1864-1920), poet and military leader.

Cypraea Gracilis A103

Sea Shells: 75c, Charonia bardayi. 1sh, Chlamys townsendi. 2sh, Cymatium ranzanii. 2.75sh, Conus argillaceus. 2.90sh, Strombus oldi.

1976, Dec. 15 **Photo.** ***Perf. 14x13½***

430 A103	50c	blue & multi	.35	.35
431 A103	75c	blue & multi	.35	.35
432 A103	1sh	blue & multi	.50	.50
433 A103	2sh	blue & multi	2.00	2.00
434 A103	2.75sh	blue & multi	7.00	7.00
435 A103	2.90sh	blue & multi	10.00	10.00
a.		Souvenir sheet of 6, #430-435	32.50	32.50
		Nos. 430-435 (6)	20.20	20.20

No. 435a sold for 11sh.

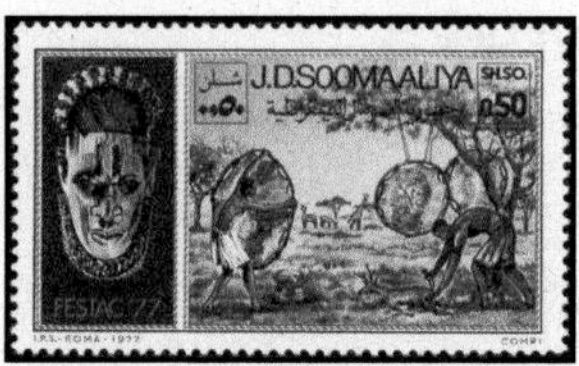
Benin Head and Hunters — A104

Benin Head and: 75c, Handicrafts. 2sh, Dancers. 2.90sh, Musicians.

1977, Aug. 30 **Photo.** ***Perf. 14x13½***

436 A104	50c	multicolored	.25	.25
437 A104	75c	multicolored	.25	.25
438 A104	2sh	multicolored	.95	.95
439 A104	2.90sh	multicolored	3.00	3.00
		Nos. 436-439 (4)	4.45	4.45

2nd World Black and African Festival, FESTAC '77, Lagos, Nigeria, Jan. 15-Feb. 12.

Arms of Somalia A105

Designs: 75c, Somali flags, vert. 1.50sh, Pres. Mohammed Siad Barre and globe. 2sh, Arms over rising sun and flags, vert.

Perf. 13½x14, 14x13½

1977, Sept. 30 **Photo.**

440 A105	75c	multicolored	.25	.25
441 A105	1sh	multicolored	.80	.80
442 A105	1.50sh	multicolored	1.10	1.10
443 A105	2sh	multicolored	2.00	2.00
		Nos. 440-443 (4)	4.15	4.15

Somali Socialist Revolutionary Party, established July 1, 1976.

Licaon Pictus A106

Protected Animals: 75c, Bush baby. 1sh, Somali ass. 1.50sh, Aardwolf. 2sh, Greater kudu. 3sh, Giraffe.

1977, Nov. 25 **Photo.** ***Perf. 14x13½***

444 A106	50c	multicolored	.40	.40
445 A106	75c	multicolored	.40	.40
446 A106	1sh	multicolored	1.25	1.25
447 A106	1.50sh	multicolored	1.75	1.75
448 A106	2sh	multicolored	3.00	3.00
449 A106	3sh	multicolored	7.50	7.50
a.		Souvenir sheet of 6, #444-449	26.00	26.00
		Nos. 444-449 (6)	14.30	14.30

Leonardo da Vinci's Flying Machine A107

ICAO Emblem and: 1.50sh, Montgolfier's balloon. 2sh, Wright brothers' plane. 2.90sh, Somali Airlines turbojet.

1977, Dec. 23 **Photo.** ***Perf. 14x13½***

450 A107	1sh	multicolored	.25	.25
451 A107	1.50sh	multicolored	.55	.55
452 A107	2sh	multicolored	1.20	1.20
453 A107	2.90sh	multicolored	2.40	2.40
a.		Souvenir sheet of 4, #450-453	14.50	14.50
		Nos. 450-453 (4)	4.40	4.40

ICAO, 30th anniv. No. 453a sold for 10sh.

Dome of the Rock — A108

Lithographed and Engraved

1978, Apr. 30 ***Perf. 13x14***

454 A108	75c multicolored	.25	.25
455 A108	2sh multicolored	1.75	1.75

Palestinian fighters and their families.

Stadium and Soccer Player — A109

Designs: 4.90sh, Stadium and goalkeeper. 5.50sh, Stadium and player.

1978, Aug. 5 **Litho.** ***Perf. 14x13½***

456 A109	1.50sh	multicolored	.80	.80
457 A109	4.90sh	multicolored	2.40	2.40
458 A109	5.50sh	multicolored	4.00	4.00
a.		Souvenir sheet of 3, #456-458	17.50	17.50
		Nos. 456-458 (3)	7.20	7.20

11th World Cup Soccer Championship, Argentina, June 1-25. No. 458a sold for 14sh.

Acacia Tortilis — A110

Trees: 50c, Ficus sycomorus, vert. 75c, Terminalia catapa, vert. 2.90sh, Baobab.

1978, Sept. 5 Photo. *Perf. 14*

459 A110 40c multicolored .25 .25
460 A110 50c multicolored .25 .25
461 A110 75c multicolored .25 .25
462 A110 2.90sh multicolored 3.25 3.25
Nos. 459-462 (4) 4.00 4.00

Forest conservation.

Hibiscus — A111

Flowers of Somalia: 1sh, Cassia baccarinii. 1.50sh, Kigelia somalensis. 2.30sh, Dichrostachys glomerata.

1978, Dec. 15 Photo. *Perf. 13½x14*

463 A111 50c multicolored .25 .25
464 A111 1sh multicolored .55 .55
465 A111 1.50sh multicolored 1.60 1.60
466 A111 2.30sh multicolored 2.40 2.40
a. Souv. sheet, #463-466, perf. 14 12.00 12.00
Nos. 463-466 (4) 4.80 4.80

Huri and Siganus Rivulatus A112

Fishery Development: 80c, Sail huri, gaterin gaterinus. 2.30sh, Fishing boats, hypacanthus amia. 2.50sh, Motorized fishing boat, mackerel.

1979, Sept. 1 Photo. *Perf. 14x13½*

467 A112 75c multicolored .55 .55
468 A112 80c multicolored .55 .55
469 A112 2.30sh multicolored 1.50 1.50
470 A112 2.50sh multicolored 3.50 3.50
Nos. 467-470 (4) 6.10 6.10

Sailing, IYC Emblem — A113

IYC Emblem, Children's Drawings: 50c, 90c, Schoolboy. 1.50sh, 2.50sh, Houses. 3sh, 4sh, Bird and flower. 1sh, as 75c.

1979, Sept. 10 Photo. *Perf. 13½x14*

471 A113 50c multicolored .30 .30
472 A113 75c multicolored .30 .30
473 A113 1.50sh multicolored .80 .80
474 A113 3sh multicolored 2.50 2.50
Nos. 471-474 (4) 3.90 3.90

Souvenir Sheet of 4

474A A113 #b.-e. 10.00 10.00

Intl. Year of the Child. No. 474A contains 90c, 1sh, 2.50sh, 4sh stamps and sold for 10sh.

University Students, Outdoor Classrooms — A114

Flower and: 50c, Housing construction. 75c, Children's recreation. 1sh, Doctor examining child, woman and man carrying grain and fish. 2.40sh, Woman and children carrying produce over dam. 3sh, Dish antenna.

1979, Nov. 30 Litho. *Perf. 14x13½*

475 A114 20c multicolored .30 .30
476 A114 50c multicolored .30 .30
477 A114 75c multicolored .65 .65
478 A114 1sh multicolored .65 .65
479 A114 2.40sh multicolored 1.90 1.90
480 A114 3sh multicolored 2.40 2.40
Nos. 475-480 (6) 6.20 6.20

Oct. 21 revolution, 10th anniversary.

Barbopsis Devecchii A115

Freshwater Fish: 90c, Phreatichthys andruzzii. 1sh, Uegitglanis zammaranoi. 2.50sh, Pardi's catfish.

1979, Dec. 12

481 A115 50c multicolored .70 .70
482 A115 90c multicolored .70 .70
483 A115 1sh multicolored 2.10 2.10
484 A115 2.50sh multicolored 2.10 2.10
a. Souvenir sheet of 4, #481-484 11.50 11.50
Nos. 481-484 (4) 5.60 5.60

No. 484a sold for 10sh.

Taleh Fortress, Congress Emblem — A116

1980, June 1 Photo. *Perf. 14x13½*

485 A116 2.25sh multicolored 1.10 1.10
486 A116 3.50sh multicolored 2.00 2.00

1st International Congress of Somalian Studies, Mogadishu, July 6-13.

View of Marka — A117

1sh, Gandershe. 2.30sh, Afgooye. 3.50sh, Muqdisho.

1980, July 1 Litho. *Perf. 14*

487 A117 75c shown .30 .30
488 A117 1sh multi + label 1.00 1.00
489 A117 2.30sh multi + label 1.00 1.00
490 A117 3.50sh multi + label 4.00 4.00
Nos. 487-490 (4) 6.30 6.30

See Nos. 502-505, 527-530.

A118

1sh, Batis perkeo. 2.25sh, Rynchostruthus socotranus louisae. 5sh, Laniarius ruficeps.

1980, July 30 Photo. *Perf. 13½x14*

491 A118 1sh multi .65 .65
492 A118 2.25sh multi 1.60 1.60
493 A118 5sh multi 3.50 3.50
a. Souvenir sheet of 3, #491-493 11.00 11.00
Nos. 491-493 (3) 5.75 5.75

A119

75c, Globe, grain. 3.25sh, Emblem, horiz.

Perf. 13½x14, 14x13½

1981, Oct. 16 Litho.

494 A119 75c multi .30 .30
495 A119 3.25sh multi 1.50 1.50
496 A119 5.50sh like No. 494 3.00 3.00
Nos. 494-496 (3) 4.80 4.80

World Food Day.

13th World Telecommunications Day — A120

1sh, Shepherdess, sheep, dish antenna. 3sh, Emblems.

1981, Oct. 10 *Perf. 13½x14*

497 A120 1sh multicolored .80 .80
498 A120 3sh multicolored 1.60 1.60
499 A120 4.60sh like No. 498 3.25 3.25
Nos. 497-499 (3) 5.65 5.65

Hegira, 1500th Anniv. — A121

1981, Oct. Photo. *Perf. 13½x14*

500 A121 1.50sh multicolored .55 .55
501 A121 3.80sh multicolored 1.90 1.90

View Type of 1980

1982, May 31 Litho. *Perf. 13½x14*

502 A117 2.25sh Balcad 1.20 1.20
503 A117 4sh Jowhar 1.60 1.60
504 A117 5.50sh Golaleey 2.40 2.40
505 A117 8.30sh Muqdisho 2.75 2.75
Nos. 502-505 (4) 7.95 7.95

Nos. 502-505 were each printed in sheets of 10 stamps and 5 labels showing regional map. Value for stamps with attached label: +25%.

1982 World Cup — A122

Designs: Various soccer players.

1982, June 13

506 A122 1sh multicolored .55 .55
507 A122 1.50sh multicolored 1.25 1.25
508 A122 3.25sh multicolored 3.00 3.00
a. Souvenir sheet of 3, #506-508 13.00 13.00
Nos. 506-508 (3) 4.80 4.80

ITU Plenipotentiaries Conference, Nairobi, Sept. — A123

1982, Oct. 15 Photo. *Perf. 14x13½*

509 A123 75c green & multi .25 .25
510 A123 3.25sh orange & multi 1.40 1.40
511 A123 5.50sh blue & multi 3.50 3.50
Nos. 509-511 (3) 5.15 5.15

Local Snakes — A124

2.80sh, Bitis arietans. 3.20sh, Psammophis punctulatus. 4.60sh, Rhamphiophis oxyrhynchus. 8.60sh, Sphalerosophis josephscorteccii.

1982, Dec. 20 Photo. *Perf. 14*

512 A124 2.80sh multicolored 1.60 1.60
513 A124 3.20sh multicolored 3.25 3.25
514 A124 4.60sh multicolored 4.75 4.75
Nos. 512-514 (3) 9.60 9.60

Souvenir Sheet

515 A124 8.60sh multicolored 20.00 20.00

Somali Woman — A125

1982, Dec. 30 *Perf. 14x13½*

516 A125 1sh yel & multi .30 .30
517 A125 5.20sh lilac & multi 1.75 1.75
518 A125 5.80sh org & multi 1.90 1.90
519 A125 6.40sh blue & multi 2.10 2.10
520 A125 9.40sh lt brn & multi 3.25 3.25
521 A125 25sh green & multi 8.00 8.00
Nos. 516-521 (6) 17.30 17.30

A126

1983, July 20 ***Perf. 13½x14***
522 A126 5.20sh multicolored 1.40 1.40
523 A126 6.40sh multicolored 2.40 2.40

World Communications Year.

2nd Intl. Congress of Somali Studies, Hamburg — A127

Various views of Hamburg.

1983, Aug. 1 ***Perf. 14***
524 A127 5.20sh multicolored .85 .85
525 A127 6.40sh multicolored 3.25 3.25

Military Uniforms — A128

Designs: a, Air Force. b, Women's Auxiliary Corps. c, Border Police. d, People's Militia. e, Army Infantry. f, Custodial Corps. g, Police. h, Navy.

1983, Oct. 21 **Litho.** ***Perf. 13½x14***
526 Strip of 8 11.00 11.00
a.-h. A128 3.20sh, any single 1.20 1.20

View Type of 1980

1983
527 A117 2.80sh Barawe .80 .80
528 A117 3.20sh Bur Hakaba .80 .80
529 A117 5.50sh Baydhabo 1.60 1.60
530 A117 8.60sh Dooy Nuunaay 4.00 4.00
Nos. 527-530 (4) 7.20 7.20

Nos. 527-530 were each printed in sheets of 10 stamps and 5 decorative labels. Value for stamps with attached label: +25%.

Sea Shells A129

No. 531, Volutocorbis rosavittoriae. No. 532, Phalium bituberculosum. No. 533, Conus milneedwarsi.
No. 534, Cypraea broderipi.

1984, Feb. 15 **Litho.** ***Perf. 14x13½***
531 A129 2.80sh multicolored .80 .80
532 A129 3.20sh multicolored 2.25 2.25
533 A129 5.50sh multicolored 5.75 5.75
Nos. 531-533 (3) 8.80 8.80

Souvenir Sheet
Perf. 14
534 A129 15sh multicolored 13.00 13.00

Olympics 1984 — A130

1984, Sept. **Litho.** ***Perf. 13½x14***
535 A130 1.50sh Runners .55 .55
536 A130 3sh Discus 1.20 1.20
537 A130 8sh Pole vaulting 3.50 3.50
a. Souvenir sheet of 3, #535-537 8.00 8.00
Nos. 535-537 (3) 5.25 5.25

No. 537a sold for 15sh.

Riccione Fair — A131

1984, Sept. **Litho.** ***Perf. 13½x14***
538 A131 5.20sh multicolored 1.75 1.75
539 A131 6.40sh multicolored 4.25 4.25

Animals A132

No. 540, Hystrix cristata. No. 541, Ichneumia albicauda. No. 542, Mungos mungo. No. 543, Mellivora capensis.

1984, Sept. **Litho.** ***Perf. 14x13½***
540 A132 1sh multicolored .35 .35
541 A132 1.50sh multicolored .35 .35
542 A132 2sh multicolored 1.75 1.75
543 A132 4sh multicolored 3.00 3.00
a. Souvenir sheet of 4, #540-543 11.00 11.00
Nos. 540-543 (4) 5.45 5.45

No. 543a sold for 10sh.

Intl. Civil Aviation Org., 40th Anniv. — A133

1984, Nov. 20 **Litho.** ***Perf. 14***
544 A133 3sh multicolored 1.20 1.20
545 A133 6.40sh multicolored 2.40 2.40

Souvenir Sheet
546 Sheet of 2 8.00 8.00
a. A133 3sh like No. 544 1.20 1.20
b. A133 6.40sh like No. 545 2.40 2.40

No. 546 contains 2 49½x46mm stamps. Sold for 10sh.

Dove — A134

Constellations from the Book of Fixed Stars, by Abd al-Rahman al-Sufi.

1985, Aug. 10 **Litho.** ***Perf. 13½x14***
547 A134 4.30sh shown 1.20 1.20
548 A134 11sh Bull 2.40 2.40
549 A134 12.50sh Rams 2.40 2.40
550 A134 13.80sh Archer 2.90 2.90
Nos. 547-550 (4) 8.90 8.90

Architecture — A135

1985, Sept. **Litho.** ***Perf. 13½x14***
551 A135 2sh Ras Kiambone .25 .25
552 A135 6.60sh Hannassa .40 .40
553 A135 10sh Mnarani 1.20 1.20
554 A135 18.60sh as #551, diff. 4.75 4.75
Nos. 551-554 (4) 6.60 6.60

Nos. 551-554 were each printed in sheets of 10 stamps and 5 decorative labels. Value for stamps with attached label: +10%.
See Nos. 572-575.

Lady Somalia Seated in Posthorn A136

1985, Oct. ***Perf. 14x14½***
555 A136 2sh multicolored .95 .95
556 A136 20sh multicolored 4.00 4.00
a. Souvenir sheet of 2, #555-556, perf. 13½ 9.50 9.50

ITALIA '85, Rome. No. 556a sold for 30sh.

Bats A137

2.50sh, Triaenops persicus. 4.50sh, Cardioderma cor. 16sh, Tadarida condylura. 18sh, Coleura afra.

1985, Dec. 25 **Litho.** ***Perf. 14x13½***
557 A137 2.50sh multi 1.00 1.00
558 A137 4.50sh multi 1.40 1.40
559 A137 16sh multi 4.00 4.00
560 A137 18sh multi 5.25 5.25
Nos. 557-560 (4) 11.65 11.65

Souvenir Sheet
561 Sheet of 4 16.00 16.00
a. A137 2.50sh like #552 1.00 1.00
b. A137 4.50sh like #553 1.40 1.40
c. A137 16sh like #554 4.00 4.00
d. A137 18sh like #555 5.25 5.25

Nos. 561a-561d printed in continuous design. No. 561 sold for 50sh.

Economic Trade Agreement with Kenya — A138

Design: Presidents Arap Moi and Barre, satellite communications.

1986, Feb. 15 ***Perf. 14***
562 A138 9sh multi 1.75 1.75
563 A138 14.50sh multi 2.75 2.75

EUROFLORA Flower Exhibition, Genoa — A139

10sh, Flower arrangement. 15sh, Arrangement, diff.

1986, Apr. 25 ***Perf. 13½x14***
564 A139 10sh multi .80 .80
565 A139 15sh multi 2.40 2.40
a. Souvenir sheet of 2, #564-565 5.25 5.25

No. 565a sold for 30sh.

3rd Intl. Congress on Somali Studies — A140

1986, May 26
566 A140 11.35sh multi .80 .80
567 A140 20sh multi 2.40 2.40

1986 World Cup Soccer Championships, Mexico — A141

Various soccer plays.

1986, June ***Perf. 14x13½***
568 A141 3.60sh multi .55 .55
569 A141 4.80sh multi .55 .55
570 A141 6.80sh multi 1.75 1.75
571 A141 22.60sh multi 2.40 2.40
a. Souvenir sheet of 4, #568-571 10.00 10.00
Nos. 568-571 (4) 5.25 5.25

No. 571a sold for 50sh.

Architecture Type of 1985

1986 **Litho.** ***Perf. 13½x14***
572 A135 10sh Bulaxaar .40 .40
573 A135 15sh Saylac .40 .40
574 A135 20sh Saylac, diff. .80 .80
575 A135 31sh Jasiiradaha Jawaay 4.75 4.75
Nos. 572-575 (4) 6.35 6.35

Nos. 572-575 were each printed in sheets of 10 stamps and 5 decorative labels. Value for stamps with attached label: +10%.

Red Crescent — Red Cross Rehabilitation Center, Mogadishu — A143

1987, May 8 **Litho.** ***Perf. 13½x13***
576 A143 56sh multi 6.75 6.75

Souvenir Sheet
577 A143 56sh multi, diff. 8.75 8.75

No. 577 sold for 60sh. See Norway No. 908.

A144

1987, Sept. 27 Litho. *Perf. 13½x14*

578 A144 20sh Running 2.10 2.10
579 A144 48sh Javelin 4.75 4.75
a. Souvenir sheet of 2, #578-579 10.00 10.00

OLYMPHILEX '87, Rome. No. 579a sold for 75sh.

A145

1987, Oct. 5 Photo. *Perf. 13½x14½*

580 A145 53sh multicolored 2.00 2.00
581 A145 72sh multicolored 3.25 3.25

Intl. Year of Shelter for the Homeless.

GEOSOM '87 — A146

Maps: 10sh, 160,000,000 years ago. 20sh, 60,000,000 years ago. 40sh, 15,000,000 years ago. 50sh, Today.

1987, Nov. 24 Litho. *Perf. 13½x14*

582 A146 10sh multi 1.25 1.25
583 A146 20sh multi, diff. 2.40 2.40
584 A146 40sh multi, diff. 4.75 4.75
585 A146 50sh multi, diff. 6.50 6.50
a. Souv. sheet of 2, #583, 585 37.50 37.50
Nos. 582-585 (4) 14.90 14.90

Symposium on the Geology of Somalia, Mogadishu, 11/24-12/1. #585a sold for 130sh.

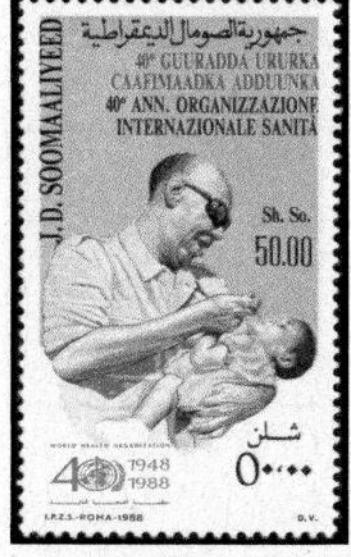

A147

1988, Dec. 31 Litho. *Perf. 13½x14*

586 A147 50sh multicolored .80 .80
587 A147 168sh multicolored 4.00 4.00

World Health Organization, 40th anniv.

Wildlife A148

No. 588, Lepus somaliensis. No. 589, Syncerus caffer. No. 590, Papio hamadryas. No. 591, Hippopotamus amphibius.

Perf. 13½x14, 14x13½

1989, Oct. 20 Litho.

588 A148 75sh multicolored .55 .55
589 A148 198sh multicolored 1.90 1.90
590 A148 200sh multicolored 3.25 3.25
591 A148 216sh multicolored 4.00 4.00
a. Souvenir sheet of 2, #590-591 13.00 13.00
Nos. 588-591 (4) 9.70 9.70

No. 591a contains 2 labels like #588-589. Sold for 700sh.

Somali Revolution, 20th Anniv. A149

Flowers, children's games: 70sh, Kick ball. 100sh, Swinging. 150sh, Teeter-totter. 300sh, Jumping rope, stick and hoop.

1989, Dec. 12 Litho. *Perf. 14x13½*

592 A149 70sh multicolored 1.40 1.40
593 A149 100sh multicolored 2.00 2.00
594 A149 150sh multicolored 3.00 3.00
595 A149 300sh multicolored 5.00 5.00
Nos. 592-595 (4) 11.40 11.40

A150

Liberation: Nos. 599-600, Dove breaking chains, horiz.

1991 Litho. *Perf. 13½x14, 14x13½*

596 A150 70sh lilac & multi *.65 .65*
597 A150 100sh grn bl & multi *.90 .90*
598 A150 150sh brt blue & multi *1.40 1.40*
599 A150 150sh yellow & multi *1.40 1.40*
600 A150 300sh yel grn & multi *2.75 2.75*
601 A150 300sh yel grn & multi *2.75 2.00*
Nos. 596-601 (6) *9.85 9.10*

Issued: Nos. 599-600, July 2; others, July 4.

No. 599 Ovptd. in Blue

1991 Litho. *Perf. 14x13½*

602 A150 150sh yellow & multi 4.00 *4.00*

Various Minarets — A151

1991 Litho. *Perf. 14*

603 A151 30sh multicolored *.30 .30*
604 A151 40sh multicolored *.45 .45*
605 A151 50sh multicolored *.75 .75*
606 A151 150sh multicolored *2.25 2.25*
Nos. 603-606 (4) *3.75 3.75*

Relief efforts have demonstrated the breakdown of government services in Somalia. It is unclear which faction has control of the Postal Service, if any is operating. The status of Scott Nos. 607-638 will be reviewed once more information is available.

Gazelles A152

500sh, Two Speke's. 700sh, One Speke's. 800sh, One Soemmering's. 1000sh, Two Soemmering's.

Inscribed in Black

1992 *Perf. 14x13½*

607 A152 500sh multicolored *3.25*
608 A152 700sh multicolored *4.50*
609 A152 800sh multicolored *6.00*
610 A152 1000sh multicolored *7.25*
Nos. 607-610 (4) *21.00*

World Wildlife Fund.

Without WWF Emblem
Inscribed in red lilac

611 A152 100sh like #607 *.85*
612 A152 200sh like #608 *1.75*
613 A152 300sh like #609 *2.40*
614 A152 400sh like #610 *3.50*

Inscribed in black

615 A152 1500sh Baboons *10.00*
616 A152 2500sh Hippopotamus *17.50*
617 A152 3000sh Giraffes *20.00*
618 A152 5000sh Leopard *30.00*
Nos. 607-618 (12) *107.00*

Nos. 607-618 are part of an expanding set. Numbers may change.
For overprints see No. 629-632.

Nos. 607-610 Ovptd. in Orange

1992 Litho. *Perf. 14x13½*

629 A152 500sh on #607 *3.50*
630 A152 700sh on #608 *5.00*
631 A152 800sh on #609 *6.50*
632 A152 1000sh on #610 *9.00*
Nos. 629-632 (4) *24.00*

Discovery of America, 500th Anniv. A153

Designs: 100sh, Sighting land from crow's nest. 200sh, Three men pointing from ship. 300sh, Columbus in his cabin. 400sh, Claiming land. 2000sh, Building fort in New World.
No. 638: a, 800sh, like #634. b, 900sh, like #635. c, 1300sh, like #633.

1992

633 A153 100sh multicolored *.40*
634 A153 200sh multicolored *1.00*
635 A153 300sh multicolored *1.25*
636 A153 400sh multicolored *1.50*
637 A153 2000sh multicolored *8.00*
Nos. 633-637 (5) *12.15*

Souvenir Sheet

638 A153 Sheet of 3, #a.-c. *12.00*

Nos. 638a-638c do not have white border. No. 638 exists imperf.

SEMI-POSTAL STAMPS

Italy Nos. B1-B3 Overprinted

Italy No. B4 Surcharged

1916 Wmk. 140 *Perf. 14*

B1 SP1 10c + 5c rose 14.50 *37.50*
B2 SP2 15c + 5c slate 60.00 *52.50*
B3 SP2 20c + 5c orange 14.50 *45.00*
B4 SP2 20c on 15c + 5c slate 60.00 *80.00*
Nos. B1-B4 (4) 149.00 *215.00*

Holy Year Issue

Italy Nos. B20-B25 Surcharged in Black or Red

1925, June 1 *Perf. 12*

B5 SP4 6b + 3b on 20c + 10c 3.75 *22.50*
B6 SP4 13b + 6b on 30c + 15c 3.75 *24.00*
B7 SP4 15b + 8b on 50c + 25c 3.75 *22.50*
B8 SP4 18b + 9b on 60c + 30c 3.75 *30.00*
B9 SP8 30b + 15b on 1 l +50c (R) 3.75 *37.50*
B10 SP8 1r + 50b on 5 l +2.50 l (R) 3.75 *57.50*
Nos. B5-B10 (6) 22.50 *194.00*

Colonial Institute Issue

"Peace" Substituting Spade for Sword — SP10

1926, June 1 Typo. *Perf. 14*

B11 SP10 5c + 5c brown .90 *7.25*
B12 SP10 10c + 5c olive grn .90 *7.25*
B13 SP10 20c + 5c blue grn .90 *7.25*
B14 SP10 40c + 5c brn red .90 *7.25*
B15 SP10 60c + 5c orange .90 *7.25*
B16 SP10 1 l + 5c blue .90 *16.00*
Nos. B11-B16 (6) 5.40 *52.25*

The surtax was for the Italian Colonial Institute.

Italian Semi-Postal Stamps of 1926 Overprinted

1927, Apr. 21 Unwmk. *Perf. 11½*

B17 SP10 40c + 20c dk brn & blk 2.75 *32.00*
B18 SP10 60c + 30c brn red & ol brn 2.75 *32.00*
B19 SP10 1.25 l + 60c dp bl & blk 2.75 *45.00*
B20 SP10 5 l + 2.50 l dk grn & blk 4.50 *70.00*
Nos. B17-B20 (4) 12.75 *179.00*

The surtax was for the charitable work of the Voluntary Militia for Italian National Defense. Nos. B19 and B20 in light blue and black and slate and black, respectively, were designed but not issued. Value, set of two, $2,500.

Allegory of Fascism and Victory — SP11

1928, Oct. 15 Wmk. 140 *Perf. 14*

B21 SP11 20c + 5c blue grn 2.25 *10.00*
B22 SP11 30c + 5c red 2.25 *10.00*
B23 SP11 50c + 10c purple 2.25 *17.00*
B24 SP11 1.25 l + 20c dk blue 2.75 *22.50*
Nos. B21-B24 (4) 9.50 *59.50*

46th anniv. of the Societa Africana d'Italia. The surtax aided that society.

Italian Semi-Postal Stamps of 1928 Overprinted

1929, Mar. 4 Unwmk. *Perf. 11*

B25 SP10 30c + 10c red & blk 3.50 *20.00*
B26 SP10 50c + 20c vio & blk 3.50 *21.00*
B27 SP10 1.25 l + 50c brn & bl 5.00 *37.50*
B28 SP10 5 l + 2 l ol grn & blk 5.00 *75.00*
Nos. B25-B28 (4) 17.00 *153.50*

The surtax was for the charitable work of the Voluntary Militia for Italian National Defense.

Italian Semi-Postal Stamps of 1926 Ovptd. in Black or Red

1930, Oct. 20 *Perf. 14*

B29 SP10 30c + 10c dk grn & bl grn (Bk) 26.00 *45.00*
B30 SP10 50c + 10c dk grn & vio (R) 26.00 *75.00*
B31 SP10 1.25 l + 30c ol brn & red brn (R) 26.00 *75.00*
B32 SP10 5 l + 1.50 l ind & grn (R) 82.50 *200.00*
Nos. B29-B32 (4) 160.50 *395.00*

The surtax was for the charitable work of the Voluntary Militia for Italian National Defense.

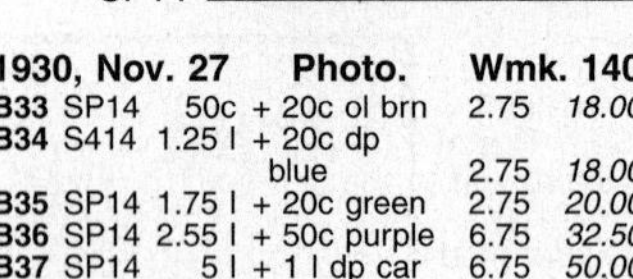
Irrigation Canal SP14

1930, Nov. 27 Photo. Wmk. 140

B33 SP14 50c + 20c ol brn 2.75 *18.00*
B34 S414 1.25 l + 20c dp blue 2.75 *18.00*
B35 SP14 1.75 l + 20c green 2.75 *20.00*
B36 SP14 2.55 l + 50c purple 6.75 *32.50*
B37 SP14 5 l + 1 l dp car 6.75 *50.00*
Nos. B33-B37 (5) 21.75 *138.50*

25th anniv. of the Italian Colonial Agricultural Institute. The surtax was for the aid of that institution.

SP15

King Victor Emmanuel III — SP16

1935, Jan. 1

B38 SP15 5c + 5c blk brn 4.50 *25.00*
B39 SP15 7½c + 7½c vio 4.50 *25.00*
B40 SP15 15c + 10c ol blk 4.50 *25.00*
B41 SP15 20c + 10c rose red 4.50 *25.00*
B42 SP15 25c + 10c dp grn 4.50 *25.00*
B43 SP15 30c + 10c brn 4.50 *25.00*
B44 SP15 50c + 10c pur 4.50 *25.00*
B45 SP15 75c + 15c rose car 4.50 *25.00*
B46 SP15 1.25 l + 15c dp bl 4.50 *25.00*
B47 SP15 1.75 l + 25c red org 4.50 *25.00*
B48 SP15 2.75 l + 25c gray 28.00 *100.00*
B49 SP15 5 l + 1 l dp cl 28.00 *100.00*
B50 SP15 10 l + 1.80 l red brn 28.00 *100.00*
B51 SP16 25 l + 2.75 l brn & red 150.00 *375.00*
Nos. B38-B51 (14) 279.00 *925.00*
Set, never hinged 815.00

Visit of King Victor Emmanuel III.

Catalogue values for unused stamps in this section, from this point to the end of the section, are for Never Hinged items.

Somalia

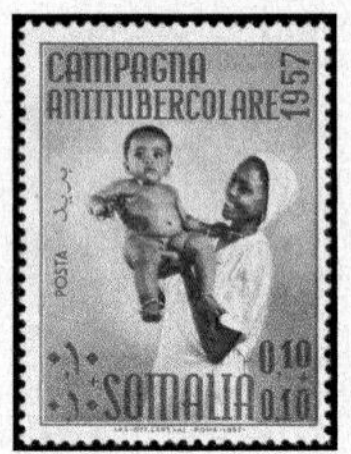
Nurse Holding Infant — SP17

1957, Nov. 30 Wmk. 303 *Perf. 14*

B52 SP17 10c + 10c red & brn .60 .60
B53 SP17 25c + 10c grn & brn .60 .60
Nos. B52-B53,CB11-CB12 (4) 2.90 3.10

The surtax was for the fight against tuberculosis.

Republic

Refugees SP18

1964, Dec. 12 Photo. *Perf. 14*

B54 SP18 25c + 10c vio bl & red .55 .30
Nos. B54,CB13-CB14 (3) 3.90 2.10

The surtax was to help refugees.

Red Cross Nurse Feeding Child — SP19

Famine Relief: 80c+20c, Nomad in parched land, horiz. 2.40sh+10c, Family with fish and produce. 2.90sh+10c, Physician and Aid Society emblem, horiz.

1976, Dec. 10 *Perf. 13x14, 14x13*

B55 SP19 75c + 25c multi .55 .55
B56 SP19 80c + 20c multi .55 .55
B57 SP19 2.40sh + 10c multi 1.75 1.75
B58 SP19 2.90sh + 10c multi 2.40 2.40
Nos. B55-B58 (4) 5.25 5.25

Refugees SP20

1981, Dec. 15 Photo. *Perf. 13½x14*

B59 SP20 2sh + 50c multi .85 .85
B60 SP20 6.80sh + 50c multi 4.00 4.00
a. Souvenir sheet of 2, #B59-B60 8.00 8.00

TB Bacillus Centenary — SP31

1982, Dec. 30 Photo. *Perf. 14*

B61 SP31 4.60sh + 60c multi 2.00 2.00
B62 SP31 5.80sh + 60c multi 2.50 2.50

AIR POST STAMPS

View of Coast AP1

Cheetahs AP2

Wmk. 140

1934, Oct. Photo. *Perf. 14*

C1 AP1 25c sl bl & red org 5.25 *21.00*
C2 AP1 50c dk grn & blue 5.25 *19.00*
C3 AP1 75c brn & red org 5.25 *19.00*
a. Imperf. 3,000.
C4 AP2 80c org brn & dk grn 5.25 *21.00*
C5 AP2 1 l scar & dark grn 5.25 *26.00*
C6 AP2 2 l dk bl & brn 5.25 *45.00*
Nos. C1-C6 (6) 31.50 *151.00*
Set, never hinged 80.00

2nd Colonial Arts Exhibition, Naples. For overprint see No. CO1.

Banana Tree and Airplane AP3

Designs: 25c, 1.50 l, Banana tree and plane. 50c, 2 l, Plane over cotton field. 60c, 5 l, Plane over orchard. 75c, 10 l, Plane over field workers. 1 l, 3 l, Small girl watching plane.

1936 Photo.

C7 AP3 25c slate green 3.50 *9.00*
C8 AP3 50c brown 2.00 .25
C9 AP3 60c red orange 4.00 *13.50*
C10 AP3 75c orange brn 3.50 2.40
C11 AP3 1 l deep blue 2.00 .25
C12 AP3 1.50 l purple 3.50 .80
C13 AP3 2 l slate blue 7.50 1.20
C14 AP3 3 l copper red 26.00 15.00
C15 AP3 5 l yellow green 30.00 18.00
C16 AP3 10 l dp rose red 37.50 34.00
Nos. C7-C16 (10) 119.50 *94.40*
Set, never hinged 260.00

Catalogue values for unused stamps in this section, from this point to the end of the section, are for Never Hinged items.

Somalia

AP8

1950-51 Wmk. 277

C17 AP8 30c yellow brn 8.00 3.75
C18 AP8 45c dk carmine 8.00 3.75
C19 AP8 65c dk blue vio 8.00 3.75
C20 AP8 70c dull blue 8.00 6.50
C21 AP8 90c olive brn 8.00 6.50
C22 AP8 1s lilac rose 9.50 3.75
C23 AP8 1.35s violet 14.50 8.00
C24 AP8 1.50s blue green 14.50 9.50
C25 AP8 3s blue 67.50 37.50
C26 AP8 5s chocolate 67.50 37.50
C27 AP8 10s red org ('51) 135.00 24.00
Nos. C17-C27 (11) 348.50 144.50

Scene in Mogadishu AP8a

1951, Oct. 4

C27A AP8a 1s vio & Prus bl 3.25 1.50
C27B AP8a 1.50s ol grn & chnt brn 8.75 *13.50*

First Territorial Council meeting.

Plane, Palm Tree and Minaret — AP9

1952, Sept. 14

C28 AP9 1.20s ol bis & dp bl 4.00 *4.00*

1st Somali Fair, Mogadishu, Sept. 14-28.

Mother and Child — AP10

1953, May 27

C29 AP10 1.20s dk grn & dk brn 2.50 *3.00*

Somali anti-tuberculosis campaign.

Fair Entrance AP11

1953, Sept. 28 Unwmk. *Perf. 11½*
C30 AP11 1.20s brn car & pink .75 1.00
C31 AP11 1.50s yel brn & buff 1.00 1.25

2nd Somali Fair, Mogadishu, Sept. 28-Oct. 12, 1953.

Plane over Map and Stamps of 1903 AP12

Perf. 13x13½
1953, Dec. 16 Engr. Wmk. 277
Early Stamps in Brn and Rose Car
C32 AP12 60c orange brown 1.25 1.75
C33 AP12 1s greenish black 1.25 2.50

1st Somali postage stamps, 50th anniv.

"UPU" among Constellations — AP13

Perf. 11½
1953, Dec. 16 Photo. Unwmk.
C34 AP13 1.20s red & cream .50 1.30
C35 AP13 1.50s brown & cream 1.00 2.25
C36 AP13 2s green & lt blue 1.00 2.25
Nos. C34-C36 (3) 2.50 5.80

UPU, 75th anniv. (in 1949).

Alexander Island Juba River — AP14

1954, June 1 *Perf. 13½x12½*
C37 AP14 1.20s dk grn & brn 1.10 1.25
C38 AP14 2s dk car & pur 1.60 1.75

See note after No. 196.

Somali Flag — AP15

Perf. 13½x13
1954, Oct. 12 Litho. Wmk. 277
C39 AP15 1.20s multicolored .45 .55

Adoption of Somali flag.

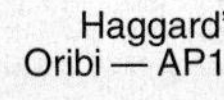
Haggard's Oribi — AP16

Designs: 45c, Phillip's dik-dik. 50c, Speke's gazelle. 75c, Gerenuk. 1.20s, Soemmering's gazelle. 1.50s, Waterbuck.

Wmk. 277
1955, Apr. 12 Photo. *Perf. 13½*
Antelopes in Natural Colors
Size: 22x33mm
C40 AP16 35c gray grn & blk .35 .80
C41 AP16 45c lilac & blk 5.50 2.25
C42 AP16 50c rose lil & blk .40 .80
C43 AP16 75c red 3.75 .80
C44 AP16 1.20s dk gray grn 3.75 5.00
C45 AP16 1.50s bright blue 5.50 7.50
Nos. C40-C45 (6) 19.25 17.15

See Nos. C57-C58.

Caravan at Water Hole AP17

Design: 1.20s, Village well.

Perf. 13½x14
1955, Sept. 24 Wmk. 303
C46 AP17 45c brown & orange .75 1.25
C47 AP17 1.20s sapphire & pink 1.25 1.25

3rd Somali Fair, Mogadishu, Sept. 1955.

Ballot Type of Regular Issue
1956, Apr. 30 Photo. *Perf. 14*
C48 A24 60c brown & ultra .75 1.00
C49 A24 1.20s brown & org .75 1.00

Opening of the territory's first democratically elected Legislative Assembly.

Arms Type of Regular Issue
Coat of Arms in Dull Yellow, Blue and Black
1957, May 6 Wmk. 303 *Perf. 13½*
C50 A25 45c blue .75 .75
C51 A25 1.20s bluish green .75 .75

Issued in honor of the new coat of arms.

Type of Regular Issue, 1957 and

Oil Well — AP18

Design: 60c, Irrigation canal construction.

1957, Sept. 28 *Perf. 14*
C52 A26 60c blue & brown 1.00 1.00
C53 AP18 1.20s black & ver 1.00 1.00

Fourth Somali Fair and Film Festival.

Sport Type of Regular Issue
60c, Runner. 1.20s, Bicyclist. 1.50s, Basketball player.

1958, Apr. 28 Wmk. 303 *Perf. 14*
C54 A27 60c brown .25 .25
C55 A27 1.20s blue .25 .40
C56 A27 1.50s rose carmine .25 .40
Nos. C54-C56 (3) .75 1.05

Animal Type of 1955
3s, Lesser kudu. 5s, Hunter's hartebeest.
Size: 20½x36½mm

1958-59 Photo.
C57 AP16 3s ocher & sepia 2.00 2.25
C58 AP16 5s gray, blk & yel ('59) 2.00 2.25

See No. CE1.

Police Bugler AP19

1959, June 19 Photo.
C59 AP19 1.20s ocher & ultra .75 1.00
C60 AP19 1.50s olive grn & ultra .75 1.00
a. Souv. sheet of 4, #228-229, C59-C60 6.00 8.00

Opening of the Constituent Assembly of Somalia.

Marabou AP20

1959, Sept. 4 Wmk. 303
C61 AP20 1.20s shown .75 .55
C62 AP20 2s Great egret .75 .55

Incense Shipment, 15th Century B.C. AP21

Design: 2s, Incense burner and view of Mogadishu harbor.

1959, Sept. 28 *Perf. 14*
C63 AP21 1.20s red & blk .50 .60
C64 AP21 2s blue, blk & org 1.00 1.00

5th Somali Fair, Mogadishu.

University Institute and Arms AP22

Design: 1.20s, Front view of Institute.

1960, Jan. 14
C65 AP22 45c grn, blk & org brn .35 .35
C66 AP22 1.20s blue, ultra & blk .55 .65

Opening of the University Institute of Somalia.

Stork and Uprooted Oak Emblem — AP23

1960, Apr. 7 Wmk. 303 *Perf. 14*
C67 AP23 1.50s lt grn, bl & red .90 1.25

World Refugee Year, 7/1/59-6/30/60.

Republic
#C42, C44 Overprinted Like #242
Wmk. 277
1960, June 26 Photo. *Perf. 13½*
Antelopes in Natural Colors
C68 AP16 50c rose lil & blk 40.00 40.00
C69 AP16 1.20s dk gray grn 29.00 32.50

See note after No. 242.

Parliament and Italian Flag AP25

1.80s, Somali flag and assembly building.

1960, July 1 Wmk. 303 *Perf. 14*
C70 AP25 1s org red, grn & red .80 .80
C71 AP25 1.80s red org, ultra & blk 3.25 3.25

Somalia's independence.

Animal Type of Regular Issue
1960, Nov. 24
C72 A37 3s Leopard 3.75 3.75

Olympic Games Type
45c, Runner, flag, Olympic rings. 1.80s, Long distance runner, flag, Olympic rings.

1960, Nov. 24
C73 A38 45c lilac & blue .85 .85
C74 A38 1.80s org ver & bl 1.75 1.75

17th Olympic Games, Rome, 8/25-9/11.

Amauris Fenestrata and Jet Plane AP26

Various Butterflies.

1961, Sept. 9
C75 AP26 60c blue, brn & yel .40 .40
C76 AP26 90c yel, blk & grn .50 .50
C77 AP26 1s multicolored 2.40 .35
C78 AP26 1.80s org, blk & red 1.10 1.10
C79 AP26 3s multicolored 2.40 2.40
C80 AP26 5s ver, blk & brt bl 8.00 3.50
C81 AP26 10s multicolored 12.50 6.50
Nos. C75-C81 (7) 27.30 14.75

Wooden Headrest, Comb and Cap AP27

Design: 1.80sh, Camel, metal sculpture.

1961, Sept. 28 Wmk. 303 *Perf. 14*
C82 AP27 1sh blk, ultra & ocher .40 .40
C83 AP27 1.80sh blk, yel & brn 2.25 2.25

6th Somali Fair, Mogadishu.

Fish Type
Fish: 2.70sh, Lutianus sebae.

1962, Apr. 26
C84 A41 2.70sh ultra, brn & rose brn 3.50 3.50

Mosquitoes and Malaria Eradication Emblem — AP28

Wmk. 303
1962, Oct. 25 Photo. *Perf. 14*
C85 AP28 1sh bis brn & blk .85 .85
C86 AP28 1.80sh lt green & blk 2.75 2.75

WHO drive to eradicate malaria.

Police Auxiliary Women — AP29

Women's Auxiliary Forces: 1.80sh, Army auxiliary women with flag.

1963, May 15 Wmk. 303 *Perf. 14*
C87 AP29 1sh dk bl, yel & org .85 .85
C88 AP29 1.80sh multicolored 2.75 2.75

Freedom from Hunger Type

Design: 1sh, Sower and wheat.

1963, June 25
C89 A44 1sh dk brn, yel & bl 2.75 2.75

President Osman Type

1963, Sept. 15 Wmk. 303 *Perf. 14*
C90 A45 1sh multicolored .70 .70
C91 A45 1.80sh multicolored 1.30 1.30

Somali Fair Type

Design: 1.80sh, Government Pavilion.

1963, Sept. 28 Photo.
C92 A46 1.80sh blue 2.00 2.00

Map of Somalia, Animals and Globe AP30

1.80sh, Somali Credit Bank emblem.

1964, May 16 Wmk. 303 *Perf. 14*
C93 AP30 1sh multicolored 1.75 1.75
C94 AP30 1.80sh blk, bl & yel 2.75 2.75

10th anniversary of Somali Credit Bank.

Olympic Type

1964, Oct. 10 Photo.
C95 A48 90c Diving .85 .85
C96 A48 1.80sh Soccer 2.75 2.75
a. Souvenir sheet, #274-275, C95-C96 *40.00*

No. C96a sold for 3.55sh.

Elephants and DC-3 AP31

Design: 1.80sh, Plane over Mogadishu.

1964, Nov. 8 Photo. *Perf. 14*
C97 AP31 1sh brown & green 2.90 2.90
C98 AP31 1.80sh black & blue 5.25 5.25

Establishment of Somali Air Lines.

ITU Type

1965, May 17 Wmk. 303 *Perf. 14*
C99 A50 1sh dp grn & blk .85 .65
C100 A50 1.80sh rose lil & brn 2.10 1.40

Somali Fair Type

Designs: 1.50sh, Sugar industry; harvesting sugar cane and refinery. 2sh, Dairy industry; bottling plant and milk cow.

1965, Sept. 28 Photo. *Perf. 14*
C101 A51 1.50sh sepia & pale bl 1.20 .55
C102 A51 2sh sepia & rose 2.50 2.10

Faisal Type

Design: 1.80sh, Ka'aba, Mecca, Pres. Abdirascid Ali Scermarche and King Faisal.

1967, Sept. 21 Wmk. 303 *Perf. 14*
C103 A60 1.80sh blk, dp rose & org 1.75 1.75

Egret — AP32

Birds: 1sh, Southern carmine bee-eater. 1.30sh, Bruce's green pigeon. 1.80sh, Broad-tailed paradise whydah.

Perf. 11½

1968, Nov. 1 Unwmk. Litho.
C104 AP32 35c blue & multi .35 .25
C105 AP32 1sh grn & multi .45 .25
C106 AP32 1.30sh vio bl & multi 1.10 .95
C107 AP32 1.80sh yel & multi 2.75 2.50
Nos. C104-C107 (4) 4.65 3.95

Somali Democratic Republic
Postal Union Type

1.30sh, Postal Union emblem and letter.

Perf. 14x13½

1972, Jan. 25 Photo. Unwmk.
C108 A81 1.30sh multicolored 1.75 1.75

AIR POST SEMI-POSTAL STAMPS

King Victor Emmanuel III SPAP1

Wmk. 140

1934, Nov. 5 Photo. *Perf. 14*

CB1	SPAP1	25c + 10c gray grn	9.00	*26.00*
CB2	SPAP1	50c + 10c brn	9.00	*26.00*
CB3	SPAP1	75c + 15c rose red	9.00	*26.00*
CB4	SPAP1	80c + 15c blk brn	9.00	*26.00*
CB5	SPAP1	1 l + 20c red brn	9.00	*26.00*
CB6	SPAP1	2 l + 20c brt bl	9.00	*26.00*
CB7	SPAP1	3 l + 25c pur	26.00	*120.00*
CB8	SPAP1	5 l + 25c org	26.00	*120.00*
CB9	SPAP1	10 l + 30c rose vio	26.00	*120.00*
CB10	SPAP1	25 l + 2 l dp grn	26.00	*120.00*
	Nos. CB1-CB10 (10)		158.00	*636.00*
	Set, never hinged		375.00	

65th birthday of King Victor Emmanuel III; non-stop flight from Rome to Mogadishu.
For overprint see No. CBO1.

Catalogue values for unused stamps in this section, from this point to the end of the section, are for Never Hinged items.

Somalia
Type of Semi-Postal Stamps, 1957

1957, Nov. 30 Wmk. 303 *Perf. 14*
CB11 SP17 55c + 20c dk bl & brn .85 *.95*
CB12 SP17 1.20s + 20c vio & brn .85 *.95*

The surtax was for the fight against tuberculosis.

Type of Semi-Postal Issue, 1964

Designs: 75c+20c, Destroyed Somali village. 1.80sh+50c, Soldier aiding children, and map of Somalia, vert.

1964, Dec. 12 Photo. *Perf. 14*
CB13 SP18 75c + 20c blk, org red & brn .85 .40
CB14 SP18 1.80sh + 50c blk, ol bis & slate 2.50 1.40

AIR POST SPECIAL DELIVERY STAMP

Catalogue value for the stamp in this section is for a Never Hinged item.

Antelopes APSD1

Wmk. 303

1958, Oct. 4 Photo. *Perf. 14*
CE1 APSD1 1.70s org ver & blk 2.75 2.25

AIR POST OFFICIAL STAMP

No. C1 Overprinted

Wmk. 140

1934, Nov. 11 Photo. *Perf. 14*
CO1 AP1 25c sl bl & red org *1,600.* *5,250.*
Never hinged 3,500.

Forgeries of this overprint exist.

AIR POST SEMI-POSTAL OFFICIAL STAMP

Air Post Semi-Postal Stamps of 1934 Overprinted in Black

1934, Nov. 5 Wmk. 140 *Perf. 14*
CBO1 SPAP1 25 l + 2 l cop red 2,950. *6,000.*
Never hinged 5,250.

SPECIAL DELIVERY STAMPS

Italy No. E3 Surcharged

1923, July 16 Wmk. 140 *Perf. 14*
E1 SD1 30b on 60c dl red 27.50 *27.50*

Italy, Type of 1908 Special Delivery Stamp Surcharged

E2 SD2 60b on 1.20 l bl & red 40.00 *47.50*

"Italia" SD3

1924, June Engr. Unwmk.
E3 SD3 30b dk red & brn 10.00 *18.00*
E4 SD3 60b dk blue & red 18.00 *27.00*

Nos. E3-E4 Surcharged in Black or Red

1926, Oct.
E5 SD3 70c on 30b (Bk) 12.00 *16.00*
E6 SD3 2.50 l on 60b (R) 13.00 *22.00*
a. Imperf., pair 1,200.

No. E3 Surcharged in Blue

1927 *Perf. 11*
E7 SD3 1.25 l on 30b 12.00 14.50
a. Perf. 14 275.00 *950.00*
b. Imperf., pair 1,050.

Catalogue values for unused stamps in this section, from this point to the end of the section, are for Never Hinged items.

Somalia

Bananas, Grant's Gazelles SD4

Wmk. 277

1950, Apr. 24 Photo. *Perf. 14*
E8 SD4 40c blue green 15.00 13.50
E9 SD4 80c violet 18.50 21.00

Gardenias SD5

Design: 1s, Eryrhina melanocantha.

1955, Feb. *Perf. 13*
E10 SD5 50c lilac & green .90 *1.10*
E11 SD5 1s bl, rose brn & grn 1.40 *1.25*

AUTHORIZED DELIVERY STAMP

Italy No. EY2 Overprinted in Black

1939 Wmk. 140 *Perf. 14*
EY1 AD2 10c brown 70.00 —

No. EY1 has yellowish gum. A 1941 printing in grayish brown, with white gum, was not issued. The overprint on the 1939 printing is located between the "OS" and "AN" of POSTE ITALIANE, while the overprint on the 1941 printing is centered. Value: unused, 80 cents; never hinged, $2.00.

POSTAGE DUE STAMPS

Values for Nos. J1-J41 are for examples with perforations touching or cutting into the design on at least one side. Examples with perforations clear of the design on all four sides are scarce and command considerable premiums.

Postage Due Stamps of Italy Overprinted

1906-08 Wmk. 140 *Perf. 14*

J1 D3 5c buff & mag 26.00 *52.50*
J2 D3 10c buff & mag 75.00 75.00
J3 D3 20c org & mag 52.50 *90.00*
J4 D3 30c buff & mag 52.50 *105.00*
J5 D3 40c buff & mag 375.00 105.00
J6 D3 50c buff & mag 82.50 *120.00*
J7 D3 60c buff & mag ('08) 75.00 *120.00*
J8 D3 1 l blue & mag 1,500. 550.00
J9 D3 2 l blue & mag 1,500. 550.00
J10 D3 5 l blue & mag 1,500. 550.00
J11 D3 10 l blue & mag 300.00 *500.00*
Nos. J1-J11 (11) 5,539. *2,818.*

Postage Due Stamps of Italy Overprinted at Top of Stamps

1909-19

J12 D3 5c buff & mag 7.50 *24.00*
J13 D3 10c buff & mag 7.50 *24.00*
J14 D3 20c buff & mag 16.00 *47.50*
J15 D3 30c buff & mag 47.50 *47.50*
J16 D3 40c buff & mag 47.50 *65.00*
J17 D3 50c buff & mag 47.50 *85.00*
J18 D3 60c buff & mag ('19) 65.00 *72.50*
J19 D3 1 l blue & mag 135.00 85.00
J20 D3 2 l blue & mag 190.00 *190.00*
J21 D3 5 l blue & mag 225.00 260.00
J22 D3 10 l blue & mag 45.00 *90.00*
Nos. J12-J22 (11) 833.50 *990.50*

Same with Overprint at Bottom of Stamps

1920

J12a D3 5c buff & magenta 120.00 180.00
b. Double overprint 550.00
J13a D3 10c buff & magenta 120.00 180.00
J14a D3 20c buff & magenta 170.00 120.00
J15a D3 30c buff & magenta 170.00 120.00
J16a D3 40c buff & magenta 170.00 180.00
J17a D3 50c buff & magenta 170.00 170.00
J18a D3 60c buff & magenta 170.00 170.00
J19a D3 1 l blue & magenta 170.00 240.00
J20a D3 2 l blue & magenta 170.00 240.00
J21a D3 5 l blue & magenta 170.00 300.00
Nos. J12a-J21a (10) 1,600. 1,900.

D4

1923, July 1

J23 D4 1b buff & black 2.40 *9.25*
J24 D4 2b buff & black 2.40 *9.25*
a. Inverted numeral and ovpt. 550.00
J25 D4 3b buff & black 2.40 *9.25*
J26 D4 5b buff & black 3.60 *9.25*
J27 D4 10b buff & black 3.60 *9.25*
J28 D4 20b buff & black 3.60 *9.25*
J29 D4 40b buff & black 3.60 *9.25*
J30 D4 1r blue & black 3.60 *50.00*
Nos. J23-J30 (8) 25.20 *114.75*

Nos. J23-J30 were overprinted on undenominated postage due stamps of Italy. They were surcharged in Somalian currencies of besas and rupees,

Type of Postage Due Stamps of Italy Overprinted

1926, Mar. 1

J31 D3 5c buff & black 23.00 *29.00*
J32 D3 10c buff & black 23.00 20.00
J33 D3 20c buff & black 23.00 *35.00*
J34 D3 30c buff & black 23.00 20.00
J35 D3 40c buff & black 23.00 20.00
J36 D3 50c buff & black 35.00 20.00
J37 D3 60c buff & black 35.00 20.00
J38 D3 1 l blue & black 52.50 35.00
J39 D3 2 l blue & black 80.00 35.00
J40 D3 5 l blue & black 87.50 47.50
J41 D3 10 l blue & black 115.00 65.00
Nos. J31-J41 (11) 520.00 346.50

Numerals and Ovpt. Invtd.

J32a D3 10c 260.00
J33a D3 20c 825.00
J34a D3 30c 260.00
J35a D3 40c 260.00
J36a D3 50c 260.00
J37a D3 60c 260.00

Postage Due Stamps of Italy, 1934, Overprinted in Black

1934, May 12

J42 D6 5c brown 1.10 *5.75*
J43 D6 10c blue 1.10 *5.75*
J44 D6 20c rose red 3.00 11.50
J45 D6 25c green 3.00 11.50
J46 D6 30c red orange 9.00 *14.50*
J47 D6 40c black brown 9.00 *20.00*
J48 D6 50c violet 15.00 6.75
J49 D6 60c black 15.00 *34.00*
J50 D7 1 l red orange 21.00 17.00
J51 D7 2 l green 37.50 34.00
J52 D7 5 l violet 40.00 *80.00*
J53 D7 10 l blue 40.00 *82.50*
J54 D7 20 l carmine 45.00 *130.00*
Nos. J42-J54 (13) 239.70 *453.25*

Catalogue values for unused stamps in this section, from this point to the end of the section, are for Never Hinged items.

Somalia

D5

1950 Wmk. 277 Photo. *Perf. 14*

J55 D5 1c dark gray violet 4.50 4.50
J56 D5 2c deep blue 4.50 4.50
J57 D5 5c blue green 4.50 4.50
J58 D5 10c rose lilac 4.50 4.50
J59 D5 40c violet 16.50 16.50
J60 D5 1s dark brown 22.50 22.50
Nos. J55-J60 (6) 57.00 57.00

PARCEL POST STAMPS

These stamps were used by affixing them to the way bill so that one half remained on it following the parcel, the other half staying on the receipt given the sender. Most used halves are right halves. Complete stamps were and are obtainable canceled, probably to order. Both unused and used values are for complete stamps.

Parcel Post Stamps of Italy, 1914-17, Overprinted

1917-19 Wmk. 140 *Perf. 13½*

Q1 PP2 5c brown 7.00 *57.50*
a. Double overprint 500.00 —
Q2 PP2 10c blue 8.00 *40.00*
Q3 PP2 20c black ('19) 325.00 190.00
Q4 PP2 25c red 13.50 *70.00*
a. Double overprint — —
Q5 PP2 50c orange 140.00 82.50
Q6 PP2 1 l lilac 45.00 *82.50*
Q7 PP2 2 l green 62.50 *82.50*
Q8 PP2 3 l bister 67.50 *145.00*
Q9 PP2 4 l slate 75.00 *145.00*
Nos. Q1-Q9 (9) 743.50 *895.00*

Halves Used

Q1 1.60
Q2 1.60
Q3 7.25
Q4 3.50
Q5 6.00
Q6 4.75
Q7 4.75
Q8 4.75
Q9 4.75

Nos. Q5-Q9 were overprinted in 1922 with a slightly different type in which the final "A" of SOMALIA is directly over the final "A" of ITALIANA. They were not regularly issued. Value for set: unused $1,600; never hinged $2,400.

Parcel Post Stamps of Italy, 1914-17, Overprinted

1923

Q10 PP2 25c red 65.00 *140.00*
Q11 PP2 50c orange 95.00 *140.00*
Q12 PP2 1 l violet 115.00 235.00
Q13 PP2 2 l green 115.00 235.00
Q14 PP2 3 l bister 175.00 235.00
Q15 PP2 4 l slate 175.00 235.00
Nos. Q10-Q15 (6) 740.00 *1,220.*

Halves Used

Q10 4.75
Q11 4.75
Q12 3.00
Q13 3.00
Q14 4.75
Q15 5.50

Parcel Post Stamps of Italy, 1914-17, Surcharged

1923

Q16 PP2 3b on 5c brown 22.50 *30.00*
Q17 PP2 5b on 5c brown 22.50 *30.00*
Q18 PP2 10b on 10c blue 22.50 27.50
Q19 PP2 25b on 25c red 22.50 42.50
Q20 PP2 50b on 50c org 28.00 *60.00*
Q21 PP2 1r on 1 l lilac 40.00 60.00
Q22 PP2 2r on 2 l green 65.00 95.00
Q23 PP2 3r on 3 l bister 65.00 95.00
Q24 PP2 4r on 4 l slate 75.00 95.00
Nos. Q16-Q24 (9) 363.00 535.00

Halves Used

Q16 1.60
Q17 1.60
Q18 1.60
Q19 3.25
Q20 3.25
Q21 3.25
Q22 3.25
Q23 3.25
Q24 3.25

No. Q16 has the numeral "3" at the left also.

Parcel Post Stamps of Italy, 1914-22 Overprinted

Nos. Q25-Q31 come with two types of overprint:

Type I — The first "I" and last "A" of ITALIANA extend slightly at both sides of SOMALIA.

Type II — Only the "I" extends.

1926-31 Red Overprint

Q25 PP2 5c brown 30.00 *75.00*
Q26 PP2 10c blue 30.00 *75.00*
Q27 PP2 20c black 65.00 75.00
Q28 PP2 25c red 65.00 75.00
Q29 PP2 50c orange 65.00 75.00
Q30 PP2 1 l violet 87.50 75.00
Q31 PP2 2 l green 145.00 75.00
Q32 PP2 3 l yellow 27.00 *75.00*
Q33 PP2 4 l slate 27.00 *75.00*
Q34 PP2 10 l vio brn ('30) 50.00 *95.00*
Q35 PP2 12 l red brn '31) 50.00 *95.00*
Q36 PP2 15 l olive ('31) 50.00 *170.00*
Q37 PP2 20 l dull vio ('31) 50.00 *170.00*
Nos. Q25-Q37 (13) 741.50 *1,205.*

Halves Used

Q25 2.00
Q26 2.00
Q27 3.25
Q28 3.25
Q29 3.25
Q30 3.25
Q31 3.25
Q32 3.25
Q33 3.25
Q34 4.00
Q35 4.00
Q36 4.00
Q37 4.00

These seven stamps with type I overprint were not regularly issued, and Nos. Q27-Q31 (type I) sell for less than with type II overprint.

Black Overprint

Q38 PP2 10 l violet brown 65.00 70.00
Q39 PP2 12 l red brown 45.00 70.00
Q40 PP2 15 l olive 45.00 70.00
Q41 PP2 20 l dull violet 45.00 70.00
Nos. Q38-Q41 (4) 200.00 280.00

Halves Used

Q38 4.00
Q39 4.00
Q40 4.00
Q41 4.00

Same Overprint on Parcel Post Stamps of Italy, 1927-38

1928-39 Black Overprint

Q42 PP3 25c red, type I ('31) 62.50 *75.00*
Never hinged 260.00
Q43 PP3 30c ultra 8.50 *10.50*
Q43A PP3 50c orange *12,750.*
Q44 PP3 60c red 8.50 *11.00*
Q45 PP3 1 l lilac brn, type II ('31) 55.00 *75.00*
Q46 PP3 2 l green, type II ('31) 55.00 *75.00*
Q47 PP3 3 l bister 21.00 *28.00*
Q48 PP3 4 l gray black 21.00 *28.00*
Q49 PP3 10 l rose lil ('34) 650.00 *950.00*
Q50 PP3 20 l lil brn ('34) 650.00 *1,050.*
Nos. Q42-Q43,Q44-Q50 (9) 1,532. *2,303.*

Halves Used

Q42 8.75
Q43 .45
Q43A 160.00
Q44 .45
Q45 2.75
Q46 2.75
Q47 .80
Q48 .80
Q49 20.00
Q50 20.00

The 25c, 1 l and 2 l come with both types of overprint (see note below No. Q37). Both types were regularly issued. Values are for type I on 25c, type II on 1 l and 2 l.

Red Overprint

Q51 PP3 5c brown ('39) 16.00
Q52 PP3 3 l bister ('30) 32.50 *80.00*
Half stamp 2.00
Q53 PP3 4 l gray black ('30) 32.50 *80.00*
Half stamp 2.00
Nos. Q51-Q53 (3) 81.00

Same Overprint in Black on Italy Nos. Q24-Q25

1940 *Perf. 13*

Q54 PP3 5c brown 8.25 *19.00*
Half stamp .50
Q55 PP3 10c deep blue 10.50 *19.00*
Half stamp .50

Catalogue values for unused stamps in this section, from this point to the end of the section, are for Never Hinged items.

Somalia

PP1

1950 Wmk. 277 Photo. *Perf. 14*

Q56 PP1 1c cerise 9.50 *9.50*
Q57 PP1 3c dark gray violet 9.50 *9.50*
Q58 PP1 5c rose lilac 9.50 *9.50*
Q59 PP1 10c red orange 9.50 *9.50*
Q60 PP1 20c dark brown 9.50 *9.50*
Q61 PP1 50c blue green 24.00 *24.00*
Q62 PP1 1s violet 67.50 *67.50*
Q63 PP1 2s brown 82.50 *82.50*
Q64 PP1 3s blue 135.00 *135.00*
Nos. Q56-Q64 (9) 356.50 *356.50*

Halves Used

Q56 .25
Q57 .25
Q58 .25
Q59 .25
Q60 .25
Q61 .25
Q62 1.60
Q63 2.00
Q64 3.25

SOMALI COAST

sō-'mä-lē 'kōst

(Djibouti)

LOCATION — Eastern Africa, bordering on the Gulf of Aden
GOVT. — French Overseas Territory
AREA — 8,500 sq. mi.
POP. — 86,000 (est. 1963)
CAPITAL — Djibouti (Jibuti)

The port of Obock, which issued postage stamps in 1892-1894, was included in the territory and began to use stamps of Somali Coast in 1902. See Obock in Vol. 4.

On Mar. 19, 1967, the territory changed its name to the French Territory of the Afars and Issas. The Republic of Djibouti was proclaimed June 27, 1977.

100 Centimes = 1 Franc

Catalogue values for unused stamps in this country are for Never Hinged items, beginning with Scott 224 in the regular postage section, Scott B13 in the semi-postal section, Scott C1 in the airpost section, Scott CB1 in the airpost semi-postal section, and Scott J39 in the postage due section.

Obock Nos. 32-33, 35, 45 with Overprint or Surcharge Handstamped in Black, Blue or Red

Navigation and Commerce
A1 A2

A3

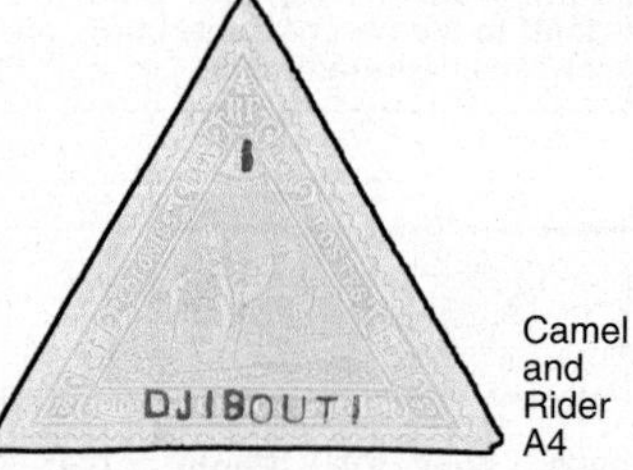

Camel and Rider
A4

1894 Unwmk. *Perf. 14x13½*

1 A1 5c grn & red, *grnsh* (with bar) 165.00 140.00
a. Without bar 1,250. 800.00
2 A2 25c on 2c brn & bl, *buff* (Bl & Bk) 350.00 225.00
a. "25" omitted 1,000. 950.00
b. "25" double 1,600.
c. "DJIBOUTI" omitted 1,000. 850.00
d. "DJIBOUTI" inverted 1,100. 975.00
e. "DJIBOUTI" double 1,600. 1,250.
3 A3 50c on 1c blk & red, *bl* (R & Bl) 350.00 250.00
a. "5" instead of "50" 1,600. 1,150.
b. "0" instead of "50" 1,600. 1,150.
c. "DJIBOUTI" omitted 1,600. 1,250.

Imperf

4 A4 1fr on 5fr car 625.00 500.00
a. "DJIBOUTI" omitted 4,500.
b. "DJIBOUTI" double 1,900. 1,650.
c. "1" double 1,900. 1,650.
5 A4 5fr carmine 1,900. 1,350.

Counterfeits exist of Nos. 4-5.

View of Djibouti, Somali Warriors — A5

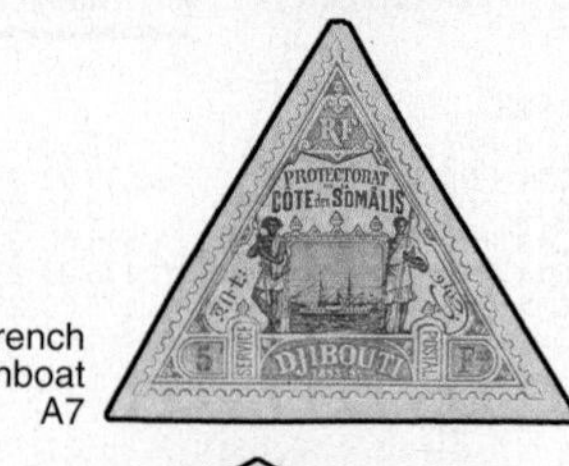

French Gunboat
A7

Crossing Desert (Size: 66mm wide, including simulated perfs.) — A8

Designs: 15c, 25c, 30c, 40c, 50c, 75c, Different views of Djibouti. 1fr, 2fr, Djibouti quay.

Imperf. (Simulated Perforations in Frame Color)

1894-1902 Typo.

Quadrille Lines Printed on Paper

6 A5 1c blk & claret 3.50 2.75
7 A5 2c claret & blk 3.50 3.50
8 A5 4c vio brn & bl 14.00 10.50
9 A5 5c bl grn & red 14.00 7.00
10 A5 5c grn & yel grn ('02) 10.50 7.75
11 A5 10c brown & grn 17.50 10.50
a. Half used as 5c on cover 200.00
12 A5 15c violet & grn 17.50 10.50
13 A5 25c rose & blue 27.50 10.50
14 A5 30c gray brn & rose 25.00 10.50
a. Half used as 15c on cover 600.00
15 A5 40c org & bl ('00) 52.50 35.00
a. Half used as 20c on cover 950.00
16 A5 50c blue & rose 27.50 17.50
a. Half used as 25c on cover 2,000.
17 A5 75c violet & org 50.00 35.00
18 A5 1fr ol grn & blk 25.00 21.00
19 A5 2fr gray brn & rose 90.00 70.00
a. Half used as 1fr on cover 2,400.
20 A7 5fr rose & blue 180.00 140.00
21 A8 25fr rose & blue 1,000. *1,050.*
22 A8 50fr blue & rose 600.00 *675.00*
Nos. 6-20 (15) 558.00 392.00

High values are found with the overprint "S" (Specimen) erased and, usually, a cancellation added.

Values for bisects are for complete covers, newspapers or other printed matter.

For surcharges see Nos. 24-27B.

1899 Black Surcharge

23 A5 40c on 4c vio brn & bl *3,000.* 32.50
a. Double surcharge *5,500.* 1,400.
b. Pair, one without surcharge 4,250.
c. Inverted surcharge 1,600.
d. Double surcharge, both inverted 3,000.

Nos. 17-20 Surcharged

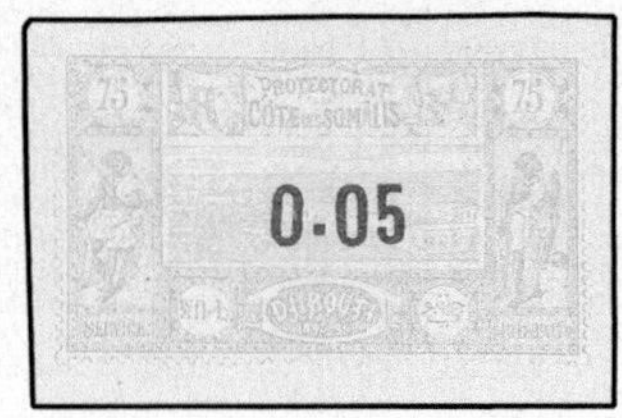

1902 Blue Surcharge

24 A5 0.05c on 75c 70.00 42.50
a. Inverted surcharge 550.00 500.00
b. Double surcharge 550.00 500.00
c. Pair, one without surcharge 2,500.
25 A5 0.10c on 1fr 80.00 62.50
a. Inverted surcharge 510.00 400.00
b. Double surcharge 510.00 400.00
26 A5 0.40c on 2fr 550.00 400.00
a. Double surcharge 2,000. 1,850.

Black Surcharge

27 A7 0.75c on 5fr 525.00 400.00
a. Inverted surcharge 2,600. 2,100.
c. Double surcharge 2,600. 2,100.

Obock No. 57 Surcharged in Blue

27B A7 0.05c on 75c gray lil & org 1,500. 1,050.

A10

Nos. 15-16 Surcharged in Black

28 A10 5c on 40c 10.50 7.00
a. Double surcharge 130.00 130.00
29 A10 10c on 50c 27.50 27.50
a. Inverted surcharge 510.00 500.00
b. Double surcharge 600.00

Stamps of Obock Surcharged

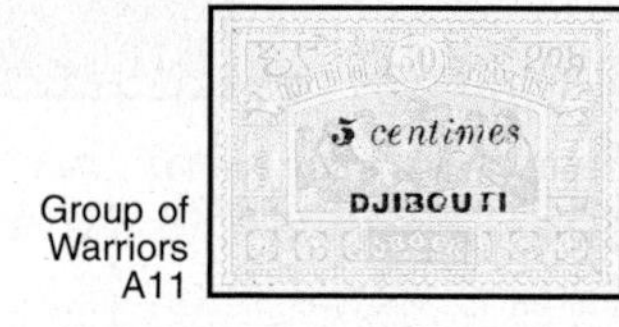

Group of Warriors
A11

Black Surcharge

30 A11 5c on 30c bis & yel grn 17.50 10.50
a. Inverted surcharge 275.00 275.00
b. Double surcharge 325.00 275.00
c. Triple surcharge 1,500.

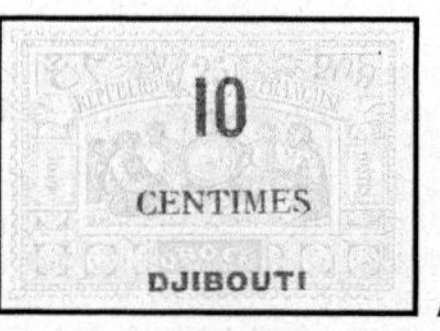

A12

Red Surcharge

31 A12 10c on 25c blk & bl 21.00 14.00
a. Inverted surcharge 275.00 275.00
b. Double surcharge 325.00 325.00
c. Triple surcharge 1,600. 1,600.
d. "Djibouti" omitted 875.00 *1,250.*

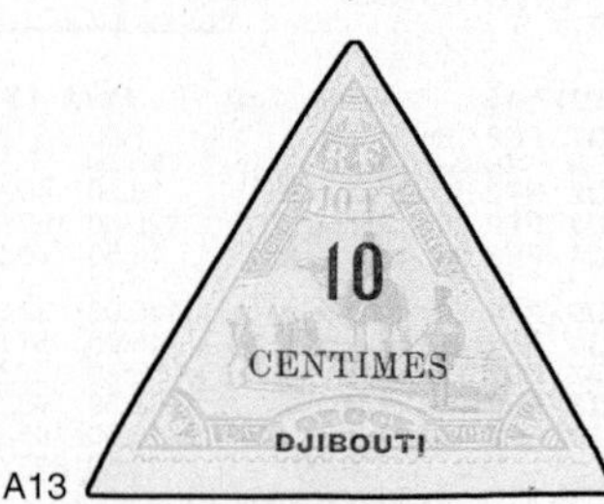

A13

Black Surcharge

32 A13 10c on 10fr org & red vio 40.00 32.50
a. Double surcharge 250.00 200.00
b. Double surch., one invtd. 2,200. 2,100.
c. Triple surcharge 1,500. 1,500.
d. "Djibouti" omitted 115.00 80.00

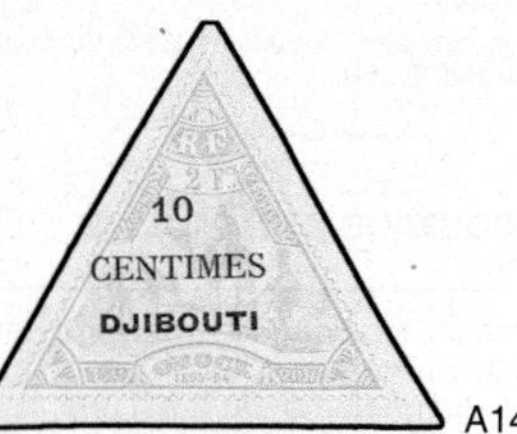

A14

Black Surcharge

33 A14 10c on 2fr dl vio & org 62.50 52.50
a. Double surcharge 450.00 435.00
b. Double surcharge, one inverted 2,200. 2,200.
c. Triple surcharge, one inverted 2,700. 2,700.
d. "DJIBOUTI" inverted 250.00 225.00
e. Large "0" in "10" 160.00 125.00

Same Surcharge on Obock No. 53 in Red

33D A7 10c on 25c blk & bl *32,500.* *22,500.*

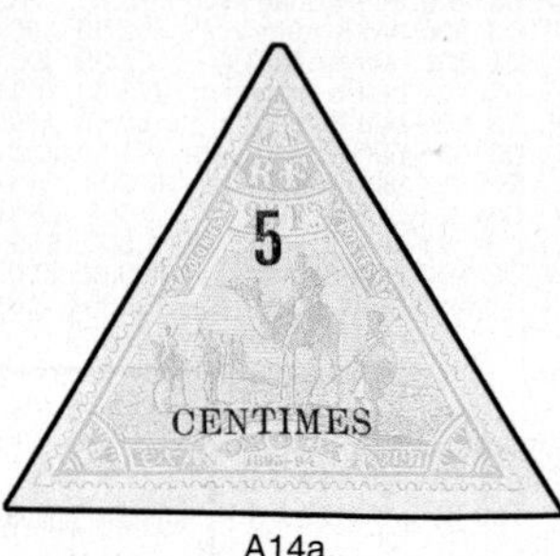

A14a

Black Surcharge on Obock Nos. 63-64

33E A14a 5c on 25fr brn & bl 62.50 55.00
33F A14a 10c on 50fr red vio & grn 80.00 60.00
g. "01" instead of "10" 225.00 210.00
h. "CENTIMES" inverted 2,750. 2,750.
i. Double surcharge 2,750. 2,100.
k. Double surcharge, one inverted 2,750. 2,250.

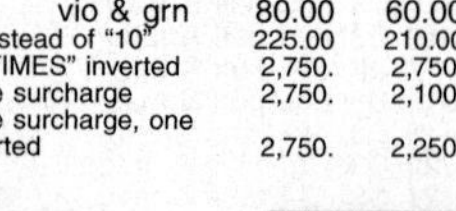

Tadjoura Mosque
A15

Somalis on Camel
A16

Warriors — A17

1902 Engr. *Perf. 11½*

34 A15 1c brn vio & org 1.40 1.10
35 A15 2c yel brn & yel grn 2.10 1.40
36 A15 4c bl & carmine 3.50 2.10
37 A15 5c bl grn & yel grn 3.50 1.75
38 A15 10c car & red org 7.00 4.25
39 A15 15c brn org & bl 7.00 4.25
40 A16 20c vio & green 17.50 7.75
41 A16 25c blue 25.00 12.50
a. 25c indigo & blue ('03) 25.00 15.00
42 A16 30c red & black 12.50 5.00
43 A16 40c orange & blue 17.50 10.00
44 A16 50c grn & red org 45.00 37.50
45 A16 75c orange & vio 10.50 7.00
46 A17 1fr red org & vio 35.00 17.50
47 A17 2fr yel grn & car 42.50 32.50
a. Without names of designer and engraver at bottom 140.00 140.00
48 A17 5fr orange & blue 35.00 27.50
Nos. 34-48 (15) 265.00 172.10

1903

49 A15 1c brn vio & blk 1.40 1.10
50 A15 2c yel brn & blk 1.40 1.10
51 A15 4c lake & blk 2.10 2.10
a. 4c red & black 2.75 2.50
52 A15 5c bl grn & blk 4.25 3.50
53 A15 10c carmine & blk 8.50 3.50

54 A15 15c org brn & blk 25.00 10.50
a. 15c brown & black 21.00 10.50
55 A16 20c dl vio & blk 25.00 17.50
56 A16 25c ultra & blk 25.00 14.00
58 A16 40c orange & blk 10.50 10.50
a. 40c bister & black 22.50 22.50
59 A16 50c green & blk 25.00 17.50
60 A16 75c buff & blk 14.00 10.50
a. 75c brown orange & black 77.50 77.50
61 A17 1fr orange & blk 21.00 21.00
62 A17 2fr yel grn & blk 14.00 10.50
a. Without names of designer and engraver at bottom 50.00 50.00
63 A17 5fr red org & blk 25.00 21.00
a. 5fr ocher & black 35.00 32.50
Nos. 49-63 (14) 202.15 144.30

Imperforates, transposed colors and inverted centers exist in the 1902 and 1903 issues. Most of these were issued from Paris and some are said to have been fraudulently printed.

Tadjoura Mosque A18

Somalis on Camel — A19

Warriors — A20

1909 **Typo.** ***Perf. 14x13½***
64 A18 1c maroon & brn 1.10 1.10
65 A18 2c vio & ol gray 1.10 1.10
66 A18 4c ol gray & bl 1.40 1.10
67 A18 5c grn & gray grn 1.75 1.10
68 A18 10c car & ver 4.50 1.75
69 A18 20c blk & red brn 7.00 5.50
70 A19 25c bl & pale bl 5.00 4.00
71 A19 30c brn & scar 7.75 5.50
72 A19 35c vio & grn 10.50 7.00
73 A19 40c rose & vio 10.50 6.25
74 A19 45c brn & bl grn 10.50 6.25
75 A19 50c maroon & brn 10.50 7.00
76 A19 75c scarlet & grn 21.00 14.00
77 A20 1fr vio & brn 27.50 22.50
78 A20 2fr brn & rose 42.50 32.50
79 A20 5fr vio brn & bl grn 70.00 45.00
Nos. 64-79 (16) 232.60 161.65

Drummer A21

Somali Girl A22

Djibouti-Addis Ababa Railroad Bridge — A23

1915-33 ***Perf. 13½x14***

Chalky Paper

80 A21 1c brt vio & red brn .25 .30
81 A21 2c ocher & ind .25 .30
82 A21 4c dk brn & red .35 .35
83 A21 5c yel grn & grn 1.10 1.10
84 A21 5c org & dl red ('22) .70 .70
85 A22 10c car & dk red 2.10 1.10
86 A22 10c ap grn & grn ('22) 1.40 1.40
87 A22 10c ver & grn ('25) .35 .70
88 A22 15c brn vio & car ('18) 1.10 .70
89 A22 20c org & blk brn .35 .35
90 A22 20c dp grn & bl grn ('25) .35 .35

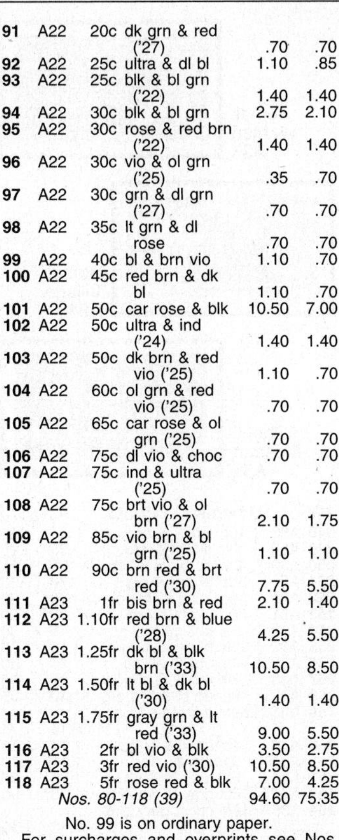

91 A22 20c dk grn & red ('27) .70 .70
92 A22 25c ultra & dl bl 1.10 .85
93 A22 25c blk & bl grn ('22) 1.40 1.40
94 A22 30c blk & bl grn 2.75 2.10
95 A22 30c rose & red brn ('22) 1.40 1.40
96 A22 30c vio & ol grn ('25) .35 .70
97 A22 30c grn & dl grn ('27) .70 .70
98 A22 35c lt grn & dl rose .70 .70
99 A22 40c bl & brn vio 1.10 .70
100 A22 45c red brn & dk bl 1.10 .70
101 A22 50c car rose & blk 10.50 7.00
102 A22 50c ultra & ind ('24) 1.40 1.40
103 A22 50c dk brn & red vio ('25) 1.10 .70
104 A22 60c ol grn & red vio ('25) .70 .70
105 A22 65c car rose & ol grn ('25) .70 .70
106 A22 75c dl vio & choc .70 .70
107 A22 75c ind & ultra ('25) .70 .70
108 A22 75c brt vio & ol brn ('27) 2.10 1.75
109 A22 85c vio brn & bl grn ('25) 1.10 1.10
110 A22 90c brn red & brt red ('30) 7.75 5.50
111 A23 1fr bis brn & red 2.10 1.40
112 A23 1.10fr red brn & blue ('28) 4.25 5.50
113 A23 1.25fr dk bl & blk brn ('33) 10.50 8.50
114 A23 1.50fr lt bl & dk bl ('30) 1.40 1.40
115 A23 1.75fr gray grn & lt red ('33) 9.00 5.50
116 A23 2fr bl vio & blk 3.50 2.75
117 A23 3fr red vio ('30) 10.50 8.50
118 A23 5fr rose red & blk 7.00 4.25
Nos. 80-118 (39) 94.60 75.35

No. 99 is on ordinary paper.
For surcharges and overprints see Nos. 119-134, 183-193.

Nos. 83, 92 Surcharged in Green or Blue

1922
119 A21 10c on 5c (G) .70 .70
a. Double surcharge 110.00
120 A22 50c on 25c (Bl) .70 .70

Type of 1915 Surcharged in Various Colors

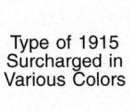

1922
121 A22 0,01c on 15c vio & rose (Bk) .35 *.45*
122 A22 0,02c on 15c vio & rose (Bl) .35 *.65*
123 A22 0,04c on 15c vio & rose (G) .70 .70
124 A22 0,05c on 15c vio & rose (R) .70 .70
Nos. 121-124 (4) 2.10 2.50

Nos. 88, 99 and Type of 1915 Surcharged

1923-27
125 A22 60c on 75c ol grn & vio .70 .70
126 A22 65c on 15c ('25) 2.75 2.75
127 A22 85c on 40c ('25) 2.10 2.10
128 A22 90c on 75c brn red & red ('27) 5.50 5.50
Nos. 125-128 (4) 11.05 11.05

No. 118 and Type of 1915-17 Surcharged with New Value and Bars in Black or Red

1924-27
129 A23 25c on 5fr 1.40 1.40
130 A23 1.25fr on 1fr dk bl & ultra (R) ('26) 1.40 1.10
131 A23 1.50fr on 1fr lt bl & dk bl ('27) 1.40 1.40
132 A23 3fr on 5fr ver & red vio ('27) 7.00 7.00
133 A23 10fr on 5fr brn red & ol brn ('27) 10.50 10.50
134 A23 20fr on 5fr gray grn & lil rose ('27) 14.00 *17.50*
Nos. 129-134 (6) 35.70 38.90

Common Design Types pictured following the introduction.

Colonial Exposition Issue

Common Design Types

Engr., Name of Country Typo. in Black

1931 ***Perf. 12½***
135 CD70 40c deep green 5.50 5.50
136 CD71 50c violet 5.50 5.50
137 CD72 90c red orange 5.50 5.50
138 CD73 1.50fr dull blue 5.50 5.50
Nos. 135-138 (4) 22.00 22.00

Paris International Exposition Issue

Common Design Types

1937 **Engr.** ***Perf. 13***
139 CD74 20c deep violet 1.90 1.90
140 CD75 30c dark green 1.90 1.90
141 CD76 40c car rose 1.90 1.90
142 CD77 50c dk brn & bl 1.90 1.90
143 CD78 90c red 1.90 1.90
144 CD79 1.50fr ultra 2.10 2.10
Nos. 139-144 (6) 11.60 11.60

Colonial Arts Exhibition Issue Souvenir Sheet

Common Design Type

1937 ***Imperf.***
145 CD75 3fr dull violet 14.00 *21.00*

Mosque of Djibouti — A24

Somali Warriors — A25

Governor Léonce Lagarde — A26

View of Djibouti — A27

1938-40 ***Perf. 12x12½, 12½***
146 A24 2c dull red vio .25 .25
147 A24 3c slate grn ('40) .25 .25
148 A24 4c dull red brn .25 .25
149 A24 5c carmine .25 .25
150 A24 10c blue gray .25 .25
151 A24 15c slate black .35 .30
152 A24 20c dark orange .35 .30
153 A25 25c dark brown .70 .70
154 A25 30c dark blue .35 .35
155 A25 35c olive grn 1.10 .70
156 A24 40c org brn ('40) .35 .35
157 A24 45c dull grn ('40) .35 .35
158 A25 50c red .70 .70
159 A25 55c dull red vio 1.10 .70
160 A25 60c black ('40) .70 .70
161 A25 65c orange brown 1.10 1.10
162 A25 70c lt violet ('40) 1.40 1.40
163 A26 80c gray blk 2.75 2.10
164 A25 90c rose vio ('39) 1.40 1.40
165 A26 1fr carmine 3.50 2.10
166 A26 1fr black ('40) .55 .55
167 A26 1.25fr magenta ('39) 1.10 1.10
168 A26 1.40fr pck bl ('40) 1.10 1.10
169 A26 1.50fr dull green 1.10 1.10
170 A26 1.60fr brn car ('40) 1.10 1.10
171 A26 1.75fr ultra 1.40 1.10
172 A26 2fr dk orange 1.10 1.10
173 A26 2.25fr ultra ('39) 1.75 1.75
174 A26 2.50fr org brn ('40) 1.75 1.75
175 A26 3fr dull violet 1.10 1.10
176 A27 5fr brn & pale cl 2.10 2.10
177 A27 10fr ind & pale bl 2.50 2.75
178 A27 20fr car lake & gray 2.50 2.75
Nos. 146-178 (33) 36.60 33.85

For types A24-A26 without "RF," see Nos. 237A-237C.
For overprints and surcharge see Nos. 194-223.

New York World's Fair Issue

Common Design Type

1939 **Engr.** ***Perf. 12½x12***
179 CD82 1.25fr car lake .70 1.40
180 CD82 2.25fr ultra .70 1.40

Mosque of Djibouti and Marshal Pétain — A28

1941, Nov. 10 **Engr.** ***Perf. 12x12½***
181 A28 1fr yellow brown .35
182 A28 2.50fr blue .35
Set, never hinged 1.40

Nos. 181-182 were issued by the Vichy government in France, but were not placed on sale in Somali Coast.
For surcharges, see Nos. B11-B12.

Nos. 80-82, 84, 88, 91, 97, 103, 105, 114-115 Overprinted in Black or Red

Perf. 13½x14, 14x13½

1943 **Unwmk.**
183 A21 1c brt vio & red brn 3.50 3.50
184 A21 2c ocher & ind 3.50 3.50
185 A21 4c dk brn & red 30.00 30.00
186 A21 5c org & dl red 3.50 3.50
187 A22 15c brn vio & car 10.50 10.50
188 A22 20c dk grn & red 3.50 3.50
189 A22 30c grn & dl grn 3.50 3.50
190 A22 50c dk brn & red vio 3.50 3.50
191 A22 65c car rose & ol grn 3.50 3.50
192 A23 1.50fr lt bl & dk bl (R) 3.50 3.50
193 A23 1.75fr gray grn & lt red 14.00 14.00
Nos. 183-193 (11) 82.50 82.50
Set, never hinged 130.00

Stamps of 1938-40 Overprinted in Black or Red

On A24

On A25

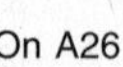

On A26

On A27

1943 *Perf. 12x12½, 12½*

No.	Type	Description	Unused	Used
194	A24	2c dl red vio	5.50	5.50
195	A24	3c sl grn (R)	5.50	5.50
196	A24	4c dl red brn	5.50	5.50
197	A24	5c carmine	5.50	5.50
198	A24	10c bl gray (R)	1.40	1.40
199	A24	15c sl blk (R)	5.50	5.50
200	A24	20c dk org	5.50	5.50
201	A25	25c dk brn (R)	5.50	5.50
202	A25	30c dk bl (R)	1.20	1.20
203	A25	35c olive (R)	5.50	5.50
204	A24	40c brn org	1.20	1.20
205	A24	45c dl grn	5.50	5.50
206	A25	55c dl red vio (R)	5.50	5.50
207	A25	60c blk (R)	1.40	1.40
208	A25	70c lt vio (R)	1.20	1.20
a.		Inverted overprint	275.00	275.00
b.		Double overprint	325.00	325.00
209	A26	80c gray blk (R)	2.10	2.10
210	A25	90c rose vio (R)	1.20	1.20
211	A26	1.25fr magenta	3.50	3.50
212	A26	1.40fr pck bl (R)	2.10	2.10
213	A26	1.50fr dl grn	3.50	3.50
214	A26	1.60fr brn car	3.50	3.50
215	A26	1.75fr ultra (R)	12.00	12.00
216	A26	2fr dk org	1.60	1.60
217	A26	2.25fr ultra (R)	3.50	3.50
218	A26	2.50fr chestnut	2.10	2.10
219	A26	3fr dl vio (R)	3.50	3.50
220	A27	5fr brn & pale cl	17.50	17.50
221	A27	10fr ind & pale bl	180.00	180.00
222	A27	20fr car lake & gray	17.50	17.50

The space between overprint on Nos. 206 and 208 measures 10½mm.

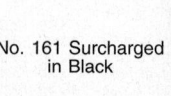

No. 161 Surcharged in Black

No.	Type	Description	Unused	Used
223	A25	50c on 65c org brn	1.60	1.60
		Nos. 194-223 (30)	316.60	316.60
		Set, never hinged	450.00	

Catalogue values for unused stamps in this section, from this point to the end of the section, are for Never Hinged items.

Locomotive and Palms — A29

1943 Unwmk. Photo. *Perf. 14½x14*

No.	Type	Description	Unused	Used
224	A29	5c royal blue	.70	.35
225	A29	10c pink	.70	.35
226	A29	25c emerald	.70	.70
227	A29	30c gray blk	.70	.70
228	A29	40c violet	.70	.70
229	A29	80c red brn	.70	.70
230	A29	1fr aqua	.70	.70
231	A29	1.50fr scarlet	.70	.70
232	A29	2fr brown	.70	.70
233	A29	2.50fr ultra	1.40	1.10
234	A29	4fr brt org	1.40	1.10
235	A29	5fr dp rose lil	1.40	1.10
236	A29	10fr lt ultra	2.10	1.75
237	A29	20fr green	2.10	1.60
		Nos. 224-237 (14)	14.70	12.25

For surcharges see Nos. 240-247.

Types of 1938-40 Without "RF"

1944, Apr. 3 Engr. *Perf. 12½*

No.	Type	Description	Unused	Used
237A	A24	40c org brn	1.10	
237B	A25	50c red	1.40	
237C	A26	1.50fr dull green	2.10	
		Nos. 237A-237C (3)	4.60	

Nos. 237A-237C were issued by the Vichy government in France, but were not placed on sale in Somali Coast.

Eboue Issue

Common Design Type

1945 Engr. *Perf. 13*

No.	Type	Description	Unused	Used
238	CD91	2fr black	.70	.70
239	CD91	25fr Prus grn	1.75	1.40

Nos. 238 and 239 exist imperforate.

Nos. 224, 226 and 233 Surcharged in Carmine or Black

1945 *Perf. 14½x14*

No.	Type	Description	Unused	Used
240	A29	50c on 5c (C)	.70	.70
a.		Inverted surcharge	310.00	
b.		Double surcharge	240.00	
241	A29	60c on 5c (C)	.70	.70
a.		Inverted surcharge	225.00	
b.		Double surcharge	190.00	
242	A29	70c on 5c (C)	.70	.70
a.		Inverted surcharge	225.00	
b.		Double surcharge, one inverted	325.00	
243	A29	1.20fr on 5c (C)	.70	.70
a.		Double surcharge, one inverted	325.00	
244	A29	2.40fr on 25c	1.10	1.40
a.		Inverted surcharge	240.00	
b.		Double surcharge	225.00	
c.		Bars doubly surcharged	125.00	
245	A29	3fr on 25c	1.10	1.40
a.		Inverted surcharge	310.00	
b.		Double surcharge, one inverted	375.00	
246	A29	4.50fr on 25c	1.40	1.40
a.		Inverted surcharge	225.00	
247	A29	15fr on 2.50fr (C)	2.10	2.10
a.		Surcharge bars omitted	180.00	
b.		Value doubly surcharged	240.00	
		Nos. 240-247 (8)	8.50	9.10

Danakil Tent — A30

Khor-Angar Outpost A31

Obock-Tadjouran Road — A32

Somali Woman A33

Somali Village A34

Djibouti Mosque A35

1947 Unwmk. Photo. *Perf. 13*

No.	Type	Description	Unused	Used
248	A30	10c vio bl & org	.35	.25
249	A30	30c ol brn & org	.35	.25
250	A30	40c dp plum & org	.35	.25
251	A31	50c bl grn & org	.70	.30
252	A31	60c choc & dp yel	.70	.30
253	A31	80c vio bl & org	.70	.30
254	A32	1fr bl & choc	.70	.30
255	A32	1.20fr bl grn & ol grn	1.10	.80
256	A32	1.50fr org & vio bl	.70	.30
257	A33	2fr red lil & bl gray	.70	.55
258	A33	3fr dp bl & brn org	1.40	.85
259	A33	3.60fr car rose & cop red	2.10	1.75
260	A33	4fr choc & bl gray	1.75	1.10
261	A34	5fr org & choc	1.10	.70
262	A34	6fr gray bl & int bl	1.75	.85
263	A34	10fr gray bl & red lil	1.75	.90
264	A35	15fr choc, gray bl & pink	2.10	1.10
265	A35	20fr dk bl, gray bl & org	2.75	1.40
266	A35	25fr vio brn, lil rose & gray bl	7.00	3.50
		Nos. 248-266 (19)	28.05	15.75

Military Medal Issue

Common Design Type

1952 Engraved and Typographed

No.	Type	Description	Unused	Used
267	CD101	15fr blk, grn, yel & dk pur	9.00	8.00

Imperforates

Most stamps of Somali Coast from 1956 onward exist imperforate in issued and trial colors, and also in small presentation sheets in issued colors.

FIDES Issue

Common Design Type and

Lighthouse, Ras-Bir — A36

15fr, Loading ship and map, Djibouti.

1956 Unwmk. Engr. *Perf. 13*

No.	Type	Description	Unused	Used
268	CD103	15fr purple	2.10	1.40
269	A36	40fr dp ultra & blue	3.25	1.75

Flower Issue

Common Design Type

Design: 10fr, Haemanthus, horiz.

1958 Photo. *Perf. 12½x12*

No.	Type	Description	Unused	Used
270	CD104	10fr grn, red & yel	4.25	1.40

Wart Hog — A37

40c, Cheetah. 50c, Gerenuk, vert.

1958 Engr. *Perf. 13*

No.	Type	Description	Unused	Used
271	A37	30c red brn & sepia	.70	.35
272	A37	40c brn & olive	.70	.35
273	A37	50c brn, grn & gray	1.10	.70
		Nos. 271-273,C21 (4)	12.50	6.40

Human Rights Issue

Common Design Type

1958, Dec. 10 Unwmk.

No.	Type	Description	Unused	Used
274	CD105	20fr brt pur & dk bl	3.50	2.10

Universal Declaration of Human Rights, 10th anniv.

Parrotfish A38

Designs: Various Tropical Fish.

1959 Engr. *Perf. 13*

No.	Type	Description	Unused	Used
275	A38	1fr brt bl, brn & red org	.85	.55
276	A38	2fr blk, lt bl, yel & grn	.85	.55
277	A38	3fr vio & blk brn	.85	.55
278	A38	4fr brt grnsh bl, org & lt brn	1.10	.70
279	A38	5fr brt grnsh bl & blk	1.75	.90
280	A38	20fr brt bl, dl red brn & rose	3.25	2.00
281	A38	25fr red, grn & ultra	5.00	2.50
282	A38	60fr bl & dk grn	11.00	5.00
		Nos. 275-282 (8)	24.65	12.75

No. 276 is vertical.

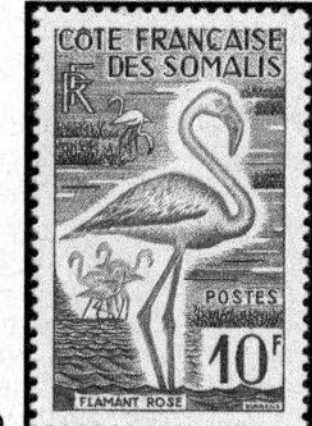

Flamingo — A39

Birds: 15fr, Bee-eater, horiz. 30fr, Sacred ibis, horiz. 75fr, Pink-backed pelican.

1960 Unwmk. *Perf. 13*

No.	Type	Description	Unused	Used
283	A39	10fr bluish grn, bis & cl	2.75	1.40
284	A39	15fr rose lil, grn & yel	3.50	1.40
285	A39	30fr bl, blk, org & brn	7.75	4.25
286	A39	75fr grn, sl grn & yel	12.00	7.00
		Nos. 283-286 (4)	26.00	14.05

Dragon Tree — A40

Klipspringer — A41

Designs: 4fr, Cony. 6fr, Large flatfish. 25fr, Fennecs. 40fr, Griffon vulture.

1962, Mar. 24 Engr. *Perf. 13*

No.	Type	Description	Unused	Used
287	A40	2fr grn, yel, org & brn	2.10	1.40
288	A40	4fr ocher & choc	2.10	1.40
289	A40	6fr brn, mar, grn & yel	4.25	2.75
290	A40	25fr red brn, ocher & grn	8.50	5.00
291	A40	40fr dk bl, brn & gray	11.00	7.00
292	A41	50fr bis, bl & lil	11.00	8.50
		Nos. 287-292 (6)	38.95	26.05

Meleagrina Margaritifera A42

Sea Shells: 10fr, Tridacna squamosa, horiz. 25fr, Strombus tricornis, horiz. 30fr, Trochus dentatus.

Shells in Natural Colors

1962, Nov. 24 **Photo.**
293 A42 8fr red & blk 1.75 .90
294 A42 10fr car rose & blk 1.75 1.10
295 A42 25fr dp bl & brn 3.75 1.60
296 A42 30fr rose lil & brn 3.75 2.00
Nos. 293-296 (4) 11.00 5.60

See Nos. C28-C29.

Red Cross Centenary Issue
Common Design Type

1963, Sept. 2 **Engr.** ***Perf. 13***
297 CD113 50fr org brn, gray & car 6.25 6.25

Astraea Coral — A43

Design: 6fr, Organ-pipe coral.

1963, Nov. 30 **Photo.** ***Perf. 13x13½***
298 A43 5fr multi 2.10 1.40
299 A43 6fr multi 2.10 1.40

See Nos. C26-C27, C30.

Human Rights Issue
Common Design Type

1963, Dec. 20 **Engr.** ***Perf. 13***
300 CD117 70fr dk brn & ultra 8.50 8.50

Philatec Issue
Common Design Type

1964, Apr. 7 **Unwmk.** ***Perf. 13***
301 CD118 80fr dp lil rose, grn & brn 7.75 7.75

Houri (Somali Sailboats) A44

Design: 25fr, Sambouk (Somali sailboats).

1964, June 9 **Engr.**
302 A44 15fr multi 1.75 1.10
303 A44 25fr multi 2.50 1.50

View of Dadwayya and Map of Somali Coast A45

Design: 20fr, View of Tadjourah and map of Somali Coast.

1965, Oct. 20 **Engr.** ***Perf. 13***
304 A45 6fr ultra, sl grn & red brn 1.00 .70
305 A45 20fr ultra, org brn & brt grn 1.00 1.00

Senna — A46

1966 **Engr.** ***Perf. 13***
306 A46 5fr shown 1.40 1.00
307 A46 8fr Poinciana 1.40 1.00
308 A46 25fr Aloe 1.75 1.75
Nos. 306-308,C41 (4) 9.55 7.00

Desert Monitor A47

1967, May 8 **Engr.** ***Perf. 13***
309 A47 20fr red brn, ocher & sepia 7.00 4.25

Stamps of Somali Coast were replaced in 1967 by those of the French Territory of the Afars and Issas.

SEMI-POSTAL STAMPS

Somali Girl — SP1

1915 **Unwmk.** ***Perf. 13½x14***
Chalky Paper
B1 SP1 10c + 5c car & dk red 9.00 8.50

Curie Issue
Common Design Type

1938 **Engr.** ***Perf. 13***
B2 CD80 1.75fr + 50c brt ultra 7.75 7.75

French Revolution Issue
Common Design Type
Photo., Name and Value Typo. in Black

1939
B3 CD83 45c + 25c green 9.00 9.00
B4 CD83 70c + 30c brown 9.00 9.00
B5 CD83 90c + 35c red org 9.00 9.00
B6 CD83 1.25fr + 1fr rose pink 9.00 9.00
B7 CD83 2.25fr + 2fr blue 9.00 9.00
Nos. B3-B7 (5) 45.00 45.00

Common Design Type and

Somali Guard SP2

Local Police — SP3

1941 **Photo.** ***Perf. 13½***
B8 SP2 1fr + 1fr red 1.40
B9 CD86 1.50fr + 3fr maroon 1.40
B10 SP3 2.50fr + 1fr blue 1.40
Nos. B8-B10 (3) 4.20
Set, never hinged 5.25

Nos. B8-B10 were issued by the Vichy government in France, but were not placed on sale in Somali Coast.

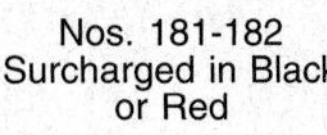

Nos. 181-182 Surcharged in Black or Red

1944 **Engr.** ***Perf. 12x12½***
B11 50c + 1.50fr on 2.50fr dp bl (R) .35
B12 + 2.50fr on 1fr yel brn .35
Set, never hinged 1.40

Colonial Development Fund.

Nos. B11-B12 were issued by the Vichy government in France, but were not placed on sale in Somali Coast.

Catalogue values for unused stamps in this section, from this point to the end of the section, are for Never Hinged items.

Red Cross Issue
Common Design Type
Inscribed "Djibouti"

1944 ***Perf. 14½x14***
B13 CD90 5fr + 20fr emerald 1.75 2.00

The surtax was for the French Red Cross and national relief.

Tropical Medicine Issue
Common Design Type

1950 **Engr.** ***Perf. 13***
B14 CD100 10fr + 2fr red brn & red 7.75 6.25

The surtax was for charitable work.

Anti-Malaria Issue
Common Design Type

1962, Apr. 7 **Unwmk.** ***Perf. 13***
B15 CD108 25fr + 5fr aqua 7.00 7.00

Infant, Sun, Chest and Skulls SP4

1965, Dec. 10 **Engr.** ***Perf. 13***
B16 SP4 25fr + 5fr ocher, sl & brt grn 2.75 2.50

Campaign against tuberculosis.

AIR POST STAMPS

Catalogue values for unused stamps in this section are for Never Hinged items.

Inscribed "Djibouti"
Common Design Type

1941 **Unwmk.** **Photo.** ***Perf. 14½x14***
C1 CD87 1fr dk orange .70 .70
C2 CD87 1.50fr brt red .70 .70
C3 CD87 5fr brown red 1.40 1.00
C4 CD87 10fr black 1.40 1.00
C5 CD87 25fr ultra 2.75 2.10
C6 CD87 50fr dark green 2.75 2.10
C7 CD87 100fr plum 4.25 3.50
Nos. C1-C7 (7) 13.95 11.10

Obock & Djibouti — AP1

1943, June 21 **Engr.** ***Perf. 13***
C7A AP1 1.50fr red brown 1.00
C7B AP1 4fr ultramarine 1.00

50th Ann. of transfer of capital from Obock to Djibouti.

Nos. C7A-C7B were issued by the Vichy government in France, but were not placed on sale in Somali Coast.

Victory Issue
Common Design Type

1946 ***Perf. 12½***
C8 CD92 8fr deep blue 1.75 1.40

Chad to Rhine Issue
Common Design Types

1946
C9 CD93 5fr gray black 2.40 1.60
C10 CD94 10fr dp orange 2.40 1.60
C11 CD95 15fr violet brn 2.40 1.60
C12 CD96 20fr brt violet 2.40 1.60
C13 CD97 25fr blue green 4.25 3.00
C14 CD98 50fr lt ultra 4.25 3.25
Nos. C9-C14 (6) 18.10 12.65

Somali Gazing Skyward — AP1a

Frontier Post, Loyada — AP2

Governor's Mansion, Djibouti — AP3

Perf. 12½x13, 13x12½
1947 **Photo.** **Unwmk.**
C15 AP1a 50fr gray bl & choc 6.25 1.40
C16 AP2 100fr multicolored 7.75 2.75
C17 AP3 200fr multicolored 10.50 4.25
Nos. C15-C17 (3) 24.50 8.40

UPU Issue
Common Design Type

1949 **Engr.** ***Perf. 13***
C18 CD99 30fr bl, dp bl, brn red & grn 14.00 10.50

Liberation Issue
Common Design Type

1954, June 6
C19 CD102 15fr indigo & pur 10.50 8.50

Somali Woman and Map of Djibouti — AP4

1956, Feb. 20 **Unwmk.**
C20 AP4 500fr dk vio & rose vio 60.00 50.00

Mountain Reedbucks — AP5

1958, July 7 **Engr.** ***Perf. 13***
C21 AP5 100fr ultra, lt grn & dk red brn 10.00 5.00

Albert Bernard, Flag and Troops — AP6

1960, Jan. 18
C22 AP6 55fr ultra, sepia & car 2.75 1.75

25th death anniv. of Administrator Albert Bernard at Moraito.

Great Bustard — AP7

1960, Oct. 24 **Unwmk.** ***Perf. 13***
C23 AP7 200fr brn, org & slate 22.50 15.00

Salt Dealers' Caravan at Assal Lake — AP8

1962, Jan. 6 **Engr.** ***Perf. 13***
C24 AP8 500fr dk bl, red brn, pink & blk 25.00 15.00

Obock — AP9

1962, Mar. 11 **Unwmk.** ***Perf. 13***
C25 AP9 100fr blue & org brn 5.00 3.50

Centenary of the founding of Obock.

Rostellaria Magna — AP10

40fr, Millepore coral. 55fr, Brain coral. 100fr, Lambis bryonia (seashell). 200fr, Branch coral.

1962-63 **Photo.** ***Perf. 13½x12½***
C26 AP10 40fr multi ('63) 3.50 1.40
C27 AP10 55fr multi ('63) 5.00 3.50
C28 AP10 60fr multi 6.25 2.75
C29 AP10 100fr multi 10.00 5.00
C30 AP10 200fr multi ('63) 12.00 7.00
Nos. C26-C30 (5) 36.75 19.65

Telstar Issue
Common Design Type

1963, Feb. 9 **Engr.** ***Perf. 13***
C31 CD111 20fr dp claret & dk grn 1.00 1.00

Zaroug (Somali Sailboats) — AP11

Designs: 50fr, Sambouk (boat) building. 300fr, Zeima sailboat.

1964-65 **Engr.** ***Perf. 13***
C32 AP11 50fr blue, ocher & choc 4.25 2.10
C33 AP11 85fr dk Prus grn, dk brn & mag 5.50 2.75
C34 AP11 300fr ultra, lt brn & bl grn ('65) 15.00 7.75
Nos. C32-C34 (3) 24.75 12.60

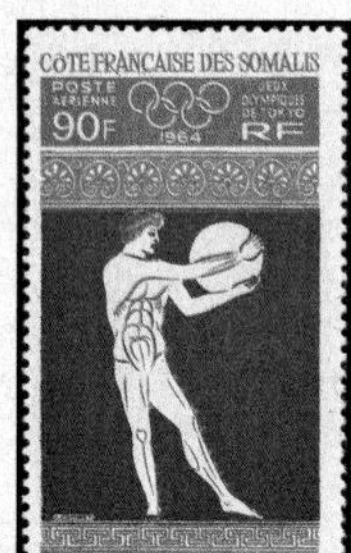

Discus Thrower — AP12

1964, Oct. 10 **Engr.**
C35 AP12 90fr rose lil, red brn & blk 10.00 7.75

18th Olympic Games, Tokyo, Oct. 10-25.

ITU Issue
Common Design Type

1965, May 17
C36 CD120 95fr lil rose, brt bl & lt brn 15.00 9.00

Camels in Ghoubet Kharab and Map of Somali Coast — AP13

1965 **Engr.** ***Perf. 13***
C37 AP13 45fr Abbe Lake 3.25 1.75
C38 AP13 65fr shown 4.00 1.75

Issue dates: 45fr, Oct. 20; 65fr, July 16.

French Satellite A-1 Issue
Common Design Type

Designs: 25fr, Diamant rocket and launching installations. 30fr, A-1 satellite.

1966, Jan. 28 **Engr.** ***Perf. 13***
C39 CD121 25fr redsh brn, ol brn & dl red 3.25 3.25
C40 CD121 30fr ol brn, dl red & redsh brn 3.25 3.25
a. Strip of 2, #C39-C40 + label 7.00 7.00

Each sheet contains 16 triptychs (2x8).

Stapelia — AP14

1966 **Engr.** ***Perf. 13***
C41 AP14 55fr sl grn, dl mag & emer 5.00 3.25

Feather Starfish and Coral — AP15

Fish: 25fr, Regal angelfish. 40fr, Pomocanthops filamentosus. 50fr, Amphiprion ephippium. 70fr, Squirrelfish. 80fr, Surgeonfish. 100fr, Pterois lunulatus.

1966 **Photo.** ***Perf. 13***
C42 AP15 8fr multicolored 3.50 3.50
C43 AP15 25fr multicolored 5.50 5.50
C44 AP15 40fr multicolored 8.50 8.50
C45 AP15 50fr multicolored 9.00 9.00
C46 AP15 70fr multicolored 14.00 14.00
C47 AP15 80fr multicolored 15.00 15.00
C48 AP15 100fr multicolored 21.00 21.00
Nos. C42-C48 (7) 76.50 76.50

French Satellite D-1 Issue
Common Design Type

1966, June 10 **Engr.** ***Perf. 13***
C49 CD122 48fr dk brn, brt bl & grn 4.25 2.75
Nos. C49 (1) 4.25 2.75

AIR POST SEMI-POSTAL STAMPS

Catalogue values for unused stamps in this section are for Never Hinged items.

SPAP1

Unwmk.
1942, June 22 **Engr.** ***Perf. 13***
CB1 SPAP1 1.50fr + 3.50fr grn .70 6.25
CB2 SPAP1 2fr + 6fr brown .70 6.25

Native children's welfare fund.
Nos. CB1-CB2 were issued by the Vichy government in France, but were not placed on sale in Somali Coast

Colonial Education Fund
Common Design Type

1942, June 22
CB3 CD86a 1.20fr + 1.80fr blue & red .70 6.25
Nos. CB3 (1) .70

No. CB3 was issued by the Vichy government in France, but was not placed on sale in Somali Coast.

Pharaoh Sacrificing before Horus and Hathor — SPAP2

Unwmk.
1964, Aug. 28 **Engr.** ***Perf. 13***
CB4 SPAP2 25fr + 5fr multi 9.00 7.75

UNESCO world campaign to save historic monuments in Nubia.

POSTAGE DUE STAMPS

D1

1915 **Unwmk.** **Typo.** ***Perf. 14x13½***
Chalky Paper
J1 D1 5c deep ultra .35 *.55*
J2 D1 10c brown red .55 *.70*
J3 D1 15c black .85 *1.20*
J4 D1 20c purple 1.75 *2.10*
J5 D1 30c orange 1.75 *2.10*
J6 D1 50c maroon 2.75 *3.25*
J7 D1 60c green 4.25 *5.00*
J8 D1 1fr dark blue 5.25 *6.25*
Nos. J1-J8 (8) 17.50 21.15

See Nos. J11-J20.

Type of 1915 Issue Surcharged

1927
J9 D1 2fr on 1fr light red 10.50 *10.50*
J10 D1 3fr on 1fr lilac rose 10.50 *10.50*

Type of 1915
1938 **Engr.** ***Perf. 12½x13***
J11 D1 5c light ultra .25 *.30*
J12 D1 10c dark carmine .25 *.30*
J13 D1 15c brown black .30 *.35*
J14 D1 20c violet .30 *.35*
J15 D1 30c orange yellow 1.00 *1.10*
J16 D1 50c brown .65 *.70*
J17 D1 60c emerald 1.00 *1.10*
J18 D1 1fr indigo 2.00 2.00
J19 D1 2fr red .90 *1.00*
J20 D1 3fr dark brown 1.25 *1.40*
Nos. J11-J20 (10) 7.90 8.60
Set, never hinged 11.00

Inscribed "Inst de Grav" below design.

Postage Due Stamps of 1915 Overprinted in Red or Black

1943 **Unwmk.** ***Perf. 14x13 ½***
J21 D1 5c ultra (R) 2.75 *2.75*
J22 D1 10c brown red 2.75 2.75
J23 D1 15c black (R) 2.75 2.75
J24 D1 20c purple 2.75 2.75
J25 D1 30c orange 2.75 2.75
J26 D1 50c maroon 2.75 2.75

J27	D1	60c green	2.75	2.75
J28	D1	1fr dark blue (R)	2.75	2.75
		Nos. J21-J28 (8)	22.00	22.00
		Set, never hinged	35.00	

Postage Due Stamps of 1938 Overprinted in Red or Black

1943 ***Perf. 12 ½x13***

J29	d1	5c lt ultra (R)	2.10	2.10
J30	D1	10c dark car	2.10	2.10
J31	D1	15c brn blk (R)	2.10	2.10
J32	D1	20c violet	2.10	2.10
J33	d1	30c org yel	2.10	2.10
J34	D1	50c brown	2.10	2.10
J35	D1	60c emerald	2.10	2.10
J36	D1	1fr indigo (R)	2.10	2.10
J37	D1	2fr red	8.50	8.50
J38	D1	3fr dk brn (R)	10.00	10.00
		Nos. J29-J38 (10)	35.30	35.30
		Set, never hinged	55.00	

For type D1 without "RF," see Nos. J38A-J38E.

Type D1 Without "RF"
Engraved, Values Typo

1944, Apr. 3

J38A	D1	30c org yel	.30
J38B	D1	50c yel brn	.30
J38C	D1	60c grn	.55
J38D	D1	2fr red	.65
J38E	D1	3fr sepia	1.00
		Nos. J38A-J38E (5)	2.80
		Set, never hinged	4.25

Nos. J38A-J38E were issued by the Vichy government in France, but were not placed on sale in Somali Coast.

Catalogue values for unused stamps in this section, from this point to the end of the section, are for Never Hinged items.

D2

1947 **Photo.** ***Perf. 13½x13***

J39	D2	10c purple	.35	.25
J40	D2	30c brown	.35	.25
J41	D2	50c green	.65	.50
J42	D2	1fr deep orange	.65	.50
J43	D2	2fr lilac rose	.90	.80
J44	D2	3fr dk org brn	.90	.80
J45	D2	4fr blue	1.10	.90
J46	D2	5fr orange red	1.10	.90
J47	D2	10fr olive green	1.10	.90
J48	D2	20fr blue violet	2.75	2.00
		Nos. J39-J48 (10)	9.85	7.80

SOMALILAND PROTECTORATE

sō-ˈmä-lē-ˌland

prə-ˈtek-t(ə-)rət

LOCATION — Eastern Africa, bordering on the Gulf of Aden
GOVT. — British Protectorate
AREA — 68,000 sq. mi.
POP. — 640,000 (estimated)
CAPITAL — Hargeisa

Formerly administered by the Indian Government, the territory was taken over by the British Foreign Office in 1898 and transferred to the Colonial Office in 1905.

Somaliland Protectorate became part of independent Somalia in 1960.

16 Annas = 1 Rupee
100 Cents = 1 Shilling (1951)

Catalogue values for unused stamps in this country are for Never Hinged items, beginning with Scott 108.

Stamps of India, 1882-1900, Overprinted at Top of Stamp

1903 **Wmk. 39** ***Perf. 14***

1	A17	½a light green	3.00	*5.00*
2	A19	1a carmine rose	3.00	*4.50*
3	A21	2a violet	2.50	1.75
a.		Double overprint	*800.00*	
4	A28	2½a ultra	2.25	*2.10*
5	A22	3a brn org	3.50	3.50
6	A23	4a olive green	4.00	3.50
7	A25	8a red violet	4.25	*6.00*
8	A26	12a brown, *red*	7.50	*9.00*
a.		Inverted overprint		*1,200.*
9	A29	1r car rose & grn	8.00	*12.50*
10	A30	2r yel brn & car rose	38.00	*60.00*
11	A30	3r grn & brn	36.00	*72.50*
12	A30	5r violet & blue	59.00	*85.00*

Wmk. Elephant's Head (38)

13	A14	6a bister	7.75	5.25
		Nos. 1-13 (13)	178.75	*270.60*

Nos. 1-5 exist without the 2nd "I" of "BRITISH."

Same, but Overprinted at Bottom of Stamp

1903 **Wmk. 39**

14	A28	2½a ultra	6.50	*8.75*
15	A26	12a violet, *red*	13.00	*15.00*
16	A29	1r car rose & grn	11.00	*16.00*
17	A30	2r yel brn & car rose	130.00	*200.00*
18	A30	3r green & brn	140.00	*200.00*
a.		Double overprint, both inverted, one albino	1,000.	
19	A30	5r violet & blue	130.00	*210.00*

Wmk. 38

20	A14	6a bister	8.50	7.50
		Nos. 14-20 (7)	439.00	*657.25*

Stamps of India, 1902-03, Ovptd.

1903 **Wmk. 39**

21	A33	½a light green	3.25	.60
22	A34	1a car rose	1.40	.35
23	A35	2a violet	2.75	*2.75*
24	A37	3a brown orange	2.75	*2.75*
25	A38	4a olive green	1.60	*3.50*
26	A40	8a red violet	3.50	*2.50*
		Nos. 21-26 (6)	15.25	*12.45*

The above overprints vary in length, also in the relative positions of the letters. Nos. 21-23 exist without the second "I" of "British."

A1

King Edward VII — A2

1904 **Wmk. 2** **Typo.**

27	A1	½a dl grn & grn	2.75	*4.50*
28	A1	1a carmine & blk	19.00	3.50
29	A1	2a red vio & dull vio	2.25	*2.60*
30	A1	2½a ultramarine	9.50	*4.00*
31	A1	3a gray grn & vio brn	2.50	*6.25*
32	A1	4a blk & gray grn	4.00	*9.00*
33	A1	6a vio & gray grn	11.50	*18.00*
34	A1	8a pale blue & blk	10.00	*9.50*
35	A1	12a ocher & blk	14.00	*12.00*

Wmk. Crown and C C (1)

36	A2	1r gray grn	22.50	*50.00*
37	A2	2r red vio & dull vio	60.00	*90.00*
38	A2	3r blk & gray grn	70.00	*130.00*
39	A2	5r carmine & blk	72.50	*140.00*
		Nos. 27-39 (13)	300.50	*479.35*

1905 **Wmk. 3**

40	A1	½a dl grn & grn	2.00	*8.00*
41	A1	1a carmine & blk	23.50	1.75
42	A1	2a red vio & dull vio	9.00	*19.00*
43	A1	2½a ultramarine	4.50	*11.00*
44	A1	3a gray grn & vio brn	2.50	*16.00*
45	A1	4a blk & gray grn	5.00	*26.00*
46	A1	6a vio & gray grn	3.00	*27.50*
47	A1	8a pale blue & blk	8.00	*12.00*
48	A1	12a ocher & black	7.25	*13.00*
		Nos. 40-48 (9)	64.75	*134.25*

Nos. 41, 42, 44-48 are on both ordinary and chalky paper, values are for lower value.

1909

49	A1	½a bluish green	45.00	*40.00*
50	A1	1a carmine	3.00	2.25

For overprints see Nos. O11-O16.

A3

King George V — A4

The ½, 1 and 2½a of type A3 are on ordinary paper, the other values of types A3 and A4 are on chalky paper.

1912-19

51	A3	½a green	.90	*14.00*
52	A3	1a carmine	3.00	.60
53	A3	2a red vio & dull vio	4.25	*16.00*
54	A3	2½a ultramarine	1.25	*9.75*
55	A3	3a gray grn & vio brn	2.75	*10.00*
56	A3	4a blk & grn ('13)	3.00	*11.50*
57	A3	6a violet & green	3.00	*11.50*
58	A3	8a lt blue & blk	4.25	*17.50*
59	A3	12a ocher & blk	4.00	*24.00*
60	A4	1r dull grn & grn	22.50	*27.50*
61	A4	2r red vio & dull vio ('19)	28.00	*80.00*
62	A4	3r blk & gray grn ('19)	87.50	*185.00*
63	A4	5r car & blk ('19)	97.50	*250.00*
		Nos. 51-63 (13)	261.90	*657.35*

1921 **Wmk. 4**

64	A3	½a blue green	3.75	*17.00*
65	A3	1a scarlet	4.25	.80
66	A3	2a vio & dull vio	5.00	1.10
67	A3	2½a ultramarine	1.25	*11.00*
68	A3	3a gray grn & vio brn	3.00	*8.50*
69	A3	4a black & grn	3.00	*15.00*
70	A3	6a violet & grn	2.00	*15.00*
71	A3	8a lt blue & blk	2.50	*12.50*
72	A3	12a ocher & blk	11.00	*17.50*
73	A4	1r dull grn & grn	10.00	*55.00*
74	A4	2r vio & dull vio	30.00	*65.00*
75	A4	3r blk & gray grn	42.50	*125.00*
76	A4	5r scarlet & blk	95.00	*200.00*
		Nos. 64-76 (13)	213.25	*543.40*

Common Design Types
pictured following the introduction.

Silver Jubilee Issue
Common Design Type

1935, May 6 **Engr.** ***Perf. 11x12***

77	CD301	1a car & dk blue	2.50	*4.00*
78	CD301	2a black & ultra	3.00	*4.25*
79	CD301	3a ultra & brown	2.50	*19.00*
80	CD301	1r brn vio & ind	9.00	*21.00*
		Nos. 77-80 (4)	17.00	*48.25*
		Set, never hinged	34.00	

Coronation Issue
Common Design Type

1937, May 13 ***Perf. 13½x14***

81	CD302	1a carmine	.25	*.50*
82	CD302	2a black	.35	*2.00*
83	CD302	3a bright ultra	.50	*1.00*
		Nos. 81-83 (3)	1.10	*3.50*
		Set, never hinged	2.00	

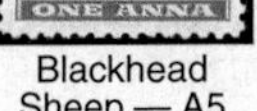
Blackhead Sheep — A5

Greater Kudu — A6

Map of Somaliland Protectorate A7

1938, May 10 **Wmk. 4** ***Perf. 12½***

84	A5	½a green	1.25	*5.75*
85	A5	1a carmine	.75	*1.75*
86	A5	2a deep claret	2.50	*4.50*
87	A5	3a ultra	10.00	*17.50*
88	A6	4a dark brown	3.50	*12.00*
89	A6	6a purple	9.00	*13.00*
90	A6	8a gray black	4.75	*13.50*
91	A6	12a orange	11.00	*35.00*
92	A7	1r green	8.50	*80.00*
93	A7	2r rose violet	15.00	*80.00*
94	A7	3r ultramarine	13.50	*45.00*
95	A7	5r black	18.00	*50.00*
a.		Horiz. pair, imperf. btwn.	*30,000.*	
		Nos. 84-95 (12)	97.75	*358.00*
		Set, never hinged	163.90	

A8

A9

A10

1942, Apr. 22

96	A8	½a green	.25	*.50*
97	A8	1a carmine	.25	.25
98	A8	2a deep claret	.45	.25
99	A8	3a ultramarine	1.50	.25
100	A9	4a dark brown	1.75	.25
101	A9	6a purple	2.00	.25
102	A9	8a gray	2.40	.25
103	A9	12a orange	2.00	*1.50*
104	A10	1r green	2.25	*2.75*
105	A10	2r rose violet	3.75	*9.50*
106	A10	3r ultra	6.75	*17.50*
107	A10	5r black	10.00	*11.00*
		Nos. 96-107 (12)	33.35	*44.25*
		Set, never hinged	55.00	

For surcharges see Nos. 116-126.

Catalogue values for unused stamps in this section, from this point to the end of the section, are for Never Hinged items.

Peace Issue
Common Design Type
Perf. 13¾x14

1946, Oct. 15 **Engr.** **Wmk. 4**

108	CD303	1a carmine	.35	.25
		Hinged	.25	
a.		Perf. 13½	19.00	*65.00*
		Hinged	11.50	
109	CD303	3a deep blue	.35	.25
		Hinged	.25	

Silver Wedding Issue
Common Design Types

1949, Jan. 28 **Photo.** ***Perf. 14x14½***

110	CD304	1a scarlet	.40	.25
		Hinged	.25	

Perf. 11½x11
Engraved; Name Typographed

111	CD305	5r gray black	8.00	*8.50*
		Hinged	6.00	

UPU Issue
Common Design Types
Surcharged in Black or Carmine with New Values in Annas

Engr.; Name Typo. on 3a, 6a

1949, Oct. 10 ***Perf. 13½, 11x11½***

112	CD306	1a on 10c rose car	.40	*.35*
		Hinged	.25	
113	CD307	3a on 30c ind (C)	2.00	*4.50*
		Hinged	1.25	
114	CD308	6a on 50c rose vio	.55	*3.25*
		Hinged	.35	

115	CD309	12a on 1sh red org	1.00	.60
		Hinged	.60	
		Nos. 112-115 (4)	3.95	8.70

Nos. 96 and 98 to 107 Surcharged with New Value in Black or Carmine

1951, Apr. 2 Wmk. 4 *Perf. 12½*

116	A8	5c on ½a green	.40	*2.25*
117	A8	10c on 2a deep claret	.40	*1.00*
118	A8	15c on 3a ultramarine	1.60	2.25
119	A9	20c on 4a dark brown	2.25	.25
120	A9	30c on 6a purple	1.80	1.50
121	A9	50c on 8a gray	2.50	.25
122	A9	70c on 12a red	4.00	*9.00*
123	A10	1sh on 1r green	2.25	2.00
124	A10	2sh on 2r rose violet	5.25	*22.50*
125	A10	2sh on 3r ultra	13.00	10.00
126	A10	5sh on 5r black (C)	22.50	15.00
		Nos. 116-126 (11)	55.95	66.00

Coronation Issue

Common Design Type

1953, June 2 Engr. *Perf. 13½x13*

127	CD312	15c dark green & blk	.40	.25

Camel Carrying Somali House
A11

Askari Militiaman
A12

Designs: 35c, 2sh, Rock Pigeon. 50c, 5sh, Martial eagle. 1sh, Blackhead sheep. 1sh30c, Tomb of Sheik Isaaq, Mait. 10sh, Taleh Fort.

1953-58 Engr. *Perf. 12½*

128	A11	5c gray	.25	*.60*
129	A12	10c red orange	2.50	.60
130	A11	15c blue green	.70	*.70*
131	A11	20c rose red	.70	.40
132	A12	30c lt chocolate	2.50	.40
133	A11	35c blue	5.75	2.00
134	A11	50c lil rose & brn	6.50	.55
135	A11	1sh grnsh blue	1.25	.30
136	A11	1sh30c dark gray & ultra ('58)	24.00	3.75
137	A11	2sh violet & brn	27.50	7.50
138	A11	5sh emer & brn	35.00	11.00
139	A11	10sh rose lilac & brn	32.50	*37.50*
		Nos. 128-139 (12)	139.15	65.30

Nos. 131 and 135 Ovptd. "Opening of the Legislative Council 1957"

1957, May 21

140	A11	20c rose red	.25	.25
141	A11	1sh greenish blue	.35	.30

Nos. 131 and 136 Ovptd. "Legislative Council Unofficial Majority, 1960"

1960, Apr. 5

142	A11	20c rose red	.25	.25
143	A11	1sh30c dk gray & ultra	1.50	.30

Changes in the Legislative Council.

Three stamps of Somalia were overprinted "Somaliland Independence 26 June 1960" and issued in Hargeisa on that day. Somaliland Protectorate became part of Somalia on July 1, 1960. These three stamps are listed in Vol. 5 as Somalia Nos. 242, C68-C69.

Stamps of Somaliland Protectorate were replaced by those of Somalia in 1960.

OFFICIAL STAMPS

Official Stamps of India, 1883-1900, Overprinted

1903, June 1 Wmk. 39 *Perf. 14*

O1	A17	½a light green	9.50	*55.00*
O2	A19	1a carmine rose	22.50	*12.50*
O3	A21	2a violet	15.00	*55.00*
O4	A25	8a red violet	19.00	*450.00*
O5	A29	1r car rose & grn	20.00	*750.00*
		Nos. O1-O5 (5)	86.00	*1,323.*

India Nos. 61-63, 68, 49 Overprinted

1903

O6	A33	½a green	.90
O7	A34	1a carmine rose	.95
O8	A35	2a violet	1.60
O9	A40	8a red violet	8.00
O10	A29	1r car rose & grn	22.50
		Nos. O6-O10 (5)	33.95

Nos. O6-O10 were not regularly issued, although used examples are known.

Regular Issue of 1904 Overprinted

1904 Wmk. Crown and C A (2)

O11	A1	½a gray green	11.00	*55.00*
O12	A1	1a carmine & blk	5.00	*8.00*
O13	A1	2a red vio & dull vio	300.00	70.00
O14	A1	8a pale blue & blk	80.00	*150.00*
		Nos. O11-O14 (4)	396.00	*283.00*

Wmk. Crown and C C (1)

O15	A2	1r gray green	300.00	*1,100.*

Same Overprint on No. 42

1905 Wmk. 3

O16	A1	2a red vio & dull vio	140.00	*1,100.*

The period after "M" may be found missing on Nos. O11-O14 and O16.

SOUTH AFRICA

sauth 'a-fri-kə

LOCATION — Southern Africa
GOVT. — Republic
AREA — 472,730 sq. mi.
POP. — 43,426,386 (1999 est.)
CAPITAL — Pretoria (administrative); Cape Town (legislative); Bloemfontein (Judicial)

The union was formed on May 31, 1910, comprising the former British colonies of Cape of Good Hope, Natal, Transvaal and the Orange Free State, which became provinces. The union became a republic in 1961.

For previous listings, see individual headings.

12 Pence = 1 Shilling
20 Shillings = 1 Pound
100 Cents = 1 Rand (1961)

Catalogue values for unused stamps in this country are for Never Hinged items, beginning with Scott 74 in the regular postage section, Scott B1 in the semi-postal section, Scott J30 in the postage due section, and Scott O21 in the officials section.

Watermarks

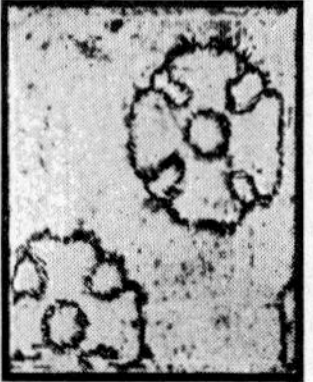
Wmk. 47 — Multiple Rosette

Wmk. 177 — Springbok's Head

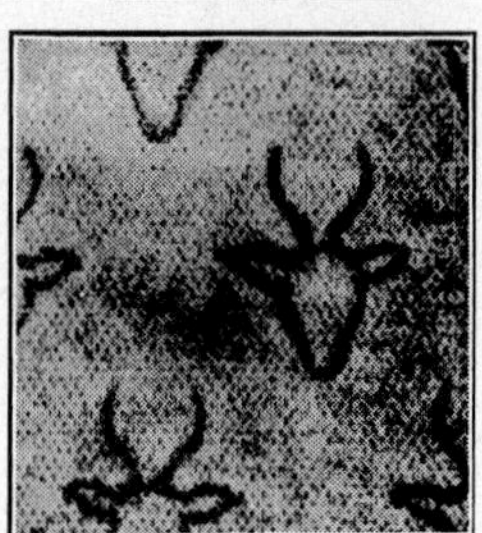
Wmk. 201 — Multiple Springbok's Head

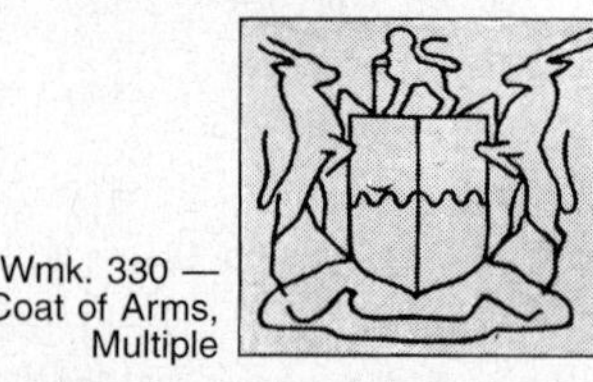
Wmk. 330 — Coat of Arms, Multiple

Wmk. 348 — RSA in Triangle, Multiple

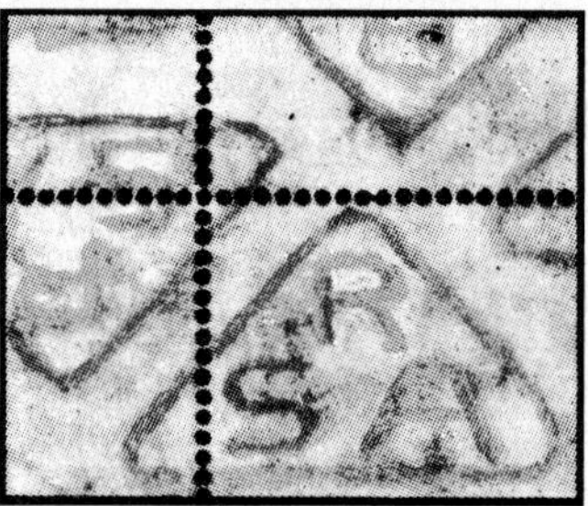
Wmk. 359 — RSA in Triangle, Tete Beche

Scott values watermarked stamps of South Africa in the normal upright position. Many issues exist with the watermark inverted, and some sideways. These varieties usually sell for a premium over the Scott values; however, in some instances the inverted watermarks sell for substantially less.

From Aug. 19, 1910, through December 31, 1937, the stamps of the provinces (Cape of Good Hope, Natal, Orange River Colony and Transvaal) were valid for postage throughout South Africa. They were demonetized effective Jan. 1, 1938.

Union of South Africa

George V — A1

1910 Engr. Wmk. 47 *Perf. 14*

1	A1	2½p blue	3.25	1.75

Union Parliament opening, Nov. 4, 1910.

Type A2 stamps have very small margins at top and bottom. Values are for examples with perfs close to, or touching the frame.

George V — A2

1913-24 Typo. Wmk. 177

2	A2	½p green	1.50	.30
a.		Double impression	*12,000.*	
e.		Printed on gummed side	*1,500.*	
3	A2	1p rose red	1.50	.25
d.		Printed on gummed side	*1,100.*	
4	A2	1½p org brn ('20)	.80	.25
a.		Tête bêche pair	2.75	*19.00*
c.		Printed on gummed side	*1,200.*	
5	A2	2p dull violet	1.50	.25
d.		Printed on gummed side	*1,200.*	
6	A2	2½p ultra	4.75	1.25
7	A2	3p brn org & blk	11.00	.45
a.		3p dull orange red & black	7.75	.30
8	A2	3p ultra ('22)	4.50	1.10
9	A2	4p ol grn & org	10.00	.75
a.		4p sage green & orange	5.75	.50
10	A2	6p violet & black	7.00	.65
11	A2	1sh orange	15.00	.75
12	A2	1sh3p violet ('20)	12.00	7.50
13	A2	2sh6p green & cl	55.00	3.75
14	A2	5sh blue & claret	130.00	9.00
15	A2	10sh ol grn & blue	260.00	10.00
16	A2	£1 red & dp grn ('16)	800.00	600.00
a.		£1 lt red & gray green ('24)	1,000.	*1,200.*
		Nos. 2-16 (15)	1,315.	636.25

The ½p, 1p and 1½p have the words "Revenue" and "Inkomst" on the stamps. On other stamps of this type these words are replaced by short vertical lines.

All values exist in many shades. No. 4a exists with and without gutter between.

Unwatermarked examples of the 1p are the result of misplaced watermarks.

Scott values watermarked stamps of South Africa in the normal upright position. Many issues exist with the watermark inverted, and some sideways. These varieties usually sell for a premium over the Scott values; however, in some instances the inverted watermarks sell for substantially less.

For overprint see No. O1.

Coil Stamps

Perf. 14 Horizontally

17	A2	½p green	6.50	1.25
18	A2	1p rose red ('14)	20.00	4.00
19	A2	1½p org brown ('20)	18.00	25.00
20	A2	2p dull violet ('21)	17.50	5.00
		Nos. 17-20 (4)	62.00	35.25

"Hope" — A3

Design: No. 22, inscribed SUIDAFRIKA.

1926 Engr. Wmk. 201 *Imperf.*

21	A3	4p blue gray	2.00	1.40
22	A3	4p blue gray	2.00	1.40

Nos. 21 and 22 were privately rouletted and perforated, but such varieties were not officially made.

No. 21 (English inscription) was printed in a separate sheet from No. 22 (Afrikaans inscription).

English-Afrikaans Se-Tenant

Stamps with English inscriptions and with Afrikaans inscriptions were printed alternately in the same sheets, starting with No. 23. Major-number listings and values are for horizontal pairs (vertical pairs sell for about one-third to one-half less) of such stamps consisting of one English and one Afrikaans-inscribed stamp, unless otherwise described.

Values are for pairs with no fold marks between stamps and no perf separations.

Beware of pairs that have been rejoined.

Springbok
A5

Jan van Riebeek's Ship, Drommedaris — A6

Orange Tree — A7

1926 Typo. *Perf. 14½x14*

No.	Description	Unused	Used
23	A5 ½p dk grn & blk, pair	2.25	4.00
a.	Single, English	.25	.25
b.	Single, Afrikaans	.25	.25
c.	Tete beche pair ('27)	1,750.	
d.	Center omitted	2,500.	
e.	Booklet pane of 6	250.00	
f.	As "e," perf. 14	375.00	
g.	Missing "1" in "1/2" (Afrikaans only)	2,400.	
h.	Perf 13½x14 ('27)	60.00	50.00
i.	As "h," single, English	8.00	4.25
j.	As "h," single, Afrikaans	8.00	4.25
k.	As "d," in pair with normal	4,000.	
m.	As "g," in pair with normal, English	3,000.	
24	A6 1p car & blk, pair	2.00	2.50
a.	Single, English	.25	.25
b.	Single, Afrikaans	.25	.25
c.	Imperf., pair	1,500.	
d.	Tete beche pair ('27)	1,900.	
f.	Booklet pane of 6	225.00	
g.	As "f," perf. 14	325.00	
h.	Imperf on three sides, vert. pair	1,200.	1,300.
i.	Perf 13½x14 ('27)	90.00	65.00
j.	As "i," single, English	9.00	4.25
k.	As "i," single, Afrikaans	9.00	4.25
25	A7 6p org & grn, pair	37.50	42.50
a.	Single, English	2.75	1.75
b.	Single, Afrikaans	2.75	1.75
	Nos. 23-25 (3)	41.75	49.00

Nos. 23c and 24d are from uncut sheets printed for the perf. 14 booklet panes of 1928, Nos. 23f and 24g.

See Nos. 33-35, 42, 45-50, 59-61, 98-99. For overprints see Nos. O2-O4, O6-O9, O12-O15, O18, O21-O25, O30-O32, O42-O45, O48.

Government Buildings, Pretoria — A8

"Groote Schuur," Rhodes's Home — A9

Native Kraal — A10

Gnu — A11

Trekking — A12

Ox Wagon — A13

Cape Town and Table Mountain — A14

Perf. 14, 14x13½

1927-28 Engr. Wmk. 201

No.	Description	Unused	Used
26	A8 2p vio brn & gray, pair	10.00	20.00
a.	Single, English	2.75	1.00
b.	Single, Afrikaans	2.75	1.00
c.	Perf. 14x13½, pair	37.50	32.50
d.	As "c," single, English	5.25	1.00
e.	As "c," single, Afrikaans	5.25	1.00
27	A9 3p red & blk, pair	20.00	30.00
a.	Single, English	2.50	.90
b.	Single, Afrikaans	2.50	.90
c.	Perf. 14x13½, pair	70.00	72.50
d.	As "c," single, English	7.50	2.00
e.	As "c," single, Afrikaans	7.50	2.00
28	A10 4p brn, pair ('28)	29.00	47.50
a.	Single, English	3.50	1.25
b.	Single, Afrikaans	3.50	1.25
c.	Perf. 14x13½, pair	55.00	62.50
d.	As "c," single, English	6.50	1.40
e.	As "c," single, Afrikaans	6.50	1.40
29	A11 1sh dp bl & bis brn, pair	37.50	60.00
a.	Single, English	7.50	1.75
b.	Single, Afrikaans	7.50	1.75
c.	Perf. 14x13½, pair ('30)	72.50	77.50
d.	As "c," single, English	8.50	2.25
e.	As "c," single, Afrikaans	8.50	2.25
30	A12 2sh6p brn & bl grn, pair	125.00	400.00
a.	Single, English	20.00	11.00
b.	Single, Afrikaans	20.00	11.00
c.	Perf. 14x13½, pair	400.00	500.00
d.	As "c," single, English	35.00	22.50
e.	As "c," single, Afrikaans	35.00	22.50
31	A13 5sh dp grn & blk, pair	300.00	725.00
a.	Single, English	35.00	35.00
b.	Single, Afrikaans	35.00	35.00
c.	Perf. 14x13½, pair	450.00	850.00
d.	As "c," single, English	60.00	45.00
e.	As "c," single, Afrikaans	60.00	45.00
32	A14 10sh ol brn & bl, pair	200.00	180.00
a.	Single, English	22.50	11.00
b.	Single, Afrikaans	22.50	11.00
c.	Perf. 14x13½, pair	250.00	200.00
d.	As "c," single, English	30.00	17.50
e.	As "c," single, Afrikaans	30.00	17.50
f.	Center inverted, single, English ('28)	22,500.	
g.	Center inverted, single, Afrikaans ('28)	22,500.	
h.	As "c," center inverted	60,000.	
	Nos. 26-32 (7)	721.50	1,463.

See Nos. 36-41, 43-44, 53-54, 58, 62-66. For overprints see Nos. O5, O10-O11, O16-O17, O19-O20, O28, O33-O35, O39, O41, O49-O53.

Types of 1926-28 Redrawn

No. 34

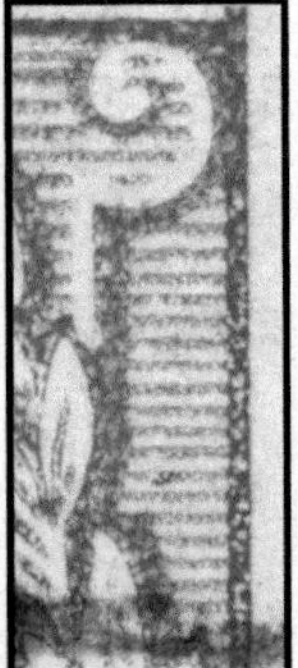

No. 35

"SUIDAFRIKA" (No Hyphen) on Afrikaans Stamps

The photogravure, unhyphenated stamps of 1930-45 are distinguished from the 1926-28 typographed or engraved stamps (also unhyphenated) by the following characteristics:

½p, 1p, 6p. Leg of "R" in AFRICA or AFRIKA ends in a straight line in the photogravure set; in a curved line in the typographed. No. 34, POSSEEL—INKOMSTE separated by ½mm; horiz. shading in side panels is close. No. 35, POSSEEL—INKOMSTE separated by 1mm; horiz. shading in side panels is wide.

2p. A memorial statue has been added just above and leftward of the "2" in value tablet on Nos. 36-37 (photogravure).

3p. Top frame on No. 38 consists of 3 heavy lines. On No. 27 it has 3 heavy and 2 very thin lines.

4p. On Nos. 40-41 the background in upper corners is solid. On No. 28 it consists of horizontal and vertical lines. No. 41 has pretzel-shaped scroll endings at bottom. On No. 40 these scroll endings enclose a solid mass of color.

1sh. No. 43 has no fine shading lines projecting from the curved top of the left inner frame, as No. 29 has. On No. 43 the shading of the last "A" of the country name partly covers the flower below it.

2sh6p. On No. 44 the shading below the country name is solid or shows signs of wear. On No. 30 it is composed of fine lines.

The engraved pictorials are much more finely executed and show details more clearly than the photogravure.

Perf. 15x14 (½p, 1p, 6p), 14

1930-45 Photo. Wmk. 201

No.	Description	Unused	Used
33	A5 ½p bl grn & blk, pair	4.00	2.75
a.	Single, English	.25	.25
b.	Single, Afrikaans	.25	.25
c.	Tete-beche pair	1,700.	
d.	As "c," gutter between	2,000.	
e.	Booklet pane of 6	75.00	60.00
f.	Vert. pair, monolingual	42.50	—
34	A6 1p car & blk, pair	4.00	2.75
a.	Single, English	.25	.25
b.	Single, Afrikaans	.25	.25
c.	Center omitted	4,500.	
d.	Frame omitted	2,500.	
e.	Tete-beche pair	1,800.	
f.	As "e," gutter between	1,500.	
g.	Booklet pane of 6	50.00	40.00
35	A6 1p rose & blk, pair ('32)	52.50	3.75
a.	Single, English	4.50	.25
b.	Single, Afrikaans	4.50	.25
c.	Center omitted	2,800.	
36	A8 2p vio & gray, pair ('31)	22.50	16.00
a.	Single, English	2.00	.40
b.	Single, Afrikaans	2.00	.40
c.	Frame omitted, single stamp (English)	6,000.	
d.	Frame omitted, single stamp (Afrikaans)	6,000.	
e.	Tete-beche pair	10,000.	
f.	Booklet pane of 4	400.00	400.00
37	A8 2p vio & ind, pair ('38)	325.00	75.00
a.	Single, English	16.00	6.00
b.	Single, Afrikaans	16.00	6.00
38	A9 3p red & blk, pair ('31)	100.00	75.00
a.	Single, English	7.00	5.50
b.	Single, Afrikaans	7.00	5.50
39	A9 3p ultra & bl, pair ('33)	17.50	7.50
a.	Single, English	1.75	.40
b.	Single, Afrikaans	1.75	.40
c.	Center omitted	34,000.	
d.	Frame omitted	17,500.	
40	A10 4p redsh brn, pair ('32)	325.00	140.00
a.	Single, English	25.00	8.50
b.	Single, Afrikaans	25.00	8.50
41	A10 4p brn, pair ('36)	4.75	3.50
a.	Single, English	.45	.30
b.	Single, Afrikaans	.45	.30
42	A7 6p org & grn, pair ('31)	60.00	17.50
a.	Single, English	4.75	.60
b.	Single, Afrikaans	4.75	.60
43	A11 1sh dl bl & yel brn, pair	115.00	45.00
a.	Single, English	8.00	1.25
b.	Single, Afrikaans	8.00	1.25
c.	1sh dp bl & brn, pair ('32)	35.00	19.00
d.	As "c," single, English	4.25	.45
e.	As "c," single, Afrikaans	4.25	.45
44	A12 2sh 6p brn & bl, pair ('45)	24.00	12.50
a.	Single, English	1.60	.50
b.	Single, Afrikaans	1.60	.50
c.	2sh6p brn & sl grn ('36), pair	275.00	225.00
d.	As "c," single, English	16.00	6.00
e.	As "c," single, Afrikaans	16.00	6.00
f.	2sh6p choc & dp grn ('37), pair	225.00	190.00
g.	As "f," single, English	3.50	1.25
h.	As "f," single, Afrikaans	3.50	1.25
i.	2sh6p red brn & grn, pair ('32)	130.00	110.00
j.	As "i," single, English	15.00	4.00
k.	As "i," single, Afrikaans	15.00	4.50
	Nos. 33-44 (12)	1,054.	401.25

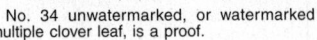

No. 34 unwatermarked, or watermarked multiple clover leaf, is a proof.

Types of 1926-28 with "SUID-AFRIKA" Hyphenated on Afrikaans Stamps, and

Gold Mine — A15

Government Buildings, Pretoria — A16

Government Buildings, Pretoria — A16a

Groote Schuur — A17

Groot Constantia — A18

½p. No. 45 shading in leaves and ornaments strengthened; 40 lines in center background. Size: 18½x22½mm.

No. 46 has 28 heavy horizontal shading lines in center background and similar thicker lines in frame. Top and bottom green bars are scored by a white horizontal line. Size: 18½x22½mm.

No. 47 is smaller, 18x22mm.

1p. No. 48, size 18½x22½mm.

No. 49, size 18x22mm.

No. 50. Size: 17½x21½mm.

2p. On Nos. 53-54, S's in SOUTH and POSTAGE are narrower than on Nos. 36-37.

5sh.On No. 64, Die I, U and A in SOUTH AFRICA have projections. Lines are contained within the design. Size 27x21¾mm.

5sh. On No. 65, Die I, dots are contained within the design, instead of lines. Size 27x21½mm.

5sh. On No. 66, Die II, U and A in SOUTH AFRICA have been redrawn to eliminate projections. Dots are contained within the design. Size 26¾x21½mm.

6p. Die I, "SUID-AFRIKA" 16½mm. Shading in leaves framing oval very faint and broken. Size: 18½x22½mm.

Die II, "SUID-AFRIKA" 17mm. Leaves strongly shaded. Heavy lines of shading in background of tree. Size: 18½x22½mm.

Die III, "question mark" scrolls below top panel are cleanly defined without intrusion of background shading. Size: 18x22mm.

Nos. 45-67 were printed in many shades. Some denominations in some printings were partly or wholly screened. Except for No. 47, the screened stamps were issued after 1947.

5sh. No. 65. Type I, letters "U" and "A" in SOUTH AFRICA have projections. Size: 27x21½mm.

No. 66. Type II, letters "U" and "A" redrawn to eliminate projections. Size: 26½x21½mm.

Perf. 15x14 (½p, 1p, 6p), 14

1933-54 Photo. Wmk. 201

No.	Description	Unused	Used
45	A5 ½p grn & gray, pair ('35)	11.00	5.00
a.	Single, English	.40	.25
b.	Single, Afrikaans	.40	.25
c.	Bklt. pane of 6, marginal ads	37.50	37.50
d.	Perf. 13½x14 (coil), pair	45.00	75.00
e.	As "d," single, English	2.00	1.00
f.	As "d," single, Afrikaans	2.00	1.00
46	A5 ½p grn & gray, redrawn, pair ('37)	10.00	1.75
a.	Single, English	.35	.25
b.	Single, Afrikaans	.35	.25
c.	Booklet pane of 6	70.00	50.00
d.	Booklet pane of 2	1.75	9.00

e. As "c," 4 blank margins 70.00 *50.00*
f. Perf. 14½x14 (coil), pair ('43) 17.50 *40.00*
g. As "f," single, English 2.00 .90
h. As "f," single, Afrikaans 2.00 .90

47 A5 ½p grn & gray, pair ('47) 2.25 *6.50*
a. Single, English .30 1.00
b. Single, Afrikaans .30 1.00
c. Bklt. pane of 6, marginal ads *8.00* *19.50*
d. As "c," no horiz. margins 8.00 *19.50*

48 A6 1p car & gray, pair ('34) 1.25 *2.00*
a. Single, English .25 .25
b. Single, Afrikaans .25 .25
c. Booklet pane of 6 47.50 47.50
d. Booklet pane of 2 2.00 *2.25*
e. Perf. 13½x14 (coil), pair 20.00 *45.00*
f. As "e," single, English 2.25 .90
g. As "e," single, Afrikaans 2.25 .90
h. Center omitted 450.00
j. Bklt. pane of 6, marginal ads 35.00 35.00
k. As "j," 4 blank margins 40.00 40.00
m. Perf. 14½x14 (coil), pair 20.00 *45.00*
n. As "m," single, English 2.25 1.00
p. As "m," single, Afrikaans 2.25 1.00
q. Pair, imperf. 225.00
r. Frame omitted 475.00

49 A6 1p rose car & gray blk, pair ('40) 1.00 .40
a. Single, English .25 .25
b. Single, Afrikaans .25 .25
c. Unwmkd., pair 300.00 300.00
d. Booklet pane of 6 6.00 5.00
e. Perf. 14½x14 (coil), pair ('43) 1.75 3.50
f. As "e," single, English .55 .25
g. As "e," single, Afrikaans .55 .25
h. As "d," marginal ads ('48) 4.25 3.50

50 A6 1p car & blk, pair ('51) .75 *1.00*
a. Single, English .25 .25
b. Single, Afrikaans .25 .25
c. Booklet pane of 6 4.50 4.50

51 A15 1½p dk grn & gold, 27x21½mm, pair ('36) 6.50 3.00
a. Single, English .30 .25
b. Single, Afrikaans .30 .25
c. Booklet pane of 4 30.00 15.00
d. Center omitted, pair 25,000. 10,000.
e. As "c," pair, one normal 3,250.

52 A15 1½p sl grn & och, 22x18mm, pair ('41) 7.50 2.25
a. Single, English .30 .25
b. Single, Afrikaans .30 .25
c. Center omitted, pair 4,750. 3,250.
d. Booklet pane of 6 7.50 4.50

53 A16 2p bl vio & dl bl, pair ('38) 45.00 30.00
a. Single, English 2.75 1.50
b. Single, Afrikaans 2.75 1.50

54 A16 2p dl vio & gray, pair ('41) 65.00 *110.00*
a. Single, English 2.00 *2.50*
b. Single, Afrikaans 2.00 *2.50*

55 A16a 2p dp reddish vio & sl, 27x21½mm, pair ('45) 5.00 2.50
a. Single, English .40 .25
b. Single, Afrikaans .40 .25

56 A16a 2p pur & sl bl, 21½ x 17¼mm, pair ('50) 4.00 *12.00*
a. Single, English .30 .40
b. Single, Afrikaans .30 .40
c. Booklet pane of 6 ('51) 13.00 *36.00*

57 A17 3p ultra, pair ('40) 5.00 2.75
a. Single, English .40 .25
b. Single, Afrikaans .40 .25
c. 3p bl, pair ('49) 3.50 *6.50*
d. As "c," single, English .30 .25
e. As "c," single, Afrikaans .30 .25

58 A10 4p choc brn, pair ('52) 4.25 *10.00*
a. Single, English .25 .50
b. Single, Afrikaans .25 .50

59 A7 6p org & bl grn, I, pair ('37) 50.00 27.50
a. Single, English 2.50 1.00
b. Single, Afrikaans 2.50 1.00

60 A7 6p org & grn, II, pair ('38) 25.00 2.25
a. Single, English .75 .25
b. Single, Afrikaans .75 .25

61 A7 6p red org & bl grn, III ('50), pair 3.25 1.25
a. Single, English .30 .25
b. Single, Afrikaans .30 .25
c. 6p org & grn, III, pair ('46) 12.50 1.75
d. As "c," single, English .75 .25
e. As "c," single, Afrikaans .75 .25

62 A11 1sh chlky bl & lt brn ('50), pair 9.00 *11.00*
a. As "f," single, English .60 .25
b. As "f," single, Afrikaans .60 .25
c. 1sh lt bl & ol brn, pair ('39) 35.00 10.00
d. As "c," single, English 1.25 .25
e. As "c," single, Afrikaans 1.25 .25
f. 1sh vio bl & brnsh blk, pair ('52) 14.50 *12.00*
g. Single, English .60 .30
h. Single, Afrikaans .60 .30

i. As "c," frame omitted, vert. pair with normal 14,000.

63 A12 2sh6p brn & brt grn, pair ('49) 14.00 *27.50*
a. Single, English 2.25 1.50
b. Single, Afrikaans 2.25 1.50

64 A13 5sh grn & blk, I, pair 62.50 70.00
a. Single, English 5.00 2.25
b. Single, Afrikaans 5.00 2.25

64C A13 5sh bl grn & blk, I, pair (photogravure) ('44) 40.00 22.50
d. Single, English 1.25 .45
e. Single, Afrikaans 1.25 .45

65 A13 5sh bl grn & blk, I, pair ('49) 45.00 *85.00*
a. Single, English 5.00 4.00
b. Single, Afrikaans 5.00 4.00

66 A13 5sh dp yel grn & blk, II, pair ('54) 60.00 *95.00*
a. Single, English 8.00 6.00
b. Single, Afrikaans 8.00 6.00

67 A18 10sh ol blk & bl, pair ('39) 45.00 12.00
a. Single, English 4.00 1.75
b. Single, Afrikaans 4.00 1.75
Nos. 45-67 (23) 482.25 520.65

See Nos. 98-99. For overprints see Nos. O26-O27, O29, O36-O38, O40, O46-O47, O54.

Imperf. examples of Nos. 57 are proofs.

George V and Springboks — A19

1935, May 1 Wmk. 201 *Perf. 15x14*

68 A19 ½p Prus grn & blk, pair 3.00 *12.00*
a. Single, English top .40 .30
b. Single, Afrikaans top .40 .30

69 A19 1p car rose & blk, pair 3.00 *8.50*
a. Single, English top .40 .25
b. Single, Afrikaans top .40 .25

70 A19 3p bl & dk bl, pair 17.50 *62.50*
a. Single, English top 3.00 3.00
b. Single, Afrikaans top 3.00 3.00

71 A19 6p org & grn, pair 34.00 *70.00*
a. Single, English top 4.75 *4.00*
b. Single, Afrikaans top 4.75 *4.00*
Nos. 68-71 (4) 57.50 *153.00*
Set, never hinged 85.00

25th anniv. of the reign of George V.

English and Afrikaans inscriptions are transposed on alternate stamps. On the ½p, 3p and 6p with "SOUTH AFRICA" at top, "SILWER JUBILEUM" is at left of medallion, but on 1p with English at top, it is at the right.

Johannesburg International Philatelic Exhibition Issue

Nos. 45c and 48j Overprinted in Black

Souvenir Sheets

1936, Nov. 2 *Perf. 15x14*

72 A5 Sheet of 6 (½p) 4.75 *8.00*
73 A6 Sheet of 6 (1p) 4.00 *5.00*
Set, never hinged 19.00

Sheets made by overprinting booklet panes Nos. 45c and 48j. Sheets exist with and without horizontal perforations through right margin. Sheet size: 81x72.

Catalogue values for unused stamps in this section, from this point to the end of the section, are for Never Hinged items.

George VI — A22

"KRONING SUID-AFRIKA" on alternate stamps.

1937, May 12 *Perf. 14*

74 A22 ½p grn & ol blk, pair .75 1.00
a. Single, English .25 .25
b. Single, Afrikaans .25 .25

75 A22 1p car & ol blk, pair .80 .85
a. Single, English .25 .25
b. Single, Afrikaans .25 .25

76 A22 1½p Prus grn & org, pair .80 .75
a. Single, English .25 .25
b. Single, Afrikaans .25 .25

77 A22 3p bl & ultra, pair 1.50 *2.75*
a. Single, English .25 .25
b. Single, Afrikaans .25 .25

78 A22 1sh Prus bl & org brn, pair 3.75 4.00
a. Single, English .40 .25
b. Single, Afrikaans .40 .25
Nos. 74-78 (5) 7.60 9.35

Coronation of George VI and Queen Elizabeth.

Wagon Wheel — A23

Voortrekker Family — A24

Alternate stamps inscribed "SOUTH AFRICA," "SUID-AFRIKA."

1938, Dec. 14 *Perf. 15x14*

79 A23 1p rose & slate, pair 8.00 3.75
a. Single, English .60 .35
b. Single, Afrikaans .60 .35

80 A24 1½p red brn & Prus bl, pair 10.00 4.25
a. Single, English 1.10 .80
b. Single, Afrikaans 1.10 .80

Issued to commemorate the Voortrekkers.

Infantry A25

Nurse and Ambulance (Barbara Palmer) A26

Airman and Spitfires (Flight Lt. Robert Kershaw) A27

Sailor (Clive Edward Peter) A28

Women's Services A29

Artillery — A30

Welder — A31

Tank Corps A32

Signal Corps — A33

Bilingual inscriptions on 2p and 1sh.

Perf. 14 (2p, 4p, 6p), 15x14

1941-43 Photo. Wmk. 201

81 A25 ½p dp bl grn, pair 1.25 *3.50*
a. Single, English .25 .25
b. Single, Afrikaans .25 .25

82 A26 1p brt rose, pair 1.60 *2.25*
a. Single, English .25 .25
b. Single, Afrikaans .25 .25

83 A27 1½p Prus grn, pair ('42) 1.25 *2.75*
a. Single, English .25 .25
b. Single, Afrikaans .25 .25

84 A28 2p dk violet .90 .60

85 A29 3p dp blue, pair 14.50 37.50
a. Single, English 2.00 1.00
b. Single, Afrikaans 2.00 1.00

86 A30 4p org brn, pair 20.00 18.00
a. Single, English 1.50 .30
b. Single, Afrikaans 1.50 .30
c. 4p red brown, pair 32.50 30.00
d. As "c," single, English 3.00 1.75
e. As "c," single, Afrikaans 3.00 1.75

87 A31 6p brt red org, pair 11.00 11.00
a. Single, English .90 .30
b. Single, Afrikaans .90 .30

88 A32 1sh dark brown 2.00 .85

89 A33 1sh3p dk ol brn, pair ('43) 12.00 9.00
a. Single, English 1.00 .50
b. Single, Afrikaans 1.00 .50
c. 1sh3p dark brown, pair 6.00 *7.50*
d. As "c," single, English .60 .30
e. As "c," single, Afrikaans .60 .30
Nos. 81-89 (9) 64.50 85.45

Infantry A34

Nurse A35

Airman — A36

Sailor — A37

Women's Services — A38

Artillery — A39

Welder — A40

Tank Corps — A41

Bilingual inscriptions on 4p and 1sh.

Pairs: Perf. 14, Roul. 6½ btwn. Strips of 3: Perf. 15x14, Roul. 6½ btwn.

1942-43 Photo. Wmk. 201

90 A34 ½p Horiz. strip of 3 1.60 1.25
- *a.* Single, English .25 .25
- *b.* Single, Afrikaans .25 .25
- *c.* As #90, imperf. between 3,000. 2,000.

91 A35 1p Horiz. strip of 3 ('43) 1.00 .85
- *a.* Single, English .25 .25
- *b.* Single, Afrikaans .25 .25
- *c.* As #91, imperf. between 2,500. 2,000.

92 A36 1½p Horiz. pair .65 *1.25*
- *a.* Single, English .25 .25
- *b.* Single, Afrikaans .25 .25
- *c.* As #92, roul. 13 2.50 *3.50*
- *d.* As #92, imperf. btwn. 400.00 425.00

93 A37 2p Horiz. pair ('43) .85 1.25
- *a.* Single, English .25 .25
- *b.* Single, Afrikaans .25 .25
- *c.* As #93, imperf. btwn. 1,500. 1,300.

94 A38 3p Vert strip of 3 7.50 *12.00*
- *a.* Single, English .30 .25
- *b.* Single, Afrikaans .30 .25

95 A39 4p Vert. strip of 3 17.00 10.00
- *a.* Single .75 .50

96 A40 6p Horiz. pair 2.00 2.00
- *a.* Single, English .25 .25
- *b.* Single, Afrikaans .25 .25

97 A41 1sh Vert. pair 15.00 4.00
- *a.* Single .55 .25

Nos. 90-97 (8) 45.60 32.60

Because of the rouletting these are collected as pairs or strips of three, even on the bilingual stamps.

Types of 1926 Redrawn
"SUID-AFRIKA" Hyphenated
Coil Stamps

1943 Photo. *Perf. 15x14*

98 A5 ½p myrtle grn, vert. pair 3.75 *5.00*
- *a.* Single, English .30 .25
- *b.* Single, Afrikaans .30 .25

99 A6 1p rose pink, vert. pair 4.75 *3.75*
- *a.* Single, English .30 .25
- *b.* Single, Afrikaans .30 .25

"Victory" — A42

"Peace" — A43

Design: 3p, Profiles of couple ("Hope").

1945, Dec. 3 Photo. *Perf. 14*

100 A42 1p rose pink & choc, pair .30 *1.00*
- *a.* Single, English .25 .25
- *b.* Single, Afrikaans .25 .25

101 A43 2p vio & sl bl, pair .30 *1.00*
- *a.* Single, English .25 .25
- *b.* Single, Afrikaans .25 .25

102 A43 3p ultra & dp ultra, pair .40 *1.25*
- *a.* Single, English .25 .25
- *b.* Single, Afrikaans .25 .25

Nos. 100-102 (3) 1.00 3.25

World War II victory of the Allies.

George VI — A44

King George VI and Queen Elizabeth A45

Princesses Margaret Rose and Elizabeth A46

Perf. 15x14

1947, Feb. 17 Wmk. 201

103 A44 1p cer & gray, pair .25 *.35*
- *a.* Single, English .25 .25
- *b.* Single, Afrikaans .25 .25

104 A45 2p purple, pair .30 *.50*
- *a.* Single, English .25 .25
- *b.* Single, Afrikaans .25 .25

105 A46 3p dk blue, pair .35 *.60*
- *a.* Single, English .25 .25
- *b.* Single, Afrikaans .25 .25

Nos. 103-105 (3) .90 1.45

Visit of the British Royal Family, Mar.-Apr., 1947.

George VI, Elizabeth — A47

1948, Apr. 26 Photo. *Perf. 14*

106 A47 3p dp chlky bl & sil, pair .80 1.00
- *a.* Single, English .25 .25
- *b.* Single, Afrikaans .25 .25

25th anniv. of the marriage of George VI and Queen Elizabeth.

Gold Mine — A48

Vertical Pairs Perf. 14 all around, Rouletted 6½ between

1948, Apr.

107 A48 1½p sl & och, vert. pair 1.25 *1.75*
- *a.* Single, English .25 .25
- *b.* Single, Afrikaans .25 .25

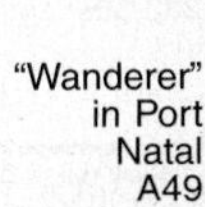

"Wanderer" in Port Natal A49

1949, May 2 Photo. *Perf. 15x14*

108 A49 1½p red brown, pair .70 .70
- *a.* Single, English .25 .25
- *b.* Single, Afrikaans .25 .25

Mercury and Globe — A50

1949, Oct. 1 *Perf. 14x15*

109 A50 ½p dk green, pair .45 *.90*
- *a.* Single, English .25 .25
- *b.* Single, Afrikaans .25 .25

110 A50 1½p dk red, pair .65 *.90*
- *a.* Single, English .25 .25
- *b.* Single, Afrikaans .25 .25

111 A50 3p ultra, pair .90 .90
- *a.* Single, English .25 .25
- *b.* Single, Afrikaans .25 .25

Nos. 109-111 (3) 2.00 2.70

75th anniv. of the UPU.

Except for Nos. 216, 310-313, 518a, 669a this is the end of bi-lingual multiples in the postage section.

Voortrekkers en Route to Natal — A51

Voortrekker Monument, Pretoria A52

Voortrekkers Looking Toward Natal, and Open Bible — A53

1949, Dec. 1 *Perf. 15x14*

112 A51 1p magenta .25 .25
113 A52 1½p dull green .25 .25
114 A53 3p dark blue .25 .25
Nos. 112-114 (3) .75 .75

Inauguration of the Voortrekker Monument at Pretoria.

Riebeeck's Seal and Dutch East India Company Monogram A54

Maria de la Quellerie — A55

2p, van Riebeeck's Ships. 4½p, Jan van Riebeeck. 1sh, Landing of van Riebeeck.

Perf. 15x14, 14x15

1952, Mar. 14 Wmk. 201

115 A54 ½p dk brn & red vio .25 .25
116 A55 1p dark green .25 .25
117 A54 2p dark purple .25 .25
118 A55 4½p dark blue .25 .25
119 A54 1sh brown .40 .40
Nos. 115-119 (5) 1.40 1.40

300th anniv. of the landing of Jan van Riebeeck at the Cape of Good Hope.

Nos. 116-117 Overprinted "SATISE" (1p) and "SADIPU" (2p)

1952, Mar. 26

120 A55 1p dark green .35 .50
121 A54 2p dark purple .40 .65

South African Tercentenary Intl. Stamp Exhib., Cape Town, Mar. 26-Apr. 5, 1952.

Coronation Issue

Queen Elizabeth II — A97

1953, June 3 *Perf. 14x15*

192 A97 2p violet blue .45 .30

Cape Triangle of 1853 A98

1953, Sept. 1 *Perf. 15x14*

193 A98 1p red & dk brown .25 .25
194 A98 4p blue & indigo .25 .25

Cent. of the introduction of postage stamps in South Africa.

Merino Ram and Sheep — A99

1953, Oct. 1 *Perf. 14*

195 A99 4½p shown .30 .25
196 A99 1sh3p Springbok 1.60 .25
197 A99 1sh6p Aloes .75 .35
Nos. 195-197 (3) 2.65 .85

Arms of Orange Free State, Pen and Scroll A100

1954, Feb. 23 *Perf. 15x14*

198 A100 2p red org & dk brown .25 .25
199 A100 4½p gray & rose violet .25 .25

Orange Free State centenary.

Wart Hog A101

White Rhinoceros A102

Lion — A103

1954, Oct. 14 *Perf. 15x14*

200 A101 ½p shown .25 .25
201 A101 1p Gnu .25 .25
202 A101 1½p Leopard .25 .25
203 A101 2p Zebra .25 .25

Perf. 14

204 A102 3p shown .70 .25
205 A102 4p Elephant .80 .25
206 A102 4½p Hippopotamus .60 .65
207 A103 6p shown .55 .25

208 A102 1sh Kudu 1.35 .25
209 A103 1sh3p Springbok 3.75 .25
210 A102 1sh6p Gemsbok 2.00 .50
211 A102 2sh6p Nyala 3.75 .30
212 A102 5sh Giraffe 11.00 1.25
213 A102 10sh Sable antelope 13.00 3.25
Nos. 200-213 (14) 38.50 8.20

See Nos. 221-228, 241-244, 247, 250-253.

Paul Kruger — A104

Portrait: 6p, Martinus Wessels Pretorius.

Perf. 14x15

1955, Oct. 21 Photo. Wmk. 201

214 A104 3p slate green .25 .25
215 A104 6p brown violet .30 .30

Centenary of Pretoria.

Andries Pretorius, Church of the Vow and Flag of Natalia — A105

Inscribed alternately in English and Afrikaans.

1955, Dec. 1 *Perf. 14*

216 A105 2p ultra & cer, pair .60 *2.75*
a. Single, English .25 .25
b. Single, Afrikaans .25 .25

Union Covenant Celebrations, Pietermaritzburg, Dec. 13-18, 1955.

German Wagon and House — A106

1958, July 1 *Perf. 14*

218 A106 2p pale lilac & brown .35 .25

Cent. of the arrival of German settlers.

Seal of Academy A107

Perf. 15x14

1959, May 1 Photo. Wmk. 201

219 A107 3p brt blue & dk blue .35 .25
a. Dark blue omitted 6,000.

50th anniv. of the South African Academy of Science and Art, Pretoria.

Globe Showing Antarctica and South Africa — A108

Perf. 14x15

1959, Nov. 16 Wmk. 330

220 A108 3p blue grn, brn & org .35 .25

South African Natl. Antarctic Expedition.

Animal Types of 1954

1959-60 Wmk. 330 *Perf. 15x14*

221 A101 ½p Wart hog ('60) .30 *3.00*
222 A101 1p Gnu .25 .25
a. Redrawn .35 .25

Perf. 14

223 A102 3p White rhino .35 .25
224 A102 4p Elephant .60 .50
225 A103 6p Lion .90 .75
226 A102 1sh Kudu 6.00 .50
227 A102 2sh6p Nyala 3.50 2.75
228 A102 5sh Giraffe ('60) 9.50 *22.50*
Nos. 221-228 (8) 21.40 30.50

On No. 222a, the numeral "1" is centered above "S." On No. 222, "1" is slightly to right of "S."

Prime Ministers Botha, Smuts, Hertzog, Malan, Strydom and Verwoerd A109

Flag and Notes from National Anthem — A110

Pushing Wheel Uphill A111

6p, Arms of the Union and of four provinces. 1sh6p, Official Union festival emblem.

Perf. 14x15, 15x14

1960 Photo. Wmk. 330

235 A109 3p chocolate .35 .25
236 A110 4p lt blue & red org .35 .25
237 A110 6p yel grn, red & brn .35 .25
238 A111 1sh yel, dk bl & blk .60 .25
239 A111 1sh6p lt blue & blk 1.25 1.25
Nos. 235-239 (5) 2.90 2.25

50th anniv. of the founding of the Union. See Nos. 245-246, 248-249.

Map, Old and New Locomotives — A112

1960, May 2 *Perf. 15x14*

240 A112 1sh3p dark blue 1.40 1.00

Centenary of railways in South Africa.

Types of 1954 and 1960

Designs: ½c, Wart hog. 1c, Gnu. 1½c, Leopard. 2c, Zebra. 2½c, Prime Ministers. 3½c, Flag and music notes. 5c, Lion. 7½c, Arms of Union and four provinces. 10c, Pushing wheel uphill. 12½c, Springbok. 20c, Gemsbok. 50c, Giraffe. 1r, Sable antelope.

Perf. 15x14, 14x15, 14 (A102, A103)

1961, Feb. 14 Photo. Wmk. 330

241 A101 ½c dk bluish grn .25 .25
242 A101 1c rose brown .25 .25
243 A101 1½c sepia .25 .25
244 A101 2c purple .25 .25
245 A109 2½c chocolate .25 .25
246 A110 3½c lt bl & red org .25 .25
247 A103 5c org & dk brn .30 .25
248 A110 7½c yel grn, red & brn .35 *.45*
249 A111 10c yel, dk bl & blk .40 .30
250 A103 12½c dull grn & dk brn 1.00 1.00
251 A102 20c pink & dk brn 2.00 1.75
252 A102 50c org yel & blk brn 4.00 *5.00*
253 A102 1r blue & black 12.50 12.50
Nos. 241-253 (13) 22.05 22.75

Republic

Natal Pigmy Kingfisher A112a

Coral Tree Flower A112b

Pouring Gold A113

Groot Constantia A114

Designs: 1½c, Afrikander bull. 3c, Crimson-breasted shrike. 5c, Baobab tree. 7½c, Corn. 10c, Castle entrance, Cape Town. 12½c, Protea flower. 20c, Secretary bird. 50c, Cape Town, harbor. 1r, Bird of Paradise flower.

Two types of 2½c:
Type I — Lines of building faint.
Type II — Lines of building very strong; strong line between bottom of building and top of name panel.

Perf. 14x15, 15x14

1961, May 31 Photo. Wmk. 330

254 A112a ½c blue, mag & brn .25 .25
a. Perf. 14x13½ ('63) .25 .25
255 A112b 1c gray & red .25 .25
256 A112a 1½c brown carmine .25 .25

Perf. 14

257 A113 2c ultra & org .25 .25
258 A114 2½c vio & grn (I) .30 .25
a. Type II .40 .25
259 A113 3c pink, dk bl & red .30 .25
260 A114 5c grnsh bl & yel .35 .25
261 A114 7½c emerald & brn .55 .25
a. Brown omitted
262 A114 10c emer & dk brn .75 .25
263 A114 12½c dk grn, red & yel 2.00 .30
a. Yellow omitted *1,750.*
264 A114 20c sal, sl bl & pink 3.50 .30
265 A113 50c ultra & blk 21.00 2.00
266 A113 1r blue, org & grn 12.50 2.00
Nos. 254-266 (13) 42.25 6.85

1961-63 Unwmk. *Perf. 15x14*

269 A112b 1c gray & red .25 .25

Perf. 14

270 A113 2c ultra & org ('63) 7.50 .35
271 A114 2½c violet & grn (II) .30 .25
272 A113 3c pink, dk bl & red .60 .25
273 A114 5c grnsh blue & yel .75 .25
274 A114 7½c emer & brn ('62) 1.10 .35
275 A114 10c green & dk brn 1.25 .65
276 A114 20c sal, sl bl & pink ('63) 10.00 2.25
277 A113 50c ultra & blk ('62) 14.00 2.75
Nos. 269-277 (9) 35.75 7.35

See Nos. 289-298, 317-322, 324, 326-338, 340-342, 376-377, 379-382, 383-385 and designs A135-A136.

Boeing 707 and Bleriot Monoplane — A115

Perf. 14x15

1961, Dec. 1 Photo. Wmk. 330

280 A115 3c blue & red .45 .25

50th anniv. of South Africa's 1st air mail.

Folk Dancers — A116

1962, Mar. 1

281 A116 2½c lt brn, choc & red org .30 .25

50th anniv. of folk dancing in South Africa.

"Chapman" Arriving in 1820 A117

Perf. 15x14

1962, Aug. 20 Photo. Wmk. 330

282 A117 2½c dp plum & bl grn .40 .25
283 A117 12½c choc & blue 2.00 1.25

Unveiling of the precinct stone of the British Settlers Monument at Grahamstown.

Red Disa Orchid, Castle Rock, Kirstenbosch Botanic Gardens — A118

1963, Mar. 14 *Perf. 14*

284 A118 2½c multicolored .35 .25

50th anniv. of the Kirstenbosch Botanic Gardens, Cape Town.

Centenary Emblem and Nurse — A119

12½c, Centenary emblem and globe, horiz.

1963, Aug. 30 Wmk. 348 *Perf. 14*

285 A119 2½c rose claret, blk & red .35 .25

Perf. 15x14

286 A119 12½c dk bl gray & red 3.00 1.50
a. Red Cross omitted *5,500.* *3,250.*

Centenary of the International Red Cross.

Assembly Seat, Bunga Building, Umtata A120

Perf. 14½x14

1963, Dec. 11 Wmk. 348

287 A120 2½c dk brn & lt grn .30 .25
a. Light green omitted *4,000.*

Transkei Legislative Assembly, 1st meeting.

Types of 1961

Perf. 15x14, 14x15

1963-67 Photo. Wmk. 348

Colors as Before

289 A112b 1c .25 .25
290 A112a 1½c ('67) 2.25 1.00

Perf. 14

291 A113 2c ('64) .40 .25
292 A114 2½c (II) ('64) .70 .25
293 A114 5c ('66) 1.00 .25
294 A114 7½c ('66) 8.00 5.00
295 A114 10c ('64) .75 .25
296 A114 20c ('64) 1.50 .60
297 A113 50c ('66) 30.00 6.50
298 A113 1r ('64) 60.00 42.00
Nos. 289-298 (10) 104.85 56.35

Rugby Board Emblem, Springbok and Ball — A121

Design: 12½c, Rugby player diving over goal line, horiz.

Perf. 14x15, 15x14

1964, May 8 Photo. Wmk. 348

301 A121 2½c dk grn & brn .35 .25
302 A121 12½c yel grn & blk 4.00 3.00

South African Rugby Board, 75th anniv.

John Calvin — A122

1964, July 10 ***Perf. 14***

303 A122 2½c choc, brt car & vio .30 .25

John Calvin (1509-64), French theologian and leader of the Reformation.

Nurse's Lamp — A123

Design: 12½c, Nurse holding lamp, horiz.

Perf. 14x15, 15x14

1964, Oct. 12 Photo. Wmk. 348

304 A123 2½c gold & ultra .25 .25
a. Clear bright lamp base (no shading) .50 .30
305 A123 12½c ultra & gold 2.75 2.00
a. Gold omitted 4,250.

South African Nursing Assoc., 50th anniv.

ITU Emblem and Satellites A124

Design: 12½c, ITU emblem, old and new communication equipment.

1965, May 17 ***Perf. 15x14***

306 A124 2½c brt blue & org .35 .25
307 A124 12½c green & claret 2.50 1.75

Cent. of the ITU.

Pulpit, Groote Kerk, Cape Town — A125

Design: 12½c, Emblem of Dutch Reformed Church of South Africa, horiz.

Perf. 14x15, 15x14

1965, Oct. 21 Photo. Wmk. 348

308 A125 2½c dp brown & yel .25 .25
309 A125 12½c lt ultra, ocher & blk 1.10 1.00

Tercentenary of the Dutch Reformed Church in South Africa.

Diamond — A126

2½c, Flying bird, symbol of freedom & the future, horiz. 3c, Corn. 7½c, Table Mountain, horiz. Inscribed alternately in English & Afrikaans.

1966, May 31 ***Perf. 14***

310 A126 1c blk, yel, dk & lt grn, pair .70 1.00
a. Single, English .25 .25
b. Single, Afrikaans .25 .25
311 A126 2½c dk bl, ultra & yel grn, pair 1.00 1.50
a. Single, English .30 .25
b. Single, Afrikaans .30 .25

Perf. 14x15, 15x14

312 A126 3c red brn, red & yel, pair 1.75 2.25
a. Single, English .30 .25
b. Single, Afrikaans .30 .25
313 A126 7½c ultra, vio bl, och & blk, pair 5.25 6.50
a. Single, English .60 .50
b. Single, Afrikaans .60 .50
Nos. 310-313 (4) 8.70 11.25

5th anniversary of the Republic.

Nos. 310-313 with watermark 359 are reprints made for U.P.U. presentation booklets.

Hendrik F. Verwoerd and Union Buildings, Pretoria A127

Designs: 3c, Verwoerd's portrait, vert. 12½c, Verwoerd and map of South Africa.

Perf. 15x14, 14x15

1966, Dec. 6 Photo. Wmk. 348

314 A127 2½c grnsh blue & blk .25 .25
315 A127 3c yellow grn & blk .25 .25
316 A127 12½c dull blue & blk .65 .65
Nos. 314-316 (3) 1.15 1.15

Dr. Verwoerd (1901-1966), Prime Minister.

Types of 1961 Redrawn and

Industry — A128

(Inscriptions in larger, bolder type)

½c, 1½c and 1r — REPUBLIEK VAN SUID-AFRIKA · REPUBLIC OF SOUTH AFRICA

On the 1r, the "N" of "VAN" is over the final "A" of "AFRIKA." On Nos. 266 and 298, the "N" is over "KA."

REPUBLIC OF SOUTH AFRICA

REPUBLIEK VAN SUID-AFRIKA

1c, 7½c and 12½c

REPUBLIC OF SOUTH AFRICA

2½c, 5c, 10c and 20c

REPUBLIC OF SOUTH AFRICA · REPUBLIEK VAN SUID-AFRIKA

2c, 3c and 50c (similar)

Perf. 13½x14, 14x15, 15x14

1964-68 Photo. Wmk. 348

Colors as Before

Chalky Paper

317 A112a ½c .25 .25
a. Imperf., pair 425.00
b. Perf. 14x15 .30 .25
318 A112b 1c .25 .25
a. Perf. 13½x14 ('68) .40 .25

Perf. 14

319 A113 2c ('68) .30 .25
320 A114 2½c .35 .25
321 A113 3c .50 .25
322 A114 12½c 1.50 .30
323 A128 15c ('67) 2.75 .30
324 A113 1r 12.00 2.25
Nos. 317-324 (8) 17.90 4.10

See No. 339.

Redrawn Types of 1964-68

4c, Groot Constantia (like 2½c). 6c, Corn (like 7½c). 9c, Protea flower (like 12½c).

1967-71 Photo. Wmk. 359

326 A112a ½c .25 .25
327 A112b 1c .25 .25
a. Perf. 15x14 ('67) .25 .25
b. Perf. 13½x14 ('68) .35 .25
328 A112a 1½c .25 .25
a. Perf. 14x13½ ('68) .30 .25
329 A113 2c ('68) 1.25 .30
330 A114 2½c .25 .25
331 A113 3c .25 .25
332 A114 4c ('71) .40 .25
333 A114 5c ('68) .25 .25
334 A114 6c ('71) .70 .25
335 A114 7½c .50 .25
336 A114 9c ('71) .85 .30
337 A114 10c ('68) 1.50 .30
338 A114 12½c ('70) 4.50 .75
339 A128 15c ('69) 1.25 .60
340 A114 20c ('68) 7.00 .90
341 A113 50c ('68) 4.50 .50
342 A113 1r ('68) 5.50 1.40
Nos. 326-342 (17) 29.45 7.30

Luminescence

Starting in 1969, South Africa began to add phosphorescent "frames" to its definitive stamps.

In 1971, stamps began to appear with the phosphorescent element throughout the paper.

Phosphorescent commemoratives include Nos. 357, 359 et cetera.

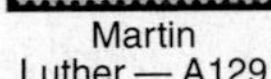

Martin Luther — A129

Door of Wittenberg Church — A130

Perf. 14x15

1967, Oct. 31 Litho. Wmk. 348

343 A129 2½c pink & black .25 .25

Wmk. 359

344 A130 12½c black & orange 1.40 1.25

450th anniversary of the Reformation.

Pres. J. J. Fouché — A133

Design: 12½c, Full-face portrait.

Perf. 14x15

1968, Apr. 10 Photo. Wmk. 348

345 A133 2½c lt rose brn & dk brn .25 .25
346 A133 12½c grysh bl & vio bl .35 .35

Wmk. 359

347 A133 12½c grysh bl & vio bl 1.40 1.25
Nos. 345-347 (3) 2.00 1.85

Pres. Jacobus Johannes Fouché, inauguration.

James B. M. Hertzog Statue — A134

Designs: 2½c, Hertzog in 1902, with hat, horiz. 3c, Hertzog in 1924, horiz.

Perf. 13½x14, 14x13½

1968, Sept. 21 Photo. Wmk. 359

348 A134 2½c dk brn, lem & blk .25 .25

Wmk. 348

349 A134 3c multicolored .25 .25
350 A134 12½c org brn, org & blk 1.25 1.10
Nos. 348-350 (3) 1.75 1.60

Unveiling of a monument in Bloemfontein honoring James Barry Munnik Hertzog (1866-1942), Boer general, prime minister of South Africa (1924-39).

Natal Pigmy Kingfisher A135

Kaffir Boom Flower A136

1969-71 Wmk. 359 Photo. ***Perf. 14***

351 A135 ½c blue & multi .25 .25
a. Perf. 14x14½ (coil) ('69) 1.75 1.00
b. Perf. 14x15 (coil) ('71) 5.00 5.00
352 A136 1c grysh brown & multi .25 .25

See Nos. 374-375.

Springbok, Torch and Rings — A137

1969, Mar. 15 ***Perf. 14x13½***

353 A137 2½c olive, ind & red .25 .25
354 A137 12½c bister, ind & red .75 .75

South African Natl. Games, Bloemfontein, Mar. 15-Apr. 19.

Groote Schuur Hospital and Dr. Barnard
A138

Hands Holding Heart
A139

Perf. 13½x14

1969, July 7 Photo. Wmk. 348

355 A138 2½c dp rose, pink & plum .25 .25

Perf. 15x14

Wmk. 359

356 A139 12½c dp bl & dp car 1.60 1.40

1st heart transplant operation (by Dr. Christiaan Barnard) and opening of the 47th South African Medical Cong., Pretoria.

Stagecoach of 1869 — A140

Transvaal No. 1 — A141

Perf. 13½x14, 14x13½

1969, Oct. 6 Photo. Wmk. 359

357 A140 2½c ocher, Prus bl & yel .35 .25
358 A141 12½c sal, grn & gold 2.75 2.50

Centenary of South African postage stamps.

Water Drop and Flower — A142

Design: 3c, Waves, horiz.

1970, Feb. 14 ***Perf. 14***

359 A142 2½c brn, brt bl & grn .25 .25
360 A142 3c pale gray, bl & ind .45 .25

Issued to publicize the Water 70 campaign of the Department of Water Affairs.

Sower — A143

"BIBLIA"
A144

1970, Aug. 24 Photo. ***Perf. 14***

361 A143 2½c multicolored .25 .25

Photo; Gold Impressed

362 A144 12½c ultra, blk & gold 2.00 1.75

150th anniv. of the South African Bible Soc.

Strijdom Tower, Johannes G. Strijdom — A145

Map of Antarctica
A146

Perf. 14x13½, 13½x14

1971, May 22 Photo. Wmk. 359

363 A145 5c blue, yel & blk .40 .25
364 A146 12½c grnsh bl, vio bl & red 2.00 2.00

Wmk. 330

365 A145 5c blue, yel & blk 2.00 1.75
Nos. 363-365 (3) 4.40 4.00

Intl. Stamp Exhib. (INTERSTEX), Cape Town, May 22-31. No. 364 also for the 10th anniv. of the Antarctic Treaty pledging peaceful uses of and scientific cooperation in Antarctica.

Landing of British Settlers, 1820, by Thomas Baines
A147

Martinus Steyn, Paul Kruger, Unification Monument — A148

1971, May 31 Wmk. 359

366 A147 2c magenta & rose red .25 .25
367 A148 4c blue green & blk .25 .25

10th anniv. of the Republic of South Africa.

Hendrik Verwoerd Dam
A149

1972, Mar. 4 Photo. ***Perf. 14***

Size: 37x22mm

368 A149 4c shown .25 .25
369 A149 5c Aerial view of dam .35 .25

Size: 57x22mm

370 A149 10c Dam, reservoir and Verwoerd 1.25 .80
Nos. 368-370 (3) 1.85 1.30

Inauguration of the Hendrik F. Verwoerd Dam of the Orange River Project.

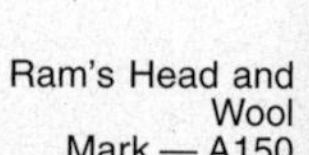

Ram's Head and Wool Mark — A150

Lamb and Wool Mark — A151

1972, May 15 Wmk. 359 ***Perf. 14***

371 A150 4c blue & multi .30 .25
372 A151 15c dull bl & dk bl 1.75 .40

South African wool industry. Issued in sheets of 100 with advertisements in margin. See Nos. 378-378A, 382A.

Cats — A152

1972, Sept. 19 Wmk. 359

373 A152 5c multicolored 1.40 .35

Centenary of the SPCA.

Redrawn Types of 1964-69 and Types of 1972

Perf. 14x15 (½c), 14 (1c, #382A), 12½

1972-74 Photo. Unwmk.

No.	Type	Description	Unused	Used
374	A135	½c blue & multi	9.00	9.00
375	A136	1c grysh brn & red	.25	.25
376	A113	2c brt blue & org	.35	.25
a.		Perf. 14 (coil) ('73)	10.00	10.00
377	A113	3c rose red & bluish black	.40	.35
378	A150	4c blue & multi	.30	.25
378A	A150	4c brown & multi	.35	.25
379	A114	5c grnsh bl & yel	1.10	.30
a.		Perf. 14 (coil) ('73)	11.00	11.00
380	A114	6c emerald & brn	3.00	3.00
381	A114	9c dk grn, red & yel	2.00	.75
382	A114	10c emer & dk brn	.90	.45
b.		Perf. 14 (coil) ('73)	13.00	13.00
382A	A151	15c dull bl & dk bl	3.25	3.00
383	A114	20c sal, sl bl & pink	2.25	.50
384	A113	50c ultra & black	5.50	1.25
385	A113	1r bl, org & grn	10.00	2.50
		Nos. 374-385 (14)	38.65	22.10

Issued: 2c, 1972; 6c, 15c, 1974; others, 1973.

Pylon — A153

Designs: 4c, Electrical usage, pylon, power plant, horiz. 15c, Smokestacks.

1973, Feb. 1 Photo. ***Perf. 12x12½***

Size: 37½x20mm

386 A153 4c blue & multi .25 .25

Size: 20x27mm

Perf. 12½

387 A153 5c blue & black .35 .25
388 A153 15c ocher & multi 3.25 1.25
Nos. 386-388 (3) 3.85 1.75

Electricity Supply Commission, 50th anniv.

Arms of University
A154

Old University, Cape Town
A156

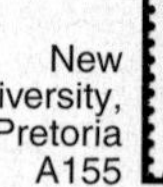

New University, Pretoria
A155

1973, Apr. 2 Unwmk. ***Perf. 12½***

389 A154 4c blue & multi .25 .25

Perf. 12x12½

Wmk. 359

390 A155 5c gold & multi .35 .25

Unwmk. ***Perf. 12½***

391 A156 15c gold & blk 2.50 1.50

Cent. of the Univ. of South Africa (UNISA).

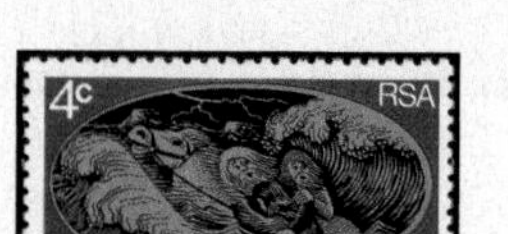

Woltemade, Sailor and Horse — A157

Designs: 5c, Sinking ship in storm. 15c, "De Jonge Thomas" sinking.

1973, June 2 Photo. ***Perf. 12x12½***

392 A157 4c brown red, ol & blk .25 .25
393 A157 5c olive, blk & citron .35 .25
394 A157 15c brown, blk & ocher 3.50 2.75
Nos. 392-394 (3) 4.10 3.25

Bicentenary of Wolraad Woltemade's heroism in saving 14 people from the ship "De Jonge Thomas" in Table Bay.

C. J. Langenhoven and Anthem — A158

4c, 5c, vert., Portrait and signature.

1973, Aug. 1 ***Perf. 12½***

Size: 27x20mm

395 A158 4c orange, blk & ultra .40 .25

Perf. 12½x12, 12x12½

Size: 21x38mm, 37x21mm

396 A158 5c orange, blk & ultra .50 .25
397 A158 15c orange, blk & ultra 4.25 1.25
Nos. 395-397 (3) 5.15 1.75

Cornelis Jacob Langenhoven (1873-1932), lawyer, writer, who worked for recognition of Afrikaans language.

World Map and Communications Network — A159

Perf. 12½

1973, Oct. 1 Photo. Unwmk.

398 A159 15c ultra & multi .55 .45
a. Wmk. 359 1.40 1.00

International Telecommunications Day.

Restored Houses, Tulbagh — A160

Design: 5c, Church Street, Tulbagh.

1974, Mar. 14 Unwmk. *Perf. 12½*

Size: 27x21mm

400 A160 4c Prus green & multi .25 .25

Size: 57x20mm

401 A160 5c ocher & multi .30 .25

Restoration of historic Church Street in Tulbagh after 1969 earthquake.

Burgerspond — A161

1974, Apr. 7 Litho. *Perf. 12½x12*

402 A161 9c multicolored .50 .40

Centenary of the first official coin struck in South Africa, 1874. The £1 gold coin shows portrait of Pres. Thomas Francois Burger.

Prime Minister D. F. Malan — A162

1974, May 22 Photo. Unwmk.

403 A162 4c lt ultra & dk blue .35 .25

Centenary of the birth of Daniel F. Malan (1874-1959), prime minister of South Africa.

Congress Emblem A163

1974, June 13 *Perf. 12x12½*

404 A163 15c silver & dk blue .60 .30

15th World Sugar Cong., Durban, 6/13-30.

"50" A164

1974, July 13 Photo. Unwmk.

405 A164 4c red & black .30 .25

50th anniversary of radio in South Africa.

Cultural Center, Grahamstown — A165

1974, July 13 *Perf. 12x12½*

406 A165 5c red & black .30 .25

Natl. Monument to British settlers of 1820.

Natal No. 78, Transvaal No. 145, Cape of Good Hope No. 28 and Orange River Colony No. 4 — A166

1974, Oct. 9 Photo. *Perf. 12½*

407 A166 15c multicolored .70 .50

Centenary of Universal Postal Union.

Wild Iris — A167

Cape Gannet — A168

Galjoen — A169

Bokmakierie (Shrike) — A170

Designs: 2c, Heather. 3c, Geranium. 4c, Calla lily. 7c, Zebrafish. 9c, Angelfish. 10c, Moorish idol. 14c, Roman fish. 15c, Greater double-collared sunbird. 20c, Yellow-billed hornbill. 25c, Barberton daisy. 50c, Blue cranes. 1r, Bateleur eagles.

Photo. and Engr.

1974, Nov. 11 Unwmk. *Perf. 12½*

408 A167 1c pink & multi .25 .25
409 A167 2c yellow & multi .25 .25
410 A167 3c multicolored .25 .25
411 A167 4c multicolored .25 .25
412 A168 5c dull blue & multi .25 .25
413 A169 6c multicolored .25 .25
414 A169 7c lilac & multi .25 .25
415 A169 9c buff & multi .30 .25
416 A169 10c lt blue & multi .25 .25
417 A169 14c salmon & multi .25 .25
418 A168 15c gray & multi .30 .25
419 A168 20c yellow & multi .45 .25
420 A167 25c dk brown & multi .60 .25

Perf. 12x12½

421 A170 30c gray & multi 5.50 .70
422 A170 50c citron & multi 1.50 .40
423 A170 1r multicolored 4.50 2.50
Nos. 408-423 (16) 15.40 6.85

The coils that follow are two colors while the above sheet stamps are multicolored.

1974 Photo. *Perf. 12½*

Coil Stamps

430 A167 1c pink & violet .40 .40
431 A167 2c yellow & grn .30 .30
432 A168 5c dull blue & blk 1.50 .60
433 A169 10c lt blue & indigo 4.25 4.00
Nos. 430-433 (4) 6.45 5.30

See note on color that follows No. 423.

1975-76 Same Designs *Perf. 14*

430a A167 1c .30 .25
431a A167 2c ('76) .30 .25
433a A169 10c ('76) 2.00 2.00
Nos. 430a-433a (3) 2.60 2.50

No. 430a has black control number on back of every fifth stamp.

Voortrekker Monument and Encampment — A171

1974, Dec. 6 Unwmk. *Perf. 12½*

438 A171 4c multicolored .30 .25

Voortrekker Monument, 25th anniversary.

Sasolburg Refinery A172

Perf. 12x12½, 12½

1975, Feb. 26 Litho.

439 A172 15c red & multi .70 .60

25th anniversary of South Africa Coal, Oil and Gas Corp., Ltd. (SASOL).

Pres. Nicolaes Diederichs — A173

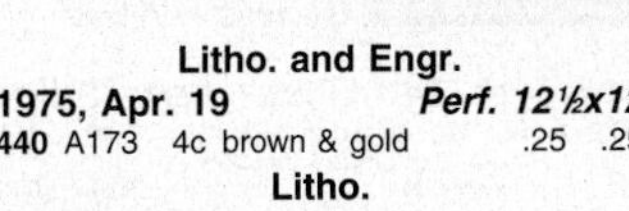

Litho. and Engr.

1975, Apr. 19 *Perf. 12½x12*

440 A173 4c brown & gold .25 .25

Litho.

441 A173 15c ultra & gold .40 .40

Installation of Dr. Nicolaes Diederichs as third State President.

Jan C. Smuts — A174

1975, May 24 Litho. and Engr.

442 A174 4c black .25 .25

Smuts (1870-1950), lawyer, gen., statesman.

Dutch East Indiaman, by Baines A175

Designs: Paintings by John Thomas Baines.

1975, June 18 Photo. *Perf. 12x12½*

443 A175 5c gold & multi .25 .25
444 A175 9c gold & multi .25 .25
445 A175 15c gold & multi .25 .25
446 A175 30c gold & multi .40 .40
a. Souvenir sheet of 4 1.10 1.10
Nos. 443-446 (4) 1.15 1.15

John Thomas Baines (1820-75), painter. #446a contains 4 litho. stamps similar to #443-446.

Gideon Malherbe House, Paarl — A176

Photo. and Engr.

1975, Aug. 14 *Perf. 12½*

447 A176 4c multicolored .25 .25

Society of Real Afrikanders (Genootskap of Regte Afrikaaners), cent.

Automatic Letter Sorting — A177

1975, Sept. 11 Photo. *Perf. 12½x12*

448 A177 4c brt blue & multi .25 .25

Postal automation.

Title Page, First Afrikaans Paper — A178

Afrikaans Monument, Paarl — A179

1975, Oct. 10 Litho. *Perf. 12½x12*

449 A178 4c black & orange .25 .25
450 A179 5c multicolored .25 .25

Inauguration of Afrikaans Language Monument.

Table Mountain — A180

No. 452, Johannesburg. No. 453, Cape vineyards. No. 454, Lions, Kruger Natl. Park.

1975, Nov. 13 Litho. *Perf. 12½*

451 A180 15c shown 1.25 1.00
452 A180 15c multi 1.25 1.00
453 A180 15c multi 1.25 1.00
454 A180 15c multi 1.25 1.00
a. Block of 4, #451-454 7.50 7.50

Tourist publicity.

Satellites, Radar and Africa on Globe — A181

1975, Dec. 3 Litho. *Perf. 12½*

455 A181 15c dk vio blue & multi .25 .25

Satellite communications.

Lawn Bowler — A182

No. 457, Cricket batsman. No. 458, Polo player. No. 459, Golfer (Gary Player).

1976 Photo. *Perf. 12½x12*

456 A182 15c green & blk .35 .25
457 A182 15c yellow grn & blk .35 .25
458 A182 15c olive & blk .35 .25
459 A182 15c brt green & blk .35 .25
a. Miniature sheet of 4, #456-459 1.75 1.75
Nos. 456-459 (4) 1.40 1.00

3rd World Bowling Championships, Zoo Lake Club, Johannesburg, Feb. 1976 (No. 456); cent. of cricket in South Africa (No. 457); intl. polo (No. 458); Gary Player, South African golf champion (No. 459).

Issue dates: #456, Feb. 18. #457, Mar. 12. #458, Aug. 16. #459, 459a, Dec. 2.

No. 456 Overprinted in Gold

1976, Apr. 6 Photo. *Perf. 12½x12*

460 A182 15c green & black .30 .45

Victory of South Africa in 3rd World Bowling championships.

Picnic under Baobab Tree A183

Paintings by Erich Mayer: 10c, Wagons at Foot of Blauberg, Transvaal. 15c, Hartbeess-port Dam, near Pretorial. 20c, Street in Doornfontein.

1976, Apr. 20 Photo. *Perf. 12x12½*

461 A183 4c ocher & multi .25 .25
462 A183 10c dk green & multi .25 .25
463 A183 15c multicolored .30 .30
464 A183 20c multicolored .45 .45
a. Souvenir sheet of 4, #461-464 1.60 1.60
Nos. 461-464 (4) 1.25 1.25

Erich Mayer (1876-1960), painter. Artist's signature in horizontal gutter between 2 se-tenant pairs.

Wildlife Protection A184

1976, June 5 Litho. *Perf. 12x12½*

465 A184 3c Cheetah .25 .25
466 A184 10c Black rhinoceros .30 .25
467 A184 15c Blesbok .40 .35
468 A184 20c Zebra .45 .45
Nos. 465-468 (4) 1.40 1.30

All values exist on yellow toned paper. Value, twice that of stamps on white paper.

Emily Hobhouse, by Johan Hoekstra — A185

1976, June 8 Photo. *Perf. 12½x12*

469 A185 4c multicolored .25 .25

Emily Hobhouse (1860-1926), the "Angel of Mercy" during Anglo-Boer War.

S.S. Dunrobin Castle, 1876 A186

1976, Oct. 5 Litho. *Perf. 12x12½*

470 A186 10c multicolored .60 .30

Ocean Mail Service contract, centenary.

Family with Globe — A187

1976, Nov. 6 Photo. *Perf. 12½x12*

471 A187 4c salmon & dull red .25 .25

Family planning.

Wine Glasses — A188

1977, Feb. 14 Litho. *Perf. 12½x12*

472 A188 15c multicolored .40 .25
a. Word "Die" omitted from left inscription 14.00 16.00

Quality of the Vintage Symposium, Cape Town, Feb. 14-21.

Jacob Daniel du Toit — A189

1977, Feb. 21 Photo.

473 A189 4c multicolored .25 .25

Dr. Jacob Daniel du Toit (Totius; 1877-1953), theologian, educator, poet.

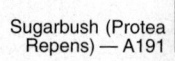

Transvaal Supreme Court A190

1977, May 18 Photo. *Perf. 12x12½*

474 A190 4c red brown .25 .25

Transvaal Supreme Court, centenary.

Sugarbush (Protea Repens) — A191

2c, P. punctata. 3c, P. neriifolia. 4c, P. longifolia. 5c, P. cynaroides. 6c, P. canaliculata. 7c, P. lorea. 8c, P. mundii. 9c, P. roupelliae. 10c, P. aristata. 15c, P. eximia. 20c, P. magnifica. 25c, P. grandiceps. 30c, P. amplexicaulis. 50c, Leucospermum cordifolium. 1r, Paranomus reflexus. 2r, Orothamnus zeyheri.

Photo. (1-5, 8, 10, 15, 20c); Litho. (others)

1977, May 27 *Perf. 12½*

475 A191 1c shown .25 .25
476 A191 2c multi .25 .25
477 A191 3c multi .25 .25
478 A191 4c multi .25 .25
479 A191 5c multi .25 .25
480 A191 6c multi .25 .25
481 A191 7c multi .25 .25
482 A191 8c multi .25 .25
483 A191 9c multi .25 .25
484 A191 10c multi .25 .25
485 A191 15c multi .25 .25
486 A191 20c multi .25 .25
487 A191 25c multi .30 .25
488 A191 30c multi .40 .25
489 A191 50c multi .50 .25
490 A191 1r multi .75 .40
491 A191 2r multi 1.25 .75
Nos. 475-491 (17) 6.20 4.90

Perf. 14

477a A191 3c Litho. .25 .25
479a A191 5c .25 .25
480a A191 6c .25 .25
481a A191 7c .25 .25
482a A191 8c .25 .25
483a A191 9c .25 .25
484a A191 10c .25 .25
486a A191 20c Litho. .85 .35
487a A191 25c .65 .35
488a A191 30c .40 .30
489a A191 50c .60 .50
490a A191 1r .60 .35
491a A191 2r .75 .95
Nos. 477a-491a (13) 5.60 4.55

Perf. 14 Vertically

Photo. Coil Stamps

492 A191 1c Silver tree .30 .25
493 A191 2c Bottle brush .30 .25
494 A191 5c Blushing bride .30 .25
495 A191 10c Leucadendrom sessile .30 .25
Nos. 492-495 (4) 1.20 1.00

Some printings have control number on back of every fifth stamp.

Gymnastics — A192

1977, Aug. 15 Litho. *Perf. 12½x12*

496 A192 15c multicolored .35 .25

8th Intl. Cong. of Physical Education and Sports for Girls and Women, Cape Town, Aug. 14-20.

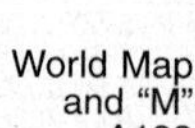

World Map and "M" A193

1977, Sept. 15 Litho. *Perf. 12x12½*

497 A193 15c multicolored .30 .25

Introduction of international metric system.

Nuclear Power Plant and Uranium Atom A194

1977, Oct. 8

498 A194 15c multicolored .30 .25

Uranium development.

Flag of South Africa A195

1977, Nov. 11

499 A195 5c multicolored .25 .25

50th anniversary of national flag.

Walvis Bay, 1878 — A196

1978, Mar. 10 Litho. *Perf. 12½*

500 A196 15c multicolored .45 .35

Centenary of Walvis Bay annexation.

Dr. Andrew Murray — A197

1978, May 9 *Perf. 12½x12*

501 A197 4c multicolored .25 .25

Dr. Andrew Murray, pioneer theologian, 150th birth anniversary.

Railroad Rail and ISCOR Emblem — A198

1978, June 5 Litho. *Perf. 12*

502 A198 15c multicolored .35 .25

50th anniversary of ISCOR (Iron and Steel Industrial Corporation).

Saldanha Bay — A199

Design: No. 504, Richard's Bay.

1978, July 21 Litho. *Perf. 12½*

503 A199 15c multicolored .55 .55
504 A199 15c multicolored .55 .55
a. Pair, #503-504 1.10 1.10

Opening of new harbors on east and west coasts of South Africa.

Landscape by Volschenk — A200

Designs: Landscapes by J. E. A. Volschenk.

1978, Aug. 21

505 A200 10c multicolored .25 .25
506 A200 15c multicolored .25 .25
507 A200 20c multicolored .30 .30

508 A200 25c multicolored .40 .40
a. Souvenir sheet of 4, #505-508 1.75 1.75
Nos. 505-508 (4) 1.20 1.20

Jan Ernst Abraham Volschenk (1853-1936), first South African professional artist.

B. J. Vorster — A201

1978, Oct. 10 Litho. *Perf. 12½x12*
509 A201 4c maroon & gold .25 .25
a. Perf. 14½x14 .55 .30

Perf. 14½x14
510 A201 15c violet & gold .25 .25

Inauguration of Balthazar John Vorster as president of South Africa.

Golden Gate Highlands National Park — A202

Designs: 15c, Blyde River Canyon, Transvaal. 20c, Amphitheater, Natal National Park. 25c, Cango Caves, Cape Province.

1978, Nov. 13 *Perf. 12½*
511 A202 10c multicolored .25 .25
512 A202 15c multicolored .25 .25
513 A202 20c multicolored .25 .25
514 A202 25c multicolored .35 .25
Nos. 511-514 (4) 1.10 1.00

Tourist publicity.

Tellurometer and Dr. I. R. Wadley — A203

1979, Feb. 12 Litho. *Perf. 12½*
515 A203 15c multicolored .25 .25

15th anniversary of the invention of the tellurometer (to measure radio distances).

South Africa No. C5 A204

1979, Mar. 30 Litho. *Perf. 14½x14*
516 A204 15c multicolored .30 .25

First stamp printed by South African Government Printer, 50th anniversary.

"Save Fuel" A205

Fuel Economy: No. 518, Language inscriptions reversed.

1979, Apr. 2 Photo. *Perf. 12x12½*
517 A205 4c red & black .25 .25
518 A205 4c red & black .25 .25
a. Pair, #517-518 .35 .40

Battle of Isandlwana, by Melton Prior — A206

15c, Battle of Ulundi, by Louis Creswicke. 20c, Battle of Rorke's Drift, by Lt. Col. Crealock.

1979, May 25 Litho. *Perf. 14x13½*
519 A206 4c red & black .25 .25
520 A206 15c red & black .30 .30
521 A206 20c red & black .40 .40
a. Souv. sheet, #519-521 + label 2.50 2.50
Nos. 519-521 (3) .95 .95

Centenary of Zulu War.

"Health Care and Service" — A207

1979, June 19 Litho. *Perf. 12½x12*
522 A207 4c multicolored .25 .25
a. Perf. 14¼x14 .30 .30

Health Year.

Boy and Girl Watching Candle — A208

1979, Sept. 13 Litho. *Perf. 14½x14*
523 A208 4c multicolored .25 .25

South African Christmas Stamp Fund, 50th anniversary.

Cape Town University, 150th Anniversary — A209

1979, Oct. 1 Litho. *Perf. 14x14½*
524 A209 4c multicolored .25 .25
a. Perf. 12x12½ .25 .25

Gary Player Rose — A210

Roses: 15c, Prof. Chris Bernard. 20c, Southern Sun. 25c, Soaring Wings.

1979, Oct. 4 Litho. *Perf. 14½x14*
525 A210 4c multicolored .25 .25
526 A210 15c multicolored .25 .25
527 A210 20c multicolored .35 .35
528 A210 25c multicolored .55 .55
a. Souvenir sheet of 4, #525-528 1.50 1.50
Nos. 525-528 (4) 1.40 1.40

Rosafari 1979, 4th World Rose Convention, Pretoria, October.

Stellenbosch University — A211

1979, Nov. 8
529 A211 4c shown .25 .25
530 A211 15c Rhenish Church .25 .25

Stellenbosch (oldest town in South Africa), 300th anniversary.

A212

1979, Dec. 18 Photo. *Perf. 12½x12*
531 A212 4c multicolored .25 .25

Federation of Afrikaans Cultural Societies, 50th anniv.

A213

Paintings by Pieter Wenning (1873-1921): 5c, Still Life with Sweet Peas. 25c, House in the Suburbs, Cape Town.

1980, May 6 Litho. *Perf. 14½x14*
532 A213 5c multicolored .25 .25

Size: 45x37mm
533 A213 25c multicolored .30 .25
a. Souvenir sheet of 2, #532-533 .90 .65

Great Star of Africa Diamond — A214

1980, May 12 Litho. *Perf. 14x14½*
534 A214 15c shown .55 .40
535 A214 20c Cullinan I diamond .65 .55

World Diamond Congress.

A215

1980, Sept. 3 Litho. *Perf. 14½x14*
536 A215 5c multicolored .25 .25

Christian Louis Leipoldt (1880-1947), writer and physician.

University of Pretoria, 50th Anniv. — A216

1980, Oct. 9 Litho.
537 A216 5c multicolored .25 .25

Marine With Ships, by Willem van de Velde — A217

Paintings: 10c, Firetail and Trainer, by George Stubbs. 15c, Lavinia, by Thomas Gainsborough, vert. 20c, Landscape, by Pieter Post.

1980, Nov. 3 *Perf. 14½x14*
538 A217 5c multicolored .25 .25
539 A217 10c multicolored .25 .25
540 A217 15c multicolored .25 .25
541 A217 20c multicolored .25 .25
a. Souvenir sheet of 4, #538-541 1.00 1.00
Nos. 538-541 (4) 1.00 1.00

Natl. Gallery, 50th anniv.

P.J. Joubert, Paul Kruger, M.W. Pretorius (First Leaders of Triumvirate Government) — A218

Design: 10c, Monument, flag of South African Republic, 1880, vert.

1980, Dec. 15 *Perf. 14x14½, 14½x14*
542 A218 5c multicolored .25 .25
543 A218 10c multicolored .25 .25

Paardekraal Monument (built on site of founding of triumverate government) centennial.

British Troops in Battle of Amajuba — A219

1981, Feb. 27 Litho. *Perf. 14x14½*
544 A219 5c Boer snipers, vert. .25 .25
545 A219 15c shown .30 .25

Battle of Amajuba centenary (led to independence of Orange Free State).

Scene from Verdi's Aida A220

1981, May 23 Litho. *Perf. 14½x14*
546 A220 20c Raka ballet scene .30 .25
547 A220 25c shown .40 .30
a. Souvenir sheet of 2, #546-547 1.10 1.10

Opening of State Theater, Pretoria.

Pres. Marais Viljoen — A221

1981, May 30 ***Perf. 14x14½***
Size: 57x21mm

548	A221	5c Former presidents	.25	.25
549	A221	15c shown	.25	.25

Deaf Girl Learning to Speak — A222

1981, June 12 ***Perf. 14½x14***

550	A222	5c shown	.25	.25
551	A222	15c Man reading braille	.25	.25

Institute for the Deaf and Blind, Worcester, centenary.

Natl. Cancer Assn. 50th Anniv. — A223

1981, July 10

552	A223	5c multicolored	.25	.25

Calanthe Natalensis — A224

1981, Sept. 11 **Litho.**

553	A224	5c shown	.25	.25
554	A224	15c Eulophia speciosa	.25	.25
555	A224	20c Disperis fanniniae	.30	.25
556	A224	25c Disa uniflora	.35	.25
a.		Souvenir sheet of 4, #553-556	1.90	1.90
		Nos. 553-556 (4)	1.15	1.00

10th World Orchid Conf., Durban, 9/11-17.

Voortrekker Movement, 50th Anniv. — A225

1981, Sept. 30 ***Perf. 14x14½***

557	A225	5c multicolored	.25	.25

Scouting Year — A226

1982, Feb. 22 **Litho.** ***Perf. 14½x14***

558	A226	15c Baden-Powell	.35	.25

TB Bacillus Centenary — A227

1982, Mar. 24 **Litho.**

559	A227	20c multicolored	.30	.25

Return of Simonstown Naval Base, 25th Anniv. — A228

1982, Apr. 2 ***Perf. 14½x14***

560	A228	8c Submarine	.25	.25
561	A228	15c Strike craft	.25	.25
562	A228	20c Mine sweeper	.25	.25
563	A228	25c Harbor patrol boats	.25	.25
a.		Souvenir sheet of 4, #560-563	2.25	2.25
		Nos. 560-563 (4)	1.00	1.00

Old Provost, Grahamstown A229

Design: 2c, Tuynhuys, Kaapstad (Cape Town). 3c, Appelhof, Bloemfontein. 4c, Raadsaal, Pretoria. 5c, Die Kasteel, Kaapstad. 6c, Goewermentsgebou, Bloemfontein. 7c, Drostdy, Graaf-Reinet. 8c, Leeuwenhof, Cape Town. 9c, Libertas, Pretoria. 10c, City Hall, Pietermaritzburg. 11c, City Hall, Kimberley. 12c, City Hall, Port Elizabeth. 14c, Johannesburg City Hall. 15c, Hotel Milner, Matjesfontein. 16c, Durban City Hall. 20c, Post Office, Durban. 25c, Melrose House, Pretoria. 30c, Old Legislative Assembly Building, Pietermaritzburg. 50c, Raadsaal, Bloemfontein. 1r, Houses of Parliament, Cape Town. 2r, Uniegebou, Pretoria.
Coils have different designs.

1982-87 **Litho.** ***Perf. 14x14½***

564	A229	1c brown ('84)	.25	.25
565	A229	2c apple green	.25	.25
566	A229	2c green	.50	.25
567	A229	2c slate grn ('85)	.40	.25
568	A229	3c purple ('85)	.90	.25
569	A229	4c olive grn ('85)	.25	.25
570	A229	5c carmine	.25	.25
571	A229	6c brt green	.25	.25
572	A229	7c gray green	.25	.25
573	A229	8c blue	.25	.25
574	A229	8c intense bl ('83)	.25	.25
575	A229	9c brt rose lilac	.25	.25
576	A229	10c lt red brown	.25	.25
577	A229	10c violet brn ('83)	.25	.25
578	A229	11c cerise ('84)	.25	.25
579	A229	12c dp ultra ('85)	.30	.25
580	A229	14c rose brn ('86)	.35	.25
581	A229	16c red ('87)	.50	.25
582	A229	20c vermilion	.25	.25
583	A229	20c black ('85)	.50	.25
584	A229	25c bister	.25	.25

Size: 45x27mm
Perf. 14½x14

586	A229	30c brown ('86)	1.00	.25
587	A229	50c Prus blue ('86)	1.50	.25
588	A229	1r violet blue ('86)	2.00	.25
589	A229	2r cerise ('85)	2.25	.60
		Nos. 564-589 (25)	13.70	6.60

For surcharge see No. B12.

Engr.

590	A229	1c dark brown	.25	.25
591	A229	2c slate grn ('83)	.25	.25
592	A229	3c violet	.25	.25
593	A229	4c olive green	.25	.25
594	A229	5c dark lake ('83)	.25	.25
595	A229	6c green blk ('84)	.35	.30
596	A229	15c blue	.25	.25
597	A229	20c black ('83)	.50	.25

Size: 45x27mm
Perf. 14½x14

598	A229	30c violet brown	.40	.25
599	A229	50c Prus blue	.50	.25
600	A229	1r violet blue	.50	.25
601	A229	2r rose carmine	.75	.25
		Nos. 590-601 (12)	4.50	3.05

In some cases there are slight design differences from litho. stamp.

Perf. 14 Horiz.
Photo. **Coil Stamps**

1c, Residence, Swellendam. 2c, City Hall, East London. 5c, Rissik St. PO, Johannesburg. 10c, Morgenster, Somerset West.

602	A229	1c brown	.25	.25
603	A229	2c green	.30	.25
604	A229	5c dark red	.35	.25
605	A229	10c brown	.35	.25
		Nos. 602-605 (4)	1.25	1.00

Bradysaurus A230

Prehistoric Animals (Karoo Fossils).

1982, Dec. 1 **Litho.** ***Perf. 14x14½***

606	A230	8c shown	.25	.25
607	A230	15c Lystrosaurus	.30	.30
608	A230	20c Euparkeria	.40	.40
609	A230	25c Thrinaxodon	.50	.50
a.		Souvenir sheet of 4, #606-609	1.75	1.75
		Nos. 606-609 (4)	1.45	1.45

Weather Station, Gough Island A231

20c, Marion Island station. 25c, Reading instruments. 40c, Weather balloon, Antarctica.

1983, Jan. 19 **Litho.**

610	A231	8c shown	.25	.25
611	A231	20c multicolored	.30	.25
612	A231	25c multicolored	.35	.25
613	A231	40c multicolored	.40	.30
		Nos. 610-613 (4)	1.30	1.05

Steam Locomotives — A232

1983, Apr. 27 **Litho.**

614	A232	10c Class S2, 1952	.25	.25
615	A232	20c Class 16E, 1935	.40	.35
616	A232	25c Class 6H, 1901	.50	.40
617	A232	40c Class 15F, 1939	.75	.65
		Nos. 614-617 (4)	1.90	1.65

Soccer — A233

Perf. 14½x14 (10c, 25c), 14x14½ (20c, 40c)
1983, July 20 **Litho.**

618	A233	10c Rugby, vert.	.25	.25
619	A233	20c shown	.25	.25
620	A233	25c Sailing, vert.	.30	.25
621	A233	40c Equestrian	.35	.25
		Nos. 618-621 (4)	1.15	1.00

Plettenberg Bay — A234

20c, Durban Beach. 25c, West Coast beach. 40c, Clifton beach scene.

1983, Oct. 12 **Litho.** ***Perf. 14½x14***

622	A234	10c shown	.25	.25
623	A234	20c multi	.25	.25
624	A234	25c multi	.25	.25
625	A234	40c multi	.30	.25
a.		Souvenir sheet of 4, #622-625	1.40	1.40
		Nos. 622-625 (4)	1.05	1.00

English Writers of South Africa — A235

Designs: 10c, Thomas Pringle (1789-1834). 20c, Pauline Smith (1882-1959). 25c, Olive Schreiner (1855-1920). 40c, Percy FitzPatrick (1862-1931).

1984, Feb. 24 **Litho.** ***Perf. 14½x14***

626	A235	10c multicolored	.25	.25
627	A235	20c multicolored	.25	.25
628	A235	25c multicolored	.25	.25
629	A235	40c multicolored	.30	.25
		Nos. 626-629 (4)	1.05	1.00

Manganese — A236

1984, June 8 **Litho.** ***Perf. 14x14½***

630	A236	11c shown	.35	.25
631	A236	20c Chromium	.40	.30
632	A236	25c Vanadium	.50	.35
633	A236	30c Titanium	.65	.40
		Nos. 630-633 (4)	1.90	1.30

Bloukrans River Bridge A237

25c, Durban 4-level Bridge Interchange. 30c, Mfolozi Railroad Bridge. 45c, Gouritz River Bridge.

1984, Aug. 24

634	A237	11c shown	.45	.25
635	A237	25c multicolored	.55	.30
636	A237	30c multicolored	.65	.45
637	A237	45c multicolored	.90	.40
		Nos. 634-637 (4)	2.55	1.40

New Constitution A238

No. 638, Preamble (English). No. 639, Preamble (Africaans). No. 640, Symbolic pillars, anthem. No. 641, Arms.

1984, Sept. 3 Litho. *Perf. 14x14½*

638	A238	11c multicolored	.35	.25
639	A238	11c multicolored	.35	.25
a.		Pair, #638-639	.75	.75
640	A238	25c multicolored	.55	.55
641	A238	30c multicolored	.60	.60
		Nos. 638-641 (4)	1.85	1.65

Military Medals — A239

11c, Pro Patria. 25c, De Wet. 30c, John Chard Decoration. 45c, Honoris Crux.

1984, Nov. 9 *Perf. 14½x14*

642	A239	11c multi	.25	.25
643	A239	25c multi	.25	.25
644	A239	30c multi	.35	.25
645	A239	45c multi	.40	.25
a.		Miniature sheet of 4, #642-645	1.20	1.20
		Nos. 642-645 (4)	1.25	1.00

Pres. Pieter Willem Botha (b. 1916) — A240

1984, Nov. 2 Litho. *Perf. 14x14½*

646	A240	11c multicolored	.30	.25
647	A240	25c multicolored	.45	.25

Frans David Oerder, Painter (1867-1944) A241

11c, Reflections. 25c, Ladies in a Garden. 30c, Still-Life with Lobster. 50c, Still-Life with Marigolds.

1985, Feb. 22 Litho. *Perf. 14½x14*

648	A241	11c multicolored	.25	.25
649	A241	25c multicolored	.25	.25
650	A241	30c multicolored	.30	.25
651	A241	50c multicolored	.35	.25
a.		Souvenir sheet of 4, #648-651	1.25	1.25
		Nos. 648-651 (4)	1.15	1.00

Cape Parliament Cent. A242

12c, Parliament. 25c, Speaker's chair. 30c, The National Convention, by Edward Roworth. 50c, South African arms.

1985, May 15 Litho.

652	A242	12c multicolored	.25	.25
653	A242	25c multicolored	.25	.25
654	A242	30c multicolored	.30	.25
655	A242	50c multicolored	.40	.30
		Nos. 652-655 (4)	1.20	1.05

Indigenous Flowers — A243

1985, Aug. 23 Litho. *Perf. 14½x14*

656	A243	12c Freesia	.25	.25
657	A243	25c Nerine	.30	.25
658	A243	30c Ixia	.35	.25
659	A243	50c Gladiolus	.40	.40
		Nos. 656-659 (4)	1.30	1.15

Cape Silver — A244

1985, Nov. 5 *Perf. 14½x14, 14x14½*

660	A244	12c Sugar bowl, horiz.	.25	.25
661	A244	25c Tea pot, horiz.	.30	.25
662	A244	30c Goblet	.35	.25
663	A244	50c Coffee pot	.40	.35
		Nos. 660-663 (4)	1.30	1.10

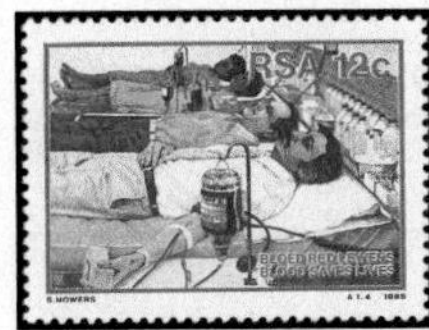

Blood Transfusion Services A245

1986, Feb. 20 *Perf. 14½x14*

664	A245	12c Blood donation	.30	.25
665	A245	20c Transfusion	.65	.30
666	A245	25c Surgery	.85	.50
667	A245	30c Emergency aid	1.00	.80
		Nos. 664-667 (4)	2.80	1.85

Republic of South Africa, 25th Anniv. A246

1986, May 30 Litho. *Perf. 14x14½*

668	A246	14c Text in Afrikaans	.65	.25
669	A246	14c Text in English	.65	.25
a.		Pair, #668-669	1.50	1.50

Cultural Heritage — A247

Restoration projects: 14c, Drostdyhof, Free Street, Graaff-Reinet, 19th cent. 20c, Pilgrim's Rest, Eastern Transvaal, 1873. 25c, J.T. Strapp and Son importers, c. 1893, Bethlehem. 30c, Palmdene, c. 1897, Pietermaritzburg.

1986, Aug. 14 *Perf. 14½x14*

670	A247	14c multicolored	.30	.25
671	A247	20c multicolored	.50	.30
672	A247	25c multicolored	.60	.40
673	A247	30c multicolored	.70	.50
		Nos. 670-673 (4)	2.10	1.45

Johannesburg, Cent. — A248

Discovery of Gold in Roodepoort, Cent. — A249

14c, Johannesburg, 1886. 20c, Gold mine. 25c, Johannesburg, 1986. 30c, Gold.

1986, Sept. 25 *Perf. 14x14½*

674	A248	14c multicolored	.40	.30
675	A249	20c multicolored	1.00	.75
676	A248	25c multicolored	.90	.65
677	A249	30c multicolored	1.50	1.00
a.		Souvenir sheet of 1	1.90	1.90
		Nos. 674-677 (4)	3.80	2.70

No. 677a for Johannesburg stamp exhibition. Sold for 50c.

Pearl Mountain — A250

20c, The Column, Drakensburg. 25c, Maltese Cross, Cedarberg. 30c, Bourke's Luck Potholes.

1986, Nov. 20 Litho. *Perf. 14x14½*

678	A250	14c multicolored	.40	.35
679	A250	20c multicolored	.65	.60
680	A250	25c multicolored	.75	.70
681	A250	30c multicolored	.85	.80
		Nos. 678-681 (4)	2.65	2.45

Beetles — A251

No. 690, Chaetodera regalis. No. 691, Trichostetha fascicularis. No. 692, Julodis viridipes. No. 693, Ceroplesis militaris.

1987, Mar. 6 Litho. *Perf. 14x14½*

690	A251	14c multicolored	.45	.40
691	A251	20c multicolored	.65	.60
692	A251	25c multicolored	.75	.70
693	A251	30c multicolored	.90	.85
		Nos. 690-693 (4)	2.75	2.55

Petroglyphs A252

16c, Eland, Sebaaieni Cave. 20c, Leaping lion, Clocolan. 25c, Black wildebeest, uMhlwazini Valley. 30c, San dance, Floukraal.

1987, June 4 *Perf. 14½x14*

694	A252	16c multi	.50	.45
695	A252	20c multi	.75	.70
696	A252	25c multi	.85	.80
697	A252	30c multi	.95	.90
		Nos. 694-697 (4)	3.05	2.85

Paarl, 300th Anniv. A253

16c, Oude Pastorie. 20c, Winegrowing. 25c, Wagon-building. 30c, KWV Cathedral Cellar.

1987, Sept. 3

698	A253	16c multi	.25	.35
699	A253	20c multi	.35	.30
700	A253	25c multi	.45	.40
701	A253	30c multi	.55	.50
		Nos. 698-701 (4)	1.60	1.55

A souvenir sheet of one, No. 701, has decorative margin picturing emblem of the natl. philatelic exhibition at Paarl, Sept. 16-19. Sold for 50c. Value $3.

Map, "The Bible" in 76 Languages — A254

Religious Paintings by Rembrandt A255

Designs: 30c, *Belshazzar's Feast.* 50c, *St. Matthew and the Angel,* vert.

Perf. 14x14½, 14½x14 (30c)

1987, Nov. 19

702	A254	16c shown	.30	.25
703	A255	30c shown	.55	.50
704	A255	50c multicolored	.85	.85
		Nos. 702-704 (3)	1.70	1.60

Bible Society of South Africa.

A 40c stamp was prepared and sent to post offices, but was not issued. Some were sold contrary to the withdrawal order, and used examples are known. Value, mint or used, $500.

For surcharge see No. B13.

Discovery of the Cape of Good Hope by Bartolomeu Dias — A256

Designs: 16c, Dias, astrolabe, Cape of Good Hope. 30c, Kwaaihoek Memorial. 40c, Caravels, 1488. 50c, Martellus Map, c. 1489.

1988, Feb. 3 *Perf. 14½x14*

706	A256	16c multicolored	.50	.25
707	A256	30c multicolored	.70	.65
708	A256	40c multicolored	1.00	.90
709	A256	50c multicolored	1.10	1.10
		Nos. 706-709 (4)	3.30	2.90

A souvenir sheet of one, No. 709, has decorative margin picturing emblem of the natl. philatelic exhibition held at Pietermaritzburg, Nov. 22-27. Sold for 70c. Value $3.50.

For surcharge see No. B14.

French Huguenot Settlement of the Cape, 300th Anniv. — A257

16c, Memorial, Franschhoek. 30c, Map of France. 40c, French-Dutch Bible, 1672. 50c, St. Bartholomew's Day Massacre, 1572.

1988, Apr. 13 *Perf. 14x14½*

710	A257	16c multicolored	.30	.25
711	A257	30c multicolored	.65	.65
712	A257	40c multicolored	.70	.70
713	A257	50c multicolored	.80	.80
		Nos. 710-713 (4)	2.45	2.40

For surcharges see Nos. B15-B18.

Lighthouses A258

16c, Pelican Point, 1932. 30c, Groenpunt, 1824. 40c, Agulhas, 1849. 50c, Umhlanga Rocks, 1954.

1988, June 9 ***Perf. 14½x14***

714	A258 16c multi		.60	.25
715	A258 30c multi		.80	.80
716	A258 40c multi		.90	.90
717	A258 50c multi		1.40	1.40
a.	Souvenir sheet of 4, #714-717		5.50	5.50
	Nos. 714-717 (4)		3.70	3.35

"Standardised Mail"
"STANDARD POSTAGE"
Stamps inscribed thus were sold for the amount shown in ( ) on date of issue.

Succulents A259

1c, Huernia zebrina. 2c, Euphorbia symmetrica. 5c, Lithops dorotheae. 7c, Gibbaeum newbrownii. 10c, Didymaotus lapidiformis. 16c, Vanheerdea divergens. 18c, Faucaria tigrina. 20c, Conophytum mundum. 21c, Gasteria armstrongii. 25c, Cheiridopsis pecularis. 30c, Tavaresia barklyi. 35c, Dinteranthus wilmotianus. 40c, Frithia pulchra. (45c), Stapelia grandiflora. 50c, Lapidaria margaretae. 90c, Dioscorea elephantipes. 1r, Trichocaulon cactiforme. 2r, Crassula columnaris. 5r, Anacampseros albissima.

No. 754, Adromischus marianiae. No. 755, Titanopsis calcarea. No. 756, Dactylopsis digitata. No. 757, Pleiospilos bolusii.

1988-93 **Litho.** ***Perf. 14x14½***

735	A259	1c multi	.25	.25
736	A259	2c multi	.25	.25
737	A259	5c multi	.25	.25
738	A259	7c multi	.25	.25
739	A259	10c multi	.25	.25
740	A259	16c multi	.25	.25
741	A259	18c multi	.25	.25
742	A259	20c multi	.25	.25
743	A259	21c multi	.25	.25
744	A259	25c multi	.25	.25
745	A259	30c multi	.25	.25
a.	Strip, 2 ea 1c, 2c, 5c, 7c, 30c		*12.00*	
746	A259	35c multi	.25	.25
747	A259	40c multi	.30	.25
748	A259	(45c) multi	.40	.25
749	A259	50c multi	.45	.30
750	A259	90c multi	.55	.45
751	A259	1r multi	.80	.40
752	A259	2r multi	1.00	.50
753	A259	5r multi	2.50	1.25
	Nos. 735-753 (19)		9.00	6.40

Coil Stamps
Photo.
Perf. 14 Horiz.

754	A259	1c multi	1.10	1.10
755	A259	2c multi	.40	.40
756	A259	5c multi	.40	.40
757	A259	10c multi	.55	.55
	Nos. 754-757 (4)		2.45	2.45

Issued: 18c, 4/1/89; 5r, 3/1/90; 21c, 4/2/90; #748, 4/1/93; others, 9/1/88.

Map and Settlers — A260

Exodus, Tapestry by W.H. Coetzer Studio — A261

Crossing the Drakensburg, Tapestry by Coetzer Studio — A262

Church of the Vow, Pietermaritzburg — A263

Perf. 14x14½, 14½x14 (50c)
1988, Nov. 21 **Litho.**

758	A260 16c multicolored	.75	.25
759	A261 30c multicolored	.90	.75
760	A262 40c multicolored	1.10	1.00
761	A263 50c multicolored	1.25	1.25
	Nos. 758-761 (4)	4.00	3.25

The Great Trek, 150th anniv.

Discovery of a Living Specimen of the Coelacanth, 50th Anniv. A264

Designs: 16c, *Latimeria chalumnae.* 30c, J. L. B. Smith, Margaret Courtenay-Latimer. 40c, Smith Institute of Ichthyology, Grahamstown. 50c, Fish, GEO two-man research submarine.

1989, Feb. 9 ***Perf. 14½x14***

762	A264 16c multicolored	.90	.35
763	A264 30c multicolored	1.25	1.25
764	A264 40c multicolored	1.60	1.60
765	A264 50c multicolored	1.75	1.75
a.	Souvenir sheet of 1	7.00	7.00
b.	Souvenir sheet of 2	1.25	1.25
	Nos. 762-765 (4)	5.50	4.95

No. 765a has decorative margin picturing emblem of the natl. philatelic exhibition WANDERERS 101, held Sept. 6-9. Sold for 1.50r.

No. 765b was issued 6/97, sold for 1r and is inscribed for Old Mutual Environmental Education Center in sheet margin.

Soil Conservation Campaign of the Natl. Grazing Strategy — A265

1989, May 3 ***Perf. 14x14½***

766	A265 18c Desertification	.45	.25
767	A265 30c Eroded gullies	.65	.65
768	A265 40c Barrage	.70	.70
769	A265 50c Verdant plain	1.00	1.00
	Nos. 766-769 (4)	2.80	2.60

Natl. Rugby Board, Cent. A266

Springboks, foreign team emblems, match scenes: 18c, France, 1980. 30c, Australia, 1963. 40c, New Zealand, 1937. 50c, British Isles, 1896.

1989, June 22

770	A266 18c multi	.70	.30
771	A266 30c multi	.90	.60
772	A266 40c multi	1.00	.90
773	A266 50c multi	1.25	1.25
	Nos. 770-773 (4)	3.85	3.05

Paintings by Jacob Hendrik Pierneef (1886-1957) A267

No. 774, Composition in Blue, 1928. No. 775, Zanzibar, 1926. No. 776, The Bushveld, 1949. No. 777, Cape Homestead, 1942.

1989, Aug. 3 ***Perf. 14½x14***

774	A267 18c multicolored	.35	.25
775	A267 30c multicolored	.65	.35
776	A267 40c multicolored	.80	.50
777	A267 50c multicolored	1.00	.75
a.	Souvenir sheet of 4, #774-777	2.75	2.75
	Nos. 774-777 (4)	2.80	1.85

Election of Pres. Frederik Willem de Klerk, Aug. 15 — A268

1989, Sept. 20 ***Perf. 14x14½***

778	A268 18c shown	.40	.25
779	A268 45c Portrait, diff.	.80	.80

Fossil Fuels, Nuclear and Thermal Power A269

18c, SOEKOR gas project, Mossel Bay. 30c, SASOL coal conversion plant. 40c, Koeberg nuclear power plant. 50c, ESKOM thermal power station.

1989, Oct. 19

780	A269 18c multicolored	.40	.25
781	A269 30c multicolored	.70	.50
782	A269 40c multicolored	.75	.60
783	A269 50c multicolored	.95	.90
	Nos. 780-783 (4)	2.80	2.25

Cooperation in Southern Africa — A270

Maps and: 18c, Cahora Bassa hydroelectric power project. 30c, Railway network. 40c, Lesotho Highlands water project. 50c, Veterinary care.

1990, Feb. 15 ***Perf. 14½x14***
Size of 18c, 40c: 68x26mm

784	A270 18c multicolored	.70	.25
785	A270 30c multicolored	.90	.65
786	A270 40c multicolored	1.10	1.10
787	A270 50c multicolored	1.25	1.25
a.	Miniature sheet of 4, #784-787	4.00	4.00
	Nos. 784-787 (4)	3.95	3.25

Stamp Day — A271

Stamps on stamps: a, Great Britain #1. b, Cape of Good Hope #2. c, Natal #4. d, Orange River Colony #10. e, Transvaal #3.

1990, May 12 **Litho.**

788	Strip of 5	2.25	2.25
a.-e.	A271 21c any single	.40	.30

Penny Black, 150th anniv.

Birds — A272

Designs: 21c, Tauraco corythaix. 35c, Cossypha natalensis. 40c, Mirafra africana. 50c, Telophorus zeylonus.

1990, Aug. 2 **Litho.** ***Perf. 14x14½***

789	A272 21c multicolored	.60	.25
790	A272 35c multicolored	.90	.65
791	A272 40c multicolored	1.10	1.00
792	A272 50c multicolored	1.40	1.40
	Nos. 789-792 (4)	4.00	3.30

A souvenir sheet of 1 #792 was sold by the Philatelic Foundation of South Africa. Value $4.50.

Karoo Landscape, Near Britstown A273

Tourism: #794, Camps Bay, Cape Peninsula. #795, Giraffes, Kruger Natl. Park. #796, Boschendal homestead, Drakenstein.

1990, Nov. 1 **Litho.** ***Perf. 14½x14***

793	A273 50c multicolored	.75	.75
794	A273 50c multicolored	.75	.75
795	A273 50c multicolored	.75	.75
796	A273 50c multicolored	.75	.75
a.	Block of 4, #793-796	4.25	4.25

A274

National Decorations: No. 797, Woltemade Cross for Bravery. No. 798, Order of the Southern Cross. No. 799, Order of the Star of South Africa. No. 800, Order for Meritorious Service. No. 801, Order of Good Hope.

1990, Dec. 6

797	A274 21c multicolored	.30	.25
798	A274 21c multicolored	.30	.25
799	A274 21c multicolored	.30	.25
800	A274 21c multicolored	.30	.25
801	A274 21c multicolored	.30	.25
a.	Souv. sheet of 5, #797-801	2.25	2.25
b.	Strip of 5, #797-801	2.00	2.00

A275

Animal Breeding: a, Boer horse. b, Bonsmara cattle. c, Dorper sheep. d, Ridgeback dog. e, Putterie racing pigeon.

1991, Feb. 21 **Litho.**

802	Strip of 5	3.50	3.50
a.-e.	A275 21c Any single	.50	.50

Achievements — A276

Designs: 25c, First heart transplant, vert. 40c, Matimba power plant. 50c, Dolos breakwater blocks. 60c, Western Deep Levels Gold Mine, world's deepest mine, vert.

Perf. 14½x14 (25c, 60c), 14x14½ (40c, 50c, #806a)

1991, May 30 **Litho.**

803	A276	25c multicolored	.30	.25
804	A276	40c multicolored	.45	.35
805	A276	50c multicolored	.55	.55
806	A276	60c multicolored	.65	.65
a.		Souvenir sheet of 1	2.25	2.25
		Nos. 803-806 (4)	1.95	1.80

30th anniv. of Republic of South Africa.

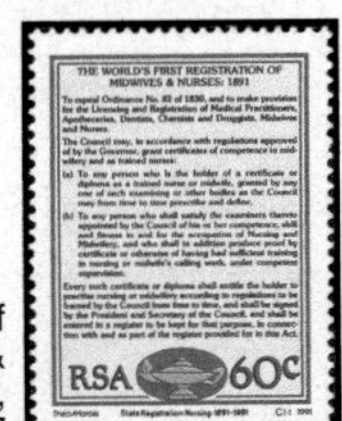

1st Registration of Nurses & Midwives, Cent. — A277

1991, Aug. 15 **Litho.** ***Perf. 14x14½***

807	A277	60c multicolored	.75	.75

Creation of South African Post Office Ltd. — A278

1991, Oct. 1 **Litho.**

808		27c Post office	.35	.25
809		27c Telkom SA Ltd.	.35	.25
a.	A278	Pair, #808-809	1.25	1.25

South African Scientists A279

Designs: 27c, Sir Arnold Theiler (1867-1936), veterinarian. 45c, Sir Basil Schonland (1896-1972), physicist. 65c, Dr. Robert Broom (1866-1951), paleontologist. 85c, Dr. Alexander L. du Toit (1878-1948), geologist.

1991, Oct. 9 ***Perf. 14½x14***

810	A279	27c multicolored	.40	.25
811	A279	45c multicolored	.85	.85
812	A279	65c multicolored	1.25	1.25
813	A279	85c multicolored	1.50	1.50
		Nos. 810-813 (4)	4.00	3.85

Antarctic Treaty, 30th Anniv. A280

27c, SA Agulhas, penguins. 65c, Meteorological chart.

1991, Dec. 5 **Litho.**

814	A280	27c multicolored	1.25	.25
815	A280	65c multicolored	2.00	1.25

Conservation — A281

1992, Feb. 6 **Litho.** ***Perf. 14x14½***

816	A281	27c Prevent erosion	.60	.25
817	A281	65c Water pollution	1.40	1.25
818	A281	85c Air pollution	1.60	1.60
		Nos. 816-818 (3)	3.60	3.10

A souvenir sheet of 1 #817 was sold by Intersapa. Value $4.

A282

Designs depicting history of postal stones: No. 819, Sailing ships at Table Bay. No. 820, Sailors going ashore at Aguada de Saldanha. No. 821, Sailors discovering postal stone near Versse River. No. 822, Finding letters under postal stones. No. 823, Reading news from other mariners.

1992, May 9 **Litho.** ***Perf. 14x14½***

819	A282	35c multicolored	.45	.45
820	A282	35c multicolored	.45	.45
821	A282	35c multicolored	.45	.45
822	A282	35c multicolored	.45	.45
823	A282	35c multicolored	.45	.45
a.		Strip of 5, #819-823	3.25	3.25

Stamp Day.

A283

Antique Cape Furniture: No. 824, Queen Anne settee, c. 1750-70. No. 825, Stinkwood settee, c. 1800. No. 826, Canopy bed, c. 1800, vert. No. 827, Rocking cradle, 19th cent. No. 828, Waterbutt, c. 1800, vert. No. 829, Flemish style cabinet, c. 1700, vert. No. 830, Armoire, c. 1780-1790, vert. No. 831, Church chair, late 17th cent, vert. No. 832, Tub chair, c. 1770-1790, vert. No. 833, Bible desk, c. 1770, vert.

Perf. 14½x14, 14x14½

1992, July 9 **Litho.**

824	A283	35c multicolored	.40	.40
825	A283	35c multicolored	.40	.40
826	A283	35c multicolored	.40	.40
827	A283	35c multicolored	.40	.40
828	A283	35c multicolored	.40	.40
829	A283	35c multicolored	.40	.40
830	A283	35c multicolored	.40	.40
831	A283	35c multicolored	.40	.40
832	A283	35c multicolored	.40	.40
833	A283	35c multicolored	.40	.40
a.		Miniature sheet of 10, #824-833	5.00	5.00

Sports A284

No. 834, Formula 1 Grand Prix. No. 835, Soccer. No. 836, Paris-le Cap Rally. No. 837, Track. No. 838, Rugby. No. 839, Cricket.

1992, July 24 ***Perf. 14x14½***

834	A284	35c multicolored	.35	.25
835	A284	35c multicolored	.35	.25
836	A284	55c multicolored	.50	.40
837	A284	70c multicolored	.70	.60
838	A284	90c multicolored	.90	.90
839	A284	1.05r multicolored	1.25	1.25
a.		Souvenir sheet of 6, #834-839	4.50	4.50
		Nos. 834-839 (6)	4.05	3.65

A285

35c, Women's Monument. 70c, Sekupu Player. 90c, The Hunter. 1.05r, Postman Lehman.

1992, Oct. 8 **Litho.** ***Perf. 14½x14***

840	A285	35c multi	.40	.30
841	A285	70c multi	.75	.60
842	A285	90c multi	.90	.80
843	A285	1.05r multi	1.10	.90
a.		Souvenir sheet of 4, #840-843	3.25	3.25
		Nos. 840-843 (4)	3.15	2.60

Sculptures by Anton van Wouw (1862-1945). No. 843a sold for 3.30r.

South African Harbors A286

1993, Jan. 28 **Litho.**

844	A286	35c Walvis Bay	.35	.30
845	A286	55c East London	.65	.45
846	A286	70c Port Elizabeth	.85	.60
847	A286	90c Cape Town	1.00	.80
848	A286	1.05r Durban	1.25	.90
a.		Souv. sheet, #844-848 + label	3.25	3.25
		Nos. 844-848 (5)	4.10	3.05

No. 848a sold for 3.90r.

A287

Aircraft: a, Bristol Boxkite, 1907. b, Voisin, 1909. c, Bleriot XI, 1911. d, Paterson No. 2 biplane, 1913. e, Henri Farman F.27, 1915. f, BE2e, 1918. g, Vickers Vimy Silver Queen, 1920. h, SE-5a, 1921. i, Avro 504K, 1921. j, Armstrong-Whitworth Atalanta, 1930. k, DH66 Hercules, 1931. l, Westland Wapiti, 1931. m, Junkers F.13, 1932. n, Handley Page HP-42, 1933. o, Junkers Ju52/3m, 1934. p, Junkers Ju86, 1936. q, Hawker Hartbees, 1936. r, Short Empire flying boat Canopus, 1937. s, Miles Master II and Airspeed AS-10 Oxford, 1940. t, Harvard Mk IIa, 1942. u, Short Sunderland, 1945. v, Avro York, 1946. w, Douglas DC-7B, 1955. x, Sikorsky S-55C, 1956. y, Boeing 707-344, 1959.

Miniature Sheet of 25

1993, May 7 **Litho.** ***Perf. 14x14½***

849	A287	45c #a.-y.	14.00	14.00

A souvenir sheet containing #849a, 849y was sold by the Philatelic Foundation of South Africa.

A288

Endangered Fauna: 1c, Heleophryne rosei. 2c, Bradypodion taeniabronchum. 5c, Cordylus giganteus. 10c, Psammobates geometricus. 20c, Atelerix frontalis. 40c, Bunolagus monticularis. (45c), Diceros bicornis. 50c, Cercopithecus mitis. 55c, Proteles cristatus. 60c, Lycaon pictus. 70c, Hippotragus equinus. 75c, Poecilogale albinucha. 80c, Otis kori. 85c, Serinus citrinipectus. 90c, Spheniscus demersus. 1r, Grus carunculatus. 2r, Hirundo atrocaerulea. 5r, Polemaetus bellicosus. 10r, Terathopius ecaudatus.

Inscriptions in Latin

1993-95 **Litho.** ***Perf. 14x14½***

850	A288	1c multicolored	.25	.25
851	A288	2c multicolored	.25	.25
852	A288	5c multicolored	.25	.25
853	A288	10c multicolored	.25	.25
854	A288	20c multicolored	.25	.25
a.		Strip, 1c, 2 ea 2c, 20c	*1.10*	
b.		Strip, 20c, 2 ea 5c, 10c	*1.10*	
c.		Strip, 20c, 2 each 5c, 10c, perf. 14½ vert.	*1.50*	
855	A288	40c multicolored	.30	.25
856	A288	(45c) multicolored	.30	.25
857	A288	50c multicolored	.30	.25
a.		Strip, #850, 852, 857, 2 #851, perf. 14½ vert.	2.25	
858	A288	55c multicolored	.30	.25
859	A288	60c multicolored	.35	.25
860	A288	70c multicolored	.40	.25
861	A288	75c multicolored	.45	.25
862	A288	80c multicolored	.50	.25
862A	A288	85c multicolored	.55	.25
863	A288	90c multicolored	.60	.30
a.		Booklet pane of 10	*10.00*	—
		Complete booklet, #863a	*12.00*	
864	A288	1r multicolored	.75	.30
865	A288	2r multicolored	1.25	.50
866	A288	5r multicolored	2.25	.60
867	A288	10r multicolored	4.25	1.50
		Nos. 850-867 (19)	13.80	6.70

#857a exists with tab showing Reader's Digest emblem in either red or black; also in different order with emblem in blue.

Issued: #854b, 8/24/94; #854c, 10/94; #857a, 9/1/95; 85c, 10/2/95; #863a, 1995; others, 9/3/93.

See designs A336 and A343 (no frames).

Wildlife Type with English Inscriptions

Designs: 1c, Table Mountain ghost frog. 2c, Smith's dwarf chameleon. 10c, Geometric tortoise. 20c, Southern African hedgehog. 40c, Riverine rabbit. (45c), Black rhinoceros. 50c, Samango monkey. 60c, Cape hunting dog. 70c, Roan antelope. 90c, Jackass penguin. 1r, Wattled crane. 2r, Blue swallow. 5r, Martial eagle. 20r, Fish Eagle.

Perf. 14x14¼, 14 Vert. on 1 or 2 sides (1c, 2c, 10c, 55c), 13x14½ (#867F)

1996-98 **Litho.**

867A	A288	1c multicolored	.25	.25
867B	A288	2c multicolored	.25	.25
867C	A288	10c multicolored	.25	.25
867D	A288	20c multicolored	.25	.25
867E	A288	40c multicolored	.25	.25
867F	A288	(45c) multicolored	.40	.25
n.		Booklet pane of 10	3.00	
		Complete booklet, #867Fn	3.00	
o.		Souvenir sheet of 1	.55	.55
867G	A288	50c multicolored	.25	.25
867H	A288	55c multicolored	.60	.60
p.		Strip of 5, 1c, 10c, 55c, 2 2c, perf 14 vert.	1.10	
867I	A288	70c multicolored	.25	.25
867J	A288	90c multicolored	.45	.25
867K	A288	1r multicolored	.45	.25
867L	A288	2r multicolored	1.00	.25
867M	A288	5r multicolored	2.00	.90

Perf. 14x14¼ Syncopated

867Q	A288	20c multicolored	.25	.25
867R	A288	(45c) multicolored	.60	.45
867S	A288	50c multicolored	.50	.25
867T	A288	60c multicolored	.25	.25
w.		With English inscription superimposed over Latin inscription	25.00	25.00
867U	A288	1r multicolored	3.50	.40

Size: 34x25mm

Perf. 14¾ Syncopated

867V	A288	20r multiicolored	9.50	4.75

No. 867Fn is inscribed in sheet margin for ExpoScience Internationale '97, and sold for 1r.

No. 867Hp has tab showing Reader's Digest emblem and release date in either green or orange.

Issued: No. 867Hp, 8/1; No. 867F, 7/7/97.

See Nos. C6A-C6E.

First Postal Services in South Africa, 190th Anniv. A289

Designs: 45c, Dragoons, Cape Town-False Bay Route. 65c, Ox train, Cape Town-Stellenbosch. 85c, Khoi-Khoin runners. 1.05r, Post riders, Cape Town-eastern districts.

1993, Oct. 8 ***Perf. 14x14½***

868	A289	45c multicolored	.45	.25
869	A289	65c multicolored	.65	.65
870	A289	85c multicolored	.85	.85
871	A289	1.05r multicolored	1.10	1.10
		Nos. 868-871 (4)	3.05	2.85

Tourism A290

a, Namaqualand. b, North Beach, Durban. c, Lion. d, Apple Express. e, Oryx gazella.

1993, Nov. 12 Litho. *Perf. 14½x14*

872 Strip of 5 3.25 3.25
a.-e. A290 85c Any single .50 .50

Export Fruits A291

1994, Jan. 28 Litho. *Perf. 14½x14*

873 A291 85c Grapes .55 .45
874 A291 90c Apples .60 .50
875 A291 1.05r Plums .70 .60
876 A291 1.25r Oranges .85 .75
877 A291 1.40r Avocados .95 .85
Nos. 873-877 (5) 3.65 3.15

A souvenir sheet of 1 #873 was sold for 3r by the Philatelic Foundation of South Africa. Value $3.

Peace and Goodwill — A292

Childrens' drawings: 45c, Smiling faces, by Nicole Davies. 70c, Dove flying toward olive tree, by Robynne Lawrie. 95c, Three girls, dove, scattered cartridge cases, by Batami Nothmann. 1.15r, Faces surrounding "peace," by Karen Uys.

1994, Apr. 8 Litho. *Perf. 14½x14*

878 A292 45c multicolored .35 .35
879 A292 70c multicolored .50 .50
880 A292 95c multicolored .65 .65
881 A292 1.15r multicolored .80 .80
a. Souvenir sheet of 1 2.50 2.50
Nos. 878-881 (4) 2.30 2.30

No. 881a was issued 8/97, sold for 1.15r and is inscribed "Chernobyl's Children, a decade later 1986-1996" in margin.

Inauguration of Pres. Nelson Mandela — A293

Perf. 14x14½, 14½x14

1994, May 10 Litho.

882 A293 45c shown .55 .30
883 A293 70c Anthems, horiz. .90 .50
884 A293 95c Flag, horiz. 1.40 1.40
885 A293 1.15r Union Bldgs., horiz. 1.60 1.60
Nos. 882-885 (4) 4.45 3.80

Tugboats — A294

1994, May 13 *Perf. 14½x14*

886 A294 45c TS McEwen .50 .40
887 A294 70c Sir William Hoy .70 .65
888 A294 95c Sir Charles Elliott .95 .90
889 A294 1.15r Eland 1.25 1.00
890 A294 1.35r Pioneer 1.40 1.25
a. Souvenir sheet of 5, #886-890 4.50 4.50
Nos. 886-890 (5) 4.80 4.20

Our Family — A295

Children's paintings: a, Mother Hands Out Work (C1.5). b, My Friends and I at Play (C2.5). c, Family Life (C3.5). d, Sunday in Church (C4.5). e, I Visit My Brother in the Hospital (C5.5).

1994, July 10 Litho. *Perf. 14x14½*

891 Strip of 5 2.25 2.25
a.-e. A295 45c Any single .35 .35

Stamp Day — A296

1994, Sept. 30 Litho. *Perf. 14*

892 A296 50c Bulk mail .40 .40
893 A296 70c Proof of delivery .55 .55
894 A296 95c Registered mail .75 .75
895 A296 1.15r Express delivery .85 .85
Nos. 892-895 (4) 2.55 2.55

Heather — A297

Designs: a, Erica tenuifolia. b, Erica urna-viridis. c, Erica decora. d, Erica aristata. e, Erica dichrus.

1994, Nov. 18 Litho. *Perf. 14*

896 Strip of 5 3.75 3.75
a.-e. A297 95c Any single .55 .55

Tourism — A298

#897, Phacochoerus aethiopicus, Eastern, Transvaal Province. #898, Lost City, Sun City, North West Province. #899, Ceratotherium simum, KwaZulu/Natal Province. #900, Waterfront, Cape Town, Western Cape Province. #901, Adansonia digitata, Northern Transvaal Province. #902, Highland Route, Free State. #903, Augrabies Falls, Northern Cape Province. #904, Addo Elephant Natl. Park, Eastern Cape Province. #905, Union Buildings, Pretoria, Gauteng.

1995-97 Litho. *Perf. 14*

897 A298 50c multicolored .50 .50
898 A298 50c multicolored .50 .50
899 A298 (60c) multicolored .60 .60
900 A298 (60c) multicolored .60 .60
901 A298 (60c) multicolored .60 .60
a. #901 + label, perf. 14 on one side 2.00 2.00
b. Souvenir sheet of 1 3.00 3.00
902 A298 (60c) multicolored .60 .60
903 A298 (60c) multicolored .60 .60
904 A298 (60c) multicolored .60 .60
905 A298 (60c) multicolored .60 .60
a. Strip of 5, #901-905 3.75 3.75
Nos. 897-905 (9) 5.20 5.20

#901a sold for 70c; #901b for 1.10r on date of issue.

Issued: #897, 1/18; #898, 2/15; #899, 4/28; #900, 5/12; #901-905, 6/30; #901a, 2/97; #901b 8/97.

South African Airforce, 75th Anniv. — A299

DeHavilland DH-9 biplane, Cheetah D fighter.

1995, Feb. 1 Litho. *Perf. 14*

906 A299 50c multicolored .60 .60

First Trans-Africa Flight, 75th Anniv. — A300

Vickers Vimy bomber Silver Queen, map of route.

1995, Feb. 1

907 A300 95c multicolored 1.25 1.25

South Africa, 1995 Rugby World Cup Champions A301

Designs: No. 908, Shown. No. 909, Player running with ball, vert. No. 910, Player holding trophy, vert. No. 911, Like #908, World Champions. No. 912, Scrum, two players.

1995 Litho. *Perf. 14*

908 A301 (60c) multicolored .30 .30
a. Perf. 14 horiz. .30 .30
909 A301 (60c) multicolored .30 .30
a. Souvenir sheet of 1 1.25 1.25
b. Perf. 14 vert. .30 .30
c. Booklet pane, 5 each #908a, 909b 5.25
Complete booklet, #909c 5.25
d. Booklet pane, 10 #909b 5.25
Complete booklet, #909d 5.25
910 A301 (60c) multicolored .30 .30
911 A301 (60c) multicolored .30 .30

Size: 68x26mm

912 A301 1.15r multicolored .55 .55
Nos. 908-912 (5) 1.75 1.75

Issued: #910-911, 6/28; others 5/25.

CSIR (Council for Scientific and Industrial Research), 50th Anniv. A302

1995, June 15

913 A302 (60c) Purifying water .60 .60

Marine Science in South Africa, Cent. A303

1995, Aug. 25 Litho. *Perf. 14*

914 A303 (60c) Dr. JDF Gilchrist .60 .60

Souvenir Sheet

Singapore '95 — A304

1995, Sept. 1

915 A304 (60c) multicolored 1.00 1.00

Masakhane Campaign A305

1995 *Perf. 14x14¼*

916 A305 (60c) multicolored .60 .60
a. Booklet pane of 10 6.00
Complete booklet, No. 916a 6.00

Booklet Stamp

Size: 29x20mm

916B A305 (60c) multicolored .60 .60
c. Booklet pane of 10 6.00
Complete booklet, #916c 6.00

Issued: #916, 9/16; #916B, 12/1.

Visit of Pope John Paul II — A306

1995, Sept. 16 *Perf. 14*

917 A306 (60c) multicolored .90 .90

Mahatma Gandhi — A307

Designs: (60c), 1906 Photograph. 1.40r, Ghandhi in later years.

1995, Oct. 2

918 A307 (60c) dull violet .85 .85
a. Souvenir sheet of 1 1.25 1.25
919 A307 1.40r brown 1.90 1.90
a. Souvenir sheet of 1 2.40 2.40

No. 918a is inscribed in sheet margin for 50th anniv. of Congress Alliance for Democratic South Africa. Issued July 1997.

Design on stamp in No. 919a extends to perforations.

See India Nos. 1534-1535.

World Post Day — A308

1995

920 A308 (60c) multicolored .70 .70

Size: 65x60mm

Imperf

921 A308 5r multicolored 2.75 2.75

Stampex '95.

Issued: (60c), 10/9; 5r, 10/19.

UN, 50th Anniv. A309

1995, Oct. 24 Litho. *Perf. 14*

922 A309 (60c) multicolored .50 .50

Souvenir Sheet

UNESCO, 50th Anniv. — A310

1995, Oct. 24

923 A310 (60c) multicolored .50 .50

Shells — A311

No. 924, Afrivoluta priglei. No. 925, Lyria africana. No. 926, Marginella mosaica. No. 927, Conus pictus. No. 928, Gypreaea fultoni.

1995, Nov. 24

924 A311 (60c) multi .55 .55
925 A311 (60c) multi .55 .55
926 A311 (60c) multi .55 .55
927 A311 (60c) multi .55 .55
928 A311 (60c) multi .55 .55
a. Strip of 5, #924-928 2.75 2.75

A312

1996 African Cup of Nations Soccer Championships: Nos. 929-933, Various soccer plays, map of Africa.

No. 934, Player in traditional uniform.

1996, Jan. 8 Litho. *Perf. 14*

Color of "RSA"

929 A312 (60c) blue .60 .60
930 A312 (60c) yellow .60 .60
931 A312 (60c) red .60 .60
932 A312 (60c) gray .60 .60
933 A312 (60c) green .60 .60
a. Strip of 5, Nos. 929-933 3.00 3.00

Souvenir Sheet

934 A312 (1.15r) multicolored .70 .70

South African Victory in African Nations Soccer Championship — A312a

1996, Feb. 8 Litho. *Perf. 14½x14*

934A A312a (60c) multicolored .70 .70

City of Bloemfontein, 150th Anniv. — A313

1996, Mar. 28 Litho. *Perf. 14*

935 A313 (60c) multicolored .80 .80

Souvenir Sheet

New Year 1996 (Year of the Rat) — A313a

1996, May 18 Litho. *Perf. 14*

940D A313a 60c multicolored 1.00 1.00

CHINA '96.

Man in a Donkey Cart, by Gerard Sekoto (1913-93) — A314

Paintings: #942, 2r, Song of the Pick. #943, 2r, Yellow Houses, Sophiatown, 1940, vert.

1996, June 1 Litho. *Perf. 14*

941 A314 1r multicolored .60 .60
942 A314 2r multicolored 1.25 1.25

Souvenir Sheet

943 A314 2r multicolored 1.50 1.50

Youth Day — A315

1996, June 8

944 A315 (60c) multicolored .50 .50

Comrades Marathon, 75th Anniv. — A316

1996, June 8 Litho. *Perf. 14*

945 A316 (60c) multicolored .50 .50

Souvenir Sheet

Parliament Building, Toronto — A316a

1996, June 8 Litho. *Perf. 14*

945A A316a 2r multicolored 1.50 1.50

CAPEX '96.

A317

1996 Summer Olympic Games, Atlanta: No. 946: a, Cycling. b, Swimming. c, Boxing. d, Running. e, Pole vault.

1.40r, South African Olympic emblem.

1996, July 5 Litho. *Perf. 14½x14*

946 A317 (70c) Strip of 5, #a.-e. 2.40 2.40

Perf. 14

947 A317 1.40r multicolored .85 .85

No. 946 was issued in sheets of 10 stamps.

New Democratic Constitution — A318

Background color: a, Vermilion & multi. b, Deep blue & multi. c, Deep yellow & multi. d, Bright blue & multi. e, Red & multi.

1996, Aug. 1 Litho. *Perf. 14*

948 Strip of 5 2.50 2.50
a.-e. A318 (70c) any single .50 .50

South African Merchant Marine, 50th Anniv. — A319

Paintings of ships, by Peter Bilas: No. 949: a, Sea Pioneer. b, SA Winterberg.

No. 950: a, Langloof. b, SA Vaal.

2r, Constantia.

1996, Aug. 5 Litho. *Perf. 14*

949 A319 Pair 1.25 1.25
a.-b. (70c) any single .60 .60
950 A319 Pair 2.75 2.75
a.-b. 1.40r any single 1.25 1.25

Souvenir Sheet

950C A319 2r multicolored 1.50 1.50

No. 950C contains one 72x30mm stamp.

Natl. Women's Day — A320

1996, Aug. 9 Litho. *Perf. 14*

951 A320 70c multicolored .50 .50

World Post Day — A321

1996, Oct. 9

952 A321 70c multicolored .50 .50

Christmas — A322

1996, Oct. 9

953 A322 70c multicolored .50 .50

No. 953 exists in a privately produced souvenir, sold at 2r for charitable purposes.

Souvenir Sheet

Bloemfontein, 150th Natl. Stamp Show — A323

1996, Oct. 9 Litho. *Perf. 14½x14*

954 A323 2r multicolored 1.50 1.50

South African Nobel Laureates, Death Cent. of Alfred Nobel — A324

a, Max Theiler, medicine, 1951. b, Albert Luthuli, peace, 1960. c, Alfred Nobel (1833-96). d, Allan Cormack, medicine, 1979. e, Aaron Klug, chemistry, 1982. f, Desmond Tutu, peace, 1984. g, Nadine Gordimer, literature, 1991. h, Symbol for Nobel Prizes 1901-96. i, Nelson R. Mandela, peace, 1993. j, F.W. de Klerk, peace, 1993.

1996, Nov. 4

955 A324 (70c) Sheet of 10, #a.-j. 4.75 4.75
k. Souvenir sheet, #955c .60 .60

First Motor Car in South Africa, Cent. A325

1997, Jan. 4 Litho. *Perf. 14*
956 A325 (70c) multicolored 1.00 1.00

Souvenir Sheet

Hong Kong '97 — A326

Perf. 14 Syncopated
1997, Feb. 12 Litho.
957 A326 3r multicolored 2.50 2.50

Natl. Water Week and Water Day — A328

Save water for: No. 959, Farming. No. 960, Gardening. No. 961, Health. No. 962, Housing. No. 963, For all.

Perf. 14 Syncopated on 2 or 3 Sides
1997, Mar. 22 Litho.
Booklet Stamps
959 A328 (70c) multicolored .60 .60
960 A328 (70c) multicolored .60 .60
961 A328 (70c) multicolored .60 .60
962 A328 (70c) multicolored .60 .60
963 A328 (70c) multicolored .60 .60
a. Booklet pane, 2 each #959-963 6.00 6.00
Complete booklet 6.00 6.00

Perf. 14x14¼ on 2 or 3 Sides
1997, Mar. Litho.
Booklet Stamps
963B A328 (70c) Like #959 .60 .60
963C A328 (70c) Like #960 .60 .60
963D A328 (70c) Like #961 .60 .60
963E A328 (70c) Like #962 .60 .60
963F A328 (70c) Like #963 .60 .60
g. Bklt. pane, 2 ea #963B-963F 6.00 6.00
Complete booklet, #963Fg 6.00 6.00

South African Navy, 75th Anniv. — A329

Warships: No. 964, Strike craft SAS Kobie Coetsee. No. 965, Survey ship SAS Protea. No. 966, Mine counter-measures ship SAS Umkomaas. No. 967, Submarine Emily Hobhouse, anti-submarine frigate SAS President Pretorius.

1997, Apr. 1 *Perf. 14 Syncopated*
964 A329 (70c) multicolored .60 .60
965 A329 (70c) multicolored .60 .60
966 A329 (70c) multicolored .60 .60
967 A329 (70c) multicolored .60 .60
a. Block of 4, #964-967 2.40 2.40

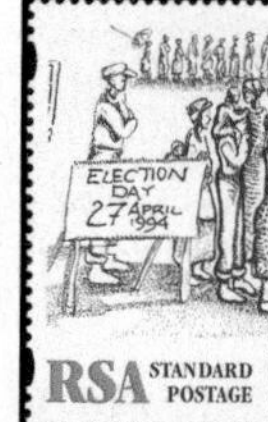

First Democratic Elections, 5th Anniv. — A330

People voting, signs saying: No. 968, "Election Day, 27, April, 1994." No. 969, "Polling Station." No. 970, "Register Here." No. 971, "Vote Here." No. 972, "Ballot Box."

Perf. 14 Syncopated
1997, Apr. 26 Litho.
968 A330 (70c) black & red .50 .50
969 A330 (70c) black & red .50 .50
970 A330 (70c) black & red .50 .50
971 A330 (70c) black & red .50 .50
972 A330 (70c) black & red .50 .50
b. Strip of 5, #968-972 2.50 2.50

Souvenir Sheet

New Year 1997 (Year of the Ox) — A330a

1997, May 2 Litho. *Perf. 14*
972A A330a 4.50r multicolored 2.25 2.25

SAPDA '97.

Cultural Artifacts — A331

No. 973, Zulu baskets. No. 974, S. Sotho figure. No. 975, S. Ndebele figure. No. 976, Venda door. No. 977, Tsonga medicine gourd. No. 978, Wooden pot, N. cape. No. 979, Khoi walking stick. No. 980, Tswana knife handle. No. 981, Xhosa pipe. No. 982, Swazi vessel.

1997, May 18 *Perf. 14*
973 A331 (70c) multi .50 .50
974 A331 (70c) multi .50 .50
975 A331 (70c) multi .50 .50
976 A331 (70c) multi .50 .50
977 A331 (70c) multi .50 .50
978 A331 (70c) multi .50 .50
979 A331 (70c) multi .50 .50
980 A331 (70c) multi .50 .50
981 A331 (70c) multi .50 .50
982 A331 (70c) multi .50 .50
a. Sheet of 10, #973-982 5.00 5.00

1997, Dec. *Perf. 14x15*
973a Zulu baskets .60 .60
974a S. Sotho figure .60 .60
975a S. Ndebele figure .60 .60
976a Venda door .60 .60
977a Tsonga medicine gourd .60 .60
978a Wooden pot, N. cape .60 .60
979a Khoi walking stick .60 .60
980a Tswana knife handle .60 .60
981a Xhosa pipe .60 .60
982a Swazi vessel .60 .60
982c Bklt. pane, #973a-981a, 982b 6.00
Complete booklet, 2 #982c 12.00

A332

Birds — No. 983, White-breasted cormorant. No. 984, Hammerkop. No. 985, Pied kingfisher. No. 986, Purple heron. No. 987, Black-headed heron. No. 988, Darter. No. 989, Green-backed heron. No. 990, White-faced duck. No. 991, Saddle-billed stork. No. 992, Water dikkop.

1997, June 5 *Perf. 14*
983 A332 (70c) multicolored .50 .50
984 A332 (70c) multicolored .50 .50
985 A332 (70c) multicolored .50 .50
986 A332 (70c) multicolored .50 .50
987 A332 (70c) multicolored .50 .50
988 A332 (70c) multicolored .50 .50
989 A332 (70c) multicolored .50 .50
990 A332 (70c) multicolored .50 .50
a. Souvenir sheet of 1 1.25 1.25
991 A332 (70c) multicolored .50 .50
992 A332 (70c) multicolored .50 .50
a. Sheet of 10, #983-992 5.00 5.00
b. Booklet pane of 10, #983-992, perf. 14x14¾ 5.00 5.00
Complete booklet, 2 #992b 10.00

Birds look bluer and browner on some stamps from No. 992b. No. 992a has Ilsapex 98 emblem in margin, which is not found on No. 992b.

No. 990a, issued 7/11/97, is inscribed in sheet margin for JUNASS '97, and sold for 2r.

Grocott's, Muirhead & Gowie Buildings, Grahamstown — A333

1997, May 29 Litho. *Perf. 14*
993 A333 5r multicolored 1.90 1.90

PACIFIC 97.

Indigenous Cattle A335

Perf. 14½ Syncopated
1997, Aug. 10
999 A335 (70c) Nguni .60 .60
1000 A335 (70c) Bonsmara .60 .60
1001 A335 (70c) Afrikander .60 .60
1002 A335 (70c) Drakensberger .60 .60
a. Block of 4, #999-1002 2.40 2.40

Antarctic Wildlife A336

1997, Aug. 27 Litho. *Perf. 14*
1003 A336 (70c) Leopard seal .50 .50
1004 A336 1.20r Antarctic skua .85 .85
1005 A336 1.70r King penguin 1.25 1.25
Nos. 1003-1005 (3) 2.60 2.60

Enoch Sontonga (1873-1905), Author of Africa's Natl. Anthem — A337

No. 1007, "Nkosi Sikelel iAfrika".

Perf. 14 Syncopated
1997, Sept. 24 Litho.
1006 A337 (70c) shown .50 .50
1007 A337 (70c) multicolored .50 .50
a. Pair, #1006-1007 1.00 1.00

Heritage Day.

Souvenir Sheet

Cape Town '97 Natl. Stamp Show — A338

1997, Oct. 8 *Perf. 14*
1008 A338 4.50r multicolored 2.25 2.25

Souvenir Sheet

World Post Day — A339

1997, Oct. 9 *Perf. 14 Syncopated*
1009 A339 (70c) multicolored .70 .70

No. 1009 sold for 1r on day of issue.

SANTA (South African Natl. Tuberculosis Assoc., 50th Anniv. — A340

Designs featuring former Christmas seals: No. 1010, Bethlehem. No. 1011, Candles on each side of Cross of Lorraine. No. 1012, Candles, angels, Cross. No. 1013, Cross, angel kneeling. No. 1014, Santa carrying Cross. No. 1015, Madonna and Child, Cross. No. 1016, Christmas trees. No. 1017, Magi. No. 1018, Bell, stained glass window. No. 1019, Native African kneeling, flag.

1997, Nov. 3 *Perf. 14 Syncopated*
1010 A340 (70c) multicolored .50 .50
1011 A340 (70c) multicolored .50 .50
1012 A340 (70c) multicolored .50 .50
1013 A340 (70c) multicolored .50 .50
1014 A340 (70c) multicolored .50 .50
1015 A340 (70c) multicolored .50 .50
1016 A340 (70c) multicolored .50 .50
1017 A340 (70c) multicolored .50 .50
1018 A340 (70c) multicolored .50 .50
1019 A340 (70c) multicolored .50 .50
a. Sheet of 10, #1010-1019 5.00 5.00

Souvenir Sheet

New Year 1998 (Year of the Tiger) — A341

1998, Jan. 28 Litho. ***Perf. 14x14½***
1020 A341 5r multicolored 2.50 2.50

Natl. Sea Rescue Institute A342

1998, Feb. 11 ***Perf. 14 Syncopated***
1021 A342 (70c) multicolored .90 .90

Fauna (no frame) — A343

5c, Giant girdle-tailed lizard. 10c, Geometric tortoise. 20c, Southern African hedgehog. 30c, Spotted hyena. 40c, Riverine rabbit. 50c, Samango monkey. 60c, Cape hunting dog. 70c, Roan antelope. 80c, Kori bustard. 90c, Jackass penguin. 1r, Wattled crane. #1032, Impala. #1033, Waterbuck. #1034, Blue wildebeest. #1035, Eland. #1036, Kudu. #1037, Black rhinoceros. #1038, White rhinoceros. #1039, Buffalo. #1040, Lion. #1041, Leopard. #1042, African elephant. #1044, Giraffe. 1.50r, Tawny eagle, vert. 2r, Blue swallow. 2.30r, Cape vulture, vert. 5r, Martial eagle. 10r, Bataleur. 20r, Fish eagle.

Perf. 14x14¼, 14x14¼, 14¼x14 Syncopated (#1043), 14x14¼ Syncopated on 2 or 3 Sides (#1036B-1036F, 1042B-1042F)

1998-2000 Litho.
1021A A343 5c multi .25 .25
1022 A343 10c multi .25 .25
1023 A343 20c multi .25 .25
1024 A343 30c multi .25 .25
1025 A343 40c multi .25 .25
1026 A343 50c multi .25 .25
1027 A343 60c multi .25 .25
1028 A343 70c multi .25 .25
1029 A343 80c multi .35 .35
1030 A343 90c multi .35 .35
1031 A343 1r multi .35 .35
1032 A343 (1.10r) multi, vert. .65 .65
1033 A343 (1.10r) multi, vert. .65 .65
1034 A343 (1.10r) multi, vert. .65 .65
1035 A343 (1.10r) multi, vert. .65 .65
1036 A343 (1.10r) multi, vert. .65 .65
a. Strip of 5, #1032-1036 3.25 3.25
h. Booklet pane, 2 each #1032-1036, "Standard" 5mm long 6.50
Booklet, #1036h 6.50
1036B A343 (1.10r) Like #1034 .40 .40
1036C A343 (1.10r) Like #1035 .40 .40
1036D A343 (1.10r) Like #1036 .40 .40
1036E A343 (1.10r) Like #1032 .40 .40
1036F A343 (1.10r) Like #1033 .40 .40
g. Booklet pane, 2 each #1036B-1036F 4.00
Booklet, #1036Fg 4.00
1037 A343 (1.10r) multi .40 .40
a. Booklet pane of 10 4.00
Complete bklt., #1037a 4.00
1038 A343 (1.30r) multi .50 .50
1039 A343 (1.30r) multi .50 .50
1040 A343 (1.30r) multi .50 .50
1041 A343 (1.30r) multi .50 .50
1042 A343 (1.30r) multi .50 .50
a. Booklet pane, 2 ea #1038-1042 5.00
Complete bklt., #1042a 5.00
1042B A343 (1.30r) Like #1038 .50 .50
1042C A343 (1.30r) Like #1039 .50 .50
1042D A343 (1.30r) Like #1040 .50 .50
1042E A343 (1.30r) Like #1041 .50 .50
1042F A343 (1.30r) Like #1042 .50 .50
g. Booklet pane, 2 each #1042B-1042F 5.00
Complete bklt., #1042Fg 5.00
1043 A343 2r multi .80 .80
1043A A343 2r multi .80 .80
1044 A343 3r multi 1.25 1.25
1045 A343 5r multi 2.25 2.25

Size: 20x38mm
Perf. 14¼x13¾
1045A A343 1.50r multi .60 .60
1045B A343 2.30r multi .90 .90

Size: 35x25mm
Perf. 14¼x14
1046 A343 10r multi 4.00 4.00
a. Perf. 14¾ 4.00 4.00

Perf. 14¾ Syncopated
1047 A343 20r multi 7.75 7.75
Nos. 1021A-1047 (40) 32.05 32.05

Self-adhesive
Die Cut Perf. 13x12¾
Litho.
1048 A343 (1.10r) like #1033 .65 .65
1049 A343 (1.10r) like #1032 .65 .65
1050 A343 (1.10r) like #1036 .65 .65
1051 A343 (1.10r) like #1035 .65 .65
1052 A343 (1.10r) like #1034 .65 .65
a. Strip of 5, #1048-1052 3.25
h. Booklet, 2 each #1048-1052 6.50

Booklet Stamps
Self-Adhesive
Serpentine Die Cut 11x11¼
1052B A343 (1.30r) Like #1035 .45 .45
1052C A343 (1.30r) Like #1036 .45 .45
1052D A343 (1.30r) Like #1032 .45 .45
1052E A343 (1.30r) Like #1034 .45 .45
1052F A343 (1.30r) Like #1033 .45 .45
g. Booklet pane, 2 each #1052B-1052F 4.50

Nos. 1038-1042F are inscribed "Airmail Postcard."

"Standard" on Nos. 1032-1036, 1036a is 5½mm long.

Nos. 1042B-1042F are booklet stamps. No. 1052Fg is a complete booklet. Nos. 1036B-1036F were issued in a booklet.

Issued: #1037, 1/98; 10c, 40c, 50c, 70c, 90c, 1r, 1/16/98; #1038-1042, 4/98; #1036B-1036F, 5/18/98; 3r, 6/24/98; 20c, 6/25/98; #1032-1036, 1048-1052, 5/18/98; 10r, 20r, 9/21/98; #1046a, 10/28/98; #1043A, 1/9/99; #1052B-1052F, 12/99; 1.50r, 2.30r, 6/5/00; 5c, 7/4/00.

Souvenir Sheet

Leopard — A344

1998, May 1 ***Perf. 14***
1053 A344 5r multicolored 2.50 2.50

SAPDA '98 Stamp Show, Johannesburg.

A345

1998, June 8
1054 A345 (1.10r) multicolored .80 .80

1998 World Cup Soccer Championships, France. No. 1054 was issued in sheets of 10.

A346

Early South African History: #1055, Early stone age hand axe. #1056, Musuku. #1057, San rock engravings. #1058, Early iron age pots. #1059, Khoekhoe pot. #1060, Florisbad skull. #1061, San rock art. #1062, Mapungubwe gold. #1063, Lydenburg head. #1064, Taung child.

1998, June 28 ***Perf. 14x14½***
1055 A346 (1.10r) multicolored .55 .55
1056 A346 (1.10r) multicolored .55 .55
1057 A346 (1.10r) multicolored .55 .55
1058 A346 (1.10r) multicolored .55 .55
1059 A346 (1.10r) multicolored .55 .55
1060 A346 (1.10r) multicolored .55 .55
1061 A346 (1.10r) multicolored .55 .55
1062 A346 (1.10r) multicolored .55 .55
1063 A346 (1.10r) multicolored .55 .55
1064 A346 (1.10r) multicolored .55 .55
a. Sheet of 10, #1055-1064 5.50 5.50
Booklet, 2 #1064a 11.00

Raptors — A347

Designs: No. 1065, Pale chanting goshawk. No. 1066, Jackal buzzard. No. 1067, Lanner falcon. No. 1068, Bearded vulture. No. 1069, Black harrier. No. 1070, Cape vulture. No. 1071, Bateleur. No. 1072, Spotted eagle owl. No. 1073, White-headed vulture. No. 1074, African fish eagle.

1998, Aug. 16 ***Perf. 14x15***
1065 A347 (1.10r) multicolored .65 .65
1066 A347 (1.10r) multicolored .65 .65
1067 A347 (1.10r) multicolored .65 .65
1068 A347 (1.10r) multicolored .65 .65
1069 A347 (1.10r) multicolored .65 .65
1070 A347 (1.10r) multicolored .65 .65
1071 A347 (1.10r) multicolored .65 .65
1072 A347 (1.10r) multicolored .65 .65
1073 A347 (1.10r) multicolored .65 .65
1074 A347 (1.10r) multicolored .65 .65
a. Sheet of 10, #1065-1074 6.50 6.50
b. Booklet pane, #1065-1074 6.50
Complete booklet, 2 #1074b + 2 prepaid postcards 14.00

Vert. and horiz. perforations extend to top, bottom and right edges of sheet on No. 1074a, but do not on No. 1074b.

Natl. Arbor Week A348

Trees: No. 1075, Baobab. No. 1076, Umbrella thorn. No. 1077, Shepherd's tree. No. 1078, Karee.

1998, Sept. 4 Litho. ***Perf. 13¾x14***
1075 A348 (1.10r) multicolored .75 .75
1076 A348 (1.10r) multicolored .75 .75
1077 A348 (1.10r) multicolored .75 .75
1078 A348 (1.10r) multicolored .75 .75
a. Block of 4, #1075-1078 3.00 3.00

Christmas — A349

1998, Oct. 9 Litho. ***Perf. 14x15***
1079 A349 (1.10r) Angel .80 .80
1080 A349 (1.10r) Bell .80 .80
1081 A349 (1.10r) Package .80 .80
1082 A349 (1.10r) Christmas tree .80 .80
1083 A349 (1.10r) Star .80 .80
a. Strip of 5, #1079-1083 4.00 4.00

Souvenir Sheet

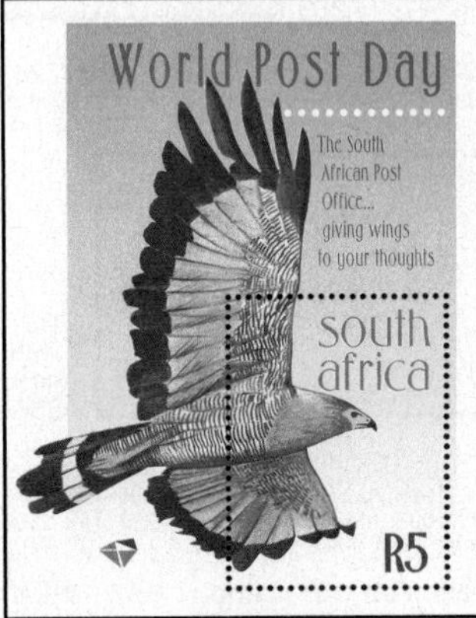

World Post Day — A351

1998, Oct. 9 Litho. ***Perf. 14x14½***
1089 A351 5r multicolored 2.50 2.50

Souvenir Sheet

ILSAPEX 1998, Midrand, South Africa — A352

Designs of unissued stamps created for 1927 definitive series in colors of: a, Red and green. b, Green and black.

1998, Oct. 20 Litho. ***Perf. 14½x14¼***
1090 A352 5r Sheet of 2, #a.-b. 4.00 4.00

Souvenir Sheet

Whales — A354

1998, Oct. 23 Litho. ***Perf. 13½x14***
1095 A354 5r multicolored 3.00 3.00

See Namibia No. 919, Norfolk Island No. 665.

Souvenir Sheet

Clover SA Limited, 100th Anniv. — A354a

1998, Nov. 15 Litho. *Perf. 14¼x14*
1095A A354a (1.10r) multicolored 2.25 2.25

Universal Declaration of Human Rights, 50th Anniv. — A355

1998, Dec. 9 *Perf. 14¼*
1096 A355 (1.10r) multicolored 1.00 1.00

UPU, 125th Anniv. A356

Designs: No. 1097, Dennis Royal Mail vehicle, 1913. No. 1098, Ford V8 Mail van, 1935. No. 1099, Mobile post office, 1937. No. 1100, Trojan post office van, 1927.

1999, Feb. 15 Litho. *Perf. 13¾x14*
1097 A356 (1.10r) multi .75 .75
1098 A356 (1.10r) multi .75 .75
1099 A356 (1.10r) multi .75 .75
1100 A356 (1.10r) multi .75 .75
a. Block of 4, #1097-1100 3.00 3.00

New Year 1999 (Year of the Rabbit) — A357

1999, Feb. 16 Litho. *Perf. 14x13½*
1101 A357 5r multicolored 2.50 2.50

Ships of the Southern Oceans — A358

1999, Mar. 19 Litho. *Perf. 13¾x14*
1102 A358 (1.10r) Endeavour .75 .75
1103 A358 (1.10r) HMS Beagle .75 .75
1104 A358 (1.10r) Discovery .75 .75
1105 A358 (1.10r) Heemskerck .75 .75
a. Block of 4, #1102-1105 3.00 3.00

Souvenir Sheet

Perf. 13¾

1106 A358 5r Lawhill, vert. 2.25 2.25

Australia 99 World Stamp Expo (No. 1106).

AIDS Awareness — A359

Perf. 14¼x14 on 3 sides

1999, Apr. 1
1107 A359 (1.20r) purple & multi .60 .60
1108 A359 (1.20r) green & multi .60 .60
a. Booklet pane, 5 each #1107-1108 6.00
Complete booklet, #1108a 6.00

Souvenir Sheets

IBRA '99, Nuremberg, Germany — A360

1999, Apr. 27 *Perf. 14¼x14*
1109 A360 5r multi 3.00 3.00

SAPDA '99, Johannesburg — A361

1999, Apr. 30 *Perf. 13¾*
1110 A361 5r multi 2.75 2.75

A362

1999, May 1 *Perf. 14x14¾*
1111 A362 (1.20r) Nurse .70 .70
1112 A362 (1.20r) Washerwoman .70 .70
1113 A362 (1.20r) Lumberjack .70 .70
1114 A362 (1.20r) Tree planter .70 .70
1115 A362 (1.20r) Cook .70 .70
1116 A362 (1.20r) Fisherman .70 .70
1117 A362 (1.20r) Construction worker .70 .70
1118 A362 (1.20r) Miner .70 .70
1119 A362 (1.20r) Mailman .70 .70
1120 A362 (1.20r) Jackhammerer .70 .70
a. Sheet of 10, #1111-1120 7.00 7.00

Labor Day.

A363

1999, June 16 *Perf. 14x14¼*
1121 A363 (1.20r) multi 1.00 1.00

Inauguration of Pres. Thabo Mbeki.

Souvenir Sheet

Order of St. John, 900th Anniv. — A364

1999, June 23 *Perf. 14x14¾*
1122 A364 2r multi 1.50 1.50

Standard Bank Arts Festival, 25th Anniv. — A365

1999, June 29 *Perf. 14x14¼*
1123 A365 (1.20r) shown .90 .90
1124 A365 (1.20r) Film .90 .90
1125 A365 (1.20r) Music .90 .90
1126 A365 (1.20r) Mask, diff. .90 .90
1127 A365 (1.20r) Painter .90 .90
a. Strip of 5, #1123-1127 4.50 4.50

Traditional Wall Art — A366

1999, Aug. 8 *Perf. 13¼x13¾*
1128 A366 (1.20r) North Ndebele .80 .80
1129 A366 (1.20r) South Ndebele .80 .80
1130 A366 (1.20r) Swazi .80 .80
1131 A366 (1.20r) Venda .80 .80
1132 A366 (1.20r) South Sotho .80 .80
1133 A366 (1.20r) Xhosa .80 .80
1134 A366 (1.20r) North Sotho .80 .80
1135 A366 (1.20r) Tsonga .80 .80
1136 A366 (1.20r) Zulu .80 .80
1137 A366 (1.20r) Tswana .80 .80
a. Sheet of 10, #1128-1137 8.00 8.00

Souvenir Sheet

China 1999 World Philatelic Exhibition — A367

1999, Aug. 21 *Perf. 14x13¼*
1138 A367 5r multi 3.00 3.00

Souvenir Sheet

JOPEX '99 — A368

1999, Sept. 8 Litho. *Perf. 14¼x14½*
1139 A368 5r Strelitzia flower 3.25 3.25

Migratory Animals — A369

No. 1140, Barn swallow. No. 1141, Great white shark. No. 1142, Lesser kestrel. No. 1143, Common dolphin. No. 1144, European bee-eater. No. 1145, Loggerhead turtle. No. 1146, Curlew sandpiper. No. 1147, Wandering albatross. No. 1148, Springbok. No. 1149, Lesser flamingo.

1999, Oct. 4 Litho. *Perf. 14x14¾*
1140 A369 (1.20r) multi .80 .80
1141 A369 (1.20r) multi .80 .80
1142 A369 (1.20r) multi .80 .80
1143 A369 (1.20r) multi .80 .80
1144 A369 (1.20r) multi .80 .80
1145 A369 (1.20r) multi .80 .80
1146 A369 (1.20r) multi .80 .80
1147 A369 (1.20r) multi .80 .80
1148 A369 (1.20r) multi .80 .80
1149 A369 (1.20r) multi .80 .80
a. Sheet of 10, #1140-1149 8.00 8.00
Complete booklet, 2 #1149a (stitched in) + 2 postal cards 20.00

Complete booklet sold for 29r.

Boer War, Cent. A370

No. 1150, Boer men, woman. No. 1151, Soldiers, ship.

1999, Oct. 11 Litho. *Perf. 13¾*
1150 A370 (1.20r) multi 1.25 1.25
1151 A370 (1.20r) multi 1.25 1.25
a. Pair, #1150-1151 2.50 2.50
b. Booklet pane, #1150-1151, perf. 13¼x13¾ ('02) 2.75 —

Issued: No. 1151b, 5/31/02. See note after No. 1282.

Millennium — A371

2000, Jan. 1 Litho. *Perf. 13¼x13¾*
1152 A371 (1.20r) multi 1.10 1.10

Start of National Lottery A372

2000, Mar. 2 Litho. *Perf. 13¼x13¾*
1153 A372 (1.20r) multi 1.00 1.00

Family Day — A373

2000, Apr. 5 Litho. *Perf. 13¼*
1154 A373 (1.30r) multi 1.00 1.00

Souvenir Sheet

The Stamp Show 2000, London — A374

2000, May 20 Litho. *Perf. 13¼*
1155 A374 4.60r multi 2.75 2.75

Frogs and Toads — A375

No. 1156: a, Banded stream frog. b, Yellow-striped reed frog. c, Natal leaf-folding frog. d, Paradise toad. e, Table Mountain ghost frog. f, Banded rubber frog. g, Dwarf grass frog. h, Long-toed tree frog. i, Namaqua rain frog. j, Bubbling kassina.
4.60r, Forest tree frog.

Perf. 13¼x13¾

2000, June 23 Litho.
1156 Sheet of 10 7.00 7.00
a.-j. A375 1.30r Any single .70 .70

Souvenir Sheet

Perf. 13¼

1157 A375 4.60r multi 2.75 2.75

Junass 2000, Boksburg (No. 1157). No. 1157 contains one 48x30mm stamp.

Medicinal Plants — A376

No. 1158: a, Stalked bulbine. b, Wild dagga. c, Wild garlic. d, Pig's ear. e, Wild ginger.
No. 1159: a, Red paintbrush. b, Cancer bush. c, Yellow star flower. d, Bitter aloe. e, Sour fig.

2000, Aug. 1 *Perf. 13¾x13¼*
1158 Horiz. strip of 5 2.50 2.50
a.-e. A376 1.30r Any single .50 .50
1159 Horiz. strip of 5 4.00 4.00
a.-e. A376 2.30r Any single .80 .80

2000 Summer Olympics, Sydney — A377

Olympic rings and: 1.30r, Flagbearer. 1.50r, Elena Meyer of South Africa and Derartu Tulu of Ethiopia. 2.20r, Joshua Thugwane. 2.30r, South African flag. 6.30r, Penny Heyns.

2000, Sept. 1 *Perf. 13¼x13¾*
1160-1164 A377 Set of 5 5.00 5.00

Intl. Year for the Culture of Peace A378

2000, Sept. 19 Litho. *Perf. 13¼*
1165 A378 1.30r multi .70 .70

World Heritage Sites — A379

Designs: No. 1166, 1.30r, Robben Island. No. 1167, 1.30r, Greater St. Lucia Wetland Park. No. 1168, 1.30r, Sterkfontein Fossil Hominid Complex.

2000, Sept. 22 *Perf. 13¼x13¾*
1166-1168 A379 Set of 3 2.00 2.00

World Post Day — A380

2000 Litho. *Perf. 13¼x13*
1169 A380 1.30r multi .70 .70
a. Perf. 13¾x13 + label .75 .75

Issued: No. 1169, 10/9; No. 1169a, 11/8. No. 1169a was issued in sheets of 20 stamps + 20 different labels depicting characters on the MTN Gladiators 3 television show that sold for 35r.

Souvenir Sheet

Year of the Dragon — A381

2000, Oct. 9 Litho. *Perf. 13½x13*
1170 A381 4.60r multi 2.10 2.10

Writers of the Boer War Era — A382

Medals and: 1.30r, Sol Plaatje, Johanna Brandt. 4.40r, Sir Arthur Conan Doyle, Sir Winston Churchill.

2000, Oct. 25 Litho. *Perf. 13¼x13¾*
1171-1172 A382 Set of 2 2.75 2.75
a. Booklet pane, #1171-1172 3.25 —

Issued: No. 1172a, 5/31/02. See note after No. 1282.

A383

Fish, Flowers, Butterflies and Birds — A384

Designs: 5c, Palette surgeonfish. 10c, Blue-banded surgeonfish. 20c, Royal angelfish. 30c, Emperor angelfish. 40c, Blackbar trigger-fish. 50c, Coral rockcod. 60c, Powder-blue surgeonfish. 70c, Threadfin butterflyfish. 80c, Longhorn cowfish. 90c, Longnose butterflyfish. 1r, Coral beauty. Nos. 1184, 1199B, 1199G, 1200, 1205, 1210, 1215, 1219A, 1220, 1225, Botterblom, vert. Nos. 1185, 1199C, 1199H, 1201, 1206, 1211, 1216, 1219B, 1221, 1226, Blue marguerite, vert. Nos. 1186, 1199D, 1199I, 1202, 1207, 1212, 1217, 1219C, 1222, 1227, Karoo violet, vert. Nos. 1187, 1199E, 1199J, 1203, 1208, 1213, 1218, 1219D, 1223, 1228, Tree pelargonium, vert. Nos. 1188, 1199F, 1199K, 1204, 1209, 1214, 1219, 1219E, 1224, 1229, Black-eyed susy, vert. 1.40r, Gold-banded forester. 1.50r, Brenton blue. 1.60r, Yellow pansy butterfly. No. 1191, Silver-barred charaxes. No. 1231, Large-spotted acraea butterfly. 2r, Lilac-breasted roller, vert. 2.10r, Koppie charaxes butterfly. 2.30r, Citrus swallowtail. 2.50r, Common grass-yellow butterfly. 3r, Woodland kingfisher, vert. 5r, White-fronted bee-eater, vert. 6.30r, Green-banded swallowtail. 7r, Southern milkweed butterfly. 10r, African green pigeon, vert. 12.60r, False dotted-border. 14r, Lilac tip butterfly. 20r, Purple-crested lourie, vert.

Non-English country name inscriptions at top: Nos. 1199B, 1199F, 1199I, 1200, 1204, 1207, 1217, 1219A, 1219E, 1220, 1224, 1227, Afrika Borwa. Nos. 1199C, 1199J, 1201, 1208, 1218, 1219B, 1221, 1228, Ningizimu Afrika. Nos. 1199D, 1202, 1219C, 1222, Suid-Afrika. Nos. 1199E, 1203, 1219D, 1223, Afrika Tshipembe. Nos. 1199G, 1205, 1215, 1225, Afrika Dzonga. Nos. 1199H, 1206, 1216, 1226, Afrika Sewula. Nos. 1199K, 1209, 1219, 1229, Mzantsi Afrika.

Perf. 14½x14¾, 14¾x14½

2000, Nov. 15 Litho.
1173 A383 5c multi .25 .25
a. Perf. 13 .25 .25
1174 A383 10c multi .25 .25
a. Perf. 13 .25 .25
1175 A383 20c multi .25 .25
a. Perf. 13 .25 .25
b. Perf. 14x13¾ .25 .25
1176 A383 30c multi .25 .25
a. Perf. 13 .25 .25
1177 A383 40c multi .25 .25
a. Perf. 13 .25 .25
1178 A383 50c multi .25 .25
a. Perf. 13 .25 .25
1179 A383 60c multi .25 .25
a. Perf. 13 .25 .25
1180 A383 70c multi .25 .25
a. Perf. 13 .25 .25
b. Perf. 14x13¾ .25 .25
1181 A383 80c multi .30 .30
a. Perf. 13 .30 .30
1182 A383 90c multi .35 .35
a. Perf. 13 .30 .30
1183 A383 1r multi .35 .35
a. Perf. 13 .35 .35
1184 A383 1.30r multi .50 .50
1185 A383 1.30r multi .50 .50
1186 A383 1.30r multi .50 .50
1187 A383 1.30r multi .50 .50
1188 A383 1.30r multi .50 .50
a. Horiz. strip of 5, #1184-1188 2.50 2.50
1189 A383 1.40r multi .55 .55
1190 A383 1.50r multi .60 .60
1191 A383 1.90r multi .70 .70
1192 A383 2r multi .80 .80
a. Perf. 13 .80 .80
1193 A383 2.30r multi .85 .85
1194 A383 3r multi 1.10 1.10
a. Perf. 13 1.10 1.10
1195 A383 5r multi 2.10 2.10
a. Perf. 13 2.10 2.10
1196 A383 6.30r multi 2.75 2.75
1197 A383 10r multi 4.00 4.00
a. Perf. 13 ('01) 4.00 4.00
1198 A383 12.60r multi 5.50 5.50
a. Perf. 13 ('01) 6.00 6.00
1199 A383 20r multi 8.00 8.00
a. Perf. 13 6.50 6.50
m. Perf. 13¾x14 5.25 5.25

Issued: Nos. 1197a, 1199a, 10/1/01. No. 1179a, 10/1/01. Nos. 1178a, 1192a, 1194a, 1195a, 2002. No. 1173a, 4/2/03; No. 1174a, 5/22/03; Nos. 1175a, 1181a, 9/22/03; Nos. 1176a, 1182a, 1199a, 2/27/03; Nos. 1177a, 1180a, 1183a, 9/23/03. Nos. 1175b, 1180b, 2/24/10; No. 1199m, 2/1/10.

Coil Stamps
Self-Adhesive

Serpentine Die Cut 13¼x13½

2000, Nov. 1 Litho.
1199B A384 1.30r multi — —
1199C A384 1.30r multi — —
1199D A384 1.30r multi — —
1199E A384 1.30r multi — —
1199F A384 1.30r multi — —
1199G A384 1.30r multi — —
1199H A384 1.30r multi — —
1199I A384 1.30r multi — —
1199J A384 1.30r multi — —
1199K A384 1.30r multi — —

Booklet Stamps
Self-Adhesive

Die Cut Perf. 13x12½ on 2 or 3 Sides

2000, Nov. 15 Litho.
1200 A384 1.30r multi .50 .50
1201 A384 1.30r multi .50 .50
1202 A384 1.30r multi .50 .50
1203 A384 1.30r multi .50 .50
1204 A384 1.30r multi .50 .50
1205 A384 1.30r multi .50 .50
1206 A384 1.30r multi .50 .50
1207 A384 1.30r multi .50 .50
1208 A384 1.30r multi .50 .50
1209 A384 1.30r multi .50 .50
a. Booklet, #1200-1209 5.00

2001, May 16 Litho. *Perf. 13*
1210 A383 1.40r multi .55 .55
1211 A383 1.40r multi .55 .55
1212 A383 1.40r multi .55 .55
1213 A383 1.40r multi .55 .55
1214 A383 1.40r multi .55 .55
a. Horiz. strip of 5, #1210-1214 2.75 2.75

"Standard Postage" in Thin Letters
Coil Stamps

Serpentine Die Cut 13½

Photo.
Self-Adhesive

1215 A384 (1.40r) multi .55 .55
1216 A384 (1.40r) multi .55 .55
1217 A384 (1.40r) multi .55 .55
1218 A384 (1.40r) multi .55 .55
1219 A384 (1.40r) multi .55 .55
1219A A384 (1.40r) multi .55 .55
1219B A384 (1.40r) multi .55 .55
1219C A384 (1.40r) multi .55 .55
1219D A384 (1.40r) multi .55 .55
1219E A384 (1.40r) multi .55 .55
f. Strip of 10, #1215-1219E 5.50

Die Cut Perf. 13x12½ on 2 or 3 Sides

Photo.
Booklet Stamps
"Standard Postage" in Thin Letters

1220 A384 (1.40r) multi .55 .55
1221 A384 (1.40r) multi .55 .55
1222 A384 (1.40r) multi .55 .55
1223 A384 (1.40r) multi .55 .55
1224 A384 (1.40r) multi .55 .55
1225 A384 (1.40r) multi .55 .55
1226 A384 (1.40r) multi .55 .55
1227 A384 (1.40r) multi .55 .55
1228 A384 (1.40r) multi .55 .55
1229 A384 (1.40r) multi .55 .55
a. Booklet, #1220-1229 5.50
Nos. 1173-1229 (66) 51.20 51.20

Designs: Nos. 1229B, 1229G, 1229M, 1229R, Botterblom, vert. Nos. 1229C, 1229H, 1229N, 1229S, Blue marguerite, vert. Nos. 1229D, 1229I, 1229O, 1229T, Karoo violet, vert. Nos. 1229E, 1229J, 1229P, 1229U, Tree pelargonium, vert. Nos. 1229F, 1229K, 1229Q, 1229V, Black-eyed susy, vert.

Non-English country name inscriptions at top: Nos. 1229B, 1229F, 1229I, 1229M, 1229Q, 1229T, Afrika Borwa. Nos. 1229C,

1229J, 1229N, 1229U, Ningizimu Afrika. Nos. 1229D, 1229O, Suid-Afrika. Nos. 1229E, 1229P, Afrika Tshipembe. Nos. 1229G, 1229R, Afrika Dzonga. Nos. 1229H, 1229S, Afrika Sewula. Nos. 1229K, 1229V, Mzantsi Afrika.

With "Standard Postage" in Thick Letters

Coil Stamps

Self-Adhesive

Serpentine Die Cut 13½x12¾

2001, May 30 **Litho.**

1229B	A384 (1.40r) multi		—	—
1229C	A384 (1.40r) multi		—	—
1229D	A384 (1.40r) multi		—	—
1229E	A384 (1.40r) multi		—	—
1229F	A384 (1.40r) multi		—	—
1229G	A384 (1.40r) multi		—	—
1229H	A384 (1.40r) multi		—	—
1229I	A384 (1.40r) multi		—	—
1229J	A384 (1.40r) multi		—	—
1229K	A384 (1.40r) multi		—	—

Booklet Stamps

Die Cut Perf. 13x12½ on 2 or 3 Sides

1229M	A384 (1.40r) multi		—	—
1229N	A384 (1.40r) multi		—	—
1229O	A384 (1.40r) multi		—	—
1229P	A384 (1.40r) multi		—	—
1229Q	A384 (1.40r) multi		—	—
1229R	A384 (1.40r) multi		—	—
1229S	A384 (1.40r) multi		—	—
1229T	A384 (1.40r) multi		—	—
1229U	A384 (1.40r) multi		—	—
1229V	A384 (1.40r) multi		—	—
w.	Booklet pane of 10, #1229M-1229V		—	—

Nos. 1215-1229 have "Standard Postage" in thin letters.

Type of 2000

2001, June 16 **Litho.** ***Perf. 13***

1230	A383	1.60r multi	.60	.60
1231	A383	1.90r multi	.75	.75
1232	A383	2.10r multi	.80	.80
1233	A383	2.50r multi	1.00	1.00
1234	A383	7r multi	2.75	2.75
1235	A383	14r multi	6.00	6.00
	Nos. 1230-1235 (6)		11.90	11.90

Myths and Legends — A385

Designs: 1.30r, The Rain Bull. 1.50r, The Treasure of the Grosvenor. 2.20r, Seven Magic Birds. 2.30r, The Hole in the Wall. 6.30r, Van Hunks and the Devil.

2001, Jan. 24 **Litho.** ***Perf. 13¾***

1236-1240 A385 Set of 5 4.50 4.50

Souvenir Sheet

Hong Kong 2001 Stamp Exhibition — A386

2001, Feb. 1 ***Perf. 14½x14***

1241 A386 4.60r Tree snake 2.75 2.75

Sports Stars A387

Designs: No. 1242, 1.40r, Ernie Els, golfer. No. 1243, 1.40r, Terence Parkin, swimmer. No. 1244, 1.40r, Hezekiel Sepeng, runner. No. 1245, 1.40r, Rosina Magola, netball player. No. 1246, 1.40r, Francois Pienaar, rugby player. No. 1247, 1.40r, Zanele Situ, javelin thrower. No. 1248, 1.40r, Hestrie Cloete, high jumper. No. 1249, 1.40r, Lucas Radebe, soccer player. No. 1250, 1.40r, Vuyani Bungu, boxer. No. 1251, 1.40r, Jonty Rhodes, cricket player.

2001, Feb. 28 ***Perf. 13¾x14***

1242-1251	A387	Set of 10	6.00	6.00
1251a		Sheet of 15 #1251 +15 labels, perf. 14½x14	8.50	

Labels on No. 1251a depict players from the 2000-01 South African World Cup Cricket team.

Kgalagadi Transfrontier Park — A388

Designs: 1.40r, Gemsboks, flags of South Africa and Botswana. 2.50r, Cheetahs. 2.90r, Sociable weaver birds. 3.60r, Meerkats.

2001, May 12 **Litho.** ***Perf. 13x13¼***

1252-1255	A388	Set of 4	4.50	4.50
1254a		Souvenir sheet, #1253-1254	3.00	3.00

See Botswana Nos. 714-717.

Campaign Against Child Abuse — A389

2001, May 16 ***Perf. 13¾***

1256 A389 1.40r multi .50 .50

Soweto Uprising, 25th Anniv. — A390

2001, June 16 **Litho.** ***Perf. 13¾***

1257 A390 1.40r multi .50 .50

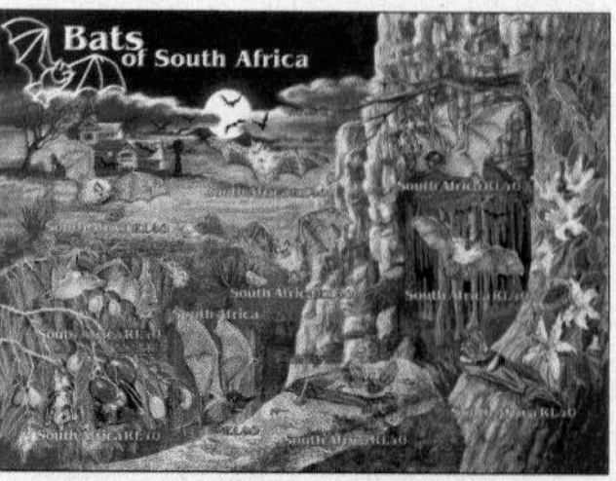

Bats — A391

No. 1258: a, Cape horseshoe bat. b, Welwitsch's hairy bat. c, Schreiber's long-fingered bat. d, Wahlberg's epauletted fruit bat. e, Short-eared trident bat. f, Common slit-faced bat. g, Egyptian fruit bat. h, Egyptian free-tailed bat, vert. i, De Winton's long-eared bat. j, Large-eared free-tailed bat.

Serpentine Die Cut 11¼

2001, June 22 **Self-Adhesive**

1258	A391	Sheet of 10, #a-j	4.50	4.50
a.-j.		1.40r Any single	.45	.45

Boer War, Cent. — A392

Designs: 1.40r, Rev. J. D. Kestell. 3r, Capt. Thomas Crean.

2001, Aug. 1 ***Perf. 13¼***

1259-1260	A392	Set of 2	2.00	2.00
a.		Booklet pane, #1259-1260, perf. 13¼x13¾	2.25	—

Issued: No. 1260a, 5/31/02. See note after No. 1282.

World Conference Against Racism, Durban — A393

No. 1262: a, Kgotlelelo le pharologantsho. b, Kubeketelelana kanye nekwehlukana. c, Verdraagsaamheid en diversiteit. d, U kondelelana na u fhambana. e, Kutlwisiso ka mefutafuta. f, Ku va ni mbilu yo leha ni kuhambana-hambana. g, Ibekezelelwano nehlukahlukano. h, Kgothlelelo le pharologano. i, Ukubekezelelana nokungafani. j, Ukunyamezelana nokungafani.

2001, Aug. 1 ***Perf. 13¾x13½***

1261	A393	2.10r shown	.75	.75
1262		Sheet of 10	6.00	6.00
a.-j.	A393	1.40r Any single	.60	.60

See Brazil No. 2809.

Musical Instruments — A394

Designs: 1.40r, Concertina. 1.90r, Trumpet. 2.50r, Electric guitar. 3r, African drum. 7r, Cello.

Litho. with Foil Application

2001, Aug. 23 ***Perf. 13¼x14***

1263-1267 A394 Set of 5 5.25 5.25

Christmas A395

Designs: 2r, Tree. 3r, Angel.

2001, Oct. 1 **Litho.** ***Perf. 13¼***

1268-1269 A395 Set of 2 1.90 1.90

Frame — A396

2001, Oct. 1 ***Serpentine Die Cut***

Self-Adhesive

1270	A396	(1.40r) multi	.60	.60
a.		Double-sided pane of 10 + 40 labels	6.00	

Volvo Round-the-World Yacht Race — A397

Designs: 1.40r, Yacht. 6r, Yacht, horiz.

2001, Oct. 23 ***Perf. 13***

1271 A397 1.40r multi .75 .75

Souvenir Sheet

Perf. 14x13¼

1272 A397 6r multi 1.25 1.25

No. 1272 contains one 40x30mm stamp.

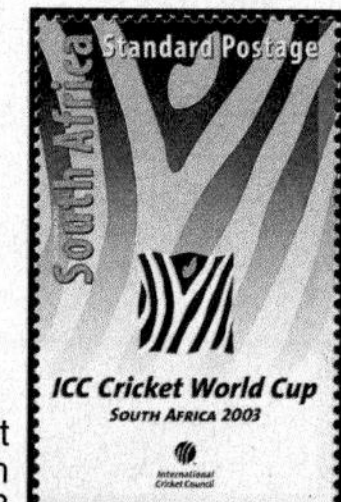

2003 ICC Cricket World Cup, South Africa — A398

2001, Nov. 1 ***Perf. 14x13¾***

1273 A398 (1.40r) multi .85 .85

Souvenir Sheet

New Year 2002 (Year of the Horse) — A399

2001, Nov. 2 ***Perf. 14x13¼***

1274 A399 6r multi 2.25 2.25

Marine Life — A400

No. 1275: a, Hammerhead shark. b, Loggerhead turtle, vert. c, Clown triggerfish, vert. d, Cape fur seal, vert. e, Bottlenosed dolphins. f, Crowned seahorse, vert. g, Blue-spotted ribbontail ray, vert. h, Moorish idol. i, Common octopus. j, Coral rock cod.

Serpentine Die Cut 12¾

2001, Nov. 2 **Self-Adhesive**

1275 A400 Sheet of 10 4.50 4.50
a.-j. (1.40r) Any single .45 .45

Johannesburg World Summit on Sustainable Development — A401

Designs: Nos. 1276a, 1281c, Prosperity, vert. Nos. 1276b, 1281a, People, vert. Nos. 1276c, 1281b, Planet, vert. (1.50r), Water, sanitation and energy for all. No. 1278, Buildings, globe. No. 1279, Clean environment for health. (3.30r), Food security for all.

Sizes: Nos. 1276a-1276c, 22x32mm, Nos. 1281a-1281c, 21x26mm.

Perf. 13¾x13¼, 13¼x13 (#1277, 1279, 1280), 13¼x13¾ (#1278)

2002 **Litho.**

1276 A401 (1.40r) Strip of 3, #a-c 1.40 1.40
1277 A401 (1.50r) multi .50 .50
1278 A401 (3r) multi .95 .95
1279 A401 (3r) multi .95 .95
1280 A401 (3.30r) multi 1.00 1.00

Booklet Stamps

Self-Adhesive

Serpentine Die Cut on 2 or 3 Sides

1281 A401 (1.40r) Strip of 3, #a-c 1.40 1.40
d. Booklet pane, 4 #1281a, 3 #1281b-1281c 4.50 4.50
Nos. 1276-1281 (6) 6.20 6.20

Issued: Nos. 1276, 1278, 1281, 4/17. Nos. 1277, 1279, 1280, 8/25. No. 1279 is airmail.

Souvenir Sheet

End of Boer War, Cent. — A402

No. 1282: a, 1.50r, Army officer. b, 3.30r, Government official.

2002, May 31 ***Perf. 13¼x13¾***

1282 A402 Sheet of 2, #a-b 1.50 1.50
c. Booklet pane, #1282 1.90 —
Complete booklet, #1151b, 1172a, 1260a, 1282c + 2 postal cards 10.50

No. 1282c has rouletting between margin of No. 1282 and the booklet pane margin. Complete booklet sold for 45r.

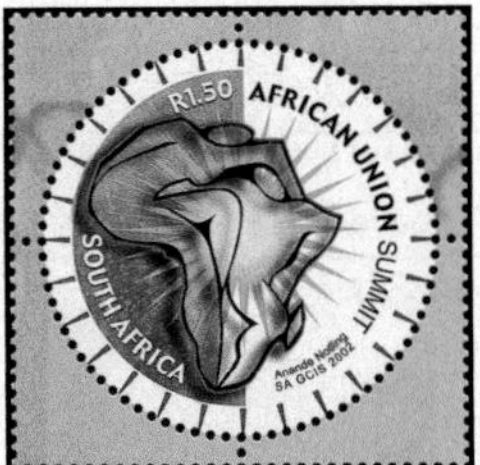

African Union Summit A403

2002, June 25 ***Perf. 13½***

1283 A403 1.50r multi .90 .90

Values are for stamps with surrounding selvage.

Type of 2000

Designs: 1.80r, Emperor moth. 2.20r, Peach moth. 2.80r, Snouted tiger moth. 9r, False tiger moth. 16r, Moon moth.

2002, Sept. 20 **Litho.** ***Perf. 13***

1284 A383 1.80r multi .55 .55
1285 A383 2.20r multi .70 .70
1286 A383 2.80r multi .85 .85
1287 A383 9r multi 2.75 2.75
1288 A383 16r multi 5.00 5.00
Nos. 1284-1288 (5) 9.85 9.85

A404 A405

A406 A407

ICC Cricket World Cup
A408 A409

2002 ***Perf. 12½x12¾***

1289 A404 (1.50r) multi .50 .50
1290 A405 (1.50r) multi .50 .50
1291 A407 (1.50r) multi .50 .50
1292 A409 (1.50r) multi .50 .50
1293 A406 (1.50r) multi .50 .50
1294 A408 (1.50r) multi .50 .50
Nos. 1289-1294 (6) 3.00 3.00

Issued: Nos. 1289, 1290, 9/23; 1292, 1294, 11/1; Nos. 1291, 1293, 12/21.

Souvenir Sheet

Steve Biko (1946-77), Anti-apartheid Leader — A410

2002, Oct. 9 ***Perf. 14¾x14½***

1295 A410 4.75r multi 1.50 1.50

See note under No. 1321.

Souvenir Sheet

World Post Day — A411

2002, Oct. 9 ***Perf. 13¼x13½***

1296 A411 4.75r multi 1.50 1.50

Christmas — A412

Stained glass patterns: 1.50r, 3r.

2002, Oct. 23 ***Perf. 14x14¾***

1297-1298 A412 Set of 2 1.40 1.40

Souvenir Sheets

Sawfish — A413

Designs: No. 1299, 7r, Pristis pectinata. No. 1300, 7r, Pristis microdon.

2002, Oct. 23 ***Perf. 13¾***

1299-1300 A413 Set of 2 4.50 4.50

JUNASS Philatelic Exhibition (#1299); Algoapex Philatelic Exhibition (#1300).

Souvenir Sheet

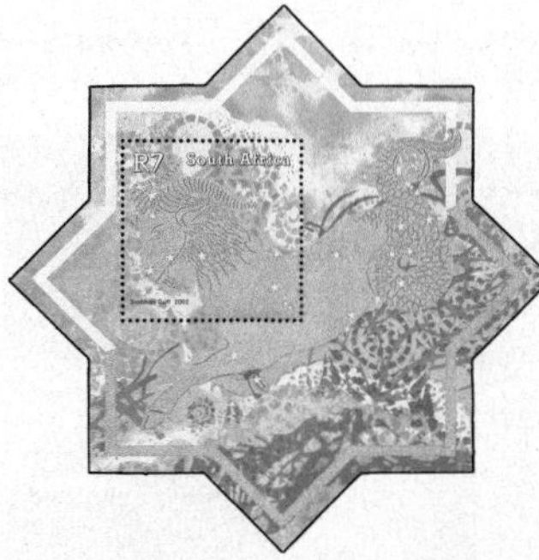

New Year 2003 (Year of the Ram) — A414

2002, Nov. 1 ***Perf. 14½***

1301 A414 7r multi 2.25 2.25

AIDS Prevention — A415

No. 1302 — AIDS prevention ribbon and: a, Man with sunglasses, male symbol. b, Woman with open mouth. c, Woman with sunglasses, female symbol. d, Hand holding candle, "Stop." e, Woman, candle. f, Hand holding candle, "Be safe." g, Candle, hand pointing at ribbon. h, Open hand. i, Face in droplet. j, Open hand, pills.

Serpentine Die Cut 11¾

2002, Nov. 29 **Self-Adhesive**

1302 Booklet of 10 5.25 5.25
a.-j. A415 (1.50r) Any single .50 .50

Souvenir Sheet

Solar Eclipse of Dec. 4, 2002 — A416

2002, Dec. 4 ***Perf. 14½***

1303 A416 4.75r multi 1.50 1.50

ICC Cricket World Cup — A417

No. 1304: a, Huts with windmill blades. b, Horseman. c, Cricket players with bats. d, Bus with people on roof. e, Mother and child. f, Double-decker bus.

2003, Feb. 28 ***Perf. 14¼x13¾***

1304 A417 (1.50r) Sheet of 6, #a-f 2.75 2.75

Souvenir Sheet

Tembisile (Chris) Hani (1942-93), African National Congress Leader — A418

2003, Apr. 27 **Litho.** ***Perf. 14¾***

1305 A418 (1.65r) multi .60 .60

See note after No. 1321.

Life in Informal Settlements — A419

No. 1306: a, Women carrying water jugs on head. b, Man with guitar. c, Man with rake. d, Woman using sewing machine. e, Two children. f, Drink vendor. g, Shoemakers. h, Woman with green cap. i, Young woman with cap and tire. j, Woman with child.

2003, May 16 ***Perf. 14x13¾***

1306 A419 (1.65r) Sheet of 10, #a-j 5.25 5.25

Souvenir Sheet

Africa Day — A420

2003, May 25 ***Perf. 14¾***
1307 A420 11.70r multi 3.75 3.75

Souvenir Sheet

Oliver Reginald Tambo (1917-93), African National Congress President — A421

2003, May 29
1308 A421 (1.65r) multi 1.25 1.25

See note after No. 1321.

Ballroom Dancing — A422

Designs: 1.65r, Salsa. 2.20r, Rumba. 2.80r, Waltz. 3.30r, Foxtrot. 3.80r, Tango.

2003, July 23 ***Perf. 13¼x13¾***
1309-1313 A422 Set of 5 4.75 4.75

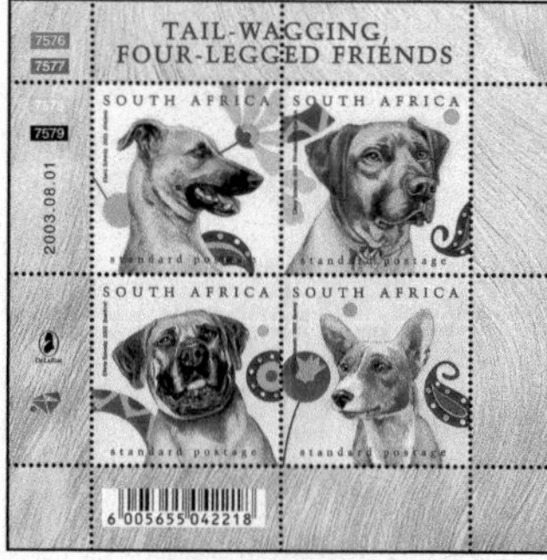

Dogs — A423

No. 1314: a, Africanis. b, Rhodesian Ridgeback. c, Boerboel. d, Basenji.

2003, Aug. 1 ***Perf. 14½***
1314 A423 (1.65r) Sheet of 4, #a-d 2.75 2.75

Type of 2000

Designs: No. 1315, Botterblom, vert. No. 1316, Blue marguerite, vert. No. 1317, Karoo violet, vert. No. 1318, Tree pelargonium, vert. No. 1319, Black-eyed susy, vert.

2003, Sept. 15 **Litho.** ***Perf. 13***

1315	A383 (1.65r) multi	.60	.60
a.	(2.40r) Perf. 14x13¾	.65	.65
b.	(2.40r) Perf. 14¾x14½	.65	.65
1316	A383 (1.65r) multi	.60	.60
a.	(2.40r) Perf. 14x13¾	.65	.65
b.	(2.40r) Perf. 14¾x14½	.65	.65
1317	A383 (1.65r) multi	.60	.60
a.	(2.40r) Perf. 14x13¾	.65	.65
b.	(2.40r) Perf. 14¾x14½	.65	.65
1318	A383 (1.65r) multi	.60	.60
a.	(2.40r) Perf. 14x13¾	.65	.65
b.	(2.40r) Perf. 14¾x14½	.65	.65
1319	A383 (1.65r) multi	.60	.60
a.	Horiz. strip of 5, #1315-1319	3.00	3.00
b.	(2.40r) Perf. 14x13¾	.65	.65
c.	Horiz. strip of 5, #1315a, 1316a, 1317a, 1318a, 1319b	3.25	3.25
d.	(2.40r) Perf. 14¾x14½	.65	.65
e.	Horiz. strip of 5, #1315b, 1316b, 1317b, 1318b, 1319d	3.25	3.25

Issued: Nos. 1315a, 1316a, 1317a, 1318a, 1319b, 2/1/10; Nos. 1315b, 1316b, 1317b, 1318b, 1319d, 2/24/10.

Souvenir Sheet

Walter Max Ulyate Sisulu (1912-2003), African National Congress Deputy President — A424

2003, Sept. 24 ***Perf. 14¾***
1320 A424 11.70r multi 4.75 4.75

See note after No. 1321.

Souvenir Sheet

Robert Mangaliso Sobukwe (1924-1978), Pan Africanist Congress President — A425

2003, Sept. 24 ***Perf. 14¾***
1321 A425 11.70r multi 4.75 4.75

Nos. 1295, 1305, 1308, 1320 and 1321 were sold in, but unattached to, a commemorative booklet that sold for 60r.

Stamp of Fortune Television Show — A426

2003, Sept. 29 ***Perf. 14¼x14***
1322 A426 (1.65r) multi .60 .60

Engineering and Postal Communication — A427

No. 1323, (3.30r): a, Shongweni Dam (60x23mm). b, Kimberley Microwave Tower (30x47mm). c, Northern Cape Legislature Building (30x23mm). d, Durban Westville highway interchange (30x47mm). e, Postal truck on Community Bridge, Limpopo (30x23mm). f, Nelson Mandela Bridge, Johannesburg (60x23mm).

2003, Oct. 9 ***Perf. 14x14¼***
1323 A427 Sheet of 6, #a-f 8.00 8.00
g. Like No. 1323, with PIARC World Road Congress inscription in margin 8.00 8.00

Souvenir Sheet

South Africa - India Diplomatic Relations, 10th Anniv. — A428

2003, Oct. 16 ***Perf. 14¾***
1324 A428 3.35r multi 1.40 1.40

Bid for Hosting 2010 World Cup Soccer Championships — A429

Emblem, soccer fan with painted face and: No. 1325, (3.80r), Map of Africa. No. 1326, (4.25r), Soccer players.

2003, Oct. 23
1325-1326 A429 Set of 2 2.40 2.40

No. 1325 is airmail.

Cape of Good Hope Triangle Stamps, 150th Anniv. A430

2003, Oct. 23 **Litho.** ***Perf. 12½x12¾***
1327 A430 (1.65r) blue .60 .60

Printed in sheets of 4.

A431

Christmas — A432

No. 1328: a, Joseph, Mary on donkey. b, Angels. c, Magi. d, Madonna and Child. e, Dove.

2003, Nov. 3 **Litho.** ***Perf. 14x14¼***
1328 Horiz. strip of 5 3.00 3.00
a.-e. A431 (1.65r) Any single .55 .55

Perf. 14¾
1329 A432 3.80r shown 1.50 1.50

Elephants — A433

No. 1330: a, African elephants. b, Asian elephant.

2003, Dec. 9 ***Perf. 14¼x14***
1330 A433 3.35r Horiz. pair, #a-b 3.25 3.25

South Africa — Thailand diplomatic relations, 10th anniv. See Thailand No. 2105.

Powered Flight, Cent. — A434

No. 1331: a, Paterson Biplane. b, "Silver Queen" Vickers Vimy. c, Wapiti. d, De Havilland DH-9. e, Junkers Ju52/53. f, Sikorsky S-55 helicopter. g, Boeing 707. h, Rooivalk helicopter. i, SUNSAT Microsatellite. j, Mark Shuttleworth, first African in space, and Space Station.

2003, Dec. 17 ***Perf. 14¼x14***
1331 A434 (1.65r) Sheet of 10, #a-j 7.00 7.00

Souvenir Sheet

New Year 2004 (Year of the Monkey) — A435

2004, Jan. 22 ***Perf. 13¾***
1332 A435 11.70r multi 4.50 4.50

Road Safety A436

No. 1333 — Inscriptions: a, Be visible. b, Don't drink and drive. c, Maintain your vehicle. d, Slow down. e, Don't drive when tired.

Perf. 13¼x13¾

2004, Mar. 24 **Litho.**
1333 Vert. strip of 5 3.00 3.00
a.-e. A436 (1.70r) Any single .60 .60

End of Apartheid, 10th Anniv. — A437

No. 1334: a, Dove, map of Africa. b, People voting. c, Women and child. d, Sports fans holding flag and trophies. e, Woman with handicrafts.

2004, Apr. 27 Litho. *Perf. 13¼*
1334 Vert. strip of 5 3.00 3.00
a.-e. A437 (1.70r) Any single .60 .60

Miniature Sheet

Legacy of Slaves — A438

No. 1335, (1.70r): a, Slave bell, Vergelegen, and slave lodge, Cape Town. b, Hidayat al-Islam, first book in Arabic-Afrikaans. c, Chair and cupboard. d, Traditional foods. e, Indian workers in sugar cane fields. f, Chinese mine workers.

2005, May 1
1335 A438 Sheet of 6, #a-f 4.25 4.25

Souvenir Sheet

FIFA (Fédération Internationale de Football Association), Cent. — A439

2004, Apr. 30 Litho. *Perf. 14¾*
1336 A439 4.35r multi 2.00 2.00

Spiders — A440

No. 1337: a, Hedgehog spider. b, Golden orb-web spider, vert. c, Lynx spider, vert. d, Black button spider, vert. e, Ladybird spider. f, Flower crab spider. g, Rain spider, vert. h, Horn baboon spider. i, Trap door spider. j, Spotted crab spider.

Serpentine Die Cut 9½x9, 9x9½
2004, July 30
Self-Adhesive
1337 A440 Sheet of 10, #a-j 7.50 7.50
a.-j. (1.70r) Any single .75 .75

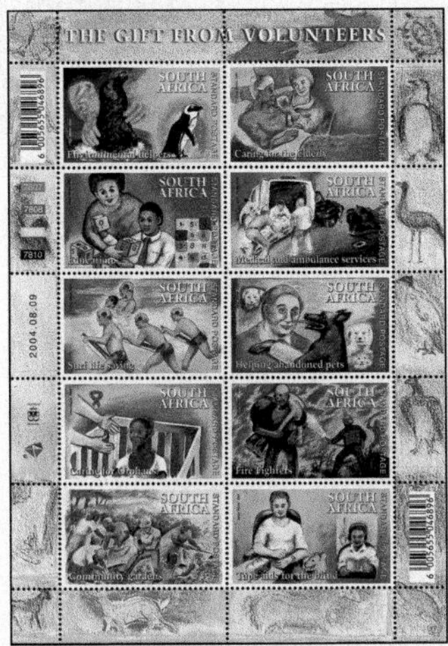

Volunteers — A441

No. 1338: a, Environmental helpers. b, Caring for the elderly. c, Education. d, Medical and ambulance services. e, Surf life saving. f, Helping abandoned pets. g, Caring for orphans. h, Fire fighters. i, Community gardens. j, Tape aids for the blind.

2004, Aug. 9 *Perf. 13½x13¾*
1338 A441 (1.70r) Sheet of 10, #a-j 7.00 7.00

Sports — A442

No. 1339: a, Archery. b, Track. c, Equestrian. d, Cycling. e, Rhythmic gymnastics. f, Canoeing. g, Soccer. h, Swimming. i, Boxing. j, Tennis.

2004, Aug. 13 *Perf. 13¾x13½*
1339 A442 (1.70r) Sheet of 10, #a-j 7.00 7.00

Christmas A443

Icons: (1.70r), Madonna and Child. (4r), Jesus Christ, Pantocrator.

2004, Oct. 1
1340-1341 A443 Set of 2 2.00 2.00

No. 1341 is inscribed "International Airmail Letter."

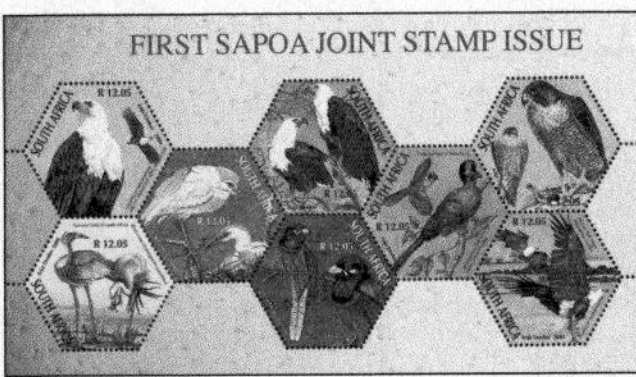

Birds — A444

No. 1342: a, African fish eagles, national bird of Namibia. b, African fish eagles, national bird of Zimbabwe. c, Peregrine falcons, national bird of Angola. d, Cattle egrets, national bird of Botswana. e, Purple-crested louries, national bird of Swaziland. f, Blue cranes, national bird of South Africa. g, Bar-tailed trogons. h, African fish eagles, national bird of Zambia.

2004, Oct. 9 *Perf. 14*
1342 A444 12.05r Sheet of 8, #a-h 32.50 32.50

See Botswana Nos. 792-793, Namibia No. 1052, Swaziland Nos. 727-735, Zambia No. 1033, and Zimbabwe No. 975.

Souvenir Sheet

Regular Air Mail Service in South Africa, 75th Anniv. — A445

Litho. with Hologram
2004, Oct. 9 *Perf. 13¾*
1343 A445 12.05r multi 4.25 4.25

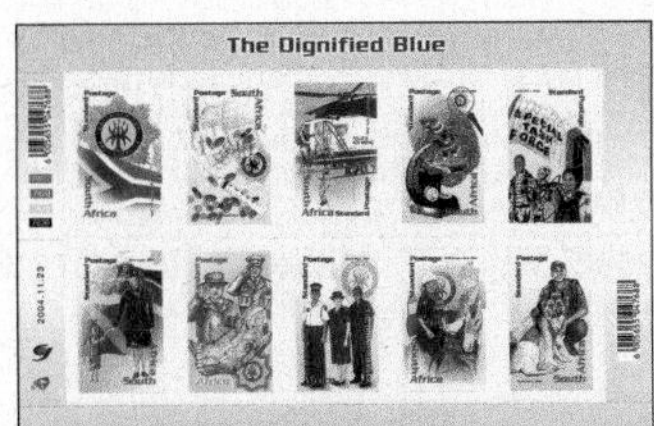

South African Police Service, 10th Anniv. — A446

No. 1344: a, South African Police Service badge, South African flag. b, Fighting drugs. c, Police air wing. d, Fingerprint and forensic science. e, Special task force. f, Protecting women and children. g, Sector policing. h, The Dignified Blue. i, SAPS mounted unit. j, Dog unit.

Serpentine Die Cut 13½x13
2004, Nov. 23 Litho.
Self-Adhesive
1344 A446 Sheet of 10 7.00 7.00
a.-j. (1.70r) Any single .70 .70

South African Large Telescope A447

No. 1345: a, Exterior of building. b, Cutaway view of building. c, Building aperture, top of telescope, Southern Cross constellation. d, Telescope. e, Building aperture, entire telescope.

2004, Dec. 1 *Perf. 13¾x13½*
1345 Horiz. strip of 5 8.00 8.00
a.-e. A447 4r Any single 1.60 1.60

Souvenir Sheet

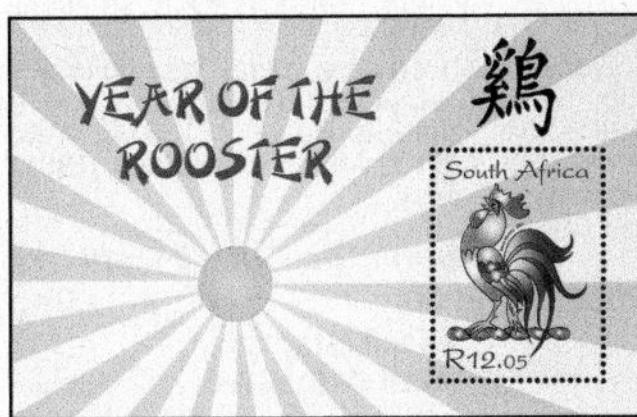

New Year 2005 (Year of the Rooster) — A448

2005, Feb. 9 *Perf. 14¾x14½*
1346 A448 12.05r multi 4.50 4.50

Souvenir Sheet

Freedom Charter, 50th Anniv. — A449

No. 1347: a, "Freedom Charter" in mirror image. b, "Freedom Charter" and "50."

Perf. 14¼x14¾
2005, June 24 Litho.
1347 A449 (1.77r) Sheet of 2, #a-b 1.40 1.40

Miniature Sheet

Legends — A450

No. 1348: a, Honeyguide's Revenge. b, How Ostrich Got His Long Neck. c, How Serval Got His Spots. d, How Zebra Got His Stripes. e, Jackal, the Tiger Eater. f, Jackal and Wolf. g, King Lion and King Eagle. h, Mantis and the Moon. i, Words as Sweet as Honey from Sankhambi. j, When Lion Could Fly.

2005, July 1
1348 A450 B5 Sheet of 10, #a-j 12.00 12.00

Nos. 1348a-11348j each sold for 3.75r on day of issue.

Miniature Sheet

Small Mammals — A451

No. 1349: a, Lesser bushbaby (24x60mm). b, Riverine rabbit (24x30mm). c, African wildcat (48x30mm). d, Yellow mongoose (24x60mm). e, Steenbok (48x30mm). f, Cape fox (24x30mm).

2005, July 15 *Perf. 14*
1349 A451 (1.77r) Sheet of 6, #a-f 4.25 4.25

Energy Sources — A452

2005, Sept. 26 *Perf. 14x14¼*
1350 A452 (1.77r) Wave .70 .70
1351 A452 (3.65r) Wind 1.40 1.40
1352 A452 (4.25r) Sun 1.75 1.75
Nos. 1350-1352 (3) 3.85 3.85

Inscription on No. 1350, Standard Postage; No. 1351, International Airmail Postcard; No. 1352, International Airmail Letter.

Christmas A453

Wire and bead sculptures: (1.77r), Candle, Christmas tree, heart. (4.25r), Angel and dove.

2005, Oct. 3

1353 A453 (1.77r) multi .70 .70
1354 A453 (4.25r) multi 1.60 1.60

Inscription on No. 1353, Standard Postage; No. 1354, International Airmail Letter.

Prevention of Blindness — A454

Litho. & Embossed

2005, Oct. 13 ***Perf. 14¼x14***

1355 A454 (1.77r) org brn & gray .70 .70

Souvenir Sheet

New Year 2006 (Year of the Dog) — A455

No. 1356: a, Seeing-eye dog. b, Drug-sniffing dog and luggage. c, Bird-chasing dog at airport.

2006, Jan. 26 ***Perf. 13¼x13***

1356 A455 B5 Sheet of 3, #a-c 4.25 4.25

Nos. 1356a-1356c each sold for 3.75r on day of issue.

Rock Art — A456

No. 1357: a, Detail of Linton Panel, Iziko South African Museum. b, Reedbuck, South African Museum of Rock Art (inscription at LR). c, San ritual specialist, South African Museum of Rock Art (inscription at LL). d, Rhinoceros, Wildebeest Kuil rock art site. e, Eland, Game Pass rock art site.

2006, Feb. 15

1357 Horiz. strip of 5 3.50 3.50
a.-e. A456 (1.77r) Any single .70 .70

Miniature Sheet

Rural Medical Outreach — A457

No. 1358: a, Helicopter and rescuer (24x60mm). b, Doctors clasping hands (24x30mm). c, Airplane, paramedics tending to man on stretcher, horiz. (48x30mm). d, Motorcycle ambulance, paramedic assisting man (24x30mm). e, Phelophepa Health Train, doctor examining woman, horiz. (72x30mm). f, Ambulance, attendants moving patient on gurney (24x30mm).

2006, May 2 Litho. ***Perf. 13¼***

1358 A457 (1.85r) Sheet of 6, #a-f 4.25 4.25

Chief Bhambatha Zondi, Leader of 1906 Rebellion — A458

2006, June 9 ***Perf. 14x13½***

1359 A458 (1.85r) multi .65 .65

Red Cross War Memorial Children's Hospital, 50th Anniv. — A459

Designs: (1.85r), Nurse and ill child. (4.40r), Hospital building, horiz.

Perf. 13¾x13½, 13½x13¾

2006, June 18

1360-1361 A459 Set of 2 2.25 2.25

Inscription on No. 1360 reads "Standard Postage;" on No. 1361, "International Letter."

Flowers Type of 2000

Designs: No, 1361A, Botterblom, vert. Nos. 1361B, 1361G, Blue marguerite, vert. No. 1361C, Karoo violet, vert. No. 1361I, Tree pelargonium, vert. No. 1361J, Black-eyed susan, vert.

Non-English country name inscriptions at top: No. 1361A, Afrika Borwa. Nos. 1361B, 1361I, Ningizimu Afrika. No. 1361C, Suid-Afrika. No. 1361G, Afrika Sewula. No. 1361J, Mzantsi Afrika.

Serpentine Die Cut 12¾x14

2008, June 30 Litho.

Coil Stamps
Self-Adhesive

1361A A384 (1.40r) multi —
1361B A384 (1.40r) multi —
1361C A384 (1.40r) multi —
1361G A384 (1.40r) multi —
1361I A384 (1.40r) multi —
1361J A384 (1.40r) multi —

Four additional stamps were issued in this set. The editors would like to examine any examples of them.

Souvenir Sheet

Women's Anti-Apartheid March to the Union Building, Pretoria, 50th Anniv. — A460

2006, Aug. 9 ***Perf. 14¾x14***

1362 A460 B5 multi 1.40 1.40

No. 1362 sold for 3.75r on day of issue.

Miniature Sheet

Clivia Flowers — A461

No. 1363, (1.85r): a, Clivia nobilis. b, Clivia miniata. c, Clivia gardenii. d, Clivia caulescens. e, Clivia mirabilis. f, Clivia robusta.

2006, Sept. 6 ***Perf. 13x13¼***

1363 A461 Sheet of 6, #a-f 3.25 3.25

Animal, Text and Tracks A462

Animal, Herd and Tracks A463

No. 1364: a, Buffalo. b, Elephant. c, Blue wildebeest. d, Hippopotamus. e, Black rhinoceros. f, Giraffe. g, Spotted hyena. h, Leopard. i, Warthog. j, Zebra.

Litho. & Embossed

2006, Sept. 15 ***Perf. 13¾x13¼***

1364 Sheet of 10 6.00 6.00
a.-e. A462 (1.85r) Any single .60 .60
f.-j. A463 (1.85r) Any single .60 .60

Christmas — A464

No. 1365: a, Antelope. b, Warthog. c, Zebra. d, Hippopotamus. e, Lion, as Santa, in sleigh. (4.40r), Lion as Santa.

2006, Oct. 2 Litho. ***Perf. 13½x13***

1365 Horiz. strip of 5 2.50 2.50
a.-e. A464 (1.85r) Any single .50 .50
1366 A464 (4.40r) multi 1.40 1.40

Inscriptions on Nos. 1365a-1365e read "Standard Postage;" on No. 1366, "International Airmail Letter."

World Post Day — A465

No. 1367 — Boy and slogan: a, "Start an Adventure." b, "Be Cool." c, "Learn More." d, "Have Fun." e, "Travel the World."

2006, Oct. 9 ***Perf. 13x13¼***

1367 Horiz. strip of 5 2.50 2.50
a.-e. A465 (1.85r) Any single .50 .50

Owls — A466

No. 1368: a, Barn owl. b, Cape eagle owl. c, African barred owlet. d, Verreaux's eagle owl. e, Pel's fishing owl.

2007, Aug. 3 Litho. ***Perf. 14½***

1368 Horiz. strip of 5 6.50 6.50
a.-e. A466 (4.64r) Any single 1.25 1.25

Souvenir Sheet

Scouting, Cent. — A467

No. 1369: a, Scout saluting. b, Scouting fleur-de-lis.

2007, Aug. 22

1369 A467 (3.90r) Sheet of 2, #a-b 2.25 2.25

Souvenir Sheet

New Year 2007 (Year of the Pig) — A468

Litho. & Embossed With Foil Application

2007, Sept. 7

1370 A468 (4.89r) green & gold 2.75 2.75

World Post Day — A469

2007, Oct. 9 Litho. ***Perf. 14x14¼***

1371 A469 (3.90r) multi 1.25 1.25

First telephone exchange in South Africa, 125th anniv.

Cheetah A470

Ostrich
A471

2007, Oct. 19 ***Perf. 14***
1372 A470 (3.90r) multi 1.25 1.25
1373 A471 (4.89r) multi 1.50 1.50
a. Perf. 14¾x14½ 1.60 1.60

Issued: No. 1373a, 9/3/09.

Miniature Sheet

Intl. Polar and Heliophysical Year — A472

No. 1374: a, King penguins (24x30mm). b, Scientists at SANAE IV Base, Antarctica (72x30mm). c, Wandering albatross (24x60mm). d, Adélie penguins (24x30mm). e, Killer whale (48x30mm). f, Weddell seal (24x30mm).

2007, Oct. 31
1374 A472 (1.93r) Sheet of 6, #a-f 3.50 3.50

Mills — A473

No. 1375: a, Mostert's Mill, Cape Town. b, La Cotte Watermill, Franschhoek. c, Witpoort Watermill, Stoffberg. d, Dwars Rivier Watermill, Cederberg. e, Colesberg Horse and Mill, Colesberg.

2007, Nov. 9 ***Perf. 14½***
1375 Vert. strip of 5 7.00 7.00
a.-e. A473 (4.64r) Any single 1.40 1.40

Union Castle Line Ships
A474

No. 1376: a, Dane. b, Kildonan Castle. c, SA Vaal. d, Edinburgh Castle. e, Windsor Castle.

2007, Dec. 5
1376 Vert. strip of 5 6.25 6.25
a.-e. A474 (4.01r) Any single 1.25 1.25

118th Inter-Parliamentary Union Assembly, Cape Town — A475

2008, Apr. 13 **Litho.** ***Perf. 13¾***
1377 A475 (2.05r) multi .55 .55

Diplomatic Relations Between South Africa and People's Republic of China — A476

No. 1378 — Flags of South Africa and People's Republic of China: a, Within circle of text. b, Above text.

2008, Apr. 24
1378 A476 Sheet of 2 1.90 1.90
a. (2.05r) multi .55 .55
b. (4.90r) multi 1.25 1.25

No. 1378a is inscribed "Standard Postage"; No. 1378b, "International Airmail Small Letter."

Miniature Sheet

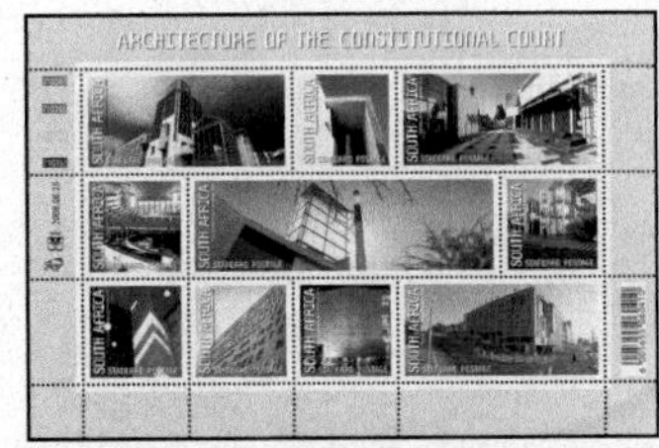
Constitutional Court Buildings — A477

No. 1379: a, Part of building, looking up from street level (56x26mm). b, Covered entranceway (26x26mm). c, Plaza between buildings (56x26mm). d, Chambers (26x26mm). e, Rectangular and cylindrical towers (86x26mm). f, Three-storied buildings and plaza (26x26mm). g, Shadows on interior column (26x26mm). h, Wall with multicolored words (26x26mm). i, Curved wall (26x26mm). j, Building and street (56x26mm).

2008, June 25 ***Perf. 14x13¼***
1379 A477 Sheet of 10 5.25 5.25
a.-j. (2.05r) Any single .50 .50

Nos. 1379a-1379j are each inscribed "Standard Postage."

Souvenir Sheets

A478

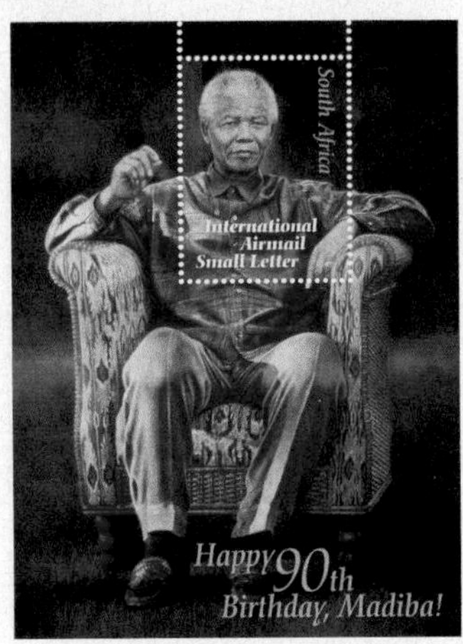

Pres. Nelson Mandela, 90th Birthday — A479

2008, July 15 ***Perf. 13¼***
1380 A478 (2.05r) multi .60 .60
1381 A479 (4.90r) multi 1.40 1.40

No. 1381 is airmail.

Souvenir Sheet

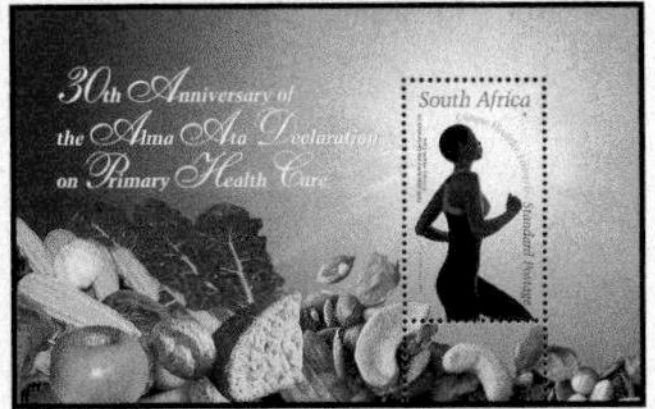

Alma Ata Declaration on Primary Health Care, 30th Anniv. — A480

2008, Sept. 6 **Litho.** ***Perf. 13¼x14***
1382 A480 (2.05r) multi .50 .50

Souvenir Sheet

Onderstepoort, Cent. — A481

Litho. With Foil Application
2008, Oct. 8 ***Perf. 13¾x13¼***
1383 A481 (2.05r) multi .45 .45

World Post Day — A482

No. 1384: a, Aberdeen Post Office. b, West Bank Post Office, East London. c, Main Post Office, Durban. d, Church Square Post Office, Pretoria. e, Frankfort Post Office.

2008, Oct. 9 **Litho.** ***Perf. 13¼x13¾***
1384 Horiz. strip of 5 2.25 2.25
a.-e. A482 (2.05r) Any single .45 .45

Nos. 1384a-1384e are each inscribed "Standard Postage."

Miniature Sheets

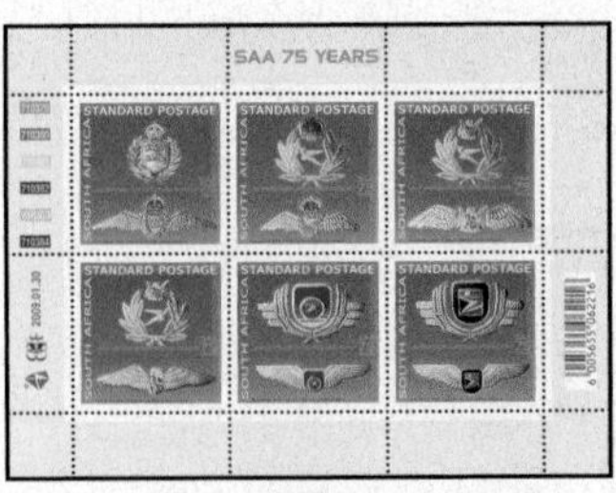

A483

South African Airways, 75th Anniv. — A484

No. 1385 — Captain's cap and uniform insignia, with cap insignia at top: a, With "S.A.A./S.A.L" in crest. b, With large crown over winged springbok flying left. c, With coat of arms above winged springbok flying left. d, With coat of arms above winged springbok flying right. e, With winged springbok in red circle. f, With crest having colors of South African flag.

No. 1386 — Airline emblem on tail of: a, Junkers Ju53/3m. b, Douglas DC-4. c, Boeing 707. d, Boeing 747 (winged springbok). e, Airbus A300. f, Boeing 747 (colors of South African flag).

Litho. & Embossed With Foil Application
2009, Jan. 30 ***Perf. 13¼***
1385 A483 Sheet of 6 2.40 2.40
a.-f. (2.05r) Any single .40 .40

Litho.
1386 A484 Sheet of 6 5.75 5.75
a.-f. (4.90r) Any single .95 .95

Nos. 1385a-1385f are inscribed "Standard Postage"; Nos. 1386a-1386f, "International Airmail Small Letter."

Rose Varieties
A485

Serpentine Die Cut
2009, Feb. 13 **Litho.**
Self-Adhesive
1387 A485 (2.05r) Johannesburg Sun .40 .40
1388 A485 (2.05r) Rina Hugo .40 .40
1389 A485 (2.05r) Beauty From Within .40 .40
1390 A485 (2.05r) Bewitched .40 .40
1391 A485 (2.05r) Cotlands Rose .40 .40
a. Miniature sheet, 2 each #1387-1391 4.00
Nos. 1387-1391 (5) 2.00 2.00

Nos. 1387-1391 are each inscribed "Standard Postage."

Souvenir Sheet

Intl. Polar Year — A486

2009, Mar. 2 ***Perf. 13¼x13¾***

1392 A486 Sheet of 2 1.40 1.40
a. (2.05r) Sooty albatrosses .40 .40
b. (4.90r) Jellyfish 1.00 1.00

No. 1392a is inscribed "Standard Postage"; No. 1392b, "International Small Letter."

Pres. Kgalema Motlanthe A487

2009, Mar. 19 ***Perf. 14½***

1393 A487 (2.05r) multi .45 .45

Occupational Health — A488

No. 1394 — Inscriptions: a, Ergonomics in the office. b, Medical surveillance. c, Personal protective equipment. d, Ensure a safe work place. e, Training in the work place.

2009, Mar. 20 ***Perf. 13¾x13¼***

1394 Vert. strip of 5 2.25 2.25
a.-e. A488 (2.05r) Any single .45 .45

Miniature Sheet

Artwork in the Constitutional Court — A489

No. 1395: a, The Benefit of the Doubt 2, tapestry by Marlene Dumas (26x35mm). b, Forgotten Family 1, by Penny Siopis (52x35mm). c, Bass Player, by Dumile Feni (26x35mm). d, Head, by William Kentridge (26x35mm). e, Hotel with Landscape (Spy), by Robert Hodgins (52x35mm). f, Hotlands, by Andrew Verster (26x70mm). g, Discussion, tapestry by Willie Bester (52x35mm). h, The Smoker, by Gerard Sekoto (52x35mm). i, Tethered Monkey, by Albert Adams (26x35mm). j, Blue Dress 3, by Judith Mason (26x35mm).

2009, June 5 **Litho.** ***Perf. 14½***

1395 A489 Sheet of 10 5.50 5.50
a.-j. (2.25r) Any single .55 .55

Nos. 1395a-1395j are inscribed "Standard Postage."

Artifacts From Mapungubwe Archaeological Site — A490

No. 1396: a, Gold bowl. b, Spouted pots. c, Gold rhinoceros. d, Terra cotta bowl. e, Gold scepter.

2009, Sept. 23

1396 Horiz. strip of 5 7.50 7.50
a.-e. A490 (5.40r) Any single 1.50 1.50

Nos. 1396a-1396e are inscribed "International Small Letter."

Souvenir Sheets

South Africa No. 1 — A491

Show Emblem — A492

2009, Oct. 9 ***Perf. 13¾***

1397 A491 (2.25r) multi .60 .60
1398 A492 (5.40r) multi 1.50 1.50

Joburg 2010 Intl. Stamp Show, Johannesburg. No. 1397 is inscribed "Standard Postage," and No. 1398, "International Small Letter."

Souvenir Sheet

Solomon Kalushi Mahlangu (1956-79), Executed African National Congress Member — A493

2009, Oct. 15 ***Perf. 13¼x13¾***

1399 A493 (2.25r) multi .60 .60

No. 1399 is inscribed "Standard Postage."

Pres. Jacob Zuma A494

2009, Nov. 10 ***Perf. 13¼***

1400 A494 (2.25r) multi .60 .60

Miniature Sheet

Bridging the Digital Divide — A495

No. 1401: a, People, cellular phone, open letter (56x28mm triangle). b, City, cellular phones, envelope (28x28mm square). c, Envelope and letter (80x40mm triangle). d, Letter box and digital code (20x60mm rhomboid). e, Computer, boat, hot-air balloons, paper airplane (80x40mm triangle).

Litho. With Foil Application

2010, Jan. 18 ***Perf. 13¾***

1401 A495 Sheet of 5 + label 5.50 5.50
a.-e. (4.05r) Any single 1.10 1.10

Nos. 1401a-1401e are inscribed "Southern Africa Small Letter."

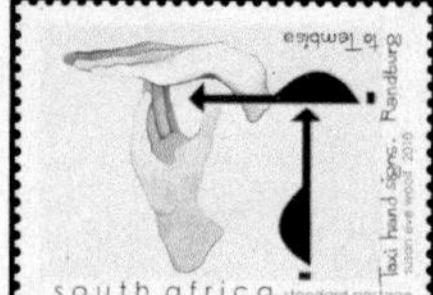

Hand Signs for Calling Taxis A496

No. 1402: a, Randberg to Tembisa. b, Tembisa to Sebenza. c, Turffontein to Mulbarton. d, Gauteng to Johannesburg Central Business District. e, Germiston to Katlehong. f, Johannesburg to Sandton. g, Alexandra to Randburg. h, Emdeni to Highgate. i, Local to the area. j, Johannesburg to Phola Park.

2010, Jan. 29 **Litho.** ***Perf. 13¾x13¼***

1402 Sheet of 10 6.00 6.00
a.-j. A496 (2.25r) Any single .60 .60

Nos. 1402a-1402j are inscribed "Standard Postage." Portions of the designs were applied by a thermographic process producing a shiny, raised effect. Sand grains were added to the thermographic ink.

Miniature Sheet

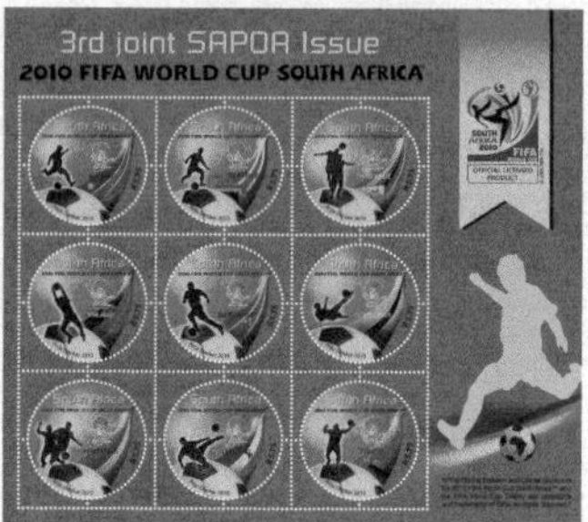

2010 World Cup Soccer Championships, South Africa — A497

No. 1403 — Soccer players, ball, 2010 World Cup mascot and flag of: a, Namibia. b, South Africa. c, Zimbabwe. d, Malawi. e, Swaziland. f, Botswana. g, Mauritius. h, Lesotho. i, Zambia.

2010, Apr. 9 ***Perf. 13¾***

1403 A497 Sheet of 9 14.50 14.50
a.-i. 5.75r Any single 1.60 1.60

See Botswana Nos. 896-905, Lesotho No. , Malawi No. 753, Mauritius No. 1086, Namibia No. 1188, Swaziland Nos. 794-803, Zambia Nos. 1115-1118, and Zimbabwe Nos. 1112-1121.

A single sheetlet of 9 omnibus issues exist containing 1403a. See footnote under Namibia 1188.

Miniature Sheet

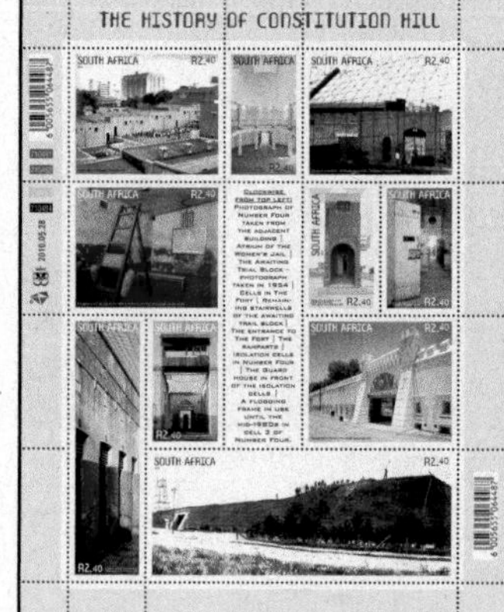

History of Constitution Hill — A498

No. 1404 — Photographs of Old Fort prison complex that housed famous political prisoners: a, Cellblock Number Four (48x40mm). b, Atrium of Women's Jail (24x40mm). c, Awaiting-Trial Block (48x40mm). d, Flogging frame in Cell 3 of Cellblock Number Four (48x40mm). e, Remaining stairwells of Awaiting-Trial Block (24x40mm). f, Cells in the Fort (24x40mm). g, Isolation cells in Cellblock Number Four (80x24mm). h, Guard house in front of isolation cells (24x40mm). i, Entrance to the Fort (48x40mm). j, Ramparts (96x40mm).

2010, May 28 ***Perf. 13½***

1404 A498 Sheet of 10 + central label 6.75 6.75
a.-j. 2.40r Any single .60 .60

A499

2010 World Cup Soccer Championships, South Africa — A500

Zakumi, official mascot of 2010 World Cup Soccer Championships: No. 1405, Holding soccer ball. No. 1406, Dribbling soccer ball, ball at right. No. 1407, Holding flag of South Africa. No. 1408, Running with soccer ball. No. 1409, With arms raised.

Designs: No. 1410, Emblem of 2010 World Cup Soccer Championships. No. 1411, Official soccer ball. No. 1412, World Cup Trophy.

2010, June 11 ***Die Cut***

Self-Adhesive

1405 A499 2.40r multi .65 .65
1406 A499 2.40r multi .65 .65
1407 A499 2.40r multi .65 .65
1408 A499 2.40r multi .65 .65
1409 A499 2.40r multi .65 .65
a. Horiz. strip of 5, #1405-1409 3.25

Serpentine Die Cut

1410 A500 4.90r multi 1.25 1.25
1411 A500 4.90r multi 1.25 1.25
1412 A500 4.90r multi 1.25 1.25
a. Sheet of 6, 2 each #1410-1412 7.50
Nos. 1405-1412 (8) 7.00 7.00

Miniature Sheet

South African Railways, 150th Anniv. — A501

No. 1413: a, Natal 0-4-0, 1860. b, Class NGC 16 Garratt 2-6-2+2-6-2, 1937. c, Class 24 2-8-4, 1948. d, Class 25 4-8-4, 1953. e, Class GMA/M Garratt 4-8-2+2-8-4, 1954. f, Class 35 Co-Co Diesel-electric locomotive, 1974. g, Class 9E Co-Co electric locomotive, 1978. h, Class 26 4-8-4, 1981. i, Class 19E Bo-Bo dual voltage electric locomotive, 2009. j, Gautrain Electrostar Bo-Bo, 2010.

2010, June 25 ***Perf. 13½x12¾***

1413 A501 Sheet of 10 6.25 6.25
a.-j. 2.40r Any single .60 .60

A531

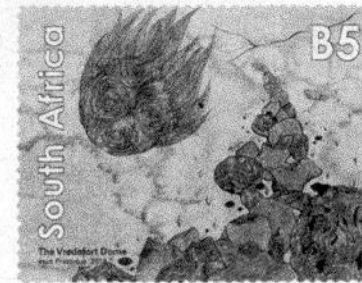
A532

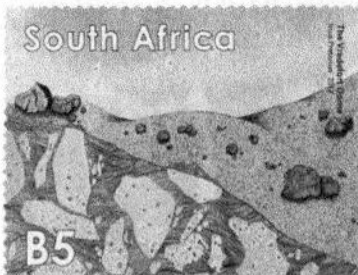
Ancient Meteorite Strike at Vredefort Dome UNESCO World Heritage Site — A533

Serpentine Die Cut 18

2012, Sept. 21 Self-Adhesive

1483	A529 (5.30r) multi		1.25	1.25
1484	A530 (5.30r) multi		1.25	1.25
1485	A531 (5.30r) multi		1.25	1.25
1486	A532 (5.30r) multi		1.25	1.25
1487	A533 (5.30r) multi		1.25	1.25
a.	Horiz. strip of 5, #1483-1487		6.25	
	Nos. 1483-1487 (5)		6.25	6.25

Nos. 1483-1487 are each inscribed "B5."

Miniature Sheet

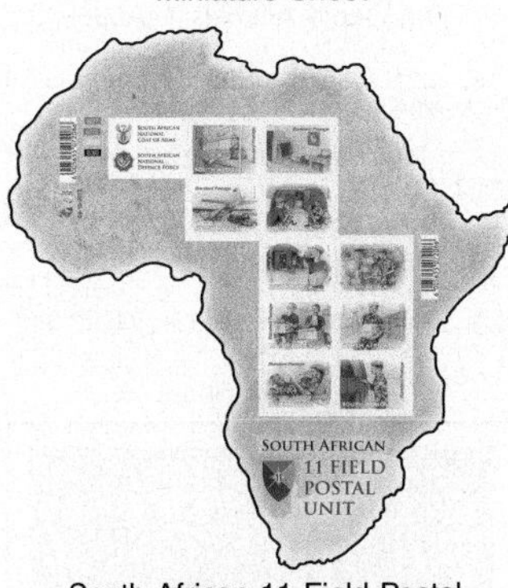

South African 11 Field Postal Unit — A534

No. 1488: a, Customer giving parcel to window clerk. b, Parcel on conveyor belt. c, Parcels on forklift near airplane. d, Five soldiers outside of field post office. e, Two soldiers with parcels at field post office. f, Soldier inventorying stack of parcels and mail bags. g, Soldiers opening parcels. h, Soldier holding parcel and letter. i, Soldier reading letter. j, Soldier placing letter in mail box.

Serpentine Die Cut 12½

2012, Oct. 9 Self-Adhesive

1488	A534	Sheet of 10	6.50	
a.-j.	(2.65r) Any single		.65	.65

Nos. 1488a-1488j each are inscribed "Standard Postage."

Miniature Sheet

Alexandra Township, Johannesburg, Cent. — A535

No. 1489 — Art: a, Alex Under Siege, by Kim Berman (40x30mm). b, Alexandra Scene, by David Koloane (40x30mm). c, Evening Township Scene, by Julian Motau (40x30mm). d, Alex Youth Collaborating, by Sipho Gwala (40x30mm). e, Alex from the Far East Bank, by Joachim schönfeldt.

2012, Oct. 26 ***Perf. 13x13¼***

1489	A535	Sheet of 5	8.00	8.00
a.-j.	(6.60r) Any single		1.60	1.60

Nos. 1489a-1489e each are inscribed "B4."

Souvenir Sheet

Go Digital — A536

2012, Nov. 23 ***Perf. 13¼x13¾***

1490	A536 (2.65r) multi		.65	.65

No. 1490 is inscribed "Standard Postage."

Souvenir Sheet

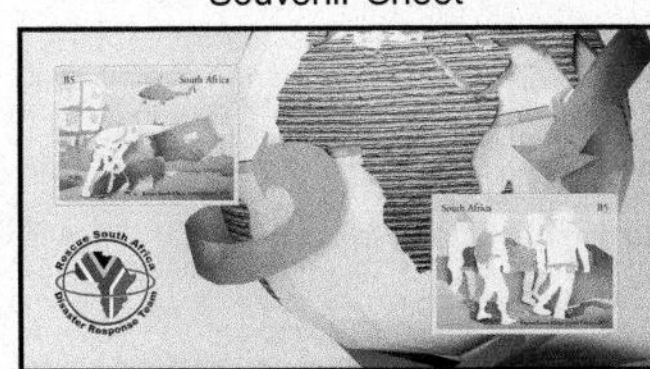
Rescue South Africa Disaster Response Team — A537

No. 1491: a, Disaster Response Team member, helicopter. b, Disaster Response Team members carrying litter.

Serpentine Die Cut 14½

2013, Feb. 22 Litho.

Self-Adhesive

1491	A537	Sheet of 2	2.50	
a.-b.	B5 Either single		1.25	1.25

Nos. 1491a-1491b each sold for 5.30r on day of issue.

Souvenir Sheet

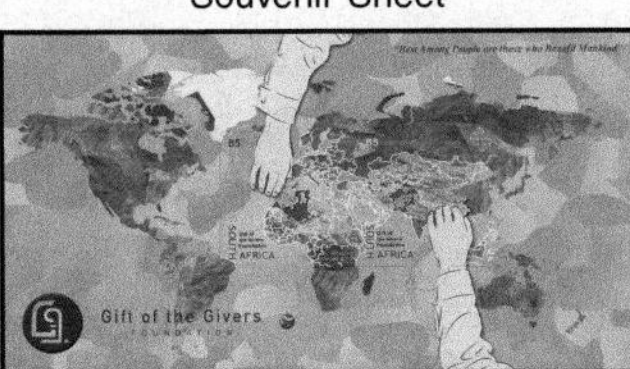

Gift of the Givers Foundation — A538

No. 1492: a, Hand, map of Europe and Africa. b, Hand, map of Asia.

2013, Feb. 22 ***Die Cut***

Self-Adhesive

1492	A538	Sheet of 2	2.50	
a.-b.	B5 Either single		1.25	1.25

Nos. 1492a-1492b each sold for 5.30r on day of issue.

Miniature Sheet

International Year of Water Cooperation — A539

No. 1493 — Inscriptions: a, Human consumption (hand holding glass under faucet). b, Working for Water Program (worker cutting log with chain saw). c, Industry (wind generators). d, Agriculture (irrigator). e, Biodiversity (fish and dragonfly).

2013, Mar. 22 ***Die Cut***

Self-Adhesive

1493	A539	Sheet of 5	7.00	
a.-e.	(6.30r) Any single		1.40	1.40

Nos. 1493a-1493e are each inscribed "International Small Letter." A rotatable cardboard disc is attached to the center of the sheet of stamps with a plastic grommet, allowing only one stamp and one block of informative text to be seen at a time. The unused value is for a sheet with the covering disc attached.

Miniature Sheet

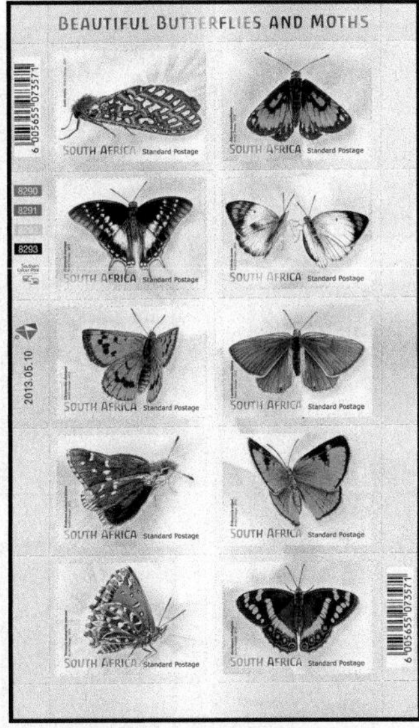

Butterflies and Moths — A540

No. 1494: a, Leto venus. b, Alaena margaritacea. c, Charaxes marieps. d, Colotis erone. e, Chrysoritis dicksoni. f, Lepidochrysops lotana. g, Kedestes barberae bunta. h, Erikssonia edgei. i, Trimenia malagrida maryae. j, Aeropetes tulbaghia.

Die Cut Perf. 14¾x14¼

2013, May 10 Self-Adhesive

1494	A540	Sheet of 10	5.50	
a.-j.	(2.80r) Any single		.55	.55

Nos. 1494a-1494j are each inscribed "Standard Postage."

Souvenir Sheet

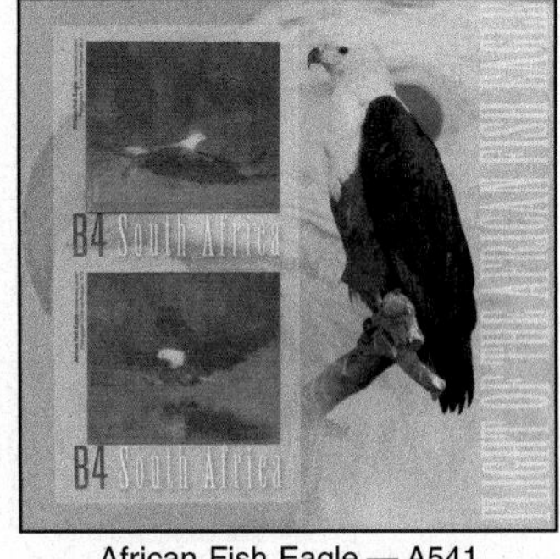
African Fish Eagle — A541

No. 1495 — Fish eagle facing: a, Right. b, Left.

Litho. With 3-Dimensional Plastic Affixed

Serpentine Die Cut 14½

2013, June 14 Self-Adhesive

1495	A541	Sheet of 2	2.80	
a.-b.	B4 Either single		1.40	1.40

Nos. 1495a-1495b each sold for 6.90r on day of issue.

Miniature Sheet

Kirstenbosch National Botanical Gardens, Cape Town, Cent. — A542

No. 1496: a, Silver tree (26x53mm). b, Natal lily (29x38mm). c, Centenary gold strelitzia amd bee (57x28mm triangular). d, Krantz aloe, bird and spider (26x53mm). e, Ninepin heath and bird (38x29mm). f, Silver restio (40x40mm triangular). g, Albany cycad (32x32mm). h, Welwitschia (57x28mm triangular). i, White gardenia (53x26mm). j, King protea and bird (32x32mm).

Litho., Sheet Margin Litho. With Foil Application

2013, July 1 ***Serpentine Die Cut 27***

Self-Adhesive

1496	A542	Sheet of 10	6.00	
a.-j.	(2.80r) Any single		.60	.60

Nos. 1496a-1496j are each inscribed "Standard Postage."

Miniature Sheet

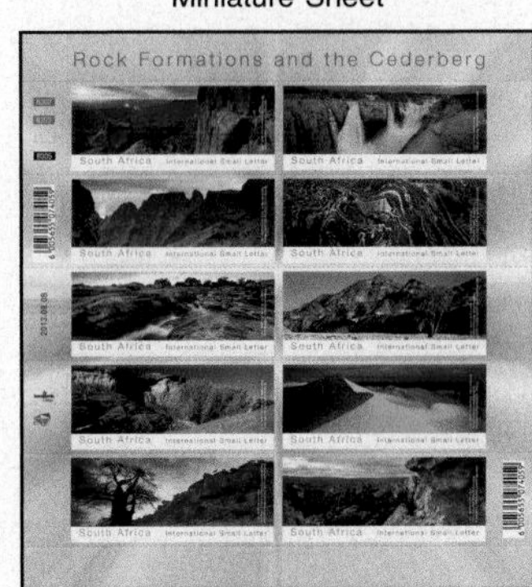

Rock Formations — A543

No. 1497: a, Igneous rock formation, Karoo National Park. b, Igneous rock formation and waterfall, Augrabies Falls National Park. c, Igneous rock formation, Gray's Pass, Drakensberg. d, Metamorphic rock formation of amphibolite in Sand River gneiss, Limpopo Province. e, Metamorphic rock formations on the Olifants River, Limpopo Province. f, Metamorphic rock formation, Ai-Ais Richtersveld National Park. g, Sedimentary rock formation, Golden Gate Highlands National Park. h, Sand dunes (future sedimentary rock formation),

Addo Elephant National Park. i, Sedimentary rock formation, Greater Mapungubwe Transfrontier Conservation Area. j, Table Mountain sandstone, Cederberg Wilderness Area.

Serpentine Die Cut 13½

2013, Aug. 8 **Litho.**

Self-Adhesive

1497 A543 Sheet of 10 14.00
a.-j. (6.60r) Any single 1.40 1.40

Nos. 1497a-1497j are each inscribed "International Small Letter."

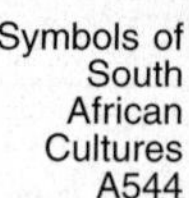

Symbols of South African Cultures A544

No. 1498: a, Blombos ochre, earliest symbolic design in South Africa. b, N'wana, symbol of fertility. c, Amasumpa, headrest symbolic of wealth. d, Ukhamba, ceremonial beer container symbolic of unity. e, Blombos shell beads, oldest symbolic ornaments in South Africa. f, Starburst engraving, symbol associated with womanhood. g, Rhinoceros engraving, symbol of rain and abundance. h, Phalaphala, horn symbolic of communication. i, Ngwenya symbol of royalty. j, Litshoba mhlope, ritual whisk symbolic of divine illumination.

Perf. 13¾x13¼

2013, Sept. 20 **Litho.**

1498 Sheet of 10 9.00 9.00
a.-j. A544 (4.50r) Any single .90 .90

Nos. 1498a-1498j are each inscribed "DL Fastmail."

Miniature Sheet

South African Post Office Achievements — A545

No. 1499 — Inscriptions: a, eBusiness boost communication. b, More people are banking on us. c, Address expansion. d, Providing third-party services of other organizations. e, Steps to reduce our carbon footprint.

Serpentine Die Cut

2013, Oct. 9 **Litho.**

Self-Adhesive

1499 A545 Sheet of 5 3.00
a.-e. (2.80r) Any single .60 .60

Nos. 1499a-1499e are each inscribed "Standard Postage."

Souvenir Sheet

Diplomatic Relations Between South Africa and Mexico, 20th Anniv. — A546

2013, Oct. 25 **Litho.** ***Perf. 12½***

1500 A546 (6.90r) multi 1.40 1.40

No. 1500 is inscribed "B4."

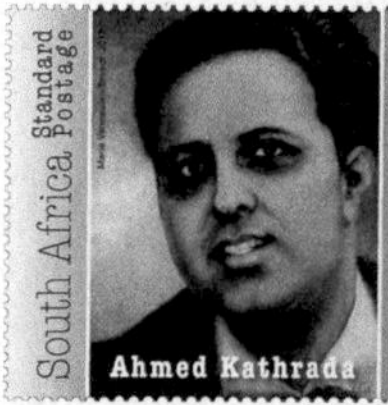

Rivonia Trial, 50th Anniv. A547

Defendants: No. 1501, Ahmed Kathrada. No. 1502, Andrew Mlangeni. No. 1503, Arthur Goldreich (1929-2011). No. 1504, Denis Goldberg. No. 1505, Elias Motsoaledi (1924-94). No. 1506, Govan Mbeki (1910-2001). No. 1507, Harold Wolpe (1926-96). No. 1508, James Kantor (1927-75). No. 1509, Lionel Bernstein (1920-2002). No. 1510, Nelson Mandela (1918-2013). No. 1511, Raymond Mhlaba (1920-2005). No. 1512, Walter Sisulu (1912-2003).

Perf. 14¾x14½

2013, Nov. 26 **Litho.**

Booklet Panes of 1

1501 A547 (2.80r) multi .55 .55
1502 A547 (2.80r) multi .55 .55
1503 A547 (2.80r) multi .55 .55
1504 A547 (2.80r) multi .55 .55
1505 A547 (2.80r) multi .55 .55
1506 A547 (2.80r) multi .55 .55
1507 A547 (2.80r) multi .55 .55
1508 A547 (2.80r) multi .55 .55
1509 A547 (2.80r) multi .55 .55
1510 A547 (2.80r) multi .55 .55
1511 A547 (2.80r) multi .55 .55
1512 A547 (2.80r) multi .55 .55
a. Complete booklet of 12, #1501-1512 6.75
Nos. 1501-1512 (12) 6.60 6.60

Nos. 1501-1512 were each inscribed "Standard Postage."

A548

A549

A550

A551

Details From Keiskamma Guernica — A552

Serpentine Die Cut 12¾x12¼ on 2 or 3 Sides

2013, Nov. 29 **Litho.**

Booklet Stamps

Self-Adhesive

1513 A548 (2.80r) multi .55 .55
1514 A549 (2.80r) multi .55 .55
1515 A550 (2.80r) multi .55 .55
1516 A551 (2.80r) multi .55 .55
1517 A552 (2.80r) multi .55 .55
a. Booklet pane of 10, 2 each #1513-1517 5.50
Nos. 1513-1517 (5) 2.75 2.75

World AIDS Day, 25th anniv. Nos. 1513-1517 are each inscribed "Standard Postage."

Miniature Sheets

A553

Union Buildings, Pretoria, Cent. — A554

No. 1518: a, Arcade around central court, with Tuscan colonnades and groin vault roof (60x30mm). b, Detail of Ionic order, loggia of West Wing (30x30mm). c, Tower Clock with Westminster chimes (30x30mm). d, Lantern, dome order and base of East Tower with Atlas sculpture, by Abraham Broadbent, on top (30x60mm). e, Hermes sculpture, by George Ness, Amphitheater (30x60mm). f, Rostrum, Amphitheater (30x60mm). g, Front view of the Union Buildings 60x30mm). h, Bronze sculpture of Southern Yellow-billed Hornbill, by Mike Edwards (30x30mm). i, Women's Memorial, iMbokodo (Grinding Stone), sculpture by Wilma Cruise (30x30mm). j, Carved stone lion's head, by Anton von Wouw (30x30mm).

No. 1519: a, Construction of building (60x30mm). b, Rostrum, Amphitheater (30x30mm). c, Construction of building, diff. (30x60mm). d, Aloe pretoriensis discovered on Meintjieskop (30x30mm). e, Carved keystone depicting cherub, by von Wouw (30x60mm). f, Construction of the Tower (30x60mm). g, Construction of building, diff. (30x30mm). h, Sir Herbert Baker (1862-1946), architect (30x30mm). i, Front view of buildings from the gardens (60x30mm). j, 1929 Armistice Day Service (30x30mm).

2013, Dec. 12 **Litho.** ***Perf. 13¼***

1518 A553 Sheet of 10 5.50 5.50
a.-j. (2.80r) Any single .55 .55
1519 A554 Sheet of 10 14.00 14.00
a.-j. (6.90r) Any single 1.40 1.40

Nos. 1518a-1519j are each inscribed "Standard Postage." Nos. 1519a-1519j are each inscribed "B4."

This stamp, released Feb. 11, 2014, had a franking value of 2.80r, but was only made available in a folder that sold for 50r.

Miniature Sheet

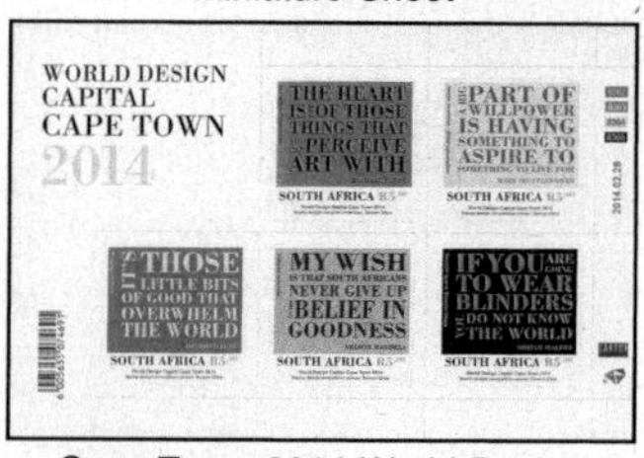

Cape Town, 2014 World Design Capital — A555

No. 1520 — Quotation from: a, Michael Elion. b, Mark Shuttleworth. c, Desmond Tutu. d, Nelson Mandela. e, Miriam Makeba.

Serpentine Die Cut 14½

2014, Feb. 28 **Litho.**

Self-Adhesive

1520 A555 Sheet of 5 4.75
a.-e. 5r Any single .95 .95

Miniature Sheet

Big Game Animals — A556

No. 1521: a, Leopard. b, Lion. c, Buffalos. d, Black rhinoceroses. e, Elephant.

Serpentine Die Cut 18

2014, May 9 **Litho.**

Self-Adhesive

1521 A556 Sheet of 5 7.00
a.-e. (7.20r) Any single 1.40 1.40

Nos. 1521a-1521e are each inscribed "B4."

Souvenir Sheet

Elephant, Fabric Art Embroidered by Tunga Embroidery Studio — A557

Litho. & Silk-Screened

2014, May 30 ***Perf. 13½x14***

1522 A557 (22.80r) multi 4.25 4.25

No. 1522 is inscribed "Econoparcel."

Souvenir Sheet

Hamilton Naki (1926-2005), Surgeon — A558

No. 1523: a, Naki, vert. b, Naki filling syringe, horiz.

Perf. 13½x13¼, 13¼x13½

2014, June 26 **Litho.**

1523 A558 Sheet of 2 6.00 6.00
a.-b. (15.25r) Either single 3.00 3.00

Nos. 1523a-1523b are each inscribed "International Small Parcel."

Popular Musicians — A559

No. 1524: a, Brenda Fassie (1964-2004). b, Solomon Linda (1909-62). c, Bernoldus Niemand (1959-95). d, Spokes Mashiyane (1933-72). e, Miriam Makeba (1932-2008). f, Johannes Kerkorrel (1960-2002). g, Lucky Dube (1964-2007). h, Simon Nkabinde (1935-99). i, Taliep Petersen (1950-2006). j, Kippie Moeketsi (1925-83).

Serpentine Die Cut 11

2014, July 3 Litho.

Self-Adhesive

1524 A559 Sheet of 10 6.00
a.-j. (3r) Any single .60 .60

Nos. 1524a-1524j are each inscribed "Standard Postage."

Miniature Sheet

World War I, Cent. — A560

No. 1525 — Inscriptions: a, German South West Africa Campaign. b, German East Africa Campaign. c, Palestine Campaign. d, S.S. Mendi. e, Delville Wood. f, Marrières Wood.

2014, July 28 Litho. *Perf. 13¼*

1525 A560 Sheet of 6 11.50 11.50
a.-f. 10r Any single 1.90 1.90

Souvenir Sheet

Democratic Elections, 20th Anniv. — A561

2014, Aug. 15 Litho. *Perf. 12½*

1526 A561 B5 multi 1.10 1.10

No. 1526 sold for 5.95r on day of issue.

Souvenir Sheet

Second Inauguration of Pres. Jacob Zuma — A562

2014, Aug. 15 Litho. *Perf. 12½*

1527 A562 (3r) multi .55 .55

No. 1527 is inscribed "Standard Postage."

Endangered Birds — A563

No. 1528: a, Damara tern. b, Taita falcon. c, Leach's storm petrel. d, White-winged flufftail. e, Tristan albatross.

2014, Sept. 1 Litho. *Perf. 12½*

1528 Horiz. strip of 5 13.00 13.00
a.-e. A563 (14r) Any single 2.60 2.60

Nos. 1528a-1528e are each inscribed "International Small Letter."

Miniature Sheet

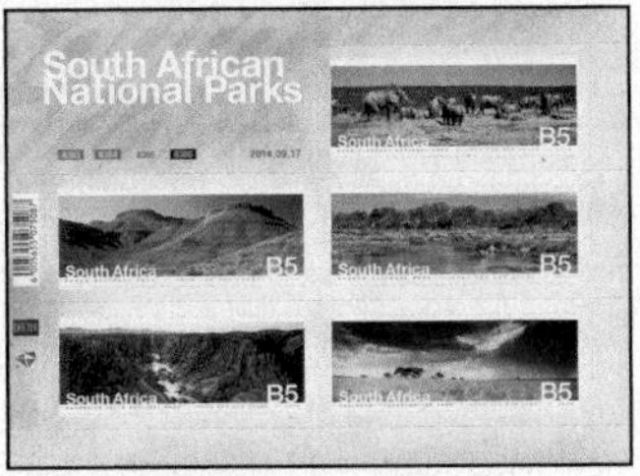

Parks — A564

No. 1529: a, Addo Elephant National Park. b, Karoo National Park. c, Kruger National Park. c, Augrabies Falls National Park. d, Kgalagadi Transfrontier Park.

Serpentine Die Cut 11

2014, Sept. 17 Litho.

Self-Adhesive

1529 A564 Sheet of 5 5.50
a.-e. B5 Any single 1.10 1.10

Nos. 1529a-1529e each sold for 5.95r on day of issue.

Miniature Sheet

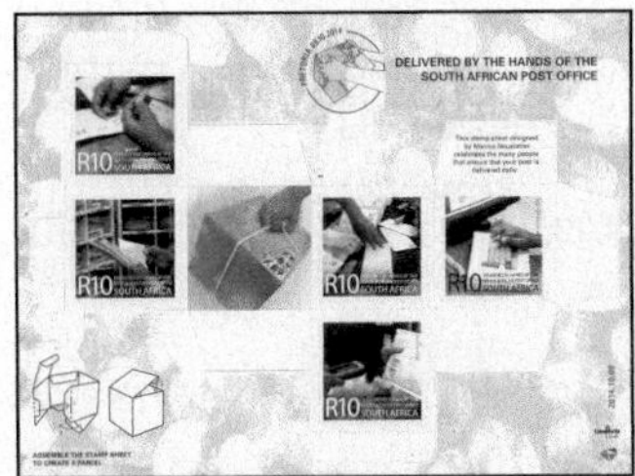

Hands of Postal Workers — A565

No. 1530: a, Hands holding twine. b, Hands sorting mail. c, Hand touching letter on counter near bin of letters. d, Hand operating keyboard. e, Hand holding electronic scanner pointed at envelope.

Serpentine Die Cut 13½

2014, Oct. 9 Litho.

Self-Adhesive

1530 A565 Sheet of 5 8.75
a.-e. 10r Any single 1.75 1.75

The outer part of the sheet can be removed and the inner part with the stamps can be folded into a small box.

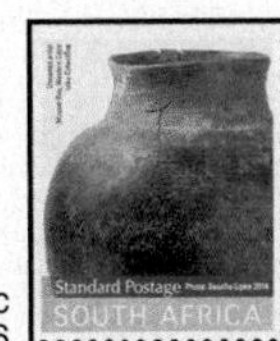

Ceramic Vessels — A566

Vessels by: No. 1531, Unnamed artist from Mossel Bay. No. 1532, Ephraim Ziqubu. No. 1533, Clive Sithole. No. 1534, Clementina van der Walt. No. 1535, Mthandeni Mkhize and Matrinah Xaba. No. 1536, Unnamed artist from Melmoth. No. 1537, Unnamed artist from Lydenburg. No. 1538, Rebecca Matibe. No. 1539, Andile Dyalvane. No. 1540, Hyme Rabinowitz.

Die Cut Perf. 12¾x12½ on 2 or 3 Sides

2014, Nov. 13 Litho.

Booklet Stamps
Self-Adhesive

1531 A566 (3r) multi .55 .55
1532 A566 (3r) multi .55 .55
1533 A566 (3r) multi .55 .55
1534 A566 (3r) multi .55 .55
1535 A566 (3r) multi .55 .55
1536 A566 (3r) multi .55 .55
1537 A566 (3r) multi .55 .55
1538 A566 (3r) multi .55 .55
1539 A566 (3r) multi .55 .55
1540 A566 (3r) multi .55 .55
a. Booklet pane of 10, #1531-1540 5.50
Nos. 1531-1540 (10) 5.50 5.50

Nos. 1531-1540 are each inscribed "Standard Postage."

Souvenir Sheet

UNI Global Union World Congress, Cape Town — A567

2014, Dec. 5 Litho. *Perf. 13x13¼*

1541 A567 5r multi .85 .85

Miniature Sheet

Endangered Animals — A568

No. 1542: a, Oribi. b, Black rhinoceros. c, Gray crowned crane. d, Ground hornbill. e, Sungazer. f, Cape parrot.

Die Cut Perf. 12¼

2015, Mar. 3 Self-Adhesive Litho.

1542 A568 Sheet of 6 3.00
a.-f. (3r) Any single .50 .50

Nos. 1542a-1542f are each inscribed "Standard Postage."

Miniature Sheet

Eighth World Congress of Nephrology, Cape Town — A569

No. 1543 — Inscriptions: a, Visit your doctor. b, Exercise. c, Healthy diet. d, Stop smoking. e, Limit alcohol.

Serpentine Die Cut 14¼

2015, Apr. 2 Self-Adhesive Litho.

1543 A569 Sheet of 5 7.00
a.-e. (7.70r) Any single 1.40 1.40

Nos. 1543a-1543e are inscribed "International Small Letter."

Miniature Sheet

Intl. Firefighters' Day — A570

No. 1544: a, 1920 Dennis fire engine. b, Turntable ladder fire engine. c, Firefighter in a fire emergency situation. d, Mountain rescue. e, Firefighters carrying a stretcher. f, Vehicle accident rescue. g, Water rescue. h, Public education.

Die Cut Perf. 12¼x12

2015, May 4 Self-Adhesive Litho.

1544 A570 Sheet of 8 4.50
a.-h. (3.30r) Any single .55 .55

Nos. 1544a-1544h are each inscribed "Standard Postage."

Souvenir Sheet

Freedom Charter, 60th Anniv. — A571

2015, June 26 Litho. ***Perf. 13¼***

1545 A571 5r multi .80 .80

Souvenir Sheet

Women's Charter, 61st Anniv. — A572

2015, Aug. 7 Litho. ***Perf. 13¼***

1546 A572 5r multi .75 .75

Miniature Sheet

Jellyfish — A573

No. 1547: a, Barrel jellyfish. b, St. Lucia jellyfish, vert. c, Box jellyfish (Carybdea branchi), vert. d, Mauve stinger, vert. e, Purple compass jellyfish. f, Cape barrel jellyfish, vert. g, Benguela compass jellyfish, vert. h, Box jellyfish (Chirodropus gorilla). i, Pink meanie. j, Helmet jellyfish.

Serpentine Die Cut 14¼x14½

2015, Aug. 12 Litho.

Self-Adhesive

1547 A573 Sheet of 10 10.00
a.-j. B5 Any single 1.00 1.00

Nos. 1547a-1547j each sold for 6.55r on day of issue.

Miniature Sheet

14th World Forestry Congress, Durban — A574

No. 1548: a, Wood carver and hikers. b, Man cutting down tree with chain saw, machine loading logs on truck. c, Man measuring tree growth. d, Indigenous forest dwellers from different South African regions. e, Forest flora and fungi.

Serpentine Die Cut 14½

2015, Sept. 7 Litho.

Self-Adhesive

1548 A574 Sheet of 5 6.25
a.-e. B4 Any single 1.25 1.25

Nos. 1548a-1548e each sold for 8r on day of issue.

Miniature Sheet

World Post Day — A575

No. 1549 — Inscriptions: a, Electronic services: Hybrid mail, Online banking, b, Parcel service. c, Electronic services: Pay a bill and Mzansi money transfer. d, Mail transport - Mail boat and Springbok Air Service. e, Cullinan diamond posted using ordinary mail.

2015, Oct. 9 Litho. ***Perf. 13¼***

1549 A575 Sheet of 5 2.50 2.50
a.-e. (3.30r) Any single .50 .50

Nos. 1549a-1549e are each inscribed "Standard Postage."

Souvenir Sheet

Oliver Tambo (1917-93), President of African National Congress — A576

2015, Oct. 27 Litho. ***Perf. 14¼x14½***

1550 A576 (3.30r) multi .50 .50

No. 1550 is inscribed "Standard Postage."

Souvenir Sheet

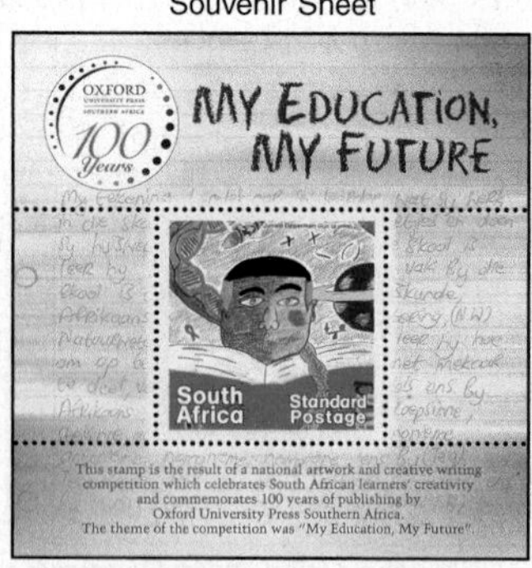

Oxford University Press Southern Africa, Cent. — A577

2015, Dec. 8 Litho. ***Perf. 13¼***

1551 A577 (3.30r) multi .45 .45

No. 1551 is inscribed "Standard Postage."

Miniature Sheet

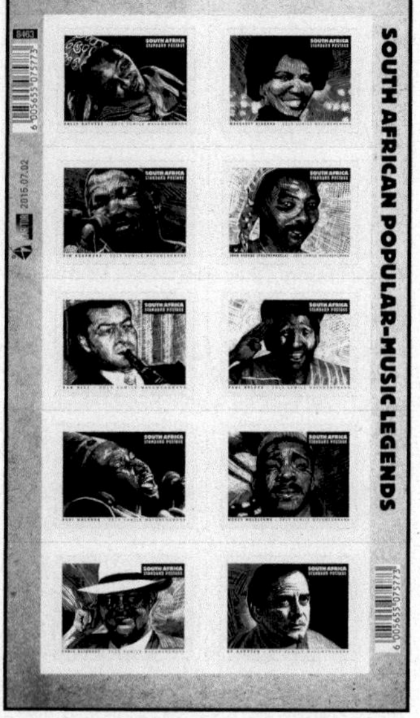

Popular Musicians — A578

No. 1552: a, Dolly Rathebe (1928-2004). b, Margaret Singana (1938-2000). c, Zim Ngqawana (1959-2011). d, John Bhengu (Phuzushukela) (1930-85). e, Dan Hill (1924-2009). f, Paul Ndlovu (d. 1986). g, Busi Mhlongo (1948-2010). h, Moses Molelekwa (1973-2001). i, Chris Blignaut (1897-1974). j, Gé Korsten (1927-99).

Serpentine Die Cut 11

2016, Jan. 8 Self-Adhesive Litho.

1552 A578 Sheet of 10 4.00
a.-j. (3.30r) Any single .40 .40

Nos. 1552a-1552j were each inscribed "Standard Postage." Dated 2015.

Miniature Sheet

35th International Geological Congress — A579

No. 1553: a, Geological cross-section of Karoo Supergroup. b, Geological cross-section of Barberton Greenstone Supergroup. c, Geological cross-section of Table Mountain World Heritage Site. d, Geological cross-section of Griqualand West Supergroup. e, Geological cross-section of Witwatersrand Supergroup. f, Geological cross-section of Vredeford Dome Meteor Impact Site. g, Geological cross-section of Bushveld Igneous Complex. h, Geological cross-section of Kimberlite volcanic pipe. i, Geological plan-view of Phalaborwa Carbonatite. j, Geological cross-section of Cradle of Humankind World Heritage Site.

Serpentine Die Cut 11

2016, Aug. 26 Litho.

Self-Adhesive

1553 A579 Sheet of 10 12.50
a.-j. (8.40r) Any single 1.25 1.25

Nos. 1553a-1553j are each inscribed "International Small Letter."

Kingfishers A580

No. 1554: a, African pygmy kingfisher. b, Giant kingfisher. c, Pied kingfisher. d, Mangrove kingfisher. e, Half-collared kingfisher.

Die Cut Perf. 12x11½

2016, Aug. 31 Litho.

Self-Adhesive

1554 Horiz. strip of 5 2.50
a.-e. A580 (3.60r) Any single .50 .50

Nos. 1554a-1554e are each inscribed "Standard Postage."

Miniature Sheet

Story Telling with Light — A581

No. 1555 (clockwise from top): a, Blue light. b, Man and white lights. c, Green and white light. d, Magenta light. e, Red and white light. f, People and white lights. g, White circle of light with lines. h, Bright magenta and white lights. i, Woman and white lights. j, Green light.

Die Cut Perf. 11½

2016, Sept. 14 Litho.

Self-Adhesive

1555 A581 Sheet of 10 12.50
a.-j. (8.40r) Any single 1.25 1.25

Nos. 1555a-1555j are each inscribed "International Small Letter."

Miniature Sheet

Pangolins — A582

No. 1556: a, Black-bellied pangolin. b, Temminck's ground pangolin. c, White-bellied pangolin. d, Giant ground pangolin.

Serpentine Die Cut 11

2016, Sept. 26 Litho.

Self-Adhesive

1556 A582 Sheet of 4 5.00
a.-d. (8.40r) Any single 1.25 1.25

Convention on International Trade in Endangered Species Conference, Johannesburg. Nos. 1556a-1556d are each inscribed "International Small Letter."

Miniature Sheet

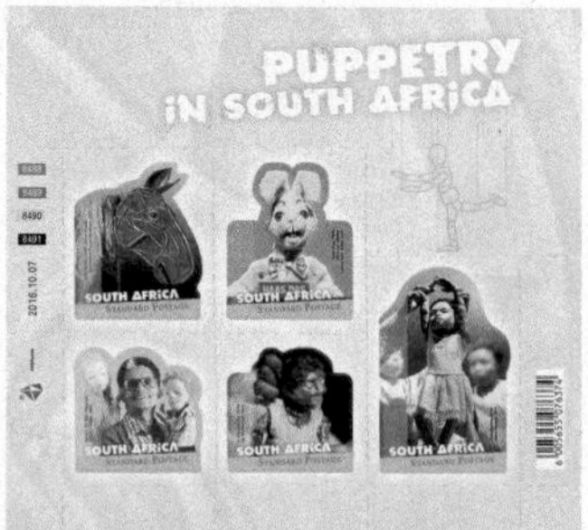

Puppetry — A583

No. 1557: a, Horse puppet from play *War Horse* (32x39mm). b, Rabbit puppet from *Haas Das* television show (32x38mm). c, Puppeteer Gawie de Wet and puppets (32x30mm). d, Puppet from *In Medea Res* puppet show (31x30mm). e, Puppet from *Ouroboros* puppet show (32x51mm).

Serpentine Die Cut 11½

2016, Oct. 7 Litho.

Self-Adhesive

1557 A583 Sheet of 5 2.75
a.-e. (3.60r) Any single .55 .55

Nos. 1557a-1557e are each inscribed "Standard Postage."

Miniature Sheet

Biospheres — A584

No. 1558: a, Cape Winelands Biosphere. b, Waterberg Biosphere. c, Cape West Coast Biosphere. d, Kruger and Canyons Biosphere. e, Kogelberg Biosphere. f, Vhembe Biosphere.

Litho. & Embossed With Foil Application

2016, Oct. 21 ***Die Cut Perf. 12½***

Self-Adhesive

1558 A584 Sheet of 6 3.50
a.-f. (3.60r) Any single .55 .55

Nos. 1558a-1558f are each inscribed "Standard Postage."

Souvenir Sheet

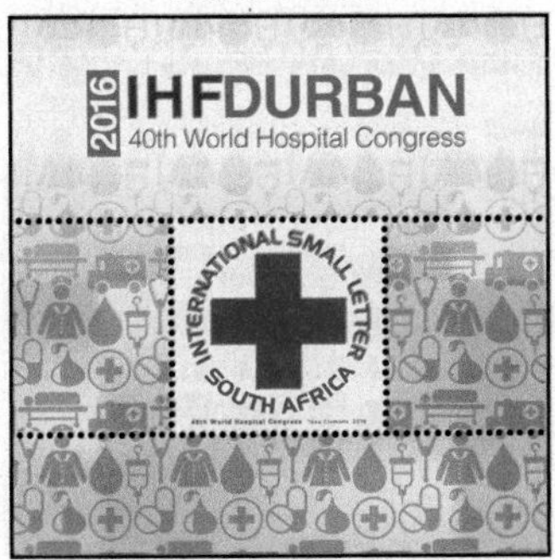

40th World Hospital Congress, Durban — A585

2016, Oct. 31 Litho. ***Perf. 14***

1559 A585 (8.40r) multi 1.25 1.25

No. 1559 is inscribed "International Small Letter."

Miniature Sheet

National Parks — A586

No. 1560: a, Marakele National Park. b, Agulhas National Park. c, Mapungubwe National Park. d, /Ai-/Ais-Richtersveld Transfrontier Park. e, Namaqua National Park. f, Tankwa Karoo National Park.

Serpentine Die Cut 11

2016, Nov. 9 Litho.

Self-Adhesive

1560 A586 Sheet of 6 3.50
a.-f. (3.60r) Any single .55 .55

Nos. 1560a-1560f are each inscribed "Standard Postage."

Souvenir Sheet

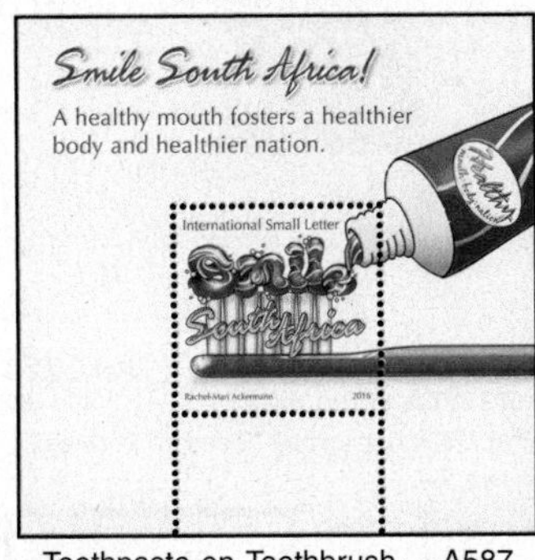

Toothpaste on Toothbrush — A587

2016, Nov. 24 Litho. ***Perf. 14***

1561 A587 (8.40r) multi 1.25 1.25

10th World Endodontic Congress, Cape Town. No. 1561 is inscribed "International Small Letter."

Souvenir Sheet

South African Airways Jet and International Flight Routes — A588

Litho. With Foil Application

2016, Dec. 2 ***Perf. 14x14¼***

1562 A588 (3.60r) multi .55 .55

No. 1562 is inscribed "Standard Postage."

Souvenir Sheet

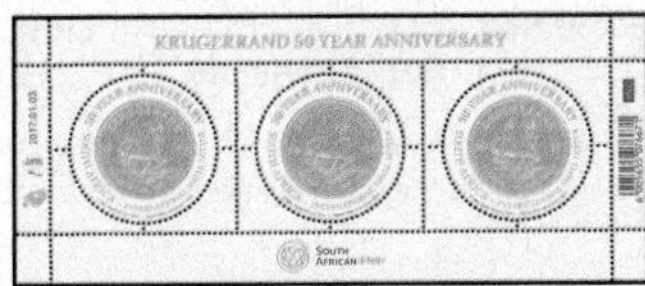

Krugerrand Gold Coins, 50th Anniv. — A589

No. 1563 — Krugerrand from: a, 1967. b, 2000. c, 2017.

Litho. & Embossed With Foil Application

2017, Jan. 3 ***Perf. 14¼***

1563 A589 Sheet of 3 3.75 3.75
a.-c. (8.40r) Any single 1.25 1.25

Nos. 1563a-1563c are each inscribed "International Small Letter."

Miniature Sheet

University of Fort Hare, Cent. (in 2016) — A590

No. 1564: a, Davidson Don Tengo Jabavu (1885-1959), professor and politician (29x36mm). b, Centenary emblem (29x36mm). c, Zachariah Keodireland Mathews (1901-68), professor (29x36mm). d, Inaugural Inter-State Native College Committee (29x36mm). e, Stylized graduate with names of famous graduates (29x36mm). f, Nursing Science Building (29x36mm). g, Christian Union Hall, c. 1930 (29x36mm). h, University blazer (29x36mm). i, Grave of Dr. James Stewart and monument (29x36mm). j, Delegates to Inter-State Native Convention, c. 1930 (102x36mm).

Serpentine Die Cut 11

2017, Feb. 8 Litho.

Self-Adhesive

1564 A590 Sheet of 10 5.50
a.-j. (3.60r) Any single .55 .55

Nos. 1564a-1564j are each inscribed "Standard Postage."

Miniature Sheet

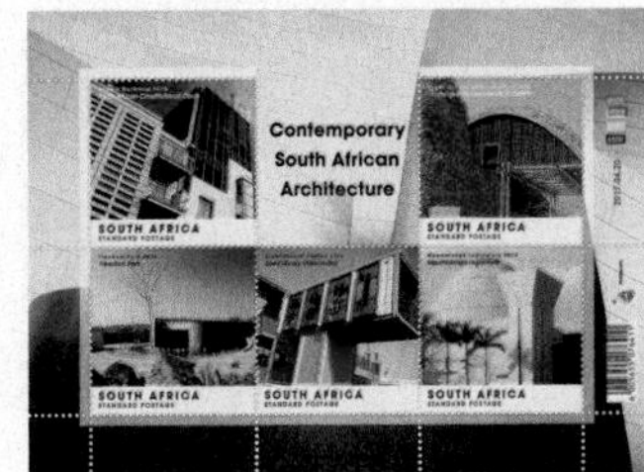

Contemporary Architecture — A591

No. 1565: a, South African Constitutional Court, Johannesburg. b, Mapungubwe Interpretation Center, Limpopo. c, Freedom Park, Pretoria. d, Seed Library, Alexandra. e, Mpumalanga Legislature, Mbombela.

2017, Apr. 20 Litho. ***Perf. 13***

1565 A591 Sheet of 5 3.00 3.00
a.-e. (3.90r) Any single .60 .60

Bee-eaters A592

No. 1566: a, European bee-eater. b, Little bee-eater. c, Southern carmine bee-eater. d, Swallow-tailed bee-eater. e, White-fronted bee-eater.

Serpentine Die Cut 10¼

2017, May 18 Litho.

Self-Adhesive

1566 Horiz. strip of 5 7.50
a.-e. A592 B4 Any single 1.50 1.50

On day of issue, Nos. 1566a-1566e each sold for 9.55r.

Bees A593

No. 1567: a, African bee. b, Cape bee. c, Pollination of crops.

Die Cut Perf. 11¾

2017, July 12 Litho.

Self-Adhesive

1567 Horiz. strip of 3 4.25
a.-c. A593 (9.15r) Any single 1.40 1.40

Nos. 1567a-1567c are each inscribed "International Small Letter."

Souvenir Sheet

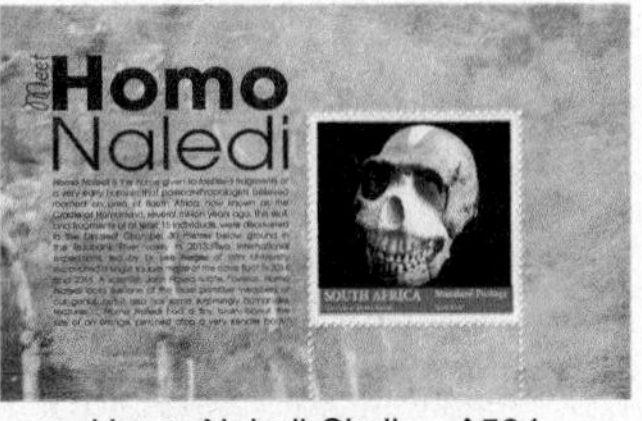

Homo Naledi Skull — A594

2017, Sept. 8 Litho. ***Perf. 14¼x14***

1568 A594 (3.90r) multi .60 .60

No. 1568 is inscribed "Standard Postage."

Souvenir Sheet

Winnie Madikizela-Mandela (1936-2018), Politician and First Lady of South Africa — A595

2017, Sept. 26 Litho. ***Perf. 13¼***

1569 A595 (3.90r) multi .60 .60

No. 1569 is inscribed "Standard Postage."

Miniature Sheet

Winemaking — A596

No. 1570: a, Bottles of 1791 Duke of Northumberland and 1821 Grand Constance wines. b, Bottle and glass of 1959 Lanzerac wine. c, Vineyard. d, Workers collecting grapes. e, Wine barrels.

Litho. With Foil Application

Serpentine Die Cut 10¼

2017, Oct. 6 Self-Adhesive

1570 A596 Sheet of 5 7.00
a.-e. (9.15r) Any single 1.40 1.40

Nos. 1570a-1570e are each inscribed "International Small Letter."

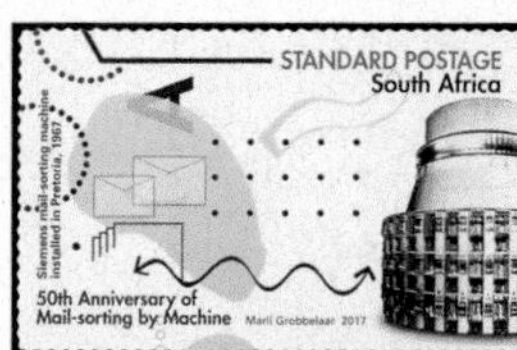

Mail Sorting by Machine in South Africa, 50th Anniv. — A597

No. 1571: a, Siemens mail sorting machine installed in Pretoria, 1967. b, Toshiba mail sorting machine in use at Tshwane Mail, Pretoria.

Serpentine Die Cut 14½

2017, Oct. 9 **Litho.**

Self-Adhesive

1571 Horiz. pair 1.10
a.-b. A597 (3.90r) Either single .55 .55

Nos. 1571a-1571b are inscribed "Standard Postage."

Souvenir Sheet

Helen Suzman (1917-2009), Anti-Apartheid Politician — A598

2017, Nov. 7 **Litho.** ***Perf. 13¼***

1572 A598 (3.90r) brnz & multi .60 .60

No. 1572 is inscribed "Standard Postage."

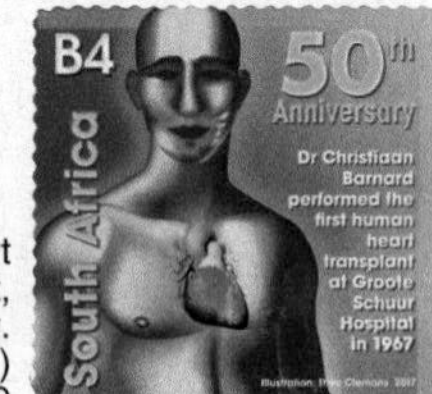

First Heart Transplant, 50th Anniv. (in 2017) A599

Serpentine Die Cut 11

2018, May 21 **Litho.**

Self-Adhesive

1573 A599 B4 multi 1.75 1.75

Dated 2017. No. 1573 sold for 10.30r on day of issue.

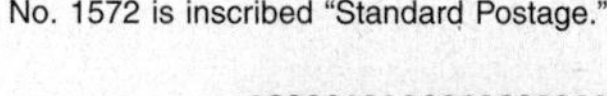

National Parks — A600

No. 1574: a, Mokala National Park. b, Mountain Zebra National Park. c, Garden Route National Park - Knysna. d, West Coast National Park. e, Garden Route National Park - Wilderness.

Serpentine Die Cut 11

2018, May 31 **Litho.**

Self-Adhesive

1574 Vert. strip of 5 3.50
a.-e. A600 (4.20r) Any single .70 .70

Nos. 1574a-1574e are each inscribed "Standard Postage."

Souvenir Sheet

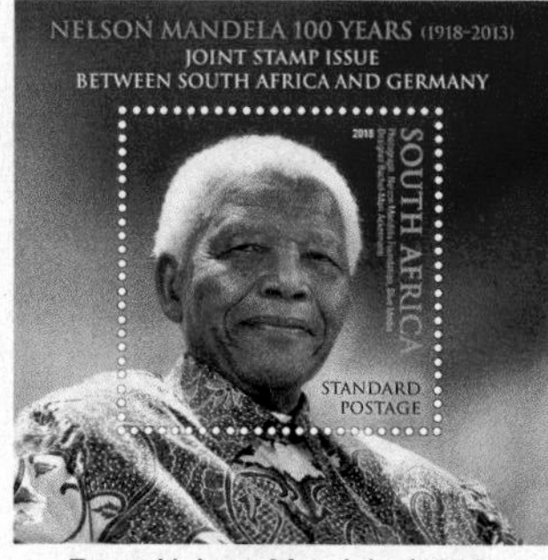

Pres. Nelson Mandela (1918-2013) — A601

2018, July 18 **Litho.** ***Perf. 13½***

1575 A601 (4.20r) multi .65 .65

No. 1575 is inscribed "Standard Postage." See Germany No. 3052.

Souvenir Sheet

Famous Men — A602

No. 1576: a, Nelson Mandela (1918-2013), President of South Africa. b, Mohandas K. Gandhi (1869-1948), Indian nationalist leader.

2018, July 26 **Litho.** ***Perf. 13½***

1576 A602 Sheet of 2 1.30 1.30
a.-b. (4.20r) Either single .65 .65

Nos. 1576a-1576b are inscribed "Standard Postage." See India Nos. 3042-3043.

A603

Pres. Cyril Ramaphosa A604

2018 **Litho.** ***Perf. 12¾***

Souvenir Sheet

1577 A603 (4.20r) multi .60 .60

Self-Adhesive

Serpentine Die Cut 11

1578 A604 (4.20r) multi .60 .60

Issued: No. 1577, 10/9; No. 1578, 10/18. Nos. 1577-1578 are inscribed "Standard Postage."

Souvenir Sheet

Pres. Nelson Mandela (1918-2013) — A605

2018, Oct. 12 **Litho.** ***Perf. 12¾***

1579 A605 (4.20r) multi .60 .60

No. 1579 is inscribed "Standard Postage."

Albertina Sisulu (1918-2011), Anti-Apartheid Activist — A606

No. 1580 — Sisulu facing: a, Left. b, Right.

Serpentine Die Cut 11

2019, Feb. 22 **Litho.**

Self-Adhesive

1580 A606 Vert. pair 1.25
a.-b. (4.20r) Either single .60 .60

Nos. 1580a-1580b are inscribed "Standard Postage."

SEMI-POSTAL STAMPS

Catalogue values for unused stamps in this section are for Never Hinged items.

English-Afrikaans Se-Tenant

Stamps with English inscriptions and with Afrikaans inscriptions of Nos. B1-B11 were printed alternately in the same sheets. Major-number listings and values are for pairs consisting of one English and one Afrikaans-inscribed stamp.

Church of the Vow — SP1

Cradock's Pass — SP2

Voortrekker — SP3

Voortrekker Woman — SP4

1933-36 **Photo.** **Wmk. 201** ***Perf. 14***

B1 SP1 ½p + ½p grn & blk, pair ('36) 9.50 4.75
a. Single, English 1.25 .75
b. Single, Afrikaans 1.25 .75
B2 SP2 1p + ½p rose & blk, pair 6.50 2.75
a. Single, English .85 .30
b. Single, Afrikaans .85 .30
B3 SP3 2p + 1p dull vio & gray, pair 11.00 5.00
a. Single, English 1.50 .55
b. Single, Afrikaans 1.50 .55
B4 SP4 3p + 1½p dp blue & gray, pair 16.50 6.00
a. Single, English 2.25 .70
b. Single, Afrikaans 2.25 .70
Nos. B1-B4 (4) 43.50 18.50

Issued to commemorate the Voortrekkers. Surtax went to the National Memorial Fund for a national Voortrekker monument.

Voortrekker Plowing — SP5

Crossing the Drakensberg — SP6

Signing Dingaan-Retief Treaty — SP7

Proposed Monument — SP8

1938, Dec. 14 ***Perf. 14***

B5 SP5 ½p + ½p dl grn & ind, pair 15.00 6.00
a. Single, English 1.25 .50
b. Single, Afrikaans 1.25 .50
B6 SP6 1p + 1p rose & sl, pair 18.00 7.00
a. Single, English 1.75 .50
b. Single, Afrikaans 1.75 .50

Perf. 15x14

B7 SP7 1½p + ½p Prus grn & choc, pair 22.50 10.00
a. Single, English 2.25 1.50
b. Single, Afrikaans 2.25 1.50

B8 SP8 3p + 3p chlky bl, pair 27.50 12.00
a. Single, English 3.25 1.75
b. Single, Afrikaans 3.25 1.75
Nos. B5-B8 (4) 83.00 35.00

Voortrekker centenary. Surtax went to the Natl. Memorial Fund for a Voortrekker monument.

"The Old Vicarage," Huguenot Museum — SP9

Rising Sun and Cross — SP10

Huguenot Dwelling, Drakenstein Mountain Valley — SP11

1939, July 17 Photo. *Perf. 14*

B9 SP9 ½p + ½p Prus grn & gray brn, pair 8.50 7.00
a. Single, English .90 .75
b. Single, Afrikaans .90 .75
B10 SP10 1p + 1p rose car & Prus grn, pair 15.00 9.00
a. Single, English 1.25 .90
b. Single, Afrikaans 1.25 .90

Perf. 15x14

B11 SP11 1½p + 1½p, vio & Prus grn, pair 30.00 14.00
a. Single, English 2.50 2.00
b. Single, Afrikaans 2.50 2.00
Nos. B9-B11 (3) 53.50 30.00

250th anniv. of the landing of the Huguenots in South Africa. Surtax went to a fund to build a Huguenot memorial at Paarl.

No. 581 Surcharged in English or Afrikaans

a

b

1987, Nov. 16 Litho. *Perf. 14x14½*

B12 Pair 1.00 1.00
a. A229(a) 16c +10c red .50 .50
b. A229(b) 16c +10c red .50 .50

Surcharge for flood relief.

No. 702 Surcharged in English or Afrikaans

1987, Dec. 1

B13 Pair 1.00 1.00
a. A254(a) 16c +10c multicolored .50 .50
b. A254(b) 16c +10c multicolored .50 .50

"+10c" is overprinted below text on Nos. B13a-B13b. Surcharge for flood relief.

No. 706 Surcharged in English or Afrikaans

1988, Mar. 1 *Perf. 14½x14*

B14 Pair 1.00 1.00
a. A256(a) 16c +10c multicolored .50 .50
b. A256(b) 16c +10c multicolored .50 .50

Surcharge for flood relief.

Nos. 710-713 Surcharged in English or Afrikaans

c

d

1988, Apr. 13 *Perf. 14x14½*

B15 Pair .85 .85
a. A257(c) 16c +10c multicolored .40 .40
b. A257(d) 16c +10c multicolored .40 .40
B16 Pair 1.60 1.60
a. A257(c) 30c +10c multicolored .80 .80
b. A257(d) 30c +10c multicolored .80 .80
B17 Pair 2.25 2.25
a. A257(c) 40c +10c multicolored 1.10 1.10
b. A257(d) 40c +10c multicolored 1.10 1.10
B18 Pair 2.75 2.75
a. A257(c) 50c +10c multicolored 1.25 1.25
b. A257(d) 50c +10c multicolored 1.25 1.25
Nos. B12-B18 (7) 10.45 10.45

Surcharge for flood relief.

On Nos. B16a, B16b, the "+ 10" is in upper left corner.

AIR POST STAMPS

Mail Plane — AP1

Unwmk.

1925, Feb. 26 Litho. *Perf. 12*

C1 AP1 1p red 4.00 *9.00*
C2 AP1 3p ultramarine 8.00 *11.50*
C3 AP1 6p violet 11.00 *22.50*
C4 AP1 9p gray green 22.00 *30.00*
Nos. C1-C4 (4) 45.00 *73.00*
Set, never hinged 150.00

Forgeries exist perf. 11, 11½ or 13.

Biplane in Flight — AP2

1929, Aug. 16 Typo. *Perf. 14x13½*

C5 AP2 4p blue green 6.50 2.75
C6 AP2 1sh orange 14.00 21.00
Set, never hinged 75.00

Catalogue values for unused stamps in this section, from this point to the end of the section, are for Never Hinged items.

"AIRMAIL POSTCARD"
"AIRMAIL POSTCARD RATE"

Stamps inscribed thus were sold for the amount shown in ( ) on date of issue.

See Nos. 1038-1042F for stamps included with postage sets.

Endangered Fauna Type of 1993

1996, May 8 Litho. *Perf. 14x14½*

C6A A288 (1r) White rhinoceros .70 .70
C6B A288 (1r) Buffalo .70 .70
C6C A288 (1r) Lion .70 .70
f. Souvenir sheet of 1 + label .80 .80
C6D A288 (1r) Leopard .70 .70
C6E A288 (1r) African elephant .70 .70
g. Strip of 5, #C6A-C6E 3.50
h. Sheet of 10, 2 each #C6A-C6E 7.00
i. Booklet pane of 5, #C6A-C6E + 5 labels 4.00
Complete booklet, #C6Ei 4.00
Nos. C6A-C6E (5) 3.50 3.50

No. C6Cf is inscribed in sheet margin for Coach House, and sold for 1r.

Issued: #C6Cf, 2/97; #C6Ei, 7/27/97.

Inauguaration of Blue Train — AP3

Designs: No. C7, Double-headed Class 6E 1, electric locomotives, Cape Town to Beaufort West. No. C8, Double-headed Class 6E 1 electric lovomotives, Hex River Valley. No. C9, 1960's Steam powered locomotives between Three Sisters and Huchinson. No. C10, Diesel locomotives, Modder River Bridge near Kimberly. No. C11, Diesel locomotives, Northern Transvaal.

1997, Aug. 1 *Perf. 14 Syncopated*

C7 AP3 (1r) multicolored .70 .70
a. Souv. sheet of 1, perf. 14 .70 .70
C8 AP3 (1r) multicolored .70 .70
C9 AP3 (1r) multicolored .70 .70
a. Souvenir sheet of 1, perf. 14 .70 .70
C10 AP3 (1r) multicolored .70 .70
C11 AP3 (1r) multicolored .70 .70
a. Strip of 5, #C7-C11 3.50 3.50

No. C7a is inscribed in sheet margin for The Cape Stamp Show and Harmers of London stamp auctioneers.

No. C9a was issued 11/97, sold for 1.30r and is inscribed for Eastgate Universal Stamps & Coins in sheet margin.

1998, Nov. Litho. *Perf. 14¾x14*

Booklet Stamps

C12 AP3 (1r) Like #C7 .70 .70
C13 AP3 (1r) Like #C8 .70 .70
C14 AP3 (1r) Like #C9 .70 .70
C15 AP3 (1r) Like #C10 .70 .70
C16 AP3 (1r) Like #C11 .70 .70
a. Bklt. pane, 2 ea #C12-C16 7.00
Complete booklet, #C16a 7.00
Nos. C12-C16 (5) 3.50 3.50

Tourism AP4

Western Cape of South Africa: No. C7, Sandstone Cliffs. No. C8, Robben Island. No. C9, Pinehurst Homestead. No. C10, Waterfront, Capetown. No. C11, Boschendal Wine Estate.

1998, Sept. 28 Litho. *Perf. 14½x14*

Booklet Stamps

C17 AP4 (1.30r) multicolored .60 .60
C18 AP4 (1.30r) multicolored .60 .60
C19 AP4 (1.30r) multicolored .60 .60
C20 AP4 (1.30r) multicolored .60 .60
C21 AP4 (1.30r) multicolored .60 .60
a. Bklt. pane, 2 ea #C17-C21 + label 6.00
Complete booklet, #C21a 6.00
Nos. C17-C21 (5) 3.00 3.00

Perf. 14¾x14 on 3 sides

1998, Sept. 28 Litho.

KwaZulu-Natal: No. C22, Drakensberge. No. C23, Zulu women and huts. No. C24, Rhinoceros and pelicans. No. C25, Rickshaw driver. No. C26, Indian dancers.

C22 AP4 (1.30r) multicolored .60 .60
C23 AP4 (1.30r) multicolored .60 .60
C24 AP4 (1.30r) multicolored .60 .60
C25 AP4 (1.30r) multicolored .60 .60
C26 AP4 (1.30r) multicolored .60 .60
a. Booklet pane, 2 ea #C22-C26 6.00
Complete booklet, #C26a 6.00

Worldwide Fund for Nature AP5

No. C27, Cuvier's beaked whale. No. C28, Minke whale. No. C29, Bryde's whale. No. C30, Pygmy right whale.

1998, Oct. 23 Litho. *Perf. 14¾x14*

C27 AP5 (1.30r) multicolored 1.00 1.00
C28 AP5 (1.30r) multicolored 1.00 1.00
C29 AP5 (1.30r) multicolored 1.00 1.00
C30 AP5 (1.30r) multicolored 1.00 1.00
a. Block of 4, #C27-C30 4.00 4.00
b. Booklet pane, 3 each #C27-C28, 2 each #C29-C30 10.00
Complete booklet 10.00
Complete booklet, 2 #C30b + 2 postal cards 30.00

No. C30b exists with and without perfs running through side and bottom pane margins.

Tourism Type of 1998

Mpumalanga and Northern Province: No. C31, Blyde River Canyon. No. C32, Lone Creek Falls. No. C33, Ndebele women. No. C34, Pilgrim's Rest historical town. No. C35, Elephants, Thulamela, Kruger National Park.

1999, Aug. Litho. *Perf. 14¾x14*

C31 AP4 (1.30r) multi .50 .50
C32 AP4 (1.30r) multi .50 .50
C33 AP4 (1.30r) multi .50 .50
C34 AP4 (1.30r) multi .50 .50
C35 AP4 (1.30r) multi .50 .50
a. Booklet pane, 2 each #C31-C35 5.00
Complete booklet, #C35a 5.00

Big Game Animals — AP6

Designs: Nos. C36, C45, Elephant. Nos. C37, C44, Lion. Nos. C38, C43, Rhinoceros. Nos. C39, C42, Leopard. Nos. C40, C41, Buffalo.

Perf. 14¾x14½ on 3 or 4 Sides

2001, Apr. 25 Litho.

Booklet Stamps

C36 AP6 (1.90r) multi .70 .70
C37 AP6 (1.90r) multi .70 .70
C38 AP6 (1.90r) multi .70 .70
C39 AP6 (1.90r) multi .70 .70
C40 AP6 (1.90r) multi .70 .70
a. Booklet pane, 2 each #C36-C40 7.00
Booklet, 2 #C40a + 2 postal cards 14.00

Self-Adhesive

Size: 30x24mm

Serpentine Die Cut 12x11½ on 2 or 3 Sides

C41 AP6 (1.90r) multi .70 .70
C42 AP6 (1.90r) multi .70 .70
C43 AP6 (1.90r) multi .70 .70
C44 AP6 (1.90r) multi .70 .70
C45 AP6 (1.90r) multi .70 .70
a. Booklet, 2 each #C41-C45 7.00

See Nos. C65-C69.

Tourism — AP7

Designs: No. C46, (2.10r), Cango Caves. No. C47, (2.10r), Table Mountain. No. C48, (2.10r), West Coast. No. C49, (2.10r), Snow-covered mountains near Elliot. No. C50, (2.10r), Augrabies Waterfall. No. C51, (2.10r), Stellenbosch vineyard country. No. C52, (2.10r), Flowers, Namaqualand. No. C53, (2.10r), Tsitsikamma Forest. No. C54, (2.10r), Cape Mountain zebras. No. C55, (2.10r), Richtersveld Desert.

2001, Sept. 6 Litho. *Perf. 13¼x13¾*

C46-C55 AP7 Set of 10 7.00 7.00

Pres. Nelson Mandela — AP8

Various photographs. Color of country name and size of stamps: a, Lilac, 31x48mm. b, Red and lilac, 50x38mm. c, Orange, 31x48mm. d, Orange, 31x31mm. e, Orange, 38x50mm. f, White, 38x50mm. g, White, 50x38mm. h, White, 31x48mm. i, Lilac, 38x50mm. j, Red, 31x31mm.

2001, Nov. 26 ***Perf. 14¾x14, 13¾***

C56 Booklet 9.00
a.-j. AP8 (2.10r) Any booklet pane .90 .90

No. C56 sold for 45r and included two postal cards.

Shaka (1785-1828), Zulu King — AP9

2003, Sept. 24 Litho. ***Perf. 13x13¼***

C57 AP9 (3.30r) multi 1.10 1.10

Miniature Sheet

Flora and Fauna of Table Mountain — AP10

No. C58: a, Cape sugarbird, vert. b, Dark opal butterflies. c, King protea. d, Cape rock hyrax. e, Cuckoo wasp. f, Table Mountain ghost frog. g, Table Mountain cockroaches. h, Staavia dodii, vert. i, Spotted skaapsteker. j, Duvalia immaculata.

Serpentine Die Cut 9x9½, 9½x9

2004, Sept. 1 **Litho.**

Self-Adhesive

C58 AP10 Sheet of 10 17.50 17.50
a.-j. (10r) Any single 1.75 1.75

World Post Day — AP11

2004, Sept. 23 ***Perf. 14***

C59 AP11 (3.45r) multi 1.25 1.25

Rotary International, Cent. — AP12

No. C60: a, Doctor listening to boy's heart-beat, infant receiving oral vaccination. b, Child at computer, welder.

2005, Feb. 23 ***Perf. 14¼x14***

C60 Horiz. pair 3.25 3.25
a.-b. AP12 (4r) Either single 1.50 1.50

Miniature Sheet

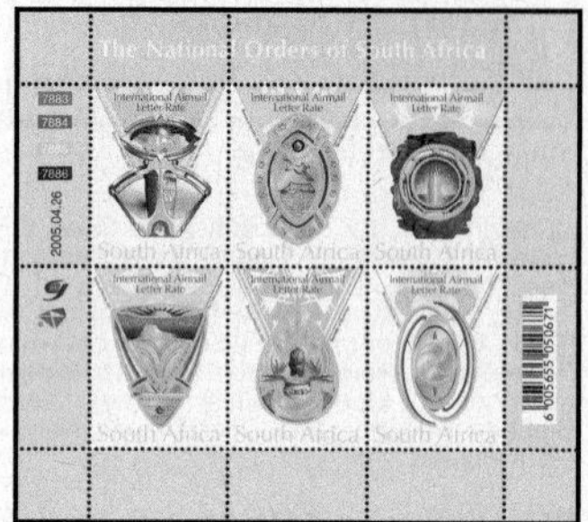

National Orders — AP13

No. C61: a, Order of Mapungubwe. b, Order of Merit for Bravery. c, Order of the Baobab. d, Order of Luthuli. e, Order of Ikhamanga. f, Order of the Companions of O. R. Tambo.

Litho. & Embossed with Foil Application

2005, Nov. 26 ***Perf. 14¾x14¼***

C61 AP13 (4.25r) Sheet of 6, #a-f 9.00 9.00

Miniature Sheet

Art — AP14

No. C62: a, Boland Winter, by Eric Laubscher. b, Table Mountain, by Maggie Laubser. c, Fishermen Drawing Nets, by Walter Battis. d, Oh, South Africa, You've Turned My World Completely Upside Down, by Lalitha Jawahirlal. e, Untitled, by Lucky Sibiya. f, Untitled, by Sophie Masiza. g, Azibuye Emasisweni, by Trevor Makhoba. h, Kontantwinkel Riebeck-Wes, by John Kramer. i, Houses in the Hills, by Gladys Mgudlandlu. j, Sequence City, by Usha Seejarim.

2005, May 6 Litho. ***Perf. 14¼x14¾***

C62 AP14 (3.65r) Sheet of 10, #a-j 13.50 13.50

Intl. Year of Physics — AP15

2005, July 7 ***Perf. 14½***

C63 AP15 (3.65r) multi 1.40 1.40

Miniature Sheet

"Hello" in Various Languages and Flag — AP16

No. C64: a, Hallo! b, Hi! c, Sawubona. d, Ndi Masiari! e, Lotjha!. f, Avuxeni. g, Dumela. h, Molo!

2005, Oct. 9

C64 AP16 (3.65r) Sheet of 8, #a-h 9.50 9.50

Big Game Animals Type of 2001

Serpentine Die Cut 12¼x12¾ on 2 or 3 Sides

2005, Oct. 10 **Self-Adhesive**

Booklet Stamps

Size: 30x24mm

C65 AP6 (3.65r) Buffalo 1.25 1.25
C66 AP6 (3.65r) Leopard 1.25 1.25
C67 AP6 (3.65r) Rhinoceros 1.25 1.25
C68 AP6 (3.65r) Lion 1.25 1.25
C69 AP6 (3.65r) Elephant 1.25 1.25
a. Booklet, 2 each # C65-C69 12.50

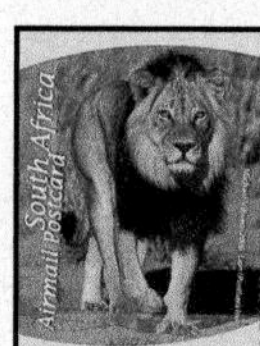

Big Game Animals — AP17

Serpentine Die Cut 12½x13½

2006, Feb. 24 **Self-Adhesive**

Booklet Stamps

C70 AP17 (3.65r) Lion 1.25 1.25
C71 AP17 (3.65r) Buffalo 1.25 1.25
C72 AP17 (3.65r) Elephant 1.25 1.25
C73 AP17 (3.65r) Rhinoceros 1.25 1.25
C74 AP17 (3.65r) Leopard 1.25 1.25
a. Booklet, 2 each #C70-C74 12.50

Cyclists — AP18

2006, Mar. 6 ***Perf. 13¼x13¾***

C75 AP18 (4.25r) multi 1.50 1.50

Souvenir Sheet

2010 World Cup Soccer Championships, South Africa — AP19

2006, July 7 Litho. ***Perf. 14¾x14½***

C76 AP19 (4.40r) multi 1.40 1.40

Miniature Sheet

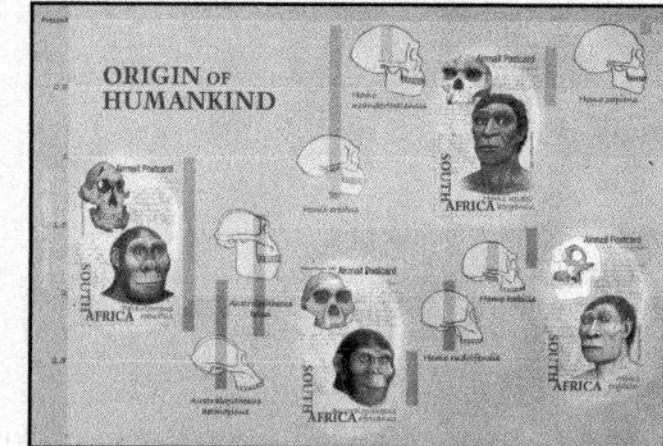

Origins of Humans — AP20

No. C77: a, Paranthropus robustus. b, Australopithecus africanus. c, Homo heidelbergensis. d, Homo ergaster.

Serpentine Die Cut 11½x11¾

2006, Nov. 10 **Self-Adhesive**

C77 AP20 (3.80r) Sheet of 4, #a-d 4.75 4.75

Big Game Animals — AP21

Serpentine Die Cut 13½x13¾ on 2 or 3 Sides

2007, Aug. 17 **Litho.**

Booklet Stamps

Self-Adhesive

C78 AP21 (4.01r) Elephant 1.10 1.10
C79 AP21 (4.01r) Leopard 1.10 1.10
C80 AP21 (4.01r) Buffalo 1.10 1.10
C81 AP21 (4.01r) Lion 1.10 1.10
C82 AP21 (4.01r) Rhinoceros 1.10 1.10
a. Booklet pane, 2 each #C78-C82 11.00
Nos. C78-C82 (5) 5.50 5.50

Souvenir Sheet

24th UPU Congress, Nairobi — AP22

2007, Oct. 9 ***Perf. 13¾***

C83 AP22 (4.64r) multi 1.40 1.40

Souvenir Sheet

2010 World Cup Soccer Championships, South Africa — AP23

2007, Nov. 23 ***Perf. 13¼x13½***

C84 AP23 (4.64r) multi 1.40 1.40

Birds — AP24

No. C85: a, Southern ground hornbill. b, Kori bustard. c, Common ostrich. d, Blue crane. e, Bearded vulture.

2008, July 1 Litho. ***Perf. 13¼x13¾***

C85 Horiz. strip of 5 6.50 6.50
a.-e. AP24 (4.90r) Any single 1.25 1.25

Nos. C85a-C85e are each inscribed "International Airmail Small Letter."

Intl. Congress of Entomology Conference, Durban — AP25

2008, July 4 ***Perf. 13¾x13¼***

C86 AP25 (4.20r) multi 1.10 1.10

Miniature Sheet

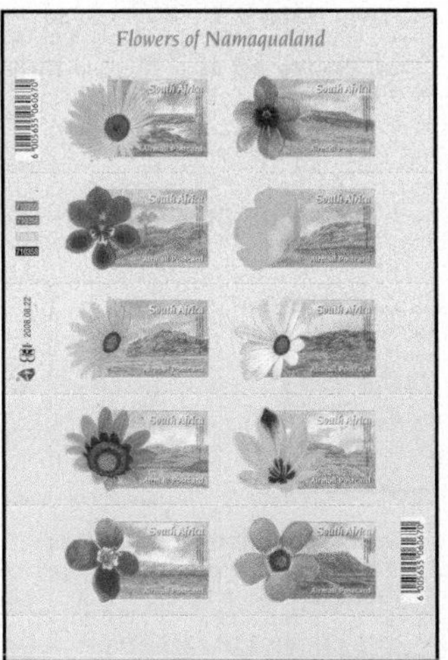

Flowers — AP26

No. C87: a, Common bokbaaivygie. b, Bokkeveld pride. c, Springbok painted petals. d, White-eyed duiker-root. e, Namaqualand daisy. f, Satin boneseed. g, Karoo gazania. h, Harlequin hesperantha. i, Showy sunflax. j, Red-eye sorrel.

2008, Aug. 22 ***Die Cut***

Self-Adhesive

C87 AP26 Sheet of 10 11.00
a.-j. (4.20r) Any single 1.10 1.10

Nos. C87a-C87j are each inscribed "Airmail Postcard."

Souvenir Sheet

2010 World Cup Soccer Championships, South Africa — AP27

2008, Sept. 5 ***Perf. 13¼x13¾***

C88 AP27 (3.70r) multi .95 .95

Miniature Sheet

uKhahlamba-Drakensberg Park — AP28

No. C89: a, View overlooking Eastern Buttress with Devils Tooth. b, View from the Sentinel overlooking the Eastern Buttress. c, Amphitheater from the Royal Natal National Park. d, View of the Sentinel and Amphitheater.

2008, Sept. 23 ***Perf. 13¼x13¾***

C89 AP28 Sheet of 4 4.75 4.75
a.-d. (4.90r) Any single 1.10 1.10

Nos. C89a-C89d are each inscribed "International Airmail Small Letter."

Big Game Animals — AP29

Booklet Stamps

Serpentine Die Cut 12¼x12¾ on 2 or 3 Sides

2008, Nov. 14 **Self-Adhesive**

C90 AP29 (4.20r) Elephant .80 .80
C91 AP29 (4.20r) Lion .80 .80
C92 AP29 (4.20r) Leopard .80 .80
C93 AP29 (4.20r) Buffalo .80 .80
C94 AP29 (4.20r) Rhinoceros .80 .80
a. Booklet pane of 10, 2 each #C90-C94 8.25
Nos. C90-C94 (5) 4.00 4.00

Nos. C90-C94 are each inscribed "Airmail Postcard."

Souvenir Sheet

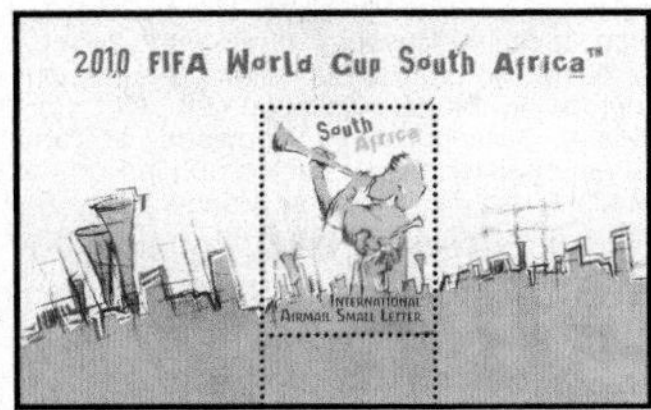

2010 World Cup Soccer Championships, South Africa — AP30

Perf. 13¼x13¾

2009, June 14 **Litho.**

C95 AP30 (5.40r) multi 1.40 1.40

No. C95 is inscribed "International Airmail Small Letter."

Miniature Sheet

Gemstones — AP31

No. C96: a, Garnet. b, Sugilite. c, Rhodocrosite. d, Jasper.

Litho. With Foil Application

2009, July 10 ***Perf. 13½***

C96 AP31 Sheet of 4 4.50 4.50
a.-d. (4.60r) Any single 1.10 1.10

Nos. C96a-C96d are each inscribed "Airmail Postcard."

Birds — AP32

No. C97: a, Jackass penguins. b, Black oyster catchers. c, Common cape gannets. d, Cape cormorants. e, Black-backed sea gull.

2009, Aug. 3 Litho. ***Perf. 14¾x14½***

C97 Horiz. strip of 5 7.00 7.00
a.-e. AP32 (5.40r) Any single 1.40 1.40

Nos. C97a-C97e are inscribed "International Airmail Small Letter."

Miniature Sheet

Dinosaurs — AP33

No. C98: a, Afrovenator. b, Afrovenator skeleton. c, Ouranosaurus. d, Ouranosaurus skeleton. e, Heterodontosaurus, vert. f, Heterodontosaurus skeleton, vert. g, Jobaria, vert. h, Jobaria skeleton, vert. i, Suchomimus, vert. j, Suchomimus skeleton, vert.

Perf. 13¼x13, 13x13¼ (#C98e-C98j)

2009, Nov. 2

C98 AP33 Sheet of 10 12.50 12.50
a.-j. (4.60r) Any single 1.25 1.25

Nos. C98a-C98j are inscribed "International Airmail Postcard." The stamp designs, when viewed through red and blue glasses, become three-dimensional.

Miniature Sheet

Life of Fishermen — AP34

No. C99: a, Fish on net, boats ashore. b, Men pushing boat in shallow water. c, Sun, house, men near boat. d, Fishemen in boat on water. e, Fishermen, boat ashore near rocks. f, Fishing community. g, Men in boat, house. h, Boat ashore, fisherman with rod. i, Fish, houses, boat. j, Man hanging fish to dry.

2010, Feb. 19 ***Perf. 13¼x13***

C99 AP34 Sheet of 10 14.00 14.00
a.-j. (5.40r) Any single 1.40 1.40

Nos. C99a-C99j are inscribed "International Airmail Small Letter."

Big Game Animals — AP35

Booklet Stamps

Die Cut Perf. 12¾x12½ on 2 or 3 Sides

2010, May 5 **Self-Adhesive**

C100 AP35 (4.90r) Elephant 1.40 1.40
C101 AP35 (4.90r) Lion 1.40 1.40
C102 AP35 (4.90r) Buffalo 1.40 1.40
C103 AP35 (4.90r) Leopard 1.40 1.40
C104 AP35 (4.90r) Rhinoceros 1.40 1.40
a. Booklet pane of 10, 2 each #C100-C104 14.00
Nos. C100-C104 (5) 7.00 7.00

Nos. C100-C104 are inscribed "Airmail Postcard."

Cats — AP36

No. C105: a, African wild cat (60x60mm). b, Serval (30x30mm). c, Caracal (30x30mm). d, Black-footed cat (30x30mm). e, African golden cat (30x30mm).

2011, Feb. 4 ***Perf. 13¼***

C105 AP36 Block of 5 6.25 6.25
a.-e. (4.30r) Any single 1.25 1.25

Nos. C105a-C015e are each inscribed "Africa Airmail." Perforations trace around the cat's head on No. C105a.

Souvenir Sheet

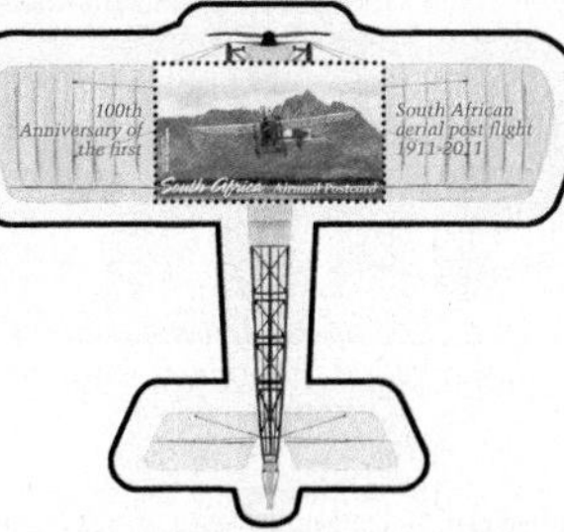

First South African Air Mail Flight, Cent. — AP37

2011, Oct. 7 ***Perf. 13x13¼***

C106 AP37 (5.10r) multi 1.40 1.40

No. C106 is inscribed "Airmail Postcard."

Souvenir Sheet

John Langalibalele Dube (1871-1946), First President of South African Native National Congress — AP38

2012, Feb. 22 Litho. ***Perf. 14½***

C107 AP38 (4.80r) black 1.40 1.40

No. C107 is inscribed "Africa Airmail."

Big Game Animals — AP39

Die Cut Perf. 12½x12¼ on 2 or 3 Sides

2012, July 12 **Self-Adhesive**

Booklet Stamps

C108 AP39 (5.40r) Buffalos 1.40 1.40
C109 AP39 (5.40r) Elephants 1.40 1.40
C110 AP39 (5.40r) Leopards 1.40 1.40
C111 AP39 (5.40r) Black rhinoceroses 1.40 1.40
C112 AP39 (5.40r) Lions 1.40 1.40
a. Booklet pane of 10, 2 each #C108-C112 14.00
Nos. C108-C112 (5) 7.00 7.00

Nos. C108-C112 are inscribed "Airmail Postcard."

Sunbirds — AP40

Designs: No. C113, White-bellied sunbird. No. C114, Dusky sunbird. No. C115, Neergaard's sunbird. No. C116, Plain-backed sunbird. No. C117, Collared sunbird.

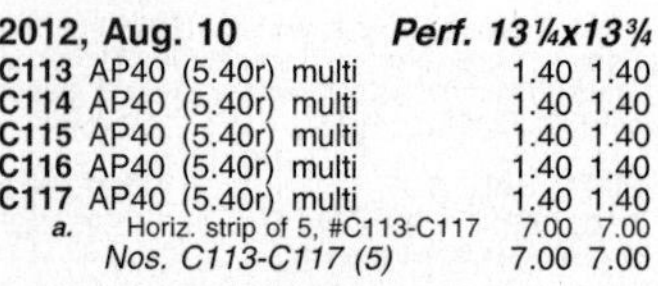

2012, Aug. 10 *Perf. 13¼x13¾*

C113 AP40 (5.40r) multi 1.40 1.40
C114 AP40 (5.40r) multi 1.40 1.40
C115 AP40 (5.40r) multi 1.40 1.40
C116 AP40 (5.40r) multi 1.40 1.40
C117 AP40 (5.40r) multi 1.40 1.40
a. Horiz. strip of 5, #C113-C117 7.00 7.00
Nos. C113-C117 (5) 7.00 7.00

Nos. C113-C117 each are inscribed "International Airmail Small Letter."

Miniature Sheet

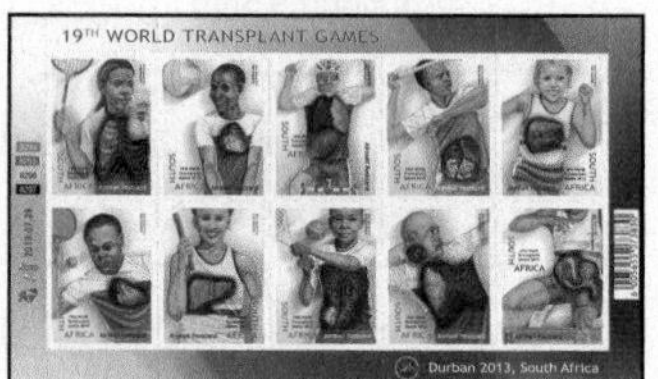

19th World Transplant Games, Durban — AP41

No. C118: a, Badminton player with lung transplant. b, Volleyball player with heart transplant. c, Cyclist with lung transplant. d, Javelin thrower with kidney transplant. e, Runner with liver transplant. f, Table tennis player with heart transplant. g, Relay runner with liver transplant. h, tennis player with kidney transplant. i, Shot putter with lung transplant. j, Hurdler with kidney and pancreas transplant.

Die Cut Perf. 14¼x14¾

2013, July 29 **Litho.**

Self-Adhesive

C118 AP41 Sheet of 10 11.00
a.-j. (5.70r) Any single 1.10 1.10

Nos. C118a-C118j are each inscribed "Airmail Postcard."

Big Game Animals — AP42

Die Cut Perf. 12¼x12¾ on 2 or 3 Sides

2014, May 9 **Litho.**

Booklet Stamps
Self-Adhesive

C119 AP42 (6.05r) Buffalo 1.10 1.10
C120 AP42 (6.05r) Elephant 1.10 1.10
C121 AP42 (6.05r) Leopard 1.10 1.10
C122 AP42 (6.05r) Black rhinoceros 1.10 1.10
C123 AP42 (6.05r) Lion 1.10 1.10
a. Booklet pane of 10, 2 each #C119-C123 11.00
Nos. C119-C123 (5) 5.50 5.50

Nos. C119-C123 are inscribed "Airmail Postcard."

Miniature Sheet

South African Aviation Corps, Cent. — AP43

No. C124: a, Pilot's wings (52x26mm). b, Shoulder title (38x26mm). c, Henry Farman biplane (52x38mm). d, 1914-15 Star (38x38mm). e, Tunic detail (38x38mm).

Die Cut Perf. 12½

2015, Feb. 5 **Litho.**

Self-Adhesive

C124 AP43 Sheet of 5 5.00
a.-e. (6.05r) Any single 1.00 1.00

Nos. C124a-C124e are each inscribed "Airmail Postcard."

Big Game Animals — AP44

Serpentine Die Cut 12¾x12¼ on 2 or 3 Sides

2018, Nov. 26 **Litho.**

Booklet Stamps
Self-Adhesive

C125 AP44 (8.50r) Lion 1.25 1.25
C126 AP44 (8.50r) Elephant 1.25 1.25
C127 AP44 (8.50r) Leopard 1.25 1.25
C128 AP44 (8.50r) White rhinoceros 1.25 1.25
C129 AP44 (8.50r) Buffalo 1.25 1.25
a. Booklet pane of 10, 2 each #C125-C129 12.50
Nos. C125-C129 (5) 6.25 6.25

Nos. C125-C129 are each inscribed "Airmail Postcard."

Miniature Sheet

Famous Diamonds From South Africa — AP45

No. C130: a, The Cullinan. b, The Star of South Africa. c, The Jubilee. d, The Eureka. e, The Golden Jubilee. f, The Centenary. g, The De Beers. h, The Heart of Eternity. i, The Blue Moon of Josephine. j, The Excelsior.

Litho. With Foil Application
Serpentine Die Cut 11

2019, June 19 **Self-Adhesive**

C130 AP45 Sheet of 10 13.00
a.-j. (9.20r) Any single 1.30 1.30

Nos. C130a-C130j are inscribed "Airmail Postcard."

REGISTRATION STAMPS

Miniature Sheet

Intl. Year of Biodiversity — R1

No. F1: a, Giant African mantis, Common lionfish. b, Black rhinoceros. c, Common chameleon, African reed frog. d, Lilac-breasted roller, Baobab tree.

Perf. 13¼x13¾

2010, Mar. 12 **Litho.**

F1 R1 Sheet of 4 18.00 18.00
a.-d. (15.85r) Any single 4.50 4.50

Nos. F1a-F1d are inscribed "Small Registered Letter."

Miniature Sheet

Port Elizabeth, Cent. — R2

No. F2: a, View of Algoa Bay From Lady Donkin's Pyramid, lithograph by George Dinsdale. b, The Donkin, photograph by Tim Hopwood. c, Port Elizabeth, painting by Ethel Sawyer. d, Coega harbor, photograph by Hopwood. e, Birth of Site and Service, watercolor by George Mnyaluza Milwa Pemba. f, Red Location Museum, photograph by Hopwood. g, Old Doll House Railway Station, photograph in Binnell Collection. h, Old Court House, photograph by Hopwood. i, Queen Street and North End, photograph in Port Elizabeth Museum. j, Nelson Mandela Bay Stadium, photograph by Hopwood.

Serpentine Die Cut 14½

2013, July 26

Self-Adhesive

F2 R2 Sheet of 10 40.00
a.-j. (19.60r) Any single 4.00 4.00

Nos. F2a-F2j each are inscribed "Registered Letter Small."

Miniature Sheet

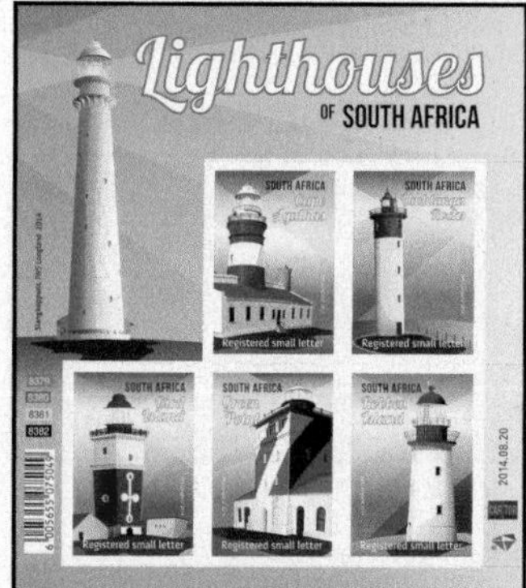

Lighthouses — R3

No. F3: a, Cape Agulhas Lighthouse. b, Umhlanga Rocks Lighthouse. c, Bird Island Lighthouse. d, Green Point Lighthouse. e, Robben Island Lighthouse.

Serpentine Die Cut 14½

2014, Aug. 20 **Litho.**

Self-Adhesive

F3 R3 Sheet of 5 20.00
a.-e. (20.80r) Any single 4.00 4.00

Nos. F3a-F3e are each inscribed "Registered small letter."

Miniature Sheet

National Parks — R4

No. F4: a, Golden Gate Highlands National Park. b, Garden Route National Park. c, Camdeboo National Park. d, Bontebok National Park. e, Table Mountain National Park.

Serpentine Die Cut 11

2017, Aug. 10 **Litho.**

Self-Adhesive

F4 R4 Sheet of 5 21.50
a.-e. (27.30r) Any single 4.25 4.25

Nos. F4a-F4e are each inscribed "Registered small letter."

POSTAGE DUE STAMPS

D1

Wmk. Springbok's Head (177)

1914-15 **Typo.** *Perf. 14*

J1 D1 ½p green & blk 2.50 4.25
J2 D1 1p red & blk 2.50 .25
J3 D1 2p vio & blk ('14) 7.50 .80
J4 D1 3p ultra & blk 2.50 .80
J5 D1 5p brown & blk 4.50 *30.00*
J6 D1 6p gray & blk 11.00 *30.00*
J7 D1 1sh black & red 77.50 *160.00*
Nos. J1-J7 (7) 108.00 *226.10*

1922 **Unwmk.** **Litho.** *Rouletted 7-8*

J8 D1 ½p blue grn & blk 1.60 *15.00*
J9 D1 1p dull red & blk 1.75 1.25
J10 D1 1½p yellow brn & blk 2.00 2.40
Nos. J8-J10 (3) 5.35 *18.65*

1922-26 *Perf. 14*

J11 D1 ½p blue grn & blk .85 1.75
J12 D1 1p rose & blk ('23) .90 .25
J13 D1 1½p yel brn & blk ('24) 1.60 1.25
J14 D1 2p vio & blk ('23) 1.40 .80
a. Imperf. pair 300.00 400.00
J15 D1 3p blue & blk ('26) 8.00 22.50
J16 D1 6p gray & blue ('23) 16.00 8.00
Nos. J11-J16 (6) 28.75 34.55

D2

1927-28 **Typo.**

J17 D2 ½p blue green & blk 1.00 3.50
J18 D2 1p rose & black 1.40 .80
J19 D2 2p violet & black 1.40 1.25
J20 D2 3p ultra & black 13.00 25.00
J21 D2 6p gray & black 24.00 20.00
Nos. J17-J21 (5) 40.80 50.55

Type of 1927-28 Redrawn
Perf. 15x14

1932-40 **Photo.** **Wmk. 201**

J22 D2 ½p blue grn & blk ('34) 2.75 1.75
J23 D2 1p rose car & blk ('34) 2.50 .95
J24 D2 2p blk violet & blk 15.00 2.50
a. 2p dark purple & black ('40) 32.50 .25
J25 D2 3p dp blue & blk 27.50 14.00
J26 D2 3p ultra & dk bl ('35) 8.00 .40
J27 D2 3p blue & dk bl ('40) 85.00 3.50
J28 D2 6p brn org & grn ('33) 25.00 6.00

J29 D2 6p red org & grn ('38) 15.00 3.50
Nos. J22-J29 (8) 180.75 32.60

The ½p No. J22 photogravure has larger but thinner numeral and the "d" is taller and thinner than on No. J17.

The 1p No. J23 photogravure has numeral with parallel sides. The "d" is taller and thicker than on No. J18.

On Nos. J25 and J27 the numeral is followed by a large "d" with thick lines and a large round period below it.

Nos. J22, J24 and J25 have frame in photogravure, value typographed.

Catalogue values for unused stamps in this section, from this point to the end of the section, are for Never Hinged items.

See "English-Afrikaans Se-tenant" note preceding No. 23.

D3

Horiz. strips of Three, Perf. 15x14 All Around, Rouletted 6½ Between

1943-44 Photo. Wmk. 201

J30 D3 ½p Prus green ('44) 15.00 *50.00*
  a. Single .25 .25
J31 D3 1p brt carmine 11.00 5.50
  a. Single .25 .25
J32 D3 2p dark purple 9.00 12.00
  a. Single .25 .25
J33 D3 3p dark blue 55.00 85.00
  a. Single .25 1.25
Nos. J30-J33 (4) 90.00 152.50

Catalogued as strips of 3 because of the perforations.

Type of 1932-38 Redrawn
Thick Numerals, Capital "D"

1948-49 ***Perf. 15x14***

J34 D2 ½p blue green & blk 9.00 13.50
J35 D2 1p deep rose & blk 16.00 6.00
J36 D2 2p dk pur & blk ('49) 17.50 9.00
J37 D2 3p ultra & dk blue 16.00 17.50
J38 D2 6p dp org & grn ('49) 37.50 8.00
Nos. J34-J38 (5) 96.00 54.00

Redrawn Type of 1948-49
Hyphen between Suid-Afrika

1950-58 ***Perf. 15x14***

J40 D2 1p car rose & blk 1.25 .45
J41 D2 2p dk pur & blk ('51) .85 .30
J42 D2 3p ultra & dk blue 6.25 2.50
J43 D2 4p emer & dk grn ('58) 14.50 15.00
J44 D2 6p dp org & grn ('52) 11.50 11.50
J45 D2 1sh brn red & dk brn ('58) 17.50 16.00
Nos. J40-J45 (6) 51.85 45.75

D4

Perf. 15x14

1961, Feb. 14 Photo. Wmk. 330

J46 D4 1c cerise & blk .25 2.50
J47 D4 2c purple & blk .25 2.50
J48 D4 4c brt & dk green 1.10 *6.00*
J49 D4 5c chalky bl & slate 2.00 *6.50*
J50 D4 6c vermilion & dk grn 8.00 *7.00*
J51 D4 10c maroon & dk brn 8.50 *10.00*
Nos. J46-J51 (6) 20.10 *34.50*

Republic

D5

Afrikaans Inscription on Top and Left Side

1961-69 ***Perf. 15x14***

J52 D5 1c cerise & blk .50 .50
J53 D5 4c brt & dk green 4.25 3.00
J54 D5 6c vermilion & dk grn 8.50 7.25

English Inscription on Top and Left Side

J55 D5 1c cerise & blk ('62) .30 3.50
J56 D5 2c purple & blk .40 .40
J57 D5 4c brt & dk grn ('69) 12.00 17.00
J58 D5 5c chlky bl & dk bl 2.40 3.00
J59 D5 5c chlky bl & blk ('62) 2.75 11.00
J60 D5 10c maroon & dk brn 4.75 3.00
Nos. J52-J60 (9) 35.85 48.65

1967-70 Photo. Wmk. 359

Afrikaans Inscription on Top and Left Side

J61 D5 1c car rose & blk .25 .25
J62 D5 2c brt pur & blk .25 .25
  a. Perf. 14 ('71) 25.00 25.00
J63 D5 4c lt grn & blk ('71) 27.50 25.00
  a. 4c bright & dark green ('70) *110.00* *110.00*
J64 D5 5c dk blue & blk .85 .85
J65 D5 6c orange & dk grn 4.25 *9.75*
J66 D5 10c dk rose brn & blk 3.50 2.10

English Inscription on Top and Left Side

J67 D5 1c car rose & blk .25 .25
J68 D5 2c brt purple & blk .40 .40
  a. Perf. 14 ('71) 25.00 25.00
J69 D5 4c lt grn & blk ('71) 27.50 25.00
  a. 4c bright & dark green ('70) *35.00* *35.00*
  b. As "a," perf. 14 ('71) *6.00* 6.00
J70 D5 5c dk blue & blk .85 .85
J71 D5 6c orange & dk grn 4.25 *9.75*
J72 D5 10c dk rose brn & blk 3.50 2.10
Nos. J61-J72 (12) 73.35 *76.55*

D6

1972, Mar. 22 ***Perf. 14x13½***

J73 D6 1c brt yellow green .55 *1.75*
J74 D6 2c orange .80 *3.00*
J75 D6 4c dull purple 2.00 *3.00*
J76 D6 6c yellow 2.00 *5.50*
J77 D6 8c bright blue 3.50 *5.50*
J78 D6 10c rose red 6.00 *8.50*
Nos. J73-J78 (6) 14.85 *27.25*

On the 2c, 6c and 10c "TO PAY" in first row at left.

OFFICIAL STAMPS

Type A2 stamps have very small margins at top and bottom. Values are for examples with perfs close to, or touching the frame.

No. 5 Overprinted in Black, Periods in Overprint

1926 Wmk. 177 ***Perf. 14***

O1 A2 2p dull violet 22.50 2.00

See "English-Afrikaans Se-tenant" note preceding No. 23.

On Nos. 23-25
Perf. 14½x14
Wmk. 201

O2 A5 ½p dk grn & blk, pair 8.00 *18.00*
  a. Single, English .75 1.50
  b. Single, Afrikaans .75 1.50
O3 A6 1p car & blk, pair 4.00 *8.50*
  a. Single, English .25 .50
  b. Single, Afrikaans .25 .50
O4 A7 6p org & grn, pair 550.00 80.00
  a. Single, English 25.00 11.00
  b. Single, Afrikaans 25.00 11.00

Nos. 26 and 25 Overprinted, No Periods in Overprint — b

(Reading Up)

1928-29 ***Perf. 14, 14½x14***

Space between words 19mm

O5 A8 2p vio brn & gray, pair ('29) 7.50 *20.00*
  a. Single, English .50 *1.50*
  b. Single, Afrikaans .50 *1.50*
  c. Space 17½mm, pair 6.00 *24.00*
  d. As "c," single, English .50 *2.00*
  e. As "c," single, Afrikaans .50 *2.00*

Space between words 11½mm

O6 A7 6p org & grn, pair 22.50 *47.50*
  a. Single, English 2.75 *2.75*
  b. Single, Afrikaans 2.75 *2.75*

Nos. 23-25 Ovptd. type "b" Reading Down

Space between words 13½-14mm

1929 ***Perf. 14½x14***

O7 A5 ½p grn & blk, pair 2.50 *4.75*
  a. Single, English .25 .35
  b. Single, Afrikaans .25 .35
  c. Period after "OFFISIEEL" on English stamp 5.00 5.00
  d. Pair, "c" + normal ½p 45.00 45.00
  e. Period after "OFFISIEEL." on Afrikaans stamp 5.00 5.00
  f. Pair, "e" + normal ½p 55.00 65.00
O8 A6 1p car & blk, pair 3.00 *6.00*
  a. Single, English .30 .50
  b. Single, Afrikaans .30 .50
O9 A7 6p org & grn, pair 8.00 *40.00*
  a. Single, English 1.25 *3.50*
  b. Single, Afrikaans 1.25 *3.50*
  c. Period after "OFFISIEEL." on English stamp 10.00 *10.00*
  d. Pair, "c" + normal 6p 75.00 *150.00*
  e. Period after "OFFISIEEL." on Afrikaans stamp 12.00 *12.00*
  f. Pair, "e" + normal 6p 90.00 *160.00*
Nos. O7-O9 (3) 13.50 *50.75*

Nos. 29-30 Ovptd. type "b" Reading Down

Space between words 17½-19mm

1931 Engr. ***Perf. 14, 14x13½***

O10 A11 1sh dp bl & bis brn, pair 40.00 *90.00*
  a. Single, English 3.00 *10.00*
  b. Single, Afrikaans 3.00 *10.00*
  c. Period after "OFFICIAL." on Afrikaans stamp 50.00 50.00
  d. Pair, "c" + normal 1sh 115.00 *240.00*
O11 A12 2sh6p brn & bl grn, pair 65.00 *150.00*
  a. Single, English 10.00 *19.00*
  b. Single, Afrikaans 10.00 *19.00*
  c. Period after "OFFICIAL." on Afrikaans stamp 72.50 100.00
  d. Pair, "c" + normal 2sh6p 300.00 *550.00*

Regular Issues of 1930-45 Overprinted type "b" Reading Down ("SUIDAFRIKA" on Afrikaans stamps)

Perf. 15x14 (½p, 1p, 6p), 14

1930-47 Photo. Wmk. 201

Space between words 9½-12mm

(Various spacings occur in same setting)

O12 A5 ½p bl grn & blk (#33), pair ('31) 2.25 *5.00*
  a. Single, English .25 *.40*
  b. Single, Afrikaans .25 *.40*
  c. Period after "OFFISIEEL." on English stamp 5.00 *5.00*
  d. Pair, "c" + normal ½p 37.50 *60.00*
  e. Period after "OFFISIEEL." on Afrikaans stamp 5.00 *5.00*
  f. Pair, "e" + normal ½p 27.50 *50.00*

Space between words 12½-13½mm

O13 A5 ½p bl grn & blk, pair (#33) 3.00 4.00
  a. Single, English .25 .50
  b. Single, Afrikaans .25 .50
O14 A6 1p car & blk, pair (#34) 6.00 6.00
  a. Single, English .50 .60
  b. Single, Afrikaans .50 .60
  c. Period after "OFFISIEEL." on English stamp 5.00 *5.00*
  d. Pair, "c" + normal 1p 50.00 *75.00*
  e. Period after "OFFISIEEL." on Afrikaans stamp 5.00 *5.00*
  f. Pair, "e" + normal 1p 35.00 *55.00*
O15 A6 1p rose & blk, pair (#35) ('33) 15.00 9.00
  a. Single, English 1.00 1.00
  b. Single, Afrikaans 1.00 1.00
  c. Double ovpt., pair 275.00 *400.00*
  d. As "c," English — —
  e. As "c," Afrikaans — —

Space between words 20½-22mm

O16 A8 2p vio & gray, pair (#36) ('31) 8.00 *11.00*
  a. Single, English .80 *1.50*
  b. Single, Afrikaans .80 *1.50*
O17 A8 2p vio & ind, pair (#37) 150.00 *100.00*
  a. Single, English 10.00 *10.00*
  b. Single, Afrikaans 10.00 *10.00*

Space between words 12½-13½mm

O18 A7 6p org & grn, pair (#42) 8.50 8.50
  a. Single, English .75 1.00
  b. Single, Afrikaans .75 1.00
  c. Period after "OFFISIEEL." on English stamp 7.00 7.00
  d. Pair, "c" + normal 6p 90.00 *100.00*
  e. Period after "OFFISIEEL." on Afrikaans stamp 5.50 5.50
  f. Pair, "e" + normal 6p 75.00 *90.00*

Space between words 21mm

O19 A11 1sh dp bl & brn, pair (#43c) ('32) 60.00 *90.00*
  a. Single, English 7.50 *7.50*
  b. Single, Afrikaans 7.50 *7.50*
  c. 1sh dk bl & yel brn (#43), 19mm, pair 50.00 *90.00*
  d. As "c," single, English 8.50 *7.50*
  e. As "c," single, Afrikaans 8.50 *7.50*
  f. As "c," spaced 21mm, pair 42.50 *65.00*
  g. As "f," single, English 6.00 *7.50*
  h. As "f," single, Afrikaans 6.00 *7.50*

Space between words 17½-18½mm

O20 A12 2sh6p brn & sl grn (#44c) ('37), pair 80.00 *140.00*
  a. Single, English 15.00 *15.00*
  b. Single, Afrikaans 15.00 *15.00*
  c. Spaced 21mm, pair 75.00 *75.00*
  d. As "c," single, English 4.50 *8.00*
  e. As "c," single, Afrikaans 4.50 *8.00*
  f. 2sh6p red brn & grn, pair (#44i) ('33) 50.00 *90.00*
  g. As "f," single, English 5.00 *8.50*
  h. As "f," single, Afrikaans 5.00 *8.50*
  j. 2sh6p brn & bl, 19-20mm (#44) ('47), pair 30.00 60.00
  k. As "j," single, English 3.00 *5.00*
  m. As "j," single, Afrikaans 3.00 *5.00*
Nos. O12-O20 (9) 332.75 *373.50*

Catalogue values for unused stamps in this section, from this point to the end of the section, are for Never Hinged items.

Regular Issue of 1933-54 Overprinted type "b" Reading Down ("SUID-AFRIKA" Hyphenated)

Space between words given with each listing

1935-50 Photo. ***Perf. 15x14, 14***

O21 A5 ½p grn & gray (#45), 12½-13mm, pair ('36) 7.00 *30.00*
  a. Single, English .25 *1.75*
  b. Single, Afrikaans .25 *1.75*
O22 A5 ½p grn & gray, (#46), 11½-13mm, pair ('38) 12.00 *12.50*
  a. Single, English .50 *1.25*
  b. Single, Afrikaans .50 *1.25*
O23 A5 ½p grn & gray (#47), 11½mm, pair ('48) 1.25 *5.00*
  a. Single, English .25 *.70*
  b. Single, Afrikaans .25 *.70*
O24 A6 1p car & gray (#48), 11-13mm, pair 4.00 3.00
  a. Single, English .25 .25
  b. Single, Afrikaans .25 .25
O25 A6 1p rose car & gray blk (#49), 11½-12mm, pair ('41) 1.00 .50
  a. Single, English .25 .25
  b. Single, Afrikaans .25 .25
O26 A15 1½p dk grn & gold (#51), 19-21mm, pair ('37) 30.00 25.00
  a. Single, English 2.25 1.75
  b. Single, Afrikaans 2.25 1.75
O27 A15 1½p sl grn & ocher (#52), 16mm, pair ('44) 50.00 *11.50*
  a. Single, English 1.25 *1.25*
  b. Single, Afrikaans 1.25 *1.25*
  c. Ovpt. spaced 14-14½mm, pair 3.00 *10.00*
  d. As "c," single, English .25 *.80*
  e. As "c," single, Afrikaans .25 *.80*
O28 A8 2p bl vio & dl bl (#53), 20-21mm, pair ('39) 150.00 40.00
  a. Single, English 7.50 2.50
  b. Single, Afrikaans 7.50 2.50
O29 A16 2p pur & sl (#55), 19-21mm, pair ('48) 5.75 *25.00*
  a. Single, English .25 *2.00*
  b. Single, Afrikaans .25 *2.00*
O30 A7 6p org & bl grn, I (#59), 12-13mm, pair ('38) 80.00 *45.00*
  a. Single, English 6.50 3.75
  b. Single, Afrikaans 6.50 3.75

No.	Type	Description	Unused	Used
O31	A7	6p org & grn, II (#60), 12-13mm, pair ('39)	14.00	10.00
a.		Single, English	1.25	1.25
b.		Single, Afrikaans	1.25	1.25
O32	A7	6p org & grn III (#61), 11½-12mm, pair ('47)	5.00	*11.00*
a.		Single, English	.85	*1.25*
b.		Single, Afrikaans	.85	*1.25*
O33	A11	1sh lt bl & ol brn (#62c), 19-21mm, pair ('40)	80.00	50.00
a.		Single, English	4.50	2.50
b.		Single, Afrikaans	4.50	2.50
c.		"OFFICIAL" on both sides	3,000.	
d.		"OFFISIEEL" on both sides	3,000.	
e.		1sh chlky bl & lt brn (#62) ('50), pair	11.00	*30.00*
f.		As "e," single, English	2.00	*2.50*
g.		As "e," single, Afrikaans	2.00	*2.50*
h.		1sh vio bl & brnsh blk (#62f), 18-19mm, pair	65.00	27.50
j.		As "h," single, English	4.50	2.00
k.		As "h," single, Afrikaans	4.50	2.00
O34	A13	5sh grn & blk (#64) 19-20mm, pair	65.00	*160.00*
a.		Single, English	3.50	*13.50*
b.		Single, Afrikaans	3.50	*13.50*
O35	A13	5sh bl grn & blk (#65), 20mm, pair	40.00	*110.00*
a.		Single, English	3.50	*12.50*
b.		Single, Afrikaans	3.50	*12.50*
O36	A18	10sh ol blk & bl (#67), 19½-20mm, pair ('48)	100.00	*275.00*
a.		Single, English	10.00	*24.00*
b.		Single, Afrikaans	10.00	*24.00*
		Nos. O21-O36 (16)	645.00	*813.50*

Nos. 52 and 56 Overprinted type "b" Reading Up

Space between words 16mm

1949-50 Size: 22x18mm *Perf. 14*

No.	Type	Description	Unused	Used
O37	A15	1½p sl grn & ocher, pair	85.00	*85.00*
a.		Single, English	5.00	*4.00*
b.		Single, Afrikaans	5.00	*4.00*

Size: 21½x17½mm

No.	Type	Description	Unused	Used
O38	A16	2p pur & sl bl, pair ('50)	*3,250.*	*3,750.*
a.		Single, English	*200.*	*275.*
b.		Single, Afrikaans	*200.*	*275.*

Nos. 64, 67 Overprinted

c

Space between words 18-19mm

1940 *Perf. 14*

No.	Type	Description	Unused	Used
O39	A13	5sh grn & blk, pair	125.00	*140.00*
a.		Single, English	12.00	*12.50*
b.		Single, Afrikaans	12.00	*12.50*
O40	A18	10sh ol brn & bl, pair	*500.00*	*525.00*
a.		Single, English	32.50	*37.50*
b.		Single, Afrikaans	32.50	*37.50*

No. 54 Overprinted type "c" Reading Up

Space between words 19mm

1945 *Perf. 14*

No.	Type	Description	Unused	Used
O41	A8	2p dl vio & gray, pair	11.00	*32.50*
a.		Single, English	1.00	*2.25*
b.		Single, Afrikaans	1.00	*2.25*

No. 47 Overprinted

1947 *Perf. 15x14*

No.	Type	Description	Unused	Used
O42	A5	½p grn & gray, pair	*22.50*	20.00
a.		Single, English	1.00	*2.00*
b.		Single, Afrikaans	1.00	*2.00*

Stamps of 1937-54 Overprinted

1950-54 *Perf. 15x14, 14*

Space between words 10mm

No.	Type	Description	Unused	Used
O43	A5	½p grn & gray, pair (#47)	.90	1.50
a.		Single, English	.25	.25
b.		Single, Afrikaans	.25	.25
O44	A6	1p rose car & gray blk, pair (#49)	1.00	*6.00*
a.		Single, English	.25	.25
b.		Single, Afrikaans	.25	.25
O45	A6	1p car & blk, pair (#50)	1.00	*3.50*
a.		Single, English	.25	.25
b.		Single, Afrikaans	.25	.25

Space between words 14½mm

No.	Type	Description	Unused	Used
O46	A15	1½p sl grn & ocher, pair (#52)	2.00	*5.00*
a.		Single, English	.25	*.35*
b.		Single, Afrikaans	.25	*.35*
O47	A16	2p pur & sl bl, pair (#56)	1.00	*2.00*
a.		Single, English	.25	*.25*
b.		Single, Afrikaans	.25	.25
c.		Ovpt. reading up, pair		

Space between words 10mm

No.	Type	Description	Unused	Used
O48	A7	6p red org & bl grn, III, pair (#61c)	2.00	*4.00*
a.		Single, English	.35	*.35*
b.		Single, Afrikaans	.35	*.35*

Space between words 19mm

No.	Type	Description	Unused	Used
O49	A11	1sh chlky bl & lt brn, pair (#62)	6.75	*18.00*
a.		Single, English	.50	*2.00*
b.		Single, Afrikaans	.50	*2.00*
c.		1sh vio bl & brnsh blk (#62f), pair	175.00	*200.00*
d.		As "c," single, English	12.50	*17.50*
e.		As "c," single, Afrikaans	12.50	*17.50*
O50	A12	2sh6p brn & brt grn, pair (#63)	10.00	*37.50*
a.		Single, English	1.00	*3.50*
b.		Single, Afrikaans	1.00	*3.50*
O51	A13	5sh bl grn & blk, pair (#64)	190.00	*125.00*
a.		Single, English	10.00	*10.00*
b.		Single, Afrikaans	10.00	*10.00*
O52	A13	5sh pale bl grn & blk, I, pair (#65)	65.00	*85.00*
a.		Single, English	5.00	*6.50*
b.		Single, Afrikaans	5.00	*6.50*
O53	A13	5sh dp yel grn & blk, II, pair (#66)	80.00	*100.00*
a.		Single, English	8.00	*9.00*
b.		Single, Afrikaans	8.00	*9.00*
O54	A18	10sh ol blk & bl, pair (#67)	80.00	*250.00*
a.		Single, English	9.00	*22.50*
b.		Single, Afrikaans	9.00	*22.50*
		Nos. O43-O54 (12)	439.65	*637.50*

BOPHUTHATSWANA

ˌbō-ˌₒpü-tät-ˈswä-nə

LOCATION — Noncontiguous enclaves, Republic of South Africa
GOVT. — Self-governing tribal homeland
AREA — 27,340 sq. mi.
POP. — 1,660,000 (1985)
CAPITAL — Mmabatho

Catalogue values for all unused stamps in this country are for Never Hinged items.

Independence from South Africa — A1

4c, Hands, dove released. 10c, Leopard (state emblem). 15c, Coat of arms. 20c, Flag.

Perf. 12½

1977, Dec. 6 Litho. Unwmk.

No.	Type	Description	Unused	Used
1	A1	4c multicolored	.60	.60
2	A1	10c multicolored	1.10	.85
3	A1	15c multicolored	2.40	1.75
4	A1	20c multicolored	3.25	2.40
		Nos. 1-4 (4)	7.35	5.60

An imperf. souvenir sheet exists containing Nos. 1-4 printed in one color (blue). Not valid for postage.

Tribal Totems — A2

Designs: 1c, African buffalo (Malete, Hwaduba). 2c, Bush pig (Kolobeng). 3c, Chacma baboon (Hurutshe, Thlaro). 4c, Leopard (state emblem). 5c, Crocodile (Kwena-Fokeng). 6c, Savanna monkey (Kgatla). 7c, Lion (Taung). 8c, Spotted hyena (Phiring). 9c, Cape porcupine (Rokologadi). 10c, Aardvark (Tlokwa). 15c, Fish (Tlhaping). 20c, Hunting dog (Tlhalerwa). 25c, Common duiker (Mfatlha). 30c, African elephant (Tlhako, Tloung). 50c, Python (Nogeng). 1r, Hippopotamus (Kubung). 2r, Greater kudu (Rolong).

1977, Dec. 6

No.	Type	Description	Unused	Used
5	A2	1c multicolored	.25	.25
6	A2	2c multicolored	.25	.25
7	A2	3c multicolored	.25	.25
8	A2	4c multicolored	4.00	1.90
9	A2	5c on 4c multi	1.10	.60
10	A2	6c multicolored	.25	.25
11	A2	7c multicolored	1.00	1.00
12	A2	8c multicolored	.25	.25
13	A2	9c multicolored	.35	.25
14	A2	10c multicolored	.25	.25
15	A2	15c multicolored	.35	.25
16	A2	20c multicolored	.35	.25
17	A2	25c multicolored	.40	.25
18	A2	30c multicolored	.45	.25
19	A2	50c multicolored	.65	.40
20	A2	1r multicolored	1.40	1.10
21	A2	2r multicolored	2.50	2.50
		Nos. 5-21 (17)	14.05	10.25

No. 9 was printed as a 4c stamp. Grass was printed over the 4c at upper right and 5c printed at upper left. Copies exist without the surcharge. No. 9A does not have the 4c.

Perf. 14

No.	Type	Description	Unused	Used
5a	A2	1c	.55	.55
6a	A2	2c	.55	.55
7a	A2	3c	.55	.55
8a	A2	4c	.55	.55
9A	A2	5c multicolored	.55	.55
11a	A2	7c	.55	.55
12a	A2	8c	.60	.60
14a	A2	10c	.60	.60
		Nos. 5a-14a (8)	4.50	4.50

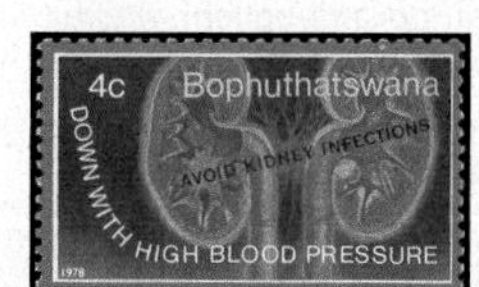

World Hypertension Month — A3

4c, Avoid kidney infections. 10c, Lower salt intake. 15c, Overeating is dangerous.

1978, Apr. 7 *Perf. 12x12½*

No.	Type	Description	Unused	Used
22	A3	4c multicolored	.55	.55
23	A3	10c multicolored	.95	.95
24	A3	15c multicolored	1.40	1.40
		Nos. 22-24 (3)	2.90	2.90

Road Safety A4

4c, Don't drink and drive. 10c, Keep children off roads. 15c, Pedestrians observe crossing signals. 20c, Observe stop signs.

1978, July 12

No.	Type	Description	Unused	Used
25	A4	4c multicolored	.55	.35
26	A4	10c multicolored	.80	.50
27	A4	15c multicolored	1.00	.60
28	A4	20c multicolored	1.60	.80
		Nos. 25-28 (4)	3.95	2.25

Cutting and Polishing Semi-precious Stones — A5

4c, Cutting slabs of travertine. 10c, Polishing travertine. 15c, Sorting stones. 20c, Factory at Taung.

1978, Oct. 3

No.	Type	Description	Unused	Used
29	A5	4c multicolored	.50	.25
30	A5	10c multicolored	1.00	.70
31	A5	15c multicolored	1.60	1.00
32	A5	20c multicolored	2.00	1.25
		Nos. 29-32 (4)	5.10	3.20

1st Airplane Flight, 75th Anniv. — A6

10c, Wright Flyer. 15c, Orville and Wilbur Wright.

1978, Dec. 1 *Perf. 12½*

No.	Type	Description	Unused	Used
33	A6	10c multicolored	1.50	1.50
34	A6	15c multicolored	2.00	2.00

Pres. Lucas M. Mangope — A7

1978, Dec. 6

No.	Type	Description	Unused	Used
35	A7	4c Profile	.40	.40
36	A7	15c Portrait	.85	.85

Sorghum Beer Production A8

4c, Drying germinated wheat. 15c, Cooking ground grain. 20c, Straining the liquid. 25c, Drinking beer.

1979, Feb. 28 *Perf. 14x14½*

No.	Type	Description	Unused	Used
37	A8	4c multicolored	.30	.30
38	A8	15c multicolored	.80	.80
39	A8	20c multicolored	1.00	1.00
40	A8	25c multicolored	1.40	1.40
		Nos. 37-40 (4)	3.50	3.50

Tate-Knoetze Boxing Match — A9

1979, June 2

No.	Type	Description	Unused	Used
41	A9	15c John Tate	.70	.70
42	A9	15c Kallie Knoetze	.70	.70
a.		Pair, #41-42	2.00	2.00

Intl. Children's Year — A10

Illustrations by local youths: 4c, Boy dazzled by sun, from a folk tale, by Hendrick Sebapo. 15c, Africans and animal silhouettes, by Daisy Morapedi. 20c, Man in profile and landscape, by Peter Tladi. 25c, Old man, boy and mule, by Sebapo.

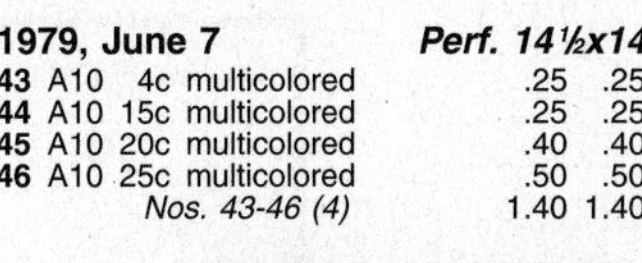

1979, June 7 *Perf. 14½x14*

43	A10	4c multicolored	.25	.25
44	A10	15c multicolored	.25	.25
45	A10	20c multicolored	.40	.40
46	A10	25c multicolored	.50	.50
		Nos. 43-46 (4)	1.40	1.40

Platinum Industry A11

Designs: 4c, Pouring molten metal. 15c, Platinum in industrial use. 20c, Telecommunications satellite in orbit. 25c, Jewelry.

1979, Aug. 15 *Perf. 14x14½*

47	A11	4c multicolored	.25	.25
48	A11	15c multicolored	.25	.25
49	A11	20c multicolored	.35	.35
50	A11	25c multicolored	.55	.55
		Nos. 47-50 (4)	1.40	1.40

Agriculture A12

5c, Cattle. 15c, Picking cotton. 20c, Researcher in corn field. 25c, Fish in net.

1979, Oct. 25

51	A12	5c multicolored	.25	.25
52	A12	15c multicolored	.25	.25
53	A12	20c multicolored	.40	.40
54	A12	25c multicolored	.45	.45
		Nos. 51-54 (4)	1.35	1.35

Stop Smoking Campaign — A13

1980, Mar. 5 *Perf. 14½x14*

55	A13	5c multicolored	.65	.65

Edible Wild Fruit — A14

5c, Landolphia capensis. 10c, Vangueria infausta. 15c, Bequaertiodendron magalismontanum. 20c, Sclerocarya caffra.

1980, June 4

56	A14	5c multicolored	.25	.25
57	A14	10c multicolored	.40	.40
58	A14	15c multicolored	.60	.60
59	A14	20c multicolored	.80	.80
		Nos. 56-59 (4)	2.05	2.05

Birds — A15

1980, Sept. 10

60	A15	5c Pied babbler	.25	.25
61	A15	10c Carmine bee-eater	.40	.40
62	A15	15c Shaft-tailed whydah	.60	.60
63	A15	20c Meyer's parrot	.75	.75
		Nos. 60-63 (4)	2.00	2.00

Sun City Tourist Attractions A16

5c, Hotel, casino, country club. 10c, Golfer at Gary Player Country Club. 15c, Casino interior. 20c, Night club dancers.

1980, Dec. 5 *Perf. 14x14½*

64	A16	5c multicolored	.25	.25
65	A16	10c multicolored	.25	.25
66	A16	15c multicolored	.40	.40
67	A16	20c multicolored	.50	.50
		Nos. 64-67 (4)	1.40	1.40

Intl. Year for the Disabled — A17

1981, Jan. 30 *Perf. 14½x14*

68	A17	5c shown	.25	.25
69	A17	15c Blind boy	.25	.25
70	A17	20c Archer in wheelchair	.40	.40
71	A17	25c X-ray (tuberculosis)	.45	.45
		Nos. 68-71 (4)	1.35	1.35

Easter A18

Bible quotes and: 5c, Lamb, sunset. 15c, Bread. 20c, Man holding lamb. 25c, Wheat field.

1981, Apr. 1 *Perf. 14x14½*

72	A18	5c multicolored	.25	.25
73	A18	15c multicolored	.25	.25
74	A18	20c multicolored	.40	.40
75	A18	25c multicolored	.45	.45
		Nos. 72-75 (4)	1.35	1.35

Telephones — A19

5c, Siemens & Halske wall telephone, 1885. 15c, Ericsson table model, 1895. 20c, Hasler table model, 1900. 25c, Mix & Genest wall model, 1904.

1981, July 31 *Perf. 14½x14*

76	A19	5c multicolored	.25	.25
77	A19	15c multicolored	.30	.30
78	A19	20c multicolored	.35	.35
79	A19	25c multicolored	.45	.45
		Nos. 76-79 (4)	1.35	1.35

Grasses — A20

5c, Themeda triandra. 15c, Rhynchelytrum repens. 20c, Eragrostis capensis. 25c, Monocymbium ceresiiforme.

1981, Nov. 25

80	A20	5c multicolored	.25	.25
81	A20	15c multicolored	.30	.30
82	A20	20c multicolored	.35	.35
83	A20	25c multicolored	.45	.45
		Nos. 80-83 (4)	1.35	1.35

Boy Scouts, 75th Anniv. — A21

5c, Scout, 1982. 15c, Mafeking Siege stamps. 20c, Scout cadet, 1907. 25c, Lord Baden-Powell.

1982, Jan. 29

84	A21	5c multicolored	.25	.25
85	A21	15c multicolored	.35	.35
86	A21	20c multicolored	.45	.45
87	A21	25c multicolored	.55	.55
		Nos. 84-87 (4)	1.60	1.60

Easter — A22

1982, Apr. 1

88	A22	15c John 12:1	.25	.25
89	A22	20c Matthew 21:1-2	.25	.25
90	A22	25c Mark 11:5-6	.50	.50
91	A22	30c Matthew 21:7	.60	.60
		Nos. 88-91 (4)	1.60	1.60

Table Telephones — A23

8c, Ericsson, 1878. 15c, Ericsson, 1885. 20c, Ericsson, 1893. 25c, Siemens & Halske, 1898.

1982, Sept. 3

92	A23	8c multicolored	.25	.25
93	A23	15c multicolored	.25	.25
94	A23	20c multicolored	.30	.30
95	A23	25c multicolored	.35	.35
		Nos. 92-95 (4)	1.15	1.15

Independence, 5th Anniv. — A24

8c, Old parliament building. 15c, New government offices. 20c, University, Mmabatho. 25c, Civic Center, Mmabatho.

1982, Dec. 6 *Perf. 14x14½*

96	A24	8c multicolored	.25	.25
97	A24	15c multicolored	.25	.25
98	A24	20c multicolored	.30	.30
99	A24	25c multicolored	.35	.35
		Nos. 96-99 (4)	1.15	1.15

Pilanesberg Nature Reserve — A25

No. 100, Ceratotherium simum. No. 101, Equus burchelli. No. 102, Hippotragus niger. No. 103, Alcelaphus caama.

1983, Jan. 5

100	A25	8c multicolored	.25	.25
101	A25	20c multicolored	.45	.45
102	A25	25c multicolored	.55	.55
103	A25	40c multicolored	.80	.80
		Nos. 100-103 (4)	2.05	2.05

Easter A26

1983, Mar. 30 *Perf. 14½x14*

104	A26	8c Matthew 21:7	.25	.25
105	A26	20c Mark 11:7	.35	.35
106	A26	25c Matthew 21:8	.40	.40
107	A26	40c Mark 11:9	.65	.65
		Nos. 104-107 (4)	1.65	1.65

Telephones — A27

10c, ATM table model, c. 1920. 20c, A/S Elektrisk wall model, c. 1900. 25c, Ericsson wall model, c. 1900. 40c, Ericsson wall model, c. 1900, diff.

1983, June 22

108	A27	10c multicolored	.25	.25
109	A27	20c multicolored	.35	.35
110	A27	25c multicolored	.45	.45
111	A27	40c multicolored	.70	.70
		Nos. 108-111 (4)	1.75	1.75

Birds of the Veld — A28

10c, Kori bustard. 20c, Black korhaan. 25c, Red-crested korhaan. 40c, Stanley bustard.

1983, Sept. 14

112	A28	10c multicolored	.25	.25
113	A28	20c multicolored	.45	.45
114	A28	25c multicolored	.60	.60
115	A28	40c multicolored	1.00	1.00
		Nos. 112-115 (4)	2.30	2.30

Grasses — A29

No. 116, Panicum maximum. No. 117, Hyparrhenia dregeana. No. 118, Cenchrus ciliaris. No. 119, Urochloa brachyura.

1984, Jan. 20

116	A29	10c multicolored	.25	.25
117	A29	20c multicolored	.30	.30
118	A29	25c multicolored	.35	.35
119	A29	40c multicolored	.50	.50
		Nos. 116-119 (4)	1.40	1.40

Easter
A30

1984, Mar. 23 ***Perf. 14½x14***

120 A30 10c Mark 11:11 .25 .25
121 A30 20c Mark 11:15 .30 .30
122 A30 25c Matthew 21:19 .40 .40
123 A30 40c Matthew 21:19, diff. .65 .65
Nos. 120-123 (4) 1.60 1.60

See Nos. 165-168, 173-176.

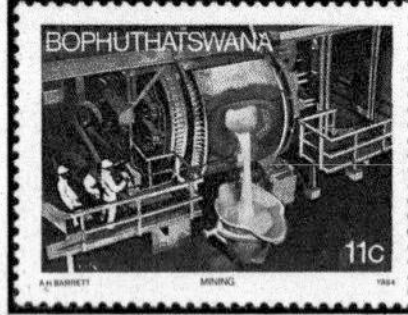

Mining Industry
A31

1984, Apr. 2 ***Perf. 14½x14***

124 A31 11c multicolored .70 .70

Telephones — A32

11c, Shuchhardt table model, c. 1905. 20c, Siemens wall model, c. 1925. 25c, Ericsson table model, c. 1900. 30c, Oki table model, c. 1930.

1984, July 20

125 A32 11c multicolored .25 .25
126 A32 20c multicolored .30 .30
127 A32 25c multicolored .40 .40
128 A32 30c multicolored .45 .45
Nos. 125-128 (4) 1.40 1.40

Lizards
A33

Designs: 11c, Yellow-throated plated lizard. 25c, Transvaal girdled lizard. 30c, Ocellated sand lizard. 45c, Bibron's thick-toed gecko.

1984, Sept. 25 ***Perf. 14x14½***

129 A33 11c multicolored .25 .25
130 A33 25c multicolored .30 .30
131 A33 30c multicolored .35 .35
132 A33 45c multicolored .50 .50
Nos. 129-132 (4) 1.40 1.40

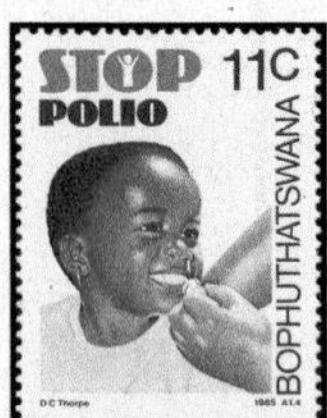

Child Health Care — A34

1985, Jan. 25

133 A34 11c Stop Polio .25 .25
134 A34 25c Stop Measles .35 .35
135 A34 30c Stop Diphtheria .45 .45
136 A34 50c Stop Whooping Cough .80 .80
Nos. 133-136 (4) 1.85 1.85

Mafeking, Cent. — A35

Portraits: 11c, Montshiwa (1814-1896), chief of the Barolong booRatshidi. 25c, Sir Charles Warren (1840-1927), army commander who established the Crown Colony and laid out the town of Mafeking.

1985, Mar. 11

137 A35 11c multicolored .25 .25
138 A35 25c multicolored .60 .60

Industries
A36

Designs: 1c, Textile mill, Bophuthatswana. 2c, Sewing cloth sacks, Selosesha. 3c, Ceramic tile production line. 4c, Processing sheepskin. 5c, Manufacture of crossbows. 6c, Automobile parts. 7c, Hosiery factory, Babelegi. 8c, Specialized bicycle factory. 9c, Lawn mower assembly line. 10c, Dress factory, Thaba Nchu. 12c, Automobile upholstery factory. 14c, Milling industry, Mafeking. 15c, Manufacturing of plastic bags. 16c, Brickworks, Mmabatho. 18c, Manufacturing of cutlery. 20c, Men's clothing factory. 25c, Chromium plating baby carriage parts. 30c, Spray-painting metal beds. 50c, Milk processing plant. 1r, Printing works. 2r, Industrial complex, Babelegi.

1985-89 ***Perf. 14½x14***

139 A36 1c multicolored .25 .25
140 A36 2c multicolored .25 .25
141 A36 3c multicolored .25 .25
142 A36 4c multicolored .25 .25
143 A36 5c multicolored .25 .25
144 A36 6c multicolored .25 .25
145 A36 7c multicolored .25 .25
146 A36 8c multicolored .25 .25
147 A36 9c multicolored .25 .25
148 A36 10c multicolored .25 .25
149 A36 12c multicolored .25 .25
150 A36 14c multicolored .30 .30
151 A36 15c multicolored .35 .35
152 A36 16c multicolored .35 .35
153 A36 18c multicolored .40 .40
154 A36 20c multicolored .45 .45
155 A36 25c multicolored .60 .60
156 A36 30c multicolored .70 .70
157 A36 50c multicolored 1.10 1.10
158 A36 1r multicolored 2.25 2.25
159 A36 2r multicolored 4.75 4.75
Nos. 139-159 (21) 14.00 14.00

Issued: 1c-10c, 15c, 20c, 25c, 30c-2r, 10/25/85; 12c, 4/1/85; 14c, 4/1/86; 16c, 4/1/87; 18c, 7/3/89.

Easter Type of 1984

1985, Apr. 2

165 A30 12c Matthew 21:14 .25 .25
166 A30 25c Matthew 21:14, diff. .30 .30
167 A30 30c Matthew 21:15 .35 .35
168 A30 50c Matthew 21:15-16 .55 .55
Nos. 165-168 (4) 1.45 1.45

Tree Conservation
A37

No. 169, Fourea saligna. No. 170, Boscia albitrunca. No. 171, Erythrina lysistemon. No. 172, Bequaertiodendron magalismontanum.

1985, July 4 ***Perf. 14x14½***

169 A37 12c multicolored .25 .25
170 A37 25c multicolored .35 .35
171 A37 30c multicolored .40 .40
172 A37 50c multicolored .65 .65
Nos. 169-172 (4) 1.65 1.65

Easter Type of 1984

1986, Mar. 6 ***Perf. 14½x14***

173 A30 12c John 12:2 .25 .25
174 A30 20c John 12:3 .35 .35
175 A30 25c John 12:3, diff. .45 .45
176 A30 30c Matthew 26:7 .60 .60
Nos. 173-176 (4) 1.65 1.65

Paintings of Thaba Nchu in the Africana Museum, Johannesburg — A38

14c, *Wesleyan Mission Station and Residence of Moroka, Chief of the Barolong, 1834,* by Charles Davidson Bell. 20c, *James Archbell's Congregation, 1834,* by Bell. 25c, *Mission Station at Thaba Nchu, 1850,* by Thomas Baines (1822-75).

1986, May 15 ***Perf. 14x14½***

177 A38 14c multicolored .25 .25
178 A38 20c multicolored .30 .30
179 A38 25c multicolored .45 .45
Nos. 177-179 (3) 1.00 1.00

Incorporation of Thaba Nchu and Bophuthatswana, Oct. 1, 1983.

A souvenir sheet of one No. 179 has decorative margin continuing the painting and picturing the emblem of the philatelic exhibition held at Johannesburg, Oct. 6-11. Sold for 50c. Value $1.

Temisano Development Projects
A39

14c, Agricultural production. 20c, Community development. 25c, Vocational training. 30c, Secondary industries.

1986, Aug. 6 ***Perf. 14½x14***

180 A39 14c multicolored .25 .25
181 A39 20c multicolored .30 .30
182 A39 25c multicolored .40 .40
183 A39 30c multicolored .45 .45
Nos. 180-183 (4) 1.40 1.40

BOP Airways, 5th Anniv.
A40

14c, Airline personnel, aircraft. 20c, Passengers. 25c, Mmabatho Intl. Airport. 30c, Cessna Citation.

1986, Oct. 16 ***Perf. 14x14½***

184 A40 14c multicolored .25 .25
185 A40 20c multicolored .40 .40
186 A40 25c multicolored .50 .50
187 A40 30c multicolored .55 .55
Nos. 184-187 (4) 1.70 1.70

Sports — A41

1987, Jan. 22

188 A41 14c Netball .25 .25
189 A41 20c Tennis .30 .30
190 A41 25c Soccer .35 .35
191 A41 30c Running .45 .45
Nos. 188-191 (4) 1.35 1.35

Wildflowers — A42

No. 192, Berkheya zeyheri. No. 193, Plumbago auriculata. No. 194, Pterodiscus speciosus. No. 195, Gazania krebsiana.

1987, Apr. 23

192 A42 16c multicolored .30 .30
193 A42 20c multicolored .35 .35
194 A42 25c multicolored .45 .45
195 A42 30c multicolored .50 .50
Nos. 192-195 (4) 1.60 1.60

A souvenir sheet of one No. 194 has decorative black and white inscribed margin picturing the emblem of the natl. philatelic exhibition held at Paarl, Sept. 16-19. Sold for 70c. Value $1.50.

Education — A43

Designs: 16c, E.M. Mokgoko Farmer Training Center, Ramatlabama. 20c, Main lecture block, University of Bophuthatswana, Mmabatho. 25c, Manpower Center. 30c, Hotel training school, Odi.

1987, Aug. 6 ***Perf. 14½x14***

196 A43 16c multicolored .25 .25
197 A43 20c multicolored .30 .30
198 A43 25c multicolored .35 .35
199 A43 30c multicolored .45 .45
Nos. 196-199 (4) 1.35 1.35

Independence, 10th Anniv. — A44

Communications.

1987, Dec. 4

200 A44 16c Postal service .25 .25
201 A44 30c Telephone .30 .30
202 A44 40c Radio .40 .40
203 A44 50c Television .50 .50
Nos. 200-203 (4) 1.45 1.45

Easter
A45

1988, Mar. 31

204 A45 16c John 12:12-14 .25 .25
205 A45 30c Mark 14:10-11 .30 .30
206 A45 40c John 13:5 .40 .40
207 A45 50c John 13:26 .45 .45
Nos. 204-207 (4) 1.40 1.40

Natl. Parks Board Activities — A46

16c, Environmental education. 30c, Conservation. 40c, Catering. 50c, Tourism.

1988, June 23 *Perf. 14½x14*

208	A46 16c multicolored	.25	.25
209	A46 30c multicolored	.40	.40
210	A46 40c multicolored	.50	.50
211	A46 50c multicolored	.65	.65
	Nos. 208-211 (4)	1.80	1.80

A souvenir sheet of one No. 211 has black and white decorative margin picturing the emblem of the natl. philatelic exhibition held at Pietermaritzburg, Nov. 22-27. Sold for 70c. Value $3.

Crops A47

1988, Sept. 15 *Perf. 14½x14*

212	A47 16c Sunflowers	.25	.25
213	A47 30c Peanuts	.40	.40
214	A47 40c Cotton	.55	.55
215	A47 50c Cabbages	.65	.65
	Nos. 212-215 (4)	1.85	1.85

Dams — A48

1988, Nov. 17

216	A48 16c Ngotwane	.30	.30
217	A48 30c Groothoek	.55	.55
218	A48 40c Sehujwane	.85	.85
219	A48 50c Molatedi	.90	.90
	Nos. 216-219 (4)	2.60	2.60

Easter A49

1989, Mar. 9

220	A49 16c Mark 26:26	.30	.30
221	A49 30c Matthew 26:39	.55	.55
222	A49 40c Mark 14:45	.85	.85
223	A49 50c John 18:10	1.00	1.00
	Nos. 220-223 (4)	2.70	2.70

Children's Art — A50

Designs: 18c, "Rooster," by Thembi Atong. 30c, "Thatched Hut in Rural Setting," by Muhammad Mahri. 40c, "Modern World," by Tshepo Mashokwe. 50c, "Cityscape," by Miles Brown.

1989, May 11

224	A50 18c multicolored	.25	.25
225	A50 30c multicolored	.40	.40
226	A50 40c multicolored	.55	.55
227	A50 50c multicolored	.70	.70
	Nos. 224-227 (4)	1.90	1.90

Birds of Prey — A51

1989, Sept. 1 *Perf. 14x14½*

228	A51 18c Elanus caeruleus	.70	.70
229	A51 30c Melierax canorus	1.10	1.10
230	A51 40c Falco naumanni	1.50	1.50
231	A51 50c Circaetus gallicus	1.90	1.90
a.	Souvenir sheet of 1	4.75	4.75
	Nos. 228-231 (4)	5.20	5.20

No. 231a has multicolored decorative margin picturing emblem of the WANDERERS 101 natl. philatelic exhibition held Sept. 6-9. Sold for 1.50r.

Traditional Thatched Dwellings A52

1989, Nov. 28 *Perf. 14½x14*

232	A52 18c shown	.25	.25
233	A52 30c multi, diff.	.40	.40
234	A52 40c multi, diff.	.45	.45
235	A52 50c multi, diff.	.55	.55
	Nos. 232-235 (4)	1.65	1.65

Community Services A53

1990, Jan. 11

236	A53 18c Playground	.25	.25
237	A53 30c Immunization clinic	.35	.35
238	A53 40c Library	.50	.50
239	A53 50c Hospital	.60	.60
	Nos. 236-239 (4)	1.70	1.70

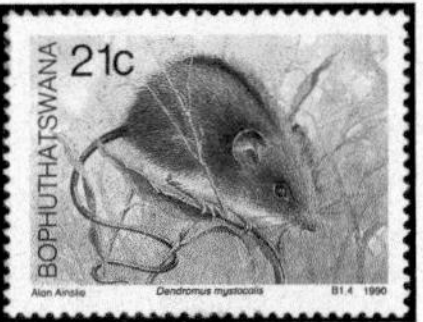

Wildlife (Small Mammals) A54

21c, Dendromus mystacalis. 30c, Ictonyx striatus. 40c, Elephantulus myurus. 50c, Procavia capensis.

1990, Apr. 11 Litho. *Perf. 14½x14*

240	A54 21c multicolored	.40	.40
241	A54 30c multicolored	.55	.55
242	A54 40c multicolored	.70	.70
243	A54 50c multicolored	.90	.90
a.	Souvenir sheet of 1	2.75	2.75
	Nos. 240-243 (4)	2.55	2.55

No. 243a has multicolored inscribed margin; text publicizes the natl. philatelic exhibition. Sold for 1.50r.

Sandgrouses — A55

1990, July 12 Litho. *Perf. 14x14½*

244	A55 21c Pterocles burchelli	.75	.75
245	A55 35c Pterocles bicinctus	1.40	1.40
246	A55 40c Pterocles namaqua	1.50	1.50
247	A55 50c Pterocles gutturalis	1.90	1.90
	Nos. 244-247 (4)	5.55	5.55

Bus Manufacturing — A56

a, Chassis welding. b, Mounting the engine. c, Body construction. d, Spray painting. e, Completed models and bare chassis.

1990, Aug. 3 *Perf. 14½x14*

248	Strip of 5	4.50	4.50
a.-e.	A56 21c any single	.90	.90

Traditional Activities — A57

1990, Oct. 4 *Perf. 14x14½*

249	A57 21c Basketry	.40	.40
250	A57 35c Tanning	.60	.60
251	A57 40c Beer making	.70	.70
252	A57 50c Pottery making	1.00	1.00
	Nos. 249-252 (4)	2.70	2.70

Bophuthatswana Air Force, 10th Anniv. — A58

Helicopters: a, Alouette III. b, BK117. Airplanes: c, Pilatus Trainer PC-7. d, Pilatus Porter PC-6. e, Casa 212.

1990, Dec. 12 *Perf. 14½x14*

253	Strip of 5	6.00	6.00
a.-e.	A58 21c any single	1.40	1.40

Edible Wild Fruit — A59

1991, Jan. 24 Litho. *Perf. 14x14½*

254	A59 21c Annona senegalensis	.40	.40
255	A59 35c Strychnos pungens	.65	.65
256	A59 40c Ficus sycomorus	.85	.85
257	A59 50c Dovyalis caffra	1.00	1.00
	Nos. 254-257 (4)	2.90	2.90

Easter A60

1991, Mar. 21 Litho. *Perf. 14½x14*

258	A60 21c Mark 14:46	.45	.45
259	A60 35c Mark 14:53	.65	.65
260	A60 40c Mark 14:65	.85	.85
261	A60 50c Mark 14:67	.95	.95
	Nos. 258-261 (4)	2.90	2.90

Locomotives A61

1991, July 4 **Litho.**
Size: 72x25mm (25c, 50c)

262	A61 25c Class 6A	.85	.85
263	A61 40c Class 7A	1.40	1.40
264	A61 50c Class 6Z	1.75	1.75
265	A61 60c Class 8	2.40	2.40
	Nos. 262-265 (4)	6.40	6.40

A souvenir sheet of 1 #265 was sold by the Philatelic Foundation of South Africa. Value $6.

See Nos. 291-294.

Maps of Africa — A62

25c, Caneiro chart, 1502. 40c, Cantino chart, 1502. 50c, Contarini map, 1506. 60c, Waldseemuller map, 1507.

1991, Sept. 12 Litho. *Perf. 14x14½*

266	A62 25c multicolored	.90	.90
267	A62 40c multicolored	1.50	1.50
268	A62 50c multicolored	1.90	1.90
269	A62 60c multicolored	2.50	2.50
	Nos. 266-269 (4)	6.80	6.80

Maps of Africa A63

27c, Fracanzano, 1508. 45c, Waldseemuller, 1513. 65c, Waldseemuller, 1516. 85c, Laurent Fries, 1522.

1992, Jan. 9 Litho. *Perf. 14½x14*

270	A63 27c multicolored	.90	.90
271	A63 45c multicolored	1.50	1.50
272	A63 65c multicolored	1.90	1.90
273	A63 85c multicolored	2.50	2.50
	Nos. 270-273 (4)	6.80	6.80

Easter A64

1992, Apr. 1 **Litho.**

274	A64 27c Mark 15:1	.25	.25
275	A64 45c Mark 15:15	.45	.45
276	A64 65c Mark 15:17-18	.60	.60
277	A64 85c Mark 15:19	.80	.80
	Nos. 274-277 (4)	2.10	2.10

Acacia Trees — A65

1992, Sept. 17 **Litho.**

278	A65 35c Karroo	.30	.30
279	A65 70c Erioloba	.65	.65
280	A65 90c Tortilis	.75	.75
281	A65 1.05r Mellifera	.85	.85
	Nos. 278-281 (4)	2.55	2.55

A souvenir sheet of 1 #279 exists. Sold for 2.50r. Value $3.75.

Lost City Hotel Complex, Sun City — A66

a, View from lake. b, Palace. c, Porte cochere. d, Lobby of Palace. e, Tusk bar.

1992, Nov. 19 Litho. *Perf. 14x14½*

282	Strip of 5	2.00	2.00
a.-e.	A66 35c any single	.50	.50

Chickens A67

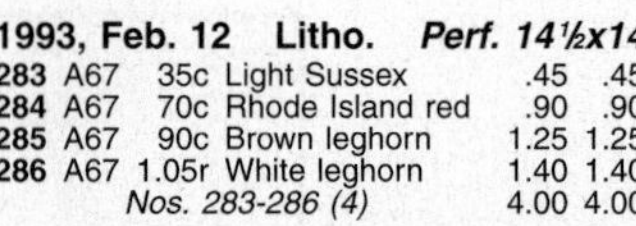

1993, Feb. 12 Litho. ***Perf. 14½x14***
283 A67 35c Light Sussex .45 .45
284 A67 70c Rhode Island red .90 .90
285 A67 90c Brown leghorn 1.25 1.25
286 A67 1.05r White leghorn 1.40 1.40
Nos. 283-286 (4) 4.00 4.00

A souvenir sheet of 1 #284 exists. Sold for 3r. Value $5.

Easter A68

1993, Mar. 5
287 A68 35c Luke 23:25 .60 .60
288 A68 70c John 19:17 1.25 1.25
289 A68 90c Mark 15:21 1.60 1.60
290 A68 1.05r Mark 15:23 1.90 1.90
Nos. 287-290 (4) 5.35 5.35

Trains Type of 1991

Designs: 45c, Mafeking locomotive shed, c. 1933, RR classes 10, 8, & 12. 65c, Locomotive No. 5. 85c, 1934 Royal visit, White Train, SAR Class 16B. 1.05r, SAR class 19D.

1993, June 18 Litho.
Size: 72x25mm (45c, 85c)
291 A61 45c multicolored .75 .75
292 A61 65c multicolored 1.10 1.10
293 A61 85c multicolored 1.40 1.40
294 A61 1.05r multicolored 1.75 1.75
a. Souvenir sheet of 4, #291-294 5.00 5.00
Nos. 291-294 (4) 5.00 5.00

Maps of Africa A69

Name of cartographer, year published: 45c, Sebastian Munster, 1540. 65c, Jacopo Gastaldi, 1564. 85c, Gerardus Mercator the Younger, 1595. 1.05r, Abraham Ortelius, 1570.

1993, Aug. 20 Litho.
295 A69 45c multicolored .60 .60
296 A69 65c multicolored .90 .90
297 A69 85c multicolored 1.25 1.25
298 A69 1.05r multicolored 1.50 1.50
Nos. 295-298 (4) 4.25 4.25

Easter A70

1994, Mar. 25 Litho. ***Perf. 14½x14***
299 A70 35c Luke 22:33 .65 .65
300 A70 65c Luke 23:35-36 1.25 1.25
301 A70 85c Luke 23:36 1.60 1.60
302 A70 1.05r Luke 23:38 1.90 1.90
Nos. 299-302 (4) 5.40 5.40

Bophuthatswana ceased to exist 4/27/94.

CISKEI

'sis-ˌkī

LOCATION — Enclave, Republic of South Africa
GOVT. — Self-governing tribal homeland
AREA — 5,592 sq. mi.
POP. — 1,000,000
CAPITAL — Bisho

Catalogue values for all unused stamps in this country are for Never Hinged Items.

Independence from South Africa — A1

Perf. 14x14½
1981, Dec. 4 Litho. Unwmk.
1 A1 5c Pres. Sebe .25 .25
2 A1 15c Coat of arms .25 .25
3 A1 20c Flag .30 .30
4 A1 25c Mace .35 .35
Nos. 1-4 (4) 1.15 1.15

An imperf. souvenir sheet exists containing Nos. 1-4 printed in one color (black). Not valid for postage.

Birds
A2 A3

1c, Tauraco corythaix. 2c, Motacilla capensis. 3c, Centropus superciliosus. 4c, Nectarinia famosa. 5c, Anthropoides paradisea. 6c, Onychognathus morio. 7c, Ceryle maxima. 8c, Bostrychia hagedash. 9c, Cuculus clamosus. 10c, Lybius torquatus. 11c, Oriolus larvatus. 12c, Alcedo cristata. 14c, Upupa epops. 15c, Haliaeetus vocifer. 16c, Batis capensis. 18c, Euplectes progne. 20c, Macronyx capensis. 21c, Aplopelia larvata. 25c, Burhinus capensis. 30c, Treron calva. 50c, Poicephalus robustus. 1r, Apaloderma narina. 2r, Bubo capensis.

1981-90 ***Perf. 14½x14***
5 A2 1c multicolored .25 .25
6 A2 2c multicolored .25 .25
7 A2 3c multicolored .25 .25
8 A2 4c multicolored .25 .25
9 A2 5c multicolored .25 .25
10 A2 6c multicolored .25 .25
11 A2 7c multicolored .25 .25
12 A2 8c multicolored .25 .25
13 A2 9c multicolored .25 .25
14 A2 10c multicolored .25 .25
15 A2 11c multicolored .55 .25
16 A2 12c multicolored .55 .25
17 A2 14c multicolored .65 .25
18 A2 15c multicolored .25 .25
19 A2 16c multicolored .65 .25
20 A3 18c multicolored 1.00 .25
21 A2 20c multicolored .35 .25
22 A2 21c multicolored 3.25 .25
23 A2 25c multicolored .40 .25
24 A2 30c multicolored .55 .35
25 A2 50c multicolored .90 .60
26 A2 1r multicolored 1.50 1.10
27 A2 2r multicolored 3.25 2.25
Nos. 5-27 (23) 16.35 9.05

Issued: 11c, 4/4/82; 12c, 4/1/85; 14c, 4/1/86; 16c, 4/1/87; 18c, 7/3/89; 21c, 7/3/90; others, 12/4/81.

Nursing A4

8c, Cecilia Makiwane, vert. 15c, Surgery, vert. 20c, Nurses pledge to serve. 25c, Hospital care.

1982, Apr. 30 ***Perf. 14½x14, 14x14½***
34 A4 8c multicolored .25 .25
35 A4 15c multicolored .30 .30
36 A4 20c multicolored .45 .45
37 A4 25c multicolored .55 .55
Nos. 34-37 (4) 1.55 1.55

Pineapple Industry A5

8c, Spraying. 15c, Harvesting. 20c, Transporting fruit to cannery. 30c, Packing.

1982, Aug. 20 ***Perf. 14x14½***
38 A5 8c multicolored .25 .25
39 A5 15c multicolored .25 .25
40 A5 20c multicolored .25 .25
41 A5 30c multicolored .40 .40
Nos. 38-41 (4) 1.15 1.15

Small Mammals A6

1982, Oct. 29
42 A6 8c Lepus capensis .25 .25
43 A6 15c Vulpes chama .35 .35
44 A6 20c Xerus inaurus .40 .40
45 A6 25c Felis caracal .45 .45
Nos. 42-45 (4) 1.45 1.45

Trees — A7

1983, Feb. 2 ***Perf. 14½x14***
46 A7 8c Cussonia spicata .25 .25
47 A7 20c Curtisia dentata .30 .30
48 A7 25c Calodendrum capense .35 .35
49 A7 40c Podocarpus falcatus .60 .60
Nos. 46-49 (4) 1.50 1.50

1984, Jan. 6
50 A7 10c Rhus chirindensis .25 .25
51 A7 20c Phoenix reclinata .30 .30
52 A7 25c Ptaeroxylon obliquum .35 .35
53 A7 40c Apodytes dimidiata .60 .60
Nos. 50-53 (4) 1.50 1.50

Sharks — A8

8c, Dusky. 20c, Ragged-tooth. 25c, Tiger. 30c, Scalloped hammerhead. 40c, Great white.

1983, Apr. 13 ***Perf. 14x14½***
54 A8 8c multicolored .25 .25
55 A8 20c multicolored .35 .35

Size: 57x21mm
56 A8 25c multicolored .40 .40
57 A8 30c multicolored .50 .50
58 A8 40c multicolored .60 .60
Nos. 54-58 (5) 2.10 2.10

Educational Institutions — A9

1983, July 6
59 A9 10c Lovedale .25 .25
60 A9 20c Fort Hare .25 .25
61 A9 25c Healdtown .30 .30
62 A9 40c Lennox Sebe .40 .40
Nos. 59-62 (4) 1.20 1.20

Military Uniforms — A10

6th Foot, 1st Warwickshire Regiment, 1821-27 (No. 63): a, White drill uniform (D1.5). b, Light Company privates (D2.5). c, Grenadier Company sergeants (D3.5). d, Light Co. Officers (D4.5). e, Officer and field officer (D5.5).

Cape Mounted Rifles, 1827-35 (No. 64): a, Trooper and sergeant, 1830 (D1.5). b, Trooper and sergeant in full dress, 1835 (D2.5). c, Officers, 1830 (D3.5). d, Officers in full dress, 1827-34 (D4.5). e, Officers in full dress, 1834 (D5.5).

1983, Sept. 28 ***Perf. 14½x14***
63 Strip of 5 2.25 2.25
a.-e. A10 20c any single .45 .45

1984, Oct. 26
64 Strip of 5 2.50 2.25
a.-e. A10 25c any single .50 .40

Sheets of 10 containing two strips of five.

Coastal Angling A11

Bait.

1984, Apr. 12 ***Perf. 14x14½***
65 A11 11c Sand prawn .25 .25
66 A11 20c Coral worm .25 .25
67 A11 25c Bloodworm .45 .45
68 A11 30c Red-bait .55 .55
Nos. 65-68 (4) 1.50 1.50

1985, Mar. 7

Game fish — 11c, Lithognathus lithognathus. 25c, Pachymetopon grande. 30c, Argyrosomus hololepidotus. 50c, Pomadasys commersonni.

69 A11 11c multicolored .25 .25
70 A11 25c multicolored .45 .30
71 A11 30c multicolored .55 .35
72 A11 50c multicolored .90 .60
Nos. 69-72 (4) 2.15 1.50

Migratory Birds and Maps — A12

11c, Banded sand martin. 25c, House martin. 30c, Greater striped swallow. 45c, European swallow.

1984, Aug. 17 ***Perf. 14½x14***
73 A12 11c multicolored .25 .25
74 A12 25c multicolored .45 .45
75 A12 30c multicolored .50 .50
76 A12 45c multicolored .75 .75
Nos. 73-76 (4) 1.95 1.95

Brownies A13

25c, Rangers planting saplings. 30c, Guide color guard. 50c, Camping.

1985, May 3

77 A13 12c shown .25 .25
78 A13 25c multicolored .25 .25
79 A13 30c multicolored .30 .30
80 A13 50c multicolored .55 .55
Nos. 77-80 (4) 1.35 1.35

Intl. Year of the Child, 75th anniv. of the Girl Guide movement.

Small Businesses A14

1985, Aug. 8 ***Perf. 14x14½***

81 A14 12c Furniture .25 .25
82 A14 25c Dress making .30 .30
83 A14 30c Welding .40 .40
84 A14 50c Basketry .70 .70
Nos. 81-84 (4) 1.65 1.65

Troop Ships — A15

1985, Nov. 15 ***Perf. 14½x14***

85 A15 12c Antelope .25 .25
86 A15 25c Pilot .40 .40
87 A15 30c Salisbury .45 .45
88 A15 50c Olive Branch .85 .85
Nos. 85-88 (4) 1.95 1.95

Miniature Sheet

Halley's Comet — A16

Comet streaking through the solar system: a, A1.10. b, A2.10. c, A3.10. d, A4.10. e, A5.10. f, A6.10. g, A7.10. h, A8.10. i, A9.10. j, A10.10.

1986, Mar. 20

89 A16 Sheet of 10 *8.00 8.00*
a.-j. 12c any single *1.00 1.00*

Military Uniforms — A17

98th Foot Regiment: 14c, Fifer in winter. 20c, Private in summer. 25c, Grenadier Company sergeant in summer. 30c, Sergeant-major in winter.

1986, June 12

90 A17 14c multicolored .25 .25
91 A17 20c multicolored .35 .35
92 A17 25c multicolored .45 .45
93 A17 30c multicolored .50 .50
a. Souvenir sheet of 1 2.00 2.00
Nos. 90-93 (4) 1.55 1.55

No. 93a for the natl. philatelic exhibition held at Johannesberg, Oct. 6-11. Sold for 50c.

Bicycle Factory, Dimbaza A18

1986, Sept. 18

94 A18 14c Welding frames .25 .25
95 A18 20c Painting .35 .35
96 A18 25c Spoke installation .40 .40
97 A18 30c Assembly .50 .50
Nos. 94-97 (4) 1.50 1.50

Independence, 5th Anniv. — A19

14c, Pres. Sebe. 20c, Natl. shrine, Ntaba kaNdoda. 25c, Legislative Assembly, Bisho. 30c, Automatic telephone exchange, Bisho.

1986, Dec. 4 ***Perf. 14x14½***

98 A19 14c multicolored .25 .25
99 A19 20c multicolored .30 .30
100 A19 25c multicolored .35 .35
101 A19 30c multicolored .45 .45
Nos. 98-101 (4) 1.35 1.35

Edible Mushrooms A20

14c, Boletus edulis. 20c, Macrolepiota zeyheri. 25c, Termitomyces. 30c, Russula capensis.

1987, Mar. 19

102 A20 14c multicolored .35 .35
103 A20 20c multicolored .45 .45
a. Souvenir sheet of 1 3.75 3.75
104 A20 25c multicolored .50 .50
105 A20 30c multicolored .65 .65
Nos. 102-105 (4) 1.95 1.95

No. 103a has fawn and black decorative margin picturing emblem of the natl. philatelic exhibition held at Paarl, Sept. 16-19. Sold for 50c.

Nkone Cattle A21

1987, June 18 ***Perf. 14½x14***

106 A21 16c Cow and calf .25 .25
107 A21 20c Cow .30 .30
108 A21 25c Bull .35 .35
109 A21 30c Herd .45 .45
Nos. 106-109 (4) 1.35 1.35

Toys — A22

Perf. 14x14½, 14½x14

1987, Sept. 17

110 A22 16c Windmill, vert. .25 .25
111 A22 20c Rag doll, vert. .30 .30
112 A22 25c Clay horse .35 .35
113 A22 30c Wire vehicle .45 .45
Nos. 110-113 (4) 1.35 1.35

Folklore A23

Legend of Sikulume: 16c, Seven birds. 20c, Sikulume escapes cannibals. 25c, Fights sea monster. 30c, Elopes and is pursued by bride's father.

1987, Nov. 6 ***Perf. 14½x14***

114 A23 16c multicolored .25 .25
115 A23 20c multicolored .30 .30
116 A23 25c multicolored .35 .35
117 A23 30c multicolored .45 .45
Nos. 114-117 (4) 1.35 1.35

See Nos. 122, 139-142, 147-150.

Endangered and Protected Plant Species — A24

16c, Clivia nobilis. 30c, Dierama pulcherrimum. 40c, Moraea reticulata. 50c, Crinum campanulatum.

1988, Mar. 17 ***Perf. 14x14½***

118 A24 16c multicolored .25 .25
119 A24 30c multicolored .45 .45
120 A24 40c multicolored .55 .55
121 A24 50c multicolored .70 .70
a. Souvenir sheet of 1 2.50 2.50
Nos. 118-121 (4) 1.95 1.95

No. 121a margin pictures the emblem of the natl. philatelic exhibition held at Pietermaritzburg, Nov. 22-27. Sold for 1r.

Folklore Type of 1987

Miniature Sheet

Legend of Mbulukazi: a, Two wives (B1.10). b, Two doves appear to Numbakatali (B2.10). c, Birth of Mbulukazi and brother (B3.10). d, Mbulukazi and brother at river (B4.10). e, Chief's son announces marriage (B5.10). f, Chief's son presents wives Mbulukazi and Mahlunguluza with huts (B6.10). g, Mahlunguluza drowns Mbulukazi (B7.10). h, Ox tears down Mahlunguluza's hut (B8.10). i, Mbulukazi revived (B9.10). j, Chief's son embraces Mbulukazi, banishes Mahlunguluza (B10.10).

1988, Aug. 26

Size of Nos. 122a-122j: 36x20mm

122 Sheet of 10 2.50 2.50
a.-j. A23 16c any single .30 .30

Citrus Farming A25

1988, Sept. 29

123 A25 16c Nursery .25 .25
124 A25 30c Grafting .40 .40
125 A25 40c Picking fruit .50 .50
126 A25 50c Grading .65 .65
Nos. 123-126 (4) 1.80 1.80

Poisonous Mushrooms A26

16c, Amanita phalloides. 30c, Chlorophyllum molybdites. 40c, Amanita muscaria. 50c, Amanita pantherina.

1988, Dec. 1

127 A26 16c multicolored .75 .75
128 A26 30c multicolored 1.50 1.50
129 A26 40c multicolored 1.90 1.90
130 A26 50c multicolored 2.40 2.40
Nos. 127-130 (4) 6.55 6.55

Dams — A27

1989, Mar. 2 ***Perf. 14½x14***

131 A27 16c Kat River .25 .25
132 A27 30c Cata .50 .50
133 A27 40c Binfield Park .60 .60
134 A27 50c Sandile .70 .70
Nos. 131-134 (4) 2.05 2.05

Trout Hatcheries A28

Artificial fertilization: 18c, Obtaining eggs from trout. 30c, Fertilized ova, alevins. 40c, Rainbow trout at 5 weeks. 40c, Adult male rainbow trout.

1989, June 8

135 A28 18c multicolored .30 .30
136 A28 30c multicolored .45 .45
137 A28 40c multicolored .65 .65
138 A28 50c multicolored .70 .70
a. Souvenir sheet of 1 4.00 4.00
Nos. 135-138 (4) 2.10 2.10

No. 138a margin pictures emblem of the natl. philatelic exhibition WANDERERS 101, held Sept. 6-9. Sold for 1.50r.

Folklore Type of 1987

Legend of the Little Jackal and the Lion: 18c, Lion and Jackal hunt large eland. 30c, Jackal and offspring climbing to lair. 40c, Lion roaring, jackal under rock. 50c, Lion falling.

1989, Sept. 21

139 A23 18c multicolored .25 .25
140 A23 30c multicolored .30 .30
141 A23 40c multicolored .40 .40
142 A23 50c multicolored .50 .50
Nos. 139-142 (4) 1.45 1.45

Early Transportation A29

1989, Dec. 7 ***Perf. 14x14½***

143 A29 18c Cape cart .25 .25
144 A29 30c Jubilee Spider .40 .40
145 A29 40c Transport wagon .45 .45
146 A29 50c Voortrekker wagon .60 .60
Nos. 143-146 (4) 1.70 1.70

Folklore Type of 1987

The Legend of Five Heads: 18c, Mpunzikazi presenting offering to Makanda Mahlanu, the 5-headed snake chief. 30c, Snake chief kills Mpunzikazi. 40c, Mpunzanyan presents offering to snake chief. 50c, Snake chief transformed into a man and marries Mpunzanyan.

1990, Mar. 15 ***Perf. 14½x14***

147 A23 18c multicolored .25 .25
148 A23 30c multicolored .30 .30
149 A23 40c multicolored .40 .40
150 A23 50c multicolored .55 .55
Nos. 147-150 (4) 1.50 1.50

Handmade Carpets — A30

1990, June 14 Litho. ***Perf. 14x14½***

151 A30 21c Hand weaving .30 .30
152 A30 35c Spinning .45 .45
153 A30 40c Dyeing yarn .55 .55

154	A30	50c Hand weaving, diff.	.65	.65
a.		Souvenir sheet of 1	2.25	2.25
		Nos. 151-154 (4)	1.95	1.95

No. 154a for the 150th anniv. of the Penny Black. Sold for 1.50r.

Plows — A31

21c, Wooden beam, c. 1855. 35c, Triple disc, c. 1895. 40c, Reversible disc, c. 1895. 50c, "Het Volk", c. 1910.

1990, Sept. 6 Litho. *Perf. 14½x14*

155	A31	21c multicolored	.25	.25
156	A31	35c multicolored	.40	.40
157	A31	40c multicolored	.50	.50
158	A31	50c multicolored	.60	.60
		Nos. 155-158 (4)	1.75	1.75

Prickly Pear — A32

21c, Vendor. 35c, Prickly pear bush. 50c, Flowering prickly pear.

1990, Nov. 29 Litho.

159	A32	21c multicolored	.45	.45
160	A32	35c multicolored	.70	.70
161	A32	40c shown	.80	.80
162	A32	50c multicolored	1.00	1.00
		Nos. 159-162 (4)	2.95	2.95

Owls — A33

1991, Feb. 2 Litho. *Perf. 14x14½*

163	A33	21c Marsh owl	.95	.95
164	A33	35c Scops owl	1.50	1.50
165	A33	40c Barn owl	1.90	1.90
166	A33	50c Wood owl	2.10	2.10
a.		Miniature sheet of 1	7.00	7.00
		Nos. 163-166 (4)	6.45	6.45

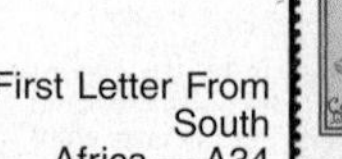

First Letter From South Africa — A34

Designs: a, Map showing location of Sao Bras (Mossel Bay), 1500. b, Storm-damaged ship off Cabo Tormentoso, 1500. c, Pedro d'Ataide lands at Sao Bras, 1501. d, D'Ataide leaves letter in boot, 1501. e, Joao da Nova finds letter, 1501.

1991, May 11 Litho.

167	A34	25c Strip of 5, #a.-e.	4.50	4.50

Inscriptions on #167a & 167b are reversed.

Solar System A35

1991, Aug. 1 Litho. *Perf. 14½x14*

168	A35	1c Comet nucleus	.25	.25
169	A35	2c Trojan asteroids	.25	.25
170	A35	5c Meteoroid	.25	.25
171	A35	7c Pluto	.25	.25
172	A35	10c Neptune	.25	.25
173	A35	20c Uranus	.25	.25
174	A35	25c Saturn	.30	.30
175	A35	30c Jupiter	.35	.35
176	A35	35c Asteroid belt	.40	.40
177	A35	40c Mars	.50	.50
178	A35	50c Earth's moon	.60	.60
179	A35	60c Earth	.70	.70
180	A35	1r Venus	1.25	1.25
181	A35	2r Mercury	2.75	2.75
182	A35	5r Sun	6.50	6.50
a.		Min. sheet of 15, #168-182	17.50	17.50
		Nos. 168-182 (15)	14.85	14.85

Frontier Forts A36

Designs: 27c, Xhosa warrior, Fort Armstrong. 45c, Sir George Grey, Keiskamma Hoek Post. 65c, Chief Sandile, Fort Hare. 85c, Cavalryman, Cavalry Barracks, Peddie.

1991, Nov. 7 Litho. *Perf. 14x14½*

183	A36	27c multicolored	.25	.25
184	A36	45c multicolored	.35	.35
185	A36	65c multicolored	.45	.45
186	A36	85c multicolored	.70	.70
		Nos. 183-186 (4)	1.75	1.75

Cloud Formations — A37

1992, Mar. 19 Litho.

187	A37	27c Cumulonimbus	.30	.30
188	A37	45c Altocumulus	.60	.60
189	A37	65c Cirrus	.75	.75
190	A37	85c Cumulus	1.10	1.10
		Nos. 187-190 (4)	2.75	2.75

Satellites A38

1992, June 4 Litho. *Perf. 14½x14*

191	A38	35c Intelsat VI	.60	.60
192	A38	70c GPS Navstar	1.10	1.10
193	A38	90c Meteosat	1.40	1.40
194	A38	1.05r Landsat VI	1.60	1.60
		Nos. 191-194 (4)	4.70	4.70

A souvenir sheet of one No. 192 exists. Sold for 2.50r. Value $2.50.

Farm Implements A39

35c, John Deere universal disc-harrow, c. 1914. 70c, John Deere clod crusher & pulverizer, c. 1914. 90c, Self-dump hay rake, c. 1910. 1.05r, McCormick hay tedder, c. 1900.

1992, Aug. 20 Litho.

195	A39	35c multicolored	.60	.60
196	A39	70c multicolored	1.10	1.10
197	A39	90c multicolored	1.40	1.40
198	A39	1.05r multicolored	1.60	1.60
		Nos. 195-198 (4)	4.70	4.70

Hotels A40

Designs: 35c, Mpekweni Sun Marine Resort. 70c, Katberg Protea Hotel. 90c, Fish River Sun Hotel. 1.05r, Amatola Sun Hotel.

1992, Nov. 5 Litho.

199	A40	35c multicolored	.60	.60
200	A40	70c multicolored	1.10	1.10
201	A40	90c multicolored	1.40	1.40
202	A40	1.05r multicolored	1.60	1.60
		Nos. 199-202 (4)	4.70	4.70

Famous Explorers A41

Map of voyage, sailing ship, and explorer: 45c, San Gabriel, 1497-98, Vasco da Gama. 65c, Endeavour, 1768-71, James Cook. 85c, Victoria, 1519, Ferdinand Magellan. 90c, Golden Hinde, 1577-80, Sir Francis Drake. 1.05r, Heemskerck, 1642, Abel Tasman.

1993, May 19 Litho.

203	A41	45c multicolored	.70	.70
204	A41	65c multicolored	1.25	1.25
205	A41	85c multicolored	1.80	1.40
206	A41	90c multicolored	1.50	1.50
207	A41	1.05r multicolored	1.75	1.75
		Nos. 203-207 (5)	7.00	6.60

Small Cage Birds — A42

Designs: 45c, Serinus canarius domesticus. 65c, Melopsittacus undulatus. 85c, Agapornis roseicollis. 90c, Nymphicus hollandicus. 1.05r, Chloebia gouldiae.

1993, July 16 Litho.

208	A42	45c multicolored	.60	.60
209	A42	65c multicolored	1.10	1.10
210	A42	85c multicolored	1.25	1.25
211	A42	90c multicolored	1.40	1.40
212	A42	1.05r multicolored	1.50	1.50
		Nos. 208-212 (5)	5.85	5.85

A souvenir sheet of one No. 210 has inscription for National Philatelic Exhibition. Sold for 3r. Value $5.75.

Churches A43

45c, Goshen Mission Church. 65c, Kamastone Mission Church. 85c, Richie Thompson Memorial Church. 1.05r, Bryce Ross Memorial Church.

1993, Sept. 17 Litho.

213	A43	45c black, buff & red	.50	.50
214	A43	65c black, blue & red	.70	.70
215	A43	85c black, tan & red	.95	.95
216	A43	1.05r blk, lt yel & red	1.25	1.25
		Nos. 213-216 (4)	3.40	3.40

Invader Plants — A44

1993, Nov. 5 Litho. *Perf. 14x14½*

217	A44	45c Opuntia aurantiaca	.60	.60
218	A44	65c Datura stramonium	.80	.80
219	A44	85c Sesbania punicea	1.10	1.10
220	A44	1.05r Nicotiana glauca	1.40	1.40
a.		Souvenir sheet, #217-220	3.75	3.75
		Nos. 217-220 (4)	3.90	3.90

Shipwrecks A45

45c, SS Losna, 1921. 65c, Catherine, 1846. 85c, Bennebroek, 1713. 1.05r, Sao Joao Bapista, 1622.

1994, Feb. 18 Litho. *Perf. 14½x14*

221	A45	45c multi	.85	.85
222	A45	65c multi	1.25	1.25
223	A45	85c multi	1.50	1.50
224	A45	1.05r multi	2.10	2.10
		Nos. 221-224 (4)	5.70	5.70

Roses A46

45c, Herman Steyn. 70c, Esther Geldenhuys. 95c, Margaret Wasserfall. 1.15r, Prof. Fred Ziady.

1994, Apr. 15 Litho. *Perf. 14½x14*

225	A46	45c multicolored	.45	.45
226	A46	70c multicolored	.75	.75
227	A46	95c multicolored	.90	.90
228	A46	1.15r multicolored	1.25	1.25
a.		Souvenir sheet of 4, #225-228	3.50	3.50
		Nos. 225-228 (4)	3.35	3.35

Ciskei ceased to exist April 27, 1994.

TRANSKEI

ˌtranˌts-ˈkī

LOCATION — Enclave, East Cape Province, Republic of South Africa
GOVT. — Self-governing tribal homeland
AREA — 16,910 sq. mi.
POP. — 2,876,122 (1985)
CAPITAL — Umtata

Catalogue values for all unused stamps in this country are for Never Hinged items.

Independence from South Africa — A1

4c, Paramount Chief K.D. Matanzima. 10c, Mace, flag. 15c, Matanzima, diff. 20c, Coat of arms.

Perf. 12½

1976, Oct. 26 Litho. Unwmk.

1	A1	4c multicolored	.40	.40
2	A1	10c multicolored	.90	.90
3	A1	15c multicolored	1.50	1.50
4	A1	20c multicolored	2.00	2.00
		Nos. 1-4 (4)	4.80	4.80

An imperf. souvenir sheet exists containing Nos. 1-4 printed in one color (black). Not valid for postage.

Lubisi Dam — A2

2c, Soil cultivation. 3c, Threshing sorghum. 4c, Transkei matron. 5c, Grinding corn. 6c, Cutting Phormium tenax. 7c, Shepherd boy. 8c, Felling timber. 9c, Agricultural school. 10c, Picking tea. 15c, Wood gathering. 20c, Weaving industry. 25c, Improving cattle breeds. 30c, Sledge transportation. 50c, Map, coat of arms. 1r, Administrative Building, Umtata. 2r, The Bunga, flag.

1976, Oct. 26 *Perf. 12x12½*

No.	Type	Value	Color	Unused	Used
5	A2	1c	multicolored	.25	.25
6	A2	2c	multicolored	.25	.25
7	A2	3c	multicolored	.25	.25
8	A2	4c	multicolored	2.75	.30
9	A2	5c	multicolored	2.75	.30
10	A2	6c	multicolored	.25	.25
11	A2	7c	multicolored	.25	.25
12	A2	8c	multicolored	.25	.25
13	A2	9c	multicolored	.25	.25
14	A2	10c	multicolored	.25	.25
15	A2	15c	multicolored	.30	.25
16	A2	20c	multicolored	.30	.25
17	A2	25c	multicolored	.35	.25
18	A2	30c	multicolored	.60	.50
19	A2	50c	multicolored	.55	.50
20	A2	1r	multicolored	1.25	1.25
21	A2	2r	multicolored	2.00	1.90
			Nos. 5-21 (17)	12.85	7.50

Perf. 14

No.	Type	Value	Unused	Used
5a	A2	1c	.25	.25
6a	A2	2c	.25	.25
7a	A2	3c	.25	.25
8a	A2	4c	.25	.25
9a	A2	5c	.25	.25
10a	A2	6c	.25	.25
12a	A2	8c	.25	.25
13a	A2	9c	.25	.25
14a	A2	10c	.40	.40
15a	A2	15c	.50	.50
16a	A2	20c	.70	.70
17a	A2	25c	1.00	1.00
18a	A2	30c	1.25	1.25
19a	A2	50c	2.00	2.00
		Nos. 5a-19a (14)	7.85	7.85

Transkei Airways Inaugural Flight, Umtata-Johannesburg — A3

1977, Feb. 11

22 A3 4c Aircraft .60 .60
23 A3 15c Aircraft, terminal 2.40 2.40

Medicinal Plants — A4

1977, May 16 *Perf. 12½x12*

24 A4 4c Artemesia affra .40 .40
25 A4 10c Bulbine natalensis 1.60 1.60
26 A4 15c Melianthus major 2.40 2.40
27 A4 20c Cotyledon orbiculata 3.25 3.25
Nos. 24-27 (4) 7.65 7.65

1978, Sept. 25

Edible fruit.

28 A4 4c Carissa bispinosa .25 .25
29 A4 10c Dovyalis caffra .35 .35
30 A4 15c Harpephyllum caffrum .50 .50
31 A4 20c Syzygium cordatum .70 .70
Nos. 28-31 (4) 1.80 1.80

1981, Apr. 15

Medicinal plants.

32 A4 5c Leonotis leonurus .25 .25
33 A4 15c Euphorbia bupleurifolia .25 .25
34 A4 20c Pelargonium reniforme .35 .35
35 A4 25c Hibiscus trionum .50 .50
Nos. 32-35 (4) 1.35 1.35

Transkei Radio, 1st Anniv. A5

1977, Oct. 26 *Perf. 12x12½*

36 A5 4c Disc jockey .40 .40
37 A5 15c Announcer 1.00 1.00

"Help the Blind" — A6

1977, Nov. 18 *Perf. 12½x12*

38 A6 4c Basket weaver .25 .25
39 A6 15c Reading Braille .60 .60
40 A6 20c Spinning wool .80 .80
Nos. 38-40 (3) 1.65 1.65

1978, Nov. 30

"Care for Cripples."

41 A6 4c Leg brace on boy .25 .25
42 A6 10c Man in wheelchair .60 .60
43 A6 15c Nurse examining boy .85 .85
Nos. 41-43 (3) 1.70 1.70

Men's Pipes A7

1978, Mar. 1 *Perf. 12x12½*

44 A7 4c shown .40 .40
45 A7 10c multi, diff. .60 .60
46 A7 15c multi, diff. 1.00 1.00
47 A7 20c Woman's and witch doctor's pipes 1.10 1.10
Nos. 44-47 (4) 3.10 3.10

Weaving Industry A8

1978, June 9

48 A8 4c Angora goat .25 .25
49 A8 10c Spinning mohair .60 .60
50 A8 15c Dyeing mohair 1.00 1.00
51 A8 20c Weaving mohair rug 1.25 1.25
Nos. 48-51 (4) 3.10 3.10

Initiation Ceremony of Xhosa Men — A9

1979, Jan. 30 *Perf. 12½*

52 A9 4c Chi Cha youth .40 .40
53 A9 10c Youths in seclusion .60 .60
54 A9 15c Umtshilo dance 1.00 1.00
55 A9 20c Leaving the Sutu 1.10 1.10
Nos. 52-55 (4) 3.10 3.10

Chief Matanzima — A10

1979, Feb. 20 *Perf. 14½x14*

56 A10 4c brn car & gold .25 .25
57 A10 15c olive grn & gold .40 .40

Inauguration of Matanzima, second state president.

Water Resources — A11

4c, Windmill. 10c, Woman filling water jar. 15c, Irrigation, Indwe River, horiz. 20c, Ncora dam, horiz.

1979, Mar. 13 *Perf. 14½x14, 14x14½*

58 A11 4c multicolored .25 .25
59 A11 10c multicolored .25 .25
60 A11 15c multicolored .35 .35
61 A11 20c multicolored .45 .45
Nos. 58-61 (4) 1.30 1.30

Waterfalls — A12

1979, Sept. 4

62 A12 4c Magwa Falls .25 .25
63 A12 10c Bawa Falls .25 .25
64 A12 15c Waterfall Bluff, horiz. .30 .30
65 A12 20c Tsitsa Falls, horiz. .40 .40
Nos. 62-65 (4) 1.20 1.20

Child Health Care — A13

5c, Pre-natal nourishment. 15c, Primary feeding. 20c, Immunization.

1979, Dec. 3 *Perf. 14½x14*

66 A13 5c multicolored .25 .25
67 A13 15c multicolored .45 .45
68 A13 20c multicolored .65 .65
Nos. 66-68 (3) 1.35 1.35

Fishing Flies — A14

a, Durham ranger. b, Colonel Bates. c, Black gnat. d, Zug bug. e, March brown.

1980, Jan. 15 *Perf. 14x14½*

69 Strip of 5 1.25 1.25
a.-e. A14 5c any single .25 .25

1981, Jan. 15

Designs: a, Kent's lightning. b, Wickham's fancy. c, Jock Scott. d, Green highlander. e, Tan nymph.

70 Strip of 5 1.50 1.50
a.-e. A14 10c any single .30 .30

1982, Jan. 6

a, Royal coachman. b, Light spruce. c, Montana nymph. d, Butcher. e, Blue charm.

71 Strip of 5 2.00 2.00
a.-e. A14 10c any single .40 .40

1983, Mar. 2

Designs: a, Alexandra. b, Kent's marbled sedge. c, White marabou. d, Mayfly nymph. e, Silver Wilkinson.

72 Strip of 5 2.00 2.00
a.-e. A14 20c any single .40 .40

1984, Feb. 10

Designs: a, Silver gray. b, Ginger quill. c, Hardy's favorite. d, March brown nymph. e, Kent's spectrum Mohawk.

73 Strip of 5 2.50 2.50
a.-e. A14 20c any single .50 .50

Rotary Intl., 75th Anniv. — A15

1980, Feb. 22 *Perf. 14½x14*

74 A15 15c blk, ultra & gold .30 .30

Cycads — A16

5c, Encephalartos altensteinii. 10c, Encephalartos princeps. 15c, Encephalartos vilosus. 20c, Encephalartos friderici-guilielmi.

1980, Apr. 30

75 A16 5c multicolored .25 .25
76 A16 10c multicolored .25 .25
77 A16 15c multicolored .30 .30
78 A16 20c multicolored .45 .45
Nos. 75-78 (4) 1.25 1.25

Birds — A17

1980, July 30

79 A17 5c Cuculus solitarius .25 .25
80 A17 10c Batis capensis .55 .55
81 A17 15c Balearica pavonina .85 .85
82 A17 20c Ploceus ocularius 1.10 1.10
Nos. 79-82 (4) 2.75 2.75

Tourism — A18

1980, Oct. 26

83 A18 5c Hole in the Wall .25 .25
84 A18 10c Port St. Johns .25 .25
85 A18 15c The Citadel .40 .40
86 A18 20c The Archway .45 .45
Nos. 83-86 (4) 1.35 1.35

Xhosa Women's Headdresses — A19

1981, Aug. 28

87 A19 5c Eyamakhwenkwe .25 .25
88 A19 15c Eyabafana .25 .25
89 A19 20c Umfazana .30 .30

90 A19 25c Ixhegokazi .40 .40
a. Souvenir sheet of 4, #87-90 1.00 1.00
Nos. 87-90 (4) 1.20 1.20

Independence, 5th Anniv. — A20

1981, Oct. 26 ***Perf. 14x14½***
91 A20 5c State House .30 .30
92 A20 15c University .50 .50

Boy Scout Movement, 75th Anniv. — A21

1982, May 14 ***Perf. 14½x14***
93 A21 8c Salute .25 .25
94 A21 10c Planting tree .25 .25
95 A21 20c Rafting .30 .30
96 A21 25c Nature hike with dog .40 .40
Nos. 93-96 (4) 1.20 1.20

Great Medical Pioneers — A22

15c, Hippocrates. 20c, Anton van Leeuwenhoek. 25c, William Harvey. 30c, Joseph Lister.

1982, Oct. 5
97 A22 15c multicolored .25 .25
98 A22 20c multicolored .25 .25
99 A22 25c multicolored .30 .30
100 A22 30c multicolored .35 .35
Nos. 97-100 (4) 1.15 1.15

1983, Aug. 17

10c, Edward Jenner. 20c, Gregor Mendel. 25c, Louis Pasteur. 40c, Florence Nightingale.

101 A22 10c multicolored .25 .25
102 A22 20c multicolored .25 .25
103 A22 25c multicolored .30 .30
104 A22 40c multicolored .40 .40
Nos. 101-104 (4) 1.20 1.20

1984, Oct. 12

11c, Nicholas of Cusa. 25c, William Morton. 30c, Wilhelm Roentgen. 45c, Karl Landsteiner.

105 A22 11c multicolored .25 .25
106 A22 25c multicolored .25 .25
107 A22 30c multicolored .30 .30
108 A22 45c multicolored .45 .45
Nos. 105-108 (4) 1.25 1.25

1985, Sept. 20

12c, Andreas Vesalius. 25c, Marcello Malpighi. 30c, Francois Magendie. 50c, William Stewart Halsted.

109 A22 12c multicolored .25 .25
110 A22 25c multicolored .30 .30
111 A22 30c multicolored .40 .40
112 A22 50c multicolored .60 .60
Nos. 109-112 (4) 1.55 1.55
Nos. 97-112 (16) 4.95 4.95

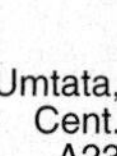

Umtata, Cent. A23

Architecture: 8c, City Hall. 15c, The Bunga. 20c, Botha Sigcau Building. 25c, Palace of Justice, Matanzima Building.

1982, Nov. 10 ***Perf. 14x14½***
113 A23 8c multicolored .25 .25
114 A23 15c multicolored .25 .25
115 A23 20c multicolored .25 .25
116 A23 25c multicolored .30 .30
Nos. 113-116 (4) 1.05 1.05

Wildcoast Holiday Resort, Mzamba A24

1983, May 25
117 A24 10c Hotel complex .25 .25
118 A24 20c Beach scene .30 .30
119 A24 25c Casino .40 .40
120 A24 40c Carousel .55 .55
Nos. 117-120 (4) 1.50 1.50

Post Offices A25

1983, Nov. 9 ***Perf. 14½x14***
121 A25 10c Lady Frere .25 .25
122 A25 20c Idutywa .25 .25
123 A25 25c Lusikisiki .25 .25
124 A25 40c Cala .35 .35
Nos. 121-124 (4) 1.10 1.10

1984, May 11
125 A25 11c Umzimkulu .25 .25
126 A25 20c Mount Fletcher .25 .25
127 A25 25c Qumbu .25 .25
128 A25 30c Umtata .35 .35
Nos. 125-128 (4) 1.10 1.10

Xhosa Lifestyle A26

1c, Amagqira. 2c, Horsemen. 3c, Mat maker. 4c, Xhosa dancers. 5c, Man, donkeys. 6c, Musicians. 7c, Fingo brides. 8c, Tasting beer. 9c, Thinning corn. 10c, Dance demonstration. 11c, Carrying water from the river. 12c, Meal preparation. 14c, Weeding. 15c, Stick fighting. 16c, Morning pasture. 20c, Abakhwetha dancers. 21c, Building initiation hut. 25c, Tribesmen singing. 30c, Matrons. 50c, Pipe maker. 1r, Intonjane women. 2r, Abakhwetha.

1984-90
129 A26 1c multicolored .25 .25
130 A26 2c multicolored .25 .25
131 A26 3c multicolored .25 .25
132 A26 4c multicolored .25 .25
133 A26 5c multicolored .25 .25
134 A26 6c multicolored .25 .25
135 A26 7c multicolored .25 .25
136 A26 8c multicolored .25 .25
137 A26 9c multicolored .25 .25
138 A26 10c multicolored .25 .25
139 A26 11c multicolored .25 .25
140 A26 12c multicolored .25 .25
141 A26 14c multicolored .25 .25
142 A26 15c multicolored .25 .25
143 A26 16c multicolored .25 .25
144 A26 20c multicolored .30 .30
145 A26 21c multicolored .30 .30
146 A26 25c multicolored .35 .35
147 A26 30c multicolored .35 .35
148 A26 50c multicolored .70 .70
149 A26 1r multicolored 1.40 1.40
150 A26 2r multicolored 3.00 3.00
Nos. 129-150 (22) 10.15 10.15

Issued: 11c, 4/2/84; 12c, 4/1/85; 14c, 4/1/86; 16c, 4/1/87; 21c, 7/3/90; others, 7/6/84.

Soil Conservation A27

Designs: 11c, Erosion from over-grazing. 25c, Wall construction to collect sediment. 30c, Regeneration of vegetation. 50c, Cattle grazing on verdant plain.

1985, Feb. 7
155 A27 11c shown .25 .25
156 A27 25c multicolored .25 .25
157 A27 30c multicolored .30 .30
158 A27 50c multicolored .45 .45
Nos. 155-158 (4) 1.25 1.25

Bridges A28

1985, Apr. 18
159 A28 12c Tsitsa .25 .25
160 A28 25c White Kei .30 .30
161 A28 30c Mitchell .35 .35
162 A28 50c Umzimvubu .55 .55
Nos. 159-162 (4) 1.45 1.45

Match Industry — A29

1985, July 25 ***Perf. 14½x14***
163 A29 12c Peeling logs .25 .25
164 A29 25c Splint chopping .25 .25
165 A29 30c VPO machine .25 .25
166 A29 50c Filling boxes .40 .40
Nos. 163-166 (4) 1.15 1.15

Port St. Johns A30

Designs: 12c, Early street scene. 20c, Coaster Umzimvubu at the Old Jetty. 25c, Unloading corn from wagons at the Jetty. 30c, View of the town, 1890's.

1986, Feb. 6
167 A30 12c multicolored .25 .25
168 A30 20c multicolored .40 .40
169 A30 25c multicolored .45 .45
170 A30 30c multicolored .50 .50
a. Souvenir sheet of 4, #167-170 1.25 1.25
Nos. 167-170 (4) 1.60 1.60

Aloes — A31

1986, May 1
171 A31 14c Aloe ferox .25 .25
172 A31 20c Aloe arborescens .30 .30
173 A31 25c Aloe maculata .40 .40
174 A31 30c Aloe ecklonis .50 .50
a. Souvenir sheet of 1 1.40 1.40
Nos. 171-174 (4) 1.45 1.45

No. 174a margin pictures emblem of the natl. philatelic exhibition held at Johannesburg, Oct. 6-11. Sold for 50c.

Hydroelectric Power Stations A32

14c, First Falls, Umtata River. 20c, Second Falls, Umtata River. 25c, Ncora, Qumanco River. 30c, Collywobbles, Mbashe River.

1986, July 24
175 A32 14c shown .25 .25
176 A32 20c multicolored .25 .25
177 A32 25c multicolored .30 .30
178 A32 30c multicolored .40 .40
Nos. 175-178 (4) 1.20 1.20

Independence, 10th Anniv. — A33

Designs: 14c, Prime Minister G. M. Matanzima. 20c, Technical College, Umtata. 25c, University of Transkei, Umtata. 30c, Palace of Justice, Umtata.

1986, Oct. 26
179 A33 14c multicolored .25 .25
180 A33 20c multicolored .25 .25
181 A33 25c multicolored .30 .30
182 A33 30c multicolored .35 .35
Nos. 179-182 (4) 1.15 1.15

Transkei Airways, 10th Anniv. — A34

1987, Feb. 5
183 A34 14c shown .25 .25
184 A34 20c Aircraft tail .40 .40
185 A34 25c Nose, propellers .50 .50
186 A34 30c Plane, control tower .60 .60
Nos. 183-186 (4) 1.75 1.75

Beadwork — A35

1987, May 22 ***Perf. 14x14½***
187 A35 16c Pondo girl .25 .25
188 A35 20c Bomvana woman .30 .30
189 A35 25c Xessibe woman .35 .35
a. Souvenir sheet of 1 1.60 1.60
190 A35 30c Xhosa man .65 .65
Nos. 187-190 (4) 1.55 1.55

No. 189a has blue and black decorative margin picturing the emblem of the natl. philatelic exhibition held at Paarl, Sept. 16-19. Sold for 50c.

Spiders — A36

16c, Latrodectus indistinctus. 20c, Nephila pilipes fenestrata. 25c, Lycosidae. 30c, Argiope nigrovittata.

1987, Aug. 24
191 A36 16c multicolored .25 .25
192 A36 20c multicolored .35 .35
193 A36 25c multicolored .40 .40
194 A36 30c multicolored .50 .50
Nos. 191-194 (4) 1.50 1.50

Domestic Animals A37

1987, Oct. 22

195 A37 16c Black pigs	.25	.25
196 A37 30c Goats	.30	.30
197 A37 40c Merino sheep	.40	.40
198 A37 50c Cattle	.50	.50
Nos. 195-198 (4)	1.45	1.45

Seaweed — A38

16c, Plocamium corallorhiza. 30c, Gelidium amanzil. 40c, Ecklonia biruncinata. 50c, Halimeda cuneata.

1988, Feb. 18

199 A38 16c multicolored	.25	.25
200 A38 30c multicolored	.30	.30
201 A38 40c multicolored	.40	.40
202 A38 50c multicolored	.50	.50
Nos. 199-202 (4)	1.45	1.45

Blanket Factory, Butterworth A39

1988, May 5 *Perf. 14½x14*

203 A39 16c Spinning machines	.25	.25
204 A39 30c Warping machine	.25	.25
205 A39 40c Weaving machine	.30	.30
206 A39 50c Raising the nap	.40	.40
Nos. 203-206 (4)	1.20	1.20

Wreck of the *Grosvenor,* 1782 — A40

Designs: 16c, Ship, map. 30c, *The Wreck of the Grosvenor,* by R. Smirke. 40c, Dirk hilt, compass and coins salvaged. 50c, *African Hospitality,* by G. Morland.

1988, Aug. 4

207 A40 16c multicolored	.35	.35
208 A40 30c multicolored	.60	.60
209 A40 40c multicolored	.80	.80
210 A40 50c multicolored	1.00	1.00
a. Souvenir sheet of 1	3.25	3.25
Nos. 207-210 (4)	2.75	2.75

No. 210a margin pictures emblem of the natl. philatelic exhibition at Pietermaritzburg, Nov. 22-27. Sold for 1r.

Endangered Species A41

16c, Felis nigripes. 30c, Philantomba monticola. 40c, Ourebia ourebi. 50c, Lycaon pictus.

1988, Oct. 20

211 A41 16c multicolored	.40	.40
212 A41 30c multicolored	.75	.75
213 A41 40c multicolored	1.00	1.00
214 A41 50c multicolored	1.25	1.25
Nos. 211-214 (4)	3.40	3.40

Locomotive, Trains and Bridges — A42

Designs: 16c, Class 14 CRB locomotive. 30c, CRB pulling train over Toleni-Halt Bridge. 40c, Train on the Great Kei River Bridge, vert. 50c, Train in the Kei Valley.

1989, Jan. 19 *Perf. 14x14½, 14½x14*

215 A42 16c multi	.30	.30
216 A42 30c multi	.55	.55
217 A42 40c multi	.85	.85
218 A42 50c multi, vert.	.95	.95
Nos. 215-218 (4)	2.65	2.65

A souvenir sheet of one No. 218 has margin picturing the emblem of the natl. philatelic exhibition WANDERERS 101, held Sept. 6-9. Sold for 1.50r. Value $5.

Basketry A43

1989, Apr. 20 *Perf. 14½x14*

219 A43 18c shown	.25	.25
220 A43 30c multi, diff.	.35	.35
221 A43 40c multi, diff.	.40	.40
222 A43 50c multi, diff.	.55	.55
Nos. 219-222 (4)	1.55	1.55

Mackerel A44

1989, July 20

223 A44 18c shown	.55	.55
224 A44 30c Squid	.90	.90
225 A44 40c Brown mussel	1.10	1.10
226 A44 50c Rock lobster	1.50	1.50
Nos. 223-226 (4)	4.05	4.05

Trees A45

1989, Oct. 5 *Perf. 14x14½*

227 A45 18c Broom cluster fig	.50	.50
228 A45 30c Natal fig	.90	.90
229 A45 40c Broad-leaved coral	1.10	1.10
230 A45 50c Cabbage tree	1.50	1.50
Nos. 227-230 (4)	4.00	4.00

Fossils A46

18c, Ginkgo koningensis. 30c, Pseudoctenis spatulata. 40c, Rissikia media. 50c, Taeniopteris anavolans.

1990, Jan. 18

231 A46 18c multicolored	.65	.65
232 A46 30c multicolored	1.25	1.25
233 A46 40c multicolored	1.60	1.60
234 A46 50c multicolored	2.25	2.25
Nos. 231-234 (4)	5.75	5.75

Great Medical Pioneers — A47

1990, Mar. 29 *Perf. 14x14½*

235 A47 18c Aretaeus	.65	.65
236 A47 30c Claude Bernard	1.10	1.10
237 A47 40c Oscar Minkowski	1.50	1.50
238 A47 50c Frederick Banting	2.00	2.00
Nos. 235-238 (4)	5.25	5.25

Diviners — A48

21c, Dancing to the Drum. 35c, Lecturing Imichetywa. 40c, Initiation ceremony. 50c, Induction ceremony.

1990, June 28 Litho. *Perf. 14x14½*

239 A48 21c multicolored	.65	.65
240 A48 35c multicolored	1.10	1.10
241 A48 40c multicolored	1.25	1.25
242 A48 50c multicolored	1.50	1.50
a. Souvenir sheet of 1	5.00	5.00
Nos. 239-242 (4)	4.50	4.50

No. 242a for the 150th anniv. of the Penny Black. Sold for 1.50r.

Flowers — A49

21c, Cyrtanthus obliquus. 35c, Disa crassicornis. 40c, Sandersonia aurantiaca. 50c, Podranea ricasoliana.

1990, Sept. 20 Litho. *Perf. 14x14½*

243 A49 21c multicolored	.70	.70
244 A49 35c multicolored	1.10	1.10
245 A49 40c multicolored	1.40	1.40
246 A49 50c multicolored	1.50	1.50
Nos. 243-246 (4)	4.70	4.70

Parasitic Plants — A50

1991, Jan. 10 Litho.

247 A50 21c Harveya pulchra	.65	.65
248 A50 35c Harveya speciosa	1.10	1.10
249 A50 40c Alectra sessiliflora	1.25	1.25
250 A50 50c Hydnora africana	1.60	1.60
Nos. 247-250 (4)	4.60	4.60

Dolphins A51

1991, Apr. 4 Litho. *Perf. 14½x14*

251 A51 25c Delphinus delphis	.95	.95
252 A51 40c Tursiops truncatus	1.50	1.50
253 A51 50c Sousa plumbea	1.90	1.90
254 A51 60c Grampus griseus	2.25	2.25
Nos. 251-254 (4)	6.60	6.60

Birds — A52

25c, Balearica regulorum. 40c, Gyps coprotheres. 50c, Grus carunculata. 60c, Neophron percnopterus.

1991, June 20 Litho.

255 A52 25c multicolored	.80	.80
256 A52 40c multicolored	1.25	1.25
257 A52 50c multicolored	1.50	1.50
258 A52 60c multicolored	1.75	1.75
a. Souvenir sheet of 1	5.50	5.50
Nos. 255-258 (4)	5.30	5.30

Medical Pioneers — A53

Developers of vaccines: 25c, Emil von Behring (1854-1917) and Shibasaburo Kitasato (1852-1931), diphtheria. 40c, Leon Albert Calmette (1863-1933) and Camille Guerin (1872-1961), tuberculosis. 50c, Jonas Salk (b. 1914), polio. 60c, John Franklin Enders (1897-1985), measles.

1991, Sept. 26 Litho. *Perf. 14x14½*

259 A53 25c multicolored	.85	.85
260 A53 40c multicolored	1.50	1.50
261 A53 50c multicolored	1.75	1.75
262 A53 60c multicolored	2.40	2.40
Nos. 259-262 (4)	6.50	6.50

Orchids — A54

27c, Eulophia speciosa. 45c, Satyrium sphaerocarpum. 65c, Disa scullyi. 85c, Disa tysonii.

1992, Feb. 20 Litho.

263 A54 27c multicolored	.30	.30
264 A54 45c multicolored	.50	.50
265 A54 65c multicolored	.75	.75
266 A54 85c multicolored	.95	.95
Nos. 263-266 (4)	2.50	2.50

Medical Pioneers A55

27c, Thomas Huckle Weller (b. 1915), developer of rubella vaccine. 45c, Ignaz Philipp Semmelweis (1818-65), diagnosed septicaemia. 65c, Sir James Young Simpson (1811-70), 1st to use chloroform in obstetrics. 85c, Rene Theophile Hyacinthe Laennec (1781-1826), inventor of stethoscope.

1992, Apr. 1 Litho. *Perf. 14½x14*

267 A55 27c multicolored	.70	.70
268 A55 45c multicolored	1.25	1.25
269 A55 65c multicolored	1.75	1.75
270 A55 85c multicolored	2.25	2.25
Nos. 267-270 (4)	5.95	5.95

Waterfowl — A56

No. 271, Anas erythrorhyncha. No. 272, Anas hottentota. No. 273, Oxyura punctata.

No. 274, Thalassornis leuconotus. No. 275, Anas sparsa. No. 276, Alopochen aegyptiacus. No. 277, Anas smithi. No. 278, Anas capensis.

1992, July 16 Litho. *Perf. 14x14½*

No.	Type	Description	Unused	Used
271	A56	35c multicolored	.60	.60
272	A56	35c multicolored	.60	.60
a.		Pair, #271-272	1.25	1.25
273	A56	70c multicolored	1.25	1.25
274	A56	70c multicolored	1.25	1.25
a.		Pair, #273-274	2.50	2.50
275	A56	90c multicolored	1.60	1.60
276	A56	90c multicolored	1.60	1.60
a.		Pair, #275-276	3.25	3.25
277	A56	1.05r multicolored	1.60	1.60
278	A56	1.05r multicolored	1.60	1.60
a.		Pair, #277-278	3.25	3.25
		Nos. 271-278 (8)	10.10	10.10

A souvenir sheet of one No. 273 was sold by the Philatelic Foundation of South Africa. Value $5.

Fossils A57

Designs: 35c, Pseudomelania sutherlandi. 70c, Gaudryceras denseplicatum. 90c, Neithea quinquecostata. 1.05r, Pugilina (Mayeria) acuticarinatus.

1992, Sept. 17 Litho. *Perf. 14½x14*

No.	Type	Description	Unused	Used
279	A57	35c multicolored	.75	.75
280	A57	70c multicolored	1.50	1.50
281	A57	90c multicolored	2.00	2.00
282	A57	1.05r multicolored	2.25	2.25
		Nos. 279-282 (4)	6.50	6.50

Dogs — A58

1993, Feb. 12 Litho.

No.	Type	Description	Unused	Used
283	A58	35c Papillon	.55	.55
284	A58	70c Pekingese	1.10	1.10
285	A58	90c Chihuahua	1.50	1.50
286	A58	1.05r Dachshund	1.75	1.75
		Nos. 283-286 (4)	4.90	4.90

A souvenir sheet of one No. 284 exists. Sold for 3r. Value $6.

Prehistoric Animals A59

1993, June 18 Litho.

No.	Type	Description	Unused	Used
287	A59	45c Fabrosaurus	1.00	1.00
288	A59	65c Diictodon	1.40	1.40
289	A59	85c Chasmatosaurus	1.75	1.75
290	A59	1.05r Rubidgea	2.25	2.25
		Nos. 287-290 (4)	6.40	6.40

Medical Pioneers A60

Designs: 45c, Sir Alexander Fleming (1881-1955), discovered penicillin and Lord Howard Walter Florey (1898-1968), purified penicillin for general use. 65c, Alexis Carrel (1873-1944), developed Carrel-Dakin fluid and method to suture blood vessels. 85c, James Lind (1716-1794), recommended citrus fruit to combat scurvy. 1.05r, Santiago Ramon y Cajal (1852-1934), established neuron as basic unit of nervous structure.

1993, Aug. 20 Litho.

No.	Type	Description	Unused	Used
291	A60	45c multicolored	1.00	1.00
292	A60	65c multicolored	1.25	1.25
293	A60	85c multicolored	1.60	1.60
294	A60	1.05r multicolored	2.00	2.00
		Nos. 291-294 (4)	5.85	5.85

Doves — A61

Designs: 45c, Streptopelia senegalensis. 65c, Turtur tympanistria. 85c, Turtur chalcospilos. 1.05r, Oena capensis.

1993, Oct. 15 Litho. *Perf. 14x14½*

No.	Type	Description	Unused	Used
295	A61	45c multicolored	.90	.90
296	A61	65c multicolored	1.25	1.25
297	A61	85c multicolored	1.60	1.60
298	A61	1.05r multicolored	1.90	1.90
a.		Souvenir sheet of 4, #295-298	5.50	5.50
		Nos. 295-298 (4)	5.65	5.65

No. 298a sold for 3.50r.

Modern Shipwrecks A62

45c, Clan Lindsay, 1898. 65c, Horizon, 1967. 85c, Oceanos, 1991. 1.05r, Forresbank, 1958.

1994, Mar. 18 Litho. *Perf. 14½x14*

No.	Type	Description	Unused	Used
299	A62	45c multicolored	1.10	1.10
300	A62	65c multicolored	1.75	1.75
301	A62	85c multicolored	2.40	2.40
302	A62	1.05r multicolored	2.75	2.75
		Nos. 299-302 (4)	8.00	8.00

A souvenir sheet of one No. 301 exists. Sold for 3r. Value $8.

Transkei ceased to exist April 27, 1994.

VENDA

'ven-də

LOCATION — Enclave, Republic of South Africa
GOVT. — Self-governing tribal homeland
AREA — 4,040 sq. mi.
POP. — 343,480 (1980)
CAPITAL — Thohoyandou

Catalogue values for all unused stamps in this country are for Never Hinged items.

Independence from South Africa — A1

Designs: 4c, Mace, flag. 15c, Administrative buildings. 20c, P.R. Mphephu, paramount chief and president. 25c, Coat of arms.

Perf. 14½x14

1979, Sept. 13 Litho. Unwmk.

No.	Type	Description	Unused	Used
1	A1	4c multicolored	.35	.35
2	A1	15c multicolored	.90	.90
3	A1	20c multicolored	1.25	1.25
4	A1	25c multicolored	1.60	1.60
		Nos. 1-4 (4)	4.10	4.10

Flowers — A2

1c, Tecomaria capensis. 2c, Catophractes alexandri. 3c, Tricliceras longipedunculatum. 4c, Dissotis princeps. 5c, Gerbera jamesonii. 6c, Hibiscus mastersianus. 7c, Nymphaea caerulaea. 8c, Crinum lugardiae. 9c, Xerophyta retinervis. 10c, Hypoxis angustifolia. 11c, Combretum microphyllum. 12c, Clivia caulescens. 15c, Pycnostachys urticifolia. 20c, Zantedeschia jucunda. 25c, Leonotis mollis. 30c, Littonia modesta. 50c, Protea caffra. 1r, Adenium multiflorum. 2r, Strelitzia caudata.

1979-85 *Perf. 12½, 14 (11c, 12c)*

No.	Type	Description	Unused	Used
5	A2	1c multicolored	.25	.25
6	A2	2c multicolored	.25	.25
7	A2	3c multicolored	.25	.25
8	A2	4c multicolored	.25	.25
9	A2	5c multicolored	1.60	.60
10	A2	6c multicolored	.25	.25
11	A2	7c multicolored	.25	.25
12	A2	8c multicolored	.30	.25
13	A2	9c multicolored	.25	.25
14	A2	10c multicolored	.25	.25
15	A2	11c multicolored	.25	.25
16	A2	12c multicolored	.35	.25
17	A2	15c multicolored	.25	.25
18	A2	20c multicolored	.25	.25
19	A2	25c multicolored	2.00	.75
20	A2	30c multicolored	.35	.25
21	A2	50c multicolored	.60	.25
22	A2	1r multicolored	.80	.40
23	A2	2r multicolored	1.75	1.00
		Nos. 5-23 (19)	10.50	6.50

Issue dates: 11c, Apr. 2, 1984; 12c, Apr. 1, 1985; others, Sept. 13, 1979.

Perf. 14

No.	Type	Description	Unused	Used
5a	A2	1c	.25	.25
6a	A2	2c	.25	.25
7a	A2	3c	.25	.25
9a	A2	5c	.25	.25
12a	A2	8c	.25	.25
14a	A2	10c	.40	.25
19a	A2	25c	1.25	.60
21a	A2	50c	2.75	1.25
		Nos. 5a-21a (8)	5.65	3.35

Wood Carvings — A3

Designs: 5c, Man with cup. 10c, Woman with corn, bowl and spoon. 15c, King Nebuchadnezzar, horiz. 20c, Python killing woman, horiz.

1980, Feb. 13 *Perf. 14½x14, 14x14½*

No.	Type	Description	Unused	Used
24	A3	5c multicolored	.25	.25
25	A3	10c multicolored	.35	.35
26	A3	15c multicolored	.50	.50
27	A3	20c multicolored	.65	.65
		Nos. 24-27 (4)	1.75	1.75

Tea Cultivation A4

1980, May 14 *Perf. 14x14½*

No.	Type	Description	Unused	Used
28	A4	5c Plants in nursery	.25	.25
29	A4	10c Harvest	.25	.25
30	A4	15c Withering	.35	.35
31	A4	20c Cut, twist, curl unit	.50	.50
		Nos. 28-31 (4)	1.35	1.35

Banana Industry A5

1980, Aug. 13

No.	Type	Description	Unused	Used
32	A5	5c Plants	.25	.25
33	A5	10c Cutting "hands"	.25	.25
34	A5	15c Sorting	.35	.35
35	A5	20c Packing	.50	.50
		Nos. 32-35 (4)	1.35	1.35

Butterflies — A6

1980, Nov. 13 *Perf. 14½x14*

No.	Type	Description	Unused	Used
36	A6	5c Precis tugela	.25	.25
37	A6	10c Charaxes bohemani	.25	.25
38	A6	15c Catacroptera cloanthe	.50	.50
39	A6	20c Papilio dardanus	.60	.60
		Nos. 36-39 (4)	1.60	1.60

Sunbirds — A7

1981, Feb. 16

No.	Type	Description	Unused	Used
40	A7	5c Anthreptes collaris	.25	.25
41	A7	15c Nectarinia mariquensis	.35	.35
42	A7	20c Nectarinia talatala	.45	.45
43	A7	25c Nectarinia senegalensis	.55	.55
		Nos. 40-43 (4)	1.60	1.60

Nwanedi Dam — A8

1981, May 6

No.	Type	Description	Unused	Used
44	A8	5c shown	.25	.25
45	A8	15c Mahovhohovho Falls	.25	.25
46	A8	20c Phiphidi Falls	.30	.30
47	A8	25c Lake Fundudzi	.40	.40
		Nos. 44-47 (4)	1.20	1.20

Orchids — A9

5c, Cynorkis kassnerana. 15c, Eulophia fridericii. 20c, Bonatea densiflora. 25c, Mystacidium brayboniae.

1981, Sept. 11

No.	Type	Description	Unused	Used
48	A9	5c multicolored	.25	.25
49	A9	15c multicolored	.25	.25
50	A9	20c multicolored	.40	.40
51	A9	25c multicolored	.45	.45
a.		Souvenir sheet of 4, #48-51	.90	.90
		Nos. 48-51 (4)	1.35	1.35

Musical Instruments A10

1981, Nov. 13 *Perf. 14x14½*

No.	Type	Description	Unused	Used
52	A10	5c Mbila	.25	.25
53	A10	15c Phalaphala	.25	.25
54	A10	20c Tshizambi	.25	.25
55	A10	25c Ngoma	.40	.40
		Nos. 52-55 (4)	1.15	1.15

Sisal Cultivation A11

1982, Feb. 26

No.	Type	Description	Unused	Used
56	A11	5c Harvesting	.25	.25
57	A11	10c Drying	.25	.25
58	A11	20c Grading	.35	.35
59	A11	25c Baling	.45	.45
		Nos. 56-59 (4)	1.30	1.30

History of Writing — A12

Designs: 8c, Bison, petroglyph, Atlamira, Spain. 15c, Animal, petroglyph, eastern California. 20c, Pictographic script on a Sumerian tablet. 25c, Bushman burial stone, Humansdorp, South Africa.

1982, June 15 *Perf. 14½x14*

60 A12 8c multicolored .25 .25
61 A12 15c multicolored .25 .25
62 A12 20c multicolored .35 .35
63 A12 25c multicolored .45 .45
Nos. 60-63 (4) 1.30 1.30

1983, May 11 **Size: 21x37mm**

10c, Indus Valley script, 3000 B.C. 20c, Sumerian cuneiform, 2000 B.C. 25c, Egyptian hieroglyphics, 1300 B.C. 40c, Chinese handscroll, A.D. 1100.

64 A12 10c multicolored .25 .25
65 A12 20c multicolored .30 .30
66 A12 25c multicolored .35 .35
67 A12 40c multicolored .40 .40
Nos. 64-67 (4) 1.30 1.30

1984, Feb. 17 *Perf. 14x14½*
Size: 37½x20½mm

Designs: 10c, Evolution of the cuneiform sign. 20c, Evolution of the Chinese character. 25c, Development of Cretan hieroglyphics. 40c, Development of Egyptian hieroglyphics.

68 A12 10c multicolored .25 .25
69 A12 20c multicolored .30 .30
70 A12 25c multicolored .35 .35
71 A12 40c multicolored .60 .60
Nos. 68-71 (4) 1.50 1.50

1985, Mar. 21 *Perf. 14½x14*
Size: 34x24½mm

Designs: 11c, Southern Arabic characters. 25c, Phoenician characters. 30c, Aramaic characters. 50c, Canaanite characters.

72 A12 11c multicolored .25 .25
73 A12 25c multicolored .30 .30
74 A12 30c multicolored .35 .35
75 A12 50c multicolored .60 .60
Nos. 72-75 (4) 1.50 1.50

1986, Apr. 10 *Perf. 14x14½*
Size: 24½x34mm

76 A12 14c Etruscan .25 .25
77 A12 20c Greek .40 .40
78 A12 25c Roman .45 .45
79 A12 30c Cyrillic .55 .55
Nos. 76-79 (4) 1.65 1.65

1988, Apr. 28 *Perf. 14½x14*
Size: 34x26mm

80 A12 16c Chinese .25 .25
81 A12 30c Hindi .30 .30
82 A12 40c Russian .40 .40
83 A12 50c Arabic .45 .45
Nos. 80-83 (4) 1.40 1.40
Nos. 60-83 (24) 8.40 8.40

See Nos. 209-212.

Trees A13

8c, Euphorbia ingens. 15c, Pterocarpus angolensis. 20c, Ficus ingens. 25c, Adansonia digitata.

1982, Sept. 17

84 A13 8c multicolored .25 .25
85 A13 15c multicolored .25 .25
86 A13 20c multicolored .35 .35
87 A13 25c multicolored .45 .45
Nos. 84-87 (4) 1.30 1.30

1983, Aug. 3

10c, Gardenia spatulifolia. 20c, Hyphaene natalensis. 25c, Albizia adianthifolia. 40c, Sesamothamnus lugardii.

88 A13 10c multicolored .25 .25
89 A13 20c multicolored .30 .30
90 A13 25c multicolored .30 .30
91 A13 40c multicolored .55 .55
Nos. 88-91 (4) 1.40 1.40

1984, June 21

11c, Afzelia quanzensis. 20c, Peltophorum africanum. 25c, Gyrocarpus americanus. 30c, Acacia sieberana.

92 A13 11c multicolored .25 .25
93 A13 20c multicolored .30 .30
94 A13 25c multicolored .35 .35
95 A13 30c multicolored .40 .40
Nos. 92-95 (4) 1.30 1.30
Nos. 84-95 (12) 3.85 3.85

Frogs — A14

8c, Rana angolensis. 15c, Chiromantis xerampelina. 20c, Leptopelis. 25c, Ptychadena anchietae.

1982, Nov. 26 *Perf. 14x14½*

96 A14 8c multicolored .25 .25
97 A14 15c multicolored .30 .30
98 A14 20c multicolored .35 .35
99 A14 25c multicolored .45 .45
Nos. 96-99 (4) 1.35 1.35

Migratory Birds and Maps — A15

8c, European bee-eater. 20c, Steppe eagle. 25c, Plum-colored starling. 40c, White-bellied stork.

1983, Feb. 16 *Perf. 14½x14*

100 A15 8c multicolored .25 .25
101 A15 20c multicolored .40 .40
102 A15 25c multicolored .50 .50
103 A15 40c multicolored .85 .85
Nos. 100-103 (4) 2.00 2.00

Subtropical Fruit A16

1983, Oct. 26 *Perf. 14x14½*

104 A16 10c Avocado .25 .25
105 A16 20c Mango .25 .25
106 A16 25c Papaya .30 .30
107 A16 40c Litchi .50 .50
Nos. 104-107 (4) 1.30 1.30

Migratory Birds — A17

1984, Apr. 26 *Perf. 14½x14*

108 A17 11c White stork .30 .30
109 A17 20c Paradise flycatcher .55 .55
110 A17 25c Yellow-billed kite .65 .65
111 A17 30c Wood sandpiper .85 .85
Nos. 108-111 (4) 2.35 2.35

Independence, 5th Anniv. — A18

1984, Sept. 13 *Perf. 14½x14*

112 A18 11c Dzata Ruins .25 .25
113 A18 25c Traditional hut .25 .25
114 A18 30c Low-income housing .30 .30
115 A18 45c Modern home .45 .45
Nos. 112-115 (4) 1.25 1.25

Songbirds — A19

11c, Heuglin's robin. 25c, Black-collared barbet. 30c, Black-headed oriole. 50c, Kurrichane thrush.

1985, Jan. 10

116 A19 11c multicolored .25 .25
117 A19 25c multicolored .40 .40
118 A19 30c multicolored .50 .50
119 A19 50c multicolored .85 .85
Nos. 116-119 (4) 2.00 2.00

Food of the Veld — A20

1985, June 21 *Perf. 14x14½*

120 A20 12c Mimusops zeyheri .25 .25
121 A20 25c Ziziphus mucronata .25 .25
122 A20 30c Citrullus lanatus .30 .30
123 A20 50c Berchemia discolor .50 .50
Nos. 120-123 (4) 1.30 1.30

See Nos. 173-176.

Ferns — A21

12c, Pellaea dura. 25c, Actiniopteris radiata. 30c, Adiantum hispidulum. 50c, Polypodium polypodioides.

1985, Sept. 5 *Perf. 14½x14*

124 A21 12c multicolored .25 .25
125 A21 25c multicolored .25 .25
126 A21 30c multicolored .30 .30
127 A21 50c multicolored .50 .50
Nos. 124-127 (4) 1.30 1.30

Reptiles A22

1c, Psammophylax tritaeniatus. 2c, Pseudaspis cana. 3c, Nucras taeniolata ornata. 4c, Bitis arietans. 5c, Mabuya capensis. 6c, Naja haje annulifera. 7c, Mabuya quinquetaeniata margaritifer. 8c, Philothamnus semivariegatus. 9c, Gerrhosaurus flavigularis. 10c, Prosymna sundevallii lineata. 14c, Platysaurus intermedius. 15c, Lacerta rupicola. 16c, Varanus niloticus. 18c, Dendroaspis polylepis. 20c, Afroedura transvaalica. 21c, Chamaeleo dilepsis. 25c, Elapsoidea sundevallii longicauda. 30c, Pachydactylus tigrinus. 50c, Mehelya capensis. 1r, Cordylus warreni depressus. 2r, Python sebae natalensis.

1986-90 *Perf. 14x14½*

128 A22 1c multicolored .25 .25
129 A22 2c multicolored .25 .25
130 A22 3c multicolored .25 .25
131 A22 4c multicolored .25 .25
132 A22 5c multicolored .25 .25
133 A22 6c multicolored .25 .25
134 A22 7c multicolored .25 .25
135 A22 8c multicolored .25 .25
136 A22 9c multicolored .25 .25
137 A22 10c multicolored .25 .25
138 A22 14c multicolored .30 .30
139 A22 15c multicolored .30 .30
140 A22 16c multicolored .35 .35
141 A22 18c multicolored .40 .40
142 A22 20c multicolored .45 .45
143 A22 21c multicolored .45 .45
144 A22 25c multicolored .55 .55
145 A22 30c multicolored .65 .65
146 A22 50c multicolored 1.10 1.10
147 A22 1r multicolored 2.25 2.25
148 A22 2r multicolored 4.50 4.50
Nos. 128-148 (21) 13.80 13.80

Issued: 14c, 4/1/86; 16c, 4/1/87; 18c, 7/3/89; 21c, 8/3/90; others, 1/16/86.

Forestry A23

Designs: 14c, Planting pine seedlings. 20c, Felling and extracting saw timber. 25c, Unloading timber at sawmill. 30c, Construction workers using pre-cut lumber.

1986, June 26 *Perf. 14x14½*

153 A23 14c multicolored .25 .25
154 A23 20c multicolored .40 .40
155 A23 25c multicolored .45 .45
156 A23 30c multicolored .55 .55
Nos. 153-156 (4) 1.65 1.65

FIVA World Classic Car Rally — A24

14c, 1910 Maxwell. 20c, 1929 Bentley 4½ l. 25c, 1933 Plymouth Coupe. 30c, 1958 Mercedes Cabriolet.

1986, Sept. 4 *Perf. 14½x14*

157 A24 14c multicolored .25 .25
158 A24 20c multicolored .25 .25
159 A24 25c multicolored .35 .35
160 A24 30c multicolored .40 .40
a. Souvenir sheet of 1 1.40 1.40
Nos. 157-160 (4) 1.25 1.25

No. 160a for the natl. philatelic exhibition held at Johannesburg, Oct. 6-11. Sold for 50c.

Waterfowl — A25

14c, Sarkidiornis melanotos. 20c, Dendrocygna viduata. 25c, Plectropterus gambensis. 30c, Alopochen aegyptiacus.

1987, Jan. 8 *Perf. 14x14½, 14½x14*
161 A25 14c multicolored .90 .90
162 A25 20c multicolored 1.40 1.40
163 A25 25c multicolored 1.60 1.60
a. Souvenir sheet of 1 4.50 4.50
164 A25 30c multicolored 2.10 2.10
Nos. 161-164 (4) 6.00 6.00

Nos. 163-164 are horiz. No. 163a margin pictures emblem of the natl. philatelic exhibition held at Paarl, Sept. 16-19. Sold for 50c.

Wood Carvings — A26

1987, Apr. 9 *Perf. 14½x14*
165 A26 16c Iron Master .35 .35
166 A26 20c Distant Drums .40 .40
167 A26 25c Sunrise .55 .55
168 A26 30c Obedience .70 .70
Nos. 165-168 (4) 2.00 2.00

Freshwater Fish — A27

16c, Hydrocynus vittatus. 20c, Opsardium zambezense. 25c, Oreochromis mossambicus. 30c, Clarias gariepinus.

1987, July 2 *Perf. 14x14½*
169 A27 16c multicolored .30 .30
170 A27 20c multicolored .35 .35
171 A27 25c multicolored .40 .40
172 A27 30c multicolored .55 .55
Nos. 169-172 (4) 1.60 1.60

Food of the Veld Type

1987, Oct. 2
173 A20 16c Grewia occidentalis .25 .25
174 A20 30c Phoenix reclinata .30 .30
175 A20 40c Halleria lucida .45 .45
176 A20 50c Cucumis africanus .55 .55
Nos. 173-176 (4) 1.55 1.55

Coffee Industry A28

1988, Jan. 21 *Perf. 14½x14*
177 A28 16c Harvesting .25 .25
178 A28 30c Weighing .30 .30
179 A28 40c Sun drying .40 .40
180 A28 50c Roasting .50 .50
Nos. 177-180 (4) 1.45 1.45

Nurse's Training College, Shayandima A29

1988, Aug. 18
181 A29 16c shown .25 .25
182 A29 30c Microscopy .30 .30
183 A29 40c Anatomy lecture .40 .40
184 A29 50c Clinical training .50 .50
Nos. 181-184 (4) 1.45 1.45

Watercolors by Kenneth Thabo A30

1988, Oct. 6
185 A30 16c Fetching Water .25 .25
186 A30 30c Grinding Maize .30 .30
187 A30 40c Offering Food .40 .40
188 A30 50c Kindling the Fire .50 .50
a. Souvenir sheet of 1 1.90 1.90
Nos. 185-188 (4) 1.45 1.45

No. 188a for the natl. philatelic exhibition held at Pietermaritzburg, Nov. 22-27. Sold for 1.50r.

See Nos. 193-196.

Traditional Kitchenware A31

1989, Jan. 5
189 A31 16c Ndongwana .25 .25
190 A31 30c Ndilo .30 .30
191 A31 40c Mufaro .40 .40
192 A31 50c Muthatha .50 .50
Nos. 189-192 (4) 1.45 1.45

Art Type of 1988

Traditional dances: watercolors by Kenneth Thabo.

1989, Apr. 5
193 A30 18c Domba .25 .25
194 A30 30c Tshinzerere .30 .30
195 A30 40c Malende .40 .40
196 A30 50c Malombo .50 .50
Nos. 193-196 (4) 1.45 1.45

Endangered Bird Species — A32

18c, Bucorvus leadbeateri. 30c, Torgos tracheliotus. 40c, Terathopius ecaudatus. 50c, Polemaetus bellicosus.

1989, June 27
197 A32 18c multicolored .90 .90
198 A32 30c multicolored 1.25 1.25
199 A32 40c multicolored 1.60 1.60
200 A32 50c multicolored 2.25 2.25
a. Souvenir sheet of 1 4.00 4.00
Nos. 197-200 (4) 6.00 6.00

No. 200a for the natl. philatelic exhibition WANDERERS 101, held Sept. 6-9. Sold for 1.50r.

Independence, 10th Anniv. — A33

18c, Pres. Ravele. 30c, Presidential office. 40c, Presidential residence. 50c, Thohoyandou Stadium.

1989, Sept. 13
201 A33 18c multicolored .25 .25
202 A33 30c multicolored .30 .30
203 A33 40c multicolored .40 .40
204 A33 50c multicolored .45 .45
Nos. 201-204 (4) 1.40 1.40

Wildlife Conservation, Nwanedi Natl. Park — A34

18c, Panthera leo. 30c, Equus burchelli. 40c, Acinonyx jubatus. 50c, Ceratotherium simum.

1990, Mar. 1
205 A34 18c multicolored .50 .50
206 A34 30c multicolored .90 .90
207 A34 40c multicolored 1.10 1.10
208 A34 50c multicolored 1.25 1.25
a. Souvenir sheet of 1 4.00 4.00
Nos. 205-208 (4) 3.75 3.75

No. 208a for the natl. philatelic exhibition. Sold for 1.50r.

History of Writing Type

Designs: 21c, Calligraphy. 30c, Musical notation, Beethoven's *Moonlight Sonata.* 40c, Computer characters. 50c, Black-and-white television picture transmitted across interstellar distances by the Arecibo radio telescope.

1990, May 23 **Litho.** *Perf. 14½x14*
209 A12 21c multicolored .25 .25
210 A12 30c multicolored .35 .35
211 A12 40c multicolored .45 .45
212 A12 50c multicolored .65 .65
Nos. 209-212 (4) 1.70 1.70

Aloe Plants — A35

1990, Aug. 23 **Litho.** *Perf. 14½x14*
213 A35 21c Aloe globuligemma .40 .40
214 A35 35c Aloe aculeata .60 .60
215 A35 40c Aloe lutescens .70 .70
216 A35 50c Aloe angelica .85 .85
Nos. 213-216 (4) 2.55 2.55

Butterflies — A36

21c, Pseudacraea boisduvalii. 35c, Papilio nireus. 40c, Charaxes jasius. 50c, Aeropetes tulbaghia.

1990, Nov. 15 *Perf. 14x14½*
217 A36 21c multicolored .60 .60
218 A36 35c multicolored 1.10 1.10
219 A36 40c multicolored 1.25 1.25
220 A36 50c multicolored 1.40 1.40
Nos. 217-220 (4) 4.35 4.35

Birds A37

21c, Batis capensis. 35c, Cossypha natalensis. 40c, Anthreptes collaris. 50c, Phyllastrephus flavostriatus.

1991, Mar. 7 **Litho.** *Perf. 14½x14*
221 A37 21c multicolored .55 .55
222 A37 35c multicolored .85 .85
223 A37 40c multicolored 1.00 1.00
224 A37 50c multicolored 1.25 1.25
Nos. 221-224 (4) 3.65 3.65

Chinese Inventions — A38

25c, Paper made from pulp. 40c, Magnetic compass. 50c, Abacus. 60c, Gunpowder.

1991, June 6 **Litho.** *Perf. 14½x14*
225 A38 25c multicolored .90 .90
226 A38 40c multicolored 1.40 1.40
227 A38 50c multicolored 1.75 1.75
228 A38 60c multicolored 2.00 2.00
a. Souvenir sheet of 1 3.25 3.25
Nos. 225-228 (4) 6.05 6.05

Hotels A39

25c, Venda Sun. 40c, Mphephu Resort. 50c, Sagole Spa. 60c, Luphephe-Nwanedi Resort.

1991, Aug. 29 **Litho.**
229 A39 25c multicolored .50 .50
230 A39 40c multicolored .90 .90
231 A39 50c multicolored 1.10 1.10
232 A39 60c multicolored 1.50 1.50
Nos. 229-232 (4) 4.00 4.00

Trees A40

27c, Acacia xanthophloea. 45c, Faurea saligna. 65c, Strelitzia caudata. 85c, Kigelia africana.

1991, Nov. 21 **Litho.**
233 A40 27c multicolored .55 .55
234 A40 45c multicolored 1.00 1.00
235 A40 65c multicolored 1.40 1.40
236 A40 85c multicolored 1.75 1.75
Nos. 233-236 (4) 4.70 4.70

Clothing Factory A41

27c, Setting the web. 45c, Knitting a pattern. 65c, Using sewing machine. 85c, Testing for flaws.

1992, Mar. 5 **Litho.**
237 A41 27c multicolored .35 .35
238 A41 45c multicolored .80 .80
239 A41 65c multicolored 1.10 1.10
240 A41 85c multicolored 1.40 1.40
Nos. 237-240 (4) 3.65 3.65

Bees A42

1992, May 21 **Litho.**
241 A42 35c Honey bee .80 .80
242 A42 70c Carder bee 1.60 1.60
243 A42 90c Leafcutter bee 1.75 1.75
244 A42 1.05r Carpenter bee 2.25 2.25
Nos. 241-244 (4) 6.40 6.40

A souvenir sheet of 1 #242 was sold by the Philatelic Foundation of South Africa. Value $3.75.

Inventions A43

Designs: 35c, Plow, Egypt 1259 B.C. 70c, Wheel, Mesopotamia, 3200 B.C. 90c, Brickmaking, Egypt, 3000 B.C. 1.05r, Sailing ship, Egypt, 1600 B.C.

1992, Aug. 13

245 A43 35c multicolored .70 .70
246 A43 70c multicolored 1.40 1.40
247 A43 90c multicolored 1.50 1.50
248 A43 1.05r multicolored 2.00 2.00
Nos. 245-248 (4) 5.60 5.60

Crocodile Farming A44

35c, Emerging from water. 70c, Egg laying. 90c, Hatchlings. 1.05r, Maternal care.

1992, Oct. 15 **Litho.**

249 A44 35c multicolored .70 .70
250 A44 70c multicolored 1.40 1.40
251 A44 90c multicolored 1.50 1.50
252 A44 1.05r multicolored 2.00 2.00
Nos. 249-252 (4) 5.60 5.60

Domestic Cats — A45

1993, Mar. 19 **Litho.**

253 A45 45c Burmese .90 .90
254 A45 65c Tabby 1.75 1.75
255 A45 85c Siamese 1.90 1.90
256 A45 1.05r Persian 2.50 2.50
Nos. 253-256 (4) 7.05 7.05

A souvenir sheet of one No. 254 has inscription for National Philatelic Exhibition. Sold for 3r. Value $6.50.

Herons A46

Designs: 45c, Butorides striatus. 65c, Nycticorax nycticorax. 85c, Ardea purpurea. 1.05r, Ardea melanocephala.

1993, July 16 **Litho.** ***Perf. 14½x14***

257 A46 45c multicolored 1.00 1.00
258 A46 65c multicolored 1.50 1.50
259 A46 85c multicolored 1.75 1.75
260 A46 1.05r multicolored 2.25 2.25
a. Souvenir sheet of 4, #257-260 6.50 6.50
Nos. 257-260 (4) 6.50 6.50

Shoe Factory — A47

45c, Punching out sole lining. 65c, Shaping heel. 85c, Joining upper to inner sole. 1.05r, Forming sole.

1993, Sept. 17 **Litho.** ***Perf. 14x14½***

261 A47 45c multicolored .45 .45
262 A47 65c multicolored .60 .60
263 A47 85c multicolored .70 .70
264 A47 1.05r multicolored 1.00 1.00
Nos. 261-264 (4) 2.75 2.75

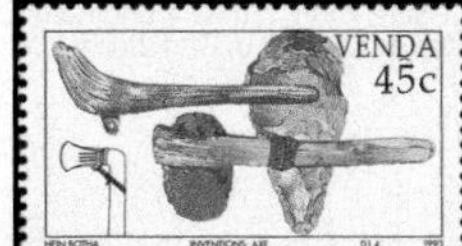

Inventions A48

1993, Nov. 5 **Litho.** ***Perf. 14x14½***

265 A48 45c Axe .60 .60
266 A48 65c Armor .90 .90
267 A48 85c Arch 1.10 1.10
268 A48 1.05r Aqueduct 1.40 1.40
Nos. 265-268 (4) 4.00 4.00

Dogs A49

1994, Jan. 14 **Litho.** ***Perf. 14½x14***

269 A49 45c Cocker spaniel 1.00 1.00
270 A49 65c Maltese 1.60 1.60
271 A49 85c Scottish terrier 1.90 1.90
272 A49 1.05r Miniature schnauzer 2.50 2.50
Nos. 269-272 (4) 7.00 7.00

A souvenir sheet of 1 #271 was sold for 3r by the Philatelic Foundation of Southern Africa and sold for 1.50r. Value $7.

Monkeys A50

Designs: 45c, Cercopithecus aethiops. 65c, Galago moholi. 85c, Cercopithecus mitis. 1.05r, Otolemur crassicaudatus.

1994, Mar. 4 **Litho.** ***Perf. 14½x14***

273 A50 45c multicolored .90 .90
274 A50 65c multicolored 1.40 1.40
275 A50 85c multicolored 1.60 1.60
276 A50 1.05r multicolored 2.10 2.10
a. Souvenir sheet of 4, #273-276 6.00 6.00
Nos. 273-276 (4) 6.00 6.00

Starlings A51

45c, Lamprotornis nitens. 70c, Cinnyricinclus leucogaster. 95c, Onychognathus morio. 1.15r, Creatophora cinerea.

1994, Apr. 29 **Litho.** ***Perf. 14½x14***

277 A51 45c multicolored 1.10 1.10
278 A51 70c multicolored 1.75 1.75
279 A51 95c multicolored 2.25 2.25
280 A51 1.15r multicolored 2.75 2.75
Nos. 277-280 (4) 7.85 7.85

Venda ceased to exist April 27, 1994.

The Venda postal service continued to operate until 1996.

SOUTH ARABIA

sauth ə-'rā-bē-ə

LOCATION — Southern Arabia
GOVT. — Federation; British dependency
AREA — 61,890 sq. mi.
POP. — 771,000 (est. 1966)
CAPITAL — Al Ittihad

The Federation of South Arabia was established in 1959 and consists of 14 states including Aden colony and part of Aden protectorate. When the Federation became independent, Nov. 30, 1967, it became the People's Republic of Southern Yemen. See People's Democratic Republic of Yemen, Vol. 6.

100 Cents = 1 Shilling
1000 Fils = 1 Dinar (1965)

Catalogue values for all unused stamps in this country are for Never Hinged items.

Common Design Types pictured following the introduction.

Red Cross Centenary Issue
Common Design Type
Wmk. 314

1963, Nov. 25 **Litho.** ***Perf. 13***

1 CD315 15c black & red .40 .40
2 CD315 1sh25c ultra & red .85 .85

Arms of Federation of South Arabia — A1

Flag of Federation — A2

Perf. 14½x14

1965, Apr. 1 **Photo.** **Unwmk.**

3 A1 5f blue .25 .25
4 A1 10f light violet blue .25 .25
5 A1 15f blue green .25 .25
6 A1 20f green .25 .25
7 A1 25f orange brown .25 .25
8 A1 30f lemon .25 .25
9 A1 35f red brown .25 .25
10 A1 50f rose red .30 .25
11 A1 65f light yellow green .30 .30
12 A1 75f rose carmine .35 .25

Perf. 14½

Flag in Black, Yellow, Green and Blue

13 A2 100f reddish brown .50 .25
14 A2 250f dark blue 4.75 1.40
15 A2 500f dark red 8.50 1.50
16 A2 1d violet 13.50 *15.00*
Nos. 3-16 (14) 29.95 20.70

For overprints, see People's Democratic Republic of Yemen.

Intl. Cooperation Year Issue
Common Design Type with Coat of Arms Replacing Queen's Portrait
Wmk. 314

1965, Oct. 24 **Litho.** ***Perf. 14½***

17 CD318 5f blue grn & claret .30 .25
18 CD318 65f lt violet & green .90 .25

Churchill Memorial Issue
Common Design Type with Coat of Arms Replacing Queen's Portrait
Design in Black, Gold and Carmine Rose
Unwmk.

1966, Jan. 24 **Photo.** ***Perf. 14***

19 CD319 5f bright blue .25 .25
20 CD319 10f green .35 .25
21 CD319 65f brown .95 .30
22 CD319 125f violet 1.40 1.40
Nos. 19-22 (4) 2.95 2.20

World Cup Soccer Issue
Common Design Type with Coat of Arms Replacing Queen's Portrait

1966, July 1 **Litho.** ***Perf. 14***

23 CD321 10f multicolored .40 .25
24 CD321 50f multicolored 1.50 .30

WHO Headquarters Issue
Common Design Type with Coat of Arms Replacing Queen's Portrait

1966, Sept. 20 **Litho.** **Unwmk.**

25 CD322 10f multicolored .60 .25
26 CD322 75f multicolored 1.50 .45

UNESCO Anniversary Issue
Common Design Type with Coat of Arms Replacing Queen's Portrait

1966, Dec. 15 **Litho.** ***Perf. 14***

27 CD323 10f "Education" .35 .35
28 CD323 65f "Science" 1.40 1.40
29 CD323 125f "Culture" 3.75 *3.75*
Nos. 27-29 (3) 5.50 5.50

SOUTHERN NIGERIA

'sə-thərn nī-'jir-ē-ə

LOCATION — In western Africa bordering on the Gulf of Guinea
GOVT. — British Crown Colony and Protectorate
AREA — 90,896 sq. mi.
POP. — 8,590,545
CAPITAL — Lagos

The Protectorate of Southern Nigeria, formed in 1900, absorbed in that year the Niger Coast Protectorate. In 1906 it united with Lagos and became the Colony and Protectorate of Southern Nigeria. An amalgamation was effected in 1914 between Northern and Southern Nigeria to form the Colony and Protectorate of Nigeria. See Nigeria, Northern Nigeria, Niger Coast Protectorate and Lagos.

12 Pence = 1 Shilling
20 Shillings = 1 Pound

Victoria — A1

Wmk. Crown and C A (2)

1901, Mar. **Typo.** ***Perf. 14***

1 A1 ½p yel grn & blk 2.00 *3.00*
a. ½p yel grn & sepia ('02) 2.50 *3.00*
2 A1 1p car rose & blk 3.00 *3.00*
a. 1p carmine rose & sepia ('02) 4.25 2.00
3 A1 2p org brn & blk 3.75 *7.25*
4 A1 4p ol grn & blk 3.75 *30.00*
5 A1 6p red vio & blk 4.75 *11.00*
6 A1 1sh blk & gray grn 10.00 *32.50*
7 A1 2sh6p brn & blk 50.00 *95.00*
8 A1 5sh yellow & blk 67.50 *135.00*
9 A1 10sh vio & blk, *yel* 150.00 *300.00*
Nos. 1-9 (9) 294.75 *616.75*

Edward VII — A2

1903-04

10 A2 ½p yel grn & blk 1.10 .35
11 A2 1p car rose & blk 1.50 .80
12 A2 2p org brn & blk 17.50 1.75
13 A2 2½p ultra & blk ('04) 2.25 2.25
14 A2 4p ol grn & blk 5.25 *6.25*
15 A2 6p red vio & blk 9.25 *9.25*
16 A2 1sh blk & gray grn 42.50 22.50
17 A2 2sh6p brown & blk 42.50 *75.00*
18 A2 5sh yellow & blk 90.00 *225.00*
19 A2 10sh vio & blk, *yel* 45.00 *150.00*
20 A2 £1 pur & gray grn 475.00 *1,000.*
Nos. 10-20 (11) 731.85 1,493.

1904-09 **Ordinary Paper** **Wmk. 3**

21 A2 ½p yel grn & blk .75 .25
22 A2 1p carmine rose & blk 18.00 .25
23 A2 2p org brn & blk ('05) 3.00 .50
24 A2 2½p ultra & blk ('09) 1.25 1.10
25 A2 4p ol grn & blk ('05) 16.00 *29.00*
26 A2 6p red vio & blk 14.50 9.00
27 A2 1sh blk & gray grn 3.75 *4.00*
28 A2 2sh6p brn & blk ('06) 27.50 *29.00*
29 A2 5sh yellow & blk ('07) 62.50 *90.00*
31 A2 £1 pur & gray grn ('06) 350.00 *425.00*
Nos. 21-31 (9) 496.00 587.00

Chalky Paper

21a A2 ½p yel grn & blk ('05) 1.25 1.00
22a A2 1p carmine rose & blk ('05) 13.00 .25
24A A2 3p vio & org brn ('07) 11.00 1.50
25a A2 4p ol grn & blk ('06) 27.50 32.50
26a A2 6p red vio & blk ('06) 14.50 *16.00*
27a A2 1sh blk & gray grn ('07) 45.00 3.50

28a	A2	2sh6p	brn & blk ('06)	55.00	20.00
29a	A2	5sh	brn & blk ('08)	90.00	110.00
30	A2	10sh	vio & blk, *yel* ('08)	175.00	225.00
31a	A2	£1	pur & gray grn ('06)	325.00	*425.00*

1907-10 Ordinary Paper

32	A2	½p	green ('08)	2.25	.25
33	A2	1p	carmine	1.00	.25
34	A2	2p	gray	3.00	.80
35	A2	2½p	ultra	8.00	4.25

Chalky Paper

36	A2	3p	violet, *yel*	2.25	.35
37	A2	4p	scar & blk, *yel*	2.50	.90
38	A2	6p	red vio & dl vio	29.00	3.75
39	A2	1sh	black, *green*	8.00	.50
40	A2	2sh6p	car & blk, *bl*	19.00	2.50
41	A2	5sh	scar & grn, *yel*	45.00	*55.00*
42	A2	10sh	red & grn, *grn*	100.00	*140.00*
43	A2	£1	blk & vio, *red*	250.00	*300.00*
			Nos. 32-43 (12)	470.00	*508.55*

1910 Ordinary Paper Redrawn

44	A2	1p	carmine	1.10	.25

In the redrawn stamp the "1" of "1d" is not as thick as in No. 33 but the "d" is taller and broader.

King George V — A3

1912

45	A3	½p	green	3.00	.25
46	A3	1p	carmine	3.00	.25
47	A3	2p	gray	1.00	.95
48	A3	2½p	ultra	5.75	3.25
49	A3	3p	violet, *yel*	1.25	.35
50	A3	4p	scar & blk, *yel*	1.60	*2.40*
51	A3	6p	red vio & dl vio	3.00	1.50
52	A3	1sh	black, *green*	3.50	1.00
53	A3	2sh6p	red & blk, *bl*	10.00	*50.00*
54	A3	5sh	red & grn, *yel*	26.00	*87.50*
55	A3	10sh	red & grn, *grn*	60.00	110.00
56	A3	£1	blk & vio, *red*	225.00	*275.00*
			Nos. 45-56 (12)	343.10	532.45

Stamps of Southern Nigeria were replaced in 1914 by those of Nigeria.

SOUTHERN RHODESIA

'sə-th̲ərn rō-'dē-zhē-ə

LOCATION — Southeastern Africa between Northern Rhodesia and Mozambique
GOVT. — British Colony
AREA — 150,333 sq. mi.
POP. — 4,010,000 (est. 1963)
CAPITAL — Salisbury

Prior to 1923 this territory was administered by the British South Africa Company. The colony was created in that year by the British Government at the request of the inhabitants. In 1953, Southern Rhodesia joined Northern Rhodesia and Nyasaland to form the Federation of Rhodesia and Nyasaland. When the Federation dissolved at the end of 1963, Southern Rhodesia again became an internally self-governing colony. See Rhodesia and Northern Rhodesia.

12 Pence = 1 Shilling
20 Shillings = 1 Pound

Catalogue values for unused stamps in this country are for Never Hinged items, beginning with Scott 56 in the regular postage section and Scott J1 in the postage due section.

King George V — A1

1924-30 Unwmk. Engr. *Perf. 14*

1	A1	½p	dark green	5.00	.75
a.			Vert. pair, imperf. btwn.	1,200.	1,300.
b.			Horiz. pair, imperf. btwn.	1,200.	1,300.
c.			Horiz. pair, imperf. vert.	1,300.	
2	A1	1p	scarlet	4.25	.25
a.			Horiz. pair, imperf. btwn.	950.00	1,100.
b.			Perf. 12½ (coil) ('30)	4.50	*92.50*
c.			Vert. pair, imperf. btwn.	1,700.	
d.			Vert. pair, imperf. horiz.	1,000.	
3	A1	1½p	bister brown	4.75	.90
a.			Horiz. pair, imperf. btwn.	*15,000.*	
b.			Vert. pair, imperf. btwn.	*8,000.*	
4	A1	2p	vio blk & blk	8.00	2.75
a.			Horiz. pair, imperf. btwn.	*17,000.*	
5	A1	3p	deep blue	7.00	7.00
6	A1	4p	org red & blk	7.00	*3.25*
7	A1	6p	lilac & blk	7.00	*9.00*
a.			Horiz. pair, imperf. btwn.	*45,000.*	
8	A1	8p	gray grn & vio	17.00	*55.00*
9	A1	10p	rose red & bl	21.00	*57.50*
10	A1	1sh	turq bl & blk	10.00	*14.00*
11	A1	1sh6p	yellow & blk	24.00	*42.50*
12	A1	2sh	brown & blk	20.00	20.00
13	A1	2sh6p	blk brn & bl	37.50	70.00
14	A1	5sh	bl grn & bl	97.50	*175.00*
			Nos. 1-14 (14)	270.00	457.90

Values for imperf between pairs are for stamps from the same pane. Stamps separated by wide margins are cross-gutter pairs and sell for much lower prices.

George V
A2

Victoria Falls
A3

1931-37 *Perf. 11½, 14 (1p)*

16	A2	½p	dp green ('33)	3.00	.25
a.			Bklt. pane of 6 ('32)	*150.00*	
b.			Perf. 12	3.50	1.10
c.			Perf. 14 ('35)	3.00	1.10
17	A2	1p	scarlet ('35)	1.50	.25
a.			Bklt. pane of 6 ('32)	*150.00*	
b.			Perf. 11½ ('33)	4.25	.25
c.			Perf. 12	3.75	1.10
18	A2	1½p	dp brown ('32)	3.00	.90
a.			Bklt. pane of 6 ('32)	*600.00*	
b.			Perf. 12 ('33)	62.50	*47.50*

Typo. *Perf. 14½x14*

19	A3	2p	blk brn & blk	13.00	1.75
20	A3	3p	dark blue	11.50	12.50

Perf. 12, 11½ (2sh6p)

Engr.

21	A2	4p	org red & blk	1.75	1.75
a.			Perf. 14 ('37)	39.00	*70.00*
b.			Perf. 11½ ('35)	20.00	6.75
22	A2	6p	rose lilac & blk	2.50	3.50
a.			Perf. 14 ('36)	8.00	2.25
b.			Perf. 11½ ('33)	17.50	2.25
23	A2	8p	green & violet	2.00	*4.50*
a.			Perf. 11½ ('34)	20.00	*37.50*
24	A2	9p	gray grn & ver ('34)	12.00	14.50
25	A2	10p	car & ultra	8.50	3.00
a.			Perf. 11½ ('33)	7.50	*15.00*
26	A2	1sh	turq bl & blk	2.25	3.00
a.			Perf. 11½ ('36)	150.00	70.00
b.			Perf. 14 ('37)	250.00	165.00
27	A2	1sh6p	ocher & blk	16.00	*28.00*
a.			Perf. 11½ ('36)	75.00	*140.00*
28	A2	2sh	dk brn & blk	37.50	9.00
a.			Perf. 11½ ('33)	42.50	35.00
29	A2	2sh6p	ol brn & ultra ('33)	40.00	52.50
a.			Perf. 12	50.00	*37.50*
30	A2	5sh	bl grn & ultra	52.50	57.50
			Nos. 16-30 (15)	207.00	192.90

Victoria Falls — A4

1932, May *Perf. 12½*

31	A4	2p	dark brn & grn	7.00	2.00
32	A4	3p	dark blue	7.00	3.00
a.			Vert. pair, imperf. horiz.	*17,000.*	*18,000.*
b.			Vert. pair, imperf. btwn.	*38,000.*	
			Set, never hinged	22.00	

See Nos. 37-37A.

Silver Jubilee Issue

Victoria Falls and George V
A5

1935, May 6 *Perf. 11x12*

33	A5	1p	car rose & olive	4.25	3.25
34	A5	2p	blk brn & lt grn	7.50	8.50
35	A5	3p	blue & violet	6.00	*11.00*
36	A5	6p	dp violet & blk	10.00	*22.50*
			Nos. 33-36 (4)	27.75	*45.25*
			Set, never hinged	42.50	

25th anniv. of the reign of George V.

"Postage and Revenue"
A6

1935-41 *Perf. 14*

37	A6	2p	dk brn & grn ('41)	3.00	.25
b.			Perf. 12½	7.00	18.00
37A	A6	3p	deep blue ('38)	4.00	1.25
			Set, never hinged	17.00	

Queen Elizabeth, George VI — A7

1937, May 12 *Perf. 12½*

38	A7	1p	carmine & gray grn	.40	*1.00*
39	A7	2p	brown & green	.40	*1.75*
40	A7	3p	lt blue & violet	1.75	*9.00*
41	A7	6p	red violet & blk	1.00	*3.75*
			Nos. 38-41 (4)	3.55	15.50
			Set, never hinged	7.00	

Coronation of George VI & Elizabeth.

King George VI — A8

1937, Nov. 25 *Perf. 14*

42	A8	½p	yellow green	.40	.25
43	A8	1p	red	.40	.25
44	A8	1½p	red brown	.75	.35
45	A8	4p	orange red	1.00	.25
46	A8	6p	dark gray	1.00	.60
47	A8	8p	blue green	1.50	4.00
48	A8	9p	blue	1.25	1.10
49	A8	10p	violet	1.50	*3.50*
50	A8	1sh	green & blk	1.75	.25
51	A8	1sh6p	ocher & blk	8.50	3.00
52	A8	2sh	brown & blk	13.00	.70
53	A8	2sh6p	violet & blue	7.00	8.00
54	A8	5sh	green & blue	13.00	3.50
			Nos. 42-54 (13)	51.05	25.75
			Set, never hinged	75.00	

Catalogue values for unused stamps in this section, from this point to the end of the section, are for Never Hinged items.

Seal of British South Africa Co. — A9

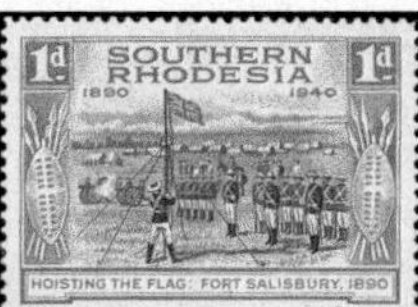

Fort Salisbury, 1890 — A10

Cecil John Rhodes — A11

Pioneer Fort and Mail Coach
A12

Rhodes Makes Peace, 1896 — A13

Victoria Falls Bridge — A14

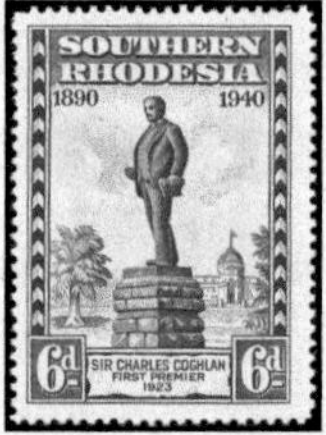

Sir Charles Coghlan — A15

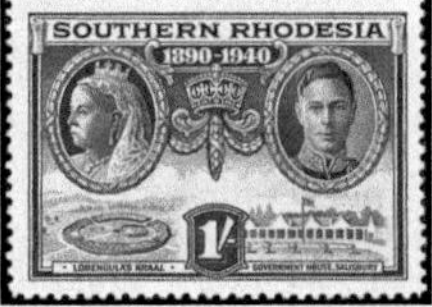

Queen Victoria, George VI, Lobengula's Kraal and Government House
A16

Unwmk.

1940, June 3 Engr. *Perf. 14*

56	A9	½p	dp grn & dull vio	.25	.65
57	A10	1p	red & vio blue	.60	.25
58	A11	1½p	cop brn & blk	.25	.80
59	A12	2p	pur & brt grn	.40	.40
60	A13	3p	dk blue & blk	1.00	1.00
61	A14	4p	brn & bl grn	2.00	*2.75*
62	A15	6p	sepia & dull grn	2.00	*2.75*
63	A16	1sh	dk bl & brt grn	3.00	*3.25*
			Nos. 56-63 (8)	9.50	*11.85*

50th anniv. of the founding of Southern Rhodesia by Cecil John Rhodes.

Pioneer — A17

1943, Nov. 1 Photo. Wmk. 201

64	A17	2p Prus grn & choc	.35	*.50*

50th anniv. of Matabeleland under British control.

Princess Elizabeth and Princess Margaret Rose A18

King George VI and Queen Elizabeth A19

Unwmk.

1947, Apr. 1 Engr. *Perf. 14*

65	A18	½p dk green & blk	.30	.60
66	A19	1p carmine & blk	.30	.60

Visit of the British Royal Family, Apr., 1947.

Victory Issue

Queen Elizabeth A20

George VI A21

Princess Elizabeth A22

Princess Margaret Rose A23

1947, May 8

67	A20	1p deep carmine	.25	.25
68	A21	2p slate black	.25	.25
69	A22	3p deep blue	.60	*.50*
70	A23	6p red orange	.30	*.75*
		Nos. 67-70 (4)	1.40	1.75

Victory of the Allied Nations in WW II.

Common Design Types pictured following the introduction.

UPU Issue

Common Design Types

Engr.; Name Typo.

1949, Oct. 10 Wmk. 4 *Perf. 11x11½*

71	CD307	2p slate black	.70	.50
72	CD308	3p slate blue	1.25	*1.75*

75th anniv. of the UPU.

Queen Victoria and King George VI A24

Unwmk.

1950, Sept. 12 Engr. *Perf. 14*

73	A24	2p choc & blue grn	.90	*1.10*

60th anniversary of Rhodesia.

Hospital, Doctor and Natives A25

Designs: 1p, African Scene. 2p, Native Houses, Modern City and Cecil Rhodes. 4½p, Dam and Natives. 1sh, Transportation.

1953, Apr. 15

74	A25	½p dk brown & blue	.25	*.40*
75	A25	1p blue grn & fawn	.25	.25
76	A25	2p vio & dk bl grn	.35	.25
77	A25	4½p dk bl & bl grn	1.50	*2.75*
78	A25	1sh chestnut & blk	3.25	1.75
		Nos. 74-78 (5)	5.60	5.40

#77 is inscribed Matabeleland Diamond Jubilee.

Type of Nyasaland Prot., 1953

1953, May 30 *Perf. 14x13½*

79	A17	6p purple	.35	.35

Nos. 74-79 were issued to commemorate the Central African Cecil Rhodes Centenary Exhibition.

Coronation Issue

Elizabeth II — A26

1953, June 1 *Perf. 12x12½*

80	A26	2sh6p cerise	7.25	*7.25*

Sable Antelope A27

Rhodes' Grave A28

Flame Lily — A29

Designs: 1p, Tobacco planter. 3p, Farm Worker. 4½p, Victoria Falls. 6p, Baobab tree. 9p, Lion. 1sh, Zimbabwe ruins. 2sh, Birchenough Bridge. 2sh6p, Kariba Gorge. 5sh, Basket maker. 10sh, Balancing rocks. £1, Arms.

Perf. 14x13½, 13½x14

1953, Aug. 31

Portrait in Various Positions

81	A27	½p rose lake & dk ol grn	.35	*.45*
82	A27	1p choc & grn	.35	.25
83	A28	2p rose vio & org brn	.35	.25

Size: 28x22½mm

84	A29	3p car & sep	.70	*1.50*
85	A29	4p gray, brn, car & grn	3.50	.40
86	A29	4½p ultra & blk	3.00	*4.50*
87	A28	6p aqua & olive	4.50	1.50
88	A29	9p org brn & dp bl	4.50	4.25
89	A29	1sh grnsh bl & rose vio	1.75	.25
90	A29	2sh red & rose vio	16.00	7.00
91	A29	2sh6p org brn & ol grn	8.00	8.00
92	A28	5s dk grn & org brn	11.00	9.00

Size: 37x27mm

93	A29	10sh ol grn & red brn	19.00	27.50
94	A29	£1 dk gray & car	25.00	32.50
		Nos. 81-94 (14)	98.00	97.35

Ansellia Orchid — A30

1964, Feb. 19 Photo. *Perf. 14½*

Size: 23x19mm

95	A30	½p Corn	.25	*2.00*
96	A30	1p Cape buffalo	.25	.25
a.		Purple omitted	*3,500.*	
97	A30	2p Tobacco	.60	.25
98	A30	3p Kudu	.25	.25
99	A30	4p Oranges	.30	.25

Perf. 13½x13

Size: 27x23mm

100	A30	6p Flame lily	.50	.25
101	A30	9p shown	2.75	1.25
102	A30	1sh Emeralds	3.75	.25
a.		Green omitted	*4,500.*	
103	A30	1sh3p Aloe	3.00	.25
104	A30	2sh Lake Kyle	2.50	2.50
105	A30	2sh6p Tiger fish	4.00	1.00
a.		Red omitted	*4,750.*	
b.		Ultra omitted	*14,000.*	

Perf. 14½x14

Size: 32x27mm

106	A30	5sh Cattle	4.00	2.75
107	A30	10sh Guinea fowl	11.50	8.50
108	A30	£1 Arms	14.00	*18.00*
		Nos. 95-108 (14)	47.65	37.75

#95-108 with overprint "Independence 11th November 1965" are listed as Rhodesia #208-221.

Stamps of Southern Rhodesia were replaced in 1965 by those of Rhodesia (formerly Southern Rhodesia).

POSTAGE DUE STAMPS

Catalogue values for unused stamps in this section are for Never Hinged items.

Great Britain Postage Due Stamps of 1938-51 Overprinted in Black

1951 Wmk. 251 *Perf. 14x14½*

J1	D1	½p emerald	3.75	*17.50*
J2	D1	1p violet blue	3.50	*2.75*
J3	D1	2p black brown	3.00	*2.25*
J4	D1	3p violet	3.25	*3.00*
J5	D1	4p brt blue	2.25	*4.00*
a.		4p slate green	275.00	*600.00*
J6	D1	1sh blue	3.00	*4.50*
		Nos. J1-J6 (6)	18.75	*34.00*

SOUTH GEORGIA

'sauth 'jor-jə

LOCATION — Island in South Atlantic Ocean, 1,100 mi. east of Tierra del Fuego

GOVT. — Dependency of Falkland Islands

AREA — 1,450 sq. mi.

POP. — Military and biological staff only.

CAPITAL — Grytviken Harbor (military garrison)

South Georgia remained a dependency of the Falkland Islands in 1962 when three other dependencies became Antarctic Territory, a separate colony. In 1985 South Georgia and the South Sandwich Islands became a separate colony. See Falkland Islands Dependencies Nos. 3L1-3L8.

12 Pence = 1 Shilling
20 Shillings = 1 Pound
100 Pence = 1 Pound (1971)

Catalogue values for all unused stamps in this country are for Never Hinged items.

Reindeer A1

Sperm Whale — A2

Designs: 1p, South Sandwich Islands map. 2½p, Penguins. 3p, Fur seals. 4p, Finback whale and ship. 5½p, Elephant seals. 6p, Sooty albatross. 9p, Whaling ship. 1sh, Leopard seal. 2sh, Shackleton's cross. 2sh6p, Wandering albatross. 5sh, Elephant and fur seals. 10sh, Plankton and krill (shrimp). No. 15, Blue whale. No. 16, King penguins.

Wmk. 314 Upright

1963-69 Engr. *Perf. 15*

1	A1	½p dull red	.50	*1.00*
a.		Perf. 14x15 ('67)	1.00	*1.40*
b.		Watermark sideways ('70)	1.40	*3.50*
2	A2	1p violet blue	3.00	1.50
3	A2	2p blue green	1.00	1.00
4	A1	2½p black	4.25	1.75
5	A2	3p olive	2.25	.30
6	A1	4p green	4.00	.60
7	A1	5½p dull violet	2.00	.30
8	A2	6p orange	.70	.40
9	A1	9p blue	5.50	1.50
10	A1	1sh lilac	.75	.30
11	A1	2sh cit & lt blue	18.50	5.00
12	A1	2sh6p blue	17.00	3.50
13	A1	5sh ocher	14.50	3.50
14	A2	10sh rose claret	35.00	9.00
15	A1	£1 ultra	90.00	45.00
16	A2	£1 slate green	8.75	*14.00*
		Nos. 1-16 (16)	207.70	88.65
		Set, hinged	95.00	

Issued: No. 16, 12/1/69; others 7/10/63.

Nos. 1-14 Surcharged with New Value (Decimal Currency) and 3 Bars

Wmk. 314 Upright; Sideways on ½p

1971-72 *Perf. 15*

17	A1	½p on ½p dull red	1.25	.90
a.		Wmk. upright ('73)	3.25	5.50
18	A2	1p on 1p vio blue	1.35	.50
a.		Wmk. sideways ('76)	.70	2.75
19	A1	1½p on 5½p dull vio	2.00	2.00
20	A2	2p on 2p blue grn	.65	.45
21	A1	2½p on 2½p black	2.00	.35
22	A2	3p on 3p olive	.90	.45
23	A1	4p on 4p green	.90	.45
24	A2	5p on 6p orange	1.90	.30
25	A1	6p on 9p blue	1.40	.65
26	A1	7½p on 1sh lilac	1.40	.65
27	A1	10p on 2sh cit & lt bl	37.50	17.50
28	A1	15p on 2sh6p blue	6.00	6.50
29	A1	25p on 5sh ocher	7.75	5.50
30	A2	50p on 10sh rose claret, glazed paper ('72)	4.75	*9.00*
a.		Wmk. sideways ('76)	7.50	*15.00*
c.		Ordinary paper	32.50	14.50
		Nos. 17-30 (14)	69.75	45.20

Two types of surcharge are found on ½p, 1p, 1½p and 50p.

Issued: Nos. 17-29, 30c, 2/15/71. No. 30, 12/1/72. No. 30a, 3/9/76.

Wmk. 373 Sideways; Upright on 3p, 50p; Inverted on 1p, 5p

1977

17b	A1	½p on ½p dull red	1.60	*1.90*
18b	A2	1p on 1p vio blue	.90	*1.90*
19b	A1	1½p on 5½p dl vio	1.20	*1.90*
21b	A1	2½p on 2½p black	12.50	3.00
22b	A2	3p on 3p olive	6.00	3.00
23b	A1	4p on 4p green	18.00	12.50
24b	A2	5p on 6p orange	3.50	2.50

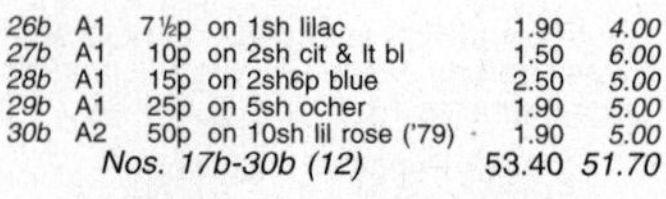

26b A1 7½p on 1sh lilac 1.90 *4.00*
27b A1 10p on 2sh cit & lt bl 1.50 *6.00*
28b A1 15p on 2sh6p blue 2.50 *5.00*
29b A1 25p on 5sh ocher 1.90 *5.00*
30b A2 50p on 10sh lil rose ('79) 1.90 *5.00*
Nos. 17b-30b (12) 53.40 *51.70*

Ernest Shackleton and "Quest" — A3

1½p, "Endurance" in ice of Weddell Sea. 5p, Launching of sailboat "James Caird." 10p, Route of "James Caird" to South Georgia.

1972, Jan. 5 Litho. *Perf. 13½*

31 A3 1½p vio bl, blk & yel .85 *1.25*
32 A3 5p bl grn, blk & yel .85 *1.50*
33 A3 10p lt blue & blk 1.25 *1.75*
34 A3 20p multicolored 1.75 *2.00*
Nos. 31-34 (4) 4.70 6.50

Sir Ernest Shackleton (1874-1922), explorer of Antarctica.

Common Design Types pictured following the introduction.

Silver Wedding Issue, 1972

Common Design Type

Design: Queen Elizabeth II, Prince Philip, elephant seal and king penguins.

1972, Nov. 20 Photo. *Perf. 14x14½*

35 CD324 5p slate grn & multi .50 .50
36 CD324 10p violet & multi .90 .90

Princess Anne's Wedding Issue

Common Design Type

1973, Dec. 1 Litho. *Perf. 14*

37 CD325 5p citron & multi .25 .25
38 CD325 15p slate & multi .50 .50

Churchill, Parliament and Big Ben — A4

Design: 25p, Churchill and battleship.

1974, Dec. 14 Litho. *Perf. 14½*

39 A4 15p vio blue & multi 1.25 1.00
40 A4 25p orange & multi 1.75 1.25
a. Souvenir sheet of 2, #39-40 6.75 6.75

Sir Winston Churchill (1874-1965).

Capt. James Cook — A5

Cook's "Possession" — A6

Design: 16p, Possession Bay.

1975, Apr. 26 Wmk. 314

41 A5 2p multicolored 2.25 1.25
42 A6 8p multicolored 3.25 1.75
43 A6 16p multicolored 3.50 2.00
Nos. 41-43 (3) 9.00 5.00

Bicentenary of Capt. Cook's discovery of South Georgia.

"Discovery" and Biological Laboratory — A7

Designs: 8p, "William Scoresby" and Nansen-Pettersson water sampling bottles. 11p, "Discovery II" and plankton net. 25p, Biological station and krill (shrimp).

Wmk. 373

1976, Dec. 21 Litho. *Perf. 14*

44 A7 2p multicolored 1.50 1.00
45 A7 8p multicolored 1.75 1.25
46 A7 11p multicolored 2.00 1.25
47 A7 25p multicolored 2.75 1.50
Nos. 44-47 (4) 8.00 5.00

50th anniversary of the biological investigations of the "Discovery."

Queen with Regalia and Westminster Abbey — A8

6p, Prince Philip visiting Shackleton Memorial, 1957. 33p, Queen in procession after coronation.

1977, Feb. 7 *Perf. 13½x14*

48 A8 6p multicolored .30 .25
49 A8 11p multicolored .40 .30
50 A8 33p multicolored .75 .70
Nos. 48-50 (3) 1.45 1.25

25th anniv. of the reign of Elizabeth II.

Elizabeth II Coronation Anniversary Issue

Common Design Types

Souvenir Sheet

Unwmk.

1978, June 2 Litho. *Perf. 15*

51 Sheet of 6 3.00 3.00
a. CD326 25p Panther of Henry VI .80 .65
b. CD327 25p Elizabeth II .80 .65
c. CD328 25p Fur seal .80 .65

No. 51 contains 2 se-tenant strips of Nos. 51a-51c, separated by horizontal gutter with commemorative and descriptive inscriptions and showing central part of coronation procession with coach.

Resolution A9

Cook's voyages: 6p, Map of South Georgia and South Sandwich Islands with Cook's route. 11p, King penguin, drawing by Forster. 25p, Cook after Flaxman/Wedgwood medallion.

1979, Feb. 14 Litho. *Perf. 11*

52 A9 3p multicolored 1.25 .90
53 A9 6p multicolored 1.50 .80
54 A9 11p multicolored 1.75 1.50

Lithographed; Embossed

55 A9 25p multicolored 2.25 1.75
Nos. 52-55 (4) 6.75 4.95

Capt. Cook's voyages.

SOUTH GEORGIA and SOUTH SANDWICH ISLANDS

Queen Elizabeth II 60th Birthday

Common Design Type

Designs: 10p, With King George and Queen Mary at christening of Prince Charles, 1948. 24p, Engagement of Prince Charles and Lady Diana, Buckingham Palace Music Room, 1981. 29p, Order of the British Empire, service at St. Paul's Cathedral, London, 1974. 45p, Banquet for Canadian Prime Minister Trudeau during the 1976 Olympics. 58p, Visiting Crown Agents' offices, 1983.

1986, Apr. 21 Wmk. 384 *Perf. 14½*

101 CD337 10p multicolored .40 .40
102 CD337 24p multicolored .60 .60
103 CD337 29p multicolored .60 .70
104 CD337 45p multicolored .85 .85
105 CD337 58p multicolored .85 1.10
Nos. 101-105 (5) 3.30 3.65

Wedding of Prince Andrew and Sarah Ferguson — A12

1986, Nov. 10 Litho. *Perf. 14½*

106 A12 17p Couple at Ascot .80 *1.10*
107 A12 22p Wedding .90 *1.15*
108 A12 29p Andrew, helicopter 1.75 2.00
Nos. 106-108 (3) 3.45 4.25

Birds A13

1p, Dominican gull. 2p, Blue-eyed cormorant. 3p, Wattled sheathbill. 4p, Brown skua. 5p, Cape pigeon. 6p, South Georgia diving petrel. 7p, South Georgia pipit. 8p, South Georgia pintail. 9p, Fairy prion. 10p, Chinstrap penguin. 20p, Macaroni penguin. 25p, Light-mantled sooty albatross. 50p, Southern giant petrel. £1, Wandering albatross. £3, King penguin.

1987, Apr. 24 Litho. Wmk. 384

109 A13 1p multicolored 1.75 *2.50*
110 A13 2p multicolored 1.75 *2.50*
111 A13 3p multicolored 1.75 *2.75*
112 A13 4p multicolored 1.75 *2.75*
113 A13 5p multicolored 1.75 *2.75*
114 A13 6p multicolored 1.75 *2.75*
115 A13 7p multicolored 2.00 *2.75*
116 A13 8p multicolored 2.00 *2.75*
117 A13 9p multicolored 2.00 *2.75*
118 A13 10p multicolored 2.25 *2.75*
119 A13 20p multicolored 2.00 *3.00*
120 A13 25p multicolored 2.00 *3.00*
121 A13 50p multicolored 2.50 *3.25*
122 A13 £1 multicolored 3.50 *4.25*
123 A13 £3 multicolored 7.00 *9.00*
Nos. 109-123 (15) 35.75 *49.50*

3, 4, 7, 8, 20, 25, 50p and £3 vert.

Intl. Geophysical Year, 30th Anniv. — A14

1987, Dec. 5 Litho. *Perf. 14½*

124 A14 24p shown .80 .65
125 A14 29p Grytviken Whaling Station .90 .80
126 A14 58p Glaciologist 1.70 1.25
Nos. 124-126 (3) 3.40 2.70

Sea Shells A15

10p, Gaimardia trapesina. 24p, Margarella tropidophoroides. 29p, Trophon scotianus. 58p, Chlanidota densesculpta.

1988, Feb. 26 Wmk. 384 *Perf. 14½*

127 A15 10p multicolored .75 .35
128 A15 24p multicolored 1.40 .65
129 A15 29p multicolored 1.50 .70
130 A15 58p multicolored 2.25 1.50
Nos. 127-130 (4) 5.90 3.20

Lloyds of London, 300th Anniv.

Common Design Type

10p, Queen Mother at the official opening of the Lloyds Building, Lime Street, 1957. 24p, Lindblad Explorer, horiz. 29p, Leith Harbor whaling station, horiz. 58p, Whale oil tanker Horatio on fire.

1988, Sept. 17 *Perf. 14*

131 CD341 10p multicolored .80 .40
132 CD341 24p multicolored 1.25 .80
133 CD341 29p multicolored 1.75 .90
134 CD341 58p multicolored 2.50 1.60
Nos. 131-134 (4) 6.30 3.70

Glacier Formations — A16

1989, July 31

135 A16 10p Glacier headwall .60 .60
136 A16 24p Accumulation area .80 .80
137 A16 29p Ablation area 1.25 1.25
138 A16 58p Calving front 2.00 2.00
Nos. 135-138 (4) 4.65 4.65

Combined Services Expedition, 1964-65 A17

10p, "Last ordeal" of the trek. 24p, Survey of Royal Bay. 29p, HMS *Protector*. 58p, 1st Ascent of Mt. Paget.

1989, Nov. 28 *Perf. 14x14½*

139 A17 10p multicolored .70 .50
140 A17 24p multicolored 1.10 .90
141 A17 29p multicolored 1.25 1.00
142 A17 58p multicolored 2.10 1.75
Nos. 139-142 (4) 5.15 4.15

Queen Mother, 90th Birthday

Common Design Types

Designs: 26p, Queen Mother. £1, King, Queen & Air Raid Wardens, 1940.

Perf. 14x15

1990, Sept. 15 Wmk. 384

143 CD343 26p multicolored 1.00 1.75

Perf. 14½

144 CD344 £1 blue & black 4.50 4.75

Shipwrecks A18

Wmk. 384

1990, Dec. 22 Litho. *Perf. 14*

145 A18 12p Brutus .65 .50
146 A18 26p Bayard 1.00 1.00
147 A18 31p Karrakatta 1.25 1.10
148 A18 62p Louise 2.50 2.75
Nos. 145-148 (4) 5.40 5.35

Elizabeth & Philip, Birthdays
Common Design Types

1991, July 2 *Perf. 14½*

149 CD345 31p multicolored 1.90 2.75
150 CD346 31p multicolored 1.90 2.75
a. Pair, #149-150 + label 4.75 7.00

No. 150a exists with two different labels.

Elephant Seals A19

12p, Two bulls. 26p, One bull. 29p, Using sand as sunscreen. 31p, Bull, close up. 34p, Harem on beach. 62p, Cow and pup.

1991, Nov. 2 Wmk. 373 *Perf. 14*

151 A19 12p multi .75 .85
152 A19 26p multi 1.25 1.50
153 A19 29p multi 1.75 1.75
154 A19 31p multi 1.75 1.75
155 A19 34p multi 1.75 2.00
156 A19 62p multi 3.00 2.50
Nos. 151-156 (6) 10.25 10.35

Queen Elizabeth II's Accession to the Throne, 40th Anniv.
Common Design Type

1992, Feb. 6

157 CD349 7p multicolored .50 .50
158 CD349 14p multicolored .75 .75
159 CD349 29p multicolored 1.10 1.10
160 CD349 34p multicolored 1.25 1.30
161 CD349 68p multicolored 2.00 2.25
Nos. 157-161 (5) 5.60 5.90

South Georgia Teal A20

1992, Mar. 22 Wmk. 384

162 A20 2p Adult, young .50 .50
163 A20 6p Adult, nest of eggs .70 .70
164 A20 12p Four swimming 1.60 1.60
165 A20 20p Adult, two chicks 2.00 2.00
Nos. 162-165 (4) 4.80 4.80

World Wildlife Fund.

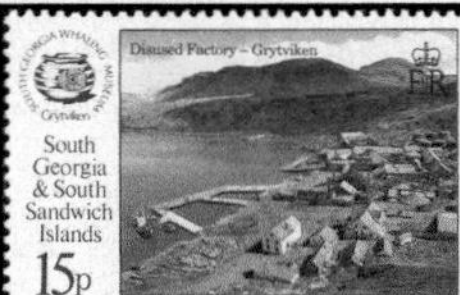

South Georgia Whaling Museum A21

Designs: 15p, Abandoned factory, Grytviken. 31p, Whaler's lighter, bones. 36p, King Edward Cove. 72p, Museum Building.

Wmk. 373

1993, June 29 Litho. *Perf. 13½*

166-169 A21 Set of 4 8.25 8.00

Macaroni Penguins A22

16p, Swimming underwater. 34p, Part of rookery. 39p, Two juveniles. 78p, Two adults.

Perf. 14x14½

1993, Dec. 10 Litho. Wmk. 373

170-173 A22 Set of 4 8.00 7.75

Ovptd. with Hong Kong '94 Emblem

1994, Feb. 18

174-177 A22 Set of 4 8.25 9.00

Whales and Dolphins A23

Designs: 1p, Hourglass dolphin. 2p, Southern right whale dolphin. 5p, Long-finned pilot whale. 8p, Southern bottlenose whale. 9p, Killer whale. 10p, Minke whale. 20p, Sei whale. 25p, Humpback whale. 50p, Southern right whale. £1, Sperm whale. £3, Fin whale. £5, Blue whale.

Wmk. 373

1994, Jan. 24 Litho. *Perf. 14*

178 A23 1p multicolored 1.50 1.10
179 A23 2p multicolored 2.00 1.50
180 A23 5p multicolored 2.50 1.75
181 A23 8p multicolored 2.60 2.00
182 A23 9p multicolored 2.60 2.00
183 A23 10p multicolored 2.60 2.00
184 A23 20p multicolored 4.00 3.00
185 A23 25p multicolored 4.00 3.00
186 A23 50p multicolored 5.00 3.25
187 A23 £1 multicolored 6.25 3.75
188 A23 £3 multicolored 11.50 7.00
189 A23 £5 multicolored 18.50 11.00
Nos. 178-189 (12) 63.05 41.35

Native Wildlife A24

17p, Bull elephant seals. 35p, Fur seal, vert. 40p, Gray-headed albatrosses. 65p, King penguins, vert.

Wmk. 384

1994, Sept. 28 Litho. *Perf. 14*

190 A24 17p multicolored .75 .90
191 A24 35p multicolored 1.50 1.80
192 A24 40p multicolored 2.00 2.25
193 A24 65p multicolored 3.00 3.25
Nos. 190-193 (4) 7.25 8.20

Capt. C. A. Larsen's First Voyage to South Georgia A25

17p, Map of Jason Harbor. 35p, Castor, 1886. 40p, Hertha, 1884. 65p, Jason, 1881.

1994, Dec. 1

194 A25 17p multi .70 .75
195 A25 35p multi 1.30 1.75
196 A25 40p multi 1.80 2.00
197 A25 65p multi 3.00 3.25
Nos. 194-197 (4) 6.80 7.75

End of World War II, 50th Anniv.
Common Design Types

#198, HMS Queen of Bermuda moored at Leith Harbor. #199, 4-inch gun, Hansen Point, four men of Norwegian Defense Force.
£1, Reverse of War Medal 1939-45.

Wmk. 384

1995, May 8 Litho. *Perf. 14*

198 CD351 50p multicolored 4.00 4.25
199 CD351 50p multicolored 4.00 4.25
a. Pair, #198-199 8.00 9.00

Souvenir Sheet

Wmk. 373

200 CD352 £1 multicolored 6.50 7.00

No. 199a is a continuous design.

Yachts — A26

Wmk. 373

1995, Nov. 16 Litho. *Perf. 14½*

201 A26 35p Damien II 1.60 1.75
202 A26 40p Curlew 2.00 2.25
203 A26 76p Mischief 3.75 4.00
Nos. 201-203 (3) 7.35 8.00

Sir Ernest Shackleton's King Haakon Bay-Stromness Trek, 80th Anniv. — A27

Designs: 15p, Shackleton, Ridge 2493 Point of No Return. 20p, Frank Worsley, King Haakon Bay from Shackleton Gap. 30p, Map of Shackleton's route. 65p, Tom Crean, Manager's Villa, Stromness Whaling Station.

Wmk. 384

1996, May 20 Litho. *Perf. 14*

204 A27 15p multicolored 1.00 1.00
205 A27 20p multicolored 1.25 1.25
206 A27 30p multicolored 2.00 2.00
207 A27 65p multicolored 3.75 3.75
Nos. 204-207 (4) 8.00 8.00

Chinstrap Penguins — A28

Perf. 14½x14

1996, Nov. 8 Litho. Wmk. 373

208 A28 17p Swimming 1.00 1.00
209 A28 35p Male, female 1.25 1.25
210 A28 40p Feeding chicks 2.00 2.00
211 A28 76p Feeding on krill 3.50 3.50
a. Souvenir sheet of 1, perf. 14x14½ 4.25 4.75
Nos. 208-211 (4) 7.75 7.75

Return of Hong Kong to China (#211a).

Queen Elizabeth and Prince Philip, 50th Wedding Anniv. — A29

#212, Queen. #213, Prince driving team of horses. #214, Queen looking at horses. #215, Prince. #216, Princess Anne on horseback, Queen. #217, Prince, child on horseback.
£1.50, Queen, Prince in open carriage, horiz.

Perf. 14½x14

1997, July 10 Litho. Wmk. 384

212 15p multicolored .90 .90
213 15p multicolored .90 .90
a. A29 Pair, #212-213 2.25 2.25
214 17p multicolored 1.00 1.00
215 17p multicolored 1.00 1.00
a. A29 Pair, #214-215 2.75 2.75
216 40p multicolored 2.50 2.50
217 40p multicolored 2.50 2.50
a. A29 Pair, #216-217 6.00 6.00
Nos. 212-217 (6) 8.80 8.80

Souvenir Sheet

218 A29 £1.50 multicolored 8.00 8.25

Flora and Fauna — A30

a, Reindeer. b, Antarctic tern. c, Gray-headed albatross. d, King penguin. e, Prickly burr. f, Fur seal.

Perf. 14½x14

1998, Mar. 16 Litho. Wmk. 373

219 A30 35p Sheet of 6, #a.-f. 10.00 9.00

Diana, Princess of Wales (1961-97)
Common Design Type

Designs: a, Looking left. b, In white evening dress. c, In red dress. d, In white.

1998, Mar. 31

220 CD355 35p Sheet of 4, #a.-d. 4.50 5.00

No. 220 sold for £1.40 + 20p, with surtax and 50% of the profits from the issue being donated to the Princess Diana Memorial Fund.

Tourism A31

Designs: 30p, MS Explorer. 35p, Wandering albatross. 40p, Elephant seal. 65p, Post Office, King Edward Point.

Wmk. 373

1998, Sept. 28 Litho. *Perf. 14½*

221 A31 30p multicolored 2.50 1.50
222 A31 35p multicolored 2.75 1.75
223 A31 40p multicolored 2.75 2.00
224 A31 65p multicolored 3.25 3.25
Nos. 221-224 (4) 11.25 8.50

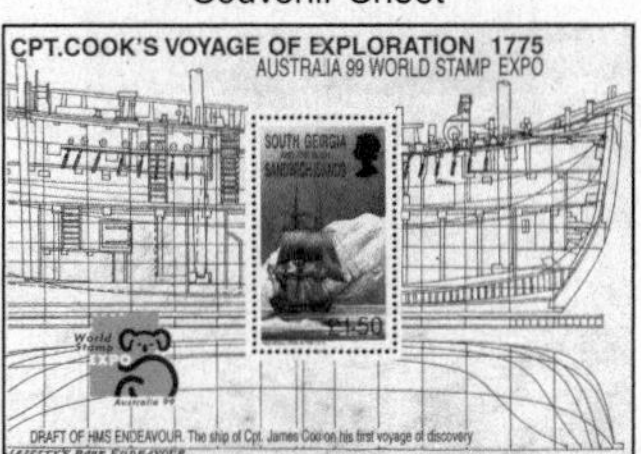

Island Views A32

Designs: 9p, Grytviken and Sugartop Mountain. 17p, Old sealing ships, Grytviken. 35p, King Edward Point. 40p, Arrival at South Georgia. 65p, Church, Grytviken.

Wmk. 384

1999, Jan. 4 Litho. *Perf. 14*

225 A32 9p multicolored 2.00 .85
226 A32 17p multicolored 2.75 1.25
227 A32 35p multicolored 3.75 1.75
228 A32 40p multicolored 3.75 1.75
229 A32 65p multicolored 5.25 2.00
Nos. 225-229 (5) 17.50 7.60

Souvenir Sheet

CPT.COOK'S VOYAGE OF EXPLORATION 1775
AUSTRALIA 99 WORLD STAMP EXPO

Capt. James Cook's Ship HMS Resolution, 1773 — A33

1999, Mar. 5 *Perf. 13½*

230 A33 £1.50 multicolored 20.00 16.00

Australia '99, World Stamp Expo.

Queen Mother's Century
Common Design Type

Queen Mother: 25p, At air raid shelter, 1940. 30p, With Prince Edward, Lady Sarah Armstrong-Jones, Viscount Linley, 70th birthday. 35p, With Prince William, 94th birthday. 40p, As colonel-in-chief of Royal Anglian Regiment.

£1, Funeral procession for Queen Victoria, portrait of Victoria.

Wmk. 384

1999, Aug. 18 Litho. *Perf. 13½*

231 CD358 25p multicolored 3.00 3.00
232 CD358 30p black 3.25 3.50
233 CD358 35p multicolored 4.00 4.00
234 CD358 40p multicolored 4.50 4.50
Nos. 231-234 (4) 14.75 15.00

Souvenir Sheet

235 CD358 £1 black 15.00 15.00

Birds — A34

Designs: 1p, Chinstrap penguin, vert. 2p, White chinned petrel. 5p, Gray backed storm petrel, vert. 10p, South Georgia pipit, vert. 11p, Gray headed albatross. 30p, Blue petrel, vert. 35p, Black browed albatross. 40p, South Georgia diving petrel. 50p, Macaroni penguin, vert. £1, Light mantled sooty albatross. £3, South Georgia pintail. £5, King penguin, vert.

Wmk. 384

1999, Nov. 15 Litho. *Perf. 14*

236 A34 1p multicolored 1.00 *1.40*
237 A34 2p multicolored 1.25 *1.40*
238 A34 5p multicolored 1.50 *1.50*
239 A34 10p multicolored 1.75 *1.75*
240 A34 11p multicolored 1.90 1.90
241 A34 30p multicolored 2.75 *3.00*
242 A34 35p multicolored 3.00 3.00
243 A34 40p multicolored 3.25 3.00
244 A34 50p multicolored 3.75 *3.75*
245 A34 £1 multicolored 6.25 *6.25*
246 A34 £3 multicolored 14.00 *15.00*
247 A34 £5 multicolored 20.00 *21.00*
Nos. 236-247 (12) 60.40 62.95

Millennium — A35

Perf. 14½x14¼

1999, Dec. 18 Litho. Wmk. 384

248 A35 11p Sunrise 2.00 2.00
249 A35 11p Church 2.00 2.00
250 A35 11p Albatrosses 2.00 2.00
251 A35 35p Penguins 3.00 3.00
252 A35 35p Reindeer 3.00 3.00
253 A35 35p Sunset 3.00 3.00
Nos. 248-253 (6) 15.00 15.00

Sir Ernest Shackleton (1874-1922), Polar Explorer — A36

Designs: 35p, Voyage across Scotia Sea, 1916. 40p, Shackleton, Thomas Crean and Frank Worsley crossing South Georgia. 65p, Shackleton's grave.

2000, Feb. 20 Wmk. 373 *Perf. 14*

254 A36 35p multi 7.00 6.00
255 A36 40p multi 8.00 6.25
256 A36 65p multi 9.00 7.50
Nos. 254-256 (3) 24.00 19.75

See British Antarctic Territory Nos. 285-287, Falkland Islands Nos. 758-760.

Prince William, 18th Birthday
Common Design Type

William: 25p, In suit, carrying bag, vert. 30p, With ski equipment, vert. 35p, Wearing suit and wearing sweater. 40p, In suit, waving. 50p, In beret, saluting.

Perf. 13¾x14¼, 14¼x13¾

2000, June 21 Litho. Wmk. 373

Stamps With White Border

257 CD359 25p multi 3.00 3.00
258 CD359 30p multi 3.00 3.00
259 CD359 35p multi 3.25 3.25
260 CD359 40p multi 3.75 3.50
Nos. 257-260 (4) 13.00 12.75

Souvenir Sheet

Stamps Without White Border

Perf. 14¼

261 Sheet of 5 16.00 16.00
a. CD359 25p multi 2.25 2.25
b. CD359 30p multi 2.50 2.50
c. CD359 35p multi 2.75 2.75
d. CD359 40p multi 3.00 3.00
e. CD359 50p multi 3.25 3.25

King Penguins — A37

#262, 37p, Penguins at sea. #263, 37p, Adult & creche. #264, 43p, Advertisement walk & courtship. #265, 43p, Nesting.

Perf. 14¾x14

2000, Oct. 16 Litho. Wmk. 373

262-265 A37 Set of 4 21.00 20.00

Royal Fleet Auxiliary Vessels A38

Designs: No. 266, 37p, RFA Sir Percivale. No. 267, 37p, RFA Tidespring. No. 268, 43p, RFA Diligence. No. 269, 43p, RFA Gold Rover.

Wmk. 373

2001, May 28 Litho. *Perf. 14*

266-269 A38 Set of 4 20.00 20.00

Marine Life — A39

Designs: 33p, Icefish. No. 271, 37p, Spiny back crab. No. 272, 37p, Krill, vert. 43p, Toothfish, vert.

Wmk. 373

2001, Oct. 22 Litho. *Perf. 13¾*

270-273 A39 Set of 4 20.00 20.00

Reign Of Queen Elizabeth II, 50th Anniv. Issue
Common Design Type

Designs: Nos. 274, 278a, 20p, With dog, 1952. Nos. 275, 278b, 37p, With Prince Philip, 1997. Nos. 276, 278c, 43p, Examining royal stamp collection, 1946. Nos. 277, 278d, 50p, Wearing blue hat, 1999. No. 278e, 50p, 1955 portrait by Annigoni (38x50mm).

Perf. 14¼x14½, 13¾ (#278e)

2002, Feb. 6 Litho. Wmk. 373

With Gold Frames

274 CD360 20p multicolored 1.50 1.50
275 CD360 37p multicolored 3.00 3.00
276 CD360 43p multicolored 3.50 3.50
277 CD360 50p multicolored 4.00 4.00
Nos. 274-277 (4) 12.00 12.00

Souvenir Sheet

Without Gold Frames

278 CD360 Sheet of 5, #a-e 16.00 16.50

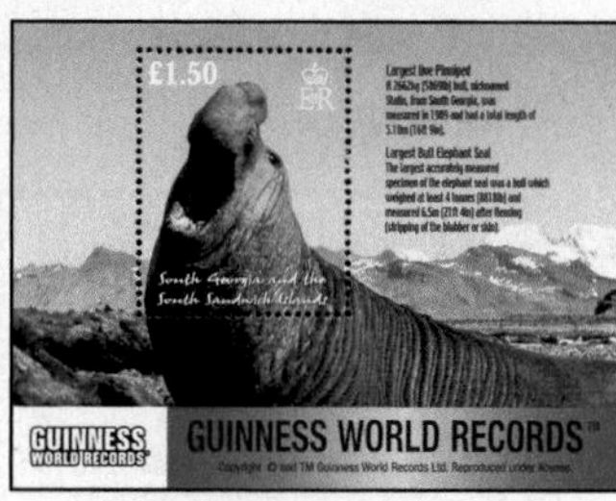

World Record Animals — A40

No. 279: a, 10p, Fin whale. b, 10p, Blue whale. c, 20p, Sperm whale. d, 37p, Leopard seal with mouth open. e, 37p, Leopard seal on ice. f, 43p, Elephant seal.

£1.50, Elephant seal, diff.

2002, Mar. 2 Litho. *Perf. 13¾*

279 A40 Sheet of 6, #a-f 18.00 18.00

Souvenir Sheet

280 A40 £1.50 multi 20.00 20.00

Queen Mother Elizabeth (1900-2002)
Common Design Type

Designs: 22p, Wearing hat (black and white photograph). 40p, Wearing tiara. Nos. 283, 285a, 45p, Holding dog (black and white photograph). Nos. 284, 285b, 95p, Wearing white stole.

Perf. 14¼, 13¾x14¼ (#283-284)

2002, Aug. 5 Litho. Wmk. 373

With Purple Frames

281 CD361 22p multicolored 1.00 1.00
282 CD361 40p multicolored 2.00 2.00
283 CD361 45p multicolored 2.25 2.25
284 CD361 95p multicolored 5.25 5.25
Nos. 281-284 (4) 10.50 10.50

Souvenir Sheet

Without Purple Frames

Perf. 14½x14¼

285 CD361 Sheet of 2, #a-b 9.00 9.00

Antarctic Fur Seals — A41

Designs: No. 286, 40p, Seal in water. No. 287, 40p, Two seals on ice. No. 288, 45p, Six seals. No. 289, 45p, One seal.

Wmk. 373

2002, Oct. 25 Litho. *Perf. 13¾*

286-289 A41 Set of 4 21.50 21.50

Worldwide Fund for Nature (WWF) — A42

Gray-headed albatross: 40p, Adults at nesting ground. No. 291, 45p, Adult and chick (WWF emblem at LL). No. 292, 45p, Two adults (WWF emblem at UL). 70p, Bird's head.

Wmk. 373

2003, Jan. 7 Litho. *Perf. 14*

290-293 A42 Set of 4 9.75 9.75
293a Strip of 4 11.00 11.00

Head of Queen Elizabeth II
Common Design Type

Wmk. 373

2003, June 2 Litho. *Perf. 13¾*

294 CD362 £2 multi 8.50 8.50

Prince William, 21st Birthday
Common Design Type

No. 295: a, Color photograph at right. b, Color photograph at left.

Wmk. 373

2003, June 21 Litho. *Perf. 14¼*

295 Horiz. pair 8.50 8.50
a.-b. CD364 70p Either single 4.00 4.00

History of South Georgia — A43

No. 296: a, HMS Sappho visits Grytviken, 1906. b, Norwegian reindeer introduced, 1911. c, Largest blue whale landed, 1912. d, Shackleton's island crossing, 1916. e, Shackleton Memorial Cross, 1922. f, Discovery investigations, 1925. g, First powered flight over South Georgia, 1938. h, Operation Tabarin, 1943. i, Duke of Edinburgh visits, 1957. j, Bird Island Research Station, 1958. k, Mt. Paget climbed, 1964. l, Liberation of the island, 1982. m, Royal charter and crest, 1985. n, Museum inaugurated, 1992. o, Applied fishery research, 2001. p, Grytviken remedial work, 2003.

Wmk. 373

2004, Feb. 6 Litho. *Perf. 13¼*

296 A43 40p Sheet of 16, #a-p 40.00 40.00

Royal Navy Ships A44

Designs: 10p, HMS Ajax. 25p, HMS Amazon. 45p, HMS Dartmouth. 50p, HMS Penelope. 70p, HMS St. Austell Bay. £1, HMS Plymouth.

Wmk. 373

2004, Apr. 26 Litho. *Perf. 14*

297-302 A44 Set of 6 21.00 16.00

Merchant Ships A45

Designs: No. 303, 42p, RMS Queen Elizabeth 2. No. 304, 42p, MS Endeavour. 50p, MS Lindblad Explorer. 75p, SS Canberra.

Perf. 13¼x13½

2004, Nov. 10 Litho.

303-306 A45 Set of 4 16.00 15.50

Animal Juveniles — A46

Designs: 1p, Skua. 2p, Reindeer. 3p, Antarctic prion, horiz. 5p, Humpback whale, horiz. 10p, Gentoo penguins. 25p, Antarctic fur seal. 50p, South Georgia pintail, horiz. 75p, Light-mantled sooty albatross. £1, Weddell seal, horiz. £2, King penguin, horiz. £3, Southern right whale, horiz. £5, Wandering albatross.

(42p), Elephant seal, horiz.

Perf. 13½x13¼, 13¼x13½

2004, Nov. 15 Wmk. 373

307	A46	1p multi	1.00	1.20
308	A46	2p multi	1.00	1.20
309	A46	3p multi	1.00	1.20
310	A46	5p multi	1.00	1.20
311	A46	10p multi	1.00	1.20
312	A46	25p multi	1.20	1.20
313	A46	50p multi	2.40	2.40
314	A46	75p multi	3.50	3.50
315	A46	£1 multi	4.75	4.75
316	A46	£2 multi	8.50	8.50
317	A46	£3 multi	12.00	12.00
318	A46	£5 multi	19.00	18.00
		Nos. 307-318 (12)	56.35	56.35

Booklet Stamp

Self-Adhesive

Unwmk.

Serpentine Die Cut 12½

319	A46 (42p) multi		2.50	2.50
a.	Booklet pane of 4		10.00	
	Complete booklet, 2 #319a		20.00	

No. 319 is inscribed "Airmail Postcard."

Grytviken, Cent. — A47

Designs: 24p, Capt. Carl Anton Larsen, founder of Grytviken. 42p, Grytviken from Mount Hodges. 50p, Whale catcher Fortuna. £1, Ski jumper.

2004, Dec. 10 Wmk. 373 *Perf. 13¾*

320-323 A47 Set of 4 11.50 11.50

Duncan Carse (1913-2004), Survey Expedition Leader — A48

Designs: No. 324, 50p, Carse. No. 325, 50p, Map of South Georgia, surveyors. 75p, Carse as radio broadcaster. £1, AMOW, Carse's hut, Undine South.

Wmk. 373

2005, Sept. 26 Litho. *Perf. 13¾*

324-327 A48 Set of 4 14.00 14.00

A49

A50

A51

A52

A53

Penguins A54

2005, Nov. 1 *Perf. 14*

328	A49	45p multi	3.25	3.25
329	A50	45p multi	3.25	3.25
330	A51	45p multi	3.25	3.25
331	A52	45p multi	3.25	3.25
332	A53	45p multi	3.25	3.25
333	A54	45p multi	3.25	3.25
		Nos. 328-333 (6)	19.50	19.50

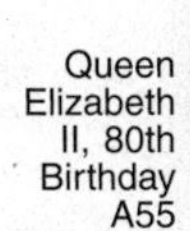

Queen Elizabeth II, 80th Birthday A55

Queen: No. 334, 50p, As child, with dog. Nos. 335, 338a, 50p, As young woman. Nos. 336, 338b, 75p, As older woman. £1, Wearing hat.

2006, Apr. 21 Litho. *Perf. 14*

With White Frames

334-337 A55 Set of 4 10.50 10.50

Souvenir Sheet

Without White Frames

338 A55 Sheet of 2, #a-b 9.00 9.00

BirdLife International A56

Birds: 24p, Black-browed albatross. 45p, Southern giant petrel. 50p, White-chinned petrel. 75p, Wandering albatross.

No. 343: a, Black-browed albatross, diff. b, White-chinned petrel, diff.

Wmk. 373

2006, Oct. 18 Litho. *Perf. 13¾*

339-342 A56 Set of 4 12.00 12.00

Souvenir Sheet

343 A56 £1 Sheet of 2, #a-b 13.00 13.00

Communications — A57

Designs: 25p, Mail drop from Royal Air Force Hercules plane. 50p, Radio/wireless room. 60p, MV Sigma. £1.05, SS Fleurus.

Perf. 14¼x14

2006, Nov. 30 Litho. Wmk. 373

344-347 A57 Set of 4 14.50 14.50

Mapping — A58

No. 348, 50p: a, Map of Neumayer Glacier, 1958. b, Map of Neumayer Glacier, 2003.

No. 349, 60p: a, Kern DKM1 theodolite and map. b, Landsat 7 satellite.

2007, Jan. 5 *Perf. 13¾*

Horiz. Pairs, #a-b

348-349 A58 Set of 2 14.50 14.50

Falkland Islands War, 25th Anniv. — A59

Designs: 25p, Ellerbeck Peak, Wasp helicopter. 50p, Stanley Peak, Wessex 3 helicopter. 60p, Sheridan Peak, Royal Marines Commandos. £1.05, Mills Peak, Royal Marines.

Perf. 12½x13

2007, Apr. 25 Litho. Wmk. 373

350-353	A59	Set of 4	14.50	14.50
353a		Souvenir sheet, #350-353	14.50	14.50

On No. 353a, the bottom perforations of Nos. 352-353 measure 13¼.

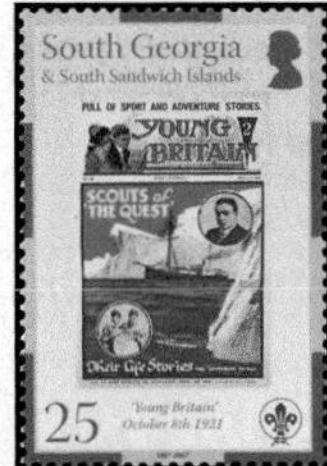

Scouting, Cent. — A60

Designs: 25p, Cover of Oct. 8, 1921 *Young Britain* magazine. 50p, Scouts James Marr and Norman Mooney raising flag on the Quest. 60p, Marr and Mooney with Sir Ernest Shackleton. 85p, Autographed postcard depicting Marr. £1.05, The Quest locked in ice.

Perf. 14¼

2007, Oct. 15 Litho. Unwmk.

354-358 A60 Set of 5 19.00 19.00

Intl. Polar Year A61

Designs: 50p, Zoological Building, Moltke Base. 60p, Meteorological Station, King Edward Point. 85p, Zooplankton. £1.05, Leopard seals.

2008, Jan. 25 Litho. *Perf. 14¼x14*

359-362 A61 Set of 4 16.00 16.00

Marine Stewardship Council — A62

Ships and marine life: 50p, Longliner, Patagonian toothfish. 60p, Trawler, Mackerel icefish. 85p, Krill trawler and refrigerator ship, Krill. £1.05, Fishery Patrol Vessel Pharos SG.

Perf. 14¼

2008, May 1 Litho. Unwmk.

363-366 A62 Set of 4 16.50 16.50

Worldwide Fund for Nature (WWF) — A63

Chinstrap penguins: No. 367, 55p, Three adults. No. 368, 55p, Two adults and a chick. 65p, Three adults in water. 90p, Two adults.

2008, July 10 Litho. *Perf. 14*

367-370	A63	Set of 4	11.00	11.00
370a		Souvenir sheet of 4, #367-370	13.50	13.50

Falkland Islands Dependencies Letter Patent, Cent. — A64

Designs: 27p, H.M.S. Sappho. 65p, Magistrate's Residence, Grytviken. 90p, James Innes Wilson, 1909-1914 Magistrate. £1.10, S.S. Coronda.

2008, Nov. 30 Litho. *Perf. 14*

371-374 A64 Set of 4 14.50 14.50

Souvenir Sheet

Preservation of Polar Regions — A65

No. 375 — Antarctic ozone map of: a, September 2008. b, September 1979.

Serpentine Die Cut

2009, Apr. 2 Litho.

Self-Adhesive

375 A65 £1.10 Sheet of 2, #a-b 11.50 11.50

Naval Aviation, Cent. A66

Royal Navy aircraft and ships: 27p, Supermarine Walrus, HMS Exeter. 65p, Westland Wasp HASI helicopter, HMS Plymouth. 90p, Westland Whirlwind HARI helicopter, HMS Protector. £1.10, Agusta Westland AW101 Merlin helicopter, HMS Lancaster.

2009, May 27 Litho. *Perf. 14*

376-379 A66 Set of 4 14.00 14.00

Ernest H. Shackleton (1874-1922), Explorer — A67

Designs: 1p, Shackleton at age 11. 2p, Shackleton at age 16. 5p, Shackleton on Discovery Expedition, 1902. 10p, Shackleton's wife, Emily, and children, Raymond, Cecily and Edward. 27p, Shackleton, Frank Wild, Dr. Eric Marshall and Jameson Adams aboard the *Nimrod*, 1909. 55p, *Endurance* trapped in ice. 65p, Launching the lifeboat *James Caird*, horiz. 90p, Shackleton, Frank Worsley and Tom Crean after crossing South Georgia, horiz. £1, Shackleton as Major. £2, Ship *Quest*. £3, Shackleton's grave, horiz. £5, Shackleton at desk, horiz.

2009, Aug. 14 Litho. *Perf. 14*

380	A67	1p multi	.25	.25
381	A67	2p multi	.30	.30
382	A67	5p multi	.40	.40
383	A67	10p multi	.50	.50
384	A67	27p multi	1.00	1.00
385	A67	55p multi	2.00	2.00
386	A67	65p multi	2.50	2.30
387	A67	90p multi	3.25	3.25
388	A67	£1 multi	3.50	3.50
389	A67	£2 multi	7.50	7.50
390	A67	£3 multi	11.00	11.00
391	A67	£5 multi	17.50	17.50
		Nos. 380-391 (12)	49.70	49.50

Corals — A68

Designs: 55p, Thouarella sp. 65p, Paragorgia sp. 90p, Stylaster sp. £1.40, Thouarella sp., diff.

2009, Nov. 9 Litho. *Perf. 13¼*

392-395 A68 Set of 4 13.00 13.00

South Georgia Post Office, Cent. — A69

No. 396, 65p: a, SS Cachelote, first mail ship. b, Old postal hut.

No. 397, 90p: a, Post Office, 2009. b, FPV Pharos SG, current mail ship.

2009, Dec. 23 Litho. *Perf. 14*

Horiz. Pairs, #a-b

396-397 A69 Set of 2 13.50 13.50

Cephalopods A70

Designs: 27p, Galiteuthis glacialis. 65p, Psychroteuthis glacialis. 90p, Thaumeledone gunteri. £1.10, Stauroteuthis gilchristi.

£2, Mesonychoteuthis hamiltoni, Physeter macrocephalus.

2010, Apr. 7 *Perf. 13¼*

398-401 A70 Set of 4 9.25 9.25

Souvenir Sheet

402 A70 £2 multi 6.50 6.50

No. 402 contains one 51x51mm stamp.

Miniature Sheet

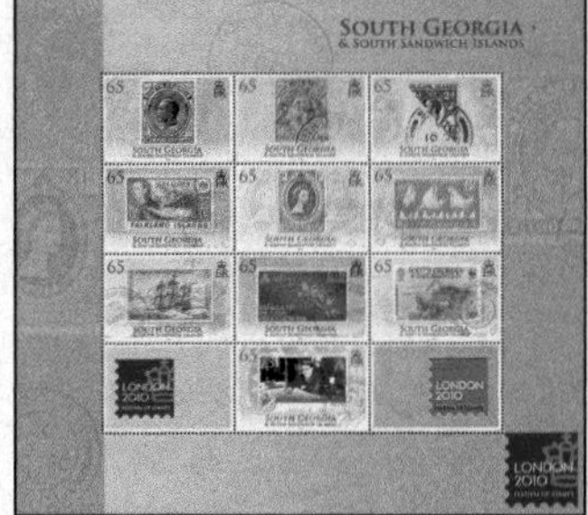

London 2010 Festival of Stamps — A71

No. 403: a, South Georgia essay depicting King George V. b, Falkland Islands #52. c, Bisect of Falkland Islands #56. d, Falkland Islands Dependencies #3L8. e, Falkland Islands Dependencies #1L18. f, South Georgia #13. g, South Georgia #42. h, Falkland Islands Dependencies #1LB1. i, South Georgia & South Sandwich Islands #165. j, South Georgia & South Sandwich Islands #391.

2010, Apr. 12 *Perf. 14x14¾*

403 A71 65p Sheet of 10, #a-j, + 2 labels 22.00 22.00

Shipwrecks and Hulks — A72

Designs: 60p, Bayard. 70p, Dias, Albatros. 95p, Karrakatta. £1.15, Petrel.

2010, June 25 *Perf. 14x14¾*

404-407 A72 Set of 4 12.00 12.00

William Hodges (1744-97), Artist on Second Pacific Expedition of Capt. James Cook — A73

Artwork by Hodges depicting: No. 408, 70p, The Resolution. No. 409, 70p, Monuments on Easter Island, horiz. 95p, Capt. Cook. £1.15, Possession Bay, South Georgia, horiz.

2010, Sept. 30 *Perf. 13¾*

408-411 A73 Set of 4 11.00 11.00

Flora — A74

Designs: 27p, Small fern. 70p, Water blinks. 95p, Antarctic pearlwort. £1.15, Adder's tongue.

2010, Dec. 15 *Perf. 13x13¼*

412-415 A74 Set of 4 13.00 13.00

Pets — A75

Designs: 45p, Vervet monkey. 60p, Anne-Marie Sorlle with puppies. 70p, Whalers with dog and fox. 95p, Nan Brown with penguin, Stugie. £1.15, Perce Blackborow and cat, Mrs. Chippy. £1.20, Sir Ernest Shackleton and puppy, Query.

2011, Feb. 15 *Perf. 13¼*

416-421 A75 Set of 6 18.50 18.50

Sir Alister Hardy (1896-1985), Marine Biologist — A76

Hardy and: 60p, Continuous plankton recorder type II. 70p, Microscope. 95p, Whaling Station, Grytviken. £1.15, RRS Discovery.

2011, Mar. 15 *Perf. 13¼x13½*

422-425 A76 Set of 4 11.50 11.50

Wedding of Prince William and Catherine Middleton — A77

Couple: 70p, Laughing at rugby match. 95p, In St. James's Palace. £1.15, At wedding ceremony.

£2, Wedding portrait, vert.

2011, July 25 Litho. *Perf. 14*

426-428 A77 Set of 3 9.50 9.50

Souvenir Sheet

Perf. 14¾x14

429 A77 £2 multi 6.75 6.75

No. 429 contains one 32x48mm stamp.

Paintings of Petrels by John Gale — A78

Designs: 60p, Southern Giant Petrel. 70p, Snow Petrels. 95p, Cape Petrel. £1.15, South Georgia Diving Petrels.

2011, Aug. 10 *Perf. 13½*

430-433 A78 Set of 4 11.50 11.50

Filming in South Georgia of *Frozen Planet* Television Series A79

Designs: 60p, Elephant seals. 70p, Wandering albatross on ground. 95p, Blonde fur seal pup. £1.15, King penguin and juveniles. £2.50, Wandering albatross in flight.

2011, Sept. 15 *Perf. 13¼x13¾*

434-437 A79 Set of 4 11.00 11.00

Souvenir Sheet

438 A79 £2.50 multi 8.00 8.00

Polar Explorers — A80

No. 439, 60p: a, Frank Wild (1873-1939), expedition ship Discovery and Polar Medal. b, Capt. Robert Falcon Scott (1868-1912) and Discovery.

No. 440, 70p: a, Wild, members of Nimrod expedition, British flag and Polar Medal. b, Ernest Shackleton (1874-1922) and expedition ship Nimrod.

No. 441, 95p: a, Wild, members of Aurora expedition and Polar Medal. b, Douglas Mawson (1882-1958) and expedition ship Aurora.

No. 442, £1.15: a, Wild, members of Endurance expedition and Polar Medal. c, Shackleton and expedition ship Endurance.

2011, Nov. 23 *Perf. 14¼*

Horiz. Pairs, #a-b

439-442 A80 Set of 4 21.50 21.50

Miniature Sheet

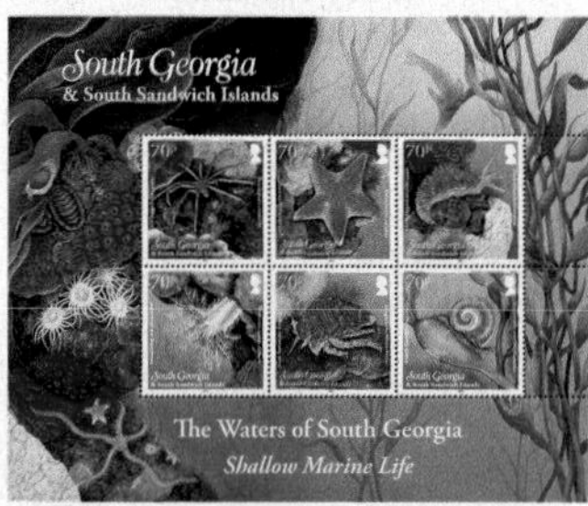

Marine Life — A81

No. 443: a, Ten-legged sea spider. b, Pink cushion seastar. c, White-tipped nudibranch. d, Branching sea cucumber. e, Giant Antarctic isopod. f, South Georgia top shell.

2012, Jan. 1 *Perf. 13¼*

443 A81 70p Sheet of 6, #a-f 13.50 13.50

Worldwide Fund for Nature (WWF) — A82

Birds: Nos. 444, 448a, 60p, Imperial shags. Nos. 445, 448b, 70p, Antarctic terns. Nos. 446, 448c, 95p, Southern skuas. Nos. 447, 448d, £1.15, Kelp gulls.

£3.50, Southern skua and chicks.

2012, Mar. 10 *Perf. 14*

Stamps With White Frames

444-447 A82 Set of 4 12.00 12.00

Stamps Without White Frame

448 A82 Strip of 4, #a-d 12.00 12.00

Souvenir Sheet

449 A82 £3.50 multi 16.00 16.00

No. 448 was printed in sheets of 16 containing four each Nos. 448a-448d.

Reign of Queen Elizabeth II, 60th Anniv. — A83

Photograph of Queen Elizabeth II from: 60p, 1952. 70p, 1977. 95p, 2002. £1.15, 2012.

£3, Queen Elizabeth II in 1957.

2012, May 28 Litho. *Perf. 13½*

450-453 A83 Set of 4 10.50 10.50

Souvenir Sheet

454 A83 £3 multi 9.25 9.25

No. 454 contains one 30x48mm stamp.

Blue Whales — A84

Blue whale: 65p, Underwater. 75p, At water's surface. £1, Blowhole, with bird in flight. £1.20, Flukes.

2012, Aug. 31 *Perf. 13¼*
455-458 A84 Set of 4 11.50 11.50

Marine Protected Area — A85

Designs: No. 459, 65p, King penguins and Fisheries Protection Vessel Pharos SG. No. 460, 65p, Elephant seals and cruise ship. No. 461, 75p, Adult gray-headed albatrosses in flight, chick on scale. No. 462, 75p, Patagonian toothfish and fishing boats. £1, Antarctic krill, lantern fish and squid. £1.20, Benthic fauna.

2012, Nov. 9 *Perf. 13¾*
459-464 A85 Set of 6 16.00 16.00

Mountains and Explorers — A86

No. 465, 65p: a, Stenhouse Peak. b, Commander Joseph R. Stenhouse (1887-1941).
No. 466, 75p: a, Mount Carse. b, Verner Duncan Carse (1913-2004).
No. 467, £1: a, Mount Paget and Allardyce Range. b, Sir William Lamond Allardyce (1861-1930).

2012, Dec. 11 *Perf. 14*
Horiz. Pairs, #a-b
465-467 A86 Set of 3 16.00 16.00

Star Trails A87

Star trails over: 65p, Harker Glacier. 75p, Maiviken Hut. £1, Shipwrecks of the Albatros and Dias. £1.20, Hope Point Memorial Cross.

2013, June 4 *Perf. 13¼x13½*
468-471 A87 Set of 4 11.50 11.50

Sir Rex Hunt (1926-2012), Governor of Falkland Islands — A88

South Georgia and South Sandwich Islands coat of arms and Hunt: 65p, At scene of helicopter crash. 75p, In front of Government House, 1982. £1, Holding coins to commemorate the 25th anniv. of the liberation of the Falkland Islands, 2007. £1.20, Wearing red jacket.

2013, June 11 *Perf. 14*
472-475 A88 Set of 4 11.50 11.50

Coronation of Queen Elizabeth II, 60th Anniv. — A89

Queen Elizabeth II: 65p, Wearing tiara before coronation. 75p, In carriage, wearing crown after coronation. £1, On balcony of Buckingham Palace. £1.20, Holding orb and scepter.

2013, July 22 *Perf. 13½x13¼*
476-479 A89 Set of 4 11.00 11.00

Shallow Marine Surveys Group A90

Marine life: Nos. 480, 484a, 65p, Chiton. Nos. 481, 484b, 75p, Anemone. Nos. 482, 484c, £1, Crocodile fish. Nos. 483, 484d, £1.20, Brittle star.
No. 485a, £1, Starfish, vert.

2013, Aug. 29 *Perf. 13¼x13½*
Stamps With White Frames
480-483 A90 Set of 4 11.50 11.50
Stamps Without White Frames
484 A90 Strip of 4, #a-d 11.50 11.50

Souvenir Sheet
Perf. 13½x13¼
485 A90 Sheet of 3 (see footnote) 9.75 9.75
a. A90 £1 multi 3.25 3.25

No. 485 contains No. 485a, Ascension No. 1104a and Falkland Islands No. 1107a. This sheet was sold in Ascension, Falkland Islands and South Georgia and the South Sandwich Islands.

Habitat Restoration A91

Emblem of South Georgia Heritage Trust and: 5p, RRS Ernest Shackleton. 30p, Bölkow BO-105 helicopters. 65p, Workers loading bait hoppers on helicopter. 75p, Rat eating bait. £1, South Georgia pintails. £1.20, South Georgia pipit.

2013, Dec. 15 **Litho.** *Perf. 13¾*
486-491 A91 Set of 6 13.00 13.00

Whalers Church, Grytviken, Cent. — A92

Designs: 30p, Church under construction. 50p, Capt. Carl A. Larsen (1860-1924), Antarctic explorer. 65p, People at church service. 75p, Church exterior. £1, Church and helicopter. £1.20, Church at night.

2013, Dec. 24 **Litho.** *Perf. 13¼*
492-497 A92 Set of 6 14.50 14.50

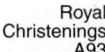

Royal Christenings A93

Photographs from christening of: 65p, Queen Elizabeth II. 75p, Prince Charles. £1, Prince William. £1.20, Prince George.

2014, June 23 **Litho.** *Perf. 13¼x13*
498-501 A93 Set of 4 12.50 12.50

Reindeer on South Georgia A94

Designs: 65p, Introduction of reindeer, 1911. 75p, Female reindeer, calf, penguin. £1, Reindeer grazing. £1.20, Reindeer eradication.

2014, Oct. 14 **Litho.** *Perf. 14*
502-505 A94 Set of 4 12.00 12.00

Frank Worsley (1872-1943), Member of Imperial Trans-Antarctic Expedition — A95

Designs: 65p, Worsley wearing captain's hat. 75p, Worsley and Reginald James observing stars. £1, Worsely and Lionel Greenstreet looking across King Edward Cove. £1.20, Worsley and expedition leader Ernest Shackleton onboard the ice-trapped ship Endurance.

2014, Nov. 5 **Litho.** *Perf. 14*
506-509 A95 Set of 4 12.00 12.00

Tom Crean (1877-1938), Member of Imperial Trans-Antarctic Expedition — A96

Designs: 65p, Crean with pipe in mouth. 75p, Crean with sled dog pups. £1, Launch of the boat James Caird. £1.20, Crean and other crew members on the Endurance.

2014, Nov. 5 **Litho.** *Perf. 14*
510-513 A96 Set of 4 12.00 12.00

Frank Hurley (1885-1962), Member of Imperial Trans-Antarctic Expedition — A97

Designs: 65p, Hurley and Alexander Macklin on the Endurance. 75p, Hurley and other crew near stove on Endurance. £1, Crew eating dinner on the Endurance, 1915. £1.20, Hurley and Dr. Leonard Hussey playing chess on the Endurance.

2014, Nov. 5 **Litho.** *Perf. 14*
514-517 A97 Set of 4 12.00 12.00

Explorers, Scientists and Ships A98

Designs: 1p, Bill Tilman (1898-1977), explorer, and the Mischief. 2p, Alister Hardy (1896-1985), marine biologist, and the William Scoresby. 5p, Stanley Kemp (1882-1945), marine biologist, and the Discovery. 10p, Ernest Shackleton (1874-1922), polar explorer, and the Endurance. 50p, Robert Cushman Murphy (1887-1973), ornithologist, and the Daisy. 70p, Wilhelm Filchner (1877-1957), explorer, and the Deutschland. 80p, Otto Nordenskjöld (1869-1928), polar explorer, and the Antarctic. £1, Carl Anton Larsen (1860-1924), Antarctic explorer, and the Jason. £1.25, Karl Schrader (1852-1930), astronomer, and the Moltke. £2, James Weddell (1787-1834), explorer, and the Jane. £3, Fabian von Bellingshausen (1778-1852), explorer, and the Vostok. £5, James Cook (1728-79), explorer, and the Resolution.

2015, Jan. 5 **Litho.** *Perf. 14*

518	A98	1p	multi	.25	.25
519	A98	2p	multi	.50	.50
520	A98	5p	multi	.75	.75
521	A98	10p	multi	1.00	1.00
522	A98	50p	multi	1.50	1.50
523	A98	70p	multi	2.10	2.10
524	A98	80p	multi	2.40	2.40
525	A98	£1	multi	3.00	3.00
526	A98	£1.25	multi	3.75	3.75
527	A98	£2	multi	6.00	6.00
528	A98	£3	multi	9.00	9.00
529	A98	£5	multi	15.00	15.00
	Nos. 518-529 (12)			45.25	45.25

Albatrosses — A99

Designs: 70p, Black-browed albatross. 80p, Gray-headed albatross. £1, Light-mantled albatross. £1.25, Wandering albatross.

2015, Jan. 30 **Litho.** *Perf. 13¼*
530-533 A99 Set of 4 11.50 11.50

Last British Steam Trawler A100

Inscription: No. 534, 70p, Viola of the Hellyer Boxing Fleet. No. 535, 70p, Viola on patrol, Farne Islands. 80p, Dias whaling off African coast. £1.25, Dias sealing, South Georgia.
£2.50, Viola pursuing UB-115.

2015, June 21 **Litho.** *Perf. 14*
534-537 A100 Set of 4 11.00 11.00

Souvenir Sheet

538 A100 £2.50 multi 7.75 7.75

The ship, originally named Viola, was later renamed Dias.

Queen Elizabeth II, Longest-Reigning British Monarch — A101

Queen Elizabeth II and events during her reign: 70p, Publications reporting on her coronation, 1953. 80p, Prince Philip visiting Leith Harbor, 1957. 90p, Hospital Ship Queen Elizabeth 2 at Grytviken, 1982. £1.25, Princess Royal at Shackleton's grave, 2009.

2015, Sept. 9 **Litho.** *Perf. 14*
539-542 A101 Set of 4 11.00 11.00

Queen Elizabeth II, 90th Birthday — A102

Photographs of Queen Elizabeth II from: 70p, 1968. 80p, 1954, white ballgown. 90p, 1954, slim-fitting white lace dress. £1.25, 2014.

£3, Queen Elizabeth II in 1968.

2016, Apr. 21 Litho. *Perf. 14*

543-546 A102 Set of 4 11.00 11.00

Souvenir Sheet

547 A102 £3 multi 9.00 9.00

International Association of Antarctica Tour Operators, 25th Anniv. — A103

Designs: 55p, M/V Lindblad Explorer. 70p, Tourists in rubber rafts near shore. 80p, Tourists on skis. £1, "IAATO" Yacht.

2016, May 4 Litho. *Perf. 14*

548-551 A103 Set of 4 9.00 9.00

Imperial Trans-Antarctic Expedition, Cent. — A104

Designs: 70p, Sir Ernest Shackleton, expedition leader, on the Endurance. 80p, Shackleton and dog on the Endurance. £1, Shackleto, diff. £1.25, Shackleton at Patience Camp.

2016, May 20 Litho. *Perf. 14*

552-555 A104 Set of 4 11.00 11.00

Sports A105

Designs: 55p, Long jump. 70p, High jump. 80p, Shot put. £1, Ski jumping.

2016, Aug. 1 Litho. *Perf. 13¼*

556-559 A105 Set of 4 8.00 8.00

Filming on Zavodovski Island of *Frozen Planet II* Television Series — A106

Designs: 70p, Macaroni penguins. 80p, Chinstrap penguins. £1.05, Chinstrap penguin chicks. £1.25, Mount Curry.

Perf. 13¼x13½

2016, Nov. 28 Litho.

560-563 A106 Set of 4 9.75 9.75

Albatross Conservation A107

Royal Society for the Protection of Birds emblem and: 70p, Black-browed albatrosses and fishing trawler. 80p, Light-mantled albatrosses and ship. £1.05, Gray-headed albatrosses, map of Antarctica. £1.25, Wandering albatrosses and researcher.

2017, June 25 Litho. *Perf. 13¼x13*

564-567 A107 Set of 4 10.00 10.00

567a Souvenir sheet of 4, #564-567 10.00 10.00

Landscapes — A108

Designs: 70p, Penguin River and Mount Paget. 80p, Nordenskjöld Glacier. £1.05, Abandoned sealing station, Leith Harbor. £1.25, Cape Rosa.

2017, Aug. 15 Litho. *Perf. 13¼*

568-571 A108 Set of 4 10.00 10.00

Worldwide Fund for Nature (WWF) — A109

Macaroni penguin: 70p, Courtship. 80p, Nest building. £1.05, On egg. £1.25, Feeding chick.

Perf. 13½x13¼

2017, Sept. 25 Litho.

572-575 A109 Set of 4 10.50 10.50

575a Souvenir sheet of 4, #572-575 10.50 10.50

70th Wedding Anniversary of Queen Elizabeth II and Prince Philip A110

Photograph of Queen Elizabeth II and Prince Philip from: 55p, 1951. 80c, 1970s. £1.05, 1977. £1.85, 2002.

2017, Nov. 20 Litho. *Perf. 13¼*

576-579 A110 Set of 4 10.00 10.00

Mapping — A111

No. 580, 70p: a, 1775 map by Capt. James Cook. b, HMS Resolution.

No. 581, 80p: a, 1958 map by Duncan Carse. b, Surveyor, 1951-57.

No. 582, £1.25: a, 2017 map by British Antarctic Survey satellite. b, Image of terrain overlaid with Geographical Information Systems contour lines.

2018, Feb. 5 Litho. *Perf. 13¼x13½*

Horiz. Pairs, #a-b

580-582 A111 Set of 3 15.00 15.00

Antarctic Fur Seals A112

Inscriptions: No. 583, 80p, Juvenile. No. 584, 80p, Juvenile diving. No. 585, 80p, Females. No. 586, 80p, Mother with pup. No. 587, 80p, Pup. No. 588, 80p, Blond male.

£3, Fur seals, diff.

2018, Mar. 15 Litho. *Perf. 12½x13*

583-588 A112 Set of 6 13.50 13.50

Souvenir Sheet

Perf. 12½

589 A112 £3 multi 8.50 8.50

Wedding of Prince Harry and Meghan Markle A113

Designs: 70p, Engagement photograph. 80p, Couple at Invictus Games Trials. £1.05, Couple holding hands after wedding. £1.25, Couple in carriage after wedding.

£3, Couple on steps of St. George's Chapel, vert.

Perf. 13¼x13½

2018, Aug. 14 Litho.

590-593 A113 Set of 4 9.75 9.75

Souvenir Sheet

Perf. 13½x13¼

594 A113 £3 multi 7.75 7.75

Migratory Whales A114

No. 595 — Blue whale and map of: a, 70p, Brazilian coast. b, 80p, Falkland Islands, South Georgia & South Sandwich Islands, Argentine and Antarctic coasts.

No. 596 — Humpback whale and map of: a, £1.05, Brazilian coast and Abrolhos Bank. b, £1.85, Falkland Islands, South Georgia & South Sandwich Islands, Argentine and Antarctic coasts.

2018, Oct. 18 Litho. *Perf. 13¼x13½*

Vert. Pairs, #a-b

595-596 A114 Set of 2 11.50 11.50

Imperial Trans-Antarctic Expedition Members and Their Medals — A115

No. 597, 80p: a, Thomas Orde-Lees (1877-1958). b, Order of the Parachute.

No. 598, £1.25: a, Frank Worsley (1872-1943). b, Distinguished Service Order for sinking of U-boat UC-33.

2018, Nov. 4 Litho. *Perf. 13½x13¼*

Horiz. Pairs, #a-b

597-598 A115 Set of 2 10.50 10.50

3-Dimensional Images of Grytviken Sites — A116

Designs: 70p, Grytviken Church. 80p, Grave of Ernest Shackleton. £1.05, Wreck of the Petrel. £1.85, Harpoon gun.

2019, May 10 Litho. *Perf. 13¼*

599-602 A116 Set of 4 11.50 11.50

The designs, when viewed through red and blue anaglyph glasses, become three-dimensional.

Food of South Georgia — A117

No. 603, 55p: a, Johann Reinhold Forster (1729-98), and son, George Forster (1754-94), botanists, and quotation. b, Greater burnet.

No. 604, 70p: a, Carl Anton Larsen (1860-1924), Antarctic explorer, and quotation. b, Reindeer.

No. 605, 80p: a, Anthony Bomford (1927-2003), surveyor, and quotation. b, Grytviken pigs.

Perf. 13¼x13½

2019, Aug. 15 Litho.

Horiz. Pairs, #a-b

603-605 A117 Set of 3 10.00 10.00

Habitat Restoration — A118

Designs: 40p, Tussock grass. 55p, South Georgia pipit. 70p, Greater burnet. 80p, White-chinned petrel. £1.05, Storm petrel. £1.25, South Georgia pintail.

Perf. 13¼x13½

2019, Sept. 20 Litho.

606-611 A118 Set of 6 12.00 12.00

A119

Design: Sir Ernest Shackleton (1874-1922), polar explorer, and his ship, Endurance.

2019, Nov. 20 Litho. *Perf. 13¼x13*

612 A119 £3.50 multi 9.25 9.25

Scott Polar Research Institute, cent.

SEMI-POSTAL STAMPS

Liberation of South Georgia, 10th Anniv. — SP1

Designs: 14p+6p, King Edward Point, Winter 1982. 29p+11p, Queen Elizabeth 2 in Cumberland Bay. 34p+16p, Royal Marines on South Sandwich Islands. 68p+32p, HMS Endurance and Wasp Helicopter.

Wmk. 384

1992, June 20 Litho. *Perf. 14*

B1 SP1 14p +6p multicolored	1.00	1.00
B2 SP1 29p +11p multicolored	1.75	1.75
B3 SP1 34p +16p multicolored	2.00	2.00
B4 SP1 68p +32p multicolored	4.00	4.00
a. Souvenir sheet of 4, #B1-B4	12.50	12.50
Nos. B1-B4 (4)	8.75	8.75

Surtax for Soldiers', Sailors' and Airmen's Families Association.

AIR POST STAMPS

See No. 319 for a stamp depicting an elephant seal that is inscribed "Airmail Postcard."

Penguins — AP1

Designs: No. C1, (60p), King penguins and chick. No. C2, (60p), Macaroni penguin. No. C3, (60p), Chinstrap penguins. No. C4, (60p), Gentoo penguin and juveniles.

2010, Oct. 25 Litho. *Perf. 13¾*

C1-C4 AP1 Set of 4	8.00	8.00
C4a Sheet of 8, 2 each #C1-C4	16.50	16.50

Biodiversity — AP2

Designs: No. C5, (70p), Greater burnet. No. C6, (70p), Tussac beetle. No. C7, (70p), Macaroni penguin. No. C8, (70p), Sea spider. No. C9, (70p), Crested bigscale. No. C10, (70p), Leopard seal.

Perf. 13½x13¼

2015, Dec. 21 Litho.

C5-C10 AP2 Set of 6	12.50	12.50

SOUTH KASAI

This part of a Congo province declared itself an autonomous state and in 1961 issued several series of stamps, some of which were overprints on Congo (ex-Belgian) stamps. Established nations did not recognize South Kasai as an independent state.

SOUTH MOLUCCAS

(Republik Maluku Selatan)

It appears that stamps of the so-called republic of South Moluccas were privately issued and had no postal use. Accordingly, they are not recognized as postage stamps.

SOUTH RUSSIA

sauth 'rəsh-ə

LOCATION — An area in southern Russia bordering on the Caspian and Black Seas.

A provisional government set up and maintained by General Denikin in opposition to the Bolshevik forces in Russia following the downfall of the Empire. The stamps were used in the field postal service established for carrying on communication between the various armies united in the revolt. These armies included the Don Cossacks, the Kuban Cossacks, and also the neighboring southern Russian people in favor of the counter-revolution against the Bolsheviks.

100 Kopecks = 1 Ruble

Values for used stamps are for canceled to order examples. Postally used stamps sell for considerably more.

Watermark

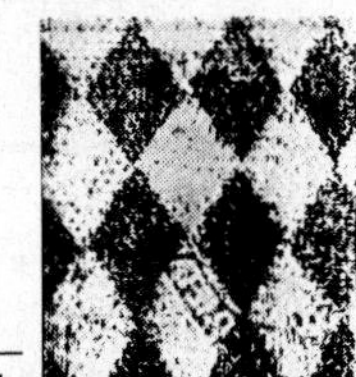
Wmk. 171 — Diamonds

Don Government (Novocherkassk) Rostov Issue

Russian Stamps of 1909-17 Surcharged

1918 Unwmk. *Perf. 14x14½*

1 A14 25k on 1k dl org yel	1.75	*1.90*
a. Inverted surcharge	100.00	*100.00*
2 A14 25k on 2k dl grn	.50	*.60*
a. Inverted surcharge	100.00	*75.00*
b. Double impression (surcharge normal)	150.00	
3 A14 25k on 3k car	.75	*.75*
a. Double surcharge	75.00	*75.00*
b. Inverted surcharge	75.00	
4 A15 25k on 4k car	2.25	*3.50*
a. Inverted surcharge	100.00	*100.00*
5 A14 50k on 7k blue	4.50	*6.50*

Imperf

6 A14 25k on 1k orange	.60	*1.25*
a. Inverted surcharge	75.00	*100.00*
7 A14 25k on 2k dull grn	6.75	*12.50*
a. Double impression (surcharge normal)	150.00	
8 A14 25k on 3k red	4.25	*3.00*
a. Inverted surcharge	100.00	
Nos. 1-8 (8)	21.35	30.00

Counterfeits exist of Nos. 1-8.

Ermak, Cossack Leader — A1

Inscription on Back

1919 *Perf. 11½*

10 A1 20k green	50.00	*85.00*

This stamp was available for both postage and currency.

Novocherkassk Issue

Russian stamps with these surcharges are bogus.

Kuban Government Ekaterinodar Issues

Russian Stamps of 1909-17 Surcharged

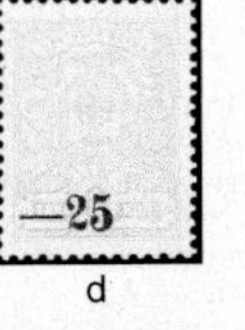
d

e

f

g

h

i

1918-20 Unwmk. *Perf. 14x14½*

20 A14(d) 25k on 1k dl org yel	.50	*2.00*
a. Inverted surcharge	75.00	*27.50*
b. Dbl. surch., one inverted	75.00	*25.00*
21 A14(d) 50k on 2k dl grn	5.00	*6.00*
a. Inverted surcharge	50.00	*27.50*
b. Double surcharge	100.00	*20.00*
c. Dbl. surcharge inverted	75.00	*20.00*
22 A14(e) 70k on 5k dk cl	2.00	*5.50*
23 A14(f) 1r on 3k car	5.00	*5.00*
a. Inverted surcharge	50.00	*20.00*
b. Double surcharge	50.00	*15.00*
c. Pair, one without surch.	50.00	*15.00*
24 A14(g) 1r on 3k car	.65	*1.00*
a. Inverted surcharge	50.00	*20.00*
b. Double surcharge	50.00	*20.00*
c. Pair, one without surcharge	100.00	*20.00*
25 A15(h) 3r on 4k rose	10.00	*15.00*
b. Inverted surcharge	100.00	*50.00*
c. Double surcharge	100.00	*60.00*
d. Dbl. surcharge inverted	100.00	*60.00*
26 A15(i) 10r on 4k rose	15.00	5.00
a. 10r on 4k carmine	20.00	*20.00*
b. Inverted surcharge	100.00	*55.00*
27 A11(i) 10r on 15k red brn & dp bl	1.00	*2.00*
a. Surchd. on face & back	40.00	15.00
b. Dbl. surch., one inverted	75.00	*60.00*
c. Inverted surcharge	100.00	
28 A14(i) 25r on 3k car	10.00	3.00
a. Inverted surcharge	100.00	*20.00*
29 A14(i) 25r on 7k bl	25.00	*50.00*
a. Inverted surcharge	75.00	*100.00*
30 A11(i) 25r on 14k bl & car	75.00	*80.00*
a. Inverted surcharge	100.00	*100.00*
31 A11(i) 25r on 25k dl grn & dk vio	25.00	*35.00*
a. Inverted surcharge	80.00	*70.00*
Nos. 20-31 (12)	174.15	209.50

Imperf

35 A14(d) 25d on 1k org	5.00	2.50
36 A14(d) 50k on 2k gray grn	1.00	*2.00*
a. Inverted surcharge	50.00	25.00
b. Double surcharge	40.00	25.00
c. Pair, one without surch.	50.00	*30.00*
37 A14(e) 70k on 5k claret	2.50	*3.25*
38 A14(f) 1r on 3k red	1.40	*2.00*
a. Inverted surcharge	40.00	20.00
b. Double surcharge	30.00	*15.00*
c. Pair, one without surch.	30.00	*15.00*
d. Double surcharge, both inverted	100.00	—
39 A14(g) 1r on 3k red	1.00	*3.00*
a. Double surcharge	20.00	*20.00*
b. Pair, one without surch.	20.00	*20.00*
c. As "a," inverted	40.00	*45.00*
d. Inverted surcharge	100.00	—
40 A11(i) 10r on 15k red brn & dp bl	4.75	*5.50*
41 A14(i) 25r on 3k red	6.00	*10.00*
a. Inverted surcharge	50.00	
Nos. 35-41 (7)	21.65	*28.25*

No. 31 is said to exist imperf.

Russian Stamps of 1909-17 Surcharged

1919 *Perf. 14, 14½x15*

45 A14 70k on 1k dl org yel	1.25	1.00
a. Inverted surcharge	100.00	

Imperf

46 A14 70k on 1k orange	1.25	*2.40*
a. Inverted surcharge	100.00	*20.00*
b. Double surch., one inverted	100.00	25.00

The 1k postal savings stamp with this surcharge inverted is a proof. Value, $500.

Counterfeits exist of Nos. 20-46.

On Russia Nos. AR1-AR3

1919 Wmk. 171 *Perf. 14½x15*

47 PF1 10r on 1k red, *buff*	50.00	*60.00*
a. Inverted surcharge	75.00	
48 PF1 10r on 5k grn, *buff*	50.00	*60.00*
a. Double surcharge	250.00	
49 PF1 10r on 10k brn, *buff*	120.00	*150.00*
Nos. 47-49 (3)	220.00	270.00

Counterfeits exist of Nos. 47-49.

Crimea

Russian Stamp of 1917 Surcharged

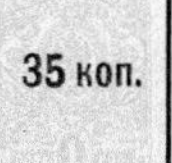

1919 Unwmk. *Imperf.*

51 A14 35k on 1k orange	2.00	*3.00*
a. Comma, instead of period in surcharge	2.00	

A3

No. 52 Back

Paper with Buff Network; Inscription on Back

1919 *Imperf.*

52 A3 50k brown	35.00	*75.00*

Available for both postage and currency.

Russia Nos. 77, 82, 123, 73, 119 Surcharged

Nos. 53-57 Nos. 58-59

1920 ***Perf. 14x14½***

53 A14 5r on 5k dk claret 1.25 *2.40*
 a. Inverted surcharge 100.00
 b. Double surcharge 100.00
54 A8 5r on 20k dl bl & dk car 1.25 *2.40*
 a. Inverted surcharge 100.00
 b. Double surcharge 100.00
 c. "5" omitted 75.00

Imperf

55 A14 5r on 5k claret 1.25 *2.40*
 a. Double surcharge 25.00

Same Surcharge on Stamp of Denikin Issue, No. 64

57 A5 5r on 35k lt bl 12.00 *14.00*
 a. Double surcharge 80.00
 Nos. 53-57 (4) 15.75 21.20

1920 ***Perf. 14x14½***

58 A14 100r on 1k dl org yel 5.00
 a. "10" in place of "100" 100.00
 b. Inverted surcharge 150.00
 c. Double surcharge 150.00

Imperf

59 A14 100r on 1k orange 5.00
 a. Inverted surcharge 150.00

Nos. 53-57 were issued at Sevastopol during the occupation by General Wrangel's army. Nos. 58-59 were prepared but not used.

Denikin Issue

A5

St. George — A6

1919 **Unwmk.** ***Imperf.***

61 A5 5k orange .30 *.25*
62 A5 10k green .30 *.25*
63 A5 15k red .30 *.35*
64 A5 35k light blue .30 *.25*
65 A5 70k dark blue .30 *.35*
 a. Tête bêche pair 90.00
66 A6 1r brown & red 1.00 *.90*
67 A6 2r gray vio & yellow 1.75 *1.60*
68 A6 3r dl rose & green 1.10 *1.25*
69 A6 5r slate & violet 1.50 *1.40*
70 A6 7r gray grn & rose 2.50 *3.25*
71 A6 10r red & gray 2.25 *2.50*
 Nos. 61-71 (11) 11.60 12.35

Perf. 11½

68a A6 3r dull rose & green 3.00 *10.00*
69a A6 5r slate & violet 4.00 *10.00*
71a A6 10r red & gray 3.00 *10.00*
 Nos. 68a-71a (3) 10.00 30.00

Nos. 61-71 were issued at Ekaterinodar and used in all parts of South Russia that were occupied by the People's Volunteer Army under Gen. Anton Ivanovich Denikin. The inscription on the stamps reads "United Russia."

Stamps of type A6 with rosettes instead of numerals in the small circles at the sides may be essays. Perforated examples of Nos. 61-67 and 70 are of private origin.

For surcharges see Russia, Offices in Turkish Empire Nos. 303-319.

SOUTH SUDAN

sauth sü-'dan

LOCATION — Central Africa, between Central Africa and Ethiopia
GOVT. — Republic
AREA — 239,285 sq. mi.
POP. — 10,625,176 (2012 estimate)
CAPITAL — Juba

South Sudan achieved independence from Sudan on July 9, 2011.

100 Piasters = 1 Pound

Catalogue values for all unused stamps in this country are for Never Hinged items.

Flag of South Sudan — A1

John Garang (1945-2005), Leader of Sudan People's Liberation Army — A2

2011, July 9 **Litho.** ***Perf. 12***

1 A1 £1 multi *5.50 5.50*
2 A2 £3.50 multi *15.00 15.00*

A £2.50 stamp depicting the coat of arms was prepared and affixed to commercially-made first day covers that were canceled, but the stamp was apparently not sold in South Sudan. Value used, $170.

For surcharges, see Nos. 9-14, 27.

A3

A4

Designs: £1, Shoe-billed storks. £2, Bearded vultures. £5, Saddle-billed storks. £10, Nile lechwe. £20, White-eared kob. £50, Arms of South Sudan.

Perf. 12¼x12 (A3), 14¾x14½ (A4)

2012 **Litho.**

3 A3 £1 multi *6.00 6.00*
4 A4 £2 multi *7.00 7.00*
5 A3 £5 multi *8.75 8.75*
6 A4 £10 multi *10.50 10.50*
7 A3 £20 multi *18.00 18.00*
8 A3 £50 multi *30.00 30.00*
 Nos. 3-8 (6) 80.25 80.25

For surcharges, see Nos. 15-26.

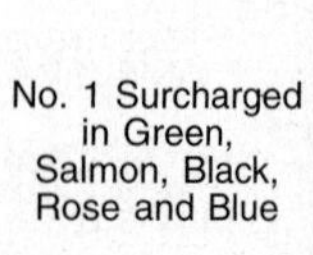

No. 1 Surcharged in Green, Salmon, Black, Rose and Blue

Method and Perf. As Before

2017, Sept. 15

Obliterator in Black

9 A1 £50 on £1 #1 (G) *8.50 8.50*
10 A1 £75 on £1 #1 (Sal) *8.50 8.50*
11 A1 £100 on £1 #1 (Bk) *8.50 8.50*
12 A1 £300 on £1 #1 (R) *8.50 8.50*
13 A1 £500 on £1 #1 (Bl) *8.50 8.50*

No. 1 Surcharged in Black

Method and Perf. As Before

2017, Sept. 15

Obliterator in Black

14 A1 £100 on £1 #1 (Bk) *8.50 8.50*

No. 4 Surcharged

Method and Perf. As Before

2017, Sept. 15

15 A4 £50 on £2 #4 *7.00 7.00*
16 A4 £75 on £2 #4 *7.00 7.00*
17 A4 £100 on £2 #4 *7.00 7.00*
18 A4 £300 on £2 #4 *7.00 7.00*

No. 4 Surcharged

Method and Perf. As Before

2017, Sept. 15

19 A4 £75 on £2 #4 *7.00 7.00*

No. 5 Surcharged

Method and Perf. As Before

2017, Sept. 15

20 A3 £50 on £5 #5 *11.00 11.00*

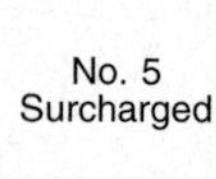

No. 5 Surcharged

Method and Perf. As Before

2017, Sept. 15

21 A3 £75 on £5 #5 *11.00 11.00*
22 A3 £150 on £5 #5 *11.00 11.00*

No. 3 Surcharged in White on Blue

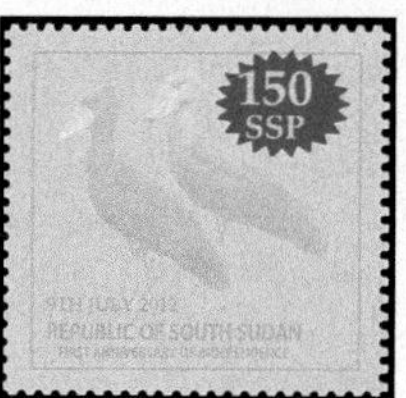

Method and Perf. As Before

2017, Sept. 15

23 A3 £150 on £1 #3 (Bl&W) *9.50 9.50*

No. 3 Surcharged in Black on Gold and Black on Silver

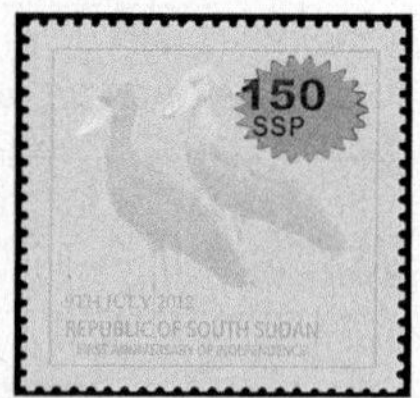

Method and Perf. As Before

2017, Sept. 15

24 A3 £150 on £1 #3 (G&Bk) *11.00 11.00*
25 A3 £200 on £1 #3 (S&Bk) *11.00 11.00*
26 A3 £250 on £1 #3 (G&Bk) *11.00 11.00*

No. 2 Surcharged in Light Brown & Black

Method and Perf. As Before

2017, Sept. 15

27 A2 £1000 on £3.50 #2 (YB&Bk) *24.00 24.00*

SOUTH WEST AFRICA

sauth 'west 'a-fri-kə

(Namibia)

LOCATION — Southwestern Africa between Angola, Botswana and South Africa, bordering on the Atlantic Ocean
GOVT. — Administered by the Republic of South Africa under a mandate of the League of Nations
AREA — 318,261 sq. mi.
POP. — 1,039,800 (1982)
CAPITAL — Windhoek

Formerly a German possession, South West Africa was occupied by South African forces in 1915 and by the Treaty of Versailles was mandated to the Union of South Africa. On March 20, 1990 it became Namibia.

12 Pence = 1 Shilling
20 Shillings = 1 Pound
100 Cents = 1 Rand (1961)

Catalogue values for unused stamps in this country are for Never Hinged items, beginning with Scott 125 in the regular postage section, Scott B1 in the semi-postal section, Scott J86 in the postage due section, and Scott O13 in the officials section.

Watermarks

Watermarks 177, 201, 330, 348 and 359 can be found at the beginning of South Africa.

Major-number listings and values of Nos. 1-40 and 85-93 are for pairs with both overprints.

Stamps of South Africa, Nos. 2-3, 5 and 9-16, Overprinted in English or Afrikaans alternately throughout the sheets.

Setting I

"South West" 14½mm wide
"Zuid-West" 13mm wide
Overprint Spaced 14mm

1923, Jan. 2 Wmk. 177 *Perf. 14*

1 A2 ½p green, pair 4.75 *10.00*
a. Single, Dutch 1.10 *.90*
2 A2 1p red, pair 8.25 *10.00*
a. Single, Dutch 1.10 *.90*
b. Inverted overprint, pair 550.00
c. As "b," single, English 125.00
d. As "b," single, Dutch 125.00
e. As #2, English "Af.rica" 190.00 325.00
f. Double overprint, pair 1,100.
g. As "f," single, English 500.00
h. As "f," single, Dutch 500.00
3 A2 2p dl vio, pair 10.00 *16.00*
a. Single, Dutch 1.75 *1.75*
b. Inverted overprint, pair 725.00 825.00
c. As "b," single, English 150.00
d. As "b," single, Dutch 150.00
4 A2 3p ultra, pair 13.00 *19.00*
a. Single, Dutch 3.00 *3.00*
5 A2 4p ol grn & org, pair 21.00 *52.50*
a. Single, Dutch 4.50 *4.50*
6 A2 6p vio & blk, pair 9.25 *52.50*
a. Single, Dutch 4.75 *4.75*
7 A2 1sh org, pair 21.00 *55.00*
a. Single, Dutch 5.75 *5.75*
b. As #7, without period after "Afrika" *7,500.*
8 A2 1sh3p violet, pair 47.50 *62.50*
a. Single, Dutch 6.50 *6.50*
b. Inverted overprint, pair 400.00
c. As "b," single, English 85.00
d. As "b," single, Dutch 85.00
9 A2 2sh6p grn & cl, pair 72.50 *150.00*
a. Single, Dutch 20.00 *20.00*
10 A2 5sh blue & cl, pair 240.00 *400.00*
a. Single, Dutch 55.00 *55.00*
11 A2 10sh ol grn & bl, pair 1,500. *2,900.*
a. Single, Dutch 425.00 *450.00*
12 A2 £1 red & dp grn, pair 800.00 *2,000.*
a. Single, Dutch 275.00 *275.00*
Nos. 1-12 (12) 2,747. *5,728.*

Most values exist with "t" of "West" partly or totally missing. Vertical displacement in overprinting accounts for the stamps with only one line of overprint.

The English overprint of Setting I is the same as that of Setting III. See Nos. 16a-27a.

Setting II

Words Same Width as Setting I
Overprint Spaced 9½-10mm

1923, Apr.

13 A2 5sh blue & cl, pair 175.00 *300.00*
a. Single, English 52.50 *52.50*
b. Single, Dutch 52.50 *52.50*
c. As #13, without period after "Afrika" 1,200. 1,400.
d. As "b," without period after "Afrika" 225.00 225.00
14 A2 10sh ol grn & bl, pair 550.00 *900.00*
a. Single, English 160.00 *160.00*
b. Single, Dutch 160.00 *160.00*
c. As #14, without period after "Afrika" 2,600. *3,250.*
d. As "b," without period after "Afrika" 550.00 550.00
15 A2 £1 red & green, pair 1,100. *1,500.*
a. Single, English 225.00 *225.00*
b. Single, Dutch 225.00 *225.00*
c. As #15, without period after "Afrika" 6,000. 5,750.
d. As "b," without period after "Afrika" 1,000. 1,000.

Setting III

English as in Setting I
"Zuidwest" 11mm wide, No Hyphen
Overprint Spaced 14mm

1923-24

16 A2 ½p grn, pair ('24) 13.00 *42.50*
a. Single, English 1.00 *4.25*
b. Single, Dutch .70 *4.25*
17 A2 1p red, pair 6.25 *10.00*
a. Single, English .85 *1.10*
b. Single, Dutch .40 *1.10*
18 A2 2p dull vio, pair 12.00 *16.50*
a. Single, English .50 *1.25*
b. Single, Dutch .50 *1.25*
c. Dbl. ovpt., pair 1,200.
d. As "c," single, English 150.00
e. As "c," single, Dutch 150.00
19 A2 3p ultra, pair 6.00 *14.50*
a. Single, English .70 *1.50*
b. Single, Dutch .70 *1.50*
20 A2 4p ol grn & org, pair 7.00 *22.50*
a. Single, English 1.00 *3.25*
b. Single, Dutch 1.00 *3.25*
21 A2 6p vio & blk, pair 14.00 *47.50*
a. Single, English 1.00 *5.50*
b. Single, Dutch 1.00 *5.50*
22 A2 1sh orange, pair 15.00 *50.00*
a. Single, English 1.50 *5.50*
b. Single, Dutch 1.50 *5.50*
23 A2 1sh3p violet, pair 27.50 *52.50*
a. Single, English 3.25 *5.50*
b. Single, Dutch 3.25 *5.50*
24 A2 2sh6p grn & cl, pair 52.50 *90.00*
a. Single, English 9.00 *10.00*
b. Single, Dutch 9.00 *10.00*
25 A2 5sh blue & cl, pair 70.00 *125.00*
a. Single, English 14.00 *20.00*
b. Single, Dutch 14.00 *20.00*
26 A2 10sh ol grn & bl, pair 190.00 *300.00*
a. Single, English 45.00 *47.50*
b. Single, Dutch 45.00 *47.50*
27 A2 £1 red & grn, pair 350.00 *500.00*
a. Single, English 60.00 *70.00*
b. Single, Dutch 60.00 *70.00*
Nos. 16-27 (12) 763.25 *1,271.*

Setting IV

Type g (on left), Type h (on right)

"South West" 16mm wide
"Zuidwest" 12mm wide
Overprint Spaced 14mm

1924, July

28 A2 2sh6p grn & cl, pair 100.00 *175.00*
a. Single, English 25.00 *32.50*
b. Single, Dutch 25.00 *32.50*

Setting VI

"South West" 16, 16½mm wide
"Zuidwest" 12½mm wide
Overprint Spaced 9½mm

1924, Dec.

29 A2 ½p green, pair 8.00 *50.00*
a. Single, English .50 *5.75*
b. Single, Dutch .50 *5.75*
30 A2 1p red, pair 5.00 *11.50*
a. Single, English .25 *1.40*
b. Single, Dutch .25 *1.40*
c. Pair, one without overprint 2,200.
31 A2 2p dull vio, pair 4.25 *22.50*
a. Single, English .30 *1.75*
b. Single, Dutch .30 *1.75*
32 A2 3p ultra, pair 5.75 *40.00*
a. Single, English .90 *3.25*
b. Single, Dutch .90 *3.25*
33 A2 4p ol grn & org, pair 7.00 *50.00*
a. Single, English .85 *4.50*
b. Single, Dutch .85 *4.50*
34 A2 6p vio & blk, pair 10.50 *50.00*
a. Single, English .80 *5.25*
b. Single, Dutch .80 *5.25*
35 A2 1sh orange, pair 9.50 *52.50*
a. Single, English 1.00 *5.50*
b. Single, Dutch 1.00 *5.50*
36 A2 1sh3p violet, pair 14.50 *52.50*
a. Single, English 1.75 *5.25*
b. Single, Dutch 1.75 *5.25*
37 A2 2sh6p grn & cl, pair 47.50 *90.00*
a. Single, English 7.50 *11.00*
b. Single, Dutch 7.50 *11.00*
38 A2 5sh blue & cl, pair 65.00 *125.00*
a. Single, English 13.00 *15.00*
b. Single, Dutch 13.00 *15.00*
39 A2 10sh ol grn & bl, pair 100.00 *180.00*
a. Single, English 17.50 *21.00*
b. Single, Dutch 17.50 *21.00*
40 A2 £1 red & grn, pair 325.00 *450.00*
a. Single, English 60.00 *60.00*
b. Single, Dutch 60.00 *60.00*
Nos. 29-40 (12) 602.00 *1,174.*

Setting VII

South Africa Nos. 21-22 Overprinted

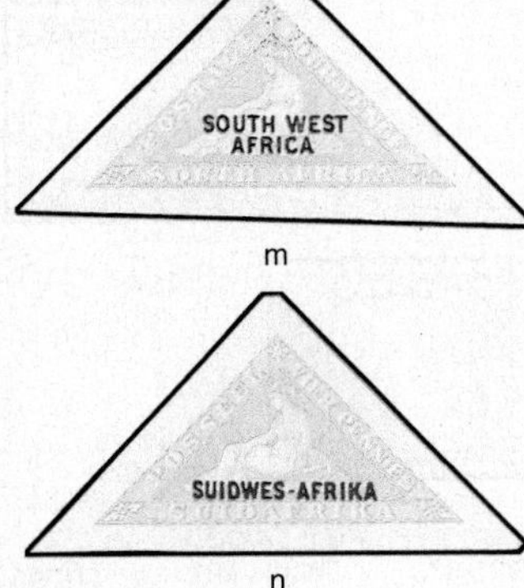

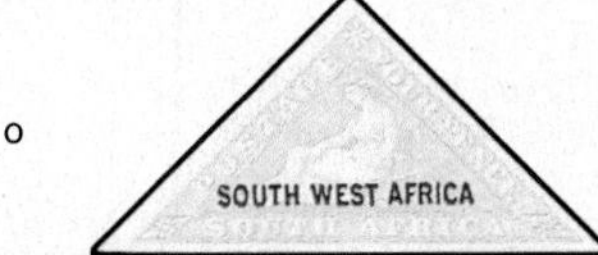

1926-27 Wmk. 201 *Imperf.*

81 A3 (m) 4p blue gray .95 *3.00*
82 A3 (n) 4p blue gray .95 *3.00*
83 A3 (o) 4p blue gray ('27) 7.50 *20.00*
Nos. 81-83 (3) 9.40 *26.00*

Nos. 81-83 were not officially perforated, but firms and individuals applied various forms of perforation and rouletting for their own convenience. Perf. 11 examples of Nos. 81-82 were made by John Meinert, Ltd., Windhoek, same values. Imperf between pairs, $60.

Setting VIII

South Africa Nos. 23-25 Overprinted Alternately with type "p" on English-inscribed Stamps and type "q" on Afrikaans-inscribed Stamps

"South West" 16½mm wide
"Suidwes" 11mm wide
Overprint Spaced 11½mm

1926 Typo. *Perf. 14½x14*

85 A5 ½p dk grn & blk, pair 4.50 *13.00*
a. Single, English .75 *1.50*
b. Single, Afrikaans .75 *1.50*
c. Ovpt. "q" on English stamp .55 *1.00*
d. Ovpt. "p" on Afrikaans stamp .55 *1.00*
e. Pair, "c" + "d" ('27) 2.75 *12.00*
f. As "e," without period after "Africa" 175.00
86 A6 1p car & blk, pair 4.00 *8.50*
a. Single, English .60 *.80*
b. Single, Afrikaans .60 *.80*
c. Ovpt. "q" on English stamp .50 *.50*
d. Ovpt. "p" on Afrikaans stamp .50 *.50*
e. Pair, "c" + "d" ('27) 3.75 *3.00*
f. As "e," without period after "Africa" 350.00
87 A7 6p org & grn, pair 24.00 *55.00*
a. Single, English 6.75 *7.25*
b. Single, Afrikaans 6.75 *7.25*
c. Ovpt. "q" on English stamp 2.50 *3.00*
d. Ovpt. "p" on Afrikaans stamp 2.50 *3.00*
e. Pair, "c" + "d" ('27) 9.50 *35.00*
f. As "e," without period after "Africa" 210.00
Nos. 85-87 (3) 32.50 *76.50*

For overprints see Nos. O1-O3.

Setting IX

South Africa Nos. 26-27, 29-32 Overprinted in Blue with types "p" and "q" Spaced 16mm

1927 Engr. *Perf. 14*

88 A8 2p vio brn & gray, pair 6.50 *16.50*
a. Single, English .85 *1.90*
b. Single, Afrikaans .85 *1.90*
89 A9 3p red & blk, pair 5.00 *32.50*
a. Single, English .70 *2.75*
b. Single, Afrikaans .70 *2.75*
90 A11 1sh dp bl & bis brn, pair 16.50 *34.00*
a. Single, English 2.50 *4.25*
b. Single, Afrikaans 2.50 *4.25*
91 A12 2sh6p brn & bl grn, pair 40.00 *100.00*
a. Single, English 9.00 *14.00*
b. Single, Afrikaans 9.00 *14.00*
92 A13 5sh dp grn & blk, pair 80.00 *200.00*
a. Single, English 19.00 *22.50*
b. Single, Afrikaans 19.00 *22.50*
93 A14 10sh ol brn & bl, pair 70.00 *165.00*
a. Single, English 15.00 *20.00*
b. Single, Afrikaans 15.00 *20.00*
Nos. 88-93 (6) 218.00 *548.00*

South Africa Nos. 12 and 16a Overprinted at Foot — r

1927 Typo. Wmk. 177

94 A2 1sh3p violet 1.40 *7.00*
 a. Without period after "A" 110.00
95 A2 £1 lt red & gray grn 100.00 180.00
 a. Without period after "A" 1,700. *2,600.*

South Africa Nos. 23-25 Overprinted type "r" at Foot

1927 Wmk. 201 *Perf. 14½x14*

96 A5 ½p green & blk, pair 2.75 *8.75*
 a. Single, English .25 *.85*
 b. Single, Afrikaans .25 *.85*
 c. As #96, without period after "A" on one stamp 45.00 80.00
97 A6 1p car & blk, pair 1.50 *4.25*
 a. Single, English .25 *.60*
 b. Single, Afrikaans .25 *.60*
 c. As #97, without period after "A" on one stamp 42.50 80.00
 d. Ovpt. at top, pair ('30) 2.00 *15.00*
 e. As "d," single, English .45 *1.75*
 f. As "d," single, Afrikaans .45 *1.75*
98 A7 6p org & grn, pair 7.50 *30.00*
 a. Single, English 2.00 *3.00*
 b. Single, Afrikaans 2.00 *3.00*
 c. As #98, without period after "A" on one stamp 125.00
 Nos. 96-98 (3) 11.75 *43.00*

For overprints see Nos. O5-O7.

South Africa Nos. 26-32 Overprinted type "r" at Top

1927-28 Engr. *Perf. 14*

99 A8 2p vio brn & gray, pair 10.00 *35.00*
 a. Single, English 1.25 *2.00*
 b. Single, Afrikaans 1.25 *2.00*
 c. As #99, without period after "A" on one stamp 85.00 150.00
 d. Double ovpt., one inverted 800.00 1,050.
100 A9 3p red & blk, pair 6.00 *32.50*
 a. Single, English 1.25 *3.25*
 b. Single, Afrikaans 1.25 *3.25*
 c. As #100, without period after "A" on one stamp 92.50 150.00
101 A10 4p brn, pair ('28) 13.50 *52.50*
 a. Single, English 1.75 *7.50*
 b. Single, Afrikaans 1.75 *7.50*
 c. As #101, without period after "A" on one stamp 95.00 *150.00*
102 A11 1sh dp bl & bis brn, pair 14.50 *52.50*
 a. Single, English 2.00 *5.00*
 b. Single, Afrikaans 2.00 *5.00*
 c. As #102, without period after "A" on one stamp 1,750. *1,950.*
103 A12 2sh6p brn & bl grn, pair 45.00 *90.00*
 a. Single, English 7.50 *12.50*
 b. Single, Afrikaans 7.50 *12.50*
 c. As #103, without period after "A" on one stamp 250.00 *375.00*
104 A13 5sh dp grn & blk, pair 67.50 *125.00*
 a. Single, English 12.50 *19.00*
 b. Single, Afrikaans 12.50 *19.00*
 c. As #104, without period after "A" on one stamp 325.00 475.00
105 A14 10sh ol brn & bl, pair 110.00 225.00
 a. Single, English 20.00 *30.00*
 b. Single, Afrikaans 20.00 *30.00*
 c. As #105, without period after "A" on one stamp 400.00 600.00
 Nos. 99-105 (7) 266.50 *612.50*

Nos. 99-102 exist perf 14x13½. Values about two times those shown.

For overprint see No. O8.

South Africa Nos. 33-34 Overprinted type "r" at Foot

1930 Photo. *Perf. 15x14*

106 A5 ½p bl grn & blk, pair 25.00 *50.00*
 a. Single, English 2.00 *4.75*
 b. Single, Afrikaans 2.00 *4.75*
107 A6 1p car rose & blk, pair 15.00 *29.00*
 a. Single, English 1.50 *3.00*
 b. Single, Afrikaans 1.50 *3.00*

Kori Bustard — A15

Cape Cross — A16

Mail Transport — A17

Bogenfels — A18

Windhoek — A19

Waterberg — A20

Lüderitz Bay — A21

Bush Scene — A22

Elands — A23

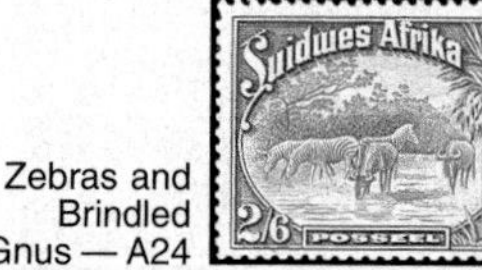

Zebras and Brindled Gnus — A24

Herero Houses — A25

Welwitschia Plant — A26

Okuwahakan Falls — A27

Perf. 14x13½

1931-37 Wmk. 201 Engr.

108 A15 ½p grn & blk, pair 3.25 2.50
 a. Single, English .25 .25
 b. Single, Afrikaans .25 .25
109 A16 1p red & ind, pair 3.00 2.50
 a. Single, English .25 .25
 b. Single, Afrikaans .25 .25
110 A17 1½p vio brn, pair ('37) 30.00 4.50
 a. Single, English 1.00 .35
 b. Single, Afrikaans 1.00 .35
111 A18 2p dk brn & dk bl, pair 1.75 *9.00*
 a. Single, English .25 .25
 b. Single, Afrikaans .25 .25
112 A19 3p dp bl & gray blk, pair 1.50 *4.50*
 a. Single, English .30 .25
 b. Single, Afrikaans .30 .25
113 A20 4p brn vio & grn, pair 1.60 *7.25*
 a. Single, English .40 .25
 b. Single, Afrikaans .40 .25
114 A21 6p ol brn & bl, pair 1.75 *10.00*
 a. Single, English .45 .25
 b. Single, Afrikaans .45 .25
115 A22 1sh bl & vio brn, pair 3.75 *17.50*
 a. Single, English .55 .30
 b. Single, Afrikaans .55 .30
116 A23 1sh3p ocher & pur, pair 6.50 11.50
 a. Single, English .75 .65
 b. Single, Afrikaans .75 .65
117 A24 2sh6p dk gray & rose, pair 28.50 25.00
 a. Single, English 3.25 2.00
 b. Single, Afrikaans 3.25 2.00
118 A25 5sh vio brn & ol grn, pair 17.00 *37.50*
 a. Single, English 4.25 3.00
 b. Single, Afrikaans 4.25 3.00
119 A26 10sh grn & brn, pair 52.50 52.50
 a. Single, English 11.50 6.50
 b. Single, Afrikaans 11.50 *6.50*
120 A27 20sh bl grn & mar, pair 77.50 *82.50*
 a. Single, English 14.00 11.00
 b. Single, Afrikaans 14.00 11.00
 Nos. 108-120 (13) 228.60 *266.75*

For overprints see Nos. O13-O27.

George V — A28

1935, May 6 *Perf. 14x13½*

121 A28 1p carmine & blk 1.00 .30
122 A28 2p dk brown & blk 1.25 .30
123 A28 3p blue & blk 7.50 *22.50*
124 A28 6p violet & blk 3.25 *13.00*
 Nos. 121-124 (4) 13.00 *36.10*
 Set, never hinged 30.00

25th anniv. of the reign of George V.

Catalogue values for unused stamps in this section, from this point to the end of the section, are for Never Hinged items.

Coronation Issue

Inscribed alternately in English and Afrikaans

George VI — A29

1937, May 12 Engr. *Perf. 13½x14*

125 A29 ½p emer & blk, pair .55 .25
 a. Single, English .25 .25
 b. Single, Afrikaans .25 .25
126 A29 1p car & blk, pair .55 .25
 a. Single, English .25 .25
 b. Single, Afrikaans .25 .25
127 A29 1½p org & blk, pair .55 .25
 a. Single, English .25 .25
 b. Single, Afrikaans .25 .25
128 A29 2p dk brn & blk, pair .55 .30
 a. Single, English .25 .25
 b. Single, Afrikaans .25 .25
129 A29 3p brt bl & blk, pair .65 .30
 a. Single, English .25 .25
 b. Single, Afrikaans .25 .25
130 A29 4p dk vio & blk, pair .65 .55
 a. Single, English .25 .25
 b. Single, Afrikaans .25 .25
131 A29 6p yel & blk, pair .70 3.00
 a. Single, English .25 .30
 b. Single, Afrikaans .25 .30
132 A29 1sh gray & blk, pair .80 *3.50*
 a. Single, English .25 .75
 b. Single, Afrikaans .25 .75
 Nos. 125-132 (8) 5.00 8.40

Coronation of George VI.

Voortrekker Issue

South Africa Nos. 79-80 Overprinted type "r"

1938, Dec. 14 Photo. *Perf. 15x14*

133 A23 1p rose & sl, pair 12.00 *22.50*
 a. Single, English 1.50 *1.75*
 b. Single, Afrikaans 1.50 *1.75*
134 A24 1½p red brn & Prus bl, pair 18.00 *27.50*
 a. Single, English 2.25 2.25
 b. Single, Afrikaans 2.25 2.25

Issued to commemorate the Voortrekkers.

South Africa Nos. 81-89 Overprinted — s

Perf. 14 (2p, 4p, 6p); 15x14

1941-43 Wmk. 201

135 A25 ½p dp blue grn, pair 1.75 2.75
 a. Single, English .25 .25
 b. Single, Afrikaans .25 .25
136 A26 1p brt rose, pair 2.75 3.75
 a. Single, English .25 .25
 b. Single, Afrikaans .25 .25
137 A27 1½p Prus grn, pair ('42) 2.25 4.00
 a. Single, English .25 .25
 b. Single, Afrikaans .25 .25
138 A28 2p dk violet .60 *1.75*
139 A29 3p dp blue, pair 24.50 *27.50*
 a. Single, English 1.25 *1.25*
 b. Single, Afrikaans 1.25 *1.25*
140 A30 4p brown, pair 10.00 *21.00*
 a. Single, English .90 *1.25*
 b. Single, Afrikaans .90 *1.25*
141 A31 6p brt red org, pair 7.50 *9.50*
 a. Single, English .85 *1.00*
 b. Single, Afrikaans .85 *1.00*
142 A32 1sh dk brown 1.60 *2.00*
143 A33 1sh3p dk ol brn, pair ('43) 14.00 *24.50*
 a. Single, English 1.50 1.50
 b. Single, Afrikaans 1.50 1.50
 Nos. 135-143 (9) 64.95 96.75

South Africa Nos. 90-97 Overprinted

t

u

Pairs or Strips of 3 Perf. 14 or 15x14 all around, Rouletted 6½ or 13 btwn.

1942-45 Wmk. 201

144 A34(t) ½p dp grn, horiz. strip of 3 .75 *8.25*
 a. Single, English .25 .25
 b. Single, Afrikaans .25 .25
 c. ½p dp bl grn, horiz. strip of 3 4.25 *8.75*
 d. As "c," single, English .25 .25
 e. As "c," single, Afrikaans .25 .25
145 A35(t) 1p brt car, horiz. strip of 3 3.50 *8.00*
 a. Single, English .25 .25
 b. Single, Afrikaans .25 .25
 c. 1p rose car, horiz. strip of 3 4.50 *8.00*
 d. As "c," single, English .25 .25
 e. As "c," single, Afrikaans .25 .25
146 A36(u) 1½p cop brn, horiz. pair .75 *1.75*
 a. Single, English .25 .25
 b. Single, Afrikaans .25 .25
147 A37(t) 2p dk vio, horiz. pair 8.50 *5.50*
 a. Single, English .25 .25
 b. Single, Afrikaans .25 .25
148 A38(t) 3p dp bl, vert. strip of 3 3.50 *25.00*
 a. Single, English .30 *.85*
 b. Single, Afrikaans .30 *.85*
149 A39(t) 4p sl grn, vert. strip of 3 2.25 *24.00*
 a. Single .40 *.75*
 b. As "c," single 80.00 70.00
 c. Invtd. ovpt., strip of 3 925.00 675.00
150 A40(t) 6p brt red org, horiz. pair 5.25 3.00
 a. Single, English .35 *.35*
 b. Single, Afrikaans .35 *.35*
 c. Inverted overprint, pair 650.00
 d. As "c," single, English 60.00 60.00
 e. As "c," single, Afrikaans 60.00 60.00
151 A41(u) 1sh dk brn, vert. pair 18.00 37.50
 a. Single 1.50 2.00
 b. As "c," single 90.00
 c. Inverted overprint, pair 825.00 475.00

152 A41(t) 1sh dk brn, vert. pair 4.00 6.00
- *a.* Single .35 *.35*
- *b.* As "c," single 62.50 45.00
- *c.* Invtd. ovpt., vert. pair 675.00 450.00

Nos. 144-152 (9) 46.50 119.00

Issue years: #144-145, 147-151, 1943; #152, 1944; #144c, 145c, 149c, 1945.

Peace Issue

South Africa Nos. 100-102 Overprinted Type "w"

1945, Dec. 3 Wmk. 201 *Perf. 14*

153 A42 1p rose pink & choc, pair .35 .75
- *a.* Single, English .25 .25
- *b.* Single, Afrikaans .25 .25
- *c.* Inverted overprint, pair 400.00 425.00
- *d.* As "c," single, English 45.00
- *e.* As "c," single, Afrikaans 45.00

154 A43 2p vio & sl bl, pair .40 .75
- *a.* Single, English .25 .25
- *b.* Single, Afrikaans .25 .25

155 A43 3p ultra & dp ultra, pair 1.10 *1.75*
- *a.* Single, English .30 .25
- *b.* Single, Afrikaans .30 .25

Nos. 153-155 (3) 1.85 3.25

WW II victory of the Allies.

Royal Visit Issue

South Africa Nos. 103-105 Overprinted

1947, Feb. 17 *Perf. 15x14*

156 A44 1p cerise & gray, pair .25 .25
- *a.* Single, English .25 .25
- *b.* Single, Afrikaans .25 .25

157 A45 2p purple, pair .30 *.60*
- *a.* Single, English .25 .25
- *b.* Single, Afrikaans .25 .25

158 A46 3p dk blue, pair .35 *.45*
- *a.* Single, English .25 .25
- *b.* Single, Afrikaans .25 .25

Nos. 156-158 (3) .90 1.30

Visit of the British Royal Family, Mar.-Apr., 1947.

South Africa No. 106 Overprinted

1948, Apr. 26 *Perf. 14*

159 A47 3p dp chalky bl & sil, pair 1.10 .35
- *a.* Single, English .25 .25
- *b.* Single, Afrikaans .25 .25

25th anniv. of the marriage of George VI and Queen Elizabeth.

UPU Issue

South Africa Nos. 109-111 Overprinted type "w" 13mm wide

1949, Oct. 1 *Perf. 14x15*

160 A50 ½p dk green, pair .75 *2.25*
- *a.* Single, English .25 *.30*
- *b.* Single, Afrikaans .25 *.30*

161 A50 1½p dk red, pair .75 *1.75*
- *a.* Single, English .25 .25
- *b.* Single, Afrikaans .25 .25

162 A50 3p ultra, pair 1.50 *1.50*
- *a.* Single, English .25 *.30*
- *b.* Single, Afrikaans .25 *.30*

Nos. 160-162 (3) 3.00 5.50

75th anniv. of the UPU.

This ends the bi-lingual multiples in the postage section.

Voortrekker Monument Issue

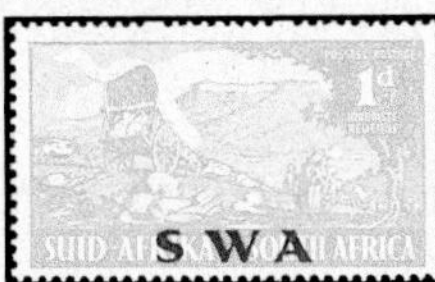

South Africa Nos. 112-114 Ovptd.

1949, Dec. 1 *Perf. 15x14*

163 A51 1p magenta .25 .25
164 A52 1½p dull green .25 .25
165 A53 3p dark blue .25 *.40*
Nos. 163-165 (3) .75 .90

Inauguration of the Voortrekker Monument at Pretoria.

South Africa Nos. 115-119 Overprinted

w

x

1952, Mar. 14 *Perf. 15x14, 14x15*

166 A54(w) ½p dk brn & red vio .25 *.30*
167 A55(x) 1p dark green .25 *.30*
168 A54(w) 2p dark purple .60 .40
169 A55(x) 4½p dark blue .55 *2.00*
170 A54(w) 1sh brown 1.10 .85
Nos. 166-170 (5) 2.75 3.85

300th anniv. of the landing of Jan van Riebeeck at the Cape of Good Hope.

Coronation Issue

Queen Elizabeth II and Flowers — A54

Various flowers.

1953, June 2 Photo. *Perf. 14*

244 A54 1p carmine rose .50 .25
245 A54 2p dark green .50 .25
246 A54 4p deep magenta .60 .40
247 A54 6p deep blue .60 .90
248 A54 1sh chestnut brown .80 .55
Nos. 244-248 (5) 3.00 2.35

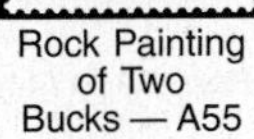

Rock Painting of Two Bucks — A55

Rhinoceros Hunt — A56

Designs: 2p, "White Lady" (rock painting). 4p, Elephant and giraffe (rock painting). 4½p, Karakul lamb. 6p, Owambo blowing Kudu horn. 1sh, Ukuanjama woman. 1sh3p, Herero woman. 1sh6p, Ukuanjama girl. 2sh6p, Lioness. 5sh, Cape Oryx. 10sh, Elephant.

1954, Nov. 15 Wmk. 201 *Perf. 14*

249 A55 1p rose brown .35 .25
250 A55 2p dk brown .45 .25
251 A56 3p brown vio 1.25 .25
252 A56 4p olive gray 1.60 .25
253 A55 4½p blue vio .90 .35
254 A55 6p gray green 1.10 .85
255 A55 1sh magenta 1.25 .85
256 A55 1sh3p rose pink 2.50 1.25
257 A55 1sh6p dull purple 2.50 1.00
258 A55 2sh6p yel brown 5.00 1.50
259 A55 5sh blue 9.00 5.50
260 A55 10sh dk green 35.00 17.50
Nos. 249-260 (12) 60.90 29.80

1960 Wmk. 330 *Perf. 14*

261 A55 1p rose brown 1.00 *1.50*
262 A55 2p dark brown 1.25 *1.50*
263 A56 3p brown vio 2.00 *4.50*
264 A56 4p olive gray 3.75 *4.00*
265 A55 1sh6p dull purple 24.00 *14.50*
Nos. 261-265 (5) 32.00 *26.00*

General Post Office, Windhoek — A57

Fishing Industry — A58

Designs: 1c, Finger Rock, Asab. 1½c, Monument, Mounted Soldier. 2c, Quivertree (aloe dichotoma Masson). 2½c, Administrator's residence. 3c, Swakopmund Lighthouse and flamingoes. 5c, Flamingo. 7½c, Christchurch. 10c, Diamonds. 12½c, Fort Namutoni. 15c, Hardap Dam. 20c, Topaz. 50c, Tourmaline. 1r, Heliodor.

1961-63 Wmk. 330 Photo. *Perf. 14*

266 A57 ½c blue & brown .50 .30
267 A58 1c pale lil & brn .25 .25
268 A58 1½c sal & dk pur .30 .25
269 A58 2c yel & green 1.00 *1.40*
270 A57 2½c lt bl & red brn .50 .25
271 A58 3c dp rose & vio bl 4.75 .75
272 A58 3½c blue grn & ind 1.00 .30
273 A58 5c bluish gray & red 8.00 .60
274 A58 7½c yellow & brn .80 .30
275 A58 10c brt blue & yel 1.75 .50
276 A57 12½c yellow & ind .60 .50
277 A57 15c dp brn & blue 13.00 3.25
278 A58 20c sal, brn & blk 4.00 .45
279 A58 50c org yel & Prus grn 4.50 1.50
280 A58 1r brt blue, mar & yel 8.50 *11.50*
Nos. 266-280 (15) 49.45 22.10

Issued: 3c, 10/1/62; 15c, 3/16/63; others, 2/14/61.

1962-73 Unwmk.

281 A57 ½c blue & brn .55 *1.25*
282 A58 1½c sal & dk pur ('63) 5.75 .40
283 A58 2c yellow & grn 4.75 3.50
284 A57 2½c lt bl & red brn ('64) 9.50 4.00
285 A58 3c dp rose & vio bl ('73) 2.75 2.25
286 A58 3½c bl grn & ind ('66) 10.00 3.50
287 A58 5c bluish gray & red 7.50 1.50
Nos. 281-287 (7) 40.80 16.40

See Nos. 304-308, 314-328.

Hardap Dam and Development — A59

1963, Mar. 16 Wmk. 330

294 A59 3c sepia green .40 .40

Opening of Hardap Dam near Mariental.

Centenary Emblem and S.W.A. Map — A60

Design: 15c, Emblem and globe.

1963, Aug. 30 Unwmk. *Perf. 14*

295 A60 7½c blue, blk & red 4.25 4.00
296 A60 15c brn org, blk & red 7.00 7.50

Centenary of the International Red Cross.

Assembly Hall — A61

1964, May 14 Photo. Wmk. 330

297 A61 3c salmon pink & vio bl .60 .60

Issued to commemorate the opening of the new hall of the Legislative Assembly.

John Calvin — A62

1964, Oct. 1 Unwmk. *Perf. 14*

298 A62 2½c magenta & gold .50 .35
299 A62 15c green & gold 3.25 *3.75*

John Calvin (1509-64), French theologian and leader of the Reformation.

Mail Runner, 1890 — A63

Kurt von François — A64

Wmk. 348

1965, Oct. 18 Photo. *Perf. 14*

300 A63 3c red & deep brown .55 .25
301 A64 15c green & deep brn 2.25 1.50

75th anniversary of Windhoek.

Dr. H. H. Vedder, Missionary, Educator and Senator, 90th Birthday — A65

1966, July 4 *Perf. 14*

302 A65 3c black & salmon .50 .25
303 A65 15c black & light blue 1.10 .70

Types of 1961-62

1966-67 Wmk. 348 Photo. *Perf. 14*

Chalky Paper

304 A57 ½c lt blue & brn *10.00* *1.00*
304A A58 1c pale lil & brn 1.50 .25
305 A58 2c brt yel & dp grn 2.50 .25
306 A57 2½c gray blue & red brn 2.50 2.00
307 A58 3½c pale grn & vio bl 4.25 2.00
308 A58 7½c brt yel & brn 4.50 .80
Nos. 304-308 (6) *25.25* *6.30*

The watermark on Nos. 304, 305-308 is very faint, and these stamps can be distinguished by the shades and by the thick chalky paper. The watermark on No. 304A is clear.

Issued: 2c, 2½c, 1966; others, 1967.

Camelthorn Tree — A66

Verwoerd — A67

Design: 3c, Waves breaking against rock.

Perf. 14, 14x15 (15c)

1967, Jan. 6 Litho. Wmk. 348

309 A66 2½c green & black .25 .25
310 A67 3c brt blue & brown .35 .25
311 A67 15c rose lilac & black .90 .70
Nos. 309-311 (3) 1.50 1.20

Dr. Hendrik F. Verwoerd (1901-1966), Prime Minister of South Africa.

Swart — A68

15c, President and Mrs. C. R. Swart.

Perf. 14x15

1968, Jan. 2 Photo. Wmk. 359

312 Strip of 3 2.75 2.75
a. A68 3c Single, English .40 .30
b. A68 3c Single, Afrikaans .40 .30
c. A68 3c Single, German .40 .30
313 Strip of 3 8.00 8.00
a. A68 15c Single, English 1.00 1.00
b. A68 15c Single, Afrikaans 1.00 1.00
c. A68 15c Single, German 1.00 1.00

Charles Robberts Swart, 1st president of South Africa, (1961-67).

Types of 1961-62

Designs: 4c, like 2½c. 6c, Christchurch. 9c, Fort Namutoni.

1968-72 Wmk. 359 Photo. *Perf. 14*

314 A57 ½c blue & brown 1.60 .25
315 A57 ½c blue & brn, redrawn ('70) 1.25 .40
316 A58 1c pale lilac & brn ('70) 1.25 .40
317 A58 1½c salmon & dk pur 5.50 .30
318 A58 1½c sal & dk pur, redrawn ('71) 14.00 17.00
319 A58 2c yel & grn, redrawn ('70) 4.50 .40
320 A57 2½c lt bl & red brn ('70) 6.75 .40
321 A58 3c dp rose & vio bl ('70) 6.00 1.50
322 A57 4c lt bl & red brn ('71) 2.25 2.00
323 A58 5c bluish gray & red 4.00 .50
324 A58 6c yel & brn ('71) 6.75 5.00
325 A57 9c yel & ind ('71) 8.00 7.00
326 A58 10c brt bl & yel ('70) 16.00 3.00
327 A57 15c dp brn & bl ('72) 17.50 6.00
328 A58 20c org, brn & blk 18.00 3.50
Nos. 314-328 (15) 113.35 47.65

Nos. 315, 318-319 are without inscription "Posgeld Incomste Postage Revenue" and the numerals have been enlarged. The ½c (#315), 2c and 10c were also issued as coils.

Water Type of South Africa, 1970

2½c, Water drop and flower. 3c, Waves, horiz.

1970, Feb. 14 *Perf. 14*

329 A142 2½c brown, brt bl & grn .40 .40
330 A142 3c pale gray, bl & indigo .75 .40

Water '70 campaign of the South African Department of Water Affairs.

Bible Society Types of South Africa

Designs: 2½c, Sower, stained glass window. 12½c, "BIBLIA" and open book.

1970, Aug. 24 Photo. *Perf. 14*

331 A143 2½c multicolored .85 .35

Photo.; Gold Impressed

332 A144 12½c ultra, blk & gold 6.00 6.00

South African Bible Soc., 150th anniv.

Stamp Exhibition Types of South Africa

Perf. 14x13½, 13½x14

1971, May 31 Photo. Wmk. 359

333 A145 5c blue, yel & blk 3.50 2.00
334 A146 12½c grnsh bl, vio bl & red 22.50 17.50

Intl. Stamp Exhib. (INTERSTEX), Cape Town, May 22-31. No. 334 also for the 10th anniv. of the Antarctic Treaty pledging peaceful uses of and scientific cooperation in Antarctica.

Republic Anniversary Types of South Africa

1971, May 31 *Perf. 14*

335 A147 2c mag, rose red & buff 2.50 .85
336 A148 4c blue green & black 3.00 .85

10th anniv. of the Republic of South Africa.

Cat Type of South Africa

1972, Sept. 19 *Perf. 14*

337 A152 5c multicolored 3.75 2.75

Cent. of the SPCA.

Landscape, by Adolph Jentsch — A69

Designs: Various landscapes by Adolph Jentsch (1888-1977). 10c, 15c, vert.

1973, Apr. 28 Litho. *Perf. 11½x12½*

338 A69 2c multicolored .75 .75
339 A69 4c multicolored 1.00 1.00
340 A69 5c multicolored 1.25 1.25
341 A69 10c multicolored 1.50 1.50
342 A69 15c multicolored 3.00 3.00
Nos. 338-342 (5) 7.50 7.50

Sarcocaulon Rigidum A70

Pachypodium Namaqua-num A71

Designs: 1c-50c, Various succulent plants. 1r, Welwitschia. 30c, 1r, horiz.

1973, Sept. 1 Litho. *Perf. 12½*

Plants in Natural Colors

343 A70 1c light blue .25 .25
344 A70 2c yellow .25 .25
345 A70 3c salmon pink .25 .25
346 A70 4c gray .25 .25
347 A70 5c blue .40 .50
348 A70 6c greenish gray 2.25 *3.50*
349 A70 7c bright yellow 1.50 *2.00*
350 A70 9c dull yellow 1.00 *1.75*
351 A70 10c blue green 1.00 .25
352 A70 14c yellow green 2.00 *3.00*
353 A70 15c light brown 1.00 .50
354 A70 20c light olive 5.00 3.50
355 A70 25c orange 5.00 2.50

Perf. 12x12½, 12½x12

356 A71 30c dull yellow .90 *1.50*
357 A71 50c light green 1.00 2.50
358 A71 1r blue green 1.75 5.00
Nos. 343-358 (16) 23.80 27.50

1979 Same Designs *Perf. 14*

344a A70 2c .30 .25
345a A70 3c .30 .30
347a A70 5c .50 .25
351a A70 10c .60 .45
356a A71 30c 1.25 1.00
357a A71 50c 1.25 *1.75*
Nos. 344a-357a (6) 4.20 4.00

Coil Stamps

1973, Sept. 1 Photo. *Perf. 14*

359 A70 1c brt pink & black .90 .75
360 A70 2c yellow & black .75 .60
361 A70 5c red & black 1.90 1.25

1978 *Perf. 14 Vertically*

361A A70 1c brt pink & black 5.00 *6.00*
362 A70 2c yellow & black 1.40 .40
362A A70 5c red & black 1.10 .95
Nos. 359-362A (6) 11.05 9.95

For overprints, see Nos. 423-428.

NOTE: coil stamps, Nos. 359-362A, are printed in two colors, sheet stamps are multicolored.

Chat-shrike — A72

Rare birds: 5c, Rosy-faced lovebirds. 10c, Damara rockjumper. 15c, Ruppell's parrot.

Perf. 12½x11½

1974, Feb. 13 Litho.

363 A72 4c shown 2.50 1.50
364 A72 5c multicolored 3.50 2.00
365 A72 10c multicolored 7.50 7.50
366 A72 15c multicolored 12.50 12.50
Nos. 363-366 (4) 26.00 23.50

Rock Carvings, Twyfelfontein — A73

1974, Apr. 10 Litho. *Perf. 12½*

367 A73 4c Giraffe & horse 1.25 .85
368 A73 5c Elephant 1.50 1.10

Perf. 12x12½

Size: 37x21½mm

369 A73 15c Deer, horiz. 6.50 5.25
Nos. 367-369 (3) 9.25 7.20

Mining — A74

10c, Diamonds. 15c, Diamond open pit mining.

1974, Sept. 30 *Perf. 12½x11½*

370 A74 10c multicolored 4.00 5.00
371 A74 15c multicolored 5.00 5.00

Map Showing Route, Covered Wagons A75

Perf. 11½x12

1974, Nov. 13 Unwmk.

372 A75 4c yellow & multi 1.00 .90

Centenary of "Thirstland Trek" from Transvaal through Kalahari Desert to Angola.

Peregrine Falcon — A76

Designs: Protected Birds of Prey.

1975, Mar. 19 *Perf. 12½x11½*

373 A76 4c shown 2.25 1.50
374 A76 5c Black eagle 3.75 1.75
375 A76 10c Martial eagle 5.00 4.25
376 A76 15c Egyptian vulture 7.00 7.00
Nos. 373-376 (4) 18.00 14.50

Kolmanskop, Ghost Diamond Mining Town — A77

Designs: 9c, German steam traction engine, 1896. 15c, Old Fort, Windhoek and statue of Colonial German trooper on horseback.

1975, July 23 Litho. *Perf. 12x12½*

377 A77 5c violet & multi .30 .30
378 A77 9c ocher & multi .65 .65
379 A77 15c yellow & multi 1.00 1.00
Nos. 377-379 (3) 1.95 1.95

Historic monuments.

Paintings by Otto Schröder (1913-75) A78

No. 380, Luderitz. No. 381, Swakopmund. No. 382, Unloading freighters. No. 383, Ships at anchor, Walvis Bay.

1975, Oct. 15 Litho. *Perf. 12x12½*

380 A78 15c multicolored .50 .50
381 A78 15c multicolored .50 .50
382 A78 15c multicolored .50 .50
383 A78 15c multicolored .50 .50
a. Souvenir sheet of 4, #380-383 3.75 3.75
b. Block of 4, #380-383 3.00 3.00

No. 383a has a horizontal gutter with black inscription on silver panel.

Elephants A79

Pre-historic Rock Paintings: 10c, Rhinoceros. 15c, Antelope and hunter. 20c, Hunter with bow and arrow.

1976, Mar. 12 Litho. *Perf. 12x12½*

384 A79 4c red brown & multi .25 .25
385 A79 10c red brown & multi .50 .50
386 A79 15c red brown & multi .75 .75
387 A79 20c red brown & multi 1.25 1.25
a. Souvenir sheet of 4, #384-387 3.75 3.75
Nos. 384-387 (4) 2.75 2.75

Schloss Duwisib A80

Castles Built by German Settlers: 10c, Schwerinsburg. 20c, Heynitzburg.

1976, May 14 Litho. *Perf. 12x12½*

388 A80 10c multicolored .45 .45
389 A80 15c multicolored .65 .65
390 A80 20c multicolored .75 .75
Nos. 388-390 (3) 1.85 1.85

Nature Protection A81

1976, July 16 Litho. *Perf. 11½x12½*
391 A81 4c Daman .30 .30
392 A81 10c Dik-diks .70 .70
393 A81 15c Tree squirrel 1.00 1.00
Nos. 391-393 (3) 2.00 2.00

Augustineum Training Institute, Windhoek — A82

20c, Katutura State Hospital, Windhoek.

1976, Sept. 17 Litho. *Perf. 12x12½*
394 A82 15c ocher & black .50 .50
395 A82 20c citron & black .75 .75

Owambo Canal System A83

20c, Ruacana Dam and hydroelectric station.

1976, Nov. 19 Litho. *Perf. 12x12½*
396 A83 15c multicolored .50 .50
397 A83 20c multicolored .75 .75

Water and electricity supply.

Sinking Ship off Namib Shore — A84

Designs: Namib Desert, various views.

1977, Mar. 29 Litho. *Perf. 12½*
398 A84 4c multicolored .25 .25
399 A84 10c multicolored .40 .40
400 A84 15c multicolored .65 .60
401 A84 20c multicolored .90 .85
Nos. 398-401 (4) 2.20 2.10

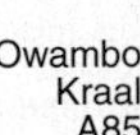
Owambo Kraal A85

Designs: 10c, Giant grain baskets. 15c, Women pounding corn. 20c, Body painting.

1977, July 15 Litho. *Perf. 12x12½*
402 A85 4c multicolored .25 .25
403 A85 10c multicolored .35 .35
404 A85 15c multicolored .50 .50
405 A85 20c multicolored .80 .80
Nos. 402-405 (4) 1.90 1.90

Traditions of the Wambo people.

J. G. Strijdom Airport, Windhoek — A86

1977, Aug. 22 *Perf. 12½*
406 A86 20c multicolored .60 .50

Drostdy, Lüderitz, 1910 A87

Historic Houses: 10c, Woermannhaus, Swakopmund, 1895. 15c, Neu-Heusis, Windhoek. 20c, Schmelenhaus, Bethanie, 1814.

1977, Nov. 4 Litho. *Perf. 12x12½*
407 A87 5c multicolored .25 .25
408 A87 10c multicolored .35 .35
409 A87 15c multicolored .55 .55
410 A87 20c multicolored .75 .75
a. Souvenir sheet of 4, #407-410 2.25 2.25
Nos. 407-410 (4) 1.90 1.90

Side-winding Adder — A88

Small Animals of the Namib Desert: 10c, Golden sand mole. 15c, Palmato gecko. 20c, Namaqua chameleon.

1978, Feb. 6 Litho. *Perf. 12½*
411 A88 4c multicolored .25 .25
412 A88 10c multicolored .35 .35
413 A88 15c multicolored .50 .50
414 A88 20c multicolored .70 .70
Nos. 411-414 (4) 1.80 1.80

Bushman Hunter Disguised as Ostrich A89

Bushmen: 10c, Woman carrying ostrich eggs on back. 15c, Making fire. 20c, Family sitting in front of hut.

1978, Apr. 14 Litho. *Perf. 12x12½*
415 A89 4c brown, buff & blk .25 .25
416 A89 10c brown, buff & blk .30 .30
417 A89 15c brown, buff & blk .50 .50
418 A89 20c brown, buff & blk .65 .65
Nos. 415-418 (4) 1.70 1.70

Lutheran Church, Windhoek — A90

Designs: 10c, Lutheran Church, Swakopmund. 15c, Rhenish Mission Church, Otjimbingwe. 20c, Rhenish Mission Church, Keetmanshoop.

1978, June 16 Litho. *Perf. 12½*
419 A90 4c ol bister & blk .25 .25
420 A90 10c bister & blk .30 .30
421 A90 15c pale red brn & blk .50 .50
422 A90 20c blue gray & blk .65 .65
a. Souvenir sheet of 4, #419-422 1.90 1.90
Nos. 419-422 (4) 1.70 1.70

Type of 1973 Inscribed in English, German or Afrikaans:

a, UNIVERSAL / SUFFRAGE
b, ALLGEMEINES / WAHLRECHT
c, ALGEMENE / STEMREG

1978, Nov. 1 Litho. *Perf. 12½*
423 Strip of 3 .25 .25
a.-c. A70 4c any single .25 .25
424 Strip of 3 .30 .30
a.-c. A70 5c any single .25 .25
425 Strip of 3 .60 .60
a.-c. A70 10c any single .25 .25
426 Strip of 3 .90 .90
a.-c. A70 15c any single .25 .25
427 Strip of 3 1.20 1.20
a.-c. A70 20c any single .35 .35
428 Strip of 3 1.60 1.60
a.-c. A70 25c any single .50 .50
Nos. 423-428 (6) 4.85 4.85

General suffrage. Printed se-tenant with inscriptions alternating horizontally and vertically in sheets of 30 (3x10).

Greater Flamingoes A91

Water Birds: 15c, White-breasted cormorants. 20c, Chestnut-banded plovers. 25c, White pelicans.

1979, Apr. 5 Litho. *Perf. 14x14½*
429 A91 4c multicolored .25 .25
430 A91 15c multicolored .40 .40
431 A91 20c multicolored .55 .55
432 A91 25c multicolored .75 .75
Nos. 429-432 (4) 1.95 1.95

Silver Topaz A92

1979, Nov. 26 Litho. *Perf. 14x14½*
433 A92 4c shown .30 .30
434 A92 15c Aquamarine .50 .50
435 A92 20c Malachite .80 .80
436 A92 25c Amethyst .95 .95
Nos. 433-436 (4) 2.55 2.55

Killer Whale — A93

5c, Humpback whale. 10c, Southern right whale. 15c, Sperm whale, giant squid. 20c, Fin whale. 25c, Blue whale, diver.

1980, Mar. 25 Litho. *Perf. 14x14½*
437 A93 4c shown .35 .30

Size: 37½x21mm

438 A93 5c multicolored .35 .30
439 A93 10c multicolored .70 .55

Size: 57½x21mm

440 A93 15c multicolored 1.10 .85
441 A93 20c multicolored 1.50 1.10

Size: 87½x21mm

442 A93 25c multicolored 1.60 1.25
a. Souvenir sheet of 6, #437-442 7.00 7.00
Nos. 437-442 (6) 5.60 4.35

Impala A94

1980, June 25 Litho. *Perf. 14½x14*
443 A94 5c shown .25 .25
444 A94 10c Tsessebe .30 .30
445 A94 15c Roan antelope .40 .40
446 A94 20c Sable antelope .55 .55
Nos. 443-446 (4) 1.50 1.50

Cape Hunting Dog — A95

1c, Black backed jackal. 3c, Hyena. 4c, Dorcas antelope. 5c, Oryx. 6c, Greater kudu. 7c, Zebra, horiz. 8c, Porcupine, horiz. 9c, Honey badger, horiz. 10c, Cheetah, horiz. 11c, Blue wildebeest ('84). 12c, Syncerus caffer, horiz. ('85). 15c, Hippopotamus, horiz. 20c, Tauro-tragus oryx, horiz. 25c, Rhinoceros, horiz. 30c, Lion, horiz. 50c, Giraffe. 1r, Leopard. 2r, Elephant.

No. 464, Suricate suricate. No. 465, Guenon. No. 466, South African chacma.

1980-85 Litho. *Perf. 14½x14*
447 A95 1c multicolored .25 .25
448 A95 2c multicolored .25 .25
449 A95 3c multicolored .25 .25
450 A95 4c multicolored .25 .25
451 A95 5c multicolored .25 .25
452 A95 6c multicolored .25 .25

Perf. 14x1414½

453 A95 7c multicolored .25 .25
454 A95 8c multicolored .25 .25
455 A95 9c multicolored .25 .25
456 A95 10c multicolored .25 .25
456A A95 11c multicolored .85 .35
456B A95 12c multicolored .55 .30
c. Booklet pane of 10 5.50
457 A95 15c multicolored .30 .30
458 A95 20c multicolored .45 .45
459 A95 25c multicolored .55 .55
460 A95 30c multicolored .65 .65

Perf. 14½x14

461 A95 50c multicolored 1.00 1.00
462 A95 1r multicolored 1.75 1.75
463 A95 2r multicolored 3.75 3.25
Nos. 447-463 (19) 12.35 11.10

Coil Stamps

1980, Oct. 1 Litho. *Perf. 14 Vert.*
464 A95 1c multicolored .40 .40
465 A95 2c multicolored .40 .40
466 A95 5c multicolored .40 .40
Nos. 464-466 (3) 1.20 1.20

See Nos. 556-557.

Von Bach Dam, Swakop River — A96

1980, Nov. 25 Litho. *Perf. 14x14½*
467 A96 5c shown .25 .25
468 A96 10c Swakoppoort Dam .25 .25
469 A96 15c Naute Dam .30 .30
470 A96 20c Hardap Dam .40 .40
Nos. 467-470 (4) 1.20 1.20

Water conservation in the desert.

Fish River Canyon — A97

Designs: Views of Fish River Canyon.

1981, Mar. 20 Litho. *Perf. 14½x14*
471 A97 5c multicolored .25 .25
472 A97 15c multicolored .30 .30
473 A97 20c multicolored .35 .35
474 A97 25c multicolored .40 .40
Nos. 471-474 (4) 1.30 1.30

Aloe Erinacea — A98

1981, Aug. 14
475 A98 5c shown .25 .25
476 A98 15c Aloe viridiflora .35 .35
477 A98 20c Aloe pearsonii .45 .45
478 A98 25c Aloe littoralis .45 .45
Nos. 475-478 (4) 1.50 1.50

Paul Weiss-Haus Building, 1909, Luderitz — A99

Historic buildings in Luderitz: 15c, Deutsche Afrika Bank, 1906. 20c, Schroederhaus, 1911. 25c, Imperial P.O., 1908.

1981, Oct. 16

479 A99 5c shown .25 .25
480 A99 15c multicolored .25 .25
481 A99 20c multicolored .30 .30
482 A99 25c multicolored .40 .40
a. Souvenir sheet of 4, #479-482 1.50 1.50
Nos. 479-482 (4) 1.20 1.20

Salt Making A100

5c, Salt pan. 15c, Dumping and washing. 20c, Stockpiling. 25c, Loading.

1981, Dec. 4 Litho. *Perf. 14x14½*

483 A100 5c multicolored .25 .25
484 A100 15c multicolored .30 .30
485 A100 20c multicolored .35 .35
486 A100 25c multicolored .40 .40
Nos. 483-486 (4) 1.30 1.30

Kalahari Starred Tortoise A101

1982, Mar. 12

487 A101 5c shown .25 .25
488 A101 15c Leopard tortoise .30 .30
489 A101 20c Angulated tortoise .45 .45
490 A101 25c Speckled padloper .55 .55
Nos. 487-490 (4) 1.55 1.55

Discoverers of South-West Africa — A102

15c, Archbishop Olaus Magnus, sea monster. 20c, Bartolomeu Dias, ships, map. 25c, Caravel. 30c, Dias erecting cross, Angra das Voltas.

1982, May 28 Litho. *Perf. 14½x14*

491 A102 15c multicolored .30 .30
492 A102 20c multicolored .45 .45
493 A102 25c multicolored .75 .75
494 A102 30c multicolored .80 .80
Nos. 491-494 (4) 2.30 2.30

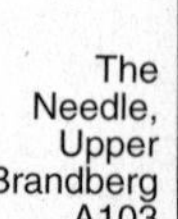

The Needle, Upper Brandberg A103

Mountain peaks: 6c, Brandberg. 15c, Omatako twin peaks. 25c, Spitzkuppe, Karakul sheep.

1982, Aug. 3 Litho. *Perf. 14x14½*

495 A103 6c multicolored .25 .25
496 A103 15c multicolored .30 .30
497 A103 20c shown .35 .35
498 A103 25c multicolored .40 .40
Nos. 495-498 (4) 1.30 1.30

Traditional Headdress, Herero Tribe — A104

1982, Oct. 15 Litho. *Perf. 14x14½*

499 A104 6c shown .25 .25
500 A104 15c Himba .35 .35
501 A104 20c Ngandjera .40 .40
502 A104 25c Kwanyama .55 .55
Nos. 499-502 (4) 1.55 1.55

See Nos. 524-527.

Fort Vogelsang A105

Bethany Chief Joseph Fredericks — A106

25c, Angra Pequena Bay. 30c, Explorer Heinrich Vogelsang. 40c, Adolf Luderitz (1834-1886).

Perf. 14x14½ (6c, 25c), 14½x14 (20c, 30-40c)

1983, Mar. 16

503 A105 6c shown .25 .25
504 A106 20c shown .25 .25
505 A105 25c multicolored .35 .35
506 A106 30c multicolored .40 .40
507 A106 40c multicolored .60 .60
Nos. 503-507 (5) 1.85 1.85

City of Luderitz centenary (1982).

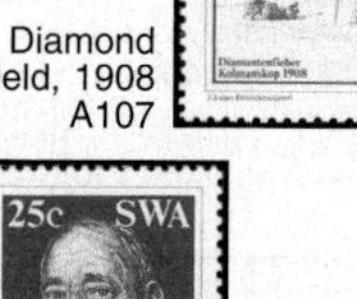

Diamond Field, 1908 A107

Ernest Oppenheimer (1880-1957), Diamond Industry Leader — A108

20c, Field, diff. 40c, August Stauch, prospector.

Perf. 14x14½ (10-20c), 14½x14 (25-40c)

1983, June 8 Litho.

508 A107 10c shown .35 .35
509 A107 20c multicolored .45 .45
510 A108 25c shown .60 .60
511 A108 40c multicolored .95 .95
Nos. 508-511 (4) 2.35 2.35

75th anniv. of discovery of diamonds at Luderitz.

Zebras Drinking, by J.J. van Ellinckhuijzen (b. 1940) — A109

Paintings: 20c, Rossing Mountain, by Herman H.-J. Henckert (b. 1906). 25c, Stampeding Buffalo, by Fritz Krampe (1913-1966). 40c, Erongo Mountains, by Johann Blatt (1905-1973).

1983, Sept. 1 *Perf. 14x14½*

512 A109 10c multicolored .30 .30
513 A109 20c multicolored .35 .35
514 A109 25c multicolored .45 .45
515 A109 40c multicolored .75 .75
Nos. 512-515 (4) 1.85 1.85

Lobster Industry A110

1983, Nov. 23 *Perf. 13½x14*

516 A110 10c Lobsters .25 .25
517 A110 20c Dinghies .30 .30
518 A110 25c Raising trap .40 .40
519 A110 40c Packaging .65 .65
Nos. 516-519 (4) 1.60 1.60

Historic Buildings, Swakopmund — A111

10c, Hohenzollern House. 20c, Railway Station. 25c, Imperial District Bureau. 30c, Ritterburg.

1984, Mar. 8 Litho. *Perf. 14x13½*

520 A111 10c multicolored .25 .25
521 A111 20c multicolored .35 .35
522 A111 25c multicolored .50 .50
523 A111 30c multicolored .55 .55
Nos. 520-523 (4) 1.65 1.65

Headdress Type of 1982

1984, May 25 Litho.

524 A104 11c Kwambi .25 .25
525 A104 20c Bushman .35 .35
526 A104 25c Kwaluudhi .50 .50
527 A104 30c Mbukushu .55 .55
Nos. 524-527 (4) 1.65 1.65

German Colonization Centenary — A112

11c, Map, flag. 25c, Flag raising. 30c, Land marker. 45c, Corvettes Elisabeth & Leipzig.

1984, Aug. 7 Litho. *Perf. 13½x14*

528 A112 11c multi .50 .50
529 A112 25c multi .85 .85
530 A112 30c multi .90 .90
531 A112 45c multi 2.10 2.10
Nos. 528-531 (4) 4.35 4.35

Spring Flowers — A113

1984, Nov. 22 Litho. *Perf. 14½x14*

532 A113 11c Sweet thorn .25 .25
533 A113 25c Camel thorn .40 .40
534 A113 30c Hook thorn .50 .50
535 A113 45c Candle-pod acacia .75 .75
Nos. 532-535 (4) 1.90 1.90

Ostrich A114

1985, Mar. 15

536 A114 11c Head of bird .40 .40
537 A114 25c Female nesting .75 .75
538 A114 30c Chick, eggs .85 .85
539 A114 50c Male mating dance 1.25 1.25
Nos. 536-539 (4) 3.25 3.25

Historic Buildings, 1900-1912, Windhoek — A115

12c, Erkrath, Gathemann Buildings, Kaiser Street. 25c, Gymnasium. 30c, Supreme Court. 50c, Railway Station.

1985, June 6

540 A115 12c multicolored .25 .25
541 A115 25c multicolored .45 .45
542 A115 30c multicolored .60 .60
543 A115 50c multicolored .80 .80
Nos. 540-543 (4) 2.10 2.10

600mm Narrow-gauge Locomotives — A116

12c, Zwilling Schmalspur, 1898. 25c, Feldspur Side-Tank. 30c, 0-6-2 Side-Tank, 1904. 50c, Henschel hd Smalspoor, 1912.

1985, Aug. 2

544 A116 12c multicolored .35 .35
545 A116 25c multicolored .70 .70
546 A116 30c multicolored .80 .80
547 A116 50c multicolored 1.50 1.50
Nos. 544-547 (4) 3.35 3.35

Swakopmund-Tsumeb Railway line, 79th anniv.

Endemic Musical Instruments A117

12c, Lidumu-dumu. 25c, Ngoma. 30c, Okambulum bumbwa. 50c, Gwashi.

1985, Oct. 17

548 A117 12c multicolored .25 .25
549 A117 25c multicolored .25 .25
550 A117 30c multicolored .30 .30
551 A117 50c multicolored .55 .55
Nos. 548-551 (4) 1.35 1.35

Diogo Cao, Portuguese Explorer, 1486 Visit to SWA A118

12c, Erecting padroes on shore. 20c, Cao coat of arms. 25c, Caravel. 30c, Portrait.

1986, Jan. 24 *Perf. 14½x14*

552 A118 12c multicolored .35 .35
553 A118 20c multicolored .55 .55
554 A118 25c multicolored .75 .75
555 A118 30c multicolored .95 .95
Nos. 552-555 (4) 2.60 2.60

Wildlife Type of 1980

1986-87 Litho. *Perf. 14x14½*

556 A95 14c Caracal, horiz. 4.00 4.00
557 A95 16c Warthog, horiz. 2.25 2.25

Issue dates: 14c, Apr. 1; 16c, Apr. 1, 1987.

Rock Formations A119

Designs: 14c, Granite bornhardt, Erongo. 20c, Vingerklip, Outjo. 25c, Aeolian sandstone, Kuiseb River. 30c, Columnar dolerite, Twyfelfontein.

1986, Apr. 24 *Perf. 14½x14*

566 A119 14c multicolored .30 .30
567 A119 20c multicolored .50 .50
568 A119 25c multicolored .65 .65
569 A119 30c multicolored .95 .95
Nos. 566-569 (4) 2.40 2.40

Karakul Wool (Swakara) Industry — A120

1986, July 10 *Perf. 14x14½*

570 A120 14c Model .30 .30
571 A120 20c Hand loom .45 .45
572 A120 25c Sheep .65 .65
573 A120 30c Rams .75 .75
a. Souvenir sheet of 1 3.50 3.50
Nos. 570-573 (4) 2.15 2.15

No. 573a margin pictures design of No. 570 and Johannesburg stamp exhib. emblem. Sold for 50c to benefit stamp exhib.

Caprivi Strip — A121

14c, Lake Liambezi. 20c, Stock and crop farming. 25c, Settlement. 30c, Map.

1986, Nov. 6 Litho. *Perf. 14½x14*

574 A121 14c multi .35 .35
575 A121 20c multi .60 .60
576 A121 25c multi .75 .75
577 A121 30c multi 1.20 1.20
Nos. 574-577 (4) 2.90 2.90

Paintings by Thomas Baines (1820-1875) A122

Designs: 14c, *Rhenish Mission Church at Gababis,* 1863. 20c, *Outspan in October,* 1861. 25c, *Outspan Under Oomahaama Tree,* 1862. 30c, *Swa-Kop River S.W. Africa,* 1861.

1987, Feb. 19 Litho. *Perf. 14½x14*

578 A122 14c multicolored .45 .45
579 A122 20c multicolored .75 .75
580 A122 25c multicolored .85 .85
a. Souvenir sheet of 1 3.25 3.25
581 A122 30c multicolored 1.00 1.00
Nos. 578-581 (4) 3.05 3.05

No. 580a for the natl. philatelic exhibition at Paarl, Sept. 16-19. Sold for 50c.

Insects A123

16c, Garreta nitens. 20c, Alcimus stenurus. 25c, Anthophora caerulea. 30c, Hemiempusa capensis.

1987, May 7

582 A123 16c multicolored .75 .75
583 A123 20c multicolored .95 .95
584 A123 25c multicolored 1.25 1.25
585 A123 30c multicolored 1.40 1.40
Nos. 582-585 (4) 4.35 4.35

Resorts — A124

16c, Okaukuejo, Etosha Natl. Park. 20c, Daan Viljoen Game Park. 25c, Ai-Ais Hot Springs. 30c, Hardap, Mariental.

1987, July 23

586 A124 16c multicolored .40 .40
587 A124 20c multicolored .55 .55
588 A124 25c multicolored .65 .65
589 A124 30c multicolored .80 .80
Nos. 586-589 (4) 2.40 2.40

Shipwrecks A125

16c, Hope, 1804. 30c, Tilly, 1885. 40c, Eduard Bohlen, 1909. 50c, Dunedin Star, 1942.

1987, Oct. 15

590 A125 16c multicolored .65 .65
591 A125 30c multicolored 1.10 1.10
592 A125 40c multicolored 1.50 1.50
593 A125 50c multicolored 1.90 1.90
Nos. 590-593 (4) 5.15 5.15

Discovery of the Cape of Good Hope by Bartolomeu Dias, 500th Anniv. — A126

30c, Caravel. 40c, The Cantino Map, 1502. 50c, King John II.

1988, Jan. 7 *Perf. 14x14½*

594 A126 16c shown .40 .40
595 A126 30c multi .70 .70
596 A126 40c multi 1.00 1.00
597 A126 50c multi 1.25 1.25
Nos. 594-597 (4) 3.35 3.35

Historic Sites A127

16c, Sossusvlei Clay Pans. 30c, Sesriem Canyon. 40c, Hoaruseb clay castles. 50c, Hoba meteorite.

1988, Mar. 3 *Perf. 14½x14*

598 A127 16c multicolored .35 .35
599 A127 30c multicolored .60 .60
600 A127 40c multicolored .85 .85
601 A127 50c multicolored 1.40 1.40
Nos. 598-601 (4) 3.20 3.20

Postal Service, Cent. A128

16c, Otyimbingue P.O., 1888. 30c, Windhoek P.O., 1904. 40c, Mail runner, 1888. 50c, Camel post, 1904.

1988, July 7 *Perf. 14x14½*

602 A128 16c multicolored .40 .40
603 A128 30c multicolored .80 .80
604 A128 40c multicolored 1.10 1.10
605 A128 50c multicolored 1.25 1.25
a. Souvenir sheet of 1 3.75 3.75
Nos. 602-605 (4) 3.55 3.55

No. 605a for the natl. philatelic exhibition held at Windhoek, July 7-9. Sold for 1r.

Birds — A129

16c, Namibornis hereo. 30c, Ammomanes grayi. 40c, Eupodotis rueppellii. 50c, Tockus monteiri.

1988, Nov. 3

606 A129 16c multicolored 1.10 1.10
607 A129 30c multicolored 1.60 1.60
608 A129 40c multicolored 1.90 1.90
609 A129 50c multicolored 2.10 2.10
Nos. 606-609 (4) 6.70 6.70

Missionaries and Mission Stations — A130

16c, Carl Hahn (1818-95) & Gross-Barmen Mission. 30c, Johann Kronlein (1826-92) & Berseba Mission. 40c, Franz Kleinschmidt (1812-64) & Rehoboth Mission. 50c, Johann Schmelen (1777-1848) & Bethanien Mission.

1989, Feb. 16

610 A130 16c multicolored .35 .35
611 A130 30c multicolored .60 .60
612 A130 40c multicolored .95 .95
613 A130 50c multicolored 1.10 1.10
Nos. 610-613 (4) 3.00 3.00

Aviation Industry, 75th Anniv. A131

Maps and aircraft — 18c, Beechcraft 1900. 30c, Ryan Navion, 1948. 40c, Junkers F13, 1930. 50c, Pfalz Otto biplane, 1914.

1989, May 18 *Perf. 14½x14*

614 A131 18c multicolored .85 .85
615 A131 30c multicolored 1.15 1.15
616 A131 40c multicolored 1.50 1.50
617 A131 50c multicolored 2.00 2.00
a. Souvenir sheet of 1 5.00 5.00
Nos. 614-617 (4) 5.50 5.50

No. 617a has decorative bright blue and black inscribed margin picturing emblem of natl. philatelic exhibition WANDERERS 101, held Sept. 6-9. Sold for 1.50r.

Namib Desert Sand Dunes — A132

1989, Aug. 14 *Perf. 14x14½*
Size of 30c, 50c: 31x21½mm

618 A132 18c Barchan dunes .25 .25
619 A132 30c Star dunes .50 .50
620 A132 40c Transverse dunes .75 .75
621 A132 50c Crescent dunes .95 .95
Nos. 618-621 (4) 2.45 2.45

Suffrage, UN Resolution 435 — A133

1989, Aug. 24

622 A133 18c dull org & gray vio .25 .25
623 A133 35c green & blue .50 .50
624 A133 45c yellow & purple .80 .80
625 A133 60c golden brn & gray grn 1.20 1.20
Nos. 622-625 (4) 2.75 2.75

Minerals — A134

Mines A135

No. 626, Gypsum. No. 627, Fluorite. No. 628, Mimetite. No. 629, Cuprite. No. 630, Azurite. No. 631, Boltwoodite. No. 632, Dioptase. No. 633, Alluvial diamond field, Oranjemund. No. 634, Lead, copper & zinc mine, Tsumeb. No. 635, Zinc mine, Rosh Pinah. No. 636, Diamonds. No. 637, Wulfenite. No. 638, Tin mine, Uis. No. 639, Uranium mine, Rossing. No. 640, Gold.

1989-90 *Perf. 14½x14*

626 A134 1c multicolored .25 .25
627 A134 2c multicolored .25 .25
628 A134 5c multicolored .25 .25
629 A134 7c multicolored .25 .25
630 A134 10c multicolored .25 .25
631 A134 18c multicolored .30 .30
631A A134 18c see footnote *14.00 8.00*
632 A134 20c multicolored .30 .30
633 A135 25c multicolored .35 .35
634 A135 30c multicolored .40 .40
635 A135 35c multicolored .50 .50
636 A134 40c multicolored .55 .55
637 A134 45c multicolored .65 .65
638 A135 50c multicolored .70 .70
639 A135 1r multicolored 1.50 1.50
640 A134 2r multicolored 3.00 3.00
Nos. 626-640 (16) *23.50* 17.50

No. 631 has formula, $K(H_3O)(UO_2)(SiO_4)$; No. 631A, $K_2(UO_2)_2(SiO_3)_2(OH)_2.5H_2O$.

Issued: No. 631A, 10/25/90; others, 11/16/89.

This set remained in use until Namibia issued a definitive set Jan. 2, 1991.

Flora — A136

18c, Adenium boehmianum. 35c, Adansonia digitata. 45c, Kigelia africana. 60c, Harpagophytum procumbens.

1990, Feb. 1 *Perf. 14½x14*

641 A136 18c multicolored .40 .40
642 A136 35c multicolored .80 .80
643 A136 45c multicolored 1.00 1.00

644 A136 60c multicolored 1.25 1.25
a. Souvenir sheet of 1 4.75 4.75
Nos. 641-644 (4) 3.45 3.45

No. 644a margin publicizes the natl. phil. exhib. Sold for 1.50r.

SEMI-POSTAL STAMPS

Catalogue values for unused stamps in this section are for Never Hinged items.

Voortrekker Monument Issue

South Africa Nos. B1-B4 Overprinted

1935-36 Wmk. 201 *Perf. 14*

B1 SP1 ½p + ½p grn & blk, pair 4.00 *6.00*
a. Single, English .55 *.75*
b. Single, Afrikaans .55 *.75*
B2 SP2 1p + ½p rose & blk, pair 4.50 3.50
a. Single, English .65 .40
b. Single, Afrikaans .65 .40
B3 SP3 2p + 1p dl vio & gray, pair 15.00 7.50
a. Single, English 2.00 1.00
b. Single, Afrikaans 2.00 1.00
B4 SP4 3p + 1½p dp bl & gray, pair 40.00 42.50
a. Single, English 4.00 *4.25*
b. Single, Afrikaans 4.00 *4.25*
Nos. B1-B4 (4) 63.50 59.50

Voortrekker Centenary Issue

South Africa Nos. B5-B8 Overprinted

1938, Dec. 14 *Perf. 14*

B5 SP5 ½p + ½p dl grn & indigo, pair 9.00 *25.00*
a. Single, English 1.25 *2.00*
b. Single, Afrikaans 1.25 *2.00*

Perf. 15x14

B6 SP6 1p + 1p rose & sl, pair 24.00 20.00
a. Single, English 1.50 1.50
b. Single, Afrikaans 1.50 1.50
B7 SP7 1½p + 1½p Prus grn & choc, pair 26.00 *35.00*
a. Single, English 2.25 *3.25*
b. Single, Afrikaans 2.25 *3.25*
B8 SP8 3p + 3p chlky bl, pair 50.00 *85.00*
a. Single, English 5.00 *8.50*
b. Single, Afrikaans 5.00 *8.50*
Nos. B5-B8 (4) 109.00 *165.00*

Same Overprint on South Africa Nos. B9-B11

1939, July 17 *Perf. 14*

B9 SP9 ½p + ½p Prus grn & gray brn, pair 14.00 *16.00*
a. Single, English 1.00 1.25
b. Single, Afrikaans 1.00 1.25
B10 SP10 1p + 1p rose car & Prus grn, pair 21.00 16.00
a. Single, English 1.25 1.25
b. Single, Afrikaans 1.25 1.25

Perf. 15x14

B11 SP11 1½p + 1½p rose vio, dk vio & Prus grn, pair 34.00 20.00
a. Single, English 2.00 1.75
b. Single, Afrikaans 2.00 1.75
Nos. B9-B11 (3) 69.00 52.00

250th anniv. of the landing of the Huguenots in South Africa. Surtax went to a fund to build a Huguenot memorial at Paarl.

AIR POST STAMPS

South Africa Nos. C5-C6 Overprinted

1930 Unwmk. *Perf. 14x13½*

C1 AP2 4p blue green 4.00 *30.00*
a. Without period after "A" 75.00 *150.00*
b. First printing 8.00 *30.00*
C2 AP2 1sh orange 6.00 *57.50*
a. Without period after "A" 475.00 *675.00*
b. First printing 75.00 *125.00*

First printings are blurred with thick lettering and rounded periods. Later printings have sharp, thinner letters and squared periods.

Overprinted

C3 AP2 4p blue green 1.50 *6.50*
a. Double overprint 200.00
b. Inverted overprint 200.00
c. Small "I" in "AIR" 7.50
C4 AP2 1sh orange 3.00 *16.00*
a. Double overprint 575.00

Monoplane over Windhoek — AP3

Biplane over Windhoek — AP4

Wmk. 201

1931, Mar. 5 Engr. *Perf. 14*

C5 AP3 3p blue & dk brn, pair 30.00 *37.50*
a. Single, English 4.00 *2.75*
b. Single, Afrikaans 4.00 *2.75*
C6 AP4 10p brn vio & blk, pair 57.50 *85.00*
a. Single, English 9.00 *7.50*
b. Single, Afrikaans 9.00 *7.50*

POSTAGE DUE STAMPS

Postage Due Stamps of South Africa and Transvaal Overprinted like Regular Issues.

Setting I

On South Africa Nos. J11, J14

1923 Unwmk. *Perf. 14*

J1 D1 ½p blue grn & blk, pair 6.75 *30.00*
a. Single, English .75 *5.50*
b. Single, Dutch .75 *5.50*
c. As #J1, without period after "Afrika" 130.00
d. Inverted ovpt., pair 600.00
J2 D1 2p violet & blk, pair 4.00 *28.00*
a. Single, English .50 *5.00*
b. Single, Dutch .50 *5.00*
c. As #J2, without period after "Afrika" 170.00 170.00

On South Africa Nos. J9-J10

Rouletted 7-8

J3 D1 1p dull red & blk, pair 8.00 *30.00*
a. Single, English .90 *5.50*
b. Single, Dutch .90 *5.50*
c. As #J3, without period after "Afrika" 150.00 150.00
d. Pair, imperf. between 1,800.
J4 D1 1½p yel brn & blk, pair 1.50 *16.00*
a. Single, English .25 *2.75*
b. Single, Dutch .25 *2.75*
c. As #J4, without period after "Afrika" 110.00 110.00

On South Africa Nos. J3-J4, J6

Perf. 14

Wmk. 177

J5 D1 2p vio & blk, pair 42.50 *55.00*
a. Single, English 3.00 *10.00*
b. Single, Dutch 3.00 *10.00*
c. As #J5, without period after "Afrika" 275.00
d. "Wes" for "West" 325.00
J6 D1 3p ultra & blk, pair 21.00 *55.00*
a. Single, English 1.50 *10.00*
b. Single, Dutch 1.50 *10.00*
J7 D1 6p gray & blk, pair 40.00 *65.00*
a. Single, English 4.00 *13.00*
b. Single, Dutch 4.00 *13.00*
Nos. J5-J7 (3) 103.50 *175.00*

On Transvaal Nos. J5-J6

Wmk. Multiple Crown and C A (3)

J8 D1 5p vio & blk, pair 4.50 *55.00*
a. Single, English .75 *11.00*
b. Single, Dutch .75 *11.00*
c. As #J8, without period after "Afrika" 130.00 130.00
J9 D1 6p red brn & blk, pair 19.00 *55.00*
a. Single, Dutch 2.50 *11.00*
b. As #J9, without period after "Afrika" 275.00

For No. J9 single in English see No. J17a and note after No. 27.

The "t" of "West" may be found partly or entirely missing on Nos. J1, J3-J6, J8-J9.

Setting II

On South Africa No. J9

Rouletted

Unwmk.

J10 D1 1p dull red & blk, pair *14,000.*
a. Single, English 800.00 1,600.
b. Single, Dutch 800.00 1,600.

On South Africa Nos. J3-J4

Perf. 14

Wmk. 177

J11 D1 2p vio & blk, pair 19.00 *50.00*
a. Single, English 1.75 *9.00*
b. Single, Dutch 1.75 *9.00*
c. As #J11, without period after "Afrika" 275.00 250.00
J12 D1 3p ultra & blk, pair 8.50 *32.50*
a. Single, English 1.00 *5.50*
b. Single, Dutch 1.00 *5.50*
c. As #J12, without period after "Afrika" 130.00 *150.00*

On Transvaal No. J5

Wmk. Multiple Crown and C A (3)

J13 D1 5p vio & blk, pair 75.00 200.00
a. Single, English 15.00 *20.00*
b. Single, Dutch 15.00 *20.00*

Setting III

On South Africa Nos. J11, J12, J9

Unwmk.

J14 D1 ½p blue grn & blk, pair 17.50 *37.50*
a. Single, Dutch 1.50 *5.50*
J15 D1 1p rose & blk, pair 27.50 *37.50*
a. Single, English 1.50 *6.00*
b. Single, Dutch 1.50 *6.00*

Rouletted 7

J16 D1 1p dull red & blk, pair 9.50 *37.50*
a. Single, Dutch 1.00 *6.00*

For Nos. J14 and J16 singles in English see Nos. J1a and J3a and note after No. 27.

On Transvaal No. J6

Perf. 14

Wmk. 3

J17 D1 6p red brn & blk, pair 23.50 *100.00*
a. Single, English 2.50 *20.00*
b. Single, Dutch 2.50 *20.00*

See note below No. 27.

Setting IV

On South Africa Nos. J11-J12, J16

1924 Unwmk.

J18 D1 ½p blue grn & blk, pair 8.50 *35.00*
a. Single, English .75 *5.50*
b. Single, Dutch .75 *5.50*
J19 D1 1p rose & blk, pair 8.50 *32.50*
a. Single, English .60 *5.50*
b. Single, Dutch .60 *5.50*
J20 D1 6p gray & blk, pair 3.00 *45.00*
a. Single, English .30 *9.00*
b. Single, Dutch .30 *9.00*

On Transvaal No. J5

Wmk. Multiple Crown and C A (3)

J21 D1 5p vio & blk, pair 800.00 *1,200.*
a. Single, English 140.00 *175.00*
b. Single, Dutch 140.00 *175.00*

Setting V

i

j

"South West" 16mm wide
"Zuidwest" 12mm wide
Overprint Spaced 12mm

On South Africa Nos. J4, J11, J13

1924 Unwmk.

J22 D1 ½p green & blk, pair 3.50 *32.50*
a. Single, English .25 *6.50*
b. Single, Dutch .25 *6.50*
J23 D1 1½p yel brown & blk 5.75 *47.50*
a. Single, English .50 *7.50*
b. Single, Dutch .50 *7.50*

Wmk. Springbok's Head (177)

J24 D1 3p ultra & black, pair 16.00 *60.00*
a. Single, English 1.75 *11.00*
b. Single, Dutch 1.75 *11.00*

On Transvaal No. J5

Wmk. Multiple Crown and C A (3)

J25 D1 5p violet & blk, pair 3.00 *25.00*
a. Single, English .40 *7.50*
b. Single, Dutch .40 *7.50*

Setting VI

On South Africa Nos. J4, J11-J16

1924, Dec. Unwmk.

J26 D1 ½p blue grn & blk, pair 14.00 *40.00*
a. Single, English 1.00 *7.50*
b. Single, Dutch 1.00 *7.50*
J27 D1 1p rose & blk, pair 2.25 *14.00*
a. Single, English .25 *1.75*
b. Single, Dutch .25 *1.75*
c. As #J27, without period after "Africa" 100.00
J28 D1 1½p yel brn & blk, pair 5.00 *35.00*
a. Single, English .30 *6.50*
b. Single, Dutch .30 *6.50*
c. As #J28, without period after "Africa" 110.00
J29 D1 2p vio & blk, pair 3.00 *19.00*
a. Single, English .35 *3.50*
b. Single, Dutch .35 *3.50*
c. As #J29, without period after "Africa" 85.00
J30 D1 3p bl & blk, pair 5.25 *20.00*
a. Single, English .85 *3.75*
b. Single, Dutch .85 *3.75*
c. As #J30, without period after "Africa" 92.50
J31 D1 6p gray & blk, pair 16.00 *57.50*
a. Single, English 2.00 *14.00*
b. Single, Dutch 2.00 *14.00*
c. As #J31, without period after "Africa" 180.00
Nos. J26-J31 (6) 45.50 *185.50*

Wmk. Springbok's Head (177)

J32 D1 3p ultra & black, pair 10.00 *65.00*
a. Single, English 1.75 *11.00*
b. Single, Dutch 1.75 *11.00*

On Transvaal No. J5

Wmk. 3

J33 D1 5p violet & blk, pair 3.25 *22.50*
a. Single, English .25 *3.50*
b. Single, Dutch .25 *3.50*
c. As #J33, without period after "Africa" 92.50 *75.00*

Setting VIII

On South Africa Nos. J18, J13-J16

1927 Unwmk.

J34 D2 1p rose & black, pair 1.25 *13.00*
a. Single, English .25 *2.25*
b. Single, Afrikaans .25 *2.25*
c. As #J34, without period after "Africa" 10.50 *17.50*
J35 D1 1½p yel brn & blk, pair 1.25 *22.50*
a. Single, English .25 *3.50*
b. Single, Afrikaans .25 *3.50*
c. As #J35, without period after "Africa" 50.00 *60.00*
J36 D1 2p vio & blk, pair 6.00 *18.00*
a. Single, English .30 *3.25*
b. Single, Afrikaans .30 *3.25*
c. As #J36, without period after "Africa" 50.00 *60.00*
J37 D1 3p bl & blk, pair 16.00 *50.00*
a. Single, English 1.75 *11.00*
b. Single, Afrikaans 1.75 *11.00*
c. As #J37, without period after "Africa" 70.00 70.00
J38 D1 6p gray & blk, pair 12.00 *40.00*
a. Single, English 1.50 *8.50*
b. Single, Afrikaans 1.50 *8.50*

c. As #J38, without period after "Africa" 100.00 115.00
Nos. J34-J38 (5) 36.50 *143.50*

On Transvaal No. J5
Wmk. Multiple Crown and C A (3)

J39 D1 5p violet & blk, pair 22.50 *97.50*
a. Single, English 3.00 *22.50*
b. Single, Afrikaans 3.00 *22.50*

South Africa Nos. J15-J16 Overprinted

1928 **Unwmk.**

J79 D1 3p blue & black 1.65 *12.00*
a. Without period after "A" 42.50 45.00
J80 D1 6p gray & black 7.50 *32.50*
a. Without period after "A" 150.00

Same Overprint on South Africa Nos. J17-J21

J81 D2 ½p blue grn & blk .65 *9.50*
J82 D2 1p rose & black .65 *4.00*
a. Without period after "A" 45.00 *50.00*
J83 D2 2p violet & black .65 *5.00*
a. Without period after "A" 62.50
J84 D2 3p ultra & black 2.75 *30.00*
J85 D2 6p gray & black 1.75 *22.50*
a. Without period after "A" 62.50 *225.00*
Nos. J81-J85 (5) 6.45 *71.00*

Catalogue values for unused stamps in this section, from this point to the end of the section, are for Never Hinged items.

D3

Wmk. 201
1931, Feb. 23 **Litho.** ***Perf. 12***
Size: 19x22mm

J86 D3 ½p yel green & blk 2.00 *8.50*
J87 D3 1p rose & black 2.00 *1.65*
J88 D3 2p violet & black 2.50 *3.25*
J89 D3 3p blue & black 5.00 *15.00*
J90 D3 6p gray & black 17.50 *30.00*
Nos. J86-J90 (5) 29.00 *58.40*

Cover values are for properly franked commercial items. Philatelic usages also exist and sell for less.

Photo. (Frame) & Typo. (Center)

1959 ***Perf. 14½x14***
Size: 17x21mm

J91 D3 1p rose & black 2.25 *15.00*
J92 D3 2p violet & black 2.25 *15.00*
J93 D3 3p blue & black 2.25 *15.00*
Nos. J91-J93 (3) 6.75 *45.00*

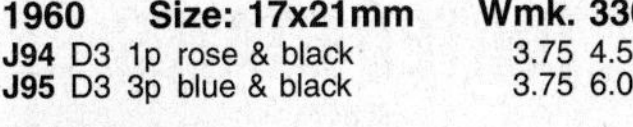

1960 **Size: 17x21mm** **Wmk. 330**

J94 D3 1p rose & black 3.75 4.50
J95 D3 3p blue & black 3.75 6.00

D4

1961, Feb. **Photo.** ***Perf. 14½x14***

J96 D4 1c green & black 1.00 *4.25*
J97 D4 2c red & black 1.00 *4.25*
J98 D4 4c lilac & black 1.00 *6.00*
J99 D4 5c blue & black 1.75 *5.25*
J100 D4 6c emerald & black 2.00 *7.50*
J101 D4 10c yellow & black 4.50 *11.00*
Nos. J96-J101 (6) 11.25 *38.25*

Type of South Africa, 1972

1972 **Wmk. 359** ***Perf. 14x13½***

J102 D6 1c bright green 1.10 *5.00*
J103 D6 8c violet blue 3.75 *8.50*

OFFICIAL STAMPS

Nos. 85-87 (Setting VIII) Overprinted at top with type "c" on English-inscribed Stamps and type "d" on Afrikaans-inscribed Stamps

c d

Without Periods after Words

1927 **Wmk. 201** ***Perf. 14½x14***

O1 A5 ½p dk grn & blk, pair 95.00 *200.00*
a. Single, English 12.50 *30.00*
b. Single, Afrikaans 12.50 *30.00*
O2 A6 1p car & blk, pair 95.00 *200.00*
a. Single, English 12.50 *30.00*
b. Single, Afrikaans 12.50 *30.00*
O3 A7 6p org & grn, pair 120.00 *225.00*
a. Single, English 15.00 *30.00*
b. Single, Afrikaans 15.00 *30.00*

South Africa No. 5 Overprinted As Nos. 85-87 plus "c" and "d"

Perf. 14
Wmk. 177

O4 A2 2p dull violet 225.00 *375.00*
a. Single, English 35.00 *45.00*
b. Single, Afrikaans 35.00 *45.00*

Nos. 96-98 Overprinted like Nos. J79-J85 at foot, Overprinted Types "c" and "d" at Top

1929 **Wmk. 201** ***Perf. 14½x14***

O5 A5 ½p green & blk, pair 1.25 *17.50*
a. Single, English .25 *2.75*
b. Single, Afrikaans .25 *2.75*
O6 A6 1p car & blk, pair 2.00 *23.00*
a. Single, English .25 *2.75*
b. Single, Afrikaans .25 *2.75*
O7 A7 6p org & grn, pair 4.50 *23.00*
a. Single, English .75 *3.75*
b. Single, Afrikaans .75 *3.75*
Nos. O5-O7 (3) 7.75 *63.50*

No. 99 Overprinted in Black

With Periods after Words

Perf. 14

O8 A8 2p vio brn & gray, pair 2.50 *22.50*
a. Single, English .35 *3.75*
b. Single, Afrikaans .35 *3.75*
c. Without period after "OFFICIAL" 7.00 *50.00*
d. Pair, "c" + normal 2p 17.00 *95.00*
e. Without period after "OFFISIEEL" 7.00 *50.00*
f. Pair, "e" + normal 2p 17.00 *95.00*
g. Pair, "c" + "e" 22.00 *95.00*

In each sheet of 120 stamps there were 12 No. O8c and 10 No. O8e.

South Africa Nos. 23-25 Overprinted

Without Periods after Words

1929 **Wmk. 201** ***Perf. 14½x14***

O9 A5 ½p green & blk, pair .85 *16.00*
a. Single, English .25 *2.75*
b. Single, Afrikaans .25 *2.75*
O10 A6 1p car & blk, pair 1.25 *17.50*
a. Single, English .25 *3.25*
b. Single, Afrikaans .25 *3.25*
O11 A7 6p org & grn, pair 3.00 *27.50*
a. Single, English .40 *6.50*
b. Single, Afrikaans .40 *6.50*
Nos. O9-O11 (3) 5.10 *61.00*

South Africa No. 26 Overprinted

With Periods after Words

Perf. 14

O12 A8 2p vio brn & gray, pair 1.50 *22.00*
a. Single, English .25 *3.50*
b. Single, Afrikaans .25 *3.50*
c. Without period after "OFFICIAL" 3.75 *45.00*
d. Pair, "c" + normal 2p 17.00 *95.00*
e. Without period after "OFFISIEEL" 6.50 *50.00*
f. Pair, "e" + normal 2p 17.00 *95.00*
g. Pair, "c" + "e" 22.00 *95.00*

Catalogue values for unused stamps in this section, from this point to the end of the section, are for Never Hinged items.

Nos. 108-109, 111 and 114 Overprinted in Red

1931

O13 A15 ½p green & blk, pair 15.00 *22.00*
a. Single, English 1.25 *3.75*
b. Single, Afrikaans 1.25 *3.75*
O14 A16 1p red & indigo, pair 1.50 *19.00*
a. Single, English .25 *3.50*
b. Single, Afrikaans .25 *3.50*
O15 A18 2p dk brn & dk bl, pair 3.75 *11.00*
a. Single, English .40 *2.25*
b. Single, Afrikaans .40 *2.25*
O16 A21 6p ol brn & bl, pair 5.75 *15.00*
a. Single, English .50 *3.25*
b. Single, Afrikaans .50 *3.25*
Nos. O13-O16 (4) 26.00 *67.00*

No. 110 Overprinted in Red

1938, July 1 **Wmk. 201**

O17 A17 1½p violet brn, pair 36.50 *50.00*
a. Single, English 3.50 *6.00*
b. Single, Afrikaans 3.50 *6.00*

Nos. 108-111, 114 Ovptd. in Red

1945-50 **Wmk. 201** ***Perf. 14x13½***

O18 A15 ½p grn & blk, pair 14.00 *35.00*
a. Single, English 1.50 *5.00*
b. Single, Afrikaans 1.50 *5.00*
O19 A16 1p red & ind, pair ('50) 14.00 *20.00*
a. Single, English .85 *3.25*
b. Single, Afrikaans .85 *3.25*
O20 A17 1½p vio brn, pair 40.00 55.00
a. Single, English 5.00 7.00
b. Single, Afrikaans 5.00 7.00
O21 A18 2p dk brn & dk bl, pair ('47) 675.00 *875.00*
a. Single, English 100.00 *100.00*
b. Single, Afrikaans 100.00 *100.00*
O22 A21 6p ol brn & bl, pair 30.00 *70.00*
a. Single, English 2.00 *8.00*
b. Single, Afrikaans 2.00 *8.00*
Nos. O18-O20,O22 (4) 98.00 *180.00*

Nos. 108-111, 114 Ovptd. in Red

1951-52

O23 A15 ½p grn & blk, pair ('52) 19.00 *25.00*
a. Single, English 2.00 *4.50*
b. Single, Afrikaans 2.00 *4.50*
O24 A16 1p red & ind, pair 6.00 *22.50*
a. Single, English .40 *2.00*
b. Single, Afrikaans .40 *2.00*
c. Ovpt. transposed, pair 110.00 *250.00*
d. As "c," single, English ovpt. 10.00
e. As "c," single, Afrikaans ovpt. 10.00
O25 A17 1½p violet brn, pair 30.00 32.50
a. Single, English 3.00 5.00
b. Single, Afrikaans 3.00 5.00
c. Ovpt. transposed, pair 80.00 *95.00*
d. As "c," single, English ovpt. 7.50
e. As "c," single, Afrikaans ovpt. 7.50
O26 A18 2p dk brn & dk bl, pair 4.00 *26.00*
a. Single, English .45 *3.50*
b. Single, Afrikaans .45 *3.50*
c. Ovpt. transposed, pair 75.00 *250.00*
d. As "c," single, English ovpt. 4.50
e. As "c," single, Afrikaans ovpt. 4.50
O27 A21 6p ol brn & blue, pair 4.00 *55.00*
a. Single, English .50 *7.50*
b. Single, Afrikaans .50 *7.50*
c. Ovpt. transposed, pair 28.00 *170.00*
d. As "c," single, English ovpt. 4.00
e. As "c," single, Afrikaans ovpt. 4.00
Nos. O23-O27 (5) 63.00 *161.00*

"Overprint transposed" means English inscription on Afrikaans stamp, or vice versa.

Use of official stamps ceased in Jan. 1955.

SPAIN

'spān

LOCATION — Southwestern Europe, Iberian Peninsula
GOVT. — Monarchy
AREA — 194,884 sq. mi.
POP. — 39,167,744 (1999 est.)
CAPITAL — Madrid

Spain was a monarchy until about 1931, when a republic was established. After the Civil War (1936-39), the Spanish State of Gen. Francisco Franco was recognized. The monarchy was restored in 1975.

32 Maravedis = 8 Cuartos = 1 Real
1000 Milesimas = 100 Centimos = 1 Escudo (1866)
100 Milesimas = 1 Real
4 Reales = 1 Peseta
100 Centimos = 1 Peseta (1872)
100 Cents = 1 Euro (2002)

Catalogue values for unused stamps in this country are for Never Hinged items, beginning with Scott 909 in the regular postage section, Scott B139 in the semi-postal section, Scott C159 in the airpost section, and Scott E21 in the special delivery section.

Watermarks

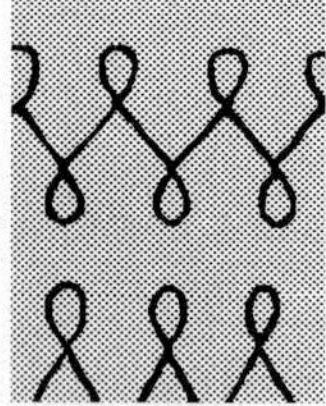

Wmk. 104 — Loops

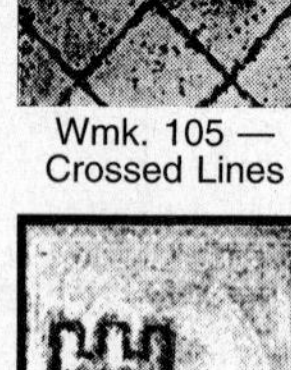

Wmk. 105 — Crossed Lines

Wmk. 116 — Crosses and Circles

Wmk. 178 — Castle

Stamps punched with a small round hole have done telegraph service. In this condition most of them sell for 20 cents to $20.

Stamps of 1854 to 1882 canceled with three parallel horizontal bars or two thin lines are remainders. Most of these are valued through No. 101 and 174 through 254. In a few cases, the bar cancels are scarcer than regular used examples and sell for more. Where no special listing is present, and if available, they sell for about the same as regular used stamps.

For additional shades see the *Scott Classic Catalogue.*

Kingdom

Queen Isabella II
A1 A2

A2a

A2b

A2c

Type I

Type II

6 CUARTOS:
Type I — "T" and "O" of CUARTOS separated.
Type II — "T" and "O" joined.

Unwmk.

1850, Jan. 1 Litho. *Imperf.*

1 A1 6c blk, thin paper (II) 650.00 17.00
a. Thick paper (II) 650.00 25.00
b. Thick paper (I) 850.00 20.00
c. Thin paper (I) 850.00 32.50
2 A2 12c lilac 2,500. 200.00
a. Thin paper *4,000.* 325.00
3 A2a 5r red 2,700. 175.00
4 A2b 6r blue 3,000. 500.00
5 A2c 10r green 4,500. 1,200.

Stamps of types A2, A3, A4, A6, A7a and A8 are inscribed "FRANCO" on the cuarto values and "CERTIFICADO," "CERTIFO" or "CERT DO" on the reales values.

A3

1851, Jan. 1 Thin Paper Typo.

6 A3 6c black 375.00 3.50
a. Thick paper 825.00 20.00
7 A3 12c lilac 7,500. 175.00
8 A3 2r red *17,000.* *5,000.*
9 A3 5r rose 2,500. 150.00
a. 5r red brown (error) *22,000.* —
10 A3 6r blue 4,500. 550.00
a. Cliche of 2r in plate of 6r — —
11 A3 10r green 3,750. 400.00

A4

1852, Jan. 1 Thick Paper

12 A4 6c rose 400.00 3.50
a. Thin paper 625.00 5.50
13 A4 12c lilac 2,400. 130.00
14 A4 2r pale red *15,000.* *2,750.*
15 A4 5r yellowish green 2,750. 100.00
16 A4 6r grnsh blue *4,250.* 400.00

Arms of Madrid — A5

Isabella II — A6

1853, Jan. 1 Thin Paper

17 A5 1c bronze 2,200. 300.00
18 A5 3c bronze *14,000.* *5,000.*
19 A6 6c carmine rose 750.00 2.25
a. Thick paper 975.00 16.00
b. Thick bluish paper 1,300. 22.50
20 A6 12c reddish purple 2,500. 135.00
21 A6 2r vermilion *12,000.* *2,000.*
22 A6 5r lt green 2,500. 130.00
23 A6 6r deep blue 3,500. 450.00

Nos. 17-18 were issued for use on Madrid city mail only. *They were reprinted on this white paper in duller colors.*

A7

A7a

Coat of Arms of Spain — A8

1854 Thin White Paper

24 A7 2c green 2,500. 450.00
c. Thick paper 3,650. 525.00
25 A7a 4c carmine 350.00 2.10
a. Thick paper 675.00 17.50
26 A8 6c carmine 300.00 1.60
27 A7a 1r indigo 3,000. 350.00
Bar cancellation 21.00
28 A8 2r scarlet 1,500. 120.00
Bar cancellation 10.00
c. Thick paper — 250.00
29 A8 5r green 1,200. 110.00
Bar cancellation 16.00
30 A8 6r blue 3,200. 325.00
Bar cancellation 25.00

See boxed note on bar cancellation before No. 1.

Thick Bluish Paper

31 A7 2c green *14,000.* *1,500.*
b. Thin paper 15,000. 2,400.
32 A7a 4c carmine 400.00 5.50
c. Thin paper 600.00 17.50
32A A8 6c carmine 700.00 19.00
d. Thin paper — 100.00
33 A7a 1r pale blue — *6,500.*
a. Thin paper — 9,500.
34 A8 2r dull red *7,000.* 600.00
a. Thin paper 7,000. 600.00

Full margins = ¾mm.

The 2c with watermark 104 is a proof.

Isabella II — A9

Blue Paper

1855, Apr. 1 Wmk. 104

36 A9 2c green *3,000.* 140.00
a. 2c yellow green *4,000.* 175.00
Bar cancellation, #36 or 36a 10.00
37 A9 4c brown red 275.00 1.00
a. 4c carmine 440.00 2.50
b. 4c lake 350.00 .90
Bar cancellation, #37, 37a or 37b 2.50
Bar cancellation 2.50
38 A9 1r green blue 1,300. 15.00
a. 1r blue 1,600. 20.00
Bar cancellation, #38 or 38a 5.00
b. Cliché of 2r in plate of 1r *25,000.* *3,250.*
Bar cancellation, #38b 850.00
39 A9 2r reddish pur 900.00 15.00
a. 2r deep violet 1,450. 20.00
Bar cancellation, #39, 39a or 39b 13.50

Rough Yellowish Paper

1856, Jan. 1 Wmk. 105

40 A9 2c green *3,500.* 200.00
Bar cancellation 15.00
41 A9 4c rose 13.50 2.25
Bar cancellation 2.50
42 A9 1r grnsh blue *5,500.* 200.00
a. 1r dull blue *5,750.* 275.00
Bar cancellation, #42 or 42a 8.50
43 A9 2r brown purple 600.00 25.00
a. 2r dark reddish purple 775.00 45.00
Bar cancellation, #43, 43a 7.50

White Smooth Paper

1856, Apr. 11 Unwmk.

44 A9 2c blue green 700.00 42.50
a. 2c yellow green 825.00 50.00
Bar cancellation, #44 or 44a 7.50
45 A9 4c rose 5.75 .35
a. 4c carmine ('59) 9.25 20.00
46 A9 1r blue 27.50 25.00
a. 1r pale greenish blue 40.00 32.50
Bar cancellation, #46 or 46a 4.00
47 A9 2r brown lilac 70.00 20.00
a. 2r dull lilac 100.00 35.00
Bar cancellation, #47 or 47a 10.00

Three types of No. 45.

1859

48 A9 12c light orange 150.
Bar cancellation 55.00
a. Tete-beche pair (#48) 500.
b. 12c dark orange 1,700.
Bar cancellation 150.00

Nos. 48-48b were never put in use. All canceled examples have the bar cancellation.

Stamps of the 1st printing (#48b), may be distinguished by shade and by a break at lower left, which is not on the 2nd printing (#48).

Reprints exist. Value, $100.

A10

1860-61 Tinted Paper

49 A10 2c green, *grn* 300.00 19.00
Bar cancellation 2.50
50 A10 4c orange, *grn* 60.00 .80
51 A10 12c car, *buff* 300.00 14.00
Bar cancellation 8.75
52 A10 19c brn, *buff* ('61) 2,500. 1,000.
53 A10 1r blue, *grn* 275.00 12.50
Bar cancellation 4.50
54 A10 2r lilac, *lil* 300.00 11.00
Bar cancellation 4.50

A11

1862, July 16

55 A11 2c dp bl, *yel* 37.50 11.00
56 A11 4c dk brn, *redsh buff* 2.40 .70
a. 4c brown, *white* 24.00 7.00
Bar cancellation 2.50
57 A11 12c blue, *pnksh* 42.50 8.50
Bar cancellation 3.25
58 A11 19c car, *lil* 200.00 225.00
a. 19c carmine, *white* 300.00 275.00
Bar cancellation, #58 or 58a 15.00
59 A11 1r brown, *yel* 57.50 17.50
Bar cancellation 3.50
60 A11 2r green, *pnksh* 37.50 11.00
Bar cancellation 3.25
Nos. 55-60 (6) 377.40 273.70

A12

1864, Jan. 1

61 A12 2c dk bl, *lil* 50.00 20.00
62 A12 4c rose, *redsh buff* 2.50 1.00
a. 4c carmine, *reddish buff* 22.50 7.50
Bar cancellation, #62 or 62a 2.50
63 A12 12c green, *pnksh* 42.50 14.50
64 A12 19c violet, *pnksh* 210.00 190.00
65 A12 1r brown, *grn* 190.00 75.00
Bar cancellation 5.00
66 A12 2r blue, *pnksh* 45.00 12.00
Bar cancellation, #66 or 66a 5.00
Nos. 61-66 (6) 540.00 312.50

A13

1865, Jan. 1 **Litho.** ***Imperf.***

67 A13 2c rose 325.00 35.00
68 A13 4c blue *2,000.*
69 A13 12c blue & rose 425.00 19.00
Bar cancellation 5.25
a. Frame inverted *12,000.* 700.00
Bar cancellation *100.00*
70 A13 19c brn & rose 1,200. 500.00
Bar cancellation 100.00
71 A13 1r yellow grn 375.00 65.00
Bar cancellation 17.50
72 A13 2r red lilac 375.00 35.00
Bar cancellation 16.00
73 A13 2r rose 450.00 65.00
Bar cancellation 17.50
a. 2r salmon 475.00 70.00
Bar cancellation 12.50

No. 68 is without gum and was never put in use.

A majority of the perforated stamps from 1865 to about 1950 are rather poorly centered. The very fine examples that are valued will be fairly well centered. Poorly centered stamps sell for less. Stamps of some issues are almost always badly centered, and our values will be for examples with fine centering. Such issues will be noted.

1865, Jan. 1 ***Perf. 14***

74 A13 2c rose red 600.00 130.00
Bar cancellation 13.50
75 A13 4c blue 60.00 1.00
76 A13 12c bl & rose 850.00 60.00
Bar cancellation 10.50
a. Frame inverted *18,000.* *2,650.*
As "a," bar cancel 50.00
77 A13 19c brn & rose *4,000.* *2,500.*
78 A13 1r yellow grn 2,000. 525.00
Bar cancellation 26.50
79 A13 2r violet 1,900. 250.00
Bar cancellation 24.00
80 A13 2r rose 1,400. 350.00
a. 2r salmon 1,400. 350.00
b. 2r dull orange 1,400. 350.00
Bar cancellation, #80, 80a or 80b 35.00

Values for Nos. 74-80 are for stamps with perforations touching the frame on at least one side.

A14

1866, Jan. 1

81 A14 2c rose 250.00 32.50
Bar cancellation 5.50
82 A14 4c blue 42.50 .80
83 A14 12c orange 260.00 12.75
a. 12c orange yellow 350.00 25.00
84 A14 19c brown 1,250. 525.00
Bar cancellation 50.00
Nos. 81-84 (4) 1,803. 571.05

A14a

1866

85 A14 10c green 300.00 27.50
Bar cancellation 4.00
86 A14 20c lilac 200.00 21.00
Bar cancellation 4.00
87 A14a 20c dull lilac 1,250. 100.00
Bar cancellation 3.00
Nos. 85-87 (3) 1,750. 148.50

For the Type A14a 20c in green, see Cuba No. 25.

A15

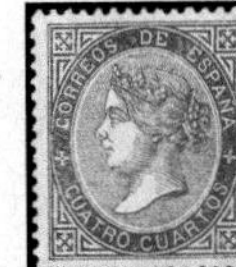
A15a

A15b

A15c

1867-68

88 A15 2c yell brn 450.00 47.50
89 A15a 4c blue 27.50 1.00
90 A15b 12c org yell 250.00 8.00
a. 12c dark orange 300.00 12.00
b. 12c red orange ('68) 1,200. 40.00
91 A15c 19c rose 1,450. 425.00
Bar cancellation 40.00

See Nos. 100-102. For overprints see Nos. 114a-115a, 124-128, 124a-128a, 124c-124c, 124e-126e.

A15d

A15e

92 A15d 10c blue green 275.00 24.50
Bar cancellation 2.50
93 A15e 20c lilac 160.00 10.50
Bar cancellation 2.50

For overprints see Nos. 116-117, 116a-117a, 116c-117c, 117d, 117e, 117f.

A16

A17

A18

94 A16 5m green 47.50 17.50
Bar cancellation 2.50
95 A17 10m brown 47.50 17.50
a. Tête bêche pair *20,000.*
96 A18 25m bl & rose 300.00 24.00
Bar cancellation 5.00
a. Frame inverted *50,000.*

97 A18 50m bis brn 22.00 .80
Bar cancellation 2.75
Nos. 94-97 (4) 417.00 59.80

See No. 98. For overprints see Nos. 118-122, 118a-122a, 120c-122c, 122d, 120e, 122e, 119f, 122f.

A19

1868-69

98 A18 25m blue 275.00 14.50
Bar cancellation 3.75
99 A19 50m violet 29.00 .60
Bar cancellation 2.50
100 A15b 100m brown 500.00 75.00
Bar cancellation 3.00
101 A15c 200m green 210.00 14.00
Bar cancellation 3.00
102 A15c 19c brown 3,000. 525.00

For overprints see #123, 123a, 123c, 123e.

Provisional Government

Excellent counterfeits exist of the provisional and provincial overprints.

For Madrid

Regular Issues Handstamped in Black

1868-69

116 A15d 10c green 50.00 16.00
117 A15e 20c lilac 50.00 12.00
118 A16 5m green 40.00 5.50
119 A17 10m brown 30.00 5.50
120 A18 25m bl & rose 100.00 14.50
g. Frame inverted *15,000.*
121 A18 25m blue 100.00 12.00
g. Double overprint (black & red) 75.00
122 A18 50m bis brn 10.00 5.00
123 A19 50m violet 10.00 5.00
124 A15b 100m brown 200.00 28.50
125 A15c 200m green 75.00 9.00
126 A15b 12c org yel (#90) 75.00 11.00
127 A15c 19c rose 800.00 140.00
128 A15c 19c brown 1,200. 165.00
Nos. 116-128 (13) 2,740. 429.00

Nos. 116-128 exist with handstamp in blue, a few in red. These sell for more.

For Andalusian Provinces

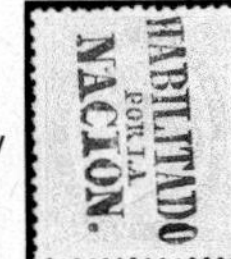

Regular Issues Handstamped Vertically in Blue

114a A15 2c brown 100.00 36.00
115a A15a 4c blue 60.00 25.00
116a A15d 10c green 100.00 15.00
117a A15e 20c lilac 100.00 16.00
118a A16 5m green 50.00 8.25
119a A17 10m brown 25.00 6.00
120a A18 25m bl & rose 100.00 15.00
b. Frame inverted *22,000.*
121a A18 25m blue 100.00 15.50
122a A18 50m bis brn 15.00 5.50
123a A19 50m violet 15.00 5.50
124a A15b 100m brown 200.00 32.50
125a A15c 200m green 100.00 12.00
126a A15b 12c org yel (#90) 75.00 13.50
127a A15c 19c rose 800.00 210.00
128a A15c 19c brown 1,400. 275.00
Nos. 114a-128a (15) 3,240. 690.75

For Valladolid Province

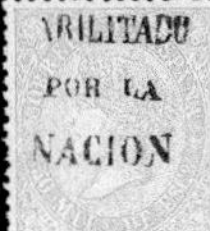

Regular Issues Handstamped in Black

(Two types of overprint)

116c A15d 10c green 100.00 16.50
117c A15e 20c lilac 100.00 19.00
120c A18 25m blue & rose 100.00 15.00
121c A18 25m blue 80.00 21.00
122c A18 50m bis brn 25.00 9.25
123c A19 50m violet 25.00 7.75
124c A15b 100m brown 200.00 38.00
125c A15c 200m green 100.00 15.00
126c A15b 12c orange 75.00 12.50

127c A15c 19c rose *800.00* *175.00*
128c A15c 19c brown *1,400.* *240.00*
Nos. 116c-126c (9) 805.00 154.00

For Asturias Province Llanes (Oviedo)

Regular Issues Handstamped in Black

117d A15e 20c lilac 210.00 125.00
122d A18 50m bister brown 230.00 125.00

For Teruel Province

Regular Issues Handstamped in Black

117e A15e 20c lilac 100.00 55.00
120e A18 25m blue & rose 150.00 55.00
122e A18 50m bister brown 85.00 32.50
123e A19 50m violet 85.00 32.50
124e A15b 100m brown 250.00 75.00
125e A15c 200m green 250.00 45.00
126e A15b 12c orange 150.00 60.00
Nos. 117e-126e (7) 1,070. 355.00

For Salamanca Province

Regular Issues Handstamped in Blue

117f A15e 20c lilac 125.00 55.00
119f A17 10m brown 125.00 42.00
122f A18 50m bister brown 125.00 50.00
Nos. 117f-122f (3) 375.00 147.00

Duke de la Torre Regency

"España" — A20

1870, Jan. 1 **Typo.**

159 A20 1m brn lil, *buff* 6.50 6.50
Bar cancellation 2.00
b. 1m brown lilac, *pinkish buff* 7.00 7.75
161 A20 2m blk, *pinkish* 7.75 8.00
a. 2m black, *buff* 8.75 9.00
163 A20 4m bister brn 16.00 13.50
164 A20 10m rose 19.00 6.00
a. 10m carmine 21.00 7.50
165 A20 25m lilac 52.50 6.50
Bar cancellation 2.00
a. 25m gray lilac 55.00 6.50
b. 25m aniline violet 85.00 8.25
166 A20 50m ultra 11.50 .35
a. 50m dull blue 125.00 5.00
167 A20 100m red brown 40.00 5.25
Bar cancellation 1.40
a. 100m claret 35.00 6.25
b. 100m orange brown 35.00 5.50
168 A20 200m pale brown 32.50 5.25
Bar cancellation 2.00
169 A20 400m green 350.00 25.00
Bar cancellation 3.00
170 A20 1e600m dull lilac 1,700. 850.00
Bar cancellation 27.50
171 A20 2e blue 1,400. 525.00
Bar cancellation 27.50
172 A20 12c red brown 325.00 7.25
173 A20 19c yel grn 450.00 225.00

The 12c carmine rose and 12c blue on pink paper were not put in use. Value $2,200. and $6,000, respectively.

Kingdom

A21

1872, Oct. 1 ***Imperf.***

174 A21 ¼c ultra 2.25 2.25
a. Complete 1c (block of 4 ¼c) 120.00 90.00
As "a," bar cancellation 5.00
b. As "a," one cliche inverted 1,800. *1,750.*

See No. 221A.

A22

King Amadeo
A23 A24

1872-73 *Perf. 14*

176 A22 2c gray lilac 20.00 8.00
a. 2c violet 32.50 18.00
b. Imperf. 75.00
177 A22 5c green 180.00 62.50
a. Imperf. 225.00
178 A23 5c rose ('73) 27.50 5.75
179 A23 6c blue 180.00 39.00
180 A23 10c brown lilac 400.00 240.00
181 A23 10c ultra ('73) 8.50 .55
Bar cancellation 3.50
182 A23 12c gray lilac 27.50 2.50
Bar cancellation 3.50
183 A23 20c gray vio ('73) 140.00 80.00
Bar cancellation 5.25
184 A23 25c brown 60.00 12.00
Bar cancellation 2.75
185 A23 40c pale red brn 80.00 10.50
Bar cancellation 2.75
186 A23 50c deep green 105.00 11.00
Bar cancellation 2.75
187 A24 1p lilac 115.00 55.00
Bar cancellation 4.00
188 A24 4p red brown 750.00 625.00
Bar cancellation 12.00
189 A24 10p deep green 2,300. 2,400.
Bar cancellation 50.00

First Republic

Mural Crown — A25

1873, July 1 *Imperf.*

190 A25 ¼c green 1.00 1.00
a. Complete 1c (block of 4 ¼c) 37.50 20.00
As "a," bar cancellation 2.50
d. As "a," ultra (error) 300.00 160.00

"España" — A26

1873, July 1 *Perf. 14*

191 A26 2c orange 13.50 6.00
192 A26 5c claret 30.00 6.00
Bar cancellation 3.00
193 A26 10c green 6.75 .35
Bar cancellation 2.00
a. Tête bêche pair *32,500.*
194 A26 20c black 150.00 25.00
Bar cancellation 3.75
195 A26 25c dp brn 35.00 6.00
Bar cancellation 2.50
196 A26 40c brown vio 42.50 6.00
Bar cancellation 2.50
197 A26 50c ultra 21.00 6.75
Bar cancellation 2.50
198 A26 1p lilac 72.50 32.50
Bar cancellation 2.50
199 A26 4p red brown 850.00 475.00
Bar cancellation 12.50
200 A26 10p violet brn 2,100. 1,750.
Bar cancellation 24.00

Only one example of No. 193a is known, and it is in a block of six stamps.

"Justice" — A27

1874, July 1

201 A27 2c yellow 22.50 8.50
Bar cancellation 2.10
202 A27 5c violet 45.00 10.00
Bar cancellation 2.10
a. 5c red violet 32.50 10.00
203 A27 10c ultra 12.50 .40
a. Imperf. 13.50
204 A27 20c dark green 225.00 45.00
Bar cancellation 4.00
205 A27 25c red brown 50.00 6.75
Bar cancellation 2.10
a. 25c lilac (error) 325.00
As "a," bar cancellation 30.00
b. Imperf. 57.50
206 A27 40c violet 450.00 8.00
Bar cancellation 2.10
a. 40c brown (error) 250.00
b. Imperf. 190.00
207 A27 50c yellow 105.00 8.25
Bar cancellation 2.10
a. Imperf. 120.00
208 A27 1p yellow green 100.00 34.00
Bar cancellation 2.10
a. 1p emerald 92.50 47.50
b. Imperf. 175.00
209 A27 4p rose 800.00 410.00
Bar cancellation 8.00
a. 4p carmine 800.00 600.00
210 A27 10p black 3,000. 1,900.
Bar cancellation 10.50

Coat of Arms — A28

1874, Oct. 1

211 A28 10c red brown 25.00 .70
Bar cancellation 1.60
a. 10c brown 42.50 3.50
b. Imperf. 90.00

Kingdom

Nos. 212-221 are almost always badly centered and are often irregularly perforated. Values are for stamps with complete perforations and fine centering. Sound stamps with average centering are worth about 50% of these values. Stamps with very fine centering sell for more.

King Alfonso XII — A29

1875, Aug. 1
Blue Framed Numbers on Back, 1-100 on Each Sheet

212 A29 2c org brn 22.50 11.00
a. 2c chocolate brown 30.00 15.00
b. Imperf. 45.00 45.00
213 A29 5c lilac 120.00 13.00
a. Imperf. 95.00 87.50
214 A29 10c blue 8.25 .40
Bar cancellation 2.00
a. Imperf. 22.50 22.50
215 A29 20c brn org 350.00 125.00
216 A29 25c rose 72.50 8.00
Bar cancellation 2.00
217 A29 40c deep brown 125.00 37.50
Bar cancellation 4.50
a. Imperf. 140.00 140.00
218 A29 50c gray lilac 200.00 42.50
Bar cancellation 5.25
219 A29 1p black 225.00 80.00
Bar cancellation 3.00
220 A29 4p dark green 600.00 525.00
221 A29 10p ultra 1,800. 1,750.

1876, June 1 *Imperf.*

221A A21 ¼c green .25 .25
b. Complete 1c (block 4 ¼c) 1.10 .30
As "b," on cover 30.00
c. As "b," two ¼c sideways, one invtd. 110.00 110.00
d. As "b," both upper ¼c invtd. 140.00 140.00
e. As "b," upper left ¼c invtd. 1,300. 500.00
f. As "b," both lower ¼c invtd. 140.00 140.00

No. 221Ac has one stamp upright, one inverted, one facing right and one facing left.

Nos. 222-230 are almost always badly centered. Values are for stamps with fine centering, fresh color and, in the case of mint stamps, full original gum. Sound stamps with average centering are worth about 50% of these values. Stamps with very fine centering sell for more.

King Alfonso XII — A30

Type I

Type II

ONE PESETA:
Type I — Thin figures of value and "PESETA" in thick letters.
Type II — Thick figures of value and "PESETA" in thin letters.

Wmk. 178
1876, June 1 **Engr.** *Perf. 14*

222 A30 5c yellow brown 15.50 3.75
223 A30 10c blue 3.75 .45
Bar cancellation 50.00
224 A30 20c bronze green 19.00 13.00
225 A30 25c brown 8.50 5.50
226 A30 40c black brown 80.00 *100.00*
227 A30 50c green 15.00 6.75
228 A30 1p dp blue, I 20.00 9.00
a. 1p ultra, II 27.50 13.00
229 A30 4p brown violet 75.00 *57.50*
230 A30 10p vermilion 200.00 125.00
Nos. 222-230 (9) 436.75 320.95

Imperf

222a A30 5c 11.50
223a A30 10c 5.75
225a A30 25c 12.50
227a A30 50c 18.00
228b A30 1p 26.00
229a A30 4p 92.50
230a A30 10p 200.00

Two plates each were used for the 5c, 10c, 25c, 50c, 1p and 10p. The 1p plates are most easily distinguished.
The 20c value also exists imperf. Value $500.

King Alfonso XII — A31

Unwmk.
1878, July 1 **Typo.** *Perf. 14*

232 A31 2c mauve 32.50 11.00
a. Imperf. 60.00
233 A31 5c orange 45.00 14.00
234 A31 10c brown 8.25 .50
Bar cancellation 3.00
235 A31 20c black 250.00 125.00
a. Imperf. 275.00
236 A31 25c olive bister 25.00 2.75
Bar cancellation 6.25
237 A31 40c red brown 190.00 140.00
238 A31 50c blue green 120.00 11.00
Bar cancellation 2.00
239 A31 1p gray 100.00 21.00
Bar cancellation 2.00
240 A31 4p violet 225.00 125.00
241 A31 10p blue 450.00 350.00
a. Imperf. 475.00
Nos. 232-241 (10) 1,446. 800.25

A32

1879, May 1

242 A32 2c black 9.50 4.50
Bar cancellation 3.00
243 A32 5c gray green 15.00 1.10
Bar cancellation 3.00
244 A32 10c rose 15.00 .45
Bar cancellation 2.00
245 A32 20c red brown 175.00 15.00
Bar cancellation 2.00
246 A32 25c bluish gray 15.50 .45
Bar cancellation 2.00
247 A32 40c brown 29.00 5.50
Bar cancellation 2.00
248 A32 50c dull buff 130.00 5.00
Bar cancellation 2.00
a. 50c yellow 190.00 7.00
249 A32 1p brt rose 150.00 2.25
Bar cancellation 2.00
250 A32 4p lilac gray 750.00 32.50
Bar cancellation 3.00
251 A32 10p olive bister 2,000. *175.00*
Bar cancellation 6.25

A33

1882, Jan. 1

252 A33 15c salmon 10.50 .25
Bar cancellation 2.00
a. 15c reddish orange 35.00 .45
253 A33 30c red lilac 310.00 5.25
Bar cancellation 2.00
254 A33 75c gray lilac 210.00 4.75
Bar cancellation 2.00
a. Imperf. 300.00

Nos. 255-270 are usually poorly centered and often exhibit defective perforations. Values are for fine to very fine examples, well centered but not very fine, fresh and without perforation faults. Average examples sell for about half these values.

King Alfonso XIII — A34

1889-99

255 A34 2c blue green 6.00 .45
256 A34 2c black ('99) 35.00 7.25
257 A34 5c blue 12.50 .25
258 A34 5c blue grn ('99) 145.00 1.40
259 A34 10c yellow brown 16.50 .25
260 A34 10c red ('99) 200.00 4.50
261 A34 15c violet brown 4.75 .25
262 A34 20c yellow green 50.00 4.75
263 A34 25c blue 20.00 .25
264 A34 30c olive gray 82.50 5.25
265 A34 40c brown 87.50 3.00
266 A34 50c rose 80.00 2.10
267 A34 75c orange 210.00 4.25
268 A34 1p dark violet 55.00 .45
a. 1p carmine rose (error) 350.00
269 A34 4p carmine rose 750.00 47.50
270 A34 10p orange red 1,300. 110.00

The 15c yellow, type A34 is an official stamp listed as No. O9.
Several values exist imperf.

Nos. 272-286 are almost always badly centered. Values are for stamps with fine centering, fresh color and, if unused, full original gum. Sound stamps with average centering sell for about half these values. Very fine stamps sell more more.

King Alfonso XIII — A35

Control Number on Back
1901-05 **Engr.** **Unwmk.**

272 A35 2c bister brown 3.25 .25
273 A35 5c dark green 5.75 .25
274 A35 10c rose red 9.50 .25
275 A35 15c blue black 17.00 .25
276 A35 15c dull lilac ('02) 13.00 .25
277 A35 15c purple ('05) 6.25 .25
278 A35 20c grnsh black 32.50 2.75
279 A35 25c blue 6.25 .40
280 A35 30c deep green 42.50 .35
281 A35 40c olive bister 150.00 5.00
282 A35 40c rose ('05) 300.00 4.50
283 A35 50c slate blue 32.50 .55
b. 50c blue green (error) *2,250.* *1,100.*
284 A35 1p lake 30.00 .80
285 A35 4p dk violet 250.00 22.50
286 A35 10p brown orange 225.00 72.50
Nos. 272-286 (15) 1,124. 110.85
Set, never hinged 3,000.

There are numerous shades and unissued colors for this issue.

Imperf

272a A35 2c 57.50
273a A35 5c 25.00
274a A35 10c 25.00
275a A35 15c 110.00
276a A35 15c 22.50
277a A35 15c 17.00
278a A35 20c 90.00
279a A35 25c 17.00
280b A35 30c 110.00
282a A35 40c 300.00

283a A35 50c 125.00
284a A35 1p 57.50
285a A35 4p 200.00
286a A35 10p 190.00

The 15c in red brown (value $850), 30c blue ($2,000), 1p olive ($2,500), 1p blue green ($2,500) and 1p dark violet ($2,500) were prepared but not issued.

Nos. 287-296 are almost always badly centered. Values are for stamps with fine centering, fresh color and, if unused, full original gum. Sound stamps with average centering sell for about half these values. Very fine stamps sell for more.

Don Quixote Starts Forth A36

10c, Don Quixote attacks windmill. 15c, Meets country girls. 25c, Sancho Panza tossed in blanket. 30c, Don Quixote knighted. 40c, Tilting at sheep. 50c, On Wooden horse. 1p, Adventure with lions. 4p, In bullock cart, 10p, The Enchanted Lady.

Control Number on Back

1905, May 1 **Typo.**

287 A36 5c dark green 1.25 1.10
  a. Imperf. 50.00
  b. Vert. pair, imperf between *100.00* *100.00*
  c. Horiz. pair, imperf between *125.00* *125.00*
288 A36 10c orange red 2.50 1.75
  b. Imperf.
289 A36 15c violet 2.50 1.75
  a. Imperf. 80.00
  c. Vert. pair, imperf between *100.00* *100.00*
290 A36 25c dark blue 6.00 3.50
  a. Horiz. pair, imperf between *200.00* *200.00*
291 A36 30c dk blue green 30.00 10.00
292 A36 40c bright rose 55.00 32.50
  a. Imperf.
293 A36 50c slate 17.50 7.00
294 A36 1p rose red 180.00 90.00
295 A36 4p dk violet 80.00 90.00
296 A36 10p brown orange 125.00 135.00
  Nos. 287-296 (10) 499.75 372.60
  Set, never hinged 2,500.

300th anniversary of the publication of Cervantes' "Don Quixote."

Counterfeits exist of Nos. 287-296.

For surcharges see Nos. 586-588, C91.

Six stamps picturing King Alfonso XIII and Queen Victoria Eugenia were put on sale Oct. 1, 1907, at the Madrid Industrial Exhibition. They were not valid for postage. Value, unused $40, mint never hinged $60.

The original labels were engraved and perf 11½. Examples printed by other methods or with other perfs are reprints. Value $2.

Alfonso XIII — A46

Blue Control Number on Back

Perf. 13x12½, 13, 13½x13, 14

1909-22 **Engr.**

297 A46 2c dark brown .55 .55
  a. No control number .55 .25
  Never hinged 2.00
298 A46 5c green 2.00 .25
299 A46 10c carmine 3.00 .25
300 A46 15c violet 9.50 .25
301 A46 20c olive green 50.00 .90
302 A46 25c deep blue 4.75 .25
303 A46 30c blue green 9.75 .25
304 A46 40c rose 15.50 .65
305 A46 50c blue ('22) 11.50 .40
  a. 50c slate blue 12.50 .40
  Never hinged 24.00
306 A46 1p lake 32.50 .40
307 A46 4p deep violet 80.00 12.00
309 A46 10p orange 100.00 26.00
  Nos. 297-309 (12) 319.05 42.15
  Set, never hinged 1,200.

Nos. 297-309 exist imperforate. Value $600.

The 5c exists in carmine; the 10c in yellow orange (value $400); the 15c in blue (value $400); the 4p in lake (value $2,000). The 5c and 15c are unissued trial colors, privately perforated and back-numbered. The 4p lake is known only with perfin "B.H.A." (Banco Hispano-Americano). 100 examples of the 4p exist, most poorly centered.

See Nos. 310, 315-317. For overprints see Nos. C1-C5, C58-C61.

Counterfeits exist.

Control Number on Back in Red or Orange

1917

310 A46 15c yellow ocher 3.50 .35
  Never hinged 6.00
  a. Control number in blue 14.50 1.10

Control Number on Back in Blue

1918

313 A46 40c light red 82.50 5.75
  Never hinged 150.00

A47

1920 **Typo.** ***Imperf.***

314 A47 1c blue green .25 .25
  Never hinged .45

Perf. 13x12½,
Litho.

315 A46 2c bister 5.00 .25
316 A46 20c violet 42.50 .25
  Nos. 314-316 (3) 47.75 .75
  Set, never hinged 175.00

Nos. 314-315 have no control number on back.

For overprints and surcharge see Nos. 358, 449, 457, 468, 10L1, 11LB1.

1921 **Engr.**

317 A46 20c violet 30.00 .25
  Never hinged 52.50

Madrid Post Office — A48

1920, Oct. 1 **Typo.** ***Perf. 13½***

Center and Portrait in Black

318 A48 1c blue green .25 *.25*
319 A48 2c olive bister .25 *.25*

Control Number on Back

320 A48 5c green .75 *1.00*
321 A48 10c red .75 *1.00*
322 A48 15c yellow 1.25 1.25
323 A48 20c violet 1.40 1.40
324 A48 25c gray blue 2.25 2.25
325 A48 30c dark green 5.50 5.50
326 A48 40c rose 21.00 7.25
327 A48 50c brt blue 24.00 20.00
328 A48 1p brown red 24.00 16.50
329 A48 4p brown violet 75.00 70.00
330 A48 10p orange 150.00 145.00
  Nos. 318-330 (13) 306.40 271.65
  Set, never hinged 1,000.

King Alfonso XIII
A49 A49a

Type I

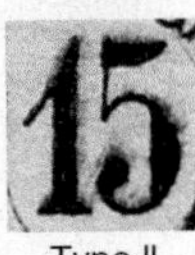

Type II

FIFTEEN CENTIMOS:
Type I — Narrow "5."
Type II — Wide "5."

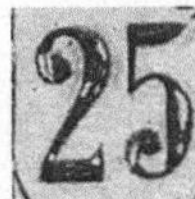

Type I Type II

TWENTY FIVE CENTIMOS:
Type I — "25" is 2¾mm high. Vertical stroke of "5" is 1mm long.
Type II — "25" is 3mm high. Vertical stroke of "5" is 1½mm long.

Perf. 11 to 14, Compound

1922-26 **Engr.** **Unwmk.**

331 A49 2c olive green .85 .25
  a. 2c deep orange (error) 87.50 *210.00*
  Never hinged *250.00*

Control Number on Back

332 A49 5c red violet 4.00 .25
333 A49 5c claret 1.60 .25
334 A49 10c carmine 1.60 1.10
335 A49 10c yellow green 1.50 .25
  a. 10c blue green ('23) 2.25 .25
  Never hinged 8.00
336 A49 15c slate bl (I) 8.00 .25
  a. 15c black green (II) 27.50 2.25
  Never hinged 82.50
337 A49 20c violet 3.50 .25
  Never hinged 13.00
338 A49 25c carmine (I) 3.50 .25
  a. 25c rose red (II) 5.50 1.00
  Never hinged 19.00
  b. 25c lilac rose (error) 100.00 160.00
  Never hinged *225.00*
339 A49 30c black brn ('26) 15.00 .25
  Never hinged 55.00
340 A49 40c deep blue 4.00 .25
341 A49 50c orange 19.50 .25
  a. 50c orange red 77.50 1.90
  Never hinged 240.00
342 A49a 1p blue black 18.00 .25
343 A49a 4p lake 85.00 4.00
344 A49a 10p brown 40.00 13.50
  Nos. 331-344 (14) 206.05 21.35
  Set, never hinged 750.00

Nos. 331 ($15), 332 ($750), 334 ($40), 336-344 ($20 to $100 each) exist imperf.

The 5c exists in vermilion (value $110); the 25c in dark blue (value $200). The 50c exists in red brown, the 4p in brown and 10p in lake; value, each $90. These five were not regularly issued.

For overprints see Nos. 359-370, 467.

Nos. 331-344 are almost always found poorly centered.

"Santa Maria" and View of Seville A50

Herald of Barcelona — A51

Exposition Buildings — A52

King Alfonso XIII and View of Barcelona A53

1929, Feb. 15 ***Perf. 11***

345 A50 1c grnsh blue 1.90 1.90
346 A51 2c pale yel grn .30 .30
347 A52 5c rose lake .35 .35

Control Number on Back

348 A53 10c green .35 .35
349 A50 15c Prus blue 2.25 2.25
350 A51 20c purple .55 .55
351 A50 25c brt rose .55 .55
352 A52 30c black brn 3.00 *3.00*
353 A53 40c dark blue 6.00 6.00
354 A51 50c deep orange 3.00 *3.00*
355 A52 1p blue black 6.00 *6.00*
356 A53 4p deep rose 26.00 26.00
357 A53 10p brown 60.00 *60.00*
  Nos. 345-357,E2 (14) 125.25 125.25
  Set, never hinged 300.00

Perf. 14

345a A50 1c greenish blue .70 .70
348a A53 10c green 20.00 37.50
349a A50 15c Prus blue 22.50 22.50
350a A51 20c purple 26.00 37.50
351a A50 25c bright rose 32.50 37.50
352a A52 30c black brown 32.50 37.50
353a A53 40c dark blue 70.00 90.00
354a A51 50c deep orange 32.50 37.50
355a A52 1p blue black 32.50 37.50
356a A53 4p deep rose 25.00 25.00
357a A53 10p brown 110.00 140.00
  Nos. 345a-357a,E2a (12) 436.70 540.70
  Set, never hinged 725.00

Seville and Barcelona Exhibitions.

Nos. 345-357 exist imperf. Value, set $2,500. See note after No. 432.

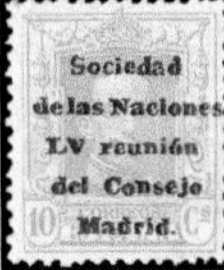

Nos. 314, 331, 333, 335-344 Overprinted in Red or Blue

1929, June 10 ***Imperf.***

358 A47 1c blue green .50 .80

Perf. 13½x12½

359 A49 2c olive green .55 *1.00*
360 A49 5c claret (Bl) .55 *1.00*
361 A49 10c yellow green .55 *1.00*
362 A49 15c slate blue .55 *1.00*
363 A49 20c violet .55 *1.00*
364 A49 25c carmine (Bl) .55 *1.00*
365 A49 30c black brown 2.25 *4.00*
366 A49 40c deep blue 2.25 *4.00*
367 A49 50c orange (Bl) 2.25 *4.00*
368 A49a 1p blue black 11.00 *19.00*
369 A49a 4p lake (Bl) 11.00 *21.00*
370 A49a 10p brown (Bl) 40.00 *70.00*
  Nos. 358-370,E4 (14) 84.55 *153.80*
  Set, never hinged 250.00

55th assembly of League of Nations at Madrid June 10-16. The stamps were available for postal use only on those days.

Nos. 359-370 values are for off-center stamps. Well centered stamps sell for about 4 times these values.

Exposition Building — A54

1930 **Litho.** ***Perf. 11***

371 A54 5c dk blue & salmon 6.25 5.00
372 A54 5c dk violet & blue 6.25 5.00
  Set, Never Hinged 22.50

Barcelona Philatelic Congress and Exhibition. "C. F. y E. F." are the initials of "Congreso Filatelico y Exposicion Filatelica." For each admission ticket, costing 2.75 pesetas, the holder was allowed to buy one of each of these stamps.

A55

Locomotives A56

1930, May 10 *Perf. 14*

373	A55	1c light blue	.55	*.55*
374	A55	2c apple green	.55	*.55*

Control Number on Back

375	A55	5c lake	.55	*.55*
376	A55	10c yellow green	.55	*.55*
377	A55	15c bluish gray	.55	*.55*
378	A55	20c purple	.55	*.55*
379	A55	25c brt rose	.55	*.55*
380	A55	30c olive gray	1.60	*1.60*
381	A55	40c dark blue	1.40	*1.40*
382	A55	50c dk orange	2.75	*2.75*
383	A56	1p dark gray	2.75	*2.75*
384	A56	4p deep rose	65.00	*65.00*
385	A56	10p bister brn	225.00	*225.00*
		Nos. 373-385,C12-C17,E6 (20)	439.35	*439.35*
		Set, never hinged	1,500.	

11th Intl. Railway Congress, Madrid, 1930.

These stamps were on sale May 10-21, 1930, exclusively at the Palace of the Senate in Madrid and at the Barcelona and Seville expositions.

Forgeries are plentiful.

Francisco de Goya at Age 80 ("1746 1828") ("1828 1928")
A57 A59

"La Maja Desnuda" — A58

1930, June 15 Litho. *Perf. 12½*

Inscribed "Correos Espana"

386	A57	1c yellow	.25	.25
387	A57	2c bister brn	.25	.25
388	A57	5c lilac rose	.25	.25
389	A57	10c green	.25	.25

Engr.

390	A57	15c lt blue	.30	.25
391	A57	20c brown violet	.30	.25
392	A57	25c red	.30	.25
393	A57	30c brown	4.25	4.00
394	A57	40c dark blue	4.25	4.00
395	A57	50c vermilion	4.25	4.00
396	A57	1p black	5.00	4.75
397	A58	1p dark violet	1.25	.75
398	A58	4p slate gray	.90	.55
399	A58	10p red brown	12.50	7.00

Inscribed "1828 Goya 1928"

Litho.

400	A59	2c olive green	.25	.25
401	A59	5c gray violet	.25	.25

Engr.

402	A59	25c rose carmine	.40	.35
		Nos. 386-402,C18-C30,CE1,E7 (32)	49.40	41.90
		Set, never hinged	66.00	

To commemorate the death of Francisco de Goya y Lucientes, painter and engraver.

Nos. 386-399 were issued in connection with the Spanish-American Exposition at Seville.

Nos. 386-402 exist imperf. Value, set $300.

See note after No. 432.

King Alfonso XIII — A61

Two types of the 40c

Type I

Type II

Type I — Middle of zero in "40" is bigger in width.

Type II — Middle of zero in "40" is smaller in width.

1930 *Perf. 11½, 12x11½*

406	A61	2c red brown	.25	.25

Control Number on Back

407	A61	5c black brown	.50	.25
408	A61	10c green	2.25	.25
409	A61	15c slate green	8.00	.25
410	A61	20c dark violet	4.50	.70
411	A61	25c carmine	.50	.25
412	A61	30c brown lake	11.50	1.75
413	A61	40c dk blue (I)	15.00	1.10
a.		Type II	27.50	1.10
414	A61	50c orange	14.00	1.90
		Nos. 406-414 (9)	56.50	6.70
		Set, never hinged	200.00	

Nos. 406-414 exist imperf. Value for set, $350.

For overprints see #450-455, 458-466, 469-487.

Bow of "Santa Maria" — A63

Stern of "Santa Maria" — A64

"Santa Maria," "Niña," "Pinta" — A65

Columbus Leaving Palos — A66

Columbus Arriving in America — A67

1930, Sept. 29 Litho. *Perf. 12½*

418	A63	1c olive gray	.25	.25
419	A64	2c olive green	.25	.25
420	A63	2c olive green	.25	.25
421	A64	5c red brown	.25	.25
422	A63	5c red brown	.25	.25
423	A64	10c blue green	.60	.60
424	A63	15c ultra	.60	.60
425	A64	20c violet	.80	.80

Engr.

426	A65	25c dark red	.80	.80
427	A66	30c bis brn, bl & blk brn	3.75	3.75
428	A65	40c ultra	3.25	3.25
429	A66	50c dk vio, bl & vio brn	5.00	5.00
430	A65	1p black	5.00	5.00
431	A67	4p blk & dk blue	6.00	6.00
432	A67	10p red brn & dk brn	23.00	23.00
		Nos. 418-432,E8 (16)	51.55	51.55
		Set, never hinged	120.00	

Christopher Columbus tribute.

Nos. 418 to 432 were privately produced. Their promoters presented a certain quantity of these labels to the Spanish Postal Authorities, who placed them on sale and allowed them to be used for three days, retaining the money obtained from the sale.

This note will also apply to Nos. 345-357, 386-402, 433-448, 557-571, B1-B105, C18-C57, C73-C87, CB1-CB5, CE1, E2, E7-E9, E15 and EB1.

Many so-called "errors" of color and perforation are known.

Nos. 418-432 exist imperf. Value, set $450. stamps.

See Nos. 2671, B194.

Arms of Spain, Bolivia, Paraguay A68

Pavilion and Map of Central America — A69

Exhibition Pavilion of Ecuador — A70

Colombia Pavilion — A71

Dominican Republic Pavilion A72

Uruguay Pavilion A73

Argentina Pavilion A74

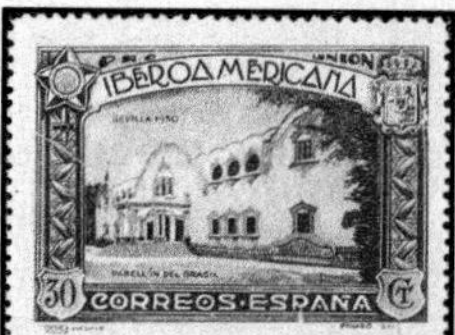

Chile Pavilion A75

Brazil Pavilion A76

Mexico Pavilion A77

Cuba Pavilion A78

Peru Pavilion A79

U.S. Pavilion A80

Exhibition Pavilion of Portugal — A81

King Alfonso XIII and Queen Victoria — A82

Unwmk.

1930, Oct. 10 Photo. *Perf. 14*

433 A68 1c blue green .25 .25
434 A69 2c bister brown .25 .25
435 A70 5c olive brown .25 .25
436 A71 10c dark green .30 .30
437 A72 15c indigo .30 .30
438 A73 20c violet .30 .30
439 A74 25c car rose .30 .30
440 A75 25c car rose .30 .30
441 A76 30c rose lilac 1.60 1.60
442 A77 40c slate blue .90 .90
443 A78 40c slate blue .90 .90
444 A79 50c brown org 1.60 1.60
445 A80 1p ultra 2.25 2.25
446 A81 4p brown violet 24.00 24.00
447 A82 10p brown 1.90 1.90

Perf. 11, 14

Engr.

448 A82 10p dk reddish brn 40.00 40.00
Nos. 433-448,C50-C57,E9 (25) 94.70 94.70
Set, never hinged 275.00

Spanish-American Union Exhibition, Seville.

The note after No. 432 will also apply to Nos. 433-448. All values exist imperforate. Value, set: hinged $250; never hinged $350.

Reprints of Nos. 433-448 have blurred colors, yellowish paper and an inferior, almost invisible gum. They sell for about one-tenth the value of originals.

Revolutionary Issues
Madrid Issue

Regular Issues of 1920-30 Overprinted in Black, Green or Red

1931 On No. 314 *Imperf.*

449 A47 1c blue green .25 .25

On Nos. 406-411
Perf. 11½

450 A61 2c red brown (G) .30 .25
451 A61 5c black brn (R) .40 .40
452 A61 10c green .70 .70
453 A61 15c slate grn (R) 1.40 1.50
454 A61 20c dk violet (R) 1.40 1.50
455 A61 25c carmine (G) 1.90 2.25
Nos. 449-455,E10 (8) 11.35 11.85
Set, never hinged 22.50

The status of Nos. 449-455, E10 has been questioned.

First Barcelona Issue

Regular Issues of 1920-30 Overprinted in Black or Red

1931 On No. 314 *Imperf.*

457 A47 1c blue green .25 .25

On Nos. 406-414
Perf. 11½

458 A61 2c red brown .25 .25
459 A61 5c black brown .25 .25
460 A61 10c green .55 .55
461 A61 15c slate grn (R) .60 .60
462 A61 20c dk violet (R) .60 .60
463 A61 25c carmine .60 .60
464 A61 30c brown lake 4.50 4.50
465 A61 40c dk blue (R) 1.25 1.25
466 A61 50c orange 1.25 1.25

On Stamp of 1922-26

467 A49a 1p blue blk (R) 7.50 6.25
Nos. 457-467,E11 (12) 23.10 21.85
Set, never hinged 45.00

Nos. 457-467 are known both with and without accent over "U."

The status of Nos. 457-467, E11 has been questioned.

Second Barcelona Issue

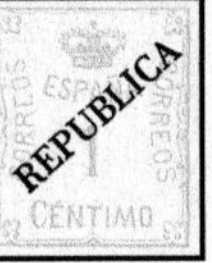

Regular Issues of 1920-30 Overprinted in Black or Red

On No. 314 *Imperf.*

468 A47 1c blue green .25 .25

On Nos. 406-414
Perf. 11½

469 A61 2c red brown .25 .25
470 A61 5c black brown (R) .25 .25
471 A61 10c green .25 .25
472 A61 15c slate grn (R) 1.40 1.25
473 A61 20c dark violet (R) .40 .45
474 A61 25c carmine .40 .45
475 A61 30c brown lake 5.75 5.75
476 A61 40c dark blue (R) 1.25 1.25
477 A61 50c orange 4.50 3.50
Nos. 468-477 (10) 14.70 13.65
Set, never hinged 27.50

The status of Nos. 469-477, C58-C61 has been questioned.

General Issue of the Republic

Nos. 406-414, 342 Overprinted in Blue or Red

1931, May 27

478 A61 2c red brown .25 .25
479 A61 5c black brn (R) .25 .25
480 A61 10c green (R) .30 .25
481 A61 15c slate grn (R) 3.50 .25
482 A61 20c dk violet (R) 1.50 1.00
483 A61 25c carmine .50 .25
484 A61 30c brown lake 4.50 1.00
485 A61 40c dk blue (R) 4.50 .55
486 A61 50c orange 7.75 .55
487 A49a 1p blue blk (R) 57.50 1.00
Nos. 478-487,E12 (11) 87.05 6.60
Set, never hinged 230.00

The setting contained 18 repetitions of "Republica Espanola" for each vertical row of 10 stamps. According to its sheet position, a stamp received different parts of the overprinted words.

Overprint position varieties include: reading down on 25c, 30c, 40c and 50c; double on 1p; double, both reading down, on 25c, 40c and 50c.

"Republica Espanola"

Stamps of various Spanish colonies overprinted "Republica Espanola" are listed with the colonies.

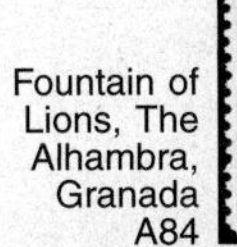

Fountain of Lions, The Alhambra, Granada A84

Interior of Mosque, Córdoba — A85

Alcántara Bridge and Alcazar, Toledo A86

Francisco García y Santos A87

Puerta del Sol, Madrid, on April 14, 1931 as Republic Was Proclaimed A88

Perf. 12½

1931, Oct. 10 Unwmk. Engr.

491 A84 5c violet brown .25 .25
492 A85 10c blue green .35 .35
493 A86 15c dark violet .35 .35
494 A85 25c deep red .35 .35
495 A87 30c olive green .35 .35
496 A84 40c indigo .90 .90
497 A85 50c orange red .90 .90
498 A86 1p black 1.60 1.60
499 A88 4p red violet 8.00 8.00
500 A88 10p red brown 25.00 *25.00*
Nos. 491-500,C62-C67,CO1-CO6,O20-O29 (32) 89.25 87.85
Set, never hinged 170.00

3rd Pan-American Postal Union Cong., Madrid.

Nos. 491-500 exist imperforate. Value, set: hinged $150; never hinged $250.

Symbolical of Montserrat Cut With a Saw — A89

Abbott Oliva and Monastery Workman — A90

"Black Virgin"
A91 A92

Montserrat Monastery — A93

1931, Dec. 9 *Perf. 11, 14*

501 A89 1c myrtle green 1.25 *1.50*
a. Perf. 14 21.00 21.00
502 A89 2c red brown .70 *1.10*
a. Perf. 14 15.00 16.00
b. Horiz. pair, imperf between *115.00* *75.00*

Control Number on Back

503 A89 5c black brown .85 *1.40*
a. Perf. 14 15.00 16.00
b. Horiz. pair, imperf between *115.00* *75.00*
504 A89 10c yellow green .95 *1.40*
a. Perf. 14 15.00 19.00
b. Horiz. pair, imperf between *115.00* *75.00*
c. Vert. pair, imperf between 200.00 *150.00*
505 A90 15c myrtle green 1.25 *1.75*
a. Perf. 14 21.00 25.00
506 A91 20c dark violet 2.25 2.25
a. Perf. 11 110.00 150.00
b. Horiz. pair, imperf between *350.00* *250.00*
c. As "a", horiz. pair, imperf between *450.00*
507 A92 25c lake 3.25 3.25
a. Perf. 14 6.25 7.25
508 A91 30c deep red 32.50 30.00
a. Perf. 14 45.00 45.00
509 A93 40c dull blue 19.00 17.00
a. Perf. 11 150.00 175.00
b. Vert. pair, imperf between *250.00* *160.00*
510 A90 50c dark orange 40.00 37.50
a. Perf. 14 70.00 80.00
511 A92 1p gray black 40.00 37.50
512 A93 4p lilac rose 300.00 300.00
a. Perf. 14 575.00 900.00
513 A92 10p deep brown 200.00 200.00
a. Perf. 14 800.00 950.00
Nos. 501-511,C68-C72,E13 (17) 211.50 216.15
Set, never hinged 350.00
Nos. 501-513,C68-C72,E13 (19) 711.50 716.15
Set, never hinged 1,600.

Commemorative of the building of the old Monastery at Montserrat, started in 1031, and of the image of the Black Virgin (said to have been carved by St. Luke) which was crowned by Pope Leo XIII in 1881.

Nos. 501-513 exist imperforate. Value, set $3,500.

For surcharges see Nos. 589, C92-C96.

Francisco Pi y Margall — A95

Joaquín Costa — A96

Nicolás Salmerón A97

Pablo Iglesias A99

Emilio Castelar — A100

1931-32 *Perf. 11½*

Control Number on Back

516 A95 5c brnsh black 2.60 .30
517 A96 10c yellow green 6.25 .30
518 A97 15c slate green 4.25 .25
520 A99 25c lake 19.50 .70
b. Imperf. 175.00
521 A99 30c carmine rose 6.25 .25
c. Imperf. 82.50
522 A100 40c dark blue 37.50 4.50
523 A97 50c orange 47.50 7.75
Nos. 516-523 (7) 123.85 14.05
Set, never hinged 300.00

Without Control Number

516a A95 5c brownish blk ('32) 4.00 .25
517a A96 10c yel grn ('32) 3.50 .25
518a A97 15c sl grn ('32) .55 .25
520a A99 25c lake 27.50 .25
521a A99 30c carmine rose 1.60 .25
522a A100 40c dark blue ('32) .25 .25
523a A97 50c orange ('32) 22.00 .50
Nos. 516a-523a (7) 59.40 2.00
Set, never hinged 110.00

Without Control Number, Imperf.

516b A95 5c 6.50
517b A96 10c 11.00
518b A97 15c 6.25
520c A99 25c *110.00*
521b A99 30c 5.50

522b	A100	40c	14.00	
523b	A97	50c	125.00	
		Nos. 516b-523b (7)	278.25	
		Set, Never Hinged	550.00	

See Nos. 532, 538, 550, 579, 579a.

For overprints and surcharges see Nos. 7LC12-7LC13, 7LC15-7LC16, 7LC18, 7LE4, 8LB6, 8LB9-8LB10, 9LC17-9LC18, 10L7, 10L10-10L12, 10L16-10L18, 10L22-10L23, 11L7, 11L10-11L12, 11LB8, 12L4, 12L8, 12L11-12L12, 13L8, 14L6, 14L10-14L12, 14L18, 14L22-14L24.

Blasco Ibáñez A103

Manuel Ruiz-Zorrilla A104

Without Control Number

1931-34 *Perf. 11½*

526	A103	2c red brown ('32)	.25	.25
528	A103	5c chocolate ('34)	.25	.25
532	A95	20c dark violet	.25	.25
534	A104	25c lake ('34)	.45	.25
538	A100	60c apple green ('32)	.25	.25
		Nos. 526-538 (5)	1.45	1.25
		Set, never hinged	2.50	

Imperf

526a	A103	2c	14.00	
528a	A103	5c	2.75	
532a	A95	20c	6.25	
534a	A104	25c	5.25	
538a	A100	60c	6.25	
		Nos. 526a-538a (5)	34.50	
		Set, never hinged	70.00	

For overprints and surcharges see Nos. 8LB3, 8LB7, 9LC3, 9LC8-9LC9, 9LC14, 10L6, 10L13, 11L4, 11L8, 11LB5, 11LB9, 12L5, 12L9, 13L5, 13L7, 14L3, 14L7, 14L15, 14L19.

Cliff Houses, Cuenca — A105

Alcázar of Segovia — A106

Gate of the Sun at Toledo — A107

1932-38 *Perf. 10*

539	A105	1p gray black ('38)	.25	.25
540	A106	4p magenta ('38)	.30	.40
541	A107	10p deep brown ('38)	.65	.70
		Nos. 539-541 (3)	1.20	1.35
		Set, never hinged	2.75	

Imperf

539a	A105	1p	5.25	2.75
540a	A106	4p	9.00	6.50
541a	A107	10p	6.50	6.00
		Nos. 539a-541a (3)	20.75	15.25
		Set, never hinged	45.00	

Perf. 11½

539b	A105	1p	.25	.25
540b	A106	4p	.70	.85
541b	A107	10p	1.90	3.00
		Nos. 539b-541b (3)	2.85	4.10
		Set, never hinged	5.00	

For overprints and surcharge see Nos. 9LC19, 10L19, 13L9, 14L25, 14L27-14L28.

Numeral — A108

1933 Unwmk. Typo. *Imperf.*

542	A108	1c blue green	.25	.25

Perf. 11½

543	A108	2c buff	.25	.25
a.		Perf. 13½x13	.65	.25
		Never hinged	1.40	
		Set, never hinged	.65	

See Nos. 592-597, 623.

For surcharges and overprints see Nos. 590-590A, 634A-634D, 8LB1-8LB2, 9LC1-9LC2, 9LC4-9LC7, 9LC11-9LC12, 9LC20, 9LC26, 10L2-10L4, 11L1-11L2, 11LB2-11LB3, 12L1-12L2, 13L1-13L3, 14L1, 14L13.

Santiago Ramón y Cajal — A109

1934 Engr. *Perf. 11½x11*

545	A109	30c black brown	6.00	1.10
		Never hinged	16.00	
a.		Perf. 14	22.50	30.00
		Never hinged	42.50	
b.		Imperf.	32.50	
		Never hinged	55.00	

Type of 1931 and

Mariana Pineda A110

Concepción Arenal A111

Gumersindo de Azcarate A112

Gaspar Melchor de Jovellanos A113

1935

546	A110	10c green	.25	.25
b.		10c blue green ('36)	.25	.25
547	A111	15c slate	.25	.25
b.		15c yellow green ('36)	.25	.25
548	A112	30c carmine rose	7.25	.25
549	A113	30c rose red	.25	.25
550	A97	50c dark blue	1.00	.30
		Nos. 546-550 (5)	9.00	1.30
		Set, never hinged	22.00	

Imperf

546a	A110	10c	1.50	
547a	A111	15c	4.75	
548a	A112	30c	22.50	
549a	A113	30c	1.75	
550a	A97	50c	*175.00*	
		Nos. 546a-550a (5)	205.50	
		Set, never hinged	400.00	

Shades exist.

For overprints and surcharges see Nos. 7LE3, 8LB4-8LB5, 8LB8, 10L8-10L9, 10L14, 10L20-10L21, 11L5-11L6, 11L9, 11LB6-11LB7, 11LB10, 12L6-12L7, 12L10, 13L6, 14L4-14L5, 14L8, 14L16-14L17, 14L20.

Lope's Bookplate A116

Lope de Vega A117

Alcántara and Alcázar, Toledo A118

1935, Oct. 12 *Perf. 11½x11, 11x11½*

552	A116	15c myrtle green	5.75	.30
553	A117	30c rose red	2.75	.30
554	A117	50c dark blue	11.00	3.00
555	A118	1p gray blue & blk	21.00	2.00
		Nos. 552-555 (4)	40.50	5.60
		Set, never hinged	75.00	

Imperf

552a	A116	15c	400.00	
553a	A117	30c	14.00	
554a	A117	50c	62.50	
555a	A118	1p	57.50	
		Nos. 552a-555a (4)	534.00	
		Set, never hinged	1,000.	

Perf. 14

553b	A117	30c	6.50	14.50
554b	A117	50c	29.00	45.00
555b	A118	1p	32.50	50.00
		Nos. 553b-555b (3)	68.00	109.50
		Set, never hinged	150.00	

Lope Felix de Vega Carpio (1562-1635), Spanish dramatist and poet.

For surcharge see No. 11LB11.

Map of Amazon by Bartolomeo Oliva, 16th Century A119

1935, Oct. 12 *Perf. 11½*

556	A119	30c rose red	2.10	.95
		Never hinged	5.50	
a.		Perf. 14	26.00	
		Never hinged	54.00	
b.		Imperf.	37.50	
		Never hinged	72.50	

Proposed Iglesias Amazon Expedition.

Miguel Moya — A120

Torcuato Luca de Tena — A121

José Francos Rodríguez A122

Alejandro Lerroux A123

Nazareth School and Rotary Press — A124

1936, Feb. 14 Photo. *Perf. 12½*

Size: 22x26mm

557	A120	1c crimson	.25	.25
558	A121	2c orange brown	.25	.25
559	A122	5c black brown	.25	.25
560	A123	10c emerald	.25	.25

Size: 24x28½mm

561	A120	15c blue green	.25	.25
562	A121	20c violet	.25	.25
563	A122	25c red violet	.25	.25
564	A123	30c crimson	.25	.25

Size: 25½x30½mm

565	A120	40c orange	.50	.40
566	A121	50c ultra	.25	.25
567	A122	60c olive green	.50	.40
568	A123	1p gray black	.50	.40
569	A124	2p lt blue	5.75	3.25
570	A124	4p lilac rose	5.75	6.50
571	A124	10p red brown	15.00	15.50
		Nos. 557-571,E15 (16)	30.50	29.00
		Set, never hinged	50.00	
		Nos. 557-571,C73-C87,E15 (31)	56.60	48.35
		Set, never hinged	95.00	

Madrid Press Association, 40th anniversary.

Nos. 557-571 exist imperf. Values about 7 times those of perf. stamps.

See note after No. 432. See Nos. C73-C87.

Arms of Madrid — A125

1936, Apr. 2 Engr. *Imperf.*

572	A125	10c brown black	30.00	30.00
573	A125	15c dark green	30.00	30.00
		Set, never hinged	90.00	

1st National Philatelic Exhibition which opened in Madrid, Apr. 2, 1936.

For overprints see Nos. C88-C89.

"Republica Espanola" — A126

1936 Litho. *Perf. 11½, 13½x13*

574	A126	2c orange brown	.25	.25
		Never hinged	.35	

For surcharges & overprints see #591, 9LC24, 10L5, 11L3, 11LB4, 12L3, 13L4, 14L2, 14L14.

Gregorio Fernández — A127

1936, Mar. 10 Engr. *Perf. 11½*

576	A127	30c carmine	1.10	.85
		Never hinged	2.25	
a.		Perf. 14	9.00	8.25
		Never hinged	17.50	
b.		Imperf.	15.00	
		Never hinged	22.50	

Tercentenary of the death of Gregorio Fernandez, sculptor.

For overprints see Nos. 7LC18-7LC19.

Type of 1931 and

Pablo Iglesias
A128 A129

Velázquez A130

Fermín Salvoechea A131

1936-38 *Perf. 11, 11½, 11½x11*

577	A128	30c rose red	.25	.25
578	A129	30c car rose	1.10	.50
579	A100	40c car rose ('37)	1.10	.50
580	A129	45c carmine ('37)	.25	.25
581	A130	50c dark blue	.25	.25

582 A131 60c indigo ('37) .75 .90
583 A131 60c dp orange ('38) 6.00 5.00
Nos. 577-583 (7) 9.70 7.65
Set, never hinged 26.00

Perf. 14

577a A128 30c rose red 6.50
578a A129 30c carmine rose 6.75
579a A100 40c carmine rose 6.50
580a A129 45c carmine 6.00
582a A131 60c indigo 6.00
583a A131 60c deep orange 9.50
Nos. 577a-583a (6) 41.25
Set, never hinged 90.00

Nos. 577-583 exist imperf. Value, set $70, never hinged $150.

For overprints see Nos. C90, 7LC17, 7LC22-7LC23, 10L15, 14L21.

Statue of Liberty, Spanish and US Flags — A132

1938, June 1 **Photo.** ***Perf. 11½***

585 A132 1p multicolored 16.50 17.50
Never hinged 32.50
a. Imperf., pair 82.50 55.00
Never hinged 110.00
b. Horiz. pair, imperf. vert. 62.50 82.50
Never hinged 92.50
c. Souvenir sheet of 1 27.50 32.50
Never hinged 44.00
d. As "c," imperf. 350.00 250.00
Never hinged 600.00

150th anniv. of the US Constitution.
For surcharge see No. C97.

No. 289 Surcharged in Black

1938 ***Perf. 14***

586 A36 45c on 15c violet 15.50 15.50
Never hinged 19.00

7th anniversary of the Republic.
Values are for examples with perforations nearly touching the design on one or two sides.

No. 289 Surcharged in Black

a

b

Fiesta del Trabajo
1 MAYO
1938
1 Peseta

1938, May 1

587 A36 45c on 15c violet 3.00 3.00
588 A36 1p on 15c violet 5.25 5.25
Set, never hinged 12.00

Issued to commemorate Labor Day.
Values are for examples with perforations nearly touching the design on one or two sides.

No. 507 Surcharged in Black

1938, Nov. 10 ***Perf. 11½***

589 A92 2.50p on 25c lake .25 .25
Never hinged .25
b. Perf. 14 3.50 6.00
Never hinged 6.00

Types of 1933-36 Surcharged in Blue or Red

1938 ***Perf. 10, 11, 13½x13, 13x14***

590 A108 45c on 1c grn (R) .40 .25
b. Imperf. 6.00 5.00
Never hinged 10.00
590A A108 45c on 2c buff (Bl) 17.00 14.00
591 A126 45c on 2c org brn (Bl) .25 .25
Nos. 590-591 (3) 17.65 14.50
Set, never hinged 29.00

Many overprint varieties exist.

Numeral Type of 1933

1938-39 **Litho.** ***Perf. 11½, 13***
White or Gray Paper

592 A108 5c gray brown .25 .25
593 A108 10c yellow green .25 .25
594 A108 15c slate green .25 .25
595 A108 20c vio, gray paper .25 .25
596 A108 25c red violet .25 .25
597 A108 30c scarlet .25 .25
Nos. 592-597 (6) 1.50 1.50
Set, never hinged 1.75

"Republic" — A133

1938 ***Perf. 11½***

598 A133 40c rose red .25 .25
599 A133 45c rose .25 .25
a. Printed on both sides 11.00 11.00
Never hinged 27.50
600 A133 50c blue .25 .25
601 A133 60c dp ultra .50 .30
Nos. 598-601 (4) 1.05
Set, never hinged 1.10

Nos. 598-601 exist imperf. Value for set $22.50

Machine Gunners A134

Infantry — A135

Perf. 11½x11, 11x11½, Imperf.

1938, Sept. 1 **Photo.**

602 A134 25c dark green 12.00 9.25
603 A135 45c red brown 12.00 9.25
Set, never hinged 50.00

43rd Division of the Republican Army. Sold only at the Philatelic Agency and for foreign exchange.
Nos. 602-603 exist imperf. Value, set $50.

Blast Furnace A136

Steel Mill and Sculpture, "Defenders of Numantia" A137

1938, Aug. 9 ***Perf. 16***

604 A136 45c black .25 .25
605 A137 1.25p dark blue .25 .25
Set, never hinged 2.00

Issued in honor of the workers of Sagunto.

Submarine — A137a

Designs: 1p, 15p, U-Boat D1. 2p, 6p, U-Boat A1. 4p, 10p, U-Boat B2.

1938, Aug. 11 ***Perf. 16***

605A A137a 1p blue 3.50 3.50
605B A137a 2p red brown 6.50 6.50
605C A137a 4p red orange 7.25 7.25
605D A137a 6p deep blue 16.00 16.00
605E A137a 10p magenta 25.00 25.00
605F A137a 15p dp gray green 250.00 250.00
Nos. 605A-605F (6) 308.25 308.25
Set, never hinged 500.00

Souvenir Sheet

Perf. 10½

605G A137a Sheet of 3 350.00 350.00
Never hinged 600.00
a. 4p carmine & gray black 85.00 85.00
b. 6p dull blue & gray black 85.00 85.00
c. 15p green & gray black 85.00 85.00

Nos. 605A-605G were issued for use on a proposed submarine mail service between Barcelona and Mahon, Minorca. One voyage was made on this mail route, carrying 300 agency-prepared covers. The stamps were also valid for ordinary mail.

Nos. 605A-605G were sold only at the Philatelic Agency in Barcelona, for double their face value.

Nos. 605A-605G exist imperf. Value: set of 6 stamps, $650 unused, $875 never hinged; souvenir sheet, $2,250 unused, $2,900, never hinged.

Riflemen A138

Machine Gunners A139

Bomb Throwing — A140

1938, Nov. 25 **Engr.** ***Perf. 10***

606 A138 5c sepia 3.25 3.25
607 A138 10c dp violet 3.25 3.25
608 A138 25c blue green 3.25 3.25
609 A139 45c rose red 3.25 3.25
610 A139 60c dark blue 6.00 6.00
611 A139 1.20p black 120.00 120.00
612 A140 2p orange 35.00 35.00
613 A140 5p dark brown 175.00 175.00
614 A140 10p dk blue grn 37.50 37.50
Nos. 606-614 (9) 386.50 386.50
Set, never hinged 750.00

Honoring the Militia. Sold only at the Philatelic Agency and for foreign exchange. Exist imperf. Value unused $1,200, never hinged $1,800.

Spanish State

Arms of Spain — A141

1936 **Litho.** ***Imperf.***
Thin Transparent Paper

615 A141 30c blue 250.00
616 A141 30c pale green 250.00

Perf. 11
Thick Wove Paper

617 A141 30c dark blue 550.00 150.00
Set, never hinged 1,500.

Issued in Granada during siege. After the city was liberated, these stamps were used throughout the province of Granada.

Well-centered copies of No. 617 are worth twice as much as the values above.

Many forgeries exist.

A143

Cathedral of Burgos — A145

University of Salamanca A146

Cathedral del Pilar, Zaragoza — A147

"La Giralda," Seville — A148

Xavier Castle, Navarre — A149

Court of Lions, Alhambra at Granada A150

Mosque, Córdoba A151

Alcántara Bridge and Alcázar, Toledo — A152

Soldier Carrying Flag — A153

Troops Landing at Algeciras A154

Type II

Two types of 30c:
Type I — Imprint 12mm long; "3" does not touch frame.
Type II — Imprint 8mm long; "3" touches frame.

1936 **Unwmk.** **Litho.** ***Imperf.***
623 A143 1c green 4.50 3.50
Perf. 11½
624 A143 2c orange brown .45 .35
625 A145 5c gray brown .45 .45
626 A146 10c green .45 .35
627 A147 15c dull green .45 .35
628 A148 25c rose lake .60 .35
629 A149 30c carmine (I) .45 .35
a. Type II .60 .50
Never hinged 1.25
630 A150 50c deep blue 10.50 7.75
631 A151 60c yellow green .70 .60
632 A152 1p black 4.00 3.50
633 A153 4p rose vio, red & yel 40.00 26.00
634 A154 10p light brown 40.00 26.00
Nos. 623-634 (12) 102.55 69.55
Set, never hinged 250.00

Nos. 624-634 exist imperf. Value, set $275. Numerous forgeries exist for Nos. 623-634.
Nos. 625-631, 633-634 were privately overprinted "VIA AEREA" and plane, supposedly for use in Ifni.
For surcharges see Nos. 9LC21, 9LC23.

Nos. 542-543 Surcharged in Two Lines

1936 ***Imperf., Perf. 11½***
634A A108 5c on 1c bl grn 2.25 3.00
634B A108 5c on 2c buff 2.25 3.00
634C A108 10c on 1c bl grn 2.25 3.00
634D A108 15c on 2c buff 2.25 3.00
Nos. 634A-634D (4) 9.00 12.00
Set, never hinged 15.00

Issued in the Balearic Islands to meet a shortage of these values. Nos. 634A and 634C are imperf., Nos. 634B and 634D are perf. 11½.

St. James of Compostela — A155

St. James Cathedral A156

Pórtico de la Gloria A157

Type I Type II

Two types of 30c:
I — No dots in "1937."
II — Dot before and after "1937."

1937 ***Perf. 11½, 11x11½***
635 A155 15c violet brown .95 1.25
636 A156 30c rose red (I) 5.00 .55
a. Type II 17.50 14.00
Never hinged 37.50
637 A157 1p blue & orange 14.50 3.25
a. Center inverted 350.00 250.00
Never hinged 500.00
Nos. 635-637 (3) 20.45 5.05
Set, never hinged 55.00

Holy Year of Compostela. Nos. 635-637 exist imperf. Value for set $175.

"Estado Espanol"
A159 A160

"El Cid" — A161

Isabella I — A162

Two types of 5c, 30c and 10p:
5 Centimos: Type I Imprint 9½mm long. Type II Imprint 14mm long.
30 Centimos: Type I Imprint, "Hija De B. Fournier Burgos." Type II Imprint, "Fournier Burgos".
10 Pesetas: Type I "10" 2½mm high. Type II "10" 3mm high.

1936-40 **With Imprint** ***Imperf.***
638 A159 1c green .25 .25
Perf. 11
640 A160 2c brown .25 .25
Perf. 11, 11½, 11½x11, 11½x10½
641 A161 5c brown (I) .35 .25
642 A161 5c brown (II) .25 .25
643 A161 10c green .25 .25
Perf. 11, 11x11½
644 A162 15c gray black .25 .25
645 A162 20c dark violet .35 .25
646 A162 25c brown lake .25 .25
647 A162 30c rose (I) .40 .25
648 A162 30c rose (II) 10.00 2.00
649 A162 40c orange 1.10 .25
650 A162 50c dark blue 1.10 .25
651 A162 60c yellow .30 .25
652 A162 1p blue 9.50 .45
653 A162 4p magenta 12.00 4.50
654 A161 10p dk bl (I) ('37) 47.50 33.00
655 A161 10p dp bl (II) ('40) 19.00 12.50
Nos. 638-655 (17) 103.10 55.45
Set, never hinged 250.00

No. 638 was privately perforated. See Nos. 662-667. For overprint and surcharges see Nos. E18, 9LC10, 9LC13, 9LC15-9LC16, 9LC22, 9LC25, 9LC27-9LC30, 9LC34-9LC53.

Ferdinand the Catholic — A163

1938 ***Perf. 10½, 11½x11***
Imprint: "Lit Fournier Vitoria"
656 A163 15c deep green 1.75 .25
657 A163 30c deep red 5.75 .25
Imprint: "Fournier Vitoria"
Perf. 10
658 A163 15c deep green 1.75 .25
659 A163 20c purple 13.00 1.40
660 A163 25c brown car .90 .25
661 A163 30c deep red 6.50 .25
Nos. 656-661 (6) 29.65 2.65
Set, never hinged 110.00

Nos. 656-661 exist imperf.; value for set, $150. Part-perf. varieties exist.
For overprints see Nos. C98-C99.

Type I

Type II

Two types of the 15 Centimos:
Type I — Medieval style numerals with diagonal line through "5."
Type II — Modern numerals. Narrower "5" without diagonal line.

Without Imprint
1938-50 ***Perf. 11, 13½***
662 A159 1c green, imperf. .25 .25
663 A160 2c brn (18½x22mm; '40) .25 .25
a. 2c bis brn (17½x21mm; '48) .25 .25
Never hinged .30
664 A161 5c gray brn ('39) .25 .25
a. Perf. 13½x13¼ ('49) .25 .25
665 A161 10c dk carmine .25 .25
a. 10c rose .35 .25
Never hinged .75
b. Perf. 13½x13¼ ('49) .25 .25
666 A161 15c dk green (I) .90 .25
666A A161 15c dk green (II) .60 .25
b. Perf 13½x13¼ ('50) .65 .25
667 A162 70c dk blue ('39) .75 .25
Nos. 662-667 (7) 3.25 1.75
Set, never hinged 4.85

Emblem of the Falange — A164

1938, July 17 ***Perf. 10***
668 A164 15c bl grn & lt grn 3.50 3.50
669 A164 25c rose red & rose 3.50 3.50
670 A164 30c bl & lt bl 2.00 2.00
671 A164 1p brown & yellow 70.00 70.00
Nos. 668-671 (4) 79.00 79.00
Set, never hinged 160.00

Second anniversary of the Civil War.
Nos. 678-681 exist imperforate, Value, set $725 hinged, $950 never hinged.

Isabella I — A165

1938-39 **Litho.** ***Perf. 10***
672 A165 20c brt violet ('39) .55 .25
673 A165 25c brown carmine 5.50 .55
674 A165 30c rose red .25 .25
675 A165 40c dull violet .30 .25
676 A165 50c indigo ('39) 25.00 2.25
677 A165 1p deep blue 8.00 .80
Nos. 672-677 (6) 39.60 4.35
Set, never hinged 110.00

Nos. 672-677 exist imperf. Value set, $225 hinged, $350 never hinged.

Gen. Francisco Franco — A166

Imprint: "Sanchez Toda"
1939-40 ***Perf. 10***
678 A166 20c brt violet .35 .25
679 A166 25c rose lake .35 .25
680 A166 30c rose carmine .25 .25
681 A166 40c slate green .25 .25
682 A166 45c vermilion ('40) 1.00 1.00
683 A166 50c indigo .30 .25
684 A166 60c orange 1.50 1.50
685 A166 70c blue .35 .25
686 A166 1p black 6.50 .25
687 A166 2p dark brown 9.00 1.00
688 A166 4p dark violet 47.50 10.00
689 A166 10p light brown 25.00 *20.00*
Nos. 678-689 (12) 92.35 35.25
Set, never hinged 200.00

Nos. 686-689 have value & "Pta." on 1 line while Nos. 702-705 have value & "Pta." on 2 lines.
Nos. 678-689 exist imperf. Value set, $525 hinged, $700 never hinged.

Without Imprint
Perf. 9½x10½
1939-47 **Litho.** **Unwmk.**
690 A166 5c dull brn vio .45 .25
691 A166 10c brown orange 1.75 .65
692 A166 15c lt green .45 .25
693 A166 20c brt violet ('40) .45 .25
694 A166 25c dp claret ('40) .45 .25
695 A166 30c blue ('40) .45 .25
697 A166 40c Prus grn ('40) .45 .25
a. 40c greenish black .60 .25
Never hinged 1.00
698 A166 45c ultra ('41) .45 .25
699 A166 50c indigo ('40) .45 .25
a. Perf. 11½ ('47) 32.50 3.00
Never hinged 55.00
700 A166 60c dull org ('40) .60 .25
701 A166 70c blue ('40) .65 .25
702 A166 1p gray blk ('40) 5.00 .25
703 A166 2p dull brn ('41) 6.00 .25
704 A166 4p dull rose ('40) 19.00 .25
705 A166 10p lt brown ('40) 100.00 2.75
Nos. 690-705 (15) 136.60 6.65
Set, never hinged 300.00

Perf. 13x13¼
1949-53 **Litho.** **Unwmk.**
693a A166 20c brt violet .25 .25
694a A166 25c dp claret .25 .25
695a A166 30c blue .25 .25
696 A166 35c aqua ('51) .25 .25
697b A166 40c Prus grn ('50) .25 .25
698a A166 45c ultra ('52) .25 .25
699b A166 50c indigo .25 .25
700a A166 60c dull org .25 .25
701a A166 70c blue ('53) 16.00 .25
702a A166 1p gray blk ('51) 8.25 .25
703a A166 2p dull brn ('50) 3.00 .25
704a A166 4p dull rose 5.00 .25
Nos. 693a-704a (12) 34.25 3.00
Set, never hinged 80.00

The 40c exists in three types, with variations in the value tablet: I. "CTS" does not touch bottom line. II. Light background in tablet. "CTS" touches bottom line. III. As type I, but with well defined lines of white and color around rectangle.
The 60c exists in two types: I. Top and left side of value tablet touch rest of design. II. Tablet separated from rest of design by white lines.
Five values exist with perf. 10: 5c, 10c, 45c, 4p and 10p.
Nos. 690-704 exist imperf. Values, set: mint, never hinged, $1,400; unused, $1,000.
The imperforate 10c dull claret, type A166, without imprint, is a postal tax stamp, RA14.

1944 **Redrawn**
706 A166 1p gray 50.00 .65
Never hinged 110.00

"PTS" instead of "PTA" as No. 702.
Nos. 690-704 and 706 exist imperforate. Value, set $925.

The value reads "PTAS" instead of "PTS"
1944 **Unwmk.** ***Perf. 9½x10½***
709 A166 10p brown 14.00 .30
Never hinged 20.00
a. Perf. 13 ('53) 1.10 .30

General Franco — A167

1942-48 Engr. *Perf. 12½x13*

712 A167 40c chestnut .40 .25
713 A167 75c dk bl, perf. 9½x10½ ('46) 3.50 .40
714 A167 90c dk green ('48) .30 .25
a. Perf. 9½x10½ ('47) 1.40 .25
715 A167 1.35p purple ('48) .90 .25
a. Perf. 9½x10½ ('46) 2.00 .40
Nos. 712-715 (4) 5.10 1.15
Set, never hinged 8.50

St. John of the Cross — A168

1942 Litho. *Perf. 9½x10½*

721 A168 20c violet .55 .25
722 A168 40c salmon 1.25 .60
723 A168 75c ultra 1.50 1.75
Nos. 721-723 (3) 3.30 2.60
Set, never hinged 5.25

St. John of the Cross (1542-1591).
Nos. 721-723 exist imperforate. Value, $65 hinged, $80 never hinged.

Holy Year Issues

Statue in St. James Cathedral A169

St. James of Compostela A170

Incense Burner — A171

Perf. 9½x10½

1943, Oct. Litho. Unwmk.

724 A169 20c deep blue .25 .25
725 A170 40c dk red brown .50 .25
726 A171 75c deep blue 2.10 2.10

Nos. 725 and 727 exist imperforate. Value, $550.

Carvings in St. James Cathedral
A172 A174

St. James — A173

1943-44 *Perf. 9½x10½, 10½x9½*

727 A172 20c rose red ('44) .25 .25
728 A173 40c dull green .50 .25
729 A174 75c dk blue ('44) 2.75 2.25

St. James' Casket A175

East Portal of Cathedral A176

St. James Cathedral — A177

1944

730 A175 20c red violet .25 .25
731 A176 40c dull brown .70 .25
732 A177 75c bright blue 30.00 *32.00*
Nos. 724-732 (9) 37.30 37.85
Set, never hinged 100.00

Millennium of Castile Issues

Arms of Soria — A178

Arms of Castile — A179

Arms of Avila A180

Fortress A181

Arms of Segovia A182

Arms of Fernan González A183

Arms of Burgos A185

Arms of Santander A186

1944 Litho. *Perf. 9½x10½*

733 A178 20c violet .30 .25
734 A179 40c dull brown 3.00 .50
735 A180 75c blue 3.00 *3.00*
736 A181 20c rose violet .25 .25
737 A182 40c dull brown 2.75 .50
738 A183 75c dull blue 2.60 *2.75*
739 A180 20c red violet .25 .25
740 A185 40c dull brown 2.10 .50
741 A186 75c blue 3.00 *3.25*
Nos. 733-741 (9) 17.25 11.25
Set, never hinged 32.50

Nos. 733, 738 and 741 exist imperforate. Value, $650. Value never hinged, $900.
No. 739 exists imperforate on grayish paper.

Francisco Gomez de Quevedo y Villegas (1580-1645), Writer — A187

1945, Sept. 8 Engr. *Perf. 10*

742 A187 40c dark brown .65 .55
Never hinged 1.10

Exists imperf. Value $80.

Type of Semi-Postal Stamp, 1940 Without Imprint at Lower Left and Right

1946, Jan. 1 Litho. *Perf. 11*

743 SP20 50c (40c + 10c) sl grn & rose vio 1.40 .25
Never hinged 2.40

No. 743 was used as an ordinary postage stamp of 50c denomination.
Exists imperf. Value $80.

Elio Antonio de Nebrija — A188

University of Salamanca and Signature of Francisco de Vitoria — A189

1946, Oct. 12 Engr. *Perf. 9½x10*

744 A188 50c deep plum .40 .30
745 A189 75c deep blue .50 .45
Nos. 744-745,C121 (3) 2.80 3.25
Set, never hinged 5.25

Stamp Day and the Day of the Race, Oct. 12, 1946.
Nos. 744-745 and C121 exist imperforate. Value set, $160 hinged, $240 never hinged.

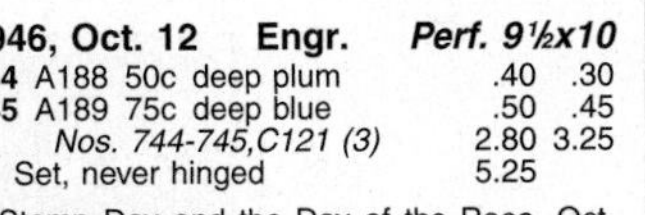

Francisco de Goya — A190

1946, Oct 26

746 A190 25c deep plum .25 .25
747 A190 50c green .25 .25
748 A190 75c dark blue .60 .75
Nos. 746-748 (3) 1.25
Set, never hinged 1.00

Francisco de Goya, birth bicentenary.
Nos. 746-748 exist imperforate. Value set, $25 hinged, $32.50 never hinged.

Benito Jeronimo Feijoo y Montenegro — A191

1947, June 1 Unwmk.

749 A191 50c deep green .45 .35
Never hinged .65

No. 749 exists imperforate. Value, $35.

Don Quixote Reading A192

"Don Quixote" by Ignacio Zuloaga A193

1947, Oct. 9 Engr. *Perf. 9½x10½*

750 A192 50c sepia .25 .25
751 A193 75c dark blue .40 .45
Nos. 750-751,C122 (3) 4.15 3.20
Set, never hinged 7.75

Stamp Day and the 400th anniv. of the birth of Miguel de Cervantes Saavedra.
Nos. 750-751 and C122 exist imperforate. Value set, $550 hinged, $650 never hinged.

General Franco
A194 A195

1948 Litho. *Perf. 12½x13*

752 A194 15c green .25 .25
753 A195 50c violet .80 .25
Set, never hinged 1.25

Nos. 752 and 753 exist imperforate. Value set, $400 hinged, $550 never hinged.
See Nos. 760-768, 780, 801-803. For surcharges see Nos. B137-B138.

Hernando Cortez — A196

Mateo Aleman — A197

1948, June 15 Engr. *Perf. 12½x13*

754 A196 35c black .25 .25

Perf. 9½x10½

755 A197 70c dk violet brn 1.40 2.00
a. Perf. 12½x13 25.00 25.00
Set, never hinged 2.25

No. 754 exists imperforate. Value set, $100 hinged, $125 never hinged.

Ferdinand III (The Saint) — A198

Grandson of Adm. Ramon de Bonifaz — A199

1948, Sept. 20 Litho. *Perf. 12½x13*

756 A198 25c rose violet .25 .25
757 A199 30c scarlet .25 .25
Set, never hinged .50

700th anniversary of the Spanish navy and of the capture of Seville by Ferdinand the Saint.

José de Salamanca y Mayol — A200

Train Crossing Pancorbo Viaduct — A201

Perf. 12½x13, 13x12½

1948, Oct. 9 Unwmk.

758 A200 50c brown .50 .25
759 A201 5p deep green 1.40 .25
Nos. 758-759,C125 (3) 3.40 2.00
Set, never hinged 6.00

Centenary of Spanish railroads.

Franco Types of 1948

1948-49 Litho. *Perf. 12½x13*

760 A194 5c brown .30 .25
761 A195 25c vermilion .30 .25
762 A195 35c blue green .30 .25
763 A195 40c red brown .65 .25

764 A195 45c car rose ('49) .40 .25
765 A194 50c bister 1.10 .25
766 A195 70c purple ('49) 1.90 .30
767 A195 75c dk vio blue 1.60 .30
768 A195 1p rose pink 5.00 .25
Nos. 760-768 (9) 11.55 2.35
Set, never hinged 17.50

Imperforates exist of Nos. 761 ($100), 762 ($300), 764 ($300) and 768 ($500)

Symbols of UPU A202

1949, Oct. 9
769 A202 50c red brown .35 .25
770 A202 75c violet blue .35 .55
Nos. 769-770,C126 (3) .95 1.25
Set, never hinged 2.25

75th anniv. of the UPU.

St. John of God — A203

1950, Mar. 8 Engr. Unwmk.
771 A203 1p dark violet 7.00 4.50
Never hinged 12.50

400th anniversary of the death of St. John of God, humanitarian.

Pedro Calderon de la Barca — A204

Designs: 10c Lope de Vega. 15c, Tirso de Molina. 20c, Juan Ruiz de Alarcon, dramatist. 50c, St. Antonio Maria Claret y Clara.

1950-53 Photo. *Perf. 12½*
772 A204 5c brown ('51) .25 .25
773 A204 10c dp rose brn ('51) .25 .25
773A A204 15c dk sl grn ('53) .25 .25
774 A204 20c violet .25 .25

Perf. 12½x13
Engr.
775 A204 50c dp bluish gray ('51) 2.50 1.50
Nos. 772-775 (5) 3.50 2.50
Set, never hinged 4.35

No. 774 exists imperforate. Value, $250.

Stamp of 1850 — A205

1950, Oct. 12 Engr. *Imperf.*
776 A205 50c purple 4.00 4.00
777 A205 75c ultra 4.00 4.00
778 A205 10p dk slate grn 47.50 *60.00*
779 A205 15p red 47.50 *60.00*
Nos. 776-779,C127-C130 (8) 202.00 227.00
Set, never hinged 375.00

Centenary of Spain's stamps.

Franco Type of 1948

1950 Litho. *Perf. 12½x13*
780 A195 45c red .60 .25
Never hinged .90

Queen Isabella I — A206

1951, Apr. 22 Photo. *Perf. 12½*
781 A206 50c brown .40 .30
782 A206 75c blue .25 .30
783 A206 90c rose brown .30 .25
784 A206 1.50p orange 5.25 5.25
785 A206 2.80p olive grn 14.00 14.00
Nos. 781-785 (5) 20.20 20.10
Set, never hinged 35.00

500th anniversary of the birth of Queen Isabella I. See Nos. C132-C136.

Ferdinand, the Catholic — A210

1952, May 10 Photo. *Perf. 13*
787 A210 50c green .40 .25
788 A210 75c indigo 2.75 1.40
789 A210 90c rose brown .30 .25
790 A210 1.50p orange 6.50 6.50
791 A210 2.80p brown 12.50 12.50
Nos. 787-791 (5) 22.45 20.90
Set, never hinged 42.50

500th anniversary of the birth of Ferdinand the Catholic of Spain. See Nos. C139-C143.

Maria Michaela Dermaisiéres A211

1952, May 26 *Perf. 12½x13*
792 A211 90c claret .25 .25
Never hinged .30

35th International Eucharistic Congress, Barcelona, 1952. See No. C137.

Dr. Santiago Ramon y Cajal — A212

Portrait: 4.50p, Dr. Jaime Ferran y Clua.

1952, July 8 Photo.
793 A212 2p bright blue 12.00 .25
794 A212 4.50p red brown .90 .90
Set, never hinged 20.00

Centenary of the births of Dr. Santiago Ramon y Cajal and Dr. Jaime Ferran y Clua.

University Seal — A213

Luis de Leon — A214

Cathedral of Salamanca A215

1953, Oct. 12 *Perf. 12½x13, 13x12½*
795 A213 50c deep magenta .50 .35
796 A214 90c dark olive gray 1.60 1.60
797 A215 2p brown 11.00 3.50
Nos. 795-797 (3) 13.10 5.45
Set, never hinged 21.00

Stamp Day, 10/12/53, and 700th anniv. of the founding of the University of Salamanca.

The Magdalene — A216

1954, Jan. 10 *Perf. 12½x13*
798 A216 1.25p deep magenta .25 .25
Never hinged .30

José de Ribera, painter, 300th death anniv.

St. James of Compostela A217

St. James Cathedral A218

1954, Mar. 1
799 A217 50c dark brown .25 .25
800 A218 3p blue 25.00 3.75
Set, never hinged 55.00

Holy year of Compostela, 1954.

Franco Types of 1948

1954 Litho. *Perf. 12½x13*
801 A194 5c olive gray .25 .25
802 A195 30c deep green .25 .25
803 A194 80c dull car rose 1.50 .25
Nos. 801-803 (3) 2.00 .75
Set, never hinged 4.75

Virgin by Alonso Cano — A219

Virgins: 15c, Begoña. 25c, Of the Abandoned. 30c, Black. 50c, Of the Pillar. 60c, Covadonga. 80c, Kings'. 1p, Almudena. 2p, Africa. 3p, Guadalupe.

1954, July 18 Photo. *Perf. 12½x13*
804 A219 10c dk car rose .25 .25
805 A219 15c olive green .25 .25
806 A219 25c purple .25 .25
807 A219 30c brown .25 .25
808 A219 50c brown olive .35 .25
809 A219 60c gray .25 .25
810 A219 80c grnsh gray 1.50 .25
811 A219 1p lilac gray 1.50 .25
812 A219 2p red brown .35 .25
813 A219 3p bright blue .60 .60
Nos. 804-813 (10) 5.55 2.85
Set, never hinged 9.00

Issued to publicize the Marian Year.

Marcelino Menendez y Pelayo — A220

1954, Oct. 12
814 A220 80c dk gray grn 5.25 .35
Never hinged 9.50

Stamp Day, October 12, 1954.

Gen. Franco — A221

Imprint: "F.N.M.T."

1954-56 *Perf. 12½x13*
815 A221 10c dk car lake .25 .25
816 A221 15c bister .25 .25
817 A221 20c dk ol grn ('55) .25 .25
818 A221 25c blue violet .25 .25
819 A221 30c brown .25 .25
820 A221 40c rose vio ('55) .25 .25
821 A221 50c dk brn olive .25 .25
822 A221 60c dk vio brown .25 .25
823 A221 70c dk green .25 .25
824 A221 80c dk blue grn .25 .25
825 A221 1p dp orange .25 .25
826 A221 1.40p lil rose ('56) .25 .25
827 A221 1.50p lt bl grn ('56) .25 .25
828 A221 1.80p emerald ('56) .25 .25
829 A221 2p red 10.00 .60
830 A221 2p red lilac ('56) .25 .25
831 A221 3p Prus blue .25 .25
832 A221 5p dk red brn .25 .25
833 A221 6p dk gray ('55) .25 .25
834 A221 8p brt vio ('56) .25 .25
835 A221 10p yel grn ('55) .25 .25
Nos. 815-835 (21) 15.00 5.60
Set, never hinged 17.00

Coils: The 1.50p, No. 830, the 3p and the 6p were issued in coils in brighter tones (the 3p in 1974, others in 1973). Every fifth stamp has a black control number on the back.

See Nos. 937-938, 1852-1855.

St. Ignatius of Loyola — A222

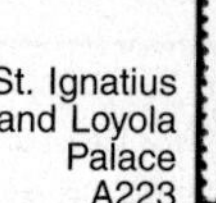

St. Ignatius and Loyola Palace A223

Perf. 13x12½, 12½x13

1955, Oct. 12 Photo. Unwmk.
836 A222 25c dull purple .25 .25
837 A223 60c bister .40 .30
838 A222 80c Prus green 1.65 .25
Nos. 836-838 (3) 2.30 .80
Set, never hinged 4.25

4th cent. of the death of St. Ignatius of Loyola, founder of the Jesuit Order, and Day of the Stamp.

Symbols of Telegraph and Radio Communi-cation A224

1955, Dec. 8 *Perf. 13x12½*
839 A224 15c dk olive bis .25 .25
840 A224 80c Prus green 3.00 .25
841 A224 3p bright blue 5.00 .75
Nos. 839-841 (3) 8.25 1.25
Set, never hinged 20.00

Spanish telegraph system centenary.

St. Vincent Ferrer — A225

1955, Dec. 20 *Perf. 13*

842 A225 15c olive bister .35 .25
Never hinged .60

Canonization of St. Vincent Ferrer, 5th cent.

"Holy Family" by El Greco — A226

1955, Dec. 24 *Perf. 13x12½*

843 A226 80c dark green 3.25 .65
Never hinged 6.00

Marching Soldiers and Dove — A227

1956, July 17 **Unwmk.**

844 A227 15c olive bis & brn .25 .25
845 A227 50c lt ol grn & ol .30 .30
846 A227 80c mag & grnsh blk 2.00 .25
847 A227 3p ultra & dp blue 3.00 1.25
Nos. 844-847 (4) 5.55 2.05
Set, never hinged 12.00

20th anniversary of Civil War.

Ciudad de Toledo A228

1956, Aug. 3 *Perf. 12½x13*

848 A228 3p blue 2.00 1.50
Never hinged 4.50

Issued to publicize the voyage of the S. S. Ciudad de Toledo to Central and South America carrying the First Floating (Industrial) Exposition.

Black Virgin of Montserrat — A229

Design: 60c, Monastery of Montserrat, mountains and crucifix.

1956, Sept. 11 *Perf. 13x12½*

849 A229 15c bister .25 .25
850 A229 60c violet black .25 .25
851 A229 80c blue green .30 .40
Nos. 849-851 (3) .80 .90
Set, never hinged .85

75th anniv. of the coronation of the Black Virgin of Montserrat.

Archangel Gabriel by Fra Angelico — A230

1956, Oct. 12 **Engr.**

852 A230 80c dull green .75 .35
Never hinged 1.00

Stamp Day, Oct. 12.

Statistical Chart A231

1956, Nov. 3 *Perf. 12½x13*

853 A231 15c dk olive bis .30 .30
854 A231 80c green 2.00 .50
855 A231 1p red orange 2.00 .50
Nos. 853-855 (3) 4.30 1.30
Set, never hinged 7.50

Centenary of Spanish Statistics.

Hermitage and Monument A232

1956, Dec. 4

856 A232 80c dull blue grn 2.00 .25
Never hinged 5.50

20th anniversary of the nomination of Gen. Franco as chief of state and commander in chief of the army.

Hungarian Children — A233

1956, Dec. 17 *Perf. 13x12½*

857 A233 10c brown lake .25 .25
858 A233 15c dk bister .25 .25
859 A233 50c olive gray .30 .25
860 A233 80c dk blue grn 1.25 .25
861 A233 1p red orange 1.25 .25
862 A233 3p brt blue 3.00 1.50
Nos. 857-862 (6) 6.30 2.75
Set, never hinged 13.00

Issued in sympathy to the children of Hungary.

St. Marguerite Alacoque's Vision of Jesus — A234

1957, Oct. 12 **Photo.** **Unwmk.**

863 A234 15c dk olive bis .25 .25
864 A234 60c violet blk .25 .25
865 A234 80c dk blue grn .30 .25
Nos. 863-865 (3) .80 .75
Set, never hinged .90

Centenary of the feast of the Sacred Heart of Jesus and for Stamp Day 1957.

Gonzalo de Cordoba — A235

1958, Feb. 28 **Engr.** *Perf. 13x12½*

866 A235 1.80p yellow green .25 .25
Never hinged .30

Issued in honor of El Gran Capitan, 15th century military leader.

"The Parasol," by Goya — A236

"Wife of the Bookseller of Carretas Street" — A237

Goya Paintings: 50c, Duke of Fernan-Nunez. 60c, The Crockery Seller. 70c, Isabel Cobos de Porcel. 80c, Goya by Vicente Lopez. 1p, "El Pelele" (Carnival Doll). 1.80p, Goya's grandson Marianito. 2p, The Vintage. 3p, The Drinker.

1958, Mar. 24 **Photo.** *Perf. 13*
Gold Frame

867 A236 15c bister .25 .25
868 A237 40c plum .25 .25
869 A237 50c olive gray .25 .25
870 A237 60c violet gray .25 .25
871 A237 70c dp yellow grn .25 .25
872 A237 80c dk slate grn .25 .25
873 A237 1p orange red .25 .25
874 A237 1.80p brt green .25 .25
875 A237 2p red lilac .30 .30
876 A236 3p brt blue .50 .50
Nos. 867-876 (10) 2.80 2.80
Set, never hinged 3.00

Issued to honor Francisco Jose de Goya and for the "Day of the Stamp," Mar. 24.
See Nos. 1111-1114. For other art types see A240a, A246a, A257, A272, A285a, A300, A310, A324, A340-A341, A360, A371 and footnote following No. 1606.

Exhibition Emblem and Globe — A238

1958, June 7 *Perf. 13x12½*

877 A238 80c car, dk brn & gray .25 .25
a. Souvenir sheet, imperf. 13.00 13.00
878 A238 3p car, vio blk & bl .85 .85
a. Souvenir sheet, imperf. 13.00 13.00
Set, never hinged 2.00
#877a-878a never hinged 45.00

No. 877a sold for 2p, No. 878a for 5p.
Universal and Intl. Exposition at Brussels.

Charles V — A239

Various Portraits of Charles V: 50c, 1.80p, with helmet. 70c, 2p, facing left. 80c, 3p, with beret.

1958, July 30 **Photo.** *Perf. 13*

879 A239 15c buff & brown .25 .25
880 A239 50c lt grn & ol brn .25 .25
881 A239 70c gray, grn & blk .25 .25
882 A239 80c pale brn & Prus grn .25 .25
883 A239 1p bis & brick red .25 .25
884 A239 1.80p pale grn & brt grn .25 .25
885 A239 2p gray & lilac .30 .30
886 A239 3p pale brn & brt bl .30 .30
Nos. 879-886 (8) 2.10 2.10
Set, never hinged 3.00

400th anniv. of the death of Charles V (Carlos I of Spain.)

Escorial and Streamlined Train — A240

Designs: 60c, 2p, Railroad bridge at Despeñaperros, vert. 80c, 3p, Train and Castle de La Mota.

1958, Sept. 29 *Perf. 12½x13*

887 A240 15c dk olive bis .25 .25
888 A240 60c dk purple .25 .25
889 A240 80c dk blue grn .25 .25
890 A240 1p red orange .25 .25
891 A240 2p red lilac .25 .25
892 A240 3p blue .70 .40
Nos. 887-892 (6) 1.95 1.65
Set, never hinged 3.00

Intl. Railroad Cong., Madrid, Sept. 28-Oct. 7.

The Spinners — A240a

Velazquez Paintings: 15c, The Drinkers, horiz. 50c, Surrender of Breda. 60c, The Little Princesses. 70c, Prince Balthazar. 80c, Velazquez Self-portrait. 1p, The Coronation of Our Lady. 1.80p, Aesop. 2p, Vulcan's Forge. 3p, Menippus.

1959, Mar. 24 **Photo.** *Perf. 13*
Gold Frame

893 A240a 15c dk brown .25 .25
894 A240a 40c rose violet .25 .25
895 A240a 50c olive .25 .25
896 A240a 60c black brown .25 .25
897 A240a 70c dp yellow grn .25 .25
898 A240a 80c dk slate grn .25 .25
899 A240a 1p orange red .25 .25
900 A240a 1.80p emerald .25 .25
901 A240a 2p red lilac .25 .25
902 A240a 3p brt blue .35 .45
Nos. 893-902 (10) 2.60 2.70
Set, never hinged 2.75

Issued to honor Diego de Silva Velazquez (1599-1660) and for Stamp Day, Mar. 24.
For other art types see A236-A237, A246a, A257, A272, A285a, A300, A310, A324, A340-A341, A360, A371 and footnote following No. 1606.

Civil War Memorial — A241

1959, Apr 1. **Litho.** **Unwmk.**

903 A241 80c yel grn & dk sl grn .25 .25
Never hinged .30

Inauguration of the war memorial at the monastery of the Holy Cross in the Valley of the Fallen.

Louis XIV and Philip IV — A242

1959, Oct. 24 Photo. *Perf. 13x12½*

904 A242 1p gold & rose brn .25 .25
Never hinged .30

300th anniv. of the signing of the Treaty of the Pyrenees. Design shows the French-Spanish meeting at Isle des Faisans in 1659, as pictured in the Lebrun Tapestry, Versailles.

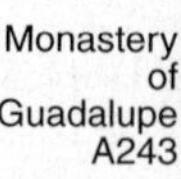

Monastery of Guadalupe A243

80c, Monastery, different view. 1p, Portals.

1959, Nov. 16 Engr. *Perf. 12½x13*

905 A243 15c lt red brown .25 .25
906 A243 80c slate .25 .25
907 A243 1p rose red .25 .25
Nos. 905-907 (3) .75 .75
Set, never hinged .80

Entrance of the Franciscan Brothers into Guadalupe monastery, 50th anniv.

Holy Family, by Goya — A244

1959, Dec. 10 Photo. *Perf. 13x12½*

908 A244 1p orange brown .25 .25
Never hinged .35

Catalogue values for unused stamps in this section, from this point to the end of the section, are for Never Hinged items.

Lidian Bull A245

Bullfighter, 19th Century — A246

Designs: 20c, Rounding up bulls. 25c, Running with the bulls, Pamplona. 30c, Bull entering arena. 50c, Bullfighting with cape. 70c, Bullfighting with banderillas. 80c, 1p, 1.40p, 1.50p, Fighting with muleta, various poses. 1.80p, Mounted bullfighter placing banderillas.

Perf. 12½x13, 13x12½

1960, Feb. 29 Engr. Unwmk.

909 A245 15c sepia & bis .25 .25
910 A245 20c vio & bl vio .25 .25
911 A246 25c gray .25 .25
912 A246 30c sepia & bister .25 .25
913 A246 50c dull vio & sep .25 .25
914 A246 70c sepia & sl grn .25 .25
915 A246 80c blue grn & grn .25 .25
916 A246 1p red & brn .25 .25
917 A246 1.40p brown & lake .25 .25
918 A246 1.50p grnsh bl & grn .25 .25
919 A245 1.80p grn & dk grn .25 .25
920 A246 5p brn & brn car .55 .45
Nos. 909-920,C159-C162 (16) 4.60 4.35

Murillo Self-portrait A246a

Murillo Paintings: 25c, The Good Shepherd. 40c, Rebecca and Eliezer. 50c, Virgin of the Rosary. 70c, Immaculate Conception. 80c, Children with Shell. 1.50p, Holy Family with a Bird, horiz. 2.50p, Children Playing Dice. 3p, Children Eating. 5p, Children counting Money.

1960, Mar. 24 Photo. *Perf. 13*

Gold Frame

921 A246a 25c dull violet .25 .25
922 A246a 40c plum .25 .25
923 A246a 50c olive gray .25 .25
924 A246a 70c dp yel grn .25 .25
925 A246a 80c deep green .25 .25
926 A246a 1p violet brown .25 .25
927 A246a 1.50p blue green .25 .25
928 A246a 2.50p rose car .25 .25
929 A246a 3p brt blue 1.25 .60
930 A246a 5p deep red brn .35 .25
Nos. 921-930 (10) 3.60 2.85

Issued to honor Bartolome Esteban Murillo (1617-1682) and for Stamp Day, Mar. 24.

For other art types see A236-A237, A240a, A257, A272, A285a, A300, A310, A324, A340-A341, A360, A371 and footnote following No. 1606.

Christ of Lepanto — A247

80c, 2.50p, 10p, Holy Family Church, Barcelona.

1960, Mar. 27 *Perf. 13x12½*

931 A247 70c brn car & grn 1.50 1.25
932 A247 80c blk & ol grn 1.50 1.25
933 A247 1p cl & brt red 1.50 1.25
934 A247 2.50p brt vio & gray vio 1.50 1.25
935 A247 5p sepia & bister 1.50 1.25
936 A247 10p sepia & bister 1.50 1.25
Nos. 931-936,C163-C166 (10) 28.00 20.50

First International Congress of Philately, Barcelona, March 26-Apr. 5. Nos. 931-936 could be bought at the exhibition upon presentation of 5p entrance ticket.

Franco Type of 1954-56
Imprint: "F.N.M.T.-B"

1960, Mar. 31 Photo. *Perf. 13*

937 A221 1p deep orange 1.40 .60
938 A221 5p dark red brown 1.40 .60

Printed and issued at the International Congress of Philately in Barcelona.

St. Juan de Ribera — A248

1960, Aug. 16 Photo. *Perf. 13*

939 A248 1p orange red .25 .25
940 A248 2.50p lilac rose .25 .25

Canonization of St. Juan de Ribera.

Common Design Types pictured following the introduction.

Europa Issue, 1960
Common Design Type

1960, Sept. 19 *Perf. 12½x13*
Size: 38½x21½mm

941 CD3 1p sl grn & ol bis *.75* .25
942 CD3 5p choc & salmon *.75* .50

St. Vincent de Paul — A249

1960, Sept. 27 Unwmk. *Perf. 13*

943 A249 25c violet .25 .25
944 A249 1p orange red .40 .25

3rd centenary of the death of St. Vincent de Paul.

Pedro Menendez de Aviles — A250

70c, 2.50p, Hernando de Soto. 80c, 3p, Ponce de Leon. 1p, 5p, Alvar Nunez Cabeza de Vaca.

1960, Oct. 12 *Perf. 13x12½*

945 A250 25c vio bl, *bl* .25 .25
946 A250 70c slate grn, *pink* .25 .25
947 A250 80c dk grn, *pale brn* .25 .25
948 A250 1p org brn, *yel* .25 .25
949 A250 2p dk car rose, *pink* .30 .25
950 A250 2.50p lil rose, *buff* .60 .25
951 A250 3p dk blue, *grnsh* 2.75 .50
952 A250 5p dk brown, *cit* 2.25 .85
Nos. 945-952 (8) 6.90 2.85

Florida's discovery & colonization, 4th cent.

Runner — A251

Sports: 40c, 2p, Bicycling, horiz. 70c, 2.50p, Soccer, horiz. 80c, 3p, Athlete with rings. 1p, 5p, Hockey on roller skates, horiz.

Perf. 13x12½, 12½x13

1960, Oct. 31 Photo.

953 A251 25c dk vio, brn & blk .25 .25
954 A251 40c purple, org & blk .25 .25
955 A251 70c brt green & red .30 .25
956 A251 80c dp grn, car & blk .25 .25
957 A251 1p red org, brt grn & blk .55 .25
958 A251 1.50p Prus grn, brn & blk .40 .25
959 A251 2p red lil, emer & blk 1.10 .25
960 A251 2.50p lil rose & green .40 .25
961 A251 3p ultra, red & blk .75 .25
962 A251 5p red brn, bl & blk .75 .35
Nos. 953-962,C167-C170 (14) 7.80 4.20

Isaac Albeniz — A252

1960, Nov. 7 *Perf. 13*

963 A252 25c dark gray .25 .25
964 A252 1p orange red .25 .25

Isaac Albeniz, composer, birth centenary.

Courtyard of Samos Monastery A253

1p, Fountain, vert. 5p, Facade, vert.

Perf. 12½x13, 13x12½

1960, Nov. 21 Engr.

965 A253 80c bl grn & Prus grn .25 .25
966 A253 1p org brn & car rose 1.10 .25
967 A253 5p sepia & ocher 1.10 .45
Nos. 965-967 (3) 2.45 .95

Issued in honor of the reconstructed Benedictine monastery at Samos, Lugo.

Adoration, by Velazquez — A254

1960, Dec. 1 Photo. *Perf. 13x12½*

968 A254 1p orange red .30 .25

Flight into Egypt by Francisco Bayeu A255

1961, Jan. 23 *Perf. 12½x13*

969 A255 1p copper red .25 .25
970 A255 5p dull red brown .45 .30

World Refugee Year.

Leandro F. de Moratin, by Goya — A256

1961, Feb. 13 *Perf. 13*

971 A256 1p henna brown .25 .25
972 A256 1.50p dk blue green .25 .25

Leandro Fernandez de Moratin (1760-1828), poet and dramatist, 200th birth anniv.

St. Peter by El Greco — A257

El Greco Paintings: 40c, Virgin Mary. 70c, Head of Christ. 80c, Knight with Hand on Chest. 1p, Self-portrait. 1.50p, Baptism of Christ. 2.50p, Holy Trinity. 3p, Burial of Count Orgaz. 5p, Christ Stripped of His Garments. 10p, St. Mauritius and the Theban Legion.

Gold Frame

1961, Mar. 24 *Perf. 13*

973 A257 25c violet black .25 .25
974 A257 40c lilac .25 .25
975 A257 70c green .25 .25
976 A257 80c Prus green .25 .25
977 A257 1p chocolate 2.00 .25
978 A257 1.50p grnsh blue .25 .25
979 A257 2.50p dk car rose .25 .25
980 A257 3p bright blue 1.75 .60
981 A257 5p black brown 3.75 1.50
982 A257 10p purple .50 .30
Nos. 973-982 (10) 9.50 4.15

El Greco and Stamp Day, March 24.

For other art types see A236-A237, A240a, A246a, A272, A285a, A300, A310, A324, A340-A341, A360, A371 and footnote following No. 1606.

Diego Velazquez — A258

Velazquez Paintings: 1p, Duke de Olivares. 2.50p, Infanta Margarita. 10p, Detail from The Spinners, horiz.

Unwmk.

1961, Apr. 17 Engr. *Perf. 13*

983 A258 80c dk blue & sl grn 1.60 .25
a. Souvenir sheet 5.00 *5.50*
984 A258 1p brn red & choc 4.50 .25
a. Souvenir sheet 5.00 *5.50*
985 A258 2.50p vio bl & bl .55 .35
a. Souvenir sheet 5.00 *5.50*
986 A258 10p grn & yel grn 7.00 2.50
a. Souvenir sheet 8.50 *8.50*
Nos. 983-986 (4) 13.65 3.35

300th anniversary (in 1960) of the death of Velazquez, painter.

Each souvenir sheet contains one imperf. stamp. The colors of the stamps have been changed: 80c, red brown & slate; 1p, blue & violet; 2.50p, green & blue; 10p, slate blue & greenish blue. The sheets were sold at a premium.

Canceled Stamp — A259

1961, May 6 Photo. *Perf. 13x12½*

987 A259 25c gray & red .25 .25
988 A259 1p orange & blk .90 .25
989 A259 10p olive grn & brn 1.00 .60
Nos. 987-989 (3) 2.15 1.10

Issued for International Stamp Day.

Juan Vazquez de Mella — A260

1961, June 8 Unwmk. *Perf. 13*

990 A260 1p henna brown .35 .25
991 A260 2.30p red lilac .25 .25

Birth centenary of Juan Vazquez de Mella y Fanjul, politician and writer.

Flag, Angel and Peace Doves — A261

Designs: 80c, Ships and Strait of Gibraltar. 1p, Alcazar and horseman. 1.50p, Ruins and triumphal arch. 2p, Horseman over Ebro. 2.30p, Victory parade. 2.50p, Ship building. 3p, Steel industry. 5p, Map of Spanish irrigation dams and statue, horiz. 6p, Dama de Elche statue and power station. 8p, Mining development. 10p, General Franco.

1961, July 10

992 A261 70c multicolored .25 .25
993 A261 80c multicolored .25 .25
994 A261 1p multicolored .25 .25
995 A261 1.50p gold, pink & brn .25 .25
996 A261 2p gold, gray & bl .25 .25
997 A261 2.30p multicolored .25 .25
998 A261 2.50p multicolored .25 .25
999 A261 3p gold, red & dk gray .35 .25
1000 A261 5p bl grn, ol gray & pink 2.00 1.10
1001 A261 6p multicolored 1.10 .75
1002 A261 8p gold, ol & sep .60 .50
1003 A261 10p gold, gray & grn .50 .50
Nos. 992-1003 (12) 6.30 4.85

25th anniversary of national uprising.

Christ, San Clemente, Tahull — A262

Designs: 25c, Bas-relief, Compostela Cathedral. 1p, Cloister of Silos. 2p, Virgin of Irache.

1961, July 24 Unwmk. *Perf. 13*

Gold Frame

1004 A262 25c blue violet .25 .25
1005 A262 1p orange brown .25 .25
1006 A262 2p deep plum .40 .25
1007 A262 3p grnsh bl, sal & blk .40 .30
Nos. 1004-1007 (4) 1.30 1.05

Seventh Exposition of the Council of Europe dedicated to Romanesque art, Barcelona-Santiago de Compostela, July 10-Oct. 10.

Luis de Argote y Gongora — A263

1961, Aug. 10 Photo. *Perf. 13*

1008 A263 25c violet black .25 .25
1009 A263 1p henna brown .25 .25

400th anniversary of the birth of Luis de Argote y Gongora, poet.

Europa Issue

Common Design Type

1961, Sept. 18 *Perf. 12½x13*

Size: 37½x21½mm

1010 CD4 1p brt vermilion .25 .25
1011 CD4 5p brown .35 .25

Cathedral at Burgos — A264

1961, Oct. 1 *Perf. 13*

1012 A264 1p gold & olive green .25 .25

25th anniversary of the nomination of Gen. Francisco Franco as Head of State.

Builders of the New World

Sebastian de Belalcazar — A265

Portraits: 70c, 2.50p, Blas de Lezo. 80c, 3p, Rodrigo de Bastidas. 1p, 5p, Nuflo de Chaves.

1961, Oct. 12 Photo. *Perf. 13x12½*

1013 A265 25c indigo, *grn* .25 .25
1014 A265 70c grn, *cream* .25 .25
1015 A265 80c sl grn, *pnksh* .25 .25
1016 A265 1p dk blue, *sal* .40 .25
1017 A265 2p dk car, *bluish* 2.00 .25
1018 A265 2.50p lil, *pale lil* .75 .45
1019 A265 3p blue, *grysh* 1.75 .75
1020 A265 5p brown, *yel* 1.75 .90
Nos. 1013-1020 (8) 7.40 3.35

Issued to honor the discoverers and conquerors of Colombia and Bolivia.

See Nos. 1131-1138, 1187-1194, 1271-1278, 1316-1323, 1377-1384, 1489-1496, 1548, 1550, 1587-1588, 1632-1633.

Views of Escorial Monastery — A266

Designs: 70c, Patio of the Kings. 80c, Patio. 1p, Garden of the Monks and Escorial, horiz. 2.50p, Staircase. 5p, General view of Escorial, horiz. 6p, Main altar.

Perf. 13x12½, 12½x13

1961, Oct. 31 Engr. Unwmk.

1021 A266 70c bl grn & ol grn .25 .25
1022 A266 80c Prus grn & ind .25 .25
1023 A266 1p ocher & dk red .55 .25
1024 A266 2.50p cl & dull vio .55 .25
1025 A266 5p bister & dk brn 1.60 .70
1026 A266 6p sl bl & dull pur 2.25 1.50
Nos. 1021-1026 (6) 5.45 3.20

Alfonso XII Monument, Retiro Park — A267

Designs: 1p, King Philip II. 2p, Town hall, horiz. 2.50p, Cibeles fountain, horiz. 3p, Alcala gate, horiz. 5p, Cervantes memorial, Plaza de Espagna.

Photogravure (25c, 2p, 5p)
Engraved (1p, 2.50p, 3p)

1961, Nov. 13 Unwmk. *Perf. 13*

1027 A267 25c gray & dull pur .25 .25
1028 A267 1p bis brn & gray .30 .25
1029 A267 2p claret & gray .30 .25
1030 A267 2.50p black & lilac .25 .25
1031 A267 3p slate & ind .60 .35
1032 A267 5p Prus grn & beige 1.10 .55
Nos. 1027-1032 (6) 2.80 1.90

400th anniv. of Madrid as capital of Spain.

Church of St. Mary, Naranco — A268

Designs: 1p, King Fruela I, founder of Oviedo. 2p, Cross of the Angels. 2.50p, King Alfonso II. 3p, King Alfonso III. 5p, Apostles from Oviedo Cathedral (sculpture).

1961, Nov. 27

1033 A268 25c pur & gray grn .25 .25
1034 A268 1p bis brn & brn .30 .25
1035 A268 2p dk brn & pale pur .75 .25
1036 A268 2.50p claret & ind .30 .25
1037 A268 3p slate & indigo .65 .35
1038 A268 5p ol & ol grn .75 .55
Nos. 1033-1038 (6) 3.00 1.90

1200th anniversary of the founding of Oviedo, capital of Asturia.

Nativity Sculptured by José Gines — A269

1961, Dec. 1 Photo. *Perf. 13x12½*

1039 A269 1p dull purple .30 .25

"La Cierva" Autogiro — A270

2p, Hydroplane "Plus Ultra.," horiz. 3p, "Jesus del Gran Poder," plane of Madrid-Manila flight, horiz. 5p, Bustard hunt by plane. 10p, Madonna of Loretto, patron saint of Spanish airmen.

1961, Dec. 11 Unwmk. *Perf. 13*

1040 A270 1p indigo & blue .25 .25
1041 A270 2p grn, dl pur & blk .25 .25
1042 A270 3p blk & ol grn 1.25 .35
1043 A270 5p dl pur, gray bl & blk 2.50 .90
1044 A270 10p blk, lt bl & ol gray 1.25 .60
Nos. 1040-1044 (5) 5.50 2.35

50th anniversary of Spanish aviation.

Provincial Arms Issue

Alava — A271

1962 Photo. *Perf. 13*

1045 A271 5p Alava .25 .25
1046 A271 5p Albacete .25 .25
1047 A271 5p Alicante .25 .25
1048 A271 5p Almeria .25 .25
1049 A271 5p Avila .25 .25
1050 A271 5p Badajoz .25 .25
1051 A271 5p Baleares .25 .25
1052 A271 5p Barcelona .25 .25
1053 A271 5p Burgos .65 .40
1054 A271 5p Caceres .35 .25
1055 A271 5p Cadiz .45 .35
1056 A271 5p Castellon de la Plana 3.50 1.50
Nos. 1045-1056 (12) 6.95 4.50

1963

1057 A271 5p Ciudad Real .45 .35
1058 A271 5p Cordoba 3.50 1.25
1059 A271 5p Coruña .55 .35
1060 A271 5p Cuenca .55 .35
1061 A271 5p Fernando Po .80 .75
1062 A271 5p Gerona .25 .25
1063 A271 5p Gran Canaria .25 .25
1064 A271 5p Granada .25 .25
1065 A271 5p Guadalajara .55 .35
1066 A271 5p Guipuzcoa .25 .25
1067 A271 5p Huelva .25 .25
1068 A271 5p Huesca .25 .25
Nos. 1057-1068 (12) 7.90 4.90

1964

1069 A271 5p Ifni .25 .25
1070 A271 5p Jaen .25 .25
1071 A271 5p Leon .25 .25
1072 A271 5p Lerida .25 .25
1073 A271 5p Logrono .25 .25
1074 A271 5p Lugo .25 .25
1075 A271 5p Madrid .25 .25
1076 A271 5p Malaga .25 .25
1077 A271 5p Murcia .25 .25
1078 A271 5p Navarra .25 .25
1079 A271 5p Orense .25 .25
1080 A271 5p Oviedo .25 .25
Nos. 1069-1080 (12) 3.00 3.00

1965

1081 A271 5p Palencia .25 .25
1082 A271 5p Pontevedra .25 .25
1083 A271 5p Rio Muni .25 .25

1084 A271 5p Sahara .25 .25
1085 A271 5p Salamanca .25 .25
1086 A271 5p Santander .25 .25
1087 A271 5p Segovia .25 .25
1088 A271 5p Seville .25 .25
1089 A271 5p Soria .25 .25
1090 A271 5p Tarragona .25 .25
1091 A271 5p Tenerife .25 .25
1092 A271 5p Teruel .25 .25
Nos. 1081-1092 (12) 3.00 3.00

Arms of Spain — A271a

1966

1093 A271 5p Toledo .25 .25
1094 A271 5p Valencia .25 .25
1094A A271 5p Valladolid .25 .25
1094B A271 5p Vizcaya .25 .25
1094C A271 5p Zamora .25 .25
1094D A271 5p Zaragoza .25 .25
1094E A271 5p Ceuta .25 .25
1094F A271 5p Melilla .25 .25
1094G A271a 10p Spain .25 .25
Nos. 1093-1094G (9) 2.25 2.25
Nos. 1045-1094G (57) 23.10 17.65

Zurbaran Self-portrait A272

Zurbaran Paintings: 25c, Martyr, horiz. 40c, Burial of St. Catherine. 70c, St. Casilda. 80c, Jesus crowning St. Joseph. 1.50p, St. Jerome. 2.50p, Virgin of Grace. 3p, The Apotheosis of St. Thomas Aquinas. 5p, The Virgin as a child. 10p, The Immaculate Virgin.

Unwmk.

1962, Mar. 24 Photo. *Perf. 13*

Gold Frame

1095 A272 25c olive gray .40 .25
1096 A272 40c purple .40 .25
1097 A272 70c green .50 .25
1098 A272 80c Prus green .40 .25
1099 A272 1p chocolate .40 .25
1100 A272 1.50p brt blue grn .50 .25
1101 A272 2.50p dk car rose 2.00 .25
1102 A272 3p bright blue 3.00 .40
1103 A272 5p deep brown 8.00 1.50
1104 A272 10p olive green 3.00 .75
Nos. 1095-1104 (10) 18.60 4.40

Issued to honor Francisco de Zurbaran (1598-1664) and for Stamp Day, March 24.

For other art types see A236-A237, A240a, A246a, A257, A285a, A300, A310, A324, A340-A341, A360, A371 and footnote following No. 1606.

San Jose Convent, Avila A272a

St. Theresa (by Velázquez?) A273

Design: 1p, St. Theresa by Bernini.

1962, Apr. 10 *Perf. 13*

1105 A272a 25c bluish blk .25 .25
1106 A272a 1p brown .25 .25

Perf. 13x12½

1107 A273 3p bright blue 1.00 .30
Nos. 1105-1107 (3) 1.50 .80

4th centenary of St. Theresa's reform of the Carmelite order.

Mercury — A274

1962, May 7

1108 A274 25c vio, rose & mag .25 .25
1109 A274 1p brn, org & lt brn .25 .25
1110 A274 10p dp grn, ol grn & brt grn 1.75 .80
Nos. 1108-1110 (3) 2.25 1.30

International Stamp Day, May 7.

Painting Type of 1958

Rubens Paintings: 25c, Ferdinand of Austria. 1p, Self-portrait. 3p, Philip II. 10p, Duke of Lerma on horseback.

1962, May 28 *Perf. 13*

Gold Frame

Size: 25x30mm

1111 A237 25c violet black .65 .30
1112 A237 1p chocolate 5.75 .30
1113 A237 3p blue 5.25 2.00

Perf. 13x12½

Size: 26x38mm

1114 A237 10p slate green 4.00 2.75
Nos. 1111-1114 (4) 15.65 5.35

St. Benedict — A275

Berruguete Sculptures: 80c, Apostle. 1p, St. Peter. 2p, St. Christopher carrying Christ Child. 3p, Ecce Homo (Christ). 10p, St. Sebastian.

1962, July 9 *Perf. 13x12½*

1115 A275 25c lt blue & plum .25 .25
1116 A275 80c sal & ol gray .35 .25
1117 A275 1p gray & red .45 .25
1118 A275 2p gray & magenta 3.00 .25
1119 A275 3p brn pink & dk bl 1.25 .85
1120 A275 10p rose & brown 1.25 .50
Nos. 1115-1120 (6) 6.55 2.35

Alonso Berruguete (1486-1561), architect, sculptor and painter.

El Cid, Statue by Cristobal — A276

2p, Equestrian statue by Anna Huntington. 3p, El Cid's treasure chest, horiz. 10p, Oath-taking ceremony at Santa Gadea, horiz.

Perf. 13x12½, 12½x13

1962, July 30 Engr.

1121 A276 1p lt green & gray .25 .25
1122 A276 2p brown & choc 1.25 .25
1123 A276 3p blue & sl grn 3.50 1.10
1124 A276 10p lt grn & sl grn 2.25 .60
Nos. 1121-1124 (4) 7.25 2.20

El Cid Campeador (Rodrigo Diaz de Vivar, 1040-99), Spain's national hero.

Europa Issue

Bee and Honeycomb — A277

1962, Sept. 13 Photo. *Perf. 12½x13*

1125 A277 1p deep rose *.25* .25
1126 A277 5p dull green *1.00* *.30*

Discus Thrower — A278

80c, Runner. 1p, Hurdler. 3p, Sprinter at start.

1962, Oct. 7 *Perf. 13x12½*

1127 A278 25c pale pink & vio blk .25 .25
1128 A278 80c pale yel & dk grn .25 .25
1129 A278 1p pale rose & brn .25 .25
1130 A278 3p pale bl & dk bl .25 .30
Nos. 1127-1130 (4) 1.00 1.05

Second Spanish-American Games, Madrid, Oct. 7-12.

Builders of the New World

Portrait Type of 1961

Portraits: 25c, 2p, Alonso de Mendoza. 70c, 2.50p, Jiménez de Quesada. 80c, 3p, Juan de Garay. 1p, 5p, Pedro de la Gasca.

1962, Oct. 12 Unwmk.

1131 A265 25c rose lil, *gray* .25 .25
1132 A265 70c grn, *pale pink* 1.00 .25
1133 A265 80c dk grn, *pale yel* .70 .25
1134 A265 1p red brn, *gray* 1.40 .25
1135 A265 2p car, *lt bl* 3.25 .25
1136 A265 2.50p dk vio,*pnksh* .70 .25
1137 A265 3p dp bl, *pale pink* 7.00 1.25
1138 A265 5p brn, *pale yel* 3.50 1.50
Nos. 1131-1138 (8) 17.80 4.25

UPAE Emblem — A279

1962, Oct. 20 Engr. *Perf. 13*

1139 A279 1p sepia & green .25 .25

50th anniv. of the founding of the Postal Union of the Americas and Spain, UPAE.

The Annunciation, by Murillo — A280

Mysteries of the Rosary: 70c, The Visitation, Correa. 80c, Nativity, Murillo. 1p, The Presentation, Pedro de Campaña. 1.50p, The Finding in the Temple, (unknown painter). 2p, The Agony in the Garden, Gianquinto. 2.50p, The Scourging at the Pillar, Alonso Cano. 3p, The Crowning with Thorns, Tiepolo. 5p, Carrying of the Cross, El Greco. 8p, The Crucifixion, Murillo. 10p, The Resurrection, Murillo.

1962, Oct. 26

1140 A280 25c lilac & brown .25 .25
1141 A280 70c grn & dk bl grn .25 .25
1142 A280 80c ol & dk bl grn .25 .25
1143 A280 1p green & gray 4.00 .70
1144 A280 1.50p green & dk bl .25 .25
1145 A280 2p brown & violet 1.10 .50
1146 A280 2.50p dk brn & rose claret .40 .25
1147 A280 3p lilac & gray .40 .25
1148 A280 5p brn & dk car .60 .35
1149 A280 8p vio brn & blk .60 .25
1150 A280 10p grn & yel grn .95 .25
Nos. 1140-1150,C171-C174 (15) 11.65 4.80

Holy Family by Pedro de Mena — A281

1962, Dec. 6 Photo. *Perf. 13x12½*

1151 A281 1p olive gray .35 .25

Malaria Eradication Emblem A282

1962, Dec. 21 *Perf. 12½x13*

1152 A282 1p blk, yel grn & yel .25 .25

WHO drive to eradicate malaria.

Pope John XXIII and St. Peter's, Rome A283

1962, Dec. 29 Engr.

1153 A283 1p dp plum & blk .25 .25

Vatican II, the 21st Ecumenical Council of the Roman Catholic Church. See No. 1199.

St. Paul, by El Greco — A284

1963, Jan. 25 *Perf. 13*

1154 A284 1p brn, blk & olive .30 .25

St. Paul's visit to Spain, 1,900th anniv.

Courtyard, Poblet Monastery — A285

Designs: 1p, Royal sepulcher. 3p, View of monastery, horiz. 5p, Gothic arch.

Perf. 12½x13, 13x12½

1963, Feb. 25 Unwmk.

1155 A285 25c choc & slate grn .25 .25
1156 A285 1p org ver & rose car .35 .25
1157 A285 3p vio bl & dk bl 1.10 .25
1158 A285 5p brown & ocher 2.40 .90
Nos. 1155-1158 (4) 4.10 1.65

Issued in honor of the Cistercian monastery of Santa Maria de Poblet.

José de Ribera, Self-portrait A285a

Ribera Paintings: 25c, Archimedes. 40c, Jacob's Flock. 70c, Triumph of Bacchus. 80c, St. Christopher. 1.50p, St. Andrew. 2.50p, St. John the Baptist. 3p, St. Onofre. 5p, St. Peter. 10p, The Immaculate Virgin.

Unwmk.
1963, Mar. 24 Photo. *Perf. 13*
Gold Frame

1159 A285a 25c violet .30 .25
1160 A285a 40c red lilac .35 .25
1161 A285a 70c green .80 .25
1162 A285a 80c dark green .80 .25
1163 A285a 1p brown .80 .25
1164 A285a 1.50p blue green .80 .25
1165 A285a 2.50p car rose 2.25 .25
1166 A285a 3p dark blue 2.40 .50
1167 A285a 5p olive 8.50 2.00
1168 A285a 10p dull red brn 3.25 1.25
Nos. 1159-1168 (10) 20.25 5.50

Issued to honor José de Ribera (1588-1652) and for Stamp Day, Mar. 24.

For other art types see A236-A237, A240a, A246a, A257, A272, A300, A310, A324, A340-A341, A360, A371 and footnote following No. 1606.

Coach — A286

1963, May 3 *Perf. 13x12½*
1169 A286 1p multicolored .25 .25

First Intl. Postal Conference, Paris, 1863.

Globe A287

1963, May 8 *Perf. 12½x13*
1170 A287 25c multicolored .25 .25
1171 A287 1p multicolored .25 .25
1172 A287 10p multicolored 1.10 .65
Nos. 1170-1172 (3) 1.60 1.15

Issued for International Stamp Day, 1963.

"Give us this Day our Daily Bread..." A288

1963, June 1 Unwmk.
1173 A288 1p multicolored .25 .25

FAO "Freedom from Hunger" campaign.

"Pillars of Hercules" and Globes — A289

Designs: 80c, Fleet of Columbus. 1p, Columbus and compass rose.

1963, June 4 *Perf. 13*
1174 A289 25c multicolored .25 .25
1175 A289 80c brn, lt grn & gold .25 .25
1176 A289 1p sl grn, sepia & gold .25 .25
Nos. 1174-1176 (3) .75 .75

Cong. of Institutions of Spanish Culture, June 5-15.

Seal of Council of San Sebastian A290

80c, Burning of city, 1813. 1p, View, 1836.

1963, June 27 Photo.
1177 A290 25c vio, grn & blk .25 .25
1178 A290 80c dk brn, gray & red .25 .25
1179 A290 1p dk grn, grn & ol .30 .25
Nos. 1177-1179 (3) .80 .75

Rebuilding of San Sebastian, 150th anniv.

Europa Issue

Our Lady of Europe — A291

1963, Sept. 16 Engr. *Perf. 13x12½*
1180 A291 1p bis brn & choc .25 .25
1181 A291 5p bluish grn & blk *.55* *.40*

Arms of Order of Mercy — A292

King James I — A293

Designs: 1p, Our Lady of Mercy. 1.50p, St. Pedro Nolasco. 3p, St. Raimundo de Penafort.

1963, Sept. 24 Photo. *Perf. 13*
1182 A292 25c blk, car rose & gold .25 .25
Engr.
1183 A293 80c sepia & green .25 .25
1184 A293 1p gray vio & brn vio .25 .25
1185 A293 1.50p dull bl & blk .25 .25
1186 A293 3p gray & black .25 .25
Nos. 1182-1186 (5) 1.25 1.25

Coronation of Our Lady of Mercy, 75th anniv.

Builders of the New World
Portrait Type of 1961

25c, 2p, Father Junipero Serra. 70c, 2.50p, Vasco Nuñez de Balboa. 80c, 3p, José de Galvez. 1p, 5p, Diego Garcia de Paredes.

1963, Oct. 12 *Perf. 13x12½*
1187 A265 25c vio bl, *bl* .25 .25
1188 A265 70c grn, *pale rose* .25 .25
1189 A265 80c dk grn, *yel* .50 .25
1190 A265 1p dk bl, *pale rose* .60 .25
1191 A265 2p magenta, *lt bl* 1.50 .25
1192 A265 2.50p vio blk, *dl rose* 1.00 .25
1193 A265 3p brt bl, *pink* 2.00 1.00
1194 A265 5p brown, *yel* 2.75 2.25
Nos. 1187-1194 (8) 8.85 4.75

The Good Samaritan — A294

1963, Oct. 28 Unwmk.
1195 A294 1p gold, pur & brt car .25 .25

Centenary of International Red Cross.

Holy Family by Alonso Berruguete (1486-1561) — A295

1963, Dec. 2 Photo. *Perf. 13x12½*
1196 A295 1p dark green .25 .25

Christmas 1963. See No. 1279.

Father Raymond Lully — A296

Portrait: 1.50p, Cardinal Luis Antonio de Belluga (1662-1743).

1963, Dec. 5 Engr.
1197 A296 1p dk violet & blk .25 .25
1198 A296 1.50p sepia & dull vio .25 .25
Nos. 1197-1198,C175-C176 (4) 3.50 1.45

Papal Type of 1962

Design: 1p, Pope Paul VI and St. Peter's, Rome.

1963, Dec. 30 *Perf. 12½x13*
1199 A283 1p dk green & blk .25 .25

Second session of Vatican II, the 21st Ecumenical Council of the Roman Catholic Church.

Alcazar, Segovia A297

Dragon Caves, Majorca — A298

Tourism: 40c, Potes, Santander. 50c, Leon Cathedral. No. 1202, Crypt of San Isidro at Leon. No. 1203, Costa Brava. 80c, Christ of the Lanterns, Cordova. No. 1206, Court of Lions, Alhambra, Granada. No. 1208, Interior of La Mezquita, Cordova. 1.50p, View of Gerona.

1964 Engr. *Perf. 13*
1200 A297 40c sepia & blue .25 .25
1201 A298 50c gray & sepia .25 .25
1202 A297 70c ind & dk bl grn .25 .25
1203 A298 70c violet & brown .25 .25
1204 A298 80c dp ultra & blk .25 .25
1205 A297 1p vio bl & pur .25 .25

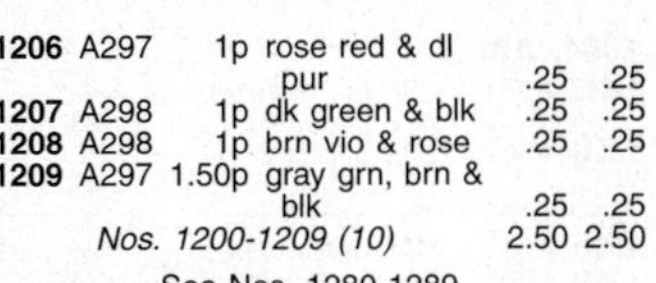
1206 A297 1p rose red & dl pur .25 .25
1207 A298 1p dk green & blk .25 .25
1208 A298 1p brn vio & rose .25 .25
1209 A297 1.50p gray grn, brn & blk .25 .25
Nos. 1200-1209 (10) 2.50 2.50

See Nos. 1280-1289.

Santa Maria de Huerta Monastery — A299

Designs: 1p, Great Hall. 5p, View of monastery with apse, horiz.

1964, Feb. 24 *Perf. 13x12½, 12½x13*
1212 A299 1p gray grn & grn .25 .25
1213 A299 2p grnsh blue & sepia .25 .25
1214 A299 5p dark blue 1.10 .60
Nos. 1212-1214 (3) 1.60 1.10

Santa Maria Monastery, Huerta, 8th cent.

Joaquin Sorolla, Self-portrait A300

Sorolla Paintings: 25c, The Jug (woman and child). 40c, Oxen and Driver, horiz. 70c, Man and Woman from La Mancha. 80c, Fisher Woman of Valencia. 1p, Self-portrait. 1.50p, Round up, horiz. 2.50p, And People Still Say Fish Are Dear (fishermen tending to wounded man), horiz. 3p, Children at the Beach, horiz. 5p, Unloading the Boat. 10p, Man and Woman on Horseback, Valencia.

Gold Frame
1964, Mar. 24 Photo. *Perf. 13*
1215 A300 25c violet .25 .25
1216 A300 40c purple .25 .25
1217 A300 70c dp yellow grn .25 .25
1218 A300 80c bluish grn .25 .25
1219 A300 1p brown .25 .25
1220 A300 1.50p Prus blue .25 .25
1221 A300 2.50p dk car rose .25 .25
1222 A300 3p violet blue .35 .35
1223 A300 5p chocolate 1.25 .75
1224 A300 10p deep green .60 .30
Nos. 1215-1224 (10) 3.95 3.15

Issued to honor Joaquin Sorolla y Bastida (1863-1923) and for Stamp Day, March 24.

For other art types see A236-A237, A240a, A246a, A257, A272, A285a, A310, A324, A340-A341, A360, A371 and footnote following No. 1606.

"Peace" A301

"Sport" — A302

Designs: 40c, Radio and television. 50c, New apartments. 70c, Agriculture. 80c, Reforestation. 1p, Economic development. 1.50p, Modern architecture. 2p, Transportation. 2.50p, Hydroelectric development. 3p, Electrification. 5p, Scientific achievements. 6p, Buildings, tourism. 10p, Generalissimo Franco.

1964, Apr. 1

No.	Type	Value	Description	Unused	Used
1225	A301	25c	blk, emer & gold	.25	.25
1226	A302	30c	blk, bl & sal pink	.25	.25
1227	A301	40c	gold & blk	.25	.25
1228	A302	50c	multicolored	.25	.25
1229	A301	70c	multicolored	.25	.25
1230	A301	80c	multicolored	.25	.25
1231	A302	1p	multicolored	.25	.25
1232	A302	1.50p	multicolored	.25	.25
1233	A301	2p	multicolored	.25	.25
1234	A302	2.50p	multicolored	.25	.25
1235	A301	3p	gold, blk & red	.70	.70
1236	A302	5p	gold, grn & red	.30	.30
1237	A301	6p	multicolored	.35	.35
1238	A302	10p	multicolored	.40	.40
			Nos. 1225-1238 (14)	4.25	4.25

Issued to commemorate 25 years of peace.

Bullfight and Unisphere — A303

Designs: 1p, Spanish pavilion, horiz. 2.50p, La Mota castle, Medina de Campo. 5p, Spanish dancer. 50p, Jai alai.

Perf. 12½x13, 13x12½

1964, Apr. 23 **Engr.**

No.	Type	Value	Description	Unused	Used
1239	A303	1p	bl grn & yel grn	.25	.25
1240	A303	1.50p	carmine & brn	.25	.25
1241	A303	2.50p	dk bl & sl grn	.25	.25
1242	A303	5p	car & dk car rose	.30	.30
1243	A303	50p	vio bl & dk bl	.65	.35
			Nos. 1239-1243 (5)	1.70	1.40

New York World's Fair, 1964-65.

Stamp of 1850 and Modern Stamps — A304

1964, May 6 ***Perf. 13x12½***

No.	Type	Value	Description	Unused	Used
1244	A304	25c	dk car rose & dl pur	.25	.25
1245	A304	1p	yel grn & dk bl	.25	.25
1246	A304	10p	orange & rose red	.35	.30
			Nos. 1244-1246 (3)	.85	.80

Issued for International Stamp Day, 1964.

Virgin of Hope — A305

1964, May 31 Photo. ***Perf. 13x12½***

No.	Type	Value	Description	Unused	Used
1247	A305	1p	dark green	.25	.25

Canonical coronation of the Virgin of Hope (La Macarena) in St. Gil's Church, Seville, May 31.

Santa Maria — A306

Designs (ships): 15c, 13th cent. ship of King Alfonso X, from medieval manuscript, vert. 25c, Carrack, from 15th cent. engraving, vert. 50c, Galley. 70c, Galleon. 80c, Xebec. 1p, Warship, Santisima Trinidad, vert. 1.50p, 18th cent. corvette, Atrevida, vert. 2p, Steamer, Isabel II. 2.50p, Frigate, Numancia, Spain's 1st armored ship. 3p, Destroyer. 5p, Submarine of Isaac Peral. 6p, Cruiser, Baleares. 10p, Training ship, Juan Sebastian Elcano.

1964, July 16 ***Perf. 13***

No.	Type	Value	Description	Unused	Used
1248	A306	15c	dp rose & vio blk	.25	.25
1249	A306	25c	org yel & gray grn	.25	.25
1250	A306	40c	ultra & dk bl	.25	.25
1251	A306	50c	slate grn & dk bl	.25	.25
1252	A306	70c	vio & dk bl	.25	.25
1253	A306	80c	dl bl grn & ultra	.25	.25
1254	A306	1p	org & vio brn	.25	.25
1255	A306	1.50p	car & sepia	.25	.25
1256	A306	2p	blk & slate grn	.55	.25
1257	A306	2.50p	rose car & dl vio	.25	.25
1258	A306	3p	sepia & indigo	.25	.25
1259	A306	5p	dk bl, lt grn & vio	.70	.70
1260	A306	6p	lt green & vio	.60	.60
1261	A306	10p	org yel & rose red	.35	.25
			Nos. 1248-1261 (14)	4.70	4.30

Issued to honor the Spanish Navy.

Europa Issue
Common Design Type

1964, Sept. 14 Photo. ***Perf. 12½x13***
Size: 21½x39mm

No.	Type	Value	Description	Unused	Used
1262	CD7	1p	bis, red & grn	.30	.25
1263	CD7	5p	brt bl, mag & grn	.85	.55

Madonna of Alcazar — A307

1964, Oct. 9 Photo. ***Perf. 13***

No.	Type	Value	Description	Unused	Used
1264	A307	25c	bister & brn	.25	.25
1265	A307	1p	gray & indigo	.25	.25

Reconquest of Jerez de la Frontera, 700th anniv.

Gold Olympic Rings

Shot Put — A308

1964, Oct. 10

No.	Type	Value	Description	Unused	Used
1266	A308	25c	shown	.25	.25
1267	A308	80c	Broad jump	.25	.25
1268	A308	1p	Slalom	.25	.25
1269	A308	3p	Judo	.25	.25
1270	A308	5p	Discus	.25	.25
			Nos. 1266-1270 (5)	1.25	1.25

1964 Olympic Games.

Builders of the New World
Portrait Type of 1961

25c, 2p, Diego de Almagro. 70c, 2.50p, Francisco de Toledo. 80c, 3p, Archbishop Toribio de Mogrovejo. 1p, 5p, Francisco Pizarro.

1964, Oct. 12 ***Perf. 13x12½***

No.	Type	Value	Description	Unused	Used
1271	A265	25c	pale grn & vio	.25	.25
1272	A265	70c	pink & ol gray	.25	.25
1273	A265	80c	buff & Prus grn	.30	.25
1274	A265	1p	buff & gray vio	.30	.25
1275	A265	2p	pale bl & ol gray	.30	.25
1276	A265	2.50p	pale grn & cl	.25	.25
1277	A265	3p	gray & dk bl	3.00	1.00
1278	A265	5p	yellow & brown	1.50	1.10
			Nos. 1271-1278 (8)	6.15	3.60

Christmas Type of 1963

Nativity by Francisco de Zurbaran (1598-1664).

1964, Dec. 4 **Photo.**

No.	Type	Value	Description	Unused	Used
1279	A295	1p	olive black	.25	.25

Tourism Types of 1964

Designs: 25c, Columbus monument, Barcelona. 30s, Facade of Santa Maria, Burgos. 50c, Santa Maria la Blanca (medieval synagogue), Toledo. 70c, Bridge, Zamora. 80c, La Giralda (tower) and Cathedral of Seville. 1p, Boat and nets in Cudillero harbor. No. 1286, Cathedral of Burgos, interior. No. 1287, View of Mogrovejo, Santander. 3p, Bridge, Cambados, Pontevedra. 6p, Silk merchants' hall (Lonja), Valencia, interior.

1965 **Engr.** ***Perf. 13***

No.	Type	Value	Description	Unused	Used
1280	A298	25c	dk blue & blk	.25	.25
1281	A298	30c	dull grn & sep	.25	.25
1282	A298	50c	cl & rose car	.25	.25
1283	A297	70c	vio bl & ind	.25	.25
1284	A298	80c	rose cl & dk pur	.25	.25
1285	A298	1p	dp cl, car & blk	.25	.25
1286	A298	2.50p	brn vio & bis	.25	.25
1287	A297	2.50p	dull bl & gray	.25	.25
1288	A298	3p	rose car & dk brn	.25	.25
1289	A298	6p	slate & black	.25	.25
			Nos. 1280-1289 (10)	2.50	2.50

Alfonso X, the Wise (1232-84) — A309

25c, Juan Donoso-Cortes (1809-53). 2.50p, Gaspar M. Jovellanos (1744-1810). 5p, St. Dominic de Guzman (1170-1221).

1965, Feb. 25 Engr. ***Perf. 13x12½***

No.	Type	Value	Description	Unused	Used
1292	A309	25c	slate bl & blk	.25	.25
1293	A309	70c	blue & indigo	.25	.25
1294	A309	2.50p	slate grn & sep	.25	.25
1295	A309	5p	dull grn & sl grn	.25	.25
			Nos. 1292-1295 (4)	1.00	1.00

Julio Romero de Torres, Self-portrait A310

De Torres Paintings: 25c, Girl with Jar. 40c, "The Song" (girl with guitar). 70c, Madonna of the Lanterns. 80c, Girl with guitar. 1.50p, "The Poem of Cordova" (pensive woman). 2.50p, Martha and Mary. 3p, "The Poem of Cordova" (two women holding statue of angel). 5p, Girl with the Charcoal. 10p, Back of woman's head.

1965, Mar. 24 Photo. ***Perf. 13***
Gold Frame

No.	Type	Value	Description	Unused	Used
1296	A310	25c	dull purple	.25	.25
1297	A310	40c	purple	.25	.25
1298	A310	70c	olive green	.25	.25
1299	A310	80c	slate green	.25	.25
1300	A310	1p	dk red brn	.25	.25
1301	A310	1.50p	blue green	.25	.25
1302	A310	2.50p	lilac rose	.25	.25
1303	A310	3p	dark blue	.35	.25
1304	A310	5p	brown	.35	.25
1305	A310	10p	slate green	.50	.30
			Nos. 1296-1305 (10)	2.95	2.55

Issued to honor Julio Romero de Torres (1880-1930) and for Stamp Day, March 24.

For other art types see A236-A237, A240a, A246a, A257, A272, A285a, A300, A324, A340-A341, A360, A371 and footnote following No. 1606.

Bull and Symbolic Stamps — A311

1965, May 6 ***Perf. 13x12½***

No.	Type	Value	Description	Unused	Used
1306	A311	25c	multicolored	.25	.25
1307	A311	1p	orange & multi	.25	.25
1308	A311	10p	multicolored	.50	.30
			Nos. 1306-1308 (3)	1.00	.80

Issued for International Stamp Day, 1965.

ITU Emblem, Old and New Communication Equipment — A312

1965, May 17 ***Perf. 12½x13***

No.	Type	Value	Description	Unused	Used
1309	A312	1p	salmon, blk & red	.25	.25

International Telecommunication Union, cent.

Pilgrim — A313

Design: 2p, Pilgrim (profile).

1965, July 25 Photo. ***Perf. 13***

No.	Type	Value	Description	Unused	Used
1310	A313	1p	multicolored	.25	.25
1311	A313	2p	multicolored	.25	.25

Issued to commemorate the Holy Year of St. James of Compostela, patron saint of Spain.

Explorer, Royal Flag of Spain and Ships — A314

1965, Aug. 28 ***Perf. 13x12½***

No.	Type	Value	Description	Unused	Used
1312	A314	3p	red, blk & yel	.25	.25

400th anniv. of the settlement of Florida, and the 1st permanent European settlement in the continental US, St. Augustine, Fla. See US No. 1271.

Europa Issue

St. Benedict — A315

1965, Sept. 27 Engr. ***Perf. 13x12½***

No.	Type	Value	Description	Unused	Used
1313	A315	1p	yel grn & sl grn	.25	.25
1314	A315	5p	lilac & violet	.40	.25

Sports Palace, Madrid — A316

1965, Oct. 9 Photo. ***Perf. 13***

No.	Type	Value	Description	Unused	Used
1315	A316	1p	gray, gold & dk brn	.25	.25

Issued to commemorate the meeting of the International Olympic Committee in Madrid.

Builders of the New World
Portrait Type of 1961

25c, 2p, Don Fadrique de Toledo. 70c, 2.50p, Father José de Anchieta. 80c, 3p, Francisco de Orellana. 1p, 5p, St. Luis Beltran.

1965, Oct. 12 Photo. *Perf. 13x12½*

1316 A265 25c pale grn & dp pur .25 .25
1317 A265 70c pink & brown .25 .25
1318 A265 80c cream & Prus grn .25 .25
1319 A265 1p buff & dk vio .25 .25
1320 A265 2p lt bl & dk ol grn .25 .25
1321 A265 2.50p lt blue & pur .25 .25
1322 A265 3p gray & dk bl 1.00 .35
1323 A265 5p yellow & brn 1.00 .30
Nos. 1316-1323 (8) 3.50 2.15

Chamber of Charles V, Yuste Monastery — A317

Yuste Monastery: 1p, Courtyard, horiz. 5p, View of monastery, horiz.

Perf. 12½x13, 13x12½

1965, Nov. 15 Engr.

1324 A317 1p bl gray & blk .25 .25
1325 A317 2p red brn & brn blk .25 .25
1326 A317 5p grayish bl & grn .25 .25
Nos. 1324-1326 (3) .75 .75

Monastery of Yuste, Estremadura.

Stamp of 1865 (No. 78) — A318

Designs: 1p, Stamp of 1865 (No. 77). 5p, Stamp of 1865 (No. 80).

1965, Nov. 22 *Perf. 13x12½*

1327 A318 80c blk & yel grn .25 .25
1328 A318 1p plum, brn & rose .25 .25
1329 A318 5p sepia & org brn .25 .25
Nos. 1327-1329 (3) .75 .75

Cent. of the 1st Spanish perforated postage stamps.

Nativity A319

1965, Dec. 1 Photo. *Perf. 12½x13*

1330 A319 1p bright green .25 .25

Virgin of Peace, Antipolo — A320

Design: 3p, Father Andres de Urdaneta.

1965, Dec. 3 *Perf. 13x12½*

1331 A320 1p pale sal & ol brn .25 .25
1332 A320 3p gray & dp blue .25 .25

Christianization of the Philippines, 400th anniv.

Globe and Four Beasts of Apocalypse — A321

1965, Dec. 29 Photo. *Perf. 13x12½*

1333 A321 1p grnsh bl, yel & brn .25 .25

Vatican II, the 21st Ecumenical Council of the Roman Catholic Church, 10/11/62-12/8/65.

Adm. Alvaro de Bazan (1526-88) — A322

2p, Daza de Valdes, scientist, 17th cent.

1966, Feb. 26 Engr. *Perf. 13x12½*

1334 A322 25c dull blue & gray .25 .25
1335 A322 2p magenta & violet .25 .25

See Nos. C177-C178.

Exhibition Emblem; Type Block "P" — A323

1966, Mar. 4 Photo. *Perf. 13*

1336 A323 1p red, grn & vio bl .25 .25

Graphic Arts and Advertising Packaging Exhibition "Graphispack," Barcelona, 3/4-13.

José Maria Sert, Self-portrait A324

Sert Paintings: 25c, The Magic Ball. 40c, Evocation of Toledo, horiz. 70c, Christ on the Cross. 80c, Parachutists. 1.50p, "Audacity." 2.50p, "Justice." 3p, Jacob Wrestling with the Angel. 5p, "The Five Continents." 10p, Sts. Peter and Paul.

1966, Mar. 24 Gold Frame

1337 A324 25c dk purple .25 .25
1338 A324 40c dp magenta .25 .25
1339 A324 70c green .25 .25
1340 A324 80c dk ol grn .25 .25
1341 A324 1p claret brn .25 .25
1342 A324 1.50p dull blue .25 .25
1343 A324 2.50p dk red .25 .25
1344 A324 3p deep blue .25 .25
1345 A324 5p sepia .25 .25
1346 A324 10p grnsh blk .25 .25
Nos. 1337-1346 (10) 2.50 2.50

Issued to honor José Maria Sert (1876-1945) and for Stamp Day, Mar. 24.

For other art types see A236-A237, A240a, A246a, A257, A272, A285a, A300, A310, A340-A341, A360, A371 and footnote following No. 1606.

Santa Maria Church, Guernica — A325

Designs: 1p, Arms of Guernica and Luno. 3p, Tree of Guernica.

1966, Apr. 28 Photo. *Perf. 13*

1347 A325 80c bl, sepia & grn .25 .25
1348 A325 1p yel grn & multi .25 .25
1349 A325 3p bl, grn & vio brn .25 .25
Nos. 1347-1349 (3) .75 .75

Founding of Guernica and Luno, 6th cent.

Cover with Stamp of 1850 (#1) A326

Designs (covers): 1p, 5r (#3). 10p, 10r (#5).

1966, May 6 *Perf. 12½x13*

1350 A326 25c rose vio, blk & red .25 .25
1351 A326 1p red brn, org & blk .25 .25
1352 A326 10p ol grn, grn & org .25 .25
Nos. 1350-1352 (3) .75 .75

Issued for International Stamp Day, 1966.

Bohi Valley — A327

Torla, Huesca A328

Tourism: 40c, Portal of Sigena Monastery, Huesca. 50c, Santo Domingo Church, Soria. 80c, Torre del Oro, Seville. 1p, Palm and view, Pico de Teyde, Santa Cruz de Tenerife. 1.50p, Monastery of Guadalupe, Caceres. 2p, Alcala de Henares University. 3p, Seo Cathedral, Lerida. 10p, Courtyard of St. Gregorio, Valladolid.

1966 Engr. *Perf. 13*

1353 A327 10c gray grn & bl grn .25 .25
1354 A328 15c gray grn & brn .25 .25
1355 A327 40c bis brn & brn .25 .25
1356 A327 50c car rose & dp cl .25 .25
1357 A327 80c lilac & rose vio .25 .25
1358 A327 1p vio bl & bl grn .25 .25
1359 A328 1.50p dk bl & blk .25 .25
1360 A328 2p sl bl & sepia .25 .25
1361 A328 3p ultra & blk .25 .25
1362 A327 10p brt bl & grnsh bl .25 .25
Nos. 1353-1362 (10) 2.50 2.50

Tree and Globe A329

1966, June 6 Photo. *Perf. 12½x13*

1363 A329 1p brn & dk grn .25 .25

6th Intl. Forestry Cong., Madrid, June 6-18.

Navy Emblem — A330

1966, July 1 Photo. *Perf. 13*

1364 A330 1p gray & dk bl .25 .25

Naval Week, Barcelona, July 1-8.

Guadamur Castle — A331

Castles: 25c, Alcazar, Segovia. 40c, La Mota. 50c, Olite. 70c, Monteagudo. 80c, Butron, vert. 1p, Manzanares. 3p, Almansa, vert.

1966, Aug. 13 Engr. *Perf. 13*

1365 A331 10c grysh bl & sep .25 .25
1366 A331 25c violet & purple .25 .25
1367 A331 40c grnsh bl & bl grn .25 .25
1368 A331 50c grnsh bl & ultra .25 .25
1369 A331 70c vio bl & ind .25 .25
1370 A331 80c vio & sl grn .25 .25
1371 A331 1p ol bis & gray .25 .25
1372 A331 3p rose & red lil .25 .25
Nos. 1365-1372 (8) 2.00 2.00

Don Quixote, Dulcinea and Aldonza Lorenzo — A332

1966, Sept. 5 Photo. *Perf. 13*

1373 A332 1.50p sal, lt grn & blk .25 .25

4th World Congress of Psychiatry, Madrid.

Europa Issue

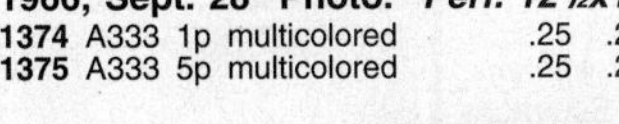

The Rape of Europa A333

1966, Sept. 28 Photo. *Perf. 12½x13*

1374 A333 1p multicolored .25 .25
1375 A333 5p multicolored .25 .25

Don Quixote and Sancho Panza on Clavileno — A334

1966, Oct. 9 *Perf. 13x12½*

1376 A334 1.50p sl bl, red brn & dk brn .25 .25

17th Cong. of the Intl. Astronautical Federation.

Builders of the New World
Types of 1961 and

Title Page of "Dotrina Christiana" — A335

30c, Antonio de Mendoza. 1p, José A. Manso de Velasco. 1.20p, Coins of Lima, 1699. 1.50p, Manuel de Castro y Padilla. 3p, Portal of Oruro Convent, Bolivia. 3.50p, Manuel de Amat. 6p, Inca courier, El Chasqui.

1966, Oct. 12
1377 A265 30c pale pink & brn .25 .25
1378 A335 50c pale bis & brn .25 .25
1379 A265 1p gray & vio .25 .25
1380 A335 1.20p gray & slate .25 .25
1381 A265 1.50p pale grn & dp grn .25 .25
1382 A335 3p pale gray & dp bl .25 .25
1383 A265 3.50p pale lil & pur .25 .25
1384 A265 6p buff & sepia .25 .25
Nos. 1377-1384 (8) 2.00 2.00

Ramon del Valle Inclan — A336

Portraits: 3p, Carlos Arniches. 6p, Jacinto Benavente y Martinez.

1966, Nov. 7 Photo. *Perf. 13*
1385 A336 1.50p blk & green .25 .25
1386 A336 3p blk & gray vio .25 .25
1387 A336 6p blk & slate .25 .25
Nos. 1385-1387 (3) .75 .75

Issued to honor Spanish writers.
See design A355.

Carthusian Monastery, Jerez A337

St. Mary Carthusian Monastery: 1p, Portal, vert. 5p, Entrance gate.

Perf. 13x12½, 12½x13
1966, Nov. 24 Engr.
1388 A337 1p grnsh bl & sl bl .25 .25
1389 A337 2p green & yel grn .25 .25
1390 A337 5p lilac & claret .25 .25
Nos. 1388-1390 (3) .75 .75

Nativity, Sculpture by Pedro Duque Cornejo A338

1966, Dec. 5 Photo. *Perf. 12½x13*
1391 A338 1.50p multicolored .25 .25

Regional Costumes Issue

Woman from Alava — A339

1967 Photo. *Perf. 13*
1392 A339 6p shown .25 .25
1393 A339 6p Albacete .25 .25
1394 A339 6p Alicante .25 .25
1395 A339 6p Almeria .25 .25
1396 A339 6p Avila .25 .25
1397 A339 6p Badajoz .25 .25
1398 A339 6p Baleares .25 .25
1399 A339 6p Barcelona .25 .25
1400 A339 6p Burgos .25 .25
1401 A339 6p Caceres .25 .25
1402 A339 6p Cadiz .25 .25
1403 A339 6p Castellon de la Plana .25 .25
Nos. 1392-1403 (12) 3.00 3.00

1968
1404 A339 6p Ciudad Real .25 .25
1405 A339 6p Cordoba .25 .25
1406 A339 6p Coruna .25 .25
1407 A339 6p Cuenca .25 .25
1408 A339 6p Fernando Po .25 .25
1409 A339 6p Gerona .25 .25
1410 A339 6p Gran Canaria, Las Palmas .25 .25
1411 A339 6p Granada .25 .25
1412 A339 6p Guadalajara .25 .25
1413 A339 6p Guipuzcoa .25 .25
1414 A339 6p Huelva .25 .25
1415 A339 6p Huesca .25 .25
Nos. 1404-1415 (12) 3.00 3.00

1969
1416 A339 6p Ifni .25 .25
1417 A339 6p Jaen .25 .25
1418 A339 6p Leon .25 .25
1419 A339 6p Lerida .25 .25
1420 A339 6p Logroño .25 .25
1421 A339 6p Lugo .25 .25
1422 A339 6p Madrid .25 .25
1423 A339 6p Malaga .25 .25
1424 A339 6p Murcia .25 .25
1425 A339 6p Navarra .25 .25
1426 A339 6p Orense .25 .25
1427 A339 6p Oviedo .25 .25
Nos. 1416-1427 (12) 3.00 3.00

1970
1428 A339 6p Palencia .25 .25
1429 A339 6p Pontevedra .25 .25
1430 A339 6p Sahara .25 .25
1431 A339 6p Salamanca .25 .25
1432 A339 6p Santa Cruz de Tenerife .25 .25
1433 A339 6p Santander .25 .25
1434 A339 6p Segovia .25 .25
1435 A339 6p Seville .25 .25
1436 A339 6p Soria .25 .25
1437 A339 6p Tarragona .25 .25
1438 A339 6p Teruel .25 .25
1439 A339 6p Toledo .25 .25
Nos. 1428-1439 (12) 3.00 3.00

1971
1440 A339 6p Valencia .25 .25
1441 A339 8p Valladolid .25 .25
1442 A339 8p Vizcaya .25 .25
1443 A339 8p Zamora .25 .25
1444 A339 8p Zaragoza .25 .25
Nos. 1440-1444 (5) 1.25 1.25
Nos. 1392-1444 (53) 13.25 13.25

Archers A340

Ornament — A341

50c, Boar hunt. 1.20p, Bison. 1.50p, Hands. 2p, Warrior. 2.50p, Deer. 3.50p, Archers. 4p, Hunters & gazelle. 6p, Hunters & deer herd.

1967, Mar. 27 Photo. *Perf. 13*
Gold Frame
1449 A340 40c ocher & car rose .25 .25
1450 A340 50c gray & dk red .25 .25
1451 A341 1p ocher & org ver .25 .25
1452 A340 1.20p gray & rose brn .25 .25
1453 A340 1.50p gray & red .25 .25
1454 A341 2p lt brn & dk car rose .25 .25
1455 A341 2.50p sky bl & rose brn .25 .25
1456 A340 3.50p yellow & blk .25 .25
1457 A341 4p citron & red .25 .25
1458 A341 6p olive & red .25 .25
Nos. 1449-1458 (10) 2.50 2.50

Issued for Stamp Day, 1967. The designs are from paleolithic and mesolithic wall paintings found in Spanish caves.

For other art types see A236-A237, A240a, A246a, A257, A272, A285a, A300, A310, A324, A360, A371 and footnote following No. 1606.

Palma Cathedral and Conference Emblem — A342

1967, Mar. 28
1459 A342 1.50p brt blue grn .25 .25

Issued to publicize the Congress of the Interparliamentary Union, Palma de Mallorca.

W. K. Röntgen, X-ray Tube and Atom — A343

1967, Apr. 3 Photo. *Perf. 13*
1460 A343 1.50p green .25 .25

7th Cong. of Latin Radiologists and 1st Cong. of European Radiologists, Barcelona, Apr. 2-8.

Averroes (1120-1198), Physician and Philosopher — A344

Portraits: 3.50p, José de Acosta (1539-1600), Jesuit, historian, poet. 4p, Moses ben Maimonides (1135-1204), Jewish philosopher and physician. 25p, Andres Laguna, 16th century physician.

1967, Apr. 6 Engr. *Perf. 13x12½*
1461 A344 1.20p lil & dl vio .25 .25
1462 A344 3.50p mag & dl pur .25 .25
1463 A344 4p brn & sep .25 .25
1464 A344 25p dl bl & blk .25 .25
Nos. 1461-1464 (4) 1.00 1.00

Europa Issue
Common Design Type
1967, May 2 Photo. *Perf. 13*
Size: 25x31mm
1465 CD10 1.50p sl grn, red brn & dl red .25 .25
1466 CD10 6p vio, brt bl & brn .25 .25

Exhibition Building and Fountain, Valencia — A345

1967, May 3
1467 A345 1.50p gray grn .25 .25

International Fair at Valencia, 50th anniv.

Numeral Postmark No. 3 of 1850 — A346

Designs: 1.50p, No. 2, 12c stamp of 1850 with crowned M postmark of Madrid. 6p, No. 4, 6r stamp of 1850 with 1r postmark.

1967, May 6
1468 A346 40c brn org, dl bl & blk .25 .25
1469 A346 1.50p brn, grn & blk .25 .25
1470 A346 6p bl, red & blk .25 .25
Nos. 1468-1470 (3) .75 .75

Intl. Stamp Day, 1967. See #1527-1528.

Guardian Angel Over Indigent Sleeper — A347

1967, May 16 *Perf. 13*
1471 A347 1.50p bl, blk, brn & red .25 .25

Issued for National Caritas Day to honor Caritas, Catholic welfare organization.

Betanzos Church, Coruña — A348

International Tourist Year Emblem A349

Tourism: 1p, Tower of St. Miguel Church, Palencia. 1.50p, Human pyramid (Castellers). 2.50p, Columbus monument, Huelva. 5p, The Enchanted City, Cuenca. 6p,Church of Our Lady, Sanlucar, Cadiz.

1967, July 26 Engr. *Perf. 13*
1472 A348 10c ultra & blk .25 .25
1473 A348 1p dl bl & blk .25 .25
1474 A348 1.50p lt brn & blk .25 .25
1475 A348 2.50p grnsh bl & dk bl .25 .25
1476 A349 3.50p dl pur & dk bl .25 .25
1477 A348 5p yel grn & dk grn .25 .25
1478 A348 6p red lil & dl lil .25 .25
Nos. 1472-1478 (7) 1.75 1.75

Balsareny Castle — A350

Castles: 1p, Jarandilla. 1.50p, Almodovar. 2p, Ponferrada, vert. 2.50p, Peniscola. 5p, Coca. 6p, Loarre. 10p, Belmonte.

1967, Aug. 11 Engr.
1479 A350 50c gray & lt brn .25 .25
1480 A350 1p bl gray & dl pur .25 .25
1481 A350 1.50p bl gray & sage grn .25 .25
1482 A350 2p brick red & bis brn .25 .25
1483 A350 2.50p grnsh bl & sep .25 .25
1484 A350 5p rose vio & vio bl .25 .25
1485 A350 6p bis brn & gray brn .25 .25
1486 A350 10p aqua & slate .25 .25
Nos. 1479-1486 (8) 2.00 2.00

Globe, Snowflake and Thermometer A351

1967, Aug. 30 **Photo.**
1487 A351 1.50p bright blue .25 .25

12th Intl. Refrigeration Cong., Madrid, Sept. 4-8.

Galleon, Map of Americas, Spain and Philippines A352

1967, Oct. 10 **Photo.** ***Perf. 13***
1488 A352 1.50p red lilac .25 .25

4th Congress of Spanish, Portuguese, American & Philippine Municipalities, Barcelona, Oct. 6-12.

Builders of the New World

Types of 1961 and

Old Map of Nootka Coast — A353

Nootka Settlement — A353a

Old Map of Coast of Northern California — A353b

Designs: 40c, Francisco de la Bodega. 1p, Francisco Antonio Mourelle. 1.50p, Esteban José Martinez. 3.50p, Cayetano Valdes. 6p, Ships, San Elias, Alaska.

1967, Oct. 12
1489 A265 40c pale pink & grnsh gray .25 .25
1490 A353 50c dp vio brn .25 .25
1491 A265 1p pale gray bl & red lil .25 .25
1492 A353a 1.20p dk ol grn .25 .25
1493 A265 1.50p pale cream & bl grn .25 .25
1494 A353b 3p buff & vio blk .25 .25
1495 A265 3.50p pink & bl .25 .25
1496 A353a 6p red brn .25 .25
Nos. 1489-1496 (8) 2.00 2.00

Issued to honor the explorers of the Northwest coast of North America.

Roman Statue and Gate — A354

Designs: 3.50p, Ancient plower with ox team, horiz. 6p, Roman coins of Caceres.

1967, Oct. 31 **Photo.** ***Perf. 13***
1497 A354 1.50p multi .25 .25
1498 A354 3.50p multi .25 .25
1499 A354 6p multi .25 .25
Nos. 1497-1499 (3) .75 .75

Founding of Caceres by the Romans, 2000th anniv.

José Bethencourt A355

1.50p, Enrique Granados (composer). 3.50p, Ruben Dario (poet). 6p, St. Ildefonso.

1967, Nov. 15
1500 A355 1.20p gray & red brn .25 .25
1501 A355 1.50p blk & grn .25 .25
1502 A355 3.50p brn & pur .25 .25
1503 A355 6p blk & slate .25 .25
Nos. 1500-1503 (4) 1.00 1.00

Issued to honor famous Spanish men. See design A336.

Santa Maria de Veruela Monastery — A356

Designs: 3.50p, Aerial view of monastery, horiz. 6p, Inside view, horiz.

1967, Nov. 24 **Engr.** ***Perf. 13***
1504 A356 1.50p ultra & ind .25 .25
1505 A356 3.50p grn & blk .25 .25
1506 A356 6p rose vio & bis brn .25 .25
Nos. 1504-1506 (3) .75 .75

St. José Receiving Last Unction, by Goya — A357

1967, Nov. 27 **Photo.**
1507 A357 1.50p multi .25 .25

200th anniversary of the canonization of St. José de Calasanz (1556-1648), founder of the first Christian Schools in Rome.

Nativity, by Francisco Salzillo — A358

1967, Dec. 5
1508 A358 1.50p multi .25 .25

Christmas, 1967.

Slalom A359

3.50p, Bobsled, vert. 6p, Ice hockey.

1968, Feb. 6 **Photo.** ***Perf. 13***
1509 A359 1.50p multi .25 .25
1510 A359 3.50p multi .25 .25
1511 A359 6p multi .25 .25
Nos. 1509-1511 (3) .75 .75

Issued to commemorate the 10th Winter Olympic Games, Grenoble, France, Feb. 6-18.

Mariano Fortuny, Self-portrait A360

Fortuny Paintings: 40c, The Vicariate, horiz. 50c, "Fantasy" (pianist). 1p, "Idyll" (piper and sheep). 1.20p, The Print Collector, horiz. 2p, Old Man in the Sun. 2.50p, Calabrian Man. 3.50p, Lady with Fan. 4p, Battle of Tetuan, 1860. 6p, Queen Christina in Carriage, horiz.

1968, Mar. 25 **Photo.** ***Perf. 13***

Gold Frame

1512 A360 40c dp red lil .25 .25
1513 A360 50c dk bl grn .25 .25
1514 A360 1p brown .25 .25
1515 A360 1.20p dp vio .25 .25
1516 A360 1.50p dp grn .25 .25
1517 A360 2p org brn .25 .25
1518 A360 2.50p car rose .25 .25
1519 A360 3.50p dk red brn .25 .25
1520 A360 4p dk ol .25 .25
1521 A360 6p brt bl .25 .25
Nos. 1512-1521 (10) 2.50 2.50

Issued to honor Mariano Fortuny y Carbo (1838-74), and for Stamp Day.

For other art types see A236-A237, A240a, A246a, A257, A272, A285a, A300, A310, A324, A340-A341, A371 and footnote following No. 1606.

Beatriz Galindo A361

Famous Women: 1.50p, Agustina de Aragon. 3.50p, Maria Pacheco. 6p, Rosalia de Castro.

1968, Apr. 8 **Engr.** ***Perf. 12½x13***
1522 A361 1.20p yel brn & blk brn .25 .25
1523 A361 1.50p bl grn & dk bl .25 .25
1524 A361 3.50p lt vio & dk vio .25 .25
1525 A361 6p gray bl & blk .25 .25
Nos. 1522-1525 (4) 1.00 1.00

Europa Issue

Common Design Type

1968, Apr. 29 **Photo.** ***Perf. 13***

Size: 38x22mm

1526 CD11 3.50p brt bl, gold & brn .25 .25

Spain No. 1 with Galicia Puebla Postmark — A362

Stamp Day: 3.50p, Spain No. 4 with Serena postmark.

1968, May 6 **Photo.** ***Perf. 13***
1527 A362 1.50p blk, bl & ocher .25 .25
1528 A362 3.50p bl, dk grn & blk .25 .25

See Nos. 1568-1569, 1608, 1677, 1754.

Map of León and Seal — A363

Designs: 1.50p, Roman legionary. 3.50p, Emperor Galba coin, horiz.

Perf. 13x12½, 12½x13

1968, June 15 **Photo.**

Size: 25x38½mm

1529 A363 1p lil, red brn & yel .25 .25

Size: 25x47½mm

1530 A363 1.50p brn, dk brn & buff .25 .25

Size: 37½x26mm

1531 A363 3.50p ocher & sl grn .25 .25
Nos. 1529-1531 (3) .75 .75

1900th anniversary of the founding of León by the Roman Legion VII Gemina.

Human Rights Emblem — A364

1968, June 25 **Photo.** ***Perf. 13x12½***
1532 A364 3.50p bl, red & grn .25 .25

International Human Rights Year, 1968.

Benavente Palace, Baeza — A365

Tourism: 1.20p, View of Salamanca with Tormes River Bridge, horiz. 1.50p, Statuary group from St. Vincent's Church, Avila (The Adoration of the Magi). 2p, Tomb of Martin Vazquez de Arce, Cathedral of Sigüenza, horiz. 3.50p, Portal of St. Mary's Church, Sangüesa, Navarre.

1968, July 15 **Engr.** ***Perf. 13***
1533 A365 50c dp rose & brn .25 .25
1534 A365 1.20p emer & sl grn .25 .25
1535 A365 1.50p dp grn & ind .25 .25
1536 A365 2p lil rose & blk .25 .25
1537 A365 3.50p brt lil & rose lil .25 .25
Nos. 1533-1537 (5) 1.25 1.25

Escalona Castle, Toledo — A366

Castles: 1.20p, Fuensaldaña, Valladolid. 1.50p, Peñafiel, Valladolid. 2.50p, Villasobroso, Pontevedra. 6p, Frias, Burgos, vert.

1968, July 29 **Engr.** ***Perf. 13***

1538 A366 40c dk bl & sepia .25 .25
1539 A366 1.20p vio brn & vio blk .25 .25
1540 A366 1.50p ol & blk .25 .25
1541 A366 2.50p ol grn & blk .25 .25
1542 A366 6p vio bl & bl grn .25 .25
Nos. 1538-1542 (5) 1.25 1.25

Rifle Shooting A367

Designs: 1.50p, Horse jumping. 3.50p, Bicycling. 6p, Sailing, vert.

Perf. 12½x13, 13x12½

1968, Sept. 24 **Photo.**

1543 A367 1p multi .25 .25
1544 A367 1.50p multi .25 .25
1545 A367 3.50p multi .25 .25
1546 A367 6p multi .25 .25
Nos. 1543-1546 (4) 1.00 1.00

19th Olympic Games, Mexico City, 10/12-27.

Builders of the New World

Types of 1961 and

Map of Capuchin Missions along Orinoco River, 1732 — A368

1p, Diego de Losada. 1.50p, Losada family coat of arms. 3.50p, Diego de Henares. 6p, Map of Caracas, drawn by Diego de Henares, 1578, horiz.

1968, Oct. 12 **Photo.** ***Perf. 13***

1547 A368 40c grnsh bl, *bluish* .25 .25
1548 A265 1p red lil, *gray* .25 .25
1549 A368 1.50p sl, *pale rose* .25 .25
1550 A265 3.50p dk bl, *pnksh* .25 .25
1551 A368 6p dk ol bis .25 .25
Nos. 1547-1551 (5) 1.25 1.25

Christianization of Venezuela and the founding of Caracas.

St. Maria del Parral Monastery, Segovia — A369

3.50p, Monastery, inside view. 6p, Madonna & Child, statue from main altar.

1968, Nov. 25 **Engr.** ***Perf. 13***

1552 A369 1.50p gray bl & rose vio .25 .25
1553 A369 3.50p brn & red brn .25 .25
1554 A369 6p rose claret & brn .25 .25
Nos. 1552-1554 (3) .75 .75

Nativity, by Federico Fiori da Urbino — A370

1968, Dec. 2 **Photo.** ***Perf. 13x12½***

1555 A370 1.50p gold & multi .25 .25

Christmas, 1968.

Alonso Cano by Velázquez A371

Cano Paintings: 40c, St. Agnes. 50c, St. John. 1p, Jesus and Angel. 2p, Holy Family. 2.50p, Circumcision of Jesus. 3p, Jesus and the Samaritan Woman. 3.50p, Madonna and Child. 4p, Sts. John Capistrano and Bernardino, horiz. 6p, Vision of St. John the Baptist.

Gold Frame

1969, Mar. 24 **Photo.** ***Perf. 13***

1556 A371 40c deep plum .25 .25
1557 A371 50c green .25 .25
1558 A371 1p sepia .25 .25
1559 A371 1.50p slate grn .25 .25
1560 A371 2p red brown .25 .25
1561 A371 2.50p dp red lil .25 .25
1562 A371 3p ultra .25 .25
1563 A371 3.50p dk rose brn .25 .25
1564 A371 4p dull lilac .25 .25
1565 A371 6p slate blue .25 .25
Nos. 1556-1565 (10) 2.50 2.50

Alonso Cano (1601-1667), and Stamp Day.
For other art types see A236-A237, A240a, A246a, A257, A272, A285a, A300, A310, A324, A340-A341, A360 and footnote following No. 1606.

DNA (Genetic Code) Molecule and Chart A372

1969, Apr. 7 **Photo.** ***Perf. 13***

1566 A372 1.50p gray & multi .25 .25

Issued to publicize the 6th European Congress of Biochemistry, Madrid, Apr. 7-11.

Europa Issue

Common Design Type

1969, Apr. 28

Size: 38x22mm

1567 CD12 3.50p multi .25 .25

Stamp Day Type of 1968

1.50p, Spain #6 with crowned M and "AL.3/1851" postmark. 3.50p, Spain #11 with Corvera postmark.

1969, May 6 **Photo.** ***Perf. 13***

1568 A362 1.50p blk, red & grn .25 .25
1569 A362 3.50p grn, bl & red .25 .25

Issued for Stamp Day, 1969.

Spectrum A373

1969, May 26

1570 A373 1.50p blk & multi .25 .25

Issued to publicize the 15th International Spectroscopy Colloquium, Madrid, May 26-30.

World Map, Red Crescent, Cross, Lion and Sun Emblems A374

1969, May 30

1571 A374 1.50p multi .25 .25

League of Red Cross Societies, 50th anniv.

Last Supper, Finial from Lugo Cathedral — A375

1969, June 4

1572 A375 1.50p grn, brn & blk .25 .25

300th anniversary of the dedication of Galicia Province to the reign of Jesus.

Turegano Castle, Segovia A376

Castles: 1.50p, Villalonso, Zamora. 2.50p, Velez Blanco, Almeria. 3.50p, Castilnovo, Segovia. 6p, Torrelobaton, Valladolid.

1969, June 24 **Engr.** ***Perf. 13***

1573 A376 1p dl grn & sl .25 .25
1574 A376 1.50p bluish lil & dk bl .25 .25
1575 A376 2.50p bl vio & bluish lil .25 .25
1576 A376 3.50p red brn & ol grn .25 .25
1577 A376 6p gray grn & dl brn .25 .25
Nos. 1573-1577 (5) 1.25 1.25

Father Junipero Serra — A377

1969, July 16 **Photo.** ***Perf. 13***

1578 A377 1.50p multi .25 .25

Bicentenary of San Diego, Calif.

Rock of Gibraltar — A378

2p, View of Gibraltar across the Bay of Algeciras.

1969, July 18

1579 A378 1.50p bl grn .25 .25
1580 A378 2p brt rose lil .25 .25

Dama de Elche — A379

Tourism: 1.50p, Alcañiz Castle, Teruel, horiz. 3p, Murcia Cathedral. 6p, St. Maria de la Redonda, Logrono.

1969, July 23 **Engr.** ***Perf. 13***

1581 A379 1.50p dl grn & blk .25 .25
1582 A379 3p yel grn & bl grn .25 .25
1583 A379 3.50p gray bl & dk bl .25 .25
1584 A379 6p yel grn & vio blk .25 .25
Nos. 1581-1584 (4) 1.00 1.00

Builders of the New World

Types of 1961 and

Santo Domingo Church, Santiago, Chile — A380

1.50p, Casa de Moneda de Chile, horiz. 2p, Ambrosio O'Higgins. 3.50p, Pedro de Valdivia. 6p, First large bridge over Mapocho River, horiz.

1969, Oct. 12 **Photo.** ***Perf. 13***

1585 A380 40c lt bl & dk red brn .25 .25
1586 A380 1.50p pale rose & dk vio .25 .25
1587 A265 2p pale pink & ol .25 .25
1588 A265 3.50p pale yel & dk Prus grn .35 .30
1589 A380 6p pale yel & blk brn .25 .25
Nos. 1585-1589 (5) 1.35 1.30

Exploration and development of Chile. See Nos. 1630-1631, 1634.

Adoration of the Magi, by Juan Bautista Mayno — A381

Christmas: 2p, Nativity, bas-relief from altar of Cathedral of Gerona.

1969, Nov. 3

1590 A381 1.50p multi .25 .25
1591 A381 2p multi .25 .25

Tomb of Alfonso VIII and Wife, Las Huelgas Monastery, Burgos — A382

Designs: 1.50p, Las Huelgas Monastery. 6p, Inside view, vert.

1969, Nov. 22 **Engr.**

1592 A382 1.50p lt bl grn & indigo .25 .25
1593 A382 3.50p ultra & vio bl .40 .35
1594 A382 6p olive & yel grn .25 .25
Nos. 1592-1594 (3) .90 .85

See Nos. 1639-1641.

St. Juan de Avila, by El Greco — A383

Design: 50p, Bishop Rodrigo Ximenez de Rada, Juan de Borgona mural.

1970, Feb. 25 Engr. *Perf. 13*

1595 A383 25p pale pur & ind 4.50 .25
1596 A383 50p brn org & brn 2.00 .25

St. Stephen, by Luis de Morales — A384

Morales Paintings: 1p, Annunciation. 1.50p, Madonna and Child with St. John. 2p, Madonna and Child. 3p, Presentation at the Temple. 3.50p, St. Jerome. 4p, St. John de Ribera. 5p, Ecce Homo. 6p, Pieta. 10p, St. Francis of Assisi.

1970, Mar. 24 Photo. *Perf. 13*

1597 A384 50c gold & multi .25 .25
1598 A384 1p gold & multi .25 .25
1599 A384 1.50p gold & multi .25 .25
1600 A384 2p gold & multi .25 .25
1601 A384 3p gold & multi .25 .25
1602 A384 3.50p gold & multi .25 .25
1603 A384 4p gold & multi .25 .25
1604 A384 5p gold & multi .25 .25
1605 A384 6p gold & multi .25 .25
1606 A384 10p gold & multi .25 .25
Nos. 1597-1606 (10) 2.50 2.50

Issued to honor Luis de Morales, "El Divino" (1509-1586), and for Stamp Day.

For other art types see A397, A410, A431, A448, A473, A501, A522, A538, A558 and footnote following No. 876.

Europa Issue
Common Design Type

1970, May 4 Photo. *Perf. 13x12½*
Size: 37½x22mm

1607 CD13 3.50p brt bl & gold .25 .25

Stamp Day Type of 1968

Stamp Day: 2p, Spain No. 51 with "Ferro Carril de Langreo" postmark.

1970, May 4 *Perf. 13x12½*

1608 A362 2p dl red, grn & blk .25 .25

Barcelona Fair Building A385

1970, May 27 *Perf. 13*

1609 A385 15p multi .25 .25

Barcelona Trade Fair, 50th anniversary.

Miguel Primo de Rivera — A386

1970, June 6 Photo. *Perf. 13*

1610 A386 2p buff, brn & ol grn .25 .25

Gen. Miguel Primo de Rivera (1870-1930), Spanish dictator, 1923-1930.

Valencia de Don Juan Castle — A387

Castles: 1.20p, Monterrey. 3.50p, Mombeltran. 6p, Sadaba. 10p, Bellver.

1970, June 24 Engr.

1611 A387 1p blk & dl bl .35 .25
1612 A387 1.20p lt grnsh bl & vio .25 .25
1613 A387 3.50p pale grn & brn .25 .25
1614 A387 6p sep & dl pur .25 .25
1615 A387 10p fawn & sepia .80 .25
Nos. 1611-1615 (5) 1.90 1.25

Alcazaba Castle, Almeria A388

Tourism: 1p, Malaga Cathedral. 1.50p, St. Mary of the Assumption, Lequemo, vert. 2p, Cloister of St. Francis of Orense. 3.50p, Market (Lonja), Zaragoza, vert. 5p, The Gate of Vitoria, vert.

1970, July 23 Engr. *Perf. 13*

1616 A388 50c bluish gray & dl pur .25 .25
1617 A388 1p red brn & ocher .25 .25
1618 A388 1.50p bluish gray & sl grn .25 .25
1619 A388 2p sl & dk bl .40 .25
1620 A388 3.50p pur & vio bl .25 .25
1621 A388 5p gray grn & red brn .80 .25
Nos. 1616-1621 (6) 2.20 1.50

Tailor, from Book Published in Madrid, 1589 A389

1970, Aug. 18 Photo. *Perf. 13*

1622 A389 2p mag, brn & dl vio .25 .25

14th Intl. Tailoring Congress, Madrid.

Diver and Map of Europe A390

1970, Aug. 25

1623 A390 2p grn & brt bl .25 .25

12th European Championships in Swimming, Diving and Water Polo, Barcelona.

Concha Espina — A391

1p, Guillen de Castro. 1.50p, Juan Ramon Jimenez. 2p, Gustavo Adolfo Becquer. 2.50p, Miguel de Unamuno. 3.50p, José M. Gabriel y Galan.

1970, Sept. 21 Photo. *Perf. 13x12½*

1624 A391 50c brn, vio bl & pale rose .25 .25
1625 A391 1p sl grn, dp rose lil & gray .25 .25
1626 A391 1.50p dk bl, brt grn & gray .25 .25
1627 A391 2p grn, dk ol & buff .25 .25
1628 A391 2.50p pur, rose lake & buff .25 .25
1629 A391 3.50p brn, dk red & gray .25 .25
Nos. 1624-1629 (6) 1.50 1.50

Issued to honor Spanish writers.

Builders of the New World
Portrait Type of 1961 and Building Type of 1969

40c, Ecala House, Queretaro, Mexico. 1.50p, Mexico Cathedral, horiz. 2p, Vasco de Quiroga. 3.50p, Brother Juan de Zumarraga. 6p, Cathedral Towers, Morelia, Mexico.

1970, Oct. 12 Photo. *Perf. 13*

1630 A380 40c lt bl & ol gray .25 .25
1631 A380 1.50p lt bl & brn .25 .25
1632 A265 2p buff & dk vio .50 .25
1633 A265 3.50p pale grn & dk grn .25 .25
1634 A380 6p pale pink & Prus bl .25 .25
Nos. 1630-1634 (5) 1.50 1.25

Exploration and development of Mexico.

Map of Western Mediterranean — A392

1970, Oct. 20 Photo. *Perf. 13*

1635 A392 2p multi .25 .25

Geographical and Statistical Institute, cent.

Adoration of the Shepherds, by El Greco — A393

Christmas: 2p, Adoration of the Shepherds, by Murillo.

1970, Oct. 30

1636 A393 1.50p multi .25 .25
1637 A393 2p multi .25 .25

UN Emblem and Headquarters — A394

1970, Nov. 3

1638 A394 8p multi .25 .25

25th anniversary of the United Nations.

Monastery Type of 1969

Ripoll Monastery: 2p, Portal. 3.50p, View of monastery. 5p, Inside court.

1970, Nov. 12 Engr.

1639 A382 2p vio & pur .50 .25
1640 A382 3.50p org & mar .25 .25
1641 A382 5p Prus grn & yel grn 1.00 .25
Nos. 1639-1641 (3) 1.75 .75

Map with Main European Pilgrimage Routes — A395

Cathedral of St. David, Wales A396

#1643, Map of main pilgrimage routes. #1644, St. Bridget statue, Vadstena, Sweden. #1645, Santiago Cathedral. #1646, Tower of St. Jacques, Paris. #1647, Pilgrim before entering Santiago de Compostela. #1648, St. James statue, Pistoia, Italy. #1649, Lugo Cathedral. 2.50p, Villafranca del Bierzo church. #1652, Astorga Cathedral. 3.50p, San Marcos de León. #1654, Charlemagne, bas-relief, Aachen Cathedral, Germany. #1655, San Tirso de Sahagun. 5p, San Martín de Fromista. 6p, Bas-relief, King's Hospital, Burgos. 7p, Portal of Santo Domingo de la Calzada. 7.50p, Cloister, Najera. 8p, Puente de la Reina (Christ on the Cross and portal). 9p, Santa Maria de Eunate. 10p, Cross of Roncesvalles.

1971 Engr. *Perf. 13*

1642 A395 50c grnsh bl & sep .25 .25
1643 A396 50c bl & dl vio .25 .25
1644 A395 1p brn & sl grn .25 .25
1645 A395 1p grn & sl grn .25 .25
1646 A395 1.50p dl grn & dp plum .25 .25
1647 A396 1.50p vio bl & lil .25 .25
1648 A395 2p dk pur & blk .25 .25
1649 A395 2p sl grn & dk bl .80 .25
1650 A396 2.50p vio brn & dl vio .25 .25
1651 A396 3p ultra & dk bl .25 .25
1652 A395 3p dl red & rose lil .40 .25
1653 A396 3.50p dp org & gray grn .25 .25
1654 A396 4p ol grn .35 .25
1655 A395 4p grnsh bl & brn .25 .25
1656 A396 5p lt grn & blk .35 .25
1657 A395 6p lt ultra .25 .25
1658 A395 7p lil & dl vio .45 .25
1659 A396 7.50p car lake & dl vio .25 .25
1660 A395 8p grn & vio blk .25 .25
1661 A396 9p grn & vio .25 .25
1662 A395 10p grn & brn .40 .25
Nos. 1642-1662 (21) 6.50 5.25

Holy Year of Compostela, 1971.

Ignacio Zuloaga, Self-portrait A397

Zuloaga Paintings: 50c, "My Uncle Daniel." 1p, View of Segovia, horiz. 1.50p, Countess of Alba. 3p, Juan Belmonte. 4p, Countess of Noailles. 5p, Pablo Uranga. 8p, Cobblers' Houses at Lerma, horiz.

1971, Mar. 24 Photo. *Perf. 13*

1663 A397 50c gold & multi .25 .25
1664 A397 1p gold & multi .25 .25
1665 A397 1.50p gold & multi .25 .25
1666 A397 2p gold & multi .25 .25
1667 A397 3p gold & multi .25 .25
1668 A397 4p gold & multi .25 .25
1669 A397 5p gold & multi .25 .25
1670 A397 8p gold & multi .25 .25
Nos. 1663-1670 (8) 2.00 2.00

Ignacio Zuloaga (1870-1945). Stamp Day.

For other art types see A384, A410, A431, A448, A473, A501, A522, A538, A558 and footnote following No. 876.

Amadeo Vives, Composer A398

2p, St. Teresa of Avila. 8p, Benito Perez Galdos, writer. 15p, Ramon Menendez Pidal, writer.

1971, Apr. 20

1671 A398 1p multicolored .25 .25
1672 A398 2p multicolored .25 .25
1673 A398 8p multicolored .25 .25
1674 A398 15p multicolored .25 .25
Nos. 1671-1674 (4) 1.00 1.00

Europa Issue
Common Design Type

1971, Apr. 29 Photo. *Perf. 13*
Size: 37x26mm

1675 CD14 2p lt bl, brn & vio bl .45 .25
1676 CD14 8p lt grn, dk brn & dk grn .30 .30

Stamp Day Type of 1968

Spain No. 1 with blue "A" cancellation.

1971, May 6

1677 A362 2p black, bl & olive .25 .25

Gymnast — A399

Design: 2p, Gymnast on bar.

1971, May 14

1678 A399 1p ocher & multi .25 .25
1679 A399 2p lt blue & multi .25 .25

9th European Gymnastic Championships for Men, Madrid, May 14-15.

Great Bustard A400

Designs: 2p, Pardine lynx. 3p, Brown bear. 5p, Red-legged partridge, vert. 8p. Spanish ibex, vert.

1971, May 24

1680 A400 1p multicolored .25 .25
1681 A400 2p multicolored .25 .25
1682 A400 3p multicolored .25 .25
1683 A400 5p multicolored .35 .25
1684 A400 8p multicolored .35 .35
Nos. 1680-1684 (5) 1.45 1.35

Legionnaires — A401

2p, Legionnaires on dress parade. 5p, Memorial service. 8p, Desert fighter and tank column.

1971, June 21 Photo. *Perf. 13*

1685 A401 1p multicolored .25 .25
1686 A401 2p multicolored .25 .25
1687 A401 5p multicolored .25 .25
1688 A401 8p multicolored .30 .30
Nos. 1685-1688 (4) 1.05 1.05

50th anniversary of the Legion, a voluntary military organization.

UNICEF Emblem, Children of Various Races — A402

1971, Sept. 10

1689 A402 8p multicolored .25 .25

25th anniv. of UNICEF.

Don Juan of Austria, Fleet Commander A403

Designs: 5p, Battle of Lepanto, horiz. 8p, Holy League banner in Cathedral.

1971, Oct. 7 Engr. *Perf. 13*

1690 A403 2p sepia & slate grn .50 .25
1691 A403 5p chocolate .90 .25
1692 A403 8p rose car & vio bl .75 .60
Nos. 1690-1692 (3) 2.15 1.10

400th anniversary of the Battle of Lepanto against the Turks.

Hockey Players, Hockey League and Games Emblems — A404

1971, Oct. 15 Photo.

1693 A404 5p multicolored .60 .25

First World Hockey Cup, Barcelona, Oct. 15-24.

De Havilland DH-9 over Seville A405

Design: 15p, Boeing 747 over Plaza de la Cibeles, Madrid.

1971, Oct. 25

1694 A405 2p multicolored .30 .25
1695 A405 15p multicolored .30 .25

50th anniversary of Spanish air mail service.

Nativity, Avia Altarpiece A406

Christmas: 8p, Nativity, Sagas altarpiece.

1971, Nov. 4 *Perf. 12½x13*

1696 A406 2p multicolored .25 .25
1697 A406 8p multicolored .25 .25

Emilia Pardo Bazan — A407

Portraits: 25p, José de Espronceda. 50p, King Fernan Gonzalez.

1972, Jan. 27 Engr. *Perf. 13*

1698 A407 15p brown & slate grn .25 .25
1699 A407 25p lt grn & slate grn .25 .25
1700 A407 50p claret & dp brn .55 .25
Nos. 1698-1700 (3) 1.05 .75

Honoring Emilia Pardo Bazan (1852-1921), novelist (15p); José de Espronceda (1808-1842), poet (25p); Fernan Gonzalez (910-970), first King of Castile (50p).

Figure Skating — A408

Design: 2p, Ski jump and Sapporo Olympic emblem, horiz.

1972, Feb. 10 Photo.

1701 A408 2p gray & multi .35 .25
1702 A408 15p blue & multi .25 .25

11th Winter Olympic Games, Sapporo, Japan, Feb. 3-13.

Don Quixote Title Page, 1605 — A409

1972, Feb. 24 Engr. *Perf. 13x12½*

1703 A409 2p brown & claret .25 .25

International Book Year 1972.

A410

Gutierrez Solana Paintings: 1p, Clowns, horiz. 2p, José Gutierrez Solana with wife and child. 3p, Balladier. 4p, Fisherman. 5p, Mask makers. 7p, The book collector. 10p, Merchant marine captain. 15p, Afterdinner speaker, horiz.

1972, Mar. 24 Photo. *Perf. 13*

1704 A410 1p gold & multi .25 .25
1705 A410 2p gold & multi .35 .25
1706 A410 3p gold & multi .40 .25
1707 A410 4p gold & multi .25 .25
1708 A410 5p gold & multi 1.25 .35
1709 A410 7p gold & multi .55 .25
1710 A410 10p gold & multi .55 .25
1711 A410 15p gold & multi .55 .25
Nos. 1704-1711 (8) 4.15 2.10

José Gutierrez Solana (1886-1945). Stamp Day 1972.

For other art types see A384, A397, A431, A448, A473, A501, A522, A538, A558 and footnote following No. 876.

Flora — A411

1972, Apr. 21

1712 A411 1p Fir .25 .25
1713 A411 2p Strawberry tree .35 .25
1714 A411 3p Cluster pine .40 .25
1715 A411 5p Evergreen oak .55 .25
1716 A411 8p Juniper .35 .30
Nos. 1712-1716 (5) 1.90 1.30

Europa Issue

Common Design Type and

Europeans Interlocking A412

1972, May 2

1717 A412 2p dull grn & ocher *1.40* .25

Size: 25x38mm

1718 CD15 8p multicolored *.50 .40*

Pre-stamp Cordoba Postmark (1824-42) A413

1972, May 6 *Perf. 12½x13*

1719 A413 2p dull yel, blk & car .25 .25

Stamp Day 1972.

Santa Catalina Castle, Jaen — A414

Castles: 1p, Sajazarra, Rioja, vert. 3p, Biar, Alicante. 5p, San Servando, Toledo. 10p, Pedraza, Segovia.

1972, June 22 Engr. *Perf. 13*

1720 A414 1p dull bl grn & brn .45 .35
1721 A414 2p gray olive & grn .85 .25
1722 A414 3p rose car & red brn .85 .25
1723 A414 5p vio bl & dull grn .85 .25
1724 A414 10p slate & lilac 2.50 .25
Nos. 1720-1724 (5) 5.50 1.35

Weight Lifting, Olympic Emblems — A415

1p, Olympic emblems, fencing, horiz. 5p, Sculling. 8p, Pole vaulting.

1972, Aug. 26 Photo. *Perf. 13*

1725 A415 1p multicolored .25 .25
1726 A415 2p shown .25 .25
1727 A415 5p multicolored .25 .25
1728 A415 8p multicolored .25 .25
Nos. 1725-1728 (4) 1.00 1.00

20th Olympic Games, Munich, 8/26-9/11.

Egyptian Mongoose A416

1972, Sept. 14

1729 A416 1p Aquatic mole, vert. .25 .25
1730 A416 2p Chamois, vert. .25 .25
1731 A416 3p Wolf, vert. .25 .25
1732 A416 5p shown .50 .25
1733 A416 7p Spotted genet .40 .25
Nos. 1729-1733 (5) 1.65 1.25

Brigadier M.A. de Ustariz — A417

San Juan, 1870
A418

1972, Oct. 12 Photo. *Perf. 13*

1734 A417 1p shown .25 .25
1735 A418 2p shown .25 .25
1736 A418 5p San Juan, 1625 .40 .25
1737 A418 8p Map of Plaza and Bay, 1792 .40 .30
Nos. 1734-1737 (4) 1.30 1.05

450th anniversary of San Juan.

St. Tomas Monastery, Avila — A419

8p, Inside view. 15p, Cloister, horiz.

1972, Oct. 26 Engr.

1738 A419 2p Prus bl & gray grn .90 .25
1739 A419 8p gray & claret .75 .30
1740 A419 15p violet & red lil .50 .25
Nos. 1738-1740 (3) 2.15 .80

Teatro del Liceo, Barcelona
A420

1972, Nov. 7 *Perf. 12½x13*

1741 A420 8p ultra & sepia .25 .25

125th anniversary of the Gran Teatro del Liceo in Barcelona.

Annunciation — A421

Christmas: 8p, Angel and shepherds. Designs are from Romanesque murals in the Collegiate Basilica of San Isidro, Leon.

1972, Nov. 14 Photo. *Perf. 13*

1742 A421 2p gold & multi .25 .25
1743 A421 8p gold & multi .25 .25

Juan de Herrera and Escorial
A422

Great Spanish Architects: 10p, Juan de Villanueva and Prado. 15p, Ventura Rodriguez and Apollo Fountain.

1973, Jan. 29 Engr. *Perf. 12½x13*

1744 A422 8p sepia & slate grn .50 .25
1745 A422 10p blk brn & bluish blk 1.60 .25
1746 A422 15p brt green & indigo .40 .25
Nos. 1744-1746 (3) 2.50 .75

Myrica Faya — A423

Flora of Canary Islands: 1p, Apollonias canariensis, horiz. 4p, Palms. 5p, Holly. 15p, Dracaena draco.

1973, Mar. 21 Photo. *Perf. 13*

1747 A423 1p multicolored .25 .25
1748 A423 2p shown .55 .25
1749 A423 4p multicolored .25 .25
1750 A423 5p multicolored .55 .25
1751 A423 15p multicolored .30 .25
Nos. 1747-1751 (5) 1.90 1.25

Europa Issue

Common Design Type and

Europa, Roman Mosaic — A424

1973, Apr. 30 Photo. *Perf. 13*

1752 A424 2p multicolored *.40* .25

Size: 37x26mm

1753 CD16 8p lt blue, blk & red *.35* .25

Stamp Day Type of 1968

Stamp Day: 2p, Spain No. 23 with red Madrid, 1853, cancellation.

1973, May 5

1754 A362 2p black, blue & red .25 .25

Iznajar Dam on Genil River — A425

1973, June 9 Photo. *Perf. 12½x13*

1755 A425 8p multicolored .25 .25

11th Congress of the International Commission on High Dams, Madrid, June 11-15.

Oñate University, Guipuzcoa
A426

Designs: 2p, Plaza del Campo and fountain, Lugo. 3p, Plaza de Llerena and fountain, Badajoz, vert. 5p, House of Columbus, Las Palmas. 8p, Windmills, La Mancha.

1973, June 11 Engr. *Perf. 13*

1756 A426 1p gray & sepia .25 .25
1757 A426 2p brt grn & sl grn .55 .25
1758 A426 3p dk brn & org brn .55 .25
1759 A426 5p dk gray & vio blk 1.40 .25
1760 A426 8p dk gray & car .60 .25
Nos. 1756-1760 (5) 3.35 1.25

Azure-winged Magpie — A427

Birds: 1p, Black-bellied sand grouse, horiz. 2p, Black stork, horiz. 7p, Imperial eagle, horiz. 15p, Red-crested pochard.

1973, July 3 Photo. *Perf. 13*

1761 A427 1p multicolored .25 .25
1762 A427 2p multicolored .35 .25
1763 A427 5p multicolored .50 .40
1764 A427 7p multicolored .60 .25
1765 A427 15p multicolored .25 .25
Nos. 1761-1765 (5) 1.95 1.40

Knight, Holy Fraternity of Castile, 1488 — A428

Uniforms: 2p, Knight, Castile, 1493, horiz. 3p, Harquebusier, 1534. 7p, Mounted rifleman, 1560. 8p, Infantry sergeants, 1567.

1973, July 17

1766 A428 1p multicolored .25 .25
1767 A428 2p multicolored .50 .25
1768 A428 3p multicolored .50 .25
1769 A428 7p multicolored .40 .25
1770 A428 8p multicolored .40 .25
Nos. 1766-1770 (5) 2.05 1.25

See Nos. 1794-1798, 1824-1828, 1869-1873, 1902-1906, 1989-1993, 2020-2024, 2051-2055, 2078-2082.

Fish in Net
A429

1973, Sept. 12 Photo. *Perf. 13*

1771 A429 2p multicolored .25 .25

6th Intl. Fishing Exhibition, Vigo, Sept. 12-19.

Conference Hall — A430

1973, Sept. 14

1772 A430 8p multicolored .25 .25

Plenipotentiary Conf. of the Intl. Telecommunications Union, Torremolinos, Sept. 1973.

Vicente López, Self-portrait
A431

Stamp Day (Paintings by Vicente López y Portana (1772-1850)): 1p, King Ferdinand VII. 3p, Señora de Carvallo. 4p, Marshal Castelldosrrius. 5p, Queen Isabella II. 7p, Francisco Goya. 10p, Maria Amalia de Sajonia. 15p, The organist Felix López.

1973, Sept. 29 Photo. *Perf. 13*

1773 A431 1p gold & multi .25 .25
1774 A431 2p gold & multi .25 .25
1775 A431 3p gold & multi .25 .25
1776 A431 4p gold & multi .25 .25
1777 A431 5p gold & multi .25 .25
1778 A431 7p gold & multi .25 .25
1779 A431 10p gold & multi .25 .25
1780 A431 15p gold & multi .25 .25
Nos. 1773-1780 (8) 2.00 2.00

For other art types see A384, A397, A410, A448, A473, A501, A522, A538, A558 and footnote following No. 876.

Leon Cathedral, Nicaragua
A432

Designs: 2p, Subtiava Church. 5p, Portal of Governor's House, vert. 8p, Rio San Juan Castle.

1973, Oct. 12

1781 A432 1p multicolored .25 .25
1782 A432 2p multicolored .30 .25
1783 A432 5p multicolored .50 .25
1784 A432 8p multicolored .35 .25
Nos. 1781-1784 (4) 1.40 1.00

Hispanic-American buildings in Nicaragua.

Pope Gregory XI and Pedro Fernandez Pecha — A433

1973, Oct. 26

1785 A433 2p multicolored .25 .25

600th anniversary of the founding of the Order of the Hermites of St. Jerome by Pedro Fernandez Pecha.

St. Domingo de Silos Monastery — A434

Designs: 8p, Cloister walk, horiz. 15p, Three saints, sculpture.

Perf. 13x12½, 12½x13

1973, Oct. 26 Engr.

1786 A434 2p brn & rose mag .45 .25
1787 A434 8p dk blue & purple .25 .25
1788 A434 15p Prus grn & indigo .25 .25
Nos. 1786-1788 (3) .95 .75

St. Domingo de Silos Monastery, Burgos.

Nativity, Column Capital, Silos Church — A435

Christmas: 8p, Adoration of the Kings, Butrera Church, horiz.

1973, Nov. 6 Photo. *Perf. 13*

1789 A435 2p multicolored .25 .25
1790 A435 8p multicolored .25 .25

Map of Spain and Americas with Dates of First Printings A436

500 years of Spanish Printing: 7p, Teacher and Pupils, woodcut from "Libros de los Sueños," Valencia, 1474, vert. 15p, Title page from "Los Sinodales," Segovia, 1472.

1973, Dec. 11 Engr. *Perf. 13*

1791	A436	1p ind & slate grn	.30	.25
1792	A436	7p violet bl & purple	.25	.25
1793	A436	15p purple & black	.25	.25
		Nos. 1791-1793 (3)	.80	.75

Uniform Type of 1973

Uniforms: 1p, Harquebusier on horseback, 1603. 2p, Harquebusiers, 1632. 3p, Cuirassier, 1635. 5p, Mounted drummer of the Dragoons, 1677. 9p, Two Musketeers, 1694.

1974, Jan. 5 Photo. *Perf. 13*

1794	A428	1p multicolored	.25	.25
1795	A428	2p multicolored	.50	.25
1796	A428	3p multicolored	.70	.25
1797	A428	5p multicolored	.90	.25
1798	A428	9p multicolored	.25	.25
		Nos. 1794-1798 (5)	2.60	1.25

Nautical Chart of Western Europe and North Africa — A437

1974, Jan. 26

1799	A437	2p multicolored	.25	.25

50th anniv. of the Superior Geographical Council of Spain. The chart is from a 14th cent. Catalan atlas.

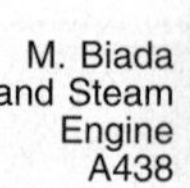

M. Biada and Steam Engine A438

1974, Apr. 2 Photo. *Perf. 13*

1800	A438	2p multicolored	.25	.25

Barcelona-Mataro Railroad, 125th anniv.

Young Collector, Album, Magnifier A439

Exhibition Emblem — A440

Design: 8p, Emblem, globe and arrows.

1974, Apr. 4 *Perf. 13*

1801	A439	2p lilac rose & multi	.25	.25

Perf. 12½

1802	A440	5p buff, blk & dull bl	.35	.30
1803	A440	8p dull green & multi	.30	.25
		Nos. 1801-1803 (3)	.90	.80

Espana 75, International Philatelic Exhibition, Madrid, Apr. 4-13, 1975.

Woman with Offering — A441

Europa: 8p, Woman from Baza, painted sculpture.

1974, Apr. 29 Photo. *Perf. 13*

1804	A441	2p multicolored	*.45*	.25
1805	A441	8p multicolored	*.25*	*.25*

No. 28 and 1854 Seville Cancel A442

1974, May 6

1806	A442	2p black, blue & red	.25	.25

World Stamp Day.

Father Jaime Balmes A443

Designs: 10p, Father Pedro Poveda. 15p, Jorge Juan y Santacilla.

1974, May 28 Engr. *Perf. 13*

1807	A443	8p blue gray & sepia	.25	.25
1808	A443	10p red brn & dk brn	.60	.25
1809	A443	15p brown & slate	.25	.25
		Nos. 1807-1809 (3)	1.10	.75

Famous Spaniards: Jaime Balmes (1810-1848), mathematician; death centenary of Pedro Poveda, pedagogue; Don Jorge Juan (1712-1773), explorer and writer.

Templeto, by Bramante, Rome — A444

1974, June 4 Photo.

1810	A444	5p multicolored	.25	.25

Cent. of the Spanish Academy of Fine Arts, Rome.

Aqueduct, Segovia A445

Designs: 2p, Tajo Bridge, Alcantara. 3p, Marcus Valerius Martial lecturing. 4p, Triumphal Arch, Tarragona, vert. 5p, Theater, Merida. 7p, Bishop Ossius of Cordoba preaching. 8p, Tribunal Arch, Talavera Forum, vert. 9p, Emperor Trajan, vert.

1974, June 25 Engr.

1811	A445	1p brown & black	.25	.25
1812	A445	2p gray grn & sepia	.30	.25
1813	A445	3p lt & dk brown	.25	.25
1814	A445	4p green & indigo	.25	.25
1815	A445	5p gray bl & choc	.25	.25
1816	A445	7p gray grn & lilac	.25	.25
1817	A445	8p dk brown & green	.25	.25
1818	A445	9p brt red lil & cl	.25	.25
		Nos. 1811-1818 (8)	2.05	2.00

Roman architecture and history in Spain.

Greek Tortoise A446

Reptiles: 2p, Common chameleon. 5p, Wall gecko. 7p, Emerald lizard. 15p, Blunt-nosed viper.

1974, July 3 Photo.

1819	A446	1p multicolored	.25	.25
1820	A446	2p multicolored	.30	.25
1821	A446	5p multicolored	.60	.50
1822	A446	7p multicolored	.40	.25
1823	A446	15p multicolored	.25	.25
		Nos. 1819-1823 (5)	1.80	1.50

Uniform Type of 1973

Uniforms: 1p, Hussar and horse, 1705. 2p, Artillery officers, 1710. 3p, Piper and drummer, Granada Regiment, 1734. 7p, Mounted standard-bearer, Numancia Dragoons, 1737. 8p, Standard-bearer and soldier, Zamora Regiment, 1739.

1974, July 17

1824	A428	1p multicolored	.25	.25
1825	A428	2p multicolored	.40	.25
1826	A428	3p multicolored	.40	.25
1827	A428	7p multicolored	.30	.25
1828	A428	8p multicolored	.25	.25
		Nos. 1824-1828 (5)	1.60	1.25

Life Saving A447

1974, Sept. 5 Photo. *Perf. 13*

1829	A447	2p multicolored	.25	.25

18th World Life Saving Championships, Barcelona, Sept. 1974.

Eduardo Rosales, by Federico Madrazo — A448

Stamp Day (Eduardo Rosales, 1836-73, Paintings): 1p, Tobias and the Angel. 3p, The Last Will of Isabella the Catholic. 4p, Nena (little girl). 5p, Presentation of John of Austria to Charles I. 7p, The First Step. 10p, St. John the Evangelist. 15p, St. Matthew.

1974, Sept. 29 Photo. *Perf. 13*

1830	A448	1p gold & multi	.25	.25
1831	A448	2p gold & multi	.25	.25
1832	A448	3p gold & multi, horiz.	.25	.25
1833	A448	4p gold & multi	.25	.25
1834	A448	5p gold & multi, horiz.	.25	.25
1835	A448	7p gold & multi, horiz.	.25	.25
1836	A448	10p gold & multi	.30	.25
1837	A448	15p gold & multi	.25	.25
		Nos. 1830-1837 (8)	2.05	2.00

For other art types see A384, A397, A410, A431, A473, A501, A522, A538, A558 and footnote following No. 876.

"International Mail" — A449

UPU Monument, Bern — A450

1974, Oct. 9

1838	A449	2p dark blue & multi	.25	.25
1839	A450	8p red & multi	.25	.25

Centenary of Universal Postal Union.

Sobremonte House, Cordoba, Argentina — A451

Ruins of San Ignacio de Mini, 18th Century — A452

The Gaucho Martin Fierro — A453

Design: 2p, Municipal Council Building, Buenos Aires, 1829.

1974, Oct. 12

1840	A451	1p multicolored	.25	.25
1841	A451	2p multicolored	.40	.25
1842	A452	5p multicolored	.30	.25
1843	A453	10p multicolored	.25	.25
		Nos. 1840-1843 (4)	1.20	1.00

Cultural ties with Latin America.

Nativity, Valdavia Church A454

Adoration of the Kings, Valcobero Church — A455

1974 Photo. *Perf. 13*

1844	A454	2p multicolored	.25	.25
1845	A455	3p lt blue & multi	.25	.25
1846	A455	8p olive & multi	.25	.25
		Nos. 1844-1846 (3)	.75	.75

Christmas 1974.
Issue dates: 2p, 8p, Nov. 4; 3p, Dec. 2.

Teucriun Lanigerum A456

Flowers: 2p, Hypericum ericoides. 4p, Thymus longiflorus. 5p, Anthyllis onobrychioides. 8p, Helianthemun paniculatum.

1974, Nov. 8

1847 A456 1p multicolored .25 .25
1848 A456 2p multicolored .25 .25
1849 A456 4p multicolored .25 .25
1850 A456 5p multicolored .25 .25
1851 A456 8p multicolored .25 .25
Nos. 1847-1851 (5) 1.25 1.25

Franco Type of 1954-56 Imprint: "F.N.M.T."

1974-75 Photo. *Perf. 12½x13*

1852 A221 4p rose car ('75) .25 .25
1853 A221 7p brt ultra .25 .25
1854 A221 12p blue green .25 .25
1855 A221 20p rose carmine .25 .25
Nos. 1852-1855 (4) 1.00 1.00

Leyre Monastery A457

8p, Column and bas-relief, vert. 15p, Crypt.

1974, Dec. 10 Engr. *Perf. 12½x13*

1862 A457 2p slate grn & bl gray .45 .25
1863 A457 8p carmine .25 .25
1864 A457 15p grnsh black .35 .25
Nos. 1862-1864 (3) 1.05 .75

Leyre Monastery, Navarre.

Spain Nos. 1 and 1802 — A458

Mail Coach, 1850 A459

Designs: 8p, Mail ship of Indian Service. 10p, Chapel of St. Mark.

Perf. 12½x13, 13x12½

1975, Jan. 2 Engr.

1865 A458 2p slate blue .35 .30
1866 A459 3p olive & brown .45 .40
1867 A459 8p lilac & slate bl 1.00 .50
1868 A458 10p brn & slate grn .50 .40
Nos. 1865-1868 (4) 2.30 1.60

125th anniversary of Spanish postage stamps.

Uniform Type of 1973

1p, Sergeant and grenadier, Toledo Regiment, 1750. 2p, Royal Artillery, 1762. 3p, Queen's Regiment, 1763. 5p, Fusiliers, Vitoria Regiment, 1766. 10p, Dragoon, Sagunto Regiment, 1775.

1975, Jan. 7 Photo. *Perf. 13*

1869 A428 1p multicolored .25 .25
1870 A428 2p multicolored .25 .25
1871 A428 3p multicolored 1.60 .25
1872 A428 5p multicolored .50 .25
1873 A428 10p multicolored 1.40 .25
Nos. 1869-1873 (5) 4.00 1.25

Antonio Gaudi A460

Designs: 10p, Antonio Palacios and Casa Guell, Barcelona. 15p, Secundino Zuazo.

1975, Feb. 25 Engr. *Perf. 13*

1874 A460 8p green & black .25 .25
1875 A460 10p carmine & dp claret .40 .25
1876 A460 15p brown & black .25 .25
Nos. 1874-1876 (3) .90 .75

Contemporary Spanish architects.

Souvenir Sheets

Spanish Goldsmiths' Works — A461

Designs: 2p, Agate box, 9th cent. 3p, Votive crown of Recesvinto. 8p, Cover of Evangelistary, Roncesvalles Collegiate Church, 12th cent. 10p, Chalice of Infanta Donna Urraca, 11th cent. 12p, Processional monstrance, St. Domingo de Silos, 16th cent. 15p, Sword of Boabdil, 15th cent. 25p, Sword and head of Charles V (Carlos I of Spain). 50p, Earring and bracelet from Aliseda, 6th-4th centuries B.C. 3p, 10p, 12p, 25p vertical (No. 1878).

1975, Apr. 4 Engr. *Perf. 13*

1877 A461 Sheet of 4 8.00 8.00
a. 2p gray & Prussian blue 2.00 2.00
b. 8p brown & Prus blue 2.00 2.00
c. 15p gray & dark carmine 2.00 2.00
d. 50p dark carmine & gray 2.00 2.00
1878 A461 Sheet of 4 8.00 8.00
a. 3p slate green & gray 2.00 2.00
b. 10p sepia & slate 2.00 2.00
c. 12p gray & bluish black 2.00 2.00
d. 25p sepia & bluish black 2.00 2.00

Espana 75 Intl. Phil. Exhib., Madrid, 4/4-13.

Pomegranates A462

1p, Almonds, nuts and blossoms, horiz. 3p, Oranges. 4p, Chestnuts. 5p, Apples.

1975, Apr. 21 Photo.

1879 A462 1p multicolored .25 .25
1880 A462 2p shown .25 .25
1881 A462 3p multicolored .25 .25
1882 A462 4p multicolored .25 .25
1883 A462 5p multicolored .25 .25
Nos. 1879-1883 (5) 1.25 1.25

Woman Gathering Honey, Arana Cave — A463

Europa: 12p, Horse, wall painting from Tito Bustillo Cave, horiz.

1975, Apr. 28 Photo. *Perf. 13*

1884 A463 3p brown & multi *.25* .25
1885 A463 12p brown & multi *.35* .25

Pre-stamp León Cancellation A464

1975, May 6 *Perf. 12½x13*

1886 A464 3p multicolored .25 .25

World Stamp Day.

World Tourism Organization Emblem — A465

1975, May 12 Photo. *Perf. 13*

1887 A465 3p dark blue .25 .25

First General Assembly of the World Tourism Organization, Madrid, May 1975.

Fair Emblem, Agricultural Symbols — A466

1975, May 14

1888 A466 3p multicolored .25 .25

25th Agricultural Fair.

Equality Between Men and Women A467

1975, June 3

1889 A467 3p multicolored .25 .25

International Women's Year.

Virgin of Cabeza Sanctuary A468

1975, June 18 Photo. *Perf. 13*

1890 A468 3p multicolored .25 .25

Virgin of Cabeza Sanctuary, site of siege during Civil War, 1937.

Cervantes' Prison Cell, Argamasilla de Alba — A469

Tourism: 2p, Bridge of St. Martin, Toledo. 3p, Church of St. Peter, Tarrasa. 4p, Arch, Alhambra, Granada, vert. 5p, Street, Mijas, Malaga, vert. 7p, Church of St. Mary, Tarrasa, vert.

1975, June 25 Engr. *Perf. 13*

1891 A469 1p purple & black .25 .25
1892 A469 2p red brn & brn .25 .25
1893 A469 3p slate & sepia .25 .25
1894 A469 4p orange & claret .25 .25
1895 A469 5p slate grn & indigo .25 .25
1896 A469 7p violet bl & indigo .40 .25
Nos. 1891-1896 (6) 1.65 1.50

Salamander — A470

1975, July 9 Photo. *Perf. 13*

1897 A470 1p shown .25 .25
1898 A470 2p Newt .25 .25
1899 A470 3p Tree toad .25 .25
1900 A470 6p Midwife toad .25 .25
1901 A470 7p Leaf frog .25 .25
Nos. 1897-1901 (5) 1.25 1.25

Uniform Type of 1973

1p, Cavalry officer, 1788. 2p, Fusilier, Asturias Regiment, 1789. 3p, Infantry Colonel, 1802. 4p, Artillery standard-bearer, 1803. 7p, Sapper, 1809.

1975, July 17

1902 A428 1p multicolored .25 .25
1903 A428 2p multicolored .50 .25
1904 A428 3p multicolored .25 .25
1905 A428 4p multicolored .25 .25
1906 A428 7p multicolored .25 .25
Nos. 1902-1906 (5) 1.50 1.25

Infant and Children Playing A471

1975, Sept. 9 Photo. *Perf. 13*

1907 A471 3p multicolored .25 .25

"Defend Life."

Scroll and Emblem A472

1975, Sept. 25

1908 A472 3p multicolored .25 .25

13th International Congress of Latin Notaries, Barcelona, Sept. 26-Oct. 4.

Blessing of the Birds A473

Scenes from Apocalypse: 2p, Angel at River of Life. 3p, Angel Guarding Gate of Paradise. 4p, Fox carrying cock. 6p, Daniel with wild bulls. 7p, The Last Judgment. 10p, Four horsemen of the Apocalypse. 12p, Bird holding snake.

1975, Sept. 29

1909 A473 1p gold & multi .25 .25
1910 A473 2p gold & multi, vert. .25 .25
1911 A473 3p gold & multi, vert. .25 .25
1912 A473 4p gold & multi .25 .25
1913 A473 6p gold & multi .25 .25
1914 A473 7p gold & multi, vert. .25 .25
1915 A473 10p gold & multi, vert. .25 .25
1916 A473 12p gold & multi, vert. .25 .25
Nos. 1909-1916 (8) 2.00 2.00

Millenium Gerona Cathedral.

For other art types see A384, A397, A410, A431, A448, A501, A522, A538, A558 and footnote following No. 876.

Symbols of Industry A474

1975, Oct. 7 Engr. *Perf. 13*

1917	A474	3p violet & lilac	.25	.25

Spanish industrialization.

Pioneers' Covered Wagon A475

Designs: 1p, El Cabildo, meeting house of 1st Uruguayan Government. 3p, Fort St. Theresa over River Plate. 8p, Montevideo Cathedral, vert.

1975, Oct. 12 Photo.

1918	A475	1p multicolored	.25	.25
1919	A475	2p multicolored	.25	.25
1920	A475	3p multicolored	.25	.25
1921	A475	8p multicolored	.25	.25
		Nos. 1918-1921 (4)	1.00	1.00

Cultural ties with Latin America; sesquicentennial of Uruguay's independence.

Ruined Columns, San Juan de la Peña — A476

3p, Monastery, horiz. 8p, Cloister, horiz.

Perf. 13x12½, 12½x13

1975, Oct. 28 Engr.

1922	A476	3p slate grn & brn	.30	.25
1923	A476	8p violet & brt lil	.25	.25
1924	A476	10p dp magenta & car	.25	.25
		Nos. 1922-1924 (3)	.80	.75

San Juan de la Pena Monastery.

Madonna, Mosaic, Navarra Cathedral — A477

Christmas: 12p, Flight into Egypt, carved capital, Navarra Cathedral, horiz.

1975, Nov. 4 Photo. *Perf. 13*

1925	A477	3p multicolored	.25	.25
1926	A477	12p multicolored	.25	.25

King Juan Carlos I — A478

Queen Sofia and King — A479

Designs: No. 1928, Queen Sofia.

1975, Dec. 29 Photo. *Perf. 13x12½*

1927	A478	3p multicolored	.25	.25
1928	A478	3p multicolored	.25	.25

Perf. 12½

1929	A479	3p multicolored	.25	.25
1930	A479	12p multicolored	.25	.25
		Nos. 1927-1930 (4)	1.00	1.00

King Juan Carlos I, accession to the throne.

Pilgrim Virgin, Pontevedra A480

1976, Jan. 2 Engr. *Perf. 13*

1931	A480	3p rose & brown	.25	.25

Holy Year of St. James of Compostela, patron saint of Spain.

Mountains and Center Emblem — A481

1976, Feb. 10 Photo.

1932	A481	6p multicolored	.25	.25

Catalunya Excursion Center, centenary.

Cosme Damian Churruca — A482

Navigators: 12p, Luis de Requesens. 50p, Juan Sebastian Elcano, horiz.

1976, Mar. 1 Engr. *Perf. 13*

1933	A482	7p vio brn & grnsh blk	1.50	.25
1934	A482	12p lt blue & violet	.25	.25
1935	A482	50p dp brn & gray ol	.55	.25
		Nos. 1933-1935 (3)	2.30	.75

A. G. Bell, Radar and Telephone A483

1976, Mar. 10 Photo.

1936	A483	3p multicolored	.25	.25

Centenary of first telephone call by Alexander Graham Bell, March 10, 1876.

"Watch at Street Crossings" A484

Road Safety: 3p, "Don't pass when in doubt," vert. 5p, "Wear seat belts."

1976, Apr. 6 Photo. *Perf. 13*

1937	A484	1p orange & multi	.25	.25
1938	A484	3p gray & multi	.35	.25
1939	A484	5p lilac & multi	.25	.25
		Nos. 1937-1939 (3)	.85	.75

St. George, Alcoy Cathedral A485

1976, Apr. 23

1940	A485	3p multicolored	.25	.25

7th centenary of the apparition of St. George in Alcoy.

Talavera Pottery A486

Europa: 12p, Lace making.

1976, May 3 Photo. *Perf. 13*

1941	A486	3p multicolored	*.65*	.25
1942	A486	12p multicolored	*.80*	*.30*

17th Conference of European Postal and Telecommunications Administrations.

6r Stamp of 1851 with Coruna Cancel — A487

1976, May 6

1943	A487	3p blue, org & blk	.25	.25

World Stamp Day.

Coin of Caesar Augustus A488

7p, Map of Roman camp on banks of Ebro, and coin. 25p, Orpheus, mosaic from Roman era, vert.

1976, May 26 Engr. *Perf. 13*

1944	A488	3p dk brn & mar	1.90	.25
1945	A488	7p dk brown & blue	1.00	.30
1946	A488	25p brown & black	.50	.25
		Nos. 1944-1946 (3)	3.40	.80

Founding of Saragossa, 2000th anniv.

Spanish-made Rifle, 1757 — A489

Designs (Bicentennial Emblem and): 3p, Bernardo de Galvez, Spanish governor. 5p, Dollar bank note, Richmond, 1861. 12p, Spanish capture of Pensacola from English.

1976, May 29

1947	A489	1p dk brn & vio bl	.25	.25
1948	A489	3p sl grn & dk brn	.90	.25
1949	A489	5p dk brn & sl grn	.40	.25
1950	A489	12p sl grn & dk brn	.40	.30
		Nos. 1947-1950 (4)	1.95	1.05

American Bicentennial.

Old Customs House, Cadiz A490

Customs Houses: 3p, Madrid. 7p, Barcelona.

1976, June 9

1951	A490	1p black & maroon	.25	.25
1952	A490	3p sepia & green	.55	.25
1953	A490	7p red brn & vio brn	1.10	.35
		Nos. 1951-1953 (3)	1.90	.85

Postal Savings Box with Symbols — A491

Railroad Post Office — A492

Rural Mailman in Winter A493

Postal Service: 10p, Automatic letter sorting machine.

1976, June 16 Photo.

1954	A491	1p multicolored	.25	.25
1955	A492	3p multicolored	.35	.25
1956	A493	6p multicolored	.25	.25
1957	A493	10p multicolored	.25	.25
		Nos. 1954-1957 (4)	1.10	1.00

King and Queen, Map of Americas A494

1976, June 25

1958	A494	12p multicolored	.25	.25

Visit of King Juan Carlos I and Queen Sofia to the Americas, June 1976.

San Marcos, León — A495

Tourism (Famous Hotels): 2p, Las Cañadas, Tenerife. 3p, Portal of R. R. Catolicos, Santiago, vert. 4p, Cruz de Tejeda, Las Palmas. 7p, Gredos, Avila. 12p, La Arruzafa, Cordoba.

1976, June 30 Engr. *Perf. 13*

1959	A495	1p	slate & sepia	.25	.25
1960	A495	2p	green & indigo	.65	.25
1961	A495	3p	brn & red brn	.45	.25
1962	A495	4p	sepia & slate	.25	.25
1963	A495	7p	slate & sepia	.85	.35
1964	A495	12p	rose brn & pur	1.00	.25
			Nos. 1959-1964 (6)	3.45	1.60

Greco-Roman Wrestling — A496

Montreal Olympic Emblem and: 1p, Men's rowing, horiz. 2p, Boxing, horiz. 12p, Basketball.

1976, July 9 Photo.

1965	A496	1p	multicolored	.25	.25
1966	A496	2p	lilac & multi	.35	.25
1967	A496	3p	multicolored	.25	.25
1968	A496	12p	multicolored	.25	.25
			Nos. 1965-1968 (4)	1.10	1.00

21st Olympic Games, Montreal, Canada, July 17-Aug. 1.

King Juan Carlos I — A497

1976-77 Photo. *Perf. 13*

1969	A497	10c	orange ('77)	.25	.25
1970	A497	25c	apple grn ('77)	.25	.25
1971	A497	30c	dp blue ('77)	.25	.25
1972	A497	50c	purple ('77)	.25	.25
1973	A497	1p	emerald ('77)	.25	.25
1974	A497	1.50p	scarlet	.25	.25
1975	A497	2p	dp blue	.25	.25
1976	A497	3p	dp green	.25	.25
1977	A497	4p	blue grn ('77)	.25	.25
1978	A497	5p	dp car rose	.25	.25
1979	A497	6p	brt green ('77)	.25	.25
1980	A497	7p	olive	.25	.25
1982	A497	8p	brt blue ('77)	.25	.25
1983	A497	10p	lilac rose ('77)	.25	.25
1984	A497	12p	golden brown	.25	.25
1985	A497	15p	vio blue ('77)	.30	.25
1986	A497	20p	brt red lil ('77)	.35	.25
			Nos. 1969-1986 (17)	4.40	4.25

Nos. 1976, 1978-1980, 1982-1983 also issued as coils with number on back of every fifth stamp.

See Nos. 2185-2194, 2268-2270.

Nos. 1969-1970, 1972-1973, 1975-1983, 1985-1986, 2185-2194 and 2268-2270 also printed on prephosphored paper. Value, mint set of 27 values, $40.

Uniform Type of 1973

Uniforms: 1p, Trumpeter, Alcantara Regiment, 1815. 2p, Sapper, 1821. 3p, Engineer in dress uniform, 1825. 7p, Artillery infantry, 1828. 25p, Infantry riflemen, 1830.

1976, July 17

1989	A428	1p	multicolored	.25	.25
1990	A428	2p	multicolored	.80	.25
1991	A428	3p	multicolored	.30	.25
1992	A428	7p	multicolored	.25	.25
1993	A428	25p	multicolored	.30	.25
			Nos. 1989-1993 (5)	1.90	1.25

Blood Donors — A498

1976, Sept. 7 Engr. *Perf. 13*

1994	A498	3p	carmine & black	.25	.25

Give blood, save a life!

Mosaic, Batitales — A499

Designs: 3p, Lugo city wall. 7p, Obverse and reverse of Roman 1st Legion coin.

1976, Sept. 22

1995	A499	1p	black & purple	.25	.25
1996	A499	3p	black & dp brn	.25	.25
1997	A499	7p	green & magenta	.45	.25
			Nos. 1995-1997 (3)	.95	.75

2000th anniversary of Lugo City.

Parliament, Madrid A500

1976, Sept. 23

1998	A500	12p	green & sepia	.25	.25

63rd Conference of Inter-parliamentary Union, Madrid.

Still Life, by L. E. Menendez — A501

Luis Eugenio Menendez Paintings: 2p, Peaches and jar. 3p, Pears, melon and barrel. 4p, Brace of pigeons and basket. 6p, Sea bream and oranges, horiz. 7p, Water melon and bread, horiz. 10p, Figs, bread and jug, horiz. 12p, Various fruits, horiz.

1976, Sept. 29 Photo. *Perf. 13*

1999	A501	1p	gold & multi	.25	.25
2000	A501	2p	gold & multi	.25	.25
2001	A501	3p	gold & multi	.25	.25
2002	A501	4p	gold & multi	.25	.25
2003	A501	6p	gold & multi	.25	.25
2004	A501	7p	gold & multi	.30	.25
2005	A501	10p	gold & multi	.25	.25
2006	A501	12p	gold & multi	.30	.25
			Nos. 1999-2006 (8)	2.10	2.00

Luis Eugenio Menendez (1716-1780). Stamp Day 1976.

For other art types see A384, A397, A410, A431, A448, A473, A522, A538, A558 and footnote following No. 876.

St. Christopher Carrying Christ Child — A502

Christmas: 3p, Nativity, horiz. Both designs after painted wood carvings.

1976, Oct. 8

2007	A502	3p	multicolored	.75	.25
2008	A502	12p	multicolored	1.50	.50

Nicoya Church, Costa Rica — A503

Juan Vazquez de Coronado — A504

Designs: 3p, Orosi Mission, Costa Rica, horiz. 12p, Tomas de Acosta.

1976, Oct. 12

2009	A503	1p	multicolored	.25	.25
2010	A504	2p	multicolored	.25	.25
2011	A503	3p	multicolored	.25	.25
2012	A504	12p	multicolored	.25	.25
			Nos. 2009-2012 (4)	1.00	1.00

Spain's link with Costa Rica.

Map of South and Central America, Santa Maria, King and Queen A505

1976, Oct. 12

2013	A505	12p	multicolored	.25	.25

Visit of King Juan Carlos I and Queen Sofia to Latin America.

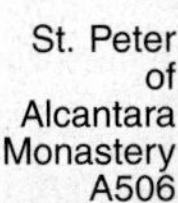

St. Peter of Alcantara Monastery A506

Tomb of Peter of Alcantara A507

St. Peter of Alcantara A508

1976, Oct. 29 Engr. *Perf. 13*

2014	A506	3p	dp brown & sepia	.30	.25
2015	A507	7p	dk purple & blk	.25	.25
2016	A508	20p	brown & dk brown	.30	.25
			Nos. 2014-2016 (3)	.85	.75

St. Peter of Alcantara (1499-1562), Franciscan reformer.

Hand Releasing Doves A509

1976, Nov. 23 Litho. *Perf. 13*

2017	A509	3p	multicolored	.25	.25

11th Philatelic Exhibition of the National Association of the Handicapped.

Casals and Cello A510

Design: 5p, Manuel de Falla and Fire Dance from El Amor Brujo.

1976, Dec. 29 Engr. *Perf. 13*

2018	A510	3p	black & vio bl	.25	.25
2019	A510	5p	slate grn & car	.25	.25

Birth centenaries of Pablo Casals (1876-1973), cellist and composer, and of Manuel de Falla (1876-1946), composer.

Uniform Type of 1973

Uniforms: 1p, Outrider, Calatrava Lancers, 1844. 2p, Sapper, 1850. 3p, Corporal, Light Infantry, 1860. 4p, Drum Major, 1861. 20p, Artillery Captain, Mounted, 1862.

1977, Jan. 5 Photo. *Perf. 13*

2020	A428	1p	multicolored	.25	.25
2021	A428	2p	multicolored	.35	.25
2022	A428	3p	multicolored	.25	.25
2023	A428	4p	multicolored	.25	.25
2024	A428	20p	multicolored	.25	.25
			Nos. 2020-2024 (5)	1.35	1.25

King James I A511

1977, Feb. 10 Engr. *Perf. 13*

2025	A511	4p	purple & ocher	.25	.25

James I, El Conquistador (1208-1276), King of Aragon, 700th death anniversary.

Jacinto Verdaguer — A512

Portraits: 7p, Miguel Servet. 12p, Pablo Sarasate. 50p, Francisco Tarrega.

1977, Feb. 22

No.	Type	Denom.	Color	Unused	Used
2026	A512	5p	purple & dk red	.25	.25
2027	A512	7p	olive & slate grn	.25	.25
2028	A512	12p	dk blue & bl grn	.25	.25
2029	A512	50p	lt green & brown	.55	.25
			Nos. 2026-2029 (4)	1.30	1.00

Honoring Jacinto Verdaguer (1845-1902), Catalan poet; Miguel Servet (1511-1553), physician and theologian; Pablo Sarasate (1844-1908), violinist and composer; Francisco Tarrega (1854-1909), creator of modern Spanish guitar music.

Marquis de Penaflorida — A513

1977, Feb. 24 Engr. *Perf. 13*

No.	Type	Denom.	Color	Unused	Used
2030	A513	4p	dull green & brn	.25	.25

Bicentenary of the Economic Society of the Friends of the Land (agricultural improvements).

Trout A514

1977, Mar. 8 Photo.

No.	Type	Denom.	Description	Unused	Used
2031	A514	1p	Salmon, vert.	.25	.25
2032	A514	2p	shown	.25	.25
2033	A514	3p	Eel	.25	.25
2034	A514	4p	Carp	.25	.25
2035	A514	6p	Barbel	.25	.25
			Nos. 2031-2035 (5)	1.25	1.25

Slalom A515

1977, Mar. 24 Engr. *Perf. 13*

No.	Type	Denom.	Color	Unused	Used
2036	A515	5p	multicolored	.25	.25

World Ski Championships, Granada, Sierra Nevada, Mar. 24-27.

La Cuadra, 1900 A516

Spanish Pioneer Automobiles: 4p, Hispano Suiza, 1916. 5p, Elizalde, 1915. 7p, Abadal, 1914.

1977, Apr. 23 Photo. *Perf. 13*

No.	Type	Denom.	Color	Unused	Used
2037	A516	2p	multicolored	.25	.25
2038	A516	4p	multicolored	.25	.25
2039	A516	5p	multicolored	.25	.25
2040	A516	7p	multicolored	.25	.25
			Nos. 2037-2040 (4)	1.00	1.00

Ordesa National Park A517

Europa: 3p, Tree in Doñana National Park.

1977, May 2 Litho.

No.	Type	Denom.	Color	Unused	Used
2041	A517	3p	multicolored	.25	.25
2042	A517	12p	multicolored	.25	.25

Plaza Mayor, Spanish Stamps, Tongs A518

1977, May 7 Engr. *Perf. 13*

No.	Type	Denom.	Color	Unused	Used
2043	A518	3p	multicolored	.25	.25

50th anniversary of Philatelic Market on Plaza Mayor, Madrid.

Enrique de Osso, St. Theresa and Book A519

1977, June 7 Photo. *Perf. 13*

No.	Type	Denom.	Color	Unused	Used
2044	A519	8p	multicolored	.25	.25

Centenary of the founding by Enrique de Osso of the Society of St. Theresa of Jesus.

Toledo Gate, Ciudad Real — A520

Tourism: 2p, Roman aqueduct, Almuñecar. 3p, Cathedral, Jaen, vert. 4p, Ronda Gorge, Malaga, vert. 7p, Ampudia Castle, Palencia. 12p, Bisagra Gate, Toledo.

1977, June 24 Engr. *Perf. 13*

No.	Type	Denom.	Color	Unused	Used
2045	A520	1p	orange & brown	.25	.25
2046	A520	2p	sepia & slate	.25	.25
2047	A520	3p	violet & purple	.25	.25
2048	A520	4p	brt & dk green	.25	.25
2049	A520	7p	brown & black	.25	.25
2050	A520	12p	vio & org brn	.25	.25
			Nos. 2045-2050 (6)	1.50	1.50

Uniform Type of 1973

Uniforms: 1p, Military Administration official, 1875. 2p, Cavalry lancers, 1883. 3p, General Staff Commander, 1884. 7p, Trumpeter, Divisional Artillery, 1887. 25p, Medical Corps official, 1895.

1977, July 16 Photo.

No.	Type	Denom.	Color	Unused	Used
2051	A428	1p	multicolored	.25	.25
2052	A428	2p	multicolored	.25	.25
2053	A428	3p	multicolored	.25	.25
2054	A428	7p	multicolored	.25	.25
2055	A428	25p	multicolored	.30	.25
			Nos. 2051-2055 (5)	1.30	1.25

A521

St. Emilian Cuculatus and earliest known Catalan manuscript.

1977, Sept. 9 Engr. *Perf. 13*

No.	Type	Denom.	Color	Unused	Used
2056	A521	5p	violet, grn & brn	.25	.25

Millennium of Catalan language.

A522

Federico Madrazo (1815-94) Portraits: 1p, The Boy Florez. 2p, Duke of San Miguel. 3p, Senora Coronado. 4p, Campoamor. 6p, Marquesa de Montelo. 7p, Rivadeneyra. 10p, Countess de Vilches. 15p, Senora Gomez de Avellaneda.

1977, Sept. 29 Photo. *Perf. 13*

No.	Type	Denom.	Color	Unused	Used
2057	A522	1p	gold & multi	.25	.25
2058	A522	2p	gold & multi	.25	.25
2059	A522	3p	gold & multi	.25	.25
2060	A522	4p	gold & multi	.25	.25
2061	A522	6p	gold & multi	.25	.25
2062	A522	7p	gold & multi	.25	.25
2063	A522	10p	gold & multi	.25	.25
2064	A522	15p	gold & multi	.25	.25
			Nos. 2057-2064 (8)	2.00	2.00

For other art types see A384, A397, A410, A431, A448, A473, A501, A538, A558 and footnote following No. 876.

Sailing Ship and Mail Routes, 18th Century — A523

1977, Oct. 7 Engr.

No.	Type	Denom.	Color	Unused	Used
2065	A523	15p	black, brn & grn	.30	.30

ESPAMER '77 Philatelic Exhibition, Barcelona, Oct. 7-13, and for the Bicentenary for regular mail routes to the Indies (Central and South America). No. 2065 issued in sheets of 8 stamps and 8 labels showing exhibition emblem.

Church of St. Francis, Guatemala City A524

Designs (Guatemala City): 3p, Modern buildings. 7p, Government Palace. 12p, Columbus Square and monument.

1977, Oct. 12 Photo. *Perf. 13*

No.	Type	Denom.	Color	Unused	Used
2066	A524	1p	multicolored	.25	.25
2067	A524	3p	multicolored	.25	.25
2068	A524	7p	multicolored	.25	.25
2069	A524	12p	multicolored	.25	.25
			Nos. 2066-2069 (4)	1.00	1.00

Spain's link with Guatemala.

San Pedro Monastery, Cardeña A525

Designs: 7p, Cloister. 20p, Tomb of El Cid and Dona Gimena.

1977, Oct. 28 Engr.

No.	Type	Denom.	Color	Unused	Used
2070	A525	3p	vio blue & slate	.25	.25
2071	A525	7p	brown & maroon	.25	.25
2072	A525	20p	green & slate	.25	.25
			Nos. 2070-2072 (3)	.75	.75

San Pedro Monastery, Cardena, Burgos.

Adoration of the Kings A526

Christmas: 12p, Flight into Egypt, vert. Designs from Romanesque paintings in Jaca Cathedral Museum.

1977, Nov. 3 Photo.

No.	Type	Denom.	Color	Unused	Used
2073	A526	5p	multicolored	.25	.25
2074	A526	12p	multicolored	.25	.25

Old and New Iberia Planes A527

1977, Nov. 3

No.	Type	Denom.	Color	Unused	Used
2075	A527	12p	multicolored	.25	.25

IBERIA, Spanish Airlines, 50th anniversary.

Felipe de Borbon, Prince of Asturias — A528

1977, Dec. 22 Photo. *Perf. 13*

No.	Type	Denom.	Color	Unused	Used
2076	A528	5p	multicolored	.25	.25

Felipe de Borbon, Spanish crown prince.

Judo, Games Emblem — A529

1977, Dec. 29

No.	Type	Denom.	Color	Unused	Used
2077	A529	3p	multicolored	.25	.25

10th World Judo Championships, Taiwan.

Uniform Type of 1973

Uniforms: 1p, Flag bearer, 1908. 2p, Lieutenant Colonel, Hussar, 1909. 3p, Mounted artillery lieutenant, 1912. 5p, Engineers' captain, 1921. 12p, Captain General, 1925.

1978, Jan. 5

No.	Type	Denom.	Color	Unused	Used
2078	A428	1p	multicolored	.25	.25
2079	A428	2p	multicolored	.25	.25
2080	A428	3p	multicolored	.25	.25
2081	A428	5p	multicolored	.25	.25
2082	A428	12p	multicolored	.25	.25
			Nos. 2078-2082 (5)	1.25	1.25

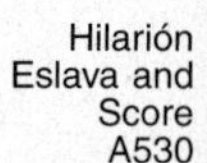

Hilarión Eslava and Score A530

8p, José Clara and sculpture. 25p, Pio Baroja and farm. 50p, Antonio Machado Ruiz and castle.

1978, Feb. 20 Engr. *Perf. 13*

No.	Type	Denom.	Color	Unused	Used
2083	A530	5p	black & dk pur	.25	.25
2084	A530	8p	blue grn & blk	.25	.25
2085	A530	25p	yel grn & blk	.30	.25
2086	A530	50p	dk pur & dk brn	.55	.25
			Nos. 2083-2086 (4)	1.35	1.00

Miguel Hilarión Eslava (1807-1878), composer; José Clara, sculptor; Pio Baroja (1872-

1956), author and physician; Antonio Machado Ruiz (1875-1939), poet and playwright.

Burial of Christ, by de Juni — A531

Detail from Burial of Christ — A532

Designs: No. 2089, Juan de Juni. No. 2090, Rape of Sabine Women, by Rubens. No. 2091, Rape (detail) and Rubens portrait. No. 2092, Rubens signature and palette. No. 2093, Judgment of Paris, by Titian. No. 2094, Judgment and Titian portrait. No. 2095, Initial "TF" and palette.

1978, Mar. 28 Engr. ***Perf. 12½x13***

2087 A532 3p multicolored .25 .25
2088 A531 3p multicolored .25 .25
2089 A532 3p multicolored .25 .25
a. Strip of 3, #2087-2089 .25 .25
2090 A532 5p multicolored .25 .25
2091 A531 5p multicolored .25 .25
2092 A532 5p multicolored .25 .25
a. Strip of 3, #2090-2092 .25 .25
2093 A532 8p multicolored .25 .25
2094 A531 8p multicolored .25 .25
2095 A532 8p multicolored .25 .25
a. Strip of 3, #2093-2095 .25 .25

Juan de Juni (1507-77), sculptor, (3p); Peter Paul Rubens (1577-1640), painter, (5p); Titian (1477-1576), painter, (8p).

Edelweiss in Pyrenees — A533

Designs: 5p, Fish and duck, wetlands. 7p, Forest, and forest destroyed by fire. 12p, Waves, oil rig, tanker and city. 20p, Sea gulls and seals, vert.

1978, Apr. 4 Photo. ***Perf. 13***

2096 A533 3p multicolored .25 .25
2097 A533 5p multicolored .25 .25
2098 A533 7p multicolored .25 .25
2099 A533 12p multicolored .25 .25
2100 A533 20p multicolored .25 .25
Nos. 2096-2100 (5) 1.25 1.25

Protection of the environment.

Palace of Charles V, Granada A534

Europa: 12p, The Lonja, Seville.

1978, May 2 Engr. ***Perf. 13***

2101 A534 5p dull grn & sl grn .25 .25
2102 A534 12p dull grn & car rose .25 .25

"España" — A535

1978, May 5 Photo. ***Perf. 12½***

2103 A535 12p multicolored .25 .25

Spain's admission to the Council of Europe.

Symbols and Emblems of Postal Service A536

1978, June 27 Engr. ***Perf. 13***

2104 A536 5p slate green .25 .25

Stamp Day.

Map of Las Palmas, 16th Century A537

5p, Hermitage of Columbus Church, vert. 12p, View of Las Palmas, 16th century.

1978, June 23 Photo.

2105 A537 3p multicolored .25 .25
2106 A537 5p multicolored .25 .25
2107 A537 12p multicolored .25 .25
Nos. 2105-2107 (3) .75 .75

Founding of Las Palmas, 500th anniv.

Pablo Picasso, Self-portrait A538

Picasso Paintings: 3p, Señora Canals. 8p, Jaime Sabartes. 10p, End of the Act (actress). 12p, Science and Charity (woman patient, doctor, nurse and child), horiz. 15p, "Las Meninas" (blue period), horiz. 20p, The Sparrows. 25p, The Painter and his Model, horiz.

1978, Sept. 29 Photo. ***Perf. 13***

2108 A538 3p gold & multi .25 .25
2109 A538 5p gold & multi .25 .25
2110 A538 8p gold & multi .25 .25
2111 A538 10p gold & multi .25 .25
2112 A538 12p gold & multi .25 .25
2113 A538 15p gold & multi .25 .25
2114 A538 20p gold & multi .25 .25
2115 A538 25p gold & multi .30 .25
Nos. 2108-2115 (8) 2.05 2.00

Pablo Picasso (1881-1973). Stamp Day 1978.

A 7p stamp like No. 2111 was not issued. Value, $29,000.

For other art types see A384, A397, A410, A431, A448, A473, A501, A522, A558 and footnote following No. 876.

José de San Martin A539

Design: 12p, Simon Bolivar.

1978, Oct. 12 Engr. ***Perf. 13***

2116 A539 7p sepia & car .25 .25
2117 A539 12p violet & car .25 .25

José de San Martin (1778-1850) and Simon Bolivar (1783-1830), South American liberators.

Flight into Egypt, Capital from St. Mary de Nieva A540

Christmas: 12p, Annunciation, capital from St. Mary de Nieva.

1978, Nov. 3 Photo. ***Perf. 13***

2118 A540 5p multicolored .25 .25
2119 A540 12p multicolored .25 .25

Mexican Calendar Stone A541

Designs (King Juan Carlos I, Queen Sofia and): No. 2121, Machu Picchu. No. 2122, Calchaqui jars from Tucuman and Angalgala.

1978

2120 A541 5p multicolored .25 .25
2121 A541 5p multicolored .25 .25
2122 A541 5p multicolored .25 .25
Nos. 2120-2122 (3) .75 .75

Royal visits to Mexico, Peru and Argentina.

Issued: #2120 (Mexico), Nov. 17; #2121 (Peru), Nov. 22; #2122 (Argentina), Nov. 26.

King Philip V — A542

Rulers of Spain: No. 2124, Louis I. 8p, Ferdinand VI. 10p, Carlos III. 12p, Carlos IV. 15p, Ferdinand VII. 20p, Isabella II. 25p, Alfonso XII. 50p, Alfonso XIII. 100p, Juan Carlos I.

1978, Nov. 22 Engr. ***Perf. 13***

2123 A542 5p dk blue & rose red .25 .25
2124 A542 5p olive & dull grn .25 .25
2125 A542 8p vio bl & red brn .25 .25
2126 A542 10p blue grn & blk .25 .25
2127 A542 12p brown & mar .25 .25
2128 A542 15p black & indigo .25 .25
2129 A542 20p olive & indigo .25 .25
2130 A542 25p ultra & vio brn .30 .25
2131 A542 50p vermilion & brn .55 .25
2132 A542 100p ultra & vio blk 1.10 .35
Nos. 2123-2132 (10) 3.70 2.60

Spanish Flag, Preamble to Constitution, Parliament — A543

1978, Dec. Photo. ***Perf. 13***

2133 A543 5p multicolored .25 .25

Proclamation of New Constitution.

Illuminated Pages from Bible and Codex — A544

1978, Dec. 27

2134 A544 5p multicolored .25 .25

Millennium of the consecration of the Basilica of Santa Maria de Ripoll.

Car and Drop of Oil — A545

Designs: 8p, Insulated house and thermometer. 10p, Hand pulling plug.

1979, Jan. 24 Photo. ***Perf. 13***

2135 A545 5p multicolored .25 .25
2136 A545 8p multicolored .25 .25
2137 A545 10p multicolored .25 .25
Nos. 2135-2137 (3) .75 .75

Energy conservation.

De La Salle, Students A546

1979, Feb. 14 Photo. ***Perf. 13***

2138 A546 5p multicolored .25 .25

Institute of Christian Brothers, founded by Jean-Baptiste de la Salle, centenary.

Jorge Manrique — A547

Portraits: 8p, Fernan Caballero (pen name of Cecilia Böhl de Faber). 10p, Francisco Villaespesa. 20p, Gregorio Marañon.

1979, Feb. 28 Engr.

2139 A547 5p green & brown .25 .25
2140 A547 8p dark red & blue .25 .25
2141 A547 10p brown & purple .25 .25
2142 A547 20p green & olive .25 .25
Nos. 2139-2142 (4) 1.00 1.00

Jorge Manrique, poet, 500th death anniversary; Fernan Caballero, Francisco Villaespesa, and Gregorio Marañon, writers, birth centenaries.

Running and Jumping A548

Sport for All: 8p, Children kicking ball and skipping rope, jogging and bicycling. 10p, Family jogging, and dog.

1979, Mar. 14 Photo. *Perf. 13*
2143 A548 5p multicolored .25 .25
2144 A548 8p multicolored .25 .25
2145 A548 10p multicolored .25 .25
Nos. 2143-2145 (3) .75 .75

Children in Library A549

1979, Apr. 27 Photo. *Perf. 13*
2146 A549 5p multicolored .25 .25

International Year of the Child.

Manuel Ysasi (1810-1855) Postal Reformer — A550

Europa: 5p, Mounted messenger and postilion, 1761 engraving, vert.

1979, Apr. 30 Engr.
2147 A550 5p brown & sepia .25 .25
2148 A550 12p red brn & sl grn .25 .25

Radar and Satellite A551

5p, Symbolic people and cables, vert.

1979, May 17 Photo. *Perf. 13*
2149 A551 5p multicolored .25 .25
2150 A551 8p multicolored .25 .25

World Telecommunications Day, May 17.

Bulgaria No. 1, Sofia Opera House, Housing Development — A552

1979, May 18
2151 A552 12p multicolored .25 .25

Philaserdica '79, International Philatelic Exhibition, Sofia, Bulgaria, May 18-27.

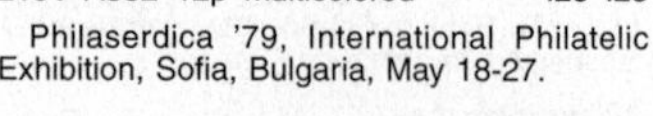

Tank, Jet and Destroyer A553

1979, May 25
2152 A553 5p multicolored .25 .25

Armed Forces Day.

Messenger Handing Letter to King — A554

1979, June 15 Litho. & Engr.
2153 A554 5p multicolored .25 .25

Stamp Day 1979.

Daroca Gate, Zaragoza — A555

Architecture: 8p, Gerona Cathedral. 10p, Interior, Carthusian Monastery Church, Granada. 20p, Portal, Palace of the Marques de Dos Aguas, Valencia.

1979, June 27 Engr.
2154 A555 5p vio bl & lilac brn .25 .25
2155 A555 8p dk blue & sepia .25 .25
2156 A555 10p black & green .25 .25
2157 A555 20p brown & sepia .25 .25
Nos. 2154-2157 (4) 1.00 1.00

Turkey Sponge A556

Fauna: 7p, Crayfish. 8p, Scorpion. 20p, Starfish. 25p, Sea anemone.

1979, July 11 Photo. *Perf. 13*
2158 A556 5p multicolored .25 .25
2159 A556 7p multicolored .25 .25
2160 A556 8p multicolored .25 .25
2161 A556 20p multicolored .25 .25
2162 A556 25p multicolored .30 .25
Nos. 2158-2162 (5) 1.30 1.25

Gen. Antonio Gutierrez and Battle A557

1979, Aug. Engr.
2163 A557 5p multicolored .25 .25

Naval defense of Tenerife, 18th century.

A558

Juan de Juanes Paintings: 8p, Immaculate Conception. 10p, Holy Family. 15p, Ecce Homo. 20p, St. Stephen in the Synagogue. 25p, The Last Supper, horiz. 50p, Adoration of the Mystic Lamb, horiz.

1979, Sept. 28 Photo. *Perf. 13x13½*
2164 A558 8p multicolored .25 .25
2165 A558 10p multicolored .25 .25
2166 A558 15p multicolored .25 .25
2167 A558 20p multicolored .25 .25
2168 A558 25p multicolored .30 .25
2169 A558 50p multicolored .55 .25
Nos. 2164-2169 (6) 1.85 1.50

For other art types see A384, A397, A410, A431, A448, A473, A501, A522, A538 and footnote following No. 876.

A559

Zaragoza Cathedral, Mother and Child statue.

1979, Oct. 3 Photo. *Perf. 13x13½*
2170 A559 5p multicolored .25 .25

8th Mariology and 15th International Marianist Congresses, Zaragoza, Oct. 3-12.

Felipe de Borbon, Hospital A560

1979, Oct. *Perf. 13½x13*
2171 A560 5p multicolored .25 .25

Hospital of the Child Jesus, centenary.

St. Bartholomew College, Bogota — A561

Hispanidad 79: 12p, University of St. Mark, Lima, coat of arms.

1979, Oct. 12 Engr. *Perf. 13*
2172 A561 7p multicolored .25 .25
2173 A561 12p multicolored .25 .25

Clasped Hands, Badge, Governor's Palace A562

Design: No. 2175, Statute book, vert.

Lithographed and Engraved

1979, Oct. 27 *Perf. 13*
2174 A562 8p multicolored .25 .25
2175 A562 8p multicolored .25 .25

Catalonian and Basque autonomy statute.

Type A54, Barcelona Coat of Arms A563

Photogravure and Engraved

1979, Nov. 6 *Perf. 13½x13*
2176 A563 5p multicolored .25 .25

Barcelona Philatelic Congress and Exhibition, 50th anniversary.

Nativity, Capital from St. Peter the Elder A564

Christmas 1979: 19p, Flight into Egypt, column from St. Peter the Elder, Huesca.

1979, Nov. 14 Photo.
2177 A564 8p multicolored .25 .25
2178 A564 19p multicolored .25 .25

Carlos I, Coat of Arms A565

Kings of the House of Austria (Hapsburg Dynasty): 20p, Philip II. 25p, Philip III. 50c, Philip IV. 100p, Carlos II.

1979, Nov. 22 Engr. *Perf. 13*
2179 A565 15p sl grn & dk bl .25 .25
2180 A565 20p dk blue & mag .25 .25
2181 A565 25p violet & yel bis .30 .25
2182 A565 50p brown & sl grn .55 .25
2183 A565 100p magenta & brn 1.10 .30
Nos. 2179-2183 (5) 2.45 1.30

2nd International Olive Oil Year — A566

1979, Dec. 4 Photo. *Perf. 13½x13*
2184 A566 8p multicolored .25 .25

King Juan Carlos I Type of 1976

1980-84 Photo. *Perf. 13*
2185 A497 13p dk red brn ('81) .25 .25
2186 A497 14p red orange ('82) .25 .25
2187 A497 16p sepia .30 .25
2188 A497 17p bluish gray ('84) .25 .25
2189 A497 19p orange .35 .25
2190 A497 30p dk green ('81) .40 .25
2191 A497 50p org ver ('81) .90 .25
2192 A497 60p blue ('81) .80 .25
2193 A497 75p brt yel grn ('81) 1.00 .30
2194 A497 85p gray ('81) 1.25 .45
Nos. 2185-2194 (10) 5.75 2.75

No. 2186 and 2187 also issued as coil with number on back of every fifth stamp.

Train and People A567

1980, Feb. 20 Engr. *Perf. 13½*
2200 A567 3p shown .25 .25
2201 A567 4p Bus .25 .25
2202 A567 5p Subway .25 .25
Nos. 2200-2202 (3) .75 .75

Public transportation.

Steel Export A568

1980, Mar. 15 Photo. *Perf. 13½x13*
2203 A568 5p shown .25 .25
2204 A568 8p Ships .25 .25
2205 A568 13p Shoes .25 .25
2206 A568 19p Machinery .25 .25
2207 A568 25p Technology .30 .25
Nos. 2203-2207 (5) 1.30 1.25

Federico Garcia Lorca (1899-1936) — A569

Europa: 19p, José Ortega y Gasset (1883-1955), philosopher and statesman.

1980, Apr. 28 Engr. *Perf. 13½*
2208 A569 8p violet & ol grn .25 .25
2209 A569 19p brown & dk grn .25 .25

Armed Forces Day A570

1980, May 24 Photo. *Perf. 13½x13*
2210 A570 8p multicolored .25 .25

Soccer Players A571

1980, May 23
2211 A571 8p shown .25 .25
2212 A571 19p Soccer ball, flags .25 .25

World Soccer Cup 1982.

Bourbon Arms, Ministry of Finance A572

1980, June 9 Engr. *Perf. 13½*
2213 A572 8p dark brown .25 .25

Public Finances in Bourbon Spain Exhibition.

Helen Keller, Sign Language A573

1980, June 27
2214 A573 19p dk yel grn & rose lake .25 .25

Helen Keller (1880-1968), deaf mute writer and lecturer.

Mounted Postman, 12th Century Panel, Barcelona — A574

Lithographed and Engraved

1980, June 28 *Perf. 13x12½*
2215 A574 8p multicolored .25 .25

Stamp Day.

King Alfonso and Count of Maceda at 1930 National Exhibition A575

1980, July 1 Photo. *Perf. 13½*
2216 A575 8p multicolored .25 .25

1st Natl. Stamp Exhibition, Barcelona, 50th anniv.

A576

Altar of the Virgin, La Palma Cathedral.

1980, July 12 Engr. *Perf. 13*
2217 A576 8p black & brown .25 .25

Appearance of the Virgin of the Snow at La Palma, 300th anniversary.

A577

1980, Aug. 9 Engr. *Perf. 13*
2218 A577 100p slate & sepia 1.10 .25

Ramon Perez de Ayala (1881-1962), novelist and diplomat.

Souvenir Sheet

La Atlantida Ruins, Mexican Bonampak Musicians — A578

Designs: b, Sun Gate, Tiahuanaco; Roman arch, Medinaceli. c, Alonso de Ercilla, Garcilaso de la Vega; title pages from La Arauca and Commentario Reales. d, Virgin of Quito, Virgin of Seafarers.

1980, Oct. 3 Engr. *Perf. 13*
2219 A578 Sheet of 4 + 2 labels 2.25 2.25
a. 25p multicolored .30 .30
b. 25p multicolored .30 .30
c. 50p multicolored .55 .45
d. 100p multicolored 1.10 .85

ESPAMER '80 Stamp Exhib., Madrid, Oct. 3-12.

400th Anniversary of Buenos Aires — A579

1980, Oct. 24
2220 A579 19p multicolored .25 .25

Miniature Sheet

The Creation, Tapestry, Gerona Cathedral — A580

1980, Nov. Litho. *Perf. 13½x13*
2221 A580 Sheet of 6 2.50 2.00
a.-c. 25p, any single .25 .25
d.-f. 50p, any single .55 .25

Conference Building, Flags of Participants A581

1980, Nov. 11 Photo. *Perf. 13½*
2222 A581 22p multicolored .25 .25

Holy Family Church of Santa Maria, Cuina — A582

Christmas 1980, 22p, Adoration of the Kings, portal, Church of Santa Maria, Cuina, horiz.

1980, Nov. 12
2223 A582 10p multicolored .25 .25
2224 A582 22p multicolored .25 .25

Pedro Vives and His Airplane A583

Aviation pioneers: 10p, Benito Loygorri. 15p, Alfonso De Orleans. 22p, Alfredo Kindelan.

1980, Dec. 10
2225 A583 5p shown .25 .25
2226 A583 10p multicolored .25 .25
2227 A583 15p multicolored .25 .25
2228 A583 22p multicolored .25 .25
Nos. 2225-2228 (4) 1.00 1.00

Winter University Games A584

1981, Mar. 4 *Perf. 13½x13*
2229 A584 30p multicolored .35 .25

Picasso's Birth Centenary Emblem, by Joan Miro — A585

1981, Mar. 27 *Perf. 13*
2230 A585 100p multicolored 1.00 .25

Pablo Picasso (1881-1973).

Galician Autonomy — A586

1981, Mar. 27 Photo. *Perf. 13*
2231 A586 12p multicolored .25 .25

Homage to the Press A587

1981, Apr. 8 Photo. *Perf. 13½x13*
2232 A587 12p multicolored .25 .25

International Year of the Disabled — A588

1981, Apr. 29 Litho.
2233 A588 30p multicolored .35 .25

Soccer Players A589

12p, Soccer players, diff., vert.

1981, May 2 Photo.
2234 A589 12p multicolored .25 .25
2235 A589 30p shown .35 .25

1982 World Cup Soccer.

Europa Issue

La Jota Folkdance A590

30p, Virgin of Rocio procession.

1981, May 4 Engr.
2236 A590 12p shown .25 .25
2237 A590 30p multicolored .35 .25

Armed Forces Day — A591

1981, May 29 Photo. *Perf. 13x13½*
2238 A591 12p multicolored .25 .25

Gabriel Miro (1879-1930), Writer — A592

Famous Men: 12p, Francisco de Quevedo (1580-1645), writer. 30p, St. Benedict (480-543), patron saint of Europe.

1981, June 17 Engr.
2239 A592 6p purple & dk grn .25 .25
2240 A592 12p brown & purple .25 .25
2241 A592 30p dk green & brown .35 .25
Nos. 2239-2241 (3) .85 .75

Mail Messenger, 14th Cent., Woodcut A593

Photogravure and Engraved
1981, June 19 *Perf. 12½x13*
2242 A593 12p multicolored .25 .25

Stamp Day.

Map of Balearic Islands, Diego Homem's Atlas, 1563 — A594

12p, Canary Islds., Prunes map, 1563.

1981, July 8 Photo. *Perf. 13x12½*
2243 A594 7p shown .25 .25
2244 A594 12p multicolored .25 .25

Kings Alfonso XII and Juan Carlos, Advocates Arms A595

1981, July 27 Engr. *Perf. 13½x13*
2245 A595 50p multicolored .55 .25

Chamber of Advocates of State (Public Prosecutor) centenary.

King Sancius VI of Navarre with City Charter, 12th Cent. Miniature A596

1981, Aug. 5 Photo. *Perf. 12½x13*
2246 A596 12p multicolored .25 .25

Vitoria, 800th anniv.

Exports A597

1981, Sept. 30 Photo. *Perf. 13½x13*
2247 A597 6p Fruit .25 .25
2248 A597 12p Wine .25 .25
2249 A597 30p Vehicles .35 .25
Nos. 2247-2249 (3) .85 .75

Congress Palace, Buenos Aires A598

1981, Oct. 12 Engr. *Perf. 13½x13*
2250 A598 12p dk bl & car rose .25 .25

ESPAMER '81 Intl. Stamp Exhibition, Buenos Aires, Nov. 13-22.

World Food Day A599

1981, Oct. 16
2251 A599 30p multicolored .35 .25

Souvenir Sheet

Guernica, by Pablo Picasso (1881-1973) — A600

1981, Oct. 25 Photo.
2252 A600 200p multicolored 2.25 2.25

Control number comes in two types.

A601

Christmas 1981: 12p, Adoration of the Kings, Cervera de Pisuerga, Palencia. 30p, Nativity, Paredes de Nava.

1981, Nov. 18 Litho. *Perf. 13*
2253 A601 12p shown .25 .25
2254 A601 30p multicolored .35 .25

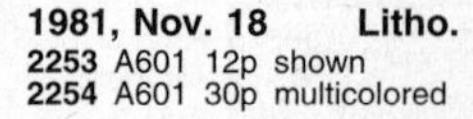

A602

King Juan Carlos I.

1981, Oct. 21 Engr. *Perf. 13x12½*
2268 A602 100p brown 1.25 .25
2269 A602 200p dark green 2.60 .25
2270 A602 500p dark blue 6.25 .55
Nos. 2268-2270 (3) 10.10 1.05

Postal Museum, Madrid A603

1981, Nov. 30 Engr. *Perf. 13*
2273 A603 7p Telegrapher .25 .25
2274 A603 12p Coach .25 .25

Souvenir Sheet
2275 Sheet of 4 1.90 1.90
c. A603 50p Emblem .55 .50
d. A603 100p Cap, posthorn, pouch 1.10 1.00

No. 2275 also contains Nos. 2273, 2274.

Royal Mint Building, Seville A604

1981, Dec. 4 Engr. *Perf. 13*
2276 A604 12p black & brown .25 .25

Spanish Administration of the Bourbons in the Indies.

A605

12p, Iparraguirre (1820-81). 30p, Juan Ramon Jimenez (1881-1958), writer. 50p, Pedro Calderon (1600-81), playwright.

1981-82
2277 A605 12p black & dk bl .25 .25
2278 A605 30p dk bl & dk grn .35 .25
2279 A605 50p black & violet .55 .25
Nos. 2277-2279 (3) 1.15 .75

Issued: 12p, 12/16; 30p, 50p, 3/10/82.

A606

1982, Feb. 24 Photo.
2280 A606 14p Poster by Joan Miro .25 .25
2281 A606 33p Cup, emblem .40 .25

Espana '82 World Cup Soccer.

Andres Bello (1782-1865), Writer — A607

1982, Mar. 10 Engr.
2282 A607 30p grn & dk grn .35 .25

St. John of Compostelo — A608

1982, Mar. 31 Photo. *Perf. 13*
2283 A608 14p multicolored .25 .25

Holy Year of Compostelo.

A609-A610

Operetta composers and scenes from their works: #2284, Manuel Fernandez Caballero (1835-1906). #2285, Gigantes and Cabezudos. #2286, Amadeo Vives Roig (1871-1932). #2287, Dona Francisquita. #2288, Tomas Breton Hernandez (1850-1923). #2289, Verbena of Paloma.

Lithographed and Engraved
1982, Apr. 28 *Perf. 13*
2284 A609 3p multicolored .25 .25
2285 A610 3p multicolored .25 .25
a. Pair, #2284-2285 .25 .25
2286 A609 6p multicolored .25 .25
2287 A610 6p multicolored .25 .25
a. Pair, #2284-2285 .25 .25
2288 A609 8p multicolored .25 .25
2289 A610 8p multicolored .25 .25
a. Pair, #2284-2285 .25 .25

See Nos. 2319-2324, 2378-2383.

Europa 1982 — A611

14p, Unification, 1512. 33p, Discovery of New World, 1492.

1982, May 3 Engr. *Perf. 12½*
2290 A611 14p multicolored .25 .25
2291 A611 33p multicolored .40 .25

Armed Forces Day — A612

1982, May 28 Photo. *Perf. 13*
2292 A612 14p multicolored .25 .25

1982 World Cup A613

Designs: Soccer players.

1982, June 13 ***Perf. 13***

2293 A613 14p multicolored .25 .25
2294 A613 33p multicolored .40 .25

Souvenir Sheets

2295 Sheets of 4, #2293-2294, 9p, 100p, each 1.75 1.75
a. A613 9p Captains' handshake .25 .25
b. A613 100p Player holding cup 1.10 1.10

#2295 has two types of margin, each showing 7 arms of the 14 host cities. One sheet has 3 blue coats of arms, the other has 2.

Stamp Day — A614

1982, July 16 **Litho.** ***Perf. 12½***

2296 A614 14p Map, postal code .25 .25

Organ Transplants A615

1982, July 28 **Photo.** ***Perf. 13***

2297 A615 14p Symbolic organs .25 .25

Storks and Express Train — A616

Locomotive, 1850 — A617

33p, Santa Fe locomotive.

Perf. 12½, 13 (A617)

1982, Sept. 27 **Photo.**

2298 A616 9p shown .25 .25
2299 A617 14p shown .25 .25
2300 A617 33p multicolored .40 .25
Nos. 2298-2300 (3) .90 .75

23rd Intl. Railways Congress, Malaga.

ESPAMER '82 Intl. Stamp Exhibition, San Juan, Oct. 12-17 A618

1982, Oct. 12 **Engr.** ***Perf. 13½x13***

2301 A618 33p dk blue & pur .40 .25

St. Teresa of Avila (1515-1582) — A619

33p, Statue by Gregorio Hernandez.

1982, Oct. 15

2302 A619 33p multicolored .40 .25

Visit of Pope John Paul II, Oct. 31-Nov. 9 — A620

1982, Oct. 31 **Engr.** ***Perf. 12½***

2303 A620 14p multicolored .25 .25

Water Wheel, Alcantarilla A621

Landscapes and Monuments: 6p, Bank of Spain, 19th cent., horiz. 9p, Crucifixion. 14p, St. Martin's Tower, Teruel. 33p, St. Andrew's Gate, Zamora.

1982, Nov. 5 ***Perf. 13x12½, 12½x13***

2304 A621 4p gray & dk blue .25 .25
2305 A621 6p dk blue & gray .25 .25
2306 A621 9p brt blue & vio .25 .25
2307 A621 14p brt blue & vio .25 .25
2308 A621 33p claret & brown .40 .25
Nos. 2304-2308 (5) 1.40 1.25

Christmas 1982 A622

14p, Nativity, wood carving, by Gil de Siloe. 33p, Flight into Egypt.

1982, Nov. 17 **Photo.** ***Perf. 13½***

2309 A622 14p multicolored .25 .25
2310 A622 33p multicolored .40 .25

Pablo Gargallo, Sculptor, Birth Centenary A623

1982, Dec. 9 **Engr.** ***Perf. 13***

2311 A623 14p blue & dk grn .25 .25

Salesian Fathers in Spain, Centenary A624

1982, Dec. 16 **Photo.** ***Perf. 12½x13***

2312 A624 14p multicolored .25 .25

Arms of King Juan Carlos I A625

1983, Feb. 9 **Photo.** ***Perf. 12½***

2313 A625 14p multicolored .25 .25

Andalusia Autonomy Statute A626

1983 **Litho.** ***Perf. 13½***

2314 A626 14p shown .25 .25
2315 A626 14p Cantabria .25 .25

Issued: #2314, Feb. 28; #2315, Mar. 15.

State Security Forces A627

9p, Natl. Police Force. 14p, Civil Guard. 33p, Superior Police Corps.

1983, Mar. 23 **Photo.**

2316 A627 9p multicolored .25 .25
2317 A627 14p multicolored .25 .25
2318 A627 33p multicolored .40 .25

Operetta Type of 1982

Designs: #2319, Scene from La Parranda. Francisco Alonso Lopez (1887-1948). #2320, Francisco Alonso Lopez (1887-1948). #2321, Jacinto Guerrero y Torres (1895-1951). #2322, Scene from La Rosa del Azafran. #2323, Jesus de Guridi Bidaola (1886-1961). #2324, Scene from El Caserio.

Lithographed and Engraved

1983, Apr. 22 ***Perf. 13***

2319 4p multicolored .25 .25
2320 4p multicolored .25 .25
a. A609 Pair, #2319-2320 .25 .25
2321 6p multicolored .25 .25
2322 6p multicolored .25 .25
a. A609 Pair, #2321-2322 .25 .25
2323 9p multicolored .25 .25
2324 9p multicolored .25 .25
a. A609 Pair, #2323-2324 .35 .35

Europa 1983 — A628

Designs: 16p, Scene from Don Quixote, by Miguel Cervantes. 38p, L. Torres Quevaedo's Niagara Spanish aerocar.

1983, May 5 **Engr.** ***Perf. 13x12½***

Granite Paper

2325 A628 16p dk grn & brn red .25 .25
2326 A628 38p brown .45 .25

Francisco Salzillo Alvarez (1707-83), Painter — A629

Designs: 38p, Antonio Soler Ramos (1729-1783), composer. 50p, Joaquin Turina Perez (1882-1949), composer. 100p, St. Isidro Labrador (1082-1170), patron saint of Madrid.

1983, May 14 ***Perf. 13***

2327 A629 16p purple & dk grn .25 .25
2328 A629 38p blue & brown .45 .25
2329 A629 50p bl grn & dk brn .55 .25
2330 A629 100p red brn & pur 1.10 .25
Nos. 2327-2330 (4) 2.35 1.00

World Communications Year — A630

1983, May 17 **Photo.** ***Perf. 13***

2331 A630 38p multicolored .45 .25

Rioja Autonomous Region — A631

Lithographed and Engraved

1983, May 25 ***Perf. 13***

2332 A631 16p multicolored .25 .25

Armed Forces Day — A632

1983, May 26 **Photo.**

2333 A632 16p multicolored .25 .25

Intl. Canine Exhibition, Madrid, June 1984 A633

Lithographed and Engraved

1983, June 8 ***Perf. 13½***

2334 A633 10p Pointer .25 .25
2335 A633 16p Mastiff .25 .25
2336 A633 26p Iberian hound .35 .25
2337 A633 38p Navarro pointer .50 .25
Nos. 2334-2337 (4) 1.35 1.00

Discovery of Tungsten Bicentenary — A634

Scouting Year A635

400th Anniv. of University of Zaragoza A636

1983, June 22 **Photo.** ***Perf. 13***

2338 A634 16p Elhuyar brothers .25 .25
2339 A635 38p multicolored .45 .25
2340 A636 50p multicolored .60 .25
Nos. 2338-2340 (3) 1.30 .75

Murcia Autonomous Region — A637

Photogravure and Engraved

1983, July 8 ***Perf. 13½***

2341 A637 16p Arms .25 .25

Asturias Autonomous Region — A638

14p, Victory Cross, Covadonga Basilica.

Lithographed and Engraved

1983, Sept. 8 ***Perf. 13***

2342 A638 14p multicolored .25 .25

Stamp Day — A640

Intl. Institute of Statistics, 44th Congress, Madrid, Sept. 12-22 A639

1983, Sept. 12 **Photo.** ***Perf. 13***

2343 A639 38p Institute building .45 .25

Lithographed and Engraved

1983, Oct. 8 ***Perf. 13x12½***

2344 A640 16p Roman mail cart .35 .30

No. 2344 se-tenant with label publicizing ESPANA '84 Philatelic Exhibition, April 27-May 6, 1984.

Valencia Autonomy Statute, 1st Anniv. A641

1983, Oct. 10 ***Perf. 13***

2345 A641 16p multicolored .25 .25

View of Seville, 16th cent. — A642

1983, Oct. 12 **Engr.** ***Perf. 12½x13***

2346 A642 38p multicolored .45 .25

Spanish-American trade in 17th century.

Stained-glass Windows A643

Designs: 10p King, Leon Cathedral. 16p, Epiphany, Gerona Cathedral. 38p, Apostle Santiago, Royal Hospital Chapel, Santiago.

Lithographed and Engraved

1983, Oct. 28 ***Perf. 12½x13***

2347 A643 10p multicolored .25 .25
2348 A643 16p multicolored .25 .25
2349 A643 38p multicolored .45 .25
Nos. 2347-2349 (3) .95 .75

Church at Llivia, Gerona — A644

Designs: 6p, Temple, Santa Maria del Mar, Barcelona. 16p, Cathedral, Ceuta. 38p, Gate of the Santiago Bridge, Melilla. 50p, Charity Hospital, Seville.

1983, Nov. 9 **Engr.** ***Perf. 13x12½***

2350 A644 3p dk bl gray & grn .25 .25
2351 A644 6p dark blue gray .25 .25
2352 A644 16p red brn & dull vio .25 .25
2353 A644 38p bis brn & rose car .45 .25
2354 A644 50p brown & org red .55 .25
Nos. 2350-2354 (5) 1.75 1.25

Christmas 1983 — A645

16p, The Nativity, Tortosa. 38p, The Adoration, Vich.

1983, Nov. 23 **Photo.** ***Perf. 13x13½***

2355 A645 16p multicolored .25 .25
2356 A645 38p multicolored .45 .25

Indalecio Prieto (1883-1962), Patriot — A646

1983, Dec. 14 **Engr.** ***Perf. 13***

2357 A646 16p red brn & blk .25 .25

Industrial Accident Prevention A647

7p, Construction worker. 10p, Fire. 16p, Electrical plug, pliers.

1984, Jan. 25 **Photo.** ***Perf. 13½***

2358 A647 7p multicolored .25 .25
2359 A647 10p multicolored .25 .25
2360 A647 16p multicolored .25 .25
Nos. 2358-2360 (3) .75 .75

Extremadura Statute of Autonomy, First Anniv. — A648

Lithographed and Engraved

1984, Feb. 25 ***Perf. 13***

2361 A648 16p multicolored .25 .25

1500th Anniv. of City of Burgos A649

1984, Mar. 1 **Engr.**

2362 A649 16p multicolored .25 .25

Carnivals A650

No. 2363, Santa Cruz de Tenerife. No. 2364, Valencia Fallas.

1984 **Photo.** ***Perf. 13½x13***

2363 A650 16p multicolored .25 .25
2364 A650 16p multicolored .25 .25

Issued: #2363, Mar. 5; #2364, Mar. 16.

Man and the Biosphere A651

38p, da Vinci's Study of Man.

1984, Apr. 11

2365 A651 38p multicolored .45 .25

Aragon Statute of Autonomy, 2nd Anniv. A652

Lithographed and Engraved

1984, Apr. 23 ***Perf. 13x13½***

2366 A652 16p Map .25 .25

Souvenir Sheet

Juan Carlos — A653

Espana '84 (Spanish Royal Family): b, Sofia of Greece. c, Cristina de Borbon. d, Prince of Asturias Felipe de Borbon. e, Elene de Borbon.

1984, Apr. 27 ***Perf. 12½x13***

2367 A653 Sheet of 5 3.25 3.25
a.-e. 38p, any single .65 .65

Congress Emblem — A654

1984, May 3 **Engr.** ***Perf. 13x13½***

2368 A654 38p purple & red .45 .25

World Philatelic Federation, 53rd Congress, Madrid, May 7-9.

Europa (1959-84) A655

1984, May 5

2369 A655 16p orange .25 .25
2370 A655 38p dark blue .45 .25

Armed Forces Day A656

Design: 17p, Monument to Hunters Regiment of Caceres, by Mariano Benlliure.

1984, May 19 Photo. ***Perf. 13½x13***
2371 A656 17p multicolored .25 .25

Canary Islds. Statute of Autonomy — A657

Lithographed and Engraved
1984, May 29 ***Perf. 13***
2372 A657 16p Arms, map .25 .25

Castilla-La Mancha Statute of Autonomy — A658

1984, May 31 ***Perf. 13***
2373 A658 17p Arms .25 .25

King Alfonso X (1252-84) A659

Design: 38p, Ignacio Barroquer (1884-1965), ophthalmologist

1984, June 20 Engr. ***Perf. 13***
2374 A659 16p multicolored .25 .25
2375 A659 38p multicolored .45 .25

Balearic Islands Statute of Autonomy — A660

1984, June 29 Litho. & Engr.
2376 A660 17p multicolored .25 .25

Feast of San Fermin of Pamplona A661

1984, July 5 Photo.
2377 A661 17p Bull runners .25 .25

Operetta Type of 1982

#2378, El Nino Judio. #2379, Pablo Luna (1880-1942). #2380, Ruperto Chapi (1851-1909). #2381, La Revoltosa. #2382, La Reina Mora. #2383, Jose Serrano (1873-1941).

Lithographed and Engraved
1984, July 20 ***Perf. 13***

2378	6p multicolored		.25	.25
2379	6p multicolored		.25	.25
a.	A609	Pair, #2378-2379	.25	.25
2380	7p multicolored		.25	.25
2381	7p multicolored		.25	.25
a.	A609	Pair, #2380-2381	.25	.25
2382	10p multicolored		.25	.25
2383	10p multicolored		.25	.25
a.	A609	Pair, #2382-2383	.30	.30

1984 Summer Olympics A662

Greek or Roman sculptures.

1984, July 27 Photo.

2384	A662	1p	Chariot race	.25	.25
2385	A662	2p	Diving, vert.	.25	.25
2386	A662	5p	Wrestling	.25	.25
2387	A662	8p	Discus, vert.	.25	.25
			Nos. 2384-2387 (4)	1.00	1.00

Navarra Statute of Autonomy A663

Lithographed and Engraved
1984, Aug. 16 ***Perf. 13***
2388 A663 17p multicolored .25 .25

Intl. Bicycling Championship, Barcelona, Aug. 27-Sept. 2 — A664

1984, Aug. 27 Photo.
2389 A664 17p multicolored .25 .25

Castilla and Leon Statute of Autonomy A665

1984, Sept. 5 Litho. & Engr.
2390 A665 17p multicolored .25 .25

Jerez Vintage Feast — A666

17p, Women picking grapes.

1984, Sept. 20 Photo. ***Perf. 13***
2391 A666 17p multicolored .25 .25

Journey to the Holy Land by Sister Egeria, 1600th Anniv. — A667

1984, Sept. 26
2392 A667 40p Map, Sister Egeria .45 .25

Stamp Day — A668

1984, Oct. 5 Litho. & Engr.
2393 A668 17p Arab postrider .25 .25

Father Junipero Serra (1713-84), Mission Founder in California A669

1984, Oct. 12 Engr. ***Perf. 13***
2394 A669 40p Map, Serra, mission .45 .25

Christmas 1984 A670

17p, Nativity. 40p, Adoration of the Kings, vert.

1984, Nov. 21 Photo.
2395 A670 17p multicolored .25 .25
2396 A670 40p multicolored .45 .25

Madrid Autonomy Statue A671

1984, Nov. 28 Litho. & Engr.
2397 A671 17p Arms, buildings .25 .25

Andean Pact, 15th Anniv. A672

Condor, Flags of Bolivia, Colombia, Ecuador, Peru and Venezuela.

1985, Jan. 16 Photo. ***Perf. 13***
2398 A672 17p multicolored .25 .25

The Virgin of Louvain, by Jan Gossaert (c. 1478-1536) A673

1985, Jan. 21 ***Perf. 13½***
2399 A673 40p multicolored .45 .25

EUROPALIA '85. See Belgium No. 1185.

Santa Cruz College, Valladolid University, 500th Anniv. — A674

1985, Feb. 20 Litho. & Engr.
2400 A674 17p Main gateway .25 .25

OLYMPHILEX '85, Lausanne, Switz. — A675

1985, Mar. 18 Photo.
2401 A675 40p multicolored .45 .25

ESPAMER '85, Cuba A676

1985, Mar. 20 Engr.
2402 A676 40p Cathedral, Havana .45 .25

Fairs A677

No. 2403, Seville. No. 2404, Alcoy. No. 2405, Arriondas-Ribadesella. No. 2406, Toledo, vert.

Perf. 13½, 13½x14 (#2405)
1985 Photo.

2403	A677	17p	multicolored	.25	.25
2404	A677	17p	multicolored	.25	.25
2405	A677	17p	multicolored	.25	.25
2406	A677	18p	multicolored	.25	.25
			Nos. 2403-2406 (4)	1.00	1.00

Issued: #2403, Apr. 16; #2404, Apr. 22; #2405, Aug. 2; #2406, June 6.

Intl. Youth Year — A678

1985, Apr. 17 Engr. ***Perf. 13½***
2407 A678 17p blk, hn brn & dk grn .25 .25

Europa '85 A680

Designs: 18p, Antonio de Cabezon (1510-1566), organist and composer, court Musician to Felipe II. 45p, Natl. Youth Orchestra.

1985, May 3 **Engr.**

2408 A680 18p dk bl, dk red & blk, *buff* .25 .25
2409 A680 45p ol grn, dk red & blk, *buff* .45 .25

Armed Forces Day A681

1985, May 24 **Photo.**

2410 A681 18p multicolored .25 .25

Natl. Flag Bicent. — A682

#2411, Arms of King Carlos III, text of 1785 Decree, sailing ship Santisima Trinidad. #2412, Natl. arms, Article No. 4 from 1978 Constitution, lion ornament from Chamber of Deputies Building.

Lithographed and Engraved

1985, May 28 ***Perf. 13x13½***

2411 18p multicolored .25 .25
2412 18p multicolored .25 .25
a. A682 Pair, #2411-2412 .50 .45

Intl. Environment Day — A683

1985, June 5 **Photo.**

2413 A683 17p multicolored .25 .25

Juan Carlos — A684

1985-92 **Photo.** ***Perf. 14***

No.	Type	Value	Color	Unused	Used
2414	A684	10c	indigo	.25	.25
2415	A684	50c	lt blue green	.25	.25
2416	A684	1p	brt blue	.25	.25
2417	A684	2p	dark green	.25	.25
2418	A684	3p	chestnut brn	.25	.25
2419	A684	4p	olive green	.25	.25
2420	A684	5p	brt rose lilac	.25	.25
2421	A684	6p	brown black	.25	.25
2422	A684	7p	brt violet	.25	.25
2423	A684	7p	apple grn	.25	.25
2424	A684	8p	gray black	.25	.25
2425	A684	10p	lake	.25	.25
2426	A684	12p	red	.25	.25
2427	A684	13p	Prus blue	.25	.25
2428	A684	15p	emerald	.25	.25
2429	A684	17p	yellow bis	.25	.25
2430	A684	18p	brt grnsh bl	.25	.25
2431	A684	19p	violet brn	.25	.25
a.			Booklet pane of 6	1.50	
2432	A684	20p	brt pink	.25	.25
2433	A684	25p	olive green	.30	.25
2434	A684	27p	deep rose lil	.35	.25
2435	A684	30p	ultra	.35	.25
2436	A684	45p	brt green	.50	.25
2437	A684	50p	violet blue	.55	.25
2438	A684	55p	black brown	.60	.25
2439	A684	60p	dark orange	.65	.25
2440	A684	75p	deep rose lil	.80	.30
			Nos. 2414-2440 (27)	8.85	6.80

Issued: 1p, 5p, 8p, 12p, 18p, 45p, 6/12; #2422, 17p, 7/16; #2423, 1/86; 2p, 3p, 4p, 10p, 4/3/86; 19p, 9/27/86; 6p, 20p, 30p, 1/26/87; 50p, 60p, 75p, 4/24/89; 10c, 50c, 13p, 15p, 5/16/89; 25p, 55p, 12/14/90; 27p, 2/92.

Astrophysical Observatory Opening, La Palma, Canary Islands — A685

1985, June 25 **Photo.** ***Perf. 14***

2441 A685 45p multicolored .50 .25

European Music Year — A686

Designs: 12p, Ataulfo Argenta, conductor. 17p, Tomas Luis de Victoria, composer. 45p, Fernando Sor, composer.

Litho. & Engr.

1985, June 26 ***Perf. 13***

2442 A686 12p multicolored .25 .25
2443 A686 17p multicolored .25 .25
2444 A686 45p multicolored .50 .25
Nos. 2442-2444 (3) 1.00 .75

Bernal Diaz del Castillo (1492-1585), Historian — A687

Famous men: 12p, Esteban Terradas (1883-1950), mathematician. 17p, Vicente Aleixandre (1898-1984), 1977 Nobel laureate in literature. 45p, Leon Felipe Camino (1884-1968), poet.

1985, July 24 **Engr.** ***Perf. 13½***

2445 A687 7p dk red, blk & dk grn, *buff* .25 .25
2446 A687 12p brt ver, dk bl & blk, *buff* .25 .25
2447 A687 17p blk, dk grn & dk red, *buff* .25 .25
2448 A687 45p bis, blk & dk grn, *buff* .55 .25
Nos. 2445-2448 (4) 1.30 1.00

Monastic Mail Delivery, 1122 — A688

Lithographed and Engraved

1985, Sept. 27 ***Perf. 13***

2449 A688 17p multicolored .25 .25

Stamp Day 1985.

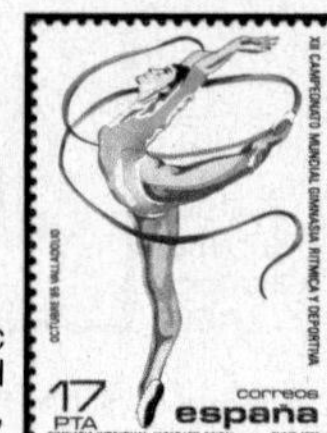

12th Rhythmic Gymnastics World Championships, Valladolid — A689

1985, Oct. 9 **Photo.** ***Perf. 13x13½***

2450 A689 17p Ribbon exercise .25 .25
2451 A689 45p Hoop exercise .50 .25

Souvenir Sheet

Prado Museum, La Alcachofa Fountain — A690

Lithographed and Engraved

1985, Oct. 18 ***Perf. 13***

2452 A690 17p multicolored .50 .50

EXFILNA '85, Madrid, Oct. 18-27.

Virgin and Child, Seville Cathedral A691

Stained glass windows: 12p, Monk, by Peter Boniface, Toledo Cathedral. 17p, King Henry II of Castile, Alcazar of Segovia.

1985, Oct. 24 ***Perf. 12½x13***

2453 A691 7p multicolored .25 .25
2454 A691 12p multicolored .25 .25
2455 A691 17p multicolored .25 .25
Nos. 2453-2455 (3) .75 .75

Christmas 1985 A692

14th-15th century paintings in the Episcopal Museum, Vich: 17p, Nativity, Guimera Altarpiece retable, 14th cent., by Ramon de Mur. 45p, Epiphany, from an embroidered frontal, 15th cent.

1985, Nov. 27 **Photo.** ***Perf. 13½***

2456 A692 17p multicolored .25 .25
2457 A692 45p multicolored .50 .25

Birds — A693

6p, Sylvia cantillans. 7p, Monticola saxatilis. 12p, Sturnus unicolor. 17p, Panurus biarmicus.

1985, Dec. 4 **Litho. & Engr.**

2458 A693 6p multicolored .25 .25
2459 A693 7p multicolored .25 .25
2460 A693 12p multicolored .25 .25
2461 A693 17p multicolored .35 .25
Nos. 2458-2461 (4) 1.10 1.00

Wildlife conservation.

Count of Penaflorida (1729-1785) — A694

1985, Dec. 11 **Engr.** ***Perf. 13½***

2462 A694 17p dark blue .25 .25

Francisco Javier de Munibe e Idiaquez, founded Natl. Economic Society of Friends in 1765.

Government Palace, Madrid, and Accession Agreement Text — A695

17p, Map and flags of EEC countries. 30p, Hall of Columns, Royal Palace. 45p, Member flags.

1986, Jan 7. **Litho.** ***Perf. 13½x13***

2463 A695 7p multicolored .25 .25
2464 A695 17p multicolored .25 .25
2465 A695 30p multicolored .35 .25
2466 A695 45p multicolored .60 .25
a. Bklt. pane of 4, #2463-2466 3.25
Nos. 2463-2466 (4) 1.45 1.00

Admission of Spain and Portugal to European Economic Community. See Portugal Nos. 1661-1662.

Tourism — A696

Historic sites: 12p, Inner courtyard, La Lupiana Monastery, Guadalajara. 35p, Balcony of Europe, Nerja.

1986, Jan. 20 **Engr.** ***Perf. 13x12½***

2467 A696 12p dk rose, brn & gray brn .25 .25
2468 A696 35p brt blue & sep .45 .25

2nd World Conference on Merino Sheep — A697

1986, Jan. 27 **Photo.** ***Perf. 13½***

2469 A697 45p multicolored .50 .25

Masquerade, 19th Cent., by F. Hohenleiter — A698

1986, Feb. 5
2470 A698 17p multicolored .25 .25

Cadiz Carnival.

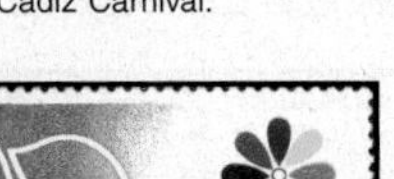

Intl. Peace Year — A699

Lithographed and Engraved

1986, Feb. 12 ***Perf. 13x13½***
2471 A699 45p multicolored .50 .25

Festival of Religious Music, Cuenca A700

1986, Mar. 26 Photo. ***Perf. 13½***
2472 A700 17p multicolored .25 .25

Chamber of Commerce, Cent. — A701

Painting detail: Swearing in of the Regent, Queen Maria Christina, Before the Spanish Parliament, 1886, by Francisco Jover and Joaquin Sorolla y Bastida, Senate Palace, Madrid.

1986, Apr. 9 Engr. ***Perf. 13½***
2473 A701 17p sage grn & grnsh blk .25 .25

Emigration of Spaniards — A702

1986, Apr. 22 Photo.
2474 A702 45p multicolored .50 .25

Europa 1986 — A703

Lithographed and Engraved

1986, May 5 ***Perf. 13x13½***
2475 A703 17p Youth feeding birds .25 .25
2476 A703 45p Girl watering tree .55 .25

Our Lady of the Dew Festival, Almonte A704

1986, May 14 Photo. ***Perf. 13½x13***
2477 A704 17p multicolored .25 .25

Army Day A705

Captains-General Building, Canary Islands.

1986, May 16 Engr. ***Perf. 13½***
2478 A705 17p pale yel brn, sep & red .25 .25

Rodrigo City Cathedral A706

Design: 35p, Calella Lighthouse.

1986, June 16 ***Perf. 12½x13½***
2479 A706 12p blue & black .25 .25
2480 A706 35p multicolored .55 .25

10th World Basketball Championships, July 5-20 — A707

1986, July 4 Photo. ***Perf. 12½***
2481 A707 45p multicolored .50 .25

Famous Men — A708

Designs: 7p, Francisco Loscos Bernal (1823-1886), botanist. 11p, Salvador Espriu (1913-1985), author. 17p, Jose Martinez Ruiz (Azorin, 1873-1967), writer. 45p, Jose Vitoriano Gonzalez (Juan Gris, 1887-1927), painter.

1986, July 16 Engr. ***Perf. 13***
2482 A708 7p olive grn & bl .25 .25
2483 A708 11p brt rose & blk .25 .25
2484 A708 17p dk brn vio & blk .25 .25
2485 A708 45p org, red vio & blk .50 .25
Nos. 2482-2485 (4) 1.25 1.00

Mystery of the Virgin's Death Festival Elche — A709

17p, Angels carrying soul.

1986, Aug. 11 Photo. ***Perf. 13x13½***
2486 A709 17p multicolored .25 .25

5th World Swimming, Water Polo, Diving and Synchronized Swimming Championships — A710

1986, Aug. 13 Engr. ***Perf. 13½***
2487 A710 45p multicolored .50 .25

10th World Pelota Championships — A711

1986, Sept. 12
2488 A711 17p multicolored .25 .25

Stamp Day — A712

Messenger, The Husband's Return, Song 63, TI1 Codex, 1979 edition, Spanish Royal Academy.

1986, Sept. 27 Litho. ***Perf. 13x12½***
2489 A712 17p multicolored .25 .25

Souvenir Sheet

EXFILNA '86, Cordova, Oct. 9-18 — A713

1986, Oct. 7 Litho. & Engr.
2490 A713 17p Man, Cordova "Mosque" .25 .25

Discovery of America, 500th Anniv. (in 1992) — A714

Men and text: 7p, Aristotle, text from De Cielo et Mundo. 12p, Seneca, text from Medea. 17p, San Isidoro, text from Etimologias. 30p, Pedro de Ailly, text from Imago Mundi. 35p, Mayan, prophesy from Libros de Chilam Balam. 45p, European, prophesy from Libros de Chilam Balam.

Lithographed and Engraved

1986, Oct. 15 ***Perf. 13x13½***
2491 A714 7p multicolored .25 .25
2492 A714 12p multicolored .25 .25
2493 A714 17p multicolored .25 .25
2494 A714 30p multicolored .35 .25
2495 A714 35p multicolored .40 .25
2496 A714 45p multicolored .50 .25
a. Bklt. pane of 6, #2491-2496 1.90
Nos. 2491-2496 (6) 2.00 1.50

Caspar de Portola y Rovira (1717-1786), Pioneer of California — A715

1986, Nov. 6 ***Perf. 13½***
2497 A715 22p multicolored .25 .25

Christmas A716

Wood carving details: 19p, The Holy Family, by Diego de Siloe (c. 1495-1563), Natl. Sculpture Museum, Valladolid, vert. 48p, Nativity, Toledo Cathedral altarpiece, by Felipe de Borgona (c. 1475-1543).

1986, Nov. 19 Photo. ***Perf. 13½***
2498 A716 19p multicolored .25 .25
2499 A716 48p multicolored .55 .25

Spanish-Islamic Cultural Heritage — A717

Famous men: 7p, Abd Al Rahman II (792-852), 4th independent emir of Cordoba. 12p, Ibn Hazm (994-1064), scholar. 17p, Al-Zarqali (1061-1100), astronomer. 45p, Alfonso VII, scholar, Toledo School of Translators.

1986, Dec. 3 Engr.
2500 A717 7p org red & dk red brn .25 .25
2501 A717 12p brn blk & red org .25 .25
2502 A717 17p black & dk blue .25 .25
2503 A717 45p green & black .50 .25
Nos. 2500-2503 (4) 1.25 1.00

Alfonso R. Castelao (1886-1950), Artist, Writer — A718

Lithographed and Engraved

1986, Dec. 11 ***Perf. 13x13½***
2504 A718 32p El Buen Cura, 1917 .40 .25

Globe, Chateau de la Muette
A719

1987, Jan. 14 ***Perf. 14***
2505 A719 48p multicolored .55 .25

Organization for Economic Cooperation and Development, OECD, 25th anniv.

EXPO '92, Seville
A720

19p, Geometric shapes. 48p, Earth, Moon's surface.

1987, Jan. 21 **Photo.**
2506 A720 19p multicolored .35 .25
2507 A720 48p multicolored .95 .25

See Nos. 2540-2541, 2550-2551.

Portrait of Vitoria, by Vera Fajardo
A721

1987, Feb. 11 **Engr.**
2508 A721 48p dark rose brown .55 .25

Francisco de Vitoria (c. 1486-1546), theologian, teacher and a founder of intl. law.

Marine Corps, 450th Anniv.
A722

Design: 18th Cent. 74-gun man-of-war, period standard bearer, corps insignia.

1987, Feb. 25
2509 A722 19p multicolored .25 .25

Deusto University, Cent. — A723

1987, Feb. 26 **Engr.** ***Perf. 14x13½***
2510 A723 19p blk, hn brn & dk grn .25 .25

UN Child Survival Campaign
A724

1987, Mar. 4 ***Perf. 13½x14***
2511 A724 19p red brown & blk .25 .25

Constitution of Cadiz, 175th Anniv. — A725

Nos. 2512a-2512c in a continuous design: The Promulgation of 1812, by Salvador Viniegra. No. 2512d, Anniv. emblem.

1987, Mar. 18 **Litho.** ***Perf. 13½***
2512 Strip of 4 1.25 1.25
a.-d. A725 25p, any single .30 .25

Ceramicware
A726

Designs: 7p, Pharmaceutical jar, 15th cent., Manises of Valencia. 14p, Abstract figurine, 20th cent., Sargadelos of Galicia. 19p, Neo-classical lidded urn, 18th cent., Buen Retiro of Madrid. 32p, Water jar, 20th cent., Salvatierra of Extremadura. 40p, Pitcher, 18th cent., Talavera of Toledo. 48p, Pitcher, 18th-19th cent., Granada of Andalucia.

Lithographed and Engraved

1987, Mar. 20 ***Perf. 12½x13***
2513 Block of 6 + 3 labels 2.75 2.75
a. A726 7p multicolored .25 .25
b. A726 14p multicolored .25 .25
c. A726 19p multicolored .30 .25
d. A726 32p multicolored .45 .30
e. A726 40p multicolored .50 .30
f. A726 48p multicolored .60 .30

See No. 2552.

Passion Week in Zamora and Seville
A727

Paintings: 19p, The Amanecer Procession, by Gallego Marquina, vert. 48p, Jesus Carrying the Cross, by Martinez Montanes, and the Gate of Forgiveness, Seville Cathedral.

1987, Apr. 13 **Photo.** ***Perf. 14x13½***
2514 A727 19p multicolored .25 .25
2515 A727 48p multicolored .55 .25

Tourism
A728

14p, Rock of Ifach, Calpe. 19p, Nave of Santa Marina d'Ozo Church, Pontevedra, before restoration. 40p, Sonanes Palace, Villacarriedo. 48p, Monastery of St. Joan de les Abadesses, Gerona, vert.

1987 **Engr.** ***Perf. 12½x13***
2515A A728 14p dp bl & sage grn .25 .25
2516 A728 19p dp grn & grnsh blk .30 .25
2516A A728 40p dp claret .50 .25
2517 A728 48p black .60 .25
Nos. 2515A-2517 (4) 1.65 1.00

Issued: 19p, 48p, 4/21; 14p, 40p, 6/10.

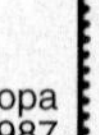

Europa 1987
A729

Modern architecture: 19p, Bilbao Bank, Madrid, designed by Saenz de Oiza, vert. 48p, Natl. Museum of Roman Art, Merida, designed by Rafael Moneo.

Lithographed and Engraved

1987, May 4 ***Perf. 14x13½***
2518 A729 19p multicolored .25 .25
2519 A729 48p multicolored .55 .25

Horse Fair, Jerez de La Frontera
A730

1987, May 6 **Photo.** ***Perf. 13½x14***
2520 A730 19p multicolored .25 .25

Ramon Carande (1887-1986), Historian — A731

1987, May 29 **Engr.**
2521 A731 40p blk & dk vio brn .45 .25

Postal Code Inauguration — A732

1987, June 1 **Litho.** ***Perf. 14***
2522 A732 19p multicolored .25 .25

Eibar Weaponry School, 75th Anniv.
A733

1987, July 2 **Litho.** ***Perf. 14***
2523 A733 20p multicolored .25 .25

1992 Summer Olympics, Barcelona
A734

32p, Casa de Battlo masonry. 65p, Athletes.

1987, July 15 **Photo.**
2524 A734 32p multicolored .50 .25
2525 A734 65p multicolored 1.00 .25

25th Folk Festival of the Pyrenees, Jaca — A735

1987, July 22
2526 A735 50p multicolored .55 .25

Monturiol and Submarine Designs
A736

1987, Sept. 9 **Engr.** ***Perf. 13½x14***
2527 A736 20p black brown .25 .25

Narcis Monturiol (d. 1887), builder of the submarine Ictineos.

Stamp Day — A737

Illuminated codex from *Constitutiones Jacobi II Regis Majoricum,* 14th cent., King Albert I Royal Library, Brussels.

Litho & Engr.

1987, Sept. 16 ***Perf. 13***
2528 A737 20p multicolored .25 .25

Postal service of Mallorca under James II.

ESPAMER '87 — A738

Designs: 8p, Handstamped letter that traveled from La Coruna to Havana, Cuba, 18th cent. 12p, La Coruna Harbor, 19th cent., engraving. 20p, Illustration of Havana harbor from *Viaje Alrededor da La Isla de Cuba,* by Francisco Mialche, 18th cent. 50p, West Indies packets.

1987, Oct. 2 **Litho. & Engr.** ***Perf. 13***
2529 Sheet of 4 3.75 3.75
a. A738 8p blk, brt blue & red .30 .30
b. A738 12p brt blue, red & blk .45 .45
c. A738 20p blk, brt blue & red .75 .75
d. A738 50p blk, brt blue & red 1.75 1.75

No. 2529 printed se-tenant (rouletted between) with ESPAMER entrance ticket. Sold for 180p. Size: 150x83mm (including ticket).

Souvenir Sheet

EXFILNA '87, Gerona, Oct. 24-Nov. 1 — A739

Greek statue, Emporion, Olympic torch-bearer.

1987, Oct. 24 Photo. ***Perf. 13x12½***
2530 A739 20p multicolored .25 .25

Discovery of America, 500th Anniv. (in 1992) — A740

Ships and: 14p, Amerigo Vespucci (1454-1512), Italian navigator. 20p, Ferdinand and Isabella. 32p, Friar Juan Perez, Queen's confessor. 40p, Juan de la Cosa (c. 1460-1510), master of the Santa Maria, cartographer who made first map of the New World. 50p, Christopher Columbus. 65p, Vicente Yanez Pinzon (c. 1460-1523) and Martin Alonso Pinzon (c. 1441-1493), brothers, navigators and ship owners, accompanied Columbus on voyage.

Litho. & Engr.

1987, Oct. 30 ***Perf. 13***
2531 A740 14p multicolored .25 .25
2532 A740 20p multicolored .25 .25
2533 A740 32p multicolored .40 .25
2534 A740 40p multicolored .45 .25
2535 A740 50p multicolored .55 .25
2536 A740 65p multicolored .75 .30
a. Bklt. pane of 6, #2531-2536 3.50 3.50
Nos. 2531-2536 (6) 2.65 1.55

Christmas — A741

1987, Nov. 17 Photo. ***Perf. 14x13½***
2537 A741 20p Ornaments .30 .25
2538 A741 50p Zambomba, tambourine .60 .25

Self-portrait, Sculpture by Victorio Macho (1887-1966) A742

1987, Dec. 23 **Engr.**
2539 A742 50p brown black .55 .25

EXPO '92 Type of 1987

1987, Dec. 29 Photo. ***Perf. 13½x14***
2540 A720 20p like No. 2506 .30 .25
2541 A720 50p like No. 2507 .55 .25

HRH Sofia and Juan Carlos, 50th Birth Annivs. — A743

1988, Jan. 5 ***Perf. 13x13½***
2542 20p Sofia .30 .25
2543 20p Juan Carlos .30 .25
a. A743 Pair, #2542-2543 + label .60 .50

Clara Campoamor (b. 1888), Suffragette — A744

1988, Feb. 12 Photo. ***Perf. 14***
2544 A744 20p multicolored .25 .25

1988 Winter Olympics, Calgary — A745

1988, Feb. 15 ***Perf. 14***
2545 A745 45p Speed skater .60 .25

Passion Week in Valladolid and Malaga — A746

Designs: 20p, Valladolid Cathedral and 17th cent. statue of Christ at the column by Gregorio Fernandez. 50p, Christ carrying the cross along Malaga procession route.

1988, Mar. 30 Photo. ***Perf. 14***
2546 A746 20p multicolored .30 .25
2547 A746 50p multicolored .60 .25

A747

Tourism — A747a

18p, Paella pan, ingredients. 45p, Covadonga Natl. Park.

1988, Apr. 7
2548 A747 18p multicolored .25 .25
2549 A747a 45p multicolored .50 .25

EXPO '92 Type of 1987

Era of Discoveries: 8p, Road to globe, rays of light, vert. 45p, Compass rose, globe.

1988, Apr. 12
2550 A720 8p multicolored .25 .25
2551 A720 45p multicolored .50 .25

Art Type of 1987

Glassware: a, Chalice, Valencia, 18th cent. b, Cadalso de los Vidrios, Madrid, 18th cent. c, Candy dish, La Granja de San Ildefonso, 18th cent. d, Castril double-handled jar, Andalucia, 18th cent. e, Jug, Catalina, 17th cent. f, Bottle, Baleares, 20th cent.

Litho. & Engr.

1988, Apr. 13 ***Perf. 12½x13***
2552 Block of 6 + 6 labels 1.75 1.75
a.-f. A726 20p any single .25 .25

Stamp Day 1988 — A748

Francis of Taxis, postmaster by royal appointment (1505) in charge of establishing communications between Spain, France, Germany, Rome, Naples.

1988, Apr. 29 Engr. ***Perf. 12½x13***
2553 A748 20p dk violet & dk brn .25 .25

General Workers' Union (UGT), Cent. A749

Emblem and Pablo Iglesias, union pioneer.

1988, May 1 Photo. ***Perf. 14***
2554 A749 20p multicolored .25 .25

Europa 1988 — A750

Transport and communication: 20p, Locomotive made in Spain and operated in Cuba, 1837. 50p, Spanish telegraph in the Philippines linking Plaza de Manila and Bagumbayan Camp, 1818.

1988, May 5 Engr. ***Perf. 13***
2555 A750 20p black & dk red *.25* .25
2556 A750 50p black & dk grn *.50* .25

Jean Monnet (1888-1979), Economist A751

1988, May 9 ***Perf. 14x13½***
2557 A751 45p blue black .50 .25

Universal Exposition, Barcelona, Cent. A752

1988, May 31 Photo. ***Perf. 13½x14***
2558 A752 50p multicolored .55 .25

Intl. Music and Dance Festival, Granada — A753

1988, June 1 ***Perf. 14x13½***
2559 A753 50p multicolored .55 .25

World Expo '88, Brisbane, Australia A754

1988, June 14 ***Perf. 13½x14***
2560 A754 50p Bull .55 .25

Coronation of the Virgin of Hope — A755

1988, June 18 ***Perf. 14x13½***
2561 A755 20p multicolored .25 .25

Holy Week in Malaga.

Souvenir Sheet

EXFILNA '88, June 25-July 3, Madrid — A756

20p, Ciudadela Fortress floor plan.

1988, June 25 ***Perf. 13x12½***
2562 A756 20p multicolored .25 .25

Tourism A757

18p, Cantabrian Coast storehouse. 45p, Dulzaina (wind instrument).

1988, July 11 Engr. ***Perf. 13½x14***
2563 A757 18p multicolored .30 .25
2564 A757 45p multicolored .60 .25

28th World Roller Hockey Championships, La Coruna — A758

1988, Sept. 7 Photo. ***Perf. 13½x14***
2565 A758 20p multicolored .25 .25

1st World Cong. of Spanish Regional Shelters — A759

1988, Sept. 9 ***Perf. 14***
2566 A759 20p multicolored .25 .25

1988 Summer Olympics, Seoul — A760

1988, Sept. 10 **Litho.**
2567 A760 50p Yachting .55 .25

Catalonia Millennium — A761

1988, Sept. 21 **Photo.** ***Perf. 12½***
2568 A761 20p multicolored .25 .25

1st Call to Session of the Leon Court, 800th Anniv. — A762

Illumination & seal of Alfonso IX, King of Leon.

1988, Sept. 26 **Photo.** ***Perf. 12½x13***
2569 A762 20p multicolored .25 .25

Federation of Spanish Philatelic Societies, 25th Anniv. A763

1988, Sept. 27 ***Perf. 14x13½***
2570 A763 20p multicolored .25 .25

1992 Summer Olympics, Barcelona A764

1988, Oct. 3 **Photo.** ***Perf. 14***
2571 A764 8p multicolored .25 .25

See Nos. B139-B141.

A765

Design: Castle in Valencia and royal seal of James I, 13th cent.

1988, Oct. 7 ***Perf. 14x13½***
2572 A765 20p multicolored .25 .25

Reconquest of Valencia by King James I, 750th anniv.

Civil Law, Cent. — A766

1988, Oct. 10 ***Perf. 13x13½***
2573 A766 20p multicolored .25 .25

Discovery of America (in 1992), 500th Anniv. — A767

Conquerors, exporers and symbols: No. 2574, Hernando Cortez, conqueror of Mexico, and serpent Quetzalcoatl. No. 2575, Vasco Nunez de Balboa, discoverer of the Pacific Ocean, and sun setting over sea. No. 2576, Francisco Pizarro, conqueror of Peru, and llama. No. 2577, Portuguese navigator Ferdinand Magellan, Juan de Elcano (c. 1476-1526) and globe symbolizing circumnavigation of the world. No. 2578, Alvar Nunez Cabeza de Vaca (c. 1490-1560), explorer, and sunrise. No. 2579, Andres de Urdaneta (1498-1568), and symbol of the west-to-east route between the Philippines and America that he discovered.

1988, Oct. 13 **Engr.** ***Perf. 13x13½***
2574 A767 10p multicolored .25 .25
2575 A767 10p multicolored .25 .25
2576 A767 20p multicolored .25 .25
2577 A767 20p multicolored .25 .25
2578 A767 50p multicolored .55 .25
2579 A767 50p multicolored .55 .25
a. Bklt. pane of 6, #2574-2579 2.75 2.75
Nos. 2574-2579 (6) 2.10 1.50

Henry III of Castile, 1st Prince of Asturias — A768

1988, Oct. 26 **Photo.** ***Perf. 13***
2580 A768 20p multicolored .25 .25

1st Bestowal of the title Prince of Asturias, 600th anniv., guaranteeing that the throne would continue to be inherited according to primogeniture.

Christmas — A769

20p, Snowflakes, horiz. 50p, Shepherd.

1988, Nov. 24 **Photo.** ***Perf. 14***
2581 A769 20p multicolored .25 .25
2582 A769 50p multicolored .55 .25

Sites and Cities Appearing on the UNESCO World Heritage List — A770

18p, Mosque de Cordoba, vert. 20p, Burgos Cathedral, vert. 45p, El Escorial Monastery. 50p, The Alhambra, Granada.

1988, Dec. 1 **Engr.** ***Perf. 12½x13***
2583 A770 18p multicolored .25 .25
2584 A770 20p multicolored .30 .25
2585 A770 45p multicolored .55 .25
2586 A770 50p multicolored .65 .25
Nos. 2583-2586 (4) 1.75 1.00

Natl. Constitution, 10th Anniv. — A771

1988, Dec. 7 **Photo.** ***Perf. 14***
2587 A771 20p multicolored .25 .25

Souvenir Sheet

Charles III (1759-1788) and the Enlightenment — A772

1988, Dec. 14 **Engr.** ***Perf. 13x12½***
2588 A772 45p black & dk grn .55 .55

Natl. Organization for the Blind, 50th Anniv. — A773

1988, Dec. 27 **Photo.** ***Perf. 14***
2589 A773 20p multicolored .25 .25

Fr. Luis de Granada (1504-1588) A774

1988, Dec. 31
2590 A774 20p multicolored .25 .25

1992 Summer Olympics, Barcelona A775

1989, Jan. 3
2591 A775 20p multicolored .25 .25

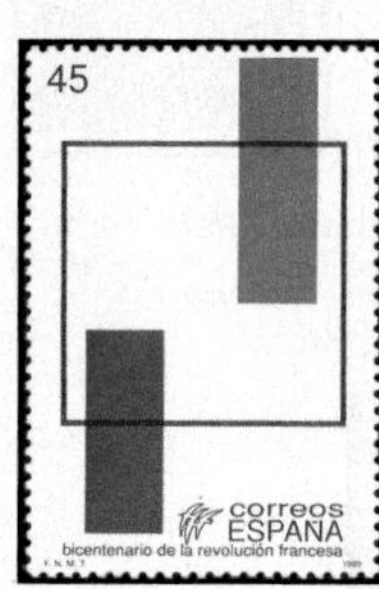

Stamp Collecting — A776

1989, Jan. 3
2592 A776 20p multicolored .25 .25

French Revolution, Bicent. — A777

1989, Jan. 24 **Photo.** ***Perf. 13***
2593 A777 45p multicolored .50 .25

Maria de Maeztu (b. 1882), Educator A778

1989, Feb. 7 **Photo.** ***Perf. 14x13½***
2594 A778 20p multicolored .25 .25

Postal Service, Cent. A779

Litho. & Engr.
1989, Mar. 11 ***Perf. 13½x14***
2595 A779 20p Uniform, 1889 .25 .25

Stamp Day — A780

Design: Intl. postal treaty negotiated with France and Italy by Franz von Taxis, 1601.

1989, Apr. 4 Engr. *Perf. 13*
2596 A780 20p black .25 .25

Casa del Cordon, Burgos — A781

1989, Apr. 22 *Perf. 14x13½*
2597 A781 20p black .25 .25

Children's Toys — A782

1989, May 5 Photo. *Perf. 13x13½*
2598 A782 40p shown *.40* .25
2599 A782 50p Top *.50* .25

Europa.

Spain's Presidency of the European Economic Community A783

1989, May 9 *Perf. 13½x14*
2600 A783 45p multicolored .50 .25

Souvenir Sheet

Holy Family with St. Anne, by El Greco — A784

1989, May 20 Litho. *Perf. 14x13½*
2601 A784 20p multicolored .25 .25

EXFILNA '89. Exists imperf in different colors.

Gabriela Mistral (1889-1957), Chilean Poet Awarded 1945 Nobel Prize for Literature — A785

Litho. & Engr.

1989, June 1 *Perf. 14x13½*
2602 A785 50p multicolored .60 .25

European Parliament 3rd Elections — A786

1989, June 12 Photo. *Perf. 13x13½*
2603 A786 45p multicolored .50 .25

Lace A787

Lace produced in: a, Catalonia. b, Andalusia. c, Extremadura. d, Canary Isls. e, Castile-La Mancha. f, Galicia.

Litho. & Engr.

1989, June 20 *Perf. 13x12½*
2604 Block of 6 + 3 labels 1.50 1.50
a.-f. A787 20p any single .25 .25

Three center labels printed in a continuous design and picture lace-making.

Pope John Paul II at the Intl. Catholic Youth Forum, Santiago — A788

1989, Aug. 19 Engr. *Perf. 13x12½*
2605 A788 50p myrtle grn, dk red brn & blk .55 .25

Athletics World Cup, Barcelona A789

1989, Sept. 1 Photo. *Perf. 13½x14*
2606 A789 50p multicolored .55 .25

A790

Litho. & Engr.

1989, Sept. 19 *Perf. 14x13½*
2607 A790 50p multicolored .55 .25

Charlie Chaplin (1889-1977), English comedian and actor.

Type A34 — A791

1989, Oct. 2 Photo. *Perf. 14x13½*
2608 A791 50p gray, ver & blk .55 .25

Cent. of the 1st Alfonso XIII issue.

A792

Fr. Andres Manjon (d. 1923), teacher.

1989, Oct. 13
2609 A792 20p multicolored .25 .25

Founding of the Ave Maria Schools by Fr. Manjon, cent.

A793

UPAE emblem and "Irrigating Corn Field in November, 17th Cent.," an illustration from the *New Chronicle and Good Government,* by Guaman Poma de Ayala.

1989, Nov. 7 Litho. & Engr.
2610 A793 50p multicolored .55 .25

America issue.

Christmas A794

20p, Star, "NAVIdAd 89," vert.

Perf. 14x13½, 13½x14

1989, Nov. 29 Photo.
2611 A794 20p multicolored .25 .25
2612 A794 45p shown .50 .25

Sites on the UNESCO World Heritage List — A795

No. 2613, Altamira Caverns. No. 2614, Santiago de Compostela. No. 2615, Roman aqueduct, Segovia. No. 2616, Guell Park and palace, Mila House.

Litho. & Engr.

1989, Dec. 5 *Perf. 13x12½*
2613 A795 20p multicolored .25 .25
2614 A795 20p multicolored .25 .25
2615 A795 20p multicolored .25 .25
2616 A795 20p multicolored .25 .25
Nos. 2613-2616 (4) 1.00 1.00

Souvenir Sheet

Sites on the World Heritage List — A796

Royal palaces: a, El Escorial. b, Aranjuez. c, Summer palace, La Granja, San Ildefonso. e, Madrid.

1989, Dec. 20 Engr. *Perf. 13x13½*
2617 A796 Sheet of 4 2.00 2.00
a.-d. 45p any single .30 .30

Illustration by Daniel Garcia Perez, Winner of the 2nd Youth Stamp Design Contest — A797

1990, Jan. 29 Photo. *Perf. 14x13½*
2618 A797 20p multicolored .25 .25

1992 Summer Olympics, Barcelona.

A798

1990, Feb. 2
2619 A798 20p multicolored .25 .25

World Cycle Cross Championship, Getzu.

A799

1990, Feb. 12 Engr.
2620 A799 20p dark purple .25 .25

Victoria Kent (1897-1987), prisons directer, reformer.

Honorary Postman Rafael Alvarez Sereix and Cancel — A800

Litho. & Engr.

1990, Apr. 18 *Perf. 13*

2621 A800 20p sepia, buff & dull grn .25 .25

Stamp Day.

Europa 1990 A801

Post offices.

Perf. 13½x14, 14x13½

1990, May 4 **Photo.**

2622 A801 20p Vitoria *.25* .25
2623 A801 50p Malaga, vert. *.50* .25

Intl. Telecommunications Union, 125th Anniv. — A802

1990, May 17 *Perf. 13½x14*

2624 A802 8p multicolored .25 .25

Wrought Iron — A803

Designs: a, 15th Cent. door knocker. b, 16th cent. lyre-shaped door knocker. c, 17th Cent. pistol. d, 17th-18th Cent. door knocker. e, 19th Cent. lock. f, Fire iron.

Litho. & Engr.

1990, May 18 *Perf. 12½*

2625 Block of 6 + 3 labels 1.75 1.75
a.-f. A803 20p any single .25 .25

Nos. 2625a-2625f printed se-tenant in a continuous design. Three labels continue the design and contain text or picture a forge.

Souvenir Sheet

Patio de La Infanta, Zaporta Palace, Zaragoza — A804

1990, May 25 **Engr.** *Perf. 14x13½*

2626 A804 20p red brown .25 .25

EXFILNA '90.

Charity, by Lopez Alonso — A805

1990, June 19 **Litho.** *Perf. 13½x13*

2627 A805 8p multicolored .25 .25

Daughters of Charity in Spain, bicentennial.

Jose Padilla, Composer, Birth Centenary — A806

1990, June 19 **Photo.** *Perf. 13x12½*

2628 A806 20p multicolored .30 .25

Town of Estella, 900th Anniv. — A807

1990, June 19 **Litho. & Engr.**

2629 A807 45p multicolored .75 .50

Novel, "Tirant lo Blanch," 500th Anniv. — A808

1990, June 19 *Perf. 12½x13*

2630 A808 50p multicolored .75 .50

Souvenir Sheet

Crypt, Palencia Cathedral — A809

1990, June 22 **Engr.** *Perf. 13½x14*

2631 A809 20p red brown .25 .25

Topical philatelic exposition.

A810

1990, Aug. 27 **Photo.** *Perf. 14x13½*

2632 A810 50p multicolored .55 .25

17th Intl. Congress of Historical Sciences.

A811

America Issue: UPAE emblem and Caribean fauna.

Litho. & Engr.

1990, Nov. 14 *Perf. 14*

2633 A811 50p multicolored .55 .25

Christmas — A812

Scenes from the film "Cosmic Poem" by Jose Antonio Sistiaga.

1990, Nov. 22 **Photo.**

2634 A812 25p multicolored .30 .25
2635 A812 45p multi, horiz. .50 .25

A813

Tapestries in Monastery of San Lorenzo: a, The Crucifixion by Jan van Roome and Bernard van Orley. b, Flamenco Soldiers by Philip Wouvermans. c, Shipwreck of the Telemac by Miguel Angel Houasse. d, Flowers by Francisco Goya.

Litho. & Engr.

1990, Nov. 28 *Perf. 13*

2636 Sheet of 4 1.25 1.25
a.-d. A813 20p any single .25 .25

European Tourism Year — A814

1990, Dec. 1 **Photo.** *Perf. 14*

2637 A814 45p multicolored .50 .25

World Heritage List — A815

Designs: No. 2638, Church of San Vicente, Avila. No. 2639, Tower of San Pedro, Teruel, vert. No. 2640, Church of San Miguel de Lillo, Oviedo, vert. No. 2641, Tower of Bujaco, Caceres.

Litho. & Engr.

1990, Dec. 10 *Perf. 13*

2638 A815 20p multicolored .30 .25
2639 A815 20p multicolored .30 .25
2640 A815 20p multicolored .30 .25
2641 A815 20p multicolored .30 .25
Nos. 2638-2641 (4) 1.20 1.00

Natl. Orchestra of Spain A816

1990, Dec. 20 **Photo.** *Perf. 13½x14*

2642 A816 25p grn, yel grn & blk .30 .25

Maria Moliner (1900-1981), Spanish Linguist — A817

1991, Jan. 21 **Photo.** *Perf. 14x13½*

2643 A817 25p multicolored .35 .25

Souvenir Sheet

Santa Fe, 500th Anniv. — A818

Litho. & Engr.

1991, Apr. 19 *Perf. 13½x14*

2644 A818 25p brown & purple .35 .35

World Philatelic Exhibition, Granada '92.

Child's Drawing — A819

25p, Olympic rings, sailboats.

1991, Apr. 12 **Photo.** *Perf. 14x13½*

2645 A819 25p multicolored .35 .25

Juan de Tassis y Peralta (1582-1622), Postal Reformer A820

1991, Apr. 26 Engr. *Perf. 12½*
2646 A820 25p black .35 .25

Stamp Day.

Souvenir Sheet

Porcelain and Ceramics — A821

a, Apothecary jar, 17th cent. b, Figurine, 18th cent. c, Vase, 19th cent. d, Plate, 19th cent.

1991, May 3 Litho. & Engr. *Perf. 13*
2647 A821 25p Sheet of 4, #a.-d. 1.50 1.50
a.-d. Any single .30 .25

See No. 2692.

Europa A822

25p, INTA-NASA ground station. 45p, Olympus I satellite.

1991, May 28 Litho. *Perf. 13½x14*
2648 A822 25p multicolored *.35* .25
2649 A822 45p multicolored *.55* .25

St. John of the Cross (1651-1695), Mystic — A823

Anniversaries: No. 2651, Fr. Luis de Leon (1527-1591), Augustinian writer, vert. No. 2652, Abd Al Rahman III (891-961), Moslem caliph, vert. No. 2653, St. Ignatius of Loyola (1451-1556), founder of Society of Jesus, vert.

Perf. 13½x14, 14x13½
1991, June 6 Litho.
2650 A823 15p multicolored .25 .25
2651 A823 15p multicolored .25 .25
2652 A823 25p multicolored .35 .25
2653 A823 25p multicolored .35 .25
Nos. 2650-2653 (4) 1.20 1.00

Antique Furniture A824

Designs: a, Wedge top armoire, 18th cent. b, Hutch cabinet, c. 19th cent. c, Ladder-back cane chair, c. 19th cent. d, Baby cradle, 19th cent. e, Round-top trunk, c. 19th cent. f, Ornate chest, c. 18th cent.

Litho. & Engr.
1991, Sept. 9 *Perf. 12½x13*
2654 Block of 6 + 3 labels 2.25 2.25
a.-f. A824 25p any single .30 .25

Orfeo Catala (Catalan Choral Society), Cent. — A825

1991, Sept. 6 Litho. *Perf. 14x13½*
2655 A825 25p multicolored .35 .25

Intl. Fishing Exposition, Vigo — A826

1991, Sept. 10
2656 A826 55p multicolored .75 .25

America Issue — A827

Litho. & Engr.
1991, Nov. 4 *Perf. 14x13½*
2657 A827 55p Nocturlabe .75 .25

Christmas — A828

25p, The Nativity, illustration from 17th cent. book. 45p, The Birth of Christ, 16th cent. icon.

1991, Nov. 22 Photo. *Perf. 14x13½*
2658 A828 25p multicolored .35 .25
2659 A828 45p multicolored .55 .25

Souvenir Sheet

The Meadowlands of St. Isidro by Goya — A829

Litho. & Engr.
1991, Dec. 12 *Perf. 13½x14*
2660 A829 25p multicolored .35 .35

EXFILNA '91, Madrid.

Sites on UNESCO World Heritage List — A830

#2661, Giralda bell tower, Seville Cathedral. #2662, Alcantara Gate, Toledo, vert. #2663, Casa de las Conchas, Salamanca, vert. #2664, Garajonay Natl. Park, Gomera, Canary Islands.

Perf. 12½x13, 13x12½
1991, Dec. 16 Engr.
2661 A830 25p brown & blue .40 .25
2662 A830 25p red brn & brn .40 .25
2663 A830 25p red brn & blk .40 .25
2664 A830 25p violet & dk grn .40 .25
Nos. 2661-2664 (4) 1.60 1.00

See Nos. 2756, 2830.

Carlos Ibanez de Ibero (1825-1891), Cartographer A831

Antarctic Treaty, Research Ship A52 — A832

1991, Dec. 27 Litho. *Perf. 14x13½*
2665 A831 25p multicolored .35 .25
2666 A832 55p multicolored .75 .25

Margarita Xirgu (1889-1969), Actress — A833

1992, Jan. 20 *Perf. 14*
2667 A833 25p lake & gold .35 .25

Child's Drawing A834

1992, Feb. 14 *Perf. 13½x14*
2668 A834 25p multicolored .35 .25

EXPO 92.

Pedro Rodriguez Campomanes (1723-1802), Historian, Postal Administrator — A835

1992, Feb. 21 *Perf. 13x12½*
2669 A835 27p multicolored .45 .25

Expo '92, Seville A836

1992, Feb. 28 *Perf. 13½x14*
2670 A836 27p gray, blk & brn .40 .25

Columbus Types of 1930
Souvenir Sheet

1992, Apr. 24 Engr. *Perf. 14*
2671 Sheet of 2 10.00 10.00
a. A65 250p black 4.50 2.50
b. A67 250p brown 4.50 2.50

Intl. Philatelic Exhibition, Granada '92.

Miniature Sheets

Expo '92, Seville — A837

#2672: a, Expo '92 World Trade Center. b, Aerial tram. c, Avenue 4. d, Barqueta Gate. e, Nature pavilion. f, Biosphere. g, Alamillo Bridge. h, Press center. i, 15th Century pavilion. j, Expo harbor. k, Tourist train. l, One day entrance ticket.

#2673: a, Cartuja Monastery. b, Arena. c, Monorail train. d, Europe Avenue. e, Discovery pavilion. f, Auditorium. g, Avenue 1. h, Plaza of the Future. i, Gate to Italy's exhibit. j, Terminal. k, Expo theater. l, Expo Mascot, Curro.

1992, Apr. 21 Litho. *Perf. 13½x14*
2672 A837 Sheet of 12 + 4 labels 6.00 6.00
a.-l. 17p any single .40 .25
2673 A837 Sheet of 12 + 4 labels 6.00 6.00
a.-l. 27p any single .60 .30

See No. B195.

1992 Paralympics, Barcelona — A838

1992, Apr. 22 Photo. *Perf. 14*
2674 A838 27p multicolored .60 .25

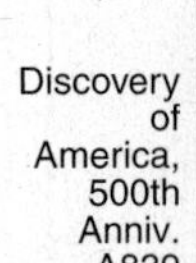

Discovery of America, 500th Anniv. A839

Europa: 17p, Preparation Before Departing from Palos, by R. Espejo. 45p, Globe, ships, and buildings at La Rabida.

1992, May 5 Photo. *Perf. 14*
2675 A839 17p multicolored .35 .25
2676 A839 45p multicolored 1.00 .25

Souvenir Sheets

Voyages of Columbus — A840

#2677, Columbus in sight of land. #2678, Landing of Columbus. #2679, Columbus soliciting aid from Isabella. #2680, Columbus welcomed at Barcelona. #2681, Columbus presenting natives. #2682, Columbus.

Borders on Nos. 2677-2682 are lithographed. Nos. 2677-2682 are similar in design to US Nos. 230-231, 234-235, 237, 245.

Litho. & Engr.

1992, May 22 *Perf. 14*
2677 A840 60p blue 1.25 1.10
2678 A840 60p brown violet 1.25 1.10
2679 A840 60p chocolate 1.25 1.10
2680 A840 60p purple 1.25 1.10
2681 A840 60p black brown 1.25 1.10
2682 A840 60p black 1.25 1.10
Nos. 2677-2682 (6) 7.50 6.60

See US Nos. 2624-2629, Italy Nos. 1883-1888 and Portugal Nos. 1918-1923.

1992 Winter & Summer Olympics, Albertville & Barcelona A841

1992, June 19 Photo. *Perf. 14*
2683 A841 45p multicolored .60 .25

World Environment Day — A842

1992, June 5 Photo. *Perf. 14x13½*
2684 A842 27p blue & yellow .40 .25

A843

1992, Oct. 29 Litho. *Perf. 14x13½*
2685 A843 17p multicolored .25 .25

Juan Luis Vives (1492-1540), Philosopher.

Pamplona Choir, Cent. A844

1992, Oct. 29 *Perf. 13½x14*
2686 A844 27p multicolored .35 .25

Unified Europe — A845

1992, Nov. 4 Photo. *Perf. 14x13½*
2687 A845 45p multicolored .60 .25

Christmas A846

1992, Nov. 5 *Perf. 13½x14*
2688 A846 27p multicolored .40 .25

1992 Special Olympics, Madrid A847

1992, Sept. 7 Photo. *Perf. 13½x14*
2689 A847 27p brown & blue .35 .25

Souvenir Sheet

St. Paul's Church, Valladolid — A848

Litho. & Engr.

1992, Oct. 9 *Perf. 14x13½*
2690 A848 27p multicolored .35 .35

Exfilna '92, Natl. Philatelic Exhibition, Valladolid.

Discovery of America, 500th Anniv. A849

1992, Oct. 15 *Perf. 13½x14*
2691 A849 60p dk brn, lt brn & bis .75 .25

Natl. Heritage Type of 1991

Miniature Sheet

Codices: a, Veitia, 18th cent. b, Trujillo of Peru, 18th cent. c, The Chess Book, 13th cent. d, General History of New Spain, 16th cent.

Litho. & Engr.

1992, Dec. 10 *Perf. 13*
2692 A821 27p Sheet of 4, #a.-d. 1.75 1.40

Road Safety A850

Environmental Protection A851

Health and Sanitation — A852

1993 Photo. *Perf. 14x13½*
2693 A850 17p green & red .35 .25
2694 A851 28p green & blue .40 .25
2695 A852 65p blue & green .90 .25
Nos. 2693-2695 (3) 1.65 .75

Issued: 17p, 4/20; 28p, 1/4; 65p, 2/12.

Maria Zambrano (1904-1991), Writer — A854

1993, Jan. 18 Photo. *Perf. 14*
2697 A854 45p buff, lil rose & brn .65 .25

Andres Segovia (1893-1987), Guitarist — A855

1993, Feb. 19 Engr. *Perf. 14x13½*
2698 A855 65p black & brown .90 .25

1908 Mailbox, Madrid Postal Museum A856

Litho. & Engr.

1993, Mar. 12 *Perf. 13½x14*
2699 A856 28p multicolored .45 .25

Stamp Day.

Mushrooms — A857

No. 2700, Amanita caesarea. No. 2701, Lepiota procera. No. 2702, Lactarius sanguifluus. No. 2703, Russula cyanoxantha.

1993, Mar. 18 Photo. *Perf. 14*
2700 A857 17p multicolored .35 .25
2701 A857 17p multicolored .35 .25
2702 A857 28p multicolored .40 .25
2703 A857 28p multicolored .40 .25
Nos. 2700-2703 (4) 1.50 1.00

See Nos. 2759-2762.

Souvenir Sheet

Holy Week Celebration — A858

1993, Apr. 2 Litho. *Perf. 14x13½*
2704 A858 100p multicolored 1.60 1.60

Exfilna '93, Alcaniz. Margin of No. 2704 is Litho. & Engr.

Fusees, by Joan Miro A859

Europa: 65p, La Bague d'Aurore, by Miro, vert.

Perf. 13½x14, 14x13½

1993, May 5 Litho.
2705 A859 45p blue & black .75 .25

Litho. & Engr.

2706 A859 65p multicolored 1.00 .25

Year of St. James A860

Designs: 17p, Transfer of St. James' body by boat. 28p, Discovery of tomb of St. James. 45p, St. James on horseback.

1993, May 13 Photo. *Perf. 13½x14*
2707 A860 17p multicolored .35 .25
2708 A860 28p multicolored .45 .25
2709 A860 45p multicolored .70 .25
Nos. 2707-2709 (3) 1.50 .75

World Telecommunications Day — A861

1993, May 17
2710 A861 28p multicolored .45 .25

Compostela '93 — A862

Stylized designs: 28p, Pilgrims paying homage to Saint James. 100p, Pilgrim under star tree while on way to Santiago de Campostela, vert.

1993, May 18 Photo. *Perf. 13½x14*

2711 A862 28p multicolored .45 .25

Souvenir Sheet

Perf. 14x13½

2712 A862 100p multicolored 1.75 1.75

World Environment Day — A863

1993, June 4 Litho. *Perf. 14x13½*

2713 A863 28p multicolored .45 .25

King Juan Carlos — A864a

A864

1993-98 Photo. *Perf. 14x13½*

A864 Gold and:

2714	A864	1p	prussian bl	.25	.25
2715	A864	2p	green	.25	.25
2716	A864	10p	magenta	.25	.25
2717	A864	15p	green	.25	.25
2718	A864	16p	brn lake	.25	.25
2719	A864	17p	yel org	.25	.25
2720	A864	18p	grn bl	.25	.25
2721	A864	19p	brown	.35	.25
2722	A864	20p	lil rose	.25	.25
2723	A864	21p	dark grn	.25	.25
2724	A864	28p	vio brn	.40	.25
2725	A864	29p	olive	.40	.25
2726	A864	30p	ultramarine	.45	.25
2727	A864	32p	green	.45	.25
2728	A864	35p	red	.40	.25
2729	A864	45p	bluish grn	.65	.25
2730	A864	55p	sepia	1.00	.50
a.			Block of 4, #2714, 2720, 2725, 2730 + 2 labels	2.00	2.00
2731	A864	60p	org brn	1.00	.50
a.			Block of 4, #2716, 2721, 2726, 2731 + 2 labels	2.50	2.50
2732	A864	65p	red org	1.00	.25
a.			Block of 4, #2719, 2724, 2729, 2732 + 2 labels	2.50	2.50
2733	A864	70p	vermilion	.90	.45

Engr.

2734	A864a	100p	brown	2.50	.30
2735	A864a	200p	green	6.25	.60
2736	A864a	300p	maroon	12.00	.90
2737	A864a	500p	blue	22.50	1.50
2738	A864a	1000p	vio blk	45.00	4.00
	Nos. 2714-2738 (25)			97.50	13.00

Issued: 17p, 28p, 45p, 65p, 5/21/93; 1p, 18p, 29p, 1/31/94; 55p, 5/27/94; 19p, 30p, 1/3/95; 10p, 60p, 6/5/95; 1000p, 11/24/95; 100p, 200p, 300p, 500p, 12/12/96; 21p, 32p, 1/27/97; 2p, 16p, 5/19/97; 15p, 3/6/98; 35p, 2/13/98; 70p, 1/30/98. 20p, 11/20/00.

Don Juan de Borbon (1913-1993), Count of Barcelona — A865

1993, June 20 Photo. *Perf. 14x13½*

2744 A865 28p multicolored .45 .25

Igualada-Martorell Railway, Cent. — A866

1993, July 4 Engr. *Perf. 13½x14*

2745 A866 45p black & green .75 .25

Natl. Mint (F.N.M.T.), Cent. A867

1993, Sept. 13

2746 A867 65p dark blue 1.10 .25

Explorers A868

Designs: 45p, Alejandro Malaspina (1754-1809), Italian explorer of South America. 65p, Jose Celestino Mutis (1732-1808), Spanish naturalist in the Americas, vert.

Perf. 13½x14, 14x13½

1993, Sept 20 Litho.

2747 A868 45p multicolored .60 .25

2748 A868 65p multicolored .90 .25

Ciconia Nigra A869

Endangered birds: No. 2750, Gypaetus barbatus (Quebrantahuesos).

Litho. & Engr.

1993, Oct. 11 *Perf. 13½x14*

2749 A869 65p pink & black .90 .25

2750 A869 65p orange & black .90 .25

Child's Painting — A870

1993, Oct. 2 Litho. *Perf. 14x13½*

2751 A870 45p multicolored .70 .25

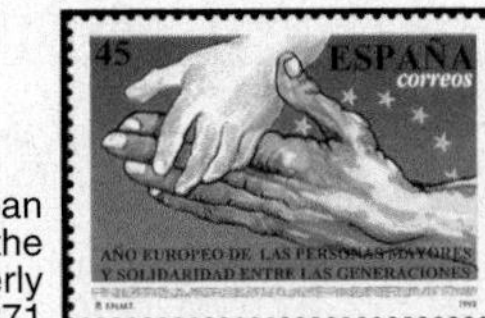

European Year of the Elderly A871

1993, Oct. 29 Photo. *Perf. 14*

2752 A871 45p multicolored .80 .25

A872

Christmas — A873

Perf. 13½x14, 14x13½

1993, Nov. 23 Photo.

2753 A872 17p multicolored .30 .25

Litho., Photo. & Engr.

2754 A873 28p multicolored .45 .25

Jorge Guillen (1893-1984), Poet — A874

1993, Nov. 29 Engr. *Perf. 14x13½*

2755 A874 28p green .45 .25

UNESCO World Heritage Type of 1991

Design: 50p, Monastery of Santa Maria of Poblet, Tarragona.

1993, Dec. 3 Engr. *Perf. 13x12½*

2756 A830 50p multicolored .90 .25

Spanish Film Industry A875

29p, Luis Bunuel (1900-83), director. 55p, Segundo de Chomon (1871-1929), film pioneer.

1994, Jan. 28 Photo. *Perf. 14*

2757 A875 29p multicolored .45 .25

2758 A875 55p multicolored .90 .25

Mushroom Type of 1993

No. 2759, Boletus satanas. No. 2760, Boletus edulis. No. 2761, Amanita phalloides. No. 2762, Lactarius deliciosus.

1994, Feb. 18 Photo. *Perf. 14*

2759	A857	18p	multi	.30	.25
2760	A857	18p	multi	.30	.25
2761	A857	29p	multi	.45	.25
2762	A857	29p	multi	.45	.25
	Nos. 2759-2762 (4)			1.50	1.00

Minerals — A876

a, Cinnabar. b, Sphalerite. c, Pyrite. d, Galena.

1994, Feb. 25

2763 A876 29p Block of 4, #a.-d., + 2 labels 2.75 2.00

Barrister's Mailbox A877

Litho. & Engr.

1994, Mar. 9 *Perf. 13½x14*

2764 A877 29p light & dark brn .45 .25

Stamp Day.

ILO, 75th Anniv. A878

1994, Apr. 7 Photo. *Perf. 13½x14*

2765 A878 65p multicolored 1.00 .25

Art of Salvador Dali (1904-89) A879

Paintings: #2766, Retrato de Gala. #2767, Poesia de America. #2768, El Gran Masturbador. #2769, Port Alguer. #2770, Self portrait. #2771, Cesta del Pan. #2772, El Enigma Sin Fin. #2173, Galatea de las Esferas.

1994, Apr. 22 *Perf. 13½x14, 14x13½*

2766	A879	18p	multi	.30	.25
2767	A879	18p	multi, vert.	.30	.25
2768	A879	29p	multi	.40	.25
2769	A879	29p	multi, vert.	.40	.25
2770	A879	55p	multi, vert.	.90	.25
2771	A879	55p	multi, vert.	.90	.25
2772	A879	65p	multi	1.10	.25
2773	A879	65p	multi, vert.	1.10	.25
	Nos. 2766-2773 (8)			5.40	2.00

Josep Pla (1897-1981), Writer — A880

1994, Apr. 23 Engr. *Perf. 13½x14*

2774 A880 65p dark grn & lake 1.00 .25

A881

Painting: Martyrdom of St. Andrew, by Rubens.

1994, Apr. 29 Photo. *Perf. 14*

2775 A881 55p multicolored .90 .25

Carlos de Amberes Foundation, 400th anniv.

A882

A883

1994, May 3 **Photo.**
2776 A882 18p multicolored .30 .25

Litho., Photo. & Engr.
2777 A883 29p multicolored .45 .25

Santa Cruz de Tenerife, 400th anniv. (#2776). Complutense University of Madrid, 700th Anniv. (#2777).

Europa A884

Designs: 55p, Severo Ochoa (1905-93), 1959 Nobel Laureate in Medicine. 65p, Miguel Angel Catalan (1894-1957), physicist.

1994, May 5 **Litho. & Engr.**
2778 A884 55p multicolored .75 .25
2779 A884 65p multicolored 1.25 .25

Spanish Literature A885

Novels by Camilo Jose Cela: 18p, The Family of Pascual Duarte. 29p, Journey to Alcarria.

1994, May 11 **Photo.**
2780 A885 18p multicolored .30 .25
2781 A885 29p multicolored .55 .25

King Sancho Ramirez, 900th Death Anniv. — A886

Treaty of Tordesillas, 500th Anniv. — A887

Design: 55p, Natl. Archives, Simancas.

Litho. & Engr.
1994, June 7 ***Perf. 14***
2782 A886 18p multicolored .30 .25
2783 A887 29p multicolored .45 .25
2784 A887 55p multicolored .90 .25
Nos. 2782-2784 (3) 1.65 .75

Souvenir Sheet

Cathedral of St. Anne, Las Palmas, Grand Canary Island — A888

1994, July 1 ***Perf. 13½x14***
2785 A888 100p multicolored 1.75 1.75

Exfilna '94, Natl. Philatelic Exhibition, Grand Canary Island.

Yachts — A889

1994, July 15 **Photo.** ***Perf. 14x13½***
2786 A889 16p Giralda .30 .25
2787 A889 29p Saltillo .45 .25

Roman City of Augusta Emerita (Merida), Badajoz — A890

Litho. & Engr.
1994, Sept. 8 ***Perf. 13***
2788 A890 55p lake, brn & buff .90 .25

UNESCO World Heritage list.

Museum of Cards, Alava — A891

Antique cards: 18p, Horse of Spades. 29p, Jack of Diamonds. 55p, King of Hearts. 65p, War god, Mars, of Diamonds.

1994, Sept. 20 **Photo.** ***Perf. 14x13½***
2789 A891 18p multicolored .30 .25
2790 A891 29p multicolored .40 .25
2791 A891 55p multicolored .90 .25
2792 A891 65p multicolored 1.10 .25
Nos. 2789-2792 (4) 2.70 1.00

Postal Transportation — A892

1994, Oct. 11 **Litho.** ***Perf. 13½***
2793 A892 65p DC-8 1.00 .25

Public Transit — A893

Civil Guard A894

1994, Oct. 17 **Photo.** ***Perf. 14x13½***
2794 A893 18p multicolored .30 .25

Perf. 13½x14
2795 A894 29p multicolored .45 .25

Western European Union A895

1994, Oct. 21 ***Perf. 13½x14***
2796 A895 55p multicolored .85 .25

Olympic Venues A896

Designs: a, Track. b, Skiing. c, Equestrian. d, Wrestling. e, Archery. f, Cycling. g, Soccer. h, Field hockey. i, Swimming. j, Sailing.

1994, Oct. 27
2797 Block of 10 + 10 labels 5.00 5.00
a.-j. A896 29p any single .50 .40

Labels inscribed with names of Spanish gold medalists and Intl. Olympic Committee cent.

See Nos. 2822, 2850.

Christmas — A897

1994, Nov. 18 ***Perf. 14x13½***
2798 A897 29p multicolored .45 .25

City of Logrono, 900th Anniv. A899

Spanish Motion Pictures A898

Designs: 30p, Belle Epoque, by Fernando Trueba. 60p Volver A Empezar (Begin the Beguine), by Jose Luis Garci.

1995, Jan. 20 **Photo.** ***Perf. 14***
2799 A898 30p multicolored .45 .25
2800 A898 60p multicolored 1.10 .25

1995, Jan. 25
2801 A899 30p multicolored .45 .25

Souvenir Sheet

SIERRA NEVADA '95, Granada — A900

130p, White star flower.

1995, Jan. 30
2802 A900 130p multicolored 2.00 2.00

World Alpine Skiing Championships.

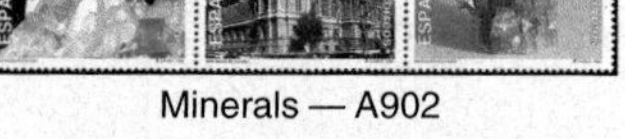

Mushrooms — A901

19p, Coprinus comatus. 30p, Dermocybe cinnamomea.

1995, Feb. 9 **Photo.** ***Perf. 13½x14***
2803 A901 19p multicolored .30 .25
2804 A901 30p multicolored .45 .25

Minerals — A902

Designs: a, Dolomite. b, Technical School for Mining Engineers, Madrid. c, Aragonite.

1995, Feb. 24
2805 A902 Strip of 3 1.40 1.40
a.-c. 30p any single .45 .25

Stamp Day A903

30p, Bronze lion's head.

1995, Mar. 9 **Engr.**
2806 A903 30p multicolored .45 .25

Alejandro Goicoechea Omar, TALGO Train — A904

Design: 60p, Young Omar, early train.

1995, Mar. 17 **Photo.** ***Perf. 14***
2807 A904 30p multicolored .45 .25
2808 A904 60p multicolored 1.00 .25

A905

1995, Apr. 6

2809 A905 60p multicolored .95 .25

Nature conservation in Europe.

A906

18th Century Sailing Ships: 19p, San Juan Nepomuceno. 30p, San Telmo.

Litho. & Engr.

1995, Apr. 7 ***Perf. 14***

2810 A906 19p multicolored .30 .25
a. Miniature sheet of 4 1.20 1.20
2811 A906 30p multicolored .70 .25
a. Miniature sheet of 4 2.80 2.80

See also Nos. 2847-2848.

Lebaniego Celebration Year — A907

60p, Mountains, St. Toribio Monastery.

1995, Apr. 21 Photo. ***Perf. 12½***

2812 A907 30p multicolored .45 .25
2813 A907 60p multicolored 1.00 .25

Spanish Literature A908

Designs: 19p, El Nino Yuntero, by Miguel Hernandez (1910-42). 30p, Juanita la Larga, by Juan Valera (1824-1905), vert.

Litho. & Engr.

1995, Apr. 27 ***Perf. 14***

2814 A908 19p multicolored .40 .25

Engr.

2815 A908 30p green & blue .55 .25

Jose Marti (1853-95), Cuban Writer A909

1995, Apr. 28 Photo.

2816 A909 60p multicolored 1.00 .25

Spanish Cartoon Characters A910

1995, May 4 Photo. ***Perf. 14***

2817 A910 30p Captain Trueno .45 .25
2818 A910 60p Carpanta, vert. 1.00 .25

See Nos. 2854-2855.

Europa A911

1995, May 5

2819 A911 60p multicolored 1.00 .25

Motion Pictures, Cent. A912

19p, Auguste and Louis Lumiere, early camera.

1995, May 12 Engr. ***Perf. 14***

2820 A912 19p brownish black .30 .25

Press Assoc. of Madrid, Cent. A913

1995, May 12 Litho.

2821 A913 30p multicolored .45 .25

Olympic Venue Type of 1994

Designs: a, Track. b, Basketball. c, Boxing. d, Soccer. e, Gymnastics. f, Equestrian. g, Field hockey. h, Canoeing. i, Polo. j, Two-man rowing. k, Tennis. l, Shooting. m, Sailing. n, Water polo.

1995, June 2 Photo. ***Perf. 14***

2822 Block of 14 + 6 labels 6.25 6.25
a.-n. A896 30p any single .45 .25

Labels are inscribed with names of Spanish silver medallists.

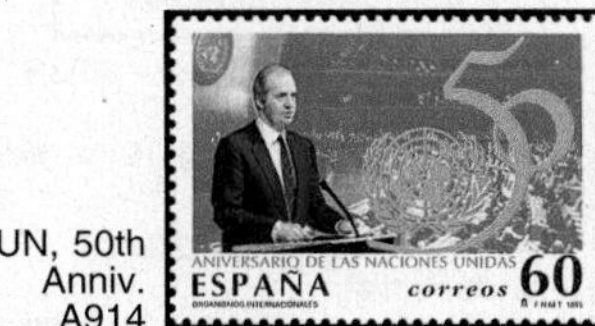

UN, 50th Anniv. A914

FAO, 50th Anniv. — A915

World Tourism Organization, 20th Anniv. — A916

1995, June 26

2823 A914 60p multicolored .90 .25
2824 A915 60p multicolored .90 .25
2825 A916 60p multicolored .90 .25
Nos. 2823-2825 (3) 2.70 .75

A917

1995, July 1

2826 A917 60p multicolored .90 .25

Spanish Presidentcy of the European Community Council of Ministers.

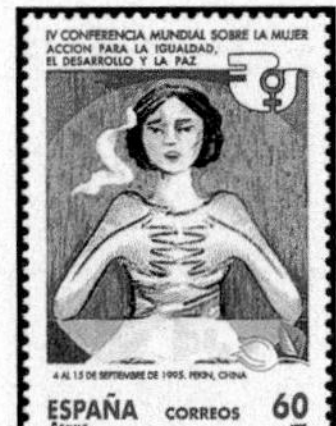

A918

1995, Sept. 4 Photo. ***Perf. 14***

2827 A918 60p multicolored .90 .25

4th World Conference on Women, Beijing.

Souvenir Sheet

17th Intl. Conference of Cartography, Barcelona — A919

1995, Sept. 5

2828 A919 130p multicolored 2.25 2.25

Santiago de Compostela University, 500th Anniv. — A920

1995, Sept. 15

2829 A920 30p multicolored .45 .25

UNESCO World Heritage Type of 1991 and

A921

No. 2830, Royal Monastery of Santa Maria de Guadalupe, vert. No. 2831, Map of Santiago de Compostela's 9th cent. route through northern Spain.

1995, Sept. 29 Engr. ***Perf. 12½***

2830 A830 60p dark brown 1.00 .25

Photo. & Engr.

2831 A921 60p multicolored 1.00 .25

Ecological Protection System, Lagunas Manchegas — A922

Ducks: 60p, Anade real, pato colorado.

1995, Oct. 11 Photo. ***Perf. 14***

2832 A922 60p multicolored .90 .25

America Issue.

Souvenir Sheet

EXFILNA '95, Nat. Philatelic Exhibition, Malaga — A923

Litho. & Engr.

1995, Oct. 6 ***Perf. 14x13½***

2833 A923 130p dark green 2.00 2.00

Archaeology — A924

#2834, Cave of Menga, Antequera, Malaga. #2835, Ruins of Torralba, Minorca.

1995, Oct. 20 Photo.

2834 A924 30p multicolored .50 .25
2835 A924 30p multicolored .50 .25

Souvenir Sheet

The Contemporary Poets, by Antonio Maria Esquivel (1806-57) — A925

Group of poets: a, Seated at left. b, One reading from paper. c, Four standing. d, Standing, seated at right.

1995, Oct. 27

2836	A925	Sheet of 4	2.75	2.75
a.		19p multicolored	.30	.25
b.		30p multicolored	.45	.45
c.-d.		60p any single	1.00	.75

Christmas A926

Design: 30p, Capital sculpture of "Adoration of the Magi," Collegiate Church of San Martin de Elines, Cantabria.

1995, Nov. 17 Photo. *Perf. 14*
2837 A926 30p multicolored .45 .25

Espamer '96, Aviation & Space Philatelic Exhibitions, Seville — A927

#2838, Sevilla-Plaza de Armas Railway Station. #2839, Lorenzo Galindez de Carvajal, Master Courier, King Fernando's Court, vert.

1995, Dec. 20 Photo. *Perf. 13*
2838 A927 60p multicolored .90 .25
2839 A927 60p multicolored .90 .25

Spanish Motion Pictures, Cent. A928

Designs: 30p, Scene from first Spanish motion picture, "Salida de los Fieles del Pilar de Zaragoza." 60p, Poster for 1952 motion picture, "Bienvenido, Mister Marshall."

1996, Jan. 30 Photo. *Perf. 14*
2840 A928 30p multicolored .45 .25
2841 A928 60p multicolored .90 .25

Spanish Mining — A929

Designs: 30p, Miner's lamp from Museum of Mining and Industry, mine shaft. 60p, Fluorite.

1996, Feb. 7
2842 A929 30p multicolored .45 .25
2843 A929 60p multicolored .90 .25

Madrid-Irun Visual Telegraph Line, 150th Anniv. — A930

1996, Mar. 8 Engr. *Perf. 14*
2844 A930 60p lake & gray grn .90 .25

Stamp Day.

Barcelona, 10th Anniv. of Urban Transformation — A931

1996, Mar. 22
2845 A931 30p multicolored .45 .25

Endangered Wildlife — A932

1996, Mar. 27 Photo.
2846 A932 30p Ursus arctos .45 .25

18th Cent. Sailing Ship Type of 1995

Designs: 30p, King Phillip. 60p, Catalán.

Litho. & Engr.

1996, Apr. 19 *Perf. 14x13½*

2847	A906	30p multicolored	.50	.25
a.		Miniature sheet of 4	2.00	2.00
2848	A906	60p multicolored	1.00	.25
a.		Miniature sheet of 4	3.50	3.50

Nos. 2847-2848 printed in miniature sheets of 4.

Madrid Bar Assoc., 400th Anniv. A933

1996, Apr. 23 Photo. *Perf. 14*
2849 A933 19p multicolored .30 .25

Olympic Venue Type of 1994

Symbols of Olympic venues, bronze ribbon: a, like #2797a. b, like #2822c. c, like #2797b. d, like 2797h. e, like #2797i. f, like 2822h. g, like #2822k. h, like #2822 l. i, like #2797j.

1996, Apr. 26 Photo. *Perf. 14*

2850		Block of 9 + 6 labels	4.50	4.50
a.-i.		A896 30p Any single	.45	.25

Labels are inscribed with names of Spanish bronze medalists.

Souvenir Sheets

A934

Royal Family — A935

Espamer '96 Philatelic Exhibition, World Aviation and Space Exposition: No. 2851a, Map of Seville-Larache Air Route, 1921. b, Zeppelin cover, Seville, 1930. c, Rocket launch. d, Hispano HA 200 SAETA aircraft.

1996, May 4

2851	a934	Sheet of 4	6.50	6.50
a.-d.		100p any single	1.60	1.40
2852	A935	400p multicolored	6.50	6.50

Carmen Amaya, Flamenco Dancer — A936

1996, May 6 *Perf. 14x13½*
2853 A936 60p multicolored 1.10 .25

Europa.

Cartoon Characters Type of 1995

19p, El Jabato, vert. 30p, El Reporter Tribulete.

1996, May 10 *Perf. 14x13½, 13½x14*
2854 A910 19p multicolored .35 .25
2855 A910 30p multicolored .65 .25

Paintings by Francisco de Goya Y Lucientes (1746-1828) — A937

19p, Gen. Don Antonio Ricardos, vert. 30p, Dairymaid of Bordeaux, vert. 60p, Boys with a Mastiff. 130p, The 3rd of May, 1808.

1996, May 31 Photo. *Perf. 14x13½*

2856	A937	19p multicolored	.35	.25
2857	A937	30p multicolored	.60	.25

Perf. 13½x14

2858	A937	60p multicolored	1.10	.25
2859	A937	130p multicolored	2.00	.40
		Nos. 2856-2859 (4)	4.05	1.15

Philatelic Service, 50th Anniv. A938

1996, June 4 *Perf. 13½x14*
2860 A938 30p multicolored .65 .25

Popular Personalities — A939

Designs: 19p, José Monge Cruz, singer, vert. 30p, Lola Flores, movie star.

Perf. 14x13½, 13½x14

1996, June 14
2861 A939 19p multicolored .30 .25
2862 A939 30p multicolored .45 .25

Lanuza Central Market, Zaragoza A940

1996, July 5 Photo. *Perf. 13½x14*
2863 A940 30p multicolored .65 .25

19th Intl. Congress of Architects, Barcelona.

Gerardo Diego (1896-1987), Poet — A941

Joaquín Costa (1846-1911), Lawyer, Teacher — A942

1996, Sept. 13 Engr.
2864 A941 19p red, black & vio .30 .25

Litho. & Engr.

2865 A942 30p multicolored .60 .25

UNICEF, 50th Anniv. — A943

1996, Sept. 13 Photo.
2866 A943 60p blue, black & red 1.00 .25

Archaeological Finds — A944

Designs: No. 2867, Naveta Des Tudons, tomb, 2000-1500BC. No. 2868, Cabezo de Alcala, reamains of Roman temple, 54-49BC.

1996, Sept. 27 Photo.
2867 A944 30p multicolored .50 .25
2868 A944 30p multicolored .50 .25

Souvenir Sheet

Exfilna '96, Natl. Philatelic Exhibition, Vitoria-Gasteiz — A945

Painting of Vitoria-Gasteiz, capital of Alava Province, by Ignacio Diaz Ruiz de Olano (1860-1937).

1996, Oct. 11 Engr. *Perf. 14x13½*
2869 A945 130p rose carmine 2.00 2.00

Sheet margin is litho.

America Issue — A946

Traditional costume of Charro Region, Salamanca.

1996, Oct. 15 Photo. ***Perf. 14***

2870 A946 60p multicolored .95 .25

Sites on UNESCO World Heritage List — A947

Designs: 19p, Albaicin, old Muslim quarter, Granada, vert. 30p, Gateway to Tiberiades Square, statue of Maimonides. 60p, Deer, De Donana Natl. Park, Huelva province, vert.

Perf. 12½x13, 13x12½

1996, Oct. 25 Engr.

2871 A947 19p dark blue violet .35 .25
2872 A947 30p deep claret .65 .25
2873 A947 60p dark blue 1.25 .25
Nos. 2871-2873 (3) 2.25 .75

Spanish Literature A948

Designs: 30p, "La Regenta," by Leopoldo Garcia-Alas Ureña (1852-1901), vert. 60p, Don Juan Tenorio, by José Zorrilla Moral (1817-93).

Perf. 14x13½, 13½x14

1996, Nov. 13 Engr.

2874 A948 30p bl, dep mag & dp vio .40 .25
2875 A948 60p dp blue & dp brn .85 .25

Christmas — A949

Birth of Christ, by Fernando Gallego.

1996, Nov. 22 Photo. ***Perf. 14***

2876 A949 30p multicolored .50 .25

Souvenir Sheet

Official Map of Spain and Its Provinces — A950

1996, Dec. 5

2877 A950 130p multicolored 2.00 2.00

Endangered Species — A951

32p, Genetta genetta.

1997, Jan. 30 Photo. ***Perf. 14x13½***

2878 A951 32p multicolored .45 .25

See Nos. 2928, 2978-2980.

A952

1997, Feb. 28 Photo. ***Perf. 14x13½***

2879 A952 32p multicolored .45 .25

Juvenia '97, Natl. Juvenile Philatelic Exhibition.

Stamp Day A953

65p, Antique letter box.

1997, Mar. 7 Engr. ***Perf. 14***

2880 A953 65p multicolored 1.00 .25

Spanish Motion Pictures — A954

1997, Mar. 12 Photo.

2881 A954 21p "Trip to Nowhere" .30 .25
2882 A954 32p "The South" .45 .25

World Day of Water — A955

1997, Mar. 22 ***Perf. 14x13½***

2883 A955 65p multicolored .95 .25

19th Cent. Sailing Ships — A956

21p, Frigate Asturias. 32p, Spanish Brigantine.

1997, Apr. 16 ***Litho. & Engr.***

2884 A956 21p multi .40 .25
a. Miniature sheet of 4 1.50 1.50
2885 A956 32p multi .60 .25
a. Miniature sheet of 4 2.50 2.50

Bilbao School of Engineering, Cent., — A957

194p, Atocha Station, High-Speed Spanish Train (AVE), 5th Anniv.

1997, Apr. 22 Photo. ***Perf. 14x13½***

2886 A957 32p multicolored .75 .25
2887 A957 194p multicolored 3.00 .70

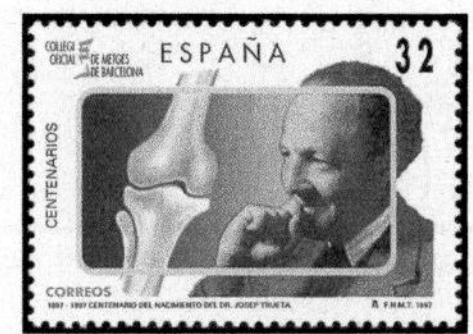

Dr. Josep Trueta (1897-1977), Orthopedic Surgeon — A958

1997, Apr. 30 ***Perf. 14***

2888 A958 32p multicolored .45 .25

Stories and Legends — A959

Europa: Princess, Prince, gnome, castle.

1997, May 5 Photo. ***Perf. 14x13½***

2889 A959 65p multicolored 1.25 .25

Fictional Characters A960

Designs: 21p, "El Lazarillo de Tormes," vert. 32p, "El Séneca," by José María Pemán.

1997, May 8 Engr. ***Perf. 14***

2890 A960 21p green & black .30 .25
2891 A960 32p black & blue .60 .25

Anxel Fole (1903-86), Poet, Writer A961

1997, May 17 Photo.

2892 A961 65p multicolored 1.00 .25

Comics A962

21p, The Ulysses Family. 32p, The Masked Warrior.

1997, May 30

2893 A962 21p multicolored .30 .25
2894 A962 32p multicolored .65 .25

Popular Personalities — A963

32p, Manuel Rodríguez Sánchez (Manolete) (1917-47), bullfighter. 65p, Charlie Rivel (Josep Andreu i Lasserre) (1896-1983), circus clown.

1997, June 5 Photo. ***Perf. 14***

2895 A963 32p multicolored .45 .25
2896 A963 65p multicolored 1.00 .25

A964

"The Age of Man" Cultural Exhibition: a, 21p, Painting, "The Annunciation," from Church of Nuestra Señora de la Peña, Agreda. b, 32p, Cathedral of El Burgo de Osma. c, 65p, Miniature from Codex titled "Commentary on the Apocalypse," by Beatus of Liebana, 786AD. d, 140p, Statue of Santo Domingo de Silos.

1997, June 13 ***Perf. 13***

2897 A964 Sheet of 4, #a.-d. 4.00 4.00

A965

1997, June 24 ***Perf. 14***

2898 A965 65p multicolored 1.00 .25

30th European Men's Basketball Championships.

NATO Summit, Madrid — A966

1997, July 8 ***Perf. 13***

2899 A966 65p multicolored 1.25 .25

A967

Design: Natl. monument to honor grape harvesting, Requena.

1997, July 11 Litho. *Perf. 14*
2900 A967 32p multicolored .50 .25

A968

Anniversaries: 21p, Don Antonio Canovas del Castillo (1828-97), politician. 32p, Roman colony of Elche, 2000th anniv. 65p, Naval defense of Tenerife, bicent., horiz.

1997, July 24 Photo.
2901 A968 21p multicolored .25 .25
2902 A968 32p multicolored .50 .25
2903 A968 65p multicolored .90 .25
Nos. 2901-2903 (3) 1.65 .75

Peace in Basque Region — A969

1997, July 30 Photo. *Perf. 14*
2904 A969 32p multicolored .45 .25

Spanish Artists — A970

Designs: 32p, Mariano Benlliure Gil (1862-1947), sculptor. 65p, Photograph of Remero Vasco, by José Ortiz Echagüe (1886-1980).

1997, Sept. 12
2905 A970 32p multicolored .50 .25
2906 A970 65p black & beige 1.00 .25

VIGO '97, World Exposition on Fisheries A971

1997, Sept. 17 Litho.
2907 A971 32p multicolored .45 .25

Anniversaries — A972

21p, City of Melilla, 500th anniv., vert. 32p, Declaration of St. Pascual Baylon as patron saint of World Eucharistic Congress, cent., vert. 65p, Ausias March (1397-1459), writer.

1997, Sept. 24 Photo.
2908 A972 21p multicolored .25 .25
2909 A972 32p multicolored .50 .25

Engr.
2910 A972 65p multicolored 1.00 .25
Nos. 2908-2910 (3) 1.75 .75

Sites on UNESCO World Heritage List — A973

Churches in Oviedo: 21p, San Julian de los Prados. 32p, Santa Cristina de Lena.

1997, Sept. 26 Engr. *Perf. 13*
2911 A973 21p multicolored .50 .25
2912 A973 32p multicolored .75 .25

29th Intl. Congress of Transport and Communications Museums, Madrid — A974

1997, Oct. 1 Litho. *Perf. 14x13½*
2913 A974 140p multicolored 2.00 .65

Souvenir Sheet

Monument to Don Pelayo, Revillagigedo Palace, Gijón — A975

1997, Oct. 4 Litho. & Engr. *Perf. 14*
2914 A975 140p multicolored 2.00 2.00

Exfilna '97, Natl. Stamp Exhibition, Gijón, Asturias

Opening of Royal Theater, Madrid — A976

Designs: 21p, Miguel Fleta (1897-1938), opera singer. 32p, Outside view of theater.

1997, Oct. 11 Engr. *Perf. 14x13½*
2915 A976 21p violet brown .30 .25
2916 A976 32p gray brown .55 .25

America Issue — A977

1997, Oct. 10 Photo.
2917 A977 65p Postman 1.00 .30

Foundation of St. Cristobal de La Laguna, 500th Anniv. — A978

1997, Oct. 17 Litho. & Engr.
2918 A978 32p multicolored .45 .25

6th World Conference on Down Syndrome, Madrid — A979

1997, Oct. 23 Photo. *Perf. 13½x14*
2919 A979 65p blue & yellow .95 .30

Veterinary College, Cordoba, 150th Anniv. A980

1997, Nov. 14 Engr. *Perf. 14*
2920 A980 21p green & blue .35 .25

Christmas — A981

Painting, Adoration of the Kings, by Pedro Berruguete.

1997, Nov. 20 Photo.
2921 A981 32p multicolored .45 .25

Jewish Heritage in Spain A982

Designs: 21p, Porta Nova, Ourense. No. 2923, Women's Gallery, Cordoba Synagogue. No. 2924, Jewish quarter, Caceres, 15th cent. 65p, Jewish Museum, Girona.

1997, Nov. 28 Engr. *Perf. 13½x14*
2922 A982 21p black & brown .30 .25
2923 A982 32p black & violet .50 .25
2924 A982 32p black & brown .50 .25
2925 A982 65p black & violet 1.00 .30
a. Strip of 4, #2922-2925 3.00 1.25

See Nos. 2969-2972.

Spanish Sports Accomplishments — A983

1997, Dec. 5 Photo.
2926 A983 32p multicolored 1.25 .25

XACOBEO 99 — A984

1998, Jan. 12 Photo. *Perf. 14x13½*
2927 A984 35p blk, org & gray .50 .25

Endangered Fauna — A985

1998, Feb. 5
2928 A985 35p Lynx pardina .45 .25

Bilbao Athletic Club, Cent. A986

1998, Feb. 10 *Perf. 13½x14*
2929 A986 35p multicolored .45 .25

Comic Book Characters A987

Designs: 35p, Mortadelo and Filemón, by Ibáñez, vert. 70p, Zipi & Zape, by Escobar.

Perf. 14x13½, 13½x14
1998, Feb. 26 Photo.
2930 A987 35p multicolored .50 .25
2931 A987 70p multicolored 1.10 .45

See Nos. 2998-2999.

Gredos State Hotel A988

1998, Mar. 12 Photo. *Perf. 13½x14*
2932 A988 35p multicolored .45 .25

Self-Government Statutes for Melilla and Ceuta — A989

1998, Mar. 16 ***Perf. 13½x14, 14x13½***
2933 A989 150p Melilla 1.90 1.00
2934 A989 150p Ceuta, vert. 1.90 1.00

"Generation of '98" Authors — A990

Design: Azorín (José Martinez Ruiz) (1873-1967), Pío Baroja (1872-1956), Miguel de Unamuno (1864-1936), Ramiro de Maetzu (1874-1936), Antonio Machado (1875-1939), Ramon Valle Inclán (1866-1936).

1998, Apr. 3 **Photo.** ***Perf. 14***
2935 A990 70p multicolored 1.10 .45

A991

Design: Pedro Abarca de Bolea, Count of Aranda (1719-98), soldier, politician.

1998, Apr. 17
2936 A991 35p multicolored .45 .25

A992

Literary characters from: 35p, Fernando de Rojas' "Le Celestina." 70p, Benito Perez Galdos' "Fortunata and Jacinta."

1998, Apr. 29 **Engr.** ***Perf. 14x13½***
2937 A992 35p multicolored .55 .25
2938 A992 70p multicolored 1.10 .45

Ships A993

1998, Apr. 30 **Litho.** ***Perf. 14***
2939 A993 35p Embarcación real .45 .25
2940 A993 70p Jabeque tajo .90 .45

Popular Festivals — A994

1998, May 5 **Photo.**
2941 A994 70p Bonfire of St. John 1.10 .45

Europa.

College of Medicine, Madrid, Cent. A995

Dr. D. Carlos Jiménez Díaz (1898-1967).

1998, May 18 ***Perf. 13½x14***
2942 A995 35p multicolored .45 .25

Popular Personalities — A996

35p, Félix Rodríguez de la Fuente (b. 1928), wildlife activist. 70p, Alfonso Aragón Bermúdez ("Fofó") (1923-76), circus comic, vert.

1998, May 28 ***Perf. 13½x14, 14x13½***
2943 A996 35p multicolored .55 .25
2944 A996 70p multicolored 1.10 .45

King Philip II (1527-98) — A997

1998, June 1 **Photo.** ***Perf. 14x13½***
2945 A997 35p multicolored .45 .25

Fedrico Garcia Lorca (1898-1936), Poet, Dramatist — A998

1998, June 2 **Litho. & Engr.**
2946 A998 35p multicolored .85 .25

Spanish Stamp Engravers A999

35p, Antonio Manso (1934-93), Spain #2129. 70p, J.L.L. Sánchez Toda (1901-), Spain #546.

1998, June 5 ***Perf. 14***
2947 A999 35p multicolored .45 .25
2948 A999 70p multicolored .90 .45

Philippine Independence, Cent. — A1000

Design: Spanish flag, Basilica of Cebu, Holy Child of Cebu, Philippine flag.

1998, June 12 **Photo.** ***Perf. 13½x14***
2949 A1000 70p multicolored .95 .50

See Philippines No. 2539.

Sculpture, "Foster Brothers," by Aniceto Marinas (1866-1953) A1000a

1998, July 10 **Photo.** ***Perf. 14***
2949A A1000a 35p multi .50 .25

Expo '98, Lisbon A1001

1998, Sept. 4
2950 A1001 70p multicolored 1.00 .50

Letter Writing — A1002

Scenes from "Don Quixote" — #2951: a, "En un lugas de la Mancha." b, "Llenósele la fantasía." c, "Armado caballero." d, "La del alba sería." e, "Le molió como cibera." f, "El donoso escrutinio." g, "Has de saber, amigo Sancho." h, "Los gigantes." i, "Viole bajar y subir con tanta gracia." j, "El escuadrón de ovejas." k, "Los galeotes." l, "Los cueros."

No. 2952: a, "El encantamiento." b, "Oh princesa del toboso." c, "El caballero de los espejos." d, "El leon." e, "La cueva de montesinos." f, "Clavileño." g, "Sancho gobernador." h, "Doña Rodríguez." i, "Compañero mío." j, "Parecioles espaciosísimo." k, "El caballero de la blanca luna." l, "La vuelta a casa."

1998, Sept. 25 ***Perf. 13***
2951 Sheet of 12 9.00 9.00
a.-l. A1002 20p any single .35 .25
2952 Sheet of 12 9.00 9.00
a.-l. A1002 20p any single .35 .25

See #3016, 3053-3954, 3121, 3175.

20th Intl. Conference on Data Protection, Santiago de Compostela — A1003

1998, Sept. 16 **Litho.** ***Perf. 14***
2953 A1003 70p multicolored 1.00 .45

Souvenir Sheet

EXFILNA '98 Natl. Philatelic Exhibition — A1004

150p, Cathedral of Barcelona.

Litho. & Engr.

1998, Sept. 18 ***Perf. 14***
2954 A1004 150p multi 2.25 2.25

UNESCO World Heritage Sites — A1005

Designs: 35p, Walled city of Cuenca. 70p, Silk Exchange, Valencia.

1998, Sept. 19 **Engr.** ***Perf. 13***
2955 A1005 35p blue & brown .60 .25
2956 A1005 70p red & brown 1.40 .45

Angel Ganivet (1865-98), Writer A1006

1998, Oct. 6 **Engr.** ***Perf. 14***
2957 A1006 35p brown & purple .50 .25

The Giralda of Seville, 800th Anniv. — A1007

1998, Oct. 6
2958 A1007 70p multicolored 1.00 .50

A1008

1998, Oct. 8 **Engr.** ***Perf. 14***
2959 A1008 35p brn & yel grn .50 .25

Aga Khan Architecture Award, Alhambra of Granada.

Stamp Day A1009

1998, Oct. 9 **Photo.**

2960 A1009 70p multicolored 1.00 .50

María Guerrero (1867-1928), Theater Actress — A1010

1998, Oct. 13

2961 A1010 70p multicolored 1.00 .50

America Issue.

Spanish Railroads, 150th Anniv. A1011

1998, Oct. 28 **Engr.**

2962 A1011 35p multicolored .50 .25

Juan Carlos I Antarctic Base A1012

1998, Nov. 6 **Photo.**

2963 A1012 35p multicolored .50 .25

A1013

Christmas (Works of art): 35p, Chestnut Seller, by Rafael Seco. 70p, Marriage of the Virgin and St. Joseph, Cathedral of Oviedo.

1998, Nov. 13

2964 A1013 35p multicolored .50 .25
2965 A1013 70p multicolored 1.00 .50

Souvenir Sheet

A1014

The Cathedral of San Salvador, Zaragoza (Details from Altarpiece: a, Holding cross, angel. b, Holy family.

1998, Nov. 11 **Photo.** ***Perf. 14***

2966 A1014 35p Sheet of 2, a.-b. 1.50 1.25

Founding of New Mexico, 400th Anniv. A1015

Designs: 35p, Expedition of Juan de Oñate. 70p, Early map of Nueva Espana (Mexico) and Nuevo Mexico.

1998, Nov. 20

2967 A1015 35p multicolored .50 .25
2968 A1015 70p multicolored 1.00 .50

Jewish Heritage in Spain Type of 1997

Designs: No. 2969, Bust of Benjamin de Tudela, Tudela Commune, Navarre. No. 2970, Residence, Hervás Community, Cáceres. No. 2971, Courtyard, Corpus Christi Church, Segovia. No. 2972, Santa Maria la Blanca Synagogue, Toledo.

1998, Nov. 23 **Engr.**

2969 A982 35p dp blue & dp ol .50 .25
2970 A982 35p dp blue & dp cl .50 .25
2971 A982 70p dp blue & dp cl 1.00 .50
2972 A982 70p dp blue & dp ol 1.00 .50
a. Strip of 4, #2969-2972 3.25 3.25

Nos. 2969, 2971 have Star of David. Nos. 2970, 2972 have menorah.

UNESCO Biosphere Reserve, Minorca A1016

1998, Dec. 2 **Photo.**

2973 A1016 35p multicolored .50 .25

Spanish Olympic Academy, 30th Anniv. A1017

70p, Bust of Plato, amphora.

1998, Dec. 9

2974 A1017 70p multi 1.00 .50

Universal Declaration of Human Rights, 50th Anniv.
A1018 A1019

Designs: 35p, Angel Sanz Briz (1910-80), Spanish ambassador. 70p, Fingerprints.

1998, Dec. 10

2975 A1018 35p multicolored .50 .25
2976 A1019 70p multicolored 1.00 .50

Carthusian Horses — A1020

Designs: a, 100p, Mare standing with colt. b, 185p, Two with heads together. c, 35p, Adult standing in grass. d, 150p, Adult standing in flowers. e, 20p, Colt lying down, mare eating grass. f, 70p, Head of adult, silhouette.

1998, Dec. 29

2977 A1020 Block of 6, #a.-f. 25.00 25.00

España 2000, Intl. Philatelic Exhibition.

Issued in sheets of two blocks, the lower one in a different order. Two of the devices shown on the coat of arms appear on each block at the intersection of the perfs. On the top block the crown is on a.-b., d.-e., while the "H" is on b.-c., e.-f. On the bottom block the location of these devices is reversed, giving all the stamps in the sheet a slightly different design.

See #3019, 3052.

Gallotia simonyi machadoi A1020a

Pandion haliaetus A1020b

Puffinus puffinus — A1020c

1999, Jan. 28 **Photo.** ***Perf. 14***

2978 A1020a 35p multicolored .50 .25
2979 A1020b 70p multicolored 1.00 .50
2980 A1020c 100p multicolored 1.40 .70
Nos. 2978-2980 (3) 2.90 1.45

Endangered fauna.

Xacobeo '99 A1021

Designs: 35p, Stone cross of Paradela, vert. 70p, Sculpture of St. James, door on Church of St. James, Sangüesa. 100p, Stone cross, Cizur Bridge, Pamplona, vert. 185p, Jurisdictional stone pillar, Boadilla del Camino, vert.

Litho. & Engr.

1999, Feb. 22 ***Perf. 13¾***

2981 A1021 35p multicolored .60 .25
2982 A1021 70p multicolored 1.25 .45
2983 A1021 100p multicolored 1.50 .65
2984 A1021 185p multicolored 2.75 1.10
Nos. 2981-2984 (4) 6.10 2.45

Barcelona Soccer Club, Cent. — A1022

1999, Mar. 11 **Photo.** ***Perf. 14***

2985 A1022 35p multicolored .50 .25

Juvenia '99, Natl. Junior Philatelic Exhibition A1023

1999, Mar. 12 **Litho.** ***Perf. 14***

2986 A1023 35p multicolored .50 .25

Spanish Police Force, 175th Anniv. A1024

1999, Mar. 26

2987 A1024 35p multicolored .50 .25

Souvenir Sheet

Palace of Alfonso I el Batallador, Zaragoza — A1025

Litho. & Engr.

1999, Apr. 9 ***Perf. 14x13½***

2988 A1025 185p multicolored 3.00 2.75

Exfilna '99, Zaragoza.

Spanish Amateur Radio Union, 50th Anniv. A1026

1999, Apr. 16 **Photo.** ***Perf. 14***

2989 A1026 70p multicolored 1.00 .50

7th World Track & Field Championships, Seville — A1027

1999, Apr. 30 **Photo.** ***Perf. 14x13½***

2990 A1027 70p multicolored 1.00 .45

Monfragüe Nature Park A1028

Litho. & Engr.

1999, May 5 ***Perf. 13½x14***

2991 A1028 70p multicolored 1.25 .45

Europa.

Barcelona Subway System, 75th Anniv. A1029

1999, May 7 Photo. *Perf. 14*
2992 A1029 70p multicolored 1.00 .45

Spanish Art — A1030

Designs: 35p, Portrait of King Solomon. 70p, Artifact from cathedral, Palencia.

1999, May 14
2993 A1030 35p multicolored .50 .25
2994 A1030 70p multicolored 1.00 .45

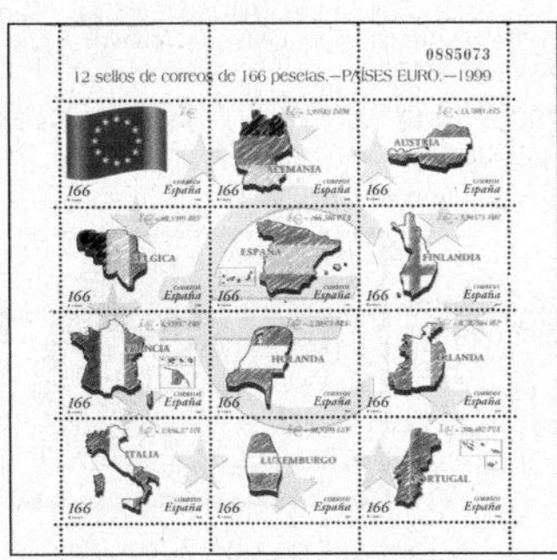
Introduction of the Euro — A1031

Design: a, European Union flag.
Maps: b, Germany. c, Austria. d, Belgium e, Spain. f, Finland. g, France. h, Netherlands. i, Ireland. j, Italy. k, Luxembourg. l, Portugal.

1999, May 28 *Perf. 13½x14*
2995 A1031 166p Sheet of 12, #a.-l. 30.00 30.00

Denomination is shown in both pesetas and euros. Each stamp shows the equivilent of 1 euro in the currency of the represented country.

Royal Recreation Club of Huelva A1032

1999, June 7
2996 A1032 35p multicolored .50 .25

Souvenir Sheet

Palma '99, Natl. Topical Philatelic Exhibition — A1033

1999, June 18 *Perf. 14x13½*
2997 A1033 185p multicolored 3.00 3.00

Comic Book Character Type of 1998

35p, Dona Urraca, by Jorge, vert. 70p, El Coyote, by José Mallorquí Figuerola, vert.

1999, June 11 Photo. *Perf. 13¾*
2998 A987 35p multicolored .50 .25
2999 A987 70p multicolored 1.00 .45

Defense of Las Palmas de Gran Canaria, 400th Anniv. — A1034

1999, June 25 Litho. & Engr.
3000 A1034 70p multicolored 1.00 .45

A1035

1999, July 2 Photo. *Perf. 13¾*
3001 A1035 35p multicolored .50 .25

San Pedro de Villanueva Benedictine Monastery.

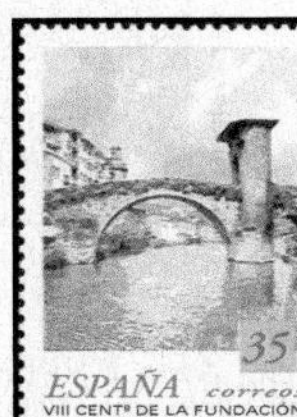
Village of Balmaseda, 800th Anniv. — A1036

1999, July 12
3002 A1036 35p multicolored .50 .25

Carlos Buigas (b. 1898), Graphic Designer A1037

1999, July 12
3003 A1037 70p multicolored 1.00 .45

General Society of Authors and Editors, Cent. — A1038

1999, July 12
3004 A1038 70p multicolored 1.00 .45

Spanish Mining Institute, 150th Anniv. A1039

1999, July 12
3005 A1039 150p multicolored 2.25 .95

El Cid (Rodrigo Diaz de Vivar) (1040-99) A1040

1999, July 16 Photo. *Perf. 13¾*
3006 A1040 35p multicolored .50 .25

Paintings by Jose Vela Zanetti (1913-99) A1041

70p, "Winter." 150p, "The Harvest."

1999, Sept. 10 Photo. *Perf. 13¾*
3007 A1041 70p multi 1.00 .45
3008 A1041 150p multi, vert. 2.00 .95

Diego Velazquez (1599-1660), Painter — A1042

Paintings: 35p, Sebastián de Morra. 70p, Sibyl.

1999, Sept. 24
3009 A1042 35p multicolored .50 .25
3010 A1042 70p multicolored 1.00 .45

Intl. Year of Older Persons A1043

1999, Sept. 30
3011 A1043 35p multicolored .50 .25

Oix Castle, Lower Pyrenees A1044

1999, Oct. 1 Engr. *Perf. 13½x14*
3012 A1044 70p blue & vio brn 1.00 .45

World Heritage Sites — A1045

Designs: 35p, San Millán de Yuso Monastery. 70p, San Millán de Suso Monastery.

1999, Oct. 8 *Perf. 13x12½*
3013 A1045 35p multicolored .65 .25
3014 A1045 70p multicolored 1.25 .45

UPU, 125th Anniv. A1046

1999, Oct. 9 Photo. *Perf. 13¾*
3015 A1046 70p multicolored 1.00 .45

Letter Writing Type of 1998

Designs: a, "Cumplimos 150 años." b, "Recorremos el mundo." c, "Llegamos juntos." d, "Escríbeme." e, "Ama la lectura." f, "Vive la naturaleza." g, "Te mostramos el patrimonio." h, "Te acercamos a la pintura." i, "Jugamos contigo." j, "Sentimos la musica." k, "Y además nos coleccionan." l, "Os esperamos."

1999, Oct. 13 Photo. *Perf. 13x12½*
3016 Sheet of 12 4.00 4.00
a.-l. A1002 20p any single .30 .25

America Issue, A New Millennium Without Arms — A1047

1999, Oct. 15 *Perf. 13¾*
3017 A1047 70p multicolored 1.00 .45

Intl. Congress of Money Museums, Madrid — A1048

1999, Oct. 18 Engr. *Perf. 13x12½*
3018 A1048 70p blue & brown 1.00 .45

Carthusian Horse Type of 1998

Designs: a, 185p, White horse, six men. b, 70p, Espana Intl. Philatelic Exhibition emblem. c, 100p, Two white horses. d, 150p, Two white horses, one with leg raised. e, 35p, Emblem, exhibition dates. f, 20p, Horse, handler.

1999, Nov. 3 Photo. *Perf. 13¾*
3019 A1020 Block of 6, #a.-f. 14.00 14.00

See footnote following No. 2977.

Christmas A1049

35p, Adoration of the Magi, Toledo Cathedral retable. 70p, Child, statue, candles.

1999, Nov. 5
3020 A1049 35p multi, vert. .50 .25
3021 A1049 70p multi 1.00 .45

Spanish Postage Stamps, 150th Anniv. A1050

a, King Juan Carlos, altered 12c design A2. b, King, altered 6c design A1. c, King, altered 5r design A2. d, King, altered 6r design A2. e, 150th anniv. emblem, altered 6c design A1. f, King, altered 10r design A2. g, King, coat of arms.

Litho. & Engr.

2000, Jan. 3 ***Perf. 13¾x14***

3022	Sheet of 12	6.00	6.00
a.-g.	A1050 35p any single	.50	.25

#3022 contains 2 ea #3022a-3022d, 3022f, 1 ea #3022e, 3022g.

Endangered Butterflies — A1051

Designs: 35p, Parnassius apollo. 70p, Agriades zullichi.

2000, Jan. 31 **Photo.** ***Perf. 13¾***

3023	A1051	35p multi	.60	.25
3024	A1051	70p multi	1.25	.45

First Printing at Montserrat Monastery, 500th Anniv. — A1052

2000, Feb. 4 **Photo.** ***Perf. 13¾***

3025	A1052	35p multi	.50	.25

Holy Roman Emperor Charles V (1500-58) A1053

2000, Feb. 24 ***Perf. 12¾x13***

3026	A1053	35p shown	.50	.25
3027	A1053	70p At age 40	1.00	.45

Souvenir Sheet

Perf. 13¼x12¾

3028	A1053	150p In armor	2.25	2.25

No. 3028 contains one 40x49mm stamp. See Belgium Nos. 1791-1793.

"Age of Man" Exhibition, Astorga — A1054

Designs: 70p, Carving of the Virgin Mary. 100p, Cross, Arab perfume bottle.

2000, Mar. 24 **Photo.** ***Perf. 14x13¾***

3029	A1054	70p multi	1.00	.40
3030	A1054	100p multi	1.50	.55

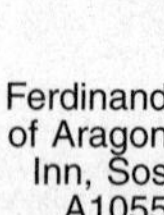

Ferdinand of Aragon Inn, Sos A1055

2000, Apr. 7 ***Perf. 13¾x14***

3031	A1055	35p multi	.60	.25

University Anniversaries — A1056

35p, Lleida, 700th anniv. 70p, Valencia, 500th anniv. (in 1999).

2000, Apr. 12 **Engr.** ***Perf. 13¾x14***

3032	A1056	35p red lil & brown	.50	.25
3033	A1056	70p blue & choc	1.00	.40

A1057

2000, Apr. 28 **Photo.** ***Perf. 14x13¾***

3034	A1057	35p multi	.60	.25

Royal Barcelona Sports Club, soccer team, cent.

A1058

2000, May 4

3035	A1058	35p multi	.60	.25

María de las Mercedes de Borbón y Orleáns (1910-2000), mother of King Juan Carlos.

Europa Issue

Common Design Type

2000, May 9

3036	CD17	70p multi	1.00	.40

Royal Academy of Medicine, Seville, 300th Anniv. A1060

Julio Rey Pastor (1888-1962), Mathematician — A1061

Pharmacy College of Granada, 150th Anniv. — A1062

Valencia, City of Arts and Sciences A1063

2000, May 25 ***Perf. 13¾x14, 14x13¾***

3037	A1060	35p multi	.60	.25
3038	A1061	70p multi	1.00	.40
3039	A1062	100p multi	1.50	.55
3040	A1063	185p multi	2.50	1.00
	Nos. 3037-3040 (4)		5.60	2.20

Intl. Mathematics Year (No. 3038).

Comic Strips A1064

Designs: 35p, Las Hermanas Gilda, by Manuel Vázquez. 70p, Roberto Alcázar y Pedrín, by Eduardo Vañó, vert.

2000, May 26 ***Perf. 13¾x14, 14x13¾***

3041	A1064	35p multi	.60	.25
3042	A1064	70p multi	1.00	.40

Guggenheim Museum, Bilbao — A1065

2000, June 2 **Photo.** ***Perf. 13¾x14***

3043	A1065	70p multi	1.00	.40

Bilbao, 700th anniv.

Angel From Prayer in the Garden, Sculpture by Francisco Salzillo (1707-73) A1066

2000, June 9 **Photo.** ***Perf. 14x13¼***

3044	A1066	70p multi	1.10	.40

Souvenir Sheet

Fountains of San Francisco, Aviles — A1067

Litho. & Engr.

2000, June 16 ***Perf. 14x13¾***

3045	A1067	185p multi	2.75	2.75

Exfilna 2000 Philatelic Exhibition, Aviles.

Trees A1068

Designs: 70p, Pinus sylvestris. 150p, Quercus ilex (encina).

Perf. 12¾x12½

2000, June 19 **Photo.**

3046-3047	A1068	Set of 2	3.00	1.10

Local Festivals A1069

Designs: 35p, Fire Walking Festival, San Pedro Manrique. 70p, Chivalry Festival of San Juan, Ciudadela.

2000, June 23 ***Perf. 13¾x14***

3048-3049	A1069	Set of 2	1.60	.55

Josemaria Escrivá de Balaguer (1902-75), Founder of Opus Dei. A1070

Litho. & Engr.

2000, June 26 ***Perf. 13¾x14***

3050	A1070	70p black & orange	1.10	.40

Souvenir Sheet

World Map of Juan de la Cosa, 500th Anniv. — A1071

2000, July 14 **Photo.** ***Perf. 13¾x14***

3051	A1071	150p multi	2.25	2.25

Carthusian Horses Type of 1998

No. 3052: a, 20p, Head of horse, five horses. b, 35p, White horse, sun partially obscured by clouds. c, 70p, Horse's head, two horses galloping. d, 100p, Heads of two horses. e, 150p, Horse's head, horse in lilac. f, 185p, Horse with bridle.

2000, July 28

3052	A1020	Block of 6, #a-f	20.00	20.00

See note following No. 2977.

Letter Writing Type of 1998

No. 3053: a, Atapuerca Man, 800,000 B.C. b, Cave paintings of Altamira, 12,000 B.C. c, Phoenecians, 1100 B.C. d, Tartessians, 800 B.C. e, Iberians and Celts, 500 B.C. f, Lady of Elche, Iberian statue, 480 B.C. g, Carthaginians, 237 B.C. h, Roman Spain, 197 B.C. i, Viriathus, Lusitanian war leader against Romans, 147 B.C. j, Siege of Numantia, 133 B.C. k, Segovia aqueduct, A.D. 50. l, Vandals, Suebis, and Alanis, 409.

No. 3054: a, Visigoths, 415. b, Conversion of Recared to Catholicism, 589. c, Arabs, 711. d, Victory over Arabs by Asturian King, Pelayo, 722. e, Discovery of alleged tomb of St. James, 813. f, Collapse of the caliphate, 1031. g, Death of El Cid, 1099. h, Alfonso VIII's victory at Las Navas de Tolosa, 1212. i, Alfonso X (the Wise) becomes King, 1252. j, Trastámara Dynasty, 1369. k, Spanish Inquisition, 1478. l, Union of Aragon and Castile, 1479.

2000, Sept. 22 *Perf. 13x12¾*

3053 Sheet of 12 4.00 4.00
a.-l. A1002 20p Any single .30 .25
3054 Sheet of 12 4.00 4.00
a.-l. A1002 20p Any single .30 .25

World Heritage Sites — A1072

Designs: 35p, Las Médulas. 70p, Pyrénées — Mt. Perdido, vert. 150p, Catalan Music Palace, Barcelona.

Perf. 13x12¾(35p), 12¾

2000, Sept. 21 Litho. (35p), Engr.

3055-3057 A1072 Set of 3 3.25 1.40

Souvenir Sheets

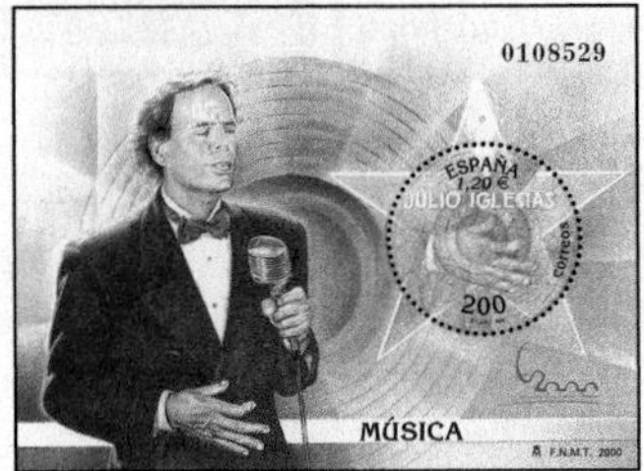

España 2000 Intl. Philatelic Exhibition — A1073

Designs: No. 3058, Hand of Julio Iglesias, singer. No. 3059, Signature of Alejandro Sanz, singer. No. 3060, Signature of Antonio Banderas, movie star. No. 3061, Mannequin, signature of Jesús del Pozo, fashion designer. No. 3062, Signature of Miguel Induráin, cyclist. No. 3063, Soccer ball, signature of Raúl González, soccer player. No. 3064, Hands of Joaquín Cortés, dancer. No. 3065, Feet of Sara Baras, dancer. No. 3066, Emblem of TVE 1 television network. No. 3067, Radio and antenna. No. 3068, Newspaper mastheads.

Illustration reduced.

Perf. 13 (round stamps), 13¾x14

2000 Photo.

3058-3068 A1073 200p Set of 11 35.00 35.00

150th anniv. of Spanish stamps, #3066.

Nos. 3060-3061, 3064-3068 each contain one 41x28mm rectangular stamp.

Exist imperf. Value $65.

Issued: #3058-3059, 10/6; #3060, 10/7; #3061, 10/8; #3062-3063, 10/9; #3064-3065, 10/10; #3066, 10/11; #3067, 10/12; #3068, 10/13.

Alfredo Kraus (1927-99), Operatic Tenor — A1074

2000, Oct. 27 *Perf. 14x13¾*

3069 A1074 70p multi 1.00 .40

America Issue, Fight Against AIDS — A1075

2000, Oct. 19 Photo. *Perf. 14x13¾*

3070 A1075 70p multi 1.00 .40

Christmas A1076

Designs: 35p, Nativity scene. 70p, Birth of Christ, by Conrad von Soest.

2000, Nov. 9 *Perf. 12¾*

3071-3072 A1076 Set of 2 1.50 .55

See Germany No. B878-B879.

Santa María la Real Church, Aranda de Duero — A1077

2000, Nov. 10 Engr. *Perf. 14x13¾*

3073 A1077 35p brown .50 .25

Spanish Literature A1078

Designs: 35p, Entre Naranjos, by Vicente Blasco Ibáñez. 70p, La Venganza de Don Mendo, by Pedro Muñoz Seca. 100p, El Alcalde Zalamea, by Pedro Calderón de la Barca.

Photo., Engr. (100p)

2000, Nov. 17 *Perf. 13¾x14*

3074-3076 A1078 Set of 3 3.25 1.50

Commercial Agents College, 75th Anniv. — A1079

2001, Jan. 8 Photo. *Perf. 14x13¾*

3077 A1079 40p multi .60 .25

Fire Fighters — A1080

2001, Jan. 19

3078 A1080 75p multi 1.10 .45

Infantry College, Toledo, 150th Anniv. A1081

2001, Feb. 16 *Perf. 13¾x14*

3079 A1081 120p multi 1.75 .65

Intl. Campaign Against Domestic Violence — A1082

2001, Feb. 22 *Perf. 14x13¾*

3080 A1082 155p multi 2.25 .85

First Spanish Mail Box, Mayorga A1083

2001, Mar. 2 Engr. *Perf. 13¾x14*

3081 A1083 155p black 2.25 .85

Stamp Day.

Juvenia 2001, Natl. Youth Philatelic Exhibition A1084

2001, Mar. 9 Photo.

3082 A1084 120p multi 1.75 .70

Placencia Inn — A1084a

2001, Mar. 16 *Perf. 14x13¾*

3083 A1084a 40p multicolored .60 .25

Famous People A1085

Designs: 40p, Joaquín Rodrigo (1901-99), musician. 75p, Rafael Alberti (1902-99), writer.

2001, Mar. 22 Engr. *Perf. 13¾x14*

3084-3085 A1085 Set of 2 1.75 .60

Castles — A1086

Designs: 40p, Zuda, Tortosa, vert. 75p, Cid, Jadraque. 155p, San Fernando, Figueres. 260p, Montesquiu, Montesquiu.

2001, Apr. 20 *Perf. 14x13¾, 13¾x14*

3086-3089 A1086 Set of 4 7.50 3.00

Book Day — A1087

2001, Apr. 23 Photo. *Perf. 14x13¾*

3090 A1087 40p multi .60 .25

Souvenir Sheet

First Flights, 75th Anniv. — A1088

No. 3091: a, 40p, Spain-Argentina. b, 75p, Spain-Philippines. c, 155p, Spain-Equatorial Guinea. d, 260p, Commemorative flight.

2001, Apr. 26 *Perf. 13¾x14*

3091 A1088 Sheet of 4, #a-d 7.50 7.50

Grand Theater, Liceu — A1089

2001, Apr. 27 *Perf. 14x13¾*

3092 A1089 120p multi 1.75 .65

King Juan Carlos — A1091

2001 Photo. *Perf. 12¾x13¼*

3093 A1091 5p sil & lil rose .25 .25
3094 A1091 40p sil & yel grn .60 .25
3095 A1091 75p sil & bl vio 1.10 .40
3096 A1091 100p sil & lt red brn 1.50 .55
Nos. 3093-3096 (4) 3.45 1.45

Issued: 40p, 5/4; 5p, 75p, 6/28; 100p, 7/15.

See also Nos. 3133-3140, 3271-3274, 3337-3343, 3387-3391.

Europa — A1092

2001, May 9 Photo. *Perf. 14x13¾*

3097 A1092 75p multi .80 .40

Architecture A1093

Designs: 40p, San Martiño Church, Noia. 75p, Santa Maria Cathedral, Tui. 155p, Villaconcha dovecote, Frechilla.

Engr., Photo. (75p)

2001, May 17 ***Perf. 14x13¾***

3098-3100 A1093 Set of 3 3.50 1.50

Luarca Harbor A1094

2001, May 26 Photo. ***Perf. 13¾x14***

3101 A1094 40p multi .60 .25

Cardinal Rodrigo de Castro (1523-1600) — A1095

2001, June 1

3102 A1095 40p multi .60 .25

Leopoldo Alas, "Clarín," (1852-1901), Writer — A1096

2001, June 13

3103 A1096 75p multi 1.10 .40

Trees A1097

Designs: 40p, Olive. 75p, Beech.

2001, June 22 ***Perf. 12¾***

3104-3105 A1097 Set of 2 1.75 .60

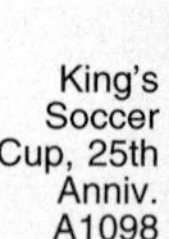

King's Soccer Cup, 25th Anniv. A1098

2001, July 6 Litho. ***Perf. 13¾x14***

3106 A1098 40p multi .60 .25

Issued in sheets of 8 + 4 labels.

Local Festivals A1099

Designs: 40p, Cipotegato, Tarazona. 120p, Giants of Pí, Barcelona, vert.

Perf. 13¾x14, 14x13¾

2001, July 10 Photo.

3107-3108 A1099 Set of 2 2.40 .80

Baltasar Gracian (1601-58), Writer A1100

2001, July 13 ***Perf. 13¾x14***

3109 A1100 120p multi 1.75 .60

"Age of Man" Exhibition — A1101

Designs: 120p, Our Lady of La Calva. 155p, Cathedral dome, Zamora.

2001, July 20 Engr. ***Perf. 14x13¾***

3110-3111 A1101 Set of 2 3.75 1.50

Grandparent's Day — A1102

Siervas de Jesús de la Caridad A1103

Perf. 14x13¾, 13¾x14

2001, July 26 Photo.

3112 A1102 40p multi .60 .25

3113 A1103 75p multi 1.00 .40

Salamanca, European City of Culture — A1104

2001, Sept. 5 Photo. ***Perf. 13x13¼***

3114 A1104 75p multi 1.10 .40

Covadonga Basilica, Cent. of Consecration — A1105

2001, Sept. 7 ***Perf. 13¾x14***

3115 A1105 40p multi .60 .25

Emblem of Privatized Postal System A1106

2001, Sept. 15

3116 A1106 40p multi .60 .25

Souvenir Sheet

Exfilna 2001 Natl. Philatelic Exhibition, Vigo — A1107

Engr. (Litho. Margin)

2001, Sept. 21

3117 A1107 260p multi 3.75 3.75

St. Dominic of Silos (c. 1000-73) — A1108

Litho. & Engr.

2001, Oct. 4 ***Perf. 14x13¾***

3118 A1108 40p multi .60 .25

a. Souvenir sheet of 1 with margin like stamp design 5.00 5.00

b. Souvenir sheet of 1 with margin differing 5.00 5.00

Year of Dialogue Among Civilizations A1109

2001, Oct. 9 Photo.

3119 A1109 120p multi 1.75 .70

Stamp Day.

Posidonia Oceanica, Ses Salines Nature Reserve A1110

2001, Oct. 15 ***Perf. 13¾x14***

3120 A1110 155p multi 2.25 .85

America issue — UNESCO World Heritage Sites.

Letter Writing Type of 1998

No. 3121: a, Christopher Columbus, 1492. b, Treaty of Tordesillas, 1494. c, Election of King Charles I as Holy Roman Emperor Charles V, 1519. d, Conquest of Mexico by Hernán Cortés, 1519. e, Circumnavigation by Juan Sebastián Elcano, 1522. f, Campaign against Incas by Francisco Pizarro, 1532. g, Ascension to throne of King Philip II, 1556. h, Start of construction of El Escoríal Monastery, 1563. i, Battle of Lepanto, 1571. j, Saints John of the Cross, Teresa of Jesus and painter El Greco, 1580. k, First play by Lope de Vega, 1593. l, Ascension to throne of King Philip III, 1598.

2001, Oct. 19 ***Perf. 13x12½***

3121 Sheet of 12 4.50 4.50

a.-l. A1002 25p Any single .35 .25

Souvenir Sheet

Bullfighter Curro Romero — A1111

2001, Oct. 25 ***Perf. 14x13¾***

3122 A1111 260p multi 3.50 3.50

Christmas A1112

Designs: 40p, Virgin With Child, by Alfredo Roldan. 75p, Adoration of the Shepherds, by José Ribera.

2001, Nov. 8 ***Perf. 12¾***

3123-3124 A1112 Set of 2 1.75 .60

a. Souvenir sheet, # 3123-3124, Germany #B895-B896, litho., perf. 13¼ 5.50 5.50

See Germany No. B896a.

Score of "El Sombrero de Tres Picos," by Manuel de Falla (1876-1946) — A1113

2001, Nov. 14 Photo. ***Perf. 13¾x14***

3125 A1113 75p multi 1.10 .40

Comic Strips A1114

Designs: 40p, Cartoon by Josep Coll i Coll. 75p, Rompetechos, by Francisco Ibañez.

2001, Nov. 20

3126-3127 A1114 Set of 2 1.75 .60

Carlos Cano (1946-2000), Singer — A1115

2001, Nov. 23 ***Perf. 14x13¾***

3128 A1115 40p black .60 .25

Intl. Volunteer Day for Economic and Social Development A1116

2001, Nov. 27
3129 A1116 120p multi 1.75 .70

World Heritage Sites — A1117

No. 3130: a, Catalan Romanesque Churches of the Vall de Boí. b, The Mystery of Elx (Elche). c, Hospital de Sant Pau, Barcelona. d, San Cristóbal de La Laguna. e, Archaeological Site of Atapuerca. f, Palmeral of Elche. g, Monuments of Oviedo. h, Roman Walls of Lugo. i, Rock Art of the Mediterranean Basin. j, Ibiza, Biodiversity and Culture. k, Archaeological Ensemble of Tarraco. l, University and Historic Precinct of Alcalá de Henares.

2001, Nov. 30 ***Perf. 12¾***
3130 Sheet of 12 7.00 7.00
a.-l. A1117 40p Any single .60 .25

Souvenir Sheet

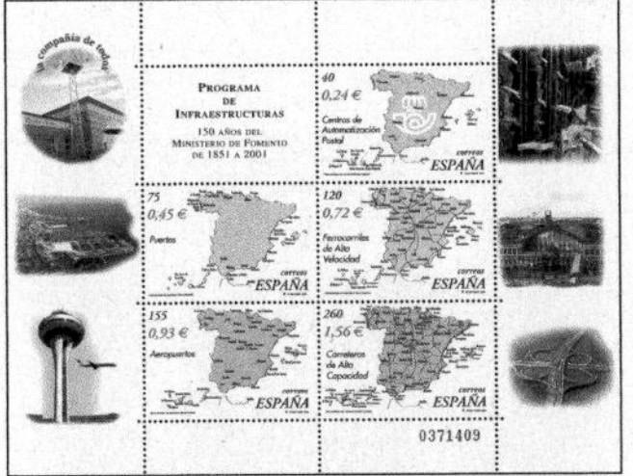

Ministry of Development, 150th Anniv. — A1118

No. 3131 — Maps showing: a, 40p, Automated postal centers. b, 75p, Ports. c, 120p, High-speed train lines. d, 155p, Airports. e, 260p, Highways.

2001, Dec. 11
3131 A1118 Sheet of 5, #a-e, + label 9.00 9.00

Souvenir Sheet

King Juan Carlos, 25th Anniv. of Reign — A1119

No. 3132: a, 40p, Crown Prince Felipe. b, 40p, Princess Elena (patterned dress). c, 40p, Royal arms. d, 40p, Princess Cristina (black dress). e, 75p, King Juan Carlos. f, 75p, Queen Sofia. g, 260p, Royal palace, Madrid (49x28mm).

2001, Dec. 14 ***Perf. 12¾x13¼***
3132 A1119 Sheet of 7, #a-g 8.00 8.00

100 Cents = 1 Euro (€)

King Juan Carlos Type of 2001 With Euro Denominations Only

2002, Jan. 2 Photo. ***Perf. 13½x14***
3133 A1091 1c sil & black .25 .25
3134 A1091 5c sil & brt blue .25 .25
3135 A1091 10c sil & gray blue .25 .25
3136 A1091 25c sil & claret .60 .25
3137 A1091 50c sil & gray 1.25 .35
3138 A1091 75c sil & red lil 1.90 .55

Perf. 12¾x13¼
3139 A1091 €1 sil & green 2.50 .75
3140 A1091 €2 sil & ver 5.00 1.50
Nos. 3133-3140 (8) 12.00 4.15

Spain's Presidency of European Union A1120

Color of star at UR: 25c, Orange. 50c, White.

2002, Jan. 2 Photo. ***Perf. 13¾x14***
3141-3142 A1120 Set of 2 1.90 .65

Trees — A1121

Designs: 50c, Savin (sabina). 75c, Elm (olmo).

2002, Jan. 25 ***Perf. 12¾***
3143-3144 A1121 Set of 2 3.00 1.10

A1122 A1123

A1124 A1125

A1126 A1127

Flowers
A1128 A1129

Die Cut Perf. 13
2002, Feb. 20 **Litho.**
Self-Adhesive
3145 Booklet of 8 10.00 10.00
a. A1122 25c multi 1.00 .25
b. A1123 25c multi 1.00 .25
c. A1124 25c multi 1.00 .25
d. A1125 25c multi 1.00 .25
e. A1126 25c multi 1.00 .25
f. A1127 25c multi 1.00 .25
g. A1128 25c multi 1.00 .25
h. A1129 25c multi 1.00 .25

España 2002 Youth Philatelic Exhibition, Salamanca A1130

Designs: 50c, Exhibition emblem. €1.80, Emblem and New Cathedral, vert.

2002, Feb. 22 Photo. ***Perf. 13¾x14***
3146 A1130 50c multi 1.25 .45

Souvenir Sheet
Perf. 14x13¾
3147 A1130 €1.80 multi 4.50 4.50

See No. 3183.

Father Francisco Piquer, Founder of Pawn Brokerage A1131

2002, Feb. 25 Litho. ***Perf. 14x13¾***
3148 A1131 25c multi .75 .25

Caja Madrid Savings Bank, 300th anniv.

Real Madrid Soccer Team, Cent. A1132

2002, Feb. 25 ***Perf. 13¾x14***
3149 A1132 75c yel & gray 1.90 .65

Souvenir Sheet

Tarazona Town Hall Portico — A1133

2002, Feb. 26
3150 A1133 €2.10 multi 5.25 5.25

Philaiberia '02, Tarazona.

Alejandro Mon (1801-82), Politician — A1134

2002, Feb. 27 ***Perf. 14x13¾***
3151 A1134 25c multi .75 .25

Retirement of Peseta Currency — A1135

2002, Feb. 28 **Litho.**
3152 A1135 25c multi .75 .25

Sil Canyons, Ribiera Sacra — A1136

Cabo de Gata Natl. Park A1137

2002, Mar. 8 ***Perf. 14x13¾, 13¾x14***
3153 A1136 75c multi 2.00 .65
3154 A1137 €2.10 multi 5.50 2.75

Zaragoza Military Academy, 75th Anniv. — A1138

2002, Mar. 15 ***Perf. 14x13¾***
3155 A1138 25c multi .75 .25

Real Unión Soccer Team, Cent. — A1139

2002, Mar. 22
3156 A1139 50c multi 1.25 .45

Stamp Day A1140

2002, Mar. 25 ***Perf. 13¾x14***
3157 A1140 25c multi .75 .25

Castle Type of 2001

Designs: 25c, Banyeres de Mariola. 50c, Soutomaior. 75c, Catalorao.

2002, Apr. 8 Engr. ***Perf. 13¾x14***
3158-3160 A1086 Set of 3 3.75 1.40

Tudela, 1200th Anniv. A1141

2002, Apr. 12 **Photo.**
3161 A1141 75c multi 1.90 .70

Monastery of Sant Cugat, 1000th Anniv. A1142

2002, Apr. 12
3162 A1142 €1.80 multi 4.50 2.25

Luis Cernuda (1902-63), Poet A1143

2002, May 8
3163 A1143 50c multi 1.25 .45

Dr. Federico Rubio (1827-1902) — A1144

2002, May 8
3164 A1144 50c multi 1.25 .45

Europa A1145

2002, May 9
3165 A1145 50c multi 1.25 .45

Reincorporation of Menorca to Spanish Crown, Bicent. — A1146

2002, May 10
3166 A1146 50c multi 1.25 .45

World Equestrian Games — A1147

No. 3167: a, Carriage driving. b, Endurance (Raid). c, Dressage (Doma). d, Reining. e, Vaulting (Volteo). f, Jumping (Saltos). g, Three-day event (Completo).

2002, May 11 ***Perf. 12¾x13¼***
3167 A1147 Sheet of 7 + 2 labels 9.50 9.50
a.-e. 25c Any single .60 .25
f. 75c multi 1.90 .70
g. €1.80 multi 4.50 2.25

Dolores Peinado (1819-94), Character From Folk Song "La Dolores" A1148

2002, May 31 ***Perf. 13¾x14***
3168 A1148 50c multi 1.25 .50

Souvenir Sheet

Exfilna 2002 Natl. Philatelic Exhibition, Salamanca — A1149

No. 3169 — Plaza Mayor, Salamanca: a, 25c, West facade. b, 25c, City Hall. c, 25c, Royal Pavilion. d, €1.80, Aerial view.

Engr. (#a-c), Litho. (#d, margin)

2002, July 7 ***Perf. 13¾x14***
3169 A1149 Sheet of 4, #a-d 6.25 6.25

Iberian Airlines, 75th Anniv. A1150

Airplanes: 25c, Rohrbach R-VIII Roland. 50c, Boeing 747.

2002, June 10 **Photo.** ***Perf. 13¾x14***
3170-3171 A1150 Set of 2 1.90 .75

Wine Producing Regions — A1151

Grapes and map of: 25c, Rías Baixas region. 50c, Rioja region. 75c, Manzanilla — Sanlúcar de Barrameda region.

2002 ***Perf. 14x13¼***
3172-3174 A1151 Set of 3 3.75 1.50

Issued: 25c, 7/27; 50c, 75c, 9/20.

Letter Writing Type of 1998

No. 3175: a, Publication of *Don Quixote,* by Miguel de Cervantes, 1605. b, Accession to throne of King Philip IV and rise in power of Conde-Duque de Olivares, 1621. c, Rivalry of poets Francisco de Quevedo and Luis de Góngora, 1620. d, Painting of "Las Meninas" by Diego Velázquez, 1656. e, Accession to throne of King Charles II, 1665. f, Accession to throne of King Philip V, 1701. g, Accesstion to throne of King Ferdinand VI, 1746. h, Accession to throne of King Charles III, 1759. i, Squillaci Riots, 1766. j, Gaspar Melchor de Jovellanos, 1787. k, Accession to throne of King Charles IV, 1788. l, Appointment of Manuel de Godoy as prime minister, 1792.

2002, Sept. 27 ***Perf. 12¾***
3175 Sheet of 12 3.50 3.50
a.-l. A1002 10c Any single .25 .25

Expiatory Temple of the Holy Family, by Architect Antonio Gaudí (1852-1926) A1152

2002, Sept. 27 **Litho.** ***Perf. 14x13¾***
3176 A1152 50c blue & black 1.25 .50

A1153

A1154

A1155

A1156

A1157

A1158

A1159

Paintings With Musical Instruments by Goyo Domínguez A1160

2002, Sept. 30 ***Die Cut Perf. 13***
Self-Adhesive

3177 Booklet pane of 8 5.00 5.00
a. A1153 25c multi .60 .25
b. A1154 25c multi .60 .25
c. A1155 25c multi .60 .25
d. A1156 25c multi .60 .25
e. A1157 25c multi .60 .25
f. A1158 25c multi .60 .25
g. A1159 25c multi .60 .25
h. A1160 25c multi .60 .25

America Issue — Youth, Education and Literacy A1161

2002, Oct. 14 **Photo.** ***Perf. 13¾x14***
3178 A1161 75c multi 1.90 .75

Almanzor (Muhammad ibn Abu Amir al-Mansur, c. 938-1002), Caliph of Córdoba — A1162

2002, Oct. 25
3179 A1162 75c multi 1.90 .75

Dijous Bó Fair, Mallorca — A1163

2002, Nov. 4 ***Perf. 14x13¾***
3180 A1163 75c multi 1.90 .75

UNESCO World Heritage Sites — A1164

No. 3181 — Architectural details of: a, Aranjuez. b, Santa Maria Church, Calatayud. c, San Martin Church, Teruel. d, Santa Maria Church, Tobed. e, Santa Tecla Church, Cervera de la Cañada. f, San Pablo Church, Zaragoza.

2002, Nov. 8
3181 A1164 Sheet of 7, #a-d, f, 2 #e, + 5 labels 17.00 17.00
a.-b. 25c Either single .60 .25
c. 50c multi 1.25 .50
d. 75c multi 1.75 .75
e. €1.80 multi 4.00 2.25
f. €2.10 multi 4.75 2.75

The two examples of No. 3181e are tete-beche in the sheet.

Alcañiz Inn — A1164a

2002, Nov. 15 ***Perf. 13¾x14***
3182 A1164a 25c multicolored .75 .25

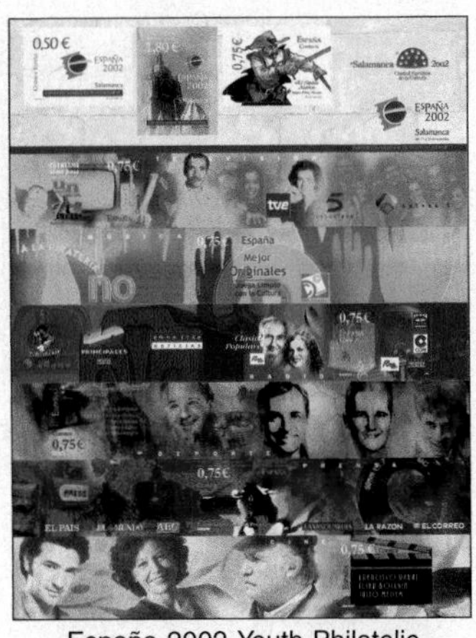

España 2002 Youth Philatelic Exhibition, Salamanca — A1165

Designs: No. 3183a, 50c, Like #3146. Nos. 3183b, 3190, 75c, Character from comic Strip "El Capitan Alatriste," by Arturo Pérez-Reverte. Nos. 3183c, 3185, 75c, Television and names of television shows. Nos. 3183d, 3189, 75c, Hand and compact disc. Nos. 3183e, 3187, 75c, Radio, musical notes and logos of Spanish radio stations. Nos. 3183f, 3188, 75c, Skier, race car, soccer ball, bicyclist and names of Spanish sports stars. Nos. 3183g, 3186, 75c, Photojournalist. Nos. 3183h, 3184, 75c, Clapboard and names of Spanish film personalities. No. 3183i, €1.80, Like #3147, vert.

2002 Litho. ***Die Cut Perf. 13***

Self-Adhesive (#3183)

3183 A1165 Sheet of 9 19.00 19.00
a. 50c multi 1.25 .50
b.-h. 75c Any single 1.90 .75
i. €1.80 multi 4.50 2.25

Souvenir Sheets

Perf. 13¾x14

3184-3190 A1165 Set of 7 11.50 11.50

Issued: No. 3183, 11/17; No. 3184, 11/18; No. 3185, 11/19; No. 3186, 11/20; No. 3187, 11/21; No. 3188, 11/22; No. 3189, 11/23; No. 3190, 11/24.

No. 3183 exists with at least three different pictures on backing paper.

San Jorge Church, Alcoy — A1166

Litho. & Engr.

2002, Nov. 25 ***Perf. 14x13¾***

3191 A1166 75c multi 1.90 .75

Compludo Forge, León A1167

2002, Nov. 27 ***Perf. 13¾x14***

3192 A1167 50c multi 1.25 .50

Souvenir Sheet

Stained Glass Window, Santa Maria Cathedral, Vitoria-Gasteiz — A1168

2002, Nov. 27 ***Perf. 14x13¾***

3193 A1168 50c multi 1.50 1.00

Crucifix, Hío — A1169

2002, Nov. 29

3194 A1169 25c multi .75 .25

Christmas A1170

Designs: 25c, Adoration of the Magi, from church altarpiece, Calzadilla de los Barros. 50c, Maternity, by Goyo Dominguez.

2002, Nov. 29 **Photo.**

3195-3196 A1170 Set of 2 1.90 .75

Opening of Somport Tunnel A1171

2003, Jan. 17 Photo. ***Perf. 13¾x14***

3197 A1171 51c multi 1.25 .55

Traditional Dress from Ansó Valley — A1172

2003, Jan. 20 ***Perf. 14x13¾***

3198 A1172 76c multi 1.75 .85

World Leprosy Day, 50th Anniv. — A1173

2003, Jan. 21

3199 A1173 26c multi .75 .30

Pedro Rodríguez de Campomanes (1723-1802), Jurist — A1174

2003, Feb. 14

3200 A1174 26c multi .75 .30

Juvenia 2003 Natl. Youth Philatelic Exhibition, Benissa A1175

2003, Feb. 21 ***Perf. 13¾x14***

3201 A1175 51c multi 1.25 .55

Práxedes Mateo Sagasta (1825-1903), Politician — A1176

2003, Mar. 11

3202 A1176 26c multi .75 .30

ABC Newspaper, Cent. A1177

2003, Mar. 17

3203 A1177 €2.15 multi 5.00 2.25

Nobel Prize Winners For Physiology or Medicine From Spain — A1178

No. 3204: a, Santiago Ramón y Cajal, 1906. b, Severo Ochoa, 1959.

Litho. & Engr.

2003, Mar. 20 ***Perf. 13x12¾***

3204 A1178 Horiz. pair 3.25 3.25
a. 51c multi 1.25 .55
b. 76c multi 1.90 .80

See Sweden No. 2460.

School of Civil Engineering, Madrid, Bicent. — A1179

Designs: 26c, Tui Bridge.

No. 3206: a, Estrecho de Puentes Dam. b, El Musel Port.

2003, Mar. 21 Photo. ***Perf. 13¾x14***

3205 A1179 26c multi .75 .30

Souvenir Sheet

3206 Sheet of 3, #3205, 3206a, 3206b 4.00 4.00
a. A1179 51c multi 1.25 .55
b. A1179 76c multi 1.75 .80

La Verdad Newspaper, Cent. A1180

2003, Mar. 26

3207 A1180 26c multi .75 .30

Paintings by Chico Montilla A1181

No. 3208: a, La Hoz de Priego. b, Fields of Gold. c, Desfiladero de los Tornos. d, Campos de Pastrana. e, Campos de Armilla. f, Nenúfar. g, De qué Color es el Vento? h, Flores Tempranas.

Die Cut Perf. 13

2003, Mar. 28 **Litho.**

Self-Adhesive

3208 Booklet pane of 8 7.50 7.50
a.-h. A1181 26c Any single .75 .30

Ramón José Sender (1901-82), Writer A1182

Litho. & Engr.

2003, Mar. 31 ***Perf. 13½x14***

3209 A1182 €2.15 multi 5.00 2.40

Rural Schools A1183

2003, Apr. 3 Photo. ***Perf. 13¾x14***

3210 A1183 26c multi .75 .30

Souvenir Sheet

EXFILNA 2003 Natl. Philatelic Exhibition, Granada — A1184

Litho. (margin) & Engr. (stamp)

2003, Apr. 7

3211 A1184 €2.15 multi 5.00 5.00

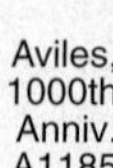

Aviles, 1000th Anniv. A1185

2003, Apr. 11 **Photo.**
3212 A1185 51c multi 1.25 .55

Stamp Day A1186

2003, Apr. 11
3213 A1186 €1.85 multi 4.50 2.00

Europa A1187

2003, Apr. 24
3214 A1187 76c multi 1.75 .85

Atlético de Madrid Soccer Team, Cent. — A1188

2003, Apr. 25 ***Perf. 14x13¾***
3215 A1188 26c red & blue .75 .30

Roman Theater, Zaragoza A1189

2003, May 5 ***Perf. 13¾x14***
3216 A1189 €1.85 multi 5.00 2.10

European Year of the Disabled A1190

2003, May 8 **Photo. & Embossed**
3217 A1190 76c multi 1.75 .85

Castles A1191

Designs: 26c, San Felipe Castle, Ferrol. 51c, Cuellar Castle, Segovia. 76c, Montilla Castle, Córdoba.

2003, May 17 **Engr.** ***Perf. 13¾x14***
3218-3220 A1191 Set of 3 3.75 1.90

Battles of Ceriñola and Garellano, 500th anniv. (No. 3220).

World Swimming Championships, Barcelona — A1192

2003, May 23 **Photo.** ***Perf. 14x13¾***
3221 A1192 Sheet of 5 + label 13.00 13.50
a. 26c Breaststroke .60 .30
b. 51c Diving 1.25 .60
c. 76c Synchronized swimming 1.75 .85
d. €1.85 Freestyle 4.25 2.10
e. €2.15 Water polo 5.00 2.50

Max Aub (1903-72), Writer — A1193

2003, June 2 **Engr.**
3222 A1193 76c black & red 1.75 .85

Sabadell Soccer Team, Cent. — A1194

2003, June 4 **Photo.**
3223 A1194 76c multi 2.25 .85

Juan Bravo Murillo (1803-73), Prime Minister — A1195

2003, June 9
3224 A1195 51c multi 1.40 .60

Diario de Cadiz Newspaper, 136th Anniv. — A1196

2003, June 16
3225 A1196 26c multi .75 .30

Souvenir Sheet

Royal Automobile Club of Spain, Cent. — A1197

2003, June 27 ***Perf. 13¾x14***
3226 A1197 Sheet of 4 8.50 8.50
a. 26c 1967 Dodge Dart Barreiros .60 .30
b. 51c 1957-73 Seat 600 1.10 .55
c. 76c 1907 Hispano-Suiza 20/30 HP 1.75 .85
d. €1.85 1953 Pegaso Z-102 Berlinetta 4.25 2.10

Chilean Postage Stamps, 150th Anniv. — A1198

2003, July 1 **Photo.** ***Perf. 14x13¾***
3227 A1198 76c Chile Type A1 1.75 .85

El Diario Montañés Newspaper, Cent. — A1199

2003, July 4
3228 A1199 26c multi .75 .30

Santa Catalina Inn, Jaén — A1200

2003, July 9 ***Perf. 13x13¼***
3229 A1200 76c multi + label 1.75 .85

Diario de Navarra Newspaper, Cent. — A1201

2003, July 11 ***Perf. 13¾x14***
3230 A1201 26c multi .75 .30

Seu Vella, Lleida, 800th Anniv. A1202

2003, July 22 **Engr.** ***Perf. 13¾x14***
3231 A1202 €1.85 pur & brn blk 4.25 2.10

El Adelanto de Salamanca Newspaper, 120th Anniv. — A1203

2003, July 24 **Photo.** ***Perf. 14x13¾***
3232 A1203 26c multi .75 .30

A1204 A1205

A1206 A1207

A1208 A1209

Paintings by Alfredo Roldán
A1210 A1211

Die Cut Perf. 13
2003, July 28 **Litho.**
Self-Adhesive
3233 Booklet pane of 8 8.00 8.00
a. A1204 A multi .60 .30
b. A1205 A multi .60 .30
c. A1206 A multi .60 .30
d. A1207 A multi .60 .30
e. A1208 A multi .60 .30
f. A1209 A multi .60 .30
g. A1210 A multi .60 .30
h. A1211 A multi .60 .30

Nos. 3233a-3233g each sold for 26c on day of issue.

El Correo Gallego Newspaper, 125th Anniv. — A1212

2003, Aug. 1 **Photo.** ***Perf. 13¾x14***
3234 A1212 26c multi .75 .30

El Comercio de Gijón Newspaper, 125th Anniv. — A1213

2003, Sept. 2
3235 A1213 26c multi .75 .30

Holy Cross of Caravaca A1214

2003, Sept. 4 *Perf. 14x13¾*
3236 A1214 76c multi 1.75 .85

Holy Year 2003.

World Sailing Championships, Gulf of Cádiz — A1215

2003, Sept. 9 *Perf. 13¾x14*
3237 A1215 76c multi 1.75 .85

Wine of Penedés Region — A1216

Wine of Montilla-Moriles Region — A1217

Wine of Valdepeñas Region — A1218

Wine of Bierzo Region — A1219

2003 *Perf. 14x13¾*
3238 A1216 26c multi .75 .30
3239 A1217 51c multi 1.25 .60
3240 A1218 76c multi 2.00 .90
3241 A1219 €1.85 multi 5.00 2.25
Nos. 3238-3241 (4) 9.00 4.05

Issued: 26c, 10/30; others, 9/22.

Academy of Military Engineering, Bicent. — A1220

2003, Sept. 24 *Perf. 13¾x14*
3242 A1220 51c multi 1.25 .60

Souvenir Sheet

Santa María Cathedral, León, 700th Anniv — A1221

2003, Sept. 26 **Litho. & Engr.**
3243 A1221 76c multi 2.00 2.00

Souvenir Sheet

Royal Geographical Society, Cent. — A1222

2003, Oct. 1
3244 A1222 €1.85 multi 4.75 4.75

Trees — A1223

Designs: 26c, Ficus macrophylla. 51c, Quercus rober.

2003, Oct. 3 **Photo.** *Perf. 14x13¾*
3245-3246 A1223 Set of 2 2.25 .95

School of Aeronautical Engineering, Madrid, 75th Anniv. — A1224

2003, Oct. 6 *Perf. 13¾x14*
3247 A1224 51c multi 1.25 .60

America Issue - Rail Transport A1225

2003, Oct. 14
3248 A1225 76c multi 1.75 .90

El Viejo y el Pájaro, by Luis Seoane (1910-79) A1226

2003, Oct. 17 *Perf. 14x13¾*
3249 A1226 €1.85 multi 4.50 2.25

El Correo de Andalucia Newspaper, Cent. — A1227

Faro de Vigo Newspaper, 150th Anniv. — A1228

La Voz de Galicia Newspaper, 121st Anniv. — A1229

2003, Nov. 3 *Perf. 13¾x14*
3250 A1227 26c multi .75 .30
3251 A1228 26c multi .75 .30
3252 A1229 26c multi .75 .30
Nos. 3250-3252 (3) 2.25 .90

Camilo José Cela (1916-2002), 1989 Nobel Laureate in Literature A1230

2003, Nov. 10 *Perf. 14x13¾*
3253 A1230 26c multi .75 .30

Parade of the Magi — A1231

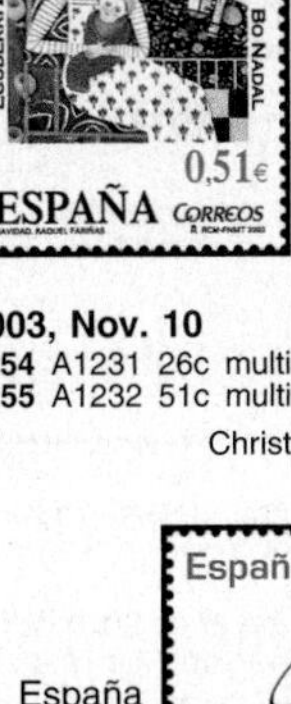

Nativity, by Raquel Fariñas — A1232

2003, Nov. 10
3254 A1231 26c multi .65 .30
3255 A1232 51c multi 1.25 .60

Christmas.

España 2004 Intl. Philatelic Exhibition A1233

Designs: 76c, Exhibition emblem. €1.85, Exhibition venue, Valencia.

2003, Nov. 14 *Perf. 13¾x14*
3256 A1233 76c multi 1.90 .95

Souvenir Sheet

3257 A1233 €1.85 multi 4.50 4.50

Organos de Montoro A1234

2003, Nov. 17
3258 A1234 51c multi 1.25 .60

Souvenir Sheet

Completion of National Geological Map — A1235

2003, Nov. 24
3259 A1235 26c multi .75 .75

Souvenir Sheets

Constitution, 25th Anniv. — A1236

Various photos or paintings with inscriptions in lower left corner of: No. 3260, 26c, RCM-FNMT. No. 3261, 26c, Miguel Torner. No. 3262, 26c, R. Seco. No. 3263, 26c, Araceli

Alarcón. No. 3264, 26c, Galicia. No. 3265, 26c, Fesanpe. No. 3266, 26c, J. Carrero. No. 3267, 26c, J. Carrero, vert. No. 3268, 26c, Goyo Domínguez, vert. No. 3269, 26c, Juan Bautista Nieto, vert.

2003, Dec. 5 ***Perf. 13¾x14, 14x13¾***
3260-3269 A1236 Set of 10 7.50 7.50

Powered Flight, Cent. A1237

2003, Dec. 17 Engr. ***Perf. 13¾x14***
3270 A1237 76c blue & brown 1.90 .95

King Juan Carlos Type of 2001 With Euro Denominations Only

2004, Jan. 2 Photo. ***Perf. 12¾x13¼***

3271	A1091	2c sil & brt pink	.25	.25
3272	A1091	27c sil & blue	.70	.35
a.		Sheet of 4 + label	2.80	2.80
3273	A1091	52c sil & bister brn	1.25	.65
3274	A1091	77c sil & dull grn	1.90	.95
		Nos. 3271-3274 (4)	4.10	2.20

No. 3272a issued 5/25.

Roman Art of Jaca — A1238

No. 3275: a, Grate. b, Huesca Cathedral Bible page. c, Painting of two apostles. d, Cloister, Monastery of San Juan de la Peña. e, Coins. f, Capital, Church of Santiago de Jaca. g, Detail of sarcophagus of Doña Sancha. h, Wooden carved crucifix.

Serpentine Die Cut 13
2004, Jan. 16 **Litho.**
Self-Adhesive

3275		Booklet pane of 8	8.00	8.00
a.-h.	A1238	A Any single	.70	.35

Nos. 3275a-3275h each sold for 27c on day of issue.

Souvenir Sheets

Paintings of Women Reading by Fabio Hurtado (1960-) — A1239

No. 3276: a, 27c, Woman reading book in rowboat. b, 52c, Woman with head on hand reading book. c, 77c, Woman reading newspaper.

No. 3277: a, 27c, Woman with legs crossed reading book. b, 52c. Woman on back reading book. c, 77c, Woman with black hat reading book.

2004, Jan. 23 Photo. ***Perf. 13¾x14***
Sheets of 3, #a-c, + label
3276-3277 A1239 Set of 2 8.00 4.50

Campaign Against Cancer A1240

2004, Feb. 2
3278 A1240 27c multi .75 .35

"La Terrona" Oak Tree, Zarza de Montánchez A1241

2004, Feb. 6 ***Perf. 14x13¾***
3279 A1241 52c multi 1.40 .70

World Rowing Championships, Banyoles — A1242

2004, Feb. 9 ***Perf. 13¾x14***
3280 A1242 77c multi 1.90 .95

School Letter Writing Campaign — A1243

No. 3281 — Scenes from comic strip Trazo de Tiza, by Miguelanxo Prado: a, Woman on cliff. b, Sailboat. c, Woman near injured gull. d, Aerial view of lighthouse.

2004, Feb. 10
3281 A1243 27c Sheet of 4, #a-d, + 12 labels 2.75 2.75

Souvenir Sheet

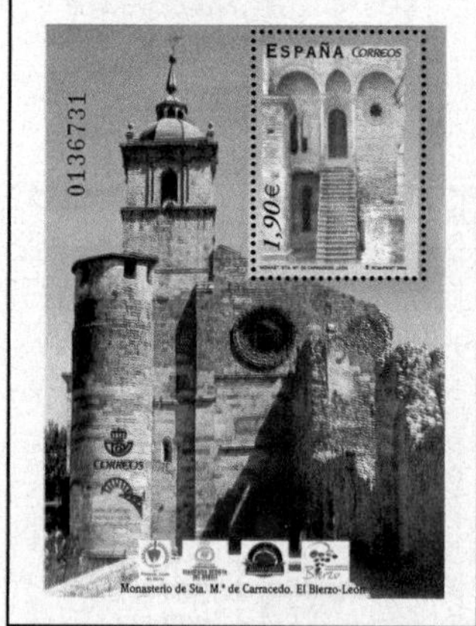

Santa María de Carracedo Monastery, Bierzo — A1244

2004, Mar. 8 ***Perf. 14x13¾***
3282 A1244 €1.90 multi 4.75 2.40

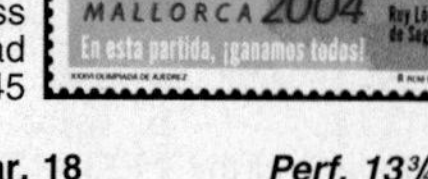

36th Chess Olympiad A1245

2004, Mar. 18 ***Perf. 13¾x14***
3283 A1245 77c multi 1.90 .95

Clocks — A1246

No. 3284: a, 27c, Clock with Muse Calliope, 19th cent. b, 52c, Clock with Cupid, 18th cent. c, 77c, Clock with Empress María Luisa, child and harp, 19th cent. d, €1.90, Clock with Venus and Cupid, 18th cent.

Perf. 13¼x12¾
2004, Mar. 31 Litho. & Engr.
3284 A1246 Sheet of 4, #a-d 8.50 4.25

Diario de Burgos Newspaper, 113th Anniv. — A1247

2004, Apr. 1 Photo. ***Perf. 14x13¾***
3285 A1247 27c multi .75 .35

March 11, 2004 Terrorist Attacks — A1248

2004, Apr. 2 Litho. ***Perf. 14x13¾***
3286 A1248 27c black & gray .75 .35

Booklet Stamp
Self-Adhesive
Size: 22x33mm
Serpentine Die Cut 13

3287	A1248	A black & gray	.75	.35
a.		Booklet pane of 8	6.00	

No. 3287 sold for 27c on day of issue.

Egg Painting Festival, Pola de Siero A1249

2004, Apr. 5 Photo. ***Perf. 13¾***
3288 A1249 27c multi .75 .35

Miniature Sheet

Paintings of Shawls, by Soledad Fernández — A1250

2004, Apr. 7 ***Perf. 14x13¾***

3289	A1250	Sheet of 4	8.50	8.50
a.		27c Shawl, shell	.65	.35
b.		52c Shawl, hands	1.25	.65
c.		77c Shawl, flowers	1.90	.95
d.		€1.90 Shawl on chair	4.50	2.25

Department of Technical Engineering of Public Works, 150th Anniv. — A1251

2004, Apr. 15 ***Perf. 13¾x14***
3290 A1251 52c multi 1.25 .60

Cable Inglés Loading Pier, Almadrabillas, Cent. — A1252

2004, Apr. 27
3291 A1252 52c multi 1.25 .60

Europa — A1253

2004, Apr. 29 ***Perf. 14x13¾***
3292 A1253 77c multi 1.90 .95

Expansion of the European Union A1254

2004, May 3 ***Perf. 13¾x14***
3293 A1254 52c multi 1.25 .60

Self-Portrait with the Neck of Rafael, by Salvador Dali (1904-89) — A1255

2004, May 11 **Photo.**
3294 A1255 77c multi 1.90 .95

FIFA (Fédération Internationale de Football Association), Cent. — A1256

2004, May 21
3295 A1256 77c multi 1.90 .95

Wedding of Prince Felipe and Letizia Ortiz Rocasolano — A1257

2004, May 22
3296 A1257 27c multi .75 .30

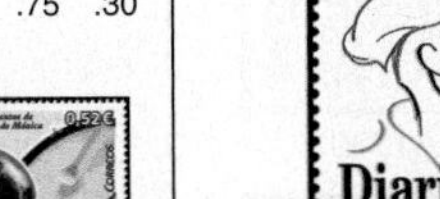

España 2004 Intl. Philatelic Exhibition — A1258

No. 3297 — Music: a, Vicente Martín y Soler (1754-1806), opera composer. b, Band instruments.

2004, May 23 **Photo.** ***Perf. 13¾x14***
3297 A1258 Horiz. pair + central label 1.90 1.90
a. 27c multi .65 .30
b. 52c multi 1.25 .60

Miniature Sheet

España 2004 Intl. Philatelic Exhibition — A1259

No. 3298 — Royalty: a, Prince Felipe and Letizia Ortiz Rocasolano. b, Prince Felipe. c, King Juan Carlos and Queen Sofia.

Litho., Litho. & Engr. (#3298c)
2004, May 24 ***Perf. 13¾x14***
3298 A1259 Sheet of 3 + 3 labels 17.00 17.00
a. 27c multi .65 .30
b. 77c multi 1.90 .95
c. €6 multi 14.00 7.00

España 2004 Intl. Philatelic Exhibition — A1260

No. 3299 — Festival of the Bulls, Valencia: a, Running of the bulls. b, Bullfighter.

2004, May 26 **Photo.** ***Perf. 13¾x14***
3299 A1260 Horiz. pair + central label 2.50 2.50
a. 27c multi .60 .30
b. 77c multi 1.90 .95

Miniature Sheet

España 2004 Intl. Philatelic Exhibition — A1261

No. 3300 — Sports: a, Tennis. b, Motorcycle racing. c, Golf.

2004, May 27 ***Perf. 12¾x13***
3300 A1261 Sheet of 3 + 3 labels 7.00 7.00
a. 35c multi .85 .40
b. 52c multi 1.25 .65
c. €1.90 multi 4.50 2.25

España 2004 Intl. Philatelic Exhibition — A1262

No. 3301 — The Sea: a, Yacht Bravo España. b, Valencia skyline.

2004, May 28 **Photo.** ***Perf. 13¾x14***
3301 A1262 Horiz. pair + central label 3.00 3.00
a. 52c multi 1.10 .65
b. 77c multi 1.75 .95

Diario de Valencia Newspaper, 214th Anniv. — A1263

2004, May 29
3302 A1263 27c multi .65 .30

Jacobean Holy Year — A1264

2004, June 11 ***Perf. 14x13¾***
3303 A1264 52c multi 1.25 .65

Lerma Inn A1265

2004, July 18 ***Perf. 13¾x14***
3304 A1265 52c multi 1.25 .65

Castles A1266

Designs: 27c, Granadilla Fortress, Granadilla. 52c, Aguas Mansas Castle, Agoncillo. 77c, Mota Fortress, Alcalá la Real. €1.90, Villafuerte de Esgueva Castle, Villafuerte de Esgueva, vert.

2004 **Engr.** ***Perf. 13¾x14, 14x13¾***
3305-3308 A1266 Set of 4 8.00 4.25

Issued: 27c, 77c, 7/1; 52c, €1.90, 7/19.

Anchor Museum, Salinas — A1267

2004, July 16 **Photo.** ***Perf. 14x13¾***
3309 A1267 €1.90 multi 4.00 2.40

Ceramics in Paintings by Antonio Miguel González — A1268

No. 3310: a, Jar with two handles and lid, oranges. b, Goblet, amphora and jar. c, Pitcher with handle at top, bread, garlic. d, Decorated pitcher with side handle. e, Pitcher with handle at top, pentagonal dodecahedron, bread, tomatoes. f, Vase. g, Pitcher with side handle, plate of pears, grapes. h, Jar with flower design and lid.

Serpentine Die Cut 13
2004, July 22 **Litho.**
Self-Adhesive
3310 Booklet pane of 8 8.00 8.00
a.-h. A1268 A Any single .65 .35

Nos. 3310a-3310h sold for 27c on day of issue.

Círculo Oscense Building, Huesca, Cent. A1269

2004, July 23 **Photo.** ***Perf. 13¾x14***
3311 A1269 52c multi 1.25 .65

Our Lady of the Snows Festival, Vitoria-Gasteiz, 50th Anniv. — A1270

2004, July 30 ***Perf. 14x13¾***
3312 A1270 27c multi .65 .30

Ribeiro Wine Grapes — A1271

Wine of Malaga — A1272

2004, Sept. 1 ***Perf. 14x13¾***
3313 A1271 27c multi .65 .35
3314 A1272 52c multi 1.25 .65

First Philippines Stamp, 150th Anniv. — A1273

2004, Sept. 6 ***Perf. 13¾x14***
3315 A1273 77c Philippines #1 1.90 .95

Heraldo de Aragón Newspaper, 109th Anniv. — A1274

2004, Sept. 20 ***Perf. 14x13¾***
3316 A1274 27c multi .70 .35

Nautical Astronomy, 250th Anniv. — A1275

2004, Sept. 24 ***Perf. 13¾x14***
3317 A1275 €1.90 multi 4.25 2.40

Souvenir Sheet

EXFILNA 2004 National Philatelic Exhibition, Valladolid — A1276

Litho. & Engr.
2004, Oct. 1 ***Perf. 14x13¾***
3318 A1276 €1.90 multi 4.25 4.25

Buildings in China and Spain — A1277

Designs: 52c, Park Guell, Barcelona. 77c, Jinmao Tower, Shanghai.

2004, Oct. 8 **Photo.**
3319-3320 A1277 Set of 2 3.00 1.60

See People's Republic of China Nos. 3406-3407.

America Issue — Environmental Protection — A1278

2004, Oct. 14 ***Perf. 13¾x14***
3321 A1278 77c multi 1.75 1.00

CERN (European Organization for Nuclear Research), 50th Anniv. — A1279

2004, Oct. 19
3322 A1279 €1.90 multi 4.50 2.50

Nature — A1280

Designs: 27c, Cíes Islands. 52c, Ebro Delta Natural Park, horiz. 77c, Taburiente Caldera National Park, horiz.

2004, Oct. 21 ***Perf. 14x13¾, 13¾x14***
3323-3325 A1280 Set of 3 3.75 2.10

Taburiente Caldera National Park, 50th anniv. (#3325).

First Registered Letter, 400th Anniv. — A1281

2004, Oct. 22 ***Perf. 13¾x14***
3326 A1281 77c multi 1.75 1.00

Stamp Day.

Ebre Observatory, Cent. — A1282

2004, Nov. 5
3327 A1282 €1.90 multi 4.25 2.50

Start of Reign of Alfonso I, King of Aragon, 900th Anniv. — A1283

Litho. & Engr.

2004, Nov. 12 ***Perf. 14x13¾***
3328 A1283 €1.90 multi 4.25 2.50

Christmas A1284

Designs: 27c, Birth of Christ, 18th cent. Neapolitan nativity scene. 52c, Nativity, by Juan Manuel Cossío.

2004, Nov. 17 **Photo.**
3329-3330 A1284 Set of 2 1.75 1.10

Queen Isabella I (1451-1504) A1285

2004, Nov. 26
3331 A1285 €2.19 multi 5.00 3.00

Royal Expedition for Smallpox Vaccination in Latin America and Philippines, Bicent. — A1286

2004, Nov. 30 **Engr.** ***Perf. 13¾x14***
3332 A1286 77c brown 1.75 1.10

Souvenir Sheet

Stained Glass, Toledo Cathedral — A1287

Litho. & Engr.

2004, Dec. 3 ***Perf. 14x13¾***
3333 A1287 €1.90 multi 4.25 4.25

Arms of the Prince of Asturias A1288

2004, Dec. 23 **Photo.** ***Perf. 13¾x14***
3334 A1288 27c multi .75 .40

Best wishes for Prince Felipe's marriage to Letizia Ortiz Rocasolano on May 22, 2004.

A1289 A1290

A1291 A1292

A1293 A1294

Paintings of Circus Performers by Manolo Elices
A1295 A1296

2005, Jan. 3 **Litho.** ***Die Cut Perf. 13***
Self-Adhesive

3335	Booklet pane of 8	6.00	
a.	A1289 A multi	.75	.35
b.	A1290 A multi	.75	.35
c.	A1291 A multi	.75	.35
d.	A1292 A multi	.75	.35
e.	A1293 A multi	.75	.35
f.	A1294 A multi	.75	.35
g.	A1295 A multi	.75	.35
h.	A1296 A multi	.75	.35

Nos. 3335a-3335h each sold for 28c on day of issue.

Signing of European Union Constitutional Treaty — A1297

2005, Jan. 12 **Photo.** ***Perf. 13¾x14***
3336 A1297 28c multi .75 .35

King Juan Carlos Type of 2001 With Euro Denominations Only

Perf. 12¾x13¼

2005, Jan. 14 **Photo.**

3337	A1091	28c sil & ol grn	.75	.35
3338	A1091	35c sil & orange	.90	.45
3339	A1091	40c sil & blue gray	1.00	.50
3340	A1091	53c sil & dull pur	1.40	.70
3341	A1091	78c sil & red	2.00	1.00
3342	A1091	€1.95 sil & yel brn	5.00	2.50
3343	A1091	€2.21 sil & ol brn	5.75	2.75
	Nos. 3337-3343 (7)		16.80	8.25

Ahuehuete Tree, Retiro Park, Madrid — A1298

2005, Jan. 17 **Photo.** ***Perf. 14x13¾***
3344 A1298 78c multi 2.00 1.00

Road Safety A1299

Blood Donation A1300

2005, Jan. 26 ***Perf. 13¾x14***
3345 A1299 28c multi .75 .35
3346 A1300 53c multi 1.40 .70

University of Seville, 500th Anniv. — A1301

2005, Feb. 3 **Engr.** ***Perf. 14x13¾***
3347 A1301 28c brn & claret .75 .35

First Royal Spanish Pharmacopoeia, 500th Anniv. — A1302

2005, Feb. 3 **Litho. & Engr.**
3348 A1302 28c multi .75 .35

Miniature Sheet

Children's Songs and Stories — A1303

No. 3349: a, Al Levantar una Lancha. b, Aquí te Espero. c, Estaba la Pájara Pinta. d, Cuatro Esquinitas. e, El Patio de mi Casa. f, Pero Mira Cómo Beben. g, Los Pollitos Cantan. h, Para Entrar en Clase.

2005, Feb. 14 **Photo.**
3349 A1303 Sheet of 8 11.00 11.00
a.-c. 28c Any single .75 .40
d.-f. 53c Any single 1.40 .70
g.-h. 78c Either single 2.10 1.10

Juvenia 2005 Youth Stamp Exhibition, Tordera — A1304

2005, Feb. 25 ***Perf. 14x13¾***
3350 A1304 28c multi .75 .35

Sevilla FC (Seville Soccer Team), Cent. A1305

Real Sporting de Gijón Soccer Team, Cent. — A1306

15th Mediterranean Games, Almería — A1307

2005, Mar. 1 ***Perf. 13¾x14***
3351 A1305 35c carmine .95 .45

Perf. 14x13¾
3352 A1306 40c multi 1.10 .55
3353 A1307 78c multi 2.10 1.10
Nos. 3351-3353 (3) 4.15 2.10

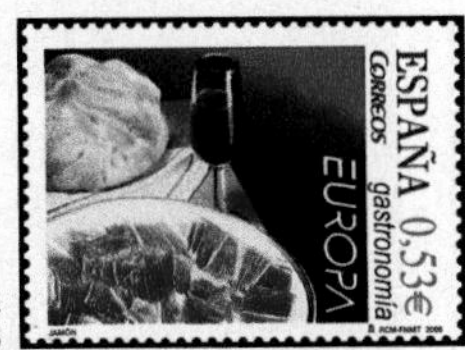
Europa A1308

2005, Apr. 15 ***Perf. 13¾x14***
3354 A1308 53c multi 1.40 .70

Juan Valera (1824-1905), Writer and Diplomat A1309

2005, Apr. 18 **Engr.** ***Perf. 14x13¾***
3355 A1309 €2.21 vio brn & blue 5.75 2.75

Souvenir Sheet

Publication of Don Quixote, 400th Anniv. — A1310

Various scenes from book.

2005, Apr. 22
3356 A1310 Sheet of 4 10.00 10.00
a. 28c black .75 .35
b. 53c black 1.40 .70
c. 78c black 2.00 1.00
d. €2.21 black 5.75 2.75

Telegraphy in Spain, 150th Anniv. — A1311

2005, Apr. 26 **Photo.** ***Perf. 13¾x14***
3357 A1311 28c multi .75 .35

Intl. Year of Physics — A1312

Die Cut Perf. 13¼
2005, Apr. 28 **Litho.**
Self-Adhesive
3358 A1312 28c multi .75 .35

Souvenir Sheet

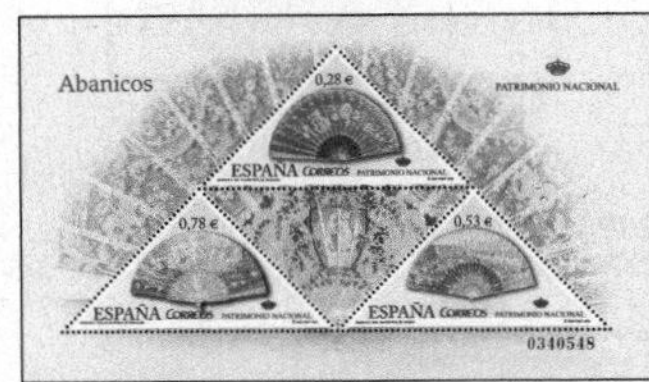
Fans — A1313

No. 3359 — Fan depicting: a, Flowers. b, Madrid street scene. c, Nymphs.

2005, May 9 **Photo.** ***Perf. 13¾***
3359 A1313 Sheet of 3 + label 4.00 4.00
a. 28c multi .70 .35
b. 53c multi 1.40 .70
c. 78c multi 1.90 .95

Diario Palentino Newspaper, 124th Anniv. — A1314

Ultima Hora Newspaper, 112th Anniv. — A1315

Diario de Ibiza Newspaper, 112th Anniv. — A1316

2005, May 16 ***Perf. 14x13¾***
3360 A1314 78c multi 1.90 .95
Perf. 13¾x14
3361 A1315 €1.95 multi 4.75 2.40
3362 A1316 €2.21 multi 5.50 2.75
Nos. 3360-3362 (3) 12.15 6.10

Inn, Oropesa A1317

2005, June 13 **Engr.** ***Perf. 13¾x14***
3363 A1317 €1.95 brown 4.75 2.40

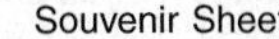
Souvenir Sheet

EXFILNA 2005, Alicante — A1318

Litho. & Engr.
2005, June 20 ***Perf. 14x13¾***
3364 A1318 €2.21 multi 5.50 5.50

Castles A1319

Designs: 78c, Alcaudete Castle. €1.95, Valderrobres Castle. €2.21, Molina de Aragón Castle.

2005, July 4 **Engr.** ***Perf. 13¾x14***
3365-3367 A1319 Set of 3 12.00 6.00

Fingerprint Registration for Newborns — A1320

2005, July 11 **Photo.**
3368 A1320 28c multi .75 .35

Stamp Day — A1321

Die Cut Perf. 13
2005, Sept. 1 **Litho.**
Self-Adhesive
3369 A1321 28c multi .75 .35

Nuestra Señora de la Asuncion Church, Pont de Suert A1322

2005, Sept. 7 **Photo.** ***Perf. 13¾x14***
3370 A1322 28c multi .75 .35

Lunnispark Building A1323

Lucho A1324

Lupita in Bed — A1325

Die Cut Perf. 13

2005, Sept. 16 Litho.

Self-Adhesive

3371	Booklet pane of 8	5.75	
a.	A1323 28c shown	.70	.35
b.	A1324 28c shown	.70	.35
c.	A1323 28c Green building	.70	.35
d.	A1324 28c Lulila	.70	.35
e.	A1324 28c Lupita	.70	.35
f.	A1325 28c shown	.70	.35
g.	A1324 28c Lublú	.70	.35
h.	A1323 28c Orange building	.70	.35

Los Lunnis children's television show.

World Cycling Championships, Madrid — A1326

2005, Sept. 20 Photo. *Perf. 13¾x14*

3372 A1326 78c multi 1.90 .95

España 2006 World Philatelic Exhibition, Malaga A1327

2005 Photo. *Perf. 13¾x14*

3373 A1327 53c multi 1.40 .70

Gardens A1328

No. 3374: a, Gardens of La Granja de San Ildefonso, Segovia. b, Bagh-e-Shahzadeh Garden, Kerman, Iran.

2005, Oct. 10

3374	Horiz. pair + central label	7.25	3.75
a.	A1328 78c multi	1.90	.95
b.	A1328 €2.21 multi	5.25	2.60

See Iran No. 2912.

15th Iberoamerican Summit, Salamanca — A1329

2005, Oct. 13

3375 A1329 78c multi 1.90 .95

America Issue, Fight Against Poverty A1330

2005, Oct. 14 *Perf. 12¾*

3376 A1330 78c multi 1.90 .95

La Orotava, 500th Anniv. — A1331

2005, Oct. 20 *Perf. 14x13¾*

3377 A1331 €2.21 multi 5.50 2.75

Colonial Postage Stamps for Cuba and Philippines, 150th Anniv. — A1332

2005, Oct. 20 *Perf. 13¾x14*

3378 A1332 €2.21 multi 5.50 2.75

Prince of Asturias Awards, 25th Anniv. — A1333

2005, Oct. 20 *Perf. 13¼x13*

3379 A1333 28c multi + label .75 .35

Printed in sheets of 8 stamps + 8 different labels.

Miniature Sheet

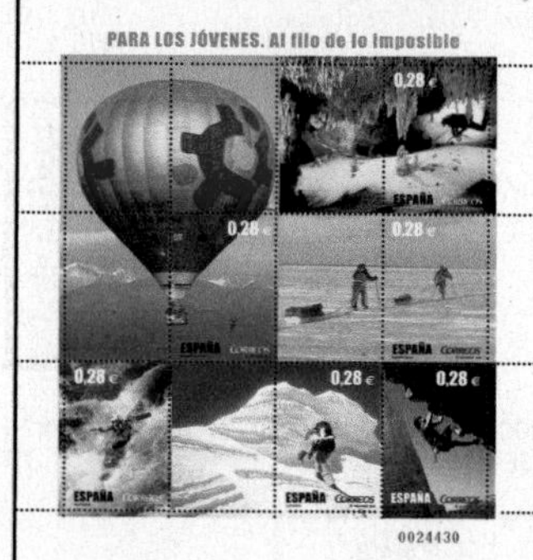
Scenes from Television Show "Al Filo de lo Imposible" — A1334

No. 3380: a, Underwater cave explorers. b, Hot-air balloon with man on rope outside of gondola. c, Man pulling sled. d, Kayaker. e, Climber on snowy mountain. f, Rock climber.

2005, Oct. 24 *Perf. 14x13¾*

3380	A1334 Sheet of 6 + 6 labels	4.25	4.25
a.-f.	28c Any single	.70	.35

See No. 3398.

A1335

Christmas A1336

2005, Oct. 31

3381	A1335 28c multi	.70	.35
3382	A1336 53c multi	1.25	.65

Souvenir Sheet

Stained Glass Window, Avila Cathedral — A1337

2005, Nov. 2 Litho. & Engr.

3383 A1337 €2.21 multi 5.25 5.25

Euromediterranean Summit, Barcelona — A1338

2005, Nov. 3 Photo. *Perf. 13¾x14*

3384 A1338 53c multi 1.25 .65

Queen Juana of Castile (1479-1555) A1339

2005, Nov. 4 *Perf. 14x13¾*

3385 A1339 28c multi .75 .35

Parliament of Toro, 500th anniv.

Toys — A1340

No. 3386: a, Marionettes. b, Tops. c, Toy car. d, Toy truck. e, Doll. f, Container of marbles. g, Toy horse and cart. h, Toy motorcycle.

2006, Jan. 2 Litho. *Die Cut Perf. 13*

Self-Adhesive

3386	Booklet pane of 8	5.50	
a.-h.	A1340 A Any single	.65	.35

Nos. 3386a-3386h each sold for 28c on day of issue.

King Juan Carlos Type of 2001 With Euro Denominations Only

2006 Photo. *Perf. 12¾x13¼*

3387	A1091	29c sil & brown	.75	.35
3388	A1091	57c sil & org	1.40	.70
3389	A1091	€2.26 sil & pur	5.50	2.75
3390	A1091	€2.33 sil & claret	5.50	2.75
3391	A1091	€2.39 sil & dull grn	5.75	2.75
	Nos. 3387-3391 (5)		18.90	9.30

Issued: 29c, 57c, 2/1; €2.26, 1/5; €2.33, €2.39, 2/13.

Carnation — A1341

Die Cut Perf. 13

2006, Jan. 20 Litho.

Self-Adhesive

3392 A1341 28c multi .75 .35

No. 3392 was printed in sheets of 10, which were bound in booklets of 10 sheets.

Bank of Spain, 150th Anniv. — A1342

2006, Jan. 27 **Engr.** ***Perf. 14x13¾***

3393 A1342 78c brown & black 1.90 .95

Cypress Tree, La Anunciada Convent, Villafranca del Bierzo — A1343

2006, Jan. 30 **Photo.**

3394 A1343 53c multi 1.40 .70

Sparrow — A1344

Die Cut Perf. 13

2006, Feb. 1 **Self-Adhesive** **Litho.**

3395 A1344 A multi .75 .35

No. 3395 sold for 29p on day of issue, and was printed in sheets of 10 which were bound in booklets of 10 sheets.

Intl. Year of Deserts and Desertification — A1345

2006, Feb. 6 **Photo.** ***Perf. 13¾x14***

3396 A1345 29c multi .75 .35

Woman Suffrage, 75th Anniv. A1346

2006, Mar. 8

3397 A1346 29c blue & sepia .75 .35

"Al Filo de lo Imposible" Type of 2005

No. 3398: a, Cyclists. b, Man in desert. c, Parachutist. d, Kayakers. e, Rafters. f, Waterfall rock climbers.

2006, Mar. 22 ***Perf. 14x13¾***

3398 A1334 Sheet of 6 + 6 labels 12.00 12.00

a.	29c multi	.70	.35
b.	38c multi	.95	.45
c.	41c multi	1.00	.50
d.	57c multi	1.40	.70
e.	78c multi	1.90	.95
f.	€2.39 multi	6.00	3.00

Goldfinch A1347

Strelitzia Flower A1348

2006, Apr. 1 **Litho.** ***Die Cut Perf. 13***

3399 A1347 29c multi .70 .35
3400 A1348 38c multi .95 .45

Nos. 3399-3400 were each printed in sheets of 10, which were bound in booklets of 10 sheets.

Civic Values — A1349

Designs: No. 3401, 29c, Water conservation. No. 3402, 29c, Man with "No Drugs" balloons. 38c, Social Security and Labor inspectors, cent., horiz. 57c, Fight against human trafficking, horiz.

Perf. 14x13¾, 13¾x14

2006, Apr. 4 **Photo.**

3401-3404 A1349 Set of 4 3.75 1.90

Diario de Pontevedra Newspaper, 117th Anniv. — A1350

Diario de Léon Newspaper, Cent. — A1351

Diario de Avila Newspaper, 108th Anniv. — A1352

El Norte de Castilla Newspaper, 150th Anniv. — A1353

Levante-El Mercantil Valenciano Newspaper, 134th Anniv. — A1354

2006, Apr. 20 ***Perf. 13¾x14, 14x13¾***

3405 A1350 41c multi 1.10 .55
3406 A1351 41c multi 1.10 .55
3407 A1352 41c multi 1.10 .55
3408 A1353 41c red & blk 1.10 .55
3409 A1354 41c multi 1.10 .55
Nos. 3405-3409 (5) 5.50 2.75

Souvenir Sheet

Christopher Columbus (1451-1506), Explorer — A1355

2006, Apr. 24 ***Perf. 14x13¾***

3410 A1355 €2.39 multi 6.25 3.00

Coronation of Santa Maria de Los Remedios Icon, Cent. — A1356

2006, Apr. 27

3411 A1356 €2.33 multi 6.00 3.00

Souvenir Sheet

Exfilna 2006 Philatelic Exhibition, Algeciras — A1357

Litho. & Engr.

2006, May 5 ***Perf. 13¾x14***

3412 A1357 €2.39 multi 6.25 3.00

Inauguration of Taxis Family Postal System in Spain, 500th Anniv. — A1358

2006, May 9 **Photo.**

3413 A1358 29c multi .75 .35

Internet Day A1359

25th Intl. Mathematics Conference, Madrid — A1360

Die Cut Perf. 13

2006, May 17 **Litho.**

3414 A1359 29c multi .75 .35
3515 A1360 57c multi 1.50 .75

Socialist Youth In Spain, Cent. A1361

2006, May 23 **Photo.** ***Perf. 13¾x14***

3416 A1361 78c multi 2.00 1.00

Souvenir Sheet

España 06 Intl. Philatelic Exhibition, Málaga — A1362

2006, May 29

3417 A1362 78c multi 2.00 2.00

San Pedro and San Marcial Festivals, Irún — A1363

2006, June 5 ***Perf. 14x13¾***

3418 A1363 29c multi .75 .35

Architecture A1364

Designs: 29c, Casa Battló, Barcelona. 38c, Vapor Aymerich, Amt y Jover, Terrassa. 41c, Depósitos del Sol Library, Albacete. 57c, Campos Eliseos Theater, Bilbao. 78c, Alfredo Kraus Auditorium, Las Palmas, horiz. €2.33, Bus station, Casar de Cáceres, horiz.

Engr., Photo. (41c, 78c, €2.33)

2006, June 8 ***Perf. 14x13¾, 13¾x14***

3419-3424 A1364 Set of 6 12.00 6.00

Al-Idrisi (c. 1100-65), Geographer A1365

2006, June 15 **Photo.** ***Perf. 14x13¾***

3425 A1365 78c multi 2.00 1.00

Greenfinch A1366

Iris A1367

2006, July 5 **Litho.** ***Die Cut Perf. 13***

Self-Adhesive

3426 A1366 29c multi .75 .35
3427 A1367 41c multi 1.10 .55

Nos. 3426-3427 were each printed in sheets of 10 which were bound in booklets of 10 sheets.

Sanlúcar de Barrameda Horse Race A1368

2006, July 6 **Photo.** ***Perf. 13¾x14***

3428 A1368 €2.33 multi 6.00 3.00

Archaeology A1369

Designs: 29c, Los Millares archaeological site. 57c, Art on vase from L'Alcudia archaeological site, horiz. 78c Moixent Warrior, bronze sculpture.

2006, July 6 ***Perf. 14x13¾, 13¾x14***

3429-3431 A1369 Set of 3 4.25 2.10

Earth Sciences A1370

Designs: No. 3432, 29c, Derived cartography. No. 3433, 29c, Vulcanology and seismology.

2006, July 13 ***Perf. 13¾x14***

3432-3433 A1370 Set of 2 1.50 .75

Benavides Thursday Market, Orbigo, 700th Anniv. A1371

Aragon-Cataluña Canal, Cent. — A1372

2006, July 20

3434 A1371 38c multi 1.00 .50
3435 A1372 38c multi 1.00 .50

Diplomatic Relations Between Spain and Israel, 20th Anniv. A1373

2006, Sept. 1

3436 A1373 78c multi 2.00 1.00

Castles A1374

Designs: 29c, Baños de la Encina Castle. €2.39, Torroella de Montgri.

2006, Sept. 8 **Engr.**

3437-3438 A1374 Set of 2 6.75 3.50

A1375

Europa — A1376

2006, Sept. 12 **Photo.** ***Perf. 14x13¾***

3439 A1375 29c multi .75 .35
3440 A1376 57c multi 1.50 .75

Bridges Between Spain and Portugal — A1377

No. 3441: a, Ayamonte International Bridge (Vila Real de Santo António). b, Alcántara Bridge.

2006, Sept. 14 ***Perf. 13x13¼***

3441 Horiz. pair 2.25 2.25
a. A1377 29c multi .75 .35
b. A1377 57c multi 1.50 .75

See Portugal Nos. 2855-2856.

Rioja Grape Harvest Festival A1378

2006, Sept. 21 ***Perf. 13¾x14***

3442 A1378 29c multi .75 .35

Real Club Deportivo La Coruna Soccer Team, Cent. A1379

2006, Sept. 25

3443 A1379 57c multi 1.50 .75

Souvenir Sheet

Victory of Spanish Team at 2006 World Basketball Championships — A1380

2006, Oct. 2 **Photo.** ***Perf. 13¾x14***

3444 A1380 29c multi .75 .75

Swallow A1381

Poinsettia A1382

2006, Oct. 4 **Litho.** ***Die Cut Perf. 13***

Self-Adhesive

3445 A1381 29c multi .75 .35
3446 A1382 29c multi .75 .35

Souvenir Sheets

España 06 World Philatelic Exhibition, Malaga — A1383

Exhibition emblem and: No. 3447, €2.33, Emblem of Vitorio & Lucchino, fashion designers. No. 3448, €2.33, Silhouette of hat and hand (cinema), vert. No. 3449, €2.33, Musical notes and staff. No. 3450, €2.33, Guitarist, vert. No. 3451, €2.33, Hand (flamenco dancing). No. 3452, €2.33, Tennis racquet and basketball, vert. No. 3453, €2.33, Pablo Picasso (1881-1973), artist.

2006 **Photo.** ***Perf. 13¾x14, 14x13¾***

3447-3453 A1383 Set of 7 42.00 21.00

Issued: No. 3447, 10/8; No. 3448, 10/9; Nos. 3449-3450, 10/10; No. 3451, 10/11; No. 3452, 10/12; No. 3453, 10/13.

America Issue, Energy Conservation — A1384

2006, Oct. 14 ***Perf. 13¾***

3454 A1384 78c multi 2.00 1.00

Appointment of First Spanish Postmen, 250th Anniv. — A1385

Die Cut Perf. 13

2006, Oct. 25 **Litho.**

Self-Adhesive

3455 A1385 29c multi .75 .35

Stamp Day.

Ramón Rubial (1906-99), Politician A1386

2006, Oct. 27 **Engr.** ***Perf. 14x13¾***

3456 A1386 57c multi 1.50 .75

A1387

Christmas A1388

Die Cut Perf. 13

2006, Nov. 2 **Self-Adhesive** **Litho.**

3457 A1387 29c multi .75 .35
3458 A1388 57c multi 1.50 .75

Souvenir Sheet

Stained Glass Window, School of Architecture, Polytechnic University of Madrid — A1389

Litho. & Engr.

2006, Nov. 3 *Perf. 14x13¾*
3459 A1389 €2.39 multi 6.25 6.25

St. Francis Xavier (1506-52) A1390

2006, Nov. 7 *Perf. 13¾x14*
3460 A1390 29c multi .80 .40

Television Broadcasting in Spain, 50th Anniv. — A1391

2006, Nov. 8 **Photo.**
3461 A1391 29c multi .80 .40

La Vanguardia Newspaper, 125th Anniv. — A1392

2006, Nov. 9 *Perf. 14x13¾*
3462 A1392 29c multi .80 .40

Pío Baroja (1872-1956), Writer — A1393

2006, Nov. 23
3463 A1393 29c multi .80 .40

Revision of Spanish Coat of Arms, 25th Anniv. — A1394

2006, Nov. 23
3464 A1394 29c multi .80 .40

A1395

Historical Memory Year A1396

2006, Nov. 30 *Perf. 13¾x14*
3465 A1395 29c multi .80 .40
3466 A1396 29c multi .80 .40

Toys — A1397

No. 3467: a, Tricycle. b, Bus. c, Train. d, Bowling game. e, Baby carriage. f, Seaplane. g, Printing kit. h, Firetruck.

2007, Jan. 2 Litho. ***Die Cut Perf. 13***
Self-Adhesive
3467 Booklet pane of 8 6.50
a.-h. A1397 A Any single .80 .40

Nos. 3467a-3467h each sold for 30c on day of issue.

King Juan Carlos — A1398

Perf. 12¾x13¼
2007, Jan. 13 **Photo.**
Color of Portrait

3468	A1398	30c blue	.80	.40
3469	A1398	58c olive grn	1.50	.75
3470	A1398	€2.43 org brn	6.25	3.25
3471	A1398	€2.49 rose pink	6.50	3.25
		Nos. 3468-3471 (4)	15.05	7.65

See Nos. 3532-3539, 3615-3618, 3688-3691, 3774-3777.

Hoopoe A1399

Red Rose A1400

Die Cut Perf. 13
2007, Jan. 20 **Litho.**
Self-Adhesive
3472 A1399 30c multi .80 .40
3473 A1400 39c multi 1.00 .50

Nos. 3472-3473 each were printed in sheets of 10, which were bound in booklets of 10 sheets.

Teacher and Pupils A1401

2007, Jan. 23 **Self-Adhesive**
3474 A1401 58c multi 1.50 .75

Las Provincias Newspaper, 140th Anniv. (in 2006) — A1402

2007, Jan. 31 Photo. *Perf. 13¾x14*
3475 A1402 42c multi 1.10 .55

Stylized Periodic Table of Elements A1403

Gregorian Calendar, 425th Anniv. — A1404

Die Cut Perf. 13
2007, Feb. 2 Self-Adhesive Litho.
3476 A1403 30c multi .80 .40
3477 A1404 42c multi 1.10 .55

Institute of Catalan Studies, Cent. A1405

2007, Feb. 5 Photo. *Perf. 13¾x14*
3478 A1405 30c multi .80 .40

2007 America's Cup Challenger Races — A1406

2007, Feb. 8
3479 A1406 30c multi .80 .40

Earth and Space Sciences A1407

Designs: 30c, Map (cartography). 78c, Yebes Astronomical Center radio telescope.

Die Cut Perf. 13
2007, Feb. 16 **Litho.**
Self-Adhesive
3480-3481 A1407 Set of 2 3.00 1.50

Fuentepiña Pine Tree — A1408

2007, Mar. 5 Photo. *Perf. 13¾x14*
3482 A1408 78c multi 2.10 1.10

Mosaic from Roman Villa, Pedrosa de la Vega A1409

Roman Baths, Campo Valdés A1410

2007, Mar. 8
3483 A1409 30c multi .80 .40
3484 A1410 30c multi .80 .40

European Economic Community, 50th Anniv. — A1411

2007, Mar. 23 *Perf. 14x13¾*
3485 A1411 58c multi 1.60 .80

Canary A1412

Violet A1413

2007, Apr. 2 Litho. ***Die Cut Perf. 13***
Self-Adhesive
3486 A1412 30c multi .80 .40
3487 A1413 42c multi 1.25 .60

Souvenir Sheet

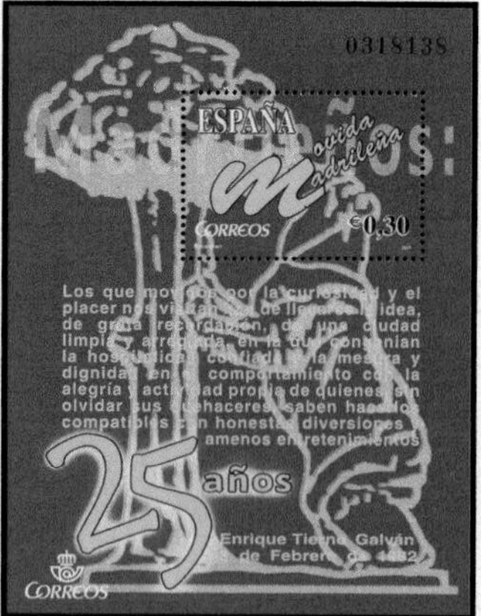

Madrid Movement, 25th Anniv. — A1414

2007, Apr. 13 Photo. *Perf. 13¾x14*
3488 A1414 30c multi .85 .85

Souvenir Sheet

Mallorca Cathedral — A1415

Engr., Litho. Margin
2007, Apr. 16
3489 A1415 €2.43 blue 6.75 6.75

Exfilna 2007 National Philatelic Exhibition, Palma de Mallorca.

Europa — A1416

2007, Apr. 23 Photo. *Perf. 14x13¾*
3490 A1416 58c multi 1.60 .80

Scouting, cent.

Architecture A1417

Designs: 30c, Valleacerón Chapel, Almadenejos. 39c, El Capricho, Comillas. 42c, Santa Caterina Market, Barcelona. 58c, Vizcaya Bridge, Las Arenas, horiz. 78c, Barajas Airport, Madrid. €2.49, Casa Lis, Salamanca, horiz.

Photo., Engr. (39c, 58c)
2007, Apr. 26 *Perf. 14x13¾, 13¾x14*
3491-3496 A1417 Set of 6 13.50 6.75

Juvenia 2007 Natl. Youth Philatelic Exhibition, Calahorra A1418

2007, Apr. 28 Photo. *Perf. 13¾x14*
3497 A1418 30c multi .85 .40

Stamp Day — A1419

2007, May 7 Litho. *Die Cut Perf. 13*
Self-Adhesive
3498 A1419 30c multi .80 .40

Song of the Cid, 800th Anniv. A1420

2007, May 9 *Die Cut Perf. 13*
Self-Adhesive
3499 A1420 30c multi .80 .40

Law of the Court of Auditors, 25th Anniv. — A1421

2007, May 12 Photo. *Perf. 14x13¾*
3500 A1421 30c multi .80 .40

Civic Values — A1422

Designs: 30c, Racial integration. 39c, No school violence. 58c, Organ donation. 78c, Equality of the sexes.

2007, May 16
3501-3504 A1422 Set of 4 5.50 2.75

Mushrooms A1423

Designs: 30c, Tricholoma equestre. 78c, Amanita muscaria.

2007, June 1
3505-3506 A1423 Set of 2 3.00 1.50

Carmen Conde (1907-96), Writer A1424

Rosa Chacel (1898-1994), Writer — A1425

2007, June 4 Engr. *Perf. 13¾x14*
3507 A1424 €2.49 red & blk 6.75 3.50
3508 A1425 €2.49 org & blk 6.75 3.50

Real Betis Balompié Soccer Team, Cent. A1426

2007, June 14 Photo. *Perf. 13¾x14*
3509 A1426 78c multi 2.10 1.10

Canonical Coronation of Blessed Mary of the O — A1427

2007, June 16 *Perf. 14x13¾*
3510 A1427 30c multi .85 .40

Nightingale A1428

Hyacinth A1429

2007, July 2 Litho. *Die Cut Perf. 13*
Self-Adhesive
3511 A1428 30c multi .85 .40
3512 A1429 30c multi .85 .40

Spanish Armed Forces Peace Missions — A1430

2007, July 4 Photo. *Perf. 13x13¼*
3513 A1430 30c multi .85 .40

Expo Zaragoza 2008 A1431

2007, July 5 Litho. *Die Cut Perf. 13*
Self-Adhesive
3514 A1431 58c multi 1.60 .80

Miniature Sheet

Scenes From Television Show "Al Filo de lo Imposible" — A1432

No. 3515: a, Diver under ice shelf. b, Skier. c, People pulling sleds. d, Sailboat in Antarctic waters. e, Kayaker in fjord. f, Iditarod dog sled team.

2007, July 12 Photo. *Perf. 14x13¾*
3515 A1432 Sheet of 6 + 6 labels 13.50 13.50
a. 30c multi .85 .40
b. 39c multi 1.00 .50
c. 42c multi 1.10 .55
d. 58c multi 1.60 .80
e. 78c multi 2.10 1.10
f. €2.43 multi 6.75 3.25

Nature Parks A1433

Designs: No. 3516, 30c, Albufera Nature Park. No. 3517, 30c, Lagunas de Ruidera Nature Park.

2007, July 19 *Perf. 13¾x14*
3516-3517 A1433 Set of 2 1.75 .85

Miniature Sheet

Lighthouses — A1434

No. 3518: a, Punta del Hidalgo Lighthouse, Tenerife. b, Cabo Mayor Lighthouse, Cantabria. c, Punta Almina Lighthouse, Ceuta. d, Melilla Lighthouse, Melilla. e, Cabo de Palos Lighthouse, Murcia. f, Gorliz Lighthouse, Vizcaya.

2007, Sept. 6
3518 A1434 Sheet of 6 + 6 labels 13.50 13.50
a. 30c multi .85 .40
b. 39c multi 1.00 .50
c. 42c multi 1.10 .55
d. 58c multi 1.60 .80
e. 78c multi 2.10 1.10
f. €2.43 multi 6.75 3.25

Castles A1435

Designs: No. 3519, €2.49, Almenar Castle. No. 3520, €2.49, Villena Castle.

2007, Sept. 10 Engr. ***Perf. 13¾x14***

3519-3520 A1435 Set of 2 14.00 7.00

Souvenir Sheet

Statues of Asclepius, Greek God of Medicine — A1436

No. 3521: a, Statue from Museum of Ampurias, Spain. b, Statue from National Archaeological Museum, Athens.

2007, Sept. 13 Photo. ***Perf. 12¾x13***

3521 A1436 Sheet of 2 2.50 2.50
a. 30c multi .85 .40
b. 58c multi 1.60 .80

See Greece No. 2319.

Dupont Lark — A1437

Daisy — A1438

2007, Oct. 1 Litho. ***Die Cut Perf. 13***

Self-Adhesive

3522 A1437 30c multi .85 .40
3523 A1438 30c multi .85 .40

El Adelantado de Segovia Newspaper, 106th Anniv. — A1439

2007, Oct. 4 Photo. ***Perf. 13¾x14***

3524 A1439 78c multi 2.25 1.10

America Issue, Education For All A1440

2007, Oct. 11

3525 A1440 78c multi 2.25 1.10

Miniature Sheet

Women's Clothing by Balenciaga In Costume Museum, Madrid — A1441

No. 3526: a, Ivory chantily lace and taffeta dress, 1948-50. b, Red silk satin two-piece party dress, 1960. c, Red morning coat and dress, 1960s. d, Yellow linen dress.

2007, Oct. 18 Photo. ***Perf. 13¼x13***

3526 A1441 Sheet of 4 6.25 6.25
a. 39c multi 1.10 .55
b. 42c multi 1.25 .60
c. 58c multi 1.60 .80
d. 78c multi 2.25 1.10

Altarpiece Sculpture Depicting Epiphany, by Damián Forment A1442

Children in Envelope A1443

Die Cut Perf. 13

2007, Oct. 31 Litho.

Self-Adhesive

3527 A1442 30c multi .90 .45
3528 A1443 58c multi 1.75 .85

Christmas.

Self-Portraits A1444

Self-portraits of: 39c, Pedro Berruguete. 42c, Mariano Salvador Maella.

2007, Nov. 5 Photo. ***Perf. 14x13¾***

3529-3530 A1444 Set of 2 2.40 1.25

Souvenir Sheet

Stained-Glass Window by Alberto Martorell — A1445

Litho. & Engr.

2007, Nov. 9 ***Perf. 13¾x14***

3531 A1445 €2.43 multi 7.25 3.75

King Juan Carlos Type of 2007

2008, Jan. 2 Photo. ***Perf. 12¾x13¼***

Color of Portrait

3532 A1398 1c black .25 .25
3533 A1398 2c lilac rose .25 .25
3534 A1398 5c blue .25 .25
3535 A1398 10c greenish blue .30 .25
3536 A1398 31c brown .90 .45
3537 A1398 60c violet blue 1.75 .90
3538 A1398 78c rose 2.40 1.25
3539 A1398 €2.60 slate green 7.75 3.50
Nos. 3532-3539 (8) 13.85 7.10

Toys — A1446

No. 3540: a, Steamship with wheels. b, Bean bag target with clown's face. c, Three sand pails. d, Stagecoach. e, Wafer container. f, Diabolo. g, Building blocks. h, Submarine.

2008, Jan. 2 Litho. ***Die Cut Perf. 13***

Self-Adhesive

3540 Booklet pane of 8 7.50
a.-h. A1446 A Any single .90 .45

Nos. 3540a-3540h each sold for 31c on day of issue.

Green Woodpecker A1447

Camellia A1448

2008, Jan. 10 ***Die Cut Perf. 13***

Self-Adhesive

3541 A1447 31c multi .90 .45
3542 A1448 60c multi 1.75 .90

Sciences A1449

Designs: 39c, Medicine. 43c, Meteorology.

2008, Jan. 17 Litho.

Self-Adhesive

3543-3544 A1449 Set of 2 2.40 1.25

See also Nos. 3613-3614.

La Voz de Avilés Newspaper, Cent. — A1450

2008, Jan. 30 Photo. ***Perf. 13¾x14***

3545 A1450 31c multi .95 .45

International Years — A1451

Designs: 78c, Intl. Polar Year. €2.60, Intl. Year of Planet Earth.

Die Cut Perf. 13

2008, Feb. 4 Litho.

Self-Adhesive

3546-3547 A1451 Set of 2 10.50 5.25

Hand and Phone Number for Abused Women's Hotline A1452

2008, Feb. 11 ***Die Cut Perf. 13***

Self-Adhesive

3548 A1452 31c multi .95 .45

Black Poplar of Horcajuelo A1453

2008, Feb. 18 Photo. ***Perf. 14x13¾***

3549 A1453 €2.44 multi 7.50 3.75

Expo Zaragoza 2008 A1454

Die Cut Perf. 13

2008, Feb. 22 Litho.

Self-Adhesive

3550 A1454 31c multi .95 .45

Civic Values A1455

Designs: 31c, Fight against child exploitation. 39c, Intergenerational solidarity. 43c, Cultural diversity.

2008, Feb. 29 Photo. ***Perf. 13¾x14***

3551-3553 A1455 Set of 3 3.50 1.75

Archaeology — A1456

Designs: No. 3554, 31c, Bicha of Balazote. No. 3555, 31c, Funerary urn of Apophis I.

2008, Mar. 3

3554-3555 A1456 Set of 2 1.90 .95

Landscapes — A1457

Designs: No. 3556, 31c, Hoces del Rio Duratón Nature Park. No. 3557, 31c, Montes de Toledo.

2008, Mar. 10

3556-3557 A1457 Set of 2 2.00 1.00

Maritime Rescue Craft A1458

Die Cut Perf. 13

2008, Mar. 12 **Litho.**

Self-Adhesive

3558 A1458 31c multi 1.00 .50

University of Oviedo, 400th Anniv. A1459

2008, Mar. 14 **Photo.** ***Perf. 13¾x14***

3559 A1459 31c multi 1.00 .50

European Parliament, 50th Anniv. — A1460

2008, Mar. 19

3560 A1460 60c multi 1.90 .95

Common Kestrel — A1461

Tulips — A1462

2008, Apr. 1 **Litho.** ***Die Cut Perf. 13***

Self-Adhesive

3561 A1461 31c multi 1.00 .50
3562 A1462 43c multi 1.40 .70

Palacio de Longoria, Madrid A1463

Casa Vicens, Barcelona A1464

Agbar Tower, Barcelona A1465

Tenerife Auditorium, Tenerife — A1466

Torrespaña, Madrid — A1467

Montjuic Communications Tower, Barcelona A1468

2008, Apr. 2 **Engr.** ***Perf. 13¾x14***

3563 A1463 31c multi 1.00 .50

Perf. 14x13¾

3564 A1464 31c multi 1.00 .50

Photo.

3565 A1465 31c multi 1.00 .50

Perf. 13¾x14

3566 A1466 31c multi 1.00 .50

Perf. 13¼x13

3567 A1467 31c multi 1.00 .50
3568 A1468 31c multi 1.00 .50
Nos. 3563-3568 (6) 6.00 3.00

Traditional Sports and Games A1469

Designs: No. 3569, Court handball (Pelota Valenciana). No. 3570, Handball (Pelota Vasca), vert. No. 3571, Stone carrying (Levantamiento de piedras), vert. No. 3572, Bar throwing (Lanzamiento de barra), vert. No. 3573, Sling hurling (Tiro con honda), vert.

No. 3574, Rowing race (regatas de traineras). No. 3575, Human tower (castillos humanos), vert.

No. 3576 — Bowling: a, Bolo leonés. b, Bolo palma. c, Bolo asturiano.

No. 3577, vert. — Martial arts: a, Stick fighting (palo canario). b, Wrestling (lucha leonesa). c, Wrestling (lucha canaria).

No. 3578 — Throwing games: a, Chito. b, Chave. c, Calva.

2008 **Photo.** ***Perf. 13¾x14, 14x13¾***

3569 A1469 43c multi + label 1.40 .70
3570 A1469 43c multi + label 1.40 .70
3571 A1469 43c multi + label 1.40 .70
3572 A1469 43c multi + label 1.40 .70
3573 A1469 43c multi + label 1.40 .70
3574 A1469 43c multi + label 1.40 .70
3575 A1469 43c multi + label 1.25 .60
Nos. 3569-3575 (7) 9.65 4.80

Miniature Sheets

3576 Sheet of 3 + 3 labels 4.25 4.25
a.-c. A1469 43c Any single 1.40 .70
3577 Sheet of 3 + 5 labels 4.25 4.25
a.-c. A1469 43c Any single 1.40 .70
3578 Sheet of 3 + 3 labels 3.50 3.50
a.-c. A1469 43c Any single 1.10 .55

Issued: Nos. 3569-3570, 4/16; No. 3571, 5/16; Nos. 3572-3573, 5/30. Nos. 3574, 3577, 7/16; No. 3575, 10/9; No. 3576, 6/5; No. 3578, 10/27.

Souvenir Sheet

Europa — A1470

2008, Apr. 23 ***Perf. 13¼x12¾***

3579 A1470 60c multi 1.90 1.90

Souvenir Sheet

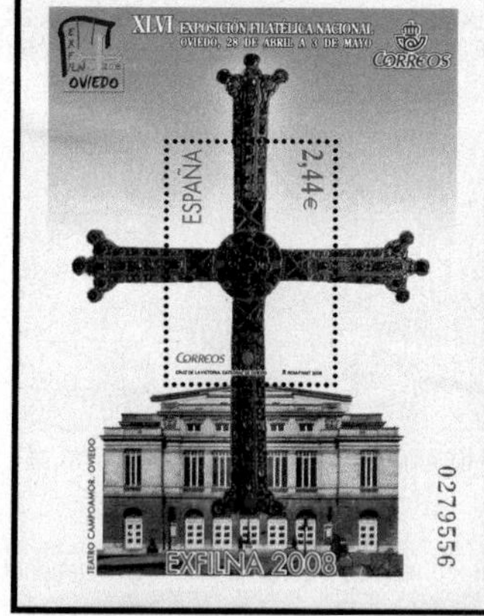

Cross of Victory, San Salvador Cathedral, Oviedo — A1471

2008. Apr. 28 ***Perf. 14x13¾***

3580 A1471 €2.44 multi 7.50 7.50

Exfilna 2008 (National Philatelic Exhibition), Oviedo.

Royal Decree of the Maritime Post — A1472

2008, May 5 **Litho.** ***Die Cut Perf. 13***

Self-Adhesive

3581 A1472 39c black & brown 1.25 .60

Stamp Day.

El Progreso Newspaper, Lugo, Cent. — A1473

2008, May 9 **Photo.** ***Perf. 13¾x14***

3582 A1473 31c multi 1.00 .50

Joan Oró (1923-2004), Biochemist A1474

Zenobia Camprubí (1887-1956), Literary Translator A1475

María Lejárraga (1874-1974), Writer — A1476

Design: No. 3586, Carmen Martín Gaite (1925-2000), writer.

2008, June 2 Engr. *Perf. 14x13¾*

3583	A1474	31c black	1.00	.50
3584	A1475	31c ver & black	1.00	.50
3585	A1476	31c black & ver	1.00	.50
3586	A1476	31c black & ver	1.00	.50
	Nos. 3583-3586 (4)		4.00	2.00

Souvenir Sheets

Francisco de Goya Monument, Zaragoza — A1477

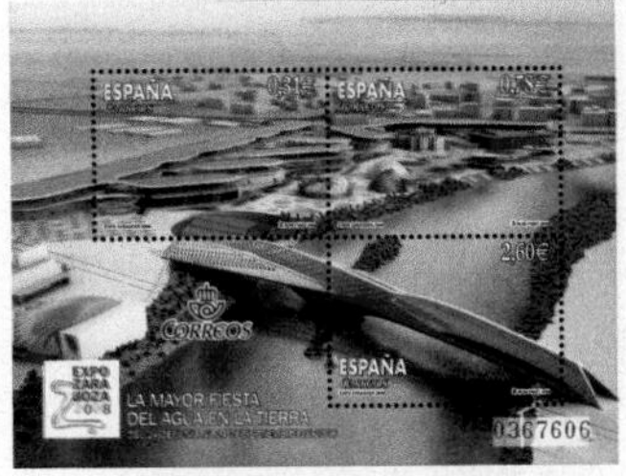

Model of Expo Zaragoza Grounds — A1478

Engr. (Litho. Margin)

2008 *Perf. 14x13¾*

3587	A1477	€2.60 Prus blue	8.00	6.00

Photo.

Perf. 13¾x14

3588	A1478	Sheet of 3	11.50	11.50
a.		31c Expo buildings	1.00	.50
b.		78c Buildings, diff.	2.40	1.25
c.		€2.60 Bridge Pavilion	8.00	4.00

Issued: No. 3587, 6/13; No. 3588, 7/4.

European Bee-eater A1479

Dahlia A1480

2008, July 1 Litho. *Die Cut Perf. 13*

Self-Adhesive

3589	A1479	31c multi	1.00	.50
3590	A1480	60c multi	1.90	.95

2008 Summer Olympics, Beijing A1481

2008, July 8 *Perf. 13¾x14*

3591	A1481	31c multi	1.00	.50

Souvenir Sheet

Spain, UEFA 2008 Soccer Champions — A1482

2008, July 24 Photo.

3592	A1482	€1 multi	3.25	3.25

Souvenir Sheets

Tapestries — A1483

Tapestries of works by Francisco de Goya: 60c, The Swing. €2.60, The Blind Man and the Guitar.

2008, July 29 *Perf. 12¾*

3593-3594	A1483	Set of 2	10.00	10.00

Miniature Sheet

Lighthouses — A1484

No. 3595: a, Barbaria Lighthouse, Isla de Formantera. b, Irta Lighthouse, Castelón. c, Pechiguera Lighthouse, Isla de Lanzarote. d, Silleiro Lighthouse, Pontevedra. e, Torredembarra Lighthouse, Tarragona. f, Punta Orchilla Lighthouse, Isla de la Hierro.

2008, Sept. 2 Photo. *Perf. 14x13¾*

3595	A1484	Sheet of 6	10.50	10.50
a.-f.		60c Any single	1.75	.85

Self-Portraits A1485

Self-portrait of: No. 3596, 31c, Antonio Maria Esquivel (1806-57). No. 3597, 43c, Darío de Regoyos (1857-1913).

2008, Sept. 8

3596-3597	A1485	Set of 2	2.10	1.10

Royal Spanish Tennis Federation, Cent. — A1486

2008, Sept. 19 Litho.

3598	A1486	31c red & orange	.90	.45

Jay A1487

Daffodil A1488

2008, Oct. 1 *Die Cut Perf. 13*

Self-Adhesive

3599	A1487	31c multi	.90	.45
3600	A1488	31c multi	.90	.45

Mushrooms — A1489

Designs: No. 3601, 31c, Lepista nuda. No. 3602, 31c, Boletus regius.

2008, Oct. 10 Photo. *Perf. 13¾x14*

3601-3602	A1489	Set of 2	1.75	.85

America Issue, National Day A1490

2008, Oct. 13

3603	A1490	78c multi	2.00	1.00

Castles A1491

Designs: No. 3604, €2.60, Maqueda Castle, Toledo. No. 3605, €2.60, La Calahorra Castle, Granada.

2008, Oct. 16 Engr.

3604-3605	A1491	Set of 2	13.50	6.75

Miniature Sheet

Women's Clothing by Pedro Rodriguez In Costume Museum, Madrid — A1492

No. 3606: a, Red ball gown, 1968-70. b, Strapless dress, c. 1947. c, V-neck chiffon dress, 1960s. d, Pink crepe dress with embroidery.

Photo. & Embossed

2008, Oct. 23 *Perf. 13¼x13*

3606	A1492	Sheet of 4	3.25	3.25
a.-d.		31c Any single	.80	.40

Creche Figures A1493

Maternity, by J. Carrero — A1494

Die Cut Perf. 13

2008, Nov. 3 Litho.

Self-Adhesive

3607	A1493	31c multi	.80	.40
3608	A1494	60c multi	1.60	.80

Souvenir Sheet

Dancers — A1495

No. 3609: a, Flamenco dancer, Spain. b, Irish dancer, Ireland.

2008, Nov. 7 Photo. *Perf. 13¼x13*

3609	A1495	Sheet of 2	3.50	3.50
a.		60c multi	1.50	.75
b.		78c multi	2.00	1.00

See Ireland Nos. 1809-1810.

Souvenir Sheet

Stained-Glass Window, by Dragant de Burdeos — A1496

Photo., Litho. & Engr.

2008, Nov. 14 ***Perf. 13¾x14***

3610 A1496 €2.60 multi 6.75 6.75

Symbols of Nation and Autonomous Communities A1497

No. 3611: a, Flag of Spain. b, Flag and map of Asturias. c, Flag and map of Galicia. d, Flag and map of Cantabria. e, Arms of Spain. f, Flag and map of Cataluña. g, Flag and map of Basque Country (Euzkadi). h, Flag and map of Andalusia.

2009, Jan. 2 Litho. ***Die Cut Perf. 13***

Self-Adhesive

3611 Booklet pane of 8 7.25
a.-h. A1497 A Any single .90 .45

On day of issue, Nos. 3611a-3611h each sold for 32c.

See Nos. 3682, 3762.

Fan and Manila Shawl A1498

2009, Jan. 2 ***Die Cut Perf. 13***

Self-Adhesive

3612 A1498 B multi 1.75 .85

Sold for 62c on day of issue.

Sciences Type of 2008

Designs: 39c, Botany. 43c, Genetics.

2009, Jan. 12 ***Die Cut Perf. 13***

Self-Adhesive

3613-3614 A1449 Set of 2 2.25 1.10

King Juan Carlos Type of 2007

Perf. 12¾x13¼

2009, Jan. 14 Photo.

Color of Portrait

3615 A1398 32c red .85 .40
3616 A1398 62c gray 1.60 .80
3617 A1398 €2.47 olive green 6.50 3.25
3618 A1398 €2.70 blue 7.00 3.50
Nos. 3615-3618 (4) 15.95 7.95

La Rioja Newspaper, 120th Anniv. — A1499

2009, Jan. 15 Photo. ***Perf. 13¾x14***

3619 A1499 32c multi .85 .40

Great Tit A1500

Hydrangea A1501

Die Cut Perf. 13

2009, Jan. 20 Litho.

Self-Adhesive

3620 A1500 32c multi .85 .40
3621 A1501 62c multi 1.60 .80

Archaeology — A1502

Roman mosaics: No. 3622, €2.70, Oceanus, from Carranque archaeological site, Toledo. No. 3623, €2.70, Oriens, from Casa del Mitreo, Mérida.

2009, Feb. 10 Photo. ***Perf. 13¾x14***

3622-3623 A1502 Set of 2 14.00 7.00

Civic Values A1503

Designs: 32c, Planting for the Planet. 62c, Balancing of work and family life. 78c, Reduction of carbon dioxide output.

2009, Feb. 17 Litho.

3624-3626 A1503 Set of 3 4.50 2.25

Renewable Energy — A1504

Designs: 32c, Hydroelectric energy. 43c, Wind energy. 62c, Solar energy. 78c, Geothermal energy.

2009, Feb. 20 Photo. ***Perf. 13***

3627-3630 A1504 Set of 4 5.50 2.75

Millennium Development Goals — A1505

2009, Mar. 2

3631 A1505 32c multi .85 .40

Nature Parks A1506

Designs: No. 3632, 43c, Cañón Río Lobos Nature Park. No. 3633, 43c, Izki Nature Park.

2009, Mar. 9 ***Perf. 13¾x14***

3632-3633 A1506 Set of 2 2.40 1.25

Gladiolus A1507

Capercaillie A1508

2009, Apr. 1 Litho. ***Die Cut Perf. 13***

Self-Adhesive

3634 A1507 32c multi .90 .45
3635 A1508 43c multi 1.25 .60

Council of Europe, 60th Anniv. A1509

2009, Apr. 6 ***Perf. 13¾x14***

3636 A1509 62c multi 1.75 .85

Miniature Sheet

Lighthouses — A1510

No. 3637: a, Porto Colom Lighthouse, Mallorca. b, Higuera Lighthouse, Huelva. c, Igeldo Lighthouse, Guipúzcoa. d, Arinaga Lighthouse, Grand Canary Island. e, Tower of Hercules Lighthouse, La Coruña. f, Torrox Lighthouse, Málaga.

2009, Apr. 15 Photo. ***Perf. 14x13¾***

3637 A1510 Sheet of 6 10.50 10.00
a.-f. 62c Any single 1.75 .85

Europa A1511

2009, Apr. 23 Litho. ***Perf. 13¾x14***

3638 A1511 62c multi 1.75 .85

Intl. Year of Astronomy.

Traditional Dances — A1512

Designs: No. 3639, Isa. No. 3640, Mateixa. No. 3641, Bolero. No. 3642, Rueda (75x29mm). No. 3643, Aurresku, vert. (29x75mm). No. 3644, Muñeira, vert. No. 3645, Fandango, vert. No. 3646, Candil, vert. No. 3648, La Sardana. No. 3647, Seguidillas, vert.

No. 3649, Sevillanas, vert. (29x41mm). No. 3650, La Jota, vert. (29x41mm).

2009 Photo. ***Perf. 13x12¾***

3639 A1512 43c multi 1.25 .60
3640 A1512 43c multi 1.25 .60
3641 A1512 43c multi + label 1.25 .60

Perf. 12¾x13¼

3642 A1512 43c multi 1.25 .60

Perf. 13¼x12¾

3643 A1512 43c multi 1.25 .60

Perf. 12¾x13

3644 A1512 43c multi + label 1.25 .60
3645 A1512 43c multi + label 1.25 .60
3646 A1512 43c multi + label 1.25 .60
3647 A1512 43c multi + label 1.25 .60

Perf. 13x12¾

3648 A1512 43c multi + label 1.25 .60
Nos. 3639-3648 (10) 12.50 6.00

Souvenir Sheet

Perf. 14x13¾

3649 A1512 43c multi 1.25 .60
3650 A1512 43c multi 1.25 .60

Issued: Nos. 3639, 3649, 4/27; Nos. 3640-3641, 5/14; Nos. 3642-3643, 6/4; Nos. 3644-3645, 7/22; Nos. 3646-3647, 9/14. Nos. 3648, 3650, 10/15.

King Alfonso VI of León and Castile (c. 1040-1109) A1513

2009, May 7 Photo. ***Perf. 14x13¾***

3651 A1513 39c multi 1.10 .55

St. Dominic de la Calzada (1019-1109) A1514

2009, May 7

3652 A1514 62c multi 1.75 .85

Souvenir Sheet

Stained-Glass Window of Spanish National Mint Paper Factory, Burgos — A1515

2009, May 29 Litho. & Engr.

3653 A1515 €2.70 multi 7.75 7.75

Miniature Sheet

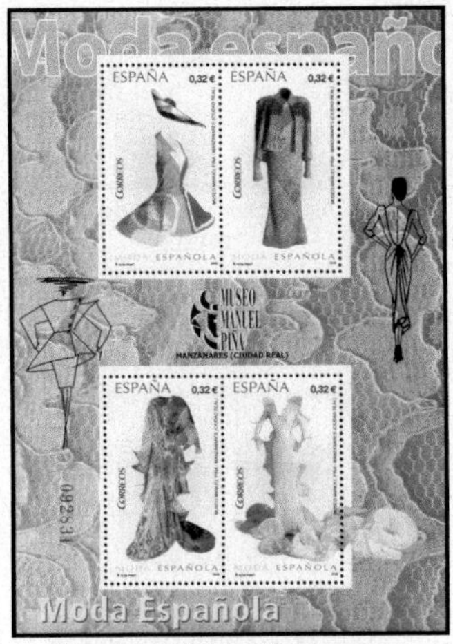

Women's Clothing Designed by Manuel Piña (1944-94) — A1516

No. 3654: a, Linen dress and hat. b, Knitted wool suit. c, Linen dress with hoops. d, Silk wedding dress.

Photo. & Embossed

2009, June 15 ***Perf. 13¼x13***

3654 A1516 Sheet of 4 3.75 3.75
a.-d. 32c Any single .90 .45

Graellsia Isabelae A1517

Geranium A1518

2009, July 1 Litho. ***Die Cut Perf. 13***
Self-Adhesive

3655 A1517 32c multi .90 .45
3656 A1518 62c multi 1.75 .85

Souvenir Sheet

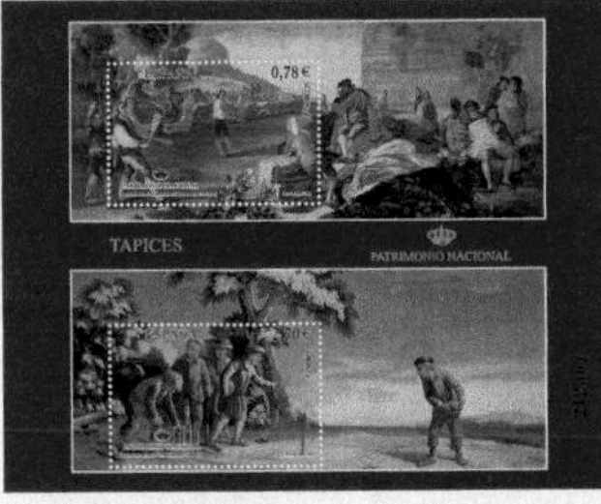

Tapestries — A1519

No. 3657 — Tapestries of sports scenes taken from painting: a, By Francisco de Goya (El Juego de Pelota a Pala). b, By Antonio González Velázquez (Juego de Bolos).

2009, July 6 Photo. ***Perf. 12¾***

3657 A1519 Sheet of 2 9.75 9.75
a. 78c multi 2.25 1.10
b. €2.70 multi 7.50 3.75

Souvenir Sheet

Introduction of the Euro, 10th Anniv. — A1520

Litho. & Engr.

2009, July 10 ***Perf. 14x13¾***

3658 A1520 €1 multi 2.75 1.40

Traffic Safety — A1521

2009, July 14 Photo. ***Perf. 13x13¼***

3659 A1521 32c multi .90 .45

Famous Men — A1522

Designs: No. 3660, 32c, Claudio Moyano (1809-90), explorer. No. 3661, 32c, Charles Darwin (1809-82), naturalist. No. 3662, 32c, Louis Braille (1809-52), educator of the blind.

Engr., Litho. & Engr. (#3662)

2009, July 15 ***Perf. 14x13¾***

3660-3662 A1522 Set of 3 2.75 1.40

Braille dots on No. 3662 were applied by a thermographic process.

First Powered Flight in Spain, Cent. A1523

2009, Sept. 5 Photo. ***Perf. 13¾x14***

3663 A1523 32c multi .95 .45

Real Sociedad Soccer Team, Cent. A1524

2009, Sept. 7 Litho.

3664 A1524 32c multi .95 .45

Canal of Castile A1525

Los Tilos Bridge, La Palma Island A1526

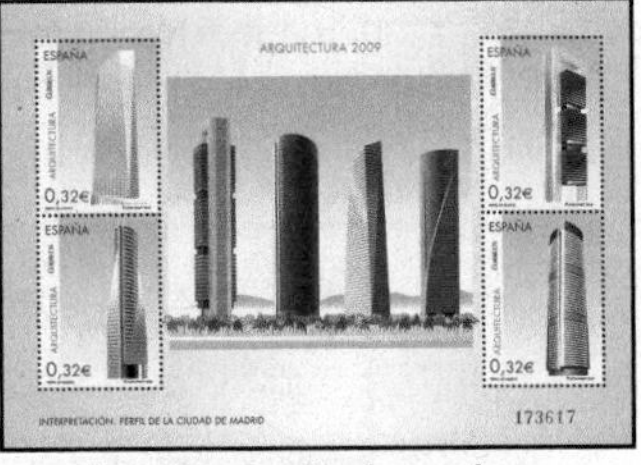

Four Towers Business Area, Madrid — A1527

No. 3667: a, Crystal Tower (with white area above top floors). b, Caja Madrid Tower (3 separate blocks in rectangular frame). c, Space Tower (with helical sides). d, Sacyr Vallehermoso Tower (with black area above top floors).

2009, Sept. 9 Photo. ***Perf. 13¾x14***

3665 A1525 32c multi .95 .45
3666 A1526 32c multi .95 .45

Souvenir Sheet
Perf. 14x13¾

3667 A1527 Sheet of 4 4.00 4.00
a.-d. 32c Any single .95 .45

Arévalo Castle, Avila A1528

Javier Castle, Navarre A1529

2009, Sept. 21 Engr. ***Perf. 13¾x14***

3668 A1528 €2.70 brn & blk 8.00 4.00
3669 A1529 €2.70 black 8.00 4.00

Hyphoraia Dejeani A1530

Pansies — A1531

2009, Oct. 1 Litho. ***Die Cut Perf. 13***
Self-Adhesive

3670 A1530 32c multi .95 .45
3671 A1531 32c multi .95 .45

Souvenir Sheet

Isla de los Faisanes, Engraving by Adam Perelle — A1532

2009, Oct. 6 Photo. ***Perf. 13¾x14***

3672 A1532 €2.47 multi 7.50 3.75

Exfilna 2009 Stamp Exhibition, Irún.

America Issue, Spanish Playing Cards A1533

2009, Oct. 8

3673 A1533 78c multi 2.40 1.25

Royal Spanish Soccer Federation, Cent. — A1534

2009, Oct. 14 Litho. ***Perf. 14x13¾***

3674 A1534 32c multi .95 .50

Mushrooms — A1535

Designs: No. 3675, 32c, Cantharellus cibarius. No. 3676, 32c, Boletus pinophilus.

2009, Oct. 16 Photo. ***Perf. 13¾x14***

3675-3676 A1535 Set of 2 1.90 .95

Compare with Type A1489.

Souvenir Sheet

Paintings by Diego Velázquez — A1536

No. 3677: a, The Royal Family of Felipe IV. b, The Infanta Margarita Teresa in a Blue Dress.

2009, Oct. 29 ***Perf. 14x13¾***

3677 A1536 Sheet of 2		4.25	4.25
a. 62c multi		1.90	.95
b. 78c multi		2.25	1.10

See Austria No. 2228.

A1537

A1538

Christmas A1539

No. 3678 — Details from Adoration of the Shepherds and Landscape with Lady in Red, by J. Carrero: a, Holy Family. b, Adoration of the Shepherds.

32c, Maternity, by Carrero. 62c, The Coming of the Three Wise Men, by Carrero.

Perf. 13¼x12¾

2009, Oct. 31 **Litho. & Engr.**

3678 A1537 Sheet of 2	15.00	15.00
a.-b. €2.47 Either single	7.50	3.75

Litho.

Self-Adhesive

Die Cut Perf. 13

3679 A1538 32c multi	.95	.50
3680 A1539 62c multi	1.90	.95

Juvenia 2009 Youth Philately Exhibition, Mieres — A1540

2009, Nov. 6 **Litho.** ***Perf. 14x13¾***

3681 A1540 39c multi	1.25	.60

Symbols of Nation and Autonomous Communities Type of 2009

No. 3682 — a, Arms and building of the Congress of Deputies. b, Flag and map of La Rioja. c, Flag and map of Castilla-La Mancha. d, Flag and map of Valencia. e, Arms and building of the Senate. f, Flag and map of the Canary Islands. g, Flag and map of Murcia. h, Flag and map of Aragon.

2010, Jan. 2 ***Die Cut Perf. 13***

Self-Adhesive

3682 Booklet pane of 8	7.75	
a.-h. A1497 A Any single	.95	.45

On day of issue, Nos. 3682a-3682h each sold for 34c.

Tourism A1541

2010, Jan. 2 **Self-Adhesive** **Litho.**

3683 A1541 B multi	1.90	.95

No. 3683 sold for 64c on day of issue.

Butterflies A1542

Designs: No. 3684, Artimelia latreillei. No. 3685, Euphydryas aurinia. No. 3686, Zygaena rhadamanthus. No. 3687, Zerynthia rumina.

2010 **Litho.** ***Die Cut Perf. 13***

Self-Adhesive

3684 A1542 34c multi	.95	.45
3685 A1542 34c multi	.95	.45
3686 A1542 64c multi	1.90	.95
3687 A1542 64c multi	1.75	.85
Nos. 3684-3687 (4)	5.55	2.70

Issued: Nos. 3684, 3686, 1/20; Nos. 3685, 3687, 4/1.

King Juan Carlos Type of 2007

2010, Feb. 5 **Photo.** ***Perf. 12¾x13¼***

Color of Portrait

3688 A1398 34c dark blue	.95	.45
3689 A1398 45c olive green	1.25	.60
3690 A1398 64c bister	1.75	.85
3691 A1398 €2.75 brt rose lil	7.50	3.75
Nos. 3688-3691 (4)	11.45	5.65

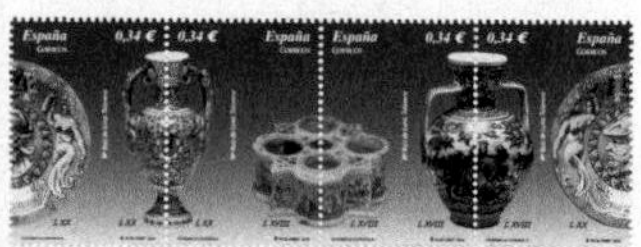

Civic Values A1543

Designs: €1, Trash recycling. €2, Responsible consumption of goods (jar with lock).

2010, Feb. 11 **Litho.** ***Perf. 13¾x14***

3692-3693 A1543 Set of 2	8.25	4.00

Ceramics — A1544

No. 3694 — Items from Ruiz de Luna Museum, Talavera: a, Plate from 1970 at left, amphora from 20th cent. at right. b, Amphora at left, inkwell from 18th cent. at right. c, Inkwell at left, pitcher from 18th cent. at right. d, Pitcher at left, plate at right.

Perf. 13¼x13¾

2010, Feb. 18 **Photo.**

3694 A1544 Horiz. strip of 4	3.75	3.75
a.-d. 34c Any single	.90	.45

Spanish Presidency of the European Union — A1545

Background color: 34c, Red. 64c, Gray.

Die Cut Perf. 13

2010, Feb. 22 **Litho.**

Self-Adhesive

3695-3696 A1545 Set of 2	2.75	1.40

Musical Instruments A1546

Design: No. 3697, Trumpet (trompeta). No. 3698, Euphonium (bombardino). 45c, Tenor saxophone. 64c, French horn.

2010 **Litho.** ***Die Cut Perf. 13***

Self-Adhesive

3697 A1546 34c multi	.95	.45
3698 A1546 34c multi	.95	.45
3699 A1546 45c multi	1.25	.60
3700 A1546 64c multi	1.60	.80
Nos. 3697-3700 (4)	4.75	2.30

Issued: No. 3697, 4/9; No. 3698, 10/5; No. 3699, 2/24; No. 3700, 7/1.

Constituent Assembly, Bicent. — A1547

2010, Mar. 1 **Litho.** ***Perf. 14x13¾***

3701 A1547 34c multi	.95	.45

Souvenir Sheet

Cathedrals of Plasencia — A1548

2010, Mar. 4 **Litho. & Engr.**

3702 A1548 €2.75 brown & blue	7.50	7.50

Goya Award, Poster for Film "Celda 211" A1549

2010, Mar. 9 **Litho.** ***Perf. 13¾x14***

3703 A1549 34c multi	.95	.45

Seven Goya Awards, Poster for Film "Agora" A1550

2010, Apr. 5 **Litho.** ***Perf. 13¾x13¼***

3704 A1550 34c multi	.95	.45

Latin American Independence, Bicent. — A1551

2010, Apr. 7 **Photo.**

3705 A1551 €2.49 multi	6.75	3.50

UNESCO World Heritage Sites — A1552

Designs: No. 3706, 45c, Patio of Casa de las Torres, Ubeda. No. 3707, 45c, Jabalquinto Palace, Baeza.

2010, Apr. 15 ***Perf. 12¾***

3706-3707 A1552 Set of 2	2.40	1.25

Urban Planners A1553

Designs: No. 3708, 34c, Carlos María de Castro (1810-93), and map of Madrid. No. 3709, 34c, Ildefonso Cerdá (1815-76), and map of Barcelona.

2010 **Photo.** ***Perf. 13¾x13¼***

3708-3709 A1553 Set of 2	1.90	.95

Issued: No. 3708, 4/20; No. 3709, 10/14.

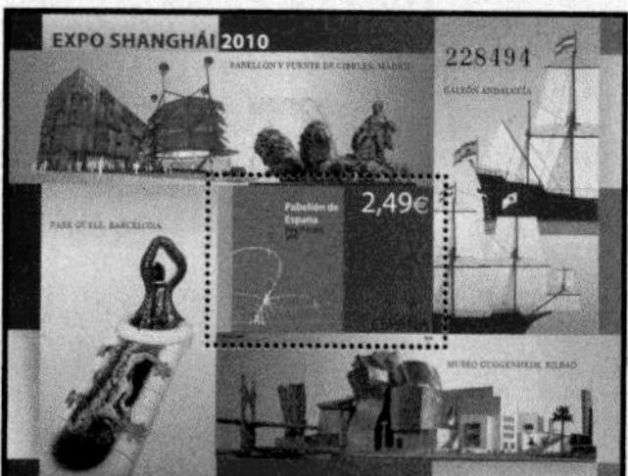

Gran Via, Madrid, Cent. — A1554

2010, Apr. 21 **Litho.** ***Perf. 13¼x13¾***

3710 A1554 34c blue & yellow	.90	.45

Souvenir Sheet

Spanish Pavilion at Expo 2010, Shanghai — A1555

Perf. 13¾x13¼

2010, Apr. 21 **Photo.**

3711 A1555 €2.49 multi	6.75	6.75

Levante U. D. Soccer Team, Cent. (in 2009) A1556

2010, Apr. 23
3712 A1556 34c multi .90 .45

El Correo Newspaper, Bilbao, Cent. — A1557

2010, Apr. 30 ***Perf. 13¼x13¾***
3713 A1557 34c multi .90 .45

Europa A1558

2010, May 6 ***Perf. 13¾x13¼***
3714 A1558 64c multi 1.75 .85

Souvenir Sheet

Kingdom of León, 1100th Anniv. — A1559

Photo. & Embossed With Foil Application
Perf. 13x12¼x12¼x13x12¾ Syncopated

2010, May 6
3715 A1559 €2.49 multi 6.50 6.50

Compostela Jubilee Year — A1560

Die Cut Perf. 13
2010, May 13 **Litho.**
Self-Adhesive
3716 A1560 34c multi .85 .40

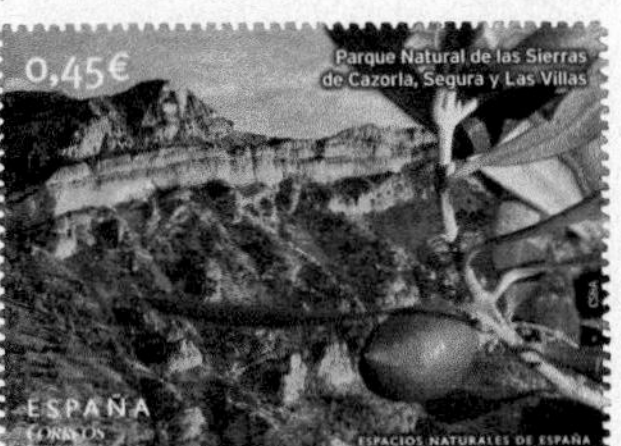

Parks — A1561

Flora or fauna and scenery from: No. 3717, 45c, Sierras de Cazoria, Segura y Las Villas Nature Park. No. 3718, 45c, Doñana National Park. No. 3719, 45c, Garajonay National Park. No. 3720, 45c, Picos de Europa National Park. No. 3721, 45c, Monfragüe National Park. No. 3722, 45c, Sierra Nevada National Park. No. 3723, 45c, Ordesa y Monte Perdido National Park. No. 3724, 45c, Lago de Sanabria Nature Park. No. 3725, 45c, Teide National Park. No. 3726, 45c, Cabrera Archipelago National Park. No. 3727, 45c, Aigüestortes y Lago de San Mauricio National Park. No. 3728, 45c, Cabo de Gata Nijar Nature Park.

2010 **Photo.** ***Perf. 13¼x13¾***
3717-3728 A1561 Set of 12 14.50 14.00

Issued: Nos. 3717-3719, 5/20; Nos. 3720-3722, 7/19; Nos. 3723-3725, 9/15; Nos. 3726-3728, 10/2.

2010 Ibero-American Athletics Championships, San Fernando A1562

2010 European Athletics Championships, Barcelona A1563

2010 World Cup Soccer Championships, South Africa — A1564

2010, June 4

3729	A1562 34c multi		.85	.40
3730	A1563 64c multi		1.60	.80
3731	A1564 78c multi		1.90	.95
	Nos. 3729-3731 (3)		4.35	2.15

Gregorio Marañón (1887-1960), Founder of Institute of Medical Pathology — A1565

Julián Arcas (1832-82), Guitarist — A1566

2010, June 11 ***Perf. 13¾x13¼***
3732 A1565 34c multi .85 .40

Perf. 13¼x13¾
3733 A1566 34c pur & orange .85 .40

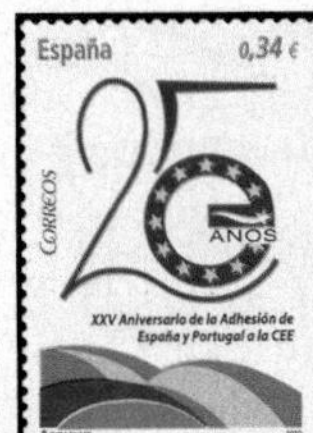

Entry Into European Community, 25th Anniv. — A1567

Die Cut Perf. 13
2010, June 12 **Litho.**
3734 A1567 34c multi .85 .45

Souvenir Sheet

Oscar Niemeyer International Cultural Center, Asturias — A1568

2010, June 19 ***Perf. 13¾x13¼***
3735 A1568 €2.49 multi 6.25 6.25

Filatem 2010 Thematic Philatelic Exhibition, Asturias.

José Luis López Vázquez (1922-2009), Actor — A1569

2010, July 6 **Photo.** ***Perf. 13¼x13¾***
3736 A1569 45c multi 1.25 .60

Souvenir Sheet

Zenobia and Emperor Aurelian, tapestry by Gerard Peemas — A1570

2010, July 12
3737 A1570 78c multi 2.10 2.10

Souvenir Sheet

Segovia Cathedral — A1571

Litho. & Engr.
2010, July 15 ***Perf. 14x13¾***
3738 A1571 €2.75 blue & brn 7.25 7.25

Renewable Energy — A1572

Designs: No. 3739, 78c, Biomass energy. No. 3740, 78c, Tidal energy (mareomotriz). No. 3741, 78c, Wave energy (undimotriz).

2010, Sept. 3 **Photo.** ***Perf. 13¼x13***
3739-3741 A1572 Set of 3 6.00 3.00

World Alzheimer's Disease Day — A1573

2010, Sept. 9 ***Perf. 13¾x13¼***
3742 A1573 34c multi .90 .45

Cádiz Soccer Team, Cent. A1574

2010, Sept. 10
3743 A1574 34c multi .90 .45

Roman Walls of Lugo UNESCO World Heritage Site — A1575

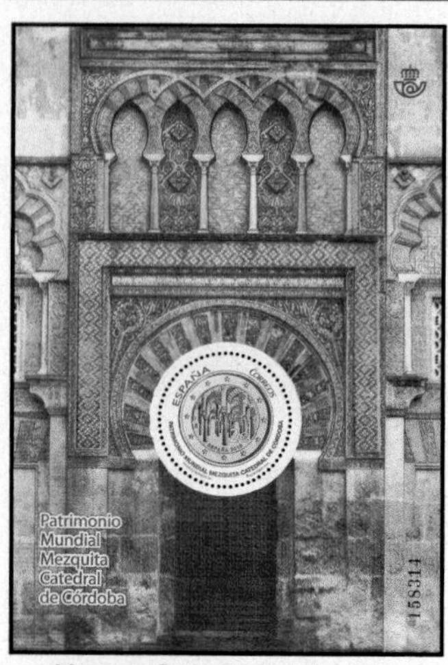

Mosque-Cathedral of Cordoba UNESCO World Heritage Site — A1576

2010, Sept. 17 Photo. *Perf. 13x12¾*
3744 A1575 34c multi .95 .45

Souvenir Sheet
Litho. & Engr.
Perf.
3745 A1576 €2 multi 5.50 5.50

Miniature Sheet

Lighthouses — A1577

No. 3746: a, Avilés Lighthouse, San Juan de Nieva, Asturias. b, Ciutadella de Menorca Lighthouse, Menorca Island. c, Cabo de Huertas Lighthouse, Alicante. d, Punta de la Polacra Lighthouse, Nijar, Almería. e, San Cibrao Lighthouse, Cervo, Lugo. f, Punta Cumplida Lighthouse, Barlovento, La Palma Island.

Perf. 13¼x13¾
2010, Sept. 20 Photo.
3746 A1577 Sheet of 6 10.50 10.00
a.-f. 64c Any single 1.75 .85

Famous Men — A1578

Designs: No. 3747, 34c, Francisco Ayala (1906-2009), writer. No. 3748, 34c, Gonzalo Torrente Ballester (1910-99), writer. No. 3749, 34c, Vicente Ferrer (1920-2009), humanitarian.

Litho. & Engr.
2010, Oct. 8 *Perf. 14x13¾*
3747-3749 A1578 Set of 3 3.00 1.50

America Issue, Spanish Arms — A1579

Perf. 13¼x13¾
2010, Oct. 11 Photo.
3750 A1579 78c multi 2.25 1.10

People, Flags of Bicentennial Group Countries — A1580

2010, Oct. 11 *Perf. 13¾x13¼*
3751 A1580 78c multi 2.25 1.10

The Bicentennial Group countries are Spain and nine Ibero-American countries (Argentina, Bolivia, Chile, Colombia, Ecuador, El Salvador, Mexico, Paraguay, and Venezuela) that achieved their independence from Spain 200 years ago.

El Día Newspaper, Santa Cruz de Tenerife, Cent. — A1581

2010, Oct. 15
3752 A1581 34c multi 1.00 .50

Miniature Sheet

Women's Clothing Designed by Manuel Pertegaz — A1582

No. 3753: a, Silk wedding dress. b, Taffeta suit and skirt. c, Taffeta cocktail dress with floral print. d, Black lace and white satin cocktail dress.

Photo. & Embossed
2010, Oct. 15 *Perf. 13¼x13*
3753 A1582 Sheet of 4 4.00 4.00
a.-d. 34c Any single 1.00 .50

Souvenir Sheet

Spain #18 and Cliché — A1583

2010, Oct. 18 Litho. *Perf. 13¼x13¾*
3754 A1583 €2.49 multi 7.00 7.00

Exfilna 2010 National Philatelic Exhibition, Madrid.

Souvenir Sheet

Religious Buildings in Spain and Turkey — A1584

No. 3755: a, Santa María de la Mayor Collegiate Church, Toro, Spain. b, Ortaköy Mosque, Istanbul, Turkey.

Perf. 13¾x13¼
2010, Oct. 18 Photo.
3755 A1584 Sheet of 2 3.50 3.50
a.-b. 64c Either single 1.75 .85

See Turkey No. 3240.

Souvenir Sheet

Victory of Spanish Team at 2010 World Cup Soccer Championships — A1585

Photo. & Embossed With Foil Application
2010, Oct. 21 *Perf. 13¼x13¾*
3756 A1585 €2 multi 5.75 5.75

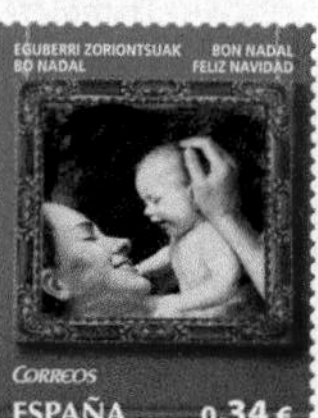

Christmas A1586

Designs: 34c, Mother holding baby. 64c, Columns, arms holding baby.

Die Cut Perf. 13
2010, Nov. 3 Litho.
Self-Adhesive
3757-3758 A1586 Set of 2 2.75 1.40

Souvenir Sheet

Sculpture From San Salvador Monastery, Oña — A1587

2010, Nov. 5 Photo. *Perf. 13¼x13¾*
3759 A1587 78c multi 2.25 2.25

San Salvador Monastery, 1000th anniv.

Souvenir Sheet

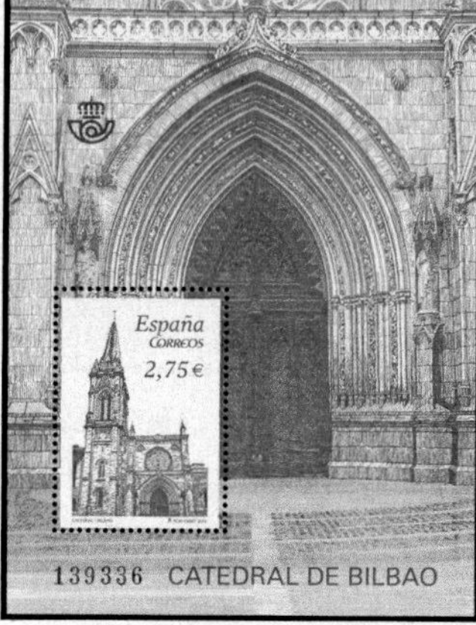

Bilbao Cathedral — A1588

Litho. & Engr.
2010, Nov. 8 *Perf. 14x13¾*
3760 A1588 €2.75 multi 7.50 7.50

Tourism A1589

2011, Jan. 3 Litho. *Die Cut Perf. 13*
Self-Adhesive
3761 A1589 B multi 1.75 .85

No. 3761 sold for 65c on day of issue.

Symbols of Nation and Autonomous Communities Type of 2009

No. 3762: a, Constitutional Court Building. b, Flag and map of Ceuta. c, Flag and map of Extremadura. d, Flag and map of Melilla. e, Flag and map of Balearic Islands. f, Flag and map of Madrid. g, Flag and map of Castilla y León. h, Flag and map of Navarra.

2011, Jan. 3 *Die Cut Perf. 13*
Self-Adhesive
3762 Booklet pane of 8 7.50
a.-h. A1497 A Any single .90 .45

On day of issue, Nos. 3762a-3762h each sold for 35c.

Butterflies A1590

Designs: No. 3763, 65c, Melanargia ines. No. 3764, 65c, Charaxes jasius. No. 3765,

65c, Papilio machaon. No. 3766, 65c, Argynnis adippe.

2011, Jan. 12 Litho.
Self-Adhesive

3763-3766 A1590 Set of 4 7.00 3.50

St. Sebastian Festival, El Pont de Suert, 425th Anniv. — A1591

2011, Jan. 20 ***Perf. 14x13¾***
3767 A1591 35c multi .95 .45

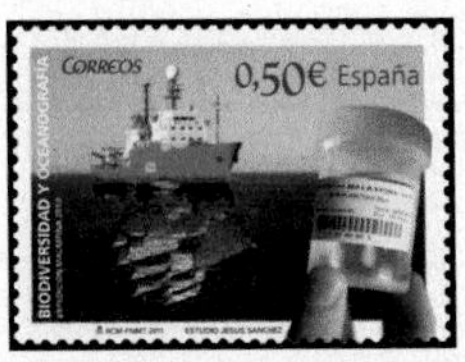

2010 Malaspina Oceanographic Expedition — A1592

2011, Jan. 20 ***Die Cut Perf. 13***
Self-Adhesive

3768 A1592 50c multi 1.40 .70

Stringed Instruments A1593

Designs: No. 3769, 35c, Guitar. No. 3770, 35c, Violin. No. 3771, 35c, Lute. No. 3772, 35c, Mandolin.

2011, Jan. 24 Litho.
Self-Adhesive

3769-3772 A1593 Set of 4 3.75 1.90

Almería Railway Station A1594

2011, Jan. 27 ***Perf. 13¾x14***
3773 A1594 35c multi .95 .50

King Juan Carlos Type of 2007

2011, Feb. 4 Photo. ***Perf. 12¾x13¼***
Color of Portrait

3774	A1398	35c lilac	.95	.50
3775	A1398	50c bright blue	1.40	.70
3776	A1398	80c brt blue grn	2.25	1.10
3777	A1398	€2.84 blue violet	7.75	4.00
		Nos. 3774-3777 (4)	12.35	6.30

Marie Curie (1867-1934), Chemist — A1595

Litho. & Engr.

2011, Feb. 7 ***Perf. 13¾x14***
3778 A1595 35c multi .95 .45

Intl. Year of Chemistry.

Property Act, 150th Anniv. A1596

2011, Feb. 8 Litho.
3779 A1596 65c multi 1.75 .90

Civic Values A1597

Designs: No. 3780, 35c, Respect on the Internet. No. 3781, 35c, Protect people with disabilities. No. 3782, 35c, Clean up and dispose of dog droppings. No. 3783, 35c, Use safety belts.

2011, Feb. 18 ***Die Cut Perf. 13***
Self-Adhesive

3780-3783 A1597 Set of 4 4.00 2.00

Souvenir Sheet

Sigüenza Cathedral — A1598

Litho. & Engr.

2011, Mar. 4 ***Perf. 13¾x14***
3784 A1598 €2.84 multi 8.00 8.00

Intl. Women's Day A1599

Die Cut Perf. 13

2011, Mar. 8 Self-Adhesive Litho.
3785 A1599 80c multi 2.25 1.10

Europa — A1600

2011, Apr. 4 Photo. ***Perf. 13¼x13¾***
3786 A1600 65c multi 1.90 .95

Intl. Year of Forests.

Jubilee Year of the Holy Cross of Canjáyar A1601

2011, Apr. 11 Litho. ***Perf. 14x13¾***
3787 A1601 65c multi 1.90 .95

Miniature Sheet

Lighthouses — A1602

No. 3788: a, Calella Lighthouse, Barcelona. b, Chipiona Lighthouse, Cádiz. c, Punta La Entallada Lighthouse, Fuerteventura Island. d, Cap Sant Sebastià Lighthoue, Girona. e, Castell de Ferro Lighthouse, Granada. f, Valencia Lighthouse, Valencia.

Perf. 13¼x13¾

2011, Apr. 11 Photo.
3788 A1602 Sheet of 6 11.50 11.50
a.-f. 65c Any single 1.90 .95

Juvenia 2011 National Youth Philatelic Exhibition, Santa Fe — A1603

2011, Apr. 12 Litho. ***Perf. 14x13¾***
3789 A1603 65c multi 1.90 .95

A1604

Goya Award — A1605

No. 3790 — Movie Poster for *Pa Negre*, Winner of 2010 Goya Award for Best Film.

2011, Apr. 26 Litho. ***Perf. 13¾x14***
3790 A1604 35c multi 1.00 .50

Souvenir Sheet
Photo.
Perf. 13¾x13¼

3791 A1605 €2.84 multi 8.25 8.25

Goya Awards, 25th anniv.

Souvenir Sheet

Alhambra of Granada UNESCO World Heritage Site — A1606

2011, May 12 Litho. & Engr. ***Perf.***
3792 A1606 €2 multi 5.75 5.75

Souvenir Sheet

Dido Bids Farewell to Aeneas, 17th Cent. Tapestry — A1607

Perf. 13¼x13¾

2011, May 16 Photo.
3793 A1607 €2.84 multi 8.25 8.25

Miniature Sheet

Military Aviation in Spain, Cent. — A1608

No. 3794: a, Aerospatiale SA-332 Super Puma helicopter (41x29mm)r. b, Two CASA-101 Aviojets (41x29mm). c, Lockheed C-130 Hercules (41x29mm). d, Eurofighter EF-2000 Typhoon (123x29mm).

2011, May 31 ***Perf. 13¾x13¼***
3794 A1608 Sheet of 4 7.75 7.75
a.-d. 65c Any single 1.90 .95

Conversion of Abandoned Railroad Lines to Greenways — A1609

2011, June 13 Litho. ***Perf. 13¾x14***
3795 A1609 35c multi 1.00 .50

Corps of Architects of the Treasury, 105th Anniv. A1610

2011, June 17

3796 A1610 80c multi 2.25 1.10

World Youth Day — A1611

2011, July 1 ***Perf. 14x13¾***

3797 A1611 80c multi 2.25 1.10

See Vatican City No. 1472.

Souvenir Sheet

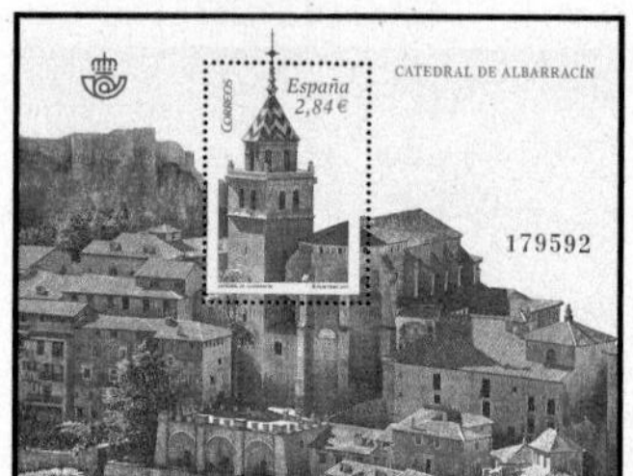

Albarracín Cathedral — A1612

2011, July 15 **Litho. & Engr.**

3798 A1612 €2.84 blue & green 8.25 8.25

Film Personalities A1613

Designs: No. 3799, 80c, Luis García Berlanga (1921-2010), director. No. 3800, 80c, Rafael Azcona (1926-2008), screenwriter.

2011, July 22 **Litho.**

3799-3800 A1613 Set of 2 4.75 2.40

Ceramics From Manises — A1614

No. 3801: a, Pitcher with lid and handle. b, Vase. c, Plate. d, Bottle.

Perf. 13¼x13¾

2011, Sept. 5 **Photo.**

3801 A1614 Horiz. strip of 4 9.00 7.00

a.-d. 80c Any single 2.25 1.10

Miniature Sheet

Art by Antoni Tàpies (1923-2012) — A1615

No. 3802 — Unnamed works depicting: a, Face and flags on blue background. b, Horizontal line across brown area. c, Chair on gray background. d, Abstract on red background.

2011, Sept. 12

3802 A1615 Sheet of 4 9.00 4.50

a.-d. 80c Any single 2.25 1.10

Miniature Sheets

Spanish National Soccer Team — A1616

No. 3803 — Soccer players from 1900-70 with Spanish text in black capitals: a, Pichichi (41x56mm). b, Zamora Parando (41x56mm). c, El Gol de Zarra (41x56mm). d, Una Excelente Delantera (82x28mm). e, El Gol de Marcelino (82x28mm).

No. 3804 — Soccer players from 1970-2010 with Spanish text in black capitals: a, Celebración del Gol Clasificatorio para Argentina 78 (41x56mm). b, Mundial España 82 (41x56mm). c, Victoria de la Selección en los Juegos Olímpicos 92 (82x28mm). d, El Gol de Torres en la Eurocopa 2008 (41x56mm). e, El Gol de Iniesta en el Mundial 2010 (82x28mm).

2011, Sept. 19 ***Perf. 13¾x13¼***

3803 A1616 Sheet of 5 + label 11.50 11.50

a.-e. 80c Any single 2.25 1.10

3804 A1616 Sheet of 5 + label 11.50 11.50

a.-e. 80c Any single 2.25 1.10

Souvenir Sheet

Exfilna 2011 National Philatelic Exposition, Valladolid — A1617

2011, Oct. 1 **Litho.** ***Perf. 13¾x14***

3805 A1617 €2.84 multi 7.75 7.75

Awarding of 2010 Nobel Prize in Literature to Mario Vargas Llosa — A1618

Litho. (Litho & Engr. Label)

2011, Oct. 3 ***Perf. 14x13¾***

3806 A1618 80c multi 2.25 1.10

Miguel Delibes (1920-2010), Writer — A1619

Gaspar Melchor de Jovellanos (1744-1811), Statesman and Writer — A1620

Luis Rosales (1910-92), Poet A1621

Miguel Servet (1511-53), Physician and Theologian — A1622

Litho. & Engr.

2011, Oct. 3 ***Perf. 14x13¾***

3807 A1619 80c multi 2.25 1.10

Perf. 13¾x14

3808 A1620 80c multi 2.25 1.10

Litho.

3809 A1621 80c multi 2.25 1.10

3810 A1622 80c multi 2.25 1.10

Nos. 3807-3810 (4) 9.00 4.40

America Issue, Mailbox — A1623

Perf. 13¼x13¾

2011, Oct. 11 **Photo.**

3811 A1623 80c multi 2.25 1.10

Miniature Sheet

Women's Clothing Designed by Elio Berhanyer — A1624

No. 3812: a, Black and white strapless ball gown. b, Green and white striped dress. c, Coat and dress. d, Black and white polka dot ball gown.

Photo. & Embossed

2011, Oct. 20 ***Perf. 13¼x13***

3812 A1624 Sheet of 4 9.00 9.00

a.-d. 80c Any single 2.25 1.10

Holy Family with Baby Jesus, Sculpture by Luisa Roldán A1625

Holy Family — A1626

Die Cut Perf. 13

2011, Nov. 3 **Self-Adhesive** **Litho.**

3813 A1625 35c multi 1.00 .50

3814 A1626 65c multi 1.90 .95

Christmas.

National Library, 300th Anniv. A1627

2011, Nov. 4 ***Perf. 13¾x14***

3815 A1627 80c multi 2.25 1.10

Barcelona Boat Show, 50th Anniv. — A1628

2011, Nov. 5 ***Perf. 14x13¾***

3816 A1628 80c multi 2.25 1.10

Souvenir Sheet

Tarazona Cathedral — A1629

2011, Nov. 8 **Litho. & Engr.**
3817 A1629 €2.84 blue & green 7.75 7.75

Year of Russia in Spain and Year of Spain in Russia A1630

2011, Nov. 10 **Litho.** ***Perf. 13¾x14***
3818 A1630 80c multi 2.25 1.10

Arches and Gates A1631

No. 3819: a, Macarena Arch, Seville. b, Alcalá Gate, Madrid. c, Santa María Arch, Burgos. d, Serrano Gate, Valencia. e, Triumphal Arch, Barcelona. f, Palmas Gate, Badajoz. g, Bisagra Gate, Toledo. h, Bará Arch, Tarragona.

2012, Jan. 2 ***Die Cut Perf. 13***
Self-Adhesive
3819 Booklet pane of 8 7.75
a.-h. A1631 A Any single .95 .45

Nos. 3819a-3819h each sold for 36c on day of issue.

Tourism A1632

2012, Jan. 2 **Litho.**
Self-Adhesive
3820 A1632 B multi 1.90 .95

No. 3820 sold for 70c on day of issue.

Lorca Tourist Attractions A1633

Designs: No. 3821, 36c, Virgin of the Orchards Sanctuary (Santuario de la Virgen de las Huertas). No. 3822, 36c, Castle (Castillo). No. 3823, 36c, Town Hall (Ayuntamiento). No. 3824, 36c, Guevara Palace (Palacio de Guevara). No. 3825, 36c, St. Patrick's Collegiate Church (Colegiata de San Patricio).

2012, Jan. 2 ***Die Cut Perf. 13***
Self-Adhesive
3821-3825 A1633 Set of 5 4.75 2.40

Civic Values A1634

Designs: 36c, No pollution. 51c, Follow speed limits. 70c, Avoid distractions while driving.

2012, Jan. 9 **Self-Adhesive** **Litho.**
3826-3828 A1634 Set of 3 4.25 2.10

Intl. Year of Sustainable Energy for All — A1635

2012, Feb. 27 ***Die Cut Perf. 13***
Self-Adhesive
3829 A1635 70c multi 1.90 .95

King Juan Carlos — A1636

Perf. 12¾x13¼
2012, Feb. 27 **Photo.**
Color of Portrait

3830	A1636	36c red	.95	.50
3831	A1636	51c green	1.40	.70
3832	A1636	85c blue	2.25	1.10
3833	A1636	€2.90 dk rose brn	7.75	4.00
	Nos. 3830-3833 (4)		12.35	6.30

See Nos. 3887-3890.

Tourism A1637

Die Cut Perf. 13
2012, Feb. 28 **Litho.**
Self-Adhesive
3834 A1637 70c multi 1.90 .95

Military Anniversaries A1638

Designs: No. 3835, 85c, Battle of Navas de Tolosa, 800th anniv. No. 3836, 85c, Conquest of Navarre, 500th anniv.

2012, Feb. 29 ***Perf. 14x13¾***
3835-3836 A1638 Set of 2 4.50 2.25

Souvenir Sheet

Matron and Warrior in Boat, Tapestry by Gerard Peemans — A1639

2012, Mar. 8 **Photo.** ***Perf. 13¼x13¾***
3837 A1639 €2.90 multi 7.75 7.75

Royal and Military Order of San Fernando, 200th Anniv. — A1640

2012, Mar. 12 **Litho.** ***Perf. 14x13¾***
3838 A1640 85c multi 2.25 1.10

1812 Constitution, Bicent. A1641

2012, Mar. 16 **Photo.** ***Perf. 12¾***
3839 A1641 36c multi .95 .45

Souvenir Sheet

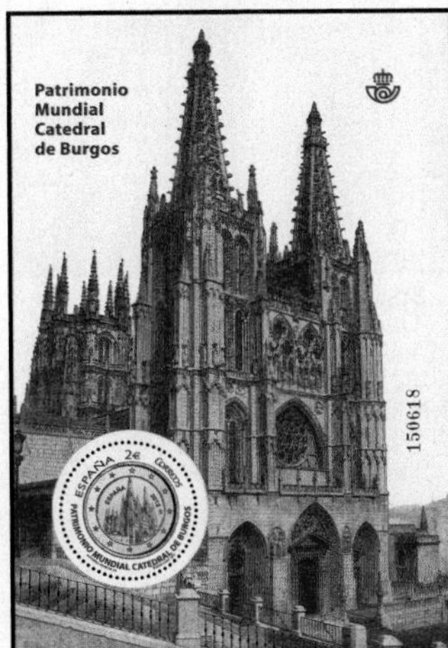

Spanish Coin Depicting Burgos Cathedral — A1642

2012, Mar. 16 **Litho. & Engr.** ***Perf.***
3840 A1642 €2 multi 5.25 5.25

Burgos Cathedral UNESCO World Heritage Site.

Stringed Instruments A1643

No. 3841: a, Harp. b, Balalaika. c, Banjo. d, Sitar. e, Rabel (rebec).

2012, Apr. 2 **Litho.** ***Die Cut Perf. 13***
Self-Adhesive
3841 Horiz. strip of 5 4.75
a.-e. A1643 36c Any single .95 .45

Europa — A1644

2012, Apr. 4 ***Perf. 14x13¾***
3842 A1644 70c multi 1.90 .95

Severiano Ballesteros (1957-2011), Golfer — A1645

José Hierro (1922-2002), Poet — A1646

Manuel Garcia Matos (1912-74), Musicologist — A1647

2012, Apr. 11 ***Perf. 13¾x14***

3843	A1645	70c multi	1.90	.95
3844	A1646	70c multi	1.90	.95
3845	A1647	70c multi	1.90	.95
	Nos. 3843-3845 (3)		5.70	2.85

Souvenir Sheet

Seville Cathedral — A1648

2012, Apr. 17
3846 A1648 €2.90 multi 7.75 7.75

Actors — A1649

No Habrá Paz para los Malvados, Winner of 2012 Goya Award for Best Film
A1650

Designs: No. 3847, Fernando Rey (1917-94). No. 3848, Francisco Rabal (1926-2001).

2012, Apr. 26 ***Perf. 14x13¾***
3847 A1649 36c multi .95 .45
3848 A1649 36c multi .95 .45

Perf. 13¾x14
3849 A1650 70c multi 1.90 .95
Nos. 3847-3849 (3) 3.80 1.85

Souvenir Sheet

Toledo Cathedral — A1651

Litho. & Engr.
2012, May 21 ***Perf. 13¾x14***
3850 A1651 €2.90 blue & brown 7.25 7.25

Notary Law, 150th Anniv. A1652

2012, May 28 **Litho.**
3851 A1652 85c multi 2.25 1.10

Antonio Mingote (1919-2012), Cartoonist
A1653

2012, May 30 ***Perf. 14x13¾***
3852 A1653 36c multi .90 .45

Miniature Sheet

Automobiles — A1654

No. 3853: a, 1934 Citröen C-11. b, 1956 Renault Dauphine. c, 1957 SEAT 600. d, 1961 Simca 1000.

2012, May 30 ***Perf. 13¾x14***
3853 A1654 Sheet of 4 9.00 9.00
a.-d. 85c Any single 2.25 1.10

Armory School, Eibar, Cent. A1655

2012, June 7
3854 A1655 85c multi 2.10 1.10

Banners of Léon — A1656

Perf. 13¼x13¾
2012, June 12 **Photo.**
3855 A1656 85c multi 2.10 1.10

Souvenir Sheet

Statue of St. James, Santiago de Compostela Cathedral — A1657

2012, June 14 **Litho.** ***Perf. 14x13¾***
3856 A1657 €2.90 multi 7.25 7.25

Emblem of State Lawyers Corps — A1658

2012, June 18
3857 A1658 85c multi 2.10 1.10

Spanish Olympic Committee, Cent. — A1659

Spanish Olympic Committee emblem and: No. 3858, 85c, Lucius Minicius Natalis, charioteer and first Spanish champion in ancient Olympics. No. 3859, 85c, Gonzalo de Figueroa y Torres (1861-1921), founder of Spanish Olympic Committee. No. 3860, 85c, Juan Antonio Samaranch (1920-2010), International Olympic Committee President.

2012, July 2 **Litho.** ***Perf. 13¾x14***
3858-3860 A1659 Set of 3 6.25 3.25

Sciences — A1660

Noi. 3861: a, Geology. b, Paleontonlogy.

2012, July 11 ***Perf. 14x13¾***
3861 A1660 Horiz. pair 1.80 .90
a.-b. 36c Either single .90 .45

Souvenir Sheet

Oviedo Cathedral — A1661

2012, July 13 **Litho. & Engr.**
3862 A1661 €2.90 multi 7.25 7.25

Churches — A1662

No. 3863: a, Episcopal Palace, Astorga, Spain. b, Church of the Savior on Spilled Blood, St. Petersburg, Russia.

2012, July 17 **Litho.**
3863 A1662 Horiz. pair 4.25 2.10
a.-b. 85c Either single 2.10 1.10

See Russia No. 7376.

Miniature Sheet

Art by Manolo Valdés — A1663

No. 3864: a, Profil con Fondo Azul (Profile with Blue Background), painting. b, La Infanta Margarita, sculpture. c, Reina Mariana XII (Queen Mariana XII), sculpture. d, Vivienne III, painting.

2012, July 18 ***Perf. 14x13¾***
3864 A1663 Sheet of 4 5.00 5.00
a.-d. 51c Any single 1.25 .60

Mushrooms — A1664

Designs: No. 3865, 51c, Entoloma lividum. No. 3866, 51c, Calocybe gambosa. No. 3867, 51c, Amanita verna.

2012, Sept. 6 ***Perf. 13¾x14***
3865-3867 A1664 Set of 3 4.00 2.00

Souvenir Sheet

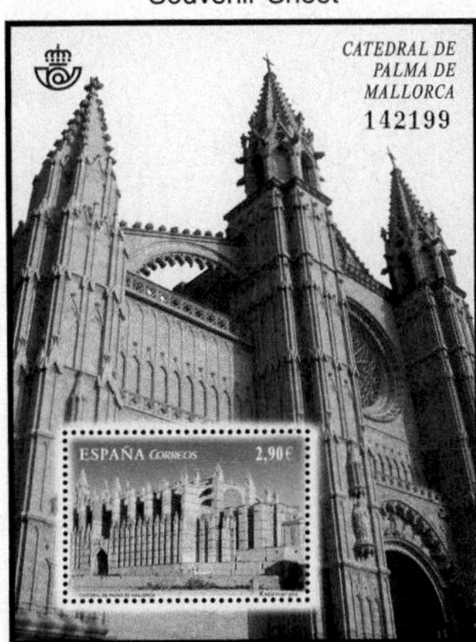

Palma de Mallorca Cathedral — A1665

2012, Sept. 10 **Litho.**
3868 A1665 €2.90 multi 7.50 7.50

A1666

Design: Old Alcaudete Train Station and Olive Oil Greenway, Jaen.

2012, Sept. 12 ***Perf. 13¾x14***
3869 A1666 70c multi 1.90 .95

Miniature Sheet

Women's Clothing Designed by Pedro del Hierro — A1667

No. 3870: a, Red violet satin dress. b, Sequined lace dress with floral pattern. c, Pink and black party dress. d, Dress with white lace and pink bodice.

Photo. & Embossed
2012, Sept. 17 ***Perf. 13¼x13***
3870 A1667 Sheet of 4 9.00 9.00
a.-d. 85c Any single 2.25 1.10

Souvenir Sheet

Lady of Calahorra — A1668

2012, Oct. 5 Litho. ***Perf. 14x13¾***
3871 A1668 €2.90 multi 7.50 7.50

Exfilna 2012 National Philatelic Exhibition, Calahorra.

Souvenir Sheet

Barcelona Cathedral — A1669

2012, Oct. 9 **Litho. & Engr.**
3872 A1669 €2.90 brown 7.50 7.50

Castilla y León Museum of Contemporary Art, Léon — A1670

National Museum of Roman Art, Mérida A1671

Queen Sofia National Museum of Art, Madrid A1672

Museum of Art and Popular Costumes, Seville A1673

2012, Oct. 11 Litho. ***Perf. 13¾x14***
3873 A1670 51c multi 1.40 .70
3874 A1671 51c multi 1.40 .70
3875 A1672 51c multi 1.40 .70
3876 A1673 51c multi 1.40 .70
Nos. 3873-3876 (4) 5.60 2.80

Colonial Postal Shelter in Andes Mountains A1674

2012, Oct. 16
3877 A1674 85c multi 2.25 1.10

Mammals — A1675

No. 3878: a, Red deer (denomination at LR). b, Ibex (denomination at LL).

2012, Oct. 19 ***Perf. 12¾***
3878 A1675 Horiz. pair 4.50 2.25
a.-b. 85c Either single 2.25 1.10

See Romania Nos. 5395-5396.

Adoration of the Magi, Mural in Chapel of St. Martin, Salamanca A1676

Madonna and Child — A1677

2012, Nov. 5 ***Die Cut Perf. 13***
Self-Adhesive
3879 A1676 36c multi .95 .45
3880 A1677 70c multi 1.75 .90

Christmas.

Souvenir Sheet

Spain, Champions of 2012 UEFA European Soccer Tournament — A1678

2012, Nov. 6 ***Perf.***
3881 A1678 €1 multi 2.60 2.60

America Issue, Legend of the Lovers of Teruel — A1679

2012, Nov. 8 ***Perf. 14x13¾***
3882 A1679 85c multi 2.25 1.10

Civil Administrators — A1680

State Comptrollers and Auditors — A1681

2012, Nov. 12 ***Perf. 13¾x14***
3883 A1680 85c multi 2.25 1.10
3884 A1681 85c multi 2.25 1.10

Souvenir Sheet

White Virgin and Child, León Cathedral — A1682

Litho. & Engr.
2012, Nov. 15 ***Perf. 14x13¾***
3885 A1682 €2.90 brown 7.50 7.50

22nd Ibero-American Summit, Cádiz — A1683

2012, Nov. 16 Litho. ***Perf. 13¾x14***
3886 A1683 36c multi .95 .45

King Juan Carlos Type of 2012
2013, Jan. 2 Photo. ***Perf. 12¾x13¼***
Color of Portrait
3887 A1636 37c Prus bl .85 .35
3888 A1636 52c orange 1.25 .60
3889 A1636 75c yel green 1.75 .85
3890 A1636 90c brown 2.00 1.00
Nos. 3887-3890 (4) 6.80 3.45

Tourism A1684

2013, Jan. 2 Litho. *Die Cut Perf. 13*
Self-Adhesive

3891 A1684 75c multi 2.00 1.00

Arches and Gates A1685

No. 3892: a, Alcázar Gate, Avila. b, Roman Arch of Cáparra, Cáceres. c, Roman Arch of Medinaceli. d, Capuchin Arch, Andújar. e, Arch of the Giants, Antequera. f, Toledo Gate, Madrid. g, Castilla Gate, Tolosa. h, Roman Arch of Cavanes, Castellón.

2013, Jan. 2 *Die Cut Perf. 13*
Self-Adhesive

3892 Booklet pane of 8 8.00
a.-h. A1685 A Any single 1.00 .50

Nos. 3892a-3892h each sold for 37c on day of issue.

International Year of Water Cooperation A1686

2013, Jan. 3 Litho.
Self-Adhesive

3893 A1686 90c multi 2.00 1.00

Setting of Boundary Stones Between Spain and France, 500th Anniv. — A1687

2013, Jan. 8 *Perf. 14x13¾*
3894 A1687 52c multi 1.25 .60

2013 Men's World Handball Championships, Spain — A1688

2013, Jan. 11 *Perf. 13¾x14*
3895 A1688 90c multi 2.00 1.00

Map of Western Hemisphere, Laws of Burgos, and Christopher Columbus — A1689

2013, Jan. 15
3896 A1689 52c multi 1.25 .60

Laws of Burgos regulating treatment of Indians and colonizers, 500th anniv.

International Equal Pay Day — A1690

2013, Feb. 22 *Die Cut Perf. 13*
Self-Adhesive

3897 A1690 52c multi 1.25 .60

Percussion Instruments A1691

No. 3898: a, Tambor (drum). b, Pandereta (tambourine). c, Castañuelas (castanets). d, Platillos (cymbals). e, Timbales (timpani).

2013, Feb. 22 Litho.
Self-Adhesive

3898 Horiz. strip of 5 4.50
a.-e. A1691 37c Any single 1.00 .50

Kingdom of Granada, 1000th Anniv. A1692

2013, Feb. 26 *Perf. 13¾x14*
3899 A1692 37c multi .85 .40

Miniature Sheet

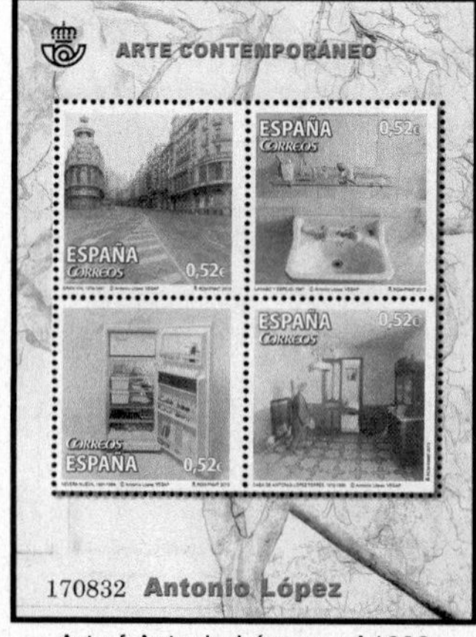

Art of Antonio López — A1693

No. 3900: a, Gran Vía, 1974-81. b, Sink and Mirror, 1967. c, New Refrigerator, 1991-94. d, House of Antonio López Torres, 1972-80.

2013, Mar. 11 Photo. *Perf. 12¾*
3900 A1693 Sheet of 4 5.00 5.00
a.-d. 52c Any single 1.25 .60

Miniature Sheet

Automobiles — A1694

No. 3901: a, 1962 Mercedes-Benz 190. b, 1948 Citroen 2CV. c, 1938 Volkswagen Beetle. d, 1963 SEAT 1500.

2013, Mar. 15 Litho. *Perf. 13¾x14*
3901 A1694 Sheet of 4 8.00 8.00
a.-d. 90c Any single 2.00 1.00

Souvenir Sheet

Spanish Coin Depicting San Lorenzo de El Escorial Royal Monastery — A1695

2013, Mar. 21 Litho. & Engr. *Perf.*
3902 A1695 €3.10 multi 7.50 7.50

San Lorenzo de El Escorial Royal Monastery UNESCO World Heritage Site.

Souvenir Sheet

Film Personalities — A1696

No. 3903: a, Rafael Gil (1913-86), director. b, Fernando Fernán Gómez (1921-2007), actor and director. c, Tony Leblanc (1922-2012), actor.

2013, Apr. 8 Photo. *Perf. 13¾x13¼*
3903 A1696 Sheet of 3 3.75 3.75
a.-c. 52c Any single 1.25 .60

Europa A1697

2013, Apr. 23 Litho.
3904 A1697 75c multi 1.75 .90

Wedding of Odotano and Zenobia, Tapestry by Workshop of Gerard Peemans — A1698

Photo. & Engr.
2013, Apr. 25 *Perf. 13¼x13¾*
3905 A1698 €3.10 multi 7.50 7.50

Spanish Federation of Philatelic Societies, 50th Anniv. A1699

2013, Apr. 29 Litho. *Perf. 13¾x13¼*
3906 A1699 37c multi .85 .40

A1700

Bridges — A1701

Designs: No. 3907, Besalú Bridge. No. 3908, Los Santos Bridge.

2013, May 4 Photo. *Perf. 13¼x13¾*
3907 A1700 €2 multi 5.00 2.50

Souvenir Sheet
Litho.
Perf. 12¾x13¼

3908 A1701 €2 multi 5.00 5.00

See Nos. 3916-3919, 3929-3932, 3936-3937.

Aviation in the Canary Islands, Cent. A1702

2013, May 7 Litho. *Perf. 13¾x13¼*
3909 A1702 52c multi 1.25 .60

Baskonia Sports Club and Baskonia Mendi Taldea, Cent. — A1703

2013, May 7 *Perf. 13¼x13¾*
3910 A1703 52c multi 1.25 .60

Marian Jubilee Year — A1704

2013, May 21
3911 A1704 90c multi 2.00 1.00

Miniature Sheet

Endangered Marine Life — A1705

No. 3912: a, Ballena Vasca (Basque whale). b, Atún rojo (Bluefin tuna). c, Foca monje (Mediterranean monk seal). d, Lamprea marina (Sea lamprey).

2013, June 3 *Perf. 13¾x13¼*
3912 A1705 Sheet of 4 3.50 3.50
a.-d. 37c Any single .85 .40

Barcelona-Sarriá Railway, 150th Anniv. — A1706

2013, June 11 **Litho.**
3913 A1706 52c multi 1.25 .60

Public Treasury Inspection Service Seal A1707

2013, June 11
3914 A1707 52c multi 1.25 .60

Emilio Aragón (1929-2012), Miliki the Clown — A1708

2013, June 12 *Perf. 13¼x13¾*
3915 A1708 37c multi .85 .40

Bridges Type of 2013

Designs: No. 3916, Piedra Bridge, Logroño. No. 3917, Tajo Bridge, Ronda, vert. No. 3918, Sancho el Mayor Bridge, Navarra. No. 3919, Puentecillas Bridge, Palencia.

Perf. 13¼x13¾, 13¼x12¾ (#3917), 12¾x13¼ (#3919)
2013 **Photo. (#3916, 3918), Litho.**
3916 A1700 €1 multi 2.50 1.25
3917 A1701 €1 multi 2.50 1.25
3918 A1700 €1 multi 2.50 1.25
3919 A1701 €2 multi 4.75 2.25
Nos. 3916-3919 (4) 12.25 6.00

Issued: Nos. 3916-3917, 6/18; Nos. 3918-3919, 6/20.

Day of Victims of Terrorism A1709

Perf. 13¾x13¼
2013, June 27 **Litho.**
3920 A1709 37c multi .85 .40

Friar Rosendo Salvado y Rotea (1814-1900), Missionary — A1710

St. Telmo (1190-1246) and Tui Cathedral A1711

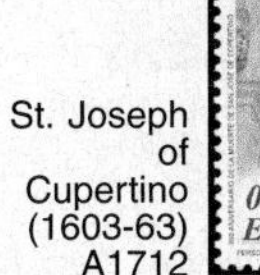

St. Joseph of Cupertino (1603-63) A1712

Perf. 13¾x13¼, 14x13¾ (#3922)
2013, July 4
3921 A1710 90c multi 2.00 1.00
3922 A1711 90c multi 2.00 1.00
3923 A1712 90c multi 2.00 1.00
Nos. 3921-3923 (3) 6.00 3.00

Souvenir Sheet

Victory of Spanish Men's Handball Team in 2013 World Championships — A1713

2013, July 9 *Perf. 13¾x13¼*
3924 A1713 €1 multi 2.50 2.50

Era Querimònia, 700th Anniv. — A1714

2013, July 11 *Perf. 13¼x13¾*
3925 A1714 52c multi 1.25 .60

Miniature Sheet

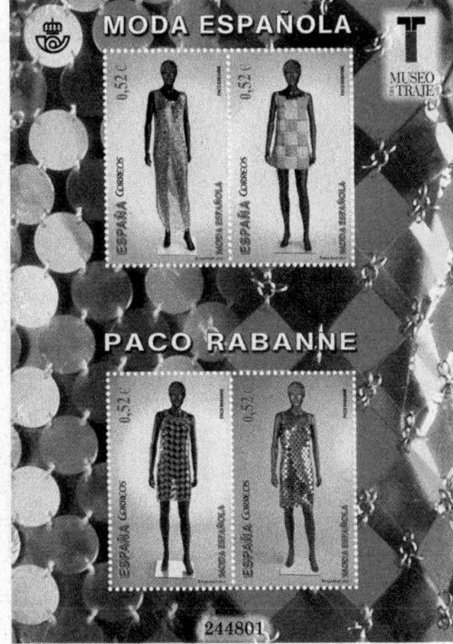

Women's Dresses by Paco Rabanne — A1715

No. 3926 — Mannequins wearing items from Rabanne's collection of unwearable dresses: a, Silver and plastic ankle-length dress. b, Yellow and blue dress made of zippers. c, See-through dress of red diamonds. d, Dress made of large golden disks.

2013, Sept. 12 Photo. *Perf. 13x12¾*
3926 A1715 Sheet of 4 5.50 5.50
a.-d 52c Any single 1.25 .60

Miniature Sheet

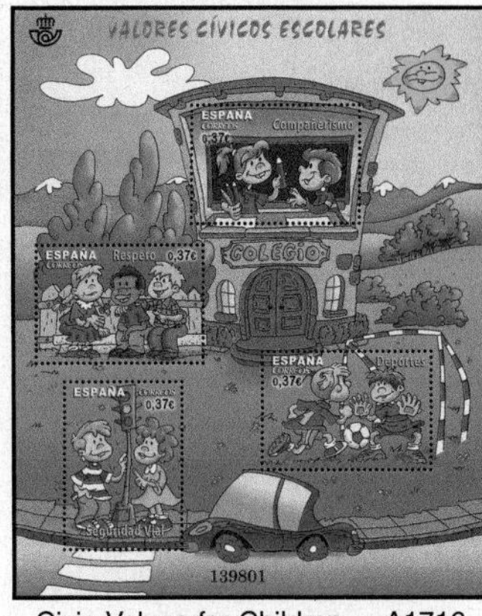

Civic Values for Children — A1716

No. 3927: a, Fellowship (compañerismo). b, Respect (respeto). c, Sportsmanship (deportes). d, Road safety (seguridad vial), vert.

Perf. 13¾x13¼, 13¼x13¾
2013, Sept. 18
3927 A1716 Sheet of 4 3.50 3.50
a.-d. 37c Any single .85 .40

Souvenir Sheet

Painting of King Fernando I, San Isidro Basilica, León — A1717

Perf. 12¾x13¼
2013, Sept. 20 **Litho.**
3928 A1717 €3.10 multi 7.50 7.50

Exfilna (National Philatelic Exhibition) 2013, León.

Bridges Type of 2013

Designs: €1, Dragon Bridge, Alcalá de Guadaíra. No. 3930, Carlos Fernández Casado Bridge, León, vert.

No. 3931, Iron Bridge (Puente del Pilar), Stone Bridge, Basilica of Our Lady of Pilar, vert. €3.10, Roman Bridge, Mérida.

Perf. 12¾x13¼
2013, Sept. 25 **Litho.**
3929 A1701 €1 multi 2.50 1.25

Perf. 13¾x13¼
3930 A1700 €2 multi 4.75 2.10

Souvenir Sheets
3931 A1700 €2 multi 4.75 2.40

Engr.
Perf. 13¼x13¾
3932 A1700 €3.10 blue & brn 7.50 3.75

Campaign Against Discrimination — A1718

2013, Oct. 3 Litho. *Die Cut Perf. 13*
3933 A1718 37c multi .85 .40

America issue.

State Lotteries, 250th Anniv. A1719

2013, Oct. 5 Litho. *Perf. 13¾x13¼*
3934 A1719 37c multi .85 .40

Mushrooms — A1720

No. 3935: a, Agaricus xanthodermus. b, Amanita pantherina. c, Marasmius oreades.

2013, Oct. 8 Litho. *Perf. 13¾x13¼*
3935 Horiz. strip of 3 2.50 2.50
a.-c. A1720 37c Any single .85 .40

Bridges Type of 2013
Souvenir Sheets

Designs: No. 3936, Frías Bridge, Burgos, vert. No. 3937, Toledo Bridge, Madrid, vert.

Litho. & Engr.
2013, Oct. 9 *Perf. 13¾*
3936 A1700 €3.10 blue & brn 7.50 7.50
3937 A1700 €3.10 blue & brn 7.50 7.50

Juvenia 2013 National Youth Philatelic Exhibition, Alicante A1721

2013, Oct. 14 Litho. *Perf. 13¾x14*
3938 A1721 75c multi 1.75 .90

Intl. Red Cross, 150th Anniv. — A1722

2013, Oct. 28 Photo. *Perf. 12¾*
3939 A1722 90c multi 2.25 1.10

No. 3939 was printed in sheets of 6 + central label. See Belgium No. 2665.

Souvenir Sheet

75th Birthdays of King Juan Carlos and Queen Sofia — A1723

Engr. (Sheet Margin Litho. & Engr.)
2013, Nov. 5 *Perf. 13¾x14*
3940 A1723 €3 black 7.00 7.00

The Nursing Virgin, by Alonso Cano — A1724

Die Cut Perf. 13
2013, Nov. 6 Litho.
Self-Adhesive
3941 A1724 A multi 1.25 .60

Christmas. No. 3941 sold for 37c on day of issue.

Puerta del Sol Clock, Madrid and Twelve Grapes — A1725

Die Cut Perf. 13
2013, Nov. 6 Litho.
Self-Adhesive
3942 A1725 B multi 3.00 1.50

New Year 2014. No. 3942 sold for 75c on day of issue.

Sports For All — A1726

No. 3943: a, Long-distance races. b, Bicycle touring. c, Hiking.

Perf. 13¾x13¼
2013, Nov. 12 Litho.
3943 A1726 Horiz. strip of 3 2.50 2.50
a.-c. 37c Any single .85 .40

Diplomatic Relations Between Spain and Japan, 400th Anniv. — A1727

No. 3944: a, Potted geraniums on decorative shelf. b, Lespedeza thunbergii.

Perf. 13¼x13¾
2013, Nov. 14 Litho.
3944 A1727 Horiz. pair 4.00 2.00
a.-b. 90c Either single 2.00 1.00

Souvenir Sheet

Adolfo Suárez Gonzalez (1932-2014), Prime Minister — A1728

Litho. & Engr.
2013, Nov. 15 *Perf. 13¾x14*
3945 A1728 €3.10 multi 7.50 7.50

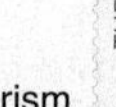

Tourism A1729

2014, Jan. 2 Litho. *Die Cut Perf. 13*
Self-Adhesive
3946 A1729 76c multi 1.75 .90

Arches and Gates — A1730

No. 3947: a, Malena Arch, Tarancón. b, Finca Miralles Gate, Barcelona. c, San Ginés Gate, Miranda del Castañar. d, Villalar Arch, Baeza. e, Estrella Arch, Cáceres. f, San Benito Arch, Sahagún. g, Bridge Gate Cordoba. h, San Lorenzo Gate, Laredo.

2014, Jan. 2 Litho. *Die Cut Perf. 13*
Self-Adhesive
3947 Booklet pane of 8 8.00
a.-h. A1730 A Any single .85 .40

Nos. 3947a-3947h each sold for 37c on day of issue.

Royal Spanish Academy, 300th Anniv. A1731

2014, Jan. 3 Litho. *Die Cut Perf. 13*
Self-Adhesive
3948 A1731 38c multi .85 .40

European Organization for Nuclear Research (CERN), 60th Anniv. — A1732

2014, Jan. 3 Litho. *Die Cut Perf. 13*
Self-Adhesive
3949 A1732 54c multi 1.25 .60

Arrival in Florida of Juan Ponce de Léon, 500th Anniv. (in 2013) A1733

2014, Jan. 3 Litho. *Die Cut Perf. 13*
Self-Adhesive
3950 A1733 92c multi 2.00 1.00

A1734

92c, Father Junípero Serra (1713-84), Founder of Missions in California.

2014, Jan. 20 Litho. *Perf. 13¾x13¼*
3951 A1734 92c multi 2.00 1.00

Statue of Pedro Cieza de Léon (c. 1520-54), Conquistador and Chronicler of Peruvian History — A1735

2014, Jan. 20 Litho. *Perf. 13¾x13¼*
3952 A1735 92c multi 2.00 1.00

Reflection of Food and Wine on Spoon — A1736

2014, Jan. 23 Litho. *Perf. 13¼x13¾*
3953 A1736 54c multi 1.25 .60

Selection of Burgos as 2013 Spanish Culinary Capital.

Real Racing Club de Santander Soccer Team, Cent. A1737

2014, Jan. 28 Litho. *Perf. 13¾x13¼*
3954 A1737 54c multi 1.25 .60

Royal Trust Housing Foundation of Seville, Cent. — A1738

2014, Jan. 28 Litho. *Perf. 13¾x13¼*
3955 A1738 54c multi 1.25 .60

Collectible Items — A1739

No. 3956: a, Lottery tickets. b, Picture postcards. c, Stickers. d, Minerals. e, Watches. f, Toy soldiers. g, Coins and currency. h, Stamps.

Die Cut Perf. 13
2014, Feb. 3 Litho.
Self-Adhesive
3956 Booklet pane of 8 8.75
a. A1739 1c multi .25 .25
b. A1739 2c multi .25 .25
c. A1739 5c multi .25 .25
d. A1739 10c multi .25 .25
e. A1739 25c multi .60 .30
f. A1739 50c multi 1.25 .60
g.-h. A1739 €1 Either single 2.50 1.25

Rural Architecture — A1740

No. 3957: a, Windmills, La Mancha. b, Granary, Asturias. c, House near water, Barranca.

2014, Feb. 6 Litho. ***Perf. 12¾x13¼***
3957 A1740 Vert. strip of 3 3.75 3.75
a.-c. 54c Any single 1.25 .60

Telgraph College, Cent. A1741

Perf. 13¾x13¼
2014, Feb. 12 Litho.
3958 A1741 54c multi 1.25 .60

Pilgrimage to Compostela of St. Francis of Assisi, 800th Anniv. — A1742

Perf. 13¾x13¼
2014, Feb. 14 Litho.
3959 A1742 54c multi 1.25 .60

Blas de Lezo y Olavarrieta (1689-1741), Admiral — A1743

Perf. 13¾x13¼
2014, Feb. 14 Litho.
3960 A1743 54c multi 1.25 .60

Kingdom of Badjoz, 1000th Anniv. A1744

Perf. 13¾x13¼
2014, Feb. 14 Litho.
3961 A1744 54c multi 1.25 .60

Launch of Submarine Designed By Isaac Peral, 125th Anniv. — A1745

Perf. 13¼x13¾
2014, Feb. 18 Litho.
3962 A1745 54c multi 1.25 .60

Souvenir Sheet

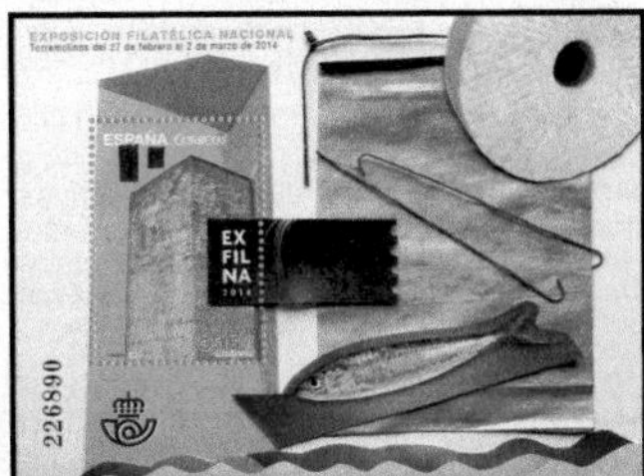

Exfilna 2014 National Philatelic Exhibition, Torremolinos — A1746

Litho. & Engr.
2014, Feb. 27 ***Perf. 14x13¾***
3963 A1746 €3.16 multi 7.50 7.50

State Society for Industrial Participation Foundation, 50th Anniv. — A1747

Perf. 13¾x13¼
2014, Mar. 10 Litho.
3964 A1747 38c multi .85 .40

Museums — A1748

Designs: No. 3965, Guadalajara Museum, decorated plaster fragment, decorated bowl, Roman sculpture. No. 3966, Museum of Spanish Abstract Art, Cuenca, painting by Fernando Zóbel.

Perf. 12¾x13¼
2014, Mar. 12 Litho.
3965 A1748 54c multi 1.25 .60
3966 A1748 54c multi 1.25 .60

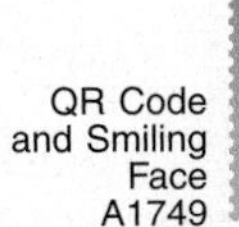

QR Code and Smiling Face A1749

Die Cut Perf. 13
2014, Mar. 14 Litho.
Self-Adhesive
3967 A1749 A multi 1.25 .60

No. 3967 sold for 37c on day of issue.

Souvenir Sheet

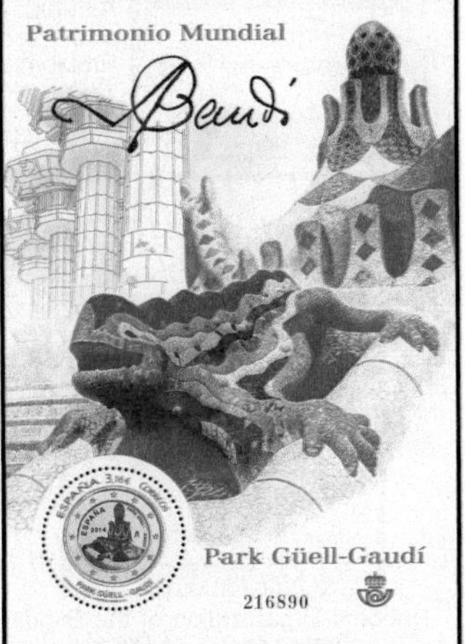

2-Euro Coin Depicting Park Güell UNESCO World Heritage Site, Barcelona — A1750

2014, Mar. 24 Litho. & Engr. ***Perf.***
3968 A1750 €3.16 multi 7.50 7.50

Establishment of Marca España Commission — A1751

Perf. 13¾x13¼
2014, Mar. 25 Litho.
3969 A1751 92c multi 2.00 1.00

Marca España A1752

Designs: No. 3970, Worker wearing air filter in factory, "E." No. 3971, Pechon Beach, "S." No. 3972, Court of the Lions, Alhambra, Granada, "P." No. 3973, Las Meninas, by Diego Velázquez, "A." No. 3974, *Don Quixote*, by Miguel de Cervantes, *The Time of the Hero*, by Mario Vargas Llosa, "N." No. 3975, Electron micoroscope, "A."

Litho. & Embossed
2014 ***Perf. 13¾x13¼***
3970 A1752 €1 multi + label 2.50 1.25
3971 A1752 €1 multi + label 2.50 1.25
3972 A1752 €1 multi + label 2.50 1.25
3973 A1752 €1 multi + label 2.50 1.25
3974 A1752 €1 multi + label 2.50 1.25
3975 A1752 €1 multi + label 2.50 1.25
Nos. 3970-3975 (6) 15.00 7.50

Issued: No. 3970, 4/14; No. 3971, 4/30; No. 3972, 5/5; No. 3973, 5/22; No. 3974, 6/5; No. 3975, 6/13.

Paco de Lucía (1947-2014), Guitarist — A1753

Die Cut Perf. 13
2014, Apr. 23 Litho.
Self-Adhesive
3976 A1753 B multi 4.00 2.00

Europa. No. 3976 sold for 76c on day of issue.

Souvenir Sheets

A1754

Spanish Cuisine — A1755

No. 3977: a, Tangerine and blossom. b, Iberian ham.
No. 3978: a, 350/ Ajo Blanco, dish by Ferran Adrià. b, Traditional Ajo Blanco (garlic and almond soup with grapes).

2014, Apr. 24 Litho. ***Perf. 13¾x13¼***
3977 A1754 Sheet of 2 15.00 15.00
a.-b. €3.15 Either single 7.50 3.75

Perf.
3978 A1755 Sheet of 2 15.00 15.00
a.-b. €3.15 Either single 7.50 3.75

Gum on No. 3977 is tangerine flavored. Gum on No. 3978 is almond flavored.

Ages of Man Eucharistic Religious Art Exhibiton, Aranda de Duero — A1756

Litho. With Foil Application
2014, May 6 ***Perf. 13¼x13½***
3979 A1756 76c multi 1.75 .90

Souvenir Sheet

UNESCO Intangible Cultural Heritage — A1757

No. 3980: a, Patio Festival, Cordoba. b, Cante de las Minas Flamenco Festival, La Unión.

2014, May 8 Photo. ***Perf. 13¾x13***
3980 A1757 Sheet of 2 9.50 9.50
a.-b. €2 Either single 4.75 2.40

Biscayne (Basque Country) Soccer Federation, Cent. A1758

2014, May 16 Litho. ***Perf. 13¾x13¼***
3981 A1758 76c multi 1.75 .90

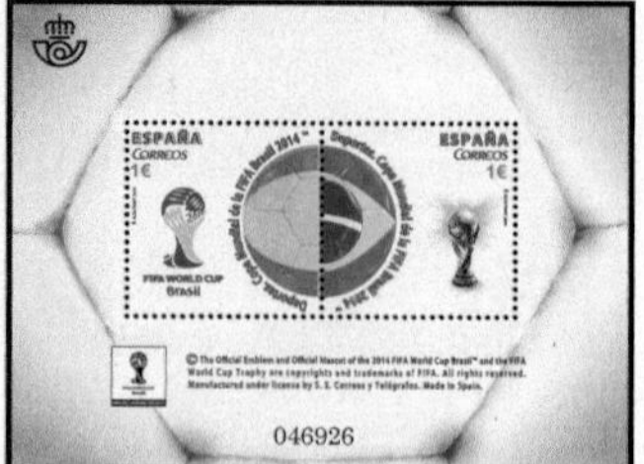
2014 World Cup Soccer Championships, Brazil — A1759

No. 3982: a, Emblem of 2014 World Cup tournament, half of soccer ball with colors of Spanish flag. b, Half of soccer ball showing Brazilian flag, World Cup.

2014, June 12 Litho. ***Perf. 12¾***
3982 A1759 Sheet of 2 5.00 5.00
a.-b. €1 Either single 2.50 1.25

Souvenir Sheet

Toledo UNESCO World Heritage Sites — A1760

No. 3983: a, Toledo Cathedral. b, Alcázar, horiz.

Perf. 13¾x13¼, 13¼x13¾ (#3983b)
2014, June 19 Litho. & Engr.
3983 A1760 Sheet of 2 5.00 5.00
a.-b. €1 Either single 2.50 1.25

Souvenir Sheet

View and Plan of Toledo, by El Greco — A1761

Photo. & Engr.
2014, June 19 ***Perf. 13¼x13¾***
3984 A1761 €2 multi 5.00 5.00

Stylized Ears of Corn and Emblem of Corps of Agricultural Engineers — A1762

Arches and Emblem of Corps of Civil Engineers A1763

Perf. 13¾x13¼
2014, June 20 Litho.
3985 A1762 54c multi 1.25 .60
3986 A1763 54c multi 1.25 .60

National Organization of the Blind, 75th Anniv. — A1764

EFE News Agency, 75th Anniv. A1765

Spanish Air Force, 75th Anniv. A1766

Perf. 13¾x13¼
2014, June 27 Litho.
3987 A1764 38c multi .85 .40
3988 A1765 38c multi .85 .40
3989 A1766 38c multi .85 .40
Nos. 3987-3989 (3) 2.55 1.20

Souvenir Sheet

Ca Va, by Miquel Barcelo — A1767

2014, July 8 Litho. ***Perf. 13¾x13¼***
3990 A1767 €3.15 multi 7.50 7.50

Movie Stars — A1768

No. 3991: a, Manolo Escobar (1931-2012). b, Sara Montiel (1928-2013). c, Alfredo Landa (1933-2013).

2014, July 11 Litho. ***Perf. 12½x12¾***
3991 Vert. strip of 3 5.25 5.25
a.-c. A1768 76c Any single 1.75 .90

Nos. 3991a-3991c each have film sprocket holes punched in the design.

Souvenir Sheet

Harley-Davidson Motorcycles — A1769

No. 3992: a, 1927 Harley-Davidson 350, front wheel of 1929 Harley-Davidson 1200J (41x58mm). b, Gas tank of 1929 Harley-Davidson 1200J (41x29mm). c, Harley-Davidson 1200J (41x29mm).

2014, July 17 Litho. ***Perf. 12½x13¼***
3992 A1769 Sheet of 3 6.00 6.00
a.-c. 92c Any single 2.00 1.00

Brotherhood of the White Virgin, 400th Anniv. — A1770

2014, July 31 Litho. ***Perf. 13¼x13¾***
3993 A1770 76c multi 1.75 .90

2014 Intl. Sailing Federation World Championships, Santander A1771

2014, Sept. 1 Litho. ***Perf. 13¼x13¾***
3994 A1771 92c multi 2.00 1.00

Royal and Military Order of San Hermenegildo, Bicent. — A1772

Center for Advanced Studies in National Defense, 50th Anniv. — A1773

Perf. 13¾x13¼
2014, Sept. 10 Litho.
3995 A1772 76c multi 1.75 .90

Perf. 13¼x13¾
3996 A1773 76c multi 1.75 .90

Souvenir Sheet

The Death of Dido Tapestry, c. 1660 — A1774

Engr., Litho. Sheet Margin
2014, Sept. 18 ***Perf. 13¼x13¾***
3997 A1774 €3.15 gray green 7.50 7.50

Saint John Paul II (1920-2005) — A1775

2014, Sept. 25 Litho. ***Perf. 13¾x14***
3998 A1775 92c multi 2.00 1.00

Arms of León, San Isisdro Basilica, Parliamentary Seating Arrangement — A1776

2014, Oct. 1 Litho. ***Perf. 13¾x13¼***
3999 A1776 76c multi 1.75 .90

León, site of first democratic parliament in Europe, 1188.

Taula of Torretrencada A1777

2014, Oct. 1 Litho. ***Perf. 14x14¼***
4000 A1777 92c multi 2.00 1.00

Faces, Map of North and South America A1778

2014, Oct. 9 Litho. ***Perf. 13¾x13¼***
4001 A1778 92c multi 2.00 1.00

America issue.

Souvenir Sheet

Cartoons by Forges — A1779

2014, Oct. 9 Litho. *Perf. 13¼x13¾*

4002 A1779 €3.15 black + 8 labels 7.50 7.50

Souvenir Sheet

King Felipe VI's Accession to the Throne — A1780

No. 4003: a, King Felipe VI. b, King Felipe VI and Queen Letizia.

Litho., Sheet Margin Litho. & Silk-Screened

2014, Oct. 12 *Perf. 13¾x13¼*

4003 A1780 Sheet of 2 5.00 5.00
a.-b. €1 Either single 2.50 1.25

Irun Railroad Station A1781

2014, Oct. 17 Litho. *Perf. 13¾x13¼*

4004 A1781 76c multi 1.75 .90

Protected Animals — A1782

No. 4005: a, Otter (nutria) (75x29mm). b, Great bustard (avutarda) (75x29mm). c, Eagle owl (bubo real) (36x58mm). d, Imperial eagle (aguila imperial) (39x58mm).

Perf. 13x13¼ on 3 or 4 Sides

2014, Oct. 20 Litho.

4005 A1782 Block of 4 6.50 4.50
a.-b. 54c Either single 1.25 .60
c.-d. 92c Either single 2.00 1.00

Peseta Currency — A1783

No. 4006: a, Back of 1953 one-peseta banknote (58x41mm). b, Obverse of 1944 one-peseta coin (41x41mm).

Litho. (#4006a), Litho & Embossed with Foil Application (#4006b)

2014, Nov. 4 *Perf. 13¼x13¾*

4006 A1783 Horiz. pair 9.50 7.50
a.-b. €2 Either single 4.50 2.25

Souvenir Sheet

Publication of Children's Book *Platero y yo,* by Juan Ramón Jiménez, Cent. — A1784

Litho. & Engr. With Foil Application

2014, Nov. 7 *Perf. 13¾x13¼*

4007 A1784 €3.15 multi 7.50 7.50

A1785

Christmas A1786

Litho. With Foil Application

2014, Nov. 11 *Die Cut Perf. 13*

Self-Adhesive

4008 A1785 A multi .85 .40

Litho.

Serpentine Die Cut 10

4009 A1786 B multi 1.75 .90
a. Tete-beche pair 2.75

On day of issue No. 4008 sold for 38c and No. 4009 sold for 76c. Parts of the design of No. 4009 were printed with thermographic ink which changes color when warmed. No. 4009 was printed in sheets of 6.

Gates A1787

No. 4010: a, Moon Gate, Cordoba. b, Chain Gate, Brihegua. c, St. Mary's Gate, Hondarribia. d, St. Peter's Gate, Peñíscola.

2015, Jan. 2 Litho. *Die Cut Perf. 13*

Booklet Stamps

Self-Adhesive

4010 Block of 4 4.00
a.-d. A1787 A Any single 1.00 .50
e. Booklet pane of 8, 2 each #4010a-4010d 8.00

On day of issue, Nos. 4010a-4010d each sold for 42c.

A1788

Tourism A1789

Litho. & Embossed

2015, Jan. 2 *Die Cut Perf. 13*

Self-Adhesive

4011 A1788 90c multi 2.00 1.00
4012 A1789 €1 multi 2.40 1.25

St. Teresa of Avila (1515-82) A1790

Litho. & Embossed

2015, Jan. 5 *Die Cut Perf. 13*

Self-Adhesive

4013 A1790 A multi .95 .50

No. 4013 sold for 42c on day of issue.

Spanish National Research Council, 75th Anniv. (in 2014) A1791

Litho. & Embossed

2015, Jan. 5 *Die Cut Perf. 13*

Self-Adhesive

4014 A1791 A2 multi 1.25 .60

No. 4014 sold for 55c on day of issue.

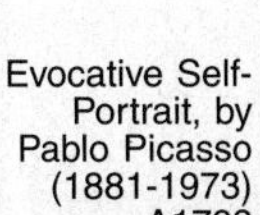

Evocative Self-Portrait, by Pablo Picasso (1881-1973) A1792

Litho. & Embossed

2015, Jan. 5 *Die Cut Perf. 13*

Self-Adhesive

4015 A1792 C multi 2.25 1.10

Exhibition of early Picasso works, A Coruña. No. 4015 sold for €1 on day of issue.

National Transplant Organization, 25th Anniv. A1793

Litho. & Embossed

2015, Jan. 16 *Die Cut Perf. 13*

Self-Adhesive

4016 A1793 B multi 2.10 1.10

No. 4016 sold for 90c on day of issue.

A1794

Winning Designs in Stamp Design Contest A1795

Litho. & Embossed

2015, Jan. 19 *Die Cut Perf. 13*

Self-Adhesive

4017 A1794 42c multi .95 .50
4018 A1795 55c multi 1.25 .60

Intl. Year of Light (No. 4017).

King Felipe VI
A1796 A1797

2015, Jan. 19 Litho. *Perf. 12¾x13¼*

Color of Portrait

4019 A1796 1c org brn .25 .25
4020 A1796 4c brown .25 .25
4021 A1796 10c blue green .25 .25
4022 A1796 €1 rose lake 2.25 1.10
4023 A1796 €2 blue 4.50 2.25

Engr. & Embossed With Foil Application

Die Cut Perf. 13

Self-Adhesive

4024 A1797 €5 black & gold 11.50 5.75
Nos. 4019-4024 (6) 19.00 9.85

Nos. 4019-4023 have a punched out "ñ."

Souvenir Sheet

Culinary Capitals of 2014 and 2015 — A1798

No. 4025: a, Tapas bar from Vitoria, 2014 Culinary Capital. b, Local foods from Caceres, 2015 Culinary Capital.

2015, Jan. 28 Litho. *Perf. 13¼x13¾*

4025 A1798 Sheet of 2 4.25 4.25
a.-b. 90c Either single 2.10 1.10

Nos. 4025a-4025b have a punched out "ñ."

Button and Badge Collecting A1799

Pipe Collecting A1800

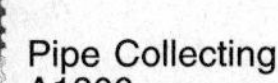

Coin Collecting A1801

Stamp Collecting A1802

Die Cut Perf. 13

2015, Feb. 3 Litho.

Booklet Stamps
Self-Adhesive

4026	Block of 4	8.50	
a.	A1799 25c multi	.55	.30
b.	A1800 50c multi	1.10	.55
c.	A1801 €1 multi	2.25	1.10
d.	A1802 €2 multi	4.50	2.25
e.	Booklet pane of 8, 2 each #4026a-4026d	17.00	

Royal Artillery College, 250th Anniv. (in 2014) A1803

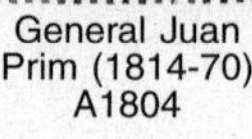

General Juan Prim (1814-70) A1804

Military Health Services, 500th Anniv. A1805

2015, Feb. 6 Litho. ***Perf. 13¾x13¼***

4027	A1803 90c multi	2.00	1.00

Perf. 13¼x13¾

4028	A1804 90c multi	2.00	1.00
4029	A1805 90c multi	2.00	1.00
	Nos. 4027-4029 (3)	6.00	3.00

Nos. 4027-4029 have a punched out "ñ."

Royal Soccer Federation of Andalusia, Cent. — A1806

Perf. 13¼x13¾

2015, Feb. 19 Litho.

4030	A1806 90c multi	2.00	1.00

No. 4030 has a punched out "ñ."

Submarine Force, Cent. A1807

Perf. 13¾x13¼

2015, Feb. 20 Litho.

4031	A1807 90c multi	2.00	1.00

No. 4031 has a punched out "ñ."

First International Congress on Bullfighting as a Cultural Heritage — A1808

Perf. 13¼x13¾

2015, Feb. 20 Litho.

4032	A1808 €1 multi	2.25	1.10

No. 4032 has a punched out "ñ."

Museums — A1809

Designs: No. 4033, 55c, National Archaeological Museum, Madrid. No. 4034, 55c, Thyssen-Bornemisza Museum, Madrid. No. 4035, 55c, Lázaro Galdiano Museum, Madrid.

2015, Mar. 3 Litho. ***Perf. 13x13¼***

4033-4035	A1809 Set of 3	3.75	1.90

Nos. 4033-4035 have punched out "ñ."

Souvenir Sheet

Exfilna 2015, National Philatelic Exhibition, Avilés — A1810

No. 4036: a, Building in color. b, Building in shades of gray and black.

Litho. (#4036a), Litho. & Engr. (#4036b)

2015, Mar. 13 ***Perf. 13¼x13¾***

4036	A1810 Sheet of 2	6.50	6.50
a.	42c multi	.95	.45
b.	€2.42 multi	5.50	2.75

Nos. 4036a-4036b have a punched out "ñ."

Lace — A1811

No. 4037: a, Flag of Croatia, lace from Lepoglava, Croatia. b, Flag colors of Spain, lace from Seville.

Perf. 13¼x13¾

2015, Mar. 31 Litho.

4037	A1811 Horiz. pair	4.50	2.25
a.-b.	€1 Either single	2.25	1.10

Nos. 4037a-4037b have numerous punched out holes. See Croatia No. 944.

Film Personalities — A1812

No. 4038: a, Francisco Martínez Soria (1902-82), actor. b, José Luis Borau (1929-2012), producer and director.

2015, Apr. 1 Litho. ***Perf. 13¼x13¾***

4038	A1812 Horiz. pair, #a-b	4.00	2.00
a.-b.	90c Either single	2.00	1.00

Nos. 4038a-4038b have a punched out "ñ."

Juvenia 2015 National Children's Stamp Exhibition, Ourense A1813

2015, Apr. 18 Litho. ***Perf. 13¾x13¼***

4039	A1813 42c multi	.95	.45

No. 4039 has a punched out "ñ."

Gabriel García Márquez (1928-2014), 1982 Nobel Literature Laureate — A1814

Luis Aragonés (1938-2014), Soccer Player — A1815

2015, Apr. 22 Litho. ***Perf. 13¼x13¾***

4040	A1814 55c multi	1.25	.60

Perf. 13¾x13¼

4041	A1815 55c multi	1.25	.60

Nos. 4040-4041 have a punched out "ñ."

Europa A1816

Litho. & Embossed

2015, Apr. 23 ***Die Cut Perf. 13***

Self-Adhesive

4042	A1816 90c multi	2.10	1.10

No. 4042 is impregnated with a pine scent.

Souvenir Sheet

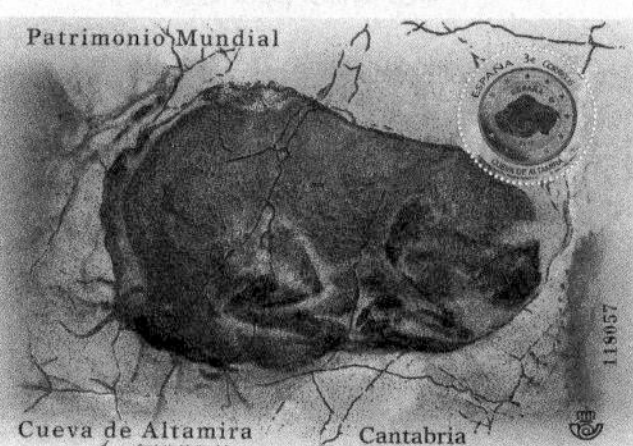

Coin Depicting Cave Painting From Altamira Cave UNESCO World Heritage Site — A1817

Litho., Engr. & Embossed

2015, Apr. 27 ***Perf.***

4043	A1817 €3 multi	6.75	6.75

Dinosaurs — A1818

Designs: No. 4044, €2, Triceratops. No. 4045, €2, Tyrannosaurus rex. No. 4046, €2, Diplodocus, vert. No. 4047, €2, Ankylosaurus.

Litho., Litho. & Thermography (#4047)

Perf. 13¼x13¾, 13¾x13¼

2015, May 7

4044-4047	A1818 Set of 4	18.00	9.00

Nos. 4044-4047 have a punched out "ñ." The designs of Nos. 4045-4046, viewed through red and blue glasses, become three-dimensional.

Souvenir Sheet

Segovia UNESCO World Heritage Site — A1819

No. 4048: a, Santa Maria Cathedral. b, Aqueduct, horiz.

Perf. 13¾x13¼, 13¼x13¾

2015, May 3 Engr.

4048	A1819 Sheet of 2	4.50	4.00
a.-b.	€1 Either single	2.25	1.10

Nos. 4048a-4048b have punched out "ñ."

Social Networks A1820

Litho & Silk-Screened

2015, May 14 ***Perf. 13¾***

4049	A1820 42c multi	.95	.45

No. 4049 has a punched out "ñ" and was printed in sheets of 6 + central label.

Devotion to Virgin of the Sea Icon, 700th Anniv. A1821

2015, May 18 Litho. ***Perf. 13¾x13¼***

4050	A1821 90c multi	2.00	1.00

No. 4050 has a punched out "ñ."

World's Largest Stamp Mosaic — A1822

2015, May 27 Litho. ***Perf. 13¼x13¾***

4051	A1822 42c multi + label	.95	.45

No. 4051 has a punched out "ñ."

World Food Program A1823

2015, June 4 Litho. ***Perf. 13¾x13¼***

4052	A1823 42c multi	.95	.45

No. 4052 has a punched out "ñ."

Souvenir Sheet

Cristóbal de Sandoval, Duke of Uceda (1581-1624), First Director of Spanish Mint — A1824

Engr., Margin Litho. & Engr. With Foil Application

2015, June 17 ***Perf. 13¼x13¾***

4053 A1824 €3.23 brown 7.25 7.25

Spanish Mint, Madrid, 400th anniv. No. 4053 has a punched out "ñ."

International Year of Soils — A1825

Litho. & Embossed

2015, June 26 ***Perf. 13¼***

4054 A1825 90c multi 2.00 1.00

Petunia seeds are sealed under a round piece of adhesive tape affixed to the face of the stamp.

Narciso Yepes (1927-97), Guitarist A1826

Litho. & Embossed

2015, July 1 ***Die Cut Perf. 13***

Self-Adhesive

4055 A1826 A2 multi 1.25 .60

No. 4055 sold for 55c on day of issue.

Souvenir Sheet

Cartoon by Peridis — A1827

2015, July 2 Litho. ***Perf. 13¾x13¼***

4056 A1827 €2.84 black 6.25 6.25

No. 4056 has a punched out "ñ."

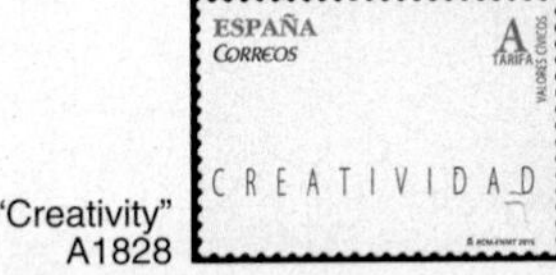

"Creativity" A1828

Litho. & Embossed

2015, July 10 ***Die Cut Perf. 13***

Self-Adhesive

4057 A1828 A multi .95 .45

No. 4057 sold for 42c on day of issue.

Souvenir Sheet

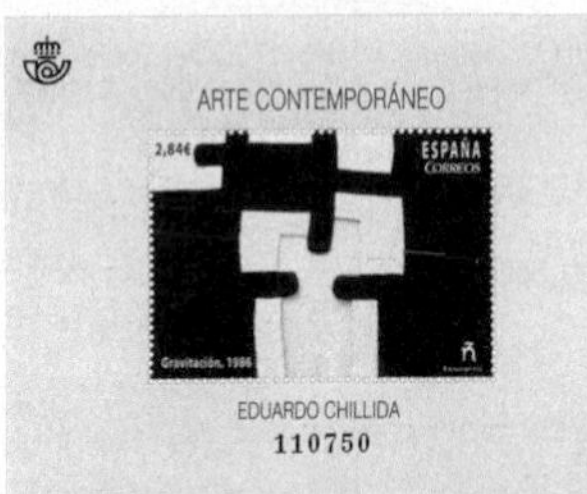

Gravitaciones, by Eduardo Chillida (1924-2002) — A1829

Litho. & Embossed

2015, July 13 ***Perf. 13¼x13¾***

4058 A1829 €2.84 multi 6.25 6.25

No. 4058 has a punched out "ñ."

61st International Habaneras and Polyphony Contest, Torrevieja — A1830

Litho. & Embossed

2015, July 19 ***Perf. 14x13½***

Self-Adhesive

4059 A1830 B multi 2.00 1.00

No. 4059 sold for 90c on day of issue.

Protected Animals — A1831

No. 4060: a, Dragonfly (libélula) (40x58mm). b, Leatherback turtle (tortuga laúd) (75x29mm). c, Long-fingered bat (Murciélago patudo) (38x58mm). d, Sturgeon (esturión) (75x29mm).

Perf. 13x13¼ on 3 or 4 Sides

2015, July 21 **Photo.**

4060 A1831 Block of 4 5.00 2.50

a.-d. 55c Any single 1.25 .60

Nos. 4060a-4060d have a punched out "ñ."

Souvenir Sheet

Constitutional Court, 35th Anniv. — A1832

Litho., Margin Litho. With Foil Application

2015, July 23 ***Perf. 13¼x13¾***

4061 A1832 €1 multi 2.25 2.25

No. 4061 has a punched out "ñ."

Silbo Gomero Language of Canary Islands — A1833

Mediterranean Diet — A1834

2015, July 28 Litho. ***Perf. 13¼x13¾***

4062 A1833 €2.84 multi 6.25 3.25

Litho. & Thermography

4063 A1834 €3.23 multi 7.25 3.75

UNESCO Intangible Cultural Heritage. Nos. 4062-4063 have a punched out "ñ."

Fermín Caballero (1800-76), Politician — A1835

Litho. With Foil Application

2015, Sept. 8 ***Perf. 13¼x13¾***

4064 A1835 42c multi .95 .45

No. 4064 has a punched out "ñ."

San Sebastián Film Festival — A1836

Litho. With Foil Application

2015, Sept. 17 ***Perf. 12¾x12½***

4065 A1836 55c multi 1.25 .65

No. 4065 has a punched out "ñ."

Juan Carreño de Miranda (1614-85), Painter — A1837

Perf. 13¼x13¾

2015, Sept. 18 **Litho.**

4066 A1837 55c multi 1.25 .60

No. 4066 has a punched out "ñ."

Founding of St. Augustine, Florida, 450th Anniv. — A1838

Litho. & Embossed

2015, Sept. 18 ***Die Cut Perf. 13***

Self-Adhesive

4067 A1838 C multi 2.25 1.10

No. 4067 sold for €1 on day of issue.

Foundation of Segobriga by Romans, 2000th Anniv. — A1839

Perf. 13¾x13¼

2015, Sept. 23 **Litho.**

4068 A1839 42c multi .95 .45

No. 4068 has a punched out "ñ."

Souvenir Sheet

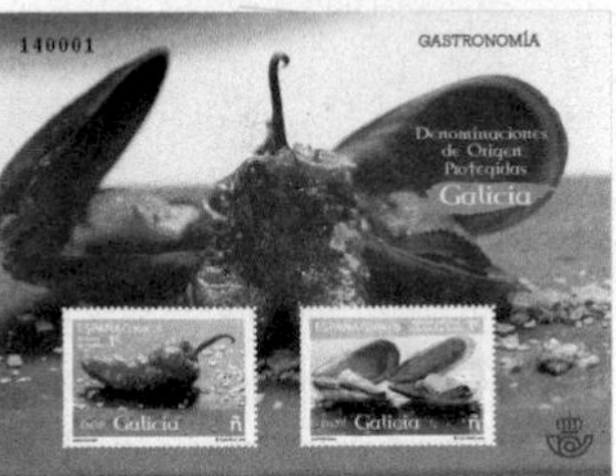

Spanish Cuisine — A1840

No. 4069 — Items with Galician protected designations of origin: a, Herbón pimento. b, Mussels.

Perf. 13¾x13¼

2015, Sept. 25 **Litho.**

4069 A1840 Sheet of 2 4.50 4.50

a.-b. €1 Either single 2.25 1.10

Nos. 4069a-4069b have a punched out "ñ."

Modern Wonders of the World — A1841

Designs: 55c, Great Wall of China, flag of People's Republic of China. 90c, Chichén Itzá, flag of Mexico. €1, Statue of Christ the Redeemer, flag of Brazil.

Perf. 12¾x13¼

2015, Sept. 30 **Litho.**

4070-4072 A1841 Set of 3 5.50 2.75

Nos. 4070-4072 have a punched out "ñ."

Princess of Asturias Awards A1842

2015, Oct. 2 Litho. ***Perf. 13¾x13¼***

4073 A1842 €1 multi 2.25 1.10

No. 4073 has a punched out "ñ."

Tarragona-Martorell Railway, 150th Anniv. — A1843

2015, Oct. 9 Litho. ***Perf. 13¾x13¼***
4074 A1843 90c multi 2.00 1.00

No. 4074 has a punched out "ñ."

International Telecommunication Union, 150th Anniv. — A1844

2015, Oct. 9 Litho. ***Perf. 13¾x13¼***
4075 A1844 90c multi 2.00 1.00

No. 4075 has a punched out "ñ."

Souvenir Sheet

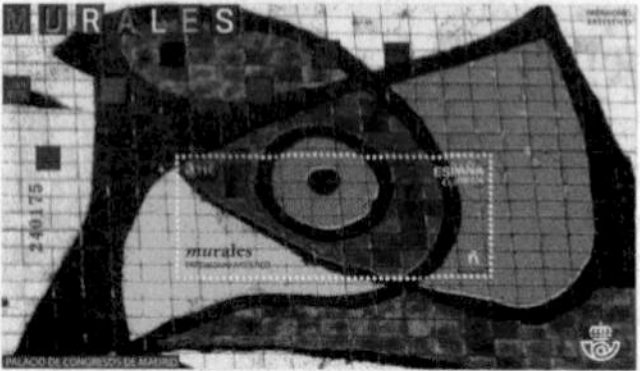

Mural by Joan Miró at Palacio de Congresos, Madrid — A1845

Litho. & Embossed
2015, Oct. 14 ***Perf. 12¾x113¼***
4076 A1845 €3.71 multi 8.25 8.25

No. 4076 has a punched out "ñ."

Francisco Alvarez de Toledo (1515-82), Viceroy of Peru A1846

2015, Oct. 23 Litho. ***Perf. 13¾x13¼***
4077 A1846 42c multi .95 .45

No. 4077 has a punched out "ñ."

United Nations, 70th Anniv. A1847

2015, Oct. 23 Litho. ***Perf. 13¾x13¼***
4078 A1847 42c multi .95 .45

No. 4078 has a punched out "ñ."

Campaign Against Human Trafficking A1848

2015, Oct. 27 Litho. ***Perf. 13¾x13¼***
4079 A1848 €1 multi 2.25 1.10

America issue. No. 4079 has a punched out "ñ."

Rural Architecture — A1849

No. 4080: a, Mountain house (Casona montañesa) and coat of arms, Cantabria. b, Silo. c, Farm building and well.

2015, Oct. 29 Litho. ***Perf. 12¾x13¼***
4080 A1849 Vert. strip of 3 6.00 6.00
a.-c. 90c Any single 2.00 1.00

Nos. 4080a-4080c have a punched out "ñ."

Christmas
A1850 A1851

Litho. & Embossed
2015, Nov. 2 ***Die Cut Perf. 13***
Self-Adhesive
4081 A1850 A multi .95 .45

Litho. With Foil Application
4082 A1851 B multi 2.00 1.00

On day of issue, No. 4081 sold for 42c; No. 4082, for 90c.

100-Peseta Currency — A1852

No. 4083: a, 1953 100-peseta banknote (58x41mm). b, 1992 100-peseta coin (41x41mm).

Litho. (#4083a), Litho & Embossed with Foil Application (#4083b)
2015, Nov. 4 ***Perf. 13¼x13¾***
4083 A1852 Horiz. pair 8.50 4.25
a.-b. €2 Either single 4.25 2.10

Nos. 4083a-4083b have a punched out "ñ."

Souvenir Sheet

Motorcycles — A1853

No. 4084: a, Bultaco motorcycle (41x58mm). b, Derbi motorcycle (41x29mm)

2015, Nov. 6 Litho. ***Perf. 13¾x13¼***
4084 A1853 Sheet of 2 + label 4.00 4.00
a.-b. 90c Either single 2.00 1.00

Nos. 4084a-4084b have a punched out "ñ."

Tourism A1854

Designs: €1.15, Mountain, lake, paraglider, bicycle, backpack, pot. €1.30, Book, paintbrush, wine glass, beach umbrella, sailboat.

Litho. & Embossed
2016, Jan. 2 ***Die Cut Perf. 13***
Self-Adhesive
4085-4086 A1854 Set of 2 5.50 2.75

King Felipe VI
A1855 A1856

2016, Jan. 2 Litho. ***Perf. 12¾x13¼***
4087 A1855 2c blue & blk .25 .25
4088 A1855 3c carmine & blk .25 .25

Litho. & Embossed With Foil Application
Self-Adhesive
Die Cut Perf. 13
4089 A1856 A sil, blk & ol grn 1.00 .50

Litho. & Embossed
4090 A1856 A2 multi 1.00 .50
4091 A1856 B multi 2.50 1.25
4092 A1856 C multi 3.00 1.50
Nos. 4089-4092 (4) 7.50 3.75

On day of issue, No. 4089 sold for 45c; No. 4090, 57c; No. 4091, €1.15; No. 4092, €1.30. Nos. 4087-4088 have a punched out "ñ."

See No. 4180.

Order of Isabel the Catholic, 200th Anniv. A1857

2016, Jan. 12 Litho. ***Perf. 13¾x13¼***
4093 A1857 €1.30 multi 3.00 1.50

No. 4093 has a punched out "ñ."

Gonzalo Fernández de Córdoba (1453-1515), General — A1858

2016, Jan. 14 Litho. ***Perf. 13¾x13¼***
4094 A1858 €1.30 multi 3.00 1.50

No. 4094 has a punched out "ñ."

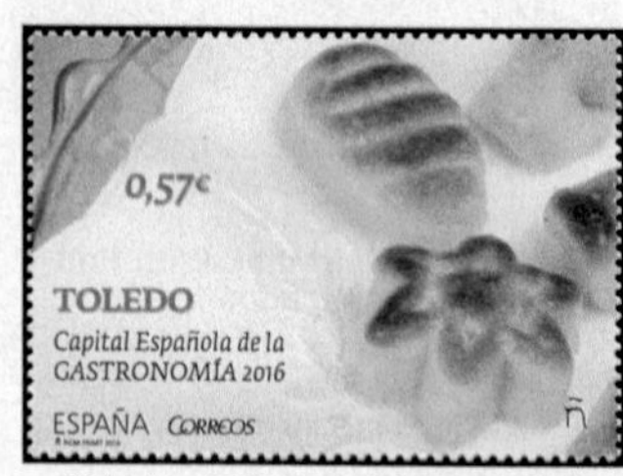

Toledo, 2016 Spanish Capital of Gastronomy — A1859

2016, Jan. 20 Litho. ***Perf. 13¼x13¾***
4095 A1859 57c multi 1.25 .60

No. 4095 has a punched out "ñ."

Kingdom of Almeria, 1000th Anniv. A1860

2016, Jan. 28 Litho. ***Perf. 13¾x13¼***
4096 A1860 57c multi 1.25 .60

No. 4096 has a punched out "ñ."

Drawing of Don Quixote, by Maximiliano Cosatti — A1861

Drawing of Don Quixote, by Carlota Artero A1862

Litho. & Embossed
2016, Jan. 29 ***Die Cut Perf. 13***
Self-Adhesive
4097 A1861 45c multi 1.00 .50
4098 A1862 57c multi 1.25 .60

Winning designs in stamp design competition.

Campaign Against Bullying — A1863

Litho. & Embossed on Foil
2016, Feb. 2 ***Die Cut Perf. 13***
Self-Adhesive
4099 A1863 45c sil & multi 1.00 .50

Diario de Avisos Newspaper, 125th Anniv. (in 2015) — A1864

2016, Feb. 5 Litho. ***Perf. 13¼x13¾***
4100 A1864 57c multi 1.25 .60

No. 4100 has a punched out "ñ."

Great Santander Fire, 75th Anniv. — A1865

2016, Feb. 15 Litho. ***Perf. 13x13¼***
4101 A1865 €1.15 multi 2.50 1.25

No. 4101 has a punched out "ñ."

Souvenir Sheet

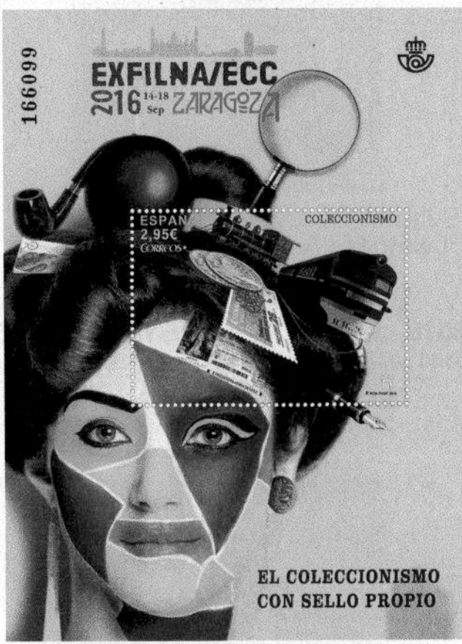

Exfilna 2016 National Philatelic Exhibition, Torremolinos — A1866

Perf. 13¼x13¾

2016, Feb. 17 **Litho.**

4102 A1866 €2.95 multi 6.50 6.50

No. 4102 has a punched out "ñ."

Migration of Refugees A1867

Litho. & Embossed

2016, Feb. 19 ***Die Cut Perf. 13***

Self-Adhesive

4103 A1867 45c multi 1.00 .50

Military Emergencies Unit, 10th Anniv. — A1868

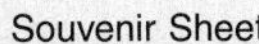

Perf. 13¼x13¾

2016, Feb. 24 **Litho.**

4104 A1868 €1.30 multi 3.00 1.50

No. 4104 has a punched out "ñ."

Souvenir Sheet

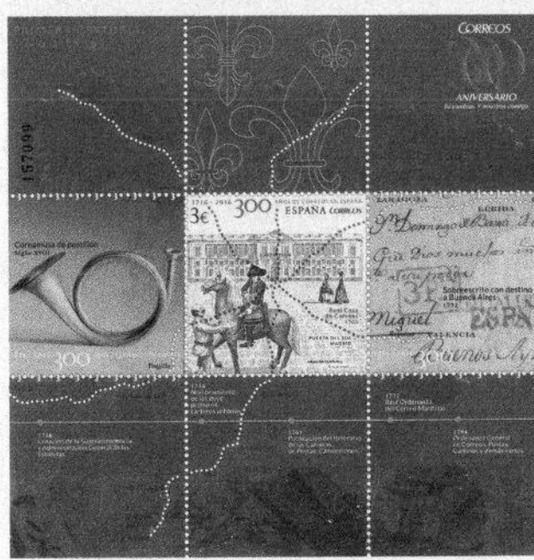

Spanish Mail Service, 300th Anniv. — A1869

Litho. & Engr., Sheet Margin Litho. & Embossed

2016, Feb. 29 ***Perf. 12½***

4105 A1869 €3 multi 6.50 6.50

Museums — A1870

Designs: No. 4106, 45c, Museum of Contemporary Art, Barcelona. No. 4107, 45c, Museum of Natural Sciences, Madrid. No. 4108, 45c, Institute of Modern Art, Valencia.

2016, Mar. 10 **Litho.** ***Perf. 13x13¼***

4106-4108 A1870 Set of 3 3.25 1.60

Nos. 4106-4108 have a punched out "ñ."

Easter Week Traditions and Customs A1871

No. 4109 — Traditions and customs in: a, Tobarra. b, Cuenca. c, Seville. d, Lorca.

Litho. & Embossed

2016, Mar. 17 ***Die Cut Perf. 13***

Booklet Stamps

Self-Adhesive

4109 Block of 4 9.00

a.-d. A1871 €1 Any single 2.25 1.10

Complete booklet, 2 each #4109a-4109d 18.00

No. 4109 is impregnated with a sandalwood incense scent. See No. 4194.

Villages — A1872

No. 4110: a, Albarrcín. b, La Alberca. c, Alcalá del Júcar. d, Santillana del Mar.

Litho. & Embossed

2016, Mar. 21 ***Die Cut Perf. 13***

Self-Adhesive

4110 Booklet pane of 4 4.50

a.-d. A1872 A Any single 1.10 .55

Nos. 4110a-4110d each sold for 45c on day of issue.

State Industrial Engineers Corps, 105th Anniv. A1873

Litho. With Foil Application

2016, Mar. 23 ***Perf. 13¾x13¼***

4111 A1873 57c sil & multi 1.40 .70

No. 4111 has a punched out "ñ."

Jerez, 2015-17 World Capital of Motorcycling A1874

Litho. & Embossed

2016, Mar. 29 ***Die Cut Perf. 13***

Self-Adhesive

4112 A1874 A multi 1.10 .55

No. 4112 sold for 45c on day of issue.

First Flight of Space Shuttle Columbia, 35th Anniv. — A1875

Litho. With Foil Application

2016, Mar. 31 ***Perf. 13¼x13¾***

4113 A1875 45c gold & multi 1.10 .55

No. 4113 has a punched out "ñ."

San Sebastián, 2016 European Capital of Culture A1876

2016, Apr. 1 **Litho.** ***Perf. 13¾x13¼***

4114 A1876 €1.15 multi 2.60 1.40

No. 4114 has a punched out "ñ."

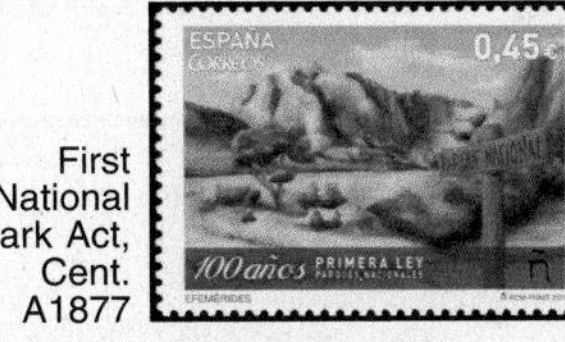

First National Park Act, Cent. A1877

2016, Apr. 5 **Litho.** ***Perf. 13¾x13¼***

4115 A1877 45c multi 1.10 .55

No. 4115 has a punched out "ñ."

First Philatelic Bourse in Barcelona, 125th Anniv. A1878

2016, Apr. 8 **Litho.** ***Perf. 13¾x13¼***

4116 A1878 57c multi 1.40 .70

No. 4116 has a punched out "ñ."

Ramón Llull (c. 1232- c. 1316), Philosopher A1879

2016, Apr. 12 **Litho.** ***Perf. 13¼x13¾***

4117 A1879 €1.30 multi 3.00 1.50

No. 4117 has a punched out "ñ."

Europa A1880

Litho. & Embossed

2016, Apr. 22 ***Die Cut Perf. 13***

Self-Adhesive

4118 A1880 A multi 1.10 .55

Think Green Issue.
No. 4117 sold for 45c on day of issue.

Rocío Jurado (1946-2006), Singer and Actress — A1881

Litho. With Foil Application

2016, Apr. 12 ***Perf. 13¾x13¼***

4119 A1881 57c multi 1.40 .70

No. 4119 has a punched out "ñ."

Chords Bridge, Jerusalem A1882

2016, Apr. 19 **Litho.** ***Perf. 13¼x13¾***

4120 A1882 C multi 3.00 1.50

Diplomatic relations between Israel and Spain, 30th anniv. No. 4120 sold for €1.30 on day of issue and has a punched out "ñ." See Israel No. 2100.

Souvenir Sheet

Telegraph Machine and Operator — A1883

Litho. & Engr., Sheet Margin Litho. & Embossed With Foil Application

2016, Apr. 21 ***Perf. 12½***

4121 A1883 €3 multi 7.00 7.00

Spanish mail service, 300th anniv. No. 4121 has a punched out "ñ."

Way of St. James A1884

Litho. & Embossed

2016, Apr. 25 ***Die Cut Perf. 13***

Self-Adhesive

4122 A1884 B multi 2.75 1.40

No. 4122 sold for €1.15 on day of issue.

Royal Soccer Federation of the Principality of Asturias, Cent. A1885

2016, May 9 Litho. *Perf. 13¾x13¼*
4123 A1885 €1.15 multi 2.60 1.40

No. 4123 has a punched out "ñ."

Souvenir Sheet

Old City of Salamanca UNESCO World Heritage Site — A1886

No. 4124: a, New Cathedral, denomination at UL. b, Old Cathedral, denomination at UR.

Perf. 13¾x13¼
2016, May 12 Litho. & Engr.
4124 A1886 Sheet of 2 4.50 4.00
a.-b. €1 Either single 2.25 1.10

Nos. 4124a-4124b have a punched out "ñ" at lower right corner.

Hispania Nostra Association, 40th Anniv. — A1887

2016, May 23 Litho. *Perf. 13¼x13¾*
4125 A1887 €1.15 multi 2.60 1.40

No. 4125 has a punched out "ñ."

Souvenir Sheet

Cartoon Depicting King Felipe VI by José María Gallego and Julio Rey — A1888

2016, May 24 Litho. *Perf. 13¾x13¼*
4126 A1888 €4 multi 9.00 9.00

No. 4126 has a punched out "ñ."

Souvenir Sheet

Spanish Gastronomy — A1889

No. 4127: a, Manchego cheese. b, Saffron and crocus from La Mancha

2016, June 9 Litho. *Perf. 13¾x13¼*
4127 A1889 Sheet of 2 6.00 6.00
a.-b. €1.30 Either single 3.00 1.50

Nos. 4127a-4127b have a punched out "ñ."

Runner, Emblem of Spanish Olympic Committee, and Pierre de Coubertin (1863-1937), Founder of International Olympic Committee A1890

Perf. 13¼x13¾
2016, June 23 Litho.
4128 A1890 €1.30 multi 3.00 1.50

America issue. No. 4128 has a punched out "ñ."

Dinosaurs — A1891

Designs: No. 4129, €2, Proa. No. 4130, €2, Turiasaurus, vert. No. 4131, €2, Pelicanimimus. No. 4132, €2, Europelta.

Litho., Litho. & Thermography (#4130), Litho. With Holographic Foil (#4131), Litho. With Three-Dimensional Plastic Affixed (#4132)
Perf. 13¼x13¾, 11¾ (#4130, 4132)
2016, June 30
4129-4132 A1891 Set of 4 18.00 9.00

Nos. 4129-4131 have a punched out "ñ." The design of No. 4129, when viewed through red and blue glasses, becomes three-dimensional. The thermographic ink on part of the design of No. 4130 changes color when warmed.

State Vehicle Fleet, 80th Anniv. A1892

2016, July 1 Litho. *Perf. 13¾x13¼*
4133 A1892 €1.15 multi 2.60 1.40

No. 4133 has a punched out "ñ."

E-Commerce A1893

2016, July 4 Litho. *Perf. 13¾*
4134 A1893 45c multi 1.00 .50

No. 4134 has a punched out "ñ."

Admission of Spain to European Union, 30th Anniv. A1894

Litho. & Embossed
2016, July 7 *Die Cut Perf. 13*
Self-Adhesive
4135 A1894 A2 multi 1.25 .65

No. 4135 sold for 57c on day of issue.

Spain as 2015-16 Member of United Nations Security Council A1895

2016, July 7 Litho. *Perf. 13¾x13¼*
4136 A1895 €1.30 multi 3.00 1.50

No. 4136 has a punched out "ñ."

Souvenir Sheet

Echo, Sculpture by Jaume Plensa — A1896

Litho. & Embossed
2016, July 14 *Perf. 12¾*
4137 A1896 €5 multi 11.50 11.00

No. 4137 has a punched out "ñ."

Protected Fauna A1897

Designs: 45c, Caballito de mar (seahorse). 57c, Visón europeo riojano (European mink). €1.15, Cangrejo de rio (crayfish, 75x37mm).

Perf. 13¾x13¼, 13 (#4140)
2016, July 18 Litho.
4138-4140 A1897 Set of 3 5.00 2.50

Nos. 4138-4140 have a punched out "ñ."

Song of the Sybil, Mallorca, UNESCO Intangible Asset of Cultural Heritage A1898

2016, July 20 Litho. *Perf. 13¾x13¼*
4141 A1898 €1.30 multi 3.00 1.50

No. 4141 has a punched out "ñ."

King Ferdinand II of Aragon (Ferdinand the Catholic), (1452-1516) — A1899

Perf. 13¾x13¼
2016, Sept. 14 Litho.
4142 A1899 45c multi 1.00 .50

No. 4142 has a punched out "ñ."

Souvenir Sheet

Skylight and Columns of Palacio de Sastago, Zaragoza — A1900

Engr., Sheet Margin Litho. & Silk-Screened
2016, Sept. 14 *Perf. 13¼x12¾*
4143 A1900 €2.95 multi 6.75 6.75

Exfilna 2016 National Philatelic Exhibition, Zaragoza. No. 4143 has a punched out "ñ."

Souvenir Sheet

Mail Truck, Sorting Equipment and Delivery — A1901

Litho. & Engr., Sheet Margin Litho. & Embossed With Foil Application

2016, Sept. 14 ***Perf. 12½***

4144 A1901 €3 multi 6.75 6.75

Spanish Mail Service, 300th anniv. No. 4144 has a punched out "ñ."

Miniature Sheet

Solidarity — A1902

No. 4145 — Words visible when letters printed in thermochromic ink are warmed, finishing phrase starting with "Solidaridad": a, "Con los enfermos." b, "Con las discapacidad." c, "Contra el maltrato." d, "Con la tercera edad." e, "Con los necesitados." f, "Contra el racismo."

Litho. & Silk-Screened

2016, Sept. 21 ***Perf. 13¾x13¼***

4145 A1902 Sheet of 6 7.50 7.50
a.-f. 57c Any single 1.25 .65

Nos. 4145a-4145f have a punched out "ñ."

Flag of India and Taj Mahal — A1903

2016, Sept. 23 Litho. ***Perf. 13x13¾***

4146 A1903 €1.30 multi 3.00 1.50

No. 4146 has a punched out "ñ."

Souvenir Sheet

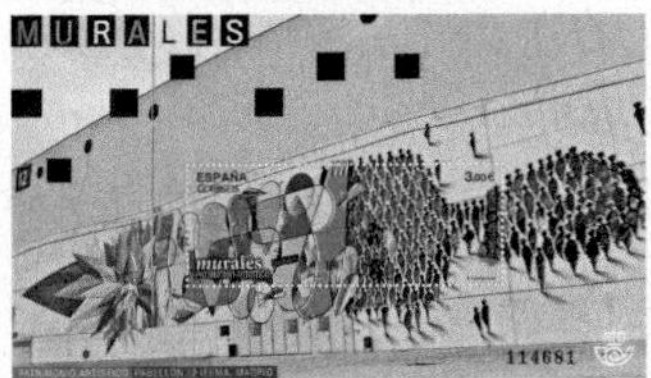

Mural by Six Graffiti Artists, Madrid — A1904

IFEMA murals on Hall 12.

2016, Sept. 23 Litho. ***Perf. 13x13¼***

4147 A1904 €3 multi 6.75 6.75

No. 4147 has a punched out "ñ."

Antonio de Ulloa (1716-95), Explorer, Scientist and First Spanish Governor of Louisiana A1905

Perf. 13¾x13¼

2016, Sept. 26 **Litho.**

4148 A1905 €1.30 multi 3.00 1.50

No. 4148 has a punched out "ñ."

Antonio Buero Vallejo (1916-2000), Playwright — A1906

2016, Oct. 3 Litho. ***Perf. 13¾x13¼***

4149 A1906 45c multi 1.00 .50

No. 4149 has a punched out "ñ."

Souvenir Sheet

2016 Two-Euro Coin Depicting Segovia Aqueduct — A1907

2016, Oct. 6 Litho. & Engr. ***Perf.***

4150 A1907 €5 multi 11.00 11.00

No. 4137 was sold folded and has a punched out "ñ."

Souvenir Sheet

Toyota Celica Race Car of Carlos Sainz — A1908

Litho. & Silk-Screened

2016, Oct. 7 ***Perf. 13¾x13¼***

4151 A1908 €3 multi 6.75 6.75

No. 4151 has a punched out "ñ."

Rural Architecture — A1909

No. 4152: a, Waterwheel, Albolafia. b, Cigarral near Toledo. c, Andalusian farm house, horse and rider, Cortijo.

2016, Oct. 10 Litho. ***Perf. 12¾x13¼***

4152 A1909 Vert. strip of 3 8.00 8.00
a.-c. €1.15 Any single 2.60 1.40

Nos. 4152a-4152c have a punched out "ñ."

Stained-Glass Window, Cathedral of Santo Domingo de la Calzada — A1910

2016, Oct. 14 Litho. ***Perf. 13¼x13¾***

4153 A1910 €1.30 multi 3.00 1.50

No. 4153 has a punched out "ñ."

Miniature Sheet

The 1950's — A1911

No. 4154: a, Vespa scooter and SEAT 600 automobile (47x35mm). b, Televisions and test patterns (46x28mm). c, Sputnik and dog, Laika (51x28mm). d, Nobel laureates Juan Ramón Jiménez (Literature, 1956), and Severo Ochoa (Physiology or Medicine, 1959) (46x38mm).

2016, Oct. 20 Photo. ***Perf. 14¼***

4154 A1911 Sheet of 4 8.00 8.00
a. 45c multi 1.00 .50
b. 57c multi 1.25 .60
c. €1.15 multi 2.60 1.40
d. €1.30 multi 3.00 1.50

Nos. 4154a-4154d have a punched out "ñ."

61st Valladolid International Film Festival (Seminci) — A1912

2016, Oct. 24 Litho. ***Perf. 12¾x12½***

4155 A1912 57c multi 1.25 .60

No. 4155 has a punched out "ñ."

Movie Stars — A1913

No. 4156: a, Amparo Rivelles (1925-2013). b, Luis Mariano (1914-70)

2016, Oct. 24 Litho. ***Perf. 13¼x13¾***

4156 A1913 Horiz. pair 6.00 3.00
a.-b. €1.30 Either single 3.00 1.50

Nos. 4156a-4156b have a punched out "ñ."

University of Salamanca, 800th Anniv. (in 2018) — A1914

2016, Oct. 26 Litho. ***Perf. 13¾x13¼***

4157 A1914 €1.30 multi 3.00 1.50

No. 4157 has a punched out "ñ."

Spanish Television, 60th Anniv. A1915

2016, Oct. 28 Litho. ***Perf. 13¾x13¼***

4158 A1915 45c multi 1.00 .50

No. 4158 has a punched out "ñ."

Bells — A1916

Virgin Mary, Santo Domingo de la Calzada Cathedral A1917

Litho. & Embossed

2016, Nov. 4 ***Die Cut Perf. 13***

Self-Adhesive

4159 A1916 A multi .95 .50
4160 A1917 B multi 2.50 1.25

Christmas. On day of issue, No. 4159 sold for 45c; No. 4160, €1.15. Die cutting surrounds the image of the Virgin Mary on No. 4160.

Currency — A1918

No. 4161: a, 1971 1000-peseta banknote (58x41mm). b, 1927 25-centimo coin (41x41mm).

Litho. (#4161a), Litho & Embossed with Foil Application (#4161b)

2016, Nov. 8 ***Perf. 13¼x13¾***

4161 A1918 Horiz. pair 8.50 4.25
a.-b. €2 Either single 4.25 2.10

Nos. 4161a-4161b have a punched out "ñ."

Abbreviations of Spanish Provinces A1919

Abbreviation: No. 4162, "GU" (Guadalajara). No. 4163, "CC" (Cáceres). No. 4164, "CA" (Cádiz). No. 4165, "B" (Barcelona). No. 4166, "A" (Asturias). No. 4167, "CO" (Córdoba). No.

4168, "T" (Tarragona). No. 4169, "TE" (Teruel). No. 4170, "SO" (Soria). No. 4171, "IB" (Balearic Islands). No. 4172, "LP" (Las Palmas). No. 4173, "TF" (Santa Cruz de Tenerife).

Litho. & Embossed

2017 ***Die Cut Perf. 13***

Self-Adhesive

4162	A1919	A multi	1.10	.55
4163	A1919	A multi	1.10	.55
4164	A1919	A multi	1.10	.55
4165	A1919	A multi	1.10	.55
4166	A1919	A multi	1.10	.55
4167	A1919	A multi	1.10	.55
4168	A1919	A multi	1.10	.55
4169	A1919	A multi	1.25	.60
4170	A1919	A multi	1.25	.60
4171	A1919	B multi	3.00	1.50
4172	A1919	C multi	3.25	1.60
4173	A1919	C multi	3.25	1.60
	Nos. 4162-4173 (10)		17.20	8.55

Issued: No. 4162, 1/2; Nos. 4163-4164, 2/1; No. 4165, 4/3; Nos. 4166-4167, 5/2; No. 4168, 6/1; No. 4169, 10/2; No. 4170, 11/2; No. 4171, 9/1; No. 4172, 7/3; No. 4173, 8/1. On day of issue, Nos. 4162-4170 each sold for 50c; No. 4171, for €1.25; Nos. 4172-4173 each sold for €1.35.

See Nos. 4239-4250. Compare type A1919 with type A2046.

Publication of *Rules of Spanish Orthography,* by Antonio de Nebrija (1444-1522), 500th Anniv. — A1920

2017, Jan. 16 Litho. ***Perf. 13¾x13¼***

4174 A1920 50c multi 1.10 .55

No. 4174 has a punched out "ñ."

International Year of Sustainable Tourism fro Development A1921

Dandelion seed head and footprints: €1.25, On beach. €1.35, In snow.

Litho. & Embossed

2017, Jan. 17 ***Die Cut Perf. 13***

Self-Adhesive

4175-4176 A1921 Set of 2 5.75 2.75

Cardinal Gonzalo Jiménez de Cisneros (1436-1517) — A1922

2017, Jan. 19 Litho. ***Perf. 13¾x13¼***

4177 A1922 B multi 2.75 1.40

No. 4177 sold for €1.25 on day of issue and has a punched out "ñ."

Huelva, 2017 Spanish Capital of Gastronomy — A1923

2017, Jan. 20 Litho. ***Perf. 13¼x13¾***

4178 A1923 A2 multi 1.40 .70

No. 4178 sold for 60c on day of issue and has a punched out "ñ."

Gabriel de Castilla Antarctic Base A1924

Litho. & Thermography

2017, Jan. 30 ***Perf. 14¼x14***

4179 A1924 C multi 3.00 1.50

No. 4179 sold for €1.35 on day of issue.

King Felipe VI Type of 2016

2017, Feb. 1 Litho. ***Perf. 12¾x13¼***

4180 A1855 5c brt grn & blk .25 .25

No. 4180 has a punched out "ñ."

Origami Elephants, by Eduardo M. Gea Martínez A1925

Broken Egg, by Alicia Esteban Esteban A1926

Litho. & Embossed

2017, Feb. 1 ***Die Cut Perf. 13***

Self-Adhesive

4181 A1925 50c multi 1.10 .55
4182 A1926 50c multi 1.10 .55

Winning designs in stamp design contest.

Houses and Pen Nib A1927

2017, Feb. 3 Litho. ***Perf. 13¾x13¼***

4183 A1927 €1 multi 1.10 .55

Vicente Blasco Ibañez (1867-1928), writer. No. 4183 has a punched out "ñ."

Souvenir Sheet

Reopening of Teatro Real Opera House, Madrid, 20th Anniv. — A1928

2017, Feb. 10 Litho. ***Perf. 12¾x13***

4184 A1928 €3.15 multi 6.75 6.75

No. 4184 was sold folded and has a punched out "ñ."

King Felipe II and Map of El Camino Español — A1929

Perf. 13¼x13¾

2017, Feb. 23 Litho.

4185 A1929 €2 multi 4.25 2.10

El Camino Español, 450th anniv. No. 4185 has a punched out "ñ."

Madonna with a Napkin, by Bartolomé Esteban Murillo (1617-82) A1930

2017, Feb. 28 Litho. ***Perf. 13¾***

4186 A1930 €1 multi 2.10 1.10

No. 4186 has a punched out "ñ." Value is for stamp with surrounding selvage.

Villages — A1931

No. 4187: a, Aínsa. b, Calatayud. c, Lastres. d, Urueña.

Litho. & Embossed

2017, Mar. 10 ***Die Cut Perf. 13***

Self-Adhesive

4187 Booklet pane of 4 4.50
a.-d. A1931 A Any single 1.10 .55

Nos. 4187a-4187d each sold for 50c on day of issue.

Málaga Film Festival — A1932

Litho. & Embossed

2017, Mar. 17 ***Die Cut Perf. 13***

Self-Adhesive On Clear Plastic Film

4188 A1932 60c multi 1.25 .65

Humanitarian Aviation — A1933

Perf. 13¾x13¼

2017, Mar. 21 Litho.

4189 A1933 €1.35 multi 3.00 1.50

No. 4189 has a punched out "ñ."

Museums — A1934

Designs: No. 4190, 60c, Pompidou Center, Málaga. No. 4191, 60c, Museum of La Rioja, Logroño. No. 4192, 60c, National Museum of Underwater Archaeology, Cartagena.

2017, Mar. 27 Litho. ***Perf. 13x13¼***

4190-4192 A1934 Set of 3 4.00 2.00

Nos. 4190-4192 have a punched out "ñ."

Souvenir Sheet

Cartoon by Quino — A1935

2017, Mar. 31 Litho. ***Perf. 12½***

4193 A1935 €3.15 multi 6.75 6.75

No. 4193 has a punched out "ñ."

Easter Week Traditions and Customs Type of 2016

No. 4194 — Traditions and customs in: a, Cáceres. b, Zamora. c, Málaga. d, Aragón.

Litho. & Embossed

2017, Apr. 5 ***Die Cut Perf. 13***

Booklet Stamps

Self-Adhesive

4194 Block of 4 9.00
a.-d. A1871 €1 Any single 2.25 1.10
Complete booklet, 2 each #4194a-4194d 18.00

Traditional Dance A1936

Litho. & Embossed

2017, Apr. 6 ***Die Cut Perf. 13***

Self-Adhesive

4195 A1936 A multi 1.10 .55

On day of issue, No. 4195 sold for 50c.

Manzanares el Real Castle, Madrid A1937

Litho. & Embossed

2017, Apr. 21 ***Die Cut Perf. 13***

Self-Adhesive

4196 A1937 B multi 2.75 1.40

Europa. On day of issue, No. 4196 sold for €1.25.

Lebaniego Jubilee Year A1938

2017, Apr. 23 Litho. ***Perf. 13¾x13¼***

4197 A1938 50c multi 1.10 .55

No. 4197 has a punched out "ñ."

Royal Company of Midshipmen, 300th Anniv. — A1939

2017, Apr. 28 Litho. *Perf. 13¼x13¾*

4198 A1939 €1.25 multi 2.75 1.40

No. 4198 has a punched out "ñ."

Souvenir Sheets

19th Century History of Spain — A1940

20th Century History of Spain — A1941

2017, May 3 Litho. *Perf. 13x13½*

4199 A1940 €3 multi + 12 labels 6.75 6.75
4200 A1941 €3 multi + 12 labels 6.75 6.75

Nos. 4199-4200 each have a punched out "ñ."

Battle of Llanos de la Victoria, 1255th Anniv. A1942

Perf. 13¾x13¼

2017, May 5 Litho. & Engr.

4201 A1942 60c multi 1.40 .70

No. 4201 has a punched out "ñ."

Miniature Sheet

La Abadia del Crimen Video Game, 30th Anniv. — A1943

No. 4202 — Image visible when gray door printed with thermochromic ink is warmed: a, Table. b, Horseman. c, Key. d, Scroll. e, Oil lamp. f, Glasses.

Litho. & Silk-Screened

2017, May 8 *Perf. 15¼*

4202 A1943 Sheet of 6 8.50 8.50
a.-f. 60c Any single 1.40 .70

Nos. 4202a-4202f each have a punched out "ñ."

Juvenia 2017 Youth Philatelic Exhibition, Avilés A1944

2017, May 10 Litho. *Perf. 13¾x13¼*

4203 A1944 50c multi 1.10 .55

No. 4203 has a punched out "ñ."

Souvenir Sheet

Obverse of 2017 Two-Euro Coin Depicting Monuments of Oviedo and the Kingdom of Asturias UNESCO World Heritage Site — A1945

2017, May 10 Litho. & Engr. *Perf.*

4204 A1945 €5 multi 11.50 11.50

No. 4204 has a punched out "ñ." Sheet was sold folded.

Jurisdiction of Najera, 1000th Anniv. A1946

2017, June 5 Litho. *Perf. 13¾x13¼*

4205 A1946 €1.25 multi 2.75 1.40

No. 4205 has a punched out "ñ."

Souvenir Sheet

Darth Vader from *Star Wars* — A1947

Litho. With 3-Dimensional Plastic Affixed

2017, May 23 *Perf. 14½*

4206 A1947 €5 multi + 5 labels 11.50 11.50

Lina Morgan (1936-2015), Actress — A1948

Vicente Aranda (1926-2015), Film Director — A1949

2017, May 25 Litho. *Perf. 13¼x13¾*

4207 A1948 50c multi 1.10 .55

Perf. 13¾x13¼

4208 A1949 50c multi 1.10 .55

Nos. 4207-4208 each have a punched out "ñ."

UNICEF, 70th Anniv. (in 2016) A1950

Litho. & Embossed

2017, June 1 *Die Cut Perf. 13*

Self-Adhesive

4209 A1950 A2 multi 1.40 .70

On day of issue, No. 4209 sold for 60c.

National Day of Spanish Sign Language A1951

Perf. 13¾x13¹³⁄₁₆

2017, June 14 Litho.

4210 A1951 50c multi 1.25 .60

No. 4210 has a punched out "ñ."

Miniature Sheets

The 1960's — A1952

The 1970's — A1953

No. 4211: a, First heart transplant by Dr. Christiaan Barnard (35x34mm). b, Footprint of first man on the Moon (33x35mm). c, May 1968 demonstrations in France (47x31mm). d, Assassination of Pres. John F. Kennedy (49x34mm).

No. 4212: a, Transition of democracy in Spain (41x32mm). b, Development of optical fiber technology (48x30mm). c, Election of Pope John Paul II (45x30mm). d, Invention of disposable syringes (49x32mm).

2017, July 10 Photo. *Perf.*

4211 A1952 Sheet of 4 9.00 9.00
a. 50c multi 1.25 .60
b. 60c multi 1.40 .70
c. €1.25 multi 3.00 1.50
d. €1.35 multi 3.25 1.60
4212 A1953 Sheet of 4 9.00 9.00
a. 50c multi 1.25 .60
b. 60c multi 1.40 .70
c. €1.25 multi 3.00 1.50
d. €1.35 multi 3.25 1.60

Nos. 4211a-4211d, 4212a-4212d have a punched out "ñ."

Tragsa Group, 40th Anniv. A1954

2017, July 12 Litho. *Perf. 13¾x13¼*

4213 A1954 €1.35 multi 3.25 1.60

No. 4213 has a punched out "ñ."

Dolmens of Antequera UNESCO World Heritage Site A1955

2017, July 14 Litho. *Perf. 13¾x13¼*

4214 A1955 €3.15 multi 7.50 3.75

No. 4214 has a punched out "ñ."

Souvenir Sheet

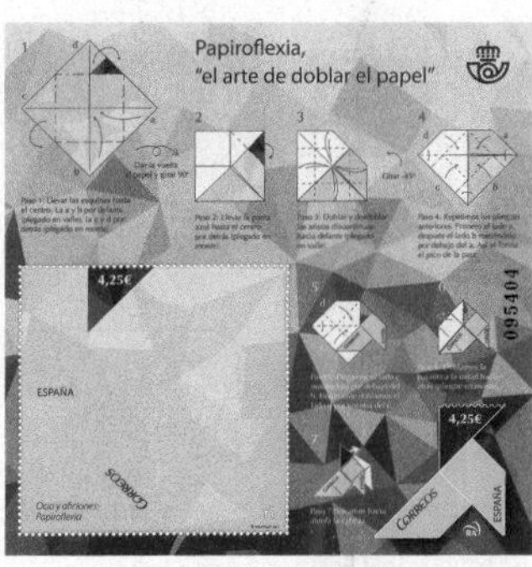

Origami — A1956

Litho. & Embossed

2017, July 17 *Perf. 13¼*

4215 A1956 €4.25 multi 10.00 10.00

No. 4215 has a punched out "ñ." The stamp can be folded to create an origami bird.

Souvenir Sheet

Se Pinta de Violeta, Photograph by Alberto Schommer (1928-2015) — A1957

Litho. With Foil Application

2017, July 20 *Perf. 13½x13¼*

4216 A1957 €4 multi 9.50 9.50

No. 4216 has a punched out "ñ."

Flag of Peru and Machu Picchu — A1958

Perf. 12¾x13¼

2017, Sept. 14 **Litho.**

4217 A1958 €1.35 multi 3.25 1.60

No. 4217 has a punched out "ñ."

Potter at Work and Finished Jar — A1959

Litho., Embossed & Silk-Screened

2017, Sept. 15 ***Perf. 12¾x13¼***

4218 A1959 €1.35 multi 3.25 1.60

No. 4218 has a punched out "ñ."

Camilo José Cela (1916-2002), 1989 Nobel Laureate in Literature — A1960

Perf. 13¾x13¼

2017, Sept. 15 **Litho.**

4219 A1960 €1.35 multi 3.25 1.60

No. 4219 has a punched out "ñ."

Miguel Hernández (1910-42), Poet A1961

Perf. 13¾x13¼

2017, Sept. 15 **Litho.**

4220 A1961 €2 multi 4.75 2.40

No. 4220 has a punched out "ñ."

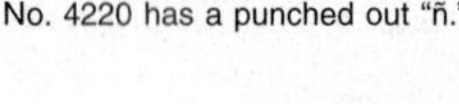

José Maximiano Zorrilla (1817-93), Poet — A1962

Perf. 13¼x13¾

2017, Sept. 15 **Litho.**

4221 A1962 €2 multi 4.75 2.40

No. 4221 has a punched out "ñ."

Souvenir Sheet

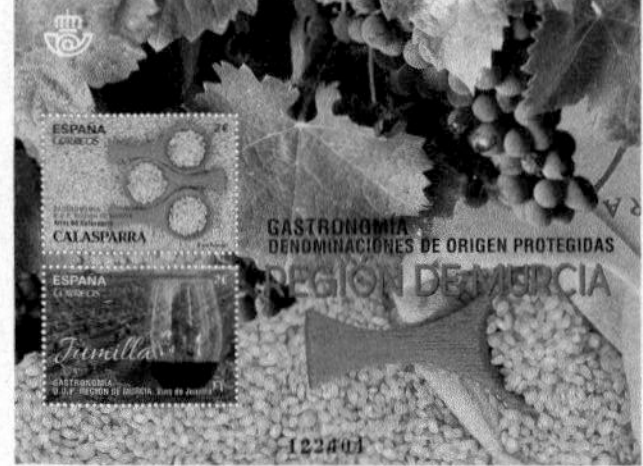

Spanish Cuisine — A1963

No. 4222 — Products of Murcia: a, Calasparra rice. b, Jumilla wine.

Perf. 13¾x13¼

2017, Sept. 20 **Litho.**

4222 A1963 Sheet of 2 9.50 9.50

a.-b. €2 Either single 4.75 2.40

Nos. 4222a-4222b have a punched out "ñ."

Erasmus Scholarships, 30th Anniv. — A1964

2017, Oct. 4 **Litho.** ***Perf. 13x13½***

4223 A1964 €1.25 multi 3.00 1.50

No. 4223 has a punched out "ñ."

Souvenir Sheet

Barros Stelae — A1965

Litho., Sheet Margin Litho. & Embossed

2017, Oct. 5 ***Perf. 13¾x14***

4224 A1965 €5 multi 12.00 12.00

A gritty substance is affixed to portions of the sheet margin.

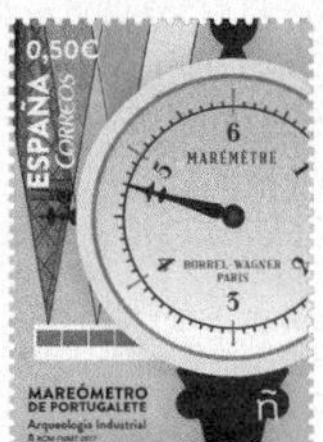

1883 Tide Gauge — A1966

2017, Oct. 9 **Litho.** ***Perf. 13¼x13¾***

4225 A1966 50c multi 1.25 .60

No. 4225 has a punched out "ñ."

Expo '92, Seville, 25th Anniv. A1967

2017, Oct. 9 **Litho.** ***Perf. 13¾x13¼***

4226 A1967 €1.35 multi 3.25 1.60

No. 4226 has a punched out "ñ."

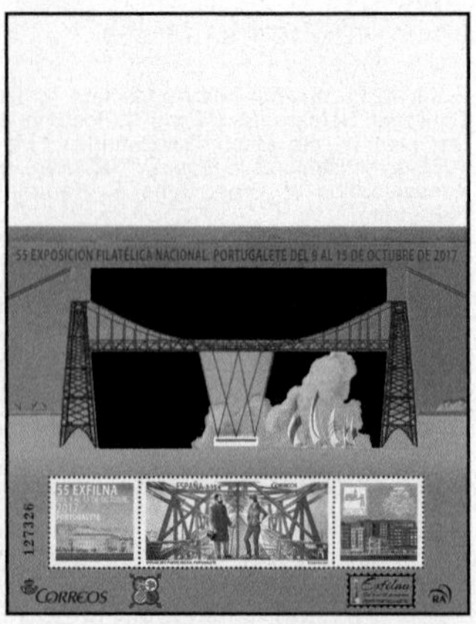

Vizcaya Bridge, Portugalete (unfolded) — A1968

Litho. & Engr.

2017, Oct. 9 ***Perf. 13x12¾***

4227 A1968 €3.15 multi 7.50 7.50

EXFILNA 2017 National Philatelic Exhibition, Portugalete. No. 4227 has a punched out "ñ" and was sold with a fold in the margin so an illustration on the back of the sheet margin would appear in the die cut window in the margin.

Spain in European Council, 40th Anniv. A1969

2017, Oct. 11 **Litho.** ***Perf. 13¾x13¼***

4228 A1969 50c multi 1.25 .60

No. 4228 has a punched out "ñ."

Carnation and Tilde — A1970

Litho. & Embossed

2017, Oct. 13 ***Die Cut Perf. 13***

Self-Adhesive

4229 A1970 C multi 3.25 1.60

America Issue. No. 4229 sold for €1.35 on day of issue.

Tuna Guitarist — A1971

2017, Oct. 18 **Litho.** ***Perf. 13¼x13¾***

4230 A1971 50c multi 1.25 .60

No. 4230 has a punched out "ñ."

Albecete Bullring, Cent. A1972

2017, Oct. 20 **Litho.** ***Perf. 13¾x13¼***

4231 A1972 €1.35 multi 3.25 1.60

No. 4231 has a punched out "ñ."

Souvenir Sheet

Granada UNESCO World Heritage Site — A1973

No. 4232 — Alhambra: a, Torre de Comares. b, Nasrid Palaces.

Engr., Sheet Margin Litho. & Engr.

2017, Oct. 27 ***Perf. 13¾x13¼***

4232 A1973 Sheet of 2 15.00 15.00

a.-b. €3.15 Either single 7.50 3.75

Nos. 4232a-4232b have a punched out "ñ."

Roman Coins Depicting Emperors Trajan and Hadrian — A1974

Litho. & Embossed With Foil Application

2017, Nov. 3 ***Perf. 13½***

4233 A1974 €3 multi 7.25 3.75

No. 4233 has a punched out "ñ." Values are for stamps with surrounding selvage.

High-Speed Trains in Spain, 25th Anniv. — A1975

Perf. 13 on 3 Sides

2017, Nov. 6 **Litho.**

4234 A1975 €1.25 multi + 2 labels 3.00 1.50

No. 4234 has a punched out "ñ."

Star — A1976

St. Joseph A1977

Litho. & Embossed

2017, Nov. 8 ***Die Cut Perf. 13***

Self-Adhesive

4235 A1976 A multi 1.25 .60

4236 A1977 B multi 3.00 1.50

Christmas. On day of issue, No. 4235 sold for 50c; No. 4236, for €1.25. Die cutting surrounds the image of the star on No. 4235 and St. Joseph on No. 4236.

Emblem and Headquarters of State Society of Industrial Participation, Madrid — A1978

2017, Nov. 9 **Litho.** ***Perf. 13***

4237 A1978 €1.35 multi 3.25 1.60

No. 4237 has a punched out "ñ."

Souvenir Sheet

Explorers of Oceania — A1979

No. 4238: a, Luis Váez de Torres, namesake of Torres Strait. b, Pedro Fernández de Quirós (1565-1614), discover of Espiritu Santo Island, Vanuatu.

Litho. & Embossed
2017, Nov. 10 ***Die Cut Perf. 13***
Self-Adhesive
On Wood Veneer

4238	A1979	Sheet of 2	6.50	6.50
a.-b.		€1.35 Either single	3.25	1.60

Abbreviations of Provinces Type of 2017

Abbreviation: No. 4239, "CU" (Cuenca). No. 4240, "GI" (Girona). No. 4241, "M" (Madrid. No. 4242, "LE" (León). No. 4243, "A" (Alicante). No. 4244, "TO" (Toledo). No. 4245, "ZA" (Zamora). No. 4246, "VA" (Valladolid). No. 4247, "MA" (Málaga). No. 4248, "NA" (Navarra). No. 4249, "SE" (Seville). No. 4250, "AV" (Avila).

Litho. & Embossed
2018 ***Die Cut Perf. 13***
Self-Adhesive

4239	A1919	A multi	1.40	.70
4240	A1919	A multi	1.40	.70
4241	A1919	A multi	1.40	.70
4242	A1919	A multi	1.40	.70
4243	A1919	A multi	1.40	.70
4244	A1919	A multi	1.40	.70
4245	A1919	A multi	1.40	.70
4246	A1919	A multi	1.40	.70
4247	A1919	A multi	1.40	.70
4248	A1919	A multi	1.40	.70
4249	A1919	A multi	1.40	.70
4250	A1919	A multi	1.25	.65
	Nos. 4239-4250 (12)		16.65	8.35

Issued: No. 4239, 1/2; No. 4240, 2/1; No. 4241, 3/1. No. 4242, 4/2; Nos. 4243-4244, 5/3; No. 4245, 6/1; No. 4246, 7/2; No. 4247, 8/1; No. 4248, 9/3; No. 4249, 10/1. No. 4250, 11/2. Nos. 4239-4250 each sold for 55c on day of issue.

Biomedical Research in Spain A1980

Litho. & Embossed
2018, Jan. 2 ***Die Cut Perf. 13***
Self-Adhesive

4251	A1980	A multi	1.40	.70

No. 4251 sold for 55c on day of issue.

Tourism — A1981

Designs: €1.35, Beach sandal. €1.45, Mountaineering boot.

Litho. & Embossed
2018, Jan. 9 ***Die Cut Perf. 13***
Self-Adhesive

4252-4253	A1981	Set of 2	7.00	3.50

Madrid Protocol on Environmental Protection to the Antarctic Treaty, 20th Anniv. — A1982

2018, Jan. 10 Litho. ***Perf. 13¾x13¼***

4254	A1982	€1.45 multi	3.75	1.90

No. 4254 has a punched out "ñ."

Festival of St. Anthony on the Balearic Islands — A1983

2018, Jan. 12 Litho. ***Perf. 13¼x13¾***

4255	A1983	A multi	1.40	.70

No. 4255 sold for 55c on day of issue and has a punched out "ñ."

Relocation of House of Trade to Cádiz, 300th Anniv. A1984

2018, Jan. 16 Litho. ***Perf. 13¾x13¼***

4256	A1984	B multi	3.50	1.75

No. 4256 sold for €1.35 on day of issue and has a punched out "ñ."

León, 2018 Spanish Capital of Gastronomy — A1985

2018, Jan. 17 Litho. ***Perf. 13¼x13¾***

4257	A1985	A2 multi	1.60	.80

No. 4257 sold for 65c on day of issue and has a punched out "ñ."

National Center of Intelligence Headquarters, Madrid A1986

Litho. & Embossed
2018, Jan. 23 ***Die Cut Perf. 13***
Self-Adhesive

4258	A1986	C multi	3.75	1.90

No. 4258 sold for €1.45 on day of issue.

Souvenir Sheet

Obverse of 2018 Two-Euro Coin Depicting St. James and Santiago de Compostela Cathedral Doors — A1987

2018, Jan. 28 Litho. & Engr. ***Perf.***

4259	A1987	€3 multi	7.50	7.00

Santiago de Compostela UNESCO World Heritage Site. No. 4259 has a punched out "ñ."

King Felipe VI, 50th Birthday A1988

Litho. With Foil Application
2018, Jan. 30 ***Perf. 13¾x13¼***

4260	A1988	€1 sil & multi	2.50	1.25

No. 4260 has a punched out "ñ."

A1989

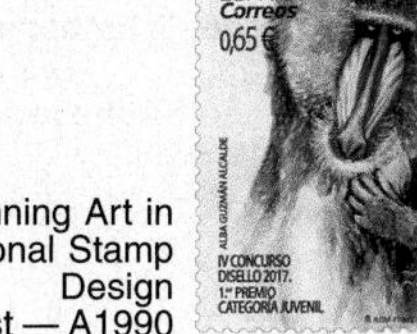

Winning Art in National Stamp Design Contest — A1990

Litho. & Embossed
2018, Feb. 5 ***Die Cut Perf. 13***
Self-Adhesive

4261	A1989	55c multi	1.40	.70
4262	A1990	65c multi	1.60	.80

Circuses, 250th Anniv. — A1991

2018, Feb. 9 Litho. ***Perf. 13¼x13¾***

4263	A1991	€1.35 multi	3.25	1.60

No. 4263 has a punched out "ñ."

Souvenir Sheet

Painting From "Parmi les Peintres" Series, by Eduardo Arroyo — A1992

2018, Feb. 14 Litho. ***Perf. 12***

4264	A1992	€5 multi	12.50	12.50

No. 4264 has a punched out "ñ."

Villages — A1993

No. 4265: a, El Castell de Guadalest. b, Villanueva de la Jara. c, Chinchón. d, Fornalutx.

Litho. & Embossed
2018, Mar. 13 ***Die Cut Perf. 13***
Self-Adhesive

4265		Booklet pane of 4	5.75	
a.-d.		A1993 A Any single	1.40	.70

Nos. 4265a-4265d each sold for 55c on day of issue.

Souvenir Sheet

Victory of Spanish National Men's Handball Team at 2018 European Championships — A1994

Perf. 13 at Left and Right
2018, Mar. 23 **Litho.**

4266	A1994	€1.35 multi	3.50	3.50

No. 4266 has a punched out "ñ."

Museums — A1995

Designs: No. 4267, 65c, Guggenheim Museum Bilbao, Bilbao. No. 4268, 65c, Cantabrian Maritime Museum, Santander. No.

4269, 65c, Museum conservators, 150th anniv.

2018, Mar. 26 Litho. *Perf. 13x13¼*
4267-4269 A1995 Set of 3 5.00 2.50

Nos. 4267-4269 have a punched out "ñ."

Northern Way of St. James A1996

No. 4270 — Map of Northern Way of St. James in: a, Galicia, and entrance to Royal Hospital of Santiago (35x25mm). b, Asturias, Church of San Salvador de Valdediós, Villaviciosa (35x24mm). c, Cantabria, Church of Santa Juliana, Santillana del Mar (35x18mm). d, Basque Country, sculpture from Zenarruza Monastery (35x17mm).

Litho. & Embossed With Foil Application
Die Cut Perf. 13 on 3 or 4 Sides
2018, Apr. 3 Self-Adhesive
Booklet Stamps

4270 Horiz. strip of 4 13.50
a.-b. A1996 €1.35 Either single 3.25 1.60
c.-d. A1996 €1.45 Either single 3.50 1.75
e. Booklet pane of 8, 2 each #4270a-4270d 27.00

Castle of San Jose de Valderas, Alcorcón A1997

Litho. & Embossed
2018, Apr. 10 *Die Cut Perf. 13*
Self-Adhesive
4271 A1997 B multi 3.25 1.60

On day of issue, No. 4271 sold for €1.35.

Souvenir Sheet

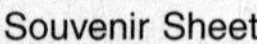

Premiere of Movie *Solo: A Star Wars Story* — A1998

Litho. With Three-Dimensional Plastic Affixed
2018, Apr. 13 *Perf. 14¾*
4272 A1998 €5 multi 12.00 12.00

Souvenir Sheet

Statue of King Philip III in Plaza Mayor, Madrid — A1999

Engr., Sheet Margin Litho.
2018, Apr. 19 *Perf. 13x13¾*
4273 A1999 €5 multi 12.00 12.00

Plaza Mayor, 400th anniv.; National Stamp Fair, 50th anniv. No. 4273 has a punched out "ñ."

La Maza Bridge, San Vicente de la Barquera — A2000

2018, Apr. 23 Litho. *Perf. 13¾x13¼*
4274 A2000 B multi 3.25 1.60

Europa. No. 4274 has a punched out "ñ" and sold for €1.35 on day of issue. The bridge in the design is laser-cut.

Souvenir Sheet

Caricature of Francisco de Quevedo (1580-1645), Writer, by Ricardo Martínez — A2001

2018, Apr. 27 Litho. *Perf. 12½*
4275 A2001 €3.30 multi 8.00 8.00

International Exhibition of Comic Art, 25th anniv. No. 4275 has a punched out "ñ."

New Ourense Bridge, Cent. A2002

2018, May 11 Litho. *Perf. 13¾x13¼*
4276 A2002 €1.35 multi 3.25 1.60

No. 4276 has a punched out "ñ."

La Celestina Festival, La Puebla de Montalbán — A2003

Litho. & Embossed
2018, May 23 *Die Cut Perf. 13*
Self-Adhesive
4277 A2003 A2 multi 1.50 .75

No. 4274 sold for 65c on day of issue.

Souvenir Sheet

Léon Cathedral — A2004

Litho. & Embossed With Foil Application
2018, May 25 *Perf. 12¾x13*
4278 A2004 A multi 1.40 1.40

No. 4278 sold for 55c on day of issue and has punched out cathedral windows and "ñ." The sheet margin depicts a revised version of No. 4242, replacing the Church of San Isidoro in Asturias with Léon Cathedral that is not valid for postage.

150th Anniv. of Visit to Spain of David G. Farragut (1801-70), U.S. Admiral A2005

2018, June 8 Litho. *Perf. 13¾x13¼*
4279 A2005 55c multi 1.25 .65

No. 4279 has a punched out "ñ."

2018 World Cup Soccer Championships, Russia — A2006

2018, June 8 Litho. *Perf. 13¾x13¼*
4280 A2006 €2 multi 4.75 2.40

No. 4280 has a punched out "ñ."

Royal Spanish Olympic Academy, 50th Anniv. A2007

Perf. 13¾x13¼
2018, June 14 Litho.
4281 A2007 €1.35 multi 3.25 1.60

No. 4281 has a punched out "ñ."

Mariemma (1917-2008), Dancer — A2008

Perf. 13¾x13¼
2018, June 18 Litho.
4282 A2008 55c multi 1.25 .65

No. 4282 has a punched out "ñ."

Gloria Fuertes (1917-98), Poet — A2009

Perf. 13¼x13¾
2018, June 18 Litho. & Engr.
4283 A2009 €1.35 multi 3.25 1.60

No. 4283 has a punched out "ñ."

Woman and Child — A2010

Perf. 13¾x13¼
2018, June 21 Litho.
4284 A2010 55c multi + label 1.25 .65

No. 4284 has a punched out "ñ." Three percent of the revenue of the sale of No. 4284 was being donated by the Spanish Post to the Manos Unidas Educational and Violence Prevention Project in Honduras.

Helen Keller (1880-1968), Deaf and Blind Writer and Activist, and Cane — A2011

Litho. & Embossed
2018, June 27 *Die Cut Perf. 13*
Self-Adhesive
4285 A2011 A multi 1.25 .65

No. 4285 sold for 55c on day of issue.

Chess Pawn A2012

Perf. 13¾x13¼
2018, June 29 Litho.
4286 A2012 €1.45 multi 3.50 1.75

No. 4286 has a punched out "ñ" and is printed with thermochromic ink that changes the pawn's color from black to white when warmed.

General Studies at Palencia University, 800th Anniv. A2013

2018, July 3 Litho. *Perf. 13¾x13¼*
4287 A2013 €1.35 multi 3.25 1.60

No. 4287 has a punched out "ñ."

Spanish Army Air Mobile Force, 50th Anniv. A2014

2018, July 3 Litho. ***Perf. 13¾x13¼***
4288 A2014 €1.35 multi 3.25 1.60

No. 4288 has a punched out "ñ."

Basic Air Academy, 25th Anniv. A2015

2018, July 3 Litho. ***Perf. 13¾x13¼***
4289 A2015 €1.35 multi 3.25 1.60

No. 4289 has a punched out "ñ."

Possessió Raixa, Mallorca — A2016

2018, July 5 Litho. ***Perf. 12¾x13¼***
4290 A2016 A2 multi 1.50 .75

No. 4289 has a punched out "ñ" and sold for 65c on day of issue.

2017-18 Volvo Ocean Race A2017

2018, July 9 Litho. ***Perf. 13¾x13¼***
4291 A2017 €1.35 multi 3.25 1.60

No. 4291 has a punched out "ñ."

Sheep and Map of the Wool Road A2018

2018, July 16 Litho. ***Perf. 13¾x13¼***
4292 A2018 €1.35 multi 3.25 1.60

No. 4292 has a punched out "ñ."

Alvaro de Mendaña y Neira (1542-95), Discoverer of Solomon Islands and Marquesas Islands — A2019

Litho. & Embossed
2018, July 25 ***Die Cut Perf. 13***
Self-Adhesive
On Wood Veneer
4293 A2019 €3.30 multi 7.75 4.00

Miniature Sheets

The 1980's — A2020

The 1990's — A2021

No. 4294: a, Félix Rodríguez de la Fuente (1928-80), environmentalist, and wild cat (29x35mm). b, Return of democracy to Spain (26x26mm). c, Entrance of Spain in European Economic Union (30x26mm). d, Improved technology (27x23mm).

No. 4295: a, Agreemernt for single European currency (28x17mm). b, Dissolution of the Soviet Union (37x33mm). c, Reunification of Germany (27x25mm). d, Emblems of 1992 Summer Olympics, Barcelona and Expo '92, Seville (35x19mm).

2018, Sept. 10 Photo. ***Perf. 14½***
4294 A2020 Sheet of 4 9.75 9.75
a. 55c multi 1.40 .70
b. 650c multi 1.50 .75
c. €1.35 multi 3.25 1.60
d. €1.45 multi 3.50 1.75
4295 A2021 Sheet of 4 9.75 9.75
a. 55c multi 1.40 .70
b. 650c multi 1.50 .75
c. €1.35 multi 3.25 1.60
d. €1.45 multi 3.50 1.75

Nos. 4294a-4294d, 4295a-4295d have a punched out "ñ."

Last Mail Train in Spain, 25th Anniv. — A2022

Litho. & Embossed
2018, Sept. 14 ***Die Cut Perf. 13***
Self-Adhesive
4296 A2022 €1.35 multi 3.25 1.60

No. 4296 has a punched out rectangle above train car.

Cosme García Sáez (1818-74), Inventor, and His Submarine — A2023

2018, Sept. 21 Litho. ***Die Cut***
Self-Adhesive
Raised Design on Rubber
4297 A2023 €1.35 red brn 3.25 1.60

Leopoldo O'Donnell (1809-67), Prime Minister A2024

Perf. 13¾x13¼
2018, Sept. 21 Litho.
4298 A2024 €1.35 multi 3.25 1.60

No. 4298 has a punched out "ñ."

Spanish Participation in Construction of Mecca-Medina High Speed Rail Line — A2025

Litho. & Thermography
2018, Sept. 24 ***Perf. 13***
4299 A2025 €1.35 multi 3.25 1.60

No. 4299 has a gritty substance added to parts of the design. No. 4299 does not have a punched out "ñ", the coloring came off of paper when embossed.

Stained Glass — A2026

Litho. & Embossed
2018, Sept. 24 ***Die Cut Perf. 13***
Self-Adhesive
On Acetate
4300 A2026 €2 multi 4.75 2.40

Souvenir Sheet

Gastronomy of the Guijuelo Area — A2027

No. 4301: a, Ribera del Duero wine. b, Guijuelo ham.

Perf. 13¾x13¼
2018, Sept. 24 Litho.
4301 A2027 Sheet of 2 9.50 9.50
a.-b. €2 Either single 4.75 2.40

No. 4301 is impregnated with a ham scent. Nos. 4301a-4301b have a punched out "ñ."

Cadastral Management and Tax Cooperation Center, 30th Anniv. — A2028

Perf. 13¾x13¼
2018, Sept. 25 Litho.
4302 A2028 55c multi 1.40 .70

No. 4302 has a punched out "ñ."

Special Operations Group, 40th Anniv. A2029

Perf. 13¾x13¼
2018, Sept. 26 Litho.
4303 A2029 55c multi 1.40 .70

No. 4303 has a punched out "ñ."

Souvenir Sheet

Houses in Cuenca — A2030

Perf. 13¼x13¾
2018, Sept. 28 Litho.
4304 A2030 €5 multi 11.50 11.00

No. 4304 has a punched out "ñ," and is folded and affixed at the sides to a cardboard backing depicting the sky. The illustration shows the sheet as sold.

2018 Sitges Fantasy and Horror Film Festival, Barcelona A2031

2018, Oct. 4 Litho. ***Perf. 12¾x13***
4305 A2031 €1.45 multi 3.50 1.75

No. 4305 has a punched out "ñ."

Monument to Pelagius (c. 685-737), and Basilica of Covadonga A2032

2018, Oct. 5 Litho. ***Perf. 13¾x13¼***
4306 A2032 55c multi 1.25 .65

Kingdom of Asturias, 1300th anniv. No. 4306 has a punched out "ñ."

Christmas
A2033 A2034

Litho. & Embossed
2018, Oct. 8 ***Die Cut Perf. 13***
Self-Adhesive
4307 A2033 A multi 1.25 .65
4308 A2034 B multi 3.25 1.60

No. 4307 sold for 55c and No. 4308 sold for €1.35 on day of issue.

Souvenir Sheet

Harry Potter — A2035

Litho. & Embossed With Foil Application
2018, Oct. 10 ***Die Cut Perf. 13***
Self-Adhesive
4309 A2035 €4 multi 9.25 9.25

No. 4309 was sold folded, allowing the folded sides of the sheet to cover the central portion containing the stamp. The illustration shows the sheet unfolded.

Gender Equality in Spanish Armed Forces, 30th Anniv. A2036

2018, Oct. 11 Litho. *Perf. 13¾x13¼*
4310 A2036 €1.45 multi 3.50 1.75

No. 4310 has a punched out "ñ."

Souvenir Sheet

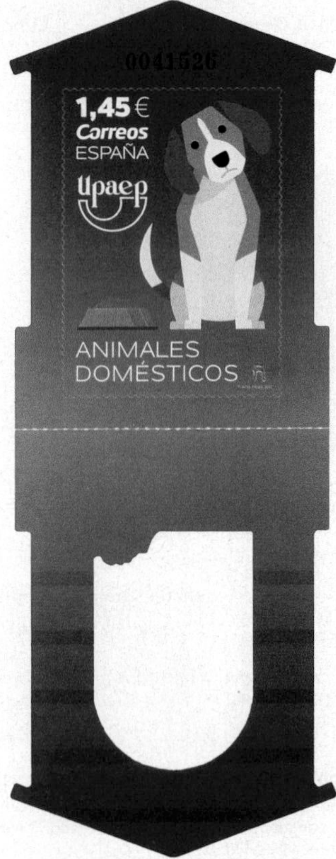
Dog and Bowl of Food — A2037

Litho. & Embossed
2018, Oct. 15 *Die Cut Perf. 13*
Self-Adhesive
4311 A2037 €1.45 multi 3.50 3.50

America issue. No. 4311 was sold folded, allowing the bottom of the sheet with cut out portion to cover the top of the sheet containing the stamp. The illustration shows the sheet unfolded.

General Archive of the Indies, Seville A2038

2018, Oct. 31 Litho. *Perf. 13¾x13¼*
4312 A2038 65c multi 1.50 .75

No. 4312 has a punched out "ñ."

Souvenir Sheet

Giraldilla Statue, Seville — A2039

Litho. & Engr.
2018, Oct. 31 *Perf. 13*
4313 A2039 €3.30 multi 7.50 7.50

EXFILNA 2018 National Philatelic Exhibition, Seville. No. 4313 has a punched out "ñ."

University and Historic District of Alcalá de Henares as UNESCO World Heritage Site, 20th Anniv. — A2040

2018, Nov. 5 Litho. *Perf. 12¾x13¼*
4314 A2040 65c multi 1.50 .75

No. 4314 has a punched out "ñ."

Eucalyptus Leaf — A2041

2018, Nov. 7 Litho. *Perf.*
4315 A2041 C multi 3.25 1.60

No. 4315 sold for €1.45 on day of issue, is impregnated with a eucalyptus scent, was printed in sheets of 6, and has a punched out "ñ."

State Volunteer Congrss, Ourense — A2042

Litho. & Embossed
2018, Nov. 8 *Die Cut Perf. 13*
Self-Adhesive
4316 A2042 A multi 1.25 .60

No. 4316 sold for 55c on day of issue.

Souvenir Sheet

Cuenca UNESCO World Heritage Site — A2043

No. 4317: a, Hanging houses. b, Cuenca Cathedral, horiz.

Perf. 13¾x13¼, 13¼x13¾
2018, Nov. 8 Litho. & Engr.
4317 A2043 Sheet of 2 23.00 23.00
a.-b. €5 Either single 11.50 5.75

Nos. 4317a-4317 b have a punched out "ñ."

Spanish Constitution, 40th Anniv. — A2044

Litho. With Foil Application
2018, Nov. 9 *Perf. 13¾x13¼*
4318 A2044 A sil & multi 1.25 .60

No. 4318 sold for 55c on day of issue. No. 4318 has a punched out "ñ."

1979 500-Peseta Bank Note Depicting Rosalía de Castro (1837-85), Writer — A2045

2018, Nov. 9 Litho. *Perf. 13¾*
4319 A2045 €3.30 multi 7.50 3.75

No. 4319 has a punched out "ñ."

Abbreviations of Spanish Provinces A2046

Abbreviation: No. 4320, "HU" (Huesca). No. 4321, "BA" (Badajoz). No. 4322, "BU" (Burgos). No. 4323, "OU" (Ourense). No. 4324, "GR" (Granada). No. 4325, "LR" (La Rioja). No. 4326, "AB" (Albacete). No. 4327, "Z" (Zaragoza). No. 4328, "AL" (Almeria). No. 4329, "V" (Valencia). No. 4330, "C" (Cantabria). No. 4331, "G" (Gipuzkoa).

Litho. & Embossed
2019 *Die Cut Perf. 13*
Self-Adhesive

4320 A2046 A multi 1.40 .70
4321 A2046 A multi 1.40 .70
4322 A2046 A multi 1.40 .70
4323 A2046 A multi 1.40 .70
4324 A2046 A multi 1.40 .70
4325 A2046 A multi 1.40 .70
4326 A2046 A multi 1.40 .70
4327 A2046 A multi 1.40 .70
4328 A2046 A multi 1.40 .70
4329 A2046 A multi 1.40 .70
4330 A2046 A multi 1.40 .70
4331 A2046 A multi 1.40 .70
Nos. 4320-4331 (12) 16.80 8.40

Issued: No. 4320, 1/2; No. 4321, 2/1; No. 4322, 3/1. No. 4323, 4/1; Nos. 4324-4325, 5/2; No. 4326, 6/3; No. 4327, 7/1; No. 4328, 8/1; No. 4329, 9/2; No. 4330, 10/1; No. 4331, 11/4. On day of issue, Nos. 4320-4331 each sold for 60c. Compare type A2046 with type A1919.

Widening of Panama Canal A2047

Litho. & Embossed
2019, Jan. 2 *Die Cut Perf. 13*
Self-Adhesive
4332 A2047 A2 multi 1.60 .80

No. 4332 sold for 70c on day of issue.

Tourism — A2048

Tourism emblem and: €1.40, Sunglasses. €1.50, Ski goggles.

Litho. & Embossed
2019, Jan. 2 *Die Cut Perf. 13*
Self-Adhesive
4333-4334 A2048 Set of 2 6.75 3.25

International Year of the Periodic Table — A2049

Litho. & Embossed
2019, Jan. 9 *Die Cut Perf. 13*
Self-Adhesive
4335 A2049 A2 multi 1.60 .80

No. 4335 sold for 70c on day of issue.

Casiodoro de Reina (c. 1520-94), Bible Translator, and "Bear Bible" A2050

2019, Jan. 14 Litho. *Perf. 13¾x13¼*
4336 A2050 A multi 1.40 .70

Protestant Reformation, 500th anniv. No. 4336 sold for 60c on day of issue, and has a punched out "ñ."

Almería, 2019 Gastronomic Capital of Spain — A2051

2019, Jan. 28 Litho. *Perf. 13¼x13¾*
4337 A2051 A2 multi 1.60 .80

No. 4337 sold for 70c on day of issue and has a punched out "ñ."

Girl in Rain Holding Love Letter, by Paula López-Berges Núñez — A2052

Badger, by Claudia Torred Martínez A2053

Litho. & Embossed
2019, Feb. 5 *Die Cut Perf. 13*
Self-Adhesive
4338 A2052 60c multi 1.40 .70
4339 A2053 70c multi 1.60 .80

Winning art in National Stamp Design Contest.

Royal Ordinances of King Charles III, 250th Anniv. — A2054

Perf. 13¼x13¾

2019, Feb. 20 **Litho.**

4340 A2054 A multi 1.40 .70

No. 4340 sold for 60c on day of issue, and has a punched out "ñ."

Spanish Diplomatic Service A2055

Perf. 13¾x13¼

2019, Mar. 11 **Litho.**

4341 A2055 €1.50 multi 3.50 1.75

No. 4341 has a punched out "ñ."

Villages — A2056

No. 4342: a, Covarrubias. b, Laguardia. c, Liérganes. d, Ujué.

Litho. & Embossed

2019, Mar. 11 ***Die Cut Perf. 13***

Self-Adhesive

4342 Booklet pane of 4 5.75

a.-d. A2056 A Any single 1.40 .70

Nos. 4342a-4342d each sold for 60c on day of issue.

2019 European Parliament Elections A2057

Perf. 13¾x13¼ on 3 Sides

2019, Mar. 15 **Litho.**

4343 A2057 €1.40 multi 3.25 1.60

No. 4343 has a punched out "ñ" and a central slit into which the tip of the ballot at top can be inserted. The illustration shows the stamp unfolded.

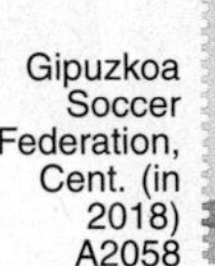

Gipuzkoa Soccer Federation, Cent. (in 2018) A2058

Perf. 13¾x13¼

2019, Mar. 18 **Litho.**

4344 A2058 €1.50 multi 3.50 1.75

No. 4344 has a punched out "ñ."

Souvenir Sheet

Valencia Soccer Team, Cent. — A2059

Litho. With Foil Application

2019, Mar. 18 ***Perf. 13¾x13¼***

4345 A2059 €5.20 multi + 4 labels 12.00 12.00

No. 4345 has a punched out "ñ."

Souvenir Sheet

Obverse of 2019 Two-Euro Coin Depicting Avila UNESCO World Heritage Site — A2060

2019, Mar. 19 **Litho. & Engr.** ***Perf.***

4346 A2060 €5.20 multi 12.00 12.00

No. 4346 has a punched out "ñ."

Treasury Department Corps of Architectural Engineers — A2061

Perf. 13¾x13¼

2019, Mar. 20 **Litho.**

4347 A2061 €1.50 multi 3.50 1.75

No. 4347 has a punched out "ñ."

Treasury and State Department Corps of Forest Engineers A2062

Perf. 13¼x13¾

2019, Mar. 20 **Litho.**

4348 A2062 €1.50 multi 3.50 1.75

No. 4348 has a punched out "ñ."

Museums — A2063

Designs: No. 4349, €1, Bilbao Museum of Fine Arts, Bilbao. No. 4350, €1, Sorolla Museum, Madrid. No. 4351, €1, Prado Museum, Madrid.

Perf. 12¾x13¼

2019, Mar. 22 **Litho.**

4349-4351 A2063 Set of 3 6.75 3.50

Nos. 4349-4351 have a punched out "ñ."

Souvenir Sheet

Mariano Bertuchi Nieto (1884-1955), Painter and Stamp Designer, and Design of Spanish Morocco No. E4 (folded) — A2064

2019, Mar. 29 **Litho.** ***Perf. 13x13½***

4352 A2064 €5.20 multi 12.00 6.00

No. 4352 has a punched out "ñ" and was sold folded. The image shown depicts only the panel with the stamp. Other panels in the sheet depict paintings and other stamp designs by Nieto, and address sides of postal cards bearing Nieto illustrations on the reverse sides.

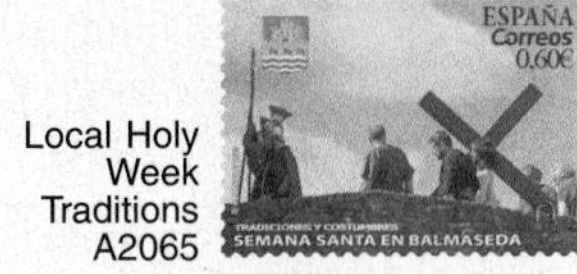

Local Holy Week Traditions A2065

No. 4353: a, Passion play and Balmaseda coat of arms. b, Parade of crucified Christ and Azuaga coat of arms. c, Crucifix in procession and Medina de Rioseco coat of arms. d, Icon of Mary holding the dead Jesus, coat of arms of Albacete.

Litho. & Embossed

2019, Apr. 4 ***Die Cut Perf. 13***

Booklet Stamps
Self-Adhesive

4353 Block of 4 9.75

a. A2065 60c multi 1.40 .70

b. A2065 70c multi 1.60 .80

c. A2065 €1.40 multi 3.25 1.60

d. A2065 €1.50 multi 3.50 1.75

e. Complete booklet, 2 #4353 19.50

Consuelo "Violeta" Alvarez (1867-1959), Telegraph Operator and Journalist — A2066

2019, Apr. 22 **Litho.** ***Perf. 13¾x13¼***

4354 A2066 60c multi 1.40 .70

No. 4354 has a punched out "ñ."

Arrival of Hernándo Cortés (1485-1547), Conquistador, in Mexico, 500th anniv. — A2067

Litho. & Embossed

2019, Apr. 22 ***Die Cut Perf. 13***

Self-Adhesive

4355 A2067 C multi 3.50 1.75

No. 4355 sold for €1.50 on day of issue.

Bearded Vultures — A2068

2019, Apr. 23 **Litho.** ***Perf. 13x12½***

4356 A2068 B multi 3.25 1.60

Europa. No. 4356 sold for €1.40 on day of issue and has a punched out "ñ."

Council of Europe, 70th Anniv. A2069

2019, May 5 **Litho.** ***Perf. 13¾x13¼***

4357 A2069 €1.40 multi 3.25 1.60

No. 4357 has a punched out "ñ."

Souvenir Sheet

Burgos Cathedral and Emblem of Juvenia 2019 Philatelic Exhibition — A2070

Litho. & Engr., Sheet Margin Litho. With Foil Application

2019, May 6 ***Perf.***

4358 A2070 €3.50 multi 8.00 4.00

No. 4358 has a punched out "ñ."

Charity Donation Box on Income Tax Return, 30th Anniv. A2071

Litho. & Embossed

2019, May 10 ***Die Cut Perf. 13***

Self-Adhesive

4359 A2071 B multi 3.25 1.60

No. 4356 sold for €1.40 on day of issue.

2019 Euroleague Basketball Final Four Tournament, Vitoria A2072

Litho. With String Netting Affixed

2019, May 17 ***Perf. 13***

4360 A2072 €1.50 multi 3.50 1.75

Souvenir Sheet

Lanzarote, by César Manrique (1919-92) — A2073

2019, May 27 **Litho.** ***Perf. 13***

4361 A2073 €5.20 multi 12.00 6.00

No. 4361 has a punched out "ñ." At the left side of the image shown is a fold, and to the left of the fold is a photograph of Manrique and a die cut rectangle which was removed. When folded, a portion of the painting appears through the rectangle.

Montserrat Caballé (1933-2018), Opera Singer — A2074

Litho. & Embossed

2019, May 31 ***Die Cut Perf. 13***

Self-Adhesive

4362 A2074 A multi 1.40 .70

No. 4362 sold for 60c on day of issue.

Coronation of the Virgin of El Rocio, Cent. — A2075

2019, June 7 **Litho.** ***Perf. 13¼x13¾***

4363 A2075 €1.50 multi 3.50 1.75

No. 4363 has a punched out "ñ."

Madrid-Yiwu, People's Republic of China Freight Train — A2076

No. 4364 — Locomotive at: a, Left. b, Right.

Litho. & Engr.

2019, June 11 ***Perf. 13¼x13***

4364 A2076 Horiz. pair 7.00 3.50

a.-b. €1.50 Either single 3.50 1.75

Nos. 4364a-4364b have a punched out "ñ." See People's Republic of China Nos.

Souvenir Sheet

Antonio Fraguas de Pablo (1942-2018), Cartoonist Known as "Forges" — A2077

Perf. 13¾x13¼

2019, June 12 **Litho.**

4365 A2077 €5.20 multi 12.00 6.00

No. 4365 has a punched out "ñ."

Souvenir Sheet

First Man on the Moon, 50th Anniv. — A2078

Litho. With Foil Application

2019, June 13 ***Perf. 12½x13¼***

4366 A2078 €3.50 multi 8.00 4.00

No. 4366 is sold folded and has a punched out "ñ."

Souvenir Sheet

Palace of Communications, Madrid — A2079

Perf. 13¼x13¾

2019, June 14 **Litho. & Engr.**

4367 A2079 €5.20 multi 12.00 6.00

No. 4367 has a punched out "ñ."

Coral de Ruada, Cent. — A2080

Perf. 13¼x13¾

2019, June 28 **Litho.**

4368 A2080 60c multi 1.40 .70

No. 4368 has a punched out "ñ."

Traditional Clothing and Map of Balearic Islands — A2081

2019, July 5 **Litho.** ***Perf. 13***

4369 A2081 €1.40 multi 3.25 1.60

No. 4369 has a punched out "ñ."

International Association of Hispanists — A2082

2019, July 7 **Litho.** ***Perf. 13¾x13¼***

4370 A2082 €1.50 multi 3.50 1.75

No. 4370 has a punched out "ñ."

Social Security, 40th Anniv. A2083

Litho. & Embossed

2019, July 12 ***Die Cut Perf. 13***

Self-Adhesive

4371 A2083 A multi 1.40 .70

No. 4371 sold for 60c on day of issue.

General Workers' Union, 130th Anniv. — A2084

2019, July 12 **Litho.** ***Perf. 13¼x13¾***

4372 A2084 €1.50 multi 3.50 1.75

No. 4372 has a punched out "ñ."

Kingdom of Nájera Historical Stage Show, 50th Anniv. — A2085

Litho. With Foil Application

Perf. 13½x13 on 3 Sides

2019, July 17

4373 A2085 60c multi 1.40 .70

No. 4373 has a punched out "ñ." The bottom part of the stamp can be folded upward to simulate an audience in front of the stage.

Directorate General of Traffic, 60th Anniv. A2086

2019, July 26 **Litho.** ***Perf. 13¾x13¼***

4374 A2086 70c multi 1.60 .80

No. 4374 has a punched out "ñ."

Casa de America at Palace of Linares, Madrid, 25th Anniv. — A2087

2019, July 29 **Litho.** ***Perf. 13¼x13¾***

4375 A2087 €1.50 multi 3.50 1.75

No. 4375 has a punched out "ñ."

Way of St. James in Northern Spain A2088

No. 4376: a, Lugo Cathedral. b, Oviedo Cathedral. c, Wayside cross, Melide. d, Statue of King Alfonso II, Oviedo, and map of the Camino Primitivo.

Litho. & Embossed

2019, Sept. 5 ***Die Cut Perf. 13***

Booklet Stamps

Self-Adhesive

4376 Horiz. strip of 4 6.00

a.-b. A2088 60c Either single 1.40 .70

c.-d. A2088 70c Either single 1.60 .80

e. Complete booklet, 2 #4376 12.00

Commercial Air Transport in Spain, Cent. — A2089

2019, Sept. 9 **Litho.** ***Perf. 13¾x13¼***

4377 A2089 €1.40 multi 3.00 1.50

No. 4377 has a punched out "ñ."

Souvenir Sheet

Juan Sebastián de Elcano (c. 1476-1526), Explorer — A2090

2019, Sept. 12 **Litho.** ***Perf. 13½***

4378 A2090 €3.50 multi 7.75 4.00

Magellan-Elcano Expedition around the world, 500th anniv. Joint Issue between Spain and Portugal.

See Portugal No. 4148.

Souvenir Sheet

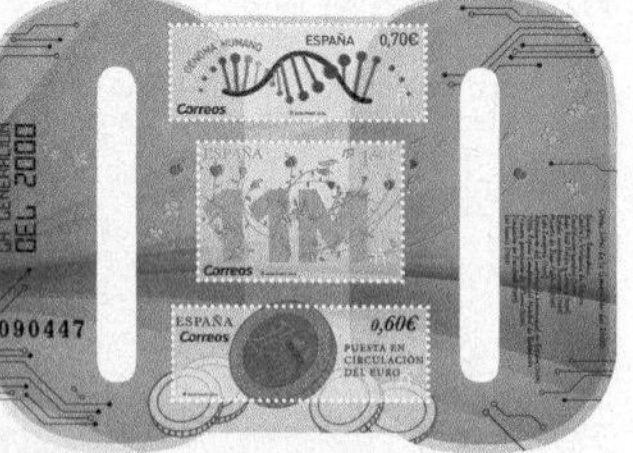

The 2000s — A2091

No. 4379: a, Introduction of Euro currency (47x18mm). b, Human Genome Project (47x18mm). c, March 11, 2004 Madrid train bombings (38x26mm).

Perf. 13¾x13½ (#4379a-4379b), 13¼x12½ (#4379c)

2019, Sept. 19 **Photo.**

4379 A2091 Sheet of 3 6.00 3.00
a. 60c multi 1.40 .70
b. 70c multi 1.60 .80
c. €1.40 multi 3.00 1.50

Nos. 4379a-4379c have a punched out "ñ."

Agenda 2030 Sustainable Development Goals — A2092

2019, Sept. 25 Litho. ***Perf. 13½x13***

4380 A2092 €1.40 multi + label 3.00 1.50

No. 4380 has a punched out "ñ." Three percent of the sales revenue of No. 4380 were donated to the Agenda 2030 project.

Souvenir Sheet

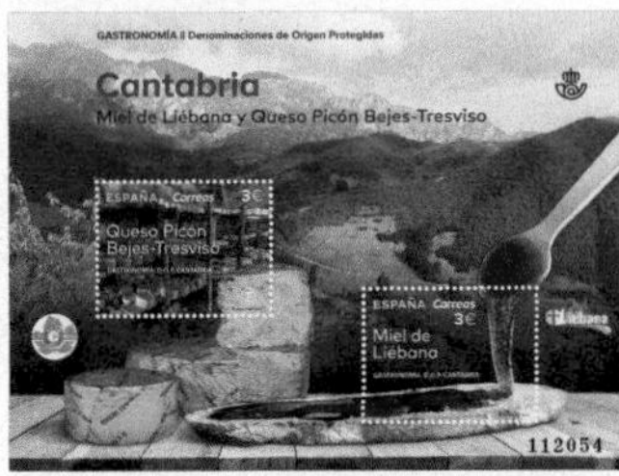

Gastronomy of Cantabria — A2093

No. 4381: a, Picón Bejes-Treviso cheese. b, Liébana honey.

2019, Sept. 26 Litho. ***Perf. 13¼x13***

4381 A2093 Sheet of 2 13.00 6.50
a.-b. €3 Either single 6.50 3.25

Nos. 4381a-4381b have a punched out "ñ."

Souvenir Sheet

Campoamor Theater, Oviedo, 125th Anniv. — A2094

Perf. 13½x13¾

2019, Sept. 27 **Litho.**

4382 A2094 €4 multi 8.75 4.50

No. 4382 has a punched out "ñ" and was sold folded. When folded, the stamp is covered by a picture of the exterior of the theater and theater seats.

Souvenir Sheet

Covadonga Mountains National Park, Cent. (in 2018) — A2095

Litho. & Engr.

2019, Sept. 30 ***Perf. 13x13¼***

4383 A2095 €5.20 multi 11.50 5.75

No. 4383 has a punched out "ñ."

Mohandas K. Gandhi (1869-1948), Indian Nationalist Leader — A2096

Indira Gandhi (1917-84), Indian Prime Minister — A2097

2019, Oct. 2 Litho. ***Perf. 13¼x13¾***

4384 A2096 €1 multi 2.25 1.10
4385 A2097 €1.50 multi 3.50 1.75

Nos. 4384-4385 have a punched out "ñ."

Paella — A2098

2019, Oct. 11 Litho. ***Perf. 13¼x13¾***

4386 A2098 €1.50 multi 3.50 1.75

America issue. No. 4386 has a punched out "ñ."

Coal Miner — A2099

Litho & Thermography With Charcoal Grit

2019, Oct. 17 ***Perf. 14***

4387 A2099 €3.50 black 8.00 4.00

Francisco Antonio Mourelle (1750-1820), Explorer of Pacific Ocean — A2100

Litho & Embossed

2019, Oct. 21 ***Die Cut Perf. 13***

On Wood Veneer

Self-Adhesive

4388 A2100 €3.50 multi 8.00 4.00

Souvenir Sheet

Ubeda and Baeza UNESCO World Heritage Sites — A2101

No. 4389: a, Assumption of the Virgin Cathedral, Baeza ("B" shape). b, Vazquez de Molina Palace, Ubeda ("U" shape).

2019, Oct. 30 Engr. ***Perf. 13***

4389 A2101 Sheet of 2 16.00 8.00
a.-b. €3.50 Either single 8.00 4.00

Nos. 4389a-4389b have a punched out "ñ."

Souvenir Sheet

The Simpsons Animated Television Show, 30th Anniv. — A2102

2019, Nov. 4 Litho. ***Perf. 13¾x13½***

4390 A2102 €4 multi 9.00 4.50

No. 4390 has a punched out "ñ" and was sold folded. When folded, the stamp is covered by a picture of the Simpson's house and automobile.

A2103

Christmas A2104

Litho. & Embossed

2019, Nov. 5 ***Die Cut Perf. 13***

Self-Adhesive

4391 A2103 A multi 1.40 .70

Litho. & Embossed With Foil Application

4392 A2104 B gold & multi 3.25 1.60

On day of issue, No. 4391 sold for 60c, and No. 4392 sold for €1.40.

D'Artacán (Dogtanian), Character From Animated Series *Dogtanian and the Three Muskehounds* — A2105

2019, Nov. 6 Litho. ***Perf.***

4393 A2105 60c multi 1.40 .70

No. 4393 has a punched out "ñ" and was printed in sheets of 6.

Gijón International Film Festival A2106

2019, Nov. 6 Litho. ***Perf. 12½x13***

4394 A2106 €1.50 multi 3.50 1.75

No. 4394 has a punched out "ñ."

Fernando Guillén (1932-2013), Actor — A2107

Litho. With Foil Application

2019, Nov. 6 ***Perf. 13¼x13¾***

4395 A2107 €1.50 sil & multi 3.50 1.75

No. 4395 has a punched out "ñ."

Cantabrian Wars of 29 B.C.-19 B.C. A2108

2019, Nov. 6 Litho. ***Perf. 13½x13¼***

4396 A2108 €1.50 multi 3.50 1.75

No. 4396 has a punched out "ñ."

Souvenir Sheet

Magdalena Palace, Santander — A2109

Litho & Engraved

2019, Nov. 6 ***Perf. 12½***

4397 A2109 €3.50 multi 7.75 4.00

EXFILNA 2019 National Philatelic Exhibition, Santander. No. 4397 has a punched out "ñ" and was sold with an acetate sleeve depicting fish.

Silbo Gomero, the Whistled Language of the Canary Islands, as UNESCO Intangible Cultural Heritage, 10th Anniv. — A2110

2019, Nov. 7 Litho. ***Perf. 13¼x13¾***
4398 A2110 €1.50 multi 3.50 1.75

No. 4398 has a punched out "ñ."

SEMI-POSTAL STAMPS

Red Cross Issue

Princesses María Cristina and Beatrice SP1

Queen as a Nurse — SP2

Queen Victoria Eugénia — SP3

Prince of Asturias — SP4

King Alfonso XIII — SP5

Perf. 12½
1926, Sept. 15 Unwmk. Engr.
B1 SP1 1c black 2.10 2.10
B2 SP2 2c ultra 2.10 2.10
B3 SP3 5c violet brn 4.75 3.75
B4 SP4 10c green 4.00 3.75
B5 SP1 15c indigo 1.50 1.25
B6 SP4 20c dull violet 1.50 1.25
a. 20c violet brown (error) 600.00 375.00
B7 SP5 25c rose red .30 .30
B8 SP1 30c blue green 35.00 32.50
B9 SP3 40c dark blue 21.00 19.00
B10 SP2 50c red orange 21.00 19.00
B11 SP4 1p slate 1.50 1.00
B12 SP3 4p magenta 1.20 .75
B13 SP5 10p brown 1.20 1.00
Nos. B1-B13,EB1 (14) 105.90 96.50
Set, never hinged 250.00

The 20c was printed in violet brown for use in the colonies (Cape Juby, Spanish Guinea, Spanish Morocco and Spanish Sahara). No. B6a, the missing overprint error, is listed here because it is not known to which colony it belongs.

For overprints see Nos. B19-B46.

Airplane and Map of Madrid-Manila Flight — SP6

1926, Sept. 15
B14 SP6 15c dp ultra & org .35 .35
B15 SP6 20c car & yel grn .35 .35
B16 SP6 30c dk brn & ultra .35 .35
B17 SP6 40c dk grn & brn org .35 .35
B18 SP6 4p magenta & yel 75.00 75.00
Nos. B14-B18,CB1-CB5 (10) 82.15 82.15
Set, never hinged 210.00

Madrid to Manila flight of Captains Eduardo G. Gallarza and Joaquim Loriga y Taboada.

Nos. B1-B18, CB1-CB5 and EB1 were used for regular postage on Sept. 15, 16, 17, 1926. Subsequently the unsold stamps were given to the Spanish Red Cross Society, by which they were sold uncanceled but they then had no franking power.

For overprints see Nos. B47-B53.

Coronation Silver Jubilee Issue

Red Cross Stamps of 1926 Overprinted "ALFONSO XIII," Dates and Ornaments in Various Colors

1927, May 27
B19 SP1 1c black (R) 5.25 5.25
B20 SP2 2c ultra (Bl) 9.75 9.75
B21 SP3 5c vio brn (R) 2.40 2.40
a. Double overprint 37.50
B22 SP4 10c green (Bl) 67.50 67.50
B23 SP1 15c indigo (R) 2.00 2.00
B24 SP4 20c dull vio (Bl) 3.50 3.50
B25 SP5 25c rose red (Bl) .50 .50
B26 SP1 30c blue grn (Bl) .90 .90
B27 SP3 40c dk blue (R) .90 .90
B28 SP2 50c red org (Bl) .90 .90
B29 SP4 1p slate (R) 2.00 2.00
B30 SP3 4p magenta (Bl) 9.75 9.75
B31 SP5 10p brown (G) 37.50 37.50
Nos. B19-B31 (13) 142.85 142.85
Set, never hinged 340.00

Same with Additional Surcharges of New Values

B32 SP2 3c on 2c (G) 8.75 8.75
B33 SP2 4c on 2c (Bk) 8.75 8.75
B34 SP5 10c on 25c (Bk) .50 .50
B35 SP5 25c on 25c (Bl) .50 .50
B36 SP2 55c on 2c (R) .95 .95
B37 SP4 55c on 10c (Bk) 50.00 50.00
B38 SP4 55c on 20c (Bk) 50.00 50.00
B39 SP1 75c on 15c (R) .70 .70
B40 SP1 75c on 30c (R) 130.00 130.00
B41 SP3 80c on 5c (R) 50.00 50.00
B42 SP3 2p on 40c (R) 1.00 1.00
B43 SP4 2p on 1p (R) 1.00 1.00
B44 SP2 5p on 50c (G) 1.75 1.75
B45 SP3 5p on 4p (Bk) 3.00 3.00
B46 SP5 10p on 10p (G) 25.00 25.00
Nos. B32-B46 (15) 331.90 331.90
Set, never hinged 650.00

Nos. B14-B18 Overprinted

B47 SP6 15c (Brn) .50 .40
a. Double overprint 30.00
B48 SP6 20c (Bl) .50 .40
a. Brown overprint (error) 65.00
b. Inverted overprint 30.00
B50 SP6 30c (R) .50 .40
a. Blue overprint (error) 65.00
b. Double overprint 30.00
B52 SP6 40c (Brn) .50 .40
a. Inverted overprint 30.00
b. Double ovpt. (Bl + Br) 95.00
B53 SP6 4p (Bl) 95.00 92.50
a. Inverted overprint 160.00

Semi-Postal Special Delivery Stamp Overprinted "ALFONSO XIII," Dates and Ornaments in Violet

B54 SPSD1 20c 5.50 5.50
Nos. B47-B54 (6) 102.50 99.60
Set, never hinged 240.00

Nos. CB1-CB5 Overprinted in Various Colors

B55 SPAP1 5c (R) 2.25 1.60
a. Inverted overprint 30.00
B56 SPAP1 10c (R) 2.50 2.25
a. Inverted overprint 30.00
B57 SPAP1 25c (Bl) .40 .40
B58 SPAP1 50c (Bl) .40 .40
a. Double ovpt., one invtd. 72.50
B59 SPAP1 1p (R) 3.00 2.50
a. Inverted overprint 95.00

Same with Additional Surcharges of New Values

B60 SPAP1 75c on 5c (R) 5.00 3.25
a. Inverted surcharge 30.00
B61 SPAP1 75c on 10c (R) 21.00 13.00
a. Inverted surcharge 30.00
B62 SPAP1 75c on 25c (Bl) 45.00 25.00
a. Double surcharge 55.00
B63 SPAP1 75c on 50c (Bl) 17.00 13.00
Nos. B55-B63 (9) 96.55 61.40
Set, never hinged 275.00

Nos. B54-B63 were available for ordinary postage.

Stamps of Spanish Offices in Morocco and Spanish Colonies, 1926 (Spain Types SP3, SP5) Surcharged in Various Colors

On Spanish Morocco

B64 SP3 55c on 4p bis (Bl) 23.00 20.00
B65 SP5 80c on 10p vio (Br) 23.00 20.00

On Spanish Tangier

B66 SP5 1p on 10p vio (Br) 130.00 100.00
B67 SP3 4p bis (G) 42.50 40.00

On Cape Juby

B68 SP3 5p on 4p bis (R) 80.00 67.50
B69 SP5 10p on 10p vio (R) 42.50 40.00

On Spanish Guinea

B70 SP5 1p on 10p vio (Bl) 23.00 20.00
B71 SP3 2p on 4p bis (G) 23.00 20.00

On Spanish Sahara

B72 SP5 80c on 10p vio (R) 37.50 31.00
B73 SP3 2p on 4p bis (R) 23.00 20.00
Nos. B64-B73 (10) 447.50 378.50
Set, never hinged 1,300.

Nos. B64-B73 were available for postage in Spain only.

Nos. B19-B73 were for the 25th year of the reign of King Alfonso XIII.

Counterfeits of Nos. B64-B73 abound.

Catacombs Restoration Issues

Pope Pius XI and King Alfonso XIII SP7

1928, Dec. 23 Engr. ***Perf. 12½***

Santiago Issue

B74 SP7 2c violet & blk .30 .30
B75 SP7 2c lake & blk .35 .35
B76 SP7 3c bl blk & vio .30 .30
B77 SP7 3c dl bl & vio .35 .35
B78 SP7 5c ol grn & vio .60 .60
B79 SP7 10c yel grn & blk 1.10 1.10
B80 SP7 15c bl grn & vio 3.00 3.00
B81 SP7 25c dp rose & vio 3.00 3.00
B82 SP7 40c ultra & blk .30 .30
B83 SP7 55c ol brn & vio .30 .30
B84 SP7 80c red & blk .30 .30
B85 SP7 1p gray blk & vio .30 .30
B86 SP7 2p red brn & blk 3.75 3.75
B87 SP7 3p pale rose & vio 3.75 3.75
B88 SP7 4p vio brn & blk 3.75 3.75
B89 SP7 5p grnsh blk & vio 3.75 3.75

Toledo Issue

B90 SP7 2c bl blk & car .30 .30
B91 SP7 2c ultra & car .35 .35
B92 SP7 3c bis brn & ultra .30 .30
B93 SP7 3c ol grn & ultra .35 .35
B94 SP7 5c red vio & car .60 .60
B95 SP7 10c yel grn & ultra 1.10 1.10
B96 SP7 15c slate bl & car 3.00 3.00
B97 SP7 25c red brn & ultra 3.00 3.00
B98 SP7 40c ultra & car .30 .30
B99 SP7 55c dk brn & ultra .30 .30
B100 SP7 80c black & car .30 .30
B101 SP7 1p yellow & car .30 .30
B102 SP7 2p dk gray & ultra 3.75 3.75
B103 SP7 3p violet & car 3.75 3.75
B104 SP7 4p vio brn & car 3.75 3.75
B105 SP7 5p bister & ultra 3.75 3.75
Nos. B74-B105 (32) 50.40 50.40
Set, never hinged 110.00

Nos. B74-B105 replaced regular stamps from Dec. 23, 1928 to Jan. 6, 1929. The proceeds from their sale were given to a fund to restore the catacombs of Saint Damasus and Saint Praetextatus at Rome.

Nos. B74-B105 exist imperf. Value set, $325 hinged, $400 never hinged.

Issues of the Republic

SP13

1938, Apr. 15 ***Perf. 11½***
B106 SP13 45c + 2p bl & grnsh bl .90 .75
a. Imperf., pair 17.50 14.50
b. Souv. sheet of 1 26.00 26.00
c. Souv. sheet of 1, imperf. 650.00 625.00

Surtax for the defenders of Madrid.

For overprint and surcharge see Nos. B108, CB6.

Nurse and Orderly Carrying Wounded Soldier — SP14

1938, June 1 Engr. ***Perf. 10***
B107 SP14 45c + 5p cop red .55 .55
a. Imperf., pair 220.00

For surcharge see No. CB7.

No. B106 Overprinted in Black

1938, Nov. 7 ***Perf. 11½***
B108 SP13 45c + 2p 3.25 3.25
Never hinged 5.00

Defense of Madrid, 2nd anniversary.

A similar but larger overprint was applied to cover blocks of four. Value, $15 hinged, $30 never hinged.

Values for souvenir sheets of 1937-38 are for examples with some faults. Undamaged sheets are very hard to find.

Spanish State

Souvenir Sheets

Alcazar, Toledo — SP15

Design: No. B108C, A patio of Alcazar after Civil War fighting.

1937 Unwmk. Photo. ***Perf. 11½***

Control Numbers on Back

B108A SP15 2p org brn 18.00 18.00
b. Imperf. 250.00 250.00
B108C SP15 2p dark green 18.00 18.00
d. Imperf. 250.00 250.00
Set, never hinged 85.00
Set, B108Ab, B108Cd, never hinged 900.00

Nos. B108A-B108C sold for 4p each.

SP16

Designs: 20c, Covadongas Cathedral. 30c, Palma Cathedral, Majorca. 50c, Alcazar of Segovia. 1p, Leon Cathedral.

1938 Unwmk. Photo. *Perf. 12½*
Control Numbers on Back

B108E SP16 Sheet of 4 35.00 35.00
f. 20c dull violet 5.00 5.00
g. 30c rose red 5.00 5.00
h. 50c bright blue 5.00 5.00
i. 1p greenish gray 5.00 5.00
j. Imperf. sheet 60.00 60.00

Each sheet sold for 4p.

SP17

Designs, alternating in sheet: Flag bearer. Battleship "Admiral Cervera." Soldiers in trenches. Moorish guard.

1938, July 1 Unwmk. *Perf. 13*
Control Numbers on Back

B108K SP17 Sheet of 20 35.00 35.00
Never hinged 50.00
l. Imperf. sheet 145.00 145.00

Sheet measures 175x132mm. Consists of five vertical rows of four 2c violet, 3c deep blue, 5c olive gray, 10c deep green and 30c red orange, with each denomination appearing in two different designs. Marginal inscription: "Homenaje al Ejercito y a la Marina" (Honoring the Army and Navy). Sold for 4p, or double face value.

Souvenir Sheets

Don Juan of Austria — SP18

Battle of Lepanto — SP19

Perf. 12½
1938, Dec. 15 Unwmk. Engr.
Control Numbers on Back

B108M SP18 30c dk car 17.00 17.00
B108N SP19 50c blue black 17.00 17.00
Nos. B108M-B108N (2) 34.00 34.00
Set, never hinged 75.00

Imperf

B108O SP18 30c black vio 250.00 *550.00*
B108P SP19 50c dk sl grn 250.00 *550.00*
Nos. B108O-B108P (2) 500.00 *1,100.*
Set, never hinged 825.00

Victory over the Turks in the Battle of Lepanto, 1571.

Nos. B108M-B108P contain one stamp. The dates "1571-1938" appear in the lower sheet margin. Size: 89x74mm. Sold for 10p a pair.

LOCAL CHARITY STAMPS

Hundreds of different charity stamps were issued by local organizations and cities during the Civil War, 1936-39. Some had limited franking value, but most were simply charity labels. They are of three kinds: 1. Local semipostals. 2. Obligatory surtax stamps. 3. Propaganda or charity labels.

Ruins of Belchite SP20

Miracle of Calanda — SP21

Designs: 10c+5c, 70c+20c, Ruins of Belchite. 15c+10c, 80c+20c, The Rosary. 20c+10c, 1.50p+50c, El Pilar Cathedral. 25c+10c, 1p+30c, Mother Raffols praying. 40c+10c, 2.50p+50c, The Little Chamber. 45c+15c, 1.40p+40c, Oath of the Besieged. 10p+4p, The Apparition.

Perf. 10½, 11½x10½, 11½
1940, Jan. 29 Litho. Unwmk.
Design SP20

B109 10c + 5c dp bl & vio brn .25 .25
B110 15c + 10c rose vio & dk grn .25 .25
B111 20c + 10c vio & dp bl .25 .25
B112 25c + 10c dp rose & vio brn .25 .25
B113 40c + 10c sl grn & rose vio .25 .25
B114 45c + 15c vio & dp rose .30 .30
B115 70c + 20c multi .30 .30
B116 80c + 20c dp rose & vio .40 .40
B117 1p + 30c dk sl grn & pur .40 .40
B118 1.40p + 40c pur & gray blk 35.00 35.00
B119 1.50p + 50c lt bl & brn vio .50 .50
B120 2.50p + 50c choc & bl .50 .50

Design SP21

B121 4p + 1p rose lil & sl grn 11.00 11.00
B122 10p + 4p ultra & chnt 175.00 175.00
Nos. B109-B122,CB8-CB17,EB2 (25) 406.70 406.60
Set, never hinged 825.00

19th centenary of the Virgin of the Pillar.

The surtax was used to help restore the Cathedral at Zaragoza, damaged during the Civil War.

No. B121 exists in violet & slate green, No. B122 in ultramarine & brown violet. Value, $42.50 each.

Nos. B109-B122 exist imperf. Value, $750.

See No. 743, CB8-CB17.

General Franco — SP23

1940, Dec. 23 Unwmk. *Perf. 10*

B123 SP23 20c + 5c dk grn & red .65 .65
B124 SP23 40c + 10c dk bl & red .90 .40
Set, never hinged 3.50

The surtax was for the tuberculosis fund. See Nos. RA15, RAC1.

Stamps of 10c denomination, types SP23 to SP28, are postal tax issues.

Knight and Lorraine Cross — SP24

1941, Dec. 23

B125 SP24 20c + 5c bl vio & red .50 .30
B126 SP24 40c + 10c sl grn & red .50 .25
Set, never hinged 1.40

The surtax was used to fight tuberculosis. See Nos. RA16, RAC2.

Cross of Lorraine — SP25

1942, Dec. 23 Litho.

B127 SP25 20c + 5c pale brn & rose red 1.40 1.25
B128 SP25 40c + 10c lt bluish grn & rose red .80 .45
Set, never hinged 4.00

The surtax was used to fight tuberculosis. See Nos. RA17, RAC3.

Cross of Lorraine — SP26

1943, Dec. 23 Photo. *Perf. 11½*

B129 SP26 20c + 5c dl sl grn & dl red 3.25 1.40
B130 SP26 40c + 10c brt bl & dl red 2.00 1.10
Set, never hinged 12.00

The surtax was used to fight tuberculosis. See Nos. RA18, RAC4.

Dragon Slaying — SP27

Perf. 9½x10
1944, Dec. 23 Litho. Unwmk.

B131 SP27 20c + 5c sl grn & red .25 .25
B132 SP27 40c + 10c dl vio & red .50 .50
B133 SP27 80c + 10c ultra & rose 7.75 7.75
Nos. B131-B133 (3) 8.50 8.50
Set, never hinged 16.00

The surtax was used to fight tuberculosis. See Nos. RA19, RAC5.

St. George Slaying the Dragon — SP28

Lorraine Cross in Red

1945, Dec. 23

B134 SP28 20c + 5c dl gray grn .25 .25
B135 SP28 40c + 10c vio .30 .25
B136 SP28 80c + 10c ultra 8.00 7.50
Nos. B134-B136 (3) 8.55 8.00
Set, never hinged 14.00

The surtax was used to fight tuberculosis. See Nos. RA20, RAC6.

Nos. 753 and 768 Surcharged in Blue

1950, Oct. 23

B137 A195 50c + 10c 29.00 29.00
a. "Caudillo" 14¾mm wide 95.00 97.50
B138 A195 1p + 10c 29.00 29.00
a. "Caudillo" 14¾mm wide 95.00 97.50
Set, never hinged 110.00
#B137a-B138a, never hinged 300.00

Visit of General Franco to Canary Islands. First printing, brighter colors and pale blue surcharge, was issued in Canary Islands. Value, $200 hinged, $300 never hinged, $200 used. Second printing was issued in Madrid Feb. 22, 1951. See No. CB18.

Catalogue values for unused stamps in this section, from this point to the end of the section, are for Never Hinged items.

1992 Summer Olympics, Barcelona SP29

No. B139, Track and field. No. B140, Badminton. No. B141, Basketball.

1988, Oct. 3 Photo. *Perf. 14*

B139 SP29 20p +5p multi .35 .35
B140 SP29 45p +5p multi .60 .60
B141 SP29 50p +5p multi .70 .70
Nos. B139-B141 (3) 1.65 1.65

See Nos. B146-B152, B163-B168, B177-B179, B184-B186, B191-B193.

EXPO '92, Seville — SP30

Globes and sites of previous exhibitions: No. B142, Crystal Palace, London, 1851. No. B143, Eiffel Tower, Paris, 1889. No. B144, "The Atom," Brussels, 1958. No. B145, Monument, Osaka, 1970.

1989, Feb. 9 Photo. *Perf. 14x13½*

B142 SP30 8p +5p multi .25 .25
B143 SP30 8p +5p multi .25 .25
B144 SP30 20p +5p multi .30 .30
B145 SP30 20p +5p multi .30 .30
Nos. B142-B145 (4) 1.10 1.10

Summer Olympics Type of 1988

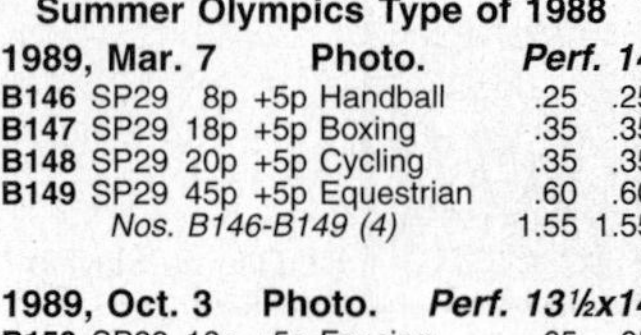

1989, Mar. 7 Photo. *Perf. 14*

B146 SP29 8p +5p Handball .25 .25
B147 SP29 18p +5p Boxing .35 .35
B148 SP29 20p +5p Cycling .35 .35
B149 SP29 45p +5p Equestrian .60 .60
Nos. B146-B149 (4) 1.55 1.55

1989, Oct. 3 Photo. *Perf. 13½x14*

B150 SP29 18p +5p Fencing .65 .65
B151 SP29 20p +5p Soccer .65 .65
B152 SP29 45p +5p Pommel horse 1.25 1.25
Nos. B150-B152 (3) 2.55 2.55

500th Anniv. Emblem and Produce or Fauna Indigenous to the Americas — SP31

1989, Oct. 16 Litho. *Perf. 13x13½*

B153 SP31 8p +5p Cocoa .25 .25
B154 SP31 8p +5p Corn .25 .25
B155 SP31 20p +5p Tomato .30 .30
B156 SP31 20p +5p Horse .30 .30
B157 SP31 50p +5p Potato .60 .60
B158 SP31 50p +5p Turkey .60 .60
a. Bklt. pane of 6, #B153-B158 2.25
Nos. B153-B158 (6) 2.30 2.30

Discovery of America, 500th anniv.

EXPO '92, Seville SP32

Curro, the character trademark, and symbols of development in Spain.

1990, Feb. 22 Photo. *Perf. 14*

B159 SP32 8p +5p multi .25 .25
B160 SP32 20p +5p multi, diff. .30 .30
B161 SP32 45p +5p multi, diff. .60 .60
B162 SP32 50p +5p multi, diff. .70 .70
Nos. B159-B162 (4) 1.85 1.85

Summer Olympics Type of 1988

1990, Mar. 7 Photo. *Perf. 13½x14*

B163 SP29 18p +5p Weight lifting .30 .30
B164 SP29 20p +5p Field hockey .30 .30
B165 SP29 45p +5p Judo .55 .55
Nos. B163-B165 (3) 1.15 1.15

1990, Oct. 3 Photo. *Perf. 13½x14*

B166 SP29 8p +5p Wrestling .25 .25
B167 SP29 18p +5p Swimming .40 .40
B168 SP29 20p +5p Baseball .50 .50
Nos. B166-B168 (3) 1.15 1.15

Discovery of America, 500th Anniv. (in 1992) — SP33

Drawings of sailing ships.

1990, Oct. 15 Litho. *Perf. 13*

B169 SP33 8p +5p "Viajes-A" .25 .25
B170 SP33 8p +5p "Viajes-B" .25 .25
B171 SP33 20p +5p "Viajes-C" .30 .30
B172 SP33 20p +5p "Viajes-D" .30 .30
a. Bklt. pane of 4, #B169-B172 1.00
Nos. B169-B172 (4) 1.10 1.10

Expo '92, Seville SP34

Designs: 15p+5p, La Cartuja, Monastery of Santa Maria de las Cuevas. 25p+5p, Amphitheater. 45p+5p, La Cartuja Bridge. 55p+5p, La Bargueta Bridge.

Litho. & Engr.

1991, Feb. 12 *Perf. 14*

B173 SP34 15p +5p multi .30 .30
B174 SP34 25p +5p multi .40 .40
B175 SP34 45p +5p multi .65 .65
B176 SP34 55p +5p multi .80 .80
Nos. B173-B176 (4) 2.15 2.15

Summer Olympics Type of 1988

No. B177, Five athletes. No. B178, Kayaking. No. B179, Rowing.

1991, Mar. 7 Litho. *Perf. 13½x14*

B177 SP29 15p + 5p multi .30 .30
B178 SP29 25p + 5p multi .40 .40
B179 SP29 45p + 5p multi .65 .65
Nos. B177-B179 (3) 1.35 1.35

Madrid, European City of Culture, 1992 SP35

Designs: 15p+5p, Fountain of Apollo. 25p+5p, Statue of Alvaro de Bazan. 45p+5p, Bank of Spain. 55p+5p, St. Isidore's Institute.

1991, July 29 Photo. *Perf. 13½x14*

B180 SP35 15p + 5p multi .30 .30
B181 SP35 25p + 5p multi .40 .40
B182 SP35 45p + 5p multi .60 .60
B183 SP35 55p + 5p multi .75 .75
Nos. B180-B183 (4) 2.05 2.05

Summer Olympics Type of 1988

1991, Oct. 3 Litho. *Perf. 14*

B184 SP29 15p +5p Tennis .45 .45
B185 SP29 25p +5p Table tennis .60 .60
B186 SP29 55p +5p Shooting 1.25 1.25
Nos. B184-B186 (3) 2.30 2.30

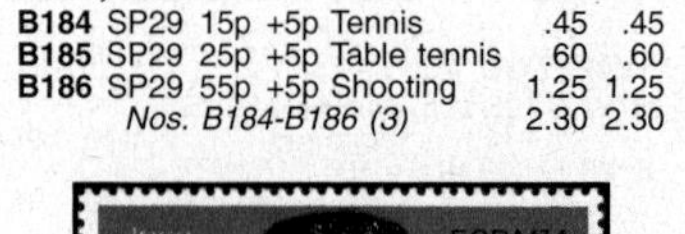

Discovery of America, 500th Anniv., 1992 — SP36

15p+5p, Garcilaso Gomez Suarez de Figueroa, the Inca, poet. 25p+5p, Pope Alexander VI. 45p+5p, Luis de Santangel, banker. 55p+5p, Friar Toribio de Paredes, monk.

1991, Oct. 15 Photo. *Perf. 13x13½*

B187 SP36 15p +5p multi .30 .30
B188 SP36 25p +5p multi .40 .40
B189 SP36 45p +5p multi .60 .60
B190 SP36 55p +5p multi .75 .75
a. Bklt. pane of 4, #B187-B190 2.00
Nos. B187-B190 (4) 2.05 2.05

Summer Olympics Type of 1988

1992, Mar. 6 Photo. *Perf. 13½x14*

B191 SP29 15p +5p Archery .40 .40
B192 SP29 25p +5p Sailing .55 .55
B193 SP29 55p +5p Volleyball 1.10 1.10
Nos. B191-B193 (3) 2.05 2.05

Columbus Type of 1930

Souvenir Sheet

1992, Mar. 31 Engr. *Perf. 14*

B194 Sheet of 3 1.00 1.00
a. A65 17p +5p dark red .30 .30
b. A65 17p +5p ultramarine .30 .30
c. A65 17p +5p black .30 .30

Discovery of America, 500th anniv.

Expo '92 Type

Design: No. B195, Seville, 16th cent.

1992, Apr. 21 Litho. *Perf. 13½x14*

Souvenir Sheet

B195 A837 17p +5p multi .35 .35

1992 Summer Olympics, Barcelona — SP37

No. B196, Mascot COBI. No. B197, Hand holding torch, horiz. No. B198, "25 Jul".

Perf. 14x13½, 13½x14

1992, July 16 Photo.

B196 SP37 17p +5p multi .40 .40
B197 SP37 17p +5p multi .40 .40
B198 SP37 17p +5p multi .40 .40
Nos. B196-B198 (3) 1.20 1.20

1992 Summer Olympics, Barcelona — SP38

Designs: a, Olympic Stadium. b, San Jordi Sports Palace. c, INEF Sports University.

1992, July 25 *Perf. 13½x14*

B199 SP38 27p +5p Triptych, #a.-c. 1.40 1.40

1992 Summer Olympics, Barcelona
SP39 SP40

No. B200, Olympic mascot as stamp collector. No. B201, Sagrada Family Church, Barcelona.

1992, July 29 Photo. *Perf. 14x13½*

B200 SP39 17p +5p multi .35 .35
B201 SP40 17p +5p multi .35 .35

Olymphilex '92 (No. B201).

Madrid, European City of Culture — SP41

#B202, Municipal Museum. #B203, Royal Theater. #B204, The Prado Museum. #B205, Queen Sofia Natl. Center for the Arts.

1992, Nov. 24 Photo. *Perf. 14x13½*

B202 SP41 17p +5p multi .35 .30
B203 SP41 17p +5p multi .35 .30
B204 SP41 17p +5p multi .35 .30
B205 SP41 17p +5p multi .35 .30
Nos. B202-B205 (4) 1.40 1.20

AIR POST STAMPS

Regular Issue of 1909-10 Overprinted in Red or Black

Perf. 13x12½, 14

1920, Apr. 4 Unwmk.

C1 A46 5c green (R) 1.40 .90
a. Imperf., pair 105.00 105.00
b. Double overprint 35.00 35.00
c. Inverted overprint 90.00 90.00
d. Double ovpt., one invtd. 35.00 35.00
e. Triple overprint 35.00 35.00
C2 A46 10c car (Bk) 1.60 1.10
a. Imperf., pair 105.00 105.00
b. Double overprint 35.00 35.00
d. Double ovpt., one invtd. 35.00 35.00
C3 A46 25c dp blue (R) 2.75 1.50
a. Inverted overprint 90.00 90.00
b. Double overprint 35.00 35.00
C4 A46 50c sl blue (R) 12.00 5.50
a. Imperf., pair 105.00 105.00
C5 A46 1p lake (Bk) 37.50 20.00
a. Imperf., pair 385.00 385.00
Nos. C1-C5 (5) 55.25 29.00
Set, never hinged 160.00

Dangerous counterfeits are plentiful.

A 30c green was authorized, but not issued. Value: hinged $650; never hinged $1,200.

For overprints see Nos. C58-C61.

"Spirit of St. Louis" over Coast of Europe — AP1

Seville-Barcelona Exposition Issue

Control Numbers on Back

1929, Feb. 15 Engr. *Perf. 11*

C6 AP1 5c brown 6.00 5.00
C7 AP1 10c rose 6.00 5.00
C8 AP1 25c dark blue 7.00 5.50
C9 AP1 50c purple 8.00 5.75
C10 AP1 1p green 37.50 25.00
C11 AP1 4p black 25.00 20.00
Nos. C6-C11 (6) 89.50 66.25
Set, never hinged 200.00

Nos. C6 to C11 exist imperforate. Value set, $800.

The so-called errors of color of Nos. C10, C18-C21, C23-C24, C28-C31, C37, C40, C42, C44, C46, C48, C50, C52, C55, C62-C67 are believed to have been irregularly produced.

Plane and Congress Seal — AP2

Railway Congress Issue

Control Numbers on Back

1930, May 10 Litho. *Perf. 14*

C12 AP2 5c bister brn 5.50 *5.50*
C13 AP2 10c rose 5.50 *5.50*
C14 AP2 25c dark blue 5.50 *5.50*
C15 AP2 50c purple 13.00 13.00
a. Vert. pair, imperf. between 300.00
Never hinged *600.00*
C16 AP2 1p yellow green 27.50 27.50
C17 AP2 4p black 30.00 30.00
Nos. C12-C17 (6) 87.00 87.00
Set, never hinged 265.00

The note after No. 385 will apply here also. Dangerous counterfeits exist.

Goya Issue

Fantasy of Flight AP3

Asmodeus and Cleofas — AP4

Fantasy of Flight AP5

Fantasy of Flight — AP6

1930, June 15 Engr. *Perf. 12½*

C18	AP3	5c brn red & yel	.25	.25
C19	AP3	15c blk & red org	.25	.25
C20	AP3	25c brn car & dp red	.25	.25
C21	AP4	5c ol grn & grnsh bl	.25	.25
C22	AP4	10c sl grn & yel grn	.25	.25
C23	AP4	20c ultra & rose red	.25	.25
C24	AP4	40c vio bl & lt bl	.30	.30
C25	AP5	30c brown & vio	.30	.30
C26	AP5	50c ver & grn	.30	.30
C27	AP5	4p brn car & blk	2.00	2.00
C28	AP6	1p vio brn & vio	.30	.30
C29	AP6	4p bl blk & sl grn	2.00	2.00
C30	AP6	10p blk brn & bis brn	7.00	7.00
		Nos. C18-C30,CE1 (14)	13.95	13.95
		Set, never hinged	21.00	

Nos. C18-C30 exist imperf. Value for set, $150.

Christopher Columbus Issue

La Rábida Monastery — AP7

Martín Alonso Pinzón — AP8

Vicente Yanez Pinzón — AP9

Columbus in His Cabin — AP10

1930, Sept. 29 Litho.

C31	AP7	5c lt red brn	.25	.25
C32	AP7	5c olive bister	.25	.25
C33	AP7	10c blue green	.25	.25
C34	AP7	15c dark violet	.25	.25
C35	AP7	20c ultra	.25	.25

Engr.

C36	AP8	25c carmine rose	.25	.25
C37	AP9	30c dp red brn	2.00	2.00
C38	AP8	40c indigo	2.00	2.00
C39	AP9	50c orange	2.00	2.00
C40	AP8	1p dull violet	2.00	2.00
C41	AP10	4p olive green	2.00	2.00
C42	AP10	10p light brown	11.00	12.00
		Nos. C31-C42 (12)	22.50	23.50
		Set, never hinged	35.00	

Nos. C31-C42 exist imperf. Value for set, $250.

Spanish-American Issue

AP11

Columbus AP12

Columbus and Pinzón Brothers AP13

1930, Sept. 29 Litho.

C43	AP11	5c lt red	.25	.25
C44	AP11	10c dull green	.25	.25

Engr.

C45	AP12	25c scarlet	.25	.25
C46	AP12	50c slate gray	2.50	2.10
C47	AP12	1p fawn	2.50	2.10
C48	AP13	4p slate blue	2.50	2.10
C49	AP13	10p brown violet	11.00	10.00
		Nos. C43-C49 (7)	19.25	17.05
		Set, never hinged	35.00	

Nos. C43-C49 exist imperf. Value for set, $250.

Spanish-American Exhibition Issue

Santos-Dumont and First Flight of His Airplane — AP14

Teodoro Fels and His Airplane AP15

Dagoberto Godoy and Pass over Andes — AP16

Sacadura Cabral and Gago Coutinho and Their Airplane AP17

Sidar of Mexico and Map of South America — AP18

Ignacio Jiménez and Francisco Iglesias — AP19

Charles A. Lindbergh, Statue of Liberty, Spirit of St. Louis and Cat AP20

Santa Maria, Plane and Torre del Oro, Seville AP21

1930, Oct. 10 Photo. *Perf. 14*

C50	AP14	5c gray black	.80	.80
C51	AP15	10c dk olive grn	.80	.80
C52	AP16	25c ultra	.80	.80
C53	AP17	50c blue gray	1.75	1.75
C54	AP18	50c black	1.75	1.75
C55	AP19	1p car lake	3.50	3.50
a.		1p brown violet	67.50	67.50
		Never hinged	160.00	
C56	AP20	1p deep green	3.50	3.50
C57	AP21	4p slate blue	6.00	6.00
		Nos. C50-C57 (8)	18.90	18.90
		Set, never hinged	65.00	

Exist imperf. Value, set $110.

Note after No. 432 also applies to Nos. C31-C57.

Reprints of Nos. C50-C57 have blurred impressions, yellowish paper. Value: one-tenth of originals. Examples of No. C56 exist with portrait of Lindbergh inverted, doubled with one inverted, and missing.

Nos. C1-C4 Overprinted in Red or Black

1931 *Perf. 13x12½*

C58	A46	5c green (R)	12.50	11.50
C59	A46	10c carmine (Bk)	12.50	11.50
C60	A46	25c deep blue (R)	17.50	16.50
C61	A46	50c slate blue (R)	35.00	26.00
		Nos. C58-C61 (4)	77.50	65.50
		Set, never hinged	160.00	

Counterfeits of overprint exist.

The status of Nos. C58-C61 has been questioned.

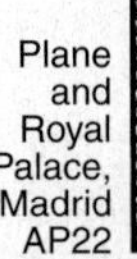

Plane and Royal Palace, Madrid AP22

Madrid Post Office and Cibeles Fountain AP23

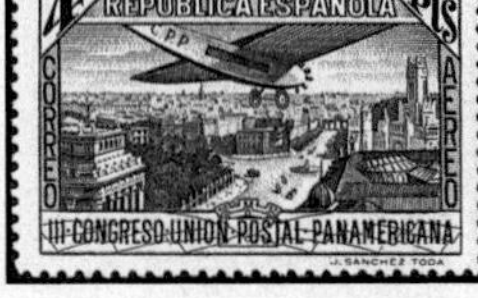

Plane over Calle de Alcalá, Madrid AP24

1931, Oct. 10 Engr. *Perf. 12*

C62	AP22	5c brown violet	.25	.30
C63	AP22	10c deep green	.25	.30
C64	AP22	25c dull red	.25	.30
C65	AP23	50c deep blue	.45	.50
C66	AP23	1p deep violet	.65	.60
C67	AP24	4p black	9.00	9.00
		Nos. C62-C67 (6)	10.85	11.00
		Set, never hinged	15.00	

3rd Pan-American Postal Union Congress, Madrid.

Exist imperf. Value, set $45.

For overprints see Nos. CO1-CO6.

Montserrat Issue

Plane over Montserrat Pass — AP25

1931, Dec. 9 *Perf. 11½*

Control Number on Back

C68	AP25	5c black brown	.50	.50
C69	AP25	10c yellow green	2.00	2.00
C70	AP25	25c deep rose	7.00	7.50
C71	AP25	50c orange	21.00	27.50
C72	AP25	1p gray black	14.00	19.00
		Nos. C68-C72 (5)	44.50	56.50
		Set, never hinged	110.00	

Perf. 14

C68a	AP25	5c	7.50	*14.50*
C69a	AP25	10c	40.00	45.00
C70a	AP25	25c	72.50	72.50
C71a	AP25	50c	72.50	72.50
C72f	AP25	1p	72.50	72.50
		Nos. C68a-C72f (5)	265.00	277.00
		Set, never hinged	275.00	

900th anniv. of Montserrat Monastery.

Nos. C68-C72 exist imperf. Value set, $525.

Autogiro over Seville — AP26

1935-39 *Perf. 11½*

C72A AP26 2p gray blue 30.00 4.50
g. Imperf., pair 600.00

Re-engraved

C72B AP26 2p dk blue ('38) .75 .25
c. Imperf., pair 20.00
d. Perf. 10 ('39) 1.50 1.10
Set, #C72A-C72B, never hinged 45.00

The sky has heavy horizontal lines of shading. Entire design is more heavily shaded than No. C72A.

No. C72B exists privately perforated 14. Value, $9 unused, $9 used.

For overprints see Nos. 7LC14, 7LC19, 14L26.

Eagle and Newspapers — AP27

Press Building, Madrid — AP28

Don Quixote and Sancho Panza Flying on the Wooden Horse — AP29

Design: 15c, 30c, 50c, 1p, Autogiro over House of Nazareth.

1936, Mar. 11 **Photo.** *Perf. 12½*

C73 AP27 1c rose car .25 .25
C74 AP28 2c dark brown .25 .25
C75 AP27 5c black brown .25 .25
C76 AP28 10c dk yellow grn .25 .25
C77 AP28 15c Prus blue .25 .25
C78 AP27 20c violet .25 .25
C79 AP28 25c magenta .25 .25
C80 AP28 30c red orange .25 .25
C81 AP27 40c orange .50 .25
C82 AP28 50c light blue .30 .25
C83 AP28 60c olive green .65 .40
C84 AP28 1p brnsh black .65 .45
C85 AP29 2p brt ultra 5.00 2.25
C86 AP29 4p lilac rose 5.00 2.75
C87 AP29 10p violet brown 12.00 11.00
Nos. C73-C87 (15) 26.10 19.35
Set, never hinged 45.00

Madrid Press Association, 40th anniv.

Exist imperf. Value, set $250 hinged, and $325 never hinged.

See note after No. 432.

Types of Regular Postage of 1936 Overprinted in Blue or Red

1936 *Imperf.*

C88 A125 10c dk red (Bl) 90.00 90.00
C89 A125 15c dk blue (R) 90.00 90.00
Set, never hinged 275.00

1st National Philatelic Exhibition which opened in Madrid, Apr. 2, 1936.

No. 577 Overprinted in Black

1936, Aug. 1 *Perf. 11½*

C90 A128 30c rose red 5.00 3.75
Never hinged 12.00
b. Imperf., pair 140.00

Issued in commemoration of the flight of aviators Antonio Arnaiz and Juan Calvo from Manila to Spain.

Counterfeit overprints exist.

Exists privately perforated 14. Value, $50 unused, $50 used.

No. 288 Surcharged in Black

1938, Apr. 13 *Perf. 14*

C91 A36 2.50p on 10c 80.00 80.00
Never hinged 160.00

7th anniversary of the Republic.

Values are for examples with perforations nearly touching the design on one or two sides.

No. 507 Surcharged in Various Colors

1938, Aug. *Perf. 11½*

C92 A92 50c on 25c (Bk) 29.00 29.00
C93 A92 1p on 25c (G) 2.25 1.50
C94 A92 1.25p on 25c (R) 2.25 1.50
C95 A92 1.50p on 25c (Bl) 2.25 1.50
C96 A92 2p on 25c (Bk & R) 40.00 34.00
Nos. C92-C96 (5) 75.75 67.50
Set, never hinged 150.00

No. 585 Surcharged

1938, June 1 *Perf. 11*

C97 A132 5p on 1p multi 225. 225.
Never hinged 450.
a. Imperf., pair 550. 525.
b. Inverted surcharge 300. 300.
c. Souvenir sheet 950. 950.
Never hinged 1,650.
d. As "c," imperf. 4,500. 4,500.
e. As "c," inverted surcharge 4,500. 4,500.

Counterfeit surcharges exist.

Type of 1938-39 Overprinted in Red or Carmine

1938, May *Perf. 10, 10½*

C98 A163 50c indigo (R) .70 .55
C99 A163 1p dk blue (C) 3.00 .70
Set, never hinged 4.50

Exist imperf. Value, each $100.

Examples without overprint are proofs.

Juan de la Cierva and his Autogiro over Madrid AP30

1939, Jan. **Unwmk.** **Litho.** *Perf. 11*

C100 AP30 20c red orange .60 .40
C101 AP30 25c dk carmine .45 .25
C102 AP30 35c brt violet .65 .40
C103 AP30 50c dk brown .65 .25
C105 AP30 1p blue .65 .25
C107 AP30 2p green 3.25 1.75
C108 AP30 4p dull blue 5.00 2.75
Nos. C100-C108 (7) 11.25 6.05
Set, never hinged 19.00

Exist imperf. Value, set $325.

1941-47 *Perf. 10*

C109 AP30 20c dk red orange .25 .25
C110 AP30 25c redsh brown .25 .25
C111 AP30 35c lilac rose 1.60 .50
C112 AP30 50c brown .45 .25
C113 AP30 1p chalky blue 1.40 .25
C114 AP30 2p lt gray grn 1.60 .25
C115 AP30 4p gray blue 5.00 .30
C116 AP30 10p brt purple ('47) 3.75 .65
Nos. C109-C116 (8) 14.30 2.70
Set, never hinged 26.00

Issued in honor of Juan de la Cierva (1895-1936), inventor of the autogiro.

Nos. C109-C115 exist imperf. Value, set $300.

The overprint "EXPOSICION NACIONAL DE FILATELIA 1948 SAN SEBASTIAN" multiple, in parallel horizontal lines, on Nos. C109 to C113 and other airmail stamps, was privately applied.

Correo Aéreo

Correo Aéreo

Nos. 625-634, 660, 676 and 677 with either of these overprints have not been established as issues of the Spanish government.

Mariano Pardo de Figueroa (Dr. Thebussem) AP31

1944, Oct. 12 **Engr.** *Perf. 10*

C117 AP31 5p brt ultra 12.50 11.50
Never hinged 21.50

"Stamp Day" and "Day of the Race," Oct. 12, 1944. Valid for franking air mail correspondence one day only.

Mail Coach, Plane and Count of St. Louis AP32

1945, Oct. 12 **Unwmk.**

C118 AP32 10p yellow green 14.00 14.00
Never hinged 22.50

"Stamp Day" and "Day of the Race," Oct. 12, 1945, and to honor Luis José Sartorius, Count of St. Louis, who issued the decree for Spain's 1st postage stamps. No. C118 was valid for franking air mail correspondence one day only.

C118 exists imperf. Value, $1,000.

Maj. Joaquin Garcia Morato AP33

1945, Nov. 27

C119 AP33 10p deep claret 17.50 5.50
Never hinged 30.00

C119 exists imperf. Value, $600 hinged, $1,000 never hinged.

Capt. Carlos Haya Gonzalez — AP34

1945, Dec. 14

C120 AP34 4p red 7.50 4.50
Never hinged 12.50

No. C120 exists imperf. Values: $600 hinged; $1,000 never hinged.

Bartolomé de las Casas — AP35

1946, Oct. 12 *Perf. 11½x11*

C121 AP35 5.50p green 1.90 2.50
Never hinged 3.00

Stamp Day and Day of the Race. Exists imperf. Value $16.

Don Quixote and Sancho Panza Astride Clavileno AP36

1947, Oct. 9 *Perf. 10*

C122 AP36 5.50p purple 3.50 2.50
Never hinged 6.75

Stamp Day and the 400th anniversary of the birth of Miguel de Cervantes Saavedra.

C122 exists imperf. Value, $1,200.

Manuel de Falla — AP37

Ignacio Zuloaga — AP38

1947, Dec. 1 *Perf. 9½x10½*

Control Number on Back

C123 AP37 25p dk vio brn 20.00 15.00
C124 AP38 50p dk carmine 100.00 40.00
Set, never hinged 200.00

Counterfeits exist.

For overprint see No. CB18.

No. C124 exists imperf. Value, $1,200.

Train and Plane — AP39

1948, Oct. 9 **Litho.** *Perf. 13x12½*

C125 AP39 2p scarlet 1.50 1.50
Never hinged 2.25

Cent. of Spanish railroads and Stamp Day.

UPU Type of Regular Issue with Pedestal and Propeller Added

1949, Oct. 9 *Perf. 12½x13*

C126 A202 4p dk olive green .25 .45
Never hinged .40

Stamp Day and the 75th anniv. of the UPU.

Stamp of 1850 — AP40

1950, Oct. 12 Engr. *Imperf.*

No.	Type	Value	Color	Unused	Used
C127	AP40	1p	rose brn	4.50	4.50
C128	AP40	2.50p	brown org	4.50	4.50
C129	AP40	20p	dark blue	45.00	45.00
C130	AP40	25p	green	45.00	45.00
			Nos. C127-C130 (4)	99.00	99.00
			Set, never hinged	175.00	

Centenary of Spanish postage stamps.

Map of Western Hemisphere — AP41

1951, Apr. 16 Photo. *Perf. 12½*

No.	Type	Value	Color	Unused	Used
C131	AP41	1p	blue	4.50	2.25
			Never hinged	7.00	

6th Congress of the Postal Union of the Americas and Spain.

Isabella I AP42

1951, Oct. 12 Engr. *Perf. 13*

No.	Type	Value	Color	Unused	Used
C132	AP42	60c	dk gray grn	5.25	.40
C133	AP42	90c	orange	.65	.50
C134	AP42	1.30p	plum	4.00	3.50
C135	AP42	1.90p	sepia	3.75	3.50
C136	AP42	2.30p	dk blue	2.25	2.25
			Nos. C132-C136 (5)	15.90	10.15
			Set, never hinged	25.00	

Stamp Day and 500th anniv. of the birth of Queen Isabella I.

"The Eucharist" by Tiepolo — AP43

1952, May 26 Photo. *Perf. 12½x13*

No.	Type	Value	Color	Unused	Used
C137	AP43	1p	gray green	3.00	.60
			Never hinged	3.50	

35th International Encharistic Congress, Barcelona, 1952.

St. Francis Xavier — AP44

1952, July 3 Engr.

No.	Type	Value	Color	Unused	Used
C138	AP44	2p	deep blue	22.50	12.00
			Never hinged	45.00	

400th anniv. of the death of St. Francis Xavier.

AP45

Design: Ferdinand the Catholic and Columbus presenting natives.

1952, Oct. 12

No.	Type	Value	Color	Unused	Used
C139	AP45	60c	dull green	.25	.25
C140	AP45	90c	orange	.25	.25
C141	AP45	1.30p	plum	.40	.30
C142	AP45	1.90p	sepia	1.60	1.60
C143	AP45	2.30p	deep blue	8.00	8.00
			Nos. C139-C143 (5)	10.50	10.40
			Set, never hinged	17.50	

500th anniversary of the birth of Ferdinand the Catholic and to publicize Stamp Day.

Joaquin Sorolla y Bastida — AP46

1953, Oct. 9 *Perf. 13x12½*

No.	Type	Value	Color	Unused	Used
C144	AP46	50p	dark violet	200.00	22.50
			Never hinged	350.00	

Issued to honor Joaquin Sorolla y Bastida (1863-1923), impressionist painter.

Miguel Lopez de Legazpi — AP47

1953, Nov. 5

No.	Type	Value	Color	Unused	Used
C145	AP47	25p	gray black	30.00	25.00
			Never hinged	100.00	

Spanish-Philippine Postal Convention of 1951.

Leonardo Torres Quevedo (1852-1939), Mathematician and Inventor — AP48

Perf. 13x12½

1955, Sept. 6 Unwmk.

No.	Type	Value	Color	Unused	Used
C146	AP48	50p	bluish gray & blk	5.00	.90
			Never hinged	11.00	

Plane and Caravel AP49

1955-56 Photo. *Perf. 12½x13*

No.	Type	Value	Color	Unused	Used
C147	AP49	20c	gray grn ('56)	.25	.25
C148	AP49	25c	gray violet	.25	.25
C149	AP49	50c	ol gray ('56)	.25	.25
C150	AP49	1p	red orange	.25	.25
C151	AP49	1.10p	emer ('56)	.25	.25
C152	AP49	1.40p	rose car	.25	.25
C153	AP49	3p	brt blue ('56)	.25	.25
C154	AP49	4.80p	yellow	.25	.25
C155	AP49	5p	redsh brown	1.50	.25
C156	AP49	7p	lilac ('56)	.45	.25
C157	AP49	10p	lt ol grn ('56)	.50	.25
			Nos. C147-C157 (11)		2.75
			Set, never hinged	4.00	

Mariano Fortuny y Carbo (1838-1874), Painter — AP50

1956, Jan. 10 Engr. *Perf. 13x12½*

No.	Type	Value	Color	Unused	Used
C158	AP50	25p	grnsh black	14.00	.90
			Never hinged	30.00	

Catalogue values for unused stamps in this section, from this point to the end of the section, are for Never Hinged items.

Bullfight Type of Regular Issue

25c, Small town arena. 50c, Fighting with cape. 1p, Dedication of the bull. 5p, Bull ring.

Perf. 13x12½, 12½x13

1960, Feb. 29 Engr. Unwmk.

No.	Type	Value	Color	Unused	Used
C159	A246	25c	brn car & dl lil	.25	.25
C160	A245	50c	blue	.25	.25
C161	A246	1p	red & dull red	.25	.25
C162	A245	5p	red lilac & vio	.55	.40
			Nos. C159-C162 (4)	1.30	1.15

Jai Alai AP51

1960, Mar. 27 Photo. *Perf. 12½x13*

No.	Type	Value	Color	Unused	Used
C163	AP51	1p	brt red & dk brn	4.75	3.25
C164	AP51	5p	dull brn & mag	4.75	3.25
C165	AP51	6p	vio blk & mag	4.75	3.25
C166	AP51	10p	grn, mag & dk brn	4.75	3.25
			Nos. C163-C166 (4)	19.00	13.00

1st Intl. Cong. of Philately, Barcelona, Mar. 26-Apr. 5. Nos. C163-C166 could be bought at the exhibition upon presentation of 5p entrance ticket.

Sport Type of Regular Issue

Sports: 1.25p, 6p, Steeplechase, horiz. 1.50p, 10p, Basque ball game.

Perf. 12½x13, 13x12½

1960, Oct. 31 Unwmk.

No.	Type	Value	Color	Unused	Used
C167	A251	1.25p	choc & car	.30	.25
C168	A251	1.50p	pur, brn & blk	.30	.25
C169	A251	6p	vio blk & car	.95	.55
C170	A251	10p	ol grn, red & blk	1.25	.55
			Nos. C167-C170 (4)	2.80	1.60

Rosary Type of Regular Issue

Mysteries of the Rosary: 25c, The Ascension, Bayeu. 1p, The Descent of the Holy Ghost, El Greco. 5p, The Assumption, Mateo Cerezo. 10p, The Coronation of the Virgin Mary, El Greco.

1962, Oct. 26 Engr. *Perf. 13*

No.	Type	Value	Color	Unused	Used
C171	A280	25c	vio & dl gray vio	.25	.25
C172	A280	1p	olive & brown	.35	.25
C173	A280	5p	brn & rose cl	.60	.25
C174	A280	10p	bluish grn & yel grn	1.40	.50
			Nos. C171-C174 (4)	2.60	1.25

Recaredo I, Visigothic King, 586-601 — AP52

Portrait: 50p, Francisco Cardinal Jimenez de Cisneros (1436-1517).

1963, Dec. 5 Engr. *Perf. 13x12½*

No.	Type	Value	Color	Unused	Used
C175	AP52	25p	dull purple	1.10	.40
C176	AP52	50p	green & black	1.90	.55

1966, Feb. 26

Portraits: 25p, Seneca (4 B.C.-65 A.D.). 50p, Pope St. Damasus I (304?-384).

No.	Type	Value	Color	Unused	Used
C177	AP52	25p	yel grn & dk grn	1.75	.25
C178	AP52	50p	sky bl & gray bl	2.75	.55

Plaza de Espana, Seville AP53

20p, Rande River Bridge, Pontevedra.

1981, Nov. 26 Engr. *Perf. 13*

No.	Type	Value	Color	Unused	Used
C179	AP53	13p	shown	.25	.25
C180	AP53	20p	multicolored	.25	.25

St. Thomas, by El Greco — AP54

13p, Sts. Andrew and Francis.

1982, July 7 Photo. *Perf. 13*

No.	Type	Value	Color	Unused	Used
C181	AP54	13p	multicolored	.25	.25
C182	AP54	20p	shown	.25	.25

Bowling AP55

1983, Apr. 13 Photo. *Perf. 13*

No.	Type	Value	Color	Unused	Used
C183	AP55	13p	Bicycling, vert.	.25	.25
C184	AP55	20p	shown	.25	.25

AIR POST SEMI-POSTAL STAMPS

Red Cross Issue

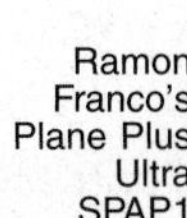

Ramon Franco's Plane Plus Ultra SPAP1

Perf. 12½, 13

1926, Sept. 15 Engr. Unwmk.

No.	Type	Value	Color	Unused	Used
CB1	SPAP1	5c	black & vio	1.40	1.40
CB2	SPAP1	10c	ultra & blk	1.40	1.40
CB3	SPAP1	25c	carmine & blk	.35	.35
CB4	SPAP1	50c	red org & blk	.35	.35
CB5	SPAP1	1p	black & green	2.25	2.25
			Nos. CB1-CB5 (5)	5.75	5.75
			Set, never hinged	8.75	

For overprints and surcharges see Nos. B55-B63.

No. B106 Surcharged in Black

1938, Apr. 15 *Perf. 11½*

No.	Type	Value	Description	Unused	Used
CB6	SP13	45c + 2p + 5p		175.	175.
			Never hinged	400.	
a.			Imperf., pair	700.	400.
b.			Souvenir sheet of 1	*3,000.*	*3,000.*
			Never hinged	*6,000.*	

c.	Souvenir sheet, imperf.	*5,500.*	*5,500.*
d.	Souv. sheet, surch. invtd.	*4,500.*	*4,500.*
	Never hinged	*6,500.*	

The surtax was used to benefit the defenders of Madrid.

This issue has been extensively counterfeited.

No. B107 Surcharged

1938, June 1 ***Perf. 10***

CB7	SP14 45c + 5p + 3p	10.00	9.75
	Never hinged	17.50	

Monument SPAP2

Dome Fresco by Goya, Cathedral of Zaragoza SPAP3

#CB9, CB14, Caravel Santa Maria. #CB10, CB12, The Ascension. #CB13, The Coronation. #CB17, Bombardment of Cathedral of Zaragoza.

Perf. 10½, 11½x10½, 11½

1940, Jan. 29 Litho. Unwmk.

Bicolored

CB8	SPAP2	25c + 5c	.40	.40
CB9	SPAP2	50c + 5c	.40	.40
CB10	SPAP2	65c + 15c	.40	.40
CB11	SPAP2	70c + 15c	.40	.40
CB12	SPAP2	90c + 20c	.40	.40
CB13	SPAP2	1.20p + 30c	.40	.40
CB14	SPAP2	1.40p + 40c	.50	.50
CB15	SPAP2	2p + 50c	.75	.75
CB16	SPAP3	4p + 1p sl grn & rose lil	13.00	13.00
CB17	SPAP3	10p + 4p chnt & ultra	165.00	165.00
	Nos. CB8-CB17 (10)		181.65	181.65
	Set, never hinged		440.00	

19th centenary of the Pillar Virgin. The surtax was used to help restore the Cathedral at Zaragoza, damaged during the Civil War.

No. CB16 exists in slate green & violet, No. CB17 in red violet & ultramarine. Value, $32.50 each.

Nos. CB8-CB17 exist imperf. Value, set $400.

No. C123 Surcharged in Black

1950-51 ***Perf. 9½x10½***

Control Number on Back

CB18	AP37 25p + 10c	175.	175.
	Never hinged	350.	
a.	Without control number	*2,400.*	*1,500.*
	Without control number, never hinged	*4,250.*	

Visit of Gen. Franco to the Canary Islands, Oct., 1950.

The control number was printed on the gum, and regummed examples of No. CB18 are frequently offered as No. CB18a.

Counterfeit surcharges exist.

Issued: #CB18a, 10/23/50; #CB18 2/22/51.

AIR POST SPECIAL DELIVERY STAMP

Goya Commemorative Issue

Type of Air Post Stamp of 1930 Overprinted

1930 Unwmk. ***Perf. 12½***

CE1	AP4 20c bl blk & lt brn (Bk)	.25	.25
	Never hinged	.25	
a.	Blue overprint	15.00	7.75
	Never hinged	21.00	
b.	Overprint omitted	15.00	22.50
	Never hinged	25.00	

See note after No. 432.

AIR POST OFFICIAL STAMPS

Pan-American Postal Union Congress Issue

Types of Air Post Stamps of 1931 Overprinted in Red or Blue

1931 Unwmk. ***Perf. 12***

CO1	AP22	5c red brown (R)	.25	.25
CO2	AP22	10c blue grn (Bl)	.25	.25
CO3	AP22	25c rose (Bl)	.25	.25
CO4	AP23	50c lt blue (R)	.25	.25
CO5	AP23	1p violet (R)	.25	.25
CO6	AP24	4p gray blk (R)	3.50	3.50
	Nos. CO1-CO6 (6)		4.75	4.75
	Set, never hinged		7.00	

Shades exist.

Nos. CO1-CO6 exist imperf. Value, set $22.50

SPECIAL DELIVERY STAMPS

Pegasus and Coat of Arms — SD1

1905-25 Unwmk. Typo. ***Perf. 14***

Control Number on Back

E1	SD1 20c deep red	45.00	.30
	Never hinged	100.00	
a.	20c rose red, litho. ('25)	38.00	.30
	Never hinged	70.00	
b.	Imperf., pair	300.00	
c.	As "a," imperf., pair	300.00	

Gazelle SD2

1929 Engr. ***Perf. 11***

Control Number on Back

E2	SD2 20c dull red	15.00	15.00
	Never hinged	37.50	
a.	Perf. 14	32.50	37.50
	Never hinged	60.00	

Seville and Barcelona Exhibitions. See note after No. 432.

Pegasus — SD3

1929-32 ***Perf. 13½x12½, 11½***

Control Number on Back

E3	SD3 20c red	21.00	4.00
	Never hinged	40.00	
a.	Imperf., pair	400.00	
b.	Without control number, perf. 11½ ('32)	60.00	1.50
	Never hinged	97.50	
c.	As "b," imperf., pair	*950.00*	

No. E3 Overprinted like Nos. 358-370

E4	SD3 20c red (Bl)	12.00	25.00
	Never hinged	30.00	

League of Nations 55th assembly.

For overprints see Nos. E5, E10-E12.

No. E3 Overprinted in Blue

1930 ***Perf. 13½x12½, 11½***

E5	SD3 20c red	13.50	.75
	Never hinged	40.00	

Railway Congress Issue

Electric Locomotive — SD4

1930, May 10 Litho. ***Perf. 14***

Control Number on Back

E6	SD4 20c brown orange	50.00	50.00
	Never hinged	105.00	

See note after No. 385.

Goya Issue

Type of Regular Issue of 1930 Overprinted

1930 ***Perf. 12½***

E7	A57 20c lilac rose	.25	.30
	Never hinged	.45	

Christopher Columbus Issue

Type of Regular Issue of 1930 Overprinted

1930 Sept. 29

E8	A64 20c brown violet	1.50	1.50
	Never hinged	2.50	

See note after No. 432.

Spanish-American Exhibition Issue

View of Seville Exhibition — SD5

1930, Oct. 10 Photo. ***Perf. 14***

E9	SD5 20c orange	.40	.40
	Never hinged	.55	.55

See note after No. 432.

Madrid Issue

No. E5 Overprinted in Green

1931 ***Perf. 11½***

E10	SD3 20c red	5.00	5.00
	Never hinged	8.00	

The status of No. E10 has been questioned.

Barcelona Issue

No. E3 Overprinted

E11	SD3 20c red	5.50	5.50
	Never hinged	12.00	

No. E11 also exists with accent over "U."

The status of No. E11 has been questioned.

No. E3 Overprinted in Blue

E12	SD3 20c red	6.50	1.25
	Never hinged	21.00	

Montserrat Issue

Pegasus — SD6

1931 Engr. ***Perf. 11***

Control Number on Back

E13	SD6 20c vermilion	25.00	25.00
	Never hinged	38.00	
a.	Perf. 14	55.00	60.00

SD7

1934 ***Perf. 10***

E14	SD7 20c vermilion	.25	.25
	Never hinged	.35	
a.	Imperf., pair	32.50	

For overprints see #10LE1, 11LE1-11LE4, 14LE1.

Newsboy — SD8

1936 Photo. *Perf. 12½*

E15 SD8 20c rose carmine .25 .30
Never hinged .50

40th anniversary of the Madrid Press Association.
See note after No. 432.

Pegasus SD9

Spanish State

1937-38 Unwmk. Litho. *Perf. 11*

With imprint "Hija. deB Fournier-Burgos"

E16 SD9 20c violet brn 7.75 4.50
Never hinged 11.00
a. Imperf., pair 77.50

Without Imprint

E17 SD9 20c dk vio brn ('38) 1.50 .30
Never hinged 3.00
a. Imperf., pair 50.00

No. 645 Overprinted in Black

1937

E18 A162 20c dark violet 11.00 11.00
Never hinged 14.50

Pegasus SD10

1939-42 *Perf. 10½*

Imprint: "SANCHEZ TODA"

E19 SD10 25c carmine 4.50 .70
Never hinged 6.25
a. Imperf., pair 50.00

Without Imprint

Perf. 10

E20 SD10 25c carmine ('42) .25 .25
Never hinged .30
a. Imperf., pair 8.50

Catalogue values for unused stamps in this section, from this point to the end of the section, are for Never Hinged items.

"Flight" SD11

Centaur — SD12

Perf. 12½x13, 13x12½

1956, Feb. 12 Photo. Unwmk.

E21 SD11 2p scarlet .25 .25
E22 SD12 4p black & magenta .25 .25

1965-66

E23 SD11 3p dp car .25 .25
E24 SD11 5p dp org ('66) .25 .25
E25 SD12 6.50p dk vio & rose brn ('66) .25 .25
Nos. E21-E25 (5) 1.25 1.25

Chariot SD13

Mail Circling Globe — SD14

1971, June 1 Photo. *Perf. 13*

E26 SD13 10p red & yel grn .25 .25
E27 SD14 15p red, bl & blk .25 .25

Communications — SD15

1993, Apr. 20 Photo. *Perf. 14x13½*

E28 SD15 180p red & yellow 2.50 .35

SEMI-POSTAL SPECIAL DELIVERY STAMPS

Red Cross Issue

Royal Family Group SPSD1

1926 Unwmk. Engr. *Perf. 12½, 13*

EB1 SPSD1 20c red vio & vio brn 8.75 8.75
Never hinged 17.00

See notes after Nos. 432 and B18.
For overprint see No. B54.

Motorcyclist and Zaragoza Cathedral — SPSD2

1940 Litho. *Perf. 11½*

EB2 SPSD2 25c + 5c rose red & buff .40 .30

19th cent. of the Pillar Virgin. The surtax was used to help restore the Cathedral at Zaragoza, damaged during the Civil War.

DELIVERY TAX STAMPS

D1

1931 Unwmk. Litho. *Perf. 11½*

ER1 D1 5c black 7.25 .25
Never hinged 12.00

For overprints see Nos. ER2-ER3, 7LE5-7LE6.

No. ER1 Overprinted in Red

1931

ER2 D1 5c black 1.25 1.40
Never hinged 2.25

No. ER2 also exists with accent over "U."

No. ER1 Overprinted in Red

ER3 D1 5c black 3.00 3.00
Never hinged 5.50

These stamps were originally issued for Postage Due purpose but were later used as regular postage stamps.

WAR TAX STAMPS

These stamps did not pay postage but represented a fiscal tax on mail matter in addition to the postal fees. Their use was obligatory.

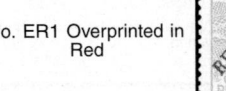

Coat of Arms — WT1

Unwmk.

1874, Jan. 1 Typo. *Perf. 14*

MR1 WT1 5c black 11.00 .95
a. Imperf., pair 14.00
MR2 WT1 10c pale blue 12.00 1.60
a. Imperf., pair 62.50

Coat of Arms — WT2

1875, Jan. 1

MR3 WT2 5c green 6.00 .60
a. Imperf., pair 27.50
MR4 WT2 10c lilac 12.00 2.75
a. Imperf., pair 55.00

King Alfonso XII — WT3

1876, June 1

MR5 WT3 5c pale green 7.50 1.00
MR6 WT3 10c blue 7.50 1.00
a. Cliche of 5c in plate of 10c 125.00
MR7 WT3 25c black 50.00 17.00
MR8 WT3 1p lilac 475.00 110.00
MR9 WT3 5p rose 900.00 300.00

Nos. MR5-MR9 exist imperforate. Value, $1,100.

King Alfonso XII — WT4

1877, Sept. 1

MR10 WT4 15c claret 27.50 1.00
a. Imperf., pair 100.00
MR11 WT4 50c yellow 900.00 110.00

WT5

1879

MR12 WT5 5c blue 65.00
MR13 WT5 10c rose 37.50
MR14 WT5 15c violet 25.00
MR15 WT5 25c brown 40.00
MR16 WT5 50c olive green 25.00
MR17 WT5 1p bister 40.00
MR18 WT5 5p gray 150.00
Nos. MR12-MR18 (7) 382.50

Nos. MR12-MR18 were never placed in use.
Nos. MR17 and MR18 exist imperforate. Value, $225.

WT6

Inscribed "1897 A 1898"

1897 *Perf. 14*

MR19 WT6 5c green 3.25 2.10
MR20 WT6 10c green 3.25 2.10
MR21 WT6 15c green 750.00 250.00
MR22 WT6 20c green 8.25 3.25

Nos. MR19-MR22 exist imperf. Value for set $825.

Inscribed

1898

MR23 WT6 5c black 2.25 1.75
MR24 WT6 10c black 2.25 1.75
MR25 WT6 15c black 50.00 9.50
MR26 WT6 20c black 3.50 3.00
Nos. MR23-MR26 (4) 58.00 16.00

Nos. MR23-MR26 exist imperf. Value about $275 a pair.

King Alfonso XIII — WT7

1898

MR27 WT7 5c black 9.00 .60
a. Imperf., pair 85.00

OFFICIAL STAMPS

Coat of Arms — O1

Unwmk.

1854, July 1 Typo. *Imperf.*

O1	O1	½o blk, *yellow*	2.10	2.75
O2	O1	1o blk, *rose*	2.75	3.25
a.		1o black, *blue*	29.00	
O3	O1	4o blk, *green*	7.50	9.25
O4	O1	1 l blk, *blue*	52.50	60.00
		Nos. O1-O4 (4)	64.85	75.25

Coat of Arms — O2

1855-63

O5	O2	½o blk, *yellow*	1.50	1.75
a.		½o black, *straw* ('63)	1.75	1.90
O6	O2	1o blk, *rose*	1.50	1.75
a.		1o black, *salmon rose*	3.25	1.90
O7	O2	4o blk, *green*	3.25	1.90
a.		4o black, *yellow green*	8.75	1.90
O8	O2	1 l blk, *gray blue*	14.50	17.50
		Nos. O5-O8 (4)	20.75	22.90

The "value indication" on Nos. O1-O8 actually is the weight of the mail in onzas (ounces, "o") and libras (pounds, "l") for which they were valid.

Type of Regular Issue of 1889

1895 *Perf. 14*

O9	A34	15c yellow	11.00	6.00
a.		Imperf., pair	250.00	

Coat of Arms — O5

1896-98

O10	O5	rose	5.25	1.75
a.		Imperf., pair	87.50	
O11	O5	dk blue ('98)	19.00	6.00

Cervantes Issue

Chamber of Deputies O6

Statue of Cervantes — O7

National Library O8

Cervantes — O9

1916, Apr. 22 Engr. *Perf. 12*

For the Senate

O12	O6	green & blk	1.10	.90
O13	O7	brown & blk	1.10	.90
O14	O8	carmine & blk	1.10	.90
O15	O9	brown & blk	1.10	.90

For the Chamber of Deputies

O16	O6	violet & blk	1.10	.90
O17	O7	carmine & blk	1.10	.90
O18	O8	green & blk	1.10	.90
O19	O9	violet & blk	1.10	.90
		Nos. O12-O19 (8)	8.80	7.20

Exist imperf. Value set of pairs, $110.

Exist with centers inverted. Value for set, $87.50

Pan-American Postal Union Congress Issue

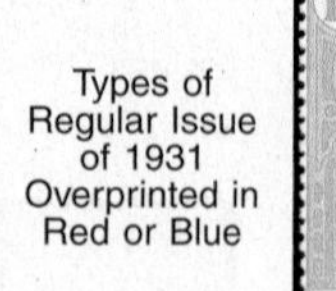

Types of Regular Issue of 1931 Overprinted in Red or Blue

1931 *Perf. 12½*

O20	A84	5c dk brown (R)	.50	.25
O21	A85	10c brt green (Bl)	.50	.25
O22	A86	15c dull violet (R)	.50	.25
O23	A85	25c deep rose (Bl)	.50	.25
O24	A87	30c olive green (Bl)	.50	.25
O25	A84	40c ultra (R)	.70	.60
O26	A85	50c deep orange (Bl)	.70	.60
O27	A86	1p blue black (R)	.70	.60
O28	A88	4p magenta (Bl)	11.00	11.00
O29	A88	10p lt brown (R)	20.00	20.00
		Nos. O20-O29 (10)	35.60	34.05
		Set, never hinged	57.50	

Nos. O22-O29 exist imperf. Values about 3 times those quoted.

Mail Coach — O9a

Decorative Mailbox Opening O10

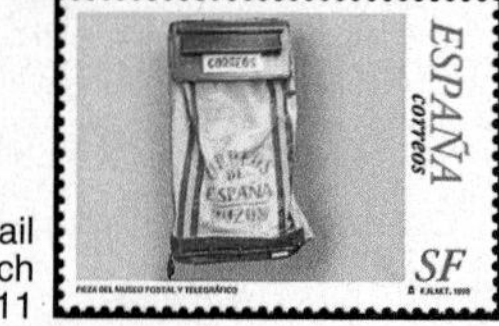

Mail Pouch O11

Bicycle for Mail Delivery O12

1999 Photo. *Perf. 13¾x14*

O30	O9a	multi	—
O31	O10	multi	—
O32	O11	multi	—
O33	O12	multi	—
a.		Horiz. strip, #O30-O33	—

For use by the Philatelic Service to any address. Not normally available unused.

POSTAL TAX STAMPS

PT5

Perf. 10½x11½

1937, Dec. 23 Litho.

RA11	PT5	10c blk, pale bl & red	8.00	5.00
		Never hinged	21.00	
a.		Imperf. pair	80.00	
		Never hinged	120.00	

The tax was for the tuberculosis fund.

PT6

1938, Dec. 23 *Perf. 11½*

RA12	PT6	10c multicolored	4.50	1.75
		Never hinged	10.00	
a.		Imperf. pair	45.00	
		Never hinged	55.00	

The tax was for the tuberculosis fund.

"Spain" Holding Wreath of Peace over Marching Soldiers PT7

1939, July 18 *Perf. 11*

RA13	PT7	10c blue	.25	.25
		Never hinged	.25	
a.		Imperf. pair	65.00	
		Never hinged	82.50	

Type of Regular Issue, 1939

Without Imprint

Unwmk.

1939, Dec. 23 Litho. *Imperf.*

RA14	A166	10c dull claret	.25	.25
		Never hinged	.25	

Tuberculosis Fund Issue

Types of Corresponding Semi-Postal Stamps

1940, Dec. 23 *Perf. 10*

RA15	SP23	10c violet & red	.25	.25
		Never hinged	.25	

1941, Dec. 23

RA16	SP24	10c black & red	.25	.25
		Never hinged	.25	

1942, Dec. 23

RA17	SP25	10c dl sal & rose red	.25	.25
		Never hinged	.25	

1943, Dec. 23 Photo. *Perf. 11*

RA18	SP26	10c purple & dl red	.30	.25
		Never hinged	.50	

Perf. 9½x10

1944, Dec. 23 Litho. Unwmk.

RA19	SP27	10c salmon & rose	.25	.25
		Never hinged	.25	

1945, Dec. 23

RA20	SP28	10c salmon & car	.25	.25
		Never hinged	.25	

Mother and Child — PT8

1946, Dec. 22 Litho. *Perf. 9½x10½*

RA21	PT8	5c violet & red	.25	.25
RA22	PT8	10c green & red	.25	.25
		Set, never hinged	.40	

See No. RAC7.

Lorraine Cross PT9

Tuberculosis Sanatorium PT10

Perf. 9½x10½

1947, Dec. 22 Unwmk.

RA23	PT9	5c dk brown & red	.25	.25
RA24	PT10	10c vio bl & red	.25	.25
		Set, never hinged	.40	

See No. RAC8.

Aesculapius — PT11

Photogravure; Cross Engraved

1948, Dec. 22 Unwmk. *Perf. 12½*

RA25	PT11	5c brown & car	.25	.25
RA26	PT11	10c dp green & car	.25	.25
		Set, never hinged	.40	

The tax on Nos. RA15-RA26 was used to fight tuberculosis. See Nos. RAB1, RAC9.

"El Cid" — PT11a

1949, Feb. 1 Litho. *Perf. 10½x9½*

RA27	PT11a	5c violet	.25	.25
		Never hinged	.25	

The tax aided displaced children. Valid for ordinary postage after Dec. 24, 1949.

Tuberculosis Fund Issues

Galleon and Lorraine Cross — PT12

Photogravure; Cross Engraved

1949, Dec. 22 *Perf. 12½*

RA28	PT12	5c violet & red	.25	.25
RA29	PT12	10c yel grn & red	.25	.25
		Set, never hinged	.40	

See Nos. RAB2, RAC10.

Pine Branch and Candle — PT13

1950, Dec. 22 Cross in Carmine

RA30	PT13	5c rose violet	.25	.25
RA31	PT13	10c deep green	.25	.25
		Set, never hinged	.35	

See Nos. RAB3, RAC11.

Children at Seashore — PT14

1951, Oct. 1 Cross in Carmine
RA32 PT14 5c rose brown .25 .25
RA33 PT14 10c dull green .35 .25
Set, never hinged .75

See No. RAC12.

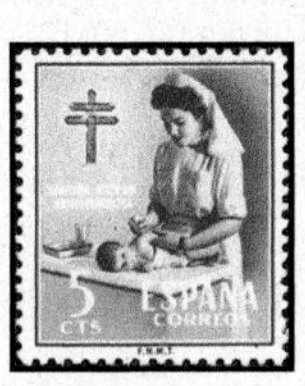
Nurse and Baby — PT15

1953, Oct. 1 Cross in Carmine
RA34 PT15 5c carmine lake .30 .25
RA35 PT15 10c gray blue .80 .25
Set, never hinged 2.25

The tax on RA28-RA35 was used to fight tuberculosis. See No. RAC13.

POSTAL TAX SEMI-POSTAL STAMPS

Types of Corresponding Postal Tax Stamps

Photogravure; Cross Engraved
1948 Unwmk. *Perf. 12½*
RAB1 PT11 50c + 10c red brn & car .80 .75
Never hinged 1.25

1949
RAB2 PT12 50c + 10c dk ol bis & red .50 .25
Never hinged .80

1950
RAB3 PT13 50c + 10c brn & car 1.25 1.25
Never hinged 2.25

The surtax on Nos. RAB1-RAB3 was used to fight tuberculosis. Combines domestic letter rate and tax obligatory Dec. 22-Jan. 3.

POSTAL TAX AIR POST STAMPS

Tuberculosis Fund Issues

Franco Type of Semi-Postal Stamps
Unwmk.
1940, Dec. 23 Litho. *Perf. 10*
RAC1 SP23 10c bright pink & red .90 .90
Never hinged 2.50

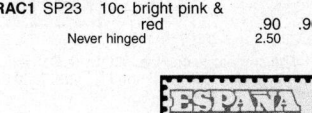

Knight and Lorraine Cross — PTAP2

1941, Dec. 23
RAC2 PTAP2 10c blue & red .25 .25
Never hinged .50

Lorraine Cross and Doves PTAP3

1942, Dec. 23
RAC3 PTAP3 10c dl sal & rose .80 .50
Never hinged 1.25

Cross of Lorraine — PTAP4

1943, Dec. 23 Photo. *Perf. 11*
RAC4 PTAP4 10c vio & dl red .90 1.00
Never hinged 1.60

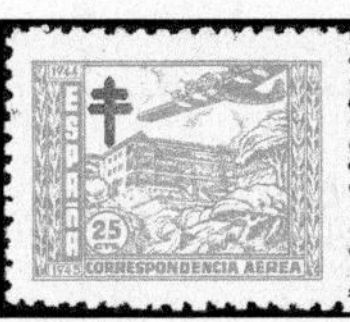
Tuberculosis Sanatorium PTAP5

1944, Dec. 23 Litho. *Perf. 10x9½*
RAC5 PTAP5 25c salmon & rose 3.75 3.75
Never hinged 5.50

Lorraine Cross and Eagle — PTAP6

1945, Dec. 23 *Perf. 10*
RAC6 PTAP6 25c red & car 1.40 1.25
Never hinged 1.75

Eagle — PTAP7

1946, Dec. 22
RAC7 PTAP7 25c red & car .25 .25
Never hinged .40

Tuberculosis Sanatorium PTAP8

1947, Dec. 22 *Perf. 11½*
RAC8 PTAP8 25c red vio .25 .25
Never hinged .40

Plane over Sanatorium PTAP9

Photogravure; Cross Engraved
1948, Dec. 22 *Perf. 12½*
RAC9 PTAP9 25c ultra & car .30 .25
Never hinged .60

Bell and Lorraine Cross — PTAP10

1949, Dec. 22
RAC10 PTAP10 25c maroon & red .25 .25
Never hinged .25

Dove and Flowers — PTAP11

1950, Dec. 22
RAC11 PTAP11 25c dk bl & car .30 .30
Never hinged .60

Mother and Child — PTAP12

1951, Oct. 1
RAC12 PTAP12 25c brn & car .50 .25
Never hinged .80

Tobias and Archangel PTAP13

1953, Oct. 1
RAC13 PTAP13 25c brn & car 3.50 5.50
Never hinged 6.50

FRANCHISE STAMPS

F1

1869 Unwmk. Litho. *Imperf.*
S1 F1 blue 52.50 38.00
a. Tête bêche pair 135.00 120.00

The franchise of No. S1 was granted to Diego Castell to use in distributing his publications on Spanish postal history.

F2

1881
S2 F2 black, *buff* 36.00 15.50

The franchise of No. S2 was granted to Antonio Fernandez Duro for his book, "Resena histórico-descriptiva de los sellos correos de Espana."

Reprints of No. S2 have been made on carmine, blue, gray, fawn and yellow paper.

CARLIST STAMPS

From the beginning of the Civil War (April 21, 1872) until separate stamps were issued on July 1, 1873, stamps of France were used on all mail from the provinces under Carlist rule.

King Carlos VII — A1

Tilde on N — A1a

Unwmk.
1873, July 1 Litho. *Imperf.*
X1 A1 1r blue 625.00
X2 A1a 1r blue 525.00 325.00

These stamps were reprinted three times in 1881 and once in 1887. The originals have 23 white lines and dots in the lower right spandrel. They are thin and of even width and spacing. The first reprint has 17 to 20 lines in the spandrel, most of them thick and of irregular width and length. The second and third reprints have 21 very thin lines, the second from the bottom being almost invisible. In the fourth reprint the lower right spandrel is an almost solid spot of color.

Originals of type A1 have the curved line above "ESPANA" broken at the left of the "E." All reprints of this type have the curved line continuous.

The reprints exist in various shades of blue, rose, red, violet and black.

King Carlos VII
A2 A3

A4

1874
X3 A2 1r violet 300.00 300.00
X4 A3 16m rose 5.50 *72.50*
X5 A4 ½r rose 125.00 125.00

Nos. X3 and X6-X7 were for use in the Basque Provinces and Navarra; No. X4 in Catalonia, and No. X5 in Valencia.

Two types of No. X5, alternating in each sheet.

No. X4 with favor cancellation (lozenge of dots) sells for same price as unused.

A5

1875 White Paper
X6 A5 50c green 8.00 *82.50*
a. 50c blue green 25.00 *100.00*
b. Bluish paper 50.00
X7 A5 1r brown 8.00 *82.50*
a. Bluish paper 50.00
Set, #X6-X7, never hinged 24.00

Fake cancellations exist on Nos. X1-X7.

REVOLUTIONARY OVERPRINTS

Issued by the Nationalist (Revolutionary) Forces

Many districts or cities made use of the stamps of the Republic overprinted in various forms. Most such overprinting was authorized by military or postal officials but some were without official sanction. These overprints were applied in patriotic celebration and partly as a protection from the use of unoverprinted stamps seized or stolen by soldiers.

BURGOS AIR POST STAMPS

Revenue Stamps Overprinted in Red, Blue or Black

RAP1

1936, Dec. 1 Unwmk. *Perf. 11½*

Control Number on Face of Stamp

7LC1	RAP1	25c gray grn & blk (R)	47.50	47.50
a.		Blue overprint	47.50	47.50
7LC2	RAP1	1.50p bl & blk (R)	6.00	6.00
7LC3	RAP1	3p rose & blk (Bl)	6.00	6.00
		Nos. 7LC1-7LC3 (3)	59.50	59.50
		Set, never hinged	105.00	

RAP2

RAP4

Perf. 13½

Blue Control Number on Back

7LC4	RAP2	15c green (R)	3.75	3.75
7LC5	RAP2	25c blue (R)	27.50	27.50
		Set, never hinged	45.00	

Perf. 11½

Without Control Number

Overprint in Black

7LC6	RAP4	1.50p dk blue	6.50	6.50
7LC7	RAP4	3p carmine	6.50	6.50
		Set, never hinged	21.00	

RAP5

RAP6

Overprint in Black

Perf. 13½, 11½

7LC8	RAP5	1.20p green	25.00	25.00
		Never hinged	37.50	

Perf. 14

Control Number on Back

7LC9	RAP6	1.20p green	25.00	25.00
7LC10	RAP6	2.40p green	25.00	25.00
		Set #7LC9-7LC10, never hinged	70.00	

No. 7LC9 is inscribed "CLASE 8a."

RAP7

1937 Unwmk. *Perf. 11½*

Control Number on Back

7LC11	RAP7	25c ultra (R)	225.00	225.00

Stamps of Spain, 1931-36, Overprinted in Red or Black (10p)

Perf. 11, 11½, 11x11½

1937 Unwmk.

Overprint 13mm high

7LC12	A100	40c blue	1.10	1.10
a.		Ovpt. 15mm high	1.10	1.10
7LC13	A97	50c dark blue	1.40	1.40
a.		Ovpt. 15mm high	1.40	1.40
7LC14	A130	50c dark blue	1.75	1.75
a.		Ovpt. 15mm high	1.75	1.75
7LC15	A100	60c apple green	2.50	2.50
a.		Ovpt. 15mm high	2.50	2.50
7LC16	AP26	2p gray blue	32.50	32.50
a.		Ovpt. 15mm high	32.50	32.50
7LC17	A49a	10p brown	82.50	82.50
a.		Ovpt. 15mm high	82.50	82.50
		Nos. 7LC12-7LC17 (6)	121.75	121.75

Issue dates: Nos. 7LC12-7LC17, 4/1. Nos. 7LC12a-7LC17a, 5/1.

Spain Nos. 576, 578 and 541b overprinted in Blue or Black

Nos. 7LC18, 7LC19

Nos. 7LC20, 7LC21

Perfs as on Basic Stamps

1937, May

7LC18	A127	30c carmine (Bk)	1.40	1.40
7LC19	A127	30c carmine (Bl)	.70	.70
7LC20	A129	30c car rose (Bk)	1.40	1.40
7LC21	A129	30c car rose (Bl)	.70	.70
7LC22	A107	10p dp brn (Bk)	11.00	11.00
		Nos. 7LC18-7LC22 (5)	15.20	15.20

Spain Nos. 539b and 540b, the 1p and 4p values, were prepared with this overprint in January, 1938, but were not issued. Value, each $4.50.

BURGOS ISSUE SPECIAL DELIVERY STAMPS

Pair of Spain No. 546 Overprinted in Black

1936 Unwmk. *Perf. 11½x11*

7LE3	A110	20c (10c+10c) emer	4.50	4.50
		Never hinged	9.00	
a.		Overprint inverted	14.00	

Type of Regular Stamp of 1931 Overprinted in Red

7LE4	A95	20c dark violet	10.00	10.00

Type of Delivery Tax Stamp of 1931 Overprinted in Red on Block of 4

Perf. 11½

7LE5	D1	20c black	8.75	8.00
		Never hinged	13.50	

Same Overprinted in Red on Block of 4

7LE6	D1	20c black	30.00	25.00
		Never hinged	50.00	

SD1

1936 Unwmk. *Perf. 11½*

7LE7	SD1	20c green & blk	7.25	5.50
7LE8	SD1	20c green & red	7.25	5.50
		Set, never hinged	25.00	

Nos. 7LE7-7LE8 exist with control number on back. Value $42.50 each.

CADIZ ISSUE SEMI-POSTAL STAMPS

Stamps of Spain, 1931-36, Surcharged in Black or Red

1936 Unwmk. *Imperf.*

8LB1	A108	1c + 5c blue grn	.25	.25

Perf. 11½x11, 11½

8LB2	A108	2c + 5c orange brn	.25	.25
8LB3	A103	5c + 5c choc (R)	.45	.45
8LB4	A110	10c + 5c green	.45	.45
8LB5	A111	15c + 5c Prus grn (R)	2.75	2.75
8LB6	A95	20c + 5c dk vio (R)	3.25	3.25
8LB7	A104	25c + 5c lake	2.50	2.50
8LB8	A113	30c + 5c rose red	1.40	1.40
8LB9	A100	40c + 5c dk blue (R)	3.25	3.25
8LB10	A97	50c + 5c dk blue (R)	6.50	6.50
		Nos. 8LB1-8LB10 (10)	21.05	21.05

CANARY ISLANDS AIR POST STAMPS

Issued for Use via the Lufthansa Service

Stamps of Spain, 1932-34, Surcharged in Blue

1936, Oct. 27 Unwmk. *Imperf.*

9LC1	A108	50c on 1c bl grn	27.50	17.50

Perf. 11½x11

9LC2	A108	80c on 2c buff	14.50	6.50
9LC3	A103	1.25p on 5c choc	30.00	17.50
		Nos. 9LC1-9LC3 (3)	72.00	41.50
		Set, never hinged	82.50	

The date July 18, 1936, in the overprints of Nos. 9LC1-9LC22 marks the beginning of the Franco insurrection.

Spain Nos. 542, 543, 528 and 641 Surcharged in Black, Red or Green

The surcharge on Nos. 9LC4 and 9LC6 exists in two types: Type I, 2½-3mm space between numerals and "Cts.". Type II, 1½-2mm space between numerals and "Cts."

1936-37 *Imperf.*

9LC4	A108	50c on 1c bl grn (I)	4.50	2.75
a.		Overprint type II	11.00	7.75
9LC5	A108	50c on 1c bl grn (R) ('37)	4.50	2.75

Perf. 11, 11½x11

9LC6	A108	80c on 2c buff (I)	2.25	1.60
a.		Overprint type II	5.50	3.25
9LC7	A108	80c on 2c buff (G) ('37)	3.25	1.60
9LC8	A103	1.25 Pts on 5c choc (R)	6.25	4.50
9LC9	A103	Pts 1.25 on 5c choc (R) ('37)	17.00	11.00
9LC10	A161	1.25p on 5c brn (G) ('37)	3.25	1.40
		Nos. 9LC4-9LC10 (7)	41.00	25.60
		Set, never hinged	65.00	

Issued: Nos. 9LC4, 9LC6, 11/28/36; No. 9LC8, 1/7/37; Nos. 9LC4a, 9LC6a, 9LC9, 2/12/37; Nos. 9LC5, 9LC7, 9LC10, 3/2/37.

Spain Nos. 542, 543 and 641 Surcharged in Blue

The surcharge on Nos. 9LC11-9LC13 exists in two types: Type I, 18mm tall. Type II, 20mm tall.

1937, Mar. 31 *Imperf.*

9LC11	A108	50c on 1c bl grn (I)	11.00	5.50
a.		Overprint type II	4.50	2.25

Perf. 11

9LC12	A108	80c on 2c buff (I)	11.00	4.50
a.		Overprint type II	2.75	1.10
9LC13	A161	1.25p on 5c brown (I)	3.25	1.10
		Nos. 9LC11-9LC13 (3)	25.25	11.10
		Set, never hinged	40.00	

Type II overprints issued 4/17/37.

Stamps of Spain, 1931-1936, Surcharged in Blue or Red (#9LC17, 9LC19)

The surcharge on Nos. 9LC15 and 9LC18 exists in two types: Type I, 2mm space between "+" and denomination. Type II, "+"

abuts surcharged denomination. Other values are Type I.

1937

9LC14 A104 25c + 50c lake 55.00 10.00
9LC15 A162 30c + 80c rose 19.50 7.75
a. Overprint type II 19.50 7.75
9LC16 A162 30c + 1.25p rose 25.00 8.25
9LC17 A97 50c + 1.25p dp bl 32.50 11.00
9LC18 A100 60c + 80c ap grn 25.00 8.75
a. Overprint type II 27.50 10.00
9LC19 A105 1p + 1.25p bl blk 80.00 22.50
Nos. 9LC14-9LC19 (6) 237.00 68.25
Set, never hinged 350.00

The surcharge represents the airmail rate and the basic stamp the postage rate.

Issued: 9LC15a, 9LC18a, 4/15. 9LC14-9LC19, 5/5.

Spain Nos. 542, 624 and 641 Surcharged in Black

1937, May 25 **Unwmk.** ***Imperf.***

9LC20 A108 50c on 1c bl grn 7.75 4.50

Perf. 11½, 11½x11

9LC21 A143 80c on 2c org brn 6.50 2.25
9LC22 A161 1.25p on 5c gray brn 6.50 2.25
Nos. 9LC20-9LC22 (3) 20.75 9.00
Set, never hinged 30.00

Stamps and Type of Spain, 1933-36, Surcharged in Black

1937, July ***Perf. 13½x13, 11, 11½***

9LC23 A143 50c on 2c org brn 3.50 2.25
9LC24 A126 80c on 2c org brn 300.00 180.00
9LC25 A161 80c on 5c gray brn 3.50 2.25
9LC26 A108 1.25p on 1c bl grn 4.25 2.25
9LC27 A161 2.50p on 10c grn 16.00 8.75

Spain Nos. 647, 650 and 652 Surcharged in Black or Red

Perf. 11

9LC28 A162 30c + 80c rose 3.00 1.40
9LC29 A162 50c + 1.25p dk bl (R) 10.50 5.00
9LC30 A162 1p + 1.25p bl (R) 16.00 8.75
Nos. 9LC23-9LC30 (8) 356.75 210.65
Set, never hinged 550.00

See note after No. 9LC19.

AP1

Perf. 14x13½

1937, July 16 **Wmk. 116**

Surcharge in Various Colors

9LC31 AP1 50c on 5c ultra (Br) 2.75 2.50
9LC32 AP1 80c on 5c ultra (G) 1.90 1.75
9LC33 AP1 1.25p on 5c ultra (V) 2.25 2.25
Nos. 9LC31-9LC33 (3) 6.90 6.50
Set, never hinged 10.00

Spain Nos. 641, 643 and 640 Surcharged in Green or Orange

1937, Oct. 29 **Unwmk.** ***Perf. 11***

9LC34 A161 50c on 5c (G) 9.25 3.75
9LC35 A161 80c on 10c (O) 5.75 2.75
9LC36 A160 1.25p on 2c (G) 10.50 7.25
Nos. 9LC34-9LC36 (3) 25.50 13.75
Set, never hinged 40.00

Spain Nos. 638, 640 and 643 Surcharged in Red, Blue or Violet

1937, Dec. 23 ***Imperf.***

9LC37 A159 50c on 1c (R) 10.50 4.50

Perf. 11, 11x11½

9LC38 A160 80c on 2c (Bl) 4.25 2.75
9LC39 A161 1.25p on 10c (V) 9.25 3.50
Nos. 9LC37-9LC39 (3) 24.00 10.75
Set, never hinged 37.50

Spain Nos. 647, 650 to 652 Surcharged in Black, Green or Brown

1937, Dec. 29

9LC40 A162 30c + 30c rose 4.50 3.75
9LC41 A162 50c + 2.50p dk bl (G) 29.00 21.00
9LC42 A162 60c + 2.30p yel (G) 29.00 21.00
9LC43 A162 1p + 5p bl (Br) 35.00 21.00
Nos. 9LC40-9LC43 (4) 97.50 66.75
Set, never hinged 110.00

See note after No. 9LC19.

Stamps of Spain, 1936, Surcharged in Black, Green, Blue or Red

No. 9LC44

No. 9LC46

1938, Feb. 2 ***Perf. 11, 11½, 11x11½***

9LC44 A160 50c on 2c brn 5.00 3.75
9LC45 A161 80c on 5c brn (G) 3.75 3.25
9LC46 A162 30c + 80c rose (Bl) 4.50 2.50
9LC47 A161 1.25p on 10c grn (Bl) 4.50 3.25
9LC48 A162 50c + 1.25p dk bl (R) 4.50 2.75
Nos. 9LC44-9LC48 (5) 22.25 15.50
Set, never hinged 27.50

Spain Nos. 645, 646 and 649 Surcharged in Brown, Green or Violet

1938, Feb. 14

9LC51 A162 2.50p on 20c (Br) 50.00 25.00
9LC52 A162 5p on 25c (G) 50.00 25.00
9LC53 A162 10p on 40c (V) 50.00 25.00
Nos. 9LC51-9LC53 (3) 150.00 75.00
Set, never hinged 175.00

MALAGA ISSUE

Stamps of 1920-36 Overprinted in Black or Red

1937 **Unwmk.** ***Imperf.***

10L1 A47 1c blue green .25 .25
10L2 A108 1c blue green .25 .25
10L3 A108 1c lt green (R) .25 .25

Perf. 13½, 13½x13, 11, 11½x11

10L4 A108 2c orange brn 14.50 14.50
10L5 A126 2c orange brn .25 .25
10L6 A103 5c chocolate (R) .25 .25
10L7 A96 10c yellow green 12.00 12.00
10L8 A110 10c emerald .30 .30
10L9 A111 15c Prus grn (R) .55 .55
10L10 A97 15c blue grn (R) .55 .55
10L11 A95 20c dk violet (R) .50 .50
10L12 A99 25c lake 1.50 1.50
10L13 A104 25c lake .50 .50
10L14 A113 30c carmine .50 .50
10L15 A129 30c carmine rose 2.50 2.50
10L16 A100 40c blue (R) .45 .45
10L17 A97 50c dk blue (R) 2.50 2.50
10L18 A100 60c apple green 1.40 1.40
10L19 A105 1p black (R) 2.75 2.75
Nos. 10L1-10L19 (19) 41.75 41.75

Stamps of 1932-35 Overprinted in Red or Black in panes of 25, reading down. "8.2.37" and "!Arriba Espana!" form the lower half of all overprints. The upper half varies.

Overprint a (1st and 2nd rows): "MALAGA AGRADECIDA A TRANQUILLO-BIANCHI"

Overprint b (3rd row): "MALAGA A SU SALVADOR QUEIPO DE LLANO"

Overprint c (4th and 5th rows): "MALAGA A SU CAUDILLO FRANCO"

Values are for vertical strips of 3 containing examples of each overprint type.

1937 ***Perf. 11½***

10L20 A111 15c Prus grn (R) 5.50 5.50
a. 15c single stamp, ovpt. a .85 .85
b. 15c single stamp, ovpt. b 1.60 1.60
c. 15c single stamp, ovpt. c .85 .85
10L21 A113 30c rose red (Bk) 5.50 5.50
a. 30c single stamp, ovpt. a .85 .85
b. 30c single stamp, ovpt. b 1.60 1.60
c. 30c single stamp, ovpt. c .85 .85
10L22 A97 50c dk blue (R) 8.75 8.75
a. 50c single stamp, ovpt. a 1.60 1.60
b. 50c single stamp, ovpt. b 3.25 3.25
c. 50c single stamp, ovpt. c 1.60 1.60
10L23 A100 60c apple grn (Bk) 11.00 11.00
a. 60c single stamp, ovpt. a 1.60 1.60
b. 60c single stamp, ovpt. b 3.25 3.25
c. 60c single stamp, ovpt. c 1.60 1.60
Nos. 10L20-10L23 (4) 30.75 30.75

SPECIAL DELIVERY STAMP

Overprinted like Nos. 10L1-10L19 on Type of Special Delivery Stamp of 1934

1937 ***Perf. 10***

10LE1 SD7 20c rose red (Bk) .45 .45

ORENSE ISSUE

Stamps of 1931-36 Overprinted in Red, Blue or Black

1936 ***Imperf.***

11L1 A108 1c blue grn (Bl) .45 .45
a. Red overprint 1.10 1.10

Perf. 11½, 13½x13

11L2 A108 2c org brn (Bk) 3.50 3.25
11L3 A126 2c org brn (Bk) .65 .65
11L4 A103 5c brown (R) 1.50 1.50
11L5 A110 10c lt green (Bl) 2.25 2.25
a. Red overprint 11.00 11.00
11L6 A111 15c Prus grn (R) 3.25 3.25
11L7 A95 20c violet (Bl) 3.25 3.25
11L8 A104 25c lake (Bk) 3.75 3.75
11L9 A113 30c rose red (Bl) 2.75 2.75
a. Black overprint 5.50 5.50
11L10 A100 40c blue (R) 3.75 3.75
a. Imperf, pair 50.00
11L11 A97 50c dark blue (R) 6.50 6.50
11L12 A100 60c apple grn (Bk) 4.75 4.75
a. Red overprint 17.00 17.00
b. As "a," imperf, pair 50.00
Nos. 11L1-11L12 (12) 36.35 36.10

SEMI-POSTAL STAMPS

Stamps of Spain, 1931-36, Surcharged in Blue on front and on back of stamp

1936-37 **Unwmk.** ***Imperf.***

11LB1 A47 1c + 5c bl grn 2.25 2.25
11LB2 A108 1c + 5c grn .40 .40

Perf. 13½x13, 11½, 11½x11

11LB3 A108 2c + 5c org brn .45 .45
11LB4 A126 2c + 5c red brn .45 .45
11LB5 A103 5c + 5c choc .65 .65
11LB6 A110 10c + 5c emer .65 .65
11LB7 A111 15c + 5c Prus grn .95 .95
11LB8 A95 20c + 5c vio .65 .65
11LB9 A104 25c + 5c lake .95 .95
11LB10 A113 30c + 5c rose red 2.75 2.75
11LB11 A117 30c + 5c rose red 42.50 42.50
11LB12 A100 60c + 5c apl grn 250.00 190.00
Nos. 11LB1-11LB12 (12) 302.65 242.65

SPECIAL DELIVERY STAMPS

Type of Special Delivery Stamp of 1934 Overprinted "!VIVA ESPANA!" in Blue or Black

1936 ***Perf. 10***

11LE1 SD7 20c rose red (Bl) 1.90 1.90
11LE2 SD7 20c rose red (Bk) 4.25 4.25

Same with Surcharge "+ 5 cts."

11LE3 SD7 20c + 5c rose red 1.00 1.00

Same Surcharge, Overprint Repeated at Right

11LE4 SD7 20c + 5c rose red 1.10 1.10
Nos. 11LE1-11LE4 (4) 8.25 8.25

SAN SEBASTIAN ISSUE

For Use in Province of Guipuzcoa

Stamps of 1931-36 Overprinted in Red or Blue

1937 **Unwmk.** ***Imperf.***

12L1 A108 1c bl grn (R) .65 .65

Perf. 11, 13½

12L2 A108 2c buff (Bl) 1.00 1.50
12L3 A126 2c org brn (Bl) 2.10 2.10
12L4 A95 5c chocolate (R) 5.00 5.00
12L5 A103 5c chocolate (R) 1.75 1.75
12L6 A110 10c emerald (R) 1.75 1.75
12L7 A111 15c Prus grn (R) 2.10 2.10
12L8 A95 20c dk violet (R) 2.75 2.75
12L9 A104 25c car lake (Bl) 2.75 2.75
12L10 A113 30c rose red (Bl) 2.75 2.75
12L11 A100 40c blue (R) 5.50 5.50
12L12 A97 50c dark blue (R) 5.50 5.50
Nos. 12L1-12L12 (12) 33.60 34.10

SANTA CRUZ DE TENERIFE ISSUE

Stamps of Spain, 1931-36 Overprinted in Black or Red

1936 **Unwmk.** ***Imperf.***

13L1 A108 1c bl grn (R) .75 .75
13L2 A108 1c bl grn (Bk) 2.75 2.75

Perf. 11, 13½

13L3	A108	2c buff (Bk)	5.50	5.50
13L4	A126	2c org brn (Bk)	.95	.95
13L5	A103	5c choc (R)	3.00	3.00
13L6	A110	10c green (R)	3.00	3.00
13L7	A104	25c lake (Bk)	11.00	11.00
13L8	A100	40c dk blue (R)	3.25	3.25
13L9	A107	10p dp brn (Bk)	300.00	225.00
		Nos. 13L1-13L9 (9)	330.20	255.20

Many forgeries of #13L9 exist.

SEVILLE ISSUE

Stamps of Spain, 1931-36, Overprinted in Black or Red

1936 *Imperf.*

14L1	A108	1c blue grn (Bk)	.30	.30

Perf. 13½x13, 11, 11½x11

14L2	A126	2c org brn (Bk)	.35	.35
14L3	A103	5c chocolate (R)	.45	.45
14L4	A110	10c emerald (Bk)	.55	.55
14L5	A111	15c Prus grn (R)	1.40	1.40
14L6	A95	20c violet (R)	1.40	1.40
14L7	A104	25c lake (Bk)	1.40	1.40
14L8	A113	30c carmine (Bk)	1.40	1.40
14L9	A128	30c rose red (Bk)	8.25	8.25
14L10	A100	40c blue (R)	5.50	5.50
14L11	A97	50c dk blue (R)	5.50	5.50
14L12	A100	60c apple grn (Bk)	6.75	6.75
		Nos. 14L1-14L12 (12)	33.25	33.25

Stamps of Spain, 1931-36, Handstamped in Black

Imperf

14L13	A108	1c blue grn	.30	.30

Perf. 13½x13, 11, 11x11½, 11½x11

14L14	A126	2c orange brn	.45	.45
14L15	A103	5c chocolate	.45	.45
14L16	A110	10c emerald	.45	.45
14L17	A111	15c Prus green	.55	.55
14L18	A95	20c violet	.55	.55
14L19	A104	25c lake	.55	.55
14L20	A113	30c carmine	.55	.55
14L21	A128	30c rose red	3.00	3.00
14L22	A100	40c blue	1.10	1.10
14L23	A97	50c dk blue	3.00	3.00
14L24	A100	60c apple grn	1.00	1.00
14L25	A105	1p black	3.00	3.00
14L26	AP26	2p gray blue	13.50	13.50
14L27	A106	4p magenta	7.25	7.25
14L28	A107	10p deep brown	10.50	10.50
		Nos. 14L13-14L28,14LE1 (17)	47.95	47.95

The date "Julio-1936" in the overprints of Nos. 14L1-14L28 and 14LE1 marks the beginning of the Franco insurrection.

SPECIAL DELIVERY STAMP

Overprinted like Nos. 14L13-14L25 on Type of Special Delivery Stamp of 1934

1936 *Perf. 10*

14LE1	SD7	20c rose red	1.75	1.75

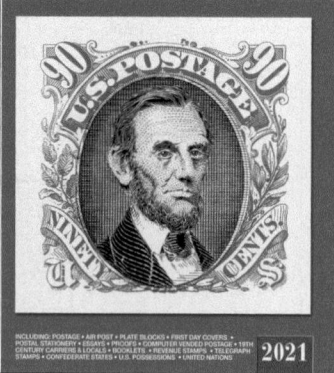

SPANISH GUINEA

'spa-nish 'gi-nē

LOCATION — In western Africa, bordering on the Gulf of Guinea
GOVT. — Spanish Colony
AREA — 10,852 sq. mi.
POP. — 212,000 (est. 1957)
CAPITAL — Santa Isabel

Spanish Guinea 1-84 were issued for and used only in the continental area later called Rio Muni. From 1909 to 1960, Spanish Guinea also included Fernando Po, Elobey, Annobon and Corisco.

Fernando Po and Rio Muni united in 1968 to become the Republic of Equatorial Guinea.

100 Centimos = 1 Peseta

Catalogue values for unused stamps in this country are for Never Hinged items, beginning with Scott 319 in the regular postage section, Scott B13 in the semi-postal section, and Scott C13 in the airpost section.

King Alfonso XIII — A1

Blue Control Numbers on Back

1902 Unwmk. Typo. *Perf. 14*

No.	Type	Description	Unused	Used
1	A1	5c dark green	12.50	6.25
2	A1	10c indigo	12.50	6.25
3	A1	25c claret	92.50	47.50
4	A1	50c deep brown	92.50	47.50
5	A1	75c violet	92.50	47.50
6	A1	1p carmine rose	140.00	47.50
7	A1	2p olive green	180.00	100.00
8	A1	5p dull red	275.00	175.00
		Nos. 1-8 (8)	897.50	477.50
		Set, never hinged	1,800.	

Exists imperf, value set $3,500.

Revenue Stamps Surcharged

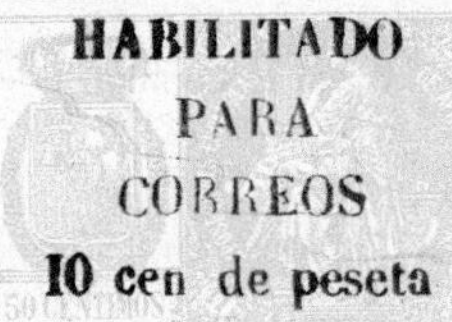

Blue or Black Control Numbers on Back

1903 *Imperf.*

No.	Description	Unused	Used
8A	10c on 25c blk (R)	450.00	200.00
8B	10c on 50c org (Bl)	120.00	30.00
8D	10c on 1p 25c car (Bk)	650.00	300.00
8F	10c on 2p cl (Bk)	700.00	500.00
g.	Blue surcharge	1,450.	800.00
8H	10c on 2p 50c red brn (Bl)	1,000.	650.00
8J	10c on 5p ol blk (R)	1,300.	450.00

Nos. 8A-8J are surcharged on stamps inscribed "Posesiones Espanolas de Africa Occidental" and "1903," with arms at left.

This surcharge was also applied to revenue stamps of 10, 15, 25, 50, 75 and 100 pesetas and in other colors.

See Nos. 98-101C.

King Alfonso XIII — A2

Blue Control Numbers on Back

1903 Typo. *Perf. 14*

No.	Type	Description	Unused	Used
9	A2	1/4c black	1.50	.85
10	A2	1/2c blue green	1.50	.85
11	A2	1c claret	1.50	.70
12	A2	2c dark olive	1.50	.70
13	A2	3c dark brown	1.50	.70
14	A2	4c vermilion	1.50	.70
15	A2	5c black brown	1.50	.70
16	A2	10c red brown	2.50	.85
17	A2	15c dark blue	8.50	6.25
18	A2	25c orange buff	8.50	6.25
19	A2	50c carmine lake	16.00	14.00
20	A2	75c violet	21.00	14.00
21	A2	1p blue green	35.00	22.00
22	A2	2p dark green	35.00	22.00
23	A2	3p scarlet	95.00	28.50
24	A2	4p dull blue	110.00	50.00
25	A2	5p dark violet	210.00	72.50
26	A2	10p carmine rose	300.00	100.00
		Nos. 9-26 (18)	852.00	341.55
		Set, never hinged	1,700.	

Blue Control Numbers on Back

1905 Same, Dated "1905"

No.	Type	Description	Unused	Used
27	A2	1c black	.30	.25
28	A2	2c blue grn	.30	.25
29	A2	3c claret	.30	.25
30	A2	4c bronze grn	.30	.25
31	A2	5c dark brown	.30	.25
32	A2	10c red	1.60	.85
33	A2	15c black brown	4.50	2.75
34	A2	25c chocolate	4.50	2.75
35	A2	50c dark blue	9.75	6.25
36	A2	75c orange buff	11.00	6.25
37	A2	1p carmine rose	11.00	6.25
38	A2	2p violet	26.00	13.00
39	A2	3p blue green	67.50	27.50
40	A2	4p dark green	67.50	39.00
40A	A2	5p vermilion	110.00	42.00
41	A2	10p dull blue	200.00	130.00
		Nos. 27-41 (16)	514.85	277.85
		Set, never hinged	950.00	

Stamps of Elobey, 1905, Overprinted in Violet or Blue

1906

No.	Type	Description	Unused	Used
42	A1	1c rose	4.00	2.25
43	A1	2c deep violet	4.00	2.25
44	A1	3c black	4.00	2.25
45	A1	4c orange red	4.00	2.25
46	A1	5c deep green	4.00	2.25
47	A1	10c blue green	9.25	5.25
48	A1	15c violet	16.00	9.00
49	A1	25c rose lake	16.00	9.00
50	A1	50c orange buff	22.50	13.00
51	A1	75c dark blue	26.00	15.00
52	A1	1p red brown	47.50	25.00
53	A1	2p black brown	67.50	37.50
54	A1	3p vermilion	97.50	55.00
55	A1	4p dark brown	475.00	250.00
56	A1	5p bronze green	475.00	250.00
57	A1	10p claret	*2,000.*	*1,100.*
		Nos. 42-54 (13)	322.25	180.00

King Alfonso XIII — A3

Blue Control Numbers on Back

1907 Typo.

No.	Type	Description	Unused	Used
58	A3	1c dark green	.75	.25
59	A3	2c dull blue	.75	.25
60	A3	3c violet	.75	.25
61	A3	4c yellow grn	.75	.25
62	A3	5c carmine lake	.75	.25
63	A3	10c orange	4.00	1.25
64	A3	15c brown	3.00	.80
65	A3	25c dark blue	3.00	.80
66	A3	50c black brown	3.00	.80
67	A3	75c blue green	3.00	.80
68	A3	1p red	6.00	1.40
69	A3	2p dark brown	9.00	6.25
70	A3	3p olive gray	9.00	6.25
71	A3	4p maroon	13.00	6.25
72	A3	5p green	13.50	9.50
73	A3	10p red violet	20.00	12.00
		Nos. 58-73 (16)	90.25	47.35
		Set, never hinged	210.00	

Issue of 1907 Surcharged in Black or Red

1908-09

No.	Type	Description	Unused	Used
74	A3	05c on 1c dk grn (R)	3.00	1.50
75	A3	05c on 2c blue (R)	3.00	1.50
76	A3	05c on 3c violet	3.00	1.50
77	A3	05c on 4c yel grn	3.00	1.50
78	A3	05c on 10c orange	3.00	1.50
a.		Red surcharge	5.25	2.75
84	A3	15c on 10c orange	14.00	9.00
		Nos. 74-84 (6)	29.00	16.50

Many stamps of this issue are found with the surcharge inverted, sideways, double and in both black and red. Other stamps of the 1907 issue are known with this surcharge but are not believed to have been put in use. Value, each $17.

King Alfonso XIII — A4

Blue Control Numbers on Back

1909 Typo. *Perf. 14½*

No.	Type	Description	Unused	Used
85	A4	1c orange brown	.25	.25
86	A4	2c rose	.25	.25
87	A4	5c dark green	1.40	.25
88	A4	10c vermilion	.40	.25
89	A4	15c dark brown	.40	.25
90	A4	20c violet	.65	.35
91	A4	25c dull blue	.65	.35
92	A4	30c chocolate	.85	.30
93	A4	40c lake	.50	.30
94	A4	50c dark violet	.50	.30
95	A4	1p blue green	13.50	7.00
96	A4	4p orange	3.50	4.25
97	A4	10p red	3.50	4.25
		Nos. 85-97 (13)	26.35	18.35
		Set, never hinged	50.00	

For overprints see Nos. 102-114.

Revenue Stamps Surcharged in Black

1909 *Imperf.*

With or Without Control Numbers on Back

No.	Description	Unused	Used
98	10c on 50c bl grn	80.00	50.00
a.	Red or violet surcharge	110.00	80.00
99	10c on 1p 25c vio	125.00	60.00
100	10c on 2p dk brn	500.00	300.00
100A	10c on 5p dk vio	500.00	300.00
101	10c on 25p red brn	*700.00*	*500.00*
101A	10c on 50p brn lil	*2,400.*	*1,500.*
101B	10c on 75p car	*2,400.*	*1,500.*
101C	10c on 100p org	*2,400.*	*1,500.*

For additional revenue stamps surcharged for postal use see Rio de Oro Nos. 44-45.

Stamps of 1909 Overprinted with Handstamp in Black, Blue, Green or Red

1911

No.	Type	Description	Unused	Used
102	A4	1c orange brn (Bl)	.40	.35
103	A4	2c rose (G)	.40	.35
104	A4	5c dk green (R)	2.00	.35
105	A4	10c vermilion	1.15	.45
106	A4	15c dk brown (R)	2.00	.75
107	A4	20c violet	2.50	1.15
108	A4	25c dull blue (R)	3.00	2.40
109	A4	30c choc (Bl)	3.75	3.50
110	A4	40c lake (Bl)	4.00	3.50
111	A4	50c dark violet	6.75	5.00
112	A4	1p blue grn (R)	55.00	40.00
113	A4	4p orange (R)	29.00	23.00
114	A4	10p red (G)	37.50	*40.00*
		Nos. 102-114 (13)	147.45	120.80
		Set, never hinged	300.00	

The date "1911" is missing from the overprint on the first stamp in each row, or ten times in each sheet of 100 stamps. This variety occurs on all stamps of the series. Value, set $550.

King Alfonso XIII — A5

Blue Control Numbers on Back

1912 Typo. *Perf. 13½*

No.	Type	Description	Unused	Used
115	A5	1c black	.30	.30
116	A5	2c dark brown	.30	.30
117	A5	5c deep green	.30	.30
118	A5	10c red	.30	.30
119	A5	15c claret	.30	.30
120	A5	20c red	.30	.30
121	A5	25c dull blue	.30	.30
122	A5	30c lake	3.50	2.00
123	A5	40c car rose	2.10	1.00
124	A5	50c brown org	2.00	.35
125	A5	1p dark violet	2.25	1.25
126	A5	4p lilac	5.00	2.50
127	A5	10p blue green	10.50	9.50
		Nos. 115-127 (13)	27.45	18.70
		Set, never hinged	50.00	

For overprints and surcharges see Nos. 141-157.

King Alfonso XIII — A6

Blue Control Numbers on Back

1914 *Perf. 13*

No.	Type	Description	Unused	Used
128	A6	1c dull violet	.35	.30
129	A6	2c car rose	.35	.30
130	A6	5c deep green	.35	.30
131	A6	10c vermilion	.35	.30
132	A6	15c dark violet	.35	.30
133	A6	20c dark brown	1.05	.55
134	A6	25c dark blue	.45	.35
135	A6	30c brown orange	1.60	.55
136	A6	40c blue green	1.60	.55
137	A6	50c dp claret	.75	.35
138	A6	1p vermilion	2.00	*2.25*
139	A6	4p maroon	7.00	4.50
140	A6	10p olive black	7.75	*8.50*
		Nos. 128-140 (13)	23.95	19.10
		Set, never hinged	60.00	

Stamps with these or similar overprints are unauthorized and fraudulent.

Stamps of 1912 Overprinted

1917 *Perf. 13½*

No.	Type	Description	Unused	Used
141	A5	1c black	125.00	85.00
142	A5	2c dark brown	125.00	85.00
143	A5	5c deep green	.40	.35
144	A5	10c red	.40	.35
145	A5	15c claret	.40	.35
146	A5	20c red	.40	.35
147	A5	25c dull blue	.40	.35
148	A5	30c lake	.40	.35
149	A5	40c carmine rose	.75	.40
150	A5	50c brown orange	.40	.35
151	A5	1p dark violet	.75	.40
152	A5	4p lilac	8.25	4.00
153	A5	10p blue green	8.25	4.00
		Nos. 141-153 (13)	270.80	181.25
		Set, never hinged	550.00	

Nos. 143-153 exist with overprint double, inverted, in dark blue, reading "9117" and in pairs one without overprint.

Stamps of 1917 Surcharged

HTADO. 1917 15 Cénts.

1918

154	A5	5c on 40c car rose	36.00	14.50
155	A5	10c on 4p lilac	36.00	14.50
156	A5	15c on 20c red	65.00	25.00
157	A5	25c on 10p bl grn	65.00	25.00
a.		"52" for "25"	*500.00*	*425.00*
		Nos. 154-157 (4)	202.00	79.00
		Set, never hinged	345.00	

The varieties "Gents" and "Censt" occur on Nos. 154-157. Values 50 percent more.

King Alfonso XIII
A7 A8

1919 **Typo.** ***Perf. 13***

Blue Control Numbers on Back

158	A7	1c lilac	1.00	.30
159	A7	2c rose	1.00	.30
160	A7	5c vermilion	1.00	.30
161	A7	10c violet	1.75	.30
162	A7	15c brown	1.75	.55
163	A7	20c blue	1.75	.80
164	A7	25c green	1.75	.80
a.		25c blue (error)	62.50	
165	A7	30c orange	2.25	.80
166	A7	40c orange	4.50	.80
167	A7	50c red	4.50	.80
168	A7	1p light green	4.50	2.75
169	A7	4p claret	10.00	*10.50*
170	A7	10p brown	20.00	19.00
		Nos. 158-170 (13)	55.75	38.00
		Set, never hinged	90.00	

1920

Blue Control Numbers on Back

171	A8	1c brown	.35	.30
172	A8	2c dull rose	.35	.30
173	A8	5c gray green	.35	.30
174	A8	10c dull rose	.35	.30
175	A8	15c orange	.35	.30
176	A8	20c yellow	.35	.35
177	A8	25c dull blue	1.15	.35
178	A8	30c greenish blue	42.50	25.00
179	A8	40c lt brown	2.00	.35
180	A8	50c lilac	2.40	.35
181	A8	1p light red	2.40	.35
182	A8	4p bright rose	6.50	6.25
183	A8	10p gray lilac	10.00	*12.50*
		Nos. 171-183 (13)	69.05	47.00
		Set, never hinged	120.00	

A9

1922

Blue Control Numbers on Back

184	A9	1c dark brown	.70	.25
185	A9	2c claret	.70	.25
186	A9	5c blue green	.70	.25
187	A9	10c pale red	4.75	1.15
188	A9	15c orange	.70	.30
189	A9	20c lilac	3.00	1.05
190	A9	25c dark blue	4.75	1.40
191	A9	30c violet	4.50	1.50
192	A9	40c turq blue	3.25	.75
193	A9	50c deep rose	3.25	.75
194	A9	1p myrtle green	3.25	.75
195	A9	4p red brown	13.00	13.00
196	A9	10p yellow	26.00	25.00
		Nos. 184-196 (13)	68.55	46.40
		Set, never hinged	130.00	

Nipa House — A10

1924

Blue Control Numbers on Back

197	A10	5c choc & bl	.25	.25
198	A10	10c gray grn & bl	.25	.25
199	A10	15c rose & blk	.25	.25
200	A10	20c violet & blk	.25	.25
201	A10	25c org red & blk	.40	.25
202	A10	30c orange & blk	.40	.25
203	A10	40c dl bl & blk	.40	.25
204	A10	50c claret & blk	.40	.25
205	A10	60c red brn & blk	.40	.25
206	A10	1p dk vio & blk	1.60	.25
a.		Center inverted	600.00	140.00
207	A10	4p brt bl & blk	3.75	2.25
208	A10	10p bl grn & blk	8.75	4.50
		Nos. 197-208 (12)	17.10	9.25
		Set, never hinged	25.00	

Seville-Barcelona Issue of Spain, 1929, Overprinted in Red or Blue

1929 ***Perf. 11***

209	A52	5c rose lake	.35	.40
210	A53	10c green (R)	.35	.40
211	A50	15c Prus bl (R)	.35	.40
212	A51	20c purple (R)	.35	.40
213	A50	25c brt rose	.35	.40
214	A52	30c black brn	.35	.40
215	A53	40c dk blue (R)	.70	.65
216	A51	50c dp orange	.70	.65
217	A52	1p blue blk (R)	6.00	6.00
218	A53	4p deep rose	12.00	11.50
219	A53	10p brown	23.00	23.00
		Nos. 209-219 (11)	44.50	44.20
		Set, never hinged	125.00	

Porter
A11

Drummers
A12

King Alfonso XIII and Queen Victoria — A13

1931 **Engr.** ***Perf. 14***

220	A11	1c blue green	.30	.25
221	A11	2c red brown	.30	.25

Blue Control Numbers on Back

222	A11	5c brown black	.30	.25
223	A11	10c light green	.30	.25
224	A11	15c dark green	.30	.25
225	A11	20c deep violet	.30	.25
226	A12	25c carmine	.30	.25
227	A12	30c lake	.40	.25
228	A12	40c dark blue	.90	.65
229	A12	50c red orange	1.75	1.25
230	A13	80c blue violet	3.25	1.90
231	A13	1p black	5.75	5.25
232	A13	4p violet rose	37.50	20.00
233	A13	5p dark brown	17.50	14.00
		Nos. 220-233 (14)	69.15	45.05
		Set, never hinged	175.00	

Exist imperf. Value for set, $300.

See Nos. 262-271. For overprints and surcharges see Nos. 234-277, 282-283, 298.

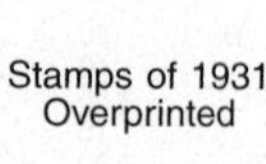

Stamps of 1931 Overprinted

1931

234	A11	1c blue green	.30	.30
235	A11	2c red brown	.30	.30
236	A11	5c brown black	.30	.30
237	A11	10c light green	.30	.30
238	A11	15c dark green	.30	.30
239	A11	20c deep violet	.30	.30
240	A12	25c carmine	.30	.30
241	A12	30c lake	.30	.30
242	A12	40c dark blue	2.25	.65
243	A12	50c red orange	14.50	7.75
244	A13	80c blue violet	4.50	2.50
245	A13	1p black	14.50	5.00
246	A13	4p violet rose	25.00	14.50
247	A13	5p dark brown	25.00	14.50
		Nos. 234-247 (14)	88.15	47.30
		Set, never hinged	200.00	

Stamps of 1931 Overprinted in Red or Blue

1933

248	A11	1c blue grn (R)	.30	.25
249	A11	2c red brown (Bl)	.30	.25
250	A11	5c brown blk (R)	.30	.25
251	A11	10c lt green (Bl)	.30	.25
252	A11	15c dk green (R)	.30	.25
253	A11	20c dp violet (R)	.30	.25
254	A12	25c carmine (Bl)	.30	.25
255	A12	30c lake (Bl)	.30	.25
256	A12	40c dk blue (R)	3.50	.95
257	A12	50c red orange (Bl)	22.00	4.75
258	A13	80c blue vio (R)	7.25	4.25
259	A13	1p black (R)	25.00	4.50
260	A13	4p violet rose (Bl)	47.50	20.00
261	A13	5p dk brown (Bl)	47.50	20.00
		Nos. 248-261 (14)	155.15	56.45
		Set, never hinged	250.00	

Types of 1931
Without Control Number

1934-35 **Engr.** ***Perf. 10***

262	A11	1c blue green ('35)	11.50	.25
263	A11	2c red brown ('35)	11.50	.25
264	A11	5c black brn	2.25	.25
265	A11	10c light green	2.25	.25
266	A11	15c dark green	3.50	.25
267	A12	30c rose red	4.50	.35
268	A12	50c indigo ('35)	9.75	1.10
		Nos. 262-268 (7)	45.25	2.70
		Set, never hinged	70.00	

Types of 1931

1941 **Litho.** **Unwmk.**

269	A11	5c olive gray	2.40	.25
270	A11	20c violet	2.40	.25
271	A12	40c gray green	.95	.25
		Nos. 269-271 (3)	5.75	.75
		Set, never hinged	7.00	

Stamps of 1931-33 Surcharged in Black

1936-37 ***Perf. 10, 14***

272	A12	30c on 40c (#228)	5.50	3.50
273	A12	30c on 40c (#242)	22.00	5.25
274	A12	30c on 40c (#256)	80.00	25.00
		Nos. 272-274 (3)	107.50	33.75
		Set, never hinged	170.00	

The surcharge on Nos. 272-274 exists in two types, differing in the "3" which is scarcer in italic.

No. 268 Surcharged in Red

275	A12	1p on 50c indigo	30.00	
276	A12	4p on 50c indigo	90.00	
277	A12	5p on 50c indigo	55.00	
		Nos. 275-277 (3)	175.00	

Nos. 275-277 were not issued.

Stamps of Spain, 1936, Overprinted in Black or Carmine

1938 ***Perf. 11***

278	A161	10c gray green	1.75	.55
279	A162	15c gray black (C)	1.75	.55
280	A162	20c dark violet	4.25	1.75
281	A162	25c brown lake	4.25	1.75
		Nos. 278-281 (4)	12.00	4.60
		Set, never hinged	16.00	

Nos. 278-281 exist imperf. Value $175.

Stamps of 1931-33, Surcharged in Black

1939

282	A13	40c on 80c (#244)	12.00	8.00
283	A13	40c on 80c (#258)	12.00	5.00
		Set, never hinged	32.50	

A14

A15

Revenue Stamps Surcharged in Black

1940-41 ***Perf. 11½***

284	A14	5c on 35c pale grn	6.00	2.10
285	A14	25c on 60c org brn	6.25	2.50
286	A14	50c on 75c blk brn	8.75	2.75
		Nos. 284-286 (3)	21.00	7.35

Red Surcharge

287	A15	10c on 75c blk brn	8.75	2.75
288	A15	15c on 1.50p lt vio	6.25	2.50
289	A15	25c on 60c org brn	11.00	3.50
		Nos. 287-289 (3)	26.00	8.75

A16

A17

Revenue Stamps Surcharged in Black or Carmine

Perf. 11

290	A16	1p on 17p deep red	52.50	15.50
291	A17	1p on 40p yel grn (C)	12.50	4.00

See No. C1

A18

A19

Black Surcharge
Perf. 11, 13x12½

292	A18	5c carmine	5.25	1.40
293	A19	1p yellow	87.50	32.50

A20

Black Surcharge

294	A20	1p on 15c gray grn	9.50	3.25

General Francisco Franco — A21

1940 *Perf. 11½, 13½*

No.	Type	Description	Unused	Used
295	A21	5c olive brown	3.75	.50
296	A21	40c blue	5.50	.50
297	A21	50c green	6.75	.50
a.		50c greenish gray	40.00	9.00
		Nos. 295-297 (3)	16.00	1.50
		Set, never hinged	75.00	

Nos. 295-297 exist imperf. Values $50.

No. 270 Surcharged in Black

1942

No.	Type	Description	Unused	Used
298	A11	3p on 20c vio	10.00	1.40

Spain, Nos. 702 and 704 Overprinted in Carmine or Black

1942 *Perf. 9½x10½*

No.	Type	Description	Unused	Used
299	A166	1p gray blk (C)	.55	.25
300	A166	4p dl rose (Bk)	7.50	.75

The overprint on No. 299 exists in two types: Spacing between lines of 2mm, and spacing of 3mm. The 3mm spacing sells for about twice as much.

For surcharges and overprint see #302-303, C3.

Spain, No. 703 Overprinted in Carmine

1943

No.	Type	Description	Unused	Used
301	A166	2p dull brown	.85	.25

Nos. 299 and 301 Surcharged in Green

1949 **Unwmk.** *Perf. 9½x10½*

No.	Type	Description	Unused	Used
302	A166	5c (cinco) on 1p gray blk	.25	.25
303	A166	15c on 2p dl brn	.25	.25

The two types of No. 299, described in footnote, also exist on No. 302.

Men Poling Canoe A22

1949, Oct. 9 **Litho.** *Perf. 12½x13*

No.	Type	Description	Unused	Used
304	A22	4p dk vio	.85	.65
		Never hinged	1.25	

UPU, 75th anniversary.

San Carlos Bay — A23

Designs: Various Views

1949-50 *Perf. 12½x13*

No.	Type	Description	Unused	Used
305	A23	2c brown	.25	.25
306	A23	5c rose vio	.25	.25
307	A23	10c Prussian bl	.25	.25
308	A23	15c dp ol gray	.25	.25
309	A23	25c red brown	.25	.25
309A	A23	30c brt yel ('50)	.25	.25
310	A23	40c olive gray	.30	.25
311	A23	45c rose lake	.30	.25
312	A23	50c brn orange	.30	.25
312A	A23	75c ultra ('50)	.30	.25
313	A23	90c dl bl grn	.35	.25
314	A23	1p gray	1.10	.25
315	A23	1.35p violet	4.00	1.10
316	A23	2p sepia	11.00	2.25
317	A23	5p lilac rose	14.00	5.75
318	A23	10p light brn	60.00	23.00
		Nos. 305-318 (16)	93.15	35.10
		Set, never hinged	180.00	

Catalogue values for unused stamps in this section, from this point to the end of the section, are for Never Hinged items.

Surveyor A24

1951, Dec. 5

No.	Type	Description	Unused	Used
319	A24	50c orange	.40	.25
320	A24	5p indigo	7.50	1.25

Intl. Conference of West Africans, 1951.

Drummer A25

1952, Mar. 10

No.	Type	Description	Unused	Used
321	A25	5c red brown	.25	.25
322	A25	50c olive gray	.40	.25
323	A25	5p violet	2.40	.25
		Nos. 321-323 (3)	3.05	.75

Musician A26

Design: 60c, Musician facing right.

1953, July 1 **Photo.**

No.	Type	Description	Unused	Used
324	A26	15c sepia	.25	.25
325	A26	60c brown	.30	.25
		Nos. 324-325,B25-B26 (4)	1.10	1.00

Woman and Dove A27

Drummer A28

1953, Sept. 5 *Perf. 13x12½*

No.	Type	Description	Unused	Used
326	A27	5c orange	.25	.25
327	A27	10c brt lilac rose	.25	.25
328	A27	60c brown	.25	.25
329	A28	1p dull purple	1.60	.25
330	A28	1.90p greenish blk	2.50	.35
		Nos. 326-330 (5)	4.85	1.35

Tragocephala Nobilis — A29

Butterfly: 60c, Papilio antimachus.

1953, Nov. 23

No.	Type	Description	Unused	Used
331	A29	15c dark green	.35	.25
332	A29	60c brown	.45	.25
		Nos. 331-332,B27-B28 (4)	1.35	1.00

Colonial Stamp Day.

Hunter A30

Design: 60c, Hunter and elephant.

1954, June 10 *Perf. 12½x13*

No.	Type	Description	Unused	Used
333	A30	15c dark gray green	.35	.25
334	A30	60c dark brown	.50	.25
		Nos. 333-334,B29-B30 (4)	1.40	1.00

Swimming Turtle A31

1954, Nov. 23

No.	Type	Description	Unused	Used
335	A31	15c shown	.30	.25
336	A31	60c Shark	.75	.25
		Nos. 335-336,B31-B32 (4)	1.65	1.00

Colonial Stamp Day.

Manuel Iradier y Bulfy, Birth Cent. (in 1954) A32

1955, Jan. 18

No.	Type	Description	Unused	Used
337	A32	60c orange brown	.50	.25
338	A32	1p dark violet	3.25	.30

Priest Saying Mass — A33

1955, June 1 **Photo.** *Perf. 13x12½*

No.	Type	Description	Unused	Used
339	A33	50c olive gray	.30	.25
		Nos. 339,B33-B34 (3)	.95	.75

Centenary of the establishment of an Apostolic Prefecture at Fernando Po.

Palace of Pardo A34

1955, July 18 *Perf. 12½x13*

No.	Type	Description	Unused	Used
340	A34	5c ol brn	.30	.25
341	A34	15c brn lake	.30	.25
342	A34	80c Prus grn	.35	.25
		Nos. 340-342 (3)	.95	.75

Treaty of Pardo, 1778.

Red-eared Guenons — A35

1955, Nov. 23 *Perf. 13x12½*

No.	Type	Description	Unused	Used
343	A35	70c gray grn & bl	.60	.25
		Nos. 343,B35-B36 (3)	1.15	.75

Colonial Stamp Day.

Orchid — A36

Flower: 50c, Strophantus Kombe.

1956, June 1 **Unwmk.**

No.	Type	Description	Unused	Used
344	A36	20c bluish green	.25	.25
345	A36	50c brown	.30	.25
		Nos. 344-345,B37-B38 (4)	1.10	1.00

See Nos. 360-361, B53-B54.

Arms of Santa Isabel — A37

1956, Nov. 23 *Perf. 13x12½*

No.	Type	Description	Unused	Used
346	A37	70c light olive green	.25	.25
		Nos. 346,B39-B40 (3)	.75	.75

Colonial Stamp Day.

African Gray Parrot — A38

1957, June 1 **Photo.**

No.	Type	Description	Unused	Used
347	A38	70c olive green	.40	.25
		Nos. 347,B41-B42 (3)	.95	.75

Elephants A39

Design: 70c, Elephant, vert.

Perf. 12½x13, 13x12½

1957, Nov. 23

No.	Type	Description	Unused	Used
348	A39	20c blue green	.35	.25
349	A39	70c emerald	.45	.25
		Nos. 348-349,B43-B44 (4)	1.45	1.00

Colonial Stamp Day.

Boxing A40

Basketball — A41

Various Sports: 15c, 2.30p, Jumping. 80c, 3p, Runner at finish line.

1958, Apr. 10 Photo. Unwmk.

350	A40	5c violet brn	.25	.25
351	A41	10c orange brn	.25	.25
352	A40	15c brown	.25	.25
353	A41	80c green	.25	.25
354	A40	1p orange red	.25	.25
355	A41	2p rose lilac	.35	.25
356	A40	2.30p dl violet	.40	.25
357	A41	3p brt blue	.45	.25
		Nos. 350-357 (8)	2.45	2.00

Preaching Missionary — A42

Design: 70c, Crucifix and missal.

1958, June 1 ***Perf. 13x12½***

358	A42	20c blue green	.30	.25
359	A42	70c green	.30	.25
		Nos. 358-359,B48-B49 (4)	1.25	1.00

Catholic missions in Spanish Guinea, 75th anniv.

Type of 1956 Inscribed: "Pro-Infancia 1959"

1959, June 1 ***Perf. 13x12½***

360	A36	20c Castor bean	.25	.25
361	A36	70c Digitalis	.30	.25
		Nos. 360-361,B53-B54 (4)	1.10	1.00

Promoting child welfare.

Stamps of Spanish Guinea were succeeded by those of Fernando Po and Rio Muni in 1960.

SEMI-POSTAL STAMPS

Red Cross Issue

Types of Semi-Postal Stamps of Spain, 1926, Ovptd. in Black or Blue

1926 Unwmk. ***Perf. 12½, 13***

B1	SP3	5c black brown	11.00	7.00
B2	SP4	10c dark green	11.00	7.00
B3	SP1	15c dark vio (Bl)	2.50	1.75
B4	SP4	20c violet brown	2.50	1.75
B5	SP5	25c deep carmine	2.50	1.75
B6	SP1	30c olive green	2.50	1.75
B7	SP3	40c ultra	.55	.25
B8	SP2	50c red brown	.55	.25
B9	SP5	60c myrtle green	.55	.25
B10	SP4	1p vermilion	.55	.25
B11	SP3	4p bister	2.25	1.50
B12	SP5	10p light violet	7.50	5.00
		Nos. B1-B12 (12)	43.95	28.50
		Set, never hinged	60.00	

See Spain No. B6a for No. B4 without overprint. For surcharges see Spain Nos. B70-B71.

Catalogue values for unused stamps in this section, from this point to the end of the section, are for Never Hinged items.

Allegory — SP1

1950, Dec. 1 Photo. ***Perf. 13x12½***

B13	SP1	50c + 10c ultra	.35	.30
B14	SP1	1p + 25c dk grn	12.00	4.00
B15	SP1	6.50p + 1.65p dp org	3.00	2.00
		Nos. B13-B15 (3)	15.35	6.30

The surtax was to help the native population.

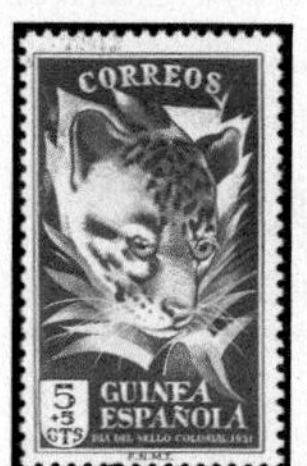

Leopard — SP2

1951, Nov. 23

B16	SP2	5c + 5c brown	.25	.25
B17	SP2	10c + 5c red orange	.25	.25
B18	SP2	60c + 15c olive brn	.35	.25
		Nos. B16-B18 (3)	.85	.75

Colonial Stamp Day, Nov. 23.

Love Lily — SP3

1952, June 1

B19	SP3	5c + 5c brown	.25	.25
B20	SP3	50c + 10c gray	.25	.25
B21	SP3	2p + 30c blue	1.50	1.00
		Nos. B19-B21 (3)	2.00	1.50

The surtax was to help the native population.

Brown-cheeked Hornbill — SP4

1952, Nov. 23 ***Perf. 12½***

B22	SP4	5c + 5c brown	.25	.25
B23	SP4	10c + 5c brown car	.25	.25
B24	SP4	60c + 15c dk green	.45	.30
		Nos. B22-B24 (3)	.95	.80

Colonial Stamp Day, Nov. 23.

Music Type of Regular Issue

1953, July 1 ***Perf. 12½x13***

B25	A26	5c + 5c like #324	.25	.25
B26	A26	10c + 5c like #325	.30	.25

The surtax was to help the native population.

Insect Type of Regular Issue

1953, Nov. 23 ***Perf. 13x12½***

B27	A29	5c + 5c like #331	.25	.25
B28	A29	10c + 5c like #332	.30	.25

Hunter Type of Regular Issue

1954, June 10 ***Perf. 12½x13***

B29	A30	5c + 5c like #333	.25	.25
B30	A30	10c + 5c like #334	.30	.25

The surtax was to help the native population.

Type of Regular Issue

1954, Nov. 23

B31	A31	5c + 5c like #335	.30	.25
B32	A31	10c + 5c like #336	.30	.25

Type of Regular Issue and

Baptism — SP5

Perf. 13x12½

1955, June 1 Photo. Unwmk.

B33	A33	10c + 5c like #339	.30	.25
B34	SP5	25c + 10c shown	.35	.25

Type of Regular Issue and

Red-eared Guenons SP6

Perf. 13x12½, 12½x13

1955, Nov. 23

B35	A35	5c + 5c like #343	.25	.25
B36	SP6	15c + 5c shown	.30	.25

Flower Type of Regular Issue

1956, June 1 ***Perf. 13x12½***

B37	A36	5c + 5c like #344	.25	.25
B38	A36	15c + 5c like #345	.30	.25

The tax was for native welfare work.

Type of Regular Issue and

Drummers and Arms of Bata SP7

Perf. 13x12½, 12½x13

1956, Nov. 23

B39	A37	5c + 5c reddish brn	.25	.25
B40	SP7	15c + 5c gray vio	.25	.25

Type of Regular Issue and

African Gray Parrot SP8

Perf. 13x12½, 12½x13

1957, June 1 Photo. Unwmk.

B41	A38	5c + 5c like #347	.25	.25
B42	SP8	15c + 5c shown	.30	.25

The surtax was for child welfare.

Type of Regular Issue, 1957

Perf. 12½x13, 13x12½

1957, Nov. 23

B43	A39	10c + 5c like #348	.30	.25
B44	A39	15c + 5c like #349	.35	.25

Pigeons and Arms of Valencia and Santa Isabel SP9

1958, Mar. 6 ***Perf. 12½x13***

B45	SP9	10c + 5c org brn	.25	.25
B46	SP9	15c + 10c bister	.25	.25
B47	SP9	50c + 10c ol gray	.25	.25
		Nos. B45-B47 (3)	.75	.75

The surtax was to aid the victims of the Valencia flood, Oct., 1957.

Type of Regular Issue, 1958

1958, June 1 Photo. ***Perf. 13x12½***

B48	A42	10c + 5c like #358	.30	.25
B49	A42	15c + 5c like #359	.35	.25

The surtax was to help the native population.

Butterflies — SP10

Stamp Day: Various butterflies.

1958, Nov. 23 Unwmk.

B50	SP10	10c + 5c brown red	.35	.25
B51	SP10	25c + 10c brt pur	.35	.25
B52	SP10	50c + 10c gray olive	.40	.25
		Nos. B50-B52 (3)	1.10	.75

Type of Regular Issue 1956 Inscribed: "Pro-Infancia 1959"

1959, June 1 Photo. ***Perf. 13x12½***

B53	A36	10c + 5c like #361	.25	.25
B54	A36	15c + 5c like #360	.30	.25

The surtax was for child welfare.

Early Bicycle — SP11

Designs: 20c+5c, Bicycle race. 50c+20c, Bicyclist winning race.

1959, Nov. 23

B55	SP11	10c + 5c lt rose brn	.25	.25
B56	SP11	20c + 5c turq blue	.25	.25
B57	SP11	50c + 20c olive gray	.30	.25
		Nos. B55-B57 (3)	.80	.75

Stamp Day.

AIR POST STAMPS

AP1

Type I — "Correo Aereo," 20½mm.
Type II — "Correo Aereo," 22mm.

Revenue Stamp Surcharged

1941 **Unwmk.** ***Perf. 11***

C1	AP1	1p on 17p dp red, I	35.00	8.00
a.		Type II	45.00	11.00

Spain No. C113 Overprinted in Red

1942, June 23

C2	AP30	1p chalky blue	1.90	.35

No. 300 Overprinted in Green

The overprint exists in two types:
Type I — The numeral 1's are lower case L's.
Type II — The numeral 1's are actual ones.

1948, Jan. 15 ***Perf. 10½x9½***

C3	A166	4p dull rose	9.00	2.75
		Never hinged	15.00	

Count of Argelejo and Frigate Catalina at Fernando Po, 1778
AP2

1949, Nov. 23 **Photo.** ***Perf. 12½x13***

C4	AP2	5p dark slate green	1.00	.75
		Never hinged	1.50	

Stamp Day, Nov. 23, 1949.

Manuel Iradier and Native Products — AP3

1950, Nov. 23 **Unwmk.** ***Perf. 12½***

C5	AP3	5p dk brn	2.50	1.00
		Never hinged	3.50	

Stamp Day, Nov. 23, 1950.

Benito Rapids
AP4

Various views.

1951, Mar. 1 **Litho.** ***Perf. 12½x13***

C6	AP4	25c	ocher	.25	.25
C7	AP4	50c	lilac rose	.25	.25
C8	AP4	1p	green	.25	.25
C9	AP4	2p	bright blue	.25	.25
C10	AP4	3.25p	rose lilac	.50	.25
C11	AP4	5p	gray brown	4.00	1.75
C12	AP4	10p	rose red	15.50	6.25
			Nos. C6-C12 (7)	21.00	9.25
			Set, never hinged	50.00	

Catalogue values for unused stamps in this section, from this point to the end of the section, are for Never Hinged items.

Woman Holding Dove — AP5

1951, Apr. 22 **Engr.** ***Perf. 10***

C13	AP5	5p dark blue	21.00	2.75

500th birth anniv. of Queen Isabella I.

Ferdinand the Catholic — AP6

1952, July 18 **Photo.** ***Perf. 13x12½***

C14	AP6	5p red brown	25.00	6.00

500th birth anniv. of Ferdinand the Catholic of Spain.

Soccer Players — AP7

1955-56 **Unwmk.**

C15	AP7	25c	blue vio ('56)	.30	.25
C16	AP7	50c	olive ('56)	.30	.25
C17	AP7	1.50p	brown ('56)	1.05	.25
C18	AP7	4p	rose car ('56)	3.25	.45
C19	AP7	10p	yellow grn	1.75	.45
			Nos. C15-C19 (5)	6.65	1.65

Planes and Arm Holding Spear — AP8

1957, Sept. 19 ***Perf. 13x12½***

C20	AP8	25p bister & sepia	15.00	.95

30th anniv. of the Atlantida Squadron flight to Spanish Guinea.

SPECIAL DELIVERY STAMP

View of Fernando Po — SD1

Perf. 12½x13

1951, Mar. 1 **Litho.** **Unwmk.**

E1	SD1	25c rose carmine	.35	.25
		Never hinged	.50	

SPANISH MOROCCO

'spa-nish mə-'rä-ˌkō

LOCATION — Northwest coast of Africa
GOVT. — Spanish Protectorate
AREA — 17,398 sq. mi. (approx.)
POP. — 1,010,117 (1950)
CAPITAL — Tetuán

Spanish authority in northern Morocco was established after Spain's invasion of the area in 1859. Spanish Morocco was a Spanish Protectorate until 1956 when it, along with the French and Tangier zones of Morocco, became the independent country, Morocco.

100 Centimos = 1 Peseta

Catalogue values for unused stamps in this country are for Never Hinged items, beginning with Scott 280 in the regular postage section, Scott B27 in the semi-postal section, Scott C24 in the airpost section, and Scott E11 in special delivery section.

Unoverprinted Spanish stamps were used in Spanish Morocco from 1860 until the appearance of separate issues for the territory in 1903. Spain No. E1 was used as a regular postage stamp in April 1914.

Spanish Offices in Morocco

Spain No. 221A Overprinted in Carmine

1903-09 **Unwmk.** ***Imperf.***

1	A21	¼c blue green	.55	.25
a.		Complete 1c (block 4 ¼c)	2.25	1.50

See Nos. 26, 39, 52, Tetuan 1, 7.

Stamps of Spain Overprinted in Carmine or Blue — a

On Stamps of 1900

Perf. 14

2	A35	2c	bister brown	1.75	1.40
3	A35	5c	green	2.10	.80
4	A35	10c	rose red (Bl)	2.25	.35
5	A35	15c	brt violet	3.25	.80
6	A35	20c	grnsh black	13.00	3.50
7	A35	25c	blue	1.00	.85
8	A35	30c	blue green	7.50	3.50
9	A35	40c	rose (Bl)	13.00	6.00
10	A35	50c	slate grn	7.75	5.75
11	A35	1p	lake (Bl)	16.00	8.00
12	A35	4p	dull violet	42.50	14.00
13	A35	10p	brown org (Bl)	42.50	35.00
			Nos. 1-13 (13)	153.15	80.20
			Set, never hinged	375.00	

Many varieties of overprint exist. Nos. 7-13 exist imperf. Value, $500.

See Tetuan Nos. 2-6, 8-15.

On Stamps of 1909-10

1909-10 ***Perf. 13x12½, 14***

14	A46	2c	dark brown	.75	.25
15	A46	5c	green	3.75	.30
16	A46	10c	carmine (Bl)	4.25	.30
17	A46	15c	violet	10.50	.65
18	A46	20c	olive green	26.00	1.25
19	A46	25c	deep blue	95.00	
20	A46	30c	blue green	8.50	.65
21	A46	40c	rose (Bl)	8.50	.65
22	A46	50c	slate blue	14.50	14.00
23	A46	1p	lake (Bl)	34.50	29.00
24	A46	4p	deep violet	95.00	
25	A46	10p	orange (Bl)	95.00	
			Nos. 14-18,20-23 (9)	111.25	47.05
			Set, never hinged	200.00	
			Nos. 14-25 (12)	396.25	

The stamps overprinted "Correo Espanol Marruecos" were used in all Morocco until the year 1914. After the issue of special stamps for the Protectorate the "Correo Espanol" stamps were continued in use solely in the city of Tangier.

Many varieties of overprint exist.

Nos. 19, 24 and 25 were not regularly issued.

See Nos. 27-38, 40-51, 53-67, 75-76, 78.

Spanish Morocco

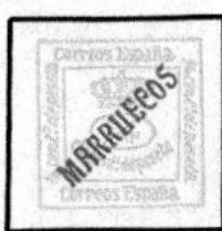

Spain No. 221A Overprinted in Carmine

1914 ***Imperf.***

26	A21	¼c green	.25	.25
a.		Complete 1c (block 4 ¼c)	1.25	.90

Stamps of Spain 1909-10 Overprinted in Carmine or Blue

Perf. 13x12½, 14

27	A46	2c	dark brown (C)	.35	.25
28	A46	5c	green (C)	.35	.25
29	A46	10c	carmine (Bl)	.35	.25
30	A46	15c	violet (C)	1.50	.90
31	A46	20c	olive grn (C)	3.00	1.90
32	A46	25c	deep blue (C)	3.00	1.50
33	A46	30c	blue grn (C)	5.75	2.75
34	A46	40c	rose (Bl)	13.00	3.75
35	A46	50c	slate blue (C)	6.50	2.75
36	A46	1p	lake (Bl)	6.50	3.75
37	A46	4p	dp violet (C)	33.00	24.00
38	A46	10p	orange (Bl)	50.00	32.00
			Nos. 26-38,E1 (14)	129.30	76.90
			Set, never hinged	350.00	

Many varieties of overprint exist, including inverted.

#27-38 exist imperf. Value for set, $525.

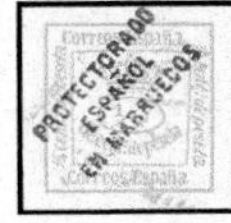

Stamps of Spain 1876 and 1909-10 Overprinted in Red or Blue

1915 ***Imperf.***

39	A21	¼c blue grn (R)	.25	.25
a.		Complete 1c (block 4 ¼c)	1.50	1.50

Perf. 13x12½, 14

40	A46	2c	dk brown (R)	.30	.30
41	A46	5c	green (R)	.35	.35
42	A46	10c	carmine (Bl)	.35	.35
43	A46	15c	violet (R)	.35	.35
44	A46	20c	olive grn (R)	1.25	.35
45	A46	25c	deep blue (R)	1.25	.55
46	A46	30c	blue grn (R)	1.40	.60
47	A46	40c	rose (Bl)	3.75	.60
48	A46	50c	slate blue (R)	6.25	.55
49	A46	1p	lake (Bl)	6.25	.60
50	A46	4p	deep violet (R)	42.50	26.00
51	A46	10p	orange (Bl)	60.00	29.00
			Nos. 39-51,E2 (14)	127.25	61.45
			Set, never hinged	350.00	

One stamp in the setting on Nos. 39-51 has the first "R" of "PROTECTORADO" inverted. Many other varieties of overprint exist, including double and inverted.

Nos. 40-51 exist imperf. Value, set $650.

ZONA DE PROTECTORADO ESPAÑOL EN MARRUECOS

Stamps of Spain 1877 and 1909-10 Overprinted in Red or Blue — b

1916-18 ***Imperf.***

52	A21	¼c blue grn (R)	1.25	.25
a.		Complete 1c (block 4 ¼c)	2.00	1.40

Perf. 13x12½, 14

53	A46	2c	dk brown (R)	1.25	.25
54	A46	5c	green (R)	5.50	.25
55	A46	10c	carmine (Bl)	6.00	.25
56	A46	15c	violet (R)	140.00	
57	A46	20c	olive grn (R)	140.00	
58	A46	25c	dp blue (R)	21.00	3.25
59	A46	30c	blue grn (R)	27.50	22.00
60	A46	40c	rose (Bl)	28.50	.50
61	A46	50c	slate blue (R)	13.50	.25
62	A46	1p	lake (Bl)	33.00	2.40
63	A46	4p	dp violet (R)	55.00	32.50
64	A46	10p	orange (Bl)	110.00	72.50
			Nos. 52-55,58-64 (11)	302.50	134.40
			Set, never hinged	440.00	
			Nos. 52-64 (13)	582.50	
			Set, never hinged	1,100.	

Nos. 56-57 were not regularly issued.

Varieties of overprint, including double and inverted, exist for several denominations.

The 5c exists in olive brown. Value $525.

Same Overprint on Spain No. 310

1920

No.	Type	Description	Unused	Used
65	A46	15c ocher (Bl)	5.50	.30

Exists imperf.; also with overprint inverted.

Nos. 44, 46 Perforated through the middle and each half Surcharged "10 céntimos" in Red

1920

No.	Type	Description	Unused	Used
66	A46	10c on half of 20c	5.00	1.90
67	A46	15c on half of 30c	11.00	7.25

No. E1 Divided and Surcharged in Black

No. 68

No. 68a

No.	Type	Description	Unused	Used
68	SD1	10c on half of 20c	12.00	7.75
a.		"10/cts." surcharge added	160.00	50.00
		Nos. 66-68 (3)	28.00	16.90

Values of Nos. 66-68 are for pairs, both halves of the stamp. Varieties were probably made deliberately.

"Justice" — A1

Revenue Stamps Perforated through the Middle and each half Surcharged in Red or Green

1920 *Perf. 11½*

No.	Type	Description	Unused	Used
69	A1	5c on 5p lt bl	12.00	2.40
70	A1	5c on 10p green	.75	.25
71	A1	10c on 25p dk grn	.75	.25
a.		Inverted surcharge	20.00	12.00
72	A1	10c on 50p indigo	.90	.40
73	A1	15c on 100p red (G)	.90	.40
74	A1	15c on 500p cl (G)	16.50	8.00
		Nos. 69-74 (6)	31.80	11.70
		Set, never hinged	60.00	

Values of Nos. 69-74 are for pairs, both halves of the stamp.

Stamps of Spain 1917-20 Overprinted Type "a" in Blue or Red

1921-24 *Perf. 13*

No.	Type	Description	Unused	Used
75	A46	15c ocher (Bl)	1.50	.25
76	A46	20c violet (R)	2.25	.25

Stamps of Spain 1920-21 Overprinted Type "b" in Red

Imperf

No.	Type	Description	Unused	Used
77	A47	1c blue green	1.50	.25

Engr.

Perf. 13

No.	Type	Description	Unused	Used
78	A46	20c violet	11.00	.25

See No. 92.

Stamps of Spain, 1922 Overprinted Type "a" in Red or Blue

1923-28 *Perf. 13½x12½*

No.	Type	Description	Unused	Used
79	A49	2c olive green (R)	4.25	.25
80	A49	5c red violet (Bl)	4.25	.25
81	A49	10c yellow green (R)	5.00	.25
82	A49	20c violet (R)	7.00	1.10
		Nos. 79-82 (4)	20.50	1.85

Same Overprinted Type "b"

1923-25

No.	Type	Description	Unused	Used
83	A49	2c olive green (R)	.75	.25
84	A49	5c red violet (Bl)	.75	.25
85	A49	10c yellow grn (R)	3.00	.25
86	A49	15c blue (R)	3.00	.25
87	A49	20c violet (R)	6.50	.25
88	A49	25c carmine (Bl)	13.00	1.50
89	A49	40c deep blue (R)	13.50	5.00
90	A49	50c orange (Bl)	35.00	8.50
91	A49a	1p blue black (R)	55.00	5.00
		Nos. 83-91,E3 (10)	142.50	31.00
		Set, never hinged	350.00	

Spain No. 314 Overprinted Type "a" in Red

1927 *Imperf.*

No.	Type	Description	Unused	Used
92	A47	1c blue green	.25	.25

Mosque of Alcazarquivir A2

Moorish Gateway at Larache A3

Well at Alhucemas A4

View of Xauen — A5

View of Tetuan — A6

1928-32 **Engr.** *Perf. 14, 14½*

No.	Type	Description	Unused	Used
93	A2	1c red ("Cs")	.25	.25
94	A2	1c car rose ("Ct") ('32)	.50	.40
95	A2	2c dark violet	.30	.25
96	A2	5c deep blue	.35	.25
97	A2	10c dark green	.35	.25
98	A2	15c orange brown	.75	.35
99	A3	20c olive green	.75	.35
100	A3	25c copper red	.80	.35
102	A3	30c black brown	2.60	.40
103	A3	40c dull blue	3.25	.40
104	A3	50c brown violet	6.75	.40
105	A4	1p yellow green	8.25	.45
106	A5	2.50p red violet	32.50	10.00
107	A6	4p ultra	24.00	7.50
		Nos. 93-107,E4 (15)	86.40	23.20
		Set, never hinged	225.00	

For surcharges see Nos. 164-167.

Seville-Barcelona Issue of Spain, 1929, Ovptd. in Red or Blue

1929 *Perf. 11, 14*

No.	Type	Description	Unused	Used
108	A50	1c greenish blue	.35	.30
109	A51	2c pale yel grn	.35	.30
110	A52	5c rose lake (Bl)	.35	.30
111	A53	10c green	.35	.30
112	A50	15c Prussian blue	.35	.30
113	A51	20c purple	.35	.30
114	A50	25c bright rose (Bl)	.35	.30
115	A52	30c black brown (bl)	.85	.75
116	A53	40c dark blue	.85	.75
117	A51	50c deep orange (Bl)	.85	.75
118	A52	1p blue black	6.75	5.75
119	A53	4p deep rose (Bl)	16.00	12.50
120	A53	10p brown (Bl)	33.00	29.00
		Nos. 108-120 (13)	60.75	51.60
		Set, never hinged	100.00	

See Nos. L1-L11.

Stamps of Spain, 1922-31, Overprinted Type "a" in Black, Blue or Red

1929-34 *Perf. 11½, 13x12½*

No.	Type	Description	Unused	Used
121	A49	5c claret (Bk)	3.50	.25
122	A61	10c green (R)	3.00	.45
123	A61	15c slate grn (R)	110.00	1.10
124	A61	20c violet (R)	3.00	.50
125	A61	30c brown lake (Bl)	3.25	1.10
126	A61	40c dark blue (R)	12.00	5.50
127	A49	50c orange (Bl)	30.00	5.25
128	A49a	10p brown (Bl)	3.00	5.75
		Nos. 121-128 (8)	167.75	19.90
		Set, never hinged	300.00	

Stamps of Spain, 1922-26, overprinted diagonally as above, and with no control number, or with "A000,000" on back, were not issued but were presented to the delegates at the 1929 UPU Congress in London. Value of complete set of 16, $3,250.

Stamps of Spain 1931-32, Overprinted in Black

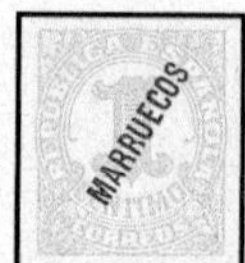

1933-34 *Imperf.*

No.	Type	Description	Unused	Used
130	A108	1c blue green	.25	.25

Perf. 11½

No.	Type	Description	Unused	Used
131	A108	2c buff	.25	.25
132	A95	5c brnsh black	.25	.25
133	A96	10c yellow green	.25	.25
134	A97	15c slate green	.25	.25
135	A95	20c dark violet	.30	.25
136	A104	25c lake	.30	.25
137	A99	30c carmine rose	60.00	6.00
138	A100	40c dark blue	.65	.25
139	A97	50c orange	1.25	.30
140	A100	60c apple green	1.25	.30
141	A105	1p blue black	1.25	.50
142	A106	4p magenta	2.75	2.50
143	A107	10p deep brown	3.50	*5.50*
		Nos. 130-143,E7 (15)	74.00	17.35
		Set, never hinged	130.00	

Street Scene in Tangier — A7

View of Xauen A8

Gate in Town Wall, Arzila — A9

Street Scene in Tangier A10

Mosque of Alcazarquivir A11

Caliph and His Guard A12

View of Tangier A13

Green Control Numbers Printed on Gum

1933-35 **Photo.** *Perf. 14, 13½*

No.	Type	Description	Unused	Used
144	A7	1c brt rose	.35	.25
145	A8	2c green ('35)	.35	.25
146	A9	5c magenta ('35)	.35	.25
147	A10	10c dark green	.45	.25
148	A11	15c yellow ('35)	3.00	.30
149	A7	20c slate green	1.25	.30
150	A12	25c crimson ('35)	29.00	.30
151	A10	30c red brown	8.00	.35
152	A13	40c deep blue	12.50	.35
153	A13	50c red orange	42.50	5.00
154	A8	1p slate blk ('35)	18.00	.35
155	A9	2.50p brown ('35)	32.50	5.00
156	A11	4p yel grn ('35)	42.50	5.00
157	A12	5p black ('35)	42.50	5.25
		Nos. 144-157,E5 (15)	234.40	23.45
		Set, never hinged	400.00	

For surcharge see No. CB1.

Mosque — A14

Landscape A15

Green Control Numbers Printed on Gum

1935

No.	Type	Description	Unused	Used
158	A14	25c violet	1.25	.25
159	A15	30c crimson	16.50	.25
160	A14	40c orange	8.50	.25
161	A15	50c bright blue	8.50	.30
162	A14	60c dk blue green	8.50	.35
163	A15	2p brown lake	42.50	6.00
		Nos. 158-163 (6)	85.75	7.40
		Set, never hinged	160.00	

Nos. 158-163 exist imperf. Value, set $250.
See No. 174.

Regular Issue and Special Delivery Stamp of 1928, Surcharged in Blue, Green or Red

Nos. 164-167

No. 168

1936

No.	Type	Description	Unused	Used
164	A6	1c on 4p ultra (Bl)	.35	.25
165	A5	2c on 2.50p red vio (G)	.35	.25
166	A3	5c on 25c cop red (R)	.35	.25
167	A4	10c on 1p yel grn (G)	10.00	4.00
168	SD2	15c on 20c blk (Bl)	7.75	2.10
		Nos. 164-168 (5)	18.80	6.85
		Set, never hinged	24.50	

Caliph and Viziers — A16

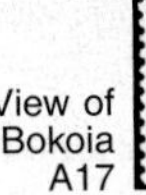

View of Bokoia A17

View of Alcazarquivir — A18

Sidi Saida Mosque A19

Caliph and Procession A20

Without Control Numbers

1937		**Photo.**		**Perf. 13½**
169	A16	1c green	.30	.25
170	A17	2c red violet	.30	.25
171	A18	5c orange	.30	.25
172	A16	15c violet	.30	.25
173	A19	30c red	.85	.25
a.		Souvenir sheet of 4, #170-173	22.00	12.00
174	A14	1p ultra	7.50	.30
a.		Souv. sheet of 4, #169-171, 174	22.00	12.00
175	A20	10p brown	60.00	17.50
		Nos. 169-175 (7)	69.55	19.05
		Set, never hinged	150.00	

Nos. 169-175 exist imperf. Value, set $250.

Nos. 173a, 174a for 1st year of the Spanish Civil War.

Nos. 173a, 174a were privately overprinted "TANGER" in black on each stamp in the sheet for "use" in the International City of Tangier, and "GUINEA" for "use" in Spanish Guinea.

Harkeno Rifleman — A21

Troops Marching A22

Designs: 2c, Legionnaires. 5c, Cavalryman leading his mount. 10c, Moroccan phalanx. 15c, Legion flag-bearer. 20c, Colonial soldier. 25c, Ifni sharpshooters. 30c, Mounted trumpeters. 40c, Cape Juby Dromedary Corps. 50c, Regular infantry. 60c, Caliphate guards. 1p, Orderly on guard. 2p, Sentry. 2.50p, Regular cavalry. 4p, Orderly.

1937				**Perf. 13½**
176	A21	1c dull blue	.35	.25
177	A21	2c orange brn	.35	.25
178	A21	5c cerise	.35	.25
179	A21	10c emerald	.35	.25
180	A21	15c brt blue	.35	.25
181	A21	20c red brown	.35	.25
182	A21	25c magenta	.35	.30
183	A21	30c red orange	.35	.30
184	A21	40c orange	.35	.35
185	A21	50c ultra	.35	.35
186	A21	60c yellow grn	.35	.35
187	A21	1p blue violet	.35	.35
188	A21	2p Prus blue	11.50	5.00
189	A21	2.50p gray black	11.50	5.00
190	A21	4p dark brown	11.50	5.00
191	A22	10p black	11.50	5.00
		Nos. 176-191,E6 (17)	50.45	23.75
		Set, never hinged	120.00	

First Year of Spanish Civil War.
Exists imperf. Value, set $300.
For overprints see Nos. 214-229.

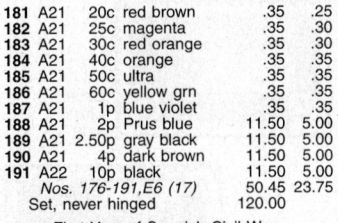

Spanish Quarter — A25

Designs: 10c, Moroccan quarter. 15c, Street scene, Larache. 20c, Tetuan.

1939		**Unwmk. Photo.**		**Perf. 13½**
194	A25	5c orange	.30	.25
195	A25	10c brt blue grn	.30	.25
196	A25	15c golden brown	.50	.30
197	A25	20c brt ultra	.50	.30
		Nos. 194-197 (4)	1.60	1.10

Postman — A26

Mail Box — A27

Landscape A28

Street Scene, Alcazarquivir A29

View of Xauen — A30

Sentry Guarding Palace at Sat — A31

The Chieftain — A32

Market Place, Larache — A33

Tetuán — A34

Ancient Gateway at Xauen — A35

Scene in Alcazarquivir A36

Post Office A37

Spanish War Veterans — A38

Victory Flag Bearers — A39

Cavalry — A40

Day of Court — A41

1940		**Unwmk. Photo.**		**Perf. 11½x11**
198	A26	1c dark brown	.35	.30
199	A27	2c olive grn	.35	.30
200	A28	5c dk blue	.35	.30
201	A29	10c dk red lilac	.35	.30
202	A30	15c dk green	.45	.35
203	A31	20c purple	.35	.35
204	A32	25c black brown	.35	.35
205	A33	30c brt green	.35	.35
206	A34	40c slate green	2.75	.35
207	A35	45c orange ver	1.10	.35
208	A36	50c brown orange	1.10	.35
209	A37	70c sapphire	1.10	.35
210	A38	1p indigo & brn	3.25	.35
211	A39	2.50p choc & dk grn	18.00	4.75
212	A40	5p dk cerise & sep	3.50	.45
213	A41	10p dk ol grn & brn org	32.50	8.00
		Nos. 198-213,E8 (17)	67.05	17.90
		Set, never hinged	120.00	

"ZONA" printed in black on back.
Exists imperf. Value, set $325.

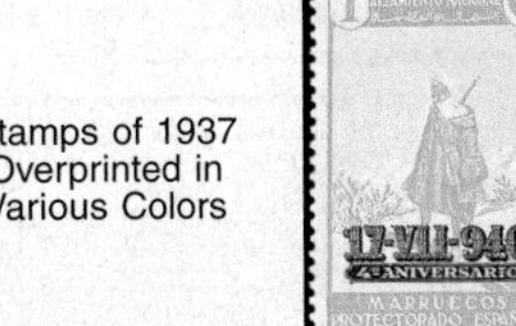

Stamps of 1937 Overprinted in Various Colors

1940		**Unwmk.**		**Perf. 13½**
214	A21	1c dull blue (Bk)	.85	.70
215	A21	2c org brn (Bk)	.85	.70
216	A21	5c cerise (Bk)	.85	.70
217	A21	10c emerald (Bk)	.85	.70
218	A21	15c brt blue (Bk)	.85	.70
219	A21	20c red brn (Bk)	.85	.70
220	A21	25c mag (Bk)	.85	.70
221	A21	30c red org (V)	.85	.70
222	A21	40c orange (V)	1.50	1.40
223	A21	50c ultra (Bk)	1.50	1.40
224	A21	60c yel grn (Bk)	1.50	1.40
225	A21	1p blue vio (V)	1.50	1.40
226	A21	2p Prus bl (Bl)	45.00	45.00
227	A21	2.50p gray blk (V)	45.00	45.00
228	A21	4p dk brn (Bl)	45.00	45.00
229	A22	10p black (R)	45.00	45.00
		Nos. 214-229,E10 (17)	204.80	200.70
		Set, never hinged	500.00	

4th anniversary of Spanish Civil War.

Larache A42

Alcazarquivir A43

Market Place, Larache — A44

Tangier

A45 A46

1941		**Unwmk. Photo.**		**Perf. 10½**
230	A42	5c dk brn & brn	.25	.25
231	A43	10c dp rose & ver	.25	.25
232	A44	15c sl grn & yel grn	.25	.25
233	A45	20c vio bl & dp bl	.55	.25
234	A46	40c dp plum & claret	1.50	.25
		Nos. 230-234 (5)	2.80	1.25
		Set, never hinged	5.00	

Exists imperf. Value, set $150.

1943				**Perf. 12x12½**
234A	A43	5c dark blue	.25	.25
235	A44	40c dull violet brn	100.00	.25

Plowing A47

Harvesting A48

Returning from Work A49

Transporting Wheat — A50

Vegetable Garden A51

Picking Oranges A52

Goat Herd — A53

1944 Unwmk. Photo. *Perf. 12½*

No.	Type	Denomination / Color	Unused	Used
236	A47	1c choc & lt bl	.25	.25
237	A48	2c sl grn & lt grn	.25	.25
238	A49	5c choc & grnsh blk	.25	.25
239	A50	10c brt ultra & red org	.25	.25
240	A51	15c sl grn & lt grn	.25	.25
241	A52	20c dp cl & blk	.25	.25
242	A53	25c lt bl & choc	.25	.25
243	A47	30c yel grn & brt ultra	.25	.25
244	A48	40c choc & red vio	.25	.25
245	A49	50c brt ultra & red brn	.65	.25
246	A50	75c yel grn & brt ultra	.90	.25
247	A51	1p brt ultra & choc	.90	.25
248	A52	2.50p blk & brt ultra	7.75	1.75
249	A53	10p sal & gray blk	11.50	3.75
		Nos. 236-249 (14)	23.95	8.50
		Set, never hinged	50.00	

Exists imperf. Value, set $125.

Potters A54

Dyers A55

Blacksmiths A56

Cobblers A57

Weavers A58

Metal Workers A59

1946 Unwmk. Litho. *Perf. 10½x10*

No.	Type	Denomination / Color	Unused	Used
250	A54	1c purple & brn	.25	.25
251	A55	2c dk Prus grn & vio blk	.25	.25
252	A54	10c dp org & vio bl	.25	.25
253	A55	15c dk bl & bl grn	.25	.25
254	A54	25c yel grn & ultra	.25	.25
255	A56	40c dk bl & brn, perf. 12½	.25	.25
256	A55	45c black & rose	.50	.25
257	A57	1p dk Prus grn & dp bl	.60	.25
258	A58	2.50p dp org & gray	1.75	.65
259	A59	10p dk bl & gray	3.00	1.50
		Nos. 250-259 (10)	7.35	4.15
		Set, never hinged	15.00	

Control letter "Z" in circle in black on back. Exists imperf. Value, set $85.

A60

Sanitorium — A61

1946, Sept. 1 *Perf. 11½x10½, 10½*

No.	Type	Denomination / Color	Unused	Used
260	A60	10c crim & bl grn	.25	.25
261	A61	25c crimson & brn	.25	.25
		Nos. 260-261,B14-B16 (5)	1.80	1.25

Issued to aid anti-tuberculosis work.

A62

A63

1947 *Perf. 10*

No.	Type	Denomination / Color	Unused	Used
262	A62	10c carmine & blue	.25	.25
263	A63	25c red & chocolate	.25	.25
		Nos. 262-263,B17-B19 (5)	1.90	1.55

Issued to aid anti-tuberculosis work.

Commerce by Railroad A64

Commerce by Truck A65

Urban Market A66

Country Market A67

Caravan A68

Maritime Commerce A69

1948 Litho. *Perf. 10, 10x10½*

No.	Type	Denomination / Color	Unused	Used
264	A64	2c purple & brn	.25	.25
265	A65	5c dp cl & vio	.25	.25
266	A66	15c brt ultra & bl grn	.25	.25
267	A67	25c blk & Prus grn	.25	.25
268	A65	35c brt ultra & gray blk	.25	.25
269	A68	50c red & violet	.25	.25
270	A66	70c dk gray grn & ultra	.25	.25
271	A67	90c cer & dk gray grn	.25	.25
272	A68	1p brt ultra & vio	.60	.25
273	A64	2.50p vio brn & sl grn	1.50	.45
274	A69	10p blk & dp ultra	2.75	1.25
		Nos. 264-274 (11)	6.85	3.95
		Set, never hinged	11.00	

Exists imperf. Value, set $120.

Emblem of Tuberculosis Association — A70

Design: 25c, Plane over sanatorium.

1948, Oct. 1 *Perf. 10*

No.	Type	Denomination / Color	Unused	Used
275	A70	10c car & green	.25	.25
276	A70	25c car & grnsh gray	1.75	.65
		Nos. 275-276,B20-B23 (6)	29.85	10.15

See No. B39.
Exists imperf. Value, set $75.

Emblem of Tuberculosis Association — A71

10c, Road of Health. 25c, Minaret and Palm.

1949

Black Control Number on Back

No.	Type	Denomination / Color	Unused	Used
277	A71	5c car & green	.25	.25
278	A71	10c car & dk vio	.25	.25
279	A71	25c car & black	.90	.30
		Nos. 277-279,B25-B26 (5)	3.35	1.50

Catalogue values for unused stamps in this section, from this point to the end of the section, are for Never Hinged items.

Mail Transport, 1890 — A72

Designs: 5c, 50c, 90c, Mail transport, 1890. 10c, 45c, 1p, Mail transport, 1906. 15c, 1.50p, Mail transport, 1913. 35c, 75c, 5p, Mail transport, 1914. 10p, Mail transport, 1918.

1950 Litho. *Perf. 10½*

Black Control Number on Back

No.	Type	Denomination / Color	Unused	Used
280	A72	5c choc & vio bl	.25	.25
281	A72	10c deep bl & sep	.25	.25
282	A72	15c grnsh blk & emer	.25	.25
283	A72	35c pur & gray blk	.25	.25
284	A72	45c dp car & rose lil	.25	.25
285	A72	50c emer & dk brn	.25	.25
286	A72	75c dk vio bl & bl	.25	.25
287	A72	90c grnsh blk & rose car	.25	.25
288	A72	1p blk brn & gray	.25	.25
289	A72	1.50p carmine & blue	1.00	.25
290	A72	5p black & vio brn	1.75	.25
291	A72	10p purple & blue	40.00	10.00
		Nos. 280-291,E11 (13)	77.50	22.75

UPU, 75th anniv. (in 1949).
Nos. 280-291 exist imperf. Value $500.

Herald — A73

Frame and Device in Carmine

1950 Unwmk. *Perf. 10*

Black Control Number on Back

No.	Type	Denomination / Color	Unused	Used
292	A73	5c gray black	.25	.25
293	A73	10c Old fort	.25	.25
294	A73	25c Sanatorium	1.00	.50
		Nos. 292-294,B27-B28 (5)	3.15	1.85

Boar Hunt A74

10c, 1p, Hunters and hounds. 50c, Boar hunt. 5p, Fishermen. 10p, Moorish fishing boat.

1950, Dec. 30 *Perf. 10½x10*

Black Control Number on Back

No.	Type	Denomination / Color	Unused	Used
295	A74	5c dk brn & rose vio	.25	.25
296	A74	10c carmine & gray	.25	.25
297	A74	50c green & sepia	.25	.25
298	A74	1p bl vio & claret	.45	.25
299	A74	5p dp claret & bl vio	.70	.25
300	A74	10p grnsh blk & dp cl	2.25	.40
		Nos. 295-300 (6)	4.15	1.65

Nos. 295-300 exist imperf. Value, set $150.

Emblem — A75

10c, Patients expressing gratitude. 25c, Plane in the Clouds.

Dated "1951"

Frame and Device in Carmine

Black Control Number on Back

1951 Litho. *Perf. 12*

301 A75 5c green .25 .25
302 A75 10c blue violet .25 .25
303 A75 25c gray black .85 .30
Nos. 301-303,B29-B32 (7) 15.00 5.65

Issued to aid anti-tuberculosis work.

Armed Attack A76

Designs: 10c, Horses on parade. 15c, Holiday procession. 20c, Road to market. 25c, "Brother-hoods." 35c, "Offering." 45c, Soldiers. 50c, On the rooftop. 75c, Teahouse. 90c, Wedding. 1p, Pilgrimage. 5p, Storyteller. 10p, Market corner.

Black Control Number on Back

1952 *Perf. 11*

304 A76 5c dk blue & brn .25 .25
305 A76 10c dk brn & lil rose .25 .25
306 A76 15c black & emer .25 .25
307 A76 20c ol grn & red vio .25 .25
308 A76 25c red & lt blue .25 .25
309 A76 35c olive & orange .25 .25
310 A76 45c red & rose red .25 .25
311 A76 50c rose car & gray grn .25 .25
312 A76 75c purple & ultra .25 .25
313 A76 90c dk bl & rose vio .25 .25
314 A76 1p dk bl & red brn .25 .25
315 A76 5p red & blue 1.25 .25
316 A76 10p dk grn & gray blk 1.75 .40
Nos. 304-316,E12 (14) 6.00 3.65

Nos. 304-316 exist imperf. Value, set $200.

Worship — A77

10c, Distributing alms. 25c, Prickly pear.

Black Control Number on Back

1952, Oct. 1 Dated "1952"

317 A77 5c car & dk ol grn .25 .25
318 A77 10c car & dk brown .25 .25
319 A77 25c car & dp blue .35 .25
Nos. 317-319,B33-B37 (8) 10.45 4.35

Nos. 317-319, B33-B37 exist imperf. Value, set of 8 $400.

Semi-Postal Types of 1948-49 Dated "1953"

1953 Litho. *Perf. 10*

Black Control Number on Back

320 SP7 5c shown .25 .25
321 SP9 10c like #B26 .25 .25
322 SP7 25c like #B23 .85 .35
Nos. 320-322,B38-B42 (8) 18.45 6.50

Issued to aid anti-tuberculosis work.

Nos. 320-322, B38-B42 exist imperf. Value, set of 8 $200.

A78

1953, Nov. 15

Black Control Number on Back

323 A78 5c red .25 .25
324 A78 10c gray green .25 .25

Nos. 323-324 exist imperf. Value, set $100.

Mountain Women — A79

50c and 2.50p, Water carrier. 90c and 2p, Mountaineers and donkey. 1p and 4.50p, Moorish women and child. 10p, Mounted dignitary.

1953, Dec. 15 Photo.

Black Control Number on Back

334 A79 35c grn & rose vio .25 .25
335 A79 50c red & green .25 .25
336 A79 90c dk bl & org .25 .25
337 A79 1p dk brn & grn .25 .25
338 A79 1.25p dk grn & car rose .25 .25
339 A79 2p dk rose vio & bl .25 .25
340 A79 2.50p black & orange .85 .25
341 A79 4.50p brt car rose & dk grn 7.50 .35
342 A79 10p green & black 9.00 .65
Nos. 334-342,E13 (10) 19.25 3.00

25th anniv. of Spanish Morocco's first definitive postage stamps.

Nos. 334-342, E13 exist imperf. Value, set of 10 $250.

Zauia — A80

10c, "The Family." 25c, Plane, Spanish coast.

1954, Nov. 1 Dated "1954"

Black Control Number on Back

343 A80 5c car & bl grn .25 .25
344 A80 10c car & dk brn .25 .25
345 A80 25c car & blue .25 .25
Nos. 343-345,B43-B45 (6) 8.55 4.90

Nos. 343-345, B43-B45 exist imperf. Value, set of 6 $300.

Queen's Gate — A81

1955 Litho. *Perf. 11*

Black Control Number on Back

Frames in Black

346 A81 15c shown .25 .25
347 A81 25c Saida .25 .25
348 A81 80c like #346 .25 .25
349 A81 1p like #347 .25 .25
350 A81 15p Ceuta 3.00 .65
Nos. 346-350,E14 (6) 4.25 1.90

Honor Guard — A82

Designs: 25c, 80c, 3p, Caliph Moulay Hassan ben el-Medi. 30c, 1p, 5p, Caliph and procession. 15p, Coat of arms.

Perf. 13x12½

1955, Nov. 8 Photo. Unwmk.

351 A82 15c ol brn & ol .25 .25
352 A82 25c lil & dp rose .25 .25
353 A82 30c brn blk & Prus grn .25 .25
354 A82 70c Prus grn & yel grn .25 .25
355 A82 80c ol & ol brn .25 .25
356 A82 1p dk bl & redsh brn .25 .25
357 A82 1.80p black & bl vio .25 .25
358 A82 3p blue & gray .25 .25
359 A82 5p dk grn & brn 1.25 .45

Engr.

360 A82 15p red brn & yel grn 2.75 1.65
Nos. 351-360 (10) 6.00 4.10

30th anniv. of accession to throne by Caliph Moulay Hassan ben el-Medi ben Ismail.

Nos. 351-360 exist imperf. Value, set $750.

Succeeding issues, released under the Kingdom, are listed under Morocco.

SEMI-POSTAL STAMPS

Types of Semi-Postal Stamps of Spain, 1926, Ovptd. in Black or Blue

1926 Unwmk. *Perf. 12½, 13*

B1 SP1 1c orange 8.50 5.50
B2 SP2 2c rose 12.00 10.00
B3 SP3 5c black brn 4.50 3.50
B4 SP4 10c dark grn 4.50 3.50
B5 SP1 15c dk violet (Bl) .80 .65
B6 SP4 20c violet brn .80 .65
B7 SP5 25c deep carmine .80 .65
B8 SP1 30c olive grn .80 .65
B9 SP3 40c ultra .25 .25
B10 SP2 50c red brown .25 .25
B11 SP4 1p vermilion .25 .25
B12 SP3 4p bister .80 .65
B13 SP5 10p light violet 3.50 2.75
Nos. B1-B13,EB1 (14) 40.50 31.65
Set, never hinged 70.00

See Spain No. B6a for No. B6 without overprint. For surcharges see Spain Nos. B64-B65.

Tuberculosis Fund Issues

SP1

SP2

SP3

Perf. 10½, 11½x10½

1946, Sept. 1 Litho. Unwmk.

B14 SP1 25c + 5c crim & rose vio .25 .25
B15 SP2 50c + 10c crim & blue .30 .25
B16 SP3 90c + 10c crim & gray brn .75 .25
Nos. B14-B16 (3) 1.25 .65

Nos. B14-B16 exist imperf. Value, set $60.

Medical Center — SP4

Nurse and Children — SP5

"Protection" — SP6

1947 *Perf. 10*

B17 SP4 25c + 5c red & violet .25 .25
B18 SP5 50c + 10c red & blue .35 .25
B19 SP6 90c + 10c red & sepia .80 .55
Nos. B17-B19 (3) 1.35 .95

Nos. B17-B19 exist imperf. Value, set $60.

Herald — SP7

Designs: No. B21, Protection. No. B22, Sun bath. No. B23, Plane over Ben Karrich.

1948, Oct. 1

B20 SP7 50c + 10c car & dk vio .35 .25
B21 SP7 90c + 10c car & dk gray 1.50 .50
B22 SP7 2.50p + 50c car & brn 10.00 3.25
B23 SP7 5p + 1p car & vio bl 16.00 5.25
Nos. B20-B23 (4) 27.85 9.25

Nos. B20-B23 exist imperf. Value, set $90.

See Nos. 320, 322.

Moulay Hassan ben el-Medi ben Ismail — SP8

1949, May 15

B24 SP8 50c + 10c lilac rose 1.10 .45

Wedding of the Caliph at Tetuan, June 5.

Tuberculosis Fund Issues

Flag — SP9

Design: No. B26, Fight with dragon.

Black Control Numbers on Back

1949
B25 SP9 50c + 10 car & brown .35 .30
B26 SP9 90c + 10 car & grnsh gray 1.60 .40

See No. 321.

Catalogue values for unused stamps in this section, from this point to the end of the section, are for Never Hinged items.

Crowd at Fountain of Life — SP10

90c+10c, Mohammedan hermit's tomb.

Black Control Numbers on Back

1950, Oct. 1 Litho. *Perf. 10*
Frame and Cross in Carmine

B27 SP10 50 + 10c dk brown .40 .30
B28 SP10 90 + 10c dk green 1.25 .55

Warrior — SP11

Designs: 90c+10c, Fort. 1p+5p, Port of Salvation. 1.10p+25c, Road to market.

Black Control Numbers on Back

1951 Unwmk. *Perf. 12*
B29 SP11 50c + 10c car & brn .25 .25
B30 SP11 90c + 10c car & bl .40 .25
B31 SP11 1p + 5p car & gray 8.25 2.75
B32 SP11 1.10p + 25c car & gray 4.75 1.60
Nos. B29-B32 (4) 13.60 4.80

See No. B40.

Pilgrimage — SP12

Designs: 60c+25c, Palmettos. 90c+10c, Fort. 1.10p+25c, Agave. 5p+2p, Warrior.

Black Control Numbers on Back

1952 *Perf. 11*
B33 SP12 50 + 10c car & gray .25 .25
B34 SP12 60 + 25c car & dk grn .80 .40
B35 SP12 90 + 10c car & vio brn .80 .40
B36 SP12 1.10p + 25c car & pur 2.25 .80
B37 SP12 5p + 2p car & gray 5.50 1.75
Nos. B33-B37 (5) 9.55 3.55

Armed Horseman in Action — SP13

#B39, As #276. #B42, Plane & clouds.

Black Control Numbers on Back

1953 *Perf. 10*
B38 SP13 50c + 10c car & vio .30 .25
B39 A70 60c + 25c car & brn 2.50 .80
B40 SP11 90c + 10c car & blk .80 .35
B41 SP13 1.10p + 25c car & vio brn 4.00 1.25
B42 A73 5p + 2p car & bl 9.50 3.00
Nos. B38-B42 (5) 17.10 5.60

Stork — SP14

50c+10c, Father & Child. 5p+2p, Tomb.

Black Control Numbers on Back

1954 Photo.
B43 SP14 5c + 5c car & rose vio .25 .25
B44 SP14 50c + 10c car & gray grn .80 .40
B45 SP14 5p + 2p car & gray 6.75 3.50
Nos. B43-B45 (3) 7.75 4.10

AIR POST STAMPS

Mosque de Baja and Plane — AP1

View of Tetuán and Plane AP2

10c, Stork of Alcazar. 25c, Shore scene, plane. 40c, Desert tribesmen watching plane. 75c, View of shoreline at Larache. 1p, Arab mailman, plane above. 1.50p, Arab farmers, stork. 2p, Plane at twilight. 3p, Shadow of plane over city.

1938 Unwmk. Photo. *Perf. 13½*
C1 AP1 5c red brown .25 .25
C2 AP1 10c emerald .25 .25
C3 AP1 25c crimson .25 .25
C4 AP1 40c dull blue 2.00 .50
C5 AP2 50c cerise .25 .25
C6 AP2 75c ultra .25 .25
C7 AP1 1p dark brown .25 .25
C8 AP1 1.50p purple .65 .35
C9 AP1 2p brown lake .40 .25
C10 AP1 3p gray black 1.75 .25
Nos. C1-C10 (10) 6.30 2.85
Set, Never Hinged 11.00

Nos. C1-C10 exist imperf. Value of set, $100.
For surcharge see No. C32.

Landscape, Ketama — AP3

Mosque, Tangier — AP4

Velez — AP5

Sanjurjo — AP6

Strait of Gibraltar — AP7

1942 *Perf. 12½*
C11 AP3 5c deep blue .25 .25
C12 AP4 10c orange brn .25 .25
C13 AP5 15c grnsh black .25 .25
C14 AP6 90c dark rose .25 .25
C15 AP7 5p black 1.50 .85
Nos. C11-C15 (5) 2.50 1.85
Set, never hinged 3.25

Exist imperf. Value, set $55.

Strait of Gibraltar — AP8

Designs: 5c, 1.75p, Strait of Gibraltar. 10c, 3p, Market day. 30c, 4p, Kebira Fortress. 6.50p, Airmail arrival. 8p, Horseman.

1949 Litho. *Perf. 10*
C16 AP8 5c vio brn & brt grn .25 .25
C17 AP8 10c blk & rose lilac .25 .25
C18 AP8 30c dk vio bl & grnsh gray .25 .25
C19 AP8 1.75p car & bl vio .25 .25
C20 AP8 3p dk blue & gray .25 .25
C21 AP8 4p grnsh blk & car rose .30 .25
C22 AP8 6.50p brt grn & brn .95 .25
C23 AP8 8p rose lil & bl vio 1.60 .40
Nos. C16-C23 (8) 4.10 2.15
Set, never hinged 5.50

Exist imperf. Value, set $80.

Catalogue values for unused stamps in this section, from this point to the end of the section, are for Never Hinged items.

Road to Tetuan — AP9

Designs: 4p, Arrival of mail from Spain. 8p, Greeting plane. 16p, Shadow of plane.

1952 *Perf. 11*
Black Frames and Inscriptions
Black Control Numbers on Back

C24 AP9 2p brt blue .25 .25
C25 AP9 4p scarlet .30 .25
C26 AP9 8p dk olive green .45 .25
C27 AP9 16p violet brown 2.25 .95
Nos. C24-C27 (4) 3.25 1.70

Part of the proceeds was used toward the establishment of a postal museum at Tetuan.

Plane over Boat — AP10

Designs: 60c, Mosques, Sidi Saidi. 1.10p, Plowing. 4.50p, Fortress, Xauen.

1953 *Perf. 10*
C28 AP10 35c dp bl & car rose .25 .25
C29 AP10 60c dk car & sl grn .25 .25
C30 AP10 1.10p dp blue & blk .30 .25
C31 AP10 4.50p dk car & dk brn 1.25 .40
Nos. C28-C31 (4) 2.05 1.15

Exist imperf. Value, set $125.

No. C6 Surcharged in Black

Type I

Type II

1953 *Perf. 13½*
C32 AP2 50c on 75c ultra (I) .50 .25
a. 50c on 75c ultra (II) .50 .25
b. Vert. gutter pair, types I and II 2.75

Sheets of 2 panes, 25 stamps each, with gutter between. Upper pane surcharged type I, lower type II.

AIR POST SEMI-POSTAL STAMPS

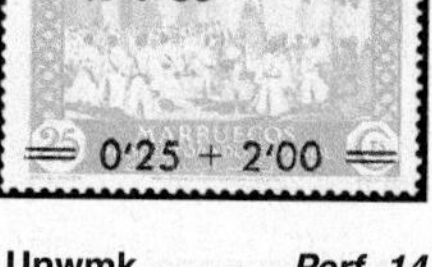

No. 150 Surcharged in Black

1936 Unwmk. *Perf. 14*
CB1 A12 25c + 2p on 25c 14.00 5.75
Never hinged 50.00
a. Bars at right omitted 57.50 42.50
b. Blue surcharge 45.00 15.00

25c was for postage, 2p for air post.

Nos. C1-C10 surcharged "Lucha Antituberculosa," a Lorraine cross and surtax are stated to be bogus.

Crowd at Palace — SPAP1

1949, May 15 Unwmk. *Perf. 10*

CB2 SPAP1 1p + 10c gray black	.75	.35

Wedding of the Caliph at Tetuan, June 5.

SPECIAL DELIVERY STAMPS

Special Delivery Stamp of Spain Overprinted in Blue

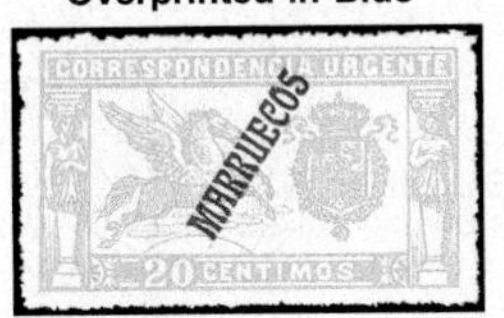

1914 Unwmk. *Perf. 14*

E1 SD1 20c red	5.75	2.60

Special Delivery Stamp of Spain Overprinted in Blue

1915

E2 SD1 20c red	3.00	1.60

For bisected surcharge see No. 68.

Special Delivery Stamp of Spain Overprinted in Blue

1923

E3 SD1 20c red	12.00	9.75

Mounted Courier SD2

1928 Engr. *Perf. 14, 14½*

E4 SD2 20c black	5.00	1.60

For surcharge see No. 168.

Moorish Postman — SD3

1935 Photo. *Perf. 14*
Green Control Number on Back

E5 SD3 20c vermilion	1.15	.25

See No. E9.

Mounted Courier — SD4

1937 *Perf. 13½*

E6 SD4 20c bright carmine	.25	.25

1st Year of the Spanish Civil War.
For surcharge see No. E10.

Spain No. E14 Overprinted in Black

1938 *Perf. 10*

E7 SD7 20c vermilion	1.50	.25

Arab Postman — SD5

1940 Photo. *Perf. 11½x11*

E8 SD5 25c scarlet	.85	.35

"ZONA" printed on back in black.

Type of 1935

1940 Litho. *Perf. 10*

E9 SD3 20c black brown	2.60	

No. E9 was prepared but not issued.
Exists imperf. Value, $10.

No. E6 Surcharged with New Value, Bars and

1940 *Perf. 13½*

E10 SD4 25c on 20c brt car	12.00	9.50

4th anniversary of Spanish Civil War.

Catalogue values for unused stamps in this section, from this point to the end of the section, are for Never Hinged items.

Airmail 1935 — SD6

1950 Unwmk. Litho. *Perf. 10½*

E11 SD6 25c carmine & gray	32.50	10.00

UPU, 75th anniv. (in 1949).

Moorish Postrider SD7

1952 *Perf. 11*
Black Control Number on Back

E12 SD7 25c car & rose car	.25	.25

Rider with Special Delivery Mail — SD8

1953 Photo. *Perf. 10*
Black Control Number on Back

E13 SD8 25c dk bl & car rose	.40	.25

25th anniv. of Spanish Morocco's first definitive postage stamps.

Gate of Tangier — SD9

1955 Litho. *Perf. 11*
Black Control Number on Back

E14 SD9 2p violet & black	.25	.25

SEMI-POSTAL SPECIAL DELIVERY STAMP

Type of Semi-Postal Special Delivery Stamp of Spain, 1926, Overprinted like #B1-B13

1926 Unwmk. *Perf. 12½, 13*

EB1 SPSD1 20c ultra & black	2.75	2.40

POSTAL TAX STAMPS

General Francisco Franco — PT1

1937-39 Unwmk. Photo. *Perf. 12½*

RA1 PT1 10c sepia	.50	.25
a. Sheet of 4, imperf.	4.50	1.75
RA2 PT1 10c copper brn ('38)	.50	.25
a. Sheet of 4, imperf.	4.50	1.75
RA3 PT1 10c blue ('39)	.50	.25
a. Sheet of 4, imperf.	4.50	1.75
Nos. RA1-RA3 (3)	1.50	.75
Set, never hinged	3.50	
Set, RA1a-RA3a	13.50	

The tax was used for the disabled soldiers in North Africa.

Soldiers PT2

1941 Litho. *Perf. 13½*

RA4 PT2 10c brt grn	4.00	.25
RA5 PT2 10c rose pink	4.00	.25
RA6 PT2 10c henna brn	4.00	.25
RA7 PT2 10c ultra	4.00	.25
Nos. RA4-RA7 (4)	16.00	1.00
Set, never hinged	25.00	

The tax was used for the disabled soldiers in North Africa.
Exist imperf. Value, set $60.

General Francisco Franco — PT3

1943 Photo. *Perf. 10*

RA8 PT3 10c chalky blue	9.00	.25
RA9 PT3 10c slate blue	9.00	.25
RA10 PT3 10c dl gray brn	9.00	.25
RA11 PT3 10c blue violet	9.00	.25
Nos. RA8-RA11 (4)	36.00	1.00
Set, never hinged	52.50	

Exists imperf. Value, set $125.

1944 *Perf. 12*

RA12 PT3 10c dp mag & brn	6.00	.25
RA13 PT3 10c dp org & dk grn	6.00	.25
Set, never hinged	16.00	

Exists imperf. Value, set $45.00.

1946 Litho.

RA14 PT3 10c ultra & brown	6.75	.25
RA15 PT3 10c gray blk & rose lil	6.75	.25
Set, never hinged	17.50	

Exists imperf. Value, set $100.

TANGIER

For the International City of Tangier
Seville-Barcelona Issue of Spain, 1929, Ovptd. in Blue or Red

1929 *Perf. 11*

L1 A52 5c rose lake	.30	.30
L2 A53 10c green (R)	.30	.30
L3 A50 15c Prus blue (R)	.30	.30
L4 A51 20c purple (R)	.30	.30
L5 A50 25c brt rose	.30	.30
L6 A52 30c black brn	.30	.30
L7 A53 40c dk blue (R)	.75	.75
L8 A51 50c deep org	.75	.75
L9 A52 1p blue blk (R)	7.75	7.75
L10 A53 4p deep rose	21.00	21.00
L11 A53 10p brown	30.00	30.00
Nos. L1-L11 (11)	62.05	62.05
Set, never hinged	105.00	

Overprints of 1937-39

The following overprints on stamps of Spain exist in black or in red:

"TANGER" vertically on Nos. 517-518, 522-523, 528, 532, 534, 539-543, 549.

"Correo Espanol Tanger" horizontally or vertically in three lines on Nos. 540, 592-597 (gray paper), 598-601.

"Tanger" horizontally on Nos. 539-541, 592-601.

"Correo Tanger" horizontally in two lines on five consular stamps.

Woman — A1

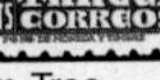
Palm Tree — A2

Man — A3

Old map of Tangier — A4

Tangier Street — A5

Moroccan Women — A6

Head of Moor — A7

Perf. 9½x10½, 12½x13 (1c, 2c, 10c, 20c)

1948-51	**Photo.**	**Unwmk.**	
L12 A1	1c blue grn ('51)	.25	.25
L13 A1	2c red org ('51)	.25	.25
	Engr.		
L14 A2	5c vio brn ('49)	.25	.25
L15 A3	10c deep blue ('51)	.25	.25
L16 A3	20c gray ('51)	.25	.25
L17 A2	25c green ('51)	.25	.25
L18 A4	30c dk slate grn	.35	.25
L19 A5	45c car rose	.35	.25
L20 A6	50c dp claret	.35	.25
L21 A7	75c deep blue	.70	.25
L22 A7	90c green	.60	.25
L23 A4	1.35p org ver	2.10	.35
L24 A6	2p purple	3.75	.35
L25 A5	10p dk grnsh bl ('49)	4.25	.65
	Nos. L12-L25,LE1 (15)	14.80	4.45
	Set, never hinged	25.00	

Nos. L18-L25, LE1 exist imperf. Value, set $500.

TANGIER SEMI-POSTAL STAMPS

Types of Semi-Postal Stamps of Spain, 1926, Overprinted

1926		***Perf. 12½, 13***	
LB1 SP1	1c orange	7.50	*8.00*
LB2 SP2	2c rose	7.50	*8.00*
LB3 SP3	5c black brn	3.75	3.75
LB4 SP4	10c dk green	3.75	3.75
LB5 SP1	15c dk violet	1.25	*1.60*
LB6 SP4	20c violet brn	1.25	*1.60*
LB7 SP5	25c dp carmine	1.25	*1.60*
LB8 SP1	30c olive grn	1.25	*1.60*
LB9 SP3	40c ultra	.35	.35
LB10 SP2	50c red brn	.35	.35
LB11 SP4	1p vermilion	.75	.75
LB12 SP3	4p bister	.75	.75
LB13 SP5	10p lt violet	3.25	3.25
	Nos. LB1-LB13,LEB1 (14)	35.95	38.35
	Set, never hinged	65.00	

For overprints & surcharges see Spain Nos. B66-B67.

TANGIER AIR POST STAMPS

Overprints of 1939

The following overprints on stamps of Spain exist in black or in red:

"Correo Aereo Tanger" in two lines on Nos. 539-541, 596 (gray paper), 600, C72B.

"Via Aerea Tanger" in three lines on Nos. 539-540, 592-597 (gray paper), 599, 601, E14.

"Correo Aereo Tanger" in three lines on four consular stamps.

"Correo Espanol Tanger" in three lines on No. C72B.

"Tanger" on No. C72B.

Plane over Shore — AP1

Twin-Engine Plane — AP2

Passenger Plane in Flight — AP3

Perf. 11x11½, 11½

1949-50	**Engr.**	**Unwmk.**	
LC1 AP1	20c violet brn ('50)	.25	.25
LC2 AP2	25c bright red	.25	.25
LC3 AP3	35c dull green	.25	.25
LC4 AP1	1p violet ('50)	.80	.25
LC5 AP2	2p deep blue	1.50	.25
LC6 AP3	10p brown violet	2.75	1.00
	Nos. LC1-LC6 (6)	5.80	2.25
	Set, never hinged	9.50	

Nos. LC1, LC4-LC6 exist imperf. Value $100 each.

TANGIER SPECIAL DELIVERY STAMP

Arab Postrider — SD1

1949	**Unwmk.**	**Engr.**	***Perf. 13***
LE1 SD1	25c red	.85	.35
	Never hinged	1.40	

TANGIER SEMI-POSTAL SPECIAL DELIVERY STAMP

Types of Semi-Postal Special Delivery Stamp of Spain, 1926, Overprinted like #LB1-LB13

1926	**Unwmk.**	***Perf. 12½, 13***	
LEB1 SPSD1	20c ultra & black	3.00	3.00
	Never hinged	5.00	

TETUAN

Spanish Offices in Morocco Nos. 1-4 & 6-7 Handstamped in Black, Blue or Violet

1908	**Unwmk.**	***Imperf.***	
1 A21	¼c blue green	13.00	10.00

Perf. 14

2 A35	2c bister brown	175.00	60.00
3 A35	5c dark green	165.00	35.00
4 A35	10c rose red	165.00	35.00
5 A35	20c grnsh black	325.00	125.00
6 A35	25c blue	125.00	35.00
	Nos. 1-6 (6)	968.00	300.00

Spain Nos. 221A, 272-274, 277-281 Handstamped in Black, Blue or Violet

1908		***Imperf.***	
7 A21	¼c deep green	7.50	3.25
	Perf. 14		
8 A35	2c bister brn	55.00	13.00
9 A35	5c dark green	70.00	22.50
10 A35	10c rose red	77.50	22.50
11 A35	15c purple	77.50	25.00
12 A35	20c grnsh black	175.00	110.00
13 A35	25c blue	95.00	35.00
14 A35	30c blue green	200.00	60.00
15 A35	40c olive bister	250.00	110.00
	Nos. 7-15 (9)	1,008.	401.25

Counterfeits of this overprint are plentiful.

SPANISH SAHARA

'spa-nish sə-'har-ə

(Spanish Western Sahara)

LOCATION — Northwest Africa, bordering on the Atlantic Ocean.
GOVT. — Spanish possession
AREA — 102,703 sq. mi.
POP. — 76,425 (1970)
CAPITAL — Aaiún

Spanish Sahara was a subdivision of Spanish West Africa. It included the colony of Rio de Oro and the territory of Saguiet el Hamra. Spanish Sahara was formerly known as Spanish Western Sahara, which superseded the older title of Rio de Oro.

In 1976, Spanish Sahara was divided between Morocco and Mauritania.

100 Centimos = 1 Peseta

Catalogue values for unused stamps in this country are for Never Hinged items, beginning with Scott 51 in the regular postage section, Scott B13 in the semi-postal section, Scott C8 in the air-post section, and Scott E1 in the special delivery section.

Tuareg and Camel — A1

1924	**Unwmk.**	**Typo.**	***Perf. 13***
	Control Number on Back		
1 A1	5c blue green	2.60	.90
2 A1	10c gray green	2.60	.90
3 A1	15c turq blue	2.60	.90
4 A1	20c dark violet	2.60	1.25
5 A1	25c red	2.60	1.25
6 A1	30c red brown	2.60	1.25
7 A1	40c dark blue	2.60	1.25
8 A1	50c orange	2.60	1.25
9 A1	60c violet	2.60	1.25
10 A1	1p rose	14.50	6.50
11 A1	4p chocolate	62.50	33.00
12 A1	10p claret	150.00	105.00
	Nos. 1-12 (12)	250.40	154.70
	Set, never hinged	400.00	

Nos. 1-12 were for use in La Aguera & Rio de Oro.

An unissued set of 10, similar to Nos. 3-12, exists perf. 10 or imperf, and no control number except on 50c. The set also exists perf 14. Value, $200.

Nos. 1-12 also exist perf 14. Value, unused $300.

For overprints see Nos. 24-35.

Seville-Barcelona Issue of Spain, 1929 Overprinted in Blue or Red

1929		***Perf. 11***	
13 A52	5c rose lake	.25	.25
14 A53	10c green (R)	.25	.25
15 A50	15c Prus blue (R)	.25	.25
16 A51	20c purple (R)	.30	.25
17 A50	25c bright rose	.30	.25
18 A52	30c black brown	.30	.25
19 A53	40c dark blue (R)	.65	.40
20 A51	50c deep orange	.65	.40
21 A52	1p blue black (R)	2.50	1.90
22 A53	4p deep rose	20.00	17.50
23 A53	10p brown	37.50	35.00
	Nos. 13-23 (11)	62.95	56.70
	Set, never hinged	100.00	

Stamps of 1924 Overprinted in Red or Blue

1931		***Perf. 13***	
24 A1	5c blue grn (R)	.95	.65
25 A1	10c gray grn (R)	.95	.65
26 A1	15c turq blue (R)	.95	.65
27 A1	20c dark violet (R)	.95	.65
28 A1	25c red	.95	.65
29 A1	30c red brown	.95	.65
30 A1	40c dark blue (R)	4.50	.90
31 A1	50c orange	4.50	2.25
32 A1	60c violet	4.50	2.25
33 A1	1p rose	4.50	2.25
34 A1	4p chocolate	45.00	22.00
35 A1	10p claret	92.50	50.00
	Nos. 24-35 (12)	161.20	83.55
	Set, never hinged	240.00	

The stamps of the 1931 issue exist with the overprint reading upward, downward, or horizontally. Some values also exist with double overprint, double overprint, one inverted and diagonal overprint.

Stamps of Spain, 1936-40, Overprinted in Carmine or Blue

1941-46	**Unwmk.**	***Imperf.***	
36 A159	1c green	2.25	1.50
	Perf. 10 to 11		
37 A160	2c org brn (Bl)	1.75	1.50
38 A161	5c gray brown	.65	.45
39 A161	10c dk car (Bl)	1.75	1.50
40 A161	15c dark green	.65	.45
41 A166	20c bright violet	.65	.45
42 A166	25c deep claret	1.50	.90
43 A166	30c light blue	1.50	1.10
44 A166	40c Prus grn	.65	.45
45 A166	50c indigo	15.00	1.25
46 A166	70c blue	10.00	1.90
47 A166	1p gray black	21.00	2.75
48 A166	2p dull brown	120.00	75.00
49 A166	4p dull rose (Bl)	350.00	225.00
50 A166	10p lt brown	1,000.	325.00
	Nos. 36-50 (15)	1,527.	639.20
	Set, never hinged	2,500.	

The stamps of this issue are normally poorly centered and are valued thus.

Counterfeit overprints exist.

Catalogue values for unused stamps in this section, from this point to the end of the section, are for Never Hinged items.

Dorcas Gazelles — A2

Designs: 2c, 20c, 45c, 3p, Caravan. 5c, 75c, 10p, Camel troops.

1943 Unwmk. *Perf. 12½*

No.	Type	Description	Unused	Used
51	A2	1c brown & lil rose	.35	.30
52	A2	2c yel grn & sl bl	.35	.30
53	A2	5c magenta & vio	.40	.30
54	A2	15c slate grn & grn	.40	.30
55	A2	20c violet & red brn	.45	.30
56	A2	40c rose vio & vio	.45	.30
57	A2	45c brn vio & red	.60	.35
58	A2	75c indigo & blue	.60	.35
59	A2	1p red & brown	2.00	1.25
60	A2	3p bl vio & sl grn	4.50	2.00
61	A2	10p black brn & blk	80.00	32.50
		Nos. 51-61,E1 (12)	91.85	39.20

Nos. 51-61, El exist imperf. Value for set, $150.

Gen. Franco and Desert Scene A5

1951 Photo. *Perf. 12½x13*

No.	Type	Description	Unused	Used
62	A5	50c deep orange	.25	.25
63	A5	1p chocolate	.25	.25
64	A5	5p blue green	20.00	10.00
		Nos. 62-64 (3)	20.50	10.50

Visit of Gen. Francisco Franco, 1950.

Allegorical Figure and Globe — A6

1953, Mar. 2 *Perf. 13x12½*

No.	Type	Description	Unused	Used
65	A6	5c red orange	.25	.25
66	A6	35c dk slate green	.25	.25
67	A6	60c brown	.35	.25
		Nos. 65-67 (3)	.85	.75

75th anniv. of the founding of the Royal Geographical Society.

Woman Musician — A7

Design: 60c, Man musician.

1953, June 1

No.	Type	Description	Unused	Used
68	A7	15c olive gray	.25	.25
69	A7	60c brown	.25	.25
		Nos. 68-69,B25-B26 (4)	1.00	1.00

Orange Scorpionfish — A8

Fish: 60c, Banded sargo.

1953, Nov. 23 *Perf. 12½x13*

No.	Type	Description	Unused	Used
70	A8	15c dk olive green	.25	.25
71	A8	60c orange	.40	.25
		Nos. 70-71,B27-B28 (4)	1.15	1.00

Colonial Stamp Day.

Hurdlers A9

Runner — A10

1954, June 1 *Perf. 12½x13, 13x12½*

No.	Type	Description	Unused	Used
72	A9	15c gray green	.25	.25
73	A10	60c brown	.30	.25
		Nos. 72-73,B29-B30 (4)	1.05	1.00

Atlantic Flyingfish A11

1954, Nov. 23 *Perf. 12½x13*

No.	Type	Description	Unused	Used
74	A11	15c shown	.25	.25
75	A11	60c Gilthead	.40	.25
		Nos. 74-75,B31-B32 (4)	1.15	1.00

Colonial Stamp Day.

Emilio Bonelli A12

1955, June 1 Photo. Unwmk.

No.	Type	Description	Unused	Used
76	A12	50c olive gray	.25	.25
		Nos. 76,B33-B34 (3)	.75	.75

Birth cent. of Emilio Bonelli, explorer.

Scimitar-horned Oryx — A13

1955, Nov. 23

No.	Type	Description	Unused	Used
77	A13	70c green	.25	.25
		Nos. 77,B35-B36 (3)	.75	.75

Colonial Stamp Day.

Antirrhinum Romosissimum A14

Design: 50c, Sesiviun portulacastrum.

1956, June 1 *Perf. 13x12½*

No.	Type	Description	Unused	Used
78	A14	20c bluish green	.25	.25
79	A14	50c brown	.35	.25
		Nos. 78-79,B37-B38 (4)	1.10	1.00

Arms of Aaiun and Camel Rider A15

1956, Nov. 23 *Perf. 12½x13*

No.	Type	Description	Unused	Used
80	A15	70c olive grn & sepia	.25	.25
		Nos. 80,B39-B40 (3)	.75	.75

Colonial Stamp Day.

Dromedaries — A16

15c, 80c, Ostrich. 50c, 1.80p, Mountain gazelle.

1957, Apr. 10 *Perf. 13x12½*

No.	Type	Description	Unused	Used
81	A16	5c purple	.25	.25
82	A16	15c bister	.25	.25
83	A16	50c dark olive	.25	.25
84	A16	70c yellow green	.70	.25
85	A16	80c blue green	.75	.25
86	A16	1.80p lilac rose	.75	.25
		Nos. 81-86 (6)	2.95	1.50

Golden Eagle — A17

1957, June 1 Photo. Unwmk.

No.	Type	Description	Unused	Used
87	A17	70c dark green	.25	.25
		Nos. 87,B41-B42 (3)	.75	.75

Striped Hyena — A18

Design: 70c, Striped Hyena, horiz.

Perf. 13x12½, 12½x13

1957, Nov. 23

No.	Type	Description	Unused	Used
88	A18	20c slate green	.25	.25
89	A18	70c yellowish green	.25	.25
		Nos. 88-89,B43-B44 (4)	1.00	1.00

Stamp Day.

Don Quixote and the Lion A19

Cervantes — A20

1958, June 1 *Perf. 12½x13, 13x12½*

No.	Type	Description	Unused	Used
90	A19	20c bister brn & grn	.25	.25
91	A20	70c dk grn & yel grn	.30	.25
		Nos. 90-91,B48-B49 (4)	1.05	1.00

Cervantes Type of 1958

Designs: 20c, Actor as "Peribanez," by Lope de Vega. 70c, Lope de Vega.

1959, June Photo. *Perf. 13x12½*

No.	Type	Description	Unused	Used
92	A20	20c lt green & brn	.25	.25
93	A20	70c yel grn & slate grn	.30	.25
		Nos. 92-93,B53-B54 (4)	1.05	1.00

Promoting child welfare.

Gray Heron — A21

Birds: 50c, 1.50p, 5p, Sparrowhawk. 75c, 2p, 10p, Sea gull.

1959, Oct. 15 *Perf. 13x12½*

No.	Type	Description	Unused	Used
94	A21	25c dull violet	.25	.25
95	A21	50c dark olive	.25	.25
96	A21	75c dark brown	.25	.25
97	A21	1p red orange	.30	.25
98	A21	1.50p brt green	.35	.25
99	A21	2p brt red lilac	1.00	.30
100	A21	3p blue	1.05	.30
101	A21	5p red brown	1.90	.35
102	A21	10p olive green	11.00	4.75
		Nos. 94-102 (9)	16.35	6.95

Scene from "The Pilferer Don Pablos" by Quevedo — A22

Francisco Gomez de Quevedo A23

1960, June *Perf. 13x12½, 12½x13*

No.	Type	Description	Unused	Used
103	A22	35c slate green	.25	.25
104	A23	80c Prussian green	.25	.25
		Nos. 103-104,B58-B59 (4)	1.00	1.00

Francisco Gomez de Quevedo, writer.

Houbara Bustard — A24

Design: 50c, 1p, 2p, 5p, Doves.

1961, Apr. 18 Photo. *Perf. 13x12½*

No.	Type	Description	Unused	Used
105	A24	25c blue violet	.25	.25
106	A24	50c olive gray	.25	.25
107	A24	75c brown violet	.25	.25
108	A24	1p orange ver	.25	.25
109	A24	1.50p blue green	.25	.25
110	A24	2p magenta	.80	.25
111	A24	3p dark blue	.95	.25
112	A24	5p red brown	1.10	.35
113	A24	10p olive	3.00	1.50
		Nos. 105-113 (9)	7.10	3.60

Map of Spanish Sahara — A25

Gen. Franco and Camel Rider A26

Design: 70c, Chapel of Aaiun.

1961, Oct. 1 ***Perf. 13x12½, 12½x13***

114 A25 25c gray violet .25 .25
115 A26 50c olive brown .25 .25
116 A25 70c brt green .25 .25
117 A26 1p red orange .25 .25
Nos. 114-117 (4) 1.00 1.00

25th anniv. of the nomination of Gen. Francisco Franco as Chief of State.

Neurada Procumbres — A27

50c, 1.50p, 10p, Anabasis articulata, flower. 70c, 2p, Euphorbia resinifera, cactus.

1962, Feb. 26 ***Perf. 13x12½***

118 A27 25c black violet .25 .25
119 A27 50c dark brown .25 .25
120 A27 70c brt green .25 .25
121 A27 1p orange ver .30 .25
122 A27 1.50p blue green .40 .25
123 A27 2p red lilac 1.25 .25
124 A27 3p slate 2.00 .30
125 A27 10p olive 4.75 1.50
Nos. 118-125 (8) 9.45 3.30

Clock Fish — A28

Design: 50c, Avia fish, horiz.

Perf. 13x12½, 12½x13

1962, July 10 **Photo.**

126 A28 25c violet black .25 .25
127 A28 50c dark green .25 .25
128 A28 1p orange brown .30 .25
Nos. 126-128 (3) .80 .75

Goats A29

Stamp Day: 35c, Sheep.

1962, Nov. 23 ***Perf. 12½x13***

129 A29 15c yellow green .25 .25
130 A29 35c magenta .25 .25
131 A29 1p orange brown .25 .25
Nos. 129-131 (3) .75 .75

Seville Cathedral Tower — A30

1963, Jan. 29 ***Perf. 13x12½***

132 A30 50c olive .25 .25
133 A30 1p brown orange .25 .25

Issued to help Seville flood victims.

Camel Riders — A31

Design: 50c, Tuareg and camel.

1963, June 1 **Unwmk.**

134 A31 25c deep violet .25 .25
135 A31 50c gray .25 .25
136 A31 1p orange red .25 .25
Nos. 134-136 (3) .75 .75

Issued for child welfare.

Hands Releasing Dove and Arms — A32

1963, July 12

137 A32 50c Prussian green .25 .25
138 A32 1p orange brown .25 .25

Issued for Barcelona flood relief.

John Dory A33

Fish: 50c, Plain bonito, vert.

Perf. 12½x13, 13x12½

1964, Mar. 6 **Photo.**

139 A33 25c purple .25 .25
140 A33 50c olive green .25 .25
141 A33 1p brown red .45 .25
Nos. 139-141 (3) .95 .75

Issued for Stamp Day 1963.

Moth and Flowers A34

Design: 50c, Two moths, vert.

Perf. 12½x13, 13x12½

1964, June 1 **Unwmk.**

142 A34 25c dull violet .25 .25
143 A34 50c brown black .25 .25
144 A34 1p orange red .45 .25
Nos. 142-144 (3) .95 .75

Issued for child welfare.

Camel Rider and Microphone — A35

Designs: 50c, 1.50p, 3p, Boy with flute and camels. 70c, 2p, 10p, Woman with drum.

1964, Sept. **Photo.** ***Perf. 13x12½***

145 A35 25c dull purple .25 .25
146 A35 50c olive .25 .25
147 A35 70c green .25 .25
148 A35 1p dull red brn .30 .25
149 A35 1.50p bright green .30 .25
150 A35 2p Prus green .35 .30
151 A35 3p dark blue .40 .30
152 A35 10p carmine lake 1.50 .70
Nos. 145-152 (8) 3.60 2.55

Squirrel — A36

Stamp Day: 1p, Squirrel's head, horiz.

1964, Nov. 23 **Unwmk.**

153 A36 50c olive gray .25 .25
154 A36 1p brown carmine .25 .25
155 A36 1.50p green .25 .25
Nos. 153-155 (3) .75 .75

Tuareg Girl — A37

Wellhead and Camel Rider — A38

25 Years of Peace: 1p, Physician examining patient, horiz.

Perf. 13x12½, 12½x13

1965, Feb. 22 **Photo.**

156 A37 50c black brown .25 .25
157 A38 1p dark red .25 .25
158 A38 1.50p deep blue .25 .25
Nos. 156-158 (3) .75 .75

Anthia Sexmaculata — A39

1p, 3p, Blepharopsis mendica, vert.

Perf. 12½x13, 13x12½

1965, June 1 **Photo.** **Unwmk.**

159 A39 50c slate blue .25 .25
160 A39 1p blue green .30 .25
161 A39 1.50p brown .35 .30
162 A39 3p dark blue 1.40 .60
Nos. 159-162 (4) 2.30 1.40

Issued for child welfare.

Basketball A40

Arms and Camels A41

1965, Nov. 23 ***Perf. 13x12½***

163 A40 50c rose claret .25 .25
164 A41 1p deep magenta .25 .25
165 A40 1.50p slate blue .25 .25
Nos. 163-165 (3) .75 .75

Issued for Stamp Day.

Ship "Rio de Oro" A42

Design: 1.50p, S.S. Fuerte Ventura.

1966, June 1 **Photo.** ***Perf. 12½x13***

166 A42 50c olive .25 .25
167 A42 1p dark red brown .25 .25
168 A42 1.50p blue green .30 .25
Nos. 166-168 (3) .80 .75

Issued for child welfare.

Ocean Sunfish — A43

Designs: 10c, 1.50p, Bigeye tuna, horiz.

1966, Nov. 23 **Photo.** ***Perf. 13***

169 A43 10c bl gray & cit .25 .25
170 A43 40c slate & pink .25 .25
171 A43 1.50p brown & olive .30 .25
172 A43 4p rose vio & gray .45 .25
Nos. 169-172 (4) 1.25 1.00

Issued for Stamp Day.

A44

Designs: 40c, 4p, Flower and leaves.

1967, June 1 **Photo.** ***Perf. 13***

173 A44 10c blk, ocher & gray grn .25 .25
174 A44 40c emerald & lilac .25 .25
175 A44 1.50p dk grn & yel grn .25 .25
176 A44 4p brt blue & org .30 .25
Nos. 173-176 (4) 1.05 1.00

Issued for child welfare.

Aaiun Harbor A45

Design: 4p, Villa Cisneros Harbor.

1967, Sept. 28 **Photo.** ***Perf. 12½x13***

177 A45 1.50p brt bl & red brn .25 .25
178 A45 4p brt bl & bis brn .25 .25

Modernization of harbor installations.

Ruddy Sheldrake
A46

Stamp Day: 1.50p, Flamingo, vert. 3.50p, Rufous bush robin.

1967, Nov. 23 Photo. *Perf. 13*

179 A46 1p bister brn & grn .25 .25
180 A46 1.50p brt rose & gray .30 .25
181 A46 3.50p brn red & sep .45 .25
Nos. 179-181 (3) 1.00 .75

Zodiac Issue

Scorpio — A47

1.50p, Aries. 2.50p, Virgo.

1968, Apr. 25 Photo. *Perf. 13*

182 A47 1p brt mag, *lt yel* .25 .25
183 A47 1.50p brown, *pink* .25 .25
184 A47 2.50p dk vio, *yel* .40 .25
Nos. 182-184 (3) .90 .75

Issued for child welfare.

Mailman — A48

Stamp Day: 1p, Post horn, pigeon, letter and Spain No. 1. 1.50p, Letter, canceller and various stamps of Spain and Ifni.

1968, Nov. Photo. *Perf. 13x12½*

185 A48 1p dp lil rose & dk bl .25 .25
186 A48 1.50p green & sl grn .30 .25
187 A48 2.50p dp org & dk bl .45 .25
Nos. 185-187 (3) 1.00 .75

Dorcas Gazelle — A49

Designs: 1.50p, Doe and fawn. 2.50p, Gazelle and camel. 6p, Leaping gazelle.

1969, June 1 Photo. *Perf. 13*

188 A49 1p gldn brn & blk .25 .25
189 A49 1.50p gldn brn & blk .30 .25
190 A49 2.50p gldn brn & blk .35 .30
191 A49 6p gldn brn & blk .55 .35
Nos. 188-191 (4) 1.45 1.15

Child welfare. See Nos. 196-199, 209-212.

Woman Playing Drum — A50

Stamp Day: 1.50p, Man with flute. 2p, Drum and camel rider, horiz. 25p, Flute, horiz.

1969, Nov. 23 Photo. *Perf. 13*

192 A50 50c brn red & lt ol .25 .25
193 A50 1.50p dk bl grn & grnsh gray .25 .25
194 A50 2p indigo & bis brn .30 .25
195 A50 25p brn & lt bl grn 1.00 .30
Nos. 192-195 (4) 1.80 1.05

Animal Type of 1969

Fennec: 50c, Sitting. 2p, Running. 2.50p, Head. 6p, Vixen and pups.

1970, June 1 Photo. *Perf. 13*

196 A49 50c dp bister & blk .25 .25
197 A49 2p org brn & blk .25 .25
198 A49 2.50p dp bister & blk .30 .25
199 A49 6p dp bister & blk .50 .25
Nos. 196-199 (4) 1.30 1.00

Issued for child welfare.

Grammodes Boisdeffrei — A51

Designs: 1p, like 50c. 2p, 5p, Danaus chrysippus. 8p, Celerio euphorbiae.

1970, Nov. 23 Photo. *Perf. 12½*

200 A51 50c red & multi .25 .25
201 A51 1p carmine & multi .30 .25
202 A51 2p green & multi .35 .25
203 A51 5p Prus bl & multi .45 .30
204 A51 8p dk blue & multi .75 .40
Nos. 200-204 (5) 2.10 1.45

Issued for Stamp Day. See Nos. 233-234.

Gazelle, Arms of Aaiun — A52

Smara Mosque — A53

Designs: 2p, Inn, horiz. 5p, Assembly building, Aaiun, horiz.

Perf. 12½x13, 13x12½

1971, June 1 Photo.

205 A52 1p multicolored .25 .25
206 A53 2p gray grn & ol .25 .25
207 A53 5p lt bl & lt red brn .30 .25
208 A53 25p lt bl & grnsh gray .90 .35
Nos. 205-208 (4) 1.70 1.10

Issued for child welfare.

Animal Type of 1969

Birds: 1.50p, 2p, Trumpeter bullfinch. 5p, Cream-colored courser. 24p, Lanner (falcon).

1971, Nov. 23 Photo. *Perf. 12½*

209 A49 1.50p black & multi .25 .25
210 A49 2p blue & multi .25 .25
211 A49 5p green & multi .30 .25
212 A49 24p black & multi .85 .35
Nos. 209-212 (4) 1.65 1.10

Stamp Day.

Saharan Woman — A55

1.50p, 2p, Saharan man. 8p, 10p, Man's head. 12p, Woman. 15p, Soldier. 24p, Dancer.

1972, Feb. 18 Photo. *Perf. 13*

213 A55 1p blue, pink & brn .25 .25
214 A55 1.50p brn, lil & blk .25 .25
215 A55 2p green, buff & sep .25 .25
216 A55 5p grn, pur & vio brn .25 .25
217 A55 8p black, lt grn & vio .30 .25
218 A55 10p blk, gray & Prus bl .35 .30
219 A55 12p multicolored .40 .35
220 A55 15p multicolored .50 .45
221 A55 24p multicolored 1.00 .60
Nos. 213-221 (9) 3.55 2.95

Tuareg Woman — A56

1972, June 1 Photo. *Perf. 13*

222 A56 8p shown .30 .25
223 A56 12p Tuareg man .40 .25

Child welfare.

Mother and Child — A57

1972, Nov. 23 Photo. *Perf. 13*

224 A57 4p shown .25 .25
225 A57 15p Saharan man .45 .25

Stamp Day. See No. 229.

Dunes A58

Design: 7p, Old Market and Gate, Aaiun.

1973, June 1 Photo. *Perf. 13*

226 A58 2p multicolored .25 .25
227 A58 7p multicolored .30 .25

Child welfare.

Type of 1972 and

View of Villa Cisneros A59

1973, Nov. 23 Photo. *Perf. 13*

228 A59 2p shown .25 .25
229 A57 7p Tuareg man .30 .25

Stamp Day.

UPU Monument, Bern — A60

1974, May Photo. *Perf. 13*

230 A60 15p multicolored .55 .25

Centenary of the Universal Postal Union.

Gate, Smara Mosque — A61

2p, Court and Minaret, Villa Cisneros Mosque.

1974, May

231 A61 1p multicolored .25 .25
232 A61 2p multicolored .25 .25

Child welfare.

Animal Type of 1970

1974, Nov. Photo. *Perf. 13*

233 A51 2p Desert eagle owl .25 .25
234 A51 5p Lappet-faced vulture .25 .25

Stamp Day.

Espana 75 Emblem, Spain No. 1084 — A63

1975, Apr. 4 Photo. *Perf. 13*

235 A63 8p olive, blk & bl .25 .25

Espana 75 Intl. Phil. Exhib., Madrid, 4/4-13.

Children A64

1975 Photo. *Perf. 13*

236 A64 1.50p shown .25 .25
237 A64 3p Children's village .25 .25

Child welfare.

Old Man — A65

1975, Nov. 7 Photo. *Perf. 13*

238 A65 3p blk, lt grn & mar .25 .25

SEMI-POSTAL STAMPS

Red Cross Issue

Types of Semi-Postal Stamps of Spain, 1926, Overprinted

1926 Unwmk. *Perf. 12½, 13*

B1	SP3	5c black brown	6.75	6.75
B2	SP4	10c dark green	6.75	6.75
B3	SP1	15c dark violet	2.10	2.10
B4	SP4	20c violet brown	2.10	2.10
B5	SP5	25c deep carmine	2.10	2.10
B6	SP1	30c olive green	2.10	2.10
B7	SP3	40c ultra	.25	.25
B8	SP2	50c red brown	.25	.25
B9	SP5	60c myrtle green	.25	.25
B10	SP4	1p vermilion	.25	.25
B11	SP3	4p bister	2.10	2.10
B12	SP5	10p light violet	6.00	6.00
		Nos. B1-B12 (12)	31.00	31.00
		Set, never hinged	50.00	

See Spain No. B6a for No. B4 without overprint. For surcharges see Spain Nos. B72-B73.

Catalogue values for unused stamps in this section, from this point to the end of the section, are for Never Hinged items.

Shepherd and Lamb — SP1

1950, Oct. 20 Photo. *Perf. 13x12½*

B13	SP1	50c + 10c brown	.35	.25
B14	SP1	1p + 25c rose brn	13.00	7.25
B15	SP1	6.50p + 1.65p dk gray grn	6.75	2.25
		Nos. B13-B15 (3)	20.10	9.75

The surtax was for child welfare.

Dromedary and Calf — SP2

1951, Nov. 23

B16	SP2	5c + 5c brown	.25	.25
B17	SP2	10c + 5 red org	.25	.25
B18	SP2	60c + 15c olive brn	.50	.30
		Nos. B16-B18 (3)	1.00	.80

Colonial Stamp Day, Nov. 23.

Child and Protector — SP3

1952, June 1

B19	SP3	5c + 5c brown	.30	.25
B20	SP3	50c + 10c gray	.35	.35
B21	SP3	2p + 30c blue	1.75	1.25
		Nos. B19-B21 (3)	2.40	1.85

The surtax was for child welfare.

Ostrich — SP4

1952, Nov. 23 *Perf. 12½*

B22	SP4	5c + 5c brn	.25	.25
B23	SP4	10c + 5c brn car	.35	.25
B24	SP4	60c + 15c dk grn	.45	.30
		Nos. B22-B24 (3)	1.05	.80

Colonial Stamp Day, Nov. 23.

Musician Type of Regular Issue

1953, June 1 *Perf. 13x12½*

B25	A7	5c + 5c like #68	.25	.25
B26	A7	10c + 5c like #69	.25	.25

The surtax was for child welfare.

Fish Type of Regular Issue

1953, Nov. 23 *Perf. 12½x13*

B27	A8	5c + 5c like #70	.25	.25
B28	A8	10c + 5c like #71	.25	.25

Athlete Types of Regular Issue

1954, June 1 *Perf. 12½x13, 13x12½*

B29	A9	5c + 5c brn org	.25	.25
B30	A10	10c + 5c purple	.25	.25

The surtax was to help the native population.

Fish Type of Regular Issue

1954, Nov. 23 *Perf. 12½x13*

B31	A11	5c + 5c like #74	.25	.25
B32	A11	10c + 5c like #75	.25	.25

Type of Regular Issue and

Emilio Bonelli SP5

1955, June 1 Photo. Unwmk.

B33	A12	10c + 5c red vio	.25	.25
B34	SP5	25c + 10c violet	.25	.25

The surtax was for child welfare.

Antelope Type of Regular Issue

15c+5c, Head of scimitar-horned oryx.

1955, Nov. 23 *Perf. 12½x13*

B35	A13	5c + 5c org brn	.25	.25
B36	A13	15c + 5c olive bister	.25	.25

Flower Type of Regular Issue

1956, June 1 *Perf. 13x12½*

B37	A14	5c + 5c like #78	.25	.25
B38	A14	15c + 5c like #79	.25	.25

The tax was for the children.

Aaiun Type of Regular Issue and

Arms of Villa Cisneros and Man — SP6

Perf. 12½x13, 13x12½

1956, Nov. 23 Unwmk.

B39	A15	5c + 5c pur & blk	.25	.25
B40	SP6	15c + 5c bis & grn	.25	.25

Eagle Type of Regular Issue

15c+5c, Lesser spotted eagle in flight.

1957, June 1 *Perf. 13x12½*

B41	A17	5c + 5c red brown	.25	.25
B42	A17	15c + 5c golden brn	.25	.25

The surtax was for child welfare.

Hyena Type of Regular Issue

Perf. 13x12½, 12½x13

1957, Nov. 23

B43	A18	10c + 5c like #88	.25	.25
B44	A18	15c + 5c like #89	.25	.25

Stork and Arms of Valencia and Aaiun SP7

1958, Mar. 6 Photo. *Perf. 12½x13*

B45	SP7	10c + 5c org brn	.25	.25
B46	SP7	15c + 10c bister	.25	.25
B47	SP7	50c + 10c brn olive	.25	.25
		Nos. B45-B47 (3)	.75	.75

The surtax was to aid the victims of the Valencia flood, Oct. 1957.

Cervantes Type of Regular Issue

15c+5c, Don Quixote & Sancho Panza.

1958, June 1 *Perf. 13x12½*

B48	A20	10c + 5c hn brn & chnt brn	.25	.25
B49	A20	15c + 5c dp org & slate grn	.25	.25

The surtax was for child welfare.

Hoopoe Lark — SP8

25c+10c, Hoopoe larks, horiz. 50c+10c, Bird.

Perf. 13x12½, 12½x13

1958, Nov. 23 Photo. Unwmk.

B50	SP8	10c + 5c brn red	.25	.25
B51	SP8	25c + 10c brt pur	.25	.25
B52	SP8	50c + 10c olive	.30	.25
		Nos. B50-B52 (3)	.80	.75

Cervantes Type of Regular Issue

10c+5c, Lope de Vega. 15c+5c, Actress from "Star of Seville," by Lope de Vega.

1959, June *Perf. 13x12½*

B53	A20	10c + 5c org brn & ol gray	.25	.25
B54	A20	15c + 5c dp ocher & choc	.25	.25

The surtax was for child welfare.

Mailman — SP9

Stamp Day: 20c+5c, Mailman. 50c+20c, Mailman on camel.

1959, Nov. 23 Photo.

B55	SP9	10c + 5c rose & brn	.25	.25
B56	SP9	20c + 5c lt grn & brn	.25	.25
B57	SP9	50c + 20c ol gray & slate	.25	.25
		Nos. B55-B57 (3)	.75	.75

Quevedo Type of Regular Issue

Designs: 10c+5c, Francisco Gomez de Quevedo. 15c+5c, Winged wheel and hourglass, symbolic of "Hora de Todas."

1960, June 1 *Perf. 12½x13, 13x12½*

B58	A23	10c + 5c maroon	.25	.25
B59	A22	15c + 5c bister brown	.25	.25

The surtax was for child welfare.

Leopard — SP10

Stamp Day: 20c+5c, Desert fox. 30c+10c, Eagle and leopard. 50c+20c, Sand fox.

1960, Nov. 23 Photo. *Perf. 13x12½*

B60	SP10	10c + 5c rose lilac	.25	.25
B61	SP10	20c + 5c dk slate grn	.25	.25
B62	SP10	30c + 10c chocolate	.30	.25
B63	SP10	50c + 20c olive gray	.40	.30
		Nos. B60-B63 (4)	1.20	1.05

Animal Type of 1961 inscribed: "Pro-Infancia 1961"

Designs: Various Mountain Gazelles.

1961, June 21 Unwmk.

B64	SP10	10c + 5c rose brn	.25	.25
B65	SP10	25c + 10c gray vio	.25	.25
B66	SP10	80c + 20c dk grn	.35	.25
		Nos. B64-B66 (3)	.85	.75

The surtax was for child welfare.

Alonso Fernandez de Lugo — SP11

Stamp Day: #B68, B70, Diego de Herrera.

1961, Nov. 23 *Perf. 13x12½*

B67	SP11	10c + 5c org red	.25	.25
B68	SP11	25c + 10c dk pur	.25	.25
B69	SP11	30c + 10c dk red brn	.25	.25
B70	SP11	1p + 10c red org	.35	.25
		Nos. B67-B70 (4)	1.10	1.00

AIR POST STAMPS

In 1942, seven air post stamps of Spain, Nos. C100-C108, were overprinted "SAHARA ESPANOL", but satisfactory information regarding their status is not available.

Catalogue values for unused stamps in this section are for Never Hinged items.

Ostriches — AP1

Desert Scene — AP2

1943 Unwmk. Litho. *Perf. 12½*

C8	AP1	5c cer & vio brn	.25	.25
C9	AP2	25c yel grn & ol grn	.25	.25
C10	AP1	50c ind & turq grn	.25	.25
C11	AP2	1p pur & grnsh bl	.30	.25
C12	AP1	1.40p gray grn & bl	.35	.25
C13	AP2	2p mag & org brn	2.50	1.40
C14	AP1	5p brown & purple	3.25	1.40
C15	AP2	6p brt bl & gray grn	62.50	25.00
		Nos. C8-C15 (8)	69.65	29.05

Nos. C8-C15 exist imperf. Value of set $125.

Diego Garcia de Herrera AP3

1950, Nov. 23 **Photo.**
C16 AP3 5p rose violet 2.75 1.10

Stamp Day.

Woman Holding Dove — AP4

1951, Apr. 22 **Engr.** ***Perf. 10***
C17 AP4 5p deep green 27.50 8.25

500th birth anniv. of Queen Isabella I.
No. C17 is valued in the grade of fine.

Helmet and Trappings — AP5

1952, July 18 **Photo.** ***Perf. 13x12½***
C18 AP5 5p brown 27.50 6.50

500th birth anniv. of Ferdinand the Catholic, of Spain.

Plane and Camel Rider — AP6

1961, May 16 **Unwmk.**
C19 AP6 25p gray brown 3.00 1.00

SPECIAL DELIVERY STAMPS

Catalogue value for unused stamps in this section are for Never Hinged items.

Type A2 Inscribed "URGENTE"

1943 **Unwmk.** ***Perf. 12½***
E1 A2 25c Camel troops 1.75 .95

Messenger on Motorcycle — SD1

Unwmk.

1971, Sept. 6 **Photo.** ***Perf. 13***
E2 SD1 10p bright rose & olive .85 .40

SPANISH WEST AFRICA

'spa-nish 'west 'a-fri-kə

LOCATION — Northwest Africa bordering on the Atlantic Ocean
GOVT. — Spanish administration
AREA — 117,000 sq. mi.
POP. — 95,000 (1950)
CAPITAL — Sidi Ifni

Spanish West Africa was the major political division of Spanish areas in northwest Africa. It included Spanish Sahara (Rio de Oro and Saguiet el Hamra) Ifni and, for administrative purposes, Southern Morocco. Separate stamp issues have been used for Rio de Oro, Ifni and La Aguera.

Catalogue values for all unused stamps in this country are for Never Hinged items.

Native — A1

Perf. 13x12½

1949, Oct. **Litho.** **Unwmk.**
1 A1 4p dark gray green 3.00 1.10

UPU, 75th anniversary.

Nomad Camp A2

5c, 30c, 75c, 2p, Tinzgarrentz Oasis. 10c, 40c, 90c, 5p, Desert well. 15c, 45c, 1p, Caravan.

1950, June 5 ***Perf. 12½x13***

No.	Type	Value	Color	Unused	Used
2	A2	2c	brown	.40	.25
3	A2	5c	rose violet	.40	.25
4	A2	10c	Prussian blue	.40	.25
5	A2	15c	dp ol gray	.40	.25
6	A2	25c	red brown	.40	.25
7	A2	30c	bright yellow	.40	.25
8	A2	40c	olive gray	.40	.25
9	A2	45c	rose lake	.40	.25
10	A2	50c	brown orange	.40	.25
11	A2	75c	ultramarine	.40	.25
12	A2	90c	dull blue grn	.50	.25
13	A2	1p	gray	.50	.25
14	A2	1.35p	violet	1.25	1.00
15	A2	2p	sepia	2.50	1.25
16	A2	5p	lilac rose	25.00	10.00
17	A2	10p	light brown	50.00	25.00
			Nos. 2-17 (16)	83.75	40.25

AIR POST STAMPS

Isabella the Catholic, Queen of Castile — AP1

Perf. 13x12½

1949, Nov. 23 **Photo.** **Unwmk.**
C1 AP1 5p yellow brown 2.25 1.00

Stamp Day, Nov. 23, 1949.

Desert Camp AP2

Designs: Various Desert Scenes.

1951, Mar. 1 **Litho.** ***Perf. 12½x13***

No.	Type	Value	Color	Unused	Used
C2	AP2	25c	ocher	.45	.25
C3	AP2	50c	lilac rose	.45	.25
C4	AP2	1p	green	.45	.25
C5	AP2	2p	bright blue	1.25	.30
C6	AP2	3.25p	rose lilac	2.25	1.00
C7	AP2	5p	gray brown	20.00	5.00
C8	AP2	10p	rose red	42.50	22.50
			Nos. C2-C8 (7)	67.35	29.55

SPECIAL DELIVERY STAMP

Tilimenzo Pass and Franco SD1

Perf. 12½x13

1951, Mar. 1 **Litho.** **Unwmk.**
E1 SD1 25c rose carmine .45 .30

SRI LANKA

ˌsrē 'läŋ-kə

LOCATION — Indian Ocean south of India
GOVT. — Democratic Socialist Republic
AREA — 26,244 sq. mi.
POP. — 19,144,875 (1999 est.)
CAPITAL — Colombo

Sri Lanka was named Ceylon until May 22, 1972. Issues inscribed "Ceylon" are listed under that name in Volume 2.

100 Cents = 1 Rupee

Catalogue values for all unused stamps in this country are for Never Hinged items.

Watermark

Wmk. 385 — CARTOR

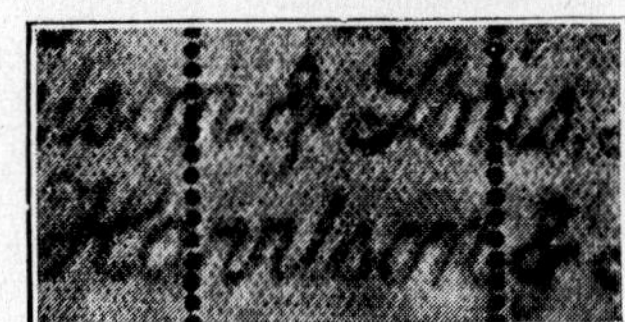
Wmk. 233 — "Harrison & Sons, London" in Script

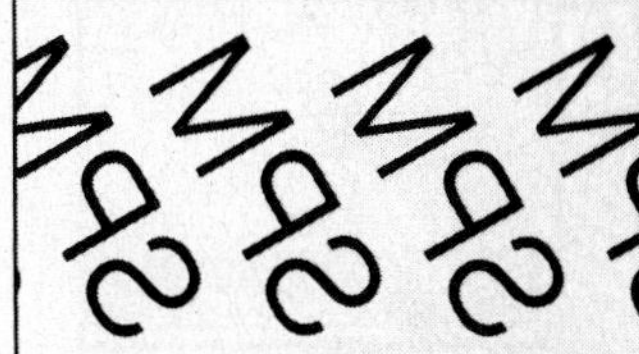
Wmk. 388 — Multiple "SPM"

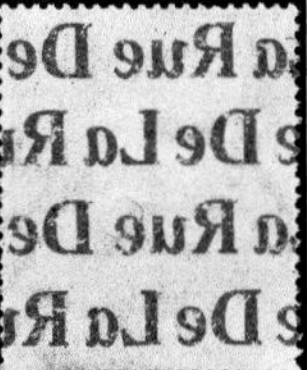
Wmk. 408

Lotus and Sunrise over Adam's Peak — A162

1972, May 22 **Litho.** ***Perf. 13½x13***
470 A162 15c blue & multi .75 .60

Inauguration of Ceylon as Republic of Sri Lanka.

A162a

Overprinted "1972" in Red

1972, May 26 ***Perf. 14x13½***
471 A162a 5c orange brn & multi .45 .60

World Fellowship of Buddhists, Sri Lanka, May 22-28.
Supposedly not issued without overprint, copies sell for 25-cents.

Book Year Emblem, Oil Lamp — A163

1972, Sept. 8 **Photo.** ***Perf. 13***
472 A163 20c yellow & dk brn .40 .50

International Book Year 1972.

Imperial Angelfish A164

Tropical Fish: 3c, Green chromide. 30c, Skipjack bonito. 2r, Black ruby barbs.

Perf. 14x13½

1972, Oct. 12 **Litho.** **Unwmk.**

No.	Type	Value	Color	Unused	Used
473	A164	2c	ultra & multi	.25	*1.00*
474	A164	3c	dp org & multi	.25	*1.00*
475	A164	30c	brt grn & multi	2.25	.45
476	A164	2r	dp green & multi	5.00	4.50
			Nos. 473-476 (4)	7.75	6.95

3rd Session of Indian Ocean Fisheries Commission, Colombo, Oct. 9-14.

Bandaranaike Memorial Hall — A165

1973, May 17 Litho. *Perf. 14*

477 A165 15c lt ultra & vio blue .45 .45

Opening of Bandaranaike Memorial International Conference Hall.

Women Holding Lotus A166

Rock and Temple Paintings: 35c, King giving away his children, Degaldoruwa Temple, near Kandy, 18th cent. 50c, Prince and gravedigger, Polonaruwa, 12th cent. 90c, Holy man holding lotus, Polonaruwa, 12th cent. Design of 1.55r is from Sigiriya, 5th cent.

1973, Sept. 3 *Perf. 13½x14*

478 A166 35c lt gray & multi .45 .25
479 A166 50c gray & multi .60 .25
480 A166 90c slate & multi .85 .85
481 A166 1.55r brown & multi 1.00 *1.75*
a. Souvenir sheet of 4, #478-481 4.50 4.50
Nos. 478-481 (4) 2.90 3.10

For surcharges see Nos. 538-540.

Bandaranaike Conference Hall — A167

1974, Sept. 6 Litho. *Perf. 14*

482 A167 85c multicolored .50 .50

20th Commonwealth Parliamentary Conference, Sri Lanka, Sept. 1-15.

S.W.R.D. Bandaranaike A168

1974, Sept. 25 Photo. *Perf. 14½*

486 A168 15c ultra & multi .45 .45

For surcharge see No. 541.

"UPU," "100" and UPU Emblem A170

1974, Oct. 9 Litho. *Perf. 13*

490 A170 50c multicolored 1.75 1.25

Parliament, Colombo A171

1975, Apr. 1 Litho. *Perf. 13½*

491 A171 1r multicolored .40 .40

Interparliamentary Union, Spring Meeting at Bandaranaike Memorial International Conference Hall, Sri Lanka, Mar. 31-Apr. 5.

Ponnambalam Ramanathan A172

1975, Sept. 4 Litho. *Perf. 13½*

492 A172 75c multicolored .45 *.70*

Sir Ponnambalam Ramanathan (1851-1930), lawyer and educator.

D. J. Wimalasurendra A173

1975, Sept. 17

493 A173 75c ultra & blue blk .45 *.70*

Devapura Jayasena Wimalasurendra (1874-1953), engineer and irrigation specialist.

Map, Mrs. Bandaranaike, Dove — A174

1975, Dec. 22 Litho. *Perf. 13½*

494 A174 1.15r blue & multi 3.75 1.90

International Women's Year 1975.

For surcharge, see No. 1579.

Rhododendron Zeylanicum A175

Flowers: 50c, Exacum trinerve. 75c, Daffodil orchid. 10r, Wormia triquetra.

1976, Jan. 1 Litho. *Perf. 13*

495 A175 25c blue & multi .25 .25
496 A175 50c ocher & multi .25 .25
497 A175 75c black & multi .25 .25
498 A175 10r black & multi 4.00 4.50
a. Souvenir sheet of 4, #495-498 17.50 17.50
Nos. 495-498 (4) 4.75 5.25

Mahaveli-ganga Sluice — A176

1976, Jan. 8 Litho. *Perf. 13x12½*

499 A176 85c multicolored .45 1.00

Mahaveli-ganga River diversion.

Radar Station — A177

1976, May 6 Litho. *Perf. 14*

500 A177 1r blue & multi .90 1.25

Opening of Satellite Earth Station, Padukka.

Prince Siddhartha as White Elephant and Sleeping Queen — A178

Birth of Buddha: 10c, King consulting astrologers. 1.50r, King entertaining astrologers at banquet. 2r, Queen taken in procession to her parents. 2.25r, Flag bearers, musicians in procession. 5r, Queen giving birth to Prince Siddhartha, the Buddha. Designs taken from 18th cent. wall paintings in Dambawa Vihara Temple.

1976, May 7 Litho. *Perf. 13½*

501 A178 5c blue & multi .25 *.75*
502 A178 10c blue & multi .25 *.75*
503 A178 1.50r blue & multi .85 *1.00*
504 A178 2r blue & multi .85 *1.00*
505 A178 2.25r blue & multi 1.75 *2.00*
506 A178 5r blue & multi 3.50 *4.80*
a. Souvenir sheet of 6, #501-506 13.50 13.50
Nos. 501-506 (6) 7.45 *10.30*

Blue Sapphire A179

Gems of Sri Lanka: 1.15r, Cat's-eye. 2r, Star sapphire. 5r, Ruby.

1976, June 16 *Perf. 12x12½*

507 A179 60c multicolored 6.50 .40
508 A179 1.15r multicolored 10.00 2.25
509 A179 2r multicolored 11.00 4.50
510 A179 5r multicolored 15.00 14.00
a. Souv. sheet of 4, #507-510 62.50 40.00
Nos. 507-510 (4) 42.50 21.15

Prime Minister Sirimavo Bandaranaike A180

1976, Aug. 3 Photo. *Perf. 14¼x14½*

511 A180 1.15r pink & multi .40 .40
512 A180 2r pink & multi .70 .70

5th Summit Conference of Non-aligned Countries, Colombo, Aug. 9-19.

For surcharges, see Nos. 1347-1348.

Statue of Liberty — A181

1976, Nov. 29 Litho. *Perf. 14*

513 A181 2.25r lt blue & indigo .85 1.25

American Bicentennial.

A. G. Bell, Telephone and Telephone Line — A182

1976, Dec. 21 Litho. *Perf. 13x13½*

514 A182 1r orange & multi .80 .35

Centenary of first telephone call by Alexander Graham Bell, Mar. 10, 1876.

Maitreya Bodhisattva — A183

Bronze Statues: 1r, Sundara Murti Swami, 11th century. 5r, Goddess Tara.

1977, Jan. 1 Litho. *Perf. 12½x13*

515 A183 50c multicolored .45 .45
516 A183 1r multicolored .45 .45
517 A183 5r multicolored 4.00 4.50
Nos. 515-517 (3) 4.90 5.40

Colombo Museum, centenary.

Kandyan Crown, 1737-1815 A184

2r, Kandyan throne and footstool, 1693-1815.

1977, Jan. 18

518 A184 1r multicolored .55 .55
519 A184 2r multicolored 1.75 *2.50*

Rahula Thero — A185

No. 521, Ponnambalam Arunachalam.

1977 Litho. *Perf. 13½*

520 A185 1r multicolored 1.00 1.00
521 A185 1r multicolored .65 .65

Sri Rahula Thero, 15th cent. poet and scholar, and Sir Ponnambalam Arunachalam (1851-1930), 1st president of Ceylon University Assoc., member of Congress.

Issue dates: No. 520, Feb. 23; No. 521, Mar. 10.

Brass Lamps — A186

Handicrafts: 25c, Jewelry box and jewelry. 50c, Caparisoned ivory elephant. 5r, Sinhala wooden mask.

1977, Apr. 7 *Perf. 13*

522 A186 20c multicolored .25 .25
523 A186 25c multicolored .25 .25
524 A186 50c multicolored .45 .45
525 A186 5r multicolored 2.50 2.75
a. Souvenir sheet of 4, #522-525 5.75 5.75
Nos. 522-525 (4) 3.45 3.70

Mohammed Cassim Siddi Lebbe — A187

1977, June 11 **Litho.** *Perf. 13*

526 A187 1r multicolored .50 .80

Lebbe (1838-98), lawyer, educator and Moslem journalist.

Girl Guide A188

1977, Dec. 13 **Litho.** *Perf. 15*

527 A188 75c multicolored 1.15 .50

60th anniversary of Sri Lanka Girl Guides.

Parliament and Wheel of Life — A189

1978, Feb. 4 **Photo.** *Perf. 12x12½*

528 A189 15c green & gold .40 .25

J.R. Jayewardene, first elected president, assumption of office. Examples of No. 528 with "1978-09-07" inscription reading down at upper right were made available only on first day covers.

See Nos. 559, 611-611A, 847. For surcharges see Nos. 542, 572, 698A-698B.

Runners — A190

1978, Apr. 27 **Litho.** *Perf. 15*

529 A190 15c multicolored .40 .60

National Youth Service Council.

For surcharge see No. 543.

Bodhisattva in Royal Attire in Lotus Position A191

Vesak Festival: 50c, Bodhisattva without royal attire cutting off his hair with sword. Both designs from rock carvings in Borobudur Temple, Java.

1978, May 16 *Perf. 13*

530 A191 15c multicolored 1.10 1.10
531 A191 50c multicolored 1.50 1.50

Veera Puran Appu and his Flag — A192

1978, Aug. 8 **Litho.** *Perf. 13*

532 A192 15c multicolored .40 .30

Veera Puran Appu (1848-1908), revolutionist, 130th birth anniversary.

Birdwing Butterfly — A193

Butterflies: 50c, Tamil lacewing. 5r, Blue oakleaf. 10r, Blue mormon.

1978, Nov. 28 **Litho.** *Perf. 14x13½*

534 A193 25c multicolored .85 .25
535 A193 50c multicolored 1.40 .25
536 A193 5r multicolored 2.60 1.75
537 A193 10r multicolored 2.60 2.75
a. Souvenir sheet of 4, #534-537 17.00 14.00
Nos. 534-537 (4) 7.45 5.00

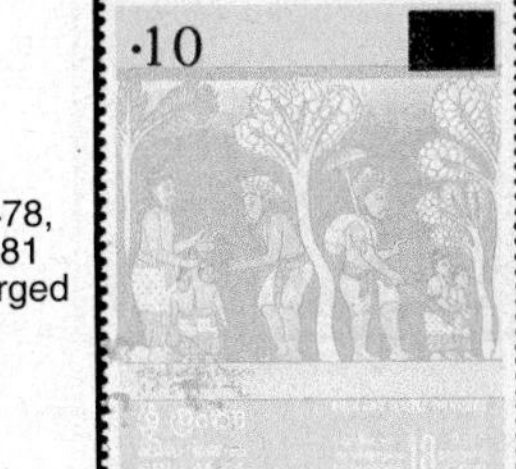

Nos. 478, 480-481 Surcharged

1978 **Litho.** *Perf. 13½x14*

538 A166 5c on 90c multi 11.50 11.50
539 A166 10c on 35c multi 4.00 4.00
540 A166 1r on 1.55r multi 8.00 8.00
Nos. 538-540 (3) 23.50 23.50

Nos. 486, 528 Surcharged

No. 529 Surcharged In Black on Pink Panel

Perf. 14½, 12x12½, 15

1979, Jan. **Litho.; Engr.**

541 A168 25c on 15c multi 7.00 7.00
542 A189 25c on 15c multi 7.00 7.00
543 A190 25c on 15c multi 7.00 7.00
Nos. 541-543 (3) 21.00 21.00

Ceylon No. 390 Overprinted Vertically "SRI LANKA" in Green and Surcharged in Black

1979, Mar. 22 **Photo.** *Perf. 11½*

Granite Paper

544 A118 15c on 10c brt green 4.50 3.00

Arrival of Sacred Tooth — A194

Wall Paintings from Kelaniya Temple: 25c, Prince Danta and Princess Hema Mala bringing Sacred Tooth from Kalinga, 4th century A.D. 1r, Princess Theri Sanghamitta bringing, by ship, the bodhi tree branch, 3rd century B.C. 10r, King Kirti offering fan of authority to supreme patriarch, 18th century.

1979, May 3 **Litho.** *Perf. 13½*

546 A194 25c multicolored .25 .25
547 A194 1r multicolored .25 .25
548 A194 10r multicolored 1.75 1.75
a. Souvenir sheet of 3, #546-548 4.25 4.25
Nos. 546-548 (3) 2.25 2.25

2523rd Vesak Festival, May 11.

Wrestlers — A195

Design: 50r, Dancer. Woodcarvings from Embekke Temple.

1979, May 18 **Litho.** *Perf. 14*

549 A195 20r multicolored 1.50 1.25
550 A195 50r multicolored 3.75 3.50

Piyadasa Sirisena — A196

1979, May 22 *Perf. 13x13½*

551 A196 1.25r deep green .60 .60

Piyadasa Sirisena (1875-1946), patriot, journalist, novelist and poet.

Dudley S. Senanayake — A197

1979, June 19 **Photo.**

552 A197 1.25r deep green .40 .40

27th death anniversary of Prime Minister Dudley S. Senanayake.

Mother Feeding Child, IYC Emblem A198

Designs: 3r, Faces and IYC emblem. 5r, Children with rope and ball, IYC emblem.

1979, July 31 **Litho.** *Perf. 12½*

553 A198 5c multicolored .25 .25
554 A198 3r multicolored .35 .90
555 A198 5r multicolored .40 1.10
Nos. 553-555 (3) 1.00 2.25

International Year of the Child.

Ceylon No. 2, Rowland Hill — A199

1979, Aug. 27 **Litho.** *Perf. 13½*

556 A199 3r multicolored .60 1.00

Sir Rowland Hill (1795-1879), originator of penny postage.

Airlanka Emblem — A200

1979, Sept. 1 **Litho.** *Perf. 12½*

557 A200 3r red, dk grn & blk 1.25 1.60

Airlanka National Airline, inaugural flight, Colombo-Bangkok.

Coconut Palm — A201

1979, Oct. 9 **Litho.** *Perf. 13½*

558 A201 2r multicolored 1.50 1.50

Asian and Pacific Coconut Community, 10th anniversary.

No. 528 Redrawn Without Date

1979, Oct. 9 **Photo.** *Perf. 13*

Size: 20x24mm

559 A189 25c green & gold .65 .25

Family in Cogwheel, Parliament A202

1979, Oct. **Litho.** *Perf. 13½*

560 A202 2r multicolored 1.25 1.50

Intl. Conf. of Parliamentarians on Population & Development, Colombo, Aug. 28-Sept. 1.

Swami Vipulananda (1892-1947), Philosopher & Theologian — A203

1979, Nov. 18 *Perf. 12½*

561 A203 1.25r multicolored .40 .50

Text and Crescent A204

1979, Nov. 22

562 A204 3.75r multicolored .60 1.50

Hegira (pilgrimage year).

Institute Emblem — A205

1979, Nov. 29 *Perf. 13*

563 A205 15c multicolored .40 .60

Ayurveda Medical Institute, 50th anniversary.

Blue Magpie — A206

15c, Lorikeet. 75c, Arrenga. 1r, Spurfowl. 5r, Yellow-fronted barbet. 10r, Yellow-eared bulbul.

1979, Dec. 13 **Litho.** *Perf. 14*

564 A206 10c shown .25 .25
565 A206 15c multicolored .25 .25
566 A206 75c multicolored .25 .25
567 A206 1r multicolored .25 .25
568 A206 5r multicolored 1.50 1.50
569 A206 10r multicolored 1.90 1.90
a. Souvenir sheet of 6, #564-569 11.00 11.00
Nos. 564-569 (6) 4.40 4.40

For surcharges, see Nos. 1062B, 1512.

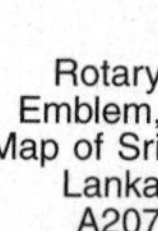

Rotary Emblem, Map of Sri Lanka A207

1979, Dec. 27 **Litho.** *Perf. 14½*

570 A207 1.50r multicolored 1.10 1.50

Rotary International, 75th anniversary.

A. Ratnayake, Educator and Pres. of Senate — A208

1980, Jan. 7 **Photo.** *Perf. 14x13½*

571 A208 1.25r slate green .40 .40

No. 559 Surcharged

1980, Mar. 17 **Photo.** *Perf. 13*

572 A189 35c on 25c multi .50 .40

One position has ".33" instead of ".35."

Leaf, Wheel, Fan (Buddhist Symbols) A209

1980, Mar. 25 **Photo.** *Perf. 13½x14*

573 A209 10c Steeple .45 1.25
574 A209 35c shown .45 .40

All Ceylon Buddhist Cong., 60th anniv.

Col. Henry Olcott, Buddhist Emblem — A210

1980, May 17 **Litho.** *Perf. 14*

575 A210 2r multicolored 1.25 1.50

Col. Henry S. Olcott (1832-1907), American theosophist and Buddhist lecturer, centenary of arrival in Sri Lanka.

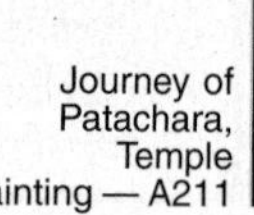

Journey of Patachara, Temple Painting — A211

Vesak Festival (Paintings, life of Buddha): 1.60r, Patachara crossing river.

1980, May 23 *Perf. 13½x14*

576 A211 35c multicolored .40 .40
577 A211 1.60r multicolored 1.90 2.10

George E. De Silva — A212

1980, June 8 *Perf. 13x13½*

578 A212 1.60r multicolored .50 .50

George E. de Silva (1879-1950), politician.

Siva Temples, Polonnaruwa — A213

No. 580, Cave Temples, Dambulla. No. 581, Sacred Tooth Temple, Kandy. No. 582, Abhayagiri Hill. No. 583, Jetavanarama Hill. No. 584, Sigiri.

1980, Aug. 25 **Litho.** *Perf. 13½*

579 A213 35c shown .25 *.40*
580 A213 35c multicolored .25 *.40*
581 A213 35c multicolored .25 *.40*
582 A213 1.60r multicolored .75 *1.25*
583 A213 1.60r multicolored .75 *1.25*
584 A213 1.60r multicolored .75 *1.25*
a. Souvenir sheet of 6, #579-584 4.00 4.00
Nos. 579-584 (6) 3.00 *4.95*

UNESCO "Cultural Triangle" Project.

Department of Cooperative Development, 50th Anniversary A214

1980, Oct. 1 **Litho.** *Perf. 13½*

585 A214 20c multicolored .40 .50

Women's Movement Emblem A215

1980, Oct. 16 **Photo.** *Perf. 14x13½*

586 A215 35c multicolored .40 .50

Mahila Samiti (Rural Women's Movement), 50th anniversary.

Nativity — A216

1980, Nov. 20 **Litho.** *Perf. 13½*

587 A216 35c shown .30 .30
588 A216 3.75r Three kings .80 .90
a. Souvenir sheet of 2, #587-588 2.00 2.00

Christmas 1980/Year of the family.

Colombo Public Library Opening A217

1980, Dec. 17 *Perf. 12x12½*

589 A217 35c multicolored .40 .40

Peacock Banner A218

Ancient flags: 25c, Elephant banner. 1.60r, Sinhalese royal flag. 20r, Kings Civil Standard.

1980, Dec. 18 *Perf. 13*

590 A218 10c shown .25 .25
591 A218 25c multi .25 .25
592 A218 1.60r multi .25 .25
593 A218 20r multi 1.50 2.10
a. Souvenir sheet of 4, #590-593 2.50 2.50
Nos. 590-593 (4) 2.25 2.85

Examples of No. 593a overprinted in the margin for the 2010 National Stamp Fair, Colombo sold for 600r.

For surcharge on No. 592, see No. 1550.

Fishing Cat — A219

No. 595, Golden palm cat. No. 596, Mouse deer. No. 597, Rusty-spotted cat.

1981, Feb. 10 **Litho.** *Perf. 14*

594 A219 2.50r on 1.60r shown .55 .25
595 A219 3r on 1.50r multi .55 .25
596 A219 4r on 2r multi .55 .45
597 A219 5r on 3.75r multi .85 .60
a. Souvenir sheet of 4, #594-597 3.00 3.00
Nos. 594-597 (4) 2.50 1.55

See Nos. 728-730A, 928. For surcharge see No. 731.

Population and Housing Census — A220

1981, Mar. 2 **Litho.** *Perf. 12½x12*

598 A220 50c multicolored .90 1.25

Ceylon Light Infantry Centenary A221

1981, Apr. 1 **Litho.** *Perf. 12*

599 A221 2r multicolored 1.40 1.40

The Death of Buddha, Carved Panel, 1st Cent. — A222

1981, May 5 *Perf. 13x13½*

600 A222 35c shown .25 .25
601 A222 50c Silk banner .25 .25
602 A222 7r Statuette 2.00 3.25
a. Souvenir sheet of 3, #600-602 5.50 5.50
Nos. 600-602 (3) 2.50 3.75

Vesak Festival.

St. John Baptist de la Salle A223

1981, May 15 **Litho.** *Perf. 12½x12*

603 A223 2r multicolored 2.25 2.25

De la Salle Brothers Order, 300th anniv.

Polwatte Sri Buddadatta A224

Famous Men: No. 605, Mohottiwatte Gunananda, Buddhist leader. No. 606, Gnanapra Kasar, Catholic missionary. No. 607, Al-Haj T.B. Jayah, Muslim teacher. No. 608, James Peiris. No. 609, N.M. Perera, founded first Marxist Party in Sri Lanka, 1935.

1981 Photo. ***Perf. 12***

604 A224 50c olive bister .75 1.00
605 A224 50c dull red brown .75 1.00
606 A224 50c lilac .75 1.00
607 A224 50c gray green .75 1.00
608 A224 50c brown .75 1.00
609 A224 50c crimson rose .75 1.00
Nos. 604-609 (6) 4.50 6.00

Issued: #604-606, 5/22; #607, 5/31; #609, 6/6; #608, 12/20.

See #623-624, 640-642, 646, 672-676, 713-717.

Intl. Year of the Disabled — A225

1981, June 19 Litho. ***Perf. 12x12½***

610 A225 2r multicolored 1.40 1.75

No. 528 Redrawn with Denomination in Upper Right Corner

1981-83 Photo. ***Perf. 13***

Size: 20x24mm

611 A189 50c green & gold 3.00 .25
611A A189 60c green & gold 11.00 1.75

Issued: 50c, June 6; 60c, Dec. 30, 1983.
For surcharges see Nos. 698A-698B.

Hand Putting Ballot in Box A226

7r, Ballot box on map, vert.

Perf. 12½x12, 12x12½

1981, July 7 Litho.

612 A226 50c shown .30 .30
613 A226 7r multicolored 2.40 3.00

Universal Franchise, 50th anniv.

Rhys Davids (Society Founder) A227

1981, July 14 ***Perf. 12½x12***

614 A227 35c multicolored 1.25 .65

All Ceylon Buddhist Students' Federation, 25th Anniv. A228

1981, July 21 Litho. ***Perf. 13½***

615 A228 2r multicolored 1.50 1.50

Family Planning — A229

1981, Sept. 25

616 A229 50c multicolored 1.50 1.50

7th World Acupuncture Cong. — A230

1981, Oct. 20 Litho. ***Perf. 12x12½***

617 A230 2r multicolored 4.00 4.00

Visit of Queen Elizabeth II, Oct. A231

Designs: Flags of Gt. Britain and Sri Lanka.

1981, Oct. 21 ***Perf. 14***

618 A231 50c multicolored .65 .65
619 A231 5r multicolored 2.00 2.00
a. Souvenir sheet of 2, #618-619 3.25 4.00

Forest Conservation A232

1981, Nov. 27 ***Perf. 13½x13***

620 A232 35c Forest .25 .25
621 A232 50c Tree planting .30 .30
622 A232 5r Jack tree 2.25 2.75
a. Souvenir sheet of 3, #620-622, perf. 14x13 2.50 3.75
Nos. 620-622 (3) 2.80 3.30

Famous Men Type of 1981

Designs: No. 623, F.R. Senanayaka (1882-1926), lawyer and politician. No. 624, Philip Gunawardhane, politician, 10th death anniv.

1982 Litho. ***Perf. 14***

623 A224 50c brown 1.00 1.00
624 A224 50c bright rose 1.00 1.00

Issue dates: No. 623, Jan. 1; No. 624, Jan. 11.

Dept. of Inland Revenue, 50th Anniv. — A233

1982, Feb. 9 Litho. ***Perf. 14***

625 A233 50c multicolored .90 .90

Natl. Television Inauguration A234

1982, Feb. 15

626 A234 2.50r multicolored 3.50 3.50

Sesquicentennial of Cricket Introduction and Centenary of Sri Lanka vs. England Match — A235

1982, Feb. 17

627 A235 2.50r multicolored 8.50 8.50

Osbeckia Wightiana A236

2r, Mesua nagassarium. 7r, Rhodomyrtus tomentosa. 20r, Phaius tancarvilleae.

1982, Apr. 1 ***Perf. 12***

628 A236 35c shown .25 .25
629 A236 2r multicolored .35 .25
630 A236 7r multicolored .80 .85
631 A236 20r multicolored 2.25 2.25
a. Souvenir sheet of 4, #628-631 10.00 10.00
Nos. 628-631 (4) 3.65 3.60

Examples of No. 631a overprinted in the margin for the 2010 National Stamp Fair, Colombo sold for 750r.

Food and Nutrition Planning A237

1982, Apr. 6 Litho. ***Perf. 13***

632 A237 50c multicolored 2.25 2.25

World Hindu Conference A238

1982, Apr. 21 ***Perf. 14x14½***

633 A238 50c multicolored 1.50 1.50

Vesak Festival 1982 A239

Scenes from Jataka Story (Pre-incarnation of Buddha), Cloth Painting, 3rd cent. B.C., Hanguranketa Temple (King Vessantara and): 35c, Giving away white elephant. 50c, Royal Family in Vankagiri Forest. 2.50r, Giving away his children to a Brahmin. 5r, Royal family in chariot.

1982, Apr. 23 ***Perf. 14***

634 A239 35c multicolored .70 .25
635 A239 50c multicolored .85 .25
636 A239 2.50r multicolored 3.00 2.75
637 A239 5r multicolored 4.00 4.00
a. Souvenir sheet of 4, #634-637 12.00 12.00
Nos. 634-637 (4) 8.55 7.25

New Parliament Building Opening A240

1982, Apr. 29

638 A240 50c multicolored 1.25 1.25

Scouting Year A241

1982, May 24 Litho. ***Perf. 12½x12***

639 A241 50c multicolored 2.25 2.25

Famous Men Type of 1981

No. 640, C.W.W. Kannangara. No. 641, G.P. Malalasekara. No. 642, John Kotelawala.

1982 ***Perf. 12x12½***

640 A224 50c multicolored 1.50 1.50
641 A224 50c multicolored 1.50 1.50
642 A224 50c multicolored 1.50 1.50
Nos. 640-642 (3) 4.50 4.50

Issued: No. 640, 5/22; No. 641, 5/26; No. 642, 6/8.

World Buddhist Leaders Conference — A242

1982, June 10 ***Perf. 12½x12***

643 A242 50c multicolored 1.50 1.50

World Environment Day — A243

1982, June 5

644 A243 50c multicolored 2.50 2.10

YMCA Centenary — A244

1982, June 24 Photo. ***Perf. 11½***

645 A244 2.50r multicolored 4.50 4.50

Famous Men Type of 1981

50c, Sir Waitialingam Duraiswamy.

1982, June 14 Litho. ***Perf. 12x12½***

646 A224 50c tan, brn blk 1.50 1.50

Weliwita Saranankara Sangharaja A245

1982, July 5
647 A245 50c orange & black 1.50 1.50

25th Anniv. of Sasana Sevaka Samithiya A246

1982, Aug. 8
648 A246 50c multicolored 2.25 2.25

TB Bacillus Centenary A247

50c, Koch, microscope, bacillus.

1982, Sept. 21
649 A247 50c multicolored 2.75 2.50

Eye Donation Society — A248

1982, Nov. 16 Litho. ***Perf. 12x12½***
650 A248 2.50r Emblems, map 4.50 *4.75*

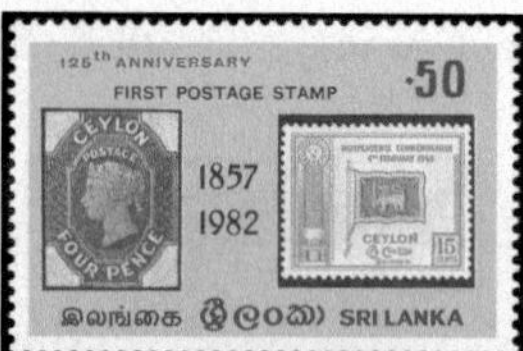

125th Anniv. of Ceylon Postage Stamps — A249

1982, Dec. 1 Litho. ***Perf. 13½***
651 A249 50c Ceylon #5, 302 .60 .60
652 A249 2.50r Ceylon #12, #611 2.25 2.25
a. Souv. sheet, #651-652, perf. 12 3.50 3.50

Natl. Stamp Exhibition.
Examples of No. 652a overprinted in the margin for the 2010 National Stamp Fair, Colombo sold for 350r.

Sir Oliver Goonetilleke A250

1982, Dec. 17 Litho. ***Perf. 12x12½***
653 A250 50c black & brown .80 1.10

25th Anniv. of Sarvodaya Social Movement A251

1983, Jan. 1 ***Perf. 13½***
654 A251 50c multicolored 1.40 1.40

55th Anniv. of Amateur Radio Society A252

1983, Jan. 17
655 A252 2.50r multicolored 4.25 4.25

Customs Cooperation Council and First Intl. Customs Day — A253

1983, Jan. 26 Litho. ***Perf. 12***
656 A253 50c orange & multi .70 .70
657 A253 5r green & multi 5.00 *6.00*

Bottlenose Dolphin A254

2r, Dugongs. 2.50r, Humpback whale. 10r, Great sperm whale.

1983, Feb. 22 ***Perf. 14½x14***
658 A254 50c shown 1.00 .25
659 A254 2r multi 1.50 1.00
660 A254 2.50r multi 4.50 2.25
661 A254 10r multi 9.00 8.00
Nos. 658-661 (4) 16.00 11.50

Ceylon Shipping Corp. A255

50c, Container ship. 2.50r, Liner services map. 5r, Conventional ship. 20r, Oil tanker.

1983, Mar. 1 ***Perf. 12x12½***
662 A255 50c multi .35 .25
663 A255 2.50r multi 1.35 .90
664 A255 5r multi 2.00 2.10
665 A255 20r multi 3.25 *5.50*
Nos. 662-665 (4) 6.95 8.75

Intl. Women's Day — A256

1983, Mar. 8 ***Perf. 13½***
666 A256 50c Woman, flag .40 .25
667 A256 5r Woman, map 1.50 *2.25*

Commonwealth Day — A257

1983, Mar. 14
668 A257 50c Waterfall .25 .25
669 A257 2.50r Tea picking .25 .25
670 A257 5r Harvesting .35 .50
671 A257 20r Cultural pageant 1.40 1.75
Nos. 668-671 (4) 2.25 2.75

Famous Men Type of 1981

No. 672, Henry W. Amarasuriya. No. 673, Charles A. Lorenz. No. 674, Simon G. Perera. No. 675, Nordeen H.M. Abdul Cader. No. 676, C.W. Tamotherampillai.

1983 Litho. ***Perf. 12***
672 A224 50c multicolored .45 .75

Size: 29x40mm

673 A224 50c multicolored .45 .75
674 A224 50c multicolored .45 .75
675 A224 50c multicolored .45 .75
676 A224 50c multicolored 1.25 1.25
Nos. 672-676 (5) 3.05 4.25

No. 676 shows Tamotherampillai looking towards the right of the stamp. A version that was to be issued May 22, showed someone labeled C. W. Tamotherampillai looking straight ahead.
Issued: No. 676, Oct. 1; others, May 22.

25th Anniv. of Lions Club A258

1983, May 7 Litho. ***Perf. 14***
677 A258 2.50r multicolored 4.00 2.75

Vesak Festival 1983 — A259

Various Colombo murals.

1983, May 13 ***Perf. 12½x12***
678 A259 35c multicolored .25 .25
679 A259 50c multicolored .25 .25
680 A259 5r multicolored 1.10 1.10
681 A259 10r multicolored 1.90 1.90
a. Souvenir sheet of 4, #678-681 3.75 *4.25*
Nos. 678-681 (4) 3.50 3.50

125th Anniv. of Telecommunication Service — A260

10r, World Communications Year.

1983, May 17 ***Perf. 12x12½***
682 A260 2r shown 1.00 .80
683 A260 10r multicolored 3.00 *4.25*

Gam Udawa Village Re-awakening Movement — A261

1983, June 23 Litho. ***Perf. 12x12½***
684 A261 50c Family .25 .30
685 A261 5r Village .60 *1.75*

Cattle Transport A262

1983, Aug. 1 Litho. ***Perf. 12***
686 A262 35c shown .30 .30
687 A262 2r Train 3.25 3.25
688 A262 2.50r Cattle cart 1.75 1.75
689 A262 5r Model T Ford 3.50 3.50
Nos. 686-689 (4) 8.80 8.80

Sir Tikiri Banda Panabokke, 20th Death Anniv. — A263

1983, Sept. 2 Litho. ***Perf. 13½x14***
690 A263 50c dark red 1.40 1.40

Ceylon Wood Pigeon A264

35c, Ceylon white-eye. 2r, Dusky-blue flycatcher. 20r, Ceylon coucal.

1983, Dec. 1 Litho. ***Perf. 14½***
691 A264 25c shown 1.10 1.10
692 A264 35c multicolored 1.10 1.10
693 A264 2r multicolored 1.50 1.50
694 A264 20r multicolored 2.40 2.40
a. Souvenir sheet of 4, #691-694 6.75 6.75
Nos. 691-694 (4) 6.10 6.10

Examples of No. 694a overprinted in the margin for the 2010 National Stamp Fair, Colombo sold for 650r.
See No. 877. For surcharge see No. 780A.

Christmas, Stone Carvings — A265

1983, Dec. 5 Litho. ***Perf. 12½x13***
695 A265 50c multicolored .25 .25
696 A265 5r ultra & bister .50 *1.75*
a. Souv. sheet, #695-696+label 1.10 2.25

A266

1983, Nov. 25 Litho. *Perf. 14x15*
697 A266 50c brown 2.10 2.10

Rev. Pelene Thero (1878-1955), Buddhist leader.

Ahamed Orabi Al-Misri — A267

1983 Litho. *Perf. 13½*
698 A267 50c green 1.40 1.40

No. 611 Surcharged in Black

No. 611A Surcharged in Green

1983-85 Photo. *Perf. 13*
698A A189 60c on 50c ('83) *17.00* 4.00

Size: 20x24mm

698B A189 75c on 60c (G) ('85) *1.00* .40

Ovpt. on No. 698A also exists with two bars. Value, *$20.*

Issue dates: both Dec. 1.

World Food Day (Oct. 16) A268

1984, Jan. 2 *Perf. 12½x12*
699 A268 3r Rice paddy .65 *1.75*

Colombo Tea Auctions Centenary A269

1984, Jan. 31
700 A269 1r Auction House .25 .25
701 A269 2r Emblem .50 .50
702 A269 5r Tea picker 1.15 *1.75*
703 A269 10r Auction 2.25 *3.50*
Nos. 700-703 (4) 4.15 6.00

Mahapola Anniversary (Educational System) — A270

60c, Students. 1r, Classroom. 5.50r, Student in library, lab. 6r, Emblem.

1984, Feb. 10 *Perf. 12*
704 A270 60c multi .25 .25
705 A270 1r multi .25 .25
706 A270 5.50r multi .35 *1.50*
707 A270 6r multi .40 *1.50*
Nos. 704-707 (4) 1.25 3.50

Vesak Festival 1984 A271

Wooden Casket Paintings, Temple Godapitiya Rajamaha Vihara, Akuressa: Scenes from Daham Sonda Jathaka legend.

1984, Apr. 27 Litho. *Perf. 14*
708 A271 35c multicolored .25 .25
709 A271 60c multicolored .70 .70
710 A271 5r multicolored 2.50 2.50
711 A271 10r multicolored 3.00 3.00
a. Souv. sheet of 4, #708-711, perf. 13x13½ 4.00 4.00
Nos. 708-711 (4) 6.45 6.45

Lions Club Intl., District 306A — A272

1984, May 5 Litho. *Perf. 14x14½*
712 A272 60c multicolored 2.00 1.50

Famous Men Type of 1981

Designs: No. 713, K. Balasingham, lawyer. No. 714, Mohamed Macan Markar (1879-1952), Muslim politician. No. 715, W. Arthur de Silva (d. 1942), industrialist. No. 716, Tissa Mahanayake Thero (1826-1907), Buddhist educator. No. 717, G.P. Wickremarachchi, medical pioneer.

1984, May 22 Litho. *Perf. 12x12½*
713 A224 60c brown .40 *.80*
714 A224 60c green .40 *.80*
715 A224 60c orange red .40 *.80*
716 A224 60c bister .40 *.80*
717 A224 60c yellow green .40 *.80*
Nos. 713-717 (5) 2.00 *4.00*

Public Service Mutual Provident Assoc. Centenary A273

1984, June 16 *Perf. 13x13½*
718 A273 4.60r Emblem .90 *2.00*

Village Re-awakening Movement A274

60c, "One Million Houses."

1984, June 23 *Perf. 12x12½*
719 A274 60c multicolored .55 *.80*

Asia-Pacific Broadcasting Union, 20th Anniv. — A275

1984, June 30 *Perf. 12½x12*
720 A275 7r Map 2.25 *3.25*

For surcharge see No. 776.

Cultural Pageant A276

Procession: a, Drummers, elephant. b, Torch bearers, 3 elephants (green or red masks). c, Torch bearers, 3 elephants (orange or yellow masks). d, Dancers. Continuous design.

1984, Aug. 11 Litho. *Perf. 12½x12*
721 Strip of 4 7.00 7.00
a.-d. A276 4.60r any single 1.50 1.50
e. Souvenir sheet of 4 *10.00 10.00*

Orchid Circle of Sri Lanka, 50th Anniversary A277

60c, Vanda memoria. 4.60r, Acanthephippium bicolor. 5r, Vanda Tessellata. 10r, Anoectochillus setaceus.

1984, Aug. 31 *Perf. 14*
722 A277 60c multi 1.60 1.60
723 A277 4.60r multi 3.25 3.25
724 A277 5r multi 2.25 2.25
725 A277 10r multi 7.00 7.00
a. Souvenir sheet of 4, #722-725 13.00 13.00
Nos. 722-725 (4) 14.10 14.10

Wildlife Type of 1981

2.50r, Felis viverrina. 3r, Paradoxurus zeylonensis. 4r, Tragulus meminna. 5r, Felis rubiginosa.

1982-89 Litho. *Perf. 14*
728 A219 2.50r multicolored .40 .30
729 A219 3r multicolored 5.50 5.50
730 A219 4r multicolored .40 .40
730A A219 5r multi, ('89) .50 .40
Nos. 728-730A (4) 6.80 6.60

No. 729 has brown inscriptions. See No. 928 for black inscriptions.

No. 728 is unwatermarked.

Issued: 2.50r, 6/1/83; 3r, 6/21/83; 4r, 11/16/82; 5r, 12/1/89.

No. 728 Surcharged in Brown

1985, Dec. 1 Litho. *Perf. 14*
731 A219 5.75r on 2.50r multi 5.25 2.75

The Observer Newspaper, 150th Anniv. A280

4.60r, Publisher, Colombo.

1984, Aug. 31 Litho. *Perf. 13x13½*
732 A280 4.60r multicolored 3.25 *4.00*

Natl. School Games — A281

1984, Oct. 5 *Perf. 13½x13*
733 A281 60c blue, gray & blk 2.50 2.25

D. S. Senanayake (1884-1952), Prime Minister — A282

35c, Irrigated field. 60c, Statue. 4.60r, Reservoir. 6r, Parliament House, Colombo.

1984, Oct. 20 *Perf. 14½x14*
734 A282 35c multicolored .25 .25
735 A282 60c multicolored .25 .25
736 A282 4.60r multicolored .40 *.55*
737 A282 6r multicolored .55 *.75*
Nos. 734-737 (4) 1.45 1.80

World Food Program — A284

7r, Globe, Sri Lankans working field.

1984, Dec. 10 Litho. *Perf. 13x13½*
738 A284 7r multicolored 2.25 1.60

Baari Arabic College, Weligama, Cent. — A285

1984, Dec. 24 *Perf. 13x12½*
739 A285 4.60r dull bl grn & blk 2.10 *2.75*

Intl. Youth Year — A286

1985, Jan. 1 *Perf. 12½x13*
740 A286 4.60r multicolored .75 .60
741 A286 20r multicolored 2.75 *3.50*

For surcharge see No. 790.

World Religion Day — A287

Design: Emblems of World religions.

1985, Jan. 20 *Perf. 12*
742 A287 4.60r multicolored 3.50 3.50

Royal College, Colombo, 150th Anniv. — A288

1985, Jan. 29 ***Perf. 13x12½***

743 A288 60c College crest .25 .30
744 A288 7r Campus 3.00 *3.75*

Mahapola Scholarship Program for Development & Education, 5th Anniv. — A289

60c, Diplomas, freighter, office buildings.

1985, Feb. 7 ***Perf. 14***

745 A289 60c multicolored 1.25 *1.75*

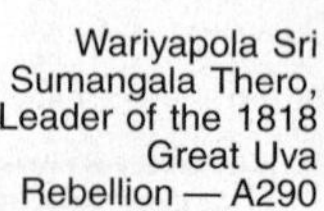

Wariyapola Sri Sumangala Thero, Leader of the 1818 Great Uva Rebellion — A290

1985, Mar. 2 ***Perf. 13x13½***

746 A290 60c brown & yellow 1.00 *1.25*

Victoria Project A291

Perf. 12½x12, 12x12½

1985, Apr. 12 **Litho.**

747 A291 60c Victoria Dam 1.10 1.10
748 A291 7r Dam, map, vert. 7.00 7.00

Vesak Festival 1985 — A292

Designs: 35c, Frontispiece of the Buddhist Annual golden jubilee issue. 60c, Women worshiping at temple, Vesak Poya Holiday cent. 6r, Bauddha Mandiraya, Colombo. 9r, Buddhist flag cent.

1985, Apr. 26 ***Perf. 13x12½***

749 A292 35c multicolored .25 .25
750 A292 60c multicolored .25 .25
751 A292 6r multicolored .85 .85
752 A292 9r multicolored 1.75 1.75
a. Souvenir sheet of 4, #749-752 7.25 7.25
Nos. 749-752 (4) 3.10 3.10

Natl. Heroes — A293

No. 753, Waskaduwe Sri Subhuthi Thero (1835-1917), Pali scholar, philologist responsible for the Sinhala dictionary. No. 754, Rev. Fr. Peter A. Pillai (1904-64), educational & social reformer. No. 755, Dr. Senarath Paranavitane (c. 1900-72), epigraphist. No. 756, A.M. Wapche Marikar (1829-1925), educational reformer, architect.

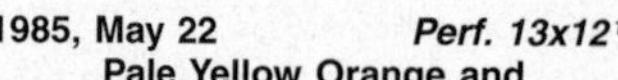

1985, May 22 ***Perf. 13x12½***

Pale Yellow Orange and

753 A293 60c tan .45 .70
754 A293 60c brt rose lilac .45 .70
755 A293 60c brown .45 .70
756 A293 60c emerald .45 .70
Nos. 753-756 (4) 1.80 2.80

Gam Udawa — Yovur Udanaya Village Reformation Movement A294

1985, June 23 ***Perf. 13½x13***

757 A294 60c multicolored 1.50 1.50

Colombo Young Poets Assoc., 50th Anniv. — A295

1985, June 25 ***Perf. 14***

758 A295 60c Emblem 1.60 1.60

Kothmale Project Commission — A296

60c, Dam, lake. 6r, Hydro-electric power station.

1985, Aug. 24

759 A296 60c multicolored .90 .90
760 A296 6r multicolored 4.50 4.50

Child Survival — A297

35c, Mother breastfeeding. 60c, Infant, oral inoculant. 6r, Weighing toddler. 9r, Infant, intravenous inoculant.

1985, Sept. 1 **Wmk. 385** ***Perf. 13½***

761 A297 35c multicolored .40 .25
762 A297 60c multicolored .60 .40
763 A297 6r multicolored 2.25 *2.75*
764 A297 9r multicolored 2.75 *3.50*
a. Souvenir sheet of 4, #761-764 7.00 7.00
Nos. 761-764 (4) 6.00 6.90

Womb, Infant — A298

1985, Sept. 2 **Unwmk.** ***Perf. 14***

765 A298 7r multi 5.50 5.50

10th Asian & Oceanic Congress of Obstetrics & Gynecology.

World Tourism Org., 10th Anniv. A299

1r, Conch shell horn. 6r, Parliament complex. 7r, Tea plantation. 10r, Buddhist monastery, Ruwanveliseya.

1985, Sept. 27 **Litho.** ***Perf. 14***

766 A299 1r multicolored .50 .25
767 A299 6r multicolored 1.35 1.35
768 A299 7r multicolored 2.00 2.00
769 A299 10r multicolored 2.50 2.50
a. Souv. sheet of 4, #766-769, perf. 13½ 8.00 8.00
Nos. 766-769 (4) 6.35 6.10

Land Development Ordinance, 50th Anniv. — A300

4.60r, Deeds presentation.

1985, Oct. 15 ***Perf. 14x15***

770 A300 4.60r multi 3.25 *3.75*

Sinhal Translation, Koran — A301

1985, Oct. 17 **Wmk. 385** ***Perf. 13½***

771 A301 60c violet & gold 3.00 2.50

Christmas — A302

60c, Our Lady of Matara. 9r, Our Lady of Madhu.

1985, Nov. 5 ***Perf. 12***

772 A302 60c multicolored .35 .25
773 A302 9r multicolored 1.75 2.25
a. Souvenir sheet of 2, #772-773 8.75 *10.00*

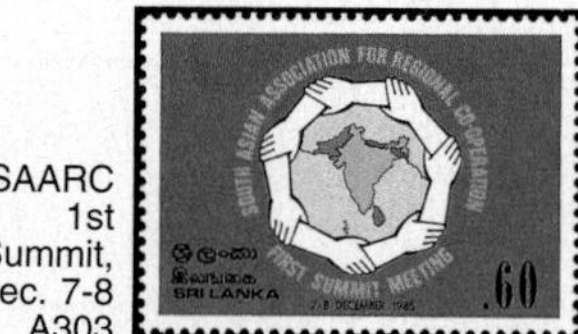

SAARC 1st Summit, Dec. 7-8 A303

5.50r, Flags on UN emblem.

1985, Dec. 8 ***Perf. 14½x14***

774 A303 60c shown 5.00 *7.00*
775 A303 5.50r multi 5.00 *6.00*

No. 720 Surcharged in Intense Blue

1986, Jan. 20 ***Perf. 12½x12***

776 A275 1r on 7r Map 12.00 4.50

Viceroy Special Train A304

1986, Feb. 2 ***Perf. 12½x13***

777 A304 1r multicolored 1.50 1.50

Colombo-Kandy line inauguration.

Students A305

1986, Feb. 14 ***Perf. 14***

778 A305 75c multicolored .80 *1.10*

Mahapola Scholarship Program for development and education, 6th anniv.

Don Richard Wijewardene (1886-1950), Newspaper Publisher — A306

1986, Feb. 23 ***Perf. 14x15***

779 A306 75c sage grn & brn .40 *1.00*

Welitara Gnanatillake Mahanayake Thero (1858-1941), Scientist — A307

1986, Feb. 26 **Wmk. 385** ***Perf. 13½***

780 A307 75c multicolored .90 *1.10*

No. 692 Surcharged

1986, Mar. 10 **Litho.** ***Perf. 14½***

780A A264 7r on 35c 8.00 1.50

Natl. Red Cross Society, 50th Anniv. A308

1986, Mar. 31 ***Perf. 12½x13***

781 A308 75c multicolored 3.00 2.50

Halley's Comet A309

50c, Comet is not an omen. 75c, Constellations. 6.50r, Trajectory diagrams. 8.50r, Edmond Halley.

1986, Apr. 5 ***Perf. 12½***

782 A309 50c multicolored .25 .25
783 A309 75c multicolored .25 .25
784 A309 6.50r multicolored .40 *1.25*
785 A309 8.50r multicolored .55 *2.00*
a. Souvenir sheet of 4, #782-785, perf. 12½x13 8.00 *10.50*
Nos. 782-785 (4) 1.45 *3.75*

Sinhalese and Tamil New Year — A310

Designs: 50c, Woman lighting lamp. 75c, Woman, holiday foods. 6.50r, Women celebrating around table. 8.50r, Food preparation, feast, anointment ritual.

1986, Apr. 10

786 A310 50c multicolored .25 .25
787 A310 75c multicolored .25 .25
788 A310 6.50r multicolored .45 1.75
789 A310 8.50r multicolored .70 2.00
a. Souvenir sheet of 4, #786-789, perf. 13x12½ 4.75 *5.50*
Nos. 786-789 (4) 1.65 4.25

No. 740 Surcharged

1986, Apr. 29 ***Perf. 12½x13***

790 A286 1r on 4.60r multi 9.00 4.50

Vesak Festival A311

Jathaka Story frescoes from the house Samudragiri Vihara, Mirissa, recounting the life of Siddhartha (583-463 B.C.): 50c, King Kurudhamma Jathakaya gives elephant to the brahman. 75c, Vasavarthi heaven. 5r, Sujatha's milk rice offering. 10d, Thapassu and Bhalluka's parched corn and honey offering.

1986, May 16

791 A311 50c multicolored .25 .25
792 A311 75c multicolored .25 .25
793 A311 5d multicolored .50 *2.00*
794 A311 10d multicolored .60 *3.00*
Nos. 791-794 (4) 1.60 5.50

Natl. Heroes — A312

No. 795, Kalukondayave Sri Prajnasekhara Mahanayaka Thero (1895-1977), theologian. No. 796, Brahmachari Walisinghe Harischandra (1876-1913), historian, social reformer. No. 797, Martin Wickramasinghe (1890-1970), author. No. 798, Ganapathipillai Gangaser Ponnambalam (1901-72), diplomat. No. 799, Aboobucker Mohammed Abdul Azeez (1911-73), scholar.

1986, May 22 ***Perf. 13x12½***

795 A312 75c multicolored .25 .70
796 A312 75c multicolored .25 .70
797 A312 75c multicolored .25 .70
798 A312 75c multicolored .25 .70
799 A312 75c multicolored .25 .70
Nos. 795-799 (5) 1.25 3.50

Natl. Cooperative Movement, 75th Anniv. — A313

1986, June 23

800 A313 1r multicolored 1.60 *2.00*

Gam Udawa, Intl. Year of Housing A314

1986, June 23 ***Perf. 13½x13***

801 A314 75c multicolored 1.90 1.90

Arthur V. Dias — A315

1986, July 31 ***Perf. 14x15***

802 A315 1r multicolored 2.25 2.25

World Wildlife Fund A316

Elephants: a, Adult with tusks. b, Adult, calf. c, Adult. d, Family in river.

1986, Aug. 5 ***Perf. 15x14***

803 Strip of 4 *57.50 20.00*
a.-d. A316 5r any single *6.50 4.00*

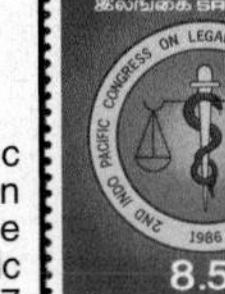

2nd Indo-Pacific Congress on Legal Medicine and Forensic Sciences — A317

1986, Aug. 14 ***Perf. 13½x13***

804 A317 8.50r multicolored 3.75 3.75

Submarine Cable — A318

1986, Sept. 8 ***Perf. 13½x14***

805 A318 5.75r Handset, map 7.25 4.75

South-East Asia, Middle East, Western Europe Submarine Cable System.

Dag Hammarskjold Award — A320

1986, Sept. 20 Litho. ***Perf. 13x12½***

808 A320 2r multicolored 1.75 1.50

Second Natl. School Games, Sept. 22-27 — A321

1986, Sept. 22 ***Perf. 12***

809 A321 1r multicolored 4.75 2.40

Natl. Surveyor's Institute, 60th Anniv. — A322

1986, Sept. 27 ***Perf. 13½x13***

810 A322 75c multicolored .90 *1.25*

Ananda College, Cent. A323

College crest and: 75c, College. 5r, Athletic field. 5.75r, Founders Migettuwatte Gunananda, Hikkaduwe Sumangala and Col. H.S. Olcott, Buddhist flag and College, 1886, 1986. 6r, Crest on flag.

1986, Nov. 1 ***Perf. 12***

811 A323 75c multicolored .25 .25
812 A323 5r multicolored .50 *.80*
813 A323 5.75r multicolored .55 *.80*
814 A323 6r multicolored .65 *1.00*
Nos. 811-814 (4) 1.95 *2.85*

Wildlife Conservation — A324

35c, Mangrove habitat. 50c, Rhizophora apiculata. 75c, Germinating flower. 6r, Fiddler crab.

1986, Nov. 11

815 A324 35c multicolored 1.25 1.25
816 A324 50c multicolored 1.40 1.40
817 A324 75c multicolored 1.50 1.50
818 A324 6r multicolored 9.00 9.00
Nos. 815-818 (4) 13.15 13.15

Preservation of mangrove habitats.

For surcharges on Nos. 815 and 818, see Nos. 1513 and 1516.

Intl. Year of Shelter for the Homeless A325

1987, Jan. 1 Litho. ***Perf. 13x13½***

819 A325 75c multicolored 3.00 .95

A.I. Thero, 19th Cent. Theologian A326

1987, Jan. 29 ***Perf. 12***

820 A326 5.75r multicolored 4.50 1.25

Proctor John De Silva (b. 1854), Lawyer and Playwright A327

1987, Jan. 31

821 A327 5.75r multicolored 1.00 1.00

Mahapola Educational Plan, 7th Anniv. — A328

1987, Feb. 6

822 A328 75c multicolored 1.15 1.15

Dr. R.L. Brohier, Historian — A329

1987, Feb. 14

823 A329 5.75r multicolored 3.75 1.75

Sri Lanka Tire Corp., 25th Anniv. A330

1987, Mar. 23 ***Perf. 14***

824 A330 5.75r multicolored .75 .75

Sri Lanka Medical Assoc., Cent. A331

1987, Mar. 24 ***Perf. 13x13½***

825 A331 5.75r multicolored 3.00 *3.50*

Farmers' Pension and Social Security Plan — A332

1987, Mar. 29 *Perf. 14*
826 A332 75c multicolored 1.60 1.60

AGRO MAHAWELI '87 Agricultural Exposition A333

1987, Apr. 2 *Perf. 12*
827 A333 75c multicolored .55 .55

Child Immunization Program — A334

1987, Apr. 7 *Perf. 13½*
828 A334 1r multicolored 4.00 1.50

World Health Day.

Sinhalese and Tamil New Year — A335

1987, Apr. 9 *Perf. 12*
829 A335 75c Three girls, swing .25 .25
830 A335 5r Lamp, women .70 .70

Vesak Festival Lanterns A336

1987, May 4 *Perf. 12*
831 A336 50c Lotus .25 .25
832 A336 75c Octagonal .25 .25
833 A336 5r Star .40 .40
834 A336 10r Gok .60 .60
a. Souvenir sheet of 4, #831-834 1.60 1.60
Nos. 831-834 (4) 1.50 1.50

Natl. Olympic Committee, 50th Anniv. — A337

1987, May 8 *Perf. 13½*
835 A337 10r multicolored 3.50 1.60

Birds A338

50c, Layard's parakeet. 1r, Legge's flowerpecker. 5r, Sri Lanka white-headed starling. 10r, Sri Lanka rufous babbler.

1987, May 18 *Perf. 14*
836 A338 50c multicolored .70 .25
837 A338 1r multicolored 1.10 .25
a. Dated "1989" 1.10 .25
838 A338 5r multicolored 1.60 1.75
839 A338 10r multicolored 2.10 2.25
a. Souvenir sheet of 4, #836-839 9.75 9.75
b. As #839, dated "1990" 2.25 2.25
Nos. 836-839 (4) 5.50 4.50

Natl. Heroes — A339

#840, Heenatiyana Sri Dhammaloka Thero, 20th cent. theologian. #841, P. de S. Kularatne, educator. #842, M.C. Abdul Rahuman, politician.

1987, May 22 *Perf. 12*
840 A339 75c multicolored .55 .40
841 A339 75c multicolored .55 .40
842 A339 75c multicolored .55 .40
Nos. 840-842 (3) 1.65 1.20

Gam Udawa A340

1987, June 23
843 A340 75c multicolored .45 .45

Village reformation movement.

Natl. Forestry Agency, Cent. A341

75c, Mesua nagassarium. 5r, Elephants in forest.

1987, June 25
844 A341 75c multicolored .30 .30
845 A341 5r multicolored 1.75 1.75

Founder H.S. Olcott and College A342

1987, June 30
846 A342 75c multicolored 3.75 .55

Dharmaraja College, cent.

No. 528 Redrawn with Denomination in Upper Right Corner

1987, July 1 Photo. *Perf. 13x13½*
Size: 20x24mm
847 A189 75c green & gold — —

Youth Services Emblem A343

1987, July 15 Litho. *Perf. 12*
848 A343 75c multicolored .35 .35

Natl. Youth Services Act, 20th anniv.

Mahaweli Games — A344

1987, Sept. 5 Litho. *Perf. 12*
849 A344 75c multicolored 5.00 2.75

Ceylon Bible Society, 175th Anniv. — A345

1987, Oct. 2
850 A345 5.75r multicolored .80 .80

Kandy Friend-in-Need Society, 150th Anniv. — A346

1987, Nov. 4 *Perf. 13½x13*
851 A346 75c multicolored .40 .40

Christmas 1987 — A347

1987, Nov. 25 Litho. *Perf. 12*
852 A347 75c Mother and Child .25 .25
853 A347 10r Infant, star, dove .45 .45
a. Souvenir sheet of 2, #852-853 1.40 1.40

Sir Ernest de Silva (1887-1957), Banker, Philatelist — A348

1987, Nov. 25 *Perf. 13x13½*
854 A348 75c multicolored .35 .35

1st Convocation Ceremony at Buddhist and Pali University — A349

1987, Dec. 14 *Perf. 12*
855 A349 75c yel, lake & org yel .40 .40

Missionary Work of Fr. Joseph Vaz (1651-1711), 300th Anniv. — A350

1987, Dec. 15
856 A350 75c multicolored .35 .35

Buddhist Publication Soc., Kandy, 30th Anniv. — A351

Design: Wheel of Life, dagaba (temple cupola) and Bo (Tree of Life) leaf.

1988, Jan. 1 Litho. *Perf. 12*
857 A351 75c multicolored .45 .45

Mahapola Dharmayatra, 5th Anniv. A352

1988, Jan. 4 *Perf. 13½x13*
858 A352 75c multicolored .55 .55

Ceylon Arts Soc., Cent. — A353

1988, Jan. 8 *Perf. 12*
859 A353 75c multicolored .90 .90

Opening of the Natl. Youth Center, Maharagama A354

1988, Jan. 31 *Perf. 13½x13*
860 A354 1r multicolored 5.50 .80

Natl. Independence, 40th Anniv. — A355

1988, Feb. 4 *Perf. 12*
861 A355 75c shown .25 .25
862 A355 8.50r Heraldic lion, "40" 1.00 1.00

Mahapola Movement, 8th Anniv. — A356

75c, Youth Education Services.

1988, Feb. 11
863 A356 75c multicolored .35 .35

Transportation Board, 30th Anniv. — A357

1988, Feb. 19
864 A357 5.75r multicolored .75 .75

Weligama Sri Sumangala Maha Nayake Thero (1825-1905), Buddhist Monk, Sanskrit Scholar — A358

1988, Mar. 13
865 A358 75c multicolored .35 .35

Artillery Regiment, Cent. A359

1988, Apr. 20
866 A359 5.75r multicolored 4.00 1.25

Chevalier I.X. Pereira (1888-1951), Politician — A360

1988, Apr. 26 **Litho.** *Perf. 12*
867 A360 5.75r multicolored .45 .45

Vesak Festival A361

Paintings in Suriyagoda Sri Narendraramaya Viharaya temple, Kandy District: 50c, Buddha inviting deities and brahmas to be born into the world as Buddhists. 75c, Buddha walking seven steps on seven lotus flowers, followers paying homage.

1988, May 13 *Perf. 12½x12*
868 A361 50c multicolored .40 .40
869 A361 75c multicolored .40 .40
a. Souvenir sheet of 2, #868-869 3.00 3.00

Natl. Heroes — A362

Designs: No. 870, Rev.-Father Ferdinand Bonnel (1873-1945), Jesuit priest who founded St. Michael's College, Batticaloa. No. 871, Sir Razik Fareed (1893-1984), political and social reformer. No. 872, W.F. Gunawardhana (b. 1861), founder of the Oriental Studies Soc. No. 873, Edward Alexander Nugawela (1898-1972), politician. No. 874, Sir Edwin Arthur Lewis Wijeyewardene (b. 1887), first Ceylonese chief justice, attorney general.

1988, May 22 *Perf. 12x12½*
870 A362 75c multicolored .25 .25
871 A362 75c multicolored .25 .25
872 A362 75c multicolored .25 .25
873 A362 75c multicolored .25 .25
874 A362 75c multicolored .25 .25
Nos. 870-874 (5) 1.25 1.25

Gam Udawa, 10th Anniv. A363

1988, June 23 **Litho.** *Perf. 12*
875 A363 75c multicolored .55 .30

Village reformation movement.

Maliyadeva College, Cent. — A364

1988, June 30 *Perf. 13½x13*
876 A364 75c multicolored .55 .30

Bird Type of 1983

1988, Sept. 28 **Litho.** *Perf. 14½*
877 A264 7r like No. 692 1.75 1.75

Mohamed J.M. Lafir (1929-1980), World Amateur Billiards Champion — A365

1988, July 5 **Litho.** *Perf. 12½x12*
878 A365 5.75r multicolored 1.25 .60

Australia Bicentennial — A366

1988, July 19 **Litho.** *Perf. 12*
879 A366 8.50r multicolored .90 .75

A367

1988, Aug. 11 *Perf. 12x12½*
880 A367 75c multicolored .45 .30

Gunaratna Maha Nayake Thero (1752-1832), Buddhist and Sinhalese language scholar.

Mahaweli Games — A368

1988, Sept. 3 *Perf. 12*
881 A368 75c multicolored .45 .30

1988 Summer Olympics, Seoul — A369

75c, Running. 1r, Swimming. 5.75r, Boxing. 8.50r, Handshake, map, emblems.

1988, Sept. 6 *Perf. 12x12½*
882 A369 75c multicolored .25 .25
883 A369 1r multicolored .25 .25
884 A369 5.75r multicolored .50 .50
885 A369 8.50r multicolored .85 .85
a. Souvenir sheet of 4, #882-885 2.00 2.00
Nos. 882-885 (4) 1.85 1.85

WHO, 40th Anniv. — A370

1988, Sept. 12 *Perf. 12*
886 A370 75c multicolored .45 .45

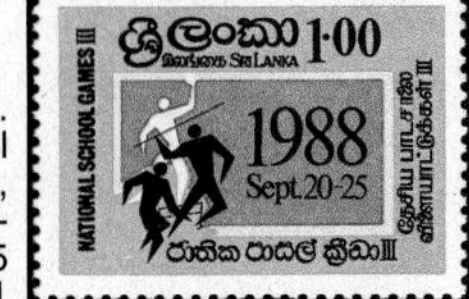

3rd Natl. School Games, Sept. 20-25 A371

1988, Sept. 20
887 A371 1r multicolored 4.00 .60

Mahatma Gandhi — A372

1988, Oct. 2 *Perf. 12*
888 A372 75c multicolored 3.75 1.10

Transportation and Communication Decade, 1978-88 — A373

Modes of transportation and: 75c, Globe. 5.75r, Communication tower.

1988, Oct. 24 **Litho.** *Perf. 12½x12*
889 A373 75c multicolored .75 .25
890 A373 5.75r multicolored 4.00 2.40

For surcharge, see No. 1580.

Randenigala Project — A374

75c, Woman, dam, power station. 5.75r, Hydrelectric dam.

1988, Oct. 31 *Perf. 12*
891 A374 75c multicolored .35 .35
892 A374 5.75r multicolored 1.05 1.05

Some stamps were distributed at the time the set was originally planned to be issued in 1986.

Opening of Gramodaya Folk Art Center — A375

1988, Nov. 17 Litho. *Perf. 13½*
893 A375 75c multicolored .45 .45

Christmas — A376

8.50r, Shepherds see star.

1988, Nov. 25 *Perf. 12x12½*
894 A376 75c shown .25 .25
895 A376 8.50r multicolored 1.00 1.00
a. Souvenir sheet of 2, #894-895 3.00 3.00

E.W. Adikaram (1905-85), Educator — A377

1988, Dec. 28 *Perf. 12*
896 A377 75c multicolored .45 .45

Waterfalls — A378

1989, Aug. 11 Litho. *Perf. 12*
897 A378 75c Dunhinda .30 .30
898 A378 1r Rawana .30 .30
899 A378 5.75r Laxapana 1.25 1.25
900 A378 8.50r Diyaluma 1.90 1.90
Nos. 897-900 (4) 3.75 3.75

Free Distribution of School Text Books, 10th Anniv. A379

1989, Jan. 23 Litho. *Perf. 13½x13*
901 A379 75c multicolored .40 .40

Poets — A380

No. 902, Wimalaratne Kumaragama. No. 903, G.H. Perera. No. 904, Sagara Palansuriya. No. 905, P.B. Alwis Perera.

1989, Jan. 27 *Perf. 13*
902 A380 75c multicolored .25 .25
903 A380 75c multicolored .25 .25
904 A380 75c multicolored .25 .25
905 A380 75c multicolored .25 .25
Nos. 902-905 (4) 1.00 1.00

Mahapola Educational Plan, 8th Anniv. — A381

1989, Feb. *Perf. 13½*
906 A381 75c multicolored .40 .25

Chamber of Commerce, 150th Anniv. — A382

1989, Mar. 25 Litho. *Perf. 12*
907 A382 75c multicolored .40 .25

AGRO Mahaweli A383

1989, Sept. 2 Litho. *Perf. 12*
908 A383 75c multicolored .65 .30

Famous Men A384

No. 909, Simon Casie Chitty. No. 910, Parawahera Sri Vajiragnana Thero. No. 911, Fr. Maurice Le Goc. No. 912, Hemapala Munidasa. No. 913, Ananda Samarakoon.

1989, May 22
909 A384 75c multicolored .35 .35
910 A384 75c multicolored .35 .35
911 A384 75c multicolored .35 .35
912 A384 75c multicolored .35 .35
913 A384 75c multicolored .35 .35
Nos. 909-913 (5) 1.75 1.75

Nos. 910-913 vert.

Hartley College, 150th Anniv. (in 1988) — A385

1989, June 5
914 A385 75c multicolored .40 .25

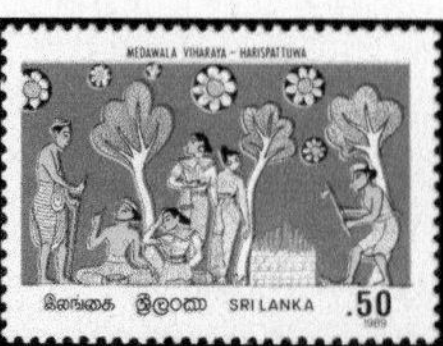
Vesak Festival A386

Various paintings in Medawala Viharaya, Harispattuwa.

1989, May 15 Litho. *Perf. 12½x12*
915 A386 50c multicolored .25 .25
916 A386 75c multicolored .25 .25
917 A386 5r multicolored .45 .40
918 A386 5.75r multicolored .55 .50
a. Souvenir sheet of 4, #915-918 3.00 3.00
Nos. 915-918 (4) 1.50 1.40

For surcharge see No. 953A.

Pres. Premadasa's Declaration Establishing the Ministry of Buddha Sasana — A387

1989, June 18 Litho. *Perf. 12½x12*
919 A387 75c multicolored .40 .40

Gam Udawa, 11th Anniv. A388

1989, June 23
920 A388 75c multicolored .50 .40

Village reformation movement.

French Revolution, Bicent. A389

1989, Aug. 26 Litho. *Perf. 13½x13*
921 A389 8.50r rose & deep blue 1.75 1.75

Bank of Ceylon, 50th Anniv. A390

75c, Old, new headquarters. 5r, Emblem, flowers.

1989, Aug. 31
922 A390 75c multicolored .25 .25
923 A390 5r multicolored .80 .65

Janasaviya Development A391

1989, June 23 Litho. *Perf. 12x11½*
924 A391 75c multicolored .70 .70

Development program to eliminate poverty and improve the standard of living through education and by providing food, health care, shelter and clothing.

See No. 953. For surcharge see No. 955.

Baptist Mission, 177th Anniv. A392

5.75r, James Chater, church, 1812.

1989, Aug. 19 *Perf. 12½x12*
925 A392 5.75r multicolored .90 .90

For surcharge, see No. 1405.

State Literary Festival — A393

1989, Sept. 22 *Perf. 12x11½*
926 A393 75c multicolored .50 .40

Wilhelm Geiger — A394

1989, Sept. 30 *Perf. 13x13½*
927 A394 75c multicolored .50 .40

Wilhelm Geiger (1856-1943), German philologist who studied Sinhalese.

Wildlife Type of 1981

1989, Oct. 11 *Perf. 14*
928 A219 3r like No. 595 4.00 .40

No. 928 has black inscriptions and is dated "1989." See No. 729 for brown inscriptions.

Famous Lawyers — A395

No. 929, H.V. Perera (1890-1969). No. 930, Sir Ivor Jennings (1903-1965).

1989, Oct. 16 *Perf. 12x11½*
929 A395 75c multicolored .25 .25
930 A395 75c multicolored .25 .25

Sir Cyril de Zoysa — A396

1989, Oct. 26 *Perf. 13x13½*
931 A396 75c multicolored .50 .40

Sir Cyril de Zoysa (1896-1978), key figure in the Buddhist cultural reformation.

Asia-Pacific Telecommunity, 10th Anniv. — A397

1989, Nov. 1 ***Perf. 12x12½***

932 A397 5.75r multicolored	.90	.60

For surcharge, see No. 1574.

Sri Sucharitha Viyaparaya Oratory Children's Soc., 50th Anniv. A398

1989, Nov. 9 ***Perf. 13***

933 A398 75c multicolored	.60	.60

1st Moon Landing, 20th Anniv. — A399

75c, Apollo 11 liftoff, crew. 1r, Astronaut descending ladder. 2r, Astronaut on lunar surface. 5.75r, Lunar surface, view of Earth.

1989, Nov. 10 ***Perf. 12x12½***

934 A399 75c multicolored	.25	.25
935 A399 1r multicolored	.25	.25
936 A399 2r multicolored	.45	.40
937 A399 5.75r multicolored	1.00	.70
a. Souvenir sheet of 4, #934-937	4.00	4.00
Nos. 934-937 (4)	1.95	1.60

For No. 937 surcharged, see No. 1515.

Christmas — A400

75c, Adoration of the Shepherds. 8.50r, Adoration of the Magi.

1989, Nov. 21 ***Perf. 13½***

938 A400 75c multicolored	.25	.25
939 A400 8.50r multicolored	.80	.80
a. Souvenir sheet of 2, #938-939	2.00	2.00

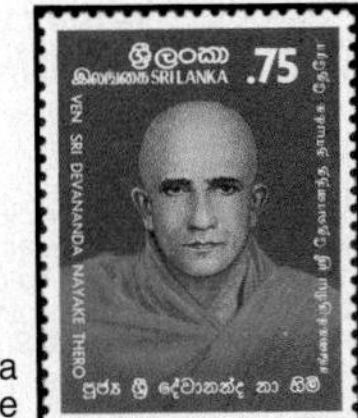

Devananda Nayake Thero — A401

1989, Nov. 25 ***Perf. 12x11½***

940 A401 75c multicolored	.50	.50

Devananda Nayake Thero (1921-1983), religious scholar, educator, reformer.

Rev. William Ault, College and Crest A402

1989, Nov. 29 ***Perf. 11½x12***

941 A402 75c multicolored	.50	.50

Batticaloa Methodist Central College, 175th anniv.

Nuwara Eliya Golf Club, Cent. A403

8.50r, Course, golf house.

1989, Dec. 8 ***Perf. 14x13½***

942 A403 75c shown	4.50	.50
943 A403 8.50r multicolored	12.00	9.50

Raja — A404

1989, Dec. 12 ***Perf. 13x13½***

944 A404 75c multicolored	7.50	1.25

Raja (1913-1988), the royal tusker of the Sri Dalada Maligawa that carried the relic casket in the Kandy Esala Procession.

Gampaha Wickamarachchi Ayurveda Medical College, 60th Anniv. — A405

1989, Dec. 14 ***Perf. 13½x13***

945 A405 75c Founder, institute	.70	.40

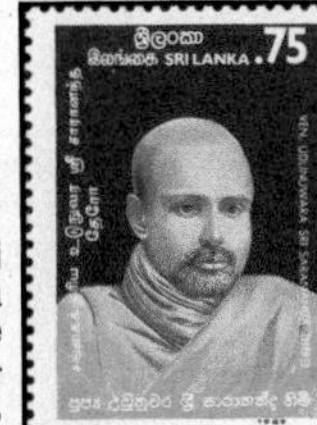

Udunuwara Sri Sarananda Mahanayake Thero (1867-1947), Educator — A406

1989, Dec. 20 ***Perf. 12x12½***

946 A406 75c multicolored	.50	.35

Railway Dept., 125th Anniv. A407

75c, Train, viaduct. 2r, Train, light signal, Maradana Station. 3r, Steam locomotive, semaphore signal. 7r, 1st train in Sri Lanka.

1989, Dec. 27 ***Perf. 11½x12, 13 (3r)***

947 A407 75c multicolored	.90	.30
948 A407 2r multicolored	2.25	.50
949 A407 3r multicolored	2.25	.85
950 A407 7r multicolored	4.25	2.00
Nos. 947-950 (4)	9.65	3.65

A408

1989, Dec. 28 ***Perf. 13x13½***

951 A408 75c multicolored	2.00	.35

Thomas Cooray (1901-88), 1st native Sri Lankan Cardinal.

A409

1990, Jan. 14 ***Perf. 12x12½***

952 A409 1r multicolored	3.00	.35

Justin Wijayawardena (1904-82), educator, politician.

Jana Saviya Grants Type of 1989

1990, Jan. 31 Litho. ***Perf. 12x11½***

953 A391 1r multicolored	1.00	.40

No. 918 Surcharged

1990, Feb. 16 Litho. ***Perf. 12½x12***

953A A386 25c on 5.75r multi	1.40	.30

Induruwe Uttarananda Mahanayake Thero — A411

1990, Mar. 15 Litho. ***Perf. 12***

954 A411 1r multicolored	2.00	1.40

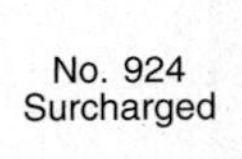

No. 924 Surcharged

1990, Mar. 22 Litho. ***Perf. 12x11½***

955 A391 1r on 75c multi	3.00	1.75

Silver Jubilee of Laksala A413

Traditional handicrafts.

1990, Apr. 2 Litho. ***Perf. 12***

956 A413 1r Drums	.40	.25
957 A413 2r Silverware	.55	.25
958 A413 3r Lacquerware	.90	.30
959 A413 8r Dumbara mats	2.40	2.75
Nos. 956-959 (4)	4.25	3.55

Vesak Festival A414

Various paintings in Wewurukannala Buduraja Maha Viharaya.

1990, May 2 ***Perf. 12½x12***

960 A414 75c multicolored	.25	.25
961 A414 1r multicolored	.25	.25
962 A414 2r multicolored	.30	.30
963 A414 8r multicolored	.90	.90
a. Souvenir sheet of 4, #960-963	2.00	2.00
Nos. 960-963 (4)	1.70	1.70

A415

Famous Men — A416

1990, May 22 ***Perf. 12***

964 A415 1r Rev. T.M.F. Long	.55	.35

Size: 25x39mm

Perf. 12x12½

965 A416 1r D.P.A. Wijewardene	.55	.35
966 A416 1r L.T.P. Manjusri	.55	.35
967 A416 1r M.D. Ratnasuriya	.55	.35
Nos. 964-967 (4)	2.20	1.40

Gam Udawa Program, 12th Anniv. A417

1990, June 23 ***Perf. 12½x12***

968 A417 1r multicolored	2.50	.60

Dept. of Archaeology, Cent. — A418

1r, Gold reliquary from Delivala Temple, c. 200 B.C. 2r, Statuette of Ganesha (the Elephant God) from Polonnaruwa. 3r, Terrace of the Bodhi-tree at Isurumuni Vihara. 8r, Stone seat with inscription of King Nissankamalle, 12th cent. A.D.

1990, July 7 ***Perf. 12***

969 A418 1r black & orange	.40	.25
970 A418 2r black & gray	.70	.25
971 A418 3r black, yel grn & gold	1.00	.40
972 A418 8r black & gold	2.10	1.50
Nos. 969-972 (4)	4.20	2.40

Sri Lanka Tennis Assoc., 75th Anniv. — A419

No. 973, Player ready to volley. No. 974, Player receiving volley. No. 975, Men players. No. 976, Women players.

1990, Aug. 14 *Perf. 13½*

973	1r multicolored	1.00	1.00
974	1r multicolored	1.00	1.00
a.	A419 Pair, #973-974	2.25	2.25
975	8r multicolored	3.50	3.50
976	8r multicolored	3.50	3.50
a.	A419 Pair, #975-976	7.75	7.75
	Nos. 973-976 (4)	9.00	9.00

Fish — A420

25c, Spotted loach. 2r, Ornate paradise fish. 8r, Mountain labeo. 20r, Cherry Barb.

1990, Sept. 14 *Perf. 11½*

977	A420 25c multicolored	.30	.30
978	A420 2r multicolored	.45	.45
979	A420 8r multicolored	1.25	1.25
980	A420 20r multicolored	2.50	2.50
a.	Souvenir sheet of 4, #977-980	5.50	5.50
	Nos. 977-980 (4)	4.50	4.50

For No. 979 surcharged, see No. 1303A.

A421

1r, Letter box, 1904. 2r, Mail runner, 1815. 5r, Mail coach, 1832. 10r, Nuwara-Eliya Post Office, 1894.

1990, Dec. 26 *Perf. 12*

981	A421 1r multicolored	.80	.60
982	A421 2r multicolored	1.50	.85
983	A421 5r multicolored	3.00	2.75
984	A421 10r multicolored	4.00	4.00
	Nos. 981-984 (4)	9.30	8.20

Sri Lanka Postal Service, 175th anniv.

A422

1990, Oct. 28 Litho. *Perf. 12*

985	A422 1r multicolored	5.75	1.75

Rukmani Devi (1923-78), actress.

Christmas A423

1r, Mary, Joseph at inn. 10r, Adoration of the Magi.

1990, Nov. 28 *Perf. 13*

986	A423 1r multicolored	.75	.45
987	A423 10r multicolored	4.75	4.75
a.	Souv. sheet of 2, #986-987, perf. 12	6.50	6.50

World AIDS Day A424

1990, Nov. 30

988	A424 1r multicolored	1.25	.25
989	A424 8r AIDS Virus	5.00	4.00

A425

1990, Dec. 8 *Perf. 12*

990	A425 1r multicolored	3.25	1.60

Dharmapala College, 50th anniv.

A426

1990, Dec. 14 Litho. *Perf. 12*

991	A426 1r olive green & brown	4.00	1.50

Peri Sunderam (b. 1890), political & social reformer.

Ceylon Institute of Chemistry, 50th anniv. — A427

1991, Jan. 25 Litho. *Perf. 12*

992	A427 1r multicolored	4.00	1.50

Vesak Festival A428

Various scenes from Buddha's life.

1991, May 17 Litho. *Perf. 12*

993	A428 75c multicolored	.40	.25
994	A428 1r multicolored	.40	.25
995	A428 2r multicolored	.75	.40
996	A428 11r multicolored	3.50	3.25
a.	Souvenir sheet of 4, #993-996	6.25	6.25
	Nos. 993-996 (4)	5.05	4.15

Mahabodhi Society, Cent. — A429

1991, May 31 *Perf. 12*

997	A429 1r multicolored	2.00	1.10

A430

Famous men — No. 998, Narada Thero. No. 999, Sir Muttu Coomaraswamy. No. 1000, Dr. Andreas Nell. No. 1001, W.A. Silva.

1991, May 22 Litho. *Perf. 12x12½*

998	A430 1r multicolored	.75	.65
999	A430 1r multicolored	.75	.65
1000	A430 1r multicolored	.75	.65
1001	A430 1r multicolored	.75	.65
	Nos. 998-1001 (4)	3.00	2.60

Gam Udawa, 13th Anniv. A431

1991, June 23 Litho. *Perf. 12½*

1002	A431 1r multicolored	3.00	.90

Henpitagedera Gnanaseeha Nayake Thero (1909-1981), Religious Leader — A432

1991, Aug. 1

1003	A432 1r multicolored	2.25	.95

Colombo Plan, 40th Anniv. A433

1991, July 1 Litho. *Perf. 12*

1004	A433 1r multicolored	3.75	1.40

Survey Dept., 190th Anniv. A434

1991, Aug. 2 *Perf. 12½*

1005	A434 1r multicolored	3.25	1.25

Police Service, 125th Anniv. A435

1991, Sept. 3 Litho. *Perf. 12½*

1006	A435 1r multicolored	1.50	.70

6th SAARC Summit A436

8r, Flags encircling building.

1991, Dec. 21 Litho. *Perf. 12½*

1007	A436 1r shown	.25	.25
1008	A436 8r multicolored	.70	*1.25*

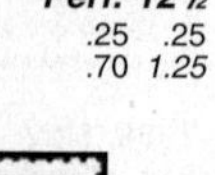

Kingswood College, Cent. — A437

1991, Oct. 26 *Perf. 12½x12*

1009	A437 1r multicolored	1.00	.50

Christmas — A439

1991, Nov. 19 Litho. *Perf. 12½*

1014	A439 1r The Annunciation	.40	.25
1015	A439 10r Nativity scene	1.50	2.00
a.	Sheet of 2, #1014-1015	2.50	2.50

A440

Telecommunications: 1r, Early telephone network. 2r, Switchboard operations. 8r, Satellite transmitters, cable network. 10r, Telephone, fiber optic cable, computer, cordless telephone, FAX machine.

1991, Nov. 23

1016	A440 1r multicolored	.25	.25
1017	A440 2r multicolored	.30	.25
1018	A440 8r multicolored	.90	1.10
1019	A440 10r multicolored	.90	1.10
	Nos. 1016-1019 (4)	2.35	2.70

5th South Asian Federation Games A441

1r, Mascot. 2r, Emblem. 4r, Stadium, Colombo. 11r, Globe and flags.

1991, Dec. 22 *Perf. 14*

1020 A441	1r multicolored	.30	.25
1021 A441	2r multicolored	.60	.25
1022 A441	4r multicolored	1.10	1.25
1023 A441	11r multicolored	2.50	3.50
	Nos. 1020-1023 (4)	4.50	5.25

Year of Exports A442

1992, Jan. 13 Litho. *Perf. 11½x12*

1024 A442 1r multicolored 3.00 1.00

Mahinda College, Cent. A443

1992, Mar. 2 Litho. *Perf. 11½x12*

1025 A443 1r multicolored .40 .40

General Ranjan Wijeratne (1931-1991) A444

1992, Mar. 2 Litho. *Perf. 12x12½*

1026 A444 1r multicolored .60 .25

Tea Production, 125th Anniv. A445

Field of tea and: 1r, Tea picker. 2r, Family, cup and glass of tea. 5r, Package of tea. 10r, James Taylor.

1992, Feb. 12 *Perf. 13½*

1027 A445	1r multicolored	.70	.25
1028 A445	2r multicolored	1.40	.30
1029 A445	5r multicolored	3.25	2.50
1030 A445	10r multicolored	4.75	4.00
	Nos. 1027-1030 (4)	10.10	7.05

Newstead College, 175th Anniv. (in 1991) A446

1992, Mar. 13 Litho. *Perf. 11½x12*

1031 A446 1r multicolored .40 .40

Dated 1991.

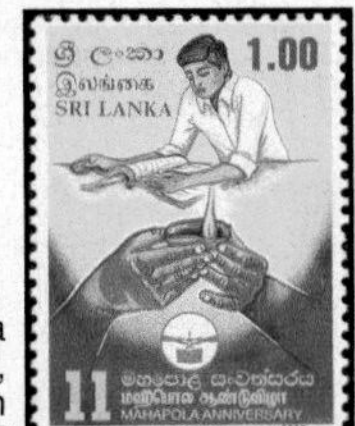

Mahapola Scholarship Fund, 11th Anniv. — A447

1992, Mar. 30 *Perf. 12*

1032 A447 1r multicolored .40 .40

Vesak Festival A448

Mural paintings from Kottimbulwala Rajamaha Vihara: 75c, Dukula and Parika retiring to forest. 1r, Sama and parents living in forest. 8r, Sama directing blind parents to hermitage. 11r, Sama's parents approach wounded son.

1992, May 5 Litho. *Perf. 11½x12*

1033 A448	75c multicolored	.25	.25
1034 A448	1r multicolored	.35	.25
1035 A448	8r multicolored	1.75	1.75
1036 A448	11r multicolored	2.50	2.50
a.	Souvenir sheet, #1033-1036	5.50	5.50
	Nos. 1033-1036 (4)	4.85	4.75

A449

National Heroes: No. 1037, Wadeebhasinha Dewamottawe Amarawansa Thero. No. 1038, R. A. Mirando. No. 1039, Gate Mudaliyar N. Canaganayagam. No. 1040, I.L.M. Abdul Azeez.

1992, May 22 *Perf. 14*

1037 A449	1r multicolored	.25	.25
1038 A449	1r multicolored	.25	.25
1039 A449	1r multicolored	.25	.25
1040 A449	1r multicolored	.25	.25
	Nos. 1037-1040 (4)	1.00	1.00

A450

1992, June 14 Litho. *Perf. 12x12½*

1041 A450 1r multicolored .70 .45

Introduction of Buddhism on Sri Lanka by Anubudu Mihindu Jayanthi, 2300th anniv.

Gam Udawa, 14th Anniv. A451

1992, June 23 *Perf. 12*

1042 A451 1r multicolored .90 .45

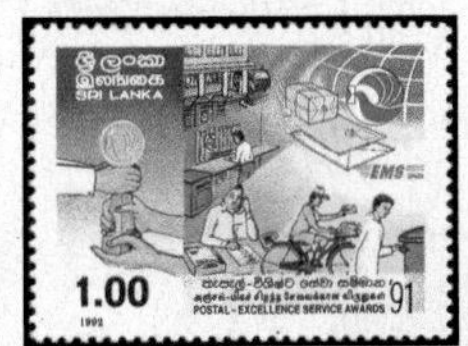

Postal Excellence Service Awards A452

Designs: 1r, Award presentation, postal work. 10r, Award of excellence medals, No. 1043 canceled on envelope.

1992, July 11 Litho. *Perf. 14*

1043 A452	1r multicolored	.75	.75
1044 A452	10r multicolored	4.50	4.50

Masks of Sri Lanka — A453

1992, Aug. 19 Litho. *Perf. 13*

1045 A453	1r Narilata	.40	.25
1046 A453	2r Mudali	.50	.40
1047 A453	5r Queen	1.00	.75
1048 A453	10r King	1.75	1.75
a.	Souvenir sheet, #1045-1048	4.50	4.50
	Nos. 1045-1048 (4)	3.65	3.15

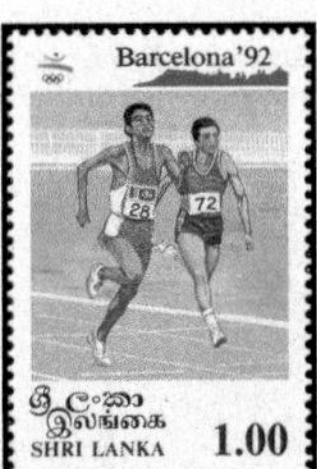

A454

1992, Sept. 15 Litho. *Perf. 14*

1049 A454	1r Running	.35	.25
1050 A454	11r Rifle shooting	2.50	2.50
1051 A454	13r Swimming	3.00	3.00
1052 A454	15r Weight lifting	3.25	3.25
a.	Souvenir sheet, #1049-1052	11.00	11.00
	Nos. 1049-1052 (4)	9.10	9.00

1992 Summer Olympics, Barcelona.

Cricket in Sri Lanka, 160th Anniv. A455

1992, Sept. 8 Litho. *Perf. 13*

1053 A455 5r multicolored 5.50 3.25

Vijaya Kumaratunga, Entertainer and Political Leader, Birth Anniv. — A456

1992, Oct. 9

1054 A456 1r multicolored .80 .50

Al-Bahjathul Ibraheemiyyah Arabic College, Cent. — A457

1992, Oct. 24 *Perf. 12*

1055 A457 1r multicolored .60 .50

A458

1992, Oct. 25 Litho. *Perf. 12x11½*

1056 A458 1r multicolored 2.00 .75

Dutch Reformed Church in Sri Lanka, 350th anniv.

Christmas A459

1992, Nov. 17 Litho. *Perf. 12x11½*

1057 A459	1r Holy Family	.50	.25
1058 A459	9r Church, family	2.50	2.50
a.	Souvenir sheet, #1057-1058	3.50	3.50

Discovery of America, 500th Anniv. A460

Designs: 1r, Ships at sea, Aug. 1492. 11r, First landing in the Americas, Oct. 1492. 13r, Santa Maria aground, Dec. 1492. 15r, Return to Spain, Apr. 1493.

1992, Dec. 1 *Perf. 14*

1059 A460	1r multicolored	1.00	.35
1060 A460	11r multicolored	2.00	2.00
1061 A460	13r multicolored	2.75	2.75
1062 A460	15r multicolored	3.00	3.00
a.	Souvenir sheet, #1059-1062	9.50	9.50
	Nos. 1059-1062 (4)	8.75	8.10

No. 564 Surcharged

1992, Dec. 1 Litho. *Perf. 14*

1062B A206 2r on 10c multi 8.25 1.00

Dambagasare Sri Sumedhankara Maha Nayake Thero (1892-1984), Buddhist Monk — A461

1992, Dec. 10 Litho. *Perf. 12*

1063 A461 1r multicolored .40 .40

University Education in Sri Lanka
A462

1992, Dec. 12 Litho. *Perf. 12*
1064 A462 1r multicolored .40 .40

No. 1064 was not available until Dec. 1993.

University of Colombo, 50th Anniv. (in 1992)
A463

1993, Mar. 23 Litho. *Perf. 13*
1065 A463 1r multicolored 1.10 .35

Zahira College, Cent.
A464

1993, Apr. 7
1066 A464 1r multicolored 1.25 .40

Vesak Festival — A465

Designs based on verses from the Dhammapada (sermons of Buddha): 75c, Magandiya being presented to Buddha. 1r, Kisa Gotami carrying dead child. 3r, Patachara, dead family members. 10r, Conversion of Angulimala, the murderer.

1993, Apr. 30 *Perf. 12x12½*
1067 A465 75c multicolored .25 .25
1068 A465 1r multicolored .30 .30
1069 A465 3r multicolored .65 .65
1070 A465 10r multicolored 1.25 1.25
a. Souvenir sheet, #1067-1070 3.25 3.25
Nos. 1067-1070 (4) 2.45 2.45

A466

1r, Guide, tent, emblem. 5r, Activities, map.

1993, May 10 *Perf. 12*
1071 A466 1r multicolored .70 .35
1072 A466 5r multicolored 2.10 2.10

Girl Guides in Sri Lanka, 75th Anniv. (in 1992).

A467

National Heroes: No. 1073, Yagirala Sri Pagnananda Maha Nayaka Thero. No. 1074, C.P. De Silva. No. 1075, Wilmot A. Perera. No. 1076, N.D.H. Abdul Caffoor.

1993, May 22 *Perf. 14*
1073 A467 1r multicolored .45 .50
1074 A467 1r multicolored .45 .50
1075 A467 1r multicolored .45 .50
1076 A467 1r multicolored .45 .50
Nos. 1073-1076 (4) 1.80 2.00

Gam Udawa, 15th Anniv.
A468

1993, June 23 Litho. *Perf. 12½*
1077 A468 1r multicolored 1.90 .50

Co-operative Consumer Service, 50th Anniv. — A469

1993, July 3 *Perf. 13*
1078 A469 1r multicolored 2.10 .50

Birds
A470

Designs: 3r, Ashy-headed laughing thrush. 4r, Ceylon brown-capped babbler. 5r, Red-faced malkoha. 10r, Ceylon hill-mynah.

1993, July 14 *Perf. 12½x12*
1079 A470 3r multicolored .50 .50
1080 A470 4r multicolored .50 .50
1081 A470 5r multicolored .90 .90
1082 A470 10r multicolored 1.75 1.75
a. Souvenir sheet, #1079-1082 4.50 4.50
Nos. 1079-1082 (4) 3.65 3.65

Talawila Church, 150th Anniv.
A471

1993, July 26 *Perf. 13*
1083 A471 1r multicolored 1.50 .50

Postal Excellence Service Awards — A472

1993, Aug. 22
1084 A472 1r multicolored 1.50 .50

Technical Education in Sri Lanka, Cent.
A473

1993, Dec. 17
1085 A473 1r multicolored 1.50 .50

Musaeus College, Cent. — A474

1993, Nov. 15
1086 A474 1r multicolored 2.50 .50

Christmas
A475

Designs: 1r, Presentation of infant Jesus in Temple of Jerusalem. 17r, Boy Jesus in Temple.

1993, Nov. 30 Litho. *Perf. 14x13½*
1087 A475 1r multicolored .25 .25
1088 A475 17r multicolored 1.40 1.40
a. Souvenir sheet, #1087-1088 3.00 3.00

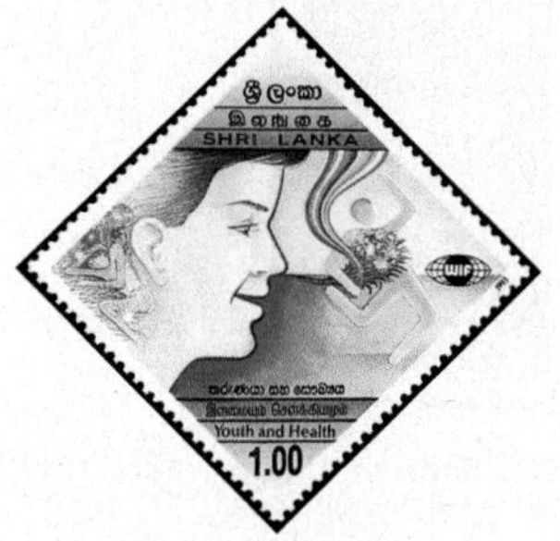

Youth and Health — A476

1993, Dec. 16 *Perf. 14*
1089 A476 1r multicolored .80 .40

Old Boy's Assoc., Trinity College, Kandy, Cent. — A478

1994, Feb. 11 Litho. *Perf. 12½*
1091 A478 1r multicolored .50 .45

St. Thomas College, Matara, 150th Anniv.
A479

1994, Mar. 10 Litho. *Perf. 13*
1092 A479 1r multicolored .50 .45

St. Joseph's College, 125th Anniv.
A480

1994, Apr. 4 Litho. *Perf. 12½*
1093 A480 1r multicolored .60 .35

Siyambalangamuwe Sri Gunaratana Thero — A481

1994, Apr. 2 Litho. *Perf. 13*
1094 A481 1r multicolored 2.25 .45

ILO, 75th Anniv. — A482

1994, May. 12
1095 A482 1r multicolored 1.60 .45

Vesak Festival
A483

Designs show actions by Bodhisatva in four of ten perfections: 1r, Dana, displaying generosity. 2r, Sila, morality. 5r, Nekkhamma, ascetic surrounded by worshippers. 17r, Panna, wisdom dispensed by Bodhisatva to others.

1994, May 7 Litho. *Perf. 12½*
1096 A483 1r multicolored .25 .25
1097 A483 2r multicolored 1.10 1.10
1098 A483 5r multicolored 1.10 1.10
1099 A483 17r multicolored 2.00 2.00
a. Souvenir sheet, #1096-1099 5.25 5.25
Nos. 1096-1099 (4) 4.45 4.45

Famous People
A484

Designs: No. 1100, Pres. Ranasinghe Premadasa. No. 1101, Ven. Mihiripanne Dhammaratana Thero. No. 1102, E. Periyathambipillai, poet. No. 1103, Dr. Colvin R. De Silva, politician.

1994, May 22 Litho. *Perf. 14*
1100 A484 1r multicolored .30 .40
1101 A484 1r multicolored .30 .40
1102 A484 1r multicolored .30 .40
1103 A484 1r multicolored .30 .40
Nos. 1100-1103 (4) 1.20 1.60

World Conference of Intl. Federation of Social Workers, Colombo
A485

1994, July 9 Litho. *Perf. 12½*

1104 A485 8r blue, lt blue & blk 3.75 3.75

Bellanwila Sri Somaratana Nayake Thero — A486

1994, Aug. 2 Litho. *Perf. 12½*

1105 A486 1r multicolored 2.40 .40

Infotel Lanka '94
A487

1994, Sept. 8

1106 A487 10r multicolored 3.00 3.00

Intl. Year of Indigenous People — A488

Designs: 1r, Veddah man making bow. 17r, Veddah man seated by rock art paintings.

1994, Sept. 12 Litho. *Perf. 12*

1107 A488 1r multicolored .50 .50
1108 A488 17r multicolored 4.75 4.75

Natl. Wildlife & Nature Protection Society, Cent.
A489

1r, Emblem. 2r, Rhino-horned lizard. 10r, Giant squirrel. 17r, Sloth bear.

1994, Nov. 24 Litho. *Perf. 12½*

1109 A489 1r multicolored .45 .25
1110 A489 2r multicolored .80 .80
1111 A489 10r multicolored 2.25 2.25
1112 A489 17r multicolored 3.25 3.25
a. Souvenir sheet, #1109-1112 7.00 7.00
Nos. 1109-1112 (4) 6.75 6.55

Gam Udawa, 16th Anniv.
A490

1994, Sept. Litho. *Perf. 13*

1113 A490 1r multicolored 1.00 .25

A491

1994, Oct. 11 Litho. *Perf. 12½*

1114 A491 1r multicolored 2.50 .90

Double entry bookkeeping, 500th anniv.

Water Lily — A492

1995, Feb. 22 *Perf. 14*

1115 A492 1r multicolored 1.25 .25

Richmond College Old Boys Assoc., Cent.
A493

1994 *Perf. 12½*

1116 A493 1r multicolored .40 .25

ICAO, 50th Anniv.
A494

1994, Dec. 7 Litho. *Perf. 13*

1117 A494 10r multicolored 4.25 3.00

Christmas
A495

Designs: 1r, Nativity. 17r, Jesus growing up, at home with Joseph and Mary.

1994, Dec. 8 Litho. *Perf. 13*

1118 A495 1r multicolored .30 .25
1119 A495 17r multicolored 3.75 3.75
a. Souvenir sheet, #1118-1119 4.50 4.50

Assoc. for Advancement of Science, 50th Anniv. — A496

1994, Dec. 19 Litho. *Perf. 13*

1120 A496 1r multicolored 3.00 .60

Orchid Circle of Ceylon, 60th Anniv. — A498

Orchids: 50c, Dendrobium maccarthiae. 1r, Cottonia peduncularis. 5r, Bulbophyllum wightii. 17r, Habenaria crinifera.

1994, Dec. 27 Litho. *Perf. 13*

1122 A498 50c multicolored .30 .25
1123 A498 1r multicolored .45 .40
1124 A498 5r multicolored .80 .80
1125 A498 17r multicolored 1.50 *3.00*
a. Souvenir sheet, #1122-1125 6.00 6.00
Nos. 1122-1125 (4) 3.05 4.45

Visit of Pope John Paul II, Beatification of Fr. Joseph Vaz — A499

1995, Jan. 20

1126 A499 1r multicolored 5.00 1.00

St. Joseph's College, Colombo, Cent.
A500

1995, Mar. 2 Litho. *Perf. 13*

1127 A500 1r multicolored 1.50 .50

Royal Asiatic Society of Sri Lanka, 150th Anniv. — A501

1995, Apr. 4

1128 A501 1r multicolored 3.25 .90

Sirimavo Bandaranaike, World's First Woman Prime Minister — A502

1995, Apr. 17 Litho. *Perf. 12*

1129 A502 2r multicolored 2.25 1.10

A503

Vesak Festival (Designs show actions by a Bodhisatva in four of ten perfections): 1r, Endeavor, standing on shore. 2r, Forebearance, one holding another. 10r, Veracity, two people listening to truths. 17r, Resolution, man holding hoe.

1995, May 5 *Perf. 12x12½*

1130 A503 1r multicolored .30 .25
1131 A503 2r multicolored .40 .25
1132 A503 10r multicolored 1.25 1.10
1133 A503 17r multicolored 2.25 2.25
a. Souvenir sheet, #1130-1133 5.00 5.00
Nos. 1130-1133 (4) 4.20 3.85

M. C. Abdul Cader — A504

1995, June 3 *Perf. 11*

1134 A504 2r multicolored 2.40 1.25

St. Aloysius College, Galle, Cent.
A506

1995, June 21 Litho. *Perf. 12½x12*

1136 A506 2r multicolored 2.40 1.25

T.B. Ilangaratna (1913-92), Politician
A507

1995, July 7 Litho. *Perf. 13*

1137 A507 2r multicolored 2.40 1.25

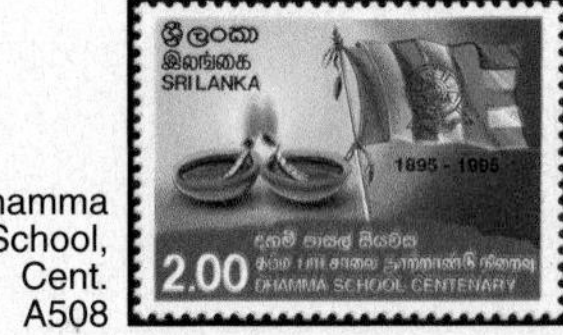

Dhamma School, Cent.
A508

1995, Aug. 3

1138 A508 2r multicolored 2.40 1.25

General Post Office, Colombo, Cent.
A509

1995, Aug. 22 Litho. *Perf. 13½*

1139 A509 1r multicolored 1.60 .45

Help the Elderly — A510

1995, Oct. 1 Litho. *Perf. 14x13½*

1140 A510 2r multicolored 2.40 1.10

41st Commonwealth Parliamentary Conference — A511

1995, Oct. 9 Litho. *Perf. 14x13½*

1141	A511	2r multicolored	2.40	1.10

UN, 50th Anniv. — A512

1995, Oct. 24 *Perf. 13½x14*

1142	A512	2r multicolored	2.40	1.10

World Thrift Day — A513

1995, Oct. 15

1143	A513	2r multicolored	2.40	1.10

Christmas A514

Designs: 2r, Arms of Colombo and Kurunegla, Persian cross from Anuradhapura, Christian church. 20r, Clasping arms, nativity scene.

1995, Nov. 10 Litho. *Perf. 13*

1144	A514	2r multicolored	.50	.25
1145	A514	20r multicolored	2.75	2.40
a.		Souvenir sheet, #1144-1145	4.00	4.00

SAARC, 10th Anniv. — A515

1995, Dec. 8

1146	A515	2r multicolored	3.50	1.25

A516

50c, Little Basses. 75c, Great Basses. 2r, Devinuwara. 20r, Galle.

1996, Jan. 22 Litho. *Perf. 12*

1147	A516	50c multicolored	.65	.50
1148	A516	75c multicolored	.65	.50
1149	A516	2r multicolored	1.50	1.00
1149A	A516	2.50r like #1149	.65	.50
1150	A516	20r multicolored	4.50	2.75
a.		Souv. sheet, #1147-1149, 1150	9.50	9.50
		Nos. 1147-1150 (5)	7.95	5.25

Lighthouses of Sri Lanka. Examples of No. 1150a overprinted in the margin for the 2010 National Stamp Fair, Colombo sold for 500r.

For surcharges see Nos. 1191-1193, 1282A.

Vincent High School, Batticaloa, 175th Anniv. — A517

1996, Jan. 17 Litho. *Perf. 13*

1151	A517	2r multicolored	2.40	1.10

Handicrafts A518

25c, Traditional sesath. 8.50r, Pottery. 10.50r, Mats. 17r,

1996, Mar. 13 *Perf. 12*

1152	A518	25c multicolored	.25	.25
1153	A518	8.50r multicolored	.45	.45
1154	A518	10.50r multicolored	.75	.70
1155	A518	17r multicolored	1.00	1.00
a.		Souvenir sheet, #1152-1155	4.25	4.25
		Nos. 1152-1155 (4)	2.45	2.40

For surcharges see Nos. 1189-1190, 1548, 1575.

A519

1996, Mar. 21

1156	A519	2r multicolored	3.00	1.10

Chundikuli Girls' College, Jaffna, cent.

A520

Vesak Festival: 1r, Capa cradling her son, teasing her husband. 2r, Dantika, mahout, elephant. 5r, Subha holding her eye in her hand, man of low morals. 10r, Punna explaining purification by water to Brahmin.

1996, Apr. 30 Litho. *Perf. 12*

1157	A520	1r multicolored	.25	.25
1158	A520	2r multicolored	.45	.45
1159	A520	5r multicolored	.55	.55
1160	A520	10r multicolored	1.10	1.10
a.		Souvenir sheet, #1157-1160	2.75	2.75
		Nos. 1157-1160 (4)	2.35	2.35

1996 Summer Olympic Games, Atlanta A521

1996, July 22 Litho. *Perf. 13½*

1161	A521	1r Diving, vert.	.30	.25
1162	A521	2r Volleyball, vert.	1.10	.55
1163	A521	5r Shooting	1.25	1.25
1164	A521	17r Running	2.75	2.75
		Nos. 1161-1164 (4)	5.40	4.80

Sri Lanka, 1996 World Cup Cricket Champions — A522

1996, Aug. 18

1165	A522	2r Bowler	.50	.50
1166	A522	10.50r Wicketkeeper	1.00	1.00
1167	A522	17r Batsman	1.50	1.50
1168	A522	20r Trophy	1.60	1.60
a.		Souvenir sheet, #1165-1168	5.00	5.00
		Nos. 1165-1168 (4)	4.60	4.60

No. 1168a contains two se-tenant pairs.

Jaffna Central College, 180th Anniv. A523

1996, Sept. 7 Litho. *Perf. 13½*

1169	A523	2r multicolored	2.50	1.10

UNESCO, 50th Anniv. — A524

1996, Nov. 4 Litho. *Perf. 13½x14*

1170	A524	2r multicolored	2.75	1.25

A525

Christmas (Scenes of parables from murals, Trinity College Chapel): 2r, Washing of the feet. 17r, Good Samaritan.

1996, Dec. 2 *Perf. 13½x13*

1171	A525	2r multicolored	.30	.25
1172	A525	17r multicolored	1.75	1.60
a.		Souvenir sheet, #1171-1172	2.00	2.00

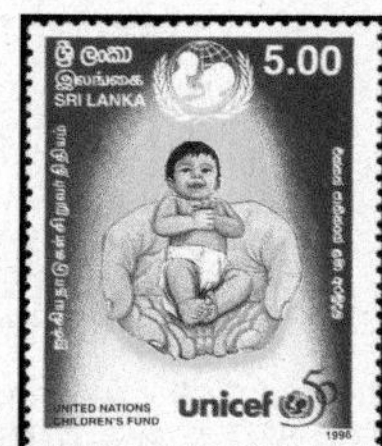

UNICEF, 50th Anniv. — A526

1996, Dec. 12 Litho. *Perf. 13½x14*

1173	A526	5r multicolored	1.00	.90

Swami Vivekananda A527

1997, Jan. 15 *Perf. 13½x13*

1174	A527	2.50r multicolored	1.25	.90

Personalities A528

Designs: No. 1175, Lt. Gen. Denzil Kobbekaduwa. No. 1176, Ven. Welivitiye Serata Thero. No. 1177, Dr. S.A. Wickremasinghe.

1997, Apr. 4 Litho. *Perf. 13½x13*

1175	A528	2r multicolored	.60	.60
1176	A528	2r multicolored	.60	.60
1177	A528	2r multicolored	.60	.60
		Nos. 1175-1177 (3)	1.80	1.80

Vesak Festival — A529

Cemeteries, monuments to the dead: 1r, Thuparama. 2.50r, Ruwanvalisaya. 3r, Abhayagiri Dagaba. 17r, Jetavana Dagaba.

1997, May 7 *Perf. 12x12½*

1178	A529	1r multicolored	.25	.25
1179	A529	2.50r multicolored	.25	.25
1180	A529	3r multicolored	.25	.25
1181	A529	17r multicolored	1.10	1.10
a.		Souvenir Sheet of 4, #1178-1181	2.25	2.25
		Nos. 1178-1181 (4)	1.85	1.85

D.J. Kumarage, Birth Cent. — A530

1997, Apr. 4 Litho. *Perf. 13½x14*

1182	A530	2.50r multicolored	1.75	.90

Medicinal Herbs — A531

2.40r, Munronia pinnata. 14r, Rauvolfia serpentina.

1997, July 22 Litho. *Perf. 13½x14*

1183	A531	2.50r multicolored	.30	.25
1184	A531	14r multicolored	1.40	1.40

Tourism A532

1997, Sept. 11 *Perf. 12*

1185	A532	20r multicolored	3.25	3.00

St. Servatius College, Matara, Cent. A533

1997, Nov. 1 *Perf. 12½x12*

1186	A533	2.50r multicolored	.80	.30

Mahagama Sekera — A534

1997, Apr. 4 Litho. *Perf. 13½x13*

1187	A534	2r multicolored	.85	.40

Asterisks obliterate portions of Mahagama Sekera's name.

Sri Jayawardenapura Vidalaya, Kotte, 175th Anniv. — A535

1997, Jan. 28 *Perf. 12½*

1188	A535	2.50r multicolored	.60	.30

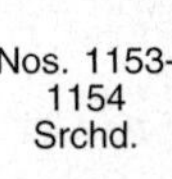

Nos. 1153-1154 Srchd.

1997, May 6 Litho. *Perf. 12*

1189	A518	1r on 8.50r, #1153	8.00	1.00
1190	A518	11r on 10.50r, #1154 (a)	6.50	6.50
a.		Surcharge type b	6.50	6.50

Surcharge Type a on #1190 is 2½mm high. Type b surcharge is 3mm high.

No. 1149 Surcharged

c

d

e

1997, Feb. 12 Litho. *Perf. 12*

1191	A516(c)	2.50r on 2r	*6.00*	*6.00*
1192	A516(d)	2.50r on 2r	*6.00*	*6.00*
1193	A516(e)	2.50r on 2r	*6.00*	*6.00*
		Nos. 1191-1193 (3)	*18.00*	*18.00*

A number has been reserved additional surcharge on No. 1149.

Reptiles A537

2.50r, Lyre head lizard. 5r, Boie's roughside. 17r, Common Lanka skink. 20r, Great forest gecko.

1997, Oct. 18 Litho. *Perf. 12*

1195	A537	2.50r multicolored	.25	.25
1196	A537	5r multicolored	.40	.40
1197	A537	17r multicolored	.75	.75
1198	A537	20r multicolored	.85	.85
a.		Souvenir sheet, #1195-1198	2.50	2.50
		Nos. 1195-1198 (4)	2.25	2.25

Christmas — A538

2.50r, Holy Family. 20r, Adoration of the Magi.

1997, Nov. 20 *Perf. 12½x13*

1199	A538	2.50r multicolored	.25	.25
1200	A538	20r multicolored	1.35	.90
a.		Souvenir sheet, #1199-1200	1.60	1.60

A539

Personalities: #1201, Hegoda Sri Indasara Thero (1932-87), religious leader. #1202, Abdul Aziz (d. 1990), politician. #1203, Subramaniam Vithiananthan (b. 1924), teacher, writer. #1204, Vivienne Goonewardene (1916-96), politician.

1997, Nov. 11 Litho. *Perf. 12½*

1201	A539	2.50r multicolored	.30	.30
1202	A539	2.50r multicolored	.30	.30
1203	A539	2.50r multicolored	.30	.30
1204	A539	2.50r multicolored	.30	.30
a.		Block of 4, #1201-1204	1.40	1.40

Young Men's Buddhist Assoc., Colombo, Cent. A540

1998, Jan. 1 Litho. *Perf. 12½*

1205	A540	2.50r multicolored	.70	.35

Traditional Jewelry and Crafts — A541

Designs: 2.50r, Chunam box. 5r, Necklace of agate. 10r, Bangle and hairpin. 17r, Sigiri earrings.

1998, Apr. 24 Litho. *Perf. 13½*

1206	A541	2.50r multicolored	.45	.25
1207	A541	5r multicolored	.70	.30
1208	A541	10r multicolored	1.25	1.25
1209	A541	17r multicolored	2.00	2.00
a.		Souvenir sheet, #1206-1209	5.00	5.00
		Nos. 1206-1209 (4)	4.40	3.80

Independence, 50th Anniv. — A542

Natl. flag and: 2r, People holding up arms, letters and symbols. No. 1211, Ceylon No. 300. No. 1212, People standing, images of industry and technology. 5r, People playing musical instruments, book, pen, television, musical instruments. 10r, People holding up items, symbols of religion, government.

Perf. 13, 13½ (#1211)

1998, Feb. 4 Litho.

1210	A542	2r multicolored	.55	.25
1211	A542	2.50r multicolored	.75	.60
1212	A542	2.50r multicolored	.75	.60
1213	A542	5r multicolored	.75	.70
1214	A542	10r multicolored	1.25	1.50
		Nos. 1210-1214 (5)	4.05	3.65

No. 1211 is 28x38mm.

William Gopallawa, 1st President A543

1998 Litho. *Perf. 13½*

1215	A543	2.50r multicolored	.60	.25

5th Natl. Scout Jamboree A544

Designs: 2.50r, Scouts holding flag, emblem, campground. 17r, Campground, flag, emblems, scout saluting.

1998, Feb. 18

1216	A544	2.50r multicolored	1.25	1.00
1217	A544	17r multicolored	3.50	2.75

World Health Organization, 50th Anniv. — A545

1998, Apr. 7 Litho. *Perf. 13x12½*

1218	A545	2.50r multicolored	.80	.25

St. John's College, Jaffna, 175th Anniv. — A546

1998, May 7 Litho. *Perf. 14½x14*

1219	A546	2.50r multicolored	.40	.25

Elephas Maximus Ceylonensis — A547

Designs: 2.50r, Wading in lake. 10r, Female, calf. 17r, Three standing in plains. 50r, Large bull.

1998, May 28 *Perf. 13*

1220	A547	2.50r multicolored	1.00	.70
1221	A547	10r multicolored	1.50	1.10
1222	A547	17r multicolored	2.10	1.40
1223	A547	50r multicolored	3.50	2.75
a.		Souvenir sheet, #1220-1223	9.00	9.00
		Nos. 1220-1223 (4)	8.10	5.95

Vesak Festival — A548

Kelaniya Rajamaha Vihara paintings: 1r, Waterfalls, tree. 2.50r, Procession of people, elephant with rider. 4r, Looking at mother with newborn baby. 17r, Presenting child for ceremony, laying stone.

1998, Apr. 30 Litho. *Perf. 12½*

1224	A548	1r multicolored	.40	.25
1225	A548	2.50r multicolored	.40	.25
1226	A548	4r multicolored	.75	.35
1227	A548	17r multicolored	1.75	1.00
a.		Souvenir sheet, #1224-1227	2.75	2.75
		Nos. 1224-1227 (4)	3.30	1.85

SAARC Summit, Colombo — A549

1998 Litho. *Perf. 14½x14*

1228	A549	2.50r multicolored	1.10	.35

1998, Year of Information Technology A550

1998 **Litho.** ***Perf. 13½***

1229 A550 2.50r multicolored 1.10 .25

Personalities A551

No. 1230, Ven. Pannakitti Nayake Thero. No. 1231, Sir Nicholas Attygalle. No. 1232, Dr. Samuel Fisk Green. No. 1233, Prof. Ediriweera Sarachchandra.

1998 ***Perf. 13***

1230 A551 2.50r multicolored .45 .35
1231 A551 2.50r multicolored .45 .35
1232 A551 2.50r multicolored .45 .35
1233 A551 2.50r multicolored .45 .35
Nos. 1230-1233 (4) 1.80 1.40

Meteorological Dept., 50th Anniv. — A552

1998 **Litho.** ***Perf. 14x13½***

1234 A552 2.50r multicolored 1.75 .55

26th Forum of South Asia, Africa & Middle East Lions Clubs Intl. — A553

1998, Nov. 20 **Litho.** ***Perf. 14x14½***

1235 A553 2.50r multicolored 3.00 1.25

Christmas A554

1998, Dec. 10 ***Perf. 13½x14***

1236 A554 2.50r Nativity .35 .25
1237 A554 20r Annunciation 1.60 1.50
a. Souvenir sheet, #1236-1237 2.00 2.00

A555

S.W.R.D. Bandaranaike, Birth Cent.: No. 1238, Wearing white scarf. No. 1239, Wearing blue scarf.

1999, Jan. 8 **Litho.** ***Perf. 12***

1238 A555 3.50r multicolored .90 .90
1239 A555 3.50r multicolored .90 .90
a. Souvenir sheet, #1238-1239, perf. 12½ 2.00 2.00

Kandyan Dancer — A556

1999, Feb. 3 **Photo.** ***Perf. 12***

1240 A556 1r brown .25 .25
1241 A556 2r green blue .25 .25
1242 A556 3r plum .25 .25
1243 A556 3.50r blue .25 .25
1244 A556 4r dark red .25 .25

Size: 21x26mm

1245 A556 5r green .25 .25
1246 A556 10r violet .30 .30
1247 A556 13.50r bright red .40 .40
1248 A556 17r blue green .45 .45
1249 A556 20r olive bister .55 .55
Nos. 1240-1249 (10) 3.20 3.20

Telecommunications, 50th Anniv. — A557

Portraits of Sir Arthur C. Clarke, diagrams of Orbital Concept: a, Rocket launch, satellites, space shuttle. b, Satellites, earth from outer space, space capsule.

1999, Feb. 10 **Litho.** ***Perf. 12***

1250 A557 3.50r Pair, #a.-b. 2.00 2.00

Dated 1998.

Salvation Army, 116th Anniv. A558

1999, Apr. 28 **Litho.** ***Perf. 11¾x12***

1251 A558 3.50r multicolored .90 .70

British Council, 50th Anniv. — A559

1999, May 20 ***Perf. 12***

1252 A559 3.50r multicolored .75 .45

Sumithrayo Organization Suicide Hot Line, 25th Anniv. — A560

1999, June 14 ***Perf. 12½***

1253 A560 3.50r multicolored .85 .50

Vesak Festival — A561

Designs: 2r, Flowers. 3.50r, Leaf, wheel. 13.50r, Nut, flower. 17r, Young people with traditional lanterns.

Unwmk.

1999, May 25 **Litho.** ***Perf. 12***

1254 A561 2r multicolored .25 .25
1255 A561 3.50r multicolored .25 .25
1256 A561 13.50r multicolored .70 .70
1257 A561 17r multicolored .90 .90
Nos. 1254-1257 (4) 2.10 2.10

Souvenir Sheet

Wmk. 388

Perf. 12½

1258 Sheet of 4 2.50 2.50
a. A561 2r like #1254 .25 .25
b. A561 3.50r like #1255 .25 .25
c. A561 13.50r like #1256 .70 .70
d. A561 17r like #1257 .90 .90

Independent Television Network, 20th Anniv. — A562

1999, June 5 **Unwmk.** ***Perf. 12¾***

1259 A562 3.50r multicolored .60 .40

Vidyodaya Pirivena, 125th Anniv. A563

Perf. 12¾

1999, Sept. 17 **Litho.** **Unwmk.**

1260 A563 3.50r multicolored .60 .30

Sri Lankan Cinema, 50th Anniv. — A564

3.50r, Handaya, 1979. 4r, Nidhanaya, 1972. 10r, Gam Peraliya, 1963. 17r, Kadawunu Poronduwa, 1947.

1999, Sept. 17 **Litho.** ***Perf. 12¾***

1261 A564 3.50r multicolored .25 .25
1262 A564 4r multicolored .30 .30
1263 A564 10r multicolored .45 .40
1264 A564 17r multicolored 1.25 1.25
a. Souvenir sheet, #1261-1264 2.75 2.75
Nos. 1261-1264 (4) 2.25 2.20

Bhakthi Prabodanaya Magazine, Cent. — A565

1999, Sept. **Litho.** ***Perf. 12x12¼***

1265 A565 3.50r multicolored .60 .30

Hector Kobbekaduwa, Politician — A566

Perf. 12¾x12½

1999, Sept. 19 **Wmk. 388** **Litho.**

1266 A566 3.50r multicolored .60 .30

National Army, 50th Anniv. — A567

1999, Oct. 10 **Unwmk.** ***Perf. 12¾***

1267 A567 3.50r multicolored .80 .40

Convention on the Rights of the Child, 10th Anniv. — A568

1999, Nov. 20 ***Perf. 12¾x12½***

1268 A568 3.50r multicolored 1.10 .70

A569

1999, Nov. 26 ***Perf. 12¾***

1269 A569 3.50r multicolored .55 .30

Balangoda Ananda Maitreya Mahanyake Thero (b. 1895), Buddhist priest.

A570

Paintings — 3.50r, By David Paynter. 4r, By Justin Daraniyagala. 17r, By Ivan Peries. 20r, By Solias Mendis.

1999, Dec. 12 ***Perf. 12¾***

1270 A570 3.50r multicolored .35 .25
1271 A570 4r multicolored .35 .25
1272 A570 17r multicolored .70 .70
1273 A570 20r multicolored 1.10 1.10
a. Souvenir sheet of 4, #1270-1273 3.50 3.50
Nos. 1270-1273 (4) 2.50 2.30

Athletic Accomplishments — A571

Designs: 1r, Kumar Anandan's swim across Palk Strait. 3.50r, World champions in cricket. 13.50r, International fame in track and field.

1999 *Perf. 12¾*

1274 A571	1r multicolored	.30	.25
1275 A571	3.50r multicolored	.70	*.75*
1276 A571	13.50r multicolored	1.40	*2.00*
	Nos. 1274-1276 (3)	2.40	*3.00*

Natl. Commission for UNESCO, 50th Anniv. — A572

Perf. 12¾x12½

1999, Nov. 16 Litho. Wmk. 388

1277 A572 13.50r multicolored 3.25 2.75

Christmas A573

1999, Nov. 30 *Perf. 12½x12¾*

1278 A573	3.50r shown	.25	.25
1279 A573	20r Magi	1.00	.80
a.	Souvenir sheet, #1278-1279	2.25	2.25

Famous People — A574

Designs: No. 1280, Dr. Pandithamani S. Kanapathipillai, Tamil scholar. No. 1281, Sunil Santha, musician. No. 1282, Dr. Al Haj Badi-udin Mahmud, Education minister.

1999, Dec. 3 *Perf. 12¾x12½*

1280 A574	3.50r multi	1.10	.70
1281 A574	3.50r multi	1.75	.90
1282 A574	3.50r multi	1.10	.70
	Nos. 1280-1282 (3)	3.95	2.30

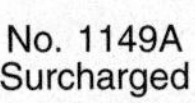

No. 1149A Surcharged

1999, Dec. 3 Litho. *Perf. 12*

1282A A516 2r on 2.50r multi *11.00 1.40*

Butterflies — A575

Designs: 3.50r, Striped albatross. 13.50r, Ceylon tiger. 17r, Three-spot grass yellow. 20r, Great orange tip.

Perf. 12x11¾

1999, Dec. 30 Unwmk.

Granite Paper

1283 A575	3.50r multi	.45	.30
1284 A575	13.50r multi	1.00	.85
1285 A575	17r multi	1.40	1.25
1286 A575	20r multi	1.60	1.40
a.	Souvenir sheet, #1283-1286	4.50	4.50
	Nos. 1283-1286 (4)	4.45	3.80

Corals A576

1999, Dec. 30 *Perf. 11¾x12*

Granite Paper

1287 A576	3.50r Boulder	.35	.40
1288 A576	13.50r Blue-tipped	1.35	1.10
1289 A576	14r Brain-boulder	1.35	1.10
1290 A576	22r Elkhorn	1.50	1.40
a.	Souvenir sheet, #1287-1290	5.25	5.25
	Nos. 1287-1290 (4)	4.55	4.00

For surcharge, see No. 1581.

Auditor General's Department, Bicent. — A576a

Perf. 12½x12¾

1999, Dec. Litho. Unwmk.

1290B A576a 3.50r multi .80 .60

Year 2000 — A577

Satellite and: 10r, Birds, religious symbols. No. 1292, Scales, girl, Red Cross, computer. No. 1293, airplane, satellite dish, man at computer. No. 1294, Hands, symbols of women's equality, crippled and blind.

2000, Jan. 1 *Perf. 11¾*

Granite Paper

1291 A577	10r multi	.30	.30
1292 A577	100r multi	3.75	3.75
1293 A577	100r multi	3.75	3.75
1294 A577	100r multi	3.75	3.75
a.	Souvenir sheet, #1291-1294	12.00	12.00
	Nos. 1291-1294 (4)	11.55	11.55

Kurunagala Diocese, 50th Anniv. A578

Unwmk.

2000, Feb. 2 Litho. *Perf. 12*

1295 A578 13.50r multi 1.40 *1.75*

Wesley College, Colombo, 125th Anniv. A579

2000, Mar. 2 *Perf. 11¾x12*

1296 A579 3.50r multi .60 .30

Panadura Pinwatte Saddharmakara Vidyayathana Pirivena, Cent. — A580

2000, Mar. 12

1297 A580 3.50r multi .60 .30

Vesak Festival — A581

2r, Arrival of Jaya Sri Maha Bodhi sapling. 3.50r, King Devanampiyatissa carrying sapling on his head. 10r, Venerating sapling. 13.50r, Royal tree planting, Anuradhapura.

2000, Apr. 28 Litho. *Perf. 12¾x12½*

1298-1301 A581	Set of 4	2.50	2.00
1301a	Souvenir sheet, #1298-1301	4.50	4.50

Sri Lanka Bar Association, 25th Anniv. (in 1999) — A582

2000, June 10 *Perf. 12*

1302 A582 3.50r multi .60 .30

Co-operative Wholesale Establishment, 50th Anniv. — A583

2000, July 1 *Perf. 12¾*

1303 A583 3.50r multi .60 .30

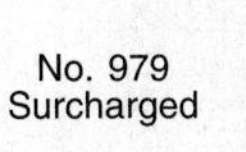

No. 979 Surcharged

2000, July 21 Litho. *Perf. 11½*

1303A A420 50c on 8r multi *7.50 3.25*

St. Patrick's College, Jaffna, 150th Anniv. A584

2000, July 21

1304 A584 3.50r multi 1.25 .70

Survey Dept., 200th Anniv. A585

2000, Aug. 2

1305 A585 3.50r multi .65 .30

Central Bank of Sri Lanka, 50th Anniv. — A586

2000, Aug. 27 *Perf. 13¼*

1306 A586 3.50r multi .60 .30

Dr. Maria Montessori (1870-1952), Educator — A587

2000, Aug. 31 *Perf. 11¾*

1307 A587 3.50r multi .65 .30

2000 Summer Olympics, Sydney — A588

Sydney Olympic Games emblem and: a, Hurdler, map. b, Shooter, runners. c, Runners. d, Hurdlers, swimmer.

2000, Sept. 7

1308 A588	10r Horiz. strip of 4, #a-d	2.75	2.75
e.	Souvenir sheet, #1308	3.50	3.50

All Ceylon Young Men's Muslim Association Conference, 50th Anniv. — A589

2000, Sept. 16

1309 A589 3.50r multi .60 .30

Hotel Industry, 25th Anniv. A590

2000, Sept. 18 ***Perf. 12¾***
1310 A590 10r multi 2.75 1.75

Immigration and Emigration Dept., 50th Anniv. A591

2000, Oct. 2 ***Perf. 11¾***
1311 A591 3.50r multi .90 .70

Traditional Dancer — A592

Perf. 13½x13 Syncopated

2000, Oct. 5 **Litho.**
1312 A592 50r multi 1.50 1.50
1313 A592 100r multi 3.25 3.25
1314 A592 200r multi 6.25 6.25
Nos. 1312-1314 (3) 11.00 11.00

All-Ceylon Buddhist Congress Natl. Awards Ceremony A593

2000, Aug. 27 **Litho.** ***Perf. 12¾***
1315 A593 3.50r multi .90 .70

Saumiyamoorthy Thondaman, Government Minister — A594

2000, Oct. 30
1316 A594 3.50r multi .60 .40

Famous People — A595

Designs: No. 1317, 3.50r, Most Ven. Baddegama Siri Piyaratana Nayake Thero, educator. No. 1318, 3.50r, Aluthgamage Simon de Silva (1874-1920), writer. No. 1319, 3.50r, Desigar Ramanujam (1907-68), politician.

Perf. 12x12¼ (#1317), 12¾x12½

2000, Nov. 14
1317-1319 A595 Set of 3 1.25 1.00

Christmas A596

Designs: 2r, Joseph, Mary, donkey. 17r, Holy family.

2000, Nov. 23 ***Perf. 12¾x12½***
1320-1321 A596 Set of 2 2.25 1.75
1321a Souvenir sheet, #1320-1321, perf. 12 2.50 2.50

Lalith Athulathmudali (1936-93), Politician — A597

2000, Nov. 30 ***Perf. 12½x12¾***
1322 A597 3.50r multi .60 .30

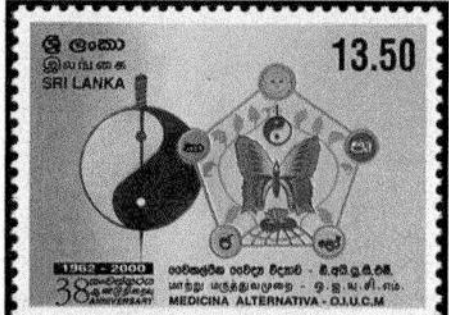

Medicina Alternativa Medical Society, 38th Anniv. A598

2000, Dec. 1 ***Perf. 12¾***
1323 A598 13.50r multi 2.25 1.50

Ladies' College, Cent. — A599

2000, Dec. 7
1324 A599 3.50r multi .75 .30

Navy, 50th Anniv. A600

2000, Dec. 9
1325 A600 3.50r multi 1.00 .50

Peliyagoda Vidyalankara Pirivena, 125th Anniv. — A601

2000, Dec. 30 ***Perf. 12x12¼***
1326 A601 3.50r multi .60 .30

Bishop's College, 125th Anniv. A602

2001, Jan. 19 **Litho.**
1327 A602 3.50r multi .60 .30

St. Thomas' College, 150th Anniv. A603

2001, Feb. 3 ***Perf. 12¾***
1328 A603 3.50r multi .60 .30

Lanka Mahila Samiti Women's Training Society, 70th Anniv. A604

2001, Feb. 15
1329 A604 3.50r multi .60 .30

Air Force, 50th Anniv. A605

2001, Mar. 9
1330 A605 3.50r multi 1.10 .50

St. Lawrence's School, Cent. A606

2001, Mar. 15
1331 A606 3.50r multi .60 .30

Bernard Soysa (1914-97), Politician — A607

2001, Mar. 20 ***Perf. 12¾***
1332 A607 3.50r multi .60 .30

Vesak Festival — A608

Designs: 2r, Sri Nagadeepa Chaithya, Jaffna. 3,50r, Muthiyangana Chaithya, Badulla. 13.50r, Kirivehera, Kataragama. 17r, Sri Dalada Maligawa, Kandy.

2001, Apr. 7 **Litho.** ***Perf. 13½x13¾***
1333 A608 2r multi .25 .25
a. Perf. 14¼ .25 .25

Perf. 14¼

1334 A608 3.50r multi .25 .25
a. Perf. 13½x13¾ .25 .25
1335 A608 13.50r multi .90 .90
1336 A608 17r multi 1.25 1.25
a. Souvenir sheet, #1333a, 1334-1336 2.75 2.75

Hansa Jataka, by George Keyt (1901-93) — A609

2001, Apr. 24 ***Perf. 13¼***
1337 A609 13.50r multi 1.60 2.00

Coins A610

Designs: 3.50r, Kahavanu gold coin, 9th cent. 13.50r, Vijayabahu I silver coin, 1055-1111. 17r, Sethu copper coin, 13th-14th cent. 20r, Buddha Jayanthi 5r commemorative silver coin, 1957.

Perf. 13¾x13½, 14¼ (17r)

2001, June 18
1338 A610 3.50r multi .25 .25
1339 A610 13.50r multi .90 .90
1340 A610 17r multi 1.25 1.25
a. Perf. 13¾x13½x14¼x13½ 1.25 1.25
1341 A610 20r multi 1.60 1.60
a. Perf. 13¾x13½x14¼x13½ 1.60 1.60
b. Souvenir sheet, #1338-1339, 1340a, 1341a 4.50 4.50

Colombo Plan, 50th Anniv. — A611

2001, July 2 ***Perf. 13½x13¾***
1342 A611 10r multi 1.00 1.00

US-Sri Lankan Diplomatic Relations, 150th Anniv. A612

2001, July 3 ***Perf. 12¾***
1343 A612 10r multi 1.25 1.00

Lance Corporal Gamini Kularatne (1966-91), Military Hero — A613

2001, July 14 ***Perf. 13¾x13½***
1344 A613 3.50r multi .60 .30

Prince and Princess of Wales College, Moratuwa, 125th Anniv. A614

2001, Sept. 14 ***Perf. 13¼***
1345 A614 3.50r multi .60 .30

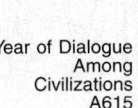

Year of Dialogue Among Civilizations A615

2001, Oct. 9 ***Perf. 13x13½***
1346 A615 10r multi 1.30 1.00

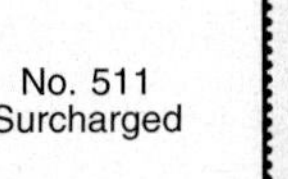

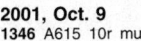

No. 511 Surcharged

2001, July 9 Photo. ***Perf. 14¼x14½***

1347 A180	5r on 1.15r multi	*5.00*	*4.00*
1348 A180	10r on 1.15r multi	*7.00*	*5.00*

An additional surcharge was released in this set. The editors would like to examine it.

13th Meeting of Parties to the Montreal Protocol — A616

2001, Oct. 18 Litho. ***Perf. 13x13¼***
1349 A616 13.50r multi .75 1.10

Ramakrishna Mission Students' Home, Batticaloa, 75th Anniv. — A617

2001, Oct. 19 ***Perf. 12¾***
1350 A617 3.50r multi .60 .30

Drummer — A618

Drummer from: 1r, 2r, 3r, 3.50r, Daul. 4r, 5r, 10r, Kandy. 13.50r, 17r, 20r, Low country.

2001, Nov. 8 Litho. ***Perf. 12½x13¼***

1351	A618	1r rose	.25	.25
1352	A618	2r emerald	.25	.25
1353	A618	3r fawn	.25	.25
1354	A618	3.50r dark blue	.25	.25

Size: 23x28mm

Perf. 13¼x12½

1355	A618	4r pink	.35	.25
1356	A618	5r orange	.35	.25
1357	A618	10r violet	.75	.30
1358	A618	13.50r dull purple	1.00	.45
1359	A618	17r yel orange	1.25	.50
1360	A618	20r Prus blue	1.50	.60
		Nos. 1351-1360 (10)	6.20	3.35

See Nos. 1389A, 1410. For surcharges, see Nos. 1409, 1514, 1549, 1582.

S.W.R.D. Bandaranaike Natl. Memorial Foundation, 25th Anniv. — A619

2001, Nov. 27 ***Perf. 13¾x13¼***
1361 A619 3.50r multi .60 .30

Christmas A620

Designs: 3.50r, Jesus and children. 17r, The Annunciation.

2001, Nov. 28 ***Perf. 13***

1362-1363 A620	Set of 2	.90	.75
1363a	Souvenir sheet, #1362-1363	1.10	1.10

Frogs A621

Designs: 3.50r, Conical wart pygmy tree frog. 13.50r, Sharp-snout saddle tree frog. 17r, Round-snout pygmy tree frog. 20r, Sri Lanka wood frog.

2001, Dec. 3 ***Perf. 13¼x13***

1364-1367 A621	Set of 4	3.25	2.75
1367a	Souvenir sheet, #1364-1367	3.50	3.50

St. Bridget's Convent, Cent. A622

2002, Feb. 1
1368 A622 3.50r multi .60 .30

Ceylon Government Gazette, 200th Anniv. — A623

2002, Mar. 15 Litho. ***Perf. 13¾x14***
1369 A623 3.50r multi .60 .30

D. S. Senanayake (1884-1952), Prime Minister — A624

2002, Mar. 22 ***Perf. 14x13¾***
1370 A624 3.50r multi .60 .30

Gamini Dissanayake (1942-94), Assassinated Government Minister — A625

2002, Mar. 27 ***Perf. 13¾x14***
1371 A625 3.50r multi .60 .30

Lester James Peries (b. 1919), Film Director A626

2002, Apr. 5 ***Perf. 13¼x13***
1372 A626 3.50r multi .60 .30

Natural Beauty of Sri Lanka — A627

Designs: 5r, Sinharaja Forest Reserve. 10r, Horton Plains National Park. 13.50r, Knuckles Range. 20r, Rumassala Cliff and Bonavista Coral Reef.

2002, Apr. 10 ***Perf. 13x13¼***
1373-1376 A627 Set of 4 2.00 2.00

Pres. Ranasinghe Premadasa (1924-93) A628

2002, Apr. 29 ***Perf. 13¾x14***
1377 A628 4.50r multi .60 .25

Sri Lanka - Japan Diplomatic Relations, 50th Anniv. — A629

2002, Apr. 29 ***Perf. 14x13¾***
1378 A629 16.50r multi 1.00 .75

Vesak Festival A630

Dambulla Raja Maha Vihara rock paintings: 3r, Queen Mahamaya's dream. 4.50r, Birth of Prince Siddhartha. 16.50r, Siddhartha's exhibition of archery talents. 23r, Ordination of Prince Siddhartha.

2002, May 17 ***Perf. 13¾x14***

1379-1382 A630	Set of 4	2.00	1.50
1382a	Souvenir sheet, #1379-1382	2.25	2.25

Most Venerable Madihe Pannasiha Maha Nayaka Thera, Religious Leader, 90th Birthday — A631

2002, June 23 ***Perf. 14x13¾***
1383 A631 4.50r multi .60 .25

Sri Lanka Oriental Studies Society, Cent. A632

2002, July 24 ***Perf. 13¾x14***
1384 A632 4.50r multi .75 .25

Rifai Thareeq Association, 125th Anniv. — A633

2002, July 26
1385 A633 4.50r multi .75 .25

14th Asian Track and Field Championships, Colombo — A634

Designs: 4.50r, Discus thrower. 16.50r, Sprinter. 23r, Hurdler. 26r, Long jumper.

2002, Aug. 8
1386-1389 A634 Set of 4 3.00 3.00

Daul Drummer Type of 2001

Perf. 12½x13¼

2002, Aug. 16 **Litho.**
1389A A618 4.50r blue violet —

For surcharge, see No. 1785.

National Museum, 125th Anniv. — A635

No. 1390: a, Carved lion (sitting). b, Carved lion (standing with head turned).

2002, Aug. 27
1390 A635 4.50r Horiz. pair, #a-b 2.00 2.00

Woman's Hand Holding Flower — A636

2002, Aug. 28 ***Perf. 14x13¾***
1391 A636 10r multi 1.10 .65

Tourism promotion.

Dr. A. C. S. Hameed (1929-99), Government Minister — A637

2002, Sept. 3
1392 A637 4.50r multi .70 .25

Freemasons' Hall, Colombo, Cent. — A638

2002, Sept. 5 ***Perf. 13¾x14***
1393 A638 4.50r multi .90 .50

Holy Cross College, Kalutara, Cent. A639

2002, Sept. 13
1394 A639 4.50r multi .70 .25

German Dharmaduta Society, 50th Anniv. — A640

2002, Sept. 21 ***Perf. 14x13¾***
1395 A640 4.50r multi 1.00 .25

Intl. Children's Day — A641

2002, Oct. 1
1396 A641 4.50r multi .70 .25

Dr. M. C. M. Kaleel (1899-1995), Government Minister — A642

2002, Oct. 18
1397 A642 4.50r green .70 .25

Uduppiddy American Mission College, 150th Anniv. A643

2002, Oct. 19 Litho. ***Perf. 13¾x14***
1398 A643 4.50r multi 1.50 1.50

Dr. Wijayananda Dahanayake (1902-97), Prime Minister — A644

2002, Oct. 22 Litho. ***Perf. 14x13¾***
1399 A644 4.50r brown .70 .25

Sri Lanka - Netherlands Relations, 400th Anniv. — A645

2002, Nov. 22 ***Perf. 13¾x14***
1400 A645 16.50r multi 1.50 1.00

Christmas — A646

Designs: 4.50r, Madonna and Child. 26r, Holy Family.

2002, Dec. 15 ***Perf. 13x13¼***
1401-1402 A646 Set of 2 2.00 1.60
1402a Souvenir sheet, #1401-1402 2.00 2.00

Sri Lanka - China Rubber and Rice Pact, 50th Anniv. A647

2002, Dec. 20 ***Perf. 13¾x14***
1403 A647 4.50r multi .75 .25

Kopay Christian College, 150th Anniv. A648

2002, Dec. 28
1404 A648 4.50r multi .70 .25

No. 925 Srchd.

2002 ? Litho. ***Perf. 12½x12***
1405 A392 25c on 5.75r multi — —

No. 1354 Surcharged

2002 ? Litho. ***Perf. 12½x13¼***
1406 A618 4.50r on 3.50r dk bl — —

Teachers' College, Maharagama, Cent. — A649

2003, Jan. 21 ***Perf. 13¾x14***
1407 A649 4.50r multi .70 .25

Holy Family Convent, Bambalapitiya, Cent. — A650

2003, Feb. 3 ***Perf. 14x13¾***
1408 A650 4.50r multi .80 .25

Drummer Type of 2001 and

No. 1359 Surcharged

Drummer from: 16.50r, Low country.

Perf. 13¼x12½
2003, Feb. 17 Litho.
1409 A618 50c on 5r org yel .50 .35
1410 A618 16.50r purple 1.30 .90

M. D. Banda (1914-74), Government Minister — A651

2003, Mar. 14 ***Perf. 13¾x14***
1411 A651 4.50r multi .90 .25

Balagalle Saraswati Maha Pirivena, Cent. A652

2003, Apr. 3
1412 A652 4.50r multi .90 .25

D. B. Welagedara, Politician — A653

2003, Apr. 22 ***Perf. 14x13¾***
1413 A653 4.50r multi .90 .25

Vesak Festival — A654

Designs: 2.50r, Paying obeisance to parents. 3r, Dhamma school. 4.50r, Going on alms round. 23r, Meditation.

2003, Apr. 26
1414-1417 A654 Set of 4 2.00 1.50
1417a Souvenir sheet, #1414-1417 2.75 2.75

Dagoba Construction Features — A655

Designs: 4.50r, Stupa. 16.50r, Guard stone, horiz. (58x28mm). 50r, Moonstone, horiz.

2003, Apr. 28 ***Perf. 13x13¼, 13¼x13***
1418-1420 A655 Set of 3 3.50 2.50
1420a Souvenir sheet, #1418-1420 4.00 4.00

Second World Hindu Conference, Colombo — A656

2003, May 2 ***Perf. 14x13¾***
1421 A656 4.50r multi .90 .25

International Nursing Day — A657

2003, May 12 ***Perf. 13¾x14***
1422 A657 4.50r multi .90 .25

Sirimavo Bandaranaike Memorial Exhibition Center — A658

2003, May 17 ***Perf. 13¼x12***
1423 A658 4.50r multi .90 .25

Al-Haj H. S. Ismail (1901-73), Parliament Speaker — A659

2003, May 18 *Perf. 14x13¾*

1424 A659 4.50r multi .65 .25

Board of Investment, 25th Anniv. — A660

2003, May 21 *Perf. 13¾x12*

1425 A660 4.50r multi .65 .25

World Biodiversity Day — A661

Designs: 4r, Pidurutalagal Mountain Range. 4.50r, Seven Maidens Mountain Range. 16.50r, Kirigalpoththa Mountain. 23r, Ritigala Mountain.

2003, May 22 *Perf. 13¾x12*

1426-1429 A661 Set of 4 3.50 1.75

Saralankara College, Gonapinuwala, Cent. — A662

2003, June 6 *Perf. 13¾x14*

1430 A662 4.50r multi .65 .25

A663

First Arab settlement, Beruwala: 4.50r, Masjidul Abrar. 23r, Masjidul Abrar, horiz. (57x22mm).

Perf. 14x13¾, 13¼x12 (23r)

2003, June 8

1431-1432 A663 Set of 2 1.50 1.10

Anti-narcotics Week — A664

2003, June 23 *Perf. 14x13¾*

1433 A664 4.50r multi .65 .25

Syamopali Maha Nikaya, 250th Anniv. A665

Designs: No. 1434, 4.50r, Asgiri Maha Viharaya. No. 1435, 4.50r, Malwathu Maha Viharaya.

2003, July 13 *Perf. 13¾x14*

1434-1435 A665 Set of 2 1.10 .75

Lanka Philex Intl. Stamp Exhibition, Colombo — A666

2003, July 31 *Perf. 13¼x12*

1436 A666 16.50r multi 1.25 .75

a. Souvenir sheet of 1 2.00 2.00

Dr. Ananda Tissa de Alwis, Government Minister — A667

2003, Aug. 21 *Perf. 13¾x14*

1437 A667 4.50r multi .70 .35

Panadura Controversy, 130th Anniv. — A668

2003, Aug. 24 *Perf. 14x13¾*

1438 A668 4.50r multi .70 .35

Venerable Haldanduwana Dhammarakkitha Thero — A669

2003, Sept. 3 **Litho.**

1439 A669 4.50r multi .70 .35

Ragama Walpola Poson Maha Perahara, 75th Anniv. A670

2003, Sept. 10 *Perf. 13¾x14*

1440 A670 4.50r multi .90 .45

M. H. M. Ashraff (1948-2000), Government Minister — A671

2003, Sept. 18 *Perf. 14x13¾*

1441 A671 4.50r multi .75 .35

Sisters of the Holy Angels, Cent. A672

2003, Sept. 27 *Perf. 13¾x14*

1442 A672 4.50r multi .75 .35

Birds — A673

No. 1443: a, Black-necked stork. b, Purple swamphen. c, Gray heron. d, White-throated kingfisher. e, Black-crowned night heron. f, Scarlet minivet. g, White-rumped shama. h, Malabar trogon. i, Asian paradise flycatcher. j, Little green bee-eater. k, Brown wood owl. l, Crested serpent eagle. m, Crested goshawk. n, Jungle owlet. o, Rufous-bellied eagle. p, Black-headed munia. q, Pompadour green pigeon. r, Plum-headed parakeet. s, Coppersmith barbet. t, Emerald dove. u, Blue-faced malkoha. v, Scimitar babbler. w, Painted francolin. x, Red-backed woodpecker. y, Malabar pied hornbill.

2003, Sept. 27 *Perf. 14x13¾*

1443 A673 4.50r Sheet of 25, #a-y 19.50 19.50

World Habitat Day — A674

2003, Oct. 6 *Perf. 13*

1444 A674 4.50r multi .70 .25

World Post Day — A675

2003, Oct. 9 *Perf. 14x13¾*

1445 A675 23r multi 2.25 1.50

Blue Sapphire — A676

2003, Oct. 21 *Perf. 12x13½*

1446 A676 4.50r multi 1.00 .25

See also No. 1497.

Ponificate of Pope John Paul II, 25th Anniv. — A677

2003, Oct. 22 *Perf. 13*

1447 A677 4.50r multi 1.75 .40

Deepavali Festival — A678

2003, Oct. 23

1448 A678 4.50r multi .70 .25

Pinnawala Elephant Orphanage A679

Designs: 4.50r, Two adult and two young elephants. 16.50r, Elephants and caretaker. 23r, Two adult elephants. 26r, Elephants in water.

2003, July 13 **Litho.** *Perf. 13½x13*

1449-1452 A679 Set of 4 5.50 3.50

1452a Souvenir sheet, #1449-1452 6.00 6.00

For surcharge, see No. 1576.

Waterfalls — A680

Designs: 2.50r, Ramboda. 4.50r, Saint Clair. 23r, Bopath Ella. 50r, Devon.

2003, Nov. 11 *Perf. 14x13¾*

1453-1456 A680 Set of 4 4.00 2.75

Ukku Banda Wanninayake (1905-73), Finance Minister — A681

2003, Nov. 23 *Perf. 13*

1457 A681 4.50r multi .65 .25

Christmas A682

Designs: 4.50r, Church. 16.50r, Shepherds and angel, vert.

2003, Nov. 30

1458-1459 A682 Set of 2 .80 .70

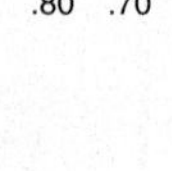

Pandith W. D. Amaradeva, Musician, 76th Birthday — A683

2003, Dec. 5

1460 A683 4.50r multi 1.00 .35

Gangarama Seemamalakaya — A684

2003, Dec. 20

1461 A684 4.50r multi .65 .25

Daham Pahana, Sri Pushparamaya, Malegoda — A685

2003, Dec. 31

1462 A685 4.50r multi .65 .25

Shazuliyathul Fassiya Tharika — A686

2004, Jan. 6

1463 A686 18r multi 1.00 .70

Chavakachcheri Hindu College, Cent. — A687

2004, Jan. 30 *Perf. 12x13½*

1464 A687 4.50r multi 1.00 .25

Royal-Thomian Cricket Match, 125th Anniv. — A688

2004, Jan. 30 *Perf. 13*

1465 A688 4.50r multi 1.10 .40

Pres. Dingiri Banda Wijetunga A689

2004, Feb. 15 **Litho.** *Perf. 13*

1466 A689 4.50r multi .75 .25

Planters Association of Ceylon, 150th Anniv. — A690

2004, Feb. 17 *Perf. 13¾x14*

1467 A690 4.50r multi .75 .40

Kalashuri Most Venerable Mapalagama Vipulasara Thero, Religious Leader — A691

Maithripala Senanayeke A692

Cathiravelu Sittampalam (1898-1964), First Posts and Telecommunications Minister — A693

M. G. Mendis, Communist Leader — A694

2004, Feb. 28 *Perf. 13x13¼*

1468 A691 3.50r multi .50 .25

1469 A692 3.50r multi .50 .25

1470 A693 3.50r multi .50 .25

1471 A694 3.50r multi .50 .25

Nos. 1468-1471 (4) 2.00 1.00

Nos. 1468-1471 are dated 2002. They were made available then, but not issued.

75th Ananda-Nalanda Cricket Match — A695

2004, Mar. 7 *Perf. 12x13¼*

1472 A695 4.50r multi 1.20 .50

St. Anthony's College, Kandy, 150th Anniv. — A696

2004, Mar. 12 *Perf. 13½x12*

1473 A696 4.50r multi .65 .25

Vesak Festival — A697

Various scenes of Sittara painting on wooden casket (with white borders on top and bottom): 4r, 4.50r, 16.50r, 20r.

26r, Scene of Sittara painting (no white borders).

2004, Apr. 30

1474-1477 A697 Set of 4 2.00 2.00

Souvenir Sheet

1478 A697 26r multi 1.50 1.50

Gongalegoda Banda (1809-49), Leader of 1848 Rebellion — A698

2004, May 22 *Perf. 14x13¾*

1479 A698 4.50r multi .65 .25

World Blood Donor Day — A699

2004, June 15 *Perf. 13*

1480 A699 4.50r multi .75 .25

2004 Summer Olympics, Athens — A700

Designs: 4.50r, Swimming. 16.50r, Women's track. 17r, Shooting. 20r, Men's track.

2004, Aug. 6 **Litho.**

1481-1484 A700 Set of 4 2.40 2.40

Sri Siddhartha Buddharakkhita, 18th Cent. Religious Leader — A701

2004, Aug. 16

1485 A701 4.50r brown .65 .25

Robert Gunawardena, Communist Leader — A702

2004, Aug. 23 *Perf. 14x13¾*

1486 A702 4.50r multi .65 .25

Pres. Junius Richard Jayewardene (1906-96) A703

2004, Sept. 27 *Perf. 13*
1487 A703 4.50r multi .65 .25

Intl. Day of Peace — A704

2004, Sept. 21
1488 A704 4.50r multi .65 .25

Sri Chandrarathna Manawasinghe, Writer — A705

2004, Oct. 6 *Perf. 12x13¼*
1489 A705 4.50r multi .65 .25

Government Service Buddhist Association, 50th Anniv. — A706

2004, Oct. 7 *Perf. 13*
1490 A706 4.50r multi .65 .25

World Post Day — A707

2004, Oct. 9 *Perf. 12x13½*
1491 A707 4.50r multi 1.00 .25

Raddelle Sri Pannaloka Anunayaka Thero, Religious Leader — A708

2004, Oct. 20 *Perf. 13*
1492 A708 4.50r multi .65 .25

Christmas A709

2004, Nov. 27 *Perf. 14x13¾*
1493 A709 5r multi .65 .25

Fathers Jacome Gonsalves and Edmond Peiris — A710

2004, Nov. 27 *Perf. 13¼x12*
1494 A710 20r multi .90 .90

Information and Communication Technology Week — A711

2004, Nov. 29 *Perf. 13¾x14*
1495 A711 5r multi .90 .25

A712

2004, Dec. 11 *Perf. 13½x14*
1496 A712 5r multi .65 .25

De Soysa Hospital for Women, Colombo, 125th Anniv.

Blue Sapphire Type of 2003

2004, Dec. 14 Litho. *Perf. 12x13½*
1497 A676 5r multi 1.50 .25

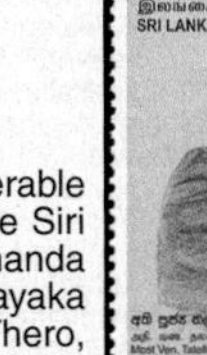

Most Venerable Talalle Siri Dhammananda Maha Nayaka Thero, Educator — A713

2005, Mar. 13 *Perf. 14x13¾*
1498 A713 5r multi .65 .25

Most Venerable Hammalawa Saddhatissa Nayaka Maha Thero (1914-90), Monk — A714

2005, Mar. 22
1499 A714 5r multi .65 .25

T. B. Tennakoon, Politician — A715

2005, Mar. 25
1500 A715 5r multi .65 .25

D. A. Rajapaksa (1905-67), Politician A716

2005, Mar. 25 *Perf. 13¾x14*
1501 A716 5r multi .65 .25

Vesak Festival — A717

Designs: 4.50r, Ambulatory meditation. 5r, Spiritual bliss through Buddhism. 10r, Meditation in standing posture. 50r, Sedentary meditation.

2005, May 12 *Perf. 14x13¾*
1502-1505 A717 Set of 4 3.00 3.00
1505a Sheet, #1502-1505 3.25 3.25

Compare with Type A723.

Rev. Marcelline Jayakody (1902-98) A718

2005, June 3 *Perf. 13*
1506 A718 20r multi 1.25 1.25

Rana Viru Day — A719

2005, June 7 *Perf. 14x13¾*
1507 A719 50r multi 1.50 1.50

Deshamanya M. A. Bakeer Markar (1917-96), Parliament Speaker — A720

2005, July 20
1508 A720 5r multi .60 .25

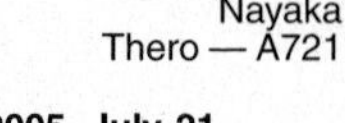

Most Venerable Matara Kithalagama Sri Seelalankara Nayaka Thero — A721

2005, July 21
1509 A721 25r multi .70 .70

South Asia Tourism Year — A722

2005, July 29 *Perf. 13*
1510 A722 100r multi 3.00 3.00

Kalutara Bodhi Trust A723

2005, Aug. 6 *Perf. 13¾x14*
1511 A723 5r multi .50 .25

Nos. 564, 815, 818, 937 and 1352 Surcharged

Methods and Perfs As Before

2005

1512	A206	50c on 10c #564	1.25	1.25
1513	A324	50c on 35c #815	1.25	1.25
1514	A618	50c on 2r #1352	1.25	1.25
1515	A399	50c on 5.75r #937	1.25	1.25
1516	A324	50c on 6r #818	1.25	1.25
		Nos. 1512-1516 (5)	6.25	6.25

Issued: No. 1514, 9/16; others, 3/21.

Postal Headquarters — A725

2005, Sept. 12 Litho. *Perf. 13½x14*
1518 A725 5r multi .40 .25

Ampitiya National Seminary A726

2005, Oct. 1
1519 A726 10r multi .40 .25

World Post Day A727

2005, Oct. 9

1520 A727 5r multi .40 .25

General Sir John Kotelawala Defense Academy, 25th Anniv. — A728

2005, Oct. 11 Litho. *Perf. 13*

1521 A728 5r multi .50 .25

Christmas A729

Cross of Blessed Joseph Vaz, Madonna and Child and: 5r, Angel. 30r, Star of Bethlehem.

2005, Dec. 3 Litho. *Perf. 13¾x14*

1522-1523 A729 Set of 2 1.10 1.10

1523a Souvenir sheet, #1522-1523 1.20 1.20

Admission to the UN, 50th Anniv. — A730

2005, Dec. 13 Litho. *Perf. 14x13½*

1524 A730 20r multi .90 .90

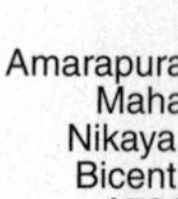

Amarapura Maha Nikaya, Bicent. A731

2005, Dec. 20 *Perf. 13½x14*

1525 A731 10r multi .50 .50

Ancient Sri Lanka — A732

Designs: 5r, Minhagalkanda and stone tools. 20r, Extinct animals in Ratnapura gem gravels and rhinoceros and hippopotamus bone fragments. 25r, Kuruwita, Batadombalena and human skull from Bellan-bandi Palassa. 30r, Agriculture on the Horton Plains, fossilized barley pollen grain.

2005, Dec. 21 *Perf. 13¼x12*

1526-1529 A732 Set of 4 2.75 2.75

Damage From Dec. 26, 2004 Tsunami A733

Designs: 5r, Damaged Kalmunai Post Office, vehicles. 20r, Train derailed near Telwatte. 30r, Giant wave breaking along coast. 33r, Lighthouse and tsunami wave.

2005, Dec. 26 Litho. *Perf. 13¾x14*

1530-1533 A733 Set of 4 1.75 1.75

1533a Souvenir sheet, #1530-1533 1.75 1.75

Animals of Wilpattu National Park — A734

Designs: 5r, Barking deer. 10r, White-bellied sea eagle. 20r, Sloth bear. 50r, Leopard.

2006, Jan. 4 Litho. *Perf. 13½x12*

1534 A734 5r multi	.60	.60
a. Souvenir sheet of 1	.60	.60
1535 A734 10r multi	.60	.60
a. Souvenir sheet of 1	.60	.60
1536 A734 20r multi	.95	.95
a. Souvenir sheet of 1	.95	.95
1537 A734 50r multi	2.40	2.40
a. Souvenir sheet of 1	2.40	2.40
Nos. 1534-1537 (4)	4.55	4.55

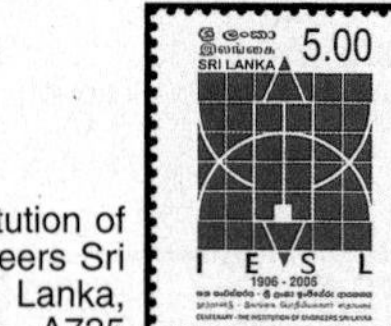

Institution of Engineers Sri Lanka, Cent. — A735

2006, Jan. 6 Litho. *Perf. 12x13¼*

1538 A735 5r black & blue .35 .25

Europa Stamps, 50th Anniv. — A736

Sri Lanka flag and: 100r, Ceylon #336. 500r, Ship, maps of Europe and Sri Lanka.

2006, Feb. 2 *Perf. 12¾x13¼*

1539-1540 A736 Set of 2 13.50 13.50

1540a Souvenir sheet, #1539-1540 13.50 13.50

Most Venerable Madithiyawala Vijithasena Anunayake Thero — A737

2006, Mar. 5 Litho. *Perf. 14x13¾*

1541 A737 17r multi .75 .75

100th Kingswood-Dharmaraja Cricket Match — A738

2006, Mar. 24 *Perf. 13¾x14*

1542 A738 4.50r multi .50 .50

Vesak — A739

No. 1543: a, Wall painting depicting a plea to the Master to descend from heaven, Tivamka Image House, Polonnaruva (1/50). b, Bas-relief of Queen Mahamaya on her way to visit her parents, Jetavana Vihara, Anuradhapura (2/50). c, Wall painting depicting birth of Prince Siddhartha, Shailabimbarama Vihara, Dodanduwa (3/50). d, Wall painting of royal teacher Asita visiting Prince Siddhartha, Purwarama Viharaya, Kataluva (4/50). e, Bas-relief of Great Renunciation, Girihandu Vihara, Ambalantota (5/50). f, Rock painting depicting defeat of evils by the Master, Hindagala Vihara, Hindagala (6/50). g, Rock painting depicting first sermon of Dhammachakka, Rangiri Dambulu Vihara, Dambulla (7/50). h, Wall painting depicting conversion of Alavaka, Sapugoda Vihara, Beruvala (8/50). i, Wall painting depicting funeral pyre of the Master, Veheragalla Samudragiri Vihara, Mirissa (9/50). j, Tapassu and Bhalluka arriving in Sri Lanka with relics of the Master, Girihandu Seya, Tiriyaya (10/50). k, Wall painting depicting perfection of generosity, Bodhirukkharama Vihara, Eluvapitiya (11/50). l, Rock painting depicting perfection of wisdom, Kaballelena Vihara, Wariyapola (12/50). m, Wall painting depicting perfection of reunification, Degaldoruva Vihara, Kandy (13/50). n, Wall painting depicting perfection of equanimity, Paramakanda Vihara, Anamaduwa (14/50). o, Wall painting depicting perfection of loving kindness, Sunandarama Vihara, Ambalangoda (15/50). p, Recitation of Chullahastpadopama Sutta by Arhat Mahinda, Stupa, Mihintale (16/50). q, Establishment of Buddhism in Sri Lanka, Rajagiri Lena, Mihintale (17/50). r, Sri Maha Bodhi entering city, Sri Maha Bodhi, Anuradhapura (18/50). s, Writing Dhamma on ola leaves, Alu Vihara, Matale (19/50). t, Arrival of tooth relic of the Master, Lankapattana, Trincomalee (20/50). u, Practice of aranyaka, Situlpavuva Vihara (21/50). v, Symbols of three traditions, Lovamahapaya, Abhayagiri Vihara, Vajra symbol and lotus (22/50). w, Emergence of katikavatas, Vatadage, Polonnaruva (23/50). x, Buddhist discourse between Sri Lanka and Southeast Asia, Tooth Relic Temple, Kandy (24/50). y, Translation of the Tripitaka into Sinhala, Buddhajayanti Vihara, Colombo (25/50). z, Vesak festival scene, Deepadutarama Vihara, Kotahena (26/50). aa, Serving of food to Buddhist clergy, Refectory at Abhayagiriya, Anuradhapura (27/50). ab, Chanting Paritta, Nishshanka Lata Mandapa, Polonnaruva (28/50). ac, Combination with village, temple tank and stupa, Tissamaharama Stupa (29/50). ad, Veneration of Bodhi tree, Bodhighara, Nillakgama (30/50). ae, Hatthikuchchi Vihara, Galgamuva, Padhanaghara, Anuradhapura (31/50). af, Ritual performance for tooth relic, Atadage, Polonnaruva (32/50). ag, Perahara, Subodharma Vihara, Karagampitiya (33/50). ah, Wall painting of a street market, Mulgirigala Vihara, local coin (34/50). ai, Sanctity of the temple, Namal Uyana, Ranava (35/50). aj, Ruvanvalisaya and Thuparama Stupas, Anuradhapura (36/50). ak, Kirivehera Stupa, Kataragama, Seruvila Stupa (37/50). al, Mahiyangana and Nagadipa Stupas, Jaffna (38/50). am, Kelaniya Stupa and Samantakuta (39/50). an, Mutiyangana Stupa, Badulla, and Deeghavapi Stupa (40/50). ao, Painted stupa, Hanguranketa Raja Maha Vihara, ancient stupas at Kandarodai, Jaffna (41/50). ap, Facade of Mihintale Stupa, bas-relief of Bahiravas (42/50). aq, Twin pond, Anuradhapura, Punkalasa lotus pond, Polonnaruva (43/50). ar, Moonstone, Mangul Maha Vihara, Lahugala (44/50). as, Bodhisattva Avalokiteshvara, Muhudumaha Vihara, Potuvil (45/50). at, Nalanda Gedige, Naula, Satmahal Prasada, Polonnaruva (46/50). au, Bas-relief of Vimana, Lankatilaka Vihara, Polonnaruva (47/50). av, Thuparama Image House, Polonnaruva, Tampita Vihara, Menikkadawara (48/50). aw, Wall painting depicting Buddhist cosmos, Omalpe Vihara, Kolonne (49/50). ax, Depiction of time in the motif of Makara, Madanvala Vihara, Hanguranketa (50/50).

2006, May 5 Litho. *Perf. 13¼x12*

1543	Sheet of 50	24.00	24.00
a.-j.	A739 2.50r Any single	.30	.30
k.-t.	A739 4.50r Any single	.35	.35
u.-ad.	A739 5r Any single	.35	.35
ae.-an.	A739 10r Any single	.55	.55
ao.-ax.	A739 17r Any single	.80	.80

Sinhala Bauddhaya Newspaper, Cent. — A740

2006, May 7 *Perf. 13¾x14*

1544 A740 5r multi .40 .25

Natl. Cadet Corps, 125th Anniv. — A741

2006, May 18 *Perf. 12x13¼*

1545 A741 2r multi .40 .25

Kotte Sri Kalyani Samagridharma Maha Sanga Sabha, 150th Anniv. — A742

2006, June 25 *Perf. 13¾x14*

1546 A742 4.50r multi .40 .25

Sri Lanka Ramanna Maha Nikaya — A743

2006, June 29 *Perf. 14x13¾*

1547 A743 4.50r multi .40 .25

Nos. 592, 1154, and 1353 Surcharged

Methods and Perfs As Before

2006

1548 A518 10r on 10.50r #1154	1.00	1.00
1549 A618 20r on 3r #1353	1.50	1.50
1550 A218 50r on 1.60r #592	3.50	3.50
Nos. 1548-1550 (3)	6.00	6.00

Size, location and style of surcharges vary.

St. Vincent Boys Home, Maggona, 125th Anniv. — A744

2006, July 15 Litho. ***Perf. 14x13¾***

1551 A744 10r multi .50 .50

Lakshman Kadiragamar (1932-2005), Foreign Minister — A745

2006, Aug. 10

1552 A745 10r multi .50 .50

St. John Dal Bastone Church, Talangama, 125th Anniv. — A746

2006, Aug. 13 ***Perf. 13¾x14***

1553 A746 5r multi .40 .25

St. John Ambulance, Cent. — A747

2006, Aug. 15

1554 A747 5r multi .50 .30

Tenth South Asian Games A748

Designs: 10r, High jump. 100r, Cycling.

2006, Aug. 17

1555-1556 A748 Set of 2 4.00 4.00

St. Joseph's Church, Wennappuwa, 125th Anniv. — A749

2006, Aug. 23

1557 A749 2r multi .35 .25

Senaka Bibile (1920-77), Pharmacologist A750

2006, Sept. 29 ***Perf. 12x13½***

1558 A750 10r multi .50 .50

World Children's Day A751

2006, Oct. 1 ***Perf. 13¾x14***

1559 A751 5r multi .35 .25

Flowers — A752

Designs: No. 1560, Indian laburnum. No. 1561, Sacred lotus. No. 1562, Foxtail orchid. No. 1563, Orange jessamine.

2006, Oct. 2 ***Perf. 14x13¾***

1560	A752	4.50r multi	.30	.30
1561	A752	4.50r multi	.30	.30
1562	A752	50r multi	1.25	1.25
a.		Miniature sheet of 8, 4 each #1560, 1562	9.00	9.00
1563	A752	50r multi	1.25	1.25
a.		Miniature sheet of 8, 4 each #1561, 1563	9.00	9.00
		Nos. 1560-1563 (4)	3.10	3.10

World Post Day A753

2006, Oct. 9 ***Perf. 13¾x14***

1564 A753 40r multi 1.50 1.50

Christmas A754

2006, Nov. 13 ***Perf. 14x13¾***

1565 A754 5r multi .35 .25

St. Anthony's Shrine, Wahakotte A755

2006, Nov. 13 ***Perf. 13¾x14***

1566 A755 20r multi .60 .60

Rugby in Sri Lanka, 125th Anniv. (in 2003) — A756

2006, Dec. 8 ***Perf. 13***

1567 A756 4.50r multi .75 .30

D. M. Rajapaksa, Politician — A757

2006, Dec. 14 ***Perf. 14x13¾***

1568 A757 5r multi .40 .25

Vee Bissakara Govijana Chaityaya, Ambuluwawa A758

Biodiversity Complex, Ambuluwawa — A759

2006, Dec. 18 ***Perf. 12x13½***

1569 A758 5r multi .40 .25

Perf. 13¾x14

1570 A759 25r multi .75 .75

Kande Viharaya A760

2007, Jan. 6 ***Perf. 13¾x14***

1571 A760 5r multi .40 .25

Ceylon Nos. 351, 352, 397, 403, and Sri Lanka Nos. 494, 890, 932, 1153, 1290, 1355, and 1452 Srchd.

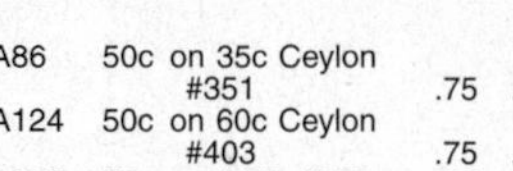

Methods and Perfs As Before

2007

1572	A86	50c on 35c Ceylon #351	.75	.75
1573	A124	50c on 60c Ceylon #403	.75	.75
1574	A397	50c on 5.75r #932	.75	.75
1575	A518	50c on 8.50r #1153	.75	.75
1576	A679	50c on 26r #1452	.75	.75
1577	A91	4.50r on 50c Ceylon #352	1.00	.75
1578	A122	4.50r on 50c Ceylon #397	1.00	.75
1579	A174	4.50r on 1.15r #494	1.00	.75
1580	A373	4.50r on 5.75r #890	1.00	.75
1581	A576	4.50r on 22r #1290	1.00	.75
1582	A618	5r on 4r #1355	1.00	.75
		Nos. 1572-1582 (11)	9.75	8.25

Issued: Nos. 1572-1576, 1582, 2/13; Nos. 1577-1581, 1/29.

Diplomatic Relations Between Sri Lanka and People's Republic of China, 50th Anniv. — A761

2007, Feb. 7 Litho. ***Perf. 13¼x12***

1583 A761 50r multi 2.50 2.50

ICC Cricket World Cup — A762

Flags of participating nations, Sri Lanka Cricket emblem and: 5r, Batsman and players. 50r, Players, Sri Lanka flag.

2007, Feb. 23 ***Perf. 13***

1584-1585 A762 Set of 2 1.50 1.50

I. M. R. A. Iriyagolle (1907-73), Education and Cultural Affairs Minister — A763

2007, Mar. 20 Litho. ***Perf. 14x13¾***

1586 A763 5r multi .40 .30

First Ceylon Postage Stamps, 150th Anniv. A764

Designs: 5r, Steamship, Ceylon #2. 10r, Mail runner, Ceylon #6, 10, 11. 20r, Mail canoe, Ceylon #3, 4. 45r, Mail coach, Ceylon #15.

2007, Apr. 1 Litho. ***Perf. 13¾x14***

1587-1590 A764 Set of 4 2.25 2.25

1590a Souvenir sheet, #1587-1590 2.50 2.50

Wall Paintings of Thelapatta Jataka — A765

No. 1591, 5r: a, House at right. b, House at center.

No. 1592, 20r: a, Flag bearer at right. b, King on throne at right.

2007, Apr. 20 Litho. *Perf. 13¾x14*
Horiz. Pairs, #a-b

1591-1592 A765 Set of 2 3.00 3.00
1592c Souvenir sheet, #1591-1592, perf. 13¾x13¼ 3.00 3.00

Sri Lankan Cricket Team, Runners-up in 2007 ICC Cricket World Cup — A766

Designs: No. 1593, 15r, Team, stadium. No. 1594, 15r, Players on field, faces of players.

2007, Apr. 30 *Perf. 13¾x14*
1593-1594 A766 Set of 2 2.75 2.75

Shells A767

Designs: 5r, Textile cone. 12r, Aquatile hairy triton. 15r, Rose-branched murex. 45r, Trapezium horse conch.

2007, May 22 Litho. *Perf. 13¾x14*
1595-1598 A767 Set of 4 5.50 5.50
1598a Souvenir sheet, #1595-1598 5.75 5.75

Scouting, Cent. — A768

2007, May 26 *Perf. 13½x12*
1599 A768 5r multi .40 .25

Sri Sangamitta Balika Maha Vidyalaya, Cent. — A769

2007, June 17 *Perf. 12x13¼*
1600 A769 5r multi .40 .25

Sri Lanka-Japan Friendship Society, 50th Anniv. — A770

2007, June 26 Litho. *Perf. 13¼x12*
1601 A770 15r multi 1.10 1.10

Ceylon Baithulmal Fund, 50th Anniv. — A771

2007, July 3 Litho. *Perf. 12x13¼*
1602 A771 5r multi .40 .25

Prisons Day — A772

2007, July 16 *Perf. 14x13¾*
1603 A772 5r multi .45 .25

Jabbar Central College, Galagedara, 104th Anniv. — A773

2007, July 27 *Perf. 13¼x12*
1604 A773 5r multi .40 .25

First Sri Lankan Buddhist Mission to Germany, 50th Anniv. — A774

2007, Aug. 22 *Perf. 13*
1605 A774 5r multi .40 .25

Diplomatic Relations Between Sri Lanka and Nepal, 50th Anniv. — A775

2007, Sept. 1 Litho. *Perf. 13*
1606 A775 15r multi 1.10 1.10

Shrine of Our Lady of Matara, Cent. A776

2007, Sept. 9 Litho. *Perf. 13*
1607 A776 5r multi .40 .25

World Tourism Day A777

2007, Sept. 27
1608 A777 5r multi .45 .25

Lions International in Sri Lanka, 50th Anniv. — A778

2007, Oct. 6 *Perf. 12x13¼*
1609 A778 5r multi .45 .25

World Post Day — A779

2007, Oct. 9 *Perf. 13¼x12*
1610 A779 5r multi .60 .25

Constellations — A780

2007, Oct. 9 Litho. *Perf. 13x12¾*
Size: 20x25mm

1611 A780 50c Aries .35 .35
1612 A780 1r Taurus .35 .35
1613 A780 2r Gemini .35 .35
1614 A780 3r Cancer .35 .35
1615 A780 4r Leo .35 .35
1616 A780 4.50r Virgo .35 .35
1617 A780 5r Libra .35 .35
a. Perf. 13x12¾ syncopated —
1618 A780 10r Scorpius .35 .35
1619 A780 12r Sagittarius .35 .35
1620 A780 15r Capricornus .40 .40
a. Perf. 13x12¾ syncopated —
1621 A780 20r Aquarius .45 .45
1622 A780 25r Pisces .60 .60
a. Sheet of 12, #1611-1622 2.50 2.50

Size: 25x30mm
Perf. 12x13½

1623 A780 30r Centaurus .70 .70
1624 A780 35r Ursa Major .80 .80
1625 A780 40r Ophiuchus .90 .90
1626 A780 45r Orion 1.05 1.05
a. Sheet of 4, #1623-1626 3.75 3.75
Nos. 1611-1626 (16) 8.05 8.05

For surcharge, see No. 2018.

Ten additional stamps were issued with syncopated perfs. The editors would like to examine any examples.

National Farmer's Day — A781

2007, Oct. 16 Litho. *Perf. 13*
1627 A781 5r multi .40 .25

Fauna of Udawalawe National Park A782

Designs: 5r, Water buffalos. 15r, Herd of elephants. 40r, Ruddy mongoose. 45r, Common langurs.

2007, Oct. 31 *Perf. 13*
1628-1631 A782 Set of 4 3.00 3.00
1630a Souvenir sheet, #1629-1630, perf. 13¾x14 3.00 3.00
1631a Souvenir sheet, #1628, 1631, perf. 13¾x14 3.00 3.00

Leslie Goonewardene (1909-83), Governmental Minister — A783

2007, Nov. 6 Litho. *Perf. 13*
1632 A783 5r multi .70 .70

Commonwealth Games Federation General Assembly, Colombo — A784

Emblem and: 5r, Man blowing into conch shell. 45r, Winged figures.

2007, Nov. 7 Litho. *Perf. 13*
1633-1634 A784 Set of 2 1.50 1.50

St. Henry's College, Ilavalai, Cent. A785

2007, Nov. 10
1635 A785 5r multi .40 .25

Christmas A786

2007, Nov. 18
1636 A786 5r multi .40 .25

St. James' Church, Mutwal A787

2007, Nov. 18
1637 A787 30r multi .75 .75

Muthiah Muralidaran, Cricket Player — A788

2007, Dec. 3 *Perf. 13¾*
Granite Paper

1638 A788 5r multi .50 .30
a. Sheet of 12 + 3 labels 6.00 6.00

Values are for stamps with surrounding selvage.

Children's Stories — A789

No. 1639 — Scenes from the Race Between the Hare and Tortoise: a, Hare and tortoise before race (green panels). b, Hare sleeping (pink panels). c, Hare leaping (blue panels).

2007, Dec. 9 ***Perf. 12x13¼***
1639 A789 Horiz. strip of 3 .75 .75
a.-c. 5r Any single .25 .25

St. Mary's Church, Maggona, 150th Anniv. A790

2007, Dec. 9 ***Perf. 13***
1640 A790 5r multi .40 .25

Intl. Anti-Corruption Day — A791

2007, Dec. 10 **Litho.**
Granite Paper
1641 A791 5r multi .40 .25

Global Knowledge to the Village — A792

2008, Jan. 4 ***Perf. 13¼x12***
1642 A792 5r multi .45 .25

Opening of 500th Nenasala Center.

Most Venerable Halgasthota Sri Devananda Mahanayaka Thero — A793

2008, Jan. 30 ***Perf. 14x13¾***
1643 A793 5r multi .40 .25

Independence, 60th Anniv. — A794

2008, Feb. 4 ***Perf. 12x13¼***
1644 A794 5r multi .40 .25

Deshamanya N. U. Jayawardena (1908-2002), Governor of Central Bank — A795

2008, Feb. 25 ***Perf. 13½x14***
1645 A795 5r multi .40 .25

7th Commonwealth Youth Ministers Meeting, Colombo — A796

Perf. 13¼x12¾ Syncopated
2008, Apr. 26
1646 A796 5r multi .40 .25

St. Mary's Convent, Matara, Cent. A797

Perf. 12¾x13¼ Syncopated
2008, Apr. 29
1647 A797 5r multi .40 .25

Ancient Sri Lanka — A798

Designs: 5r, Megalithic cist, bead necklace, Ibbankatuwa, 600-400 B.C. 10r, Basawakkulama Veva (reservoir), 3rd cent. B.C. 12r, Inscribed Vallipuram gold plate, 1st cent. 15r, Alakolavela iron furnace, 1st-2nd cent. 30r, Gajalakshmi coin, 1st cent. B.C.-A.D. 4th cent., punch mark coin, 3rd cent. B.C.-A.D. 4th cent. 40r, Sigiri painting, 5th cent.

2008, Apr. 30 ***Perf. 12x13¼***
1648-1653 A798 Set of 6 3.50 3.50

Vesak A799

Various Dahamsonda Jataka wall paintings from Reswehere Raja Maha Vihara, Kudakatnoruwa: 4.50r, 5r, 15r, 40r.

2008, May 9 ***Perf. 13¾x14***
1654-1657 A799 Set of 4 2.50 2.50
1657a Souvenir sheet, #1654-1657, perf. 13¾x13½ 3.00 3.00

2008 Summer Olympics, Beijing — A800

Designs: 5r, Shooting. 15r, Javelin. 40r, Boxing. 45r, Running.

2008, July 23 ***Perf. 12¾x13***
1658-1661 A800 Set of 4 3.25 3.25
1658a Tete-beche pair .40 .40
1659a Tete-beche pair 1.00 1.00
1660a Tete-beche pair 2.50 2.50
1661a Tete-beche pair 3.00 3.00

15th South Asian Association for Regional Cooperation Summit, Colombo — A801

2008, Aug. 2 ***Perf. 13***
Granite Paper
1662 A801 15r multi .75 .75

Takiko Yoshida, Philantropist A802

Perf. 13¼x12¾ Syncopated
2008, Aug. 16
1663 A802 5r multi .45 .25

Employees' Provident Fund, 50th Anniv. — A803

2008, Sept. 11 ***Perf. 14x13¾***
1664 A803 5r multi .45 .25

Ancient Sri Lanka — A804

Designs: 5r, Gold ingot, coin and mold, 8th-10th cents. 10r, Medirigiriya Vatadage ruins and conjectural drawing of structure, 7th cent. 15r, Urinal stone from Western monastery, Anuradhapura, cross section of sanitary system, 7th-8th cents. 20r, Jewelry, 6th-9th cents. 30r, Bodhisattva Vajrapani, Avalokithesvara, and sculpture of royal family, Isurumuniya, 8th-9th cents.

2008, Sept. 16 ***Perf. 13¼x12***
1665-1669 A804 Set of 5 3.00 3.00

Lion — A805

Perf. 12½ Syncopated
2008, Sept. 24 **Photo. & Engr.**
Granite Paper
Color of Denomination

1670	A805	50r red violet	1.05	1.05
1671	A805	70r blue	1.60	1.60
1672	A805	100r olive green	2.10	2.10
1673	A805	500r orange	10.00	10.00
1674	A805	1000r purple	21.00	21.00
1675	A805	2000r blue green	42.50	42.50
		Nos. 1670-1675 (6)	78.25	78.25

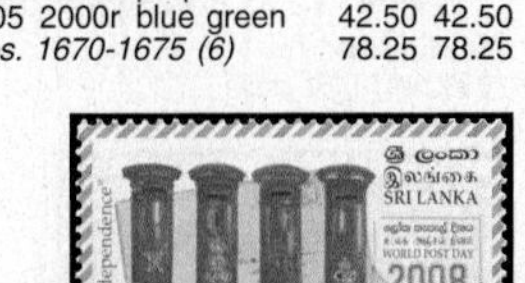

World Post Day A806

2008, Oct. 9 **Litho.** ***Perf. 13½x14***
1676 A806 5r multi .45 .25

Dutch Burgher Union of Ceylon, Cent. A807

2008, Oct. 22
1677 A807 5r multi .45 .25

Anton Jayasuriya (1930-2005), Acupuncturist A808

Perf. 13¼x12¾ Syncopated
2008, Nov. 7
1678 A808 5r multi .45 .25

Pieter Keuneman (1917-97), Politician — A809

2008, Dec. 1
1679 A809 5r multi .45 .25

The Two Men and the Bear — A810

Perf. 12¾x13¼ Syncopated
2008, Dec. 5
1680 A810 5r multi .60 .25

Most Venerable Weweldeniye Medhalankara Mahanayake Mahathero A811

Perf. 13¼x12¾ Syncopated
2008, Dec. 7
1681 A811 5r multi .45 .25

Christmas A812

Perf. 12¾x13¼ Syncopated
2008, Dec. 9
1682 A812 5r multi .45 .25

St. Mary's Cathedral, Kaluwella A813

Perf. 13¼x12¾ Syncopated
2008, Dec. 9
1683 A813 30r multi 1.00 1.00

Universal Declaration of Human Rights, 60th Anniv. A814

2008, Dec. 10 ***Perf. 13¾x14***
1684 A814 5r multi .45 .25

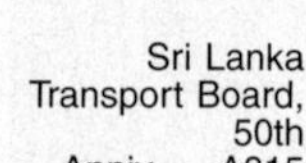
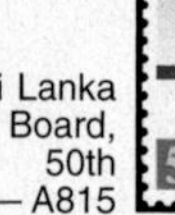
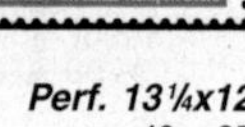

Sri Lanka Transport Board, 50th Anniv. — A815

2008, Dec. 30 ***Perf. 13¼x12***
1685 A815 5r multi .40 .25

Madu Ganga Wetlands A816

Designs: 5r, Lumnitzera littorea flowers, river. 25r, Mangroves and river.

2009, Feb. 2 Litho. ***Perf. 13¾x14***
1686-1687 A816 Set of 2 .80 .80

Year of English and Information Technology A817

2009, Feb. 13 ***Perf. 14x13¾***
1688 A817 5r multi .40 .25

University of Sri Jayewardenepura, Nugegoda, 50th Anniv. — A818

2009, Feb. 18 ***Perf. 13¾x14***
1689 A818 5r multi .40 .25

F. R. Jayasuriya (1909-84), Economics Professor at Kelaniya University — A819

2009, Feb. 25 ***Perf. 14x13¾***
1690 A819 5r multi .40 .25

A. P. de Zoysa (1890-1968), Buddhist Scholar — A820

2009, Mar. 5 ***Perf. 13¾x14***
1691 A820 5r multi .40 .25

Moors Sports Club (Cricket Team), Cent. A821

Perf. 12¾x13¼ Syncopated
2009, Mar. 5
1692 A821 5r multi .40 .25

Sri Lanka Railway Running Shed, Dematagoda, Cent. — A822

2009, Mar. 9 **Litho.**
1693 A822 5r multi .40 .25

Mahmoud Shamsuddeen Kariapper, Politician — A823

2009, Mar. 13 ***Perf. 12x13¼***
1694 A823 5r multi .40 .25

University of Vocational Technology A824

Perf. 13¼x12¾ Syncopated
2009, Mar. 31
1695 A824 5r multi .40 .25

Natural Rubber Research and Development in Sri Lanka, Cent. — A825

Perf. 12¾x13¼ Syncopated
2009, Apr. 2
1696 A825 5r multi .40 .25

Jeyaraj Fernandopulle (1953-2008), Politician — A826

Perf. 13¼x12¾ Syncopated
2009, Apr. 7
1697 A826 5r multi .40 .25

Leprosy Hospital, Hendala, 300th Anniv. (in 2008) A827

2009, Apr. 23 ***Perf. 13¾x14***
1698 A827 5r multi .40 .25

Sri Sumangala College, Panadura, Cent. A828

Perf. 12¾x13¼ Syncopated
2009, Apr. 23
1699 A828 5r multi .40 .25

Handupelpola Sri Punnaratana Nayaka Maha Thero, Politician — A829

Perf. 13¼x12¾ Syncopated
2009, May 2
1700 A829 5r multi .40 .25

Most Venerable Welithara Sri Gnanawimala Tissa Mahanayake Thero (1766-1833), Religious Leader — A830

2009, May 5
1701 A830 5r multi .40 .25

Vesak Festival A831

Designs 4r, Visit to the temple. 5r, Meditation.

2009, May 5 ***Perf. 13¾x14***
1702 A831 4r multi .45 .45

Perf. 12¾x13¼ Syncopated
1703 A831 5r multi .55 .55

Nimal S. de Silva, President of 2009-10 World Health Assembly A832

2009, June 8 ***Perf. 13¾x14***
1704 A832 5r multi .40 .25

Polonnaruwa Era — A833

Designs: 5r, Galpotha inscription of King Nissankamalla, obverse and reverse of coin of Queen Leelawathi. 10r, Siva Temple and adornments.15r, Parakrama Samudra Reservoir and statue of King Parakramabahu or of a sage. 25r, Palace of King Parakramabahu and Audience Hall of King Nissankamalla. 30r, Ancient hospital, medical trough, surgical instrument and grinding stone. 40r, Scupltures of Siva, Uma, and Saiva Saint Karaikkal Ammaiyar.

Perf. 12¾x13¼ Syncopated

2009, June 23
1705-1710 A833 Set of 6 3.25 3.25

Mahmood Hasarath, Educator — A834

2009, July 25 ***Perf. 14x13¾***
1711 A834 5r slate blue .40 .25

Hameed Al Husseinie College Colombo, 125th Anniv. A835

2009, July 30 ***Perf. 13¾x14***
1712 A835 5r multi .40 .25

University of Kelaniya, 50th Anniv. — A836

2009, July 31 ***Perf. 13¼x12***
1713 A836 5r multi .40 .25

Bank of Ceylon, 70th Anniv. — A837

2009, Aug. 3 ***Perf. 14x13¾***
1714 A837 5r multi .40 .25

Retirement of Colombo Archbishop Oswald Gomis — A838

2009, Aug. 10 **Litho.**
1715 A838 15r multi .50 .50

Sri Lanka Customs, 200th Anniv. A839

Perf. 12¾x13¼ Syncopated

2009, Aug. 25
1716 A839 15r multi .70 .70

Sree Narayana Gurudev (1856-1924), Religious Leader — A840

2009, Sept. 4 ***Perf. 14x13¾***
1717 A840 5r multi .40 .25

Sivali Central College, Ratnapura, Cent. — A841

2009, Sept. 25 ***Perf. 13¼x12***
1718 A841 15r multi .60 .60

World Post Day — A842

2009, Oct. 9 ***Perf. 14x13¾***
1719 A842 15r multi .80 .80

Sri Lanka Army, 60th Anniv. A843

2009, Oct. 10 ***Perf. 13***
1720 A843 15r multi .70 .70

Humane Eradication of Rabies — A844

2009, Nov. 5 ***Perf. 14x13¾***
1721 A844 15r multi .70 .70

A845

Christmas A846

2009, Nov. 8 ***Perf. 14x13¾***
1722 A845 5r multi .35 .25
a. Souvenir sheet of 2 .50 .50

Perf. 13¾x14

1723 A846 15r multi .65 .65
a. Souvenir sheet of 2 1.00 1.00

No. 1722a sold for 20r; No. 1723a for 40r.

Diplomatic Relations Between Sri Lanka and Cuba, 50th Anniv. — A847

2009, Nov. 9 ***Perf. 12x13¼***
1724 A847 5r multi .55 .25

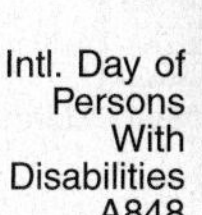
Intl. Day of Persons With Disabilities A848

2009, Dec. 3 ***Perf. 13¾x14***
1725 A848 10r multi .50 .50

Voet Lights Society, 110th Anniv. A849

2009, Dec. 4
1726 A849 15r multi .60 .60

Peduru Hewage William de Silva (1908-88), Politician — A850

Perf. 13¼x12¾ Syncopated

2009, Dec. 15 **Litho.**
1727 A850 10r multi .50 .50

Dr. Hudson Silva (1929-99), Founder of Intl. Eye Bank — A851

2009, Dec. 21 ***Perf. 14x13¾***
1728 A851 10r multi .50 .50

D. M. Dasanayake (1953-2008), Politician — A852

2010, Jan. 8 ***Perf. 14x13¾***
1729 A852 10r multi .50 .50

Thurstan College, Colombo, 60th Anniv. — A853

2010, Jan. 11 ***Perf. 13¼x12***
1730 A853 10r multi .50 .50

Ceylon-German Technical Training Institute, 50th Anniv. — A855

2010, Feb. 15 **Litho.** ***Perf. 13¾x14***
1733 A855 10r multi .50 .50

Government Officers' Benefit Association, Cent. (in 2009) — A856

2010, Feb. 24
1734 A856 5r multi .35 .25

Rotary International in Sri Lanka, 80th Anniv. (in 2009) — A857

2010, Mar. 18 ***Perf. 14x13¾***
1735 A857 10r multi .50 .50

M. J. C. Fernando (1885-1939), Buddhist Leader — A858

2010, Mar. 27 ***Perf. 13¾x14***
1736 A858 10r multi .50 .50

Buddhist Flag, 125th Anniv. — A859

2010, Apr. 28 ***Perf. 14x13¾***
1737 A859 5r multi .35 .25

Vesak Festival — A860

Designs: 4r, Arrival of Lord Buddha at Mahiyanganaya. 5r, Mahiyangana Stupa. 10r, Mirisawetiya Stupa, Anuradhapura, horiz. 30r, Jetawana Stupa, Anuradhapura, horiz.

2010, May 24 ***Perf. 14x13¾, 13¾x14***
1738-1741 A860 Set of 4 2.00 2.00
1741a Souvenir sheet of 4, #1738-1741 2.00 2.00

St. Anthony's Shrine, Kochchikade, 175th Anniv. — A861

2010, June 12 ***Perf. 14x13¾***
1742 A861 5r multi .35 .25

Sri Kalyaniwansa Nikaya Buddhist Order, 200th Anniv. — A862

2010, June 17 ***Perf. 13¾x14***
1743 A862 10r multi .50 .50

Mahajana College, Tellippalai, Cent. A863

2010, June 18 **Litho.**
1744 A863 10r multi .50 .50

Pepiliyana Sunethra Mahadevi Piriven Rajamaha Viharaya, 600th Anniv. — A864

2010, June 20 ***Perf. 13¼x12***
1745 A864 5r multi .35 .25

Victory and Peace — A865

2010, July 6 ***Perf. 14x13¾***
1746 A865 5r multi .35 .25

Postal History — A866

No. 1747: a, National Postal Museum. b, Philatelic Exhibition Center.

2010, July 6 ***Perf. 13¾x14***
1747 A866 5r Horiz. pair, #a-b .50 .50

A souvenir sheet containing Nos. 1747a-1747b sold for 60r.

Anuradhapura Teaching Hospital, 50th Anniv. — A867

2010, July 10
1748 A867 5r multi .35 .25

Royal College, Colombo, 175th Anniv. A868

2010, July 16 **Litho.**
1749 A868 10r multi .50 .50

Kokuvil Hindu College, Cent. A869

2010, July 22
1750 A869 10r multi .50 .50

M. P. De Zoysa, Politician, Cent. of Birth — A870

2010, Aug. 9 ***Perf. 14x13¾***
1751 A870 10r multi .50 .50

2010 Youth Olympics, Singapore — A871

Perf. 12¾x13¼ Syncopated
2010, Aug. 12
1752 A871 10r multi .50 .50

World Indigenous People's Day — A872

No. 1753: a, Indigenous people. b, Art by indigenous people.

2010, Aug. 25 ***Perf. 13¾x14***
1753 A872 5r Horiz. pair, #a-b .50 .50

A souvenir sheet containing Nos. 1753a-1753b sold for 60r.

Central Bank of Sri Lanka, 60th Anniv. — A873

2010, Aug. 27 ***Perf. 13¼x12***
1754 A873 10r multi .50 .50

Beaches — A874

Designs: 15r, Pasikudah Beach. 25r, Trincomalee Beach. 40r, Arugam Bay Beach.

2010, Sept. 7 ***Perf. 13¼***
1755-1757 A874 Set of 3 2.50 2.50

Souvenir sheets of 1 of Nos. 1755-1757 each sold for 100r.

Horton Plains National Park — A875

Designs: 5r, Sri Lanka whistling thrush. 15r, Sambur, horiz. 25r, Rhinohorn lizard, horiz. 40r, Purple-faced leaf monkey.

2010, Sept. 7 ***Perf. 13¼***
1758-1761 A875 Set of 4 3.00 3.00

Four souvenir sheets each containing one of Nos. 1758 -1761 sold for 15r, 25r, 35r and 50r, respectively.

University of Peradeniya Faculty of Engineering, 60th Anniv. — A876

2010, Sept. 9 **Litho.** ***Perf. 13¾x14***
1762 A876 15r multi .60 .60

Vienna Convention for Ozone Layer Protection, 25th Anniv. — A877

2010, Sept. 16 ***Perf. 14x13¾***
1763 A877 5r multi .35 .25

St. Michael's Church, Koralawella, 150th Anniv. — A878

2010, Sept. 29
1764 A878 5r multi .35 .25

World Children's Day — A879

2010, Oct. 3 ***Perf. 13***
1765 A879 5r multi .35 .25

Children's Story, "The Story of How the Tortoise Flew" — A880

2010, Oct. 3 ***Perf. 13¾x14***
1766 A880 5r multi .35 .25

World Post Day A881

2010, Oct. 9 **Litho.**
1767 A881 5r multi .35 .25

Rankot Viharaya, Panadura, 200th Anniv. A882

2010, Oct. 10
1768 A882 5r multi .35 .25

Diocese of Colombo Diocesan Council, 125th Anniv. A883

2010, Oct. 14
1769 A883 5r multi .35 .25

Louis Braille (1809-52), Educator of the Blind A884

2010, Oct. 15
1770 A884 5r multi .35 .25

World Fellowship of Buddhists, 60th Anniv. — A885

2010, Nov. 14 **Litho.** ***Perf. 13½x12***
1771 A885 5r multi .25 .25

Magam Ruhunupura Rajapaksa Port — A886

2010, Nov. 18 ***Perf. 13¾x14***
1772 A886 5r multi .25 .25

Christmas A887

Designs: 5r, People around Christmas tree. 15r, St. Mary's Church, Kegalle.

2010, Nov. 28
1773-1774 A887 Set of 2 .35 .35
1774a Souvenir sheet of 2, #1773-1774 1.00 1.00

No. 1774a sold for 35r.

Sri Lanka Navy, 60th Anniv. A888

2010, Dec. 9 ***Perf. 13***
1775 A888 5r multi .40 .40

Holy Emmanuel Church, Moratuwa, 150th Anniv. — A889

2010, Dec. 27 ***Perf. 14x13¾***
1776 A889 5r multi .40 .40

Labugama Reservoir, 125th Anniv. — A890

2011, Jan. 18 ***Perf. 13½x12***
1777 A890 5r multi .40 .40

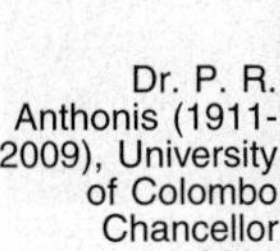

Dr. P. R. Anthonis (1911-2009), University of Colombo Chancellor A891

2011, Jan. 21 ***Perf. 14x13¾***
1778 A891 5r multi .40 .40

Intl. Year of Chemistry A892

2011, Jan. 30 ***Perf. 12x13½***
1779 A892 5r multi .40 .40

Trains A893

No. 1780: a, Viceroy Special steam locomotive BB 240. b, Viceroy Special locomotive B2 213. c, Sentinel Camel steam rail car V2 331. d, Narrow gauge steam locomotive JI 220.
45r, Viceroy Special steam train B1 251.

Perf. 12¾x13½ Syncopated
2011, Feb. 2 **Granite Paper**
1780 Horiz. strip of 4 .75 .75
a.-d. A893 5r Any single .25 .25

Souvenir Sheet
Perf. 13¾x14
1781 A893 45r multi 2.50 2.50

Viceroy Special steam train, 25th anniv. No. 1781 contains one 123x30mm stamp and sold for 60r.

St. Mary's Church, Dehiwala, 175th Anniv. A894

2011, Feb. 6 ***Perf. 13¾x14***
1782 A894 5r multi .40 .40

Southlands College, Galle, 125th Anniv. — A895

2011, Feb. 18 ***Perf. 13½x12***
1783 A895 5r multi .40 .40

Sri Lanka Air Force, 60th Anniv. A896

2011, Mar. 2 ***Perf. 13¾x14***
1784 A896 5r multi .40 .40

No. 1389A Surcharged

Method and Perf As Before
2011, Apr. 1
1785 A618 15r on 4.50r #1389A .30 .30

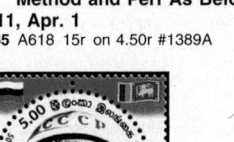

First Man in Space, 50th Anniv. A897

2011, Apr. 26 **Litho.** ***Perf. 13¾***
1787 A897 5r multi .40 .40

Values are for stamp with surrounding selvage.

Sambuddhatva Jayanthi (Enlightenment of Buddha) Festival, 2600th Anniv. — A898

No. 1788 — Inscriptions at bottom: a, Buddhism is a universal doctrine. b, Let us practice Buddhist principles. c, Let us take care of our parents and respect them. d, Let us help the sick. e, Person who practices Buddhism illuminates the entire world. f, Let us build an antinarcotic society.

2011, Apr. 29 ***Perf. 13½x12***
Granite Paper
1788 A898 5r Block of 6, #a-f 1.00 1.00

Rabindranath Tagore (1861-1941), Poet — A899

2011, May 7 ***Perf. 14x13¾***
1789 A899 5r multi .40 .40

Vesak Festival — A900

No. 1790 — Map of India and Sri Lanka, Sambuddhatva Jayanthi Festival 2600th anniversary emblem and Buddhist temples at: a, Lumbini, Nepal. b, Buddhagaya, India. c, Baranesa Isipathanarama, India. d, Kusinara, India.

2011, May 14 ***Perf. 14x13¾***
1790 A900 5r Block of 4, #a-d — —
e. Souvenir sheet, #1790a-1790d — —

No. 1790e sold for 35r.

Bridges — A901

No. 1791: a, Ancient stone bridge, Mahakanadarawa. b, Suspension bridge, Peradeniya.
No. 1792: a, Wooden bridge, Bogoda. b, Steel arch bridge, Ruwanwella.

2011, May 27 ***Perf. 13½x12***
1791 A901 10r Vert. pair, #a-b .80 .80
1792 A901 15r Vert. pair, #a-b 1.10 1.10
c. Souvenir sheet of 2, #1791a, 1792a, perf. 13½ 1.50 1.50
d. Souvenir sheet of 2, #1791b, 1792b, perf. 13½ 1.50 1.50

Nos. 1792c and 1792d each sold for 40r.

People's Bank, 50th Anniv. A902

Perf. 12¾x13½ Syncopated
2011, July 1
1793 A902 5r multi .40 .40

Radampala Sri Sumangala Central College, Cent. — A903

2011, July 15 ***Perf. 13¾x14***
1794 A903 5r multi .40 .40

Non-aligned Movement, 50th Anniv. — A904

Perf. 13½x12¾ Syncopated
2011, July 21
1795 A904 5r multi .40 .40

World Tourism Day A905

Designs: No. 1796, 5r, Buddhist stupa ("Heritage" at left). No. 1797, 5r, Sigiriya Rock ("Heritage" at right). No. 1798, 5r, Dancers and drummers. No. 1799, 5r, Sri Lankan women and flag. No. 1800, 15r, Woman bathing under floating flowers. No. 1801, 15r, Waterfall. 30r, Elephants. 35r, Leopard. 40r, Sailboat near shore. 45r, Whitewater rafters.

2011, Sept. 27 **Litho.** ***Perf. 13***
1796-1805 A905 Set of 10 5.00 5.00
1805a Souvenir sheet of 10, #1796-1805, + 2 central labels 5.00 5.00

World Children's Day — A906

Perf. 13½x12¾ Syncopated
2011, Oct. 1
1806 A906 5r multi .40 .40

World Post Day A907

Perf. 12¾x13½ Syncopated
2011, Oct. 9
1807 A907 5r multi .40 .40

First South Asian Beach Games, Hambantota — A908

2011, Oct. 11 ***Perf. 13¾x14***
1808 A908 5r multi .40 .40

Dudley Senanayake (1911-73), Prime Minister — A909

Perf. 13½x12¾ Syncopated
2011, Oct. 14
1809 A909 5r black & brown .40 .40

Telephone and Number for Government Information Center — A910

Perf. 12¾x13½ Syncopated
2011, Oct. 17
1810 A910 5r multi .40 .40

Old Automobiles — A911

Designs: No. 1811, 5r, 1928 Austin 12. No. 1812, 5r, 1934 Rolls Royce 20/25. No. 1813, 5r, 1937 Jaguar SS 100. No. 1814, 5r, 1949 Morris Minor.

Perf. 12¾x13¼ Syncopated
2011, Oct. 28
1811-1814 A911 Set of 4 .80 .80

Christmas A912

Designs: 5r, Shrine of Our Lady of Lourdes, Kalaoya. 20r, Holy Family, dove with flags of Sri Lanka and Vatican City on wings.

Perf. 13¼x12¾ Syncopated
2011, Nov. 27
1815-1816 A912 Set of 2 .80 .80
1816a Souvenir sheet of 2, #1815-1816, perf. 14x13¾ 1.50 1.50

No. 1816a sold for 45r.

Most Venerable Kotagama Wachissara Thero, Religious Figure — A913

Perf. 13¼x12¾ Syncopated
2011, Nov. 28
1817 A913 5r multi .40 .40

World AIDS Day — A914

2011, Dec. 1 **Litho.**
1818 A914 5r multi .40 .40

Sri Lankan Film Personalities A915

Designs: No. 1819, 5r, Eddy Jayamanna (1915-81), comedian. No. 1820, 5r, Sandaya Kumari, actress. No. 1821, 5r, Titus Thotawatta (1929-2011), director. 10r, Joe Abewickrama (1927-2011), actor. 15r, Malini Fonseka, actress. 20r, Gamini Fonseka (1936-2004), actor.

2012, Jan. 21 ***Perf. 14x13¾***
1819-1824 A915 Set of 6 1.10 1.10
1824a Souvenir sheet of 6, #1819-1824, imperf. 1.10 1.10

Sri Lankan Branch of Institute of Chartered Ship Brokers, 25th Anniv. — A916

Perf. 12¾x13¼ Syncopated
2012, Feb. 9
1825 A916 5r black & brown .25 .25

Scouting in Sri Lanka, Cent. A917

2012, Feb. 22 ***Perf. 13***
1826 A917 5r multi .25 .25
a. Souvenir sheet of 4 #1826, imperf. .35 .35

Peonies — A918

No. 1827: a, Denomination at LL. b, Denomination at LR.

2012, Mar. 10 **Litho.** ***Perf. 13¾x14***
1827 A918 30r Horiz. pair, #a-b .95 .95

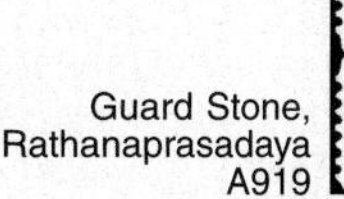

Guard Stone, Rathanaprasadaya
A919

Perf. 13 Syncopated

2012, Mar. 10 **Litho.**

1828 A919 50r mar & multi 1.25 1.25
1829 A919 100r bl vio & multi 2.50 2.50

Sustainable Energy For All — A920

2012, Mar. 20 ***Perf. 13¼x12***

1830 A920 5r multi .25 .25

Asian-Pacific Postal Union, 50th Anniv. — A921

2012, Apr. 1 ***Perf. 13¾x14***

1831 A921 5r multi .25 .25

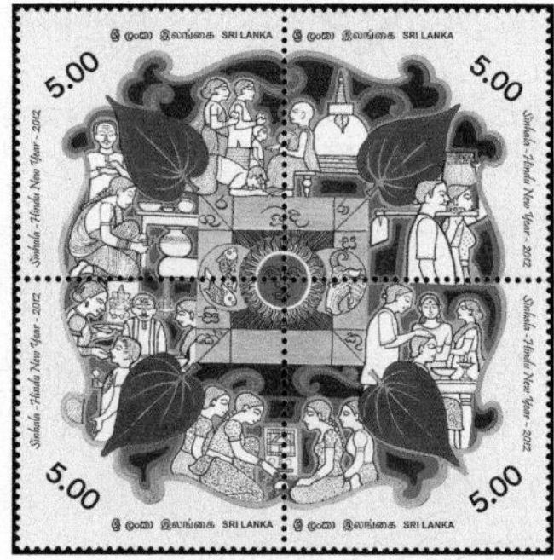

Sinhala (Hindu New Year) — A922

No. 1832 — People and leaves with denomination at: a, UL. b, UR. c, LL. d, LR.

2012, Apr. 10 ***Perf. 13***

Granite Paper

1832 A922 5r Block of 4, #a-d .35 .35

Sapugaskanda Petroleum Refinery — A923

2012, Apr. 30 ***Perf. 13¾x14***

1833 A923 5r multi .25 .25

Ceylon Petroleum Corporation, 50th anniv.

Sambuddhatva Jayantiya (Enlightenment of Buddha), 2600th Anniv. — A924

2012, May 3 ***Perf. 13¼x12***

1834 A924 5r multi .25 .25

Vesak Festival
A925

Leaves, religious symbols and emblems, with denomination at: 5r, Left. 12r, Right.

2012, May 6 ***Perf. 13¾x14***

1835-1836 A925 Set of 2 .30 .30
1836a Souvenir sheet of 2, #1835-1836 .30 .30

Professor Walpola Sri Rahula Thero (1907-97), Buddhist Historian — A926

2012, May 15 ***Perf. 14x13¾***

1837 A926 5r multi .25 .25

St. Philip Neri's Church, Udammita South, 225th Anniv. — A927

2012, May 26 **Litho.**

1838 A927 5r multi .25 .25

Kusuma Gunawardena (1912-85), Abettor in Jail Break of Anti-Colonial Leaders — A928

2012, May 28 ***Perf. 14x13¾***

1839 A928 5r multi .25 .25

Asgiri Maha Viharaya, 700th Anniv.
A929

2012, June 12 ***Perf. 13¾x14***

1840 A929 5r multi .25 .25

Ceylon School for the Deaf and Blind, Cent. — A930

Perf. 12¾x13¼ Syncopated

2012, June 17 **Litho. & Embossed**

1841 A930 5r multi .25 .25

Terra Cotta Figure, Sigiriya — A931

Perf. 13½x12¾ Syncopated

2012, July 16 **Litho.**

1842 A931 5r multi .25 .25

Natl. Archaeology Week.

Department of Agriculture, Cent. — A932

2012, July 22 ***Perf. 13¼x12***

1843 A932 5r multi .25 .25

2012 Summer Olympics, London — A933

Big Ben and: 5r, Running. 15r, Swimming. 25r, Shooting. 75r, Badminton.

Perf. 13½x12¾ Syncopated

2012, July 23

1844-1847 A933 Set of 4 1.90 1.90
1847a Souvenir sheet of 4, #1844-1847, perf. 14x13¾ 1.90 1.90

58th Commonwealth Parliamentary Conference, Colombo — A934

Perf. 12¾x13½ Syncopated

2012, Sept. 11

1848 A934 5r multi .25 .25

Colonial Buildings — A935

Designs: No. 1849, 15r, Galle Face Hotel, Colombo. No. 1850, 15r, National Museum. No. 1851, 15r, Colombo Municipal Council Building. No. 1852, 15r, Old Parliament Building.

2012, Sept. 11 ***Perf. 13¼x12***

1849-1852 A935 Set of 4 .90 .90
1850a Souvenir sheet of 2, #1849-1850, perf. 13¼ .45 .45
1852a Souvenir sheet of 2, #1851-1852, perf. 13¼ .45 .45

World Children's Day
A936

2012, Oct. 1 **Litho.** ***Perf. 13***

1853 A936 5r multi .25 .25

World Post Day — A937

2012, Oct. 6 ***Perf. 12x13¼***

1854 A937 5r multi .25 .25

Flowers
A938

Designs: No. 1855, 5r, Exacum trinevirum. No. 1856, 5r, Plumeria rubra. No. 1857, 5r, Hibiscus rosa-sinensis. No. 1858, 5r, Helianthus annuus.

2012, Oct. 7 ***Perf. 13¾x14***

1855-1858 A938 Set of 4 .30 .30
1858a Souvenir sheet of 4, #1855-1858 .30 .30

2012 World Post Day Stamp Exhibition (#1858a).

World Health Organization Service in Sri Lanka, 60th Anniv. — A939

2012, Oct. 16 ***Perf. 14x13¾***

1859 A939 12r multi .25 .25

Sri Lanka Insurance, 50th Anniv.
A940

Perf. 12¾x13½ Syncopated

2012, Oct. 31

1860 A940 5r multi .25 .25

Christmas
A941

Designs: 5r, Holy Family, doves and children. 25r, Flight into Egypt, man pulling woman and children in cart.

Perf. 12¾x13½ Syncopated

2012, Dec. 2

1861-1862 A941 Set of 2 .50 .50
1862a Souvenir sheet of 2, #1861-1862, perf. 13¾x14 .50 .50

Aviation in Sri Lanka, Cent. A942

Designs: 5r, Blériot monoplane. 12r, Air Ceylon jet. 15r, Sri Lankan Airlines jet. 25r, Mihin Lanka Airlines jet.

Perf. 12¾x13¼ Syncopated

2012, Dec. 7

1863-1866 A942 Set of 4 .90 .90
1866a Souvenir sheet of 4, #1863-1866, perf. 13¾x14 .90 .90

Moonstones, Guard Stones and Balustrades — A943

Designs: 50c, Vishnu Dewala moonstone, Kandy. 1r, Watadage moonstone, Polonnaruwa. 2r, Rajamaha Vihara moonstone, Beligala. 3r, Abayagiri Vihara moonstone, Anuradhapura. 4r, Jethawana Vihara guard stone, Anuradhapura, vert. 4.50r, Rajamaha Vihara guard stone, Arattana, vert. 5r, Tissamaharamaya guard stone, vert. 10r, Abayagiri Rathnaprasadaya guard stone, Anuradhapura, vert. 12r, Abayagiri Stupa guard stone, Anuradhapura, vert. 15r, Dematamal Vihara guard stone, Buttala, vert. 20r, Mahavihara balustrade, Anuradhapura. 25r, Lankathilaka Image House balustrade, Polonnaruwa. 30r, Jethawanarama Vihara balustrade, Anuradhapura. 40r, Mahavihara balustrade, Anuradhapura, diff. 55r, Mahavihara balustrade, Anuradhapura, diff. 75r, Yapahuwa balustrade.

2012, Dec. 12 ***Perf. 13 Syncopated***

Granite Paper

1867 A943 50c multi .25 .25
1868 A943 1r multi .25 .25
1869 A943 2r multi .25 .25
1870 A943 3r multi .25 .25
a. Souvenir sheet of 4, #1867-1870 .25 .25
1871 A943 4r multi .25 .25
1872 A943 4.50r multi .25 .25
1873 A943 5r multi .25 .25
1874 A943 10r multi .25 .25
1875 A943 12r multi .25 .25
1876 A943 15r multi .25 .25
a. Souvenir sheet of 6, #1871-1876 .80 .80
1877 A943 20r multi .30 .30
1878 A943 25r multi .40 .40
1879 A943 30r multi .50 .50
1880 A943 40r multi .65 .65
1881 A943 55r multi .90 .90
1882 A943 75r multi 1.25 1.25
a. Souvenir sheet of 6, #1877-1882 4.00 4.00
Nos. 1867-1882 (16) 6.50 6.50

For surcharges, see Nos. 2019-2021.

Rajans International Scout Centennial Gathering, Kandy — A945

Perf. 12¾x13¼ Syncopated

2013, Feb. 18

1885 A945 25r multi .40 .40

Opening of Mattala Rajapaksa International Airport — A946

2013, Mar. 18

1886 A946 5r gray & black .25 .25

Sri Lanka Peace Pada Yatra (Peace March) — A947

2013, Apr. 5 ***Perf. 13¼x12***

1887 A947 5r multi .25 .25

Dharmasoka College, Ambalangoda, Cent. — A948

Perf. 12¾x13¼ Syncopated

2013, May 4

1888 A948 5r multi .25 .25

Vesak Festival A949

Encounters of Prince Siddhartha with: 4r, Old man. 5r, Diseased man. 15r, Decaying corpse. 50r, Ascetic.

Perf. 12¾x13¼ Syncopated

2013, May 18

1889-1892 A949 Set of 4 1.25 1.25
1892a Souvenir sheet of 4, #1889-1892, perf. 13½x14 1.25 1.25

Dambegoda Bodhisattva Statue — A950

2013, May 25 ***Perf. 12x13¼***

1893 A950 5r multi .25 .25

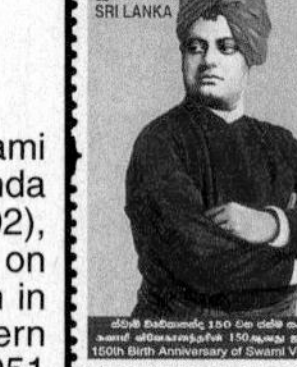

Swami Vivekananda (1863-1902), Lecturer on Hinduism in Western Countries — A951

Perf. 13¼x12½ Syncopated

2013, June 7

1894 A951 25r multi .40 .40

Christ Church Girls' College, Baddegama, 125th Anniv. — A952

Perf. 12¾x13½ Syncopated

2013, July 5 **Litho.**

1895 A952 5r multi .25 .25

Wildlife in Yala National Park A953

Designs: 5r, Hawksbill turtle. 15r, Swamp crocodile. 25r, Elephant, vert. 30r, Black-necked stork, vert. 40r, Wild boar. 50r, Spotted deer.

Perf. 13¾x14, 14x13¾

2013, July 28 **Litho.**

1896 A953 5r multi .25 .25
1897 A953 15r multi .25 .25
1898 A953 25r multi .40 .40
1899 A953 30r multi .45 .45
a. Souvenir sheet of 2, #1898-1899 .85 .85
b. As "a," with Thailand 2013 World Stamp Exhibition emblem in sheet margin *.85 .85*
1900 A953 40r multi .60 .60
a. Souvenir sheet of 2, #1897, 1900 .85 .85
b. As "a," with Thailand 2013 World Stamp Exhibition emblem in sheet margin *.85 .85*
1901 A953 50r multi .75 .75
a. Souvenir sheet of 2, #1896, 1901 .85 .85
b. As "a," with Thailand 2013 World Stamp Exhibition emblem in sheet margin *.85 .85*
Nos. 1896-1901 (6) 2.70 2.70

Father Tissa Balasuriya (1924-2013), Founder of Center for Society and Religion — A954

Perf. 13½x12¾ Syncopated

2013, Aug. 29 **Litho.**

1902 A954 5r multi .25 .25

World Children's Day — A955

No. 1903 — The Umbrella Thief, by Sybil Wettasinghe, with word balloon at left beginning with: a, "In the village of Kirimama. . ." b, "What are you looking for?" c, "Ha. . .ha. . !"

Perf. 12¾x13½ Syncopated

2013, Oct. 1 **Litho.**

1903 A955 Horiz. strip of 3 .25 .25
a.-c. 5r Any single .25 .25

World Post Day A956

2013, Oct. 9 **Litho.** ***Perf. 12x13½***

1904 A956 5r multi .25 .25

Sigiriya UNESCO World Heritage Site A957

Stilt Fishermen A958

2013, Oct. 9 **Litho.** ***Perf. 13½x14***

Granite Paper

1905 A957 15r multi *.40 .40*
1906 A958 15r multi *.40 .40*

The right parts of Nos. 1905-1906 could be personalized. The generic image depicting the emblem of Sri Lanka Post is shown.

Opening of Colombo-Katunayake Expressway — A959

Perf. 13½x12¾ Syncopated

2013, Oct. 27 **Litho.**

1907 A959 5r multi .25 .25

Deshabandu Alec Robertson (1928-2002), President of Servants of Buddha Society — A960

Perf. 13½x12¾ Syncopated

2013, Oct. 30 **Litho.**

1908 A960 5r multi .25 .25

Dr. Premasiri Khemadasa (1937-2008), Composer A961

Perf. 13½x12¾ Syncopated

2013, Nov. 1 **Litho.**

1909 A961 5r multi .25 .25

Excise Department, Cent. — A962

Perf. 12¾x13½ Syncopated

2013, Nov. 6 **Litho.**

1910 A962 5r multi .25 .25

Commonwealth Heads of Government Meeting, Colombo — A963

Emblem, girl with flowers with background colors of: 5r, Red and purple. 25r, Blue and green.

2013, Nov. 14 **Litho.** ***Perf. 13½x14***

1911-1912 A963 Set of 2 .45 .45

1912a Souvenir sheet of 2, #1911-1912 .45 .45

Dr. Tissa Abeysekara (1939-2009), Film Maker — A964

Perf. 12¾x13¼ Syncopated

2013, Nov. 27 **Litho.**

1913 A964 5r multi .25 .25

Christmas A965

Designs: 5r, People in circle around Holy Family. 30r, People, Madonna and child.

2013, Dec. 1 **Litho.** ***Perf. 14x13½***

1914-1915 A965 Set of 2 .55 .55

1915a Souvenir sheet of 2, #1914-1915 .55 .55

All Ceylon Moor's Association, Cent. — A966

Perf. 12¾x13½ Syncopated

2013, Dec. 2 **Litho.**

1916 A966 5r blk & red .25 .25

Dharmadasa Walpola (1927-83), Singer — A967

Perf. 13½x12¾ Syncopated

2013, Dec. 19 **Litho.**

1917 A967 5r multi .25 .25

Venerable Baddegama Wimalawansa Nayaka Thero (1913-93), Buddhist Monk and Writer — A968

Perf. 13½x12¾ Syncopated

2013, Dec. 21 **Litho.**

1918 A968 5r multi .25 .25

Sri Lanka Administrative Service, 50th Anniv. — A969

Perf. 13½x12¾ Syncopated

2013, Dec. 23 **Litho.**

1919 A969 5r multi .25 .25

Thai Pongal Farmer's Festival A970

Designs: 5r, Farmer with ox-drawn plow. 25r, Man and woman cooking pongal.

2014, Jan. 12 **Litho.** ***Perf. 13½x14***

1920-1921 A970 Set of 2 .45 .45

1921a Souvenir sheet of 2, #1920-1921 .45 .45

Deyata Kirula Exhibition, Kuliyapitiya A971

Perf. 13½x12¾ Syncopated

2014, Feb. 21 **Litho.**

1922 A971 5r multi .25 .25

Sri Lankan Railway Civil Engineering Projects — A972

Designs: No. 1923, 5r, Nine Arch Viaduct, Gotuwala. No. 1924, 5r, Spiral railway, Demodara.

2014, Feb. 28 **Litho.** ***Perf. 13***

Granite Paper

1923-1924 A972 Set of 2 .25 .25

Mountain Hourglass Tree Frog — A973

Perf. 13½x12¾ Syncopated

2014, Mar. 3 **Litho.**

1925 A973 5r multi .25 .25

World Wildlife Day.

H. Sri Nissanka (1898-1954), Jurist — A974

Perf. 13¼x12¾ Syncopated

2014, Apr. 4 **Litho.**

1926 A974 5r multi .25 .25

Ceylon Fertilizer Company, Cent. A975

Perf. 12¾x13¼ Syncopated

2014, Apr. 4 **Litho.**

1927 A975 5r multi .25 .25

Ho Chi Minh (1890-1969), President of North Viet Nam — A976

2014, Apr. 28 **Litho.** ***Perf. 12x13¼***

1928 A976 5r multi .25 .25

World Conference on Youth, Colombo — A977

Perf. 12¾x13¼ Syncopated

2014, May 7 **Litho.**

1929 A977 5r multi .25 .25

Vesak Festival — A978

Prince Siddhartha on the eve of renunciation: 5r, Sees the repulsive sight of sleeping dancers. 10r, Looking at his wife, Yasodhara, and son, Rahula. 15r, Crossing the River Anoma. 20r, Cutting off his hair.

2014, May 12 **Litho.** ***Perf. 14x13½***

1930-1933 A978 Set of 4 .80 .80

1933a Souvenir sheet of 4, #1930-1933 .80 .80

Carey College, Cent. A979

Perf. 12¾x13¼ Syncopated

2014, May 29 **Litho.**

1934 A979 5r multi .25 .25

World Environment Day — A980

Perf. 13¼x12¾ Syncopated

2014, June 5 **Litho.**

1935 A980 5r multi .25 .25

Arrival of Methodist Missionaries in Sri Lanka, 200th Anniv. — A981

2014, June 29 Litho. *Perf. 13*

1936 A981 5r multi .25 .25

Pigeon Island Marine National Park A982

Designs: 7r, Rock pigeons. 10r, Sperm whale. 15r, Blacktip reef shark. 25r, Blackwedged butterflyfish. 35r, Scaly rock crab. 50r, Knotted fan coral.

2014, Aug. 22 Litho. *Perf. 13½x14*

Granite Paper

1937-1942 A982 Set of 6 2.25 2.25

1942a Souvenir sheet of 6, #1937-1942 2.25 2.25

Dr. R. L. Spittel (1881-1969), Surgeon — A983

Perf. 13¼x12¾ Syncopated

2014, Sept. 3 Litho.

1943 A983 10r multi .25 .25

Asian-Pacific Postal Union Executive Council Meeting, Colombo — A984

Designs: 7r, Executive Council Meeting emblem. 10r, Executive Council Meeting Emblem, Asian-Pacific Postal Union Emblem, arms of Sri Lanka, map of Sri Lanka, emblem of Sri Lanka Post. 35r, Executive Council Meeting emblem, mail box, men and women. 50r, Executive Council Meeting emblem, map and flags of Asian-Pacific Postal Union members.

2014, Sept. 15 Litho. *Perf. 13½x14*

1944-1947 A984 Set of 4 1.60 1.60

1947a Souvenir sheet of 4, #1944-1947 1.60 1.60

Anagarika Dharmapala (1864-1933), Buddhist Missionary — A985

2014, Sept. 17 Litho. *Perf. 13x12¾*

1948 A985 10r multi .25 .25

World Children's Day — A986

Perf. 13¼x12¾ Syncopated

2014, Oct. 1 Litho.

Granite Paper

1949 A986 10r multi .25 .25

World Post Day A987

Perf. 12¾x13¼ Syncopated

2014, Oct. 9 Litho.

Granite Paper

1950 A987 10r multi .25 .25

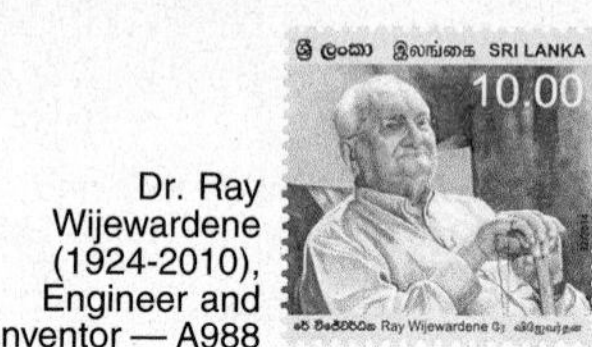

Dr. Ray Wijewardene (1924-2010), Engineer and Inventor — A988

2014, Oct. 31 Litho. *Perf. 12x13¼*

Granite Paper

1951 A988 10r multi .25 .25

Christmas — A989

No. 1952 — Winning art in stamp design contest depicting Nativity scenes with Christmas tree and denomination at: a, Right. b, Left.

2014, Nov. 30 Litho. *Perf. 13½x14*

Granite Paper

1952 A989 10r Horiz. pair, #a-b .30 .30

c. Souvenir sheet of 2, #1952a-1952b .30 .30

Sri Lanka Standards Institution, 50th Anniv. — A990

2014, Dec. 3 Litho. *Perf. 12x13¼*

Granite Paper

1953 A990 10r multi .25 .25

Solar System — A991

Designs: 7r, Sun. 8r, Mercury. 10r, Venus. 12r, Earth. 15r, Moon. 20r, Mars. 25r, Jupiter. 30r, Saturn. 35r, Uranus. 40r, Neptune.

2014, Dec. 5 Litho. *Perf. 12x13¼*

Granite Paper

1954-1963 A991 Set of 10 3.25 3.25

1963a Souvenir sheet of 10, #1954-1963, perf. 13¼x12 3.25 3.25

1963b As "a," with "National Stamp Exhibition 2014" inscription in sheet margin, perf. 13¼x12 3.25 3.25

Visit of Pope Francis to Sri Lanka A992

Pope Francis and: 10r, St. Peter's Basilica. 75r, Holding cross.

2015, Jan. 13 Litho. *Perf. 13½x14*

Granite Paper

1964-1965 A992 Set of 2 1.40 1.40

1965a Souvenir sheet of 2, #1964-1965 1.40 1.40

National Hospital of Sri Lanka, 150th Anniv. — A993

2015, Mar. 20 Litho. *Perf. 13*

1966 A993 10r multi .25 .25

Vesak Festival A994

Designs: 8r, Proceeding in Dana Ceremony. 10r, Offering to the sacred Bodhi tree. 50r, Meditation.

2015, Apr. 20 Litho. *Perf. 13¾x14*

Granite Paper

1967-1969 A994 Set of 3 1.10 1.10

1969a Souvenir sheet of 3, #1967-1969 1.10 1.10

Mahiyangana Dagoba Relic Chamber Painting — A995

Perf. 12¾x13¼ Syncopated

2015, May 4 Litho.

Granite Paper

1970 A995 10r multi .25 .25

World Day Against Child Labor — A996

Perf. 13¼x12¾ Syncopated

2015, June 12 Litho.

Granite Paper

1971 A996 10r multi .25 .25

H. C. P. Bell (1851-1937), First Archaeological Commisioner and Dig Site — A997

Perf. 12¾x13¼ Syncopated

2015, July 8 Litho.

Granite Paper

1972 A997 10r multi .25 .25

Department of Archaeology, 125th anniv.

Ancient Stone Carvings — A998

Carving from: 10r, Wijesundararama Temple, Dambadeniya. 15r, Decorated entrance of Citadel of Yapahuwa. 35r, Door jamb at Tooth Relic Temple, Kurunegala. 40r, Gadaladeniya Temple, Pilimatalawa.

2015, July 8 Litho. *Perf. 14x13¾*

Granite Paper

1973-1976 A998 Set of 4 1.50 1.50

1976a Souvenir sheet of 4, #1973-1976 1.50 1.50

Gems — A999

Designs: 10r, Star sapphire. 25r, Blue sapphire. 35r, Cat's eye. 40r, Padparadscha.

2015, Sept. 3 Litho. *Perf. 14x13¾*

Granite Paper

1977-1980 A999 Set of 4 1.75 1.75

1980a Souvenir sheet of 4, #1977-1980 1.75 1.75

World Maritime Day — A1000

2015, Sept. 24 Litho. *Perf. 13½x12*

1981 A1000 5r multi .25 .25

Department of Elections, 60th Anniv. — A1001

Designs: 10r, Three hands with raised pinkies. 15r, People with raised pinkies. 25r, Man with loudspeaker, people with banner. 35r, Polling place.

2015, Sept. 28 Litho. *Perf. 13¾x14*
Granite Paper

1982-1985 A1001 Set of 4 1.25 1.25
1985a Souvenir sheet of 4, #1982-1985 1.25 1.25

World Post Day A1002

Perf. 12¾x13¼ Syncopated

2015, Oct. 9 Litho.
1986 A1002 10r multi .25 .25

United Nations, 70th Anniv. A1003

Perf. 12¾x13¼ Syncopated

2015, Oct. 24 Litho.
1987 A1003 10r multi .25 .25

Sri Lankan admittance to United Nations, 60th anniv.

Diplomatic Relations Between Thailand and Sri Lanka, 60th Anniv. — A1004

Designs: 10r, Jethavana Stupa, flag of Sri Lanka. 50r, Phrapathomchedi Pagoda, flag of Thailand.

2015, Nov. 2 Litho. *Perf. 14x13¾*
1988-1989 A1004 Set of 2 .85 .85
1989a Souvenir sheet of 2, #1988-1989 .85 .85

See Thailand No. 2883.

Deepavali — A1005

2015, Nov. 10 Litho. *Perf. 13¼x12*
1990 A1005 10r multi .25 .25

Anton Chekhov (1860-1904), Writer, and Scene From *The Cherry Orchard* — A1006

Perf. 13¼x12¾ Syncopated

2015, Nov. 23 Litho.
1991 A1006 10r multi .25 .25

125th Anniv. of the visit of Anton Chekhov to Sri Lanka.

Christmas A1007

Designs: 10r, Holy Family and shepherd, Sri Lankan Christmas celebration. 35r, Holy Family, people and angels.

2015, Dec. 6 Litho. *Perf. 14x13¾*
1992-1993 A1007 Set of 2 .65 .65
1993a Souvenir sheet of 2, #1992-1993 .65 .65

Colombo Municipal Council, 150th Anniv. — A1008

2015, Dec. 14 Litho. *Perf. 12¾x13*
1994 A1008 10r multi .25 .25

Most Venerable Davuldena Gnanissara Mahanayake Thero, Chief Prelate of Amarapura Sect, 100th Birthday — A1009

Perf. 13¼x12¾ Syncopated

2015, Dec. 31 Litho.
1995 A1009 10r multi .25 .25

Wilson Hegoda (1915-84), Photographer A1010

Perf. 13¼x12¾ Syncopated

2016, Jan. 11 Litho.
1996 A1010 10r multi .25 .25

Sri Lanka School of Agriculture, Cent. — A1011

Perf. 12¾x13¼ Syncopated

2016, Jan. 16 Litho.
1997 A1011 10r multi .25 .25

Wildlife of Kumana National Park A1012

Designs: 7r, Blue whale. 10r, Leatherback sea turtle. 15r, Black-necked stork, vert. 20r, Saltwater crocodile. 25r, Asian elephant, vert. 35r, Leopard, vert. 40r, Sloth bear, vert.

Perf. 13¾x14, 14x13¾

2016, Jan. 26 Litho.
1998-2004 A1012 Set of 7 2.10 2.10
2004a Souvenir sheet of 7, #1998-2004 2.10 2.10

World Wetlands Day — A1013

Designs: 7r, Fulvous whistling duck. 10r, Greater flamingo. 35r, Western spot-billed duck. 50r, Caspian tern.

2016, Feb. 2 Litho. *Perf. 13¼x12*
2005 A1013 7r multi .25 .25
a. Souvenir sheet of 1, perf. 13¼ .25 .25
2006 A1013 10r multi .25 .25
a. Souvenir sheet of 1, perf. 13¼ .25 .25
2007 A1013 35r multi .50 .50
a. Souvenir sheet of 1, perf. 13¼ .50 .50
2008 A1013 50r multi .70 .70
a. Souvenir sheet of 1, perf. 13¼ .70 .70
Nos. 2005-2008 (4) 1.70 1.70

H. R. Jothipala (1936-87), Singer — A1014

Perf. 13¼x12¾ Syncopated

2016, Feb. 12 Litho.
2009 A1014 10r multi .25 .25

D. B. Wijetunga (1916-2008), President and Prime Minister — A1015

Perf. 12¾x13¼ Syncopated

2016, Feb. 14 Litho.
2010 A1015 10r multi .25 .25

D. R. Wijewardena (1886-1950), Founder of Ceylon Daily News — A1016

Perf. 12¾x13¼ Syncopated

2016, Feb. 26 Litho.
2011 A1016 10r multi .25 .25

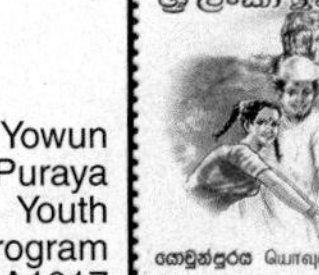

Yowun Puraya Youth Program A1017

Perf. 12¾x13¼ Syncopated

2016, Apr. 2 Litho.
2012 A1017 10r multi .25 .25

Sirimavo Bandaranaike (1916-2000), Prime Minister — A1018

2016, Apr. 7 Litho. *Perf. 13*
Granite Paper

2013 A1018 15r lake brown .25 .25

People's Victory, 60th Anniv. — A1019

2016, Apr. 8 Litho. *Perf. 12x13¼*
Granite Paper

2014 A1019 15r multi .25 .25

1956 election of Prime Minister S. R. W. D. Bandaranaike.

Vesak A1020

Designs: 8r, Situlpawwa Viharaya. 10r, Yatala Stupa. 35r, Sandagiri Stupa.

2016, May 2 Litho. *Perf. 13½x14*
Granite Paper

2015-2017 A1020 Set of 3 .75 .75
2017a Souvenir sheet of 3, #2015-2017 .75 .75

No. 1626 Surcharged in Black and Silver

Method and Perf. As Before

2016, May 9
2018 A780 5r on 45r #1626 .25 .25

Nos. 1872, 1881, 1882 Surcharged

Method and Perf. As Before

2016, May 9
2019 A943 3r on 4.50r #1872 .25 .25
2020 A943 10r on 55r #1881 .25 .25
2021 A943 20r on 75r #1882 .30 .30
Nos. 2019-2021 (3) .80 .80

Cub Scouts, Cent. — A1021

2016, May 13 Litho. *Perf. 13*
Granite Paper

2022 A1021 10r multi .25 .25

Paintings of Four Gods of Protection on Ancient Wooden Box — A1022

2016, May 22 Litho. *Perf. 13¼x12*

2023 A1022 10r multi .25 .25

State Vesak Festival.

Visvalingam Veerasingam (1892-1964), President of Cooperative Societies Federation A1023

Perf. 13¼x12¾ Syncopated
2016, May 27 Litho.
Granite Paper

2024 A1023 10r multi .25 .25

Sri Lanka Tourism, 50th Anniv. — A1024

Perf. 13¼x12¾ Syncopated
2016, May 27 Litho.
Granite Paper

2025 A1024 15r multi .25 .25

C.V. Gunaratne, Minister of Industry Killed in 2000 Terrorist Bombing A1025

2016, June 7 Litho. *Perf. 12x13¼*
Granite Paper

2026 A1025 15r multi .25 .25

International Day Against Drug Abuse and Illicit Trafficking — A1026

Perf. 12½x13¼ Syncopated
2016, June 26 Litho.
Granite Paper

2027 A1026 15r multi .25 .25

Chitrasena (1921-2005), Dancer — A1027

Perf. 12½x13¼ Syncopated
2016, July 18 Litho.
Granite Paper

2028 A1027 15r multi .25 .25

2016 Summer Olympics, Rio de Janeiro A1028

Sri Lanka Olympic Committee emblem, Christ the Redeemer Statue, Rio de Janeiro, and: 8r, Swimming. 10r, Judo. 35r, Javelin. 50r, Weight lifting.

2016, July 21 Litho. *Perf. 13½x14*
Granite Paper

2029-2032 A1028 Set of 4 1.50 1.50
2032a Souvenir sheet of 4, #2029-2032 1.50 1.50

Dharmasiri Senanayake (1933-2000), Politician — A1029

2016, July 24 Litho. *Perf. 13½x14*
Granite Paper

2033 A1029 10r multi .25 .25

2016 Lawasia Conference, Colombo — A1030

Perf. 12½x13¼ Syncopated
2016, Aug. 12 Litho.
Granite Paper

2034 A1030 15r multi .25 .25

Sri Lanka Police, 150th Anniv. — A1031

Perf. 13¼x12½ Syncopated
2016, Sept. 3 Litho.
Granite Paper

2035 A1031 15r multi .25 .25

Archaeological Society of Sri Lanka, 50th Anniv. — A1032

Perf. 13¼x12½ Syncopated
2016, Sept. 8 Litho.
Granite Paper

2036 A1032 15r multi .25 .25

World Children's Day A1033

Perf. 12½x13¼ Syncopated
2016, Oct. 1 Litho.
Granite Paper

2037 A1033 15r multi .25 .25

Flowers — A1034

Designs: 1r, Impatiens elongata. 2r, Ranunculus sagittifolius. 5r, Rhynchoglossum notonianum. 7r, Strobilanthes viscosa. 10r, Impatiens repens. 15r, Gordonia speciosa. 20r, Schumacheria alnifolia. 25r, Osbeckia parvifolia. 30r, Adrorhizon purpurascens. 35r, Habenaria accuminata. 40r, Luisia teretifolia. 50r, Impatiens henslowiana.

Perf. 13x12¾ Syncopated
2016, Oct. 7 Litho.
Granite Paper

2038 A1034 1r multi .25 .25
2039 A1034 2r multi .25 .25
2040 A1034 5r multi .25 .25
2041 A1034 7r multi .25 .25
2042 A1034 10r multi .25 .25
2043 A1034 15r multi .25 .25
2044 A1034 20r multi .30 .30
2045 A1034 25r multi .35 .35
a. Souvenir sheet of 8, #2038-2045 1.25 1.25

Size: 25x30mm
Perf. 13x13¼ Syncopated

2046 A1034 30r multi .40 .40
2047 A1034 35r multi .50 .50
2048 A1034 40r multi .55 .55
2049 A1034 50r multi .70 .70
a. Souvenir sheet of 4, #2046-2049 2.25 2.25
Nos. 2038-2049 (12) 4.30 4.30

World Post Day A1035

Designs: 5r, Pigeon post, 1850. 10r, Mail coach, 1820. 15r, Clipper ship, 1850.

2016, Oct. 9 Litho. *Perf. 13½x14*
Granite Paper

2050-2052 A1035 Set of 3 .40 .40
2052a Souvenir sheet of 3, #2050-2052 .40 .40

Dr. Arumadura N. S. Kulasinghe (1919-2006), Engineer — A1036

Perf. 12½x13¼ Syncopated
2016, Oct. 26 Litho.
Granite Paper

2053 A1036 10r multi .25 .25

Lions Clubs International, Cent. — A1037

2016, Dec. 1 Litho. *Perf. 12x13¼*
Granite Paper

2054 A1037 10r multi .25 .25

Tourist Attractions A1038

Designs: No. 2055, Bambarakanda Falls, Kalupahana. No. 2056, Ruins of Sir Frederick North's Bungalow, Arippu. No. 2057, Fort Hammenhiel, Jaffna. No. 2058, Hummanaya Blowhole, Kudawella. No. 2059, Sand dunes, Kawtharimunai. No. 2060, Wild Horse Sanctuary, Delft Island. No. 2061, Govinda Hela, Siyambalanduwa. No. 2062, Mini World's End, Pitamaruwa. No. 2063, Queen's Tower, Delft Island. No. 2064, Senanayake Samudraya, Inginiyagala. No. 2065, Lighthouse and old pier, Talaimannar. No. 2066, Kudiramalai Point, Wilpattu.

2016, Dec. 2 Litho. *Perf. 13¾x14*
Granite Paper

2055 A1038 25r multi .35 .35
2056 A1038 25r multi .35 .35
2057 A1038 25r multi .35 .35
2058 A1038 25r multi .35 .35
2059 A1038 25r multi .35 .35
2060 A1038 25r multi .35 .35
2061 A1038 25r multi .35 .35
2062 A1038 25r multi .35 .35
2063 A1038 25r multi .35 .35
2064 A1038 25r multi .35 .35
a Souvenir sheet of 4, #2055, 2058, 2061, 2064 1.40 1.40
2065 A1038 25r multi .35 .35
a Souvenir sheet of 4, #2056, 2059, 2062, 2065 1.40 1.40
2066 A1038 25r multi .35 .35
a Souvenir sheet of 4, #2057, 2060, 2063, 2066 1.40 1.40
b. Sheet of 12, #2055-2066 4.25 4.25
Nos. 2055-2066 (12) 4.20 4.20

Christmas A1039

Designs: 10r, Adoration of the Shepherds. 35r, Holy Family, dove and worshipers.

2016, Dec. 4 Litho. *Perf. 13¾x14*
Granite Paper

2067-2068 A1039 Set of 2 .60 .60
2068a Souvenir sheet of 2, #2067-2068 .60 .60

Volleyball in Sri Lanka, Cent. — A1040

2016, Dec. 7 Litho. *Perf. 13¾*
Granite Paper

2069 A1040 10r multi .25 .25

Values are for stamps with surrounding selvage.

National Meelad-Un-Nabi Festival — A1041

Perf. 13¼x12½ Syncopated
2016, Dec. 12 Litho.
Granite Paper

2070 A1041 10r multi .25 .25

Sri Lanka Broadcasting Corporation, 50th Anniv. — A1042

2017, Jan. 5 Litho. *Perf. 13¼x12*
Granite Paper

2071 A1042 10r multi .25 .25

International Year of Shelter for the Homeless, 30th Anniv. — A1043

Perf. 13¼x12½ Syncopated
2017, Jan. 12 Litho.
Granite Paper

2072 A1043 10r multi .25 .25

Visakha Vidyalaya Girls' School, Cent. A1044

Perf. 12½x13¼ Syncopated
2017, Jan. 16 Litho.
Granite Paper

2073 A1044 10r multi .25 .25

National Integration and Reconciliation Week — A1045

Perf. 13¼x12½ Syncopated
2017, Feb. 3 Litho.
Granite Paper

2074 A1045 10r multi .25 .25

Asian Development Bank, 50th Anniv. — A1046

2017, Feb. 6 Litho. *Perf. 12x13¼*
Granite Paper

2075 A1046 10r multi .25 .25

Montague Jayewickreme (1911-2001), Politician — A1047

Perf. 12½x13¼ Syncopated
2017, Mar. 20 Litho.
Granite Paper

2076 A1047 10r multi .25 .25

Girl Guides in Sri Lanka, Cent. A1048

Perf. 12¾x13¼ Syncopated
2017, Mar. 21 Litho.
Granite Paper

2077 A1048 15r multi .25 .25

Ferguson High School, Rathnapura, Cent. — A1049

Perf. 12½x13¼ Syncopated
2017, Mar. 27 Litho.
Granite Paper

2078 A1049 15r multi .25 .25

First Postage Stamps of Ceylon, 160th Anniv. — A1050

Designs: No. 2079, 15r, Ceylon #2. No. 2080, 15r, Ceylon #5. No. 2081, 15r, Ceylon #8. No. 2082, 15r, Ceylon #9.

2017, Apr. 1 Litho. *Perf. 14x13½*
Granite Paper

2079-2082 A1050 Set of 4 .80 .80
2082a Souvenir sheet of 4, #2079-2082 .80 .80

Vesak — A1051

Inscriptions: 8r, Dhamma preaching and listening. 10r, Offering of alms piously. 15r, Love of environment.

2017, May 3 Litho. *Perf. 14x13½*
Granite Paper

2083-2085 A1051 Set of 3 .45 .45
2085a Souvenir sheet of 3, #2083-2085 .45 .45

Vattarama Sri Arahatta Maliyadeva Raja Maha Viharaya, Site of State Vesak Festival — A1052

Perf. 13¼x12 Syncopated
2017, May 9 Litho.
Granite Paper

2086 A1052 15r multi .25 .25

United Nations Day of Vesak — A1053

Buddhist sites in various countries: No. 2087, 15r, Mes Aynak, Afghanistan. No. 2088, 15r, Somapur Maha Vihara, Paharpur, Bangladesh. No. 2089, 15r, Paro Taktsang, Bhutan. No. 2090, 15r, Angkor Archaeological Site, Cambodia. No. 2091, 15r, Yungang Grottoes, China. No. 2092, 15r, Buddhist Monuments at Sanchi, India. No. 2093, 15r, Borobudur Temple Compounds, Indonesia. No. 2094, 15r, Horyu-ji Temple, Japan. No. 2095, 15r, Town of Luang Prabang, Laos. No. 2096, 15r, Kek Lok Si, Malaysia. No. 2097, 15r, Gandantegchinlen Monastery, Mongolia. No. 2098, 15r, Bagan Archaeological Zone, Myanmar. No. 2099, 15r, Lumbini, Nepal. No. 2100, 15r, Taxila, Pakistan. No. 2101, 15r, Ivolginsky Datsan, Russia. No. 2102, 15r, Kong Meng San Phor Kark See Monastery, Singapore. No. 2103, 15r, Haeinsa Temple Complex, South Korea. No. 2104, 15r Lankathilaka Temple, Kandy, Sri Lanka. No. 2105, 15r, Sukhothai Ancient City, Thailand. No. 2016, 15r, One Pillar Pagoda, Viet Nam.

Perf. 13¼x12¾ Syncopated
2017, May 12 Litho.
Granite Paper

2087-2106 A1053 Set of 20 4.00 4.00
2106a Sheet of 20, #2087-2106 .25 .25

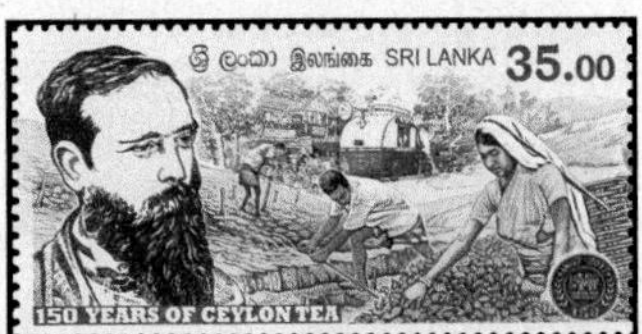

Ceylon Tea, 150th Anniv. — A1054

No. 2107: a, James Taylor (1835-92), tea planter, and workers in field. b, Factory worker, tea taster, ship and train.

2017, July 13 Litho. *Perf. 13¼x12*

2107 Horiz. pair .90 .90
a.-b. A1054 35r Either single .45 .45
c. Souvenir sheet of 2, #2107a-2107b, perf. 13¼ .90 .90

Most Venerable Boosse Dhammarakkhitha Mahanayaka Thero (1890-1982), Monk — A1055

Perf. 13¼x12½ Syncopated
2017, Aug. 3 Litho.
Granite Paper

2108 A1055 10r multi .25 .25

Kandyan Dancer — A1056

Punkalasa A1057

Dondra Head Lighthouse A1058

Perf. 13x12¾ Syncopated
2017, Sept. 13 Litho.
Granite Paper

2109 A1056 10r multi .25 .25
2110 A1057 15r multi .25 .25
2111 A1058 25r multi .35 .35
Nos. 2109-2111 (3) .85 .85

World Children's Day — A1059

Perf. 13¼x12½ Syncopated
2017, Oct. 1 Litho.
Granite Paper

2112 A1059 10r multi .25 .25

Parliamentary Democracy in Sri Lanka, 70th Anniv. — A1060

Perf. 13¼x12½ Syncopated
2017, Oct. 3 Litho.
Granite Paper

2113 A1060 12r multi .25 .25

Colombo Fort Railway Station, Cent. — A1061

2017, Oct. 4 Litho. *Perf. 13¼x12*
Granite Paper

2114 A1061 10r multi .25 .25

8th Conference of South Asian Association for Regional Cooperation Speakers and Parliamentarians, Colombo — A1062

Perf. 12½x13¼ Syncopated
2017, Oct. 4 Litho.
Granite Paper

2115 A1062 12r multi .25 .25

World Post Day — A1063

Designs: 15r, Landing of the English Mail at Talaimannar Pier, 1955. 35r, Inside of Traveling Post Office.

2017, Oct. 9 Litho. *Perf. 13¼x12*
Granite Paper

2116-2117 A1063 Set of 2 .65 .65
2117a Souvenir sheet of 2, #2116-2117, perf. 13¼ .65 .65

Diyogu B. Dhanapala (1905-71), Writer A1064

Perf. 12½x13¼ Syncopated
2017, Oct. 19 Litho.
Granite Paper

2118 A1064 10r multi .25 .25

7th Buddhist Summit, Colombo — A1065

2017, Nov. 2 Litho. *Perf. 13¼x12*
Granite Paper

2119 A1065 25r multi .35 .35
a. Souvenir sheet of 1, perf. 13¼ .35 .35

Sri Lanka Philatelic Bureau, 50th Anniv. A1066

2017, Nov. 8 Litho. *Perf. 13¾*
Granite Paper

2120 A1066 35r multi .45 .45

Values are for stamps with surrounding selvage.

Diplomatic Relations Between Sri Lanka and South Korea, 40th Anniv. — A1067

Designs: 10r, Female Kandyan dancer, Sri Lanka. 50r, Dance of the Spring Nightingale, South Korea.

Perf. 13¼x12½ Syncopated
2017, Nov. 14 Litho.
Granite Paper

2121-2122 A1067 Set of 2 .80 .80
2122a Souvenir sheet of 2, #2121-2122, perf. 14x13½ syncopated .80 .80

See South Korea No. 2508.

Christmas A1068

Designs: 15r, Holy Family, Shepherds and Magi. 35r, Nativity.

Perf. 12½x13¼ Syncopated
2017, Nov. 26 Litho.
Granite Paper

2123-2124 A1068 Set of 2 .65 .65
2124a Souvenir sheet of 2, #2123-2124, perf. 13½x14 syncopated .65 .65

Birds — A1069

Designs: 4r, Sri Lanka black-capped bulbul. 10r, Sri Lanka chestnut-backed owlet. 15r, Sri Lanka warbler. 35r, Sri Lanka drongo.

Perf. 13¼x12½ Syncopated
2017, Dec. 16 Litho.
Granite Paper

2125-2128 A1069 Set of 4 .85 .85
2128a Souvenir sheet of 4, #2125-2128, perf. 14x13½ syncopated .85 .85

Muhammadiya Jumma Mosque, Jaffna — A1070

2017, Dec. 23 Litho. *Perf. 13¼x12*
Granite Paper

2129 A1070 15r multi .25 .25

National Meelad-Un-Nabi.

Independence, 70th Anniv. — A1071

2018, Feb. 4 Litho. *Perf. 13*
Granite Paper

2130 A1071 15r multi .25 .25

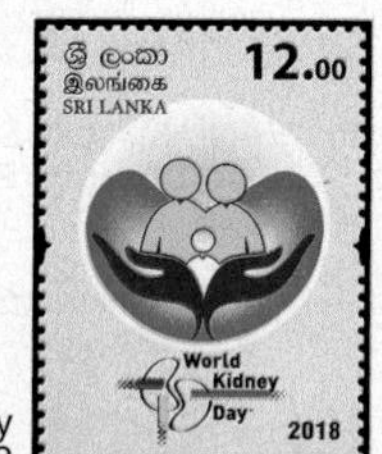

World Kidney Day — A1072

Perf. 13¼x12½ Syncopated
2018, Mar. 8 Litho.
Granite Paper

2131 A1072 12r multi .25 .25

Ambalamas (Traveler Shelters) — A1073

Designs: 10r, Marassana Gama Meda Ambalama. 15r, Karagahagedara Ambalama. 35r, Panavitiya Ambalama. 50r, Godamunna Ambalama.

Perf. 12½x13¼ Syncopated
2018, Mar. 23 Litho.
Granite Paper

2132-2135 A1073 Set of 4 1.50 1.50
2135a Souvenir sheet of 4, #2132-2135, perf. 13½x14 syncopated 1.50 1.50

World Health Day, 70th Anniv. — A1074

Perf. 13¼x12½ Syncopated
2018, Apr. 7 Litho.
Granite Paper

2136 A1074 12r multi .25 .25

Vesak A1075

Various scenes from *Chulla Suthasoma Jathaka*: 10r, 15r, 35r.

Perf. 12½x13¼ Syncopated
2018, Apr. 9 Litho.
Granite Paper

2137-2139 A1075 Set of 3 .75 .75
2139a Souvenir sheet of 3, #2137-2139, perf. 13½x14 syncopated .75 .75

Devagiri Rajamaha Viharaya, Bingiriya — A1076

2018, Apr. 28 Litho. *Perf. 13¼x12*
Granite Paper

2140 A1076 12r multi .25 .25

Fauna — A1077

Designs: 3r, Sri Lankan birdwing butterfly. 12r, Grizzled giant squirrel. 100r, Sri Lankan jungle fowl.

Perf. 13 Syncopated
2018, May 24 Litho.
Granite Paper

2141-2143 A1077 Set of 3 1.50 1.50
2143a Souvenir sheet of 3, #2141-2143 1.50 1.50

A1078

A1079

A1080

A1081

A1082

A1083

A1084

A1085

A1086

A1087

A1088

A1089

A1090

A1091

A1092

A1093

A1094

Traditional Sinhalese Exorcism Ritual Dancers A1095

Perf. 12¾x13¼ Syncopated

2018, Aug. 8 Litho.

Granite Paper

2144 A1078 15r multi .25 .25
2145 A1079 15r multi .25 .25
2146 A1080 15r multi .25 .25
2147 A1081 15r multi .25 .25
2148 A1082 15r multi .25 .25
2149 A1083 15r multi .25 .25
2150 A1084 15r multi .25 .25
2151 A1085 15r multi .25 .25
2152 A1086 15r multi .25 .25
2153 A1087 15r multi .25 .25
2154 A1088 15r multi .25 .25
2155 A1089 15r multi .25 .25
2156 A1090 15r multi .25 .25
2157 A1091 15r multi .25 .25
a. Souvenir sheet of 6, #2144, 2145, 2149, 2150, 2153, 2157, perf. 13½x13¾ syncopated 1.50 1.50
2158 A1092 15r multi .25 .25
2159 A1093 15r multi .25 .25
2160 A1094 15r multi .25 .25
a. Souvenir sheet of 6, #2146, 2154, 2155, 2158, 2159, 2160, perf. 13½x13¾ syncopated 1.50 1.50
2161 A1095 15r multi .25 .25
a. Souvenir sheet of 6, #2147, 2148, 2151, 21528, 2156, 2161, perf. 13½x13¾ syncopated 1.50 1.50
Nos. 2144-2161 (18) 4.50 4.50

Bishop Charles de Forbin-Janson (1785-1844), Founder of Pontifical Society of the Holy Childhood — A1096

2018, Sept. 29 Litho. *Perf. 13¼x12*

Granite Paper

2162 A1096 45r multi .55 .55

Pontifical Society of the Holy Childhood, 175th anniv.

World Children's Day A1097

Perf. 12¾x13¼ Syncopated

2018, Oct. 1 Litho.

Granite Paper

2163 A1097 45r multi .55 .55

World Post Day — A1098

2018, Oct. 9 Litho. *Perf. 13¼x12*

Granite Paper

2164 A1098 15r multi .25 .25

Lighthouses A1099

Designs: No. 2165, Oluvil Lighthouse. No. 2166, Barberyn Lighthouse. No. 2167, Point Pedro Lighthouse. No. 2168, Galbokka Point Lighthouse.

2018, Oct. 26 Litho. *Perf. 12x13¼*

Granite Paper

2165 A1099 45r multi .55 .55
a. Souvenir sheet of 1, perf. 13¼ .55 .55
b. As "a," with Thailand 2018 Philatelic Exhibition emblem overprinted in gold in sheet margin *.55 .55*
2166 A1099 45r multi .55 .55
a. Souvenir sheet of 1, perf. 13¼ .55 .55
b. As "a," with Thailand 2018 Philatelic Exhibition emblem overprinted in gold in sheet margin *.55 .55*
2167 A1099 45r multi .55 .55
a. Souvenir sheet of 1, perf. 13¼ .55 .55
b. As "a," with Thailand 2018 Philatelic Exhibition emblem overprinted in gold in sheet margin *.55 .55*
2168 A1099 45r multi .55 .55
a. Souvenir sheet of 1, perf. 13¼ .55 .55
b. As "a," with Thailand 2018 Philatelic Exhibition emblem overprinted in gold in sheet margin *.55 .55*
Nos. 2165-2168 (4) 2.20 2.20

Rubber Trade in Sri Lanka, Cent. — A1100

2018, Oct. 27 Litho. *Perf. 13¼x12*

Granite Paper

2169 A1100 15r multi .25 .25

Uva-Wellassa Uprising, 200th Anniv. — A1101

2018, Nov. 30 Litho. *Perf. 13¼x12*

Granite Paper

2170 A1101 15r multi .25 .25

Most Venerable Rathmalane Sri Dharmarama Nayaka Thero (1853-1918), Monk and Literary Scholar — A1102

Perf. 13¼x12¾ Syncopated

2018, Dec. 2 Litho.

Granite Paper

2171 A1102 15r multi .25 .25

Visit to Sri Lanka of Lions Club International President Gudrun Yngvadottir — A1103

Perf. 12¾x13¼ Syncopated

2018, Dec. 3 Litho.

Granite Paper

2172 A1103 45r multi .50 .50

Christmas A1104

Designs: 15r, Adoration of the Shepherds. 45r, Holy Family.

Perf. 12¾x13¼ Syncopated

2018, Dec. 9 Litho.

Granite Paper

2173-2174 A1104 Set of 2 .65 .65
2174a Souvenir sheet of 2, #2173-2174, perf. 13½x13¾ syncopated .65 .65

Proposal to Declare the Theravada Tripitaka a UNESCO Memory of the World Document — A1105

2019, Jan. 5 Litho. *Perf. 13¼x12*

Granite Paper

2175 A1105 15r multi .25 .25

Spices A1106

Designs: No. 2176, 15r, Cinnamon. No. 2177, 15r, Pepper. No. 2178, 15r, Cloves. No. 2179, 15r, Nutmeg.

Perf. 12¾x13¼ Syncopated

2019, Feb. 26 Litho.

Granite Paper

2176-2179 A1106 Set of 4 .70 .70
2179a Souvenir sheet of 4, #2176-2179, perf. 13¾ syncopated .70 .70

Tripitaka Week — A1107

Perf. 13x12¾ Syncopated

2019, Mar. 23 Litho.

2180 A1107 45r multi .55 .55

Dr. Cyril Ponnamperuma (1923-94), Exobiologist, Examining Moon Rock — A1108

Perf. 13¼x12½ Syncopated

2019, Mar. 28 **Litho.**
2181 A1108 15r multi .25 .25

International Labor Organization, Cent. — A1109

Perf. 13x12¾ Syncopated

2019, Apr. 11 **Litho.**
2182 A1109 15r multi .25 .25

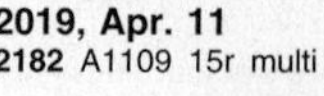

A1110

A1111

Kuddala Jathaka A1112

Perf. 13x13¼ Syncopated

2019, May 7 **Litho.**
2183 A1110 10r multi .25 .25
2184 A1111 15r multi .25 .25
2185 A1112 45r multi .50 .50
a. Souvenir sheet of 3, #2183-2185, perf. 13½x13¾ syncopated .80 .80
Nos. 2183-2185 (3) 1.00 1.00

Vesak Festival.

World Thalassemia Day — A1113

Perf. 13¼x12½ Syncopated

2019, May 8 **Litho.**
2186 A1113 15r multi .25 .25

Thotagamu Rathpath Raja Maha Vihara Wall Painting — A1114

Perf. 13¼x12¾ Syncopated

2019, May 17 **Litho.**
2187 A1114 15r multi .25 .25

State Vesak Festival.

Kataragama Festival — A1115

Various festival participants.

Perf. 13¼x12½ Syncopated

2019, July 8 **Litho.**
2188 A1115 15r multi .25 .25
a. Souvenir sheet of 1, perf. 14x13¾ syncopated .25 .25
2189 A1115 35r multi .40 .40
a. Souvenir sheet of 1, perf. 14x13¾ syncopated .40 .40
2190 A1115 45r multi .50 .50
a. Souvenir sheet of 1, perf. 14x13¾ syncopated .50 .50
Nos. 2188-2190 (3) 1.15 1.15

Express Mail Service, 20th Anniv. A1116

Perf. 13x13¼ Syncopated

2019, Sept. 10 **Litho.**
2191 A1116 45r multi .50 .50

Lotus Tower, Colombo A1117

2019, Sept. 16 **Litho.** ***Perf. 12x13***
2192 A1117 45r multi .50 .50
a. Souvenir sheet of 1, perf. 13¼ .50 .50

World Children's Day A1118

Perf. 13x13¼ Syncopated

2019, Oct. 1 **Litho.**
2193 A1118 15r multi .25 .25

Mohandas K. Gandhi (1869-1948), Indian Nationalist Leader — A1119

Gandhi: 45r, Without eyeglasses. 100r, With eyeglasses.

Perf. 13¼x13 Syncopated

2019, Oct. 2 **Litho.**
2194-2195 A1119 Set of 2 1.60 1.60
2195a Souvenir sheet of 2, #2194-2195, perf. 14x13½ syncopated 1.60 1.60

Fauna of Wasgamuwa National Park — A1120

Designs: No. 2196, Painted-lipped lizard. No. 2197, Five-bar swordtail. No. 2198, Sri Lanka combtail. No. 2199, Sri Lanka purple-face langur. No. 2200, Asian elephant. No. 2201, Sri Lanka red-faced malkoha.

2019, Oct. 5 **Litho.** ***Perf. 13½x12***
2196 A1120 12r multi .25 .25
a. Souvenir sheet of 1, perf. 13½x13¼ .25 .25
2197 A1120 12r multi .25 .25
a. Souvenir sheet of 1, perf. 13½x13¼ .25 .25
2198 A1120 15r multi .25 .25
a. Souvenir sheet of 1, perf. 13½x13¼ .25 .25
2199 A1120 15r multi .25 .25
a. Souvenir sheet of 1, perf. 13½x13¼ .25 .25
2200 A1120 45r multi .50 .50
a. Souvenir sheet of 1, perf. 13½x13¼ .50 .50
2201 A1120 45r multi .50 .50
a. Souvenir sheet of 1, perf. 13½x13¼ .50 .50
Nos. 2196-2201 (6) 2.00 2.00

International Year of the Periodic Table — A1121

2019, Oct. 6 **Litho.** ***Perf. 13½x12***
2202 A1121 45r multi .50 .50

International Year of Indigenous Languages A1122

Perf. 13 Syncopated

2019, Oct. 7 **Litho.**
2203 A1122 15r multi .25 .25

Solias Mendis (1897-1975), Painter — A1123

Perf. 13x13¼ Syncopated

2019, Oct. 8 **Litho.**
2204 A1123 15r multi .25 .25

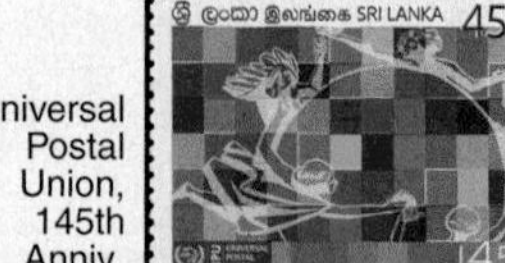

Universal Postal Union, 145th Anniv. A1124

Perf. 13x13¼ Syncopated

2019, Oct. 9 **Litho.**
2205 A1124 45r multi .50 .50

World Post Day A1125

Perf. 13x13¼ Syncopated

2019, Oct. 9 **Litho.**
2206 A1125 45r multi .50 .50

Christmas A1126

Designs: 15r, Family distributing gifts. 45r, Nativity.

Perf. 13x13¼ Syncopated

2019, Dec. 1 **Litho.**
2207-2208 A1126 Set of 2 .70 .70
2208a Souvenir sheet of 2, #2207-2208, perf. 13¼x14 syncopated .70 .70

POSTAL-FISCAL STAMPS

The editors believe that six additional revenue stamps were authorized for postal use during 1979-98 and would like to examine them.

National Coat of Arms With Sinhalese Characters at Left and Right — PF1

Perf. 13x12

1979, May 28 **Engr.** **Wmk. 233**
AR2 PF1 20r dark green —
AR3 PF1 50r violet —

Nos. AR2 and AR3 were issued in 1974 for revenue purposes, and were usable on mail starting on May 28, 1979.

Coat of Arms Type of 1979

Perf. 13x12

1983, Oct. 14 **Engr.** **Wmk. 233**
AR4 PF1 100r carmine 26.00 32.00

National Coat of Arms — PF2

1984 **Engr.** ***Perf. 14½x14***
AR6 PF2 50r vermilion 2.00 2.00
AR7 PF2 100r deep claret 3.75 3.75

A lithographed 500r value exists but was not authorized for postal use.

Arms Type of 1984

Perf. 14½x14¼

1998, Dec. 16 **Engr.** **Wmk. 408**
AR9 PF2 100r chocolate —

An additional stamp was issued in this set. The editors would like to examine it.

National Coat of Arms — PF3

Granite Paper
Color of Denomination

Perf. 12½ Syncopated

2002, May 28 **Litho. & Engr.**

No.	Type	Description	Unused	Used
AR10	PF3	50r brown	—	

Stamps of type PF3 with denominations of 500r and 1000r were not valid for postage.

An additional stamp was issued in this set. The editors would like to examine it.

National Coat of Arms — PF4

Granite Paper
Color of Denomination

Perf. 12¾x12½ Syncopated

2007, Nov. 23 **Photo. & Engr.**

No.	Type	Description	Unused	Used
AR13	PF4	50r blue	1.15	1.15
AR14	PF4	100r gray green	2.50	2.50
AR15	PF4	200r lilac	5.00	5.00
		Nos. AR13-AR15 (3)	8.65	8.65

OFFICIAL STAMP

Parliament Building and Arms of Sri Lanka O1

2005, June 8 **Litho.** ***Perf. 14***

No.	Type	Description	Unused	Used
O25	O1	5r multi	—	—

No. O25 was for use by members of Parliament.

STELLALAND

ˈste-lə-ˌland

LOCATION — South Africa
GOVT. — Republic
AREA — 5,000 sq. mi. (approx.)
CAPITAL — Vryburg

This short-lived republic was set up by the Boers in an effort to annex territory ruled by the Bechuana chiefs. Great Britain refused to recognize it and in 1885 sent an expeditionary force which ended the political career of the country.

Stellaland was annexed by Great Britain in 1885 and became a part of British Bechuanaland.

12 Pence = 1 Shilling

Coat of Arms — A1

1884, Feb. **Unwmk.** **Litho.** ***Perf. 12***

No.	Type	Description	Unused	Used
1	A1	1p red	225.00	*375.00*
a.		Horiz. pair, imperf. between	4,500.	
b.		Vert. pair, imperf. between	5,000.	
2	A1	3p orange	37.50	*375.00*
a.		Horiz. pair, imperf. vert.	1,400.	
b.		Vert. pair, imperf. between	2,200.	
c.		Horiz. pair, imperf. between	1,100.	
3	A1	4p gray	32.50	*400.00*
a.		Horiz. pair, imperf. between	850.00	
b.		Vert. pair, imperf. between	*2,400.*	
4	A1	6p lilac	40.00	*400.00*
a.		Horiz. pair, imperf. between	1,750.	
b.		Vert. pair, imperf. between	2,000.	
5	A1	1sh green	92.50	*850.00*
		Nos. 1-5 (5)	427.50	2,400.

Imperf. varieties are believed to be proofs.

Used values are for examples with manuscript cancellations or postmaster's initials. Many used stamps went uncanceled.

No. 3 Handstamped in Lake Violet

1885

No.	Type	Description	Unused	Used
6	A1	2p on 4p olive gray	*3,500.*	

The status of No. 6 has long been questioned.

STRAITS SETTLEMENTS

ˈstrāts ˈse-təl-mənts

LOCATION — Malay Peninsula in southeastern Asia
GOVT. — British Colony
AREA — 1,356 sq. mi.
POP. — 1,435,895 (estimated)
CAPITAL — Singapore

The colony comprised the settlements of Malacca, Singapore and Penang, which were incorporated under one government in 1826 and the administration transferred from India to the Secretary of State for the Colonies in 1867.

The colony was dissolved in 1946 when Singapore became a separate crown colony. Malacca and Penang were incorporated into the Malayan Union, which became the Federation of Malaya in 1948.

Stamps of India were used in Malacca, Penang and Singapore, 1854-67.

See Malaya for stamps of the Federated Malay States, the Federation of Malaya, Johore, Kedah, Kelantan, Malacca, Negri Sembilan, Pahang, Penang, Perak, Perlis, Selangor, Sungei Ujong and Trengganu.

100 Cents = 1 Dollar

Stamps of India Surcharged in Red, Blue, Black Violet or Green

Nos. 1-7

Nos. 8-9

1867, Sept. 1 **Wmk. 38** ***Perf. 14***

No.	Type	Description	Unused	Used
1	A7	1½c on ½a bl (R)	130.00	*200.00*
2	A7	2c on 1a brn (R)	200.00	100.00
3	A7	3c on 1a brn (Bl)	190.00	100.00
4	A7	4c on 1a brn (Bk)	325.00	275.00
5	A7	6c on 2a yel (V)	925.00	250.00
6	A7	8c on 2a yel (G)	360.00	42.50
7	A9	12c on 4a grn (R)	1,600.	325.00
a.		Double surcharge	4,500.	
8	A7	24c on 8a rose (Bl)	775.00	110.00
9	A7	32c on 2a yel (Bk)	525.00	120.00

Manuscript Surcharge, Pen Bar Across "THREE HALF" of No. 1

No.	Type	Description	Unused	Used
9A	A7	2(c) on 1½c on ½a	*20,000.*	*6,500.*

Values for Nos. 1-9A are for stamps with perforations touching the frame line on one or two sides. Used values for Nos. 1-9 are for stamps with company chops in addition to postal cancellations. Examples with postal cancels only sell for somewhat higher prices. For detailed listings, see the Scott Classic Specialized catalogue.

A2

A3

A4

A5

1867-72 **Typo.** **Wmk. 1** ***Perf. 14***

No.	Type	Description	Unused	Used
10	A2	2c bister brown	60.00	8.50
11	A2	4c rose	87.50	13.50
12	A2	6c violet	165.00	22.50
13	A3	8c yellow	260.00	18.00
a.		8c orange	260.00	20.00
14	A3	12c blue	230.00	12.50
15	A3	24c green	210.00	8.00
16	A4	30c claret ('72)	425.00	17.50
17	A5	32c pale red	675.00	70.00
18	A5	96c olive gray	425.00	55.00
		Nos. 10-18 (9)	2,538.	225.50

Corner ornaments of types A2, A3 and A5 differ for each value.

See Nos. 19, 40-44, 48-50, 52-57. For surcharges see Nos. 20-35, 58-59, 61-66, 73-82, 91. For overprints see Malaya, Johore No. 1, Perak Nos. 1, O1-O2, Selangor Nos. 1-2, Sungei Ujong Nos. 2-3.

See the *Scott Classic Catalogue* for other shades.

Stamps of Straits Settlements, 1867-82, overprinted "B" are listed under Bangkok.

1871 ***Perf. 12½***

No.	Type	Description	Unused	Used
19	A5	96c olive gray	2,750.	275.00

Stamps of 1867-72 Surcharged

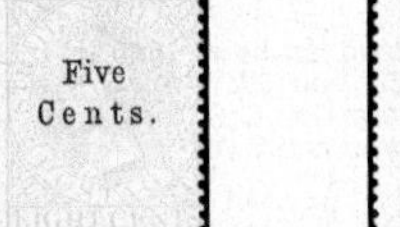

1879, May ***Perf. 14***

No.	Type	Description	Unused	Used
20	A3	5c on 8c yellow	150.00	*190.00*
a.		No period after "CENTS"	1,100.	*1,300.*
21	A5	7c on 32c pale red	180.00	*200.00*
a.		No period after "CENTS"	1,800.	*2,200.*

No. 16 Surcharged

e f g j

k

m

h

1880

No.	Type	Description	Unused	Used
22	A4(e)	10c on 30c	325.00	62.50
23	A4(f)	10c on 30c	925.00	130.00
24	A4(g)	10c on 30c	325.00	62.50
25	A4(h)	10c on 30c	—	24,000.
25A	A4(j)	10c on 30c	8,750.	1,100.
25B	A4(k)	10c on 30c	8,750.	1,100.
25C	A4(m)	10c on 30c	8,750.	1,100.

Surcharges e & f and g, h, j & m are similar and require expert identification. Values are for examples with a certificate of authenticity from a reputable source.

Unused examples are valued without gum.

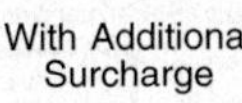

With Additional Surcharge

No.	Type	Description	Unused	Used
26	A4(e)	10c on 30c	600.	100.
27	A4(f)	10c on 30c	11,000.	1,100.
27A	A4(g)	10c on 30c	6,500.	650.
28	A4(h)	10c on 30c	*20,000.*	2,250.
28A	A4(j)	10c on 30c	*20,000.*	2,250.
28B	A4(k)	10c on 30c	*20,000.*	2,250.
28C	A4(m)	10c on 30c	*20,000.*	2,250.

Unused examples are valued without gum.

No. 13 Surcharged

n o p

1880

No.	Type	Description	Unused	Used
29	A3(n)	5c on 8c yellow	200.00	*225.00*
30	A3(o)	5c on 8c yellow	700.00	*925.00*
31	A3(p)	5c on 8c yellow	210.00	*250.00*

No. 11 Surcharged

1882, Jan.

No.	Type	Description	Unused	Used
32	A2	5c on 4c rose	375.00	*400.00*

Nos. 12 and 16 Surcharged

1880-81

No.	Type	Description	Unused	Used
33	A2	10c on 6c violet ('81)	90.00	7.50
a.		Double surcharge	—	3,250.
34	A3	10c on 12c blue ('81)	77.50	12.00
35	A4	10c on 30c claret	500.00	100.00
		Nos. 33-35 (3)	667.50	119.50

A6

A7

1882, Jan. Typo. *Perf. 14*

No.	Type	Description	Unused	Used
38	A6	5c violet brown	120.00	*140.00*
39	A7	10c slate	575.00	80.00
		Ovptd. "SPECIMEN"	1,000.	

See Nos. 45-47, 51. For surcharges see Nos. 60, 67-72, 89-92.

1882-99 Wmk. Crown and C A (2)

No.	Type	Description	Unused	Used
40	A2	2c bister brown	400.00	52.50
41	A2	2c car rose ('83)	13.00	1.00
a.		2c rose	52.50	4.75
42	A2	4c rose	170.00	14.00
43	A2	4c car rose ('99)	16.00	1.40
44	A2	4c bister brn ('83)	57.50	6.25
45	A6	5c ultra ('83)	19.00	1.40
46	A6	5c brown ('94)	17.50	1.10
47	A6	5c magenta ('99)	5.00	*2.40*
48	A2	6c violet	2.75	*16.00*
49	A3	8c orange	6.50	1.10
50	A3	8c ultra ('94)	5.25	.60
51	A7	10c slate	16.00	1.50
52	A3	12c vio brn ('83)	87.50	20.00
53	A3	12c claret ('94)	29.00	*16.00*
54	A3	24c blue grn ('83)	11.00	*7.00*
a.		24c yellow green ('84)	85.00	13.00
55	A4	30c claret ('91)	22.50	24.00
56	A5	32c red org ('87)	16.00	5.50
57	A5	96c olive gray ('88)	80.00	70.00
		Nos. 40-57 (18)	974.50	241.75

For overprints see Malaya, Perak Nos. O3-O9, Selangor Nos. 3-4, Sungei Ujong Nos. 6-7, 11.

Preceding Issues Surcharged

Surcharged Vertically

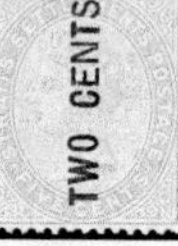

1883-84 Wmk. 2, 1

No.	Type	Description	Unused	Used
58	A3	2c on 8c orange	190.00	90.00
a.		Double surcharge	*3,750.*	*1,350.*
59	A5	2c on 32c pale red	900.00	300.00
a.		Double surcharge		
60	A6	2c on 5c ultra ('84)	175.00	180.00
a.		Pair, one without surcharge		
b.		Double surcharge		
		Nos. 58-60 (3)	1,265.	570.00

Five types of surcharge on No. 58, two types on No. 59 and three types on No. 60.

Surcharged in Black

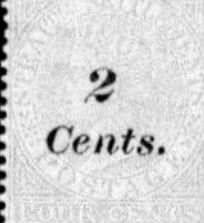

1883 Wmk. 2

No.	Type	Description	Unused	Used
61	A2	2c on 4c rose	100.00	*100.00*
b.		"s" of "Cents." inverted	1,700.	1,900.

Wmk. 1

No.	Type	Description	Unused	Used
62	A3	2c on 12c blue	500.00	180.00
a.		"s" of "Cents." inverted	8,000.	3,750.

Surcharged in Black or Blue

1884

No.	Type	Description	Unused	Used
63	A3	8c on 12c blue	1,300.	175.00

Wmk. 2

No.	Type	Description	Unused	Used
64	A3	8c on 12c vio brn	725.00	175.00

With Additional Surcharge Handstamped in Red

No.	Type	Description	Unused	Used
65	A3	8c on 8c on 12c vio brn (R + Bk)	575.00	500.00
66	A3	8c on 8c on 12c vio brn (R + Bl)	11,000.	

Surcharged in Black or Red

1884

No.	Type	Description	Unused	Used
67	A6	4c on 5c ultra (Bk)	3,500.	*5,750.*
68	A6	4c on 5c ultra (R)	190.00	150.00

No. 68 Surcharged in Red

No.	Type	Description	Unused	Used
69	A6	4c on 4c on 5c ultra		*42,500.*

No. 69 may be a trial printing. "Usage" seems to been restricted to less than 10 letters known sent from the Postmaster General to his wife.

Surcharged in Black

1885-87

No.	Type	Description	Unused	Used
70	A6	3c on 5c ultra	175.00	*280.00*
a.		Double surcharge	3,500.	

Surcharged in Black

No.	Type	Description	Unused	Used
71	A6	3c on 5c vio brn ('86)	350.00	*360.00*

Surcharged

No.	Type	Description	Unused	Used
72	A6	2c on 5c ultra ('87)	50.00	*110.00*
a.		Double surcharge	1,700.	1,600.
b.		"C" omitted		*4,500.*

In the surcharged issues of 1883 to 1887, Nos. 59, 62, 63 and 71 are on stamps watermarked Crown and C C, the others are watermarked Crown and C A.

Surcharged

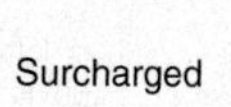

1885-94 Wmk. Crown and C A (2)

No.	Type	Description	Unused	Used
73	A5	3c on 32c magenta	2.25	1.10
74	A5	3c on 32c rose ('94)	2.75	.85
a.		Without surcharge	*6,500.*	

No. 74a value is for a stamp with perfs touching frame line.

Surcharged

1891

No.	Type	Description	Unused	Used
75	A3	10c on 24c green	8.25	1.40
a.		Narrow "0" in "10"	32.50	37.50

Surcharged

No.	Type	Description	Unused	Used
76	A5	30c on 32c red orange	16.50	4.25

Surcharged

1892

No.	Type	Description	Unused	Used
77	A2	1c on 2c rose	2.25	*5.00*
78	A2	1c on 4c bister brn	9.50	*7.50*
a.		Double surcharge	1,800.	
79	A2	1c on 6c violet	2.75	*12.50*
a.		Dbl. surch., one invtd.	2,300.	2,100.
80	A3	1c on 8c orange	1.25	4.25
81	A3	1c on 12c vio brown	5.75	*10.50*
		Nos. 77-81 (5)	21.50	39.75

Surcharged

No.	Type	Description	Unused	Used
82	A3	1c on 8c gray green	1.10	*1.75*

Queen Victoria — A13

1892-99 Typo.

No.	Type	Description	Unused	Used
83	A13	1c gray green	9.50	.80
84	A13	3c car rose ('95)	13.00	.55
85	A13	3c brown ('99)	17.50	.70
86	A13	25c dk vio & grn	37.50	7.50
87	A13	50c ol grn & car	29.00	3.50
88	A13	$5 org & car ('98)	500.00	275.00
		Nos. 83-88 (6)	606.50	288.05

Denomination of $5, is in color on plain tablet.

Stamps of 1883-94 Surcharged

1899

No.	Type	Description	Unused	Used
89	A6	4c on 5c ultra	14.00	*32.50*
a.		Double surcharge	—	3,750.
90	A6	4c on 5c brown	3.25	*5.25*
91	A3	4c on 8c brt blue	3.75	*2.00*
a.		4c on 8c ultra	4.00	*4.00*
b.		Double surcharge	*1,600.*	*1,500.*
		Nos. 89-91 (3)	21.00	*39.75*

Type of 1882 Issue Surcharged

No.	Type	Description	Unused	Used
92	A6	4c on 5c rose	1.10	.40
a.		Without surcharge	*40,000.*	

King Edward VII — A14

Numerals of 5c, 8c, 10c, 30c, $1 and $5, type A14, are in color on plain tablet.

1902 Wmk. 2 Typo.

No.	Type	Description	Unused	Used
93	A14	1c green	3.00	*5.00*
94	A14	3c vio & org	3.75	.25
95	A14	4c violet, *red*	5.00	.35
96	A14	5c violet	6.00	2.40
97	A14	8c violet, *blue*	4.75	.30
98	A14	10c vio & blk, *yel*	29.00	1.60
99	A14	25c violet & grn	19.00	13.00
100	A14	30c gray & car rose	25.00	10.00
101	A14	50c grn & car rose	24.00	22.50
102	A14	$1 green & blk	25.00	*80.00*
103	A14	$2 violet & blk	87.50	80.00
104	A14	$5 grn & brn org	215.00	180.00
104A	A14	$100 dl vio & grn, *yel*	*16,000.*	
		Nos. 93-104 (12)	447.00	395.40

High values of the 1902 and 1904 issues with revenue cancellations are of minimal value. No. 104A is inscribed "Postage & Revenue" but the limit of weight probably precluded its use postally.

See Nos. 113, 115-128B, 133.

A15

A16

A17

A18

1903-04

No.	Type	Description	Unused	Used
105	A15	1c gray green	4.25	9.25
106	A16	3c dull violet	12.00	4.75
107	A17	4c violet, *red*	17.50	.35
108	A18	8c violet, *blue*	52.50	1.50
		Nos. 105-108 (4)	86.25	15.85

See Nos. 109-112, 114, 129-132, 134.

1904-11 Chalky Paper Wmk. 3

No.	Type	Description	Unused	Used
109	A15	1c gray green	5.25	.25
110	A16	3c dull violet	3.00	.35
111	A17	4c violet, *red*	24.00	.80
112	A17	4c dull vio ('08)	6.50	.25
113	A14	5c violet ('06)	30.00	2.75
114	A18	8c violet, *bl*	57.50	1.60
115	A14	10c vio & blk, *yel*	9.00	.85
116	A14	10c vio, *yel* ('08)	15.00	1.10
117	A14	25c vio & grn	60.00	40.00
118	A14	25c violet ('09)	22.50	9.00
119	A14	30c gray & car rose	55.00	3.25
120	A14	30c vio & org ('09)	60.00	4.50
121	A14	50c grn & car rose	65.00	22.00
122	A14	50c blk, *grn* ('10)	9.50	5.25
123	A14	$1 green & blk	75.00	45.00
124	A14	$1 blk & red, *bl* ('11)	16.00	6.50
125	A14	$2 violet & blk	120.00	95.00
		Revenue cancel		15.00
126	A14	$2 grn & red, *yel* ('09)	27.50	25.00
127	A14	$5 grn & brn org	325.00	210.00
128	A14	$5 grn & red, *grn* ('10)	150.00	80.00
		Revenue cancel		6.50
128A	A14	$25 green & blk	3,600.	3,600.
		Revenue cancel		55.00
128B	A14	$100 dl vio & grn, *yel*	*22,000.*	
		Revenue cancel		200.00
		Nos. 109-128 (20)	1,136.	553.45

Nos. 125, 128A and 128B are on chalky paper, the other values are on both ordinary and chalky. The note about No. 104A will apply to No. 128B.

1906-11 Ordinary Paper

No.	Type	Description	Unused	Used
129	A15	1c blue grn ('10)	25.00	1.25
130	A16	3c carmine ('08)	9.25	.25
131	A17	4c carmine ('07)	8.50	3.00
132	A17	4c lake ('11)	3.50	.95
133	A14	5c orange ('09)	3.00	2.75
134	A18	8c ultra ('06)	4.50	.65
		Nos. 129-134 (6)	53.75	8.85

Stamps of Labuan 1902-03, Overprinted or Surcharged in Red or Black

a

b

c

Perf. 12½ to 16 and Compound

1907 **Unwmk.**

134A A38(a) 1c violet & blk 75.00 *190.00*
135 A38(a) 2c grn & blk 425.00 *500.00*
136 A38(a) 3c brn & blk 27.50 *95.00*
137 A38(c) 4c on 12c yel & blk 4.00 *14.00*
a. No period after "CENTS" 650.00 —
138 A38(c) 4c on 16c org brn & grn (Bk) 12.00 *15.00*
a. With additional name in red 700.00 1,100.
b. As "a," in pair with #138 9,000.
139 A38(c) 4c on 18c bis & blk 3.00 *14.00*
a. No period after "CENTS" 425.00 675.00
b. "FOUR CENTS." & bar double 17,500.
140 A38(a) 8c org & blk 7.25 *13.50*
141 A38(b) 10c sl bl & brn 12.50 *16.00*
a. No period after "Settlements" 775.00 *800.00*
142 A38(a) 25c grnsh bl & grn 35.00 *52.50*
143 A38(a) 50c gray lil & vio 25.00 *75.00*
144 A38(a) $1 org & red brn 50.00 *125.00*
Nos. 134A-144 (11) 676.25 *1,110.*

A19

1908-11 **Typo.** **Wmk. 3** ***Perf. 14***

Chalky Paper

145 A19 $25 bl & vio, *bl* ('11) 3,600. 2,300.
Revenue cancel 200.
146 A19 $500 violet & org *175,000.*
Revenue cancel 1,000.

No. 146 is inscribed "Postage-Revenue" but was probably used only for revenue.

Excellent forgeries of No. 146 exist.

A20

1910 **Chalky Paper**

147 A20 21c maroon & vio 7.00 *40.00*
148 A20 45c black, *green* 3.75 4.50

King George V
A21 A22

A23 A24

A25 A26

Die I (Type A24)

For description of dies I and II see front section of the Catalogue.

The 25c, 50c and $2 denominations of type A24 show the numeral on horizontally-lined tablet.

1912-23 **Chalky Paper** **Wmk. 3**

149 A21 1c green 14.50 1.60
150 A21 1c black ('18) 4.00 2.40
151 A25 2c dp green ('18) 2.25 .55
152 A22 3c scarlet 3.25 .25
a. 3c carmine 3.50 1.35
153 A23 4c gray violet 4.50 .65
154 A23 4c scarlet ('18) 4.00 .25
a. Booklet pane of 1
b. Booklet pane of 12
c. 4c carmine ('18) 2.00 .25
155 A24 5c orange 2.25 1.10
156 A25 6c dull claret ('20) 2.25 .55
157 A25 8c ultra 3.75 .85
158 A24 10c violet, *yel* 1.60 1.10
159 A24 10c brt blue ('19) 4.25 .50
160 A26 21c maroon & vio 16.00 *16.00*
161 A24 25c vio & red vio 17.00 15.00
162 A24 30c vio & org ('14) 8.50 6.75
163 A26 45c blk, *bl grn,* ol back ('14) 7.50 *27.50*
Ovptd. "SPECIMEN" 85.00
a. 45c black, *emerald* ('17) 7.25 *13.75*
164 A24 50c black, *grn* ('14) 6.50 5.25
a. 50c blk, *bl grn,* olive back ('18) 32.50 13.50
b. 50c black, *emerald* ('21) 14.50 10.50
c. Die II ('22) 3.25 *5.00*
165 A24 $1 blk & red, *bl* ('14) 21.00 17.50
166 A24 $2 grn & red, *yel* ('15) 20.00 52.50
167 A24 $5 grn & red, *grn* ('15) 120.00 85.00
a. $5 grn & red, *bl grn,* ol back 190.00 115.00
b. $5 grn & red, *emer* ('15) 240.00 140.00
c. Die II ('23) 145.00 90.00
Nos. 149-167 (19) 263.10 235.30

The 1c, 3c, 5c and 8c are on ordinary paper.

Surface-colored Paper

168 A24 10c violet, *yel* 2.40 1.25
169 A26 45c black, *grn* ('14) 7.50 *22.50*
170 A24 $2 grn & red, *yel* ('14) 16.00 *52.50*
171 A24 $5 grn & red, *grn* 120.00 60.00
Nos. 168-171 (4) 145.90 *136.25*

See Nos. 179-201. For surcharges see Nos. B1-B2.

A27

1915

172 A27 $25 bl & vio, *bl* 2,150. 650.00
Revenue cancel 5.75
173 A27 $100 red & blk, *bl* *8,500.*
Revenue cancel *90.00*
174 A27 $500 org & dl vio *90,000.*
Revenue cancel *200.00*

Although Nos. 173 and 174 were available for postage, it is probable that they were used only for fiscal purposes.

See Nos. 202-204, AR1.

Die II (Type A24)

1921-32 **Ordinary Paper** **Wmk. 4**

179 A21 1c black .65 .25
180 A25 2c green .65 .25
181 A25 2c brown 8.00 4.75
182 A22 3c green 1.75 .90
183 A23 4c scarlet 2.25 *6.25*
184 A23 4c dp violet ('25) .70 .25
185 A23 4c orange ('29) 1.10 .25
186 A24 5c orange ('23) 2.75 1.50
a. Die I 3.75 .25
187 A24 5c dk brown ('32) 3.25 .25
a. Die I ('32) 5.75 .25
188 A25 6c claret 2.50 .25
189 A25 6c scarlet ('27) 3.00 .25
a. 6c rose red ('25) 30.00 11.00
190 A24 10c ultra (I) 2.00 4.25

Chalky Paper

191 A24 10c vio, *yel* ('27) 3.25 .35
a. Die I ('25) 3.00 *14.00*
192 A25 12c ultra 1.35 .25
193 A26 21c mar & vio 7.00 *60.00*
194 A24 25c vio & red vio 5.75 2.00
a. Die I 35.00 90.00
195 A24 30c violet & org 2.25 1.50
a. Die I 29.00 *60.00*
196 A26 35c org & vio 14.00 7.00
197 A26 35c vio & car ('31) 11.50 8.00
198 A24 50c blk, *emer* 2.00 .45
199 A24 $1 blk & red, *bl* 7.00 1.80
200 A24 $2 grn & red, *yel* 11.50 9.25
201 A24 $5 grn & red, *grn* 125.00 45.00
202 A27 $25 bl & vio, *bl* 1,450. 200.00
203 A27 $100 red & blk, *bl* 10,000. 3,100.
Revenue cancel 175.00
204 A27 $500 org & dl vio *75,000.*
Revenue cancel 700.00
Nos. 179-201 (23) 219.20 155.00

No. 192 is on ordinary paper.

Nos. 203 and 204 were probably used only for fiscal purposes.

Stamps of 1912-21 Overprinted in Black

1922 **Wmk. 3**

151d A25 2c deep green 50.00 *28.00*
154d A23 4c scarlet 12.00 *26.00*
155d A24 5c orange 12.00 *22.50*
157d A25 8c ultra 2.75 *12.50*
161d A24 25c vio & red vio 5.50 *52.50*
163d A26 45c blk, *bl grn,* ol back 4.00 *50.00*
165d A24 $1 blk & red, *bl* 675.00 *1,800.*
166d A24 $2 grn & red, *yel* 30.00 *160.00*
167d A24 $5 grn & red, *grn* 475.00 *825.00*

Wmk. 4

179d A21 1c black 3.50 *27.50*
180d A25 2c green 2.75 *16.00*
183d A23 4c scarlet 5.00 *52.50*
186d A24 5c orange (II) 3.25 *52.50*
190d A24 10c ultra 2.75 *29.00*
199d A24 $1 blk & red, *bl* 22.50 *160.00*
Nos. 151d-199d (15) 1,306. *3,314.*

Industrial fair at Singapore, Mar. 31-Apr. 15, 1922.

Common Design Types

pictured following the introduction.

Silver Jubilee Issue

Common Design Type

1935, May 6 **Engr.** ***Perf. 11x12***

213 CD301 5c black & ultra 3.50 .35
214 CD301 8c indigo & green 3.75 *3.50*
215 CD301 12c ultra & brown 3.75 8.50
216 CD301 25c brn vio & ind 4.00 *12.75*
Nos. 213-216 (4) 15.00 *25.10*
Set, never hinged 25.00
Set, perf. "SPECIMEN" 240.00

George V — A28

1936-37 **Typo.** ***Perf. 14***

Chalky Paper

217 A28 1c black ('37) 1.60 .25
218 A28 2c green 1.60 .80
220 A28 4c orange brn 2.40 .80
221 A28 5c brown 1.10 .35
222 A28 6c rose red 1.35 1.25
223 A28 8c gray 3.75 .80
224 A28 10c dull vio 2.40 .70
225 A28 12c ultra 2.25 3.00
226 A28 25c rose red & vio 1.60 .60
227 A28 30c org & dk vio 1.40 3.50
229 A28 40c dk vio & car 1.40 2.75
230 A28 50c blk, *emerald* 4.75 1.40
232 A28 $1 red & blk, *blue* 20.00 1.90
233 A28 $2 rose red & gray grn 57.50 11.50
234 A28 $5 grn & red, *grn* ('37) 140.00 11.50
Nos. 217-234 (15) 243.10 41.10
Set, never hinged 325.00
Set, perf. "SPECIMEN" 525.00

Coronation Issue

Common Design Type

1937, May 12 **Engr.** ***Perf. 13½x14***

235 CD302 4c deep orange .65 .25
236 CD302 8c gray black .80 .25
237 CD302 12c bright ultra 1.80 1.10
Nos. 235-237 (3) 3.25 1.60
Set, never hinged 6.00
Set, perf. "SPECIMEN" 240.00

George VI — A29

Die I

Die II

Two Dies

Die I. Printed in two operations. Lines of background touch outside of central oval. Foliage of palms touches outer frame line. Palm frond in front of King's eye has two points.

Die II. Printed from a single plate. Lines of background separated from central oval by a white line. Foliage of palms does not touch outer frame line. Palm frond in front of King's eye has one point.

1937-41 **Typo.** ***Perf. 14***

238 A29 1c black (I) 6.00 .25
239 A29 2c green (I) 11.00 .25
c. Die II ('38) 35.00 .45
239A A29 2c brn org ('41) (II) 1.25 *20.00*
239B A29 3c green ('41) (II) 5.00 4.25
240 A29 4c brown org (I) 13.50 .25
a. Die II ('38) 50.00 .25
241 A29 5c brown (I) 12.00 .35
a. Die II ('39) 20.00 .25
242 A29 6c rose red ('38) (I) 5.50 .65
243 A29 8c gray ('38) (I) 19.00 .25
244 A29 10c dull vio (I) 6.00 .25
245 A29 12c ultra ('38) (I) 6.00 .35
245A A29 15c ultra ('41) (II) 5.00 *10.50*
246 A29 25c rose red & vio (I) 25.00 1.10
247 A29 30c org & vio (I) 11.00 2.00
248 A29 40c dk vio & rose red (I) 10.00 2.50
249 A29 50c blk, *emer* ('38) (I) 10.00 .45
250 A29 $1 red & blk, *bl* ('38) (I) 15.00 .40
251 A29 $2 rose red & gray grn ('38) (I) 30.00 12.50
252 A29 $5 grn & red, *grn* ('38) (I) 15.00 7.50
Nos. 238-252 (18) 206.25 63.80
Set, never hinged 375.00
Set, perf. "SPECIMEN" 900.00

For overprints see Nos. 256-271, N1-N29 and Malaya, Malacca Nos. N1-N14, Penang Nos. N1-N26.

Stamps and Type of 1937-41 Overprinted in Red or Black

1945-48

256 A29 1c black (R) .25 .25
257 A29 2c brown org (II) .25 .25
a. Die I ('46) 7.50 *3.75*
258 A29 3c green .25 .25
259 A29 5c brown .75 .60
260 A29 6c gray .25 .25
261 A29 8c rose red .25 .25
262 A29 10c dull vio (I) .30 .25
a. 10c claret (II) ('48) *10.00* 1.25
263 A29 12c ultra 1.75 *3.25*
264 A29 15c ultra (Bk) 2.25 *4.75*
265 A29 15c ultra (R) .25 .25
266 A29 25c rose red & vio 1.40 .25
a. Double overprint 400.00

267 A29 50c blk, *emer* (R) .60 .25
268 A29 $1 rose red & blk 2.00 .25
269 A29 $2 rose red & gray grn 2.50 .65
270 A29 $5 grn & red, *grn* 72.50 72.50
271 A29 $5 brn org & vio 3.75 2.75
Nos. 256-271 (16) 89.30 87.00
Set, never hinged 140.00

The letters "B M A" are initials of "British Military Administration".

An 8c gray with BMA overprint was prepared but not issued. Value $5.

The 6c gray, 8c rose red and $5 brown orange & violet exist without BMA overprint, but were issued only with it.

No. 262a does not exist without overprint. No. 262 exists in at least three shades.

POSTAL-FISCAL STAMP

Type of 1915 with head George VI Inscribed "REVENUE" at each side

1938
AR1 A27 $25 Blue & purple, *blue* 1,450. 675.00

Although documentation authorizing its postal use has not been found, No. AR1 was frequently used as a postage stamp throughout 1941.

SEMI-POSTAL STAMPS

Nos. 152-153 Surcharged

1917 **Wmk. 3** ***Perf. 14***
B1 A22 3c + 2c scarlet 3.00 *32.50*
a. No period after "C" 575.00 *975.00*
B2 A23 4c + 2c gray violet 4.00 *35.00*
a. No period after "C" 525.00 *900.00*

POSTAGE DUE STAMPS

D1

1924-26 **Typo.** **Wmk. 4** ***Perf. 14***
J1 D1 1c violet 12.50 *5.75*
J2 D1 2c black 3.75 1.25
J3 D1 4c green ('26) 2.25 *3.00*
J4 D1 8c red 4.75 .60
J5 D1 10c orange 6.50 .90
J6 D1 12c ultramarine 7.50 .75
Nos. J1-J6 (6) 37.25 *12.25*
Set never hinged 55.00
Set, ovptd. "SPECIMEN" 350.00

OCCUPATION STAMPS

Issued Under Japanese Occupation

Nos. 238, 239A-B, 243 and 245A Hstmpd. in Red

1942, Mar. 16 **Wmk. 4** ***Perf. 14***
N1 A29 1c black 22.50 22.50
N2 A29 2c brown orange 16.00 16.00
N3 A29 3c green 70.00 *85.00*
N4 A29 8c gray 27.50 22.50
N5 A29 15c ultra 21.00 20.00
Nos. N1-N5 (5) 157.00 166.00
Set, never hinged 200.00

Other denominations with this handstamp are believed to be proofs.

The handstamp reads: "Seal of Post Office of Malayan Military Department."

Stamps of 1937-41, Handstamped in Red, Black, Violet or Brown

1942, Apr. 3

Handstamped in Red

N6 A29 1c black 4.00 4.00
N7 A29 2c orange 3.50 2.50
N8 A29 3c green 4.00 2.50
N9 A29 5c brown 30.00 32.50
N10 A29 8c gray 9.00 2.50
N11 A29 10c dull violet 80.00 52.50
N12 A29 12c ultramarine 120.00 160.00
N13 A29 15c ultramarine 3.75 4.00
N14 A29 30c orange & vio 4,500. 4,500.
N15 A29 40c dk vio & rose red 170.00 110.00
N16 A29 50c blk, *emerald* 80.00 60.00
N17 A29 $1 red & blk, *bl* 110.00 80.00
N18 A29 $2 rose red & gray grn 190.00 240.00
N19 A29 $5 grn & red, *grn* 260.00 300.00

Handstamp in Black

N6b A29 1c black 425.00 425.00
N7b A29 2c orange 140.00 150.00
N8b A29 3c green 450.00 475.00
N9b A29 5c brown 625.00 625.00
N10b A29 8c gray 290.00 290.00

Handstamp in Violet

N6c A29 1c black 1,700. 800.00
N7c A29 2c orange 275.00 250.00
N7D A29 2c green 4,250. 2,900.
N8c A29 3c green 1,700. 850.00
N13c A29 15c ultramarine 1,000. 850.00

Handstamp in Brown

N7e A29 2c orange 1,300. 800.00
N11e A29 10c dull violet 1,500. 900.00
N15e A29 40c dk vio & rose red 1,200. 550.00

Nos. N6-N7, N9, N11-N12, N15-N19 with red handstamp were used in Sumatra. The 2c green with red handstamp was not regularly issued. Value, $400.

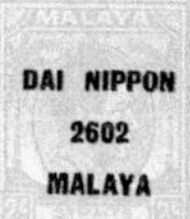

Straits Settlements Nos. 239A, 239B, 243 and 245A Ovptd. in Black

1942
N20 A29 2c brown orange 4.00 1.00
a. Inverted overprint 17.50 27.50
b. Dbl. ovpt., one invtd. 60.00 70.00
N21 A29 3c green 62.50 *75.00*
N22 A29 8c gray 11.00 4.75
a. Inverted overprint 22.50 45.00
N23 A29 15c ultra 26.00 16.00
Nos. N20-N23 (4) 103.50 96.75
Set never hinged 165.00

Straits Settlements Nos. 239A and 243 Overprinted in Black

1942, Nov. 3
N24 A29 2c brown orange 14.00 *25.00*
a. Inverted overprint 375.00 425.00
N25 A29 8c gray 15.00 *25.00*
a. Inverted overprint 375.00 425.00

Agricultural-Horticultural Exhibition held at Kuala Lumpur, Selangor, Nov. 1-2, 1942. Sold only at a temporary post office at the exhibition.

Straits Settlements Nos. 243, 245 and 248 Ovptd. in Black or Red

1943
N26 A29 8c gray (Bk) 1.60 1.00
a. Inverted overprint 60.00 75.00
b. Pair, ovpt. omitted on one stamp 900.00
N27 A29 8c gray (R) 2.75 4.00
N28 A29 12c ultramarine 2.00 16.00
N29 A29 40c dk vio & rose red 4.25 8.00
Nos. N26-N29 (4) 10.60 29.00
Set never hinged 17.00

The Japanese characters read: "Japanese Postal Service."

SUDAN

sü-'dan

LOCATION — Northeastern Africa, south of Egypt
GOVT. — Republic
AREA — 967,500 sq. mi.
POP. — 27,953,000 (1997 est.)
CAPITAL — Khartoum

10 Milliemes = 1 Piaster
100 Piasters = 1 Pound
Dinar (1992)
100 Qirsh = 1 Pound (2007)

Catalogue values for unused stamps in this country are for Never Hinged items, beginning with Scott 79 in the regular postage section, Scott C35 in the air post section, Scott CO1 in the air post official section, Scott J12 in the postage due section, and Scott O28 in the officials section.

Watermarks

Wmk. 71 — Rosette

Wmk. 179 — Multiple Crescent and Star

Wmk. 214 — Multiple S G

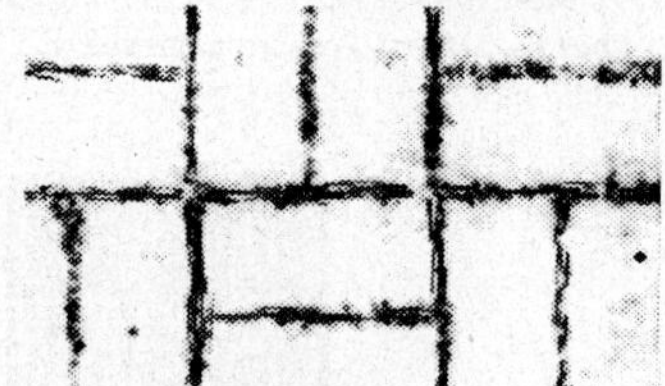
Wmk. 334 — Rectangles

Wmk. 345 — Rhinoceros

Egyptian Stamps of 1884-93 Overprinted in Black

1897, Mar. 1 **Wmk. 119** ***Perf. 14***
1 A18 1m brown 3.25 *1.75*
a. Inverted overprint 250.00
2 A19 2m green 1.25 *1.75*
3 A20 3m orange 1.50 *1.50*
4 A22 5m carmine rose 2.00 .70
a. Inverted overprint 325.00 275.00
5 A14 1p ultra 7.00 2.00
6 A15 2p orange brown 65.00 16.00
7 A16 5p gray 65.00 25.00
a. Double overprint *6,000.*
8 A23 10p violet 50.00 *65.00*
Nos. 1-8 (8) 195.00 113.70

Unofficial reprints exist. Counterfeits of Nos. 1-8 are plentiful.

Camel Post — A1

1898, Mar. 1 **Typo.** **Wmk. 71**
9 A1 1m rose & brn 1.00 *3.00*
10 A1 2m brown & grn 2.00 2.75
11 A1 3m green & vio 2.00 2.50
12 A1 5m black & rose 2.00 1.75
13 A1 1p yel brn & ultra 17.00 3.25
14 A1 2p ultra & blk 42.50 4.00
15 A1 5p grn & org brn 42.50 17.50
16 A1 10p dp vio & blk 35.00 5.00
Nos. 9-16 (8) 144.00 39.75

See Nos. 17-27, 43-50. For overprints see Nos. C3, MO1-MO15, O1-O9, O17-O24. For surcharges see Nos. 28, 62, C16.

1902-21 **Wmk. 179**
17 A1 1m car rose & brn ('05) 1.00 .50
18 A1 2m brown & grn 1.50 .25
19 A1 3m grn & vio ('03) 2.00 .25
20 A1 4m ol brn & bl ('07) 1.25 *2.25*
21 A1 4m brn & red ('07) 1.25 .75
22 A1 5m blk & rose red ('03) 1.75 .25
23 A1 1p brn & ultra ('03) 2.00 .30
24 A1 2p ultra & blk ('08) 40.00 1.25
25 A1 2p org & vio brn, chalky paper ('21) 11.00 *13.00*
26 A1 5p grn & org brn ('08) 30.00 .50
27 A1 10p dp vio & blk ('11) 25.00 3.75
Nos. 17-27 (11) 116.75 23.05

No. 15 Surcharged in Black

1903, Sept. **Wmk. 71**
28 A1 5m on 5p 8.50 *9.50*
a. Inverted surcharge 350.00 *275.00*

A2

1921-22 **Typo.** **Wmk. 179**
29 A2 1m orange & blk ('22) 1.00 *5.75*
30 A2 2m dk brn & org ('22) 9.00 *13.50*
31 A2 3m green & vio ('22) 2.50 *11.00*
32 A2 4m brown & grn ('22) 7.50 9.00
33 A2 5m blk & ol brn ('22) 2.25 .30
34 A2 10m black & car ('22) 5.75 .30
35 A2 15m org brn & ultra 7.00 1.25
Nos. 29-35 (7) 35.00 41.10

See Nos. 36-42. For overprints see Nos. C1-C2, O10-O16.

For surcharges see Nos. 60-61.

1927-40 **Wmk. 214**
36 A2 1m org yel & blk .40 .30
37 A2 2m dk brn & org .40 .25
38 A2 3m green & violet .40 .25
39 A2 4m brown & green .30 .25
40 A2 5m blk & ol brn .30 .25
a. Booklet pane of 4
41 A2 10m black & car .85 .25
42a A2 15m org brn & ultra 2.25 .25
43 A1 2p orange & vio brn 2.60 .25

44 A1 3p dk bl & red brn ('40) 5.50 .25
45 A1 4p blk & ultra ('36) 2.50 .25
46 A1 5p dk grn & org brn 1.00 .25
47 A1 6p blk & pale bl ('36) 10.00 2.25
48 A1 8p blk & pck grn ('36) 11.00 4.00
49 A1 10p dp vio & blk 5.50 .35
50a A1 20p bl & lt blue 8.00 .40
Nos. 36-50a (15) 51.00 9.80

Charles George Gordon — A3

Gordon Memorial College A4

Memorial Service at Khartoum — A5

1935, Jan. 1 Engr. *Perf. 13½x14*

51 A3 5m deep green .30 .25
52 A3 10m brown .75 .25
53 A3 13m ultra .80 *12.00*
54 A3 15m carmine 1.50 .25
55 A4 2p deep blue 1.90 .25
56 A4 5p orange 2.00 .85
57 A4 10p dull violet 7.75 *8.00*
58 A5 20p black 27.50 *72.50*
59 A5 50p red brown 85.00 *155.00*
Nos. 51-59 (9) 127.50 249.35
Set, never hinged 325.00

50th anniv. of the death of Gen. Charles George ("Chinese") Gordon (1833-85).

No. 41 Surcharged in Black

Wmk. Multiple S G (214)

1940, Feb. 25 Typo. *Perf. 14*

60 A2 5m on 10m black & car 1.50 1.50

Nos. 40 and 48 Surcharged in Black

a

b

1940-41

61 A2(a) 4½p on 5m ('41) 47.50 12.00
62 A1(b) 4½p on 8p 42.50 9.00

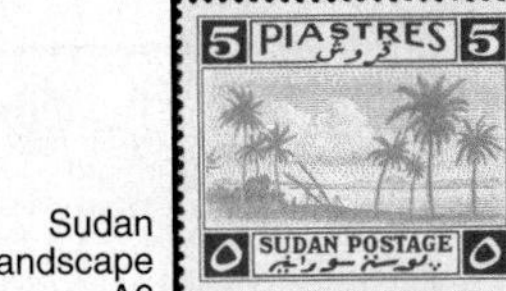

Sudan Landscape A6

Perf. 13½, 14x13½

1941 Litho. Unwmk.

Size: 21½x17½mm

63 A6 1m org & sl bl 2.50 *6.00*
64 A6 2m chocolate & org 2.50 *6.00*
65 A6 3m grn & rose vio 2.75 .25
66 A6 4m choc & bl grn .60 *.90*
67 A6 5m indigo & ol bis .25 .25
68 A6 10m indigo & rose pink 12.00 4.50
69 A6 15m chestnut & ultra 1.00 .25

Size: 29x25mm

71 A6 2p orange & claret 4.50 .90
72 A6 3p dk blue & fawn .85 .25
73 A6 4p blk & brt ultra 2.75 .25
74 A6 5p dk grn & brn org 5.00 *13.50*
75 A6 6p ind & turq bl 15.00 1.25
76 A6 8p black & green 15.00 1.00
77 A6 10p rose vio & gray 57.50 1.10
78 A6 20p dk & lt blue 55.00 45.00
Nos. 63-78 (15) 177.20 81.40
Set, never hinged 275.00

Catalogue values for unused stamps in this section, from this point to the end of the section, are for Never Hinged items.

Types of 1898-1940 with Changed Arabic Wording Below Camel

A7

A8

Wmk. 214

1948, Jan. 1 Typo. *Perf. 14*

79 A7 1m dk org & blk .25 *5.25*
80 A7 2m choc & org .60 *4.50*
81 A7 3m grn & rose lil .25 *7.25*
82 A7 4m choc & sl grn .40 *3.00*
83 A7 5m black & ol brn 9.00 2.25
84 A7 10m black & car 4.25 .25
a. Center inverted 50,000.
85 A7 15m org brn & ultra 3.75 .25
86 A8 2p org yel & vio 9.00 3.75
87 A8 3p dk bl & red brn 5.75 .25
88 A8 4p black & ultra 3.00 1.40
89 A8 5p dk grn & org 3.25 *5.25*
90 A8 6p blk & pale bl 3.50 2.75
91 A8 8p blk & pck grn 3.50 *4.50*
92 A8 10p dp rose lil & blk 12.00 7.50
93 A8 20p dk blue & blue 3.50 .40
a. Perf. 13 70.00 *210.00*
94 A8 50p ultra & car 6.00 2.25
Nos. 79-94 (16) 68.00 50.80

Arabic inscription, types A7 and A8: "Berid es-Sudan"; types A1 and A2; "Postai-Sudaniye."

For overprints see Nos. O28-O43.

Stamp of 1898 — A9

1948, Oct. 1 *Perf. 12½x13*

95 A9 2p dull blue & gray blk .75 .25

50th anniv. of Sudan's 1st postage stamp.

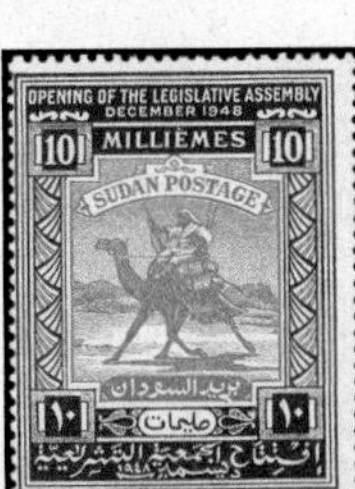

A10

1948, Dec. 19 *Perf. 13*

96 A10 10m black & carmine .75 .25
97 A10 5p dk green & orange 1.50 *2.00*

Legislative Assembly opening, Dec., 1948.

Nubian Ibex — A11

Cotton Picking — A12

Camel Post — A13

Designs: 2m, Shoebill. 3m, Giraffe. 4m, Baggara girl. 5m, Shilluk warrior. 10m, Hadendowa. 15m, Sudan policeman. 3p, Ambatch canoe. 3½p, Nuba wrestlers. 4p, Weaving. 5p, Saluka farming. 6p, Gum tapping. 8p, Darfur chief. 10p, Stack laboratory. 20p, Nile lechwe.

1951, Sept. 1 Typo. *Perf. 14*

Center in Black (#98-104)

98 A11 1m orange 2.00 1.25
99 A11 2m ultra 2.00 .75
100 A11 3m dark green 6.50 3.50
101 A11 4m emerald 1.75 *3.50*
102 A11 5m plum 1.25 .25
103 A11 10m light blue .25 .25
104 A11 15m dp orange brn 5.50 .25

Perf. 13

105 A12 2p lt bl & dk bl .25 .25
106 A12 3p vio blue & brn 6.50 .25
107 A12 3½p brown & bl grn 1.50 .25
108 A12 4p blk & dp bl 3.75 .25
109 A12 5p emer & org brn 2.00 .25
110 A12 6p black & blue 4.25 1.75
111 A12 8p brown & dp bl 7.00 2.50
112 A12 10p green & black .75 .75
113 A12 20p blk & bl grn 6.00 2.00
114 A13 50p blk & car 10.00 2.50
Nos. 98-114 (17) 61.25 20.50

See #159. For overprints see #O44-O61, O75.

Camel Post — A14

1954, Jan. 9 *Perf. 12½x13*

115 A14 15m emerald & brn org .55 *1.00*
116 A14 3p black & blue .65 *3.00*
117 A14 5p red violet & blk .80 *1.75*
Nos. 115-117 (3) 2.00 5.75

Self-government in the Sudan.

A quantity of these sets inscribed "1953" was sold in London. They were not valid for postage. Value, set $25.

Independent Republic

Map of Sudan and Sun — A15

Wmk. 214

1956, Sept. 15 Engr. *Perf. 14*

118 A15 15m rose lilac & org .40 .40
119 A15 3p dk blue & org .60 .60
120 A15 5p green & org .60 .60
Nos. 118-120 (3) 1.60 1.60

Independence Day, Jan. 1, 1956.

Rhinoceros Carrying Globe — A16

1958, Aug. 2 Center in Orange

121 A16 15m plum .50 .25
122 A16 3p blue .75 .35
123 A16 5p green 1.10 .75
Nos. 121-123 (3) 2.35 1.35

APU Cong., Khartoum, Aug. 2, 1958.

Soldier, Farmer and Map of Nile — A17

Lithographed and Engraved

1959, Nov. 17 Unwmk. *Perf. 14*

124 A17 15m brown, yel & ultra .30 .25
125 A17 3p multicolored .70 .40
126 A17 55m multicolored .80 .60
Nos. 124-126 (3) 1.80 1.25

Sudanese army revolution, 1st anniv.

Arab League Center A17a

Perf. 13x13½

1960, Mar. 22 Photo. Wmk. 328

127 A17a 15m dull green & blk .60 .40

Opening of the Arab League Center and the Arab Postal Museum in Cairo.

Uprooted Oak Emblem, Refugee Man and Child — A18

Wmk. 214

1960, Apr. 7 Litho. *Perf. 14*

128 A18 15m black, buff & ultra .25 .25
129 A18 55m black, beige & org .75 .50

World Refugee Year, 7/1/59-6/30/60.

Soccer Player — A19

1960, Aug. 25 Wmk. 214 *Perf. 14*

130 A19 15m ultra, blk & yel .30 .25
131 A19 3p yellow, blk & grn .65 .40
132 A19 55m emerald, blk & yel .75 .50
Nos. 130-132 (3) 1.70 1.15

17th Olympic Games, Rome, 8/25-9/11.

Forest — A20

1960, Sept. 6

133 A20 15m multicolored .30 .25
134 A20 3p multicolored .65 .25
135 A20 55m multicolored .75 .50
Nos. 133-135 (3) 1.70 1.00

5th World Forestry Cong., Seattle, WA, Aug. 29-Sept. 10.

King Tirhaqah, 689-663 B.C. — A21

Unwmk.

1961, Mar. 1 Engr. *Perf. 14*

136 A21 15m yellow grn & brown .30 .25
137 A21 3p salmon & violet .60 .50
138 A21 55m lt blue & red brown 1.10 .70
Nos. 136-138 (3) 2.00 1.45

Save historic monuments in Nubia.

An imperf. souvenir sheet exists, not sold at post offices, containing one each of Nos. 136-138. Size: 154x97mm. The sheet was not issued for postal purposes and cancellation requests are declined. Value $9.

Girl with Book — A22

1961, Nov. 17 Litho. Wmk. 214

139 A22 15m violet, claret & pink .30 .25
140 A22 3p orange, blk & blue .65 .40
141 A22 55m gray grn, blk & och .90 .65
Nos. 139-141 (3) 1.85 1.30

50 years of girls' education in the Sudan.

Malaria Eradication Emblem — A23

1962, Apr. 7 Unwmk. *Perf. 14*

142 A23 15m black, pur & blue .55 .25
143 A23 55m dk brown & green 1.10 .65

WHO drive to eradicate malaria.

Arab League Building, Cairo — A24

1962, Apr. 22 Photo. *Perf. 13½x13*

144 A24 15m deep orange .30 .25
145 A24 55m blue green .70 .50

Arab League Week, Mar. 22-28.

Type of 1951 and

Palace of the Republic, Khartoum — A25

Cotton Picker — A26

Designs: 15m, Straw cover. 35m, 4p, Wild animals. 55m, 6p, Cattle. 8p, Date palms. 10p, Sailboat. 20p, Bohein Temple, 1500 B.C. 50p, Sennar Dam. £1, Camel Post (A13 redrawn).

Perf. 14½x14, 14x14½

1962, Oct. 1 Litho. Wmk. 345

Size: 23x19mm, 19x23mm

146 A25 5m blue .25 .25
147 A26 10m blue & lilac .25 .25
148 A25 15m multicolored .25 .25
149 A25 2p lt purple .25 .25
150 A26 3p bl grn, red brn & brn .40 .25
151 A26 35m yel grn, brn & org brn .75 .25
152 A26 4p red, lt bl & lil .75 .25
153 A25 55m gray & yel ol .75 .30
154 A25 6p brown & lt blue .90 .30
155 A25 8p green .90 .30

Perf. 14x14½, 13x13½, 14x13½, 13½x14

Size: 24½x30mm, 30x24½mm

156 A26 10p lt bl, red brn & blk 1.00 .50
157 A25 20p gray ol & yel grn 2.50 1.10
158 A25 50p dk gray, ol & bl 6.00 1.75

Engr.

159 A13 £1 green & brn org 12.00 6.50
b. Wmk 334 — —
Nos. 146-159 (14) 26.95 12.50

The frame of No. 159 has been altered with Arabic inscription on top and English at bottom.

See Nos. 420, 427-428. For surcharge and overprints see Nos. 430, O62-O74, O92, O99-O100.

1975-79 Unwmk.

Perfs, Sizes and Printing Methods as Before

146a	A25	5m	('76)	.25	.25
147a	A26	10m	('76)	.25	.25
148a	A25	15m		.25	.25
149a	A25	2p		.25	.25
150a	A26	3p	('76)	.30	.25
151a	A26	35m		.50	.25
152a	A26	4p		.50	.25
153a	A25	55m	('79)	.50	.25
154a	A25	6p		.60	.25
155a	A25	8p	('77)	.75	.25
156a	A26	10p		1.00	.40
157a	A25	20p		2.00	.90
158a	A25	50p		5.50	1.25
159a	A13	£1		—	*6.00*
	Nos. 146a-158a (13)			12.65	5.05

For surcharges, see Nos. 368A-368D, 656-657, 667-672.

Corn and Millet — A27

1963, Mar. 21 Litho. Wmk. 345

160 A27 15m. emer, gray & brn .30 .25
161 A27 55m violet, lt & dk blue .70 .40

FAO "Freedom from Hunger" campaign.

Centenary Emblem and Medals — A28

1963, Oct. 1 *Perf. 14*

162 A28 15m blk, red, gray & gold .50 .25
163 A28 55m grn, gray, red & gold 1.00 .50

Centenary of the International Red Cross.

Melchior — A29

Designs: 30m, St. Joseph seated, with cross and manuscript, horiz. 55m, Archangel with cross. Designs from frescoes in excavated Faras Church.

1964, Mar. 8 Litho. *Perf. 14*

164 A29 15m multicolored .40 .30
165 A29 30m red brn, blk & brn .55 .35
166 A29 55m red brn, blk & brn 1.25 .80
Nos. 164-166 (3) 2.20 1.45

UNESCO world campaign to save historic monuments in Nubia.

Khashm El Girba Dam — A30

New York World's Fair, 1964-65: 3p, Pavilion. 55m, Illustrated map of Sudan, vert.

Perf. 14x14½, 14½x14

1964, Apr. 22 Wmk. 345

167 A30 15m lt vio bl & vio brn .25 .25
168 A30 3p multicolored .30 .30
169 A30 55m multicolored .80 .35
Nos. 167-169 (3) 1.35 .90

Eleanor Roosevelt and People Breaking Chains — A31

1964, Dec. 10 *Perf. 14*

170 A31 15m grnsh blue & blk .25 .25
171 A31 3p violet & black .40 .25
172 A31 55m orange brn & blk .65 .65
Nos. 170-172 (3) 1.30 1.15

Eleanor Roosevelt (1884-1962), on the 16th anniv. of the Universal Declaration of Human Rights.

Arab Postal Union Emblem — A32

1964, Dec. 30 Litho.

173 A32 15m brick red, blk & gold .25 .25
174 A32 3p gray green, blk & gold .40 .30
175 A32 55m violet, blk & gold .85 .50
Nos. 173-175 (3) 1.50 1.05

10th anniv. of the Permanent Office of the Arab Postal Union.

ITU Emblem, Old and New Communication Equipment — A33

1965, May 17 Wmk. 345 *Perf. 13½*

176 A33 15m brown & gold .30 .25
177 A33 3p black & gold .65 .30
178 A33 55m green & gold 2.25 .60
Nos. 176-178 (3) 3.20 1.15

Cent. of the ITU.

"Gurashi" and Revolutionists — A34

1965, Nov. 10 Litho. *Perf. 12*

179 A34 15m deep ocher & black .30 .25
180 A34 3p bright red & black .40 .25
181 A34 55m dark gray & black .85 .50
Nos. 179-181 (3) 1.55 1.00

1st anniv. of the October 21st Revolution and to honor "Gurashi," one of its heroes.

ICY Emblem — A35

Perf. 14½x14

1965, Dec. 10 Litho. Wmk. 345

182 A35 15m violet & blk .45 .25
183 A35 3p yellow green & blk .55 .30
184 A35 55m vermilion & blk 1.25 .55
Nos. 182-184 (3) 2.25 1.10

International Cooperation Year, 1965.

El Siddig el Mahdi — A36

1966, Jan. 1 *Perf. 13*

185 A36 15m lt blue & vio blue .50 .25
186 A36 3p orange & brown .75 .30
187 A36 55m gray & red brown 1.75 .90
Nos. 185-187 (3) 3.00 1.45

El Siddig el Mahdi (1911-61), imam of Ansar region and political leader.

Mubarak Zaroug A37

1966, Jan. 1 Litho.

188 A37 15m pink & lt olive grn .50 .25
189 A37 3p brt yel grn & dk grn .75 .50
190 A37 55m org brn & dk brn 1.40 .85
Nos. 188-190 (3) 2.65 1.60

Issued in memory of Mubarak Zaroug (1917-65), lawyer and political leader.

WHO Headquarters, Geneva — A38

1966, June 11 Photo. *Perf. 11½x11*

191 A38 15m blue .30 .25
192 A38 3p magenta .40 .30
193 A38 55m brown 1.25 .50
Nos. 191-193 (3) 1.95 1.05

Inauguration of WHO Headquarters, Geneva.

Map of Sudan and Crests of Upper Nile, Blue Nile and Kassala Provinces — A39

Designs: 3p, Map of Sudan and crests of Equatoria, Kordofan and Khartoum Provinces. 55m, Map of Sudan and crests of Bahr El Gazal, Darfur and Northern Provinces.

1967, Apr. 1 Litho. *Perf. 14*

194 A39 15m org, pur & lt bl grn .25 .25
195 A39 3p dp org, vio & lt bl .50 .35
196 A39 55m yel, dp clar & yel grn 1.10 .60
Nos. 194-196 (3) 1.85 1.20

Month of the South.

Giraffe and ITY Emblem — A40

Perf. 12½x13

1967, Aug. 15 Litho. Wmk. 345

197 A40 15m multicolored .40 .25
198 A40 3p multicolored 1.00 .35
199 A40 55m multicolored 2.25 .60
Nos. 197-199 (3) 3.65 1.20

International Tourist Year 1967.

Clasped Hands and Arab League Emblem — A41

Perf. 11x11½

1967, Aug. 29 Photo. Unwmk.

200 A41 15m orange & ultra .30 .25
201 A41 3p brown org & emer .35 .35
202 A41 55m lemon & violet .60 .40
Nos. 200-202 (3) 1.25 1.00

Arab League Summit Conference.

Emblem of Palestine Liberation Organization — A42

1967, Aug. 29 *Perf. 11½x11*

203 A42 15m olive, car & yel .50 .30
204 A42 3p green, car & yel 1.25 .40
205 A42 55m brt green, car & yel 1.50 .50
Nos. 203-205 (3) 3.25 1.20

Palestine Liberation Organization.

Abdullahi el Fadil el Mahdi A43

Perf. 11½x11

1968, Feb. 15 Photo. Unwmk.

206 A43 15m ultra & brt purple .40 .25
207 A43 3p dp ultra & brt grn .55 .30
208 A43 55m orange & green 1.20 .55
Nos. 206-208 (3) 2.15 1.10

Issued in memory of Abdullahi el Fadil el Mahdi (1892-1966), political leader.

Mohammed Nur el Din — A44

1968, Feb. 15

209 A44 15m sl blue & apple grn .40 .25
210 A44 3p blue & olive .55 .30
211 A44 55m blue & violet blue 1.20 .50
Nos. 209-211 (3) 2.15 1.05

Issued in memory of Mohammed Nur el Din (1898-1964), political leader.

Ahmed Yousif Hashim A45

Perf. 11½x11

1968, Mar. 5 Photo. Unwmk.

212 A45 15m green & brown .40 .25
213 A45 3p brt blue & sepia .55 .30
214 A45 55m indigo & violet 1.20 .50
Nos. 212-214 (3) 2.15 1.05

Ahmed Yousif Hashim (1906-1958), journalist.

Mohammed Ahmed el Mardi (1905-1966), Political Leader — A46

Perf. 11x11½

1968, Mar. 5 Photo. Unwmk.

215 A46 15m Prus bl & vio bl .50 .30
216 A46 3p ultra, och & dl rose .75 .50
217 A46 55m dk blue & brown 1.40 .60
Nos. 215-217 (3) 2.65 1.40

DC-3 A47

20th anniv. of Sudan Airways: 2p, De Havilland Dove. 3p, Fokker Friendship. 55m, De Havilland Comet 4C.

1968, Dec. 15 Litho. *Perf. 13½x13*

218 A47 15m multicolored .50 .25
219 A47 2p multicolored 1.00 .25
220 A47 3p multicolored 1.25 .30
221 A47 55m multicolored 1.75 .50
Nos. 218-221 (4) 4.50 1.30

African Development Bank Emblem (right) — A48

Wmk. Rectangles (334)

1969, Dec. 20 Photo. *Perf. 13*

222 A48 2p black, gray & gold .35 .25
223 A48 4p dark red & gold .50 .30
224 A48 65m green & gold 1.00 .35
Nos. 222-224 (3) 1.85 .90

5th anniv. of the African Development Bank.

ILO Emblem A49

Unwmk.

1969, Dec. 27 Litho. *Perf. 14*

225 A49 2p blue, blk & pink .35 .25
226 A49 4p yellow, blk & silver .45 .30
227 A49 65m green, blk & lilac .90 .35
Nos. 225-227 (3) 1.70 .90

50th anniv. of the ILO.

Citizens A50

1970, May 25 *Perf. 11½x11*

228 A50 2p multicolored
228A A50 4p multicolored
228B A50 65m multicolored
Set, 228-228B 100.00 —

First anniv. of May 25th Revolution.

This set was withdrawn on day of issue; 1721 sets of the 2p, 4p and 65m stamps in same design were sold through the Philatelic service. A few copies of No. 228 were sold at Post offices. Nos. 229-231 were issued in October to replace this set.

Citizens A51

1970, Oct. 21 Photo. *Perf. 11½x11*

229 A51 2p brown, olive & red .35 .25
230 A51 4p lt blue, olive & red .55 .30
231 A51 65m olive, dk blue & red .90 .40
Nos. 229-231 (3) 1.80 .95

1st anniv. of the May 25th Revolution.

Map and Flags of UAR, Libya, Sudan A52

1971, Jan. 2 Unwmk. *Perf. 11½*

232 A52 2p lt green, car & blk .50 .25

Signing of the Charter of Tripoli affirming the unity of UAR, Libya and the Sudan, Dec. 27, 1970.

Education Year Emblem — A53

1971, May 2 Photo. *Perf. 11x11½*

233 A53 2p blue, blk & brn .30 .25
234 A53 4p carmine, blk & brn .45 .30
235 A53 65m vio brn, blk & brn .85 .40
Nos. 233-235 (3) 1.60 .95

International Education Year.

Emblem — A54

1971, Nov. 10 *Perf. 11x11½*

236 A54 2p yellow, grn & blk .35 .25
237 A54 4p blue, grn & blk .75 .35
238 A54 10½p gray, grn & blk 2.00 .55
Nos. 236-238 (3) 3.10 1.15

2nd anniversary of May 25th Revolution.

Arab League and Sudanese Emblems — A55

1972, Feb. 10 Photo. *Perf. 11x11½*

239 A55 2p yellow, grn & blk .40 .25
240 A55 4p orange, bl & blk .70 .30
241 A55 10½p orange, brn & blk 1.75 .55
Nos. 239-241 (3) 2.85 1.10

25th anniv. (in 1971) of the Arab League.

UN Emblem — A56

1972, Mar. 12 Photo. *Perf. 11x11½*

242 A56 2p emer, rose red & org .40 .25
243 A56 4p ultra, rose red & org .70 .30
244 A56 10½p blk, rose red & org 1.75 .55
Nos. 242-244 (3) 2.85 1.10

25th anniv. (in 1970) of the UN.

Emblems and Measure A57

1972, Apr. 22 Photo. *Perf. 11½x11*

245 A57 2p multicolored .40 .25
246 A57 4p lt blue & multi .70 .30
247 A57 10½p pink & multi 1.75 .55
Nos. 245-247 (3) 2.85 1.10

World Standards Day, Oct. 14, 1970.

Pres. Nimeiry and Arms of Sudan A58

1972, May 2 Litho. *Perf. 13x13½*

248 A58 2p vio bl, blk & gold .40 .25
249 A58 4p dp org, blk & gold .70 .25
250 A58 10½p ol grn, blk & gold 1.75 .55
Nos. 248-250 (3) 2.85 1.05

Election of Gaafar al-Nimeiry as President, Oct. 1971.

Arms of Sudan and Congress Emblem A59

1972, Oct. 15 Photo. *Perf. 11½x11*

251 A59 2p blue & multi .30 .25
252 A59 4p multicolored .60 .35
253 A59 10½p lt olive & multi 1.75 .45
Nos. 251-253 (3) 2.65 1.05

Founding Congress of the Sudanese Socialist Union.

Letter and African Postal Union Emblem A60

1972, Dec. 16

254 A60 2p yellow & multi .30 .25
255 A60 4p multicolored .55 .30
256 A60 10½p blue & multi 1.75 .45
Nos. 254-256 (3) 2.60 1.00

10th anniv. (in 1971) of the APU.

Emblems of Sudanese Provinces A61

Designs: 4p, Governing Council of Sudan. 10½p, Nat'l Coat of Arms and Unity emblem, vert.

1973, Jan. 1 Litho. *Perf. 13*

257 A61 2p gold & multi .30 .25
258 A61 4p dk red brn & blk .40 .25
259 A61 10½p silver, org & grn 2.00 .40
Nos. 257-259 (3) 2.70 .90

National Unity Day, March 3, 1972.

Emperor Haile Selassie — A62

1973, June 25 Unwmk. *Perf. 13*

260 A62 2p tan & multi .60 .30
261 A62 4p silver & multi 1.00 .40
262 A62 10½p gold & multi 2.00 .60
Nos. 260-262 (3) 3.60 1.30

80th birthday of Haile Selassie, Emperor of Ethiopia.

Nasser and Crowd A63

1973, July 15 Photo. *Perf. 11½x11*

263 A63 2p black .50 .25
264 A63 4p pale green & blk .75 .25
265 A63 10½p lilac & blk 1.75 .45
Nos. 263-265 (3) 3.00 .95

Gamal Abdel Nasser (1918-70), President of Egypt.

UN and FAO Emblems, Portal and Map of Resettlement Project — A64

1973, Dec. 30 Litho. *Perf. 13*

266 A64 2p multicolored .30 .25
267 A64 4p multicolored .60 .25
268 A64 10½p multicolored 2.25 .50
Nos. 266-268 (3) 3.15 1.00

World Food Program, 10th anniversary.

Scout Emblem, Knotted Rope and Stave — A65

1974, Jan. 15

269 A65 2p multicolored .60 .25
270 A65 4p multicolored .75 .35
271 A65 10½p multicolored 2.10 .65
Nos. 269-271 (3) 3.45 1.25

24th World Boy Scout Conference.

INTERPOL Emblem A66

1974, Feb. 16 Litho. *Perf. 13x13½*

272 A66 2p orange & multi .70 .25
273 A66 4p gray & multi 1.00 .25
274 A66 10½p lt blue & multi 1.75 .50
Nos. 272-274 (3) 3.45 1.00

50th anniv. of Intl. Criminal Police Org.

K.S.M. Building A67

1974, July 1 Litho. *Perf. 13x13½*

275 A67 2p lilac rose & multi .50 .25
276 A67 4p lt green & multi .75 .25
277 A67 10½p vermilion & multi 2.50 .55
Nos. 275-277 (3) 3.75 1.05

50th anniversary of the Faculty of Medicine, University of Khartoum.

African Postal Union and UPU Emblems — A68

4p, Letters, Arab Postal Union and UPU emblems. 10½p, Letters, UPU and African Postal Union emblems.

1974, Sept. 9 Litho. *Perf. 13½*

278 A68 2p multicolored .25 .25
279 A68 4p lt blue & multi .40 .30
280 A68 10½p lilac & multi 1.25 .45
Nos. 278-280 (3) 1.90 1.00

Centenary of Universal Postal Union.

Ali Abdel Latif, Abdel Fadil Elmaz, Revolutionary Flag and Nile — A69

1975, July 26 Litho. *Perf. 14x13½*

281 A69 2½p green & vio blue .25 .25
282 A69 4p rose & vio blue .40 .25
283 A69 10½p sepia & vio blue 1.00 .50
Nos. 281-283 (3) 1.65 1.00

50th anniversary of 1924 revolution. Portraits show political and military leaders of the revolution.

ADB Emblem with Map of Africa A70

1975, July 26

284 A70 2½p multicolored .25 .25
285 A70 4p multicolored .40 .25
286 A70 10½p multicolored 1.00 .50
Nos. 284-286 (3) 1.65 1.00

African Development Bank, 10th anniv.

Radar Station and Camel Rider — A71

1976, Feb. 2 Litho. *Perf. 13½x14*

287 A71 2½p lt green & multi .25 .25
288 A71 4p lilac & multi .40 .25
289 A71 10½p vio blue & multi 1.25 .50
Nos. 287-289 (3) 1.90 1.00

Umm Haraz Satellite Station.

IWY Emblem, Flag and Woman A72

1976, May 10 Litho. *Perf. 14x13½*

290 A72 2½p multicolored .25 .25
291 A72 4p multicolored .35 .25
292 A72 10½p dk blue & multi .90 .50
Nos. 290-292 (3) 1.50 1.00

International Women's Year 1975.

Arms of Sudan, Olympic Rings, Track — A73

1976, July 17 Litho. *Perf. 13½x14*

293 A73 2½p green & multi .35 .25
294 A73 4p green & multi .50 .30
295 A73 10½p green & multi 1.25 .60
Nos. 293-295 (3) 2.10 1.15

21st Olympic Games, Montreal, Canada, July 17-Aug. 1.

Education, Engineering, Forestry, Agriculture and Defense — A74

1977, July 20 Litho. *Perf. 13½x14*

296 A74 2½p multicolored .25 .25
297 A74 4p multicolored .25 .35
298 A74 10½p multicolored .85 .35
Nos. 296-298 (3) 1.35 .95

5th anniversary of national unity.

Archbishop Capucci — A75

1977, Oct. 22 Photo. *Perf. 11x11½*

299 A75 2½p black .75 .25
300 A75 4p black & green 1.00 .35
301 A75 10½p black & red 2.00 .60
Nos. 299-301 (3) 3.75 1.20

Palestinian Archbishop Hilarion Capucci, jailed by Israel in 1974.

Fair Emblem, Sudanese Flag A76

Perf. 11½x 11

1978, Jan. 19 Photo. Wmk. 342

302 A76 3p multicolored .25 .25
303 A76 4p multicolored .40 .25
304 A76 10½p multicolored .65 .40
Nos. 302-304 (3) 1.30 .90

International Khartoum Fair, Jan. 19-27.

APU Emblem A77

1978, Mar. 8 Litho. *Perf. 14x13½*

305 A77 3p black, car & sil .25 .25
306 A77 4p dk green, blk & sil .30 .25
307 A77 10½p ultra, blk & sil .75 .40
Nos. 305-307 (3) 1.30 .90

APU, 25th anniv. (in 1977).

Jinnah and Sudanese Flag A78

1978, May 6 Litho. *Perf. 13*
308 A78 3p multicolored .25 .25
309 A78 4p multicolored .40 .25
310 A78 10½p multicolored .70 .40
Nos. 308-310 (3) 1.35 .90

Mohammed Ali Jinnah (1876-1948), first Governor General of Pakistan.

Desert A79

1978, May 6 *Perf. 14x13½*
311 A79 3p multicolored .25 .25
312 A79 4p multicolored .45 .25
313 A79 10½p multicolored 1.25 .65
Nos. 311-313 (3) 1.95 1.15

UN Desertification Conference.

Lion God Apedemek, African Unity Emblems — A80

1978, July 18 Litho. *Perf. 13½x14*
314 A80 3p multicolored .25 .25
315 A80 4p multicolored .50 .25
316 A80 10½p multicolored 1.10 .40
Nos. 314-316 (3) 1.85 .90

15th African Summit Conference, Khartoum, July 18-21.

May Revolution, 10th Anniv. — A81

1979, Oct. 1 Litho. *Perf. 13½x14*
317 A81 3½p multicolored .25 .25
318 A81 6p multicolored .40 .25
319 A81 13p multicolored .85 .45
Nos. 317-319 (3) 1.50 .95

A82

1980, Jan. 19 Litho. *Perf. 13½x14*
320 A82 4½p orange & black .25 .25
321 A82 8p olive green & blk .40 .35
322 A82 15½p blue & black .85 .50
Nos. 320-322 (3) 1.50 1.10

UNESCO emblem, children holding globe.

IYC Emblem, Hands Protecting Child A83

1980, Mar. 15 *Perf. 14x13½*
323 A83 4½p multicolored .30 .25
324 A83 8p multicolored .40 .40
325 A83 15½p multicolored 1.50 .50
Nos. 323-325 (3) 2.20 1.15

International Year of the Child (1979).

25th Anniv. of Independence — A84

1982, Mar. 4 Photo. *Perf. 11½*
326 A84 60m multicolored .70 .30
327 A84 120m multicolored 1.50 .50
328 A84 250m multicolored 3.00 1.00
Nos. 326-328 (3) 5.20 1.80

World Food Day, Oct. 16, 1981 A85

60m, Emblem on map, reaching hands. 120m, Produce. 250m, Map, grain.

1983, Jan. 15 Photo. *Perf. 11½*
329 A85 60m multi .35 .25
330 A85 120m multi .60 .30
331 A85 250m multi 1.25 .60
Nos. 329-331 (3) 2.20 1.15

A86

1984, Feb. 20 Litho. *Perf. 13½*
332 A86 10p pink & silver .25 .25
333 A86 25p lt blue & silver .55 .40
334 A86 40p green & silver 1.00 .75
Nos. 332-334 (3) 1.80 1.40

25th Anniv. of Economic Commission for Africa (1983).

A87

1984, June 16 Litho. *Perf. 14*
335 A87 10p multicolored .30 .25
336 A87 25p multicolored .70 .50
337 A87 40p multicolored 1.25 .65
Nos. 335-337 (3) 2.25 1.40

Cent. of Shaykan Battle, Kordofan (1983).

Olympic Week A88

1984, Dec. 1 Litho. *Perf. 14*
338 A88 10p multicolored .40 .25
339 A88 25p multicolored .75 .40
340 A88 40p multicolored 1.40 .65
Nos. 338-340 (3) 2.55 1.30

Sudan-Egypt Integration Charter, 2nd Anniv. — A89

1985, Mar. 16 Photo. *Perf. 13½x13*
341 A89 10p multicolored .35 .25
342 A89 25p multicolored .70 .50
343 A89 40p multicolored 1.40 .65
Nos. 341-343 (3) 2.45 1.40

Bakht Erruda, Teacher Training Institute — A90

1985, Apr. 1
344 A90 10p multicolored .30 .25
345 A90 25p multicolored .70 .50
346 A90 40p multicolored 1.10 .65
Nos. 344-346 (3) 2.10 1.40

April 6 Uprising, 1st Anniv. A91

1986, Apr. 1 Litho. *Perf. 14*
347 A91 5p multicolored .25 .25
348 A91 25p multicolored .65 .35
349 A91 40p multicolored 1.25 .65
Nos. 347-349 (3) 2.15 1.25

World Food Day 1986 A92

25p, Net fishermen. 30p, Two fish, vert. 50p, Globe. 75p, Stylized fish on wave. 300p, Fish in sea.

Perf. 13x13½, 13½x13 (30p), 14 (50p)

1988, Jan. 1 Litho.
350 A92 25p multi .45 .25
351 A92 30p multi .40 .25
352 A92 50p multi .65 .45
353 A92 75p multi 1.50 .75
354 A92 300p multi 5.00 2.25
Nos. 350-354 (5) 8.00 3.95

Souvenir Sheet

Imperf

354A A92 75p like 25p 3.50 3.50

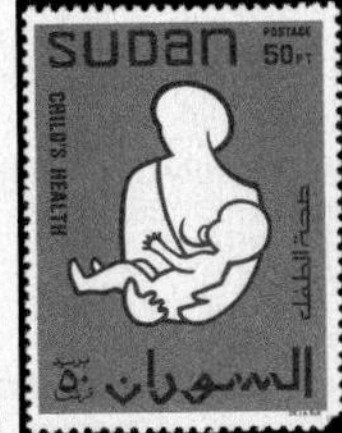

Child Survival — A93

No. 355, Breast-feeding, vert. No. 356, Oral rehydration. No. 358, Oral vaccine. No. 359, Growth monitoring.

Perf. 14, Imperf. (No. 357)

1988, Mar. 15 Litho.
355 A93 50p brt pur & blk .50 .30
356 A93 75p multi 1.00 .40
357 A93 75p like 50p, vert. 1.75 1.75
358 A93 100p multi 1.40 .60
359 A93 150p multi 2.10 .90
Nos. 355-359 (5) 6.75 3.95

No. 357 issued without gum. Size: 63x84mm.

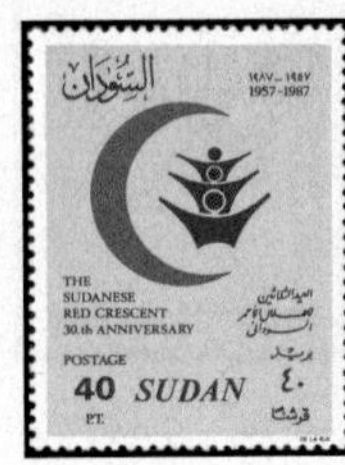

Red Crescent in Sudan, 30th Anniv. (in 1987) — A94

Designs: 100p, Crescent, candle. 150p, Crescent, stylized figure of a man.

1988, Oct. 31 Litho. *Perf. 14*
360 A94 40p org yel, blk & dk red .50 .30
361 A94 100p blk, blue grn & dk red 1.50 .75
362 A94 150p blk, brt blue & dk red 2.00 1.25
Nos. 360-362 (3) 4.00 2.30

Nos. 361-362 horiz.

World Food Day, Oct. 16, 1987, and the Small Farmer — A95

FAO emblem and: 40p, Early farming tools, horiz. 100p, Ox-drawn plow. 150p, Crude public water supply.

1988, Oct. 31 *Perf. 13x13½, 13½x13*
363 A95 40p multicolored .50 .30
364 A95 100p shown 1.50 .75
365 A95 150p multicolored 2.00 1.20
Nos. 363-365 (3) 4.00 2.25

Khartoum Bank, 75th Anniv. A96

Designs: 40p, Anniv. emblem. 100p, Spheres, emblem, medallion on ribbon. 150p, Text, emblem.

1988, Oct. 31 *Perf. 14*
366 A96 40p multicolored .50 .30
367 A96 100p multicolored 1.50 .75
368 A96 150p multicolored 2.00 1.20
Nos. 366-368 (3) 4.00 2.25

Nos. 156a, 157a, O72a, O73c Handstamp Surcharged in Various Colors

Methods and Perfs As Before

1988 ? Unwmk.
368A A26 £5 on 10p #156a — —
368B A25 £5 on 20p #157a — —
368C A26 £10 on 10p #156a — —
368D A25 £10 on 20p #157a — —

On Official Stamps

368E A26 £5 on 10p #O72a — —
368F A25 £5 on 20p #O73c — —
368G A26 £10 on 10p #O72a — —
368H A25 £10 on 20p #O73c — —

The illustration shown is that of the £10 surcharge. The £5 surcharge has an oval representing "5" at the right side. Surcharge colors are known in blue, black, red and blends of these colors.

Declaration of Palestinian State, 1st Anniv. — A97

Nos. 370, 372, 374, Crowd of demonstrators.

1989, Dec. 10 Litho. *Perf. 14*

369 A97 100p yellow grn & multi 1.75 .50
370 A97 100p buff & multi 2.00 .50
371 A97 150p lt vio & multi 2.50 1.00
372 A97 150p lt blue & multi 2.75 1.00
373 A97 200p pink & multi 3.50 1.25
374 A97 200p lt green & multi 3.50 1.25
Nos. 369-374 (6) 16.00 5.50

Palestinian Uprising (Nos. 370, 372, 374).

African Development Bank, 25th Anniv. — A99

1989, Dec. 28 *Perf. 13x13½*

375 A99 100p yel grn, blk & sil 1.50 .50
376 A99 150p blue, blk & sil 2.50 .75
377 A99 200p plum, blk & sil 3.25 1.00
Nos. 375-377 (3) 7.25 2.25

Independence, 33rd Anniv. (in 1989) — A100

1990, Jan. 22 Litho. *Perf. 13½x13*

378 A100 50p blue & yellow .50 .25
379 A100 100p deep claret & yel 1.25 .40
380 A100 150p brt rose & yel 1.75 .60
381 A100 200p dp rose lil & yel 2.50 .90
Nos. 378-381 (4) 6.00 2.15

Mammals A101

25p, Leopard. 50p, Elephant. 75p, Giraffe, vert. 100p, White rhinoceros. 125p, Addax, vert.

1990, Feb. 20 *Perf. 13x13½*

382 A101 25p multicolored .80 .25
383 A101 50p multicolored 1.25 .50

Perf. 14

384 A101 75p multicolored 2.00 .75
385 A101 100p multicolored 2.50 1.00
386 A101 125p multicolored 3.50 1.25
Nos. 382-386 (5) 10.05 3.75

No. 385 inscribed "Rino."

Birds — A102

25p, Zande hornbill. 50p, Marabou stork. 75p, Buff-crested bustard. 100p, Saddle-bill. 150p, Bald-headed ibis.

1990, Mar. 25 *Perf. 13½x13*

387 A102 25p multicolored .75 .25
388 A102 50p multicolored 1.40 .50
389 A102 75p multicolored 2.00 .80
390 A102 100p multicolored 2.75 1.00

Perf. 14

391 A102 150p multicolored 3.50 1.25
Nos. 387-391 (5) 10.40 3.80

Traditional Dances A103

Perf. 13x13½, 13½x13

1990, May 10 Litho.

392 A103 25p Mardoum .45 .30
393 A103 50p Zandi, vert. 1.00 .40
394 A103 75p Kambala, vert. 1.50 .60
395 A103 100p Nubian, vert. 1.75 .75
396 A103 125p Sword 2.25 .95
Nos. 392-396 (5) 6.95 3.00

Natl. Salvation Revolution, 1st Anniv. — A104

1991, Apr. 14 Litho. *Perf. 13*

399 A104 150p multicolored 1.25 .75
400 A104 200p multicolored 1.75 1.00
401 A104 250p multicolored 2.00 1.25
402 A104 £5 multicolored 3.75 2.50
403 A104 £10 multicolored 7.50 4.75
Nos. 399-403 (5) 16.25 10.25

For surcharge see No. 438.

Shoebill A105

Camel Postman A109

Designs: 50p, Sunflower. 75p, Gum arabic. 100p, Cotton. 125p, Crowned crane. 150p, Kenana Sugar Company, horiz. (30x24mm). 175p, Secretary bird (24x30mm). £2, Atbara cement factory, horiz. (30x24mm). 250p, Statue of King Taharqa (26x37mm). £3, Republican Palace (26x37mm). £4, Hug jar (24x30mm). No. 415, Gabana coffee pot (24x30mm). £8, Pterois volitans, horiz. (36x27mm). £10, Animal wealth, horiz. (36x27mm). £15, Nubian ibex.

1991, July 1 Litho. *Perf. 13½x13*

404 A105 25p shown .25 .25
405 A105 50p multi .40 .25
406 A105 75p multi .60 .40
407 A105 100p multi .80 .50
408 A105 125p multi 1.00 .55

Perf. 14x14½, 13½x14

409 A105 150p multi 1.25 .75
410 A105 175p multi 1.50 .85
411 A105 £2 multi 2.00 .95

Perf. 14

412 A105 250p multi 2.50 1.25
413 A105 £3 multi 3.00 1.50

Perf. 13½x14

414 A105 £4 multi 3.50 2.00
415 A105 £5 multi 4.25 2.40

Litho. & Engr.

Perf. 14

Wmk. 334

416 A109 £8 multi 6.00 4.00
417 A109 £10 multi 7.50 4.75
418 A109 £15 multi 11.00 7.00
419 A109 £20 shown 16.00 9.50
Nos. 404-419 (16) 61.55 36.90

For surcharges on No. 416, 605-606, 673-675.

Types of 1962

Designs: 25p, Cattle. £5, Bohein temple. £10, Sailboat.

Perf. 14½x14

1990-92 Litho. Unwmk.

420 A25 25p multi ('92) — 10.00

Perf. 14x13½

427 A25 £5 multi 14.50 10.00

Perf. 13½x14

428 A26 £10 multi 24.00 15.00

See Nos. O76-O100. For surcharges see Nos. 430, 436-453, O104-O111.

No. 156a Handstamp Surcharged in Blue Violet

1990, Sept. *Perf. 13½x14*

430 A26 £1 on 10p #156a 75.00 10.00

Surcharge on No. 430 is often incomplete.

Pan-African Rinderpest Campaign A114

Perf. 13½x13

1991, July 27 Litho. Unwmk.

431 A114 £1 black & brt grn 1.25 .50
432 A114 £2 dp violet & emer 2.50 1.75
433 A114 £5 org & blue grn 6.50 2.50
Nos. 431-433 (3) 10.25 4.75

Nos. 404-409, 411-414, 416 Surcharged in Black, Blue Violet or Red

c

d

e

f

g

h

i

j

k

1992?-97

Perfs. & Printing Methods as Before

436 A105(c) 1d on 100p #407 (Blk) 5.00 2.50
437 A105(c) 2d on £2 #411 (BV) 9.00 4.75
438 A105(c) 2.50d on 25p #404 (BV) 12.50 5.75
438A A25(d) 2.50d on 25p #420 (Blk) 2.50 1.75
439 A105(c) 3d on £3 #413 (BV) 15.00 7.00
440 A105(c) 4d on £4 #414 (Blk) 17.50 9.50
441 A105(e) 5d on 50p #405 (Blk) 2.75 .90
443 A105(d) 7.50d on 75p #406 (Blk) 7.50 5.00
446 A105(d) 1.50d on 150p #409 (Blk) 1.50 1.00
447 A105(f) 15d on 150p #409 (Blk) 4.00 —
448 A105(g) 25d on 75p #406 (Blk) — —
448A A105(k) 25d on 75p #406 (Blk) — —
449 A105(h) 25d on 250p #412 (R) 7.00 4.00
451 A105(i) 35d on £8 #416 (Blk) 8.00 5.00
a. Inverted surcharge — —
452 A105(j) 100d on 125p #408 (Blk) 5.75 5.75
453 A105(j) 100d on 125p #408 (R) 50.00 —
Nos. 436-453 (15) 148.00 52.90

Intl. Human Rights Day — A115

Designs: £5, Chain links, rainbow of colors, horiz. 750p, Trellis, rose, inscription.

1993, Dec. 20 Litho. *Perf. 14*

454 A115 £4 multicolored 1.00 .65
455 A115 £5 multicolored 1.25 .90
456 A115 750p multicolored 1.75 1.25
Nos. 454-456 (3) 4.00 2.80

Fung Sultanate, 5th Cent. — A116

Designs: £5, Inscription on tablet. 750p, Inscription in circle, helmet, horiz.

1993, Dec. 20

457	A116	£4 multicolored	1.00	.65
458	A116	£5 multicolored	1.25	.90
459	A116	750p multicolored	1.75	1.25
		Nos. 457-459 (3)	4.00	2.80

Wild Ass — A117

1994, July 15 **Litho.** ***Perf. 14½***

460	A117	4d With young	1.00	.50
461	A117	8d Standing	1.50	1.00
462	A117	10d Running	1.75	1.25
463	A117	15d Up close	2.50	2.00
		Nos. 460-463 (4)	6.75	4.75

Intl. Olympic Committee, Cent. — A118

1994, Aug. 1 **Litho.** ***Perf. 14***

464	A118	5d vermilion & multi	.50	.40
465	A118	7d green & multi	1.00	.55
466	A118	15d gray & multi	2.00	1.10
		Nos. 464-466 (3)	3.50	2.05

ICAO, 50th Anniv. — A119

1994, Dec. 7 **Litho.** ***Perf. 13½***

467	A119	5d lilac & multi	.35	.25
468	A119	7d brown & multi	.60	.45
469	A119	15d blue & multi	1.25	.95
		Nos. 467-469 (3)	2.20	1.65

A120

1994 World Cup Soccer Championships, US: 4d, Goalie, green vest. 5d, Like 4d, blue vest. 7d, Player about to kick ball, green shirt. 8d, Like 7d, brown shirt. 10d, Player, long-sleeved shirt. 15d, Player, yellow shirt. 20d, Player, magenta & blue background. 25d, Player, white shirt & pants. 35d, Like 20d, blue & green background.

75d, Goalie, orange shirt, horiz. 100d, Player kicking ball, horiz.

1995, July 15 **Litho.** ***Perf. 14***

470	A120	4d multicolored	.40	.25
471	A120	5d multicolored	.40	.25
472	A120	7d multicolored	.60	.35
473	A120	8d multicolored	.70	.35
474	A120	10d multicolored	.85	.50
475	A120	15d multicolored	1.00	.50
476	A120	20d multicolored	1.75	1.00
477	A120	25d multicolored	2.00	1.25
478	A120	35d multicolored	3.00	1.50
		Nos. 470-478 (9)	10.70	5.95

Souvenir Sheets

479	A120	75d multicolored	7.50	7.50
480	A120	100d multicolored	11.50	11.50

Arab League, 50th Anniv. — A121

1995, Dec. 16 **Litho.** ***Perf. 13½***

481	A121	15d apple grn & blk	1.50	1.00
482	A121	25d blue & black	2.75	1.50
483	A121	30d purple & black	3.25	2.00
		Nos. 481-483 (3)	7.50	4.50

A122

1996, May 4 **Litho.** ***Perf. 13½***

484	A122	15d orange & multi	1.50	1.00
485	A122	25d apple grn & multi	2.75	1.50
486	A122	30d black & multi	3.50	2.00
		Nos. 484-486 (3)	7.75	4.50

Common Market for East and South Africa (COMESA).

Abdel Rahman el Mahdi, (1885-1959) — A123

1997, Jan. 22 **Photo.** ***Perf. 13½***

487	A123	25d black & violet	2.00	1.75
488	A123	35d black & red brown	3.25	2.00
489	A123	50d black & brown	4.25	3.00
		Nos. 487-489 (3)	9.50	6.75

Waiting For Peace — A124

1997, June 1 **Photo.** ***Perf. 13½x13***

490	A124	5d multicolored	.75	.40

A125

1997, Oct. 15 **Photo.** ***Perf. 13½***

491	A125	25d lilac & multi	2.00	1.75
492	A125	35d apple grn & multi	3.00	2.75
493	A125	50d grn, blk & sil	4.00	3.50
		Nos. 491-493 (3)	9.00	8.00

Police Commanders, Arab Security Conference, 25th anniv.

A126

Al-Shaykh Qaribulla's Mosque: Various views of mosque.

1997, Nov. 1

494	A126	25d blue & multi	1.50	1.25
495	A126	35d yellow & multi	2.50	1.75
496	A126	50d buff & multi, vert.	3.50	2.50
		Nos. 494-496 (3)	7.50	5.50

A127

1998, Jan. 18 **Litho.** ***Perf. 13½***

497	A127	25d multicolored	1.75	1.25
498	A127	35d violet & multi	2.75	2.25
499	A127	50d multicolored	3.50	2.75
		Nos. 497-499 (3)	8.00	6.25

Pan African Postal Union, 18th anniv.

Sudanese Archeology A128

No. 500, Kerma pottery, 2500 BC. No. 501, Fresco, Faras church, 11th cent. No. 502, Close-up of fresco, Faras Church, 11th cent. 60d, C Group pottery, 2000 BC. No. 504, Meroe pottery, 4000 BC. No. 505, Tomb of Natakamani Meroitic king, 1st cent. BC, vert. 100d, C Group pottery, 2000 BC, diff.

1998, Jan. 25 ***Perf. 13½x13, 13x13½***

500	A128	50d multicolored	2.25	2.00
501	A128	50d multicolored	2.25	2.00
502	A128	50d multicolored	2.25	2.00
503	A128	60d multicolored	2.50	2.25
504	A128	75d multicolored	3.25	2.50
505	A128	75d multicolored	3.25	2.50
506	A128	100d multicolored	4.25	3.50
		Nos. 500-506 (7)	20.00	16.75

Ruins, Camel Post Rider — A129

1998, Mar. 1 ***Perf. 13x13½***

507	A129	100d multicolored	7.00	6.00

First Sudanese Postage Stamp, cent.

Battle of Kerreri, Cent. — A130

1999, May 15 **Litho.** ***Perf. 13¼x13½***

508	A130	75d multicolored	*4.50*	*3.75*
509	A130	100d green & multi	*6.00*	*5.50*
510	A130	150d blue & multi	*9.00*	*8.00*
		Nos. 508-510 (3)	*19.50*	*17.25*

American Bombing of Elshifa Pharmaceuticals Factory, Aug. 20, 1998 — A131

75d, Bomb damage. 100d, Company emblem, falling bombs. 150d, Casualties.

Perf. 13¾x13½, 13¾x13¼

1999, July 1 **Litho.**

511	A131	75d multi	*4.50*	*3.75*
512	A131	100d multi, vert.	*6.00*	*5.50*
513	A131	150d multi	*9.00*	*8.00*
		Nos. 511-513 (3)	*19.50*	*17.25*

A132 A133

Perf. 13¼x13½, 13½x13¼

1999, Oct. 20 **Litho.**

514	A132	75d shown	*4.50*	*3.75*
515	A133	100d shown	*6.00*	*5.50*
516	A132	150d 7 people	*9.00*	*8.00*
		Nos. 514-516 (3)	*19.50*	*17.25*

Intl. Year of the Elderly.

SOS Children's Villages, 50th Anniv. — A134

1999, Oct. 31 ***Perf. 13½x13¼***

517	A134	75d brn & multi	*4.50*	*3.75*
518	A134	100d grn & multi	*6.00*	*5.50*
519	A134	150d blue & multi	*9.00*	*8.00*
		Nos. 517-519 (3)	*19.50*	*17.25*

UPU, 125th Anniv. (in 1999) — A134a

2000, Mar. 1 **Litho.** ***Perf. 13½x13¼***

Denomination Color

519A	A134a	75d red	5.00	4.50
519B	A134a	100d violet	6.00	5.25
519C	A134a	150d black	10.00	8.00
		Nos. 519A-519C (3)	21.00	17.75

Common Market for Eastern and Southern Africa Free Trade Area — A135

Panel color: 100d, White. 150d, Pink. 200d, Yellow.

2000, Oct. 31 **Litho.** ***Perf. 13¼x13¾***

520-522	A135	Set of 3	*27.50*	*27.50*

UN High Commissioner for Refugees, 50th Anniv. — A136

Frame color: 100d, Green. 150d, Red. 200d, Violet.

Perf. 13¼x13½

2001, Aug. 15 **Litho.**

523-525	A136	Set of 3	*27.50*	*27.50*

Al-Zubair Prize for Innovation and Scientific Excellence A137

Frame color: 100d, Yellow. 150d, Red. 200d, Green.

2002, Feb. 14 ***Perf. 13¼***

526-528	A137	Set of 3	*30.00*	*30.00*

Association for the Promotion of Scientific Innovation — A138

Frame color: 100d, Black. 150d, Red. 200d, Green.

2002, Feb. 14
529-531 A138 Set of 3 *30.00 30.00*

Year of Dialogue Among Civilizations A139

Country name in: 100d, Red. 150d, Orange. 200d, Black.

2002, Jan. 28 Litho. *Perf. 13¼x13¾*
532-534 A139 Set of 3 *32.50 32.50*

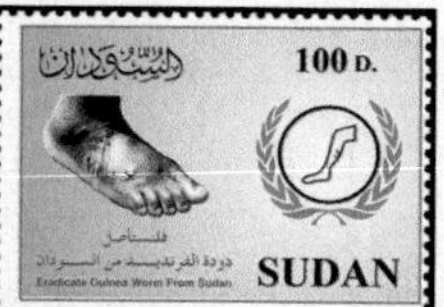

Guinea Worm Eradication Campaign A140

Designs: 100d, Infested foot, campaign emblem. 150d, Campaign emblem. 200d, Child, campaign emblem.

2002, Mar. 3 Litho. *Perf. 13¼*
535-537 A140 Set of 3 *30.00 30.00*

Palestinian Intifada — A141

Country name in: 100d, Green. 150d, Red. 200d, Black.

Perf. 13½x13¼
2002, Feb. 14 Litho.
538-540 A141 Set of 3 *30.00 30.00*

Sudanese postal officials have declared as illegal the following items:
Sheets of six stamps depicting Pope John Paul II (2 different)
Miniature sheet of two stamps depicting Pope John Paul II (2 different).

Association of African Banknote and Security Document Printers 11th Annual Conference — A142

Conference emblem and: 100d, Association emblem, circular design. 150d, Banknote rosettes. 200d, Archaeological ruins.

2003, May 10 Litho. *Perf. 13½x13¼*
541-543 A142 Set of 3 *37.50 37.50*

Mango — A143

Nile Perch — A144

Cattle — A145

Soldiers — A146

Muhammad Ahmad (Al-Mahdi, 1844-85), Religious Leader — A147

Butterflyfish — A148

Temple of Amun Ra — A149

Baobab Tree — A150

Doum Palm Tree — A151

Sheep — A152

Grapefruit A153

Oil Rigs A154

Tomb of Sheikh El-Mursi A155

Camel Postman A156

Perf. 13½x13¼, 13¼x13½
2003, July 15

544	A143	50d multi	*.75*	*.75*
545	A144	50d multi	*.75*	*.75*
546	A145	75d multi	*1.25*	*1.25*
547	A146	100d multi	*1.50*	*1.50*
548	A147	100d multi	*1.50*	*1.50*
549	A148	125d multi	*2.00*	*2.00*
550	A149	150d multi	*2.25*	*2.25*
551	A150	150d multi	*2.25*	*2.25*
552	A151	150d multi	*2.25*	*2.25*
553	A152	150d multi	*2.25*	*2.25*
554	A153	200d multi	*3.00*	*3.00*
555	A154	200d multi	*3.00*	*3.00*
556	A155	300d multi	*4.50*	*4.50*
557	A156	500d multi	*7.50*	*7.50*
a.		Souvenir sheet, #544-557, imperf.	*35.00*	*35.00*
		Nos. 544-557 (14)	*34.75*	*34.75*

For surcharges, see Nos. 638-639.

Parliament, 50th Anniv. — A157

Panel colors: 100d, Lilac. 200d, Yellow orange. 250d, Pink.

2004, Jan. 5 *Perf. 13½x13¼*
558-560 A157 Set of 3 *9.25 9.25*

General Secretariat for Council of Ministers, 50th Anniv. — A158

Panel colors: 100d, Light blue. 200d, Yellow. 250d, Pink.

2004, Jan. 8
561-563 A158 Set of 3 *9.25 9.25*

Rural Women's Innovation — A159

Panel colors: 100d, Light blue. 200d, Yellow. 250d, Lilac.

2004, Jan. 26
564-566 A159 Set of 3 *9.25 9.25*

Armed Forces, 50th Anniv. — A160

Background color: 100d, Orange. 200d, Red. 250d, Purple.

Perf. 13¼x13½
2004, Aug. 14 Litho.
567-569 A160 Set of 3 *12.00 12.00*

Peace — A161

Background color: 200d, Dark blue. 300d, Green and yellow, 400d, Light blue.

2005, Jan. 9 *Perf. 13½x13¼*
570-572 A161 Set of 3 *15.50 15.50*

7th Conference of Sudanese Women's General Union — A162

Panel color: 200d, White. 300d, Lilac. 400d, Light blue.

Perf. 13½x13¼
2005, June 29 Litho.
573-575 A162 Set of 3 *14.00 14.00*

Merowe Dam Project — A163

Background color: 200d, Light blue. 300d, Light green. 400d, Lilac.

2005, June 30
576-578 A163 Set of 3 *13.00 13.00*

World Summit on the Information Society, Tunis — A164

Background color: 200d, Yellow green. 300d, Blue. 400d, Yellow orange.

2005, Sept. 24
579-581 A164 Set of 3 *13.00 13.00*

Merowe Dam Housing Rehabilitation Projects — A165

Denomination in: 200d, Black. 300d, Green. 400d, Red.

2005, Oct. 1 Litho. *Perf. 13¼x13¾*
582-584 A165 Set of 3 *12.50 12.50*

Merowe Dam Archaeology Project — A166

Map and clay pot: 200d, Shown. 300d, With blue panel. 400d, With peach panel.

2005, Dec. 20 *Perf. 13¾x13¼*
585-587 A166 Set of 3 *12.50 12.50*

A167

A168

Independence, 50th Anniv. — A169

Perf. 13¼x13¾, 13¾x13¼

2006, Jan. 15

588 A167 200d multi		3.25	3.25
589 A168 300d multi		4.75	4.75
590 A169 400d multi		6.25	6.25
a.	Souvenir sheet, #588-590, imperf.	35.00	35.00
	Nos. 588-590 (3)	14.25	14.25

OPEC Intl. Development Fund, 30th Anniv. — A170

Background color: 200d, Red. 300d, Green. 400d, Blue.

2006, Oct. 12 **Litho.** ***Perf. 13¾x13½***
591-593 A170 Set of 3 *11.50 11.50*

100 qirsh = 1 pound

African Soccer Confederation, 50th Anniv. — A171

Background colors; £2, Pink. £3.50, Pale yellow. £4.50, White.

Perf. 13¾x13½

2007, Feb. 11 **Litho.**
594-596 A171 Set of 3 *14.00 14.00*

10th Meeting of Regional African Satellite Communications Organization A172

Background colors: £1, Lilac. £2, Light green. £3.50, Yellow. £4.50, Blue.

2007 ***Perf. 13½x13¾***
597-600 A172 Set of 4 *15.00 15.00*

24th Universal Postal Union Congress, Nairobi — A173

Panel color: £1, Lilac. £2, Brown. £3.50, Blue. £4.50, Ocher.

2008 ***Perf. 13¾x13½***
601-604 A173 Set of 4 *15.00 15.00*

Due to political unrest in Kenya, the UPU Congress was moved to Geneva, Switzerland.

No. 416 Srchd. in Black or Red

Methods, Perfs and Watermarks As Before

2008
605 A109 £2 on £8 #416 (Bk) *12.00 12.00*
606 A109 £2 on £8 #416 (R) *7.00 7.00*

Comprehensive Peace Agreement, 3rd Anniv. — A174

Panel color in: £1, Blue. £2, Black. £3.50, Green. £4.50, Brown.

Perf. 13¾x13½

2008, Jan. 22 **Litho.** **Unwmk.**
607-610 A174 Set of 4 *17.50 17.50*

Population and Housing Census — A175

Background colors: £1, Blue. £2, Yellow. £3.50, Lilac. £4.50, Green.

2008, Jan. 22 **Litho.** ***Perf. 13¾x13½***
611-614 A175 Set of 4 *17.00 17.00*

Arab Postal Day — A176

Emblem and: £2, Camel caravan. £3.50, World map, pigeon.

2008, Aug. 3
615-616 A176 Set of 2 *8.75 8.75*

Diplomatic Relations Between Sudan and People's Republic of China, 50th Anniv. — A177

Background color: £2.50, Pink. £5, Pale green. £6, Gray.

Perf. 13¾x13½

2009, Feb. 19 **Litho.**
617-619 A177 Set of 3 *20.00 20.00*

Merowe Dam Transmission Lines — A178

Background color: £2.50, Purple. £5, Green. £6, Blue.

2009
620-622 A178 Set of 3 *20.00 20.00*

Inauguration of Merowe Dam — A179

Panel color: £2.50, Pink. £5, Light blue. £6, Buff.

2009
623-625 A179 Set of 3 *20.00 20.00*

Completion of Merowe Dam — A180

Frame color: £3, Blue. £5.50, Orange brown. £7, Green.

2010, Apr. 7
626-628 A180 Set of 3 *20.00 20.00*

Solidarity — A181

Color of country name: £3, Green. £5.50, Yellow. £7, Orange brown.

2010, Sept. 7 ***Perf. 13½x13¾***
629-631 A181 Set of 3 *20.00 20.00*

Sudan Radio — A182

Background color: £3, Green. £5.50, Blue. £7, Red.

2010, Sept. 26 ***Perf. 13¾x13½***
632-634 A182 Set of 3 *20.00 20.00*

Sudan E-Government A183

Frame color: £3, Red. £5.50, Blue. £7, Blue green.

2011, July 27 **Litho.** ***Perf. 13½x13¾***
635-637 A183 Set of 3 *20.00 20.00*

No. 547 Surcharged in Black

No. 548 Surcharged in Black

Methods and Perfs As Before

2012
638 A146 £7 on 100d #547 *13.00 13.00*
639 A147 £7 on 100d #548 *13.00 13.00*

Arab Postal Day — A184

Denomination color: £3, Blue. £5.50, Red. £7, Black.

2012 **Litho.** ***Perf. 13¾x13½***
640-642 A184 Set of 3 *18.00 18.00*

Roseires Dam Heightening Project — A185

Color of top panel: £2, White. £3, Green. £5.50, Red. £7, Black.

2013
643-646 A185 Set of 4 *18.00 18.00*

National Telecommunications Day — A186

Head, globe and satellite with background color at top of: £10, White. £15, Blue. £25, Green.

2015, June 1 Litho. *Perf. 13½x13¼*

647-649	A186	Set of 3	*26.00 26.00*

World Standards Day — A187

Panel color of: £10, Yellow. £15, Turquoise green. £25, Red.

2015 Litho. *Perf. 13½x13¼*

650-652	A187	Set of 3	— —

Nos. 153a, 156a Surcharged

No. 656

No. 657

Methods and Perfs. As Before

2016

656	A25	£8 on 55m #153a	3.75	3.75
657	A26	£10 on 10p #156a	4.75	4.75

National Army — A188

Emblem and: £10, Soldiers (light blue background). £15, Doctor examining child. £25, Soldiers (light green background).

2017 Litho. *Perf. 13¾x13½*

658-660	A188	Set of 3	*19.00 19.00*

Arab Postal Day — A190

Globe at: £10, Right. £15, Right. £25, Left.

2017 Litho. *Perf. 13¾x13½*

661-663	A190	Set of 3	*26.00 26.00*

Sinnar, Capital of Islamic Culture — A191

Emblem and various buildings in Sinnar with background dots in: £10, Light blue. £15, Sage green. £25, Gray.

2017 Litho. *Perf. 13¾x13½*

664-666	A191	Set of 3	*26.00 26.00*

No. 155a Surcharged

No. 154a Surcharged

No. 149a Surcharged

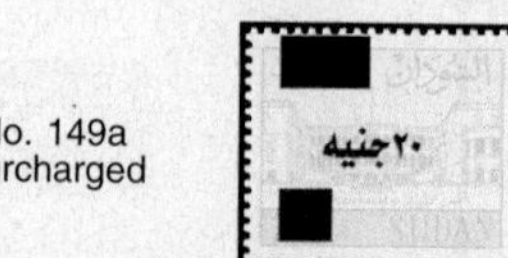

No. 156a Surcharged

Methods and Perfs. As Before

2018

667	A25	£10 on 8p #155a	2.25	2.25
668	A25	£15 on 6p #154a	3.25	3.25
669	A25	£20 on 2p #149a	4.50	4.50
670	A25	£25 on 10p #156a	5.25	5.25
		Nos. 667-670 (4)	15.25	15.25

No. 157a Surcharged

No. 158a Surcharged

No. 408 Surcharged

No. 410 Surcharged

No. 412 Surcharged

Methods and Perfs. As Before

2019

671	A25	£50 on 20p #157a	*4.00*	*4.00*
672	A25	£100 on 50p #158a	*8.00*	*8.00*
673	A105	£200 on 125p #408	*16.00*	*16.00*
674	A105	£250 on 175p #410	*20.00*	*20.00*
675	A105	£300 on 250p #412	*24.00*	*24.00*
		Nos. 671-675 (5)	*72.00*	*72.00*

A192

A193

Mohandas K. Gandhi (1869-1948), Indian Nationalist Leader — A194

2019, Sept. Litho. *Perf. 13½*

676	A192	£100 multi	*12.00*	*12.00*
677	A193	£150 dp turq blue	*18.00*	*18.00*
678	A194	£200 brown	*24.00*	*24.00*
		Nos. 676-678 (3)	*54.00*	*54.00*

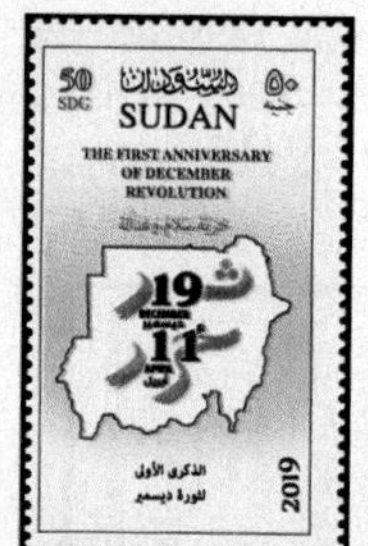

December Revolution, 1st Anniv. — A195

Stamps with varying background shading in denominations of £50, £100, £150.

2019 Litho. *Perf. 13½x13¾*

679-681	A195	Set of 3	*25.00 25.00*

December Revolution, 1st Anniv. — A196

Background color: £50, White. £100, Light blue. £150, Green.

2019 Litho. *Perf. 13½x13¾*

682-684	A196	Set of 3	*25.00 25.00*

December Revolution, 1st Anniv. — A197

Denominations: £50, £100, £150.

2019 Litho. *Perf. 13½x13¾*

685-687	A197	Set of 3	*25.00 25.00*

December Revolution, 1st Anniv. — A198

Denominations: £50, £100, £150.

2019 Litho. *Perf. 13¾x13½*

688-690	A198	Set of 3	— —

December Revolution, 1st Anniv. — A199

Background color: £50, Blue. £100, Green. £150, Black purple.

2019 Litho. *Perf. 13¾x13½*

691-693	A199	Set of 3	— —

AIR POST STAMPS

Nos. 40-41, 43 Overprinted in Black

Nos. C1-C2

No. C3

1931 Wmk. 214 *Perf. 11½x12½, 14*

C1	A2	5m blk & olive brown	.50	*1.00*
C2	A2	10m blk & carmine	1.50	*6.00*
C3	A1	2p org & vio brown	1.00	*5.00*
		Nos. C1-C3 (3)	3.00	*12.00*

Statue of Gen. C. G. Gordon AP3

1931-35 Engr. *Perf. 14*

C4	AP3	3m dk brn & grn ('33)	3.50	*7.25*
C5	AP3	5m grn & blk	1.50	.25
C6	AP3	10m car rose & blk	1.50	.25
C7	AP3	15m dk brn & brn	.75	.25
C8	AP3	2p org & blk	.65	.25
C9	AP3	2½p bl & red vio ('33)	4.75	.25
C10	AP3	3p gray & blk	1.00	.25
C11	AP3	3½p dl vio & blk	2.25	.90
C12	AP3	4½p gray & brn	12.50	*16.50*
C13	AP3	5p ultra & blk	1.75	.35
C14	AP3	7½p pck grn & dk grn ('35)	12.00	6.00

C15 AP3 10p pck bl & sep ('35) 11.50 2.00
Nos. C4-C15 (12) 53.65 34.50

See Nos. C23-C30. For surcharges see Nos. C17-C22, C31-C34.

No. 43 Surcharged in Black

1932, July 18 **Typo.**
C16 A1 2½p on 2p 2.00 *4.00*

Nos. C6, C4-C5, C12 Surcharged

1935 **Engr.** ***Perf. 14***
C17 AP3 15m on 10m .40 .25
a. Double surcharge 1,000. *1,400.*
b. Arabic characters omitted 750.00
C18 AP3 2½p on 3m 1.00 *6.00*
a. "½" 2¼mm high instead of 3mm 5.00 *25.00*
b. Second Arabic character of surcharge omitted 50.00 *125.00*
C19 AP3 2½p on 5m .50 *1.00*
a. "½" 2¼mm high instead of 3mm 1.50 *3.00*
b. Second Arabic character of surcharge omitted 40.00 *60.00*
c. Inverted surcharge 1,000. *1,400.*
d. As "a," inverted 30,000. *30,000.*
e. As "b," inverted 4,500. *6,000.*
f. Pair, C19c and C19d 52,000.
C20 AP3 3p on 4½p 1.75 *22.00*
C21 AP3 7½p on 4½p 6.50 *55.00*
a. "7¼" instead of "7½"
C22 AP3 10p on 4½p 6.50 *55.00*
Nos. C17-C22 (6) 16.65 *139.25*

Type of 1931-35

1936-37 ***Perf. 11½x12½***
C23 AP3 15m dk brn & brn ('37) 4.50 .25
C24 AP3 2p org & blk ('37) 5.00 *18.00*
C25 AP3 2½p bl & red vio 2.75 .25
C26 AP3 3p gray & blk ('37) .75 .40
C27 AP3 3½p dl vio & blk ('37) 2.25 *15.00*
C28 AP3 5p ultra & blk ('37) 4.00 .40
C29 AP3 7½p pck grn & dk grn ('37) 4.25 *11.00*
C30 AP3 10p pck bl & sep ('37) 6.50 *30.00*
Nos. C23-C30 (8) 30.00 *75.30*

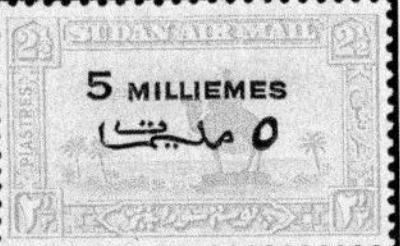

Nos. C25, C11, C14 and C15 Srchd. as in 1935

1938 **Wmk. 214** ***Perf. 11½x12½, 14***
C31 AP3 5m on 2½p 1.50 .30
C32 AP3 3p on 3½p 27.50 *60.00*
a. On No. C27 700.00 *750.00*
C33 AP3 3p on 7½p 5.00 *7.25*
a. On No. C29 700.00 *750.00*
C34 AP3 5p on 10p 1.50 *5.50*
a. On No. C30 700.00 *750.00*
Nos. C31-C34 (4) 35.50 73.05

A 5p on 2½p (No. C25) exists from a trial printing. Value, $425 unused and used.

Catalogue values for unused stamps in this section, from this point to the end of the section, are for Never Hinged items.

Bridge Over Blue Nile, Khartoum
AP4

Designs: 2½p, Kassala Jebel. 3p, Water wheel. 3½p, Port Sudan. 4p, Gordon Memorial College. 4½p, Nile post boat. 6p, Suakin. 20p, General Post Office, Khartoum.

1950, July 1 **Engr.** ***Perf. 12***
C35 AP4 2p dk bl grn & blk 5.75 1.75
C36 AP4 2½p red org & bl 1.00 1.50
C37 AP4 3p dp bl & plum 4.50 1.50
C38 AP4 3½p chnt & choc 4.50 *5.00*
C39 AP4 4p bl & brn 1.75 *3.50*
C40 AP4 4½p ultra & blk 3.00 *5.00*
C41 AP4 6p car & blk 3.50 *4.00*
C42 AP4 20p plum & blk 3.00 *6.75*
Nos. C35-C42 (8) 27.00 *29.00*

For overprints see Nos. CO1-CO8.

AIR POST OFFICIAL STAMPS

Catalogue values for unused stamps in this section are for Never Hinged items.

Nos. C35 to C42 Overprinted in Carmine or Black

1950, July 1 **Wmk. 214** ***Perf. 12***
CO1 AP4 2p dk bl grn & blk (C) 16.00 3.75
CO2 AP4 2½p red org & bl 1.50 *2.00*
CO3 AP4 3p dp bl & plum 1.00 *1.25*
CO4 AP4 3½p chnt & choc 1.00 *10.00*
CO5 AP4 4p bl & brn 1.00 *9.50*
CO6 AP4 4½p ultra & blk (C) 4.75 *21.00*
CO7 AP4 6p car & blk (C) 1.00 *5.50*
CO8 AP4 20p plum & blk (C) 4.50 *15.00*
Nos. CO1-CO8 (8) 30.75 68.00

POSTAGE DUE STAMPS

Postage Due Stamps of Egypt, 1889, Overprinted in Black

1897 **Wmk. 119** ***Perf. 14***
J1 D3 2m green 2.50 *6.00*
J2 D3 4m maroon 2.50 *6.00*
J3 D3 1p ultra 14.00 *5.00*
J4 D3 2p orange 14.00 *10.00*
Nos. J1-J4 (4) 33.00 27.00

Steamboat on Nile River — D1

1901 **Typo.** **Wmk. 179**
J5 D1 2m orange brn & blk 1.00 .85
J6 D1 4m blue green & brn 3.00 1.25
J7 D1 10m bl vio & bl grn 6.00 5.00
J8 D1 20m car rose & ultra 5.00 4.75
Nos. J5-J8 (4) 15.00 11.85

1927-30 **Wmk. Multiple S G (214)**
J9 D1 2m org brn & blk ('30) 3.00 3.00
J10 D1 4m blue grn & brn 1.50 1.00
J11 D1 10m violet & blue grn 2.50 *2.00*
Nos. J9-J11 (3) 7.00 6.00

Catalogue values for unused stamps in this section, from this point to the end of the section, are for Never Hinged items.

Redrawn

Bottom inscription altered — D2

1948, Jan. 1
J12 D2 2m dp orange & blk 2.75 *50.00*
J13 D2 4m blue grn & choc 4.50 *37.50*
J14 D2 10m rose lil & bl grn 20.00 *19.00*
a. Wmk. 345 ('71?)
J15 D2 20m brt car rose & ultra 21.00 *30.00*
a. Wmk. 345 ('73)
Nos. J12-J15 (4) 48.25 *136.50*

ARMY OFFICIAL STAMPS

Regular Issues of 1898 and 1902-08 Overprinted in Black

Nos. MO1, MO3 and MO2, MO4

1905 **Wmk. 71** ***Perf. 14***
MO1 A1 1m rose & brown 190.00 *200.00*
a. "OFFICIAL" 4,750. 3,250.
b. Pair, #MO1 and #MO2 4,500.
MO2 A1 1m rose & brown 3,000. *3,000.*

Wmk. 179
MO3 A1 1m car rose & brn 6.50 3.00
a. "OFFICIAL" 90.00 55.00
b. Inverted overprint 70.00 60.00
c. Horizontal overprint 475.00
MO4 A1 1m car rose & brn 60.00 30.00
a. Inverted overprint 350.00 375.00

Regular Issues of 1902-11 Overprinted in Black

1906-11
MO5 A1 1m car rose & brn 3.00 .50
a. "Army" and "Service" 14mm apart 550.00 400.00
b. Inverted overprint 650.00 *700.00*
c. Pair, one without ovpt. *7,000.*
d. Double overprint *1,750.*
e. "Service" omitted *4,500.*
MO6 A1 2m brn & grn 22.50 1.25
a. Pair, one without ovpt. 4,000.
b. "Army" omitted 4,200. *4,200.*
MO7 A1 3m grn & vio 22.50 .50
a. Inverted overprint 2,200.
MO8 A1 5m blk & rose red 3.50 .25
a. Inverted overprint 375.00
b. Double overprint 325.00 250.00
c. Double ovpt., one invtd. 1,500. 550.00
MO9 A1 1p yel brn & ultra 22.50 .40
a. "Army" omitted 3,250. 3,250.
MO10 A1 2p ultra & blk ('09) 85.00 15.00
a. Double overprint 3,400.
MO11 A1 5p grn & org brn ('08) 175.00 75.00
MO12 A1 10p dp vio & blk ('11) 625.00 *750.00*
Nos. MO5-MO12 (8) 959.00 842.90

Same Overprint On Regular Issue of 1898

Wmk. 71
MO13 A1 2p ultra & blk 90.00 11.50
a. Inverted overprint
MO14 A1 5p grn & org brn 130.00 *250.00*
MO15 A1 10p dp vio & blk 175.00 475.00

There are two types of this overprint which may be distinguished by the size and shape of the "y."

OFFICIAL STAMPS

Regular Issue of 1898 Overprinted in Black

1902-06 **Wmk. 71** ***Perf. 14***
O1 A1 1m rose & brn 3.50 *11.00*
Never hinged 7.00
a. Inverted overprint 325.00 *450.00*
b. Round periods 8.00 *45.00*
c. Double overprint 650.00
d. Oval "O" in overprint 90.00
e. As "d," inverted overprint 5,500.
O2 A1 10p dp vio & blk ('06) 16.00 *27.50*
Never hinged 32.50

Same Ovpt. on Stamps of 1902-11

1903-12 **Wmk. 179**
O3 A1 1m car rose & brn ('04) .60 .25
Never hinged 1.20
a. Double overprint
O4 A1 3m grn & vio ('04) 2.50 .25
Never hinged 5.00
a. Double overprint
O5 A1 5m blk & rose red 2.50 .25
Never hinged 5.00
O6 A1 1p yel brn & ultra 6.00 .25
Never hinged 12.00
O7 A1 2p ultra & blk 24.00 .25
Never hinged 48.00
O8 A1 5p grn & org brn 2.50 .40
Never hinged 5.00
O9 A1 10p dp vio & blk 5.00 70.00
Never hinged 10.00
Nos. O3-O9 (7) 43.10 71.65

Regular Issue of 1927-40 Overprinted in Black

Perf. 14, 13½x 14
1936-46 **Wmk. 214**
O10 A2 1m dk org & int blk ('46) 2.25 *12.50*
O11 A2 2m dk brn & dk org ('45) 2.25 *8.00*
O12 A2 3m green & vio ('37) 2.00 .25
O13 A2 4m brown & green 3.25 *4.00*
O14 A2 5m blk & ol brn ('40) 3.00 .25
O15 A2 10m blk & car ('46) .90 .25
O16 A2 15m org brn & ultra ('37) 7.50 .35

Regular Issue of 1927-40 Overprinted in Black

O17 A1 2p org & vio brn ('37) 11.50 .25
O18 A1 3p dk bl & red brn ('46) 5.25 3.00
O19 A1 4p blk & ultra ('46) 22.00 5.50
O20 A1 5p dk grn & org brn 8.50 *9.00*
O21 A1 6p blk & pale bl ('46) 6.00 7.00
O22 A1 8p blk & pck grn ('46) 4.00 *22.50*
O23 A1 10p dp vio & blk ('37) 37.50 6.50
O24 A1 20p bl & lt bl ('46) 25.00 *32.50*
Nos. O10-O24 (15) 140.90 111.85

Catalogue values for unused stamps in this section, from this point to the end of the section, are for Never Hinged items.

Nos. 79-85 Overprinted Like #O10-O16

1948, Jan. 1
O28 A7 1m dk org & blk .50 *4.50*
O29 A7 2m choc & org 2.00 .25
O30 A7 3m grn & rose lil 5.00 *10.00*
O31 A7 4m choc & sl grn 4.75 *6.00*
O32 A7 5m blk & ol brn 4.75 .25
O33 A7 10m blk & car 4.25 1.00
O34 A7 15m org brn & ultra 5.00 .25

Nos. 86-94 Overprinted Like Nos. O17-O24

O35 A8 2p org yel & vio brn 5.00 .25
O36 A8 3p dk bl & red brn 6.00 .25
O37 A8 4p blk & ultra 4.25 .25
a. Perf. 13 13.00 *18.00*
O38 A8 5p dk grn & org 6.50 .25
O39 A8 6p blk & pale bl 4.25 .25
O40 A8 8p blk & pck grn 4.25 *6.50*
O41 A8 10p dp rose lil & blk 7.75 .25
O42 A8 20p dk bl & bl 5.75 1.00
a. Perf. 13
O43 A8 50p ultra & car 82.50 70.00
Nos. O28-O43 (16) 152.50 101.25

Nos. 98-104 Overprinted Liked Nos. O10-O16 in Red

1951, Sept. 1 Wmk. 214 *Perf. 14*

Center in Black

O44 A11 1m orange .75 *5.00*
O45 A11 2m ultra .75 *2.00*
O46 A11 3m dk grn 12.00 *18.00*
O47 A11 4m emerald .25 6.00
O48 A11 5m plum .25 .25
O49 A11 10m light blue .25 .25
O50 A11 15m dp org brn 1.00 .25

Nos. 105-114 Overprinted Like Nos. O17-O24 in Black or Red

Perf. 13

O51 A12 2p lt bl & dk bl .25 .25
a. Inverted overprint 1,100.
O52 A12 3p vio bl & brn 22.50 .25
O53 A12 3½p brn & bl grn .85 .40
O54 A12 4p blk & dp bl 5.00 .25
O55 A12 5p emer & org brn .90 .25
O56 A12 6p blk & bl 1.10 *4.50*
O57 A12 8p brn & dp bl 1.50 .35
O58 A12 10p grn & blk (R) 1.75 .35
O59 A12 20p blk & bl grn 2.75 1.25
a. Inverted overprint 3,500.
O60 A13 50p blk & car 8.50 4.00
Nos. O44-O60 (17) 60.35 43.60

No. 112 Overprinted Like Nos.O17-O24 in Black

1958

O61 A12 10p green & black 22.50 3.75

Nos. 146-159 Overprinted

Size: 23x19mm, 19x23mm

Perf. 14½x14, 14x14½

1962, Oct. 1 Litho. Wmk. 345

O62 A25 5m blue .30 .25
O63 A26 10m blue & lilac .30 .25
O64 A25 15m yel, vio, org & brn .30 .25
O65 A25 2p lt pur .35 .25
O66 A26 3p bl grn, red brn & brn .60 .25
O67 A26 35m yel grn, brn & org brn .75 .25
O68 A26 4p red, lt bl & lil .90 .30
O69 A25 55m gray & yel ol 1.20 .50
O70 A25 6p brn & lt bl 1.20 .50
O71 A25 8p green 1.50 .60

Size: 24½x30mm, 30x24½mm

O72 A26 10p lt bl, red brn & blk 1.90 .65
O73 A25 20p gray ol & yel grn 4.00 1.50
a. Perf. 13½x12½ 4.00 1.25
b. Perf. 13½x14 9.00 2.25
O74 A25 50p dk gray, ol & bl 8.25 3.50
a. Perf. 13½x14 8.25 3.25

Engr.

O75 A13 £1 grn & brn org 25.00 15.00
Nos. O62-O75 (14) 46.55 24.05

The overprint measures 12x4½mm on Nos. O62-O71; 16x6mm on Nos. O72-O75.

Same Perfs., Sizes and Printing Methods as Before

1975-79 Unwmk.

O62a A25 5m .25 .25
O63a A26 10m ('76) .25 .25
O64a A25 15m .25 .25
O65a A25 2p .25 .25
O66a A26 3p .35 .25
O67a A26 35m .40 .25
O68a A26 4p .45 .25
O69a A25 55m .75 .45
O70a A25 6p ('76) .80 .45
O71a A25 8p 1.10 .55
O72a A26 10p 1.50 .70
O73c A25 20p 4.00 1.25
O74b A25 50p 7.00 3.00
O75a A13 £1 ('79) 25.00 14.00
Nos. O62a-O75a (14) 42.35 22.15

For surcharges, see Nos. 368E-368H.

Nos. 404-419 Overprinted

Perf. 13½x13

1991, July 1 Litho. Unwmk.

O76 A105 25p on #404 .30 .25
O77 A105 50p on #405 .60 .50
O78 A105 75p on #406 .75 .50
O79 A105 100p on #407 1.00 1.00
O80 A105 125p on #408 1.25 1.25

Size: 30x24mm

Perf. 14x14½, 13½x14

O81 A105 150p on #409 1.50 1.50
O82 A105 175p on #410 1.75 1.75
O83 A105 £2 on #411 2.00 2.00

Size: 26x37mm

Perf. 14

O84 A105 250p on #412 2.50 2.50
O85 A105 £3 on #413 3.00 3.00

Size: 24x30mm

Perf. 13½x14

O86 A105 £4 on #414 4.00 4.00
O87 A105 £5 on #415 5.00 5.00

Size: 36x27mm

Perf. 14

Wmk. 334

O88 A105 £8 on #416 8.00 7.00
O89 A105 £10 on #417 10.00 8.00
O90 A105 £15 on #418 15.00 12.00
O91 A105 £20 on #419 20.00 18.00
Nos. O76-O91 (16) 76.65 68.25

For surcharges see Nos. O104-O111.

Nos. 420, 427-428 Overprinted

1992 Litho. Unwmk. *Perf. 14½*

O92 A25 25p on #420 .35 .25

Perf. 14x13½, 13½x14

O99 A25 £5 on #427 10.00 8.00
O100 A25 £10 on #428 20.00 15.00
Nos. O92-O100 (3) 30.35 23.25

Nos. O79, O81, O83, O85-O87 Srchd. in Blue Violet or Black

Perf. 13½x13

1993? Litho. Unwmk.

O104 A105 1d on 100p #O79 1.25 .65

Perf. 13½x14

O105 A105 1.50d on 150p #O81 1.75 1.00
O107 A105 2d on £2 #O83 2.25 1.25

Perf. 14

O109 A105 3d on £3 #O85 3.25 2.00

Perf. 14½x14

O110 A105 4d on £4 #O86 4.25 2.75

Perf. 13½x14

O111 A105 5d on £5 #O87 (Blk) 5.50 3.25

Perf. 14

Size: 36x27mm

O112 A109 35d on £8 #O88 20.00 20.00
Nos. O104-O112 (7) 38.25 30.90

Coat of Arms — O1

2003 Litho. *Perf. 13½x13¼*

O113 O1 50d multi *4.25 4.00*
O114 O1 100d multi *6.50 6.00*
O115 O1 200d multi *15.00 13.00*
O116 O1 300d multi *22.50 19.00*
Nos. O113-O116 (4) 48.25 42.00

SURINAM

ˈsur-ə-ˌnam

(Dutch Guiana)

LOCATION — On the northeast coast of South America, bordering on the Atlantic Ocean
GOVT. — Republic
AREA — 63,234 sq. mi.
POP. — 431,156 (1999 est.)
CAPITAL — Paramaribo

The Dutch colony of Surinam became an integral part of the Kingdom of the Netherlands under the Constitution of 1954. It became an independent state November 25, 1975.

100 Cents = 1 Gulden (Florin)
100 Cents = 1 Dollar (2004)

Catalogue values for unused stamps in this country are for Never Hinged items, beginning with Scott 168 in the regular postage section, Scott B34 in the semi-postal section, Scott C23 in the airpost section, Scott CB1 in the airpost semi-postal section, and Scott J33 in the postage due section.

Watermark

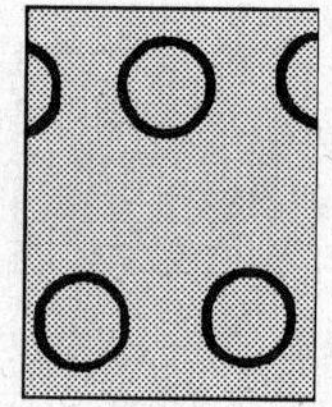

Wmk. 202 — Circles

Early issues of Surinam were sent to the colony without gum. Many of these were subsequently gummed locally.

King William III — A1

Perf. 11½, 11½x12, 12½x12, 13½, 14

1873-89 Typo. Unwmk.

Without Gum

1 A1 1c lil gray ('85) 2.50 *3.00*
2 A1 2c yellow ('85) 1.60 1.60
3 A1 2½c rose 1.60 1.60
4 A1 3c green 20.00 18.00
5 A1 5c dull violet 20.00 5.75
6 A1 10c bister 6.50 3.00
7 A1 12½c sl bl ('85) 20.00 8.00
8 A1 15c gray ('89) 24.00 8.00
9 A1 20c green ('89) 37.50 32.00
10 A1 25c grnsh blue 80.00 9.75
11 A1 25c ultra 280.00 24.00
12 A1 30c red brn ('88) 35.00 *40.00*
13 A1 40c dk brn ('89) 32.50 32.50
14 A1 50c brown org 32.50 20.00
15 A1 1g red brn & gray ('89) 52.50 52.50
16 A1 2.50g grn & org ('79) 77.50 70.00
Nos. 1-16 (16) 723.70 329.70

Perf. 14, Small Holes

3b A1 2½c rose 12.00 *14.00*
4b A1 3c green 22.00 *28.00*
5b A1 5c dull violet 22.00 18.00
6b A1 10c bister 20.00 *24.00*
11b A1 25c ultra 280.00 72.50
14b A1 50c brown org 57.50 50.00
Nos. 3b-14b (6) 413.50 206.50

The paper of Nos. 3-6, 11 and 14 sometimes has an accidental bluish tinge of varying strength. During its manufacture a chemical whitener (bluing agent) was added in varying quantities. No particular printing was made on bluish paper.

"Small hole" varieties have the spaces between the holes wider than the diameter of the holes.

Nos. 1-16 and 3b-14b exist with gum.

For surcharges see Nos. 23, 31-35, 39-42.

Numeral of Value — A2

1890 *Perf. 11½x11, 12½*

Without Gum

17 A2 1c gray 2.00 1.20
18 A2 2c yellow brn 3.25 2.50
19 A2 2½c carmine 3.00 2.00
20 A2 3c green 6.00 4.00
21 A2 5c ultra 52.50 1.60
Nos. 17-21 (5) 66.75 11.30

Nos. 17-21 exist with gum.

For surcharges see Nos. 63-64.

A3

1892, Aug. 11 *Perf. 10½*

Without Gum

No.	Type	Description	Unused	Used
22	A3	2½c black & org	2.00	1.25
a.		First and fifth vertical words have fancy "F"	26.00	16.00
b.		Imperf.	2.25	
c.		As "a," imperf.	30.00	

No. 14 Surcharged in Black

1892, Aug. 1 *Perf. 14*

Without Gum

No.	Type	Description	Unused	Used
23	A1	2½c on 50c	320.00	15.00
a.		Perf. 12½x12	400.00	12.00
b.		Perf. 11½x12	475.00	17.50
c.		As "b," double surcharge	400.00	300.00
d.		Perf. 14, small holes	340.00	15.00
e.		As "b," double surcharge	525.00	—

Nos. 23-23c were issued without gum.

Queen Wilhelmina — A5

1892-93 **Typo.** *Perf. 12½*

Without Gum

No.	Type	Description	Unused	Used
25	A5	10c bister	45.00	3.50
26	A5	12½c rose lilac	52.50	6.00
27	A5	15c gray	4.00	2.75
28	A5	20c green	4.50	3.25
29	A5	25c blue	10.00	5.75
30	A5	30c red brown	5.75	5.00
		Nos. 25-30 (6)	121.75	26.25

Nos. 25-30 exist with gum.

For surcharges see Nos. 65-66.

Nos. 7-12 Surcharged

1898 *Perf. 11½x12, 12½x12, 13½*

Without Gum

No.	Type	Description	Unused	Used
31	A1	10c on 12½c sl bl	26.00	4.00
32	A1	10c on 15c gray	72.50	60.00
33	A1	10c on 20c green	5.25	5.00
34	A1	10c on 25c grnsh bl	12.00	6.50
c.		Perf. 11½x12	12.00	12.00
34A	A1	10c on 25c ultra	575.00	500.00
b.		Perf. 11½x12	675.00	600.00
35	A1	10c on 30c red brn	5.25	5.00
a.		Double surcharge	325.00	

Dangerous counterfeits exist.

Netherlands Nos. 80, 83-84 Surcharged

No. 36

Nos. 37-38

1900, Jan. 8 *Perf. 12½*

Without Gum

No.	Type	Description	Unused	Used
36	A11	50c on 50c	28.00	8.00

Engr.

Perf. 11½x11

No.	Type	Description	Unused	Used
37	A12	100c on 1g dk grn	26.00	14.50
38	A12	2.50g on 2½g brn lil	26.00	14.00
		Nos. 36-38 (3)	80.00	36.50

For surcharge see No. 67.

Nos. 13-16 Surcharged

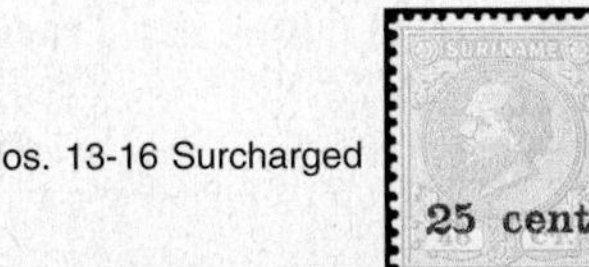

Perf. 11½, 11½x12, 12½x12, 14

1900 **Typo.**

Without Gum

No.	Type	Description	Unused	Used
39	A1	25c on 40c	4.00	3.00
40	A1	25c on 50c	4.00	3.00
a.		Perf. 14, small holes	140.00	*140.00*
b.		Perf. 11½x12	4.50	4.50
41	A1	50c on 1g	32.00	28.00
42	A1	50c on 2.50g	140.00	*150.00*
		Nos. 39-42 (4)	180.00	184.00

Counterfeits of No. 42 exist.

A9

Queen Wilhelmina

A10 A11

1902-08 **Typo.** *Perf. 12½*

Without Gum

No.	Type	Description	Unused	Used
44	A9	½c violet	.80	.80
45	A9	1c olive grn	2.00	1.25
46	A9	2c yellow brn	10.00	4.00
47	A9	2½c blue grn	4.50	.40
48	A9	3c orange	7.25	5.00
49	A9	5c red	7.75	.40
50	A9	7½c gray ('08)	16.00	7.25
51	A10	10c slate	10.00	.80
52	A10	12½c deep blue	3.75	.40
53	A10	15c dp brown	28.00	9.25
54	A10	20c olive grn	24.00	5.00
55	A10	22½c brn & ol grn	20.00	11.50
56	A10	25c violet	18.50	1.25
57	A10	30c orange brn	40.00	13.00
58	A10	50c lake brown	32.00	8.00

Engr.

Perf. 11

No.	Type	Description	Unused	Used
59	A11	1g violet	60.00	16.00
60	A11	2½g slate blue	52.50	60.00
		Nos. 44-60 (17)	337.05	144.30

Nos. 44-60 exist with gum.

A12

1909 **Typeset** *Serrate Roulette 13½*

Without Gum

No.	Type	Description	Unused	Used
61	A12	5c red	10.00	8.00
a.		Tête bêche pair	190.00	175.00

Perf. 11½x10½

No.	Type	Description	Unused	Used
62	A12	5c red	12.00	10.00
a.		Tête bêche pair	140.00	140.00

Nos. 17-18, 29-30, 38 Surcharged in Red

Nos. 63-64

Nos. 65-66

No. 67

1911, July 15 **Typo.** *Perf. 12½*

Without Gum

No.	Type	Description	Unused	Used
63	A2	½c on 1c	1.60	1.60
64	A2	½c on 2c	9.25	7.25
65	A5	15c on 25c	72.50	57.50
66	A5	20c on 30c	10.00	7.25

Engr.

Perf. 11½x11

No.	Type	Description	Unused	Used
67	A12	30c on 2.50g on 2½g	130.00	130.00
		Nos. 63-67 (5)	223.35	203.60

A13

1912, July **Typeset** *Perf. 11½*

Without Gum

No.	Type	Description	Unused	Used
70	A13	½c lilac	1.00	1.00
a.		Horiz. pair, imperf. btwn.	225.00	
71	A13	2½c dk green	1.00	.80
72	A13	5c pale red	7.75	7.75
a.		Vert. pair, imperf. btwn.	275.00	
73	A13	12½c deep blue	11.00	11.00
		Nos. 70-73 (4)	20.75	20.55

Numeral of Value — A14

A15

Queen Wilhelmina — A16

1913-31 **Typo.** *Perf. 12½*

No.	Type	Description	Unused	Used
74	A14	½c violet	.40	.25
75	A14	1c olive green	.40	.25
76	A14	1½c bl, perf 11 ½ ('21)	.40	.25
a.		Perf. 12½ ('32)	1.20	.80
77	A14	2c yellow brn	1.60	1.20
78	A14	2½c green	.80	.25
79	A14	3c yellow	.80	.60
80	A14	3c green ('26)	3.00	2.40
81	A14	4c chlky bl ('26)	7.25	4.50
82	A14	5c rose	1.60	.25
83	A14	5c green ('22)	2.00	1.00
84	A14	5c lilac ('26)	1.60	.25
85	A14	6c bister ('26)	2.40	2.40
86	A14	6c red org ('31)	2.00	.60
87	A14	7½c drab	1.20	.40
a.		Perf. 11x11½	1.60	.60
88	A14	7½c orange ('27)	1.20	.40
89	A14	7½c yellow ('31)	8.00	8.00
90	A14	10c violet ('22)	4.50	4.50
91	A14	10c rose ('26)	3.75	.80
92	A15	10c car rose	1.20	.50
93	A15	12½c blue	1.60	.60
94	A15	12½c red ('22)	2.00	2.00
95	A15	15c olive grn	.80	.65
96	A15	15c lt blue ('26)	7.00	4.25
97	A15	20c green	3.25	3.25
98	A15	20c blue ('22)	2.40	2.00
99	A15	20c ol grn ('26)	3.25	3.00
100	A15	22½c orange	2.40	2.40
101	A15	25c red violet	3.75	.40
102	A15	30c slate	4.50	1.00
103	A15	32½c vio & org ('22)	14.00	16.00
104	A15	35c sl & red ('26)	4.50	4.50

Perf. 11, 11½, 11½x11, 12½

Engr.

No.	Type	Description	Unused	Used
105	A16	50c green	4.00	.80
a.		Perf. 12½ ('32)	12.00	1.60
106	A16	1g brown	6.00	.80
a.		Perf. 12½ ('32)	14.00	1.60
107	A16	1½g dp vio ('26)	34.00	32.00
108	A16	2½g carmine ('23)	26.00	24.00
a.		Perf. 11½x11	34.00	32.50
		Nos. 74-108 (35)	163.55	126.45

Nos. 74, 75, 77-79, 82, 87, 105, 106 and 108 were issued both with and without gum.

Early printings of Nos. 74-104 had water soluble ink.

For surcharges see Nos. 116-120, 139.

Queen Wilhelmina — A17

1923, Oct. 5 *Perf. 11, 11x11½, 11½*

No.	Type	Description	Unused	Used
109	A17	5c green	.80	.65
110	A17	10c car rose	1.60	1.40
111	A17	20c indigo	3.75	3.00
112	A17	50c brown org	18.00	40.00
113	A17	1g brown vio	24.00	40.00
114	A17	2½g gray blk	72.50	*190.00*
115	A17	5g brown	100.00	*230.00*
		Nos. 109-115 (7)	220.65	*505.05*

25th anniv. of the assumption of the government of the Netherlands by Queen Wilhelmina, at age 18.

Values for Nos. 114-115 used are for stamps with postmarks clearly dated before July 15, 1924.

Nos. 83, 93-94, 98 Surcharged in Black or Red

j

k

m

1925, Dec. 19 **Typo.** *Perf. 12½*

No.	Type	Description	Unused	Used
116	A14	3c on 5c green	.80	.80
117	A15	10c on 12½c red	2.40	2.40
118	A15	15c on 12½c blue (R)	1.20	1.20
119	A15	15c on 20c blue	1.20	1.20
		Nos. 116-119 (4)	5.60	5.60

No. 100 Surcharged in Blue

1926, Jan. 1

No.	Type	Description	Unused	Used
120	A15	12½c on 22½c org	22.00	24.00

Postage Due Stamps Nos. J14 and J29 Surcharged in Blue or Black

o

p

No.	Type	Description	Unused	Used
121	D2(o)	12½c on 40c (Bl)	3.75	3.75
122	D2(p)	12½c on 40c (Bk)	26.00	26.00
		Nos. 120-122 (3)	51.75	53.75

No. 121 issued without gum.

Queen Wilhelmina — A21

1927-30 **Engr.** *Perf. 11½*

No.	Type	Description	Unused	Used
123	A21	10c carmine	.80	.40
124	A21	12½c red orange	1.60	1.60
125	A21	15c dark blue	1.90	.65
126	A21	20c indigo	1.90	.80
127	A21	21c dk brown ('30)	19.00	19.00
128	A21	22½c brown ('28)	7.50	9.25

No.	Type	Description	Unused	Used
129	A21	25c dk violet	2.60	.80
130	A21	30c dk green	2.60	1.00
131	A21	35c black brown	2.75	3.00
		Nos. 123-131 (9)	40.65	36.50

Types of Netherlands Marine Insurance Stamps Inscribed and Surcharged

Nos. 132-134, 138

Nos. 135-136

No. 137

1927, Oct. 26

No.	Type	Description	Unused	Used
132	MI1	3c on 15c dk grn	.60	.80
133	MI1	10c on 60c car rose	.65	.80
134	MI1	12½c on 75c gray brn	.80	.80
135	MI2	15c on 1.50 dk blue	2.40	2.40
136	MI2	25c on 2.25g org brn	6.50	6.50
137	MI3	30c on 4½g black	8.00	6.50
138	MI3	50c on 7½g red	6.50	6.50
		Nos. 132-138 (7)	25.45	24.30

No. 88 Surcharged

1930, Mar. 1 Typo. *Perf. 12½*

No.	Type	Description	Unused	Used
139	A14	6c on 7½c orange	1.90	1.00

Prince William I (Portrait by Van Key) — A22

1933, Apr. 24 Photo.

No.	Type	Description	Unused	Used
141	A22	6c deep orange	5.75	1.60

400th birth anniv. of Prince William I, Count of Nassau and Prince of Orange, frequently referred to as William the Silent.

Van Walbeeck's Ship A23

Queen Wilhelmina A24

1936-41 Litho. *Perf. 13½x12½*

No.	Type	Description	Unused	Used
142	A23	½c yellow brn	.25	.40
143	A23	1c lt yellow grn	.35	.25
144	A23	1½c brt blue	.50	.40
145	A23	2c black brown	.60	.40
146	A23	2½c green	.25	.25
a.		Perf. 13 ('41)	7.25	3.00
147	A23	3c dark ultra	.60	.40
148	A23	4c orange	.60	.65
149	A23	5c gray	.60	.25
150	A23	6c red	2.25	1.60
151	A23	7½c red violet	.25	.25
a.		7½c plum, perf. 13 ('41)	2.00	.25

Engr.

Perf. 14, 12½

Size: 20x30mm

No.	Type	Description	Unused	Used
152	A24	10c vermilion	.80	.25
a.		Perf. 12½ ('39)	52.50	10.00
153	A24	12½c dull green	3.00	1.25
154	A24	15c dark blue	1.25	.60
155	A24	20c yellow org	2.00	.65
156	A24	21c dk gray	3.25	3.00
a.		Perf. 12½ ('39)	3.25	3.25
157	A24	25c brown lake	2.00	1.00
158	A24	30c brown vio	3.25	1.00
159	A24	35c olive brown	3.75	3.75

Perf. 12½x14

Size: 22x33mm

No.	Type	Description	Unused	Used
160	A24	50c dull yel grn	3.75	1.60
161	A24	1g dull blue	6.50	2.00
162	A24	1.50g black brown	19.50	15.00
163	A24	2.50g rose lake	11.00	7.25
		Nos. 142-163 (22)	66.30	42.20

For surcharges see Nos. 181-183, B37-B40.

Queen Wilhelmina — A25

Perf. 12½x12

1938, Aug. 30 Photo. Wmk. 202

No.	Type	Description	Unused	Used
164	A25	2c dull purple	.40	.40
165	A25	7½c red orange	.80	.80
166	A25	15c royal blue	2.40	2.40
		Nos. 164-166 (3)	3.60	3.60

Reign of Queen Wilhelmina, 40th anniv.

Catalogue values for unused stamps in this section, from this point to the end of the section, are for Never Hinged items.

Van Walbeeck's Ship — A26

1941 Unwmk. Typo. *Perf. 12*

No.	Type	Description	Unused	Used
168	A26	1c lt yellow grn	.85	.40
169	A26	2c black brown	2.00	2.00

Type A26 is similar to type A23 except for the white side frame lines which extend to the base.

For surcharges see No. 180.

Queen Wilhelmina — A27

1941-46 Photo. *Perf. 13½x12½*

Size: 18x22½mm

No.	Type	Description	Unused	Used
174	A27	12½c royal blue ('46)	1.25	.25

Perf. 12½

No.	Type	Description	Unused	Used
175	A27	15c ultra	24.00	10.00

Royal Family — A28

1943, Nov. 2 Engr. *Perf. 13½x13*

No.	Type	Description	Unused	Used
176	A28	2½c deep orange	.55	.45
177	A28	7½c red	.55	.30
178	A28	15c black	2.25	1.75
179	A28	40c deep blue	3.00	2.00
		Nos. 176-179 (4)	6.35	4.50

Birth of Princess Margriet Francisca of the Netherlands.

No. 168 Surcharged in Black

No. 151 Surcharged in Black

No. 152 Surcharged in Black

1945 Unwmk. *Perf. 13, 14, 12*

No.	Type	Description	Unused	Used
180	A26	½c on 1c	.80	.80
181	A23	2½c on 7½c	3.50	3.25
182	A24	5c on 10c	.80	.80
183	A24	7½c on 10c	.80	.80
a.		Double surcharge, one inverted	240.00	240.00
		Nos. 180-183 (4)	5.90	5.65

Bauxite Mine, Moengo A29

Queen Wilhelmina
A30 A31

Designs: 1½c, Bush Negroes on Cottica River near Moengo. 2c, Waterfall in interior. 2½c, Road scene, Coronie District. 3c, Surinam River near Berg en Dahl Plantation. 4c, Government Square, Paramaribo. 5c, Mining gold. 6c, Street in Paramaribo. 7½c, Sugar cane train.

1945, Nov. 5 Engr. *Perf. 12*

No.	Type	Description	Unused	Used
184	A29	1c rose carmine	.80	.35
185	A29	1½c rose lake	2.00	1.15
186	A29	2c violet	1.00	.35
187	A29	2½c olive brn	1.00	.35
188	A29	3c dull green	2.00	.80
189	A29	4c brown	2.00	.80
190	A29	5c blue	2.00	.35
191	A29	6c olive	4.00	1.30
192	A29	7½c deep orange	1.30	.35
193	A30	10c blue	2.00	.25
194	A30	15c brown	3.25	.35
195	A30	20c dull green	4.00	.25
196	A30	22½c gray	5.00	.80
197	A30	25c carmine	10.00	4.00
198	A30	30c olive green	10.00	1.60
199	A30	35c brt blue grn	16.00	6.50
200	A30	40c rose lake	10.00	.40
201	A30	50c red orange	10.00	.40
202	A30	60c violet	10.00	.80
203	A31	1g red brown	12.00	.40
204	A31	1.50g lilac	10.00	1.25
205	A31	2.50g olive brn	24.00	1.25
206	A31	5g rose carmine	45.00	14.00
207	A31	10g red orange	70.00	27.00
		Nos. 184-207 (24)	257.35	65.05

For surcharges see #240, B41-B46, CB2-CB3.

No. 151 Surcharged in Blue

No. 152 Surcharged in Black

1947 *Perf. 13½x12½, 14*

No.	Type	Description	Unused	Used
209	A23	1½(c) on 7½c (Bl)	.40	.35
a.		Double surcharge, one inverted	240.00	
210	A24	2½c on 10c (Bk)	1.25	.35

Numeral A32

Queen Wilhelmina A33

Perf. 12½x13½

1948, July 21 Unwmk. Photo.

No.	Type	Description	Unused	Used
211	A32	1c dark red	.40	.25
212	A32	1½c plum	.40	.35
213	A32	2c purple	.40	.25
214	A32	2½c olive grn	1.75	.25
215	A32	3c dark green	.40	.25
216	A32	4c red brown	.40	.25

Perf. 13½x12½

No.	Type	Description	Unused	Used
217	A33	5c deep blue	.45	.25
218	A33	6c dark olive	1.10	.65
219	A33	7½c scarlet	.45	.25
220	A33	10c blue	.65	.25
221	A33	12½c dark blue	1.25	1.00
222	A33	15c henna brown	1.75	.40
223	A33	17½c dk vio brn	1.90	1.20
224	A33	20c dk blue grn	1.45	.25
225	A33	22½c slate blue	1.45	.65
226	A33	25c crimson	1.45	.35
227	A33	27½c car lake	1.45	.25
228	A33	30c olive green	2.10	.25
229	A33	37½c olive brn	3.00	1.75
230	A33	40c lilac rose	2.25	.35
231	A33	50c red orange	2.50	.35
232	A33	60c purple	2.50	.40
233	A33	70c black	3.25	.60
		Nos. 211-233 (23)	32.70	10.80

See Nos. 241-242.

Wilhelmina — A34

1948, Aug. 30 Engr. *Perf. 12½x14*

No.	Type	Description	Unused	Used
234	A34	7½c vermilion	1.20	.75
235	A34	12½c deep blue	1.20	.75

Reign of Queen Wilhelmina, 50th anniv.

Juliana — A35

Perf. 14x13

1948, Sept. 10 Wmk. 202 Photo.

No.	Type	Description	Unused	Used
236	A35	7½c deep orange	3.00	3.00
237	A35	12½c ultra	3.00	3.00

Investiture of Queen Juliana, Sept. 6, 1948.

For surcharges see Nos. B53-B54.

Post Horns Entwined — A36

1949, Oct. 1 Unwmk. *Perf. 11½x12*

238 A36 7½c brown red 6.00 3.00
239 A36 27½c dull blue 6.00 2.00

UPU, 75th anniversary.

No. 192 Surcharged with New Value, Square and Bar in Black

1950, Aug. 9 *Perf. 12*

240 A29 1c on 7½c dp org 1.20 .80

Numeral Type of 1948

1951, Apr. 5 *Perf. 12½x13½*

241 A32 5c deep blue 1.60 .25
242 A32 7½c deep orange 3.25 1.15

A37

Queen Juliana — A38

1951, Apr. 5 *Perf. 13½x13*

243 A37 10c blue .65 .25
244 A37 15c henna brn 1.40 .35
245 A37 20c dk blue grn 2.40 .25
246 A37 25c crimson 1.75 .40
247 A37 27½c carmine lake 1.75 .25
248 A37 30c olive green 1.75 .40
249 A37 35c olive brown 2.00 1.00
250 A37 40c lilac rose 2.40 .40
251 A37 50c red orange 3.25 .40

Engr.

Perf. 12½x12

252 A38 1g red brown 25.00 .50
Nos. 243-252 (10) 42.35 4.20

For surcharge see No. 271.

Shooting Fish A39

Fisherman A40

Designs: 5c, Bauxite mining. 6c, Log raft. 7½c, Plowing with Water Buffalo. 10c, Woman picking fruit. 12½c, Armored catfish. 15c, Macaw. 17½c, Armadillo. 20c, Poling canoe. 25c, Common iguana.

1953-55 Photo. *Perf. 14x13, 13x14*

253 A39 2c olive green .25 .25
254 A40 2½c blue green .35 .25
255 A40 5c gray .35 .25
256 A40 6c bright blue 1.60 1.15
257 A40 7½c purple .25 .25
258 A40 10c bright red .25 .25
259 A40 12½c dk gray blue 1.75 1.30
260 A40 15c crimson .60 .35
261 A40 17½c red brown 2.60 1.90
262 A40 20c Prus green .50 .25
263 A40 25c olive green 2.60 .80
a. Min. sheet of 4, #259-261, 263 65.00 40.00
Nos. 253-263 (11) 11.10 7.00

Issued: 2c, 7½c, 10c, 20c, 5/9/53; #263a, 2/14/55;.others, 12/1/54.

Queen Juliana — A41

1954, Dec. 15 *Perf. 13½*

264 A41 7½c dark red brown .80 .80

Charter of the Kingdom, adopted Dec. 15, 1954.

See Netherlands No. 366, Netherlands Antilles No. 232.

Harvesting Bananas — A46

Designs: 7½c, Pounding rice. 10c, Preparing cassava. 15c, Fishing.

1955, May 12 *Perf. 14x13*

265 A46 2c dark green 1.60 1.15
266 A46 7½c dull yellow 2.60 1.90
267 A46 10c orange brown 2.60 1.90
268 A46 15c ultra 2.75 1.90
Nos. 265-268 (4) 9.55 6.85

4th anniv. of the establishment of the Caribbean Tourist Assoc.

Globe and Mercury's Rod — A47

1955, Sept. 19 Unwmk. *Perf. 13x12*

269 A47 5c bright ultra .40 .40

Paramaribo Trade Fair, Oct. 1955.

Flags and Map of Caribbean — A48

1956, Dec. 6 Litho. *Perf. 13x14*

270 A48 10c lt blue & red .40 .40

10th anniv. of Caribbean Commission.

No. 247 Surcharged

1958, Nov. 11 Photo. *Perf. 13½x13*

271 A37 8c on 27½c car lake .25 .25

Queen Juliana — A49

Perf. 12½x12

1959, Oct. 15 Unwmk. Litho.

272 A49 1g magenta 1.60 .25
273 A49 1.50g olive bister 2.25 .50
274 A49 2.50g dk carmine 3.00 .35
275 A49 5g dull blue 6.25 .40
Nos. 272-275 (4) 13.10 1.50

Symbolic Flowers — A50

1959, Dec. 15 Photo. *Perf. 12½x13*

276 A50 20c multicolored 3.00 1.60

5th anniv. of the constitution. Flowers in design symbolize Netherlands, Surinam and Netherlands Antilles.

Charles Lindbergh's Plane — A51

10c, De Snip plane. 15c, Cessna 170B. 20c, Super Constellation. 40c, Boeing 707 Jet.

1960, Mar. 12 *Perf. 12½*

277 A51 8c chalky blue 1.25 1.25
278 A51 10c bright green 1.75 1.75
279 A51 15c rose red 1.75 1.75
280 A51 20c pale violet 2.00 2.00
281 A51 40c light brown 3.00 3.00
Nos. 277-281 (5) 9.75 9.75

Inauguration of Zanderij Airport, Mar. 12. Nos. 277-281 show 25 years of Surinam's civil aviation.

Flag of Surinam and Map — A52

Arms of Surinam — A53

1960, July 1 Litho. *Perf. 12½x13*

282 A52 10c multicolored .65 .65

Perf. 13x12½

283 A53 15c multicolored .65 .65

Day of Freedom, July 1.

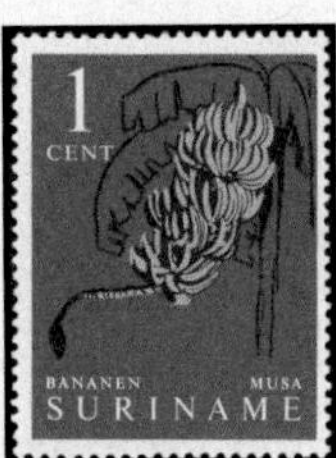

Bananas — A54

1961, Mar. 1 Litho. *Perf. 13½*

284 A54 1c shown .25 .25
285 A54 2c Citrus fruit .25 .25
286 A54 3c Cacao .25 .25
287 A54 4c Sugar cane .25 .25
288 A54 5c Coffee .25 .25
289 A54 6c Coconuts .25 .25
290 A54 8c Rice .25 .25
Nos. 284-290 (7) 1.75 1.75

Finance Building — A55

Buildings: 15c, Court of Justice. 20c, Concordia Lodge (Masons). 25c, Neve Shalom Synagogue, Paramaribo, horiz. 30c, Old Dutch lock in New Amsterdam. 35c, Government office, horiz. 40c, Governor's palace, horiz. 50c, Legislative Council, horiz. 60c, Old Dutch Reformed Church, horiz. 70c, Zeelandia Fortress, horiz.

1961 *Perf. 13½x14, 14x13½*

291 A55 10c multi .30 .25
292 A55 15c multi .25 .25
293 A55 20c multi .30 .25
294 A55 25c multi .55 .40
295 A55 30c multi 1.50 1.20
296 A55 35c multi 1.50 1.30
297 A55 40c multi .75 .60
298 A55 50c multi .75 .30
299 A55 60c multi .85 .85
300 A55 70c multi .90 1.00
Nos. 291-300 (10) 7.65 6.40

Issued: 10c, 20c, 25c, 50c, 70c, 4/1; others, 5/15.

Dag Hammarskjold (1905-1961) A56

1962, Jan. 2 Litho. *Perf. 11¾, 12½*

301 A56 10c brt blue & blk .25 .25
302 A56 20c lilac & blk .25 .25

Dag Hammarskjold, Secretary General of the United Nations, 1953-61.

Sheets of both perfs. exist either with or without extension of perforations through the margins.

A56a

1962, Feb. 1 Photo. *Perf. 14x13*

303 A56a 20c olive green .40 .35

Silver wedding anniversary of Queen Juliana and Prince Bernhard.

A57

Malaria eradication emblem.

1962, May 2 Litho. *Perf. 13x14*

304 A57 8c bright red .25 .25
305 A57 10c blue .25 .25

WHO drive to eradicate malaria.

Stoelmans Guesthouse — A58

Design: 15c, Torarica Hotel.

1962, July 4 ***Perf. 14x13½***

306	A58 10c multicolored	.40	.40
307	A58 15c multicolored	.40	.40

Opening of the Torarica Hotel in Paramaribo and Stoelmans Guesthouse on Stoelman Island.

Deaconess Residence and Recreation Area — A59

Design: 20c, Deaconess Hospital.

1962, Nov. 30

308	A59 10c multicolored	.40	.40
309	A59 20c multicolored	.40	.40

Hands Holding Wheat Emblem A60

20c, Farmer harvesting & wheat emblem, vert.

Perf. 14x13, 13x14

1963, Mar. 21 **Photo.**

310	A60 10c deep carmine	.25	.25
311	A60 20c dark blue	.25	.25

FAO "Freedom from Hunger" campaign.

Broken Chain — A61

1963, June 28 **Litho.** ***Perf. 14x13***

312	A61 10c red & blk	.25	.25
313	A61 20c green & blk	.25	.25

Centenary of emancipation of the slaves.

Prince William of Orange Landing at Scheveningen A61a

1963, Nov. 21 **Photo.** ***Perf. 13½x14***
Size: 26x26mm

314	A61a 10c dull bl, blk & brn	.25	.25

Founding of the Kingdom of the Netherlands, 150th anniv.

Faja Lobbi Wreath — A62

1964, Dec. 15 **Litho.** ***Perf. 12½x13***

315	A62 25c multicolored	.25	.25

Charter of the Kingdom of the Netherlands, 10th anniv.

Abraham Lincoln (1809-1865) — A63

1965, Apr. 14 **Litho.** ***Perf. 12½x13***

316	A63 25c olive bister & brn	.25	.25

ICY Emblem A64

1965, May 26 ***Perf. 13x12½***

317	A64 10c orange & blue	.25	.25
318	A64 15c red & violet bl	.25	.25

International Cooperation Year.

Bauxite Mine, Moengo A65

Designs: 15c, Alum Pottery Works, Paranam. 20c, Hydroelectric plant, Afobaka. 25c, Aluminum smeltery, Paranam.

1965, Oct. 9 **Photo.** **Unwmk.**

319	A65 10c ocher	.35	.25
320	A65 15c dark green	.35	.25
321	A65 20c dark blue	.35	.25
322	A65 25c carmine	.35	.25
	Nos. 319-322 (4)	1.40	1.00

Opening of the Brokopondo Power Station.

Red-breasted Blackbird — A66

2c, Great kiskadee. 3c, Silver-beaked tanager. 4c, Ruddy ground dove. 5c, Blue-gray tanager. 6c, Glittering-throated emerald (hummingbird). 8c, Turquoise tanager. 10c, Pale-breasted robin.

1966, Feb. 16 **Litho.** ***Perf. 13x14***

323	A66 1c brt grn, blk & red	.45	.25
324	A66 2c lt ultra, yel & brn	.45	.25
325	A66 3c multi	.45	.25
326	A66 4c lt ol grn, red brn & blk	.45	.25
327	A66 5c org, ultra & blk	.45	.25
328	A66 6c multi	.45	.25
329	A66 8c gray, vio bl & blk	.45	.25
330	A66 10c multi	.45	.25
	Nos. 323-330 (8)	3.60	2.00

Central Hospital A67

Design: 15c, Hospital, side view.

1966, Mar. 9 **Litho.** ***Perf. 13x12½***

331	A67 10c multi	.25	.25
332	A67 15c multi	.25	.25

Opening of Central Hospital, Paramaribo.

Father Petrus Donders — A68

Designs: 10c, Church and parsonage, Batavia. 15c, Msgr. Joannes B. Swinkels. 25c, Cathedral, Paramaribo.

1966, Mar. 26 **Photo.** ***Perf. 12½x13***

333	A68 4c org brn & blk	.25	.25
334	A68 10c rose brn & blk	.25	.25
335	A68 15c yel brn & blk	.25	.25
336	A68 25c lt vio & blk	.25	.25
	Nos. 333-336 (4)	1.00	1.00

Centenary of the Redemptorist Mission in Surinam (Congregation of the Most Holy Redeemer).

100-Year-Old Tree — A69

1966, May 9 **Litho.** ***Perf. 13x12½***

337	A69 25c grn, dp org & blk	.25	.25
338	A69 30c red org, grn & blk	.25	.25

Centenary of the Surinam Parliament.

Television Transmitter, Eye and Globe — A70

1966, Oct. 20 **Litho.** ***Perf. 12½x13***

339	A70 25c dk bl & ver	.25	.25
340	A70 30c brn & ver	.25	.25

Inauguration of television service.

Bauxite Industry, 1916 — A71

Design: 25c, Bauxite industry, 1966.

1966, Dec. 19 **Litho.** ***Perf. 13x12½***

341	A71 20c yel, org & blk	.25	.25
342	A71 25c org, bl & blk	.25	.25

50th anniversary of bauxite industry.

Central Bank, Paramaribo A72

Design: 25c, Central Bank, different view.

1967, Apr. 1 **Litho.** ***Perf. 13x12½***

343	A72 10c dp yel & blk	.25	.25
344	A72 25c lil & blk	.25	.25

Central Bank of Surinam, 10th anniv.

Amelia Earhart, Lockheed Electra and Paramaribo A73

1967, June 3 **Photo.** ***Perf. 13x12½***

345	A73 20c yel & dk car	.35	.25
346	A73 25c yel & grn	.35	.25

30th anniv. of Amelia Earhart's visit to Surinam, June 3-4, 1937.

Siva Nataraja, God of Dance, and Ballerina's Foot — A74

Design: 25c, Drummer's mask "Bashi Lele," and scroll of violin.

1967, June 21 **Litho.** ***Perf. 12½x13***

347	A74 10c yel grn & bl	.25	.25
348	A74 25c yel grn & brn	.25	.25

20th anniv. of the Surinam Cultural Center Foundation.

New Amsterdam, 1660 (New York City) — A75

Designs after 17th Century Engravings: 10c, Fort Zeelandia, Paramaribo, 1670. 25c, Breda Castle, Netherlands, 1667.

1967, July 31 **Litho.** ***Perf. 13½x13***

349	A75 10c yel, blk & bl	.35	.25
350	A75 20c red brn, yel & blk	.35	.25
351	A75 25c bl grn, yel & blk	.35	.25
	Nos. 349-351 (3)	1.05	.75

300th anniv. of the Treaty of Breda between Britain, France and the Netherlands.

WHO Emblem A76

1968, Apr. 7 **Litho.** ***Perf. 13x12½***

352	A76 10c magenta & dk bl	.25	.25
353	A76 25c bl & dk pur	.25	.25

WHO, 20th anniversary.

Chandelier and Christian Symbols A77

15c, like 10c, reversed. Brass chandelier from the Reformed Church, Paramaribo.

1968, May 29 **Litho.** ***Perf. 13x12½***

354	A77 10c dark blue	.25	.25
355	A77 25c dp yel grn	.25	.25

Reformed Church of Paramaribo, 300th anniv.

Missionary Store, 1768 — A78

Designs: 25c, Main Church and store, Paramaribo, 1868. 30c, C. Kersten & Co., 1968.

1968, June 29 Litho. *Perf. 13x12½*

356 A78 10c yel & blk .25 .25
357 A78 25c lt grnsh bl & blk .25 .25
358 A78 30c lilac rose & blk .25 .25
Nos. 356-358 (3) .75 .75

200th anniv. of C. Kersten & Co., which is partially owned by the Evangelical Brotherhood Missionary Society.

Joden Savanne Synagogue — A79

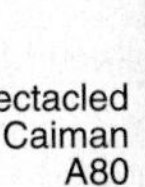

Designs: 20c, Map of Joden Savanne and Surinam River. 30c, Gravestone, 1733. The Hebrew inscriptions are quotations from the Bible: 20c, Joshua 24:2; 25c, Isaiah 56:7; 30c, Genesis 31:52.

1968, Aug. 28 *Perf. 12½x13*

359 A79 20c multi .40 .40
360 A79 25c multi .40 .40
361 A79 30c multi .40 .40
Nos. 359-361 (3) 1.20 1.20

Founding of the first synagogue in the Western Hemisphere in 1685 in Joden Savanne, Surinam.

Spectacled Caiman A80

20c, Squirrel monkey, vert. 25c, Armadillo.

Perf. 13x12½, 12½x13

1969, Aug. 20 Litho.

362 A80 10c grn & multi .65 .40
363 A80 20c bl gray & multi .65 .40
364 A80 25c vio & multi .65 .40
Nos. 362-364 (3) 1.95 1.20

Mahatma Gandhi — A81

1969, Oct. 2 Litho. *Perf. 12½x13*

365 A81 25c red & blk 1.20 .80

Mohandas K. Gandhi (1869-1948), leader in India's fight for independence.

ILO Emblem A82

1969, Oct. 29 Litho. *Perf. 13x12½*

366 A82 10c brt bl grn & blk .25 .25
367 A82 25c red & blk .35 .35

ILO, 50th anniversary.

Queen Juliana and Rising Sun — A82a

1969, Dec. 15 Photo. *Perf. 14x13*

368 A82a 25c blue & multi .35 .35

15th anniv. of the Charter of the Kingdom of the Netherlands. Phosphorescent paper.

"1950-1970" A83

1970, Apr. 3 Litho. *Perf. 13x12½*

369 A83 10c brn, grn & org .25 .25
370 A83 25c emer, dk bl & org .25 .25

20th anniv. of secondary education in Surinam.

Inauguration of UPU Headquarters, Bern — A84

Design: 25c, UPU Headquarters, sideview and UPU emblem.

1970, May 20 Litho. *Perf. 13x12½*

371 A84 10c sky bl & dk pur .25 .25
372 A84 25c red & blk .25 .25

"UNO" — A85

1970, June 26 Litho. *Perf. 12½x13*

373 A85 10c ocher & yel .25 .25
374 A85 25c dp bl & ultra .25 .25

25th anniversary of the United Nations.

Plane over Paramaribo — A86

Designs: 20c, Plane over map of Totness, 25c, Plane over Nieuw-Nickerie.

1970, July 15

375 A86 10c bl, vio bl & gray .40 .35
376 A86 20c yel, red & gray .40 .35
377 A86 25c pink, dk red & gray .40 .35
Nos. 375-377 (3) 1.20 1.05

40th anniv. of domestic airmail service.

Cocoi Heron A88

Birds in Flight: 20c, Flamingo. 25c, Scarlet macaw.

1971, Feb. 14 Litho. *Perf. 13x12½*

382 A88 15c gray & multi .50 .40
383 A88 20c ultra & multi .50 .40
384 A88 25c pale grn & multi .50 .40
Nos. 382-384 (3) 1.50 1.20

25th anniversary of regular air service between the Netherlands, Surinam and Netherlands Antilles.

Morse Key — A89

Designs: 20c, Telephone. 25c, Lunar landing module, telescope.

1971, May 17 Photo. *Perf. 12½x13*

385 A89 15c light green & multi .40 .40
386 A89 20c blue & multi .40 .40
387 A89 25c lilac & multi .40 .40
Nos. 385-387 (3) 1.20 1.20

3rd World Telecommunications Day.

Prince Bernhard, Fokker F27, Boeing 747B — A89a

1971, June 29 Photo. *Perf. 13x14*

388 A89a 25c multi .35 .35

60th birthday of Prince Bernhard.

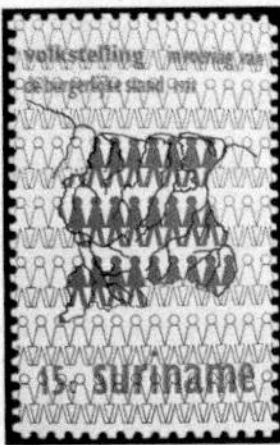

Map of Surinam, Population Chart — A90

Design: 30c, Map of Surinam and individual representing population.

1971, July 31 Litho. *Perf. 12½x13*

389 A90 15c gray bl, blk & ver .25 .25
390 A90 30c ver, gray bl & blk .35 .35

50th anniv. of the first census; introduction of civil registration in Surinam.

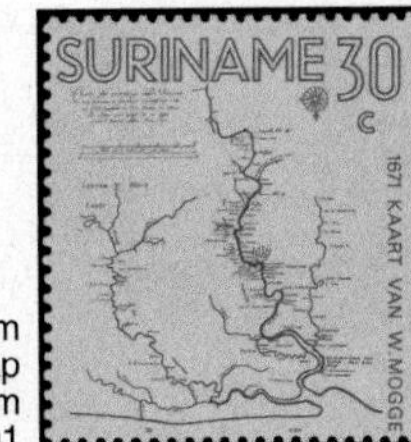

William Mogge's Map of Surinam A91

1971, Oct. 27 *Perf. 11½x11*

391 A91 30c dull yel & dk brn .60 .50

300th anniv. of the first map of Surinam.

Map of Albina — A92

August Kappler — A93

20c, View of Albina from Maroni River.

1971, Dec. 13 *Perf. 13x12½, 12½x13*

392 A92 15c sapphire & blk .40 .40
393 A92 20c brt grn & blk .40 .40
394 A93 25c yel & blk .40 .40
Nos. 392-394 (3) 1.20 1.20

125th anniv. of the founding of Albina by August Kappler (1815-1887).

Drop of Water — A94

Design: 30c, Faucet and water tower.

1972, Feb. 2 *Perf. 12½x13*

395 A94 15c vio & blk .35 .35
396 A94 30c bl & blk .40 .40

Surinam water works, 40th anniversary.

Air Mail Envelope A95

1972, Aug. 2 Litho. *Perf. 13x12½*

397 A95 15c red & blue .25 .25
398 A95 30c blue & red .35 .35

Arrival of the 1st airmail in Surinam, carried by Capt. Dutertre from French Guiana, 50th anniv.

Giant Tree — A96

Designs: 20c, Wood transport by air lift. 30c, Hands tending seedling.

1972, Dec. 20 Photo. *Perf. 12½x13*

399 A96 15c yel & dk brn .25 .25
400 A96 20c bl & dp brn .25 .25
401 A96 30c brt grn & dp brn .40 .40
Nos. 399-401 (3) .90 .90

Surinam Forestry Commission, 25th anniv.

Hindu Woman in Rice Field — A97

25c, J. F. A. Cateau van Rosevelt with map of Surinam, ship "Lalla Rookh." 30c, Symbolic bird, flower, sun, flag, factories.

1973, June 5 Litho. *Perf. 13½x14*

402 A97 15c purple & yel .35 .35
403 A97 25c maroon & gray .35 .35
404 A97 30c yel & light blue .40 .40
Nos. 402-404 (3) 1.10 1.10

1st immigrants from India, cent.

Queen Juliana, Surinam and House of Orange Colors A97a

Engr. & Photo.

1973, Sept. 4 *Perf. 12½x12*

405 A97a 30c sil, blk & org .65 .60

25th anniversary of reign of Queen Juliana.

INTERPOL Emblem — A98

Design: 30c, INTERPOL emblem, Surinam visa handstamp.

1973, Nov. 7 Litho. *Perf. 14x14½*

406 A98 15c vio bl & multi .25 .25
407 A98 30c lt bl, lil & blk .35 .35

50th anniv. of Intl. Criminal Police Org.

Mailman — A99

15c, Pigeons carrying Letters. 30c, Map of Surinam, plane, ship, train and truck.

1973, Dec. 12 Litho. *Perf. 12½x13*

408 A99 15c lt yel grn & bl .25 .25
409 A99 25c sal, blk & bl .35 .35
410 A99 30c ver & multi .50 .50
Nos. 408-410 (3) 1.10 1.10

Centenary of stamps of Surinam.

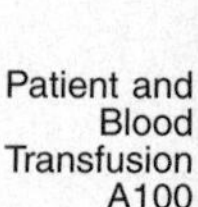

Patient and Blood Transfusion A100

30c, Cross section of tissue and oscilloscope.

1974, June 1 Litho. *Perf. 14½x14*

411 A100 15c red brn & multi .25 .25
412 A100 30c lemon & multi .35 .35

75th anniversary of the Medical College.

Crop Dusting A101

1974, July 17 Litho. *Perf. 13½*

413 A101 15c shown .25 .25
414 A101 30c Fertilizer plant .35 .35

Foundation for Development of Mechanical Agriculture in Surinam, 25th anniv.

Old Title Page — A102

1974, July 31 *Perf. 14x14½*

415 A102 15c multicolored .25 .25
416 A102 30c multicolored .35 .35

"Weekly Wednesday Surinam Newspaper," bicent. 1st editor was Beeldsnijder Matroos.

Paramaribo Main Post Office A103

Design: 30c, Post Office, different view.

1974, Sept. 11 Litho. *Perf. 14½x14*

417 A103 15c brown & blk .25 .25
418 A103 30c blue & blk .35 .35

Centenary of Universal Postal Union.

Gold Panner A104

Design: 30c, Modern excavator.

1975, Feb. 5 Litho. *Perf. 13x12½*

419 A104 15c brown & olive bis .40 .25
420 A104 30c vermilion & maroon .40 .35

Centenary of prospecting policy granting concessions for winning of raw materials.

Symbolic Design A105

1975, June 25 Litho. *Perf. 13x12½*

421 A105 15c green & multi .40 .40
422 A105 25c blue & multi .40 .40
423 A105 30c red & multi .40 .40
Nos. 421-423 (3) 1.20 1.20

Cent. of Intl. Meter Convention, Paris, 1875.

Hands Holding Saw — A106

Designs: 50c, Book with notes and letter "a." 75c, Hands holding ball.

1975, Nov. 25 Litho. *Perf. 13½x14*

424 A106 25c yellow, red & brn .45 .35
425 A106 50c yellow, red & pur 1.05 .80
426 A106 75c dk bl, org & emer 1.50 1.15
Nos. 424-426 (3) 3.00 2.30

Independence. Sheets of 10 (5x2) with ornamental margins.

Oncidium Lanceanum A107

Central Bank, Paramaribo A109

Orchids: 2c, Epidendrum stenopetalum. 3c, Brassia lanceana. 4c, Epidendrum ibaguense. 5c, Epidendrum fragrans.

1975-76 Litho. *Perf. 14½x13½*

427 A107 1c multicolored .30 .25
428 A107 2c multicolored .30 .25
429 A107 3c multicolored .30 .25
430 A107 4c multicolored .30 .25
431 A107 5c multicolored .30 .25

Perf. 14x13½

436 A109 1g rose lil & blk 1.50 .25
437 A109 1½g brn, dp org & blk 2.60 .25
438 A109 2½g red brn, org red & blk 4.00 .25
439 A109 5g grn, yel grn & blk 7.50 .25
440 A109 10g dk vio bl & blk 16.50 .55
Nos. 427-431,436-440 (10) 33.60 2.80

Issued: #436-439, Nov. 25, 1975; #427-431, Feb. 18, 1976; #440, May 5, 1976.
For surcharges see Nos. 772-774, 810.

Flag of Surinam — A110

Design: 35c, Coat of Arms.

1976, Mar. 3 *Perf. 14x13½*

445 A110 25c emerald & multi .55 .50
446 A110 35c red orange & multi .75 .70

Sheets of 12 (6x2) with ornamental margins.

Pomacanthus Semicirculatus — A111

Fish: 2c, Adioryx diadema. 3c, Pogonoculius zebra. 4c, Balistes vetula. 5c, Myripristis jacobus.

1976, June 2 Litho. *Perf. 12½x13*

447 A111 1c multicolored .25 .25
448 A111 2c multicolored .25 .25
449 A111 3c multicolored .25 .25
450 A111 4c multicolored .25 .25
451 A111 5c multicolored .25 .25
Nos. 447-451,C55-C57 (8) 5.15 3.30

See #471-475, 504-508, C72-C74, C85-C87.

19th Century Switchboard and Telephone — A112

35c, Satellite, globe and 1976 telephone.

1976, Aug. 5 Litho. *Perf. 13½x14*

452 A112 20c yellow & multi .40 .40
453 A112 35c ultra & multi .80 .80

Centenary of first telephone call by Alexander Graham Bell, Mar. 10, 1876.

The Story of Anansi Tori, by A. Baag — A113

Designs: 30c, "Surinam Now" (young people), by R. Chang. 35c, Lamentation, by Nola Hatterman, vert. 50c, Chess Players, by Q. Jan Telting.

Perf. 13½x14, 14x13½

1976, Sept. 29 Photo.

454 A113 20c multicolored .35 .30
455 A113 30c multicolored .60 .45
456 A113 35c multicolored .80 .50
457 A113 50c multicolored 1.10 .85
Nos. 454-457 (4) 2.85 2.10

Paintings by Surinam artists.

Franklin's Divided Snake Poster, 1754 — A114

1976, Nov. 10 Litho. *Perf. 13½x14*

458 A114 20c green & blk .40 .30
459 A114 60c orange & blk 1.15 1.00

American Bicentennial.

Ionopsis Utricularioides A115

Orchids: 30c, Rodiguezia secunda. 35c, Oncidium pusillum. 55c, Sobralia sessilis. 60c, Octomeria surinamensis.

1977, Jan. 19 Litho. *Perf. 14½x13½*

460 A115 20c vermilion & multi .35 .25
461 A115 30c ultra & multi .50 .25
462 A115 35c magenta & multi .50 .45
463 A115 55c yellow & multi 1.00 .80
464 A115 60c green & multi 1.00 .90
Nos. 460-464 (5) 3.35 2.65

Surinam Costume A116

Various Surinamese women's costumes.

1977, Mar. 2 Litho. *Perf. 14x13½*

465 A116 10c brt blue & multi .25 .25
466 A116 15c green & multi .25 .25
467 A116 35c violet & multi .35 .25
468 A116 60c orange & multi .70 .55
469 A116 75c ultra & multi .90 .70
470 A116 1g yellow & multi 1.15 .90
Nos. 465-470 (6) 3.60 2.90

Fish Type of 1976

Tropical Fish: 1c, Liopropoma carmabi. 2c, Holacanthus ciliaris. 3c, Opistognathus aurifrons. 4c, Anisotremus virginicus. 5c, Gramma loreto.

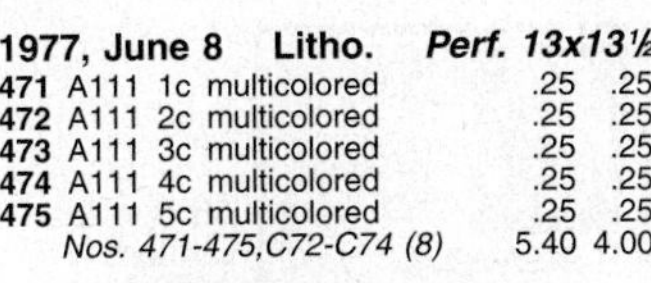

1977, June 8 Litho. *Perf. 13x13½*

471 A111 1c multicolored .25 .25
472 A111 2c multicolored .25 .25
473 A111 3c multicolored .25 .25
474 A111 4c multicolored .25 .25
475 A111 5c multicolored .25 .25
Nos. 471-475,C72-C74 (8) 5.40 4.00

Edison's Phonograph, 1877 — A117

Design: 60c, Modern turntable.

1977, Aug. 24 Litho. *Perf. 13½x14*

476 A117 20c multicolored .35 .30
477 A117 60c multicolored .85 .70

Invention of the phonograph, cent.

Packet Curacao, 1827 A118

Designs: 15c, Hellevoetsluis Harbor and postmark, 1827. 30c, Sea chart and technical details of packet Curacao. 35c, Logbook and compass rose. 60c, Map of Paramaribo harbor and 1852 postmark. 95c, Modern liner Stuyvesant.

1977, Sept. 28 Litho. *Perf. 14x13½*

478 A118 5c grnsh bl & dk bl .25 .25
479 A118 15c orange & mar .25 .25
480 A118 30c lt brn & blk .25 .25
481 A118 35c olive & blk .25 .25
482 A118 60c lilac & blk .30 .25
483 A118 95c yel grn & dk grn .65 .60
Nos. 478-483 (6) 1.95 1.85

Regular steamer connection between the Netherlands and Surinam, 150th anniversary.

Passiflora Quadrangularis A119

Flowers: 30c, Centropogon surinamensis. 55c, Gloxinia perennis. 60c, Hydrocleis nymphoides. 75c, Clusia grandiflora.

1978, Feb. 8 Litho. *Perf. 13x14*

484 A119 20c multicolored .40 .45
485 A119 30c multicolored .40 .45
486 A119 55c multicolored .65 .55
487 A119 60c multicolored .75 .70
488 A119 75c multicolored .85 .80
Nos. 484-488 (5) 3.05 2.95

Javanese Costume — A120

People of Surinam, Costumes: 20c, Forest black. 35c, Chinese. 60c, Creole. 75c, Aborigine Indian. 1g, Hindustani.

1978, Mar. 1 Litho. *Perf. 13x14*

489 A120 10c multicolored .30 .30
490 A120 20c multicolored .30 .30
491 A120 35c multicolored .30 .30
492 A120 60c multicolored .50 .50
493 A120 75c multicolored .55 .55
494 A120 1g multicolored .85 .85
Nos. 489-494 (6) 2.80 2.80

Air Post Stamps of 1972 Surcharged

1977, Nov. 15 Litho. *Perf. 13½x14*

495 AP6 1c on 25c #C44 .25 .25
496 AP6 4c on 15c #C42 .25 .25
497 AP6 4c on 30c #C45 .25 .25
498 AP6 5c on 40c #C47 .40 .25
499 AP6 10c on 75c #C54 .55 .25
Nos. 495-499 (5) 1.70 1.25

"Luchtpost" obliterated with 2 bars.

Old Municipal Church A121

Johannes King — A122

Designs: 55c, New Municipal Church. 60c, Johannes Raillard.

1978, May 31 Litho. *Perf. 14x13*

500 A121 10c blue, blk & gray .30 .25
501 A122 20c gray & blk .30 .25
502 A121 55c rose lil & blk .50 .40
503 A122 60c orange & blk .50 .45
Nos. 500-503 (4) 1.60 1.35

Evangelical Brothers Community Church, Paramaribo, bicentenary.

Fish Type of 1976

Tropical Fish: 1c, Nannacara Anomala. 2c, Leporinus fasciatus. 3c, Pristella riddlei. 4c, Nannostomus beckfordi. 5c, Rivulus agilae.

1978, June 21 *Perf. 12½x13½*

504 A111 1c multicolored .25 .25
505 A111 2c multicolored .25 .25
506 A111 3c multicolored .25 .25
507 A111 4c multicolored .25 .25
508 A111 5c multicolored .25 .25
Nos. 504-508,C85-C87 (8) 5.00 4.55

Souvenir Sheet

Commewijne River Development — A124

Development: 60c, Map of Surinam and dam. 95c, Planes and world map.

1978, Oct. 18 Litho. *Perf. 14x13*

509 A124 Sheet of 3 1.90 1.90
a. 20c multi .35 .25
b. 60c multi .50 .40
c. 95c multi .75 .60

Coconuts — A125

1978-85 Litho. *Perf. 13½x13*

510 A125 5c shown .25 .25
a. Bklt. pane, 4 #510, 3 #511, 5 #515 ('80) 2.00
511 A125 10c Oranges .25 .25
512 A125 15c Papayas .25 .25
a. Bklt. pane, 5 #512, 6 #514 + label ('79) 2.00
513 A125 20c Bananas .25 .25
514 A125 25c Soursop .25 .25
514A A125 30c Cocoa beans ('85) .85 .85
b. Bklt. pane, 6 #514A, 1 #513 + label ('85) 3.25 3.25
515 A125 35c Watermelon .55 .55
Nos. 510-515 (7) 2.65 2.65

Wright Brothers' Flyer 1 — A126

Designs: 20c, Daedalus and Icarus, vert. 95c, DC 8. 125c, Concorde.

Perf. 13x14, 14x13

1978, Dec. 13 Litho.

516 A126 20c multicolored .30 .25
517 A126 60c multicolored .65 .60
518 A126 95c multicolored .95 .90
519 A126 125c multicolored 1.20 1.10
Nos. 516-519 (4) 3.10 2.85

75th anniversary of 1st powered flight.

Rodriguezia Candida — A127

Flowers: 20c, Stanhopea grandiflora. 35c, Scuticaria steelei. 60c, Bollea violacea.

1979, Feb. 7 Litho. *Perf. 13x14*

520 A127 10c multicolored .40 .40
521 A127 20c multicolored .40 .40
522 A127 35c multicolored .70 .50
523 A127 60c multicolored .90 .75
Nos. 520-523 (4) 2.40 2.05

Javanese Dancer — A128

Dancing Costumes: 10c, Forest Negro. 15c, Chinese. 20c, Creole. 25c, Aborigine Indian. 35c, Hindustani.

1979, Feb. 28

524 A128 5c multicolored .25 .25
525 A128 10c multicolored .25 .25
526 A128 15c multicolored .25 .25
527 A128 20c multicolored .25 .25
528 A128 25c multicolored .25 .25
529 A128 35c multicolored .45 .45
Nos. 524-529 (6) 1.70 1.70

Equetus Pulchellus A129

Tropical Fish: 2c, Apogon binotatus. 3c, Anisotremus virginicus. 5c, Bodianus rufus. 35c, Microspathodon chrysurus.

1979, May 30 Photo. *Perf. 14x13*

530 A129 1c multicolored .25 .25
531 A129 2c multicolored .25 .25
532 A129 3c multicolored .25 .25
533 A129 5c multicolored .25 .25
534 A129 35c multicolored .45 .30
Nos. 530-534,C89-C91 (8) 4.80 3.25

See Nos. 557-561, C92-C94.

Javanese Wooden Head — A130

Folkart: 35c, Head ornament, Indian. 60c, Horse's head, Javanese.

1979, Aug. 29 Litho. *Perf. 14x13*

535 A130 20c multicolored .30 .25
536 A130 35c multicolored .50 .35
537 A130 60c multicolored .85 .60
Nos. 535-537 (3) 1.65 1.20

Sir Rowland Hill — A131

1979, Oct. 3 Litho. *Perf. 13x14*

538 A131 1g yellow & olive 1.25 .85

Sir Rowland Hill (1795-1879), originator of penny postage.

SOS Emblem, House A132

Design: 60c, SOS emblem and buildings.

1979, Oct. 3 *Perf. 13x14*

539 A132 20c multicolored .35 .25
540 A132 60c multicolored .80 .55

Intl. Year of the Child; SOS Children's Villages, 30th anniv.

Javanese Girl's Costume — A133

1980, Feb. 6 Photo. *Perf. 13x14*

541 A133 10c Javanese girl .35 .30
542 A133 15c Forest Black boy .35 .30
543 A133 25c Chinese girl .35 .30
544 A133 60c Creole girl .75 .50
545 A133 90c Indian girl .90 .70
546 A133 1g Hindustani boy 1.00 .75
Nos. 541-546 (6) 3.70 2.85

Rotary Intl., 75th Anniversary A134

20c, Handshake, Rotary emblem, vert.

Perf. 13x14, 14x13

1980, Feb. 23 Litho.

547 A134 20c ultra & yellow .30 .30
548 A134 60c ultra & yellow .85 .65

Rowland Hill — A135

50c, Mailcoach. 2g, People mailing letters.

1980, May 6 Litho. *Perf. 13x14*

549 A135 50c multicolored .35 .25
550 A135 1g shown .85 .60
a. Souvenir sheet 1.00 .70
551 A135 2g multicolored 1.90 1.25
Nos. 549-551 (3) 3.10 2.10

London 1980 Intl. Stamp Exhibition, May 6-14. No. 550a contains No. 550 in changed colors. Blue and black margin shows designs of Nos. 549, 551, London 1980 emblem. (No.

550 in lilac rose and multicolored; stamps of No. 550a in light green and multicolored).

Weight Lifting — A136

1980, June 17

552 A136 20c shown .25 .25
553 A136 30c Diving .35 .30
554 A136 50c Gymnast .40 .40
555 A136 75c Basketball .75 .65
556 A136 150c Running 1.45 1.30
a. Souvenir sheet of 3, #554-556 2.60 2.40
Nos. 552-556 (5) 3.20 2.90

22nd Summer Olympic Games, Moscow, July 19-Aug. 3.

Fish Type of 1979

Tropical Fish: 10c, Osteoglossum bicirrhosum. 15c, Colossoma species. 25c, Hemigrammus pulcher. 30c, Petitella georgiae. 45c, Copeina guttata.

1980, Sept. 10 Photo. *Perf. 14x13*

557 A129 10c multicolored .25 .25
558 A129 15c multicolored .25 .25
559 A129 25c multicolored .25 .25
560 A129 30c multicolored .25 .25
561 A129 45c multicolored .55 .55
Nos. 557-561,C92-C94 (8) 4.65 3.65

Souvenir Sheet

Open Hands (Reflection) — A137

1g, Shaking hands (cooperation). 2g, Victory sign.

1980, Nov. 19 Litho. *Perf. 13x14*

562 Sheet of 3 4.25 4.25
a. A137 50c shown .50 .35
b. A137 1g multicolored .75 .60
c. A137 2g multicolored 1.50 1.25

5th anniv. of independence.

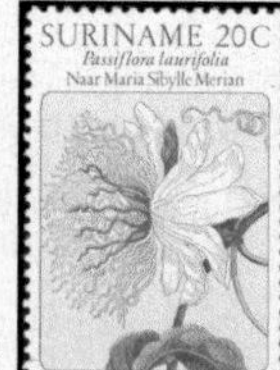
Passiflora Laurifolia — A138

Designs: Flower paintings by Maria Sibylle Merian (1647-1717) — 30c, Aphelandra pectinata. 60c, Caesalpinia pulcherrima. 75c, Hibiscus mutabilis. 1.25g, Hippeastrum puniceum.

1981, Jan. 14 Litho. *Perf. 13x14*

563 A138 20c shown .25 .25
564 A138 30c multicolored .35 .25
565 A138 60c multicolored .70 .55
566 A138 75c multicolored .80 .65
567 A138 1.25g multicolored 1.50 1.20
Nos. 563-567 (5) 3.60 2.90

Renovation of the Economic Order A139

1981, Feb. 25 *Perf. 14x13*

568 A139 30c shown .25 .25
569 A139 60c Educational Order .65 .50
570 A139 75c Social Order .75 .60
571 A139 1g Political Order 1.00 .80
a. Souvenir sheet of 2, #569, 571 2.00 2.00
Nos. 568-571 (4) 2.65 2.15

Government renovation.

Miniature Sheet

Youths — A140

1981, Apr. 29 Litho. *Perf. 14x13½*

572 A140 Sheet of 2 2.40 2.25
a. 1g shown .95 .95
b. 1.50g Youths, diff. .95 .95

Youth and its future. Entire sheet in continuous design.

Souvenir Sheet

No. 424, Exhibition Hall — A141

1981, May 22 Litho. *Perf. 13½x14*

573 Sheet of 3 3.50 3.50
a. A141 50c shown .50 .50
b. A141 1g Penny Black 1.00 1.00
c. A141 2g Austria #5 1.75 1.75

WIPA '81 Intl. Philatelic Exhibition, Vienna, May 22-31.

Leptodactylus Pentadactylus A142

40c, Phyllomedusa hypochondrialis. 60c, Hyla boans.

1981, June 24 Photo. *Perf. 14x13*

574 A142 40c multicolored .60 .45
575 A142 50c shown .75 .60
576 A142 60c multicolored .90 .75
Nos. 574-576,C95-C97 (6) 7.10 5.55

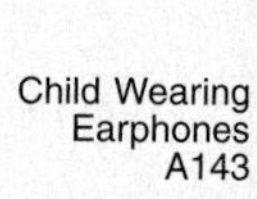
Child Wearing Earphones A143

100c, Child reading Braille. 150c, Woman in wheelchair.

1981, Sept. 16 Litho. *Perf. 14x13*

580 A143 50c shown .40 .40
581 A143 100c multicolored 1.00 .95
582 A143 150c multicolored 1.60 1.50
Nos. 580-582 (3) 3.00 2.85

Intl. Year of the Disabled.

Planter's House on Parakreek River — A144

Designs: Illustrations from Voyage to Surinam, by P.I. Benoit — 30c, Sarameca St., Paramaribo. 75c, Negro Hamlet, Paramaribo. 1g, Fish Market, Paramaribo. 1.25g, Blaauwe Berg Cascade.

1981, Oct. 21 Photo. *Perf. 14x13*

583 A144 20c shown .25 .25
584 A144 30c multicolored .30 .25
585 A144 75c multicolored .70 .55
586 A144 1g multicolored 1.00 .80
a. Miniature sheet of 1, perf 13½x13 1.60 1.60
587 A144 1.25g multicolored 1.40 1.10
Nos. 583-587 (5) 3.65 2.95

Research and Peaceful Uses of Space A145

35c, Satellites. 65c, Columbia space shuttle. 1g, Apollo-Soyuz.

1982, Jan. 13 Litho.

588 A145 35c multi .55 .35
589 A145 65c multi 1.15 .70
590 A145 1g multi 1.60 1.00
Nos. 588-590 (3) 3.30 2.05

Caretta Caretta A146

10c, Chelonia mydas. 20c, Dermochelys coriacea. 25c, Eretmochelys imbricata. 35c, Lepidochelys olivacea.

1982, Feb. 17 Photo. *Perf. 14x13*

591 A146 5c multicolored .30 .25
592 A146 10c multicolored .30 .25
593 A146 20c multicolored .40 .35
594 A146 25c multicolored .55 .45
595 A146 35c multicolored .70 .60
Nos. 591-595,C98-C100 (8) 6.25 4.65

25th Anniv. of Lions Intl. in Surinam A147

1982, May 7 Litho.

596 A147 35c multicolored .60 .55
597 A147 70c multicolored 1.20 1.10

A148

1982, May 18 Litho. *Perf. 13x14*

598 A148 35c Helping the sick .95 .70
599 A148 65c Birthplace, map 1.75 1.25
a. Souvenir sheet 1.90 1.90

Beatification of Father Petrus Donders, May 23.

A149

1982, June 9 Litho. *Perf. 13x14*

600 A149 50c Stamp designing .50 .50
601 A149 100c Printing 1.00 .95
602 A149 150c Collecting 1.50 1.40
a. Souvenir sheet of 3, #600-602 3.00 3.00
Nos. 600-602 (3) 3.00 2.85

PHILEXFRANCE '82 Stamp Exhibition, Paris, June 11-21. Nos. 600-602 in continuous design.

TB Bacillus Centenary A150

1982, Sept. 15 Litho. *Perf. 14x13*

603 A150 35c Text .35 .25
604 A150 65c Microscope .90 .70
605 A150 150c Bacillus 2.40 1.90
Nos. 603-605 (3) 3.65 2.85

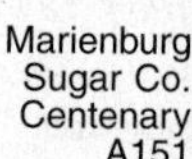

Marienburg Sugar Co. Centenary A151

1982, Oct. 20

606 A151 35c Mill .45 .30
607 A151 65c Gathering cane .80 .55
608 A151 100c Rail transport 1.40 .95
609 A151 150c Gears 2.10 1.50
Nos. 606-609 (4) 4.75 3.30

A152

EBG Missionaries, 250th Anniv. in Caribbean: 35c, Municipal Church, horiz. 65c, St. Thomas Monastery, horiz. 150c, Johan Leonhardt Dober (1706-1766).

Perf. 14x13, 13x14

1982, Dec. 13 Litho.

610 A152 35c multicolored .50 .35
611 A152 65c multicolored .95 .70
612 A152 150c multicolored 2.40 1.75
Nos. 610-612 (3) 3.85 2.80

Inga Edulis — A153

Flower Paintings by Maria Sibylle Merian (1647-1717) — 1c, Erythrina fusca, horiz. 2c, Ipomoea acuminata, horiz. 3c, Heliconia psittacorum, horiz. 5c, Ipomoea, horiz. 10c, Herba non denominata, horiz. 15c, Anacardium occidentale, horiz. 25c, Abelmoschus moschatus. 30c, Argemone mexicana. 35c, Costus arabicus. 45c, Muellera frutescens. 65c, Punica granatum.

1983, Jan. 12

613 A153 1c multicolored .25 .25
614 A153 2c multicolored .25 .25
615 A153 3c multicolored .25 .25
616 A153 5c multicolored .25 .25
617 A153 10c multicolored .25 .25
618 A153 15c multicolored .35 .30
619 A153 20c shown .45 .35
620 A153 25c multicolored .65 .50
621 A153 30c multicolored .80 .65
622 A153 35c multicolored .85 .70
623 A153 45c multicolored 1.00 .80
624 A153 65c multicolored 1.60 1.30
Nos. 613-624 (12) 6.95 5.85

Scouting Year — A154

1983, Feb. 22 Litho. *Perf. 13x14*
625 A154 40c Anniv. emblem .85 .70
626 A154 65c Baden-Powell 1.30 1.00
627 A154 70c Tent, campfire 1.35 1.10
628 A154 80c Ax in log 1.50 1.25
Nos. 625-628 (4) 5.00 4.05

500th Birth Anniv. of Raphael — A155

Crayon sketches.

1983, Apr. 13 Photo.
629 A155 5c multicolored .30 .25
630 A155 10c multicolored .30 .25
631 A155 40c multicolored .75 .50
632 A155 65c multicolored 1.10 .80
633 A155 70c multicolored 1.10 .80
634 A155 80c multicolored 1.35 .95
Nos. 629-634 (6) 4.90 3.55

1982 Coins and Banknotes A156

1983, June 1 Litho. *Perf. 14x13*
635 A156 5c 1-cent coin .25 .25
636 A156 10c 5-cent coin .25 .25
637 A156 40c 10-cent coin .65 .45
638 A156 65c 25-cent coin 1.05 .75
639 A156 70c 1g note 1.20 .85
640 A156 80c 2.50g note 1.45 1.00
Nos. 635-640 (6) 4.85 3.55

For surcharge & overprints see Nos. 751, J59-J60.

25th Anniv. of Dept. of Construction — A157

1983, June 15 Litho. *Perf. 13x14*
641 A157 25c Map .50 .40
642 A157 50c Map, bulldozers 1.10 .90

Local Butterflies A158

Drawings by Maria Sibylle Merian (1647-1717) — 1c, Papile anchisiades esper, vert. 2c, Urania leilus, vert. 3c, Morpho deidamia, vert. 5c, Thysania aguippina, vert. 10c, Morpho sp., vert. 15c, Metamorpha dido, vert. 20c, Morpho menelaus. 25c, Manduca rustica. 30c, Rothschildia sp. 35c, Catopsilia ebule. 45c, Pailio androgeos. 65c, Eumorpha vitis.

Perf. 13x14, 14x13
1983, Sept. 14 Litho.
643 A158 1c multicolored .25 .25
644 A158 2c multicolored .25 .25
645 A158 3c multicolored .25 .25
646 A158 5c multicolored .25 .25
647 A158 10c multicolored .30 .30
648 A158 15c multicolored .45 .35
649 A158 20c multicolored .60 .45
650 A158 25c multicolored 1.00 .75
651 A158 30c multicolored 1.25 .75
652 A158 35c multicolored 1.50 1.00
653 A158 45c multicolored 1.75 1.40
654 A158 65c multicolored 3.00 2.10
Nos. 643-654 (12) 10.85 8.10

Manned Ballooning, 200th Anniv. — A159

Designs: 5c, 1783, sheep, cock and duck. 10c, first manned flight, d'Arlandes and Pilatre de Rozier. 40c, first hydrogen balloon, Jacques Charles. 65c, 1870, Paris flight, minister Gambetta. 70c, Double Eagle II, transatlantic flight. 80c, Intl. Balloon Festival, Albuquerque.

1983, Oct. 19 Litho. *Perf. 13x14*
655 A159 5c multicolored .25 .25
656 A159 10c multicolored .25 .25
657 A159 40c multicolored .75 .50
658 A159 65c multicolored 1.15 .75
659 A159 70c multicolored 1.20 .80
660 A159 80c multicolored 1.60 1.00
Nos. 655-660 (6) 5.20 3.55

Martin Luther, 500th Birth Anniv. — A160

1983, Dec. 7 Litho.
661 A160 25c Portrait .50 .45
662 A160 50c Engraving 1.15 1.00

Local Flowers — A161

5c, Catasetum discolor. 10c, Menadenium labiosum. 40c, Comparettia falcata. 50c, Rodriquezia decora. 70c, Oncidium papilio. 75c, Epidendrum porpax.

1984, Jan. 11 Litho.
663 A161 5c multicolored .25 .25
664 A161 10c multicolored .25 .25
665 A161 40c multicolored .70 .60
666 A161 50c multicolored 1.00 .75
667 A161 70c multicolored 1.15 .85
668 A161 75c multicolored 1.35 .90
Nos. 663-668 (6) 4.70 3.60

Local Seashells — A162

40c, Arca zebra. 65c, Trachycardium egmontianum. 70c, Tellina radiata. 80c, Vermicularia knorrii

1984, Feb. 22 Litho.
669 A162 40c multicolored .85 .65
670 A162 65c multicolored 1.40 1.10
671 A162 70c multicolored 1.40 1.10
672 A162 80c multicolored 1.75 1.25
Nos. 669-672 (4) 5.40 4.10

Intl. Civil Aviation Org., 40th Anniv. A163

35c, Sea plane. 65c, Surinam Airways jet.

1984, May 16 Litho. *Perf. 14x13*
673 A163 35c multicolored .65 .45
674 A163 65c multicolored 1.40 1.00

A164

Greek Art and Artifacts, Ancient Games: 2c, Running. 3c, Javelin, discus, long jump. 5c, Massage. 10c, Ointment massage. 15c, Wrestling. 20c, Boxing. 30c, Horse racing. 35c, Chariot racing. 45c, Temple of Olympia. 50c, Crypt entrance. 65c, Olympia Stadium. 75c, Zeus (bust).

1984, June 13 *Perf. 13x14*
675 A164 2c multi .25 .25
676 A164 3c multi .25 .25
677 A164 5c multi .25 .25
678 A164 10c multi .25 .25
679 A164 15c multi .25 .25
680 A164 20c multi .25 .25
681 A164 30c multi .70 .50
682 A164 35c multi .80 .60
683 A164 45c multi .90 .70
684 A164 50c multi 1.00 .75
685 A164 65c multi 1.75 1.30
686 A164 75c multi 1.75 1.30
a. Min. sheet of 3, #675, 682, 686 2.75 2.75
Nos. 675-686 (12) 8.40 6.65

1984 Summer Olympics.
For overprint see No. 843.

A165

1984, Sept. 18 Litho. *Perf. 13x14*
687 A165 50c Ball, net 1.00 .75
688 A165 90c Ball in net 1.60 1.30

Intl. Council of Military Sports basketball championship.

World Chess Championship, Moscow — A166

1984, Oct. 10 Litho. *Perf. 14x13*
689 A166 10c Red Square .40 .25
690 A166 15c Knight, king, pawn .40 .25
691 A166 30c Kasparov .65 .45
692 A166 50c Board 1.25 .75
693 A166 75c Karpov 1.75 1.10
a. Souv. sheet of 3 (30c, 50c, 75c), perf 13½x13 5.25 5.25
694 A166 90c Game 2.00 1.40
Nos. 689-694 (6) 6.45 4.20

For overprints see Nos. 742, 796.

World Food Day, Oct. 16 — A167

50c, Children receiving milk. 90c, Food.

1984, Oct. 10
695 A167 50c multicolored 1.00 .65
696 A167 90c multicolored 1.60 1.00

Cacti — A168

1985, Jan. 9 Litho. *Perf. 13x14*
697 A168 5c Leaf .25 .25
698 A168 10c Melon .25 .25
699 A168 30c Pillar .80 .55
700 A168 50c Fig 1.20 .75
701 A168 75c Nightqueen 1.90 1.20
702 A168 90c Segment 2.00 1.30
Nos. 697-702 (6) 6.40 4.30

A169

Independence, 5th Anniv.: 5c, Star, red stripe from national flag. 30c, Unified labor. 50c, Perpetual flowering plant. 75c, Growth of agriculture. 90c, Peace dove and plant.

1985, Feb. 22
703 A169 5c multicolored .25 .25
704 A169 30c multicolored .45 .40
705 A169 50c multicolored .75 .65
a. Min. sheet of 3, 2 #703, #705 1.60
706 A169 75c multicolored 1.25 1.00
707 A169 90c multicolored 1.60 1.25
Nos. 703-707 (5) 4.30 3.55

Chamber of Commerce and Industry, 75th Anniv. A170

1985, Apr. 17 Litho. *Perf. 14x13*
708 A170 50c Chamber emblem .75 .60
709 A170 90c Chamber, factories 1.75 1.40

UN Emblem, Natl. Coat of Arms — A171

1985, Apr. 29 Litho. *Perf. 13x14*
710 A171 50c multicolored .80 .55
711 A171 90c multicolored 1.75 1.25

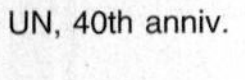
UN, 40th anniv.

Trains — A172

No. 712, Surinam No. 192. No. 713, Monaco, No. J50. No. 714, Locomotive "Dam". No. 715, Diesel locomotive. No. 716, Steam locomotive "No. 3737". No. 717, Netherlands locomotive "IC III". No. 718, Stephenson's locomotive "Rocket". No. 719, French Railways high-speed TGV. No. 720, Stephenson's locomotive "Adler". No. 721, French Railways commuter train. No. 722, Locomotive "General". No. 723, Japanese bullet train "Shinkansen".

1985, June 5 Litho. *Perf. 13½*
712 A172 5c multicolored .25 .25
713 A172 5c multicolored .25 .25
a. Pair, #712-713 .40 .30
714 A172 10c multicolored .25 .25
715 A172 10c multicolored .25 .25
a. Pair, #714-715 .55 .45

716 A172 20c multicolored .45 .40
717 A172 20c multicolored .45 .40
a. Pair, #716-717 .90 .75
718 A172 30c multicolored .75 .65
719 A172 30c multicolored .75 .65
a. Pair, #716-717 1.45 1.15
720 A172 50c multicolored 1.15 .90
721 A172 50c multicolored 1.15 .90
a. Pair, #720-721 2.40 2.00
722 A172 75c multicolored 1.75 1.45
723 A172 75c multicolored 1.75 1.45
a. Pair, #722-723 3.75 3.00
Nos. 712-723 (12) 9.20 7.80

For surcharges see Nos. 749-750, 808-809, 928-929.

Birds — A173

10c, Toucan. 1g, American purple fowl. 1.50g, Tiger bird. 2.50g, Red ibis. 5g, Guyana red cockerel. 10g, Harpy eagle. 15g, Parrot. 25g, Owl. 1300g, Rose lepelaar. 1780g, Toucan. 2225g, Hummingbird. 2995g, Hoatzin.

1985-95 Litho. *Perf. 14x13*
724 A173 10c multi .25 .25
725 A173 1g multi 1.75 1.75
a. Miniature sheet of 1 4.00 4.00
726 A173 1.50g multi 3.25 3.25
727 A173 2.50g multi 5.00 5.00
728 A173 5g multi 9.50 9.50
729 A173 10g multi *14.00 14.00*
730 A173 15g multi *22.50 22.50*
731 A173 25g multi *35.00 35.00*
732 A173 1300g multi *37.50 37.50*
733 A173 1780g multi *9.25 9.25*
734 A173 2225g multi *11.50 11.50*
735 A173 2995g multi *16.00 16.00*
Nos. 724-735 (12) 165.50 165.50

Nos. 724, 730 inscribed 1990.
Issued: 1g, 1.50g, 2.50g, 8/21; #725a, 5g, 1/2/86; 10g, 10/1/86; 10c, 15g, 1/30/91; 25g, 1/20/93; 1300g, 3/31/94; 1780g, 2225g, 2995g, 9/6/95.
See #1040, 1053-1055, 1108-1111, 1136-1138, 1160, 1194-1195, 1220-1221. For surcharges & overprint see #963-964, J63.

Mailboxes — A174

1985, Oct. 2 Litho. *Perf. 13x14*
736 A174 15c Germany, 1900 .35 .35
737 A174 30c France, 1900 .55 .50
738 A174 50c England, 1932 .95 .85
739 A174 90c Netherlands, 1850 1.75 1.60
Nos. 736-739 (4) 3.60 3.30

Natl. Independence, 10th Anniv. — A175

1985, Nov. 22
740 A175 50c Agriculture .95 .65
741 A175 90c Industry 1.50 1.00
a. Miniature sheet of 2, #740-741 2.40 2.40

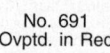

No. 691 Ovptd. in Red

1985, Nov. 22 Litho. *Perf. 14x13*
742 A166 30c multi 3.00 2.00

Orchids, World Wildlife Fund — A177

5c, Epidendrum ciliare. 15c, Cycnoches chlorochilon. 30c, Epidendrum anceps. 50c, Epidendrum vespa.

1986, Feb. 19 Litho. *Perf. 14x13*
743 A177 5c multicolored 1.75 .70
744 A177 15c multicolored 4.75 1.60
745 A177 30c multicolored 9.25 3.50
746 A177 50c multicolored 15.00 5.50
Nos. 743-746 (4) 30.75 11.30

Halley's Comet A178

Designs: 50c, The Bayeux Tapestry, c. 1092, France. 110c, Halley's Comet.

1986, Mar. 5 Litho. *Perf. 14x13*
747 A178 50c multi 1.00 .75
748 A178 110c multi 1.90 1.35

Nos. 720-721 Surcharged in Red

1986, May 28 Litho. *Perf. 13½*
749 A172 15c on 50c #720 2.60 2.00
750 A172 15c on 50c #721 2.60 2.00
a. Pair, #749-750 6.00 6.00

No. 639 Surcharged

1986, June 25 Litho. *Perf. 14x13*
751 A156 30c on 70c multi 2.75 2.75

Finance Building, Paramaribo, 150th anniv.

Surinam Shipping Co., 50th Anniv. A179

50c, Emblem. 110c, Freighter Saramacca.

1986, Sept. 1 Litho. *Perf. 14x13*
752 A179 50c multicolored .65 .65
753 A179 110c multicolored 1.75 1.75

Monkeys A180

1987, Jan. 7 Litho.
755 A180 35c Alouatta .55 .45
756 A180 60c Aotus .90 .70
757 A180 110c Saimiri 1.75 1.40
758 A180 120c Cacajao 1.90 1.55
Nos. 755-758 (4) 5.10 4.10

Esperanto, Cent. — A181

110c, World map, doves. 120c, L.L. Zamenhof.

1987, Feb. 4 Litho.
759 A181 60c shown .85 .70
760 A181 110c multicolored 1.60 1.30
761 A181 120c multicolored 1.75 1.45
Nos. 759-761 (3) 4.20 3.45

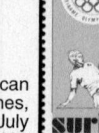

10th Pan-American Games, Indianapolis, July 23 — A182

1987, June 3 Litho. *Perf. 13x14*
763 A182 90c Soccer 1.10 .95
764 A182 110c Swimming 1.30 1.10
765 A182 150c Basketball 1.60 1.40
Nos. 763-765 (3) 4.00 3.45

Forestry Commission, 40th Anniv. — A183

90c, Emblem. 120c, Logging. 150c, Parrot in virgin forest.

1987, July 21 Litho. *Perf. 13x14*
766 A183 90c multi 1.00 .85
767 A183 120c multi 1.30 1.10
768 A183 150c multi 1.75 1.50
Nos. 766-768 (3) 4.05 3.45

Intl. Year of Shelter for the Homeless A184

90c, Distressed boy, encampment. 120c, Man, ghetto.

1987, Sept. 2 Litho. *Perf. 14x13*
769 A184 90c multi 1.25 1.25
770 A184 120c multi 1.90 1.90

Founders Catherine and William Booth — A185

1987, Sept. 2 *Perf. 14x13*
771 A185 150c multi 2.00 2.00

Salvation Army in the Caribbean, cent.

Nos. 436-438 Surcharged

1986, Dec. 29 Litho. *Perf. 13½x13*
772 A109 35c on 1g 2.75 2.75
773 A109 50c on 1.50g 4.25 4.25
774 A109 60c on 2.50g 5.50 5.50
Nos. 772-774 (3) 12.50 12.50

Fruits — A186

1987, Oct. 14 Litho. *Perf. 13x13½*
775 A186 10c Bananas .25 .25
776 A186 15c Cacao .25 .25
777 A186 20c Pineapple .25 .25
778 A186 25c Papaya .50 .35
779 A186 35c Oranges .75 .55
Nos. 775-779 (5) 2.00 1.65

Aircraft and Aircraft on Stamps — A187

No. 784, Degen, 1808. No. 785, Ultra Light. No. 786, J.C.H. Ellehammer, 1906. No. 787, Concorde jet . No. 788, Fokker F7, 1924. No. 789, Fokker F28 jet. No. 790, Spin Fokker, 1910. No. 791, DC-10. No. 792, Orion, 1932. No. 793, Boeing 747.

1987, Oct. 14 Litho. *Perf. 13½*
784 A187 25c multi .25 .25
785 A187 25c multi .25 .25
a. Pair, #784-785 .80 .80
786 A187 35c multi .50 .45
787 A187 35c multi .50 .45
a. Pair, #786-787 1.15 1.15
788 A187 60c multi .80 .75
789 A187 60c multi .80 .75
a. Pair, #788-789 1.90 1.90
790 A187 90c multi 1.25 1.15
791 A187 90c multi 1.25 1.15
a. Pair, #790-791 2.60 2.60
792 A187 110c multi 1.60 1.50
793 A187 110c multi 1.60 1.50
a. Pair, #792-793 3.50 3.50
794 A187 120c No. 346 1.75 1.60
795 A187 120c No. 518 1.75 1.60
a. Pair, #794-795 3.75 3.75
Nos. 784-795 (12) 12.30 11.40

No. 693a Overprinted "3e match sevilla 1987" on Stamps in 3 or 4 Lines and with Bar and "sevilla 1987" in Sheet Margin

1987, Nov. 2 Litho. *Perf. 13½x13*

Souvenir Sheet

796 Sheet of 3 *30.00 30.00*
a. A166 30c Kasparov *3.50 3.50*
b. A166 50c Board *6.00 6.00*
c. A166 75c Karpov *9.00 9.00*

Alligators and Crocodiles A188

50c, Gavialis gangeticus. 60c, Crocodylus niloticus. 90c, Melanosuchus niger. 110c, Mississippi alligator.

1988, Jan. 20 Litho. *Perf. 14x13*
797 A188 50c multicolored .60 .60
798 A188 60c multicolored .80 .80
799 A188 90c multicolored 1.10 1.10
800 A188 110c multicolored 1.60 1.60
Nos. 797-800 (4) 4.10 4.10

Traditional Wedding Costumes — A189

1988, Feb. 24 Litho. *Perf. 13x14*
801 A189 35c Javanese .35 .35
802 A189 60c Bushman .70 .60
803 A189 80c Chinese .80 .70
804 A189 110c Creole 1.15 1.00
805 A189 120c Indian 1.25 1.10
806 A189 130c Hindustan 1.50 1.35
Nos. 801-806 (6) 5.75 5.10

Nos. 722-723 and 440 Surcharged in Black or Silver

No. 808

No. 810

Perf. 13½x13, 13½

1988, Mar. 23 **Litho.**

808 A172 60c on 75c #722 *5.00 4.00*
809 A172 60c on 75c #723 *5.00 4.00*
a. Pair, #808-809 *9.75 9.75*
810 A109 125c on 10g #440 (S) *10.50 7.50*
Nos. 808-810 (3) 20.50 15.50

1988 Summer Olympics, Seoul — A190

90c, Relay. 110c, Soccer. 120c, Pole vault. 250c, Women's tennis.

1988, May 4 **Litho.** ***Perf. 13x14***

812 A190 90c multi .80 .75
813 A190 110c multi 1.30 1.20
814 A190 120c multi 1.40 1.30
a. Souvenir sheet of 3, #812-814 4.00 4.00
815 A190 250c multi 3.25 3.00
Nos. 812-815 (4) 6.75 6.25

Abolition of Slavery, 125th Anniv. — A191

50c, Abaisa Monument. 110c, Kwakoe Monument. 120c, Home of Anton de Kom.

1988, June 29 **Litho.**

816 A191 50c multicolored .50 .40
817 A191 110c multicolored 1.25 1.10
818 A191 120c multicolored 1.50 1.25
Nos. 816-818 (3) 3.25 2.75

See Netherlands Antilles Nos. 597-598.

Intl. Fund for Agricultural Development (IFAD), 10th Anniv. A192

105c, Crop harvest. 110c, Net fishing. 125c, Agricultural research.

1988, Sept. 21 ***Perf. 14x13***

819 A192 105c multi 1.25 1.00
820 A192 110c multi 1.25 1.00
821 A192 125c multi 1.60 1.30
Nos. 819-821 (3) 4.10 3.30

FILACEPT '88, The Netherlands, Oct. 18-23 — A193

120c, Egypt #49. 150c, Netherlands #334. 250c, Surinam #238.

1988, Oct. 18 **Litho.** ***Perf. 13x14***

822 A193 120c multi 1.20 1.15
823 A193 150c multi 1.75 1.75
824 A193 250c multi 3.00 2.60
Nos. 822-824 (3) 5.95 5.50

Souvenir Sheet

Same Types, Colors Changed (120c, 150c)

825 Sheet of 3 10.00 10.00
a. A193 120c Egypt Type A23 (4m green) 1.10 1.10
b. A193 150c Netherlands Type A81 (10c red brown) 1.40 1.40
c. A193 250c Surinam No. 239 2.40 2.40

Stylized Butterfly Stroke A194

1988, Nov. 1 **Litho.** ***Perf. 14x13***

826 A194 110c multi 1.60 1.60

Anthony Nesty, swimmer and 1st Olympic gold medalist from Surinam.

Otters A195

1989, Jan. 18 **Litho.** ***Perf. 14x13***

827 A195 10c Otter .25 .25
828 A195 20c Two on land .25 .25
829 A195 25c Two crossing log .50 .50
830 A195 30c Fishing .60 .60
Nos. 827-830,C107 (5) 4.60 4.60

Classic and Modern Automobiles — A196

No. 831, 1930 Mercedes Tourenwagen. No. 832, 1985 Mercedes-Benz 300E. No. 833, 1897 Daimler. No. 834, 1986 Jaguar Sovereign. No. 835, 1898 Renault Voiturette. No. 836, 1989 Renault 25TX. No. 837, 1927 Volvo Jacob. No. 838, 1989 Volvo 440. No. 839, Left half of Monaco #484. No. 840, Right half of Monaco #484. No. 841, 1936 Toyota AA. No. 842, 1988 Toyota Corolla sedan.

1989, June 7 **Litho.** ***Perf. 13½***

831 A196 25c multi .60 .60
832 A196 25c multi .60 .60
a. Pair, #831-832 1.00 1.00
833 A196 60c multi 1.25 1.25
834 A196 60c multi 1.25 1.25
a. Pair, #833-834 2.50 2.50
835 A196 90c multi 2.00 2.00
836 A196 90c multi 2.00 2.00
a. Pair, #835-836 3.75 3.75
837 A196 105c multi 2.25 2.25
838 A196 105c multi 2.25 2.25
a. Pair, #837-838 4.50 4.50
839 A196 110c multi 2.40 2.40
840 A196 110c multi 2.40 2.40
a. Pair, #839-840 5.00 5.00
841 A196 120c multi 2.75 2.75
842 A196 120c multi 2.75 2.75
a. Pair, #841-842 5.75 5.75
Nos. 831-842 (12) 22.50 22.50

No. 686a Ovptd. "PHILEXFRANCE 7t/m 17 juli 1989" on Margin, with Exhibition Emblem on Stamps in Gold

1989, July 7 **Litho.** ***Perf. 13x14***

Miniature Sheet

843 Sheet of 3 6.25 6.25
a. A164 2c on No. 675 .25 .25
b. A164 35c on No. 682 .40 .40
c. A164 75c on No. 686 .95 .95

PHILEXFRANCE '89.

Photography, 150th Anniv. A197

60c, Joseph Niepce. 110c, Daguerreotype camera. 120c, Louis Daguerre.

1989, Sept. 6 **Litho.** ***Perf. 14x13***

844 A197 60c multi 1.00 1.00
845 A197 110c multi 1.90 1.90
846 A197 120c multi 2.10 2.10
Nos. 844-846 (3) 5.00 5.00

America Issue — A198

UPAE emblem and pre-Columbian amulets — 60c, Amazon or Jade Stones. 110c, Bisque fertility statue.

1989, Oct. 12 **Litho.** ***Perf. 13x14***

847 A198 60c multicolored 10.00 10.00
848 A198 110c multicolored 10.00 10.00

The White House, Washington, DC, and Stamps on Stamps A199

Perf. 13x14, 14x13

1989, Nov. 17 **Litho.**

849 A199 110c No. 445, vert. 1.50 1.45
850 A199 150c US No. 990 1.90 1.75
851 A199 250c No. 459 3.00 3.00
a. Souv. sheet, #849-851, perf 13x14, 14 7.25 6.50
Nos. 849-851 (3) 6.40 6.20

World Stamp Expo '89 and 20th UPU Congress, Washington, DC.

UNESCO Intl. Literacy Year — A200

110c, Emblems. 120c, Emblems, youth reading.

1990, Jan. 19 **Photo.** ***Perf. 13x14***

852 A200 60c shown .75 .60
853 A200 110c multi 1.35 1.10
854 A200 120c multi 1.45 1.25
Nos. 852-854 (3) 3.55 2.95

Arya Dewaker Temple, 60th Anniv. — A201

1990, Feb. 14 **Litho.**

855 A201 60c dk red brn, blk & red .70 .70
856 A201 110c vio blue & blk 1.30 1.30
857 A201 200c emer grn & blk 2.10 2.10
Nos. 855-857 (3) 4.10 4.10

A202

110c, Surinam #C1. 200c, Great Britain #1. 250c, Great Britain #208.

1990, May 4

858 A202 110c multicolored 1.30 1.20
859 A202 200c multicolored 2.10 2.00
860 A202 250c multicolored 3.25 3.00
a. Souvenir sheet of 3, #858-860 8.00 7.50
Nos. 858-860 (3) 6.65 6.20

Penny Black, 150th anniv. Stamps World London '90.

A203

60c, Couple carrying baskets. 110c, Woman carrying bundle. 120c, Man carrying baskets.

1990, Aug. 9

861 A203 60c multicolored .75 .70
862 A203 110c multicolored 1.45 1.30
863 A203 120c multicolored 1.60 1.50
Nos. 861-863 (3) 3.80 3.50

Javanese Immigration, cent.

Flowers — A204

No. 864, Punica granatum. No. 865, Passiflora laurifolia. No. 866, Hippeastrum puniceum. No. 867, Ipomaea batatas. No. 868, Hibiscus syriacus. No. 869, Jasminum officinale. No. 870, Musa serapionis. No. 871, Hibiscus mutabilis. No. 872, Plumiria rubra. No. 873, Hibiscus diversifolius. No. 874, Bixa orellana. Nol. 875, Ceasalpinia pulcherima.

1990, Sept. 5 ***Perf. 13½***

864 A204 25c multicolored .45 .35
865 A204 25c multicolored .45 .35
a. Pair, #864-865 .90 .90
866 A204 35c multicolored .55 .45
867 A204 35c multicolored .55 .45
a. Pair, #866-867 1.10 1.10
868 A204 60c multicolored 1.00 .75
869 A204 60c multicolored 1.00 .75
a. Pair, #868-869 2.10 2.10
870 A204 105c multicolored 1.60 1.30
871 A204 105c multicolored 1.60 1.30
a. Pair, #870-871 3.50 3.50
872 A204 110c multicolored 1.60 1.30
873 A204 110c multicolored 1.60 1.30
a. Pair, #872-873 3.50 3.50
874 A204 120c multicolored 1.90 1.50
875 A204 120c multicolored 1.90 1.50
a. Pair, #874-875 4.00 4.00
Nos. 864-875 (12) 14.20 11.30

America Issue — A205

1990, Oct. 10 **Litho.** ***Perf. 14x13***

876 A205 60c bluish grn & blk 4.25 3.50
877 A205 110c brn & blk 8.00 6.00

Organization of American States, Cent. — A206

1990, Oct. 10

878 A206 110c multicolored 1.60 1.40

Independence, 15th Anniv. — A207

60c, Passion flower. 110c, Dove with olive branch.

1990, Nov. 21 Litho. *Perf. 13x14*

879	A207	10c shown	.25	.25
880	A207	60c multi	.75	.60
881	A207	110c multi	1.60	1.25
		Nos. 879-881 (3)	2.60	2.10

Architecture A208

Buildings: 35c, Waterfront warehouse. 60c, Upper class residence. 75c, Labor inspection building. 105c, Plantation supervisor's residence. 110c, Ministry of Labor. 200c, Small residences.

1991, May 15 Litho. *Perf. 14x13*

882	A208	35c multicolored	.50	.50
883	A208	60c multicolored	.70	.70
884	A208	75c multicolored	.90	.90
885	A208	105c multicolored	1.30	1.30
886	A208	110c multicolored	1.35	1.35
887	A208	200c multicolored	2.40	2.40
		Nos. 882-887 (6)	7.15	7.15

Nos. 714-715, 720-721 Surcharged

Methods and Perfs as Before

1991

888	A172	2c on 10c #714	*2.50*	*2.50*
889	A172	2c on 10c #715	*2.50*	*2.50*
a.		Pair, #888-889	*6.00*	*6.00*
890	A172	3c on 50c #720	*2.50*	*2.50*
891	A172	3c on 50c #721	*2.50*	*2.50*
a.		Pair, #890-891	*6.00*	*6.00*
		Nos. 888-891 (4)	*10.00*	*10.00*

Puma Concolor A209

Various pictures of pumas.

Perf. 13x14, 14x13

1991, Sept. 12 Litho.

892	A209	10c multi, vert.	.25	.25
893	A209	20c multi, vert.	.25	.25
894	A209	25c multi, vert.	.35	.35
895	A209	30c multi, vert.	.45	.40
896	A209	125c multi	1.60	1.50
897	A209	500c multi	5.75	5.50
		Nos. 892-897 (6)	8.65	8.25

Nos. 896-897 are airmail.

Discovery of America, 500th Anniv. (in 1991) — A210

Diagram showing Columbus' route: 60c, Western Atlantic and Caribbean Sea. 110c, Eastern Atlantic.

1991, Oct. 11 *Perf. 13x14*

898		60c lt bl, red & blk	2.10	1.75
899		110c lt bl, red & blk	4.75	4.00
a.	A210	Pair, #898-899	9.75	9.75

UPAEP. No. 899a has continous design.

Snakes — A211

#900, Corallus enydris. #901, Corallus caninus. #902, Lachesis muta. #903, Boa constrictor. #904, Micrurus surinamensis. #905, Crotalus durissus. #906, Eunectes murinus. #907, Clelia cloelia. #908, Epicrates cenchris. #909, Chironius carinatus. #910, Oxybelis argentieus. #911, Spilotes pullatus.

1991, Nov. 14 *Perf. 13½*

900	A211	25c multicolored	.30	.25
901	A211	25c multicolored	.30	.25
a.		Pair, #900-901	.80	.80
902	A211	35c multicolored	.55	.45
903	A211	35c multicolored	.55	.45
a.		Pair, #902-903	1.10	1.10
904	A211	60c multicolored	.90	.70
905	A211	60c multicolored	.90	.70
a.		Pair, #904-905	2.10	2.10
906	A211	75c multicolored	1.25	.95
907	A211	75c multicolored	1.25	.95
a.		Pair, #906-907	2.50	2.50
908	A211	110c multicolored	1.75	1.35
909	A211	110c multicolored	1.75	1.35
a.		Pair, #908-909	3.75	3.75
910	A211	200c multicolored	3.25	2.40
911	A211	200c multicolored	3.25	2.40
a.		Pair, #910-911	6.75	6.75
		Nos. 900-911 (12)	16.00	12.20

Orchids — A212

Designs: 50c, Cycnoches haagii. 60c, Lycaste cristata. 75c, Galeandra dives, horiz. 125c, Vanilla mexicana. 150c, Cyrtopodium glutiniferum. 250c, Gongora quinquenervis.

1992, Feb. 12 *Perf. 13x14, 14x13*

912	A212	50c multicolored	.60	.50
913	A212	60c multicolored	.80	.65
914	A212	75c multicolored	.90	.75
915	A212	125c multicolored	1.75	1.50
916	A212	150c multicolored	2.25	1.75
917	A212	250c multicolored	3.75	3.00
		Nos. 912-917 (6)	10.05	8.15

Souvenir Sheet

A213

Designs: a, 75c, #847. b, 125c, #848. c, 150c, #898. d. 250c, #899.

1992, Mar. 24 Litho. *Perf. 13x13½*

918	A213	Sheet of 4, #a.-d.	9.75	9.75

Granada '92, Intl. Philatelic Exibition.

1992 Summer Olympics, Barcelona — A214

1992, Apr. 8 Litho. *Perf. 13x14*

919	A214	35c Basketball	.50	.50
920	A214	60c Volleyball	.85	.85
921	A214	75c Running	1.00	1.00
922	A214	125c Soccer	1.75	1.75
923	A214	150c Cycling	2.00	2.00
924	A214	250c Swimming	4.00	4.00
a.		Souvenir sheet of 3, #921, 922, 924, perf 13x13½	6.75	6.75
		Nos. 919-924 (6)	10.10	10.10

YWCA, 50th Anniv. A215

1992, June 12 Litho. *Perf. 14x13*

925	A215	60c red brown & multi	.70	.70
926	A215	250c purple & multi	3.00	3.00

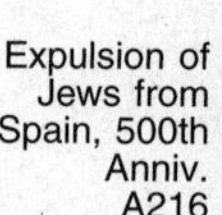

Expulsion of Jews from Spain, 500th Anniv. A216

1992, Aug. 17

927	A216	250c multicolored	3.00	2.75

Nos. 712-713 Surcharged

1992, Aug. 17 *Perf. 13½*

928	A172	1c on 5c multi	1.50	1.50
929	A172	1c on 5c multi	1.50	1.50
a.		Pair, #928-929	3.75	3.75

A217

1992, Sept. 15 *Perf. 13x14*

930	A217	60c green & multi	.70	.70
931	A217	250c pink & multi	3.00	3.00

Jan E. Matzeliger (1852-1889), inventor of shoe lasting machine.

A218

1992, Oct. 12

932	A218	60c blue grn & multi	1.30	1.25
933	A218	250c dp org & multi	5.25	5.00

Discovery of America, 500th anniv.

Christmas — A219

Various abstract designs.

1992, Nov. 15

934	A219	10c multicolored	.40	.35
935	A219	60c multicolored	.75	.65
936	A219	250c multicolored	2.60	2.10
937	A219	400c multicolored	4.50	3.75
		Nos. 934-937 (4)	8.25	6.85

Medicinal Plants A220

Designs: 50c, Costus arabicus, vert. 75c, Quassia amara, vert. 125c, Combretum rotundifolium. 500c, Bixa orellana.

Perf. 13x14, 14x13

1993, Feb. 3 Litho.

938	A220	50c multicolored	.60	.55
939	A220	75c multicolored	1.00	.85
940	A220	125c multicolored	1.55	1.35
941	A220	500c multicolored	6.25	5.50
		Nos. 938-941 (4)	9.40	8.25

Beetles and Grasshoppers — A221

Designs: No. 942, Macrodontia cervicornis. No. 943, Acrididae. No. 944, Curculionidae. No. 945, Acrididae, diff. No. 946, Euchroma gigantea. No. 947, Tettigonidae. No. 948, Tettigonidae. No. 949, Phanaeus festivus. No. 950, Gryllidae. No. 951, Phanaeus lancifer. No. 952, Tettigonidae. No. 953, Batus barbicornis.

1993, June 30 Litho. *Perf. 13½*

942	A221	25c multicolored	.40	.35
943	A221	25c multicolored	.40	.35
a.		Pair, #942-943	.85	.85
944	A221	35c multicolored	.50	.45
945	A221	35c multicolored	.50	.45
a.		Pair, #944-945	1.60	1.60
946	A221	50c multicolored	.70	.60
947	A221	50c multicolored	.70	.60
a.		Pair, #946-947	1.90	1.90
948	A221	100c multicolored	1.40	1.20
949	A221	100c multicolored	1.40	1.20
a.		Pair, #948-949	3.75	3.25
950	A221	175c multicolored	2.60	2.25
951	A221	175c multicolored	2.60	2.25
a.		Pair, #950-951	6.50	5.50
952	A221	220c multicolored	3.25	2.60
953	A221	220c multicolored	3.25	2.60
a.		Pair, #952-953	8.50	6.50
		Nos. 942-953 (12)	17.70	14.90

A222

#956b, 250c, like #955. #956c, 500c, like #956.

1993, July 30 *Perf. 13x14*

954	A222	50c Brazil No. 3	.25	.25
955	A222	250c Brazil No. 2	1.00	1.00
956	A222	500c Brazil No. 1	2.25	2.10
		Nos. 954-956 (3)	3.50	3.35

Souvenir Sheet

956A	A222	Sheet of 2, #b.-c.	9.00	9.00

1st Brazilian postage stamps, 150th Anniv. Brasiliana '93 (#956A).

Nos. 956b-956c have purple border.

A223

America issue: Paleosuchus palpebrosus.

1993, Oct. 12 *Perf. 14x13*

957	A223	50g brown & multi		3.25	2.40
958	A223	100g green & multi		7.00	5.25

Christmas Angels — A224

25g, African angel with drum. 45g, Asian angel holding lamp. 50g, Oriental angel holding lantern. 150g, American Indian angel holding wand.

1993, Nov. 15 Litho. *Perf. 13x14*

959	A224	25g multicolored	.75	.65
960	A224	45g multicolored	1.25	1.10
961	A224	50g multicolored	1.50	1.25
962	A224	150g multicolored	4.75	4.00
		Nos. 959-962 (4)	8.25	7.00

The foreign exchange rate of the Surinam florin was allowed to float freely against foreign currencies on Oct. 19, 1994. The florin's value against the dollar has fluctuated dramatically. Stamps may sell for values significantly different from those quoted in the Scott listings.

Nos. 729-730 Surcharged

1993 Litho. *Perf. 14x13*

963	A173	5g on 10g Harpy eagle	*2.40*	*1.60*
964	A173	5g on 15g Parrot	2.40	1.60

Surchanges differ slightly. Issued: #963, 12/16. #964, 12/28.

Traditional Musical Instruments — A225

25g, Indian drum. 50g, Bosland Creooise drum. 75g, Tambourine. 100g, Hindu drum.

1994, Feb. 16 Litho. *Perf. 13x14*

965	A225	25g multicolored	.90	.75
966	A225	50g multicolored	1.75	1.50
967	A225	75g multicolored	3.00	2.50
968	A225	100g multicolored	4.00	3.25
		Nos. 965-968 (4)	9.65	8.00

Environmental Protection A226

1994, June 8 Litho. *Perf. 14x13*

969	A226	50g Smoke stacks	.65	.60
970	A226	350g Dying fish	5.50	5.00

Intl. Olympic Committee, Cent. — A227

1994, July 4 Litho. *Perf. 14x13*

971	A227	250g multicolored	6.50	4.00

1994 World Cup Soccer Championships, U.S. — A228

100g, Goalkeeper's hands. 250g, Soccer shoe. 300g, Goal.

1994, July 4 *Perf. 13x14*

972	A228	100g multi	1.05	1.00
973	A228	250g multi	3.75	3.50
974	A228	300g multi	5.50	5.25
a.		Souvenir sheet of 2, #973-974	12.00	12.00
		Nos. 972-974 (3)	10.30	9.75

Butterflies — A229

No. 975, Dulcedo. No. 976, Ithomia. No. 977, Danaus. No. 978, Danaus, diff. No. 979, Echenais. No. 980, Bithijs. No. 981, Junonia evarette. No. 982, Anartia jatrophae. No. 983, Heliconius. No. 984, Heliconius erato. No. 985, Eurytides. No. 986, Parides.

1994, Sept. 7 Litho. *Perf. 13½*

975	A229	25g multicolored	.45	.35
976	A229	25g multicolored	.45	.35
a.		Pair, #975-976	.85	.85
977	A229	30g multicolored	.50	.35
978	A229	30g multicolored	.50	.35
a.		Pair, #977-978	.95	.95
979	A229	45g multicolored	.70	.55
980	A229	45g multicolored	.70	.55
a.		Pair #979-980	1.40	1.40
981	A229	75g multicolored	1.20	.85
982	A229	75g multicolored	1.20	.85
a.		Pair, #981-982	2.25	2.25
983	A229	250g multicolored	3.75	2.75
984	A229	250g multicolored	3.75	2.75
a.		Pair, #983-984	7.75	7.75
985	A229	300g multicolored	4.75	3.50
986	A229	300g multicolored	4.75	3.50
a.		Pair, #985-986	9.25	9.25
		Nos. 975-986 (12)	22.70	16.70

For surcharges see #1088-1091.

FEPAPOST '94 — A230

1994, Oct. 1 Litho. *Perf. 14x13*

987	A230	250g Netherlands #B148	3.50	3.50
988	A230	300g #168	4.00	4.00
a.		Souvenir sheet of 2, #987-988, perf. 13½x13	7.50	7.50

America Issue A231

Post vehicles: 50g, Airplane, canoe. 400g, Van, donkey cart.

1994, Oct. 12 Litho. *Perf. 13½*

989	A231	50g multicolored	1.25	.60
990	A231	400g multicolored	10.50	5.00

A232

Christmas: (A), Angel in sky. 250g, Mother reading to children. 625g, Woman kneeling in prayer.

1994, Nov. 22 *Perf. 13x14*

991	A232	(A) multicolored	.50	.45
992	A232	250g multicolored	1.50	1.35
993	A232	625g multicolored	4.00	3.50
a.		Souvenir sheet, #992-993	8.00	8.00
		Nos. 991-993 (3)	6.00	5.30

No. 991 sold for 37g on day of issue.

Volleyball, Cent. — A233

1995, Jan. 31

994	A233	375g shown	2.50	2.10
995	A233	650g Volleyballs	4.25	3.75
a.		Souvenir sheet, #994-995	7.00	7.00

Medicinal Plants — A234

Designs: No. 998, Stachytarpheta jamaicense. No. 999, Ruellia tuberosa. No. 1000, Peperomia pellucida. No. 1001, Ocimum sanctum. No. 1002, Phyllanthus amarus. No. 1003, Portulaca oleracea. No. 1004, Wulffia baccata. No. 1005, Sesamum indicum. No. 1006, Ascelepias curassavica. No. 1007, Heliotropium indicum. No. 1008, Wedelia trilobata. No. 1009, Lantana camara.

1995, Mar. 31 Litho. *Perf. 13½*

998	A234	30g multicolored	.35	.25
999	A234	30g multicolored	.35	.25
a.		Pair, #998-999	.75	.75
1000	A234	50g multicolored	.50	.35
1001	A234	50g multicolored	.50	.35
a.		Pair, #1000-1001	1.00	1.00
1002	A234	75g multicolored	.75	.55
1003	A234	75g multicolored	.75	.55
a.		Pair, #1002-1003	1.50	1.50
1004	A234	250g multicolored	2.25	1.60
1005	A234	250g multicolored	2.25	1.60
a.		Pair, #1004-1005	4.75	4.75
1006	A234	500g multicolored	4.75	3.50
1007	A234	500g multicolored	4.75	3.50
a.		Pair, #1006-1007	9.25	9.25
1008	A234	600g multicolored	5.50	4.00
1009	A234	600g multicolored	5.50	4.00
a.		Pair, #1008-1009	11.50	11.50
		Nos. 998-1009 (12)	28.20	20.50

World Wildlife Fund — A235

25g, Herpailurus yaguarondi. 30g, same up close. 50g, Leopardus tigrinus. 100g, same up close. 1000g, Leopardus wiedi. 1200g, same up close.

1995, May 31 *Perf. 14x13*

1010	A235	25g multicolored	.75	.75
1011	A235	30g multicolored	.75	.75
1012	A235	50g multicolored	.75	.75
1013	A235	100g multicolored	1.90	1.90
1014	A235	1000g multicolored	4.75	4.75
1015	A235	1200g multicolored	5.75	5.75
		Nos. 1010-1015 (6)	14.65	14.65

Nos. 1014-1015 are airmail and do not contain WWF emblem.

UN, 50th Anniv. — A236

1995, June 26 Litho. *Perf. 13x14*

1016	A236	135g green & multi	.60	.55
1017	A236	740g blue & multi	4.00	3.75

Surinam Police Force, Cent. — A237

1995, June 21 *Perf. 14x13*

1018	A237	875g multicolored	5.00	4.75

Nilom Junior Chamber, 25th Anniv. A238

1995, Sept. 6 Litho. *Perf. 14x13*

1019	A238	700g multicolored	3.50	2.75

Environmental Protection A239

1995, Oct. 12

1020	A239	135f multicolored	1.00	.75
1021	A239	1500f multicolored	11.00	9.00

America issue.

Christmas — A240

70g, Shepherds, star. 135g, Flight into Egypt. 295g, Magi. 1000g, Nativity, horiz.

1995, Nov. 15 *Perf. 13x14, 14x13*

1022	A240	70g multicolored	.30	.25
1023	A240	135g multicolored	.65	.55
1024	A240	295g multicolored	1.25	1.05
1025	A240	1000g multicolored	5.25	4.25
a.		Souvenir sheet of 1	4.75	3.75
		Nos. 1022-1025 (4)	7.45	6.10

For surcharges see Nos. 1065A-1065B.

A241

Paintings of Jesters, by Corneille.

1995, Dec. 5 *Perf. 13x14*

1026	A241	135f With bird	.75	.70
1027	A241	615f With cat	3.75	3.50

Orchids — A242

No. 1028, Cyrtopodium cristatum. No. 1029, Epidendrum cristatum. No. 1030, Otostylis lepida. No. 1031, Cochleanthes guianensis. No. 1032, Rudolfiella aurantiaca. No. 1033, Catasetum longifolium. No. 1034, Maxillaria splendens. No. 1035, Encyclia granitica. No. 1036, Catasetum macrocarpum. No. 1037, Brassia caudata. No. 1038, Vanilla grandiflora. No. 1039, Maxillaria rufescens.

1996, Feb. 29 Litho. *Perf. 13½*

1028 A242 10g multicolored .25 .25
1029 A242 10g multicolored .25 .25
a. Pair, #1028-1029 .30 .30
1030 A242 75g multicolored .50 .45
1031 A242 75g multicolored .50 .45
a. Pair, #1030-1031 1.00 1.00
1032 A242 135g multicolored .85 .75
1033 A242 135g multicolored .85 .75
a. Pair, #1032-1033 1.75 1.75
1034 A242 250g multicolored 1.60 1.45
1035 A242 250g multicolored 1.60 1.45
a. Pair, #1034-1035 3.50 3.50
1036 A242 300g multicolored 2.00 1.75
1037 A242 300g multicolored 2.00 1.75
a. Pair, #1036-1037 4.50 4.50
1038 A242 750g multicolored 4.75 4.25
1039 A242 750g multicolored 4.75 4.25
a. Pair, #1038-1039 11.00 11.00
Nos. 1028-1039 (12) 19.90 17.80

Bird Type of 1985

2000f, Kraagpapegaai.

1996, Apr. 16 Litho. *Perf. 14x13*

1040 A173 2000f multi 12.50 12.50

Ecotourism A243

Designs: No. 1041, Traditional huts. No. 1042, Butterfly in rain forest. No. 1043, Two natives. No. 1044, Native woman.

Perf. 13½x13 on 3 Sides

1996, Apr. 30 Litho.

Booklet Stamps

1041 A243 70g multicolored 1.25 1.10
1042 A243 70g multicolored 1.25 1.10
1043 A243 135g multicolored 2.75 2.10
1044 A243 135g multicolored 2.75 2.10
a. Booklet pane of 4, #1041-1044 8.00
Complete booklet, #1044a 9.00

Radio, Cent. — A244

135g, First wireless radio communication device, vert. 615g, Guglielmo Marconi.

Perf. 13x14, 14x13

1996, May 17 Litho.

1045 A244 135g multicolored 1.00 .75
1046 A244 615g multicolored 4.50 3.75

1996 Summer Olympic Games, Atlanta — A245

Olymphilex '96, Atlanta — A245a

70g, Basketball. 135g, Athletics. 195g, Badminton. 200g, Swimming. 900g, Cycling. 1000g, Hurdles.

Stamp on stamp: No. 1052Ab, 135f, #678. No. 1052Ac, 865f, #683.

1996, June 27 Litho. *Perf. 13x14*

1047 A245 70g multi .50 .35
1048 A245 135g multi .90 .70
1049 A245 195g multi 1.30 1.00
1050 A245 200g multi 1.50 1.15
1051 A245 900g multi 6.50 5.00
1052 A245 1000g multi 7.00 5.25
Nos. 1047-1052 (6) 17.70 13.45

Souvenir Sheet

1052A A245a Sheet of 2, #b.-c. 6.75 5.50

Bird Type of 1985

Designs: 75f, Fisman. 160f, Fremusu-aka. 1765f, Roodpoot honingzuiger.

1996, Oct. 2 Litho. *Perf. 14x13*

1053 A173 75f multicolored .45 .25
1054 A173 160f multicolored 1.00 .55
1055 A173 1765f multicolored 11.00 5.75
Nos. 1053-1055 (3) 12.45 6.55

A246

Women's Traditional Costumes: Various styles.

1996, Oct. 9 Litho. *Perf. 13x14*

1056 135f multicolored 1.00 1.00
1057 990f multicolored 6.50 6.00
a. A246 Pair, #1056-1057 8.25 8.25

America issue.

A247

Christmas: Various stylized designs of Madonna and Child.

1996, Oct. 30 Litho. *Perf. 13x14*

1058 A247 10f multicolored .25 .25
1059 A247 70f multicolored .40 .35
1060 A247 135f multicolored .75 .60
1061 A247 285f multicolored 1.90 1.60
1062 A247 750f multicolored 5.00 4.00
a. Souvenir sheet, #1062 5.00 5.00
Nos. 1058-1062 (5) 8.30 6.80

A248

Youth Care: Paintings, by Jan Telting: 135f, Brown dog, child. 865f, White dog, child.

1996, Dec. 4 Litho. *Perf. 13x14*

1063 A248 135f multicolored .90 .85
1064 A248 865f multicolored 7.25 5.50

A249

City of Albina, 150th Anniv.: August Kappler (1815-87), founder.

1996, Dec. 13

1065 A249 875f multicolored 6.00 4.75

Nos. 1024, 1025 Surcharged in Black or Silver

Methods and perfs as before

1996, Dec. 16

1065A A240 (125g) on 295g 3.00 3.00
1065B A240 (125g) on 1000g (S) 3.00 3.00

SURALCO (Surinam Aluminum Co.) — A250

10f, Opening of aluminum smelter, Paranam, 1965. 70f, Drilling blasting holes for ore exploration, Moengo, 1947. 130f, Workers' housing, Moengo, 1919. 150f, Dust-free loading of alumina, Paranam dock, 1995. 160f, Constructing dam, power station, 1960. 730f, Schooner Moengo, 1922.

Perf. 13½x13 on 2 or 3 Sides

1996, Dec. 18 Booklet Stamps

1066 A250 10f multicolored .25 .25
1067 A250 70f multicolored .65 .60
1068 A250 130f multicolored 1.10 1.00
1069 A250 150f multicolored 1.25 1.10
1070 A250 160f multicolored 1.40 1.25
1071 A250 730f multicolored 6.50 6.50
a. Booklet pane, #1066-1071 + label 11.50
Complete booklet, #1071a 12.50

Heinrich von Stephan (1831-97) — A251

1997, Jan. 31 Litho. *Perf. 13x14*

1072 A251 275f brown & multi 2.50 2.00
1073 A251 475f dk blue & multi 3.75 3.00

Fauna — A252

#1074, Cebus nigrivittatus. #1075, Cebus apella. #1076, Saguinus midas. #1077, Ateles paniscus. #1078, Ateles geoffroyi panamensis. #1079, Ateles geoffroyi frontatus. #1080, Cacajao calvus. #1081, Lagothrix flavicauda. #1082, Saguinus bicolor. #1083, Saguinus oedipus. #1084, Alouatta seniculus. #1085, Saimiri sciureus.

1997, Feb. 12 Litho. *Perf. 13½*

1074 A252 25f multicolored .25 .25
1075 A252 25f multicolored .25 .25
a. Pair, #1074-1075 .40 .40
1076 A252 75f multicolored .55 .45
1077 A252 75f multicolored .55 .45
a. Pair, #1076-1077 1.25 1.25
1078 A252 100f multicolored .75 .60
1079 A252 100f multicolored .75 .60
a. Pair, #1078-1079 1.60 1.60
1080 A252 275f multicolored 2.00 1.60
1081 A252 275f multicolored 2.00 1.60
a. Pair, #1080-1081 4.50 4.50
1082 A252 300f multicolored 2.50 1.90
1083 A252 300f multicolored 2.50 1.90
a. Pair, #1082-1083 5.25 4.25
1084 A252 725f multicolored 5.25 4.25
1085 A252 725f multicolored 5.25 5.25
a. Pair, #1084-1085 12.00 12.00
Nos. 1074-1085 (12) 22.60 19.10

Retracing and Completion of Amelia Earhart's Trans-Global Flight by Linda Finch — A253

1997, Mar. 30 Litho. *Perf. 14x13*

1086 A253 275f multicolored 2.40 2.00

Surinam Museum, 50th Anniv. A254

1997, Apr. 3

1087 A254 625f multicolored 4.75 4.75

Nos. 983-986 Surcharged in Black or Silver

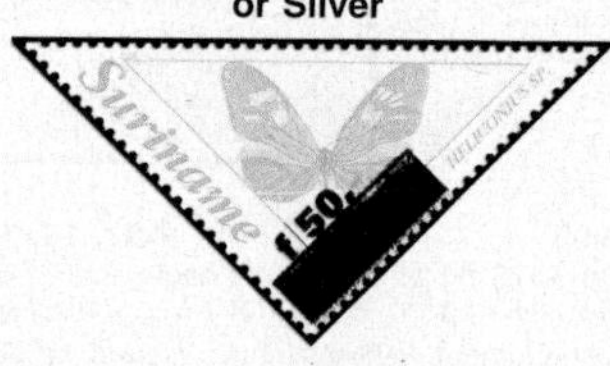

1996-97 Litho. *Perf. 13½*

1088 A229 50f on 250g #983 1.10 1.10
1089 A229 50f on 250g #984 1.10 1.10
a. Pair, #1088-1089 5.50 5.50
1090 A229 100f on 300g #985 (S) 2.10 2.10
1091 A229 100f on 300g #986 (S) 2.10 2.10
a. Pair, #1090-1091 7.25 7.25
Nos. 1088-1091 (4) 6.40 6.40

Issued; #1089a, 11/1; #1091a, 1/1/97.

Orchids — A255

Designs: 25f, Selenipedium steyermarkii. 50f, Phragmipedium schlimii. 75f, Criosantes arietina. 200f, Cypripedium margaritaceum. 775f, Paphiopedilum gratrixianum.

1997, Apr. 3 Litho. *Perf. 13x14*

1092 A255 25f multicolored .25 .25
1093 A255 50f multicolored .35 .35
1094 A255 75f multicolored .50 .50
1095 A255 200f multicolored 1.35 1.35
1096 A255 775f multicolored 5.25 5.25
Nos. 1092-1096 (5) 7.70 7.70

Souvenir Sheet

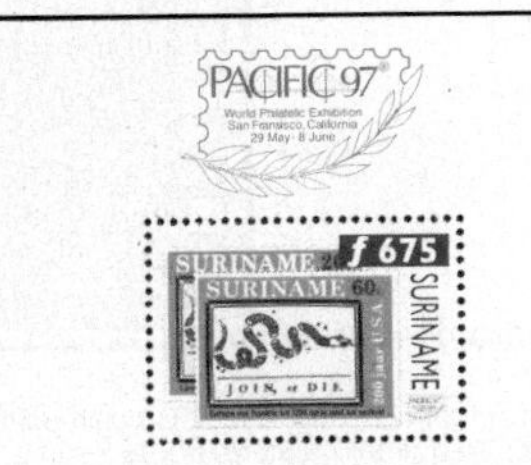

PACIFIC 97, San Francisco — A256

1997, May 29 Litho. *Perf. 13½x13*

1097 A256 675f #458-459 5.00 5.00

A257

Mosques: 50f, Great Mosque, Isfahan, Iran. 125f, Dome of the Rock, Jerusalem. 175f, Madrasa of Ulugh beg, Samarkand. 225f, Taj Mahal, Agra, India. 275f, Kaiser St. Mosque, Paramaribo. 325f, Sülcjamiye, Istanbul.

1997, July 7 *Perf. 13x14*

Background Color

1098 A257 50f pink .35 .35
1099 A257 125f olive .85 .80
1100 A257 175f blue 1.15 1.10
1101 A257 225f purple 1.50 1.40
1102 A257 275f green 1.90 1.75
1103 A257 325f brown 2.25 2.10
a. Souvenir sheet of 1 2.50 2.40
Nos. 1098-1103 (6) 8.00 7.50

A258

State Oil Co. Refinery, Saramacca: 50f, Pumping station. 125f, Derrick, butterfly. #1106, Storage tanks. #1107, Gauge, testing mechanism.

Booklet Stamps

Perf. 13x13½ on 3 Sides

1997, Aug. 16 Litho.

1104 A258 50f multicolored .40 .55
1105 A258 125f multicolored 1.10 1.60
1106 A258 275f multicolored 2.25 3.75
1107 A258 275f multicolored 2.25 3.75
a. Booklet pane, #1104-1107 7.00
Complete booklet, #1107a 8.00

Bird Type of 1985

1997, Sept. 17 Litho. *Perf. 14x13*

1108 A173 50f Krabu-owrukuku .50 .50
1109 A173 125f Mangrodoifi 1.50 1.50
1110 A173 275f Peprefowru 2.00 2.00
1111 A173 3150f Kroonvink 25.00 25.00
Nos. 1108-1111 (4) 29.00 29.00

A259

Child Care: 50f, Right side of boy's face. 100f, Left side of boy's face, 175f, Right side of girl's face. 225f, Left side of girl's face. 350f, 675f, Boy's face upside down, girl's face.

1997, Dec. 4 Litho. *Perf. 13x14*

1112 A259 50f multicolored .40 .40
1113 A259 100f multicolored .75 .75
1114 A259 175f multicolored 1.20 1.20
1115 A259 225f multicolored 1.60 1.60
1116 A259 350f multicolored 2.60 2.60
Nos. 1112-1116 (5) 6.55 6.55

Souvenir Sheet

1117 A259 675f multicolored 4.75 4.25

A260

Christmas: 125f, Madonna and Child. 225f, Children looking at baby. 450f, Angel. 675f, Children singing, horiz.

1997, Dec. 4

1118 A260 125f multicolored .85 .85
1119 A260 225f multicolored 1.50 1.50
1120 A260 450f multicolored 3.00 3.00
Nos. 1118-1120 (3) 5.35 5.35

Souvenir Sheet

1121 A260 675f multicolored 4.25 4.25

America Issue — A261

Designs: 170f, Postal worker, motorcycle. 230f, Postal worker carrying package.

1997, Dec. 10 Litho. *Perf. 13x14*

1122 170f multicolored 1.00 1.00
1123 230f multicolored 1.40 1.40
a. A261 Pair, #1122-1123 4.00 4.00

Moths & Butterflies — A262

1998, Jan. 26 *Perf. 13½*

1124 A262 50f Alcandor .40 .25
1125 A262 50f Achilles .40 .25
a. Pair, #1124-1125 1.00 1.00
1126 A262 75f Alphenor .55 .40
1127 A262 75f Ceres .55 .40
a. Pair, #1126-1127 1.75 1.75
1128 A262 100f Cecropia .75 .50
1129 A262 100f Helenor .75 .50
a. Pair, #1128-1129 2.25 2.25
1130 A262 175f Promothea 1.25 .85
1131 A262 175f Cassiae 1.25 .85
a. Pair, #1130-1131 4.00 4.00
1132 A262 275f Ino 2.50 1.75
1133 A262 275f Phidippus 2.50 1.75
a. Pair, #1132-1133 7.25 7.25
1134 A262 725f Palamedes 6.75 4.50
1135 A262 725f Helenor, diff. 6.75 4.50
a. Pair, #1134-1135 18.50 18.50
Nos. 1124-1135 (12) 24.40 16.50

Bird Type of 1985

50f, Marjrietje. 225f, Aka. 2425f, Timmerman, vert.

1998, Mar. 12 *Perf. 14x13, 13x14*

1136 A173 50f multi .40 .25
1137 A173 225f multi 2.00 1.25
1138 A173 2425f multi 20.00 13.50
Nos. 1136-1138 (3) 22.40 15.00

Hindustani Immigration, 125th Anniv. A263

Designs: 175f, Painting showing first immigrants from boat, "Lala Rooch." 200f, Statue of Baba and Mai, first immigrants from India.

1998, June 4 Litho. *Perf. 14x13*

1139 A263 175f multicolored 1.50 1.50
1140 A263 200f multicolored 1.90 1.90

Temples A264

Designs: 50f, Sri Lanka. 75f, Golden Pagoda, Burma, vert. 275f, Swayambhunath, Nepal, vert. 325f, Borobudur, Indonesia. 400f, Wat Phra Kaew, Thailand, vert. 450f, Peking Temple, China, vert.
675f, Statue, Borobudur, Indonesia, vert.

Perf. 13½x12½, 12½x13½

1998, June 4

1141 A264 50f multicolored .40 .35
1142 A264 75f multicolored .55 .50
1143 A264 275f multicolored 2.00 1.75
1144 A264 325f multicolored 2.50 2.10
1145 A264 400f multicolored 2.75 2.25
1146 A264 450f multicolored 3.50 3.00
Nos. 1141-1146 (6) 11.70 9.95

Souvenir Sheet

1147 A264 675f multicolored 6.00 6.00

No. 1147 is a continuous design.

Ferry Boat and Surinam Flag A265

1998, Oct. 31 *Perf. 13½x14*

1148 A265 275f blue & multi 2.00 2.00
1149 A265 400f sepia & multi 3.00 3.00

See Guyana Nos. 3360A-3360B.

America Issue — A266

Outstanding women: 400f, Sophie Redmond (1907-55). 1000f, Grace Ruth Schneiders-Howard (1869-1968).

1998, Oct. 8 Litho. *Perf. 13x14*

1150 A266 400f multicolored 3.50 2.50
1151 A266 1000f multicolored 7.75 5.50

World Stamp Exhibition, The Hague, Netherlands A267

Designs: 400f, #245, portions of #174, #141. 800f, #174, portions of #245, #141. 2400f, #141, portions of #245, #174.

1998, Oct. Litho. *Perf. 14x13*

1152 A267 400f multicolored 2.50 2.50
1153 A267 800f multicolored 5.00 5.00

Souvenir Sheet

1154 A267 2400f multicolored 17.00 17.00

A268

Christmas: Various nativity scenes.

1998, Nov. 1 *Perf. 13x14*

1155 A268 50f multicolored .35 .25
1156 A268 325f multicolored 1.30 1.00
1157 A268 400f multicolored 1.60 1.25
1158 A268 1225f multicolored 5.75 4.25
Nos. 1155-1158 (4) 9.00 6.75

Souvenir Sheet

1159 A268 1400f multicolored 6.50 6.50

Bird Type of 1985

3800f, Butarides striatus.

1998, Nov. 16 Litho. *Perf. 14x13*

1160 A173 3800f multi 14.50 12.00

A269

400f, Mother, child, foods. 1000f, Mother, child, flower.

1998, Dec. 4 Litho. *Perf. 13x14*

1161 A269 400f multicolored 1.50 1.25
1162 A269 1000f multicolored 4.00 3.25

World Health Organization, 50th anniv.

Child Care — A270

400f, Flying kite, diff. 1225f, Holding kite.

1998, Dec. 4 Litho. *Perf. 14x13*

1163 A270 375f shown 1.60 1.50
1164 A270 400f multi 1.60 1.50
1165 A270 1225f multi 5.75 5.25
Nos. 1163-1165 (3) 8.95 8.25

Heliconia — A271

No. 1166, Caribaea kawauchi. No. 1167, Pastazae. No. 1168, Rostrata. No. 1169, Sexy pink. No. 1170, Collinsiana. No. 1171, Wagneriana. No. 1172, Bihai-nappi. No. 1173, Jaded forest. No. 1174, Golden torch. No. 1175, Latispatha-red yellow gyro. No. 1176, Sexy pink, diff. No. 1177, Nappi yellow.

1999, Jan. 27 Litho. *Perf. 13½*

1166 A271 50f multicolored .25 .25
1167 A271 50f multicolored .25 .25
a. Pair, #1166-1167 .35 .35
1168 A271 200f multicolored .75 .60
1169 A271 200f multicolored .75 .60
a. Pair, #1168-1169 1.60 1.60
1170 A271 300f multicolored 1.10 .90
1171 A271 300f multicolored 1.10 .90
a. Pair, #1170-1171 2.75 2.75
1172 A271 400f multicolored 1.40 1.15
1173 A271 400f multicolored 1.40 1.15
a. Pair, 1172-1173 3.75 3.75
1174 A271 750f multicolored 2.75 2.25
1175 A271 750f multicolored 2.75 2.25
a. Pair, #1174-1175 7.25 7.25
1176 A271 1300f multicolored 4.75 4.00
1177 A271 1300f multicolored 4.75 4.00
a. Pair, #1176-1177 12.00 12.00
Nos. 1166-1177 (12) 22.00 18.30

Old Plantation Houses A272

1999, Mar. 17 Litho. *Perf. 14x13*

1178 A272 75f Katwijk .30 .30
1179 A272 300f Sorgvliet 1.20 1.10
1180 A272 400f Peperpot 1.40 1.30
1181 A272 2225f Spiering-shoek 8.25 7.50
Nos. 1178-1181 (4) 11.15 10.20

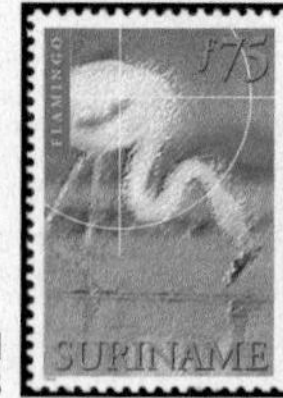

Endangered Species — A273

1999, June 30 Litho. *Perf. 13x14*
1182 A273 75f Flamingo .25 .25
1183 A273 375f Orangutan .70 .55
1184 A273 450f Elephant .85 .65
1185 A273 500f Whale .90 .70
1186 A273 850f Frog 1.45 1.15
1187 A273 900f Rhinoceros 1.60 1.25
1188 A273 1600f Giant panda 2.75 2.10
1189 A273 7250f Tiger 13.00 10.00
Nos. 1182-1189 (8) 21.50 16.65

Coppename Bridge A274

1999, June 30 *Perf. 14x13*
1190 A274 850f black & green 1.40 1.40
1191 A274 2250f black & blue 3.75 3.75

A275

A276

1999, July 9 *Perf. 13x14*
1192 A275 850f multicolored 1.25 1.25
1193 A276 2650f multicolored 3.50 3.50
a. Souvenir sheet, #1192-1193, perf. 13x13½ 4.75 4.75

Surinam Conservation Foundation, 30th anniv. (No. 1192), Central Surinam Nature Preserve, 1st anniv. (No. 1193).

Bird Type of 1985-95

1999, Aug. 21 *Perf. 14x13*
1194 A173 1000f Blauwtje 1.75 1.75
1195 A173 5500f Kepanki 8.25 8.25

UPU, 125th Anniv. — A277

1999, Oct. 9 *Perf. 13x14*
1196 A277 950f Earth 1.60 1.60
1197 A277 1000f Saturn 1.75 1.75

A278

1999, Oct. 9
1198 1000f Gun 1.60 1.60
1199 2250f Flower 3.00 3.00
a. A278 Pair, #1198-1199 5.50 5.50

America issue, A New Millennium Without Arms.

Christmas — A279

500f, Star, stable. 850f, Christmas tree. 900f, Angel. 1000f, Candle.
2275f, Mother and child.

1999, Nov. 3 *Perf. 13x14*
1200 A279 500f multi .80 .80
1201 A279 850f multi 1.35 1.35
1202 A279 900f multi 1.45 1.45
1203 A279 1000f multi 1.50 1.50
Nos. 1200-1203 (4) 5.10 5.10

Souvenir Sheet

1204 A279 2275f multi 3.75 3.75

Children's Pictures A280

1999, Dec. 3 Litho. *Perf. 14x13*
1205 A280 1100f multi 1.60 1.60
1206 A280 1400f multi, diff. 2.10 2.10
1207 A280 1600f multi, diff. 2.25 2.25
a. Souvenir sheet of 1 2.50 2.50
Nos. 1205-1207 (3) 5.95 5.95

Children's Drawings A281

1000f, By Tahirih van Kanten. 2500f, By Tirsa Braaf.

2000, Jan. 3 Litho. *Perf. 14x13*
1208 A281 1000f multi 1.75 1.75
1209 A281 2500f multi 5.00 5.00

See No. 1224.

Traffic Signs — A282

2000 *Perf. 13x14*
1210 A282 2000f Turn right 3.50 3.50
1211 A282 2000f No passing 3.50 3.50
1212 A282 2000f Sharp turns 3.50 3.50
1213 A282 2000f Traffic circle 3.50 3.50
Nos. 1210-1213 (4) 14.00 14.00

Issued: #1210, 1/3; #1211, 4/3; #1212, 5/18. #1213, 9/29.

See Nos. 1246-1248, 1267-1268, 1275-1278, 1311-1312.

Fruits A283

No. 1214, 50f: a, Citrullus vulgaris. b, Carica papaya.
No. 1215, 175f: a, Mangifera indica. b, Garcinia mangostana.
No. 1216, 200f: a, Musa nana. b, Citrus paradisi.
No. 1217, 250f: a, Punika granatum. b, Ananas comosus.
No. 1218, 325f: a, Cocos nucifera. b, Passiflora quadrangularis.
No. 1219, 5000f: a, Citrus sinensis. b, Persea gratissima.

2000, Feb. 29 Litho. *Perf. 13¼*
Pairs, #a-b
1214-1219 A283 Set of 6 18.00 18.00

No. 1219 is airmail.

Bird Type of 1985

Designs: 1100f, Dendrocygna autumnalis. 4425f, Ceryle torquata.

2000, Apr. 3 *Perf. 14x13*
1220 A173 1100f multi 1.60 1.60
1221 A173 4425f multi 7.25 7.25

Surinam River Bridge A284

Lettering in: 1100f, Red. 1700f, Blue.

2000, May 18
1222-1223 A284 Set of 2 4.25 4.25

Children's Drawings Type
Souvenir Sheet

2000 *Perf. 13¼x13*
1224 A281 3575f #1208, 1209 5.75 5.75

World Stamp Expo 2000, Anaheim, Stampin' the Future children's stamp design contest.

2000 Summer Olympic, Sydney A285

No. 1225, 1100f: a, Soccer. b, Track and field.
No. 1226, 3900f: a, Tennis. b, Swimming.
No. 1227: a, Soccer, diff. b, Swimming, diff.

2000, Aug. 8 Litho. *Perf. 13¼*
Pairs, #a-b
1225-1226 A285 Set of 2 16.00 16.00

Souvenir Sheet

1227 A285 2500f Sheet of 2, #a-b 7.25 7.25

America Issue, Fight Against AIDS — A286

No. 1228: a, 1100f, Foot with condom stamping out AIDS, horiz. b, 6400f, People holding condoms.

2000 *Perf. 13x14*
1228 A286 Pair, #a-b 12.00 12.00

25th Anniv. of International Agencies Ltd. as Philatelic and Numismatic Agent — A287

Designs: 125f, Paper money. 5900f, Stamps.

2000, Nov. 24
1229-1230 A287 Set of 2 5.00 5.00
1230a Souvenir sheet, #1229-1230 6.00 6.00

Children — A288

Child: 1100f, Walking. 3900f, Breastfeeding. 2000f, With umbilical cord, horiz.

2000, Dec. 5 *Perf. 13x14*
1231-1232 A288 Set of 2 5.50 5.50

Souvenir Sheet
Perf. 14x13

1233 A288 2000f multi 2.50 2.50

Fight Against Poverty A289

Country name in: 1100f, Green. 4900f, Red.

2000 *Perf. 14x13*
1234-1235 A289 Set of 2 5.50 5.50

Christmas — A290

Designs: 1100f, Star of Bethlehem. 3900f, Madonna and Child.
3000f, Magi with gifts, horiz.

2000 *Perf. 13x14*
1236-1237 A290 Set of 2 6.00 6.00

Souvenir Sheet
Perf. 14x13

1238 A290 3000f multi 3.75 3.75

No. 945a Surcharged

Methods and Perfs as Before

2000 (?)
1238A Pair 4.00 4.00
b. A221 1000f on 25c No. 942 1.75 1.75
c. A221 1000f on 25c No. 943 1.75 1.75
1239 Pair 5.50 5.50
a. A221 3100f on 35c No. 944 2.50 2.50
b. A221 3100f on 35c No. 945 2.50 2.50

Birds A291

No. 1240, 50f: a, Rood zwart vink tagara. b, Tyarman.
No. 1241, 175f: a, Sabaku. b, Kolibrie.
No. 1242, 200f: a, Aka. b, Timmerman.
No. 1243, 250f: a, Paarskeel cotinga. b, Zwarte kraag donfowru.
No. 1244, 825f: a, Kees. b, Stonkuyake.
No. 1245, 7500f: a, Guyanese rood cotinga. b, Butabuta.

2001, Jan. 31 Litho. *Perf. 13¼*
Pairs, #a-b

1240-1245 A291 Set of 6 18.00 18.00

No. 1245 is airmail.

Traffic Signs Type of 2000

2001 Litho. *Perf. 13x14*

1246 A282 2000f No parking 3.75 3.75
1247 A282 4000f Drawbridge 4.50 4.50
1248 A282 4000f Tractor, No entry 4.50 4.50

Issued: 2000f, 3/8; No. 1247, 4/25; No. 1248, 9/12.

UN Women's Human Rights Campaign — A292

Designs: 1400f, Female and male symbols. 4600f, Woman.

2001, Mar. 15 Litho. *Perf. 13x14*

1249-1250 A292 Set of 2 5.75 5.75

Youth Philately — A293

Children's art by: 650f, Bhoelai Surender Kumar. 5350f, Sharon Cameron.

2001, Apr. 25

1251-1252 A293 Set of 2 5.50 5.50

Bird Type of 1985

Designs: 4500f, Charadrius collaris. 9000f, Bubo virginianus.

2001, May 10 *Perf. 14x13*

1253 A173 4500f multi 5.00 5.00
1254 A173 9000f multi 10.00 10.00

Fruit — A294

Designs: 150f, Sapotille. 200f, Noni vrucht. 800fr, Baby bananas. 1200f, Mope. 1700f, Pommerak.

2001, July 20 Litho. *Perf. 12¾x13½*

1255-1259 A294 Set of 5 4.75 4.75

America Issue — A295

Paramaribo buildings: Nos. 1260a, 1261a, 1700f, Bishop's house. Nos. 1260b, 1261b, 7300f, Presidential palace.

2001, Sept. 12 Litho. *Perf. 14x13*
Country Name in Red

1260 A295 Pair, #a-b 9.50 9.50

Souvenir Sheet
Country Name in Green
Perf. 13¼x13

1261 A295 Sheet of 2, #a-b 9.50 9.50

Stamp Day — A296

Designs: No. 1262a, 3750f, #648 (green background). No. 1262b, 5250f, #29 (red background).

No. 1263a, 3750f, #648 (red background). No. 1263b, 5250f, #29 (orange background).

2001, Oct. 19 *Perf. 13x14*

1262 A296 Pair, #a-b 9.50 9.50

Souvenir Sheet
Perf. 13x13¼

1263 A296 Sheet of 2, #a-b 9.50 9.50

Christmas A297

Children's Sports — A298

2001, Nov. 2 *Perf. 13¼*

1264 A297 1700f blue & multi 2.00 2.00

Perf. 14x13

1265 A298 5000f red & multi 5.75 5.75

Souvenir Sheet
Perf. 13¼x13

1266 Sheet of 2 7.75 7.75
a. A297 1700f green & multi 2.10 2.10
b. A298 5000f blue & multi 5.75 5.75

No. 947a Surcharged in Gold

2001, Dec. 7 Litho. *Perf. 13½*

1266C Pair 6.00 6.00
d. A221 2500f on 50c No. 946 3.00 3.00
e. A221 2500f on 50c No. 947 3.00 3.00

Traffic Signs Type of 2000

2001-02 *Perf. 13x14*

1267 A282 4000f Pedestrian crossing 4.50 4.50
1268 A282 4000f Yield 4.50 4.50

Issued: No. 1267, 12/7/01; No. 1268, 2/13/02.

Parrots A299

No. 1269, 150f: a, Deroptyus accipitrinus. b, Amazona achrocephala.

No. 1270, 200f: a, Ara manilata. b, Amazona dufresniana.

No. 1271, 800f: a, Ara severa. b, Pionites melanocephala.

No. 1272, 1200f: a, Ara nobilis. b, Pionus fiscus.

No. 1273, 1700f: a, Ara chloroptera. b, Pionopsitta caicca.

No. 1274, 5325f: a, Ara macao. b, Amazona farinosa.

2002, Jan. 9 *Perf. 13¼*
Pairs, #a-b

1269-1274 A299 Set of 6 19.50 19.50

No. 1274 is airmail.

Traffic Signs Type of 2000

No. 1275, U turn. No. 1276, Pedestrian path. No. 1277, Train crossing without barriers. No. 1278, Motorcycles.

2002-03 Litho. *Perf. 13x14*

1275 A282 4000f multicolored 4.50 4.50

Perf. 12¾x14

1276 A282 4000f multicolored 4.50 4.50
1277 A282 4000f multicolored 4.50 4.50
1278 A282 4000f multicolored 4.00 4.00
Nos. 1275-1278 (4) 17.50 17.50

Issued: No. 1275, 4/17/02; No. 1276, 6/19/02; No. 1277, 9/20/02; No. 1278, 2/13/03.

Costumes — A300

Costumes of: Nos. 1279a, 1279c, 1279e, 1279g, 1279i, 1279k, Various men. Nos. 1279b, 1279d, 1279f, 1279h, 1279j, 1279l, Various women.

2002, May 15 *Perf. 12¾x13¼*

1279 Horiz. strip of 12 16.00 16.00
a.-b. A300 150f Either single .25 .25
c.-d. A300 200f Either single .25 .25
e.-f. A300 800f Either single .75 .75
g.-h. A300 1200f Either single 1.10 1.10
i.-j. A300 1700f Either single 1.60 1.60
k.-l. A300 4950f Either single 4.50 4.50

Birds — A301

5000f, Royal flycatcher. 8500f, Swampufowru.

2002, June 19 *Perf. 12¾x14*

1280 A301 5000f multicolored 5.50 5.50
1281 A301 8500f multicolored 9.25 9.25

Amphilex 2002 Intl. Stamp Exhibition, Amsterdam — A302

No. 1282: a, 1700f, Netherlands #244 (yellow background). b, 6800f, Netherlands #103 (maroon background).

No. 1283: a, 1700f, Like No. 1282a (maroon background). b, 6800f, Like No. 1282b (yellow background).

2002, Aug. 30 *Perf. 13¼x12¾*

1282 A302 Horiz. pair, #a-b 8.25 8.25

Souvenir Sheet

1283 A302 Sheet of 2, #a-b 8.25 8.25

No. 1230a Overprinted in Gold
Souvenir Sheet

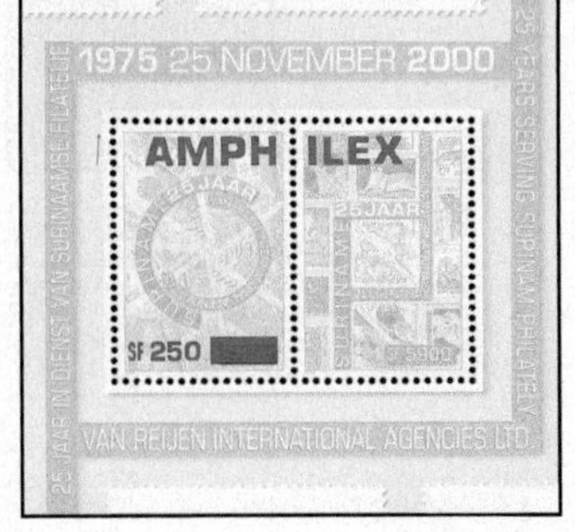

2002, Aug. 30 Litho. *Perf. 13x14*

1284 A287 Sheet of 2 8.50 8.50
a. 250f on 125f #1229 .45 .45
b. 5900f #1230 overprinted 8.00 8.00

America Issue - Youth, Education and Literacy — A303

No. 1285 — Letters, numbers and: a, 1700f, Stylized head and question mark. b, 7300f, "X" in signature box.

2002, Sept. 20 *Perf. 13¼x12¾*

1285 A303 Horiz. pair, #a-b 10.00 10.00

Christmas A304

Designs: No. 1286, 1700f, Unclothed Santa Claus and clothing (light blue background). No. 1287, 5000f, Christmas tree, decorations and gifts (green background).

No. 1288: a, 1700f, Like No. 1286 (yellow background). b, 5000f, Like No. 1287 (blue background).

2002, Nov. 6

1286-1287 A304 Set of 2 6.25 6.25

Souvenir Sheet

1288 A304 Sheet of 2, #a-b 6.25 6.25

Nos. 949a, 953a Surcharged Like No. 1266C in Gold or Silver

2002 ? Litho. *Perf. 13½*

1289 Pair 5.25 5.25
a. A221 2500f on 100c #948 2.50 2.50
b. A221 2500f on 100c #949 2.50 2.50
1290 Pair 8.00 8.00
a. A221 3750f on 220c #952 (S) 4.00 4.00
b. A221 3750f on 220c #953 (S) 4.00 4.00

Birds — A305

No. 1291: a, Falco deiroleucus. b, Lophornis ornatus. c, Touit purpurata. d, Thanlurania furcata. e, Myrmeciza ferruginea. f, Pteroglossus aracari. g, Cotinga cotinga. h, Granatellus pelzelni. i, Euphonia musica. j, Pitangus lictor. k, Cacicus haemorrhous. l, Columba speciosa.

2003, Jan. 9 *Perf. 13¼x14*

1291 Block of 12 19.00 19.00
a.-b. A305 150f Either single .25 .25
c.-d. A305 200f Either single .25 .25
e.-f. A305 800f Either single .90 .90
g.-h. A305 1200f Either single 1.25 1.25
i.-j. A305 1700f Either single 1.90 1.90
k.-l. A305 4950f Either single 5.00 5.00

No. 951a Surcharged in Silver Like No. 1266C

2002, Dec. 30 Litho. *Perf. 13½*

1292 Pair 6.75 6.75
a. A221 2750f on 175c #950 3.25 3.25
b. A221 2750f on 175c #951 3.25 3.25

Dolls — A306

No. 1293: a, A. M. 352/1030. b, S&H 1079, 1892. c, Jumeau, 1895 (denomination in white). d, Jumeau, 1895 (denomination in red). e, A. M. 390, 1900. f, Minerva, 1900. g, K&R 126, 1905. h, K&R, 1905. i, Handwerck, 1905. j, SFBJ, 1907. k, A. M. 980, 1920. l, K&R, 1910.

2003, May 12 ***Perf. 13½x14***

1293 Block of 12 12.00 12.00
a.-l. A306 1000f Any single 1.00 1.00

A307

Designs: 150f, Izaak Enschedé. 800f, Old building of Johann Enschedé Printers, horiz. 1700f, Surinam #7. 3850f, First Surinam banknote printed by Enschedé, horiz.
7500f, Like 150f.

Perf. 12¾x13½, 13½x12¾

2003, June 3

1294-1297 A307 Set of 4 7.00 7.00

Souvenir Sheet

1298 A307 7500f multi 7.00 7.00

Johann Enschedé and Sons, printers, 300th anniv.

A308

Birds: 5400f, Anthracothorax viridigula. 6600f, Campephilus melanoleucos.

2003, Sept. 3 ***Perf. 12¾x14***

1299 A308 5400f multi 5.75 5.75
1300 A308 6600f multi 6.50 6.50

Traffic Signs Type of 2000

2003, Sept. 3 Litho. ***Perf. 12¾x14***

1301 A282 4000f 10% grade 4.00 4.00

America Issue - Flora and Fauna — A309

No. 1302: a, 1700f, Faya lobi. b, 8500f, Puma.

2003, Sept. 20 Litho. ***Perf. 14x12¾***

1302 A309 Horiz. pair, #a-b 12.00 12.00
c. Souvenir sheet, #1302 12.00 12.00

Nos. 889a, 929a Surcharged

Methods and Perfs as Before

2003

1303 Pair 8.00 8.00
a. A172 3500f on 1c on 5c #928 4.00 4.00
b. A172 3500f on 1c on 5c #929 4.00 4.00

1304 Pair 7.50 7.50
a. A172 3500f on 2c on 10c #888 3.75 3.75
b. A172 3500f on 2c on 10c #889 3.75 3.75

Issued: No. 1303, 11/1; No. 1304, 12/1.

Christmas — A310

Designs: 1700f, Children, dog, toy horse. 5300f, Woman holding candle.

2003, Nov. 6 Litho. ***Perf. 12¾x14***

1306 A310 1700f multi 1.40 1.40
1307 A310 5300f multi 4.25 4.25
a. Horiz. pair, #1306-1307 + central label 7.00 7.00
b. Souvenir sheet, #1306-1307 7.00 7.00

Powered Flight, Cent. A311

Designs: 1700f, Santos-Dumont 14bis, first European flight, 1906. 5300f, Replica of 1903 aircraft by Richard Pearse, New Zealand.

2003, Dec. 13 ***Perf. 14x12¾***

1308 A311 1700f multi 1.75 1.75
1309 A311 5300f multi 5.00 5.00
a. Souvenir sheet, #1308-1309 6.75 6.75

The Surinam dollar replaced the florin in January 2004 at an exchange rate of 1000 florins to 1 dollar. Nos. 1310-1313, though issued after the introduction of the new currency, have denominations expressed in florins.

Butterflies A312

No. 1310: a, Anartia amathea. b, Vanessa carye. c, Papilio demetrius. d, Precis octavia. e, Papilio blumei. f, Papilio aritodemus ponceanus. g, Zerynthia rumina. h, Parides gundlachianus. i, Ornithoptera priamus. j, Lyropteryx apollonia. k, Agrias narcissus. l, Elzunia bonplandii.

2004, Jan. 12 ***Perf. 12¾x14***

1310 Block of 12 21.00 21.00
a.-b. A312 150f Either single .25 .25
c.-d. A312 200f Either single .25 .25
e.-f. A312 800f Either single .65 .65
g.-h. A312 1200f Either single .95 .95
i.-j. A312 1700f Either single 1.40 1.40
k.-l. A312 L Either single 7.00 7.00

Nos. 1310k-1310l sold for 9500f on day of issue.

Traffic Signs Type of 2000

No. 1311, Horse and rider crossing. No. 1312, Large vehicles prohibited.

2004 Litho. ***Perf. 12¾x14***

1311 A282 4000f multi 7.75 7.75
1312 A282 4000f multi 7.75 7.75
a. Souvenir sheet, #1278, 1301, 1311, 1312 16.50 16.50

Issued: Nos. 1311-1312, 3/31; No. 1312a, 10/1.

Mailboxes of the World — A313

No. 1313: a, Indonesia. b, Brazil. c, Macao. d, Germany. e, Uruguay. f, Republic of Korea. g, Oman. h, Mexico. i, Australia. j, Switzerland. k, Hong Kong. l, United States.

2004, May 6

1313 Block of 12 22.00 22.00
a.-b. A313 150f Either single .25 .25
c.-d. A313 200f Either single .25 .25
e.-f. A313 800f Either single .60 .60
g.-h. A313 1200f Either single .90 .90
i.-j. A313 1700f Either single 1.25 1.25
k.-l. A313 K Either single 8.00 8.00

Nos. 1313k-1313l each sold for 11,500f ($11.50) on day of issue.

Greek Amphorae — A314

No. 1314 — Inscriptions: a, Athena en Poseidon. b, Wedren. c, Athena Promachus, 363/62 v. C. d, Hippodamia ontvoerd door Pelops, 415 v. C. e, Winnaar muziekconcours, 440-430 v. C. f, Wedren 485-470 v. C. g, Vaashals: speer-en discuswerpers. h, Wedren vier paarden. i, Heracles met leeuw van Nemea, 520 v. C. j, Amfoor, 566 v. C. k, Winnaar muziekconcours (no handles). l, Winnaar muziekconcours (with handles).

No. 1315 — Portions of an amphora: a, $2, Left. b, $3, Center. c, $5, Right.

2004, July 1

1314 Block of 12 28.00 28.00
a.-b. A314 5c Either single .25 .25
c.-d. A314 15c Either single .25 .25
e.-f. A314 20c Either single .25 .25
g.-h. A314 45c Either single .35 .35
i.-j. A314 80c Either single .60 .60
k.-l. A314 M Either single 12.50 12.50

Souvenir Sheet

1315 A314 Sheet of 3, #a-c 8.00 8.00

2004 Summer Olympics, Athens (No. 1315). Nos. 1314k-1314l each sold for $16 on day of issue, and are airmail.

America Issue - Birds — A315

Designs: $1.70, Duck. $12, Parrots.

2004, Sept. 16 ***Perf. 14x12¾***

1316-1317 A315 Set of 2 10.00 10.00
1317a Souvenir sheet, #1316-1317 11.00 11.00

Birds — A316

No. 1318: a, Chloroceryle inda. b, Brotogeris chrysoperus. c, Buteo magnisrostris. d, Buteo albicaudatus. e, Calliphlox amethystina (facing left). f, Calliphlox amethystina (facing right). g, Harpagus diodon. h, Aratinga pertinax. i, Chlorocersyle amazona. j, Galbula galbula. k, Buteogallus aequinoctialis. l, Polyborus plancus.

2004, Oct. 21 ***Perf. 12¾x14***

1318 Block of 12 27.50 27.50
a.-b. A316 5c Either single .25 .25
c.-d. A316 15c Either single .25 .25
e.-f. A316 20c Either single .25 .25
g.-h. A316 45c Either single .35 .35
i.-j. A316 80c Either single .60 .60
k.-l. A316 M Either single 12.00 12.00

Nos. 1318k-1318l each sold for $16 on day of issue, and are airmail.

See Nos. 1329, 1350.

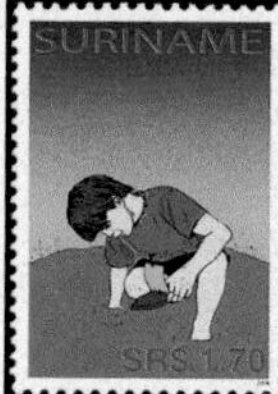

Child Care A317

Christmas A318

2004, Nov. 18 Litho. ***Perf. 12¾x14***

1319 A317 $1.70 multi 1.25 1.25
1320 A318 $7.70 multi 5.75 5.75
a. Souvenir sheet, #1319-1320 7.00 7.00

Teddy Bears — A319

No. 1321: a, Bing, 1919. b, Steiff "Teddy Clown," 1926. c, Steiff "Teddy Girl," 1905. d, Steiff, 1905. e, Steif "Elliot," 1907. f, Ideal "Aloysius," 1907. g, Steiff, 1936. h, Steif "Zotty," 1951. i, Steiff, 1910. j, Steiff "Titanic," 1912. k, Steiff "Berlin," 1985. l, Aux Nations, 1903.

No. 1322: a, Blue mohair, 1938-52. b, Musical bear, 1937. c, Red mohair, 1908. d, Shaggy beige mohair, 1908. e, Ally bear, 1916. f, National bear, 1917. g, Cowboy, 1940s. h, Coronation bear, 1953. i, Tumbling bear, 1920-30s. j, Messenger bear, 1923. k, Bear on a tricycle, 1958. l, Michi Takahashi, 1999.

2004-05 Litho. ***Perf. 12¾x14***

1321 Block of 12 19.00 19.00
a.-b. A319 5c Either single .25 .25
c.-d. A319 15c Either single .25 .25
e.-f. A319 20c Either single .25 .25
g.-h. A319 45c Either single .35 .35
i.-j. A319 80c Either single .65 .65
k.-l. A319 K Either single 8.50 8.50

1322 Block of 12 28.00 28.00
a.-b. A319 5c Either single .25 .25
c.-d. A319 15c Either single .25 .25
e.-f. A319 20c Either single .25 .25
g.-h. A319 45c Either single .35 .35
i.-j. A319 80c Either single .50 .50
k.-l. A319 N Either single 12.50 12.50

Issued: No. 1321, 2004; No. 1322, 3/1/05. Nos. 1321k-1321l each sold for $11.50 on day of issue, and are airmail. Nos. 1322k-1322l each sold for $17 on day of issue, and are airmail.

Butterflies — A320

No. 1323: a, Papilio chikae. b, Iphiclides podalirius. c, Paraphnaeus. d, Morpho didius. e, Delias eucharis. f, Parides sesostris. g, Baronia brevicornis. h, Graphium agamemnon. i, Papilio palinurus. j, Ornithoptera meridionalis. k, Battus bhilenor. l, Eurytides bellerophon.

2005, Jan. 5

1323 Block of 12 28.00 28.00
a.-b. A320 5c Either single .25 .25
c.-d. A320 15c Either single .25 .25
e.-f. A320 20c Either single .25 .25
g.-h. A320 45c Either single .35 .35
i.-j. A320 80c Either single .50 .50
k.-l. A320 N Either single 12.50 12.50

Nos. 1323k-1323l each sold for $17 on day of issue, and are airmail.

Ships A321

No. 1324: a, Louis Roux, Altana. b, Fanerom Eni. c, Nafsika. d, Aristeidis Glykas. e, G. D'Esposito. f, G. D'Esposito, diff.

2005, May 4 Litho. *Perf. 14x12¾*

1324	Block of 6	16.00	16.00
a.	A321 5c multi	.25	.25
b.	A321 15c multi	.25	.25
c.	A321 20c multi	.25	.25
d.	A321 80c multi	.50	.50
e.	A321 $1.70 multi	1.25	1.25
f.	A321 P multi	13.50	13.50

No. 1324f is airmail and sold for $18 on day of issue.

Orchids — A322

No. 1325: a, Vanda hybrid. b, Phalaenopsis hybrid, dark pink flowers. c, Dendrobium hybrid, pink flowers. d, Dendrobium hybrid, dark red flowers with foliage in background. e, Vanda hybrid, diff. f, Peristeria elata. g, Spathoglottis hybrid. h, Dendrobium hybrid, yellow orange flowers. i, Vanda sanderiana. j, Phalaenopsis hybrid, peach flowers. k, Phalaenopsis hybrid, pink flowers. l, Phalaenopsis hybrid, white flowers.

2005, June 29 *Perf. 12¾x14*

1325	Block of 12	25.00	25.00
a.-b.	A322 5c Either single	.25	.25
c.-d.	A322 15c Either single	.25	.25
e.-f.	A322 20c Either single	.25	.25
g.-h.	A322 45c Either single	.40	.40
i.-j.	A322 80c Either single	.70	.70
k.-l.	A322 Q Either single	10.00	10.00

Nos. 1325k and 1325 l are airmail and each sold for $12.50 on day of issue. See No. 1337.

America Issue, Fight Against Poverty A323

Designs: $1.70, Teacher and children. $14.50, Farmer, oxen and plow.
$14, Teacher and children, diff.

Perf. 14x12¾, 12¾x14

2005, Sept. 14

1326-1327	A323	Set of 2	12.50	12.50

Souvenir Sheet

Perf. 12¾x13¼

1328	A323 $14 multi	11.00	11.00

Birds Type of 2004

No. 1329: a, Porphyrula flavirostris. b, Asio clamator. c, Herpetotheres cashinnans. d, Jacana jacana. e, Touit batavica. f, Dendrocygna autumnalis. g, Coccyzus minor. h, Busarellus nigricollis. i, Lophostrix cristata. j, Otus choliba. k, Chrysolampis mosquitus. l, Pyrrhula picta.

2005, Oct. 19 *Perf. 12¾x14*

1329	Block of 12	32.50	32.50
a.-b.	A316 5c Either single	.25	.25
c.-d.	A316 15c Either single	.25	.25
e.-f.	A316 20c Either single	.25	.25
g.-h.	A316 80c Either single	.65	.65
i.-j.	A316 $1.80 Either single	1.25	1.25
k.-l.	A316 P Either single	13.50	13.50

Nos. 1329k and 1329 l are airmail and each sold for $18 on day of issue.

Children — A324

Designs (country name in red): 80c, Girl jumping rope. $9.50, Boy on swing.
No. 1332 — Country name in white: a, Girl jumping rope, diff. b, Boy on swing, diff.

2005, Nov. 16 *Perf. 12¾x13¼*

1330-1331	A324	Set of 2	8.50	8.50

Souvenir Sheet

1332	A324 $5 Sheet of 2, #a-b	8.50	8.50

No. 891a Surcharged

Methods and Perfs as Before

2005, Dec. 1

1333	Pair	6.00	6.00
a.	A172 $3.50 on 3c on 50c #891a	3.00	3.00
b.	A172 $3.50 on 3c on 50c #891b	3.00	3.00

Europa Stamps, 50th Anniv. — A325

Designs: $1, Netherlands #379. $2, Netherlands #369. $9, Netherlands #375.

2006, Jan. 4 Litho. *Perf. 12¾x13¼*

1334-1336	A325	Set of 3	8.75	8.75
1336a	Souvenir sheet, #1334-1336		8.75	8.75

Orchids Type of 2005

No. 1337: a, Dendrobium hybrid, yellow flowers. b, Dendrobium hybrid, white flowers. c, Phalaenopsis hybrid, light purple flowers. d, Phalaenopsis hybrid, pink flowers. e, Vanda hybrid, white flowers. f, Vanda hybrid, purple flowers. g, Dendrobium hybrid, purple and white flowers. h, Arachnis hybrid. i, Vanda hybrid, light orange flowers. j, Vanda hybrid, speckled purple flowers. k, Complex hybrid, orange flowers. l, Vanda hybrid, purple and white flowers.

2006, Feb. 15 *Perf. 12¾x14*

1337	Block of 12	30.00	30.00
a.-b.	A322 5c Either single	.25	.25
c.-d.	A322 15c Either single	.25	.25
e.-f.	A322 20c Either single	.25	.25
g.-h.	A322 45c Either single	.35	.35
i.-j.	A322 80c Either single	.60	.60
k.-l.	A322 Q Either single	13.50	13.50

Nos. 1337k and 1337 l are airmail and each sold for $17.50 on day of issue.

Birds — A326

No. 1338: a, Phaethornis ruber. b, Threnetes leucurus. c, Podager nacunda. d, Columbina passerina. e, Leptotila rufaxilla. f, Claravis pretiosa. g, Campylopterus largipennis. h, Otus choliba. i, Porzana albicollis. j, Amazilia fimbriata. k, Ciccata virgata. l, Nyctidromus albicollis.

2006, May 15 Litho. *Perf. 14x12¾*

1338	Block of 12	30.00	30.00
a.-b.	A326 5c Either single	.25	.25
c.-d.	A326 15c Either single	.25	.25
e.-f.	A326 20c Either single	.25	.25
g.-h.	A326 45c Either single	.35	.35
i.-j.	A326 80c Either single	.60	.60
k.-l.	A326 Q Either single	13.50	13.50

Nos. 1338k-1338l each sold for $17.50, and are airmail.

Nobel Laureates — A327

No. 1339: a, Aung San Suu Kyi, Peace, 1991. b, Milton Friedman, Economics, 1976. c, Marie Curie, Chemistry, 1911. d, Johannes Diderik van der Waals, Physics, 1910. e, Selma Lagerlöf, Literature, 1909. f, Gary S. Becker, Economics, 1992.

2006, June 26 *Perf. 12¾x13¼*

1339	Block of 6	8.50	8.50
a.	A327 20c multi	.25	.25
b.	A327 $1.20 multi	.85	.85
c.	A327 $1.70 multi	1.25	1.25
d.	A327 $2 multi	1.40	1.40
e.	A327 $3 multi	2.25	2.25
f.	A327 $3.50 multi	2.50	2.50

America Issue, Energy Conservation A328

Designs: 80c, Solar-powered airplane. $16.20, Windmill.
No. 1342: a, $3.50, Glider. b, $12.50, Windmills.

2006, Sept. 15 *Perf. 14*

1340-1341	A328	Set of 2	13.00	13.00

Souvenir Sheet

1342	A328	Sheet of 2, #a-b	12.00	12.00

Fish — A329

No. 1343: a, Crown betta. b, Barbus barilioides. c, Macropodus opercularis. d, Xiphophorus maculatus. e, Acanthurus lineatus. f, Carassius auratus.

2006, Oct. 15 *Perf. 13¼x12¾*

1343	Block of 6	15.00	15.00
a.	A329 $1.20 multi	1.00	1.00
b.	A329 $1.70 multi	1.25	1.25
c.	A329 $2 multi	1.50	1.50
d.	A329 $3 multi	2.25	2.25
e.	A329 $3.50 multi	2.50	2.50
f.	A329 $8.60 multi	6.25	6.25

Child Care — A330

Christmas A331

2006, Nov. 6 *Perf. 14*

1344	A330	$4 shown	3.00	3.00
1345	A331	$9.20 shown	6.75	6.75

Souvenir Sheet

1346	Sheet of 2	5.25	5.25
a.	A330 80c Children with ball	.60	.60
b.	A331 $6 Stained glass, diff.	4.25	4.25

No. 447 Surcharged in Brown

Methods and Perfs As Before

2006, Dec. 1

1347	A111 $3.25 on 1c #447	2.40	2.40
1348	A111 $3.75 on 1c #447	2.75	2.75

Primates — A332

No. 1349: a, Hylobates lar. b, Leontopithecus rosalia. c, Saguinus imperator. d, Callithrix geoffroyi. e, Callithrix argentata. f, Pygathrix nemaeus nemaeus. g, Saimiri sciureus. h, Douc langur. i, Cercopithecus neglectus. j, Alouatta caraya. k, Verreaux sitaka. l, Pan troglodytes.

2006, Dec. 13 *Perf. 12¾x13¼*

1349	Block of 12	24.00	24.00
a.	A332 R multi	.25	.25
b.	A332 20c multi	.25	.25
c.	A332 45c multi	.35	.35
d.	A332 80c multi	.60	.60
e.	A332 $1.20 multi	.90	.90
f.	A332 $1.70 multi	1.25	1.25
g.	A332 $2 multi	1.40	1.40
h.	A332 $3 multi	2.25	2.25
i.	A332 $3.50 multi	2.50	2.50
j.	A332 $4 multi	3.00	3.00
k.	A332 $5 multi	3.75	3.75
l.	A332 $10 multi	7.25	7.25

No. 1349a sold for 15c on day of issue.

Bird Type of 2004

$10, Phaethornis superciliosus.

2006, Dec. 20 *Perf. 12¾x14*

1350	A316 $10 multi	7.50	7.50

Printed in sheets of 2 + label.

Orchids — A333

No. 1351: a, Cattleya labiata. b, Vuylstekeara. c, Cymbidium. d, Odontoglossum pestcatorei. e, Odontocidium f, Odontioda. g, Vanda. h, Cattleya. i, Paphiopedilum insigne. j, Phalaenopsis. k, Thunia. l, Oncidium.

2007, Jan. 3 *Perf. 12¾x13¼*

1351	Block of 12	24.00	24.00
a.	A333 S multi	.25	.25
b.	A333 20c multi	.25	.25
c.	A333 45c multi	.35	.35
d.	A333 80c multi	.60	.60
e.	A333 $1.20 multi	.90	.90
f.	A333 $1.70 multi	1.25	1.25
g.	A333 $2 multi	1.40	1.40
h.	A333 $3 multi	2.25	2.25
i.	A333 $3.50 multi	2.50	2.50
j.	A333 $4 multi	3.00	3.00
k.	A333 $5 multi	3.75	3.75
l.	A333 $10 multi	7.25	7.25

No. 1351a sold for 10c on day of issue.

Butterflies A334

No. 1352: a, Great spangled fritillary. b, Peacock pansy. c, Viceroy. d, Unidentified taxco. e, Tropical buckeye. f, Limenitis popul.

2007, Feb. 14 *Perf. 14*

1352	Block of 6	9.00	9.00
a.	A334 T multi	.25	.25
b.	A334 $1.20 multi	.85	.85
c.	A334 $1.70 multi	1.25	1.25
d.	A334 $2 multi	1.40	1.40
e.	A334 $3 multi	2.25	2.25
f.	A334 $4 multi	3.00	3.00

No. 1352a sold for 5c on day of issue.
See No. 1366.

Reptiles A335

No. 1353: a, Terapene carolina. b, Cuora flavomarginata. c, Chelonia mydas. d, Testudo hermanni. e, Uromastyx acanthinura. f, Physignathus cocincinus. g, Iguana iguana. h, Amblyrhynchus cristatus. i, Chamaeleo jacksoni. j, Crocodylus niloticus. k, Caiman crocodilus. l, Varanus komodensis.

Perf. 13¼x12¾

2007, Mar. 21 Litho.

1353	Block of 12	24.00	24.00
a.	A335 S multi	.25	.25
b.	A335 20c multi	.25	.25
c.	A335 45c multi	.30	.30
d.	A335 80c multi	.60	.60
e.	A335 $1.20 multi	.90	.90
f.	A335 $1.70 multi	1.25	1.25
g.	A335 $2 multi	1.50	1.50
h.	A335 $3 multi	2.25	2.25
i.	A335 $3.50 multi	2.60	2.60
j.	A335 $4 multi	3.00	3.00
k.	A335 $5 multi	3.75	3.75
l.	A335 $10 multi	7.25	7.25

No. 1353a sold for 10c on day of issue.

Parrots — A336

No. 1354: a, Callocephalon fimbriatum. b, Cacatua ophthalmica. c, Cacatua galerita. d, Cacatua sulphure amazone. e, Calyporhychus magunificus. f, Cacatua sulphure amazone, diff. g, Eolophus rosicapillus. h, Cacatua sulphure amazone, diff. i, Parrot (inscribed "Pan troglodytes" in error).

2007, Apr. 26 *Perf. 14*

1354	Block of 9	11.50	11.50
a.	A336 T multi	.25	.25
b.	A336 25c multi	.25	.25
c.	A336 55c multi	.40	.40
d.	A336 80c multi	.60	.60
e.	A336 $1.10 multi	.80	.80
f.	A336 $1.20 multi	.90	.90
g.	A336 $2 multi	1.50	1.50
h.	A336 $4 multi	3.00	3.00
i.	A336 $5 multi	3.75	3.75

No. 1354a sold for 5c on day of issue.

Birds — A337

No. 1355: a, Agamia agami. b, Botaurus pinnatus. c, Rallus maculatus. d, Melanerpes cruentatus. e, Piculus chrysochloros. f, Paroaria gularis. g, Gyanicterus cyanicterus. h, Tersina viridis. i, Sicalis floreola.

2007, May 23 *Perf. 12¾x13¼*

1355	Block of 9	18.00	18.00
a.	A337 T multi	.25	.25
b.	A337 20c multi	.25	.25
c.	A337 45c multi	.35	.35
d.	A337 80c multi	.60	.60
e.	A337 $1.20 multi	.90	.90
f.	A337 $2 multi	1.50	1.50
g.	A337 $4 multi	3.00	3.00
h.	A337 $5 multi	3.75	3.75
i.	A337 $10 multi	7.25	7.25

No. 1355a sold for 5c on day of issue.
See Nos. 1373, 1388.

Fish — A338

No. 1356: a, Brachydanio rerio. b, Pterois miles. c, Pomacanthus annularis. d, Balsitoides conspicillum. e, Plectorhynchus orientalis. f, Chaetodon auriga.

Perf. 13¼x12¾

2007, June 27 Litho.

1356	Block of 6	15.00	15.00
a.	A338 $1.20 multi	.90	.90
b.	A338 $1.70 multi	1.25	1.25
c.	A338 $2 multi	1.50	1.50
d.	A338 $3 multi	2.25	2.25
e.	A338 $3.50 multi	2.60	2.60
f.	A338 $8.60 multi	6.25	6.25

Ferrari Automobiles A339

No. 1357: a, 1947 125 S. b, 1962 250 GTO. c, 1984 GTO. d, 1999 F399. e, 1983 Mondial Cabriolet. f, 1994 F 333 SP. g, 1971 365 GT4 BB. h, 2006 FXX.

2007, July 11 *Perf. 14*

1357	Block of 8 + label	9.75	9.75
a.	A339 10c multi	.25	.25
b.	A339 20c multi	.25	.25
c.	A339 50c multi	.35	.35
d.	A339 $1 multi	.75	.75
e.	A339 $1.60 multi	1.10	1.10
f.	A339 $1.75 multi	1.25	1.25
g.	A339 $3 multi	2.25	2.25
h.	A339 $5 multi	3.50	3.50

No. 1357 was issued in sheets containing two blocks, one of which had the label in the lower right corner, and the other with the label in the upper left corner.

Primates — A340

No. 1358: a, Pan troglodytes. b, Cercopithecus neglectus. c, Nasalis larvatus. d, Macaca fascicularis. e, Mandrillus sphinx. f, Rhinopithecus roxellana.

2007, Aug. 15 Litho. *Perf. 14*

1358	Block of 6	15.00	15.00
a.	A340 $1.20 multi	.90	.90
b.	A340 $1.70 multi	1.25	1.25
c.	A340 $2 multi	1.50	1.50
d.	A340 $3 multi	2.25	2.25
e.	A340 $3.50 multi	2.60	2.60
f.	A340 $8.60 multi	6.25	6.25

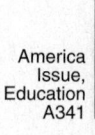

America Issue, Education A341

Designs: 80c, Children in classroom. $16.20, Children in classroom, diff.

No. 1361: a, $7, Boy at blackboard. b, $9, Two children.

2007, Sept. 19

1359-1360	A341	Set of 2	12.50	12.50

Souvenir Sheet

1361	A341	Sheet of 2, #a-b	12.00	12.00

Christmas — A342

Designs: $4, Four children at desks. $6, Holy Family.

No. 1364: a, 80c, Children, words and letters. b, $9.20, Holy Family, sheep.

2007, Nov. 7

1362-1363	A342	Set of 2	7.25	7.25

Souvenir Sheet

1364	A342	Sheet of 2, #a-b	7.25	7.25

Frogs A343

No. 1365: a, Agalychnis callidryas. b, Dendrobates pumilio. c, Sphaeramia nematoptera. d, Hoffmanni. e, Sphaeramia nematoptera, diff. f, Dendrobates histrionicus.

2007, Dec. 12 Litho. *Perf. 14x12¾*

1365	Block of 6	11.00	11.00
a.	A343 T multi	.25	.25
b.	A343 $1.20 multi	.85	.85
c.	A343 $1.70 multi	1.25	1.25
d.	A343 $2 multi	1.40	1.40
e.	A343 $3 multi	2.25	2.25
f.	A343 $7 multi	5.00	5.00

On day of issue, No. 1365a sold for 5c.

Butterflies Type of 2007

No. 1366: a, Anthocharis bella. b, Satyr angelwing. c, Red lacewing. d, Inachis io. e, Purple sapphire. f, Pearly crescentspot. g, Monarch. h, Marpesia berania. i, Darkmuseum swallowtail. j, Byasa alcinous. k, Brown peacock. l, Brown and orange Mexican.

2008, Jan. 2 Litho. *Perf. 14*

1366	Block of 12	24.00	24.00
a.	A334 T multi	.25	.25
b.	A334 25c multi	.25	.25
c.	A334 45c multi	.30	.30
d.	A334 80c multi	.60	.60
e.	A334 $1.20 multi	.90	.90
f.	A334 $1.70 multi	1.25	1.25
g.	A334 $2 multi	1.50	1.50
h.	A334 $3 multi	2.25	2.25
i.	A334 $3.50 multi	2.60	2.60
j.	A334 $4 multi	3.00	3.00
k.	A334 $5 multi	3.75	3.75
l.	A334 $10 multi	7.25	7.25

No. 1366a sold for 5c on day of issue.

Fish — A344

No. 1367: a, Sphaeramia nematoptera. b, Neophrynichthys latus. c, Cheilodipterus isostigmus.

2008, Feb. 13

1367 A344	Horiz. strip of 3	8.75	8.75
a.	$1.20 multi	.90	.90
b.	$3 multi	2.25	2.25
c.	$7.80 multi	5.50	5.50

Children in Native Costumes — A345

Children in various costumes.

2008, Mar. 19 Litho. *Perf. 14*

1368 A345	Block of 12	24.00	24.00
a.	T multi	.25	.25
b.	25c multi	.25	.25
c.	45c multi	.35	.35
d.	80c multi	.60	.60
e.	$1.20 multi	.90	.90
f.	$1.70 multi	1.25	1.25
g.	$2 multi	1.50	1.50
h.	$3 multi	2.25	2.25
i.	$3.50 multi	2.60	2.60
j.	$4 multi	3.00	3.00
k.	$5 multi	3.75	3.75
l.	$10 multi	7.25	7.25

No. 1368a sold for 5c on day of issue.

2008 Summer Olympics, Beijing — A346

No. 1369: a, Archery. b, Weight lifting. c, Basketball. d, Runner crossing finish line.

2008, Apr. 9 Litho. *Perf. 14*

1369	Horiz. strip of 4	5.25	5.25
a.	A346 $1 multi	.75	.75
b	A346 $1.50 multi	1.10	1.10
c.	A346 $2 multi	1.50	1.50
d.	A346 $2.50 multi	1.90	1.90

Stamp Passion Philatelic Exhibition, the Netherlands A347

No. 1370: a, Netherlands #104. b, Surinam #120. c, Netherlands #43. d, Netherlands #103. e, Netherlands #B85. f, Netherlands #C9. g, Netherlands #J27. h, Netherlands #O25. i, Surinam #B10. j, Surinam #C14. k, Netherlands #160. l, Netherlands #96.

2008, Apr. 9 Litho. *Perf. 14*

1370	Block of 12	37.50	37.50
a.	A347 $1 multi	.75	.75
b.	A347 $1.50 multi	1.10	1.10
c.	A347 $2 multi	1.50	1.50
d.	A347 $2.50 multi	1.90	1.90
e.	A347 $3 multi	2.25	2.25
f.	A347 $3.50 multi	2.60	2.60
g.	A347 $4 multi	3.00	3.00
h.	A347 $5 multi	3.75	3.75
i.	A347 $5.50 multi	4.00	4.00
j.	A347 $6 multi	4.50	4.50
k.	A347 $7 multi	5.25	5.25
l.	A347 $9 multi	6.75	6.75

Images of some stamps are distorted.

Buildings — A348

No. 1371: a, F.H.R. Lim A Postraat 34A. b, Combékerk. c, Waterkant 10. d, Waterkant 14. e, Waterkant 12. f, Officierswoning 6. g, Grote Combéweg 33. h, Officierswoning 5. i, Officierswoning 9.

2008, Apr. 23

1371	Block of 9	16.50	16.50
a.	A348 V multi	.25	.25
b.	A348 40c multi	.30	.30
c.	A348 50c multi	.35	.35
d.	A348 80c multi	.60	.60
e.	A348 $1.20 multi	.90	.90
f.	A348 $2 multi	1.50	1.50
g.	A348 $4 multi	3.00	3.00
h.	A348 $5 multi	3.75	3.75
i.	A348 $8 multi	5.75	5.75

No. 1371a sold for 15c on day of issue.

Snakes A349

No. 1372: a, Candoia carinata. b, Viper. c, Yellow Chondropython viridis. d, Red juvenile Chondropython viridis. e, Eyelash viper. f, Green mamba. g, Emerald tree boa. h, Tiger rat snake.

2008, May 21

1372	Block of 8 + label	33.00	33.00
a.	A349 $1 multi	.75	.75
b.	A349 $1.50 multi	1.10	1.10
c.	A349 $2 multi	1.50	1.50
d.	A349 $3 multi	2.25	2.25
e.	A349 $5 multi	3.75	3.75
f.	A349 $7.50 multi	5.25	5.25
g.	A349 $10 multi	7.25	7.25
h.	A349 $15 multi	11.00	11.00

Bird Type of 2007

No. 1373: a, Ceryle torquata. b, Tangara velia. c, Florisuga mellivora. d, Psarocollus viridis. e, Pionus fuscus. f, Chloroceryle aenea. g, Caryothraustes canadensis. h, Campephilus rubricollis.

Perf. 13¼x13¾

2008, Aug. 15 **Litho.**

Size: 16x21mm

1373 Horiz. strip of 8 8.00 8.00
a. A337 30c multi .25 .25
b. A337 45c multi .30 .30
c. A337 50c multi .35 .35
d. A337 75c multi .55 .55
e. A337 90c multi .65 .65
f. A337 $1.40 multi 1.00 1.00
g. A337 $2.50 multi 1.90 1.90
h. A337 $4 multi 3.00 3.00
i. Souvenir sheet, 2 each #1373e, 1373f + central label 6.75 6.75

America Issue, Festivals — A350

No. 1374: a, Two Carifesta participants. b, Surinam flag at Carifesta.
No. 1375: a, $7, Woman in Carnaval costume. b, $15, Woman wearing Carnaval hat.

2008, Sept. 17 **Litho.** ***Perf. 14***

1374 A350 Horiz. pair + central label 16.00 16.00
a. $9 multi 6.75 6.75
b. $12.50 multi 9.25 9.25

Souvenir Sheet

1375 A350 Sheet of 2, #a-b 16.50 16.50

Birds — A351

No. 1376: a, Ceryle rudis. b, Copsychus saularis. c, Dicaeum cruetatum. d, Garrulax perspicillatus. e, Halcyon smyrnensis. f, Leiothrix lutea.

2008, Oct. 15

1376 Block of 6 11.50 11.50
a. A351 V multi .25 .25
b. A351 $1.10 multi .80 .80
c. A351 $1.80 multi 1.40 1.40
d. A351 $3 multi 2.25 2.25
e. A351 $4 multi 3.00 3.00
f. A351 $5 multi 3.75 3.75

No. 1376a sold for 15c on day of issue. Bird names are misspelled on Nos. 1376c and 1376e.

Children and Adults — A352

No. 1377: a, Woman swinging girl by arms. b, Boy in soap box derby car.
No. 1378: a, $5, Woman and girl with cut flowers. b, $7, Woman and girl painting birdhouse.

2008, Nov. 5

1377 A352 Horiz. pair + central label 9.00 9.00
a. 80c multi .60 .60
b. $11.20 multi 8.25 8.25

Souvenir Sheet

1378 A352 Sheet of 2, #a-b 9.00 9.00

Flowers — A353

No. 1379: a, Ixora Nora Grant White. b, Ixora Bonnie Lynn. c, Ixora coccinea. d, Ixora Dwarf Pink. e, Ixora Dwarf Orange. f, Ixora Maui Pink

2008, Dec. 10

1379 Block of 6 15.00 15.00
a. A353 $1.10 multi .80 .80
b. A353 $1.80 multi 1.40 1.40
c. A353 $2 multi 1.50 1.50
d. A353 $3 multi 2.25 2.25
e. A353 X multi 3.75 3.75
f. A353 $7 multi 5.25 5.25

No. 1379e sold for $5.10 on day of issue.

Souvenir Sheet

Streptopelia Orientalis — A354

2009, Jan. 7 **Litho.** ***Perf. 14***

1380 A354 $9.50 multi 7.00 7.00

Frogs — A355

Designs: $1, Ceratophrys cornuta. $2, Bufo marinus. $2.50, Eleutherodactylus counouspeus. $3.50, Gastrotheca monticola. $5, Leptodactylus pentadactylus. $6, Pipa pipa. $7, Pseudis paradoxa.

2009, Feb. 15 **Litho.** ***Perf. 14***

1381-1387 A355 Set of 7 20.00 20.00

Nos. 1381-1387 were printed in a sheet containing 2 of each stamp + a central label.

Birds Type of 2007

No. 1388: a, Tinamus major. b, Crypturellus erythropus. c, Crypturellus variegatus. d, Crypturellus cinereus. e, Aburria pipile. f, Bucco capensis. g, Crypturellus soui. h, Ortalis motmot. i, Penelope marail. j, Chelidoptera tenebrosa.

2009, Mar. 18 **Litho.** ***Perf. 14***

1388 Block of 10 33.00 33.00
a. A337 Z multi .90 .90
b. A337 $1.50 multi 1.10 1.10
c. A337 $2.50 multi 1.75 1.75
d. A337 $3 multi 2.25 2.25
e. A337 $3.50 multi 2.50 2.50
f. A337 $4 multi 3.00 3.00
g. A337 $5 multi 3.50 3.50
h. A337 $5.50 multi 4.00 4.00
i. A337 $7 multi 5.25 5.25
j. A337 $12 multi 8.75 8.75

No. 1388a sold for $1.25 on day of issue.

Electricity, 200th Anniv. — A356

No. 1389: a, Sir Humphry Davy (1778-1829), chemist. b, Diagram of light bulb. c, Thomas Alva Edison (1847-1931), inventor.

2009, Mar. 21 **Litho.** ***Perf. 14***

1389 Vert. strip of 3 11.00 11.00
a. A356 $2 blk & red 1.50 1.50
b. A356 $5 blk & red 3.75 3.75
c. A356 $8 blk & red 5.75 5.75

Mailboxes From Around the World — A357

2009, May 27 **Litho.** ***Perf. 14***

1390 Block of 10 29.00 29.00
a. A357 Z Argentina .90 .90
b. A357 $2 Canada 1.50 1.50
c. A357 $2.50 China 1.75 1.75
d. A357 $3 India 2.25 2.25
e. A357 $3.25 Ireland 2.40 2.40
f. A357 $3.75 Russia 2.75 2.75
g. A357 $5 Turkey 3.50 3.50
h. A357 $5.50 Venezuela 4.00 4.00
i. A357 $6.50 Yemen 4.50 4.50
j. A357 $7 Great Britain 5.25 5.25

No. 1390a sold for $1.25 on day of issue.

Fish — A358

No. 1391: a, Cephalopholis miniata. b, Epinephelus fasciatus. c, Pomacanthus xanthocephalus. d, Anampses meleagrides. e, Chaetodon bennetti. f, Cephalopholis argus. g, Chaetodon xanthocephalus. h, Scarus frenatus. i, Priacanthus hamrur. j, Cephalopholis polieni. k, Pomacanthus semicirculatus. l, Ostracion cubicus.

2009, July 8

1391 Block of 12 33.50 33.50
a. A358 Z multi .90 .90
b. A358 $1.25 multi .90 .90
c. A358 $1.50 multi 1.10 1.10
d. A358 $2 multi 1.50 1.50
e. A358 $2.50 multi 1.75 1.75
f. A358 $3 multi 2.25 2.25
g. A358 $3.50 multi 2.50 2.50
h. A358 $4 multi 3.00 3.00
i. A358 $5.75 multi 4.25 4.25
j. A358 $6 multi 4.50 4.50
k. A358 $7 multi 5.25 5.25
l. A358 $7.50 multi 5.50 5.50

No. 1391a sold for $1.25 on day of issue.

Children at Play — A359

No. 1392: a, $8, Knikkeren (marbles). b, $15, Hoepelen (hoop rolling).
No. 1393: a, $10, Hoelahoep (hula hoop). b, $12, Vijfsteentje (five girls in circle).

2009, Sept. 16

1392 A359 Horiz. pair, #a-b 17.00 17.00

Souvenir Sheet

1393 A359 Sheet of 2, #a-b 16.00 16.00

Miniature Sheet

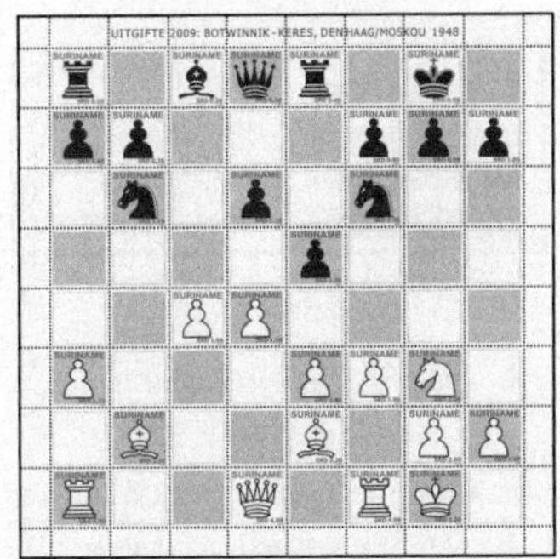

Chess Board — A360

No. 1394: a, 10c, Black rook. b, 20c, Black bishop. c, 30c, Black queen. d, 40c, Black rook. e, 50c, Black king. f, 60c, Black pawn. g, 70c, Black pawn. h, 80c, Black pawn. i, 90c, Black pawn. j, $1, Black pawn. k, $1.10, Black knight. l, $1.20, Black pawn. m, $1.30, Black knight. n, $1.40, Black pawn. o, $1.50, White pawn. p, $1.60, White pawn. q, $1.70, White pawn. r, $1.80, White pawn. s, $1.90, White pawn. t, $2, White knight. u, $2.10, White bishop. v, $2.20, White bishop. w, $2.50, White pawn. x, $3, White pawn. y, $4.50, White rook. z, $4.80, White queen. aa, $4.90, White rook. ab, $5, White king.

2009, Oct. 21 **Litho.** ***Perf. 14***

1394 A360 Sheet of 28, #a-ab, + 36 labels 37.00 37.00

No. 1394 shows position of pieces of 1948 match between Paul Keres and Mikhail Botvinnik. Compare with No. 1428.

Endangered Primates — A361

No. 1395: a, $1, Aotus trivirgatus. b, $1.50, Alouatta palliata. c, $2, Cacajao calvus. d, $2.50, Lagothrix lagotricha. e, $3, Pithecia pithecia. f, $5, Callithrix mauesi. g, $7, Alouatta seniculus. h, $8, Gorilla. i, $9, Cercopithecus diana.

2009, Nov. 4

1395 A361 Block of 9, #a-i 29.00 29.00

Flowers — A362

No. 1396: a, Pulsatilla vernalis. b, Crisanthemum maximum. c, Abronia villosa. d, Aquilegia caerulea. e, Zinnia elegans. f, Bougainvillea glabra. g, Daffodil. h, Victoria cruziana. i, Rosa palustris. j, Nymphaea.

2009, Dec. 9 ***Perf. 14***

1396 Block of 10 30.00 30.00
a. A362 Z multi .90 .90
b. A362 $2 multi 1.50 1.50
c. A362 $2.50 multi 1.90 1.90
d. A362 $3 multi 2.25 2.25
e. A362 $3.25 multi 2.40 2.40
f. A362 $3.75 multi 2.75 2.75
g. A362 $5 multi 3.75 3.75
h. A362 $5.50 multi 4.00 4.00
i. A362 $6.50 multi 4.75 4.75
j. A362 $7 multi 5.25 5.25

No. 1396a sold for $1.25 on day of issue.

Miniature Sheet

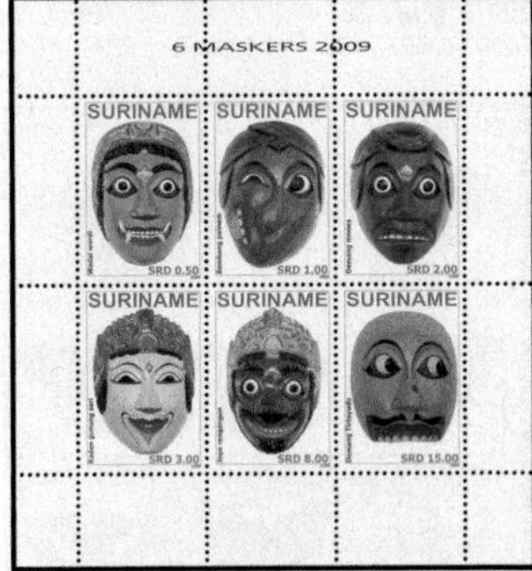

Masks — A363

No. 1397: a, 50c, Wadal werdi. b, $1, Bambang painem. c, $2, Demang mones. d, $3, Raden gunung sari. e, $8, Joyo rengangon. f, $15, Demang tirtoyudo.

2009, Dec. 30 ***Perf. 12¾x13¼***

1397 A363 Sheet of 6, #a-f 22.00 22.00

Shells — A364

No. 1398: a, Cardita megastropha. b, Frangum unedo. c, Galeodea echinophora. d, Architectonica maxima. e, Opeatostoma pseudodon. f, Haliotis queketti. g, Cymatium hepaticum. h, Clanculus pharaonius. i, Harpa harpa. j, Hydatina nobilis.

2010, Jan. 20 ***Perf. 14***

1398	Block of 10	30.00	30.00
a.	A364 $1 multi	.75	.75
b.	A364 $1.50 multi	1.10	1.10
c.	A364 $2 multi	1.50	1.50
d.	A364 $2.50 multi	1.90	1.90
e.	A364 $3 multi	2.25	2.25
f.	A364 $4 multi	3.00	3.00
g.	A364 $5 multi	3.75	3.75
h.	A364 $6 multi	4.50	4.50
i.	A364 $7 multi	5.25	5.25
j.	A364 $8 multi	6.00	6.00

No. 1398 was printed in a sheet containing two irregular blocks of 10 + a central label.

Souvenir Sheet

Mushrooms — A365

No. 1399: a, $2, Amanita muscaria. b, $5, Boletus edulis. c, $8, Agaricus xanthoderma.

2010, Feb. 24 ***Perf. 13¼x12¾***

1399 A365 Sheet of 3, #a-c 11.00 11.00

Cuckoo Clocks A366

No. 1400 — Clock from: a, $1.50, 1760. b, $2.50, 1890. c, $3.50, 1900. d, $4.50, 1910. e, $5, 1920. f, $8, 1950.

2010, Mar. 25 ***Perf. 14***

1400 A366 Block of 6, #a-f 18.50 18.50

Butterflies — A367

No. 1401: a, Maniola jurtina. b, Melanargia galathea. c, Argynnis adippe. d, Apatura iris. e, Lasiommata megera. f, Pararge aegeria. g, Argynnis paphia. h, Vanessa atalanta. i, Limenitis camilla. j, Polyommatus bellargus. k, Argynnis aglaja. l, Pyronia tithonus.

$12, Apatura ilia, horiz.

2010, Apr. 28

1401	A367 Block of 12	32.00	32.00
a.	70c multi	.50	.50
b.	$1.25 multi	.90	.90
c.	$1.75 multi	1.25	1.25
d.	$2.50 multi	1.90	1.90
e.	$2.75 multi	2.00	2.00
f.	$3 multi	2.25	2.25
g.	$3.75 multi	2.75	2.75
h.	$4.25 multi	3.00	3.00
i.	$4.50 multi	3.25	3.25
j.	$5 multi	3.75	3.75
k.	$6 multi	4.50	4.50
l.	$7 multi	5.25	5.25

Souvenir Sheet

Perf. 13¼x12¾

1402 A367 $12 multi 8.75 8.75

No. 1402 contains one 34x23mm stamp.

Birds — A368

No. 1403: a, Tangara chilensis. b, Leptopogon amaurocephalus. c, Xolmis cinerea. d, Tangara cayana. e, Conopophaga aurita. f, Megarhynchus pitangua. g, Tangara mexicana. h, Picumnus exilis. i, Hirundinea ferruginea. j, Galbula albirostris. k, Tyrannopsis sulphurea. l, Tangara varia.

2010, May 26 ***Perf. 14***

1403	Block of 12	37.00	37.00
a.	A368 50c multi	.35	.35
b.	A368 $1 multi	.75	.75
c.	A368 $1.50 multi	1.10	1.10
d.	A368 $2 multi	1.50	1.50
e.	A368 $2.50 multi	1.90	1.90
f.	A368 $3 multi	2.25	2.25
g.	A368 $3.50 multi	2.60	2.60
h.	A368 $4 multi	3.00	3.00
i.	A368 $5 multi	3.75	3.75
j.	A368 $7 multi	5.25	5.25
k.	A368 $9 multi	6.50	6.50
l.	A368 $11 multi	8.00	8.00

Orchids A369

No. 1404: a, Laeliocattleya. b, Coelogyne mooreana. c, Phalaenopsis. d, Calanthe. e, Maxillaria fucata. f, Cymbidium erythrostylum. g, Cymbidium beaumont. h, Cattleya portia. i, Miltoniopsis portelet. j, Sophrolaeliacattleya marion. k, Dendrobium thwaitesii. l, Ascocenda vernon.

2010, July 7

1404	Block of 12	34.00	34.00
a.	A369 A multi	.35	.35
b.	A369 55c multi	.40	.40
c.	A369 $1 multi	.75	.75
d.	A369 $1.50 multi	1.10	1.10
e.	A369 $2 multi	1.50	1.50
f.	A369 $2.50 multi	1.90	1.90
g.	A369 $3 multi	2.25	2.25
h.	A369 $4.50 multi	3.25	3.25
i.	A369 $5 multi	3.75	3.75
j.	A369 $6.50 multi	4.75	4.75
k.	A369 $7 multi	5.25	5.25
l.	A369 $11 multi	8.00	8.00

No. 1404a sold for 45c on day of issue.

America Issue, National Symbols — A370

No. 1406: a, $11, Presidential Palace. b, $13, National anthem.

2010, Sept. 15

1405	A370 Horiz. pair	20.50	20.50
a.	$13 National flag	9.50	9.50
b.	$15 National arms	11.00	11.00

Souvenir Sheet

1406 A370 Sheet of 2, #a-b 17.50 17.50

Primates — A371

No. 1407: a, A, Theropithecus gelada. b, 55c, Gorilla beringei. c, $1, Cercopithecus nictitans. d, $1.50, Microcebus myoxinus. e, $2, Macaca silenus. f, $2.50, Lemur catta. g, $3, Propithecus verrauxi. h, $4, Galago crassicaudatus. i, $4.50, Cacajao melanocephalus. j, $5, Pan paniscus. k, $6.50, Lagothrix cana. l, $9, Capucinus albifrons.

2010, Oct. 20 Litho. ***Perf. 12¾x13¼***

1407 A371 Block of 12, #a-l 29.00 29.00

No. 1407a sold for 45c on day of issue.

Fish — A372

No. 1408: a, Amphiprion ocellaris. b, Pomacentrus caeruleus. c, Barbus tetrazona. d, Betta smaragdina. e, Calisa lalia. f, Geophagus brasiliensis. g, Astronotus ocellatus. h, Microgeophagus ramirezi.

2010, Dec. 1 Litho. ***Perf. 13¼x12¾***

1408	Block of 8	33.00	33.00
a.	A372 A multi	.35	.35
b.	A372 $1.55 multi	1.10	1.10
c.	A372 $3 multi	2.25	2.25
d.	A372 $5 multi	3.75	3.75
e.	A372 $7 multi	5.25	5.25
f.	A372 $8 multi	5.75	5.75
g.	A372 $9 multi	6.50	6.50
h.	A372 $11 multi	8.00	8.00

No. 1408a sold for 45c on day of issue.

Masks — A373

No. 1409: a, Begawan wiro sekti. b, Dewi kilisuci. c, Kartolo. d, Bilung. e, Panji amerdadu. f, Betara kalla.

2010, Dec. 29 ***Perf. 14***

1409	Block of 6	22.00	22.00
a.	A373 50c multi	.35	.35
b.	A373 $1.50 multi	1.10	1.10
c.	A373 $3.50 multi	2.60	2.60
d.	A373 $6 multi	4.50	4.50
e.	A373 $8 multi	5.75	5.75
f.	A373 $10 multi	7.25	7.25

Shells A374

Designs: 50c, Tonicella lineata. $1, Chione paphia. $3.50, Callanaitis disjecta. $5, Angaria tyria. $8, Epitonium pallasi. $9, Strombus pipus. $13, Haliotis marmorata.

2011, Jan. 19 ***Perf. 13¼x12¾***

1410-1416 A374 Set of 7 29.00 29.00

Nos. 1410-1416 were printed in a sheet containing 2 of each stamp + a central label.

Mushrooms — A375

No. 1417: a, $8, Russula paludosa. b, $10, Phaeolepiota aurea.

2011, Feb. 16 ***Perf. 14***

1417 A375 Horiz. pair, #a-b 11.00 11.00

No. 1417 was printed in sheets containing two pairs + two labels.

Postal Union of the Americas, Spain and Portugal (UPAEP), Cent. — A376

No. 1418 — Arc of circles containing flags of member nations: a, $5. b, $7. c, $9. d, $11.

2011, Mar. 16

1418 A376 Block of 4, #a-d 19.50 19.50

Maastricht Paper Money Fair — A377

No. 1419: a, Malaysia 100-ringit note. b, Vanuatu 500-vatu note. c, Nepal 500-rupee note. d, Samoa 20-tala note. e, Oman 1-rial note. f, French Polynesia 10,000-franc note. g, Gibraltar 1-pound note. h, Bhutan 1-ngultrum note. i, Tonga 5-pa'anga note. j, Argentina 1,000,000-peso note. k, Surinam #751. l, Iceland 5000-kronur note.

2011, Apr. 4 ***Perf. 13½x12¾***

1419	Block of 12	31.00	31.00
a.	A377 A multi	.30	.30
b.	A377 55c multi	.35	.35
c.	A377 $1 multi	.60	.60
d.	A377 $2.50 multi	1.50	1.50
e.	A377 $3 multi	1.90	1.90
f.	A377 $3.50 multi	2.10	2.10
g.	A377 $4 multi	2.50	2.50
h.	A377 $5 multi	3.00	3.00
i.	A377 $6 multi	3.75	3.75
j.	A377 $7 multi	4.25	4.25
k.	A377 $8 multi	5.00	5.00
l.	A377 $9 multi	5.50	5.50

No. 1419a sold for 45c on day of issue.

Peonies — A378

No. 1420: a, Red peony, denomination at LR reading across. b, White peony, denomination at LL reading across. c, Pink peonies, denomination at LL reading up. d, Red and white peonies, denomination at LR reading down.

$7, Pink peony.

2011, Apr. 20 ***Perf. 14***

1420 A378 $2 Sheet of 4, #a-d 5.00 5.00

Souvenir Sheet

1421 A378 $7 multi 4.25 4.25

Birds — A379

No. 1422: a, Suiriri suiriri. b, Pitangus sulphuratus. c, Pipra serena. d, Schiffornis turdinus. e, Euphonia violacea. f, Ochthoeca littoralis. g, Amazona farinosa. h, Anthracothorax nigricollis. i, Psophia crepitans. j, Euphonia plumbea. k, Piprites chloris. l, Neopipo cinnamomea.

2011, May 25

1422		Block of 12	32.00	32.00
a.	A379	A multi	.30	.30
b.	A379	55c multi	.35	.35
c.	A379	$1 multi	.65	.65
d.	A379	$2.25 multi	1.40	1.40
e.	A379	$3.25 multi	2.00	2.00
f.	A379	$3.50 multi	2.25	2.25
g.	A379	$4.25 multi	2.75	2.75
h.	A379	$4.75 multi	3.00	3.00
i.	A379	$6 multi	3.75	3.75
j.	A379	$7 multi	4.50	4.50
k.	A379	$8 multi	5.00	5.00
l.	A379	$9 multi	5.50	5.50

Orchids — A380

No. 1423: a, Pink Phalaenopsis hybrid, bright green background. b, Dendrobium mousmee. c, Dendrobium densiflorum. d, Laelia purpurata. e, Encyclia vitellina. f, Miltoniopsis rozel. g, Yellow Cymbidium hybrid. h, Dendrobium hybrid. i, Ascocenda. j, Red Cymbidium hybrid. k, Laeliocattleya hybrid. l, Pink Phalaenopsis hybrid, olive green background.

2011, June 29

1423		Block of 12	26.00	26.00
a.	A380	A multi	.30	.30
b.	A380	55c multi	.35	.35
c.	A380	$1 multi	.65	.65
d.	A380	$1.50 multi	.95	.95
e.	A380	$2 multi	1.25	1.25
f.	A380	$2.50 multi	1.60	1.60
g.	A380	$3 multi	1.90	1.90
h.	A380	$4 multi	2.50	2.50
i.	A380	$4.50 multi	2.75	2.75
j.	A380	$5.50 multi	3.50	3.50
k.	A380	$7 multi	4.50	4.50
l.	A380	$8 multi	5.00	5.00

No. 1423a sold for 45c on day of issue.

Primates — A381

No. 1424: a, A, Papio hamadryas. b, $2.55, Saguinus oedipus. c, $4, Cebus apella. d, $6, Erythrocebus patas. e, $8, Macaca nemestrina. f, $9, Chlorocebus pygerythrus.

2011, Aug. 10 *Perf. 12¾x13¼*

1424 A381 Block of 6, #a-f 18.50 18.50

No. 1424a sold for 45c on day of issue.

Azaleas A382

No. 1425: a, Country name at UL, denomination adjacent to vignette. b, Country name adjacent to vignette, denomination at LR.

2011, Sept. 14 *Perf. 14¼x13¾*

1425 A382 $1.50 Vert. pair, #a-b 1.90 1.90

America Issue, Mailboxes — A383

No. 1426: a, $11, Mailbox on black pedestal near wall. b, $15, Rectangular mailbox.

No. 1427: a, $11, Mailbox on black pedestal. b, $13, Top of mailbox.

2011, Sept. 14 *Perf. 14*

1426 A383 Horiz. pair, #a-b 17.00 17.00

Souvenir Sheet

1427 A383 Sheet of 2, #a-b 15.00 15.00

Miniature Sheet

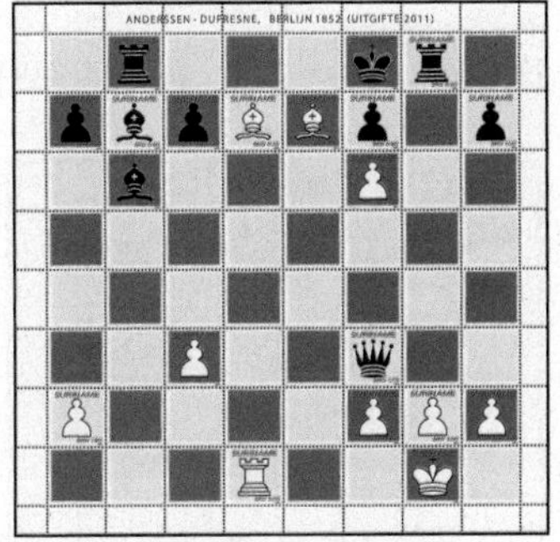
Chess Board — A384

No. 1428: a, 10c, Black rook. b, 20c, Black king. c, 30c, Black rook. d, 40c, Black pawn. e, 50c, Black bishop. f, 60c, Black pawn. g, 70c, White bishop. h, 80c, White bishop. i, 90c, Black pawn. j, $1, Black pawn. k, $1.20, Black bishop. l, $1.40, White pawn. m, $1.60, White pawn. n, $1.75, Black queen. o, $1.90, White pawn. p, $2.15, White pawn. q, $3, White pawn. r, $4.50, White pawn. s, $5, White rook. t, $6, White king.

2011, Oct. 26

1428 A384 Sheet of 20, #a-t, + 44 labels 21.00 21.00

No. 1428 shows position of pieces at end of 1852 match between Adolf Anderssen and Jean Dufresne. Compare with No. 1394.

Masks — A385

No. 1429: a, $1, Botu terong. b, $2, Demang mundu. c, $3, Emban dawala. d, $7, Jarodeh. e, $8, Kelono baron sakeber. f, $9, Maheso suro.

2011, Dec. 7 *Perf. 14*

1429 A385 Block of 6, #a-f 18.50 18.50

Butterflies A386

No. 1430: a. Memphis aureola. b, Delias bagoe. c, Ornithoptera tithonus. d, Ogyris genoveva gela. e, Parnassius apollo. f, Dismorphia cordillera. g, Bhutannitis mansfieldi. h, Anthene definita. i, Papilio demoleus. j, Parides orellana. k, Papilio pelaus atkinsi. l. Mellicta britomartis.

2012, Jan. 18

1430		Block of 12	32.00	32.00
a.	A386	B multi	.35	.35
b.	A386	75c multi	.45	.45
c.	A386	90c multi	.55	.55
d.	A386	$1.25 multi	.75	.75
e.	A386	$1.55 multi	.95	.95
f.	A386	$3.50 multi	2.25	2.25
g.	A386	$4.50 multi	2.75	2.75
h.	A386	$5 multi	3.25	3.25
i.	A386	$6 multi	3.75	3.75
j.	A386	$8 multi	5.00	5.00
k.	A386	$8.50 multi	5.25	5.25
l.	A386	$9.50 multi	6.00	6.00

No. 1430a sold for 55c on day of issue.

New Year 2012 (Year of the Dragon) — A387

No. 1431 — Dragon and flower: a, $2. b, $3.

2012, Jan. 25 *Perf. 13¾*

1431 A387 Pair, #a-b 3.25 3.25

No. 1431 printed in sheets containing 2 pairs.

Churches — A388

No. 1432: a, $1, Martin Luther Church. b, $3, Seventh Day Adventist Church Center. c, $5, Christian and Missionary Alliance Church of Surinam. d, $6, Interior of Saints Peter and Paul Cathedral. e, $7, Exterior of Saints Peter and Paul Cathedral, vert. f, $8, Steeple of Saints Peter and Paul Cathedral, vert.

2012, Feb. 15 *Perf. 14*

1432 A388 Block of 6, #a-f 18.50 18.50

Flowers A389

Designs: $1, Allamanda. $2, Anemone. $3, Amaryllis. $4, Wedelia. $5.50, Thunbergia. $7.50, Crossandra. $8, Dahlia. $9, Heliconia.

2012, Mar. 21

1433	A389	$1 multi	.60	.60
1434	A389	$2 multi	1.25	1.25
1435	A389	$3 multi	1.90	1.90
1436	A389	$4 multi	2.50	2.50
1437	A389	$5.50 multi	3.50	3.50
1438	A389	$7.50 multi	4.75	4.75
1439	A389	$8 multi	5.00	5.00
1440	A389	$9 multi	5.50	5.50
		Nos. 1433-1440 (8)	25.00	25.00

Nos. 1433-1440 were printed in sheets of 14 containing two of each stamp + 2 labels.

Birds — A390

No. 1441: a, Rostrhamus sociabilis. b, Thamnophilus murinus. c, Xiphorhynchus guttatus. d, Odontophorus gujanensis. e, Dryocopus lineatus. f, Bucco tamatia. g, Celeus undatus. h, Phaethornis longuemareus. i, Glaucis hirsuta. j, Elanus leucurus. k, Heliothryx aurita. l, Nonnula rubecula.

2012, May 23

1441		Block of 12	31.00	31.00
a.	A390	B multi	.35	.35
b.	A390	$1 multi	.65	.65
c.	A390	$1.45 multi	.90	.90
d.	A390	$2 multi	1.25	1.25
e.	A390	$2.50 multi	1.50	1.50
f.	A390	$3 multi	1.90	1.90
g.	A390	$3.50 multi	2.25	2.25
h.	A390	$4 multi	2.50	2.50
i.	A390	$5 multi	3.00	3.00
j.	A390	$7 multi	4.25	4.25
k.	A390	$9 multi	5.50	5.50
l.	A390	$11 multi	6.75	6.75

No. 1441a sold for 55c on day of issue.

Miniature Sheet

Fish — A391

No. 1442: a, $1, Crenimugil crenilabrus. b, $1.50, Myripristis vittata. c, $2, Neoniphon sammara. d, $3, Epinephelus ongus. e, $3.50, Plectropomus laevis. f, $4, Aphareus furca. g, $4.50, Sargocentron diadema. h, $5, Plectropomus areolatus. i, $7.50, Pterocaesio tile. j, $8, Lethrinus obsoletus.

2012, June 20

1442 A391 Sheet of 10, #a-j 25.00 25.00

2012 Summer Olympics, London A392

No. 1443: a, Badminton. b, Cycling. c, Diving. d, Equestrian. e, Gymnastics. f, Hammer throw. g, Javelin. h, Long jump. i, Relay race. j, Rowing. k, Swimming. l, Tennis.

No. 1444, vert.: a, Volleyball. b, Running. c, Hurdles.

2012, Aug. 15

1443		Block of 12	25.00	25.00
a.	A392	50c multi	.30	.30
b.	A392	$1 multi	.60	.60
c.	A392	$1.50 multi	.95	.95
d.	A392	$2 multi	1.25	1.25
e.	A392	$2.50 multi	1.50	1.50
f.	A392	$3 multi	1.90	1.90
g.	A392	$3.50 multi	2.25	2.25
h.	A392	$4 multi	2.50	2.50
i.	A392	$4.50 multi	2.75	2.75
j.	A392	$5 multi	3.25	3.25
k.	A392	$5.50 multi	3.50	3.50
l.	A392	$7 multi	4.25	4.25

Souvenir Sheet

1444		Sheet of 3	6.50	6.50
a.	A392	$2 multi	1.25	1.25
b.	A392	$3 multi	1.90	1.90
c.	A392	$5 multi	3.25	3.25

America Issue — A393

No. 1445: a, $13, Maluana. b, $15, Malohkoh.
No. 1446: a, $11, Maluana, diff. b, $13, Malohkoh, diff.

2012, Sept. 19

1445 A393 Horiz. pair, #a-b 17.00 17.00

Souvenir Sheet

1446 A393 Sheet of 2, #a-b 15.00 15.00

Lighthouses — A394

No. 1447: a, $1, Cabo Raper Lighthouse, Chile. b, $3, Punta Huacho Lighthouse, Peru. c, $5, Piedra Diamante Lighthouse, Argentina. d, $6, Manta Lighthouse, Ecuador. e, $7, Sao Joao Lighthouse, Brazil. f, $8, Santa Marta Lighthouse, Colombia.

2012, Oct. 24 ***Perf. 14***

1447 A394 Block of 6, #a-f 18.50 18.50

Masks — A395

No. 1448: a, $1.50, Brojonoto. b, $2.50, Kelono sewandono. c, $4, Dewi walang wati. d, $6, Panji amiluhur. e, $8, Panji banyaksasi. f, 10, Rasonto.

2012, Dec. 5 **Litho.**

1448 A395 Block of 6, #a-f 19.50 19.50

Butterflies A396

No. 1449: a, Graphium antheus. b, Atrophaneura luchti. c, Pandemos pasiphae.

2013, Jan. 13

1449	Sheet of 3	3.75 3.75
a.	A396 $1 multi	.60 .60
b.	A396 $2 multi	1.25 1.25
c.	A396 $3 multi	1.90 1.90

Birds — A397

No. 1450: a, Aratinga aurea. b, Polytmus guainumbi. c, Terenotriccus erythrurus. d, Synallaxis albescens. e, Zonotrichia capensis. f, Synallaxis macconnelli. g, Thraupis palmarum. h, Certhiaxis gutturata. i, Tapera naevia. j, Automolus rubiginosus. k, Euscarthmus rufomarginatus. l, Thraupis episcopus.

2013, Feb. 20

1450	Sheet of 12	34.00 34.00
a.	A397 B multi	.35 .35
b.	A397 $1.45 multi	.90 .90
c.	A397 $1.75 multi	1.10 1.10
d.	A397 $2.25 multi	1.40 1.40
e.	A397 $2.75 multi	1.75 1.75
f.	A397 $3.25 multi	2.00 2.00
g.	A397 $3.75 multi	2.25 2.25
h.	A397 $4.25 multi	2.60 2.60
i.	A397 $5.50 multi	3.50 3.50
j.	A397 $7.50 multi	4.50 4.50
k.	A397 $9.50 multi	5.75 5.75
l.	A397 $12.50 multi	7.75 7.75

No. 1450a sold for 55c on day of issue.

Miniature Sheet

Flowers — A398

No. 1451: a, B, Agapanthus africanus. b, $1.35, Anthurium andraeanum. c, $1.85, Aquilegia vulgaris. d, $2.25, Ferocactus wislizenii. e, $2.50, Crocus vernus. f, $3.50, Gazania rigens. g, $3.75, Leucospermum, h, $4.25, Saguaro cactus. i, $5.50, Sempervivum grandiflorum. j, $7.50, Telopea speciosissima. k, $10.50, Tulipa gesneriana. l, $11.50, Zantedeschia aethiopica.

2013, Mar. 13

1451 A398 Sheet of 12, #a-l 34.00 34.00

No. 1451a sold for 55c on day of issue.

Fish — A399

No. 1452: a, Cephalopholiss fulva. b, Epinephelus guttatus. c, Hypoplectrus puella. d, Hypoplectrus unicolor. e, Liopropoma carmabi. f, Serranus annularis. g, Serranus tabacarius. h, Petrometopon cruentatum. i, Mycteroperca venenosa. j, Serranus baldwini.

2013, May 15

1452	Sheet of 10	31.00 31.00
a.	A399 B multi	.30 .30
b.	A399 $1.45 multi	.85 .85
c.	A399 $2.50 multi	1.50 1.50
d.	A399 $3.50 multi	2.10 2.10
e.	A399 $4.50 multi	2.75 2.75
f.	A399 $5.50 multi	3.50 3.50
g.	A399 $6.50 multi	4.00 4.00
h.	A399 $7.50 multi	4.75 4.75
i.	A399 $8.50 multi	5.25 5.25
j.	A399 $9.50 multi	6.00 6.00

No. 1452a sold for 55c on day of issue.

Miniature Sheet

Thailand 2013 World Stamp Exhibition, Bangkok — A400

No. 1453: a, $2.50, Grand Palace, Bangkok. b, $4.50, Saints Peter and Paul Cathedral, Paramaribo. c, $5.50, Lophura diardi. d, $7.50, Ramphastos vitellinus. e, $9, Dendrobium. f, $11, Ixora.

2013, June 19

1453 A400 Sheet of 6, #a-f 25.00 25.00

Miniature Sheet

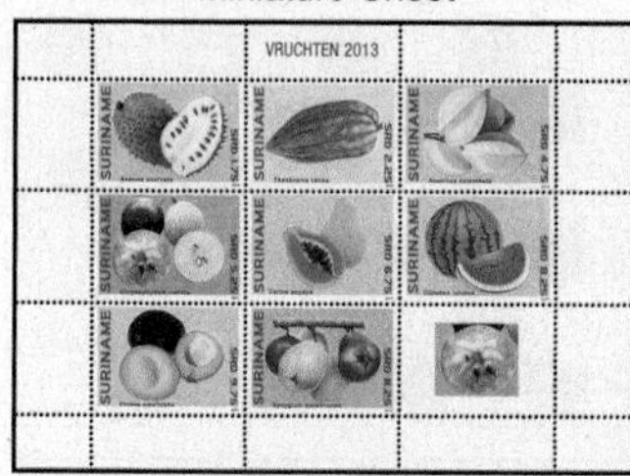

Fruit — A401

No. 1454: a, $1.75, Annona muricata. b, $2.25, Theobroma cacao. c, $4.75, Averrhoa carambola. d, $5.25, Chrysophyllum cainito. e, $6.75, Carica papaya. f, $8.25, Citrullus lanatus. g, $9.75, Persea americana. h, $11.25, Syzygium malaccense.

2013, Aug. 14 **Litho.** ***Perf. 14***

1454 A401 Sheet of 8, #a-h, + label 31.00 31.00

Souvenir Sheets

A402

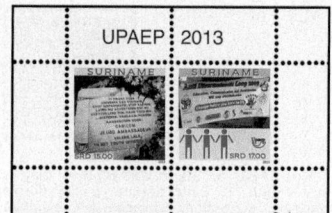

America Issue — A403

No. 1455: a, $13, Anti-discrimination marchers. b, $15, Anti-discriminiation poster with hand.
No. 1456: a, $15, Anti-discrimination monument and flowers. b, $17, Anti-discrimination parade banner.

2013, Sept. 18 **Litho.** ***Perf. 14***

1455 A402 Sheet of 2, #a-b 17.00 17.00
1456 A403 Sheet of 2, #a-b 19.50 19.50

Miniature Sheet

Monuments in Paramaribo — A404

No. 1457: a, $7, Mama Sranan Monument. b, $9, Statenmonument. c, $11, Helstone Mounument. d, $13, Monument to the Fallen.

2013, Oct. 23 **Litho.** ***Perf. 14***

1457 A404 Sheet of 4, #a-d 25.00 25.00

Unity — A405

No. 1458: a, $1.25, Ceiba pentandra. b, $1.75, *Wan Bon,* poem by Robin Dobru Raveles.

2013, Nov. 10 **Litho.** ***Perf. 14***

1458 A405 Vert. pair, #a-b, + central label 1.90 1.90

Masks — A406

No. 1459 — Inscriptions: a, $1, Dewi sekartaji. b, $2.50, Klono garudo lelono. c, $3.50, Kollo tekik salagonjo. d, $7.50, Kraeng sengkollo. e, $9.50, Panji amisani. f, $11, Patih dandang mangkurat.

2013, Dec. 4 Litho. *Perf. 14*

1459	A406	Block of 6, #a-f	21.50	21.50

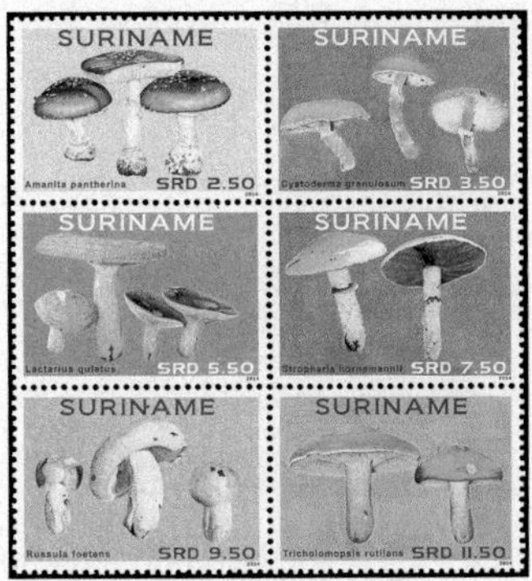

Mushrooms — A407

No. 1460: a, $2.50: a, Amanita pantherina. b, $3.50, Cystoderma granulosum. c, $5.50, Lactarius quietus. d, $7.50, Stropharia hornemannii. e, $9.50, Russula foetens. f, $11.50, Tricholomopsis rutilans.

2014, Jan. 15 Litho. *Perf. 14*

1460	A407	Block of 6, #a-f	25.00	25.00

Birds — A408

No. 1461: a, Hylophilus muscicapinus. b, Euphonia plumbea. c, Columbina talpacoti. d, Lophrotriccus vitiosus. e, Myrmotherula brachyra. f, Icterus nigrogularis. g, Passerina cyanoides. h, Pipra erythrocephala. i, Pithys albifrons. j, Xenops menutus. k, Terenura spodioptila. l, Scierurus mexicanus.

2014, Feb. 19 Litho. *Perf. 14*

1461	Block of 12	37.50	37.50
a.	A408 B multi	.35	.35
b.	A408 $1.45 multi	.90	.90
c.	A408 $2 multi	1.25	1.25
d.	A408 $2.50 multi	1.50	1.50
e.	A408 $3.50 multi	2.10	2.10
f.	A408 $4.50 multi	2.75	2.75
g.	A408 $5.50 multi	3.50	3.50
h.	A408 $6 multi	3.75	3.75
i.	A408 $7 multi	4.25	4.25
j.	A408 $8 multi	5.00	5.00
k.	A408 $9 multi	5.50	5.50
l.	A408 $10 multi	6.25	6.25

No. 1461a sold for 55c on day of issue.

Flowers A409

Designs: B, Dendrobium nobile. $1.45, Hemerocallis fulva. $2, Laeliocattleya. $2.50, Lycaste cruenta. $3.50, Ophrys apifera. $4.50, Paphiopedilum. $5, Phalaenopsis fuscata. $5.50, Sophrolaeliocattleya. $7, Vanda arcuata. $8, Vanda bensonii.

2014, Mar. 12 Litho. *Perf. 14*

1462	A409	B multi	.35	.35
1463	A409	$1.45 multi	.90	.90
1464	A409	$2 multi	1.25	1.25
1465	A409	$2.50 multi	1.60	1.60
1466	A409	$3.50 multi	2.10	2.10
1467	A409	$4.50 multi	2.75	2.75
1468	A409	$5 multi	3.25	3.25
1469	A409	$5.50 multi	3.50	3.50
1470	A409	$7 multi	4.25	4.25
1471	A409	$8 multi	5.00	5.00
		Nos. 1462-1471 (10)	24.95	24.95

Nos. 1462-1471 were printed in sheets of 20, containing 2 of each stamp + central label.

50th Wandelmars Day — A410

No. 1472 — Wandelmars parade participants: a, $2, Three women. b, $4, Two women, vert.

2014, Apr. 1 Litho. *Perf. 14*

1472	A410	Pair, #a-b	3.75	3.75

Butterflies A411

No. 1473: a, Araschnia levana. b, Automeris moloneyi. c, Cercyonis pegala. d, Euchloe ausonides. e, Hypanartia lethe. f, Speyeria cybele. g, Lasaia sula. h, Lycaena epixanthe. i, Mylothris rhodope. j, Parthenos sylvia. k, Sallya amulia. l, Vanessa gonerilla.

2014, May 14 Litho. *Perf. 14*

1473	Block of 12	37.50	37.50
a.	A411 B multi	.35	.35
b.	A411 $1.45 multi	.90	.90
c.	A411 $2 multi	1.25	1.25
d.	A411 $2.50 multi	1.60	1.60
e.	A411 $3.50 multi	2.10	2.10
f.	A411 $4.50 multi	2.75	2.75
g.	A411 $5.50 multi	3.50	3.50
h.	A411 $6 multi	3.75	3.75
i.	A411 $7 multi	4.25	4.25
j.	A411 $8 multi	5.00	5.00
k.	A411 $9 multi	5.50	5.50
l.	A411 $10 multi	6.25	6.25

No. 1473a sold for 55c on day of issue.

2014 World Cup Soccer Championships, Brazil — A412

No. 1474 — Soccer ball and: a, Two players. b, One player. c, One player, diff. d, One player, diff.

2014, June 11 Litho. *Perf. 14*

1474	Block of 4	12.50	12.50
a.	A412 $2 multi	1.25	1.25
b.	A412 $4 multi	2.50	2.50
c.	A412 $6 multi	3.75	3.75
d.	A412 $8 multi	5.00	5.00

Fish — A413

No. 1475: a, Chaetodon capistratus. b, Chaetodon striatus. c, Gramma loreto. d, Holacanthus isabelita. e, Halichoeres bivittatus. f, Holacanthus ciliaris. g, Lachnolaimus maximus. h, Mulloidichthys martinicus. i, Pempheris schomburgki. j, Pomacanthus arcuatus. k, Scarus croicensis. l, Pseudupeneus maculatus.

2014, July 16 Litho. *Perf. 14*

1475	Block of 12	34.00	34.00
a.	A413 B multi	.35	.35
b.	A413 $1.45 multi	.90	.90
c.	A413 $2 multi	1.25	1.25
d.	A413 $2.50 multi	1.50	1.50
e.	A413 $3.50 multi	2.10	2.10
f.	A413 $4.50 multi	2.75	2.75
g.	A413 $5 multi	3.00	3.00
h.	A413 $5.50 multi	3.50	3.50
i.	A413 $6 multi	3.75	3.75
j.	A413 $7 multi	4.25	4.25
k.	A413 $8 multi	5.00	5.00
l.	A413 $9 multi	5.50	5.50

No. 1475a sold for 55c on day of issue.

A414

Airplanes — A415

No. 1476: a, $1.25, Walden III, U.S., 1909. b, $2.50, Chiribiri No. 5, Italy, 1912. c, $2.75, Fokker T-2, Netherlands, 1921. d, $3.50, Fokker F. VIIa-3m, Netherlands, 1925. e, $4.75, Potez 25A-2, France, 1925. f, $5.25, Albatros L73, Germany, 1926. g, $5.50, Douglas M-4, U.S., 1927. h, $6.50, Junkers G24, Germany, 1927.

No. 1477 — Flowers and part of Surinam Airways jet: a, $8, Tail section. b, $9, Fuselage, rear door, landing gear. c, $11, Fuselage, front door.

2014, July 17 Litho. *Perf. 14*

1476	A414	Sheet of 8, #a-h, + central label	19.50	19.50

Souvenir Sheet

1477	A415	Sheet of 3, #a-c	17.00	17.00

Panama Canal, Cent. — A416

No. 1478: a, $2.50, Ship. b, $3.50, Ship, diff. c, $5.50, Ship, diff. d, $6.50, Ship near locks. e, $8, Ship, diff. f, $9, Locks.

2014, Oct. 22 Litho. *Perf. 14*

1478	A416	Block of 6, #a-f	21.50	21.50

Masks — A417

No. 1479: a, $2.50, Dewi ragil kuning. b, $3.50, Patih gajah meto. c, $5.50, Kollo marko mamang. d, $7.50, Panji kudonowarongso. e, $9.50, Patih talang segoro. f, $11.50, Panji amiseno.

2014, Dec. 3 Litho. *Perf. 14*

1479	A417	Block of 6, #a-f	24.50	24.50

Souvenir Sheet

Birds — A418

No. 1480: a, $13, Mimus saturninus. b, $16, Colinus cristatus.

2014, Dec. 31 Litho. *Perf. 14*

1480	A418	Sheet of 2, #a-b	18.00	18.00

Butterflies A419

No. 1481: a, Agrias claudina sardanapalus. b, Phoebis sennae. c, Hemithea aestivaria. d, Palaeochrysophanus hippothoe. e, Thecla betulae. f, Antheraea polyphemus. g, Geometra papilionaria. h, Limenitis lorquini. i, Eacles imperialis. j, Boloria thore. k, Callithea leprieurii. l, Automeris io.

2015, Jan. 14 Litho. *Perf. 14*

1481	Block of 12	37.00	37.00
a.	A419 $2.25 multi	1.40	1.40
b.	A419 $2.75 multi	1.75	1.75
c.	A419 $3.25 multi	2.00	2.00
d.	A419 $3.75 multi	2.25	2.25
e.	A419 $4.25 multi	2.60	2.60
f.	A419 $4.75 multi	3.00	3.00
g.	A419 $5.25 multi	3.25	3.25
h.	A419 $5.75 multi	3.50	3.50
i.	A419 $6.25 multi	3.75	3.75
j.	A419 $6.75 multi	4.25	4.25
k.	A419 $7.25 multi	4.50	4.50
l.	A419 $7.75 multi	4.75	4.75

Miniature Sheet

Fruit — A420

No. 1482: a, $2, Anacardium occidentale (cashews). b, $4, Artocarpus heterophyllus (jackfruit). c, $5, Blighia sapida (ackee). d, $7, Citrus paradisi (grapefruit). e, $8, Musa (bananas). f, $9, Psidium guajava (guava).

2015, Feb. 11 Litho. *Perf. 14*

1482	A420	Sheet of 6, #a-f	21.50	21.50

Miniature Sheet

Birds — A421

No. 1483: a, $2.25, Daptrius ater. b, $2.75, Circus buffoni. c, $3.25, Buteogallus meridionalis. d, $3.75, Buteogallus urubitinga. e, $4.25, Dendrocygna autumnalis. f, $4.75, Ciccaba huhula. g, $5.25, Harpagus bidentatus. h, $5.75, Micrastur mirandollei. i, $6.25, Nyctibius griseus. j, $6.75, Spizaetus melanoleucus. k, $7.25, Ictinia plumbea. l, $7.75, Asturina nitida.

2015, Mar. 18 Litho. *Perf. 14*
1483 A421 Sheet of 12, #a-l 37.00 37.00

Fish — A422

No. 1484: a, $2, Hemigrammus erythrozonus. b, $3, Paracheirodon innesi. c, $4, Poecilia reticulata. d, $6, Pterophyllum scalare. e, $7, Poecilia velifera. f, $8, Pygocentrus piraya.

2015, May 20 Litho. *Perf. 14*
1484 A422 Block of 6, #a-f 18.50 18.50

Women's Costumes — A423

No. 1485 — Various costumes with background colors of: a, $2, Light blue. b, $3, Green. c, $4, Light blue. d, $6, Peach. e, $7, Light blue. f, $8, Dull rose.

2015, June 17 Litho. *Perf. 14*
1485 A423 Block of 6, #a-f 18.50 18.50

Flowers — A424

No. 1486: a, $2.25, Bauhinia purpurea. b, $2.75, Catharanthus roseus. c, $3.25, Couroupita guianensis. d, $3.75, Lantana camara. e, $4.25, Datura candida. f, $4.75, Passiflora. g, $5.25, Euphorbia pulcherrima. h, $5.75, Solandra nitida. i, $6.25, Nerium oleander. j, $6.75, Strelitzia reginae. k, $7.25, Punica granatum. l, $7.75, Thunbergia grandiflora.

2015, July 15 Litho. *Perf. 14*
1486 A424 Block of 12, #a-l 36.50 36.50

A425

America Issue — A426

No. 1487: a, $15, Woman with tape on mouth. b, $17. Woman with "Be Human Stop Trafficking" sign.

No. 1488: a, $13, Raised hand. b, $15, Person behind prison bars.

2015, Sept. 16 Litho. *Perf. 14*
1487 A425 Vert. pair, #a-b 19.50 19.50

Souvenir Sheet

1488 A426 Sheet of 2, #a-b 17.00 17.00

Souvenir Sheet

Independence, 40th Anniv. — A427

No. 1489: a, $5, National Assembly Building. b, $7, Coat of arms. c, $8, Court House.

2015, Nov. 24 Litho. *Perf. 14*
1489 A427 Sheet of 3, #a-c 10.50 10.50

Souvenir Sheet

Surinam's Association With Van Reijen International Agencies Ltd. (Philatelic Agent), 40th Anniv. — A428

No. 1490 — Various Surinam postage stamps: a, $4. b, $6.

2015, Nov. 24 Litho. *Perf. 14*
1490 A428 Sheet of 2, #a-b 5.25 5.25

Masks — A429

No. 1491: a, $1, B. Joyo sentiko. b, $3, Panji asmoro bangun. c, $5, Panji gadingan. d, $6, Panji laras. e, $7, Panji maleko kusumo. f, $8, Panji pambelah.

2015, Dec. 2 Litho. *Perf. 14*
1491 A429 Block of 6, #a-f 15.00 15.00

Souvenir Sheet

Mushrooms — A430

No. 1492: a, $7, Lactarius torminosus. b, $9, Cortinarius varius. c, $12, Cortinarius variecolor.

2016, Jan. 13 Litho. *Perf. 14*
1492 A430 Sheet of 3, #a-c 14.00 14.00

Birds — A431

No. 1493: a, $2.25, Ajaja ajaja. b, $2.75, Ardea alba. c, $3.25, Ardea cocoi. d, $3.75, Chauna torquata. e, $4.25, Dendrocygna viduata. f, $4.75, Egretta thula. g, $5.25, Fregata magnificens. h, $5.75, Mycteria americana. i, $6.25, Phalacrocorax brasilianus. j, $6.75, Spheniscus magellanicus. k, $7.25, Syrigma sibilatrix. l, $7.75, Theristicus caerulescens.

2016, Feb. 17 Litho. *Perf. 14*
1493 A431 Block of 12, #a-l 30.00 30.00

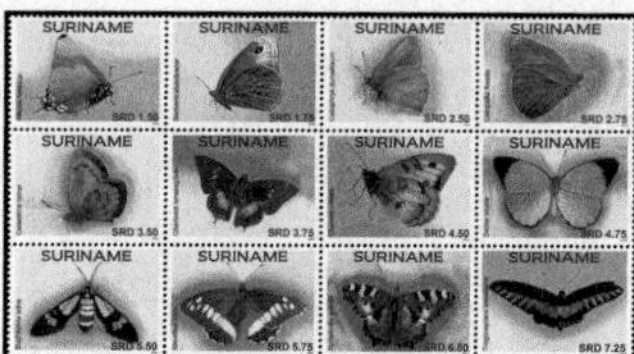

Butterflies — A432

No. 1494: a, $1.50, Atlides halesus. b, $1.75, Berberia abdelkader. c, $2.50, Callophrys dumetorum. d, $2.75, Catopsilla florella. e, $3.50, Celastrina ladon. f, $3.75, Charaxes smaragdalis. g, $4.50, Chazara briseis. h, $4.75, Delias aruna. i, $5.50, Euchromia lethe. j, $5.75, Kanetisa circe. k, $6.50, Nymphalis urticae. l, $7.25, Trogonoptera brookiana.

2016, Mar. 16 Litho. *Perf. 14*
1494 A432 Block of 12, #a-l 25.00 25.00

Fish — A433

No. 1495: a, $1.50, Acipenser fulvescens. b, $1.75, Acipenser transmontanus. c, $2.50, Amia calva. d, $2.75, Atractosteus spatula. e, $3.50, Lampetra appendix. f, $3.75, Lepisosteus oculatus. g, $4.50, Oncorhynchus clarki. h, $4.75, Oncorhynchus kisutch. i, $5.50, Oncorhynchus nerka. j, $5.75, Oncorhynchus tshawytscha. k, $6.50, Polyodon spathula. l, $7.25, Scaphirhynchus albus.

2016, May 18 Litho. *Perf. 14*
1495 A433 Block of 12, #a-l 18.00 18.00

Inventions of 1816 — A434

No. 1496: a, Metronome. b, Miner's safety lamp, c, Stethoscope. d, Stirling air engine.

2016, June 15 Litho. *Perf. 14*

1496	Vert. strip of 4	6.75	6.75
a.	A434 $4 multi	1.10	1.10
b.	A434 $5 multi	1.40	1.40
c.	A434 $7 multi	2.00	2.00
d.	A434 $8 multi	2.25	2.25

Flowers — A435

No. 1497: a, $1.50, Adonis annua. b, $1.75, Capparis spinosa. c, $2.50, Convallaria majalis. d, $2.75, Erythronium dens-canis. e, $3.50, Hyacinthoides. f, $3.75, Iris latifolia. g, $4.50, Iris persica. h, $4.75, Muscari latifolium. i, $5.50, Papaver somniferum. j, $5.75, Polianthes tuberosa. k, $6.50, Spartium junceum. l, $7.25, Tropaeolum majus.

2016, July 13 Litho. *Perf. 14*
1497 A435 Block of 12, #a-l 14.50 14.50

Easter Island Moai — A436

No. 1498: a, $2, Seven moai on platform. b, $3, People looking at unraised moai. c, $4, Unraised moai. d, $6, Uncompleted moai. e, $7, Three moai, vert. f, $8, Moai, vert.

2016, Aug. 17 Litho. *Perf. 14*
1498 A436 Block of 6, #a-f 8.00 8.00

A437

2016 Summer Olympics, Rio de Janeiro — A438

No. 1499 — Amphora depicting: a, $15, Hercules and Geryon. b, $17, Athlete.

No. 1500 — Part of amphora depicting runners: a, $4, UL. b, $5, UR. c, $6, Left center. d, $8, Right center. e, $10, LL. f, $11, LR.

2016, Sept. 14 Litho. *Perf. 14*
1499 A437 Vert. pair, #a-b 8.50 8.50

Miniature Sheet

1500 A438 Sheet of 6, #a-f 12.00 12.00

America issue.

Frogs — A439

No. 1501: a, $1, Boophis bottae. b, $2, Boophis tephraeomystax. c, $3, Cochranella spinosa. d, $4, Dendrobates tinctorius. e, $7, Hyloscirtus lindae. f, $8, Polypedates otilophus.

2016, Oct. 19 Litho. *Perf. 14*
1501 A439 Block of 6, #a-f 6.50 6.50

Airplanes — A440

No. 1502: a, $2, Blériot VII, 1907. b, $3, Breguet III, 1912. c, $4, De Pischoff 1, 1907. d, $6, Fokker Spider, 1911. e, $7, Santos-Dumont 14bis, 1906. f, $8, Short S.41, 1912.

2016, Nov. 16 Litho. *Perf. 14*
1502 A440 Block of 6, #a-f 8.00 8.00

Masks — A441

No. 1503 — Inscriptions: a, $2, Patih carang lampit. b, $3, Patih kalla renggut muko. c, $4, Patih kollo dinemprang. d, $6, Patih kollo memreng. e, $7, Patih kraeng projo. f, $8, Patih kudono warongso.

2016, Dec. 7 Litho. *Perf. 14*
1503 A441 Block of 6, #a-f 8.25 8.25

Paintings by Aloi Pilioko — A442

No. 1504: a, $3, Allegory. b, $4, Three Cats. c, $5, Beloved in the Market. d, $7, Person with Cat. e, $8, Two Girls. f, $9, Entangled Pair.

2017, Jan. 11 Litho. *Perf. 14*
1504 A442 Block of 6, #a-f 9.75 9.75

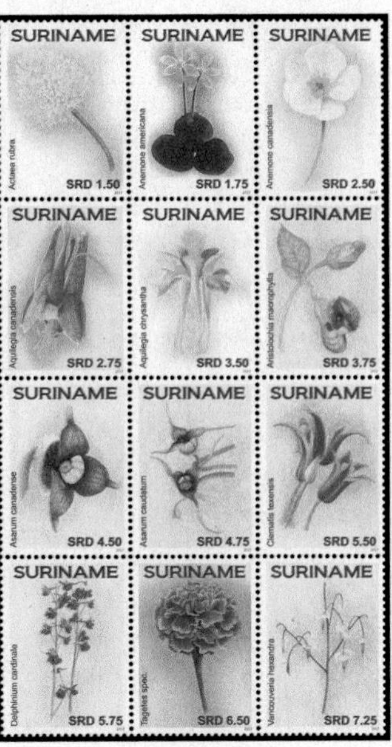

Flowers — A443

No. 1505: a, $1.50, Actaea rubra. b, $1.75, Anemone americana. c, $2.50, Anemone canadensis. d, $2.75, Aquilegia canadensis. e, $3.50, Aquilegia chrysantha. f, $3.75, Aristolochia macrophylla. g, $4.50, Asarum canadense. h, $4.75, Asarum caudatum. i, $5.50, Clematis texensis. j, $5.75, Delphinium cardinale. k, $6.50, Tagetes spec. l, $7.25, Vancouveria hexandra.

2017, Feb. 15 Litho. *Perf. 14*
1505 A443 Block of 12, #a-l 13.50 13.50

Birds — A444

No. 1506: a, $1.50, Buteo albonotatus. b, $1.75, Buteo brachyurous. c, $2.50, Caracara cheriway. d, $2.75, Cathartes aura. e, $3.50, Cathartes burrovianus. f, $3.75, Coragyps atratus. g, $4.50, Crax fasciolata. h, $4.75, Falco femoralis. i, $5.50, Geranoaetus melanoleucus. j, $5.75, Harpia harpyja. k, $6.50, Ortalis canicollis. l, $7.25, Penelope obscura.

2017, Mar. 15 Litho. *Perf. 14*
1506 A444 Block of 12, #a-l 13.50 13.50

Shells — A445

No. 1507: a, $2, Aporrhais pespelicanis. b, $3, Aporrhais seresianus. c, $4, Babylonia areolata. d, $6, Babylonia papillaris. e, $7, Conus gloriamaris. f, $8, Strombus labiatus.

2017, May 17 Litho. *Perf. 14*
1507 A445 Block of 6, #a-f 8.00 8.00

Fish — A446

No. 1508: a, $1.50, Ameiurus brunneus. b, $1.75, Ameiurus catus. c, $2.50, Ameiurus melas. d, $2.75, Ameiurus serracanthus. e, $3.50, Ictalurus punctatus. f, $3.75, Noturus flavus. g, $4.50, Oncorhynchus mykiss. h, $4.75, Pylodictis olivaris. i, $5.50, Salvelinus fontinalis. j, $5.75, Salvelinus malma. k, $6.50, Satan eurystomus. l, $7.25, Thymallus arcticus.

2017, June 14 Litho. *Perf. 14*
1508 A446 Block of 12, #a-l 13.50 13.50

Butterflies — A447

No. 1509: a, $1.50, Adelpha cocala. b, $1.75, Anaea aidea. c, $2.50, Chlosyne lacinia. d, $2.75, Colobura dirce. e, $3.50, Danaus eresimus. f, $3.75, Doxocopa elis. g, $4.50, Dynamine artemisia glauce. h, $4.75, Heliconius charitonius. i, $5.50, Heliconius sara. j, $5.75, Papilio aristodemus ponceaus. k, $6.50, Papilio astyalus. l, $7.25, Papilio thoas.

2017, July 12 Litho. *Perf. 14*
1509 A447 Block of 12, #a-l 13.50 13.50

Mushrooms — A448

No. 1510: a, $1, Boletus erythropus. b, $2, Boletus luridus. c, $3, Boletus pinophilus. d, $4, Boletus queletti. e, $7, Boletus reticulatus. f, $8, Tylopilus felleus.

2017, Aug. 16 Litho. *Perf. 14*
1510 A448 Block of 6, #a-f 6.75 6.75

Souvenir Sheets

A449

Tourism — A450

No. 1511: a, $11, Brownsberg Nature Park. b, $17, Fort Zeelandia.

No. 1512: a, $17, Brokopondo. b, $19, Tafelberg.

2017, Sept. 13 Litho. *Perf. 14*

1511 A449 Sheet of 2, #a-b, + central label 7.75 7.75
1512 A450 Sheet of 2, #a-b 9.75 9.75

America issue.

Fruit — A451

No. 1513: a, $3, Annona reticulata. b, $5, Citrus aurantifolia. c, $6, Cocos nucifera. d, $7, Malpighia glabra. e, $8, Mammea americana. f, $9, Mangifera indica.

2017, Oct. 11 Litho. *Perf. 14*

1513 A451 Block of 6, #a-f 10.50 10.50

Miniature Sheet

Frogs — A452

No. 1514: a, $3, Cruziohyla calcarifer. b, $5, Hyla geographica. c, $6, Litoria wollastoni. d, $7, Megophrys nasuta. e, $8, Rana catesbeiana. f, $9, Rhacophorus pardalis.

2017, Nov. 15 Litho. *Perf. 14*

1514 A452 Sheet of 6, #a-f 10.50 10.50

Masks — A453

No. 1515: a, $4, Panji pamecut. b, $5, Panji parang tejo. c, $6, Panji walang sumirang. d, $8, Patih mising jiwo. e, $9, Patih suro dwi panggo. f, $10, Potrojoyo.

2017, Dec, 6 Litho. *Perf. 14*

1515 A453 Block of 6, #a-f 11.50 11.50

Souvenir Sheets

Flora and Fauna — A454

Designs: No. 1516, $5, Thamnophilus amazonicus. No. 1517, $5, Morelia bredli. No. 1518, $5, Lepidocolaptes angustirostris. No. 1519, $5, Rana catesbeiana. No. 1520, $5, Selenidera culik. No. 1521, $5, Chloceryle americana. No. 1522, $5, Encyclia diurna. No. 1523, $5, Ixobrychus involucris. No. 1524, $5, Eulepte gastralis. No. 1525, $5, Galago crassicaudatus. No. 1526, $5, Brachymesia sp. No. 1527, $5, Tupaia minor.

2017, Dec. 19 Litho. *Perf. 14*

1516-1527 A454 Set of 12 16.50 16.50

Owls — A455

No. 1528: a, A, Asio abyssinicus. b, $5.50, Bubo leucostictus. c, $6, Glaucidium albertinum. d, $7, Glaucidium capense. e, $9, Glaucidium hardyi. f, $10, Ninox affinis. g, $11, Otus balli. h, $12, Otus senegalensis. i, $14, Phodilus assimilis. j, $18, Phodilus badius. k, $20, Phodilus prigoginei. l, $22, Strix woodfordii.

2018, Jan. 3 Litho. *Perf. 14*

1528 A455 Block of 12, #a-l 36.00 36.00

No. 1528a sold for 50c on day of issue.

Ships — A456

No. 1529: a, A, Argo, 1984. b, $15.50, Brendan, 1976. c, $19, Hsu Fu, 1993. d, $20, Sutton Hoo, 1939.

2018, Feb. 14 Litho. *Perf. 14*

1529 A456 Block of 4, #a-d 15.00 15.00

No. 1529a sold for 50c on day of issue.

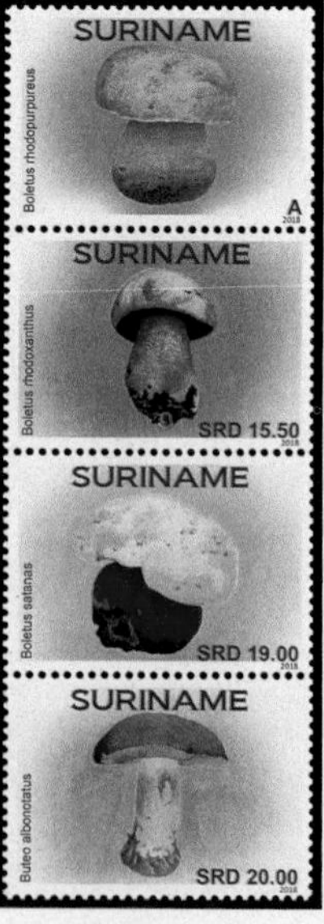

Mushrooms A457

No. 1530: a, A, Boletus rhodopurpureus, b, $15, Boletus rhodoxanthus. c, $19, Boletus satanas. d, $20, Buteo albonotatus (incorrect inscription).

2018, Mar. 14 Litho. *Perf. 14*

1530 A457 Vert. strip of 4, #a-d 15.00 15.00

On day of issue, No. 1530a sold for 50c.

Butterflies — A458

No. 1531: a, A, Graphium antheus, b, $5.50, Graphium delesserti. c, $6, Graphium epaminondas. d, $7, Graphium mendana. e, $9, Graphium stresemanni. f, $10, Iphiclides podalirius. g, $11, Ornithoptera alexandrae. h, $12, Ornithoptera meridionalis. i, $14, Ornithoptera victoriae. j, $18, Papilio alexanor. k, $20, Papilio antimachus. l, $22, Papilio eurymedon.

2018, Apr. 11 Litho. *Perf. 14*

1531 A458 Block of 12, #a-l 36.00 36.00

On day of issue, No. 1531a sold for 50c.

Marine Life of the Mariana Trench A459

Designs: A, Argyropelecus hemigymnus. $9.50, Benthocodon. $10, Caulophryne jordani. $11, Chauliodus. $15, Chlamydoselachus anguineus. $20, Chondrochladia lampadiglobus. $34, Grimpoteuthis abyssicola.

2018, May 16 Litho. *Perf. 14*

1532	A459	A multi		.25	.25
1533	A459	$9.50 multi		2.60	2.60
1534	A459	$10 multi		2.75	2.75
1535	A459	$11 multi		3.00	3.00
1536	A459	$15 multi		4.00	4.00
1537	A459	$20 multi		5.50	5.50
1538	A459	$34 multi		9.25	9.25
		Nos. 1532-1538 (7)		27.35	27.35

On day of issue No. 1532 sold for 50c. Nos. 1532-1538 were printed in sheets of 14 (2 of each stamp) + central label.

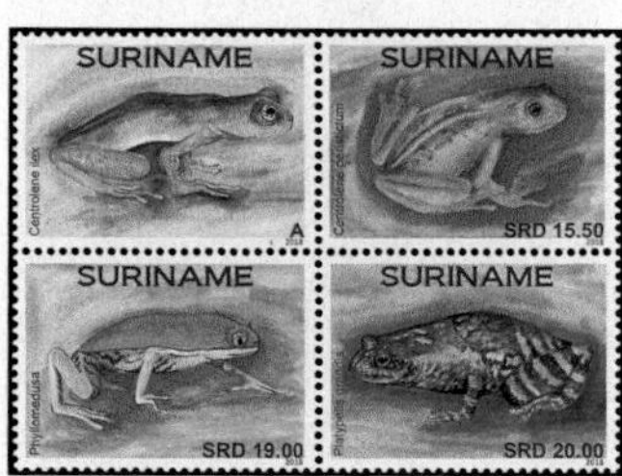

Frogs — A460

No. 1539: a, A, Centrolene ilex. b, $15.50, Centrolene peristictum. c, $19, Phyllomedusa. d, $20, Platypelis grandis.

2018, June 20 Litho. *Perf. 14*

1539 A460 Block of 4, #a-d 15.00 15.00

Cockatoos — A461

No. 1540: a, $1, Cacatua alba. b, $5, Cacatua ducorpsii. c, $6, Cacatua galerita eleonora. d, $7, Cacatua galerita fitzroyi. e, $9, Cacatua galerita triton. f, $10, Cacatua galerita. g, $11, Cacatua goffiniana. h, $12, Cacatua haematuropygia. i, $14, Cacatua leadbeateri. j, $18, Cacatua moluccensis. k, $20, Cacatua ophthalmica. l, $22, Cacatua sanguinea.

2018, July 18 Litho. *Perf. 14*
1540 A461 Block of 12, #a-l 36.00 36.00

Birds — A462

No. 1541: a, $25, Sialia sialis. b, $70, Taeniopygia guttata.
No. 1542, vert.: a, $35, Agapornis. b, $60, Erythrura gouldiae.

2018, Sept. 12 Litho. *Perf. 14*
1541 A462 Horiz. pair, #a-b 25.50 25.50

Souvenir Sheet

1542 A462 Sheet of 2, #a-b 25.50 25.50

America issue.

Birds of Prey — A463

No. 1543: a, $1, Aquila africanus. b, $5, Aquila fasciatus. c, $6, Aquila heliaca. d, $7, Circaetus beaudouini. e, $9, Circaetus cinerascens. f, $10, Circaetus cinereus. g, $11, Circaetus pectoralis. h, $12, Dryotriorchis spectabilis. i, $14, Haliaeetus leucocephalus. j, $18, Haliaeetus vocifer. k, $20, Harpyhaliaetus coronatus. l, $22, Hieraaetus ayresii.

2018, Oct. 10 Litho. *Perf. 14*
1543 A463 Block of 12, #a-l 36.00 36.00

Fruit — A464

No. 1544: a, $1, Ananas comosus. b, $14, Citrus sinensis. c, $20, Manilkara zapota. d, $21, Myristica fragrans. e, $24, Passiflora edulis. f, $25, Punica granatum.

2018, Nov. 14 Litho. *Perf. 14*
1544 A464 Block of 6, #a-f 28.00 28.00

Masks — A465

No. 1545: a, $1, Dewi anjani. b, $9, Klana sewandana. c, $20, Panji pangending. d, $21, Patih kudono warso. e, $24, Patih lindu sekti. f, $25, Walang semirang.

2018, Dec. 12 Litho. *Perf. 14*
1545 A465 Block of 6, #a-f 27.00 27.00

Souvenir Sheets

Flora and Fauna — A466

Designs: No. 1546, X, Ramphastos tucanus. No. 1547, $5, Loris tardigratus. No. 1548, $5, Galbula galbula. No. 1549, $5, Boophis viridis. No. 1550, $5, Cebus olivaceus. No. 1551, $5, Monasa atra. No. 1552, $5, Trogon melanurus. No. 1553, $5, Thalurania furcata. No. 1554, $5, Ciccaba huhula. No. 1555, $5, Litoria infrafrenata. No. 1556, $5, Zygosepalum labiosum. No. 1557, $5, Dacnis lineata.

2018, Dec. 29 Litho. *Perf. 14*
1546-1557 A466 Set of 12 16.00 16.00

No. 1546 sold for $5 on day of issue.

Composers — A467

No. 1558: a, C, Béla Bartók (1881-1945). b, $9.50, Géza Frid (1904-89). c, $14, György Ligeti (1923-2006). d, $15, Pál Hermann (1902-44). e, $25, Zoltán Kodály (1882-1967). f, $30, Zoltán Székely (1903-2001).

2019, Jan. 16 Litho. *Perf. 14*
1558 A467 Block of 6, #a-f 25.50 25.50

No. 1558a sold for $1.50 on day of issue.

Eagles — A468

No. 1559: a, C, Hieraeetus pennatus. b, $4.50, Hieraeetus spilogaster. c, $6, Ictinaetus malayensis. d, $7, Morphnus guianensis. e, $9, Nisaetus alboniger. f, $10, Nisaetus cirrhatus. g, $11, Nisaetus floris. h, $12, Spilornis cheela. i, $14, Spilornis elgini leucocephalus. j, $18, Spizaetus isidori. k, $20, Stephanoaetus coronatus. l, $22, Terathopius ecaudatus.

2019, Feb. 13 Litho. *Perf. 14*
1559 A468 Block of 12, #a-l 36.00 36.00

No. 1559a sold for $1.50 on day of issue.

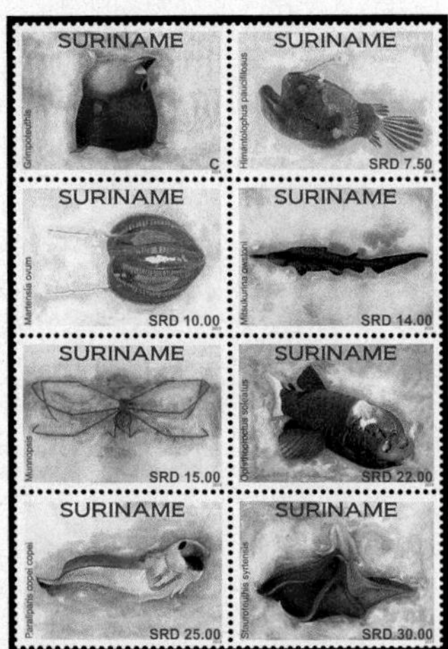

Marine Life of the Mariana Trench — A469

No. 1560: a, C, Grimpoteuthis. b, $7.50, Himantolophus paucifilosus. c, $10, Martensia ovum. d, $14, Mitsukurina owstoni. e, $15, Munnopsis. f, $22, Opisthoproctus soleatus. g, $25, Paraliparis copei copei. h, $30, Stauroteuthis syrtensis.

2019, Mar. 13 Litho. *Perf. 14*
1560 A469 Block of 8, #a-h 33.50 33.50

No. 1560a sold for $1.50 on day of issue.

Owls — A470

No. 1561: a, C, Tyto almae. b, $4.50, Tyto aurantia. c, $6, Tyto capensis. d, $7, Tyto glaucops. e, $9, Tyto inexspectata. f, $10, Tyto longimembris. g, $11, Tyto multipunctata. h, $12, Tyto nigrobrunnea. i, $14, Tyto novaehollandiae. j, $18, Tyto rosenbergii. k, $20, Tyto soumagnei. l, $22, Tyto tenebricosa.

2019, Apr. 10 Litho. *Perf. 14*
1561 A470 Block of 12, #a-l 36.00 36.00

No. 1561a sold for $1.50 on day of issue.

Ships — A471

No. 1561: a, C, Aileach, 1991. b, $5.50, Cutty Sark, 1840. c, $7, H.M.S. Victory, 1759. d, $8, Mary Rose, 1509. e, $9, Matthew, 1497. f, $10, Sohar, 1980. g, $14, T. S. Royalist, 1971.

2019, May 15 Litho. *Perf. 14*
1562 A471 Block of 7, #a-g, + label 15.00 15.00

No. 1562a sold for $1.50 on day of issue.

Butterflies — A472

No. 1563: a, C, Anteos maerula. b, $4.50, Appias nero. c, $6, Catopsilia scylla. d, $7, Colias nastes. e, $9, Colias vautieri. f, $10, Colostis celimene. g, $11, Colostis danae. h, $12, Colostis ione. i, $14, Colostis regina. j, $18, Papilio lorimeri. k, $20, Papilio pericles. l, $22, Papilio pilumnus.

2019, June 12 Litho. *Perf. 14*
1563 A472 Block of 12, #a-l 36.00 36.00

No. 1563a sold for $1.50 on day of issue.

Frogs — A473

Designs: D, Dendropsophus leucophyllatus. $7, Dendropsophus triangulum. $12, Hyla meridionalis. $14, Litoria caerulea. $15, Litoria splendida. $20, Pyxicephalus adspersus. $25, Trachycephalus resinifictrix.

2019, July 10 Litho. *Perf. 14*

1564	A473	D multi	.55	.55
1565	A473	$7 multi	1.90	1.90
1566	A473	$12 multi	3.25	3.25
1567	A473	$14 multi	3.75	3.75
1568	A473	$15 multi	4.00	4.00
1569	A473	$20 multi	5.50	5.50
1570	A473	$25 multi	6.75	6.75
		Nos. 1564-1570 (7)	25.70	25.70

On day of issue, No. 1564 sold for $2. Nos. 1564-1570 were printed in sheets containing two of each stamp + a central label.

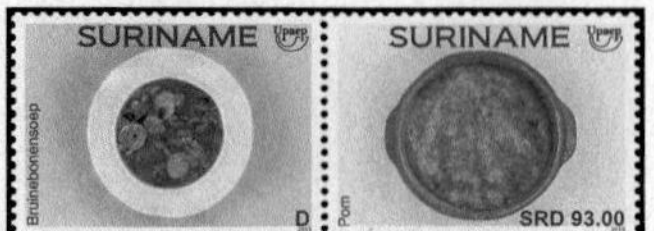

Traditional Dishes — A474

No. 1571: a, D, Bruinebonensoep. b, $93, Pom.
No. 1572: a, F, Pepre watra. b, $93, Roti.

2019, Sept. 11 Litho. *Perf. 14*

1571 A474 Horiz. pair, #a-b 25.50 25.50

Souvenir Sheet

1572 A474 Sheet of 2, #a-b 25.50 25.50

America issue. Nos. 1571a and 1572a each sold for $2 on day of issue.

Statue Depicting Mohandas K. Gandhi (1869-1948), Indian Nationalist Leader — A475

No. 1573 — Background color: a, $6.20, White. b, $8, Pale blue.

2019, Oct. 2 Litho. *Perf. 14*

1573 A475 Horiz. pair, #a-b 4.00 4.00

Parrots — A476

No. 1574: a, D, Cacatua sulphurea citrinocristata. b, $4, Cacatua sulphurea. c, $6, Cacatua tenuirostris. d, $7, Callocephalon fimbriatum. e, $8, Calyptorhynchus banksii. f, $10, Calyptorhynchus baudinii. g, $11, Calyptorhynchus funereus. h, $12, Calyptorhynchus lathami. i, $14, Calyptorhynchus latirostris. j, $18, Eolophus roseicapilla. k, $20, Nymphicus hollandicus. l, $22, Probosciger atterimus.

2019, Oct. 9 Litho. *Perf. 14*

1574 A476 Block of 12, #a-l 36.00 36.00

No. 1574a sold for $2 on day of issue.

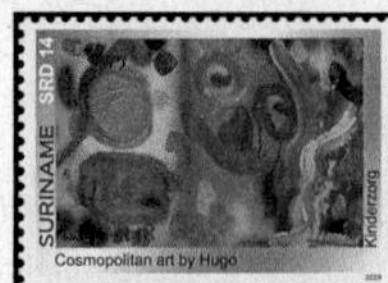

Paintings by Hugo — A477

No. 1575: a, Apen in Jigokudani. b, Buurtschap. c, Dans rond Zonnebloem. d, Denken aan de Toekomst. e, Droefenis. f, Grenzen. g, Homo videns. h, Kind en Teddybeer. i, Kinderzorg. j, Observatie. k, Op de Spooktrein. l, Rotsbloem.

2019, Nov. 13 Litho. *Perf. 14*

1575	Block of 12	36.50	36.50
a.	A477 $2 multi	.50	.50
b.	A477 $4 multi	1.10	1.10
c.	A477 $6 multi	1.60	1.60
d.	A477 $7 multi	1.90	1.90
e.	A477 $9 multi	2.40	2.40
f.	A477 $10 multi	2.75	2.75
g.	A477 $11 multi	3.00	3.00
h.	A477 $12 multi	3.25	3.25
i.	A477 $14 multi	3.75	3.75
j.	A477 $18 multi	4.75	4.75
k.	A477 $20 multi	5.50	5.50
l.	A477 $22 multi	6.00	6.00

Shadow Puppets — A478

No. 1576: a, D, Abimanyu. b, $9, Abiyoso. c, $14, Anggodo. d, $15, Anilo. e, $20, Anoman. f, $30, Asuotomo.

2019, Dec. 11 Litho. *Perf. 14*

1576 A478 Block of 6, #a-f 24.00 24.00

No. 1576a sold for $2 on day of issue.

Souvenir Sheets

Flora and Fauna — A479

Designs: No. 1577, Y, Boophis viridis. No. 1578, $5, Tangara cayana. No. 1579, $5, Granatellus pelzelni. No. 1580, $5, Spoladea recurvalis. No. 1581, $5, Anolis gingivinus. No. 1582, $5, Pionopsitta caica. No. 1583, $5, Agelaius icterocephalus. No. 1584, $5, Tangara punctata. No. 1585, $5, Kallima paralekta. No. 1586, $5, Forpus passerinus. No. 1587, $5, Sobralia sessilis. No. 1588, $5, Varecia variegata. No. 1589, $5, Amazona amazonica. No. 1590, $5, Cheirogaleus medius. No. 1591, $5, Vanessa cardui. No. 1592, $5, Papilio demoleus.

2019, Dec. 27 Litho. *Perf. 14*

1577-1592 A479 Set of 16 21.50 21.50

No. 1577 sold for $5 on day of issue.

Butterflies — A481

No. 1594: a, F, Arcas imperialis. b, $9, Danaus melanippus. c, $12, Heliconius aoede. d, $13, Heliconius hecale. e, $14, Hypolimnas bolina. f, $15, Junonia hierta. g, $16, Morpho rhetenor. h, $23, Prothoe calydonia.

2020, Feb. 5 Litho. *Perf. 14*

1594 A481 Block of 8, #a-h 28.00 28.00

No. 1594a sold for $3 on day of issue.

February 25, 1980 Coup d'Etat, 40th Anniv. — A482

2020, Feb. 25 Litho. *Perf. 14*

1595 A482 $40 multi 11.00 11.00

Flowers — A483

No. 1596: a, F, Chamaesyce albomarginata. b, $6, Cucurbita foetidissima. c, $9, Echinocystis lobata. d, $10, Erodium cicutarium. e, $11, Geranium erianthum. f, $12, Geranium maculatum. g, $13, Geranium richardsonii. h, $14, Hibiscus coccineus. i, $15, Hibiscus coulteri. j, $16, Ibervillea lindheimeri. k, $20, Iliamna grandiflora. l, $21, Marah fabaceus.

2020, Mar. 4 Litho. *Perf. 14*

1596 A483 Block of 12, #a-l 40.00 40.00

No. 1596a sold for $3 on day of issue.

SEMI-POSTAL STAMPS

SP1

SP2

Green Cross — SP3

Perf. 12½

1927, Aug. 1 Unwmk. Photo.

B1	SP1	2c (+ 2c) bl blk & grn	1.00	1.00
B2	SP2	5c (+ 3c) vio & grn	1.00	1.00
B3	SP3	10c (+ 3c) ver & grn	2.10	1.75
		Nos. B1-B3 (3)	4.10	3.75
		Set, never hinged	10.50	

Surtax was given to the Green Cross Society, which promotes public health services.

Nurse and Patient — SP4

1928, Dec. 1 *Perf. 11½*

B4	SP4	1½c (+ 1½c) ultra	4.50	4.50
B5	SP4	2c (+ 2c) bl grn	4.50	4.50
B6	SP4	5c (+ 3c) vio	5.00	5.00
B7	SP4	7½c (+ 2½c) ver	5.00	5.00
		Nos. B4-B7 (4)	19.00	19.00
		Set, never hinged	70.00	

The surtax on these stamps was for a fund to combat indigenous diseases.

Good Samaritan — SP5

1929, Dec. 1 *Perf. 12½*

B8	SP5	1½c (+ 1½c) grn	6.00	6.00
B9	SP5	2c (+ 2c) scar	6.00	6.00
B10	SP5	5c (+ 3c) ultra	6.50	6.50
B11	SP5	6c (+ 4c) blk	6.50	6.50
		Nos. B8-B11 (4)	25.00	25.00
		Set, never hinged	72.50	

Surtax for the Green Cross Society.

Surinam Mother and Child — SP6

1931, Dec. 14

B12	SP6	1½c (+ 1½c) blk	4.50	4.50
B13	SP6	2c (+ 2c) car rose	4.50	4.50
B14	SP6	5c (+ 3c) ultra	4.50	4.50
B15	SP6	6c (+ 4c) dp grn	4.50	4.50
		Nos. B12-B15 (4)	18.00	18.00
		Set, never hinged	55.00	

The surtax was for Child Welfare Societies.

Designs Symbolical of the Creed of the Moravians
SP7 SP8

1935, Aug. 1 ***Perf. 13x14***

B16 SP7 1c (+ ½c) dk brn 2.00 2.00
B17 SP7 2c (+ 1c) dp ultra 2.40 2.40
B18 SP8 3c (+ 1½c) grn 2.40 2.40
B19 SP8 4c (+ 2c) red org 3.00 3.00
B20 SP8 5c (+ 2½c) blk brn 3.25 3.25
B21 SP7 10c (+ 5c) car 3.25 3.25
Nos. B16-B21 (6) 16.30 16.30
Set, never hinged 72.50

200th anniv. of the founding of the Moravian Mission in Surinam.

Surinam Child — SP9

1936, Dec. 14 ***Perf. 12½***

B22 SP9 2c (+ 1c) dk grn 2.25 2.25
B23 SP9 3c (+ 1½c) dk bl 2.25 2.25
B24 SP9 5c (+ 2½c) brn blk 3.00 3.00
B25 SP9 10c (+ 5c) lake 3.00 3.00
Nos. B22-B25 (4) 10.50 10.50
Set, never hinged 29.00

Surtax for baby food and the Green Cross Society.

"Emancipation" SP10

Surinam Girl SP11

1938, June 1 **Litho.** ***Perf. 12½x12***

B26 SP10 2½c (+ 2c) dk bl grn 1.60 1.45

Photo.

B27 SP11 3c (+ 2c) vio blk 1.60 1.45
B28 SP11 5c (+ 3c) dk brn 2.00 1.75
B29 SP11 7½c (+ 5c) indigo 2.00 1.75
Nos. B26-B29 (4) 7.20 6.40
Set, never hinged 16.50

75th anniv. of the abolition of slavery in Surinam. Surtax to Slavery Remembrance Committee.

Creole Woman — SP12

Javanese Woman — SP13

Hindustani Woman — SP14

American Indian Woman — SP15

1940, Jan. 8 **Engr.** ***Perf. 13x14***

B30 SP12 2½c (+ 2c) dk grn 1.75 2.00
B31 SP13 3c (+ 2c) red org 1.75 2.00
B32 SP14 5c (+ 3c) dp bl 1.90 2.00
B33 SP15 7½c (+ 5c) henna brn 1.90 2.00
Nos. B30-B33 (4) 7.30 8.00
Set, never hinged 12.00

Surtax to leper care and baby food.

Catalogue values for unused stamps in this section, from this point to the end of the section, are for Never Hinged items.

Netherlands Coat of Arms and Inscription, "Netherlands Shall Rise Again" — SP16

1941, Aug. 30 **Litho.** ***Perf. 12½***

B34 SP16 7½c + 7½c dp org, ultra & blk 5.75 5.75
B35 SP16 15c + 15c scar, ultra & blk 6.50 6.50
B36 SP16 1g + 1g gray & ultra 24.00 20.00
Nos. B34-B36 (3) 36.25 32.25

The surtax was used to buy fighters for Dutch pilots in the Royal Air Force of Great Britain.

Nos. 145, 169, 146, 151 Surcharged in Red

I

+2c +5c +5c +5c
II III IV V

1942, Jan. 2

B37 A23 2c + 2c blk brn, I 2.50 2.10
a. Type II 2.50 2.10
B38 A26 2c + 2c blk brn, I 60.00 50.00
a. Type II 60.00 50.00
B39 A23 2½c + 2c green, I 2.50 2.10
a. Type II 2.50 2.10
B40 A23 7½c + 5c red vio, III 2.50 2.10
a. Type IV 10.00 8.50
b. Type V 25.00 21.00
Nos. B37-B40,CB1 (5) 73.75 62.55

The surtax was for the Red Cross.

In type III, the "c" may be "large," as illustrated, or "small," as in type II. Value is the same.

The distinctive feature of type IV is the pointed ending of the lower part of the "5."

Types of Regular Issue of 1945 Surcharged in Black

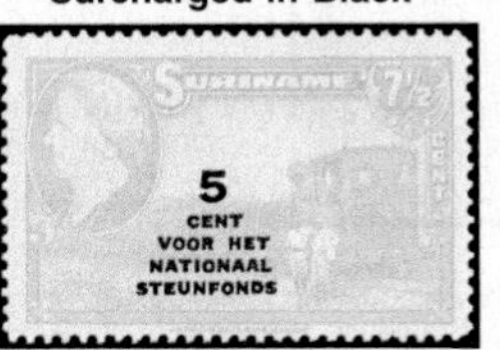

Unwmk.

1945, July 23 **Engr.** ***Perf. 12***

B41 A29 7½c + 5c dp org 5.75 2.60
B42 A30 15c + 10c brn 3.25 2.60
B43 A30 20c + 15c dl grn 3.25 2.60
B44 A30 22½c + 20c gray 3.25 2.60
B45 A30 40c + 35c rose lake 3.25 2.60
B46 A30 60c + 50c vio 3.25 2.60
Nos. B41-B46 (6) 22.00 15.60

Surtax for the National Welfare Fund.

Star — SP17

1947, Dec. 16 **Photo.** ***Perf. 13½x13***

B47 SP17 7½c + 12½c red org 3.75 3.00
B48 SP17 12½c + 37½c blue 3.75 3.00
Nos. B47-B48,CB4-CB5 (4) 15.00 12.00

The surtax was used to combat leprosy.

Marie Curie — SP18

7½c+22½c, 27½c+12½c, Wm. Roentgen.

1950, May 15 ***Perf. 14x13***

B49 SP18 7½c + 7½c 16.00 9.00
B50 SP18 7½c + 22½c 16.00 9.00
B51 SP18 27½c + 12½c 16.00 9.00
B52 SP18 27½c + 97½c 16.00 9.00
Nos. B49-B52 (4) 64.00 36.00

The surtax was used to combat cancer.

Nos. 236-237 Surcharged in Black (#B53) or Red (#B54)

1953, Feb. 18 **Wmk. 202**

B53 A35 12½c + 7½c on 7½c 3.25 2.75
B54 A35 20c + 10c on 12½c 3.25 2.75

The surtax was for flood relief in the Netherlands.

Stadium, Paramaribo — SP19

1953, Aug. 29 **Unwmk.** ***Perf. 13½***

B55 SP19 10c + 5c claret 11.50 8.25
B56 SP19 15c + 7½c brn 11.50 8.25
B57 SP19 30c + 15c dk grn 11.50 8.25
Nos. B55-B57 (3) 34.50 24.75

Opening of the new stadium.

Surinam Children — SP20

1954, Nov. 1 ***Perf. 13x14***

B58 SP20 7½c + 3c sepia 5.75 4.75
B59 SP20 10c + 5c bl grn 5.75 4.75
B60 SP20 15c + 7½c red brn 5.75 4.75
B61 SP20 30c + 15c blue 5.75 4.75
Nos. B58-B61 (4) 23.00 19.00

Surtax for the youth center of the Moravian Church.

Doves — SP21

1955, May 5 ***Perf. 14x13***

B62 SP21 7½c + 3½c brt red 2.40 2.40
B63 SP21 15c + 8c ultra 2.40 2.40

The Netherlands' liberation, 10th anniv.

Queen Juliana and Prince Bernhard SP22

1955, Oct. 27 **Unwmk.**

B64 SP22 7½c + 2½c dk olive .60 .60

Royal visit to Surinam, 1955. Surtax for the Royal present.

Theater, 1837 — SP23

Designs: 10c+5c, Theater and car, circa 1920. 15c+7½c, Theater and car, circa 1958. 20c+10c, Theater interior.

1958, Feb. 15 **Litho.** ***Perf. 13x12½***

B65 SP23 7½c + 3c lt bl & blk .50 .40
B66 SP23 10c + 5c rose lil & blk .50 .40
B67 SP23 15c + 7½c lt grn & blk .50 .40
B68 SP23 20c + 10c org & blk .50 .40
Nos. B65-B68 (4) 2.00 1.60

120th anniv. of the "Thalia" theatrical society.

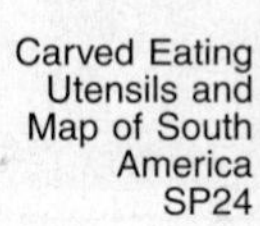
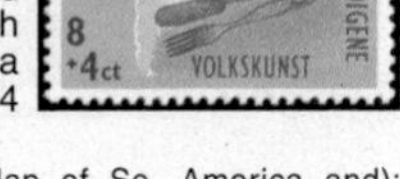

Carved Eating Utensils and Map of South America SP24

Native Art (Map of So. America and): 10c+5c, Feather headgear. 15c+7c, Clay pottery. 20c+10c, Carved wooden stool.

1960, Jan. 15

B69 SP24 8c + 4c multi 1.00 1.00
B70 SP24 10c + 5c salmon, red & bl 1.00 1.00
B71 SP24 15c + 7c red org, grn & sepia 1.00 1.00
B72 SP24 20c + 10c lt bl, ultra & bis 1.00 1.00
Nos. B69-B72 (4) 4.00 4.00

SP25

Design: Uprooted Oak emblem of WRY.

1960, Apr. 7 ***Perf. 13x14***

B73 SP25 8c + 4c choc & grn .25 .25
B74 SP25 10c + 5c vio bl & ol grn .25 .25

World Refugee Year, July 1, 1959-June 30, 1960. The surtax was for aid to refugees.

SP26

1960, Aug. 10 Litho. *Perf. 14x13*

B75 SP26	8c + 4c Shot put	.75	.75
B76 SP26	10c + 5c Basketball	.75	.75
B77 SP26	15c + 7c Runner	1.00	1.00
B78 SP26	20c + 10c Swimmer	1.00	1.00
B79 SP26	40c + 20c Soccer	1.05	1.05
	Nos. B75-B79 (5)	4.55	4.55

17th Olympic Games, Rome, 8/25-9/11. Surtax for Olympic Committee.

Girl Scout Signaling SP27

Designs: 10c+3c, Scout Saluting, vert. 15c+4c, Brownies around toadstool. 20c+5c, Scouts around campfire, vert. 25c+6c, Scouts cooking outdoors.

Perf. 14x13, 13x14

1961, Aug. 19 Litho.

Multicolored Designs

B80 SP27	8c + 2c blue	.45	.30
B81 SP27	10c + 3c lilac	.45	.30
B82 SP27	15c + 4c yellow	.45	.30
B83 SP27	20c + 5c brn red	.50	.50
B84 SP27	25c + 6c aqua	.50	.50
	Nos. B80-B84 (5)	2.35	1.90

Caribbean Girl Scout Jamborette. Surtax for various charities.

Hibiscus SP28

Flowers: 10c+5c, Caesalpinia pulcherrima. 15c+6c, Heliconia psittacorum. 20c+10c, Lochnera rosea. 25c+12c, Ixora macrothyrsa.

1962, Mar. 7 Photo. *Perf. 14x13*

Cross in Red

B85 SP28	8c + 4c dk ol & scar	.50	.30
B86 SP28	10c + 5c dk bl & org	.50	.30
B87 SP28	15c + 6c multi	.50	.30
B88 SP28	20c + 10c multi	.50	.30
B89 SP28	25c + 12c dk bl grn, red & yel	.50	.30
	Nos. B85-B89 (5)	2.50	1.50

The surtax was for the Red Cross.

Hands Protecting Duck — SP29

1962, Dec. 15 Litho. *Perf. 13x14*

B90 SP29	2c + 1c shown	.40	.30
B91 SP29	8c + 2c Dog	.40	.30
B92 SP29	10c + 3c Donkey	.40	.30
B93 SP29	15c + 4c Horse	.40	.30
	Nos. B90-B93 (4)	1.60	1.20

The surtax was for the Organization for Animal Protection.

American Indian Girl — SP30

Girls: 10c+4c, Negro. 15c+10c, East Indian. 20c+10c, Indonesian. 40c+20c, Caucasian.

1963, Oct. 30 Photo. Unwmk.

B94 SP30	8c + 3c Prus grn	.25	.25
B95 SP30	10c + 4c red brn	.25	.25
a.	Min. sheet, 2 each #B94-B95	1.40	1.40
B96 SP30	15c + 10c dp blue	.25	.25
B97 SP30	20c + 10c brn red	.25	.25
B98 SP30	40c + 20c red vio	.35	.25
	Nos. B94-B98 (5)	1.35	1.25

The surtax was for Child Welfare.

X-15 SP31

Designs: 8c+4c, Flag of the Aeronautical and Astronautical Foundation. 10c+5c, 20c+10c, Agena B Ranger rocket.

1964, Apr. 15 *Perf. 13x12½*

B99 SP31	3c + 2c blk & rose lake	.40	.25
B100 SP31	8c + 4c blk, ultra & lt ultra	.40	.25
B101 SP31	10c + 5c blk & grn	.40	.25
B102 SP31	15c + 7c blk & yel brn	.40	.25
B103 SP31	20c + 10c blk & vio	.40	.25
	Nos. B99-B103 (5)	2.00	1.25

Surtax for the Aeronautical and Astronautical Foundation of Surinam.

Stylized Campfire amid Trees — SP32

1964, July 29 Litho. *Perf. 13x14*

B104 SP32	3c + 1c brn ol, yel bis & lem	.30	.25
B105 SP32	8c + 4c bluish blk, vio bl & yel bis	.30	.25
B106 SP32	10c + 5c dk red, red & yel bis	.30	.25
B107 SP32	20c + 10c grnsh blk, ol grn & yel bis	.30	.25
	Nos. B104-B107 (4)	1.20	1.00

Jamborette at Paramaribo, Aug. 20-30, marking the 40th anniv. of the Surinam Boy Scout Association.

Surtax for various charities.

Girls Skipping Rope — SP33

10c+4c, Children on swings. 15c+9c, Girl on scooter. 20c+10c, Boy rolling hoop.

1964, Nov. 30 Photo. *Perf. 14x13*

B108 SP33	8c + 3c dk blue	.25	.25
B109 SP33	10c + 4c red	.25	.25
a.	Min. sheet, 2 each #B108-B109	1.00	1.00
B110 SP33	15c + 9c olive grn	.25	.25
B111 SP33	20c + 10c magenta	.25	.25
	Nos. B108-B111 (4)	1.00	1.00

Issued for Child Welfare.

Mother and Child — SP34

Designs: 4c+2c, Pregnant woman. 15c+7c, Child. 25c+12c, Old man.

1965, Feb. 27 Photo. *Perf. 13x14*

B112 SP34	4c + 2c green	.25	.25
B113 SP34	10c + 5c brn & grn	.25	.25
B114 SP34	15c + 7c Prus bl & grn	.25	.25
B115 SP34	25c + 12c brt pur & grn	.25	.25
	Nos. B112-B115 (4)	1.00	1.00

50th anniv. of the Green Cross Assoc. which promotes public health services.

Girl with Leopard and Spider SP35

Designs: 10c+5c, Boy with monkey and spider. 15c+7c, Girl with tortoise and spider. 25c+10c, Boy with rabbit and spider.

Perf. 13x12½

1965, Nov. 26 Litho. Unwmk.

B116 SP35	4c + 4c lt grn & blk	.25	.25
B117 SP35	10c + 5c ocher & blk	.25	.25
B118 SP35	15c + 7c dp org & blk	.25	.25
a.	Min. sheet, 2 each #B116, B118	1.20	1.20
B119 SP35	25c + 10c lt ultra & blk	.25	.25
	Nos. B116-B119 (4)	1.00	1.00

Issued for Child Welfare.

"Help them to a safe haven" SP35a

1966, Jan. 31 Photo. *Perf. 14x13*

B120 SP35a	10c + 5c blk & grn	.25	.25
B121 SP35a	25c + 10c blk & rose brn	.25	.25
a.	Min. sheet of 3, 2 #B120, B121	.60	.60

The surtax was for the Intergovernmental Committee for European Migration (ICEM). The message on the stamps was given and signed by Queen Juliana.

Mary Magdalene, Disciples and "Round Table" Emblem — SP36

Mary Magdalene (John 20:18), and Service Club Emblems: 15c+8c, Toastmasters Intl. 20c+10c, Junior Chamber, Surinam. 25c+12c, Rotary Intl. 30c+15c, Lions Intl.

1966, Apr. 13 Photo. *Perf. 12½x13*

B122 SP36	10c + 5c dp crim, blk & gold	.25	.25
B123 SP36	15c + 8c dp vio, blk & bl	.25	.25
B124 SP36	20c + 10c yel org, blk & ultra	.25	.25
B125 SP36	25c + 12c grn, blk & gold	.25	.25
B126 SP36	30c + 15c ultra, blk & gold	.25	.25
	Nos. B122-B126 (5)	1.25	1.25

Easter charities.

"New Year's Eve" Boys with Bamboo Gun — SP37

Designs: 15c+8c, "The End of Lent," boys pouring paint over each other. 20c+10c, "Liberation Day," parading children. 25c+12c, "Queen's Birthday," children on hobbyhorses. 30c+15c, "Christmas," Children decorating room with star.

1966, Nov. 25 Litho. *Perf. 12½x13*

B127 SP37	10c + 5c multi	.25	.25
B128 SP37	15c + 8c multi	.25	.25
B129 SP37	20c + 10c multi	.25	.25
a.	Min. sheet of 3, 2 #B127, B129	.90	.80
B130 SP37	25c + 12c multi	.25	.25
B131 SP37	30c + 15c multi	.25	.25
	Nos. B127-B131 (5)	1.25	1.25

Child welfare.

Good Samaritan Giving His Coat — SP38

The Good Samaritan: 15c+8c, Dressing the wounds. 20c+10c, Feeding the poor man. 25c+12c, Poor man riding Samaritan's horse. 30c+15c, Samaritan taking poor man to the inn.

1967, Mar. 22

B132 SP38	10c + 5c yellow & blk	.25	.25
B133 SP38	15c + 8c lt blue & blk	.25	.25
B134 SP38	20c + 10c buff & blk	.25	.25
B135 SP38	25c + 12c pale rose & blk	.25	.25
B136 SP38	30c + 15c grn & blk	.25	.25
	Nos. B132-B136 (5)	1.25	1.25

Easter charities.

Children Stilt-walking — SP39

Children's Games: 15c+8c, Boys playing with marbles. 20c+10c, Girl playing dibs (five stones). 25c+12c, Boy making kite. 30c+15c, Girls play-cooking.

1967, Nov. 21 Litho. *Perf. 12½x13*

B137 SP39	10c + 5c multi	.25	.25
B138 SP39	15c + 8c multi	.25	.25
B139 SP39	20c + 10c multi	.25	.25
a.	Min. sheet, #B139, 2 #B137	1.00	.80
B140 SP39	25c + 12c multi	.25	.25
B141 SP39	30c + 15c multi	.25	.25
	Nos. B137-B141 (5)	1.25	1.25

Child welfare.

Cross, Ash Wednesday — SP40

Easter Symbols: 15c+8c, Palms, Palm Sunday. 20c+10c, Bread and Wine, Maundy Thursday. 25c+12c, Cross, Good Friday. 30c+15c, Chrismon, Easter Sunday.

1968, Mar. 27 Litho. ***Perf. 12½x13***

B142	SP40 10c + 5c lilac & gray	.25	.25
B143	SP40 15c + 8c brick red & grn	.25	.25
B144	SP40 20c + 10c yellow & dk grn	.25	.25
B145	SP40 25c + 12c gray & blk	.25	.25
B146	SP40 30c + 15c brt yel & brn	.25	.25
	Nos. B142-B146 (5)	1.25	1.25

Easter charities.

Hopscotch — SP41

15c+8c, Balancing pyramid. 20c+10c, Handball. 25c+12c, Handicraft. 30c+15c, Tug-of-war.

1968, Nov. 22 Litho. ***Perf. 12½x13***

B147	SP41 10c + 5c fawn & blk	.25	.25
B148	SP41 15c + 8c lt ultra & blk	.25	.25
B149	SP41 20c + 10c pink & blk	.25	.25
a.	Min. sheet, #B149, 2 #B147	1.00	.80
B150	SP41 25c + 12c yel grn & blk	.25	.25
B151	SP41 30c + 15c bluish lil & blk	.30	.25
	Nos. B147-B151 (5)	1.30	1.25

Child welfare.

Globe with Map of South America — SP42

1969, Apr. 2 Litho. ***Perf. 12½x13***

B152	SP42 10c + 5c bl & lt bl	.30	.30
B153	SP42 15c + 8c sl grn & yel	.30	.30
B154	SP42 20c + 10c sl grn & gray grn	.30	.30
B155	SP42 25c + 12c brn & bis	.30	.30
B156	SP42 30c + 15c vio & gray	.30	.30
	Nos. B152-B156 (5)	1.50	1.50

Easter charities.

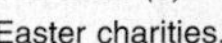

Pillow Fight — SP43

15c+8c, Eating contest. 20c+10c, Pole climbing. 25c+12c, Sack race. 30c+15c, Obstacle race.

1969, Nov. 21 Litho. ***Perf. 12½x13***

B157	SP43 10c + 5c lt ultra & mag	.25	.25
B158	SP43 15c + 8c yel & brn	.25	.25
B159	SP43 20c + 10c gray & dp bl	.25	.25
a.	Min. sheet, #B159, 2 B157	1.00	1.00
B160	SP43 25c + 12c pink & brt bl	.25	.25
B161	SP43 30c + 15c emer & brn	.25	.25
	Nos. B157-B161 (5)	1.25	1.25

Child welfare.

Butterfly — SP44

Designs: 10c+5c, Flower. 20c+10c, Flying bird. 25c+12c, Sun. 30c+15c, Star.

1970, Mar. 25 Litho. ***Perf. 12½x13***

B162	SP44 10c + 5c multi	.50	.50
B163	SP44 15c + 8c multi	.50	.50
B164	SP44 20c + 10c multi	.50	.50
B165	SP44 25c + 12c multi	.50	.50
B166	SP44 30c + 15c multi	.50	.50
	Nos. B162-B166 (5)	2.50	2.50

Easter.

Ludwig van Beethoven, 1786 — SP45

Various Portraits of Beethoven: 15c+8c, In 1804. 20c+10c, In 1812. 25c+12c, In 1814. 30c+15c, In 1827 (death mask).

Portrait and Inscription in Gray and Ocher

1970, Nov. 25 Litho. ***Perf. 12½x13***

B167	SP45 10c + 5c green	.55	.50
B168	SP45 15c + 8c scarlet	.55	.50
B169	SP45 20c + 10c blue	.55	.50
a.	Min. sheet, #B169, 2 #B167	1.50	1.50
B170	SP45 25c + 12c red org	.55	.50
B171	SP45 30c + 15c purple	.55	.50
	Nos. B167-B171 (5)	2.75	2.50

Ludwig van Beethoven (1770-1827), composer. The surtax was for child welfare.

Donkey and Palm — SP46

Easter: 15c+8c, Cock. 20c+10c, Lamb of God. 25c+12c, Cross and Crown of Thorns. 30c+15c, Sun.

1971, Apr. 7 Litho. ***Perf. 12½x13***

B172	SP46 10c + 5c multi	.50	.50
B173	SP46 15c + 8c blue & multi	.50	.50
B174	SP46 20c + 10c multi	.50	.50
B175	SP46 25c + 12c multi	.50	.50
B176	SP46 30c + 15c multi	.50	.50
	Nos. B172-B176 (5)	2.50	2.50

Easter charities.

Leapfrog, by Peter Brueghel — SP47

Children's Games, by Peter Brueghel: 15c+8c, Girl strewing flowers. 20c+10c, Spinning the hoop. 25c+12c, Ball players. 30c+15c, Stilt walker.

1971, Nov. 24 Photo. ***Perf. 13x14***

B177	SP47 10c + 5c multi	.55	.55
B178	SP47 15c + 8c multi	.55	.55
B179	SP47 20c + 10c multi	.55	.55
a.	Min. sheet, #B179, 2 #B177	1.75	1.75
B180	SP47 25c + 12c multi	.55	.55
B181	SP47 30c + 15c multi	.55	.55
	Nos. B177-B181 (5)	2.75	2.75

Child welfare.

Easter Candle — SP48

Easter: 15c+8c, Christ teaching Apostles, and crosses. 20c+10c, Cup and folded hands. 25c+12c, Fish in net. 30c+15c, Judas' bag of silver.

1972, Mar. 29 Litho. ***Perf. 12½x13***

B182	SP48 10c + 5c multi	.50	.50
B183	SP48 15c + 8c multi	.50	.50
B184	SP48 20c + 10c multi	.50	.50
B185	SP48 25c + 12c multi	.50	.50
B186	SP48 30c + 15c multi	.50	.50
	Nos. B182-B186 (5)	2.50	2.50

Easter charities.

Toys — SP49

Designs: 15c+8c, Abacus and clock. 20c+10c, Pythagorean theorem. 25c+12c, Model of molecule. 30c+15c, Monkey wrench and drill. Each design represents a different stage of education.

1972, Nov. 29 Litho. ***Perf. 12½x13***

B187	SP49 10c + 5c multi	.50	.50
B188	SP49 15c + 8c multi	.50	.50
B189	SP49 20c + 10c multi	.50	.50
a.	Min. sheet, #B189, 2 #B187	1.60	1.60
B190	SP49 25c + 12c multi	.50	.50
B191	SP49 30c + 15c multi	.50	.50
	Nos. B187-B191 (5)	2.50	2.50

Child welfare.

Jesus Calming the Waves — SP50

Easter: 15c+8c, The washing of the feet. 20c+10c, Jesus carrying Cross. 25c+12c, Cross and "ELI, ELI, LAMA SABACHTHANI?" 30c+15c, on the road to Emmaus.

1973, Apr. 4 Litho. ***Perf. 12½x13***

B192	SP50 10c + 5c multi	.45	.45
B193	SP50 15c + 8c multi	.45	.45
B194	SP50 20c + 10c multi	.45	.45
B195	SP50 25c + 12c multi	.45	.45
B196	SP50 30c + 15c multi	.45	.45
	Nos. B192-B196 (5)	2.25	2.25

Easter charities.

Red Cross and Florence Nightingale SP51

1973, Oct. 3 Litho. ***Perf. 14½x14***

B197	SP51 30c + 10c multi	1.00	1.00

30th anniversary of Surinam Red Cross.

Flower — SP52

1973, Nov. 28 Litho. ***Perf. 14x14½***

B198	SP52 10c + 5c shown	.55	.50
B199	SP52 15c + 8c Tree	.55	.50
B200	SP52 20c + 10c Dog	.55	.50
a.	Min. sheet, #B200, 2 #B198	1.40	1.25
B201	SP52 25c + 12c House	.55	.50
B202	SP52 30c + 15c Girl	.55	.50
	Nos. B198-B202 (5)	2.75	2.50

Child welfare.

Bitterwood — SP53

Tropical Flowers: 15c+8c, Passion flower. 20c+10c, Wild angelica. 25c+12c, Candlestick senna. 30c+15c, Blood flower.

1974, Apr. 3 Litho. ***Perf. 14x14½***

B203	SP53 10c + 5c multi	.50	.50
B204	SP53 15c + 8c multi	.50	.50
B205	SP53 20c + 10c multi	.50	.50
B206	SP53 25c + 12c multi	.50	.50
B207	SP53 30c + 15c multi	.50	.50
	Nos. B203-B207 (5)	2.50	2.50

Easter charities.

Boy Scout, Tent and Trees — SP54

Designs: 15c+8c, 5th Caribbean Jamboree emblem. 20c+10c, Scouts and emblem.

1974, Aug. 21 Litho. ***Perf. 14x14½***

B208	SP54 10c + 5c multi	.55	.40
B209	SP54 10c + 8c multi	.55	.40
B210	SP54 20c + 10c multi	.55	.40
	Nos. B208-B210 (3)	1.65	1.20

50th anniversary of Surinam Boy Scouts.

Fruit — SP55

Designs: 15c+8c, Children, birds and nest (security). 20c+10c, Flower, mother and child (protection). 25c+12c, Child and corn (good food). 30c+15c, Dancing children (child care).

1974, Nov. 27 Litho. ***Perf. 14½x14***

B211	SP55 10c + 5c multi	.50	.50
B212	SP55 15c + 8c multi	.50	.50
B213	SP55 20c + 10c multi	.50	.50
a.	Min. sheet, #B213, 2 #B211	1.60	1.40
B214	SP55 25c + 12c multi	.50	.50
B215	SP55 30c + 15c multi	.50	.50
	Nos. B211-B215 (5)	2.50	2.50

Child welfare.

The Good Shepherd — SP56

Designs: 20c+10c, Peter's denial. 30c+15c, The Women at the Tomb. 35c+20c, Jesus showing His wounds to Thomas.

1975, Mar. 26 Litho. ***Perf. 12½x13***

B216 SP56 15c + 5c yel grn & grn .50 .50
B217 SP56 20c + 10c org & dk bl .50 .50
B218 SP56 30c + 15c yel & red .50 .50
B219 SP56 35c + 20c bl & pur .50 .50
Nos. B216-B219 (4) 2.00 2.00

Easter charities.

Woman and IWY Emblem — SP57

1975, May 14 Litho. ***Perf. 12½x13***

B220 SP57 15c + 5c multi .65 .65
B221 SP57 30c + 15c multi .65 .65

International Women's Year.

Carib Indian Water Jug — SP58

Designs: 20c+10c, 35c+20c, Indian arrow head, diff. 30c+15c, Wayana board with animal figures.

1975, Nov. 12 Litho. ***Perf. 12½x13***

B222 SP58 15c + 5c multi .50 .50
B223 SP58 20c + 10c multi .50 .50
a. Min. sheet, #B223, 2 #B222 1.60 1.50
B224 SP58 30c + 15c multi .50 .50
B225 SP58 35c + 20c multi .50 .50
Nos. B222-B225 (4) 2.00 2.00

Child welfare.

Feeding the Hungry — SP59

Paintings: 25c+15c, Visiting the Sick. 30c+15c, Clothing the Naked. 35c+15c, Burying the Dead. 50c+25c, Giving Water to the Thirsty. Designs after panels in Alkmaar Church, 1504.

Perf. 14½x13½

1976, Apr. 14 **Photo.**

B226 SP59 20c + 10c multi .65 .50
B227 SP59 25c + 15c multi .80 .55
B228 SP59 30c + 15c multi 1.15 .85
a. Souv. sheet, #B228, 2 #B226 3.25 3.25
B229 SP59 35c + 15c multi 1.15 .85
B230 SP59 50c + 25c multi 1.60 1.15
Nos. B226-B230 (5) 5.35 3.90

Easter.

Pekingese and Boy's Head — SP60

25c+10c, German shepherd. 30c+15c, Dachshund. 35c+15c, Retriever. 50c+25c, Terrier.

1976 Litho. ***Perf. 13½***

B231 SP60 20c + 10c multi .80 .65
B232 SP60 25c + 10c multi 1.10 .85
B233 SP60 30c + 15c multi 1.30 1.00
a. Min. sheet, #B233, 2 #B231 6.25 6.25
B234 SP60 35c + 15c multi 1.30 1.10
B235 SP60 50c + 25c multi 2.10 1.50
Nos. B231-B235 (5) 6.60 5.10

Surtax was for child welfare.

St. Veronica's Veil — SP61

Descent from the Cross — SP62

Easter: Religious scenes, side panels, front and back, from triptych by Jan Mostaert (1473-1555).

1977, Apr. 6 Litho. ***Perf. 13½x14***

B236 SP61 20c + 10c multi .25 .25
B237 SP61 25c + 15c multi .50 .40
B238 SP61 30c + 15c multi .50 .40
B239 SP62 35c + 15c multi .60 .50
B240 SP61 50c + 25c multi .75 .60
Nos. B236-B240 (5) 2.60 2.15

Dog and Girl's Head — SP63

Child's Head and: 25c+15c, Monkey. 30c+15c, Rabbit. 35c+15c, Cat. 50c+25c, Parrot.

1977, Nov. 23 Litho. ***Perf. 13x14***

B241 SP63 20c + 10c multi .45 .40
B242 SP63 25c + 15c multi .55 .45
B243 SP63 30c + 15c multi .65 .50
a. Min. sheet, #B243, 2 #B241 1.60 1.60
B244 SP63 35c + 15c multi .80 .60
B245 SP63 50c + 25c multi 1.15 .90
Nos. B241-B245 (5) 3.60 2.85

Surtax was for child welfare.

Crosses, Luke 23:43 — SP64

Easter: 25c+15c, Serpent and Cross, John 3:14. 30c+15c, Lamb and blood, Exodus 12:13. 35c+15c, Passover plate, chalice and bread. 60c+30c, Cross and solar eclipse.

1978, Mar. 22 Litho. ***Perf. 12½x14***

B246 SP64 20c + 10c multi .25 .25
B247 SP64 25c + 15c multi .35 .30
B248 SP64 30c + 15c multi .40 .35
B249 SP64 35c + 15c multi .45 .40
B250 SP64 60c + 30c multi .90 .80
Nos. B246-B250 (5) 2.35 2.10

Child's Head and White Cat — SP65

Child's head and cats in various positions.

1978, Nov. 22 Litho. ***Perf. 14x13***

B251 SP65 20c + 10c multi .30 .30
B252 SP65 25c + 15c multi .45 .35
B253 SP65 30c + 15c multi .50 .40
a. Min. sheet, #B253, 2 #B251 1.60 1.60
B254 SP65 35c + 15c multi .55 .50
B255 SP65 60c + 30c multi .95 .80
Nos. B251-B255 (5) 2.75 2.35

Surtax was for child welfare.

Church, Cross and Chalice — SP66

Easter: Cross, chalice and various churches.

1979, Apr. 11 Litho. ***Perf. 13x14***

B256 SP66 20c + 10c multi .25 .25
B257 SP66 30c + 15c multi .40 .30
B258 SP66 35c + 15c multi .50 .40
B259 SP66 40c + 20c multi .60 .45
B260 SP66 60c + 30c multi .85 .65
Nos. B256-B260 (5) 2.60 2.05

Boy, Bird, Red Cross, Blood Transfusion Bottle — SP67

1979, Nov. 21 Litho. ***Perf. 13x14***

B261 SP67 20c + 10c multi .25 .25
B262 SP67 30c + 15c multi .40 .25
B263 SP67 35c + 15c multi .55 .35
a. Min. sheet, #B263, 2 #B261 2.25 1.45
B264 SP67 40c + 20c multi .65 .45
B265 SP67 60c + 30c multi .95 .60
Nos. B261-B265 (5) 2.80 1.90

Surtax was for child welfare.

Cross — SP68

Easter: Various symbols.

1980, Mar. 26 Litho. ***Perf. 13x14***

B266 SP68 20c + 10c multi .30 .30
B267 SP68 30c + 15c multi .45 .45
B268 SP68 40c + 20c multi .55 .50
B269 SP68 50c + 25c multi .75 .75
B270 SP68 60c + 30c multi .85 .85
Nos. B266-B270 (5) 2.90 2.85

Anansi — SP69

Characters from Anansi and His Creditors: No. B272, Ba Tigri. No. B273, Kakafowroe. No. B274, Ontiman. No. B275, Mat Kalaka.

1980, Nov. 5 Litho. ***Perf. 13x14***

B271 SP69 20c + 10c shown .30 .25
B272 SP69 25c + 15c multi .45 .30
B273 SP69 30c + 15c multi .50 .35
B274 SP69 35c + 15c multi .50 .35
B275 SP69 60c + 30c multi .90 .65
a. Min. sheet, #B275, 2 #B271 1.60 1.60
Nos. B271-B275 (5) 2.65 1.90

Surtax was for child welfare.

Woman Reading SP70

No. B277, Gardening. No. B278, With grandchildren.

1980, Dec. 10 ***Perf. 14x13***

B276 SP70 25c + 10c shown .40 .35
B277 SP70 50c + 15c multi .70 .60
B278 SP70 75c + 20c multi 1.00 .85
Nos. B276-B278 (3) 2.10 1.80

Surtax was for the elderly.

Crucifixion — SP71

Easter: Scenes from the Passion of Christ.

1981, Apr. 8 Litho. ***Perf. 13x14***

B279 SP71 20c + 10c multi .25 .25
B280 SP71 30c + 15c multi .35 .35
B281 SP71 50c + 25c multi .75 .75
B282 SP71 60c + 30c multi .80 .80
B283 SP71 75c + 35c multi .95 .95
Nos. B279-B283 (5) 3.10 3.10

Surtax was for the elderly.

Indian Girl — SP72

1981, Nov. 26 **Litho.**

B284 SP72 20c + 10c shown .25 .25
B285 SP72 30c + 15c Black .45 .45
B286 SP72 50c + 25c Hindustani .70 .70
B287 SP72 60c + 30c Javanese .75 .75
B288 SP72 75c + 35c Chinese .85 .85
a. Souv. sheet, #B288, 2 #B285 2.75 2.75
Nos. B284-B288 (5) 3.00 3.00

Surtax was for child welfare.

Easter — SP73

Designs: Stained-glass windows, Sts. Peter and Paul Church, Paramaribo.

1982, Apr. 7 Litho. ***Perf. 13x14***

B289 SP73 20c + 10c multi .35 .35
B290 SP73 35c + 15c multi .65 .65
B291 SP73 50c + 25c multi .95 .95
B292 SP73 65c + 30c multi .95 .95
B293 SP73 75c + 35c multi 1.20 1.20
Nos. B289-B293 (5) 4.10 4.10

Man Pushing Wheelbarrow SP74

Children's Drawings of City Cleaning Activities.

1982, Nov. 17 **Litho.**

B294 SP74 20c + 10c multi .35 .30
B295 SP74 35c + 15c multi .60 .50
B296 SP74 50c + 25c multi 1.15 .95
B297 SP74 65c + 30c multi 1.15 .95
B298 SP74 75c + 35c multi 1.35 1.15
a. Souv. sheet, #B298, 2 #B295 3.00 3.00
Nos. B294-B298 (5) 4.60 3.85

Surtax was for child welfare.

Easter — SP75

Mosaic Symbols.

1983, Mar. 23 **Litho.** ***Perf. 13x14***

B299 SP75 10c + 5c Dove .25 .25
B300 SP75 15c + 5c Bread .35 .25
B301 SP75 25c + 10c Fish .75 .60
B302 SP75 50c + 25c Eye 1.60 1.25
B303 SP75 65c + 30c Wine cup 1.75 1.35
Nos. B299-B303 (5) 4.70 3.70

Pitcher — SP76

No. B305, Headdress. No. B306, Medicine rattle. No. B307, Sieve. No. B308, Basket.

1983, Nov. 16 **Litho.** ***Perf. 13x14***

B304 SP76 10c + 5c shown .35 .25
B305 SP76 15c + 5c multi .35 .25
B306 SP76 25c + 10c multi .55 .45
B307 SP76 50c + 25c multi 1.60 1.25
B308 SP76 65c + 30c multi 1.75 1.35
a. Min. sheet, #B305, B306, B308 3.25 3.25
Nos. B304-B308 (5) 4.60 3.55

Easter — SP77

No. B309, Cross, rose. No. B310, Cemetery. No. B311, Candles. No. B312, Cross, crown of thorns. No. B313, Candle.

1984, Apr. 4 **Litho.** ***Perf. 13x14***

B309 SP77 10c + 5c multi .30 .25
B310 SP77 15c + 15c multi .30 .25
B311 SP77 25c + 10c multi .55 .50
B312 SP77 50c + 25c multi 1.50 1.25
B313 SP77 65c + 30c multi 1.75 1.25
Nos. B309-B313 (5) 4.40 3.50

SP78

Boy Scouts in Surinam, 60th Anniv.: 30c+10c, 8th Caribbean Jamboree emblem. 35c+10c, Salute. 50c+10c, Gardening. 90c+10c, Campfire in map of Surinam. Surtax was for Boy Scouts.

1984, Aug. 15 **Litho.** ***Perf. 13x14***

B314 SP78 30c + 10c multi .85 .70
B315 SP78 35c + 10c multi 1.05 .85
B316 SP78 50c + 10c multi 1.35 1.10
B317 SP78 90c + 10c multi 2.10 1.75
Nos. B314-B317 (4) 5.35 4.40

Children's Games — SP79

No. B318, Kites. No. B319, Kites, diff. No. B320, Pingi-pingi-kasi. No. B321, Cricket. No. B322, Peroen, peroen.

1984, Nov. 14 **Litho.** ***Perf. 13x14***

B318 SP79 5c + 5c multi .30 .25
B319 SP79 10c + 5c multi .30 .25
B320 SP79 30c + 10c multi .65 .50
B321 SP79 50c + 25c multi 1.30 1.00
a. Souv. sheet of 3, #B319-B321 2.25 2.25
B322 SP79 90c + 30c multi 1.90 1.50
Nos. B318-B322 (5) 4.45 3.50

Surtax was for child welfare.

Easter — SP80

1985, Mar. 27 **Litho.** ***Perf. 12½x14***

B323 SP80 5c + 5c multi .30 .25
B324 SP80 10c + 5c multi .30 .25
B325 SP80 30c + 15c multi .75 .55
B326 SP80 50c + 25c multi 1.15 .85
B327 SP80 90c + 30c multi 1.90 1.40
Nos. B323-B327 (5) 4.40 3.30

Surtax for child welfare.

Map, Emblem — SP81

No. B329, Crucifix, missionaries. No. B330, Scroll.

1985, Oct. 22 **Litho.** ***Perf. 13x14***

B328 SP81 30c + 10c shown .70 .55
B329 SP81 50c + 10c multi 1.00 .85
B330 SP81 90c + 20c multi 1.75 1.40
Nos. B328-B330 (3) 3.45 2.80

Evangelical Brotherhood Mission in Surinam, 250th anniv. Surtax for mission medical and social work.

Literacy — SP82

5c+5c, Boy reading. 10c+5c, Learning alphabet. 30c+10c, Writing. 50c+25c, Girl reading. 90c+30c, Studying.

1985, Nov. 6

B331 SP82 5c + 5c multi .35 .25
B332 SP82 10c + 5c multi .35 .25
B333 SP82 30c + 10c multi .55 .45
B334 SP82 50c + 25c multi 1.15 .90
a. Min. sheet of 3, #B332-B334 2.25 2.25
B335 SP82 90c + 30c multi 2.00 1.60
Nos. B331-B335 (5) 4.40 3.45

Surtax for child welfare.

Easter — SP83

1986, Mar. 19 **Litho.** ***Perf. 13x14***

B336 SP83 5c + 5c multi .25 .25
B337 SP83 10c + 5c multi .25 .25
B338 SP83 30c + 15c multi .60 .50
B339 SP83 50c + 25c multi 1.00 .80
B340 SP83 90c + 30c multi 1.50 1.15
Nos. B336-B340 (5) 3.60 2.95

Sts. Peter and Paul Cathedral, Cent. — SP84

No. B341, Exterior. No. B342, Saints, bas-relief. No. B343, Baptismal font.

1986, May 28 **Litho.**

B341 SP84 30c + 10c multi .50 .45
B342 SP84 50c + 10c multi .75 .60
B343 SP84 110c + 30c multi 1.75 1.50
Nos. B341-B343 (3) 3.00 2.55

Ancient Order of Foresters Court Charity, Cent. — SP85

50c+20c, Foresters emblem. 110c+30c, Court building.

1986, July 29 **Litho.** ***Perf. 14x13***

B344 SP85 50c + 20c multi .90 .55
B345 SP85 110c + 30c multi 2.00 1.25

Youth Activities SP86

No. B346, Hopscotch. No. B347, Ballet. No. B348, Mobile library. No. B349, Crafts. No. B350, Education.

1986, Nov. 5 **Litho.** ***Perf. 14x13***

B346 SP86 5c + 5c multi .30 .30
B347 SP86 10c + 5c multi .30 .30
B348 SP86 30c + 10c multi .55 .55
B349 SP86 50c + 25c multi 1.00 1.00
a. Min. sheet of 3, #B347-B349 2.50 2.50
B350 SP86 110c + 30c multi 2.10 2.10
Nos. B346-B350 (5) 4.25 4.25

Surtax for Children's Charities.

Easter — SP87

Stations of the cross — 5c+5c, Crucifixion. 10c+5c, Christ on cross. 35c+15c, Descent from cross. 60c+30c, Funeral procession. 110c+50c, Entombment.

1987, Apr. 8 **Litho.** ***Perf. 13x14***

B351 SP87 5c + 5c multi .25 .25
B352 SP87 10c + 5c multi .25 .25
B353 SP87 35c + 15c multi .55 .45
B354 SP87 60c + 30c multi 1.05 .85
B355 SP87 110c + 50c multi 1.75 1.40
Nos. B351-B355 (5) 3.85 3.20

Surtax for annual Easter Charity programs.

Natl. Girl Guides Movement, 40th Anniv. — SP88

Designs: 15c+10c, Mushroom, Brownie's emblem. 60c+10c, Clover, Guides' emblem. 110c+10c, Campfire, Rangers' emblem. 120c+10c, Ivy, Captain's emblem.

1987, May 7 **Litho.**

B356 SP88 15c + 10c multi .45 .35
B357 SP88 60c + 10c multi 1.00 .80
B358 SP88 110c + 10c multi 1.75 1.40
B359 SP88 120c + 10c multi 2.00 1.55
Nos. B356-B359 (4) 5.20 4.10

Surtax for the Surinam Girl Guides.

Caribbean Manari — SP89

50c+25c, Herring bone. 60c+30c, Tortoise-back. 110c+50c, Whirlpool (squares).

1987, Nov. 4 **Litho.** ***Perf. 13x14***

B360 SP89 50c + 25c multi .90 .85
B361 SP89 60c + 30c multi .95 .85
B362 SP89 110c + 50c multi 1.75 1.60
a. Min. sheet of 2, #B360, B362 2.50 2.40
Nos. B360-B362 (3) 3.60 3.30

Surtax to benefit child welfare organizations.

Easter — SP90

1988, Mar. 23 ***Perf. 13x13½***

B363 SP90 50c + 25c multi .75 .70
B364 SP90 60c + 30c multi 1.00 .95
B365 SP90 110c + 50c multi 1.75 1.60
Nos. B363-B365 (3) 3.50 3.25

Surtax for annual Easter Charity programs.

Intl. Red Cross and Red Crescent Organizations, 125th Annivs. — SP91

#B367, Anniv. & blood donation emblems.

1988, Oct. 26 Litho. *Perf. 13x14*

B366	SP91	60c + 30c multi	1.60	1.30
B367	SP91	120c + 60c multi	2.50	2.00

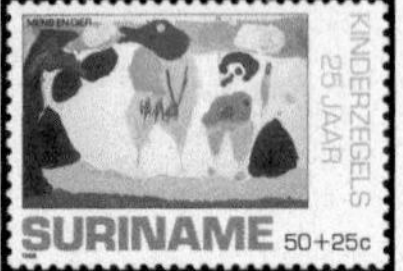

Children's Drawings SP92

50c+25c, Man and animal. 60c+30c, Children and nature. 110c+50c, Stop drugs.

1988, Dec. 5 Litho. *Perf. 14x13*

B368	SP92	50c + 25c multi	.90	.80
B369	SP92	60c + 30c multi	.95	.90
B370	SP92	110c + 50c multi	1.90	1.75
a.		Souv. sheet of 2, #B368, B370, perf 13½x13	3.75	3.75
		Nos. B368-B370 (3)	3.75	3.45

Surtax to benefit children's charities.

Easter 1989 — SP93

Details from Hungarian altarpieces: 60c+30c, Scenes of the Passion, by M.S., 1506. 105c+50c, Crucifixion, by Tamas of Koszvar, 1427. 110c+55c, Miracles, by Tamas of Koszvar, 1427.

1989, Mar. 21 Litho. *Perf. 13½*

Size: No. B372, 28½x36½mm

B371	SP93	60c + 30c multi	1.00	.85
B372	SP93	105c + 50c multi	1.90	1.50
B373	SP93	110c + 55c multi	2.10	1.75
		Nos. B371-B373 (3)	5.00	4.10

Surtax for annual East Charity programs.

Children's Drawings SP94

No. B374, Helping each other. No. B375, Child and nature. No. B376, In the school bus.

1989, Dec. 6 Litho. *Perf. 14x13*

B374	SP94	60c +30c multi	1.30	1.30
B375	SP94	105c +50c multi	2.25	2.25
B376	SP94	110c +55c multi	2.25	2.25
a.		Souv. sheet of 2, #B374, B376	3.50	3.50
		Nos. B374-B376 (3)	5.80	5.80

Surtax for children's charities.

Easter — SP95

Designs: No. B377, Mother holding Christ child. No. B378, Christ, follower. No. B379, Mary holding martyred Christ.

1990, Mar. 28 Litho. *Perf. 13x14*

B377	SP95	60c +30c multi	.95	.90
B378	SP95	105c +50c multi	1.60	1.55
B379	SP95	110c +55c multi	1.75	1.60
		Nos. B377-B379 (3)	4.30	4.05

Children's Drawings SP96

60c+30c, Children, hammock. 105c+50c, Child, animal, palm tree. 110c+55c, Child, bird in tree.

1990, Dec. 4 Litho. *Perf. 14x13*

B380	SP96	60c +30c multi	1.20	1.10
B381	SP96	105c +50c multi	1.90	1.75
B382	SP96	110c +55c multi	2.10	2.00
a.		Souv. sheet of 2, #B380, B382, perf. 13½x13	3.50	3.50
		Nos. B380-B382 (3)	5.20	4.85

SP97

Easter: 60c+30c, Christ carrying cross. 105c+50c, The Crucifixion. 110c+55c, Woman cradling Christ's body.

1991, Mar. 20 Litho. *Perf. 13x14*

B383	SP97	60c +30c multi	1.15	1.00
B384	SP97	105c +50c multi	1.35	1.20
B385	SP97	110c +55c multi	2.00	1.75
a.		Souv. sheet of 2, #B383, B385	3.75	3.75
		Nos. B383-B385 (3)	4.50	3.95

SP98

Children's Drawings: 60c+30c, Child in wheelchair. 105c+50c, Child beside trees. 110c+55c, Children playing outdoors.

1991, Dec. 4 Litho. *Perf. 13x14*

B386	SP98	60c +30c multi	1.15	.85
B387	SP98	105c +50c multi	2.10	1.50
B388	SP98	110c +55c multi	2.25	1.60
a.		Souv. sheet of 2, #B386, B388	3.00	3.00
		Nos. B386-B388 (3)	5.50	3.95

SP99

Easter: 60c+30c, Crucifixion. 105c+50c, Taking away body of Christ. 110c+55c, Resurrection.

1992, Mar. 18

B389	SP99	60c +30c multi	.90	.80
B390	SP99	105c +50c multi	1.75	1.55
B391	SP99	110c +55c multi	1.90	1.75
		Nos. B389-B391 (3)	4.55	4.10

SP100

Children's Drawings: 60c + 30c, Child as tree. 105c + 50c, Face as tree. 110c, + 55c, Boy and girl hanging from tree.

1992, Dec. 3 Litho. *Perf. 13x14*

B392	SP100	60c +30c multi	.90	.80
B393	SP100	105c +50c multi	1.75	1.55
B394	SP100	110c +55c multi	1.90	1.75
a.		Souv. sheet, #B392, B394	3.25	3.25
		Nos. B392-B394 (3)	4.55	4.10

Surtax for Child Welfare.

SP101

Easter: 60c+30c, Message from Christ. 110c+50c, Crucifixion. 125c+60c, Resurrection.

1993, Mar. 31 Litho. *Perf. 13x14*

B395	SP101	60c +30c multi	1.10	.85
B396	SP101	110c +50c multi	2.00	1.50
B397	SP101	125c +60c multi	2.25	1.60
		Nos. B395-B397 (3)	5.35	3.95

SP102

Children Playing Hopscotch: 25c+10c, 2 children. 35c+10c, 3 children. 50c+25c, 8 children. 75c+25c, 7 children.

1993, Dec. 3

B398	SP102	25c +10c grn & multi	1.00	.90
B399	SP102	35c +10c bl & multi	1.30	1.10
B400	SP102	50c +25c grn & multi	2.00	1.75
a.		Souvenir sheet of 2, #B399-B400	3.50	3.50
B401	SP102	75c +25c bl & multi	2.75	2.40
		Nos. B398-B401 (4)	7.05	6.15

Surtax for Child Welfare.

Stamps in No. B400a do not have the 1993 date in lower left corner.

AIR POST STAMPS

Allegory of Flight — AP1

Perf. 12½

1930, Sept. 3 Unwmk. Engr.

C1	AP1	10c dull red	3.25	.50
C2	AP1	15c ultra	3.25	.65
C3	AP1	20c dull green	.25	.25
C4	AP1	40c orange	.25	.40
C5	AP1	60c brown violet	.75	.40
C6	AP1	1g gray black	1.20	1.45
C7	AP1	1½g deep brown	1.60	1.60
		Nos. C1-C7 (7)	10.55	5.25

Nos. C1-C7 Overprinted in Black or Red

1931, Aug. 8

C8	AP1	10c red (Bk)	18.50	14.50
a.		Double overprint	650.00	
C9	AP1	15c ultra (Bk)	19.00	16.00
C10	AP1	20c dull grn (R)	19.00	18.50
C11	AP1	40c orange (Bk)	28.00	23.00
a.		Double overprint	650.00	
C12	AP1	60c brn vio (R)	57.50	57.50
C13	AP1	1g gray blk (R)	70.00	70.00
C14	AP1	1½g deep brn (Bk)	72.50	65.00
		Nos. C8-C14 (7)	284.50	264.50

The variety with period omitted after "Do" occurs twice on each sheet.

Warning: The red overprint may dissolve in water.

Type of 1930
Thick Paper

1941, Sept. 25 Litho. *Perf. 13*

C15	AP1	20c lt green	3.75	1.50
C16	AP1	40c lt orange	13.00	4.50
C17	AP1	2½g yellow	17.00	11.50
C18	AP1	5g blue green	300.00	320.00
C19	AP1	10g lt bister	50.00	52.50
		Nos. C15-C19 (5)	383.75	390.00

The lines of shading on Nos. C15 and C16 are not as heavy as on Nos. C3 and C4. For surcharges see Nos. C24-C25.

Type of 1930
Redrawn

1941 Engr. *Perf. 12*

C20	AP1	10c light red	2.00	.60
C21	AP1	60c dl brn vio	1.50	.90
C22	AP1	1g black	19.00	22.50
		Nos. C20-C22 (3)	22.50	24.00

Redrawn stamps have three horizontal lines through post horn and many minor variations. For surcharges see Nos. C23, CB1.

Catalogue values for unused stamps in this section, from this point to the end of the section, are for Never Hinged items.

Nos. C21, C17, C19 Surcharged with New Values and Bars in Carmine

1945, Mar. 12 *Perf. 13, 12*

C23	AP1	22½c on 60c	3.00	3.00
a.		Inverted surcharge	300.00	300.00
C24	AP1	1g on 2½g	21.00	21.00
C25	AP1	5g on 10g	21.00	21.00
		Nos. C23-C25 (3)	45.00	45.00

Women of Netherlands and Surinam — AP2

Perf. 12x12½

1949, May 10 Photo. Unwmk.

C26	AP2	27½c henna brown	6.25	3.25

Valid only on first flight of Paramaribo-Amsterdam service.

Globe and Winged Post Horn — AP3

1954, Sept. 25 *Perf. 13½x12½*

C27	AP3	15c dp ultra & ultra	1.60	1.20

Establishment of airmail service in Surinam, 25th anniv.

Redstone Mercury Rocket and Comdr. Alan B. Shepard, Jr. — AP4

15c, Cosmonaut Gagarin in capsule and globe.

1961, July 3 Litho. *Perf. 12*

C28	AP4	15c multicolored	1.00	1.00
C29	AP4	20c multicolored	1.00	1.00

"Man in Space," Major Yuri A. Gagarin, USSR, and Comdr. Alan B. Shepard, Jr., US.

Printed in sheets of 12 (4x3) with ornamental borders and inscriptions. Two printings differ in shades and selvage perforations.

Water Tower — AP5

Designs: 15c, 65c, Brewery. 20c, Boat on lake. 25c, 75c, Wood industry. 30c, Bauxite mine. 35c, 50c, Poelepantje bridge. 40c, Ship in harbor. 45c, Wharf.

1965, July 31 Photo. *Perf. 14x13½*

Size: 25x18mm

C30	AP5	10c olive grn	.25	.25
C31	AP5	15c ocher	.25	.25
C32	AP5	20c slate grn	.25	.25
C33	AP5	25c violet blue	.25	.25
C34	AP5	30c blue green	.25	.25
C35	AP5	35c red orange	.30	.25
C36	AP5	40c orange	.30	.25
C37	AP5	45c dk carmine	.30	.30
C38	AP5	50c vermilion	.30	.25
C39	AP5	55c emerald	.35	.35
C40	AP5	65c bister	.40	.35
C41	AP5	75c blue	.40	.35
		Nos. C30-C41 (12)	3.60	3.35

See Nos. C75-C82.

Eucyane Bicolor — AP6

1972, July 26 Litho. *Perf. 13½x14*

C42	AP6	15c shown	.40	.25
C43	AP6	20c Helicopis cupido	.40	.25
C44	AP6	25c Papilio thoas thoas	.40	.25
C45	AP6	30c Urania leilus	.50	.25
C46	AP6	35c Stalachtis calliope	.50	.25
C47	AP6	40c Stalachtis phlegia	.50	.25
C48	AP6	45c Victorina steneles	.50	.25
C49	AP6	50c Papilio neophilus	.60	.25
C50	AP6	55c Anartia amathea	.75	.60
C51	AP6	60c Adelpha cytherea	.75	.75
C52	AP6	65c Heliconius doris metharmina	.75	.40
C53	AP6	70c Nessaea obrinus	.80	.60
C54	AP6	75c Ageronia feronia	.80	.40
		Nos. C42-C54 (13)	7.65	4.75

Surinam butterflies. Valid for regular postage also. For surcharges, see Nos. 495-499.

#C42, C45 exist perf 14 with redrawn design.

Fish Type of 1976

Fish: 35c, Chaetodon unimaculatus. 60c, Centropyge loriculus. 95c, Caetodon collare.

1976, June 2 Litho. *Perf. 12½x13*

C55	A111	35c multicolored	.70	.40
C56	A111	60c multicolored	1.20	.65
C57	A111	95c multicolored	2.00	1.00
		Nos. C55-C57 (3)	3.90	2.05

Black-headed Sugarbird AP7

Birds of Surinam: 20c, Leistes militaris. 30c, Paradise tangara. 40c, Whippoorwill. 45c, Hemitraupis flavicollis. 50c, White-tailed gold-throated hummingbird. 55c, Saberwing. 60c, Blackcap parrot, vert. 65c, Toucan, vert. 70c, Manakin, vert. 75c, Collared parrot, vert. 80c, Cayenne cotinga, vert. 85c, Trogon, vert. 95c, Black-striped tropical tree owl, vert.

1977 Litho. *Perf. 14x13, 13x14*

C58	AP7	20c multi	.25	.25
C59	AP7	25c multi	.35	.25
C60	AP7	30c multi	.35	.25
a.		Min. sheet of 4, 2 each #C59-C60, perf. 13½x14	3.50	2.00
C61	AP7	40c multi	.65	.30
C62	AP7	45c multi	.65	.30
C63	AP7	50c multi	.70	.35
C64	AP7	55c multi	.85	.45
C65	AP7	60c multi	.90	.45
C66	AP7	65c multi	1.00	.50
C67	AP7	70c multi	1.10	.60
C68	AP7	75c multi	1.10	.60
C69	AP7	80c multi	1.10	.60
C70	AP7	85c multi	1.25	.65
C71	AP7	95c multi	1.60	.80
		Nos. C58-C71 (14)	11.85	6.35

A souv. sheet of 4 with same stamps and perf. as No. C60a has marginal inscription "Amphilex 77" with magnifier over No. 424. Sold in folder at phil. exhib. in Amsterdam May 26-June 5, 1977. Value $5.75.

Issued: 25c, 30c, 50c, 60c, 75c, 80c, 95c, Apr. 27; #C60a, May 26; others, Aug. 24.

See Nos. C88, C101. For surcharges and overprints see Nos. C102-C105, C108-C111, J58, J62.

Tropical Fish Type of 1976

60c, Chaetodon striatus. 90c, Bodianus pulchellus. 120c, Centropyge argi.

1977, June 8 Litho. *Perf. 13x13½*

C72	A111	60c multi	.75	.60
C73	A111	90c multi	1.40	.75
C74	A111	120c multi	2.00	1.40
		Nos. C72-C74 (3)	4.15	2.75

Type of 1965 Redrawn

Designs: 5c, Brewery. 10c, Water tower. 20c, Boat on lake. 25c, Wood industry. 30c, Bauxite mine. 35c, Poelepantje bridge. 40c, Ship in harbor. 60c, Wharf.

1976-78 Photo. *Perf. 12½x13½*

Size: 22x18mm

C75	AP5	5c ocher	.25	.25
a.		Bklt. pane, 4 #C75, 3 #C82 + label	2.50	
C76	AP5	10c olive green	.55	.55
a.		Bklt. pane, 1 #C76, 4 #C80 + label	2.75	
C77	AP5	20c slate green	.25	.25
a.		Bklt. pane, 2 ea #C77-C79	2.75	
b.		Bklt. pane, 6 #C77, 2 #C81	2.50	
C78	AP5	25c vio bl	.55	.55
C79	AP5	30c bl grn	.65	.65
C80	AP5	35c red org	.55	.55
C81	AP5	40c org	.90	.90
C82	AP5	60c dk car	.75	.75
		Nos. C75-C82 (8)	4.45	4.45

Nos. C75-C82 issued in booklets only. Nos. C75a and C77b have inscribed selvage the size of 4 stamps; Nos. C76a and C77a the size of 6 stamps.

Issued: 10c-35c, 12/8; 5c, 40c, 60c, #C77b, 1/11/78.

Tropical Fish Type of 1976

60c, Astyanax species. 90c, Corydoras wotroi. 120c, Gasteropelecus sternicla.

1978, June 21 Litho. *Perf. 13x13½*

C85	A111	60c multi	.75	.60
C86	A111	90c multi	1.25	1.10
C87	A111	120c multi	1.75	1.60
		Nos. C85-C87 (3)	3.75	3.30

Bird Type of 1977

Design: 5g, Crested curassow, vert.

1979, Jan. 10 Engr. *Perf. 13x13½*

C88	AP7	5g violet	5.25	4.00

Tropical Fish Type of 1979

60c, Cantherinus macrocerus. 90c, Holocenthrus rufus. 120c, Holacanthus tricolor.

1979, May 30 Photo. *Perf. 14x13*

C89	A129	60c multi	.65	.25
C90	A129	90c multi	1.10	.60
C91	A129	120c multi	1.60	1.10
		Nos. C89-C91 (3)	3.35	1.95

Tropical Fish Type of 1979

60c, Symphysodon discus. 75c, Aeqidens curviceps. 90c, Catoprion mento.

1980, Sept. 10 Photo. *Perf. 14x13*

C92	A129	60c multi	.70	.50
C93	A129	75c multi	1.20	.80
C94	A129	90c multi	1.20	.80
		Nos. C92-C94 (3)	3.10	2.10

Frog Type of 1981

75c, Phyllomedusa burmeisteri, vert. 1g, Dendrobates tinctorius, vert. 1.25g, Bufo guttatus, vert.

1981, June 24 *Perf. 13x14*

C95	A142	75c multi	1.25	1.00
C96	A142	1g multi	1.60	1.25
C97	A142	1.25g multi	2.00	1.50
		Nos. C95-C97 (3)	4.85	3.75

Turtle Type of 1982

65c, Platemys platycephala. 75c, Phrynops gibba. 125c, Rhinoclemys punctularia.

1982, Feb. 17 Photo. *Perf. 14x13*

C98	A146	65c multi	.90	.60
C99	A146	75c multi	1.10	.75
C100	A146	125c multi	2.00	1.40
		Nos. C98-C100 (3)	4.00	2.75

Bird Type of 1977

90c, Venezuelan Amazon, vert.

1985, Jan. 9 Litho. *Perf. 13x14*

C101	AP7	90c multi	4.75	2.10

For overprint see No. J61.

No. C60 Surcharged in Brown

1986, Oct. 1 Litho. *Perf. 14x13*

C102	AP7	15c on 30c multi	4.00	3.40

Nos. C70-C71 and C67 Surcharged

1987, Mar. Litho. *Perf. 13x14*

C103	AP7	10c on 85c No. C70	2.00	2.00
C104	AP7	10c on 95c No. C71	2.00	2.00
C105	AP7	25c on 70c No. C67	6.00	6.00
		Nos. C103-C105 (3)	10.00	10.00

Otter Type of 1989

1989, Jan. 18 Litho. *Perf. 13x14*

C107	A195	185c Otters, vert.	3.00	3.00

No. C63 Surcharged

1993, Jan. 20 Litho. *Perf. 14x13*

C108	AP7	35c on 50c multi	.40	.40

Nos. C62, C64-C65 Surcharged

1994, Apr. 11 *Perf. 14x13, 13x14*

C109	AP7	( ) on 60c #C65	.25	.25
C110	AP7	( ) on 45c #C62	2.00	2.00
C111	AP7	( ) on 55c #C64	3.00	3.00
		Nos. C109-C111 (3)	5.25	5.25

The face value of Nos. C109-C111 fluctuates with postal rate changes. Face values on day of issue were: No. C109, 2.50f; No. C110, 10f; No. C111, 25f. No. C109 paid the additional 5 grams letter rate to the Netherlands. No. C110 paid the basic rate to North and South America and the Caribbean. No. C111 paid the basic 10-gram letter rate to the Netherlands.

Size and location of surcharge varies.

AIR POST SEMI-POSTAL STAMPS

Catalogue values for unused stamps in this section are for Never Hinged items.

No. C20 Srchd. in Red

Unwmk.

1942, Jan. 2 Engr. *Perf. 12*

CB1	AP1	10c + 5c lt red, III	6.25	6.25
a.		Type IV	9.75	9.75
b.		Type V	27.50	27.50

The surtax was for the Red Cross.

See note on types III and IV below No. B40.

Nos. 193 and 194 Surcharged in Carmine

1946, Feb. 24 *Perf. 12*

CB2	A30	10c + 40c blue	2.10	1.75
CB3	A30	15c + 60c brown	2.10	1.75

The surtax was for the Red Cross.

Star Type of Semi-Postals

Perf. 13½x12½

1947, Dec. 16 Photo.

CB4	SP17	22½c + 27½c gray	3.75	3.00
CB5	SP17	27½c + 47½c grn	3.75	3.00

POSTAGE DUE STAMPS

D1

D2

Type I — 34 loops. "T" of "BETALEN" over center of loop; top branch of "E" of "TE" shorter than lower branch.

Type II — 33 loops. "T" of "BETALEN" over space between two loops.

Type III — 32 loops. "T" of "BETALEN" slightly to the left of center of loop; top branch of first "E" of "BETALEN" shorter than lower branch.

Type IV — 37 loops and letters of "PORT" larger than in the other 3 types.

Value in Black

Perf. 12½x12

1886-88 Typo. Unwmk.

Type III

J1	D1	2½c lilac	4.00	4.00
J2	D1	5c lilac	11.00	11.00
J3	D1	10c lilac	150.00	120.00
J4	D1	20c lilac	16.00	16.00
J5	D1	25c lilac	21.00	21.00
J6	D1	30c lilac ('88)	6.00	6.00
J7	D1	40c lilac	8.00	8.00
J8	D1	50c lilac ('88)	6.50	6.50
		Nos. J1-J8 (8)	222.50	192.50

Type I

J1a	D1	2½c	6.00	6.00
J2a	D1	5c	13.00	13.00
J3a	D1	10c	160.00	140.00
J4a	D1	20c	22.50	22.50
J5a	D1	25c	21.00	21.00
J6a	D1	30c	22.50	22.50
J7a	D1	40c	12.50	12.50
J8a	D1	50c	7.25	7.25
		Nos. J1a-J8a (8)	264.75	244.75

Type II

J1b	D1	2½c	5.00	5.00
J2b	D1	5c	12.00	12.00
J3b	D1	10c	1,600.	1,600.
J4b	D1	20c	17.00	17.00
J5b	D1	25c	450.00	450.00

No.	Type	Description	Unused	Used
J6b	D1	30c	85.00	85.00
J7b	D1	40c	400.00	400.00
J8b	D1	50c	7.75	7.75

Type IV

No.	Type	Description	Unused	Used
J3c	D1	10c	575.00	320.00
J5c	D1	25c	220.00	220.00
J7c	D1	40c	220.00	220.00
		Nos. J3c-J7c (3)	1,015.	760.00

Nos. J1-J16 were issued without gum. For surcharges, see Nos. J15-J16.

1892-96 Value in Black *Perf. 12½*

Type III

No.	Type	Description	Unused	Used
J9	D2	2½c lilac	.80	.80
J10	D2	5c lilac	1.25	1.20
J11	D2	10c lilac	26.00	26.00
J12	D2	20c lilac	2.40	2.00
J13	D2	25c lilac	8.00	7.25

Type I

No.	Type	Description	Unused	Used
J9a	D2	2½c	.80	.80
J10a	D2	5c	2.00	2.00
J11a	D2	10c	24.00	22.50
J12a	D2	20c	5.00	5.00
J13a	D2	25c	13.00	12.50
J14	D2	40c ('96)	3.25	4.50

Type II

No.	Type	Description	Unused	Used
J9b	D2	2½c	1.20	1.20
J10b	D2	5c	3.00	3.00
J11b	D2	10c	40.00	42.50
J12b	D2	20c	92.50	90.00
J13b	D2	25c	100.00	100.00

For surcharges, see Nos. 121-122.

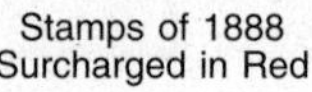
Stamps of 1888 Surcharged in Red

1911, July 15

No.	Type	Description	Unused	Used
J15	D1	10c on 30c lil (III)	97.50	97.50
a.		10c on 30c lilac (I)	225.00	260.00
b.		10c on 30c lilac (II)	*2,000.*	*2,000.*
J16	D1	10c on 50c lil (III)	120.00	120.00
a.		10c on 50c lilac (I)	140.00	140.00
b.		10c on 50c lilac (II)	140.00	140.00

D3

Type I

Value in Color of Stamp

1913-31 *Perf. 12½, 13½x12½*

No.	Type	Description	Unused	Used
J17	D2	½c lilac ('30)	.25	2.00
J18	D2	1c lilac ('31)	.25	2.00
J19	D2	2c lilac ('31)	.25	2.00
J20	D2	2½c lilac	.25	2.00
J21	D2	5c lilac	.25	2.00
J22	D2	10c lilac	.25	2.00
J23	D2	12c lilac ('31)	.25	2.00
J24	D2	12½c lilac ('22)	.25	2.00
J25	D2	15c lilac ('26)	.55	2.00
J26	D2	20c lilac	.85	2.00
J27	D2	25c lilac	.45	2.00
J28	D2	30c lilac ('26)	.45	2.00
J29	D2	40c lilac	14.50	14.00
J30	D2	50c lilac ('26)	1.25	2.00
J31	D2	75c lilac ('26)	1.50	2.00
J32	D3	1g lilac ('26)	1.75	2.00
		Nos. J17-J32 (16)	23.30	44.00

Catalogue values for unused stamps in this section, from this point to the end of the section, are for Never Hinged items.

D4

1945 Litho. *Perf. 12*

No.	Type	Description	Unused	Used
J33	D4	1c light brown violet	2.40	1.20
J34	D4	5c light brown violet	6.50	2.50
J35	D4	25c light brown violet	10.50	.80
		Nos. J33-J35 (3)	19.40	4.50

D5

Perf. 13½x12½

1950 Unwmk. Photo.

No.	Type	Description	Unused	Used
J36	D5	1c purple	12.00	8.00
J37	D5	2c purple	12.00	8.00
J38	D5	2½c purple	12.00	8.00
J39	D5	5c purple	8.00	1.60
J40	D5	10c purple	8.00	1.60
J41	D5	15c purple	12.00	8.00
J42	D5	20c purple	4.00	8.00
J43	D5	25c purple	24.00	1.60
J44	D5	50c purple	32.00	8.00
J45	D5	75c purple	45.00	45.00
J46	D5	1g purple	32.00	20.00
		Nos. J36-J46 (11)	201.00	117.80

D6

1956

No.	Type	Description	Unused	Used
J47	D6	1c purple	.80	.80
J48	D6	2c purple	.80	.80
J49	D6	2½c purple	.80	.80
J50	D6	5c purple	.80	.80
J51	D6	10c purple	.80	.80
J52	D6	15c purple	1.20	1.20
J53	D6	20c purple	1.20	1.20
J54	D6	25c purple	1.20	.40
J55	D6	50c purple	2.00	.50
J56	D6	75c purple	2.40	1.60
J57	D6	1g purple	3.25	1.25
		Nos. J47-J57 (11)	15.25	10.15

For surcharges, see Nos. J64-J69.

Stamps of 1977-1985 Overprinted

Perf. 13x14, 14x13

1987, July Litho.

No.	Type	Description	Unused	Used
J58	AP7	65c No. C66	3.00	3.00
J59	A156	65c No. 638	3.00	3.00
J60	A156	80c No. 640	3.75	3.75
J61	AP7	90c No. C101	4.25	4.25
J62	AP7	95c No. C71	5.00	5.00
J63	A173	1g No. 725	5.25	5.25
		Nos. J58-J63 (6)	24.25	24.25

Nos. J47, J50, J55 and J57 Surcharged

Methods and Perfs. As Before

2007, Dec. 3

No.	Type	Description	Unused	Used
J64	D6	$1 on 1c #J47	.75	.75
J65	D6	$1.50 on 1g #J57	1.10	1.10
J66	D6	$2 on 5c #J50	1.50	1.50
J67	D6	$3 on 50c #J55	2.25	2.25
J68	D6	$3.50 on 1g #J57	2.60	2.60
J69	D6	$4 on 1g #J57	3.00	3.00
		Nos. J64-J69 (6)	11.20	11.20

SWAZILAND

'swə-zē-ˌland

LOCATION — Southeast Africa bordered by the Transvaal and Zululand in South Africa and by Mozambique

GOVT. — Constitutional monarchy

AREA — 6,705 sq. mi.

POP. — 985,335 (1999 est.)

CAPITAL — Mbabane

An independent state in the 19th century, Swaziland was administered by Transvaal from 1894 to 1906, when the administration was transferred to the British High Commissioner for South Africa. In 1934 Swaziland and Bechuanaland Protectorate came under the administration of the British High Commissioner for Basutoland. The issuing of individual postage stamps had been resumed in 1933. Internal self-government was introduced in 1967. Independence was proclaimed September 6, 1968.

12 Pence = 1 Shilling

20 Shillings = 1 Pound

100 Cents = 1 Rand (1961)

100 Cents = 1 Emalangeni (1975)

Catalogue values for unused stamps in this country are for Never Hinged items, beginning with Scott 38 in the regular postage section and Scott J1 in the postage due section.

Coat of Arms — A1

Black Overprint

1889 Unwmk. *Perf. 12½, 12½x12*

No.	Type	Description	Unused	Used
1	A1	½p gray	10.50	*27.00*
a.		Inverted overprint	1,250.	850.00
b.		"Swazielan"	2,100.	1,200.
c.		As "b," inverted overprint		8,000.
2	A1	1p rose	25.00	25.00
a.		Inverted overprint	800.00	*750.00*
3	A1	2p olive bister	32.50	18.00
a.		Inverted overprint	950.00	575.00
b.		"Swazielan"	550.00	475.00
c.		Perf. 12½x12	100.00	40.00
d.		As "c," "Swazielan"	1,250.	725.00
e.		As "d," inverted overprint		1,750.
f.		As "b," inverted overprint	7,500.	5,000.
g.		Double overprint	2,600.	
4	A1	6p gray blue	47.50	*62.50*
5	A1	1sh green	21.00	*16.00*
a.		Inverted overprint	1,000.	525.00
6	A1	2sh6p yellow	325.00	*500.00*
7	A1	5sh slate	175.00	*340.00*
a.		Inverted overprint	*1,900.*	*3,000.*
b.		"Swazielan"	*5,250.*	
c.		As "b," inverted overprint	*5,750.*	
8	A1	10sh lt brown	*7,250.*	*5,000.*

1892 Red Overprint

No.	Type	Description	Unused	Used
9	A1	½p gray	8.50	19.00
a.		Inverted overprint	575.00	
b.		Double overprint	525.00	*525.00*
c.		Pair, one without overprint		2,000.

Beware of counterfeits.

Reprints have a period after "Swazieland."

Stamps of Swaziland were replaced by those of Transvaal in 1895. Swaziland issues were resumed in 1933.

George V — A2

Perf. 14

1933, Jan. 2 Engr. Wmk. 4

No.	Type	Description	Unused	Used
10	A2	½p green	.40	*.35*
11	A2	1p carmine	.40	.25
12	A2	2p lt brown	.40	.50
13	A2	3p ultra	.55	*3.75*
14	A2	4p orange	3.50	*4.25*
15	A2	6p rose violet	1.60	*1.30*
16	A2	1sh olive green	1.75	*3.25*
17	A2	2sh6p violet	16.00	*25.00*
18	A2	5sh gray	40.00	*57.50*
19	A2	10sh black brown	145.00	*185.00*
		Nos. 10-19 (10)	209.60	*281.15*
		Set, never hinged	500.00	

The ½, 1p, 2p and 6p values were prepared overprinted "OFFICIAL". They were withdrawn before they were used. Value, set of 4, $50,000.

Common Design Types pictured following the introduction.

Silver Jubilee Issue

Common Design Type

1935, May 4 *Perf. 11x12*

No.	Type	Description	Unused	Used
20	CD301	1p carmine & blue	.55	*1.75*
21	CD301	2p black & ultra	2.00	*3.50*
22	CD301	3p ultra & brown	1.00	*8.00*
23	CD301	6p brn, vio & ind	3.25	*5.00*
		Nos. 20-23 (4)	6.80	18.25
		Set, never hinged	11.00	

Coronation Issue

Common Design Type

1937, May 12 *Perf. 11x11½*

No.	Type	Description	Unused	Used
24	CD302	1p dark carmine	.25	*1.50*
25	CD302	2p brown	.25	*.30*
26	CD302	3p deep ultra	.25	.90
		Nos. 24-26 (3)	.75	2.70
		Set, never hinged	1.60	

George VI — A3

1938, Apr. 1 *Perf. 13, 13x13½*

No.	Type	Description	Unused	Used
27	A3	½p green	.25	*1.60*
28	A3	1p rose carmine	.55	*1.10*
29	A3	1½p light blue	.25	*.65*
a.		Perf. 14 ('42)	1.90	.70
30	A3	2p brown	.25	*.35*
31	A3	3p ultra	5.00	6.25
32	A3	4p red orange	.65	*.90*
33	A3	6p rose violet	2.25	.95
34	A3	1sh olive green	.65	.40
35	A3	2sh6p dark violet	13.00	11.00
36	A3	5sh gray	26.00	12.50
37	A3	10sh black brown	5.25	*4.50*
		Nos. 27-37 (11)	54.10	40.20
		Set, never hinged	85.00	

Catalogue values for unused stamps in this section, from this point to the end of the section, are for Never Hinged items.

Peace Issue

South Africa, Nos. 100-102 Overprinted

Basic stamps inscribed alternately in English and Afrikaans.

1945, Dec. 3 Wmk. 201 *Perf. 14*

No.	Type	Description	Unused	Used
38	A42	1p rose pink & choc, pair	.80	*1.25*
a.		Single, English	.25	.25
b.		Single, Afrikaans	.25	.25
39	A43	2p vio & sl blue, pair	.80	*1.25*
a.		Single, English	.25	.25
b.		Single, Afrikaans	.25	.25
40	A43	3p ultra & dp ultra, pair	.80	*3.00*
a.		Single, English	.25	.25
b.		Single, Afrikaans	.25	.25
		Nos. 38-40 (3)	2.40	*5.50*

World War II victory of the Allies.

Royal Visit Issue

Type of Basutoland, 1947

Perf. 12½

1947, Feb. 17 Wmk. 4 Engr.

No.	Type	Description	Unused	Used
44	A3	1p red	.25	.25
45	A4	2p green	.25	.25
46	A5	3p ultramarine	.25	.25
47	A6	1sh dark violet	.25	.25
		Nos. 44-47 (4)	1.00	1.00

Visit of the British Royal Family, 3/25/47.

Silver Wedding Issue

Common Design Types

1948, Dec. 1 Photo. *Perf. 14x14½*

No.	Type	Description	Unused	Used
48	CD304	1½p bright ultra	.30	.25

Perf. 11½x11

Engraved; Name Typographed

No.	Type	Description	Unused	Used
49	CD305	10sh violet brown	40.00	*47.50*

UPU Issue
Common Design Types
Engr.; Name Typo. on 3p, 6p
Perf. 13½, 11x11½

1949, Oct. 10 Wmk. 4

50	CD306	1½p blue	.30	.25
51	CD307	3p indigo	1.60	2.00
52	CD308	6p red lilac	.40	1.75
53	CD309	1sh olive	.50	.65
		Nos. 50-53 (4)	2.80	4.65

Coronation Issue
Common Design Type

1953, June 3 Engr. *Perf. 13½x13*

54	CD312	2p yel brn & blk	.30	.25

Asbestos Mine — A4

Married Woman — A5

1p, 2sh6p, Highveld view. 3p, 1sh3p, Courting couple. 4½p, 5sh, Warrior. 6p, £1, Kudu. 1sh, Asbestos mine. 10sh, Married woman.

Perf. 13x13½, 13½x13

1956, July 2 Engr. Wmk. 4
Center in Black, except Nos. 63-64

55	A4	½p orange	.40	.25
56	A4	1p emerald	.25	.25
57	A5	2p redsh brown	.40	.25
58	A5	3p rose red	.30	.25
59	A5	4½p ultra	.85	.25
60	A5	6p magenta	2.75	.25
61	A4	1sh gray olive	.40	.25
62	A5	1sh3p brown	4.50	*4.50*
63	A4	2sh6p car & brt grn	3.25	3.25
64	A5	5sh blue gray & vio	12.00	8.00
65	A5	10sh dull violet	25.00	20.00
66	A5	£1 turquoise	60.00	40.00
		Nos. 55-66 (12)	110.10	77.50

Nos. 55-61 and 63-66 Surcharged with New Value

2½c I, 2½c II, 4c I, 4c II

5c I, 5c II, 25c I, 25c II

50c I, 50c II, 50c III

R1 I, R1 II, R1 III

R2 I, R2 II

1961

67	A4	½c on ½p	3.50	6.50
a.		Inverted surcharge	1,300.	
68	A4	1c on 1p	.25	.25
a.		"1c" at center	35.00	
b.		Double surcharge	1,500.	
69	A5	2c on 2p	.25	.25
70	A5	2½c on 2p	.25	.25
71	A5	2½c on 3p (I)	.25	.25
a.		Type II	.25	.25
72	A5	3½c on 2p	.25	.25
73	A5	4c on 4½p (II)	.25	.25
a.		Type I	.25	.25
74	A5	5c on 6p (II)	.25	.25
a.		Type I	.25	.25
75	A4	10c on 1sh	40.00	11.00
a.		Double surcharge	1,600.	
76	A4	25c on 2sh6p (I)	.40	1.50
a.		Type II, "25c" centered	1.60	1.00
b.		Type II, "25c" at lower left	450.00	*600.00*
77	A5	50c on 5sh (I)	.45	*1.50*
a.		Type II	9.50	3.00
b.		Type III	725.00	*850.00*
78	A5	1r on 10sh (I)	1.75	1.50
a.		Type II	4.00	*6.00*
b.		Type III	85.00	*120.00*

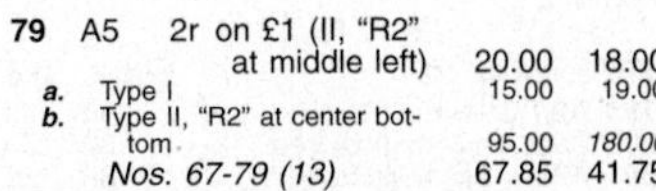

79	A5	2r on £1 (II, "R2" at middle left)	20.00	18.00
a.		Type I	15.00	19.00
b.		Type II, "R2" at center bottom	95.00	*180.00*
		Nos. 67-79 (13)	67.85	41.75

The type II "25c" surcharge is nearly centered in the sky on No. 76a, and is at lower left touching the value tablet on No. 76b.

Surcharge types are numbered chronologically.

For surcharges see Nos. J3-J6.

Types of 1956

½c, 10c, Asbestos mine. 1c, 25c, Highveld view. 2c, 1r, Married woman. 2½c, 12½c, Courting couple. 4c, 50c, Warrior. 5c, 2r, Kudu.

Perf. 13x13½, 13½x13

1961 Engr. Wmk. 4
Center in Black, except Nos. 88-89

80	A4	½c orange	.25	*1.25*
81	A4	1c emerald	.25	.25
82	A5	2c redsh brown	.25	*2.75*
83	A5	2½c rose red	.25	.25
84	A4	4c ultra	.25	*1.50*
85	A5	5c magenta	1.25	.25
86	A4	10c gray olive	.25	.25
87	A5	12½c brown	1.25	.70
88	A4	25c car & brt green	4.50	*6.50*
89	A5	50c blue gray & vio	5.50	3.00
90	A5	1r dull violet	13.50	*16.00*
91	A5	2r turquoise	21.00	14.00
		Nos. 80-91 (12)	48.50	46.70

Swazi Shields — A6

Designs: 1c, Battle axe. 2c, Forestry. 2½c, Ceremonial headdress. 3½c, Musical instrument. 4c, Irrigation. 5c, Widow bird. 7½c, Rock paintings. 10c, Secretary bird. 12½c, Pink arum lily. 15c, Married woman. 20c, Malaria control. 25c, Swazi warrior. 50c, Ground hornbill, horiz. 1r, Aloes. 2r, Msinsi (flame tree), horiz.

Perf. 12½x14, 14x12½

1962, Apr. 24 Photo. Wmk. 314

92	A6	½c ocher, blk & brn	.25	.25
93	A6	1c gray & orange	.25	*.25*
94	A6	2c lt yel grn, dk grn & blk	.25	*1.25*
95	A6	2½c vermilion & blk	.25	.25
96	A6	3½c gray & emerald	.25	*.70*
97	A6	4c aqua & black	.25	.25
98	A6	5c orange red & blk	1.50	.25
99	A6	7½c dull ocher & brn	2.00	.40
100	A6	10c lt blue & black	4.00	.25
101	A6	12½c lt olive & dp car	2.25	*3.50*
102	A6	15c red lilac & blk	1.75	1.25
103	A6	20c emerald & blk	.50	*1.50*
104	A6	25c ultra & blk	.60	*1.25*
105	A6	50c rose red & dk brn	18.00	7.00
106	A6	1r bister & emer	3.25	2.50
107	A6	2r ultra & scar	22.50	15.00
		Nos. 92-107 (16)	57.85	35.85

For surcharge & overprints see #138, 143-159.

Freedom from Hunger Issue
Common Design Type

1963, June 4 *Perf. 14x14½*

108	CD314	15c lilac	.50	.50

Red Cross Centenary Issue
Common Design Type

1963, Sept. 2 Litho. *Perf. 13*

109	CD315	2½c black & red	.30	.30
110	CD315	15c ultra & red	.80	.80

Train and Railroad Map — A7

Perf. 11½x12

1964, Nov. 5 Engr. Wmk. 314

111	A7	2½c purple & brt grn	.60	.25
112	A7	3½c dk olive & blue	.65	*1.10*
113	A7	15c dk brown & orange	.80	.70
114	A7	25c dk blue & yellow	1.00	.80
		Nos. 111-114 (4)	3.05	2.85

Opening of the Swaziland Railroad linking Ka Dake with Lourenco Marques.

ITU Issue
Common Design Type
Perf. 11x11½

1965, May 17 Litho. Wmk. 314

115	CD317	2½c blue & bister	.25	.25
116	CD317	15c red lil & rose red	.45	.45

Intl. Cooperation Year Issue
Common Design Type

1965, Oct. 25 *Perf. 14½*

117	CD318	½c bl grn & claret	.25	.25
118	CD318	15c lt violet & grn	.50	.50

Churchill Memorial Issue
Common Design Type

1966, Jan. 24 Photo. *Perf. 14*
Design in Black, Gold and Carmine Rose

119	CD319	½c brt blue	.25	.50
120	CD319	2½c green	.25	*.90*
121	CD319	15c brown	.50	.25
122	CD319	25c violet	.70	*.90*
		Nos. 119-122 (4)	1.70	2.55

UNESCO Anniversary Issue
Common Design Type

1966, Dec. 1 Litho. *Perf. 14*

123	CD323	2½c "Education"	.25	.25
124	CD323	7½c "Science"	.40	.40
125	CD323	15c "Culture"	.75	.75
		Nos. 123-125 (3)	1.40	1.40

King Sobhuza II and Map of Swaziland A8

Design: 7½c, 25c, King Sobhuza II, vert.

Perf. 14½x14, 14x14½

1967, Apr. 25 Photo. Wmk. 314

126	A8	2½c multicolored	.25	.25
127	A8	7½c multicolored	.25	.25
128	A8	15c multicolored	.25	.25
129	A8	25c multicolored	.30	.30
		Nos. 126-129 (4)	1.05	1.05

Attainment of internal self-government.

King Sobhuza II, University Buildings and Graduates — A9

Perf. 14x14½

1967, Sept. 1 Photo. Unwmk.

130	A9	2½c yel, sepia & dp bl	.25	.25
131	A9	7½c blue, sepia & dp bl	.25	.25
132	A9	15c dl rose, sepia & dp bl	.25	.25
133	A9	25c lt vio, sepia & dp bl	.30	.30
		Nos. 130-133 (4)	1.05	1.05

1st conferment of degrees by the University of Botswana, Lesotho and Swaziland at Roma, Lesotho.

Swazi Reed Dance (Umhlanga) — A10

Designs: 3c, 15c, Feast of the First Fruits, Incwala (bull, sun and king), horiz.

Perf. 14½x14, 14x14½

1968, Jan. 5 Photo. Wmk. 314

134	A10	3c red, blk & silver	.25	.25
135	A10	10c brown, blk, org & sil	.25	.25
136	A10	15c red, blk & gold	.25	.25
137	A10	25c brown, blk, org & gold	.30	.30
		Nos. 134-137 (4)	1.05	1.05

No. 98 Surcharged with New Value

1968, May 1 *Perf. 12½x14*

138	A6	3c on 5c org red & blk	.60	.60

Independent Kingdom

Plowing and King Sobhuza II A11

Designs: 4½c, Cable lift carrying asbestos. 17½c, Worker cutting sugar cane. 25c, Iron ore mining and map showing Swaziland railroad.

Perf. 14x12½

1968, Sept. 6 Photo. Wmk. 314

139	A11	3c gold & multi	.25	.25
140	A11	4½c gold & multi	.25	.25
141	A11	17½c gold & multi	.25	.25
142	A11	25c slate & gold	.30	.30
a.		Strip of 4, #139-142	4.00	4.00
		Nos. 139-142 (4)	1.05	1.05

Swaziland's independence.

Nos. 139-142 printed in sheets of 50. No. 142a printed in sheets of 20 (4x5).

Nos. 92-107 Overprinted; No. 96 Surcharged

1968, Sept. 6 *Perf. 12½x14, 14x12½*

143	A6	½c ocher, blk & brn	.25	.25
144	A6	1c gray & orange	.25	.25
145	A6	2c multicolored	.25	.25
146	A6	2½c vermilion & blk	1.25	*2.25*
147	A6	3c on 2½c #146	.25	.25
148	A6	3½c gray & emerald	.25	.25
149	A6	4c aqua & black	.25	.25
150	A6	5c org red & blk	4.75	.25
151	A6	7½c dull ocher & brn	.75	.25
152	A6	10c lt blue & blk	5.00	.25
153	A6	12½c lt olive & dp car	.45	*.90*
154	A6	15c red lilac & blk	.45	*1.25*
155	A6	20c emerald & blk	1.25	*2.00*
156	A6	25c ultra & blk	.55	*1.10*
157	A6	50c rose red & dk brn	8.50	5.00
a.		Wmk. sideways	3.75	*10.00*
158	A6	1r bister & emerald	3.25	*5.00*
159	A6	2r ultra & scarlet	6.50	*11.50*
a.		Wmk. sideways	8.50	5.50
		Nos. 143-159 (17)	34.20	31.25

Caracal (African Lynx) — A12

Waterbuck — A12a

1c, Cape porcupine. 2c, Crocodile. 3c, Lion. 3½c, African elephants. 5c, Bush pig. 7½c, Impalas. 10c, Chacma baboon. 12½c, Ratel (honey badger). 15c, Leopard. 20c, Blue wildebeest (brindled gnu). 25c, White (square-lipped) rhinoceros. 50c, Burchell's zebra. 2r, Giraffe.

Perf. 13x12½, 12½x13

1969, Aug. 1 Litho. Wmk. 314

Size: 30½x21½mm

160 A12 ½c multicolored .25 .25
161 A12 1c multicolored .25 .25
162 A12 2c multicolored .25 .25
a. Perf. 12½x12 ('75) 4.00 *5.50*

Size: 35x25mm

163 A12 3c multicolored .90 .25
a. Wmk. upright ('75) 5.00 5.00
164 A12 3½c multicolored 1.00 .25

Size: 30½x21½mm, 21½x30½mm

165 A12 5c multicolored .35 .25
166 A12 7½c multicolored .45 .25
167 A12 10c multicolored .65 .25
168 A12 12½c multicolored .75 *4.00*
169 A12 15c multicolored 1.25 .90
170 A12 20c multicolored 1.00 .75
171 A12 25c multicolored 1.50 *2.00*
172 A12 50c multicolored 1.75 *3.25*
173 A12a 1r multicolored 4.50 *6.50*
174 A12a 2r multicolored 9.50 *11.50*
Nos. 160-174 (15) 24.35 30.90

See #228-229. For surcharges see #259-260.

King Sobhuza II and Flags — A13

Designs: 7½c, 25c, UN emblem, UN Headquarters, NY, and King Sobhuza II.

1969, Sept. 24 Litho. *Perf. 13½*

175 A13 3c dp blue & multi .25 .25
176 A13 7½c pink & multi .25 .25
177 A13 12½c yellow & multi .25 .25
178 A13 25c lt blue & multi .30 .30
Nos. 175-178 (4) 1.05 1.05

1st anniv. of admission to the UN.

Walking Racer, Shield and King — A14

Designs: 7½c, Runner. 12½c, Hurdler. 25c, Parade of Swaziland team with flag bearer.

Perf. 14x14½

1970, July 16 Litho. Wmk. 314

179 A14 3c red org & multi .25 .25
180 A14 7½c yellow & multi .25 .25
181 A14 12½c lt blue & multi .30 .30
182 A14 25c multicolored .40 .40
Nos. 179-182 (4) 1.20 1.20

Issued to publicize the 9th Commonwealth Games, Edinburgh, July 16-25.

Bauhinia Galpinii and King — A15

Flowers of Swaziland: 10c, Crocosmia aurea. 15c, Gloriosa superba. 25c, Watsonia densiflora.

Perf. 14x14½

1971, Feb. 1 Litho. Wmk. 314

183 A15 3c bister & multi .30 .35
184 A15 10c pale salmon & multi .35 .35
185 A15 15c pale green & multi .55 .55
186 A15 25c multicolored 1.00 1.00
Nos. 183-186 (4) 2.20 2.25

King Sobhuza II — A16

Designs (King Sobhuza II): 3½c, In 1971. 7½c, In tribal costume at gathering of chiefs (Incwala). 25c, Opening Swazi parliament.

1971, Dec. 22

187 A16 3c blue & multi .25 .25
188 A16 3½c gold, blk, bl & brn .25 .25
189 A16 7½c gold & multi .25 .25
190 A16 25c lilac & multi .25 .25
Nos. 187-190 (4) 1.00 1.00

50th anniv. of the reign of Sobhuza II.

UNICEF Emblem, King Sobhuza II — A17

1972, Apr. 17 *Perf. 14½x14*

191 A17 15c violet & black .25 .25
192 A17 25c olive & black .35 *.60*

25th anniv. (in 1971) of UNICEF.

Traditional Reed Dancers — A18

Perf. 13½x14

1972, Sept. 11 Wmk. 314

193 A18 3½c shown .25 .25
194 A18 7½c Swazi beehive hut .25 .25
195 A18 15c Ezulwini Valley .35 .35
196 A18 25c Usutu River fishing .65 .65
Nos. 193-196 (4) 1.50 1.50

Tourist publicity.

Mosquito Control A19

7½c, Anti-malaria vaccination.

1973, May 21 Litho. *Perf. 14½*

197 A19 3½c shown .25 .25
198 A19 7½c multicolored .60 .50

25th anniv. of WHO.

Mpaka Coal Mines — A20

7½c, Oxen pulling plow. 15c, Weir over Komati River. 25c, Experimental rice plantation.

Perf. 13½x14

1973, June 21 Wmk. 314

199 A20 3½c multicolored .55 .25
200 A20 7½c multicolored .30 .25
201 A20 15c multicolored .35 .25
202 A20 25c multicolored .50 .50
Nos. 199-202 (4) 1.70 1.25

Development of natural resources.

Swaziland Coat of Arms — A21

10c, King Sobhuza II in dress uniform. 15c, Parliament. 25c, National Somhlolo Stadium.

1973, Sept. 7 Litho. *Perf. 14*

203 A21 3c brick red & black .25 .25
204 A21 10c dull orange & multi .25 .25
205 A21 15c blue & multi .35 *.50*
206 A21 25c yellow & multi .40 *1.00*
Nos. 203-206 (4) 1.25 2.00

5th anniversary of independence.

Botswana, Lesotho, Swaziland Flags and Cap — A22

12½c, Kwaluseni Campus. 15c, Map of Africa & location of Botswana, Lesotho & Swaziland. 25c, Shield of University.

1974, Mar. 29 Litho. *Perf. 14*

207 A22 7½c orange & multi .25 .25
208 A22 12½c emerald & multi .30 .25
209 A22 15c yellow & multi .35 .30
210 A22 25c ultra & multi .40 .40
Nos. 207-210 (4) 1.30 1.20

10th anniversary of the University of Botswana, Lesotho and Swaziland.

Sobhuza as Student at Lovedale College, South Africa — A23

1974, July 22 Litho. *Perf. 13x11*

211 A23 3c shown .25 .25
212 A23 9c Sobhuza as middle-aged man .25 .25
213 A23 50c As old man .70 .60
Nos. 211-213 (3) 1.20 1.10

75th birthday of King Sobhuza II.

Mail Carried by Overhead Cable A24

4c, Post Office, Lobamba. 10c, Mbabane temporary P.O., 1902. 25c, Mule-drawn mail coach.

1974, Oct. 9 *Perf. 14*

214 A24 4c multicolored .25 .25
215 A24 10c multicolored .25 .25
216 A24 15c shown .30 .30
217 A24 25c multicolored .40 .40
Nos. 214-217 (4) 1.20 1.20

Centenary of Universal Postal Union.

Animal Type of 1969

"E" instead of "R"

Designs as before.

1975, Jan. 2 Litho. *Perf. 12½x13*

228 A12a 1e multicolored *1.00* 1.00
229 A12a 2e multicolored *2.50 6.00*

Girl's Umcwasho Ceremony — A26

Swazi youth: 10c, Butimba, hunting ceremony. 15c, Lusekwane, ceremony of preparation, horiz. 25c, Gcina Regiment marching with flags.

1975, Mar. 20 Wmk. 314 *Perf. 14*

232 A26 3c lt green & multi .25 .25
233 A26 10c lt violet & multi .25 .25
234 A26 15c brown org & multi .45 .45
235 A26 25c yellow & multi .55 .55
Nos. 232-235 (4) 1.50 1.50

Matsapa Airport Control Tower A27

5c, Fire brigade car and staff. 15c, Douglas C-47 Dakota. 25c, Hawker Siddeley 748.

1975, Aug. 18 Litho. *Perf. 14½*

236 A27 4c multicolored .40 .25
237 A27 5c multicolored .70 .25
238 A27 15c multicolored 1.50 1.50
239 A27 25c multicolored 2.40 2.40
Nos. 236-239 (4) 5.00 4.40

10th anniversary of internal air service.

Women in Service — A28

4c, Elephant with IWY emblem, horiz. 5c, Queen Labotsibeni, grandmother of King Sobhuza II, horiz. 15c, Handicrafts women.

Wmk. 373

1975, Dec. 22 Litho. *Perf. 14*

240 A28 4c ultra, blk & gray .25 .25
241 A28 5c bister & multi .25 .25
242 A28 15c multicolored .35 .35
243 A28 25c multicolored .40 *.70*
Nos. 240-243 (4) 1.25 1.55

International Women's Year 1975.

Green Pigeon — A29

Birds: 1c, Black-headed oriole, horiz. 3c, Melba finch, horiz. 4c, Plum-colored starling. 5c, Black-headed heron. 6c, Stonechat. 7c, Chorister robin. 10c, Gorgeous bush shrike. 15c, Black-collared barbet. 20c, Gray heron. 25c, Giant kingfisher. 30c, Black eagle. 50c, Red bishop. 1e, Pin-tailed whydah. 2e, Lilac-breasted roller, horiz.

1976, Jan. 2 Wmk. 373 *Perf. 14*

244 A29 1c orange & multi .85 *2.25*
245 A29 2c lilac & multi 1.00 *2.25*
246 A29 3c yel grn & multi 1.45 1.05
247 A29 4c gray blue & multi 1.05 .35
248 A29 5c orange & multi 1.15 1.75
249 A29 6c orange & multi 2.00 2.25
250 A29 7c orange & multi 1.75 2.25
251 A29 10c slate & multi 1.75 1.75
252 A29 15c lt green & multi 3.00 1.05
253 A29 20c ocher & multi 4.00 2.60
254 A29 25c orange & multi 4.50 2.60
255 A29 30c orange & multi 4.50 3.00
256 A29 50c sepia & multi 1.75 *1.75*
257 A29 1e vermilion & multi 3.00 *4.00*
258 A29 2e lt blue & multi 5.25 *7.50*
Nos. 244-258 (15) 37.00 36.40

Nos. 166 and 168 Surcharged in Ultra or Brown

1976 Wmk. 314 *Perf. 13x12½*

259 A12 3c on 7½c multi (U) 1.00 *1.25*
260 A12 6c on 12½c multi (B) 1.75 1.75

Denomination at lower left on No. 260.

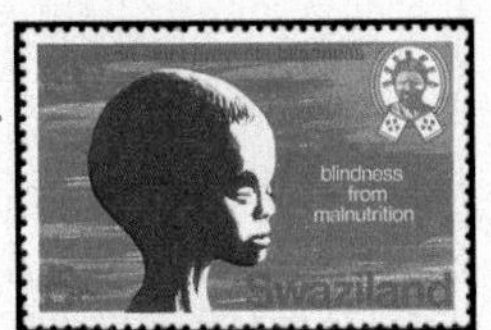

Blindness from Malnutrition — A30

Designs (WHO Emblem and): 10c, Retina, "Operation prevents blindness." 20c, Blind eye, "Blindness from trachoma." 25c, Medicine and syringe, "Medicine and rehabilitation."

Wmk. 373

1976, June 15 Litho. *Perf. 14*

261 A30 5c multicolored .25 .25
262 A30 10c multicolored .40 .25
263 A30 20c multicolored .65 .65
264 A30 25c multicolored .70 .70
Nos. 261-264 (4) 2.00 1.85

World Health Day: Foresight prevents blindness.

Marathon Runner — A31

Designs (Olympic Rings and): 6c, Boxing. 20c, Soccer. 25c, Olympic torch and flame.

1976, July 17 Litho. Wmk. 373

265 A31 5c lt blue & multi .25 .25
266 A31 6c olive & multi .25 .25
267 A31 20c lt violet & multi .50 .50
268 A31 25c dull orange & multi .60 .60
Nos. 265-268 (4) 1.60 1.60

21st Olympic Games, Montreal, Canada, July 17-Aug. 1.

Soccer — A32

Designs: 5c, Player heading ball. 20c, Goalkeeper catching ball. 25c, Player kicking ball.

1976, Sept. 13 Litho. *Perf. 14½*

269 A32 4c blue & multi .25 .25
270 A32 5c olive & multi .25 .25
271 A32 20c red & multi .45 .45
272 A32 25c multicolored .55 .55
Nos. 269-272 (4) 1.50 1.50

FIFA membership for Swaziland in 1976 (Federation Internationale de Football Associations).

A. G. Bell and 1976 Telephone A33

Designs (A. G. Bell and Telephone): 5c, 1895. 10c, 1876. 15c, 1877. 20c, 1905.

1976, Nov. 22 *Perf. 14*

273 A33 4c multicolored .25 .25
274 A33 5c multicolored .25 .25
275 A33 10c multicolored .25 .25
276 A33 15c multicolored .25 .25
277 A33 20c multicolored .30 .30
Nos. 273-277 (5) 1.30 1.30

Centenary of first telephone call by Alexander Graham Bell, Mar. 10, 1876.

Elizabeth II and Sobhuza II — A34

Designs: 25c, Queen's coach at Admiralty Arch. 50c, Queen seated in coach.

1977, Feb. 7 *Perf. 13½*

278 A34 20c silver & multi .25 .25
279 A34 25c silver & multi .25 .25
280 A34 50c silver & multi .30 .30
Nos. 278-280 (3) .80 .80

25th anniv. of the reign of Elizabeth II.

Matsapa College A35

10c, Men's & Women's uniforms & jeep. 20c, Police badge. 25c, Dog handler & dog.

1977, May 2 Litho. *Perf. 14*

281 A35 5c multi .40 .40
282 A35 10c multi .55 .35
283 A35 20c multi, vert. .75 .75
284 A35 25c multi 1.35 1.35
Nos. 281-284 (4) 3.05 2.85

50 years of police training in Swaziland.

Various Animals A36

Rock Paintings: 10c, 20c, Groups of men. 15c, Cattle and herdsman.

Perf. 14x14½

1977, Aug. 8 Wmk. 373

285 A36 5c multicolored .30 .25
286 A36 10c multicolored .35 .30
287 A36 15c multicolored .60 .50
288 A36 20c multicolored .75 .60
a. Souvenir sheet of 4, #285-288 3.00 3.00
Nos. 285-288 (4) 2.00 1.65

Rock paintings from Highveld area, c. 1700-1850.

Evergreens, Timber, Map of Highveld — A37

Designs: 10c, Pineapple and map of Middleveld. 15c, Map of Lowveld, orange and lemon. 20c, Map of Lubombo and grazing cattle. No. 293, Map of Swaziland and produce, vert.: UL, Evergreens; UR, Orange and lemon; LL, Pineapple; LR, Cattle.

1977, Oct. 17 Litho. *Perf. 13½*

289 A37 5c multicolored .25 .25
290 A37 10c multicolored .70 .70
291 A37 15c multicolored .95 .95
292 A37 20c multicolored 1.35 1.35
Nos. 289-292 (4) 3.25 3.25

Souvenir Sheet

293 Sheet of 4 2.50 2.50
a.-d. A37 25c single stamp .65 .65

Nos. 293a-293d are vertical.

Cussonia Spicata Thunb. — A38

Trees: 10c, Sclerocarya birrea. 20c, Pterocarpus angolensis. 25c, Erythrina lysistemon.

1978, Jan. 12 Litho. Wmk. 373

294 A38 5c multicolored .25 .25
295 A38 10c multicolored .35 .25
296 A38 20c multicolored .45 .45
297 A38 25c multicolored .65 *1.00*
Nos. 294-297 (4) 1.70 1.95

Rural Electrification, Lobamba — A39

Hydroelectric Power: 10c, Edwaleni Power Station. 20c, Switchgear, Magududza Power Station. 25c, Hydroturbine hall, Edwaleni.

1978, Mar. 6 Litho. *Perf. 13½*

298 A39 5c black & ocher .25 .25
299 A39 10c black & yel grn .25 .25
300 A39 20c black & blue .25 .25
301 A39 25c black & rose mag .30 *.30*
Nos. 298-301 (4) 1.05 1.05

Elizabeth II Coronation Anniversary Issue

Souvenir Sheet

Common Design Types

1978, Apr. 21 Unwmk. *Perf. 15*

302 Sheet of 6 1.60 1.60
a. CD326 25c Queen's lion .25 .25
b. CD327 25c Elizabeth II .25 .25
c. CD328 25c African Elephant .25 .25

No. 302 contains 2 se-tenant strips of Nos. 302a-302c, separated by horizontal gutter with commemorative and descriptive inscriptions and showing central part of coronation procession with coach.

Clay Pots A40

Handicrafts: 10c, Basketwork. 20c, Wooden utensils. 30c, Wooden pot with lid.

Wmk. 373

1978, June 26 Litho. *Perf. 13½*

303 A40 5c multicolored .25 .25
304 A40 10c multicolored .25 .25
305 A40 20c multicolored .25 .25
306 A40 30c multicolored .25 .25
Nos. 303-306 (4) 1.00 1.00

See Nos. 317-320.

Defense Force A41

Designs: 6c, King's Regiment. 10c, Tinkabi tractor and ox-drawn plow. 15c, Laying water pipe. 25c, Adult literacy class. 50c, Fire engine and ambulance.

1978, Sept. 6 Litho. *Perf. 14*

307 A41 4c multicolored .25 .25
308 A41 6c multicolored .25 .25
309 A41 10c multicolored .25 .25
310 A41 15c multicolored .30 .25
311 A41 25c multicolored .40 .35
312 A41 50c multicolored 1.00 .40
Nos. 307-312 (6) 2.45 1.75

10th anniversary of independence.

Angel Appearing to the Shepherds — A42

Christmas: 10c, Adoration of the Kings. 15c, Angel warning Joseph in a dream. 25c, Flight into Egypt.

1978, Dec. 12 Litho. *Perf. 14*

313 A42 5c multicolored .25 .25
314 A42 10c multicolored .25 .25
315 A42 15c multicolored .25 .25
316 A42 25c multicolored .25 .25
Nos. 313-316 (4) 1.00 1.00

Handicrafts Type of 1978

1979, Jan. 10 *Perf. 13½*

317 A40 5c Sisal bowls .25 .25
318 A40 15c Clay pots .25 .25
319 A40 20c Basketwork .30 .30
320 A40 30c Hide shield .35 .35
Nos. 317-320 (4) 1.15 1.15

Prospecting at Phophonyane A43

15c, Early 3-stamp battery mill. 25c, Cyanide tanks at Piggs Peak. 50c, Pouring off molten gold.

Wmk. 373

1979, Mar. 27 Litho. *Perf. 14*

321 A43 5c blue & gold .35 .30
322 A43 15c brown & gold .65 .30
323 A43 25c green & gold .75 .55
324 A43 50c red & gold 1.20 1.20
Nos. 321-324 (4) 2.95 2.35

Centenary of discovery of gold in Swaziland.

Girls at Piano, 1892, by Renoir — A44

Paintings by Renoir: 15c, Madame Charpentier and her Children, 1878. 25c, Girls Picking Flowers, 1889. 50c, Girl with Watering Can, 1876.

1979, May 8 *Perf. 13½*

325	A44	5c multicolored	.25	.25
326	A44	15c multicolored	.25	.25
327	A44	25c multicolored	.40	.40
328	A44	50c multicolored	.75	.75
a.		Souvenir sheet of 4, #325-328	2.10	2.10
		Nos. 325-328 (4)	1.65	1.65

International Year of the Child.

Swaziland No. 40 and Rowland Hill — A45

Rowland Hill and: 20c, Swaziland #18. 25c, Swaziland #142. 50c, Swaziland #60.

1979, July 17 **Litho.** *Perf. 14½*

329	A45	10c multicolored	.25	.25
330	A45	20c multicolored	.25	.25
331	A45	25c multicolored	.35	.35
		Nos. 329-331 (3)	.85	.85

Souvenir Sheet

332	A45	50c multicolored	1.10	1.10

Sir Rowland Hill (1795-1879), originator of penny postage.

5c Cupro-Nickel Coin — A46

Coins: 10c, King Sobhuza II and sugar cane. 20c, King and elephant head. 50c, Coat of arms. 1e, Mother and son.

Perf. 13½x14

1979, Sept. 6 **Litho.** **Wmk. 373**

333	A46	5c multicolored	.25	.25
334	A46	10c multicolored	.25	.25
335	A46	20c multicolored	.35	.25
336	A46	50c multicolored	.50	.50
337	A46	1e multicolored	1.00	1.00
		Nos. 333-337 (5)	2.35	2.25

Big Bend Post Office A47

15c, Mount Ntondozi microwave station, vert. 20c, Swaziland #53. 50c, Swaziland #217.

1979, Nov. 22

338	A47	5c multicolored	.25	.25
339	A47	15c multicolored	.25	.25
340	A47	20c multicolored	.25	.25
341	A47	50c multicolored	.30	.30
		Nos. 338-341 (4)	1.05	1.05

25th anniv. of Post and Telecommunications service (5c, 15c); 10th anniv. of UPU membership (20c, 50c).

Rotary International, 75th Anniversary A48

15c, Hospital equipment. 50c, Rotary principles. 1e, Headquarters, Evanston, IL.

Wmk. 373

1980, Feb. 23 **Litho.** *Perf. 14*

342	A48	5c shown	.25	.25
343	A48	15c multicolored	.40	.40
344	A48	50c multicolored	.70	.70
345	A48	1e multicolored	1.45	1.45
		Nos. 342-345 (4)	2.80	2.80

Flowers A49

Designs: 1c, Brunsvigia radulosa, vert. 2c, Aloe suprafoliata, vert. 3c, Haemanthus magificus, vert. 4c, Aloe marlothii, vert. 5c, Dicoma zeyheri, vert. 6c, Aloe kniphofioides, vert. 7c, Cyrtanthus bicolor, vert. 10c, Eucomis autumnalis. 15c, Leucospermum gerrardii. 20c, Haemanthus multiflorus. 30c, Acridocarpus natalitius. 50c, Adenium swazicum. 1e, Protea simplex, vert. 2e, Calodendrum capense, vert. 5e, Gladiolus ecklonii, vert.

1980, Apr. 28 **Unwmk.** *Perf. 13½*

Without Year Inscription

346	A49	1c multicolored	.25	.25
347	A49	2c multicolored	.25	.25
348	A49	3c multicolored	.25	.25
a.		Perf. 12	*3.50*	*3.50*
349	A49	4c multicolored	.25	.25
350	A49	5c multicolored	.25	.25
a.		Perf. 12	*4.00*	*2.50*
351	A49	6c multicolored	.25	.25
352	A49	7c multicolored	.25	.25
353	A49	10c multicolored	.25	.25
354	A49	15c multicolored	.25	.25
355	A49	20c multicolored	.30	.30
356	A49	30c multicolored	.40	.40
357	A49	50c multicolored	.40	.40

Size: 22x37½mm

358	A49	1e multicolored	.95	.95
359	A49	2e multicolored	2.40	2.40
360	A49	5e multicolored	4.75	4.75
		Nos. 346-360 (15)	11.45	11.45

1983 **Inscribed "1983"** *Perf. 12*

346a	A49	1c	1.00	.75
347a	A49	2c	1.00	.75
349a	A49	4c	1.25	1.25
b.		As "a," without date inscription below design		—
351a	A49	6c	1.90	1.50
353a	A49	10c	2.40	1.00
355a	A49	20c	2.60	1.75
		Nos. 346a-355a (6)	*10.15*	*7.00*

For surcharges see Nos. 465-470.

Mail Runner, London 1980 Emblem A50

1980, May 6 **Wmk. 373** *Perf. 14*

361	A50	10c shown	.25	.25
362	A50	20c Mail truck	.30	.25
363	A50	25c Mail sorting	.35	.30
364	A50	50c Mail ropeway	.70	.70
		Nos. 361-364 (4)	1.60	1.50

London 80 Intl. Stamp Exhib., May 6-14.

Yellow Fish A51

1980, Aug. 25 **Litho.** *Perf. 14*

365	A51	5c shown	.40	.25
366	A51	10c Silver barbel	.40	.25
367	A51	15c Tigerfish	.70	.30
368	A51	30c Squeaker fish	.85	.50
369	A51	1e Bream	1.60	1.60
		Nos. 365-369 (5)	3.95	2.90

Oribi Antelope A52

1980, Oct. 1 **Litho.** *Perf. 14*

370	A52	5c shown	.30	.25
371	A52	10c Nile crocodile, vert.	.65	.25
372	A52	50c Pangolin	1.00	1.00
373	A52	1e Leopard, vert.	2.25	2.25
		Nos. 370-373 (4)	4.20	3.75

Bus A53

1981, Jan. 5 **Litho.** *Perf. 14½*

374	A53	5c shown	.25	.25
375	A53	25c Jet	.40	.25
376	A53	30c Truck	.50	.35
377	A53	1e Train	1.10	1.10
		Nos. 374-377 (4)	2.25	1.95

Mantenga Falls A54

15c, Mananga Yacht Club. 30c, White rhinoceri, Mlilwane Game Sanctuary. 1e, Gambling.

1981, Apr. 16 **Litho.** *Perf. 14*

378	A54	5c shown	.30	.30
379	A54	15c multicolored	.35	.35
380	A54	30c multicolored	.75	.50
381	A54	1e multicolored	1.00	*1.25*
		Nos. 378-381 (4)	2.40	2.40

Royal Wedding Issue

Common Design Type

Wmk. 373

1981, July 21 **Litho.** *Perf. 14*

382	CD331	10c Bouquet	.25	.25
383	CD331	25c Charles	.30	.25
384	CD331	1e Couple	.75	.75
		Nos. 382-384 (3)	1.30	1.25

Installation of King Sobhuza II, 1921 — A55

60th Anniv. of King Sobhuza II's Reign (King and): 10c, Visit of Royal Family, 1947. 15c, Coronation of Queen Elizabeth II, 1953. 25c, Independence ceremony, 1968. 30c, Early portrait. 1e, Parliament buildings.

Wmk. 373

1981, Aug. 24 **Litho.** *Perf. 14½*

385	A55	5c multicolored	.25	.25
386	A55	10c multicolored	.25	.25
387	A55	15c multicolored	.25	.25
388	A55	25c multicolored	.30	.30
389	A55	30c multicolored	.35	.35
390	A55	1e multicolored	.85	.85
		Nos. 385-390 (6)	2.25	2.25

Duke of Edinburgh's Awards, 25th Anniv. — A56

1981, Nov. 5 **Litho.** *Perf. 14*

391	A56	5c Basketball	.25	.25
392	A56	20c Compass reading	.25	.35
393	A56	50c Square	.50	.90
394	A56	1e Duke of Edinburgh	1.10	1.10
		Nos. 391-394 (4)	2.10	2.60

Intl. Year of the Disabled — A57

5c, Men learning carpentry, horiz. 15c, Boy learning Braille. 25c, Carpentry, diff. 1e, Driving, horiz.

1981, Dec. 7 *Perf. 14x14½, 14½x14*

395	A57	5c multi	.35	.25
396	A57	15c multi	.60	.40
397	A57	25c multi	.90	.65
398	A57	1e multi	2.50	2.50
		Nos. 395-398 (4)	4.35	3.80

Papilio Demodocus — A58

1982, Jan. 6 **Litho.** *Perf. 14*

399	A58	5c shown	.75	.30
400	A58	10c Charaxes candiope	.75	.30
401	A58	50c Papilio nireus	1.90	1.50
402	A58	1e Eurema desjardinsii	4.75	2.50
		Nos. 399-402 (4)	8.15	4.60

Non-smoker, Flowers — A59

10c, Smoker, non-smoker.

1982, Apr. 27 **Litho.** *Perf. 14*

403	A59	5c multicolored	.75	.75
404	A59	10c multicolored	1.00	1.00

First Intl. Conference on Smoking and Health, Apr. 25-29

A60

a, Female fishing owl. b, Pair. c, Owl in nest, egg. d, Adult and young owls. e, Male.

Perf. 13½x13

1982, June 16 **Litho.** **Wmk. 373**

405		Strip of 5	*105.00*	*80.00*
a.-e.		A60 35c, any single	*13.00*	*7.50*

Princess Diana Issue

Common Design Type

1982, July 1 *Perf. 14½*

406	CD333	5c Arms	.25	.30
407	CD333	20c Diana	.85	.30
408	CD333	50c Wedding	1.00	.40
409	CD333	1e Portrait	1.75	1.25
		Nos. 406-409 (4)	3.85	2.25

Sugar Industry A61

1982, Sept. 1 Litho.

410 A61 5c Planting sugar cane .25 .25
411 A61 20c Harvesting cane .35 .25
412 A61 30c Mhlume Mills .50 .35
413 A61 1e Rail transport 1.60 1.60
Nos. 410-413 (4) 2.70 2.45

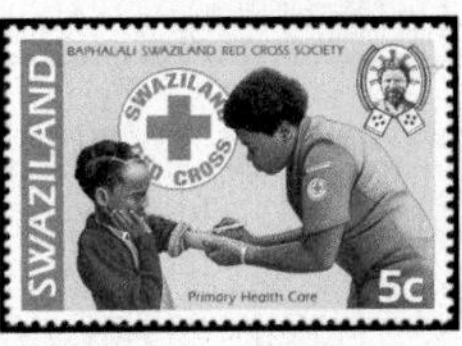

Baphalali Red Cross Society A62

5c, Immunization. 20c, Red Cross Juniors. 50c, Disaster relief. 1e, Red Cross founder Henry Dunant.

1982, Nov. 9 ***Perf. 14***

414 A62 5c multi .25 .25
415 A62 20c multi .35 .35
416 A62 50c multi .75 .75
417 A62 1e multi 1.75 1.75
Nos. 414-417 (4) 3.10 3.10

Scouting Year — A63

5c, Reciting promise. 10c, Hiking. 25c, Community development. 75c, Baden-Powell. 1e, Emblem.

Perf. 14½x14

1982, Dec. 6 Litho. Wmk. 373

418 A63 5c multi .25 .25
419 A63 10c multi .25 .25
420 A63 25c multi .40 .40
421 A63 75c multi 1.50 1.50
Nos. 418-421 (4) 2.40 2.40

Souvenir Sheet

422 A63 1e multi 2.60 2.60

Commonwealth Day — A64

6c, Satellite view. 10c, King Sobhuza II, flag. 50c, Beehive huts, horiz. 1e, Spraying sugar crop, horiz.

1983, Mar. 14 Litho. ***Perf. 14***

423 A64 6c multicolored .25 .25
424 A64 10c multicolored .25 .25
425 A64 50c multicolored .55 .55
426 A64 1e multicolored 1.50 1.50
Nos. 423-426 (4) 2.55 2.55

Bearded Vulture — A65

Designs: a, Male. b, Pair. c, Nest, egg. d, Female at nest. e, Adult, fledgeling.

Perf. 13½x13

1983, May 16 Litho. Wmk. 373

427 Strip of 5 22.00 20.00
a.-e. A65 35c, any single 2.40 2.25

Souvenir Sheets

Soccer Tour of Swaziland 1983 — A66

1983, Aug. 20 Litho. ***Perf. 14x13½***

428 A66 75c Natl. team 1.25 1.25
429 A66 75c Tottenham Hotspur 1.25 1.25
430 A66 75c Manchester United 1.25 1.25
Nos. 428-430 (3) 3.75 3.75

Manned Flight Bicentenary — A67

5c, Montgolfiere, 1783, vert. 10c, Wright brothers' plane. 25c, Royal Swazi Fokker Fellowship. 50c, Bell X-1 jet. 1e, Columbia space shuttle take-off, vert.

1983, Sept. 22 Litho. ***Perf. 14***

431 A67 5c multicolored .25 .25
432 A67 10c multicolored .25 .25
433 A67 25c multicolored .45 .45
434 A67 50c multicolored .75 .75
Nos. 431-434 (4) 1.70 1.70

Souvenir Sheet

435 A67 1e multicolored 2.50 2.50

Alfred Nobel, 150th Birth Anniv. A68

6c, Albert Schweitzer. 10c, Dag Hammarskjold. 50c, Albert Einstein.

1983, Oct. 21

436 A68 6c multi 2.75 1.00
437 A68 10c multi 1.25 .50
438 A68 50c multi 5.00 2.75
439 A68 1e shown 6.00 6.00
Nos. 436-439 (4) 15.00 10.25

World Food Program A69

1983, Nov. 29

440 A69 6c Maize .25 .25
441 A69 10c Rice .40 .40
442 A69 50c Cattle 1.25 1.25
443 A69 1e Tractor 2.00 2.00
Nos. 440-443 (4) 3.90 3.90

Women's College A70

15c, Technical training school. 50c, University. 1e, Primary school.

Wmk. 373

1984, Mar. 12 Litho. ***Perf. 14***

444 A70 5c shown .25 .25
445 A70 15c multi .30 .30
446 A70 50c multi .60 .60
447 A70 1e multi 1.10 1.10
Nos. 444-447 (4) 2.25 2.25

Bald Ibis — A71

Designs: a, Male. b, Male, female. c, Nest, egg. d, Female at nest. e, Adult, fledgeling.

1984, May 18 Litho. ***Perf. 13½x13***

448 Strip of 5 27.50 27.50
a.-e. A71 35c, any single 3.75 3.00

1984 UPU Congress — A72

Mail Coaches: 7c, Mule-drawn coach. 15c, Oxen-drawn post wagon. 50c, Mule-drawn, diff. 1e, Bristol-London.

1984, June 15 Litho. ***Perf. 14½***

449 A72 7c multi .45 .25
450 A72 15c multi .55 .30
451 A72 50c multi 1.25 1.00
452 A72 1e multi 1.90 1.90
Nos. 449-452 (4) 4.15 3.45

1984 Summer Olympics A73

1984, July 28 ***Perf. 14***

453 A73 7c Running .25 .25
454 A73 10c Swimming .25 .25
455 A73 50c Shooting .80 .80
456 A73 1e Boxing 1.40 1.40
a. Souvenir sheet of 4, #453-456 4.75 4.75
Nos. 453-456 (4) 2.70 2.70

Local Fungi A74

10c, Suillus bovinus. 15c, Langermannia gigantea, vert. 50c, Coriolus versicolor, vert. 1e, Boletus edulis.

1984, Sept. 19 Litho. ***Perf. 14***

457 A74 10c multicolored 2.25 .40
458 A74 15c multicolored 3.00 .65
459 A74 50c multicolored 3.25 2.50
460 A74 1e multicolored 4.50 4.50
Nos. 457-460 (4) 13.00 8.05

20th Anniv. of Swazi Railways A75

10c, Opening ceremony. 25c, Type 15A locomotive, Siweni Exchange Yard. 30c, Container loading, Matsapha Station. 1e, No. 268, Alto Tunnel.

1984, Nov. 5 Litho. Wmk. 373

461 A75 10c multicolored .40 .25
462 A75 25c multicolored .75 .60
463 A75 30c multicolored .85 .75
464 A75 1e multicolored 2.50 2.25
a. Souvenir sheet of 4, #461-464 6.00 6.00
Nos. 461-464 (4) 4.50 3.85

Nos. 346a, 346-349, 351-352 Surcharged

1984, Dec. 15 Litho. ***Perf. 12***

465 A49 10c on 4c #349a 3.00 3.00
a. Perf. 13½ (#349) 35.00 35.00
b. On No. 349b (perf. 12, without date inscription below design) 45.00 45.00

Perf. 13½, 12 (#469)

466 A49 15c on 7c #352 .90 .30
467 A49 20c on 3c #348 .90 .40
a. Perf 12 —
468 A49 25c on 6c #351 .90 .40
469 A49 30c on 1c #346a 1.00 .60
470 A49 30c on 2c #347 2.75 1.50
Nos. 465-470 (6) 9.45 6.20

Rotary Intl., 80th Anniv. A76

10c, Rotary emblem, world map. 15c, Training scholarships. 50c, Two children. 1e, Nurse, children.

1985, Feb. 23 Wmk. 373 ***Perf. 14***

471 A76 10c multicolored .90 .45
472 A76 15c multicolored 1.50 .45
473 A76 50c multicolored 2.00 2.00
474 A76 1e multicolored 3.75 3.75
Nos. 471-474 (4) 8.15 6.65

Life Cycle of the Ground Hornbill — A77

Audubon birth bicentenary.

1985, May 15 Wmk. 373

475 Strip of 5 16.00 16.00
a.-e. A77 25c, any single 2.25 2.25

Queen Mother 85th Birthday
Common Design Type

10c, Visit to South Africa, 1947. 15c, With Elizabeth II and Margaret. 50c, 75th birthday celebration. 1e, Holding Prince Henry. 2e, Greeting Prince Andrew.

Perf. 14½x14

1985, June 7 Litho. Wmk. 384

476 CD336 10c multicolored .50 .25
477 CD336 15c multicolored .50 .25
478 CD336 50c multicolored 1.25 1.25
479 CD336 1e multicolored 1.75 1.75
Nos. 476-479 (4) 4.00 3.50

Souvenir Sheet

480 CD336 2e multicolored 3.75 3.75

Classic Automobiles — A78

Wmk. 373

1985, Sept. 16 Litho. ***Perf. 14***

481 A78 10c Buick Tourer .85 .40
482 A78 15c Four-cylinder Rover .90 .50
483 A78 50c De Dion Bouton 2.00 1.75
484 A78 1e Ford Model-T 3.25 3.25
Nos. 481-484 (4) 7.00 5.90

Intl. Youth Year
A79

10c, Bridge-building. 20c, Girl Guides camping. 50c, Recreation. 1e, Guides collecting branches.

1985, Dec. 2

485	A79	10c multi	.25	.25
486	A79	20c multi	.25	.25
487	A79	50c multi	.75	.65
488	A79	1e multi	1.40	1.40
		Nos. 485-488 (4)	2.65	2.55

Girl Guide Movement, 20c, 1e. IYY, 10c, 50c.

Halley's Comet
A80

1986, Feb. 27 Wmk. 384 *Perf. 14½*

489	A80	1.50e multicolored	4.50	4.50

Queen Elizabeth II 60th Birthday
Common Design Type

10c, Princess Anne's christening, 1950. 30c, Wedding of Prince Charles and Lady Diana, 1981. 45c, With George VI, the Dutchess of York and Sobhuza II at Nhlangano, 1947. 1e, At Windsor Polo Ground, 1984. 2e, Visiting Crown Agents' offices, 1983.

1986, Apr. 21 *Perf. 14x14½*

490	CD337	10c scar, blk & sil	.25	.25
491	CD337	30c ultra & multi	.25	.25
492	CD337	45c green, blk & sil	.30	.30
493	CD337	1e violet & multi	.45	.45
494	CD337	2e rose vio & multi	.90	.90
		Nos. 490-494 (5)	2.15	2.15

For overprints see Nos. 527-530.

Coronation of Crown Prince Makhosetive
A81

10c, Portrait, vert. 20c, Prince and King Sobhuza II at an Incwala ceremony. 25c, Prince at primary school. 30c, At school in England. 40c, Escorted from Matsapha Airport by Guard of Honor. 2e, Dancing the Simemo.

1986, Apr. 25 *Perf. 14½*

495	A81	10c multicolored	.50	.50
496	A81	20c multicolored	.75	.55
497	A81	25c multicolored	.80	.60
498	A81	30c multicolored	1.05	.70
499	A81	40c multicolored	2.40	2.00
500	A81	2e multicolored	5.00	5.00
		Nos. 495-500 (6)	10.50	9.35

Assoc. of Round Tables in Central Africa, 50th Anniv. — A82

Club emblems.

Wmk. 384

1986, Oct. 4 Litho. *Perf. 14*

501	A82	15c Orbis	.40	.25
502	A82	25c Ehlanzeni 51	.50	.45
503	A82	55c Mbabane 30	1.10	.90
504	A82	70c Bulembu 54	1.20	*1.25*
505	A82	2e Manzini 44	2.60	*2.75*
		Nos. 501-505 (5)	5.80	5.60

Butterflies
A83

10c, Yellow pansy. 15c, Guineafowl. 20c, Red forest charaxes. 25c, Paradise skipper. 30c, Broad-bordered acraea. 35c, Veined swallowtail. 45c, Large striped swordtail. 50c, Eyed pansy. 55c, Zebra white. 70c, Gaudy commodore. 1e, Common dotted border. 5e, Queen purple tip. 10e, Natal barred blue.

Unwmk.

1987, Mar. 17 Litho. *Perf. 14*

506	A83	10c multicolored	.55	.50
507	A83	15c multicolored	.65	.50
508	A83	20c multicolored	.65	.30
509	A83	25c multicolored	.65	.60
510	A83	30c multicolored	.65	.50
511	A83	35c multicolored	.65	.50
512	A83	45c multicolored	.70	.65
513	A83	50c multicolored	.75	.50
514	A83	55c multicolored	.75	.50
515	A83	70c multicolored	1.00	1.25
516	A83	1e multicolored	1.50	3.00
517	A83	5e multicolored	3.50	2.00
518	A83	10e multicolored	5.00	5.00
		Nos. 506-518 (13)	17.00	15.80

See Nos. 600-611. For surcharges see Nos. 574-577. Compare with design A101.

White Rhinoceros
A84

1987, July 1 Wmk. 384 *Perf. 14½*

519	A84	15c Two adults	3.00	1.25
520	A84	25c Adult, calf	4.25	2.00
521	A84	45c Adult walking	7.25	3.50
522	A84	70c Adult in mud	9.00	6.25
		Nos. 519-522 (4)	23.50	13.00

World Wildlife Fund.

Flowers — A85

1987, Oct. 19 Litho. *Perf. 14½*

523	A85	15c Blue moon	1.50	.75
524	A85	35c Danse de feu	2.25	1.00
525	A85	55c Odin	2.50	2.00
526	A85	2e Lilium davidii	7.75	7.75
		Nos. 523-526 (4)	14.00	11.50

Nos. 491-494 Ovptd. "40TH WEDDING ANNIVERSARY" in Silver

Perf. 14x14½

1987, Dec. 9 Litho. Wmk. 384

527	CD337	30c ultra & multi	.40	.30
528	CD337	45c green, blk & sil	.50	.45
529	CD337	1e violet & multi	1.00	1.00
530	CD337	2e rose vio & multi	1.10	1.10
		Nos. 527-530 (4)	3.00	2.85

Insects
A86

15c, Zabalius aridus. 55c, Callidea bohemani. 1e, Phymateus viridipes. 2e, Nomadacris septemfasciata.

Wmk. 384

1988, Mar. 14 Litho. *Perf. 14*

531	A86	15c multicolored	1.60	.30
532	A86	55c multicolored	3.25	1.25
533	A86	1e multicolored	5.50	*5.75*
534	A86	2e multicolored	8.75	*9.00*
		Nos. 531-534 (4)	19.10	16.30

1988 Summer Olympics, Seoul
A87

15c, Flag-bearer, stadium. 35c, Tae kwon do. 1e, Boxing. 2e, Tennis.

1988, Aug. 22 Litho. Wmk. 384

535	A87	15c multi	1.25	.45
536	A87	35c multi	1.75	.95
537	A87	1e multi	2.50	2.50
538	A87	2e multi	4.50	4.50
		Nos. 535-538 (4)	10.00	8.40

Intl. Tennis Federation, 75th anniv. (2e).

Small Mammals
A88

Wmk. 384

1989, Jan. 16 Litho. *Perf. 14*

539	A88	35c Green monkey	2.00	.40
540	A88	55c Rock dassie	2.60	.95
541	A88	1e Zorilla	4.50	*4.75*
542	A88	2e African wildcat	7.25	*7.75*
		Nos. 539-542 (4)	16.35	13.85

Intl. Red Cross and Red Crescent Organizations, 125th Annivs. — A89

Wmk. 373

1989, Sept. 21 Litho. *Perf. 12*

543	A89	15c David Hynd	.35	.25
544	A89	60c First aid	.90	.60
545	A89	1e Sigombeni Clinic	1.50	1.50
546	A89	2e Relief work	2.10	2.10
		Nos. 543-546 (4)	4.85	4.45

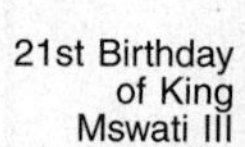

21st Birthday of King Mswati III
A90

King Mswati III: 15c, With Prince of Wales, 1987. 60c, With Pope John Paul II, 1988. 1e, Introduction to the nation while crown prince. 2e, With queen mother.

Perf. 14½x14

1989, Nov. 15 Unwmk.

547	A90	15c multicolored	.25	.25
548	A90	60c multicolored	.55	.55
549	A90	1e multicolored	.95	.95
550	A90	2e multicolored	1.40	1.40
		Nos. 547-550 (4)	3.15	3.15

African Development Bank, 25th Anniv.
A91

15c, Manzini-Mahamba Road. 60c, Mbabane microwave radio link. 1e, Mbabane Government Hospital. 2e, Ezulwini Power Switching Station.

Perf. 14x14½

1989, Dec. 18 Wmk. 384

551	A91	15c multicolored	.40	.25
552	A91	60c multicolored	.70	.50
553	A91	1e multicolored	1.20	1.20
554	A91	2e multicolored	1.90	1.90
		Nos. 551-554 (4)	4.20	3.85

Stamp World London '90 — A92

15c, Intl. priority mail. 60c, Facsimile service. 1e, Post office. No. 558, Ezulwini Earth Satellite Station.

No. 559, Mail runner.

Wmk. 384

1990, May 3 Litho. *Perf. 12½*

555	A92	15c multi	.35	.30
556	A92	60c multi	.80	.65
557	A92	1e multi	1.20	1.20
558	A92	2e multi	2.40	2.40
		Nos. 555-558 (4)	4.75	4.55

Souvenir Sheet

559	A92	2e multi	8.75	8.75

150th anniv. of the Penny Black.

Queen Mother, 90th Birthday
Common Design Types

75c, Queen Mother. 4e, King, Queen visiting Hatfield House.

1990, Aug. 4 Wmk. 384 *Perf. 14x15*

565	CD343	75c multicolored	.60	.60

Perf. 14½

566	CD344	4e multicolored	3.50	3.50

Intl. Literacy Year
A94

Wmk. 373

1990, Sept. 21 Litho. *Perf. 14*

567	A94	15c shown	.25	.25
568	A94	75c Outdoor class	.65	.65
569	A94	1e Modern instruction	.80	.80
570	A94	2e Receiving diploma	1.25	1.25
		Nos. 567-570 (4)	2.95	2.95

UN Development Program, 40th Anniv. — A95

Perf. 13½x14

1990, Dec. 10 Litho. Wmk. 373

571	A95	60c Rural water supply	.75	.75
572	A95	1e Seed production	1.05	1.05
573	A95	2e Low cost housing	1.90	1.90
		Nos. 571-573 (3)	3.70	3.70

Nos. 509-510, 512, 514 Surcharged

Unwmk.

1990, Dec. 17 Litho. *Perf. 14*

574 A83 10c on 25c multi .50 .50
575 A83 15c on 30c multi .75 .75
575A A83 15c on 45c multi *55.00 55.00*
576 A83 20c on 45c multi .75 .75
577 A83 40c on 55c multi 1.00 1.00

National Heritage A96

No. 578, Lobamba Hot Spring. No. 579, Sibebe Rock. No. 580, Jolobela Falls. No. 581, Mantjolo Sacred Pool.
No. 581A, Usushwana River.

Perf. 14x14½

1991, Feb. 11 Wmk. 233

578 A96 15c multicolored .75 .35
579 A96 60c multicolored 1.75 .85
580 A96 1e multicolored 2.25 2.25
581 A96 2e multicolored 3.25 3.25
Nos. 578-581 (4) 8.00 6.70

Souvenir Sheet

Perf. 14

581A A96 2e multicolored 8.75 8.75

Coronation of King Mswati III, 5th Anniv. — A97

15c, King making radio address. 75c, Butimba royal hunt. 1e, King, schoolmates, 1986. 2e, King opening parliament.

Perf. 14x13½

1991, Apr. 24 Litho. Wmk. 373

582 A97 15c multicolored .35 .25
583 A97 75c multicolored 1.25 .95
584 A97 1e multicolored 1.25 1.25
585 A97 2e multicolored 2.60 2.60
Nos. 582-585 (4) 5.45 5.05

Elizabeth & Philip, Birthdays
Common Design Types

Wmk. 384

1991, June 17 Litho. *Perf. 14½*

586 CD346 1e multicolored 1.40 1.40
587 CD345 2e multicolored 2.25 2.25
a. Pair, #586-587 + label 4.00 4.00

Flowers — A98

15c, Xerophyta retinervis. 75c, Bauhinia galpinii. 1e, Dombeya rotundifolia. 2e, Kigelia africana.

1991, Sept. 30 Wmk. 373 *Perf. 14*

588 A98 15c multicolored .65 .40
589 A98 75c multicolored 1.50 1.25
590 A98 1e multicolored 1.90 1.90
591 A98 2e multicolored 3.00 3.00
Nos. 588-591 (4) 7.05 6.55

Christmas — A99

20c, Santa Claus, children. 70c, Carolers. 1e, Priest reading Bible. 2e, Nativity Scene.

Wmk. 373

1991, Dec. 18 Litho. *Perf. 13½*

592 A99 20c multicolored .30 .25
593 A99 70c multicolored .85 .75
594 A99 1e multicolored 1.10 1.10
595 A99 2e multicolored 2.25 2.25
Nos. 592-595 (4) 4.50 4.35

Reptiles A100

20c, Lubombo flat lizard. 70c, Natal hinged tortoise. 1e, Swazi thick-toed gecko. 2e, Nile monitor.

1992, Feb. 25

596 A100 20c multicolored 1.25 .25
597 A100 70c multicolored 2.75 1.50
598 A100 1e multicolored 3.50 3.50
599 A100 2e multicolored 4.75 4.75
Nos. 596-599 (4) 12.25 10.00

Butterflies A101

1992-2000 Litho. Unwmk. *Perf. 14*

600 A101 5c Red tip .25 .25
601 A101 10c like #506 .25 .25
602 A101 15c like #507 .25 .25
603 A101 20c like #508 .25 .25
604 A101 25c like #509 .25 .25
605 A101 30c like #510 .30 .25
606 A101 35c like #511 .35 .30
607 A101 45c like #512 .40 .35
608 A101 50c like #513 .45 .40
609 A101 55c like #514 .50 .45
a. Dated "2000" *6.75 6.75*
610 A101 70c like #515 .55 .55
611 A101 1e like #516 1.00 1.00
612 A101 5e Like #517 *20.00 7.00*
613 A101 10e Like #518 *20.00 9.00*
Nos. 600-611 (12) 4.80 4.55

Issued: Nos. 600-611, 8/26/92. No. 612, 2000.
Nos. 600-611 dated 1991. Nos. 612 and 613 dated 2000.
Nos. 600-612 have different portrait of King Mswati III from Nos. 506-517.

A102

Designs: 20c, Missionaries with royal family. 1e, Pioneer missionaries.

1992, Dec. 16 Litho. *Perf. 13½x14*

614 A102 20c multicolored .65 .55
615 A102 1e multicolored 2.75 2.75

Evangelical Alliance Mission in Swaziland, cent.

Cooking Utensils — A103

20c, Calabashes. 70c, Contemporary pottery for cooking. 1e, Wooden bowls. 2e, Quern for grinding seeds.

1993, Mar. 18 Litho. *Perf. 13½x14*

616 A103 20c multicolored .65 .25
617 A103 70c multicolored 1.50 .95
618 A103 1e multicolored 2.00 2.00
619 A103 2e multicolored 2.75 2.75
Nos. 616-619 (4) 6.90 5.95

Independence, 25th Anniv. — A104

King Mswati, 25th Birthday: 25c, King Mswati as baby with mother. 40c, King Mswati III addressing PTA meeting. 1e, King Sobhuza II receiving Instrument of Independence, 1968. 2e, King Mswati III delivering first speech on Coronation Day, 1986.

1993, Sept. 6 Litho. *Perf. 13½x14*

620 A104 25c multicolored .25 .25
621 A104 40c multicolored .35 .25
622 A104 1e multicolored .90 .90
623 A104 2e multicolored 1.75 1.75
Nos. 620-623 (4) 3.25 3.15

Common Waxbill — A105

1993, Nov. 25 *Perf. 13½*

624 A105 25c Male & female .50 .30
625 A105 40c Nest & eggs .80 .35
626 A105 1e Incubating 1.75 1.75
627 A105 2e Feeding nestlings 3.00 3.00
Nos. 624-627 (4) 6.05 5.40

US Peace Corps, 25th Anniv. — A106

1994, Feb. 22 Litho. *Perf. 13½*

628 A106 25c Education .40 .25
629 A106 40c Rural services .55 .25
630 A106 1e Swazi culture 2.00 2.00
631 A106 2e People to people 2.25 2.25
Nos. 628-631 (4) 5.20 4.75

US Peace Corps, 25th anniv.

Mushrooms A107

1994, Sept. 15 *Perf. 13½x14*

632 A107 30c Horse mushroom 1.40 .60
633 A107 40c Penny bun bolete 1.40 .60
634 A107 1e Rusulla verdigris 3.00 2.00
635 A107 2e Honey fungus 4.00 4.00
Nos. 632-635 (4) 9.80 7.20

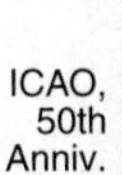

ICAO, 50th Anniv. A108

1994, Nov. 30 Litho. *Perf. 14*

636 A108 30c Natl. airline .50 .25
637 A108 40c Control tower .55 .30
638 A108 1e Air rescue service 1.25 1.25
639 A108 2e Air traffic control 2.00 2.00
Nos. 636-639 (4) 4.30 3.80

Traditional Handicrafts A109

1995, Apr. 7 Litho. *Perf. 13½*

640 A109 35c Wooden bowls .65 .40
641 A109 50c Chicken nests .85 .60
642 A109 1e Leather crafts 1.75 1.75
643 A109 2e Wood carvings 3.25 3.25
Nos. 640-643 (4) 6.50 6.00

A110

FAO, 50th anniv.: 35c, Corn harvest. 50c, Planting vegetables. 1e, Herd of cattle. 2e, Sorghum harvest.

1995, June 5 Litho. *Perf. 13½*

644 A110 35c multicolored .25 .25
645 A110 50c multicolored .45 .45
646 A110 1e multicolored .80 .80
647 A110 2e multicolored 1.60 1.60
Nos. 644-647 (4) 3.10 3.10

Lourie A111

35c, Knysna lourie. 50c, Lourie in flight. 1e, Purple crested lourie. 2e, Gray lourie.

1995, Sept. 27 Litho. *Perf. 13½x13*

648 A111 35c multi .65 .30
649 A111 50c multi .85 .50
650 A111 1e multi 1.20 1.20
651 A111 2e multi 1.60 1.60
Nos. 648-651 (4) 4.30 3.60

Reptiles A112

1996, Jan. 17 Litho. *Perf. 13½x13*

652 A112 35c Chameleon .65 .30
653 A112 50c Rock monitor .85 .50
654 A112 1e African python 1.40 1.40
655 A112 2e Tree agama 2.10 2.10
Nos. 652-655 (4) 5.00 4.30

Trees — A113

1996, Apr. 23 Litho. *Perf. 13*

656 A113 40c Waterberry	.40	.25
657 A113 60c Sycamore fig	.50	.40
658 A113 1e Stem fruit	.90	.90
659 A113 2e Wild medlar	1.10	1.10
Nos. 656-659 (4)	2.90	2.65

Local Landmarks — A114

Designs: 40c, First church, Mahamba Methodist. 60c, Colonial Secretariat, Mbabane. 1e, King Sobhuza II Memorial Monument. 2e, First High Court Building, Hlatikulu.

1996, Aug. 26 Litho. *Perf. 13½x13*

660 A114 40c multicolored	.60	.30
661 A114 60c multicolored	.75	.50
662 A114 1e multicolored	1.35	1.35
663 A114 2e multicolored	2.10	2.10
Nos. 660-663 (4)	4.80	4.25

UNICEF, 50th Anniv. A115

Designs: 40c, Basic education for all. 60c, Universal child immunization, vert. 1e, No more polio, vert. 2e, Children first, vert.

1996, Dec. 31 Litho. *Perf. 13½x14*

664 A115 40c multicolored	.30	.30

Perf. 14x13½

665 A115 60c multicolored	.60	.60
666 A115 1e multicolored	.80	.80
667 A115 2e multicolored	1.40	1.40
Nos. 664-667 (4)	3.10	3.10

Wild Animals A116

50c, Klipspringer, vert. 70c, Gray duiker, vert. 1e, Antbear. 2e, Cape clawless otter.

Perf. 14x13½, 13½x14

1997, Sept. 22 Litho.

668 A116 50c multicolored	.50	.40
669 A116 70c multicolored	.60	.50
670 A116 1e multicolored	1.00	1.00
671 A116 2e multicolored	1.75	1.75
Nos. 668-671 (4)	3.85	3.65

Traditional Costumes — A117

1997, Dec. 1 Litho. *Perf. 13x13½*

672 A117 50c Umgaco	.30	.30
673 A117 70c Sigeja	.55	.55
674 A117 1e Umdada	.85	.85
675 A117 2e Ligcebesha	1.60	1.60
Nos. 672-675 (4)	3.30	3.30

Toads and Frogs A118

1998, June 1 Litho. *Perf. 14*

676 A118 55c Olive toad	.45	.25
677 A118 75c African bullfrog	.60	.35
678 A118 1e Water lily frog	1.10	1.10
679 A118 2e Bushveld rain frog	1.90	1.90
Nos. 676-679 (4)	4.05	3.60

Independence, 30th Anniv., King Mswati III, 30th Birthday — A119

55c, King Sobhuza II Memorial Park. 75c, King Mswati III taking oath. 1e, King Mswati III delivering 1st speech. 2e, King Sobhuza II receiving instrument of independence.

Perf. 13½x14, 14x13½

1998, Sept. 3 Litho.

680 A119 55c multicolored	.45	.30
681 A119 75c multicolored	.80	.75
682 A119 1e multicolored	1.25	1.10
683 A119 2e multicolored	1.60	1.60
Nos. 680-683 (4)	4.10	3.75

Traditional Utensils — A120

1999, May 17 Litho. *Perf. 13¾x13¼*

684 A120 60c Grinding stone	.50	.30
685 A120 75c Stirring sticks	.60	.45
686 A120 80c Clay pot	.60	.50
687 A120 95c Swazi spoons	.70	.60
688 A120 1.75e Beer cup	1.10	1.10
689 A120 2.40e Mortar and pestle	1.60	1.60
Nos. 684-689 (6)	5.10	4.55

UPU, 125th Anniv. A121

60c, Internet service, vert. 80c, Cellular phone service, vert. 1e, Intl. mail exchange. 2.40e, Training school.

Perf. 13¾x13½

1999, Oct. 9 Litho. Unwmk.

690 A121 60c multicolored	.40	.30
691 A121 80c multicolored	.55	.40

Perf. 13½x13¾

692 A121 1e multicolored	2.00	1.50
693 A121 2.40e multicolored	3.00	3.00
Nos. 690-693 (4)	5.95	5.20

Wildlife A122

Designs: 65c, Lion, vert. 90c, Leopard. 1.50e, Rhinoceros. 2.50e, Buffalo, vert.

Perf. 13½x13¼, 13¼x13½

2000. July 3 Litho. Unwmk.

694 A122 65c multi	.65	.30
695 A122 90c multi	.90	.40
696 A122 1.50e multi	3.00	2.75
697 A122 2.50e multi	2.50	2.50
Nos. 694-697 (4)	7.05	5.95

Worldwide Fund for Nature (WWF) — A123

Designs: 65c, Oribi with young. 90c, Oribi. 1.50e, Klipspringers. 2.50e, Klipspringers, diff.

Wmk. 373

2001, Feb. 1 Litho. *Perf. 14*

698-701 A123 Set of 4	4.50	4.50
701a Sheet, 4 each #698-701	17.50	17.50

Environmental Protection — A124

Designs: 70c, Fighting forest fires. 95c, Tree planting. 2.05e Construction of Maguga Dam. 2.80e, Building embankment.

2001, July 30 Litho. *Perf. 14*

702-705 A124 Set of 4	5.25	5.25

Reign Of Queen Elizabeth II, 50th Anniv. Issue

Common Design Type

Designs: Nos. 706, 710a, 70c, Princess Elizabeth, Princess Anne, Princes Philip and Charles, 1947. Nos. 707, 710b, 95c, Wearing purple hat. Nos. 708, 710c, 2.05e, Wearing crown. Nos. 709, 710d, 2.80e, Wearing yellow hat, 2001. No. 710e, 22.50e, 1955 portrait by Annigoni (38x50mm).

Perf. 14¼x14½, 13¾ (#710e)

2002, Feb. 6 Litho. Wmk. 373

With Gold Frames

706 CD360 70c multicolored	.50	.50
707 CD360 95c multicolored	.75	.75
708 CD360 2.05e multicolored	1.50	1.50
709 CD360 2.80e multicolored	2.00	2.00
Nos. 706-709 (4)	4.75	4.75

Souvenir Sheet

Without Gold Frames

710 CD360 Sheet of 5, #a-e	7.75	7.75

Tourism A125

Designs: 75c, Swazi chalets. 1e, King Mswati III facing lions, vert. 2.05e, Crocodile. 2.80e, Ostriches.

Perf. 13¼x13¾, 13¾x13¼

2002, Dec. 23 Litho.

711-714 A125 Set of 4	4.75	4.75

Musical Instruments A126

Designs: 80c, Mouth organ, vert. 1.05e, Rattles. 2.35e, Kudu horn trumpet. 2.80e, Chordphone, vert.

2003, Aug. 12 Litho. *Perf. 14*

715-718 A126 Set of 4	3.75	3.75

AIDS Prevention A127

Designs: 85c, Community home-based care. 1.10e, Know your HIV status. 2.45e, Testing blood samples, vert. 3.35e, Unsterilized instruments can transmit HIV and AIDS, vert.

Perf. 13¼x13¾, 13¾x13¼

2004, Mar. 9 Litho.

719-722 A127 Set of 4	4.75	4.75

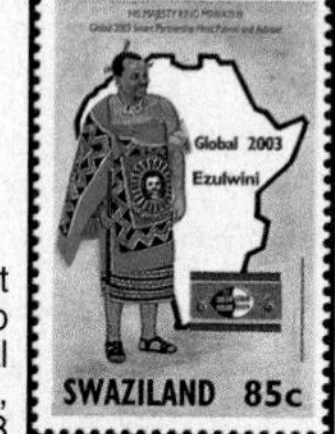

Global 2003 Smart Partnership International Dialogue, Ezulwini — A128

Designs: 85c, King Mswati III, Swaziland flag, map of Africa. 1.10e, Map of Africa, Swaziland flag, Smart Partnership International Movement emblems, horiz. 2.45e, Sharing ideas. 3.35e, Man, woman at microphone.

Perf. 13¾x13¼, 13¼x13¾

2004, June 14 Litho.

723-726 A128 Set of 4	3.75	3.75

Birds A129

Designs: 85c, Purple-crested louries, national bird of Swaziland. 1.10e, Blue cranes, national bird of South Africa. 1.35e, Cattle egrets, national bird of Botswana. 1.90e, African fish eagles, national bird of Zimbabwe. 2e, African fish eagles, national bird of Namibia. 2.45e, Bar-tailed trogons. 3e, African fish eagles, national bird of Zambia. 3.35e, Peregrine falcons, national bird of Angola.

No. 735: a, Cattle egrets, national bird of Botswana. b, African fish eagles, national bird of Namibia. c, Bar-tailed trogons. d, African fish eagles, national bird of Zambia. e, Peregrine falcons, national bird of Angola.

2004, Oct. 11 Litho. *Perf. 14*

727-734 A129 Set of 8	*12.50*	*12.50*
735 Sheet of 8, #727, 728, 730, #735a-735e	*16.00*	*16.00*
a.-b. A129 1.90e Either single	*2.00*	*2.00*
c. A129 2.25e multi	*2.50*	*2.50*
d.-e. A129 2.30e Either single	*2.50*	*2.50*

See Botswana Nos. 792-793, Namibia No. 1052, South Africa No. 1342, Zambia No. 1033, and Zimbabwe No. 975.

Road Safety Council A130

Inscriptions: 85c, Stop Killing Them In Traffic. 1.10e, Avoid Accidents. 2.45e, Safe Crossing. 3.35e, No Overloading.

2005, Jan. 25 Litho. *Perf. 13¼x13¾*

736-739 A130 Set of 4	2.75	2.75

Snakes A131

Designs: 85c, Black mamba. 1.10e, Python. 2.45e, Boomslang. 3.35e, Puff adder.

2005, Apr. 5 Litho. *Perf. 13¼x13¾*
740-743 A131 Set of 4 4.00 4.00

Pope John Paul II (1920-2005) A132

2005, Aug. 18 Litho. *Perf. 14*
744 A132 4.50e multi 1.75 1.75

Locusts A133

Designs: 85c, Schistocerca solitaria. 1.10e, Red locust. 2.45e, Southern Africa desert locust. 3.35e, African migratory locust.

2005, Oct. 11 Litho. *Perf. 13¼x13¾*
745-748 A133 Set of 4 6.50 6.50

Queen Mothers — A134

Designs: 85c, Ntombi Tfwala. 1.10e, Dzeliwe Shongwe. 2e, Lomawa Ndwandwe. 2.45e, Labotsibeni Mdluli. 3.35e, Tibati Nkambule.

2006, Jan. 10 *Perf. 13¾x13¼*
749-753 A134 Set of 5 *8.50 8.50*

Postal History A135

Designs: 90c, Manzini District Office and Post Office, 1920s. 1.15e, Ox wagon. 2e, Bremersdorp Post Office, 1893. 2.55e, Mail runner, vert. 3.50e, Mbabane Temporary Post Office, 1902.

Perf. 13¾

2006, May 8 Litho. Unwmk.
754-758 A135 Set of 5 *8.75 8.75*

Waterfalls — A136

Designs: 90c, Mgubudla Falls. 1.15e, Phophonyane Falls. 1.40e, Mantenga Falls, horiz. 2e, Malolotja Falls. 2.55e, Mabhudlweni Falls. 3.50e, Manzamnyama Falls.

2006, Sept. 26
759-764 A136 Set of 6 *10.50 10.50*

Trees A137

Designs: 70c, Common cabbage tree. 85c, Broom cluster fig. 90c, Scented thorn. 1.05e, Natal mahogany. 1.15e, Marula. 1.40e, Stem fruit tree. 2e, Fever tree. 2.40e, Large-leaved coral tree. 2.55e, African teak. 3.50e, Red ivory. 5e, Common coral tree. 10e, Jacket-plum. 20e, Sausage tree.

2007, Jan. 23 Litho. *Perf. 13¼x13¾*

765	A137	70c multi	.35	.25
766	A137	85c multi	.35	.25
767	A137	90c multi	.40	.25
768	A137	1.05e multi	.50	.30
769	A137	1.15e multi	.55	.35
770	A137	1.40e multi	.60	.40
771	A137	2e multi	.70	.45
772	A137	2.40e multi	.80	.50
773	A137	2.55e multi	1.25	.80
774	A137	3.50e multi	1.50	1.25
775	A137	5e multi	2.00	2.00
776	A137	10e multi	4.00	4.00
777	A137	20e multi	7.50	7.50
		Nos. 765-777 (13)	20.50	18.30

Community-based Tourism — A138

Designs: 1e, Rock art at Nsangwini Rock Art Center. 1.20e, Mahamba Gorge Lodge. 2.70e, Shewula Mountain Camp. 3.70e, Khopo Camp, Ngwempisi Hiking Trails.

2008, Jan. 22 Litho. *Perf. 13½x13¾*
778-781 A138 Set of 4 *7.00 7.00*

Decorations and Jewelry for Warriors — A139

Designs: 1e, Shoulder strap. 2.70e, Beaded necklace, horiz. 3.70e, Anklets, horiz.

Perf. 13¾x13¼, 13¼x13¾

2008, May 27 Litho.
782-784 A139 Set of 3 *6.25 6.25*

Independence, 40th Anniv. and 40th Birthday of King Mswati III — A140

Designs: 1e, Transportation infrastructure. 1.05e, King Mswati III receives constitution, vert. 1.30e, Maguga Dam. 1.60e, Maidens at reed dance, vert. 2.15e, First lilangeni currency. 2.40e, Health and social welfare. 2.75e, Information and communications technology. 2.90e, King Mswati III's 40th birthday. 3.95e, King Sobhuza at Independence ceremony, 1968, vert.

Perf. 13¼x13¾, 13¾x13¼

2008, Oct. 28 Litho.
785-793 A140 Set of 9 *9.25 9.25*

2010 World Cup Soccer Championships, South Africa — A141

Soccer players, ball, 2010 World Cup mascot and flag of: Nos. 794, 803a, 1e, Zimbabwe. Nos. 795, 803b, 1.25e, South Africa. Nos. 796, 803c, 1.50e, Mauritius. Nos. 797, 803d, 1.90e, Namibia. Nos. 798, 803e, 2.50e, Zambia. Nos. 799, 803f, 3.40e, Swaziland. Nos. 800, 803g, 3.80e, Malawi. Nos. 801, 803h, 4.60e, Botswana. Nos. 802, 803i, 4.90e, Lesotho.

On Plain Paper With Olive Brown Background

2010, Apr. 9 *Perf. 13½*
794-802 A141 Set of 9 9.00 9.00

On Gold-faced Paper

803 A141 Sheet of 9, #a-i 18.00 18.00

No. 803 sold for 45e.

See Botswana Nos. 896-905, Lesotho No. , Malawi No. 753, Mauritius No. 1086, Namibia No. 1188, South Africa No. 1403, Zambia Nos. 1115-1118, and Zimbabwe Nos. 1112-1121.

A single sheetlet of 9 omnibus issues exist containing 1121a. See footnote under Namibia 1188.

Locusts A142

Designs: No. 804, A, Southern African desert locust. No. 805, B, Schistocerca solitaria. No. 806, C, African migratory locust. No. 807, D, Red locust.

2012, Apr. 2 *Perf. 13¼x13¾*
804-807 A142 Set of 4 4.25 4.25

On day of issue, Nos. 804-807 sold for 1.35e, 1.70e, 3.30e and 4.90e, respectively.

Towards 2022 First World Vision A143

Designs: I, First national soccer team, 1968. II, National clinical laboratory services. III, Free primary education. IV, Lubovane Dam. V, Emergency preparedness and response. VI, Sikhuphe International Airport Air Traffic Control Tower and Fire Station.

2013, Sept. 4 Litho. *Perf. 14¼x14*
808-813 A143 Set of 6 4.75 4.75

On day of issue, Nos. 808-813 sold for 1.45e, 2.10e, 2.90e, 3.50e, 3.90e and 5.25e respectively.

A144

Designs: I, Maps and flags of member nations. II, SADC and Swaziland emblems. III, SADC emblem and flags of member nations. IV, Ring of stylized people around SADC emblem. V, Swaziland and SADC flags.

2016, Aug. 22 Litho. *Perf. 14¼*
814-818 A144 Set of 5 3.25 3.25

36th Ordinary Southern Africa Development Community Summit of Heads of State and Governments, Lozitha.

On day of issue, Nos. 814-818 sold for 1.75e, 2.50e, 2.65e, 4.70e, and 6.35e respectively

Ibrahim Index of African Governance A145

Inscriptions: I, Governance. II, Elderly grants. III, Anti-corruption. IV, Bringing clean water closer to communities. V, Human development, Participation & Human rights, Sustainable economic opportunity, Safety & Rule of law.

2017, Feb. 27 Litho. *Perf. 14¼*
819-823 A145 Set of 5 6.00 6.00

On day of issue, Nos. 819-823 sold for 2e, 2.90e, 4e, 5e and 5.40e respectively.

Animals A146

Designs: I, Lion. II, Elephants. III, Buffalos. IV, Leopard. V, Rhinoceros.

2017, Aug. 21 Litho. *Perf. 14¼*
825-829 A146 Set of 5 6.00 6.00

On day of issue, Nos. 825-829 sold for 2e, 2.90e, 4e, 5e and 5.40e respectively.

POSTAGE DUE STAMPS

Catalogue values for unused stamps in this section are for Never Hinged items.

D1

1933 Typo. Wmk. 4 *Perf. 14*

J1	D1	1p carmine rose	4.00	*17.50*
a.		Wmk. 4a (error)	275.00	
J2	D1	2p violet	12.00	*35.00*

Value, Nos. J1-J2 hinged $6.

No. 57 Surcharged

I

II

1961 Engr. *Perf. 13½x13*

J3	A5	(2d) on 2p, type I	8.00	*12.00*
a.		Type II	.40	
J4	A5	1c on 2p, type I	2.50	*4.00*
a.		Type II	1.50	*3.00*
J5	A5	2c on 2p, type I	2.50	*4.00*
a.		Type II	1.10	*2.00*
J6	A5	5c on 2p, type I	2.50	*4.00*
a.		Type II	2.00	*3.00*
		Nos. J3-J6 (4)	15.50	24.00
		Nos. J3a-J6a (4)	5.00	
		Nos. J4a-J6a (3)	4.35	

No. J3a was surcharged after decimal currency was introduced.

Type of 1933

1961 Typo. *Perf. 14*

J7	D1	1c carmine rose	.25	*1.00*
J8	D1	2c violet	.30	*1.25*
J9	D1	5c green	.75	*2.00*
		Nos. J7-J9 (3)	1.30	*4.25*

D2

Wmk. 314

1971, Feb. 1 Litho. ***Perf. 11½***

J10 D2 1c carmine rose	.80	*4.00*
J11 D2 2c dull purple	1.25	*4.50*
J12 D2 5c green	2.00	*6.00*
Nos. J10-J12 (3)	4.05	*14.50*

1977, Jan. 17 **Wmk. 373**

J10a D2 1c carmine rose	.80	*4.50*
J11a D2 2c dull purple	1.25	*5.00*
J12a D2 5c green	2.00	*6.50*
Nos. J10a-J12a (3)	4.05	*16.00*

1978-91 ***Perf. 15x14***

Size: 17½x21mm

J13 D2 1c carmine lake	.60	*1.25*
J14 D2 2c purple	.60	*.80*
a. Dated "1991"	.30	*.75*
J15 D2 5c green	.50	*.80*
a. Dated "1991"	.30	*.75*
J16 D2 10c sky blue	.50	*.80*
J17 D2 25c brown	.70	*1.00*
Nos. J13-J17 (5)	2.90	*4.65*

Issued: 1c-5c, 4/20; 10c-25c, 7/17/91.

SWEDEN

'swē-dən

LOCATION — Northern Europe, occupying the eastern half of the Scandinavian Peninsula
GOVT. — Constitutional Monarchy
AREA — 173,341 sq. mi.
POP. — 9,182,927 (2007 est.)
CAPITAL — Stockholm

48 skilling banco = 1 riksdaler banco (until 1858)
100 öre = 1 riksdaler (1858 to 1874)
100 öre = 1 krona (since 1874)

Catalogue values for unused stamps in this country are for Never Hinged items, beginning with Scott 358 in the regular postage section, and Scott B37 in the semi-postal section.

Watermarks

Wmk. 180 — Crown

Wmk. 307 — Crown and 1955

Wmk. 181 — Wavy Lines

Values for unused stamps are for examples with original gum as defined in the catalogue introduction except Nos. 1-5, excluding reprints, and LX1 which are valued without gum.

Coat of Arms — A1

1855 Unwmk. Typo. *Perf. 14*

1	A1	3s blue green	*10,000.*	*5,000.*
a.		3s orange (error)		*3,000,000.*
2	A1	4s lt blue	1,600.	100.00
e.		4s grayish ultramarine, thick paper ('57)	—	550.00
3	A1	6s gray	*10,000.*	1,600.
f.		Imperf.		—
4	A1	8s red org	5,500.	650.00
h.		Imperf.		5,750.
5	A1	24s dull red	*8,000.*	2,200.

Nos. 1-5 were reprinted from new blocks in 1868 (twice), 1871 (No. 1 only) and 1885. The 1868 and 1871 printings were perf 14, and the 1885 printing was perf 13. These later printings were made after Nos. 1-5 were withdrawn, but before being demonetized. The post office did not distinguish between these and earlier printings, although most saw little, if any, postal use. See the Scott Specialized Catalogue of Stamps and Covers 1840-1940 for detailed listings.

Coat of Arms — A2

1858-62 *Perf. 14*

6	A2	5o green	210.00	20.00
a.		5o deep green	575.00	250.00
7	A2	9o violet	425.00	250.00
a.		9o red lilac	625.00	325.00
8	A2	12o blue	225.00	2.00
9	A2	12o ultra ('61)	450.00	12.50
10	A2	24o orange	500.00	30.00
a.		24o yellow	750.00	60.00
11	A2	30o brown	500.00	30.00
a.		30o dark red brown	750.00	87.50
12	A2	50o rose	600.00	100.00
a.		50o carmine	750.00	110.00
		Nos. 6-12 (7)	2,910.	444.50

Nos. 6 and 8 exist with double impressions. No. 8 is known printed on both sides. No. 11 exists imperf.

Nos. 6-8, 10-12 were reprinted in 1885, perf. 13. See the Scott Specialized Catalogue of Stamps and Covers 1840-1940 for detailed listings. Also reprinted in 1963, perf. 13½, with lines in stamp color crossing denominations, and affixed to book page. Value $12.50 each.

Lion and Arms
A3 A4

1862-69

13	A3	3o bister brown	275.00	14.00
a.		Printed on both sides		*3,700.*
14	A4	17o red vio ('66)	800.00	160.00
15	A4	17o gray ('69)	850.00	*800.00*
16	A4	20o vermilion ('66)	300.00	20.00
		Nos. 13-16 (4)	2,225.	994.00

Nos. 13-15 were reprinted in 1885, perf. 13. See the Scott Specialized Catalogue of Stamps and Covers 1840-1940 for detailed listings.

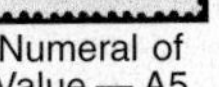

Numeral of Value — A5

Coat of Arms — A6

1872-77 *Perf. 14*

17	A5	3o bister brown	70.00	8.00
18	A5	4o gray ('76)	450.00	150.00
19	A5	5o blue green	400.00	5.00
a.		5o emerald	500.00	25.00
20	A5	6o violet	400.00	40.00
a.		6o dark violet	1,250.	300.00
21	A5	6o gray ('74)	1,100.	95.00
22	A5	12o blue	225.00	1.00
23	A5	20o vermilion	1,000.	8.00
a.		20o pale org ('75)	3,500.	50.00
b.		Double impression, dull yel & ver ('76)	3,500.	55.00
24	A5	24o orange	950.00	35.00
a.		24o yellow	950.00	35.00
25	A5	30o brown	825.00	11.00
a.		30o black brown	875.00	14.00
26	A5	50o rose	875.00	50.00
a.		50o carmine	900.00	50.00
27	A6	1rd bister & blue	1,000.	95.00
a.		1rd bister & ultra	1,000.	95.00
		Nos. 17-27 (11)	7,295.	498.00

1877-79 *Perf. 13*

28	A5	3o yellow brown	125.00	6.00
29	A5	4o gray ('79)	225.00	3.50
30	A5	5o dark green	140.00	1.00
31	A5	6o lilac	150.00	5.00
a.		6o red lilac	375.00	14.00
32	A5	12o blue	35.00	1.00
33	A5	20o vermilion	275.00	1.00
a.		"TRETIO" instead of "TJUGO" ('79)	12,000.	7,500.
34	A5	24o orange ('78)	75.00	25.00
a.		24o lemon yellow ('83)	625.00	25.00
35	A5	30o brown	450.00	2.00
a.		30o black brown	875.00	3.00
36	A5	50o carmine ('78)	325.00	9.00
37	A6	1rd bister & blue	2,400.	500.00
38	A6	1k bis & bl ('78)	625.00	20.00
		Nos. 28-36,38 (10)	2,425.	73.50

Imperf., Pairs

28a	A5	3o	1,000.	
29a	A5	4o	1,000.	
30a	A5	5o	1,000.	
31b	A5	6o	1,000.	
32a	A5	12o	1,000.	
33b	A5	20o	1,000.	
34b	A5	24o	1,000.	
35b	A5	30o	1,000.	*4,000.*
36a	A5	50o	1,000.	
38a	A6	1k	1,000.	

See Nos. 40-44, 46-49. For surcharges see Nos. B1-B10, B22-B31.

No. 37 has been reprinted in yellow brown and dark blue; perforated 13. Value, $325.

King Oscar II — A7

1885 Typo.

39	A7	10o dull rose	225.00	1.00
a.		Imperf., pair	*2,500.*	

Numeral Type with Post Horn on Back

1886-91

40	A5	2o orange ('91)	2.50	*8.00*
a.		Period before "FRIMARKE"	12.00	*22.50*
b.		Imperf., pair	725.00	
41	A5	3o yellow brn ('87)	15.00	*25.00*
42	A5	4o gray	30.00	2.00
43	A5	5o green	60.00	1.00
44	A5	6o red lilac ('88)	30.00	*62.50*
a.		6o violet	35.00	*62.50*
45	A7	10o pink	87.50	.50
a.		10o rose	87.50	.25
b.		Imperf.		3,250.
46	A5	20o vermilion	125.00	1.00
47	A5	30o brown	210.00	2.00
48	A5	50o rose	190.00	5.00
49	A6	1k bister & dk bl	100.00	3.00
a.		Imperf., pair	700.00	
		Nos. 40-49 (10)	850.00	110.00

Nos. 32, 34 with Blue Surcharge

1889, Oct. 1

50	A5	10o on 12o blue	3.75	*4.00*
51	A5	10o on 24o orange	9.00	*40.00*

A9

King Oscar II
A10 A11

Wmk. 180

1891-1904 Typo. *Perf. 13*

52	A9	1o brown & ultra ('92)	1.40	.65
53	A9	2o blue & yellow org	3.25	.40
54	A9	3o brn & org ('92)	.60	1.75
55	A9	4o car & ultra ('92)	4.75	.50

Engr.

56	A10	5o yellow green	2.75	.30
a.		5o blue green	11.50	.30
d.		5o brown (error)	*7,500.*	—
e.		Booklet pane of 6	140.00	
57	A10	8o red vio ('03)	3.25	1.25
58	A10	10o carmine	4.50	.30
c.		Booklet pane of 6	240.00	
59	A10	15o red brn ('96)	27.50	.50
60	A10	20o blue	28.00	.40
61	A10	25o red org ('96)	37.50	.50
62	A10	30o brown	55.00	.40
63	A10	50o slate	125.00	.85
64	A10	50o ol gray ('04)	100.00	.85
65	A11	1k car & sl ('00)	175.00	2.25
		Nos. 52-65 (14)	568.50	10.90

Imperf., Pairs

52a	A9	1o	87.50
53a	A9	2o	*325.00*
54a	A9	3o	*325.00*
55a	A9	4o	325.00
56b	A10	5o No. 56	85.00
c.		No. 56a	300.00
57a	A10	8o	500.00
58a	A10	10o	52.50
59a	A10	15o	500.00
60a	A10	20o	150.00
61a	A10	25o	600.00
62a	A10	30o	600.00
63a	A10	50o	650.00
64a	A10	50o	500.00
65a	A11	1k	625.00

No. 56d may be a color proof.

A booklet pane of 6 invalid stamps similar to No. 56 but with engraved lines through the denominations was released in 2004 to commemorate the 100th anniversary of the first Swedish booklet. This booklet pane is unwatermarked.

See Nos. 75-76.

Stockholm Post Office — A12

1903, Oct. 26

66	A12	5k blue	240.00	10.00
a.		Imperf., pair	3,000.	

Opening of the new General Post Office at Stockholm.

For surcharge see No. B11.

Arms — A13

Gustaf V — A14

Perf. 13, 13x13½

1910-14 Typo. Wmk. 180

67	A13	1o black ('11)	.65	*1.50*
68	A13	2o orange	1.75	*4.00*
69	A13	4o violet	2.50	1.10

Engr.

70 A14 5o green ('11) 14.00 *29.00*
71 A14 10o carmine 10.00 .50
72 A14 1k black, *yel* ('11) 95.00 .50
73 A14 5k claret, *yel* ('14) 1.50 *3.00*
Nos. 67-73 (7) 125.40 *39.60*

See #77-98. For surcharges see #99-104, Q1-Q2.

1911 Unwmk.

75 A10 20o blue 22.50 15.00
76 A10 25o red orange 27.50 4.00

1910-19

77 A14 5o green ('11) 2.00 .30
a. Booklet pane of 10 225.00
b. Booklet pane of 4 125.00
78 A14 7o gray grn ('18) .30 .30
a. Booklet pane of 10 8.75
79 A14 8o mag ('12) .30 .30
80 A14 10o car ('10) 2.00 .30
a. Booklet pane of 10 225.00
b. Booklet pane of 4 135.00
81 A14 12o rose lake ('18) .30 .30
a. Booklet pane of 10 10.00
82 A14 15o red brn ('11) 6.00 .30
a. Booklet pane of 10 375.00
83 A14 20o dp bl ('11) 9.50 .30
a. Booklet pane of 10 400.00
84 A14 25o org red ('11) .30 .30
85 A14 27o pale bl ('18) .40 .90
86 A14 30o clar brn ('11) 20.00 .30
87 A14 35o dk vio ('11) 17.00 .30
88 A14 40o ol grn ('17) 25.00 .30
89 A14 50o gray ('12) 50.00 .30
90 A14 55o pale bl ('18) *2,100.* *6,500.*
91 A14 65o pale ol grn ('18) .65 2.00
92 A14 80o black ('18) *2,100.* *6,500.*
93 A14 90o gray grn ('18) .60 .65
94 A14 1k blk, *yel* ('19) 92.50 .30
Nos. 77-89,91,93-94 (16) 226.85 7.45

Excellent forgeries of Nos. 90 and 92 exist.

1911-19 Typo. Wmk. 181 *Perf. 13*

95 A13 1o black .30 .30
96 A13 2o orange .30 .30
97 A13 3o pale brown ('19) .30 .30
98 A13 4o pale violet .30 .30
Nos. 95-98 (4) 1.20 1.20

Remainders of Nos. 95-98 received various private overprints, mostly as publicity for stamp exhibitions. They were not postally valid.

Unwatermarked Stamps with Watermarks

Stamps of these and later issues through the UPU Congress issue of 1924, are frequently found with watermark showing parts of the words "Kungl Postverket" in double-lined capitals. This watermark is normally located in the margins of the sheets of unwatermarked paper or paper watermarked wavy lines or crown.

Nos. 80, 84, 91, 90, 92 Surcharged

a b

1918 Unwmk.

99 A14(a) 7o on 10o .30 *.40*
100 A14(b) 12o on 25o 1.90 .40
a. Inverted surcharge 625.00 1,200.
101 A14(a) 12o on 65o .85 *1.40*
102 A14(a) 27o on 55o .75 *1.60*
103 A14(a) 27o on 65o 1.40 *3.50*
104 A14(a) 27o on 80o .85 *1.60*
Nos. 99-104 (6) 6.05 8.90

Arms
A15

Heraldic Lion Supporting Arms of Sweden
A16

Two types each of 5o green, 5o copper red and 10o violet, type A16.

Perf. 10 Vertically

1920-25 Engr. Unwmk.

115 A15 3o copper red .25 *.40*
116 A16 5o green ('25) 3.25 .40
117 A16 5o cop red ('21) 4.00 .40
118 A16 10o green ('21) 18.00 .40
a. Tête bêche pair *1,650.* *3,250.*
119 A16 10o violet ('25) 4.00 .40
120 A16 25o orange ('21) 10.00 .40
121 A16 30o brown .45 .45

Wmk. 181

122 A16 5o green 2.20 1.30
123 A16 5o cop red ('21) 7.50 1.00
124 A16 10o green ('21) 2.00 1.30
125 A16 30o brown 7.50 18.00
Nos. 115-125 (11) 59.15 24.45

Coil Stamps

Unless part of a booklet pane any stamp perforated only horizontally or vertically is a coil stamp.

1920-26 Unwmk. *Perf. 10*

126 A16 5o green 3.50 1.00
a. Booklet pane of 10 80.00
127 A16 10o green ('21) 10.00 3.50
a. Booklet pane of 10 225.00
128 A16 10o violet ('25) 6.00 .85
a. Booklet pane of 10 180.00
129 A16 30o brown 30.00 4.00

Wmk. 181

130 A16 5o green 10.00 30.00
131 A16 10o green ('21) 40.00 *100.00*
a. Booklet pane of 10 425.00

Perf. 13 Vertically

Unwmk.

132 A16 5o green ('25) 3.50 1.50
133 A16 5o cop red ('21) 300.00 160.00
134 A16 10o violet ('26) 20.00 37.50

Wmk. 181

135 A16 5o green ('25) 1.80 *8.00*
136 A16 5o cop red ('22) 1.80 7.00
137 A16 10o green ('24) 8.00 *40.00*
138 A16 10o violet ('25) 7.25 *25.00*
Nos. 126-138 (13) 441.85 418.35

The paper used for the earlier printings of types A16, A17, A18, A18a and A20 is usually tinted by the color of the stamp. Printings of 1934 and later are on white paper in slightly different shades.

King Gustaf V — A17

1920-21 Unwmk. *Perf. 10 Vertically*

139 A17 10o rose 20.00 .40
140 A17 15o claret .30 .45
141 A17 20o blue 25.00 .50

Perf. 10

142 A17 10o rose 10.00 6.00
143 A17 20o blue ('21) 25.00 11.00
a. Booklet pane of 10 550.00
Nos. 139-143 (5) 80.30 18.35

Wmk. 181

144 A17 20o blue *4,000.*

A18

Crown and Post Horn — A18a

See note after No. 138 regarding paper. There are 2 types of the 35, 40, 45 and 60o.

1920-34 Unwmk. *Perf. 10 Vert.*

145 A18 35o yellow ('22) 40.00 .75
146 A18 40o olive green 30.00 .75
147 A18 45o brown ('22) 1.25 .55
148 A18 60o claret 17.00 .40
149 A18 70o red brn ('22) .60 2.50
150 A18 80o deep green .40 .40
151 A18 85o myr grn ('29) 4.50 .45
152 A18 90o lt blue ('25) 45.00 .30
153 A18a 1kr dp org ('21) 7.00 .40
154 A18 110o ultra .50 .40
155 A18 115o red brn ('29) 8.00 .45
156 A18 120o gray blk ('25) 52.50 .60
157 A18 120o lil rose ('33) 14.00 .60
158 A18 140o gray black .90 .30
159 A18 145o brt grn ('30) 8.50 .55

Wmk. 181

160 A18 35o yellow ('23) 50.00 7.50
161 A18 60o red violet 80.00 *150.00*
162 A18 80o blue green 8.25 15.00
163 A18 110o ultra 3.50 4.50
Nos. 145-163 (19) 371.90 186.40

The value for #147 is for the 2nd type, issued in 1925.

Gustavus Adolphus — A19

Perf. 10 Vertically

1920, July 28 Unwmk.

164 A19 20o deep blue 2.00 .40

Wmk. 181

165 A19 20o blue 130.00 35.00

Unwmk.

Perf. 10

166 A19 20o blue 5.50 2.25
a. Booklet pane of 10 130.00
Nos. 164-166 (3) 137.50 37.65

Tercentenary of Swedish post which first ran between Stockholm and Hamburg.

King Gustaf V — A20

See note after No. 138 regarding paper.
There are two types each of the 15o rose and 40o olive green.

1921-36 Unwmk. *Perf. 10 Vert.*

167 A20 15o vio ('22) 12.00 .40
168 A20 15o rose ('28) 5.00 .45
169 A20 15o brn ('36) 4.00 .45
170 A20 20o violet .25 .30
171 A20 20o rose ('22) 17.50 .60
172 A20 20o org ('25) .25 .45
174 A20 25o rose red ('22) .55 1.50
175 A20 25o dk bl ('25) 11.00 .40
176 A20 25o ultra ('34) 11.00 .80
177 A20 25o yel org ('36) 25.00 .45
178 A20 30o blue ('23) 15.00 .45
179 A20 30o brn ('25) 17.50 .35
180 A20 30o lt ultra ('36) 6.00 .70
181 A20 35o red vio ('30) 17.50 .45
182 A20 40o blue .45 .70
183 A20 40o ol grn ('29) 35.00 2.00
184 A20 45o brn ('29) 4.00 .90
185 A20 50o gray 1.50 1.00
186 A20 85o myr grn ('25) 15.00 2.00
187 A20 115o brn red ('25) 10.00 2.00
188 A20 145o apl grn ('25) 7.50 2.00
Nos. 167-188 (21) 216.00 18.35

Wmk. 181

189 A20 15o vio ('22) 3,500. 1,000.
189A A20 20o violet *4,750.*

1922-36 Unwmk. *Perf. 10*

190 A20 15o violet 14.00 .70
a. Booklet pane of 10 400.00
191 A20 15o rose red ('25) 18.00 .90
a. Booklet pane of 10 600.00
192 A20 15o brown ('36) 4.50 1.25
a. Booklet pane of 10 175.00
193 A20 20o violet ('22) .40 *1.50*
a. Booklet pane of 10 10.00
Nos. 190-193 (4) 36.90 4.35

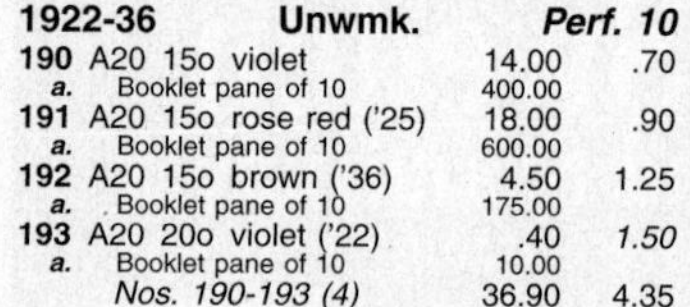

Gustavus Vasa — A21

1921, June 6 *Perf. 10 Vertically*

194 A21 20o violet 12.50 *30.00*
195 A21 110o ultra 45.00 8.00
196 A21 140o gray black 22.50 8.00
Nos. 194-196 (3) 80.00 46.00
Set, never hinged 275.00

400th anniversary of Gustavus Vasa's war of independence from the Danes.

Universal Postal Union Congress

Composite View of Stockholm's Skyline
A22

King Gustaf V — A23

1924, July 4 Unwmk. *Perf. 10*

197 A22 5o red brown 1.60 *3.25*
198 A22 10o green 1.60 *3.25*
199 A22 15o dk violet 1.60 *2.50*
200 A22 20o rose red 12.50 *21.00*
201 A22 25o dp orange 15.00 *21.00*
202 A22 30o deep blue 15.00 *21.00*
a. 30o greenish blue 75.00 110.00
203 A22 35o black 17.50 *28.00*
204 A22 40o olive green 22.50 *32.50*
205 A22 45o deep brown 22.50 32.50
206 A22 50o gray 22.50 32.50
207 A22 60o violet brn 37.50 *55.00*
208 A22 80o myrtle grn 32.50 37.50
209 A23 1k green 50.00 *87.50*
210 A23 2k rose red 110.00 *250.00*
211 A23 5k deep blue 250.00 *450.00*

Wmk. 181

212 A22 10o green 15.00 *65.00*
Nos. 197-212 (16) 627.30 *1,143.*
Set, never hinged 1,250.

Postrider Watching Airplane
A24

Carrier Pigeon and Globe — A25

1924, Aug. 16 Engr. Unwmk.

213 A24 5o red brown 2.50 4.50
214 A24 10o green 2.50 5.75
215 A24 15o dk violet 2.75 3.00
216 A24 20o rose red 19.00 32.50
217 A24 25o deep orange 20.00 32.50
218 A24 30o deep blue 20.00 32.50
a. 30o greenish blue 75.00 52.50
219 A24 35o black 22.50 47.50
220 A24 40o olive green 22.50 32.50
221 A24 45o deep brown 27.50 35.00
222 A24 50o gray 37.50 62.50
223 A24 60o violet brown 40.00 77.50
224 A24 80o myrtle green 32.50 37.50
225 A25 1k green 65.00 87.50
226 A25 2k rose red 110.00 75.00
227 A25 5k deep blue 225.00 225.00

Wmk. 181

228 A24 10o green 35.00 *65.00*
Nos. 213-228 (16) 684.25 855.75
Set, never hinged 1,500.

Universal Postal Union issue.

Royal Palace at Stockholm
A26

1931, Nov. 26 Unwmk. *Perf. 10*

229	A26 5k dark green	85.00	12.50
	Never hinged	250.00	
a.	Booklet pane of 10	3,100.	

Death of Gustavus Adolphus — A27

1932, Nov. 1

230	A27 10o dark violet	2.20	5.50
a.	Booklet pane of 10	40.00	
231	A27 15o dark red	4.00	2.00
a.	Booklet pane of 10	110.00	

Perf. 10 Vertically

232	A27 10o dark violet	1.70	.40
233	A27 15o dark red	2.00	.40
234	A27 25o dark blue	5.00	.95
235	A27 90o dark green	17.50	2.25
	Nos. 230-235 (6)	32.40	11.50
	Set, never hinged	85.00	

300th anniv. of the death of King Gustavus Adolphus II who was killed on the battlefield of Lützen, Nov. 6, 1632.

Catching Sunlight in Bowl — A28

1933, Dec. 6 *Perf. 10*

236	A28 5o green	2.25	2.00
a.	Booklet pane of 10	60.00	

There are two types of No. 236.

Perf. 10 Vertically

237	A28 5o green	2.25	.40

Perf. 13 Vertically

238	A28 5o green	3.00	7.25
	Nos. 236-238 (3)	7.50	9.65
	Set, never hinged	17.50	

50th anniv. of the Swedish Postal Savings Bank.

The Old Law Courts — A29

The "Four Estates" and Arms of Engelbrekt
A34

Designs: 10o, Stock exchange. 15o, Parish church (Storkyrkan). 25o, House of the Nobility. 35o, House of Parliament.

1935, Jan. 10 *Perf. 10*

239	A29 5o green	1.75	1.40
a.	Booklet pane of 10	100.00	
240	A29 10o dull violet	3.50	*5.75*
a.	Booklet pane of 10	110.00	
241	A29 15o carmine	4.00	1.10
a.	Booklet pane of 10	200.00	

Perf. 10 Vertically

242	A29 5o green	.75	.40
243	A29 10o dull violet	4.50	.40
244	A29 15o carmine	1.75	.40
245	A29 25o ultra	4.75	.60
246	A29 35o deep claret	9.50	2.25
247	A34 60o deep claret	14.00	2.50
	Nos. 239-247 (9)	44.50	14.80
	Set, never hinged	100.00	

500th anniv. of the Swedish Parliament.

Chancellor Axel Oxenstierna
A35

Post Runner — A36

Mounted Courier — A37

Old Sailing Packet — A38

Mail Paddle Steamship
A39

Mail Coach — A40

1855 Stamp Model — A41

Mail Train — A42

Postmaster General A. W. Roos — A43

Mail Truck and Trailer — A44

Modern Swedish Liner — A45

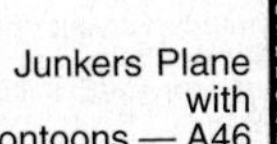

Junkers Plane with Pontoons — A46

1936, Feb. 20 Engr. *Perf. 10*

248	A35 5o green	1.60	.85
a.	Booklet pane of 18	72.50	
249	A36 10o dk violet	1.90	3.00
a.	Booklet pane of 18	95.00	
250	A37 15o dk carmine	2.75	.55
a.	Booklet pane of 18	250.00	

Perf. 10 Vertically

251	A35 5o green	1.60	.25
252	A36 10o dk violet	1.60	.25
253	A37 15o dk carmine	3.00	.25
254	A38 20o lt blue	7.50	5.00
255	A39 25o lt ultra	4.75	.50
256	A40 30o yellow brn	14.50	3.25
257	A41 35o plum	5.00	1.25
258	A42 40o olive grn	5.25	2.75
259	A43 45o myrtle grn	7.00	1.50
260	A44 50o gray	18.00	2.75
261	A45 60o maroon	22.50	.70
262	A46 1k deep blue	7.50	8.50
	Nos. 248-262 (15)	104.45	31.35
	Set, never hinged	300.00	

300th anniv. of the Swedish Postal Service. See Nos. 946-950, B55-B56.

Airplane over Bromma Airport
A47

Design Size: 33.25mm x 25.5mm

1936, May 23 *Perf. 10 Vert.*

263	A47 50o ultra	4.00	8.50
	Never hinged	10.00	

Opening of Bromma Airport near Stockholm.

Swedish Booklets

Before 1940, booklets were handmade and usually held two panes of 10 stamps (2x5). About every third booklet contained one row of stamps with straight edges at right or left side. Se-tenant pairs may be obtained with one stamp perforated on 4 sides and one perforated on 3 sides.

Starting in 1940, booklet stamps have one or more straight edges.

Some combination booklets containing multiple face-different stamps may exist with different configurations of those stamps. The most common configuration has been valued.

Emanuel Swedenborg — A48

1938, Jan. 29 *Perf. 12½*

264	A48 10o violet	.90	.35
a.	Perf. on 3 sides	8.00	4.00
	Never hinged	17.00	
b.	Booklet pane of 10	30.00	

Perf. 12½ Vertically

266	A48 10o violet	.80	.25
267	A48 100o green	1.75	1.40
	Nos. 264-267 (3)	3.45	2.00
	Set, never hinged	14.00	

250th anniv. of the birth of Swedenborg, scientist, philosopher and religious writer.

Johann Printz and Indian Chief — A49

"Kalmar Nyckel" Sailing from Gothenburg
A50

Symbolizing the Settlement of New Sweden — A51

Holy Trinity Church, Wilmington, Del. — A52

Queen Christina — A53

1938, Apr. 8 *Perf. 12½ Vert.*

268	A49 5o green	.55	.30
269	A50 15o brown	.55	.30
270	A51 20o red	.90	.70
271	A52 30o ultra	2.00	.85
272	A53 60o brown lake	2.75	.35

Perf. 12½

273	A49 5o green	.90	1.00
a.	Perf. on 3 sides	5.00	*7.50*
	Never hinged	17.00	
b.	Booklet pane of 18	67.50	
274	A50 15o brown	1.35	.70
a.	Perf. on 3 sides	10.00	4.75
	Never hinged	29.00	
b.	Booklet pane of 18	115.00	
	Nos. 268-274 (7)	9.00	4.20
	Set, never hinged	34.00	

Tercentenary of the Swedish settlement at Wilmington, Del. See No. B54.

King Gustaf V — A54

1938, June 16 *Perf. 12½ Vert.*

275	A54 5o green	.35	.30
276	A54 15(o) brown	.40	.30
277	A54 30(o) ultra	9.00	.75

Perf. 12½

278	A54 5o green	.75	.40
a.	Perf. on 3 sides	5.00	5.50
	Never hinged	22.50	
b.	Booklet pane of 10	45.00	
279	A54 15(o) brown	.90	.40
a.	Perf. on 3 sides	7.00	1.40
	Never hinged	35.00	
b.	Booklet pane of 10	37.50	
	Nos. 275-279 (5)	11.40	2.15
	Set, never hinged	37.00	

80th birthday of King Gustaf V.

King Gustaf V — A55

Three Crowns — A56

1939 *Perf. 12½ Vertically*

280	A55 10o violet	.40	.40
281	A55 20o carmine	1.00	.60
282	A56 60o lake	.40	.30
283	A56 85o dk green	.30	.30
284	A56 90o peacock blue	.30	.30
285	A56 1k orange	.30	.30
286	A56 1.15k henna brn	.30	.30
287	A56 1.20k brt rose vio	1.25	.30
288	A56 1.45k lt yel grn	1.25	.80

Perf. 12½

289	A55 10o violet	1.00	4.00
a.	Perf. on 3 sides	30.00	65.00
	Never hinged	80.00	

b. Bklt. pane of 10, perf. on 4 sides 30.00
Nos. 280-289 (10) 6.50 7.60
Set, never hinged 20.00

See Nos. 394-398, 416-417, 425-426, 431, 439-441, 473, 588-591, 656-664.

Per Henrik Ling — A57

1939, Feb. 25 ***Perf. 12½ Vert.***
290 A57 5o green .25 .25
291 A57 25(o) brown .40 .40

Perf. 12½

292 A57 5o green .40 .40
a. Perf. on 3 sides 6.00 6.00
Never hinged 29.00
b. Booklet pane of 10 37.50
Nos. 290-292 (3) 1.05 1.05
Set, never hinged 4.00

Centenary of the death of P. H. Ling, father of Swedish gymnastics.

J. J. Berzelius A58

Carl von Linné A59

Perf. 12½ Vertically

1939, June 2 **Engr.**
293 A58 10o violet .90 .40
294 A59 15o fawn .25 .30
295 A58 30o ultra 5.50 .45
296 A59 50o gray 6.00 1.00

Perf. 12½

297 A58 10o violet .80 .65
a. Perf. on 3 sides 25.00 19.00
Never hinged 125.00
b. Booklet pane of 10 65.00
298 A59 15o fawn .90 .50
a. Perf. on 3 sides 5.00 .45
Never hinged 20.00
b. Booklet pane of 10 100.00
c. As "a," bklt. pane of 20 450.00
Nos. 293-298 (6) 14.35 3.30
Set, never hinged 62.50

200th anniv. of the founding of the Royal Academy of Science at Stockholm.

King Gustaf V — A60

Type A55 Re-engraved

1939-46 ***Perf. 12½***
299 A60 5o dp green ('46) .25 .25
b. Perf. on 3 sides ('41) .30 .30
Never hinged .50
c. As "b," bklt. pane of 20 12.00
300 A60 10(o) violet ('46) .25 .25
a. Bklt. pane of 10, perf. on 4 sides 45.00
Never hinged .50
c. Perf. on 3 sides 2.00 .30
i. As "c," booklet pane of 20 50.00
300D A60 15(o) chestnut ('46) .25 .25
f. Perf. on 3 sides ('45) .30 .30
Never hinged .65
j. As "f," booklet pane of 20 7.75
300G A60 20(o) red ('42) .25 .25
h. Booklet pane of 20 6.50
Nos. 299-300G (4) 1.00 1.00
Set, never hinged 1.50

No. 300 differs slightly from the original due to deeper engraving. No. 300G was issued only in booklets; all examples have one straight edge.

Nos. 299, 300, 300D exist in booklet panes of 20 made from sheets of stamps. These can be collected as booklets.

1940-42 ***Perf. 12½ Vertically***
301 A60 5o dp green ('41) .25 .30
302 A60 10(o) violet .25 .30
302A A60 15(o) chestnut ('42) .25 .30
303 A60 20(o) red .25 .30
304 A60 25(o) orange .40 .30
305 A60 30(o) ultra .40 .30
306 A60 35(o) red vio ('41) .40 .30
307 A60 40(o) olive grn .40 .30
308 A60 45(o) dk brown .40 .30
309 A60 50(o) gray blk ('41) 2.75 .30
Nos. 301-309 (10) 5.75 3.00
Set, never hinged 10.00

Numerals measure 4½mm high. Less shading around head gives a lighter effect. Horizontal lines only as background for "SVERIGE."

See Nos. 391-393, 399.

Carl Michael Bellman — A61

1940, Feb. 4 **Engr.** ***Perf. 12½ Vert.***
310 A61 5o green .25 .25
311 A61 35(o) rose red .40 .40

Perf. 12½

312 A61 5o green .50 *.60*
a. Perf. on 3 sides 2.25 .75
Never hinged 20.00
b. Booklet pane of 10 50.00
c. As "a," bklt. pane of 20 425.00
Nos. 310-312 (3) 1.15 1.25
Set, never hinged 3.75

Bellman (1740-95), lyric poet.

Tobias Sergel — A62

1940, Sept. 5 ***Perf. 12½ on 3 Sides***
313 A62 15o lt brown 4.00 .50
a. Booklet pane of 20 275.00

Perf. 12½ Vertically

314 A62 15o lt brown 1.00 .40
315 A62 50o gray black 5.00 1.40
Nos. 313-315 (3) 10.00 2.30
Set, never hinged 60.00

Bicentenary of birth of Johan Tobias von Sergel (1740-1814), sculptor.

Reformers Presenting Bible to Gustavus Vasa — A63

1941, May 11 ***Perf. 12½ on 3 Sides***
316 A63 15o brown 2.50 .45
a. Booklet pane of 18 90.00

Perf. 12½ Vertically

317 A63 15o brown .25 .25
318 A63 90o ultra 17.50 .95
Nos. 316-318 (3) 20.25 1.65
Set, never hinged 40.00

400th anniv. of the 1st authorized version of the Bible in Swedish.

View of Skansen — A64

1941, June 18 ***Perf. 12½ on 3 Sides***
319 A64 10o violet 2.25 .65
a. Booklet pane of 20 85.00

Perf. 12½ Vertically

320 A64 10o violet 2.75 .25
321 A64 60o red lilac 7.25 .60
Nos. 319-321 (3) 12.25 1.50
Set, never hinged 32.50

50th anniv. of Skansen, an open air extension of the Nordic Museum.

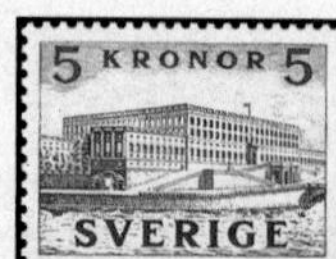

Royal Palace at Stockholm — A65

1941 ***Perf. 12½ on 3 Sides***
322 A65 5k blue 1.50 .25
Never hinged 3.00
a. Perf. on 4 sides 25.00 1.00
Never hinged 55.00
b. Bklt. pane of 20, perf. 3 sides 50.00
c. Bklt. pane of 10, perf. 4 sides 575.00

For coil stamp see No. 537.

Artur Hazelius — A66

1941, Aug. 30 ***Perf. 12½ on 3 Sides***
323 A66 5o lt green 2.25 .55
a. Booklet pane of 20 100.00

Perf. 12½ Vertically

324 A66 5o lt green .25 .25
325 A66 1k lt orange 6.25 4.00
Nos. 323-325 (3) 8.75 4.80
Set, never hinged 25.00

Issued to honor Artur Hazelius, founder of Skansen, Nordic museum.

St. Bridget of Sweden — A67

Perf. 12½ on 3 Sides

1941, Oct. 7 **Engr.**
326 A67 15o deep brown 1.60 .40
a. Booklet pane of 18 60.00

Perf. 12½ Horiz.

327 A67 15o deep brown .25 .25
328 A67 1.20k red vio 18.00 10.50
Nos. 326-328 (3) 19.85 11.15
Set, never hinged 50.00

King Gustavus III — A68

K. G. Tessin, Architect — A69

1942, June 29 ***Perf. 12½ on 3 Sides***
329 A68 20o red 1.00 .45
a. Booklet pane of 20 45.00

Perf. 12½ Vertically

330 A68 20o red .50 .25
331 A69 40o olive green 12.50 1.25
Nos. 329-331 (3) 14.00 1.95
Set, never hinged 35.00

Sesquicentennial of the Swedish National Museum, Stockholm.

Torsten Rudenschold and Nils Mansson — A70

1942, July 1 ***Perf. 12½ Horiz.***
332 A70 10o magenta .25 .40
a. Booklet pane of 10 3.50

Perf. 12½ Vertically

333 A70 10o magenta .25 .35
334 A70 90o light blue 2.50 6.00
Nos. 332-334 (3) 3.00 6.75
Set, never hinged 5.00

Swedish Public School System, 100th anniv.

Carl Wilhelm Scheele — A71

1942, Dec. 9 ***Perf. 12½ on 3 Sides***
335 A71 5o green 1.25 1.00
a. Booklet pane of 20 45.00

Perf. 12½ Vertically

336 A71 5o green .25 .25
337 A71 60o deep magenta 6.25 .60
Nos. 335-337 (3) 7.75 1.85
Set, never hinged 15.00

200th anniv. of the birth of Carl Wilhelm Scheele, chemist.

King Gustaf V — A72

Perf. 12½ Horizontally

1943, June 16
338 A72 20o red .45 .45
339 A72 30o ultra .75 2.50
340 A72 60o brt red vio .90 3.25

Perf. 12½ on 3 Sides

341 A72 20o red 3.75 1.10
a. Booklet pane of 20 160.00
Nos. 338-341 (4) 5.85 7.30
Set, never hinged 12.50

85th birthday of King Gustaf V, June 16.

Rifle Federation Emblem — A73

1943, July 22 ***Perf. 12½ Vert.***
342 A73 10o rose violet .25 .25
343 A73 90o dp ultra 3.50 .45

Perf. 12½ on 3 Sides

344 A73 10o rose violet .35 .40
a. Booklet pane of 20 10.00
Nos. 342-344 (3) 4.10 1.10
Set, never hinged 10.00

50th anniversary of the Swedish Voluntary Rifle Associations.

Oscar Montelius — A74

1943, Sept. 9 **Engr.** ***Perf. 12½ Vert.***
345 A74 5o green .25 .25
346 A74 1.20k brt red vio 6.00 2.50

Perf. 12½ on 3 Sides

347 A74 5o green .55 .40
a. Booklet pane of 20 17.50
Nos. 345-347 (3) 6.80 3.15
Set, never hinged 11.50

Montelius (1843-1921), archaeologist.

Johan Mansson's Chart of Baltic, 1644 — A75

Perf. 12½ on 3 Sides

1944, Apr. 15 **Engr.** **Unwmk.**
348 A75 5o green .60 *.80*
a. Booklet pane of 20 25.00

Perf. 12½ Vertically

349 A75 5o green .25 .25
350 A75 60o lake 4.25 .80
Nos. 348-350 (3) 5.10 1.85
Set, never hinged 10.00

1st Swedish Marine Chart, tercentenary.

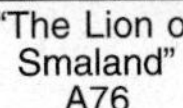

"The Lion of Smaland" A76

Clas Fleming A77

30o, "Kung Karl." 40o,Stern of "Amphion," Flagship of Gustavus III. 90o, "Gustaf V."

1944, Oct. 13 *Perf. 12½ Vert.*

351 A76 10o purple .35 .35
352 A77 20o red .30 .25
353 A76 30o blue .50 *.80*
354 A76 40o olive green .60 *1.25*
355 A76 90o gray black 6.00 2.25

Perf. 12½ on 3 Sides

356 A76 10o purple .60 *2.00*
a. Booklet pane of 20 22.50
357 A77 20o red 2.00 .35
a. Booklet pane of 20 75.00
Nos. 351-357 (7) 10.35 7.25
Set, never hinged 25.00

Issued to honor the Swedish Fleet and mark the tercentenary of the Swedish naval victory at Femern, 1644.

See Nos. B53, B57-B58.

Catalogue values for unused stamps in this section, from this point to the end of the section, are for Never Hinged items.

Red Cross — A81

1945, Feb. 27 *Perf. 12½ Vert.*

358 A81 20o red .50 .25

Perf. 12½ on 3 Sides

359 A81 20o red 2.60 .40
a. Booklet pane of 20 65.00

Swedish Red Cross Society, 80th anniv.

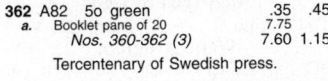

Torch and Quill Pen — A82

1945, May 29 *Perf. 12½ Vert.*

360 A82 5o green .25 .25
361 A82 60o carmine rose 7.00 .45

Perf. 12½ on 3 Sides

362 A82 5o green .35 .45
a. Booklet pane of 20 7.75
Nos. 360-362 (3) 7.60 1.15

Tercentenary of Swedish press.

Rydberg — A83

1945, Sept. 21 *Perf. 12½ Vert.*

363 A83 20o red .50 .25
364 A83 90o blue 7.00 .45

Perf. 12½ on 3 Sides

365 A83 20o red 1.50 .45
a. Booklet pane of 20 30.00
Nos. 363-365 (3) 9.00 1.15

Viktor Rydberg (1828-95), author.

Oak Tree — A84

1945, Oct. 27 *Perf. 12½ Vert.*

366 A84 10o violet .25 .35
367 A84 40o olive 1.50 1.25

Perf. 12½ on 3 Sides

368 A84 10o violet .30 *.70*
a. Booklet pane of 20 8.00
Nos. 366-368 (3) 2.05 2.30

125th anniv. of the Savings Bank movement.

Angel and Lund Cathedral A85

View of Lund Cathedral A86

Perf. 12½ Vertically

1946, May 28 **Unwmk.**

369 A85 15o orange brn 1.00 .55
370 A86 20o red .50 .25
371 A85 90o ultra 9.50 .85

Perf. 12½ on 3 Sides

372 A85 15o orange brn 1.00 1.10
a. Booklet pane of 20 16.00
373 A86 20o red 2.00 .45
a. Booklet pane of 20 40.00
Nos. 369-373 (5) 14.00 3.20

Lund Cathedral, 800th anniversary.

Mare and Colt — A87

1946, June 8 *Perf. 12½ Vert.*

374 A87 5o green .25 .25
375 A87 60o carmine rose 7.00 .40

Perf. 12½ on 3 Sides

376 A87 5o green .25 .45
a. Booklet pane of 20 5.00
Nos. 374-376 (3) 7.50 1.10

Centenary of Swedish agricultural shows.

Esaias Tegner — A88

Perf. 12½ Vertically

1946, Nov. 2 **Engr.** **Unwmk.**

377 A88 10o deep violet .25 .25
378 A88 40o dk olive grn 1.25 .45

Perf. 12½ on 3 Sides

379 A88 10o dp violet .25 .25
a. Booklet pane of 20 6.00
Nos. 377-379 (3) 1.75 .95

Esaias Tegner (1782-1846), poet.

Nobel — A89

1946, Dec. 10 *Perf. 12½ Vert.*

380 A89 20o red .80 .25
381 A89 30o ultra 2.25 .60

Perf. 12½ on 3 Sides

382 A89 20o red 1.90 .55
a. Booklet pane of 20 45.00
Nos. 380-382 (3) 4.95 1.40

50th anniversary of the death of Alfred Nobel, inventor and philanthropist.

Geijer — A90

1947, Apr. 23 *Perf. 12½ Vert.*

383 A90 5o dk yellow grn .25 .25
384 A90 90o ultra 5.00 .25

Perf. 12½ on 3 Sides

385 A90 5o dk yellow grn .30 .45
a. Booklet pane of 20 5.00
Nos. 383-385 (3) 5.55 .95

Centenary of the death of Erik Gustaf Geijer, historian, philosopher and poet.

King Gustaf V — A91

1947, Dec. 8 **Engr.** *Perf. 12½ Horiz.*

386 A91 10o deep violet .25 .25
387 A91 20o red .25 .25
388 A91 60o red violet 1.25 1.40

Perf. 12½ on 3 Sides

389 A91 10o deep violet .25 .30
a. Booklet pane of 20 3.50
390 A91 20o red .30 .40
a. Booklet pane of 20 7.50
Nos. 386-390 (5) 2.30 2.60

40th anniv. of the reign of King Gustaf V.

King and 3-Crown Types of 1939

1948 **Unwmk.** *Perf. 12½ Vertically*

391 A60 5o orange .25 .25
392 A60 10o green .30 .25
393 A60 25o violet 1.50 .25
394 A56 55o orange brown 1.40 .25
395 A56 80o olive green .80 .25
396 A56 1.10k violet 7.00 .25
397 A56 1.40k dk blue green .80 .25
398 A56 1.75k brt grnsh blue 12.50 6.75

Perf. 12½ on 3 Sides

399 A60 10o green .25 .25
a. Booklet pane of 20 5.00
Nos. 391-399 (9) 24.80 8.75

Plowman, Early and Modern Buildings — A92

1948, Apr. 26 *Perf. 12½ Vert.*

400 A92 15o orange brown .50 .25
401 A92 30o ultra .60 .55
402 A92 1k orange 2.00 1.25

Perf. 12½ on 3 Sides

403 A92 15o orange brown .50 *.50*
a. Booklet pane of 20 10.00
Nos. 400-403 (4) 3.60 2.55

Centenary of the Swedish pioneers' settlement in the United States.

August Strindberg — A93

1949, Jan. 22 *Perf. 12½ Vert.*

404 A93 20o red .60 .25
405 A93 30o blue .80 .75
406 A93 80o olive green 3.00 .45

Perf. 12½ on 3 Sides

407 A93 20o red 1.00 .35
a. Booklet pane of 20 16.00
Nos. 404-407 (4) 5.40 1.80

Birth centenary of August Strindberg (1849-1912), author and playwright.

Girl and Boy Gymnasts — A94

Perf. 12½ Horiz.

1949, July 27 **Engr.**

408 A94 5o ultra .25 *.45*
409 A94 15o brown .25 .25

Perf. 12½ on 3 Sides

410 A94 15o brown .45 .65
a. Booklet pane of 20 9.00
Nos. 408-410 (3) .95 1.35

2nd Lingiad or World Gymnastics Festival, Stockholm, July-August 1949.

A95

Symbols of UPU — A96

1949, Oct. 9 *Perf. 12½ Vert.*

411 A95 10o green .25 .25
412 A95 20o red .25 .25

Perf. 12½ Horizontally

413 A96 30o lt blue .40 .65

Perf. 12½ on 3 sides

414 A95 10o green .25 .25
a. Booklet pane of 20 3.50
415 A95 20o red .25 .25
a. Booklet pane of 20 4.00
Nos. 411-415 (5) 1.40 1.65

75th anniv. of the formation of the UPU.

Three-Crown Type of 1939

Perf. 12½ Vertically

1949, Nov. 11 **Unwmk.**

416 A56 65o lt yellow grn .75 .30
417 A56 70o peacock blue 3.50 1.25

Gustaf VI Adolf (Letters in color) — A97

Without Imprint

1951, June 6 *Perf. 12½ Vert.*

418 A97 10o dull green .25 .25
419 A97 15o chestnut brown .35 .25
420 A97 20o carmine rose .35 .25
421 A97 25o gray .65 .25
422 A97 30o ultra .45 .25

Perf. 12½ on 3 sides

423 A97 10o dull green .40 .25
a. Booklet pane of 20 7.50
424 A97 25o gray .50 .25
a. Booklet pane of 20 9.00
Nos. 418-424 (7) 2.95 1.75

See Nos. 435-438, 442-443, 456-461, 502, 505-509, 515-517.

Three-Crown Type of 1939

1951, June 1 *Perf. 12½ Vert.*

425 A56 85o orange brown 4.00 1.60
426 A56 1.70k red .75 .25

Christopher Polhem — A98

1951, Aug. 30 *Perf. 12½ Vert.*

427 A98 25o gray 1.50 .25
428 A98 45o brown .75 .40

Perf. 12½ on 3 sides

429 A98 25o gray .40 .30
a. Booklet pane of 20 7.50
Nos. 427-429 (3) 2.65 .95

200th anniversary of the death of Christopher Polhem, engineer and technician.

Three Crown Type of 1939 and

Numeral (Lettering in color) — A99

1951, Nov. Engr. *Perf. 12½ Vert.*
430 A99 5o rose carmine .25 .25
431 A56 1.50k red violet 1.25 1.25

For other stamps similar to type A99, see type A115a, Nos. 503-504, 513-514, 570, 580, 666-667.

Olaus Petri Preaching — A100

1952, Apr. 19 *Perf. 12½ Horiz.*
432 A100 25o gray black .35 .25
433 A100 1.40k brown 2.75 .80

Perf. 12½ on 3 sides
434 A100 25o gray black 1.75 2.60
a. Booklet pane of 20 45.00
Nos. 432-434 (3) 4.85 3.65

Olaus Petri (1493-1552), Lutheran clergyman, historian and Bible translator.

King and 3-Crown Types of 1951 and 1939

1952 *Perf. 12½ Vertically*
Without Imprint
435 A97 20o gray .25 .25
436 A97 25o car rose 1.00 .25
437 A97 30o dk brown .35 .40
438 A97 40o blue .80 .40
439 A56 50o gray 1.50 .25
440 A56 75o orange brown 2.25 .80
441 A56 2k red violet .75 .25

Perf. 12½ on 3 sides
442 A97 20o gray .40 .60
a. Booklet pane of 20 12.50
443 A97 25o carmine rose 1.00 .40
a. Booklet pane of 20 22.50
Nos. 435-443 (9) 8.30 3.60

Ski Jump A101

Ice Hockey A102

40o, Woman throwing slingball. 1.40kr, Wrestlers.

Perf. 12½ Vert. (V), Horiz. (H)
1953, May 27
444 A101 10o green (V) .40 .25
445 A102 15o brown (H) .60 *1.10*
446 A102 40o deep blue (H) 1.25 *1.60*
447 A101 1.40k red violet (V) 3.75 1.25

Perf. 12½ on 3 sides
448 A101 10o green .60 1.10
a. Booklet pane of 20 15.00
Nos. 444-448 (5) 6.60 5.30

50th anniv. of Swedish Athletic Association.

Old Stockholm A103

Original and Present Seals of Stockholm A104

1953, June 17 *Perf. 12½ Vert.*
449 A103 25o blue .30 .25
450 A104 1.70k red 2.75 .75

Perf. 12½ on 3 sides
451 A103 25o blue .65 .30
a. Booklet pane of 20 17.50
Nos. 449-451 (3) 3.70 1.30

700th anniv. of the founding of Stockholm.

"Telephone" — A105

1953, Nov. 2 *Perf. 12½ Horiz.*
452 A105 25o shown .25 .25
453 A105 40o "Radio" 1.25 1.40
454 A105 60o "Telegraph" 2.75 2.50

Perf. 12½ on 3 sides
455 A105 25o shown .75 .50
a. Booklet pane of 20 17.50
Nos. 452-455 (4) 5.00 4.65

Centenary of the foundation of the Swedish Telegraph Service.

King Type of 1951

1954 *Perf. 12½ Vertically*
Without Imprint
456 A97 10o dark brown .25 .25
457 A97 25o ultra .25 .25
458 A97 30o red 7.50 .25
459 A97 40o olive green .50 .25

Perf. 12½ on 3 sides
460 A97 10o dark brown .25 .25
a. Booklet pane of 10 7.00
b. Booklet pane of 20 7.50
461 A97 25o ultra .25 .25
a. Booklet pane of 4 10.00 11.00
b. Booklet pane of 8 90.00 —
c. Booklet pane of 20 10.00 —
Nos. 456-461 (6) 9.00 1.50

The booklet pane of 4 contains two copies of No. 461 which are perforated on two adjoining sides.

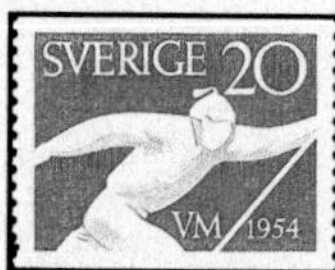

Skier — A106

1954, Feb. 13 *Perf. 12½ Vert.*
462 A106 20o shown .50 .45
463 A106 1k Girl skier 6.50 1.25

Perf. 12½ on 3 sides
464 A106 20o shown 1.10 1.75
a. Booklet pane of 20 30.00
Nos. 462-464 (3) 8.10 3.45

World Ski Championship Matches, 1954.

Anna Maria Lenngren — A107

1954, June 18 *Perf. 12½ Horiz.*
465 A107 20o gray .50 .30
466 A107 65o dark brown 5.00 3.25

Perf. 12½ on 3 sides
467 A107 20o gray 1.10 1.50
a. Booklet pane of 20 32.50
Nos. 465-467 (3) 6.60 5.05

200th anniversary of the birth of Anna Maria Lenngren, author.

Rock Carvings — A108

1954, Nov. 8 *Perf. 12½ Vert.*
468 A108 50o gray .25 .25
469 A108 60o dp carmine .40 .25
470 A108 65o dk olive grn 1.00 .25
471 A108 75o dk brown 1.75 .25
472 A108 90o dk blue .45 .25
Nos. 468-472 (5) 3.85 1.25

See Nos. 510-512, 655.

Three-Crown Type of 1939

1954, Dec. 10 *Perf. 12½ Vert.*
473 A56 2.10k dp ultra 6.50 .50

Coat of Arms — A109

1955, May 16 *Perf. 12½ Vert.*
474 A109 25o blue .25 .25
475 A109 40o green 1.25 .35

Perf. 12½ on 3 sides
476 A109 25o blue .25 .25
a. Booklet pane of 4 7.00 8.50
b. Booklet pane of 20 3.75 —
Nos. 474-476 (3) 1.75 .85

Centenary of Sweden's 1st postage stamps.
The booklet pane of 4 contains two copies of No. 476 which are perforated on two adjoining sides.

Crown and Flag — A110

Perf. 12½
1955, June 6 Unwmk. Litho.
477 A110 10o green, bl & yel .25 .25
478 A110 15o lake, bl & yel .25 .30

National Flag Day.

A111

Wmk. 307
1955, July 1 Typo. *Perf. 13*
479 A111 3o yellow green 2.00 *5.00*
480 A111 4o blue 2.00 *5.00*
481 A111 6o gray 2.00 *5.00*
482 A111 8o orange yellow 2.00 *5.00*
483 A111 24o salmon 2.00 *5.00*
Nos. 479-483 (5) 10.00 25.00

Cent. of the 1st Swedish postage stamps. Nos. 479-483 were printed in sheets of nine. They were sold in complete sets at the Stockholmia Philatelic Exhibition, July 1-10, 1955. A set cost 45 ore (face value) plus 2k (entrance fee). Value, $90.

Per Atterbom — A112

Perf. 12½ Horizontally
1955, July 21 Engr. Unwmk.
484 A112 20o dark blue .30 .30
485 A112 1.40k sepia 3.50 .80

Perf. 12½ on 3 sides
486 A112 20o dark blue 1.00 *1.40*
a. Booklet pane of 20 35.00
Nos. 484-486 (3) 4.80 2.50

Cent. of the death of Per Daniel Amadeus Atterbom, poet.

Greek Horseman A113

1956, Apr. 16 *Perf. 12½ Vert.*
487 A113 20o carmine .75 .40
488 A113 25o ultra .75 .25
489 A113 40o gray green 3.00 1.90

Perf. 12½ on 3 sides
490 A113 20o carmine .30 .50
a. Booklet pane of 20 9.00
491 A113 25o ultra .30 .25
a. Booklet pane of 20 9.00
Nos. 487-491 (5) 5.10 3.30

Issued to publicize the Olympic Equestrian Competitions, Stockholm, June 10-17, 1956.

Northern Countries Issue

Whooper Swans — A113a

Perf. 12½ Vertically
1956, Oct. 30 Engr. Unwmk.
492 A113a 25o rose red .25 .25
493 A113a 40o ultra .75 .65

See footnote after Norway No. 354.

Railroad Builders — A114

Designs: 25o, First Swedish locomotive and passenger car. 40o, Express train crossing Arsta bridge.

1956, Dec. 1 *Perf. 12½ Vert.*
494 A114 10o olive green .60 .25
495 A114 25o ultra .25 .25
496 A114 40o orange 3.00 *3.00*

Perf. 12½ on 3 sides
497 A114 10o olive green .45 .45
a. Booklet pane of 20 10.00
498 A114 25o ultra .75 .45
a. Booklet pane of 20 16.00
Nos. 494-498 (5) 5.05 4.40

Centenary of Swedish railroads.

Ship in Distress and Lifeboat — A115

Perf. 12½ Vertically
1957, June 1 Engr. Unwmk.
499 A115 30o blue 4.00 .25
500 A115 1.40k deep rose 5.00 1.10

Perf. 12½ on 3 sides
501 A115 30o blue 1.25 1.50
a. Booklet pane of 20 45.00
Nos. 499-501 (3) 10.25 2.85

Swedish Life Saving Society, 50th anniv.

King Type of 1951

1957, June 1 *Perf. 12½ Vert.*
Without Imprint
502 A97 25o dark brown 1.10 *1.75*

Re-engraved Types of 1951 & 1954 with Imprint, and

Numeral (Letters in white) — A115a

1957-64 *Perf. 12½ Vertically*
503 A115a 5o red ('61) .25 .25
a. 5o dark red .25 .25
504 A115a 10o blue ('61) .25 .25
a. 10o dark blue .30 .25
505 A97 15o dark red .25 .25
506 A97 20o gray .25 .25
507 A97 25o brown .60 .25
508 A97 30o blue .45 .25
509 A97 40o olive green .75 .25
510 A108 55o vermilion .75 .25
511 A108 70o orange .60 .25
512 A108 80o yellow green .80 .25

Perf. 12½ on 3 sides
513 A115a 5o red ('61) .25 .25
a. Bklt. pane of 20 ('64) 1.50
Complete booklet, #513a 1.50
b. 5o dark red 4.00 1.00
c. Bklt. pane, 5 #513b, 5 #515 22.50
514 A115a 10o blue ('61) .25 .25
a. 10o dark blue 20.00 2.50
b. Bklt. pane, #514a, 3 #517 32.50 18.00

515 A97 15o dark red .60 .25
a. Bklt. pane of 20 10.00
516 A97 20o gray 1.00 .60
a. Bklt. pane of 20 25.00
517 A97 30o blue .75 .25
a. Bklt. pane of 20 30.00
Nos. 503-517 (15) 7.80 4.10

In the redrawn Numeral type A99, "Sverige, ore" and the "g" tail flourishes are white instead of in color.

Booklet pane including #513 is listed as #581b.

The booklet pane of 4, No. 514b, contains two copies of No. 517 which are imperf. on two adjoining sides. No. 514a was issued only in booklet pane No. 514b.

See Nos. 570, 580, 580a, 581b, 584b, 586b-586c, 666-667, 668a, 669b-669c.

Helicopter Mail Service — A116

Perf. 12½ Vertically

1958, Feb. 10 Engr. Unwmk.
518 A116 30o blue .35 .25
519 A116 1.40k brown 4.25 1.00

Perf. 12½ on 3 sides

520 A116 30o blue .70 .55
a. Booklet pane of 20 17.50
Nos. 518-520 (3) 5.30 1.80

10th anniversary of helicopter mail service to the Stockholm archipelago, Feb. 10.

Modern and 17th Century Vessels — A117

1958, Feb. 10 *Perf. 12½ Vert.*
521 A117 15o dark red .25 .25
522 A117 40o gray olive 4.25 3.00

Perf. 12½ on 3 sides

523 A117 15o dark red .40 .50
a. Booklet pane of 20 11.00
Nos. 521-523 (3) 4.90 3.75

3 centuries of transatlantic mail service.

Soccer Player — A118

1958, May 8 *Perf. 12½ Vert.*
524 A118 15o vermilion .75 .25
525 A118 20o yellow green .40 .25
526 A118 1.20k dark blue 1.60 1.10

Perf. 12½ on 3 sides

527 A118 15o vermilion .45 .45
a. Booklet pane of 20 8.00
528 A118 20o yellow green .40 *.65*
a. Booklet pane of 20 10.00
Nos. 524-528 (5) 3.60 2.70

Issued to publicize the 6th World Soccer Championships, Stockholm, June 8-29.

Bessemer Converter — A119

Perf. 12½ Horizontally

1958, July 18 Engr. Unwmk.
529 A119 30o gray blue .25 .25
530 A119 1.70k dull red brown 3.00 .95

Perf. 12½ on 3 sides

531 A119 30o gray blue .65 .55
a. Booklet pane of 20 14.00
Nos. 529-531 (3) 3.90 1.75

Centenary of the first successful Bessemer blow in Sweden, July 18, 1858.

Selma Lagerlof — A120

1958, Nov. 20 *Perf. 12½ Horiz.*
532 A120 20o dark red .30 .30
533 A120 30o blue .40 .25
534 A120 80o olive green .80 .80

Perf. 12½ on 3 Sides

535 A120 20o dark red .40 .65
a. Booklet pane of 20 11.00
536 A120 30o blue .40 .50
a. Booklet pane of 20 14.00
Nos. 532-536 (5) 2.30 2.50

Selma Lagerlof, writer, birth cent.

Palace Type of 1941

1958, Sept. 17 *Perf. 12½ Vert.*
537 A65 5k blue 2.50 .25

Electric Power Line — A121

Hydroelectric Plant and Dam — A122

Perf. 12½ Horiz. (H), Vert. (V)

1959, Jan. 20 Unwmk.
538 A121 30o ultra (H) .45 .25
539 A122 90o carmine rose (V) 3.25 2.25

Perf. 12½ on 3 sides

540 A121 30o ultra .50 .50
a. Booklet pane of 20 13.00
Nos. 538-540 (3) 4.20 3.00

50th anniv. of the establishment of the State Power Board.

Verner von Heidenstam — A123

Perf. 12½ Horizontally

1959, July 6 Engr. Unwmk.
541 A123 15o rose carmine 1.00 .35
542 A123 1k slate 3.50 .85

Perf. 12½ on 3 Sides

543 A123 15o rose carmine .50 .85
a. Booklet pane of 20 11.00
Nos. 541-543 (3) 5.00 2.05

Verner von Heidenstam, poet, birth cent.

Forest — A124

Design: 1.40k, Felling tree.

1959, Sept. 4 *Perf. 12½ Horiz.*
544 A124 30o green 1.50 .25
545 A124 1.40k brown red 3.50 .50

Perf. 12½ on 3 sides

546 A124 30o green .90 *1.10*
a. Booklet pane of 20 22.50
Nos. 544-546 (3) 5.90 1.85

Administration of crown lands and forests, cent.

Svante Arrhenius — A125

Perf. 12½ Horizontally

1959, Dec. 10 Engr. Unwmk.
547 A125 15o dull red brown .25 .25
548 A125 1.70k dark blue 3.25 .40

Perf. 12½ on 3 sides

549 A125 15o dull red brown .40 .50
a. Booklet pane of 20 7.50
Nos. 547-549 (3) 3.90 1.15

Arrhenius (1859-1927), chemist and physicist.

Anders Zorn — A126

1960, Feb. 18 *Perf. 12½ Horiz.*
550 A126 30o gray .35 .25
551 A126 80o sepia 3.75 2.00

Perf. 12½ on 3 sides

552 A126 30o gray 1.00 .50
a. Booklet pane of 20 35.00
Nos. 550-552 (3) 5.10 2.75

Zorn (1860-1920), painter and sculptor.

Uprooted Oak Emblem A127

People of Various Races, WRY Emblem A128

Perf. 12½ Vert. (V), Horiz. (H)

1960, Apr. 7 Engr. Unwmk.
553 A127 20o red brown (V) .25 .25
554 A128 40o purple (H) .30 .30

Perf. 12½ on 3 sides

555 A127 20o red brown .50 .40
a. Booklet pane of 20 9.00
Nos. 553-555 (3) 1.05 .95

World Refugee Year, 7/1/59-6/30/60.

Target Shooting A129

Design: 90o, Parade of riflemen.

1960, June 30 *Perf. 12½ Vert.*
556 A129 15o rose carmine .30 .25
557 A129 90o grnsh blue 2.50 2.00

Perf. 12½ on 3 sides

558 A129 15o rose carmine .25 .40
a. Booklet pane of 20 6.50
Nos. 556-558 (3) 3.05 2.65

Centenary of the founding of the Voluntary Shooting Organization.

Gustaf Froding — A130

1960, Aug. 22 *Perf. 12½ Horiz.*
559 A130 30o red brown .30 .25
560 A130 1.40k slate green 2.80 .35

Perf. 12½ on 3 sides

561 A130 30o red brown .45 .35
a. Booklet pane of 20 9.00
Complete booklet, #561a 10.00
Nos. 559-561 (3) 3.55 .95

Gustaf Froding (1860-1911), poet.

Common Design Types pictured following the introduction.

Europa Issue, 1960
Common Design Type

1960, Sept. 19 *Perf. 12½ Vert.*
Size: 27x21mm
562 CD3 40o blue .25 .25
563 CD3 1k red *.80* .30

Hjalmar Branting (1860-1925), Labor Party Leader and Prime Minister — A131

Perf. 12½ Horiz.

1960, Nov. 23 Engr.
564 A131 15o rose carmine .25 .25
565 A131 1.70k slate blue 3.00 .65

Perf. 12½ on 3 sides

566 A131 15o rose carmine .45 .25
a. Booklet pane of 20 4.00
Nos. 564-566 (3) 3.70 1.15

SAS Issue

DC-8 Airliner — A131a

Perf. 12½ Vertically

1961, Feb. 24 Unwmk.
567 A131a 40o blue .25 .25

Perf. 12½ on 3 sides

568 A131a 40o blue .75 1.00
a. Booklet pane of 10 8.00

Scandinavian Airlines System, SAS, 10th anniv.

Numeral Type of 1957, Three-Crown Type of 1939 and

Gustaf VI Adolf (Letters, numerals in white) A132

Rune Stone, Oland, 11th Century A133

1961-65 *Perf. 12½ Vert.*
570 A115a 15o green ('62) .30 .25
571 A132 15o red .35 .25
572 A132 20o gray .35 .25
573 A132 25o brown .65 .25
574 A132 30o ultra 1.50 .25
575 A132 30o lilac ('62) .55 .25
576 A132 35o lilac .55 .25
577 A132 35o ultra ('62) 1.10 .25
578 A132 40o emerald 1.00 .25
579 A132 50o gray grn ('62) .65 .25

Perf. 12½ on 3 sides

580 A115a 15o grn ('65) .30 .30
a. Bklt. pane, 2 each #514, 580, 583 2.00
Complete booklet, #580a 2.00
581 A132 15o red .25 .25
a. Bklt. pane of 20 5.00
Complete booklet, #581a 6.75
b. Bklt. pane, 5 #513, 5 #581 2.50
Complete booklet, #581b 2.50
582 A132 20o gray 1.25 .85
a. Bklt. pane of 20 25.00
Complete booklet, #582a 25.00
583 A132 25o brown ('62) .35 .25
a. Bklt. pane of 20 15.00
b. Bklt. pane of 4 2.25
Complete booklet, #583b 2.25

584 A132 30o ultra .65 .25
a. Bklt. pane of 20 7.50
Complete booklet, #584a 9.00
b. Bklt. pane, #514 + 3 #584 4.00
Complete booklet, #584b 4.00
585 A132 30o lilac ('64) .65 .50
a. Bklt. pane of 20 14.00
Complete booklet, #585a 22.00
586 A132 35o ultra ('62) .55 .25
a. Bklt. pane of 20 12.50
b. Bklt. pane, 3 #514, 2 #586 + blank label 5.00 3.50
Complete booklet, #586b 5.00
c. As "b," inscribed label 3.50 1.50

Perf. 12½ Vertically

588 A56 1.05k Prus grn ('62) 1.10 .40
589 A56 1.50k brown ('62) .80 .30
590 A56 2.15k dk sl grn ('62) 4.00 .80
591 A56 2.50k emerald 1.50 .25

Perf. 12½ on 3 sides

592 A133 10k dl red brn 23.00 .65
a. Bklt. pane of 10 ('68) 250.00
b. Bklt. pane of 20 800.00
Nos. 570-592 (22) 41.40 7.55

Booklet panes of 4, 5 or 6 (Nos. 580a, 583b, 584b, 586b, 586c) contain two stamps which are imperf. on two adjoining sides.

Combination panes (Nos. 580a, 581b, 584b, 586b, 586c) come in different arrangements of the denominations.

The label of No. 586c is inscribed "ett brev / betyder / sa / mycket" ("a letter means so much"). The label inscription "nord 63 / 5-13 oktober / GÖTEBORG" was privately applied to No. 586b by the Gothenburg Philatelic Society to raise funds for Nord 63 Philatelic Exhibition in Gothenburg. The pane was sold for the equivalent of $1 US, 5 times face value.

See Nos. 648-654A, 666a, 668-672F.

K.-G. Pilo, Self-portrait — A134

1961, Apr. 17 ***Perf. 12½ Horiz.***

594 A134 30o brown .25 .25
595 A134 1.40k Prus blue 3.25 1.30

Perf. 12½ on 3 sides

596 A134 30o brown .90 .45
a. Booklet pane of 20 25.00
Complete booklet, #596a 25.00
Nos. 594-596 (3) 4.40 2.00

Karl-Gustaf Pilo (1711-1793), painter. Self-portrait from "The Coronation of Gustavus III."

Jonas Alstromer A135

1961, June 2 ***Perf. 12½ Vert.***

597 A135 15o dull claret .25 .25
598 A135 90o grnsh blue 1.40 2.00

Perf. 12½ on 3 sides

599 A135 15o dull claret .25 *.40*
a. Booklet pane of 20 6.00
Nos. 597-599 (3) 1.90 2.65

200th anniversary of the birth of Jonas Alstromer, pioneer of agriculture and industry.

17th Century Printer and Student in Library — A136

Perf. 12½ Vert.

1961, Sept. 22 **Engr.**

600 A136 20o dark red .30 .30
601 A136 1k blue 7.00 1.50

Perf. 12½ on 3 sides

602 A136 20o dark red .30 .55
a. Booklet pane of 20 6.00
Nos. 600-602 (3) 7.60 2.35

300th anniversary of the regulation requiring copies of all Swedish printed works to be deposited in the Royal Library.

Roentgen, Prudhomme, von Behring, van't Hoff — A137

1961, Dec. 9 ***Perf. 12½ Vertically***

603 A137 20o vermilion .25 .25
604 A137 40o blue .25 .25
605 A137 50o green .40 .25

Perf. 12½ on 3 sides

606 A137 20o vermilion .25 .25
a. Booklet pane of 20 5.00
Nos. 603-606 (4) 1.15 1.00

Winners of the 1901 Nobel Prize; Wilhelm K. Roentgen, Rene Sully Prudhomme, Emil von Behring, Jacob van't Hoff.

See Nos. 617-619, 637-639, 673-676, 689-692, 710-713, 769-772, 804-807.

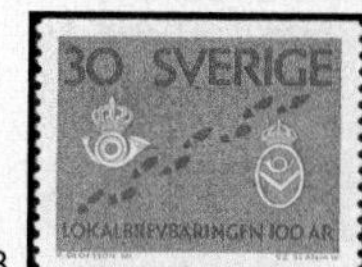

A138

Footsteps and postmen's badges.

1962, Jan. 29 **Engr.** ***Perf. 12½ Vert.***

607 A138 30o lilac .30 .25
608 A138 1.70k rose red 3.25 .65

Perf. 12½ on 3 sides

609 A138 30o lilac .40 .50
a. Booklet pane of 20 9.00
Complete booklet, #609a 10.00
Nos. 607-609 (3) 3.95 1.40

Local mail delivery service in Sweden, cent.

A139

Voting Tool (Budkavle), Codex of Law and Gavel

1962, Mar. 21 ***Perf. 12½ Horiz.***

610 A139 30o dark blue .25 .25
611 A139 2k red 4.50 .35

Perf. 12½ on 3 sides

612 A139 30o dark blue .40 .40
a. Booklet pane of 20 9.00
Complete booklet, #612a 12.00
Nos. 610-612 (3) 5.15 1.00

Centenary of the municipal reform laws.

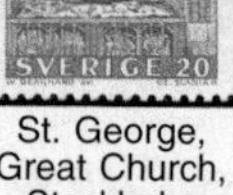
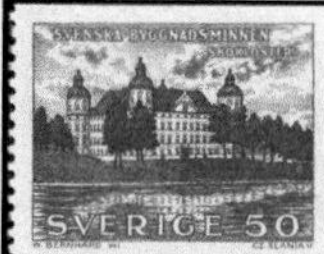

St. George, Great Church, Stockholm A140

Skokloster Castle A141

Perf. 12½ Horiz. (H), Vert. (V)

1962, Sept. 24

613 A140 20o rose lake (H) .25 .25
614 A141 50o dk slate grn (V) .55 .35

Perf. 12½ on 3 sides

615 A140 20o rose lake .25 .25
a. Booklet pane of 20 5.50
Complete booklet, #615a 7.00
616 A141 50o dk slate grn 1.00 *1.25*
a. Booklet pane of 10 8.00
Complete booklet, #616a 10.00
Nos. 613-616 (4) 2.05 2.10

Nobel Prize Winners Type of 1961

Designs: 25o, Theodor Mommsen and Sir Ronald Ross. 50o, Hermann Emil Fischer, Pieter Zeeman and Hendrik Antoon Lorentz.

1962, Dec. 10 ***Perf. 12½ Vert.***

617 A137 25o dark red .25 .25
618 A137 50o blue .40 .40

Perf. 12½ on 3 sides

619 A137 25o dark red .40 .65
a. Booklet pane of 20 8.00
Complete booklet, #619a 8.00
Nos. 617-619 (3) 1.05 1.30

Winners of the 1902 Nobel Prize.

Ice Hockey — A143

1963, Feb. 15 ***Perf. 12½ Horiz.***

620 A143 25o green .40 .30
621 A143 1.70k violet bl 3.00 .70

Perf. 12½ on 3 sides

622 A143 25o green .25 .65
a. Booklet pane of 20 6.00
Nos. 620-622 (3) 3.65 1.65

1963 Ice Hockey World Championships.

Wheat Emblem and Stylized Hands — A144

1963, Mar. 21 ***Perf. 12½ Vertically***

623 A144 35o lilac rose .35 .25
624 A144 50o violet .50 .35

Perf. 12½ on 3 sides

625 A144 35o lilac rose .30 .40
a. Booklet pane of 20 5.00
Complete booklet, #625a 8.00
Nos. 623-625 (3) 1.15 1.00

FAO "Freedom from Hunger" campaign.

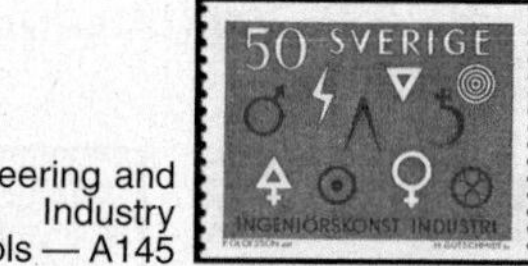

Engineering and Industry Symbols — A145

1963, May 27 ***Perf. 12½ Vertically***

626 A145 50o gray .70 .35
627 A145 1.05k orange 3.25 3.00

Perf. 12½ on 3 sides

628 A145 50o gray 2.00 2.75
a. Booklet pane of 10 20.00
Complete booklet, #628a 25.00
Nos. 626-628 (3) 5.95 6.10

Gregoire François Du Reitz — A146

Perf. 12½ Vertically

1963, Sept. 16 **Engr.** **Unwmk.**

629 A146 25o brown .40 .45
630 A146 35o dark blue .30 .25
631 A146 2k dark red 4.00 .55

Perf. 12½ on 3 sides

632 A146 25o brown .65 .75
a. Booklet pane of 20 12.00
Complete booklet, #632a 15.00
633 A146 35o dark blue .40 .30
a. Booklet pane of 20 8.00
Complete booklet, #633a 14.00
Nos. 629-633 (5) 5.75 2.30

300th anniversary of the Swedish Board of Health. Dr. Du Rietz (1607-1682) was first president of the "Collegium Medicorum," forerunner of the Board of Health.

Hammarby, Home of Carl von Linné (Linnaeus) A147

1963, Oct. 25 ***Perf. 12½ Vert.***

634 A147 20o orange red .25 .25
635 A147 50o yellow grn .30 .25

Perf. 12½ on 3 sides

636 A147 20o orange red .25 .25
a. Booklet pane of 20 5.00
Nos. 634-636 (3) .80 .75

Nobel Prize Winners Type of 1961

Designs: 25o, Svante Arrhenius, Niels Finsen, Bjornstjerne Bjornson. 50o, Antoine Henri Becquerel, Pierre and Marie Curie.

Perf. 12½ Vertically

1963, Dec. 10 **Engr.** **Unwmk.**

637 A137 25o gray olive .75 .70
638 A137 50o chocolate .40 .50

Perf. 12½ on 3 sides

639 A137 25o gray olive .75 1.10
a. Booklet pane of 20 11.00
Complete booklet, #639a 15.00
Nos. 637-639 (3) 1.90 2.30

Winners of the 1903 Nobel Prize.

A149

"The Assumption of Elijah."

1964, Feb. 3 ***Perf. 12½ Horiz.***

640 A149 35o lt ultra .65 .25
641 A149 1.05k dull red 3.75 3.75

Perf. 12½ on 3 sides

642 A149 35o lt ultra .45 .35
a. Booklet pane of 20 6.75
Complete booklet, #642a 9.00
Nos. 640-642 (3) 4.85 4.35

Erik Axel Karlfeldt (1864-1931), poet.

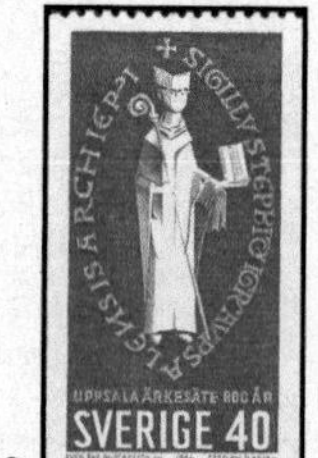

A150

Seal of Archbishop Stephen.

1964, June 12 ***Perf. 12½ Horiz.***

643 A150 40o slate green .25 .30
644 A150 60o orange brown .25 .35

Perf. 12½ Vertically

645 A150 40o slate green .30 .30
a. Booklet pane of 10 2.40
Complete booklet, #645a 2.75
646 A150 60o orange brown .35 .55
a. Booklet pane of 10 2.00
Complete booklet, #646a 3.50
Nos. 643-646 (4) 1.15 1.50

800th anniv. of the Archbishopric of Uppsala.

Types of Regular Issues, 1939-61, and

Post Horns — A151

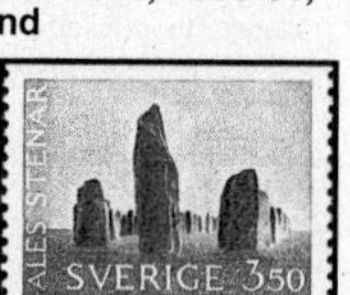

Ship Grave, Skane (Bronze Age) — A152

1964-71 **Engr.** ***Perf. 12½ Vert.***

647 A151 20o sl bl & org yel ('65) .25 .25
648 A132 35o gray .60 .25
649 A132 40o ultra .60 .25
650 A132 45o orange .60 .25
651 A132 45o violet bl ('67) .60 .25
652 A132 50o green ('68) .55 .25
652A A132 55o dk red ('69) .40 .25
653 A132 60o rose car .65 *.65*
653A A132 65o dull grn ('71) .80 .25
654 A132 70o lil rose ('67) .50 .25
654A A132 85o dp cl ('71) .80 .30
655 A108 95o violet 3.00 *4.00*
656 A56 1.20k lt blue 3.50 3.50
657 A56 1.80k dk blue ('67) 1.25 .50
658 A56 1.85k blue ('67) 3.00 1.00
659 A56 2k dp car ('69) .75 .25

660 A56 2.30k choc ('65) 5.50 .25
661 A56 2.55k red 2.10 *2.60*
662 A56 2.80k red ('67) 1.40 .25
663 A56 2.85k orange ('65) 2.75 *4.00*
664 A56 3k brt ultra 1.75 .25
665 A152 3.50k grnsh gray ('66) 3.00 .25

Perf. 12½ on 3 Sides

666 A115a 10o brown .25 .25
a. Bklt. pane, 2 each #666, 667, 583 2.25
Complete booklet, #666a 2.25
667 A115a 15o brown .50 *.80*
668 A132 30o rose red ('66) .85 *.85*
a. Bklt. pane, 2 each #513, 580, 668 1.40
Complete booklet, #668a 2.50
b. Perf. on 3 sides 1.10 1.10

No. 668 is perf. on 2 adjoining sides.

669 A132 40o ultra .25 .25
a. Bklt. pane of 20 16.00
Complete booklet, #669a 27.00
b. Bklt. pane, 2 ea #514, 669 1.50
Complete booklet, #669b 2.50
c. Bklt. pane, 2 each #513-514, 580, 668b-669 4.00
Complete booklet, #669c 8.00
670 A132 45o org ('67) .65 .25
a. Bklt. pane of 20 14.00
671 A132 45o vio bl ('67) .70 .25
a. Bklt. pane of 20 12.50
Complete booklet, #671a 20.00
672 A132 50o green ('69) .50 *.60*
a. Bklt. pane of 10 5.00
672B A132 55o dk red ('69) .50 .25
c. Bklt. pane of 10 5.00
672D A132 65o dull grn ('71) .85 .50
e. Bklt. pane of 10 9.00
672F A132 85o dp cl ('71) .90 *1.25*
g. Bklt. pane of 10 9.50
Nos. 647-672F (32) 40.30 25.30

Some combination booklet panes of 4, 6 or 10 contain two stamps which are imperf. on two adjoining sides. Combination panes come in different arrangements of the denominations.

Fluorescent Paper

Starting in 1967, fluorescent paper was used in printing both definitive and commemorative issues. Its use was gradually eliminated starting in 1976. Numerous definitives and a few commemoratives were printed on both ordinary and fluorescent paper.

Nobel Prize Winners Type of 1961

30o, José Echegaray y Eizaguirre, Frédéric Mistral and John William Strutt, Lord Rayleigh. 40o, Sir William Ramsey and Ivan Petrovich Pavlov.

Perf. 12½ Vertically

1964, Dec. 10 **Engr.**
673 A137 30o blue .45 .45
674 A137 40o red .70 .25

Perf. 12½ on 3 Sides

675 A137 30o blue .45 .75
a. Booklet pane of 20 7.50
Complete booklet, #675a 7.50
676 A137 40o red .75 .35
a. Booklet pane of 20 15.00
Nos. 673-676 (4) 2.35 1.80

Winners of the 1904 Nobel Prize.

Visby Town Wall — A154

1965, Apr. 5 ***Perf. 12½ Horiz.***
677 A154 30o dk car rose .30 .25
678 A154 2k brt ultra 4.25 .35

Perf. 12½ on 3 Sides

679 A154 30o dk car rose .40 .35
a. Booklet pane of 20 9.00
Nos. 677-679 (3) 4.95 .95

Antenna — A155

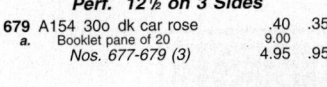

1965, May 17 ***Perf. 12½ Horiz.***
680 A155 60o lilac .45 .45
681 A155 1.40k bluish blk 2.25 1.90

Perf. 12½ on 3 Sides

682 A155 60o lilac 1.10 1.60
a. Booklet pane of 10 10.00
Complete booklet, #682a 11.00
Nos. 680-682 (3) 3.80 3.95

Centenary of the ITU.

Prince Eugen — A156

1965, July 5 ***Perf. 12½ Horiz.***
683 A156 40o black .25 .25
684 A156 1k brown 2.10 .35

Perf. 12½ on 3 Sides

685 A156 40o black .25 .25
a. Booklet pane of 20 4.50
Complete booklet, #685a 5.00
Nos. 683-685 (3) 2.60 .85

Prince Eugen (1865-1947), painter and patron of the arts.

Fredrika Bremer (1801-65), Novelist — A157

Perf. 12½ Vertically

1965, Oct. 25 **Engr.**
686 A157 25o violet .25 .25
687 A157 3k gray green 4.00 .25

Perf. 12½ on 3 Sides

688 A157 25o violet .25 .25
a. Booklet pane of 20 3.75
Complete booklet, #688a 7.50
Nos. 686-688 (3) 4.50 .75

Nobel Prize Winners Type of 1961

30o, Philipp von Lenard, Adolf von Baeyer. 40o, Robert Koch, Henryk Sienkiewicz.

Perf. 12½ Vertically

1965, Dec. 10 **Unwmk.**
689 A137 30o ultra .35 .45
690 A137 40o dark red .40 .25

Perf. 12½ on 3 Sides

691 A137 30o ultra .45 .75
a. Booklet pane of 20 7.50
Complete booklet, #691a 9.00
692 A137 40o dark red .85 .30
a. Booklet pane of 20 13.00
Complete booklet, #692a 15.00
Nos. 689-692 (4) 2.05 1.75

Winners of the 1905 Nobel Prize.

Nathan Soderblom — A158

1966, Jan. 15 ***Perf. 12½ Horiz.***
693 A158 60o brown .35 .25
694 A158 80o green .75 .25

Perf. 12½ on 3 Sides

695 A158 60o brown .75 .75
a. Booklet pane of 10 5.75
Complete booklet, #695a 7.50
Nos. 693-695 (3) 1.85 1.25

Nathan Soderblom (1866-1931), Protestant theologian, who worked for the union of Christian churches and received 1930 Nobel Peace Prize.

Speed Skater — A159

Perf. 12½ on 3 Sides

1966, Feb. 18 **Engr.**
696 A159 5o rose red .25 .25
697 A159 25o slate green .25 .25
698 A159 40o dark blue .35 *.70*
a. Bklt. pane, 4 ea #696-697, 2 #698 1.90
Complete booklet, #698a 2.00
Nos. 696-698 (3) .85 1.20

World Speed Skating Championships for Men, Gothenburg, Feb. 18-20, and 75th anniversary of World Skating Championships.

National Museum, Staircase, 1866 — A160

1966, Mar. 26 ***Perf. 12½ Vert.***
699 A160 30o violet .25 .25
a. Booklet pane of 10 2.00
Complete booklet, #699a 2.00
700 A160 2.30k olive green 1.40 1.75
a. Booklet pane of 10 10.50
Complete booklet, #700a 20.00

National Gallery, Blasieholmen, Stockholm, cent. The design is from an 1866 woodcut showing the inauguration of the Museum.

Baron Louis Gerhard De Geer — A161

1966, May 12 ***Perf. 12½ Vertically***
701 A161 40o dark blue .25 .25
702 A161 3k brown carmine 4.00 .65

Perf. 12½ on 3 Sides

703 A161 40o dark blue .25 .35
a. Booklet pane of 20 7.00
Nos. 701-703 (3) 4.50 1.25

Cent. of the reform of the Representative Assembly under the leadership of Minister of Justice (1858-70) Baron Louis Gerhard De Geer (1818-96).

Stage, Drottningholm Court Theater — A162

Perf. 12½ on 3 Sides

1966, June 15 **Engr.**
Salmon Paper
704 A162 5o vermilion .25 .25
705 A162 25o olive bister .25 .25
706 A162 40o dark purple .40 .50
a. Bklt. pane, 4 ea #704-705, 2 #706 1.75
Complete booklet, #706a 2.00
Nos. 704-706 (3) .90 1.00

Drottningholm Court Theater, 200th anniv.

Almqvist and Wild Rose — A163

Perf. 12½ Horizontally

1966, Sept. 26 **Engr.**
707 A163 25o magenta .25 .25
708 A163 1k green 2.25 .30

Perf. 12½ on 3 Sides

709 A163 25o magenta .25 .25
a. Booklet pane of 20 3.50
Complete booklet, #709a 6.00
Nos. 707-709 (3) 2.75 .80

Carl Jonas Love Almqvist (1793-1866), writer and poet.

Nobel Prize Winner Type of 1961

Designs: 30o, Joseph John Thomson and Giosue Carducci. 40o, Henri Moissan, Camillo Golgi and Santiago Ramon y Cajal.

Perf. 12½ Vertically

1966, Dec. 10 **Engr.**
710 A137 30o rose lake .50 .25
711 A137 40o dark green .50 .25

Perf. 12½ on 3 Sides

712 A137 30o rose lake .50 .45
a. Booklet pane of 20 8.00
Complete booklet, #712a 10.00
713 A137 40o dark green .50 .45
a. Booklet pane of 20 9.00
Complete booklet, #713a 10.00
Nos. 710-713 (4) 2.00 1.40

Winners of the 1906 Nobel Prize.

Field Ball Player — A164

1967, Jan. 12 ***Perf. 12½ Horiz.***
714 A164 45o dk violet blue .25 .25
715 A164 2.70k dp rose lilac 2.75 1.20

Perf. 12½ on 3 Sides

716 A164 45o dk violet blue .25 .25
a. Booklet pane of 20 4.50
Complete booklet, #716a 6.00
Nos. 714-716 (3) 3.25 1.70

World Field Ball Championships, Jan. 12-21.

EFTA Emblem — A165

1967, Feb. 15 ***Perf. 12½ Horiz.***
717 A165 70o orange .45 .40

Perf. 12½ on 3 Sides

718 A165 70o orange 1.10 1.10
a. Booklet pane of 10 12.00
Complete booklet, #718a 14.00

European Free Trade Association. Tariffs were abolished Dec. 31, 1966, among EFTA members: Austria, Denmark, Finland, Great Britain, Norway, Portugal, Sweden, Switzerland.

"The Fjeld," by Sixten Lundbohm A166

Lion Fortress, Gothenburg A167

Uppsala Cathedral A168

Gripsholm Castle A169

1967 **Engr.** ***Perf. 12½ Vert.***
719 A166 35o dl bl & blk brn .25 .25

Perf. 12½ Horiz.

720 A167 3.70k violet 2.10 .25
721 A168 4.50k dull red 2.75 .25

Perf. 12½ Vert.

722 A169 7k vio bl & rose red 3.50 .55

Perf. 12½ on 3 Sides

723 A166 35o dl bl & blk brn .25 .25
a. Booklet pane of 10 1.50
Complete booklet, #723a 2.50
Nos. 719-723 (5) 8.85 1.55

Issued: #719, 721, 723, 3/15; #720, 2/15; #722, 4/11.

Table Tennis — A170

1967, Apr. 11 **Perf. 12½ Horiz.**
724 A170 35o bright magenta .30 .25
725 A170 90o greenish blue 1.30 .50

Perf. 12½ on 3 Sides

726 A170 35o bright magenta .35 .40
a. Booklet pane of 20 5.25
Complete booklet, #726a 7.50
Nos. 724-726 (3) 1.95 1.15

World Table Tennis Championships, Stockholm.

Man with Axe and Fettered Beast — A171

Designs: 15o, Man fighting two bears. 30o, Warrior disguised as wolf pursuing enemy. 35o, Two warriors with swords and lances. The designs are taken from 6th century bronze plates (1¾in. x 2½in.) used to decorate helmets; now in Swedish Museum of National Antiquities.

Perf. 12½ on 3 Sides

1967, May 17 **Engr.**
727 A171 10o dk brown & dp bl .25 .25
728 A171 15o dp blue & dk brn .25 .25
729 A171 30o brt pink & dk brn .25 .25
730 A171 35o dk brown & brt pink .25 .25
a. Bklt. pane, 4 #727, 2 ea #728-730 1.60 *2.75*
Nos. 727-730 (4) 1.00 1.00

Double Mortise Corner — A172

Lithographed and Photogravure

1967, June 16 **Perf. 12½**
731 A172 10o olive & multi .25 .25
732 A172 35o dk blue multi .25 .25
a. Bklt. pane, 6 #731, 4 #732 1.50 *2.00*

Issued to honor generations of Finnish settlers in Sweden.

Right-hand Driving as Seen Through Windshield — A173

1967, Sept. 2 **Engr.** **Perf. 12½ Vert.**
733 A173 35o dp bl, ocher & blk .25 .35
734 A173 45o yel grn, ocher & blk .35 .45

Perf. 12½ Horiz.

735 A173 35o dp bl, ocher & blk .30 .45
a. Booklet pane of 10 2.00
736 A173 45o yel grn, ocher & blk .25 .25
a. Booklet pane of 10 2.00
Nos. 733-736 (4) 1.15 1.50

Issued to publicize the introduction of right-hand driving in Sweden, Sept. 3, 1967.

Postrider A174

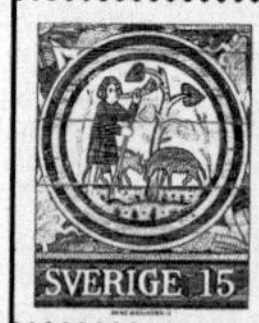

The Prodigal Son, 13th cent., Rada Church A174a

Griffin A174b

Rocky Isles in Bloom, by Harald Lindberg A175

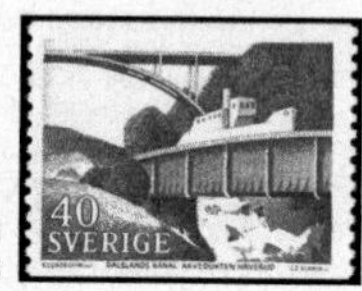

Dalsland Canal — A176

Log roller — A176a

Gothenburg Harbor — A176b

Horse-drawn timber sled — A176c

Nils Holgersson Riding Wild Goose — A176d

Windmills, Ölana Island — A176e

Steamer Storskar and Royal Palace, Stockholm A176f

Moose — A177

Roe deer — A177a

Dancing cranes — A177b

Mail Coach, by Eigil Schwab — A177c 751A

Illustration from Lapponia, by Johannes Schefferus — A177d

Blood-money Coins and Old Map of Sweden A177e

Great Seal, 1439 (St. Erik with Banner and Shield) — A177f

10o, Merchant vessel in Oresund, 1661. 20o, St. Stephen as a boy tending horses, medallion from Dädesio Church. #742, Lion, from Grodinge tapestry, 15th cent. 2.55k, Seal of Magnus Ladulas, 1285 (King Magnus Birgersson on throne with lily scepter and orb). 3k, Seal of Duke Erik Magnusson, 1306 (Duke on horseback with standard of Folkunga dynasty). 6k, Gustavus Vasa's silver daler.

1967-72 **Perf. 12½ Horiz. or Vert.**
737 A174 5o red & blk .25 .25
738 A174 10o blue & blk .25 .25
739 A174a 15o sl grn, *grnsh* ('71) .25 .25
740 A174 20o sep, *buff* ('70) .25 .25
741 A174b 25o bis & blk ('71) .25 .25
742 A174b 25o blk & bis ('71) .25 .25
a. Pair, #741-742 .40 .50
743 A175 30o ultra & ver .25 .25
744 A176 40o blk, dk grn & ultra ('68) .30 .25
745 A176a 45o bl & brn blk ('70) .30 .25
746 A176b 55o bl & vio, vert. ('71) .40 .25
747 A176c 60o black brn ('71) .30 .25
747A A176d 65o brt blue ('71) .30 .25
748 A176e 75o slate grn ('71) .30 .25
749 A176f 80o blue & blk ('71) .40 .25
750 A177 90o sep & bl gray .55 .25
750A A177a 95o sepia ('72) .40 .25
751 A177b 1k slate grn ('68) .55 .25
751A A177c 1.20k multi ('71) .65 .25
751B A177d 1.40k lt bl & red ('72) .75 .25
752 A177f 2.55k brt blue ('70) 1.75 .65
753 A177f 3k dk gray bl ('70) 1.25 .25
754 A177e 4k black ('71) 1.80 .25
755 A177f 5k Prus grn ('70) 2.00 .25
755A A177e 6k indigo ('72) 3.00 .25

Perf. 12½ on 3 Sides, 12½ Horiz. (#761)

756 A174 5o red & blk .25 .25
a. Booklet pane of 20 .75
757 A174 10o bl & blk ('69) .25 .25
a. Booklet pane of 20 1.90
758 A175 30o ultra & ver .30 .30
a. Booklet pane of 10 3.25
759 A176 40o blk, dk grn & ultra ('68) .25 .30
a. Booklet pane of 10 2.75
760 A176a 45o bl & brn blk ('70) .25 .25
a. Booklet pane of 10 2.25
761 A176b 55o bl & vio ('71) .35 .25
a. Booklet pane of 10 2.00
762 A176d 65o brt blue ('71) .40 .40
a. Booklet pane of 10 2.50
763 A176e 75o slate grn ('72) .50 .25
a. Booklet pane of 10 7.50
764 A177 90o sepia & bl gray 1.00 1.00
a. Booklet pane of 10 11.00
Nos. 737-764 (33) 20.30 9.65

King Gustaf VI Adolf — A178

Perf. 12½ Horiz.

1967, Nov. 11 **Engr.**
765 A178 45o lt ultra .30 .25
766 A178 70o green .30 .30

Perf. 12½ on 3 Sides

767 A178 45o lt ultra .25 .25
a. Booklet pane of 20 5.00
768 A178 70o green .65 .95
a. Booklet pane of 10 6.50
Nos. 765-768 (4) 1.50 1.75

85th birthday of King Gustaf VI Adolf.

Nobel Prize Winners Type of 1961

35o, Eduard Buchner (Chemistry), Albert A. Michelson (Physics). 45o, Charles L. A. Laveran (Medicine), Rudyard Kipling (Literature).

1967, Dec. 9 **Perf. 12½ Vert.**
769 A137 35o vermilion .65 .50
770 A137 45o dark blue .55 .25

Perf. 12½ on 3 Sides

771 A142 35o vermilion .70 *.95*
a. Booklet pane of 10 7.00
772 A142 45o dark blue .45 *.50*
a. Booklet pane of 10 6.00
Nos. 769-772 (4) 2.35 2.20

Winners of the 1907 Nobel Prize.

Franz Berwald, Violin and His Music — A179

1968, Apr. 3 **Perf. 12½ Horiz.**
773 A179 35o black & red .35 .25
774 A179 2k blk, vio bl & org yel 3.00 .80

Perf. 12½ on 3 Sides

775 A179 35o black & red .45 .60
a. Booklet pane of 10 3.25
Nos. 773-775 (3) 3.80 1.65

Franz Berwald (1796-1868), composer. Design includes opening bar of overture to his opera, "The Queen of Golconda."

National Bank Seal — A180

Perf. 12½ Vertically

1968, May 15 **Engr.**
776 A180 45o dull blue .25 .25
777 A180 70o black, *pink* .30 .35

Perf. 12½ on 3 Sides

778 A180 45o dull blue .35 *.50*
a. Booklet pane of 10 3.00
779 A180 70o black, *pink* .55 *.85*
a. Booklet pane of 10 5.50
Nos. 776-779 (4) 1.45 1.95

300th anniv. of the National Bank of Sweden. Nos. 777, 779 are on non-fluorescent paper.

Seal of Lund University A181

1968, June 4 **Perf. 12½ on 3 sides**
780 A181 10o deep blue .25 .25
781 A181 35o red .25 *.50*
a. Bklt. pane, 6 #780, 4 #781 1.70 *2.75*

300th anniversary of University of Lund.

Butterfly Orchid — A182

Nordic Wild Flowers: No. 783, Wood anemone. No. 784, Dog rose. No. 785, Prune Cherry. No. 786, Lily of the valley.

1968, June 4

782 A182 45o slate green .80 .45
783 A182 45o gray green .80 .45
784 A182 45o sl grn & rose car .80 .45
785 A182 45o gray green .80 .45
786 A182 45o slate green .80 .45
a. Bklt. pane, 2 each #782-786 8.50
Nos. 782-786 (5) 4.00 2.25

World Council of Churches' Emblem — A183

1968, July 4 ***Perf. 12½ Horiz.***

787 A183 70o plum .55 *.60*
788 A183 90o Prus green 1.00 .50

Perf. 12½ on 3 Sides

789 A183 70o plum .65 *.95*
a. Booklet pane of 10 6.50
Nos. 787-789 (3) 2.20 2.05

4th General Assembly of the World Council of Churches, Uppsala, July 4-19.

Electron Orbits — A184

Perf. 12½ Horizontally

1968, Aug. 9 **Engr.**

790 A184 45o rose carmine .65 .25
791 A184 2k dark blue 3.00 .40

Perf. 12½ on 3 Sides

792 A184 45o rose carmine .65 .45
a. Booklet pane of 10 4.00
Nos. 790-792 (3) 4.30 1.10

Establishment of the 1st 3 People's Colleges, cent.

"Orienteer" Finding Way through Forest — A185

Perf. 12½ Horizontally

1968, Sept. 5 **Engr.**

793 A185 40o violet & red brn .35 .40
794 A185 2.80k green & violet 3.00 2.50

Perf. 12½ on 3 Sides

795 A185 40o violet & red brn .40 .65
a. Booklet pane of 10 4.00
Nos. 793-795 (3) 3.75 3.55

Issued to publicize the World Championships in Orienteering, Linkoping, Sept. 28-29.

"Fingerkrok" by Axel Petersson A186

Perf. 12½ on 3 Sides

1968, Oct. 28 **Engr.**

796 A186 5o green .25 .25
797 A186 25o sepia .90 .90
798 A186 45o blk brn & red brn .25 .25
a. Bklt. pane, 3 #796, 2 #797, 3 #798 2.00
Nos. 796-798 (3) 1.40 1.40

Axel Petersson, called "Doderhultarn" (1868-1925), sculptor.

Black-backed Gull — A187

Designs: No. 799, Varying hare. No. 801, Red fox. No. 802, Hooded crows harassing golden eagle. No. 803, Weasel.

Perf. 12½ on 3 Sides

1968, Nov. 9 **Engr.**

799 A187 30o blue .60 *.70*
800 A187 30o black .60 *.70*
801 A187 30o dark brown .60 *.70*
802 A187 30o black .60 *.70*
803 A187 30o blue .60 *.70*
a. Bklt. pane, 2 each #799-803 6.00
Nos. 799-803 (5) 3.00 3.50

See Nos. 873-877.

Nobel Prize Winners Type of 1961

35o, Elie Metchnikoff, Paul Ehrlich, Ernest Rutherford. 45o, Gabriel Lippmann, Rudolf Eucken.

1968, Dec. 10 ***Perf. 12½ Vertically***

804 A137 35o maroon .55 .25
805 A137 45o dark green .50 .25

Perf. 12½ on 3 Sides

806 A137 35o maroon .50 .90
a. Booklet pane of 10 5.00
807 A137 45o dark green .45 .40
a. Booklet pane of 10 4.50
Nos. 804-807 (4) 2.00 1.80

Nordic Cooperation Issue

Five Ancient Ships — A187a

1969, Feb. 28 **Engr.** ***Perf. 12½ Vert.***

808 A187a 45o dark gray .25 .25
809 A187a 70o blue .55 *.75*

Perf. 12½ on 3 Sides

810 A187a 45o dark gray .50 *.75*
a. Booklet pane of 10 10.00
Nos. 808-810 (3) 1.30 1.75

50th anniv. of the Nordic Society and centenary of postal cooperation among the northern countries. The design is taken from a coin found at the site of Birka, an ancient Swedish town. See also Denmark Nos. 454-455, Finland No. 481, Iceland Nos. 404-405 and Norway Nos. 523-524.

Worker, by Albin Amelin — A188

Perf. 12½ Horiz.

1969, Mar. 31 **Engr.**

811 A188 55o dk carmine rose .45 .25
812 A188 70o dk blue .90 .65

Perf. 12½ on 3 Sides

813 A188 55o dk carmine rose .35 .25
a. Booklet pane of 10 4.00
Nos. 811-813 (3) 1.70 1.15

50th anniv. of the ILO.

Europa Issue, 1969

Common Design Type

1969, Apr. 28 **Photo.** ***Perf. 14 Vert.***

Size: 27x22mm

814 CD12 70o orange & multi *1.50* .45
815 CD12 1k vio blue & multi *1.00* .40

Perf. 14 on 3 Sides

816 CD12 70o orange & multi *1.50* *2.00*
a. Booklet pane of 10 *17.50*
Nos. 814-816 (3) 4.00 2.85

Not fluorescent.

Albert Engstrom with Owl, Self-portrait A189

1969, May 12 **Engr.** ***Perf. 12½ Vert.***

817 A189 35o black brown .30 .25
818 A189 55o blue gray .30 .25

Perf. 12½ on 3 Sides

819 A189 35o black brown .35 .55
a. Booklet pane of 10 2.75
820 A189 55o blue gray .30 .30
a. Booklet pane of 10 2.50
Nos. 817-820 (4) 1.25 1.35

Albert Engstrom (1869-1940), cartoonist.

Souvenir Sheet

Paintings by Ivan Agueli — A190

1969, June 6 **Litho.** ***Perf. 13½***

821 A190 Sheet of 6 2.25 *4.25*
a. 45o Landscape .40 *.45*
b. 45o Still life .40 *.45*
c. 45o Near East town .40 *.45*
d. 55o Young woman .40 *.45*
e. 55o Sunny landscape .40 *.45*
f. 55o Street at night .40 *.45*

Ivan Agueli (1869-1917), painter. Size: #821a-821c, 35x28mm. #821d-821e, 28x44mm. #821f, 48x44mm. Not fluorescent.

Tjorn Bridges — A191

Designs: 15o, 30o, Various bridges.

Size: 20x19mm

Perf. 12½ on 3 Sides

1969, Sept. 3 **Bluish Paper** **Engr.**

822 A191 15o deep blue 1.10 .45
823 A191 30o dk grn & blk 1.10 .45

Size: 41x19mm

824 A191 55o blk & dp bl 1.10 .45
a. Bklt. pane, 2 each #822-824 8.00
Nos. 822-824 (3) 3.30 1.35

Tjorn highway bridges connecting the Islands of Orust and Tjorn in the Gothenburg Archipelago with the mainland.

Man's Head, Woodcarving — A192

Warship Wasa, 1628 — A193

Designs: No. 826, Crowned lion. No. 827, Great Swedish coat of arms. No. 828, Lion, front view. No. 829, Man's head (different from No. 825).

1969, Sept. 3 ***Perf. 12½ on 3 Sides***

825 A192 55o dark red .30 .25
826 A192 55o brown .30 .25
827 A193 55o dark blue .45 .60
828 A192 55o brown .30 .25
829 A192 55o dark red .30 .25
830 A193 55o dark blue .45 .60
a. Bklt. pane, #827, #830, 2 each #825-826, 828-829 3.00
Nos. 825-830 (6) 2.10 2.20

Salvaging in 1961 of the warship Wasa, sunk on her maiden voyage, Aug. 10, 1628.

Soderberg A194

Bo Bergman A195

Perf. 12½ Horiz.

1969, Oct. 13 **Engr.**

831 A194 45o brown, *buff* .50 .30

Perf. 12½ Vert.

832 A195 55o green, *grnsh* .50 .25

Perf. 12½ on 3 Sides

833 A194 45o brown, *buff* .40 *.85*
a. Booklet pane of 10 3.25
Complete booklet, #833a 4.00
834 A195 55o green, *grnsh* .25 .40
a. Booklet pane of 10 3.75
Complete booklet, #834a 5.00
Nos. 831-834 (4) 1.65 1.80

Hjalmar Soderberg (1869-1941), writer; Bo Bergman (1869-1967), poet.

Lever Light, Lightship, Landsort and Svenska Lighthouses — A196

Perf. 12½ Vert.

1969, Nov. 17 **Photo.**

835 A196 30o gray, blk & pink .25 .25
836 A196 55o lt bl, blk & brn .25 .25

300th anniversary of Swedish lighthouses.

Pelle's New Suit — A197

The Adventures of Nils — A198

Swedish Fairy Tales: No. 839, Pippi Longstocking (little girl, horse and monkey). No. 840, Vill-Vallareman (boy blowing horn). No. 841, Kattresan (child riding on back of cat).

Perf. 12½ on 3 Sides

1969, Nov. 17 **Engr.**

837 A197 35o org, red & dk brn 1.50 1.40
838 A198 35o dark brown 1.50 1.40
839 A197 35o org, red & dk brn 1.50 1.40
840 A198 35o dark brown 1.50 1.40
841 A197 35o org, red & dk brn 1.50 1.40
a. Bklt. pane, 2 each #837-841 14.00 16.00
Nos. 837-841 (5) 7.50 7.00

Issued for use in Christmas cards.

Dr. Emil T. Kocher and Wilhelm Ostwald — A199

55o, Selma Lagerlof, open book. 70o, Guglielmo Marconi, Carl Ferdinand Braun.

1969, Dec. 10 ***Perf. 12½ Vert.***

842 A199 45o dull green .75 .35
843 A199 55o blk, *pale sal* .60 .25
844 A199 70o black .75 1.25

Perf. 12½ on 3 Sides

845 A199 45o dull green .45 .55
a. Booklet pane of 10 5.00
846 A199 55o blk, *pale sal* .40 .30
a. Booklet pane of 10 6.00
Nos. 842-846 (5) 2.95 2.70

Winners of the 1909 Nobel Prize.

Weather Vane, Soderala Church A200

Door with Iron Fittings, Bjorksta Church, Vastmanland A201

Swedish Art Forgings: 10o, like 5o, facing right. 30o, Memorial cross, Ekshärad churchyard, Varmland.

Perf. 12½ on 3 sides

1970, Feb. 9 **Engr.**

847 A200 5o dp grn & brn .25 .25
848 A200 10o dp grn & brn .25 .25
849 A200 30o blk & dp grn .25 .25

Perf. 12½ Vert.

850 A201 55o brn & dp grn .25 .25
a. Bklt. pane, 2 each #847-850 1.75 *3.75*
Complete booklet, #850a 2.00
Nos. 847-850 (4) 1.00 1.00

Ljusman River Rapids A202

1970, May 11 **Engr.** ***Perf. 12½ Vert.***

851 A202 55o black & multi .30 .25
852 A202 70o black & multi .65 .60

European Nature Conservation Year, 1970.

Skiing — A203

"Around the Arctic Circle": No. 853, View of Kiruna. No. 855, Boat on mountain lake in Stora Sjofellet National Park. No. 856, Reindeer herd and herdsman. No. 857, Rocket probe under northern lights.

Perf. 12½ Horiz.

1970, June 5 **Engr.**

853 A203 45o sepia .50 *.85*
854 A203 45o violet blue .50 *.85*
855 A203 45o dull green .50 *.85*
856 A203 45o sepia .50 *.85*
857 A203 45o violet blue .50 *.85*
a. Bklt. pane, 2 each #853-857 5.50
Nos. 853-857 (5) 2.50 4.25

China Palace, Drottningholm Park, 1769 — A204

Perf. 12½ Vert.

1970, Aug. 28 **Photo.**

858 A204 2k yel, grn & pink 1.50 .25

Glimmingehus, Skane Province, 15th Century — A205

Perf. 12½ Horiz.

1970, Aug. 28 **Engr.**

859 A205 55o gray green .30 .25

Perf. 12½ on 3 Sides

860 A205 55o gray green .25 .25
a. Booklet pane of 10 3.50

Timber Industry A206

Miner A208

Shipping Industry — A207

Designs: No. 863, Heavy industry (propeller). No. 864, Hydroelectric power (dam and diesel). No. 865, Mining (freight train and mine). No. 866, Technical research.

Perf. 12½ on 3 sides

1970, Sept. 28 **Engr.**

861 A206 70o indigo & lt brn 2.00 *2.50*
862 A207 70o ind, lt brn & dp plum 2.00 *2.50*
863 A206 70o ind & dp plum 2.00 *2.50*
864 A206 70o ind & dp plum 2.00 *2.50*
865 A207 70o ind & dp plum 2.00 *2.50*
866 A206 70o dp plum & lt brn 2.00 *2.50*
a. Booklet pane of 6, #861-866 14.00 *20.00*
867 A208 1k black, *buff* .40 .25
a. Booklet pane of 10 4.00

Perf. 12½ Vertically

868 A208 1k black, *buff* .90 .25
Nos. 861-868 (8) 13.30 15.50

Swedish trade and industry.

"Love, Not War" A209

Design: 70o, Four-leaf clovers symbolizing efforts for equality and brotherhood.

Engraved and Lithographed

1970, Oct. 24 ***Perf. 12½ Horiz.***

869 A209 55o rose red, yel & blk .25 .35
a. Booklet pane of 4 1.50
870 A209 70o emerald, yel & blk .40 .45
a. Booklet pane of 4 2.00

Perf. 12½ Vert.

871 A209 55o rose red, yel & blk .35 .25
872 A209 70o emerald, yel & blk .40 *.35*
Nos. 869-872 (4) 1.40 1.40

25th anniversary of the United Nations.

Bird Type of 1968

Birds: No. 873, Blackbird. No. 874, Great titmouse. No. 875, Bullfinch. No. 876, Greenfinch. No. 877, Blue titmouse.

Perf. 12½ on 3 Sides

1970, Nov. 20 **Photo.**

873 A187 30o blue grn & multi .85 1.00
874 A187 30o bister & multi .85 1.00
875 A187 30o blue & multi .85 1.00
876 A187 30o pink & multi .85 1.00
877 A187 30o org yel & multi .85 1.00
a. Bklt. pane, 2 each #873-877 8.50 *14.00*
Nos. 873-877 (5) 4.25 5.00

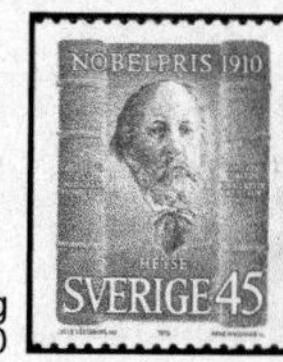

Paul Johann Ludwig Heyse — A210

Designs: 55o, Otto Wallach and Johannes Diderik van der Waals. 70o, Albrecht Kossel.

Perf. 12½ Horiz.

1970, Dec. 10 **Engr.**

878 A210 45o violet .80 .40
879 A210 55o slate blue .50 .30
880 A210 70o gray 1.25 1.10

Perf. 12½ on 3 Sides

881 A210 45o violet .60 *1.10*
a. Booklet pane of 10 6.50
882 A210 55o slate blue .65 .35
a. Booklet pane of 10 6.50
Nos. 878-882 (5) 3.80 3.25

Winners of the 1910 Nobel Prize.

Kerstin Hesselgren — A211

Perf. 12½ Horiz.

1971, Feb. 19 **Engr.**

883 A211 45o dp claret, *gray* .45 .40
884 A211 1k dp brn, *buff* .65 .25

Perf. 12½ on 3 Sides

885 A211 45o dp claret, *gray* .30 *.85*
a. Booklet pane of 10 3.25
Nos. 883-885 (3) 1.40 1.50

50th anniv. of woman suffrage; Kerstin Hesselgren, was 1st woman member of Swedish Upper House.

Terns in Flight — A212

1971, Mar. 26 ***Perf. 13½ Vert.***

886 A212 40o dark red .40 .35
887 A212 55o violet blue .80 .25

Perf. 12½ on 3 Sides

888 A212 55o violet blue .40 .25
a. Booklet pane of 10 4.50
Nos. 886-888 (3) 1.60 .85

Joint northern campaign for the benefit of refugees.

Abstract Music, by Ingvar Lidholm — A213

Perf. 12½ Horiz.

1971, Aug. 27 **Engr.**

889 A213 55o deep lilac .40 .25
890 A213 85o green .45 .30

Perf. 12½ on 3 Sides

891 A213 55o deep lilac .30 *.30*
a. Booklet pane of 10 2.50
Nos. 889-891 (3) 1.15 .85

The Three Kings, Grotlingbo Church — A214

Flight into Egypt, Stanga Church A215

Designs: 10o, Adam and Eve, Gammelgarn Church. 55o, Saint on horseback and Samson with the lion, Hogrän Church.

Perf. 12½ on 3 Sides

1971, Sept. 28 **Engr.**

892 A214 5o violet & brn .50 .40
893 A214 10o violet & sl grn .50 .40

Perf. 12½ Horiz.

894 A215 55o slate grn & brn .50 .35
895 A215 65o brown & vio blk .30 .25
a. Bklt. pane, #892-894, 2 #895 1.75 *4.50*
Nos. 892-895 (4) 1.80 1.40

Art of medieval stonemasons in Gotland.

Toddler and Automobile Wheel — A216

1971, Oct. 20 ***Perf. 12½ Vert.***

896 A216 35o black & red .25 .25
897 A216 65o dp blue & multi .80 .25

Perf. 12½ on 3 Sides

898 A216 65o dp blue & multi .40 .25
a. Booklet pane of 10 5.75
Nos. 896-898 (3) 1.45 .75

Publicity for road safety.

King Gustavus Vasa's Sword, c. 1500 — A217

Swedish Crown Regalia: No. 900, Scepter. No. 901, Crown. No. 902, Orb (Scepter, crown and orb were made in 1561 for Erik XIV). No. 903, Karl IX's anointing horn, 1606.

Perf. 12½ on 3 Sides

1971, Oct. 20 **Engr.**

899 A217 65o lt blue & multi .50 .40
900 A217 65o lt ol grn & multi .50 .40
901 A217 65o dk blue & multi .50 .40
902 A217 65o lt ol grn & multi .50 .40
903 A217 65o lt blue & multi .50 .40
a. Bklt. pane, 2 each #899-903 5.50 *10.00*
Nos. 899-903 (5) 2.50 2.00

Christmas Elf and Goat Bringing Gifts — A218

Christmas Customs (Old Prints): No. 905, Christmas market. No. 906, Dancing children and father playing fiddle. No. 907, Ice-skating on frozen waterways in Stockholm. No. 908, Sleigh ride to church.

1971, Nov. 10

904 A218 35o deep carmine 1.25 1.20
905 A218 35o violet blue 1.25 1.20
906 A218 35o violet brown 1.25 1.20
907 A218 35o violet blue 1.25 1.20
908 A218 35o slate green 1.25 1.20
a. Bklt. pane, 2 each #904-908 12.50 *16.00*
Nos. 904-908 (5) 6.25 6.00

Maurice Maeterlinck — A219

Designs: 65o, Wilhelm Wien and Allvar Gullstrand. 85o, Marie Sklodovska Curie.

1971, Dec. 10 ***Perf. 12½ Horiz.***

909 A219 55o orange .65 .55
910 A219 65o green .65 .25
911 A219 85o dk carmine .65 .60

Perf. 12½ on 3 Sides

912 A219 55o orange .60 *.80*
a. Booklet pane of 10 6.00
913 A219 65o green .65 .40
a. Booklet pane of 10 6.50
Nos. 909-913 (5) 3.20 2.60

Winners of the 1911 Nobel Prize.

Women Athletes — A220

1972, Feb. 23 ***Perf. 12½ on 3 Sides***

914 A220 55o Fencing .65 *.75*
915 A220 55o Diving .65 *.75*
916 A220 55o Gymnastics .65 *.75*
917 A220 55o Tennis .65 *.75*
918 A220 55o Figure skating .65 *.75*
a. Bklt. pane, 2 each #914-918 5.50 *12.00*
Nos. 914-918 (5) 3.25 3.75

Lars Johan Hierta, by Christian Eriksson — A221

Frans Michael Franzen, by Soderberg and Hultstrom — A222

Hugo Alfven, by Carl Milles — A223

Georg Stiernhielm, by David K. Ehrenstrahl — A224

Photo., Perf 12½ Horiz. (35, 85o); Engr., Perf. 12½ Vert. (50, 65o)

1972 Feb. 23

919 A221 35o multicolored .30 .25
920 A222 50o violet .30 .25
921 A223 65o bluish black .40 .25
922 A224 85o multicolored .50 .50
Nos. 919-922 (4) 1.50 1.25

Hierta (1801-72), journalist. Franzen (1772-1847), poet. Alfven (1872-1960), composer. Stiernhielm (1598-1672), poet, writer, scientist.

Lifting Molten Glass A225

Swedish Glassmaking: No. 924, Glass blower. No. 925, Decorating vase. No. 926, Annealing vase. No. 927, Polishing jug.

Perf. 12½ Horiz.

1972, Mar. 22 **Engr.**

923 A225 65o black .80 .90
924 A225 65o violet blue .80 .90
925 A225 65o carmine .80 .90
926 A225 65o black .80 .90
927 A225 65o violet blue .80 .90
a. Bklt. pane, 2 each #923-927 8.00
Nos. 923-927 (5) 4.00 4.50

Horses and Ruin of Borgholm Castle — A226

Designs: No. 929, Oland Island Bridge. No. 930, Kalmar Castle. No. 931, Salmon fishing. No. 932, Schooner Falken, Karlskrona.

1972, May 8 ***Perf. 12½ Horiz.***

928 A226 55o chocolate .40 .75
929 A226 55o dk violet blue .40 .75
930 A226 55o chocolate .40 .75
931 A226 55o blue green .40 .75
932 A226 55o dk violet blue .40 .75
a. Bklt. pane, 2 each #928-932 4.00
Nos. 928-932 (5) 2.00 3.75

Tourist attractions in Southeast Sweden.

"Only one Earth" Environment Emblem — A227

"Spring," Bror Hjorth — A228

1972, June 5 **Engr.** ***Perf. 12½ Vert.***

933 A227 65o blue & carmine .25 .25

Perf. 12½ Horiz.

934 A227 65o blue & carmine .25 .25
a. Booklet pane of 10 2.00
Complete booklet, #934a 4.00

Perf. 12½ Vert.

935 A228 85o brown & multi .45 .30
a. Booklet pane of 4 1.80
Complete booklet, #935a 4.00
Nos. 933-935 (3) .95 .80

UN Conference on Human Environment, Stockholm, June 5-16.

Junkers JU52 — A229

Historic Planes: 5o, Junkers F13. 25o, Friedrichshafen FF49. 75o, Douglas DC-3.

1972, Sept. 8 ***Perf. 12½ on 3 Sides***

Size: 20x19mm

936 A229 5o lilac .25 .25

Size: 44x19mm

937 A229 15o blue .45 .50
938 A229 25o blue .45 .50
939 A229 75o gray green .30 .30
a. Bklt. pane, #937-938, 2 ea #936, 939 1.60 *3.00*
Complete booklet, #939a 3.00
Nos. 936-939 (4) 1.45 1.55

Stockholm from the South, by Johan Fredrik Martin — A230

Amphion Figurehead, by Per Ljung — A231

Lady with Veil, by Alexander Roslin — A232

#941, Anchor Forge, by Pehr Hillestrom. #943, Quadriga, by Johan Tobias von Sergel. #945, (Queen) Sofia Magdalena, by Carl Gustaf Pilo.

1972, Oct. 7 **Engr.** ***Perf. 12½ Horiz.***

940 A230 75o greenish black .40 *.60*
941 A230 75o dark brown .40 *.60*

Perf. 12½ on 3 Sides

942 A231 75o dark carmine .45 *.55*
943 A231 75o dark carmine .45 *.55*

Perf. 12½ on 2 Sides

944 A232 75o dk brn, blk & dk car .45 *.60*
945 A232 75o dk brn, blk & dk car .45 *.60*
a. Booklet pane of 6, #940-945 3.00 *4.75*
Complete booklet, #945a 3.50

18th century Swedish art.

Types of 1936

Imprint: "1972"

1972, Oct. 7 ***Perf. 12½ on 3 Sides***

946 A36 10o dark carmine .30 *.50*
947 A37 15o yellow green .30 *.50*
948 A42 40o deep blue .30 *.50*
949 A44 50o deep claret .30 *.50*
950 A45 60o deep blue .30 *.50*
a. Bklt. pane, 2 each #946-950 3.00 *7.00*
Nos. 946-950 (5) 1.50 2.50

Olle Hjortzberg (1872-1959), stamp designer. Booklet sold for 5k of which 1.50k was for Stockholmia 74, Intl. Phil. Exhib., Sept. 21-29, 1973.

Santa Claus — A233

St. Lucia Singers A234

Perf. 14 on 3 Sides

1972, Nov. 6 **Photo.**

951 A233 45o Candles .30 .25
952 A233 45o shown .30 .25
a. Bklt. pane, 5 each #951-952 3.00

Perf. 12½ Vert.

953 A234 75o gray & multi .55 .25
Nos. 951-953 (3) 1.15 .75

Christmas 1972 (children's drawings).

Horse — A235

Viking Ship — A236

Willows, by Peter A. Persson A237

Trosa, by Reinhold Ljunggren A238

Spring Birches, by Oskar Bergman A239

King Gustaf VI Adolf — A240

Perf. 12½ Horiz. or Vert.

1972-73 **Engr.**

954 A235 5o maroon ('73) .25 .25
955 A236 10o dk blue ('73) .25 .25
956 A237 40o sepia ('73) .25 .25
957 A238 50o blk & brn ('73) .30 .25
958 A239 55o yel grn ('73) .35 .25
959 A240 75o indigo .40 .25
960 A240 1k dp carmine .65 .25

1973 ***Perf. 12½ on 3 Sides***

961 A235 5o maroon .25 .25
a. Booklet pane of 20 .75
962 A236 10o dark blue .25 .25
a. Booklet pane of 20 .75
Complete booklet, #962a .75
963 A240 75o indigo .30 .25
a. Booklet pane of 10 3.00
Nos. 954-963 (10) 3.25 2.50

King Gustaf VI Adolf — A245

Chinese Objects — A246

Designs: No. 983, King opening Parliament. No. 984, Etruscan vase and dish. No. 985, King with flowers.

1972, Nov. 11 ***Perf. 12½ Vert.***

981 A245 75o violet blue 1.15 2.50
982 A246 75o slate green 1.15 2.50
983 A245 75o maroon 1.15 2.50
984 A246 75o violet blue 1.15 2.50
985 A245 75o slate green 1.15 2.50
a. Bklt. pane of 5, #981-985 6.75 15.00
Complete booklet, #985a 8.00

90th birthday of King Gustaf VI Adolf. Booklet sold for 4.75k of which 1k was for the King Gustaf VI Adolf Foundation for Swedish Cultural Activities.

Paul Sabatier and Victor Grignard — A247

Dr. Alexis Carrel — A248

75o, Nils Gustaf Dalen. 1k, Gerhart Hauptmann.

1972, Dec. 8 Engr. *Perf. 12½ Vert.*

986 A247 60o olive bister .60 .40

Perf. 12½ Horiz.

987 A248 65o dark blue .70 .40
988 A248 75o violet .90 .25
989 A248 1k redsh brown 1.10 .30
Nos. 986-989 (4) 3.30 1.35

Winners of the 1912 Nobel Prize.

Mail Coach, 1923 — A249

Design: 70o, Postal autobus, 1972.

Perf. 12½ on 3 Sides

1973, Jan. 18 Engr.

990 A249 60o black, *yellow* .25 .25
a. Booklet pane of 10 2.75

Perf. 12½ Vert.

991 A249 70o blue, orange & grn .50 .25

Tintomara, by Lars Johan Werle — A250

Orpheus and Eurydice, by Christoph W. Gluck — A251

1973, Jan. 18 *Perf. 12½ Horiz.*

992 A250 75o green .80 .25

Booklet Stamp

993 A251 1k red lilac .55 .35
a. Booklet pane of 5 3.00

Bicentenary of the Royal Theater in Stockholm. The 75o shows a stage setting by Bo-Ruben Hedwall for Tintomara, a new opera, performed for the bicentenary celebration. The 1k shows painting by Pehr Hillestrom of Orpheus and Eurydice, which was first opera performed in Royal Theater.

Vaasa Ski Race, Dalecarlia — A252

Designs: No. 995, "Going to Church in Mora" (church boats), by Anders Zorn. No. 996, Church stables, Rättvik. No. 997, Falun copper mine. No. 998, Midsummer Dance, by Bengt Nordenberg.

1973, Mar. 2 *Perf. 12½ Horiz.*

994 A252 65o slate green .40 .40
995 A252 65o slate green .40 .40
996 A252 65o black .40 .40
997 A252 65o slate green .40 .40
998 A252 65o claret .40 .40
a. Bklt. pane, 2 each #994-998 4.00
Nos. 994-998 (5) 2.00 2.00

Tourist attractions in Dalecarlia.

Worker, Confederation Emblem — A253

1973, Apr. 26 *Perf. 12½ Vert.*

999 A253 75o dark carmine .40 .25
1000 A253 1.40k slate blue .75 .25

75th anniversary of the Swedish Confederation of Trade Unions (LO).

Observer Reading Temperature A254

Design: No. 1002, Clouds, photographed by US weather satellite.

1973, May 24 Engr. *Perf. 12½ Vert.*

1001 A254 65o slate green .75 .65
1002 A254 65o black & ultra .75 .65
a. Pair, #1001-1002 1.50 *2.50*

Cent. of the Swedish Weather Organization and of Intl. Meteorological Cooperation.

Nordic Cooperation Issue

Nordic House, Reykjavik A254a

1973, June 26 *Perf. 12½ Vert.*

1003 A254a 75o multicolored .45 .25
1004 A254a 1k multicolored .65 .25

A century of postal cooperation among Denmark, Finland, Iceland, Norway and Sweden and in connection with the Nordic Postal Conference, Reykjavik, Iceland.

Carl Peter Thunberg (1743-1828) — A255

Swedish Explorers: No. 1006, Anders Sparrman (1748-1820) and Polynesian double canoe. No. 1007, Nils Adolf Erik Nordenskjold (1832-1901) and ship in pack ice. No. 1008, Salomon August Andrée (1854-1897) and balloon on snow field. No. 1009, Sven Hedin (1865-1952) and camel riders.

1973, Sept. 22 *Perf. 12½ Horiz.*

1005 A255 1k sl grn, bl & brn 1.20 1.00
1006 A255 1k bl, sl grn & brn 1.20 1.00
1007 A255 1k bl, sl grn & brn 1.20 1.00
1008 A255 1k black & multi 1.20 1.00
1009 A255 1k black & multi 1.20 1.00
a. Bklt. pane of 5, #1005-1009 6.00 *8.25*
Complete booklet, #1009a 7.00

Plower with Ox Team A256

Designs: No. 1011, Woman working flax brake. No. 1012, Farm couple planting potatoes. No. 1013, Women baking bread. No. 1014, Man with horse-drawn sower.

1973, Oct. 24 *Perf. 12½ Horiz.*

1010 A256 75o grnsh black 1.20 .45
1011 A256 75o red brown 1.20 .45
1012 A256 75o grnsh black 1.20 .45
1013 A256 75o plum 1.20 .45
1014 A256 75o red brown 1.20 .45
a. Bklt. pane, 2 ea #1010-1014 12.00
Nos. 1010-1014 (5) 6.00 2.25

Centenary of Nordic Museum, Stockholm.

Gray Seal — A257

Protected Animals: 20o, Peregrine falcon. 25o, Lynx. 55o, Otter. 65o, Wolf. 75o, White-tailed sea eagle.

1973, Oct. 24 *Perf. 12½ on 3 Sides*

1015 A257 10o slate green .25 .25
1016 A257 20o violet .25 .25
1017 A257 25o Prus green .25 .25
1018 A257 55o Prus green .25 .25
1019 A257 65o violet .25 .25
1020 A257 75o slate green .35 .35
a. Bklt. pane, 2 each #1015-1020 2.50 *3.00*
Nos. 1015-1020 (6) 1.60 1.60

King Gustaf VI Adolf — A258

1973, Oct. 24 *Perf. 12½ Vert.*

1021 A258 75o dk violet blue .50 .25
1022 A258 1k purple .75 .25

King Gustaf VI Adolf (1882-1973).

The Three Kings A259

Charles XIV John — A260

No. 1024, Merry country dance. No. 1026, Basket with stylized Dalecarlian gourd plant.

Perf. 14 Horiz.

1973, Nov. 12 Photo.

1023 A259 45o multicolored .35 .25
1024 A259 45o multicolored .35 .25
a. Bklt. pane, 5 each #1023-1024 3.50

Coil Stamps

1025 A260 75o multicolored 1.25 .25
1026 A260 75o multicolored 1.25 .25
a. Pair, #1025-1026 2.75 *5.00*
Nos. 1023-1026 (4) 3.20 1.00

Christmas 1973. Designs are from Swedish peasant paintings.

The Goosegirl, by Josephson — A261

Perf. 12½ Horiz.

1973, Nov. 12 Engr.

1027 A261 10k multicolored 4.25 .35

Ernst Josephson (1851-1906), painter.

Alfred Werner and Heike Kamerlingh-Onnes A262

Charles Robert Richet A263

Design: 1.40k, Rabindranath Tagore.

1973, Dec. 10 Engr. *Perf. 12½ Vert.*

1028 A262 75o dark violet .75 .25

Perf. 12½ Horiz.

1029 A263 1k dark brown .75 .30
1030 A263 1.40k green .65 .25
Nos. 1028-1030 (3) 2.15 .80

Winners of 1913 Nobel Prize.

Ski Jump A264

Skiing: No. 1032, Cross-country race. No. 1033, Relay race. No. 1034, Slalom. No. 1035, Women's cross-country race.

Perf. 12½ Horiz.

1974, Jan. 23 Engr.

1031 A264 65o slate green .50 .45
1032 A264 65o violet blue .50 .45
1033 A264 65o slate green .50 .45
1034 A264 65o dk carmine .50 .45
1035 A264 65o violet blue .50 .45
a. Bklt. pane, 2 each #1031-1035 5.00
Nos. 1031-1035 (5) 2.50 2.25

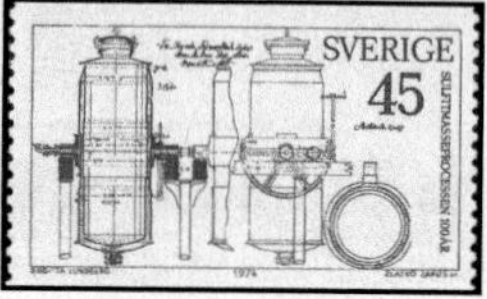

Drawing of First Industrial Digester A265

Hans Järta and Quotation from 1809 — A266

Samuel Owen and 19th Century Factory A267

1974, Mar. 5 Engr. *Perf. 12½ Vert.*

1036 A265 45o sepia .25 .25
1037 A266 60o green .30 .30
1038 A267 75o dull red 1.00 .25
Nos. 1036-1038 (3) 1.55 .80

Centenary of sulphite pulp process (45o); Hans Järta (1774-1847), statesman responsible for the Instrument of Government Act of 1809 (60o); Samuel Owen (1774-1854), English-born industrialist who introduced new production methods (75o).

Stora Sjofallet (Great Falls) — A268

Street in Ystad — A269

1974, Apr. 2 *Perf. 12½ Horiz.*

1039 A268 35o blue grn & blk .45 .25

Perf. 12½ on 3 Sides

1040 A269 75o dull claret .30 .25
a. Booklet pane of 10 3.00
Complete booklet, #1040a 6.75

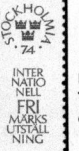

UPU Type of 1924 A270

1974 Engr. *Perf. 12½ on 3 Sides*

1041 A270 20o green .25 .25
1042 A270 25o ultra .25 .25
1043 A270 30o dark brown .25 .25
1044 A270 35o dark red .25 .25
a. Bklt. pane, 2 each #1041-1044 1.75 *3.50*
Complete booklet, #1044a 2.00
Nos. 1041-1044 (4) 1.00 1.00

Miniature Sheets

Perf. 12½

1045 Sheet of 4 1.00 *3.50*
a. A270 20o ocher, single stamp .40 *.75*
1046 Sheet of 4 1.00 *3.50*
a. A270 25o dk vio, single stamp .40 *.75*
1047 Sheet of 4 1.00 *3.50*
a. A270 30o dk red, single stamp .40 *.75*
1048 Sheet of 4 2.00 *3.50*
a. A270 35o yel grn, single stamp .40 *.75*

Stockholmia 74 philatelic exhibition, Stockholm, Sept. 21-29. Booklet sold for 3k with surtax going toward financing the exhibition.

Nos. 1045-1048 sold during exhibition in folder with 5k entrance ticket.

Issued: #1041-1044, 4/2; #1045-1048, 9/21.

"Man in Storm," by Bror Marklund — A271

Europa: 1k, Sculpture by Picasso, Lake Vanern, Kristinehamm.

Perf. 12½ Horiz.

1974, Apr. 29 Engr.

1049 A271 75o violet brown *1.00* .25
1050 A271 1k slate green *1.10* .30

King Carl XVI Gustaf — A272

1974-78 Engr. *Perf. 12½ Vert.*

1068 A272 75o slate grn .40 .25
1069 A272 90o brt blue ('75) .35 .25
1070 A272 1k maroon .45 .25
1071 A272 1.10k rose red ('75) .40 .25
1072 A272 1.30k green ('76) .50 .25
1073 A272 1.40k violet bl ('77) .75 .25
1074 A272 1.50k red lilac ('80) .60 .25
1075 A272 1.70k orange ('78) 1.00 .25
1076 A272 2k dk brown ('80) 1.00 .25

Perf. 12½ on 3 Sides

1077 A272 75o slate green .30 .25
a. Booklet pane of 10 3.00
Complete booklet, #1077a 4.50
1078 A272 90o brt blue ('75) .30 .25
a. Booklet pane of 10 3.00
Complete booklet, #1078a 5.50
1079 A272 1k maroon ('76) .40 .25
a. Booklet pane of 10 4.00
Complete booklet, #1079a 5.50
1080 A272 1.10k rose red ('77) .40 .25
a. Booklet pane of 10 4.00
Complete booklet, #1080a 5.50
1081 A272 1.30k green ('78) .50 .25
a. Booklet pane of 10 5.00
Complete booklet, #1081a 6.50
1082 A272 1.50k red lilac ('80) .60 .25
a. Booklet pane of 10 6.00
Complete booklet, #1082a 7.50
Nos. 1068-1082 (15) 7.95 3.75

A273

Central Post Office, Stockholm A274

Mailman, Northernmost Rural Delivery Route — A275

Perf. 12½ on 3 Sides

1974, June 7 Engr.

1084 A273 75o violet brown .70 .40
1085 A274 75o violet brown .70 .40
a. Bklt. pane, 5 ea #1084-1085 7.00
Complete booklet, #1085a 8.00

Perf. 12½ Vert.

1086 A275 1k slate green .65 .25
Nos. 1084-1086 (3) 2.05 1.05

Centenary of Universal Postal Union.

Regatta A276

Scenes from Sweden's West Coast: No. 1088, Vinga Lighthouse. No. 1089, Varberg Fortress. No. 1090, Seine fishing. No. 1091, Fishing village Mollosund.

1974, June 7 *Perf. 12½ Horiz.*

1087 A276 65o crimson .65 .45
1088 A276 65o blue .65 .45
1089 A276 65o dk olive green .65 .45
1090 A276 65o slate green .65 .45
1091 A276 65o brown .65 .45
a. Bklt. pane, 2 each #1087-1091 6.50
Complete booklet, #1091a 10.00
Nos. 1087-1091 (5) 3.25 2.25

Mr. Simmons, by Axel Fridell — A277

Perf. 12½ on 3 Sides

1974, Aug. 28 Engr.

1092 A277 45o black .25 .25
a. Booklet pane of 10 3.00
Complete booklet, #1092a 4.00

Perf. 12½ Horiz.

1093 A277 1.40k deep claret .75 .25

Swedish Publicists' Club, centenary.

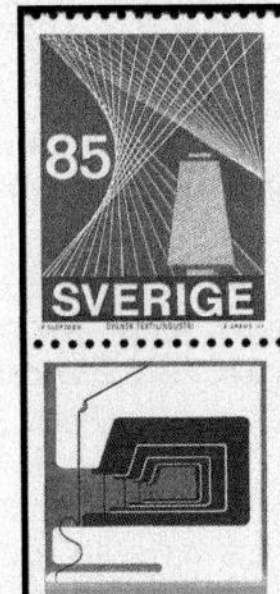

Swedish Textile & Clothing Industries — A278

No. 1094, Thread and spool. No. 1095, Sewing machines (abstract).

1974, Aug. 28 *Perf. 12½ Horiz.*

1094 85o deep violet .40 .25
1095 85o black & org .40 .25
a. A278 Pair, #1094-1095 1.00 .80

Tugs in Stockholm Harbor — A279

No. 1096, Tanker. No. 1097, Liner "Snow Storm." No. 1098, Ice breakers Tor and Atle. No. 1099, Skane Train Ferry, Trelleborg-Sassnitz.

1974, Nov. 16 *Perf. 12½ Horiz.*

1096 A279 1k dark blue .60 .80
1097 A279 1k dark blue .60 .80
1098 A279 1k dark blue .60 .80
1099 A279 1k dark blue .60 .80
1100 A279 1k dark blue .60 .80
a. Bklt. pane of 5, #1096-1100 3.00 7.00
Complete booklet, #1100a 5.75

Swedish shipping industry.

Miniature Sheet

Quilt from Skepptuna Church — A280

Deer, Quilt from Hog Church — A281

Designs are from woolen quilts, 15th-16th centuries. Motifs shown on No. 1101 are stylized deer, griffins, lions, unicorn and horses.

1974, Nov. 16 Photo. *Perf. 14*

1101 A280 Sheet of 10 9.00 *13.00*
a.-j. 45o, single stamp .90 1.00

Perf. 13 Horiz.

1102 A281 75o bl blk, red & yel .45 .25

Max von Laue — A282

Designs: 70o, Theodore William Richards. 1k, Robert Bárány.

1974, Dec. 10 Engr. *Perf. 12½ Vert.*

1103 A282 65o rose red .30 .25
1104 A282 70o slate .40 .30
1105 A282 1k indigo .90 .25
Nos. 1103-1105 (3) 1.60 .80

Winners of 1914 Nobel Prize.

A283

No. 1106, Sven Jerring's children's program. No. 1107, Televising parliamentary debate.

1974, Dec. 10 *Perf. 12½ Vert.*

1106 75o dk blue & brn .65 .25
1107 75o brown & dk bl .65 .25
a. A283 Pair, #1106-1107 1.25 *2.00*

Swedish Broadcasting Corp., 50th anniv.

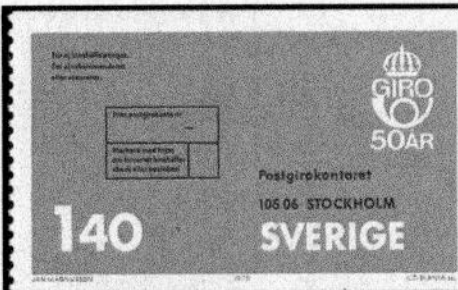

Account Holder's Envelope A285

Photogravure and Engraved

1975, Jan. 21 *Perf. 14 Vert.*

1108 A285 1.40k ocher & blk .75 .25

Swedish Postal Giro Office, 50th anniv.

Male and Female Architects, New Parliament A286

Jenny Lind (1820-87), by J. O. Sodermark A287

1975, Mar. 25 Engr. *Perf. 12½ Vert.*

1109 A286 75o slate green .35 .25

Perf. 12½ Horiz.

1110 A287 1k claret .50 .25

Perf. 12½ on 3 Sides

1111 A286 75o slate green .30 .25
a. Booklet pane of 10 3.00
Complete booklet, #1111a 3.50
Nos. 1109-1111 (3) 1.15 .75

International Women's Year 1975.

Horseman, Helmet Decoration A288

"Gold Men" A289

Designs: 15o, Scabbard and hilt. 20o, Shield buckle. 55o, Iron helmet.

1975, Mar. 25 *Perf. 12½ on 3 sides*

1112 A288 10o dull red .25 .25
1113 A288 15o slate green .25 .25
1114 A288 20o violet .25 .25
1115 A288 55o violet brown .25 .25
a. Bklt. pane, 2 each #1112-1115 .75 *1.60*
Complete booklet, #1115a 1.50

Perf. 12½ Horiz.

1116 A289 25o deep yellow .25 .25
Nos. 1112-1116 (5) 1.25 1.25

Treasures from tombs of the Vendel period (550-800 A.D.), and "gold men" (25o) from Eketorp II excavations (400-700 A.D.).

Europa Issue

New Year's Eve at Skansen, by Eric Hallstrom — A290

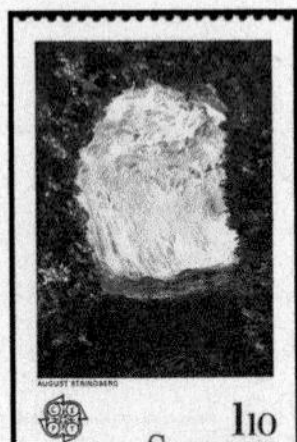

Inferno, by August Strindberg — A291

Perf. 12½ Vert.

1975, Apr. 28 Photo.

1117 A290 90o multi *1.00* .25

Perf. 14¼ Horiz.

1118 A291 1.10k multi *1.00* .25

Capercaillie
A292

Rok Stone, 9th Century
A293

1975, May 20 Engr. *Perf. 12½ Vert.*
1119 A292 170o indigo .70 .25

Perf. 12½ Horiz.
1120 A293 2k deep claret .85 .25

Metric Tape Measure — A294

Folke Filbyter Statue, by Milles — A296

Hernqvist by Per Krafft the Younger — A295

1975, May 20 *Perf. 12½ Vert.*
1121 A294 55o deep blue .35 .25
1122 A295 70o yel brn & dk brn .40 .25

Perf. 12½ Horiz.
1123 A296 75o violet .40 .25
Nos. 1121-1123 (3) 1.15 .75

Cent. of Intl. Meter Convention, Paris, 1875; bicent. of Swedish veterinary medicine, founded by Peter Hernqvist (1726-1808); Carl Milles (1875-1955), sculptor.

Officers' Mess, Rommehed, 1798 — A297

No. 1124, Skelleftea Church Village, 17th cent. No. 1125, Foundry and furnace, Engelsberg, 18th cent. No. 1126, Gunpowder Tower, Visby. No. 1127, Falun Mine pithead gear, 1852.

1975, June 13 *Perf. 12½ Horiz.*
1124 A297 75o black .40 *.75*
1125 A297 75o dk carmine .40 *.75*
1126 A297 75o black .40 *.75*
1127 A297 75o dk carmine .40 *.75*
1128 A297 75o violet blue .40 *.75*
a. Bklt. pane, 2 each #1124-1128 4.50
Complete booklet, #1128a 5.00
Nos. 1124-1128 (5) 2.00 3.75

European Architectural Heritage Year 1975.

Rescue at Sea: Helicopter over Ice-covered Tanker — A298

Designs: No. 1129, Fire fighters: firemen fighting fire. No. 1130, Customs narcotics service: trained dogs checking cargo. No. 1131, Police: Officer talking to boy on bridge. No. 1132, Hospital Service: patient arriving by ambulance.

1975, Aug. 27 *Perf. 12½ Horiz.*
1129 A298 90o dk car rose .50 .50
1130 A298 90o dk bl .50 .50
1131 A298 90o dk car rose .50 .50
1132 A298 90o dk bl .50 .50
1133 A298 90o green .50 .50
a. Bklt. pane, 2 each #1129-1133 5.50
Complete booklet, #1133a 7.50
Nos. 1129-1133 (5) 2.50 2.50

Public service organizations watching, guarding, helping.

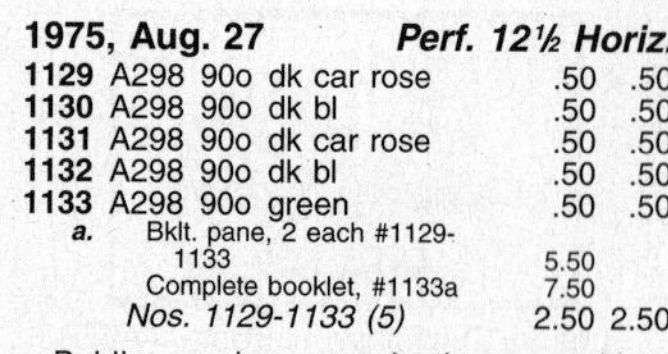

"Fryckstad"
A299

"Gotland"
A300

Design: 90o, "Prins August."

1975, Aug. 27 *Perf. 12½ on 3 Sides*
Size: 20x19mm
1134 A299 5o green .25 .25
1135 A300 5o dark blue .25 .25

Size: 45x19mm
1136 A299 90o slate green .45 .25
a. Bklt. pane, 2 each #1134-1136 1.75 *2.50*
Complete booklet, #1136a 2.50
Nos. 1134-1136 (3) .95 .75

Scouts — A302

1975, Oct. 11 Photo. *Perf. 14 Vert.*
1137 90o Around campfire .50 .25
1138 90o In canoes .50 .25
a. A301 Pair, #1137-1138 1.25 *2.00*

Nordjamb 75, 14th World Boy Scout Jamboree, Lillehammer, Norway, July 29-Aug. 7.

Hedgehog
A303

Old Man Playing Key Fiddle — A304

Romeo and Juliet Ballet — A305

1975, Oct. 11 Engr. *Perf. 12½ Vert.*
1139 A303 55o black .25 .25
1140 A304 75o dk red .50 .25

Perf. 12½ Horiz.
1141 A305 7k blue green 3.00 .25

Perf. 12½ on 3 Sides
1142 A303 55o black .25 .25
a. Booklet pane of 10 2.50
Complete booklet, #1142a 4.00
Nos. 1139-1142 (4) 4.00 1.00

See No. 2642c.

Virgin Mary, 12th Cent. Statue — A306

Chariot of the Sun, from 12th Cent. Altar — A307

Mourning Mary, c. 1280 — A308

Jesse at Foot of Genealogical Tree, c. 1510 — A309

Christmas: #1145, Nativity, from 12th cent. gilt-copper altar. #1148, like #1147.

Perf. 14 Horiz.
1975, Nov. 11 Photo.
1143 A306 55o multi .30 .25

Perf. 12½ on 3 Sides
1144 A307 55o gold & multi .35 .25
1145 A307 55o gold & multi .35 .25
a. Bklt. pane, 5 each #1144-1145 3.00
Complete booklet, #1145a 4.00

Perf. 12½ Horiz.
Engr.
1146 A308 90o brown .50 .25

Perf. 12½ on 3 Sides
1147 A309 90o red .60 .25
1148 A309 90o blue .60 .25
a. Bklt. pane, 5 ea #1147-1148 6.00
Complete booklet, #1148a 7.00
Nos. 1143-1148 (6) 2.70 1.50

No. 1145a was issued with top row of 5 either No. 1144 or No. 1145.

William H. and William L. Bragg — A310

Designs: 90o, Richard Willstätter. 1.10k, Romain Rolland.

1975, Dec. 10 Engr. *Perf. 12½ Vert.*
1149 A310 75o claret .35 *.45*
1150 A310 90o violet blue .40 .25
1151 A310 1.10k slate green .50 .35
Nos. 1149-1151 (3) 1.25 1.05

Winners of 1915 Nobel Prize.

Cave of the Winds, by Eric Grate — A311

1976, Jan. 27 *Perf. 12½ Vert.*
1152 A311 1.90k slate green .80 .25

The sculpture by Eric Grate (b. 1896) stands in front of the Town Hall of Vasteras.

Razor-billed Auks and Black Guillemot
A312

Bobbin Lace Maker from Vadstena
A313

1976, Mar. 10 Engr. *Perf. 12½ Vert.*
1153 A312 85o dark blue .55 .25

Perf. 12½ Horiz.
1154 A313 1k claret brn .45 .30

Perf. 12½ on 3 Sides
1155 A312 85o dk bl .30 .30
a. Booklet pane of 10 3.00
Complete booklet, #1155a 5.00
1156 A313 1k claret brn .30 .30
a. Booklet pane of 10 3.00
Complete booklet, #1156a 4.00
Nos. 1153-1156 (4) 1.60 1.15

Old and New Telephones, Relays — A314

1976, Mar. 10 *Perf. 12½ Vert.*
1157 A314 1.30k brt violet .50 .25
1158 A314 3.40k red 1.00 .50

Centenary of first telephone call by Alexander Graham Bell, March 10, 1876.

Europa Issue

Lapp Elk Horn Spoon — A315

Tile Stove — A316

Perf. 14½ Horiz.
1976, May 3 Photo.
1159 A315 1k multi *.65 .25*
1160 A316 1.30k multi *.65 .45*

Wheat and Cornflower Seeds — A317

Viable and Nonviable Seedlings
A318

1976, May 3 Engr. *Perf. 12½ Vert.*
1161 A317 65o brown .30 .25
1162 A318 65o choc & grn .30 .25
a. Pair, #1161-1162 .90 .90

Swedish seed testing centenary.

King Carl XVI Gustaf and Queen Silvia — A319

Perf. 12½ Vert.
1976, June 19 Engr.
1163 A319 1k rose car .30 .25
1164 A319 1.30k slate grn .40 .25

Perf. 12½ on 3 Sides
1165 A319 1k rose car .30 .25
a. Booklet pane of 10 3.00
Complete booklet, #1165a 6.00
Nos. 1163-1165 (3) 1.00 .75

Wedding of King Carl XVI Gustaf and Silvia Sommerlath.

View from Ringkallen, by Helmer Osslund — A320

Views in Angermanland Province: No. 1167, Tugboat pulling timber. No. 1168, Hay-drying racks. No. 1169, Granvagsnipan slope, Angerman River. No. 1170, Seine fishing.

1976, June 19 ***Perf. 12½ Horiz.***

1166 A320 85o slate grn .35 .30
1167 A320 85o vio bl .35 .30
1168 A320 85o dp brn .35 .30
1169 A320 85o vio bl .35 .30
1170 A320 85o brn red .35 .30
a. Bklt. pane, 2 each #1166-1170 3.50
Complete booklet, #1170a 6.00
Nos. 1166-1170 (5) 1.75 1.50

Roman Cross and Ship's Wheel — A321

1976, June 19 ***Perf. 12½ Horiz.***

1171 A321 85o brt bl & bl .55 *.40*

Swedish Seamen's Church, centenary.

Torgny Segerstedt and 1917 Page of Gothenburg Journal — A322

1976, June 19 ***Perf. 12½ Vert.***

1172 A322 1.90k brn & blk .70 .30

Torgny Segerstedt (1876-1945), editor in chief of the Gothenburg Journal of Commerce and Shipping, birth centenary.

Coiled Snake, Bronze Buckle — A323

Pilgrim's Badge, Adoration of the Magi — A324

Drinking Horn, 14th Century — A325

Chimney Sweep — A326

Girl's Head, by Bror Hjorth, 1922 — A327

Perf. 12½ Horiz., Vert. (30o)

1976, Sept. 8 **Engr.**

1173 A323 15o bister .25 .25
1174 A324 20o green .25 .25
1175 A325 30o dk rose brn .25 .25
1176 A326 90o indigo .40 .25
1177 A327 9k yel grn & sl grn 4.00 .25
Nos. 1173-1177 (5) 5.15 1.25

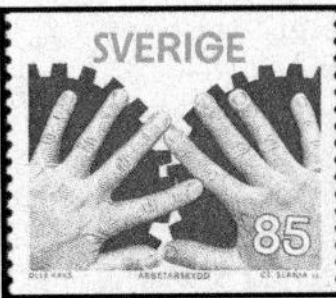

Inventors A328

No. 1178, John Ericsson (1803-1889), ship propeller and "Monitor". No. 1179, Helge Palmcrantz (1842-80) & reaper. No. 1180, Lars Magnus Ericsson (1846-1926) & switchboard. No. 1181, Sven Wingquist (1876-1953) & ball bearing. No. 1182, Gustaf de Laval (1845-1913) & milk separator.

1976, Oct. 9 **Engr.** ***Perf. 12½ Horiz.***

1178 A328 1.30k multi .60 .60
1179 A328 1.30k multi .60 .60
1180 A328 1.30k multi .60 .60
1181 A328 1.30k multi .60 .60
1182 A328 1.30k multi .60 .60
a. Bklt. pane of 5, #1178-1182 3.50 *6.00*

Swedish inventors and their technological inventions.

Hands and Cogwheels A329

1976, Oct. 9 ***Perf. 12½ Vert.***

1183 A329 85o org & dk vio .30 .25
1184 A329 1k yel grn & brn .45 .25

Industrial safety.

Verner von Heidenstam, Lake Vattern — A330

1976, Nov. 17 ***Perf. 12½ Vert.***

1185 A330 1k yellow green .40 .25
1186 A330 1.30k blue .60 .45

Verner von Heidenstam (1859-1940), Swedish poet, 1916 Nobel Prize winner.

Archangel Michael A331

Virgin Mary Visiting St. Elizabeth A332

Christmas: No. 1189, like No. 1187. No. 1190, St. Nicholas saving 3 children. No. 1191, like No. 1188. No. 1192, Illuminated page, prayer to Virgin Mary. 65o, stamps are from Flemish prayer book, c. 1500. 1k stamps are from Austrian prayer book, late 15th century.

Perf. 12½ Horiz.

1976, Nov. 17 **Photo.**

1187 A331 65o blue & multi .30 .25
1188 A332 1k gold & multi .30 .25

Perf. 12½ on 3 Sides

1189 A331 65o blue & multi .25 *.40*
1190 A331 65o blue & multi .25 *.40*
a. Bklt. pane, 5 each #1189-1190 2.00
Complete booklet, #1190a 3.00

Perf. 12½ Vert.

1191 A332 1k gold & multi .30 .25
1192 A332 1k gold & multi .30 .25
a. Bklt. pane, 5 each #1191-1192 3.00
Complete booklet, #1192a 6.00
Nos. 1187-1192 (6) 1.70 1.80

Five Water Lilies — A333

Photogravure and Engraved

1977, Feb. 2 ***Perf. 12½ Horiz.***

1193 A333 1k brt grn & multi .45 .25
1194 A333 1.30k ultra & multi .55 *.55*

Nordic countries cooperation for protection of the environment and 25th Session of Nordic Council, Helsinki, Feb. 19.

Tailor — A334

1977, Feb. 24 ***Perf. 12½ Vert.***

1195 A334 2.10k red brn .75 .25

Longdistance Skating — A335

Perf. 12½ Horiz.

1977, Mar. 24 **Engr.**

1196 A335 95o shown .40 *.55*
1197 A335 95o Swimming .40 *.55*
1198 A335 95o Bicycling .40 *.55*
1199 A335 95o Jogging .40 *.55*
1200 A335 95o Badminton .40 *.55*
a. Bklt. pane, 2 each #1196-1200 4.00
Complete booklet, #1200a 6.00
Nos. 1196-1200 (5) 2.00 2.75

Physical fitness.

Politeness, by "OA," 1905 — A336

1977, Mar. 24 ***Perf. 12½ on 3 Sides***

1201 A336 75o black .35 .25
a. Booklet pane of 10 2.50
Complete booklet, #1201a 5.00

Perf. 12½ Horiz.

1202 A336 3.80k red 2.00 .45

Oskar Andersson (1877-1906), cartoonist.

Calle Schewen A337

No. 1204, Seagull. No. 1205, Dancers and accordionist. No. 1206, Fishermen in boat. No. 1207, Tree on shore at sunset.

Designs are illustrations for poem The Calle Schewen Waltz, by Evert Taube, and include bars of music of this song.

1977, May 2 **Engr.** ***Perf. 12½ Horiz.***

1203 A337 95o slate grn .35 .45
1204 A337 95o vio bl .35 .45
1205 A337 95o grn & blk .35 .45
1206 A337 95o dark blue .35 .45
1207 A337 95o red .35 .45
a. Bklt. pane, 2 each #1203-1207 3.50
Complete booklet, #1207a 7.00
Nos. 1203-1207 (5) 1.75 2.25

Tourist publicity for Roslagen (archipelago) and to honor Evert Taube (1890-1976), poet.

Gustavianum, Uppsala University A338

1977, May 2 **Photo.** ***Perf. 14 Vert.***

1208 A338 1.10k multi .55 .25

Perf. 14 on 3 Sides

1209 A338 1.10k multi .35 .25
a. Booklet pane of 10 3.50
Complete booklet, #1209a 6.00

Uppsala University, 500th anniversary.

Europa Issue

Forest in Snow A339

Rapadalen Valley — A340

1977, May 2 ***Perf. 14 Vert.***

1210 A339 1.10k multi 1.10 .30
1211 A340 1.40k multi 1.10 .65

Owl — A341

Cast-iron Stove Decoration — A342

Gotland Ponies A343

1977, Sept. 8 **Engr.** ***Perf. 12½ Vert.***

1212 A341 45o dk slate grn .50 .40

Perf. 12½ Horiz.

1213 A342 70o dk vio bl .45 .25

Booklet Stamp

1214 A343 1.40k brown .40 .35
a. Booklet pane of 5 2.00
Complete booklet, #1214a 3.50
Nos. 1212-1214 (3) 1.35 1.00

Wild Berries — A344

Perf. 14 on 3 Sides

1977, Sept. 8 **Photo.**

1215 A344 75o Blackberry .30 .30
1216 A344 75o Cranberry .30 .30
1217 A344 75o Raspberry .30 .30
1218 A344 75o Whortleberry .30 .30
1219 A344 75o Alpine strawberry .30 .30
a. Bklt. pane, 2 each #1215-1219 3.00 *6.50*
Complete booklet, #1219a 6.00
Nos. 1215-1219 (5) 1.50 1.50

Horse-drawn Trolley — A345

Designs: Public transportation.

1977, Oct. 8 **Engr.** ***Perf. 12½ Horiz.***

1220 A345 1.10k shown .60 *.50*
1221 A345 1.10k Electric trolley .60 *.50*
1222 A345 1.10k Ferry .60 *.50*
1223 A345 1.10k Tandem bus .60 *.50*
1224 A345 1.10k Subway .60 *.50*
a. Bklt. pane of 5, #1220-1224 3.00 *6.50*
Complete booklet, #1224a 3.50

Putting up Sheaf for the Birds — A346

Preparing Dried Soaked Fish — A347

Traditional Christmas Preparations: No. 1227, Children baking ginger snaps. No. 1228, Bringing in Yule tree. No. 1229, Making straw goat. No. 1230, Candle dipping.

Perf. 12½ Horiz.

1977, Nov. 17 **Engr.**

1225 A346 75o violet .30 .25
1226 A347 1.10k yel grn .50 .25

Perf. 12½ on 3 Sides

1227 A346 75o ocher .30 .25
1228 A346 75o slate grn .30 .25
a. Bklt. pane, 5 each #1227-1228 2.00
Complete booklet, #1228a 4.00
1229 A347 1.10k dk red .35 .25
1230 A347 1.10k dk bl .35 .25
a. Bklt. pane, 5 each #1229-1230 3.25
Complete booklet, #1230a 6.00
Nos. 1225-1230 (6) 2.10 1.50

Christmas 1977.

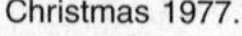

Henrik Pontoppidan, Karl Adolph Gjellerup A348

Design: 1.40k, Charles Glover Barkla.

1977, Nov. 17 ***Perf. 12½ Vert.***

1231 A348 1.10k red brn .45 .25
1232 A348 1.40k yel grn .50 .50

1917 Nobel Prize winners: Henrik Pontoppidan (1857-1943) and Karl Adolph Gjellerup (1857-1919), Danish writers; Charles Glover Barkla (1877-1944), English X-ray pioneer.

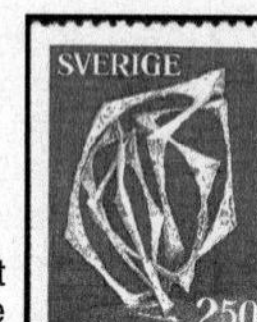

Space Without Affiliation, by Arne Jones — A349

1978, Jan. 25 ***Perf. 12½ Horiz.***

1233 A349 2.50k vio bl .85 .25

Brown Bear — A350

1978, Apr. 11 ***Perf. 12½ Horiz.***

1234 A350 1.15k dark brown .50 .25

Europa Issue

Örebro Castle — A351

Arch and Stairs — A352

1978, Apr. 11 ***Perf. 12½ Vert.***

1235 A351 1.30k slate green 1.25 .25

Perf. 12½ Horiz.

1236 A352 1.70k dull red 1.60 .50

Pentecostal Preacher and Congregation A353

Free Churches: No. 1238, Swedish Missionary Society. No. 1239, Evangelical National Missionary Society. No. 1240, Baptist Society. No. 1241, Salvation Army.

1978, Apr. 11 ***Perf. 12½ on 3 sides***

1237 A353 90o purple .40 .40
1238 A353 90o slate .40 .40
1239 A353 90o violet .40 .40
1240 A353 90o slate .40 .40
1241 A353 90o purple .40 .40
a. Bklt. pane, 2 each #1237-1241 4.00 7.50
Complete booklet, #1241a 7.00
Nos. 1237-1241 (5) 2.00 2.00

Independent Christian Associations.

Brosarp Hills — A354

Grindstone Production A355

Red Limestone Cliff — A356

Designs: No. 1243, Avocets. No. 1245, Linnaea borealis (Linné's favorite flower.) No. 1247, Linné with Lapp drum, wearing Lapp clothes and Dutch doctor's hat.

Perf. 12½ Horiz.

1978, May 23 **Engr.**

1242 A354 1.30k gray green .65 .50
1243 A354 1.30k violet blue .65 .50

Perf. 12½ on 3 Sides

1244 A355 1.30k violet brown .65 .60
1245 A355 1.30k brown red .65 .60

Perf. 12½ on 2 Sides

1246 A356 1.30k violet blue .65 .60
1247 A356 1.30k violet brown .65 .60
a. Bklt. pane of 6, #1242-1247 3.75 *5.50*
Complete booklet, #1247a 6.00

Travels of Carl von Linné (1707-1778), botanist.

Cranes, Lake Hornborgasjon — A357

Designs: No. 1248, Gliding School, Alleberg. No. 1250, Skara Church, Lacko Island. No. 1251, Ancient rock tomb, Luttra. No. 1252, Cloth merchants, sculpture by Nils Sjogren.

1978, May 23 ***Perf. 12½ Horiz.***

1248 A357 1.15k dull green .40 .35
1249 A357 1.15k maroon .40 .35
1250 A357 1.15k violet blue .40 .35
1251 A357 1.15k dk gray grn .40 .35
1252 A357 1.15k brn & gray grn .40 .35
a. Bklt. pane, 2 each #1284-1252 4.00
Complete booklet, #1252a 8.00
Nos. 1248-1252 (5) 2.00 1.75

Tourist publicity for Vastergotland.

Laurel and Scroll — A358

1978, May 23 ***Perf. 12½ Vert.***

1253 A358 2.50k gray & sl grn .85 .25

Stockholm University, centenary.

Homecoming, by Carl Kylberg — A359

Nude, by Karl Isakson A360

Self-portrait, by Ivar Arosenius A361

1978, Sept. 5 **Engr.** ***Perf. 12½ Vert.***

1254 A359 90o multicolored .35 .35

Perf. 12½ Horiz.

1255 A360 1.15k multi .50 .30
1256 A361 4.50k multi .60 .50
Nos. 1254-1256 (3) 1.45 1.15

Swedish painters: Carl Kylberg (1878-1952); Karl Isakson (1878-1922); Ivar Arosenius (1878-1909).

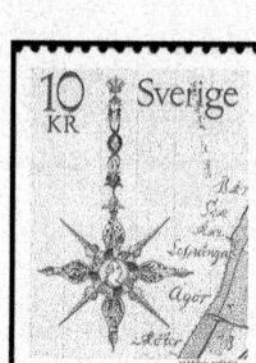

North Arrow (Compass Rose), Map, 1769 — A362

1978, Sept. 5 ***Perf. 12½ Horiz.***

1257 A362 10k lilac 2.25 .25

Coronation Coach, 1699 — A363

1978, Oct. 7 **Engr.** ***Perf. 12½ Horiz.***

1258 A363 1.70k dk red, *yel* .75 .40
a. Booklet pane of 5 3.50
Complete booklet, #1258a 6.00

Orange Russula — A364

Edible mushrooms — No. 1260, Lycoperdon perlatum. No. 1261, Macrolepiota procera. No. 1262, Cantharellus cibarius. No. 1263, Boletus edulis. No. 1264, Ramaria botrytis.

1978, Oct. 7 ***Perf. 12½ on 3 Sides***

1259 A364 1.15k shown .50 .50
1260 A364 1.15k multicolored .50 .50
1261 A364 1.15k multicolored .50 .50
1262 A364 1.15k multicolored .50 .50
1263 A364 1.15k multicolored .50 .50
1264 A364 1.15k multicolored .50 .50
a. Bklt. pane of 6, #1259-1264 3.00 *7.50*
Complete booklet, #1264a 5.00

Toy Ferris Wheel — A365

Teddy Bear — A365a

Dalecarlian Wooden Horse — A365b

Doll — A365c

Spinning Tops — A366

Rider Drawing Water Cart — A366a

Perf. 12½ Horiz.

1978, Nov. 14 **Engr.**

1265 A365 90o dk red & grn .40 .25
1266 A365a 1.30k brt ultra .60 .25

Perf. 12½ on 3 Sides

Photo.

1267 A365b 90o multicolored .30 .25
1268 A365c 90o multicolored .30 .25
a. Bklt. pane, 5 each #1267-1268 2.50
Complete booklet, #1268a 6.00
1269 A366 1.30k multicolored .50 .25
1270 A366a 1.30k multicolored .50 .25
a. Bklt. pane, 5 each #1269-1270 4.00
Complete booklet, #1270a 7.00
Nos. 1265-1270 (6) 2.60 1.50

Christmas 1978.

Fritz Haber — A367

Design: 1.70k, Max Planck.

1978, Nov. 14 **Engr.** ***Perf. 12½ Vert.***

1271 A367 1.30k dark brown .65 .50
1272 A367 1.70k dark violet bl .85 .65

1918 Nobel Prize winners: Fritz Haber (1868-1934), German chemist; Max Planck (1858-1947), German physicist.

See #1310-1312, 1341-1344, 1387-1389.

Bandy — A368

1979, Jan. 25 **Engr.** ***Perf. 12½ Vert.***

1273 A368 1.05k violet blue .40 .30
1274 A368 2.50k orange .80 .50

Child Wearing Gas Mask in Heavy Traffic — A369

1979, Mar. 13 ***Perf. 12½ Vert.***
1275 A369 1.70k dark blue .75 .75

International Year of the Child.

Drill-weave Tapestry, c. 1855-1860 — A370

1979, Mar. 13 ***Perf. 12½ Horiz.***
1276 A370 4k gray & red 1.50 .25

Carrier Pigeon, Hand with Quill — A371

Perf. 14x14½ on 3 Sides
1979, Apr. 2 **Photo.**
1277 A371 (1k) ultra & yel 1.40 .25
a. Booklet pane of 20 27.50
Complete booklet, #1277a 40.00

Price of booklet 20k.

DISCOUNT BOOKLETS

Every Swedish household received during Apr. 1979, 2 coupons for the purchase of 2 discount booklets, #1277a. The stamps were for use on post cards and letters within Sweden. The stamps are inscribed "INRIKES POST."

The program continued with numerous changes. The Inscription changed to "PRIVATPOST" in 1981, the same year that denominations were added. At some point the stamps could also be used to Denmark, Norway, Finland and Iceland. In 1991 the discount value of the stamps ended July, 1.

The last stamps inscribed "PRIVAT POST" were issued in 1993.

Mail Service by Boat, Grisslehamn to Echero A372

Europa: 1.70k, Hand on telegraph.

1979, May 7 **Engr.** ***Perf. 12½ Vert.***
1278 A372 1.30k slate grn & blk 2.00 .50
1279 A372 1.70k ocher & blk 2.00 1.00

Woodcutter, Winter — A373

Designs: No. 1281, Sowing, spring. No. 1282, Grazing cattle, summer. No. 1283, Harvester, summer. No. 1284, Plowing, autumn.

1979, May 7 ***Perf. 12½ Horiz.***
1280 A373 1.30k multicolored .40 .35
1281 A373 1.30k sl grn & dk brn .40 .35
1282 A373 1.30k dk brn & sl grn .40 .35
1283 A373 1.30k sl grn & ocher .40 .35
1284 A373 1.30k multicolored .40 .35
a. Bklt. pane, 2 each #1280-1284 4.50
Complete booklet, #1284a 8.00
Nos. 1280-1284 (5) 2.00 1.75

Tourist Steamer Juno — A374

Roller Bridge, Hajstorp — A375

Sailing Ship — A376

Gota Canal: No. 1286, Borenshult Lock. No. 1288, Hand-drawn gate. No. 1290, Rowboat in Forsvik lock.

1979, May 7 ***Perf. 12½ Horiz.***
1285 A374 1.15k violet blue .55 *.75*
1286 A374 1.15k slate green .55 *.75*

Perf. 12½ on 3 Sides
1287 A375 1.15k dull purple .55 *.85*
1288 A375 1.15k carmine .55 *.85*

Perf. 12½ on 2 Sides
1289 A376 1.15k violet blue .55 *.85*
1290 A376 1.15k slate green .55 *.85*
a. Bklt. pane of 6, #1285-1290 3.50 *5.75*
Complete booklet, #1290a 4.00
Nos. 1285-1290 (6) 3.30 4.90

Strikers and Sawmill A377

Temperance Movement Banner — A378

Jons Jacob Berzelius A379

Johan Olof Wallin A380

1979, Sept. 6 **Engr.** ***Perf. 12½ Vert.***
1291 A377 90o car & dp brn .50 *.35*

Perf. 12½ Horiz.
Litho.
1292 A378 1.30k multi .50 .30
Engr.
1293 A379 1.70k brown & grn .70 .40
1294 A380 4.50k slate blue 1.90 .50
Nos. 1291-1294 (4) 3.60 1.55

Centenaries of Sundsvall strike and Swedish Temperance Movement; birth bicentennials of Jons Jacob Berzelius (1779-1848), physician and chemist; Johan Olof Wallin (1779-1839), Archbishop and poet.

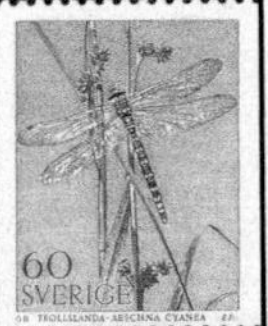
Dragonfly A381

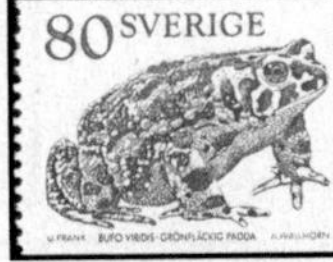
Green Spotted Toad A383

Pike A382

1979, Sept. 6 ***Perf. 12½ Horiz.***
1295 A381 60o violet .40 .40

Perf. 12½ Vert.
1296 A382 65o gray .50 .35
1297 A383 80o olive green .50 .55
Nos. 1295-1297 (3) 1.40 1.30

Souvenir Sheet

Swedish Rococo — A384

Designs: 90o, Potpourri pot. 1.15k, Portrait, by Johan Henrik Scheffel. 1.30k, Silver coffee-pot. 1.70k, Bust of Carl Johan Cronstedt.

Engraved and Photogravure
1979, Oct. 6 ***Perf. 12x12½***
1298 A384 Sheet of 4 2.00 *3.25*
a.-d. Any single .50 *.60*

No. 1298 sold for 6k; surtax was for philately.

Herrings, Age Determination — A386

Sea Research: No. 1300, Acoustic survey of sea bottom. No. 1301, Water bloom of algae in Baltic Sea. No. 1302, Computer map of herring distribution in South Baltic Sea. No. 1303, Research ship Argos.

1979, Oct. 6 **Engr.** ***Perf. 12½ Horiz.***
1299 A386 1.70k multicolored .75 .75
1300 A386 1.70k sepia .75 .75
1301 A386 1.70k multicolored .75 .75
1302 A386 1.70k sepia .75 .75
1303 A386 1.70k multicolored .75 .75
a. Bklt. pane of 5, #1299-1303 5.25 *6.50*
Complete booklet, #1303a 6.00

Brooch from Jamtland A387

Ljusdal Costume A388

Christmas (Costumes and Jewelry from): No. 1305, Pendant, Smaland. No. 1307, Osteraker. No. 1308, Goinge. No. 1309, Mora.

Perf. 12½ Horiz.
1979, Nov. 15 **Engr.**
1304 A387 90o dk Prus blue .40 .30
1305 A387 1.30k dull red .40 .25

Perf. 12½ on 3 Sides
Photo.
Size: 22x27mm
1306 A388 90o multicolored .30 .30
1307 A388 90o multicolored .30 .30
a. Bklt. pane, 5 each #1306-1307 2.50
Complete booklet, #1307a 5.00

Perf. 12½ Vert.
Size: 26x44mm
1308 A388 1.30k multicolored .40 .25
1309 A388 1.30k multicolored .40 .25
a. Bklt. pane, 5 each #1308-1309 3.50
Complete booklet, #1309a 7.00
Nos. 1304-1309 (6) 2.20 1.65

Nobel Prize Winner Type of 1978

1919 Winners: 1.30k, Jules Bordet (1870-1961), Belgian bacteriologist. 1.70k, Johannes Stark (1874-1957), German physicist. 2.50k, Carl Spitteler (1845-1924), Swiss poet.

1979, Nov. 15 **Engr.** ***Perf. 12½ Vert.***
1310 A367 1.30k lilac .60 .30
1311 A367 1.70k ultra .75 .90
1312 A367 2.50k olive green 1.00 .40
Nos. 1310-1312 (3) 2.35 1.60

Wind Power — A389

Renewable Energy Sources: No. 1314, Biodegradable material. No. 1315, Solar energy. No. 1316, Geothermal energy. No. 1317, Hydro power.

1980, Jan. 29 ***Perf. 12½ on 3 sides***
1313 A389 1.15k dark blue .60 .85
1314 A389 1.15k dk grn & bis .60 .85
1315 A389 1.15k yellow orange .60 .85
1316 A389 1.15k dark green .60 .85
1317 A389 1.15k dk bl & dk grn .60 .85
a. Bklt. pane, 2 each #1313-1317 6.00 *12.50*
Complete booklet, #1317a 7.00
Nos. 1313-1317 (5) 3.00 4.25

Crown Princess Victoria and King Carl XVI Gustaf — A390

1980, Feb. 26 ***Perf. 12½ on 3 sides***
1318 A390 1.30k brt blue .45 .25
a. Booklet pane of 10 4.50
Complete booklet, #1318a 8.00

Perf. 12½ Vert.
1319 A390 1.30k brt blue .70 .25
1320 A390 1.70k carmine rose .90 .40
Nos. 1318-1320 (3) 2.05 .90

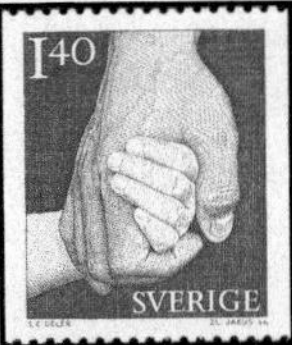
Child Holding Adult's Hand — A391

Hand Holding Cane — A392

1980, Apr. 22 ***Perf. 12½ Horiz.***
1321 A391 1.40k red brown .65 .25
1322 A392 1.60k slate green .75 .25

Parents' insurance system; care for the elderly.

Squirrel — A393

Perf. 15 on 3 Sides
1980, May 12 **Photo.**
1323 A393 (1k) ultra & yellow 1.25 .25
a. Booklet pane of 20 25.00
Complete booklet, #1323a 40.00

See note after No. 1277.

Elise Ottesen-Jensen (1886-1973), Journalist A394

Europa: 1.70k, Joe Hill (1879-1915), member of American Workers' Movement and poet.

1980, June 4 Engr. ***Perf. 12½ Vert.***

1324 A394 1.30k green 1.10 .25
1325 A394 1.70k red 1.30 1.10

Banga Farm, Alfta, Halsingland Province — A395

Tourism (Halsingland Province): No. 1327, Iron Works, Iggesund. No. 1328, Blaxas Ridge, Forsa. No. 1329, Tybling farm, Tyby. No. 1330, Sunds Canal, Hudiksvall.

1980, June 4 ***Perf. 12½ Horiz.***

1326 A395 1.15k red .50 .65
1327 A395 1.15k dark blue .50 .65
1328 A395 1.15k dark green .50 .65
1329 A395 1.15k chocolate .50 .65
1330 A395 1.15k dark blue .50 .65
a. Bklt. pane, 2 each #1326-1330 5.50
Complete booklet, #1330a 8.00
Nos. 1326-1330 (5) 2.50 3.25

Chair, Scania, 1831 — A396

Cradle, North Bothnia, 19th Century — A397

Perf. 12½ Horiz.

1980, Sept. 9 Engr.

1331 A396 1.50k grnsh blue .50 .25

Perf. 12½ Vert.

1332 A397 2k dk red brown .75 .45

Norden 80.

Scene from "Diagonal Symphony," 1924 — A398

1980, Sept. 9 ***Perf. 12½ Horiz.***

1333 A398 3k dark blue 1.10 .25

Viking Eggeling (1880-1925), artist and film maker.

Souvenir Sheet

Swedish Automobile History — A399

90o, Gustaf Erikson's carriage. 1.15k, Vabis, 1909. 1.30k, Thulin, 1923. 1.40k, Scania, 1903. 1.50k, Tidaholm, 1917. 1.70k, Volvo, 1927.

Photogravure and Engraved

1980, Oct. 11 ***Perf. 12½***

1334 A399 Sheet of 6 3.00 5.00
a.-f. Any single .50 .60

No. 1334 sold for 9k.

Bamse the Bear — A401

Farmer Kronblom — A402

Christmas 1980 (Comic Strip Characters): No. 1336, Mandel Karlsson, vert. No. 1337, Adamson, vert.

1980, Oct. 11 Engr. ***Perf. 12½ Vert.***

1335 A401 1.15k multicolored .45 .30

Perf. 12½ on 3 sides

Photo.

1336 A401 1.15k multicolored .40 .40
a. Booklet pane of 10 4.00

Perf. 12½ Horiz.

Complete booklet, #1336a 7.00

Engr.

1337 A401 1.50k black .70 .25

Photo.

1338 A402 1.50k multicolored .40 .25
a. Booklet pane of 10 4.00
Complete booklet, #1338a 8.00
Nos. 1335-1338 (4) 1.95 1.20

Angel Blowing Horn — A403

Perf. on 3 Sides

1980, Nov. 18 Engr.

1339 A403 1.25k multicolored .50 .25
a. Booklet pane of 12 5.00

Christmas 1980.

Necken, by Ernst Josephson — A404

1980, Nov. 18 ***Perf. 12½ Horiz.***

1340 A404 8k multicolored 3.00 .25

Nobel Prize Winner Type of 1978

1920 Winners: #1341, Knut Hamsun (1859-1953), Norwegian writer. #1342, August Krogh (1874-1949), Danish Physiologist, #1343, Charles-Edouard Guillaume (1861-1938), French physicist. #1344, Walther Nernst (1864-1941), German chemist.

1980, Nov. 18 ***Perf. 13 on 3 Sides***

1341 A367 1.40k dk blue gray .50 .40
1342 A367 1.40k red .50 .40
a. Bklt. pane, 5 each #1341-1342 5.00
Complete booklet, #1342a 8.00
1343 A367 2k green .65 .55
1344 A367 2k brown .65 .55
a. Bklt. pane, 5 each #1343-1344 6.50
Complete booklet, #1344a 12.00
Nos. 1341-1344 (4) 2.30 1.90

Ernst Wigforss (1881-1977), Politician & Writer — A405

1981, Jan. 29 Engr. ***Perf. 12½ Vert.***

1345 A405 5k rose carmine 1.50 .25

Freya (Fertility Goddess) — A406

Norse Mythological Characters: 10o, Thor (thunder god). 15o, Heimdall (rainbow god). 50o, Frey (god of peace, fertility, weather). 1k, Odin.

1981, Jan. 29 ***Perf. 12½ on 3 Sides***

1346 A406 10o blue black .25 .25
1347 A406 15o dk carmine .25 .25
1348 A406 50o dk carmine .25 .25
1349 A406 75o deep green .25 .25
1350 A406 1k blue black .25 .25
a. Bklt. pane, 2 each #1346-1350 2.25
Complete booklet, #1350a 3.00
Nos. 1346-1350 (5) 1.25 1.25

Gyrfalcon A407

1981, Feb. 26 Engr. ***Perf. 12½ Vert.***

1351 A407 50k multicolored 12.50 .75
a. Booklet pane of 4 *50.00*
Complete booklet, #1351a *75.00*

Troll Chasing Boy — A408

Europa: 2k, Lady of the Woods.

1981, Apr. 28 Engr.

1352 A408 1.50k dk blue & red 1.30 .50
1353 A408 2k dk green & red 1.30 .60

Intl. Year of the Disabled — A409

1981, Apr. 28

1354 A409 1.50k dk green .50 .30
1355 A409 3.50k purple 1.25 .70

Arms of Oster-gotland Province — A410

Perf. 14½ on 3 Sides

1981, May 18 Photo.

1356 A410 1.40k shown 1.00 .25
1357 A410 1.40k Jamtland 1.00 .25
1358 A410 1.40k Dalarna 1.00 .25
1359 A410 1.40k Bohuslan 1.00 .25
a. Bklt. pane, 5 each #1356-1359 20.00
Nos. 1356-1359 (4) 4.00 1.00

See note after No. 1277. See Nos. 1403-1406, 1456-1459, 1492-1495, 1534-1537, 1592-1595.

Sail Boat, Bohuslan A411

Perf. 12½ on 3 Sides

1981, May 26 Engr.

1360 A411 1.65k shown .60 .55
1361 A411 1.65k Blekinge .60 .55
1362 A411 1.65k Norrbotten .60 .55
1363 A411 1.65k Halsingland .60 .55
1364 A411 1.65k Gotland .60 .55
1365 A411 1.65k Skane .60 .55
a. Bklt. pane of 6, #1360-1365 4.00 *8.00*
Complete booklet, #1365a 6.00

King Carl XVI Gustaf A412

Queen Silvia A413

1981-84 ***Perf. 12½ Vert.***

1366 A412 1.65k dark green .85 .25
1367 A413 1.75k dark blue .85 .35
1368 A412 1.80k dark blue ('83) .70 .25
1369 A412 1.90k red ('84) 1.00 .25
1370 A412 2.40k violet brn .90 .60
1371 A413 2.40k grnsh black ('84) 1.00 .80
1372 A412 2.70k brt lilac ('83) 1.05 .90
1373 A413 3.20k red ('83) 1.35 1.00
Nos. 1366-1373 (8) 7.70 4.40

Day and Night — A414

Perf. 12½ on 3 Sides

1981, Sept. 9 Engr.

1376 A414 1.65k dark blue .50 .25
a. Booklet pane of 10 5.00
Complete booklet, #1376a 10.50

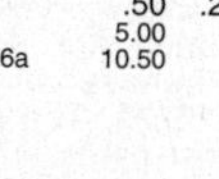

Scene from Par Lagerkvist's Autobiography Guest of Reality — A415

1981, Sept. 9 ***Perf. 12½ Horiz.***

1377 A415 1.50k dark green .55 .25

Conductor Sixten Ehrling and Opera Singer Birgit Nilsson — A416

Bjorn Borg, Tennis Player — A417

Designs: No. 1378, Electric locomotive. No. 1379, Trucks. No. 1381, Oil rig. No. 1383, Ingemar Stenmark, skier.

Perf. 12½ on 2 (Type A416) or 3 (Type A417) sides

1981, Sept. 9

1378 A416 2.40k rose carmine .95 .85
1379 A416 2.40k red .95 .85
1380 A416 2.40k rose lilac .95 .85
1381 A416 2.40k deep violet .95 .85
1382 A417 2.40k dark blue .95 .85
1383 A417 2.40k dark blue .95 .85
a. Bklt. pane of 6, #1378-1383 5.25 12.00
Complete booklet, #1383a 7.50

Baker's Sign — A418

1981, Sept. 9 *Perf. 12½ Vert.*

1384 A418 2.30k shown 2.00 .25
1385 A418 2.30k Pewter shop sign 2.00 .25
a. Pair, #1384-1385 5.00 2.25

A419

Swedish Films: a, Olof Ahs in The Coachman. b, Ingrid Bergman and Gosta Ekman in Intermezzo. c, Greta Garbo in The Gosta Berling Saga, d, Stig Jarrel and Alf Kjellin in Persecution. e, Kari Sylwan and Harriet Andersson in Cries and Whispers

Photogravure and Engraved

1981, Oct. 10 *Perf. 13½*

1386 A419 Sheet of 5 3.00 3.50
a.-e. Any single .45 .40

No. 1386 sold for 10k.

Nobel Prize Winner Type of 1978

1921 Winners: 1.35k, Albert Einstein (1879-1955), German physicist. 1.65k, Anatole France (1844-1924), French writer. 2.70k, Frederick Soddy (1877-1956), British chemist.

1981, Nov. 24 Engr. *Perf. 12½ Vert.*

1387 A367 1.35k red .55 .25
1388 A367 1.65k green .75 .25
1389 A367 2.70k blue .90 .50
Nos. 1387-1389 (3) 2.20 1.00

Christmas 1981 — A421

Designs: Wooden birds.

1981, Nov. 24 *Perf. 12½ on 3 Sides*

1390 A421 1.40k red .60 .25
1391 A421 1.40k green .60 .25
a. Bklt. pane, 5 each #1390-1391 5.50
Complete booklet, #1391a 7.00

Knight on Horseback, John Bauer's Fairy Tales — A422

John Bauer (1882-1918), Fairytale Illustrator: No. 1393, "What a Miserable Little Paleface, said the Troll Mother." No. 1394, Marsh Princess. No. 1395, Now the Dusk of the Night is already Upon Us.

Perf. 12x12½ on 3 sides

1982, Feb. 16 **Engr.**

1392 A422 1.65k multicolored .85 .75
1393 A422 1.65k multicolored .85 .75
1394 A422 1.65k multicolored .85 .75
1395 A422 1.65k multicolored .85 .75
a. Bklt. pane of 4, #1392-1395 3.00 *4.75*
Complete booklet, #1395a 4.00

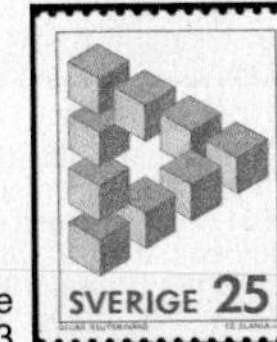

Impossible Figures — A423

Designs: Geometric figures.

1982, Feb. 16 *Perf. 12½ Horiz.*

1396 A423 25o violet brown .25 .25
1397 A423 50o brown olive .25 .25
1398 A423 75o dark blue .30 .25
Nos. 1396-1398 (3) .80 .75

Newspaper Distributor, by Svenolov Ehren A424

Graziella, by Carl Larsson A425

1982, Feb. 16

1399 A424 1.35k deep violet .55 .25
1400 A425 5k violet brown 1.50 .25

Europa Issue

Land Reform, 19th Cent. A426

Anders Celsius (1701-1744), Inventor of Temperature Scale — A427

1982, Apr. 26 Engr. *Perf. 12½ Vert.*

1401 A426 1.65k dk olive grn 2.25 .25

Perf. 12½ on 3 Sides

1402 A427 2.40k dark green 1.00 .80
a. Booklet pane of 6 6.00
Complete booklet, #1402a 7.00

Provincial Arms Type of 1981

Perf. 14 on 3 Sides

1982, Apr. 26 **Photo.**

1403 A410 1.40k Dalsland 1.00 .25
1404 A410 1.40k Oland 1.00 .25
1405 A410 1.40k Vastmandland 1.00 .25
1406 A410 1.40k Halsingland 1.00 .25
a. Bklt. pane, 5 each #1403-1406 20.00
Complete booklet, #1406a 27.50
Nos. 1403-1406 (4) 4.00 1.00

See note after No. 1277.

Elin Wagner (1882-1949), Writer — A428

1.35k, Sketch by Siri Derkert.

Perf. 12½ Horiz.

1982, June 3 **Engr.**

1407 A428 1.35k purple brown .55 .30

Burgher House — A429

Embroidered Lace Ribbon, 19th Cent. — A430

1982, June 3 *Perf. 12½ Vert.*

1408 A429 1.65k brown 1.00 .25

Perf. 12½ Horiz.

1409 A430 2.70k bister 1.40 1.10

Cent. of Museum of Cultural History, Lund.

1982 Intl. Buoyage System A431

Various buoy signals: No. 1411, Ferry. No. 1412, Six sailboats. No. 1413, One-globed buoy. No. 1414, Two-globed buoy.

1982, June 3 *Perf. 13 Horiz.*

1410 A431 1.65k shown .50 .55
1411 A431 1.65k multi .50 .55
1412 A431 1.65k multi .50 .55
1413 A431 1.65k multi .50 .55
1414 A431 1.65k multi .50 .55
a. Bklt. pane, 2 each #1410-1414 5.50
Nos. 1410-1414 (5) 2.50 2.75

Vietnamese Workers in Sweden — A432

Living Together: Swedish emigration and immigration: No. 1415, Leaving Sweden, 1880. No. 1417, Local voting right. No. 1418, Girls.

1982, Aug. 26 Engr. *Perf. 13 Horiz.*

1415 A432 1.65k multi .70 .55
1416 A432 1.65k shown .70 .55
1417 A432 1.65k multi .70 .55
1418 A432 1.65k multi .70 .55
a. Bklt. pane, 2 each #1415-1418 6.00
Complete booklet, #1418a 8.00
Nos. 1415-1418 (4) 2.80 2.20

Wild Orchids — A433

Wild Orchids: 1.65k (No. 1419a), Orchis mascula. 1.65k (No. 1419d), Cypripedium calcéolus. 2.40k, Epipactis palustris. 2.70k, Dactylorhiza sambucina.

Photogravure and Engraved

1982, Oct. 9 *Perf. 12x13*

1419 A433 Sheet of 4 4.00 *5.00*
a.-d. Any single .75 1.00

Sold for 10k for benefit of stamp collecting.

Christmas 1982 — A434

Stained-glass Windows, Church at Lye, Gotland, 14th cent. — No. 1420, Angel. No. 1421, Child in the Temple. No. 1422, Adoration of the Kings. No. 1423, Tidings to the Shepherds. No. 1424, Birth of Christ.

Perf. 13 on 3 Sides

1982, Nov. 24 **Photo.**

1420 A434 1.40k multi .50 .35
1421 A434 1.40k multi .50 .35
1422 A434 1.40k multi .50 .35
1423 A434 1.40k multi .50 .35
1424 A434 1.40k multi .50 .35
a. Bklt. pane, 2 each #1420-1424 5.00 *7.50*
Complete booklet, #1424a 8.00
Nos. 1420-1424 (5) 2.50 1.75

Signature, Atomic Model — A435

Nobel Prizewinners in Physics (Quantum Mechanics). Various Atomic Models: No. 1425, Niels Bohr, Denmark, 1922. No. 1426, Erwin Schrodinger, Austria, 1933. No. 1427, Louis de Broglie, France, 1929. No. 1428, Paul Dirac, England, 1933. No. 1429, Werner Heisenberg, Germany, 1932.

1982, Nov. 24 Engr. *Perf. 13 Horiz.*

1425 A435 2.40k multi 1.00 .70
1426 A435 2.40k multi 1.00 .70
1427 A435 2.40k multi 1.00 .70
1428 A435 2.40k multi 1.00 .70
1429 A435 2.40k multi 1.00 .70
a. Bklt. pane of 5, #1425-1429 5.50 *8.00*
Complete booklet, #1429a 7.50
Nos. 1425-1429 (5) 5.00 3.50

Fruit A436

Games A436a

Crown and Posthorn A436b

King Carl XVI Gustaf A436c

Queen Silvia A436d

Games A436e

5o, Horse chestnut. 10o, Norway maple. 15o, Dogrose. 20o, Sloe. 50o, Fox and cheese. 60o, Dominoes. 70o, Ludo. 80o, Chinese checkers. 90o, Backgammon. 3k, Chess.

1983-85 Engr. *Perf. 12½ Vert.*

1430 A436 5o brown .25 .25
1431 A436 10o green .25 .25
1432 A436 15o red .25 .25
1433 A436 20o blue .25 .25
1434 A436a 50o brt blue .25 .25
1435 A436a 60o green .25 .25
1436 A436a 70o yellow .25 .25
1437 A436a 80o red .25 .25
1438 A436a 90o mauve .30 .25
1439 A436b 1.60k deep blue .50 .25
1440 A436c 2k black .55 .25
1441 A436b 2.50k bister .75 .45
1442 A436c 2.70k dull red brn .75 1.00

Perf. 12½ Horiz.

1443 A436e 3k purple 1.00 .25

Perf. 12½ Vert.

1444 A436d 3.20k brt blue 1.10 1.60
1445 A436b 4k dp car 1.10 .25
Nos. 1430-1445 (16) 8.05 6.30

Issued: #1430-1433, 2/10/83; #1434-1438, 1443, 10/12/85; #1439-1442, 1444-1445, 1/24/85.

See Nos. 1567-1580, 1783.

Peace Movement Centenary A437

1983, Feb. 10

1446 A437 1.35k blue .55 .35

Nils Ferlin (1898-1961), Poet — A438

1983, Feb. 10
1447 A438 6k dk grn 1.60 .25

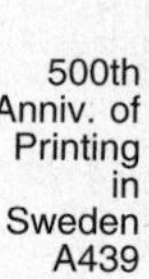

500th Anniv. of Printing in Sweden A439

No. 1448, Lead type. No. 1449, Dialogus Creaturarum, 1483. No. 1450, Carolus XII Bible, 1703. No. 1451, ABC Books, 1760s. No. 1452, Laser photo composition.

1983, Feb. 10 ***Perf. 13 Horiz.***
1448 A439 1.65k multi .85 .45
1449 A439 1.65k multi .85 .45
1450 A439 1.65k multi .85 .45
1451 A439 1.65k multi .85 .45
1452 A439 1.65k multi .85 .45
a. Bklt. pane, 2 each #1448-1452 9.50
Complete booklet, #1452a 11.00
Nos. 1448-1452 (5) 4.25 2.25

Sweden-US Relations Bicentenary — A440

2.70k, Ben Franklin, Swedish Arms.

1983, Mar. 24
1453 A440 2.70k multi .90 .65
a. Booklet pane of 5 4.75
Complete booklet, #1453a 5.00

See US No. 2036.

Nordic Cooperation Issue — A441

Perf. 12½ Horiz.
1983, Mar. 24 **Engr.**
Size: 21x27mm
1454 A441 1.65k Bicycling .50 .25
Perf. 13 Vert.
1455 A441 2.40k Sailing .80 .75

Provincial Arms Type of 1981

1983, Apr. 25 **Photo.** ***Perf. 14½x14***
1456 A410 1.60k Vastergotland 1.00 .25
1457 A410 1.60k Medelpad 1.00 .25
1458 A410 1.60k Gotland 1.00 .25
1459 A410 1.60k Gastrikland 1.00 .25
a. Bklt. pane, 5 each #1456-1459 20.00
Complete booklet, #1459a 25.00
Nos. 1456-1459 (4) 4.00 1.00

See note after No. 1277.

Europa — A442

1.65k, Swedish Ballet Co. 2.70k, Sliding-jaw wrench.

Perf. 12½ Horiz.
1983, Apr. 25 **Engr.**
1460 A442 1.65k multi *1.50* .50
1461 A442 2.70k multi *1.50* *1.50*

A443

Designs: 1k, 3k, 10-ore King Oscar II definitive essays, 1884. 2k, No. 39. 4k, No. 58.

1983, May 25 ***Perf. 12½***
1462 A443 1k blue .80 .40
1463 A443 2k red .85 .45
1464 A443 3k blue 1.00 .50
1465 A443 4k green 1.15 .60
a. Bklt. pane of 4, #1462-1465 3.75 *5.25*
Complete booklet, #1465a 5.50

STOCKHOLMIA Intl. Stamp Exhibition, Aug. 28-Sept. 7, 1986

Red Cross — A444

Greater Karlso — A445

1983, Aug. 24 ***Perf. 12½ Horiz.***
1466 A444 1.50k red .55 .25
1467 A445 1.60k dk blue .65 .25

Planorbis Snail — A446

Arctic Fox — A447

1983, Aug. 24 ***Perf. 12½ on 3 Sides***
1468 A446 1.80k green .55 .25
a. Booklet pane of 10 6.00
Complete booklet, #1468a 9.50
Perf. 12½ Horiz.
1469 A447 2.10k grnsh blk .90 .45

See Nos. 1488-1489, 1526-1527, 1623-1626, 1678-1680, 1762-1763.

Hjalmar Bergman (1883-1931), Writer — A448

No. 1470, Portrait. No. 1471, Jac the Clown illustration by Nisse Skoog.

1983, Aug. 24 ***Perf. 13 Horiz.***
1470 A448 1.80k multi .65 .25
1471 A448 1.80k multi .65 .25
a. Pair, #1470-1471 1.30 1.25

View of Helgeandsholmen, Stockholm, by Franz Hogenberg, 1580 — A449

1983, Aug. 24 ***Perf. 12½ Vert.***
1472 A449 2.70k dl pur & dk bl .90 .55

A450

Designs: a, Wilhelm Stenhammar, pianist. b, Aniara (opera). c, Lars Gullin, jazz saxophonist. d, ABBA, pop music group. e, Hins Anders, violinist.

Photogravure and Engraved

1983, Oct. 1 ***Perf. 13½***
1473 A450 Sheet of 5 4.00 5.00
a. 1.80k multicolored .65 .45
b. 1.80k multicolored .65 .45
c. 1.80k multicolored .65 .45
d. 1.80k multicolored .65 .45
e. 2.70k multicolored .85 .85

Sold for 11.50k.

Christmas 1983 — A452

Postcard designs: No. 1474, Christmas Gnomes around the tree. No. 1475, on straw goats. No. 1476, Folk children, Christmas porridge and gingerbread. No. 1477, Gnomes carrying Christmas gifts on a pole.

Perf. 12½x14 on 3 sides
1983, Nov. 22 **Photo.**
1474 A452 1.60k multi .50 .25
1475 A452 1.60k multi .50 .25
1476 A452 1.60k multi .50 .25
1477 A452 1.60k multi .50 .25
a. Bklt. pane, 3 each #1474-1477 6.00
Complete booklet, #1477a 12.00
Nos. 1474-1477 (4) 2.00 1.00

Chemistry, Nobel Prize Winners — A453

Designs: No. 1478, Arne Tiselius (1902-1971), Electrophoresis Studies. No. 1479, George De Hevesy (1885-1966), Radioactive isotope tracers. No. 1480 Svante Arrhenius (1859-1927), Theory of Electrolytic Dissociation. No. 1481, Theodor Svedberg (1884-1971), Colloid Studies. No. 1482, Hans Von Euler-Chelpin (1873-1964). Enzyme and Vitamin Structures.

Photogravure and Engraved

1983, Nov. 22 ***Perf. 12½ Horiz.***
1478 A453 2.70k slate .90 .85
1479 A453 2.70k dp bl vio .90 .85
1480 A453 2.70k red lilac .90 .85
1481 A453 2.70k blue blk .90 .85
1482 A453 2.70k grnsh blk .90 .85
a. Bklt. pane of 5, #1478-1482 4.50 *8.50*

Postal Savings Centenary — A454

Design: 100o, Three crowns.

1984, Feb. 9 **Engr.** ***Perf. 12½ Vert.***
1483 A454 100o orange .35 .35
1484 A454 1.60k purple .50 .55
1485 A454 1.80k pink .75 .25
Nos. 1483-1485 (3) 1.60 1.15

Europa 1984 A455

Symbolic bridge of communications exchange.

1984, Feb. 9 ***Perf. 12½ Horiz.***
1486 A455 1.80k red .65 .25
a. Booklet pane of 10 7.00
Complete booklet, #1486a 10.00
Perf. 13 Vert.
1487 A455 2.70k dp ultra 2.75 1.50

Conservation Type of 1983 and

Angelica — A457

1984, Mar. 27 ***Perf. 12½ on 3 Sides***
1488 A447 1.90k Lemmings .45 .25
1489 A447 1.90k Musk ox .45 .25
a. Bklt. pane, 5 each #1488-1489 4.50
Complete booklet, #1489a 8.00
Perf. 12½ Horiz.
1490 A457 2k shown .90 .25
1491 A457 2.25k Alpine birch 1.00 .75
Nos. 1488-1491 (4) 2.80 1.50

Provincial Arms Type of 1981

1984, Apr. 24 **Photo.** ***Perf. 14½x14***
1492 A410 1.60k Sodermanland 1.00 .25
1493 A410 1.60k Blekinge 1.00 .25
1494 A410 1.60k Vasterbotten 1.00 .25
1495 A410 1.60k Skane 1.00 .25
a. Bklt. pane, 5 ea #1492-1495 20.00
Complete booklet, #1495a 30.00
Nos. 1492-1495 (4) 4.00 1.00

See note after No. 1277.

A458

Swedish Patent System Centenary: No. 1496, Paraffin stove, F.W. Lindqvist, 1892. No. 1497, Industrial robot ASEA-IRB 6. No. 1498, Fan suction vacuum cleaner, Axel Wenner-gren, 1912. No. 1499, Inboard-outboard motor, AQ-200, No. 1500, SLIC integrated electronic circuit. No. 1501, Tetrahedron container, 1948, 1951.

Perf. 12½ on 3 Sides
1984, June 6 **Engr.**
1496 A458 2.70k red 1.15 1.15
1497 A458 2.70k sepia 1.15 1.15
1498 A458 2.70k green 1.15 1.15
1499 A458 2.70k green 1.15 1.15
1500 A458 2.70k sepia 1.15 1.15
1501 A458 2.70k blue 1.15 1.15
a. Bklt. pane of 6, #1496-1501 7.00 9.50
Complete booklet, #1501a 8.50

A459

Stockholmia '86 (Famous Letters): 1k, Erik XIV's marriage proposal to Queen Elizabeth I, 1561. 2k, Erik Dahlbergh to Sten Bielke, 1684. 3k, Feather letter, 1834. 4k, August Strindberg to Harriet Bosse, 1905.

Lithographed and Engraved

1984, June 6 *Perf. 12½*

1502 A459 1k multi .30 .25
1503 A459 2k multi .60 .50
1504 A459 3k multi .90 .75
1505 A459 4k multi 1.20 1.00
a. Bklt. pane of 4, #1502-1505 3.00 *6.00*
Complete booklet, #1505a 3.00

Fredrika Bremer Assn. (Women's Rights) Centenary A460

Perf. 12½ Vert.

1984, Aug. 28 **Engr.**

1506 A460 1.50k pink .50 .25
1507 A460 6.50k red 2.00 .75

Medieval Towns A461

Engravings by E. Dahlbergh or M. Karl.

1984, Aug. 28 *Perf. 12½x13*

1508 A461 1.90k Jonkoping .60 .55
1509 A461 1.90k Karlstad .60 .55
1510 A461 1.90k Gavle .60 .55
1511 A461 1.90k Sigtuna .60 .55
1512 A461 1.90k Norrkoping .60 .55
1513 A461 1.90k Vadstena .60 .55
a. Bklt. pane of 6, #1508-1513 3.75 *8.25*
Complete booklet, #1513a 3.75

Viking Satellite, 1985 A462

1.90k, Satellite. 3.20k, Receiving station.

1984, Oct. 13 *Perf. 12½ Vert.*

1514 A462 1.90k multi .50 .25
1515 A462 3.20k multi 1.00 .90

Souvenir Sheet

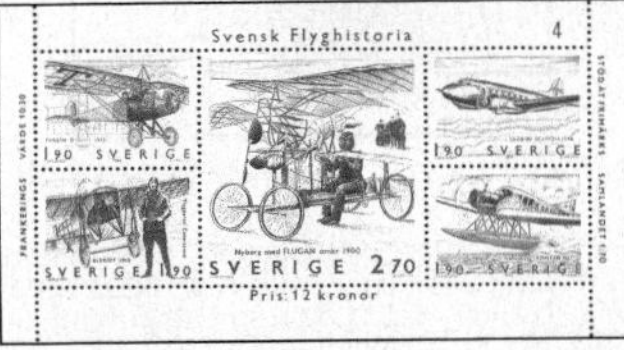

Swedish Aviation History — A463

Designs: a, Thulin D Two-Seater, 1915. b, SAAB-90 Scandia, 1946. c, Carl Gustaf Cederstrom (1867-1918, "The Flying Baron"), Bleriot, 1910. d, Tomten, 1927. e, Carl Nyberg's Flugan, 1900.

1984, Oct. 13 *Perf. 12½*

1516 A463 Sheet of 5 3.75 3.75
a.-d. 1.90k, any single .60 .60
e. 2.70k, multi .75 .75

Sold for 12k.

Christmas 1984 — A465

Birds — No. 1517, Coccothraustes coccothraustes. No. 1518, Bombycilla garrulus. No. 1519, Dendrocopos major. No. 1520, Sitta europaea.

Lithographed and Engraved

1984, Nov. 29 *Perf. 12½ on 3 Sides*

1517 A465 1.60k multi .50 .25
1518 A465 1.60k multi .50 .25
1519 A465 1.60k multi .50 .25
1520 A465 1.60k multi .50 .25
a. Bklt. pane, 3 each #1517-1520 6.00
Complete booklet, #1520a 6.00
Nos. 1517-1520 (4) 2.00 1.00

Inner Ear A466

Nobel Prize Winners in Physiology or Medicine: No. 1521, Georg von Bekesy, 1961, hearing. No. 1522, John Eccles, Alan Hodgkin & Andrew Huxley, 1963, Nerve cell activation. No. 1523, Julius Axelrod, Bernard Katz & Ulf von Euler, 1970, nerve cell storage and release. No. 1524, Roger Sperry, 1981, brain functions. No. 1525, David Hubel, Torsten Wiesel, 1981, Visual information processing.

Perf. 12½ Horiz.

1984, Nov. 29 **Engr.**

1521 A466 2.70k shown .90 .90
1522 A466 2.70k Nerve, arrows .90 .90
1523 A466 2.70k Nerve (front, side) .90 .90
1524 A466 2.70k Brain halves .90 .90
1525 A466 2.70k Eye .90 .90
a. Bklt. pane of 5, #1521-1525 4.50 *8.00*
Complete booklet, #1525a 4.50

Conservation Type of 1983 and

A467

No. 1526, Muscardinus avellanarius. No. 1527, Salvelinus salvelinus. No. 1528, Nigritella nigra. No. 1529, Nymphaea alba.

Perf. 13 on 3 Sides

1985, Mar. 14 **Engr.**

1526 A447 2k multicolored .60 .30
1527 A447 2k multicolored .60 .30
a. Bklt. pane, 5 each #1526-1527 6.00
Complete booklet, #1527a 6.00

Perf. 12½ Horiz.

1528 A467 2.20k multi .40 .40
1529 A467 3.50k multi 1.00 .65
Nos. 1526-1529 (4) 2.60 1.65

World Wildlife Fund.

World Table Tennis Championships A468

2.70k, Jan-Ove Waldner, Sweden. 3.20k, Cai Zhenhua, China.

1985, Mar. 14 *Perf. 12½ Vert.*

1530 A468 2.70k blue .90 .50
1531 A468 3.20k mauve 1.20 .65

Clavichord — A469

Key Harp — A470

1985, Apr. 24 *Perf. 13 Vert.*

1532 A469 2k bluish blk, *buff* 3.75 .50

Perf. 13 on 3 Sides

1533 A470 2.70k dl red brn, *buff* .90 .75
a. Booklet pane of 6 5.50

Europa 1985.

Provincial Arms Type of 1981

Perf. 14½x14 on 3 Sides

1985, Apr. 24 **Photo.**

1534 A410 1.80k Narke 1.00 .25
1535 A410 1.80k Angermanland 1.00 .25
1536 A410 1.80k Varmland 1.00 .25
1537 A410 1.80k Smaland 1.00 .25
a. Bklt. pane, 5 ea #1534-1537 20.00
Complete booklet, #1537a 25.00
Nos. 1534-1537 (4) 4.00 1.00

See note after No. 1277.

St. Cnut's Land Grant to Lund Cathedral, 900th Anniv. — A471

Seal of St. Cnut and: No. 1538, Lund Cathedral. No. 1539, City of Helsingdorg.

Perf. 12½ on 3 Sides

1985, May 21 **Engr.**

1538 A471 2k bluish blk & blk .60 .25
1539 A471 2k blk & dk red .60 .25
a. Bklt. pane, 5 each, #1538-1539 6.00
Complete booklet, #1539a 7.50

See Denmark Nos. 777-778.

Stockholmia '86 — A472

Paintings of old Stockholm: No. 1540, A View of Slussen, by Sigrid Hjerten (1919). No. 1541, Skeppsholmen, Winter, by Gosta Adrian-Nilsson (1919). No. 1542, A Summer's Night by the Riddarholmen, by Hilding Linnqvist (1945). No. 1543, Klara Church Tower, by Otte Skold (1927).

Lithographed and Engraved

1985, May 21 *Perf. 12½*

1540 A472 2k multi 1.00 .90
1541 A472 2k multi 1.00 .90
1542 A472 3k multi 1.00 .90
1543 A472 4k multi 1.00 .90
a. Bklt. pane of 4, #1540-1543 4.00 *7.50*
Complete booklet, #1543a 4.50

Swedish Touring Club Cent. — A473

#1544, Touring Club Syl Station (c. 1920). #1545, Af Chapman Hostel, Stockholm.

1985, May 21 **Engr.** *Perf. 12½ Vert.*

1544 2k blk & dp bl .70 .35

Size: 58x23mm

1545 2k dp bl & blk .70 .50
a. A473 Pair, #1544-1545 1.50 1.00

Trade Signs — A474

No. 1546, Music Shop, Slottsgatan. No. 1547, Furrier, Stockholm. No. 1548, Coppersmith, Landskrona. No. 1549, Haberdasher, Stockholm. No. 1550, Shoemaker, Norrkoping.

Perf. 12½ on 3 Sides

1985, Aug. 28 **Engr.**

1546 A474 10o dark blue .25 .25
1547 A474 20o brn lake .25 .25
1548 A474 20o brn lake .25 .25
1549 A474 50o dark blue .25 .25
1550 A474 2k green .60 .25
a. Bklt. pane, #1546-1549, 2 #1550 1.75 *3.00*
Complete booklet, #1550a 2.00
Nos. 1546-1550 (5) 1.60 1.25

The Dying Spartan Hero, Otryades, 1779, by Johan Tobias Sergel — A475

Baron Carl Frederik Adelcrantz, Academy Pres., 1754, by Alexander Roslin (1718-1793) — A476

1985, Aug. 28 *Perf. 12½ Vert.*

1551 A475 2k slate blue .50 .25

Perf. 12½ Horiz.

1552 A476 7k dk red brn 2.00 .40

Royal Academy of Fine Arts, 250th anniv.

Intl. Youth Year — A477

Children's drawings: 2k, Participation, by Marina Karlsson. 2.70k, Development, by Madeleine Andersson. 3.20k, Peace, by Charlotta Ankar.

Lithographed and Engraved

1985, Oct. 12 *Perf. 12½x13*

1553 A477 Sheet of 3 3.25 *3.75*
a. 2k multi .90 .45
b. 2.70k multi .90 .45
c. 3.20k multi 1.00 .50

Sold for 10k.

Prime Minister Per Albin Hansson (1885-1946) — A478

Birger Sjoberg (1885-1929), Journalist, Novelist, Poet — A479

1985, Oct. 12 **Engr.** *Perf. 12½ Vert.*

1556 A478 1.60k black & red .50 .35

Perf. 12½ Horiz.

1557 A479 4k dk blue grn 1.30 .30

Christmas 1985 — A480

15th cent. religious paintings by Albertus Pictor — No. 1558, Annunciation. No. 1559, Birth of Christ. No. 1560, Adoration of the Magi. No. 1561, Mary as the Apocalyptic Virgin.

Perf. 13x12½ on 3 Sides

1985, Nov. 21 **Engr.**

1558 A480 1.80k multicolored .55 .35
1559 A480 1.80k multicolored .55 .35
1560 A480 1.80k multicolored .55 .35
1561 A480 1.80k multicolored .55 .35
a. Bklt. pane, 3 each #1558-1561 6.50
Complete booklet, #1561a 6.75
Nos. 1558-1561 (4) 2.20 1.40

Nobel Laureates in Literature — A481

Authors: No. 1562, William Faulkner (1897-1962), 1949, Southern United States. No. 1563, Halldor Kiljan Laxness (b.1902), 1955, Iceland. No. 1564, Miguel Angel Asturias (1899-1974), 1967, Guatemala. No. 1565, Yasunari Kawabata (1899-1972), 1968, Japan. No. 1566, Patrick White (b. 1912), 1973, Australia.

Lithographed and Engraved

1985, Nov. 21 ***Perf. 13 Horiz.***

1562 A481 2.70k myr grn 1.00 .60
1563 A481 2.70k dp brn, chlky bl & myr grn 1.00 .60
1564 A481 2.70k myr grn & tan 1.00 .60
1565 A481 2.70k chlky bl & myr grn 1.00 .60
1566 A481 2.70k chlky bl & ocher 1.00 .60
a. Bklt. pane of 5, #1562-1566 5.00 *6.25*
Complete booklet, #1566a 5.50

Types of 1983-85

Engr., Litho. (1.80k, 3.20k, 6k)

1986-89 ***Perf. 12½ Vert.***

1567 A436b 1.70k dk violet .60 .25
1568 A436b 1.80k brt violet .70 .25
1569 A436c 2.10k dk blue .85 .25
1570 A436c 2.20k int blue .85 .25
1571 A436c 2.30k dk ol grn .85 .25
1572 A436b 2.80k emerald .90 .80
1573 A436c 2.90k dk green 1.10 .60
1574 A436c 3.10k dk brown 1.10 .65
1575 A436b 3.20k yellow brn 1.10 .85
1576 A436c 3.30k dk rose brn 1.10 1.00
1577 A436d 3.40k dk red 1.20 .55
1578 A436d 3.60k green 1.40 .60
1579 A436d 3.90k violet blue 1.40 1.50
1580 A436b 6k blue green 1.60 .35
Nos. 1567-1580 (14) 14.75 8.15

Issued: 2.10, 2.90, 3.40k, 1/23'; 1.70, 2.80k, 2/20; 1.80, 3.10, 3.20, 3.60, 6k, 1/27/87; 2.20k, 1/29/88; 2.30, 3.30, 3.90k, 4/20/89.
See No. 1796.

Waterbirds A484

Perf. 13 on 2 or 3 Sides

1986, Jan. 23 **Engr.**

1582 A484 2.10k Eider .50 .25
1583 A484 2.10k Smaspov .50 .25
a. Bklt. pane, 5 each #1582-1583 5.00
Complete booklet, #1583a 6.00
1584 A484 2.30k Storlom .85 .25
Nos. 1582-1584 (3) 1.85 .75

STOCKHOLMIA '86 — A485

Lithographed and Engraved

1986, Jan. 23 ***Perf. 13***

1585 A485 2k #33a, cancel .65 .55
1586 A485 2k Stamp engraver .65 .55
1587 A485 3k #268, 271, US #836 .95 .85
1588 A485 4k Boy soaking stamps 1.20 1.10
a. Bklt. pane of 4, #1585-1588 3.50 *6.50*
Complete booklet, #1588a 3.75

See US Nos. 2198-2201a.

Swedish PO, 350th Anniv. — A486

Lithographed and Engraved

1986, Feb. 20 ***Perf. 13x12½***

1589 A486 2.10k org yel & dk bl .75 .25
a. Bklt pane of 8 6.00
Complete booklet, #1589a 7.00

Sundial — A487

No. 1591, Motto of the Swedish Academy.

1986, Feb. 20 **Engr.** ***Perf. 13 Horiz.***

1590 A487 1.70k dk bl & lake, *gray* .65 .35
1591 A487 1.70k grn & dk red, *gray* .65 .35
a. Pair, #1590-1591 1.50 *.90*

Royal Swedish Academy of Letters, History and Antiquities, and Swedish Academy, bicents.

Provincial Arms Type of 1981

Perf. 15x14½ on 3 Sides

1986, Apr. 23 **Photo.**

1592 A410 1.90k Harjedalen 1.25 .25
1593 A410 1.90k Uppland 1.25 .25
1594 A410 1.90k Halland 1.25 .25
1595 A410 1.90k Lapland 1.25 .25
a. Bklt. pane, 5 each #1592-1595 20.00
Complete booklet, #1595a 25.00
Nos. 1592-1595 (4) 5.00 1.00

See note after No. 1277.

King Carl XVI Gustaf — A488

Royal Cipher — A489

40th birthday: No. 1598, King presenting Nobel Prize for literature to Czeslaw Milosz, 1980. No. 1600, Royal family at Soldien palace

Lithographed and Engraved

1986, Apr. 23 ***Perf. 12 on 3 Sides***

1596 A488 2.10k grnsh blk & pale grn .75 .30
1597 A489 2.10k dk bl, pink & gold .75 .30
1598 A488 2.10k dk bl & pale bl .75 .30
1599 A489 2.10k dk bl, pale grn & gold .75 .30
1600 A488 2.10k blk & pale pink .75 .30
a. Bklt. pane, 2 each #1596-1600 7.50 11.00
Complete booklet, #1600a 8.00
Nos. 1596-1600 (5) 3.75 1.50

Olof Palme (1927-1986), Prime Minister — A490

Perf. 13 on 3 Sides

1986, Apr. 11 **Engr.**

1601 A490 2.10k dk lilac rose .85 .85
1602 A490 2.90k grnsh black 1.00 1.00
a. Bklt. pane, 5 ea #1601-1602 10.00
Complete booklet, #1602a 11.00

Nordic Cooperation Issue — A491

Sister towns.

1986, May 27 **Engr.** ***Perf. 13 Vert.***

1603 A491 2.10k Uppsala .75 .25
1604 A491 2.90k Eskilstuna 1.20 .60

Europa 1986 — A492

2.10k, Automotive pollutants. 2.90k, Industrial pollutants.

1986, May 27 ***Perf. 13 Horiz.***

1605 A492 2.10k multi 1.75 .50

Perf. 13 on 3 Sides

1606 A492 2.90k multi 1.10 1.25
a. Booklet pane of 6 6.75
Complete booklet, #1606a 12.50

STOCKHOLMIA '86 — A493

Designs: No. 1607, Mail handling terminal, Tomteboda, 1986. No. 1608, Railroad mail car, 19th cent. No. 1609, Post Office, 18th cent. No. 1610, Postman, 17th cent.

Lithographed and Engraved

1986, Aug. 29 ***Perf. 13***

1607 A493 2.10k multi 3.00 *3.00*
1608 A493 2.10k multi 3.00 *3.00*
1609 A493 2.90k multi 3.00 *3.00*
1610 A493 2.90k multi 3.00 *3.00*
a. Bklt. pane of 4, #1607-1610 12.00 *16.00*
Complete booklet, #1610a 16.00

Bklt. sold for 40k, including 30k ticket to STOCKHOLMIA '86.

Souvenir Sheet

World Class Athletes in Track and Field — A494

Designs: a, Ann-Louise Skoglund, 400-meter hurdle, 1982. b, Dag Wennlund, 1986, and Eric Lemming, c. 1900, javelin. c, Standing high jumper and Patrik Sjoberg, high jump, 1985. d, Anders Garderud, 300-meter steeplechase record-holder.

1986, Oct. 18 **Engr.** ***Perf. 12½***

1611 A494 Sheet of 4 4.00 3.50
a.-d. 2.10k, any single .85 .80

No. 1611 sold for 11k to benefit philatelic organizations.

Intl. Peace Year — A495

Amnesty Intl., 25th Anniv. — A496

1986, Oct. 18 ***Perf. 13 Vert.***

1612 A495 3.40k bluish blk & emer grn 1.25 1.25
1613 A496 3.40k dk red & bluish blk 1.25 1.25
a. Pair, #1612-1613 2.50 2.50

Christmas — A497

Winter village scenes.

Perf. 13x12½ on 3 Sides

1986, Nov. 25 **Litho. & Engr.**

1614 1.90k Postal van .70 .30
1615 1.90k Postman on bicycle .70 .30
1616 1.90k Children, sled .70 .30
1617 1.90k Child mailing letter .70 .30
a. A497 Block of 4, #1614-1617 2.80 3.50
b. Bklt. pane of 12, 3 #1617a 8.50 —
Complete booklet, #1617b 9.00

Nobel Peace Prize Laureates — A498

#1618, Bertha von Suttner, 1905. #1619, Carl von Ossietzky, 1935. #1620, Albert Luthuli, 1960. #1621, Martin Luther King, Jr., 1964. #1622, Mother Teresa, 1979.

1986, Nov. 25 **Engr.** ***Perf. 13 Horiz.***

1618 A498 2.90k brt bl, blk & hn brn 1.25 1.00
1619 A498 2.90k blk & hn brn 1.25 1.00
1620 A498 2.90k brt bl, blk & brn blk 1.25 1.00
1621 A498 2.90k brn blk & hn brn 1.25 1.00
1622 A498 2.90k blk, brt bl & hn brn 1.25 1.00
a. Bklt. pane of 5, #1618-1622 6.25 *9.50*
Complete booklet, #1622a 7.00

Conservation Type of 1983

No. 1623, Parnassius mnemosyne. No. 1624, Gentianella campestris. No. 1625, Osmoderma eremita. No. 1626, Arnica montana.

Perf. 13 on 3 Sides

1987, Mar. 10 **Engr.**

1623 A447 2.10k multicolored .70 .25
1624 A447 2.10k multicolored .70 .25
a. Booklet pane, 5 ea #1623-1624 7.00
Complete booklet, #1624a 7.50

Perf. 13 Horiz.

1625 A447 2.50k multicolored .90 .25
1626 A447 4.20k multicolored 1.45 .50
Nos. 1623-1626 (4) 3.75 1.25

Swedish Aviation Industry A500

1987, Mar. 10 *Perf. 13 Vert.*
1627 A500 25k Saab SF340 16.00 .40

Europa 1987 — A501

Nos. 1628-1629, City Library, Asplund. No. 1630, Lewerentz Marcus Church.

1987, May 14 **Engr.** *Perf. 13 Vert.*
1628 A501 2.10k int blk & grn 3.25 .30

Perf. 13 on 3 Sides

1629 A501 3.10k emer grn & red brn 1.00 .90
1630 A501 3.10k emer grn & sep 1.00 .90
a. Bklt. pane, 3 each #1629-1630 6.00
Nos. 1628-1630 (3) 5.25 2.10

Illustrations from Children's Novels by Astrid Lindgren (b. 1907) — A502

No. 1631, Karlsson Pa Taket. No. 1632, Barnen and Bullerbyn. No. 1633, Madicken. No. 1634, Mio, Min Mio. No. 1635, Nils Karlsson-Pyssling. No. 1636, Emil and Lonneberga. No. 1637, Ronja Rovardotter. No. 1638, Pippi Longstocking. No. 1639, Broderna Lejonhjarta. No. 1640, Lotta Pa Brakmakargatan.

Perf. 13x12½ on 3 Sides

1987, May 14 **Litho. & Engr.**
1631 A502 1.90k multi 1.25 .25
1632 A502 1.90k multi 1.25 .25
1633 A502 1.90k multi 1.25 .25
1634 A502 1.90k multi 1.25 .25
1635 A502 1.90k multi 1.25 .25
1636 A502 1.90k multi 1.25 .25
1637 A502 1.90k multi 1.25 .25
1638 A502 1.90k multi 1.25 .25
1639 A502 1.90k multi 1.25 .25
1640 A502 1.90k multi 1.25 .25
a. Bklt. pane, 2 ea #1631-1640 25.00
Nos. 1631-1640 (10) 12.50 2.50

See note after No. 1277.

Medieval Towns — A503

No. 1641, 2.10k, Hans Brask, Bishop of Linkoping, 16th cent. No. 1642, 2.10k, Nykopingshus Castle.

1987, May 14 **Engr.** *Perf. 12½ Vert.*
1641 A503 blk, dk vio & yel bis .75 .40
1642 A503 dk vio, blk & yel bis .75 .40
a. Pair, #1641-1642 1.60 1.50

Swedes in the Service of Mankind A504

Designs: No. 1643, Raoul Wallenberg, Swedish diplomat in Budapest during World War II. No. 1644, Dag Hammarskjold (1905-1961), UN secretary-general. No. 1645, Folke Bernadotte af Wisborg (1895-1948), organizer of the Red Cross operation that saved thousands from Nazi death camps.

Perf. 12½ Horiz.

1987, Aug. 10 **Engr.**
1643 A504 3.10k blue 1.10 .75
1644 A504 3.10k green 1.10 .75
1645 A504 3.10k brown violet 1.10 .75
a. Bklt. pane, 2 each #1643-1645 7.00
Complete booklet, #1645a 7.50
Nos. 1643-1645 (3) 3.30 2.25

Gripsholm Castle, 450th Anniv. — A505

Paintings from the Royal Castle Collection, Gripsholm: No. 1646, King Gustav I Vasa (d. 1560), artist unknown. No. 1647, Blue Tiger, 1673, favorite horse of King Charles XI, by D.K. Ehrenstrahl. No. 1648, Hedvig Charlotta Nordenflycht (1718-1763), poet, by Kopia J.H. Scheffel. No. 1649, Gripsholm Castle Outer Courtyard, 17th Cent., 19th cent. lithograph by C.J. Billmark.

1987, Aug. 10 *Perf. 13 Vert.*
1646 A505 2.10k multi .75 .30
1647 A505 2.10k multi .75 .30
1648 A505 2.10k multi .75 .30
1649 A505 2.10k multi .75 .30
a. Bklt. pane of 8, 2 strips of #1646-1649 with gutter btwn. 6.00
Complete booklet, #1649a 6.50
Nos. 1646-1649 (4) 3.00 1.20

Botanical Gardens A506

Designs: No. 1650, Victoria cruziana (water lily), Victoria House, Bergian Garden, c. 1790, Stockholm University. No. 1651, Layout of baroque palace garden, by Carl Harleman (1700-1753), Uppsala University. No. 1652, White anemones, rock garden, Gothenberg Botanical Gardens, 1923. No. 1653, Tulip tree blossoms, Academy Garden, c. 1860, Lund University.

1987, Oct. 10 **Engr.** *Perf. 13 Vert.*
1650 A506 2.10k multi .75 .30
1651 A506 2.10k multi .75 .30
1652 A506 2.10k multi .75 .30
1653 A506 2.10k multi .75 .30
a. Bklt. pane, 2 each #1650-1653 with gutter between 6.00
Nos. 1650-1653 (4) 3.00 1.20

The Circus in Sweden, Bicent. — A507

Litho. & Engr.

1987, Oct. 10 *Perf. 13*
1654 A507 2.10k Juggler, clown 1.25 *1.00*
1655 A507 2.10k High wire 1.25 *1.00*
1656 A507 2.10k Equestrian 1.25 *1.00*
a. Bklt. pane of 3, #1654-1656 3.75 *4.00*
Complete booklet, 2 #1656a 9.00

Stamp Day. Sold for 8k.

Christmas A508

Customs: No. 1657, Putting porridge in the stable for the gray Christmas elf. No. 1658, Watering horses at a north-running stream on Boxing Day. No. 1659, Sled-race home from church on Christmas Day. No. 1660, Hanging out sheaves of wheat to foretell a good harvest.

Perf. 13 on 3 Sides

1987, Nov. 25 **Litho.**
1657 A508 2k multi .75 .30
1658 A508 2k multi .75 .30
1659 A508 2k multi .75 .30
1660 A508 2k multi .75 .30
a. Bklt. pane, 3 each #1657-1660 9.00
Complete booklet, #1660a 9.50
Nos. 1657-1660 (4) 3.00 1.20

Nobel Prize Winners in Physics A509

Space and diagram or formula: No. 1661, Antony Hewish, Great Britain, 1974. No. 1662, Subrahmanyan Chandrasekhar, US, 1983. No. 1663, William Fowler, US, 1983. No. 1664, Arno Penzias and Robert Wilson, US, 1978. No. 1665, Martin Ryle, Great Britain, 1974.

1987, Nov. 25 **Engr.** *Perf. 13*
1661 A509 2.90k dark blue 1.00 .85
1662 A509 2.90k blk 1.00 .85
1663 A509 2.90k dark blue 1.00 .85
1664 A509 2.90k dark blue 1.00 .85
1665 A509 2.90k blk 1.00 .85
a. Bklt. pane of 5, #1661-1665 5.00 *10.00*
Complete booklet, #1665a 5.50

Inland Boats A510

No. 1666, Skiff, Lake Hjalmaren. No. 1667, Village boat, Lake Vattern. No. 1668, Rowboat, Byske. No. 1669, Flat-bottomed rowboat, Asnen. No. 1670, Ice boat, Lake Vanern. No. 1671, Church boat, Lake Locknesjon.

1988, Jan. 29 **Engr.** *Perf. 13*
1666 A510 3.10k multi 1.00 .70
1667 A510 3.10k multi 1.00 .70
1668 A510 3.10k multi 1.00 .70
1669 A510 3.10k multi 1.00 .70
1670 A510 3.10k multi 1.00 .70
1671 A510 3.10k multi 1.00 .70
a. Bklt. pane of 6, #1666-1671 6.00 *9.50*
Complete booklet, #1671a 6.50

A511

A512

Settling of New Sweden, 350th Anniv. — A513

Designs: No. 1672, 17th Cent. European settlers negotiating with American Indians, map of New Sweden, the Swedish ships *Kalmar Nyckel* and *Fogel Grip*, based on an 18th cent. illustration from a Swedish book about the American Colonies. No. 1673, Bishop Hill and painter Olof Krans. No. 1674, Carl Sandburg (1878-1967), author, and Jenny Lind (1820-1867), opera singer known as the "Swedish Nightingale." No. 1675, Charles Lindbergh (1902-1974), and *The Spirit of St. Louis*. No. 1676, American astronaut with Swedish Hasselblad camera on the Moon. No. 1677, Swedish players in National Hockey League.

Litho. & Engr., Engr. (#1674-1675)

1988, Mar. 29 *Perf. 13x12½ Horiz*
1672 A511 3.60k multi 1.50 1.25
1673 A511 3.60k multi 1.50 1.25

Perf. 13x12½ on 3 Sides

1674 A512 3.60k brn 1.50 1.25
1675 A512 3.60k dk bl & brn 1.50 1.25

Perf. 13x12½ on 2

1676 A513 3.60k dk bl & yel 1.50 1.25
1677 A513 3.60k dk red, dk bl & blk 1.50 1.25
a. Bklt. pane of 6, #1672-1677 9.00 *12.50*
Complete booklet, #1677a 10.00

See US No. C117 and Finland No. 768.

Conservation Type of 1983

Species Inhabiting Coastal Waters — No. 1678, Haliaetus albicilla. No. 1679, Halichoerus grypus. No. 1680, Anguilla anguilla.

Perf. 13 on 3 Sides

1988, Mar. 29 **Engr.**
1678 A447 2.20k multicolored .75 .25
1679 A447 2.20k multicolored .75 .25
a. Bklt. pane, 5 #1678, 5 #1679 7.50
Complete booklet, #1679a 9.00

Perf. 13 Horiz.

1680 A447 4.40k multicolored 1.60 .25
Nos. 1678-1680 (3) 3.10 .75

Midsummer Celebration — A515

No. 1681, Wildflowers in meadow. No. 1682, Rowing. No. 1683, Children making wreaths. No. 1684, Raising maypole. No. 1685, Fiddlers. No. 1686, Ferry. No. 1687, Dancing. No. 1688, Accordion player. No. 1689, Maypole, residence. No. 1690, Bouquet of flowers.

Perf. 12½ on 3 Sides

1988, May 17 **Litho. & Engr.**
1681 A515 2k multicolored 1.20 .25
1682 A515 2k multicolored 1.20 .25
1683 A515 2k multicolored 1.20 .25
1684 A515 2k multicolored 1.20 .25
1685 A515 2k multicolored 1.20 .25
1686 A515 2k multicolored 1.20 .25
1687 A515 2k multicolored 1.20 .25
1688 A515 2k multicolored 1.20 .25
1689 A515 2k multicolored 1.20 .25
1690 A515 2k multicolored 1.20 .25
a. Bklt. pane, 2 ea #1681-1690 24.00
Complete booklet, #1690a 27.50
Nos. 1681-1690 (10) 12.00 2.50

See note after No. 1277.

Skara Township Millennium A516

Design: Detail from Creation, a Skara Cathedral stained-glass window by Bo Beskow, 20th cent.

1988, May 17 ***Perf. 13 Horiz.***

1691 A516 2.20k multi .75 .35

Stora Mining Co., 700th Anniv. — A517

1988, May 17 **Engr.**

1692 A517 4.40k Mine, 18th cent. 1.25 .75

Royal Dramatic Theater, Stockholm, Founded by King Gustav III in 1788 — A518

Design: Scene fron *The Queen's Diamond Ornament,* about the murder of King Gustav III at the Royal Opera in 1792.

1988, May 17

1693 A518 8k grn, red & blk 2.50 1.25

Self-portrait, 1923, by Nils Dardel (1888-1943) A519

Paintings: No. 1695, *Old Age Home in Autumn,* c. 1930, by Vera Nilsson (1888-1979). No. 1696, *Self-portrait,* 1912, by Isaac Grunewald (1899-1979). No. 1697, *Visit of an Eccentric Lady,* 1921, by Dardel. No. 1698, *Soap Bubbles,* 1927, by Nilsson. No. 1699, *The Fair,* 1915, by Grunewald.

Perf. 13 on 3 Sides

1988, Aug. 25 **Litho. & Engr.**

Size: 33x35mm (Nos. 1695, 1698)

1694 A519 2.20k shown .80 .60
1695 A519 2.20k multi .80 .60
1696 A519 2.20k multi .80 .60
1697 A519 2.20k multi .80 .60
1698 A519 2.20k multi .80 .60
1699 A519 2.20k multi .80 .60
a. Bklt. pane of 6, #1694-1699 5.00 *7.50*

Europa — A520

Transport and communication — No. 1700, X2 high-speed train. No. 1701, X2 high-speed train, diff. No. 1702, Steam locomotive, 1887.

1988, Aug. 25 **Engr.** ***Perf. 13 Vert.***

1700 A520 2.20k multi 2.75 .90

Perf. 13 on 3 Sides

1701 A520 3.10k multi 1.00 .95
1702 A520 3.10k multi 1.00 .95
a. Bklt. pane, 3 each #1701-1702 6.00
Complete booklet, #1702a 6.50
Nos. 1700-1702 (3) 4.75 2.80

Common Swift — A521

1988, Aug. 25 ***Perf. 12½ Vert.***

1703 A521 20k brt vio & dk vio 7.50 .25

Dan Andersson (1888-1920), Poet, and Manuscript A522

Forest and Pond, Finnmarken — A523

1988, Oct. 8 **Engr.** ***Perf. 13 Vert.***

1704 A522 2.20k vio, dk bl & dk bl grn .80 .35
1705 A523 2.20k vio, dk bl & dk bl grn .80 .45
a. Pair, #1704-1705 1.75 .95

Soccer — A524

Match scenes: No. 1706, Dribble (Torbjorn Nilsson representing local club matches). No. 1707, Heading the ball (Ralf Edstrom of the national league). No. 1708, Kick (Pia Sundhage, women's soccer).

1988, Oct. 8 **Litho. & Engr.** ***Perf. 13***

1706 A524 2.20k multi 1.00 .75
1707 A524 2.20k multi 1.00 .75
1708 A524 2.20k multi 1.00 .75
a. Bklt. pane of 3, #1706-1708 3.00 3.50
Complete booklet, #1708a 7.50

No. 1708a sold for 8.50k; surtax benefited stamp collecting.

Nobel Laureates in Chemistry A525

Designs: No. 1709, Willard F. Libby, US, 1960, carbon-14 method of dating artifacts. No. 1710, Karl Ziegler, West Germany, and Guilio Natta, Italy, 1963, catalysts. No. 1711, Aaron Klug, South Africa, 1982, electron microscopy. No. 1712, Ilya Prigogine, Belgium, 1977, proof that molecular order can occur spontaneously out of chaos.

1988, Nov. 29 ***Perf. 12½ Vert.***

1709 A525 3.10k multi 1.00 .80
1710 A525 3.10k multi 1.00 .80
1711 A525 3.10k multi 1.00 .80
1712 A525 3.10k multi 1.00 .80
a. Bklt. pane, 2 each #1709-1712 9.00
Complete booklet, #1712a 10.00
Nos. 1709-1712 (4) 4.00 3.20

Christmas — A526

Story of Christ's birth according to Luke (2:7-20): No. 1713, Angels appear to inform shepherds of Christ's birth. No. 1714, Star of Bethlehem, angel, horse. No. 1715, Birds singing. No. 1716, Magi offering gifts. No. 1717, Holy family. No. 1718, Shepherds with palm offering.

Perf. 12½x13 on 3 Sides

1988, Nov. 29

1713 A526 2k multi .70 .50
1714 A526 2k multi .70 .50
1715 A526 2k multi .70 .50
1716 A526 2k multi .70 .50
1717 A526 2k multi .70 .50
1718 A526 2k multi .70 .50
a. Bklt. pane, 2 each #1713-1718 9.00
Complete booklet, #1718a 10.00
Nos. 1713-1718 (6) 4.20 3.00

Nos. 1713 and 1716, 1714 and 1717, 1715 and 1718 have continuous designs.

Lighthouses A527

Designs: 1.90k, Twin masonry lighthouses, 1832, and concrete lighthouse, 1946, Nidingen, Kattegat Is. 2.70k, Soderarm, Uppland, 1839. 3.80k, Sydostbrotten, Gulf of Bothnia, 1963. 3.90k, Sandhammaren, Skane, c. 1860.

1989, Jan. 31 **Engr.** ***Perf. 13 Vert.***

1719 A527 1.90k multi .75 .30
1720 A527 2.70k multi 1.15 .60
1721 A527 3.80k multi 1.30 .90
1722 A527 3.90k multi 1.75 1.00
Nos. 1719-1722 (4) 4.95 2.80

Endangered Species — A528

No. 1723, Gulo gulo. No. 1724, Strix uralensis. No. 1725, Dendrocopos minor. No. 1726, Calidris alpina schinzii. No. 1727, Hyla arborea. No. 1728, Ficedula parva.

1989, Jan. 31 ***Perf. 13 on 3 Sides***

1723 A528 2.30k multicolored .70 .25
1724 A528 2.30k multicolored .70 .25
a. Bklt. pane, 5 each #1723-1724 7.50
Complete booklet, #1724a 8.00

Perf. 13 Horiz.

1725 A528 2.40k multicolored .70 .30
1726 A528 2.60k multicolored 1.05 .60
1727 A528 3.30k multicolored 1.05 .80
1728 A528 4.60k multicolored 1.60 .35
Nos. 1723-1728 (6) 5.80 2.55

Opening of The Globe Arena, Stockholm — A529

Perf. 13 Horiz.

1989, Apr. 14 **Litho. & Engr.**

1729 A529 2.30k Exterior 1.00 .35
1730 A529 2.30k Ice hockey 1.00 .35
1731 A529 2.30k Gymnastics 1.00 .35
1732 A529 2.30k Concert 1.00 .35
a. Bklt. pane of 4, #1729-1732 4.00
Complete booklet, 2 #1732a separated by gutter 9.00

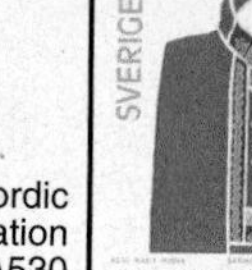

Nordic Cooperation Issue — A530

Folk costumes.

Perf. 13 Horiz.

1989, Apr. 20 **Litho. & Engr.**

1733 A530 2.30k Woman's wool waist .80 .25
1734 A530 3.30k Belt pouch 1.20 .40

Natl. Labor Movement, Cent. — A531

1989, May 17 **Engr.** ***Perf. 13 Horiz.***

1735 A531 2.30k dk red & blk 1.10 .75

Europa 1989 — A532

Children's games: 2.30k, No. 1738, Sailing toy boats. No. 1737, Kick-sledding.

1989, May 17 ***Perf. 13 Vert.***

1736 A532 2.30k car lake 2.50 .60

Perf. 13

1737 A532 3.30k greenish blue .85 .70
1738 A532 3.30k lilac .85 .70
a. Bklt. pane, 3 #1737, 3 #1738 5.50
Complete booklet, #1738a 6.00
Nos. 1736-1738 (3) 4.20 2.00

Summer — A533

Perf. 13 on 3 Sides

1989, May 17 **Litho.**

1739 A533 2.10k Sailing 1.25 .25
1740 A533 2.10k Beach ball 1.25 .25
1741 A533 2.10k Cycling 1.25 .25
1742 A533 2.10k Canoeing 1.25 .25
1743 A533 2.10k Angling 1.25 .25
1744 A533 2.10k Camping 1.25 .25
1745 A533 2.10k Croquet 1.25 .25
1746 A533 2.10k Badminton 1.25 .25
1747 A533 2.10k Gardening 1.25 .25
1748 A533 2.10k Sand sculpture 1.25 .25
a. Bklt. pane, 2 ea #1739-1748 25.00
Complete booklet, #1748a 27.50
Nos. 1739-1748 (10) 12.50 2.50

See note after No. 1277.

Polar Exploration A534

Swedish polar techniques used in the Arctic (Nos. 1749-1751) and Antarctic: No. 1749, Aircraft, temperature experiment. No. 1750, Settlement, Arctic pass. No. 1751, Icebreaker, experiment. No. 1752, Penguins, tall ship and longboat. No. 1753, Antarctic transports, helicopter. No. 1754, Surveying, albatross.

Perf. 13 on 3 Sides

1989, Aug. 22 **Litho. & Engr.**

Size: 40x43mm (Nos. 1750, 1753)

1749	A534 3.30k multi		1.25	1.05
1750	A534 3.30k multi		1.25	1.05
1751	A534 3.30k multi		1.25	1.05
1752	A534 3.30k multi		1.25	1.05
1753	A534 3.30k multi		1.25	1.05
1754	A534 3.30k multi		1.25	1.05
a.	Bklt. pane of 6, #1749-1754		7.50	*14.00*

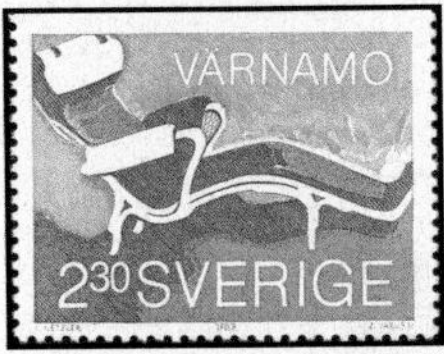

Smaland Businesses A535

No. 1755, Furniture. No. 1756, Assembly equipment. No. 1757, Sewing machines. No. 1758, Glassware. No. 1759, Metal springs. No. 1760, Matchsticks.

Perf. 12½x12 on 3 Sides

1989, Aug. 22 **Engr.**

1755	A535 2.30k multi	.80	.65
1756	A535 2.30k multi	.80	.65
1757	A535 2.30k multi	.80	.65
1758	A535 2.30k multi	.80	.65
1759	A535 2.30k multi	.80	.65
1760	A535 2.30k multi	.80	.65
a.	Bklt. pane of 6, #1755-1760	5.00	*10.50*
	Complete booklet, #1760a	5.50	

Eagle Owl, *Bubo bubo* A536

1989, Aug. 22 ***Perf. 13 Vert.***

1761	A536 30k vio, blk & grn blk	7.50	.40

A536a

Birds and Coastline, Bla Jungfrun Natl. Park — A537

No. 1762, Rhododendron lapponicum. No. 1763, Calypso bulbosa.

Perf. 13x12½ on 3 Sides

1989, Sept. 12 **Engr.**

1762	A536a 2.40k multicolored	.75	.25
1763	A536a 2.40k multicolored	.75	.25
a.	Bklt. pane, 5 ea #1762-1763	7.50	
	Complete booklet, #1763a	8.00	

Perf. 12½ Vert.

1764	A537 4.30k dark blue, blk & brn vio	1.25	.95
	Nos. 1762-1764 (3)	2.75	1.45

See Nos. 1776-1780.

Swedish Kennel Club, Cent. — A538

a, Large spitz. b, Fox hound. c, Small spitz.

1989, Oct. 7 **Litho.** ***Perf. 13x12½***

1765	A538 Bklt. pane of 3	3.00	3.75
a.-c.	2.40k any single	.90	.75
	Complete booklet, 2 #1765	7.00	

Sold for 9.50k.

Christmas — A539

Holiday symbols: No. 1766, Top of Christmas tree, wreath. No. 1767, Candelabrum, foods. No. 1768, Star, poinsettia plant, grot pot. No. 1769, Bottom of tree, straw goat, gifts. No. 1770, Gifts, television, girl. No. 1771, Boy, grandfather, girl opening gift.

Perf. 12½x13 on 3 Sides

1989, Nov. 24 **Litho.**

1766	A539 2.10k multi	1.00	.30
1767	A539 2.10k multi	1.00	.30
1768	A539 2.10k multi	1.00	.30
1769	A539 2.10k multi	1.00	.30
1770	A539 2.10k multi	1.00	.30
1771	A539 2.10k multi	1.00	.30
a.	Bklt. pane, 2 each #1766-1771	12.50	
	Complete booklet, #1771a	13.00	
	Nos. 1766-1771 (6)	6.00	1.80

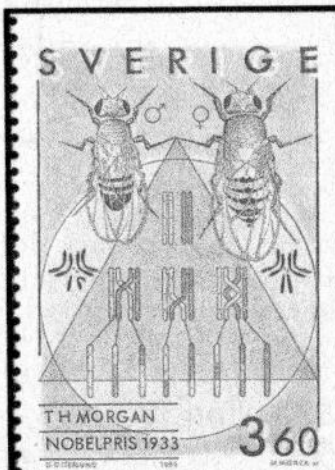

Nobel Laureates in Physiology A540

Genetics: No. 1772, Thomas Morgan (1866-1945), US, 1933, chromosomal study of fruit flies to determine laws and mechanism of heredity. No. 1773, James Watson, US, and Francis Crick with Maurice Wilkins, Great Britain, 1962, molecular structure of DNA. No. 1774, Werner Arber, Switzerland, Daniel Nathans and Hamilton Smith, US, 1978, enzymatic cutting of nucleotides to create gene hybrids. No. 1775, Barbara McClintock, botanist, US, 1983, corn color studies that led to theory of gene jumping.

Perf. 12½ Vert.

1989, Nov. 24 **Litho. & Engr.**

1772	A540 3.60k multi	1.25	.60
1773	A540 3.60k multi	1.25	.60
1774	A540 3.60k multi	1.25	.60
1775	A540 3.60k multi	1.25	.60
a.	Bklt. pane, 2 each #1772-1775 with gutter between	10.00	
	Complete booklet, #1775a	11.00	
	Nos. 1772-1775 (4)	5.00	2.40

Natl. Parks Type of 1989

Designs: No. 1776, Campground, sailboat on lake, Angso Park. No. 1777, Hiking, Pieljekaise Park. 3.70k, Three whooper swans over wetlands, Muddus Park. 4.10k, Deer, lake, Padjelanta Park. 4.80k, Bears, forest, Sanfjallet Park.

Perf. 13 on 3 Sides

1990, Jan. 26 **Engr.**

1776	A537 2.50k multicolored	.75	.25
1777	A537 2.50k multicolored	.75	.25
a.	Bklt. pane, 5 each #1776-1777	7.50	
	Complete booklet, #1777a	8.00	

Perf. 13 Vert.

1778	A537 3.70k multicolored	1.60	.25
1779	A537 4.10k multicolored	1.75	1.05
1780	A537 4.80k multicolored	1.75	1.05
	Nos. 1776-1780 (5)	6.60	2.85

King and Queen Types of 1985-86 and

Queen Silvia — A541

King Carl XVI Gustaf — A542

King Carl XVI Gustav A543

Queen Silvia A544

King Carl XVI Gustaf — A545

Perf. 12½ Vert., Horiz. (A541, A542, A545)

1990-97 **Engr.**

1783	A436c 2.50k deep claret	1.00	.25
1784	A542 2.80k dk blue	1.10	.25
1785	A542 2.90k deep green	1.30	.25
1786	A542 3.20k violet	1.50	.25
1787	A543 3.70k dark red brown	1.50	.25
1788	A543 3.85k black	1.75	.30
1789	A436d 4.60k bright org	2.00	1.75
1790	A541 5k deep rose vio	2.00	.40
1791	A545 (5k) deep blue	2.10	.30
1792	A541 6k deep claret	2.25	.60
1793	A544 6k dark green	2.75	1.25
1794	A541 6.50k purple	3.50	2.00
1795	A544 7.50k purple	3.10	1.65
1796	A544 8k brown red	3.10	1.00
	Nos. 1783-1796 (14)	28.95	10.50

Issued: 2.50k, 4.60k, 1/26; 5k, 3/20/91; 2.80k, 11/20/91; 2.90k, #1792, 1/2/93; 3.20k, 1/17/94; 6.50k, 3/18/94; 3.70k, #1793, 1/2/95; 3.85k, 7.50k, 1/2/96; (5k), 8k, 2/28/97.

No. 1791 is inscribed "BREV."

Viking Heritage A546

Designs: No. 1801, Viking head of carved bone, dragon carving from a molding found in Birka. No. 1802, Three viking longships. No. 1803, Viking town. No. 1804, Bronze statue of pagan fertility god, silver filigree cross. No. 1805, Bishop's crosier, southern Russian carved statue of a deer. No. 1806, Viking longship (stern). No. 1807, Viking longship (bow), horsemen, woman, warrior, wolf. No. 1808, Sword hilts.

Perf. 12x13 on 3 Sides

1990, Mar. 28 **Litho. & Engr.**

1801	A546 2.50k multicolored	.75	.50
1802	A546 2.50k multicolored	.75	.50
1803	A546 2.50k multicolored	.75	.50
1804	A546 2.50k multicolored	.75	.50
1805	A546 2.50k multicolored	.75	.50
1806	A546 2.50k multicolored	.75	.50
1807	A546 2.50k multicolored	.75	.50
1808	A546 2.50k multicolored	.75	.50
a.	Bklt. pane of 8, #1801-1808	6.00	*10.00*
	Complete booklet, #1808a	6.50	

Nos. 1802-1803, 1806-1807 printed in a continuous design.

Swedish Industrial Safety, Cent. — A547

1990, Mar. 28 **Engr.** ***Perf. 13 Horiz.***

1809	A547 2.50k Lumberjack	1.00	.25

Europa 1990 — A548

Post offices — No. 1810, Postal Museum, 1720. No. 1811, Sollebrunn, 1985. No. 1812, Vasteras, 1956.

1990, Mar. 28 ***Perf. 13 Vert.***

1810	A548 2.50k multi	3.50	.40

Perf. 13 on 3 Sides

1811	A548 3.80k multi	1.75	.90
1812	A548 3.80k multi	1.75	.90
a.	Bklt. pane, 3 each #1811-1812	10.50	
	Complete booklet, #1812a	11.00	
	Nos. 1810-1812 (3)	7.00	2.20

World Equestrian Games, Stockholm A549

No. 1813, Endurance riding. No. 1814, Combined training. No. 1815, Show jumping. No. 1816, Dressage. No. 1817, Volting. No. 1818, Four-in-hand.

Litho. & Engr.

1990, May 15 ***Perf. 12½x13***

1813	A549 3.80k multicolored	1.20	.80
1814	A549 3.80k multicolored	1.20	.80
1815	A549 3.80k multicolored	1.20	.80
1816	A549 3.80k multicolored	1.20	.80
1817	A549 3.80k multicolored	1.20	.80
1818	A549 3.80k multicolored	1.20	.80
a.	Bklt. pane of 6, #1813-1818	7.25	*11.50*
	Complete booklet, #1818a	7.50	

Apiculture — A550

#1819, Worker bee collecting nectar. #1820, Bee, bilberry flower. #1821, Worker bee. #1822, Apiary hive. #1823, Two bees in honeycomb. #1824, Drone, 7 cells, blue green panel. #1825, Queen bee, 7 cells, yellow panel. #1826, Swarm hanging from tree. #1827, Beekeeper. #1828, Honey.

1990, May 15 **Litho.**

1819	A550 2.30k multicolored	1.00	.30
1820	A550 2.30k multicolored	1.00	.30
1821	A550 2.30k multicolored	1.00	.30
1822	A550 2.30k multicolored	1.00	.30
1823	A550 2.30k multicolored	1.00	.30
1824	A550 2.30k multicolored	1.00	.30
1825	A550 2.30k multicolored	1.00	.30
1826	A550 2.30k multicolored	1.00	.30
1827	A550 2.30k multicolored	1.00	.30
1828	A550 2.30k multicolored	1.00	.30
a.	Bklt. pane, 2 ea #1819-1828	20.00	
	Complete booklet, #1828a	25.00	
	Nos. 1819-1828 (10)	10.00	3.00

See note after No. 1277.

Wasa Nautical Museum — A551

Man-of-war *Wasa:* 2.50k, Bow. 4.60k, Stern.

1990, May 15 **Engr.** ***Perf. 13 Vert.***

1829	A551 2.50k org & blk	.75	.25
1830	A551 4.60k dk bl & org	1.50	.75

Dearest Brothers, Sisters and Friends — A552

Proud City A553

Allusions to poetry verses of Carl Michael Bellman (No. 1833) and Evert Taube: No. 1833, Fredmen in the gutter. No. 1834, Happy baker in San Remo. No. 1835, At sea. No. 1836, Violava.

Perf. 13 on 3 Sides

1990, Aug. 8 **Litho. & Engr.**

1831 A552 2.50k multicolored 1.25 1.25
1832 A553 2.50k multicolored 1.25 1.25
1833 A552 2.50k multicolored 1.25 1.25
1834 A552 2.50k multicolored 1.25 1.25
1835 A553 2.50k multicolored 1.25 1.25
1836 A552 2.50k multicolored 1.25 1.25
a. Bklt. pane of 6, #1831-1836 6.00 *12.00*

Paper Production A554

#1837, Paper production c. 1600. #1838, Watermark. #1839, Newspaper mastheads. #1840, Modern paper production.

1990, Aug. 8 ***Perf. 12½ Vert.***

1837 A554 2.50k multicolored .90 .25
1838 A554 2.50k multicolored .90 .25
1839 A554 2.50k multicolored .90 .25
1840 A554 2.50k multicolored .90 .25
a. Bklt. pane, 2 each #1837-1840 with gutter between 7.25
Complete booklet, #1840a 8.00
Nos. 1837-1840 (4) 3.60 1.00

Ovedskloster Palace — A555

1990, Aug. 8 **Engr.** ***Perf. 13 Vert.***

1841 A555 40k multicolored 10.00 .30

See Nos. 1874-1877.

Photography A556

No. 1842, Bellows camera. No. 1843, August Strindberg. No. 1844, 35mm camera.

Litho. & Engr.

1990, Oct. 6 ***Perf. 12½***

1842 A556 2.50k multi 1.00 .80
1843 A556 2.50k multi 1.00 .80
1844 A556 2.50k multi 1.00 .80
a. Bklt. pane of 3, #1842-1844 3.00 *4.00*
Complete booklet, 2 #1844a 6.50

Stamp Day. Booklet of two panes sold for 20k. Surtax benefited stamp collecting.

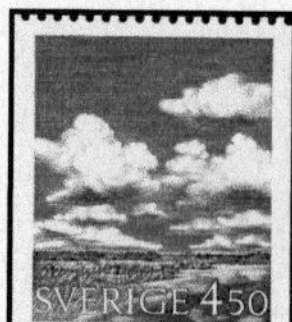

Clouds — A557

1990, Oct. 6 **Engr.** ***Perf. 12½ Horiz.***

1845 A557 4.50k Cumulus 1.20 .25
1846 A557 4.70k Cumulonimbus 1.45 .60
1847 A557 4.90k Cirrus 1.70 .60
1848 A557 5.20k Alto cumulus 1.95 .85
Nos. 1845-1848 (4) 6.30 2.30

A558

1990, Oct. 6 ***Perf. 12½ Vert.***

1849 A558 2.50k shown .80 .30
1850 A558 2.50k Women bathing .80 .30
a. Pair, #1849-1850 1.75 .75

Moa Martinson (1890-1964), author.

Nobel Laureates in Literature — A559

No. 1851, Par Lagerkvist, 1951. No. 1852, Ernest Hemingway, 1954. No. 1853, Albert Camus, 1957. No. 1854, Boris Pasternak, 1958.

Perf. 13 on 2 Sides

1990, Nov. 27 **Engr.**

1851 A559 3.80k multicolored 1.25 .75
1852 A559 3.80k multicolored 1.25 .75
1853 A559 3.80k multicolored 1.25 .75
1854 A559 3.80k multicolored 1.25 .75
a. Bklt. pane, 2 each #1851-1854 with gutter between 10.00
Complete booklet, #1854a 11.00
Nos. 1851-1854 (4) 5.00 3.00

See Nos. 1914-1917.

Christmas — A560

Flowers — No. 1855, Schlumbergera x buckleyi. No. 1856, Helleborus niger. No. 1857, Rhododendron simsii. No. 1858, Hippeastrum x hortorum. No. 1859, Hyacinthus orientalis. No. 1860, Euphorbia pulcherrima.

Perf. 13 on 3 Sides

1990, Nov. 27 **Litho.**

1855 A560 2.30k multi .75 .45
1856 A560 2.30k multi .75 .45
1857 A560 2.30k multi .75 .45
1858 A560 2.30k multi .75 .45
1859 A560 2.30k multi .75 .45
1860 A560 2.30k multi .75 .45
a. Bklt. pane, 2 each #1855-1860 9.00
Complete booklet, #1860a 10.00
Nos. 1855-1860 (6) 4.50 2.70

Carta Marina by Olaus Magnus, 1572 — A561

Scandanavia by A. Bureas and J. Blaeus, 1662 — A562

Maps: No. 1863, Celestial globe by Anders Akerman, 1759. No. 1864, Contour map, 1938. No. 1865, Stockholm, 1989. No. 1866, Bedrock Map, Geological Survey, 1984.

Perf. 13 on 3 Sides

1991, Jan. 30 **Litho. & Engr.**

1861 A561 5k multicolored 1.30 .75
1862 A562 5k multicolored 1.30 .75
1863 A561 5k multicolored 1.30 .75
1864 A561 5k multicolored 1.30 .75
1865 A562 5k multicolored 1.30 .75
1866 A561 5k multicolored 1.30 .75
a. Bklt. pane of 6, #1861-1866 8.00 *18.00*

Fish — A563

No. 1868, Siluris glanis, diff. No. 1869, Cobitis taenia. No. 1870, Gobio gobio. No. 1871, Noemacheilus barbatulus. No. 1872, Leucaspius delineatus.

Perf. 13 on 3 Sides

1991, Jan. 30 **Engr.**

1867 A563 2.50k shown .75 .25
1868 A563 2.50k multi .75 .25
b. Bklt. pane, 5 each #1867-1868 7.50
Complete booklet, #1868b 8.00

Perf. 13 Vert.

1869 A563 5k multi 1.00 .25
1870 A563 5.40k multi 1.75 1.75
1871 A563 5.50k multi 1.45 .25
1872 A563 5.60k multi 1.45 .85
Nos. 1867-1872 (6) 7.15 3.60

Palace Type of 1990

Designs: 10k, Stromsholm Castle. 20k, Karlberg Castle. 25k, Drottningholm Palace.

1991-92 **Engr.** ***Perf. 13 Vert.***

1874 A555 10k blk & olive brn 2.75 .25
1876 A555 20k multicolored 6.00 .25

Size: 58x23mm

1877 A555 25k multicolored 7.50 .45
Nos. 1874-1877 (3) 16.25 .95

Issued: 10k, 4/27; 25k, 3/20; 20k, 5/21/92.

A564

No. 1883, Seglora church. No. 1884, Flag above park. No. 1885, Wedding. No. 1886, Animals.

Perf. 12½x13 on 3 Sides

1991, May 15 **Litho.**

1883 A564 2.40k multi .85 .25
1884 A564 2.40k multi .85 .25
1885 A564 2.40k multi .85 .25
1886 A564 2.40k multi .85 .25
b. Bklt. pane, 5 ea #1883-1886 17.00
Complete booklet, #1886b 17.50
Nos. 1883-1886 (4) 3.40 1.00

Skansen Park, Stockholm, 100th anniv. See note after No. 1277. Complete booklet of 20 stamps sold for 46k.

Kolmarden Zoological Park, Ostergotland A565

Perf. 12½ Horiz.

1991, May 15 **Engr.**

1887 A565 2.50k Polar bears 1.00 .25
1888 A565 4k Dolphin show 1.50 .60

Norden '91.

A566

Public Parks, cent.: #1890, Dancing in park.

1991, May 15 ***Perf. 13 Vert.***

1889 A566 2.50k dark blue .90 .40
1890 A566 2.50k dark blue .90 .40
a. Pair, #1889-1890 2.00 1.75

Europa — A567

Litho. & Engr.

1991, May 15 ***Perf. 13***

1891 A567 4k Hermes space plane *1.75 1.75*
1892 A567 4k Freja satellite *1.75 1.75*
1893 A567 4k Tele-X satellite *1.75 1.75*
a. Bklt. pane of 3, #1891-1893 *5.50 8.50*

Olympic Champions A568

Designs: No. 1894, Magda Julin, figure skating, Antwerp, 1920. No. 1895, Toini Gustaffson, cross country skiing, Grenoble, 1968. No. 1896, Agneta Andersson, Anna Olsson, two-person kayak, Los Angeles, 1984. No. 1897, Ulrika Knape, diving, Munich, 1972.

Perf. 12x13 on 3 Sides

1991, Aug. 27 **Litho. & Engr.**

1894 A568 2.50k multicolored 1.00 .55
1895 A568 2.50k multicolored 1.00 .55
1896 A568 2.50k multicolored 1.00 .55
1897 A568 2.50k multicolored 1.00 .55
a. Bklt. pane, 2 each #1894-1897 8.50
Complete booklet, #1897a 9.50
Nos. 1894-1897 (4) 4.00 2.20

See Nos. 1937-1940, 1953-1956.

Iron Mining — A569

#1898, Spetal Mine, Norberg. #1899, Forsmark Mill. #1900, Ironworks forge. #1901, Forge welding. #1902, Dannemora Mine. #1903, Blast furnace, Pershyttan.

Perf. 13 on 2 or 3 Sides

1991, Aug. 27 **Engr.**

1898 A569 2.50k multicolored .80 .50
1899 A569 2.50k multicolored .80 .50

Size: 31x26mm

1900 A569 2.50k multicolored .80 *.60*
1901 A569 2.50k multicolored .80 *.60*

Size: 31x40mm

1902 A569 2.50k multicolored .80 *.60*
1903 A569 2.50k multicolored .80 *.60*
a. Bklt. pane of 6, #1898-1903 5.00 6.75
Complete booklet, #1903a 5.50

Coronation of King Gustavus III, by Carl Gustaf Pilo — A570

Details from painting: No. 1904, King Gustavus III. No. 1905, Gustavus with crown held above head. No. 1906, Chancellor Arvid Horn, Archbishop Mattias Beronius holding crown above Gustavus III.

1991, Oct. 5 Engr. *Perf. 13*

1904 A570 10k blue 3.25 2.25
1905 A570 10k violet 3.25 2.25

Size: 76x44mm

1906 A570 10k greenish black 3.25 2.25
a. Bklt. pane of 3, #1904-1906 10.00 11.00

Czeslaw Slania, engraver, 70th birthday. No. 1906a sold for 35k to benefit stamp collecting.

Rock Musicians A571

1991, Oct. 5 Litho. & Engr.

1907 A571 2.50k Lena Philipsson 1.50 .80
1908 A571 2.50k Roxette 1.50 .80
1909 A571 2.50k Jerry Williams 1.50 .80
a. Bklt. pane of 3, #1907-1909 5.00 4.00

A572

Christmas: No. 1910, Boy with star, girl with snacks. No. 1911, Family dancing around Christmas tree. No. 1912, Cat beside tree. No. 1913, Child beside bed.

Perf. 12½x13 on 3 Sides

1991, Nov. 20 Litho.

1910 A572 2.30k multicolored .80 .25
1911 A572 2.30k multicolored .80 .25
1912 A572 2.30k multicolored .80 .25
1913 A572 2.30k multicolored .80 .25
b. Bklt. pane, 3 ea #1910-1913 10.00
Complete booklet, #1913b 12.50
Nos. 1910-1913 (4) 3.20 1.00

Nobel Laureates Type of 1990

Nobel Peace Prize Winners: No. 1914, Jean Henri Dunant, founder of Red Cross. No. 1915, Albert Schweitzer, physician and theologian. No. 1916, Alva Myrdal, disarmament negotiator. No. 1917, Andrei Sakharov, physicist.

1991, Nov. 20 Engr. *Perf. 13 Horiz.*

1914 A559 4k carmine 1.50 1.15
1915 A559 4k dk green 1.50 1.15
1916 A559 4k dk ultra 1.50 1.15
1917 A559 4k dk violet 1.50 1.15
a. Bklt. pane, 2 each #1914-1917 with gutter between 12.00
Complete booklet, #1917a 12.50
Nos. 1914-1917 (4) 6.00 4.60

A573

1992, Jan. 30 Engr. *Perf. 13 Horiz.*

1918 A573 2.30k red, grn & blk .90 .30

Outdoor Life Assoc., cent.

A574

A575

Wild Animals: No. 1920, Capreolus capreolus. No. 1921, Capreolus capreolus (with fawn). No. 1922, Ursus arctos (2 cubs). No. 1923, Ursus arctos (adult). No. 1924, Mustela erminea. No. 1925, Lutra lutra. No. 1926, Erinaeceus eropaeus. No. 1929, Mustela putorius. No. 1930, Castor fiber. No. 1932, Canis lupus. No. 1933, Sciurus vulgaris. No. 1934, Alces alces. No. 1935, Vulpes vulpes. No. 1936, Lynx lynx. No. 1936A, Lynx lynx.

Perf. 13 on 3 Sides

1992-2009 Engr.

1920 A574 2.80k multi .80 .25
1921 A574 2.80k multi .80 .25
b. Bklt. pane, 5 ea #1920-1921 8.00
Complete booklet, #1921b 9.00
1922 A574 2.90k multi .90 .25
1923 A574 2.90k multi .90 .25
b. Bklt. pane, 5 ea #1922-1923 9.00
Complete booklet, #1923b 10.00
1924 A574 3.85k multi 1.00 .25
1925 A574 3.85k multi 1.00 .25
a. Bklt. pane, 5 ea #1924-1925 16.00
Complete booklet, 1 #1925a 16.00

Perf. 13 Vert. (A574), Horiz. (A575)

1926 A574 1k multi .40 .25
1927 A574 2.80k like #1921 1.00 .25
1928 A574 2.90k like #1922 1.25 .25
1929 A574 3k multi 1.25 .45
1930 A575 3.20k multi 1.50 1.25
1931 A574 3.85k like #1924 1.50 .25
1932 A574 5.80k multi 2.75 .40
1933 A575 6k multi 2.50 .50
1934 A575 7k multi 3.00 .50
1935 A574 7.70k multi 3.00 .30
1936 A575 12k multi 3.75 .85

Perf. 12 Horiz. Syncopated

1936A A575 12k multi *2.50 6.25*
Nos. 1920-1936 (17) 27.30 6.75

Issued: #1920-1921, 1930, 6k, 7k, Jan. 30; #1922-1923, 1928-1929, 1932, 1936, Jan. 28, 1993; 1k, 3.20k, 3.85k, 7.70k, 1/2/96. No. 1936A, 1/1/2009.

See Nos. 2207-2209, 2238.

Olympic Champions Type of 1991

No. 1937, Gunde Svan, cross-country skiing, Sarajevo, 1984. No. 1938, Thomas Wassberg, cross-country skiing, Lake Placid, 1980. No. 1939, Tomas Gustafson, speed skating, Sarajevo, 1984. No. 1940, Ingemar Stenmark, slalom skiing, Lake Placid, 1980.

Perf. 12x13 on 3 Sides

1992, Jan. 30 Litho. & Engr.

1937 A568 2.80k multicolored .90 .40
1938 A568 2.80k multicolored .90 .40
1939 A568 2.80k multicolored .90 .40
1940 A568 2.80k multicolored .90 .40
a. Bklt. pane, 2 each #1937-1940 7.50
Complete booklet, 1 #1940a 8.00
Nos. 1937-1940 (4) 3.60 1.60

European Soccer Championships, Sweden — A576

1992, Mar. 26 Engr. *Perf. 13 Vert.*

1941 A576 2.80k shown .90 .25
1942 A576 2.80k Two players .90 .25
a. Pair, #1941-1942 2.00 1.40

Sweden No. 1a A577

Litho. & Engr.

1992, Mar. 26 *Perf. 13*

1943 A577 2.80k No. 1 3.00 2.50
1944 A577 4.50k No. 1 3.00 2.50
1945 A577 5.50k shown 2.50 1.25
a. Bklt. pane, #1943-1944, 2 #1945 11.00 *11.00*
Complete booklet, 1 #1945a 12.50
Nos. 1943-1945 (3) 8.50 6.25

No. 1945a sold for 25k. Surtax benefited stamp collecting.

Sailing Ships — A578

1992, Mar. 26

1946 A578 4.50k Sprengtporten, 1785 *2.10* 1.25
1947 A578 4.50k Superb, 1855 *2.10* 1.25
1948 A578 4.50k Big T *2.10* 1.25
a. Bklt. pane of 3, #1946-1948 *6.50 6.50*

Europa. Discovery Race, Spain-Florida (No. 1948).

Children's Drawings A579

Perf. 13x12½ on 3 Sides

1992, May 21 Litho.

1949 A579 2.50k Rabbit .75 .25
1950 A579 2.50k Horses .75 .25
1951 A579 2.50k Cat .75 .25
1952 A579 2.50k Elephant .75 .25
a. Bklt. pane, 5 ea #1949-1952 15.00
Complete booklet, 1 #1952a 17.50
Nos. 1949-1952 (4) 3.00 1.00

See note after No. 1277.

Olympic Champions Type of 1991

Designs: No. 1953, Gunnar Larsson, swimming, 1972. No. 1954, Bernt Johansson, cycling, 1976. No. 1955, Anders Garderud, steeplechase, 1976. No. 1956, Gert Fredriksson, kayaking, 1948-1956.

Perf. 12x13 on 3 Sides

1992, May 21 Litho. & Engr.

1953 A568 5.50k multicolored 1.75 1.75
1954 A568 5.50k multicolored 1.75 1.75
1955 A568 5.50k multicolored 1.75 1.75
1956 A568 5.50k multicolored 1.75 1.75
a. Bklt. pane, 2 ea #1953-1956 14.00
Complete booklet, 1 #1956a 15.00
Nos. 1953-1956 (4) 7.00 7.00

Greetings Stamps — A580

No. 1957, Hand with flower. No. 1958, Cheese. No. 1959, Baby. No. 1960, Hand holding pen.

Perf. 13x12 on 3 Sides

1992, Aug. 14 Litho.

1957 A580 2.80k multi .90 .60
1958 A580 2.80k multi .90 .60
1959 A580 2.80k multi .90 .60
1960 A580 2.80k multi .90 .60
b. Bklt. pane, 2 each #1957-1960 7.25
Complete booklet, 1 #1960b 8.00
Nos. 1957-1960 (4) 3.60 2.40

88th Inter-Parliamentary Union Conference, Stockholm — A581

Swedish Patent and Registration Office, Cent. — A582

#1961, Riksdag building. #1962, First automatic lighthouse, Gustaf Dalén's sun valve.

Perf. 12½ Vert.

1992, Aug. 27 Engr.

1961 A581 2.80k violet, *tan* 1.00 .25

Perf. 13 Horiz.

1962 A582 2.80k blue & black 1.00 .25

Kitchen Maid, by Rembrandt A583

The Triumph of Venus, by Francois Boucher A584

Paintings: No. 1965, Portrait of a Girl, by Albrecht Durer. No. 1966, Rorstrand Vase, by Erik Wahlberg. No. 1967, Motif from the Seine/The Tree and the River Bend III, by Carl Fredrik Hill. No. 1968, Sergel in his Studio, by Carl Larsson.

Perf. 12½ on 3 Sides

1992, Aug. 27 Litho. & Engr.

1963 A583 5.50k multicolored 2.00 1.90
1964 A584 5.50k multicolored 2.00 1.90
1965 A583 5.50k multicolored 2.00 1.90
1966 A583 5.50k multicolored 2.00 1.90
1967 A584 5.50k multicolored 2.00 1.90
1968 A583 5.50k multicolored 2.00 1.90
a. Bklt. pane of 6, #1963-1968 12.50 *20.00*

National Museum of Fine Arts, 200th anniv.

Prehistoric Animals — A585

No. 1969, Plateosaurus. No. 1970, Thoracosaurus scanicus. No. 1971, Coelodonta antiquitatis. No. 1972, Mammuthus primigenius.

Perf. 13x12½ on 3 Sides

1992, Oct. 3 Litho. & Engr.

1969 A585 2.80k multi 1.25 .75
1970 A585 2.80k multi 1.25 .75
1971 A585 2.80k multi 1.25 .75

1972	A585	2.80k multi	1.25	.75
a.		Bklt. pane, 2 ea #1969-1972	10.00	
		Complete booklet, 1 #1972a	11.00	
		Nos. 1969-1972 (4)	5.00	3.00

No. 1972a sold for 27k to benefit stamp collecting.

1950 Automobiles — A586

1992, Oct. 3 Engr. *Perf. 12½ Vert.*

1973		4k Saab 92	1.40	1.20
1974		4k Volvo P 831	1.40	1.20
a.	A586	Pair, #1973-1974	3.00	2.50

Birds of the Baltic Shores — A587

No. 1975, Pandion haliaetus. No. 1976, Limosa limosa. No. 1977, Mergus merganser. No. 1978, Tadorna tadorna.

1992, Oct. 3 Litho. & Engr. *Perf. 13*

1975	A587	4.50k multi	1.75	.85
1976	A587	4.50k multi	1.75	.85
1977	A587	4.50k multi	1.75	.85
1978	A587	4.50k multi	1.75	.85
a.		Bklt. pane of 4, #1975-1978	7.00	*7.50*
		Complete booklet, 2 #1978a with vertical gutter	15.00	

See Estonia Nos. 231-234, Latvis Nos. 332-335, and Lithuania Nos. 427-430.

A588 A589

A590 A591

Christmas

Icons: No. 1979, Joachim and Anna, 16th cent. No. 1980, Madonna and Child, 14th cent. No. 1981, Archangel Gabriel, 12th cent. No. 1982, St. Nicholas, 16th cent.

Perf. 12½x13 on 3 Sides

1992, Nov. 27 Litho. & Engr.

1979	A588	2.30k multicolored	1.00	.35
1980	A589	2.30k multicolored	1.00	.35
1981	A590	2.30k multicolored	1.00	.35
1982	A591	2.30k multicolored	1.00	.35
a.		Bklt. pane, 3 ea #1979-1982	12.00	
		Complete booklet, #1982a	13.00	
		Nos. 1979-1982 (4)	4.00	1.40

See Russia Nos. 6103-6106.

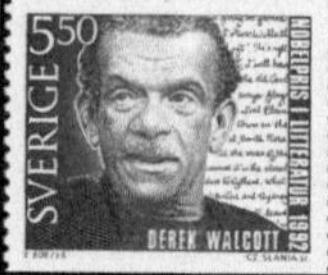

Derek Walcott, Nobel Laureate in Literature, 1992 — A592

1992, Nov. 27 Engr. *Perf. 12½ Vert.*

1983	A592	5.50k Text	1.75	1.00
1984	A592	5.50k Portrait	1.75	1.00
a.		Pair, #1983-1984	4.00	2.50

1993 Sports Championships — A593

Perf. 12½x13 on 3 Sides

1993, Jan. 28 Litho. & Engr.

1985	A593	6k Gliding	2.00	1.45
1986	A593	6k Wrestling	2.00	1.45
1987	A593	6k Table tennis	2.00	1.45
1988	A593	6k Bowling	2.00	1.45
1989	A593	6k Team handball	2.00	1.45
1990	A593	6k Cross-country skiing	2.00	1.45
a.		Booklet pane, #1985-1990	12.00	13.50
		Complete booklet, #1990a	13.00	

World Gliding Championships, Borlange (#1985). World Wrestling Championships, Stockholm (#1986). World Table Tennis Championships, Gothenburg (#1987). European Bowling Championships, Malmo (#1988). World Team Handball Championships, Gothenburg (#1989). World Cross-Country Skiing Championships, Falun (#1990).

Uppsala Convocation, 400th Anniversary A594

Litho. & Engr.

1993, Mar. 25 *Perf. 13 Vert.*

1991	A594	2.90k Stone carving	1.25	.30
1992	A594	2.90k Uppsala Cathedral	1.25	.30
a.		Pair, #1991-1992	2.50	1.50

A595

Tourist Attractions in Gothenburg: No. 1993, Roller coaster Liseberg Loop, Liseburg Amusement Park. No. 1994, Fountain of Poseidon, by Carl Milles.

1993, Mar. 25

1993	A595	3.50k multicolored	1.40	.95
1994	A595	3.50k multicolored	1.40	.95
a.		Pair, #1993-1994	3.00	2.25

A596

A596a

Fruit — A596b

No. 1995, Ribes uva crispa. No. 1996, Pyrus communis. No. 1997, Victoria plum. No. 1998, Opal plum. No. 2001, Ribes nigrum. No. 2002, Rubus idaeus. No. 2004, Prunus avium. No. 2005, James Grieve apple. No. 2008, Fragaria ananassa.

Perf. 12½ on 3 Sides

1993-95 Engr.

1995	A596	2.40k multi	.85	.45
1996	A596	2.40k multi	.85	.45
b.		Bklt. pane, 5 ea #1996-1996	8.50	
		Complete booklet, #1996b	9.00	
1997	A596a	2.80k multi	1.00	.50
1998	A596a	2.80k multi	1.00	.50
b.		Bklt. pane, 5 ea #1997-1998	10.00	
		Complete booklet, #1998b	11.00	
2001	A596b	3.35k multi	1.15	.35
2002	A596b	3.35k multi	1.15	.35
a.		Bklt. pane, 5 ea #2001-2002	11.50	
		Complete booklet, #2002a	12.00	

Perf. 12½ Vert.

2004	A596	2.40k multi	.80	.50
2005	A596a	2.80k multi	1.10	.60

Perf. 12½ Horiz.

2008	A596b	3.35k multi	1.15	.40
		Nos. 1995-2008 (9)	9.05	4.10

Issued: #1995-1996, 2004, 3/25/93; #1997-1998, 2005, 1/17/94; #2000-2001, 2008, 1/2/95.

Oxe-eye Daisy — A597

Poppy — A598

Buttercup A599

Bluebell A600

Perf. 12½x13 on 3 Sides

1993, May 21 Litho.

2013	A597	2.60k multicolored	.90	.25
2014	A598	2.60k multicolored	.90	.25
2015	A599	2.60k multicolored	.90	.25
2016	A600	2.60k multicolored	.90	.25
b.		Bklt. pane, 5 ea #2013-2016	18.00	
		Complete booklet, #2016b	20.00	
		Nos. 2013-2016 (4)	3.60	1.00

See note after No. 1277.

Contemporary Art — A601

Europa: No. 2017, Oguasark, by Olle Baertling (1911-81). No. 2018, Ade-Lidic-Nander II, by Oyvind Fahlstrom (1928-76), horiz. No. 2019, The Cubist Chair, by Otto G. Carlsund (1897-1948).

Litho. & Engr.

1993, May 21 *Perf. 13*

2017	A601	5k multicolored	1.75	1.45
2018	A601	5k multicolored	1.75	1.45
2019	A601	5k multicolored	1.75	1.45
a.		Booklet pane of 3, #2017-2019	5.50	*7.50*

Butterflies — A602

No. 2020, Papilio machaon. No. 2021, Nymphalis antiopa. No. 2022, Colias palaeno. No. 2023, Euphydryas maturna.

1993, May 21 *Perf. 12½ Horiz.*

2020	A602	6k multicolored	1.90	1.50
2021	A602	6k multicolored	1.90	1.50
2022	A602	6k multicolored	1.90	1.50
2023	A602	6k multicolored	1.90	1.50
a.		Booklet pane, 2 each #2020-2023 with gutter between	15.00	
		Complete booklet, #2023a	16.00	
		Nos. 2020-2023 (4)	7.60	6.00

A603 A604

A605 A606

Greetings

Perf. 13 on 3 Sides

1993, Aug. 6 Litho.

2024	A603	2.90k multicolored	.80	.30
2025	A604	2.90k multicolored	.80	.45
2026	A605	2.90k multicolored	.80	.30
2027	A606	2.90k multicolored	.80	.45
b.		Booklet pane, 3 each #2024, 2026, 2 each #2025, 2027	8.00	
		Complete booklet, #2027b	9.00	
		Nos. 2024-2027 (4)	3.20	1.50

Sea Birds A607

No. 2028, Mergus serrator. No. 2029, Melanitta fusca. No. 2030, Aythya fuligula. No. 2031, Somateria mollissima.

Perf. 12½ Horiz.

1993, Aug. 26 Engr.

2028	A607	5k multi	1.50	1.20
2029	A607	5k multi	1.50	1.20
2030	A607	5k multi	1.50	1.20
2031	A607	5k multi	1.50	1.20
a.		Booklet pane, 2 each #2028-2031 with gutter between	12.00	
		Complete booklet, #2031a	13.00	
		Nos. 2028-2031 (4)	6.00	4.80

A608

No. 2032, Modern echo sounding. No. 2033, 1643 Method.

1993, Oct. 2 Engr. *Perf. 13 Vert.*

2032		2.90k multi	1.00	.30
2033		2.90k multi	1.00	.30
a.	A608	Pair, #2032-2033	2.50	1.45

Hydrographic survey.

King Holding Flag — A609

No. 2035, King Carl XVI Gustaf. No. 2036, Queen Silvia. No. 2037, Royal family.

1993, Oct. 2 Engr. *Perf. 13*

2034	A609	8k multi	3.00	1.60
2035	A609	10k multi	3.00	1.75
2036	A609	10k multi	3.00	1.75

Size: 75x43mm

2037	A609	12k multi	3.00	2.75
a.		Booklet pane, #2034-2037	12.50	14.00
		Nos. 2034-2037 (4)	12.00	7.85

Reign of King Carl XVI Gustaf, 20th anniv.

Christmas — A610

Perf. 12½ on 3 Sides

1993, Nov. 25 **Engr.**

2038 A610 2.40k Plaited heart .80 .25
2039 A610 2.40k Straw goat .80 .25
b. Bklt pane, 5 ea #2038-2039 8.00
Complete booklet, #2039b 9.00

Toni Morrison, Nobel laureate in Literature, 1993 — A611

#2041, Stockholm City Hall.

1993, Nov. 25 **Engr.** ***Perf. 12½ Vert.***

2040 A611 6k red brown & brown 2.00 1.00
2041 A611 6k multicolored 2.00 1.00
a. Pair, #2040-2041 5.00 5.00

European Economic Assoc. Agreement A612

1994, Jan. 17 ***Perf. 12½ Vert.***

2042 A612 5k Mother Svea 1.75 .35

Domestic Animals — A613

No. 2047, North Sweden horse, vert. No. 2048, Two horses, vert. No. 2049, Red polled cattle, vert. No. 2050, Goat, vert. No. 2054, Swedish dwarf poultry. No. 2055, Gotland sheep. No. 2059, Mountain cow. No. 2060, Scanian goose. No. 2060A, Yellow duck.

1994-95 **Engr.** ***Perf. 13 on 3 Sides***

2047 A613 3.20k multicolored .90 .30
2048 A613 3.20k multicolored .90 .30
a. Bklt. pane, 5 ea #2047-2048 9.00
2049 A613 3.70k multicolored 1.25 .30
2050 A613 3.70k multicolored 1.25 .30
a. Bklt. pane, 5 ea #2049-2050 12.50
Complete booklet, #2050a 12.50

Perf. 13 Vert.

2054 A613 3.10k multicolored 1.40 .25
2055 A613 3.20k multicolored .90 .25
2059 A613 6.40k multicolored 2.40 .35
2060 A613 7.40k multicolored 3.25 .35
2060A A613 7.50k multicolored 3.25 1.75
Nos. 2047-2060A (9) 15.50 4.15

Issued: #2047-2048, 2055, 2059, 1/17/94; #2049-2050, 2054, 1/2/95; 2060-2060A, 3/17/95.

Cats — A614

Litho. & Engr.

1994, Mar. 18 ***Perf. 13***

2061 A614 4.50k Siamese 1.50 1.15
2062 A614 4.50k Persian 1.50 1.15
2063 A614 4.50k European 1.50 1.15
2064 A614 4.50k Abyssinian 1.50 1.15
a. Booklet pane of 4, #2061-2064 7.00 8.00

Roman De La Rose — A615

Swedish, French Flags A616

Swedish-French cultural relations: No. 2067, House of the Nobility, designed by Simon and Jean de la Vallee. No. 2068, Household Chores, by Hillestrom. No. 2069, Banquet for Gustavus III at the Trianon, 1784, by Lafrensen. No. 2070, Charles XIV John, by Gerard.

Litho. & Engr., Litho. (#2066)

1994, Mar. 18 ***Perf. 13 on 3 Sides***

2065 A615 5k multicolored 1.50 1.25
2066 A616 5k multicolored 1.50 1.25
2067 A615 5k multicolored 1.50 1.25
2068 A615 5k multicolored 1.50 1.25
2069 A616 5k multicolored 1.50 1.25
2070 A615 5k multicolored 1.50 1.25
a. Booklet pane of 6, #2065-2070 9.00 10.00

See France Nos. 2410-2415.

Roses — A617

No. 2071, Nyponros rosa dumalis. No. 2072, Rosa alba maxima. No. 2073, Tuscany superb. No. 2074, Peace. No. 2075, Quatre saisons.

Perf. 12½x13 on 3 Sides

1994, May 11 **Litho.**

2071 A617 3.20k multicolored .90 .25
2072 A617 3.20k multicolored .90 .25
2073 A617 3.20k multicolored .90 .25
2074 A617 3.20k multicolored .90 .25
2075 A617 3.20k multicolored .90 .25
a. Bklt. pane, 2 ea #2071-2075 9.00
Nos. 2071-2075 (5) 4.50 1.25

Swedish Design — A618

#2076, Vase with Irises, by Gunnar Wennerberg, 1897. #2077, Table and Chair, by Carl Malmsten; Wallpaper, by Uno Ahren, 1917. #2078, Cabinet, 1940s, and textile, 1920s, by Josef Franck. #2079, Fireworks Bowl, by Edward Hald, 1921. #2080, Silver water jug, by Wiwen Nilsson, 1941. #2081, Towel, by Astrid Sampe; Plate, by Stig Lindberg; Fork and Spoon, by Sigurd Persson, 1955.

Perf. 12½ on 3 Sides

1994, May 11 **Litho. & Engr.**

2076 A618 6.50k multicolored 2.00 2.00
2077 A618 6.50k multicolored 2.00 2.00
2078 A618 6.50k multicolored 2.00 2.00
2079 A618 6.50k multicolored 2.00 2.00
2080 A618 6.50k multicolored 2.00 2.00
2081 A618 6.50k multicolored 2.00 2.00
a. Bklt. pane, #2076-2081 12.50 *12.00*

1994 World Cup Soccer Championships, US — A619

1994, May 11 **Engr.** ***Perf. 12½ Vert.***

2082 A619 3.20k red & blue 1.25 .30

First Manned Moon Landing, 25th Anniv. A620

1994, May 11

2083 A620 6.50k multicolored 2.00 1.15

Greetings A621

Perf. 12½ on 3 Sides

1994, Aug. 5 **Litho.**

2084 A621 3.20k Cat 1.10 .25
2085 A621 3.20k Snail 1.10 .25
2086 A621 3.20k Frog 1.20 .70
2087 A621 3.20k Dog 1.20 .70
a. Booklet pane, 3 each #2084-2085, 2 each #2086-2087 10.00
Nos. 2084-2087 (4) 4.60 1.90

Swedish Explorers A622

Europa: No. 2088, Erland Nordenskiold (1877-1932), explored South America. No. 2089, Eric Von Rosen (1879-1948), explored Africa. No. 2090, Sten Bergman (1895-1975), explored Asia and the Pacific.

Litho. & Engr.

1994, Aug. 26 ***Perf. 12½***

2088 A622 5.50k multicolored 1.75 1.40
2089 A622 5.50k multicolored 1.75 1.40
2090 A622 5.50k multicolored 1.75 1.40
a. Booklet pane of 3, #2088-2090 5.50 6.50

Finland-Sweden Track and Field Meet — A623

#2091, Seppo Raty, Finland, javelin. #2092, Patrick Sjoberg, Sweden, high jump.

1994, Aug. 26 ***Perf. 12½ on 3 Sides***

2091 A623 4.50k multicolored 1.50 1.35
2092 A623 4.50k multicolored 1.50 1.35
a. Bklt. pane, 2 ea #2091-2092 7.00 7.25

See Finland Nos. 942-943.

Johan Helmich Roman (1694-1758), Composer A624

No. 2094, Opera House, Gothenburg.

Perf. 12½ Vert.

1994, Aug. 26 **Engr.**

2093 A624 3.20k multicolored 1.00 .25
2094 A624 3.20k multicolored 1.00 .25

Yes & No Stamps — A625

1994, Oct. 1 **Litho.** ***Perf. 12½ Vert.***

2095 A625 3.20k Ja 1.00 .30
2096 A625 3.20k Nej 1.00 .30

See Nos. 2107-2108.

World Wildlife Fund — A626

#2097, Sterna caspia. #2098, Haliaeetus albicilla. #2099, Dendrocopos leucotos. #2100, Anser erythropus.

Litho. & Engr.

1994, Oct. 1 ***Perf. 12½***

2097 A626 5.50k multicolored 2.00 .90
2098 A626 5.50k multicolored 2.00 .90
2099 A626 5.50k multicolored 2.00 .90
2100 A626 5.50k multicolored 2.00 .90
a. Booklet pane of 4, #2097-2100 8.00 *10.00*

Frans G. Bengtsson (1894-1954), Writer — A627

1994, Oct. 1 **Engr.** ***Perf. 12½ Vert.***

2101 A627 6.40k multicolored 2.00 1.00

Nobel Laureates in Literature A628

Designs: 4.50k, Erik Axel Karlfeldt (1864-1931). 5.50k, Eyvind Johnson (1900-76). 6.50k, Harry Martinson (1904-78).

1994, Nov. 11

2102 A628 4.50k multicolored 1.35 .55
2103 A628 5.50k multicolored 1.70 .80
2104 A628 6.50k multicolored 2.00 .70
Nos. 2102-2104 (3) 5.05 2.05

Christmas — A629

Scenes from medieval altar pieces: No. 2105, Annunciation. No. 2106, Flight to Egypt.

Perf. 12½x13 on 3 Sides

1994, Nov. 11 **Litho. & Engr.**

2105 A629 2.80k multicolored 1.00 .25
2106 A629 2.80k multicolored 1.00 .25
a. Bklt. pane, 5 ea #2105-2106 10.00

Yes & No Type of 1994

1995, Jan. 2 **Litho.** ***Perf. 12½ Vert.***

2107 A625 3.70k Ja 1.00 .30
2108 A625 3.70k Nej 1.00 .30

Houses A630

Designs: No. 2109, Country cottage. No. 2110, Soldier's log house. No. 2111, Farmhouse courtyard. No. 2112, Timbered farmhouse. No. 2113, Manor house.

Perf. 14 Horiz.

1995, Mar. 17 **Litho. & Engr.**

2109	A630	3.70k multicolored	1.00	.30
2110	A630	3.70k multicolored	1.00	.30
2111	A630	3.70k multicolored	1.00	.30
2112	A630	3.70k multicolored	1.00	.30
2113	A630	3.70k multicolored	1.00	.30
a.		Booklet pane of 5, #2109-2113	5.00	8.00
		Complete booklet, #2113a	6.00	

1995 Ice Hockey World Championships — A631

1995 World Track & Field Championships A632

Litho. & Engr.

1995, Mar. 17 ***Perf. 13 Vert.***

2114	A631	3.70k multicolored	1.50	.60

Perf. 13 Horiz.

2115	A632	3.70k multicolored	1.00	.30

See No. 2702.

A633

Wood Sculptures, by Bror Hjorth — A634

Europa: Nos. 2116, 2118, Walt Whitman, Christ, Socrates. Nos. 2117, 2119, Patrice Lumumba, Albert Schweitzer, children dancing.

1995, Mar. 17 **Litho.** ***Perf. 13***

2116	A633	5k multicolored	1.70	1.30
2117	A634	5k multicolored	1.70	1.30
2118	A633	6k multicolored	2.00	1.45
2119	A634	6k multicolored	2.00	1.45
a.		Bklt. pane of 4, #2116-2119	7.40	*10.00*
		Complete booklet, 2 #2119a	15.00	

Swedish Membership in European Union — A635

1995, Mar. 17 ***Perf. 13 Vert.***

2120	A635	6k multicolored	2.00	.55

Rock Speedwell A636

Cloudberry A637

Mountain Heath — A638

Alpine Arnica — A639

Perf. 13 on 3 Sides

1995, May 12 **Litho.**

2121	A636	3.70k multicolored	1.00	.35
2122	A637	3.70k multicolored	1.25	.35
2123	A638	3.70k multicolored	1.00	.35
2124	A639	3.70k multicolored	1.25	.35
a.		Booklet pane, 3 each #2121, 2123, 2 each #2122, 2124	9.00	
		Complete booklet, #2124a	9.00	
		Nos. 2121-2124 (4)	4.50	1.40

Tourist Attractions — A640

No. 2125, Canal boat Wilhelm Tham on Gota Canal. No. 2126, Sail boat anchored on Lake Vattern.

1995, May 12 **Engr.**

2125	A640	5k dark green	1.50	1.00
2126	A640	5k dark violet	1.50	1.00
a.		Bklt. pane, 2 ea #2125-2126	6.00	
		Complete booklet, #2126a	6.00	

Trams A641

#2127, Gothenburg, c. 1900. #2128, Norrkoping, 1905. #2129, Helsingborg, 1921. #2130, Kiruna, 1958. #2131, Stockholm, 1967.

1995, May 12 ***Perf. 13 Horiz.***

2127	A641	7.50k rose claret	2.00	2.00
2128	A641	7.50k dp brown vio	2.00	2.00
2129	A641	7.50k dk green	2.00	2.00
2130	A641	7.50k dk gray violet	2.00	2.00
2131	A641	7.50k dk violet blue	2.00	2.00
a.		Bklt. pane of 5, #2127-2131	10.00	11.00
		Complete booklet, #2131a	10.00	

UN, 50th Anniv. A642

1995, Aug. 3 **Engr.** ***Perf. 13 Vert.***

2132	A642	3.70k multicolored	1.00	.25

Greetings A643

Children's drawings: No. 2133, "The Ball is Yours," by M. Angesjo. No. 2134, Happy man, by E. Sandstrom. No. 2135, Teddy Bear saying "I miss you," by L. Nordenhem. No. 2136, Mussel saying "Hello," by C. Stenbom.

1995, Aug. 3 **Litho.** ***Perf. 13x12½***

2133	A643	3.70k multicolored	1.20	.25
2134	A643	3.70k multicolored	1.20	.25
2135	A643	3.70k multicolored	1.40	.55
2136	A643	3.70k multicolored	1.40	.55
a.		Booklet pane, 3 each #2133-2134, 2 each #2135-2136	12.75	
		Complete booklet, No. #2136a	13.00	
		Nos. 2133-2136 (4)	5.20	1.60

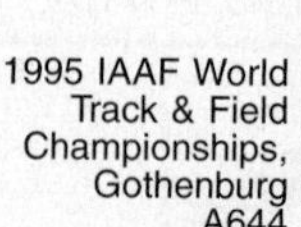

1995 IAAF World Track & Field Championships, Gothenburg A644

Perf. 13 Horiz.

1995, Aug. 3 **Litho. & Engr.**

2137	A644	7.50k Maria Akraka	2.00	1.15

Motion Picture, Cent. A645

Scenes from films: No. 2138, Soldier Bom, 1948. No. 2139, Sir Arne's Treasure, 1919. No. 2140, Wild Strawberries, 1957. No. 2141, House of Angels, 1992. No. 2142, One Summer of Happiness, 1951. No. 2143, The Apple War, 1971.

Litho. & Engr.

1995, Oct. 7 ***Perf. 12½x13***

Booklet Stamps

2138	A645	6k multicolored	2.00	1.45
2139	A645	6k multicolored	2.00	1.45
2140	A645	6k multicolored	2.00	1.45
2141	A645	6k multicolored	2.00	1.45
2142	A645	6k multicolored	2.00	1.45
2143	A645	6k multicolored	2.00	1.45
a.		Booklet pane, #2138-2143	12.00	*18.00*
		Complete booklet, #2143a	12.50	

Fritiof Nilsson (1895-1972), Writer — A646

Litho. & Engr.

1995, Oct. 27 ***Perf. 13 Vert.***

2144	A646	3.70k blue & claret	1.00	.25

Ancient Artifacts — A647

Designs: No. 2145, Bronze cult figures of man with beak, nude woman, Bronze Age. No. 2146, Detail of gold collar, Great Migration period. No. 2147, Bracteate pendant picturing figure on horse, Great Migration period. No. 2148, Circular bronze cult object, Bronze Age.

1995, Oct. 27 ***Perf. 13***

2145	A647	3.70k multicolored	1.00	.65
2146	A647	3.70k multicolored	1.00	.65
2147	A647	3.70k multicolored	1.00	.65
2148	A647	3.70k multicolored	1.00	.65
a.		Booklet pane of 4, #2145-2148	4.00	*7.50*
		Complete booklet, 2 #2148a	8.00	

A648

Tycho Brache (1546-1601), Astronomer: 5k, Uranienborg Observatory, Ven Island. 6k, Sextant.

Litho. & Engr.

1995, Oct. 27 ***Perf. 13 Vert.***

2149	A648	5k multicolored	1.35	.65
2150	A648	6k multicolored	1.90	1.15

See Denmark Nos. 1035-1036.

A649

Christmas candlesticks.

Perf. 12½x13 on 3 Sides

1995, Nov. 9 **Litho.**

2151	A649	3.35k Santa	.85	.25
2152	A649	3.35k Apple	1.15	.40
2153	A649	3.35k Wrought iron	.85	.25
2154	A649	3.35k Red wooden	1.15	.40
a.		Booklet pane, 3 ea #2151, 2153, 2 ea #2152, 2154	9.75	
		Complete booklet, No. 2151a	9.75	
		Nos. 2151-2154 (4)	4.00	1.30

Nobel Prize Fund Established, Cent. — A650

Designs: No. 2155, Alfred Nobel, last will and testament. No. 2156, Nobel's home, 59 Avenue de de Malakoff, Paris. No. 2157, Björkborn Laboratory, Karlkoga. No. 2158, Wilhelm Röntgen receiving the first physics prize, 1901.

Photo. & Engr.

1995, Nov. 9 ***Perf. 13 Horiz.***

2155	A650	6k multicolored	1.75	1.45
2156	A650	6k multicolored	1.75	1.45
2157	A650	6k multicolored	1.75	1.45
2158	A650	6k multicolored	1.75	1.45
a.		Booklet pane, #2155-2158	7.00	7.50
		Complete booklet, No. 2158a	7.00	

Holly — A651

Rowan Berries — A652

Rose Hips & Juniper — A653

Lingonberries & Sloe — A654

1996, Jan. 2 **Litho.** ***Perf. 13 Horiz.***

2159	A651	3.50k multicolored	1.10	.40
2160	A652	7.50k multicolored	2.50	.85

Perf. 13 on 3 Sides

2161	A653	3.50k multicolored	1.00	.40
2162	A654	3.50k multicolored	1.00	.40
a.		Bklt. pane, 5 ea, #2161-2162	10.00	
		Complete booklet, #2162a	10.00	
		Nos. 2159-2162 (4)	5.60	2.05

End of Railway Mail Sorting — A655

1996, Mar. 29 Engr. *Perf. 13 Vert.*

2163 A655 6k multicolored 2.00 .80

King Carl XVI Gustaf, 50th Birthday — A656

King Carl XVI Gustaf: No. 2164, In forest. No. 2165, In front of portrait of King Charles XIV John. No. 2166, In carriage with King Albert of Belgium, 1994. 20kr, With family.

Litho. & Engr.

1996, Apr. 19 *Perf. 13x12½*

2164 A656 10k multicolored 3.00 3.00
2165 A656 10k multicolored 3.00 3.00
2166 A656 10k multicolored 3.00 3.00

Size: 80x48mm

2167 A656 20k multicolored 6.00 5.50
a. Booklet pane, #2164-2167 15.00 19.50

Historic Buildings — A657

Designs: No. 2168, Railway station, Halsingland. No. 2169, Motala Assembly Hall, Ostergotland. No. 2170, Parish storehouse, Smaland. No. 2171, Half-timbered barn, Vasterbotten. No. 2172, Sheep shelter, Gotland. No. 2173, Old Town Hall, Lidkoping.

Perf. 13 on 2 or 3 Sides

1996, Apr. 19

2168 A657 3.85k multicolored 1.25 .50
2169 A657 3.85k multicolored 1.25 .50

Size: 28x29mm

2170 A657 3.85k multicolored 1.25 .60
2171 A657 3.85k multicolored 1.25 .60

Size: 28x38mm

2172 A657 3.85k multicolored 1.25 .60
2173 A657 3.85k multicolored 1.25 .60
a. Booklet pane of 6, #2168-2173 7.50 7.50

Famous Women — A658

Europa: No. 2174, Karin Kock (1891-1976), economist. No. 2175, Astrid Lindgren (b. 1907), creator of Pippi Longstocking.

Perf. 13 on 3 Sides

1996, May 3 Engr.

2174 A658 6k multicolored 2.75 1.40
2175 A658 6k multicolored 2.75 1.40
a. Bklt. pane, 2 ea #2174-2175 11.00
Complete booklet, #2175a 11.00

Summer Scenes A659

Paintings by: No. 2176, Sven X:Et Erixson (1899-1970). No. 2177, Roland Svensson (b. 1910). No. 2178, Eric Hallström (1893-1946), No. 2179, Thage Nordholm (1927-90). No. 2180, Ragnar Sandberg (1902-72).

Perf. 13 on 2 Sides

1996, May 24 Litho.

2176 A659 3.85k multicolored 1.20 .25
2177 A659 3.85k multicolored 1.20 .25
2178 A659 3.85k multicolored 1.20 .25
2179 A659 3.85k multicolored 1.20 .25
2180 A659 3.85k multicolored 1.20 .25
a. Bklt. pane, 2 ea #2176-2180 12.00
Complete booklet, #2180a 12.00
Nos. 2176-2180 (5) 6.00 1.25

Golf — A660

1996, Aug. 23 Engr. *Perf. 13 Horiz.*

2181 A660 3.50k dark green, *buff* 1.50 .60

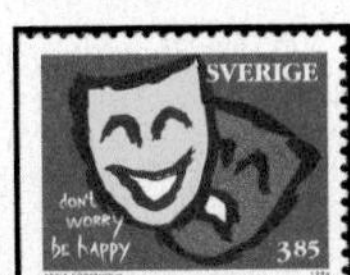

Greetings Stamps — A661

Designs: No. 2182, Masks of comedy, tragedy, "don't worry, be happy." No. 2183, Hearts, "Var Glad (Be happy)," vert. No. 2184, Posthorn. No. 2185, Hearts, person, "Minns du mig? (Do you remember me?)."

Perf. 13x12½ on 3 Sides

1996, Aug. 23 Litho.

2182 A661 3.85k multicolored 1.10 .25
2183 A661 3.85k multicolored 1.10 .25
2184 A661 3.85k multicolored 1.25 .30
2185 A661 3.85k multicolored 1.25 .30
a. Booklet pane, 3 each #2182-2183, 2 each #2184-2185 12.00
Complete booklet, #2185a 12.00
Nos. 2182-2185 (4) 4.70 1.10

Mushrooms — A662

3.85k, Boletus edulis. #2187, Russula integra. #2188, Cantharellus cibarius. #2189, Craterellus cornucopioides. #2190, Coprinus comatus.

Perf. 13 Horiz.

1996, Aug. 23 Litho. & Engr.

2186 A662 3.85k multicolored 1.60 .25

Perf. 12½x13 on 3 Sides

2187 A662 5k multicolored 1.60 .80
2188 A662 5k multicolored 1.60 .80
2189 A662 5k multicolored 1.60 .80
2190 A662 5k multicolored 1.60 .80
a. Booklet pane of 4, #2187-2190 6.40 7.00
Complete booklet, #2190a 6.40
Nos. 2186-2190 (5) 8.00 3.45

Ecopark, Stockholm A663

Designs: No. 2191, Pelousen, grassy area, Haga Park. No. 2192, Copper tents, Haga Park. No. 2193, Rosendals Palace, roe deer. No. 2194, Isbladskarret, marsh birds.

Litho. & Engr.

1996, Aug. 23 *Perf. 12½Vert.*

2191 A663 7.50k multicolored 2.50 2.10
2192 A663 7.50k multicolored 2.50 2.10
2193 A663 7.50k multicolored 2.50 2.10
2194 A663 7.50k multicolored 2.50 2.10
a. Booklet pane of 4, #2191-2194 10.00 10.75
Complete booklet, #2194a 10.00

Four Decades A664

Designs: No. 2195, Errand boy, 1930's. No. 2196, Flower child, 1960's. No. 2197, Zootsuiter, 1940's. No. 2198, Biker, 1950's.

Perf. 12½x13 on 3 Sides

1996, Oct. 5 Litho. & Engr.

2195 A664 3.85k multicolored 1.15 .30
2196 A664 3.85k multicolored 1.50 .90
2197 A664 3.85k multicolored 1.15 .30
2198 A664 3.85k multicolored 1.50 .90
a. Bklt. pane, 3 ea #2195, 2197, 2 ea #2196, 2198 13.00
Complete booklet, #2198a 13.00
Nos. 2195-2198 (4) 5.30 2.40

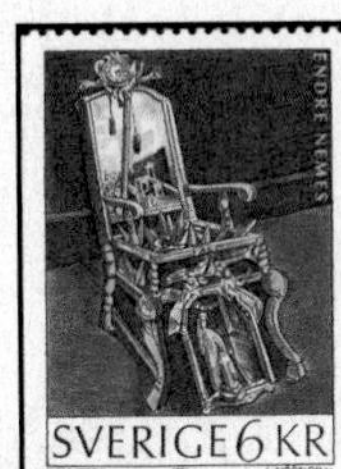

The Baroque Chair, by Endre Nemes — A665

1996, Oct. 5 *Perf. 12½ Horiz.*

2199 A665 6k multicolored 2.00 1.00

See Czech Republic #2995, Slovakia #255.

Christmas A666

Illustrations from Book of Hours (15th cent.): No. 2200, The Annunciation. No. 2201, The Birth. No. 2202, Adoration of the Magi.

Perf. 12½ Vert.

1996, Nov. 8 Litho. & Engr.

2200 A666 3.50k multicolored 1.15 .65

Perf. 12½x13 on 3 Sides

2201 A666 3.50k multicolored 1.00 .25
2202 A666 3.50k multicolored 1.00 .25
a. Bklt. pane, 5 ea #2201-2202 10.00
Complete booklet, #2202a 10.00
Nos. 2200-2202 (3) 3.15 1.15

Nobel Laureates in Physiology or Medicine — A667

#2203, Sune Bergström (b. 1916), medical chemist. #2204, Bengt Samuelsson (b. 1934), medical chemist. #2205, Hugo Theorell (1903-82), biochemist. #2206, Ragnar Granit (1900-91), neurophysiologist.

Perf. 13x12½ on 3 Sides

1996, Nov. 8 Engr.

2203 A667 5k bl, grn & blk + label 1.50 .75
2204 A667 5k grn, bl & blk + label 1.50 .75
2205 A667 5k bl, grn & blk + label 2.00 1.25
2206 A667 5k grn & blk + label 2.00 1.25
a. Booklet pane, 3 each #2203-#2204, 2 each #2205-2206 17.00
Complete booklet, #2206a 17.00
Nos. 2203-2206 (4) 7.00 4.00

Wild Animal Types of 1992

1997, Jan. 2 Engr. *Perf. 13 Vert.*

2207 A574 3.20k Gulo gulo 1.25 1.10
2208 A574 3.50k Nyclea scandiaca 1.25 .70

Perf. 13 Horiz.

2209 A575 7.70k Ciconia ciconia 4.25 4.25
Nos. 2207-2209 (3) 6.75 6.05

Churches — A668

Perf. 13 Horiz.

1997, Jan. 2 Litho. & Engr.

2210 A668 3.85k Dalby 1.30 1.00
2211 A668 3.85k Vendel 1.30 1.00

Size: 27x23mm

Perf. 13x12½ on 2 or 3 Sides

2212 A668 3.85k Hagby 1.30 1.00
2213 A668 3.85k Overtornea 1.30 1.00

Size: 27x37mm

2214 A668 3.85k Varnhem 1.30 1.00
2215 A668 3.85k Ostra Amtervik 1.30 1.00
a. Booklet pane of 6, #2210-2215 8.00 8.00
Complete booklet, #2215a 8.00

Kalmar Union, 600th Anniv. — A669

Design: Queen Margareta, Erik of Pomerania, coronation document.

1997, Jan. 2 Engr. *Perf. 12½ Vert.*

2216 A669 3.85k dark blue 1.25 .25

Valentine's Day — A670

Perf. 13x12½ on 3 Sides

1997, Jan. 2 Litho.

2217 A670 3.85k gray & multi 1.25 .45
2218 A670 3.85k yellow & multi 1.25 .45
a. Bklt. pane, 5 ea #2217-2218 12.50
Complete booklet, #2218a 12.50

Stamps that follow, with denominations in parenthesis, are inscribed "Brev," "Ekonomibrev," "Foreningsbrev," etc.

Wild Animals — A671

No. 2219, Alopex lagopus. No. 2220, Equus przewalskii. No. 2221, Panthera uncia, adult. No. 2222, same, cubs.

Perf. 13 on 2 Sides

1997, Feb. 28 Engr.

2219 A671 (4.50k) multi 1.10 .30
2220 A671 (5k) multi 1.80 .25

Perf. 13 on 3 Sides

2221 A671 (5k) multi 1.80 .25
2222 A671 (5k) multi 1.80 .25
a. Bklt. pane, 3 ea #2221-2222 11.00
Complete booklet, #2222a 11.00
Complete booklet, 1 ea #2221-2222 6.00
Nos. 2219-2222 (4) 6.50 1.05

No. 2220 is 28x21mm.

Easter Stamps — A672

Perf. 13x12½ on 3 Sides

1997, Feb. 28 **Litho.**

2223 A672 (5k) Rooster 2.25 .30
2224 A672 (5k) Daffodils 2.25 .30
a. Bklt. pane, 3 ea #2223-2224 13.50
Complete booklet, #2224a 13.50

Pheasants A673

Designs: No. 2225, Phasianus colchicus. No. 2226, Chrysolophus amherstiae.

Perf. 12½ Horiz.

1997, May 9 **Litho. & Engr.**

2225 A673 2k multicolored 1.00 .30
2226 A673 2k multicolored 1.00 .30
a. Pair, #2225-2226 2.25 1.10

See China (PRC) Nos. 2763-2764.

Garden Flowers — A674

#2227, Iris sibirica. #2228, Lonicera periclymenum. #2229, Aquilegia vulgaris. #2230, Hemerocallis flava. #2231, Viola x wittrokiana.

1997, May 9 **Litho.** ***Perf. 12½x13***

2227 A674 (5k) multicolored 1.50 .25
2228 A674 (5k) multicolored 1.50 .25
2229 A674 (5k) multicolored 1.50 .25
2230 A674 (5k) multicolored 1.50 .25
2231 A674 (5k) multicolored 1.50 .25
a. Bklt. pane, 2 ea #2227-2231 15.00
Complete booklet, #2231a 15.00
Nos. 2227-2231 (5) 7.50 1.25

A675

A676

6k, Ship's figurehead, 18th cent., Naval Museum, Karlskrona. 7k, Compass rose, 18th cent. atlas. 8k, Compass rose, 1568 atlas.

Perf. 12½ Vert.

1997, May 9 **Litho. & Engr.**

2232 A675 6k multicolored 2.50 1.25

Litho.

Perf. 12½ Horiz.

2233 A676 7k multicolored 2.50 1.60
2234 A676 8k multicolored 3.00 4.65
Nos. 2232-2234 (3) 8.00 7.50

18th Intl. Cartographic Conf. (#2233-2234).

Gnomes and Trolls — A677

Illustrations from "Among Trolls and Sprites," by John Bauer: No. 2235, Troll looking through treasure chest, gnome. No. 2236, Trolls looking at girl seated on rock. No. 2237, Troll talking with boy.

Litho. & Engr.

1997, May 9 ***Perf. 12x13***

2235 A677 7k multicolored 2.00 1.00
2236 A677 7k multicolored 2.00 1.00
2237 A677 7k multicolored 2.00 1.00
a. Bklt. pane, 2 ea, #2235-2237 12.00
Complete booklet, #2237a 12.00
Nos. 2235-2237 (3) 6.00 3.00

Europa.

Wild Animal Type of 1992

No. 2238, Ailurus fulgens, vert.

Perf. 12½ Horiz.

1997, Aug. 21 **Engr.**

2238 A575 (3.50k) multi 2.00 1.50

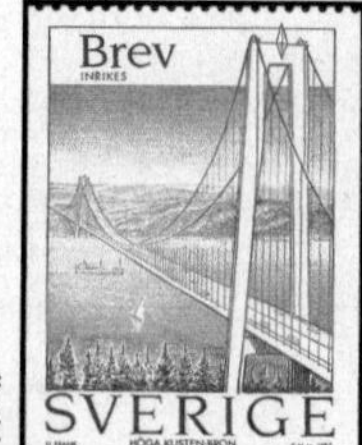

Construction of High Coast Bridge — A678

1997, Aug. 21

2239 A678 (5k) multicolored 1.75 1.05

Swedish Elk A679

Designs: No. 2240, Elk as fantasy character. No. 2241, Bar code elk. No. 2242, Swedish elk, yellow bars. No. 2243, Forest elk, green background. No. 2244, Road sign elk, black silhouette against yellow. No. 2245, Old Norse elks, adult & calf.

1997, Aug. 21 **Litho.** ***Perf. 13***

2240 A679 (5k) multicolored 1.80 .60
2241 A679 (5k) multicolored 1.80 .60
2242 A679 (5k) multicolored 1.80 .60
2243 A679 (5k) multicolored 1.80 .60
2244 A679 (5k) multicolored 1.80 .60
2245 A679 (5k) multicolored 1.80 .60
a. Booklet pane, #2240-2245 12.00 10.50
Complete booklet, #2245a 12.00

Perforations at each corner of Nos. 2240-2245 end in a large hole within the pane or semi-circles at the edges of the pane, giving the corners of each stamp a slightly concave appearance.

King Gustav III's Museum of Antiquities, Stockholm Palace — A680

Perf. 13x12½ on 3 Sides

1997, Aug. 21 **Engr.**

2246 A680 8k Muses Gallery 3.00 2.40
2247 A680 8k Endymion 3.00 2.40
a. Booklet pane, 2 each #2246-2247 + 4 labels 12.00
Complete booklet, #2247a 12.00

Classic Cars A681

#2248, 1958 Volvo Duett. #2249, 1955 Chevrolet Bel-Air. #2250, 1959 Porsche 356A Coupé. #2251, 1952, Citroen B11. #2252, 1963 Saab 96. #2253, 1961 E-Type Jaguar.

Perf. 12½x13 on 3 Sides

1997, Oct. 4 **Litho. & Engr.**

Booklet Stamps

2248 A681 (5k) multicolored 2.00 1.75
2249 A681 (5k) multicolored 2.00 1.75
2250 A681 (5k) multicolored 2.00 1.75
2251 A681 (5k) multicolored 2.00 1.75
2252 A681 (5k) multicolored 2.00 1.75
2253 A681 (5k) multicolored 2.00 1.75
a. Booklet pane, #2248-2253 12.00 12.00
Complete booklet, #2253a 12.00

Alfred Nobel (1833-1896), Founder of Nobel Prize — A682

Design: No. 2255, Paul Karrer (1889-1971), winner of Nobel prize for chemistry, 1937.

Perf. 12½x13 on 3 Sides

1997, Nov. 13 **Litho. & Engr.**

2254 A682 7k lt pink & black 2.50 2.00
2255 A682 7k gray & black 2.50 2.00
a. Bklt. pane, 2 ea #2254-2255 10.00 11.00
Complete booklet, #2255a 10.00

See Switzerland Nos. 1004-1005.

Christmas Gingerbread A683

Perf. 12½ Vert.

1997, Nov. 20 **Litho.**

2256 A683 (3.50k) Heart 2.00 1.00

Perf. 12½ on 3 Sides

2257 A683 (3.50k) Animals 1.25 .60
2258 A683 (3.50k) People 1.25 .60
a. Bklt. pane, 5 ea #2257-2258 12.50
Complete booklet, #2258a 12.50

Christmas Angels — A684

Angels from altarpiece, Litslena Church: No. 2259, Playing horn, mandolin. No. 2260, Playing pipes, harp.

1997, Nov. 20 ***Perf. 13x12½***

2259 A684 6k multicolored 2.25 1.50
2260 A684 6k multicolored 2.25 1.50
a. Booklet pane, 5 each #2259-2260 + 10 labels 22.50
Complete booklet, #2260a 22.50

Photographer Jan Lindblad (1932-87) and His Tigers — A685

Design: No. 2262, Two tigers on rock.

Perf. 12½ Horiz.

1998, Jan. 15 **Litho. & Engr.**

2261 A685 (3.50k) shown 1.50 .75
2262 A685 (3.50k) multi 1.50 .75
a. Pair, #2261-2262 3.00 2.40

New Modern Museum of Art, Stockholm A686

#2263, Fungus Sculpture, by Yves Klein. #2264, Skeppsholmen, by Göran Gidenstam. #2265, Monogram, by Robert Rauschenberg.

1998, Jan. 15 ***Perf. 12½ Vert.***

2263 A686 (5k) multicolored 1.50 .35
2264 A686 (5k) multicolored 1.50 .35
2265 A686 (5k) multicolored 1.50 .35
a. Booklet pane of 3, #2263-2265 4.50 4.50
Complete booklet, 2 #2265a 9.00

Valentine's Day — A687

Perf. 13 (on 3 Sides)

1998, Jan. 15 **Litho.**

2266 A687 (5k) dp grn & org red 1.75 .30
2267 A687 (5k) dp blue & rose red 1.75 .30
a. Bklt. pane, 3 ea #2266-2267 10.50
Complete booklet, #2267a 10.50

Swedish Confederation of Trade Unions, Cent. — A688

Perf. 12½ Horiz.

1998, Mar. 19 **Engr.**

2268 A688 (5k) multicolored 1.50 .30

Public Buildings A689

#2269, Fire station, Gävle. #2270, Shoe shop, Askersund. #2271, Fish halls, Gothenburg. #2272, Rödalvarm (Red Mill) Cinema, Halmstad. #2273, Town Hotel, Eksjö.

1998, Mar. 19 ***Perf. 12½ Horiz.***

2269 A689 (5k) multicolored 1.50 .30
2270 A689 (5k) multicolored 1.50 .30
2271 A689 (5k) multicolored 1.50 .30
2272 A689 (5k) multicolored 1.50 .30
2273 A689 (5k) multicolored 1.50 .30
a. Booklet pane, #2269-2273 7.50
Complete booklet, #2273a 7.50

Queen Christina, Medallion Commemorating the Peace of Westphalia, 1648 — A690

1998, Mar. 19 **Engr.** ***Perf. 12½ Vert.***

2274 A690 7k rose brn & dp grn 2.25 1.00

Handicrafts
A691

Designs: (4.50k), Apron from costume, Dalecarlia. (5k), Wrought iron ornamental designs. No. 2277, Lovikka mitten. No. 2278, Boxes made from wood shavings.

1998, Mar. 19 ***Perf. 13 Vert.***

2275 A691 (4.50k) multicolored 1.60 .65
2276 A691 (5k) multicolored 1.75 .25

Perf. 12½ on 3 Sides

2277 A691 8k multicolored 2.50 3.00
2278 A691 8k multicolored 2.50 3.00
a. Bklt. pane, 2 ea #2277-2278 10.00
Complete booklet, #2278a + 4 labels 10.00

Wetland Flowers
A692 A693

Perf. 13 on 3 Sides

1998, May 14 **Litho.**

2279 A692 (5k) Marsh violet 2.25 .25
2280 A693 (5k) Great willow-herb 2.25 .25
a. Bklt pane, 5 ea #2279-2280 22.50
Complete booklet, #2280a 22.50

City of Stockholm — A694

Designs: Nos. 2281, 2287, Stockholm Palace. Nos. 2282, 2288, Skerry boats. No. 2283, Opera House, cent. No. 2284, Sail boats. No. 2285, Langholmen Beach, vert. No. 2286, Fireworks over City Hall, vert.

Perf. 13 on 2 or 3 Sides

1998, May 14 **Litho. & Engr.**

2281 A694 (5k) multicolored 1.40 .55
2282 A694 (5k) multicolored 1.40 .55

Size: 27x22mm

2283 A694 (5k) multicolored 1.60 .65
2284 A694 (5k) multicolored 1.60 .65

Size: 27x36mm

2285 A694 (5k) multicolored 1.60 .65
2286 A694 (5k) multicolored 1.60 .65
a. Booklet pane, #2281-2286 9.50 7.50
Complete booklet, #2286a 9.50 7.50

Size: 58x23mm

2287 A694 7k multicolored 2.00 1.50
2288 A694 7k multicolored 2.00 1.50
a. Bklt. pane, 2 ea #2287-2288 8.00
Complete booklet, #2288a 8.00

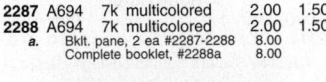

Cruise Ship Albatros in Stockholm Harbor — A695

1998, May 14 ***Perf. 13 Vert.***

Coil Stamp

2289 A695 6k multicolored 1.75 1.05

Festivals and Holidays — A696

Europa: No. 2290, Crayfish party, paper moon. No. 2291, Dancing around maypole, Midsummer in June.

Perf. 13 on 3 Sides

1998, May 14 **Litho.**

2290 A696 7k multicolored *2.00* 1.75
2291 A696 7k multicolored *2.00* 1.75
a. Bklt. pane, 2 ea #2289-2290 *8.00* 8.00
Complete booklet, #2291a + 4 labels *8.00* 8.00

King Carl XVI Gustaf, 25th Anniv. of Accession to the Throne — A697

1998, May 14 **Engr.** ***Perf. 13 Vert.***

2292 A697 (5k) multicolored 1.50 .25

Vilhelm Moberg (1898-1973), Writer — A698

Litho. & Engr.

1998, Aug. 20 ***Perf. 13 Vert.***

Coil Stamp

2293 A698 (5k) multicolored 1.50 .40

Pastries
A699

Designs: No. 2294, Princess cake. No. 2295, Gustav Adolf pastry. No. 2296, Napoleon pastry. No. 2297, Mocha cake. No. 2298, National pastry. No. 2299, Lent bun (semla).

Perf. 13 on 3 Sides

1998, Aug. 20 **Litho.**

2294 A699 (5k) multicolored 1.50 .50
2295 A699 (5k) multicolored 1.50 .50
2296 A699 (5k) multicolored 1.50 .50
2297 A699 (5k) multicolored 1.50 .50
2298 A699 (5k) multicolored 1.50 .50
2299 A699 (5k) multicolored 1.50 .50
a. Booklet pane, #2294-2299 9.00 8.00
Complete booklet, #2299a 9.00

The Millennium — A700

Swedish developments during 1900's: No. 2300, Painting, "Flowers on the Window Sill," by Carl Larsson. No. 2301, Stockholm Stadium, poster for 1912 Olympic Games. No. 2302, Power plant, Porjus, Lapland. No. 2303, Inventions; zippers, ball bearings, vacuum cleaners, refrigerators. No. 2304, Johnson (shipping) Line. No. 2305, AB Radiotjänst, 1924. No. 2306, Jazz music, Charleston dance. No. 2307, Ellen Key, Kerstin Hesselgren, pioneers for women's rights. No. 2308, Arne Borg, swimmer, Gillis Grafström, figure skater, world champions. No. 2309, Ernst Rolf, entertainer, 1920's.

Perf. 12½ Horiz.

1998, Oct. 3 **Litho. & Engr.**

2300 A700 (5k) multicolored 2.00 1.35
2301 A700 (5k) multicolored 2.00 1.35
2302 A700 (5k) multicolored 2.00 1.35
2303 A700 (5k) multicolored 2.00 1.35
2304 A700 (5k) multicolored 2.00 1.35
2305 A700 (5k) multicolored 2.00 1.35
2306 A700 (5k) multicolored 2.00 1.35
2307 A700 (5k) multicolored 2.00 1.35
2308 A700 (5k) multicolored 2.00 1.35
2309 A700 (5k) multicolored 2.00 1.35
a. Booklet pane, #2300-2309 20.00 *20.00*
Complete booklet, #2309a 20.00

See Nos. 2327-2336, 2379-2388.

Nobel Laureates
A701

Perf. 13x12½ on 3 Sides

1998, Oct. 3 **Engr.**

2310 A701 6k Nadine Gordimer, 1991 1.75 1.40
2311 A701 6k Sigrid Undset, 1928 1.75 1.40
a. Bklt. pane, 2 ea #2310-2311 7.00
Complete booklet, #2311a + 4 labels 7.00

Sigismund (1566-1632), King of Sweden and Poland — A702

Perf. 12½ Horiz.

1998, Oct. 3 **Litho. & Engr.**

2312 A702 7k multicolored 2.25 1.60

See Poland No. 3421.

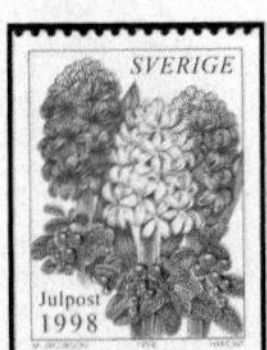

A703

Perf. 12½ Horiz.

1998, Nov. 19 **Litho.**

2313 A703 (4k) Hyacinth 1.40 .45

Perf. 12½ on 3 Sides

2314 A703 (4k) Mistletoe 1.10 .35
2315 A703 (4k) Amaryllis 1.10 .35
a. Bklt. pane, 5 ea #2314-2315 11.00
Complete booklet, #2315a 11.00
2316 A703 6k Wreath 2.00 1.40
2317 A703 6k Azalea 2.00 1.40
a. Bklt. pane, 5 ea #2316--2317 20.00
Complete booklet, #2317a 20.00
Nos. 2313-2317 (5) 7.60 3.95

Christmas.

A704

1999, Jan. 14 **Litho.** ***Perf. 13 Vert.***

2318 A704 (5k) multicolored 1.75 .25

Swedish Cooperative Union, cent.

A705

Swedish Coins: No. 2319, Gustav Vasa Daler. No. 2320, Carl XIV John Riksdaler.

1999, Jan. 14 **Engr.** ***Perf. 12½ Vert.***

2319 A705 (4.50k) dark green 1.30 .50
2320 A705 (5k) dark blue 1.60 .25

A706

Easter Eggs: No. 2321, Sugar egg. No. 2322, Egg filled with marzipan chicks.

Perf. 12½ on 3 Sides

1999, Jan. 14 **Litho.** **Panel Color**

2321 A706 (5k) green 1.60 .55
2322 A706 (5k) red 1.60 .55
a. Bklt. pane, 3 ea #2321-2322 10.00
Complete booklet, #2322a 10.00

"Little Sister Rabbit," by Ulf Nilsson — A707

Rabbits: No. 2323, Preparing meal over fireplace. No. 2324, Feeding Little Sister. No. 2325, Dancing to music. No. 2326, Hopping through thicket.

Perf. 12½ Vert.

1999, Jan. 14 **Litho. & Engr.**

2323 A707 (5k) multicolored 1.50 .50
2324 A707 (5k) multicolored 1.50 .50
2325 A707 (5k) multicolored 1.50 .50
2326 A707 (5k) multicolored 1.50 .50
a. Booklet pane, #2323-2326 6.00 7.50
Complete booklet, #2326a 6.00

The Millennium Type of 1998

Sweden in years 1939-1969: No. 2327, Scene from Bergman's film "Smiles of a Summer Night," 1955. No. 2328, Vällingby Centre. No. 2329, Silhouette of soldier, singer Ulla Bilquist. No. 2330, Cobra telephone, three-point seat belt, ASEA high voltage cables and breakers, Tetra Pak's milk carton. No. 2331, Scandinavian Airlines System formed, DC-4 over New York City, 1946. No. 2332, "Hyland's Corner," Carl-Gustaf Lindstedt, Prime Minister Tage Erlander on television. No. 2333, Protests of the 60's, Hep Stars band. No. 2334, Volvo Amazon car, family picnic. No. 2335, Ingemar Johansson, heavy-weight boxing champion, 1959, Mora-Nisse Karlsson, skiing champion, Gunder Hägg, running champion, 1941-45. No. 2336, Jazz singer Alice Babs, opera singer Jussi Björling.

Perf. 12½ Horiz.

1999, Mar. 11 **Litho.**

2327 A700 (5k) multicolored 2.00 1.00
2328 A700 (5k) multicolored 2.00 1.00
2329 A700 (5k) multicolored 2.00 1.00
2330 A700 (5k) multicolored 2.00 1.00
2331 A700 (5k) multicolored 2.00 1.00
2332 A700 (5k) multicolored 2.00 1.00
2333 A700 (5k) multicolored 2.00 1.00
2334 A700 (5k) multicolored 2.00 1.00
2335 A700 (5k) multicolored 2.00 1.00
2336 A700 (5k) multicolored 2.00 1.00
a. Booklet pane, #2327-2336 21.00 21.00
Complete booklet, #2336a 21.00

Construction of the Oresund Bridge — A708

(5k), Swan Pontoon Crane. 6k, Building bridge.

1999, Mar. 11 ***Perf. 12½ Vert.***

2337 A708 (5k) multicolored 1.80 .25
2338 A708 6k multicolored 2.20 1.00

Swedish Ships A709

Perf. 12½x13 on 3 Sides

1999, Mar. 11 Litho. & Engr.

2339 A709 8k East Indiaman	2.50	2.00
2340 A709 8k Mary Anne	2.50	2.00
2341 A709 8k Beatrice	2.50	2.00
2342 A709 8k SS Austalic	2.50	2.00
a. Booklet pane, #2339-2342	10.00	11.00
Complete booklet, #2342a + 4 labels	10.00	

Australia '99 World Stamp Expo.

Pyramid Orchid — A710

Lady's Slipper — A711

Marsh Helleborine A712

Green-Winged Ordhid A713

Perf. 12½ on 3 Sides

1999, May 20 Litho.

2343 A710 (5k) multicolored	2.00	.25
2344 A711 (5k) multicolored	2.00	.25
2345 A712 (5k) multicolored	2.00	.25
2346 A713 (5k) multicolored	2.00	.25
a. Booklet pane, 3 each #2343, 2345, 2 each #2344, #2346	20.00	
Complete booket, #2346a	20.00	
Nos. 2343-2346 (4)	8.00	1.00

Council of Europe, 50th Anniv. — A714

1999, May 20 *Perf. 12½ Horiz.*

2347 A714 7k multicolored	2.50	2.00

Europa — A715

No. 2348, Tyresta Natl. Park. No. 2349, Gotska Sandön Natl. Park.

Perf. 12½x13 on 3 Sides

1999, May 20

2348 A715 7k multicolored	*2.50*	2.00
2349 A715 7k multicolored	*2.50*	2.00
a. Bklt. pane, 2 ea #2348-2349	*10.00*	*11.00*
Complete bklt., #2349a+4 labels	*10.00*	

Post Bike — A716

Racing Bike — A717

Town Bike — A718

Messenger Bike — A719

Engr., Litho. (#2351)

1999, May 20 *Perf. 12½ Horiz.*

2350 A716 (3.50k) multicolored	1.60	1.10
Perf. 12½ Vert.		
2351 A717 (5k) multicolored	1.60	.50
2352 A718 6k multicolored	1.90	.95
2353 A719 8k multicolored	2.40	*1.60*
Nos. 2350-2353 (4)	7.50	4.15

Signs of the Zodiac A720

No. 2354: a, Aquarius. b, Pisces. c, Aries. d, Taurus. e, Gemini. f, Cancer.

No. 2355: a, Leo. b, Virgo. c, Libra. d, Scorpio. e, Sagittarius. f, Capricorn.

Litho. & Engr.

1999, Aug. 12 *Perf. 13*

2354 Booklet pane of 6	12.50	12.50
a.-f. A720 (5k) any single	2.00	1.20
2355 Booklet pane of 6	12.50	12.50
a.-f. A720 (5k) any single	2.00	1.20
Complete booklet, #2354-2355	25.00	

Perforations at each corner of Nos. 2354a-2354f, 2355a-2355f end in a large hole within the pane or semi-circles at the edges of the pane, giving the corners of each stamp a slightly concave appearance.

Butterflies A721

a, Inachis io. b, Junonia orithya wallacei. c, Hypolimnas bolina. d, Vanessa atalanta.

1999, Aug. 12 *Perf. 12½x13*

2356 Booklet pane of 4	8.00	*4.00*
a.-d. A721 6k any single	2.00	1.00
Complete bklt., #2356 + 4 labels	8.00	8.00

See Singapore Nos. 903-907.

Nobel Laureates in Peace — A722

#2357, Auguste Beernaert (1829-1912). #2358, Henri La Fontaine (1854-1943).

Perf. 13x12½ on 3 sides

1999, Sept. 30 Litho. & Engr.

2357 A722 7k gold & blue	2.75	2.25
2358 A722 7k gold & red	2.75	2.25
a. Bklt. pane, 2 ea #2357-2358	11.00	
Complete booklet, #2358a + 4 labels	11.00	

See Belgium Nos. 1749-1750.

Dance Bands A723

Designs: a, Thorleifs. b, Arvingarna. c, Lotta Engbergs. d, Sten & Stanley.

Litho. & Engr.

1999, Oct. 2 *Perf. 12¾*

2359 Booklet pane of 4	8.00	8.00
a.-d. A723 (5k) any single	2.00	1.50
Complete booklet, 2 #2359	16.00	

A724

Christmas A725

Stained glass: No. 2360, Nativity, Klinte Church. No. 2361, Nativity, Hablingbro Church. No. 2362, Three kings, Hablingbro Church.

Madonna and child icons from: No. 2363, Bälinge Church. No. 2364, Skänninge Church.

Perf. 12½ Vert.

1999, Nov. 18 Litho.

2360 A724 (4.50k) multicolored	1.40	.60
Perf. 12¾ on 3 sides		
2361 A724 (4.50k) multicolored	1.20	.30
2362 A724 (4.50k) multicolored	1.20	.30
a. Bklt. pane, 5 ea #2361-2362	12.00	
Complete booklet, # 2362a	12.00	
Litho. & Engr.		
2363 A725 6k multicolored	1.75	1.10
2364 A725 6k multicolored	1.75	1.10
a. Booklet pane, 5 each #2363-2364 + 10 labels	17.50	
Complete booklet, # 2364a	17.50	
Nos. 2360-2364 (5)	7.30	3.40

Millennium — A726

Sun rays touching Heligholmen Island: No. 2365, Island rocks. No. 2366, Island map.

Perf. 12¾ Horiz.

1999, Dec. 27 Litho. & Engr.

2365 A726 5k multicolored	2.25	1.15
2366 A726 5k multicolored	2.25	1.15
a. Bklt. pane, 2 ea #2365-2366	9.00	
Complete booklet, 2 #2366a	18.00	

New Year 2000 (Year of the Dragon) A727

Dragon from children's book "The Dragon with Red Eyes," by Astrid Lindgren: No. 2367, In flight (shown). No. 2368, With basket. No. 2369, In flight, diff.

Perf. 12¾ Horiz.

2000, Jan. 13 Litho.

2367 A727 (5k) multi	1.90	.60
2368 A727 (5k) multi	1.90	.60
2369 A727 (5k) multi	1.90	.60
a. Bklt. pane, 2 ea #2367-2369	11.50	
Complete booklet, #2369a	11.50	

A728

Love.

2000, Jan. 13 *Perf. 12¾ on 3 sides*

2370 A728 (5k) shown	1.50	.35
2371 A728 (5k) Heart, diff.	1.50	.35
a. Bklt. pane, 3 ea #2370-2371	9.00	
Complete booklet, #2371a	9.00	

A729

Watch of King Karl XII, 1701: (4.50k), Works. (5k), Face.

2000, Jan. 13 Engr. *Perf. 12½ Vert.*

2372 A729 (4.50k) blue	1.25	.60
2373 A729 (5k) claret brown	1.75	.25

Souvenir Sheet

Detail of "Great Deeds by Swedish Kings," by David Ehrenstrahl — A730

Litho. & Engr.

2000, Mar. 17 *Perf. 12¾*

2374 A730 50k multi	15.00	9.00

Czeslaw Slania's 1000th postage stamp.

Forests — A731

Designs: (3.80k), People in forest. No. 2376, Elk in forest. No. 2377, Bird in forest. 6k, Birch forest.

Perf. 12¾ Vert.

2000, Mar. 17 Litho.

2375 A731 (3.80k) multi	2.00	1.75
2376 A731 (5k) multi	1.90	.55
2377 A731 (5k) multi	1.90	.55
a. Pair, #2376-2377	3.75	3.50
2378 A731 6k multi	2.50	2.00
Nos. 2375-2378 (4)	8.30	4.85

Millennium Type of 1998

Sweden in the years 1970-99: No. 2379, Art in Stockholm subway stations. No. 2380, Swedish UN forces, postal clerk. No. 2381, Computer, mouse and mobile phone. No. 2382, Cullberg Ballet, Svenska Ord repertory company. No. 2383, Jönköping railway station. No. 2384, Youth with spiked hair, musical group ABBA. No. 2385, European Union flag, map of member countries. No. 2386, Scene from film, "The Apple War." No. 2387, Skiiers Pernilla Wiberg, Ingemar Stenmark, tennis player Björn Borg. No. 2388, Photo of child in womb, taken by Lennart Nilsson.

Perf. 12¾ Horiz.

2000, Mar. 17 **Litho.**

2379	A700 (5k) multi		2.00	.60
2380	A700 (5k) multi		2.00	.60
2381	A700 (5k) multi		2.00	.60
2382	A700 (5k) multi		2.00	.60
2383	A700 (5k) multi		2.00	.60
2384	A700 (5k) multi		2.00	.60
2385	A700 (5k) multi		2.00	.60
2386	A700 (5k) multi		2.00	.60
2387	A700 (5k) multi		2.00	.60
2388	A700 (5k) multi		2.00	.60
a.	Booklet pane, #2379-2388		20.00	20.00
	Complete booklet, #2388a		20.00	

Art by Philip von Schantz (1928-98) — A732

Designs: No. 2389, A Peck of Apples. No. 2390, A Bowl of Blueberries.

Perf. 12¾ on 3 sides

2000, May 9 **Litho.**

2389	A732 (5k) multi	1.50	.25
2390	A732 (5k) multi	1.50	.25
a.	Bklt. pane, 5 ea #2389-2390	15.00	
	Complete booklet, #2390a	15.00	

A733

Oresund Bridge, Sweden-Denmark — A734

2000, May 9 **Engr.** ***Perf. 12½ Vert.***

2391	A733 (5k) blue & ultra	1.90	.45

Litho.

Perf. 12¾ Horiz.

2392	A734 6k shown	2.10	1.35
2393	A734 6k Map	2.10	1.35
a.	Booklet pane, 2 each #2392-2393, + 4 etiquettes	8.50	
	Complete booklet, #2393a	8.50	

See Denmark Nos. 1187-1188.

Europa Issue

Common Design Type

2000, May 9 **Litho.** ***Perf. 12¾ Horiz.***

2394	CD17 7k multi	*3.00*	*1.50*

2000 Summer Olympics, Sydney — A735

No. 2395: a, Hurdler Ludmila Engquist. b, Archer Magnus Petersson. c, Windsurfer Fredrik Palm. d, Beach volleyball player Lena Malm.

Perf. 12¾x12½ on 3 sides

2000, Aug. 17 **Litho.**

2395	A735 Booklet pane of 4	10.00	11.00
a.-d.	8k Any single	2.50	2.25
	Booklet, #2395 + 4 etiquettes	10.00	

Sky Conditions A736

No. 2396: a, Clouds and sun. b, Clouds and lightning. c, Clouds and rainstorm. d, Aurora borealis. e, Rainbow. f, Cumulus clouds.

2000, Aug. 17 ***Die Cut Perf. 9¾x10***

Self-Adhesive

2396	Booklet of 6	12.00	
a.-f.	A736 (5k) Any single	2.00	.75

King Carl XVI Gustaf — A737

Design: 8k, Queen Silvia.

Perf. 12¾ Vert.

2000, Aug. 17 **Engr.**

2397	A737 (5k) blue	2.25	.30
2398	A737 8k red	2.75	1.25

See Nos. 2466-2467.

Nobel Laureates for Literature — A738

a, Wislawa Szymborska. b, Nelly Sachs.

Perf. 12¾x12½ on 3 sides

2000, Oct. 7 **Engr.**

2399	A738 Pair	5.00	3.50
a.-b.	7k Any single	2.50	1.75
c.	Booklet pane, 2 #2399	10.00	
	Booklet, #2399c + 4 etiquettes	10.00	

Toys — A739

No. 2400: a, Doll, tea set, teddy bear. b, Marbles, tin soldier, yo-yo, jump rope. c, Pine cone cow, doll, horse-drawn wagon. d, Cars and policeman. e, Model train, mechanical men. f, Lego car, robot, Furbee.

Perf. 12¾ on 3 sides

2000, Oct. 7 **Litho. & Engr.**

2400	Booklet of 6	12.00	13.50
a.-f.	A739 (5k) Any single	2.00	2.25

Christmas Songs — A740

Christmas Snowflakes — A741

Designs: No. 2401, Hey, Santas.

No. 2402, vert.: a, It's Christmas Again (four children, tree). b, Three Gingerbread Men. c, The Fox Runs Over the Ice. d, Christmas Has Come to Our House (three children, candles).

No. 2403: a, White background. b, Blue background.

Perf. 12¾ Vert.

2000, Nov. 16 **Litho.**

2401	A740 (4.30k) multi	1.50	.50

Perf. 12¾ on 3 sides

2402	Block of 4	4.75	4.75
a.-d.	A740 (4.30k) Any single	1.20	.30
e.	Booklet pane, 3 ea #2402a, 2402c, 2 ea #2402b, 2402d	12.00	
	Booklet, #2402e	12.00	
2403	A741 Pair	2.50	*2.00*
a.-b.	6k Any single	1.25	1.00
c.	Booklet pane, 5 #2403 + 10 etiquettes	12.50	
	Booklet, #2403c	12.50	
	Nos. 2401-2403 (3)	8.75	7.25

Rock Carvings, Tanum World Heritage Site — A742

Swedish World Heritage Site A743

Designs: (4.50k), Rock carvings of animals and people. (5k), Rock carvings of ships.

No. 2406: a, Gammelstad Church Village. b, Karlskrona Naval Port. c, Theater, Drottningholm Palace. d, Engelsberg Ironworks.

2001, Jan. 31 **Engr.** ***Perf. 12½ Vert.***

2404	A742 (4.50k) blue, *gray*	1.50	.75
2405	A742 (5k) red, *gray*	1.50	.25

Litho.

Perf. 12½x12¾ on 3 sides

2406	Booklet pane of 4	7.50	9.00
a.-d.	A743 6k Any single	1.90	1.25
	Booklet, #2406 + 4 etiquettes	7.50	

New Year 2001 (Year of the Snake) — A744

No. 2407: a, Snake with tongue extended. b, Snake curled up.

Perf. 12¾ on 3 sides

2001, Jan. 31 **Litho.**

2407	A744 Pair	3.50	1.15
a.-b.	(5k) Any single	1.75	.50
c.	Booklet pane, 3 #2407	10.50	
	Booklet, #2407c	10.50	

Dogs — A745

No. 2408: a, Golden retriever. b, German shepherd. c, Labrador retriever. d, Dachshund.

2001, Jan. 31 ***Perf. 12¾ Vert.***

2408	A745 Booklet of 4	7.50	8.25
a.-d.	(5k) Any single	1.80	.75

Birds — A746

Designs: (3.80k), Vanellus vanellus. (5k), Pica pica. 6k, Larus argentatus. 7k, Aegithalos caudatus.

2001, Mar. 22 **Engr.** ***Perf. 12¾ Vert.***

2409	A746 (3.80k) multi	1.40	.85
2410	A746 (5k) multi	1.50	.25
2411	A746 6k multi	1.60	.95
2412	A746 7k multi	1.80	1.25
	Nos. 2409-2412 (4)	6.30	3.30

Europa — A747

No. 2413: a, Waterways of northern Sweden. b, Large ship in Trollhätte Canal, trees. c, Waterways of southern Sweden. d, Ship "Juno" in Trollhätte Canal, duck.

Perf. 12¾ on 3 Sides

2001, Mar. 22 **Litho.**

2413	A747 Booklet pane of 4	*10.00*	*10.50*
a.-d.	7k Any single	*2.50*	1.90
	Booklet, #2413 + 4 etiquettes	*10.00*	

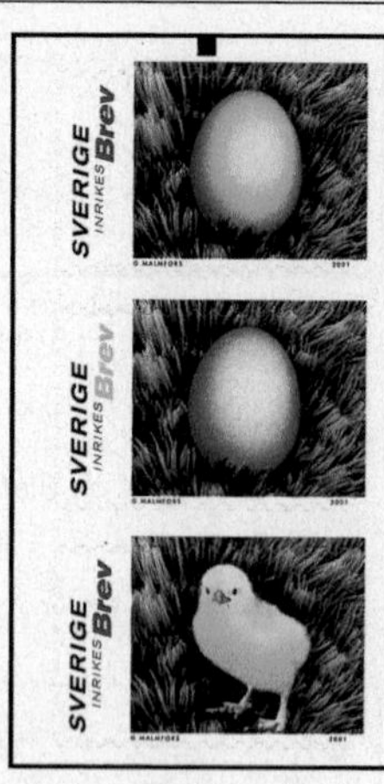

Easter A748

No. 2414: a, Orange egg. b, Purple egg. c, Chick.

2001, Mar. 22 ***Die Cut Perf. 9¾x10***

Self-Adhesive

2414 A748 Booklet pane of 3 6.00 6.00
a.-c. (5k) Any single 1.90 .95
Booklet, 2 #2414 12.00

Nobel Prize, Cent. A749

No. 2415: a, Alfred Nobel, Peace medal, obverse of Physics, Chemistry, Physiology or Medicine, Literature medal. b, Reverse of Physiology or Medicine medal. c, Reverse of medal for Physics or Chemistry. d, Reverse of Literature medal.

Perf. 12¾x13½ on 3 Sides

2001, Mar. 22 **Litho. & Engr.**

2415 Vert. strip of 4 10.00 11.00
a.-d. A749 8k Any single 2.50 1.90
e. Booklet pane, #2415 + 4 etiquettes + 4 blank labels 10.00
Booklet, #2415e 10.00

See United States No. 3504.

Ivar Lo-Johansson (1901-90), Writer — A750

No. 2416: a, Portrait. b, Lo-Johansson, truck.

2001, May 17 **Engr.** ***Perf. 12¾ Vert.***

2416 A750 Pair 3.00 1.00
a.-b. (5k) Any single 1.50 .50

Peonies — A751

No. 2417: a, Fernleaf peony (two flowers, one bud). b, Chinese peony "Mons Jules Elie." c, Herbaceous peony (yellow). d, Common peony (flower and bud). e, Tree peony.

Perf. 12¾ on 3 Sides

2001, May 17 **Litho.**

2417 Horiz. strip of 5 7.50 2.40
a.-e. A751 (5k) Any single 1.50 .50
f. Booklet pane, 2 #2417 15.00
Booklet, #2417f 15.00

Nobel Prize, Cent. — A752

Past winners: a, Doctors Without Borders. b, Red Cross.

Perf. 12¾ Vert.

2001, Aug. 16 **Litho.**

2418 A752 Horiz. pair 5.00 5.00
a.-b. 8k Any single 2.50 1.75

Daniel Solander (1733-82), Botanist on Endeavour A753

No. 2419: a, Barringtonia calyptrata and Solander. b, Cochlospermum gillivraei and Endeavour.

Perf. 12½x12¾ on 3 Sides

2001, Aug. 16 **Litho. & Engr.**

2419 A753 Vert. pair 6.00 *6.00*
a.-b. 8k Any single 3.00 2.00
c. Booklet pane, 2 #2419 12.00
Booklet, #2419c + 4 etiquettes 12.00

See Australia Nos. 1996-1997.

Fish A754

Designs: a, Perca fluviatilis. b, Abramis brama. c, Triglopsis quadricornis.

Die Cut Perf. 13½ Horiz.

2001, Aug. 16 **Litho. & Engr.**

Self-Adhesive

2420 Booklet pane of 3 5.50 5.50
a.-c. A754 (5k) Any single 1.80 .65
d. Booklet, 2 #2420 11.00

Souvenir Sheet

Aviation — A755

No. 2421: a, Lilienthal glider, 1895. b, Royal Swedish Aero Club. c, Saab J-29, 1962. d, Friedrichshafen FF49. e, Trike ultralight, 1999. f, Douglas DC-3, 1938.

Perf. 12½x12¾

2001, Oct. 6 **Litho. & Engr.**

2421 A755 Sheet of 6 11.00 13.00
a.-f. 5k Any single 1.90 1.50

Stamp Design Contest Winners — A756

No. 2422: a, Rollerblader, by Emilie Kilström, Kikebo School, Oskarshamn. b, The Letter, by Thomas Fröhling.

Perf. 12¾ on 3 Sides

2001, Oct. 6 **Litho.**

2422 A756 Horiz. pair 3.75 3.00
a.-b. (5k) Any single 1.80 1.10
c. Booklet pane, 3 #2422 11.25
Booklet, #2422c 11.25

A757

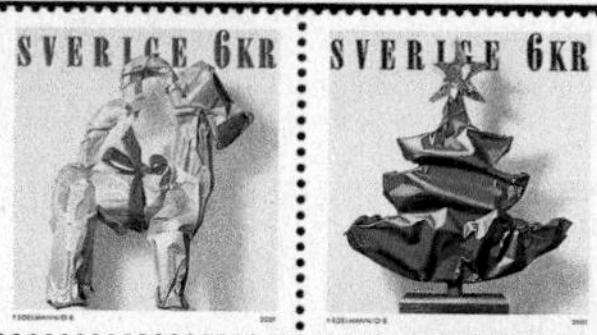

Christmas — A758

Designs: No. 2423, Christmas tree.
No. 2424 — Tree ornaments (26x20mm): a, Star. b, Cracker. c, Angel. d, Heart e, Cone.
No. 2425 — Crumpled paper art by Yrjö Edelmann: a, Straw goat. b, Christmas tree.

Perf. 12¾ Vert.

2001, Nov. 21 **Litho.**

2423 A757 (4.50k) multi 1.20 .75

Self-Adhesive

Die Cut Perf. 10¾x11¼

2424 Vert. strip of 5 6.00 5.00
a.-e. A757 (4.50k) Any single 1.10 .50
Booklet, 2 #2424 12.00

Water-Activated Gum

Perf. 12¾ on 3 Sides

2425 A758 Horiz. pair 3.00 3.75
a.-b. 6k Any single 1.50 1.20
c. Booklet pane, 5 #2425 + 10 etiquettes 15.00
Booklet, #2425c 15.00
Nos. 2423-2425 (3) 10.20

World Ice Hockey Championships A759

2002, Jan. 24 **Litho.** ***Perf. 12¾ Vert.***

2426 A759 (5k) multi 1.75 .70

Pandion Haliaetus A760

2002, Jan. 24 **Engr.**

2427 A760 10k multi 2.50 .85

New Year 2002 (Year of the Horse) — A761

No. 2428 — The Stones Family, by Bertil Almqvist: a, Boy and girl on horse. b, Girl on, and boy leading horse, dog running.

Perf. 12¾ on 3 Sides

2002, Jan. 24 **Litho.**

2428 A761 Horiz. pair 3.50 2.50
a.-b. (5k) Any single 1.75 .70
c. Booklet pane, 5 #2428 17.50 —
Booklet, #2428c 17.50

Love and Miss Terrified, by Joanna Rubin Dranger A762

No. 2429: a, "Det tror. . ." b, "Men jag. . ." c, "Anej!!!"

Die Cut Perf. 13¾ Horiz.

2002, Jan. 24 **Litho.**

Self-Adhesive

2429 A762 Booklet pane of 3 5.00 5.25
a.-c. (5k) Any single 1.60 .75
d. Booklet, 2 #2429 10.00

Antarctic Expedition of Otto Nordenskjöld, Cent. — A763

No. 2430: a, Scientists, ship, gull. b, Ship, penguin.

Litho. & Engr., Litho. (#2430b)

2002, Jan. 24 ***Perf. 12¾ Horiz.***

2430 A763 Vert. pair 6.00 *6.25*
a.-b. 10k Any single 3.00 2.75
c. Booklet pane, 2 #2430 12.00 —
Booklet, #2430c + 4 etiquettes 12.00

Astrid Lindgren (1907-2002), Children's Book Writer — A764

Designs: a, Pippi Langstrump (Pippi Longstocking). b, Karlsson pa Taket. c, Bröderna Lejonhjärta, vert. d, Lindgren (24x29mm). e, Emil i Lönneberga, vert. f, Lotta pa Brakmakargatan. g, Madicken.

2002, Mar. 5 Litho. *Perf. 13x13¼*

2431	A764	Booklet pane of 7	12.50	14.50
a.-g.		5k Any single	1.75	1.25
		Booklet, #2431	12.50	

Stockholm, 750th Anniv. — A765

Painting of Stockholm, 1535: (5k), Town and Lake Mälaren. 10k, Close-up view of Cathedral and palace.

2002, Mar. 21 Engr. *Perf. 12¾ Vert.*

2432	A765	(5k) shown	1.75	.80

Size: 28x28mm

2433	A765	10k claret	3.00	1.75

A766

Swedish World Heritage Sites A767

Artifacts from Birka archaeological site: (3.80k), Cross. (4.50k), Runic stone. (5k), Man's face.

No. 2437 — Scenes from Visby: a, Town and ring wall. b, Wall towers. c, Burmeister building, flowers. d, Square, walls of St. Catherine's Church.

2002, Mar. 21 Engr. *Perf. 12½ Vert.*

2434	A766	(3.80k) purple	1.25	.80
2435	A766	(4.50k) blue	1.50	.70
2436	A766	(5k) brn & claret	1.70	.60
		Nos. 2434-2436 (3)	4.45	2.10

Litho. & Engr.

Perf. 12½x12¾ on 3 Sides

2437		Booklet pane of 4	6.75	7.00
a.-d.		A767 (5k) Any single	1.60	.90
		Booklet, #2437	6.75	

Kristianstad Sculptures — A768

No. 2438: a, Structure by Takashi Naraha. b, Sprung From, by Pal Svensson.

Perf. 12¾ Vert.

2002, Mar. 23 Litho. & Engr.

2438	A768	Horiz. pair	5.00	4.25
a.-b.		8k Any single	2.50	2.00

Europa — A769

No. 2439: a, Charlie Rivel (1896-1983), clown. b, Clowns Without Borders (boy and clown). c, Cirkus Cirkör (performer with balloon). d, Cirkus Scott (woman on elephant).

Perf. 12¾ on 3 Sides

2002, May 2 Litho.

2439	A769	Booklet pane of 4	*11.00*	*12.50*
a.-d.		8k Any single	*2.75*	*3.00*
		Booklet, #2439 + 4 etiquettes	*11.00*	

Art From Sweden and New Zealand A770

No. 2440: a, Rain Forest, glass vase blown by Ola Höglund, Sweden. b, Maori basket, by Willa Rogers, New Zealand.

Perf. 12½x12¾ on 3 Sides

2002, May 2 Litho. & Engr.

2440	A770	Vert. pair	6.00	*6.75*
a.-b.		10k Any single	3.00	2.75
c.		Booklet pane, 2 #2440	12.00	—
		Booklet, #2440c + 4 etiquettes	12.00	

See New Zealand Nos. 1780, 1786.

A771

Summer in Bohuslän — A772

Designs: No. 2441, Waterfront building.

No. 2442: a, Lighthouse and gull. b, Lighthouse and three birds. c, Bridge, sailboat, waterfront buildings. d, Boat with outboard motor.

2002, May 10 Engr. *Perf. 12¾ Vert.*

2441	A771	(5k) multi	1.75	.60

Litho.

Self-Adhesive

Serpentine Die Cut 6¾

2442	A772	Block of 4	7.00	6.75
a.-d.		(5k) Any single	1.75	1.00
e.		Booklet, #2442c-2442d, 2 #2442	17.50	

Grönköpings Veckoblad Satirical Newspaper, Cent. — A773

No. 2443: a, Newspaper and fictitious Postmaster of Grönköping. b, Fictitious police chief and criminal.

Perf. 12¾ Vert.

2002, Aug. 29 Litho. & Engr.

2443	A773	Pair	4.00	3.75
a.-b.		(5k) Either single	2.00	1.75

Chefs A774

No. 2444: a, Charles Emil Hagdahl (1809-97) and Cajsa Warg (1703-69). b, Marit "Hiram" Huldt, cook with cauldron and bird, flowers. c, Tore Wretman and medal. d, Leif Mannerström, fish and lobster. e, Gert Klötzke and Swedish Culinary Team. f, Christer Lingström, poultry, peas and apples.

Perf. 12½x12¾ on 3 Sides

2002, Aug. 29 Litho.

2444		Booklet pane of 6	10.50	*10.50*
a.-f.		A774 (5k) Any single	1.75	1.25
		Booklet, #2444	10.50	

Royal Palaces A775

No. 2445: a, Sweden. b, Thailand.

Perf. 12½x13 on 3 Sides

2002, Oct. 5 Litho. & Engr.

2445	A775	Vert. pair	6.50	7.25
a.-b.		5k Either single	3.25	3.00
c.		Booklet pane, 2 #2445	13.00	—
		Booklet, #2445c	13.00	

See Thailand Nos. 2040-2041.

Motorcycle Racers — A776

No. 2446: a, Hakan Carlqvist. b, Sten Lundin. c, Anders Eriksson. d, Ulf Karlsson.

No. 2447: a, Ove Fundin. b, Tony Rickardsson. c, Peter Linden. d, Varg-Olle Nygren.

2002, Oct. 5 Litho. *Perf. 12¾*

2446	A776	Booklet pane of 4	6.50	8.00
a.-d.		5k Any single	1.60	1.60

Litho. & Engr.

2447	A776	Booklet pane of 4	6.50	8.00
a.-d.		5k Any single	1.60	1.60
		Booklet, #2446-2447	13.00	

Animated Film *Karl-Bertil Jonsson's Christmas* A777

Designs: No. 2448, Man with arm on Karl-Bertil's shoulder.

No. 2449: a, Karl-Bertil and mail sack of Christmas parcels. b, Karl-Bertil asleep with Robin Hood hat. c, Karl-Bertil giving parcel to poor man. d, Karl-Bertil with man, woman and child.

Perf. 12¾ Vert.

2002, Nov. 21 Litho.

2448	A777	(4.50k) multi	1.50	1.00

Self-Adhesive

Serpentine Die Cut 6½x6 on 3 Sides

2449		Block of 4	5.50	6.00
a.-d.		A777 (4.50k) Any single	1.40	.85
e.		Booklet pane, 3 #2449a-2449b, 2 #2449c-2449d	14.00	

Churches — A778

No. 2450: a, Kiruna Church. b, Habo Church. c, Sundborn Church. d, Tensta Bell Tower.

2002, Nov. 21 *Perf. 12¾ on 3 Sides*

2450	A778	Block of 4	11.00	13.50
a.-d.		8k Any single	2.50	1.75
e.		Booklet pane, 3 #2450a-2450b, 2 #2450c-2450d	27.50	—
		Booklet, #2450e	27.50	

St. Bridget (1303-73) — A779

2003, Jan. 20 Engr. *Perf. 12¾ Vert.*

2451	A779	(5.50k) red & brown	1.90	.75

Swedish Sports Federation, Cent. — A780

No. 2452: a, Woman and child. b, Wheelchair racer. c, Snowboarder and sign language. d, Girl running.

Serpentine Die Cut 8½

2003, Jan. 20 Litho.

Self-Adhesive

2452		Booklet pane, 3 each #2452a, 2452c, 2 each #2452b, 2452d	17.50	
a.-d.		A780 (5.50k) Any single	1.75	.85

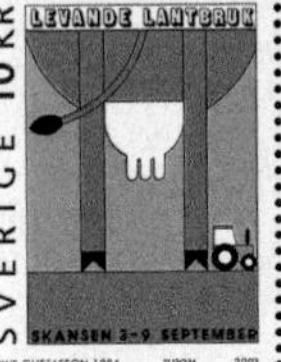

Europa — A781

Posters by: a, Anders Beckman, 1935. b, Georg Magnusson, 1930. c, Owe Gustafson, 1984. d, Carina Länk, 1993.

Perf. 12¾x12½ on 3 Sides

2003, Jan. 20

2453 A781 Booklet pane of 4 *11.00* *12.50*
a.-d. 10k Any single *2.75* 2.50
Booklet, #2453 + 4 etiquettes *11.00*

Knots — A782

Various knots.

2003, Jan. 20 Engr. *Perf. 12½ Vert.*

2454 A782 (4.80k) green 1.40 1.30
2455 A782 (5k) blue 1.50 .75
2456 A782 (5.50k) red 1.75 .30
Nos. 2454-2456 (3) 4.65 2.35

Regional Houses — A783

Perf. 12¼ Vert. Syncopated

2003, Mar. 20 Engr.

2457 A783 2k Närke .75 .55
2458 A783 4k Bohuslän 1.25 .85
2459 A783 5k Medelpad 1.50 .95
Nos. 2457-2459 (3) 3.50 2.35

Nobel Prize Winners For Physiology or Medicine From Spain — A784

No. 2460: a, Santiago Ramón y Cajal, 1906. b, Severo Ochoa, 1959.

Perf. 12 Vert. Syncopated

2003, Mar. 20 Litho. & Engr.

2460 A784 Horiz. pair 5.50 *6.00*
a.-b. 10k Either single 2.75 2.75

See Spain No. 3204.

Flowers — A785

No. 2461: a, Hepatica nobilis. b, Primula veris. c, Tussilago farfara.

Die Cut Perf. 9¾x10

2003, Mar. 20 Litho.

Self-Adhesive

2461 Booklet pane of 3 4.50 *5.50*
a.-c. A785 (5.50k) Any single 1.50 1.25
Booklet, 2 #2461 9.00

Oland Moorland, UNESCO World Heritage Site A786

No. 2462: a, Windmills. b, Megaliths and windmill. c, Cow and linear village. d, Sheep and lighthouse.

Perf. 12¾ Horiz.

2003, Mar. 20 Litho. & Engr.

2462 Booklet pane of 4 7.00 6.25
a.-d. A786 (5.50k) Any single 1.75 1.05
Booklet, #2462 7.00

A787

Garden Pavilions A788

Designs: No. 2463, 1820s pavilion, by Frederik Blom.

No. 2464: a, Pavilion of Emanuel Swedenborg. b, Pavilion of Ebba Brahe. c, Västana farm pavilion, Borensberg. d, Godegard pavilion.

Perf. 12½ Vert. Syncopated

2003, May 16 Engr.

2463 A787 (5.50k) multi 1.75 1.05

Litho.

Self-Adhesive

Serpentine Die Cut 6½ on 3 Sides

2464 Block of 4 7.00 *7.50*
a.-d. A788 (5.50k) Any single 1.75 1.25
e. Booklet pane, 3 #2464a-2464b, 2 #2464c-2464d 17.50

Souvenir Sheet

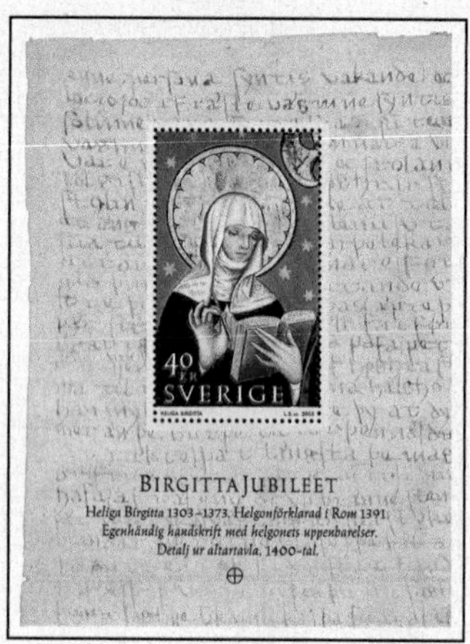

St. Bridget (1303-73) — A789

Litho. & Engr.

2003, May 31 *Perf. 13*

2465 A789 40k multi 12.50 14.00

No. 2465 exists with and without numbers printed in LL and LR corners of the margin.

Royalty Type of 2000

Designs: (5.50k), King Carl XVI Gustaf. 10k, Queen Silvia.

Perf. 13 Vert. Syncopated

2003, Aug. 21 Engr.

2466 A737 (5.50k) red brown 2.00 .75
2467 A737 10k purple 3.50 2.00

Harvest Time — A790

No. 2468: a, Tree, radicchio, parsnip, cucumber, beet, onion. b, Pitchfork, artichoke, pear, gourd, raspberries, apple, plum, pumpkin, eggplant. c, Trowel, garlic, peas, cabbage, tomato, potato, turnip, carrots. d, Strawberries, sunflower, cherries, plums, apple, pear.

Serpentine Die Cut 6½ on 3 Sides

2003, Aug. 21 Litho.

Self-Adhesive

2468 A790 Block of 4 7.25 *7.50*
a.-d. (5.50k) Any single 1.75 1.25
e. Booklet pane, 3 each #2468a-2468b, 2 each #2468c-2468d 18.00

Birds — A791

No. 2469: a, Recurvirostra avosetta. b, Podiceps auritus. c, Gavia arctica. d, Podiceps cristatus.

Perf. 12½x12¾ on 3 Sides

2003, Oct. 4 Litho. & Engr.

2469 A791 Booklet pane of 4 12.00 12.00
a.-d. 10k Any single 3.00 2.10
Complete booklet, #2469 + 4 etiquettes 12.00

See Hong Kong Nos. 1052-1055.

Building of East Indiaman "Götheborg" — A792

No. 2470: a, Figurehead (19x23mm). b, Ship under construction (19x23mm). c, Side view of ship, horiz. (23x40mm). d, Ship at sea (39x50mm).

2003, Oct. 4 *Perf. 12½x12¾*

2470 A792 Booklet pane of 4 17.50 22.00
a.-b. 5.50k Either single 2.25 2.25
c. 10k multi 3.25 3.25
d. 30k multi 9.00 9.00
Complete booklet, #2470 + label 17.50

Christmas at Sundborn, by Carl Larsson — A793

No. 2471: a, Martina med Frukostbrickan. b, Kerstis Slädfärd.

Perf. 12¾ on 3 Sides

2003, Nov. 10 Litho.

2471 A793 Horiz. pair 5.25 5.25
a.-b. 9k Either single 2.50 1.75
c. Booklet pane, 5 #2471 +10 etiquettes 26.50
Complete booklet, #2471c 26.50

Christmas Paintings by Carl Larsson — A794

Designs: No. 2472, Aftonvarden.

No. 2473, vert.: a, Esbjörn pa Skidor. b, Brita med Julljus. c, Farfar och Esbjörn. d, Garden och Brygghuset.

Perf. 12¾ Vert. Syncopated

2003, Nov. 10

2472 A794 (5k) multi 1.75 .85

Self-Adhesive

Serpentine Die Cut 6½x6 on 3 Sides

2473 A794 Block of 4 6.50 7.25
a.-d. (5k) Any single 1.60 1.40
e. Booklet pane, #2473b, 2473d, 2 #2473 16.00

Anna Lindh (1957-2003), Murdered Minister of Foreign Affairs — A795

Perf. 12¾ on 3 Sides

2003, Nov. 11 Engr.

2474 A795 Pair 5.25 5.25
a. (5.50k) claret 2.00 1.20
b. 10k blue 3.00 2.10
c. Booklet pane, 2 each #2474a-2474b 10.00 —
Complete booklet, #2474c 10.00

No. 2474c sold for 35k, 4k of which went to the Anna Lindh Memorial Fund.

Woodworking Tools — A796

Designs: (4.80k), Brace and bit. (5k), Saw. (5.50k), Plane.

Perf. 12 Vert. Syncopated

2004, Jan. 26 Engr.

2475 A796 (4.80k) green 1.40 1.20
2476 A796 (5k) blue 1.40 1.00
2477 A796 (5.50k) claret 1.60 .30
Nos. 2475-2477 (3) 4.40 2.50

Flowers A797

No. 2478: a, Tulip. b, Lily. c, Hibiscus. d, Amaryllis. e, Calla lily.

Perf. 12¾ Horiz.

2004, Jan. 26 Litho.

2478 Vert. strip of 5 8.50 6.75
a.-e. A797 (5.50k) Any single 1.60 .80
f. Booklet pane, 2 #2478 17.00 —
Complete booklet, #2478f 17.00

Europa A798

No. 2479 — Views of Lapland: a, Mountain with purple sky. b, Tents near lake.

Perf. 12¾x13½ on 3 Sides

2004, Jan. 26

2479 A798 Pair 5.75 6.25
a.-b. 10k Either single 2.75 2.75
c. Booklet pane, 2 #2479 11.50 —
Complete booklet, #2479c + 4 etiquettes 11.50

Souvenir Sheet

Norse Mythology — A799

No. 2480 — Return to Valhalla: a, Return of a warrior (denomination at LR). b, Welcoming Valkyrie (denomination at UR).

Litho. & Engr.

2004, Mar. 26 ***Perf. 12¾***

2480 A799 Sheet of 2 5.75 7.50
a.-b. 10k Either single 2.75 2.75

Falun, UNESCO World Heritage Site — A800

No. 2481: a, Excavation pit, red mine shaft entrance building. b, Yellow green and green copper weighing building, red, white and purple mining operations building. c, Gray mine entrance building. d, Miners and houses.

Perf. 12½x12¾ on 3 Sides

2004, Mar. 26 **Litho.**

2481 A800 Block of 4 9.50 7.25
a.-d. (5.50k) Any single 1.75 1.05
e. Booklet pane, #2481b, 2481d, 2 each #2481a, 2481c 9.50 —
Complete booklet, #2481e 9.50

Swedish Soccer Association, Cent. — A801

No. 2482: a, Nils Liedholm. b, Hanna Ljungberg. c, Fredrik Ljungberg. d, Henrik Larsson. e, Victoria Svensson. f, Thomas Ravelli.

Serpentine Die Cut 7x6¼ on 3 Sides

2004, Mar. 26

Self-Adhesive

2482 Booklet pane of 6 10.50 8.75
a.-f. A801 (5.50k) Any single 1.75 1.05

Sunset Scenes — A802

No. 2483: a, Fisherman. b, Lighthouse.

Perf. 12½ Vert. Syncopated

2004, May 13 **Engr.**

2483 A802 Horiz. pair 3.50 2.75
a.-b. (5.50k) Either single 1.75 .65

Stockholm Archipelago A803

No. 2484: a, Sailboat, red house, Gillöga. b, Rowboat, houses, Langviksskär. c, Ferry, Stora Nassa. d, Sailboat, lighthouse, Nämdöfjärden.

Serpentine Die Cut 6¾ on 3 Sides

2004, May 13 **Litho.**

Self-Adhesive

2484 Block of 4 7.00 8.00
a.-d. A803 (5.50k) Any single 1.75 1.50
e. Booklet pane, 3 #2484a-2484b, 2 #2484c-2484d 15.00

Cottages A804

Designs: 3k, Blacksmith's cottage, Uppland. 6k, Dalsland cottage. 8k, Stone cottage, Gotland.

Perf. 12¾ Vert. Syncopated

2004, Aug. 19 **Engr.**

2485 A804 3k multi .80 .50
2486 A804 6k multi 1.60 .80
2487 A804 8k multi 2.10 1.35
Nos. 2485-2487 (3) 4.50 2.65

Birds — A805

Designs: (5k), Streptopelia decaocto. (5.50k), Swedish tumbler. 10k, Columba palumbus.

2004, Aug. 19

2488 A805 (5k) multi 1.40 1.20
2489 A805 (5.50k) multi 1.50 .35
2490 A805 10k multi 2.75 1.90
Nos. 2488-2490 (3) 5.65 3.45

Forest Larder — A806

No. 2491: a, Mushrooms, lingonberries. b, Wild strawberries, butterfly, basket of blueberries. c, Juniper berries, basket of mushrooms. d, Cloudberries, cranberries.

Serpentine Die Cut 6½ on 3 Sides

2004, Aug. 19 **Litho.**

Self-Adhesive

2491 A806 Block of 4 7.25 8.00
a.-d. (5.50k) Any single 1.75 1.25
e. Booklet pane, 3 each #2491a-2491b, 2 each #2491c-2491d 15.00

Nobel Prize Winners for Literature from Ireland — A807

No. 2492: a, William Butler Yeats, 1923. b, George Bernard Shaw, 1925. c, Samuel Beckett, 1969. d, Seamus Heaney, 1995.

Perf. 12½x13½ on 3 Sides

2004, Oct. 1 **Litho. & Engr.**

2492 A807 Booklet pane of 4 11.00 11.50
a.-d. 10k Any single 2.75 2.25
Complete booklet, #2492 + 4 etiquettes 11.00

See Ireland Nos. 1576-1579.

Rock Music, 50th Anniv. — A808

No. 2493: a, Jerry Williams (29x39mm). b, Elvis Presley (36x39mm). c, Eva Dahlgren (29x39mm). d, Ulf Lundell (36x39mm). e, Tomas Ledin (29x39mm). f, Pugh Rogefeldt (29x33mm). g, Sahara Hotnights (36x33mm). h, Louise Hoffsten (29x33mm).

Litho., Litho. & Engr. (#2493b, 2493d)

2004, Oct. 2 ***Perf. 12x12¾***

2493 A808 Booklet pane of 8 + 2 labels 14.00 14.50
a.-h. 5.50k Any single 1.75 1.30
Complete booklet, #2493 14.00
i. Sheet of 9 #2493b 20.00 —

Labels and margins of Nos. 2493 and 2493i have perforations reading "Rock 54-04." No. 2493i sold for 55k.

Regional Houses Type of 2003 and

Log Cabin — A809

Scanian Farm House — A810

Designs: 1k, Miner's house. 9k, Blekinge cottage.

Perf. 12 Vert. Syncopated

2004, Nov. 11 **Engr.**

2494 A809 50o multi .25 .25

Perf. 12¼ Vert. Syncopated

2495 A783 1k multi .25 .25
2496 A810 7k multi 2.00 1.25
2497 A810 9k multi 2.75 2.00
Nos. 2494-2497 (4) 5.25 3.75

Birds — A811

No. 2498: a, Parus major. b, Emberiza citrinella. c, Pinicola enucleator. d, Pyrrhula pyrrhula.

Perf. 12¾ on 3 Sides

2004, Nov. 11 **Litho.**

2498 A811 Booklet pane of 4 12.00 14.50
a.-d. 10k Any single 3.00 2.75
Complete booklet, #2498 + 4 etiquettes 12.00

Christmas A812

Designs: No. 2499, Gnomes playing leap frog.

No. 2500: a, Three gnomes. b, Gnome with Christmas tree. c, Two gnomes with chair on skis. d, Gnome, birds at mail box.

Perf. 12¼ Vert. Syncopated

2004, Nov. 11

2499 A812 (5k) multi 1.50 1.05

Self-Adhesive

Serpentine Die Cut 6¼x6 on 3 Sides

2500 Block of 4 6.00 *6.75*
a.-d. A812 (5k) Any single 1.50 1.50
e. Booklet pane, 3 each #2500a-2500b, 2 each #2500c-2500d 15.00

King Carl XVI Gustaf — A813

Queen Silvia — A814

Perf. 12½ Vert. Syncopated

2005, Jan. 27 **Engr.**

2501 A813 (5.50k) multi 1.60 .25
2502 A814 10k multi 3.00 2.50

See No. 2560.

High Coast, UNESCO World Heritage Site — A815

No. 2503: a, Högbonden Lighthouse, birds on rocks. b, Cliffs and eagles, Storön Nature Reserve. c, Fishing boat at dock, Ulvön. d, Lakes near Häggvik.

Perf. 12¾x13½ on 3 Sides

2005, Jan. 27 **Litho. & Engr.**

2503 A815 Booklet pane of 4 12.00 *14.00*
a.-d. 10k Any single 3.00 3.00
Complete booklet, #2503 + 4 etiquettes 12.00

Swedish Design A816

No. 2504: a, Glassware, by Ingegerd Raman. b, Turn-o-matic number ticket machine, by A/E Design. c, Speedway 9000 welding helmet, by Carl-Göran Crafoord and Hakan Bergkvist. d, Camilla chair and Pilaster shelving unit, by John Kandell. e, Women's watch, by Vivianna Torun Bülow-Hübe. f, Streamliner toy car, by Ulf Hanses.

Die Cut Perf. 12½ Horiz.

2005, Jan. 27 **Self-Adhesive**

2504 Booklet pane of 6 10.00 10.00
a.-f. A816 (5.50k) Any single 1.75 1.25

Oriolus Oriolus A817

Perf. 12½ Vert. Syncopated

2005, Mar. 10 **Litho. & Engr.**

2505 A817 11k multi 3.25 2.25

Dag Hammarskjold (1905-61), UN Secretary General — A818

No. 2506: a, Hammarskjold. b, United Nations flag.

2005, Mar. 10 Engr.

2506	A818 Horiz. pair	3.25	2.75
a.-b.	(5.50k) Either single	1.60	1.00

Europa A819

No. 2507: a, Lemon, star anise, elderberry marmalade. b, Apples, rosemary, Jerusalem artichokes. c, Chives, goat cheese, beets.

Perf. 12¾ Horiz.

2005, Mar. 10 Litho.

2507	A819 Vert. strip of 3	*5.00*	5.00
a.-c.	(5.50k) Any single	*1.75*	1.00
d.	Booklet pane, 2 #2507	*10.00*	—
	Complete booklet, #2507d	*10.00*	

Spring Flowers A820

No. 2508: a, Convallaria majalis. b, Gagea lutea. c, Pulsatilla vulgaris. d, Anemone nemorosa.

Serpentine Die Cut 10 on 3 Sides

2005, Mar. 10

Self-Adhesive

2508	Block of 4	6.50	6.00
a.-d.	A820 (5.50k) Any single	1.60	.80
e.	Booklet pane, 3 each #2508a-2508b, 2 each #2508c-2508d	16.00	12.50
f.	As "a," serpentine die cut 6¾ on 3 sides	*12.50*	*2.00*
g.	As "b," serpentine die cut 6¾ on 3 sides	*12.50*	*2.00*
h.	As "c," serpentine die cut 6¾ on 3 sides	*12.50*	*2.00*
i.	As "d," serpentine die cut 6¾ on 3 sides	*12.50*	*2.00*
j.	Booklet pane, 3 each #2508f-2508g, 2 each #2508h-2508i	*125.00*	

Nos. 2508f-2508i issued 9/6.

Mother Svea A821

Perf. 12½ Vert. Syncopated

2005, May 26 Litho. & Engr.

2509	A821 15k multi	4.00	3.00

Tumba Bruk, manufacturer of Swedish banknotes, 250th anniv.

A822

Allotment Gardens — A823

No. 2510, Woman digging in garden.

No. 2511: a, Girl near shrub, man tending vegetable garden. b, Woman at table. c, Man tending garden, woman with basket of vegetables. d, Man watering garden.

Perf. 12¾ Vert. Syncopated

2005, May 26 Litho.

2510	A822 (5.50k) multi	1.50	1.15

Self-Adhesive

Serpentine Die Cut 10 on 3 Sides

2511	A823 Block of 4	6.00	6.00
a.-d.	(5.50k) Any single	1.50	.75
e.	Complete booklet, 3 each #2511a, 2511c, 2 each #2511b, 2511d	15.00	

A824

Swedish Postage Stamps, 150th Anniv. — A825

No. 2512 — Details from stamps: a, #944 (1972). b, #430 (1951). c, #250 (1936). d, #1490 (1984).

No. 2513: a, Count Pehr Ambjörn Sparre, #2, printing press. b, Woman reading letter, cover. c, Airplane, train. d, Mailman in van at mailbox.

2005, May 26 Litho. *Perf. 12¾*

2512	A824 Booklet pane of 4	7.50	*7.50*
a.-d.	(5.50k) Any single	1.90	1.15

Litho. & Engr.

2513	A825 Booklet pane of 4	7.50	*7.50*
a.-d.	(5.50k) Any single	1.90	1.15
e.	Miniature sheet, 9 #2513a	20.00	—
	Complete booklet, #2512-2513	15.00	

No. 2513e sold for 55k.

Souvenir Sheet

Dissolution of Union of Sweden and Norway, Cent. — A826

No. 2514 — Svinesund Bridge: a, View of roadway with cars. b, View from valley.

Perf. 12½x12¾

2005, May 27 Litho. & Engr.

2514	A826 Sheet of 2	6.00	7.50
a.-b.	10k Either single	3.00	3.00

See Norway Nos. 1430-1431.

Varberg Radio Station World Heritage Site — A827

Skogskyrkogarden Cemetery World Heritage Site — A828

Perf. 12½ Vert. Syncopated

2005, Sept. 23 Engr.

2515	A827 (4.80k) grn & violet	1.40	1.40
2516	A828 (5k) multi	1.60	.50

Greta Garbo (1905-90), Actress — A829

No. 2517: a, Portrait. b, Caricature and "Greta."

Perf. 12¾x12½ on 3 Sides

2005, Sept. 23 Litho. & Engr.

2517	A829 Pair	5.50	5.50
a.-b.	10k Either single	2.75	2.25
c.	Booklet pane, 2 each #2517a-2517b	11.00	—
	Complete booklet, #2517c + 4 etiquettes	11.00	
d.	Souvenir sheet of 4 #2517a, perf. 12¾x12½	*80.00*	*95.00*

No. 2517d sold for 45k and has a lithographed sheet margin. Single stamps from #2517d are perforated on all four sides.

See United States No. 3943.

Juvenile Wild Animals — A830

No. 2518: a, Lynx. b, Bear. c, Wolf. d, Fox.

Serpentine Die Cut 10 on 3 Sides

2005, Sept. 23 Litho.

Self-Adhesive

2518	A830 Block of 4	6.00	
a.-d.	(5.50k) Any single	1.60	1.00
e.	Complete booklet, 3 each #2518a-2518b, 2 each #2518c-2518d	16.00	

A831

Mopeds — A832

No. 2519: a, Man, woman, Fram moped. b, Husqvarna moped. c, Kuli moped engine and wheel. d, Two men sitting on mopeds.

No. 2520: a, Man repairing hoisted moped. b, Three-wheeled platform scooter. c, Zundapp moped engine. d, Man riding moped.

Litho., Litho. & Engr. (#2519b, 2519c, 2520b, 2520c)

2005, Sept. 24 *Perf. 12¾*

2519	A831 Booklet pane of 4	6.00	7.50
a.-d.	5.50k Any single	1.50	1.15
e.	Sheet of 9 #2519d	20.00	20.00
2520	A832 Booklet pane of 4	6.00	7.50
a.-d.	5.50k Any single	1.50	1.50
	Complete booklet, #2519-2520	12.00	

No. 2519e sold for 55k.

Christmas A833

Illustrations from Christmas in a Noisy Village, by Astrid Lindgren: No. 2521, Dog, child on skis.

No. 2522: a, Children near fence. b, Dog, children with sled. c, Girl wrapping gifts. d, Children looking at Christmas tree.

Perf. 12¾ Vert. Syncopated

2005, Nov. 10 **Litho.**

2521 A833 (5k) multi 1.25 .75

Self-Adhesive

Serpentine Die Cut 10 on 3 Sides

2522 Block of 4 6.50 8.00
a.-d. A833 (5k) Any single 1.50 1.25
e. Booklet pane, 3 each #2522a-2522b, 2 each #2522c-2522d 12.50

Angel Musicians, Sculptures by Carl Milles — A834

No. 2523: a, Angel with horn facing right. b, Angel with horn facing left. c, Angel with flute facing right. d, Angel with flute facing forward.

Perf. 12¾ on 3 Sides

2005, Nov. 10 **Litho. & Engr.**

2523 A834 Booklet pane of 4 10.00 13.00
a.-d. 10k Any single 2.50 2.50
Complete booklet, #2523 + 4 etiquettes 10.00

Swedish Railroads, 150th Anniv. — A835

Designs: 10k, X40 train.

No. 2525: a, Mallet steam locomotive (green). b, Gasoline-powered Rail bus (tan). c, SJ Class D electric locomotive (orange). d, R steam locomotive (black). e, RC electric locomotive (red).

Perf. 12½ Vert. Syncopated

2006, Jan. 26 **Litho.**

2524 A835 10k multi 2.50 2.50

Litho. & Engr.

Booklet Stamps

Perf. 12½ Horiz.

2525 Vert. strip of 5 8.00 7.25
a.-e. A835 (5.50k) Any single 1.60 1.00
f. Booklet pane, 2 #2525 16.00 —
Complete booklet, #2525f 16.00

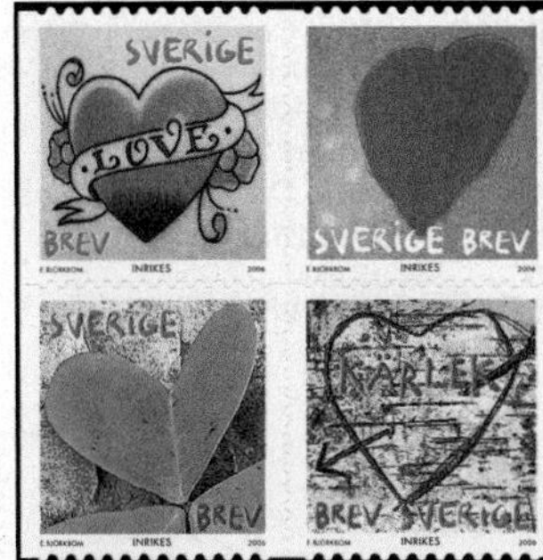

Hearts — A836

No. 2526: a, Tattooed heart. b, Red heart. c, Heart-shaped leaf. d, Heart carved in tree trunk.

Serpentine Die Cut 10 on 3 Sides

2006, Jan. 26 **Litho.**

Self-Adhesive

2526 A836 Block of 4, #a-d 6.00 5.00
a.-d. (5.50k) Any single 1.50 1.00
e. Booklet pane, 2 each #2526c-2526d, 3 each #2526a-2526b 15.00

Souvenir Sheet

Norse Mythology — A837

No. 2527: a, Skogsraet, reindeer, goats and bird. b, Näcken, horse and violin.

Litho. & Engr.

2006, Mar. 29 *Perf. 12¾*

2527 A837 Sheet of 2 5.25 6.50
a.-b. 10k Either single 2.50 2.50

Souvenir Sheet

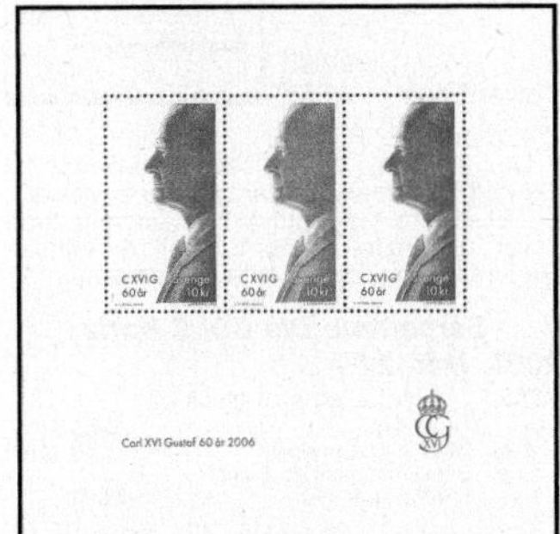

King Carl XVI Gustaf, 60th Birthday — A838

2006, Mar. 29 **Engr.** *Perf. 13x12¾*

2528 A838 Sheet, 2 #2528a, 1 #2528b 8.00 10.50
a. 10k black 3.00 2.50
b. 10k blue 2.60 2.60

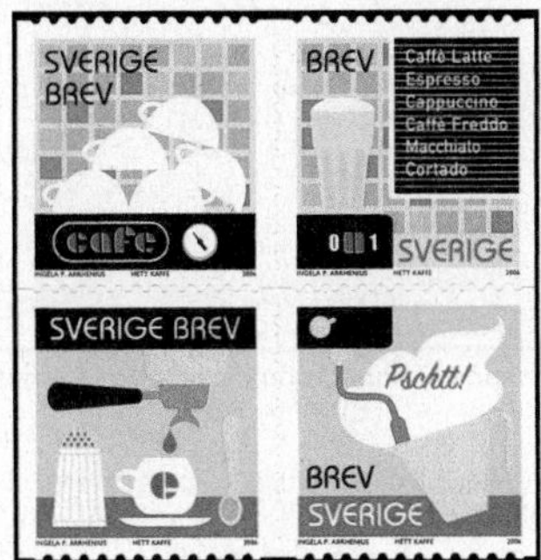

Coffee — A839

No. 2529: a, Coffee cups stacked on coffeemaker. b, Glass of cappucino. c, Espresso machine and cup, sugar dispenser and spoon. d, Steamed milk dispenser and measuring cup.

Serpentine Die Cut 10 on 3 Sides

2006, Mar. 29 **Litho.**

Self-Adhesive

2529 A839 Block of 4 6.25 5.50
a.-d. (5.50k) Any single 1.60 1.00
e. Booklet pane, 3 each #2529a-2529b, 2 each #2529c-2529d 15.50

Suomenlinna (Sveaborg) Fortress, Helsinki, Finland — A840

No. 2530: a, Ship without oars, flagpole at fortress. b, Ship with oars facing fortress. c, Ship with oars, windmill.

Litho. & Engr.

2006, May 4 *Perf. 12¾*

2530 A840 Booklet pane of 3 8.25 9.00
a.-c. 10k Any single 2.75 3.25
Complete booklet, #2530 8.25

See Finland No. 1266.

Track and Field Athletes — A841

Designs: (4.80k), Stefan Holm, high jump. 10k, Christian Olsson, triple jump.

No. 2533: a, Carolina Klüft, heptathlon. b, Kajsa Bergqvist, high jump.

Perf. 13¼ Vert. Syncopated

2006, May 4 **Litho.**

2531 A841 (4.80k) grn & multi 1.40 1.15
2532 A841 10k gray & multi 3.00 2.50
2533 Horiz. pair 3.00 2.25
a.-b. A841 (5.50k) Either single 1.50 .60
Nos. 2531-2533 (3) 7.40 5.90

Europa A842

No. 2534 — Children's art by: a, Alexandros Terzis. b, Linda Wong.

Perf. 12¾x13¼ on 3 Sides

2006, May 4

2534 A842 Pair 5.50 5.50
a.-b. 10k Either single 2.75 2.25
c. Booklet pane, 2 each #2534a-2534b 11.00
Complete booklet, #2534c + 4 etiquettes 11.00

Summer by the Lake — A843

No. 2536: a, Elk and immigrant women's picnic. b, Father and daughter fishing. c, Dog watching swimmers. d, Frog and boaters.

Perf. 12¼ Vert. Syncopated

2006, May 4

2535 A843 (5.50k) shown 1.50 1.00

Self-Adhesive

Size: 34x24mm

Serpentine Die Cut 10 on 3 Sides

2536 Block of 4 6.00 6.75
a.-d. A843 (5.50k) Any single 1.50 .85
e. Booklet pane, 3 each #2536a-2536b, 2 each #2536c-2536d 15.00

Famous Men — A844

Designs: (4.80k,) Carl Michael Bellman (1740-95), poet. (5k), Joseph Martin Kraus (1756-92), composer. (5.50k), Wolfgang Amadeus Mozart (1756-91), composer.

2006, Sept. 7 **Engr.** *Perf. 12¾*

2537 A844 (5.50k) multi 3.00 3.00

Coil Stamps

Perf. 12½ Vert. Syncopated

2538 A844 (4.80k) multi 1.40 1.40
2539 A844 (5k) multi 1.40 1.20
2540 A844 (5.50k) multi 1.50 .85
Nos. 2537-2540 (4) 7.30 6.45

No. 2537 was issued in a sheet of 6 stamps that sold for 38k. Value, $15.

Hanseatic League, 650th Anniv. — A845

Designs: No. 2541, Hanseatic cog, 1380. No. 2542, Building and ships, Visby. No. 2543, City seal, shopper and salesman, Stockholm.

Perf. 12½x13½ on 3 Sides

2006, Sept. 7 **Litho. & Engr.**

2541 A845 10k multi 2.75 2.50
2542 A845 10k multi 2.75 2.50
2543 A845 10k multi 2.75 2.50
a. Booklet pane, #2542-2543, 2 #2541 11.00 —
Complete booklet, #2543a 11.00

See Germany No. 2394.

Souvenir Sheets

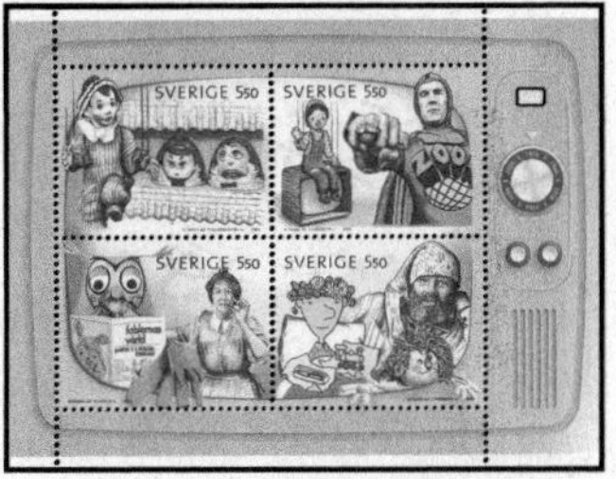

A846

Characters from Swedish Children's Television Shows — A847

No. 2544: a, Andy Pandy (marionette), Humle and Dumle (puppets). b, Anita on Television, Captain Zoom. c, Fablernas Värld (owl), Teskedsgumman (woman). d, Kalles Klätterträd (cartoon), Beppe Wolgers Godnattstunden (man in pajamas).

No. 2545: a, Trazan and Banarne, pink elephant. b, Pippi Longstockings, bear. c, Dinosaur, characters from Tjet och Allram Eest. d, Loophole, Bananas in Pajamas.

Litho. & Engr.

2006, Sept. 30 *Perf. 12½x13*

2544 A846 Sheet of 4 6.00 8.50
a.-d. 5.50k Any single 1.50 1.20

2545 A847 Sheet of 4 6.00 8.50
a.-d. 5.50k Any single 1.50 1.20
e. Booklet pane, #2544-2545 12.00 —
Complete booklet, #2545e 12.00
f. Sheet of 9 #2545a 30.00 30.00

No. 2545e has a row of rouletting separating No. 2544 from No. 2545, and has a wider margin where the pane is attached to the booklet cover.

Winter Scenes in Art — A848

No. 2546: a, Bourdelle's Heracles in Snow, by Prince Eugen. b, Lelle-Kalle, by Sven Ljundberg. c, Modification of a Winter Landscape by W. O. Petersen, by Philip von Schantz. d, Rime Frost on Ice, by Gustaf Adolf Fjaestad.

Perf. 12¾ on 3 Sides

2006, Nov. 9 **Litho.**

2546 A848 Booklet pane of 4 12.00 14.00
a.-d. 10k Any single 3.00 2.00
Complete booklet, #2546 + 4 etiquettes 12.00

Christmas A849

Designs: No. 2547, Santa Claus, New Year's ornament, candles.

No. 2548: a, Star ornament. b, Spherical and New Year's ornaments. c, Bird at feeder, poinsettia. d, Candles.

Perf. 12½ Vert. Syncopated

2006, Nov. 9

2547 A849 (5k) multi 1.50 1.05

Self-Adhesive

Size: 25x25mm

Serpentine Die Cut 10 on 3 Sides

2548 Block of 4 6.00
a.-d. A849 (5k) Any single 1.50 .90
e. Booklet pane, 3 each #2548a-2548b, 2 each #2548c-2548d 15.00

Linnaea Borealis — A850

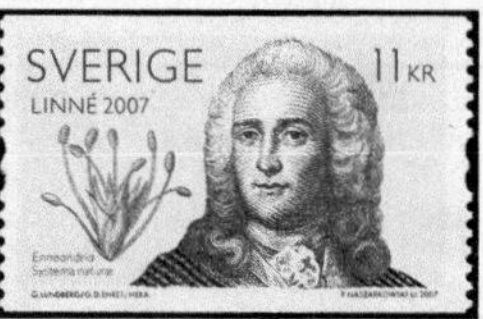

Enneandria and Carl von Linné (1707-78), Creator of Linnaean Taxonomic System — A851

Perf. 12½ Vert. Syncopated

2007, Jan. 25 **Engr.**

2549 A850 (5.50k) multi 1.60 .90

Litho. & Engr.

2550 A851 11k multi 3.25 2.50

Spring — A852

No. 2551: a, Birds, heart, musical notes. b, Sun, cloud, person. c, Flower, heart, person. d, Bird, sun, musical notes.

Serpentine Die Cut 10 on 3 Sides

2007, Jan. 25 **Litho.**

2551 A852 Block of 4 6.25 5.50
a.-d. (5.50k) Any single 1.50 .90
e. Booklet pane, 3 each #2551a-2551b, 2 each #2551c-2551d 15.50

Souvenir Sheet

Intl. Polar Year — A853

No. 2552: a, Stenfragment I, etching by Svenerik Jakobsson. b, Arctic Ocean 2001 88 Degrees North, 145 Degrees East, by Johan Petterson.

Perf. 13, 12¾x13¼ (#2552b)

2007, Jan. 25 **Litho. & Engr.**

2552 A853 Sheet of 2 5.75 7.50
a.-b. 10k Either single 2.75 3.25

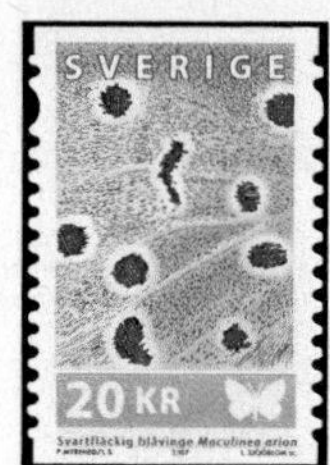

Wing of Maculinea Arion Butterfly — A854

Serpentine Die Cut 9 Vert. Syncopated

2007, Mar. 22 **Litho. & Engr.**

Self-Adhesive

2553 A854 20k multi 5.75 3.00

Printed in sheets of 40.

Swedish Sea Rescue Society, Cent. — A855

Designs: (4.80k), Rowboat, rescuer on jet-ski. (5k), Helicopter rescue. (5.50k), Nautical chart, rescue boat.

Litho. & Engr., Engr. (#2554, 2557)

2007, Mar. 22 ***Perf. 13x12¾***

2554 A855 (5.50k) multi 1.90 1.30

Perf. 12½ Vert. Syncopated

2555 A855 (4.80k) multi 1.40 1.40
2556 A855 (5k) multi 1.40 1.40
2557 A855 (5.50k) multi 1.60 1.10
Nos. 2554-2557 (4) 6.30 5.20

No. 2554 was printed in sheets of 6 that sold for 38k. Value, $15.

Europa A856

No. 2558: a, "Jamboree", globe and airplane. b, Scouts.

Perf. 12½x13¼ on 3 Sides

2007, Mar. 22 **Litho.**

2558 A856 Horiz. or vert. pair 3.25 3.25
a.-b. (5.50k) Either single 1.60 1.35
c. Booklet pane, 2 each #2558a-2558b 6.50 —

Scouting, cent.

Swedish Inventions — A857

No. 2559: a, Wall anchor for screws, by Oswald Thorsman. b, Allergy globe for flowers, by Elisabeth Gagnemyhr. c, Cooling food cover, by Birgitta Folcker-Sundell. d, Adjustable wrench, by Johan Petter Johansson.

Serpentine Die Cut 9 Horiz.

2007, Mar. 22

2559 Horiz. strip or block of 4 5.75
a.-d. A857 (5k) Any single 1.40 1.40
e. Booklet paneof 20, 5 each #2559a-2559d 29.00

Queen Silvia Type of 2005

Perf. 12½ Vert. Syncopated

2007, May 10 **Engr.**

2560 A814 11k grn & blue 3.25 2.25

Souvenir Sheet

Botanical Illustrations by Georg Dionys Ehret — A858

No. 2561: a, Musa x paradisiaca. b, Podophyllum peltatum.

Litho. & Engr.

2007, May 10 ***Perf. 13***

2561 A858 Sheet of 2 6.50 6.50
a.-b. 11k Either single 3.25 3.25

Exists with serial number in margin.

Children Fishing — A859

Designs: No. 2562, Boy fishing in pail.

No. 2563: a, Boy on dock. b, Child kissing fish. c, Girls holding caught fish. d, Boys with fishing pole and caught fish.

Perf. 12½ Vert. Syncopated

2007, May 10 **Litho.**

2562 A859 (5.50k) multi 1.60 .75

Size: 34x24mm

Self-Adhesive

Booklet Stamps

Serpentine Die Cut 10 on 3 Sides

2563 Block of 4 6.50
a.-d. A859 (5.50k) Any single 1.60 .90
e. Booklet pane, 3 each #2563a-2563b, 2 each #2563c-2563d 16.00

Landscapes — A860

No. 2564: a, Rape field and house, Skane. b, Duck on lake, Muddus National Park. c, Elk in forest, Sveafallen. d, Hay field and Kallsjön Lake, Jämtland.

Perf. 12¾x13½

2007, May 10 **Litho. & Engr.**

2564 A860 Booklet pane of 4 13.00 —
a.-d. 11k Any single 3.25 3.25
Complete booklet, #2564 + 4 etiquettes 13.00

Wing of Papilio Machaon A861

Serpentine Die Cut 9¼ Vert. Syncopated

2007, Sept. 27 **Litho. & Engr.**

Self-Adhesive

2565 A861 50k multi 15.00 6.00

Chocolate A862

Designs: No. 2566, Chocolate candy.

No. 2567: a, Chocolate bonbon with whipped cream and cherry. b, Chocolate-dipped strawberry. c, Cacao pod. d, Cup of cocoa.

Perf. 12½ Vert. Syncopated

2007, Sept. 27 **Coil Stamp** **Litho.**

2566 A862 (5.50k) multi 1.75 .85

Self-Adhesive

Booklet Stamps

Serpentine Die Cut 10 on 3 Sides

Size: 25x26mm

2567 Block of 4 7.00
a.-d. A862 (5.50k) Any single 1.75 .85
e. Booklet pane of 10, 3 each #2567a-2567b, 2 each #2567c-2567d 17.50

Swedish Fashion — A863

No. 2568 — Clothing designs by: a, Lars Wallin. b, Ann-Sofie Back. c, Katja of Sweden.

d, Behnaz Aram. e, Gunilla Pontén. f, Carin Rodebjer. g, Rohdi Heintz. h, Nakkna.

Litho. & Engr.

2007, Sept. 29 *Perf. 12½x13*
2568 Booklet pane of 8 12.00 —
a.-h. A863 5.50k Any single 1.50 .95
Complete booklet, #2568 12.00
i. Miniature sheet, 4 each #2568a, 2568g 15.00 15.00

No. 2568i sold for 49k.

Sami Culture A864

Designs: No. 2569, Reindeer from ceremonial drum, country name in red. No. 2570, Silver button, country name in green. No. 2571, Glass dish, country name in blue.

2007, Nov. 8 *Perf. 12¾x13*
2569 A864 11k multi 3.25 3.25

Booklet Stamps

Perf. 12¾x13 on 3 Sides

2570 A864 11k multi 3.00 3.00
2571 A864 11k multi 3.00 3.00
a. Booklet pane of 6, 2 each #2569-2571 17.50 —
Complete booklet, #2571a 17.50
Nos. 2569-2571 (3) 9.25 9.25

No. 2569 was printed in sheets of 4 that sold for 49k. Examples of No. 2569 from booklet pane are perforated on 3 sides like Nos. 2570-2571. No. 2571a sold for 66k.

Souvenir Sheet

Astrid Lindgren (1907-2002), Writer — A865

Litho. & Engr.

2007, Nov. 8 *Perf. 12¾*
2572 A865 11k multi 5.00 5.00

See Germany No. 2462.

Christmas A866

Scenes from children's stories by Astrid Lindgren: No. 2573, Pippi Longstocking rolling gingerbread dough on floor.

No. 2574: a, Houses in winter. b, Children in snowball fight. c, Lotta and father roping Christmas tree to sled. d, Children and horse-drawn sleigh.

Perf. 12½ Vert. Syncopated

2007, Nov. 8 **Coil Stamp** **Litho.**
2573 A866 (5k) multi 1.60 .95

Self-Adhesive

Booklet Stamps

Serpentine Die Cut 10 on 3 Sides

2574 Block of 4 6.50
a.-d. A866 (5k) Any single 1.60 .95
e. Booklet pane of 10, 3 each #2574a-2574b, 2 each #2574c-2574d 16.00

Olof von Dalin (1708-63), Historian — A867

No. 2575: a, Illuminated letter "D." b, Illustration from first edition of *The Swedish Argus.*

Perf. 13¼ Vert. Syncopated

2008, Jan. 24 **Engr.**
2575 A867 Horiz. pair 6.00 6.00
a.-b. 11k Either single 3.00 3.00

Ingmar Bergman (1918-2007), Film Director — A868

Scene From "Fanny and Alexander" — A869

Perf. 13 Vert. Syncopated

2008, Jan. 24 **Engr.**
2576 A868 (5.50k) indigo 1.75 .50

Souvenir Sheet

Litho. & Engr.

Perf. 12¾x13¼

2577 A869 11k multi 4.00 4.00

A book containing an imperf example of No. 2577, an imperf example of the litho portions of No. 2577 and an imperf example of the engraved portions of No. 2577 sold for 299k.

A870

Insects — A871

Designs: (4.80k), Bombus hypnorum (bee). (5k), Formica rufa (ants). (5.50k), Coccinella (ladybug).

2008, Jan. 24 **Litho.** *Perf. 13½*
2578 A870 (5.50k) multi 2.00 1.20

Coil Stamps

Engr.

Perf. 12½ Vert. Syncopated

Size: 27x21mm

2579 A871 (4.80k) multi 1.50 1.50

Size: 28x24mm

2580 A871 (5k) multi 1.60 1.35

Litho.

Perf. 13¼ Vert. Syncopated

Size: 27x28mm

2581 A870 (5.50k) multi 1.75 .50
Nos. 2578-2581 (4) 6.85 4.55

Coil Stamp

Perf. 13¼ Horiz. Syncopated

2581A A870 (5.50k) multi 1.75 .50

No. 2578 was printed in a sheet of 6 that sold for 38k. Value, $15.

Dogs — A872

No. 2582: a, Lagotto Romagnolo (light green background). b, Saluki (pink background). c, Pug (yellow background). d, Great Dane (light blue background).

Serpentine Die Cut 10 on 3 Sides

2008, Jan. 24 **Litho.**
2582 A872 Block of 4 7.00
a.-d. (5.50k) Any single 1.75 .90
e. Booklet pane of 10, 3 each # 2582a, 2582c, 2 each #2582b, 2582d 17.50

Trees — A873

No. 2583: a, Juniperus communis tree. b, Juniperus communis berries.

No. 2584: a, Betula pendula tree. b, Betula pendula catkins.

Perf. 12 Vert. Syncopated

2008, Mar. 27 **Litho.**
2583 A873 Horiz. pair .60 .60
a.-b. 1k Either single .30 .25
2584 A873 Horiz. pair 1.20 1.00
a.-b. 2k Either single .50 .25

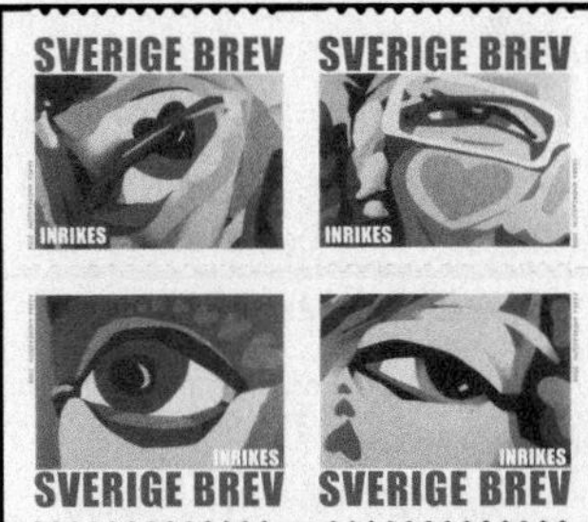

Eyes and Hearts — A874

No. 2585: a, Eye with heart-shaped pupil. b, Eye with heart on cheek. c, Eye with hearts as eyebrow. d, Eye with hearts as teardrops.

Serpentine Die Cut 10 on 3 Sides

2008, Mar. 27 **Self-Adhesive**
2585 A874 Block of 4 7.00
a.-d. (5.50k) Any single 1.75 .90
e. Booklet pane of 10, 3 each #2585a-2585b, 2 each #2585c-2585d 17.50

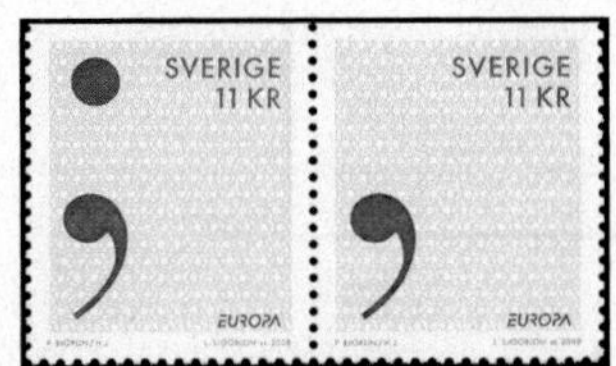

Europa — A875

No. 2586: a, Semicolon. b, Comma.

Perf. 12¾ on 3 Sides

2008, Mar. 27 **Litho. & Engr.**
2586 A875 Pair 5.00 5.00
a.-b. 11k Either single 2.50 2.50
c. Booklet pane of 4, 2 each #2586a-2586b 10.00
Complete booklet, #2586c + 4 etiquettes 10.00

Souvenir Sheet

Blakulla — A876

No. 2587: a, Woman riding backwards on ram. b, Bats.

2008, Mar. 27 *Perf. 12¾*
2587 A876 Sheet of 2 6.50 6.50
a.-b. 11k Either single 3.25 3.25

Butterfly Wings — A877

Wings of: 5k, Argynnis aglaja. 10k, Parnassius apollo.

Serpentine Die Cut 9¼ Vert. Syncopated

2008, May 15 **Litho. & Engr.**

Self-Adhesive

2588 A877 5k multi 1.50 1.00

Size: 24x34mm

2589 A877 10k multi 2.50 1.50

Food Served Outdoors A878

Designs: No. 2590, Plate of crawfish, glasses of wine.

No. 2591: a, Strawberry cake, potatoes, cheese, pickled herring in sour cream and chives. b, Fish on grill. c, Coffee and pastries. d, Ham, bread, watermelon, tomatoes, wine.

Perf. 12¾ Vert. Syncopated

2008, May 15 **Coil Stamp** **Litho.**
2590 A878 (5.50k) multi 1.75 .80

Booklet Stamps

Self-Adhesive

Size: 34x23mm

Serpentine Die Cut 10 on 3 Sides

2591 Block of 4 7.00
a.-d. A878 (5.50k) Any single 1.75 .95
e. Booklet pane of 10, 3 each #2591a-2591b, 2 each #2591c-2591d 18.00

Sailing Ships A879

Designs: No. 2592, Tre Kronor af Stockholm.

No. 2593: a, Training ship Gunilla. b, Like #2592. c, Gratitude. d, Gladan and Falken.

Perf. 12½x12¾

2008, May 15 **Litho. & Engr.**
2592 A879 11k multi 3.50 3.50

Perf. 12½x12¾ on 3 Sides

2593 Booklet pane of 4 12.50 —
a.-d. A879 11k Any single 3.00 3.00
Complete booklet, #2593 + 4 etiquettes 12.50

No. 2592 was printed in sheets of 4 that sold for 49k. Value, $17.50.

Organic Fruits and Vegetables A880

Designs: No. 2594, Apples. 11k, Carrots.
No. 2596, vert.: a, Beets. b, Cabbages. c, Pumpkin. d, Potatoes.

Perf. 12½ Vert. Syncopated

2008, Sept. 25 **Litho.**

Coil Stamps

2594 A880 (5.50k) multi 1.75 .85

Size: 27x21mm

2595 A880 11k multi 2.50 1.50

Booklet Stamps

Self-Adhesive

Serpentine Die Cut 10 on 3 Sides

Size: 23x27mm

2596 Block of 4 7.00
a.-d. A880 (5.50k) Any single 1.75 1.00
e. Booklet pane of 10, 3 each #2596a, 2596c, 2 each #2596b, 2596d 17.50

A881

Comic Strips — A882

No. 2597: a, Assar, by Ulf Lundkvist. b, Ensamma Mamman, by Cecilia Torudd. c, Arne Anka, by Charlie Christensen. d, Rocky, by Martin Kellerman.
No. 2598: a, Nameless Gloomy Girl, by Nina Hemmingsson. b, Hälge, by Lars Mortimer. c, Socker-Conny, by Joakim Pirinen. d, Swedish Manga, by Asa Ekström.

Litho. & Engr.

2008, Sept. 25 ***Perf. 12½x13***

2597 A881 Sheet of 4 6.00 8.50
a.-d. 5.50k Any single 1.50 1.20
2598 A882 Sheet of 4 6.00 8.50
a.-d. 5.50k Any single 1.50 1.20
e. Booklet pane, #2597-2598 12.00 —
Complete booklet, #2598e 12.00
f. Miniature sheet of 9, 5 #2597a, 4 #2598b 15.00 15.00

No. 2598e has a row of rouletting separating No. 2597 from No. 2598, and has a wider margin where the pane is attached to the booklet cover. No. 2598f sold for 54.50k.

Souvenir Sheet

Dario Fo, 1997 Nobel Laureate for Literature — A883

No. 2599: a, Fo (31x39mm). b, Illustration on Fo's Nobel diploma (34x50mm).

Litho. & Engr.

2008, Nov. 13 ***Perf. 12¾***

2599 A883 Sheet of 2 4.75 4.75
a.-b. 11k Either single 2.25 2.25

Winter Activities — A884

No. 2600: a, Child sledding. b, Snowball lantern and house. c, Children making snowman.

2008, Nov. 13 ***Perf. 12¾ on 3 Sides***

Booklet Stamps

2600 A884 Horiz. strip of 3 8.00 8.00
a.-c. 11k Any single 2.60 2.60
d. Booklet pane of 6, 2 each #2600a-2600c 16.00 —
Complete booklet, #2600d + 6 etiquettes 16.00

A885

Christmas — A886

No. 2602 — Various wreaths with background color of: a, Green. b, Gray. c, Blue. d, Brown.

Perf. 12¾ Vert. Syncopated

2008, Nov. 13 **Coil Stamp** **Litho.**

2601 A885 (5k) multi 1.70 1.00

Booklet Stamps

Self-Adhesive

2602 A886 Block of 4 6.75
a.-d. (5k) Any single 1.70 .90
e. Complete booklet, 3 each #2602a-2602b, 2 each #2602c-2602d 17.00

A887

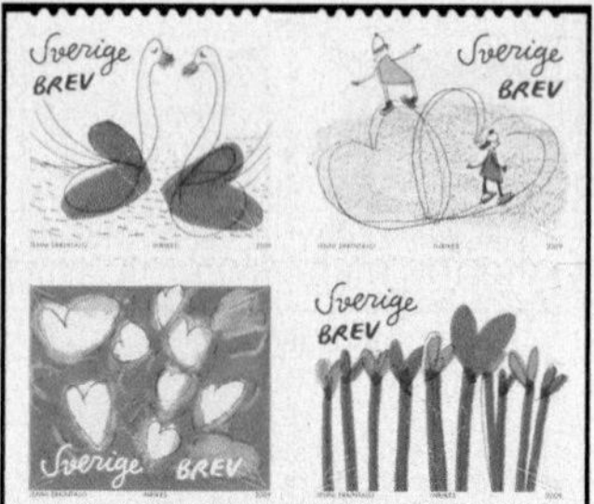

Greetings — A888

No. 2604: a, Swans. b, Skaters making hearts in ice. c, White hearts. d, Hearts as flowers.

Perf. 12¾ Vert. Syncopated

2009, Jan. 29 **Litho. & Engr.**

Coil Stamp

2603 A887 (6k) red & pink 1.50 .60

Booklet Stamps

Self-Adhesive

Serpentine Die Cut 10 on 3 Sides

2604 A888 Block of 4 7.00
a.-d. (6k) Any single 1.75 .75
e. Booklet pane of 10, 3 each #2604a-2604b, 2 each #2604c-2604d 17.50

Die cuts and rouletting are found on face of Nos. 2604a-2604d to prevent reuse of stamps.

Europa — A889

No. 2605: a, Polarimeter. b, Star chart of Crab Nebula, balloon.

Perf. 12¾ on 3 Sides

2009, Jan. 29 **Litho.**

Booklet Stamps

2605 A889 Horiz. or vert. pair 5.50 5.00
a.-b. 12k Either single 2.50 2.25
c. Booklet pane of 4, 2 each #2605a-2605b 11.00 —
Complete booklet, #2605c + 4 etiquettes 11.00

A small star-shaped hole is punched into No. 2605b.

Automobiles — A890

Designs: Nos. 2606, 2608e, Ford Mustang convertible. 12k, Volvo Amazon and trailer.
No. 2608: a, Volkswagen 1200. b, Volvo PV 444. c, Cadillac Coupe de Ville. d, Citroen DS 19.

Litho. & Engr.

2009, Jan. 29 ***Perf. 12¾***

2606 A890 (6k) multi 2.50 2.00

Coil Stamp

Engr.

Perf. 12¾ Vert. Syncopated

2607 A890 12k multi 3.00 2.00

Booklet Stamps

Perf. 12¾ Horiz.

2608 Vert. strip of 5 10.00 10.00
a.-e. A890 (6k) Any single 2.00 2.00
f. Booklet pane of 10, 2 each #2608a-2608e 20.00 —
Complete booklet, #2608f 20.00

No. 2606 was printed in sheets of 6 that sold for 41k. Value, $15.

A891

A892

Birds — A893

Designs: (5k), Pandion haliaetus. (5.50k), Accipiter nisus.
No. 2611: a, Haliaeetus albicilla. b, Asio flammeus.

Perf. 12¾ Vert. Syncopated

2009, Mar. 26 **Engr.**

Coil Stamps

2609 A891 (5k) multi 1.25 1.25
2610 A892 (5.50k) multi 1.40 .70

Perf. 13¼ Vert. Syncopated

2611 A893 Horiz. pair 3.00 2.00
a.-b. (6k) Either single 1.50 .70
Nos. 2609-2611 (3) 5.65 3.95

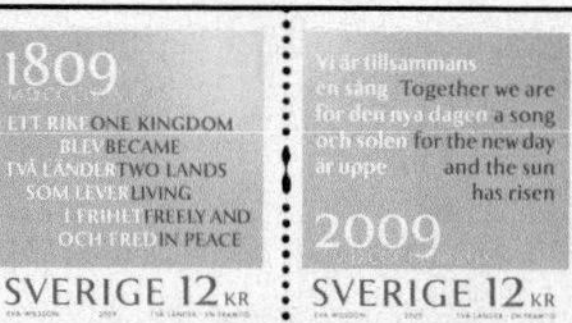

Creation of the Grand Duchy of Finland, Bicent. — A894

No. 2612 — Text and date: a, 1809. b, 2009.

Perf. 13¼ Vert. Syncopated

2009, Mar. 26 **Litho.**

Coil Stamps

2612 A894 Horiz. pair 5.50 5.00
a.-b. 12k Either single 2.75 2.50

Souvenir Sheet

Wheel of Life, by Albertus Pictor (c. 1440-1509) — A895

No. 2613: a, Musician, man riding wheel. b, Man at top of wheel. c, Man falling off wheel, corpse.

Litho. & Engr.

2009, Mar. 26 ***Perf. 12¾x13***

2613 A895 Sheet of 3 8.00 7.50
a.-c. 12k Any single 2.75 2.50

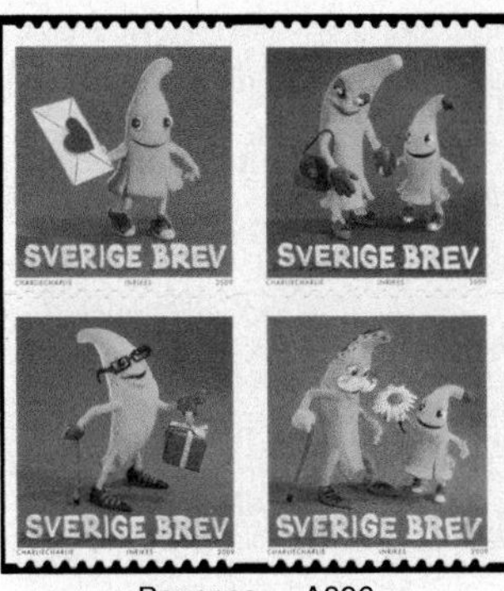

Bananas — A896

No. 2614 — Clay figures: a, Young banana with love letter. b, Banana mother and child. c, Banana holding gift. d, Young banana giving flower to old banana.

Serpentine Die Cut 10 on 3 Sides

2009, Mar. 26 Litho.

Booklet Stamps

Self-Adhesive

2614 A896 Block of 4 6.50
a.-d. (6k) Any single 1.80 .90
e. Booklet pane of 10, 3 each #2614a-2614b, 2 each #2614c-2614d 16.00

Queen Silvia Type of 2005

Perf. 12½ Vert. Syncopated

2009, May 14 Coil Stamp Engr.

2615 A814 12k multi 3.00 1.50

Architecture — A897

Designs: No. 2616, Turning Torso, Malmö.
No. 2617: a, Kaknäs Tower, Stockholm. b, Lugnet ski jump, Falun. c, Balder roller coaster, Gothenburg. d, Like #2616.

2009, May 14 Engr. *Perf. 12½x12¾*

2616 A897 12k dark blue 3.25 3.25

Booklet Stamps

Perf. 12½x12¾ on 3 Sides

2617 Booklet pane of 4 11.00 10.50
a.-d. A897 12k Any single 2.75 2.50
e. Complete booklet, #2617 + 4 etiquettes 11.00

No. 2616 was printed in a sheet of 4 stamps that sold for 53k.

Flora and Fauna A898

Designs: No. 2618, Sand star, Kosterhavet Park.
No. 2619: a, Globeflowers, Abisko National Park. b, Tree frog, Stenshuvud National Park. c, Dormouse, Garphyttan National Park. d, Cranberries, Store Mosse National Park.

Perf. 12¼ Vert. Syncopated

2009, May 14 Coil Stamp Litho.

2618 A898 (6k) multi 1.50 1.00

Booklet Stamps

Self-Adhesive

Size: 37x26mm

Serpentine Die Cut 10 on 3 Sides

2619 Block of 4 6.00
a.-d. A898 (6k) Any single 1.50 1.50
e. Booklet pane of 10, 3 each #2619a-2619b, 2 each #2619c-2619d 15.00

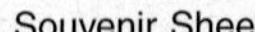
Souvenir Sheet

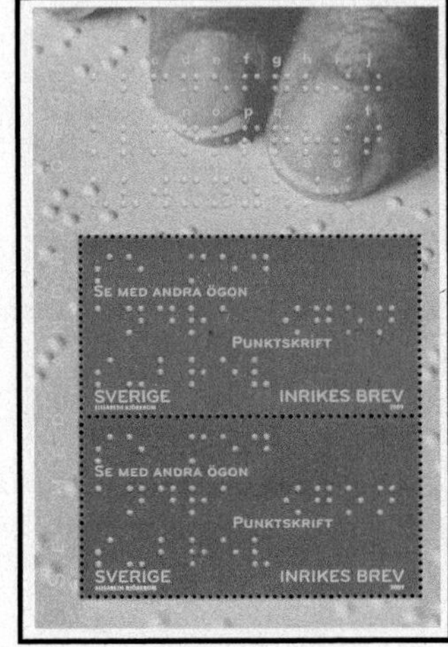

Braille Text — A899

No. 2620 — Text in Swedish and Braille with background color of: a, Red violet. b, Purple.

2009, May 14 Litho. *Perf. 12¾x12½*

2620 A899 Sheet of 2 3.00 3.00
a.-b. (6k) Either single 1.50 .75

Louis Braille (1809-52), educator of the blind. Braille dots were applied by a thermographic process.

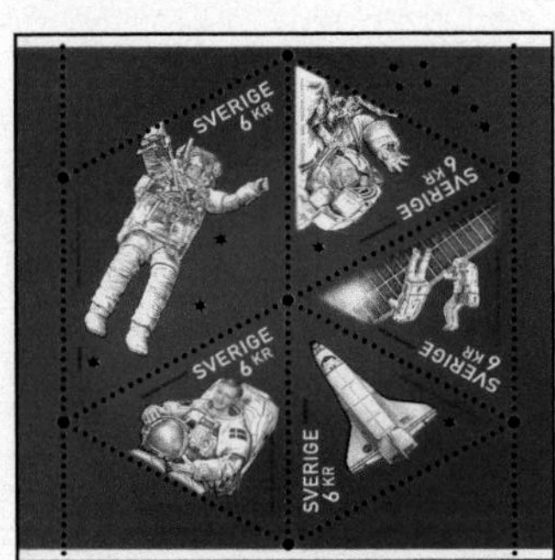

Christer Fugelsang, First Swede in Space — A900

No. 2621: a, Fugelsang waving (39x33mm). b, Fugelsang and Astronaut Robert Curbeam repairing solar panel (39x33mm). c, Space Shuttle Discovery (39x33mm). d, Fugelsang with helmet on lap (39x33mm). e, Fugelsang on space walk (39x66mm).

Litho. & Engr.

2009, Sept. 24 *Perf. 12¾*

2621 A900 Block of 5 7.50 7.50
a.-e. 6k Any single 1.50 1.00
f. Booklet pane, 2 #2621 15.00 —
Complete booklet, #2621f 15.00
g. Sheet of 9 #2621d 15.00 15.00

Star-shaped holes are punched into Nos. 2621a, 2621c and 2621e. No. 2621g sold for 59k.

A901

A902

Spices — A903

Designs: No. 2622, Anethum graveolens (dill). 12k, Allium schoenoprasum (chives).
No. 2624: a, Ocimum basilicum (basil). b, Capsicum (chili peppers). c, Rosmarinus officinalis (rosemary). d, Allium sativum (garlic).

Perf. 12½ Vert. Syncopated

2009, Sept. 24 Coil Stamps Engr.

2622 A901 (6k) multi 1.75 .80
2623 A902 12k multi 2.75 2.00

Booklet Stamps

Litho.

Serpentine Die Cut 10 on 3 Sides

2624 A903 Block of 4 6.00 5.25
a.-d. (6k) Any single 1.50 .75
e. Booklet pane of 10, 3 each #2624a-2624b, 2 each #2624c-2624d 15.00

White Animals A910

No. 2625: a, Lagopus muta. b, Mustela erminea. c, Lepus timidus.

Perf. 12¾ on 3 Sides

2009, Nov. 19 Engr.

Booklet Stamps

2625 Horiz. strip of 3 10.00 8.50
a.-c. A910 12k Any single 3.25 2.75
d. Booklet pane of 6, 2 each #2625a-2625c, + 6 etiquettes 20.00 —
Complete booklet, #2625d 20.00

A911

Christmas — A912

No. 2627 — Various wrapped gifts including: a, Lamp and bottle. b, Large ball and saw. c, Teddy bear and rolling pin. d, Toy train and flower.

Perf. 13¼ Vert. Syncopated

2009, Nov. 19 Coil Stamp Litho.

2626 A911 (5.50k) multi 1.50 .90

Booklet Stamps

Self-Adhesive

Serpentine Die Cut 10 on 3 Sides

2627 A912 Block of 4 6.40
a.-d. (5.50k) Any single 1.60 1.60
e. Booklet pane of 10, 3 each #2627a-2627b, 2 each #2627c-2627d 16.00

A913

Castles and Palaces — A914

Designs: Nos. 2628, 2629d, Läckö Castle. No. 2629a, Vadstena Castle. No. 2629b, Ulriksdal Palace. No. 2629c, Tjolöholm Castle. No. 2629e, Sofiero Palace.

2010, Jan. 28 Engr. *Perf. 12¾x12½*

2628 A913 12k blue & green 3.50 3.50

Booklet Stamps

Self-Adhesive

Serpentine Die Cut 10 Horiz. (A914), Serpentine Die Cut 10 on 3 Sides (A913)

2629 Booklet pane of 5 + 5 etiquettes 16.50
a.-c. A914 12k Any single 3.25 1.90
d.-e. A913 12k Either single 3.25 1.90

No. 2628 was printed in sheets of 4 that sold for 53k. Value, $15.

Europa — A915

No. 2630 — Illustrations from children's books: a, Maja's Alphabet, by Lena Andersson. b, Children of the Forest, by Elsa Beskow.

Perf. 13¼ Vert. Syncopated

2010, Jan. 28 Litho. & Engr.

Coil Stamps

2630 A915 Horiz. pair 6.00 5.50
a.-b. 12k Either single 3.00 2.25

Black Cats — A916

No. 2631 — Cat: a, Drinking from saucer. b, Playing with ball. c, Arching back. d, Stretching.

Serpentine Die Cut 10

2010, Jan. 28 **Litho.**

Booklet Stamps

Self-Adhesive

2631 A916 Block of 4 7.50 7.50
a.-d. (6k) Any single 2.00 1.00
e. Booklet pane of 10, 3 each #2631a-2631b, 2 each #2631c-2631d 18.50

King Carl XVI Gustaf — A917

Queen Silvia — A918

Perf. 13¼ Vert. Syncopated

2010, Mar. 24 **Coil Stamps** **Engr.**

2632 A917 (6k) dark green 1.75 .40
2633 A918 12k dark brown 2.80 1.00

Wedding Rings — A919

Celebrations — A920

No. 2635: a, Cake. b, Birds. c, Hands and hearts. d, Champagne bottle and glasses.

Perf. 13¼ Vert. Syncopated

2010, Mar. 24 **Coil Stamp** **Litho.**

2634 A919 (6k) multi 1.75 .50

Booklet Stamps

Self-Adhesive

Serpentine Die Cut 10 on 3 Sides

2635 A920 Block of 4 7.00 7.00
a.-d. (6k) Any single 1.75 .90
e. Booklet pane of 10, 3 each #2635a-2635b, 2 each #2635c-2635d 17.50

Souvenir Sheet

Life on the Coast — A921

No. 2636: a, Mytilus edulis. b, Fishing boat SD141 Emelie.

Litho. & Engr.

2010, Mar. 24 ***Perf. 13x12½***

2636 A921 Sheet of 2 7.00 7.50
a.-b. 12k Either single 3.50 3.50

Karolinska Institutet, Bicent. — A922

No. 2637 — Electron microscope photographs by Lennart Nilsson of: a, Silicon (blue crystals) b, Selenium (red violet crystals).

Perf. 13¼ Vert. Syncopated

2010, May 13 **Engr.**

Coil Stamps

2637 A922 Horiz. pair 3.00 2.50
a.-b. (5.50k) Any single 1.50 1.00

Sea Mammals — A923

No. 2638: a, Phocoena phocoena. b, Enhydra lutris. c, Balaenoptera musculus. d, Pusa hispida.

Perf. 13x12¾ on 3 Sides

2010, May 13 **Litho. & Engr.**

Booklet Stamps

2638 A923 Block of 4 12.50 11.50
a.-d. 12k Any single 3.00 2.75
e. Booklet pane, #2638a-2638d + 4 etiquettes 12.50
Complete booklet, #2638e 12.50

See Canada No. 2387.

A924

Pansies — A925

No. 2640 — Flower color: a, Yellow and red, green petal showing. b, Blue violet. c, Red. d, Purple and red.

Perf. 12½ Vert. Syncopated

2010, May 13 **Litho.**

Coil Stamp

2639 A924 (6k) multi 1.80 1.20

Booklet Stamps

Self-Adhesive

Serpentine Die Cut 10 on 3 Sides

2640 A925 Block of 4 7.25 7.00
a.-d. (6k) Any single 1.80 .90
e. Booklet pane of 10, 3 each #2640a-2640b, 2 each #2640c-2640d 18.00

Souvenir Sheet

Wedding of Crown Princess Victoria and Daniel Westling — A926

No. 2641: a, Crown Princess Victoria (27x36mm). b, Royal monogram of Crown Princess Victoria (27x36mm). c, Crown Princess Victoria and Daniel Westling (54x40mm).

Perf. 13¼x12¾

2010, May 13 **Litho. & Engr.**

2641 A926 Sheet of 3 4.50 4.50
a.-c. 6k Any single 1.50 1.50

Souvenir Sheet

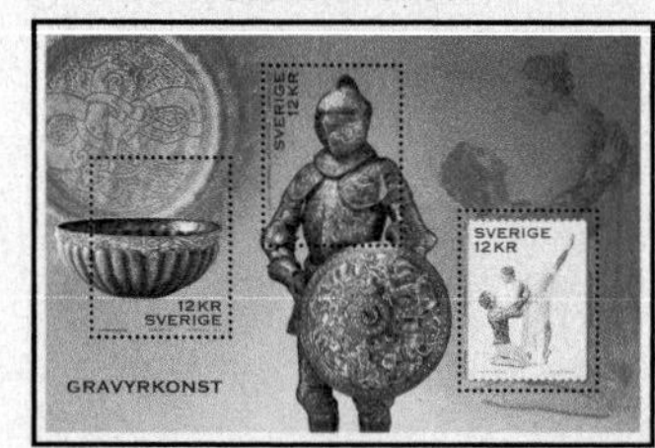

Art of Engraving — A927

No. 2642: a, Viking era silver bowl, engraved by Martin Mörck. b, Armor of King Erik XIV, engraved by Lars Sjööblom. c, Sweden Type A305, engraved by Czeslaw Slania.

Litho. & Engr.

2010, Aug. 26 ***Perf. 12¾***

2642 A927 Sheet of 3 9.50 8.75
a.-c. 12k Any single 3.00 2.75

See Ireland No. 1895.

A928

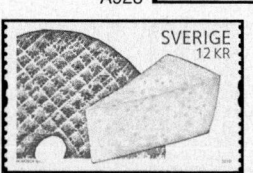

A929

Swedish Foods — A930

Designs: No. 2643, Waffles and cloudberries. 12k, Crispbread and Västerbotten cheese.

No. 2645: a, Girl eating peppermint stick. b, Hand holding gravlax (marinated salmon). c, Man cutting pyramid cake. d, Man sniffing can of fermented herring.

Perf. 12½ Vert. Syncopated

2010, Aug. 26 **Engr.**

Coil Stamps

2643 A928 (6k) bis & org 1.75 1.20

Perf. 12¾ Vert. Syncopated

2644 A929 12k brn & bis 2.70 1.50

Booklet Stamps

Litho.

Serpentine Die Cut 10 on 3 Sides

Self-Adhesive

2645 A930 Block of 4 7.00
a.-d. (6k) Any single 1.75 .90
e. Booklet pane of 10, 3 each #2645a-2645b, 2 each #2645c-2645d 17.50

Crime Novelists — A931

No. 2646: a, Maj Sjöwall, Per Wahlöö (1926-75), helicopter and handcuffs (66x27mm). b, Henning Mankell, dead body, handcuffs, gavel (66x27mm). c, Liza Marklund and police car (66x27mm). d, Hakan Nesser and pistol (33x30mm). e, Stieg Larsson (1954-2004) and laptop computer (33x30mm).

Litho. & Engr.

2010, Aug. 26 ***Perf. 13x12¾***

2646 A931 Block of 5 7.50 7.50
a.-e. 6k Any single 1.50 1.00
f. Booklet pane, 2 #2646 15.00 —
Complete booklet, #2646f 15.00
g. Sheet of 9 #2646d 15.00 15.00

Nos. 2646a-2646c each have two holes and Nos. 2646d-2646e each have one hole drilled through stamp. No. 2646g sold for 59k.

A932

A933

A934

A935

Snowflakes A936

Perf. 12¾x12½

2010, Nov. 18 Litho. & Engr.

2647 A932 12k multi 3.50 3.50

Self-Adhesive

Serpentine Die Cut 10 on 3 Sides, Serpentine Die Cut 10 Horiz. (A933)

2648 Booklet pane of 5 + 5 etiquettes 13.50
a. A933 12k multi 2.70 1.50
b. A934 12k multi 2.70 1.50
c. A932 12k multi 2.70 1.50
d. A935 12k multi 2.70 1.50
e. A936 12k multi 2.70 1.50

No. 2647 was printed in a sheet of 4 that sold for 53k. Value, $16.

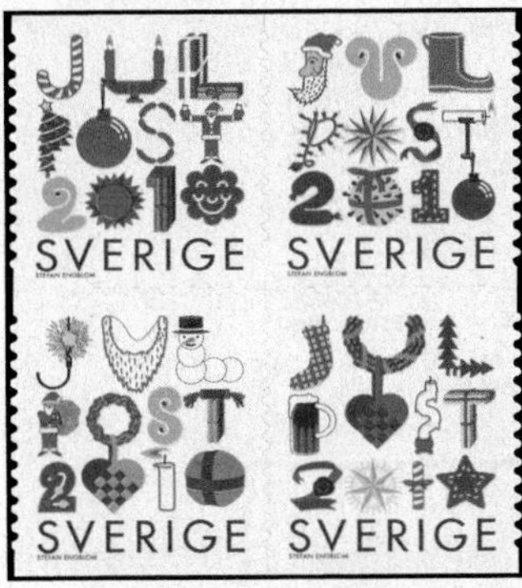
Christmas — A937

No. 2649 — "J" as: a, Candy cane. b, Santa Claus. c, Christmas light. d, Stocking.

Serpentine Die Cut 10 on 3 Sides

2010, Nov. 18 Litho.

Booklet Stamps

Self-Adhesive

2649 A937 Block of 4 6.40
a.-d. (5.50k) Any single 1.60 .80
e. Booklet pane of 10, 3 each #2649a, 2649c, 2 each #2649b, 2649d 16.00

Fossils — A938

Fossils of: 30k, Molluscs. 40k, Cuttlefish.

Serpentine Die Cut 9 Horiz.

2011, Jan. 27 Litho. & Engr.

Self-Adhesive

2650 A938 30k multi 8.00 1.00

Serpentine Die Cut 9 Vert.

Size: 28x28mm

2651 A938 40k multi 9.50 1.50

Bicycles and Tricycles A939

No. 2652: a, Tricycle and air pump. b, Bicycle and helmet. c, Bicycle and chain guard. d, Bicycle and chain ring. e, Tricycle and horn.

2011, Jan. 27 ***Perf. 12¾ Horiz.***

Booklet Stamps

2652 Vert. strip of 5 9.00 9.00
a.-e. A939 (6k) Any single 1.80 1.00
f. Booklet pane, 2 #2652 18.00 —
Complete booklet, #2652f 18.00

A940

Flag of Sweden — A941

No. 2654: a, Flag on flagpole. b, People waving flags. c, Flag on person's forehead. d, Flag on vehicle.

Perf. 12½ Vert. Syncopated

2011, Jan. 27 Litho.

Coil Stamp

2653 A940 (6k) multi 1.80 1.20

Booklet Stamps

Self-Adhesive

Serpentine Die Cut 10 on 3 Sides

2654 A941 Block of 4 7.50 7.25
a.-d. (6k) Any single 1.90 .95
e. Booklet pane of 10, 3 each #2654a-2654b, 2 each #2654c-2654d 18.50

Compare types A940 and A1015.

Hands and Curved Lines — A942

No. 2655 — Hands and lines in: a, Red. b, Blue.

Perf. 13¼ Vert. Syncopated

2011, Mar. 24 Litho. & Engr.

Coil Stamps

2655 A942 Horiz. pair, #a-b 2.50 2.75
a.-b. (5k) Either single 1.25 1.25

Europa — A943

No. 2655 — Wood of: a, Betula. b, Pica abies.

2011, Mar. 24 Coil Stamps

2656 A943 Horiz. pair, #a-b 6.00 5.50
a.-b. 12k Either single 3.00 1.10

Intl. Year of Forests.

A944

Renewable Energy — A945

No. 2658: a, Clouds, solar panels. b, Field, wind turbine. c, Trees, bioenergy tank. d, Underwater scene, wave energy converter.

Perf. 13 Vert. Syncopated

2011, Mar. 24 Coil Stamp Litho.

2657 A944 (6k) multi 1.60 1.00

Booklet Stamps

Self-Adhesive

Serpentine Die Cut 10 on 3 Sides

2658 A945 Block of 4 7.50
a.-d. (6k) Any single 1.80 .90
e. Booklet pane of 10, 3 each #2658a-2658b, 2 each #2658c-2658d 18.00

Scenes From Industrial Towns — A946

Buildings or workers in: Nos. 2659, 2660e, Mackmyra. No. 2660a, Forsvik, horiz. (58x29mm). No. 2660b, Glasriket. No. 2660c, Avesta. No. 2660d, Jonsered.

2011, Mar. 24 Engr. ***Perf. 12¾x12½***

2659 A946 12k dk brn & brn 3.50 2.00

Self-Adhesive

Serpentine Die Cut10 on 2 or 3 Sides

2660 Booklet pane of 5 + 5 etiquettes 17.50
a.-e. A946 12k Any single 3.50 2.00

No. 2659 was printed in sheets of 4 that sold for 53k. Value, $15.

Souvenir Sheet

Struve Geodetic Arc UNESCO World Heritage Site — A947

No. 2661: a, Theodolite. b, Wilhelm Struve (1793-1864), astronomer.

2011, May 6 Litho. & Engr. ***Perf. 13***

2661 A947 Sheet of 2 6.00 6.00
a.-b. 12k Either single 3.00 3.00

Water Lilies — A948

No. 2662: a, Four red water lilies, one white water lily, dragonfly. b, Four white water lilies, three yellow water lilies, dragonfly. c, Yellow water lily. d, White water lily.

Perf. 12¾ on 3 Sides

2011, May 12 Litho.

Booklet Stamps

2662 A948 Block of 4 11.00 10.25
a.-d. 12k Any single 2.70 2.50
e. Booklet pane, #2662a-2662d + 4 etiquettes 11.00
Complete booklet, #2662e 11.00

Banana Split A949

Ice Cream — A950

No. 2664: a, Ice cream bar. b, Vanilla ice cream cone. c, Sundae with cherries. d, Chocolate-coated ice cream cone.

Perf. 12½ Vert. Syncopated

2011, May 12 Litho. Coil Stamp

2663 A949 (6k) multi 1.90 1.20

Booklet Stamps
Self-Adhesive

Serpentine Die Cut 10 on 3 Sides

2664 A950 Block of 4 9.00
a.-d. (6k) Any single 1.80 1.00
e. Booklet pane of 10, 3 each #2664a-2664b, 2 each #2664c-2664d 18.00

Equestrian Sports — A951

Designs: Nos. 2665, 2666a, Harness racing (Stig H. Johannson driving Victory Tilly). No. 2666b, Show jumping (Malin Baryard-Johnsson on Butterfly Flip). No. 2666c, Pony racing (Ebba Stigenberg on Norrskenets Grim). No. 2666d, Dressage (Jan Brink on Briar). No. 2666e, Eventing (Hannes Melin on Gaston KLG).

Perf. 12¾x12½

2011, Aug. 25 Litho. & Engr.

2665 A951 6k multi 2.00 2.00

Booklet Stamps

Perf. 12¾ Horiz.

2666 Vert. strip of 5 7.50 7.50
a.-e. A951 6k Any single 1.50 1.00
f. Booklet pane, 2 #2666 15.00 —
Complete booklet, #2666f 15.00

No. 2665 was printed in sheets of 9 that sold for 59k. Value, $15.

Poppy, Rye and Barley Seed Capsules A952

Conifer Cones A953

A954

A955

A956

Seed Capsules A957

Perf. 12¼ Vert. Syncopated

2011, Aug. 25 Engr.

Coil Stamps

2667 A952 (6k) multi 1.90 .85
2668 A953 12k multi 2.70 2.00

Booklet Stamps
Self-Adhesive
Litho.

Serpentine Die Cut 10 on 3 Sides

2669 Block of 4 7.50
a. A954 (6k) multi 1.80 .90
b. A955 (6k) multi 1.80 .90
c. A956 (6k) multi 1.80 .90
d. A957 (6k) multi 1.80 .90
e. Booklet pane of 10, 3 each #2669a-2669b, 2 each #2669c-2669d 18.00

Winter Clothing — A958

Designs: Nos. 2670, 2671e, Mittens. No. 2671a, Socks, horiz. (62x32mm). No. 2671b, Hats (31x39mm). No. 2671c, Scarf (31x39mm). No. 2671d, Sweater (31x39mm).

Perf. 12¾x12½

2011, Nov. 17 Litho. & Engr.

2670 A958 12k multi 3.50 3.50

Booklet Stamps
Self-Adhesive

Serpentine Die Cut 10 on 2 or 3 Sides

2671 Booklet pane of 5 + 5 etiquettes 16.00
a.-e. A958 12k Any single 3.00 1.60

No. 2670 was printed in a sheet of 4 that sold for 53k. Value, $16.

Souvenir Sheet

Intl. Year of Chemistry — A959

No. 2672: a, Marie Curie (1867-1934), 1911 Nobel laureate for Chemistry (40x55mm). b, Nobel medal and radium, horiz. (36x28mm).

Perf. 13x12¾ (#2672a), 12¾ (#2672b)

2011, Nov. 17

2672 A959 Sheet of 2 6.00 6.00
a.-b. 12k Either single 3.00 3.00

See Poland No. 4024.

Christmas Cactus — A960

Poinsettia A961

Amaryllis A962

Hellebore A963

Serpentine Die Cut 10 on 3 Sides

2011, Nov. 17 Litho.

Booklet Stamps

2673 Block of 4 7.00
a. A960 (5.50k) multi 1.75 .85
b. A961 (5.50k) multi 1.75 .85
c. A962 (5.50k) multi 1.75 .85
d. A963 (5.50k) multi 1.75 .85
e. Booklet pane of 10, 3 each #2673a-2673b, 2 each #2673c-2673d 17.50

Christmas.

Europa — A964

No. 2674 — Tourist attractions: a, Dalarna. b, Ericsson Globe Arena, Stockholm.

Perf. 12½ Vert. Syncopated

2012, Jan. 12 Engr.

Coil Stamps

2674 A964 Horiz. pair 6.50 6.00
a. 12k green 3.25 1.20
b. 12k blue 3.25 1.20

A965

Octahedrons

A966 A967

Perf. 12½ Vert. Syncopated

2012, Jan. 12 Coil Stamp

2675 A965 (5.50k) green 1.50 1.50

Booklet Stamps
Self-Adhesive

Serpentine Die Cut 9 Horiz.

2676 Block or horiz. strip of 4 5.50
a. A966 (5.50k) blue 1.25 1.25
b. A967 (5.50k) red 1.25 1.25
c. A967 (5.50k) blue 1.25 1.25
d. A966 (5.50k) red 1.25 1.25
e. Booklet pane of 20, 5 each #2676a-2676d 27.50

Lill-Babs Performing at People's Park A968

Entrance to People's Park, Borlänge — A969

Entrance to People's Park, Björneborg A970

Dance Floor at People's Park, Arvika A971

Chocolate Wheel at People's Park, Kolsnäs A972

2012, Jan. 12 ***Perf. 12¾***

2677 A968 (6k) claret 2.50 2.50

Coil Stamp

Perf. 12½ Vert. Syncopated

2678 A969 (6k) purple 1.90 1.20

Booklet Stamps
Self-Adhesive

Serpentine Die Cut 10 on 3 Sides

2679 Block of 4 7.25
a. A970 (6k) red 1.80 .90
b. A971 (6k) blue 1.80 .90
c. A968 (6k) blue 1.80 .90
d. A972 (6k) red 1.80 .90
e. Booklet pane of 10, 3 each #2679a-2679b, 2 each #2679c-2679d 17.00

No. 2677 was printed in a sheet of six that sold for 41k. Value, $15.

Fishing Pole With Ambassadeur Reel — A973

Salmon Fly — A974

Hi-Lo Wobbler and Toby Spoon Spinner Lures A975

Coil Stamps

Die Cut Perf. 11¾x11½

2012, Mar. 21 Self-Adhesive

2680 A973 5k multi 1.25 .50

Die Cut Perf. 11¾

2681 A974 10k multi 2.50 1.00
2682 A975 20k multi 5.00 1.50
Nos. 2680-2682 (3) 10.50 10.50

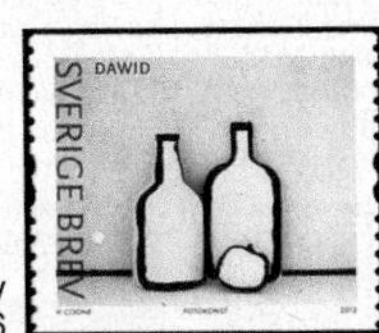

Art Photography
A976

Designs: (6k), 2680, by Dawid.

No. 2684: a, Dreamer in the Blue House, by Sune Jonsson (man with open book, 58x29mm). b, At Home, by Gunnar Smoliansky (plant cutting in glass, 27x36mm). c, Agneta, Finland, by Denise Grünstein (woman swimming, 27x36mm). d, Attempting to Deal With Time and Space, by Annika von Hausswolff (person squeezing balloon, 27x36mm). e, Paris, by Christer Strömholm (people kissing, 27x36mm).

Perf. 12¼ Vert. Syncopated

2012, Mar. 21 Coil Stamp Litho.

2683 A976 (6k) shown 1.80 .50

Serpentine Die Cut 10 Horiz., Serpentine Die Cut 10 on 3 Sides (#2684b-2684d)

2684 Booklet pane of 5 + 5 etiquettes 16.00
a.-e. A976 12k Any single 3.00 1.75

Poultry Breeds — A977

No. 2685: a, Hedemora hens (Hedemorahöna). b, Old Swedish dwarf hens (Gammalsvensk dvärghöna). c, Swedish spotted hens (Skansk blommehöna). d, Orust hens (Orusthöna).

Booklet Stamps

Serpentine Die Cut 10 on 3 Sides

2012, Mar. 21 Self-Adhesive

2685 A977 Block of 4 7.75
a.-d. (6k) Any single 1.90 .95
e. Booklet pane of 10, 3 each #2685a-2685b, 2 each #2685c-2685d 19.00

Souvenir Sheet

Life on the Coast — A978

No. 2686: a, Häradskär Lighthouse, Arkö 833 pilot boat. b, Dash 8Q-300 surveillance airplane.

Litho. & Engr.

2012, Mar. 21 ***Perf. 12¾***

2686 A978 Sheet of 2 6.50 7.00
a.-b 12k Either single 3.25 3.25

Type
Fonts — A979

No. 2687: a, Berling Antiqua. b, Indigo Antiqua. c, Sispos. d, Satura. e, Traffic.

Serpentine Die Cut 9 Horiz.

2012, May 10 Engr.

Self-Adhesive

2687 Vert. strip of 5 15.00
a.-e. A979 12k Any single 3.00 1.10

A980

Olympic Gold Medalists — A981

Designs: 12k, Eric Lemming (1880-1930), javelin gold medalist, 1912 Olympics.

No. 2689: a, Ragnar Skanaker, pistol shooting gold medalist, 1972 Olympics. b, Carolina Klüft, heptathlon gold medalist, 2004 Olympics.

Litho. & Engr. (12k), Litho.

2012, May 10 ***Perf. 12¾***

2688 A980 12k multi 4.00 4.00

Coil Stamps

Perf. 13¼ Vert. Syncopated

2689 A981 Horiz. pair 3.00 3.00
a.-b. (6k) Either single 1.50 .80

Perf. 12¾ Vert. Syncopated

2690 A980 12k multi 3.00 1.75

No. 2688 was printed in sheets of 4 that sold for 53k. Value, $16.

Flowers — A982

Designs: No. 2691: Cowslip, hairy violet, mountain everlasting, meadow saxifrage.

No. 2692: a, Cowslip (gullviva). b, Hairy violet (buskviol). c, Mountain everlasting (kattfot). d, Meadow saxifrage (mandelblomma).

Perf. 13¼ Vert. Syncopated

2012, May 10 Litho. Coil Stamp

2691 A982 (6k) multi 1.75 .80

Booklet Stamps

Self-Adhesive

Serpentine Die Cut 10 on 3 Sides

2692 Block of 4 7.00
a.-d. A982 (6k) Any single 1.75 .80
e. Booklet pane of 10, 3 each #2692a-2692b, 2 each #2692c-2692d 17.50

Souvenir Sheet

Raoul Wallenberg (1912-47), Diplomat — A983

Litho. & Engr.

2012, May 10 ***Perf. 12¾***

2693 A983 12k multi 3.50 3.50

See Hungary No. 4241.

Textile
Art
A984

Details from: Nos. 2694, 2695d, Peace in the Valley — At Last, by Teresa Oscarsson. No. 2695a, June Flowers, by Märta Maas-Fjetterström. No. 2695b, Hommage à Tuskaft, by Laris Strunke. No. 2695c, Oomph, by Viola Grasten. No. 2695e, Signs in an Archive, by Lennart Rohde.

2012, Aug. 16 ***Perf. 12¾***

2694 A984 (6k) multi 2.10 2.10

Booklet Stamps

Perf. 12¾ Horiz.

2695 Vert. strip of 5 9.00 7.00
a.-e. A984 (6k) Any single 1.80 1.00
f. Booklet pane of 10, 2 each #2695a-2695e 18.00 —
Complete booklet, #2695f 18.00

No. 2694 was printed in a sheet of six that sold for 41k. Value, $15.

Youths Writing — A985

No. 2696: a, Girl with pen and letter. b, Boy writing letter under desk lamp. c, Girl writing letter on computer. d, Girl with letter and envelopes.

Serpentine Die Cut 10 on 3 Sides

2012, Aug. 16 Litho.

Booklet Stamps

Self-Adhesive

2696 A985 Block of 4 7.25
a.-d. (6k) Any single 1.80 .90
e. Booklet pane of 10, 3 each #2696a, 2696c, 2 each #2696b, 2696d 18.00

Souvenir Sheet

The Masked Ball, Opera by Daniel Auber — A986

No. 2697: a, Auber (1782-1871). b, King Gustav III of Sweden (1746-92), main character in opera.

Litho. & Engr.

2012, Nov. 9 ***Perf. 12¾***

2697 A986 Sheet of 2 6.00 5.50
a.-b. 12k Either single 3.00 2.75

See France No. 4298.

Christmas — A987

No. 2698 — Christmas tree and ornaments: a, Small orange ball, large red ball with star. b, Star with ribbon, small red ball. c, Candle and heart. d, Candle and angel.

Serpentine Die Cut 10 on 3 Sides

2012, Nov. 12 Litho.

Booklet Stamps

Self-Adhesive

2698 A987 Block of 4 7.00
a.-d. (5.50k) Any single 1.75 .85
e. Booklet pane of 10, 3 each #2698a-2698b, 2 each #2698c-2698d 17.50

Water and
Horizon — A988

Hearts in Nature — A989

No. 2700: a, Heart on rock. b, Three heart-shaped leaves and moss. c, Hear-shaped water droplet on leaf. d, Tulip petals.

Perf. 13 Vert. Syncopated

2013, Jan. 10 Coil Stamp

2699 A988 (6k) multi 1.90 1.20

Booklet Stamps

Self-Adhesive

2700 A989 Block of 4 7.60
a.-d. (6k) Any single 1.90 .90
e. Booklet pane of 10, 3 each #2700a-2700b, 2 each #2700c-2700d 19.00

Insects — A990

No. 2701: a, Lygaeus equestris. b, Bryodema tuberculata. c, Melolontha melolontha. d, Aeshna serrata.

Die Cut Perf. 11¾x11½

2013, Jan. 10 Engr.

Coil Stamps

Self-Adhesive

2701 Vert. strip of 4 12.50
a.-d. A990 12k Any single 3.00 2.75

See No. 2727.

Ice Hockey Type of 1995 and

Ice Hockey Players — A991

No. 2703: a, Henrik Lundqvist. b, Jörgen Jönsson. c, Börje Salming. d, Nicklas Lidström.

Litho. & Engr.

2013, Mar. 13 *Perf. 12¾*

2702 A631 6k multi 2.00 2.00

Booklet Stamps Self-Adhesive Litho.

Serpentine Die Cut 10 on 3 Sides

2703 A991 Block of 4 7.50
a.-d. (6k) Any single 1.90 .90
e. Booklet pane of 10, 2 each #2703a,-2703b, 3 each #2703c-2703d 19.00

No. 2702 was printed in sheets of 9 that sold for 59k. Value, $18.

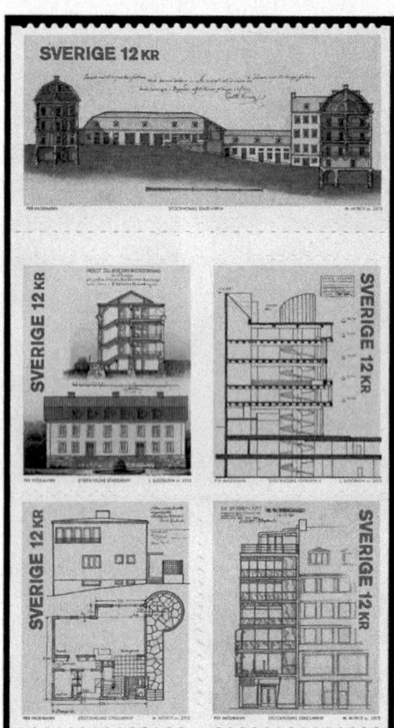
Stockholm Building Designs — A992

No. 2704 — Building blueprint drawings from Stockholm city archives: a, Spice merchant's building, 1795 (58x28mm). b, Three-story Gröna Garden worker's house, by J. F. Abom, 1854 (27x36mm). c, Kulturhuset (with spiral staircase), by Peter Celsing, 1970 (27x36mm). d, House in Bromma, by Edvin Engström, 1935 (27x36mm). e, Bredenberg's Department Store, by Gunnar Asplund, 1934 (27x36mm).

Serpentine Die Cut 10 on 2 or 3 Sides

2013, Mar. 14 **Litho. & Engr.**

Booklet Stamps Self-Adhesive

2704 A992 Booklet pane of 5 + 5 etiquettes 15.00
a.-e. 12k Any single 3.00 1.75

Souvenir Sheet

Europa — A993

No. 2705 — Postal worker and mail vehicle: a, Electric bicyle. b, Club Car electric vehicle, horiz.

Perf. 12½x13¼

2013, Mar. 14 **Litho. & Engr.**

2705 A993 Sheet of 2 6.00 6.50
a.-b. 12k Either single 3.00 3.00

Measuring Devices — A994

Designs: 30k, Aneroid barometer. 40k, Sundial. 50k, Compass.

Die Cut Perf. 11½ Syncopated

2013 **Self-Adhesive** **Engr.**

Coil Stamps

2706 A994 30k blk & red 7.50 1.00

Die Cut Perf. 11¾ Syncopated

Size: 27x28mm

2707 A994 40k blk & blue 9.00 1.50

Size: 34x28mm

2708 A994 50k blk & blue 12.50 3.00
Nos. 2706-2708 (3) 37.25 37.25

Issued: 30k, 40k, 5/8; 50k, 3/14.

A995

Cookies — A996

No. 2710 — Background color: a, Blue. b, Green. c, Red lilac. d, Orange brown.

Perf. 12½ Vert. Syncopated

2013, May 8 **Coil Stamp** **Litho.**

2709 A995 (6k) multi 1.90 1.25

Booklet Stamps Self-Adhesive

Serpentine Die Cut 10 on 3 Sides

2710 A996 Block of 4 7.50
a.-d. (6k) Any single 1.90 .95
e. Booklet pane of 10, 3 each #2710a-2710b, 2 each #2710c-2710d 18.00

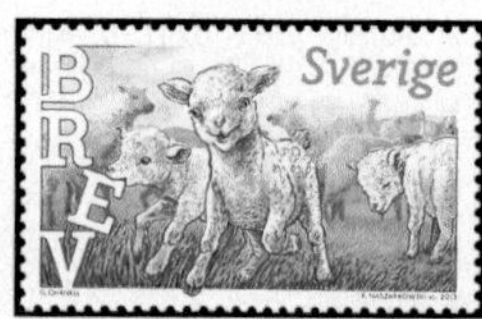
Baby Animals A997

Designs: Nos. 2711, 2712b, Lambs. No. 2712a, Calves. No. 2712c, Ducklings. No. 2712d, Kids. No. 2712e, Piglets.

Litho. & Engr.

2013, Aug. 22 *Perf. 12¾*

2711 A997 (6k) multi 2.00 1.50

Booklet Stamps

Perf. 12¾ Horiz.

2712 Vert. strip of 5 9.50 9.50
a.-e. A997 (6k) Any single 1.90 .95
f. Booklet pane of 10, 2 each #2712a-2712e 19.00 —
Complete booklet, #2712f 19.00

No. 2711 was printed in sheets of nine that sold for 59k. Value, $20.

Dahlias — A998

No. 2713: a, Decorative dahlia (orange red flower, country name at left). b, Ball dahlias (purple flowers, country name at right). c, Ruffle dahlia (pinkish violet flower and bud, country name at left). d, Waterlily dahlia (red flowers and bud, country name at right).

Serpentine Die Cut 10 on 3 Sides

2013, Aug. 22 **Litho.**

Booklet Stamps Self-Adhesive

2713 A998 Block of 4 7.50
a.-d. (6k) Any single 1.90 .95
e. Booklet pane of 10, 3 each #2713a-2713b, 2 each #2713c-2713d 18.00

Souvenir Sheet

Reign of King Carl XVI Gustav, 40th Anniv. — A999

No. 2714: a, Monogram of King Carl XVI Gustav (27½x36mm). b, King Carl XVI Gustav (27½x36mm). c, King Carl XVI Gustav, Crown Princess Victoria and Princess Estelle (55x41mm).

Litho. & Engr.

2013, Aug. 22 *Perf. 13x12¾*

2714 A999 Sheet of 3 5.00 5.00
a.-c. 6k Any single 1.60 1.60

Souvenir Sheet

Table Tennis — A1000

No. 2715 — Players: a, Woman. b, Man.

2013, Sept. 27 **Litho.** *Perf. 12¾*

2715 A1000 Sheet of 2 3.50 3.50
a.-b. 6k Either single 1.75 1.75

See People's Republic of China Nos. 4152-4153. A souvenir sheet containing Nos. 2715a and 2715b but having a different sheet margin was produced in limited quantities and sold only at the 2013 China International Collection Expo.

Top of 18th Century Tile Stove Made at Rörstrand Porcelain Factory — A1001

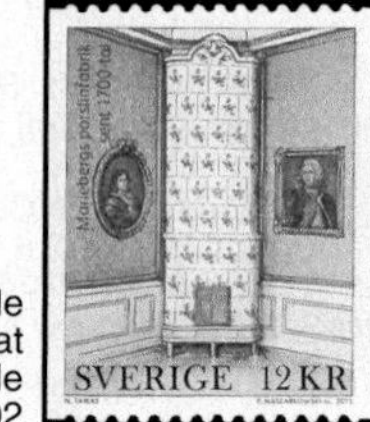
19th Century Tile Stove Made at Akerlindska Tile Factory — A1002

18th Century Tile Stove Made at Marieberg Porcelain Factory — A1003

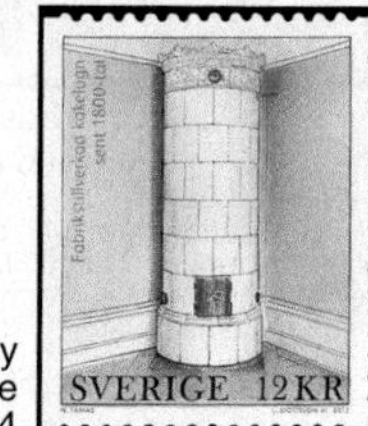
19th Century White Tile Stove — A1004

Door of 18th Century Tile Stove — A1005

Serpentine Die Cut 10 on 2 or 3 Sides

2013, Nov. 14 **Litho. & Engr.**

Self-Adhesive

2716 Booklet pane of 5 + 5 etiquettes 15.00
a. A1001 12k multi 3.00 1.75
b. A1002 12k multi 3.00 1.75
c. A1003 12k multi 3.00 1.75
d. A1004 12k multi 3.00 1.75
e. A1005 12k multi 3.00 1.75

Souvenir Sheet

Awarding of 2011 Nobel Prize for Literature to Tomas Tranströmer — A1006

No. 2717: a, Tranströmer (31x39mm). b, Musical score from a sonata by Franz Schubert (34x50mm).

Litho. & Engr.

2013, Nov. 14 *Perf. 13x12¾*

2717 A1006 Sheet of 2 6.50 7.00
a.-b. 12k Either single 3.25 3.25

A1007

Christmas — A1008

No. 2718, Reindeer on hill. No. 2719: a, Two birds carrying heart on string. b, Foxes and Christmas tree. c, Hibernating bears and gift boxes. d, Squirrel and gingerbread man cookie.

Die Cut Perf. 11¾x11½

2013, Nov. 14 Coil Stamp Litho.

Self-Adhesive

2718 A1007 (5.50k) multi 1.75 .80

Booklet Stamps

Serpentine Die Cut 10 on 3 Sides

2719 A1008 Block of 4 7.00
a.-d. (5.50k) Any single 1.75 .85
e. Booklet pane of 10, 3 each #2719a-2719b, 2 each #2719c-2719d 17.50

Bildmuseet, Umea, Sweden A1009

National Library, Riga, Latvia A1010

Die Cut Perf. 13x13½ Syncopated

2014, Jan. 16 Litho.

Coil Stamps

Self-Adhesive

2720 A1009 12k multi 3.00 1.75
2721 A1010 12k multi 3.00 1.75

Selecition of Umea and Riga as European Capitals of Culture. See Latvia Nos. 857-858.

Sporting Events A1011

Designs: Nos. 2722, 2723a, Vasaloppet 90-kilometer cross-country skiing race. No. 2723b, Lidingöloppet 30-kilometer race. No. 2723c, Vansbrosimningen 3-kilometer swimming race. No. 2723d, Vatternrundan 300-kilometer bicycle race. No. 2723e, Engelbrektsloppet 60-kilometer cross-country skiing race.

Litho. & Engr.

2014, Jan. 16 *Perf. 13x13½*

2722 A1011 (6k) multi 2.00 1.50

Booklet Stamps

Self-Adhesive

Die Cut Perf. 13x13½ Syncopated

2723 Vert. strip of 5 9.50
a.-e. A1011 (6k) Any single 1.90 .95
f. Booklet pane of 10, 2 each #2723a-2723e 19.00

No. 2722 was printed in sheets of 9 that sold for 59k. Value, $22.50.

Souvenir Sheet

Icebreakers — A1012

No. 2724: a, Icebreaker Atle. b, Icebreaker Ymer, vert.

Perf. 12¾x13, 13x12¾

2014, Mar. 17 Litho. & Engr.

2724 A1012 Sheet of 2 6.00 6.00
a.-b. 12k Either single 3.00 3.00

Carl Michael Bellman (1740-95), Composer — A1013

Die Cut Perf. 13¼ Syncopated

2014, Mar. 27 Litho. & Engr.

Coil Stamp

Self-Adhesive

2725 A1013 100k multi 25.00 5.00

Zlatan Ibrahimovic, Soccer Player A1014

No. 2726 — Ibrahimovic: a, Scissor kicking, "Zlatan" at left. b, With soccer ball. c, Making leaping kick, "Zlatan" at upper right. d, With arms extended. e, In blue shirt, smiling.

Die Cut Perf. 13x13¼ Syncopated

2014, Mar. 27 Litho.

Booklet Stamps

Self-Adhesive

2726 Vert. strip of 5 9.50
a.-e. A1014 (6k) Any single 1.90 1.05
f. Booklet pane of 10, 2 each #2726a-2726e 19.00

Insects Type of 2013

Die Cut Perf. 11¾x11½

2014, Apr. 1 Coil Stamp Engr.

Self-Adhesive

2727 A990 14k Aeshna serrata 3.00 1.50

Flag of Sweden A1015

Die Cut Perf. 13x13¼ Syncopated

2014, May 8 Coil Stamp Litho.

Self-Adhesive

2728 A1015 (7k) multi 2.00 1.10

Compare types A1015 and A940.

Summer Greetings — A1016

No. 2729: a, Flowers in paper airplane, ribbon. b, Gift box, trumpet under parachute, piece of candy and ladybug under balloons. c, Piece of candy under balloon, flower in bottle. d, Candles on cake, flowers, ribbon. e, Bouquet of flowers, ribbon.

Die Cut Perf. 13½ Syncopated

2014, May 8 Litho.

Booklet Stamps

Self-Adhesive

2729 Vert. strip of 5 10.00
a.-e. A1016 (7k) Any single 2.00 1.10
f. Booklet pane of 10, 2 each #2729a-2729e 20.00

Church Art A1017

Designs: No. 2730, 2731a, Skara Missal, baptismal font from Ottum Church. No. 2731b, Angel from Brahe Church, Visingsö, organ from Askeryd Church. No. 2731c, Room in monastery, Stockholm, candle holder from Torsaker Church. No. 2731d, Movement and face of clock in tower or German Church, Stockholm. No. 2731e, Baptismal font and candles from St. Peter's Church, Klippan.

Litho. & Engr.

2014, May 8 *Perf. 12¾*

2730 A1017 (7k) multi 2.40 1.50

Booklet Stamps

Perf. 12¾ Horiz.

2731 Vert. strip of 5 10.00 11.25
a.-e. A1017 (7k) Any single 2.00 1.10
f. Booklet pane of 10, 2 each #2731a-2731e 20.00 —
Complete booklet, #2731f 20.00

No. 2730 was printed in sheets of 9 that sold for 68k. Value, $22.50.

Souvenir Sheet

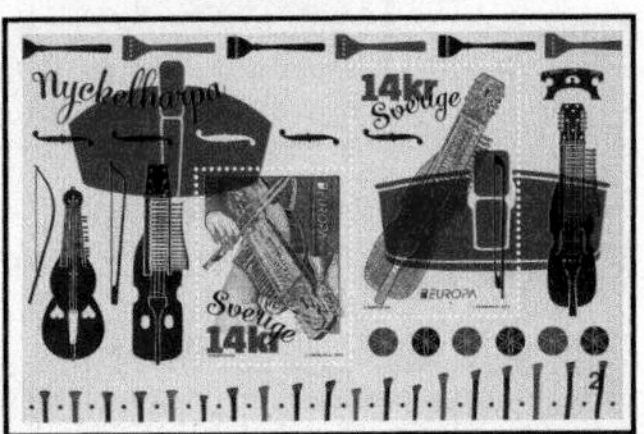

Europa — A1018

No. 2732: a, Musician playing nyckelharpa (31x39mm). b, Nyckelharpa and bow (34x50mm).

Litho. & Engr.

2014, May 8 *Perf. 13x12¾*

2732 A1018 Sheet of 2 6.50 6.50
a.-b. 14k Either single 3.25 3.25

A1019

A1020

A1021

A1022

A1023

A1024

Berries and Leaves A1025

Die Cut Perf. 13¾ Syncopated

2014, Aug. 21 Engr.

Coil Stamps

Self-Adhesive

2733 A1019 (6.50k) multi 1.90 1.90

Die Cut Perf. 13¼x13½ Syncopated

2734 A1020 (7k) multi 1.90 1.00

Litho.

Booklet Stamps

2735 Vert. strip of 5 9.00
a. A1021 (7k) multi 1.90 1.00
b. A1022 (7k) multi 1.90 1.00
c. A1023 (7k) multi 1.90 1.00
d. A1024 (7k) multi 1.90 1.00
e. A1025 (7k) multi 1.90 1.00
f. Booklet pane of 10, 2 each #2735a-2735e 18.00

Chairs A1026

No. 2736: a, Hug chair, designed by Anna von Schewen, 2002. b, Lilla Aland chair, designed by Carl Malmsten, 1940. c, Lamino chair, designed by Yngve Ekström, 1956. d, Cinema chair, designed by Gunilla Allard, 1993. e, Aluminiumfatöljen chair, designed by Mats Theselius, 1990.

Die Cut Perf. 13¼x13½ Syncopated

2014, Aug. 21 Litho. & Engr.

Self-Adhesive

2736 Booklet pane of 5 + 5 etiquettes 17.50
a.-e. A1026 14k Any single 3.50 1.75

Souvenir Sheet

Alice Tegnér (1864-1943), Composer of Children's Songs — A1027

No. 2737: a, Tegnér. b, Children in ring, horiz.

Litho. & Engr.

2014, Nov. 13 ***Perf. 12¾x13***

2737 A1027 Sheet of 2 6.50 6.50
a.-b. 14k Either single 3.25 3.25

A1028

Christmas — A1029

Designs: No. 2738, Mugs of mulled wine.
No. 2739: a, Gingerbread house. b, Orange spiked with cloves. c, Lussebulle bun. d, Candy apple on stick. e, Marzipan pig.

Die Cut Perf. 13¼x13½ Syncopated

2014, Nov. 13 Litho.

Coil Stamp
Self-Adhesive

2738 A1028 (6.50k) multi 1.75 1.00

Booklet Stamps

2739 Vert. strip of 5 8.75
a.-e. A1029 (6.50k) Any single 1.75 .85
f. Booklet pane of 10, 2 each #2739a-2739e 17.50

King Carl XVI Gustaf — A1030

Queen Silvia — A1031

Die Cut Perf. 13¾ Syncopated

2015, Jan. 15 Coil Stamps Litho.

Self-Adhesive

2740 A1030 (7k) dp car & car 1.75 .80
2741 A1031 14k purple & lilac 3.25 1.00

See Nos. 2782-2783, 2797.

Popular Music
A1032

No. 2742: a, Avicii, record producer and disc jockey. b, Robyn, singer. c, Max Martin, songwriter and producer. d, First Aid Kit, folk singers. e, Seinabo Sey, singer and songwriter.

Die Cut Perf. 13¼x13½ Syncopated

2015, Jan. 15 Litho.

Booklet Stamps
Self-Adhesive

2742 Vert. strip of 5 8.75
a.-e. A1032 (7k) Any single 1.75 .95
f. Booklet pane of 10, 2 each #2742a-2742e 17.50

Paintings by Prince Eugen of Sweden (1865-1947)
A1033

No. 2743: a, Molnet (Cloud), 1896. b, Det Gamla Slottet (The Old Castle), 1893. c, Hagastämningar, 1898. d, Oljekvarnen (Mill, Autumn Evening), 1908. e, Lyckans Tempel, 1892.

Die Cut Perf. 13¾ Syncopated

2015, Jan. 15 Litho.

Self-Adhesive

2743 Booklet pane of 5, #a-e, + 5 etiquettes 17.50
a.-e. A1033 14k Any single 3.50 1.75

A1034

A1035

A1036

A1037

A1038

A1039

Bees
A1040

Die Cut Perf. 13¾ Syncopated

2015, Mar. 26 Coil Stamps Litho.

Self-Adhesive

2744 Horiz. pair, #a-b 3.00
a. A1034 (6.50k) multi 1.50 1.50
b. A1035 (6.50k) multi 1.50 1.50

Booklet Stamps

Die Cut Perf. 13¼x13½ Syncopated

2745 Vert. strip of 5, #a-e 8.75
a. A1036 (7k) multi 1.75 1.00
b. A1037 (7k) multi 1.75 1.00
c. A1038 (7k) multi 1.75 1.00
d. A1039 (7k) multi 1.75 1.00
e. A1040 (7k) multi 1.75 1.00
f. Booklet pane of 10, 2 each #2745a-2745e 17.50

Viking Artifacts
A1041

Artifact and location where found: Nos. 2746, 2747c, Fitting for horse's bridle, Broa. No. 2747a, Three gold figurines, Lunda. No. 2747b, Silver jewelry, Aska. No. 2747d, Bronze Buddha, Helgö. No. 2747e, Gilded figurine depicting flying man. Uppakra.

Litho. & Engr.

2015, Mar. 26 ***Perf. 12¾***

2746 A1041 (7k) multi 2.25 1.50

Booklet Stamps

Perf. 12¾ Horiz.

2747 Vert. strip of 5 8.75 8.75
a.-e. A1041 (7k) Any single 1.75 1.00
f. Booklet pane of 10, 2 each #2747a-2747e 17.50 —
Complete booklet, #2747f 17.50

No. 2746 was printed in sheets of 9 that sold for 73k. Value, $22.50.

Souvenir Sheet

Europa — A1042

No. 2748 — Old toys: a, Skoglund & Olson cast iron airplane, 1920s. b. Metal horse on cart, 1910s, Brio wooden donkey, 1950s.

Litho. & Engr.

2015, Mar. 26 ***Perf. 13***

2748 A1042 Sheet of 2 6.00 6.00
a.-b. 14k Either single 3.00 3.00

A1043

Decorated Farmhouses of Hälsingland UNESCO World Heritage Site — A1044

Designs: 1k, Wall decoration, Bortom farmhouse. 2k, Peony wallpaper, Bommars farmhouse. 5k, Room in Bommars farmhouse, and wall decoration, Gästgivars farmhouse. 10k, Doorway, Bortom farmhouse, and wall decoration, Gästgivars farmhouse. 20k, Jon-Lars farmhouse, decoration from Kristofers farmhouse.

Die Cut Perf. 13¾x13¼ Syncopated

2015, May 7 Coil Stamps Litho.

Self-Adhesive

2749 A1043 1k multi .25 .25
2750 A1043 2k multi .50 .25

Engr.

Die Cut Perf. 13¼x13¾ Syncopated

2751 A1044 5k blue & brn 1.25 .50
2752 A1044 10k red brn & bl 2.40 .95
2753 A1044 20k blue & green 4.75 1.90
Nos. 2749-2753 (5) 9.15 3.85

A1045

A1046

A1047

A1048

A1049

Magnolias — A1050

Die Cut Perf. 13¼x13¾ Syncopated

2015, May 7 Coil Stamp Litho.

Self-Adhesive

2754 A1045 (7k) multi 1.75 1.00

Booklet Stamps

Die Cut Perf. 13¾x13¼ Syncopated

2755 Horiz. strip of 5, #a-e 8.75 7.25
a. A1046 (7k) multi 1.75 .95
b. A1047 (7k) multi 1.75 .95
c. A1048 (7k) multi 1.75 .95
d. A1049 (7k) multi 1.75 .95
e. A1050 (7k) multi 1.75 .95
f. Booklet pane of 10, 2 each #2755a-2755e 17.50

A1051

Ingrid Bergman (1915-82), Actress — A1052

Litho. & Engr.

2015, Aug. 20 ***Perf. 12½x13***

Stamp With White Frame

2756 A1051 14k multi 3.75 3.75

Coil Stamps
Stamps Without White Frame
Self-Adhesive

2757 A1051 14k multi 3.00 3.00

Litho.

2758 A1052 14k multi 3.00 3.00
a. Vert. pair, #2757-2758 6.00

No. 2756 was printed in sheets of 6 that sold for 94k. Value, $25.

See United States No. 5012.

A1053

Mushrooms
A1054

Inscriptions: No. 2759, Fjällig bläcksvamp (shaggy ink cap). No. 2760, Kantarell (chantarelle).
No. 2761: a, Mandelriska (weeping milk cap). b, Karljohan (porcini). c, Gul fingerswamp (white coral fungus). d, Scharlakansröd vaxskivling (scarlet waxy cap). e, Trattkantarell (funnel chanterelle).

Die Cut Perf. 13¾x13½ Syncopated
2015, Aug. 20 Coil Stamps Litho.
Self-Adhesive

2759	A1053 (7k) multi		1.75	1.45
2760	A1053 (7k) multi		1.75	1.45
a.	Horiz. pair, #2759-2760		3.50	

Booklet Stamps

2761	Horiz. strip of 5	8.75	
a.-e.	A1054 (7k) Any single	1.75	1.75
f.	Booklet pane of 10, 2 each #2761a-2761e	17.50	

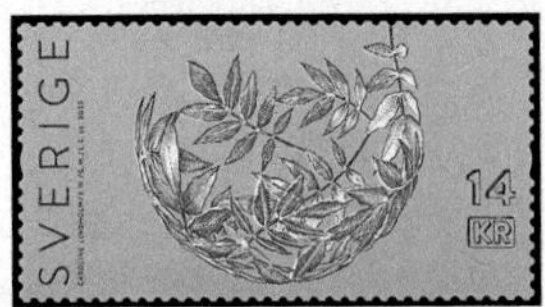

Items Made by Blacksmiths and Silversmiths — A1055

No. 2762: a, Decorative bowl by Caroline Lindholm. b, Chandelier by Jon Olofsson. c, Tea pot by Petronella Eriksson. d, Bowl by Tore Svensson. e, Bracelet by Erik Tidång.

Die Cut Perf. 13½ Syncopated
2015, Nov. 12 Litho. & Engr.
Self-Adhesive

2762	Booklet pane of 5 + 5 etiquettes	16.50	
a.-e.	A1055 14k Any single	3.25	1.60

A1056

A1057

A1058 A1059

Trees in Winter — A1060

Die Cut Perf. 13½x13 Syncopated
2015, Nov. 12 Engr.
Self-Adhesive
Booklet Stamps

2763	Horiz. strip of 5	8.00	
a.	A1056 (7k) dark blue	1.60	.90
b.	A1057 (7k) blue	1.60	.90
c.	A1058 (7k) dark blue	1.60	.90
d.	A1059 (7k) blue	1.60	.90
e.	A1060 (7k) dark blue	1.60	.90
f.	Booklet pane of 10, 2 each #2763a-2763e	16.00	

Christmas Ornament A1061

Die Cut Perf. 13x13½ Syncopated
2015, Nov. 12 Litho.
Coil Stamp
Self-Adhesive

2764	A1061 (7k) multi	1.60	.90

Christmas — A1062

No. 2765: a, Snowflake. b, Lit candle. c, Ribbon bow on gift. d, Star of Bethlehem. d, Conifer tree star with garland and ornament.

Die Cut Perf. 13½ Syncopated
2015, Nov. 12 Litho.
Self-Adhesive
Booklet Stamps

2765	Vert. strip of 5	8.00	
a.-e.	A1062 (6.50k) Any single	1.60	.95
f.	Booklet pane of 10, 2 each #2765a-2765e	16.00	

Europa A1063

Die Cut Perf. 13x13½ Syncopated
2016, Jan. 14 Coil Stamp Litho.
Self-Adhesive

2766	A1063 14k multi	3.25	3.25

Think Green Issue.

White-tailed Eagle A1064

Die Cut Perf. 13x13½ Syncopated
2016, Jan. 14 Litho. & Engr.
Coil Stamp
Self-Adhesive

2767	A1064 50k multi	12.00	3.00

Swedish Museum of Natural History, Cent. A1065

No. 2768: a, Quagga fetus, dome of museum. b, Dinosaur hatching from egg, fern. c, Silvianthemum suecicum flower fossil, pollen grains of dandelion, masur birch and amaranth. d, Diving beetle, diatoms. e, Siberian mammoth, double helix strands.

Die Cut Perf. 13x13½ Syncopated
2016, Jan. 14 Litho. & Engr.
Booklet Stamps
Self-Adhesive

2768	Vert. strip of 5	8.75	
a.-e.	A1065 (7k) Any single	1.75	.95
f.	Booklet pane of 10, 2 each #2768a-2768e	17.50	

Bridges A1066

Designs: Nos. 2769, 2770c, Tullbron. No. 2770a, Tallbergsbroarna. No. 2770b, Sölvesborgsbron. No. 2770d, Uddevallabron. No. 2770e, Lejonströmsbron.

Litho. & Engr.
2016, Mar. 17 *Perf. 13x12½*

2769	A1066 (7k) multi	2.25	1.75

Booklet Stamps
Self-Adhesive
Die Cut Perf. 13x13½ Syncopated

2770	Vert. strip of 5	8.75	
a.-e.	A1066 (7k) Any single	1.75	.95
f.	Booklet pane of 10, 2 each #2770a-2770e	17.50	

No. 2769 was printed in sheets of 6 that sold for 52k. Value, $15.

International Foods A1067

Designs: 13k, Nordic foods (fish, potato, chives, cheese, crisp bread, egg).

No. 2772: a, Italian foods (spaghetti, olives, mushroom, clam, cheese, tomato). b, Japanese food (sushi). c, Mexican foods (taco, lime, pepper, avocado and onion). d, Mediterranean foods (kebabs, stuffed grape leaves, eggplants). e, American foods (hamburger, tomato and corn).

Die Cut Perf. 13x13½ Syncopated
2016, Mar. 17 Coil Stamp Litho.
Self-Adhesive

2771	A1067 13k multi	3.25	1.10

Booklet Stamps

2772	Vert. strip of 5	8.75	
a.-e.	A1067 (7k) Any single	1.75	.95
f.	Booklet pane of 10, 2 each #2772a-2772e	17.50	

Souvenir Sheet

Swedish Royalty — A1068

No. 2773: a, Queen Silvia (31x53mm). b, King Carl XVI Gustaf, Crown Princess Victoria, Princess Estelle (70x49mm). c, King Carl XVI Gustaf (31x53mm).

Perf. 13x12¾, 12¾x13 (#2773b)
2016, Mar. 17 Litho.

2773	A1068 Sheet of 3	5.25	4.75
a.-c.	(7k) Any single	1.75	.95

King Carl XVI Gustaf, 70th birthday; 40th wedding anniversary of King Carl XVI Gustaf and Queen Silvia.

Rainbow Flag of Gay Rights Movement A1069

Die Cut Perf. 13x13½ Syncopated
2016, May 4 Coil Stamp Litho.
Self-Adhesive

2774	A1069 (6.50k) multi	1.60	.90

A1070

Vacation Activities — A1071

Die Cut Perf. 13x13½ Syncopated
2016, May 4 Engr.
Coil Stamps
Self-Adhesive

2775	A1070 (6k) multi	1.50	1.00

Die Cut Perf. 13½x13 Syncopated

2776	A1071 (6.50k) multi	1.80	1.00

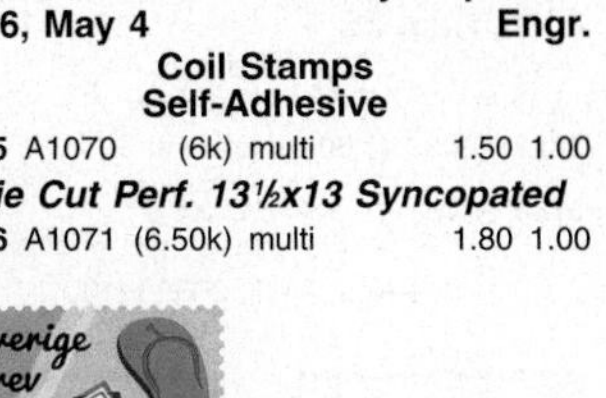

Beach Vacation Items — A1072

No. 2777: a, Seaweed, sandal, deck of cards, beach hat. b, Beach hat, sea shell, phone with earbuds, starfish. c, Crab, suntan lotion, snorkel. d, Sea shells, beach ball, sunglasses, pail, juice box. e, Seaweed, shovel, mussels, picnic basket, thermos, apple.

Die Cut Perf. 13½ Syncopated
2016, May 4 Litho.
Self-Adhesive

2777	Vert. strip of 5	8.00	
a.-e.	A1072 (6.50k) Any single	1.60	.90
f.	Booklet pane of 10, 2 each #2777a-2777e	16.00	

Old Town (Gamla Stan) of Stockholm — A1073

Inscriptions: Nos. 2778, 2779b, Skeppsbron / Gamla stan. No. 2779a, Gamla stan / Stockholm. No. 2779c, Stortorget / Gamla stan. No. 2779d, Brända tomten / Gamla stan. No. 2779e, Storkyrkan / Gamla stan.

2016, May 4 Litho. *Perf. 13x12½*

2778	A1073 13k multi	4.00	4.00

Self-Adhesive
Die Cut Perf. 13½ Syncopated

2779	Booklet pane of 5 + 5 etiquettes	16.00	
a.-e.	13k Any single	3.00	1.50

No. 2778 was printed in sheets of 4 that sold for 60k. Value, $15.

Birds — A1074

Designs: 30k, Acanthis flammea. 40k, Upupa epops.

Die Cut Perf. 13½x13 Syncopated
2016, Aug. 25 Litho. & Engr.
Coil Stamps
Self-Adhesive

2780	A1074 30k multi	7.00	2.50
2781	A1074 40k multi	9.50	3.50

King and Queen Types of 2015

King Carl XVI Gustaf — A1075

Queen Silvia — A1076

Die Cut Perf. 13¾x13½ Syncopated
2016, Aug. 25 Litho.
Coil Stamps
Self-Adhesive

2782 A1030 (6.50k) blue & dark blue 1.50 .85
2783 A1031 13k org brn & brn 3.00 1.50

See Nos. 2797, 2832-2833.

A1077

A1078

A1079

A1080

A1081

Trees in Autumn — A1082

Die Cut Perf. 13¾x13½ Syncopated
2016, Aug. 25 Litho.
Coil Stamp
Self-Adhesive

2784 A1077 (6.50k) multi 1.50 1.00

Booklet Stampa

2785 Vert. strip of 5 8.50
a. A1078 (6.50k) multi 1.70 .95
b. A1079 (6.50k) multi 1.70 .95
c. A1080 (6.50k) multi 1.70 .95
d. A1081 (6.50k) multi 1.70 .95
e. A1082 (6.50k) multi 1.70 .95
f. Booklet pane of 10, 2 each #2785a-2785e 17.00

Ungulates — A1083

No. 2786: a, Cervus elaphus. b, Alces alces. c, Rangifer tarandus. d, Dama dama. e, Capreolus capreolus.

Die Cut Perf. 13½x13 Syncopated
2016, Nov. 10 Litho.
Booklet Stamps
Self-Adhesive

2786 Horiz. strip of 5 8.00
a.-e. A1083 (6.50k) Any single 1.60 .90
f. Booklet pane of 10, 2 each #2786a-2786e 16.00

Aurora Borealis — A1084

No. 2787 — Photograph of Aurora Boralis taken at: a, 63 degrees, 9 minutes, 44 seconds north, 14 degrees, 31 minutes, 42 seconds east. b, 63 degrees, 58 minutes, 58 seconds north, 13 degrees, 58 minutes, 4 seconds east. c, 63 degrees, 7 minutes, 45 seconds north, 14 degrees, 25 minutes, 53 seconds east. d, 63 degrees, 14 minutes, 26 seconds north, 14 degrees, 27 minutes, 10 seconds east. e, 63 degrees, 11 minutes, 18 seconds north, 14 degrees, 30 minutes, 16 seconds east.

Die Cut Perf. 13¼ Syncopated
2016, Nov. 10 Litho.
Self-Adhesive

2787 Booklet pane of 5 + 5 etiquettes 15.00
a.-e. A1084 13k Any single 3.00 1.50

Souvenir Sheet

Lund University, 350th Anniv. — A1085

No. 2788: a, Researchers and MAX IV ring. b, Sphinx statues, Main University building.

Litho. & Engr.
2016, Nov. 10 ***Perf. 13x12¾***

2788 A1085 Sheet of 2 6.00 6.00
a.-b. 13k Either single 3.00 3.00

A1086

Christmas A1087

Designs: (6.50k), Elf with porridge bowl and spoon.
No. 2790 — Elf and: a, Cat. b, Rabbit and carrots. c, Dog in doghouse. d, Moose. e, Fox.

Die Cut Perf. 13¾x13½ Syncopated
2016, Nov. 10 Litho.
Coil Stamp
Self-Adhesive

2789 A1086 (6.50k) multi 1.50 .85

Booklet Stamps
Die Cut Perf. 13x13½ Syncopated

2790 Vert. strip of 5 7.50
a.-e. A1087 (6k) Any single 1.50 .90
f. Booklet pane of 10, 2 each #2790a-2790e 15.00

A1088

Household Items and Storage A1089

Designs: 19.50k, Items on shelves.
No. 2793: a, Clothes hanging in closet. b, Kitchen cabinet and stove. c, Coffee pot and other items on kitchen table. d, Items on desk. e, Items on coffee table.

2017, Jan. 12 Litho. ***Perf. 13x12¾***

2791 A1088 19.50k multi 5.00 2.50

Coil Stamp
Self-Adhesive
Die Cut Perf. 13¾x13½ Syncopated

2792 A1088 19.50k multi 5.50 5.50

Booklet Stamps
Die Cut Perf. 13¼x13½ Syncopated

2793 Vert. strip of 5 8.00
a.-e. A1089 (6.50k) Any single 1.60 .90
f. Booklet pane of 10, 2 each #2793a-2793e 16.00

No. 2791 was printed in sheets of 6 that sold for 125k. Value, $35.

Butterflies A1090

Designs: No. 2794, Nässelfjäril (Tortoiseshell butterfly).
No. 2795: a, Hagtornsfjäril (Black-veined white butterfly). b, Aurorafjäril (Orange tip butterfly). c, Angsblavinge (Mazarine blue butterfly). d, Angsnätfjäril (Glanville fritillary butterfly). e, Citronfjäril (Brimstone butterfly).

Die Cut Perf. 13x13½ Syncopated
2017, Mar. 16 Litho.
Self-Adhesive
Coil Stamp

2794 A1090 (6.50k) multi 1.75 1.00

Booklet Stamps

2795 Vert. strip of 5 8.00
a.-e. A1090 (6.50k) Any single 1.60 .90
f. Booklet pane of 10, 2 each #2795a-2795e 16.00

Souvenir Sheet

Europa — A1091

No. 2796: a, Wanas Castle, Skane. b, Double Dribble, sculpture by Anne Thulin at Wanas Castle.

2017, Mar. 16 Litho. ***Perf. 13***

2796 A1091 Sheet of 2 3.50 3.00
a.-b. (6.50k) Either single 1.75 1.50

Queen Silvia Type of 2016
Die Cut Perf. 13¾x13½ Syncopated
2017, Apr. 1 Litho.
Coil Stamp
Self-Adhesive

2797 A1031 21k blue & dark blue 4.00 1.50

Scenes From *City of My Dreams,* Novel by Per Anders Fogelström (1917-98) — A1092

Designs: No. 2798, Hammarby Sjö (with added text at top of stamp).
No. 2799: a, Katarinahissen. b, Hammarby Sjö (no text at top of stamp). c, Barnängens Fabrik. d, Kornhamnstorg. e, Stigbergsgatan.

2017, June 1 Litho. ***Perf. 13x12½***

2798 A1092 21k multi 4.50 2.25

Self-Adhesive
Die Cut Perf. 13½ Syncopated

2799 Booklet pane of 5, + 5 etiquettes 22.50
a.-e. A1092 21k Any single 4.50 2.25

No. 2798 was printed in sheets of 4 that sold for 92k. Value, $18.50.

Winning Photographs in Instagram Pictures Contest — A1093

Photographs of: No. 2800, Cat on dock, by Madelene Peterson. No. 2801, Boat, by Orjan Jalava.

No. 2802: a, Elk, by Bertram S. Fridell. b, Amusement park ride, by Johanna Mörtberg. c, Tattooed man holding child, by Fredrik Thomasson. d, Boats and dock-side cabins, by Jeppe Gustafsson. e, Forest, by Monica Thelin.

Die Cut Perf. 13¼ Syncopated
2017, June 1 Litho.
Self-Adhesive
Coil Stamps

2800 A1093 (7k) multi 1.75 1.00
2801 A1093 (7k) multi 1.75 1.00
a. Vert. coil pair, #2800-2801 3.50

Booklet Stamps

2802 Horiz. strip of 5 9.00
a.-e. A1093 (7k) Any single 1.75 .95
f. Booklet pane of 10, 2 each #2802a-2802e 18.00

Apple — A1094

Apples — A1095

No. 2804 — Apples and: a, Seeds, peeled apple, bottles of cider and jars of applesauce. b, Seeds, peel, apple slices on skewer, shaved apple curls. c, Seeds, peel, halved apples and apple prints. d, Halved apples used for printing, cards with apple impressions. e, Apple pie and pie server.

Die Cut Perf. 13¾x13½ Syncopated
2017, Aug. 24 Photo.
Self-Adhesive
Coil Stamp

2803 A1094 5k multi 1.00 .40

Self-Adhesive
Litho.
Die Cut Perf. 13½ Syncopated

2804 Booklet pane of 5, + 5 etiquettes 22.50
a.-e. A1095 21k Any single 4.50 2.25

A1096

A1097

A1098

A1099

Watercolors by Lars Lerin A1100

Die Cut Perf. 13x13½ Syncopated
2017, Aug. 24 Litho.
Booklet Stamps
Self-Adhesive

2805	Vert. strip of 5	8.75	
a.	A1096 (7k) multi	1.75	.95
b.	A1097 (7k) multi	1.75	.95
c.	A1098 (7k) multi	1.75	.95
d.	A1099 (7k) multi	1.75	.95
e.	A1100 (7k) multi	1.75	.95
f.	Booklet pane of 10, 2 each $2805a-2805e	17.50	

Souvenir Sheet

Medicinal Plants — A1101

No. 2806: a, Plantago major. b, Hypericum perforatum. c, Digitalis purpurea.

2017, Aug. 24 Litho. *Perf. 13*

2806	A1101 Sheet of 3	15.00	15.00
a.-c.	21k Any single	5.00	5.00

Digital Innovations — A1102

Die Cut Perf. 13¼x13½ Syncopated
2017, Nov. 16 Photo.
Self-Adhesive
Coil Stamp

2807	A1102 100k multi	22.50	5.50

A1103

A1104

A1105

A1106

Christmas Roses — A1107

Die Cut Perf. 13½x13 Syncopated
2017, Nov. 16 Litho.
Booklet Stamps
Self-Adhesive

2808	Horiz. strip of 5	8.75	
a.	A1103 (7k) multi	1.75	.95
b.	A1104 (7k) multi	1.75	.95
c.	A1105 (7k) multi	1.75	.95
d.	A1106 (7k) multi	1.75	.95
e.	A1107 (7k) multi	1.75	.95
f.	Booklet pane of 10, 2 each #2808a-2808e	15.00	

A1108

A1109

A1110

A1111

A1112

Christmas — A1113

Die Cut Perf. 13x13¼ Syncopated
2017, Nov. 16 Photo.
Coil Stamp
Self-Adhesive

2809	A1108 (7k) multi	1.75	1.00

Booklet Stamps
Die Cut Perf. 13¾ Syncopated

2810	Horiz. strip of 5	8.00	
a.	A1109 (6.50k) multi	1.60	.90
b.	A1110 (6.50k) multi	1.60	.90
c.	A1111 (6.50k) multi	1.60	.90
d.	A1112 (6.50k) multi	1.60	.90
e.	A1113 (6.50k) multi	1.60	.90
f.	Booklet pane of 10, 2 each #2810a-2810e	15.00	

A1114

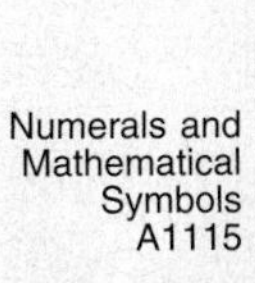

Numerals and Mathematical Symbols A1115

Die Cut Perf. 13¾x13½ Syncopated
2018, Jan. 4 Litho.
Coil Stamps
Self-Adhesive

2811	A1114 10k multi	2.00	.50

Die Cut Perf. 13x13¼ Syncopated

2812	A1115 20k multi	4.00	1.00

Riksbank, 350th anniv.

Lighthouses A1116

Designs: Nos. 2813, 2815c, Vinga Lighthouse. No. 2814, Lange Jan Lighthouse. No. 2815a, Falsterbo Lighthouse. No. 2815b, Pite-Rönneskär Lighthouse. No. 2815d, När Lighthouse. No. 2815e, Orskär Lighthouse.

2018, Jan. 4 Litho. *Perf. 14¼*

2813	A1116 (9k) multi	2.00	1.10

Coil Stamp
Self-Adhesive
Die Cut Perf. 13¼x13 Syncopated

2814	A1116 (9k) multi	2.25	2.25

Booklet Stamps

2815	Horiz. strip of 5	10.00	
a.-e.	A1116 (9k) Any single	2.00	1.10
f.	Booklet pane of 10, 2 each #2815a-2815e	20.00	

No. 2813 was printed in a sheet of 6 that sold for 62k. Value, $15.

Souvenir Sheet

Swedish National Archives, 400th Anniv. — A1117

No. 2816: a, 1641 map. b, Books. c, Page from registry and magnifying glass.

2018, Jan. 4 Litho. *Perf. 13*

2816	A1117 Sheet of 3	13.50	13.50
a.-c.	21k Any single	4.50	2.25

A1118

A1119

Designs: No. 2817, Bibi Andersson (1935-2019) and Liv Ullmann in *Persona,* Directed by Ingmar Bergman (1918-2007). No. 2818, Pernilla August and Bergman, Director of 2000 Production of *Mary Stuart.*

Die Cut Perf. 13x13½ Syncopated
2018, May 3 Litho.
Coil Stamps
Self-Adhesive

2817	A1118 21k multi	4.00	2.00
2818	A1119 21k multi	4.00	2.00
a.	Horiz. pair, #2817-2818	8.00	

A1120

Fish A1121

Designs: No. 2819: a, Gasterosteus aculeatus.

No. 2820: a, Labrus mixtus. b, Cyclopterus lumpus. c, Gobiusculus flavescens. d, Pholis gunnellus. e, Myoxocephalus scorpius.

Die Cut Perf. 13x13½ Syncopated
2018, May 3 Litho.
Coil Stamp
Self-Adhesive

2819	A1120 21k multi	4.00	1.50

Booklet Stamps

2820	Booklet pane of 5 + 5 etiquettes	20.00	
a.-e.	A1121 21k Any single	4.00	2.00

Edible Plants and Flowers — A1122

No. 2821 — Inscriptions: a, Löktrav (garlic mustard), Luktviol (sweet violet). b, Ramslök (wild garlic), Tusensköna (daisy). c, Vatarv (chickweed), Jordreva (ground ivy). d, Maskros (dandelion), Alm (elm seeds). e, Sommargyllen (bittercress), Brännässla (stinging nettle).

Die Cut Perf. 13½x13¾ Syncopated
2018, May 3 Litho.
Booklet Stamps
Self-Adhesive

2821	Horiz. strip of 5	10.00	
a.-e.	A1122 (9k) Any single	2.00	1.10
f.	Booklet pane of 10, 2 each #2821a-2821e	20.00	

Souvenir Sheet

Europa — A1123

No. 2822 — Oresund Bridge: a, Approach. b, Spires.

2018, May 3 Litho. *Perf. 13*

2822	A1123 Sheet of 2	8.00	8.00
a.-b.	21k Either single	4.00	4.00

Flag of Sweden A1124

2018, Aug. 23 Litho. *Perf. 14¼*

2823	A1124 (9k) multi	2.00	1.10

Coil Stamp
Self-Adhesive
Die Cut Perf. 13x13½ Syncopated

2824	A1124 (9k) multi	2.00	2.00

No. 2823 was printed in sheets of 6 that sold for 62k. Value, $12.50.

Bank Vole — A1125

Marten A1126

Brown Bear — A1127

Die Cut Perf. 13¾ Syncopated
2018, Aug. 23 Litho.
Coil Stamps
Self-Adhesive

2825	A1125 1k multi	.25	.25

Die Cut Perf. 13x13½ Syncopated

2826 A1126 2k multi .45 .45

Die Cut Perf. 13½x13¼ Syncopated

2827 A1127 50k multi 11.00 5.50
Nos. 2825-2827 (3) 11.70 6.20

Good Luck Symbols — A1128

No. 2828: a, Rainbow over clouds, four-leaf clover. b, Stars, ladybug, yin-yang. c, Four-leaf clovers, elephants. d, Yin-yang, hamsas, dice. e, Maneki-neko (Japanese cat), horseshoes.

Die Cut Perf. 13¾x13½ Syncopated

2018, Aug. 23 **Litho.**

Booklet Stamps
Self-Adhesive

2828 Vert. strip of 5 10.00
a.-e. A1128 (9k) Any single 2.00 1.10
f. Booklet pane of 10, 2 each #2828a-2828e 20.00

Birds in Winter — A1129

No. 2829: a, Talgoxe (great tit). b, Sidenswans (waxwing). c, Domherre facing right (bullfinch). d, Domherre facing left. e, Steglits (goldfinch). f, Grönfink (greenfinch). g, Rödhake (robin). h, Blames (blue tit). i, Pilfink facing right (tree sparrow). j, Pilfink facing left.

Die Cut Perf. 13¾x13½ Syncopated

2018, Nov. 1 **Litho.**

Self-Adhesive

2829 Booklet pane of 10 20.00
a.-j. A1129 (9k) Any single 2.00 1.10

A1130

Christmas — A1131

No. 2831: a, Elf writing on gift label. b, Girl holding Christmas gift. c, Bearded man carrying child in basket. d, Elves in balloon dropping Christmas cards. e, Elf with basket of gifts near window.

Die Cut Perf. 13x13½ Syncopated

2018, Nov. 1 **Litho.**

Coil Stamp
Self-Adhesive

2830 A1130 (9k) multi 1.80 1.05

Booklet Stamps

Die Cut Perf. 13½x13¼ Syncopated

2831 Horiz. strip of 5 8.50
a.-e. A1131 (8.50k) Any single 1.70 1.00
f. Booklet pane of 10, 2 each #2831a-2831e 17.00

King and Queen Types of 2016

Die Cut Perf. 13¾ Syncopated

2019, Jan. 10 **Litho.**

Coil Stamps
Self-Adhesive

2832 A1030 (9k) olive bister & blk 1.80 1.00
2833 A1031 21k silver & blk 4.00 2.00

A1132

A1133

A1134

A1135

A1136

A1137

Tulips — A1138

Die Cut Perf. 13¾ Syncopated

2019, Jan. 10 **Litho.**

Coil Stamps
Self-Adhesive

2834 A1132 5k multi 1.00 .50

Die Cut Perf. 13x13½ Syncopated

2835 A1133 21k multi 4.25 2.00

Booklet Stamps

Die Cut Perf. 13½x13 Syncopated

2836 Horiz. strip of 5 9.00
a. A1134 (9k) multi 1.80 1.00
b. A1135 (9k) multi 1.80 1.00
c. A1136 (9k) multi 1.80 1.00
d. A1137 (9k) multi 1.80 1.00
e. A1138 (9k) multi 1.80 1.00
f. Booklet pane of 10, 2 each #2836a-2836e 18.00

A1139

A1140

A1141

A1142

A1143

Embroidery — A1144

2019, Jan. 10 **Litho.** *Perf. 14*

2837 A1139 21k multi 4.25 2.00

Coil Stamp
Self-Adhesive

Die Cut Perf. 13x13½ Syncopated

2838 A1140 (9k) multi 1.80 1.00

Booklet Stamps

Die Cut Perf. 13½x13¼ Syncopated

2839 Booklet pane of 5 + 5 etiquettes 21.00
a. A1141 21k multi 4.25 2.00
b. A1142 21k multi 4.25 2.00
c. A1143 21k multi 4.25 2.00
d. A1139 21k multi 4.25 2.00
e. A1144 21k multi 4.25 2.00

No. 2837 was printed in sheets of 4 that sold for 92k.

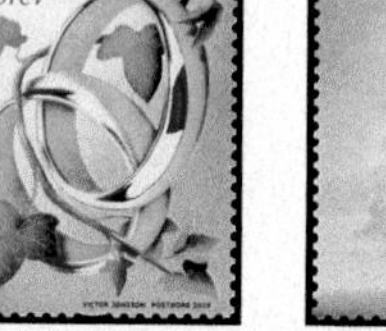

Wedding Rings — A1145

Clouds — A1146

Party Hats — A1147

Gift — A1148

Party Balloons A1149

Streamers A1150

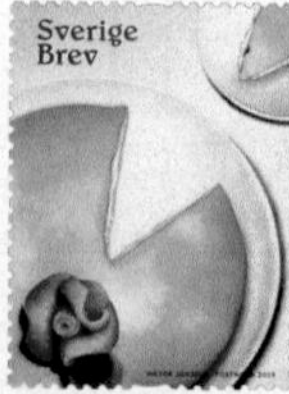

Cake — A1151

Die Cut Perf. 13½x13 Syncopated

2019, May 9 **Litho.**

Self-Adhesive
Coil Stamps

2840 A1145 (9k) multi 1.80 1.00
2841 A1146 (9k) multi 1.80 1.00

Booklet Stamps

2842 Horiz. strip of 5 9.00
a. A1147 (9k) multi 1.80 1.00
b. A1148 (9k) multi 1.80 1.00
c. A1149 (9k) multi 1.80 1.00
d. A1150 (9k) multi 1.80 1.00
e. A1151 (9k) multi 1.80 1.00
f. Booklet pane of 10, 2 each #2842a-2842e 18.00

Souvenir Sheet

Europa — A1152

No. 2843 — Turdus merula facing: a, Right. b, Left.

2019, May 9 **Litho.** *Perf. 13½*

2843 A1152 Sheet of 2 8.50 8.50
a.-b. 21k Either single 4.25 2.00

Souvenir Sheet

First Man on the Moon, 50th Anniv. — A1153

No. 2844: a, Launch of Apollo 11. b, Lunar Module above Moon. c, Astronaut's footprint on Moon.

2019, May 9 **Litho.** *Perf. 14x14¼*

2844 A1153 Sheet of 3 12.75 12.75
a.-c. 21k Any single 4.25 2.00

A 130x90mm souvenir sheet with cut out squares in the sheet margin simulating film sprocket holes, a gold inscription in the sheet margin, and an example of No. 2844c with added embossing was printed in limited quantities and made available only to attendees of the Stockholmia 2019 Philatelic Exhibition and standing order customers.

Clothing by Swedish Designers — A1154

Clothing designed by: Nos, 2845, 2846a, Gudrun Sjödén. No. 2846b, Arket. No. 2846c, Whyred. No. 2846d, Filippa K. No. 2846e, Hope.

2019, Aug. 11 **Litho.** *Perf. 14*

2845 A1154 (9k) multi 2.10 2.10

Booklet Stamps
Self-Adhesive

Die Cut Perf. 13¾x13¼ Syncopated

2846 Horiz. strip of 5 9.50
a.-e. A1154 (9k) Any single 1.90 1.90
f. Booklet pane of 10, 2 each #2846a-2846e 19.00

No. 2845 was printed in sheets of 6 that sold for 62k.

Train Stations A1155

No. 2847 — Station at: a, Haparanda. b, Järle. c, Alvesta. d, Asarna. e, Jörn.

Die Cut Perf. 13x13½ Syncopated
2019, Nov. 7 Litho.

Booklet Stamps
Self-Adhesive

2847 Vert. strip of 5 9.50
a.-e. A1155 (9k) Any single 1.90 1.90
f. Booklet pane of 10, 2 each #2847a-2847e 19.00

A1156

Christmas — A1157

Designs: (9k), Birds on vine, children building snowman.

No. 2849: a, Angel and dog ornaments. b, Bird and apple ornament. c, Cat, star and blue spherical ornaments. d, Elf, pink spherical ornament and heart-shaped ornament. e, Two spherical ornaments and Christmas tree-shaped ornament. f, Candy cane, striped spherical ornament, unicorn ornament, house and snowman ornament. g, Angel, gingerbread man and red spherical ornament. h, Clown, gift box and blue and white ornaments. i, Gifts at base of Christmas tree. j, Elf and straw ram.

Die Cut Perf. 13x13¾ Syncopated
2019, Nov. 7 Litho.

Coil Stamp
Self-Adhesive

2848 A1156 (9k) multi 1.90 1.90

Booklet Stamps

Die Cut Perf. 13¾ Syncopated

2849 A1157 Booklet pane of 10 17.50
a.-j. (8.50k) Any single 1.75 1.75

Door at Villa Edstrand, Falsterbo
A1158

Door at Zorngarden, Mora
A1159

Die Cut Perf. 13½x13¼ Syncopated
2020, Jan. 9 Litho.

Coil Stamps
Self-Adhesive

2850 A1158 20k multi 4.25 4.25
2851 A1159 50k multi 10.50 10.50

A1160

A1161

A1162

A1163

A1164

A1165

Flowers — A1166

Die Cut Perf. 13½ Syncopated, Die Cut Perf. 13½x13¼ Syncopated (#2853)
2020, Jan. 9 Litho.

Coil Stamps
Self-Adhesive

2852 A1160 (11k) multi 2.25 2.25
2853 A1161 22k multi 4.50 4.50

Booklet Stamps

2854 Vert. strip of 5 11.50
a. A1162 (11k) multi 2.25 2.25
b. A1163 (11k) multi 2.25 2.25
c. A1164 (11k) multi 2.25 2.25
d. A1165 (11k) multi 2.25 2.25
e. A1166 (11k) multi 2.25 2.25
f. Booklet pane of 10, 2 each #2854a-2854e 23.00

SEMI-POSTAL STAMPS

Type of 1872-91 Issues Surcharged in Dark Blue

Perf. 13x13½
1916, Dec. 21 Wmk. 181

B1 A5 5o + 5o on 2o org 4.75 *7.25*
B2 A5 5o + 5o on 3o yel brn 4.75 *7.25*
B3 A5 5o + 5o on 4o gray 4.75 *7.25*
B4 A5 5o + 5o on 5o grn 4.75 *7.25*
B5 A5 5o + 5o on 6o lilac 4.75 *7.25*
B6 A5 10o + 10o on 12o pale bl 4.75 *7.25*
B7 A5 10o + 10o on 20o red org 4.75 *7.25*
B8 A5 10o + 10o on 24o yel 4.75 *7.25*
B9 A5 10o + 10o on 30o brn 4.75 *7.25*
B10 A5 10o + 10o on 50o rose red 4.75 *7.25*
Nos. B1-B10 (10) 47.50 72.50
Set, never hinged 122.50

The surtax on Nos. B1-B31 was for the militia. See note after No. B21.

For surcharges see Nos. B22-B31.

No. 66 Surcharged in Dark Blue

1916, Dec. 21 Wmk. 180 *Perf. 13*

B11 A12 10o + 4.90k on 5k 150.00 *375.00*
Never hinged 225.00

Nos. J12-J22 Surcharged in Dark Blue

1916, Dec. 21 Unwmk. *Perf. 13*

B12 D1 5o + 5o on 1o 25.00 18.00
B13 D1 5o + 5o on 3o 5.00 7.00
B14 D1 5o + 5o on 5o 18.00 7.00
B15 D1 5o + 10o on 6o 5.00 8.00
B16 D1 5o + 15o on 12o 42.50 32.50
B17 D1 10o + 20o on 20o 15.00 25.00
B18 D1 10o + 40o on 24o 55.00 *100.00*
B19 D1 10o + 20o on 30o 6.50 6.00
B20 D1 10o + 40o on 50o 20.00 *42.50*
B21 D1 10o + 90o on 1kr 150.00 *375.00*
Nos. B12-B21 (10) 342.00 *621.00*
Set, never hinged 900.00

The surtax on Nos. B12-B21 is indicated not in figures, but in words at bottom of surcharge: Fem, 5; Tio, 10; Femton, 15; Tjugo, 20; Fyrtio, 40; Nittio, 90.

Nos. B1-B10 Surcharged

1918, Dec. 18 Wmk. 181

B22 A5 7o + 3o on #B1 8.00 *9.00*
B23 A5 7o + 3o on #B2 2.75 1.25
B24 A5 7o + 3o on #B3 2.75 1.25
B25 A5 7o + 3o on #B4 2.75 1.25
B26 A5 7o + 3o on #B5 2.75 1.25
B27 A5 12o + 8o on #B6 2.75 1.25
B28 A5 12o + 8o on #B7 2.75 1.25
B29 A5 12o + 8o on #B8 2.75 1.25
B30 A5 12o + 8o on #B9 2.75 1.25
B31 A5 12o + 8o on #B10 2.75 1.25
Nos. B22-B31 (10) 32.75 20.25
Set, never hinged 100.00

The 12o+8o surcharge exists on Nos. B1-B5 and the 7o+3o surcharge exists on Nos. B6-B10. Value, each $72.50.

Nos. B24, B26, B28 and B30 exist with surcharge inverted. Value unused, each $140.

King Gustaf V — SP1

Unwmk.
1928, June 16 Engr. *Perf. 10*

B32 SP1 5o (+ 5o) yel grn 1.50 4.50
B33 SP1 10o (+ 5o) dk vio 1.50 4.50
B34 SP1 15o (+ 5o) car 1.50 3.25
Complete booklet, pane of 8 ea. #B32, B33, B34 250.00
B35 SP1 20o (+ 5o) org 3.00 2.00
B36 SP1 25o (+ 5o) dk bl 3.00 2.50
Nos. B32-B36 (5) 10.50 *16.75*
Set, never hinged 25.00

70th birthday of King Gustaf V. The surtax was used for anti-cancer work.

Catalogue values for unused stamps in this section, from this point to the end of the section, are for Never Hinged items.

King Gustaf V — SP2

1948, June 16 *Perf. 12½ Vertically*

B37 SP2 10o + 10o green .50 .55
B38 SP2 20o + 10o red .75 .70
B39 SP2 30o + 10o ultra .50 .55

Perf. 12½ on 3 Sides

B40 SP2 10o + 10o green .60 .65
a. Booklet pane of 20 9.00
B41 SP2 20o + 10o red .75 .85
a. Booklet pane of 20 10.00
Nos. B37-B41 (5) 3.10 3.30

90th anniv. of the birth of King Gustaf V. The surtax provided aid for Swedish youth.

King Gustaf VI Adolf — SP3

1952, Nov. 11 *Perf. 12½ Horiz.*

B42 SP3 10o + 10o green .25 *.35*
B43 SP3 25o + 10o car rose .25 *.35*
B44 SP3 40o + 10o ultra .50 *.50*

Perf. 12½ on 3 Sides

B45 SP3 10o + 10o green .25 *.35*
a. Booklet pane of 20 6.00
B46 SP3 25o + 10o car rose .25 *.35*
a. Booklet pane of 20 6.00
Nos. B42-B46 (5) 1.50 1.90

70th birthday of King Gustaf VI Adolf. The surtax was used to promote Swedish culture.

Henri Dunant — SP4

1959, May 8 *Perf. 12½ Horizontally*

B47 SP4 30o + 10o red .50 *.75*

Perf. 12½ on 3 Sides

B48 SP4 30o + 10o red .80 1.00
a. Booklet pane of 20 16.50

Centenary of the Red Cross idea. The surtax went to the Swedish Red Cross.

King Gustav VI Adolf — SP5

Perf. 12½ Vertically
1962, Nov. 10 Engr. Unwmk.
Size: 58x24mm

B49 SP5 20o + 10o brown .25 .30
B50 SP5 35o + 10o blue .25 .30

Perf. 12½ Horizontally

B51 SP5 20o + 10o brown .25 .30
a. Booklet pane of 10 2.50
B52 SP5 35o + 10o blue .25 .30
a. Booklet pane of 10 2.50
Nos. B49-B52 (4) 1.00 1.20

80th birthday of King Gustav VI Adolf. The surtax went to the King Gustav VI Adolf 80th anniv. Foundation for Swedish Cultural Activities.

Ship Types of Regular Issues

Imprint: "1966"

Designs (Ships): 10o, "The Lion of Småland." 15o, "Kalmar Nyckel." 20o, Old Sailing Packet. 25o, Mail Paddle Steamship. 30o, "Kung Karl." 40o, Stern of "Amphion."

1966, Nov. 15 ***Perf. 12½ on 3 Sides***

B53 A76 10o vermilion .25 .40
B54 A50 15o vermilion .25 .40
B55 A38 20o slate grn .25 .40
B56 A39 25o ultra .25 .25
B57 A76 30o vermilion .25 .50
B58 A76 40o vermilion .25 .50
a. Bklt. pane. #B53-B54, B57-B58, 2 #B55, 4 #B56 2.75
Nos. B53-B58 (6) 1.50 2.45

The booklet sold for 3.50k and the surtax of 1.15k went to the National Cancer Fund.

Save the Children Sweden — SP6

No. B59 — Three children, birds with tree at center and: a, Right. b, Left.

Serpentine Die Cut 10 on 3 Sides

2011, Mar. 24 **Litho.**

Booklet Stamps
Self-Adhesive

B59 SP6 Horiz. pair 4.00
a.-b. (6k+1k) Either single 2.00 1.50
c. Booklet pane of 10, 5 each #B59a-B59b 20.00

Surtax for Save the Children Sweden.

Swedish Cancer Society — SP7

No. B60: a, Silhouette of man. b, Abstract design.

Booklet Stamps

2012, Jan. 12 **Self-Adhesive**

B60 SP7 Horiz. pair 4.00
a.-b. (6k+1k) Either single 2.00 1.50
c. Booklet pane of 10, 5 each #B60a-B60b 18.00

Surtax for Swedish Cancer Society.

SOS Children's Villages — SP8

No. B61: a, Woman and three children. b, Woman and child.

Booklet Stamps

2013, Jan. 10 **Self-Adhesive**

B61 SP8 Horiz. pair 4.00
a.-b. (6k+1k) Either single 2.00 1.75
c. Booklet pane of 10, 5 each #B61a-B61b 20.00

Surtax for SOS Children's Villages in Cambodia and Ukraine.

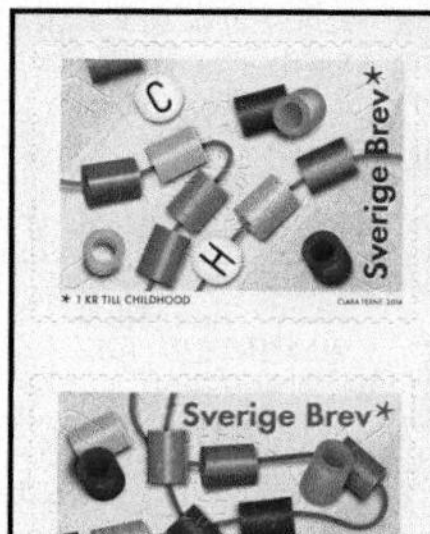

Beads SP9

No. B62 — Beads with letters: a, "C" and "H." b, "O" and "D."

Die Cut Perf. 13x13½ Syncopated

2014, Jan. 16 **Litho.**

Booklet Stamps
Self-Adhesive

B62 SP9 Vert. pair 3.75 3.00
a.-b. (6k+1k) Either single 1.80 1.50
c. Booklet pane of 10, 6 #B62a, 4 #B62b 19.00

Surtax for World Childhood Foundation.

Worldwide Fund for Nature (WWF) — SP10

No. B63 — Sun, bird and: a, Deer. b, Farmhouses and wind generator.

Die Cut Perf. 13¾x13¼ Syncopated

2015, May 7 **Self-Adhesive** **Litho.**

Booklet Stamps

B63 Horiz. pair, #a-b 4.00
a.-b. SP10 (7k)+1k Either single 2.00 1.35
c. Booklet pane of 10, 6 #B63a, 4 #B63b 18.00

Surtax for Worldwide Fund for Nature. See Denmark Nos. B109-B110.

AIR POST STAMPS

Official Stamps Surcharged in Dark Blue

1920, Sept. 17 **Wmk. 181** ***Perf. 13***

C1 O3 10o on 3o brn 1.50 6.50
a. Inverted surcharge 375.00 *1,350.*
C2 O3 20o on 2o org 2.50 9.50
a. Inverted surcharge 375.00 *1,100.*
C3 O3 50o on 4o vio 15.00 22.00
a. Inverted surcharge 375.00 *1,350.*
Nos. C1-C3 (3) 19.00 *38.00*
Set, never hinged 50.00

Wmk. 180

C4 O3 20o on 2o org 2,750.
Never hinged 5,000.
C5 O3 50o on 4o vio 175.00 *500.00*
Never hinged 325.00

Airplane over Stockholm AP2

Perf. 10 Vertically

1930, May 9 **Engr.** **Unwmk.**

C6 AP2 10o deep blue .25 .50
C7 AP2 50o dark violet .50 1.50
Set, never hinged 1.25

Flying Swans — AP3

1942-53 ***Perf. 12½ on 3 Sides***

C8 AP3 20k brt ultra ('53) 3.50 .65
Never hinged 6.00
a. Bklt. pane of 20 ('53) 725.00
b. Bklt. pane of 10 ('68) 55.00
c. Perf. on 4 sides 40.00 13.50
Never hinged 110.00
d. As "c," bklt. pane of 10 1,350.

Issued: #C8c, May 4, 1942; #C8, July 7.

POSTAGE DUE STAMPS

D1

1874 **Unwmk.** **Typo.** ***Perf. 14***

J1 D1 1o black 75.00 40.00
J2 D1 3o rose 75.00 40.00
J3 D1 5o brown 75.00 35.00
J4 D1 6o yellow 150.00 95.00
J5 D1 12o pale red 7.75 6.00
J6 D1 20o blue 80.00 37.50
J7 D1 24o violet 625.00 375.00
J8 D1 24o gray 75.00 52.50
J9 D1 30o dk grn 87.50 40.00
J10 D1 50o brown 275.00 60.00
J11 D1 1k blue & bister 300.00 75.00
Nos. J1-J11 (11) 1,825. 856.00

1877-86 ***Perf. 13***

J12 D1 1o black ('80) 2.75 4.00
J13 D1 3o rose 6.25 7.25
J14 D1 5o brown 4.50 4.50
J15 D1 6o yellow 4.50 4.50
a. Printed on both sides 1,600.
J16 D1 12o pale red ('82) 14.50 17.00
J17 D1 20o pale blue ('78) 5.25 4.50
J18 D1 24o red lilac ('86) 26.00 29.00
a. 24o violet ('84) 26.00 29.00
J19 D1 24o gray lil ('82) 190.00 *240.00*
J20 D1 30o yellow green 6.50 4.50
J21 D1 50o yellow brown 10.50 5.75
J22 D1 1k blue & bister 30.00 17.50
Nos. J12-J22 (11) 300.75 338.50

Nos. J12-J17, J19-J22 exist imperf. Value, pairs, each $400.

For surcharges see Nos. B12-B21.

STAMPS FOR CITY POSTAGE

S1

1856-62 **Typo.** **Unwmk.** ***Perf. 14***

LX1 S1 (1sk) (3o) blk ('58) 1,100. 550.00
LX2 S1 (3o) bis brn ('62) 600.00 550.00

From 1856 to 1858 No. LX1 was sold at 1sk, from 1858 to 1862 at 3o. The paper of the 1sk black is thin while the paper of the 3o black is medium thick.

No. LX1 was reprinted three times with perf. 14, once with perf. 13. No. LX2 was reprinted once with each perforation. Value of lowest cost Perf. 14 reprints, $250 each. See the Scott Specialized Catalogue of Stamps and Covers 1840-1940 for detailed listings.

OFFICIAL STAMPS

O1

1874-77 **Unwmk.** **Typo.** ***Perf. 14***

O1 O1 3o bister 90.00 42.50
O2 O1 4o gray ('77) 300.00 75.00
O3 O1 5o yel green 140.00 52.50
O4 O1 6o lilac 275.00 65.00
O5 O1 6o gray 525.00 175.00
O6 O1 12o blue 200.00 3.00
O7 O1 20o pale red 1,050. 90.00
O8 O1 24o yellow 1,050. 20.00
a. 24o orange 1,050. 22.50
O9 O1 30o pale brn 425.00 37.50
O10 O1 50o rose 600.00 125.00
O11 O1 1k bl & bis 1,700. 65.00
Nos. O1-O11 (11) 6,355. 750.50

Imperf., Pairs

O1a O1 3o 1,500.
O2a O1 4o 1,500.
O3a O1 5o 1,500.
O4a O1 6o 1,500.
O6a O1 12o 1,500.
O7a O1 20o 1,500.
O8b O1 24o 1,500.
O9a O1 30o 1,500.
O10a O1 50o 1,500.
O11a O1 1k 2,500.

1881-96 ***Perf. 13***

O12 O1 2o org ('91) 1.40 2.00
O13 O1 3o bis brn 1.40 2.25
O14 O1 4o gray blk ('93) 2.50 .70
a. 4o gray ('82) 20.00 2.75
O15 O1 5o grn ('84) 5.25 .60
O16 O1 6o red lil ('82) 40.00 60.00
a. 6o lilac ('81) 45.00 65.00
O17 O1 10o car ('95) 3.00 .25
b. 10o rose ('85) 45.00 1.25
O18 O1 12o blue 57.50 22.50
O19 O1 20o ver ('82) 200.00 2.50
O20 O1 20o dk bl ('91) 5.75 .60
O21 O1 24o yellow 72.50 25.00
a. 24o orange 65.00 25.00
O22 O1 30o brown 26.00 .70
O23 O1 50o pale rose 140.00 25.00
O24 O1 50o pale gray ('93) 18.00 3.00
O25 O1 1k dk bl & yel brn, square periods ('96) 9.00 2.50
a. blue & brn, round periods ('81) 500.00 6.50
Nos. O12-O25 (14) 582.30 147.60

No. O25 has square periods. No. O25a has round periods.

Imperf., Pairs

O12a O1 2o 400.00
O17a O1 10o No. O17 400.00
c. No. O17b 400.00
O20a O1 20o 50.00
O24a O1 50o 400.00

Surcharged in Dark Blue

1889

O26 O1 10o on 12o blue 13.00 *18.00*
a. Inverted surcharge *2,100.* *5,000.*
b. Perf. 14 *5,500.* *5,500.*
O27 O1 10o on 24o yel 16.00 *25.00*
a. Inverted surcharge *7,000.* *5,500.*
b. Perf. 14 *5,500.* *5,500.*

O3

1910-12 **Wmk. 180** **Typo.**

O28 O3 1o black .30 .45
O29 O3 2o orange 1.40 *4.50*
O30 O3 4o pale violet 1.75 *4.00*
O31 O3 5o green .50 *1.10*
O32 O3 8o claret .40 *1.10*
O33 O3 10o red 11.00 .70
O34 O3 15o red brown .80 .80
O35 O3 20o deep blue 7.00 1.75
O36 O3 25o red orange 7.00 2.50
O37 O3 30o chocolate 7.00 3.50
O38 O3 50o gray 7.00 3.50
O39 O3 1k black, *yellow* 7.75 7.75
O40 O3 5k claret, *yellow* 10.00 4.00
Nos. O28-O40 (13) 61.90 35.65
Set, never hinged 145.00

1910-19 **Wmk. Wavy Lines (181)**

O41 O3 1o black 2.00 *3.75*
O42 O3 2o orange .30 *.40*
O43 O3 3o pale brown .40 *1.00*
O44 O3 4o pale violet .30 *.40*
O45 O3 5o green .30 *.40*
O46 O3 7o gray green .40 *1.25*
O47 O3 8o rose 18.00 *27.50*
O48 O3 10o red .30 .25
O49 O3 12o rose red .30 .40
O50 O3 15o org brown .30 .30
O51 O3 20o deep blue .45 .30

O52	O3	25o orange	.80	.50
O53	O3	30o chocolate	.55	.55
O54	O3	35o dark violet	.85	*1.00*
O55	O3	50o gray	3.25	2.25
		Nos. O41-O55 (15)	28.50	40.25
		Set, never hinged	60.00	

For surcharges see Nos. C1-C5.

Use of official stamps ceased on July 1, 1920.

PARCEL POST STAMPS

Regular Issue of 1914 Surcharged

1917 **Wmk. 180** ***Perf. 13***

Q1	A14	1.98k on 5k claret, *yel*	1.40	*6.00*
Q2	A14	2.12k on 5k claret, *yel*	1.40	*6.00*
		Set, never hinged	5.50	

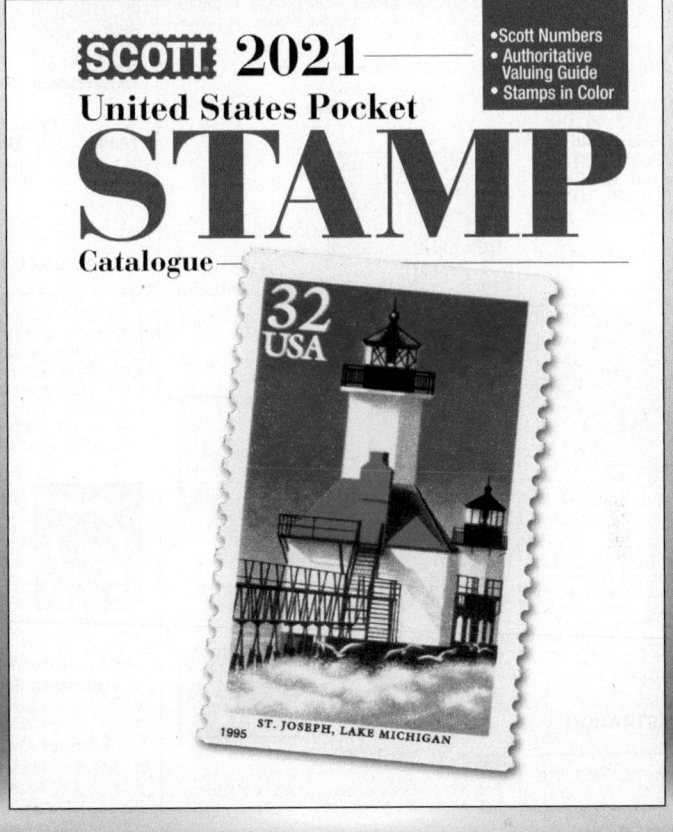

SWITZERLAND

'swit-sər-lənd

(Helvetia)

LOCATION — Central Europe, between France, Germany and Italy
GOVT. — Republic
AREA — 15,943 sq. mi.
POP. — 7,062,400 (1998 est.)
CAPITAL — Bern

100 Rappen or Centimes = 1 Franc

Catalogue values for unused stamps in this country are for Never Hinged items, beginning with Scott 365 in the regular postage section, Scott B272 in the semi-postal section, Scott C46 in the airpost section, Scott CB1 in the airpost semi-postal section, and Scott 3O94, 4O40, 5O26, 7O31, 8O1, 9O1, 10O1, 11O1, 12O1 in the official sections.

Watermarks

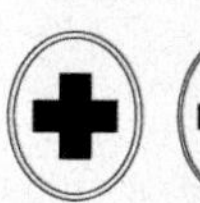

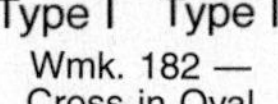
Type I Type II

Wmk. 182 — Cross in Oval

Wmk. 183 — Swiss Cross

Watermark 182 is not a true watermark, having been impressed after the paper was manufactured. There are two types: I- width just under 9mm; heighth just under 11mm; double oval lines nearly 1mm apart; cross has short, thick arms. II- width just under 8½mm; double oval lines very close together; cross has longer, thinner arms than Type I.

CANTONAL ADMINISTRATION

Unused values of Nos. 1L1-3L1 are for stamps without gum.

Counterfeit and repaired copies of Nos. 1L1-3L1 abound.

Zurich

A1 A2
Numerals of Value

1843 Unwmk. Litho. *Imperf.*
Red Vertical Lines

1L1 A1 4r black *27,000. 18,500.*
1L2 A2 6r black *7,700. 1,950.*

1846 Red Horizontal Lines

1L3 A1 4r black *18,500. 25,000.*
1L4 A2 6r black 2,175. 1,775.

Five varieties of each value.

Reprints of the Zurich stamps show signs of wear and lack the red lines. Values 4r, $7,000; 6r, $2,350.

Coat of Arms — A3

1850 Unwmk. *Imperf.*

1L5 A3 2½r black & red *7,750. 4,200.*

No. 1L5 has separation designs in the margins between stamps as shown. Values are for stamps showing part of the separation design on all four sides.

Geneva

Coat of Arms — A4

1843 Unwmk. Litho. *Imperf.*

2L1 A4 10c blk, *yel grn* *77,500. 42,500.*
a. Either half *24,750. 9,250.*
b. Stamp composed of right half at left & left half at right *77,500. 60,000.*

A5

A6

1845-48

2L2 A5 5c blk, *yel grn* 3,400. 1,900.
2L3 A6 5c blk, *yel grn* ('46) 2,350. 2,000.
2L4 A6 5c blk, *dk grn* ('48) 4,500. 3,000.

A7

1849-50

2L5 A7 4c black & red *46,000. 20,750.*
2L6 A7 5c blk & red ('50) 2,750. 1,950.

Coat of Arms — A8

1851

2L7 A8 5c black & red *10,500. 4,150.*

ENVELOPE STAMP USED AS ADHESIVE

E1

1847 Unwmk. *Imperf.*

2LU1 E1 5c yel grn, see footnote *22,500.*

Value is for cut-out stamp used on folded letters. This use was authorized and is known from Feb. 19, 1847. Value of unused envelope cut-out, $475. Value of used cut-out off cover, $3,850.

Basel

Dove of Basel — A9

Typo. & Embossed
1845 Unwmk. *Imperf.*

3L1 A1 2½r blk, crim & bl *17,500. 15,500.*

FEDERAL ADMINISTRATION

Due to its tendency to damage the paper and/or the color of the stamps, the gum on Nos. 1-40 very often is removed. Unused values for Nos. 1-40 are for stamps without gum. Stamps with original gum sell for about the same prices.

A10

A11

1850 Unwmk. Litho. *Imperf.*
Full Black Frame Around Cross

1 A10 2½r black & red 3,500. 1,500.
2 A11 2½r black & red 3,100. 1,600.

Without Frame Around Cross

3 A10 2½r black & red 7,000. 2,950.
4 A11 2½r blk & red *52,500. 27,000.*

Forty types of each.

A12

A13

1850
Full Black Frame Around Cross

5 A12 5r dk bl, blk & red 6,200. 1,375.
a. 5r dk grayish bl, blk & red 6,200. 1,375.
6 A13 10r yel, blk & red *130,000.*

No. 6 used, with only parts of frame around cross showing, value $175 to $900.

Without Frame Around Cross

7 A12 5r lt bl, blk & red 1,925. 575.
a. 5r dp bl, blk & red *1,925.* 575.
b. 5r pur bl, blk & red — *4,650.*
c. 5r grnsh bl, blk & red 2,300. 650.
8 A13 10r yel, blk & red 1,000. 160.
a. 10r buff, blk & red 1,275. 225.
b. 10r org yel, blk & red 1,250. 250.
d. Half used as 5r on cover, 5r rate *16,000.*

Beware of examples of Nos. 7-8 with faked frame added.

1851
Full Blue Frame Around Cross

9 A12 5r light blue & red *210,000.*

No. 9 used, with only parts of frame around cross showing, value $180 to $3,750.

Without Frame Around Cross

10 A12 5r lt blue & red 625. 160.

Beware of examples of No. 10 with faked frame added.

Forty types of each.

A14

A15

A16

1852
Vermilion Frame Around Cross

11 A14 15r vermilion *20,000.* 775.
12 A15 15r vermilion 2,700. 160.
13 A16 15c vermilion *18,500.* 1,150.

Ten types of each.

On October 1st, 1854, all stamps of the preceding issues were declared obsolete.

The Sitting Helvetia type (Scott Nos. 14-40) are valued with three margins clear of frame lines, with the fourth margin touching or lightly cutting into the frame line. Stamps with four margins clear of all frame lines are rare and command sustantial premiums.

Helvetia — A17

1854 Embossed. Unwmk.
Thin Paper, Fine Impressions
Emerald Silk Threads

14 A17 5r orange brn *14,000. 1,750.*
15 A17 5r red brown 625.00 160.00
16 A17 10r blue 850.00 85.00
17 A17 15r car rose 1,400. 190.00
a. 15r pale rose 1,350. 190.00
18 A17 40r pale yel grn *11,600.* 1,300.
19 A17 40r yellow grn 1,850. 375.00

1854-55

Emerald Silk Threads
Medium Thick Paper
Fine Impressions

20 A17 5r pale yel brn 775.00 170.00
21 A17 10r blue 2,300. 125.00
22 A17 15r rose 1,150. 110.00
23 A17 20r pale orange 1,700. 200.00

1855-57

Colored ( ) Silk Threads
Medium Thick Paper
Fine to Rough Impressions

24 A17 5r yel brn (yel) 625.00 115.00
25 A17 5r dk brn (blk) 350.00 40.00
26 A17 10r mlky bl (red) 1,550. 230.00
27 A17 10r blue (car) 325.00 47.50
 a. Thin paper 5,400. 475.00
28 A17 15r rose (bl) 575.00 70.00
29 A17 40r yel grn (mar) 1,100. 110.00
30 A17 1fr lav (blk) 1,775. 1,000.
31 A17 1fr lav (yel) 1,550. 1,000.
 a. Thin paper *21,250.* 7,725.

1857

Thin (Emergency) Paper
Rough Impressions
Green Silk Threads

32 A17 5r pale gray brn 5,400. 1,100.
32A A17 10r blue 7,000. 1,000.
33 A17 15r pale dl rose 3,475. 350.
34 A17 20r pale dl org 4,250. 290.

1858-62

Thick Ordinary Paper
Rough Impressions
Green Silk Threads

35 A17 2r gray 275.00 *575.00*
 a. One and one-half used as 3r on newspaper or wrapper *12,500.*
 c. Half used as 1r on cover
36 A17 5r brown 250.00 30.00
 a. 5r black brown 275.00 47.50
 b. 5r gray brown 250.00 27.50
 c. Half used as 2r on cover *1,550.*
37 A17 10r blue 260.00 32.50
 a. Half used as 5r on cover *7,250.*
 b. 10r pale blue 260.00 27.50
 c. 10r dark blue 250.00 24.00
 d. 10r greenish blue 310.00 45.00
38 A17 15r dark rose 400.00 70.00
 a. 15r pale rose 400.00 72.50
39 A17 20r dk org 525.00 77.50
 a. Half used as 10r on cover *17,500.*
 b. 20r yel orange 525.00 80.00
40 A17 40r grn (to dp grn) 475.00 92.50
 a. Half used as 20r on cover *27,500.*
 b. 40r yellow green 475.00 100.00
 Nos. 35-40 (6) 2,185. 877.50

Helvetia — A18

Double transfer errors, Nos. 43c, 44a, 55b, 60a, 61a, 61b, 67b, have the design impressed twice. These do not refer to the "embossed" watermark.

1862-64 Wmk. 182 *Perf. 11½*

White Wove Paper

41 A18 2c gray 175.00 4.75
42 A18 3c black 12.00 *160.00*
43 A18 5c dark brown 3.90 1.00
 a. 5c bister brown 115.00 2.40
 b. 5c gray brown 115.00 32.50
 c. Dbl. transfer, one invtd. 4,250. 470.00
 d. Dbl. transfer of lower left "5" 1,550.
44 A18 10c blue 700.00 1.00
 a. Dbl. transfer, one invtd. *8,500.*
45 A18 20c orange 2.40 3.90
 a. 20c yellow orange 390.00 3.90
46 A18 30c vermilion 1,850. 47.50
47 A18 40c green 1,700. 77.50
48 A18 60c bronze 1,550. 215.00
50 A18 1fr gold 22.50 *130.00*
 a. 1fr yellowish bronze ('64) 1,775. 620.00

1867-78

52 A18 2c bister brown 2.40 2.00
 a. 2c red brown 775.00 290.00
53 A18 10c carmine 7.75 1.20
54 A18 15c lemon 6.25 *47.50*
55 A18 25c blue green 1.60 *4.75*
 a. 25c yellow green 60.00 40.00
 b. Dbl. transfer, one invtd. 600.00
56 A18 30c ultra 620.00 16.00
 a. 30c blue *2,300.* 270.00
58 A18 40c gray 1.60 *170.00*
59 A18 50c violet 62.50 77.50
 Nos. 52-59 (7) *702.10* *318.95*

1881 Granite Paper

60 A18 2c bister .80 *30.00*
 a. Dbl. transfer, one invtd. 390.00
61 A18 5c brown .75 *16.00*
 a. Dbl. transfer, one invtd. 24.00 *475.00*
 b. Double transfer of lower left "5" *1,250.*
62 A18 10c rose 6.25 *16.00*
63 A18 15c lemon 9.25 *540.00*
64 A18 20c orange .80 *170.00*
65 A18 25c green .75 *110.00*
66 A18 40c gray 1.60 *3,875.*
67 A18 50c deep violet 13.00 *625.00*
 b. Dbl. transfer, one invtd. 200.00 *5,000.*
68 A18 1fr gold 17.50 *1,400.*

The granite paper contains fragments of blue and red silk threads.

Forged or backdated cancellations are found frequently on Nos. 42, 50, 54, 58 and 60-68.

All stamps of the preceding issues were declared obsolete on October 1st, 1883. Some of the remainders of Nos. 41-68 were overprinted "AUSSER KURS" (Obsolete) diagonally in black.

Numeral — A19

Wmk. 182 (Type II)

1882-89 Typo. *Perf. 11½*

Granite Paper

69 A19 2c bister 2.40 1.25
70 A19 3c gray brown 3.10 *16.00*
 a. 3c gray 65.00 72.50
71 A19 5c maroon 24.00 .80
 a. Tête bêche pair —
72 A19 5c deep grn ('99) 12.00 .75
73 A19 10c red 9.25 .80
74 A19 12c ultra 12.00 1.15
 a. 12c dull blue 390.00 42.50
76 A19 15c lilac ('89) 77.50 5.75
 Nos. 69-76 (7) 140.25 *26.50*
 Set, never hinged 291.00

Wmk. 182 (Type I)

69a A19 2c olive brown 40.00 5.50
70b A19 3c gray 62.50 70.00
71b A19 5c brownish lilac 92.50 3.10
73a A19 10c carmine 110.00 2.00
73b A19 10c light rose 650.00 12.00
74c A19 12c ultramarine 160.00 6.25
75 A19 15c yellow 160.00 40.00
75a A19 15c yellow-orange *18,500.* *5,400.*
76b A19 15c dull purple 4750.00 32.50

Wmk. 182 (Type II)

1882 White Paper

77 A19 2c olive brown 500.00 425.00
78 A19 5c brownish lilac 1,350. 115.00
79 A19 10c pale rose 2,700. 75.00
80 A19 12c grayish ultra 290.00 30.00
81 A19 15c yellow 370.00 *375.00*

Nos. 77-81 were the first stamps issued in the Numeral series.

See Nos. 113-118.

Helvetia (Large numerals) A20

Helvetia (Small numerals) A21

Wmk. 182 (Type I)

1882-1904 Engr. *Perf. 11½ - 11¾*

82 A20 20c orange 350.00 7.75
83 A20 25c green 200.00 4.00
95b A20 30c brown — *27,000.*
84 A20 40c gray 310.00 60.00
86 A20 50c blue 310.00 27.50
87 A20 1fr claret 470.00 16.00
88 A20 3fr yel brn ('91) 310.00 32.50

Wmk. 182 (Type II)

85 A21 40c gray ('04) 50.00 40.00
88d A20 3fr yellow brown ('04) *7,500.*

1888 Wmk. 182 (Type I) *Perf. 9½*

89 A20 20c orange 1,150. 125.00
90 A20 25c yellow grn 230.00 24.00
91 A20 40c gray 1,100. 925.00
92 A20 50c blue 1,700. 450.00
93 A20 1fr claret 1,300. 115.00

Values for Nos. 89-93 are for well-centered stamps with slightly uneven perforations. Stamps missing perforations sell for much less.

Wmk. 182 (Type I)

1891-1903 *Perf. 11½x11*

82c A20 20c orange *925.00* 11.50
83b A20 25c green *350.00* 7.75
95c A20 30c red brown ('92) *620.00* 62.50
84c A20 40c gray *1,150.* 115.00
86b A20 50c blue *70.00* 37.50
87c A20 1fr claret *1,175.* 32.50
88c A20 3fr olive brown *23,250.*

Wmk. 182 (Type II)

82a A20 20c orange 160.00 2.40
83a A20 25c green 19.00 2.40
94 A20 25c blue ('99) 22.00 6.25
95 A20 30c red brn ('92) 23.00 2.40
84a A20 40c gray 100.00 7.75
86a A20 50c blue 70.00 23.00
96 A20 50c green ('99) 100.00 50.00
87a A20 1fr claret 62.50 6.25
97 A20 1fr carmine ('03) 97.50 12.50
88a A20 3fr yellow brown 200.00 37.50

Wmk. 182 (Type II)

1901-03 *Perf. 11½x12*

82b A20 20c orange 47.50 2.40
94a A20 25c blue 20.00 1.60
95a A20 30c red brown 47.50 2.75
84b A20 40c gray 125.00 47.50
96a A20 50c green 85.00 20.00
87b A20 1fr claret *2,500.* 350.00
97a A20 1fr carmine ('03) 620.00 55.00
88b A20 3fr yellow brown 230.00 32.50

Numerous retouches and plate flaws exist on all values of this issue.

The small numerals illustrated by A21 are only present in the 40c gray. The denomination does not touch the inner frame line on the small numeral issues.

Nos. 82-88 are ½mm taller (paper size) than Nos. 82b-88b.

See Nos. 105-112, 119-125.

UPU Allegory — A22

1900 *Perf. 11½*

98 A22 5c gray green 40.00 3.00
99 A22 10c carmine rose 12.50 3.00
100 A22 25c blue 32.00 47.50
 Nos. 98-100 (3) 84.50 53.50

Re-engraved

101 A22 5c gray green 4.00 3.00
102 A22 10c carmine rose 62.50 57.50
103 A22 25c blue 800.00 *16,250.*

Universal Postal Union, 25th anniv.

The impression of the re-engraved stamps is much clearer, especially the horizontally lined background. The figures of value are lined instead of being solid.

Helvetia Types of 1882-1904

1905 Wmk. 183 *Perf. 11½x11*

White Paper

105 A20 20c orange 6.25 4.00
106 A20 25c blue 11.50 *16.00*
107 A20 30c brown 11.50 3.00
108a A21 40c gray 195.00 *230.00*
109 A20 50c green 92.50 16.00
110 A20 1fr carmine 160.00 6.25
111 A20 3fr yellow brn 350.00 230.00

Some clichés in the plates of the 20c, 25c, 30c, 50c and 3fr have been retouched.

1906 Re-engraved *Perf. 11½x11*

112 A20 25c pale blue 9.25 2.75

In the re-engraved stamp the stars are larger and the background below "FRANCO" is of horiz. or horiz. and vert. crossed lines, instead of horiz. and curved lines.

1906 *Perf. 11½*

112a A20 25c pale blue 195.00 14.00
108 A21 40c gray 47.50 23.00

1907 *Perf. 11½x12*

105a A20 20c orange 11.00 9.00
109a A20 50c green 77.50 32.50
110a A20 1fr carmine 135.00 18.00
111a A20 3fr yellow brown 425.00 310.00

Numeral Type of 1882-99

1905 Typo. *Perf. 11½*

Granite Paper

113 A19 2c dull bister 9.50 2.75
114 A19 3c gray brown 11.00 *140.00*
115 A19 5c green 10.00 .75
116 A19 10c scarlet 9.25 .75
117 A19 12c ultra 14.00 4.75
118 A19 15c brown vio 95.00 27.50
 Nos. 113-118 (6) 148.75 *176.50*

Helvetia Types of 1882-1904

1907 Engr. *Perf. 11½x12*

Granite Paper

119 A20 20c orange 4.00 6.25
120 A20 25c blue 24.00 *24.00*
121 A20 30c red brown 9.25 *32.50*
122 A21 40c gray 32.50 *77.50*
 a. Helvetia without diadem 375.00 *1,650.*
123 A20 50c gray green 7.75 *32.50*
124 A20 1fr carmine 47.50 16.00
125a A20 3fr yellow brown *15,500.*

There are retouches and plate flaws on all values.

Perf. 11½x11

120a A20 25c deep blue 16.00 11.50
121a A20 30c red brown 250.00 *500.00*
122b A21 40c gray *20,000.*
124a A20 1fr carmine *19,500.* *7,750.*
125 A20 3fr yel brn 170.00 110.00

William Tell's Son — A23

A24

Helvetia — A25

No. 136 No. 136a

No. 136 has two leaves and "CL" below sword hilt. No. 136a has three leaves and designer's full name below hilt.

1907-25 Typo. *Perf. 11½*

Granite Paper

126 A23 2c pale bister .40 *1.55*
127 A23 3c lilac brn .40 *16.00*
128 A23 5c yellow grn 4.75 .75
 Never hinged 16.00
 On cover 1.60
129 A24 10c rose red 2.40 .75
130 A24 12c ocher .40 *6.25*
131 A24 15c red vio 4.75 *20.00*
132 A25 20c red & yel ('08) 4.00 1.55
133 A25 25c dp blue ('08) 3.00 1.15
 a. Tête bêche pair 32.50 *195.00*
134 A25 30c yel brn & pale grn ('08) 2.40 .75
135 A25 35c yel grn & yel ('08) 3.00 3.50
136 A25 40c red vio & yel ('08) 22.50 1.55
 a. Designer's name in full on the rock ('08) 12.00 *124.00*
137 A25 40c deep blue ('22) 2.40 .75
 a. 40c light blue ('21) 9.25 3.00
138 A25 40c red vio & grn ('25) 57.50 .75
139 A25 50c dp grn & pale grn ('08) 16.00 .75
140 A25 60c brn org & buff ('18) 19.00 1.55
141 A25 70c dk brn & buff ('08) 77.50 27.50
142 A25 70c vio & buff ('24) 20.00 5.50
143 A25 80c slate & buff ('15) 20.00 2.75

No.	Type	Description	Unused	Used
144	A25	1fr dp cl & pale grn ('08)	12.00	.75
145	A25	3fr bis & yel ('08)	465.00	3.90
		Nos. 126-145 (20)	737.40	*98.00*

For surcharges and overprints see Nos. 189, 199, O10-O13, O15, 1O6-1O8, 1O14-1O16, 2O18-2O26, 3O14-3O22.

1933 With Grilled Gum

No.	Type	Description	Unused	Used
135a	A25	35c yel grn & yel	1.55	*19.00*
138a	A25	40c red vio & grn	55.00	2.40
139a	A25	50c dp grn & pale grn	12.00	2.40
		Never hinged	37.50	
		On cover		16.00
140a	A25	60c brn org & buff	16.00	2.40
142a	A25	70c vio & buff	19.00	7.75
143a	A25	80c slate & buff	16.00	6.25
144a	A25	1fr dp cl & pale grn	24.00	10.00
		Nos. 135a-144a (7)	143.55	50.20

"Grilled" Gum

In 1930-44 many Swiss stamps were treated with a light grilling process, applied with the gumming to counteract the tendency to curl. It resembles a faint grill of vertical and horizontal ribs covering the entire back of the stamp, and can be seen after the gum has been removed. Listings of the grilled gum varieties begin with No. 135a.

William Tell's Son — A26

Bow-string in front of stock

1909 *Perf. 11½, 12*

Granite Paper

No.	Type	Description	Unused	Used
146	A26	2c bister	.40	2.00
a.		Tête bêche pair	3.10	*47.50*
147	A26	3c dark violet	.40	*16.00*
148	A26	5c green	11.50	.75
a.		Tête bêche pair	35.00	*85.00*
		Nos. 146-148 (3)	12.30	*18.75*

See Nos. 149-163.

First Redrawing

Bow-string behind stock. Thin loop above crossbow. Letters of "HELVETIA" without serifs.

1910-17 Granite Paper

No.	Type	Description	Unused	Used
149	A26	2c bister ('10)	16.00	11.00
150	A26	3c dk violet ('10)	.40	.75
a.		Tête bêche pair	3.10	16.00
b.		Booklet pane of 6	30.00	
151	A26	3c brown org ('17)	.40	.75
a.		Tête bêche pair	7.75	23.00
152	A26	5c green ('10)	32.50	11.00
a.		Tête bêche pair	155.00	500.00
		Nos. 149-152 (4)	49.30	23.50

Second Redrawing

Bow-string behind stock. Thick loop above crossbow. Letters of "HELVETIA" have serifs.

7½ CENTIMES:

Type I — Top of "7" is ½mm thick. The "1" of "½" has only traces of serifs. The two base plates of the statue are of even thickness.

Type II — Top of "7" is 1mm thick. The "1" of "½" has distinct serifs. The upper base plate is thinner than the lower.

1911-30 Granite Paper

No.	Type	Description	Unused	Used
153	A26	2c bister ('11)	.40	.75
a.		Tête bêche pair	3.10	27.50
154	A26	2½c claret ('18)	.40	*2.00*
155	A26	2½c ol, *buff* ('28)	.40	*4.00*
156	A26	3c ultra, *buff* ('30)	5.50	*16.00*
157	A26	5c green ('11)	1.10	.75
a.		Tête bêche pair	6.25	*23.00*
158	A26	5c org, *buff* ('21)	.40	.75
a.		Bklt. pane of 6 (5 #158, 168)	27.50	*75.00*
159	A26	5c gray vio, *buff* ('24)	.40	.95
a.		Bklt. pane of 6 (5 #159, 168)	12.50	*37.50*
160	A26	5c red vio, *buff* ('27)	.40	.75
a.		Bklt. pane 6 (5 #160, 168)	55.00	*100.00*
161	A26	5c dk grn, *buff* ('30)	.40	.60
a.		Bklt. pane 6 (5 #161, 169)	55.00	*125.00*
162	A26	7½c gray (I) ('18)	6.25	4.75
a.		Tête bêche pair	19.00	*77.50*
c.		7½c slate (II)	6.25	4.75
163	A26	7½c dp grn, *buff* (I) ('28)	.40	*7.75*
		Nos. 153-163 (11)	16.05	*39.05*

For surcharges and overprints see Nos. 186, 193-195, 207-208, 1O1-1O3, 1O9-1O11, 2O1-2O7, 3O1-3O5.

1933 With Grilled Gum

No.	Type	Description	Unused	Used
156a	A26	3c ultra, *buff*	7.75	*32.50*
161b	A26	5c dark green, *buff*	1.60	*16.00*

Helvetia — A27

1909 Granite Paper

No.	Type	Description	Unused	Used
164	A27	10c carmine	1.55	.75
		Never hinged	3.00	
		On cover		1.50
a.		Tête bêche pair	4.00	*24.00*
165	A27	12c bister brn	.75	1.55
166	A27	15c red violet	37.50	1.55
		Nos. 164-166 (3)	39.80	3.85

For surcharge see No. 187.

William Tell — A28

TEN CENTIMES:

Type I — Bust 16½mm high. "HELVETIA" 15½mm wide. Cross bar of "H" at middle of the letter.

Type II — Bust 15mm high. "HELVETIA" 15mm wide. Cross bar of "H" above middle of the letter.

1914-30 Granite Paper *Perf. 11½*

No.	Type	Description	Unused	Used
167	A28	10c red, *buff* (type II)	.75	.75
a.		10c red, *buff* (type I)	3.10	*24.00*
b.		Tête bêche pair (II)	3.10	16.00
d.		Bklt. pane 6 (5 #167, 172)	60.00	*160.00*
168	A28	10c grn, *buff* (type II) ('21)	.40	.75
a.		Tête bêche pair	1.15	3.10
168C	A28	10c bl grn, *buff* (type II) ('28)	.40	.75
d.		Tête bêche pair	1.55	4.75
169	A28	10c vio, *buff* (type II) ('30)	1.55	.75
a.		Tête bêche pair	7.00	7.75
170	A28	12c brn, *buff*	.75	*7.00*
		Never hinged	1.55	
		On cover, single franking		375.00
171	A28	13c ol grn, *buff* ('15)	2.40	.75
172	A28	15c vio, *buff*	6.25	.75
b.		15c dk vio, *buff*	55.00	16.00
c.		Tête bêche pair	125.00	*215.00*
173	A28	15c brn red, *buff* ('28)	4.75	7.00
174	A28	20c red vio, *buff* ('21)	2.40	.75
a.		Tête bêche pair	7.75	*16.00*
175	A28	20c ver, *buff* ('24)	.75	.75
a.		Tête bêche pair	4.75	*16.00*
176	A28	20c car, *buff* ('25)	.75	.75
a.		Tête bêche pair	4.00	4.75
177	A28	25c ver, *buff* ('21)	1.55	3.25
178	A28	25c car, *buff* ('22)	.75	1.55
179	A28	25c brn, *buff* ('25)	6.25	2.40
180	A28	30c dp bl, *buff* ('24)	16.00	.75
		Nos. 167-180 (15)	45.70	28.70

1932-33 With Grilled Gum

No.	Type	Description	Unused	Used
169c	A28	10c violet, *buff*	4.75	2.40
173a	A28	15c brn red, *buff* ('33)	92.50	*92.50*
176c	A28	20c carmine, *buff*	7.75	2.40
179a	A28	25c brown, *buff* ('33)	92.50	55.00
180a	A28	30c deep blue, *buff*	77.50	4.00
		Nos. 169c-180a (5)	275.00	156.30

For surcharges and overprints see Nos. 188, 196-198, 1O4-1O5, 1O12-1O13, 2O8-2O17, 3O6-3O13.

The Mythen A29

The Rütli — A30

The Jungfrau A31

1914-30 Engr. Granite Paper

No.	Type	Description	Unused	Used
181	A29	3fr Pruss green	775.00	9.25
182	A29	3fr red ('18)	125.00	2.40
183	A30	5fr dp ultra	52.50	4.00
184	A31	10fr dull violet	155.00	4.00
185	A31	10fr gray grn ('30)	275.00	57.50
		Nos. 181-185 (5)	1,383.	77.15

See No. 206. For overprints see Nos. 2O27-2O30, 3O23-3O26.

Stamps of 1909-14 Surcharged

a

b

c

1915

No.	Type	Description	Unused	Used
186	A26(a)	1c on 2c bister	.40	*1.55*
187	A27(b)	13c on 12c bis brn	.40	*16.00*
188	A28(c)	13c on 12c brn, *buff*	.40	*1.55*
		Nos. 186-188 (3)	1.20	*19.10*

No. 141 Surcharged

No.	Type	Description	Unused	Used
189	A25	80c on 70c	37.50	32.50

Significant of Peace A32

"Peace" A33

"Dawn of Peace" A34

Perf. 11½

1919, Aug. 1 Typo. Unwmk.

No.	Type	Description	Unused	Used
190	A32	7½c olive drab & blk	2.40	*4.00*
191	A33	10c red & yel	2.40	*9.25*
192	A34	15c violet & yel	3.00	4.00
		Nos. 190-192 (3)	7.80	17.25

Commemorating Peace after World War I.

Nos. 151, 149, 162, 171-172, 133 Surcharged in Black, Red or Dark Blue

a

b

c

1921 Wmk. 183

No.	Type	Description	Unused	Used
193	A26(a)	2½c on 3c (Bl)	.40	*1.55*
a.		Tête bêche pair	1.15	*7.75*
b.		Inverted surcharge	775.00	*1,575.*
c.		Double surcharge	*775.00*	*1,575.*
194	A26(a)	5c on 2c (R)	.40	*7.00*
a.		Double surcharge	*450.00*	*450.00*
195	A26(a)	5c on 7½c (R)	.40	.75
		Never hinged	.75	
		On cover		2.50
a.		Tête bêche pair	7.00	*100.00*
		Never hinged	14.00	
		On cover		140.00
b.		Double surcharge	*400.00*	*775.00*

c.	5c on 7½c slate (II)	3,100.	*7,500.*
	Never hinged	6,600.	
196	A28(b) 10c on 13c (R)	.40	*4.00*
a.	Double surcharge	*625.00*	*1,400.*
197	A28(c) 20c on 15c (Bk)	.75	*4.00*
a.	Tête bêche pair	3.00	*110.00*
b.	Double surcharge	*875.00*	*875.00*
198	A28(c) 20c on 15c (Bl)	3.00	*9.50*
b.	Double surcharge	*875.00*	*875.00*
199	A25(c) 20c on 25c dp bl (R)	.40	*.75*
a.	Tête bêche pair	1.55	*17.50*
	Nos. 193-199 (7)	5.75	*27.55*

A36

1924 Typo. *Perf. 11½*

Granite Paper, Surface Colored

200	A36 90c grn & red, *grn*	24.00	4.00
201	A36 1.20fr brn rose & red, *rose*	7.75	7.75
202	A36 1.50fr bl & red, *bl*	55.00	9.25
203	A36 2fr gray blk & red, *gray*	70.00	10.00
	Nos. 200-203 (4)	156.75	31.00
	Set, never hinged	467.50	

1933 With Grilled Gum

200a	A36 90c	27.50	4.75
201a	A36 1.20fr	70.00	8.50
202a	A36 1.50fr	24.00	9.25
203a	A36 2fr	42.50	13.50
	Nos. 200a-203a (4)	164.00	36.00
	Set, never hinged	425.00	

For overprints see Nos. O16-O18, 2O31-2O34, 3O27-3O30.

1940 With Smooth Gum

Ordinary Paper

200b	A36 90c	24.00	*77.50*
	On cover		235.00
201b	A36 1.20fr	24.00	*115.00*
202b	A36 1.50fr	24.00	*725.00*
	On cover		*5,750.*
	Nos. 200b-202b (3)	72.00	917.50
	Set, never hinged	120.00	

Building in Bern, Location of 1st UPU Congress, 1874

A37 A38

1924, Oct. 9 Engr. Wmk. 183

Granite Paper

204	A37 20c vermilion	.75	*2.40*
205	A38 30c dull blue	1.55	*9.25*
	Set, never hinged	5.55	

50th anniv. of the UPU.

Type of 1914 Issue

The Rütli — A39

1928 Re-engraved *Perf. 11½*

206	A39 5fr blue	165.00	16.00
	Never hinged	475.00	
	On cover		*400.00*
a.	Imperf., pair, never hinged	*9,000.*	

In the re-engraved stamp the picture is clearer and lighter than on No. 183. "HELVETIA" is in smaller letters. The names at foot of the stamp are "Grasset-J. Sprenger" instead of "E. GRASSET-A. BURKHARD."

For overprints see Nos. 2O35, 3O31.

Nos. 155 and 163 Surcharged

1930, June *Perf. 11½*

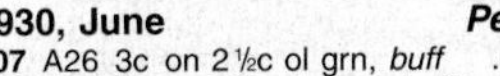

207	A26 3c on 2½c ol grn, *buff*	.40	*4.75*
208	A26 5c on 7½c dp grn, *buff*	.40	*16.00*
	Set, never hinged	1.50	

The Mythen A40

1931 Engr. Granite Paper

209	A40 3fr orange brown	65.00	7.75
	Never hinged	200.00	
	On cover		*115.00*

For overprints see Nos. 2O56, 3O47.

Dove on Broken Sword — A41

"Peace" A42

1932, Feb. 2 Typo. *Perf. 11½*

Granite Paper

210	A41 5c peacock blue	.40	.75
211	A41 10c orange	.40	.75
212	A41 20c cerise	.40	.75
213	A41 30c ultra	2.25	1.60
214	A41 60c olive brown	17.50	8.75

Unwmk.

Photo.

215	A42 1fr olive gray & bl	24.00	15.00
	Never hinged	150.00	
	On cover		*115.00*
	Nos. 210-215 (6)	44.95	27.60
	Set, never hinged	*118.00*	

Intl. Disarmament Conf., Geneva, Feb. 1932.

For overprints see #2O36-2O41, 3O32-3O37.

Louis Favre — A43

Alfred Escher — A44

Design: 30c, Emil Welti.

Wmk. 183

1932, May 31 Engr. *Perf. 11½*

Granite Paper

216	A43 10c red brown	.40	.75
217	A44 20c vermilion	.40	.75
218	A44 30c deep ultra	.75	*4.75*
	Nos. 216-218 (3)	1.55	*6.25*
	Set, never hinged	4.70	

Completion of the St. Gotthard tunnel, 50th anniv.

Nos. 216-218 exist imperforate.

Staubbach Falls A46

Mt. Pilatus A47

Chillon Castle A48

Rhone Glacier A49

St. Gotthard Railroad A50

Via Mala Gorge A51

Rhine Falls — A52

1934, July 2 Typo. *Perf. 11½*

Grilled Gum, Ordinary Paper

219	A46 3c olive	.25	*4.50*
220	A47 5c emerald	.25	.25
221	A48 10c brt violet	.55	.25
222	A49 15c orange	.65	3.75
223	A50 20c red	1.00	.25
224	A51 25c brown	8.50	8.25
225	A52 30c ultra	24.00	1.55
	Nos. 219-225 (7)	35.20	18.80
	Set, never hinged	124.00	

Tête bêche Pairs

220a	A47 5c	3.50	5.25
221a	A48 10c	3.25	8.00
222a	A49 15c	3.50	12.00
223a	A50 20c	4.50	12.00

Souvenir Sheet

A52a

1934, Sept. 29

226	A52a Sheet of 4	350.00	*600.00*

No. 226 was issued in connection with the Swiss National Philatelic Exhibition at Zurich, Sept. 29 to Oct. 7, 1934. It contains one each of Nos. 220-223. Size: 62x72mm.

For overprints see Nos. 2O42-2O46, 3O48.

Staubbach Falls A53

Mt. Pilatus A54

Chillon Castle A55

Rhone Glacier A56

St. Gotthard Railroad A57

Via Mala Gorge A58

Rhine Falls — A59

Balsthal Pass — A60

Alpine Lake of Säntis — A61

Type I

Type II

Type I

Type II

Two types of 10c red violet:

I — Shading inside "0" of 10 has only vertical lines.

II — Shading in "0" includes two diagonal lines.

Two types of 20c:

I — Small bollards marking the edge of the road.

II — Thicker and higher bollards marking the edge of the road. Shading and lines are more pronounced around the terminals.

1936-42 Unwmk. Engr. *Perf. 11½*

227	A53 3c olive	.25	.50
228	A54 5c blue green	.25	.25
229	A55 10c red vio (II)	.40	.40
b.	Type I	.85	.30
230	A55 10c dk red brn ('39)	.25	.40
230B	A55 10c org brn ('42)	.25	.25
231	A56 15c orange	.60	1.75
232	A57 20c carmine (I)	5.75	.25
b.	Type II	5.00	.25
233	A58 25c lt brown	.65	1.50
234	A59 30c ultra	1.15	.25
235	A60 35c yellow grn	1.15	2.50
236	A61 40c gray	8.50	.25
	Nos. 227-236 (11)	19.20	8.30
	Set, never hinged	42.50	

See Nos. 316-321.

For overprints see Nos. O1-O4, O6-O9, O19-O19-O22, O24-O27, 2O47-2O55, 2O68-2O68A, 2O70-2O73, 2O75-2O78, 3O38-3O46, 3O60-3O60A, 3O62-3O65, 3O67-3O70, 4O1-4O4, 4O6-4O9, 4O23-4O24, 4O27-4O28, 5O1-5O2, 5O5.

Tête bêche Pairs

228a	A54	5c	blue green	.35	.45
229a	A55	10c	red violet (II)	1.60	1.35
230a	A55	10c	dark red brown	.70	2.40
230Bd	A55	10c	orange brown	.60	1.00
232a	A57	20c	carmine	29.00	50.00

1936-40 With Grilled Gum

227a	A53	3c	olive	.80	*6.00*
228d	A54	5c	blue green	.25	.25
229d	A55	10c	red violet (II)	.75	.25
e.	Type I			.75	.25
230e	A55	10c	dk red brn ('40)	.95	*15.50*
231a	A56	15c	orange	.40	.25
232c	A57	20c	carmine	6.25	.90
233a	A58	25c	light brown	.70	*3.50*
234a	A59	30c	ultra	1.20	.25
235a	A60	35c	yellow green	1.35	2.25
236a	A61	40c	gray	10.00	.25
	Nos. 227a-236a (10)			22.65	*29.40*
	Set, never hinged			50.00	

Tête bêche Pairs

228e	As "d,"	1.00	.50
229f	As "d,"	6.00	5.00
229g	As "e,"	4.00	2.00
232d	As "c,"	4.50	2.25

Mobile Post Office A62

1937, Sept. 5 Photo.

Granite Paper

237	A62	10c	black & yellow	.50	*1.00*

No. 237 was sold exclusively by the traveling post office. It exists on two kinds of granite paper, black and red fibers or blue and red fibers. See No. 307 for type A62 redrawn.

View of Labor Building from Lake Geneva A63

Palace of League of Nations A64

Main Building, Palace of League of Nations A65

Labor Building and Albert Thomas Monument A66

1938, May 2 ***Perf. 11½***

Granite Paper

238	A63	20c	red & buff	.30	.25
239	A64	30c	blue & lt blue	.45	.50
240	A65	60c	brown & buff	1.50	*3.00*
241	A66	1fr	black & buff	7.50	*21.00*
	Nos. 238-241 (4)			9.75	*24.75*
	Set, never hinged			25.00	

Opening of Assembly Hall of the Palace of the League of Nations.

For overprints see Nos. 2O57-2O64, 3O49-3O56.

Souvenir Sheet

A67

Engraved and Typographed

1938, Sept. 17 Unwmk. ***Perf. 11½***

Granite Paper

242	A67 Sheet of 3		40.00	35.00
	Never hinged		70.00	
a.	AP4 10c on 65c gray bl & dp bl		24.00	*24.00*
	Never hinged		45.00	
b.	A68 20c red		2.00	*2.00*
	Never hinged		4.00	

Natl. Phil. Exhib. at Aarau, Sept. 17-25, and 25th anniv. of Swiss air mail. No. 242 contains 2 No. 243, but on granite paper, and a 10c on 65c similar to No. C22 but redrawn, with wing tips 1½mm from side frame lines; overall size 37x20½mm; no watermark.

On No. C22, wing tips touch frame lines; size is 36x21½mm; Wmk. 183.

Lake Lugano — A68

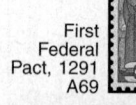

First Federal Pact, 1291 A69

Diet of Stans, 1481 A70

Citizens Voting A71

1938, Sept. 17 Engr. ***Perf. 11½***

243	A68 20c red		.40	.65
a.	"c,"tête bêche pair		.95	*1.15*
c.	Grilled gum		.50	*1.25*
d.	As "c," tête bêche pair		2.10	*17.00*

Granite Paper

244	A69	3fr	brn car, *grnsh*	13.50	10.50
245	A70	5fr	slate bl, *grnsh*	13.50	9.75
246	A71	10fr	grn, *grnsh*	55.00	60.00
	Nos. 243-246 (4)			82.40	80.90
	Set, never hinged			200.00	

No. 243 is printed on ordinary paper. Nos. 244-246 are on granite surface-colored paper. The greenish surface coating has faded on most examples.

For type A68 in orange brown, see No. 318.

See Nos. 242b, 284-286. For overprints see Nos. O5, O23, 2O65-2O67, 2O69, 2O74, 2O88-2O90, 3O57-3O59, 3O61, 3O66, 3O80-3O82, 4O5, 4O19-4O21, O4O25, 5O3, 5O23-5O25, 7O18-7O20.

Deputation of Trades and Professions — A72

Swiss Family A73

Alpine Scenery A74

German

Italian

Engr., Photo. (30c)

1939, Feb. 1 ***Perf. 11½***

Inscribed in French

247	A72	10c	dl pur & red	.25	.25
248	A73	20c	lake & red	1.00	.25
249	A74	30c	dp blue & red	3.50	*7.75*

Inscribed in German

250	A72	10c	dl pur & red	.25	.25
251	A73	20c	lake & red	.60	.25
252	A74	30c	dp blue & red	2.40	*3.00*

Inscribed in Italian

253	A72	10c	dl pur & red	.25	.25
254	A73	20c	lake & red	2.00	.30
255	A74	30c	dp blue & red	3.25	*8.75*
	Nos. 247-255 (9)			13.50	*21.05*
	Set, never hinged			35.00	

National Exposition of 1939, Zurich.

Tree and Crossbow — A75

1939, May 6 Photo. ***Perf. 11½***

Granite Paper

Inscribed in French

256	A75	5c	deep green	.75	*2.50*
257	A75	10c	gray brown	.95	*3.25*
258	A75	20c	brt carmine	1.60	*14.50*
259	A75	30c	violet blue	1.75	*6.00*

Inscribed in German

260	A75	5c	deep green	.75	*2.50*
261	A75	10c	gray brown	.30	*.90*
262	A75	20c	brt carmine	1.60	*14.50*
263	A75	30c	violet blue	1.75	*4.75*

Inscribed in Italian

264	A75	5c	deep green	.75	*2.50*
265	A75	10c	gray brown	.95	*3.25*
266	A75	20c	brt carmine	1.60	*14.50*
267	A75	30c	violet blue	2.25	*6.50*
	Nos. 256-267 (12)			15.00	*75.65*
	Set, never hinged			35.00	

National Exposition of 1939.

The 5c, 10c and 20c stamps in the three languages exist se-tenant in coils. On the 10c coil stamp, the inscription "COURVOISIER S.A." beneath is design is smaller, with the "A" just left of the point on the "V" of "HELVETIA". On the sheet stamp, the "A" is just right of the "V". Value about three times that of the sheet stamp.

1939 With Grilled Gum

256a	A75	5c	deep green	.75	*3.25*
257a	A75	10c	gray brown	.85	*3.25*
258a	A75	20c	bright carmine	2.10	*4.25*
260a	A75	5c	deep green	.75	*2.40*
262a	A75	20c	bright carmine	1.45	2.40
264a	A75	5c	deep green	1.25	*5.00*
265a	A75	10c	gray brown	1.00	*4.25*
266a	A75	20c	bright carmine	2.40	*5.75*
	Nos. 256a-266a (8)			10.55	*30.55*
	Set, never hinged			35.00	

View of Geneva A76

Perf. 11½

1939, Aug. 22 Photo. Unwmk.

Granite Paper

268	A76 20c red, car & buff	.40	.50
269	A76 30c blue, car & gray	.50	*4.00*
	Set, never hinged	1.90	

75th anniv. of the founding of the Intl. Red Cross Society.

"The Three Swiss" — A77

William Tell — A78

Fighting Soldier — A79

Dying Warrior — A80

Standard Bearer — A81

Ludwig Pfyffer — A82

Jürg Jenatsch — A83

Francois de Reynold — A84

Joachim Forrer — A85

1941-59 Engr. *Perf. 11½*

Granite Paper

270	A77 50c dp pur, *grnsh*	4.25	.30
271	A78 60c red brn, *buff*	6.00	.25
272	A79 70c rose vio, *pale lil*	3.00	1.20
273	A80 80c blk, *pale gray*	1.20	.25
a.	80c black, *pale lilac* ('58)	1.20	.60
274	A81 90c dk red, *pale rose*	.60	.25
a.	90c dark red, *buff* ('59)	1.20	*1.20*
275	A82 1fr dk grn, *grnsh*	1.20	.25
276	A83 1.20fr red vio, *pale gray*	1.50	.30
a.	1.20fr red vio, *pale lil* ('58)	1.50	2.10
277	A84 1.50fr dk bl, *buff*	1.75	.30
278	A85 2fr mar, *pale rose*	2.10	.25
a.	2fr maroon, *buff* ('59)	2.10	.60
	Nos. 270-278 (9)	21.60	3.35
	Set, never hinged	50.00	

For overprints see Nos. O28-O36, 2O79-2O87, 3O71-3O79, 4O10-4O18, 5O17-5O22, 6O6-6O8, 7O12-7O17.

Farmer Plowing A86

1941, Mar. 21 Photo.

Granite Paper

279	A86 10c brown & buff	.25	*.40*
	Never hinged	.25	

Natl. Agriculture Development Plan of 1941.

Masons, Knight and Bern Coat of Arms A87

1941, Sept. 6 Granite Paper

280	A87 10c multicolored	.25	*.90*
	Never hinged	.40	

750th anniversary of Bern.

A88

Design: "In order to Endure, Reclaim Used Materials" Inscribed in French.

1942, Mar. 21 Unwmk. *Perf. 11½*

281	A88 10c shown	.25	*.35*
282	A88 10c German	.60	*1.10*
283	A88 10c Italian	6.00	4.50
	Nos. 281-283 (3)	6.85	5.95
	Set, never hinged	14.00	
	Sheet of 25	100.00	*550.00*

Printed in sheets of 25, containing 8 No. 281, 12 No. 282 and 5 No. 283.

Types of 1938

1954-55 Engr.

Cream-surfaced Granite Paper

284	A69 3fr brown car	6.25	.85
285	A70 5fr slate blue	5.50	.85
286	A71 10fr green	7.25	3.00
	Nos. 284-286 (3)	19.00	4.70
	Set, never hinged	37.50	

1942, May 11 Cream paper

284a	A69 3fr	22.50	.75
285a	A70 5fr	12.50	.75
286a	A71 10fr	30.00	1.50
	Nos. 284a-286a (3)	65.00	3.00
	Set, never hinged	150.00	

The 1955 set is on cream-surfaced granite paper with white back, and blue and red fibers. The 1942 set is on colored-through cream paper with black and red fibers.

See note after No. 246.

Zurich Stamps of 1843 A91

1943, Feb. 26

287	A91 10c blk & salmon	.25	.25
	Never hinged	.25	

Centenary of postage stamps of Switzerland. See Nos. B130-B131.

Apollo Statue — A94

1944, Mar. 21 Photo.

Granite Paper

290	A94 10c org yel & gray blk	.30	*.50*
291	A94 20c cer & gray blk	.40	*.50*
292	A94 30c lt bl & gray blk	.60	*4.75*
	Nos. 290-292 (3)	1.30	*5.75*
	Set, never hinged	2.50	

Olympic Jubilee.

Numeral of Value — A95

Olive Branch A96

Field of Crocus A97

Aged Couple A98

Designs: 60c, Keys of peace. 80c, Horn of plenty. 1fr, Dove of peace. 2fr, Plowing. 5fr, Clasped hands.

1945, May 9 Unwmk. *Perf. 12*

Granite Paper

293	A95 5c gray & green	.25	*.40*
294	A95 10c gray & brown	.25	.25
295	A95 20c gray & car rose	.35	.25
296	A95 30c gray & ultra	.65	*3.25*
297	A95 40c gray & orange	2.60	*9.00*
298	A96 50c dark red	3.00	*21.00*
299	A96 60c dull gray	4.50	*12.00*
300	A96 80c slate green	7.00	*85.00*
301	A96 1fr blue	8.75	*95.00*
302	A96 2fr red brown	26.00	*160.00*

Engr.

303	A97 3fr dk sl grn, *buff*	33.00	*70.00*
304	A98 5fr brn lake, *buff*	80.00	*250.00*
305	A98 10fr rose vio, *buff*	100.00	*100.00*
	Nos. 293-305,B145 (14)	266.65	*806.90*
	Set, never hinged	525.00	

End of war in Europe.

Johann Heinrich Pestalozzi — A104

1946, Jan. 12 Engr. *Perf. 11½*

306	A104 10c rose violet	.25	.25
	Never hinged	.25	

200th anniversary of the birth of J. H. Pestalozzi, educational reformer.

For overprint see No. 4O22.

Mobile P.O. Type of 1937

Redrawn

1946, July 6 Photo.

Granite Paper

307	A62 10c black & yellow	1.25	.60
	Never hinged	3.00	

The designer's and printer's names are larger on the redrawn stamp. There are many minor differences in the two designs. Sizes: 1937, 37½x21mm. 1946, 38x22½mm.

First Swiss Steam Locomotive — A105

Modern Steam Locomotive — A106

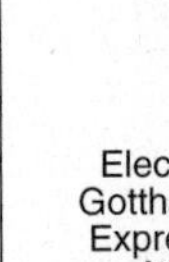

Electric Gotthard Express A107

Electric Trains Passing on Bridge A108

1947, Aug. 6 Photo. *Perf. 11½*

Granite Paper

308	A105 5c dk grn, blk & yel	.30	*.30*
309	A106 10c dk brn, gray & blk	.30	*.30*
310	A107 20c dk red & red	.35	*.35*
311	A108 30c dk bl & bl gray	1.10	*2.50*
	Nos. 308-311 (4)	2.05	*3.45*
	Set, never hinged	4.00	

Centenary of the opening of the first Swiss railroad, between Zurich and Baden.

Johann Rudolf Wettstein A109

Castle at Neuchatel A110

"Helvetia" A111

Symbol of Swiss Federal State A112

1948, Feb. 27 Granite Paper

312	A109 5c dp grn	.25	*.50*
313	A110 10c gray blk	.25	.25
314	A111 20c dk red	.30	.25
315	A112 30c dk bl & red	.50	*1.25*
	Nos. 312-315 (4)	1.30	*2.25*
	Set, never hinged	2.00	

Tercentenary of the acknowledgment of independence of the Swiss Confederation, and the centenaries of the Neuchatel Revolution and the Swiss Federal State.

See Nos. B178a and B178b for 10c and 20c denominations, type A109.

Types of 1936-42 and

Grisons National Park — A113

1948, Mar. 1 **Engr.**

316 A54 5c chocolate .25 .25
a. Tête bêche pair .80 1.05
317 A55 10c green .25 .25
a. Tête bêche pair .80 .95
318 A68 20c org brn .25 .25
a. Tête bêche pair 1.10 1.90
319 A113 25c carmine .95 2.60
320 A59 30c grnsh bl 3.75 3.75
321 A61 40c ultra 14.00 1.90
Nos. 316-321 (6) 19.45 9.00
Set, never hinged 42.50

For overprints see Nos. 4O26, 5O4.

Figures Encircling Globe A114

Designs: 25c, Globe and inscribed ribbon. 40c, Globe and pigeons.

Perf. 11½

1949, May 16 **Photo.** **Unwmk.**

322 A114 10c green .25 .50
323 A114 25c dark red .40 *.25*
324 A114 40c brt blue .50 *7.00*
Nos. 322-324 (3) 1.15 *7.75*
Set, never hinged 2.00

75th anniv. of the UPU.

Post Horn A115

Horse Drawn Mail Coach A116

Design: 30c, Post bus with trailer.

1949, May 16

325 A115 5c gray, yel & pink .25 *.25*
326 A116 20c pur, gray & yel .30 *1.75*
327 A116 30c dk org brn, gray & yel .45 *2.10*
Nos. 325-327 (3) 1.00 *4.10*
Set, never hinged 1.50

Centenary of the establishment of the Federal Post in Switzerland.

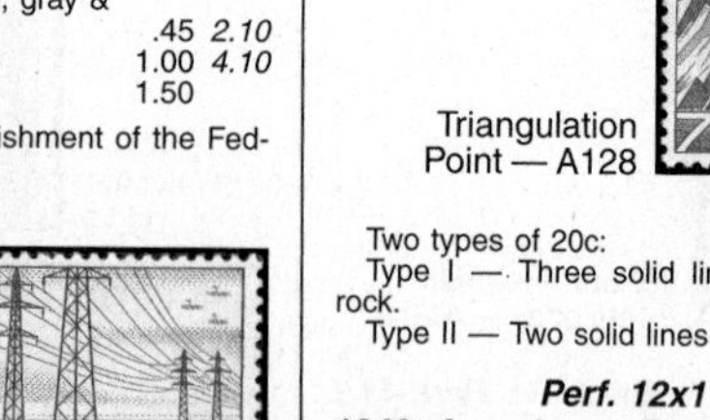

High Tension Conductors A117

Viaducts — A118

Mountain Railway — A119

Rotary Snow Plow — A120

Reservoir, Grimsel — A121

Lake Dam — A122

Dam and Power Station — A123

Alpine Postal Road — A124

Harbor of the Rhine — A125

Suspension Railway — A126

Railway Viaduct — A127

Triangulation Point — A128

Two types of 20c:
Type I — Three solid lines above curved rock.
Type II — Two solid lines above rock.

Perf. 12x11½

1949, Aug. 1 **Engr.** **Unwmk.**

328 A117 3c gray .90 *2.00*
329 A118 5c orange .25 .25
a. Tête bêche pair .50 .35
330 A119 10c yel grn .25 .25
a. Tête bêche pair .50 .35
331 A120 15c aqua .25 *.35*
332 A121 20c brown car (II) .25 .25
a. Tête bêche pair 1.00 1.00
c. Type I 2,000. *67.50*
Type I, never hinged 3,750.
333 A122 25c red .25 .25
334 A123 30c olive .40 .25
335 A124 35c red brown .90 *2.40*
336 A125 40c deep blue 1.20 .25
337 A126 50c slate gray 1.50 .30
338 A127 60c blue green 3.00 .25
339 A128 70c purple 1.50 .40
Nos. 328-339 (12) 10.65 7.20
Set, never hinged 20.00

For use in vending machines, some printings of the 5c, 10c, 20c (II), 25c, 30c and 40c carry a control number on the back of every fifth stamp. The number was applied on top of the gum.

For overprints see Nos. O37-O47, 3O83-3O93, 4O29-4O39, 5O6-5O16, 6O1-6O5, 7O1-7O11.

Symbolical of the Telegraph — A129

10c, Telephone. 20c, Radio. 40c, Television.

1952, Feb. 1 **Photo.** ***Perf. 11½***

340 A129 5c org & yel .25 .65
341 A129 10c brt grn & pink .25 .25
342 A129 20c dp red lil & gray bl .60 .25
343 A129 40c dp bl & lt bl 1.50 *4.25*
Nos. 340-343 (4) 2.60 *5.40*
Set, never hinged 5.25

"A century of telecommunications."

Zurich Airport and Tail of Plane A130

1953, Aug. 29

344 A130 40c blue, red & gray 1.90 *7.50*
Never hinged 4.00

Opening of Zurich-Kloten airport.

Alpine Post Bus, Winter Background — A131

Design: 20c, Same, summer background.

1953, Oct. 8

345 A131 10c dk grn, grn & yel .25 .25
346 A131 20c dk red, red brn & yel .30 .25
Set, never hinged .90

Sold only on Swiss alpine post buses.

Symbols of Agriculture, Forestry and Horticulture — A132

Map and Nautical Emblems — A133

20c, Winged spoon. 40c, Football and map.

1954, Mar. 15 ***Perf. 11½***

347 A132 10c multicolored .35 .25
348 A132 20c multicolored .65 .25
349 A133 25c red, dk ol grn & gray 1.00 *3.25*
350 A132 40c bl, yel & brn 1.30 *2.75*
Nos. 347-350 (4) 3.30 *6.50*
Set, never hinged 6.00

Nos. 347-348 were issued to publicize exhibitions at Lucerne and Bern; No. 349, fifty years of navigation on the Rhine; No. 350, the 1954 World Soccer Championships in Switzerland.

Lausanne Cathedral A134

Alphorn Blower — A135

Designs: 10c, Vaud costume hat. 40c, Automobile steering wheel.

1955, Feb. 15 ***Perf. 11½***

351 A134 5c multi .30 *.60*
352 A134 10c grn, yel & red .30 *.25*
a. Souvenir sheet of 2 55.00 *70.00*
Never hinged 80.00
353 A135 20c red & sepia .30 .25
354 A134 40c bl, pink & gray 1.55 *3.00*
Nos. 351-354 (4) 2.45 *4.10*
Set, never hinged 5.00

No. 352a contains 10c and 20c multicolored, imperf. stamps of Cathedral type A134. Size: 104x52mm.

National Philatelic Exhibition (5c, #352a), Winegrowers' Festival (10c), Alpine Herdsman and Costume Festival (20c) and 25th Intl. Automobile Show (40c).

First Swiss Post Bus — A136

10c, North Gate of Simplon Tunnel and Stockalper Palace. 20c, Children crossing street and road signs. 40c, Planes and emblem of Swissair, vert.

1956, Mar. 1 **Photo.**
Granite Paper

355 A136 5c ol gray, blk & yel .25 *.45*
356 A136 10c brt grn, gray & red .25 .25
357 A136 20c multi .35 *.30*
358 A136 40c blue & red 1.35 *1.75*
Nos. 355-358 (4) 2.20 *2.75*
Set, never hinged 4.00

50th anniv. of the Swiss Motor Coach Service (#355); 50th anniv. of the opening of Simplon Tunnel (#356); Accident prevention (#357); 25th anniv. of the founding of Swissair (#358).

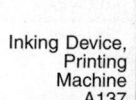

Inking Device, Printing Machine A137

Type I

Type II

10c, Train on southern ramp of Gotthard Railroad. 20c, Shield of civil defense and coat of arms. 40c, Munatius Plancus and view of Basel.

Two types of 10c:
I — "Black" bottom line on train.
II — Brown bottom line.

1957, Feb. 27 ***Perf. 11½***
Granite Paper

359 A137 5c multicolored .25 .25
360 A137 10c lt bl grn, dk grn & red brn (I) .85 .25
a. Type II 1.25 .40

361 A137 20c red org & gray .35 *.25*
362 A137 40c multi .85 *1.00*
Nos. 359-362 (4) 2.30 *1.75*
Set, never hinged 4.00

Intl. Exhibition for Graphic Arts, Lausanne, June 1-16, 1957 (#359). 75th anniv. of St. Gotthard railroad (#360). Civil defense (#361). 2000th anniv. of Basel (#362).

Rope and Symbol of European Unity — A138

1957, July 15 **Engr.** ***Perf. 11½***
363 A138 25c lt red .65 .75
364 A138 40c blue 1.30 .50
Set, never hinged *3.75*

Issued to emphasize European unity.

Catalogue values for unused stamps in this section, from this point to the end of the section, are for Never Hinged items.

Nyon Castle and Corinthian Capital A139

Designs: 10c, Woman's head and ribbons in Swiss colors. 20c, Crossbow emblem. 40c, Salvation Army hat.

1958, Mar. 5 **Photo.** **Unwmk.**
Granite Paper
365 A139 5c ol bis & dl pur .30 .30
366 A139 10c grn, dk grn & red .30 .25
367 A139 20c ver, lil & car .35 .25
368 A139 40c multicolored 1.40 1.40
Nos. 365-368 (4) 2.35 2.20

2000th anniv. of Nyon (#365). Saffa Exhibition, Zurich, July 17-Sept. 15 (#366). 25th anniv. of Swiss manufacturing emblem (#367). 75th anniv. of the Salvation Army in Switzerland (#368).

Symbol of Nuclear Fission A140

1958, Aug. 25 ***Perf. 11½***
Granite Paper
369 A140 40c blue, yel & red .50 .50

2nd UN Atomic Conf. for peaceful uses of atomic power, Geneva, Sept. 1958.

"Transportation" — A141

Designs: 10c, Fasces and post horn. 20c, Owl, rabbit and fish. 50c, Jean Calvin, Theodore de Beze and University of Geneva.

1959, Mar. 9 **Photo.** **Unwmk.**
Granite Paper
370 A141 5c multicolored .25 .25
371 A141 10c emer, yel & lt gray .40 .25
a. Souvenir sheet of 2, imperf. 13.00 13.00
372 A141 20c multicolored .65 .25
373 A141 50c multicolored 1.20 1.10
Nos. 370-373 (4) 2.50 1.85

Opening of the Swiss House of Transport and Communications (5c). Natl. Phil. Exhib., St. Gall, Aug. 21-30 (10c and #371a). Protection of animals (20c). 400th anniv. of the University of Geneva (50c).

No. 371a contains a 10c green, gold and light gray and a 20c deep carmine. Sold for 2fr; the money went for the St. Gall Phil. Exhib.

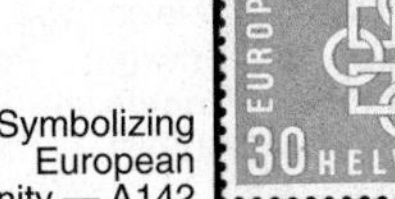

Chain Symbolizing European Unity — A142

1959, June 22 **Engr.** ***Perf. 11½***
374 A142 30c brick red *1.30* .30
375 A142 50c lt ultra *1.75* .50

Issued to emphasize European Unity.

Overprinted "REUNION DES PTT D'EUROPE 1959" in Ultramarine or Red

1959, June 22
376 A142 30c brick red *20.00 6.50*
377 A142 50c lt ultra *20.00 6.50*

European Conference of PTT Administrations, Montreux, June 22-July 31. Nos. 376-377 were on sale only during the conference at a special P. O. in Montreux.

"Cancer Control" A143

Designs: 20c, Founding charter and scepter of University of Basel. 50c, Uprooted Oak Emblem. 75c, Swissair Jet DC-8.

1960, Apr. 7 **Photo.** ***Perf. 11½***
Granite Paper
378 A143 10c brt grn & red .45 .25
379 A143 20c car rose, gray blk & yel .60 .25
380 A143 50c ultra & yel .85 1.20
381 A143 75c lt bl, gray & red 2.25 2.25
Nos. 378-381 (4) 4.15 3.95

50th anniv. of the Swiss League for Cancer Control (10c). 500th anniv. of the University of Basel (20c). World Refugee Year, July 1, 1959-June 30, 1960 (50c). Swissair's entry into the jet age (75c).

Messenger, Fribourg A144

Cathedral, Lausanne A145

Designs: 10c, Messenger, Schwyz. 15c, Messenger and pack animal. 20c, Postilion on horseback. 30c, Grossmünster (church), Zürich. 35c, 1.30fr, Woodcutters' Guildhall, Biel. 40c, Cathedral, Geneva. 50c, Spalen Gate, Basel. 60c, Clock Tower, Berne. 70c, 2.80fr, Sts. Peter and Stephen Church, Bellinzona (tower omitted on 2.80fr). 75c, Bridge and water tower, Lucerne. 80c, Cathedral, St. Gallen. 90c, Munot tower, Schaffhausen. 1fr, Townhall, Fribourg. 1.20fr, Basel gate, Solothurn. 1.50fr, Reding house, Schwyz. 1.70fr, 2fr, 2.20fr, Church, Einsiedeln.

Two types of 5c, 10c, 20c, 50c:
5 Centimes:
Type I — Four lines on pike at left of hand.
Type II — Three lines.
10 Centimes:
Type I — Dot on pike below head.
Type II — No dot.
20 Centimes:
Type I — Ten dots on horiz. harness strip.
Type II — Nine dots.
50 Centimes:
Type I — 3 shading lines at right above arch.
Type II — 2 shading lines.

1960-63 **Engr.** ***Perf. 11½***
1.30fr, 1.70fr, 2.20fr, 2.80fr on Granite Paper, Red and Blue Fibers
382 A144 5c lt ultra (I) .25 .25
c. Tête bêche pair .35 .35
383 A144 10c blue grn (I) .25 .25
c. Tête bêche pair .40 .40
384 A144 15c lt red brn .25 .25
385 A144 20c rose pink (I) .35 .25
c. Tête bêche pair .70 .70
386 A145 25c emerald .55 .25
387 A145 30c vermilion .55 .25
388 A145 35c orange red .70 .85
389 A145 40c lilac .70 .25
390 A145 50c lt vio bl (I) .85 .25
c. Tête bêche pair 2.00 2.00
391 A145 60c rose red 1.05 .25
392 A145 70c orange 1.05 .60
393 A145 75c lt blue 1.40 .80
394 A145 80c dp claret 1.10 .30
395 A145 90c olive green 1.40 .25
396 A144 1fr dull orange 1.40 .25
397 A144 1.20fr dull red 1.75 .25
397A A145 1.30fr red brn, *pink* ('63) 1.75 .25
398 A144 1.50fr brt green 2.00 .50
398A A144 1.70fr rose lil, *pink* ('63) 2.25 .25
399 A144 2fr brt blue 3.50 1.00
399A A144 2.20fr bl grn, *grn* ('63) 3.00 .50
399B A145 2.80fr org, *buff* ('63) 4.00 .40
Nos. 382-399B (22) 30.10 8.45

See Nos. 440-455.

1963-76
Violet Fibers, Fluorescent Paper
382d A144 5c lt ultra (I) .25 .25
g. Tête bêche pair ('68) .25 .25
383d A144 10c bl grn (I) .25 .25
e. Bklt. pane of 2 + 2 labels ('68) .65 .65
g. Tête bêche pair ('68) .35 .25
384a A144 15c lt red brn .45 .30
385d A144 20c rose pink (I) .25 .25
g. Tête bêche pair ('68) .50 .40
386a A145 25c emerald .25 .25
387a A145 30c vermilion .25 .25
c. Tête bêche pair ('68) .50 .40
389a A145 40c lilac ('67) .35 .25
c. Tête bêche pair ('76) .70 .50
390d A145 50c lt vio bl (I) .50 .25
391a A145 60c rose red ('67) .50 .25
393a A145 75c lt blue ('68) 1.00 .60
394a A145 80c dp claret 1.00 .25
395a A145 90c olive grn ('67) 1.00 .25
396a A144 1fr dull org ('67) 1.00 .30
397b A144 1.20fr dl red ('68) 2.10 1.50
398b A144 1.50fr brt green ('68) 2.10 1.50
Nos. 382d-398b (15) 11.25 6.70

Coil Stamps

1960 **White Paper**
382b A144 5c lt ultra (II) 1.20 1.15
383b A144 10c blue grn (II) .60 .55
385b A144 20c rose pink (II) .60 .55
390b A145 50c lt vio bl (II) 4.75 4.50
Nos. 382b-390b (4) 7.15 6.75

The coil stamps were printed in sheets (available to collectors) and pasted into coils. Every fifth stamp has a control number on the back.

Other denominations issued in coils on white paper are: 40c, 60c, 90c, 1fr, 1.30fr, 1.70fr, 2.20fr and 2.80fr.

Denominations issued in coils on granite paper (red & blue fibers) are: 1.30fr, 1.70fr, 2.20fr and 2.80fr.

Violet Fibers, Fluorescent Paper
1965-68 **Coil Stamps**
382e A144 5c lt ultra (II) 1.10 .90
383h A144 10c blue grn (II) .80 .70
385e A144 20c rose pink (II) .80 .70
390e A145 50c lt vio bl (II) 4.25 3.75
Nos. 382e-390e (4) 6.95 6.05

Other denominations issued in coils on violet-fiber paper are: 40c, 60c, 90c and 1fr.

Common Design Types pictured following the introduction.

Europa Issue
Common Design Type

1960, Sept. 19 **Unwmk.** ***Perf. 11½***
Size: 33x23mm
400 CD3 30c vermilion .75 .25
401 CD3 50c ultra 1.00 .50

Wall under Construction and Globe — A146

Designs: 10c, Symbolic sun (HYSPA Emblem). 20c, Ice hockey stick and puck. 50c, Wiring diagram on map of Switzerland.

1961, Feb. 20 **Photo.** ***Perf. 11½***
Granite Paper
402 A146 5c gray, brick red & grnsh bl .25 .25
403 A146 10c aqua & yel .40 .25
404 A146 20c multicolored .40 .35
405 A146 50c ultra, gray & car rose 2.00 1.00
Nos. 402-405 (4) 3.05 1.85

Development aid to new nations (5c). HYSPA 1961, Health and Sports Exhibition, Bern, May 18-July 17 (10c). Intl. Ice Hockey Championships, Lausanne and Geneva, Mar. 2-12 (20c). Fully automatic Swiss telephone service (50c).

St. Matthew and Angel — A147

Evangelists: 5fr, St. Mark and winged lion. 10fr, St. Luke and winged ox. 20fr, St. John and eagle.

Perf. 11½
1961, Sept. 18 **Unwmk.** **Engr.**
Granite Paper
406 A147 3fr rose carmine 4.75 .25
407 A147 5fr dark blue 4.75 .25
408 A147 10fr dark brown 8.75 .50
409 A147 20fr red 17.50 2.50
Nos. 406-409 (4) 35.75 3.50

Designs are after 15th century wood carvings from St. Oswald's church, Zug.

Europa Issue
Common Design Type

1961, Sept. 18 **Size: 26x21mm**
410 CD4 30c vermilion .65 .25
411 CD4 50c blue 1.25 .35

Trans-Europe Express A148

10c, Rower. 20c, Jungfrau railroad station and Mönch. 50c, WHO Anti-malaria emblem.

1962, Mar. 19 **Photo.** ***Perf. 11½***
412 A148 5c multicolored .55 .25
413 A148 10c brt grn, lem & lil .45 .25
414 A148 20c rose lil, pale bl & bis .70 .25
415 A148 50c ultra, lt grn & rose lil .90 .60
Nos. 412-415 (4) 2.60 1.35

Introduction of Swiss electric TEE trains (5c). Rowing world championship, Lucerne, Sept. 6-9 (10c). 50th anniv. of the railroad station on the Jungfrau mountain (20c). WHO Anti-Malaria campaign (50c).

Europa Issue
Common Design Type

1962, Sept. 17 **Unwmk.** ***Perf. 11½***
Size: 33x23mm
416 CD5 30c orange, yel & brn .65 .40
417 CD5 50c ultra, lt grn & brn 1.00 .60

Boy Scout — A149

Designs: 10c, Swiss Alpine Club emblem. 20c, Luegelkinn viaduct. 30c, Wheat Emblem. No. 426, 428a, Red Cross Jubilee Emblem. No. 427, Post Office Building, Paris, 1863.

1963, Mar. 21 **Photo.**
422 A149 5c gray, dk red & brn .30 .30
423 A149 10c dk grn, gray & red .45 .30
424 A149 20c dk car, brn & gray .55 .30
425 A149 30c yel grn, yel & org 1.60 .80
426 A149 50c blue, sil & red 1.10 .80
427 A149 50c ultra, pink, yel & gray 1.10 1.05
Nos. 422-427 (6) 5.10 3.55

Souvenir Sheet
Imperf
428 Sheet of 4 7.00 6.00
a. A149 50c bl, lt bl, sil & red 1.75 1.50

50 years of Swiss Boy Scouts (5c). Cent. of Swiss Alpine Club (10c). 50 years Lötschberg Railroad (20c). FAO "Freedom from Hunger"

campaign (30c). Red Cross Cent. (#426, 428). 1st Intl. Postal Conf., Paris 1863 (#427).
No. 428 sold for 3fr.

Europa Issue
Common Design Type

1963, Sept. 16 Unwmk. *Perf. 11½*
Granite Paper
Size: 26x21mm

429 CD6 50c ultra & ocher .90 .60

EXPO Emblem A150

50c, EXPO emblem on globe & moon ("Outlook"). 75c, EXPO emblem on globe ("Insight").

1963, Sept. 16 Unwmk. *Perf. 11½*
Granite Paper

430 A150 10c brt grn & dk grn .25 .25
431 A150 20c red & maroon .30 .25
432 A150 50c ultra & red .60 .40
433 A150 75c purple & red .70 .45
Nos. 430-433 (4) 1.85 1.35

Issued to publicize the Swiss National Exhibition, Lausanne, Apr. 30-Oct. 25, 1964.

Road Tunnel Through Great St. Bernard A151

10c, Symbolic water god & waves. 20c, Soldiers of 1864 & 1964. 50c, Standards of Swiss Confederation & Geneva.

1964, Mar. 9 Photo.
Granite Paper

434 A151 5c ol, ultra & red .25 .25
435 A151 10c Prus bl & grn .30 .25
436 A151 20c red, ultra, blk & sal .60 .25
437 A151 50c ultra, red, yel & blk .80 .65
Nos. 434-437 (4) 1.95 1.40

1st Trans-Alpine Automobile route from Switzerland to Italy (5c). "Pro Aqua" water conservation campaign (10c). Centenary of the Swiss Noncommissioned Officers' Association (20c). Sesqui. of union of Geneva with Swiss Confederation (50c).

Europa Issue
Common Design Type

1964, Sept. 14 Engr. *Perf. 11½*
Size: 21x26mm
Violet Fibers, Fluorescent Paper

438 CD7 20c vermilion *.55* .25
439 CD7 50c ultra *1.10* .25

Type of Regular Issue, 1960-63

Designs: 5c, Lenzburg. 10c, Freuler Mansion, Näfels. 15c, St. Mauritius Church, Appenzell. 20c, Planta House, Samedan. 30c, Gabled houses, Gais. 50c, Castle and Abbey Church, Neuchâtel. 70c, Lussy House, Wolfenschiessen. 1fr, Santa Croce Church, Riva San Vitale. 1.20fr, Abbey Church, Payerne. 1.30fr, Church of St. Pierre de Clages. 1.50fr, La Porte de France, Porrentruy. 1.70fr, Frauenfeld Castle. 2fr, A Pro Castle, Seedorf. 2.20fr, Thomas Tower and Gate, Liestal. 2.50fr, St. Oswald's Church, Zug. 3.50fr, Benedictine Abbey, Engelberg.

1964-68 Engr. *Perf. 11½*
Violet Fibers, Fluorescent Paper

440 A144 5c car rose ('68) .25 .25
441 A144 10c violet bl ('68) .25 .25
b. Tête bêche pair .40 .25
c. Booklet pane of 2 + 2 labels .70
442 A144 15c brown red ('68) .25 .25
b. Tête bêche pair .50 .25
443 A144 20c blue grn ('68) .30 .25
b. Tête bêche pair .60 .35
444 A144 30c vermilion ('68) .45 .25
b. Tête bêche pair .95 .50
445 A144 50c ultra ('68) .75 .25
446 A145 70c brown ('67) .95 .25
447 A145 1fr dk green ('68) 1.40 .25
448 A145 1.20fr brown red ('68) 1.75 .25
449 A145 1.30fr violet bl ('66) 2.00 .60
450 A145 1.50fr green ('68) 2.10 .25
451 A145 1.70fr brown org ('66) 2.25 1.25
452 A145 2fr orange ('67) 2.75 .25
453 A145 2.20fr green 3.00 .60
454 A145 2.50fr Prus grn ('67) 3.25 .25
455 A145 3.50fr purple ('67) 4.75 .35
Nos. 440-455 (16) 26.45 5.80

The 15c was issued in coils in 1972 (?) with control number on the back of every fifth stamp.

Nurse and Patient A152

Seated Helvetia, 1854 — A153

Women's Army Auxiliary A154

Intercontinental Communications Map — A155

1965, Mar. 8 Photo. *Perf. 11½*
Violet Fibers, Fluorescent Paper

462 A152 5c lt ultra & red .25 .25
463 A153 10c emer, brn & blk .25 .25
464 A154 20c red & multi .45 .25

Granite Paper, Red and Blue Fibers

465 A155 50c dl bl grn & mar .70 .50
Nos. 462-465 (4) 1.65 1.25

Nursing and auxiliary medical professions (5c). Natl. Postage Stamp Exhibition, NABRA, Bern, Aug. 27-Sept. 5, 1965 (10c). 20th anniv. of Women's Army Auxiliary Corps (20c). Cent. of ITU (50c).
See No. B344.

Swiss Arms, Cantonal Emblems of Valais, Neuchatel, Geneva A156

1965, June 1 Unwmk. *Perf. 11½*
Granite Paper, Red and Blue Fibers

466 A156 20c multicolored .45 .25

150th anniversary of the entry of the cantons of Valais, Neuchatel and Geneva in the Swiss Confederation.

Matterhorn A157

30c, like 10c but inscribed in French "Cervin."

1965, June 1 Photo.
Granite Paper, Red and Blue Fibers

467 A157 10c grn, slate & dk red .25 .25

Violet Fibers, Fluorescent Paper

468 A157 30c dk red, grn & slate .70 .50

Year of the Alps; the cent. of the 1st winter-time visitors to the Alps and cent. of the 1st ascent of the Matterhorn. Nos. 467-468 on sale only at Swiss Alpine post buses.

Europa Issue
Common Design Type

1965, Sept. 14 Unwmk. *Perf. 11½*
Violet Fibers, Fluorescent Paper

469 CD8 50c bl, dk bl & grn 1.15 .50

Figure Skating A159

1965, Sept. 14 Photo.
Violet Fibers, Fluorescent Paper

470 A159 5c grn, dl bl & blk .25 .25

Issued to publicize the World Figure Skating Championships, Davos, Feb. 22-27, 1966.

ITU Emblem and Atom Diagram A160

Cent. of the ITU: 30c, Symbol of communications, waves.

1965, Sept. 14
Violet Fibers, Fluorescent Paper

471 A160 10c ultra & multi .25 .25

Granite Paper, Red and Blue Fibers

472 A160 30c org, red & gray .50 .25

Violet Fibers, Fluorescent Paper
Paper from No. 473 onward is fluorescent and has violet fibers, unless otherwise noted.

European Kingfisher A161

Mercury's Helmet and Laurel A162

Flags of 13 Member Nations and Nuclear Fission A163

1966, Feb. 21 Photo.

473 A161 10c emer & multi .30 .25
474 A162 20c dp mag, red & brt grn .30 .25
475 A163 50c slate blue & multi .70 .40
Nos. 473-475 (3) 1.30 .90

Intl. Cong. for Conservation "Pro Natura," Lucerne (10c). 50th anniv. of Swiss Trade Fair, Basel, Apr. 16-26 (20c). European Organization for Nuclear Research, CERN (50c).

Emblem of Society of Swiss Abroad — A164

1966, June 1 Photo. *Perf. 11½*

476 A164 20c ultra & ver .40 .25

50th anniv. of the Society of Swiss Abroad.

Europa Issue
Common Design Type

1966, Sept. 26 Engr. *Perf. 11½*
Size: 21x26mm

477 CD9 20c vermilion .40 .25
478 CD9 50c ultra 1.00 .35

Finsteraarhorn — A165

1966, Sept. 26 Photo.

479 A165 10c lt grnsh bl, dk bl & dk red .35 .25

Automobile Wheels and White Cane — A166

Flags of EFTA Members A167

1967, Mar. 13 Photo. *Perf. 11½*

480 A166 10c bl grn, blk & yel .25 .25
481 A167 20c multicolored .40 .25

No. 480 issued to publicize the white cane as a distinguishing mark for blind pedestrians. No. 481 publicizes the European Free Trade Association, EFTA. See note after Norway No. 501.

Europa Issue
Common Design Type

1967, Mar. 13 Engr.

482 CD10 30c blue gray .60 .30

Cogwheel and Swiss Emblem A169

Hourglass and Sun — A170

San Bernardino, from North — A171

Railroad Wheel A172

1967, Sept. 18 Photo. *Perf. 11½*

483 A169 10c multicolored .25 .25
484 A170 20c red, yel & blk .30 .25
485 A171 30c multicolored .40 .25
486 A172 50c multicolored .75 .50
Nos. 483-486 (4) 1.70 1.25

50th anniv. of Swiss Week (10c). 50th anniv. of the Foundation for the Aged (20c). Opening of the San Bernardino Road Tunnel (30c). 75th anniv. of the Central Office for Intl. Railroad Transportation (50c).

Mountains and Club's Emblem
A173

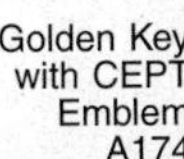

Golden Key with CEPT Emblem
A174

Rook and Chessboard
A175

Aircraft Tail and Satellites
A176

1968, Mar. 14 Photo. *Perf. 11½*

487	A173	10c grn, lt ultra & red	.25	.25
488	A174	20c Prus bl, yel & brn	.40	.25
489	A175	30c dk ol bis & vio bl	.50	.25
490	A176	50c dk blue & red	.80	.50
		Nos. 487-490 (4)	1.95	1.25

50th anniv. of the Swiss Women's Alpine Club (10c). A unified Europe through postal cooperation (20c). 18th Chess Olympics, Lugano, Oct. 17-Nov. 6 (30c). Inauguration of the new Geneva-Cointrin Air Terminal (50c).

Worker's Protective Helmet
A177

Double Geneva and Zurich Stamps of 1843 — A178

Map Showing Systematic Planning
A179

Flag of Rhine Navigation Committee
A180

1968, Sept. 12 Photo. *Perf. 11½*

491	A177	10c bl grn & yel	.25	.25
492	A178	20c dp car, blk & yel grn	.35	.25
493	A179	30c multicolored	.40	.25
494	A180	50c bl, yel & blk	.80	.50
		Nos. 491-494 (4)	1.80	1.25

50th anniv. of the Swiss Accident Insurance comp., SUVA (10c). 125th anniv. of 1st Swiss postage stamps (20c). 25th anniv. of the Swiss Society for Territorial Planning (30c). Cent. of the Rhine Navigation Act (50c).

Swiss Girl Scouts' Emblem and Camp — A181

Pegasus Constellation
A182

Comptoir Suisse Emblem and Beaulieu Building, Lausanne
A183

Gymnaestrada Emblem (Man in Circle) — A184

Swissair DC-8 and DH-3 — A185

1969, Feb. 12 Photo. *Perf. 11½*

495	A181	10c multicolored	.30	.25
496	A182	20c dark blue	.40	.25
497	A183	30c red, ocher, grn & gray	.50	.25
498	A184	50c vio bl, bl, red, grn & sil	1.00	.50
499	A185	2fr bl, dk bl & red	4.00	2.00
		Nos. 495-499 (5)	6.20	3.25

50th anniv. of Swiss Girl Scouts (10c). Opening of 1st Swiss Planetarium, Lucerne, July 1 (20c). 50th anniv. of the Comptoir Suisse (trade fair, 30c). 5th Gymnaestrada (gymnastic meet), Basel, July 1-5 (50c). 50th anniv. of Swiss airmail service (2fr).

Europa Issue
Common Design Type

1969, Apr. 28 Size: 32½x23mm

500	CD12	30c brn org & multi	.70	.25
501	CD12	50c chlky bl & multi	1.15	.75

Huldreich Zwingli (1484-1531)
A186

Famous Swiss: 20c, Gen. Henri Guisan (1874-1960). 30c, Francesco Borromini, architect (1599-1667). 50c, Othmar Schoeck, musician (1886-1957). 80c, Germaine de Stael, writer (1766-1817).

1969, Sept. 18 Engr. *Perf. 11½*

502	A186	10c brt purple	.25	.25
503	A186	20c green	.45	.25
504	A186	30c deep carmine	.65	.25
505	A186	50c deep blue	1.05	.75
506	A186	80c red brown	1.55	.85
		Nos. 502-506 (5)	3.95	2.35

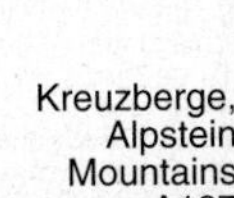

Kreuzberge, Alpstein Mountains
A187

Children Crossing Street — A188

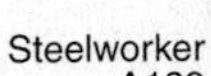

Steelworker
A189

1969, Sept. 18 Photo.

507	A187	20c blue & multi	.45	.25
508	A188	30c car & multi	.50	.25
509	A189	50c violet & multi	.85	.45
		Nos. 507-509 (3)	1.80	.95

No. 508 publicizes the traffic safety campaign; No. 509 for 50th anniv. of the ILO.

Telex Tape — A190

Fireman Rescuing Child — A191

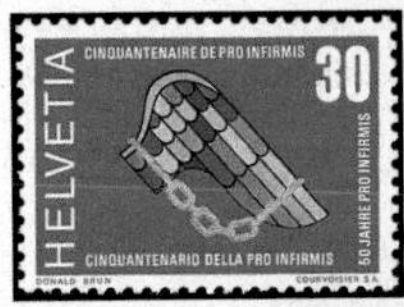

Pro Infirmis Emblem
A192

United Nations Emblem
A193

New UPU Headquarters
A194

1970, Feb. 26 Photo. *Perf. 11½*

510	A190	20c dk grn, yel & blk	.30	.25
511	A191	30c dk car & multi	.45	.25
512	A192	30c red & multi	.45	.25
513	A193	50c dk bl, lt grnsh bl & sil	.70	.70
514	A194	80c dk pur, sep & tan	1.15	.70
		Nos. 510-514 (5)	3.05	2.15

75th anniv. of the Swiss Telegraph Agency (20c). Cent. of the Swiss Firemen's Assoc. (No. 511). 50th anniv. of the Pro Infirmis Foundation (No. 512). UN, 25th anniv. (50c). New Headquarters of the UPU in Bern (80c).

Europa Issue
Common Design Type

1970, May 4 Engr. *Perf. 11½*
Size: 21x26mm

515	CD13	30c vermilion	.70	.25
516	CD13	50c brt blue	1.15	.45

Soccer
A195

Census Form — A196

Piz Palu, Grisons
A197

"Nature Conservation"
A198

1970, Sept. 17 Photo. *Perf. 11½*

517	A195	10c green & multi	.25	.25
518	A196	20c dk grn & multi	.35	.25
519	A197	30c slate bl & multi	.65	.25
520	A198	50c dk bl & multi	.85	.80
		Nos. 517-520 (4)	2.10	1.55

75th anniv. of Swiss Soccer Association (10c). Federal Census of 1970 (20c). Swiss Alps (30c). Nature Conservation Year (50c).

Numeral — A199

Coil Stamps

1970, Sept. 17 Engr. *Perf. 11½*

521	A199	10c brown lake	.25	.25
522	A199	20c olive grn	.35	.25
523	A199	50c ultra	.80	.50
		Nos. 521-523 (3)	1.40	1.00

Control number in stamp's color on back of every fifth stamp. Nos. 521-523 were regularly issued only in coils, but exist in sheets of 50.

Gymnastic Trio — A200

Rose — A201

Switzerland No. 8 — A202

Rising Spiral — A203

Intelsat 4 Satellite
A204

Adaptation of 1850 Design — A205

Design: No. 525, Runners (men).

1971, Mar. 11 Photo. *Perf. 11½*

524	A200	10c ol, brn & bl	.30	.25
525	A200	10c gray, brn & yel	.30	.25
a.		Pair, #524-525	1.20	1.20
526	A201	20c dk grn & multi	.40	.25
527	A202	30c dp car & multi	.60	.25
528	A203	50c dk bl & bis	.90	.65
529	A204	80c multicolored	1.90	1.10
		Nos. 524-529 (6)	4.40	2.75

Souvenir Sheet

Typo.

Imperf

530	A205	2fr blue & multi	4.00	4.00

New article on gymnastics and sports in Swiss Constitution (10c); Intl. Child Welfare Org. (20c); NABA Natl. Postage Stamp Exhibition, Basel, June 4-13 (30c, 2fr); 2nd decade of development aid (50c); Intl. Space Communications Conf., Geneva, June-July, 1971 (80c).

#525a printed checkerwise. #530 sold for 3fr.

Europa Issue

Common Design Type

1971, May 3 Engr. *Perf. 11½*

Size: 26x21mm

531	CD14	30c rose car & org	.70	.25
532	CD14	50c blue & org	1.15	.40

Les Diablerets, Vaud — A206

Telecommunications Symbols — A207

1971, Sept. 23 Photo. *Perf. 11½*

533	A206	30c rose lil & bl gray	.60	.30
534	A207	40c ultra, yel & brt pink	.70	.55

No. 534 for the 50th anniv. of Radio-Suisse, which is also in charge of air traffic control.

Alexandre Yersin (1863-1943) Bacteriologist A208

Physicians: 20c, Auguste Forel (1848-1931), psychiatrist. 30c, Jules Gonin (1870-1935), ophthalmologist. 40c, Robert Koch (1843-1910), German bacteriologist. 80c, Frederick G. Banting (1891-1941), Canadian physiologist.

1971, Sept. 23 Engr.

535	A208	10c gray olive	.25	.25
536	A208	20c bluish green	.35	.25
537	A208	30c carmine rose	.50	.25
538	A208	40c dark blue	.65	.50
539	A208	80c brt purple	1.25	.85
		Nos. 535-539 (5)	3.00	2.10

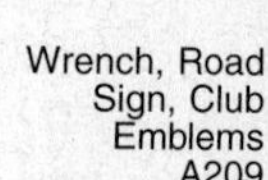

Wrench, Road Sign, Club Emblems A209

Electronic Switch Panel — A210

Boy's Head and Radio Waves A211

Symbolic Tree — A212

1972, Feb. 17 Photo. *Perf. 11½*

540	A209	10c multicolored	.25	.25
541	A210	20c olive & multi	.30	.25
542	A211	30c orange & maroon	.45	.25
543	A212	40c blue, grn & pur	.60	.50
		Nos. 540-543 (4)	1.60	1.25

75th anniv. of the touring and automobile clubs of Switzerland (10c). 125th anniv. of Swiss railroads (20c). 50th anniv. of Swiss radio (30c). 50th annual congress of Swiss citizens living abroad, Bern, Aug. 25-27 (40c).

Europa Issue

Common Design Type

1972, May. 2 Size: 21x26mm

544	CD15	30c multicolored	.70	.25
545	CD15	40c multicolored	.95	.35

Alberto Giacometti (1901-66), Painter and Sculptor — A213

Portraits and Signatures: 20c, Charles Ferdinand Ramuz (1878-1947), writer. 30c, Le Corbusier (Charles Edouard Jeanneret; 1887-1965) architect. 40c, Albert Einstein (1879-1955), physicist. 80c, Arthur Honegger (1892-1955), composer.

Engraved & Photogravure

1972, Sept. 21 *Perf. 11½*

546	A213	10c ocher & blk	.25	.25
547	A213	20c lt olive & blk	.45	.25
548	A213	30c pink & blk	.70	.25
549	A213	40c lt blue & blk	.90	.55
550	A213	80c lil rose & blk	1.35	.70
		Nos. 546-550 (5)	3.65	2.00

Civil Defense Emblem A214

Spannörter, Swiss Alps — A215

Red Cross Rescue Helicopter A216

Clean Air, Fire, Earth and Water — A217

1972, Sept. 21 Photo.

551	A214	10c org, bl & yel	.65	.25
552	A215	20c bl grn & multi	.25	.25
553	A216	30c lilac, red & indigo	.65	.25
554	A217	40c lt blue & multi	.65	.55
		Nos. 551-554 (4)	2.20	1.30

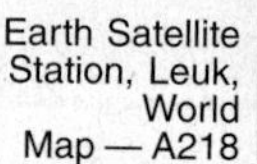

Earth Satellite Station, Leuk, World Map — A218

Quill Pen and Arrows in Circle — A219

INTERPOL Emblem A220

1973, Feb. 15 Photo. *Perf. 11½*

555	A218	15c gray, yel & bl	.25	.25
556	A219	30c multicolored	.45	.25
557	A220	40c dp bl, lt bl & gray	.60	.50
		Nos. 555-557 (3)	1.30	1.00

Opening of the satellite station at Leuk; Swiss Association of Commercial Employees, cent. (30c); International Criminal Police Organization (INTERPOL), 50th anniv.

Sottoceneri A221

Sign of Inn "Zur Sonne," Toggenburg A222

Villages: 10c, Graubunden. 15c, Central Switzerland. 25c, Jura. 30c, Simme Valley. 35c, Central Switzerland (2 buildings). 40c, Vaud. 50c, Valais. 60c, Engadine. 70c, Sopraceneri. 80c, Eastern Switzerland.

Designs: 1fr, Rose window, Lausanne Cathedral. 1.10fr, Gallus Portal, Basel Cathedral. 1.20fr, Romanesque capital (eagle), St. Jean Baptiste Church, Grandson. 1.50fr, Ceiling medallion (bird feeding nestlings), Stein am Rhein Convent. 1.70fr, Romanesque capital (St. George and dragon), St. Jean Baptiste, Grandson. 1.80fr, Gargoyle, Bern Cathedral. 2fr, Bay window, Schaffhausen. 2.50fr, Cock weather vane, St. Ursus Cathedral, Solothurn. 3fr, Font, St. Maurice Church, Saanen. 3.50fr, Astronomical clock, Bern clock tower.

1973-80 Engr. *Perf. 11½*

Fluorescent, No Violet Fibers

558	A221	5c dl yel & dk bl	.25	.25
559	A221	10c rose lil & ol grn	.25	.25
560	A221	15c org & vio bl	.25	.25
561	A221	25c emer & vio bl	.40	.35
562	A221	30c brick red & dk bl	.50	.25
563	A221	35c red org & brt vio ('75)	.60	.45
564	A221	40c brt bl & blk	.65	.25
565	A221	50c ol grn & org	.85	.25
566	A221	60c yel brn & gray	.85	.25
567	A221	70c sep & dk grn	1.00	.25
568	A221	80c brt grn & brick red	1.20	.40

Violet Fibers, Fluorescent Paper

569	A222	1fr pur ('74)	1.60	.25
a.		Without fibers, fluorescent paper ('78)	1.60	.35
570	A222	1.10fr Prus bl ('75)	1.90	.25
571	A222	1.20fr rose red ('74)	2.10	1.00
572	A222	1.30fr ocher	2.25	.25
573	A222	1.50fr grn ('74)	2.50	.25
574	A222	1.70fr gray	2.50	.40
575	A222	1.80fr dp org	3.00	.25
576	A222	2fr ultra ('74)	3.25	.25
a.		Without fibers, fluorescent paper ('78)	3.25	1.75
577	A222	2.50fr gldn brn ('75)	4.25	.50
578	A222	3fr dk car ('79)	5.00	.70
579	A222	3.50fr ol grn ('80)	5.00	2.00
		Nos. 558-579 (22)	40.15	9.30

No. 577 exists without tagging. Value, $60 unused, $30 used.

Europa Issue

Common Design Type

1973, Apr. 30 Engr. and Photo.

Size: 38x28mm

580	CD16	25c brown & yel	.60	.25
581	CD16	40c ultra & yel	.95	.35

"Man and Time" — A223

Skier and Championship Emblem A224

Child — A225

1973, Aug. 30 Photo. *Perf. 11½*

582	A223	15c multicolored	.30	.25
583	A224	30c pink & multi	.40	.25
584	A225	40c blue vio & blk	.60	.50
		Nos. 582-584 (3)	1.30	1.00

Opening of the Intl. Clock Museum, La Chaux-de-Fonds, 1974 (15c); Intl. Alpine Skiing Championships, St. Moritz, Feb. 2-10, 1974 (30c); "Terre des hommes" children's aid program (40c).

Souvenir Sheet

Medieval Postal Couriers — A226

1974, Jan. 29 Photo. *Perf. 11½*

585	A226	Sheet of 4	5.50	5.50
a.		30c Basel (with staff)	1.00	1.00
b.		30c Zug (without staff)	1.00	1.00
c.		60c Uri	1.00	1.00
d.		80c Schwyz	1.00	1.00

Cent. of UPU and for INTERNABA 74 Intl. Phil. Exhib., Basel, June 7-16. No. 585 sold for 3fr.

Pine and Cabin on Globe — A227

Gymnast and Hurdlers A228

Target and Pistol — A229

1974, Jan. 29

586	A227	15c lt green & multi	.25	.25
587	A228	30c red & multi	.45	.25
588	A229	40c blue & multi	.65	.65
		Nos. 586-588 (3)	1.35	1.15

50th anniv. of Swiss Youth Hostels (15c); Cent. of Swiss Workers' Gymnast and Sports Association (SATUS) (30c); World Marksmanship Championships, Thun and Bern, Sept. 1974 (40c).

Old Houses, Parliament RR Station, Bern — A230

Eugéne Borel — A231

Designs: No. 590, Castle, Town Hall, Chauderon Center, Lausanne. 40c, Heinrich von Stephan. 80c, Montgomery Blair.

1974, Mar. 28 Photo. *Perf. 11½*

589	A230	30c orange & multi	.55	.25
590	A230	30c scarlet & multi	.55	.25
a.		Pair, #589-590	1.20	.50

Engr.

591	A231	30c rose & blk	.50	.25
592	A231	40c gray & blk	.65	.50
593	A231	80c lt yel grn & blk	.95	.75
		Nos. 589-593 (5)	3.20	2.00

Cent. of the UPU. Nos. 589-590 publicize the Cent. Cong., Lausanne, May 22-July 5; Nos. 591-593 honor the founders of the UPU.

"Continuity," by Max Bill — A232

Europa: 40c, "Amazon," bronze sculpture by Carl Burckhardt.

1974, Mar. 28 Photo.

594	A232	30c red & black	.60	.30
595	A232	40c ultra & sepia	1.00	.70

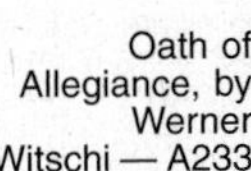

Oath of Allegiance, by Werner Witschi — A233

Sports Foundation Emblem A234

Conveyor Belts, Paths of Mail Transport and Delivery A235

1974, Sept. 19 Photo. *Perf. 11½*

596	A233	15c lil, ol & dk ol	.35	.25
597	A234	30c silver & multi	.40	.25
598	A235	30c plum & multi	.50	.25
		Nos. 596-598 (3)	1.25	.75

Centenary of Swiss Constitution (15c); Swiss Sports Foundation (No. 597); 125th anniversary of Swiss Federal Post (No. 598).

Standard Meter, Krypton Spectrum A236

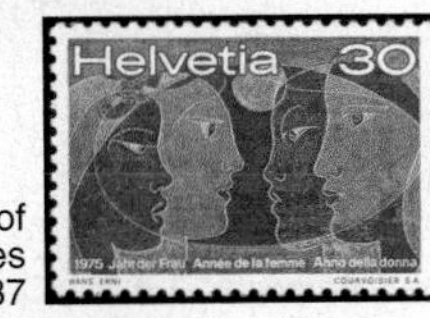

Women of Four Races A237

Red Cross Flag, Barbed Wire — A238

"Ville de Lucerne" Dirigible A239

1975, Feb. 13 Photo. *Perf. 11½*

599	A236	15c grn, org & ultra	.25	.25
600	A237	30c brown & multi	.40	.25
601	A238	60c ultra, blk & red	.80	.60
602	A239	90c blue & multi	1.25	.80
		Nos. 599-602 (4)	2.70	1.90

Cent. of Intl. Meter Convention, Paris, 1875 (15c); Intl. Women's Year 1975 (30c); 2nd Session of Diplomatic Conf. on Humanitarian Intl. Law, Geneva, Feb. 1975 (60c); Aviation and Space Travel exhibition in Museum of Transport and Communications, Lucerne (90c).

Mönch, by Ferdinand Hodler — A240

Vineyard Worker, by Maurice Barraud — A241

Europa: 50c, Still Life with Guitar, by René Auberjonois.

1975, Apr. 28 Photo. *Perf. 12x11½*

603	A240	30c gray & multi	*.50*	*.25*
604	A241	50c multicolored	*.85*	*.60*
605	A241	60c bl gray & multi	1.00	.60
		Nos. 603-605 (3)	2.35	1.45

Man Pulling Wheel Chair Upstairs A242

"The Helping Hand" A243

Architectural Heritage Year Emblem A244

Beat Fischer von Reichenbach A245

1975, Sept. 11 Photo.

606	A242	15c lilac, blk & grn	.25	.25
607	A243	30c red, blk & car	.45	.25
608	A244	50c yel brn & mar	.75	.65
609	A245	60c blue & multi	.90	.70
		Nos. 606-609 (4)	2.35	1.85

Special building features for the handicapped (15c); interdenominational telephone pastoral counseling (30c); European Architectural Heritage Year 1975 (50c); Fischer Post, Bern, tercentenary (60c).

Forest A246

Fruits and Vegetables A247

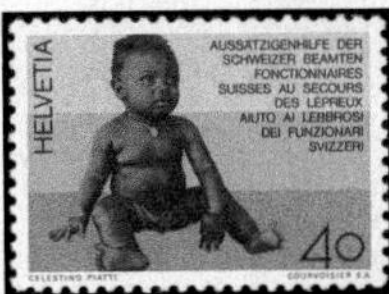

Black Infant — A248

Telephones of 1876 and 1976 — A249

1976, Feb. 12 Photo. *Perf. 11½*

Fluorescent, No Violet Fibers

610	A246	20c green & multi	.35	.25
611	A247	40c car & multi	.65	.25
612	A248	40c lil rose & multi	.65	.25

Engr.

Violet Fibers, Fluorescent Paper

613	A249	80c lt bl & dk bl	1.25	1.00
		Nos. 610-613 (4)	2.90	1.75

Centenary of Federal forest laws (20c); healthy nutrition to combat alcoholism (No. 611); fight against leprosy (No. 612); telephone centenary (80c).

Cotton and Gold Lace, St. Gall — A250

Pocket Watch, 18th Century — A251

1976, May 3 Engr. *Perf. 11½*

614	A250	40c red brn & multi	.80	.25
615	A251	80c black & multi	1.60	.90

Europa. Both 40c and 80c are on fluorescent paper, the 80c having violet fibers.

Fawn, Frog and Swallow A252

"Conserve Energy" A253

St. Gotthard Mountains A254

Skater A255

1976, Sept. 16 Photo. *Perf. 11½*

Fluorescent, No Violet Fibers

616	A252	20c multicolored	.45	.25
617	A253	40c multicolored	.60	.25
618	A254	40c multicolored	.75	.25
619	A255	80c multicolored	1.20	1.00
		Nos. 616-619 (4)	3.00	1.75

Wildlife protection (20c); energy conservation (No. 617); Pizzo Lucendro to Pizzo Rotondo, seen from Altanca (No. 618); World Men's Skating Championships, Davos, Feb. 5-6, 1977 (80c).

Oskar Bider, Bleriot Monoplane A256

Swiss Aviation Pioneers: 80c, Eduard Spelterini and balloon gondola. 100c, Armand Dufaux and Dufaux plane. 150c, Walter Mittelholzer and Dornier hydroplane.

1977, Jan. 27 Engr. *Perf. 11½*

620	A256	40c multicolored	.60	.45
621	A256	80c multicolored	1.20	.90
622	A256	100c multicolored	1.50	1.35
623	A256	150c multicolored	2.25	1.75
		Nos. 620-623 (4)	5.55	4.45

Blue Cross — A257

Festival Emblem A258

Balloons Carrying Letters A259

1977, Jan. 27 **Photo.**

624 A257 20c gray, bl & blk	.30	.25
625 A258 40c red, gold & brn	.55	.25
626 A259 80c lt bl & multi	1.10	1.00
Nos. 624-626 (3)	1.95	1.50

Blue Cross Society (care of alcoholics and fight against alcoholism), centenary (20c); Vintage Festival, Vevey, July 30-Aug. 14 (40c); JUPHILEX 77 Youth Philatelic Exhibition, Bern, Apr. 7-11 (80c).

Fluorescent Paper

From No. 624 onward the paper lacks violet fibers but is fluorescent, unless otherwise noted.

St. Ursanne on Doubs River — A260

Europa: 80c, Sils-Baselgia on Inn River.

1977, May 2 **Engr.** ***Perf. 11½***

627 A260 40c multicolored	.80	.25
628 A260 80c multicolored	1.60	.70

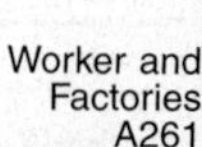

Worker and Factories A261

Ionic Column and Shield A262

Swiss Cross, Arrow and Butterfly A263

1977, Aug. 25 **Photo.** ***Perf. 11½***

629 A261 20c multicolored	.35	.30
630 A262 40c multicolored	.50	.30
631 A263 80c multicolored	1.25	1.05
Nos. 629-631 (3)	2.10	1.65

Federal Factories Act, centenary (20c); protection of cultural monuments (40c); Swiss hiking trails (80c).

Star Singer, Bergün — A264

Folk Customs: 10c, Horse race, Zürich. 20c, New Year's Eve costumes, Herisau. 25c, Chesslete, Solothurn. 30c, Rollelibutzen, Altstatten. 35c, Cutting off the goose, Sursee. 40c, Herald reading proclamation and men scaling wall, Geneva. 45c, Klausjagen, Kussnacht. 50c, Masked men, Laupen. 60c, Schnabelgeissen, Ottenbach. 70c, Procession (horse and masked men), Mendrisio. 80c, Griffins, Basel. 90c, Masked men, Lotschental.

1977-84 **Engr.** ***Perf. 11½***

632 A264 5c blue grn	.25	.25
a. Bklt. pane of 4 ('84)	1.50	.75
633 A264 10c dark red	.25	.25
a. Bklt. pane of 2 + 2 labels ('79)	6.00	3.00
b. Bklt. pane of 4 ('84)	2.25	1.50
634 A264 20c orange	.30	.25
a. Booklet pane of 4 ('79)	3.50	3.50
635 A264 25c brown	.40	.40
636 A264 30c brt green	.45	.25
637 A264 35c olive	.55	.25
a. Bklt. pane of 4 ('84)	4.25	2.60
638 A264 40c brown lake	.60	.25
a. Booklet pane of 4 ('79)	5.75	5.75
b. Violet fibers, flourescent paper ('78)	1.10	1.10
639 A264 45c gray blue	.75	.75
640 A264 50c red brown	.60	.25
a. Bklt. pane of 2+2 labels ('84)	3.00	2.25
b. Bklt. pane of 4 ('84)	5.25	4.25
641 A264 60c gray brown	.75	.75
642 A264 70c purple	1.05	.30
643 A264 80c steel blue	1.20	.75
644 A264 90c deep brown	1.35	1.15
Nos. 632-644 (13)	8.50	5.85

Issue dates: 30c, Nov. 25, 1982; 25c, 45c, 60c, Sept. 11, 1984; others, Aug. 25, 1977.

Arms of Vaud Canton A265

Old Lucerne A266

Title Page of "Melusine" A267

Stylized Lens and Bellows A268

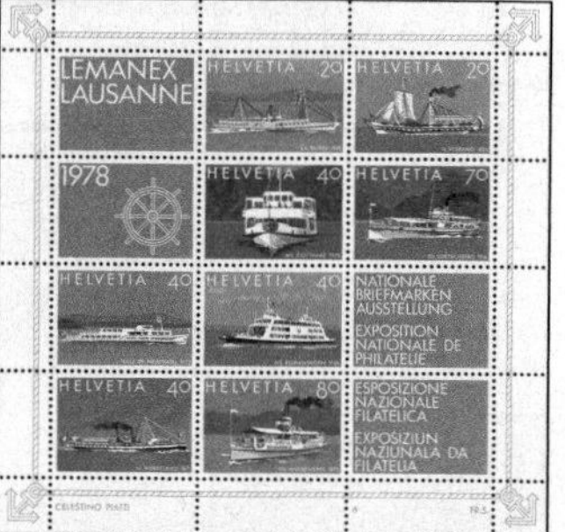

Steamers on Swiss Lakes — A269

1978, Mar. 9 **Photo.** ***Perf. 11½***

652 A265 20c multicolored	.30	.25
653 A266 40c multicolored	.60	.25
654 A267 70c multicolored	1.00	.80
655 A268 80c multicolored	1.15	1.00
Nos. 652-655 (4)	3.05	2.30

Miniature Sheet

656 A269 Sheet of 8	8.00	8.00
a. 20c La Suisse, 1910	.40	.40
b. 20c Il Verbano, 1826	.40	.40
c. 40c MS Gotthard, 1970	.80	.80
d. 40c Ville de Neuchatel, 1972	.80	.80
e. 40c MS Romanshorn, 1958	.80	.80
f. 40c Le Winkelried, 1871	.80	.80
g. 70c DS Loetschberg, 1914	1.00	1.00
h. 80c DS Waedenswil, 1895	1.20	1.20

LEMANEX 78 Philatelic Exhibition, Lausanne, May 26-June 4 (#652); Founding of Lucerne, 800th anniv. (#653); printing in Geneva, 500th anniv. (#654); 2nd Intl. Triennial Photography Exhibition, Fribourg, June 17-Oct. 22 (#655).

Size of No. 656: 134x129mm. Sold for 5fr.

Stockalper Palace, Brig — A270

Europa: 80c, Diet Hall, Bern.

1978, May 2 **Engr.** ***Perf. 11½***

657 A270 40c multicolored	.95	.30
658 A270 80c multicolored	1.90	1.20

Machinist A271

#660, Chemical worker (French inscription). #661, Construction worker (Italian inscription).

1978, Sept. 14 **Photo.** ***Perf. 11½***

659 A271 40c multicolored	.90	.45
660 A271 40c multicolored	.90	.45
661 A271 40c multicolored	.90	.45
a. Strip of 3, #659-661	2.75	2.75

Industrial safety.

Joseph Bovet (1879-1951), Composer — A272

Portraits: 40c, Henri Dunant (1828-1910), founder of Red Cross. 70c, Carl Gustave Jung (1875-1961), psychologist. 80c, Auguste Piccard (1884-1962), physicist and balloonist.

1978, Sept. 14 **Engr.**

662 A272 20c dull green	.30	.25
663 A272 40c rose lake	.60	.25
664 A272 70c gray	1.00	.75
665 A272 80c blue gray	1.15	.90
Nos. 662-665 (4)	3.05	2.15

Arms of Switzerland and Jura — A273

1978, Sept. 25 **Photo.** ***Perf. 11½***

666 A273 40c buff, red & blk	.80	.25

Admission of Jura as 23rd Canton.

Rainer Maria Rilke (1875-1926), Poet, Muzot Castle — A274

Designs: 40c, Paul Klee (1879-1940), painter and "heroic roses." 70c, Hermann Hesse (1877-1962), writer, and vines. 80c, Thomas Mann (1875-1955), writer, and Lubeck buildings.

1979, Feb. 21 **Engr.** ***Perf. 11½***

667 A274 20c gray green	.30	.25
668 A274 40c red	.60	.30
669 A274 70c brown	1.00	.70
670 A274 80c gray blue	1.15	1.00
Nos. 667-670 (4)	3.05	2.25

O. H. Ammann, Verrazano-Narrows Bridge, NY — A275

Target Hit with Pole and Lucerne Flag — A276

Hot Air Balloon A277

Airport, Swissair and Air France Jets — A278

1979, Feb. 21 **Photo.**

671 A275 20c multicolored	.35	.25
672 A276 40c multicolored	.65	.25
673 A277 70c multicolored	.80	.70
674 A278 80c multicolored	1.30	1.00
Nos. 671-674 (4)	3.10	2.20

Othmar H. Ammann (1879-1965), engineer, bridge builder in US; 50th Federal Riflemen's Festival, Lucerne, July 7-22; World Esperanto Congress, Lucerne; new runway at Basel-Mulhouse Intl. Airport.

Letter Box, 1845, Spalentor, Basel — A279

Europa: 80c, Microwave radio relay station on Jungfraujoch.

1979, Apr. 30 **Engr.** ***Perf. 11½***

675 A279 40c multicolored	.80	.25
676 A279 80c multicolored	1.30	.90

Helvetian Gold Quarter Stater, 2nd Century B.C. — A280

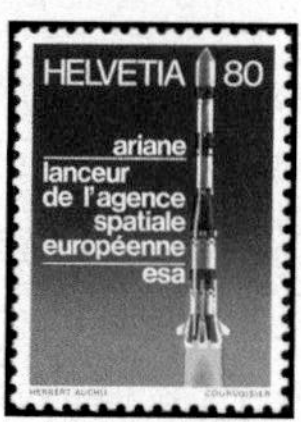

Three-stage Launcher Ariane — A283

Child and Dove — A281

Morse Key and Satellite A282

1979, Sept. 6 **Photo.**

677 A280 20c multicolored	.30	.25
678 A281 40c multicolored	.60	.25
679 A282 70c multicolored	.75	.70
680 A283 80c multicolored	1.20	.90
Nos. 677-680 (4)	2.85	2.10

Centenary of Swiss Numismatic Society; International Year of the Child; Union of Swiss Radio Amateurs, 50th anniv.; European Space Agency (ESA).

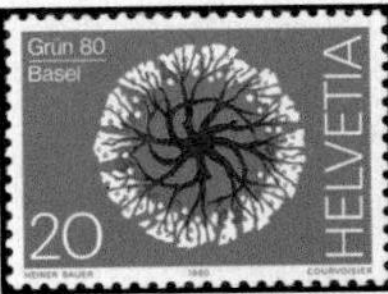

Tree in Bloom
A284

Hand Carved
Milk Bucket
A285

Winterthur
Town
Hall — A286

"Pic-Pic,"
1930 — A287

1980, Feb. 21 **Photo.**

681	A284 20c multicolored	.30	.25
682	A285 40c multicolored	.60	.25
683	A286 70c multicolored	1.00	.80
684	A287 80c multicolored	1.15	1.00
	Nos. 681-684 (4)	3.05	2.30

Green '80, Swiss Horticultural & Gardening Expo., Basel, 4/12-9/9/12; Swiss Arts Crafts Centers, 50th anniv.; Soc. for Swiss Art History, cent.; 50th Intl. Automobile Show, Geneva, 3/16.

Johann Konrad
Kern (1808-
1888), Politician
A288

Europa: 80c, Gustav Adolf Hasler (1830-1900), communications pioneer.

1980, Apr. 28 **Lith. & Engr.**

Granite Paper

685	A288 40c multicolored	.80	.25
686	A288 80c multicolored	1.60	.90

Postal Giro
System
A289

Postal Bus
System
A290

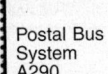

Security
Printing Plant,
50th
Anniversary
A291

Swiss
Telephone
Service
Centenary
A292

Photo., Photo. & Engr. (70c)

1980, Sept. 5 ***Perf. 12***

687	A289 20c multicolored	.30	.25
688	A290 40c multicolored	.60	.25
689	A291 70c multicolored	1.00	.75
690	A292 80c multicolored	1.15	1.10
	Nos. 687-690 (4)	3.05	2.35

Swiss
Meteorological
Office
Centenary
A293

Swiss Trade
Union
Federation
Centenary
A294

Opening of
St. Gotthard
Tunnel for
Year-round
Traffic — A295

1980, Sept. 5 **Photo.**

691	A293 20c multicolored	.35	.25
692	A294 40c multicolored	.55	.25
693	A295 80c multicolored	1.25	1.00
	Nos. 691-693 (3)	2.15	1.50

Granary,
Kiesen, 17th
Century
A296

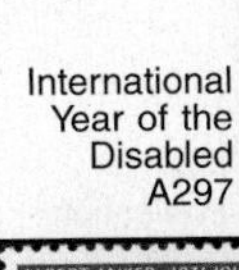

International
Year of the
Disabled
A297

The Parish Clerk, by
Albert
Anker — A298

Theodolite
and
Rod — A299

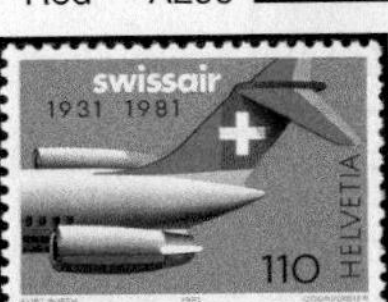

DC-9 (50th
Anniversary of
Swissair)
A300

1981, Mar. 9 **Photo.** ***Perf. 11½***

694	A296 20c multicolored	.35	.25
695	A297 40c multicolored	.70	.25
696	A298 70c multicolored	1.00	.80
697	A299 80c multicolored	1.15	.90
698	A300 110c multicolored	1.60	1.20
	Nos. 694-698 (5)	4.80	3.40

Ballenberg Open-air Museum of Rural Architecture, Furnishing and Crafts; Albert Anker (1831-1910), artist (70c); 16th Congress of the International Federation of Surveyors, Montreux, Aug. (80c).

Europa Issue

Couple Dancing in
Native
Costumes — A301

1981, May 4 **Photo.** ***Perf. 11½***

699	A301 40c shown	.95	.25
700	A301 80c Stone putting	1.60	1.00

Seal of
Fribourg
A302

1981, Sept. 3 **Photo. & Engr.**

701	A302 40c shown	.60	.25
702	A302 40c Seal of Solothurn	.60	.25
703	A302 80c Old Town Hall, Stans	1.15	1.00
	Nos. 701-703 (3)	2.35	1.50

Diet of Stans, 500th anniv., and entry of Fribourg & Solothurn into the Swiss Confederation.

Voltage
Regulator
A303

Crossbow
Quality
Emblem
A304

Youths
A305

Flower
Mosaic, St.
Peter's
Cathedral,
Geneva
A306

1981, Sept. 3 **Photo.**

704	A303 20c multi	.35	.25
705	A304 40c multi	.50	.30
706	A305 70c multi	.95	.75
707	A306 1.10fr multi	1.55	1.25
	Nos. 704-707 (4)	3.35	2.55

Technorama Industrial Fair, Winterthur; Crossbow Quality Emblem, 50th anniv.; Swiss Youth Assoc., 50th anniv.; restoration of St. Peter's Cathedral.

Gotthard
Railway
Centenary
A307

Designs: Locomotives.

1982, Feb. 18 **Photo.**

708	A307 40c Steam	.60	.30
709	A307 40c Electric	.60	.30
a.	Pair, #708-709 + central label	1.25	.60

Nos. 708-709 were issued as a miniature sheet of 10 with central label.

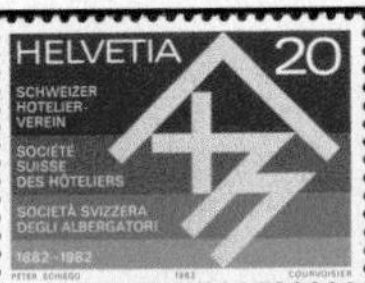

Swiss
Hoteliers'
Assoc.
Centenary
A308

Federal Gymnastic Society
Sesquicentennial — A309

Intl. Gas
Union, 50th
Anniv.
Convention,
Lausanne
A310

Bern Museum of Natural History
Sesquicentennial — A311

Society of
Chemical
Industries
Centenary
A312

1982, Feb. 18

710	A308 20c multicolored	.35	.25
711	A309 40c multicolored	.65	.30
712	A310 70c multicolored	.85	.75
713	A311 80c multicolored	1.25	1.10
714	A312 110c multicolored	1.55	1.20
	Nos. 710-714 (5)	4.65	3.60

Europa
1982 — A313

1982, May 3 **Photo.** ***Perf. 11½***

715	A313 40c Oath of Eternal Fealty	.45	.30
716	A313 80c Pact of 1291	1.90	1.00

Virgo, Schwarzee
above
Zermatt — A314

Signs of the Zodiac and City Views — 1fr, Aquarius, Old Bern. 1.10fr, Pisces, Nax near Sion. 1.20fr, Aries, Graustock. 1.40fr, Gemini, Bischofszell. 1.50fr, Taurus, Basel Cathedral. 1.60fr, Gemini, Schonengrund. 1.70fr, Cancer, Wetterhorn, Grindelwald. 1.80fr, Leo, Areuse Gorge, Neuchatel. No. 724, 2fr, Virgo, Jungfrau Monch Eiger Mts. 2.50fr, Libra, Fechy. 3fr, Scorpio, Corippo. 4fr, Sagittarius, Glarus. 4.50fr, Capricorn, Schuls.

Photogravure and Engraved

1982-86 ***Perf. 11½***

717	A314	1fr multi	1.75	.25
718	A314	1.10fr multi	2.00	.25
719	A314	1.20fr multi	2.10	.35
719A	A314	1.40fr multi	2.75	.35
720	A314	1.50fr multi	2.75	.45
721	A314	1.60fr multi	3.75	1.75
722	A314	1.70fr multi	3.25	.25
723	A314	1.80fr multi	3.75	3.50
724	A314	2fr multi	4.75	3.50
725	A314	2fr shown	3.75	.45
726	A314	2.50fr multi	4.75	.90
727	A314	3fr multi	5.50	.35

728	A314	4fr multi	7.25	.25
728A	A314	4.50fr multi	8.25	2.25
		Nos. 717-728A (14)	56.35	14.85

Issued: #717-719, 720-721, 8/23/82; #719A, 2/11/86; #722-724, 2/17/83; #725, 11/24/83; #726-727, 2/19/85; #728-728A, 2/21/84.

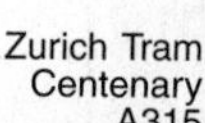
Zurich Tram Centenary A315

Centenary of Salvation Army in Switzerland A316

World Dressage Championship, Lausanne, Aug. 25-29 — A317

Intl. Water Supply Assoc., 14th World Congress, Zurich, Sept. 6-10 — A318

1982, Aug. 23 **Photo.**

729	A315	20c multicolored	.30	.25
730	A316	40c multicolored	.60	.25
731	A317	70c multicolored	1.00	.90
732	A318	80c multicolored	1.15	1.00
		Nos. 729-732 (4)	3.05	2.40

Fishing and Pisciculture Fed. Centenary A319

Zurich University Sesquicentennial — A320

Journalists' Fed. Centenary A321

Machine Manufacturers' Assoc. Centenary — A322

20c, Perch. 70c, Computer printouts. 80c, Micrometer, cycloidal computer pattern.

1983, Feb. 17 **Photo.**

Granite Paper

733	A319	20c multicolored	.30	.25
734	A320	40c multicolored	.60	.30
735	A321	70c multicolored	1.00	.90
736	A322	80c multicolored	1.15	1.00
		Nos. 733-736 (4)	3.05	2.45

Europa 1983 — A323

Photogravure and Engraved

1983, May 3 ***Perf. 11½***

737	A323	40c Celestial globe, 1594	.80	.25
738	A323	80c Cog railway, 1871	1.75	1.00

Basel Seal, 1832-1848 — A324

1983, May 26 **Photo.**

739	A324	40c multicolored	.75	.25

Basel Canton sesquicentennial (land division).

Octodurus Martigny Bimillenium A325

Swiss Kennel Club Centenary A326

Bicycle and Motorcycle Federation Centenary A327

World Communications Year — A328

1983, Aug. 22 **Photo.**

740	A325	20c multicolored	.30	.25
741	A326	40c multicolored	.60	.25
742	A327	70c multicolored	1.00	.90
743	A328	80c multicolored	1.15	1.00
		Nos. 740-743 (4)	3.05	2.40

NABA-ZURI'84 Natl. Stamp Show, Zurich, June 22-July 1 — A329

1100th Anniv. of Saint Imier — A330

Upper City, Lausanne A331

1984, Feb. 21 **Photo.**

744	A329	25c multicolored	.60	.25
745	A330	50c multicolored	1.15	.25
746	A331	80c multicolored	1.90	1.10
		Nos. 744-746 (3)	3.65	1.60

Selection of Lausanne as permanent headquarters for the Intl. Olympic Committee (80c).

Europa (1959-1984) A332

1984, May 2 **Photo.** ***Perf. 11½***

747	A332	50c lilac rose	1.10	.50
748	A332	80c ultra	1.90	1.00

Souvenir Sheet

Panoramic View of Zurich — A333

1984, May 24

749	A333	Sheet of 4	5.00	5.00
a.-d.		50c any single	1.10	1.10

NABA-ZURI '84 Stamp Show. Sold for 3fr.

Fire Prevention A334

1984, Sept. 11 **Photo.**

750	A334	50c Flames, match	.70	.25

Railway Staff Association, Cent. — A335

Rheto-Roman Culture Bimillennium A336

Lake Geneva Rescue Soc., Cent. — A337

Intl. Congress on Large Dams, Lausanne A338

35c, Conductor's hat, paraphernalia. 50c, Engraved artifact, Chur. 70c, Rescuing drowning victim. 80c, Grande Dizence Dam, Canton Valais.

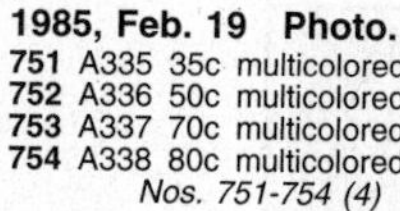

1985, Feb. 19 **Photo.** ***Perf. 12x11½***

751	A335	35c multicolored	.65	.25
752	A336	50c multicolored	.85	.25
753	A337	70c multicolored	1.20	.90
754	A338	80c multicolored	1.35	1.10
		Nos. 751-754 (4)	4.05	2.50

Europa 1985 — A339

Designs: 50c, Ernest Ansermet (1883-1969), composer, conductor. 80c, Frank Martin (1890-1974), composer.

1985, May 7 **Photo.** ***Perf. 11½x12***

755	A339	50c multicolored	1.00	.25
756	A339	80c multicolored	1.60	1.00

Swiss Master Bakers and Confectioners Federation, Bern, Cent. — A340

Swiss Radio Intl., 50th Anniv. A341

Postal, Telegraph & Telephone Intl. Congress, Sept. 16-21, Interlaken A342

1985, Sept. 10 **Photo.** ***Perf. 12x11½***

757	A340	50c Baker	.85	.25
758	A341	70c multi	1.00	1.00
759	A342	80c PTTI 75th anniv.	1.25	1.25
		Nos. 757-759 (3)	3.10	2.50

Swiss Worker's Relief Org., 50th Anniv. A343

Battle of Sempach, 600th Anniv. A344

Roman Chur Bimillennium A345

Vindonissa Bimillennium A346

Zurich Bimillennium A347

1986, Feb. 11 Photo. *Perf. 12*

772 A343 35c Knot .50 .40
773 A344 50c Military map, 1698 .80 .25
774 A345 80c Mercury statue 1.10 .90
775 A346 90c Gallic head 1.25 1.00
776 A347 1.10fr Augustus coin 1.55 1.25
Nos. 772-776 (5) 5.20 3.80

Europa 1986 — A348

1986, Apr. 22 Photo. *Perf. 13½*

777 A348 50c Woman 1.00 .30
778 A348 90c Man 2.00 1.25

Mail Handling — A349

5c, Franz mail van, 1911. 10c, Parcel sorting. 20c, Mule post. 25c, Letter-facing, canceling. 30c, Mail coach, 1735-1960. 35c, Counter service. 45c, Packet steamer, 1837-40. 50c, Postman, 1986. 60c, Loading airmail, 1986. 75c, 17th Cent. courier. 80c, Postman, ca. 1900. 90c, Railroad mail car.

Photo. & Engr.

1986-89 *Perf. 13½x13*

779 A349 5c multicolored .45 .35
780 A349 10c multicolored .45 .25
781 A349 20c multicolored .35 .25
782 A349 25c multicolored .70 .25
783 A349 30c multicolored .80 .25
784 A349 35c multicolored .90 .35
785 A349 45c multicolored .80 .50
786 A349 50c multicolored .90 .25
a. Bklt. pane of 10 ('88) 20.00
787 A349 60c multicolored 1.10 .50
788 A349 75c multicolored 1.35 .85
789 A349 80c multicolored 1.75 1.25
790 A349 90c multicolored 1.75 1.25
Nos. 779-790 (12) 11.30 6.30

Nos. 779, 780, 782, 784, 789, 790 exist on chalky phosphored paper. Regular stamps are on white fluorescent paper.

Issued: 5c, 10c, 25c, 35c, 80c, 90c, 9/9/86; 20c, 30c, 45c, 50c, 60c, 3/10/87; 75c, 3/7/89.

For surcharge see No. B535.

Intl. Peace Year — A351

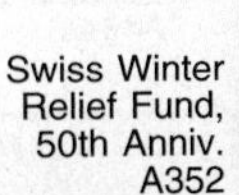

Swiss Winter Relief Fund, 50th Anniv. A352

Berne Convention for the Protection of Literary and Artistic Copyrights, Cent. — A353

25th Intl. Red Cross Conference, Geneva, Oct. 23-31 A354

1986, Sept. 9 Photo. *Perf. 12x11½*

799 A351 35c multicolored .60 .60
800 A352 50c multicolored .85 .25
801 A353 80c multicolored 1.00 1.00
802 A354 90c multicolored 1.35 1.35
Nos. 799-802 (4) 3.80 3.20

Mobile P.O., 50th Anniv. A355

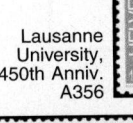

Lausanne University, 450th Anniv. A356

Swiss Engineers & Architects Assoc., Sesquicent. A357

Cointrin Airport-Geneva, Rail Link Opening, June 1, 1987 — A358

Baden Hot Springs, 2000th Anniv. A359

1987, Mar. 10 Photo.

803 A355 35c multicolored .55 .35
804 A356 50c multicolored .80 .25
805 A357 80c multicolored 1.10 1.15
806 A358 90c multicolored 1.25 1.30
807 A359 1.10fr multicolored 1.60 1.60
Nos. 803-807 (5) 5.30 4.65

Europa 1987 — A360

Sculpture: 50fr, Scarabaeus, 1979, by Bernard Luginbuhl. 90fr, Carnival Fountain, 1977, by Jean Tinguely, Basel Theater.

1987, May 26 Photo. *Perf. 11½*

808 A360 50c multicolored 1.15 .30
809 A360 90c multicolored 2.10 1.25

Swiss Master Butchers' Federation, Cent. — A361

Stamp Day, 50th Anniv. A362

Swiss Dairy Assoc., Cent. — A363

1987, Sept. 4 Photo. *Perf. 12x11½*

810 A361 35c multicolored .55 .40
811 A362 50c multicolored .80 .40
812 A363 90c Cheesemaker 1.45 1.00
Nos. 810-812 (3) 2.80 1.80

Tourism Industry, Bicent. — A364

Switzerland's four language regions: 50c, Clock Tower, Zug, German. 80c, Church of San Carlo, Blenio Valley, Italian. 90c, Witches' Tower, Sion Castle, French. 140c, Jorgenberg Castle ruins, Waltensburg/Vuorz, Surselva, Rhaeto-Romansh.

1987, Sept. 4 *Perf. 11½*

813 A364 50c multicolored .75 .40
814 A364 80c multicolored 1.05 .90
815 A364 90c multicolored 1.20 1.00
816 A364 140c multicolored 2.10 1.75
a. Souvenir sheet of 4, #813-816 4.50 3.75
Nos. 813-816 (4) 5.10 4.05

Stamps from No. 816a are on phosphored paper.

Swiss Women's Benevolent Soc., Cent. — A365

Swiss Hairdressers Assoc., Cent. — A366

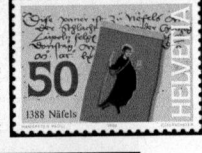

Battle of Naefels, 600th Anniv. A367

European Campaign to Protect Undeveloped and Developing Lands A368

Intl. Music Festival, Lucerne, 50th Anniv. A369

50c, Banner of St. Fridolin, medieval manuscript. 90c, Girl playing a shawm.

1988, Mar. 8 Photo. *Perf. 12x11½*

817 A365 25c multicolored .50 .25
818 A366 35c multicolored .70 .40
819 A367 50c multicolored 1.00 .75
820 A368 80c multicolored 1.60 .90
821 A369 90c multicolored 1.75 1.25
Nos. 817-821 (5) 5.55 3.05

Europa 1988 — A370

50c, Arrows (transport). 90c, Circuitry (communication).

1988, May 24 Photo. *Perf. 11½*

822 A370 50c multicolored 1.00 .40
823 A370 90c multicolored 2.00 1.25

Swiss Accident Prevention Office, 50th Anniv. A371

Assoc. of Metalworkers and Watchmakers, Cent. — A372

Federal Topography Office, 150th Anniv. A373

Intl. Red Cross Museum, Geneva A374

80c, Triangulation pyramid, theodolite, map.

1988, Sept. 13 Photo. *Perf. 12x11½*

824 A371 35c multicolored .55 .40
825 A372 50c multicolored .75 .25
826 A373 80c multicolored 1.20 .90
827 A374 90c multicolored 1.35 1.10
Nos. 824-827 (4) 3.85 2.65

Metamecanique, by Jean Tinguely — A375

1988, Nov. 25 Photo. *Perf. 13x12½*

828 A375 90c multicolored 4.25 3.00

See France No. 2137.

Military Post, Cent. — A376

Delemont Municipal Charter, 700th Anniv. A377

Public Transport Assoc., Cent. — A378

Rhaetian Railway, Cent. — A379

Great St. Bernard Pass Bimillennium A380

25c, Army postman. 35c, Fontaine du Sauvage & the Porte au Loup, Delemont. 50c, Eye, modes of transportation. 80c, Train, viaduct. 90c, St. Bernard dog, statue of saint, hospice on summit.

1989, Mar. 2 Photo. ***Perf. 12x11½***

829	A376	25c multicolored	.50	.25
830	A377	35c multicolored	.65	.40
831	A378	50c multicolored	.95	.25
832	A379	80c multicolored	1.50	1.00
833	A380	90c multicolored	2.00	1.10
		Nos. 829-833 (5)	5.60	3.00

Europa — A381

Children's games: 50c, Hopscotch. 90c, Blindman's buff.

1989, May 23 ***Perf. 11½***

834	A381	50c multicolored	1.00	.50
835	A381	90c multicolored	2.10	1.25

Industry — A382

2.75fr, Bricklayer. 2.80fr, Cook. 3fr, Cabinet maker. 3.60fr, Pharmacist. 3.75fr, Fisherman. 4fr, Wine grower. 5fr, Cheesemaker. 5.50fr, Dressmaker.

Engr., Litho. & Eng. (2.80, 3, 3.60, 4, 5fr)

1989-94 ***Perf. 13x13½***

842	A382	2.75fr multi	5.50	1.90
843	A382	2.80fr multi	5.50	3.00
844	A382	3fr multi	6.00	3.00
845	A382	3.60fr multi	7.00	4.00
846	A382	3.75fr multi	7.50	3.50
847	A382	4fr multi	8.00	2.40
848	A382	5fr multi	10.00	.95
849	A382	5.50fr multi	11.00	5.25
		Nos. 842-849 (8)	60.50	24.00

Issued: 2.75fr, 5.50fr, 8/29/89; 3.75fr, 3/6/90; 2.80fr, 3.60fr, 1/24/92; 5fr, 9/7/93; 4fr, 3/15/94; 3fr, 7/5/94.

Swiss Electricians' Assoc., Cent. — A383

Swiss Travel Fund, 50th Anniv. A384

Fribourg University, Cent. — A385

Opening of the Natl. Sound-Recording Archives, 1st Anniv. — A386

Interparliamentary Union, Cent. — A387

80c, "Wisdom" and "Science".

1989, Aug. 25 Photo. ***Perf. 11½***

851	A383	35c multicolored	.70	.45
852	A384	50c multicolored	1.00	.25
853	A385	80c multicolored	1.20	.75
854	A386	90c multicolored	1.55	1.00
855	A387	140c multicolored	2.75	1.75
		Nos. 851-855 (5)	7.20	4.20

Union of Swiss Philatelic Societies, Cent. — A388

Urban Railway System, Zurich A389

Assistance for Mountain Communities, 50th Anniv. A390

1990 World Ice Hockey Championships — A391

1990, Mar. 6

856	A388	25c No. 71, & type of A20	.45	.25
857	A389	35c Locomotives	.60	.40
858	A390	50c Mountain farmer	.85	.30
859	A391	90c Athletes	1.60	1.00
		Nos. 856-859 (4)	3.50	1.95

Europa 1990 — A393

Post offices.

Litho. & Engr.

1990, May 22 ***Perf. 13½***

861	A393	50c Lucerne	1.00	.25
862	A393	90c Geneva	2.10	1.25

Conrad Ferdinand Meyer (1825-1898), Writer — A394

Designs: 50c, Angelika Kaufmann (1741-1807), painter. 80c, Blaise Cendrars (1887-1961), journalist. 90c, Frank Buchser (1828-1890), artist.

1990, Sept. 5 **Litho.**

863	A394	35c green & blk	.70	.40
864	A394	50c blue & blk	.95	.30
865	A394	80c yellow & blk	1.55	.80
866	A394	90c vermilion & blk	1.90	1.10
		Nos. 863-866 (4)	5.10	2.60

Swiss Confederation, 700th Anniv. in 1991 — A395

1990, Sept. 5 Photo. ***Perf. 11½***

867	A395	50c shown	1.00	.40
868	A395	90c multi, diff.	2.10	1.25

Natl. Census A396

1990, Nov. 20

869	A396	50c multicolored	1.00	.40

Animals — A397

1990-95 Litho. & Engr. ***Perf. 13***

870	A397	10c Cow	.25	.25
871	A397	50c House cats	.85	.30
872	A397	70c Rabbit	1.00	.65
a.		Booklet pane of 10	16.00	
		Complete booklet, #872a	16.00	
873	A397	80c Barn owls	1.15	.60
874	A397	100c Horses	1.50	.80
875	A397	110c Geese	2.50	.60
876	A397	120c Dog	1.75	1.00
877	A397	140c Sheep	2.25	.75
878	A397	150c Goats	2.50	.75
879	A397	160c Turkey	2.50	1.25
880	A397	170c Donkey	3.00	.90
881	A397	200c Chickens	3.50	1.75
		Nos. 870-881 (12)	22.75	9.60

Issued: 50c, 3/6/90; 70c, 80c, 1/15/91; 10c, 160c, 1/24/92; 100c, 120c, 3/16/93; 150c, 200c, 7/5/94; #872a, 110c, 140c, 170c, 11/28/95.

Swiss Confederation, 700th Anniv. — A398

Swiss Parliament, US Capitol A399

1991, Feb. 22 Photo. ***Perf. 12***

884	A398	50c "700 jahre"	1.00	.50
885	A398	50c "700 onns"	1.00	.50
886	A398	50c "700 ans"	1.00	.50
887	A398	50c "700 anni"	1.00	.50
a.		Block of 4, #884-887	4.00	2.00
888	A399	1.60fr multicolored	3.25	2.00
		Nos. 884-888 (5)	7.25	4.00

See US No. 2532.

Bern, 800th Anniv. — A400

1991, Feb. 22 ***Perf. 11½***

889	A400	80c multicolored	1.60	.90

Europa — A401

1991, May 14 Litho. ***Perf. 11½***

890	A401	50c Ariane payload fairing	1.00	.25
891	A401	90c Giotto probe	1.75	1.00

Union of Postal, Telephone and Telegraph Officials, Cent. — A402

1991, Sept. 10 Photo. ***Perf. 11½***

892	A402	80c multicolored	1.60	1.00

Bridges A403

Designs: 50c, Stone bridge near Lavertezzo. 70c, Wooden "New Bridge" near Bremgarten. 80c, Railway bridge between Koblenz and Felsenau. 90c, Ganter Bridge, Simplon Pass.

1991, Sept. 10

893	A403	50c multicolored	1.00	.25
894	A403	70c multicolored	1.35	.70
895	A403	80c multicolored	1.55	.80
896	A403	90c multicolored	1.90	1.00
		Nos. 893-896 (4)	5.80	2.75

Mountain Lakes — A404

A404a

A404b

Design: 50c, Lago Moesola. 60c, Lac de Tanay. 80c, Melchsee.

Litho., Litho. & Engr. (#905, 908)

1991-95 ***Perf. 13½x13***

904	A404	50c shown	1.15	.25
905	A404	60c blue & multi	1.40	.25
a.		Booklet pane of 10	22.50	

905B	A404	60c bl & multi, dated "2015"	1.25	1.50
907	A404	80c red & multi	1.90	.30
908	A404a	80c reddish orange	1.90	.25
909	A404b	90c multicolored	2.10	.50
a.		Booklet pane of 10	21.00	
		Complete booklet, #909a	21.00	
		Nos. 904-909 (5)	8.45	1.55

Issued: 50c, No. 907, 12/16/91; Nos. 905, 908, 1/19/93; 90c, 11/28/95; No. 905B, 9/3/2015.

See No. 1102.

Bird Over Rhine River — A405

Faces of Parents, Child — A406

Molecular Formula, Structure and Model A407

1992, Mar. 24 Photo. *Perf. 11½*

911	A405	50c multicolored	.90	.35
912	A406	80c multicolored	1.35	.65
913	A407	90c multicolored	2.00	.95
		Nos. 911-913 (3)	4.25	1.95

Intl. Rhine Regulation, cent. (No. 911), Pro Familia Switzerland, 50th anniv. (No. 912), Intl. Chemical Nomenclature Conf., Geneva, cent. (No. 913).

Discovery of America, 500th Anniv — A408

Europa: 90c, Columbus, map of voyage.

1992, Mar. 24

914	A408	50c multicolored	1.15	.50
915	A408	90c multicolored	2.10	1.10

Protect the Alps — A409

1992, May 22 Photo. *Perf. 12*

916	A409	90c multicolored	1.75	1.10

See Austria No. 1571.

Comic Strips A410

1992, May 22 *Perf. 11½*

917	A410	50c Cosey	.95	.25
918	A410	80c Zep	1.50	.80
919	A410	90c Aloys	1.90	1.20
		Nos. 917-919 (3)	4.35	2.25

World of the Circus A411

50c, Clowns on trapeze. 70c, Sea lion, clown. 80c, Clown, elephant. 90c, Lipizzaner, harlequin.

1992, Aug. 25 Photo. *Perf. 12x11½*

920	A411	50c multicolored	1.00	.30
921	A411	70c multicolored	1.40	.60
922	A411	80c multicolored	1.60	.60
923	A411	90c multicolored	1.75	1.00
		Nos. 920-923 (4)	5.75	2.50

Central Office for Intl. Carriage by Rail, Cent. (in 1993) — A412

1992, Nov. 24 Photo. *Perf. 11½*

924	A412	90c multicolored	1.75	1.00

First Swiss Postage Stamps, 150th Anniv. — A413

Designs: 60c, Zurich Types A1, A2, Geneva Type A1. 80c, Stylized canceled stamp. 100c, Stylized stamps on album page.

1993, Mar. 16 Photo. *Perf. 11½*

925	A413	60c multicolored	1.20	.35
926	A413	80c multicolored	1.60	.65
927	A413	100c multicolored	2.00	1.30
		Nos. 925-927 (3)	4.80	2.30

Paracelsus (1493-1541), Physician A414

Opening of Olympic Museum, Lausanne A415

Intl. Metalworkers' Federation, Cent. — A416

1993, Mar. 16 Photo. *Perf. 11½*

928	A414	60c blue & sepia	1.10	.40
929	A415	80c multicolored	1.45	.75
930	A416	180c multicolored	3.75	2.10
		Nos. 928-930 (3)	6.30	3.25

Lake Constance Steamer Hohentwiel A417

1993, May 5 Photo. *Perf. 11½x12*

931	A417	60c multicolored	1.40	.80

See Austria No. 1598, Germany No. 1786.

Contemporary Architecture A418

Europa: 60c, Media House, Villeurbanne, France. 80c, House, Breganzona, Switzerland.

Litho. & Engr.

1993, May 5 *Perf. 13½*

932	A418	60c multicolored	1.40	.40
933	A418	80c red & black	1.90	.90

Works of Art by Swiss Women A419

Designs: 60c, Work No. 095, by Emma Kunz. 80c, Grande Cantatrice Lilas Goergens, by Aloise Corbaz. 100c, Under the Rain Cloud, by Meret Oppenheim. 120c, Four Spaces in Horizontal Bands, by Sophie Taeuber-Arp.

1993, Sept. 7 Photo. *Perf. 11½*

934	A419	60c multicolored	1.10	.40

Size: 33x33½mm

935	A419	80c multicolored	1.45	.75
936	A419	100c multicolored	2.25	1.00
937	A419	120c multicolored	2.75	1.25
		Nos. 934-937 (4)	7.55	3.40

Swiss Sports School, 50th Anniv. A420

Jakob Bernoulli (1654-1705), Mathematician A421

Swiss Telecom PTT Participation in Unisource A422

ICAO, 50th Anniv. A423

1994, Mar. 15 Photo. *Perf. 11½*

938	A420	60c multicolored	1.10	.30
939	A421	80c multicolored	1.40	.60
940	A422	100c multicolored	2.10	1.20
941	A423	180c multicolored	3.50	1.75
		Nos. 938-941 (4)	8.10	3.85

Intl. Congress of Mathematicians, Zurich (#939).

"Books and the Press" Exhibition, Geneva A424

1994, Mar. 15

942	A424	60c Early manuscripts	1.20	.35
943	A424	80c Letterpress	1.60	.70
944	A424	100c Electronic publishing	2.00	1.35
		Nos. 942-944 (3)	4.80	2.40

1994 World Cup Soccer Championships, U.S. — A425

1994, Mar. 15

945	A425	80c multicolored	1.60	.95

Research Vehicles of August & Jacques Piccard — A426

Europa: 60c, Bathyscaphe Trieste. 100c, Stratospheric balloon.

1994, May 17 Photo. *Perf. 12*

946	A426	60c multicolored	1.60	.50
947	A426	100c multicolored	2.00	1.45

Georges Simenon (1903-89), Writer A427

Litho. & Engr.

1994, Oct. 15 *Perf. 13*

948	A427	100c multicolored	2.00	1.20

See Belgium No. 1567, France No. 2443.

Campaign to stop AIDS — A428

1994, Oct. 15 Photo. *Perf. 11½*

949	A428	60c multicolored	1.40	.35

Endangered Species — A429

1995, Mar. 7 Photo. *Perf. 11½*

950	A429	60c European beaver	.80	.40
951	A429	80c Map butterfly	1.30	.75
952	A429	100c Green tree frog	1.60	1.05
953	A429	120c Litte owl	1.90	1.75
		Nos. 950-953 (4)	5.60	3.95

Swiss Wrestling Assoc., Cent. — A430

Swiss Assoc. of Producers & Distributors of Electricity, Cent. — A431

Swiss News Agency, Cent. — A432

UN, 50th Anniv. A433

1995, Mar. 7

954	A430	60c blue & black	1.20	.55
955	A431	60c multicolored	1.20	.55
956	A432	80c multicolored	1.60	1.50
957	A433	180c multicolored	3.75	1.75
		Nos. 954-957 (4)	7.75	4.35

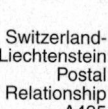

Peace & Freedom A434

Europa: 60c, Dove, faces. 100c, Zeus disguised as bull, abducting Europa, daughter of King of Phoenicia.

Litho., Engr. & Embossed

1995, May 16 ***Perf. 13***

958	A434	60c lt blue & dk blue	1.40	.40
959	A434	100c orange & brown	2.25	.85

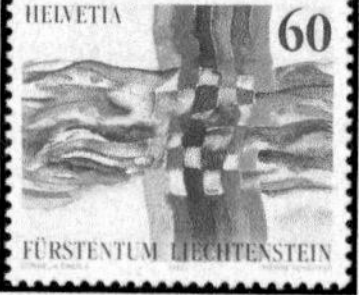

Switzerland-Liechtenstein Postal Relationship A435

Litho. & Engr.

1995, Sept. 5 ***Perf. 13½***

960	A435	60c multicolored	1.40	.50

See Liechtenstein No. 1055.

No. 960 and Liechtenstein No. 1055 are identical. This issue was valid for postage in both countries.

Motion Pictures, Cent. — A436

Scenes from motion pictures: 60c, La Vocation d'Andre Carrel. 80c, Anna Goldin-The Last Witch. 150c, Pipilotti's Mistakes-Absolution.

1995, Sept. 5 **Photo.** ***Perf. 11½***

961	A436	60c multicolored	1.20	.40
962	A436	80c multicolored	1.60	.75
963	A436	150c multicolored	3.00	1.90
		Nos. 961-963 (3)	5.80	3.05

Telecom '95, Geneva — A437

1995, Sept. 5

964	A437	180c multicolored	3.50	1.90

Swiss Charities, Solidarity Chain, 50th Anniv. A438

Touring Club, Cent. — A439

Federal Music Festival, Interlaken A440

Swiss Natl. Assoc. Pro Filia, Cent. — A441

Jean Piaget (1896-1980), Psychologist A442

1996, Mar. 12 **Photo.** ***Perf. 11½***

965	A438	70c multicolored	1.40	.55
966	A439	70c multicolored	1.40	.55
967	A440	90c multicolored	1.75	.70
968	A441	90c multicolored	1.75	.70
969	A442	180c multicolored	3.75	2.40
		Nos. 965-969 (5)	10.05	4.90

Famous Women — A443

Europa: 70c, S. Corinna Bille (1912-79), author. 110c, Iris von Roten-Meyer (1917-90), writer, painter.

Litho. & Engr.

1996, May 14 ***Perf. 13½***

970	A443	70c multicolored	1.40	.50
971	A443	110c multicolored	2.00	1.10

Modern Olympic Games, Cent. — A444

1996, May 14 **Litho.** ***Perf. 13½***

972	A444	180c multicolored	3.75	2.00

Guinness Record Stamp — A445

Design: Aerial view of 11,000 gymnasts arranged as No. 909, making record as world's largest living postage stamp.

1996, June 27 **Litho.** ***Perf. 13½x13***

973	A445	90c multicolored	2.50	1.25

Greeting Stamps A446

Various ornate or floral patterns.

Serpentine Die Cut 7 Vert.

1996, Sept. 10 **Typo.**

Self-Adhesive

Booklet Stamps

974	A446	90c yellow & black	1.90	1.00
975	A446	90c blue & multi	1.90	1.00
976	A446	90c red & multi	1.90	1.00
977	A446	90c green & multi	1.90	1.00
a.		Booklet pane of 4, #974-977	7.50	
		Complete booklet, 2 #977a	15.00	

Music Boxes and Automata A447

Designs: 70c, Ring with mechanical figures, musical movement, by Isaac-Daniel Piguet. 90c, Basso-piccolo mandolin cylinder music box, by Eduard Jaccard. 110c, Station automaton, by Paillard and Co. 180c, Kalliope disk music box.

1996, Sept. 10 **Photo.** ***Perf. 11½***

978	A447	70c multicolored	1.45	.35
979	A447	90c multicolored	1.90	.70
980	A447	110c multicolored	2.00	1.35
981	A447	180c multicolored	3.75	2.00
		Nos. 978-981 (4)	9.10	4.40

Stamp Design Competition Winners — A448

Designs: 70c, Golden cow. 90c, Smiling creature. 110c, Leaves. 180c, Dove.

1996, Nov. 26 **Photo.** ***Perf. 11½***

982	A448	70c blue & bister	1.40	.55
983	A448	90c multicolored	1.75	.80
984	A448	110c multicolored	2.00	1.00
985	A448	180c multicolored	3.75	1.75
		Nos. 982-985 (4)	8.90	4.10

"Globi" as Postman A449

1997, Mar. 11 **Litho.** ***Perf. 13x13½***

986	A449	70c multicolored	1.50	.50

Swiss Railways, 150th Anniv. A450

Designs: 70c, Locomotive 2000, 1990's. 90c, Red Arrow, 1930's. 140c, Pullman coach, 1920's-30's. 170c, Limmat steam locomotive, 1800's.

1997, Mar. 11 **Photo.** ***Perf. 11½***

987	A450	70c multicolored	1.20	.50
988	A450	90c multicolored	1.60	.95
989	A450	140c multicolored	3.00	1.35
990	A450	170c multicolored	3.50	2.25
		Nos. 987-990 (4)	9.30	5.05

Gallo-Roman Art — A451

Archaeological finds: 70c, Venus of Octodurus. 90c, Bronze bust of Bacchus. 110c, Ceramic fragment depicting Victoria. 180c, Mosaic theatrical mask.

1997, Mar. 11

991	A451	70c multicolored	1.40	.50
992	A451	90c multicolored	1.75	.95
993	A451	110c multicolored	2.00	1.45
994	A451	180c multicolored	3.75	2.10
		Nos. 991-994 (4)	8.90	5.00

Swiss Air's North Atlantic Service, 50th Anniv. — A452

1997, Mar. 11 **Litho.** ***Perf. 13½***

995	A452	180c multicolored	3.50	1.75

Swiss Farmers' Union, Cent. — A453

1997, May 13 **Litho.** ***Perf. 13½***

996	A453	70c shown	1.40	.55
997	A453	90c Street map	1.75	.85

Swiss Municipalities' Union, cent. (#997).

Stories and Legends — A454

Europa: Devil and Billy Goat from legend of the "Devil's Bridge."

1997, May 13 **Litho. & Engr.**

998	A454	90c multicolored	2.10	1.10

King of Thailand's Visit to Switzerland, Cent. — A455

King Chulalongkorn (Rama V), Pres. Adolf Deucher.

1997, Sept. 12 Litho. *Perf. 13½*

999 A455 90c multicolored 2.10 1.50

Energy 2000 — A456

1997, Sept. 12 Photo. *Perf. 11½*

1000 A456 70c Air (clouds) 1.25 .55
1001 A456 90c Fire 1.60 1.25
1002 A456 110c Water 2.25 1.40
1003 A456 180c Earth 3.75 1.90
Nos. 1000-1003 (4) 8.85 5.10

Paul Karrer (1889-1971), Winner of Nobel Prize for Chemistry, 1937 — A457

Design: 110c, Alfred Nobel (1833-96), founder of Nobel Prize.

Litho. & Engr.

1997, Nov. 13 *Perf. 13*

1004 A457 90c gray & blk 2.00 .95
1005 A457 110c lt gray brn & blk 3.00 1.20

Nos. 1004-1005 each issued in sheets of 8.
See Sweden Nos. 2254-2255.

Swiss Postal Service A458

Various people from different generations, cultures. Each stamp inscribed in one of Switzerland's four national languages with message to keep in touch.

1997, Nov. 20 Litho. *Perf. 13*

Color of Denomination

1006 A458 70c blue 1.40 .40
1007 A458 70c yellow 1.40 .40
1008 A458 70c green 1.40 .40
1009 A458 70c red 1.40 .40
a. Strip of 4, #1006-1009 5.75 5.75

Division of Swiss PTT — A459

1998, Jan. 7 Litho. *Perf. 13½*

1010 A459 90c Swisscom 1.75 .90
1011 A459 90c Swiss Post 1.75 .90

Confederation, 150th Anniv. and Helvetic Republic, Bicent. — A460

Stylized design, proclamation in one of four languages, location of denomination: No. 1012, German, LL. No. 1013, Romansch, LR. No. 1014, French, UL. No. 1015, Italian, UR.

1998, Mar. 10 Photo. *Perf. 11½*

1012 A460 90c multicolored 1.75 1.00
1013 A460 90c multicolored 1.75 1.00
1014 A460 90c multicolored 1.75 1.00
1015 A460 90c multicolored 1.75 1.00
a. Block of 4, #1012-1015 7.50 5.00

Printed in continuous design.

Swiss Old Age and Survivors' Insurance, 50th Anniv. A461

Opening of Natl. Museum, Prangins Castle A462

St. Gallen University, Cent. — A463

1998, Mar. 10

1016 A461 70c multicolored 1.35 .65
1017 A462 70c multicolored 1.35 .65
1018 A463 90c multicolored 1.90 1.00
Nos. 1016-1018 (3) 4.60 2.30

View of Switzerland A464

Designs: 10c, Simplon Pass. 20c, Snow-covered winter scene. 50c, Fence posts along country road. 70c, Hobbyhorses, posts. 90c, Stream, route marker. 110c, Lake, shoreline.

1998, Mar. 10 Litho. *Perf. 13x13½*

1019 A464 10c multicolored .40 .25
1020 A464 20c multicolored .60 .35
1021 A464 50c multicolored .95 .50
1022 A464 70c multicolored 1.35 .35
1023 A464 90c multicolored 1.75 .35
1024 A464 110c multicolored 2.10 .95
Nos. 1019-1024 (6) 7.15 2.75

See Nos. 1027-1029.

Sion, Candidate for 2006 Winter Olympic Games — A465

1998, Feb. 12 Litho. *Perf. 13½*

1025 A465 90c multicolored 1.90 1.00

National Day — A466

1998, May 12

1026 A466 90c multicolored 1.90 1.25

Europa.

View of Switzerland Type of 1998

140c, City of Zug. 170c, Olive grove, Castagnola. 180c, Road, mountains outside Reutigen.

1998, Sept. 8 Litho. *Perf. 13*

1027 A464 140c multicolored 2.25 .90
1028 A464 170c multicolored 2.75 1.00
1029 A464 180c multicolored 3.00 1.20
Nos. 1027-1029 (3) 8.00 3.10

Youth Sports — A467

Die Cut x Serpentine Die Cut

1998, Sept. 8 Photo.

Self-Adhesive

Booklet Stamps

1030 A467 70c Roller blading 1.40 1.00
1031 A467 70c Snow boarding 1.40 1.00
1032 A467 70c Mountain biking 1.40 1.00
1033 A467 70c Street basketball 1.40 1.00
1034 A467 70c Beach volleyball 1.40 1.00
a. Booklet pane, #1030-1034 + label 7.00
Complete booklet, 2 #1034a 14.00

Universal Declaration of Human Rights, 50th Anniv. — A468

1998, Nov. 25 Litho. *Perf. 13½*

1035 A468 70c multicolored 1.40 .60

Christmas A469

1998, Nov. 25

1036 A469 90c multicolored 1.75 .85

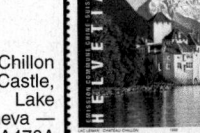

Bridge 24, Slender West Lake, Yangzhou A470

Chillon Castle, Lake Geneva — A470A

Photo. & Engr.

1998, Nov. 25 *Perf. 13½*

1037 A470 20c multicolored .40 .40

Photo.

1038 A470a 70c multicolored 1.40 1.00
a. Sheet of 4 each, #1038-1039 12.00 12.00

Souvenir Sheet

Perf. 11½

1039 A470a 90c Castle, Bridge 24 2.00 2.00

No. 1039 contains one 53x45mm stamp. See China (PRC) Nos. 2920-2921.

No. 1039 exists with China 1999 World Philatelic Exhibition emblem and a hologram in margin. These were sold for 3.50fr only canceled on cover.

Switzerland Post, 150th Anniv. A471

1999, Jan. 21 Photo. *Perf. 12*

1040 A471 90c multicolored 2.00 1.00

Pingu the Penguin as Postman A472

1999, Mar. 9 Litho. *Perf. 13½*

1041 A472 70c Carrying package 1.45 .60
1042 A472 90c In delivery cart 1.75 .90

See Nos. 1064-1065 for redrawn designs.

Comic Book, "Les Amours de Monsieur Vieux Bois," by Rodolphe Töpffer (1799-1846) — A473

Vieux Bois: No. 1043, Waving out of window, lady walking away. No. 1044, Down on knees, lady. No. 1045, In air after knocking over furniture. No. 1046, Pulling lady up to lift her over wall. No. 1047, Standing with his lady to be married.

Booklet Stamps

Die Cut x Serpentine Die Cut

1999, Mar. 9 Self-Adhesive

1043 A473 90c multicolored 2.10 .75
1044 A473 90c multicolored 2.10 .75
1045 A473 90c multicolored 2.10 .75
1046 A473 90c multicolored 2.10 .75
1047 A473 90c multicolored 2.10 .75
a. Booklet pane, #1043-1047 + label 10.50
Complete booklet, 2 #1047a 21.00

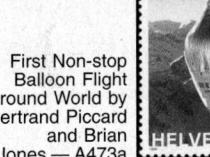

First Non-stop Balloon Flight Around World by Bertrand Piccard and Brian Jones — A473a

1999, Mar. 24 Litho. *Perf. 13½*

1047B A473a 90c multicolored 2.10 .90

UPU, 125th Anniv. — A474

1999, May 5 Photo. *Perf. 12*

1048 A474 20c shown .45 .25
1049 A474 70c UPU emblem 1.60 .65
a. Pair, #1048-1049 2.10 1.25

No. 1049 is 56x30mm. Issued in sheets of 8 stamps.

SOS Children's Village, Wabern, 50th Anniv. — A475

1999, May 5 Litho. *Perf. 13½*

1050 A475 70c multicolored 1.45 1.00

Vintners Festival, Vevey — A476

1999, May 5

1051 A476 90c multicolored 1.90 1.10
Complete booklet, 10 #1051 19.00

Council of Europe, 50th Anniv. — A477

1999, May 5 Photo. *Perf. 11½*

1052 A477 90c multicolored 2.10 .90

Swiss National Park — A478

1999, May 5 Litho. *Perf. 13½*

1053 A478 90c Horns of an ibex 2.10 1.10

Europa.

Geneva Convention, 50th Anniv. — A479

1999, May 5

1054 A479 110c multicolored 2.50 1.10

A481

Designs: 70c, Suvorov and soldiers, monument at Schöllenen Gorge. 110c, Suvorov's vanguard by Lake Klöntal.

1999, Sept. 24 Photo. *Perf. 11¾*

1056 A481 70c multicolored 1.60 .80
1057 A481 110c multicolored 2.50 1.25

Field Marshal Aleksandr Suvorov's Alpine Campaign, 200th Anniv.

Nos. 1056-1057 each issued in sheets of 8 stamps.

See Russia Nos. 6534-6535.

Rights of the Child — A482

1999, Sept. 24 Litho. *Perf. 13½*

1058 A482 70c multicolored 1.60 .70

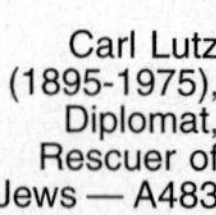

Carl Lutz (1895-1975), Diplomat, Rescuer of Jews — A483

1999, Sept. 24

1059 A483 90c multicolored 2.10 .90

Christian Friedrich Schönbein (1799-1868), Discoverer of Ozone — A484

1999, Sept. 24

1060 A484 1.10fr multicolored 2.50 1.10

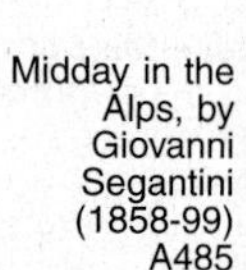

Midday in the Alps, by Giovanni Segantini (1858-99) A485

1999, Sept. 24

1061 A485 180c multicolored 4.25 1.75

Christmas — A486

Perf. 13½x13¼

1999, Nov. 23 Litho.

1062 A486 90c multicolored 2.10 .90

Millennium A487

Perf. 11¾x11½

1999, Nov. 23 Photo.

1063 A487 90c multicolored 1.40 .70

No. 1063 was printed in sheets of 8 stamps and 8 se-tenant labels with text or blank. Swiss Post offered to print photos or artwork sent in by customers on the blank labels. Personalized sheets sold for 14fr per sheet.

Pingu The Penguin Type of 1999

Redrawn to Omit Strings on Packages

1999, Dec. 6 Litho. *Perf. 13¼x13½*

1064 A472 70c Like #1041 1.60 .70
1065 A472 90c Like #1042 2.10 .90

Intl. Cycling Union, Cent. — A488

2000, Mar. 7 Litho. *Perf. 13¼x13½*

1066 A488 70c multicolored 1.60 .80

Swiss Souvenirs — A489

Souvenirs in snow domes: 10c, Alphorn. 20c, Fondue pot. 30c, Wine pitchers. 50c, Figurine of ibex. 60c, Neuchâtel "Pendule" wall clock. 70c, St. Bernard dog.

2000, Mar. 7 Litho. *Perf. 13x13¼*

1067 A489 10c multicolored .25 .25
1068 A489 20c multicolored .45 .25
1069 A489 30c multicolored .70 .35
1070 A489 50c multicolored 1.15 .60
1071 A489 60c multicolored 1.40 .70
1072 A489 70c multicolored 1.10 .60
Nos. 1067-1072 (6) 5.05 2.75

See No. 1101.

National Council of Women, Cent. A490

2000, May 10 Litho. *Perf. 13¼*

1073 A490 70c multi 1.60 .80

Europa Issue

Common Design Type

2000, May 10

1074 CD17 90c multi 2.10 1.05

Embroidery — A491

Embroidered

2000, June 21 *Imperf.*

Self-Adhesive

1075 A491 5fr multi 16.00 16.00
a. Sheet of 4 225.00 225.00

A492

Designs: 120c, Payerne Church, violin. 130c, Church of St. Saphorin, waiter's tray. 180c, Vals hot springs, bather.

2000, June 21 Litho. *Perf. 13x13¼*

1076 A492 120c multi 2.75 1.20
1077 A492 130c multi 3.00 1.30
1078 A492 180c multi 4.25 1.75
Nos. 1076-1078 (3) 10.00 4.25

See Nos. 1089-1092, 1103-1105.

2000 Census — A493

2000, Sept. 15 *Perf. 13¼x13½*

1079 A493 70c multi 1.60 .80

A Perfect World, by Sandra Dobler A494

My Town, by Stephanie Aerschmann A495

Stampin' the Future children's stamp design contest winners: No. 1080, Alien From Outer Space, by Yannik Kehrli. No. 1081, Looks Below the Sun, by Charlotte Bättig.

Booklet Stamps

Serpentine Die Cut 5¾ Vert.

2000, June 15 Self-Adhesive

1080 A494 70c multi 1.60 .80
1081 A494 70c multi 1.60 .80
1082 A494 70c shown 1.60 .80
1083 A495 70c shown 1.60 .80
a. Booklet pane, #1080-1083 6.50
Booklet, 2 #1083a 13.00

The booklet, which was sold unfolded, has rouletting between panes.

2000 Summer Olympics, Sydney A496

2000, Sept. 15 Photo. *Die Cut*

Booklet Stamps

Self-Adhesive

1084 A496 90c Swimmer 2.10 1.05
1085 A496 90c Cyclist 2.10 1.05
1086 A496 90c Runner 2.10 1.05
a. Booklet pane, #1084-1086 6.50
Booklet, #1086a 6.50

No. 1086a is separated from booklet cover by rouletting. The booklet was sold folded.

See Nos. 1201-1202.

Stamp Day — A497

Perf. 13¼x13½

2000, Nov. 21 Litho.

1087 A497 70c multi 1.60 .80

Christmas — A498

2000, Nov. 21 Photo. *Perf. 11½*

Granite Paper

1088 A498 90c multi 2.10 1.05

See No. 1197c.

Type of 2000

Designs: 200c, Mountain, hiker. 220c, Postbus, children. 300c, Cyclist, bridge and church, Biasca. 400c, Airplane at airport, tourist with suitcase.

2000-01 Litho. *Perf. 13x13¼*

1089 A492 200c multi 4.50 2.25
1090 A492 220c multi 5.00 2.50
1091 A492 300c multi 7.00 3.00
1092 A492 400c multi 9.25 4.75

Issued: 200c, 300c, 11/21/00. 220c, 400c, 3/13/01.

Alice Rivaz (1901-98), Writer — A499

Perf. 13¼x13½

2001, Mar. 13 Litho. & Engr.

1093 A499 70c multi 1.60 .80

Aero Club, Cent. A500

2001, Mar. 13 Litho. *Perf. 13¼*

1094 A500 90c multi 2.10 1.05

Congratulations A501

2001, Mar. 13 *Perf. 13¼x13½*

1095 A501 90c multi 2.10 1.05

Caritas, Cent. — A502

2001, Mar. 13

1096 A502 110c multi 2.50 1.25

UN High Commissioner for Refugees, 50th Anniv. — A503

2001, Mar. 13

1097 A503 130c multi 3.00 1.50

Vela Museum, Ligornetto A504

2001, May 9

1098 A504 70c multi 1.60 .80

Europa — A505

2001, May 9

1099 A505 90c multi 2.10 1.05

Chocosuisse, Cent. — A506

2001, May 9 Photo. *Perf. 11½*

Granite Paper

1100 A506 90c brown 2.10 1.05

No. 1100 has a scratch-and-sniff coating with a chocolate aroma.

Swiss Souvenirs Type of 2000

Serpentine Die Cut 5¾ Horiz.

2001, May 9 Self-Adhesive Litho.

1101 A489 70c Like #1072 1.60 .80
a. Booklet of 12 19.50

No. 1101 was issued in coil rolls of 100 with backing paper wider than the stamp and the stamps spaced. Also issued in booklets with different backing paper with stamps adjoining. Used examples of each variety are identical.

Type of 1995

Serpentine Die Cut 5¾ Vert.

2001, May 9 Self-Adhesive Typo.

1102 A404b 90c multi 2.10 1.05
a. Booklet of 12 25.00

Type of 2000

Designs: 90c, Farm house, Willisau, people feeding horse. 100c, Boat on Lake Geneva, woman at water's edge. 110c, Kleine Matterhorn Glacier, skier.

2001, Sept. 20 Litho. *Perf. 13x13¼*

1103 A492 90c multi 2.10 1.05
1104 A492 100c multi 2.25 1.15
1105 A492 110c multi 2.50 1.25
Nos. 1103-1105 (3) 6.85 3.45

The Birth of Venus, by Arnold Böcklin (1827-1901) A507

2001, Sept. 20 *Perf. 13½*

1106 A507 180c multi 4.25 2.10

Souvenir Sheet

Flowers — A508

70c, Melastoma malabathricum. 90c, Saraca cauliflora. 110c, Leontopodium alpinum. 130c, Gentiana clusii.

2001, Sept. 20 *Perf. 13¼x12¾*

1107 A508 Sheet of 4 11.00 11.00
a. 70c multicolored 1.60 .80
b. 90c multicolored 2.10 1.05
c. 110c multicolored 2.50 1.25
d. 130c multicolored 3.00 1.50

See Singapore Nos. 984-988.

Illustrations from Children's Book, "The Rainbow Fish," by Marcus Pfister — A509

2001, Sept. 20 Photo. *Perf. 12¾x14*

1108 A509 70c Fish, coral 1.60 .80
1109 A509 90c Fish, starfish 2.10 1.05

Stamp Day Stamp Design Competition Winner — A510

Perf. 13¼x13½

2001, Nov. 20 Litho.

1110 A510 70c multi 1.60 .80

Christmas — A511

2001, Nov. 20 *Perf. 11½*

Granite Paper

1111 A511 90c multi 2.10 1.05

See No. 1197a.

Geneva Escalade, 400th Anniv. — A512

Perf. 13¼x13½

2002, Mar. 12 Litho.

1112 A512 70c multi 1.60 .80

Federal Parliament Building, Cent. — A513

2002, Mar. 12

1113 A513 90c multi 2.10 1.05

Rega Air Rescue Foundation A514

Litho. with Hologram Affixed

2002, Mar. 12 *Perf. 13x13¾*

1114 A514 180c multi 4.25 2.10

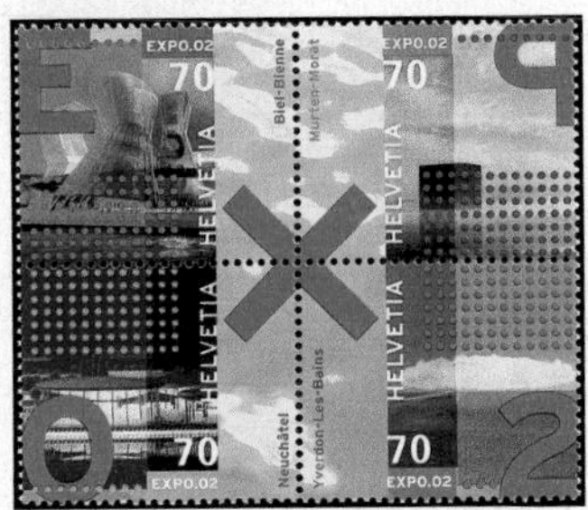

Expo.02, Switzerland — A515

No. 1115: a, "E." b, Backwards "P." c, "0." d, "2."

2002, Mar. 12 Photo. *Perf. 14x14¼*

Granite Paper

1115 A515 Block of 4 6.50 4.50
a.-d. 70c Any single 1.60 .80

Swiss Railways, Cent. — A516

Designs: 70c, RABDe 500 Inter-city tilting train. 90c, Inter-city 2000 double-deck train. 120c, Seetal line railcar. 130c, Re 460 locomotive.

2002, Mar. 12 *Perf. 12¾x14*

1116 A516 70c multi 1.60 .80
1117 A516 90c multi 2.10 1.05
1118 A516 120c multi 2.75 1.40
1119 A516 130c multi 3.00 1.50
Nos. 1116-1119 (4) 9.45 4.75

Souvenir Sheet

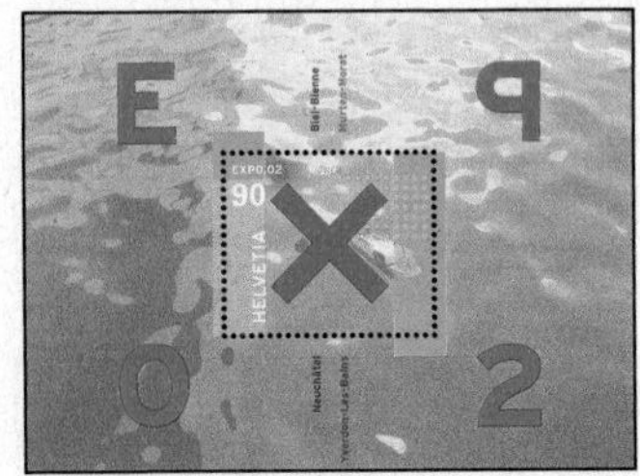

Arteplage Mobile du Jura — A517

2002, May 15 Photo. *Perf. 14*

1120 A517 90c multi 2.10 1.25

Expo.02, Switzerland.

Europa A518

2002, May 15 Litho. *Perf. 13¼*

1121 A518 70c Clown 1.60 .80
1122 A518 90c Clown, diff. 2.10 1.05

Teddy Bears, Cent. — A519

No. 1123 — Teddy bear from: a, France, 1925 (round, with tan frame, 26mm diameter). b, Switzerland, 1950s (square with cut in corners, 25x25mm). c, Germany, 1904 (oval, 23x33mm). d, Switzerland, 2002 (rectangular, 26x23mm). e, England, c. 1920 (round, with blue and red frame, 26mm diameter).

2002, May 15 *Die Cut*

Self-Adhesive

1123 A519 Booklet pane of 5 10.50
a.-e. 90c Any single 2.10 1.05
f. Booklet, 2 #1123 21.00

Cessation of Production at Swiss Post Stamp Printers A520

Litho. & Engr.

2002, Sept. 17 *Perf. 13¼*

1124 A520 70c multi 1.60 .80

Ladybug — A521

Serpentine Die Cut 12¼ Vert.

2002, Sept. 17 Litho.

Self-Adhesive

1125 A521 90c multi + label 2.10 1.05
a. Booklet pane of 10 21.00

Insects — A522

Designs: 10c, Anax imperator. 20c, Mesoacidalia aglaja. 50c, Rosalia alpina. 100c, Graphosoma lineatum.

Perf. 13¾x14¼

2002, Sept. 17 **Litho.**

1126	A522	10c multi	.25	.25
1127	A522	20c multi	.45	.25
1128	A522	50c multi	1.15	.60
1129	A522	100c multi	2.25	1.15
		Nos. 1126-1129 (4)	4.10	2.25

Minerals — A523

Designs: 200c, Quartz crystal. 500c, Titanite.

2002-05 **Litho.** ***Perf. 13¼***

1130	A523	200c multi	4.50	2.25
1131	A523	500c multi	11.50	5.75
a.		Perf. 13¾x14¼	11.50	5.75

Issued: Nos. 1130-1131, 9/17/02. No. 1131a, 5/10/05.

Switzerland's Entry Into United Nations — A524

Perf. 13¾x14¼

2002, Sept. 10 **Litho.**

1132	A524	90c multi	2.10	1.05

Stamp Day — A525

2002, Nov. 19 ***Perf. 13¾x14***

1133	A525	70c multi	1.60	.80

World Alpine Skiing Championships, St. Moritz — A526

2002, Nov. 19 ***Perf. 14x13¾***

1134	A526	90c multi	2.10	1.05

Emblem of Switzerland Tourism — A527

Serpentine Die Cut 13¼ Vert.

2002, Nov. 19 **Self-Adhesive**

1135	A527	(1.30fr) blue & multi	3.00	1.50
a.		Booklet pane of 6	18.00	
1136	A527	(1.80fr) red & multi	4.25	2.10
a.		Booklet pane of 6	25.00	

Nos. 1135-1136 were valid only on post cards sent to European (#1135) or non-European (#1136) addresses, and could not be used in combination with other stamps. No. 1135a sold for 7.20fr, and No. 1136a for 10fr.

Christmas — A528

2002, Nov. 19 **Photo.** ***Perf. 11½***

Granite Paper

1137	A528	90c multi	2.10	1.05

See No. 1197b.

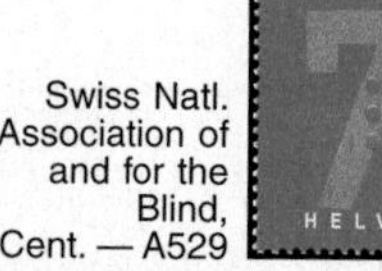

Swiss Natl. Association of and for the Blind, Cent. — A529

Litho. & Embossed

2003, Mar. 6 ***Perf. 14¾x14½***

1138	A529	70c red & carmine	1.60	.80

100th Natl. Horse Market and Show, Saignelégier — A530

2003, Mar. 6 **Litho.** ***Perf. 13¼x13½***

1139	A530	90c multi	2.10	1.05

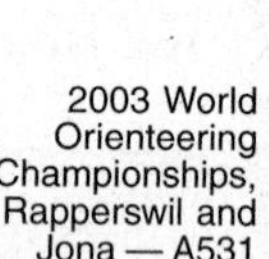

2003 World Orienteering Championships, Rapperswil and Jona — A531

2003, Mar. 6

1140	A531	90c multi	2.10	1.05

Intl. Year of Water — A532

2003, Mar. 6 ***Perf. 13x13¼***

1141	A532	90c multi	2.10	1.05

Medicinal Plants — A533

Designs: 70c, Hypericum perforatum. 90c, Vinca minor. 110c, Valeriana officinalis. 120c, Arnica montana. 130c, Centaurium minus. 180c, Malva sylvestris. 220c, Matricaria chamomilla.

2003-05 ***Perf. 14x13¾***

1142	A533	70c multi	1.60	.80
1143	A533	90c multi	2.10	1.05
1144	A533	110c multi	2.50	1.25
1145	A533	120c multi	2.75	1.40
a.		Perf. 14x14½	2.75	1.40
1146	A533	130c multi	3.00	1.50
1147	A533	180c multi	4.25	2.10
a.		Perf. 14x14½	4.25	2.10
1148	A533	220c multi	5.00	2.50
a.		Perf. 14x14½	5.00	2.50
		Nos. 1142-1148 (7)	21.20	10.60

Issued: Nos. 1142-1148, 3/6/03; Nos. 1145a, 1147a, 1148a, 2005.

Europa — A534

2003, May 8 **Litho.** ***Perf. 13¼x13***

1149	A534	90c multi	2.10	1.05

Comic Strip Art — A535

No. 1150 — Envelope and: a, Woman, birthday cake. b, Man, heart. c, Man, thunder cloud. d, Woman, musical note.

90c, Envelope, woman, duck.

2003, May 8 ***Perf. 14¾***

1150	A535	Block of 4	6.50	4.00
a.-d.		70c Any single	1.60	.80

Souvenir Sheet

1151	A535	90c multi	2.50	1.25

20th Intl. Comics Festival, Sierre.

Souvenir Sheet

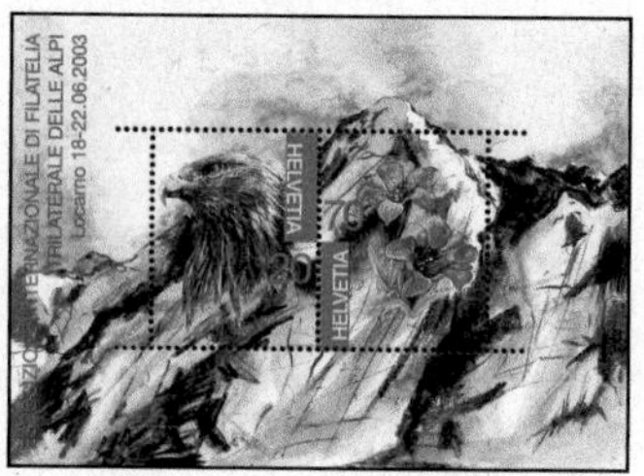

Trilateral Stamp Exhibition, Ticino — A536

2003, May 8 ***Perf. 14¾***

1152	A536	Sheet of 2	2.50	2.50
a.		20c Eagle	.45	.25
b.		70c Gentian	1.60	.80

Switzerland's Victory in 2003 America's Cup Yacht Races — A537

2003, Mar 7 **Litho.** ***Perf. 13x13¼***

1153	A537	90c multi	2.10	1.05

No. 1153 was not sent to standing order subscribers until September.

Minerals Type of 2002

Designs: 300c, Rutilated quartz. 400c, Green fluorite.

2003, Sept. 9 ***Perf. 13¾x14¼***

1154	A523	300c multi	7.00	3.50
1155	A523	400c multi	9.25	4.75

Comic Strip "Diddl," by Thomas Goletz — A538

Designs: 70c, Mice reading love letters. 90c, Mouse chasing flying envelopes.

2003, Sept. 9 ***Perf. 13¼x13½***

1156	A538	70c multi	1.60	.80
1157	A538	90c multi	2.10	1.05

See Nos. 1184-1185.

UNESCO World Heritage Sites — A539

Designs: No. 1158, Jungfrau-Aletsch-Bietschhorn. No. 1159, Three Castles, Bellinzona. No. 1160, Old City, Bern. No. 1161, Convent of St. Gall. No. 1162, Benedictine Convent of St. John, Müstair.

2003, Sept. 9 ***Perf. 12¾***

1158	A539	90c multi	2.10	1.05
1159	A539	90c multi	2.10	1.05
1160	A539	90c multi	2.10	1.05
1161	A539	90c multi	2.10	1.05
1162	A539	90c multi	2.10	1.05
		Nos. 1158-1162 (5)	10.50	5.25

Nos. 1158-1162 each issued in sheets of 6.

See NO. 1186.

Stamp Day — A540

Perf. 13¼x13½

2003, Nov. 19 **Litho.**

1163	A540	70c multi	1.60	.80

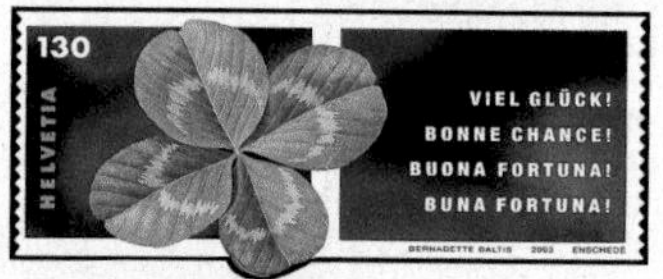

Four-leaf Clover — A541

Serpentine Die Cut 12¼ Vert.

2003, Nov. 19 **Self-Adhesive**

1164	A541	130c multi + label	3.00	1.50
a.		Booklet of 10	30.00	

Christmas — A542

Ornaments: 70c, Horseman. 90c, Santa Claus.

2003, Nov. 19 **Photo.** ***Perf. 11½***

1165	A542	70c multi	1.60	.80
1166	A542	90c multi	2.10	1.05

See Nos. 1197d-1197e.

Swiss Design — A543

Designs: 15c, Rex potato peeler, 1947, designed by Alfred Neweczeral. 50c, Zipper, 1924, designed by M.O. Winterthaler. 85c, Station clock, 1944, designed by Hanls Hilfiker. No. 1169, Le Fauteuil Grand Confort (black armchair), 1928, designed by Le Corbusier. No. 1170, Landi chair (aluminum chair), 1938, designed by Hans Coray.

Serpentine Die Cut 12

2003-04 **Self-Adhesive** **Litho.**

1167	A543	15c multi	.35	.25
a.		Booklet pane of 10	3.50	

1168 A543 85c multi 2.00 1.00
a. Booklet pane of 10 19.50
1169 A543 100c multi + etiquette 2.25 1.15
a. Booklet pane of 10 + 10 etiquettes 25.00
b. Nos. 1167-1169 on translucent paper 4.50
1170 A543 100c multi + etiquette 2.25 1.15
a. Booklet pane of 10 + 10 etiquettes 25.00

Coil Stamp

1171 A543 50c multi 1.15 .60
Nos. 1167-1171 (5) 8.00 4.15

Issued: 15c, 85c, No. 1169, 12/30; No. 1170, 3/31/04; 50c, 9/7/04.

See No. 1206.

FIFA (Fédération Internationale de Football Association), Cent. — A544

2004, Mar. 9 ***Perf. 13¼***
1172 A544 100c multi 2.25 1.15

UEFA (European Football Union), 50th Anniv. — A545

2004, Mar. 9 ***Perf. 13¼x13½***
1173 A545 130c multi 3.00 1.50

CERN (European Organization for Nuclear Research), 50th Anniv. — A546

2004, Mar. 9 ***Perf. 13½x13¼***
1174 A546 180c multi 4.25 2.10

Comic Strip "Titeuf," by Zep — A547

Titeuf: No. 1175, Giving spring flower to Nadia. No. 1176, Sitting in refrigerator. No. 1177, Running through raked leaves. No. 1178, Pointing at snowman.

2004, Mar. 9 ***Perf. 14x13½***
1175 A547 85c multi 2.00 1.00
1176 A547 85c multi 2.00 1.00
1177 A547 85c multi 2.00 1.00
1178 A547 85c multi 2.00 1.00
Nos. 1175-1178 (4) 8.00 4.00

Souvenir Sheet

Cycling — A548

No. 1179 — Cyclists and marker for: a, Route 5. b, Route 3.

2004, Mar. 9 ***Perf. 14x13½***
1179 A548 Sheet of 2 5.50 5.50
a.-b. 100c Either single 2.25 1.15

Doorbell Button — A549

2004, May 6 ***Perf. 14½x14¼***
1180 A549 85c multi 2.00 1.00

Europa A550

2004, May 6 ***Perf. 14¼x14½***
1181 A550 100c multi 2.25 1.15

2004 Summer Olympics, Athens A551

2004, May 6 ***Perf. 13x13¼***
1182 A551 100c multi 2.25 1.15

See No. 1203.

Zeppelin NT — A552

2004, May 6 ***Perf. 14x13½***
1183 A552 180c multi 4.25 2.10

Diddl Type of 2003

Designs: 85c, Diddl with teddy bear, Pimboli, and butterflies. 100c, Diddl with flower.

2004, May 6 ***Perf. 13¼x13½***
1184 A538 85c multi 2.00 1.00
1185 A538 100c multi 2.25 1.15

UNESCO World Heritage Type of 2003

Design: Monte San Giorgio.

2004, Sept. 7 ***Perf. 13¾x14¼***
1186 A539 100c multi 2.25 1.15

Issued in sheets of 6.

Suisse Balance Health Program A553

2004, Sept. 7 ***Perf. 13¼x13½***
1187 A553 85c multi 2.00 1.00

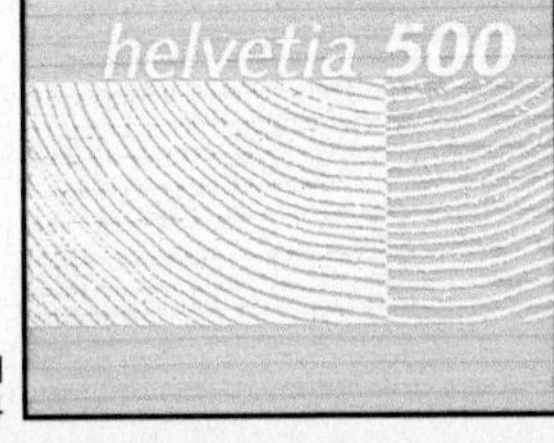

Wood A554

Silk-screened on Wood

2004, Sept. 7 ***Imperf.***

Self-Adhesive

1188 A554 500c white 11.50 5.75

Cheesemaking A555

Designs: 100c, Cheesemaker inspecting curds and whey. 130c, Cheeses, grapes and nuts.

2004, Sept. 7 Litho. ***Perf. 13¼x13½***
1189 A555 100c multi 2.25 1.15
1190 A555 130c multi 3.00 1.50

Animal Protection A556

2004, Sept. 7 ***Perf. 14x13½***
1191 A556 85c Cat 2.00 1.00
1192 A556 100c Hedgehog 2.25 1.15
1193 A556 130c Pig 3.00 1.50
Nos. 1191-1193 (3) 7.25 3.65

Nos. 1191-1193 each issued in sheets of 6.

Souvenir Sheet

Sitting Helvetia Stamps and Coins, 150th Anniv. — A557

No. 1194: a, Type A17. b, Coin.

Litho. (#1194a), Litho. & Embossed (#1194b)

Perf. 14¼x13¾ on 3 Sides

2004, Sept. 7
1194 A557 Sheet of 2 4.50 4.50
a.-b. 85c Either single 2.00 1.00

Stamp Day — A558

Perf. 13¼x13½

2004, Nov. 23 **Litho.**
1195 A558 85c multi 2.00 1.00

Sports A559

2004, Nov. 23 Litho. ***Perf. 13x13½***
1196 A559 180c multi 4.25 2.10

No. 1196 is identical to United Nations Offices in Geneva No. 433. The stamp, available for use throughout Switzerland, also served as an official stamp for the International Olympic Committee.

Christmas Ornaments Types of 2000-2003

2004, Nov. 23 Photo. ***Perf. 13x13½***
1197 Sheet of 5 12.50 12.50
a. A511 85c Snowflake 2.00 1.00
b. A528 85c Church 2.00 1.00
c. A498 100c Angel 2.25 1.15
d. A542 100c Horseman 2.25 1.00
e. A542 100c Santa Claus 2.25 1.15

Photographs by René Burri — A560

No. 1198: a, Children kissing, German inscription. b, Teenagers on bicycle, French inscription. c, Man and woman kissing, Italian inscription. d, Man and woman in bumper car, Romansch inscription.

Serpentine Die Cut 12

2005, Jan. 3 Self-Adhesive Litho.
1198 Block of 4, #a-d + 4 etiquettes 9.25
a.-d. A560 100c Any single 2.25 1.15
e. Booklet pane, 2 each #1198a-1198d + 8 etiquettes 18.50

No. 1198 lacks self-adhesive selvage, and is on a translucent paper that is rouletted on the left and right sides. No. 1198e has a white paper backing, has each stamp and its se-tenant etiquette surrounded by self-adhesive selvage, and is rouletted through the selvage and backing paper.

Swiss Federal Institute of Technology, Zurich, 150th Anniv. A561

2005, Mar. 8 ***Perf. 13***
1199 A561 85c multi 2.00 1.00

Matterhorn Superimposed Over Inverted Map of Africa — A562

2005, Mar. 8 ***Perf. 13x13¼***
1200 A562 85c multi 2.00 1.00

Discovery of rocks from Africa making up top of the Matterhorn.

Unspunnen Traditional Costume and Alpine Herdsman's Festival, Bicent. — A563

2005, Mar. 8 ***Perf. 13¼x13***
1201 A563 100c multi 2.25 1.15

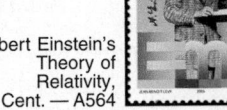

Albert Einstein's Theory of Relativity, Cent. — A564

2005, Mar. 8 ***Perf. 13½x13¼***
1202 A564 130c multi 3.00 1.50

Cartoon Mouse, by Uli Stein — A565

Mouse with: 85c, Slice of Swiss cheese in typewriter. 100c, Golf club and letter on tee.

2005, Mar. 8 ***Perf. 13¼x13½***

1203 A565 85c multi 2.00 1.00
1204 A565 100c multi 2.25 1.15

Souvenir Sheet

Geneva International Auto Show, Cent. — A566

2005, Mar. 8 ***Perf. 13¾x14¼***

1205 A566 Sheet of 2 14.50 14.50
a. 100c Front of car 2.25 1.15
b. 130c Side of car 3.00 1.50

Swiss Design Type of 2003-04

Design: Fixpencil, by Caran d'Ache.

2005, May 10 ***Serpentine Die Cut 12***
Self-Adhesive

1206 A543 220c multi + etiquette 5.00 2.50
a. Serpentine die cut 12¼x12 + etiquette 5.00 2.50
b. Booklet pane, 6 #1206, 4 #1206a + 10 etiquettes 50.00

Europa A567

2005, May 10 ***Perf. 13x13¼***

1207 A567 100c multi 2.25 1.15

Soccer for the Visually Impaired A568

2005, May 10 ***Perf. 13¾x14¼***

1208 A568 100c multi 2.25 1.15

Printed in sheets of 6.

Opening of Paul Klee Center, Bern — A569

2005, May 10 ***Perf. 13¼x14***

1209 A569 100c multi 2.25 1.15

Printed in sheets of 6.

Stylized Butterflies A570

Serpentine Die Cut 11¾

2005, May 10 **Self-Adhesive**

1210 A570 100c multi 2.25 1.15
a. Booklet pane of 10 + 10 labels 25.00

Felix the Bunny, by Annette Langen A571

Felix and: 85c, Lambs, cows. 100c, Swans and Chillon Castle.

2005, May 10 ***Perf. 13x13¼***

1211 A571 85c multi 2.00 1.00
1212 A571 100c multi 2.25 1.15

Subtractive Color Combinations — A572

Additive Color Combinations — A573

Serpentine Die Cut 12½

2005, Sept. 6 **Litho.**
Self-Adhesive

1213 A572 50c multi 1.15 .60
1214 A573 100c multi 2.25 1.15

Swiss Timepieces A574

Designs: 100c, Watchmaker, pocket watch and mechanism. 130c, Woman, wristwatches.

2005, Sept. 6 ***Perf. 13¼x13½***

1215 A574 100c multi 2.25 1.15
1216 A574 130c multi 3.00 1.50

Cell Phone Pictures — A575

Images: 85c, On Horseback, by Brigit Rohrbach. 100c, Mountain Hike, by Peter Schumacher. 130c, On Top of the World, by Rémy Sager. 180c, Tracks in the Snow, by Debora Ronchi.

2005, Sept. 6 ***Perf. 14¼x14***

1217 A575 85c multi 2.00 1.00
1218 A575 100c multi 2.25 1.15
1219 A575 130c multi 3.00 1.50
1220 A575 180c multi 4.25 2.10
Nos. 1217-1220 (4) 11.50 5.75

Souvenir Sheet

Friends of Nature Switzerland, Cent. — A576

2005, Sept. 6 ***Perf. 13½***

1221 A576 Sheet of 4 11.50 11.50
a. 85c Skiers 2.00 1.40
b. 100c Chalet, vert. 2.25 1.60
c. 110c People fording stream 2.50 1.75
d. 130c Mountain climber, vert. 3.00 2.10

Stamp Day — A577

Perf. 13¼x13½

2005, Nov. 22 **Litho.**

1222 A577 85c multi 2.00 1.00

2006 Winter Olympics, Turin, Italy — A578

2005, Nov. 22 ***Perf. 13¾***

1223 A578 100c Curling 2.25 1.15

Issued in sheets of 6. See No. 1204.

Swiss Papal Guards, 500th Anniv. A579

Designs: 85c, Guard and drummers. 100c, Guards and St. Peter's Basilica.

2005, Nov. 22 ***Perf. 14x14¼***

1224 A579 85c multi 2.00 1.00
1225 A579 100c multi 2.25 1.15

Nos. 1224-1225 each issued in sheets of 6. See Vatican City Nos. 1315-1316.

Christmas — A580

Designs: 85c, Crozier and miter. 100c, Gingerbread man.

2005, Nov. 22 ***Perf. 13½x13¼***

1226 A580 85c multi 2.00 1.00
1227 A580 100c multi 2.25 1.15

Reintroduction of Alpine Ibex in Switzerland, Cent. — A581

2006, Mar. 7 **Litho.** ***Perf. 13¼x13***

1228 A581 85c multi 2.00 1.00

Youth Soccer — A582

2006, Mar. 7 ***Perf. 13¼x13½***

1229 A582 85c multi 2.00 1.00

Cuculus Canorus A583

Serpentine Die Cut 12

2006, Mar. 7 **Photo.**
Self-Adhesive

1230 A583 240c multi + etiquette 5.50 2.75
a. Block of 10 + 10 etiquettes 55.00

No. 1230a is on a backing paper with bar codes on the reverse.
See Nos. 1273-1276, 1306-1308, 1341-1342.

Railroad Anniversaries A584

Designs: 85c, Simplon Tunnel, cent. 100c, Bern-Lötschberg-Simplon Railway, cent.

2006, Mar. 7 **Litho.** ***Perf. 14x13¾***

1231 A584 85c multi 2.00 1.00
1232 A584 100c multi 2.25 1.15

Art Nouveau Exhibition, La Chaux-de-Fonds — A585

Designs: 100c, "Fir." 180c, "Petal."

2006, Mar. 7

1233 A585 100c multi 2.25 1.15
1234 A585 180c multi 4.25 2.10

Post Buses, Cent. — A586

Various post buses and passengers.

Serpentine Die Cut 10¾x11

2006, Mar. 7 **Self-Adhesive** **Litho.**

1235 A586 85c blue & multi 2.00 1.00
a. Block of 4 on backing paper 7.75

1236 A586 100c red & multi 2.25 1.15
a. Block of 4 on backing paper 9.25
1237 A586 130c grn & multi 3.00 1.50
a. Block of 4 on backing paper 12.00
b. Block of 3, #1235-1237 on backing paper 7.25
Nos. 1235-1237 (3) 7.25 3.65

Nos. 1235-1237 each were issued in sheets of 20. Stamps are adjacent on Nos. 1235a-1237a and on a shiny, but opaque backing paper.

Kasperli, Children's Theater Puppet — A587

2006, May 9 Litho. *Perf. 14x13¾*
1238 A587 85c multi 2.00 1.00

Europa A588

2006, May 9 *Perf. 13x13¼*
1239 A588 100c multi 2.25 1.15

Mountains — A589

No. 1240: a, Eiger (35x36mm). b, Monch (30x36mm). c, Jungfrau (39x36mm).

2006, May 9 *Perf. 13¼x13½*
1240 A589 Horiz. strip of 3 6.00 6.00
a.-c. 85c Any single 2.00 1.00

Caricatures of Cows by Patrice Killoffer — A590

Cow: 85c, On back. 100c, In water. 130c, Seated. 180c, In snow.

2006, May 9 *Perf. 14x14¼*
1241 A590 85c multi 2.00 1.00
1242 A590 100c multi 2.25 1.15
1243 A590 130c multi 3.00 1.50
1244 A590 180c multi 4.25 2.10
Nos. 1241-1244 (4) 11.50 5.75

First Session of United Nations Human Rights Council — A591

Perf. 13¾x14¼
2006, June 19 Litho.
1245 A591 100c multi 2.25 1.15

Dimitri the Clown — A592

2006, Sept. 7 *Perf. 13¼x13*
1246 A592 100c multi 2.25 1.15

Victorinox Swiss Army Knives — A593

Designs: 100c, First model, 1897, khaki pants. 130c, Modern model, blue jeans.

2006, Sept. 7 *Perf. 14x13¾*
1247 A593 100c multi 2.25 1.15
1248 A593 130c multi 3.00 1.50

Cocolino the Cooking Cat, by Oskar Weiss — A594

Serpentine Die Cut 10¾x11
2006, Sept. 7 Self-Adhesive
1249 A594 85c multi 2.00 1.00
a. Booklet pane of 10 19.50

Fruit — A595

Designs: 200c, Gelterkinder cherries. 300c, Spätlauber apple. 400c, Hauszwetschge plums.

2006 Photo. *Serpentine Die Cut 12*
Self-Adhesive
1250 A595 200c multi 4.60 2.25
1251 A595 300c multi 6.90 3.50
a. Pair, #1250-1251 on backing paper 13.80
1252 A595 400c multi 9.20 4.75
Nos. 1250-1252 (3) 20.70 10.50

Issued: 200c, 300c, 9/7; 400c, 11/21.Nos. 1250-1252 each were printed in sheets of 50. See also No. 1314.

Town of Olten, Boy Wearing Train Conductor's Hat — A596

Perf. 13½x13¼
2006, Nov. 21 Litho.
1253 A596 85c multi 2.00 1.00

Stamp Day.

Christmas — A597

Designs: 85c, Star singers. 100c, Advent wreath.

2006, Nov. 21
1254 A597 85c multi 2.00 1.00
1255 A597 100c multi 2.25 1.15

Women's Soccer — A598

2007, Mar. 6 Litho. *Perf. 13¼x13½*
1256 A598 85c multi 2.00 1.00

Printed in sheets of 6.

Leonhard Euler (1707-83), Mathematician A599

2007, Mar. 6
1257 A599 130c multi 3.00 1.50

Stein am Rhein, 1000th Anniv. — A600

No. 1258: a, Town Hall (28x36mm). b, Houses on Town Hall Square (40x36mm). c, Municipal Fountain (34x36mm).

2007, Mar. 6 *Perf. 13¾x13½*
1258 A600 Horiz. strip of 3 6.00 6.00
a.-c. 85c Any single 2.00 1.00

Legends A601

Designs: 85c, Charlemagne and the Snake. 100c, Fenetta, the Island Maiden. 130c, The Judge of Bellinzona. 180c, Margaretha.

2007, Mar. 6 *Perf. 13½x14*
1259 A601 85c multi 2.00 1.00
1260 A601 100c multi 2.25 1.15
1261 A601 130c multi 3.00 1.50
1262 A601 180c multi 4.25 2.10
Nos. 1259-1262 (4) 11.50 5.75

Swiss Club for Bernese Mountain Dogs, Cent. — A602

Serpentine Die Cut 11x10¾
2007, Mar. 6 Self-Adhesive
1263 A602 85c multi 2.00 1.00
a. Block of 4 on backing paper 8.00

No. 1263 was issued in sheets of 20.

Swiss National Bank, Cent. — A603

Designs: 85c, Banknote security devices. 100c, Artwork from 100-franc banknote.

2007, Mar. 6 Self-Adhesive Litho.
1264 A603 85c multi 2.00 1.00
a. Block of 4 on backing paper 8.00
1265 A603 100c multi 2.25 1.15
a. Horiz. pair, #1264-1265 4.25
b. Block of 4 on backing paper 9.25

Nos. 1264-1265 each were printed in sheets of 12.

Roger Federer, Tennis Player — A604

2007, Apr. 10 *Perf. 13¾x14¼*
1266 A604 100c multi 2.25 1.15

Swiss Assoc. of Day Care Centers, Cent. — A605

2007, Apr. 27 *Perf. 13½x13¾*
1267 A605 85c multi 2.00 1.00

Europa — A606

2007, Apr. 27 *Perf. 14*
1268 A606 100c multi 2.25 1.15

Scouting, cent. Printed in sheets of 18 + 12 labels.

Art Brut Movement — A607

Designs: 100c, Saint Adolf-Throne-Rock Face-Flower, by Adolf Wölfli. 180c, Untitled work by Carlo Zinelli.

2007, Apr. 27 *Perf. 14¼x14*
1269 A607 100c multi 2.25 1.15
1270 A607 180c multi 4.25 2.10

Museum of Communications, Cent. — A608

People with: 85c, Lake in background. 100c, Building in background.

Litho. With Three-Dimensional Plastic Affixed
Serpentine Die Cut 10½
2007, Apr. 27 Self-Adhesive
1271 A608 85c multi 2.00 1.00
1272 A608 100c multi 2.25 1.15

Bird Type of 2006

Designs: 85c, Fringilla coelebs. 100c, Parus major. 110c, Tichodroma muraria. 180c, Aegolius funereus.

Serpentine Die Cut 12
2007, Sept. 6 Photo.
Self-Adhesive
1273 A583 85c multi 2.00 1.00
a. Booklet pane of 10 20.00

1274 A583 100c multi + etiquette 2.25 1.15
a. Booklet pane of 10 + 10 etiquettes 24.00
1275 A583 110c multi 2.50 1.25
1276 A583 180c multi 4.25 2.10
a. Block of 4, #1273-1276, + 2 etiquettes on backing paper 11.00
Nos. 1273-1276 (4) 11.00 5.50

No. 1276 was printed with and without an etiquette.

The Dance, by Nina Corti — A609

2007, Sept. 6 Litho. *Perf. 14¼x14*
1277 A609 85c multi 2.00 1.00

Illustration for Children's Book "Schnellen-Ursli," by Alois Carigiet — A610

Serpentine Die Cut 10½x11
2007, Sept. 6 Self-Adhesive
1278 A610 85c multi 2.00 1.00
a. Booklet pane of 10 20.00

Congratulations A611

Designs: 85c, Children and hearts. 100c, Boy and stars. 130c, Woman and starbursts.

2007, Sept. 6 Litho.
Self-Adhesive
1279 A611 85c multi 2.00 1.00
1280 A611 100c multi 2.25 1.15
1281 A611 130c multi 3.00 1.50
a. Block of 3, #1279-1281, on backing paper 7.25
Nos. 1279-1281 (3) 7.25 3.65

Swiss Settings in British Literature A612

Designs: 85c, Mönch, from *Frankenstein,* by Mary Shelley. 100c, Staubbach Falls, from "At Staubbach Falls," by William Wordsworth, vert. 130c, Lake Leman, from "The Prisoner of Chillon," by Lord Byron, vert. 180c, Reichenbach Waterfall, from *The Final Problem,* by Sir Arthur Conan Doyle.

Litho. With Foil Application
Perf. 13¼x13½, 13½x13¼
2007, Sept. 6
1282 A612 85c black & silver 2.00 1.00
1283 A612 100c black & silver 2.25 1.15
1284 A612 130c black & silver 3.00 1.50
1285 A612 180c black & silver 4.25 2.10
Nos. 1282-1285 (4) 11.50 5.75

Skiers and Swiss Post BeeTagg — A613

Serpentine Die Cut 10¾x10½
2007, Oct. 31 Litho.
Self-Adhesive
1286 A613 100c multi 2.25 1.15

The BeeTagg design can be read by camera phones to connect the phones to client websites.

Souvenir Sheet

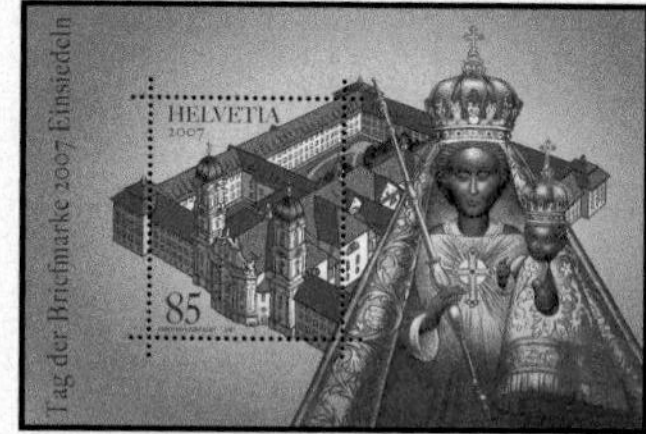

Einsiedeln Abbey — A614

2007, Nov. 20 *Perf. 13¼x14*
1287 A614 85c multi 2.00 1.50

Paper Cuttings A615

Paper cuttings: 85c, Heart, by Christian Schwizgebel. 100c, Spring, by Pia Arm. 130c, Family Trip, by Christiane and Jacqueline Saugy. 180c, Minuet, by Verena Kühni.

Serpentine Die Cut 10¾
2007, Nov. 20 Self-Adhesive
1288 A615 85c red & black 2.00 1.00
a. Block of 4 #1288 on backing paper 8.00
1289 A615 100c green & black 2.25 1.15
a. Block of 4 #1289 on backing paper 9.25
1290 A615 130c blue & black 3.00 1.50
a. Block of 4 #1290 on backing paper 12.00
1291 A615 180c org & black 4.25 2.10
a. Block of 4 #1291 on backing paper 17.00
b. Block of 4, #1288-1291 on backing paper 11.50
Nos. 1288-1291 (4) 11.50 5.75

Christmas — A616

Designs: 85c, Berne Christmas Fair. 100c, Christmas tree. 130c, Gifts.

2007, Nov. 20 *Perf. 13½x13¼*
1292 A616 85c multi 2.00 1.00
1293 A616 100c multi 2.25 1.15
1294 A616 130c multi 3.00 1.50
Nos. 1292-1294 (3) 7.25 3.65

Intl. Year of the Potato — A617

2008, Mar. 4 Litho.
1295 A617 85c multi 2.00 1.00

Albrecht von Haller (1708-77), Physiologist A618

2008, Mar. 4 *Perf. 13¼x13½*
1296 A618 85c multi 2.00 1.00

The Little Polar Bear, by Hans de Beer — A619

Serpentine Die Cut 10½x11
2008, Mar. 4 Self-Adhesive
1297 A619 85c multi 2.00 1.00
a. Booklet pane of 10 20.00

Euro 2008 Soccer Championships, Austria and Switzerland — A620

Serpentine Die Cut 12x12¼
2008, Mar. 4 Photo.
Self-Adhesive
1298 A620 100c green & black 2.25 1.15

Printed in sheets of 10.

Men's Soccer — A621

2008, Mar. 4 Litho. *Perf. 13¾x14¼*
1299 A621 100c multi 2.25 1.15

Printed in sheets of 6.

Ice Hockey in Switzerland, Cent. — A622

2008, Mar. 4 *Perf. 13x13¼*
1300 A622 100c multi 2.25 1.15

Horse Foundation, 50th Anniv. — A623

No. 1301 — Horses and: a, Sun (35x37mm). b, Path and fence (38x37mm). c, Building (31x37mm)

2008, Mar. 4 *Perf. 13½*
1301 A623 Horiz. strip of 3 6.00 6.00
a.-c. 85c Any single 2.00 1.00

Musical Instruments A624

Designs: 85c, Violin. 100c, Swiss accordion. 130c, Electric guitar. 180c, Saxophone.

2008, Mar. 4 Litho. *Perf. 13x14*
1302 A624 85c multi 2.00 1.00
1303 A624 100c multi 2.25 1.15
1304 A624 130c multi 3.00 1.50
1305 A624 180c multi 4.25 2.10
Nos. 1302-1305 (4) 11.50 5.75

Birds Type of 2006

Designs: 120c, Picus canus. 130c, Monticola saxatilis. 220c, Podiceps cristatus.

Serpentine Die Cut 12
2008, May 8 Photo.
Self-Adhesive
1306 A583 120c multi 2.75 1.40
1307 A583 130c multi 3.00 1.50
1308 A583 220c multi + etiquette 5.00 2.50
a. Block of 3, #1306-1308, on backing paper 11.00
Nos. 1306-1308 (3) 10.75 5.40

No. 1307 was printed with and without etiquette.

UEFA Euro 2008 Soccer Championships, Austria and Switzerland A625

Serpentine Die Cut 10½x11
2008, May 8 Litho.
Self-Adhesive
1309 A625 85c multi 2.00 1.00

No. 1309 was printed in sheets of 10 with a rouletted and slit backing paper. Single stamps also were available on an unslit translucent backing paper.

Swiss Lifesaving Society, 75th Anniv. — A626

2008, May 8 *Perf. 13¼x13½*
1310 A626 100c multi 2.25 1.15

2008 Summer Olympics, Beijing — A627

2008, May 8 *Perf. 14x14¼*
1311 A627 100c Mountain biking 2.25 1.15

See No. 1205.

Europa
A628

2008, May 8 ***Perf. 13x13¼***
1312 A628 100c multi 2.25 1.15

24th Universal Postal Congress, Geneva — A629

2008, July 23 ***Perf. 14x13***
1313 A629 130c multi 3.00 1.50

Fruit Type of 2006

Serpentine Die Cut 12

2008, Sept. 4 **Photo.**

Self-Adhesive

1314 A595 500c Catillac pear 11.50 5.75

No. 1314 was printed in sheets of 50. Single stamps also were available on a translucent paper.

Grains — A630

2008, Sept. 4 ***Serpentine Die Cut 12***

Self-Adhesive

1315 A630 10c Wheat	.25	.25
1316 A630 15c Barley	.35	.25
1317 A630 20c Rye	.45	.25
1318 A630 50c Oats	1.15	.60
a. Block of 4, #1315-1318 on backing paper	2.25	
Nos. 1315-1318 (4)	2.20	1.35

Nos. 1315-1318 were each printed in sheets of 50.

Old Rhine Bridge, Bad Sackingen, Germany - Stein, Switzerland — A631

2008, Sept. 4 **Litho.** ***Perf. 14***
1319 A631 100c multi 2.25 1.15

Printed in sheets of 10. See Germany No. 2503.

Drawing by Film Maker Fredi M. Murer A632

2008, Sept. 4 ***Perf. 13x13¼***
1320 A632 100c multi 2.25 1.15

Swiss Products A633

Designs: 85c, Swiss cheese. 100c, Chocolate. 130c, Clock. 180c, Swiss Army knife tools.

2008, Sept. 4 ***Perf. 13¾x13***

1321 A633 85c multi	2.00	1.50
1322 A633 100c multi	2.25	1.75
1323 A633 130c multi	3.00	2.25
1324 A633 180c multi	4.25	3.25
Nos. 1321-1324 (4)	11.50	8.75

Red Square, by Max Bill (1908-94) — A634

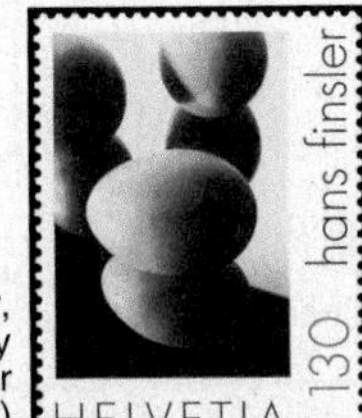

Eggs in a Mirror, Photograph by Hans Finsler (1891-1972) A635

2008, Nov. 21 **Litho.** ***Perf. 13½***
1325 A634 100c black & red 2.25 1.75
1326 A635 130c black & red 3.00 2.25

Souvenir Sheet

Stamp Day — A636

2008, Nov. 21 ***Perf. 14x13¼***
1327 A636 85c multi 2.00 1.50

Christmas — A637

Silver star and: 85c, Christmas ornament. 100c, Gold star. 130c, Bell.

Litho. With Foil Application

2008, Nov. 21 ***Perf. 13½x13¼***

1328 A637 85c multi	2.00	1.50
1329 A637 100c multi	2.25	1.75
1330 A637 130c multi	3.00	2.25
Nos. 1328-1330 (3)	7.25	5.50

European Brown Bear — A638

2009, Mar. 5 **Litho.**
1331 A638 85c multi 2.00 1.50

Pro Natura, Cent.

Hans Ulrich Grubenmann (1709-83), Architect, and Rhine Bridge, Schaffhausen A639

2009, Mar. 5 ***Perf. 13¼x13½***
1332 A639 85c multi 2.00 1.50

2009 Intl. Ice Hockey Federation World Championships, Bern and Zurich — A640

2009, Mar. 5 ***Perf. 13¾x14¼***

Self-Adhesive

1333 A640 100c multi 2.25 1.75

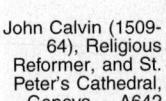

Morteratsch Glacier and Lines Showing Glacier's Retreat A641

Litho. & Silk-screened

2009, Mar. 5 ***Perf. 14***
1334 A641 100c multi 2.25 1.75

John Calvin (1509-64), Religious Reformer, and St. Peter's Cathedral, Geneva — A642

2009, Mar. 5 **Litho.** ***Perf. 13½x13¼***
1335 A642 100c multi 2.25 1.75

Hans Erni, 100th Birthday — A643

Paintings by Erni: 100c, The Human Mind. 130c, Human Hands.

2009, Mar. 5 ***Perf. 14¼x13¾***
1336 A643 100c multi 2.25 1.75
1337 A643 130c multi 3.00 2.25

Swiss Museum of Transport, 50th Anniv. A644

Designs: 85c, Steamship Rigi. 100c, Dufaux race car. 130c, Lockheed Orion 9C Special.

2009, Mar. 5 ***Perf. 13x13½***

1338 A644 85c multi	2.00	1.50
1339 A644 100c multi	2.25	1.75
1340 A644 130c multi	3.00	2.25
Nos. 1338-1340 (3)	7.25	5.50

Birds Type of 2006

Designs: 140c, Alectoris graeca. 190c, Milvus milvus.

Serpentine Die Cut 12¼x12

2009, May 8 **Self-Adhesive**

1341 A583 140c multi + etiquette	3.25	2.40
1342 A583 190c multi + etiquette	4.50	3.50
a. Pair, #1341-1342 + 2 etiquettes on backing paper	7.75	

European Wildcat — A645

2009. May 8 ***Perf. 13¾x14¼***
1343 A645 85c multi 2.00 1.50

Type Slug and "@" Symbol on Printed Page — A646

2009, May 8 ***Perf. 14x13***
1344 A646 100c multi 2.25 1.75

Graphics industry in Switzerland, 550th anniv.

See Luxembourg No. 1283.

Location of Helvetia Asteroid — A647

2009, May 8 ***Perf. 12¾x13½***
1345 A647 100c multi 2.25 1.75

Europa.

Contemporary Architecture A648

Designs: 100c, Stiva da Morts, Vrin, by Gion A. Caminada. 180c, Pentorama Community Center, Amriswil, by Müller/Sigrist Architects.

2009, May 8 ***Perf. 14x13***
1346 A648 100c multi 2.25 1.75
1347 A648 180c multi 4.25 3.25

Trees — A649

2009, May 8 ***Perf. 13½***

Self-Adhesive

1348 A649 85c Birch	2.00	1.50
1349 A649 100c Oak	2.25	1.75
1350 A649 130c Willow	3.00	2.25
Nos. 1348-1350 (3)	7.25	5.50

Princess Lillifee, by Monika Finsterbusch A650

Litho. & Silk-screened
2009, Sept. 3 ***Serpentine Die Cut 12***
Self-Adhesive

1351 A650 85c multi 2.00 1.50
a. Booklet pane of 10 20.00

Swiss Stamp Dealers Association, Cent. — A651

2009, Sept. 3 Litho. ***Perf. 13¼x13½***
1352 A651 100c multi 2.25 1.75

Printed in sheets of 12 + 8 labels.

Geneva Conventions, 60th Anniv. — A652

2009, Sept. 3 ***Perf. 14x13***
1353 A652 100c multi 2.25 1.75

Wedding A653

Anniversary A654

Birth — A655

2009, Sept. 3 ***Perf. 13¾x14¼***
Self-Adhesive

1354 A653 100c multi 2.25 1.75
1355 A654 100c multi 2.25 1.75
1356 A655 100c multi 2.25 1.75
Nos. 1354-1356 (3) 6.75 5.25

Red Flowers With White Crosses A656

Various red flowers with white crosses and German text.

2009, Sept. 3 ***Perf. 14x13, 13x14***
1357 A656 85c multi 2.00 1.50
1358 A656 100c multi, vert. 2.25 1.75
1359 A656 130c multi, vert. 3.00 2.25
1360 A656 180c multi 4.25 3.25
Nos. 1357-1360 (4) 11.50 8.75

Movement of Livestock to New Pastures — A657

No. 1361: a, Sheep and cattle (38x36mm). b, Cattle (32x36mm). c, Cow and horse (34x36mm).

2009, Sept. 3 ***Perf. 13¼x13½***
1361 A657 Horiz. strip of 3 6.00 6.00
a.-c. 85c Any single 2.00 1.50

2010 Paralympics, Vancouver A658

2009, Nov. 20 ***Perf. 13½***
1362 A658 130c multi 3.00 2.25

2010 Winter Olympics, Vancouver — A658a

Perf. 13¼x13½
2009, Nov. 20 Litho.
1362A A658a 100c multi 2.25 2.00

Souvenir Sheet

Gruyères Castle and Crane — A659

2009, Nov. 20 ***Perf. 14x13¼***
1363 A659 85c multi 2.40 2.40

Stamp Day.

Christmas — A660

Star and: 85c, Cap of Santa Claus. 100c, Christmas tree. 130c, Gift box.

Litho. With Hologram
2009, Nov. 20 ***Perf. 13½x13¼***
1364 A660 85c multi 2.00 1.50
1365 A660 100c multi 2.25 1.75
1366 A660 130c multi 3.00 2.25
Nos. 1364-1366 (3) 7.25 5.50

Basel Carnival Committee, Cent. — A661

No. 1367: a, Four marchers, two carrying parade lantern and sign, Spalentor in background (30x36mm). b, Fifer, drum major, drummer, wagon, Town Hall in background (43x36mm). c, Four musicians, Münster Cathedral in background (30x36mm).

2010, Jan. 12 Litho. ***Perf. 13¾x13½***
1367 A661 Horiz. strip of 3 7.00 7.00
a.-c. 100c Any single 2.25 1.75

University of Basel, 550th Anniv. — A662

2010, Mar. 4 ***Perf. 14x13***
1368 A662 85c multi 2.00 1.50

Intl. Year of Biodiversity A663

2010, Mar. 4 ***Perf. 14¼x13¾***
Self-Adhesive

1369 A663 85c multi 2.00 1.50

Swiss Cancer League, Cent. — A664

2010, Mar. 4 ***Perf. 14x13***
1370 A664 100c multi 2.25 1.75

Powered Flight in Switzerland, Cent. — A665

Designs: 85c, Ernest Failloubaz, first holder of pilot's license, and Grandjean monoplane. 100c, Airbus A340 and Zurich Airport. 130c, Jorge "Géo" Chavez, first man to fly across the Alps, and Blériot XI monoplane. 180c, Sport airplane, glider and hot-air balloons.

2010, Mar. 4 ***Perf. 13¼x13¾***
1371 A665 85c multi 2.00 1.50
1372 A665 100c multi 2.25 1.75
1373 A665 130c multi 3.00 2.25
1374 A665 180c multi 4.25 3.25
Nos. 1371-1374 (4) 11.50 8.75

2010 Federal Marksmen's Festival, Aarau — A666

2010 Federal Drumming and Piping Festival, Interlaken A667

Swiss Yodeling Association, Cent. — A668

2010 Federal Costume Festival, Schwyz A669

2010, Mar. 4 Litho. ***Perf. 13¾x14¼***
1375 A666 100c multi 2.25 1.75

Litho. & Embossed With Foil Application

1376 A667 100c multi 2.25 1.75

Litho. & Embossed

1377 A668 100c multi 2.25 1.75
1378 A669 100c multi 2.25 1.75
Nos. 1375-1378 (4) 9.00 7.00

No. 1375 has a hole drilled into target in vignette.

Johann Peter Hebel (1760-1826), Poet — A670

2010, May 6 Litho. ***Perf. 13¼x13½***
1379 A670 85c multi 2.00 1.50

School Boy with Slate, by Albert Anker (1831-1910) A671

2010, May 6 ***Perf. 13½x13***
1380 A671 85c multi 2.00 1.50

Heidi and Goats — A672

2010, May 6 ***Perf. 13¼x13***
1381 A672 100c multi 2.25 1.75

Europa.

Kunsthaus Zurich, Cent. A673

2010, May 6 ***Perf. 13¼x13½***
Self-Adhesive

1382 A673 100c multi 2.25 1.75

Swiss Public Welfare Society, Bicent. — A674

2010, May 6 ***Perf. 13½x13¼***
1383 A674 100c multi 2.25 1.75

Circus World Geneva 2010 Circus Festival — A675

2010, May 6

1384 A675 140c multi 3.25 2.40

Railway Centenaries A676

Designs: 85c, Niesen Funicular. 100c, Bernina Railway, horiz.

2010, May 6 ***Perf. 14¼x13¾***

1385 A676 85c multi 2.00 1.50

Perf. 13¾x14¼

1386 A676 100c multi 2.25 1.75

Jimmy Flitz, Character From Children's Book by Roland Zoss — A677

Serpentine Die Cut 12

2010, Sept. 3 **Litho.**

Self-Adhesive

1387 A677 85c multi 1.75 1.35
a. Booklet pane of 10 17.50

Jeanne Hersch (1910-2000), Philosopher A678

2010, Sept. 3 ***Perf. 13¼x13½***

1388 A678 100c multi 2.00 1.50

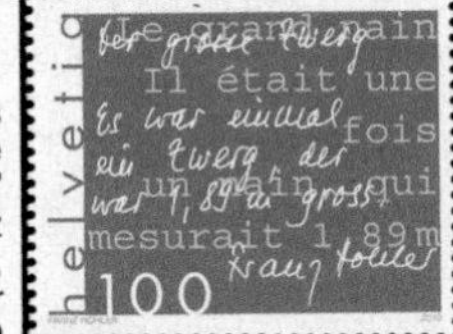

Words From "The Big Dwarf," by Franz Hohler, Writer A679

2010, Sept. 3 ***Perf. 13x13¼***

1389 A679 100c green & black 2.00 1.50

European Free Trade Association, 50th Anniv. — A680

2010, Sept. 3 ***Perf. 14x13¾***

1390 A680 140c yellow & black 2.75 2.10

Gustave Moynier (1826-1910) and Henri Dunant (1828-1910), Founders of Intl. Red Cross — A681

2010, Sept. 3 ***Perf. 13¼x13½***

1391 A681 190c multi 3.75 3.00

Composers A682

Designs: 100c, Rolf Liebermann (1910-99). 140c, Heinrich Sutermeister (1910-95).

2010, Sept. 3 ***Perf. 13x13¼***

1392 A682 100c lilac & black 2.00 1.50
1393 A682 140c ol brn & blk 2.75 2.10

Prehistoric Animals A683

Designs: 85c, Theropod. 100c, Ichthyosaur. 140c, Pterosaur.

2010, Sept. 3 ***Perf. 13¼x13½***

1394 A683 85c multi 1.75 1.35
1395 A683 100c multi 2.00 1.50
1396 A683 140c multi 2.75 2.10
Nos. 1394-1396 (3) 6.50 4.95

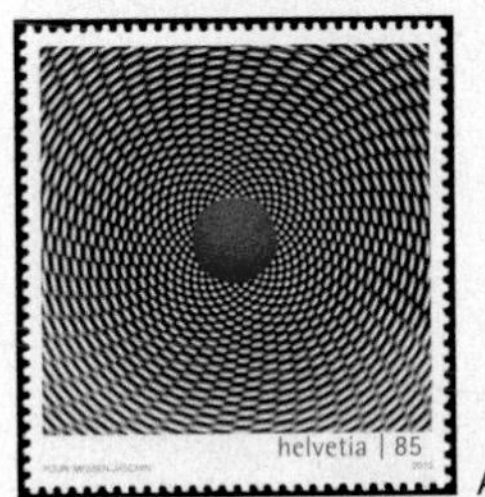

A684

A685

Optical Art by Youri Messen-Jaschin — A686

2010, Sept. 3 ***Perf. 14x13¼***

Self-Adhesive

1397 A684 85c multi 1.75 1.35
1398 A685 100c multi 2.00 1.50
1399 A686 140c black & red 2.75 2.10
Nos. 1397-1399 (3) 6.50 4.95

Souvenir Sheet

Zähringer Fountain, Bern — A687

2010, Nov. 4 ***Perf. 14x13¼***

1400 A687 85c multi 1.75 1.35

Stamp Day.

Handicrafts A688

Designs: 200c, Bobbin lacemaking. 300c, Wood carving.

2010, Nov. 4 ***Serpentine Die Cut 12***

Self-Adhesive

1401 A688 200c multi 4.25 3.25
1402 A688 300c multi 6.25 4.75
a. Pair, #1401-1402 10.50

Nos. 1401-1402 also were printed in sheets of 10. See Nos. 1418-1419.

Christmas — A689

Designs: 85c, Star, candle, conifer sprigs. 100c, Snowflake. 140c, Star, angel.

Litho. With Hologram

2010, Nov. 4 ***Perf. 13½x13¼***

1403 A689 85c multi 1.75 1.35
1404 A689 100c multi 2.10 1.60
1405 A689 140c multi 3.00 2.25
Nos. 1403-1405 (3) 6.85 5.20

Pettersson and Findus, Children's Book Characters by Sven Nordqvist A690

Serpentine Die Cut 12

2011, Mar. 3 **Self-Adhesive** **Litho.**

1406 A690 85c multi 1.90 1.45
a. Booklet pane of 10 19.00

Honeybee and Flower A691

2011, Mar. 3 ***Perf. 11¾***

1407 A691 85c multi 1.90 1.45

Cerebral Foundation, 50th Anniv. — A692

2011, Mar. 3 ***Perf. 13¼x13½***

1408 A692 85c multi 1.90 1.45

14th World Gymnaestrada, Lausanne A693

2011, Mar. 3

1409 A693 85c multi 1.90 1.45

Neuchatel, 1000th Anniv. — A694

2011, Mar. 3

1410 A694 100c multi 2.25 1.75

Worldwide Fund for Nature (WWF), 50th Anniv. — A695

2011, Mar. 3

1411 A695 100c multi 2.25 1.75

Max Frisch (1911-91), Playwright & Novelist — A696

2011, Mar. 3

1412 A696 100c gray & black 2.25 1.75

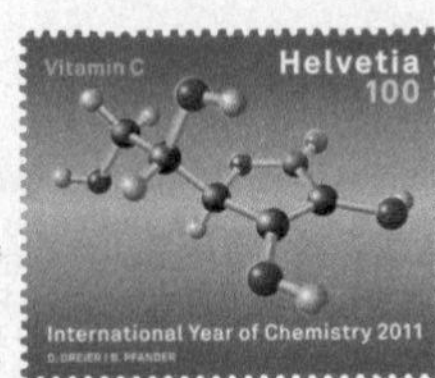

Model of Vitamin C Molecule A697

Litho. & Embossed

2011, Mar. 3 ***Perf. 13x13¼***

1413 A697 100c multi 2.25 1.75

Intl. Year of Chemistry.

Flowers — A698

Designs: 85c, Cucurbita pepo. 100c, Pisum sativum. 110c, Allium ursinum. 260c, Cynara scolymus.

Serpentine Die Cut 12

2011, Mar. 3 Self-Adhesive Litho.

1414	A698 85c multi		1.90	1.45
a.	Booklet pane of 10		19.00	
1415	A698 100c multi + etiquette		2.25	1.75
a.	Booklet pane of 10 + 10 etiquettes		22.50	
1416	A698 110c multi		2.40	1.75
1417	A698 260c multi		5.75	4.50
a.	Block of 4, #1414-1417		12.50	
	Nos. 1414-1417 (4)		12.30	9.45

Nos. 1414-1415 also were printed in sheets of 50. Nos. 1416-1417 also were printed in sheets of 10. See Nos. 1440-1442, 1481-1482.

Handicrafts Type of 2010

Designs: 400c, Potter shaping pot on wheel. 500c, Blacksmith hammering work on anvil.

Serpentine Die Cut 12

2011, May 5 Self-Adhesive Litho.

1418	A688 400c multi	9.25	7.00
1419	A688 500c multi	11.50	8.75
a.	Pair, #1418-1419	21.00	

Nos. 1418-1419 also were printed in sheets of 10.

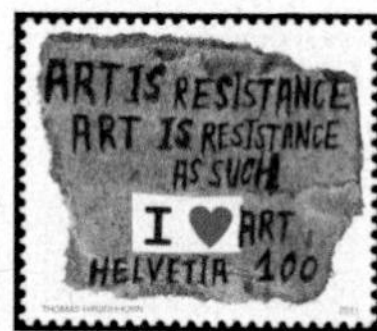

Art Is Resistance, by Thomas Hirschhorn A699

2011, May 5 *Perf. 13¾x14¼*

1420	A699 100c multi	2.40	1.75

Venice Art Biennale.

Europa A700

2011, May 5 *Perf. 13½*

1421	A700 100c multi	2.40	1.75

Intl. Year of Forests.

Miniature Sheet

Provisional Declaration Naming "Swiss Psalm" as National Anthem, 50th Anniv. — A701

No. 1422: a, Urnerboden (red panels at bottom and right). b, Urnersee bei Flüelen (red panels at left and bottom). c, Urigen (red panels at top and right). d, Schächentaler Windgällen (red panels at left and top).

2011, May 5 *Perf. 13½*

1422	A701 Sheet of 4	2.40	2.40
a.-d.	25c Any single	.80	.60

On each of the four stamps in the sheet, the first verse of the anthem is printed in fluorescent ink in one of Switzerland's four official languages.

Fruit, by Shirana Shahbazi A702

2011, Sept. 2 *Perf. 13¼x13½*

1423	A702 100c multi	2.25	1.75

See Liechtenstein No. 1522.

Paul Burkhard (1911-77), Composer A703

2011, Sept. 2 *Perf. 13½*

1424	A703 100c multi	2.25	1.75

Works of Handicapped Artists — A704

Designs: 85c, Untitled painting by Bajram Mahmuti. 100c, Emmental, painting by Claudia Aebi-Torre, horiz. 140c, Untitled dot picture, by Christian Oppliger, horiz. 190c, Photograph of dancer and wood sculpture, by Flavia Trachsel.

2011, Sept. 2

1425	A704 85c multi	2.00	1.50
1426	A704 100c multi	2.25	1.75
1427	A704 140c black	3.25	2.40
1428	A704 190c multi	4.50	3.50
	Nos. 1425-1428 (4)	12.00	4.00

Lavaux Vineyard Terraces UNESCO World Heritage Site — A705

No. 1429: a, Vineyard terraces and steps (26x37mm). b, Village, vineyards, Lake Geneva (41x37mm). c, Open gate and stone wall overlooking Lake Geneva (37x37mm).

2011, Sept. 2 **Litho.**

1429	A705 Horiz. strip of 3	6.75	6.75
a.-c.	100c Any single	2.25	1.75

Muggestutz, King of the Dwarves, Book Illustration by Susanna Schmid-Germann A706

2011, Sept. 2 *Serpentine Die Cut 12*

Self-Adhesive

1430	A706 85c multi	2.00	1.50
a.	Booklet pane of 10	20.00	

Single examples of No. 1430 on a translucent paper also were made available.

Greetings Stamps A707

Designs: No. 1431, Champagne flutes. No. 1432, Heart. No. 1433, Engagement and wedding rings. No. 1434, Baby's pacifier.

2011, Sept. 2 *Perf. 13¼x13½*

Self-Adhesive

1431	A707 100c multi	2.25	1.75
1432	A707 100c multi	2.25	1.75
1433	A707 100c multi	2.25	1.75
1434	A707 100c multi	2.25	1.75
	Nos. 1431-1434 (4)	9.00	3.00

A708

Design: Drawing of Swiss flag, machine, clouds, rainbow and musical notes, by rap musician Stress.

2011, Nov. 17 *Perf. 13½*

1435	A708 100c multi	2.25	1.75

Souvenir Sheet

Château de Villa, Sierre — A709

2011, Nov. 17

1436	A709 85c multi	1.90	1.45

Stamp Day.

Christmas A710

Christmas trees and: 85c, Chapel. 100c, Gifts on sleigh, village. 140c, Wreath, chalet.

2011, Nov. 17 *Perf. 13¼x13½*

Self-Adhesive

1437	A710 85c multi	1.90	1.45
1438	A710 100c multi	2.25	1.75
1439	A710 140c multi	3.25	2.40
	Nos. 1437-1439 (3)	7.40	2.50

Flowers Type of 2011

Designs: 140c, Lycopersicon lucopersicum. 180c, Phaeolus coccineus. 190c, Allium cepa.

2012, Mar. 1 *Serpentine Die Cut 12*

Self-Adhesive

1440	A698 140c multi	3.25	2.40
1441	A698 180c multi	4.00	3.00
1442	A698 190c multi	4.25	3.25
a.	Nos. 1440-1442 on translucent paper	11.50	
	Nos. 1440-1442 (3)	11.50	2.30

Nos. 1440-1442 each were printed in sheets of 10 stamps.

Swiss Brass Band Association, 150th Anniv. — A711

Litho. With Foil Application

2012, Mar. 1 *Perf. 14¼x13¾*

1443	A711 100c multi	2.25	1.75

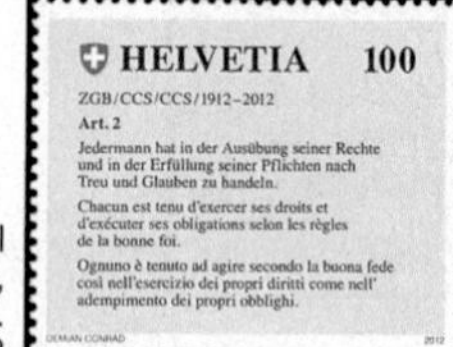

Swiss Civil Code, Cent. A712

2012, Mar. 1 Litho. *Perf. 13½*

1444	A712 100c multi	2.25	1.75

Building of Hermitage in the Steinach Valley by St. Gall (c. 550- c. 645), 1400th Anniv. — A713

2012, Mar. 1 *Perf. 13¼x13½*

1445	A713 100c multi	2.25	1.75

Jungfrau Railway, Cent. — A714

2012, Mar. 1

1446	A714 100c multi	2.25	1.75

Swiss Tectonic Arena Sardona UNESCO World Heritage Site — A715

No. 1447: a, Buildings in Elm (30x47mm). b, Sun shining through Martinsloch (hole in mountain) (44x47mm). c, Sunshine on Elm Church Tower clock face (30x47mm).

2012, Mar. 1 *Perf. 13½*

1447	A715 Horiz. strip of 3	6.75	6.75
a.-c.	100c Any single	2.25	1.75

Beaver — A716

2012, Mar. 1 *Perf. 13½x13¼*

Self-Adhesive

1448	A716 100c multi	2.25	1.75

Children's Book Illustration by Janosch (Horst Eckert) — A717

Serpentine Die Cut 12

2012, Mar. 12 **Self-Adhesive**

1449 A717 100c multi 2.25 1.75
a. Serpentine die cut 12¼x12 2.25 1.75
b. Booklet pane of 10 #1449 22.50

Single examples of No. 1449 were made available on a translucent paper. No.1449a is available only on translucent paper.

Cadastral Surveying in Switzerland, Cent. — A718

2012, May 9 ***Perf. 13¾x14¼***
1450 A718 100c multi 2.25 1.75

Inauguration of Stanserhorn Cabrio Cable Car — A719

2012, May 9 ***Perf. 13¼x13½***
1451 A719 100c multi 2.25 1.75

Tidying Up Art, by Ursus Wehrli — A720

2012, May 9 **Litho.** ***Perf. 13½***
1452 A720 100c multi 2.25 1.75

Blood Donation — A721

2012, May 9 ***Perf. 13½x13¼***
1453 A721 100c multi 2.25 1.75

Europa — A722

2012, May 9 ***Perf. 13½***
1454 A722 100c multi 2.25 1.75

Tell Theaters A723

Actors at: No. 1455, Tell Theater in Altdorf. No. 1456, Open-air Tell Theater in Interlaken.

2012, May 9 ***Perf. 13***
Self-Adhesive
1455 A723 100c multi 2.25 1.75
1456 A723 100c multi 2.25 1.75

Tell Theaters in Altdorf, 500th anniv.; in Interlaken, cent.

Swimmers in Rhine River Near Basel — A724

Symbols From Arms of Geneva and Colors From International Flags — A725

Intersection in Zurich — A726

2012, Sept. 6 ***Perf. 13¼x13½***
Self-Adhesive
1457 A724 100c multi 2.10 1.60
1458 A725 100c multi 2.10 1.60
1459 A726 100c multi 2.10 1.60
Nos. 1457-1459 (3) 6.30 4.80

Pop Art by Peter Stämpfli A727

Designs: 85c, James Bond (hands on steering wheel). 100c, Bond Street (hand holding bowler hat). 200c, Pudding (molded chocolate pudding and whipped cream).

2012, Sept. 6 ***Perf. 14x13½***
Self-Adhesive
1460 A727 85c black 1.90 1.45
1461 A727 100c black 2.10 1.60
1462 A727 200c multi 4.25 3.25
Nos. 1460-1462 (3) 8.25 6.30

Woodcuttings of Nature Scenes by Franz Gertsch A728

Designs: 85c, Butterbur. 100c, Grasses. 140c, Black Water Triptych.

2012, Sept. 6 ***Perf. 13½***
Self-Adhesive
1463 A728 85c lt grn & green 1.90 1.45
1464 A728 100c lt grn & red 2.10 1.60
1465 A728 140c lt grn & gray blue 3.00 2.25
Nos. 1463-1465 (3) 7.00 5.30

Souvenir Sheet

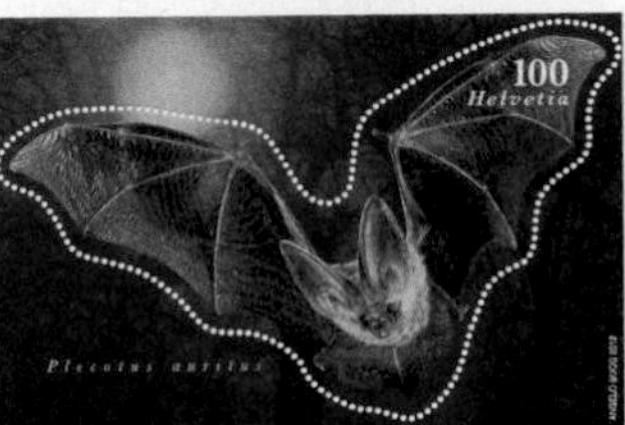

Plecotus Auritus — A729

Litho. & Embossed
2012, Sept. 6 ***Perf.***
1466 A729 100c multi 2.10 1.60

Yakari, Comic Strip by Derib and Job — A730

Yakari and: No. 1467, Butterfly and flower. No. 1468, Horse and bird.

Serpentine Die Cut 12
2012, Nov. 22 **Litho.**
Self-Adhesive
1467 A730 100c multi 2.25 1.75
1468 A730 100c multi 2.25 1.75
a. Horiz. pair, #1467-1468, on translucent backing paper 4.50
b. Booklet pane of 10, 5 each #1467-1468 22.50

Souvenir Sheet

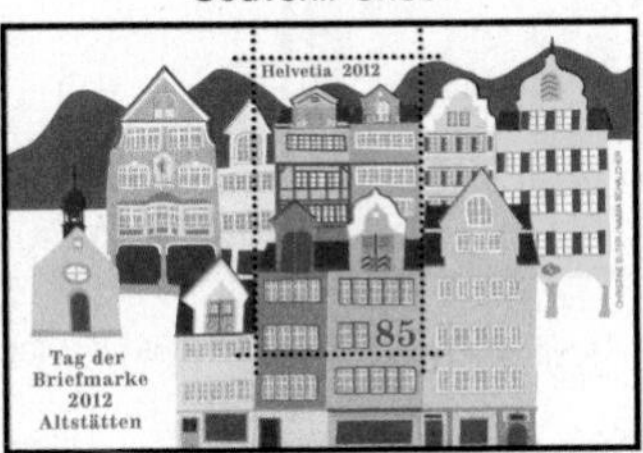

Altstätten — A731

2012, Nov. 22 ***Perf. 13¾***
1469 A731 85c multi 1.90 1.45

Stamp Day.

Christmas — A732

Christmas lights and: 85c, Stars, ribbon. 100c, Star, angel, Christmas tree. 140c, Violin, open book, Christmas ornament.

2012, Nov. 22 ***Perf. 13½x13¼***
Self-Adhesive
1470 A732 85c multi 1.90 1.45
1471 A732 100c multi 2.25 1.75
1472 A732 140c multi 3.00 2.25
Nos. 1470-1472 (3) 7.15 5.45

Swiss Council for Accident Prevention, 75th Anniv. — A733

2013, Mar. 7 ***Perf. 13¼x13½***
1473 A733 85c multi 1.90 1.45

Swiss Protection and Support Services, 50th Anniv. — A734

2013, Mar. 7
1474 A734 85c multi 1.90 1.45

Lötschberg Railway, Cent. — A735

2013, Mar. 7
1475 A735 100c multi 2.10 1.60

Gottlieb Duttweiler (1888-1962), Founder of Migros Supermarkets, and Delivery Van — A736

2013, Mar. 7 ***Perf. 13½***
1476 A736 100c multi 2.10 1.60

Appenzell Cantons in Swiss Confederation, 500th Anniv. — A737

2013, Mar. 7
1477 A737 100c multi 2.10 1.60

A738

Children's Book Illustrations by Ernst Kreidolf (1863-1956) A739

2013, Mar. 7 ***Serpentine Die Cut 12***
Self-Adhesive
1478 A738 100c multi 2.10 1.60
1479 A739 100c multi 2.10 1.60
a. Horiz. pair, #1478-1479, on translucent paper 4.20
b. Booklet pane of 10, 5 each #1478-1479 21.00

Miniature Sheet

Swiss Alpine Club, 150th Anniv. — A740

No. 1480: a, Line of skiers and mountain (50x42mm). b, Mountain climber on rock face (28x70mm). c, Hikers on mountain path (78x28mm). d, Mountain hut and Swiss flag (28x42mm).

Perf. 12 on 1, 2, or 3 Sides
2013, Mar. 7
1480 A740 Sheet of 4 11.00 8.25
a. 85c multi 1.90 1.45
b. 100c multi 2.10 1.60
c. 140c multi 3.00 2.25
d. 190c multi 4.00 3.00

Flowers Type of 2011

Designs: 130c, Capsicum annuum. 220c, Allium porrum.

2013, May 7 ***Serpentine Die Cut 12***
Self-Adhesive

1481 A698 130c multi 2.75 2.10
1482 A698 220c multi 4.75 3.75
a. Horiz. pair, #1481-1482, on translucent paper 7.50

Nos. 1481-1482 each were printed in sheets of 10 stamps.

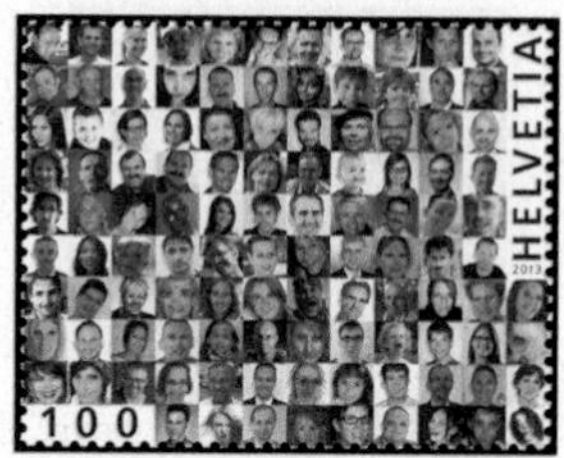

Faces of Swiss People — A741

2013, May 7 ***Perf. 12***
1483 A741 100c multi 2.10 1.60

White Stork — A742

2013, May 7 ***Perf. 14¼x13¾***
Self-Adhesive

1484 A742 100c multi 2.10 1.60

"You They They I You" Sculpture by Valentin Carron — A743

2013, May 7 ***Perf. 13¼x13½***
1485 A743 100c multi 2.10 1.60

2013 Venice Art Biennale.

Europa A744

Postal vehicles: No. 1486, Tribelhorn delivery van (denomination in blue). No. 1487, Kyburz DXP electric three-wheeler (denomination in brown orange).

2013, May 7 ***Perf. 13½***
1486 A744 100c multi 2.10 1.60
1487 A744 100c multi 2.10 1.60

Swiss Men's Ice Hockey Team's Second-Place Finish in 2013 World Championships A745

2013, May 31 **Litho.** ***Perf. 13¼x13½***
1488 A745 100c multi 2.25 1.75

Hillside Buildings, Lausanne A746

Bear, Heraldic Animal of Bern — A747

Buildings and Symbols of Winterthur A748

2013, Sept. 5 ***Perf. 13¾x14¼***
Self-Adhesive

1489 A746 100c multi 2.25 1.75
1490 A747 100c multi 2.25 1.75
1491 A748 100c multi 2.25 1.75
Nos. 1489-1491 (3) 6.75 5.25

Baby Animals A749

Designs: 85c, Chicks. 100c, Calves. 140c, Lambs. 190c, Piglets.

2013, Sept. 5 **Litho.**
Self-Adhesive

1492 A749 85c multi 1.90 1.45
1493 A749 100c multi 2.25 1.75
1494 A749 140c multi 3.00 2.25
1495 A749 190c multi 4.25 3.25
Nos. 1492-1495 (4) 11.40 8.70

Smurfs — A750

Designs: No. 1496, Smurfs kissing. No.1497, Papa Smurf.

2013, Sept. 5 ***Serpentine Die Cut 12***
Self-Adhesive

1496 A750 100c multi 2.25 1.75
1497 A750 100c multi 2.25 1.75
a. Horiz. pair, #1496-1497 on translucent paper 4.50
b. Booklet pane of 10, 5 each #1496-1497 22.50

Restoration of Waterways — A751

No. 1498 — Waterway and: a, Butterfly (37x37mm). b, Bird (32x37mm). d, Fish (37x37mm).

2013, Sept. 5 ***Perf. 13¾x14***
1498 A751 Horiz. strip of 3 6.75 6.75
a.-c. 100c Any single 2.25 1.75

Souvenir Sheet

Obverse of Swiss Gold Vreneli Coin — A752

Litho. & Embossed With Foil Application

2013, Sept. 5 ***Perf.***
1499 A752 600c gold & multi 13.00 9.75

Goose With Body of Guitar, by Polo Hofer A753

2013, Nov. 14 **Litho.** ***Perf. 13½***
1500 A753 100c multi 2.25 1.75

Souvenir Sheet

Bell — A754

Litho. & Embossed

2013, Nov. 14 ***Perf. 13¼***
1501 A754 85c multi 1.90 1.45

Stamp Day.

Souvenir Sheet

Matter Valley Cabins — A755

2013, Nov. 14 **Litho.** ***Perf. 13¼x14***
1502 A755 200c multi 4.50 3.50

Christmas A756

Designs: 85c, Fox, Christmas ornament on tree. 100c, Fawn, lantern. 140c, Owl, Christmas ornament on tree. 190c, Squirrel, lantern.

Perf. 13¾x14¼
2013, Nov. 14 **Litho.**
Self-Adhesive

1503 A756 85c multi 1.90 1.45
1504 A756 100c multi 2.25 1.75
1505 A756 140c multi 3.25 2.40
1506 A756 190c multi 4.25 3.25
Nos. 1503-1506 (4) 11.65 8.85

Diplomatic Relations Between Switzerland and Japan, 150th Anniv. — A757

Designs: 100c, Mount Fuji, Japan. 190c, Mountain valley, Switzerland.

2014, Feb. 6 **Litho.** ***Perf. 12¾x13***
1507 A757 100c multi 2.25 1.75
1508 A757 190c multi 4.25 3.25
a. Horiz. pair, #1507-1508 6.50 6.50

See Japan No. 3646.

Swiss Army Post, 125th Anniv. — A758

2014, Mar. 6 **Litho.** ***Perf. 13¼x13½***
1509 A758 100c multi 2.25 1.75

Intl. Year of Crystallography — A759

Litho. With Foil Application

2014, Mar. 6 ***Perf. 13x13¼***
1510 A759 85c Epidote 1.90 1.45
1511 A759 100c Amethyst 2.25 1.75

Swiss Air Force, Cent. — A760

Designs: 100c, F/A-18 Hornets. 140c, F-5 Tigers.

2014, Mar. 6 **Litho.** ***Perf. 13¼x13½***
1512 A760 100c multi 2.25 1.75
1513 A760 140c multi 3.25 2.40

Swiss National Park — A761

No. 1514: a, Tree trunk, hiker, text in German (37x37mm). b, Bird, mountain, text in Romansh (32x37mm). c, Mountain, text in Italian (35x37mm).

2014, Mar. 6 **Litho.** ***Perf. 13¾x14***
1514 A761 Horiz. strip of 3 6.75 6.75
a.-c. 100c Any single 2.25 1.75

Mushrooms A762

Designs: 10c, Cantharellus cibarius. 15c, Lactarius lignyotus. 20c, Hydnellum caeruleum. 50c, Strobilomyces strobilaceus.

Serpentine Die Cut 12
2014, Mar. 6 **Litho.**
Self-Adhesive

1515 A762 10c multi .25 .25
1516 A762 15c multi .35 .30
1517 A762 20c multi .45 .35
1518 A762 50c multi 1.10 .85
a. Block of 4, #1515-1518, on translucent paper 2.25
Nos. 1515-1518 (4) 2.15 1.75

Nos. 1515-1518 each were printed in sheets of 10.

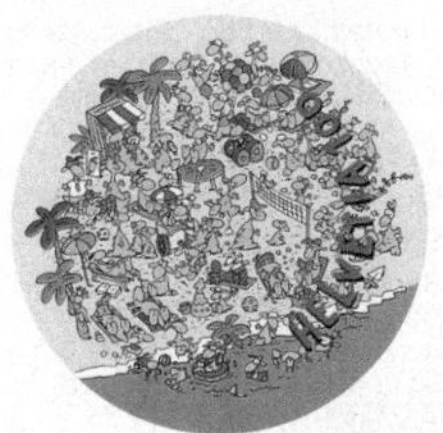

Dinosaurs on Beach
A763

Fred the Dinosaur
A764

2014, Mar. 6 Litho. *Die Cut*
Self-Adhesive

1519 A763 100c multi 2.25 1.75

Serpentine Die Cut 12

1520 A764 100c multi 2.25 1.75
a. Pair, #1519-1520 on translucent paper 4.50
b. Booklet pane of 9, #1519, 8 #1520 20.50

Renewable Energy
A765

2014, May 8 Litho. *Perf. 13½*

1521 A765 100c multi 2.25 1.75

Pilatus Cogwheel Railway, 125th Anniv. — A766

2014, May 8 Litho. *Perf. 13x14*

1522 A766 100c multi 2.25 1.75

Special Olympics National Games, Bern — A767

2014, May 8 Litho. *Perf. 13½x13¼*
Self-Adhesive

1523 A767 100c multi 2.25 1.75

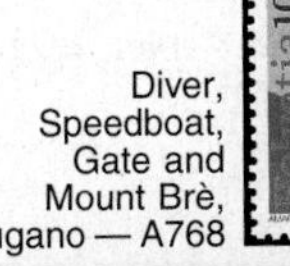

Diver, Speedboat, Gate and Mount Brè, Lugano — A768

Woman, Lake Lucerne and Chapel Bridge, Lucerne
A769

Abbey Cathedral and Tree in Planter, St. Gallen — A770

2014, May 8 Litho. *Perf. 13¼x13½*
Self-Adhesive

1524 A768 100c multi 2.25 1.75
1525 A769 100c multi 2.25 1.75
1526 A770 100c multi 2.25 1.75
Nos. 1524-1526 (3) 6.75 5.25

Europa — A771

No. 1527: a, Dulcimer and accordion. b, Accordion and alphorn.

2014, May 8 Litho. *Perf. 13½*

1527 A771 Horiz. pair 4.50 4.50
a.-b. 100c Either single 2.25 1.75

Clock Towers and Clocks
A772

Designs: 100c, Zytglogge, Bern. 140c, Kazansky Tower, Moscow, Russia.

2014, May 21 Litho. *Perf. 13x13½*

1528 A772 100c multi 2.25 1.75
1529 A772 140c multi 3.25 2.40

See Russia No. 7531.

2014 Swiss Skills Competition, Bern — A773

2014, Sept. 4 Litho. *Perf. 13½*

1530 A773 100c multi 2.25 1.75

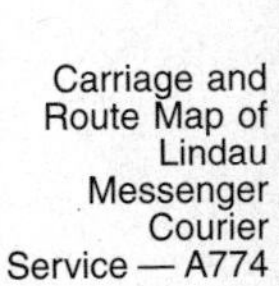

Carriage and Route Map of Lindau Messenger Courier Service — A774

2014, Sept. 4 Litho. *Perf. 13¼x13½*

1531 A774 140c multi 3.00 2.25

Wildlife — A775

Designs: 85c, Mouse weasel. 100c, Alpine marmot. 140c, Nutcracker. 190c, Red deer.

2014, Sept. 4 Litho. *Perf. 13¼x13½*

1532 A775 85c multi 1.90 1.45
1533 A775 100c multi 2.25 1.75
1534 A775 140c multi 3.00 2.25
1535 A775 190c multi 4.25 3.25
Nos. 1532-1535 (4) 11.40 8.70

Garfield, Comic Strip Characters by Jim Davis — A776

Designs: No. 1536, Garfield and Odie making fondue. No. 1537, Garfield eating chocolate, Swiss flag and mountains.

Serpentine Die Cut 12

2014, Sept. 4 Litho.
Self-Adhesive

1536 A776 100c multi 2.25 1.75
1537 A776 100c multi 2.25 1.75
a. Pair, #1536-1537 on translucent paper 4.50
b. Booklet pane of 10, 5 each #1536-1537 22.50

Souvenir Sheet

Record Label — A777

2014, Sept. 4 Litho. *Rouletted*
On Cardboard

1538 A777 500c multi 11.00 8.25

The stamp from No. 1538 has a circular hole in the center. The sheet margin is coated with a varnish upon which phonograph record grooves have been impressed. The 33⅓rpm recording features a brass band playing the Swiss national anthem.

Tongues — A778

2014, Nov. 13 Litho. *Perf. 12¾x13*

1539 A778 100c multi 2.10 1.60

Souvenir Sheet

Houses in Emmental Region — A779

2014, Nov. 13 Litho. *Perf. 12*

1540 A779 200c multi 4.25 3.25

Christmas
A780

Garland and: 85c, Star, gifts, Christmas tree, creche. 100c, Bow, Santa Claus, Christmas stockings hung near fireplace. 140c, Holly, star, candles, dinner table. 190c, Ornament, kitchen, cookies.

Perf. 13¼x13½

2014. Nov. 13 Litho.
Self-Adhesive

1541 A780 85c multi 1.75 1.35
1542 A780 100c multi 2.10 1.60
1543 A780 140c multi 3.00 2.25
1544 A780 190c multi 4.00 3.00
Nos. 1541-1544 (4) 10.85 8.20

Expo 2015, Milan
A781

Litho. With Foil Application

2015, Mar. 5 *Perf. 13x13¼*

1545 A781 100c multi 2.10 1.60

Stairs, Martinsberg Community Center, Baden, and Murals, Convent of St. John, Müstair — A782

2015, Mar. 5 Litho. *Perf. 13½*

1546 A782 100c multi 2.10 1.60

Swiss Federal Commission for Monument Preservation, cent.

Swiss Federal Tax Administration, Cent. — A783

2015, Mar. 5 Litho. *Perf. 13½x13¼*

1547 A783 100c multi 2.10 1.60

Battles
A784

Designs: No. 1548, Battle of Morgarten, 1315. No. 1549, Battle of Marignano, 1515.

2015, Mar. 5 Litho. *Perf. 13½*

1548 A784 100c multi 2.10 1.60
1549 A784 100c multi 2.10 1.60

Pets — A785

2015, Mar. 5 Litho. *Perf. 13¾x14¼*
Self-Adhesive

1550 A785 85c Dog 1.75 1.35
1551 A785 100c Cat 2.10 1.60
1552 A785 140c Rabbit 3.00 2.25
1553 A785 190c Hamster 4.00 3.00
Nos. 1550-1553 (4) 10.85 8.20

Abbey of St. Maurice, 1500th Anniv. — A786

Designs: No. 1554, Martolet archaeological site. No. 1555, Reliquary of the Children of St. Sigismund. No. 1556, Document and pen. No. 1557, Stained-glass window.

2015, Mar. 5 Litho. *Perf. 13¼x13½*
1554 A786 100c multi 2.10 1.60
1555 A786 100c multi 2.10 1.60
a. Horiz. pair, #1554-1555 4.25 3.25
1556 A786 100c multi 2.10 1.60
1557 A786 100c multi 2.10 1.60
a. Horiz. pair, #1556-1557 4.25 3.25
Nos. 1554-1557 (4) 8.40 6.40

Rhein Falls — A787

No. 1558: a, Falls, buildings and tour boat (37x37mm), b, Falls, bridge and viewing platform (35x37mm). c, Falls and Laufen Castle (32x37mm).

2015, Mar. 5 Litho. *Perf. 13¾x14*
1558 A787 Horiz. strip of 3 6.50 6.50
a.-c. 100c Any single 2.10 1.60

Souvenir Sheet

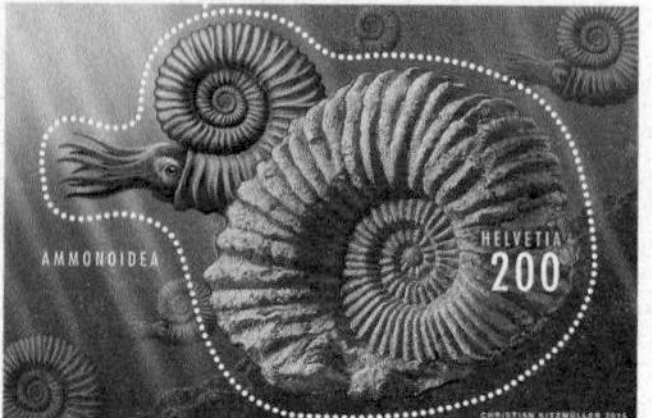

Ammonite and Fossil — A788

Litho. & Embossed

2015, Mar. 5 *Perf.*
1559 A788 200c multi 4.25 3.25

Swiss Sponsorship for Mountain Communities, 75th Anniv. — A789

2015, May 7 Litho. *Perf. 13½*
1560 A789 100c multi 2.10 1.60

Skin — A790

2015, May 7 Litho. *Perf. 13¼x13½*
Flocked Granite Paper With Ripples
1561 A790 100c multi 2.10 1.60

Exhibition of the works of Pamela Rosenkranz at Venice Biennale. No. 1561 is printed in sheets of 10. The rippling on each stamp in the sheet is different.

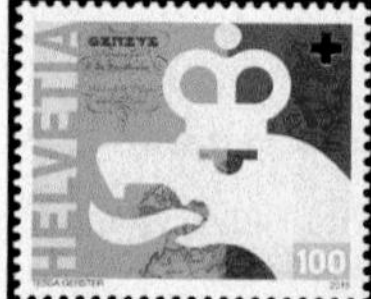

Admission of Geneva to Swiss Federation, 200th Anniv. — A791

Admission of Valais to Swiss Federation, 200th Anniv. — A792

Admission of Neuchâtel to Swiss Federation, 200th Anniv. — A793

2015, May 7 Litho. *Perf. 13¼x13½*
1562 A791 100c multi 2.10 1.60
1563 A792 100c multi 2.10 1.60
1564 A793 100c multi 2.10 1.60
Nos. 1562-1564 (3) 6.30 4.80

Nos. 1562-1564 each have cross-shaped hole in upper right corner of stamp.

Europa — A794

Toys: a, Wisa-Gloria rocking duck, 1957. b, Helvetia tricycle, 1949.

2015, May 7 Litho. *Perf. 13½*
1565 A794 Horiz. pair 4.25 3.25
a.-b. 100c Either single 2.10 1.60

Penny Black, 175th Anniv. A795

2015, Sept. 3 Litho. *Perf. 13½*
1566 A795 100c multi 2.10 1.60

Union of Swiss Philatelic Societies, 125th Anniv. — A796

2015, Sept. 3 Litho. *Perf. 13¼x13½*
1567 A796 100c multi 2.10 1.60

No. 1567 was printed in sheets of 12 + 8 labels.

Silver Jewelry — A797

Designs: 100c, Brooch from Bern, Switzerland. 140c, Buckle from Aland Islands.

Litho. & Embossed

2015, Sept. 3 *Perf. 13¼*
1568 A797 100c multi 2.10 1.60
1569 A797 140c multi 3.00 2.25

See Aland Islands Nos. 371-372.

Antique Automobiles — A798

Desings: 85c, 1906 Pic-Pic. 100c, 1897 Martini. 140c, 1902 Tribelhorn. 190c, 1908 Fischer.

2015, Sept. 3 Litho. *Perf. 13½*
Self-Adhesive
1570 A798 85c multi 1.75 1.35
1571 A798 100c multi 2.10 1.60
1572 A798 140c multi 3.00 2.25
1573 A798 190c multi 4.00 3.00
Nos. 1570-1573 (4) 10.85 8.20

Greetings A799

First names and: No. 1574, Rose. No. 1575, Snail. No. 1576, Ladybug. No. 1577, Feather.

Serpentine Die Cut 12

2015, Sept. 3 Litho.
Self-Adhesive
1574 A799 85c multi 1.75 1.35
a. Block of 4 on translucent paper 7.00
1575 A799 85c multi 1.75 1.35
a. Block of 4 on translucent paper 7.00
1576 A799 100c multi 2.10 1.60
a. Block of 4 on translucent paper 8.50
1577 A799 100c multi 2.10 1.60
a. Block of 4 #1574-1577 on translucent paper 7.75
b. Block of 4 on translucent paper 8.50
Nos. 1574-1577 (4) 7.70 5.90

A800

Marsupilami A801

Serpentine Die Cut 12

2015, Sept. 3 Litho.
Self-Adhesive
1578 A800 100c multi 2.10 1.60
a. Block of 4 on translucent paper 8.50
1579 A801 100c multi 2.10 1.60
a. Horiz. pair, #1578-1579 on translucent paper 4.25
b. Booklet pane of 10, 5 each #1578-1579 21.00
c. Block of 4 on translucent paper 8.50

Jonny Fischer and Manu Burkart, Members of Cabaret DivertiMento Comedy Duo — A802

2015, Nov. 12 Litho. *Perf. 14*
1580 A802 50c multi + label 1.00 .75

Christmas — A803

Snowglobes containing: 85c, Gifts. 100c, Christmas tree and snowman. 140c, Christmas ornaments. 190c, Candles and holly.

Litho. With Foil Application

2015, Nov. 12 *Perf. 13½x13¼*
Self-Adhesive
1581 A803 85c multi 1.75 1.35
1582 A803 100c multi 2.00 1.50
1583 A803 140c multi 2.75 2.10
1584 A803 190c multi 3.75 3.00
Nos. 1581-1584 (4) 10.25 7.95

Organization of the Swiss Abroad, Cent. — A804

2016, Mar. 3 Litho. *Perf. 13½*
1585 A804 100c multi 2.00 1.50

Marie Heim-Vögtlin (1845-1916), First Female Physician in Switzerland A805

2016, Mar. 3 Litho. *Perf. 13½x13¼*
1586 A805 100c multi 2.00 1.50

Swiss Red Cross, 150th Anniv. — A806

2016, Mar. 3 Litho. *Perf. 13¼x13½*
1587 A806 100c multi 2.00 1.50

145 Poison Information Emergency Number, 50th Anniv. — A807

2016, Mar. 3 Litho. *Perf. 14x13*
1588 A807 100c multi 2.00 1.50

Henri Nestlé (1814-90), Founder of Nestlé S.A. — A808

2016, Mar. 3 Litho. *Perf. 14x14¼*
Self-Adhesive
1589 A808 100c multi 2.00 1.50

Nestlé S.A., 150th anniv.

Dada Art Movement, Cent. — A809

Designs: No. 1590, Hugo Ball in a Cubist Costume, by Hugo Ball, 1916-17. No. 1591, Portrait of Jean Arp, by Sophie Tauber-Arp, 1918.

2016, Mar. 3 Litho. *Perf. 13½*
1590 A809 100c multi 2.00 1.50
1591 A809 100c multi 2.00 1.50

Swiss Merchant Fleet, 75th Anniv. — A810

Ships: 85c, Lavaux. 100c, Lugano. 150c, Lausanne. 200c, Stockhorn.

2016, Mar. 3 Litho. *Perf. 13¼x13½*
1592 A810 85c multi 1.75 1.35
1593 A810 100c multi 2.00 1.50
1594 A810 150c multi 3.00 2.25
1595 A810 200c multi 4.00 3.00
Nos. 1592-1595 (4) 10.75 8.10

A811

Molly Monster A812

Serpentine Die Cut 12
2016, Mar. 3 Litho.
Self-Adhesive
1596 A811 100c multi 2.00 1.50
a. Block of 4 on translucent paper 8.00
1597 A812 100c multi 2.00 1.50
a. Horiz. pair, #1596-1597 on translucent paper 4.00
b. Booklet pane of 10, 5 each #1596-1597 20.00
c. Block of 4 on translucent paper 8.00

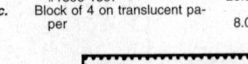

Swiss Wrestling Festival, Estavayer A813

2016, May 12 Litho. *Perf. 13½*
1598 A813 100c multi 2.10 1.60

Printed in sheets of 12 + 5 labels.

A814

Europa A815

2016, May 12 Litho. *Perf. 13½*
1599 A814 100c multi 2.10 1.60
1600 A815 100c multi 2.10 1.60
a. Horiz. pair, #1599-1600 4.25 3.25

Think Green Issue.

Nocturnal Animals A816

Designs: 85c, Tawny owl. 100c, Garden dormouse. 150c, European glowworm. 200c, Hedgehog.

2016, May 12 Litho. *Perf. 13¼x13½*
1601 A816 85c multi 1.75 1.35
1602 A816 100c multi 2.10 1.60
1603 A816 150c multi 3.00 2.25
1604 A816 200c multi 4.00 3.00
Nos. 1601-1604 (4) 10.85 8.20

Lake Constance — A817

No. 1605: a, Säntis and Romanshorn, swans, waterbirds, stern of boat. b, Obersee, dock, bow of boat, sailboats, Zeppelin. c, Untersee and Ermatingen, gull on piling, reeds.

2016, May 12 Litho. *Perf. 14½*
1605 A817 Horiz. strip of 3 5.25 4.00
a.-c. 85c Any single 1.75 1.35

Opening of Gotthard Base Tunnel — A818

No. 1606: a, Erstfeld end of tunnel, SBB Cargo train (33x37mm). b, Bodio end of tunnel, Swiss Federal Railways train (33x37mm).

2016, May 12 Litho. *Perf. 14*
1606 A818 Horiz. pair + central label 4.25 3.25
a.-b. 100c Either single 2.10 1.60

A varnish containing powdered stone from the tunnel construction was applied to parts of the design.

Aerophilately Day, 50th Anniv. — A819

2016, Sept. 8 Litho. *Perf. 13½*
1607 A819 100c multi 2.10 1.60

Railroad Stations A820

Station in: 85c, Brig. 100c, Lucerne (Luzern). 150c, Bellinzona. 200c, Geneve (Genève), 530c, Basel.

2016 Litho. *Serpentine Die Cut 12*
Self-Adhesive
1608 A820 85c multi 1.75 1.35
a. Serpentine die cut 12¼x12 1.75 1.35
b. Booklet pane of 10 #1608a 17.50
c. Block of 4 #1608 on translucent paper 7.00
1609 A820 100c multi + etiquette 2.10 1.60
a. Serpentine die cut 12¼x12 + etiquette 2.10 1.60
b. Booklet pane of 10 #1609a + 10 etiquettes 21.00
c. Block of 4 #1609 + 4 etiquettes on translucent paper 8.50
1610 A820 150c multi 3.00 2.25
a. Block of 4 on translucent paper 12.00
1611 A820 200c multi 4.00 3.00
a. Block of 4, #1608-1611, + etiquette on translucent paper 11.00
b. Block of 4 #1611 on translucent paper 16.00
1612 A820 530c multi 10.50 8.00
a. Block of 4 on translucent paper 42.00
Nos. 1608-1612 (5) 21.35 16.20

Issued:, 85c, 100c, 150c, 200c, 9/8. Nos. 1608c, 1609c, 1610a, 1611b, 9/18, 530c, 11/17. See Nos. 1639-1642, 1654, 1684-1687, 1700.

Souvenir Sheet

Flower and Butterfly — A821

No. 1613: a, Flower (49x40mm). b, Butterfly (79x43mm).

2016, Sept. 8 Litho. *Perf.*
1613 A821 Sheet of 2 4.25 3.25
a.-b. 100c Either single 2.10 1.60

Numerous laser-cut holes are found in Nos. 1613a-1613b.

Souvenir Sheet

Verzasca Valley — A822

2016, Sept. 8 Litho. *Perf. 13¼x14*
1614 A822 200c multi 4.25 3.25

Circumnavigation of Solar Impulse 2 Solar Powered Airplane — A823

2016, July 27 Litho. *Perf. 13x13¼*
1615 A823 100c multi 2.10 1.60

Yello Musical Group, 37th Anniv. — A824

Perf. 13¼x13½
2016, Nov. 17 Litho.
1616 A824 100c multi 2.00 1.50

Landscapes — A825

No. 1617: a, Flag of Switzerland, Lacs de Fenêtre. b, Flag of Dominican Republic, Playa Bavaro.

2016, Nov. 17 Litho. *Perf. 13½*
1617 A825 Horiz. pair 4.00 3.00
a.-b. 100c Either single 2.00 1.50

Diplomatic relations between Switzerland and Dominican Republic, 80th anniv. See Dominican Republic No. 1602.

Christmas A826

Designs: 85c, Christmas tree. 100c, Snowman. 150c, Angel. 200c, Sled.

Serpentine Die Cut 11
2016, Nov. 17 Litho.
Self-Adhesive
1618 A826 85c multi 1.75 1.35
a. Block of 4 on translucent paper 7.00
1619 A826 100c multi 2.00 1.50
a. Block of 4 on translucent paper 8.00
1620 A826 150c multi 3.00 2.25
a. Block of 4 on translucent paper 12.00
1621 A826 200c multi 4.00 3.00
a. Block of 4, #1618-1621, on translucent paper 11.00
b. Block of 4 on translucent paper 16.00
Nos. 1618-1621 (4) 10.75 8.10

Swiss Heart Foundation, 50th Anniv. — A827

2017, Mar. 2 Litho. *Perf. 13½*
1622 A827 85c silver & multi 1.75 1.35

Glassblowing in Hergiswil, 200th Anniv. — A828

2017, Mar. 2 Litho. *Perf. 13½*
1623 A828 100c multi 2.00 1.50

St. Niklaus of Flüe (1417-87) — A829

2017, Mar. 2 Litho. *Perf. 13½x13¼*
1624 A829 100c multi 2.00 1.50

Schilthorn Cable Car, 50th Anniv. — A830

Piz Gloria Revolving Restaurant, 50th Anniv. — A831

2017, Mar. 2 Litho. *Perf. 13¾x14¼*

1625 A830 100c multi 2.00 1.50
1626 A831 100c multi 2.00 1.50

Draisine A832

Modern Bicycle — A833

2017, Mar. 2 Litho. *Perf. 13¼x13½*

1627 A832 100c black 2.00 1.50
1628 A833 100c black 2.00 1.50

Juvenile Animals A834

Designs: 85c, Otter pup. 100c, Lynx cub. 150c, Wolf cub. 200c, Bear cub.

2017, Mar. 2 Litho. *Perf. 13¼x13½*
Self-Adhesive

1629 A834 85c multi 1.75 1.35
1630 A834 100c multi 2.00 1.50
1631 A834 150c multi 3.00 2.25
1632 A834 200c multi 4.00 3.00
Nos. 1629-1632 (4) 10.75 8.10

Unspunnen Festival — A835

2017, May 11 Litho. *Perf. 13¼x13½*

1633 A835 100c multi 2.00 1.50

70th Locarno Film Festival A836

2017, May 11 Litho. *Perf. 13¼x13½*

1634 A836 100c multi 2.00 1.50

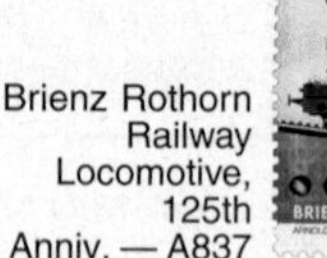

Brienz Rothorn Railway Locomotive, 125th Anniv. — A837

2017, May 11 Litho. *Perf. 13¾x13½*

1635 A837 100c multi 2.00 1.50

CH Foundation for Federal Cooperation, 50th Anniv. — A838

2017, May 11 Litho. *Perf. 13½*

1636 A838 100c multi 2.00 1.50

Europa — A839

No. 1637 — Castles in Bellinzona: a, Sasso Corbaro and Montebello. b, Castelgrande.

2017, May 11 Litho. *Perf. 13½*

1637 A839 Horiz. pair 4.00 3.00
a.-b. 100c Either single 2.00 1.50

Selun and Frümsel A840

Brisi and Zuestoll A841

Schibenstoll and Hinderrugg A842

Chäserrugg A843

2017, May 11 Litho. *Perf. 13¼*

1638 Horiz. strip of 4 7.00 5.25
a. A840 85c multi 1.75 1.35
b. A841 85c multi 1.75 1.35
c. A842 85c multi 1.75 1.35
d. A843 85c multi 1.75 1.35

Peaks in the Churfirsten Range.

Railroad Stations Type of 2016

Station in: 110c, Appenzell. 130c, Zug. 140c, Interlaken Ost. 180c, Scuol-Tarasp.

Serpentine Die Cut 12
2017, Sept. 17 Litho.
Self-Adhesive

1639 A820 110c multi 2.40 1.75
a. Block of 4 on translucent paper 9.75
1640 A820 130c multi 2.75 2.10
a. Block of 4 on translucent paper 11.00
1641 A820 140c multi 3.00 2.25
a. Block of 4 on translucent paper 12.00
1642 A820 180c multi 3.75 3.00
a. Block of 4, #1639-1642, on translucent paper 12.00
b. Block of 4 on translucent paper 15.00
Nos. 1639-1642 (4) 11.90 9.10

Selfie — A844

2017, Sept. 7 Litho. *Perf. 13½*
On Paper Faced With Silver Foil

1643 A844 100c black & green 2.10 1.60

Statue of St. Sebastian and Bern Cathedral Ceiling — A845

Bern Coat of Arms on Bern Cathedral Ceiling — A846

2017, Sept. 7 Litho. *Perf. 13¼x13½*

1644 A845 100c multi 2.10 1.60
1645 A846 100c multi 2.10 1.60

Completion of Bern Cathedral vaulted ceiling, 500th anniv.

Postcrossing A847

Post cards in air and: 100c, Swiss family and dog on mountain. 150c, European people surrounded by ring of stars. 200c, African, Asian and Mexican people.

2017, Sept. 7 Litho. *Perf. 13¼x13½*

1646 A847 100c multi 2.10 1.60
1647 A847 150c multi 3.25 2.40
1648 A847 200c multi 4.25 3.25
Nos. 1646-1648 (3) 9.60 7.25

Emojis — A848

Designs: 85c, 25 different emojis. 100c, Smiley face with sunglasses.

Serpentine Die Cut 12
2017, Sept. 7 Litho.
Self-Adhesive

1649 A848 85c multi 1.75 1.35
1650 A848 100c multi 2.10 1.60
a. Horiz. pair, #1649-1650, on translucent paper 4.00
b. Booklet pane of 10, 5 each #1649-1650 19.50

Souvenir Sheet

1867 Tübli Stamped Envelopes — A849

2017, Sept. 7 Litho. *Perf. 14*

1651 A849 85c multi 1.75 1.35

Souvenir Sheet

Creux du Van Rock Formation — A850

2017, Sept. 7 Litho. *Perf. 13½x13¼*

1652 A850 100c multi 2.10 1.60

Souvenir Sheet

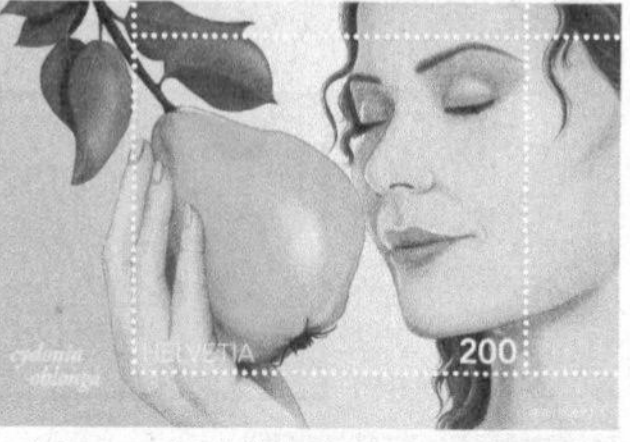
Woman Holding Quince — A851

2017, Sept. 7 Litho. *Perf. 12*

1653 A851 200c multi 4.25 3.25

No. 1653 is impregnated with a quince scent.

Railroad Stations Type of 2016

Station in: 400c, Zurich.

Serpentine Die Cut 12
2017, Nov. 16 Litho.
Self-Adhesive

1654 A820 400c multi 8.25 6.25
a. Block of 4 on translucent paper 33.00

Heart — A852

Litho. With Foil Application
2017, Nov. 16 *Perf. 13¾x14¼*

1655 A852 100c sil & multi 2.10 1.60

Simmental Cow, Flag and Map of Switzerland A853

2017, Nov. 16 Litho. *Perf. 13½*

1656 A853 100c multi 2.10 1.60

Christmas A854

Designs: 85c, Snowman on sled holding lantern. 100c, Globe and bell Christmas ornaments. 150c Santa Claus with cell phone. 200c, Traffic light covered in snow.

Serpentine Die Cut 12
2017, Nov. 16 Litho.
Self-Adhesive

1657 A854 85c multi 1.75 1.35
a. Block of 4 on translucent paper 7.00
1658 A854 100c multi 2.10 1.60
a. Block of 4 on translucent paper 8.50
1659 A854 150c multi 3.25 2.40
a. Block of 4 on translucent paper 13.00

1660 A854 200c multi 4.25 3.25
a. Block of 4, #1657-1660, on translucent paper 11.50
b. Block of 4 #1660 on translucent paper 17.00
Nos. 1657-1660 (4) 11.35 8.60

2018 Winter Olympics, PyeongChang, South Korea — A855

2018, Jan. 29 Litho. ***Perf. 13¾x14¼***
1661 A855 100c multi 2.25 1.75

Swiss League Against Rheumatism, 60th Anniv. — A856

2018, Mar. 1 Litho. ***Perf. 13½x13¼***
1662 A856 85c multi 1.90 1.45

Swiss Mountain Aid, 75th Anniv. A857

2018, Mar. 1 Litho. ***Perf. 13½***
1663 A857 100c multi 2.10 1.60

Swiss National Accident Insurance Fund (SUVA), Cent. A858

2018, Mar. 1 Litho. ***Perf. 13½***
1664 A858 100c multi 2.10 1.60

Swiss Year of Cultural Heritage — A859

Designs: 85c, Prehistoric pot. 100c, St. Benedict Chapel, Sumvitg.

2018, Mar. 1 Litho. ***Perf. 13½x13¼***
1665 A859 85c dk gray & brt vio 1.90 1.45
1666 A859 100c dk gray & org brn 2.10 1.60

Forest Animals A860

Designs: 85c, Great spotted woodpecker. 100c, Red squirrel. 150c. Roe deer. 200c, European badger.

Serpentine Die Cut 12
2018, Mar. 1 Litho.
Self-Adhesive
1667 A860 85c multi 1.90 1.45
1668 A860 100c multi 2.10 1.60
1669 A860 150c multi 3.25 2.40
1670 A860 200c multi 4.25 3.25
a. Block of 4, #1667-1670, on translucent paper 11.50
Nos. 1667-1670 (4) 11.50 8.70

Schyinge Platte Railway, 125th Anniv. — A861

Wengernalp Railway, 125th Anniv. — A862

Stanserhorn Railway, 125th Anniv. — A863

2018 Litho. ***Perf. 13¾x14¼***
1671 A861 100c multi 2.10 1.60
1672 A862 100c multi 2.10 1.60
1673 A863 100c multi 2.00 1.50
Nos. 1671-1673 (3) 6.20 4.70

Issued: Nos. 1671-1672, 3/1; No. 1673, 5/17. No. 1673 was printed in sheets of 10 + 2 labels.

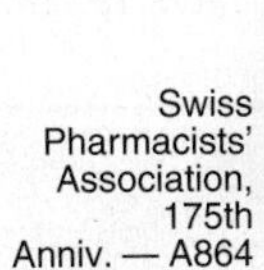

Swiss Pharmacists' Association, 175th Anniv. — A864

2018, May 17 Litho. ***Perf. 13½x13¼***
1674 A864 100c multi 2.00 1.50

2018 Mountain Bike World Championships, Lenzerheide A865

2018, May 17 Litho. ***Perf. 13½x13¼***
1675 A865 100c multi 2.00 1.50

Hornussen A866

2018, May 17 Litho. ***Perf. 14¼***
1676 A866 100c multi 2.00 1.50

Ballenberg Open-Air Museum Foundation, 50th Anniv. — A867

Museum buildings: No. 1677, Public laundry, Rüschlikon. No. 1678, Hay barn, Vals. No. 1679, Houses, Cugnasco. No. 1680, Farmhouse with pigeonry, Lancy.

2018, May 17 Litho. ***Perf. 13¼x13½***
1677 A867 85c multi 1.75 1.35
1678 A867 85c multi 1.75 1.35
1679 A867 100c multi 2.00 1.50
1680 A867 100c multi 2.00 1.50
Nos. 1677-1680 (4) 7.50 5.70

Europa A868

Bridges: No. 1681, Spreuer Bridge, Lucerne. No. 1682, Trift Bridge, Gadmental.

2018, May 17 Litho. ***Perf. 13½***
1681 A868 100c multi 2.00 1.50
1682 A868 100c multi 2.00 1.50

Visit of Pope Francis to Switzerland A869

Perf. 13½x13¾
2018, June 21 Litho.
1683 A869 100c multi 2.00 1.00

Railroad Stations Type of 2016

Station in: 10c, Zweisimmen. 15c, Huttwil. 20c, Alp Grüm. 50c, Fleurier.

Serpentine Die Cut 12
2018, Sept. 6 Litho.
Self-Adhesive
1684 A820 10c multi .25 .25
a. Block of 4 on translucent paper without back printing 1.00
1685 A820 15c multi .30 .25
a. Block of 4 on translucent paper without back printing 1.25
1686 A820 20c multi .40 .25
a. Block of 4 on translucent paper without back printing 1.60
1687 A820 50c multi 1.00 .35
a. Block of 4, #1684-1687, on translucent paper 2.00
b. Block of 4 #1687 on translucent paper without back printing 4.00
Nos. 1684-1687 (4) 1.95 1.10

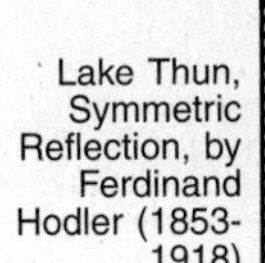

Lake Thun, Symmetric Reflection, by Ferdinand Hodler (1853-1918) A870

2018, Sept. 6 Litho. ***Perf. 13¼x13½***
1688 A870 100c multi 2.10 1.10

Fairy Tale Characters in Forest A871

Fairy Tale Characters Near Bridge A872

2018, Sept. 6 Litho. ***Perf. 13½***
1689 A871 100c multi 2.10 1.10
1690 A872 100c multi 2.10 1.10

Jass Cards — A873

Designs: No. 1691, King of Acorns. No. 1692, Jack of Bells. No. 1693, King of Clubs. No. 1694, Queen of Hearts.

2018, Sept. 6 Litho. ***Perf. 13½***
1691 A873 100c multi 2.10 1.10
1692 A873 100c multi 2.10 1.10
1693 A873 100c multi 2.10 1.10
1694 A873 100c multi 2.10 1.10
a. Horiz. strip of 4, #1691-1694 8.40 4.40
Nos. 1691-1694 (4) 8.40 4.40

Greeting Stamps — A874

Designs: No. 1695, Four-leaf clover and clover flowers. No. 1696, Bird with letter. No. 1697, Ladybug. No. 1698, Fern in envelope.

Serpentine Die Cut 12
2018, Sept. 6 Litho.
Self-Adhesive
1695 A874 85c multi 1.75 .85
a. Block of 4 on translucent paper without back printing 7.00
1696 A874 85c multi 1.75 .85
a. Block of 4 on translucent paper without back printing 7.00
1697 A874 100c multi 2.10 1.10
a. Block of 4 on translucent paper without back printing 8.50
1698 A874 100c multi 2.10 1.10
a. Block of 4, #1695-1698, on translucent paper 7.75
b. Block of 4 #1698 on translucent paper without back printing 8.50
Nos. 1695-1698 (4) 7.70 3.90

Souvenir Sheet

Alpstein — A875

2018, Sept. 6 Litho. ***Perf. 13½***
1699 A875 100c multi 2.10 1.10

Railroad Stations Type of 2016

Station in: 360c, Bern.

Serpentine Die Cut 12
2018, Nov. 15 Litho.
Self-Adhesive
1700 A820 360c multi 7.25 3.75
a. Block of 4 on translucent paper 29.00

Wedge of Swiss Cheese — A876

Fondue Pot — A877

2018, Nov. 15 Litho. ***Perf. 13¾***
1701 A876 100c multi 2.00 1.00
1702 A877 100c multi 2.00 1.00
a. Pair, #1701-1702 4.00 2.00

Miniature Sheet

Medicinal Plants — A878

No. 1703: a, Auricula muris. b, Aconitum. c, Tithymalus paralius. d, Scolymus non aculeatus.

Litho. & Engr.

2018, Nov. 15 ***Perf. 14¼***

1703 A878 Sheet of 4 8.00 4.00
a.-d. 100c Any single 2.00 1.00

Christmas Lights — A879

Designs: 85c, Bottmingen Water Castle. 100c, Kandersteg Church. 150c, Bedretto. 200c, Saint-Ursanne Bridge.

Serpentine Die Cut 11

2018, Nov. 15 **Litho.**

Self-Adhesive

1704 A879 85c multi 1.75 .85
a. Block of 4 on translucent paper 7.00
1705 A879 100c multi 2.00 1.00
a. Block of 4 on translucent paper 8.00
1706 A879 150c multi 3.00 1.50
a. Block of 4 on translucent paper 12.00
1707 A879 200c multi 4.00 2.00
a. Block of 4, #1704-1707 on translucent paper 11.00
b. Block of 4 #1707 on translucent paper 16.00
Nos. 1704-1707 (4) 10.75 5.35

Alfred Escher (1819-82), Politician and Chairman of Railway Companies A880

2019, Mar. 7 **Litho.** ***Perf. 13¼x13½***

1708 A880 100c multi 2.00 1.50

Pig With Four-Leaf Clover — A881

2019, Mar. 7 **Litho.** ***Die Cut***

Flocked Paper

Self-Adhesive

1709 A881 100c multi 2.00 1.50

Addition of Basel Carnival to UNESCO Intangible Cultural Heritage List A882

2019, Mar. 7 **Litho.** ***Perf. 13½***

1710 A882 100c multi 2.00 1.50

Swiss Air Transport, Cent. — A883

2019, Mar. 7 **Litho.** ***Perf. 13½***

1711 A883 100c multi 2.00 1.50

Post Bus Routes, Cent. — A884

Post bus for: 85c, Chur-Laax route. 100c, Brig-Domodossola route.

2019, Mar. 7 **Litho.** ***Perf. 13¼x13½***

1712 A884 85c multi 1.75 1.40
1713 A884 100c multi 2.00 1.50

A885

National Circus Knie, Cent. — A886

2019, Mar. 7 **Litho.** ***Perf. 13½***

1714 A885 100c multi 2.00 1.50
1715 A886 100c multi 2.00 1.50
a. Horiz. pair, #1714-1715 4.00 3.00

Fumetto Comic Festival — A887

No. 1716 — Cartoon character and: a, Map of Switzerland and cheese wheels. b, Mountain, cow and goose. c, Chocolate bar, Swiss Army knife, wristwatch.

2019, Mar. 7 **Litho.** ***Perf. 14¼***

1716 A887 Horiz. strip of 3 6.00 4.50
a.-c. 100c Any single 2.00 1.50

Faces of Animals — A888

Face of: 85c, Dog. 100c, Cat. 150c, Rabbit. 200c, Horse.

Serpentine Die Cut 12

2019, Mar. 7 **Litho.**

Self-Adhesive

1717 A888 85c multi 1.75 1.40
a. Block of 4 on translucent paper 7.00
1718 A888 100c multi 2.00 1.50
a. Block of 4 on translucent paper 8.00
1719 A888 150c multi 3.00 2.25
a. Block of 4 on translucent paper 12.00
1720 A888 200c multi 4.00 3.00
a. Block of 4, #1717-1720 on translucent paper 11.00
b. Block of 4 #1720 on translucent paper 16.00
Nos. 1717-1720 (4) 10.75 8.15

Huldrych Zwingli (1484-1531), Religious Reformer A889

2019, May 2 **Litho.** ***Perf. 14***

1721 A889 85c multi 1.75 1.40

See Germany No. 3099.

First Man on the Moon, 50th Anniv. — A890

2019, May 2 **Litho.** ***Perf. 13¾x14¼***

1722 A890 100c multi 2.00 1.50

Lake Constance Transportation A891

Designs: 100c, Romanshorn-Friedrichshafen train ferry, 150th anniv. 150c, Romanshorn-Rorschach rail line and vehicle ferry, 150th anniv.

2019, May 2 **Litho.** ***Perf. 13½***

1723 A891 100c multi 2.00 1.50
1724 A891 150c multi 3.00 2.25

Europa A892

Birds: No. 1725, Aquila chrysaetos. No. 1726, Calidris alba.

2019, May 2 **Litho.** ***Perf. 13½***

1725 A892 100c multi 2.00 1.50
1726 A892 100c multi 2.00 1.50
a. Horiz. pair, #1725-1726 4.00 3.00

Vintner's Festival A893

No. 1727: a, Bunch of grapes. b, Sun. c, Bird.

2019, May 2 **Litho.** ***Perf. 14¼***

1727 Horiz. strip of 3 6.00 4.50
a.-c. A893 100c Any single 2.00 1.50

Land Art by Ivo Moosberger A894

Designs: 85c, Buttercup rings, Ticino. 100c, Willow rod spheres, Zug. 150c, Stone spiral, Uri. 200c, Stone arch, Graubünden.

Serpentine Die Cut 9¾x10¼

2019, May 2 **Litho.**

Self-Adhesive

1728 A894 85c multi 1.75 1.40
a. Block of 4 on translucent paper 7.00
1729 A894 100c multi 2.00 1.50
a. Block of 4 on translucent paper 8.00
1730 A894 150c multi 3.00 2.25
a. Block of 4 on translucent paper 12.00
1731 A894 200c multi 4.00 3.00
a. Block of 4, #1728-1731 on translucent paper 11.00
b. Block of 4 #1731 on translucent paper 16.00
Nos. 1728-1731 (4) 10.75 8.15

Carl Spitteler (1845-1924), 1919 Nobel Laureate in Literature A895

2019, Sept. 5 **Litho.** ***Perf. 13½***

1732 A895 100c multi 2.00 1.50

Basel Cathedral, 1000th Anniv. — A896

2019, Sept. 5 **Litho.** ***Perf. 13¾x14¼***

1733 A896 100c multi 2.00 1.50

Calligraphy by Rebekka Moser — A897

2019, Sept. 5 **Litho.** ***Perf. 13½***

1734 A897 100c multi 2.00 1.50

Lager Beer in Mug — A898

Dark Beer in Glass — A899

2019, Sept. 5 **Litho.** ***Perf. 13½x13¼***

1735 A898 100c multi 2.00 1.50
1736 A899 100c multi 2.00 1.50
a. Horiz. pair, #1735-1736 4.00 3.00

Animals — A900

Designs: No. 1737, Giraffe. No. 1738, Zebra, horiz. No. 1739, Flamingo, horiz. No. 1740, Meerkat.

Serpentine Die Cut 12

2019, Sept. 5 Litho.

Self-Adhesive

1737	A900	85c multi	1.75	1.40
a.		Block of 4 on translucent paper	7.00	
1738	A900	85c gold & multi	1.75	1.40
a.		Block of 4 on translucent paper	7.00	
1739	A900	100c multi	2.00	1.50
a.		Block of 4 on translucent paper	8.00	
1740	A900	100c multi	2.00	1.50
a.		Block of 4, #1737-1740, on translucent paper	7.50	
b.		Block of 4 on translucent paper	8.00	
		Nos. 1737-1740 (4)	7.50	5.80

Traditional Women's Clothing A901

No. 1741 — Clothing from: a, Lötschental. b, Fribourg. c, Valle Verzasca. d, Engiadina.

2019, Sept. 5 Litho. *Perf. 14¼*

1741		Sheet of 4	8.00	6.00
a.-d.	A901	100c Any single	2.00	1.50

2020 Winter Youth Olympics, Lausanne A902

Perf. 13¼x13½

2019, Nov. 14 Litho.

1742	A902	100c multi	2.00	1.50

A903

Diversity A904

Perf. 13½x13¼

2019, Nov. 14 Litho.

1743	A903	85c multi	1.75	1.40

Perf. 13¼x13½

1744	A904	100c multi	2.00	1.50

Joint Issue between Switzerland and Liechtenstein.

See Liechtenstein Nos. 1802-1803.

Souvenir Sheet

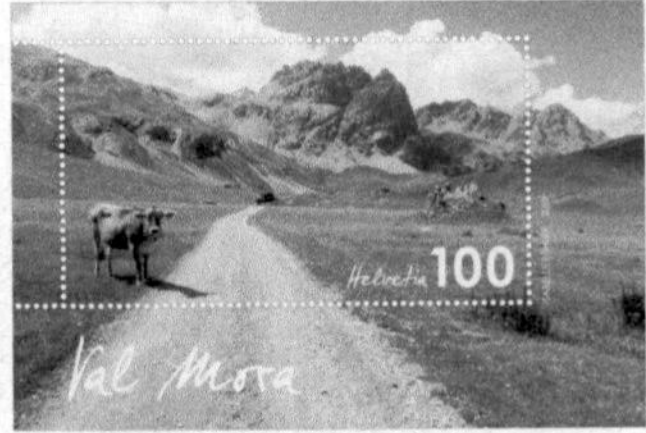

Val Mora — A905

2019, Nov. 14 Litho. *Perf. 13¼*

1745	A905	100c multi	2.00	1.50

Christmas — A906

Designs: 85c, Gift. 100c, Snowflake. 150c, Candle. 200c, Star.

Serpentine Die Cut 12

2019, Nov. 14 Litho.

Self-Adhesive

1746	A906	85c gold & multi	1.75	1.40
1747	A906	100c sil & multi	2.00	1.50
1748	A906	150c gold & multi	3.00	2.25
1749	A906	200c sil & multi	4.00	3.00
a.		Block of 4, #1746-1749, on translucent paper	11.00	
		Nos. 1746-1749 (4)	10.75	8.15

Japanese Beetle — A907

2020, Mar. 5 Litho. *Perf. 13¼x13½*

1750	A907	85c multi	1.75	1.40

International Year of Plant Health.

Hérens Cattle — A908

2020, Mar. 5 Litho. *Perf. 13¼x13½*

1751	A908	100c multi	2.10	1.60

Swiss Federation of Hérens Cattle Breeders, Cent.

National Library, 125th Anniv. — A909

2020, Mar. 5 Litho. *Perf. 13½x13¼*

1752	A909	100c multi	2.10	1.60

Swiss Fire Brigade Association, 150th Anniv. — A910

2020, Mar. 5 Litho. *Perf. 13½x13¼*

1753	A910	100c multi	2.10	1.60

Solothurn, 2000th Anniv. — A911

2020, Mar. 5 Litho. *Perf. 13½x13¼*

1754	A911	100c multi	2.10	1.60

Swiss Soccer Association, 125th Anniv. — A912

2020, Mar. 5 Litho. *Perf. 13½x13¼*

1755	A912	100c multi	2.10	1.60

2020 World Ice Hockey Championships, Switzerland — A913

Designs: 85c, Swiss player and puck. 100c, Swiss hockey players.

Serpentine Die Cut 9¾x10¼

2020, Mar. 5 Litho.

Self-Adhesive

1756	A913	85c multi	1.75	1.40
1757	A913	100c multi	2.10	1.60
a.		Horiz. pair, #1756-1757, on translucent paper	4.00	

The 2020 World Ice Hockey Championships were canceled because of the coronavirus pandemic.

Souvenir Sheet

Engelberg Abbey, 900th Anniv. — A914

2020, Mar. 5 Litho. *Perf. 12*

1758	A914	100c multi	2.10	1.60

Magnified Forget-me-not Pollen Grains — A915

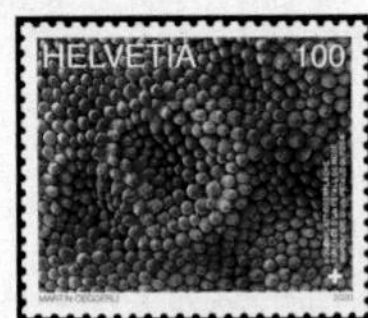

Magnified Rose Petal — A916

2020, May 7 Litho. *Perf. 13¼x13½*

1759	A915	85c multi	1.75	1.40
1760	A916	100c multi	2.10	1.60

Geneva Airport, Cent. — A917

2020, May 7 Litho. *Perf. 13¼x13½*

1761	A917	100c multi	2.10	1.60

Swiss Foundation for Landscape Conservation, 50th Anniv. — A918

2020, May 7 Litho. *Perf. 13½*

1762	A918	100c multi	2.10	1.60

Society for the History of Swiss Art, 140th Anniv. A919

2020, May 7 Litho. *Perf. 13½*

1763	A919	100c multi	2.10	1.60

Mail Carrier on Rheinhausen-Mantua Postal Route — A920

Post Rider on Rheinhausen-Mantua Postal Route — A921

2020, May 7 Litho. *Perf. 13½*

1764	A920	100c multi	2.10	1.60
1765	A921	100c multi	2.10	1.60
a.		Vert. pair, #1764-1765	4.25	3.25

Europa.

Swiss Florists' Association (florist.ch), Cent. — A922

Serpentine Die Cut 12

2020, May 7 Litho.

Self-Adhesive

1766	A922	100c multi	2.10	1.60

Adult and Juvenile Animals A923

Adult and juvenile: 85c, Mergansers. 100c, Marmots. 150c, Lynx. 200c, Ibex.

Serpentine Die Cut 12

2020, May 7 Litho.

Self-Adhesive

1767	A923	85c multi	1.75	1.40
1768	A923	100c multi	2.10	1.60
1769	A923	150c multi	3.25	2.50
1770	A923	200c multi	4.25	3.25
a.		Block of 4, #1767-1770, on translucent paper	11.50	
		Nos. 1767-1770 (4)	11.35	8.75

SEMI-POSTAL STAMPS

Nos. B1-B76, B81-B84 were sold at premiums of 2c for 3c stamps, 5c for 5c-20c stamps and 10c for 30c-40c stamps.

Helvetia and Matterhorn — SP2

Perf. 11½, 12

1913, Dec. 1 Typo. Wmk. 183

Granite Paper

B1 SP2 5c green 3.75 *11.50*
Never hinged 10.00

Boy (Appenzell) SP3

Girl (Lucerne) SP4

1915, Dec. 1 ***Perf. 11½***

B2 SP3 5c green, *buff* 3.75 *16.00*
a. Tête bêche pair 77.50 *1,400.*
B3 SP4 10c red, *buff* 77.50 100.00
Set, never hinged 356.50

Girl (Fribourg) SP5

Dairy Boy (Bern) SP6

Girl (Vaud) — SP7

1916, Dec. 1

B4 SP5 3c vio, *buff* 7.75 *37.50*
B5 SP6 5c grn, *buff* 16.00 11.50
B6 SP7 10c brn red, *buff* 62.50 *77.50*
Nos. B4-B6 (3) 86.25 *126.50*
Set, never hinged 170.00

Girl (Valais) SP8

Girl (Unterwalden) SP9

Girl (Ticino) — SP10

1917, Dec. 1

B7 SP8 3c vio, *buff* 3.75 *57.50*
B8 SP9 5c green, *buff* 9.25 7.75
B9 SP10 10c red, *buff* 24.00 30.00
Nos. B7-B9 (3) 37.00 *95.25*
Set, never hinged 94.00

Uri SP11

Geneva SP12

Straw-Surfaced Paper

1918, Dec. 1

B10 SP11 10c red, org & blk 11.50 *35.00*
B11 SP12 15c vio, red, org & blk 16.00 *19.50*
Set, never hinged 66.50

Nidwalden SP13

Vaud SP14

Obwalden — SP15

Cream-Surfaced Paper

1919, Dec. 1

B12 SP13 7½c gray, red & blk 3.75 *22.00*
B13 SP14 10c lake, grn & blk 3.75 *22.00*
B14 SP15 15c pur, red & blk 7.75 *11.00*
Nos. B12-B14 (3) 15.25 *55.00*
Set, never hinged 47.00

Schwyz SP16

Zürich SP17

Ticino — SP18

Cream-Surfaced Paper

1920, Dec. 1

B15 SP16 7½c gray & red 4.75 *24.00*
B16 SP17 10c red & lt bl 7.75 *25.00*
B17 SP18 15c violet, red & bl 3.75 *11.50*
Nos. B15-B17 (3) 16.25 *60.50*
Set, never hinged 46.50
Set, on first day cover 2,330.

Valais SP19

Bern SP20

Switzerland — SP21

Cream-Surfaced Paper

1921, Dec. 1

B18 SP19 10c grn, red & blk .75 *4.75*
B19 SP20 20c vio, red, org & blk 3.00 *7.00*
B20 SP21 40c blue & red 12.50 *85.00*
Nos. B18-B20 (3) 16.25 *96.75*
Set, never hinged 40.50

Zug SP22

Fribourg SP23

Lucerne SP24

Switzerland SP25

Cream-Surfaced Paper

1922, Dec. 1

B21 SP22 5c org, pale bl & blk .75 *9.25*
B22 SP23 10c ol grn & blk .75 *3.00*
B23 SP24 20c vio, pale bl & blk 1.60 *3.00*
B24 SP25 40c bl & red 14.00 *92.50*
Nos. B21-B24 (4) 17.10 *107.75*
Set, never hinged 40.00

Basel SP26

Glarus (St. Fridolin) SP27

Neuchâtel SP28

Switzerland SP29

Cream-Surfaced Paper

1923, Dec. 1

B25 SP26 5c org & blk .40 *7.75*
B26 SP27 10c multi .40 *3.75*
B27 SP28 20c multi .75 *3.75*
B28 SP29 40c dk bl & red 11.00 *70.00*
Nos. B25-B28 (4) 12.55 *85.25*
Set, never hinged 30.00
Set, on first day cover 1,800.

Appenzell SP30

Solothurn SP31

Schaffhausen SP32

Switzerland SP33

Cream-Surfaced Paper

1924, Dec. 1

B29 SP30 5c dk vio & blk .40 *2.50*
B30 SP31 10c grn, red & blk .75 *1.15*
B31 SP32 20c car, yel & blk .75 *2.00*
B32 SP33 30c bl, red & blk 2.50 *21.00*
Nos. B29-B32 (4) 4.40 *26.65*
Set, never hinged 11.00

St. Gallen (Canton) SP34

Appenzell-Ausser-Rhoden SP35

Grisons SP36

Switzerland SP37

Cream-Surfaced Paper

1925, Dec. 1

B33 SP34 5c vio, grn & blk .40 *2.50*
B34 SP35 10c grn & blk .40 *1.60*
B35 SP36 20c multi .55 *1.60*
B36 SP37 30c dk bl, red & blk 1.40 *14.00*
Nos. B33-B36 (4) 2.75 *19.70*
Set, never hinged 7.50

Thurgau SP38

Basel SP39

Aargau SP40

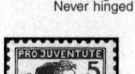

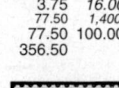

Switzerland SP41

Cream-Surfaced Paper

1926, Dec. 1

B37 SP38 5c vio, bis & grn .40 *2.00*
B38 SP39 10c gray grn, red & blk .40 *2.00*
B39 SP40 20c red, blk & bl .55 *2.50*
B40 SP41 30c dk bl & red 1.40 *16.00*
Nos. B37-B40 (4) 2.75 *22.50*
Set, never hinged 7.50

Orphan SP42

Orphan at Pestalozzi School SP43

SP44

J. H. Pestalozzi SP45

1927, Dec. 1 Typo. Wmk. 183

Granite Paper

B41 SP42 5c brn pur & yel, *grysh* .40 *2.50*
B42 SP43 10c grn & brn rose, *grnsh* .40 *.75*

Engr.

B43 SP44 20c red .55 *.75*

Unwmk.

Photo.

B44 SP45 30c gray bl & blk 1.40 *11.50*
Nos. B41-B44 (4) 2.75 *15.50*
Set, never hinged 5.75

Nos. B43-B44 for the centenary of the death of Johann Heinrich Pestalozzi, the Swiss educational reformer.

Lausanne
SP46

Winterthur
SP47

St. Gallen (City) — SP48

J. H. Dunant
SP49

1928, Dec. 1 Typo. Wmk. 183

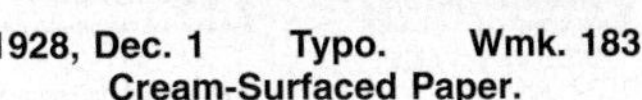

Cream-Surfaced Paper.

B45 SP46 5c dk vio, red & blk .40 *2.50*
B46 SP47 10c bl grn, org red & blk .40 *1.60*
B47 SP48 20c brn red, blk & yel .25 *.70*

Unwmk.

Photo.

Thick White Paper

B48 SP49 30c dl bl & red 1.60 *10.00*
Nos. B45-B48 (4) 2.65 *14.80*
Set, never hinged 6.75
Set, on first day cover 530.00

No. B48 for the centenary of the birth of Jean Henri Dunant, Swiss author, philanthropist and founder of the Red Cross Society.

Lake Lugano and Mt. Salvatore
SP50

Lake Engstlen and Mt. Titlis
SP51

Mt. Lyskamm
SP52

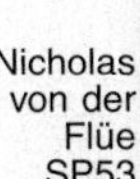

Nicholas von der Flüe
SP53

1929, Dec. 1 ***Perf. 11x11½***

B49 SP50 5c dk vio & red org .40 *2.00*
B50 SP51 10c ol brn & gray bl .40 *1.60*
B51 SP52 20c brn garnet & bl .40 *2.00*
B52 SP53 30c dk blue 1.70 *20.00*
Nos. B49-B52 (4) 2.90 *25.60*
Set, never hinged 6.75

No. B52 for Nicholas von der Flüe, the Swiss patriot. By his advice the Swiss Confederation was continued and Swiss independence was saved.

Fribourg
SP54

Altdorf
SP55

Schaffhausen
SP56

Jeremias Gotthelf
SP57

Wmk. 183

1930, Dec. 1 Typo. ***Perf. 11½***

Cream-Surfaced Paper

B53 SP54 5c dp grn, dl bl & blk .40 *1.60*
B54 SP55 10c multicolored .40 *1.15*
B55 SP56 20c multicolored .40 *1.15*

Engr.

White Paper

B56 SP57 30c slate blue 1.60 *7.75*
Nos. B53-B56 (4) 2.80 *11.65*
Set, never hinged 6.75

No. B56 for Jeremias Gotthelf, pen name of Albrecht Bitzius, pastor and author.

Lakes Silvaplana and Sils
SP58

Wetterhorn
SP59

Lake Geneva
SP60

Alexandre Vinet
SP61

1931, Dec. 1 Photo. Unwmk.

Granite Paper

B57 SP58 5c dp grn .60 *2.00*
B58 SP59 10c dk vio .40 *1.15*
B59 SP60 20c brn red .95 *1.60*

Wmk. 183

Engr.

B60 SP61 30c ultra 6.25 *27.00*
Never hinged 16.00
On cover 55.00
Nos. B57-B60 (4) 8.20 *31.75*
Set, never hinged 19.00

No. B60 for Alexandre Rudolph Vinet, critic and theologian.

Flag Swinger
SP62

Putting the Stone
SP63

Wrestling
SP64

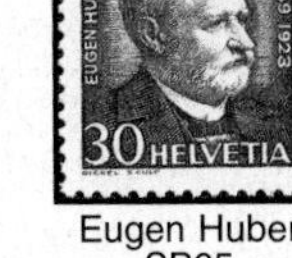

Eugen Huber
SP65

1932, Dec. 1 Typo. Unwmk.

Granite Paper

B61 SP62 5c dk grn & red .45 *2.75*
B62 SP63 10c orange .60 *2.75*
B63 SP64 20c scarlet .75 *2.75*

Wmk. 183

Engr.

B64 SP65 30c ultra 2.75 *11.00*
Nos. B61-B64 (4) 4.55 *19.25*
Set, never hinged 12.50

No. B64 for Eugen Huber, jurist and author of the Swiss Civil Law Book.

Girl of Vaud — SP66

Girl of Bern — SP67

Girl of Ticino
SP68

Jean Baptiste Girard (Le Père Grégoire)
SP69

1933, Dec. 1 Photo. Unwmk.

Granite Paper

B65 SP66 5c grn & buff .45 *2.40*
B66 SP67 10c vio & buff .45 *1.55*
B67 SP68 20c red & buff .60 *3.00*

Wmk. 183

Engr.

B68 SP69 30c ultra 3.00 *13.00*
Nos. B65-B68 (4) 4.50 *19.95*
Set, never hinged 11.00

Girl of Appenzell
SP70

Girl of Valais
SP71

Girl of Grisons
SP72

Albrecht von Haller
SP73

1934, Dec. 1 Photo. Unwmk.

B69 SP70 5c grn & buff .40 *2.40*
B70 SP71 10c vio & buff .55 *1.55*
B71 SP72 20c red & buff .60 *2.40*

Wmk. 183

Engr.

B72 SP73 30c ultra 3.00 *16.00*
Nos. B69-B72 (4) 4.55 *22.35*
Set, never hinged 11.00

Girl of Basel
SP74

Girl of Lucerne
SP75

Girl of Geneva
SP76

Stefano Franscini
SP77

1935, Dec. 1 Photo. Unwmk.

Granite Paper

B73 SP74 5c grn & buff .40 *2.40*
B74 SP75 10c vio & buff .55 *1.55*
B75 SP76 20c red & buff .60 *3.75*

Wmk. 183

Engr.

B76 SP77 30c ultra 3.00 *16.00*
Nos. B73-B76 (4) 4.55 *23.70*
Set, never hinged 11.00

No. B76 honors Stefano Franscini (1796-1857), political economist and educator.

Alpine Herdsman — SP78

Perf. 11½

1936, Oct. 1 Photo. Unwmk.

Granite Paper

B77 SP78 10c + 5c vio .75 *1.55*
B78 SP78 20c + 10c dk red 1.15 *6.00*
B79 SP78 30c + 10c ultra 5.50 *27.50*
Nos. B77-B79 (3) 7.40 *35.05*
Set, never hinged 15.50

Souvenir Sheet

B80 SP78 Sheet of 3 60.00 *240.00*
Never hinged 105.00
a. Block of 4 sheets 240.00 *1,250.*
Never hinged 460.00

Swiss National Defense Fund Drive.

No. B80 contains stamps similar to Nos. B77-B79, but on grilled granite paper with blue and red fibers instead of black and red. Sold for 2fr. Size: 120x130mm.

Johann Georg Nägeli
SP79

Girl of Neuchâtel
SP80

Girl of Schwyz
SP81

Girl of Zurich
SP82

Wmk. 183

1936, Dec. 1 Engr. *Perf. 11½*

Granite Paper

B81 SP79 5c grn .40 *1.15*

Unwmk.

Photo.

B82 SP80 10c vio & buff .75 *1.15*
B83 SP81 20c red & buff .45 *3.00*
B84 SP82 30c ultra & buff 5.00 *40.00*
Nos. B81-B84 (4) 6.60 *45.30*
Set, never hinged 14.00

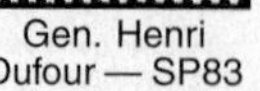

Gen. Henri Dufour — SP83

Nicholas von der Flüe — SP84

Boy SP85

Girl SP86

Perf. 11½

1937, Dec. 1 Unwmk. Engr.

B85 SP83 5c + 5c bl grn .40 *.75*
B86 SP84 10c + 5c red vio .40 *.75*

Photo.

Granite Paper

B87 SP85 20c + 5c red & silver .60 *.75*
B88 SP86 30c + 10c ultra & sil 1.70 *7.75*
Nos. B85-B88 (4) 3.10 *10.00*
Set, never hinged 6.50

25th anniv. of the Pro Juventute (child welfare) stamps.

Souvenir Sheet

1937, Dec. 20 *Imperf.*

B89 Sheet of 2 4.00 *62.50*
a. SP85 20c + 5c red & silver 1.30 *17.00*
b. SP86 30c + 10c ultra & silver 1.30 *17.00*
Never hinged 2.25

Simulated perforation in silver. Sheet sold for 1fr.

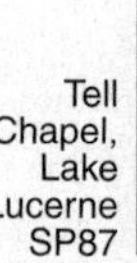

Tell Chapel, Lake Lucerne SP87

1938, June 15 *Perf. 11½*

Granite Paper

B90 SP87 10c + 10c brt vio & yel .45 *2.75*
Never hinged 2.00
a. Grilled gum 11.50 *70.00*
Never hinged 23.00

National Fête Day.

Salomon Gessner SP88

Girl of St. Gallen SP89

Girl of Uri — SP90

Girl of Aargau — SP91

1938, Dec. 1 Engr. *Perf. 11½*

B91 SP88 5c + 5c dp bl grn .40 *.75*

Photo.

Granite Paper

B92 SP89 10c + 5c pur & buff .40 *.75*
B93 SP90 20c + 5c red & buff .55 *.75*
B94 SP91 30c + 10c ultra 2.10 *9.25*
Nos. B91-B94 (4) 3.45 *11.50*
Set, never hinged 7.50
Set, on first day cover 400.00

Castle at Laupen SP92

1939, June 15

B95 SP92 10c + 10c brn, gray & red .40 *2.00*
Never hinged 1.60

600th anniversary of the Battle of Laupen. The surtax was used to aid needy mothers.

Hans Herzog SP93

Girl of Fribourg SP94

Girl of Nidwalden SP95

Girl of Basel SP96

Perf. 11½

1939, Dec. 1 Unwmk. Engr.

B96 SP93 5c + 5c dk grn .40 *.75*

Photo.

Granite Paper

B97 SP94 10c + 5c rose vio & buff .40 *.75*
B98 SP95 20c + 5c org red .40 *1.60*
B99 SP96 30c + 10c ultra & buff 2.00 *22.00*
Nos. B96-B99 (4) 3.20 *25.10*
Set, never hinged 7.50

Sempach, 1386 — SP97

Giornico, 1478 — SP98

Calven, 1499 SP99

WWI Ranger SP100

1940, Mar. 20 Photo.

Granite Paper

B100 SP97 5c + 5c emer, blk & red .40 *1.60*
B101 SP98 10c + 5c brn org, blk & car .40 *.75*
B102 SP99 20c + 5c brn red, blk & car 2.40 1.60
B103 SP100 30c + 10c brt bl, brn blk & red 2.00 *11.50*

National Fête Day. The surtax was for the National Fund and the Red Cross.

Redrawn

B104 SP99 20c + 5c brn red, blk & car 6.25 9.00
Nos. B100-B104 (5) 11.45 *24.45*
Set, never hinged 35.00

The base of statue has been heavily shaded. "Calven 1499" moved nearer to bottom line of base. Top line of base removed.

Souvenir Sheet

Unwmk.

1940, July 16 Photo. *Imperf.*

Granite Paper

B105 Sheet of 4 175.00 *500.00*
Never hinged 325.00
a. SP97 5c+5c yel grn, blk & red 16.00 *35.00*
Never hinged 27.50
b. SP98 10c+5c org yel, blk & red 57.50 *175.00*
Never hinged 77.50
c. SP99 20c+5c brn red, blk & red (redrawn) 57.50 *175.00*
Never hinged 77.50
d. SP100 30c+10c chlky bl, blk & red 16.00 *35.00*
Never hinged 27.50

National Fete Day. Sheets measure 125x65mm and sold for 5fr.

Gottfried Keller SP102

Girl of Thurgau SP103

Girl of Solothurn SP104

Girl of Zug SP105

1940, Dec. 1 Engr. *Perf. 11½*

B106 SP102 5c + 5c dk bl grn .40 *.75*

Photo.

B107 SP103 10c + 5c brn & buff .40 *.75*
B108 SP104 20c + 5c org red & buff .45 *.75*
B109 SP105 30c + 10c dp ultra & buff 1.70 *13.00*
Nos. B106-B109 (4) 2.95 *15.25*
Set, never hinged 7.50

Lake Lucerne, Arms of Cantons SP106

Tell Chapel at Chemin Creux SP107

1941, June 15

B110 SP106 10c + 10c multi .30 *.75*
B111 SP107 20c + 10c org, red & lt buff .40 *1.25*
Set, never hinged 2.00

Natl. Fête Day and 650th anniv. of Swiss Independence.

Johann Lavater SP108

Girl of Schaffhausen SP109

Girl of Obwalden SP110

Daniel Jean Richard SP111

1941, Dec. 1 Engr.

B112 SP108 5c + 5c dk grn .30 *.30*
B113 SP111 30c + 10c dp ultra .30 *5.00*

Photo.

B114 SP109 10c + 5c chnt & buff .35 *.40*
B115 SP110 20c + 5c ver & buff 1.05 *.40*
Nos. B112-B115 (4) 2.00 *6.10*
Set, never hinged 3.50

Souvenir Sheet

Imperf

B116 Sheet of 2 50.00 *350.00*
a. SP109 10c +5c chnt & buff 17.00 *125.00*
b. SP110 20c +5c ver & buff 17.00 *125.00*
Never hinged 95.00

Issued in sheets measuring 75x70mm and sold for 2fr. The surtax was used for charity.

Ancient Geneva SP113

Soldiers' Monument, Forch SP114

1942, June 15 *Perf. 11½*

B117 SP113 10c + 10c gray blk, red & yel .25 *.50*
B118 SP114 20c + 10c cop red, red & buff .25 *.85*
Set, never hinged 1.20

National Fête Day, 1942. No. B117 for the 2000th anniv. of the City of Geneva.

Souvenir Sheet

Imperf

B119 Sheet of 2 40.00 *225.00*
a. SP113 10c +10c gray black, red & yellow 14.00 *80.00*

b. SP113 20c +10c copper red, red & buff 14.00 *80.00*
Never hinged 85.00

Issued in sheets measuring 105x63mm in commemoration of National Fete and the 2000th anniv. of the City of Geneva. Sold for 2fr. The surtax was divided between the Swiss Alliance of Samaritans and the National Community Chest.

Niklaus Riggenbach SP116

Girl of Appenzell SP117

Girl of Glarus SP118

Konrad Escher von der Linth SP119

1942, Dec. 1 **Engr.** ***Perf. 11½***

B120 SP116 5c + 5c deep grn .25 *.40*
B121 SP119 30c + 10c royal bl .25 *.40*

Photo.

B122 SP117 10c + 5c dp brn & buff .35 *.40*
B123 SP118 20c + 5c org red 1.25 *3.75*
Nos. B120-B123 (4) 2.10 *4.95*
Set, never hinged 4.00

Intragna SP120

Parliament Buildings, Bern SP121

1943, June 15 **Photo.** ***Perf. 11½***

B124 SP120 10c + 10c blk brn, buff & dk red .25 *.75*
B125 SP121 20c + 10c cop red, buff & dk red .30 *1.50*
Set, never hinged 1.40

National Fête Day, 1943.

Emanuel von Fellenberg SP122

Silver Thistle SP123

20c+5c, Lady slipper. 30c+10c, Gentian.

1943, Dec. 1 **Engr.**

B126 SP122 5c + 5c green .25 *.35*

Photo.

B127 SP123 10c + 5c sl grn & ocher .25 *.35*
B128 SP123 20c + 5c copper red & yel .25 *.35*
B129 SP123 30c + 10c royal bl & lt bl 1.10 *6.00*
Nos. B126-B129 (4) 1.85 *7.05*
Set, never hinged 3.25

Souvenir Sheets

SP126

1943 **Engr.** ***Imperf.***

B130 SP126 Sheet of 12 35.00 *60.00*
a. 10c black, single stamp 1.10 *3.75*
Never hinged 70.00

Sold for 5fr. Size: 165x140mm.

SP127

Red Horizontal Lines

B131 SP127 Sheet of 2 35.00 *52.50*
a. 4c black & red 12.50 *18.00*
b. 6c black & red 12.50 *18.00*
Never hinged 70.00

Sold for 3fr. Size: 70x75mm.

Arms of Geneva — SP128

B132 SP128 Sheet of 2 32.50 *40.00*
a. 5c green & black 11.00 *13.00*
Never hinged 65.00

Sold for 3fr. Size: 72x72mm. Centenary of Swiss postage stamps. The surtax aided the Swiss Red Cross.

Heiden SP129

St. Jacob SP130

Mesocco SP131

Basel SP132

Perf. 11½

1944, June 15 **Photo.** **Unwmk.**

B133 SP129 5c + 5c dk bl grn, red & buff .25 *1.60*
B134 SP130 10c + 10c gray blk, red & buff .25 *.45*
B135 SP131 20c + 10c hn, red & buff .30 *.45*
B136 SP132 30c + 10c brt ultra & red 2.10 *12.50*
Nos. B133-B136 (4) 2.90 *15.00*
Set, never hinged 5.50

National Fete Day.

Numa Droz SP133

Edelweiss SP134

Designs: 20c+5c, Lilium martagon. 30c+10c, Aquilegia alpina.

1944, Dec. 1 **Engr.**

B137 SP133 5c + 5c green .25 *.30*

Photo.

B138 SP134 10c + 5c dk sl grn, yel & gray .25 *.35*
B139 SP134 20c + 5c red, yel & gray .35 *.40*
B140 SP134 30c + 10c bl, gray & lt bl 1.15 *5.75*
Nos. B137-B140 (4) 2.00 *6.80*
Set, never hinged 4.00

Symbol of Faith, Hope and Love — SP137

Lifeboat Making a Rescue — SP138

1945, Feb. 20 ***Perf. 11½***

B141 SP137 10c + 10c multi .30 *.50*
B142 SP137 20c + 60c multi .90 *5.00*
Set, never hinged 2.75

Imperf

Souvenir Sheet

B143 SP138 3fr + 7fr bl gray 130.00 *240.00*
Never hinged 225.00

Issued in sheets measuring 70x110mm. Surtax for the benefit of war victims.

Souvenir Sheet

Dove of Basel — SP139

1945, Apr. 14 **Typo.**

B144 SP139 Sheet of 2 55.00 *95.00*
a. 10c gray, maroon & black 18.50 *27.50*
Never hinged 110.00

Cent. of the Basel Cantonal Stamp. The sheets measure 71x63mm and sold for 3fr. The surtax was for the Pro Juventute Foundation.

Numeral of Value and Red Cross — SP140

1945 **Photo.** ***Perf. 12***

B145 SP140 5c + 10c grn & red .30 *.75*
Never hinged .65

Weaver SP141

Farm of Jura SP142

Farm of Emmental SP143

Frame House, Eastern Switzerland — SP144

1945, June 15 **Engr.** ***Perf. 11½***

B146 SP141 5c + 5c bl grn & red .40 *1.40*

Photo.

B147 SP142 10c + 10c brn, gray bl & red .35 *.50*
B148 SP143 20c + 10c hn brn, buff & red .50 *.50*
B149 SP144 30c + 10c saph & red 5.50 *22.50*
Nos. B146-B149 (4) 6.75 *24.90*
Set, never hinged 14.00

The surtax was for needy mothers.

Ludwig Forrer — SP145

Susanna Orelli — SP146

Alpine Dog-Rose SP147

Crocus SP148

1945, Dec. 1 **Engr.**
B150 SP145 5c + 5c dk grn .25 *.40*
B151 SP146 10c + 10c dk red brn .25 *.30*

Photo.
B152 SP147 20c + 10c rose brn, rose & yel org .50 *.30*
B153 SP148 30c + 10c dk bl, gray & lil 1.25 *5.75*
Nos. B150-B153 (4) 2.25 *6.75*
Set, never hinged 4.00

Cheese Making SP149

Farm Buildings and Vineyards SP150

House in Appenzell SP151

House in Engadine SP152

1946, June 15 **Engr.**
B154 SP149 5c + 5c bl grn & red .45 *1.60*

Photo.
B155 SP150 10c + 10c brn, buff & red .35 *.50*
B156 SP151 20c + 10c henna, buff & red .50 *.50*
B157 SP152 30c + 10c saph & red 2.75 *7.50*
Nos. B154-B157 (4) 4.05 *10.10*
Set, never hinged 8.00

Rodolphe Toepffer SP153

Narcissus SP154

20c+10c, Mountain sengreen. 30c+10c, Blue thistle.

1946, Nov. 30 **Engr.**
B158 SP153 5c + 5c green .25 *.35*

Photo.
B159 SP154 10c + 10c dk sl grn, gray & red org .25 *.35*
B160 SP154 20c + 10c brn car, gray & yel .25 *.35*
B161 SP154 30c + 10c dk bl, gray & pink 1.55 *5.50*
Nos. B158-B161 (4) 2.30 *6.55*
Set, never hinged 3.75

Railroad Laborers SP157

Railroad Station, Rorschach SP158

Lüen-Castiel Station — SP159

Flüelen Station SP160

Perf. 11½
1947, June 14 **Engr.** **Unwmk.**
B162 SP157 5c + 5c dk grn & red .55 *1.60*

Photo.
B163 SP158 10c + 10c gray blk, cream & red .55 *.45*
B164 SP159 20c + 10c rose lil, cream & red .75 *.45*
B165 SP160 30c + 10c bl, gray & red 2.50 *7.50*
Nos. B162-B165 (4) 4.35 *10.00*
Set, never hinged 8.00

The surtax was for professional education of invalids and for the fight against cancer.

Jakob Burckhardt SP161

Auricula Primrose SP162

20c+10c, Red lily. 30c+10c, Cyclamen.

1947, Dec. 1 **Engr.**
B166 SP161 5c + 5c dk grn .25 *.30*

Photo.
B167 SP162 10c + 10c sl blk, gray & yel .25 *.30*
B168 SP162 20c + 10c red brn, gray & cop red .30 *.30*
B169 SP162 30c + 10c dk bl, gray & pink 1.25 *5.00*
Nos. B166-B169 (4) 2.05 *5.90*
Set, never hinged 3.50

Sun and Olympic Emblem SP165

Icehockey Player SP167

10c+10c, Snowflake and Olympic Emblem. 30c+10c, Ski-runner.

1948, Jan. 15
B170 SP165 5c + 5c dk bl grn & yel .30 *1.20*
B171 SP165 10c + 10c choc & bl .30 *.80*
B172 SP167 20c + 10c dp mag, gray & org yel .40 *1.20*
B173 SP167 30c + 10c dk bl, bl & gray blk 1.25 *4.00*
Nos. B170-B173 (4) 2.25 *7.20*
Set, never hinged 5.25

Issued to publicize the 5th Olympic Winter Games, St. Moritz, Jan. 30-Feb. 8, 1948.

Frontier Guard SP169

House of Fribourg SP170

House of Valais SP171

House of Ticino SP172

1948, June 15 **Engr.**
B174 SP169 5c + 5c dk grn & red .30 *.90*

Photo.
B175 SP170 10c + 10c sl & gray .30 *.50*
B176 SP171 20c + 10c brn red & pink .30 *.60*
B177 SP172 30c + 10c bl & gray 2.00 *6.00*
Nos. B174-B177 (4) 2.90 *8.00*
Set, never hinged 5.75

Johann R. Wettstein — SP173

1948, Aug. 21 ***Perf. 11x12½***
B178 SP173 Sheet of 2 40.00 *65.00*
a. 10c rose lilac 13.00 *25.00*
b. 20c chalky blue 13.00 *25.00*
Never hinged 75.00

Intl. Phil. Expo., Basel, Aug. 21-29, 1948. Sheet, size 110x60mm, sold for 3fr, of which the surtax was used for the exhibition and charitable purposes.

Gen. Ulrich Wille SP174

Foxglove SP175

20c+10c, Alpine rose. 40c+10c, Lily of paradise.

1948, Dec. 1 **Engr.** ***Perf. 11½***
B179 SP174 5c + 5c dk vio brn .25 *.25*

Photo.
B180 SP175 10c + 10c dk grn, yel grn & yel .25 *.25*
B181 SP175 20c + 10c brn, crim & buff .25 *.25*
B182 SP175 40c + 10c bl, gray & org 1.25 *4.75*
Nos. B179-B182 (4) 2.00 *5.50*
Set, never hinged 3.75

Postman SP176

Mountain Farmhouse SP177

House of Lucerne SP178

House of Prattigau SP179

Engraved and Photogravure
1949, June 15 **Shield in Carmine**
B183 SP176 5c + 5c rose vio .30 *1.20*

Photo.
B184 SP177 10c + 10c bl grn & car .30 *.60*
B185 SP178 20c + 10c dk brn & cr .30 *.60*
B186 SP179 40c + 10c bl & pale bl 2.50 *7.75*
Nos. B183-B186 (4) 3.40 *10.15*
Set, never hinged 7.25

The surtax was for professional education of Swiss youth.

Niklaus Wengi SP180

Anemone Sulphureous SP181

20c+10c, Alpine clematis. 40c+10c, Superb pink.

1949, Dec. 1 **Engr.** ***Perf. 11½***
B187 SP180 5c + 5c vio brn .25 *.25*

Photo.
B188 SP181 10c + 10c grn, gray & yel .25 *.25*
B189 SP181 20c + 10c brn, bl & yel .25 *.25*
B190 SP181 40c + 10c bl, lav & yel 1.40 *4.25*
Nos. B187-B190 (4) 2.15 *5.00*
Set, never hinged 3.75

Adaptation of 1850 Design SP182

Putting the Stone SP183

Designs: 20c+10c, Wrestlers. 30c+10c, Runners. 40c+10c, Target shooting.

1950, June 1 **Engr. & Photo.**

Shield in Red

B191 SP182 5c + 5c black .35 *.50*

Photo.

Inscribed: "I. VIII. 1950"

B192 SP183 10c + 10c green .80 *.50*
B193 SP183 20c + 10c brn ol .95 *.75*
B194 SP183 30c + 10c rose lil 3.50 *12.50*
B195 SP183 40c + 10c dull bl 3.50 *9.00*
Nos. B191-B195 (5) 9.10 *23.25*
Set, never hinged 16.00

The surtax was for the Red Cross and the Society of Swiss History of Art.

Theophil Sprecher von Bernegg SP184

Admiral Butterfly SP185

Designs: 20c+10c, Blue Underwing Butterfly. 30c+10c, Bee. 40c+10c, Sulphur Butterfly.

1950, Dec. 1 **Engr.**

B196 SP184 5c + 5c sepia .25 *.30*

Photo.

B197 SP185 10c + 10c multi .30 *.25*
B198 SP185 20c + 10c multi .40 *.35*
B199 SP185 30c + 10c rose lil, gray & dk brn 3.00 *11.50*
B200 SP185 40c + 10c bl, dk brn & yel 3.00 *8.50*
Nos. B196-B200 (5) 6.95 *20.90*
Set, never hinged 11.50

Arms of Switzerland and Zurich — SP186

Valaisan Polka SP187

20c+10c, Flag-swinging. 30c+10c, Hornussen (natl. game). 40c+10c, Blowing alphorn.

1951, June 1 **Engr.**

Shield in Red

B201 SP186 5c + 5c gray .35 *.50*

Photo.

Inscribed: "1. VIII. 1951"

Shield in Red, Figure Shaded in Gray

B202 SP187 10c + 10c green .65 *.60*
B203 SP187 20c + 10c ol bis .65 *.60*
B204 SP187 30c + 10c red vio 3.75 *9.00*
B205 SP187 40c + 10c brt blue 4.75 *9.75*
Nos. B201-B205 (5) 10.15 *20.45*
Set, never hinged 18.50

The surtax was used primarily for needy mothers.

Souvenir Sheet

1951, Sept. 29 ***Imperf.***

B206 SP187 40c brt bl, sheet 175.00 *190.00*
Never hinged 275.00

No. B206 sold for 3fr, size: 74x56mm. Natl. Phil. Exhib., LUNABA, Sept. 29-Oct. 7, 1951, Lucerne. The net proceeds were used for Swiss schools abroad.

Johanna Spyri SP189

Dragonfly SP190

Butterflies: 20c+10c, Black-Veined. 30c+10c Orange-Tip. 40c+10c, Saturnia pyri.

1951, Dec. 1 **Engr.** ***Perf. 11½***

B207 SP189 5c + 5c red brn .25 *.30*

Photo.

B208 SP190 10c + 10c grn & dk bl .25 *.25*
B209 SP190 20c + 10c rose lil, cr & blk .30 *.35*
B210 SP190 30c + 10c ol grn, gray & org 2.00 *6.75*
B211 SP190 40c + 10c bl, dk brn & car 2.50 *6.75*
Nos. B207-B211 (5) 5.30 *14.40*
Set, never hinged 10.00

Arms of Switzerland, Glarus and Zug — SP191

Doubs River — SP192

Designs: 20c+10c, Lake of St. Gotthard. 30c+10c, Moesa River. 40c+10c, Lake of Marjelen.

1952, May 31 **Engr. & Typo.**

B212 SP191 5c + 5c gray & red .25 *.90*

Photo.

B213 SP192 10c + 10c bl grn .25 *.50*
B214 SP192 20c + 10c brn car .30 *.50*
B215 SP192 30c + 10c brown 2.50 *6.00*
B216 SP192 40c + 10c blue 3.00 *6.00*
Nos. B212-B216 (5) 6.30 *13.90*
Set, never hinged 11.00

The surtax was used primarily for historical research and popular culture.

See Nos. B222-B226, B233-B236, B243-B246, B253-B256.

Portrait of a Boy, by Albert Anker SP193

Ladybug SP194

20c+10c, Barred-wing butterfly. 30c+10c, Argus butterfly. 40c+10c, Silkworm moth.

Perf. 11½

1952, Dec. 1 **Unwmk.** **Engr.**

B217 SP193 5c + 5c brn car .25 *.30*

Photo.

B218 SP194 10c + 10c bluish grn, blk & org red .25 *.25*
B219 SP194 20c + 10c rose lil, cr & blk .30 *.35*
B220 SP194 30c + 10c brn, blk & gray bl 2.00 *6.25*
B221 SP194 40c + 10c pale vio, brn & buff 1.90 *5.75*
Nos. B217-B221 (5) 4.70 *12.90*
Set, never hinged 10.00

See Nos. B227-B231, B238-B241.

Types Similar to 1952

Designs: 5c+5c, Arms of Switzerland and Bern. 10c+10c, Reuss River. 20c+10c, Sihl Lake. 30c+10c, Bisse River. 40c+10c, Lake of Geneva.

Engraved and Photogravure

1953, June 1

B222 SP191 5c + 5c gray & red .25 *.30*

Photo.

B223 SP192 10c + 10c bl grn .35 *.25*
B224 SP192 20c + 10c brn car .45 *.25*
B225 SP192 30c + 10c brown 2.25 *5.75*
B226 SP192 40c + 10c blue 2.25 *6.25*
Nos. B222-B226 (5) 5.55 *12.80*
Set, never hinged 12.00

The surtax was used for Swiss nationals abroad and for disabled persons.

Booklet Panes

Panes consisting of blocks, strips or pairs removed from large sheets of regular issue and fastened or enclosed within a cover or folder, often by stapling or sewing in the sheet margin, are no longer being listed. Such panes contain no straight edges and can easily be made privately.

Types Similar to 1952, Dated "1953"

5c+5c, Portrait of a girl, by Albert Anker. 10c+10c, Nun moth. 20c+10c, Camberwell beauty butterfly. 30c+10c, Purple longicorn beetle. 40c+10c, Self-portrait, Ferdinand Hodler, facing left.

1953, Dec. 1 **Engr.** ***Perf. 11½***

B227 SP193 5c + 5c rose brn .35 *.75*

Photo.

B228 SP194 10c + 10c multi .35 *.40*
B229 SP194 20c + 10c multi .35 *.40*
a. Sheet of 24 240.00 *1,150.*
Never hinged 375.00
b. Bklt. pane, 4 #B229, 2 #B230 32.50
B230 SP194 30c + 10c ol, blk & red 2.10 *5.50*

Engr.

B231 SP193 40c + 10c blue 2.10 *5.50*
Nos. B227-B231 (5) 5.25 *12.55*
Set, never hinged 11.50

No. B229a consists of 16 No. B229 and 8 No. B230, arranged to include four se-tenant pairs and four pairs which are both se-tenant and tête bêche.

Types Similar to 1952, Dated "1954" and

Opening Bars of "Swiss Hymn" — SP195

Views: 10c+10c, Neuchatel lake. 20c+10c, Maggia river. 30c+10c, Cascade, Taubenloch gorge. 40c+10c, Sils lake.

1954, June 1 **Engr.** ***Perf. 11½***

B232 SP195 5c + 5c dk grn .30 *.85*

Photo.

B233 SP192 10c + 10c bl grn .30 *.45*
B234 SP192 20c + 10c dp plum .30 *.45*
B235 SP192 30c + 10c dk brn 2.00 *5.00*
B236 SP192 40c + 10c dp bl 2.25 *5.50*
Nos. B232-B236 (5) 5.15 *12.25*
Set, never hinged 11.00

The surtax was used to aid vocational training and home nursing.

No. B232 commemorates the centenary of the death of Alberik Zwyssig, composer of the "Swiss Hymn."

Types Similar to 1952, Dated "1954" and

Jeremias Gotthelf — SP196

Insects: 10c+10c, Garden tiger. 20c+10c, Bumble bee. 30c+10c, Ascalaphus. 40c+10c, Swallow-tail.

1954, Dec. 1 **Engr.**

B237 SP196 5c + 5c dk red brn .25 *.30*

Photo.

B238 SP194 10c + 10c multi .40 *.45*
B239 SP194 20c + 10c multi .40 *.45*
B240 SP194 30c + 10c rose vio, brn & yel 2.00 *5.50*
B241 SP194 40c + 10c multi 2.00 *5.50*
Nos. B237-B241 (5) 5.05 *12.20*
Set, never hinged 11.00

Type Similar to 1952, Dated "1955" and

Federal Institute of Technology, Zurich — SP197

Views: 10c+10c, Saane river. 20c+10c, Lake of Aegeri. 30c+10c, Grappelen Lake. 40c+10c, Lake of Bienne.

1955, June 1 **Engr.** ***Perf. 11½***

B242 SP197 5c + 5c gray .35 *.70*

Photo.

B243 SP192 10c + 10c dp grn .35 *.40*
B244 SP192 20c + 10c rose brn .35 *.40*
B245 SP192 30c + 10c brown 1.75 *5.00*
B246 SP192 40c + 10c dp bl 2.00 *5.00*
Nos. B242-B246 (5) 4.80 *11.50*
Set, never hinged 9.75

The surtax aided mountain dwellers.

No. B242 for the centenary of the Federal Institute of Technology in Zurich.

Charles Pictet de Rochemont SP198

Peacock Butterfly SP199

Insects: 20c+10c, Great Horntail. 30c+10c, Yellow Bear moth. 40c+10c, Apollo butterfly.

1955, Dec. 1 **Engr.** **Unwmk.**

B247 SP198 5c + 5c brn car .25 *.30*

Photo.

Insects in Natural Colors

B248 SP199 10c + 10c yel grn .40 *.30*
B249 SP199 20c + 10c red .40 *.35*
B250 SP199 30c + 10c dk ocher 1.90 *3.25*
B251 SP199 40c + 10c ultra 1.90 *5.25*
Nos. B247-B251 (5) 4.85 *9.45*
Set, never hinged 9.50

Types Similar to 1952, Dated "1956" and

"Woman's Work" — SP200

Designs: 10c+10c, Rhone at St. Maurice. 20c+10c, Katzensee. 30c+10c, Rhine at Trin. 40c+10c, Lake Wallen.

1956, June 1 **Engr.** ***Perf. 11½***

B252 SP200 5c + 5c turq bl .45 *.75*

Photo.

B253 SP192 10c + 10c green .45 *.40*
B254 SP192 20c + 10c brn car .45 *.50*
B255 SP192 30c + 10c brown 1.60 *3.75*
B256 SP192 40c + 10c ultra 2.00 *4.25*
Nos. B252-B256 (5) 4.95 *9.65*
Set, never hinged 10.00

The surtax was for the National Day Collection, the National Library and Academy of Arts and Letters. No. B252 was issued in honor of Swiss women.

Carlo Maderno SP201

Burnet Moth SP202

Insects: 20c+10c, Purple Emperor. 30c+10c, Blue ground beetle. 40c+10c, Cabbage butterfly.

1956, Dec. 1 **Engr.** ***Perf. 11½***
B257 SP201 5c + 5c brn car .25 *.25*

Photo.

Granite Paper

B258 SP202 10c + 10c grn, dk grn & car rose .25 *.25*
B259 SP202 20c + 10c multi .30 *.25*
B260 SP202 30c + 10c yel & dp bl 1.40 *3.50*
B261 SP202 40c + 10c lt ultra, pale yel & sep 1.40 *4.00*
Nos. B257-B261 (5) 3.60 *8.25*
Set, never hinged 7.50

Red Cross and Swiss Emblems SP203

"Charity" — SP204

Engraved and Photogravure

1957, June 1 **Unwmk.** ***Perf. 11½***
B262 SP203 5c + 5c gray & red .40 *.75*

Photo.

Granite Paper

Cross in Deep Carmine

B263 SP204 10c + 10c brt grn & gray .40 *.45*
B264 SP204 20c + 10c red & bl gray .40 *.45*
B265 SP204 30c + 10c brn & vio gray 1.45 *3.50*
B266 SP204 40c + 10c brt bl & bis 1.75 *3.50*
Nos. B262-B266 (5) 4.40 *8.65*
Set, never hinged 8.75

The surtax went to the Red Cross for the needs of the sick and to combat cancer.

Leonhard Euler — SP205

Clouded Yellow — SP206

Insects: 20c+10c, Magpie moth. 30c+10c, Rose Chafer. 40c+10c, Red Underwing.

1957, Nov. 30 **Engr.** ***Perf. 11½***
B267 SP205 5c + 5c brn car .30 *.25*

Photo.

Granite Paper

B268 SP206 10c + 10c multi .30 *.25*
B269 SP206 20c + 10c lil rose, blk & yel .40 *.25*
B270 SP206 30c + 10c rose brn, ind & brt grn 1.25 *3.75*
B271 SP206 40c + 10c multi 1.25 *2.60*
Nos. B267-B271 (5) 3.50 *7.10*
Set, never hinged 7.00

Catalogue values for unused stamps in this section, from this point to the end of the section, are for Never Hinged items.

Mother and Child — SP207

Fluorite — SP208

Designs: 20c+10c, Ammonite. 30c+10c, Garnet. 40c+10c, Rock Crystal.

Perf. 11½

1958, May 31 **Unwmk.** **Engr.**
B272 SP207 5c + 5c brn car .60 *.65*

Photo.

Granite Paper

B273 SP208 10c + 10c multi .75 *.35*
B274 SP208 20c + 10c blk, red & ol bis .75 *.35*
B275 SP208 30c + 10c blk, dl yel & mag 2.25 *3.50*
B276 SP208 40c + 10c blk, chlky bl & sl bl 3.00 *2.60*
Nos. B272-B276 (5) 7.35 *7.45*

The surtax was for needy mothers.
See #B283-B286, B292-B295, B304-B307.

Albrecht von Haller — SP209

Pansy — SP210

Flowers: 20c+10c, China aster. 30c+10c, Morning glory. 40c+10c, Christmas rose.

1958, Dec. 1 **Engr.** ***Perf. 11½***
B277 SP209 5c + 5c brn car .40 *.30*

Photo.

Granite Paper

B278 SP210 10c + 10c grn, yel & brn .70 *.30*
B279 SP210 20c + 10c multi .70 .30
B280 SP210 30c + 10c multi 1.60 *2.10*
B281 SP210 40c + 10c dk bl, yel & grn 1.60 *2.60*
Nos. B277-B281 (5) 5.00 *5.60*

See Nos. B287-B291.

Mineral Type of 1958 and

Globe and Swiss Flags — SP211

Designs: 10c+10c, Agate. 20c+10c, Tourmaline. 30c+10c, Amethyst. 40c+10c, Fossil salamander (andrias).

1959, June 1 **Engr.** ***Perf. 11½***
B282 SP211 5c + 5c dl grn & red .55 *.90*

Photo.

Granite Paper

B283 SP208 10c + 10c gray, yel grn & ver .75 *.55*
B284 SP208 20c + 10c blk, lil rose & bl grn .75 .55
B285 SP208 30c + 10c blk, lt brn & vio 1.45 *2.10*
B286 SP208 40c + 10c blk, bl & gray 2.10 *2.10*
Nos. B282-B286 (5) 5.60 *6.20*

Types of 1958

Designs: 5c+5c, Karl Hilty. 10c+10c, Marigold. 20c+10c, Poppy. 30c+10c, Nasturtium. 50c+10c, Sweet pea.

1959, Dec. 1 **Engr.** ***Perf. 11½***
B287 SP209 5c +5c brn car .35 *.35*

Photo.

Granite Paper

B288 SP210 10c + 10c dk grn, grn & yel .55 .35
B289 SP210 20c + 10c mag, red & grn .55 .35
B290 SP210 30c + 10c multi 1.75 *2.00*
B291 SP210 50c + 10c multi 1.75 *2.60*
Nos. B287-B291 (5) 4.95 *5.65*

Mineral Type of 1958 and

Owl, T-Square and Hammer — SP212

Designs: 5c+5c, Smoky quartz. 10c+10c, Feldspar. 20c+10c, Gryphaea, fossil. 30c+10c, Azurite.

1960, June 1 **Photo.** ***Perf. 11½***

Granite Paper

B292 SP208 5c + 5c blk, bl & ocher .70 *.60*
B293 SP208 10c + 10c blk, yel grn & pink .70 .45
B294 SP208 20c + 10c blk, lil rose & yel .85 .45
B295 SP208 30c + 10c multi 3.50 4.00

Engr.

B296 SP212 50c + 10c bl & gold 3.50 4.00
Nos. B292-B296 (5) 9.25 9.50

Souvenir Sheet

Imperf

Typo.

B297 Sheet of 4 40.00 20.00

No. B297 contains 4 50c+10c stamps of design SP212 in gold & blue. Size: 84x75mm. Sold for 3fr.

Alexandre Calame SP213

Dandelion SP214

Flowers: 20c+10c, Phlox. 30c+10c, Larkspur. 50c+10c, Thorn apple.

1960, Dec. 1 **Engr.** **Unwmk.**
B298 SP213 5c + 5c grnsh bl .50 .30

Photo.

Granite Paper

B299 SP214 10c + 10c grn, yel & gray .50 .30
B300 SP214 20c + 10c mag, grn & gray 1.00 .55
B301 SP214 30c + 10c org brn, grn & bl 1.50 2.25
B302 SP214 50c + 10c ultra & grn 2.50 2.75
Nos. B298-B302 (5) 6.00 6.15

See Nos. B308-B312, B329-B333, B339-B343.

Mineral Type of 1958 and

Book of History with Symbols of Time and Eternity — SP215

Designs: 10c+10c, Fluorite. 20c+10c, Petrified fish. 30c+10c, Lazulite. 50c+10c, Petrified fern.

1961, June 1 **Engr.** ***Perf. 11½***
B303 SP215 5c + 5c lt blue .45 *.50*

Photo.

Granite Paper

B304 SP208 10c + 10c gray, grn & pink .45 .40
B305 SP208 20c + 10c gray & car rose .60 .40
B306 SP208 30c + 10c gray, org & grnsh bl 1.20 *2.00*
B307 SP208 50c + 10c gray, bl & bis 1.75 *2.50*
Nos. B303-B307 (5) 4.45 *5.80*

Types of 1960

Designs: 5c+5c, Jonas Furrer. 10c+10c, Sunflower. 20c+10c, Lily of the valley. 30c+10c, Iris. 50c+10c, Silverweed.

1961, Dec. 1 **Engr.** ***Perf. 11½***
B308 SP213 5c + 5c dk blue .35 .30

Photo.

Granite Paper

B309 SP214 10c + 10c grn, yel & org .40 .30
B310 SP214 20c + 10c dk red, grn & gray .40 .30
B311 SP214 30c + 10c multi 1.15 *1.15*
B312 SP214 50c + 10c dk bl, yel & grn 1.55 *2.00*
Nos. B308-B312 (5) 3.85 *4.05*

Jean Jacques Rousseau SP216

Half-Thaler, Obwalden, 1732 SP217

Coins: 20c+10c, Ducat, Schwyz, ca. 1653. 30c+10c, "Steer Head" Batzen, Uri, 1659. 50c+10c, Nidwalden Batzen.

Perf. 11½

1962, June 1 **Unwmk.** **Engr.**
B313 SP216 5c + 5c dk blue .35 .30

Photo.

Granite Paper

B314 SP217 10c + 10c grn & stl bl .50 *.40*
B315 SP217 20c + 10c car rose & yel .50 *.55*
B316 SP217 30c + 10c org & sl bl 1.00 *1.05*
B317 SP217 50c + 10c ultra & vio bl 1.00 *1.05*
Nos. B313-B317 (5) 3.35 *3.35*

Apple Blossoms SP218

Mother and Child SP219

Designs: 10c+10c, Boy chasing duck. 30c+10c, Girl and sunflowers. 50c+10c, Forsythia. 1fr+20c, Mother and child, facing right.

1962, Dec. 1 ***Perf. 11½***

Granite Paper

B318 SP218 5c + 5c bl gray, pink, grn & yel .30 .35
B319 SP218 10c + 10c grn, pink & dk grn .35 .35
B320 SP219 20c + 10c org red, brn, grn & pink .35 .70
B321 SP218 30c + 10c org, red & yel 1.00 *1.35*
B322 SP218 50c + 10c dp bl, yel & brn 1.35 *1.35*
Nos. B318-B322 (5) 3.35 *4.10*

Souvenir Sheet

Imperf

B323 SP219 1fr + 20c Sheet of 2 5.25 5.25

50th anniv. of the Pro Juventute (Youth Aid) Foundation. No. B323 sold for 3fr.

Anna Heer, M.D. — SP220

Bandage Roll — SP221

Designs: 20c+10c, Gift parcel. 30c+10c, Plasma bottles. 50c+10c, Red Cross armband.

1963, June 1 Engr. *Perf. 11½*

B324 SP220 5c + 5c dk blue .30 .55

Photo.

Granite Paper

Cross in Red

B325 SP221 10c + 10c lt & dk grn & gray .35 .35
B326 SP221 20c + 10c rose, gray & blk .40 .35
B327 SP221 30c + 10c multi .85 *1.20*
B328 SP221 50c + 10c bl, gray & blk 1.10 *1.40*
Nos. B324-B328 (5) 3.00 *3.85*

Types of 1960

Designs: 5c+5c, Portrait of a Boy by Albert Anker. 10c+10c, Daisy. 20c+10c, Geranium. 30c+10c, Cornflower. 50c+10c, Carnation.

1963, Nov. 30 Engr. *Perf. 11½*

B329 SP213 5c + 5c blue .25 *.25*
a. Booklet pane of 4 3.00

Photo.

B330 SP214 10c + 10c grn, gray & yel .40 *1.10*
a. Booklet pane of 4 4.00
B331 SP214 20c + 10c multi .75 *1.60*
a. Booklet pane of 4 5.75
B332 SP214 30c + 10c multi 1.25 *.55*
B333 SP214 50c + 10c ultra, lil rose & grn 1.25 .55
Nos. B329-B333 (5) 3.90 *4.05*

Nos. B329-B331 were printed on two kinds of paper: I. Fluorescent, with violet fibers. II. Non-fluorescent, the 10c+10c and 20c+10c with mixed red and blue fibers. Nos. B332-B333 exist only on violet-fibered, fluorescent paper. The booklet panes, Nos. B329a, B330a and B331a, exist only on non-fluorescent paper.

Johann Georg Bodmer SP222

Copper Coin, Zurich SP223

Coins: 20c+10c, Doppeldicken, Basel. 30c+10c, Silver taler, Geneva. 50c+10c, Gold half florin, Bern.

Violet Fibers, Fluorescent Paper

1964, June 1 Engr. *Perf. 11½*

B334 SP222 5c + 5c blue .25 .25

Photo.

B335 SP223 10c + 10c grn, bis & blk .25 .30
B336 SP223 20c + 10c rose car, gray & blk .35 .40
B337 SP223 30c + 10c org, gray & blk .50 .60

Granite Paper, Red and Blue Fibers

B338 SP223 50c + 10c ultra, yel & brn .75 .60
Nos. B334-B338 (5) 2.10 2.15

Fluorescent Paper

Paper of Nos. B334-B425, B427 and B429 is fluorescent and has violet fibers.

Nos. B426, B428 and all semipostals from No. B430 onward are fluorescent but lack violet fibers, unless otherwise noted.

Types of 1960

Designs: 5c+5c, Portrait of a Girl by Albert Anker. 10c+10c, Daffodil. 20c+10c, Rose. 30c+10c, Clover. 50c+10c, Water lily.

1964, Dec. 1 Engr. *Perf. 11½*

B339 SP213 5c + 5c grnsh bl .25 .25

Photo.

B340 SP214 10c + 10c dp grn, yel & org .25 .25
B341 SP214 20c + 10c dp car, rose & grn .30 .25
B342 SP214 30c + 10c brn, lil & grn .50 .55
B343 SP214 50c + 10c multi .75 .65
Nos. B339-B343 (5) 2.05 1.95

Type of Regular Issue, 1965

Souvenir Sheet

10c, 20r Seated Helvetia. 20c, 40r Seated Helvetia.

1965, Mar. 8 Photo. *Imperf.*

Granite Paper, Nonfluorescent

B344 A153 Sheet of 2 1.50 1.00
a. 10c grn, pale orange & blk .75 .50
b. 20c dark red, yel grn & blk .75 .50

Natl. Postage Stamp Exhib., NABRA, Bern, Aug. 27-Sept. 5, 1965. Sold for 3fr, the net proceeds were used to cover expenses of the exhibition and to promote philately.

Father Theodosius Florentini SP224

The Temptation of Christ SP225

Ceiling Paintings from Church of St. Martin at Zillis, 12th century: 10c+10c, Symbol of evil (goose with fishtail). 20c+10c, Magi on horseback. 30c+10c, Fishermen on Sea of Galilee.

Perf. 11½

1965, June 1 Unwmk. Engr.

B345 SP224 5c + 5c blue .25 .25

Photo.

B346 SP225 10c + 10c ol grn, ocher & bl .30 .25
B347 SP225 20c + 10c dk brn, red & buff .40 .25
B348 SP225 30c + 10c dk brn, sep & bl .55 .30
B349 SP225 50c + 10c vio bl, bl & brn .65 .30
Nos. B345-B349 (5) 2.15 1.35

See Nos. B355-B359, B365-B369.

Hedgehogs — SP226

Designs: 10c+10c, Alpine marmots. 20c+10c, Red deer. 30c+10c, European badgers. 50c+10c, Varying hares.

1965, Dec. 1 Photo. *Perf. 11½*

B350 SP226 5c + 5c multi .25 .25
B351 SP226 10c + 10c multi .25 .25
B352 SP226 20c + 10c multi .30 .25
B353 SP226 30c + 10c multi .55 .25
B354 SP226 50c + 10c multi .80 .30
Nos. B350-B354 (5) 2.15 1.30

See Nos. B360-B364.

Types of 1965

5c+5c, Heinrich Federer (1866-1928), writer. 10c+10c, Joseph's dream. 20c+10c, Joseph on his way. 30c+10c, Virgin and Child fleeing to Egypt. 50c+10c, Angel leading the way. Nos. B356-B359 from ceiling paintings, Church of St. Martin at Zillis.

1966, June 1 Engr. *Perf. 11½*

B355 SP224 5c + 5c dp blue .25 .25

Photo.

B356 SP225 10c + 10c multi .25 .25
B357 SP225 20c + 10c multi .35 .25
B358 SP225 30c + 10c multi .50 .25
B359 SP225 50c + 10c multi .60 .35
Nos. B355-B359 (5) 1.95 1.35

Animal Type of 1965

5c+5c, Ermine. 10c+10c, Red squirrel. 20c+10c, Red fox. 30c+10c, Hares. 50c+10c, Two chamois.

1966, Dec. 1 Photo. *Perf. 11½*

Animals in Natural Colors

B360 SP226 5c + 5c grnsh bl .25 .25
B361 SP226 10c + 10c emer .25 .25
B362 SP226 20c + 10c ver .35 .25
B363 SP226 30c + 10c brt lemon .60 .25
B364 SP226 50c + 10c ultra .70 .40
Nos. B360-B364 (5) 2.15 1.40

Types of 1965

Designs: 5c+5c, Dr. Theodor Kocher. 10c+10c, Annunciation to the Shepherds. 20c+10c, Jesus and the Samaritan Woman at the Well. 30c+10c, Adoration of the Magi. 50c+10c St. Joseph. (Ceiling paintings, St. Martin at Zillis).

Perf. 11½

1967, June 1 Unwmk. Engr.

B365 SP224 5c + 5c blue .25 .25

Photo.

B366 SP225 10c + 10c multi .30 .25
B367 SP225 20c + 10c multi .40 .25
B368 SP225 30c + 10c multi .55 .25
B369 SP225 50c + 10c multi .65 .35
Nos. B365-B369 (5) 2.15 1.35

Roe Deer — SP227

Designs: 20c+10c, Pine marten. 30c+10c, Alpine ibex. 50c+20c, Otter.

1967, Dec. 1 Photo. *Perf. 11½*

Animals in Natural Colors

B370 SP227 10c + 10c yel grn .25 .25
B371 SP227 20c + 10c dp car .35 .25
B372 SP227 30c + 10c ol bis .50 .25
B373 SP227 50c + 20c ultra .75 .50
Nos. B370-B373 (4) 1.85 1.25

Hunter, Month of May — SP228

Designs from Rose Window, Lausanne Cathedral: 20c+10c, Leo. 30c+10c, Libra. 50c+20c, Pisces.

1968, May 30 Photo. *Perf. 11½*

B374 SP228 10c + 10c multi .25 .25
B375 SP228 20c + 10c multi .40 .25
B376 SP228 30c + 10c multi .50 .30
B377 SP228 50c + 20c multi .65 .60
Nos. B374-B377 (4) 1.80 1.40

Capercaillie — SP229

Birds: 20c+10c, Bullfinch. 30c+10c, Woodchat shrike. 50c+20c, Firecrest.

1968, Nov. 28 Photo. *Perf. 11½*

Birds in Natural Colors

B378 SP229 10c + 10c dull yel .25 .25
B379 SP229 20c + 10c olive grn .35 .25
B380 SP229 30c + 10c lilac rose .45 .25
B381 SP229 50c + 20c dp violet .80 .50
Nos. B378-B381 (4) 1.85 1.25

See Nos. B386-B389.

St. Francis — SP230

Designs: 10c+10c, St. Francis Preaching to the Birds, Königsfelden Convent Church. 20c+10c, Israelites Drinking from Spring of Moses, Berne Cathedral. 30c+10c, St. Christopher, Laufelfinger Church (now Basel Museum). 50c+20c, Virgin and Child, Chapel at Grapplang (now National Museum).

1969, May 29 Photo. *Perf. 11½*

B382 SP230 10c + 10c multi .25 .25
B383 SP230 20c + 10c multi .40 .25
B384 SP230 30c + 10c multi .50 .25
B385 SP230 50c + 20c multi .65 .45
Nos. B382-B385 (4) 1.80 1.20

Bird Type of 1968

Birds: 10c+10c, European goldfinch. 20c+10c, Golden oriole. 30c+10c, Wall creeper. 50c+20c, Eurasian jay.

1969, Dec. 1 Photo. *Perf. 11½*

Birds in Natural Colors

B386 SP229 10c + 10c gray .25 .25
B387 SP229 20c + 10c green .40 .25
B388 SP229 30c + 10c plum .50 .25
B389 SP229 50c + 20c ultra .90 .55
Nos. B386-B389 (4) 2.05 1.30

Sailor, by Gian Casty, Gellert Schoolhouse, Basel — SP231

Contemporary Stained Glass Windows: 20c+10c, Abstract composition, by Celestino Piatti. 30c+10c, Bull (Assyrian god Marduk), by Hans Stocker. 50c+20c, Man and Woman, by Max Hunziker and Karl Ganz.

1970, May 29 Photo. *Perf. 11½*

B390 SP231 10c + 10c multi .30 .25
B391 SP231 20c + 10c multi .45 .25
B392 SP231 30c + 10c multi .55 .25
B393 SP231 50c + 20c multi .70 .50
Nos. B390-B393 (4) 2.00 1.25

See Nos. B398-B401.

Blue Titmice — SP232

Birds: 20c+10c, Hoopoe. 30c+10c, Greater spotted woodpecker. 50c+20c, Crested grebes.

Birds in Natural Colors

1970, Dec. 1 Photo. *Perf. 11½*

B394 SP232 10c + 10c orange .25 .25
B395 SP232 20c + 10c emerald .40 .25
B396 SP232 30c + 10c brt rose .50 .25
B397 SP232 50c + 20c blue .95 .60
Nos. B394-B397 (4) 2.10 1.35

See Nos. B402-B405.

Art Type of 1970

Contemporary Stained Glass Windows: 10c+10c, "Composition," by Jean-François Comment. 20c+10c, Cock, by Jean Prahin. 30c+10c, Fox, by Kurt Volk. 50c+20c, "Composition," by Bernard Schorderet.

1971, May 27 Photo. *Perf. 11½*

B398 SP231 10c + 10c multi .30 .25
B399 SP231 20c + 10c multi .45 .25
B400 SP231 30c + 10c multi .60 .25
B401 SP231 50c + 20c multi .75 .50
Nos. B398-B401 (4) 2.10 1.25

Bird Type of 1970

Birds: 10c+10c, European redstarts. 20c+10c, White-spotted bluethroats. 30c+10c, Peregrine falcon. 40c+20c, Mallards.

1971, Dec. 1

B402 SP232 10c + 10c multi .30 .25
B403 SP232 20c + 10c multi .40 .25
B404 SP232 30c + 10c multi .55 .25
B405 SP232 40c + 20c multi .80 .60
Nos. B402-B405 (4) 2.05 1.35

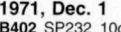

Harpoon Heads, Late Stone Age — SP233

Archaeological Treasures: 20c+10c, Bronze hydria, Hallstadt period. 30c+10c, Gold bust of Emperor Marcus Aurelius, Roman period. 40c+20c, Horseback rider (decorative disk), early Middle Ages.

1972, June 1

B406 SP233 10c + 10c multi .25 .25
B407 SP233 20c + 10c multi .45 .25
B408 SP233 30c + 10c multi .70 .40
B409 SP233 40c + 20c multi .95 .75
Nos. B406-B409 (4) 2.35 1.65

McGredy's Sunset — SP234

Famous Roses: 20c+10c, Miracle. 30c+10c, Papa Meilland. 40c+20c, Madame Dimitriu.

1972, Dec. 1 Photo. *Perf. 11½*

B410 SP234 10c + 10c multi .30 .25
B411 SP234 20c + 10c multi .50 .25
B412 SP234 30c + 10c multi .65 .25
B413 SP234 40c + 20c multi .95 1.10
Nos. B410-B413 (4) 2.40 1.85

Rauraric (Gallic) Jug — SP235

Archeologic Finds: 30c+10c, Bronze head of a Gaul. 40c+20c, Alemannic dress fasteners (fish), 6th century. 60c+20c, Gold bowl, 6th century B.C.

1973, May 29 Photo. *Perf. 11½*

B414 SP235 15c + 5c multi .30 .25
B415 SP235 30c + 10c multi .55 .25
B416 SP235 40c + 20c multi .85 .70
B417 SP235 60c + 20c multi 1.40 1.15
Nos. B414-B417 (4) 3.10 2.35

See Nos. B422-B425.

Chestnut — SP236

Fruits of the Forest: 30c+10c, Sweet cherries. 40c+20c, Blackberries. 60c+20c, Blueberries.

1973, Nov. 29 Photo. *Perf. 11½*

B418 SP236 15c + 5c multi .30 .25
B419 SP236 30c + 10c multi .55 .25
B420 SP236 40c + 20c multi .80 .50
B421 SP236 60c + 20c multi 1.00 .80
Nos. B418-B421 (4) 2.65 1.80

Archaeological Type of 1973

Archaeological Finds: 15c+5c, Polychrome glass bowl. 30c+10c, Bull's head. 40c+20c, Gold fibula. 60c+20c, Ceramic bird.

1974, May 30 Photo. *Perf. 11½*

B422 SP235 15c + 5c multi .30 .25
B423 SP235 30c + 10c multi .55 .25
B424 SP235 40c + 20c multi .85 .75
B425 SP235 60c + 20c multi .90 .80
Nos. B422-B425 (4) 2.60 2.05

Laurel — SP237

Designs: 30c+20c, Belladonna. 50c+20c, Laburnum. 60c+25c, Mistletoe.

1974, Nov. 29 Photo. *Perf. 11½*

B426 SP237 15c + 10c multi .40 .25
B427 SP237 30c + 20c multi .65 .25
B428 SP237 50c + 20c multi .65 .60
B429 SP237 60c + 25c multi .95 .80
Nos. B426-B429 (4) 2.65 1.90

Gold Fibula, 6th Century — SP238

Archaeological Treasures: 30c+20c, Bronze head of Bacchus, 2nd century. 50c+20c, Bronze daggers, 1800-1600 B.C. 60c+25c, Colored glass bottle, 1st century.

1975, May 30 Photo. *Perf. 11½*

B430 SP238 15c + 10c multi .35 .35
B431 SP238 30c + 20c multi .65 .65
B432 SP238 50c + 20c multi .75 .75
B433 SP238 60c + 25c multi 1.00 1.00
Nos. B430-B433 (4) 2.75 2.75

Mail Bucket SP239

Hepatica SP240

Forest Plants: 30c+20c, Mountain ash berries. 50c+20c, Yellow nettle. 60c+25c, Sycamore maple.

1975, Nov. 27 Photo. *Perf. 11½*

B434 SP239 10c + 5c multi .30 .25
B435 SP240 15c + 10c multi .35 .25
B436 SP240 30c + 20c multi .70 .30
B437 SP240 50c + 20c multi .70 .65
B438 SP240 60c + 25c multi 1.05 .75
Nos. B434-B438 (5) 3.10 2.20

See Nos. B443-B446.

Castles SP241

1976, May 28 Photo. *Perf. 11½*

B439 SP241 20c + 10 Kyburg .50 .40
B440 SP241 40c + 20 Grandson .80 .25
B441 SP241 40c + 20 Murten .80 .25
B442 SP241 80c + 40 Bellinzona 1.55 1.20
Nos. B439-B442 (4) 3.65 2.10

See #B447-B450, B455-B458, B463-B466.

Plant Type of 1975

Medicinal Forest Plants: 20c+10c, Barberry. No. B444, Black elder. No. B445, Linden. 80+40c, Pulmonaria.

1976, Nov. 29 Photo. *Perf. 11½*

B443 SP240 20c + 10c multi .35 .25
B444 SP240 40c + 20c lil & multi .65 .25
B445 SP240 40c + 20c terra cotta & multi .65 .25
B446 SP240 80c + 40c multi 1.25 1.00
Nos. B443-B446 (4) 2.90 1.75

Castle Type of 1976

1977, May 26 Photo. *Perf. 11½*

B447 SP241 20c + 10c Aigle .40 .30
B448 SP241 40c + 20c Pratteln .65 .25
B449 SP241 70c + 30c Sargans 1.25 1.00
B450 SP241 80c + 40c Hallwil 1.55 1.25
Nos. B447-B450 (4) 3.85 2.80

Wild Rose — SP242

Designs: Roses.

1977, Nov. 28 Photo. *Perf. 11½*

B451 SP242 20c + 10c multi .40 .25
B452 SP242 40c + 20c multi .65 .25
B453 SP242 70c + 30c multi .95 .75
B454 SP242 80c + 40c multi 1.55 1.00
Nos. B451-B454 (4) 3.55 2.25

See Nos. B492-B496.

Castle Type of 1976

1978, May 26 Photo. *Perf. 11½*

B455 SP241 20c + 10c Hagenwil .35 .30
B456 SP241 40c + 20c Burgdorf .70 .25
B457 SP241 70c + 30c Tarasp 1.15 1.00
B458 SP241 80c + 40c Chillon 1.45 1.25
Nos. B455-B458 (4) 3.65 2.80

Communal Arms — SP243

20c+10c, Aarburg. 40c+20c, Gruyeres. 70c+30c, Castasegna. 80c+40c, Wangen an der Aare.

1978, Nov. 28 Photo. *Perf. 11½*

B459 SP243 20c + 10c multi .35 .25
B460 SP243 40c + 20c multi .50 .25
B461 SP243 70c + 30c multi .80 .75
B462 SP243 80c + 40c multi 1.35 1.25
Nos. B459-B462 (4) 3.00 2.50

See #B467-B470, B475-B478, B484-B487.

Castle Type of 1976

20c+10c, Oron. 40c+20c, Spiez. 70c+30c, Porrentruy. 80c+40c, Rapperswil.

1979, May 25 Photo. *Perf. 11½*

B463 SP241 20c + 10c multi .35 .35
B464 SP241 40c + 20c multi .60 .30
B465 SP241 70c + 30c multi 1.15 1.05
B466 SP241 80c + 40c multi 1.25 1.20
Nos. B463-B466 (4) 3.35 2.90

Arms Type of 1978

20c+10c, Cadro. 40c+20c, Rute. 70c+30c, Schwamendingen. 80c+40c, Perroy.

1979, Nov. 28 Photo. *Perf. 11*

B467 SP243 20c + 10c multi .40 .25
B468 SP243 40c + 20c multi .65 .25
B469 SP243 70c + 30c multi 1.00 .75
B470 SP243 80c + 40c multi 1.30 1.10
Nos. B467-B470 (4) 3.35 2.35

Masons' and Carpenters' Sign — SP244

40c+20c, Barber. 70c+30c, Hat maker. 80c+40c, Baker.

1980, May 29 Photo. *Perf. 11½*

B471 SP244 20c + 10c shown .35 .30
B472 SP244 40c + 20c multi .60 .25
B473 SP244 70c + 30c multi 1.15 1.00
B474 SP244 80c + 40c multi 1.25 1.00
Nos. B471-B474 (4) 3.35 2.55

Arms Type of 1978

20c+10c, Cortaillod. 40c+20c, Sierre. 70c+30c, Scuol. 80c+40c, Wolfenschiessen.

1980, Nov. 26 Photo. *Perf. 11½*

B475 SP243 20c + 10c multi .40 .25
B476 SP243 40c + 20c multi .65 .25
B477 SP243 70c + 30c multi 1.00 .75
B478 SP243 80c + 40c multi 1.30 1.10
Nos. B475-B478 (4) 3.35 2.35

Icarus in Flight SP245

1981, Mar. 9 Photo.

B479 SP245 2fr + 1fr multi 3.00 2.25

Swissair, 50th Anniversary. Surtax was for Pro Aero Foundation Issued in sheet of 8.

Post Office Sign, Aarburg, 1685 — SP246

Post Office Signs (c. 1849).

1981, May 4 Photo.

B480 SP246 20c + 10c shown .35 .40
B481 SP246 40c + 20c Fribourg .55 .25
B482 SP246 70c + 30c Gordola 1.10 1.00
B483 SP246 80c + 40c Splugen 1.30 1.00
Nos. B480-B483 (4) 3.30 2.65

Arms Type of 1978

1981, Nov. 26 Photo. *Perf. 11½*

B484 SP243 20c + 10c Uffikon .40 .25
B485 SP243 40c + 20c Torre .65 .25
B486 SP243 70c + 30c Benken 1.00 1.10
B487 SP243 80c + 40c Preverenges 1.30 1.10
Nos. B484-B487 (4) 3.35 2.70

Sonne Inn Sign, Willisau SP247

40c+20c, A L'Onde, St. Saphorin. 70c+30c, Three Kings, Rheinfelden. 80c+40c, Krone, Winterthur.

1982, May 27 Photo. *Perf. 11½*

B488 SP247 20c + 10c shown .35 .40
B489 SP247 40c + 20c multi .65 .25
B490 SP247 70c + 30c multi 1.05 1.00
B491 SP247 80c + 40c multi 1.30 1.00
Nos. B488-B491 (4) 3.35 2.65

See Nos. B497-B500.

Rose Type of 1977

Designs: 10c+10c, Letter balance. 20c+10c, La Belle Portugaise. 40c+20c, Hugh Dickson. 70c+30c, Mermaid. 80c+40c, Madame Caroline.

1982, Nov. 25 Photo.

B492 SP242 10c + 10c multi .25 .25
B493 SP242 20c + 10c multi .40 .25
B494 SP242 40c + 20c multi .80 .25
B495 SP242 70c + 30c multi 1.35 .90
B496 SP242 80c + 40c multi 1.60 1.15
Nos. B492-B496 (5) 4.40 2.80

Inn Sign Type of 1982

20c+10c, Lion Inn, Heimiswil, 1669. 40c+20c, Cross Hotel, Sachseln, 1489. 70c+30c, Tankard Inn, 1830. 80c+40c, Au Cavalier Inn, Vaud.

1983, May 26 Photo.

B497 SP247 20c + 10c multi .35 .25
B498 SP247 40c + 20c multi .70 .25
B499 SP247 70c + 30c multi 1.15 1.00
B500 SP247 80c + 40c multi 1.40 1.00
Nos. B497-B500 (4) 3.60 2.50

Antique Toys — SP248

20c+10c, Kitchen stove, 1850. 40c+20c, Rocking horse, 1826. 70c+30c, Doll, 1870. 80c+40c, Steam locomotive, 1900.

1983, Nov. 24

B501 SP248 20c + 10c multi .45 .25
B502 SP248 40c + 20c multi .75 .25
B503 SP248 70c + 30c multi 1.45 .90
B504 SP248 80c + 40c multi 1.45 1.20
Nos. B501-B504 (4) 4.10 2.60

Ceramic Tiled Stoves — SP249

1984, May 24 Photo. *Perf. 11½*

B505 SP249 35c + 15c 1566 .65 .50
B506 SP249 50c + 20c 1646 .95 .25
B507 SP249 70c + 30c 1768 1.25 1.00
B508 SP249 80c + 40c 18th cent. 1.50 1.20
Nos. B505-B508 (4) 4.35 2.95

See Nos. B660-B663.

Children's Stories SP250

35c+15c, Heidi. 50c+20c, Pinocchio. 70c+30c, Pippi Longstocking. 80c+40c, Max and Moritz.

1984, Nov. 26 Photo.

B509 SP250 35c + 15c multi .65 .55
B510 SP250 50c + 20c multi .90 .25
B511 SP250 70c + 30c multi 1.25 1.10
B512 SP260 80c + 40c multi 1.50 1.10
Nos. B509-B512 (4) 4.30 3.00

Musical Museum Exhibits SP251

25c+10c, Music box, 1895. 35c+15c, Rattle box, 18th cent. 50c+20c, Emmenthal necked zither, 1828. 70c+30c, Drum, 1571. 80c+40c, Diatonic accordion, 20th cent.

1985, May 28 Photo. *Perf. 11½*

B513 SP251 25c + 10c multi .50 .45
B514 SP251 35c + 15c multi .70 .55
B515 SP251 50c + 20c multi 1.00 .30
B516 SP251 70c + 30c multi 1.40 1.05
B517 SP251 80c + 40c multi 1.75 1.25
Nos. B513-B517 (5) 5.35 3.60

Surtax for Swiss cultural programs.

Hansel and Gretel SP252

Fairy tales by Jakob (1785-1863) and Wilhelm (1786-1859) Grimm — 50c+20c, Snow White. 80c+40c, Little Red Riding Hood. 90c+40c, Cinderella.

1985, Nov. 26 Photo.

B518 SP252 35c + 15c shown .70 .60
B519 SP252 50c + 20c multi .95 .25
B520 SP252 80c + 40c multi 1.60 1.15
B521 SP252 90c + 40c multi 1.60 1.15
Nos. B518-B521 (4) 4.85 3.15

Surtax for Pro Juventute Foundation and youth welfare orgs.

Man, Vitality and Movement SP253

1986, Feb. 11 Photo. *Perf. 12*

B522 SP253 50c + 20c multi 1.00 .75

Surtax for Natl. Sports Federation and cultural programs.

Paintings in Natl. Museums SP254

Swiss art: 35c+15c, Bridge in the Sun, 1907, by Giovanni Giacometti (1868-1933). 50c+20c, The Violet Hat, 1907, by Cuno Amiet (1868-1961). 80c+40c, After the Funeral, 1905, by Max Buri (1868-1915). 90c+40c, Still Life, 1914, by Felix Valloton (1865-1925).

1986, Apr. 22 Photo. *Perf. 11½*

B523 SP254 35c + 15c multi .85 .70
B524 SP254 50c + 20c multi 1.10 .30
B525 SP254 80c + 40c multi 1.45 1.20
B526 SP254 90c + 40c multi 1.60 1.40
Nos. B523-B526 (4) 5.00 3.60

Surtax for Natl. Day Collection &monuments preservation, social & cultural organizations.

Children's Toys — SP255

35c+15c, Teddy bear. 50c+20c, Top. 80c+40c, Steamroller. 90c+40c, Doll.

1986, Nov. 25 Photo.

B527 SP255 35c + 15c multi .70 .50
B528 SP255 50c + 20c multi .95 .25
B529 SP255 80c + 40c multi 1.60 1.35
B530 SP255 90c + 40c multi 1.75 1.50
Nos. B527-B530 (4) 5.00 3.60

Surtax was for youth welfare organizations and the Pro Juventute Foundation.

Antique Furniture SP256

Designs: 35c+15c, Saane Valley wall cabinet, 1764, Vieux Pays d'Enhaut Museum, Chateau d'Oex. 50c+20c, Raised chest, 16th cent., Rhaetian Museum, Chur. 80c+40c, Ticino canton cradle, 1782, Valmaggia Museum, Cevio. 90c+40c, Appenzell region wardrobe, 1698, St. Gallen Historical Museum.

1987, May 26 Photo.

B531 SP256 35c + 15c multi .85 .70
B532 SP256 50c + 20c multi .90 .30
B533 SP256 80c + 40c multi 1.55 1.25
B534 SP256 90c + 40c multi 2.00 1.60
Nos. B531-B534 (4) 5.30 3.85

Surtax for Red Cross and patriotic funds.

No. 786 Surcharged in Red

Photo. & Engr.

1987, Sept. 7 *Perf. 13½x13*

B535 A349 50c + 50c multi 1.25 .90

Surtaxed to benefit flood victims.

Christmas SP257

Child Development SP258

50c+20c, Boy, building blocks. 80c+40c, Boy, girl in sandbox. 90c+40c, Father, child.

1987, Nov. 24 Photo. *Perf. 11½*

B536 SP257 25c +10c shown .65 .30
B537 SP258 35c +15c shown .85 .60
B538 SP258 50c +20c multi .85 .25
B539 SP258 80c +40c multi 1.55 1.20
B540 SP258 90c +40c multi 1.60 1.20
Nos. B536-B540 (5) 5.50 3.55

Surtax for national youth welfare projects and the Pro Juventute Foundation.
See Nos. B555-B558.

Junkers JU-52, 1939, and the Matterhorn SP259

1988, Mar. 8 Photo.

B541 SP259 140c +60c multi 2.75 2.25

Pro Aero Foundation, Zurich, 50th Anniv. Issued in sheets of 8.

SP260

Minnesingers — 35c+15c, Count Rudolf of Neuchatel. 50c+20c, Rudolf von Rotenburg. 80c+40c, Master Johannes Hadlaub. 90c+40c, The Hardegger.

1988, May 24 Photo.

B542 SP260 35c +15c multi .85 .65
B543 SP260 50c +20c multi .95 .30
B544 SP260 80c +40c multi 1.60 1.25
B545 SP260 90c +40c multi 1.75 1.35
Nos. B542-B545 (4) 5.15 3.55

700 Years of art and culture.

SP261

1988, Nov. 25 *Perf. 11½*

B546 SP261 35c +15c Reading .90 .35
B547 SP261 50c +20c Music .90 .45
B548 SP261 80c +40c Math 1.60 1.40
B549 SP261 90c +40c Art 1.75 1.40
Nos. B546-B549 (4) 5.15 3.60

Child development. Surtax for natl. youth welfare projects and the Pro Juventute Foundation.

700 Years of Art and Culture SP262

Illuminations in Zurich Central, Bern Burgher and Lucerne Central libraries: No. B550, King Friedrich II presenting Bern municipal charter, 1218, *Bendicht Tschachtlan Chronicle,* 1470. No. B551, Capt. Adrian von Bubenberg and troops passing through Murten town gate, 1476, *Bern Chronicle,* by Diebold Schilling, 1483. No. B552, Official messenger of Schwyz before the Council of Zurich, c. 1440, *Gerold Edlibach Chronicle,* 1485. No. B553, Schilling presenting manuscript to the mayor and councilmen in the council chamber, Lucerne, c. 1500, *Diebold Schilling's Lucerne Chronicle,* 1513.

1989, May 23

B550 SP262 35c +15c multi .75 .60
B551 SP262 50c +20c multi 1.00 .30
B552 SP262 80c +40c multi 1.75 1.40
B553 SP262 90c +40c multi 1.90 1.50
Nos. B550-B553 (4) 5.40 3.80

Surtax to benefit women's and cultural organizations.

Gymnastics SP263

1989, Aug. 25 Photo. *Perf. 11½*

B554 SP263 50c +20c multi 1.25 1.00

Surtax to benefit Swiss Natl. Sports Federation, cultural and social work.

Child Development Type of 1987

35c+15c, Community work. 50c+20c, Friendship. 80c+40c, Vocational training. 90c+40c, Higher education and research.

1989, Nov. 24

B555 SP258 35c +15c multi .90 .65
B556 SP258 50c +20c multi 1.05 .45
B557 SP258 80c +40c multi 1.60 1.25
B558 SP258 90c +40c multi 1.75 1.25
Nos. B555-B558 (4) 5.30 3.60

Surtax for natl. youth welfare projects and the Pro Juventute Foundation.

700 Years of Art and Culture — SP264

Street criers: No. B559, Fly swatter and starch-sprinkler vendor. No. B560, Clock vendor. No. B561, Knife grinder. No. B562, Pinewood sellers.

1990, May 22 Photo.

B559 SP264 35c +15c multi .75 .65
B560 SP264 50c +20c multi 1.05 .35
B561 SP264 80c +40c multi 1.75 1.50
B562 SP264 90c +40c multi 1.90 1.60
Nos. B559-B562 (4) 5.45 4.10

Souvenir Sheet

Natl. Philatelic Exhibition, Geneva '90 — SP265

a, Brass badge worn by Geneva Cantonal post drivers before 1849. b, Place du Bourgde-Four and entrance to Rue Etienne-Dumont. c, Ile Rousseau and Pont des Bergues. d, No. 2L1 on cover.

1990, Sept. 5

B563	SP265	Sheet of 4	4.50	4.50
a.-d.		50c +25c any single	1.00	1.00

Child Development SP266

No. B564, Model making. No. B565, Youth groups. No. B566, Sports. No. B567, Music.

1990, Nov. 20

B564	SP266	35c +15c multi	.90	.65
B565	SP266	50c +20c multi	1.05	.50
B566	SP266	80c +40c multi	1.60	1.25
B567	SP266	90c +40c multi	1.75	1.25
		Nos. B564-B567 (4)	5.30	3.65

700 Years of Art and Culture SP267

Contemporary paintings by: 50c+20c, Wolf Barth. 70c+30c, Helmut Federle. 80c+40c, Matthias Bosshart. 90c+40c, Werner Otto Leuenberger.

1991, May 14 Photo. *Perf. 11½*

B568	SP267	50c +20c multi	1.00	.75
B569	SP267	70c +30c multi	1.40	.30
B570	SP267	80c +40c multi	1.75	1.40
B571	SP267	90c +40c multi	1.90	1.60
		Nos. B568-B571 (4)	6.05	4.05

Woodland Flowers SP268

50c+25c, Allium ursinum. 70c+30c, Geranium sylvaticum. 80c+40c, Campanula trachelium. 90c+40c, Hieracium murorum.

1991, Nov. 26

B572	SP268	50c +25c multi	.95	.30
B573	SP268	70c +30c multi	1.50	.90
B574	SP268	80c +40c multi	1.50	1.20
B575	SP268	90c +40c multi	1.90	1.45
		Nos. B572-B575 (4)	5.85	3.85

Surtax for youth and family welfare projects and the Pro Juventute Foundation.

Swiss Folk Art — SP269

50c + 20c, Earthenware plate, Heimberg, 18th cent. 70c + 40c, Paper cutout by Johann Jakob Hauswirth (1809-1871). 80c + 40c, Cream spoon, Gruyeres. 90c + 40c, Embroidered silk carnation, Grisons.

1992, May 22 Photo. *Perf. 11½*

B576	SP269	50c +20c multi	1.00	.25
B577	SP269	70c +30c multi	1.40	1.00
B578	SP269	80c +40c multi	1.60	1.20
B579	SP269	90c +40c multi	1.75	1.30
		Nos. B576-B579 (4)	5.75	3.75

Surtax for preservation of cultural heritage.

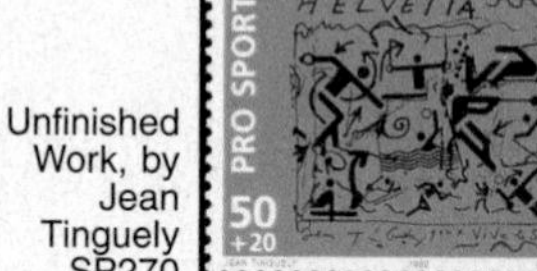

Unfinished Work, by Jean Tinguely SP270

1992, Aug. 25 Photo. *Perf. 12*

B580	SP270	50c +20c bl & blk	1.15	1.00

Surtax for Natl. Sports Federation and sports-related social and cultural activities.

Wood Puppet of Melchior, 18th Cent. — SP271

Trees — SP272

No. B582, Copper beech. No. B583, Norway maple. No. B584, Common oak. No. B585, Spruce.

1992, Nov. 24 Photo. *Perf. 11½*

B581	SP271	50c +25c multi	1.00	.40
B582	SP272	50c +25c multi	1.00	.40
B583	SP272	70c +30c multi	1.40	1.30
B584	SP272	80c +40c multi	1.60	1.50
B585	SP272	90c +40c multi	1.60	1.50
		Nos. B581-B585 (5)	6.60	5.10

Christmas. Surtax for youth and family welfare projects and the Pro Juventute Foundation.

Swiss Folk Art — SP273

Designs: No. B586, Appenzell dairyman's earring. No. B587, Fluhli glassware. 80c + 40c, Painting of cattle drive, by Sylvestre Pidoux. 100c + 40c, Straw hat ornament.

1993, May 5 Photo. *Perf. 11½*

B586	SP273	60c +30c multi	1.20	.45
B587	SP273	60c +30c multi	1.20	.45
B588	SP273	80c +40c multi	1.60	1.45
B589	SP273	100c +40c multi	1.90	1.60
		Nos. B586-B589 (4)	5.90	3.95

Architectural Heritage Type of 1960

Design: 80c+20c, Kapell Bridge and Water Tower, Lucerne.

1993, Sept. 7 Litho. *Perf. 13½x13*

B590	A145	80c +20c org & red	1.50	1.00

Surtax for reconstruction of Kapell Bridge with any excess for preservation of architectural heritage.

SP274

Woodland plants — No. B591, Christmas wreath. No. B592, Male fern. No. B593, Guelder rose. No. B594, Mnium punctatum.

1993, Nov. 23 Photo. *Perf. 11½*

B591	SP274	60c +30c multi	.90	.40
B592	SP274	60c +30c multi	1.30	.40
B593	SP274	80c +40c multi	1.75	1.35
B594	SP274	100c +50c multi	2.10	1.60
		Nos. B591-B594 (4)	6.05	3.75

Christmas. Surtax for youth and family welfare projects and the Pro Juventute Foundation.

SP275

Swiss Folk Art: No. B595, Weight-driven Neuchatel clock. No. B596, Linen-embroidered pomegranate. 80c+40c, Biscuit mold for Krafli. 100c+40c, Paper bird mobile for child's cradle.

1994, May 17 Photo. *Perf. 11½*

B595	SP275	60c +30c multi	1.30	.55
B596	SP275	60c +30c multi	1.30	.55
B597	SP275	80c +40c multi	1.75	1.60
B598	SP275	100c +40c multi	2.00	1.90
		Nos. B595-B598 (4)	6.35	4.60

Christmas SP276

Mushrooms SP277

Designs: No. B600, Wood blewit. 80c+40c, Red boletus. 100c+50c, Shaggy pholiota.

1994, Nov. 28 Litho. *Perf. 11½*

B599	SP276	60c +30c multi	1.40	.40
B600	SP277	60c +30c multi	1.40	.40
B601	SP277	80c +40c multi	1.90	1.30
B602	SP277	100c +50c multi	2.25	1.90
		Nos. B599-B602 (4)	6.95	4.00

Surtax for youth and family welfare projects and the Pro Juventute Foundation.

Swiss Folk Art — SP278

Designs: No. B603, Wooden cream pail. No. B604, Straw hat. 80c+40c, Chest lock, c. 1580. 100c+40c, Langnau pottery sugar bowl.

1995, May 16 Photo. *Perf. 11½*

B603	SP278	60c +30c multi	1.40	.45
B604	SP278	60c +30c multi	1.40	.45
B605	SP278	80c +40c multi	1.90	1.45
		Complete booklet, 10 #B605	15.00	
B606	SP278	100c +40c multi	2.25	1.60
		Nos. B603-B606 (4)	6.95	3.95

Surtax for Swiss Pro Patria Foundation and special cultural, social projects.

Souvenir Sheet

Basler Taube '95 Philatelic Exhibition, Basel — SP279

Designs: a, 80c+30c, like Switzerland #3L1. Engraved panorama of Basel, by Matthaus Merian, 17th cent.: b, 60c+30c, Buildings, twin church steeples. c, 100c+50c, Buildings. d, 100c+50c, Buildings, bridge.

1995, May 16 Photo. *Perf. 13x14*

B607	SP279	Sheet of 4	8.00	8.00
a.		80c +30c multi	1.90	.60
b.		60c +30c black & blue	1.40	.55
c.-d.		100c +50c any single	2.25	.90

Nos. B607b-B607d are a continuous design.

Christmas SP280

Life In and Around Water — SP281

#B608, Angel from "The Annunciation," by Bartolome. #B609, River trout. 80c+40c, Grey wagtail. 100c+50c, Spotted salamander.

1995, Nov. 28 Photo. *Perf. 11½*

B608	SP280	60c +30c multi	1.40	.45
		Complete booklet, 10 #B608	14.00	
B609	SP281	60c +30c multi	1.40	.45
B610	SP281	80c +40c multi	1.90	1.50
B611	SP281	100c +50c multi	2.25	2.10
		Nos. B608-B611 (4)	6.95	4.50

Surtax for Pro Juventute Foundation.

For Sports SP282

1996, Mar. 12 Photo. *Perf. 11½*

B612	SP282	70c +30c multi	1.60	1.25
		Complete booklet, 10 #B612	16.00	

SP283

Restorations, projects: No. B613, Magdalena Chapel, Wolfenschiessen. No. B614, Underground mills, Col-des-Roches. 90c+40c, Pfäfers Baroque spa complex. 110c+50c, Roman road over Great St. Bernhard.

1996, May 14 Photo. *Perf. 11½*

B613 SP283 70c +35c multi 1.75 .50
B614 SP283 70c +35c multi 1.75 .50
B615 SP283 90c +40c multi 2.10 1.25
Complete booklet, 10 #B615 19.00
B616 SP283 110c +50c multi 2.50 1.50
Nos. B613-B616 (4) 8.10 3.75

Christmas SP284

Life In and Around Water — SP285

No. B617, Star, constellations. No. B618, Grayling. No. B619, Crayfish. No. B620, Otter.

1996, Nov. 26 Photo. *Perf. 11½*

B617 SP284 70c +35c multi 1.60 .60
B618 SP285 70c +35c multi 1.60 .60
Complete booklet, 10 #B618 16.00
B619 SP285 90c +45c multi 2.10 1.50
B620 SP285 110c +55c multi 2.50 1.75
Nos. B617-B620 (4) 7.80 4.45

SP286

Designs: No. B621, St. Valbert Church, Soubey. No. B622, Culture Mill, Lützelflüh. 90c+40c, Ittingen Charterhouse, Thurgau. 110c+50c, Municipal Building, Onsernone Valley.

1997, May 13 Photo. *Perf. 11½*

B621 SP286 70c +35c multi 1.50 1.20
B622 SP286 70c +35c multi 1.50 1.20
B623 SP286 90c +40c multi 1.75 1.50
Complete booklet, 10 #B623 17.00
B624 SP286 110c +50c multi 2.25 1.75
Nos. B621-B624 (4) 7.00 5.65

Christmas SP287

Life In and Around Water — SP288

Designs: No. B625, Misteltoe twig. No. B626, Three-spined stickleback. 90c+45c, Yellow-bellied toad. 110c+55c, Ruff.

1997, Nov. 20 Photo. *Perf. 11½*

B625 SP287 70c +35c multi 1.60 1.25
B626 SP288 70c +35c multi 1.60 1.25
Complete booklet, 10 #B626 14.00
B627 SP288 90c +45c multi 2.10 1.60
B628 SP288 110c +55c multi 2.50 1.90
Nos. B625-B628 (4) 7.80 6.00

Surtax for Pro Juventute Foundation.

Pro Patria Stamps, 60th Anniv. SP289

Heritage and landscapes: No. B629, St. Gall Rhine Valley. No. B630, Round Church, Saas Balen. No. B631, Natural forest preserves, Bödmeren. No. B632, St. Gotthard Refuge. 110c +50c, Blacksmiths, Corcelles.

1998, May 12 Photo. *Perf. 11½*

B629 SP289 70c + 35c multi 1.50 .90
B630 SP289 70c + 35c multi 1.50 .90
B631 SP289 90c + 40c multi 1.75 1.30
Complete booklet, 10 #B631 15.00
B632 SP289 90c + 40c multi 1.75 1.30
B633 SP289 110c + 50c multi 2.25 1.60
Nos. B629-B633 (5) 8.75 6.00

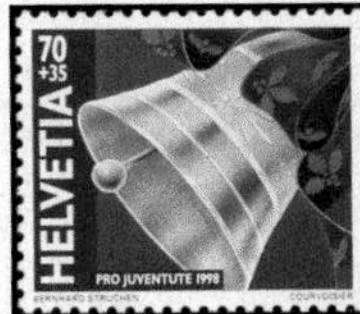

Christmas SP290

Life Near Water — SP291

No. B634, Bell, holly on ribbon. No. B635, Ramshorn snail. 90c+45c, Great crested grebe. 110c+55c, Pike.

1998, Nov. 25 Photo. *Perf. 11½*

B634 SP290 70c +35c multi 1.40 1.10
B635 SP291 70c +35c multi 1.40 1.10
B636 SP291 90c +45c multi 2.10 1.50
Complete booklet, 6 #B634, 4 #B636 15.00
B637 SP291 110c +55c multi 2.50 1.90
Nos. B634-B637 (4) 7.40 5.60

Pro Patria — SP292

Heritage and landscapes: No. B638, Chestnut groves, Malcantone. No. B639, La Sarraz Castle. 90c+40c, Lake Lucerne steamship. 110c+50c, St. Paul's Chapel, Rhäzüns.

1999, May 5 Litho. *Perf. 13½*

B638 SP292 70c +35c multi 1.60 1.40
B639 SP292 70c +35c multi 1.60 1.40
B640 SP292 90c +40c multi 2.10 1.75
Complete booklet, 10 #B640 21.00
B641 SP292 110c +50c multi 2.50 2.10
Nos. B638-B641 (4) 7.80 6.65

Souvenir Sheet

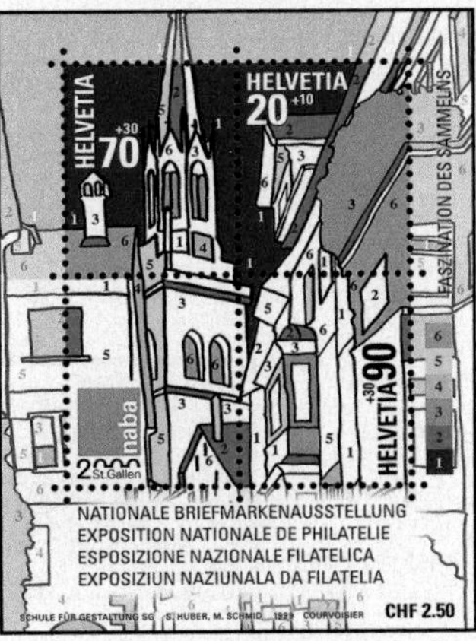

NABA 2000 Philatelic Exhibition, St. Gallen — SP293

a, 70c+30c, St. Laurenzen Church spire. b, 20c+10c, Top of town house. c, 90c+30c, Oriel window.

1999, Sept. 9 Photo. *Perf. 11¾*
Sheet of 3

B642 SP293 #a.-c. + label 6.00 6.00
a. 70c+30c multicolored 1.60 1.25
b. 20c+10c multicolored .45 .40
c. 90c+30c multicolored 2.10 1.60

Christmas SP294

Nicolo the Clown From Children's Book by Verena Pavoni SP295

Designs: No. B643, Children, snowman. No. B644, Nicolo, circus tent. 90c+45c, Nicolo and his father. 110c+55c, Nicolo and donkey.

Perf. 13½x13¼
1999, Nov. 23 Litho.

B643 SP294 70c +35c multi 1.60 1.40
B644 SP295 70c +35c multi 1.60 1.40
B645 SP295 90c +45c multi 2.10 1.75
Complete booklet, 6 #B644, 4 #B645 18.00
B646 SP295 110c +55c multi 2.50 2.10
Nos. B643-B646 (4) 7.80 6.65

Surtax for Pro Juventute Foundation.
See Nos. B660-B663.

Cities With Pro Patria Foundation Renovation Projects SP296

Perf. 13¼x13½
2000, May 10 Litho. & Engr.

B647 SP296 70c +35c Näfles 1.60 1.25
B648 SP296 70c +35c Tengia 1.60 1.25
B649 SP296 90c +40c Brugg 2.10 1.60
B650 SP296 90c +40c Carouge 2.10 1.60
Booklet, 10 #B650 21.00
Nos. B647-B650 (4) 7.40 5.70

Souvenir Sheet

NABA 2000 Philatelic Exhibition, St. Gallen — SP297

Quadrants of stylized No. 5: a, UL. b, UR. c, LL. d, LR.

2000, May 10 Photo. *Perf. 11¾*

B651 SP297 Sheet of 4 5.50 5.50
a. 70c+35c multicolored 1.60 1.25
b.-c. 20c+10c any single .45 .35
d. 90c+45c multicolored 2.10 1.75

Christmas SP298

Illustrations from Little Albert, by Albert Manser SP299

Designs: No. B652, St. Nicholas and Schmutzli in sleigh. No. B653, Children at fence. No. B654, Little Albert with umbrella. No. B655, Children on sleds.

Perf. 13¼x13½
2000, Nov. 21 Litho.

B652 SP298 70c +35c multi 1.60 1.25
B653 SP299 70c +35c multi 1.60 1.25
B654 SP299 90c +45c multi 2.10 1.50
Booklet, 6 #B653, 4 #B654 18.00
B655 SP299 90c +45c multi 2.10 1.50
Nos. B652-B655 (4) 7.40 5.50

Surtax for Pro Juventute Foundation.

Landmarks SP300

Designs: No. B656, Hauterive Abbey. No. B657, La Chaux-de-Fonds Theater. No. B658, Granary, Rorschach. No. B659, Bishop's Castle, Leuk.

2001, May 9 Litho. *Perf. 13¼x13½*

B656 SP300 70c +35c multi 1.60 1.25
B657 SP300 70c +35c multi 1.60 1.25
B658 SP300 90c +40c multi 2.10 1.50
B659 SP300 90c +40c multi 2.10 1.50
Booklet, 10 #B659 21.00
Nos. B656-B659 (4) 7.40 5.50

Surtax for Pro Patria Foundation.

Pro Juventute Types of 1999

Art from children's books: No. B660, What's Santa Claus Doing?, by Karin von Oldershausen. No. B661, Leopold the Leopard, from Leopold and the Sun, by Stephan Brülhart. No. B662, Honeybear, from Leopold and the Sun. No. B663, Tom the Monkey, from Leopold and the Sun.

Perf. 13½x13¼
2001, Nov. 20 Litho.

B660 SP294 70c +35c multi 1.60 1.25
B661 SP295 70c +35c multi 1.60 1.25
B662 SP295 90c +45c multi 2.10 1.60
Booklet, 6 #B661, 4 #B662 18.00
B663 SP295 90c +45c multi 2.10 1.60
Nos. B660-B663 (4) 7.40 5.70

Surtax for Pro Juventute Foundation.

Mills — SP301

Location: No. B664, Bruzella. No. B665, Oberdorf. No. B666, Büren an der Aare. No. B667, Lussery-Villars.

2002, May 15 Litho. *Perf. 13¼x13½*

B664 SP301 70c +35c multi 1.60 1.40
B665 SP301 70c +35c multi 1.60 1.40
B666 SP301 90c +40c multi 2.10 1.60
Booklet, 10 #B666 21.00
B667 SP301 90c +40c multi 2.10 1.60
Nos. B664-B667 (4) 7.40 6.00

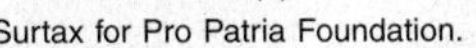
Surtax for Pro Patria Foundation.

Roses — SP302

Designs: No. B668, Christmas rose (gold background). No. B669, Ingrid Bergman rose (white background). No. B670, Belle Vaudoise rose (orange petals). No. B671, Charmian rose (pink petals). 130c+65c, Frühlingsgold rose.

Perf. 13¾x13¼
2002, Nov. 19 Litho.

B668 SP302 70c +35c multi 1.60 1.40
B669 SP302 70c +35c multi 1.60 1.40
B670 SP302 90c +45c multi 2.10 1.90
Booklet, 6 #B669, 4 #B670 18.00

B671 SP302 90c +45c multi 2.10 1.90
B672 SP302 130c +65c multi 3.00 2.60
Nos. B668-B672 (5) 10.40 9.20

Surtax for Pro Juventute Foundation. No. B668 is impregnated with a pine needle, cinnamon and clove scent, and Nos. B669-B672 with a rose scent.

Bridges
SP303

Designs: No. B673, Wynigen Bridge, Burgdorf, 1776. No. B674, Salginatobel Bridge, Schiers, 1929. No. B675, Pont St. Jean, Saint Ursanne, 15th cent. No. B676, Reuss Bridge, Rottenschwil, 1907.

2003, May 8 Litho. ***Perf. 13¼x13½***

B673 SP303 70c +35c multi 1.60 1.60
B674 SP303 70c +35c multi 1.60 1.60
B675 SP303 90c +40c multi 2.10 2.00
Booklet, 10 #B675 21.00
B676 SP303 90c +40c multi 2.10 2.00
Nos. B673-B676 (4) 7.40 7.20

Rights of the Child — SP304

Children: 70c+35c, Christmas tree, toy tractor, gift. 85c+35c, Playing as storekeeper and shopper. 90c+45c, Skateboarding with dog. 100c+45c, Playing guitar and drums.

Serpentine Die Cut 10½x11

2003, Nov. 19 Litho.

Self-Adhesive

B677 SP304 70c +35c multi 1.75 1.75
a. Block of 4 on translucent backing paper 7.00
B678 SP304 85c +35c multi 2.00 1.90
a. Block of 4 on translucent backing paper 8.00
B679 SP304 90c +45c multi 2.10 2.10
a. Block of 4 on translucent backing paper 8.40
B680 SP304 100c +45c multi 2.25 2.25
a. Block of 4 on translucent backing paper 9.00
b. Nos. B677-B680 on translucent backing paper 8.00
c. Booklet, 6 each #B678, B680 22.50
Nos. B677-B680 (4) 8.10 8.00

Nos. B677-B680 each were printed in sheets of 20 stamps with a white paper backing.

Small Buildings
SP305

Designs: No. B681, Bathing pavilion, Gorgier. No. B682, Granary, Oberramsern. No. B683, Ossuary, Gentilino. No. B684, Dock house, Lucerne.

2004, May 6 Litho. ***Perf. 13¾x14¼***

B681 SP305 85c +40c multi 2.00 1.90
B682 SP305 85c +40c multi 2.00 1.90
B683 SP305 100c +50c multi 2.40 2.40
B684 SP305 100c +50c multi 2.40 2.40
Complete booklet, 6 #B681, 4 #B684 22.50

Complete booklet sold for 14.50fr.

Rights of the Child — SP306

Designs: No. B685, Children playing card game. No. B686, Children, man, giraffe. No. B687, Children, teacher. No. B688, Child, elderly man and woman.

Serpentine Die Cut 10½x11

2004, Nov. 23 Litho.

Self-Adhesive

B685 SP306 85c +40c multi 2.25 2.25
a. Block of 4 on translucent paper 9.00
B686 SP306 85c +40c multi 2.25 2.25
a. Block of 4 on translucent paper 9.00
B687 SP306 100c +50c multi 2.75 2.75
a. Block of 4 on translucent paper 11.00
b. Booklet pane, 6 each #B685, B687 30.00
B688 SP306 100c +50c multi 2.75 2.75
a. Block of 4 on translucent paper 11.00
b. Nos. B685-B688 on translucent paper 10.00
Nos. B685-B688 (4) 10.00 10.00

Nos. B685-B688 were each printed in sheets of 20 stamps. No. B687b sold for 17fr.

Historic
Buildings
SP307

Designs: No. B689, Rotach Houses, Zurich. No. B690, Monte Carasso Abbey, Monte Carasso. No. B691, St. Katharinental Abbey, Diessenhofen. No. B692, Palais Wilson, Geneva.

2005, May 10 Litho. ***Perf. 13¼x13½***

B689 SP307 85c +40c multi 2.10 2.10
B690 SP307 85c +40c multi 2.10 2.10
B691 SP307 100c +50c multi 2.50 2.50
Complete booklet, 6 #B690, 4 #B691 23.00
B692 SP307 100c +50c multi 2.50 2.50
Nos. B689-B692 (4) 9.20 9.20

Surtax for Pro Patria Foundation.

Children's
Rights
SP308

Children and: No. B693, Life preserver. No. B694, Cherries. No. B695, Computer. No. B696 Candle in window.

Serpentine Die Cut 10½x11

2005, Nov. 22 Photo.

Self-Adhesive

B693 SP308 85c +40c multi 2.00 1.90
a. Block of 4 on translucent paper 8.00
B694 SP308 85c +40c multi 2.00 1.90
a. Block of 4 on translucent paper 8.00
B695 SP308 100c +50c multi 2.25 2.25
a. Block of 4 on translucent paper 9.00
b. Booklet pane, 2 each #B693, B695 8.50
Complete booklet, 3 #B695b 26.00
B696 SP308 100c +50c multi 2.25 2.25
a. Block of 4 on translucent paper 9.00
b. Nos. B693-B696 on translucent paper 8.50
Nos. B693-B696 (4) 8.50 8.30

Nos. B693-B696 were each printed in sheets of 20. Complete booklet sold for 17 fr.

Gardens and
Parks — SP309

Designs: No. B697, Prangins Castle, Prangins. No. B698, Heidegg Castle, Gelfingen. No. B699, Birseck Castle, Arlesheim. No. B700, Villa Garbald, Castasegna.

2006, May 9 Litho. ***Perf. 14x13¾***

B697 SP309 85c +40c multi 2.10 2.10
B698 SP309 85c +40c multi 2.10 2.10
B699 SP309 100c +50c multi 2.50 2.50
B700 SP309 100c +50c multi 2.50 2.50
Complete booklet, 6 #B698, 4 #B700 24.00
Nos. B697-B700 (4) 9.20 9.20

Complete booklet sold for 14.50 fr.

Souvenir Sheet

Wettingen Monastery — SP310

No. B701: a, Building, country name at left. b, Building and bridge, country name at right. c, Main building.

2006, May 9 ***Perf. 13¾x14¼***

B701 SP310 Sheet of 3 7.25 7.25
a.-b. 85c+15c Either single 2.00 1.75
c. 100c+50c multi 2.25 2.50

NABA Baden 2006.

Souvenir Sheet

NABA Baden 2006 Philatelic Exhibition — SP311

No. B702: a, Baden City Tower. b, Fountain.

Perf. 14¼x13¾ on 3 Sides

2006, Sept. 7 Litho.

B702 SP311 Sheet of 2 5.50 5.50
a.-b. 100c +50c Either single 2.25 2.50

Children's Art
Competition
SP312

Designs: No. B703, Singer, by Veronica Jesus Garcia Pinto. No. B704, Car in garage, by Stephane Arada. No. B705, Bandaged dog, by Lea Mayer. No. B706, Angel, by Ted Scapa, judge of competition.

Serpentine Die Cut 10¾x11

2006, Nov. 21

Self-Adhesive

B703 SP312 85c +40c multi 2.10 2.10
a. Block of 4, #B703 8.50
B704 SP312 85c +40c multi 2.10 2.10
a. Block of 4, #B704 8.50
B705 SP312 100c +50c multi 2.50 2.50
a. Booklet pane, 6 each #B704-B705 28.00
b. Block of 4, #B705 10.00
B706 SP312 100c +50c multi 2.50 2.50
a. Block of 4, #B703-B706 9.25
b. Block of 4, #B706 10.00
Nos. B703-B706 (4) 9.20 9.20

Surtax for Pro Juventute Foundation.
See also Nos. B711-B714, B719-B722.

Historic Roads
SP313

Designs: No. B707, Via Jura, Chateau de Vorbourg. No. B708, Via Jacobi, Chapel of St. Apollonia. No. B709, Via Cook, Grandhotel Giessbach. No. B710, Via Gottardo, Alte Sust.

2007, Apr. 27 Litho. ***Perf. 13½x13¼***

B707 SP313 85c +40c multi 2.10 2.10
B708 SP313 85c +40c multi 2.10 2.10
B709 SP313 100c +50c multi 2.50 2.50
Complete booklet, 6 #B708, 4 #B709 23.00
B710 SP313 100c +50c multi 2.50 2.50
Nos. B707-B710 (4) 9.20 9.20

Surtax for Pro Patria Foundation.
See also Nos. B715-B718, B723-B726.

Children's Art Competition Type of 2006

Designs: No. B711, Camping, by Christine Fischer. No. B712, Mountains, by Jonathan Balest. No. B713, Sunshine, by Morena Rufatti. No. B714, Angels, by Ted Scapa, judge of competition.

Serpentine Die Cut 10½x11

2007, Nov. 20 Litho.

Self-Adhesive

B711 SP312 85c +40c multi 2.25 2.25
a. Block of 4 #B711 on backing paper 9.00
B712 SP312 85c +40c multi 2.25 2.25
a. Block of 4 #B712 on backing paper 9.00
B713 SP312 100c +50c multi 2.75 2.75
a. Block of 4 #B713 on backing paper 11.00
b. Booklet pane, 6 each #B711, B713 30.00
B714 SP312 100c +50c multi 2.75 2.75
a. Block of 4 #B714 on backing paper 11.00
b. Block of 4, #B711-B714 on backing paper 10.00 10.00
Nos. B711-B714 (4) 10.00 10.00

Surtax for Pro Juventute Foundation.

Historic Roads Type of 2007

Designs: No. B715, Via Romana, East Gate, Avenches, and columns, Nyon. No. B716, Via Sbrinz, Schnitzturm Tower. No. B717, Via Stockalper, Old Hospice, Simplon. No. B718, Via Valtellina, Dürrboden Restaurant, Grisons.

2008, May 8 Litho. ***Perf. 13½x13¼***

B715 SP313 85c +40c multi 2.40 2.40
B716 SP313 85c +40c multi 2.40 2.40
B717 SP313 100c +50c multi 3.00 3.00
Complete booklet, 6 #B716, 4 #B717 27.00
B718 SP313 100c +50c multi 3.00 3.00
Nos. B715-B718 (4) 10.80 10.80

Surtax for Pro Patria Foundation.

Children's Art Competition Type of 2006

Designs: No. B719, Friendship Unites (Sun and Moon), by Andrea Andreazzi. No. B720, Friendship Provides Support (boy, girl, child in wheelchair), by Manon Peng. No. B721, Friendship is the Source of Happiness (girls and four-leaf clover), by Delia Candolo. No. B722, Friendship is Uplifting (angels), by Ted Scapa, judge of competition.

Serpentine Die Cut 10¾x11

2008, Nov. 21 Litho.

Self-Adhesive

B719 SP312 85c +40c multi 2.10 2.10
B720 SP312 85c +40c multi 2.10 2.10
B721 SP312 100c +50c multi 2.50 2.50
a. Booklet pane, 6 each #B719, B721 28.00
B722 SP312 100c +50c multi 2.50 2.50
a. Block of 4, #B719-B722 on backing paper 9.25
Nos. B719-B722 (4) 9.20 9.20

No. B721a sold for 17fr. Surtax for Pro Juventute Foundation.

Historic Roads Type of 2003

Designs: No. B723, Via Salina and Bern Gate, Murten. No. B724, Via Francigena and Great St. Bernhard Hospice, Bourg-Saint-Pierre. No. B725, Via Rhenana and salt drilling towers, Rheinfelden. No. B726, Via Spluga and Albertini House, Splügen.

2009, May 8 ***Perf. 13½x13¼***

B723 SP313 85c +40c multi 2.25 2.25
B724 SP313 85c +40c multi 2.25 2.25
B725 SP313 100c +50c multi 2.75 2.75
Complete booklet, 6 #B724, 4 #B725 26.00
B726 SP313 100c +50c multi 2.75 2.75
Nos. B723-B726 (4) 10.00 10.00

Complete booklet sold for 14.50fr. Surtax for Pro Patria Foundation.

Souvenir Sheet

Pro Patria Foundation, Cent. — SP314

2009, May 8 Litho. *Perf. 14x13¼*

B727 SP314 100c +50c multi 2.75 2.75

Surtax for Pro Patria Foundation.

Services of the Pro Juventute Foundation SP315

Designs: No. B728, Letters to Parents (family and arrows). No. B729, Vacation Pass programs (children and tree). No. B730, Advice 147 counseling (boy and girl). No. B731, Semi-postal stamp sales (four children and stylized stamps).

Serpentine Die Cut 12

2009, Nov. 20 Litho.

Self-Adhesive

B728 SP315 85c +40c multi 2.50 2.50
- *a.* Block of 4 #B728 on backing paper 10.00

B729 SP315 85c +40c multi 2.50 2.50
- *a.* Block of 4 #B729 on backing paper 10.00

B730 SP315 100c +50c multi 3.00 3.00
- *a.* Booklet pane of 12, 6 each #B728, B730 34.00
- *b.* Block of 4 #B730 on backing paper 12.00

B731 SP315 100c +50c multi 3.00 3.00
- *a.* Block of 4, #B728-B731, on translucent paper 11.00
- *b.* Block of 4 #B731 on backing paper 12.00

Nos. B728-B731 (4) 11.00 11.00

Complete booklet sold for 17fr. Surtax for Pro Juventute Foundation.

Details From Panorama of Battle of Murten, by Louis Braun — SP316

Desings: No. B732, Retreat of Charles the Bold on caparisoned horse. No. B733, Death of Duke of Somerset near tents. No. B734, Confederate troops with flags and halberds. No. B735, Burgundian Cavalry being attacked by Confederate troops.

2010, May 6 Litho. *Perf. 14*

B732 SP316 85c +40c multi 2.25 2.25
B733 SP316 85c +40c multi 2.25 2.25
B734 SP316 100c +50c multi 2.75 2.75
- Complete booklet, 6 #B732, 4 #B734 27.00

B735 SP316 100c +50c multi 2.75 2.75

Nos. B732-B735 (4) 10.00 10.00

Surtax for Pro Patria Foundation. Complete booklet sold for 14.50fr.

Boy Saving Money SP317

Designs: No. B736, Boy thinking of teddy bear, piggy bank. No. B737, Boy and piggy bank. No. B738, Boy, teddy bear and piggy bank. No. B739, Piggy bank, boy holding gift.

Serpentine Die Cut 12

2010, Nov. 4 Litho.

Self-Adhesive

B736 SP317 85c +40c multi 2.60 2.60
- *a.* Block of 4 on translucent backing paper 10.50

B737 SP317 85c +40c multi 2.60 2.60
- *a.* Block of 4 on translucent backing paper 10.50

B738 SP317 100c +50c multi 3.25 3.25
- *a.* Block of 4 on translucent backing paper 13.00

B739 SP317 100c +50c multi 3.25 3.25
- *a.* Block of 4, #B736-B739 12.00
- *b.* Booklet pane of 12, 6 each #B736, B739 36.00
- *c.* Block of 4 on translucent backing paper 13.00

Nos. B736-B739 (4) 11.70 11.70

Surtax for Pro Juventute Foundation. No. B739b sold for 17fr.

Lake Steamships SP318

Designs: No. B740, PS Gallia. No. B741, PS Piemonte. No. B742, PS Blümlisalp. No. B743, PS La Suisse.

2011, May 5 Litho. *Perf. 13½*

Color of Denomination

B740 SP318 85c+40c green 3.00 3.00
B741 SP318 85c+40c orange 3.00 3.00
B742 SP318 100c+50c yellow 3.50 3.50
- Complete booklet, 6 #B741, 4 #B742 35.00

B743 SP318 100c+50c brt pink 3.50 3.50

Nos. B740-B743 (4) 13.00 13.00

Complete booklet sold for 14.50fr. Surtax for Pro Patria Foundation.

Children SP319

Stylized flowers and: No. B744, Young boy, duck, sheep, bear, leaf, crescent moon. No. B745, Two girls, happy face, musical notes, envelope, ice cream cone, heart. No. B746, Two young girls, gift, stars, bell, Christmas tree. No. B747, Boy, sun, fish, ball, paw print.

Color of Denomination

Serpentine Die Cut 12

2011, Nov. 17 Self-Adhesive

B744 SP319 85c +40c blue 2.75 2.75
B745 SP319 85c +40c rose lil 2.75 2.75
B746 SP319 100c +50c dl org 3.50 3.50
B747 SP319 100c +50c green 3.50 3.50
- *a.* Block of 4, #B744-B747, on translucent paper 12.50
- *b.* Booklet pane of 12, 3 each #B744-B747 37.50

Nos. B744-B747 (4) 12.50 12.50

Stamps do not touch on No. B747a, but touch in No. B747b. No. B747b sold for 17fr. Surtax for Pro Juventute Foundation.

Girls on Swing SP320

2012, Mar. 1 *Serpentine Die Cut 12*

Self-Adhesive

B748 SP320 100c +50c multi 3.25 3.25

Pro Juventute Foundation, cent. Surtax for Pro Juventute Foundation.

Architectural Preservation SP321

Designs: No. B749, Eichberg Estate Lion Fountain, Uetendorf. No. B750, Ferme des Troncs storehouse, Mézières. No. B751, Domed stone cellar, Brusio. No. B752, Villa Abendstern summer house, Wädenswil.

2012, May 9 *Perf. 14¼x13¾*

B749 SP321 85c +40c multi 2.75 2.75
B750 SP321 85c +40c multi 2.75 2.75
B751 SP321 100c +50c multi 3.25 3.25
- Complete booklet, 6 #B749, 4 #B751 32.50

B752 SP321 100c +50c multi 3.25 3.25

Nos. B749-B752 (4) 12.00 12.00

Complete booklet sold for 14.50fr. Surtax for Pro Patria Foundation.

2012 National Stamp Exhibiton, Stans — SP322

No. B753: a, Buildings on Stans village square, statue base, mountain peak in background (34x42mm). b, Buildings on village square, clouds in background (34x42mm). c, Statue, exhibition emblem (37x70mm). d, Airplane (68x28mm).

Perf. 13 on 1, 2 or 3 Sides

2012, Sept. 6 Litho.

B753 SP322 Sheet of 4 12.00 12.00
- *a.-b.* 85c+45c Either single 2.75 2.75
- *c.-d.* 100c+55c Either single 3.25 3.25

Pro Juventute Posters — SP323

Designs: 85c+40c, Children Playing, by Margarethe Lipps, 1959. No. B755, Girl with Doll, by Victor Rutz, 1952. No. B756, Child in High Chair, by Celestino Piatti, 1955.

Serpentine Die Cut 12

2012, Nov. 22 Self-Adhesive

B754 SP323 85c +40c multi 2.75 2.75
- *a.* Block of 4 #B754 on translucent paper 11.00

B755 SP323 100c +50c multi 3.25 3.25
- *a.* Block of 4 #B755 on translucent paper 13.00

B756 SP323 100c +50c multi 3.25 3.25
- *a.* Nos. B754-B756 on translucent backing paper 9.25
- *b.* Booklet pane of 12, 4 each #B754-B756 37.50
- *c.* Block of 4 #B756 on translucent paper 13.00

Nos. B754-B756 (3) 9.25 9.25

No. B756b sold for 17.50fr. Surtax for Pro Juventute Foundation.

Exhibits in Local Museums SP324

Designs: No. B757, Wax toad, Fram Museum, Einsiedeln. No. B758, Straw hat, Stroh Museum, Wohlen. No. B759, Carved wooden cow, Toggenburger Museum, Lichtensteig. No. B760, Carpenter's plane, Bagnes Museum, Villette.

2013, May 7 *Perf. 13¼x13½*

B757 SP324 85c +40c multi 2.75 2.75
B758 SP324 85c +40c multi 2.75 2.75
B759 SP324 100c +50c multi 3.25 3.25
B760 SP324 100c +50c multi 3.25 3.25
- Complete booklet, 6 #B758, 4 #B760 31.00

Surtax for Pro Patria Foundation. Complete booklet sold for 14.50fr.

See Nos. B764-B767, B772-B775.

Children and Swiss Railway Locomotives SP325

Designs: 85c+40c, Girl and Red Arrow RAe 2/4. No. B762, Boy with glasses, Krokodil Ce 6/8. No. B763, Boy, stars, Gotthard Line Ae6/6.

Serpentine Die Cut 12

2013, Nov. 14 Litho.

Self-Adhesive

B761 SP325 85c +40c multi 3.00 3.00
B762 SP325 100c +50c multi 3.50 3.50
B763 SP325 100c +50c multi 3.50 3.50
- *a.* Sheet of 3, #B761-B763, on translucent paper 10.00
- *b.* Booklet pane of 12, 4 each #B761-B763 40.00

Nos. B761-B763 (3) 10.00 10.00

Surtax for Pro Juventute Foundation. No. B763b sold for 17.50fr.

Exhibits in Local Museums Type of 2013

Designs: No. B764, Roof tile, Malcantone Museum, Curio. No. B765, Painted larval mask, Ortsmuseum, Binningen. No. B766, Hurdy-gurdy, Musical Instrument Collection, Willisau. No. B767, Apprentice watch by Emile Juillard, Museum Hôtel-Dieu, Porrentruy.

2014, May 8 Litho. *Perf. 13¾x14¼*

B764 SP324 85c +40c multi 3.00 3.00
B765 SP324 85c +40c multi 3.00 3.00
B766 SP324 100c +50c multi 3.50 3.50
B767 SP324 100c +50c multi 3.50 3.50
- Complete booklet, 6 #B765, 4 #B767 33.00

Nos. B764-B767 (4) 13.00 13.00

Surtax for Pro Patria Foundation. Complete booklet sold for 14.50fr.

Swiss Family Traditions SP326

Designs: 85c+40c, St. Martin's Day lantern procession. No. B769, Adult reading story to children. No. B770, Family making Christmas cookies.

Serpentine Die Cut 12

2014, Nov. 13 Litho.

Self-Adhesive

B768 SP326 85c +40c multi 2.60 2.60
B769 SP326 100c +50c multi 3.25 3.25
B770 SP326 100c +50c multi 3.25 3.25
- *a.* Sheet of 3, #B768-B770, on translucent paper 9.25
- *b.* Booklet pane of 12, 4 each #B768-B770 37.00

Nos. B768-B770 (3) 9.10 9.10

Surtax for Pro Juventute Foundation. No. B770b sold for 17.50fr. See Nos. B776-B778.

Souvenir Sheet

Horses at Saignelégier Horse Market — SP327

2014, Nov. 13 Litho. ***Perf. 14x13½***
B771 SP327 100c +50c multi 3.25 3.25

Stamp Day. Surtax for Foundation for the Promotion of Philately.

Exhibits in Local Museums Type of 2013

Designs: No. B772, Tobacco pouch, Appenzell Museum, Appenzell. No. B773, Wine barrel, Wine and Vine Museum, Aigle. No. B774, Carved butter board, 18th cent., Saanen Museum of the Countryside, Saanen. No. B775, Merovingian Period disc brooch from Steckborn-Chilestigli burial ground, Archaeology Museum. Frauenfeld.

2015, May 7 Litho. ***Perf. 13¼x13½***
B772 SP324 85c +40c multi 2.75 2.75
B773 SP324 85c +40c multi 2.75 2.75
B774 SP324 100c +50c multi 3.25 3.25
B775 SP324 100c +50c multi 3.25 3.25
Complete booklet, 6 #B773, 4 #B775 32.00
Nos. B772-B775 (4) 12.00 12.00

Surtax for Pro Patria Foundation. Complete booklet sold for 14.50fr.

Family Traditions Type of 2014

Designs: 85c+40c, Christmas meal. No. B777, Family making Christmas arts and crafts. No. B778, Family and Christmas tree.

Serpentine Die Cut 12
2015, Nov. 12 Litho.
Self-Adhesive
B776 SP326 85c +40c multi 2.50 2.50
a. Block of 4 on translucent paper 10.00
B777 SP326 100c +50c multi 3.00 3.00
a. Block of 4 on translucent paper 12.00
B778 SP326 100c +50c multi 3.00 3.00
a. Sheet of 3, #B776-B778 on translucent paper. 8.50
b. Booklet pane of 12, 4 each #B776-B778 34.00
c. Block of 4 on translucent paper 12.00
Nos. B776-B778 (3) 8.50 8.50

Surtax for Pro Juventute Foundation. No. B778b sold for 17.50fr.

Souvenir Sheet

Architectural Landmarks — SP328

No. B779: a, Lake Gruyère Viaduct (53x32mm). b, Gibloux Radio Tower (36x41mm).

2015, Nov. 12 Litho. ***Perf. 14x13¾***
B779 SP328 Sheet of 2 3.00 3.00
a.-b. 50c+25c Either single 1.50 1.50

Stamp Day. Surtax for Foundation for the Promotion of Philately.

Fortresses and Castles SP329

Designs: 85c+40c, Zug Castle. 100c+50c, Neu-Bechburg Castle.

2016, May 12 Litho. ***Perf. 13¼x13½***
B780 SP329 85c +40c multi 2.60 2.60
B781 SP329 100c +50c multi 3.00 3.00
Complete booklet, 4 #B780, 6 #B781 28.50

Surtax for Pro Patria Foundation. See Nos. B786-B787.

Face and Poppies SP330

2016, Sept. 8 Litho. ***Perf. 13x13¼***
Self-Adhesive
B782 SP330 100c +50c multi 3.00 3.00

Surtax for Emergency Aid Fund for Victims of Compulsory Social Measures and Forced Fostering.

Souvenir Sheet

Oberaargau — SP331

No. B783: a, Aarwangen Castle. b, Flowers and irrigation system.

2016, Nov. 17 Litho. ***Perf.***
B783 SP331 Sheet of 2 + central label 3.00 3.00
a.-b. 50c +25c Either single 1.50 1.50

Stamp Day.

Children With Chalk — SP332

School children: 85c+40c, Playing hopscotch. 100c+50c, At blackboard.

Serpentine Die Cut 12
2016, Nov. 17 Litho.
Self-Adhesive
B784 SP332 85c +40c multi 2.50 2.50
B785 SP332 100c +50c multi 3.00 3.00
a. Horiz. pair, #B784-B785 on translucent paper 5.50
b. Booklet pane of 12, 6 each #B784-B785 33.00

Surtax for Pro Junventute Foundation.

Fortresses and Castles Type of 2016

Designs: 85c+40c, Visconti Castle. 100c+50c, Oberhofen Castle.

2017, May 11 Litho. ***Perf. 13¼x13½***
B786 SP329 85c +40c multi 2.50 2.50
B787 SP329 100c +50c multi 3.00 3.00
Complete booklet, 4 #B786, 6 #B787 28.00

Surtax for Pro Partia Foundation.

Pro Senectute Foundation, Cent. — SP333

2017, May 11 Litho. ***Perf. 13¼x13½***
B788 SP333 100c +50c multi 3.00 3.00

Surtax for Pro Senectute Foundation.

Children at School SP334

Children: 85c+40c, With teacher and globe. 100c+50c, Singing in choir.

Serpentine Die Cut 12
2017, Nov. 16 Litho.
Self-Adhesive
B789 SP334 85c +40c multi 2.60 2.60
a. Block of 4 on translucent paper 10.50
B790 SP334 100c +50c multi 3.25 3.25
a. Horiz. pair, #B789-B790 on translucent paper 6.00
b. Booklet pane of 12, 6 each #B789-B790 35.50
c. Block of 4 #B790 on translucent paper 13.00

Surtax for Pro Junventute Foundation.

Souvenir Sheet

Sainte-Croix — SP335

No. B791: a, Aerial view of Sainte-Croix. b, Music box mechanism.

2017, Nov. 16 Litho. ***Perf. 14x14½***
B791 SP335 Sheet of 2 3.25 3.25
a.-b. 50c+25c Either single 1.60 1.60

Stamp Day. Surtax for Foundation for the Promotion of Philately.

Switzerland Nos. 1L1 and 1L2 SP336

2018, Mar. 1 Litho. ***Perf. 13½***
B792 SP336 100c +50c multi 3.25 3.25

Swiss postage stamps, 175th anniv. Surtax for Foundation for the Promotion of Philately.

Fortresses and Castles Type of 2016

Designs: 85c+40c, Hagenwil Water Castle. 100c+50c, Romont Castle.

2018, May 17 Litho. ***Perf. 13¼x13½***
B793 SP329 85c +40c multi 2.50 2.50
B794 SP329 100c +50c multi 3.00 3.00
Complete booklet, 4 #B793, 6 #B794 28.00

Surtax for Pro Partia Foundation.

2018 National Stamp Exhibition, Lugano SP337

2018, May 17 Litho. ***Perf. 13½***
B795 SP337 100c +50c multi 3.00 3.00

Surtax for NABA Stamp Exhibition and Foundation for the Promotion of Philately.

Souvenir Sheet

Allschwil — SP338

Perf. 13¼x13¾
2018, Nov. 15 Litho.
B796 SP338 100c +50c multi 3.00 3.00

Stamp Day. Surtax for Foundation for the Promotion of Philately.

Children at Play — SP339

Designs: 85c+40c, Boy playing with blocks. 100c+50c, Girl blowing bubbles.

Serpentine Die Cut 12
2018, Nov. 15 Litho.
Self-Adhesive
B797 SP339 85c +40c multi 2.50 2.50
a. Block of 4 on translucent paper 10.00
B798 SP339 100c +50c multi 3.00 3.00
a. Horiz. pair, #B797-B798, on translucent paper without back printing 5.50
b. Booklet pane of 12, 6 each #B797-B798 33.00
c. Block of 4 #B798 on translucent paper 12.00

Surtax for Pro Juventute Foundation.

White Cross of Swiss Flag and Definitions of Red Color — SP340

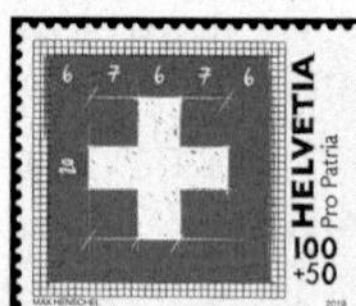

Dimensions of Swiss Flag — SP341

2019, May 2 Litho. ***Perf. 13¼x13½***
B799 SP340 85c +40c multi 2.50 2.50
B800 SP341 100c +50c multi 3.00 3.00
Complete booklet, 4 #B799, 6 #B800 28.00

Surtax for Pro Patria Foundation.

SP342

United Nations Convention on the Rights of the Child, 30th Anniv. — SP343

Serpentine Die Cut 12
2019, Nov. 14 Litho.
Self-Adhesive
B801 SP342 85c +40c multi 2.50 2.50
B802 SP343 100c +50c multi 3.00 3.00
a. Horiz. pair, #B801-B802, on translucent paper without back printing 5.50
b. Booklet pane of 12, 6 each #B801-B802 33.00

Surtax for the Pro Juventute Foundation.

Souvenir Sheet

Bulle — SP344

2019, Nov. 28 Litho. *Perf. 14x14¼*
B803 SP344 100c +50c multi 3.00 3.00

Stamp Day.

Pro Infirmis Foundation, Cent. — SP345

2020, Mar. 5 Litho. *Perf. 13½*
B804 SP345 100c +50c multi 3.25 3.25

Surtax for Pro Infirmis Foundation and Postage Stamp Fund for Cultural and Social Commitment.

COVID-19 Solidarity SP346

2020, Apr. 6 Litho. *Perf. 13¾x14¼*
B805 SP346 100c +500c red 12.50 12.50

Surtax for Swiss Solidarity and Swiss Red Cross.

Cultural Institutions SP347

Designs: 85c+40c, Sitterwerk Foundation Art Library, St. Gallen. 100c+50c, Weaver, Tessanda Foundation, Val Müstair.

2020, May 7 Litho. *Perf. 13¼x13½*
B806 SP347 85c +40c multi 2.60 2.60
B807 SP347 100c +50c multi 3.25 3.25
Complete booklet, 4 #B806, 6 #807 30.00

Surtax for the Pro Patria Foundation.

AIR POST STAMPS

Nos. 134 and 139 Overprinted in Carmine

1919-20 Wmk. 183 *Perf. 11½*
Granite Paper
C1 A25 30c yel brn & pale grn ('20) 110.00 *1,250.*
C2 A25 50c dp & pale grn 32.50 110.00
Set, never hinged 350.00

Counterfeits of overprint and fraudulent cancellations exist.

Airplane AP1

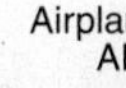

Pilot at Controls of Airplane AP2

Biplane against Sky — AP3

Allegorical Figure of Flight AP4

Perf. 11½, 12 and Compound
1923-25 Typo.
C3 AP1 15c brn red & ap grn 2.75 6.25
C4 AP1 20c grn & lt grn ('25) .90 *4.00*
C5 AP1 25c dk bl & bl 6.50 *16.00*
C6 AP2 35c brn & buff 9.75 *30.00*
C7 AP2 40c vio & gray vio 11.00 *35.00*
C8 AP3 45c red & ind 1.50 *5.00*
C9 AP3 50c blk & red 10.00 13.00

Perf. 11½
C10 AP4 65c gray bl & dp bl ('24) 3.00 *12.00*
C11 AP4 75c org & brn red ('24) 12.00 *55.00*
C12 AP4 1fr vio & dp vio ('24) 30.00 23.00
Nos. C3-C12 (10) 87.40 *199.25*
Set, never hinged 300.00

For surcharges see Nos. C19, C22, C26.

1933-37 With Grilled Gum
C4a AP1 20c grn & lt grn ('37) .30 .40
C5a AP1 25c dk bl & bl ('34) 5.00 *50.00*
C8a AP3 45c red & indigo ('37) 2.50 *52.50*
C9a AP3 50c gray grn & scar ('35) 1.25 1.60
C10a AP4 65c gray bl & dp bl ('37) 2.10 *8.50*
C11a AP4 75c org & brn red ('36) 27.50 *175.00*
C12a AP4 1fr vio & deep vio 2.10 3.00
Nos. C4a-C12a (7) 40.75 *291.00*
Set, never hinged 80.00

See Grilled Gum note after No. 145.

Allegory of Air Mail — AP5

Bird Carrying Letter AP6

1929-30 Granite Paper
C13 AP5 35c red brn, bis & claret 15.00 35.00
C14 AP5 40c dl grn, yel grn & bl 52.50 60.00
C15 AP6 2fr blk brn & red brn, *gray* ('30) 65.00 65.00
Nos. C13-C15 (3) 132.50 160.00
Set, never hinged 300.00

1933-35 With Grilled Gum
C13a AP5 35c red brn, bis & cl 5.00 *27.50*
C14a AP5 40c dk grn, yel grn & bl 37.50 37.50
C15a AP6 2fr blk brn & red brn ('35) 7.25 7.50
Nos. C13a-C15a (3) 49.75 *72.50*
Set, never hinged 140.00

Front View of Airplane AP7

1932, Feb. 2 Granite Paper
C16 AP7 15c dp grn & lt grn .70 *1.60*
C17 AP7 20c dk red & buff 1.10 *2.00*
C18 AP7 90c dp bl & gray 7.75 *25.00*
Nos. C16-C18 (3) 9.55 *28.60*
Set, never hinged 22.50

Intl. Disarmament Conf., Geneva, Feb. 1932.
For surcharges see Nos. C20-C21, C23-C25.

Nos. C3, C10, C16-C18 Surcharged with New Values and Bars in Black or Red

1935-38
C19 AP1 10c on 15c 4.75 *21.00*
C20 AP7 10c on 15c .40 .40
a. Inverted surcharge *6,500. 12,000.*
C21 AP7 10c on 20c ('36) .45 *1.10*
C22 AP4 10c on 65c ('38) .25 .40
C23 AP7 30c on 90c ('36) 3.00 *8.75*
C24 AP7 40c on 20c ('37) 3.75 *11.00*
C25 AP7 40c on 90c ('36) (R) 3.25 *11.00*
a. Vermilion surcharge 85.00 *800.00*
Never hinged, #C25a 150.00
Nos. C19-C25 (7) 15.85 *53.65*
Set, never hinged 40.00

Stamp similar to No. C22, but from souvenir sheet, is listed as No. 242a.

Type of Air Post Stamp of 1923 Srchd. in Black

1938, May 22 Wmk. 183 *Perf. 11½*
C26 AP3 75c on 50c gray & red 6.00

"Pro Aero" Meeting, May 21-22.
No. C26 was not sold to the public in the ordinary way, but affixed to air mail letters by postal officials. While it was not regularly obtainable unused, unused examples exist. Value, $1,000.

Jungfrau — AP8

Designs: 40c, View of Valais. 50c, Lake Geneva. 60c, Alpstein. 70c, View of Ticino. 1fr, Lake Lucerne. 2fr, The Engadine. 5fr, Churfirsten.

Perf. 11½
1941, May 1 Unwmk. Engr.
Tinted Granite Paper
C27 AP8 30c ultra .55 .25
C28 AP8 40c gray blk .55 .25
C29 AP8 50c slate grn .55 .30
C30 AP8 60c chestnut .85 .30
C31 AP8 70c plum .90 .55
C32 AP8 1fr Prus grn 1.75 .85
C33 AP8 2fr car lake 5.75 2.75
C34 AP8 5fr deep blue 19.00 12.00
Nos. C27-C34 (8) 29.90 17.25
Set, never hinged 80.00

See Nos. C43-C44.

Type of 1941 Overprinted in Red

1941, May 12
C35 AP8 1fr blue green 5.50 *15.00*
Never hinged 10.00

Issued to commemorate special flights between Payerne and Buochs, May 28, 1941.

Parliament Buildings, Bern AP16

1943, July 13 Photo.
C36 AP16 1fr cop red, buff & blk 1.60 *8.00*
Never hinged 3.75

30th anniv. of the 1st Alpine flight, by Oscar Bider, July 13, 1913.

DH-3 Haefeli AP17

Fokker AP18

Lockheed-Orion — AP19

1944, Sept. 1
C37 AP17 10c gray brn & pale grn .25 *.35*
C38 AP18 20c rose car & buff .30 *.35*
C39 AP19 30c ultra & pale gray .35 *1.25*
Nos. C37-C39 (3) .90 *1.95*
Set, never hinged 1.90

25th anniv. of the 1st regular air route in Switzerland.

Douglas DC-3 AP20

1944, Sept. 20 Granite Paper
C40 AP20 1.50fr multi 6.00 *15.50*
Never hinged 11.00

25th anniv. of the Zurich-Geneva air route.

Zoegling Training Glider AP21

1946, May 1 Granite Paper
C41 AP21 1.50fr henna brn & gray 11.50 *22.50*
Never hinged 20.00

Valid for use only on two special flights.

Douglas DC-4 Linking Geneva and New York AP22

1947, Mar. 17 Granite Paper
C42 AP22 2.50fr bl gray, dk bl & red 7.25 *16.00*
Never hinged 14.00

Valid only on the Geneva-New York flight of May 2, 1947.
Because of bad weather at NYC the flight ended at Washington.

Types of 1941

1948, Oct. 1 **Engr.**

Tinted Granite Paper

C43 AP8 30c dk slate bl 4.50 *10.00*
C44 AP8 40c deep ultra 21.00 1.50
Set, never hinged 57.50

Glider in Symbolized Aerodynamic Buoyancy — AP23

1949, Apr. 11 **Engr. & Typo.**

C45 AP23 1.50fr dk vio & yel 16.00 *28.00*
Never hinged 28.00

Valid only on special flights, Apr. 27-29, 1949. Proceeds were for the advancement of national aviation.

Catalogue values for unused stamps in this section, from this point to the end of the section, are for Never Hinged items.

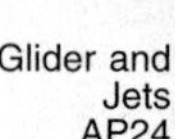

Glider and Jets AP24

1963, June 1 **Photo.** ***Perf. 11½***

Granite Paper

C46 AP24 2fr multicolored 4.00 3.50

50th anniversary of the first Alpine flight by Oscar Bider, July 13, 1913. Valid for postage on July 13, 1963, on flights from Bern to Locarno and Langenbruck to Bern. Proceeds went to the Pro Aero Foundation.

AIR POST SEMI-POSTAL STAMP

Catalogue values for unused stamps in this section are for Never Hinged items.

Boeing 747 — SPAP1

1972, Feb. 17 **Photo.** ***Perf. 12½***

Violet Fibers, Fluorescent Paper

CB1 SPAP1 2fr + 1fr dp bl, red & gray 2.75 2.25

50th anniv. of 1st Swiss Intl. flight, Zurich to Nuremberg, and 25th anniv. of 1st Swissair trans-Atlantic flight, Zurich to NYC. Valid on all mail but obligatory on special flights from Geneva to NYC in May, and from Geneva to Nuremberg in June, 1972.

Surtax was for Pro Aero Foundation and the training of young airmen, and for the Swiss Air Rescue Service.

POSTAGE DUE STAMPS

D1

D2

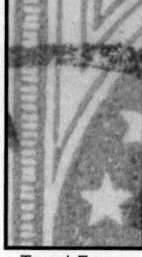

Type I Frame Normal - UR Ornament

Type I Frame Normal - UL Triangle

Type I Frame Normal: Ornament at UR is undamaged. UL triangle tip and star tip align horizontally. LR triangle tip aligns horizontally with the center of the star.

Wmk. 182 Type I

1878 **Typo.** ***Perf. 11½***

Type I Frame Normal

J1 D1 1c blue 1.75 1.50
J2 D2 2c blue 1.75 1.50
J3 D2 3c blue 16.00 *17.50*
J4 D2 5c blue 16.00 9.50
f. Design as #J1 —
J5 D2 10c blue 175.00 7.50
J6 D2 20c blue 200.00 6.75
J7 D2 50c blue 575.00 18.50
J8 D2 100c blue 500.00 15.50
J9 D2 500c blue 450.00 26.00
Nos. J1-J9 (9) 1,936. 104.25

A 5c in design D1 exists.

Type I Frame Inverted - UL Triangle

Type I Frame Inverted: Ornament at LL is undamaged. UL triangle tip aligns horizontally with star center. LR triangle tip and star tip align horizontally.

1878 **Typo.** **Wmk. 182** ***Perf. 11½***

Type I Frame Inverted

J1a 1c blue 12.00 *15.00*
J2a 2c blue 1.75 1.75
J3a 3c blue 16.00 *16.50*
J4a 5c blue 21.00 10.00
J5a 10c blue 180.00 14.00
J6a 20c blue 200.00 8.75
J7a 50c blue 280.00 25.00
J8a 100c blue 500.00 15.50
J9a 500c blue 450.00 26.00
Nos. J1a-J9a (9) 1,661. 132.50

Type II Frame Normal - UR Ornament

Type II Frame Normal: Ornament at UR is broken with a white gap in center. UL triangle tip and star tip align horizontally. LR triangle tip aligns horizontally with the center of the star.

Wmk. 182

1878-81 **Typo.** ***Perf. 11½***

Type II Frame Normal

J3b 3c blue 12.00 10.50
J4b 5c blue 16.50 12.00
J5b 10c blue 175.00 7.75
J6d 20c ultra ('79) 200.00 5.00
J7b 50c blue ('79) 425.00 23.00
J8d 100c ultra ('81) 950.00 120.00
J9d 500c ultra ('81) 475.00 62.50
Nos. J3b-J9b (7) 2,254. 240.75

Type II Frame Inverted - LL Ornament

Type II Frame Inverted: Ornament at LL is broken with a white gap in center. UL triangle tip aligns horizontally with star center. LR triangle tip and star tip align horizontally.

Wmk. 182

1878-81 **Typo.** ***Perf. 11½***

Type II Frame Inverted

J3c 3c blue 13.00 12.00
J4c 5c blue 14.50 7.25
J5c 10c blue 190.00 8.75
J6c 20c ultra ('79) 220.00 6.50
J7c 50c blue ('79) 450.00 28.00
J8c 100c ultra ('81) — 1,700.
J9c 500c ultra ('81) 450.00 55.00

Type II Frame Normal

1882 **Granite Paper**

J10 D2 10c ultra 160.00 40.00
J11 D2 20c ultra 375.00 50.00
J12 D2 50c ultra 2,100. 500.00
J13 D2 100c ultra 725.00 350.00
J14 D2 500c ultra *13,500.* 210.00

1882 **Granite Paper**

Type II Frame Inverted

J10a 10c ultra 160.00 42.50
J11a 20c ultra 400.00 60.00
J12a 50c ultra 2,250. 550.00
J13a 100c ultra 775.00 400.00
J14a 500c ultra *14,000.* 225.00

1883-93 **Numerals in Red**

Type II Frame Inverted

J14B D2 3c ol grn ('92) 4.75 *5.50*
J15 D2 5c ol grn ('92) 17.00 3.00
J16 D2 10c ol grn ('92) 23.00 2.50
J17 D2 20c ol grn ('92) 26.00 1.90
J18 D2 50c ol grn ('92) 65.00 5.50
J19 D2 100c ol grn ('92) 85.00 12.00
J20 D2 500c ol grn ('92) 120.00 14.50

1883-93 **Numerals in Red**

Type II Frame Normal

J14Bc 3c olive green ('92) 100.00 115.00
J15a 5c olive green ('92) 200.00 105.00
J16a 10c olive green ('92) 250.00 92.50
J17a 20c olive green ('92) 210.00 100.00
J18a 50c olive green ('92) 375.00 125.00
J19a 100c olive green ('92) 425.00 125.00
J20a 500c olive green ('92) 525.00 160.00

1888-93 **Numerals in Red**

Type I Frame Inverted

J14Bd 3c olive green ('92) 400.00 300.00
J15b 5c olive green ('92) 225.00 190.00
J16b 10c olive green ('92) 250.00 210.00
J17b 20c olive green ('92) 225.00 190.00
J18b 50c olive green ('92) 350.00 240.00
J19b 100c olive green ('92) 350.00 240.00
J20b 500c olive green ('92) 950.00 450.00

1897-1907 **Wmk. 182 Type II**

Numerals in Vermilion

Type II Frame Normal

J21 D2 1c olive ('05) .95 .95
J23 D2 5c olive ('03) 1.60 .60
J24 D2 10c olive ('03) 4.00 .90
J25 D2 20c olive ('03) 8.00 1.40
J26 D2 50c olive ('03) 12.00 3.00
J27 D2 100c olive ('05) 14.00 2.50
J28 D2 500c bright olive ('99) 150.00 175.00

1897-1907

Numerals in Vermilion

Type II Frame Inverted

J21a 1c olive ('05) .95 .95
J23a 5c olive ('03) 1.60 .60
J24a 10c olive ('03) 3.75 .90
J25a 20c olive ('03) 8.00 1.35
J26a 50c olive ('03) 12.50 3.00
J27a 100c olive ('05) 14.00 2.50
J28j 500c bright olive ('99) 160.00 160.00

1897-1901

Numerals in Vermilion

Type I Frame Normal

J21k 1c bright olive 180.00 180.00
J23k 5c bright olive ('98) 175.00 190.00
J24k 10c bright olive ('98) 160.00 130.00
J25k 20c bright olive 190.00 135.00
J26k 50c bright olive ('98) 290.00 160.00
J27k 100c bright olive ('98) 500.00 240.00
J28k 500c bright olive ('99) 1,400. 1,050.

1897-1901

Numerals in Vermilion

Type I Frame Inverted

J21h 1c green 525.00 475.00
J23h 5c green 350.00 300.00
J24h 10c green 500.00 325.00
J25h 20c green 600.00 325.00
J26h 50c green 725.00 500.00
J27h 100c green 900.00 925.00
J28h 500c green 1,700. 1,000.

1894-96

Type II Frame Normal

Numerals in Red

J23b 5c olive green 16.50 3.50
J24b 10c olive green ('95) 22.00 4.50
J25b 20c olive green ('95) 22.00 6.50
J26b 50c olive green ('95) 82.50 55.00
J27b 100c olive green ('95) 160.00 140.00

1894-96

Type II Frame Inverted

Numerals in Red

J23c 5c olive green 12.00 1.90
J24c 10c olive green ('95) 16.50 2.25
J25c 20c olive green ('95) 17.50 3.00
J26c 50c olive green ('95) 60.00 16.00
J27c 100c olive green ('95) 82.50 35.00

1895-96

Type I Frame Normal

Numerals in Red

J23d 5c olive green 225.00 190.00
J24d 10c olive green ('96) 275.00 200.00
J25d 20c olive green ('96) 275.00 175.00

1894-95

Type I Frame Inverted

Numerals in Red

J23e 5c olive green 275.00 210.00
J24e 10c olive green ('95) 350.00 225.00
J25e 20c olive green ('95) 275.00 175.00
J26e 50c olive green ('95) 750.00 375.00
J27e 100c olive green ('95) 800.00 450.00

1907-10 **Wmk. 183**

Numerals in Vermilion

Type II Frame Normal

J29 D2 1c brnsh ol ('08) .30 .85
J30 D2 5c brnsh ol ('08) .75 1.00
J31 D2 10c brnsh ol ('09) 3.00 2.10
J32 D2 20c brnsh ol ('09) 7.75 5.75
J33 D2 50c brnsh ol ('09) 33.00 1.00
J34 D2 100c brownish olive ('09) 52.50 2.25
Nos. J29-J34 (6) 97.30 12.95

1907-10 **Wmk. 183**

Numerals in Vermilion

Type II Frame Inverted

J29a 1c brownish olive ('08) .30 .85
J30a 5c brownish olive ('08) .75 1.00
J31a 10c brownish olive ('09) 3.00 2.25
J32a 20c brownish olive ('09) 7.75 5.75
J33a 50c brownish olive ('09) 32.00 1.00
J34a 100c brownish olive ('09) 50.00 2.10

D3

1910 ***Perf. 11½, 12***

Numerals in Red

J35 D3 1c blue green .25 .25
J36 D3 3c blue green .25 .25
J37 D3 5c blue green .25 .25
J38 D3 10c blue green 11.00 .25
J39 D3 15c blue green .65 1.10
J40 D3 20c blue green 17.50 .25
J41 D3 25c blue green 1.25 .65
J42 D3 30c blue green 1.25 .55
J43 D3 50c blue green 1.50 1.10
Nos. J35-J43 (9) 33.90 4.65

See Nos. S1-S12.

No. J36 Surcharged

1916

J44 D3 5c on 3c bl grn & red .40 .25

Nos. J35-J36, J43 Surcharged

1924

J45 D3 10c on 1c .25 *8.25*
J46 D3 10c on 3c .25 *1.50*
J47 D3 20c on 50c .95 1.50
Nos. J45-J47 (3) 1.45 11.25

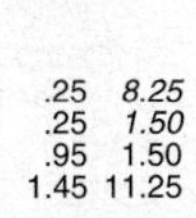

D4

Wmk. 183

1924-26 Typo. *Perf. 11½*

Granite Paper

J48 D4 5c ol grn & red .65 .25
J49 D4 10c ol grn & red 2.75 .25
J50 D4 15c ol grn & red ('26) 2.50 .55
J51 D4 20c ol grn & red 6.00 .25
J52 D4 25c ol grn & red 2.75 .55
J53 D4 30c ol grn & red 2.75 .85
J54 D4 40c ol grn & red ('26) 3.75 .70
J55 D4 50c ol grn & red 3.75 .70
Nos. J48-J55 (8) 24.90 4.10

1924 With Grilled Gum

J48a D4 5c olive green & red .65 .60
J49a D4 10c olive green & red 2.50 1.10
J51a D4 20c olive green & red 4.75 1.50
J52a D4 25c olive green & red 7.25 *65.00*
Nos. J48a-J52a (4) 15.15 *68.20*

See Grilled Gum note after No. 145.

Nos. J50, J53 & J55 Surcharged in Black

1937

J56 D4 5c on 15c .90 *4.25*
J57 D4 10c on 30c .90 *1.50*
J58 D4 20c on 50c 1.50 *5.00*
J59 D4 40c on 50c 2.50 *12.00*
Nos. J56-J59 (4) 5.80 *22.75*
Set, never hinged 10.50

D5

1938 Engr. Unwmk.

J60 D5 5c scarlet .40 .25
J61 D5 10c scarlet .55 .25
J62 D5 15c scarlet 1.25 *2.25*
J63 D5 20c scarlet .95 .25
J64 D5 25c scarlet 1.40 *1.90*
J65 D5 30c scarlet 1.40 1.25
J66 D5 40c scarlet 1.60 .45
J67 D5 50c scarlet 1.90 2.25
Nos. J60-J67 (8) 9.45 *8.85*
Set, never hinged 19.00

1938 With Grilled Gum

J60a D5 5c scarlet .65 *1.60*
J61a D5 10c scarlet .65 *1.25*
J62a D5 15c scarlet 1.40 *2.50*
J63a D5 20c scarlet 1.25 .55
J64a D5 25c scarlet 1.40 *9.50*
J65a D5 30c scarlet 1.40 *2.25*
J66a D5 40c scarlet 2.10 2.10
J67a D5 50c scarlet 2.50 *3.50*
Nos. J60a-J67a (8) 11.35 *23.25*
Set, never hinged 29.00

See Grilled Gum note after No. 145.

OFFICIAL STAMPS

Switzerland perforated Official stamps are listed in the Scott *Classic Specialized Catalogue 1840-1940.*

Values for canceled Official Stamps are for those canceled to order. Postally used stamps sell for considerably more. This note does not apply to Nos. 1O1-1O16, 2O27-2O30, 3O23-3O26.

Counterfeit overprints exist of most Official stamps.

Official stamps without unused values were not made available to the public unused.

For General Use

Regular Issues of 1908-36 Overprinted in Black

1938 Unwmk. *Perf. 11½*

O1 A53 3c olive .25 .25
O2 A54 5c blue green .25 .25
O3 A55 10c red violet 1.10 .45
O4 A56 15c orange .55 *1.60*
O5 A68 20c red .55 .25
O6 A58 25c brown .55 *1.40*
O7 A59 30c ultra .65 *1.00*
O8 A60 35c yellow green .65 *1.25*
O9 A61 40c gray .65 *1.00*

Wmk. 183

With Grilled Gum

O10 A25 50c dp grn & pale grn 1.10 *1.50*
O11 A25 60c brn org & buff 1.50 *2.50*
O12 A25 70c vio & buff 2.40 *4.25*
O13 A25 80c sl & buff 1.50 *3.25*
O14 A36 90c grn & red, *grn* 1.50 *3.25*
O15 A25 1fr dp cl & pale grn 1.50 *3.25*
O16 A36 1.20fr brn rose & red, *rose* 1.50 *4.50*
O17 A36 1.50fr bl & red, *bl* 2.75 *6.00*
O18 A36 2fr gray blk & red, *gray* 3.25 *7.00*
Nos. O1-O18 (18) 22.20 *42.95*
Set, never hinged 65.00

Nos. O14, O16, O17 and O18 are on surface-colored paper.

1938 Unwmk. With Grilled Gum

O1a A53 3c olive 5.25 .45
O2a A54 5c blue green 1.75 .45
O3a A55 10c red violet 2.00 .55
O4a A56 15c orange 3.50 1.25
O5a A68 20c red 2.00 .70
O6a A58 25c brown 75.00 7.75
O7a A59 30c ultra 3.25 1.10
O8a A60 35c yellow green 2.50 1.90
O9a A61 40c gray 3.25 1.00
Nos. O1a-O9a (9) 98.50 15.15
Set, never hinged 190.00

See Grilled Gum note after No. 145.

Postage Stamps of 1936-42 Overprinted in Black

1942-45 Unwmk. *Perf. 11½*

O19 A53 3c olive .30 *1.10*
O20 A54 5c blue green .30 .25
a. Grilled gum *1,500.*
O21 A55 10c dk red brn .40 .45
O21A A55 10c org brn ('45) .30 *.50*
O22 A56 15c orange .40 *1.00*
O23 A68 20c red .40 .45
O24 A58 25c lt brown .40 *1.25*
O25 A59 30c ultra .50 .50
a. Grilled gum *500.00*
O26 A60 35c yellow grn .75 *1.75*
O27 A61 40c gray .75 1.00
O28 A77 50c dp pur, *grnsh* 4.00 *3.75*
O29 A78 60c red brn, *buff* 4.50 3.75
O30 A79 70c rose vio, *pale lil* 4.75 *7.75*
O31 A80 80c blk, *pale gray* .95 *1.50*
O32 A81 90c dk red, *pale rose* 1.25 *1.50*
O33 A82 1fr dk grn, *grnsh* 1.25 2.00
O34 A83 1.20fr red vio, *pale gray* 1.75 *2.75*
O35 A84 1.50fr dk bl, *buff* 2.00 *2.75*
O36 A85 2fr mar, *pale rose* 2.75 *3.25*
Nos. O19-O36 (19) 27.70 *37.25*
Set, never hinged 60.00

Same Overprint on Nos. 329-339

1950 Unwmk. *Perf. 12x11½*

O37 A118 5c orange .35 *.60*
O38 A119 10c yellow grn .50 .60
O39 A120 15c aqua 5.75 *12.50*
O40 A121 20c brown car 1.90 .60
O41 A122 25c red 3.00 *7.50*
O42 A123 30c olive 2.25 *3.25*
O43 A124 35c red brown 3.00 *7.50*
O44 A125 40c deep blue 2.25 *3.75*
O45 A126 50c slate gray 3.75 *5.00*
O46 A127 60c blue green 4.50 *5.00*
O47 A128 70c purple 13.00 *18.50*
Nos. O37-O47 (11) 40.25 *64.80*
Set, never hinged 70.00

FOR THE WAR BOARD OF TRADE

Regular Issues of 1908-18 Overprinted

1918 Wmk. 183 *Perf. 11½, 12*

1O1 A26 3c brown org 110.00 *225.00*
1O2 A26 5c green 10.00 *32.50*
1O3 A26 7½c gray (I) 300.00 *450.00*
a. 7½c slate (II) 550.00 *950.00*
1O4 A28 10c red, *buff* 15.00 *40.00*
1O5 A28 15c vio, *buff* 12.50 *45.00*
1O6 A25 20c red & yel 125.00 *500.00*
1O7 A25 25c dp bl 125.00 *500.00*
1O8 A25 30c yel brn & pale grn 125.00 *450.00*
Nos. 1O1-1O8 (8) 822.50 *2,243.*

Most unused examples of Nos. 1O1-1O8 are reprints made using the original overprint forms.

Counterfeits exist.

Overprinted

1918

1O9 A26 3c brn org 4.25 *35.00*
1O10 A26 5c green 12.00 *52.50*
1O11 A26 7½c gray 4.50 *22.50*
1O12 A28 10c red, *buff* 45.00 *87.50*
1O13 A28 15c vio, *buff* 82.50
1O14 A25 20c red & yel 8.75 *52.50*
1O15 A25 25c dp blue 8.75 *52.50*
1O16 A25 30c yel brn & pale grn 14.50 *87.50*
Nos. 1O9-1O16 (8) 180.25 390.00

No. 1O13 was never placed in use.

Fraudulent cancellations are found on Nos. 1O1-1O16.

FOR THE LEAGUE OF NATIONS

Regular Issues Overprinted

On 1908-30 Issues

1922-31 Wmk. 183 *Perf. 11½, 12*

2O1 A26 2½c ol, *buff* ('28) — .45
2O2 A26 3c ultra, *buff* ('30) — 6.75
2O3 A26 5c orange, *buff* — 3.25
2O4 A26 5c gray vio, *buff* ('26) — 4.00
2O5 A26 5c red vio, *buff* ('27) — 1.50
2O6 A26 5c dk grn, *buff* ('31) — 20.00
2O7 A26 7½c dp grn, *buff* ('28) — .60
2O8 A28 10c green, *buff* — .60
2O9 A28 10c bl grn, *buff* ('28) — 1.75
2O10 A28 10c vio, *buff* ('31) — 2.25
2O11 A28 15c brn red, *buff* ('28) — 1.75
2O12 A28 20c red vio, *buff* — 5.50
2O13 A28 20c car, *buff* ('26) — 2.50
2O14 A28 25c ver, *buff* — 8.00
2O15 A28 25c car, *buff* — 1.25
2O16 A28 25c brn, *buff* ('27) — 15.50
2O17 A28 30c dp bl, *buff* ('25) — 9.25
2O18 A25 30c yel brn & pale grn — 4.25
2O19 A25 35c yel grn & yel — 5.50
2O20 A25 40c deep blue — 1.50
2O21 A25 40c red vio & grn ('28) — 12.25
2O22 A25 50c dp grn & pale grn — 9.75
2O23 A25 60c brn org & buff 30.00 1.25
2O24 A25 70c vio & buff ('25) — 26.00
2O25 A25 80c slate & buff — 6.25
2O26 A25 1fr dp cl & pale grn — 6.75
2O27 A29 3fr red — 27.50
2O28 A30 5fr ultra — 67.50
2O29 A31 10fr dull violet — 120.00
2O30 A31 10fr gray grn ('30) — 137.50
Nos. 2O1-2O30 (30) 510.90

1930-44 With Grilled Gum

2O2a A26 3c ultra, *buff* ('33) — 10.00
2O6a A26 5c dk grn, *buff* ('33) — 22.00
2O17a A28 30c dp bl,*buff* — 425.00
2O22a A25 50c dp grn & pale grn ('35) 1.50 1.75
2O23a A25 60c brn org & buff ('44) 25.00 *225.00*
2O24a A25 70c violet & buff ('32) 1.60 2.00
2O25a A25 80c slate & buff ('42) 2.75 2.25
2O26a A25 1fr dp cl & pale grn ('42) 3.50

1935-36 With Grilled Gum

2O31 A36 90c grn & red, *grn* ('36) 175.00 5.00
2O32 A36 1.20fr brn rose & red, *rose* ('36) 2.75 *4.50*
2O33 A36 1.50fr bl & red, *bl* 2.75 *4.50*
2O34 A36 2fr gray blk & red, *gray* ('36) 2.75 *5.25*

1922-25 Ordinary Gum

2O31a A36 90c — 11.50
2O32a A36 1.20fr ('25) — 5.00
b. Inverted overprint *4,250.*
2O33a A36 1.50fr ('25) — 12.50
2O34a A36 2fr ('25) — 12.50

1928

2O35 A39 5fr blue — 80.00

1932 On 1932 Issue

2O36 A41 5c peacock bl — 17.00
2O37 A41 10c orange — 1.60
2O38 A41 20c cerise — 1.60
2O39 A41 30c ultra — 47.50
2O40 A41 60c olive brn — 17.00

Unwmk.

2O41 A42 1fr ol gray & bl — 10.00
Nos. 2O36-2O41 (6) 94.70

On 1934 Issue

1934-35 Wmk. 183

2O42 A46 3c olive — .25
2O43 A47 5c emerald — .65
2O44 A49 15c orange ('35) — .95
2O45 A51 25c brown — 19.00
2O46 A52 30c ultra — 1.75
Nos. 2O42-2O46 (5) 22.60

1937 On 1936 Issue Unwmk.

2O47 A53 3c olive .25 .25
2O48 A54 5c blue green .25 .25
2O49 A55 10c red violet (II) — 1.10
b. Type I — 8.00
2O50 A56 15c orange .45 .55
2O51 A57 20c carmine — 1.90
2O52 A58 25c brown .65 1.10
2O53 A59 30c ultra .65 1.00
2O54 A60 35c yellow green .65 1.00
2O55 A61 40c gray .95 1.25
Nos. 2O47-2O55 (9) 8.40

1937 With Grilled Gum

2O47a A53 3c olive — .25
2O48a A54 5c blue green — .30
2O49a A55 10c red violet (II) — 6.25
c. Type I — 6.00
2O50a A56 15c orange — .50
2O51a A57 20c carmine — 1.25
2O52a A58 25c brown — 1.25
2O53a A59 30c ultra — 1.25
2O54a A60 35c yellow green — 2.50
2O55a A61 40c gray — 1.25
Nos. 2O47a-2O55a (9) 14.80

1937 On 1931 Issue Wmk. 183

2O56 A40 3fr orange brown — 190.00

On 1938 Issue

1938 **Unwmk.** ***Perf. 11½***

Granite Paper

2O57 A63 20c red & buff — 1.90
2O58 A64 30c blue & lt blue — 3.00
2O59 A65 60c brown & buff — 5.75
2O60 A66 1fr black & buff — 9.25
Nos. 2O57-2O60 (4) 19.90

Regular Issue of 1938 Overprinted in Black or Red

Granite Paper

2O61 A63 20c red & buff — 3.25
2O62 A64 30c blue & lt blue — 4.00
a. Inverted ovpt. 2,500.
2O63 A65 60c brown & buff — 4.75
2O64 A66 1fr black & buff (R) — 9.75
Nos. 2O61-2O64 (4) 21.75

Regular Issue of 1938 Overprinted in Black

1939

2O65 A69 3fr brn car, *buff* 6.75 *11.00*
2O66 A70 5fr slate bl, *buff* 9.50 *15.00*
2O67 A71 10fr green, *buff* 16.50 *32.50*
Nos. 2O65-2O67 (3) 32.75 *58.50*

Same Overprint in Black on Regular Issues of 1939-42

1942-43

2O68 A55 10c dk red brown — .85
2O68A A55 10c orange brn ('43) .60 *.85*
2O69 A68 20c red .70 *1.10*
Nos. 2O68-2O69 (3) *2.80*

Stamps of 1936-42 Overprinted in Black

1944

2O70 A53 3c olive .25 *.25*
2O71 A54 5c blue green .25 *.25*
2O72 A55 10c orange brown .25 .40
2O73 A56 15c orange .25 *.50*
2O74 A68 20c red .40 *.75*
2O75 A58 25c lt brown .50 *.90*
2O76 A59 30c ultra .55 *1.00*
2O77 A60 35c yellow green .55 *1.00*
2O78 A61 40c gray .65 *1.25*

Nos. 2O73-2O75 and 2O78 exist with grilled gum. Value each $2,000 unused, $2,250 used.

Stamps of 1941 Overprinted in Black

2O79 A77 50c dp pur, *grnsh* 1.10 *2.10*
2O80 A78 60c red brn, *buff* 1.40 *2.60*
2O81 A79 70c rose vio, *pale lil* 1.40 *3.00*
2O82 A80 80c blk, *pale gray* 1.25 *2.40*
2O83 A81 90c dk red, *pale rose* 1.25 *2.40*
2O84 A82 1fr dk grn, *grnsh* 1.35 *2.60*
2O85 A83 1.20fr red vio, *pale gray* 1.75 *3.75*
2O86 A84 1.50fr dk bl, *buff* 2.25 *4.50*
2O87 A85 2fr mar, *pale rose* 2.75 *5.00*

Stamps of 1942 Overprinted in Black

Unwmk. ***Perf. 11½***

2O88 A69 3fr brn car, *cr* 4.50 *9.50*
2O89 A70 5fr slate bl, *cr* 7.00 *13.00*
2O90 A71 10fr green, *cr* 10.50 *19.00*
Nos. 2O70-2O90 (21) 40.15 *76.15*
Set, never hinged 65.00

FOR THE INTERNATIONAL LABOR BUREAU

Regular Issues Overprinted

On 1908-30 Issues

1923-30 **Wmk. 183** ***Perf. 11½, 12***

3O1 A26 2½c ol grn, *buff* ('28) — .30
3O2 A26 3c ultra, *buff* ('30) — 1.10
3O3 A26 5c org, *buff* — .55
3O4 A26 5c red vio, *buff* ('28) — .25
3O5 A26 7½c dp grn, *buff* ('28) — .45
3O6 A28 10c grn, *buff* — .55
3O7 A28 10c bl grn, *buff* ('28) — 1.10
3O8 A28 15c brn red, *buff* ('28) — 1.10
3O9 A28 20c red vio, *buff* — 13.00
3O10 A28 20c car, *buff* ('27) — 5.00
3O11 A28 25c car, *buff* — 1.25
3O12 A28 25c brn, *buff* ('28) — 3.00
3O13 A28 30c dp bl, *buff* ('25) — 2.50
3O14 A25 30c yel brn & pale grn — 60.00
3O15 A25 35c yel grn & yel — 11.00
3O16 A25 40c deep blue — 1.25
3O17 A25 40c red vio & grn ('28) — 17.00
3O18 A25 50c dp grn & pale grn — 5.00
3O19 A25 60c brn org & buff 2.25 *1.90*
3O20 A25 70c vio & buff ('24) — 26.00
3O21 A25 80c slate & buff 14.00 2.25
3O22 A25 1fr dp cl & pale grn — 2.75
3O23 A29 3fr red — 25.00
3O24 A30 5fr ultra — 37.50
3O25 A31 10fr dull violet — 150.00
3O26 A31 10fr gray grn ('30) — 150.00
Nos. 3O1-3O26 (26) 519.80

1937-44 **With Grilled Gum**

3O18a A25 50c dp grn & pale grn ('42) 2.00 3.00
3O20a A25 70c vio & buff 2.00 1.75
3O21a A25 80c slate & buff ('44) 25.00 *175.00*
3O22a A25 1fr dp cl & pale grn ('42) — 3.25

1925-42 **With Grilled Gum**

3O27 A36 90c grn & red, *grn* ('37) — 9.75
a. Ordinary gum — 5.00
3O28 A36 1.20fr brn rose & red, *rose* ('42) 14.00 4.00
a. Ordinary gum — 4.50
3O29 A36 1.50fr bl & red, *bl* ('37) 2.75 *3.00*
a. Ordinary gum — 10.00
3O30 A36 2fr gray blk & red, *gray* ('36) 3.25 *6.25*
a. Ordinary gum — 32.50
Nos. 3O27-3O30 (4) 23.00

1928

3O31 A39 5fr blue — 95.00

1932 **On 1932 Issue**

3O32 A41 5c peacock blue — 1.10
3O33 A41 10c orange — .90
3O34 A41 20c cerise — 1.25
3O35 A41 30c ultra — 7.75
3O36 A41 60c olive brown — 7.75

Unwmk.

3O37 A42 1fr ol gray & bl — 10.00
Nos. 3O32-3O37 (6) 28.75

1937 **On 1936 Issue**

3O38 A53 3c olive .25 .55
3O39 A54 5c blue green .25 .55
3O40 A55 10c red violet (I) — 2.75
b. Type II — 5.00
3O41 A56 15c orange .45 1.10
3O42 A57 20c carmine — 2.25
3O43 A58 25c brown .60 *1.40*
3O44 A59 30c ultra .60 *1.10*
3O45 A60 35c yellow green .60 *1.60*
3O46 A61 40c gray .95 *1.90*
Nos. 3O38-3O46 (9) 3.70 *13.20*

1937 **With Grilled Gum**

3O38a A53 3c olive — .75
3O39a A54 5c blue green — .60
3O40a A55 10c red violet (I) — 1.25
3O41a A56 15c orange — .90
3O42a A57 20c carmine — 1.25
3O43a A58 25c brown — 2.40
3O44a A59 30c ultra — 1.75
3O45a A60 35c yellow green — 1.75
3O46a A61 40c gray — 2.40
Nos. 3O38a-3O46a (9) 13.05

1937 **On 1931 Issue** **Wmk. 183**

3O47 A40 3fr orange brown — 175.00

On 1934 Issue

3O48 A46 3c olive — 5.75

On 1938 Issue

Granite Paper

1938 **Unwmk.** ***Perf. 11½***

3O49 A63 20c red & buff — 1.50
3O50 A64 30c blue & lt blue — 2.25
3O51 A65 60c brown & buff — 7.50
3O52 A66 1fr black & buff — 7.50
Nos. 3O49-3O52 (4) 18.75

Regular Issue of 1938 Overprinted in Black or Red

3O53 A63 20c red & buff (Bk) — 4.25
3O54 A64 30c bl & lt bl (Bk) — 3.25
3O55 A65 60c brn & buff (Bk) — 6.25
3O56 A66 1fr blk & buff (R) — 6.25
Nos. 3O53-3O56 (4) 20.00

Regular Issue of 1938 Overprinted in Black

1939

3O57 A69 3fr brn car, *buff* 7.25 *7.75*
3O58 A70 5fr slate bl, *buff* 8.50 *13.00*
3O59 A71 10fr green, *buff* 14.50 *26.00*
Nos. 3O57-3O59 (3) 30.25 *46.75*

Same Overprint in Black on Regular Issues of 1939-42

1942-43

3O60 A55 10c dark red brown — .80
3O60A A55 10c orange brn ('43) .50 *.80*
3O61 A68 20c red .55 *.80*
Nos. 3O60-3O61 (3) *2.40*

Stamps of 1936-42 Overprinted in Black

1944

3O62 A53 3c olive .25 .25
3O63 A54 5c blue green .25 .25
3O64 A55 10c orange brn .25 .35
3O65 A56 15c orange .50 .60
3O66 A68 20c red .35 *.75*
3O67 A58 25c lt brown .55 *.90*
3O68 A59 30c ultra .50 *1.25*
3O69 A60 35c yellow grn .70 *2.00*
3O70 A61 40c gray .75 *2.25*

Stamps of 1941 Overprinted

3O71 A77 50c dp pur, *grnsh* 1.50 *4.25*
3O72 A78 60c red brn, *buff* 1.50 *4.25*
3O73 A79 70c rose vio, *pale lil* 1.75 *4.25*
3O74 A80 80c blk, *pale gray* .45 *1.25*
3O75 A81 90c dk red, *pale rose* .45 *1.25*
3O76 A82 1fr dk grn, *grnsh* .45 *1.25*
3O77 A83 1.20fr red vio, *pale gray* .75 *1.50*
3O78 A84 1.50fr dull bl, *buff* 1.00 *2.25*
3O79 A85 2fr mar, *pale rose* 1.25 *3.25*

Stamps of 1942 Overprinted

3O80 A69 3fr brown car, *cr* 3.25 *6.50*
3O81 A70 5fr slate blue, *cr* 5.00 *10.50*
3O82 A71 10fr green, *cr* 10.00 *21.00*
Nos. 3O62-3O82 (21) 31.45 *70.10*
Set, never hinged 60.00

Nos. 329-339 Overprinted in Black

1950 **Unwmk.** ***Perf. 12x11½***

3O83 A118 5c orange 3.50 *3.50*
3O84 A119 10c yellow green 3.50 *3.50*
3O85 A120 15c aqua 5.25 *5.25*
3O86 A121 20c brn car 5.25 *5.25*
3O87 A122 25c red 5.50 *5.50*
3O88 A123 30c olive 2.00 *2.00*
3O89 A124 35c red brown 6.00 *6.00*
3O90 A125 40c deep blue 6.00 *6.00*
3O91 A126 50c slate gray 7.50 *7.50*
3O92 A127 60c blue green 8.00 *8.00*
3O93 A128 70c purple 9.50 *9.50*
Nos. 3O83-3O93 (11) 62.00 *62.00*
Set, never hinged 125.00

Catalogue values for unused stamps in this section, from this point to the end of the section, are for Never Hinged items.

Miners — O1

Globe, Chimney and Wheel — O2

1956-60 **Unwmk.** **Engr.** ***Perf. 11½***

3O94 O1 5c dark gray .25 .25
3O95 O1 10c green .25 .25
3O96 O2 20c vermilion 1.25 *1.75*
3O97 O2 20c car rose ('60) .25 .25
3O98 O2 30c orange ver ('60) .25 *.25*
3O99 O1 40c blue 1.25 *1.75*
3O100 O1 50c lt ultra ('60) .30 *.40*
3O101 O2 60c reddish brown .30 *.35*
3O102 O2 2fr rose violet 1.10 *1.00*
Nos. 3O94-3O102 (9) 5.20 *6.25*

Type of 1960 Overprinted: "Visite du / Pape Paul VI / Genève / 10 juin 1969"

Violet Fibers, Fluorescent Paper

1969, June 10

3O103 O2 30c orange vermilion .30 .30

Visit of Pope Paul VI to the Intl. Labor Bureau to celebrate its 50th anniv., Geneva, June 10.

ILO Headquarters, Geneva — O3

Violet Fibers, Fluorescent Paper

1974, May 30 Photo. *Perf. 11½*

3O104 O3 80c blue, yel & gray 1.90 .80

Inauguration of the new International Labor Organization Building.

Young Man at Lathe, Cogwheels O4

Designs: 60c, Woman at drilling machine. 90c, Welder and lab assistant using protective devices and clothing. 100c, Surveyor with theodolite and topographical map. 120c, Professional education for youth.

1975-88 Photo. *Perf. 11½*

3O105 O4 30c red brn & dk brn .60 .30
3O106 O4 60c ultra & blk 1.20 .60
3O107 O4 100c dk green & blk 2.00 1.00
3O108 O4 120c multicolored 2.40 1.25

Perf. 12x11½

3O109 O4 90c multicolored 1.80 1.00
Nos. 3O105-3O109 (5) 8.00 4.15

Issued: 30c-100c, 2/13; 120c, 8/22/83; 90c, 9/13/88.

ILO, 75th Anniv. — O5

1994, May 17 Litho. *Perf. 13*

3O110 O5 180c multicolored 3.00 2.00

ILO, Cent. — O6

2019, May 2 Litho. *Perf. 13¼*

3O111 O6 100c multi 2.00 2.00

FOR THE INTERNATIONAL BUREAU OF EDUCATION

Regular Issues of 1936-42, Overprinted in Black

1944 Unwmk. *Perf. 11½*

4O1 A53 3c olive .45 *.85*
4O2 A54 5c blue grn .60 *1.10*
4O3 A55 10c orange brn .60 *1.10*
4O4 A56 15c orange .60 *1.10*
4O5 A68 20c red .60 *1.10*
4O6 A58 25c lt brown .60 *1.10*
4O7 A59 30c ultra .90 *1.60*
4O8 A60 35c yellow grn .90 *1.60*
4O9 A61 40c gray 1.20 *2.25*

Regular Issue of 1941, Overprinted in Black

4O10 A77 50c dp pur, *grnsh* 4.00 *10.00*
4O11 A78 60c red brn, *buff* 4.00 *10.00*
4O12 A79 70c rose vio, *pale lil* 4.00 *10.00*
4O13 A80 80c blk, *pale gray* .75 *1.60*
4O14 A81 90c dk red, *pale rose* .90 *1.90*
4O15 A82 1fr dk grn, *grnsh* 1.20 *2.75*
4O16 A83 1.20fr red vio, *pale gray* 1.20 *2.75*
4O17 A84 1.50fr dk bl, *buff* 1.60 *3.00*
4O18 A85 2fr mar, *pale rose* 2.00 *4.25*

Regular Issue of 1942, Overprinted in Black

4O19 A69 3fr brn car, *cr* 6.50 *17.50*
4O20 A70 5fr slate bl, *cr* 8.25 *24.00*
4O21 A71 10fr green, *cr* 13.00 *42.50*
Nos. 4O1-4O21 (21) 53.85 *142.05*
Set, never hinged 110.00

No. 306 Overprinted in Carmine

1946

4O22 A104 10c rose violet .25 *.50*
Never hinged .50

Nos. 316-321 Overprinted in Black

1948 Unwmk. *Perf. 11½*

4O23 A54 5c chocolate 1.75 *3.00*
4O24 A55 10c green 1.75 *3.00*
4O25 A68 20c orange brn 1.75 *3.00*
4O26 A113 25c carmine 1.75 *3.00*
4O27 A59 30c grnsh blue 2.00 *3.00*
4O28 A61 40c ultra 2.00 *3.00*
Nos. 4O23-4O28 (6) 11.00 18.00
Set, never hinged 20.00

Same Overprint on Nos. 329-339

1950 *Perf. 12x11½*

Overprint 18mm wide

4O29 A118 5c orange .30 *.75*
4O30 A119 10c yellow grn .50 *.90*
4O31 A120 15c aqua .55 *1.00*
4O32 A121 20c brown car 2.40 *3.50*
4O33 A122 25c red 7.00 *13.00*
4O34 A123 30c olive 7.00 *13.00*
4O35 A124 35c red brn 3.00 *7.25*
4O36 A125 40c deep blue 3.00 *7.25*
4O37 A126 50c slate gray 3.75 *8.25*
4O38 A127 60c blue green 4.50 *9.50*
4O39 A128 70c purple 5.00 *11.00*
Nos. 4O29-4O39 (11) 37.00 *75.40*
Set, never hinged 60.00

Catalogue values for unused stamps in this section, from this point to the end of the section, are for Never Hinged items.

Globe and Books — O1

Designs: 20c, 30c, 60c, 2fr, Pestalozzi Monument at Yverdon.

1958-60 Engr. *Perf. 11½*

4O40 O1 5c dark gray .25 .25
4O41 O1 10c green .25 .25
4O42 O1 20c vermilion 2.25 2.25
4O43 O1 20c car rose ('60) .25 .25
4O44 O1 30c org ver ('60) .25 *.35*
4O45 O1 40c blue 2.75 2.75
4O46 O1 50c lt ultra ('60) .30 *.50*
4O47 O1 60c reddish brn .30 *.50*
4O48 O1 2fr rose violet 1.10 *1.50*
Nos. 4O40-4O48 (9) 7.70 8.60

FOR THE WORLD HEALTH ORGANIZATION

No. 316-319, 321 Overprinted in Black

1948 Unwmk. *Perf. 11½*

5O1 A54 5c chocolate 1.75 *1.75*
5O2 A55 10c green 2.25 *3.50*
5O3 A68 20c orange brn 2.25 *3.50*
5O4 A113 25c carmine 2.25 *4.50*
5O5 A61 40c ultra 2.25 *5.00*
Nos. 5O1-5O5 (5) 10.75 *18.25*
Set, never hinged 20.00

Regular Issues of 1941, 1942 and 1949 Overprinted in Black

1948-50

5O6 A118 5c orange .30 *.45*
5O7 A119 10c yellow grn .60 *1.20*
5O8 A120 15c aqua .95 *2.60*
5O9 A121 20c brown car 4.00 *5.00*
5O10 A122 25c red 4.00 *7.50*
5O11 A123 30c olive .95 *3.25*
5O12 A124 35c red brown .95 *5.00*
5O13 A125 40c deep blue .95 *3.25*
5O14 A126 50c slate gray 1.25 *5.00*
5O15 A127 60c blue green 1.25 *5.50*
5O16 A128 70c purple 2.60 *5.50*
5O17 A80 80c blk, *pale gray* ('48) 2.40 *4.50*
5O18 A81 90c dk red, *pale rose* 3.50 *6.50*
5O19 A82 1fr dk grn, *grnsh* ('48) 2.40 4.50
5O20 A83 1.20fr red vio, *pale gray* 4.00 12.50
5O21 A84 1.50fr dk bl, *buff* 11.50 15.50
5O22 A85 2fr mar, *pale rose* ('48) 3.50 6.50
5O23 A69 3fr brn car, *cr* 22.00 40.00
5O24 A70 5fr sl bl, *cr* ('48) 8.50 15.50
5O25 A71 10fr grn, *cr* 45.00 55.00
Nos. 5O6-5O25 (20) 120.60 *204.75*
Set, never hinged 250.00

Catalogue values for unused stamps in this section, from this point to the end of the section, are for Never Hinged items.

WHO Emblem — O2

1957-60 Unwmk. Engr. *Perf. 11½*

5O26 O2 5c gray .25 .25
5O27 O2 10c lt grn .25 .25
5O28 O2 20c vermilion 2.40 2.40
5O29 O2 20c car rose ('60) .25 .25
5O30 O2 30c org ver ('60) .25 .25
5O31 O2 40c blue 2.40 2.40
5O32 O2 50c lt ultra ('60) .45 .45
5O33 O2 60c red brn .40 .40
5O34 O2 2fr rose lilac 1.10 1.10
Nos. 5O26-5O34 (9) 7.75 7.75

No. 5O32 Overprinted

1962, Mar. 19

5O35 O2 50c lt ultra .75 .75

WHO drive to eradicate malaria.

O3

World Health Organization Emblem — O3a

1975-95 Typo. *Perf. 11½*

5O36 O3 30c multi .70 .30
5O37 O3 60c lt bl & multi 1.40 .30
5O38 O3 90c lilac & multi 2.10 .90
5O39 O3 100c orange & multi 2.25 1.00

Litho.

Perf. 12

5O40 O3 140c lt grn, scar & grn 3.25 1.50

Perf. 13½x13

5O41 O3a 180c multicolored 4.25 2.10
Nos. 5O36-5O41 (6) 13.95 6.10

Issued: 140c, 5/27/86; 180c, 11/28/95; others, 2/13/75.

FOR THE INTERNATIONAL ORGANIZATION FOR REFUGEES

Stamps of 1941 and 1949 Overprinted in Black

1950 Unwmk. *Perf. 12x11½, 11½*

6O1 A118 5c orange 11.00 *14.00*
6O2 A119 10c yellow green 11.00 *14.00*
6O3 A121 20c brn car 11.00 *14.00*
6O4 A122 25c red 11.00 *14.00*
6O5 A125 40c deep blue 11.00 *14.00*
6O6 A80 80c blk, *pale gray* 11.00 *14.00*
6O7 A82 1fr dk grn, *grnsh* 11.00 *14.00*
6O8 A85 2fr mar, *pale rose* 11.00 *14.00*
Nos. 6O1-6O8 (8) 88.00 *112.00*
Set, never hinged 150.00

FOR THE UNITED NATIONS EUROPEAN OFFICE

See No. 513 for postage issue commemorating the United Nations.

Stamps of 1941-49 Overprinted in Black

1950 Unwmk. *Perf. 12x11½, 11½*

7O1 A118 5c orange .40 *1.25*
7O2 A119 10c yellow grn .40 *1.25*
7O3 A120 15c aqua .80 *2.50*
7O4 A121 20c brown car 1.20 *3.50*
7O5 A122 25c red 1.60 *5.25*
7O6 A123 30c olive 1.60 *5.25*

7O7 A124 35c red brown 1.60 *5.25*
7O8 A125 40c deep blue 2.25 *6.75*
7O9 A126 50c slate gray 3.00 *9.50*
7O10 A127 60c blue green 3.50 *10.00*
7O11 A128 70c purple 3.50 *12.00*
7O12 A80 80c blk, *pale gray* 7.50 *12.00*
7O13 A81 90c dk red, *pale rose* 7.50 *12.00*
7O14 A82 1fr dk grn, *grnsh* 7.50 *12.00*
7O15 A83 1.20fr red vio, *pale gray* 8.00 *15.00*
7O16 A84 1.50fr dk bl, *buff* 8.00 *15.00*
7O17 A85 2fr mar, *pale rose* 8.00 *15.00*
7O18 A69 3fr brn car, *cr* 55.00 *95.00*
7O19 A70 5fr sl bl, *cr* 55.00 *95.00*
7O20 A71 10fr grn, *cr* 87.50 *170.00*
Nos. 7O1-7O20 (20) 263.85 *503.50*
Set, never hinged 500.00

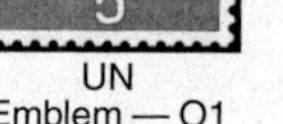

UN Emblem — O1

Statue from UN Building, Geneva — O2

1955-59 Engr. *Perf. 11½*

7O21 O1 5c dk violet brn .25 .25
7O22 O1 10c green .25 .25
7O23 O2 20c vermilion 2.00 4.00
7O24 O2 20c car rose ('59) .25 .25
7O25 O2 30c org ver ('59) .25 .30
7O26 O1 40c ultra 2.00 4.50
7O27 O1 50c ultra ('59) .30 .40
7O28 O2 60c red brown .30 .50
7O29 O2 2fr lilac 1.00 1.60
Nos. 7O21-7O29 (9) 6.60 12.05
Set, never hinged 12.50

See Nos. 7O34-7O37. For overprints see Nos. 7O31-7O32.

United Nations Emblem — O3

1955, Oct. 24 Photo.

7O30 O3 40c dark blue & bister 1.75 *3.75*
Never hinged 4.00

10th anniv. of the UN, Oct. 24, 1955.

Catalogue values for unused stamps in this section, from this point to the end of the section, are for Never Hinged items.

Nos. 7O24 Overprinted in Black

Nos. 7O27 Overprinted in Red

1960

7O31 O2 20c carmine rose .25 .25
7O32 O1 50c ultra (R) .50 .50

World Refugee Year, 7/1/59-6/30/60.

Palace of Nations, Geneva O4

1960 Granite Paper *Perf. 11½*

7O33 O4 5fr blue 4.50 *4.00*

No. 7O34

No. 7O35

Types of 1955 Inscribed

Engraved; Inscription Typographed

1962, Oct. 24 Unwmk. *Perf. 11½*

7O34 O1 10c green & red .25 .25
7O35 O2 30c org ver & ultra .30 .30
7O36 O1 50c ultra & org .50 .50
7O37 O2 60c red brn & emer .60 .60
Nos. 7O34-7O37 (4) 1.65 1.65

Opening of the Philatelic Museum, UN European Office, Geneva.

O5 O6

UNCSAT Emblem

1963, Feb. 4 Engr. *Perf. 11½*

7O38 O5 50c ultra & car rose .40 .40
7O39 O6 2fr lilac & emer 2.00 2.00

UN Conf. on the Application of Science and Technology for the Benefit of the Less Developed Areas (UNCSAT), Geneva, Feb. 4-20.

Stamps issued, starting Oct. 4, 1969, by the UN in Swiss currency for use by UN staff members or the public are listed under "United Nations" in Vol. 1 of this catalogue and in Scott's U.S. Specialized Catalogue. These stamps are on sale in various UN post offices, but are valid only in the UN enclave in Geneva. They are not inscribed "Helvetia."

FOR THE WORLD METEOROLOGICAL ORGANIZATION

Catalogue values for unused stamps in this section are for Never Hinged items.

Sun, Cloud, Rain and Snow — O1

Design: 20c, 30c, 60c, 2fr, Direction indicator and anemometer.

1956-60 Unwmk. Engr. *Perf. 11½*

8O1 O1 5c dark gray .25 .25
8O2 O1 10c green .25 .25
8O3 O1 20c vermilion 2.25 2.25
8O4 O1 20c car rose ('60) .25 .25
8O5 O1 30c org ver ('60) .35 .35
8O6 O1 40c blue 2.75 2.75
8O7 O1 50c lt ultra ('60) .50 .50
8O8 O1 60c reddish brn .60 .60
8O9 O1 2fr rose violet 2.00 2.00
Nos. 8O1-8O9 (9) 9.20 9.20

WMO Emblem O2

1973, Aug. 30 Engr. *Perf. 11½*

Violet Fibers, Fluorescent Paper

8O10 O2 30c carmine .45 *.30*
8O11 O2 40c blue .60 *.40*
8O12 O2 1fr ocher 1.20 1.00
Nos. 8O10-8O12 (3) 2.25 1.70

O2a

1973, Aug. 30 Photo. *Perf. 11½*

Violet Fibers, Fluorescent Paper

8O13 O2a 80c deep violet & gold 2.00 1.00

Intl. meteorological cooperation, cent.

FOR THE INTERNATIONAL BUREAU OF THE UNIVERSAL POSTAL UNION

Catalogue values for unused stamps in this section are for Never Hinged items.

See Nos. 98-103, 204-205, 514, 589-590 for postage issues commemorating the UPU.

UPU Monument, Bern — O1

Design: 10c, 20c, 30c, 60c, Pegasus.

1957-60 Unwmk. Engr. *Perf. 11½*

9O1 O1 5c gray .25 .25
9O2 O1 10c lt grn .25 .25
9O3 O1 20c vermilion 2.25 2.25
9O4 O1 20c car rose ('60) .25 .25
9O5 O1 30c org ver ('60) .35 .35
9O6 O1 40c blue 2.75 2.75
9O7 O1 50c lt ultra ('60) .50 .50
9O8 O1 60c red brn .60 .60
9O9 O1 2fr rose lilac 2.00 2.00
Nos. 9O1-9O9 (9) 9.20 9.20

First Class Mail — O2

Parcel Post — O3

Money Orders — O4

Technical Cooperation O5

Intl. Reply and Notication Service — O6

Express Mail Service — O7

Post NET System O8

1976-95 Photo. *Perf. 11½*

Fluorescent Paper

9O10 O2 40c multi .55 .50
9O11 O3 80c multi 1.10 1.00
9O12 O4 90c multi 1.35 1.25
9O13 O5 100c multi 1.75 1.60
9O14 O6 120c multi 2.10 2.00
9O15 O7 140c multi 2.60 2.40

Perf. 13½x13

9O16 O8 180c multicolored 3.75 3.25
Nos. 9O10-9O16 (7) 13.20 12.00

Issued: 120c, 8/22/83; 140c, 3/7/89; 180c, 11/28/95; others, 9/16/76.

UPU, 125th Anniv. O9

1999, Mar. 9 *Perf. 13*

9O17 O9 20c shown .50 .30
9O18 O9 70c Hand holding rainbow 1.75 1.00

Service Quality Improvement O10

2003, Sept. 9 Litho. *Perf. 13¾x14¼*

9O19 O10 90c multi 2.10 1.25

Methods of Mail Transport O11

2005, Sept. 6 Litho. *Perf. 13½x14¼*

9O20 O11 100c multi 2.25 2.00

Postman O12

2007, Sept. 6 Litho. *Perf. 13¼x13½*

9O21 O12 180c multi 4.25 4.00

See United Nations No. 944, United Nations Offices in Geneva No. 475, and United Nations Offices in Vienna No. 403.

René de Saint-Marceaux (1845-1915), Sculptor of UPU Monument — O13

Litho. & Engr.

2009, Oct. 9 *Perf. 13x13¼*
9O22 O13 180c multi 4.25 4.00

See France No. 3724.

Dove — O14

2012, Oct. 9 Litho. *Perf. 13¼x13½*
9O23 O14 190c multi 4.00 4.00

25th Universal Postal Congress, Doha, Qatar.

FOR THE INTERNATIONAL TELECOMMUNICATION UNION

Catalogue values for unused stamps in this section are for Never Hinged items.

Transmitter — O1

Designs: 20c, 30c, 60c, 2fr, Antenna.

1958-60 Unwmk. Engr. *Perf. 11½*
1O1 O1 5c dark gray .25 .25
1O2 O1 10c green .25 .25
1O3 O1 20c vermilion 2.25 2.25
1O4 O1 20c car rose ('60) .25 .25
1O5 O1 30c org ver ('60) .35 .35
1O6 O1 40c blue 2.75 2.75
1O7 O1 50c lt ultra ('60) .50 .50
1O8 O1 60c redsh brn .60 .60
1O9 O1 2fr rose vio 2.00 2.00
Nos. 1O1-1O9 (9) 9.20 9.20

ITU Headquarters, Geneva — O2

1973, Aug. 30 Photo. *Perf. 11½*
Violet Fibers, Fluorescent Paper
1O10 O2 80c blue & black .80 .80

Sound Waves, ITU Emblem O3

Airplane, Ocean Liner — O4

Radio Waves, Face on TV, Microphone O5

Photogravure and Engraved

1976, Feb. 12 *Perf. 11½*
Violet Fibers, Fluorescent Paper
1O11 O3 40c dp org & vio bl .75 .60
1O12 O4 90c bl, vio bl & yel 1.40 1.20
1O13 O5 1fr grn & multi 1.60 1.40
Nos. 1O11-1O13 (3) 3.75 3.20

ITU activities: world telecommunications, mobile radio and mass media.

Fiber Optic Communication Links — O6

1988, Sept. 13 Litho. *Perf. 12x11½*
1O14 O6 1.40fr multi 2.75 1.50

Radio Waves, ITU Emblem — O7

1994, May 17 Litho. *Perf. 13½*
1O15 O7 1.80fr multicolored 3.25 1.90

Telecommunications — O8

1999, Mar. 9 Photo. *Perf. 11½*
1O16 O8 10c Teleeducation .25 .25
1O17 O8 100c Telemedicine 1.75 1.60

Stylized Face — O9

2003, Sept. 9 Litho. *Perf. 13¾x14¼*
1O18 O9 90c multi 2.10 1.25

FOR THE WORLD INTELLECTUAL PROPERTY ORGANIZATION

Catalogue values for unused stamps in this section are for Never Hinged items.

WIPO Emblem O1

80c, Headquarters, Geneva. 100c, Industrial symbols. 120c, Educational and artistic symbols.

1982, May 27 Photo. *Perf. 12x11½*
11O1 O1 40c shown .50 .40
11O2 O1 80c multicolored 1.00 .90
11O3 O1 100c multicolored 1.25 1.10
11O4 O1 120c multicolored 1.50 1.25

1985, Sept. 10 Photo. *Perf. 12x11½*

50c, Mind in action.

11O5 O1 50c multicolored 1.15 .75
Nos. 11O1-11O5 (5) 5.40 4.40

FOR THE INTERNATIONAL OLYMPIC COMMITTEE

Catalogue values for unused stamps in this section are for Never Hinged items.

Olympics Type of Regular Issue

Hand and plant with leaves of Olympic rings and: 20c, Orange frame. 70c, Green frame.

2000, Sept. 15 Photo. ***Die Cut***
Booklet Stamps
Self-Adhesive
12O1 A496 20c multi .45 .40
12O2 A496 70c multi 1.90 1.50
a. Booklet pane, #12O1-12O2 2.40
Booklet, #12O2a 2.40

No. 12O2a is separated from booklet cover by rouletting. The booklet was sold folded.

Olympics Type of Regular Issue, 2004

Design: Runner, "40," Olympic rings, scene from 1896 Athens Olympics.

2004, May 6 Litho. *Perf. 13x13¼*
12O3 A551 100c multi 2.75 2.25

2006 Winter Olympics Type of 2005

2005, Nov. 22 Litho. *Perf. 13½x13*
12O4 A578 130c Ice hockey 3.25 2.50

Issued in sheets of 6.

Summer Olympics Type of 2008

2008, May 8 Litho. *Perf. 14x14¼*
12O5 A627 180c BMX cycling 4.50 3.75

FRANCHISE STAMPS

These stamps were distributed to many institutions and charitable societies for franking their correspondence.

F1

Control Figures Overprinted in Black
214

Perf. 11½, 12
1911-21 Typo. Wmk. 183
Blue Granite Paper
S1 F1 2c ol grn & red .25 .25
S2 F1 3c ol grn & red 2.50 .55
S3 F1 5c ol grn & red 1.10 .25
S4 F1 10c ol grn & red 1.40 .25
S5 F1 15c ol grn & red 21.00 4.00
S6 F1 20c ol grn & red 5.00 .60
Nos. S1-S6 (6) 31.25 5.90

Without Control Figures

S1a F1 2c olive green & red .55 *19.00*
S2a F1 3c olive green & red .55 *25.00*
S3a F1 5c olive green & red 4.75 *32.50*
S4a F1 10c olive green & red 8.25 *50.00*
S5a F1 15c olive green & red 5.25 *125.00*
S6a F1 20c olive green & red 9.50 *50.00*
Nos. S1a-S6a (6) 28.85 *301.50*

Control Figures Overprinted in Black

1926
S7 F1 5c ol grn & red 12.50 4.50
S8 F1 10c ol grn & red 7.75 3.25
S9 F1 20c ol grn & red 10.00 3.75
Nos. S7-S9 (3) 30.25 11.50

Control Figures Overprinted in Black

1927 White Granite Paper
S10 F1 5c green & red 5.00 .40
S11 F1 10c green & red 2.50 .25
b. Grilled gum 325.00 *725.00*
S12 F1 20c green & red 3.50 .30
Nos. S10-S12 (3) 11.00 .95

Without Control Figures

S10a F1 5c green & red 32.50 *140.00*
S11a F1 10c green & red 32.50 *140.00*
c. Grilled gum 150.00 *650.00*
S12a F1 20c green & red 32.50 *140.00*

Nurse — F2

Nun — F3

J. H. Dunant — F4

Control Figures Overprinted in Black

1935 *Perf. 11½*
S13 F2 5c turq green 2.25 *5.50*
b. Grilled gum 3.25 .40
S14 F3 10c lt violet 2.25 *5.50*
b. Grilled gum 3.25 .25
S15 F4 20c scarlet 2.25 *6.50*
b. Grilled gum 3.75 .45
Nos. S13-S15 (3) 6.75 *17.50*
Nos. S13b-S15b (3) 10.25 1.10

Without Control Figures

S13a F2 5c turquoise green 1.40 *3.75*
c. Grilled gum 15.00 1.40
S14a F3 10c light violet 1.40 *3.75*
c. Grilled gum 15.00 1.40
S15a F4 20c scarlet 1.40 *5.00*
c. Grilled gum 15.00 1.50
Nos. S13a-S15a (3) 4.20 *12.50*
Nos. S13c-S15c (3) 45.00 4.30

SYRIA

'sir-ē-ə

LOCATION — Asia Minor, bordering on Turkey, Iraq, Lebanon, Israel and the Mediterranean Sea
GOVT. — Republic
AREA — 71,498 sq. mi.
POP. — 14,972,000 (1997 est.)
CAPITAL — Damascus

Syria was originally part of the Turkish province of Sourya conquered by British and Arab forces in late 1918 and later partitioned. The British assumed control of the Palestine and Transjordan regions; the French were permitted to occupy the sanjaks of Lebanon, Alaouites and Alexandretta; and the remaining territory, including the vilayets of Damascus and Aleppo, was established as an independent Arab kingdom, under which the first Syrian stamps were issued.

French forces from Beirut deposed King Faisal in July 1920, and two years of military occupation followed until Syria was mandated to France in July 1922. Syrian autonomy was substituted for the mandate in 1934, but full independence was not again achieved until 1946. In 1958, Syria and Egypt merged to form the United Arab Republic. Syria left this union in 1961, adopting the name Syrian Arab Republic. UAR issues for Syria are listed following Syria's 1919-20 Issues of the Arabian Government.

10 Milliemes = 1 Piaster
40 Paras = 1 Piaster (Arabian Govt.)
100 Centimes = 1 Piaster (1920)
100 Piasters = 1 Syrian Pound

Catalogue values for unused stamps in this country are for Never Hinged items, beginning with Scott 314 in the regular postage section, Scott B13 in the semi-postal section, Scott C124 in the airpost section, Scott CB5 in the airpost semipostal section, Scott J40 in the postage due section, and all of the items in the UAR sections.

Watermarks

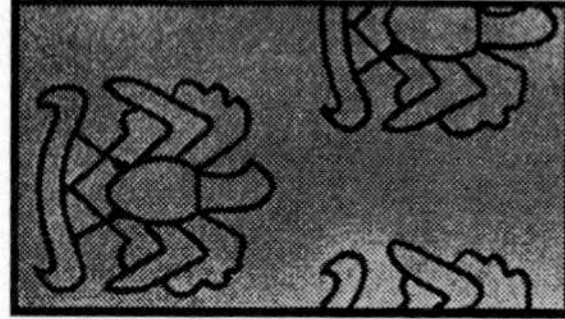

Wmk. 291 — National Emblem Multiple

Carrier Pigeon — Wmk. 403

Issued under French Occupation

Stamps of France, 1900-07, Surcharged

Perf. 14x13½

1919, Nov. 21 Unwmk.

1 A16 1m on 1c gray 250.00 200.00
2 A16 2m on 2c vio brn 600.00 *550.00*
3 A16 3m on 3c red org 300.00 240.00
4 A20 4m on 15c gray grn 60.00 47.50
5 A22 5m on 5c dp grn 35.00 22.50
6 A22 1p on 10c red 50.00 32.50
7 A22 2p on 25c blue 25.00 15.00
8 A18 5p on 40c red & pale bl 32.50 22.50
9 A18 9p on 50c bis brn & lav 65.00 50.00
10 A18 10p on 1fr cl & ol grn 110.00 80.00
Nos. 1-10 (10) 1,528. 1,260.

The letters "T.E.O." are the initials of "Territoires Ennemis Occupés." There are two types of the numerals in the surcharges on Nos. 2, 3, 8 and 9.

Stamps of French Offices in Turkey, 1902-03, Surcharged

1919

11 A2 1m on 1c gray 1.50 .80
a. Inverted surcharge 40.00
12 A2 2m on 2c violet brn 1.50 .80
a. Inverted surcharge 40.00
13 A2 3m on 3c red orange 3.25 1.40
14 A3 4m on 15c pale red 1.50 .80
a. Inverted surcharge 40.00
15 A2 5m on 5c green 1.50 .80

Overprinted

16 A5 1p on 25c blue 1.50 .75
a. Inverted overprint 40.00
17 A6 2p on 50c bis brn & lav 2.50 1.25
18 A6 4p on 1fr claret & ol grn 4.00 2.50
19 A6 8p on 2fr gray vio & yel 12.50 8.00
a. "T.E.O." double 110.00 110.00
20 A6 20p on 5fr dk bl & buff 350.00 210.00
Nos. 11-20 (10) 379.75 227.10

On Nos. 17-20 "T.E.O." reads vertically up.

Nos. 1-20 were issued in Beirut and mainly used in Lebanon. Nos. 16-20 were also used in Cilicia.

Inverted surcharges exist on several values of this issue.

Stamps of France, 1900-07, Surcharged

1920

21 A16 1m on 1c gray 5.50 4.50
a. Inverted surcharge 60.00
b. Double surcharge 67.50
22 A16 2m on 2c vio brn 6.50 4.75
a. Double surcharge 67.50
b. Inverted surcharge 60.00
23 A22 3m on 5c green 13.00 12.00
a. Double surcharge 82.50
b. Inverted surcharge 100.00
24 A18 20p on 5fr dk bl & buff 475.00 450.00
Nos. 21-23 (3) 25.00 21.25

The letters "O.M.F." are the initials of "Occupation Militaire Francaise."

Stamps of France, 1900-07, Surcharged in Black or Red

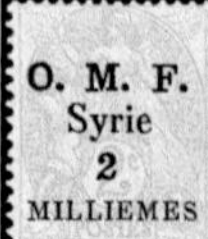

1920

25 A16 1m on 1c gray 1.25 .95
26 A16 2m on 2c vio brn 1.50 1.00
27 A22 3m on 5c green 2.25 2.00
a. Double surcharge 67.50
28 A22 5m on 10c red 2.50 2.25
a. Inverted surcharge 65.00 65.00
b. Double surcharge 65.00 65.00
29 A18 20p on 5fr dk bl & buff 72.50 70.00
30 A18 20p on 5fr dk bl & buff (R) 300.00 250.00
Nos. 25-30 (6) 380.00 326.20

Stamps of France, 1900-21, Surcharged in Black or Red

1920-22

31 A16 25c on 1c gray 2.00 1.00
32 A16 50c on 2c vio brn 2.00 1.00
33 A16 75c on 3c red org 2.00 1.00
a. Inverted surcharge 52.50 52.50
b. Double surcharge 60.00 60.00
34 A22 1p on 5c grn (R) 2.25 2.00
a. Double surcharge 60.00 60.00
35 A22 1p on 5c green 1.25 1.00
a. Inverted surcharge 35.00 35.00
b. Double surcharge 45.00 45.00
36 A22 1p on 20c red brn ('21) .75 .25
a. Inverted surcharge 35.00 35.00
b. Double surcharge 35.00 35.00
37 A22 1.25p on 25c bl ('22) 1.50 .95
a. Inverted surcharge 40.00 40.00
b. Double surcharge 37.50 37.50
38 A22 1.50p on 30c org ('22) 1.60 .80
a. Inverted surcharge 27.50 40.00
39 A22 2p on 10c red 1.25 1.00
a. Inverted surcharge 50.00 50.00
40 A22 2p on 25c bl (R) 1.25 1.00
a. Inverted surcharge 45.00 45.00
b. Double surcharge 35.00 35.00
41 A18 2p on 40c red & pale bl ('21) 1.60 .75
42 A20 2.50p on 50c dl bl ('22) 1.40 1.10
a. Final "S" of "Piastres" omitted 24.00 24.00
b. Inverted surcharge 30.00 30.00
c. Double surcharge 35.00 35.00
43 A22 3p on 25c bl (R) 1.40 1.10
a. Inverted surcharge 45.00 45.00
44 A18 3p on 60c vio & ultra ('21) 1.75 1.10
a. Inverted surcharge 37.50 37.50
45 A20 5p on 15c gray grn 2.50 2.25
a. Double surcharge 140.00 *150.00*
46 A18 5p on 1fr cl & ol grn ('21) 3.00 1.50
47 A18 10p on 40c red & pale bl 3.75 3.25
48 A18 10p on 2fr org & pale bl ('21) 6.00 3.00
49 A18 25p on 50c bis brn & lav 5.50 4.00
a. Inverted surcharge 100.00 100.00
50 A18 25p on 5fr dk bl & buff ('21) 110.00 95.00
51 A18 50p on 1fr cl & ol grn 25.00 20.00
a. "PIASRTES" *1,650.* *1,650.*
b. Double surcharge *1,700.* *1,900.*
52 A18 100p on 5fr dk bl & buff (R) 47.50 45.00
53 A18 100p on 5fr dk bl & buff (Bk) 250.00 225.00
a. "PIASRTES" *1,650.* *1,650.*
Nos. 31-53 (23) 475.25 413.05

In first printing, space between "Syrie" and numeral is 2mm, second printing, 1mm.

For overprints see Nos. C1-C9.

Surcharged in Black or Red

1920-23

54 A16 10c on 2c violet ('23) 1.40 .90
a. Inverted surcharge 35.00 35.00
55 A22 10c on 5c org (R) ('23) 1.00 .65
a. Inverted surcharge 35.00 35.00
56 A16 25c on 1c dk gray 1.10 .90
a. Inverted surcharge 40.00 40.00
b. Double surcharge 52.50 52.50
c. 50c on 1c dk gray (error) 4.50 4.50
57 A22 25c on 5c green ('21) 1.10 .60
a. Inverted surcharge 35.00 35.00
b. Double surcharge 35.00 35.00
58 A22 25c on 5c org ('22) 1.00 .80
a. "CENTIEMES" omitted 37.50 37.50
b. Inverted surcharge 35.00 35.00
c. Double surcharge 37.50 37.50
59 A16 50c on 2c vio brn 1.10 .90
a. Inverted surcharge 35.00 35.00
b. Double surcharge 45.00 45.00
60 A22 50c on 10c red ('21) 1.25 .55
a. Inverted surcharge 35.00 35.00
b. Double surcharge 35.00 35.00
61 A22 50c on 10c grn ('22) 1.50 1.25
a. Inverted surcharge 35.00 35.00
b. Double surcharge 37.50 37.50
c. Double surcharge, one inverted 50.00 50.00
62 A16 75c on 3c red orange 3.00 2.00
a. Inverted surcharge 35.00 35.00
b. Double surcharge 45.00 45.00
63 A20 75c on 15c sl grn ('21) 1.40 .90
a. Double surcharge 35.00 35.00
Nos. 54-63 (10) 13.85 9.45

Preceding Issues Overprinted

1920 Black Overprint

64 A16 25c on 1c sl gray 12.00 10.00
a. Double overprint 45.00
65 A16 50c on 2c vio brn 13.00 11.00
a. Double overprint 45.00
66 A22 1p on 5c grn 11.00 9.00
a. Double overprint 45.00
67 A22 2p on 25c blue 18.00 14.50
a. Double overprint 82.50
68 A20 5p on 15c gray grn 55.00 47.50
a. Double overprint 140.00 *150.00*
69 A18 10p on 40c red & pale bl 80.00 75.00
a. Double overprint 325.00
70 A18 25p on 50c bis brn & lav 225.00 190.00
a. Double overprint 600.00
71 A18 50p on 1fr cl & ol grn 650.00 625.00
a. Double overprint 2,100.
72 A18 100p on 5fr dk bl & buff 2,000. 1,900.
a. Double overprint 3,900. *4,300.*
Nos. 64-72 (9) 3,064. 2,882.

Red Overprint

73 A16 25c on 1c sl gray 12.50 10.00
74 A16 50c on 2c vio brn 11.00 8.50
75 A22 1p on 5c grn 11.00 8.50
76 A22 2p on 25c bl 9.00 6.50
77 A20 5p on 15c gray grn 55.00 47.50
a. Double overprint 190.00
78 A18 10p on 40c red & pale bl 85.00 75.00
a. Double overprint 170.00
79 A18 25p on 50c bis brn & lav 225.00 180.00
a. Double overprint 450.00 *475.00*
80 A18 50p on 1fr cl & ol grn 475.00 425.00
a. Double surcharge 1,700. *1,900.*
81 A18 100p on 5fr dk bl & buff 1,650. 1,650.
a. Double overprint 3,500. *3,750.*
Nos. 73-81 (9) 2,534. 2,411.

Nos. 64-81 were used only in the vilayet of Aleppo where Egyptian gold currency was still in use.

A1

Black or Red Surcharge

1921 *Perf. 11½*

82 A1 25c on 1/10p lt brn 1.25 .85
a. "25 Centiemes" omitted
83 A1 50c on 2/10p grn 1.25 .85
84 A1 1p on 3/10p yel 1.75 .85
a. "2/10" for "3/10" 12.50 12.50
b. Inverted surcharge 60.00 60.00
85 A1 1p on 5m rose 2.00 1.10
86 A1 2p on 5m rose 2.50 1.25
a. Tête bêche pair 160.00 160.00
b. Inverted surcharge 40.00 40.00
c. Double surcharge 45.00 45.00
87 A1 3p on 1p gray bl 3.00 1.25
a. Inverted surcharge 40.00 40.00
88 A1 5p on 2p bl grn 5.00 3.50
a. Inverted surcharge 45.00 45.00

89 A1 10p on 5p vio brn 11.00 5.75
90 A1 25p on 10p gray (R) 13.00 8.00
a. Inverted surcharge 45.00 45.00
Nos. 82-90 (9) 40.75 23.40

Nos. 82-90 are surcharged on stamps of the Arabian Government Nos. 85, 87-93 and have the designs and sizes of those stamps.

Kilis Issue

A2

Sewing Machine Perf. 9

1921 Pelure Paper Handstamped

91 A2 (1p) violet *50.00 45.00*

Issued at Kilis to meet a shortage of the regular issue, caused by the sudden influx of a large number of Armenian refugees from Turkey. The Kilis area was restored to Turkey in Oct. 1923.

Stamps of France, Surcharged

1921-22 ***Perf. 14x13½***

92 A18 2p on 40c red & pale bl 1.25 .90
a. Inverted surcharge 35.00 35.00
b. Double surcharge 35.00 35.00
c. Triple surcharge 82.50
93 A18 2.50p on 50c bis brn & lav ('22) 1.40 1.00
a. Double surcharge 37.50 37.50
b. 2p on 50c bister brown & lavender (error) 82.50 67.50
94 A18 3p on 60c vio & ultra 1.25 .90
a. Inverted surcharge 35.00 35.00
b. Double surcharge 35.00 35.00
95 A18 5p on 1fr cl & ol grn 7.00 6.00
a. Inverted surcharge 40.00 40.00
96 A18 10p on 2fr org & pale bl 15.00 11.00
97 A18 25p on 5fr dk bl & buff 13.00 10.00
Nos. 92-97 (6) 38.90 29.80

On No. 93 the surcharge reads: "2 PIASTRES 50."
For overprints see Nos. C10-C17.

French Mandate

French Stamps of 1900-23 Surcharged

1923

104 A16 10c on 2c vio brn .40 .25
a. Inverted surcharge 27.50 27.50
b. Double surcharge 35.00 35.00
105 A22 25c on 5c orange .75 .75
a. Inverted surcharge 27.50 27.50
106 A22 50c on 10c green .90 .85
a. Inverted surcharge 27.50 27.50
b. Double surcharge 35.00 35.00
c. 25c on 10c green (error) 240.00 240.00
107 A20 75c on 15c sl grn 1.60 1.50
a. Inverted surcharge 35.00 35.00
b. Double surcharge 37.50 37.50
108 A22 1p on 20c red brn .75 .70
a. Inverted surcharge 27.50 27.50
b. Double surcharge 35.00 35.00
109 A22 1.25p on 25c blue 1.40 1.25
a. Inverted surcharge 40.00 40.00
b. Double surcharge 37.50 37.50
110 A22 1.50p on 30c org 1.10 .90
a. Inverted surcharge 27.50 27.50
111 A22 1.50p on 30c red 1.10 .90
112 A20 2.50p on 50c dl bl .70 .60
a. Inverted surcharge 60.00 60.00
b. Double surcharge 35.00 35.00

On Pasteur Stamps of 1923

113 A23 50c on 10c green 2.00 1.75
114 A23 1.50p on 30c red 1.75 1.50
115 A23 2.50p on 50c blue 2.00 1.75

Surcharged

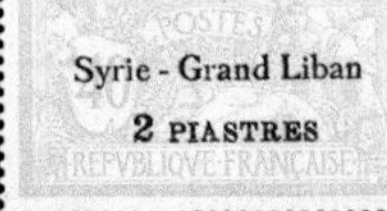

116 A18 2p on 40c red & pale bl .75 .70
a. Inverted surcharge 35.00 35.00
b. Double surcharge 37.50 37.50
c. "Liabn" 450.00 450.00
117 A18 3p on 60c vio & ultra 1.50 1.25
a. Inverted surcharge 40.00 40.00
b. Double surcharge 75.00 75.00
c. "Liabn" 450.00 450.00
118 A18 5p on 1fr cl & ol grn 2.00 1.50
a. Inverted surcharge 75.00 75.00
b. "Liabn" 450.00 450.00
119 A18 10p on 2fr org & pale bl 7.50 7.00
a. "Liabn" 450.00 450.00
120 A18 25p on 5fr dk bl & buff 22.50 20.00
Nos. 104-120 (17) 48.70 43.15

Stamps of France, 1900-21, Surcharged

1924 ***Perf. 14x13½***

121 A16 10c on 2c vio brn .40 .25
a. Inverted surcharge 35.00 35.00
122 A22 25c on 5c orange .70 .60
a. "25" omitted 24.00
123 A22 50c on 10c green .70 .60
a. Inverted surcharge 35.00 35.00
124 A20 75c on 15c sl grn .70 .60
125 A22 1p on 20c red brn .60 .50
a. "1 PIASTRES" 24.00
126 A22 1.25p on 25c blue 1.10 .90
127 A22 1.50p on 30c orange 1.10 .90
128 A22 1.50p on 30c red 1.00 .85
129 A20 2.50p on 50c dl bl 1.00 .85

Same on Pasteur Stamps of France, 1923

1924

130 A23 50c on 10c grn .90 .70
a. Inverted surcharge 47.50 47.50
131 A23 1.50p on 30c red 1.40 1.10
132 A23 2.50p on 50c blue .75 .70
a. Inverted surcharge 35.00 35.00
Nos. 121-132 (12) 10.35 8.55

Olympic Games Issue

Stamps of France, 1924, Surcharged

1924

133 A24 50c on 10c gray grn & yel grn 30.00 27.50
134 A25 1.25p on 25c rose & dk rose 30.00 27.50
135 A26 1.50p on 30c brn red & blk 30.00 27.50
136 A27 2.50p on 50c ultra & dk bl 30.00 27.50
Nos. 133-136 (4) 120.00 110.00

See Nos. 166-169.

Stamps of France 1900-20 Surcharged

137 A18 2p on 40c red & pale bl .90 .50
138 A18 3p on 60c vio & ultra .70 .65
139 A18 5p on 1fr claret & ol grn 3.50 3.25
140 A18 10p on 2fr org & pale bl 3.50 3.00
141 A18 25p on 5fr dk bl & buff 5.25 4.50
Nos. 137-141 (5) 13.85 11.90

For overprints see Nos. C18-C21.

Stamps of France 1900-21, Surcharged

or

1924-25

143 A16 10c on 2c vio brn .40 .25
a. Double surcharge 35.00 35.00
b. Inverted surcharge 30.00 30.00
144 A22 25c on 5c orange .40 .25
a. Double surcharge 35.00 35.00
145 A22 50c on 10c green .75 .50
a. Double surcharge 35.00 35.00
b. Inverted surcharge 30.00 30.00
146 A20 75c on 15c gray grn .90 .70
a. Double surcharge 35.00 35.00
b. Inverted surcharge 30.00 30.00
147 A22 1p on 20c red brn .60 .40
a. Inverted surcharge 26.00 26.00
148 A22 1.25p on 25c blue .95 .75
a. Inverted surcharge 30.00 30.00
149 A22 1.50p on 30c red .90 .70
a. Double surcharge 35.00 35.00
150 A22 1.50p on 30c orange 26.00 25.00
151 A22 2p on 35c violet ('25) 1.00 .80
152 A18 2p on 40c red & pale bl .75 .50
a. Arabic "Piastre" in singular 1.75 1.75
153 A18 2p on 45c grn & bl ('25) 5.00 4.00
154 A18 3p on 60c vio & ultra 1.10 .75
155 A20 3p on 60c lt vio ('25) 1.25 .75
156 A20 4p on 85c ver .45 .25
157 A18 5p on 1fr cl & ol grn 1.25 .75
158 A18 10p on 2fr org & pale bl 2.00 1.50
159 A18 25p on 5fr dk bl & buff 2.75 1.50
Nos. 143-159 (17) 46.45 39.35

On No. 152a, the surcharge is as illustrated. The correct fourth line ("2 Piastres" -plural), as it appears on Nos. 151, 152 and 153, has four characters, the third resembling "9."
For overprints see Nos. C22-C25.

Same Surcharge on Pasteur Stamps of France

1924-25

160 A23 50c on 10c green 1.25 1.00
161 A23 75c on 15c grn ('25) 1.25 1.00
162 A23 1.50p on 30c red 1.25 1.00
163 A23 2p on 45c red ('25) 1.25 1.00
164 A23 2.50p on 50c blue 1.75 1.25
165 A23 4p on 75c blue 1.75 1.25
Nos. 160-165 (6) 8.50 6.50

Olympic Games Issue

Stamps of France, 1924, Surcharged in French and Arabic

1924 **Same Colors as #133-136**

166 A24 50c on 10c 29.00 29.00
167 A25 1.25p on 25c 29.00 29.00
168 A26 1.50p on 30c 29.00 29.00
169 A27 2.50p on 50c 29.00 29.00
Nos. 166-169 (4) 116.00 116.00

Ronsard Issue

Same Surcharge on France No. 219

1925

170 A28 4p on 75c bl, *bluish* 1.00 .75

Mosque at Hama
A3

Mosque at Damascus
A5

View of Merkab
A4

Designs: 50c, View of Alexandretta. 75c, View of Hama. 1p, Omayyad Mosque, Damascus. 1.25p, Latakia Harbor. 1.50p, View of Damascus. 2p, View of Palmyra. 2.50p, View of Kalat Yamoun. 3p, Bridge of Daphne. 5p, View of Aleppo. 10p, View of Aleppo. 25p, Columns at Palmyra.

Perf. 12½, 13½

1925 Litho. Unwmk.

173 A3 10c dark violet .35 .25

Photo.

174 A4 25c olive black 1.00 .55
175 A4 50c yellow green .50 .25
176 A4 75c brown orange .60 .25
177 A5 1p magenta .60 .25
178 A4 1.25p deep green 2.25 1.10
179 A4 1.50p rose red .75 .25
180 A4 2p dark brown 2.00 .25
181 A4 2.50p peacock blue 1.50 .50
182 A4 3p orange brn 1.50 .25
183 A4 5p violet 1.25 .25
184 A4 10p violet brown 3.50 .30
185 A4 25p ultra 5.75 4.50
Nos. 173-185 (13) 21.55 8.95

For surcharges see Nos. 186-206, B1-B12, C26-C45, CB1-CB4.

Surcharged in Black or Red

1926-30

186 A4 1p on 3pi org brn ('30) 2.00 .50
187 A4 2p on 1p25 dp grn (R) ('28) 1.25 .40
a. Double surcharge 16.00 16.00
188 A4 3.50p on 75c org brn 1.00 .35
a. Double surcharge 16.00 16.00
189 A4 4p on 25c ol blk 1.50 .35
190 A4 4p on 25c ol blk ('27) 1.40 .45
191 A4 4p on 25c ol blk (R) ('28) 1.25 .35
192 A4 4.50p on 75c brn org 1.40 .35
193 A4 6p on 2p50 pck bl 1.00 .35
194 A4 7.50p on 2p50 pck bl 1.10 .35
195 A4 7.50p on 2p50 pck bl (R) ('28) 3.50 .90
a. Double surcharge 29.00
196 A4 12p on 1p25 dp grn 1.50 .40
a. Surcharge on face and back 50.00 42.50
197 A4 15p on 25p ultra 2.75 .90
198 A4 20p on 1p25 dp grn 2.25 .70
Nos. 186-198 (13) 21.90 6.35

Size of numerals and arrangement of this surcharge varies on the different denominations.
No. 189 has slanting foot on "4."
No. 190, foot straight.

No. 173 Surcharged in Red

1928

199 A3 05c on 10c dk vio 1.00 .25

Stamps of 1925 Ovptd. in Red or Blue

1929 ***Perf. 13½***

No.	Type	Denom.	Color	Unused	Used
200	A4	50c	yellow grn (R)	3.50	2.75
201	A5	1p	magenta (Bl)	3.50	2.75
202	A4	1.50p	rose red (Bl)	3.50	2.75
203	A4	3p	orange brn (Bl)	3.50	2.75
204	A4	5p	violet (R)	3.50	2.75
205	A4	10p	violet brn (Bl)	3.50	2.75
206	A4	25p	ultra (R)	3.50	2.75
			Nos. 200-206 (7)	24.50	19.25

Industrial Exhibition, Damascus, Sept. 1929.

View of Hama — A6

View of Alexandretta — A9

Citadel at Aleppo A10

Great Mosque of Damascus A11

Ruins of Bosra A13

Mosque at Homs A15

View of Sednaya A16

Citadel at Aleppo A17

Ancient Bridge at Antioch A18

Mosque at Damascus A22

Designs: 20c, Great Mosque, Aleppo. 25c, Minaret, Hama. 2p, View of Antioch. 4p, Square at Damascus. 15p, Mosque at Hama. 25p, Monastery of St. Simeon the Stylite (ruins). 50p, Sun Temple (ruins), Palmyra.

Perf. 12x12½

1930-36 **Litho.** **Unwmk.**

No.	Type	Denom.	Color	Unused	Used
208	A6	10c	red violet	.50	.25
209	A6	10c	vio brn ('33)	.50	.35
209A	A6	10c	vio brn, redrawn ('35)	.50	.25
210	A6	20c	dark blue	.50	.25
211	A6	20c	brn org ('33)	.50	.25
212	A6	25c	gray green	.50	.25
213	A6	25c	dk bl gray ('33)	.80	.45

Photo.

Perf. 13

No.	Type	Denom.	Color	Unused	Used
214	A9	50c	violet	.50	.25
215	A15	75c	org red ('32)	.50	.25
216	A10	1p	green	.75	.25
217	A10	1p	bis brn ('36)	1.75	.40
218	A11	1.50p	bister brown	7.50	3.00
219	A11	1.50p	dp grn ('33)	1.00	.50
220	A9	2p	dark violet	.75	.25
221	A13	3p	yellow green	2.00	.70
222	A10	4p	yellow orange	.75	.25
223	A15	4.50p	rose carmine	1.75	.55
224	A16	6p	grnsh black	2.25	.50
225	A17	7.50p	dull blue	2.25	.70
226	A18	10p	dark brown	2.00	.50
227	A10	15p	deep green	3.50	1.00
228	A18	25p	violet brown	5.00	1.10
229	A15	50p	olive brown	17.50	7.00
230	A22	100p	red orange	35.00	15.00
			Nos. 208-230 (24)	88.55	34.25

On No. 209A Arabic inscriptions, upper right, are entirely redrawn with lighter lines. Hyphen added in "Helio-Vaugirard" imprint. Lines in buildings and background more distinct.

On No. 215 the letters of "VAUGIRARD" in the imprint are reversed as in a mirror.

For overprints and surcharges see Nos. 253-268, 346, M1-M2.

Autonomous Republic

Parliament Building A23

abu-al-Ala al-Maarri — A24

President Ali Bek el Abed — A25

Saladin — A26

1934, Aug. 2 **Engr.** ***Perf. 12½***

No.	Type	Denom.	Color	Unused	Used
232	A23	10c	olive green	2.00	*2.00*
233	A23	20c	black	2.00	*2.00*
234	A23	25c	red orange	2.50	*2.50*
235	A23	50c	ultra	3.00	*3.00*
236	A23	75c	plum	3.00	*3.00*
237	A24	1p	vermilion	5.50	5.50
238	A24	1.50p	green	6.50	6.50
239	A24	2p	red brown	6.50	6.50
240	A24	3p	Prus blue	6.50	6.50
241	A24	4p	brt violet	6.75	6.75
242	A24	4.50p	carmine	7.00	7.00
243	A24	5p	dark blue	7.00	7.00
244	A24	6p	dark brown	8.00	8.00
245	A24	7.50p	dark ultra	10.00	10.00
246	A25	10p	dark brown	15.00	15.00
247	A25	15p	dull blue	25.00	25.00
248	A25	25p	rose red	25.00	13.00
249	A26	50p	dark brown	50.00	35.00
250	A26	100p	lake	60.00	60.00
			Nos. 232-250 (19)	251.25	224.25

Proclamation of the Republic. See Nos. C57-C66. For surcharge see No. M3.

Nos. 232-250 exist imperf. Value: $1,000.

Stamps of 1930-36 Overprinted in Red or Black

1936, Apr. 15

No.	Type	Denom.	Color	Unused	Used
253	A9	50c	violet (R)	2.75	1.50
254	A10	1p	bister brn (Bk)	2.75	1.50
255	A9	2p	dk violet (R)	2.75	1.50
256	A13	3p	yellow grn (Bk)	3.25	1.50
257	A10	4p	yellow org (Bk)	3.25	1.50
258	A15	4.50p	rose car (Bk)	3.25	1.50
259	A16	6p	grnsh blk (R)	4.00	2.00
260	A17	7.50p	dull blue (R)	4.75	2.75
261	A18	10p	dk brown (Bk)	5.75	3.75
			Nos. 253-261 (9)	32.50	17.50

Industrial Exhibition, Damascus, May 1936. See Nos. C67-C71.

Stamps of 1930 Srchd. in Black

1937-38 ***Perf. 13½x13***

No.	Type	Denom.	Color	Unused	Used
262	A10	2.50p	on 4p yel org ('38)	.55	.40
263	A22	10p	on 100p red org	1.00	.90

Stamps of 1930-33 Srchd. in Red or Black

1938 ***Perf. 13½***

No.	Type	Denom.	Color	Unused	Used
264	A15	25c	on 75c org red (Bk)	.50	.25
265	A11	50c	on 1.50p dp grn (R)	.60	.30
266	A17	2p	on 7.50p dl bl (R)	1.00	.60
267	A17	5p	on 7.50p dl bl (R)	1.75	.90
268	A15	10p	on 50p ol brn (Bk)	2.25	.95
			Nos. 264-268 (5)	6.10	3.00

President Hashem Bek el Atassi — A27

1938-43 **Photo.** **Unwmk.**

No.	Type	Denom.	Color	Unused	Used
268A	A27	10p	dp blue ('42)	1.25	.85
269	A27	12.50p	on 10p dp bl (R)	1.50	.90
270	A27	20p	dark brown	1.25	.85
			Nos. 268A-270 (3)	4.00	2.60

The 10pi and 20pi exist imperf.

Columns at Palmyra A28

1940 **Litho.** ***Perf. 11½***

No.	Type	Denom.	Color	Unused	Used
271	A28	5p	pale rose	2.00	.65

Exists imperf.

Museum at Damascus — A29

Hotel at Bloudan A30

Kasr-el-Heir A31

1940 **Typo.** ***Perf. 13x14***

No.	Type	Denom.	Color	Unused	Used
272	A29	10c	bright rose	.70	.25
273	A29	20c	light blue	.70	.25
274	A29	25c	fawn	.75	.25
275	A29	50c	ultra	.75	.25

Engr.

Perf. 13

No.	Type	Denom.	Color	Unused	Used
276	A30	1p	peacock blue	1.00	.25
277	A30	1.50p	chocolate	1.50	.70
278	A30	2.50p	dark green	1.00	.30
279	A31	5p	violet	1.10	.40
280	A31	7.50p	vermilion	2.00	.40
281	A31	50p	sepia	3.50	1.25
			Nos. 272-281 (10)	13.00	4.30

For overprints see Nos. 298-299.

President Taj Eddin Hassani A32

1942, Apr. 6 **Litho.** ***Perf. 11½***

No.	Type	Denom.	Color	Unused	Used
282	A32	50c	sage green	4.50	2.50
283	A32	1.50p	dull gray brn	4.75	2.50
284	A32	6p	fawn	5.00	2.50
285	A32	15p	light blue	5.50	2.50
			Nos. 282-285,C96-C97 (6)	28.00	18.25

Proclamation of independence by the Allies, Sept. 27, 1941.

President Taj Eddin Hassani — A33

1942 **Photo.** **Unwmk.**

No.	Type	Denom.	Color	Unused	Used
286	A33	6p	rose lake & salmon rose	4.00	1.25
287	A33	15p	dull blue & blue	4.00	1.50
			Nos. 286-287,C98 (3)	12.00	6.50

Nos. 286-287 exist imperf.

President Hassani and Map of Syria — A34

1943 **Litho.**

No.	Type	Denom.	Color	Unused	Used
288	A34	1p	light green	4.00	1.50
289	A34	4p	buff	4.00	1.50
290	A34	8p	pale violet	4.00	1.50
291	A34	10p	salmon	4.00	1.50
292	A34	20p	dull chalky blue	4.00	1.50
			Nos. 288-292,C99-C102 (9)	32.00	19.50

Proclamation of a United Syria. Exist imperf.

Stamps of 1943 Overprinted with Border in Black

1943

No.	Type	Denom.	Color	Unused	Used
293	A34	1p	light green	4.00	1.50
294	A34	4p	buff	4.00	1.50
295	A34	8p	pale violet	4.00	1.50

296 A34 10p salmon 4.00 1.50
297 A34 20p dl chalky bl 4.25 1.50
Nos. 293-297,C103-C106 (9) 32.25 19.50

Mourning for President Hassani. Exist imperf.

Nos. 278 and 280 Overprinted in Carmine or Black

1944 Unwmk. *Perf. 13*

298 A30 2.50p dk green (C) 4.50 2.50
299 A31 7.50p vermilion (Bk) 4.75 2.75
Nos. 298-299,C114-C116 (5) 37.75 33.75

1000th anniv. of the Arab poet and philosopher, abu-al-Ala al-Maarri.

President Shukri el Kouatly — A35

1945, Mar. 15 Litho. *Perf. 11½*

300 A35 4p pale lilac 1.00 .35
301 A35 6p dull blue 1.25 .40
302 A35 10p salmon 1.25 .40
303 A35 15p dark brown 2.00 .50
304 A35 20p slate green 2.00 .50
305 A35 40p orange 3.00 1.00
Nos. 300-305,C117-C123 (13) 26.60 10.35

Resumption of constitutional government.

Fiscal Stamps Overprinted or Surcharged in Black

A36

A37

A38

A39

1945 Typo. *Perf. 11, 11½x11*

306 A36 12½p on 15p yel grn 4.25 1.25
307 A37 25p buff 8.25 1.75
307A A38 25p on 25s lt vio brn 5.25 1.40
308 A39 50p on 75p brn org 9.50 2.50
309 A39 75p brown org 12.00 3.25
310 A37 100p yellow grn 19.00 4.00
Nos. 306-310 (6) 58.25 14.15

Type of 1945 and Nos. 308 and 310 Overprinted in Black

a

b

1945 Unwmk. *Perf. 11*

311 A37(b) 50p magenta 6.00 1.50
312 A39(a) 50p on 75p brn org 4.50 .90
313 A37(b) 100p yellow green 7.75 1.50
Nos. 311-313 (3) 18.25 3.90

Catalogue values for unused stamps in this section, from this point to the end of the section, are for Never Hinged items.

Independent Republic

A40

Fiscal Stamp Overprinted in Carmine

1946

314 A40 200p light blue 35.00 10.00

Sun and Ears of Wheat — A41

President Shukri el Kouatly — A42

1946 Litho. *Perf. 13x13½*

315 A41 50c brown orange .60 .25
316 A41 1p violet 1.00 .25
317 A41 2.50p blue gray 1.25 .30
318 A41 5p lt blue green 1.10 .25

Photo.

Perf. 13½x13, 13x13½

319 A42 7.50p dark brown .60 .25
320 A42 10p Prussian green .85 .25
321 A42 12.50p deep violet 2.25 .25
Nos. 315-321 (7) 7.65 1.80

For overprints see Nos. 328-329, 335-336.

Arab Horse A44

1946-47 Litho.

325 A44 50p olive brown 5.75 .90
326 A44 100p dk blue grn ('47) 12.50 2.00
327 A44 200p rose violet ('47) 65.00 5.50
Nos. 325-327 (3) 83.25 8.40

For overprints and surcharges see Nos. 330, 337, 347, 356-357.

Nos. 320, 321 and 325 Overprinted in Black or Green

1946, Apr. 17

328 A42 10p Prus green 1.25 .45
329 A42 12.50p deep violet 1.75 .65
330 A44 50p olive brown (G) 4.00 1.60
Nos. 328-330,C135 (4) 9.50 3.70

Evacuation of British and French troops from Syria. For surcharge see No. 347.

President Shukri el Kouatly — A45

1946 Unwmk. Litho. *Perf. 13½x13*

331 A45 15p red 1.00 .25
332 A45 20p violet 1.50 .25
333 A45 25p ultra 2.25 .30
Nos. 331-333 (3) 4.75 .80

No. 333 Overprinted in Magenta

1946, Aug. 28

334 A45 25p ultra 3.00 1.10
Nos. 334,C136-C138 (4) 14.50 7.10

8th Arab Medical Cong., Aleppo, 8/28-9/4.

Nos. 328 to 330 With Additional Overprint in Black

e

f

Perf. 13½x13, 13x13½

1947, June 10

335 A42(e) 10p Prus green 1.50 .25
336 A42(e) 12.50p deep violet 1.60 .25
337 A44(f) 50p olive brown 4.50 .75
Nos. 335-337,C139 (4) 10.10 2.50

Evacuation of British and French troops, 1st anniv.

Hercules and the Lion — A46

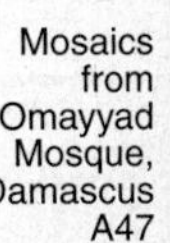

Mosaics from Omayyad Mosque, Damascus A47

1947, Nov. 15 Litho. *Perf. 11½*

338 A46 12.50p slate green 3.00 .40
339 A47 25p gray blue 4.25 .85
Nos. 338-339,C140-C141 (4) 13.75 3.75

1st Arab Archaeological Cong., Damascus, Nov.

See No. C141a.

Courtyard of Azem Palace A48

Telephone Building A49

1947, Nov. 15

340 A48 12.50p deep claret 2.50 .50
341 A49 25p brt blue 3.25 .70
Nos. 340-341,C142-C143 (4) 11.25 3.95

3rd Congress of Arab Engineers, Damascus, Nov.
See No. C143a.

House of Parliament A50

Pres. Shukri el Kouatly — A51

1948, June 23 Unwmk. *Perf. 10½*

342 A50 12.50p black & org 1.00 .25
343 A51 25p deep rose 2.00 .45
Nos. 342-343,C144-C145 (4) 6.15 1.95

Reelection of Pres. Shukri el Kouatly. See No. C145a.

National Emblem — A52

Syrian Flag and Soldier — A53

1948, June 23 Litho.

344 A52 12.50p gray & choc 1.50 .25
345 A53 25p multicolored 2.00 .45
Nos. 344-345,C146-C147 (4) 6.25 1.75

Inauguration of compulsory military training. See No. C147a.

Nos. 215 and 327 Surcharged with New Value and Bars in Black

1948 *Perf. 13, 13x13½*

346 A15 50c on 75c org red .50 .25
347 A44 25p on 200p rose vio 2.75 .30

Col. Husni Zayim — A54

1949, June 20 Litho. *Perf. 11½*

348 A54 25p blue 2.00 .40

Revolution of Mar. 30, 1949. See No. C153.

A souvenir sheet comprises Nos. 348 and C153, imperf. Value $80.

Ain el Arous A55

Palmyra — A56

1949, June 20

349 A55 12.50p violet 3.75 1.50
350 A56 25p blue 6.50 2.75
Nos. 349-350,C154-C155 (4) 36.75 22.75

UPU, 75th anniv. See note after No. C155.

Pres. Husni Zayim and Map — A57

Wmk. 291

1949, Aug. 6 Litho. *Perf. 11½*

351 A57 25p blue & brown 6.50 1.25

Election of President Husni Zayim. See Nos. C156, C156a.

Tel-Chehab Waterfall — A58

Damascus Scene A59

1949

352 A58 5p gray .75 .25
353 A58 7.50p olive gray 1.00 .25
354 A59 12.50p violet brown 1.25 .25
355 A59 25p blue 2.00 .40
Nos. 352-355 (4) 5.00 1.15

See No. 376.

Nos. 327 and 326 Surcharged with New Value and Bars in Black

1950 Unwmk. *Perf. 13x13½*

356 A44 2.50p on 200p rose vio .40 .25
357 A44 10p on 100p dk bl grn .50 .25

National Emblem — A60

Road to Damascus A61

Postal Administration Building, Damascus — A62

1950-51 Litho. *Perf. 11½*

358 A60 50c orange brn .30 .25
359 A60 2.50p pink .40 .25
360 A61 10p purple ('51) .50 .25
361 A61 12.50p sage grn ('51) .75 .40
362 A62 25p blue ('51) 1.75 .25
363 A62 50p black ('51) 5.25 .60
Nos. 358-363 (6) 8.95 2.00

Nos. 358 to 363 exist imperforate.

Parliament Building, Damascus A63

1951, Apr. 14

364 A63 12.50p gray blk .40 .25
365 A63 25p blue .75 .35
Nos. 364-365,C162-C163 (4) 2.80 1.85

New constitution adopted Sept. 5, 1950. Nos. 364-365 exist imperforate.

Water Wheel, Hama A64

Palace of Justice, Damascus A65

Perf. 11½

1952, Apr. 22 Litho. Unwmk.

366 A64 50c dark brown .30 .25
367 A64 2.50p dark blue .35 .25
368 A64 5p blue green .40 .25
369 A64 10p red .45 .25
370 A65 12.50p gray black .75 .25
371 A65 15p lilac rose 4.00 .25
372 A65 25p deep blue 2.00 .35
373 A65 100p olive brown 7.50 2.00
Nos. 366-373 (8) 15.75 3.85

Nos. 366-373 exist imperforate.

Type of 1949 and

Crusaders' Fort — A66

Crusaders' Fort — A67

1953 Photo.

374 A67 50c rose red .40 .25
375 A66 2.50p dark brown .40 .25
376 A58 7.50p green .50 .25
377 A67 12.50p deep blue 1.75 .25
Nos. 374-377 (4) 3.05 1.00

Farm Workers — A68

Family Group A69

Designs: 1pi, 5pi, Farm workers. 10pi, 12½p, Family group. 20pi, 25pi, 50pi, Factory and construction workers.

1954 *Perf. 11½*

378 A68 1p olive .25 .25
379 A68 2½p brown red .30 .25
380 A68 5p deep blue .40 .25
381 A69 7½p brown red .50 .25
382 A69 10p black .60 .25
383 A69 12½p violet .70 .25
384 A69 20p deep plum .85 .25
385 A69 25p violet 1.25 .35
386 A69 50p dark green 3.00 .75
Nos. 378-386 (9) 7.85 2.85

For overprints see Nos. 387-388, UAR 20, 34.

Nos. 382 and 385 Overprinted in Carmine

1954, Oct. 9

387 A69 10p black 1.25 .35
388 A69 25p violet 1.50 .45
Nos. 387-388,C185-C186 (4) 5.85 3.40

Cotton Festival, Aleppo, October 1954.

Globe — A69a

Arab Postal Union Issue

1955 Photo. *Perf. 13½x13*

389 A69a 12½p green .50 .25
390 A69a 25p violet .95 .35
Nos. 389-390,C191 (3) 1.85 .85

Founding of the APU, 7/1/54. Exist imperf. For overprints see Nos. 396-399, C203, C207.

Mother and Child — A70

1955, May 13 Litho. *Perf. 11½*

391 A70 25p red .80 .25
Nos. 391,C194-C195 (3) 3.30 1.80

Mother's Day.

United Nations Emblem A71

1955 Photo.

392 A71 7½p crimson .50 .25
393 A71 12½p Prus green 1.00 .50
Nos. 392-393,C200-C201 (4) 3.75 1.75

UN, 10th anniv., Oct. 24. For overprints see Nos. 401-402.

Aqueduct at Aleppo A72

1955 Litho. Unwmk.

394 A72 7.50p lilac .55 .25
395 A72 12.50p carmine 1.00 .35
Nos. 394-395,C202 (3) 3.55 1.70

New aqueduct bringing water from the Euphrates to Northern Syria. Exist imperf.

Nos. 389-390 Overprinted in Ultramarine or Green

1955 Photo. *Perf. 13½x13*

396 A69a 12½p green .40 .25
397 A69a 25p vio (G) 1.25 .40
Nos. 396-397,C203 (3) 2.15 .90

APU Congress held at Cairo, Mar. 15.

Nos. 389-390 Overprinted in Black

1956

398 A69a 12½p green .50 .25
399 A69a 25p violet 1.25 .55
Nos. 398-399,C207 (3) 2.25 1.05

Visit of King Hussein of Jordan to Damascus, Apr. 1956.

Cotton — A73

1956 Unwmk. Litho. *Perf. 11½*

400 A73 2½p bluish green .50 .25

Issued to publicize a Cotton Festival.

Nos. 392-393 Overprinted in Black

1956 Photo. *Perf. 11½*

401 A71 7½p crimson .50 .25
402 A71 12½p Prussian green .75 .35
Nos. 401-402,C221-C222 (4) 4.00 2.45

UN, 11th anniv.

People's Army A74

1957 Litho. *Perf. 11½*

403 A74 5p lilac rose .30 .25
404 A74 20p gray green .50 .25

Formation of the Popular Resistance Movement.

For overprints see Nos. 405-406, 413-414.

Nos. 403-404 Overprinted in Black or Red

1957

405 A74 5p lilac rose .30 .25

406 A74 20p gray green (R) .65 .30

Evacuation of Port Said by British and French troops, Dec. 22, 1956.

Azem Palace, Damascus A75

1957 Litho. *Perf. 11½*

407 A75 12½p lilac .30 .25

408 A75 15p gray .50 .25

For overprint see UAR No. 33.

Map of Near East, Scales and Damascus Skyline — A76

1957 Wmk. 291 *Perf. 11½*

409 A76 12½p bright green .40 .25

Nos. 409,C240-C241 (3) 1.70 1.05

3rd Congress of the Union of Arab Lawyers, Damascus, Sept. 21-25.

Cotton, Bale and Ship — A77

1957

410 A77 12½p lt bl grn & blk .50 .25

Nos. 410,C242-C243 (3) 2.50 1.15

Cotton Festival, Aleppo, Oct. 3-5.

Children — A78

1957, Oct. 7

411 A78 12½p olive 1.00 .25

Nos. 411,C244-C245 (3) 3.75 1.25

Intl. Children's Day, Oct. 7.
For overprint see UAR Nos. 13A, C10-C11.

Mailing and Receiving Letter A79

1957 Unwmk.

412 A79 5p magenta .50 .25

Intl. Letter Writing Week, Oct. 6-12. See No. C246.

Nos. 403-404 Overprinted in Black or Red

1957 *Perf. 11½*

413 A74 5p lilac rose .40 .25

414 A74 20p gray green (R) .50 .25

Digging of fortifications along the Syrian-Israeli frontier.

Scales, Torch and Map A80

1957, Nov. 8 Wmk. 291

415 A80 20p olive gray .55 .25

Nos. 415,C247-C248 (3) 1.80 1.10

Congress of Afro-Asian Jurists, Damascus.

Glider A81

1957, Nov. 8 Litho. *Perf. 11½*

416 A81 25p red brown 1.10 .30

417 A81 35p green 1.50 .40

418 A81 40p ultra 3.00 .70

Nos. 416-418 (3) 5.60 1.40

Issued to commemorate a glider festival.

Khaled ibn el Walid Mosque, Homs — A82

1957 Unwmk. *Perf. 12*

419 A82 2½p dull brown .40 .25

Scroll, Communications Building and Telephone — A83

1958 Wmk. 291 *Perf. 11½*

420 A83 25p ultra .30 .25

Nos. 420,C249-C250 (3) 1.05 .75

Issues of 1958-61 released by the United Arab Republic are listed following the listings of Syria, Issues of the Arabian Government.

Syrian Arab Republic

Hall of Parliament, Damascus A83a

1961 Unwmk. Litho. *Perf. 12*

420A A83a 15p magenta .40 .25

420B A83a 35p olive gray .75 .25

Establishment of Syrian Arab Republic.

Water Wheel, Hama — A84

Roman Arch of Triumph, Latakia — A85

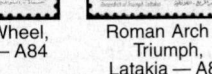

Qalb Lozah Church, Aleppo A86

7½p, 10p, Khaled ibn el Walid Mosque, Homs.

Perf. 11½x11

1961-62 Unwmk. Litho.

421 A84 2½p rose red .30 .25

422 A84 5p blue .30 .25

423 A84 7½p blue grn ('62) .30 .25

424 A84 10p orange ('62) .35 .25

Perf. 12x11½

425 A85 12½p gray brn .60 .25

426 A86 17½p olive gray ('62) .50 .25

427 A85 25p dull red brown .70 .25

428 A86 35p dull green ('62) .65 .25

Nos. 421-428 (8) 3.70 2.00

Types of 1961, Regular and Air Post

Designs: 2½p, 5p, 7½p, 10p, Arch, Jupiter Temple. 12½p, 15p, 17½p, 22½p, "The Beauty of Palmyra."

1962 *Perf. 11½x11*

429 A84 2½p gray blue .30 .25

430 A84 5p brown orange .30 .25

431 A84 7½p olive bister .30 .25

432 A84 10p claret .30 .25

Perf. 12x11½

Size: 26x38mm

433 AP68 12½p gray olive .35 .25

434 AP68 15p ultra .50 .25

435 AP68 17½p brown .50 .25

436 AP68 22½p grnsh blue .70 .25

Nos. 429-436 (8) 3.25 2.00

Martyrs' Memorial — A87

1962, June 11 Litho.

440 A87 12½p tan & sepia .30 .25

441 A87 35p green & bl grn .35 .25

1925 Revolution.

Pres. Nazem el-Kodsi — A88

1962, Dec. 14 *Perf. 12x11½*

442 A88 12½p sepia & lt bl .30 .25

1st anniv. of the election of Pres. Nazem el-Kodsi. See No. C278.

Queen Zenobia — A89

Central Bank of Syria A90

Designs: 2½p, 5p, "The Beauty of Palmyra." 17½p, Hejaz Railway Station, Damascus. 22½p, Mouassat Hospital, Damascus. 35p, P.T.T. Jalaa Avenue Office, Damascus.

1963 Unwmk. *Perf. 11½x11*

443 A89 2½p dk bl gray .30 .25

444 A89 5p rose lilac .30 .25

445 A89 7½p dull blue .35 .25

446 A89 10p olive gray .70 .25

447 A89 12½p ultra 1.00 .25

448 A89 15p violet brn 1.50 .25

Perf. 11½x12

449 A90 17½p dull violet .60 .25

450 A90 22½p brt violet .30 .25

451 A90 25p bister brown .30 .25

452 A90 35p bright pink .35 .25

Nos. 443-452 (10) 5.70 2.50

Wheat Emblem and Globe — A91

1963, Mar. 21 Litho. *Perf. 12x11½*

453 A91 12½p ultra & blk .30 .25

FAO "Freedom from Hunger" Campaign. See No. C291 and souvenir sheet No. C291a.

Cotton Festival Type of Air Post Issue, 1962, Inscribed "1963"

1963, Sept. 26 *Perf. 12x11½*

455 AP75 17½p multi .30 .25

456 AP75 22½p multi .35 .25

The 1963 Cotton Festival, Aleppo.

Boy Playing Ball and UN Emblem — A92

1963, Oct. 24 *Perf. 12x11½*
457 A92 12½p emer & sl grn .30 .25
458 A92 22½p rose red & dk grn .30 .25

Issued for International Children's Day.

Ugharit Princess — A93

1964 **Litho.** *Perf. 11½x11*
459 A93 2½p gray .30 .25
460 A93 5p brown .30 .25
461 A93 7½p rose claret .30 .25
462 A93 10p emerald .30 .25
463 A93 12½p light violet .30 .25
464 A93 17½p ultra .30 .25
465 A93 20p rose carmine .45 .25
466 A93 25p orange .75 .25
Nos. 459-466 (8) 3.00 2.00

A94

Designs: Map of North Africa and Middle East, flag of Syria, and crowd.

1965, Mar. 8 **Litho.** *Perf. 11½x12*
467 A94 12½p multicolored .30 .25
468 A94 17½p multicolored .30 .25
469 A94 20p multicolored .30 .25
Nos. 467-469 (3) .90 .75

Mar. 8 Revolution, 2nd anniv.

Weather Map and Anemometer — A95

1965, Mar. 23 **Litho.** **Unwmk.**
470 A95 12½p dl lilac & blk .30 .25
471 A95 27½p lt blue & blk .30 .25

Fifth World Meteorological Day.

"Evacuation of Apr. 17, 1946" — A96

1965, Apr. 17 **Litho.** *Perf. 12x11½*
472 A96 12½p bl & brt yel grn .30 .25
473 A96 27½p rose red & lt lil .30 .25

19th anniv. of the evacuation of British and French troops from Syria.

Peasants' Union Emblem — A97

1965, Aug. **Unwmk.** *Perf. 11½x11*
474 A97 2½p blue green .30 .25
475 A97 12½p purple .30 .25
476 A97 15p maroon .30 .25
Nos. 474-476 (3) .90 .75

Issued to publicize the Peasants' Union.

Torch, Map of Arab Countries and Farmer, Soldier, Woman, Intellectual and Worker — A98

1965, Nov. 23 *Perf. 12x11½*
477 A98 12½p multicolored .30 .25
478 A98 25p multicolored .30 .25

National Council of the Revolution, a legislative body working for a socialist and democratic society.

Workers, Factory and Emblem — A99

1966, Jan. **Litho.** *Perf. 11½x11*
479 A99 12½p blue .30 .25
480 A99 15p carmine .30 .25
481 A99 20p dull violet .30 .25
482 A99 25p olive gray .30 .25
Nos. 479-482 (4) 1.20 1.00

Establishment of the General Union of Trade Unions.

Roman Lamp A100

Islamic Vessel, 12th Century A101

1966 **Litho.** *Perf. 11½x11*
483 A100 2½p slate green .30 .25
484 A100 5p magenta .30 .25
485 A101 7½p brown .30 .25
486 A101 10p brt rose lilac .30 .25
Nos. 483-486 (4) 1.20 1.00

"Evacuation of Troops" — A102

1966, Apr. 17 **Litho.** *Perf. 12x11½*
487 A102 12½p multi .30 .25
488 A102 27½p multi .30 .25

20th anniv. of the evacuation of British and French troops from Syria.

Bust of Core, Terra Cotta Vase — A103

Design: 15p, 20p, 25p, 27½p, Bronze vase in form of seated African woman.

1967 *Perf. 11½x11*
489 A103 2½p brt green .30 .25
490 A103 5p salmon pink .30 .25
491 A103 10p grnsh blue .30 .25
492 A103 12½p dull brown .30 .25
493 A103 15p brt pink .30 .25
494 A103 20p brt blue .30 .25
495 A103 25p green .30 .25
496 A103 27½p violet blue .30 .25
Nos. 489-496 (8) 2.40 2.00

Arab Revolution Monument, Damascus A104

1968, Mar. 8 **Litho.** *Perf. 12x12½*
497 A104 12½p black, yel & brn .30 .25
498 A104 25p blk, pink & car rose .30 .25
499 A104 27½p blk, lt grn & grn .30 .25
Nos. 497-499 (3) .90 .75

Mar. 8 Revolution, 5th anniversary.

Map of Syria — A105

1968, Apr. 4 **Litho.** *Perf. 12x12½*
500 A105 12½p pink & multi .30 .25
501 A105 60p gray & multi .40 .25

Arab Baath Socialist Party, 21st anniv.

Hands Holding Wrench, Gun and Torch — A106

1968, Apr. 13
502 A106 12½p tan & multi .30 .25
503 A106 17½p rose & multi .30 .25
504 A106 25p yellow & multi .30 .25
Nos. 502-504 (3) .90 .75

Issued to publicize the mobilization effort.

Rising Sun, Power Lines and Railroad Tracks A107

1968, Apr. 17 **Litho.** *Perf. 12½x12*
505 A107 12½p multicolored .30 .25
506 A107 27½p violet & multi .30 .25

22nd anniv. of the evacuation of British and French troops from Syria.

Oil Wells and Oil Pipe Line on Map — A108

1968, May 1
507 A108 12½p lt & dk grn & ultra .30 .25
508 A108 17½p pink, brn & ultra .30 .25

Syrian oil exploitation; completion of the oil pipe line to Tartus.

Map of Palestine and Torch — A109

1968, May **Litho.** *Perf. 12x12½*
509 A109 12½p ultra, blk & red .75 .35
510 A109 25p ol bis, blk & red 1.00 .35
511 A109 27½p gray, blk & red 1.50 .50
Nos. 509-511 (3) 3.25 1.20

Issued for Palestine Day.

Citadel of Aleppo, Wheat and Cogwheel A110

1968, July 18 **Litho.** *Perf. 12x12½*
512 A110 12½p multi .30 .25
513 A110 27½p multi .30 .25

Industrial and Agricultural Fair, Aleppo.

Fair Emblem, Globe, Grain, Wheel and Horse — A111

Design: 27½p, Syrian flag, hand with torch, fair emblem, globe, grain and wheel.

Perf. 12x12½, 12½x12

1968, Aug. 25 **Litho.**
514 A111 12½p dp brn, blk & emer .30 .25
515 A111 27½p multicolored .30 .25
516 A111 60p bl gray, blk & dp org .30 .25
Nos. 514-516 (3) .90 .75

15th Intl. Damascus Fair, Aug. 25-Sept. 20.

Woman Carrying Cotton, and Castle of Aleppo — A112

1968, Oct. 3 **Litho.** *Perf. 12x12½*
517 A112 12½p multi .30 .25
518 A112 27½p multi .30 .25

13th Cotton Festival, Aleppo.

Al Jahez — A113

1968, Nov. 9 Litho. *Perf. 12x12½*

519 A113 12½p black & buff .30 .25
520 A113 27½p black & gray .60 .25

9th Science Week; Al Jahez Abu Uthman Amr ben Bahr (776-868).

Oil Derrick and Pipe Line — A114

1968 *Perf. 12x11*

521 A114 2½p grnsh bl & dk grn .30 .25
522 A114 5p grn & vio bl .30 .25
523 A114 7½p lt yel grn & bl .30 .25
524 A114 10p brt yel & grn .30 .25
525 A114 12½p yellow & ver .30 .25
526 A114 15p ol bis & dk brn .30 .25
527 A114 27½p dl org & dk red brn .30 .25
Nos. 521-527 (7) 2.10 1.75

Broken Chains and Sun A115

1969, Mar. 8 Litho. *Perf. 12½x12*
Sun in Yellow and Red

528 A115 12½p vio bl & blk .30 .25
529 A115 25p gray & blk .30 .25
530 A115 27½p dull grn & blk .30 .25
Nos. 528-530 (3) .90 .75

March 8 Revolution, 6th anniversary.

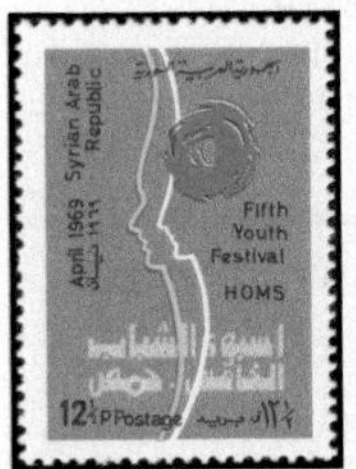

"Sun of Freedom, Young Man and Woman" — A116

1969, Mar. 29 *Perf. 12x12½*

531 A116 12½p multi .30 .25
532 A116 25p multi .30 .25

Youth Week; 5th Youth Festival, Homs, 4/18-24.

Liberation through Knowledge and Construction A117

1969, Apr. 17 Litho. *Perf. 12x12½*

533 A117 12½p yellow & multi .30 .25
534 A117 27½p gray & multi .30 .25

23rd anniv. of the evacuation of British and French troops from Syria.

Mahatma Gandhi — A118

1969, Oct. 7 Litho. *Perf. 12x12½*

535 A118 12½p brown & dull yel .30 .25
536 A118 27½p green & yellow .30 .25

Mohandas K. Gandhi (1869-1948), leader in India's fight for independence.

Cotton — A119

1969, Oct. 10

537 A119 12½p multi .30 .25
538 A119 17½p multi .30 .25
539 A119 25p multi .30 .25
Nos. 537-539 (3) .90 .75

14th Cotton Festival, Aleppo.

Map of Arab Countries A120

Designs: 25p, Arab Academy. 27½p, Damascus University.

1969, Nov. 2 Litho. *Perf. 12½x12*

540 A120 12½p ultra & lt grn .30 .25
541 A120 25p dk pur & dp pink .30 .25
542 A120 27½p dp bis & yel grn .30 .25
Nos. 540-542 (3) .90 .75

10th Science Week, and 6th Arab Scientific Conf. No. 541 also for 50th anniv. of the Arab Academy and No. 542, the 50th anniv. of the Medical School of the Damascus University.

Symbols of Progress A121

1970, Mar. 8 Litho. *Perf. 12½x12*

543 A121 12½p brt bl, blk & bis brn .30 .25
544 A121 25p red, blk & dp bl .30 .25
545 A121 27½p lt grn, blk & tan .30 .25
Nos. 543-545 (3) .90 .75

March 8 Revolution, 7th anniversary.

Map of Arab League Countries, Flag and Emblem A122

1970, Mar. 22

546 A122 12½p multi .30 .25
547 A122 25p gray & multi .30 .25
548 A122 27½p multi .35 .25
Nos. 546-548 (3) .95 .75

25th anniversary of the Arab League.

Sultan Saladin and Battle of Hattin, 1187, between Saracens and Crusaders — A123

1970, Apr. 17 Litho. *Perf. 12½x12*

549 A123 15p brn & buff .30 .25
550 A123 35p lilac & buff .35 .25

24th anniv. of the evacuation of British and French troops from Syria.

Development of Agriculture and Industry — A124

1970-71 Litho. *Perf. 11x11½*

551 A124 2½p brn & red ('71) .30 .25
552 A124 5p orange & bl .30 .25
553 A124 7½p lil & gray ('71) .30 .25
554 A124 10p lt & dk brn .30 .25
555 A124 12½p blue & org ('71) .30 .25
556 A124 15p grn & red lil .30 .25
557 A124 20p vio & red brn .30 .25
558 A124 22½p red brn & blk ('71) .30 .25
559 A124 25p gray & vio bl ('71) .30 .25
560 A124 27½p brt grn & dk brn ('71) .30 .25
561 A124 35p rose red & emer ('71) .35 .25
Nos. 551-561 (11) 3.35 2.75

Young Man and Woman, Map of Arab Countries A125

1970, May 7 Unwmk. *Perf. 12½x12*

569 A125 15p green & ocher .30 .25
570 A125 25p brown & ocher .30 .25

First Youth Week, Latakia, Apr. 23-29. Inscribed "Youth's First Weak" (sic.).

Refugee Family A126

1970, May 15

571 A126 15p multicolored .30 .25
572 A126 25p gray & multi .30 .25
573 A126 35p green & multi .30 .25
Nos. 571-573 (3) .90 .75

Issued for Arab Refugee Week.

Cotton — A127

1970, Aug. 18 Litho. *Perf. 12½*

574 A127 5p shown .30 .25
575 A127 10p Tomatoes .30 .25
576 A127 15p Tobacco .30 .25
577 A127 20p Beets .30 .25
578 A127 35p Wheat .75 .25
a. Strip of 5, #574-578 2.00 2.00

Industrial and Agricultural Fair, Aleppo.

Boy Scout, Tent, Emblem and Map of Arab Countries A128

1970, Aug. 25 *Perf. 12½x12*

579 A128 15p gray green .40 .25

9th Pan-Arab Boy Scout Jamboree, Damascus.

Olive Tree and Emblem A129

1970, Sept. 28 Litho. *Perf. 11½x12*

580 A129 15p gray grn, yel & blk .30 .25
581 A129 25p red brn, yel & blk .50 .25

Issued to publicize World Olive Year.

Protection of Industry, Agriculture, Arts and Commerce — A130

1971, Mar. 8 Litho. *Perf. 12½x12*

582 A130 15p olive, yel & bl .30 .25
583 A130 22½p red brn, yel & ol .30 .25
584 A130 27½p bl, yel & red brn .30 .25
Nos. 582-584 (3) .90 .75

March 8 Revolution, 8th anniversary.

Workers Memorial, Hands with Wrench and Olive Branch A131

1971, May 1 Litho. *Perf. 12½x12*

585 A131 15p brn vio, yel & bl .30 .25
586 A131 25p dk bl, bl & yel .30 .25

Labor Day.

Child and Traffic Lights A132

World Traffic Day: 25p, Road signs, traffic lights, children, vert.

1971, May 4 *Perf. 11½x12, 12x11½*

587 A132 15p black, red & bl .30 .25
588 A132 25p gray & multi .30 .25
589 A132 45p black, red & yel .30 .25
Nos. 587-589 (3) .90 .75

Factories, Cogwheel and Cotton A133

1971, July 15 Litho. *Perf. 12½x12*

590 A133 15p lt grn, bl & blk .30 .25
591 A133 30p red & black .30 .25

11th Industrial and Agricultural Fair, Aleppo.

Arab Postal Union Emblem — A134

1971, Sep. 1 ***Perf. 12x12½***

592 A134 15p claret & multi .30 .25
593 A134 20p vio bl & multi .30 .25

25th anniv. of the Conference of Sofar, Lebanon, establishing the APU.

Flag, Map of Syria, Egypt and Libya — A135

1971, Aug. 13 ***Perf. 12x11½***

594 A135 15p car, dl grn & blk .30 .25

Confederation of the Arab states of Syria, Libya and Egypt.

Red Pepper and Chemical Factory (Fertilizer Industry) — A136

18th Intl. Damascus Fair: 15p, Electronics industry (TV, telephone, computer). 35p, Glass industry (old map and glass manufacture). 50p, Carpet industry (carpet and looms).

1971, Aug. 25 ***Perf. 12½***

595 A136 5p violet & multi .30 .25
596 A136 15p dull grn & multi .30 .25
597 A136 35p multicolored .30 .25
598 A136 50p yel grn & multi .50 .25
Nos. 595-598 (4) 1.40 1.00

Pres. Hafez al Assad and Crowd — A137

1971, Nov. **Litho.** ***Perf. 12x12½***

599 A137 15p vio bl, blk & car .30 .25
600 A137 20p dk & lt grn, car & blk .30 .25

1st anniv. of Correctionist Movement of Nov. 16, 1970.

UNESCO Emblem, Radar, Spacecraft, Telephone A138

1971, Dec. 8

601 A138 15p vio bl & multi .30 .25
602 A138 50p green & multi .30 .25

25th anniv. of UNESCO.

UNICEF Emblem and Playing Children — A139

1971, Dec. 21

603 A139 15p ultra, dk bl & dp car .30 .25
604 A139 25p grnsh bl, ocher & dk bl .30 .25

UNICEF, 25th anniv.

Conference Emblem — A140

1971, Dec. ***Perf. 12½x12***

605 A140 15p blk, grnsh bl & org .30 .25

Scholars' Conference.

Book Year Emblem A141

1972, Jan. 2

606 A141 15p tan, lt bl & vio .30 .25
607 A141 20p brn, lt grn & grn .30 .25

International Book Year.

Wheel, "8" and Scales of Justice — A142

1972, Mar. 8 **Litho.** ***Perf. 12x12½***

608 A142 15p blue grn & vio .30 .25
609 A142 20p olive bis & car .30 .25

March 8 Revolution, 9th anniversary.

Baath Party Emblem — A143

1972, Mar. 7

610 A143 15p dk blue & multi .30 .25
611 A143 20p violet & multi .30 .25

Arab Baath Socialist Party, 25th anniv.

Eagle, Chimneys, Grain and Oil Rigs — A144

1972, Apr. 17 ***Perf. 12½x12***

612 A144 15p gold, blk & car .30 .25

Federation of Arab Republics, 1st anniv.

Symbolic Flower, Broken Chain — A145

1972, Apr. 17 ***Perf. 12x11½***

613 A145 15p rose red & gray .30 .25
614 A145 50p pale bl grn & gray .30 .25

26th anniv. of the evacuation of British and French troops from Syria.

Hand Holding Wrench and Spade — A146

1972, May 1

615 A146 15p ol grn, bl & blk .30 .25
616 A146 50p vio bl, brn & blk .30 .25

Labor Day.

Environment Emblem, Crystals, Microscope A147

1972, June 5

617 A147 15p multicolored .30 .25
618 A147 50p blue & multi .35 .25

UN Conference on Human Environment, Stockholm, June 5-16.

Dove over Factory — A148

1972, July 17 **Litho.** ***Perf. 12x11½***

619 A148 15p yellow & multi .30 .25
620 A148 20p yellow & multi .30 .25

Agricultural and Industrial Fair, Aleppo.

Folk Dance — A149

20p, Women and tambourine player. 50p, Men and drummer.

1972, Aug. 25 **Litho.** ***Perf. 12x12½***

621 A149 15p shown .30 .25
622 A149 20p multicolored .30 .25
623 A149 50p multicolored .50 .25
Nos. 621-623 (3) 1.10 .75

19th International Damascus Fair.

Olympic Rings, Discus, Soccer, Swimming — A150

Warriors on Horseback, Olympic Emblems — A151

Design: 60p, Olympic rings, running, gymnastics, fencing.

1972 **Litho.** ***Perf. 12½x12***

624 A150 15p ol bis, blk & vio .50 .25
625 A150 60p dull bl, blk & org .60 .25

Souvenir Sheet

Imperf

626 A151 75p lt grn, bl & blk 2.00 2.00

20th Olympic Games, Munich, Aug. 26-Sept. 11, 1972.

Emblem of Revolution and Prancing Horse A152

1973, Mar. 8 **Litho.** ***Perf. 11½x12***

627 A152 15p brt grn, blk & red .30 .25
628 A152 20p dull org, blk & red .30 .25
629 A152 25p blue, blk & red .30 .25
Nos. 627-629 (3) .90 .75

March 8 Revolution, 10th anniversary.

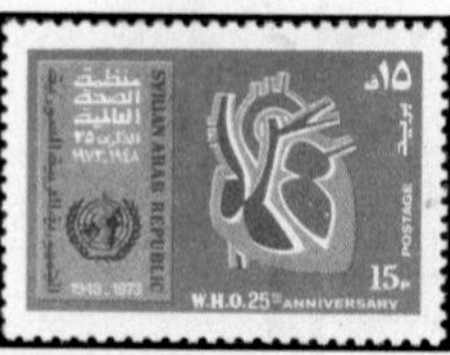

Heart and WHO Emblem A153

1973, Mar. 21

630 A153 15p gray & multi .30 .25
631 A153 50p lt brown & multi .35 .25

WHO, 25th anniversary.

Cogwheel and Grain Emblem — A154

1973, Apr. 17 *Perf. 12x12½*

632	A154 15p blue & multi		.30	.25
633	A154 20p multicolored		.30	.25

27th anniv. of the evacuation of British and French troops from Syria.

Workers and Globe A155

1973, May 1 *Perf. 11½x12*

634	A155 15p rose & multi	.30	.25
635	A155 50p blue & multi	.35	.25

Labor Day.

UN, FAO Emblems, People and Symbols — A156

1973, May 7 *Perf. 12x11½*

636	A156 15p lt grn & red brn	.30	.25
637	A156 50p lilac & blue	.35	.25

World food program, 10th anniv.

Stock — A157

1973, May 15

638	A157 5p shown	.30	.25
639	A157 10p Gardenia	.30	.25
640	A157 15p Jasmine	.30	.25
641	A157 20p Rose	.30	.25
642	A157 25p Narcissus	.30	.25
a.	Strip of 5, #638-642	1.50	1.50

Intl. Flower Show, Damascus.

A158

Children and Flame — A158a

Children's Day: 3 children's heads and flame in different arrangements; 25p, 35p, 70p, vertical.

Perf. 11½x12, 12x11½

1973-74 **Litho.**

643	A158 2½p lt olive grn	.30	.25
644	A158 5p orange	.30	.25
645	A158a 7½p dk brown	.30	.25
646	A158a 10p crimson	.30	.25
647	A158 15p ultra	.30	.25
648	A158a 25p gray	.30	.25
649	A158a 35p brt blue	.30	.25
650	A158a 55p green	.30	.25
651	A158a 70p rose lilac	.35	.25
	Nos. 643-651 (9)	2.75	2.25

Issued: 15p, 55p, 70p, 5/73; others, 3/74.

Fair Emblem A159

1973, June 17 *Perf. 11½x12*

652	A159 15p multicolored	.30	.25

13th Agricultural and Industrial Fair, Aleppo.

Euphrates Dam and Power Plant — A160

1973, July 5 *Perf. 12½x12*

653	A160 15p green & multi	.30	.25
654	A160 50p brown & multi	.30	.25

Euphrates River diversion and dam project.

Woman from Deir Ezzor — A161

Women's Costumes from: 10p, Hassaké. 20p, As Sahel. 25p, Zakié. 50p, Sarakeb.

1973, July 25 **Litho.** *Perf. 12*

655	A161 5p multicolored	.30	.25
656	A161 10p multicolored	.30	.25
657	A161 20p multicolored	.30	.25
658	A161 25p multicolored	.30	.25
659	A161 50p multicolored	.30	.25
a.	Strip of 5, #655-659	1.50	1.50

20th International Damascus Fair.

Map of Palestine, Barbed Wire, Human Rights Emblem — A162

1973, Aug. 20 *Perf. 12x11½*

660	A162 15p lt green & multi	.90	.50
661	A162 50p lt blue & multi	1.75	.50

25th anniversary of the Universal Declaration of Human Rights.

Citadel of Ja'abar A163

15p, Minaret of Meskeneh, vert. 25p, Statue of Psyche at Anab al Safinah, vert.

Perf. 11½x12, 12x11½

1973, Sept. 5 **Litho.**

662	A163 10p black, org & blue	.30	.25
663	A163 15p black, org & blue	.30	.25
664	A163 25p black, org & blue	.30	.25
	Nos. 662-664 (3)	.90	.75

Salvage of monuments threatened by Euphrates Dam.

WMO Emblem A164

1973, Sept. 12 *Perf. 11½x12*

665	A164 70p yellow & multi	.50	.25

Intl. meteorological cooperation, cent.

Maalula A165

Design: 50p, Ruins of Afamia.

1973, Oct. 22 **Litho.** *Perf. 11½x12*

666	A165 15p gray blue & blk	.30	.25
667	A165 50p brown & blk	.30	.25

Arab Emigrants' Congress, Buenos Aires.

Workers and Soldiers A166

1973, Nov. 16 **Litho.** *Perf. 12½x12*

668	A166 15p ultra & yellow	.30	.25
669	A166 25p purple & red brn	.30	.25

3rd anniv. of Correctionist Movement of Nov. 16, 1970.

Nicolaus Copernicus A167

Design: 25p, Abu-al-Rayhan al-Biruni.

1973, Dec. 15 *Perf. 12x11½*

670	A167 15p gold & black	.30	.25
671	A167 25p gold & black	.30	.25

14th Science Week.

Arms of Syria and Emblems A168

1974, Mar. 8 *Perf. 11x12*

672	A168 20p gray & blue	.30	.25
673	A168 25p lt green & vio	.30	.25

11th anniversary of March 8th Revolution.

UPU Emblem — A169

Air Mail Letter & UPU Emblem — A169a

1974, Mar. 15 *Perf. 12x11½, 11½x12*

674	A169 15p gray & multi	.30	.25
675	A169a 20p multicolored	.30	.25
676	A169 70p gray & multi	.50	.25
	Nos. 674-676 (3)	1.10	.75

Centenary of Universal Postal Union.

Arab Postal Institute A170

1974, Apr. 10 *Perf. 11½x12*

677	A170 15p multicolored	.30	.25

Inauguration of the Higher Arab Postal Institute, Damascus, Apr. 10.

Sun and Monument A171

1974, Apr. 10

678	A171 15p emerald, blk & org	.30	.25
679	A171 20p dp org, blk & org	.30	.25

28th anniversary of the evacuation of British and French troops from Syria.

Machine Shop Worker — A172

1974, May 1 *Perf. 12x12½*

680	A172 15p black, yel & bl	.30	.25
681	A172 50p black, buff & bl	.30	.25

Labor Day.

Abulfeda — A173

Design: 200p, al-Farabi.

1974 Litho. *Perf. 11½x11*

682 A173 100p pale green .50 .25
683 A173 200p lt brown 1.00 .45

Damascus Fair Emblem — A174

Design: 25p, Cog wheel and sun.

1974, July 25 *Perf. 11½x11*

684 A174 15p multicolored .30 .25
685 A174 25p blue, blk & yel .30 .25

21st International Damascus Fair.

Figs — A175

Fruits: 15p, Grapes. 20p, Pomegranates. 25p, Cherries. 35p, Rose hips.

1974, Aug. 21 *Perf. 12x12½*

686 A175 5p gray & multi .30 .25
687 A175 15p gray & multi .30 .25
688 A175 20p gray & multi .30 .25
689 A175 25p gray & multi .30 .25
690 A175 35p gray & multi .30 .25
a. Strip of 5, #686-690 2.50 2.50

Agricultural and Industrial Fair, Aleppo.

Burning Fuse and Flowers — A176

20p, Bomb and star-shaped holes in target.

1974, Oct. 6 Litho. *Perf. 12x12½*

691 A176 15p multicolored .75 .25
692 A176 20p multicolored 1.00 .25

First anniv. of October Liberation War (Yom Kippur War).

Rook and Knight — A177

Design: 50p, Knight and chess board.

1974, Nov. 23

693 A177 15p blue & black .75 .25
694 A177 50p orange, blk & bl 2.25 .80

Chess Federation, 50th anniversary.

WPY Emblem — A178

1974, Dec. 4 Litho. *Perf. 12x12½*

695 A178 50p black, slate & red .30 .25

World Population Year.

Ishtup, Ilum — A179

Ancient Statuettes: 55p, Woman holding pitcher. 70p, Ur-Nina.

1975 *Perf. 12x11½*

696 A179 20p brt green .30 .25
697 A179 55p brown .30 .25
698 A179 70p gray blue .50 .25
Nos. 696-698 (3) 1.10 .75

"A," People and Sun — A180

1975, Mar. 8 Litho. *Perf. 12x11½*

699 A180 15p gray & multi .30 .25

12th anniversary, March 8th Revolution.

Postal Savings Bank Emblem, Family — A181

Design: 20p, Family depositing money, and stamped envelope.

1975, Mar. 17

700 A181 15p brt green & multi .30 .25
701 A181 20p orange & black .30 .25

Publicity for Savings Certificates and Postal Savings Bank.

"Sun" and Dove — A182

1975, Apr. 17 Litho. *Perf. 12x11½*

702 A182 15p bister, red & blk .30 .25
703 A182 25p bister, grn & blk .30 .25

29th anniversary of the evacuation of British and French troops from Syria.

"Worker and Industry" — A183

1975, May 1 Litho. *Perf. 12x11½*

704 A183 15p blue grn & blk .30 .25
705 A183 25p brown, yel & blk .30 .25

Labor Day.

Camomile A184

Flowers: 10p, Chincherinchi. 15p, Carnation. 20p, Poppy. 25p, Honeysuckle.

1975, May 17

706 A184 5p ultra & multi .30 .25
707 A184 10p lilac & multi .30 .25
708 A184 15p blue & multi .35 .25
709 A184 20p gray grn & multi .40 .25
710 A184 25p vio bl & multi .75 .25
a. Strip of 5, #706-710 2.10 2.10

International Flower Show, Damascus.

Kuneitra Destroyed and Rebuilt — A185

1975, June 5 *Perf. 12½*

711 A185 50p black & multi .35 .25

Re-occupation of Kuneitra by Syria.

Apples A186

1975, July 7

712 A186 5p shown .30 .25
713 A186 10p Quince .30 .25
714 A186 15p Apricots .35 .25
715 A186 20p Grapes .40 .25
716 A186 25p Figs .50 .25
a. Strip of 5, #712-716 1.90 1.90

Agricultural and Industrial Fair, Aleppo.

22nd Intl. Damascus Fair — A187

1975, July 25 Litho. *Perf. 12x11½*

717 A187 15p olive grn & multi .30 .25
718 A187 35p brown & multi .30 .25

Pres. Hafez al Assad A188

1975, Nov. 29 Litho. *Perf. 11½x12*

719 A188 15p green & multi .30 .25
720 A188 50p blue & multi .30 .25

5th anniv. of Correctionist Movement of Nov. 16, 1970.

Farm Woman — A189

IWY Emblem and: 15p, Mother. 25p, Student. 50p, Laboratory technician.

1975, Nov. 29 *Perf. 12x11½*

721 A189 10p buff & multi .30 .25
722 A189 15p rose & black .30 .25
723 A189 25p dull green & blk .35 .25
724 A189 50p orange & blk .50 .25
Nos. 721-724 (4) 1.45 1.00

International Women's Year.

Horse-shaped Bronze Lamp A190

Man's Head Inkstand A191

Designs: 10p, 25p, like 20p. 35p, like 30p. 50p, 60p, Nike. 75p, Hera. 100p, Imdugug-Mari (winged animal). 500p, Palmyrene coin of Vasalathus. 1000p, Abraxas coin.

1976 *Perf. 11½x12, 12x11½*

725 A190 10p brt bluish grn .30 .25
726 A190 20p lilac rose .30 .25
727 A190 25p violet blue .30 .25
728 A191 30p brown .30 .25
729 A191 35p olive .30 .25
730 A191 50p brt blue .30 .25
731 A191 60p violet .30 .25
732 A191 75p orange .35 .25
733 A191 100p lilac rose .50 .25
734 A191 500p grnsh gray 2.00 1.75
735 A191 1000p dk green 4.00 2.25
Nos. 725-735 (11) 8.95 6.25

See Nos. 798-803.

National Theater, Damascus and Pres. al Assad A192

1976, Mar. 8 Litho. *Perf. 11½x12*
736 A192 25p brt grn, sil & blk .30 .25
737 A192 35p olive, sil & blk .30 .25

13th anniversary of March 8 Revolution.

Syria, Arabian Government #85 — A193

1976, Apr. 12 *Perf. 12x12½*
738 A193 25p brt green & multi .30 .25
739 A193 35p blue & multi .30 .25

Post's Day.

Nurse and Emblem — A194

1976, Apr. 8 *Perf. 12x11½*
740 A194 25p blue, blk & red .30 .25
741 A194 100p violet, blk & red .50 .30

Arab Red Cross and Red Crescent Societies, 8th Conference, Damascus.

Eagle and Stars — A195

1976, Apr. 17
742 A195 25p blk, red & brt grn .30 .25
743 A195 35p blk, red & brt grn .30 .25

30th anniversary of the evacuation of British and French troops from Syria.

Hand Holding Wrench — A196

May Day: 60p, Hand holding globe.

1976, May 1
744 A196 25p blue & black .30 .25
745 A196 60p citron & multi .40 .25

Cotton and Factory — A197

1976, July 1
746 A197 25p vio & multi .30 .25
747 A197 35p bl & multi .30 .25

Agricultural and Industrial Fair, Aleppo.

Tulips — A198

1976, July 26
748 A198 5p shown .30 .25
749 A198 15p Yellow daisies .30 .25
750 A198 20p Turk's-cap lilies .30 .25
751 A198 25p Irises .50 .25
752 A198 35p Freesia .75 .25
a. Strip of 5, #748-752 2.25 2.25

Intl. Flower Show, Damascus.

People, Globe and Olive Branch A199

60p, Symbolic arrow piercing darkness.

1976, Sept. 2 *Perf. 11½x12*
753 A199 40p yel & multi .30 .25
754 A199 60p multi .35 .25

5th Summit Conference of Non-aligned Countries, Colombo, Sri Lanka, Aug. 9-19.

Soccer, Pan Arab Games Emblem A200

1976, Oct. 6 Litho. *Perf. 12½*
755 A200 5p shown .30 .25
756 A200 10p Swimming .30 .25
757 A200 25p Running .30 .25
758 A200 35p Basketball .30 .25
759 A200 50p Javelin .30 .25
a. Strip of 5, #755-759 1.50 1.50

Souvenir Sheet

Imperf

760 A200 100p Steeplechase 2.00 2.00

5th Pan Arab Sports Tournament. Size of stamp of No. 760: 55x35mm.

"Development" A201

1976, Nov. 16 *Perf. 12½x12½*
761 A201 35p multi .30 .25

Correctionist Movement pof Nov. 16, 1970.

The Fox and the Crow — A202

Fairy Tales: 15p, The Hare and the Tortoise, horiz. 20p, Little Red Riding Hood. 25p, The Lamb and the Wolf, horiz. 35p, The Lamb and the Wolf.

1976, Dec. 7 *Perf. 12x12½, 12½x12*
762 A202 10p multi .30 .25
763 A202 15p multi .30 .25
764 A202 20p multi .30 .25
765 A202 25p multi .30 .25
766 A202 35p multi .30 .25
a. Strip of 5, #762-766 1.50 1.50

Children's literature.

Syrian Airlines Boeing 747 — A203

1977, Feb. Litho. *Perf. 12½x12*
767 A203 35p multi .30 .25

Civil Aviation Day.

Muhammad Kurd-Ali (1876-1953), Philosopher, Birth Cent. — A204

1977, Feb. *Perf. 12x12½*
768 A204 25p lt grn & multi .30 .25

Woman Holding Syrian Flag — A205

1977, Mar. 8 Litho. *Perf. 12x12½*
769 A205 35p multi .30 .25

14th anniversary of March 8 Revolution.

Warrior on Horseback — A206

1977, Apr. 10 Litho. *Perf. 12½*
770 A206 100p multi .30 .25

31st anniversary of the evacuation of British and French troops from Syria.

APU Emblem — A207

1977, Apr. 12 Litho. *Perf. 12x12½*
771 A207 35p silver & multi .30 .25

Arab Postal Union, 25th anniversary.

Tools and Factories A208

1977, May 1 *Perf. 12½x12*
772 A208 60p multi .35 .25

Labor Day.

ICAO Emblem, Plane and Globe A209

1977, May 11
773 A209 100p multi .50 .25

Intl. Civil Aviation Org., 30th anniv.

Pioneers — A210

1977, Aug. 15 Litho. *Perf. 12x12½*
774 A210 35p multi .30 .25

Al Baath Pioneer Organization.

Citrus Fruit — A211

1977, Aug. 1
775 A211 10p Lemon .30 .25
776 A211 20p Lime .30 .25
777 A211 25p Grapefruit .30 .25
778 A211 35p Oranges .30 .25
779 A211 60p Tangerines .40 .25
a. Strip of 5, #775-779 1.60 1.60

Agricultural and Industrial Fair, Aleppo.

Flowers A212

1977, Aug. 6 Litho. *Perf. 12½x12*

780 A212 10p Mallow .30 .25
781 A212 20p Coxcomb .30 .25
782 A212 25p Morning glories .30 .25
783 A212 35p Almond blossoms .30 .25
784 A212 60p Lilacs .30 .25
a. Strip of 5, #780-784 1.50 1.50

Intl. Flower Show, Damascus.

Coffeepot and Ornament A213

1977, Sept. 10 *Perf. 12x12½*

785 A213 25p blk, bl & red .30 .25
786 A213 60p blk, grn & brn .35 .25

24th Intl. Damascus Fair.

Blind Man, Globe and Eye — A214

1977, Nov. 17 Litho. *Perf. 12x12½*

787 A214 55p multi .30 .25
788 A214 70p multi .30 .25

World Blind Week.

Globe and Measures A215

1977, Nov. 5

789 A215 15p grn & multi .30 .25

World Standards Day, Oct. 14.

Microscope, Book, Harp, UNESCO Emblem — A216

1977, Nov. 5 *Perf. 12½x12*

790 A216 25p multi .30 .25

30th anniversary of UNESCO.

Archbishop Capucci, Map of Palestine, Bars — A217

1977, Nov. 17 *Perf. 12x12½*

791 A217 60p multi 2.00 .50

Palestinian Archbishop Hilarion Capucci, jailed by Israel in 1974.

Fight Cancer Shield, Crab and Surgeon — A218

1977, Nov. 17

792 A218 100p multi 1.00 .50

Fight Cancer Week.

Dome of the Rock, Jerusalem — A219

1977, Dec. 6 *Perf. 12*

793 A219 5p multi .50 .25
794 A219 10p multi .75 .25

Palestinian fighters and their families.

Mural — A220

Designs: 10p, 15p, Murals from Dura-Europos, in National Museum, Damascus.

1978, Jan. 22 Litho. *Perf. 12x11½*

795 A220 5p gray grn .30 .25
796 A220 10p vio bl .30 .25
797 A220 15p brown, horiz. .30 .25
Nos. 795-797 (3) .90 .75

Types of 1976

Designs: 40p, Man's head inkstand. 55p, Nike. 70p, 80p, Hera. 200p, Arab-Islamic astrolabe. 300p, Palmyrene (Herod) coin.

1978 Litho. *Perf. 12x11½, 11½x12*

798 A191 40p pale org .30 .25
799 A191 55p brt rose .30 .25
800 A191 70p vermilion .35 .25
801 A191 80p green .35 .25
802 A191 200p lt ultra 1.00 .30
803 A190 300p rose lil 1.50 .50
Nos. 798-803 (6) 3.80 1.80

Pres. Hafez al Assad — A221

1978 *Perf. 12x11½*

805 A221 50p multi .40 .25

Anniversary of "Correction Movement."

Blood Circulation, WHO Emblem — A222

1978, Apr. 7 Litho. *Perf. 12x11½*

806 A222 100p multi .50 .25

World Health Day, fight against hypertension.

Factory — A223

1978, Apr. 17

807 A223 35p multi .30 .25

32nd anniversary of the evacuation of British and French troops from Syria.

Rosette — A224

1978, Apr. 21

808 A224 25p blk & grn .30 .25

14th Arab Engineering Conference, Damascus, Apr. 21-26.

Map of Arab Countries, Police, Flag and Eye — A225

1978, May

809 A225 35p multi .30 .25

6th Conf. of Arab Police Commanders.

European Goldfinch A226

Birds: 20p, Peregrine falcon. 25p, Rock dove. 35p, Eurasian hoopoe. 60p, Old World quail.

1978 *Perf. 11½x12*

810 A226 10p multi .40 .25
811 A226 20p multi .40 .25
812 A226 25p multi .40 .25
813 A226 35p multi .50 .25
814 A226 60p multi .60 .25
a. Strip of 5, #810-814 2.40 2.40

Trout A227

Designs: Various fish.

1978, July Litho. *Perf. 11½x12*

815 A227 10p multi .40 .25
816 A227 20p multi .40 .25
817 A227 25p multi .40 .25
818 A227 35p multi .50 .25
819 A227 60p multi .55 .25
a. Strip of 5, #815-819 2.25 2.25

Pres. Assad Type of Air Post, 1978

Miniature Sheet

1978, Sept. Litho. *Imperf.*

820 AP161 100p gold & multi 1.00 1.00

Reelection of President Assad. Size of stamp: 58x80mm.

Flowering Cactus A228

Designs: Flowering cacti.

1978 Litho. *Perf. 12½*

821 A228 25p multi .50 .25
822 A228 30p multi .50 .25
823 A228 35p multi .50 .25
824 A228 50p multi .50 .25
825 A228 60p multi .50 .25
a. Strip of 5, #821-825 2.50 2.50

International Flower Show, Damascus.

Fair Emblem — A229

1978 Litho. *Perf. 12x12½*

826 A229 25p sil & multi .30 .25
827 A229 35p sil & multi .30 .25

Miniature Sheet

Imperf

828 A229 100p sil & multi 1.00 1.00

25th Intl. Damascus Fair. No. 828 shows different ornament, size of stamp: 40x46mm.

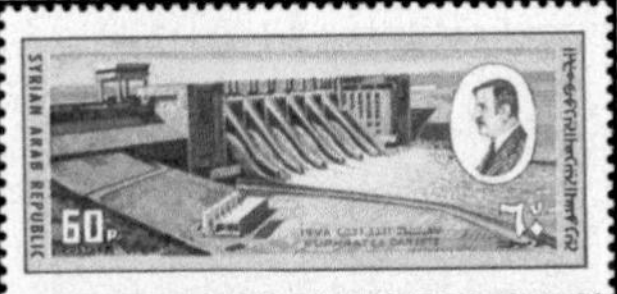

Euphrates Dam and Pres. Assad — A230

1978, Dec. Litho. ***Perf. 12½x12***
829 A230 60p multi .50 .25

Inauguration of Euphrates Dam.

Pres. Hafez al Assad — A231

1978, Nov. 16 Litho. ***Perf. 12x12½***
830 A231 60p multi .40 .25

Nov. 16 Movement.

Racial Equality Emblem A232

1978, Mar. Litho. ***Perf. 12½***
831 A232 35p multi .40 .25

International Year to Combat Racism.

Averroes — A233

1979, Mar.
832 A233 100p multi .75 .25

Averroes (1126-1198), Spanish-Arabian philosopher and physician.

Human Rights Flame and Globe — A234

1978, Dec. ***Perf. 12x12½***
833 A234 60p multi .50 .25

30th anniversary of Universal Declaration of Human Rights (in 1978).

Symbolic Design — A235

1979, Mar.
834 A235 100p multi .50 .25

16th anniversary of March 8 Revolution.

Princess, 2nd Century Shield — A236

Designs: 20p, Helmet of Homs. 35p, Ishtar.

1979 Litho. ***Perf. 11½***
836 A236 20p green .30 .25
837 A236 25p rose car .30 .25
838 A236 35p sepia .30 .25
Nos. 836-838 (3) .90 .75

Flame Emblem — A237

1979 Litho. ***Perf. 12x11½***
846 A237 35p multi .30 .25

Intl. Middle East Dental Congress.

Flame Emblem — A238

1979
847 A238 35p multi .30 .25

33rd anniversary of evacuation.

Ibn Assaker, 900th Anniv. A239

1979 ***Perf. 11½x12***
848 A239 75p multi .30 .25

Telephone Lineman — A240

1979, May 1 Litho. ***Perf. 12x11½***
849 A240 50p multi .30 .25
850 A240 75p multi .30 .25

May Day.

Wright Brothers' Plane A241

Designs: 75p, Bleriot's plane crossing English Channel. 100p, Spirit of St. Louis.

1979 ***Perf. 11½x12***
851 A241 50p multi .30 .25
852 A241 75p multi .30 .25
853 A241 100p multi .50 .25
Nos. 851-853 (3) 1.10 .75

75th anniversary of 1st powered flight.

Girl with IYC Emblem — A242

Design: 15p, Boy, globe, IYC emblem.

1979 ***Perf. 12x11½***
854 A242 10p multi .30 .25
855 A242 15p multi .35 .25

International Year of the Child.

Power Plant — A243

1979 ***Perf. 11x11½***
856 A243 5p blue .30 .25
857 A243 10p lil rose .30 .25
858 A243 15p gray grn .30 .25
Nos. 856-858 (3) .90 .75

Flags and Pavilion — A244

Design: 75p, Lamppost and flags.

1979 Photo. ***Perf. 12x11½***
859 A244 60p multi .30 .25
860 A244 75p multi .35 .25

26th International Damascus Fair.

Correction Movement, 9th Anniversary — A245

1979 Photo. ***Perf. 11½x12***
861 A245 100p multi .50 .25

Games Emblem, Running A246

1979, Nov.
862 A246 25p shown .30 .25
863 A246 35p Diving .30 .25
864 A246 50p Soccer .30 .25
Nos. 862-864 (3) .90 .75

8th Mediterranean Games, Split, Yugoslavia, Sept. 15-29.

Butterfly — A247

Designs: Various butterflies.

1979, Dec. Litho. ***Perf. 12x11½***
865 A247 20p multi .50 .25
866 A247 25p multi .50 .25
867 A247 30p multi .50 .25
868 A247 35p multi .50 .25
869 A247 50p multi .50 .25
Nos. 865-869 (5) 2.50 1.25

Damascus Intl. Flower Show A248

Design: Roses.

1980, Jan. 9 Litho. ***Perf. 12½***
870 A248 5p multi .50 .25
871 A248 10p multi .50 .25
872 A248 15p multi .50 .25
873 A248 50p multi .50 .25
874 A248 75p multi .50 .25
875 A248 100p multi .80 .25
Nos. 870-875 (6) 3.30 1.50

March 8 Revolution, 17th Anniv. — A249

1980, Mar. 25 Litho. ***Perf. 12x11½***
876 A249 40p multi .30 .25

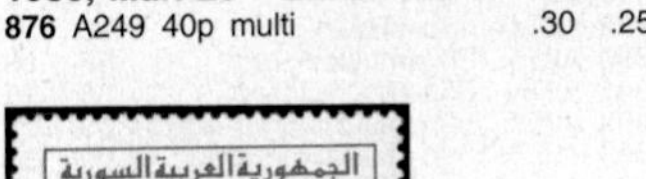

Astrolabe A250

1980, May 2 ***Perf. 12½***

877	A250	50p violet	.30	.25
878	A250	100p sepia	.50	.25
879	A250	1000p gray grn	4.00	1.25
		Nos. 877-879 (3)	4.80	1.75

2nd International History of Arabic Sciences Symposium, Apr. 5.

Lit Cigarette, Skull — A251

1980, June 25 Photo. ***Perf. 12x11½***

880	A251	60p Smoker	.60	.25
881	A251	100p shown	1.00	.30

World Health Day; anti-smoking campaign.

Evacuation, 34th Anniversary A252

1980, June 25 **Litho.**

882	A252	40p multi	.30	.25
883	A252	60p multi	.35	.25

Moscow '80 Emblem and Wrestling A253

1980, July Litho. ***Perf. 11½x12***

884	A253	15p shown	.30	.25
885	A253	25p Fencing	.30	.25
886	A253	35p Weight lifting	.35	.25
887	A253	50p Judo	.50	.25
888	A253	75p Boxing	1.00	.25
a.		Strip of 5, #884-888	2.50	2.50

Souvenir Sheet

Imperf

888B	A253	300p Discus, running	5.00	5.00

22nd Summer Olympic Games, Moscow, July 19-Aug. 3.

Sinbad the Sailor A254

25p, Scheherezade and Shahrayar. 35p, Ali Baba and the Forty Thieves. 50p, Hassan the Clever. 100p, Aladdin's Lamp.

1980 Litho. ***Perf. 11½x12***

889	A254	15p shown	.30	.25
890	A254	25p multicolored	.30	.25
891	A254	35p multicolored	.35	.25
892	A254	50p multicolored	.50	.25
893	A254	100p multicolored	1.00	.30
a.		Strip of 5, #889-893	2.50	2.50

Popular stories.

Savings Certificates — A255

1980

894	A255	25p multicolored	.30	.25

Hegira, 1500th Anniv. — A256

1980 ***Perf. 12½x12***

895	A256	35p multicolored	.35	.25

Intl. Flower Show, Damascus A257

1980 ***Perf. 12x11½***

896	A257	20p Daffodils	.50	.25
897	A257	30p Chrysanthemums	.50	.25
898	A257	40p Clematis	.55	.25
899	A257	60p Yellow roses	.60	.25
900	A257	100p Chrysanthemums, diff.	.75	.25
a.		Strip of 5, #896-900	3.00	3.00

May Day — A258

1980, May

901	A258	35p multicolored	.40	.25

Children's Day — A259

1980

902	A259	25p multicolored	.40	.25

November 16th Movement, 10th Anniv. — A260

1980 ***Perf. 11½x12***

903	A260	100p multicolored	1.00	.25

Steam-powered Passenger Wagon — A261

1980

904	A261	25p shown	.35	.25
905	A261	35p Benz, 1899	.40	.25
906	A261	40p Rolls-Royce, 1903	.60	.25
907	A261	50p Mercedes, 1906	.75	.25
908	A261	60p Austin, 1915	1.00	.30
a.		Strip of 5, #904-908	3.25	3.25

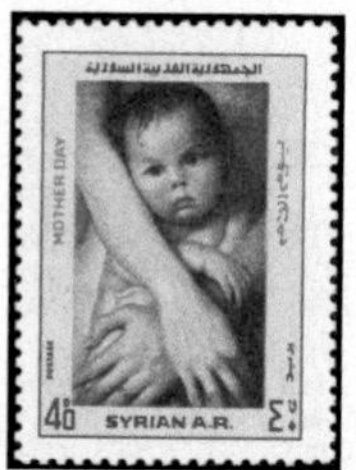

Mother's Day — A262

1980 ***Perf. 12x11½***

909	A262	40p shown	.50	.25
910	A262	100p Mother and child	1.00	.25

27th International Damascus Fair — A263

1981, Jan. 24 ***Perf. 11½x12***

911	A263	50p multi	.45	.25
912	A263	100p multi	.80	.25

Army Day — A264

1981, Jan. 24 ***Perf. 12½x12***

913	A264	50p multi	.45	.25

A265

1981, Mar. 8 Litho. ***Perf. 12x11½***

914	A265	50p multi	.35	.25

18th anniv. of March 8th revolution.

A266

1981, Apr. 17 Litho. ***Perf. 12x11½***

915	A266	50p multi	.35	.25

35th anniversary of evacuation.

World Conference on History of Arab and Islamic Civilization, Damascus — A267

1981, May 30 Photo. ***Perf. 12½x12***

916	A267	100p multi	.60	.25

Intl. Workers' Solidarity Day — A268

1981, May 30 Litho. ***Perf. 12x11½***

917	A268	100p multi	.60	.25

Housing and Population Census — A269

1981, June 1

918	A269	50p multi	.35	.25

Umayyad Window A270

Abdul Malik Gold Coin A270a

10p, figurine. 15p, Rakkla's cavalier, Abbcid ceramic. 160p, like 5p. 500p, Umar B. Abdul Aziz gold coin.

1981 ***Perf. 12x11½, 11½x12***

919	A270	5p crim rose	.25	.25
920	A270	10p brt grn	.25	.25
921	A270	15p dp rose lil	.25	.25
922	A270a	75p blue	.35	.25
923	A270	160p dk grn	.70	.35
924	A270a	500p dk brn	2.50	1.10
		Nos. 919-924 (6)	4.30	2.45

Olives
A270b

Harbor
A270c

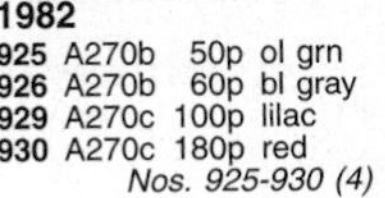
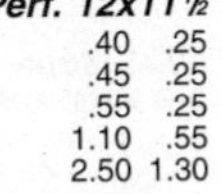

1982 *Perf. 12x11½*
925 A270b 50p ol grn .40 .25
926 A270b 60p bl gray .45 .25
929 A270c 100p lilac .55 .25
930 A270c 180p red 1.10 .55
Nos. 925-930 (4) 2.50 1.30

Saving Certificates Plan — A271

1981, June 22
931 A271 50p gldn brn & blk .35 .25

Avicenna (980-1037), Philosopher and Physician
A272

1981, Aug.
932 A272 100p multi .60 .25

Syria-P.L.O. Solidarity, Intl. Conference
A273

1981, June 22
933 A273 160p multi 3.50 .90

Grand Mosque, Damascus — A274

1981 *Perf. 12½*
934 A274 50p Glass lamp, 13th cent. .30 .25
935 A274 180p shown 1.40 .40
936 A274 180p Hunter 1.40 .40
Nos. 934-936 (3) 3.10 1.05

Youth Festival
A275

1981 *Perf. 12½*
937 A275 60p multi .40 .25

28th Intl. Damascus Fair — A276

1981 *Perf. 12x11½*
938 A276 50p Ornament .30 .25
939 A276 160p Emblem 1.00 .45

Intl. Palestinian Solidarity Day — A277

1981
940 A277 100p multi .75 .25

1300th Anniv. of Bulgaria
A278

1981 *Perf. 11½x12*
941 A278 380p multi 2.25 1.00

Intl. Children's Day
A279

1981
942 A279 180p multi 1.10 .45

World Food Day, Oct. 16
A280

1981
943 A280 180p multi 1.10 .45

9th Intl. Flower Show, Damascus
A281

Designs: Flowers.

1981 *Perf. 12x11½*
944 A281 25p multi .25 .25
945 A281 40p multi .40 .25
946 A281 50p multi .50 .30
947 A281 60p multi .75 .35
948 A281 100p multi 1.10 .50
a. Strip of 5, #944-948 3.00 2.00

Souvenir Sheet

Koran Competition — A282

1981 **Litho.** *Imperf.*
949 A282 500p multi 5.00 5.00

11th Anniv. of Correction Movement
A283

1981, Nov. *Perf. 12x11½*
950 A283 60p multi .45 .30

TB Bacillus Centenary
A284

1982 **Litho.** *Perf. 11½x12*
951 A284 180p multi 1.25 .65

Mothers' Day — A285

1982 *Perf. 11½*
952 A285 40p green .25 .25
953 A285 75p brown .50 .25

Mar. 8th Revolution, 19th Anniv. — A286

1982, Mar. *Perf. 12x11½*
954 A286 50p multi .35 .25

Intl. Year of the Disabled (1981) — A287

1982 *Perf. 12x11½*
955 A287 90p multi .75 .30

Pres. Hafez al Assad — A288

1982 *Perf. 11½*
956 A288 150p ultra .90 .50

36th Anniv. of Evacuation
A289

1982 *Perf. 12x11½*
957 A289 70p multi .50 .25

World Traffic Day — A290

1982
958 A290 180p multi 1.25 .65

Intl. Workers' Solidarity Day — A291

1982
959 A291 180p multi 1.25 .65

World Telecommunication Day, May 17 — A292

1982

960 A292 180p multi 1.25 .65

Soldier Holding Rifles — A293

1982 Photo. *Perf. 12x11½*

961 A293 50p multi .30 .25

Arab Postal Union, 30th Anniv. — A294

1982

962 A294 60p multi .45 .25

1982 World Cup — A295

Various soccer players. 300p, Ball.

1982, July *Perf. 12½*

963	A295 40p multi		.25	.25
964	A295 60p multi		.40	.25
965	A295 100p multi		.65	.40
	Nos. 963-965 (3)		1.30	.90

Size: 75x55mm

Imperf

966 A295 300p multi *10.00 10.00*

10th Intl. Flower Show, Damascus A297

1982 *Perf. 12x11½*

967 A297 50p Honeysuckle .45 .25
968 A297 60p Geraniums .60 .30

Scouting Year A298

1982, Nov. 4 *Perf. 11½x12*

969 A298 160p green 1.40 .75

Ladybug A299

1982 *Perf. 12x12½*

970	Strip of 5	.75	.40
a.	A299 5p Dragonfly	.25	.25
b.	A299 10p Stag Beetle	.25	.25
c.	A299 20p shown	.25	.25
d.	A299 40p Grasshopper	.25	.25
e.	A299 50p Honeybee	.30	.25

ITU Plenipotentiaries Conference, Nairobi, Sept — A300

1982 *Perf. 11½x12*

971 A300 50p Map .30 .25
972 A300 180p Dish antenna 1.40 .75

12th Anniv. of Correction Movement A301

1982, Nov.

973 A301 50p dk bl & sil .35 .25

A302

Factory — A302a

Walled Arch — A302b

Ruins — A302c

1982-83 Litho. *Perf. 11½*

974	A302	30p brown	.25	.25
975	A302a	50p grnish blk	.25	.25
976	A302b	70p green	.35	.25
977	A302c	200p red	1.00	.55
		Nos. 974-977 (4)	1.85	1.30

Issued: 50p, 11/16/83; others, 11/4/82.

Dove and Satellite — A303

1982 Litho. *Perf. 12x11½*

978 A303 50p multi .50 .30

2nd UN Conference on Peaceful Uses of Outer Space, Vienna, Aug. 9-21.

Intl. Palestinian Solidarity Day — A304

1982

979 A304 50p multi .90 .25

20th Anniv. of March 8th Revolution — A305

1983 *Perf. 12½x12*

980 A305 60p multi 1.00 .50

World Communications Year — A305a

1983

981 A305a 180p multi 1.25 .65

9th Anniv. of Liberation of Al-Kuneitra — A306

1983, June 26 Litho. *Perf. 11½*

982 A306 50p View 1.50 .50
983 A306 100p View, diff. 3.00 .65

Arab Pharmacists' Day, Apr. 2 — A307

1983, Apr. 2 *Perf. 11½x12*

984 A307 100p multi .75 .30

25th Anniv. of Intl. Maritime Org. — A308

1983, June *Perf. 12x11½*

985 A308 180p multi 1.40 .75

Namibia Day, Aug. 26 A309

1983, Aug. 26 *Perf. 11½x12*

986 A309 180p multi 1.40 .75

Eibla Sculpture, 3rd Cent. BC A310

1983

987 A310 380p ol & brn 2.50 1.40

World Standards Day — A311

50p, Factory, emblem. 100p, Measuring equipment.

1983, Oct. 14 Photo. *Perf. 11½*

988 A311 50p multicolored .40 .25
989 A311 100p multicolored .80 .40

11th Intl. Flower Show, Damascus A312

1983, Oct. 14 Litho. *Perf. 11½*

990 A312 50p multi .40 .25
991 A312 60p multi, diff. .50 .25

World Heritage Day — A313

1983, Oct. 14 Photo. *Perf. 11½*

992 A313 60p dk brn .50 .25

World Food Day A313a

1983, Oct. 16 Litho. ***Perf. 11½x12***
992A A313a 180p multi 1.50 .75

Waterwheels of Hama — A314

Perf. 11x11½, 11½x11

1982-84 Litho.

993	A314	5p sepia	.25	.25
994	A314	10p violet	.25	.25
995	A314	20p red	.25	.25
997	A314	50p blkish grn	.60	.30
		Nos. 993-997 (4)	1.35	1.05

Issued: 50p, 11/25/82; others, 1/15/84.
On No. 997 "50" is in outlined numbers.

Statue — A316

1983 ***Perf. 12***
1003 A316 225p brown 2.00 1.00

Intl. Symposium on History and Archaeology of Deir Ez-zor.

View of Aleppo — A317

1983 ***Perf. 12x12½***
1004 A317 245p multi 2.25 1.10

Intl. Symposium on Conservation of Old City of Aleppo, Sept. 26-30.

Mar. 8th Revolution, 21st Anniv. — A318

1984, Mar. 8 ***Perf. 12½x12***
1005 A318 60p Alassad Library .75 .35

Massacre at Sabra and Shatilla A319

1983 Litho. ***Perf. 11½x12***
1006 A319 225p Victims, mother & child 2.00 .50

Mothers' Day — A320

1984, Mar. 21 ***Perf. 12x11½***
1007 A320 245p Mother & child 2.50 1.25

12th Intl. Flower Show, Damascus A321

Various flowers.

1984, May 25

1008	A321	245p multi	2.50	1.25
1009	A321	285p multi	2.75	1.40

1984 Summer Olympics — A322

1984 Litho. ***Perf. 12x11½***

1010		Strip of 5	3.00	2.40
a.	A322	30p Swimming	.30	.25
b.	A322	50p Wrestling	.50	.25
c.	A322	60p Running	.60	.30
d.	A322	70p Boxing	.65	.35
e.	A322	90p Soccer	.90	.45

Souvenir Sheet

Imperf

1011 A322 200p Soccer, diff. 3.50 3.50

9th Regional Pioneers' Festival A323

1984 ***Perf. 11½x12***

1012	A323	50p Pioneers	.50	.25
1013	A323	60p Pioneers, diff.	.60	.30

Aleppo Agricultural & Industrial Fair — A324

1984, June 12 Litho. ***Perf. 12x12½***
1014 A324 150p Peppers, Aleppo Castle 1.25 .50

Supreme Council of Science, 25th Anniv. A325

1985, Feb. 23 ***Perf. 12½x12***
1015 A325 65p multi .40 .25

Aleppo University, 25th Anniv. A326

1985, Feb. 23
1016 A326 45p multi .25 .25

Syrian Arab Army, 39th Anniv. A327

1985, Feb. 23
1017 A327 65p brn & gldn brn .40 .25

Pres. Assad, Soldier Saluting, Troops A328

1984, Aug. 1 ***Perf. 11½x12***
1018 A328 60p multi .60 .30

4th General Revolutionary Youth Conference.

ITU Emblem, Satellite Dish, Telephone A329

1984, Oct. 2 ***Perf. 12½***
1019 A329 245p multi 1.75 .90

Intl. Telecommunications Day.

APU Emblem and Administration Building, Damascus — A330

1984, Oct. 9
1020 A330 60p multi .60 .30

Arab Postal Union Day.

Gearwheel, Arabesque Pattern — A331

Gold Necklace — A332

1984, Oct. 27 ***Perf. 12x12½, 12x11½***

1021	A331	45p multi	.45	.25
1022	A332	100p multi	1.00	.45

Intl. Fair, Damascus.

Intl. Civil Aviation Org., 40th Anniv. A333

1984, Oct. 27 ***Perf. 11½x12***

1023	A333	45p brt bl & lt bl	.25	.25
1024	A333	245p brt ultra, brt bl & lt bl	1.25	.60

14th Anniv. of 11-16-70 Movement A334

1984, Dec. 3 ***Perf. 12½x12***
1025 A334 65p red brn, blk & org .65 .35

Pres. Assad, Text on Scroll A335

1984, Nov. 29 ***Perf. 12½***
1026 A335 50p grn, brn org & sep .50 .25

Vow of Dedication taken by Youth of the Revolution.

Agricultural Exhibition — A336

1984, June 12 ***Perf. 12½x12***
1027 A336 65p multi .65 .35

Al-Kuneitra Memorial, Rose — A337

1984

1028 A337 70p multi 1.25 .35

Roman Arch and Colonnades, Palmyra — A338

1984, Dec. 3

1029 A338 100p multi 1.00 .50

Intl. Tourism Day.

Woodland Conservation — A339

1984

1030 A339 45p multi .25 .25

March 8 Revolution, 22nd Anniv. — A340

1985, Apr. 27

1031 A340 60p multi .40 .25

UPU Emblem, Postal Headquarters, Damascus A341

1985, Apr. 27

1032 A341 285p multi 3.00 1.50

World Post Day.

APU Building, Damascus — A342

1985, Apr. 27 ***Perf. 12½***

1033 A342 245p multi 2.50 1.25

Arab Parliamentary Union, 10th Anniv.

Natl. Flag, Map of Arab Countries A343

1985 ***Perf. 12½x12***

1034 A343 50p multi .50 .25

Arab League.

Re-election of President Assad A344

1985, Mar. 12 ***Perf. 12½***

1035 A344 200p multi 1.25 .70

1036 A344 300p multi 2.00 1.00

1037 A344 500p multi 3.25 1.75

a. Souvenir sheet of 3, #1035-1037, imperf. 7.00 5.50

Nos. 1035-1037 (3) 6.50 3.45

Arab Postal Union, 12th Congress, Damascus A345

1985, Aug. 12 ***Perf. 12x12½***

1038 A345 60p multi .60 .30

Labor Day — A346

1985, Aug. 12 ***Perf. 12½***

1039 A346 60p Order of Labor .60 .30

32nd Intl. Fair, Damascus A347

1986, Feb. 1 **Litho.** ***Perf. 12½***

1040 A347 60p multi .50 .25

2nd Scientific Symposium — A348

1985, Nov. 16 ***Perf. 12½***

1041 A348 60p Locomotives .60 .30

UN Child Survival Campaign A349

1985, Nov. 16 ***Perf. 12½x12***

1042 A349 60p Malnourished child .50 .25

UN, 40th Anniv. — A350

1985, Nov. 16 ***Perf. 12x12½***

1043 A350 245p multi 2.25 1.10

November 16th Movement, 15th Anniv. — A351

Design: Pres. Assad, highway.

1985, Nov. 16 ***Perf. 12½***

1044 A351 60p multi .50 .25

Abdul Rahman Dakhei in Andalusia, 1200th Anniv. A352

1986, Feb. 1 ***Perf. 12½x12***

1045 A352 60p beige & brn .60 .30

Tulips — A353

1986, Feb. 1 ***Perf. 12½***

1046 A353 30p multi .30 .25

1047 A353 60p multi, diff. .60 .30

Intl. Flower Show, Damascus.

Dental Congress, Damascus — A354

1986 ***Perf. 12½x12***

1048 A354 110p yel, grysh grn & bl 1.10 .55

World Traffic Day — A355

1986 ***Perf. 12x12½***

1049 A355 330p multi 3.00 1.50

Syrian Investment Certificates, 15th Anniv. — A357

1986 **Litho.** ***Perf. 12x11½***

1055 A357 100p multi 1.00 .50

Liberation of Al-Quneitra, 12th Anniv. — A358

1986 **Litho.** ***Perf. 11½x12***

1056 A358 110p Government Building .75 .40

Day of Internal Security Forces — A359

1986 ***Perf. 12x11½***

1057 A359 110p multi .75 .40

Labor Day — A360

1986, Aug. 12

1058 A360 330p multi 1.25 .60

1986 World Cup Soccer Championships, Mexico — A361

500p, Hemispheres, ball.

1986, July 7

1059 A361 330p multi	3.25	1.75
1060 A361 370p multi	3.50	1.90

Booklet Stamp
Size: 105x80mm
Imperf

1061 A361 500p multi	5.00	2.50
Nos. 1059-1061 (3)	11.75	6.15

Pres. Hafez al Assad — A362

1986-90 Litho. *Perf. 12x11½*

1068 A362	10p rose	.25	.25
1069 A362	30p dl ultra	.25	.25
1070 A362	50p claret	.40	.25
1071 A362	100p brt lt bl	.65	.30
1072 A362	150p brn vio	1.40	.65
1073 A362	175p violet	1.60	.80
1074 A362	200p pale red brn	1.40	.65
1075 A362	300p brt rose lil	2.00	1.00
1076 A362	500p orange	3.25	1.60
1077 A362	550p pink	5.00	2.50
1078 A362	600p dull grn	5.25	2.75
1079 A362	1000p brt pink	6.50	3.25
1080 A362	2000p pale grn	13.00	6.50
Nos. 1068-1080 (13)		40.95	20.75

Issued: 150p, 175p, 550p, 600p, 1988; 50p, 9/30/90.

Intl. Day for Solidarity with the Palestinian People — A363

1986, Aug. 7 Litho.

1081 A363 110p multi 1.10 .55

Mothers' Day — A364

1986, Aug. 7

1082 A364 100p multi 1.00 .50

March 8 Revolution, 23rd Anniv. — A365

1986, Aug. 7 *Perf. 11½x12*

1083 A365 110p multi 1.10 .55

Arab Post Day A366

1986, Aug. 7

1084 A366 110p multi 1.10 .55

A367

33rd Intl. Damascus Fair A368

1986, Dec. 9 Litho. *Perf. 11½x12*

1085 A367 110p multi	.90	.45
1086 A368 330p multi	2.50	.60

14th Intl. Flower Show, Damascus — A369

Various flowers.

1986, Oct. 11 *Perf. 12½*

1087 Strip of 5	6.50	5.00
a. A369 10p multi	.25	.25
b. A369 50p multi	.50	.25
c. A369 100p multi	1.00	.50
d. A369 110p multi	1.10	.60
e. A369 330p multi	3.50	1.75

Syria-Soviet Joint Space Project — A370

1986, Nov. 16 Litho. *Perf. 12½*

1088 A370 330p multi 3.50 1.75

World Children's Day — A371

No. 1090, Youth art exhibition, horiz.

1986 *Perf. 12x12½, 12½x12*

1089 A371 330p shown	1.75	.90
1090 A371 330p multi	1.75	.90

World Post Day A372

1986, Jan. 28 *Perf. 12½x12*

1091 A372 330p multi 1.75 .90

Intl. Tourism Day A373

Women wearing folk costumes, landmarks.

1986

1092 A373 330p multi	1.75	.90
1093 A373 370p multi	2.00	1.00

Pres. Assad, Tishreen Palace — A374

1986, Nov. 16 Litho. *Perf. 12½*

1094 A374 110p multi 1.25 .60

Nov. 16 Corrective Movement.

March 8th Revolution, 24th Anniv. — A375

1987, Mar. 6

1095 A375 100p multi .60 .30

Intl. Peace Year — A376

1987, Mar. 8 *Perf. 12x11½*

1096 A376 370p multi 2.25 1.25

Arab Baath Socialist Party, 40th Anniv. A377

1987, Apr. 7 Litho. *Perf. 12½*

1097 A377 100p multi .60 .30

Arab Post Day, 35th Anniv. A378

1987, May 1 *Perf. 11½x12*

1098 A378 110p multi .70 .35

Evacuation, Day, 41st Anniv. — A379

1987, Apr. 17 *Perf. 12½x12*

1099 A379 100p multi .60 .30

Labor Day — A380

1987, May 1 *Perf. 12x11½*

1100 A380 330p multi 2.00 1.00

Hitteen's Battle, 800th Anniv. — A381

1987, June 25 Litho. *Perf. 12½*

1101 A381 110p multi 1.00 .45

Al-Kuneitra Monument A382

1987, June 25 *Perf. 12x11½*

1102 A382 100p multi .65 .30

Child Vaccination Campaign — A383

1987, June 25 *Perf. 11½x12*

1103 A383 100p multi	.50	.30
1104 A383 330p multi	2.00	1.10

A384

A385

Syrian-Soviet Joint Space Flight, July 22-30 — A386

Designs: No. 1105, Launch, July 22. No. 1106, Docking at space station, July 24. No. 1107, Landing, July 30, vert. No. 1108a, Lift-off. No. 1108b, Parachute landing. No. 1108c, Docked at space station. No. 1108d, Cosmonauts.

Perf. 12½, 11½x12, 12x11½

1987 **Litho.**

1105 A384 330p multi 2.00 1.00
1106 A385 330p multi 2.00 1.00
1107 A385 330p multi 2.00 1.00
Nos. 1105-1107 (3) 6.00 3.00

Souvenir Sheet

Imperf

1108 A386 Sheet of 4 10.00 10.00
a.-d. 300p, any single 2.25 2.25

6th Conference of Arab Ministers of Culture A387

1987, Apr. 21 **Litho.** ***Perf. 12½***

1109 A387 330p dull blue grn & blk 3.00 1.50

President Assad Conversing with Syrian Cosmonaut — A388

1987, Aug. 12

1110 A388 500p multi 3.50 1.75

10th Mediterranean Games, Latakia — A389

Designs: 100p, Gymnastic rings, weight lifting, vert. 330p, Phoenician sailing ship. 370p, Flags spelling "SYRIA." No. 1115a, Emblem, gymnastics. No. 1115b, Emblem, weight lifting. No. 1115c, Emblem, tennis. No. 1115d, Emblem, soccer.

Perf. 12x11½, 11½x12

1987, Sept. 10

1111 A389 100p brt rose lil & blk .70 .35
1112 A389 110p shown .75 .40

Size: 58x28mm

Perf. 12½

1113 A389 330p multi 2.25 1.10
1114 A389 370p multi 2.50 1.25
Nos. 1111-1114 (4) 6.20 3.10

Souvenir Sheet

Imperf

1115 Sheet of 4 7.75 7.75
a.-d. A389 300p any single 1.90 1.90

34th Intl. Damascus Fair — A390

1987 ***Perf. 12x11½***

1116 A390 330p multi 2.00 1.00

Intl. Flower Show, Damascus A391

1987, Oct. 20 ***Perf. 11½x12***

1117 A391 330p Poppies 1.90 1.00
1118 A391 370p Gentian 2.00 1.00

Arbor Day — A392

1987, Oct. 20 ***Perf. 12x11½***

1119 A392 330p multi 2.00 1.00

Army Day — A393

1987, Oct. 20 **Litho.** ***Perf. 12x11½***

1120 A393 100p multi .60 .30

Intl. Palestine Day — A394

1987, Nov. 16

1121 A394 500p multi 3.50 1.75

Corrective Movement, 17th Anniv. — A395

Design: Assad waving to crowd.

1987, Nov. 16 ***Perf. 12½***

1122 A395 150p multi 1.00 .50

World Post Day — A396

1988, Mar. 8 **Litho.** ***Perf. 12½x12***

1123 A396 500p multi 3.00 1.50

Intl. Tourism Day A397

Women wearing folk costumes and: No. 1124, Palmyra Ruins. No. 1125, Reconstructed Roman amphitheater, Busra.

1988, Feb. 25 **Litho.** ***Perf. 11½x12***

1124 A397 500p multi 3.00 1.50
1125 A397 500p multi 3.00 1.50

See Nos. 1147-1148, 1178-1179.

Intl. Children's Day — A398

1988, Feb. 27 ***Perf. 12½***

1126 A398 500p multi 3.00 1.50

March 8th Revolution, 25th Anniv. — A399

1988, Mar. 15 **Litho.** ***Perf. 12x11½***

1127 A399 150p multi 1.00 .50

Size: 110x81mm

Imperf

1128 A399 500p multi, diff. 4.75 4.75

No. 1128 pictures vignette like 150p without denomination, in diff. colors, and Arab Revolt flag, text, outline map; denomination at LR in sheet.

Mothers' Day — A400

1988, Apr. 12 **Litho.** ***Perf. 12x12½***

1129 A400 500p multi 3.00 1.50

Arab Post Day A401

1988, Apr. 17 ***Perf. 12½x12***

1130 A401 150p multi 1.00 .50

1946 Evacuation A402

1988, Apr. 17 ***Perf. 12x12½***

1131 A402 150p multi 1.00 .50

Labor Day — A403

1988, May 1

1132 A403 550p multi 3.00 1.50

Intl. Flower Show, Damascus A404

1988, May 25 ***Perf. 12x11½***

1133 A404 550p Tiger Lily 3.25 1.60
1134 A404 600p Carnations 3.75 1.90

Arab Engineers' Union — A405

1988, May 25

1135 A405 150p multi 1.00 .50

A406

1988, Aug. 28 Litho. ***Perf. 12x11½***
1136 A406 600p blk, grn & olive 3.50 1.75

Intl. Children's Day.

A407

1988, Aug. 28 ***Perf. 12½***
1137 A407 550p multi 3.00 1.50

Restoration of San'a, Yemen Arab Republic.

Ebla Intl. Symposium on Archaeology of Idlib — A408

175p, Hieroglyphic tablet. 550p, Bas-relief (votive basin). 600p, Gold statue, 3000 B.C.

1988, Aug. 28
1138 A408 175p multicolored 1.00 .50
1139 A408 550p multicolored 3.00 1.50
1140 A408 600p multicolored 3.50 1.75
Nos. 1138-1140 (3) 7.50 3.75

1988 Summer Olympics, Seoul A409

550p, Cycling. 600p, Soccer. 1200p, Emblem, character trademark.

1988, Sept. 17 ***Perf. 11½x12***
1141 A409 550p multi 3.50 1.60
1142 A409 600p multi 3.75 1.75

Size: 81x61mm

Imperf

1143 A409 1200p multi 12.50 12.50
Nos. 1141-1143 (3) 19.75 15.85

35th Intl. Fair, Damascus A410

1988, Aug. 28 ***Perf. 12x11½***
1144 A410 600p multi 3.50 1.75

WHO, 40th Anniv. — A411

1988, Aug. 28 Litho. ***Perf. 12x11½***
1145 A411 600p multi 3.25 1.60

Arab Scouting Movement, 50th Anniv. — A412

1988, Sept. 17 ***Perf. 12½x12***
1146 A412 150p multi 1.50 .75

Tourism Type of 1988

Women wearing folk costumes and: 550p, Euphrates Bridge, Deir-ez-Zor. 600p, The Tetrapylon, Latakia.

1988, Oct. 18
1147 A397 550p multi 3.25 1.60
1148 A397 600p multi 3.50 1.75

World Post Day — A413

1988, Dec. 7 Litho. ***Perf. 12x12½***
1149 A413 600p multi 3.50 1.75

Arbor Day — A414

1988, Nov. 16
1150 A414 600p multi 3.50 1.75

Shelter for the Homeless — A415

150p, Arab Housing Day. 175p, Intl. Year of Shelter for the Homeless. 550p, World Housing Day.

1988-89 ***Perf. 12½x12***
1151 A415 150p multicolored .65 .35
1151A A415 175p multicolored 1.25 .60
1152 A415 550p multicolored 2.50 1.25
1153 A415 600p as No. 1151A 2.75 1.50
Nos. 1151-1153 (4) 7.15 3.70

The IYSH emblem is pictured on the 175p, 550p and 600p.

Issued: 175p, 2/6/89; others, 10/18/88.

Al-Assad University Hospital — A416

1988, Nov. 16 Litho. ***Perf. 12½***
1154 A416 150p multi .90 .45

Corrective Movement, 18th anniv.

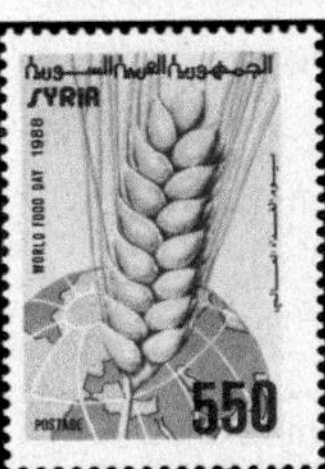

World Food Day — A417

1988, Oct. 18 ***Perf. 12x12½***
1155 A417 550p multi 2.75 1.40

Birds A418

1989, Mar. 21 Litho. ***Perf. 11½x12***
1156 A418 600p Goldfinch 1.50 .75
1157 A418 600p Turtledove 1.50 .75
1158 A418 600p Bee eater 1.50 .75
Nos. 1156-1158 (3) 4.50 2.25

Jawaharlal Nehru, 1st Prime Minister of Independent India — A419

1989, Mar. 8 ***Perf. 12½***
1159 A419 550p brn & chest 1.10 .55

Mothers' Day — A420

1989, Mar. 21
1160 A420 550p multi 1.10 .55

Teacher's Day A421

1989, Mar. 8 Litho. ***Perf. 11½x12***
1161 A421 175p multi .70 .35

5th General Congress of the Union of Women A422

1989, Mar. 8 ***Perf. 12½***
1162 A422 150p multi .30 .25

March 8th Revolution, 26th Anniv. — A423

1989, Mar. 8 ***Perf. 11½x12***
1163 A423 150p multi .30 .25

Arab Board for Medical Specializations, 10th Anniv. — A424

1989, Feb. 6 ***Perf. 12½***
1164 A424 175p multi .60 .30

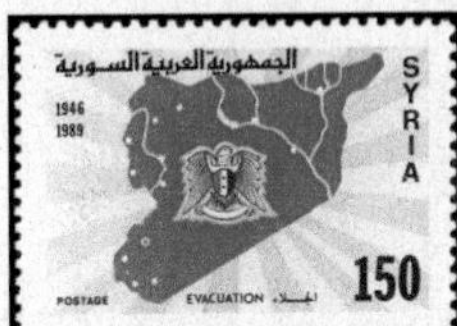

1946 Evacuation of British and French Troops — A425

1989, Apr. 17 Litho. ***Perf. 11½x12***
1165 A425 150p multi .40 .25

Intl. Flower Show, Damascus A426

1989, June 3 ***Perf. 12½***
1166 Strip of 5 5.00 4.00
a. A426 150p Snapdragon .30 .25
b. A426 150p Canaria .30 .25
c. A426 450p Compositae .90 .45
d. A426 850p Clematis sackmani 1.75 .85
e. A426 900p Gesneriaceae 1.75 .90

A427

1989, May 1 ***Perf. 12x11½***
1167 A427 850p blue grn & blk 1.75 .90

Labor Day.

A428

1989, June 6 Litho. ***Perf. 12x11½***
1168 A428 175p multi .50 .25

13th General Congress of the Arab Teachers' Union.

Arab Post Day — A429

1989, June 6
1169 A429 175p multi .50 .25

Liberation of Al-Kuneitra, 15th Anniv. — A430

1989, June 26
1170 A430 450p multi 1.25 .60

17th Congress of the Arab Advocates Union A431

1989, June 19 ***Perf. 11½x12***
1171 A431 175p multi .50 .25

World Post Day A432

1989, June 26
1172 A432 550p multi 1.50 .75

World Telecommunications Day — A433

1989, June 6
1173 A433 550p multi 1.50 .75

Interparliamentary Union, Cent. — A434

1989. July 12 ***Perf. 12½***
1174 A434 900p multi 2.50 1.25

Butterflies A435

1989, June 6
1175 A435 550p Small white 1.50 .75
1176 A435 550p Clouded yellow 1.50 .75
1177 A435 550p Painted Lady 1.50 .75
Nos. 1175-1177 (3) 4.50 2.25

Intl. Tourism Day Type of 1988

Women wearing folk costumes and: 550p, Jaabar Castle, Rakka. 600p, Temple of the Bell, Palmyra.

1989, Oct. 16 Litho. ***Perf. 11½x12***
1178 A397 550p multicolored 3.75 1.75
1179 A397 600p multicolored 4.00 2.00

36th Intl. Fair, Damascus A436

1989, Oct. 16 ***Perf. 12x11½***
1180 A436 450p multicolored 3.00 1.50

Fish A437

1989, Oct. 24 ***Perf. 11½x12***
1181 A437 550p Carp 3.75 1.75
1182 A437 600p Trout 4.00 2.00

2nd Anniv. of the Palestinian Uprising — A438

1989, Oct. 24 ***Perf. 12x11½***
1183 A438 550p Child's drawing 3.75 1.75

Corrective Movement, 19th Anniv. — A439

1989, Nov. 16 Litho. ***Perf. 12½x12***
1184 A439 150p multicolored 1.00 .50

World Children's Day — A440

1990, Feb. 13 Litho. ***Perf. 12x11½***
1185 A440 850p multicolored 1.00 .50

March 8th Revolution, 27th Anniv. — A441

1990
1186 A441 600p multicolored .70 .35

Revolutionary Youth Union A442

1990 ***Perf. 12½***
1187 A442 150p multicolored .25 .25

World Food Day A443

1990, Feb. 13 Litho. ***Perf. 11½x12***
1188 A443 850p multicolored 1.00 .50

Dated 1989.

Evacuation of British and French Troops, 1946 — A444

1990, Apr. 17 ***Perf. 12x11½***
1189 A444 175p multicolored .25 .25

Mother's Day — A445

1990, Apr. 17 ***Perf. 12½***
1190 A445 550p multicolored .65 .30

Labor Day — A446

1990, May 1 Litho. ***Perf. 12x12½***
1191 A446 550p multicolored .75 .35

World Cup Soccer Championships, Italy — A447

550p, Denomination at right. 600p, Map, soccer ball, vert. 1300p, Stadium.

Perf. 11½x12, 12x11½

1990, June 8 **Litho.**
1192 A447 550p shown .40 .25
1193 A447 550p multi .40 .25
1194 A447 600p multi .45 .25
Nos. 1192-1194 (3) 1.25 .75

Miniature Sheet

Imperf

1195 A447 1300p multi 3.50 1.75

Intl. Flower Show, Damascus A448

1990, May 27 ***Perf. 12x11½***
1196 A448 600p Lily 1.10 .50
1197 A448 600p Pastelkleurig 1.10 .50
1198 A448 600p Marigold 1.10 .50
1199 A448 600p Viburnum opulus 1.10 .50
1200 A448 600p Swan river daisy 1.10 .50
Nos. 1196-1200 (5) 5.50 2.50

World Health Day — A449

1990, May 1 Litho. ***Perf. 12½***
1201 A449 600p multicolored 2.50 1.25

Liberation of Al-Kuneitra, 16th Anniv. — A450

1990, June 26 ***Perf. 12x11½***
1202 A450 550p multicolored 2.50 1.25

Intl. Literacy Year — A451

1990, June 26
1203 A451 550p multicolored 2.25 1.10

UN Conference on Least Developed Countries — A452

1990, July 10 ***Perf. 11½x12***
1204 A452 600p multicolored 2.40 1.25

37th Damascus Intl. Fair — A453

1990, Aug. 28 ***Perf. 12x11½***
1205 A453 550p multicolored 2.25 1.10

World Meteorology Day — A454

1990, Aug. 28 ***Perf. 11½x12***
1206 A454 450p multicolored 1.90 .95

Arbor Day — A455

1990, Oct. 30 ***Perf. 12x11½***
1207 A455 550p multicolored 2.25 1.10

World Food Day — A456

1990, Oct. 30 ***Perf. 12½***
1208 A456 850p multicolored 3.25 1.75

Al Maqdisi, Cartographer A457

1990, Nov. 6 ***Perf. 12x11½***
1209 A457 550p multicolored 2.25 1.10

A458

A459

Pres. Hafez al Assad A460

1990, Nov. 16 Litho. ***Perf. 11½***

1210	A458	50p	claret	.25	.25
1211	A458	70p	gray	.25	.25
1212	A458	100p	blue	.35	.25
1213	A458	150p	brown	.60	.30

Perf. 12x11½

1214	A459	175p	multicolored	.70	.35
1215	A459	300p	multicolored	1.25	.55
1216	A459	550p	multicolored	2.25	1.10
1217	A459	600p	multicolored	2.40	1.25

Perf. 11½x12

1219	A460	1000p	multicolored	4.00	2.00
1220	A460	1500p	multicolored	6.00	3.00
1222	A460	2000p	multicolored	8.00	4.00
1224	A460	2500p	multicolored	10.00	5.00
	Nos. 1210-1224 (12)			36.05	18.30

1992, May 19 Litho. ***Perf. 11½***
Without Date at Right

1225	A458	150p	brown	.60	.30
1225A	A458	300p	violet	1.25	.60
1225B	A458	350p	gray	1.40	.70
1225C	A458	400p	red	1.60	.80
	Nos. 1225-1225C (4)			4.85	2.40

Souvenir Sheet

Corrective Movement, 20th Anniv. — A461

a, Pres. Assad with children. b, Assad addressing crowd. c, Assad, memorial. d, Assad, dam.

1990, Nov. 16 ***Imperf.***
1227 A461 550p Sheet of 4, #a.-d. 9.00 9.00

UN Development Program, 40th Anniv. — A462

1990, Dec. 11 ***Perf. 11½x12***
1228 A462 550p multicolored 2.25 1.10

Arab Civil Aviation Day A463

1990, Dec. 11
1229 A463 175p multicolored 1.00 .50

World Post Day — A464

1990, Dec. 11 ***Perf. 12x11½***
1230 A464 550p multicolored 2.25 1.10

Intl. Children's Day — A465

1990, Dec. 11
1231 A465 550p multicolored 2.25 1.10

Arab-Spanish Cultural Symposium A466

1990, Dec. 24
1232 A466 550p multicolored 2.25 1.10

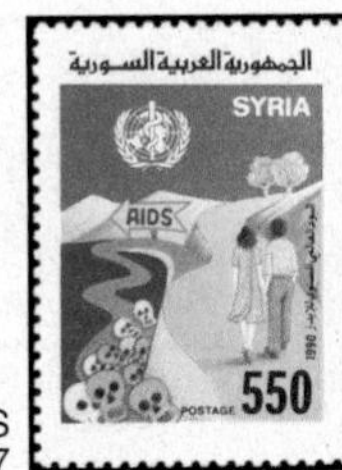
World AIDS Day — A467

1990, Dec. 24
1233 A467 550p multicolored 2.25 1.10

March 8th Revolution, 28th Anniv. — A468

1991, Mar. 8 Litho. ***Perf. 11½x12***
1234 A468 150p multicolored .60 .30

Butterflies A469

No. 1235, Small tortoiseshell. No. 1236, Changeful great mars. No. 1237, Papillion machaon.

1991, Mar. 17 ***Perf. 12½***

1235	A469	550p	multicolored	2.25	1.10
1236	A469	550p	multicolored	2.25	1.10
1237	A469	550p	multicolored	2.25	1.10
	Nos. 1235-1237 (3)			6.75	3.30

Birds — A470

1991, Mar. 17 ***Perf. 12x11½***

1238	A470	600p	Golden oriole	2.40	1.25
1239	A470	600p	European roller	2.40	1.25
1240	A470	600p	House sparrow	2.40	1.25
	Nos. 1238-1240 (3)			7.20	3.75

Mother's Day — A471

1991, Mar. 21
1241 A471 550p multicolored 2.25 1.10

1946 Evacuation of British and French Troops — A472

1991, Apr. 17 ***Perf. 11½x12***
1242 A472 150p multicolored .60 .30

Labor Day A473

1991, May 1
1243 A473 550p multicolored 2.25 1.10

Intl. Flower Show, Damascus — A474

550p, Narcissus. 600p, Monarda didyma.

1991, July 8 ***Perf. 12x12½***
1244 A474 550p multi 2.25 1.10
1245 A474 600p multi 2.40 1.25

Liberation of Kuneitra, 17th Anniv. A475

1991, July 22 ***Perf. 11½x12***
1246 A475 550p multicolored 2.25 1.10

11th Mediterranean Games, Athens — A476

No. 1247, Running. No. 1248, Soccer. No. 1249, Equestrian. No. 1250, Dolphins playing water polo.

1991, July 22
1247 A476 550p multi 2.25 1.10
1248 A476 550p multi 2.25 1.10
1249 A476 600p multi 2.25 1.25

Size: 80x64mm

Imperf

1250 A476 1300p multi 5.25 5.25
Nos. 1247-1250 (4) 12.00 8.70

38th Damascus Intl. Fair — A477

1991, Aug. 28 ***Perf. 12x12½***
1251 A477 550p multicolored 2.25 1.10

Intl. Tourism Day A478

Designs: 450p, Woman at Khan Asaad Pasha El Azem. 550p, Woman at Castle of Arwad Island.

1991, Sept. 27 ***Perf. 11½x12***
1252 A478 450p multicolored 1.90 .95
1253 A478 550p multicolored 2.25 1.10

Housing Day — A479

1991, Oct. 7 ***Perf. 12x11½***
1254 A479 175p multicolored 1.00 .50

Intl. Children's Day — A480

1991, Oct. 16
1255 A480 600p multicolored 2.40 1.25

Physician Abu Bakr Al Razi (Rhazes), Patient A481

1991, Nov. 2 **Litho.** ***Perf. 12½x12***
1256 A481 550p multicolored 2.25 1.10

31st Science Week.

World Post Day A482

1991, Nov. 12
1257 A482 550p multicolored 2.25 1.10

World Food Day A483

1991, Nov. 12
1258 A483 550p multicolored 2.25 1.10

Tomb of Unknown Soldier, Damascus A484

1991, Nov. 16 ***Perf. 12½***
1259 A484 600p multicolored 2.40 1.25

Size: 65x80mm

Imperf

1260 A484 1000p multicolored 4.00 2.00

Corrective Movement, 21st Anniv. — A485

1991, Nov. 16 ***Imperf.***
1261 A485 2500p multicolored 10.00 5.00

Protect the Environment — A486

1991, Nov. 20 ***Perf. 12½x12***
1262 A486 175p multicolored .70 .35

World Telecommunications Fair — A487

1991, Nov. 20 ***Perf. 12x12½***
1263 A487 600p multicolored 2.40 1.25

March 8th Revolution, 29th Anniv. A488

1992, Mar. 8 **Litho.** ***Perf. 12½***
1264 A488 600p multicolored 2.40 1.25

Re-election of Pres. Assad — A489

1992, Mar. 12 **Litho.** ***Imperf.***
1265 A489 5000p shown 20.00 10.00

Size: 100x85mm

1266 A489 5000p inscription at right 20.00 10.00

Nos. 1265-1266 incorporate designs of Nos. 1036, C496 & C506.

Baath Party, 45th Anniv. A490

1992, Apr. 7 ***Perf. 12½x12***
1267 A490 850p multicolored 3.50 1.75

Labor Day — A491

1992, May 1 *Perf. 12x12½*
1268 A491 900p multicolored 3.50 1.75

Mother's Day — A492

1992, May 19
1269 A492 900p multicolored 3.50 1.75

Evacuation of British and French Troops, 46th Anniv. — A493

1992, May 19 *Perf. 12½x12*
1270 A493 900p multicolored 3.50 1.75

Traffic Safety Day — A494

1992, May 19 *Perf. 12x12½*
1271 A494 850p multicolored 3.50 1.75

Intl. Flower Show, Damascus A495

Designs: 300p, Linum mucronatum, horiz. 800p, Yucca filamentosa. 900p, Zinnia elegans.

Perf. 11½x12, 12x11½
1992, July 5 **Litho.**
1272 A495 300p multicolored 1.25 .65
1273 A495 800p blue & multi 3.25 1.60
1274 A495 900p multicolored 3.50 1.75
Nos. 1272-1274 (3) 8.00 4.00

1992 Summer Olympics, Barcelona A496

No. 1275: a, 150p, Team handball. b, 150p, Running. c, 450p, Swimming. d, 750p, Wrestling. 5000p, Incorporates designs of Nos. 1275a-1275d.

1992, July 25 Litho. *Perf. 12x11½*
1275 A496 Strip of 4, #a.-d. 6.00 5.00

Imperf

Size: 80x124mm

1276 A496 5000p multicolored 20.00 10.00

Anti-Smoking Campaign A497

1992, Aug. 28 *Perf. 12x12½*
1277 A497 750p multicolored 3.00 1.50

39th Intl. Damascus Fair — A498

1992, Aug. 28
1278 A498 900p multicolored 3.50 1.75

7th Arab Games, Damascus — A499

Designs: a, 750p, Soccer. b, 850p, Pommel horse. c, 900p, Pole vault.

1992, Sept. 4 *Perf. 12½*
1279 A499 Strip of 3, #a.-c. 10.00 5.00

World Post Day — A500

1992, Oct. 9 *Perf. 12x12½*
1280 A500 600p multicolored 2.40 1.25

World Children's Day — A501

1992, Nov. 7 *Perf. 12x11½*
1281 A501 850p multicolored 3.50 1.75

Sebtt El Mardini (826-912) A502

1992, Nov. 7 Litho. *Perf. 12x11½*
1282 A502 850p multicolored 3.50 1.75

1992 Special Olympics, Madrid A503

1992, Nov. 7 *Perf. 12½*
1283 A503 850p multicolored 3.50 1.75

Corrective Movement, 22nd Anniv. — A504

1992, Nov. 16 *Perf. 11½x12*
1284 A504 450p multicolored 1.75 .90

Arbor Day — A505

1992, Dec. 31 *Perf. 12x12½*
1285 A505 600p multicolored 2.40 1.25

2nd Intl. Conference of PACO — A506

Design: 1150p, Eye surrounded by scenes of day and night, rainbow.

1993, May 12 Litho. *Perf. 12*
1286 A506 1100p multicolored 1.00 .50

Size: 35½x24mm

Perf. 11½x12

1287 A506 1150p multicolored 1.10 .55

Syrian Ophthamological Society, 25th anniv. (No. 1287).

March 8th Revolution, 30th Anniv. — A507

1993, Mar. 8 Litho. *Perf. 11½x12*
1288 A507 1100p multicolored .80 .40

Butterflies A508

Designs: a, 1000p, Common blue. b, 1500p, Silver-washed fritillary. c, 2500p, Precis orithya.

1993, Mar. 13
1289 A508 Strip of 3, #a.-c. 4.75 4.75

Mother's Day — A509

1993, Apr. 17 *Perf. 12x11½*
1290 A509 1100p multicolored .80 .40

Evacuation of British and French Troops, 47th Anniv. — A510

1993, Apr. 17 *Perf. 11½x12*
1291 A510 1100p multicolored .80 .40

A511

1993, Apr. 17 Litho. *Perf. 11½x12*
1292 A511 2500p multicolored 1.75 .85

Agricultural Reform, 25th Anniv. — A512

1993, Apr. 20 Litho. *Perf. 11½x12*
1293 A512 1150p multicolored .90 .45

Labor Day — A513

1993, May 1 *Perf. 12x11½*
1294 A513 1100p multicolored .80 .40

Intl. Flower Show, Damascus — A514

a, 1000p, Alcea setosa. b, 1100p, Primulaceae. c, 1150p, Gesneriaceae.

1993, June 17 Litho. *Perf. 12x11½*
1295 A514 Strip of 3, #a.-c. 2.25 2.25

Tourism A515

1993, Sept. 27 *Perf. 11½x12*
1296 A515 1000p Woman, prism tomb 1.00 .50

World Post Day A516

1993, Oct. 9 *Perf. 12½x12*
1297 A516 1000p multicolored 1.00 .50

World Child Day A517

1993, Nov. 6 *Perf. 11½x12*
1298 A517 1150p multicolored 1.10 .55

Ibn El Bittar, Chemist — A518

1993, Nov. 6 *Perf. 12x11½*
1299 A518 1150p multicolored 1.10 .55

Corrective Movement, 23rd Anniv. — A519

1993, Nov. 16 Litho. *Imperf.*
1300 A519 2500p multicolored 2.50 2.50

Arabian Horses A520

1994, Jan. Litho. *Perf. 12½*
1301 A520 1000p shown .60 .30
1302 A520 1000p White horse .60 .30
1303 A520 1500p Tan horse .90 .45
1304 A520 1500p Black horse .90 .45
a. Strip of 4, #1301-1304 3.00 3.00

Arbor Day A521

1994, Jan. Litho. *Perf. 12½x12*
1305 A521 1100p multicolored 1.75 .85

40th Intl. Damascus Fair A522

1994, Jan.
1306 A522 1100p multicolored 1.75 .85

Basel Al Assad (1962-94) — A523

1994, Mar. 1 *Perf. 12x12½*
1307 A523 2500p multicolored 4.00 2.00

March 8th Revolution, 31st Anniv. — A524

a, Oranges. b, Mandarin oranges. c, Lemons.

1994, Mar. 8 *Perf. 12½x12*
1308 A524 1500p Strip of 3, #a.-c. 7.50 7.50

Evacuation of British and French Troops, 48th Anniv. — A525

1994, Apr. 17
1309 A525 1800p multicolored 2.75 1.40

Mother's Day A526

1994, May 1 Litho. *Perf. 12½x12*
1310 A526 1800p multicolored 2.75 1.40

Labor Day A527

1994, May 1
1311 A527 1700p multicolored 2.75 1.40

ILO, 75th Anniv. A528

1994, June 1
1312 A528 1700p multicolored 2.75 1.40

1994 World Cup Soccer Championships, U.S. — A529

Various soccer plays.

1994, June 17 *Perf. 12½*
1313 A529 1700p Pair, #a.-b. 5.75 2.75

Size: 80x80mm

Imperf

1314 A529 4000p multicolored 6.75 6.75

41st Intl. Fair, Damascus A530

1994, Aug. 3 Litho. *Perf. 12x12½*
1315 A530 1800p multicolored 1.60 .80

Intl. Flower Show, Damascus — A531

a, Daisies. b, Red flowers. c. Yellow flowers.

1994, Aug. 3 *Perf. 12x11½*
1316 A531 1800p Strip of 3, #a.-c. 4.50 4.50

Intl. Olympic Committee, Cent. — A532

1994, Aug. 3 *Perf. 11½x12*
1317 A532 1700p multicolored 1.50 .75

Butterflies — A533

a, Apollo (shown). b, Purple emperor, value at right. c, Birdwing, value at left.

1994, Aug. 9 Litho. ***Perf. 11½x12***
1318 A533 1700p Strip of 3, #a.-c. 8.25 8.25

4th Natl. Census A534

1994, Aug. 15
1319 A534 1000p multicolored 1.50 .75

Science Week A535

Design: £10, Al Kindi, philosopher.

1994, Nov. 5 ***Perf. 12½***
1320 A535 £10 multicolored 1.50 .75

Corrective Movement, 24th Anniv. — A536

1994, Nov. 16 ***Imperf.***
1321 A536 £25 multicolored 6.50 6.50

ICAO, 50th Anniv. — A537

1994, Dec. 7 Litho. ***Perf. 12½***
1322 A537 17p multicolored 1.50 .75

Martyr's Square A538

1994, Dec. 7 Litho. ***Perf. 11½x12***
1323 A538 £50 purple 7.25 3.75

See Nos. 1472-1474, 1518, 1538.

Intl. Children's Day — A539

1994, Dec. 19 ***Perf. 12x11½***
1324 A539 £10 multicolored 1.50 .75

World Post Day — A540

1994, Dec. 19
1325 A540 £10 multicolored 1.50 .75

Intl. Tourism Day — A541

1994, Dec. 19
1326 A541 £17 multicolored 2.50 1.25

March 8 Revolution, 32nd Anniv. — A542

1995, Mar. 8 Litho. ***Perf. 11½x12***
1327 A542 £18 multicolored 2.75 1.40

Arab League, 50th Anniv. A543

1995, Mar. 22 ***Perf. 12½***
1328 A543 £17 multicolored 2.50 1.25

World Water Day — A544

1995, Apr. 9 Litho. ***Perf. 12x12½***
1329 A544 £17 multicolored 1.25 .60

Mother's Day A545

1995, Apr. 9 Litho. ***Perf. 12½x12***
1330 A545 £17 multicolored 2.00 1.00

Arbor Day — A546

1995, Apr. 9 Litho. ***Perf. 12x12½***
1331 A546 1800p multicolored 1.50 .75

UN, 50th Anniv. — A547

1995, Aug. 13 Litho. ***Perf. 12x11½***
1332 A547 £18 multicolored 2.75 1.40

A548

1995, Aug. 21
1333 A548 £18 multicolored 2.75 1.40

4th World Conference on Women, Beijing.

Desert Festival, Tourism Day A549

1995, June 25 ***Perf. 12½x12***
1334 A549 £18 multicolored 1.25 .65

Labor Day — A550

1995, June 25 ***Perf. 12x12½***
1335 A550 £10 multicolored .75 .40

A551

1995, Apr. 30 Litho. ***Perf. 12x11½***
1336 A551 £17 multicolored 1.25 .60

Evacuation of British & French Troops, 49th anniv.

Intl. Year of the Family — A552

1995, Apr. 30 Litho. ***Perf. 12x11½***
1337 A552 £17 multicolored 1.40 .70

Arab Apiculture Union, 1st Anniv. — A553

1995, Apr. 30 Litho. ***Perf. 12x12½***
1338 A553 £17 multicolored 2.00 1.00

FAO, 50th Anniv. A554

1995, June 25 ***Perf. 12½x12***
1339 A554 £15 multicolored 1.75 .85

42nd Intl. Fair, Damascus A555

1995, Aug. 28 Litho. ***Perf. 11½x12***
1340 A555 £15 multicolored 1.50 .75

Int'l Flower Show, Damascus A556

No. 1341, Astilbe. No. 1342, Evening primrose. No. 1343, Blue carpet.

1995, July 30 Litho. ***Perf. 12½***
1341 A556 £10 multicolored .50 .25
1342 A556 £10 multicolored .50 .25
1343 A556 £10 multicolored .50 .25
a. Strip of 3, #1341-1343 1.50 1.50

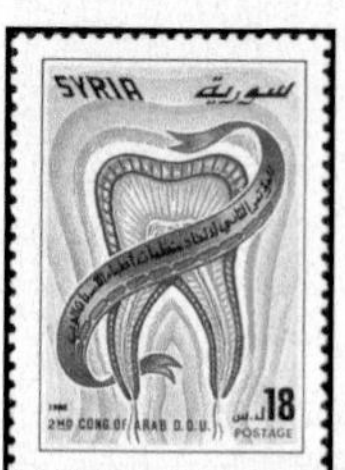

Second Congress of Arab Dentists' Assoc. — A557

1995, Sept. 16 Litho. ***Perf. 12x11½***
1344 A557 £18 multicolored 1.50 .75

Syrian Army, 50th Anniv. A558

1995, Oct. 2 Litho. ***Perf. 11½x12***
1345 A558 £18 multicolored 1.40 .70

World Post Day A559

1995, Oct. 2 Litho. ***Perf. 11½x12***
1346 A559 £15 multicolored 1.60 .85

World Children's Day — A560

1995, Oct. 2 ***Perf. 12x11½***
1347 A560 £18 multicolored 2.00 1.00

Ahmed ben Maged, Cartographer, 500th Death Anniv. — A561

1995, Nov. 4 Litho. ***Perf. 11½x12***
1348 A561 £18 multicolored 2.00 1.00

Corrective Movement, 25th Anniv. A562

Design: £50, like No. 1349 with #1044, 720, 1227b, 903.

1995, Nov. 11 Litho. ***Perf. 12½***
1349 A562 £10 multicolored 1.10 .55

Imperf
Size: 100x64mm
1350 A562 £50 multicolored 5.50 2.75

Songbirds — A563

Designs: a, Group on tree branch. b, One in snow, flower. c, One on fence rail.

1995, Dec. 5 Litho. ***Perf. 12½***
1351 A563 £18 Strip of 3, #a.-c. 7.25 7.25

Louis Pasteur (1822-95) A564

1995, Dec. 21 ***Perf. 12½x12***
1352 A564 £18 multicolored 2.00 1.00

March 8 Revolution, 33rd Anniv. — A565

Design: Hydro-electric plant.

1996, Mar. 8 Litho. ***Perf. 11½x12***
1353 A565 £25 multicolored 2.00 1.00

Evacuation Day, 50th Anniv. — A566

1996, Apr. 17 ***Perf. 12½***
1354 A566 £10 black & multi .85 .40
1355 A566 £25 bister & multi 2.00 1.00

Size: 57x46mm
Imperf
1356 A566 £25 bis, blk, & multi *5.25 2.75*

Liberation of Kuneitra A567

1996, June 26 Litho. ***Perf. 11½x12***
1357 A567 £10 multicolored .60 .30

1996 Summer Olympic Games, Atlanta A568

1996, July 19 ***Perf. 11½x12***
1358 A568 £17 Wrestling 1.10 .55
1359 A568 £17 Swimming 1.10 .55
1360 A568 £17 Running 1.10 .55
a. Strip of 3, #1358-1360 3.25 3.25

Size: 55x41mm
Imperf
1361 A568 £25 Soccer 1.60 .80
Nos. 1358-1361 (4) 4.90 2.45

Intl. Flower Show, Damascus A569

Cactus: No. 1362, Notocactus graessnerii. No. 1363, Mammilaria erythosperma.

1996, July 1 Litho. ***Perf. 12½***
1362 A569 £18 multicolored 1.25 .65
1363 A569 £18 multicolored 1.25 .65

Ba'ath Party, 50th Anniv. A570

1996, July 1 ***Perf. 11½x12***
1364 A570 £18 multicolored 1.25 .65

Pres. Hafez al-Assad — A571

1995 Litho. ***Perf. 11½***
1365 A571 100p bright blue .25 .25
1366 A571 500p bright orange .55 .25
1367 A571 £10 bright lilac 1.10 .55
1368 A571 £17 rose lake 1.90 .95
1369 A571 £18 slate green 2.00 1.00
Nos. 1365-1369 (5) 5.80 3.00

Issued: £10, 5/3; 100p, 500p, £17, £18, 12/31.

Arbor Day — A572

1996, Mar. 8 Litho. ***Perf. 12¼x12½***
1370 A572 £17 multicolored .80 .40

Mother's Day — A573

1996, May 1 ***Perf. 12x11½***
1370A A573 £10 multicolored .50 .25

Labor Day — A574

1996, May 1 ***Perf. 12¼x12½***
1371 A574 £15 multicolored .70 .35

Radio, Cent. — A575

1996, Aug. 18 Litho. ***Perf. 12½***
1372 A575 £17 multicolored 1.10 .55

World AIDS Day — A576

1996, Aug. 18 ***Perf. 12x11½***
1373 A576 £17 multicolored 1.10 .55

43rd Intl. Fair, Damascus A577

1996, Aug. 28
1374 A577 £17 multicolored 1.10 .55

NICE, 5th Anniv. A578

1996, Sept. 5 ***Perf. 11½x12***
1375 A578 £18 multicolored 1.10 .60

World Child Day — A579

1996, Oct. 9 ***Perf. 12x11½***
1376 A579 £10 multicolored .65 .30

World Post Day — A580

1996, Oct. 9
1377 A580 £17 multicolored 1.10 .55

UNICEF, 50th Anniv. — A581

1996, Nov. 20
1378 A581 £17 multicolored 1.10 .55

36th Science Week — A582

Design: Musa Iben Shaker's sons.

1996, Nov. 2 ***Perf. 12½x12***
1379 A582 £10 multicolored .65 .35

Corrective Movement, 26th Anniv. A583

1996, Nov. 16 ***Perf. 12½***
1380 A583 £10 multicolored .65 .35

Size: 65x90mm

Imperf

1381 A583 £50 like No. 1380 3.25 1.60

Natl. Advance Party — A584

1997, Mar. 7 Litho. ***Perf. 12x11½***
1382 A584 £3 multicolored .25 .25

March 8 Revolution, 34th Anniv. — A585

1997, Mar. 8
1383 A585 £15 multicolored 1.00 .50

Arbor Day — A586

1997, Apr. 8 Litho. ***Perf. 12x12½***
1384 A586 £10 multicolored .75 .40

Fish — A587

1997, Apr. 8 ***Perf. 12½x12***
1385 £17 Two dorsal fins 1.00 .50
1386 £17 One dorsal fin 1.00 .50
a. A587 Pair, #1385-1386 2.00 2.00

Mother's Day — A588

1997, Apr. 8 ***Perf. 12x11½***
1387 A588 £15 multicolored 1.00 .50

Baath Party Revolution, 50th Anniv. A589

1997, Apr. 3 ***Perf. 12½***
1388 A589 £25 multicolored 1.60 .80

Size: 90x65mm

Imperf

1389 A589 £25 multicolored 1.60 .80

World Tourism Day — A590

1997, Apr. 8 ***Perf. 12x11½***
1390 A590 £17 multicolored 1.10 .60

Evacuation Day, 51st Anniv. — A591

1997, Apr. 17 ***Perf. 11½x12***
1391 A591 £15 multicolored 1.00 .50

Labor Day — A592

1997, May 1 ***Perf. 12x11½***
1392 A592 £15 multicolored 1.00 .50

World Book Day — A592a

1997, June 16 Litho. ***Perf. 12½***
1392A A592a £10 multicolored .50 .25

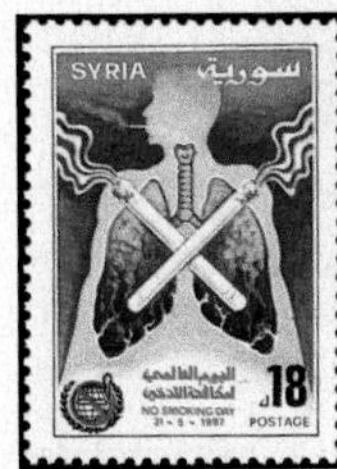
A592b

1997, June 16 ***Perf. 12x11½***
1392B A592b £18 multicolored .70 .35

No smoking day.

Intl. Flower Show, Damascus — A593

No. 1393, Echino ereus. No. 1394, Iris.

1997, June 21 Litho. ***Perf. 12x11½***
1393 £18 multicolored 1.10 .60
1394 £18 multicolored 1.10 .60
a. A593 Pair, #1393-1394 2.25 2.25

See Nos. 1412-1413.

4th Congress of Arab Denistry — A594

1997, Sept. 4
1395 A594 £10 multicolored .65 .35

44th Intl. Fair, Damascus A595

1997, Sept. 4
1396 A595 £17 multicolored 1.10 .55

World Post Day A596

1997, Sept. 27 ***Perf. 11½x12***
1397 A596 £17 multicolored 1.10 .55

World Children's Day A597

1997, Sept. 27
1398 A597 £17 multicolored 1.10 .55

Intl. Tourism Day A598

1997, Sept. 27
1399 A598 £17 multicolored 1.10 .55

37th Science Week — A599

1997, Nov. 1 **Litho.** ***Perf. 12x11½***
1400 A599 £17 multicolored 1.10 .55

Corrective Movement, 27th Anniv. A600

1997, Nov. 16 ***Perf. 12½***
1401 A600 £10 multicolored .70 .35

Size: 92x67mm

Imperf

1402 A600 £50 like #1401 3.25 3.25

Islamic Conference, 30th Anniv. — A601

1997, Dec. 9 **Litho.** ***Perf. 11½x12***
1403 A601 £10 multicolored .70 .35

March 8 Revolution, 35th Anniv. — A602

1998, Mar. 8 **Litho.** ***Perf. 12½x12***
1404 A602 £17 multicolored 1.10 .55

Mother's Day A603

1998, March 21 ***Perf. 11½x12***
1405 A603 £10 multicolored .70 .35

Evacuation Day, 52nd Anniv. — A604

1998, Apr. 17 **Litho.** ***Perf. 12x11½***
1406 A604 £10 multicolored .70 .35

Labor Day — A605

1998, May 1
1407 A605 £18 multicolored 1.10 .55

World Tourism Day — A606

Design: Princess of Banias.

1998, July 22 **Litho.** ***Perf. 12x11½***
1408 A606 £17 multicolored 1.10 .55

Mother Teresa (1910-97) A607

1998, July 22
1409 A607 £18 multicolored 1.10 .55

1998 World Cup Soccer Championships, France — A608

£25, Soccer players, diff.

1998, June 22 ***Perf. 12x12½***
1410 A608 £10 shown .60 .30

Size: 60x55mm

Imperf

1411 A608 £25 multicolored 2.25 1.10

Intl. Flower Show Type of 1997

Flowers: No. 1412, Plum-colored with yellow centers. No. 1413, Red hibiscus.

1998, June 22 ***Perf. 12x11½***
1412 A593 £17 multicolored 1.10 1.10
1413 A593 £17 multicolored 1.10 1.10
a. Pair, #1412-1413 2.25 2.25

45th Intl. Damascus Fair A609

1998, Sept. 26 **Litho.** ***Perf. 11½x12***
1414 A609 £18 multicolored 1.10 .55

World Children's Day — A610

1998, Sept. 26 ***Perf. 12x11½***
1415 A610 £18 multicolored 1.10 .55

World Post Day A611

1998, Sept. 26 **Litho.** ***Perf. 11½x12***
1416 A611 £18 multicolored 1.10 .55

Day to Stop Smoking — A612

1998, Sept. 26 ***Perf. 12x11½***
1417 A612 £15 multicolored .95 .50

Arab Post Day — A613

1998, Sept. 26 ***Perf. 12½***
1418 A613 £10 multicolored .60 .30

Arab-Israeli October War, 25th Anniv. — A614

1998, Oct. 6 ***Imperf.***
1419 A614 £25 multicolored 1.60 .80

Science Week A615

1998, Nov. 3 ***Perf. 11½x12***
1420 A615 £10 multicolored .65 .35

Camels A616

1998, Nov. 25 ***Perf. 12½***
1421 A616 £17 multicolored 1.10 .55

Corrective Movement, 28th Anniv. A617

1998, Nov. 16 **Litho.** ***Perf. 12½***
1422 A617 £10 multicolored .65 .30

Size: 99x65mm

Imperf

1423 A617 £25 multicolored .65 .30

Jerusalem — A618

1998, Nov. 25 ***Perf. 12½***
1424 A618 £10 multicolored .65 .30

Re-election of Pres. Assad
A619

£50, Portrait with designs from Nos. 1036, C496, C506, & portrait from No. 1265.

1999, Feb. 11 Litho. *Perf. 12½*
1425 A619 £10 red brn & multi .50 .25
1426 A619 £17 pale yel & multi .90 .45
1427 A619 £18 pale grn & multi .95 .45

Size: 140x110mm
Imperf

1428 A619 £50 pale grn & multi 2.50 2.50
Nos. 1425-1428 (4) 4.85 3.65

Arbor Day — A620

1999, Apr. 29 Litho. *Perf. 12½*
1429 A620 £17 multicolored 1.10 .55

Evacuation Day, 53rd. Anniv. — A621

1999, Apr. 29 *Perf. 12x11½*
1430 A621 £18 multicolored 1.10 .55

Mother's Day — A622

1999, Apr. 29
1431 A622 £17 multicolored 1.10 .55

Intl. Flower Show, Damascus — A623

Designs: a, Jasminum. b, Acanthaceae.

1999, June 20 Litho. *Perf. 12x11½*
1432 A623 £10 Pair, #a.-b. .85 .45

March 8 Revolution, 36th Anniv. — A624

No. 1434, Building, monument.

1999, Mar. 8 Litho. *Perf. 12¼x12½*
1433 A624 £25 shown 1.50 .75

Size: 75x110mm
Imperf

1434 A624 £25 multicolored 1.50 .75

Declaration of Human Rights, 50th Anniv. — A625

1999, June 5 *Perf. 11½x12*
1435 A625 £18 multicolored .95 .45

Labor Day — A626

1999, June 5 Litho. *Perf. 12x11½*
1436 A626 £10 multicolored .55 .30

10th Amity Festival
A627

1999, Aug. 1 Litho. *Perf. 11½x12*
1437 A627 £10 multicolored .65 .30

Arab Post Day — A628

1999, Oct. 12 Litho. *Perf. 12x11½*
1438 A628 £10 multicolored .65 .30

46th Intl. Fair, Damascus
A629

1999, Aug. 28 *Perf. 11½x12*
1439 A629 £15 multicolored .95 .45

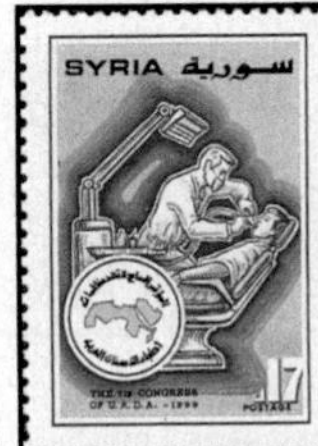
A630

1999, Sept. 21 *Perf. 12x11½*
1440 A630 £17 multicolored 1.10 .55

Arab Dentists Assoc., 7th Congress.

World Children's Day — A631

1999, Nov. 16
1441 A631 £18 multicolored 1.10 .55

UPU, 125th Anniv. — A632

1999, Oct. 12
1442 A632 £17 multicolored 1.10 .55

Corrective Movement, 29th Anniv. — A633

No. 1443, Building, statue. No. 1444, Close-up of statue. £25, Building statue, fountain.

1999, Nov. 16 *Perf. 12½*
1443 A633 £17 multicolored 1.10 .55
1444 A633 £17 multi, vert. 1.10 .55

Imperf
Size: 115x76mm

1445 A633 £25 multicolored 1.60 1.60
Nos. 1443-1445 (3) 3.80 2.70

Abu Hanifah al-Deilouri, Botanist — A634

1999, Oct. 12 *Perf. 11½x12*
1446 A634 £17 multicolored 1.10 .55

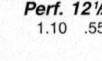

Christianity, 2000th Anniv. — A635

1999, Nov. 16 *Perf. 12½*
1447 A635 £17 multicolored 1.10 .55

March 8 Revolution, 37th Anniv.
A636

2000, Mar. 8 Litho. *Perf. 12½*
1448 A636 £18 multicolored 1.10 .55

Mother's Day — A637

2000, Mar. 21
1449 A637 £17 multicolored 1.00 .50

Evacuation Day, 54th Anniv. — A638

2000, Apr. 17 *Imperf.*
1450 A638 £25 multicolored 1.50 1.50

Labor Day — A639

2000, May 1 Litho. *Perf. 12x11½*
1451 A639 £10 multicolored .40 .25

Installation of Bashar al-Assad as President A640

2000, July 17 ***Perf. 12¼***

1452	Strip of 4	1.90	1.90
a.	A640 £3 lt blue & multi	.25	.25
b.	A640 £10 tan & multi	.40	.25
c.	A640 £17 bl gray & multi	.65	.30
d.	A640 £18 gray & multi	.65	.35

Imperf

Size: 110x74mm

1453 A640 £50 multi 1.90 1.90

Arab Post Day A641

2000, Aug. 20 Litho. ***Perf. 11½x12***

1454 A641 £18 multicolored 1.10 .55

47th Damascus Fair — A642

2000, Aug. 20

1455 A642 £15 multicolored .90 .45

2000 Summer Olympics, Sydney — A643

No. 1456: a, £17, Weight lifting. b, £18, Women's shot put.

2000, Oct. 1 Litho. ***Perf. 12x11½***

1456 A643 Pair, #a-b 1.40 .70

Imperf

Size: 80x77mm

1457 A643 £25 Javelin .95 .50

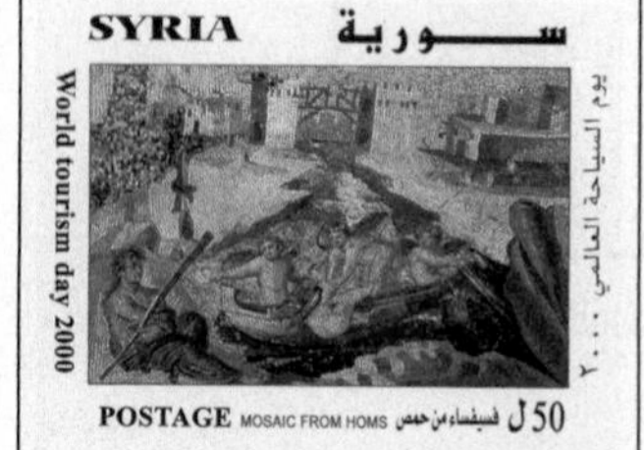

World Tourism Day — A644

2000, Dec. 6 Litho. ***Imperf.***

1458 A644 £50 Mosaic 3.00 3.00

World Post Day A645

2000, Aug. 20 ***Perf. 11½x12***

1459 A645 £18 multicolored 1.10 .55

Nasir ad-Din at-Tusi (1201-74), Scientist A646

2000, Nov. 1 Litho. ***Perf. 12½x12¼***

1460 A646 £15 multicolored .60 .30

Science week.

Arbor Day — A647

2000, May 15 ***Perf. 12x11½***

1461 A647 £18 multicolored .65 .35

Butterflies — A648

a, £17, Charaxes jasius. b, £18, Apaturairis.

2000, May 15 ***Perf. 12½***

1462 A648 Pair, #a-b 1.40 .70

World Children's Day — A649

2000, Aug. 20 Litho. ***Perf. 12x11½***

1463 A649 £10 multicolored .60 .30

World Meteorological Organization, 50th Anniv. — A650

2000, Dec. 6

1464 A650 £10 multicolored .60 .30

March 8 Revolution, 38th Anniv. — A651

2001 Litho. ***Perf. 12x11½***

1465 A651 £25 multicolored .95 .50

Mother's Day — A652

2001

1466 A652 £10 multicolored .40 .25

Evacuation Day, 55th Anniv. — A653

2001

1467 A653 £25 multicolored .95 .50

Book and Author's Rights — A654

2001

1468 A654 £10 multi .40 .25

Intl. Flower Show, Damascus — A655

No. 1469: a, Weigela. b, Mertensia.

2001

1469 A655 £10 Horiz. pair, #a-b .75 .40

Syrian Engineering Syndicate, 50th Anniv. A656

2001, Feb. 1 Litho. ***Perf. 12½***

1470 A656 £17 multi .65 .35

Size: 95x85mm

Imperf

1471 A656 £25 multi .95 .50

Martyr's Square Type of 1994

2001 ***Perf. 11½x12***

1472	A538	100p brt blue grn	.25	.25
1473	A538	£10 red	.35	.25
1474	A538	£50 blue	1.90	.95
		Nos. 1472-1474 (3)	2.50	1.45

Labor Day — A657

2001 Litho. ***Perf. 12x11½***

1475 A657 £18 multi .75 .40

48th Damascus Fair — A658

2001 Litho. ***Perf. 12x11½***

1476 A658 £10 multi .40 .25

Re-occupation of Kuneitra by Syria, 27th Anniv. — A659

2001 ***Perf. 11½x12***

1477 A659 £17 multi .65 .35

Anti-Smoking Campaign — A660

2001

1478 A660 £18 multi .70 .35

UN High Commissioner for Refugees, 50th Anniv. — A661

2001

1479 A661 £17 multi .65 .35

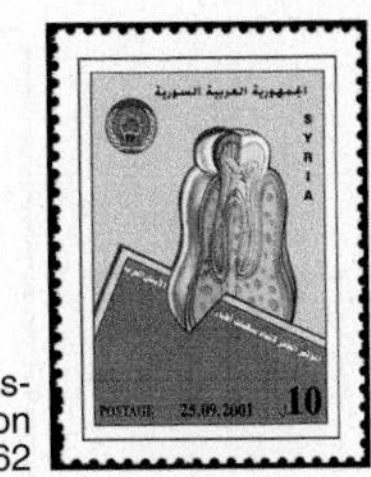

Tooth Cross-section A662

2001 ***Perf. 12x11½***

1480 A662 £10 multi .40 .25

World Children's Day — A663

2001 ***Perf. 12x11½***

1481 A663 £18 multi .70 .35

A664

2001 ***Perf. 12x11½***

1482 A664 £10 multi .40 .25

Size: 84x111mm

Imperf

1483 A664 £25 multi 1.00 1.00

A665

Aga Khan Award for Architecture — A666

2001 ***Perf. 11½x12***

1484 A665 £10 multi .40 .25

1485 A666 £17 multi .65 .35

1486 A666 £18 multi .70 .35

Nos. 1484-1486 (3) 1.75 .95

Installation of Bashar al-Assad as President, 1st Anniv. — A667

Assad and: a, £10, Silver frame. b, £17, Gold frame.

2001 **Litho.** ***Perf. 12½x12¼***

1487 A667 Horiz. pair, #a-b 1.10 .55

Arab Post Day A668

2001 ***Perf. 11½x12***

1488 A668 £18 multi .75 .35

World Post Day A669

2001

1489 A669 £10 multi .40 .25

Arbor Day — A670

2001 ***Perf. 12x11½***

1490 A670 £5 multi .25 .25

World Tourism Day — A671

2001 ***Perf. 12½***

1491 A671 £17 multi .70 .35

Palestinian Intifada — A672

2001 ***Perf. 12x11½***

1492 A672 £17 multi .70 .35

Pres. Hafez al-Assad (1930-2000) — A673

2001 ***Perf. 12¼x12½***

1493 A673 £25 multi 1.00 .50

Correctionist Movement, 31st Anniv. — A674

Text color: £5, Black. £15, Red.

2001 ***Perf. 11½x12***

1494-1495 A674 Set of 2 .80 .40

Evacuation Day, 56th Anniv. — A675

2002, Apr. 7 **Litho.** ***Perf. 12x11½***

1496 A675 £15 multi .65 .30

Labor Day — A676

2002, May 1 ***Perf. 12x12½***

1497 A676 £10 multi .45 .25

Intl. Flower Show, Damascus — A677

No. 1498: a, £15, Yellow flowers. b, £17, White lilies.

2002, May 1 ***Perf. 12x11½***

1498 A677 Horiz. pair, #a-b 1.40 .70

March 8 Revolution, 39th Anniv. A678

2002, Mar. 8 **Litho.** ***Perf. 11½x12***

1499 A678 £15 multi .65 .30

Mother's Day — A679

2002, Mar. 21 ***Perf. 12x11½***

1500 A679 £25 multi 1.10 .55

Gazelle A680

2002, Mar. 8 ***Perf. 12½***

1501 A680 £15 multi .65 .30

Baath Party, 55th Anniv. A681

2002, Apr. 7 ***Perf. 11½x12***

1502 A681 £15 multi .65 .30

2002 World Cup Soccer Championships, Japan and Korea — A682

No. 1503 — Various players: a, £5. b, £10. £25, Goalie making save, horiz.

2002, May 31 ***Perf. 12½***

1503 A682 Horiz. pair, #a-b .65 .30

Size: 78x65mm

Imperf

1504 A682 £25 multi 1.10 .55

World Tourism Day — A683

2002, Sept. 27 ***Perf. 12½***

1505 A683 £10 multi .40 .25

First Syrian Railroad, Cent. — A684

2002, Nov. 9

1506 A684 £10 multi .40 .25

Abd al-Rahman al-Kawakibi (1849-1902), Arab Nationalist — A685

2002, Aug. 13 ***Perf. 12x11½***
1507 A685 £10 multi .40 .25

Intifada — A686

Designs: £10, Flag bearer, four rock throwers, tank.
£25, Flag bearer, rock thrower, tank.

2002, Sept. 28 ***Perf. 12x11½***
1508 A686 £10 multi .40 .25

Size: 66x79mm

Imperf

1509 A686 £25 multi 1.10 .55

Birds A687

2002, Sep. 27 ***Perf. 11½x12***
1510 Vert. strip of 4 1.40 .70
a. A687 £3 Sand grouse .25 .25
b. A687 £5 Francolin .25 .25
c. A687 £10 Duck .40 .25
d. A687 £15 Goose .65 .30

Arab Post Day A688

Frame color: £5, Blue. £10, Red violet.

2002, Aug. 3 ***Perf. 11½x12***
1511-1512 A688 Set of 2 .65 .30

49th Intl. Damascus Fair — A689

Emblem and: a, £5, "X's." b, £10, Squares and diamonds.

2002, Aug. 28 ***Perf. 12x11½***
1513 A689 Horiz. pair, #a-b .65 .30

World Post Day — A690

No. 1514: a, Dove, envelope, rainbow. b, Envelope, UPU emblem, horiz.

Perf. 12x11½, 11½x12 (#1514b)

2002, Oct. 9
1514 A690 £10 Horiz. pair, #a-b .80 .40

Arbor Day — A691

2002, Dec. 26 ***Perf. 12x11½***
1515 A691 £10 multi .40 .25

Intl. Children's Day — A692

2002, Oct. 16 ***Perf. 12½***
1516 A692 £10 multi .40 .25

Corrective Movement, 32nd Anniv. A693

2002, Oct. 16 ***Perf. 11½x12***
1517 A693 £10 multi .40 .25

Martyr's Square Type of 1994

2003, May 5 Litho. ***Perf. 11½x12***
1518 A538 300p brown .25 .25

March 8 Revolution, 40th Anniv. — A694

2003, Mar. 8 ***Perf. 12¼x12½***
1519 A694 £15 multi .65 .30

Teacher's Day — A695

2003, Mar. 8 ***Perf. 12x11½***
1520 A695 £17 multi .75 .40

Mother's Day — A696

2003, Mar. 21
1521 A696 £32 multi 1.40 .70

Evacuation Day, 57th Anniv. — A697

2003, Apr. 17
1522 A697 £15 multi .65 .30

Labor Day — A698

2003, May 1
1523 A698 £25 multi 1.10 .55

Intl. Flower Show, Damascus A699

No. 1524: a, Damask roses and violets. b, Anemones. c, Daisies. d, Damask roses and gillyflowers. e, Sunflowers.

2003, June 15 ***Perf. 12½x12¼***
1524 Horiz. strip of 5 2.25 1.10
a.-e. A699 £10 Any single .45 .25

50th Intl. Damascus Fair — A700

Designs: £32, Flags, emblems. £50, Open orbs, horiz.

2003, Sep. 3 ***Perf. 12x12½***
1525 A700 £32 multi 1.40 .70

Size: 89x66mm

Imperf

1526 A700 £50 multi 2.25 2.25

World Tourism Day — A701

2003, Sep. 27 ***Perf. 12¼x12½***
1527 A701 £32 multi 1.40 .70

Election of Pope John Paul II, 25th Anniv. — A702

2003, Oct. 16 ***Perf. 12½x12¼***
1528 A702 £32 multi 1.40 .70

World Post Day A703

2003, Oct. 14 Litho. ***Perf. 11½x12***
1529 A703 £10 multi .45 .25

Corrective Movement, 33rd Anniv. — A704

2003, Nov. 16 ***Perf. 12x11½***
1530 A704 £15 multi .65 .30

Intl. Children's Day A705

2003, Dec. 8 *Perf. 11½x12*

1531 A705 £15 multi .65 .30

Birds A706

2003, Dec. 8 *Perf. 12½x12¼*

1532	Horiz. strip of 5	2.75	2.75
a.	A706 £5 Woodcock	.25	.25
b.	A706 £10 Lapwing	.45	.25
c.	A706 £15 European roller	.65	.30
d.	A706 £17 Teal	.70	.35
e.	A706 £18 Bustard	.75	.40

Pres. Bashar al-Assad — A707

Perf. 11¾x11¼

2003, Dec. 8 **Unwmk.**

1533	A707	£15 brt blue green	.65	.30
1534	A707	£25 blue	1.10	.55
1535	A707	£50 lilac	2.10	1.10
		Nos. 1533-1535 (3)	3.85	1.95

See Nos. 1585-1594. Compare with Nos. 1652-1654.

World Summit on the Information Society, Geneva — A708

2003, Dec. 10 *Perf. 12x11½*

1536 A708 £15 multi .65 .30

Arbor Day — A709

2003, Dec. 25 **Litho.**

1537 A709 £25 multi 1.10 .55

Martyr's Square Type of 1994

2004 *Perf. 11½x12*

1538 A538 £5 blue .25 .25

March 8 Revolution, 41st Anniv. — A710

2004, Mar 8 *Perf. 12½x12*

1539 A710 £10 multi .40 .25

Teacher's Day — A711

2004, Mar. 13 *Perf. 12x11½*

1540 A711 £5 multi .25 .25

Mother's Day A712

2004, Mar. 21 *Perf. 11½x12*

1541 A712 £15 multi .65 .30

Evacuation Day, 58th Anniv. — A713

2004, Apr. 17 **Litho.**

1542 A713 £10 multi .40 .25

Labor Day A714

2004, May 1

1543 A714 £10 multi .40 .25

A715

A716

A717

A718

FIFA (Fédération Internationale de Football Association), Cent. — A719

2004, May 21 *Perf. 11½x12*

1544	A715	£5 multi	.25	.25
1545	A716	£10 multi	.40	.25

Perf. 12½x12¼

1546	A717	£15 multi	.60	.30

Perf. 12¼x12½

1547	A718	£32 multi	1.25	.60
		Nos. 1544-1547 (4)	2.50	1.40

Imperf

1548	A719	£25 multi	1.00	1.00

Intl. Flower Show, Damascus A720

No. 1549: a, Gladiola lavender. b, Jasmine. c, Iris. d, Orange nesrien. e, Tulip.

2004, June 15 *Perf. 12x11½*

1549	Horiz. strip of 5	1.00	1.00
a.-e.	A720 £5 Any single	.25	.25

Children and War Campaign of Intl. Committee of the Red Cross — A721

2004, June 17 *Perf. 12¼x12½*

1550 A721 £32 red & black 1.25 .60

2004 Summer Olympics, Athens — A722

Designs: £5, Track. £10, Boxing, horiz. £25, Swimming, horiz.

Perf. 12x11½, 11½x12

2004, Aug. 13

1551-1553 A722 Set of 3 1.60 .80

51st Intl. Damascus Fair — A723

2004, Sept. 3 *Perf. 12x11½*

1554 A723 £25 multi 1.00 .50

2004 Census A724

2004, Sept. 14 *Perf. 12½*

1555 A724 £10 multi .45 .25

World Tourism Day A725

Designs: £5, Locomotive. No. 1557, £10, Building. No. 1558, £10, Train.

Perf. 11½x12

2004, Sept. 27 **Litho.** **Unwmk.**

1556-1558 A725 Set of 3 1.00 .50

World Post Day — A726

2004, Oct. 9 **Litho.** *Perf. 12x11½*

1559 A726 £17 multi .70 .35

Intl. Children's Day A727

2004, Oct. 16 *Perf. 11½x12*

1560 A727 £18 multi .70 .35

Corrective Movement, 34th Anniv. — A728

2004, Nov. 16 ***Perf. 12½x12***
1561 A728 £25 multi 1.00 .50

Arbor Day — A729

2004, Dec. 30 ***Perf. 12x11½***
1562 A729 £10 multi .40 .25

Northern Bald Ibis — A730

Perf. 12½x12¼
2004, Dec. 30 **Litho.** **Unwmk.**
1563 A730 £10 multi .40 .25

Farm Animals A731

2004, Dec. 30 ***Perf. 11½x12***
1564 Vert. strip of 4 2.10 1.10
a. A731 £5 Shami goat .25 .25
b. A731 £15 Awassi ewe .55 .25
c. A731 £17 Bull .65 .30
d. A731 £18 Shami cow .70 .35

March 8 Revolution, 42nd Anniv. — A732

Perf. 12¼x12½
2005, Mar. 8 **Wmk. 403**
1565 A732 £17 multi .65 .30

Teacher's Day A733

2005, Mar. 13 ***Perf. 11½x12***
1566 A733 £25 multi 1.00 .50

Mother's Day — A734

2005, Mar. 21 ***Perf. 12x11½***
1567 A734 £18 multi .70 .35

Arab League, 60th Anniv. — A735

2005, Mar. 22
1568 A735 £10 multi .40 .25

National Day — A736

2005, Apr. 17
1569 A736 £17 multi .65 .30

Labor Day — A737

2005, May 1 **Wmk. 403**
1570 A737 £15 multi .60 .30

Intl. Flower Show, Damascus A738

2005, June 15 **Litho.**
1571 Horiz. strip of 5 2.50 1.25
a. A738 £5 Hyacinth .25 .25
b. A738 £10 Sternbergia clusiana .40 .25
c. A738 £15 Primula obconica .55 .30
d. A738 £17 Primula malacoides .65 .30
e. A738 £18 Canaria .70 .35

Butterflies A739

No. 1572: a, Papilio ulysses. b, Monarch. c, Baeotus baeotus. d, Lacewing. e, Tiger swallowtail.

2005, Aug. 7 ***Perf. 12½***
1572 Horiz. strip of 5 2.00 1.00
a.-e. A739 £10 Any single .40 .25

52nd Intl. Damascus Fair — A740

2005, Sept. 3 ***Perf. 12x11½***
1573 A740 £15 multi .60 .30

Mevlana Jalal ad-Din ar-Rumi (1207-73), Islamic Philosopher A741

2005, Sept. 25 ***Perf. 12½x12¼***
1574 A741 £25 multi 1.00 .50

See Afghanistan Nos. 1449-1451, Iran No. 2911, and Turkey No. 2971.

World Tourism Day A742

2005, Sept. 27 ***Perf. 11½x12***
1575 A742 £17 multi .65 .30

World Post Day — A743

2005, Oct. 9 ***Perf. 12x11½***
1576 A743 £18 multi .70 .35

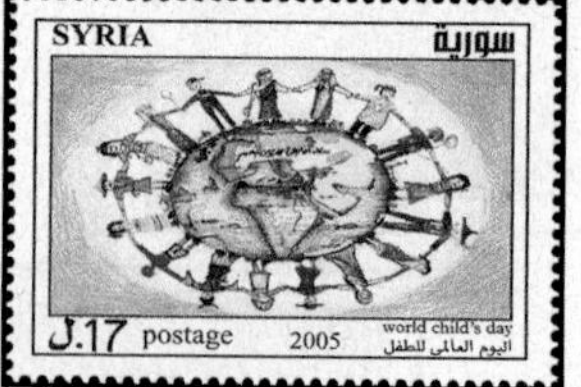

Intl. Children's Day — A744

2005, Oct. 16 ***Perf. 12¼x12½***
1577 A744 £17 multi .65 .30

Corrective Movement, 35th Anniv. — A745

2005, Nov. 16 ***Perf. 11½x12***
1578 A745 £25 multi 1.00 .50

World Summit on the Information Society, Tunis — A746

2005, Nov. 16 ***Perf. 12¼x12½***
1579 A746 £17 multi .65 .30

Poets — A747

No. 1580: a, Nizar Kabbani (1923-98). b, Sadalah Wannous (1941-97). c, Omar Abu Reisheh (1910-90).

2005, Dec. 20 ***Perf. 12½x12¼***
1580 A747 Horiz. strip of 3 1.75 .85
a. £10 multi .40 .25
b. £17 multi .65 .30
c. £18 multi .70 .35

Arbor Day — A748

2005, Dec. 25 **Wmk. 403**
1581 A748 £17 multi .65 .30

March 8 Revolution, 43rd Anniv. — A749

Perf. 12x11½
2006, Mar. 8 **Litho.** **Wmk. 403**
1582 A749 £18 multi .70 .35

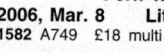

Aleppo, 2006 Capital of Islamic Culture A750

No. 1583: a, £17, Aleppo Castle. b, £18, Mosque, vert.
£25, Emblem and buildings.

2006, Mar. 16 ***Perf. 11½x12, 12x11½***
1583 A750 Pair, #a-b 1.40 .70

Imperf

Size: 79x60mm

1584 A750 £25 multi .95 .50

Pres. Bashir al-Assad Type of 2003

2006 **Wmk. 403** ***Perf. 11¾x11¼***

1585	A707	£1 brt blue	.25	.25
a.		Dated "2008"	.25	.25
1586	A707	£3 lilac rose	.25	.25
1587	A707	£5 brown	.25	.25
a.		Dated "2008"	.25	.25
1588	A707	£10 purple	.40	.25
1589	A707	£15 brt blue grn	.60	.30
1590	A707	£17 orange brn	.65	.35
1591	A707	£18 dark blue	.70	.35
1592	A707	£25 blue	.95	.50
1593	A707	£50 lilac	1.90	.95
1594	A707	£100 green	4.00	2.00
		Nos. 1585-1594 (10)	9.95	5.45

Issued: £1, 9/7; £3, 8/24; £5, 8/1; £10, 6/2; £15, £25, £50, 3/19; £17, 5/11; £18, 6/8; £100, 9/27.

Mother's Day — A751

Perf. 12x11½

2006, Mar. 21 **Wmk. 403**
1595 A751 £17 multi .65 .35

National Day — A752

No. 1596: a, Sultan Pasha al-Atrach (1889-1982). b, Yousef al-Azmeh (1884-1920). c, Sheikh Saleh al-Ali (1885-1950). d, Ibrahim Hanano (1889-1935). e, Ahmad Moraiwed (1886-1926).

2006, Apr. 17
1596 Horiz. strip of 5 1.90 .95
a.-e. A752 £10 Any single .35 .25

Labor Day — A753

2006, May 1
1597 A753 £17 multi .65 .35

Intl. Flower Show, Damascus A754

No. 1598: a, £5, Hyoscyamus aureus. b, £10, Cistus salviaefolius.

2006, May 15 ***Perf. 11½x12***
1598 A754 Vert. pair, #a-b .60 .30

2006 World Cup Soccer Championships, Germany — A755

No. 1599: a, £17, Players, aerial view of stadium. b, £18, Players under stadium roof.
£50, Players, vert.

2006, June 25 ***Perf. 11½x12***
1599 A755 Vert. pair, #a-b 1.40 .70

Imperf

Size: 60x80mm

1600 A755 £50 multi 1.90 .95

Diplomatic Relations Between Syria and People's Republic of China, 50th Anniv. — A756

2006, Aug. 1 ***Perf. 12½x12¼***
1601 A756 £10 multi .40 .25

Intl. Year of Deserts and Desertification — A757

2006, Aug. 13 **Wmk. 403**
1602 A757 £10 multi .40 .25

53rd Intl. Damascus Fair — A758

2006, Sept. 3 ***Perf. 12x11½***
1603 A758 £10 multi .40 .25

A759

World Tourism Day — A760

2006, Sept. 27 ***Perf. 11½x12***
1604 A759 £10 multi .40 .25

Perf. 12¼x12½

1605 A760 £10 multi .40 .25

World Post Day — A761

2006, Oct. 19 ***Perf. 12x11½***
1606 A761 £17 multi .65 .35

Artists — A762

No. 1607: a, Fateh Almudarres (1922-99). b, Adham Ismail (1922-63). c, Saeed Makhlouf (1925-2000). d, Burhan Karkutli (1932-2003). e, Michael Kirsheh (1900-73).

2006, Nov. 12 **Litho.**
1607 Horiz. strip of 5 1.90 .95
a.-e. A762 £10 Any single .35 .25

Corrective Movement, 36th Anniv. — A763

2006, Nov. 16 ***Perf. 12½x12¼***
1608 A763 £15 multi .60 .30

Arbor Day — A764

2006, Dec. 28 ***Perf. 12¼x12½***
1609 A764 £15 multi .60 .30

Fish A765

No. 1610: a, Light-colored fish, green and violet seaweed. b, Dark-colored fish, green and violet seaweed. c, Light-colored fish, green seaweed.

2006, Dec. 28 ***Perf. 11½x12***
1610 A765 £15 Vert. strip of 3, #a-c 1.75 .85

March 8 Revolution, 44th Anniv. — A766

Perf. 12¼x12½

2007, Mar. 8 **Litho.** **Wmk. 403**
1611 A766 £17 multi .65 .35

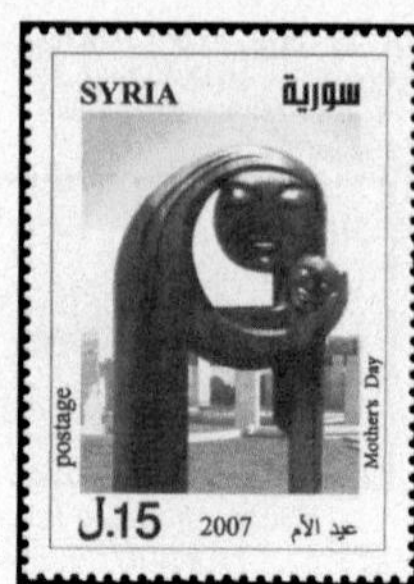

Mother's Day — A767

2007, Mar. 21 ***Perf. 12½x12¼***
1612 A767 £15 multi .60 .30

Baath Party, 60th Anniv. A768

2007, Apr. 7
1613 A768 £25 multi 1.00 .50

National Day — A769

2007, Apr. 14
1614 A769 £15 multi .60 .30

Labor Day — A770

2007, May 1 ***Perf. 12½***
1615 A770 £10 multi .40 .25

Intl. Flower Show, Damascus — A771

No. 1616: a, Freesia. b, Ipomoea purpurea. c, Plumbago capensis.

2007, June 27 ***Perf. 12¼x12½***
1616 A771 £15 Vert. strip of 3, #a-c 1.75 .90

Second Term of Pres. Bashar al-Assad — A772

No. 1617: a, £10, Portrait of Assad. b, £15, Portrait of Assad, diff.
£25, Assad taking oath, horiz.

Perf. 12½x12¼
2007, July 17 **Litho.** **Wmk. 403**
1617 A772 Horiz. pair, #a-b 1.00 .50

Size: 85x70mm

Imperf

1618 A772 £25 multi 1.00 .50

54th Intl. Damascus Fair — A773

Perf. 12x11½
2007, Aug. 15 **Litho.** **Wmk. 403**
1619 A773 £15 multi .60 .30

Launch of Sputnik 1, 50th Anniv. — A774

No. 1620 — Sputnik 1, rocket, "50" and background color of: a, £15, Green. b, £25, Brown.

2007, Oct. 4
1620 A774 Horiz. pair, #a-b 1.60 .80

World Tourism Day A775

2007, Nov. 4 ***Perf. 11½x12***
1621 A775 £10 multi .40 .25

World Post Day — A776

2007, Nov. 4 ***Perf. 12½***
1622 A776 £25 multi 1.00 .50

Correctionist Movement, 37th Anniv. — A777

2007, Nov. 16 ***Perf. 12½x12¼***
1623 A777 £15 multi .60 .30

Arbor Day A778

2007, Dec. 25 ***Perf. 11½x12***
1624 A778 £18 multi .70 .35

Doctors — A779

No. 1625: a, Dr. Hussny Sabah (1900-86). b, Dr. Wajieh Al-Barudy (1906-96). c, Dr. Nadim Shoman (1903-84). d, Dr. Tawfik Izzed-din (1912-75). e, Dr. Abdussalam Al-Ojaily (1918-2006).

2007, Dec. 25 ***Perf. 12x11½***
1625 Horiz. strip of 5 2.00 1.00
a.-e. A779 £10 Any single .40 .25

Birds — A780

No. 1626: a, White stork. b, Syrian woodpeckers. c, Shoveler ducks. d, Bee-eater. e, Turtle dove.

2007, Dec. 30 ***Perf. 12½x12¼***
1626 Horiz. strip of 5 2.00 1.00
a.-e. A780 £10 Any single .40 .25

March 8 Revolution, 45th Anniv. A781

2008, Mar. 8 **Litho.**
1627 A781 £15 multi .60 .30

Mother's Day — A782

2008, Mar. 21 ***Perf. 12x11½***
1628 A782 £10 multi .40 .25

20th Arab Summit, Damascus A783

Emblem, flags and: £10, Map. £25, Horseman.

2008, Mar. 29 ***Perf. 12½x12¼***
1629 A783 £10 multi .40 .25

Imperf

Size: 70x85mm

1630 A783 £25 multi 1.00 .50

Damascus, 2008 Arab Capital of Culture — A784

Designs: £10, Al-Shamieh School. £15, Al-Thaheria Library.
£25, Damascus University, vert.

2008, Mar. 30 ***Perf. 12¼x12½***
1631-1632 A784 Set of 2 1.00 .50

Imperf
Size: 70x84mm

1633 A784 £25 multi 1.00 1.00

National Day — A785

2008, Apr. 17 ***Perf. 12½***
1634 A785 £10 multi .40 .25

Labor Day — A786

2008, May 1 ***Perf. 12x11½***
1635 A786 £20 multi .80 .40

Aleppo University, 50th Anniv. — A787

2008, May 4 **Wmk. 403**
1636 A787 £15 multi .60 .30

Intl. Flower Show, Damascus A788

No. 1637: a, Roses. b, Thistles. c, Dahlias. d, Wallflowers. e, Daisies (margreet).

2008, June 25 ***Perf. 12½x12¼***
1637 Horiz. strip of 5 2.00 1.00
a.-e. A788 £10 Any single .40 .25

Arab Postal Day — A789

No. 1638 — Emblem and: a, Camel caravan. b, Map and pigeon.

2008, Aug. 3 ***Perf. 11½***
1638 A789 Horiz. pair 1.40 .70
a. £15 multi .60 .30
b. £20 multi .80 .40

55th Intl. Damascus Fair — A790

2008, Aug. 15 ***Perf. 12x11½***
1639 A790 £25 multi 1.00 .50

Hejaz Railway, Cent. — A791

Emblem and: £25, Train on bridge. £50, Train in tunnel, railway map, vert.

2008, Aug. 19 ***Perf. 12½x12¼***
1640 A791 £25 multi 1.00 .50

Imperf
Size: 70x85mm

1641 A791 £50 multi 2.00 1.00

2008 Summer Olympics, Beijing — A792

Designs: £5, Weight lifting. £10, Long jump, vert.
£25, Swimming.

Perf. 12¼x12½, 12½x12¼
2008, Aug. 19
1642-1643 A792 Set of 2 .60 .30

Imperf
Size: 85x63mm

1644 A792 £25 multi 1.00 .50

Snakes A793

No. 1645: a, Golan snake. b, Eryx jaculus. c, Telescopus fallax syriacus.

2008, Sept. 16 ***Perf. 12½***
1645 Horiz. strip of 3 2.40 1.25
a.-c. A793 £20 Any single .80 .40

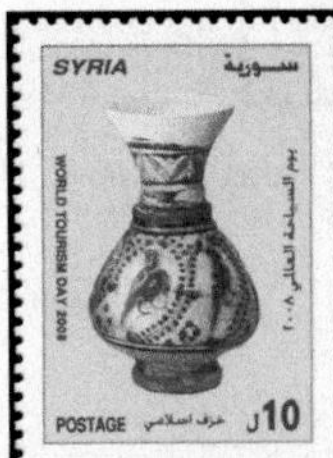

World Tourism Day — A794

Designs: £10, Vase. £15, Plate.

2008, Sept. 27 ***Perf. 12x11½***
1646 A794 £10 multi .40 .25

Size: 32x32mm
Perf. 12½

1647 A794 £15 multi .60 .30

World Post Day — A795

2008, Oct. 19 ***Perf. 12x11½***
1648 A795 £18 multi .80 .40

Corrective Movement, 38th Anniv. — A796

2008, Nov. 16 ***Perf. 12¼x12½***
1649 A796 £10 multi .45 .25

Arbor Day A797

Perf. 11½x12
2008, Dec. 25 **Litho.** **Wmk. 403**
1650 A797 £17 multi .75 .35

Louis Braille (1809-52), Educator of the Blind A798

2008, Dec. 27
1651 A798 £17 multi .75 .35

Pres. Bashir al-Assad Type of 2003 Redrawn With Sans-Serif Numerals

Perf. 11¾x11¼
2008-09 **Litho.** **Wmk. 403**
1652 A707 £5 brown .25 .25
a. Dated "2010" .25 .25
1653 A707 £10 purple .45 .25
a. Dated "2010" .45 .25
b. Dated "2011" .40 .25
1654 A707 £25 blue 1.10 .55
a. grn blue, dated "2011" 1.00 .50
Nos. 1652-1654 (3) 1.80 1.05

Issued: £25, 2008; £5, £10, 2009. Nos. 1587-1588, 1592 have serifed numerals.

Famous People A799

No. 1655: a, Mustafa Alaakad (1930-2005), film director and producer. b, Nihad Kalaai (1926-93), artist. c, Maha Al-Saleh (1945-2008), artist. d, Abd Allateef Fathy (1916-86), artist. e, Fahd Kaaekati (1924-82), artist.

2009, Feb. 22 ***Perf. 12½x12¼***
1655 Horiz. strip of 5 4.50 2.25
a.-e. A799 £20 Any single .90 .45

March 8 Revolution, 46th Anniv. — A800

2009, Mar. 8 ***Perf. 12x11½***
1656 A800 £10 multi .45 .25

Mother's Day — A801

2009, Mar. 21 ***Perf. 12½***
1657 A801 £18 multi .80 .40

National Day — A802

2009, Apr. 17 ***Perf. 12¼x12½***
1658 A802 £17 multi .75 .35

Labor Day A803

2009, May 1 ***Perf. 11½x12***
1659 A803 £15 multi .65 .35

Intl. Flower Fair, Damascus A804

No. 1660: a, Wallflowers. b, Maemozas. c, Irises d, Lilies. e Adalias.

2009, June 15 **Wmk. 403** ***Perf. 12***
1660 Horiz. strip of 5 4.50 2.25
a.-e. A804 £20 Any single .90 .45

Jerusalem, Capital of Arab Culture A805

2009, Aug. 3 ***Perf. 12½x12¼***
1661 A805 £10 multi .45 .25

56th Intl. Damascus Fair — A806

2009, Aug. 15 ***Perf. 12x11½***
1662 A806 £15 multi .65 .35

World Tourism Day — A807

No. 1663 — Sites in Bosra: a, Bab Al-Hawa. b, Mabrak Al-Naqa Mosque. c, Amphitheater.

2009, Sept. 27 ***Perf. 12¼x12½***
1663 A807 £25 Vert. strip of 3, #a-c 3.25 1.60

Birds — A808

No. 1664: a, Thrasher. b, Redstart. c, Blue-headed yellow wagtail. d, Honeyeater. e, Syrian serin.

2009, Oct. 8 **Litho.** ***Perf. 12***
1664 Vert. strip of 5 4.50 2.25
a.-e. A808 £20 Any single .90 .45

World Post Day — A809

2009, Oct. 9 ***Perf. 12½***
1665 A809 £50 multi 2.25 1.10

Corrective Movement, 39th Anniv. — A810

2009, Nov. 16 ***Perf. 12***
1666 A810 £10 multi .45 .25

Arbor Day — A811

2009, Dec. 31 **Wmk. 403**
1667 A811 £15 multi .65 .35

March 8 Revolution, 47th Anniv. A812

2010, Mar. 8 **Wmk. 403** ***Perf. 12½***
1668 A812 £25 multi 1.10 .55

Mother's Day — A813

2010, Mar. 21 ***Perf. 12***
1669 A813 £10 multi .45 .25

National Day — A814

2010, Apr. 17 ***Perf. 12x11½***
1670 A814 £50 multi 2.25 1.10

Labor Day — A815

2010, May 1 ***Perf. 12½x12¼***
1671 A815 £25 multi 1.10 .55

Intl. Year of Biodiversity — A816

2010, May 1 ***Perf. 12¼x12½***
1672 A816 £50 multi 2.25 1.10

2010 World Cup Soccer Championships, South Africa — A817

No. 1673 — Emblem and: a, Players with blue shirts celebrating. b, Players chasing ball. £50, Emblem, World Cup, horiz.

2010, May 1 ***Perf. 12¼x12½***
1673 A817 £25 Vert. pair, #a-b 2.25 1.10

Size: 85x67mm

Imperf

1674 A817 £50 multi 2.25 1.10

50th Aleppo Industrial and Agricultural Production Fair — A818

2010, June 24 **Litho.** ***Perf. 12***
1675 A818 £15 multi .65 .30

Intl. Flower Fair, Damascus A819

No. 1676: a, Calendula. b, Cyclamen. c, Rose. d, Fuchsia. e, Rosa bracteata.

2010, June 25 ***Perf. 12½x12¼***
1676 Horiz. strip of 5 5.50 2.75
a.-e. A819 £25 Any single 1.10 .55

Historical and Tourism Sites of Brazil and Syria — A820

2010, June 28 ***Perf. 12½x12¼***
1677 A820 £50 multi 2.25 1.10

See Brazil No. 3132.

57th Intl. Damascus Fair — A821

2010, July 14 ***Perf. 12x11½***
1678 A821 £50 multi 2.25 1.10

Friendship Between Syria and Chile, 200th Anniv. A822

2010, Sept. 23 **Wmk. 403** ***Perf. 12½***
1679 A822 £25 multi 1.10 .55

Mammals A823

No. 1680: a, Squirrel. b, Hedgehog. c, Ichneumon.

2010, Sept. 23 **Litho.**
1680 Horiz. strip of 3 4.50 2.25
a.-b. A823 £30 Either single 1.25 .65
c. A823 £40 multi 1.75 .85

World Tourism Day — A824

No. 1681: a, Small plaza with flowers. b, Building, dervishes.

2010, Sept. 27 *Perf. 12*
1681 A824 £25 Horiz. pair, #a-b 2.25 1.10

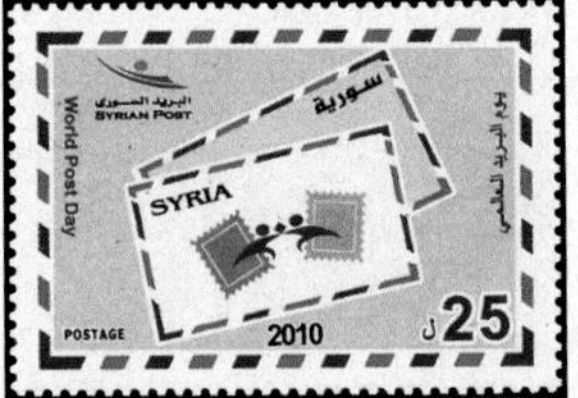
World Post Day — A825

2010, Oct. 9 **Wmk. 403**
1682 A825 £25 multi 1.10 .55

Corrective Movement, 40th Anniv. A826

2010, Nov. 16
1683 A826 £25 multi 1.10 .55

Miniature Sheet

Lawyers — A827

No. 1684: a, Fatihullah al-Sakal (1893-1970). b, Faris al-Khoubi (1877-1962). c, Saeed al-Gazi (1877-1967). d, Abd-el-Salam al-Tirmanini (1913-2006). e, Mohammad al-Fadel (1919-77). f, Ahmad Fouad al-Koudmani (1905-81)

2010, Dec. 31 *Perf. 12x11½*
1684 A827 £25 Sheet of 6, #a-f 6.50 3.25

March 8 Revolution, 48th Anniv. — A829

Perf. 12x11½
2011, Mar. 8 **Litho.** **Wmk. 403**
1686 A829 £25 multi 1.10 .55

Mother's Day — A830

2011, Mar. 21
1687 A830 £25 multi 1.10 .55

National Day A831

2011, Apr. 17 *Perf. 11½x12*
1688 A831 £25 multi 1.10 .55

Labor Day A832

2011, May 1 **Wmk. 403**
1689 A832 £50 multi 2.10 1.10

Cetaceans — A836

No. 1693: a, Physeter macrocephalus. b, Globiocephala melas. c, Stenella coeruleoalba. d, Grampus griseus. e, Tursiops truncatus. f, Killer whales.

Perf. 11½x12
2011, Sept. 18 **Litho.** **Wmk. 403**
1693 A836 £25 Block of 6, #a-f 6.50 3.25

Labor Day — A845

Perf. 12x11½
2012, May 1 **Litho.** **Wmk. 403**
1702 A845 £50 multi 2.50 1.25

Syrian Eagle — A847

No. 1704: a, Eagle standing on rock. b, Head of eagle. c, Eagle on rock with wings extended. d, Eagle in flight.

Wmk. 403
2012, July 26 **Litho.** *Perf. 12½*
1704 A847 £50 Block of 4, #a-d — —

Writers — A851

No. 1708: a, Abed Alkareem Alyafy (1919-2010). b, Kamar Kaeilany (1928-2012). c, Kostaky Al Houmsy (1858-1941). d, Sedky Ismail (1924-72). e, Alfat El Edelby (1912-2007). f, Midhat Akash (1923-2012).

Perf. 12x11½
2012, Dec. 25 **Litho.** **Wmk. 403**
1708 A851 £50 Block of 6, #a-f 12.00 6.00

Birds — A859

No. 1716: a, Serinus syriacus. b, Starling. c, Erithacus rubecula. d, Yellow-breasted chat. e, Megarhynchos luscinia. f, Cinereous bunting.

Perf. 12x11½
2013 **Litho.** **Wmk. 403**
1716 A859 £75 Block of 6, #a-f 13.00 6.50

Directors of Arab Academy of Damascus — A860

No. 1717: a, Mustapha Al Shehabi (1893-1968). b, Khalil Mardam Beyk (1895-1959). c, Mohammed Kurd Ali (1876-1953). d, Marwan Al Mahasseni. e, Shaker Al Fahham (1921-2008). f, Husni Sabah (1900-86).

Perf. 12x11½
2013 **Litho.** **Wmk. 403**
1717 A860 £100 Block of 6, #a-f 10.50 5.25

March 8 Revolution, 51st Anniv. — A865

Perf. 12½x13
2014, Mar. 8 **Litho.** **Wmk. 403**
1722 A865 £80 multi 1.10 .55

Labor Day — A868

Wmk. 403
2014, May 1 **Litho.** *Perf. 12½*
1725 A868 £75 multi 1.00 .50

2014 World Cup Soccer Championships, Brazil — A872

No. 1729 — Soccer players wearing: a, £100, Red and white shirts. b, £150, Orange and blue shirts.

Perf. 12¼x12½
2014, May 1 **Litho.** **Wmk. 403**
1729 A872 Vert. pair, #a-b 3.50 1.75

Arabic Language Day A873

2014 **Litho.** **Wmk. 403** *Perf. 13*
1730 A873 £180 multi 2.25 1.10

Values are for stamps with surrounding selvage.

Mammals A874

No. 1731: a, £75, Mustela frenata. b, £80, Fox. c, £170, Jackal.

Perf. 11½x12

2014, Sept. 23 Litho. Wmk. 403
1731 A874 Vert. strip of 3, #a-c *4.00 2.00*

2014 Youth Olympic Games, Nanjing, People's Republic of China — A875

Wmk. 403

2014, Aug. 16 Litho. *Perf. 12½*
1732 A875 £200 multi *4.00 2.00*

World Post Day — A878

Wmk. 405

2014, Oct. 9 Litho. *Perf. 12½*
1735 A878 £80 multi *1.00 .50*

Corrective Movement, 44th Anniv. — A879

Wmk. 403

2014, Nov. 16 Litho. *Perf. 12*
1736 A879 £60 multi *.70 .35*

Arbor Day — A880

Wmk. 403

2014, Dec. 31 Litho. *Perf. 12*
1737 A880 £245 multi *2.75 1.40*

March 8 Revolution, 52nd Anniv. — A881

Wmk. 403

2015, Mar. 8 Litho. *Perf. 12*
1738 A881 £300 multi *3.25 1.60*

Mother's Day A882

Wmk. 403

2015, Mar. 21 Litho. *Perf. 13*
1739 A882 £110 multi *1.25 .60*

Values are for stamps with surrounding selvage.

National Day — A883

Perf. 12¼x12½

2015, Apr. 17 Litho. Wmk. 403
1740 A883 £60 multi *.65 .35*

Labor Day — A884

Perf. 12½x12¼

2015, May 1 Litho. Wmk. 403
1741 A884 £235 multi *2.50 1.25*

Martyr's Star Monument A885

Perf. 12½x12¼

2015 Litho. Wmk. 403
1742 A885 £260 multi *2.75 1.40*

Animals A886

No. 1743: a, Lynx. b, Arab deer. c, Syrian bear.

Perf. 11½x12

2015, Jan. 1 Litho. Wmk. 403
1743 A886 £110 Vert. strip of 3, #a-c *4.00 2.00*

Musicians A887

No. 1744: a, Fuad Ghazi (1955-2011). b, Abd Al Fattah Sukar (1930-2008). c, Sameer Hilmi (1939-97). d, Adnan Abi Al Shamat (1934-2011). e, Fahed Ballan (1933-97).

Wmk. 403

2015, Jan. 1 Litho. *Perf. 12*
1744 Horiz. strip of 5 *5.75 3.00*
a.-e. A887 £100 Any single *1.10 .60*

Syrian Arab Army Day — A888

Perf. 12x12½

2015, Aug. 1 Litho. Wmk. 403
1745 A888 £110 multi *1.75 .85*

World Tourism Day — A889

No. 1746 — Sculptures depicting: a, Tambourine beater, Ugharit. b, Man, Palmyra.

Wmk. 403

2015, Sept. 27 Litho. *Perf. 12½*
1746 A889 £150 Horiz. pair, #a-b *3.50 1.75*

World Post Day — A890

Perf. 12x11¾

2015, Oct. 9 Litho. Wmk. 403
1747 A890 £60 multi *.75 .35*

Corrective Movement, 45th Anniv. — A891

Perf. 12½x12

2015, Nov. 16 Litho. Wmk. 403
1748 A891 £60 multi *.75 .35*

National Environment Day — A892

Wmk. 403

2015, Nov. 25 Litho. *Perf. 12*
1749 A892 £100 multi *1.25 .60*

Tree Day — A893

Wmk. 403

2015, Dec. 31 Litho. *Perf. 12*
1750 A893 £250 multi *3.00 1.50*

March 8 Revolution, 53rd Anniv. — A894

Perf. 12x11½

2016, Mar. 8 Litho. Wmk. 403
1751 A894 £200 multi *2.75 1.40*

International Women's Day — A895

Wmk. 403

2016, Mar. 8 Litho. *Perf. 12¼*

1752 A895 £100 multi *1.40 .70*

Mother's Day — A896

Perf. 12¼x12½

2016, Mar. 21 Litho. Wmk. 403

1753 A896 £150 multi *1.25 .60*

Labor Day A897

Wmk. 403

2016, May 1 Litho. *Perf. 13*

1754 A897 £300 multi *2.50 1.25*

Values are for stamp with surrounding selvage.

2016 Summer Olympics, Rio de Janeiro — A898

No. 1755: a, Weight lifting. b, Track. c, Swimming. d, Table tennis. e, Judo.

Perf. 12x11½

2016, Aug. 6 Litho. Wmk. 403

1755 Horiz. strip of 5 *8.75 4.25*

a.-e. A898 £200 Any single *1.75 .85*

World Post Day — A899

Wmk. 403

2016, Oct. 9 Litho. *Perf. 12½*

1757 A899 £250 multi *2.50 1.25*

Ancient Artifacts — A900

Designs: No. 1758, Decorated ewer from Abbasid period.

No. 1759: a, Clay cup. b, Marble bowl, horiz. c, Necklace, horiz. d, Figurine of hawk standing erect. e, Female fertility statue.

Perf. 11½x11¼, 11¼x11½

2016-17 Litho. Wmk. 403

1758 A900 £25 multi *.25 .25*

1759 A900 Strip of 5, dated "2017" *1.90 1.90*

a.	£25 multi	*.25*	*.25*
b.	£50 multi	*.25*	*.25*
c.	£75 multi	*.30*	*.30*
d.	£100 multi	*.40*	*.40*
e.	£155 multi	*.60*	*.60*
f.	Strip of 5, dated "2018"	*1.90*	*1.90*
g.	£25 multi, dated "2018"	*.25*	*.25*
h.	£50 multi, dated "2018"	*.25*	*.25*
i.	£75 multi, dated "2018"	*.30*	*.30*
j.	£100 multi, dated "2018"	*.40*	*.40*
k.	£155 multi, dated "2018"	*.60*	*.60*

Issued: No. 1758, 11/14.

59th Damascus International Fair — A901

No. 1760 — Denomination color: a, £200, Brown red. b, £300, Deep violet.

£500, Deep violet denomination, no frame line.

Perf. 12x11½

2017, Aug. 17 Litho. Wmk. 403

1760 A901 Horiz. pair, #a-b *2.00 2.00*

Size: 64x85mm

Imperf

1761 A901 £500 multi *2.00 2.00*

60th Damascus International Fair — A902

No. 1762: a, £200, Partial rosette. b, £300, Complete rosette.

Perf. 12x11½

2018, Sept. 6 Litho. Wmk. 403

1762 A902 Horiz. pair #a-b 5.25 2.60

World Post Day A903

Perf. 11½x12

2018, Oct. 9 Litho. Wmk. 403

1764 A903 £200 multi 3.00 1.50

Bust of an Ugarit Princess — A904

2018 Litho. Wmk. 403 *Perf. 11½*

Background Color

1765	A904	£5	org brn	.25	.25
1766	A904	£10	blue	.25	.25
1767	A904	£25	olive bister	.35	.25
1768	A904	£50	yel grn	.70	.35
1769	A904	£100	red brown	1.40	.70
1770	A904	£155	violet	1.40	.70
	Nos. 1765-1770 (6)			4.35	2.50

National Environment Day — A905

Perf. 12x11½

2018 Litho. Wmk. 403

1771 A905 £450 multi 4.25 2.10

International Day of Tourism A906

2018 Litho. Wmk. 403 *Perf. 12½*

1772 A906 £500 multi 4.50 2.25

Aleppo Provisional Stamps, Cent. — A907

2018 Litho. Wmk. 403 *Perf. 12*

1773 A907 £500 multi 4.50 2.25

Merops Oreobates — A908

Vanellus A909

Oriolus A910

Sylvia Atricapilla A911

Vanellus A912

Perf. 11½x12

2018 Litho. Wmk. 403

1774 Vert. strip of 5 14.00 7.00

a.	A908 2.75 multi	2.75	1.40
b.	A909 2.75 multi	2.75	1.40
c.	A910 2.75 multi	2.75	1.40
d.	A911 2.75 multi	2.75	1.40
e.	A912 2.75 multi	2.75	1.40

Corrective Movement, 48th Anniv. — A913

Perf. 12½x12

2018 Litho. Wmk. 403

1775 A913 £175 multi 3.00 1.50

Musicians of the 4th Century — A914

2019 Litho. Wmk. 403 *Perf. 12*

1776 A914 £300 multi 3.50 1.75

Day of Culture. Dated 2018.

March 8 Revolution, 56th Anniv. — A915

Perf. 12½x12

2019 Litho. Wmk. 403

1778 A915 £155 multi 1.75 .85

Syrian Sports Day — A916

Perf. 12x11½

2019 Litho. Wmk. 403
1779 A916 £400 multi 5.00 2.50

Motherhood, by Louay Kayali — A917

Perf. 11½x12

2019 Litho. Wmk. 403
1780 A917 £200 multi 3.00 1.50

Mother's Day.

Express Mail Service in Syria, 20th Anniv. — A918

2019 Litho. Wmk. 403 ***Perf. 12***
1781 A918 £250 multi 3.00 1.50

National Day — A919

Perf. 12x12½

2019, Apr. 17 Litho. Wmk. 403
1782 A919 £200 multi 2.75 2.75

Labor Day — A920

Perf. 12½x12

2019, May 1 Litho. Wmk. 403
1783 A920 £300 multi 3.50 3.50

Martyrs' Day — A921

Wmk. 403

2019, May 6 Litho. ***Perf. 12***
1784 A921 £250 multi 2.40 2.40

Flowers A922

No. 1785: a, Lawsonia. b, Saffron. c, Dahlias. d, Salvia officinalis. e, Jasminum sambac.

Wmk. 403

2019, July Litho. ***Perf. 12¼***
1785 Horiz. strip of 5 15.00 15.00
a.-e. A922 £400 Any single 3.00 3.00

Syrian Arab Army Day — A923

Wmk. 403

2019, Aug. 1 Litho. ***Perf. 12***
1786 A923 £155 multi 1.90 1.90

61st International Damascus Fair — A924

No. 1787 — Denomination color: a, £200, Scarlet. b, £300, Dark blue.

Perf. 12x11½

2019, Aug. 28 Litho. Wmk. 403
1787 A924 Horiz. pair, #a-b 4.25 4.25

2019 Mediterranean Beach Games, Greece — A925

No. 1789: a, Beach wrestling. b, Beach soccer. c, Long-distance swimming. d, Aquathlon.

Perf. 11½x12

2019, Sept. Litho. Wmk. 403
1789 Vert. strip of 4 9.00 9.00
a.-d. A925 £250 Any single 2.25 2.25

Burning of Al-Aqsa Mosque, Jerusalem, 50th Anniv. A926

Wmk. 403

2019, Sept. Litho. ***Perf. 13***
1791 A926 £300 multi 2.60 2.60

Values are for stamps with surrounding selvage.

International Year of Indigenous Languages — A927

Perf. 11½x12

2019, Sept. Litho. Wmk. 403
1793 A927 £300 multi 2.60 2.60

A928

A929

A930

International Day of Tourism — A931

Wmk. 403

2019, Sept. 27 Litho. ***Perf. 12***
1795 Vert. strip of 4 5.75 5.75
a. A928 £150 multi 1.40 1.40
b. A929 £150 multi 1.40 1.40
c. A930 £150 multi 1.40 1.40
d. A931 £150 multi 1.40 1.40

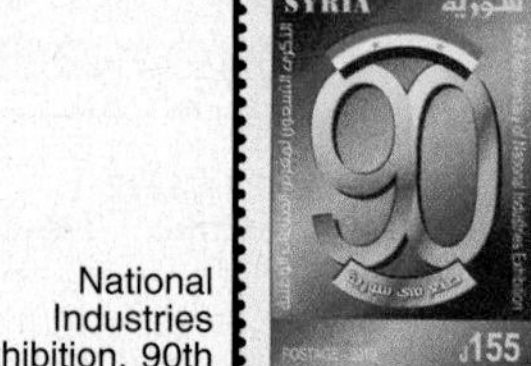
National Industries Exhibition, 90th Anniv. — A932

Perf. 12x11½

2019, Oct. Litho. Wmk. 403
1796 A932 £155 multi 1.50 1.50

Universal Postal Union, 145th Anniv. — A933

Wmk. 403

2019, Oct. 9 Litho. ***Perf. 12***
1797 A933 £300 multi 3.00 3.00

2019 World Beach Games, Qatar — A934

Wmk. 403

2019, Nov. Litho. ***Perf. 12***
1799 A934 £500 multi 5.25 5.25

World Environment Day — A935

Wmk. 403

2019, Nov. Litho. ***Perf. 12***
1801 A935 £250 multi 3.00 3.00

Corrective Movement, 49th Anniv. — A936

Perf. 12½x12

2019, Dec. Litho. Wmk. 403
1802 A936 £200 multi 2.40 2.40

Ancient Amphitheaters — A937

No. 1803: a, Bosra Amphitheater. b, Palmyra Amphitheater. c, Jableh Amphitheater.

2019 Litho. Wmk. 403 ***Perf. 12***
1803 Vert. strip of 3 6.75 6.75
a.-c. A937 £300 Any single 2.25 2.25

Culture Day — A938

2019 **Litho.** ***Perf. 12x11½*** **Wmk. 403**

1804 A938 £250 multi 3.00 3.00

Decorated Urn — A939

2019 Litho. Wmk. 403 *Perf. 11½*

Denomination Color

1805 A939 £5 purple .25 .25
1806 A939 £10 red brn .25 .25
1807 A939 £25 redsh lilac .25 .25
1808 A939 £50 white .50 .50
1809 A939 £100 violet .95 .95
1810 A939 £155 grnsh yel 1.50 1.50
Nos. 1805-1810 (6) 3.70 3.70

SEMI-POSTAL STAMPS

Nos. 174-185 Srchd. in Red or Black

1926 Unwmk. *Perf. 12½, 13½*

B1 A4 25c + 25c ol blk (R) 2.25 2.00
B2 A4 50c + 25c yel grn 2.25 2.00
B3 A4 75c + 25c brown org 2.25 2.00
B4 A5 1p + 50c magenta 2.25 2.00
B5 A4 1.25p + 50c dp grn (R) 2.25 2.00
B6 A4 1.50p + 50c rose red 2.25 2.00
B7 A4 2p + 75c dk brn (R) 2.25 2.00
B8 A4 2.50p + 75c pck bl (R) 2.25 2.00
B9 A4 3p + 1p org brn (R) 2.25 2.00
B10 A4 5p + 1p violet 2.25 2.00
B11 A4 10p + 2p vio brn 2.25 2.00
B12 A4 25p + 5p ultra (R) 2.25 2.00
Nos. B1-B12 (12) 27.00 24.00
Set, never hinged 36.00

On No. B4 the surcharge is set in six lines to fit the shape of the stamp.

The surcharge was a contribution to the relief of refugees from the Djebel Druze War.

See Nos. CB1-CB4.

Catalogue values for unused stamps in this section, from this point to the end of the section, are for Never Hinged items.

Syrian Arab Republic

Jordanian Flags on Map of Israel, and Arabs — SP1

1965, June 12 Litho. *Perf. 12x11½*

B13 SP1 12½p + 5p multi .25 .25
B14 SP1 25p + 5p multi .25 .25

Issued for Palestine Week.

Father with Children and Red Crescent SP2

1968, May Litho. *Perf. 12½x12*

B15 SP2 12½p + 2½p multi .25 .25
B16 SP2 27½p + 7½p multi .25 .25

The surtax was for refugees.

AIR POST STAMPS

Nos. 35, 45, 47 Hstmpd. in Violet — a

1920, Dec. Unwmk. *Perf. 13½*

C1 A22 1p on 5c 175.00 40.00
C2 A20 5p on 15c 300.00 47.50
C3 A18 10p on 40c 450.00 77.50
Nos. C1-C3 (3) 925.00 165.00

Nos. 36, 46, 48 Overprinted Type "a" in Violet

1921, June 12

C4 A22 1p on 20c 90.00 40.00
C5 A18 5p on 1fr 450.00 150.00
C6 A18 10p on 40c 450.00 150.00
Nos. C4-C6 (3) 990.00 340.00

Excellent counterfeits exist of Nos. C1-C6.

Nos. 36, 46, 48 Overprinted — b

1921, Oct. 5

C7 A22 1p on 20c 65.00 18.50
C8 A18 5p on 1fr 160.00 37.50
a. Inverted overprint 325.00 250.00
C9 A18 10p on 2fr 200.00 60.00
a. Double overprint 475.00 425.00
Nos. C7-C9 (3) 425.00 116.00

Nos. 92, 94-96 Ovptd. — c

1922, May 28

C10 A18 2p on 40c 30.00 30.00
a. Inverted overprint
C11 A18 3p on 60c 30.00 30.00
C12 A18 5p on 1fr 30.00 30.00
C13 A18 10p on 2fr 30.00 30.00
Nos. C10-C13 (4) 120.00 120.00

Nos. 116-119 Overprinted Type "c"

1923, Nov. 22

C14 A18 2p on 40c 35.00 35.00
b. Inverted surcharge
C15 A18 3p on 60c 35.00 35.00
C16 A18 5p on 1fr 35.00 35.00
C17 A18 10p on 2fr 35.00 35.00
b. Double overprint
Nos. C14-C17 (4) 140.00 140.00

Overprinted "Liabn"

C14a A18 2p on 40c 400.00 400.00
C15a A18 3p on 60c 400.00 400.00
C16a A18 5p on 1fr 400.00 400.00
C17a A18 10p on 2fr 400.00 400.00

Nos. 137-140 Overprinted Type c

1924, Jan. 13

C18 A18 2p on 40c 6.00 6.00
a. Double overprint 30.00
C19 A18 3p on 60c 6.00 6.00
a. Inverted overprint 50.00
C20 A18 5p on 1fr 6.00 6.00
a. Double overprint 60.00 30.00
C21 A18 10p on 2fr 6.00 6.00
Nos. C18-C21 (4) 24.00 24.00

Nos. 152, 154, 157-158 Overprinted

1924, July 17

C22 A18 2p on 40c 9.00 9.00
a. Inverted overprint 35.00
C23 A18 3p on 60c 9.00 9.00
a. Inverted overprint 35.00
b. Double overprint 25.00
C24 A18 5p on 1fr 9.00 9.00
C25 A18 10p on 2fr 9.00 9.00
a. Inverted overprint 35.00
Nos. C22-C25 (4) 36.00 36.00

Regular Issue of 1925 Overprinted in Green

1925, Mar. 1

C26 A4 2p dark brown 2.50 2.50
C27 A4 3p orange brown 2.50 2.50
C28 A4 5p violet 2.50 2.50
C29 A4 10p violet brown 2.50 2.50
Nos. C26-C29 (4) 10.00 10.00

Nos.180, 182, 183-184 Ovptd. in Red — f

1926

C30 A4 2p dark brown 2.25 2.25
a. Inverted overprint 42.50 42.50
C31 A4 3p orange brown 2.25 2.25
C32 A4 5p violet 2.75 2.75
a. Inverted overprint 42.50 42.50
b. Double overprint 67.50 67.50
C33 A4 10p violet brown 2.75 2.75
a. Inverted overprint 42.50 42.50
b. Double overprint 70.00 70.00
Nos. C30-C33 (4) 10.00 10.00

Nos. C30-C33 received their first airmail use June 16, 1929, at the opening of the Beirut-Marseille line.

For surcharges see Nos. CB1-CB4.

Regular Issue of 1925 Overprinted Type "f" in Red or Black

1929

C34 A4 50c yellow green (R) 1.50 1.50
a. Inverted overprint 42.50
b. Overprinted on face and back 25.00
c. Double overprint 42.50
d. Double overprint, one inverted 62.50
e. Pair, one without overprint
C35 A5 1p magenta (Bk) 2.00 2.00
a. Reversed overprint
b. Red overprint
C36 A4 25p ultra (R) 5.75 5.75
a. Inverted overprint 87.50
b. Pair, one without overprint
Nos. C34-C36 (3) 9.25 9.25

On No. C35, the overprint is vertical, with plane nose down.

No. 197 Overprinted Type "f" in Red

1929, July 9

C37 A4 15p on 25p ultra 4.50 4.50
a. Inverted overprint

Air Post Stamps of 1926-29 Ovptd. in Various Colors

1929, Sept. 5

C38 A4 50c yellow grn (R) 3.00 3.00
C39 A5 1p magenta (Bl) 3.00 3.00
C40 A4 2p dk brown (V) 3.00 3.00
C41 A4 3p orange brn (Bl) 3.00 3.00
a. Inverted overprint 70.00
C42 A4 5p violet (R) 3.00 3.00
C43 A4 10p violet brn (Bl) 3.00 3.00
C44 A4 25p ultra (R) 3.00 3.00
Nos. C38-C44 (7) 21.00 21.00

Damascus Industrial Exhibition.

AP1

1930, Jan. 30 Red Surcharge

C45 AP1 2p on 1.25p dp grn 3.00 3.00
a. Inverted surcharge
b. Double surcharge 60.00

Plane over Homs AP2

Designs: 1pi, City Wall, Damascus. 2pi, Euphrates River. 3pi, Temple Ruins, Palmyra. 5pi, Deir-el-Zor. 10pi, Damascus. 15pi, Aleppo, Citadel. 25pi, Hama. 50pi, Zebdani. 100pi, Telebisse.

1931-33 Photo. Unwmk.

C46 AP2 50c ocher 1.00 .90
C47 AP2 50c black brn ('33) 1.25 1.00
C48 AP2 1p chestnut brown 1.10 .95
C49 AP2 2p Prus blue 2.75 1.75
C50 AP2 3p blue grn 1.75 1.25
C51 AP2 5p red violet 1.25 1.25
C52 AP2 10p slate grn 1.25 1.25
C53 AP2 15p orange red 2.10 1.50
C54 AP2 25p orange brn 2.75 2.00
C55 AP2 50p black 3.00 2.25
C56 AP2 100p magenta 3.75 2.50
Nos. C46-C56 (11) 21.95 16.60

Nos. C46 to C56 exist imperforate. Value, $425.

For overprints see Nos. C67-C71, C110-C112, C114-C115, MC1-MC4.

Village of Bloudan AP12

1934, Aug. 2 Engr. *Perf. 12½*

C57 AP12 50c yel brown 2.50 2.50
C58 AP12 1p green 3.00 3.00
C59 AP12 2p peacock bl 3.00 3.00
C60 AP12 3p red 3.50 3.50
C61 AP12 5p plum 3.50 3.50
C62 AP12 10p brt violet 30.00 30.00
C63 AP12 15p orange brn 32.50 32.50
C64 AP12 25p dk ultra 37.50 37.50
C65 AP12 50p black 50.00 50.00
C66 AP12 100p red brown 110.00 110.00
Nos. C57-C66 (10) 275.50 275.50

Proclamation of the Republic. Nos. C57-C66 exist imperf. Value, set $1,100. Also exists without figures of value. Value, set $1,500.

Complete set of 29 (Nos. 232-250, C57-66) exist imperf. Value, $2,600.

No. C58 exists without values, imperf. Value, $125.

Air Post Stamps of 1931-33 Overprinted in Red or Black

1936, Apr. 15 *Perf. 13½x13, 13½*

C67 AP2 50c black brown 5.25 4.75
C68 AP2 1p chnt brown (Bk) 5.25 4.75
C69 AP2 2p Prus blue 5.25 4.75
C70 AP2 3p blue green 5.25 4.75
C71 AP2 5p red violet (Bk) 5.25 4.75
Nos. C67-C71 (5) 26.25 23.75

Damascus Fair, May 1936.

Syrian Pavilion at Paris Exposition AP13

1937, July 1 Photo. *Perf. 13½*

C72 AP13 ½p yellow green 2.75 2.75
C73 AP13 1p green 2.75 2.75
C74 AP13 2p lt brown 2.75 2.75
C75 AP13 3p rose red 2.75 2.75
C76 AP13 5p brown orange 2.75 2.75
C77 AP13 10p grnsh black 4.75 4.75
C78 AP13 15p blue 5.25 5.25
C79 AP13 25p dark violet 6.25 6.25
Nos. C72-C79 (8) 30.00 30.00

Paris International Exposition. Exist imperf.

Ancient Citadel at Aleppo AP14

Omayyad Mosque and Minaret of Jesus at Damascus AP15

1937 Engr. *Perf. 13*

C80 AP14 ½p dark violet .65 .65
C81 AP15 1p black .65 .65
C82 AP14 2p deep green .65 .65
C83 AP15 3p deep ultra .65 .65
C84 AP14 5p rose lake 2.00 2.00
C85 AP15 10p red brown 1.10 1.10
C86 AP14 15p lake brown 4.75 4.75
C87 AP15 25p dark blue 6.00 6.00
Nos. C80-C87 (8) 16.45 16.45

No. C80 to C87 exist imperforate. Value, set $175.
For overprint see No. C109.

Maurice Noguès and Route of France-Syria Flight — AP16

1938, July Photo. *Perf. 11½*

C88 AP16 10p dark green 5.00 4.50
a. Souv. sheet of 4, perf. 13½ 50.00 45.00
b. Perf. 13½ 8.00 8.00

10th anniversary of first Marseille-Beirut flight, by Maurice Noguès.
No. C88a exists imperf.; value $800.

Bridge at Deir-el-Zor AP17

1940 Engr. *Perf. 13*

C89 AP17 25c brown black .25 .25
C90 AP17 50c peacock blue .25 .25
C91 AP17 1p deep ultra .30 .30
C92 AP17 2p dk orange brn .45 .45
C93 AP17 5p green .95 .95
C94 AP17 10p rose carmine 1.40 1.00
C95 AP17 50p dark violet 3.00 2.25
Nos. C89-C95 (7) 6.60 5.45

Exist imperf. Value, set $175.

President Taj Eddin Hassani AP18

1942 Litho. *Perf. 11½*

C96 AP18 10p blue gray 4.00 4.00
C97 AP18 50p gray lilac 4.25 4.25

Proclamation of Independence by the Allies, Sept. 27, 1941.

President Taj Eddin Hassani — AP19

1942 Photo.

C98 AP19 10p sl grn & yel grn 4.00 4.00

Exists imperforate. Value, $30.

President Hassani and Map of Syria — AP20

1943 Litho.

C99 AP20 2p dull brown 3.00 3.00
C100 AP20 10p red violet 3.00 3.00
C101 AP20 20p aqua 3.00 3.00
C102 AP20 50p rose pink 3.00 3.00
Nos. C99-C102 (4) 12.00 12.00

Proclamation of United Syria.

Overprinted with Black Border

1943, May 5

C103 AP20 2p dull brown 3.00 3.00
C104 AP20 10p red violet 3.00 3.00
C105 AP20 20p aqua 3.00 3.00
C106 AP20 50p rose pink 3.00 3.00
Nos. C103-C106 (4) 12.00 12.00

Mourning for President Hassani. Exist imperf.

President Shukri el Kouatly — AP21

1944

C107 AP21 200p sepia 9.50 7.50
C108 AP21 500p dull blue 14.00 11.00

For overprints see Nos. C113, C116.

Stamps of 1931-44 Overprinted in Black, Blue or Carmine

1944 *Perf. 13, 13½, 11½*

C109 AP15 10p red brn (Bk) 2.50 2.50
C110 AP2 15p orange red 2.75 2.75
C111 AP2 25p org brown 2.75 2.75
C112 AP2 100p magenta 8.00 6.75
C113 AP21 200p sepia (C) 15.00 12.00
Nos. C109-C113 (5) 31.00 26.75
Set, never hinged 50.00

1st congress of Arab lawyers held in Damascus, Sept. 1944.

Nos. C53-C54, C108 Overprinted in Black or Orange

1944

C114 AP2 15p orange red 3.00 3.00
C115 AP2 25p org brown 3.00 3.00
C116 AP21 500p dull blue (O) 22.50 22.50
Nos. C114-C116 (3) 28.50 28.50
Set, never hinged 40.00

See note after No. 299.

President Shukri el Kouatly AP22

1945, Mar. 15 Litho. *Perf. 11½*

C117 AP22 5p pale green .50 .25
C118 AP22 10p dull red .50 .25
C119 AP22 15p orange .60 .25
C120 AP22 25p lt blue 1.25 .50
C121 AP22 50p lt violet 1.75 .70
C122 AP22 100p deep brown 3.50 1.25
C123 AP22 200p fawn 8.00 4.00
Nos. C117-C123 (7) 16.10 7.10
Set, never hinged 25.00

Resumption of constitutional government.

Catalogue values for unused stamps in this section, from this point to the end of the section, are for Never Hinged items.

Plane and Flock of Sheep AP23

Kattineh Dam AP24

Kanawat, Djebel Druze AP25

Sultan Ibrahim Mosque AP26

1946-47 *Perf. 13x13½*

C124 AP23 3p rose brown .50 .25
C125 AP23 5p lt bl grn ('47) .50 .25
C126 AP23 6p dp org ('47) .50 .25
C127 AP24 10p sl gray ('47) .35 .25
C128 AP24 15p scarlet ('47) .35 .25
C129 AP24 25p blue .45 .25
C130 AP25 50p violet .75 .25
C131 AP25 100p blue green 1.75 .40
C132 AP25 200p brown ('47) 4.00 1.25
C133 AP26 300p red brn ('47) 16.00 2.50
C134 AP26 500p ol gray ('47) 17.50 3.50
Nos. C124-C134 (11) 42.65 9.40

For overprints and surcharges see Nos. C135-C139, C148-C152, C157, C172.

No. C129 Overprinted in Red

1946, Apr. 17

C135 AP24 25p blue 2.50 1.00

Evacuation of British and French troops from Syria.

Nos. C129-C131 Overprinted in Magenta

1946, Aug. 28

C136 AP24 25p blue 2.50 1.25
C137 AP25 50p violet 3.00 1.75
C138 AP25 100p blue green 6.00 3.00
Nos. C136-C138 (3) 11.50 6.00

See note after No. 334.

No. C135 with Additional Overprint in Black

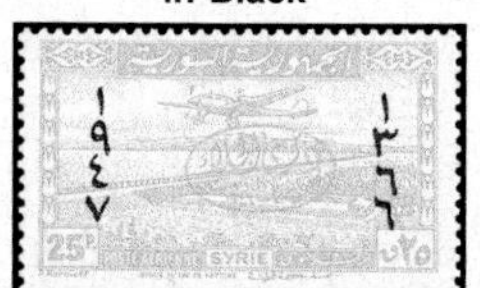

1947, June 10 *Perf. 13x13½*

C139 AP24 25p blue 2.50 1.25

1st anniv. of the evacuation of British and French troops from Syria.

Window at Kasr El-Heir El-Gharbi AP27

Ram-headed Sphinxes Carved in Ivory, from King Hazael's Bed — AP28

1947, Nov. 15 Litho. *Perf. 11½*

C140 AP27 12.50p dark violet 1.50 .50
C141 AP28 50p brown 5.00 2.00
a. Souv. sheet of 4, #338-339, C140-C141 65.00 65.00

1st Arab Archaeological Cong., Damascus, Nov.
No. C141a sold for 125 piasters.

Kasr El-Heir El-Charqui AP29

Congress Emblem — AP30

1947, Nov. 15

C142	AP29	12.50p olive black	1.00	.50
C143	AP30	50p dull violet	4.50	2.25
a.		Souv. sheet of 4, #340, 341, C142, C143	65.00	65.00

3rd Cong. of Arab Engineers, Damascus, Nov.

No. C143a sold for 125 piasters.

Kouatly Types of Regular Issue

1948, June 22 Litho. *Perf. 10½*

C144	A50	12.50p dp bl & vio brn	.65	.25
C145	A51	50p violet brn & grn	2.50	1.00
a.		Souv. sheet, #342, 343, C144, C145, imperf	150.00	150.00

Reelection of Pres. Shukri el Kouatly.

Military Training Types of Regular Issue

1948, June 22

C146	A52	12.50p blue & dk bl	.75	.25
C147	A53	50p green, car & blk	2.00	.80
a.		Souv. sheet of 4, #344, 345, C146, C147, imperf.	140.00	140.00

Inauguration of compulsory military training.

Nos. C124, C126 & C132 to C134 Srchd. in Black or Carmine

No. C148

No. C151

1948, Oct. 18 *Perf. 13x13½*

C148	AP23	2.50p on 3p	.30	.25
C149	AP23	2.50p on 6p	.35	.25
C150	AP25	25p on 200p (C)	.80	.25
C151	AP26	50p on 300p	*10.00*	.75
C152	AP26	50p on 500p	*10.00*	.75
		Nos. C148-C152 (5)	21.45	2.25

Husni Zayim Type of Regular Issue

1949, June 20 Litho. *Perf. 11½*

C153	A54	50p brown	3.75	2.50

Revolution of March 30, 1949.

Pigeons and Globe AP36

Husni Zayim and View of Damascus AP37

1949, June 20 Unwmk.

C154	AP36	12.50p claret	7.50	6.00
C155	AP37	50p gray black	19.00	12.50

UPU, 75th anniv. A souvenir sheet of 4 contains #349, 350, C154, C155. Value $125.

Election Type of Regular Issue Wmk. 291

1949, Aug. 6 Litho. *Perf. 11½*

C156	A57	50p car rose & dk grnsh bl	3.75	2.50
a.		Souv. sheet of 2, #351, C156, imperf.	175.00	175.00

Election of Pres. Husni Zayim.

No. C131 Surcharged in Black

1950 Unwmk. *Perf. 13x13½*

C157	AP25	2.50p on 100p bl grn	.40	.25

Port of Latakia AP38

1950, Dec. 25 *Perf. 11½*

C158	AP38	2.50p dull lilac	.50	.25
C159	AP38	10p grnsh blue	1.10	.25
C160	AP38	15p orange brown	2.50	.40
C161	AP38	25p bright blue	5.50	.35
		Nos. C158-C161 (4)	9.60	1.25

Exist imperf. Value, $35. See No. C173. For overprint see No. C169.

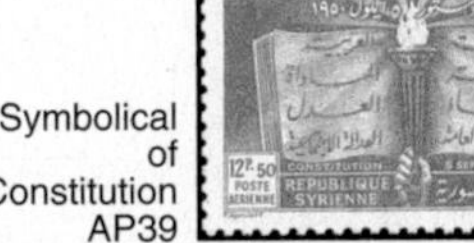
Symbolical of Constitution AP39

1951, Apr. 14 Unwmk.

C162	AP39	12.50p crimson rose	.40	.25
C163	AP39	50p brown violet	1.25	1.00

New constitution adopted Sept. 5, 1950. Exist imperf.

Ruins, Palmyra AP40

Citadel at Aleppo AP41

1952, Apr. 22 Litho. *Perf. 11½*

C164	AP40	2.50p vermilion	.30	.25
C165	AP40	5p green	.35	.25
C166	AP40	15p violet	.50	.25
C167	AP41	25p deep blue	.75	.35
C168	AP41	100p lilac rose	5.50	1.00
		Nos. C164-C168 (5)	7.40	2.10

Nos. C164-C168 exist imperforate. For overprints see Nos. C170-C171, C186.

Stamps of 1946-52 Overprinted in Black

1953, Feb. 16 *Perf. 13x13½, 11½*

C169	AP38	10p grnsh blue	2.00	1.00
C170	AP40	15p violet	2.25	1.10
C171	AP41	25p deep blue	3.25	1.60
C172	AP25	50p violet	8.00	2.25
		Nos. C169-C172 (4)	15.50	5.95

UN Social Welfare Seminar, Damascus, Dec. 8-20, 1952.

Type of 1950 and

Post Office, Aleppo AP42

1953, Oct. Photo. *Perf. 11½*

C173	AP38	10p violet blue	.50	.25
C174	AP42	50p red brown	1.60	.30

For overprint see No. C185.

Building at Hama and PTT Emblem — AP43

University of Syria, Damascus AP44

1954

C175	AP43	5p violet	.25	.25
C176	AP43	10p brown	.30	.25
C177	AP43	15p dull green	.35	.25
C178	AP44	30p dark brown	.45	.25
C179	AP44	35p blue	.80	.25
C180	AP44	40p orange	1.75	.40
C181	AP44	50p deep plum	1.25	.60
C182	AP44	70p purple	3.25	.70
		Nos. C175-C182 (8)	8.40	2.95

For overprints see UAR Nos. C27-C28.

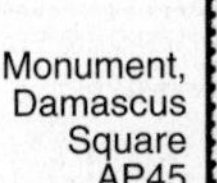

Monument, Damascus Square AP45

Mosque and Syrian Flag — AP46

1954, Sept. 2

C183	AP45	40p carmine rose	1.00	.45
C184	AP46	50p green	1.25	.55

Damascus Fair, Sept. 1954. Nos. C183-C184 exist imperforate.

Nos. C174 and C168 Overprinted in Blue or Black

1954, Oct. 9

C185	AP42	50p red brown (Bl)	1.10	1.00
C186	AP41	100p lilac rose	2.00	1.60

Cotton Festival, Aleppo, October 1954.

Virgin of Sednaya Convent — AP47

1955, Mar. 27 Photo. *Perf. 11½*

C187	AP47	25p deep purple	.60	.40
C188	AP47	75p deep blue green	1.75	1.25

50th anniv. of the founding of Rotary Intl. Exist imperforate.

Omayyad Mosque — AP48

1955, Mar. 26

C189	AP48	35p cerise	.95	.60
C190	AP48	65p deep green	1.75	1.10

1955 Regional Cong. of Rotary Intl., Damascus.

Arab Postal Union Type of Regular Issue

1955, Jan. 1 *Perf. 13½x13*

C191	A69a	5p yellow brown	.40	.25

Founding of the APU, July 1, 1954. For overprints see Nos. C203, C207.

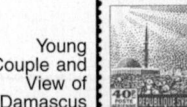

Young Couple and View of Damascus AP49

60p, Tank and planes leading advancing troops.

1955, Apr. 16 Litho. *Perf. 11½*

C192	AP49	40p dark rose lake	.60	.30
C193	AP49	60p ultra	2.25	.35

9th anniv. of the evacuation of British and French troops from Syria.

Mother's Day Type of Regular Issue

1955, May 13 Unwmk.

C194	A70	35p violet	1.00	.60
C195	A70	40p black	1.50	.95

Issued to publicize Mother's Day.

Emigrants under Syrian Flag — AP51

15p, Airplane over globe and fountain.

1955, July 26 *Perf. 11½*

C196	AP51	5p magenta	.55	.25
C197	AP51	15p light blue	.75	.40

Emigrants' Congress. Exist imperf.

Mother and Child — AP52

1955, Oct. 3 **Photo.**

C198 AP52 25p deep blue .75 .50
C199 AP52 50p plum 1.25 .90

International Children's Day.

Globe, Scales and Dove AP53

1955, Oct. 30

C200 AP53 15p ultra .75 .40
C201 AP53 35p brown black 1.50 .60

10th anniv. of the UN, Oct. 24, 1955.
For overprints see Nos. C221-C222.

Aqueduct Type of Regular Issue

1955, Nov. 21 **Litho.** **Unwmk.**

C202 A72 30p dark blue 2.00 1.10

No. C191 Overprinted in Ultramarine

1955, Dec. 29 **Photo.** ***Perf. 13½x13***

C203 A69a 5p yellow brown .50 .25

APU Congress, Cairo, Mar. 15, 1955.

Liberation Monument — AP54

Designs: 65p, Winged figure with shield and sword. 75p, President Shukri el Kouatly.

1956, Apr. 17 **Litho.** ***Perf. 11½***

C204 AP54 35p black brown .60 .40
C205 AP54 65p rose red 1.00 .60
C206 AP54 75p dk slate green 1.90 1.00
Nos. C204-C206 (3) 3.50 2.00

10th anniv. of the evacuation of British and French troops from Syria.

No. C191 Overprinted in Black

1956, Apr. 11 **Photo.** ***Perf. 13½x13***

C207 A69a 5p yellow brown .50 .25

Visit of King Hussein of Jordan to Damascus, Apr. 1956.

President Shukri el Kouatly — AP55

1956, July 7 **Litho.** ***Perf. 11½***

C208 AP55 100p black 1.25 1.00
C209 AP55 200p violet 2.50 1.25
C210 AP55 300p dull rose 4.00 2.75
C211 AP55 500p dk bl grn 7.50 5.00
Nos. C208-C211 (4) 15.25 10.00

Nos. CB5-CB8 Overprinted with 3 Bars Obliterating Surtax

1956

C212 SPAP1 25p gray black .60 .25
C213 SPAP1 35p ultra .75 .25
C214 SPAP2 40p rose lilac 1.50 .60
C215 SPAP1 70p Prus green 1.75 .90
Nos. C212-C215 (4) 4.60 2.00

Gate of Kasr el Heir, Palmyra — AP56

Designs: 20p, Hand loom and modern mill. 30p, Ox-drawn plow and tractor. 35p, Cog-wheels and galley. 50p, Textiles and vase.

1956, Sept. 1 **Unwmk.**

C216 AP56 15p gray .50 .50
C217 AP56 20p brt ultra .75 .75
C218 AP56 30p blue green 1.00 1.00
C219 AP56 35p blue 1.25 1.25
C220 AP56 50p rose lilac 1.50 1.50
Nos. C216-C220 (5) 5.00 5.00

3rd International Fair, Damascus.

Nos. C200-C201 Ovptd. in Red or Green

1956, Oct. 30 **Photo.** ***Perf. 11½***

C221 AP53 15p ultra (R) 1.00 .60
C222 AP53 35p brown blk (G) 1.75 1.25

United Nations, 11th anniversary.

Clay Tablet with First Alphabet AP57

Helmet of Syrian Legionary and Ornament — AP58

50p, Lintel from Temple of the Sun, Palmyra.

1956, Oct. 8 **Typo.**

C223 AP57 20p gray 1.00 .40
C224 AP58 30p magenta 1.25 .50
C225 AP57 50p gray brown 1.90 1.00
Nos. C223-C225 (3) 4.15 1.90

Intl. Museum Week (UNESCO), Oct. 8-14.

Trees and Mosque AP59

1956, Dec. 27 **Litho.** ***Perf. 11½***

C226 AP59 10p olive bister .40 .25
C227 AP59 40p slate green .90 .45

Day of the Tree, Dec. 27, 1956.
See UAR No. 36. For overprint see UAR No. 49.

Mother and Child — AP60

Design: 60p, Mother holding infant.

1957, Mar. 21 **Unwmk.**

C228 AP60 40p ultra .75 .60
C229 AP60 60p vermilion 1.25 .85

Mother's Day, 1957.

Sword and Shields — AP61

Designs: 15p, 35p, Map and "Syria" holding torch. 25p, Pres. Kouatly.

1957, Apr. 20 **Wmk. 291**

C230 AP61 10p redsh brn .30 .25
C231 AP61 15p bl grn .40 .25
C232 AP61 25p violet .50 .35
C233 AP61 35p cerise .75 .50
C234 AP61 40p gray 1.10 .60
Nos. C230-C234 (5) 3.05 1.95

British-French troop evacuation, 11th anniv.

Ship Loading — AP62

Sugar Production AP63

30p, 40p, Harvesting grain and cotton.

1957, Sept. 1 **Unwmk.** ***Perf. 11½***

C235 AP62 25p magenta .50 .30
C236 AP62 30p light red brown .60 .35
C237 AP63 35p light blue .75 .40
C238 AP62 40p blue green 1.00 .50
C239 AP62 70p olive bister 1.25 .90
Nos. C235-C239 (5) 4.10 2.45

4th International Fair, Damascus.

Arab Lawyers Type of Regular Issue

1957, Sept. 21 **Litho.** **Wmk. 291**

C240 A76 17½p red .40 .30
C241 A76 40p black .90 .50

Cotton Festival Type of Regular Issue

1957, Oct. 17

C242 A77 17½p org & blk .75 .40
C243 A77 40p lt bl & blk 1.25 .50

Children's Day Type of Regular Issue

1957, Oct. 3

C244 A78 17½p ultra 1.25 .50
C245 A78 20p red brn 1.50 .50

International Children's Day, Oct. 7.
For overprints see UAR Nos. C10-C11.

Family Writing and Reading Letters AP64

1957, Oct. 18 **Litho.** **Unwmk.**

C246 AP64 5p brt grn .40 .25

Intl. Letter Writing Week Oct. 6-12.
For overprint see UAR No. C26.

Afro-Asian Jurists Type of Regular Issue

1957, Nov. **Wmk. 291** ***Perf. 11½***

C247 A80 30p lt bl grn .50 .35
C248 A80 50p lt vio .75 .50

Type of Regular Issue and

Radio, Telegraph and Telephone — AP65

1958, Feb. 12 ***Perf. 11½***

C249 A83 10p brt grn .35 .25
C250 AP65 15p brown .40 .25

Syrian Arab Republic

Souvenir Sheet

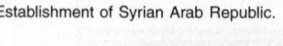

Syrian Flag — AP67

1961 **Unwmk.** **Litho.** ***Imperf.***

C253 AP67 50p multi 2.75 2.75

Establishment of Syrian Arab Republic.

"The Beauty of Palmyra" — AP68

Archway, Palmyra — AP69

Design: 200p, 300p, 500p, 1000p, Niche, King Zahir Bibar's tomb.

1961-63 Litho. *Perf. 12x11½*

C255	AP68	45p	citron	.40	.25
C256	AP68	50p	red org	.50	.25
C257	AP69	85p	sepia	1.00	.30
C258	AP69	100p	lilac	1.25	.35
C259	AP69	200p	sl grn ('62)	2.25	.65
C260	AP69	300p	dk bl ('62)	2.75	.75
C261	AP69	500p	lilac ('63)	4.00	1.50
C262	AP69	1000p	dk gray ('63)	8.25	2.75
	Nos. C255-C262 (8)			20.40	6.80

See Nos. 433-436.

Arab League Building, Cairo, and Emblem — AP70

1962, Apr. 1 *Perf. 12x11½*

C264	AP70	17½p	Prus grn & yel grn	.30	.25
C265	AP70	22½p	dk & lt bl	.30	.25
C266	AP70	50p	dk brn & dl org	.75	.30
	Nos. C264-C266 (3)			1.35	.80

Arab League Week, Mar. 22-28.

Malaria Eradication Emblem — AP71

1962, Apr. 7

C267	AP71	12½p	ol, lt bl & pur	.40	.25
C268	AP71	50p	brn, yel & grn	.75	.40

WHO drive to eradicate malaria.

Rearing Horse — AP72

Gen. Yusef al-Azmeh AP73

1962, Apr. 17

C269	AP72	45p	vio & org	.55	.25
C270	AP73	55p	vio bl & lt bl	.75	.25

Evacuation Day, 1962.

Martyrs' Square Memorial, Globe and Handshake AP74

Design: 40p, 45p, Eastern Gate at Fair.

1962, Aug. 25 Litho. *Perf. 12x11½*

C271	AP74	17½p	rose cl & brn	.30	.25
C272	AP74	22½p	ver & magenta	.30	.25
C273	AP74	40p	vio brn & lt brn	.30	.25
C274	AP74	45p	grnsh bl & lt grn	.50	.25
	Nos. C271-C274 (4)			1.40	1.00

9th International Damascus Fair.

Cotton and Cogwheel AP75

1962, Sept. 20 *Perf. 12x11½*

C275	AP75	12½p	multi	.35	.25
C276	AP75	50p	multi	.50	.25

Cotton Festival, Aleppo. See Nos. 455-456.

President Type of Regular Issue

1962, Dec. 14 Unwmk.

C278	A88	50p	bl gray & tan	.75	.25

1st anniv. of the election of Pres. Nazem el-Kodsi.

Queen Zenobia of Palmyra — AP76

1962, Dec. 28 *Perf. 12x11½*

C279	AP76	45p	violet	1.00	.25
C280	AP76	50p	rose red	1.00	.25
C281	AP76	85p	blue green	1.00	.30
C282	AP76	100p	rose claret	1.25	.55
	Nos. C279-C282 (4)			4.25	1.35

Saad Allah El Jabri — AP77

1962, Dec. 30 Litho.

C283	AP77	50p	dull blue	.50	.25

Saad Allah El Jabri (1894-1947), a leader in Syria's struggle for independence.

Woman from Mohardé — AP78

Regional Costumes: 40p, Marje Sultan. 45p, Kalamoun. 55p, Jabal-Al-Arab. 60p, Afrine. 65p, Hauran.

1963 *Perf. 12*

Costumes in Original Colors

C285	AP78	40p	pale lil & blk	.55	.25
C286	AP78	45p	pink & blk	.60	.25
C287	AP78	50p	lt grn & blk	.60	.25
C288	AP78	55p	lt bl & blk	.75	.30
C289	AP78	60p	tan & blk	.80	.30
C290	AP78	65p	pale grn & blk	1.00	.40
	Nos. C285-C290 (6)			4.30	1.75

Hunger Type of Regular Issue

50p, Wheat emblem & bird feeding nestlings.

Perf. 12x11½

1963, Mar. 21 Unwmk.

C291	A91	50p	ver & blk	.45	.25
a.	Souv. sheet of 2, #453, C291, imperf.			1.50	1.50

FAO "Freedom from Hunger" campaign.

Eagle in Flight — AP79

1963, Apr. 18 Litho.

C292	AP79	12½p	brt grn	.30	.25
C293	AP79	50p	lilac rose	.35	.25

Revolution of Mar. 8, 1963.

Faris el Khouri — AP80

Arms and Wreath — AP81

1963, Apr. 27 *Perf. 12x11½*

C294	AP80	17½p	gray	.30	.25
C295	AP81	22½p	bl grn & blk	.30	.25

Evacuation Day, 1963.

abu-al-Ala al-Maarri — AP82

1963, Aug. 19 *Perf. 12x11½*

C296	AP82	50p	violet blue	.40	.25

abu-al-Ala al-Maarri (973-1057), poet and philosopher.

Copper Pitcher, Arch and Fair — AP83

1963, Aug. 25

C297	AP83	37½p	ultra, yel & brn	.45	.25
C298	AP83	50p	brt bl, yel & brn	.50	.25

10th International Damascus Fair.

Centenary Emblem — AP84

50p, Centenary emblem and globe.

1963, Sept. 19 Litho.

C299	AP84	15p	chlky bl, red & blk	.40	.25
C300	AP84	50p	yel grn, blk & red	.50	.25

Centenary of the International Red Cross.

Abou Feras al Hamadani AP85

1963, Nov. 13 *Perf. 12x11½*

C301	AP85	50p	yel ol & dk brn	.50	.25

Abou Feras (932-968), poet.

Heads of Three Races and Flame — AP86

1964, Jan. 6 Unwmk.

C302	AP86	17½p	multi	.30	.25
C303	AP86	22½p	grn, blk & red	.30	.25
C304	AP86	50p	vio, blk & red	.40	.25
a.	Souv. sheet of 3			1.10	1.10
	Nos. C302-C304 (3)			1.00	.75

Universal Declaration of Human Rights, 15th anniv. No. C304a contains 3 imperf. stamps similar to Nos. C302-C304 with simulated perforations.

Flag, Torch and Map of Arab Countries AP87

1964, Mar. 8 Unwmk. *Perf. 11½*

C305	AP87	15p multi	.30	.25
C306	AP87	17½p multi	.30	.25
C307	AP87	22½p multi	.30	.25
		Nos. C305-C307 (3)	.90	.75

Revolution of Mar. 8, 1963, 1st anniv.

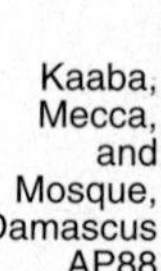

Kaaba, Mecca, and Mosque, Damascus AP88

1964, Mar. 14 Litho. *Perf. 11½x12*

C308	AP88	12½p bl & blk	.30	.25
C309	AP88	22½p rose lil & blk	.30	.25
C310	AP88	50p lt grn & blk	.35	.25
		Nos. C308-C310 (3)	.95	.75

First Arab Conference of Moslem Wakf Ministers, Damascus.

Young Couple and View of Damascus AP89

1964, Apr. 17 Unwmk.

C311	AP89	20p blue	.30	.25
C312	AP89	25p rose car	.30	.25
C313	AP89	60p emerald	.35	.25
		Nos. C311-C313 (3)	.95	.75

Evacuation Day, Apr. 17, 1964.

Abul Kasim (Albucasis) AP90

1964, Apr. 21 *Perf. 12x11½*

C314	AP90	60p brown	.40	.25

4th Arab Congress of Dental and Oral Surgery, Damascus.

Mosaic, Chahba, Thalassa AP91

Perf. 11½x12

1964, June-July Litho.

C315	AP91	27½p car rose	.30	.25
C316	AP91	45p gray	.30	.25
C317	AP91	50p brt grn	.40	.25
C318	AP91	55p slate grn	.40	.25
C319	AP91	60p ultra	.50	.25
		Nos. C315-C319 (5)	1.90	1.25

Hanging Lamp, Fair Emblem — AP92

Globe and Fair Emblem — AP93

1964, Aug. 28 *Perf. 12x11½*

C320	AP92	20p multi	.30	.25
C321	AP93	25p multi	.30	.25

11th International Damascus Fair.

Industrial and Agricultural Symbols — AP94

1964, Sept. 22 Litho. Unwmk.

C322	AP94	25p multi	.30	.25

No. C322 Overprinted in Red and Arabic

C323	AP94	25p multi	.30	.25

Cotton Festival, Aleppo. Overprint on No. C323 translates: "Market for Industrial and Agricultural Products."

Arms of Syria and Aero Club Emblem AP95

1964, Oct. 8 Litho. *Perf. 11½x12*

C324	AP95	12½p emer & blk	.30	.25
C325	AP95	17½p crim & blk	.30	.25
C326	AP95	20p brt bl & blk	.40	.25
		Nos. C324-C326 (3)	1.00	.75

10th anniversary of Syrian Aero Club.

Arab Postal Union Emblem — AP96

1964, Nov. 12 Litho. *Perf. 12x11½*

C327	AP96	12½p org & blk	.30	.25
C328	AP96	20p emer & blk	.30	.25
C329	AP96	25p dp lil rose & blk	.30	.25
		Nos. C327-C329 (3)	.90	.75

10th anniv. of the permanent office of the APU.

Grain and Hands Holding Book — AP97

1964, Nov. 30 Unwmk.

C330	AP97	12½p emer & blk	.30	.25
C331	AP97	17½p mar & blk	.30	.25
C332	AP97	20p dp bl & blk	.30	.25
		Nos. C330-C332 (3)	.90	.75

Burning of the library of Algiers, 6/7/62.

Tennis Player — AP98

17½p, Wrestlers and drummer. 20p, Weight lifter. 100p, Wrestlers and drummer.

1965, Feb. 7 *Perf. 12x11½*

C333	AP98	12½p multi	.30	.25
C334	AP98	17½p multi	.30	.25
C335	AP98	20p multi, horiz.	.30	.25
		Nos. C333-C335 (3)	.90	.75

Souvenir Sheet

Imperf

C336	AP98	100p multi	1.25	1.25

18th Olympic Games, Tokyo, 10/10-25/64. No. C336 contains one 45x33mm stamp.

Ramses Battling the Hittites AP99

Design: 50p, Two statues of Ramses II.

1965, Mar. 21 Litho. *Perf. 11x12*

C337	AP99	22½p emer, ultra & blk	.30	.25
C338	AP99	50p ultra, emer & blk	.40	.25

UNESCO world campaign to save historic monuments in Nubia.

Al-Sharif Al-Radi — AP100

1965, Apr. 3 Litho. *Perf. 12x11½*

C339	AP100	50p gray brn	.50	.25

5th Poetry Festival held in Latakia; Al-Sharif Al-Radi (970-1015), poet.

Hippocrates and Avicenna — AP101

1965, Apr. 19 *Perf. 11½*

C340	AP101	60p dl bl grn & blk	.55	.30

"Medical Days of the Near and Middle East," a convention held at Damascus Apr. 19-25.

Dagger in Map of Palestine AP102

1965, May 15

C341	AP102	12½p multi	.90	.25
C342	AP102	60p multi	1.00	.25

Deir Yassin massacre, Apr. 9, 1948.

ITU Emblem, Old and New Communication Equipment — AP103

Perf. 11½x12

1965, May 24 Litho. Unwmk.

C343	AP103	12½p multi	.30	.25
C344	AP103	27½p multi	.30	.25
C345	AP103	60p multi	.50	.25
		Nos. C343-C345 (3)	1.10	.75

ITU, centenary.

Syrian Welcoming AP104

1965, Aug. Unwmk. *Perf. 12x11½*

C346	AP104	25p pur & multi	.30	.25
C347	AP104	100p blk & multi	.75	.25

Issued to welcome Arab immigrants.

Bridge and Gate — AP105

27½p, Fair emblem. 60p, Jug & ornaments.

1965, Aug. 28 Litho.

C348	AP105	12½p blk, brt ultra & brn	.30	.25
C349	AP105	27½p multi	.30	.25
C350	AP105	60p multi	.40	.25
		Nos. C348-C350 (3)	1.00	.75

12th International Damascus Fair.

Fair Emblem and Cotton Pickers — AP106

1965, Sept. 30 ***Perf. 12x11½***
C351 AP106 25p olive & multi .30 .25

10th Cotton Festival, Aleppo.

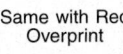

Same with Red Overprint

1965, Sept. 30
C352 AP106 25p olive & multi .30 .25

Industrial and Agricultural Fair, Aleppo.

View of Damascus and ICY Emblem AP107

1965, Oct. 24 ***Perf. 11½x12***
C353 AP107 25p multi .30 .25

International Cooperation Year.

Radio Transmitter, Globe, Syrian Flag and View of Damascus AP108

1966, Feb. 16 **Litho.** ***Perf. 12x11½***
C354 AP108 25p multi .30 .25
C355 AP108 60p multi .35 .25

3rd Conference of Arab Information Ministers, Damascus, Feb. 14-18.

Hand (shaped like a dove) Holding Flower — AP109

Design: 17½p, Stylized people, horiz.

1966, Mar. 8 ***Perf. 12x11½, 11½x12***
C356 AP109 12½p multi .30 .25
C357 AP109 17½p multi .30 .25
C358 AP109 50p multi .75 .25
Nos. C356-C358 (3) 1.35 .75

March 8 Revolution, 3rd anniversary.

Statues of Ramses II from Abu Simbel — AP110

1966, Mar. 15 ***Perf. 12x11½***
C359 AP110 25p dark blue .30 .25
C360 AP110 60p dark slate green .40 .25

Arab "Save the Nubian Monument Week."

UN Headquarters Building and Emblem — AP111

Design: 100p, UN Flag.

1966, Apr. 11 **Litho.** ***Perf. 11½x12***
C361 AP111 25p blk & gray .30 .25
C362 AP111 50p blk & pale grn .35 .25

Souvenir Sheet

Imperf

C363 AP111 100p yel, brt bl & blk 1.25 1.25

20th anniv. (in 1965) of the UN. No. C363 contains one stamp 42x36mm.

Marching Workers AP112

1966, May 1 **Litho.** ***Perf. 11½x12***
C364 AP112 60p multi .40 .25

Issued for May Day.

Inauguration of WHO Headquarters, Geneva — AP113

1966, May 3
C365 AP113 60p blk, bl & yel .40 .25

Map of Arab Countries and Traffic Signals — AP114

1966, May 4 ***Perf. 12x11½***
C366 AP114 25p gray & multi .30 .25

Issued to publicize Traffic Day.

Astarte & Tyche, 1st cent. Basrelief, Palmyra AP115

1966, July 26 **Litho.** ***Perf. 12x11½***
C367 AP115 50p pale brn .35 .25
C368 AP115 60p slate .50 .25

Symbolic Flag, Wheat, Globe and Fair Emblem AP116

1966, Aug. 25 **Litho.** ***Perf. 12x11½***
C369 AP116 12½p multi .35 .25
C370 AP116 60p multi .35 .25

13th Intl. Damascus Fair, Aug. 25-Sept. 20.

Shuttle and Symbols of Agriculture, Industry and Cotton — AP117

1966, Sept. 9 **Litho.** ***Perf. 12x11½***
C371 AP117 50p sil, blk & plum .35 .25

11th Cotton Festival, Aleppo.

Symbolic Water Cycle — AP118

1966, Oct. 24 **Litho.** ***Perf. 12x11½***
C372 AP118 12½p emer, blk & org .30 .25
C373 AP118 60p ultra, blk & org .35 .25

Hydrological Decade (UNESCO), 1965-74.

Abd-el Kader — AP119

1966, Nov. 7
C374 AP119 12½p brt grn & blk .30 .25
C375 AP119 50p brt grn & red brn .35 .25

Transfer from Damascus to Algiers of the ashes of Abd-el Kader (1807?-1883), Emir of Mascara.

Clasped Hands over Map of South Arabia — AP120

1967, Feb. 8 **Litho.** ***Perf. 12x11½***
C376 AP120 20p pink & multi .30 .25
C377 AP120 25p multi .30 .25

3rd Congress of Solidarity with the Workers and People of Aden, Damascus, Jan. 15-18.

Pipelines and Pigeons AP121

1967, Mar. 8 **Litho.** ***Perf. 12x11½***
C378 AP121 17½p multi .30 .25
C379 AP121 25p multi .30 .25
C380 AP121 27½p multi .30 .25
Nos. C378-C380 (3) .90 .75

4th anniversary of March 8 Revolution.

Soldier, Woman and Man Holding Flag — AP122

1967, Apr. 17 **Litho.** ***Perf. 12x11½***
C381 AP122 17½p green .30 .25
C382 AP122 25p dp claret .30 .25
C383 AP122 27½p vio blue .30 .25
Nos. C381-C383 (3) .90 .75

21st anniv. of the evacuation of British and French troops from Syria.

Workers' Monument, Damascus AP123

1967, May 1
C384 AP123 12½p bl grn .30 .25
C385 AP123 50p brt pink .35 .25

Issued for Labor Day, May 1.

Fair Emblem and Gate, Minaret, Omayyad Mosque — AP124

1967, Aug. 25 **Litho.** ***Perf. 12x12½***
C386 AP124 12½p multi .30 .25
C387 AP124 60p multi .35 .25

14th Intl. Damascus Fair, Aug. 25-Sept. 20.

Statue of Ur-Nina and ITY Emblem AP125

1967, Sept. 2 ***Perf. 12½x12***

C388 AP125 12½p lt bl, brt rose lil & blk .30 .25
C389 AP125 25p lt bl, ver & blk .30 .25
C390 AP125 27½p lt bl, dk bl & blk .30 .25
Nos. C388-C390 (3) .90 .75

Souvenir Sheet

Imperf

C391 AP125 60p lt bl & vio bl 1.00 1.00

Intl. Tourist Year.

Cotton Boll and Cogwheel Segment AP126

1967, Sept. 28 **Litho.** ***Perf. 12x12½***

C392 AP126 12½p ocher, brn & blk .30 .25
C393 AP126 60p ap grn, brn & blk .40 .25

12th Cotton Festival, Aleppo.

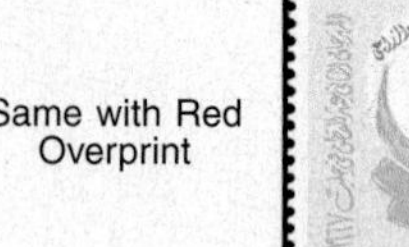

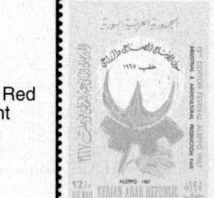

Same with Red Overprint

1967, Sept. 28

C394 AP126 12½p multi .30 .25
C395 AP126 60p multi .35 .25

Industrial and Agricultural Production Fair, Aleppo.

Head of Young Man, Amrith, 4th-5th Century B.C. — AP127

100p, 500p, Bronze bust of a Princess, 2nd cent.

1967, Oct. 7

C396 AP127 45p orange .30 .25
C397 AP127 50p brt pink .40 .25
C398 AP127 60p grnsh bl .50 .25
C399 AP127 100p green .60 .30
C400 AP127 500p brn red 2.25 1.50
Nos. C396-C400 (5) 4.05 2.55

Ibn el-Naphis AP128

1967, Dec. 28 **Litho.** ***Perf. 12x12½***

C401 AP128 12½p grn & org .30 .25
C402 AP128 27½p dk bl & lil rose .30 .25

700th death anniv. of Ibn el-Naphis (1210-1288), Arab physician.

Human Rights Flame and People AP129

Design: 100p, Heads of various races and Human Rights flame.

1968, Feb. 21 **Litho.** ***Perf. 12½x12***

C403 AP129 12½p lt grnsh bl, bl & blk .30 .25
C404 AP129 60p pink, blk & dl red .40 .25

Souvenir Sheet

Imperf

C405 AP129 100p multi 1.00 1.00

20th anniv. of the Declaration of Human Rights; Intl. Human Rights Year.

Old Man and Woman Reading AP130

Design: 17½p, 45p, Torch and book.

1968, Mar. 3 ***Perf. 12x12½***

C406 AP130 12½p rose car, blk & org .30 .25
C407 AP130 17½p multi .30 .25
C408 AP130 25p grn, blk & org .30 .25
C409 AP130 45p bl & multi .30 .25
Nos. C406-C409 (4) 1.20 1.00

Issued to publicize the literacy campaign.

Euphrates Dam Project — AP131

1968, Apr. 11 **Litho.** ***Perf. 12½x12***

C410 AP131 12½p multi .30 .25
C411 AP131 17½p multi .30 .25
C412 AP131 25p multi .30 .25
Nos. C410-C412 (3) .90 .75

Proposed dam across Euphrates River.

WHO Emblem and Avenzoar (1091-1162) — AP132

WHO Emblem and: 25p, Rhazes (Razi, 850-923). 60p, Geber (Jabir 721-776).

1968, June 10 **Litho.** ***Perf. 12½x12***

C413 AP132 12½p brn, grn & sal .30 .25
C414 AP132 25p brn, gray & sal .30 .25
C415 AP132 60p brn, gray bl & sal .40 .25
Nos. C413-C415 (3) 1.00 .75

WHO, 20th anniv.

Monastery of St. Simeon the Stylite AP133

Designs: 17½p, El Tekkieh Mosque, Damascus, vert. 22½p, Columns, Palmyra, vert. 45p, Chapel of St. Paul, Bab Kisan. 50p, Theater of Bosra.

Perf. 12½x12, 12x12½

1968, Oct. 10 **Litho.**

C416 AP133 15p pale grn & rose brn .30 .25
C417 AP133 17½p redsh brn & dk red brn .30 .25
C418 AP133 22½p grn gray & dk red brn .30 .25
C419 AP133 45p yel & dk red brn .30 .25
C420 AP133 50p lt bl & dk red brn .30 .25
Nos. C416-C420 (5) 1.50 1.25

Hammer Throw — AP134

Designs: 25p, Discus. 27½p, Running. 60p, Basketball. 50p, Polo, horiz.

1968, Dec. 19 **Litho.** ***Perf. 12x12½***

C421 AP134 12½p brt pink, blk & grn .30 .25
C422 AP134 25p red, grn & blk .30 .25
C423 AP134 27½p blk, gray & grn .30 .25
C424 AP134 60p multi .30 .25
Nos. C421-C424 (4) 1.20 1.00

Souvenir Sheet

Imperf

C425 AP134 50p multi 1.00 1.00

19th Olympic Games, Mexico City, Oct. 12-27. No. C425 contains one 52x80mm horiz. stamp.

Construction of Damascus Intl. Airport — AP135

1969, Jan. 20 **Litho.** ***Perf. 12½x12***

C426 AP135 12½p yel, brt bl & grn .30 .25
C427 AP135 17½p org, pur & lt grn .30 .25
C428 AP135 60p car, blk & yel .40 .25
Nos. C426-C428 (3) 1.00 .75

Baal Shamin Temple, Palmyra AP136

Designs: 45p, Interior of Omayyad Mosque, Damascus, vert. 50p, Amphitheater, Palmyra. 60p, Khaled ibn al-Walid Mosque, Homs, vert. 100p, Ruins of St. Simeon, Djebel Samaan.

1969, Jan. 20 **Photo.** ***Perf. 12x11½***

C429 AP136 25p multi .30 .25
C430 AP136 45p bl & multi .30 .25
C431 AP136 50p multi .30 .25
C432 AP136 60p multi .30 .25
C433 AP136 100p vio & multi .60 .25
Nos. C429-C433 (5) 1.80 1.25

Workers, ILO Emblem, Cogwheel AP137

Design: 60p, ILO emblem.

1969, May 1 **Litho.** ***Perf. 12½x12***

C434 AP137 12½p multi .30 .25
C435 AP137 27½p multi .30 .25

Miniature Sheet

Imperf

C436 AP137 60p multi .60 .60

ILO, 50th anniv. No. C436 contains one stamp 53½x47mm.

Ballet Dancers AP138

Designs: 12½p, Russian dancers. 45p, Lebanese singer and dancers. 55p, Egyptian dancer and musicians. 60p, Bulgarian dancers.

1969, Aug. 25 **Litho.** ***Perf. 12½x12***

C437 AP138 12½p multi .30 .25
C438 AP138 27½p bl & multi .30 .25
C439 AP138 45p multi .30 .25
C440 AP138 55p multi .30 .25
C441 AP138 60p multi .40 .25
a. Strip of 5, #C437-C441 1.75 1.75

16th Intl. Fair, Damascus, Aug. 25-Sept. 20.

Children Playing — AP139

1969, Oct. 6 **Litho.** ***Perf. 12x12½***

C442 AP139 12½p aqua, dk bl & emer .30 .25
C443 AP139 25p brn red, dk bl & lt vio .30 .25
C444 AP139 27½p ultra, dk bl & gray .30 .25
Nos. C442-C444 (3) .90 .75

Issued for Children's Day.

Fortuna — AP140

Designs: 25p, Seated woman from Palmyra. 60p, Motherhood. All sculptures from Greco-Roman period.

1969, Oct. 10

C445 AP140 17½p blk, yel grn & grn .30 .25
C446 AP140 25p dk brn, red brn & lt grn .30 .25

C447 AP140 60p blk, lt gray & bl gray .40 .25
Nos. C445-C447 (3) 1.00 .75

9th Intl. Congress for Classical Archaeology, Oct. 11-20.

Damascus Agricultural Museum — AP141

1969, Dec. 24 Litho. *Perf. 12½x12*
C448 AP141 12p Cock .30 .25
C449 AP141 17½p Cow .30 .25
C450 AP141 20p Corn .30 .25
C451 AP141 50p Olives .30 .25
a. Strip of 4, #C448-C451 + label 1.25 1.25

Weather Balloon Tracking and UN Emblem AP142

1970, Mar. 23 Litho. *Perf. 12½x12*
C452 AP142 25p blk, sl grn & yel .30 .25
C453 AP142 60p blk, dk bl & yel .35 .25

10th World Meteorological Day.

Lenin (1870-1924) AP143

1970, Apr. 15 Litho. *Perf. 12x12½*
C454 AP143 15p red & dk brn .30 .25
C455 AP143 60p red & grn .35 .25

Workers' Syndicate Emblem AP144

1970, May 1 Litho. *Perf. 12½x12*
C456 AP144 15p dk brn & brt grn .30 .25
C457 AP144 60p dk brn & org .35 .25

Issued for Labor Day.

Radar and Open Book AP145

1970, May 17
C458 AP145 15p brt pink & blk .30 .25
C459 AP145 60p bl & blk .35 .25

International Telecommunications Day.

Opening of UPU Headquarters, Bern — AP146

1970, May 30
C460 AP146 15p multi .30 .25
C461 AP146 60p multi .35 .25

"Zahier Piebers and Maarouf" — AP147

Folk Tales: 10p, Two warriors on horseback. 15p, Two warriors on white horses. 20p, Lady and warrior on horseback. 60p, Warriors, woman and lion.

1970, Aug. 12 Litho. *Perf. 12½*
C462 AP147 5p lt bl & multi .30 .25
C463 AP147 10p lt bl & multi .30 .25
C464 AP147 15p lt bl & multi .30 .25
C465 AP147 20p lt bl & multi .30 .25
C466 AP147 60p lt bl & multi .50 .25
a. Strip of 5, #C462-C466 1.75 1.75

Al Aqsa Mosque on Fire AP148

1970, Aug. 21 *Perf. 12½x12*
C467 AP148 15p multi .30 .25
C468 AP148 60p multi .35 .25

1st anniv. of the burning of Al Aqsa Mosque, Jerusalem.

Wood Carving — AP149

Handicrafts: 20p, Jewelry. 25p, Glass making. 30p, Copper engraving. 60p, Shellwork.

1970, Aug. 25 *Perf. 12½*
C469 AP149 15p vio & multi .30 .25
C470 AP149 20p ol & multi .30 .25
C471 AP149 25p multi .30 .25
C472 AP149 30p multi .30 .25
C473 AP149 60p multi .50 .25
a. Strip of 5, #C469-C473 1.75 1.75

17th Intl. Fair, Damascus.

Education Year Emblem AP150

1970, Nov. 2 Litho. *Perf. 12*
C474 AP150 15p dl grn & dk brn .30 .25
C475 AP150 60p vio bl & dk brn .35 .25

International Education Year.

AP151

Design: UN Emblem, Symbols of Progress, Justice and Peace.

1970, Nov. 3
C476 AP151 15p lt ultra, red & blk .30 .25
C477 AP151 60p bl, yel & blk .35 .25

United Nations, 25th anniversary.

Khaled ibn-al-Walid AP152

1970-71 *Perf. 12x11½, 12½x12½*
C478 AP152 45p brt pink .30 .25
C479 AP152 50p green .35 .25
C480 AP152 60p vio brn .50 .25
C481 AP152 100p dk bl .60 .25
C482 AP152 200p grnsh gray ('71) 1.10 .50
C483 AP152 300p lil ('71) 1.50 .95
C484 AP152 500p gray ('71) 3.00 1.60
Nos. C478-C484 (7) 7.35 4.05

Woman with Garland AP153

1971, Apr. 17 Litho. *Perf. 12*
C485 AP153 15p dl red, blk & grn .30 .25
C486 AP153 60p grn, blk & dk red .35 .25

25th anniv. of the evacuation of British and French troops from Syria.

People Dancing Around Globe AP154

1971, Apr. 28 Litho. *Perf. 12½x12*
C487 AP154 15p vio & multi .30 .25
C488 AP154 60p grn & multi .30 .25

Intl. Year against Racial Discrimination.

Pres. Hafez al Assad and Council Chamber — AP155

1971, Sept. 30 Litho. *Perf. 12½x12*
C489 AP155 15p grn & multi .30 .25
C490 AP155 65p bl & multi .60 .25

People's Council and presidential election.

Gamal Abdel Nasser (1918-1970), President of Egypt — AP156

1971, Oct. 17 *Perf. 12x12½*
C491 AP156 15p lt ol grn & brn .30 .25
C492 AP156 20p gray & brn .30 .25

Globe and Arrows AP157

1972, May 17 Litho. *Perf. 11½*
C493 AP157 15p bl, vio bl & pink .30 .25
C494 AP157 50p org, yel & sep .30 .25

4th World Telecommunications Day.

Pres. Hafez al Assad — AP158

1972, July Litho. *Perf. 12x11½*
C495 AP158 100p dk grn .60 .25
C496 AP158 500p dk brn 3.00 1.10

Airline Emblem, Eastern Hemisphere AP159

1972, Sept. 16 Litho. *Perf. 12x11½*
C497 AP159 15p blk, lt bl & Prus bl .30 .25
C498 AP159 50p blk, gray & Prus bl .30 .25

Syrianair, Syrian airline, 25th anniversary.

Pottery — AP160

Handicraft Industries: 25p, Rugs. 30p, Metal (weapons). 35p, Straw (baskets, mats). 100p, Wood carving.

1976, July Litho. *Perf. 12x12½*
C499 AP160 10p multi .30 .25
C500 AP160 25p multi .30 .25
C501 AP160 30p multi .30 .25
C502 AP160 35p multi .30 .25
C503 AP160 100p multi .50 .30
a. Strip of 5, #C499-C503 1.75 1.75

23rd Intl. Damascus Fair.

Pres. Hafez al Assad AP161

1978, Sept. Litho. *Perf. 12½x12*

C504 AP161 25p sil & multi .50 .25
C505 AP161 35p grn & multi .50 .25
C506 AP161 60p gold & multi .50 .25
Nos. C504-C506 (3) 1.50 .75

Reelection of Pres. Assad. See No. 820.

AIR POST SEMI-POSTAL STAMPS

Nos. C30-C33 Surcharged Like Nos. B1-B12 in Black and Red

1926, Apr. 1 Unwmk. *Perf. 13½*

CB1 A4 2p + 1p dk brown 3.00 2.75
CB2 A4 3p + 2p org brn 2.75 2.75
CB3 A4 5p + 3p violet 2.75 2.75
CB4 A4 10p + 5p vio brn 2.75 2.75
Nos. CB1-CB4 (4) 11.25 11.00

The new value is in red and rest of the surcharge in black on Nos. CB1-CB3. The entire surcharge is black on No. CB4.
See note following Nos. B1-B12.

Catalogue values for unused stamps in this section, from this point to the end of the section, are for Never Hinged items.

Fair Entrance SPAP1

Industry, Handicraft and Farming SPAP2

Design: 70p+10p, Fairgrounds.

Perf. 11½, Imperf.

1955 Litho. Unwmk.

CB5 SPAP1 25p + 5p gray black .40 .40
CB6 SPAP2 35p + 5p ultra .40 .40
CB7 SPAP2 40p + 10p rose lilac .60 .60
CB8 SPAP1 70p + 10p Prus grn 1.10 1.10
Nos. CB5-CB8 (4) 2.50 2.50

Intl. Fair, Damascus, Sept. 1955.
For overprint see Nos. C212-C215.

United Nations Refugee Emblem SPAP3

1966, Dec. 12 Litho. *Perf. 11½x12*

CB9 SPAP3 12½p + 2½p ultra & blk .25 .25
CB10 SPAP3 50p + 5p grn & blk .50 .25

UN Day, 21st anniv.; Refugee Week, Oct. 24-31.

POSTAGE DUE STAMPS

Under French Occupation

French Offices in the Turkish Empire, 1902-03, Surcharged

1920 Unwmk. *Perf. 14x13½*

J1 A3 1p on 10c rose red 160.00 160.00
J2 A3 2p on 20c brn vio 160.00 160.00
J3 A3 3p on 30c lil 160.00 160.00
J4 A4 4p on 40c red & pale bl 160.00 160.00
Nos. J1-J4 (4) 640.00 640.00

Postage Due Stamps of France, 1893-1920, Surcharged in Black or Red

1920

J5 D2 1p on 10c brown 3.25 3.25
J6 D2 2p on 20c ol grn (R) 3.25 3.25
a. "PIASTRE" 900.00 900.00
J7 D2 3p on 30c red 3.25 3.25
a. "PIASTRE"
J8 D2 4p on 50c brn vio 4.75 4.75
a. 3p in setting of 4p 525.00 525.00
Nos. J5-J8 (4) 14.50 14.50

1921-22

J9 D2 50c on 10c brown 1.40 1.40
a. "75" instead of "50" 90.00
b. "CENTI MES" instead of "CENTIEMES" 7.50
J10 D2 1p on 20c ol grn 1.40 1.40
J11 D2 2p on 30c red 3.25 3.25
J12 D2 3p on 50c brn vio 3.50 3.50
J13 D2 5p on 1fr red brn, *straw* 5.00 5.00
Nos. J9-J13 (5) 14.55 14.55

D3

1921 Red Surcharge *Perf. 11½*

J14 D3 50c on 1p black 3.75 3.75
J15 D3 1p on 1p black 3.75 3.75

D4

1922

J16 D4 2p on 5m rose 10.00 6.50
a. "AX" of "TAXE" inverted 175.00 175.00
J17 D4 3p on 1p gray bl 15.00 12.00

French Mandate

Postage Due Stamps of France, 1893-1920, Surcharged

1923

J18 D2 50c on 10c brown 1.50 1.50
J19 D2 1p on 20c ol grn 2.25 2.25
J20 D2 2p on 30c red 1.90 1.90
J21 D2 3p on 50c vio brn 1.90 1.90
J22 D2 5p on 1fr red brn, *straw* 3.75 3.75
Nos. J18-J22 (5) 11.30 11.30

Postage Due Stamps of France, 1893-1920, Surcharged

1924

J23 D2 50c on 10c brown 1.00 1.00
J24 D2 1p on 20c ol grn 1.00 1.00
J25 D2 2p on 30c red 1.10 1.10
J26 D2 3p on 50c vio brn 1.50 1.50
J27 D2 5p on 1fr red brn, *straw* 1.50 1.50
Nos. J23-J27 (5) 6.10 6.10

Postage Due Stamps of France, 1893-1920, Surcharged

1924

J28 D2 50c on 10c brown .75 .75
J29 D2 1p on 20c ol grn .75 .75
J30 D2 2p on 30c red 1.00 1.00
J31 D2 3p on 50c vio brn 1.40 1.40
J32 D2 5p on 1fr red brn, *straw* 1.75 1.75
Nos. J28-J32 (5) 5.65 5.65

Water Wheel at Hama D5

Bridge at Antioch — D6

Designs: 2p, The Tartous. 3p, View of Banias. 5p, Chevaliers' Castle.

1925 Photo. *Perf. 13½*

J33 D5 50c brown, *yel* .25 .25
J34 D6 1p violet, *rose* .25 .25
J35 D5 2p black, *blue* .55 .55
J36 D5 3p black, *red org* 1.25 1.25
J37 D5 5p black, *bl grn* 1.50 1.50
Nos. J33-J37 (5) 3.80 3.80

D7

Lion — D8

1931

J38 D7 8p black, *gray blue* 3.50 3.50
J39 D8 15p black, *dull rose* 6.00 6.00

Catalogue values for unused stamps in this section, from this point to the end of the section, are for Never Hinged items.

Syrian Arab Republic

D9

1965 Unwmk. Litho. *Perf. 11½x11*

J40 D9 2½p violet blue .25 .25
J41 D9 5p black brown .25 .25
J42 D9 10p green .25 .25
J43 D9 17½p carmine rose .25 .25
J44 D9 25p blue .25 .25
Nos. J40-J44 (5) 1.25 1.25

MILITARY STAMPS

Free French Administration

Syria No. 222 Surcharged in Black

1942 Unwmk. *Perf. 13*

M1 A10 50c on 4p yel org 10.00 8.00

Lebanon Nos. 155 and 142A Surcharged in Carmine

M2 A13 1fr on 5p grnsh bl 10.00 8.00
M3 A25 2.50fr on 12½p dp ultra 10.00 8.00

Camel Corps, Palmyra — M1

Perf. 11½x11¾

1942 Unwmk. Litho.

Bistre Background

M4 M1 1fr deep rose 1.00 .55
M5 M1 1.50fr bright violet 1.00 .55
M6 M1 2fr orange 1.00 .55
M7 M1 2.50fr brown gray 1.10 .85
M8 M1 3fr Prussian blue 1.50 1.10
M9 M1 4fr deep green 2.25 1.60
M10 M1 5fr deep claret 2.75 1.75
Nos. M4-M10 (7) 10.60 6.95

Nos. M4 to M10 exist imperforate. Value: unused $125; never hinged $200.
For surcharges see Nos. MB1-MB2, MC10.

MILITARY SEMI-POSTAL STAMPS

Free French Administration

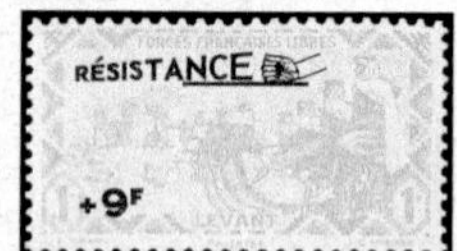

Military Stamps of 1942 Srchd. in Black

1943 Unwmk. *Perf. 11½*

MB1 M1 1fr + 9fr deep rose 17.50 *17.50*
MB2 M1 5fr + 20fr deep claret 17.50 *17.50*

MILITARY AIR POST STAMPS

Free French Administration

Syria Nos. C55-C56 Srchd. in Black, Carmine or Orange

1942 Unwmk. *Perf. 13*

MC1 AP2 4fr on 50p blk (C) 9.00 8.25
MC2 AP2 6.50fr on 50p blk (C) 9.00 8.25
MC3 AP2 8fr on 50p blk (O) 9.00 8.25
MC4 AP2 10fr on 100p mag 9.00 8.25
Nos. MC1-MC4 (4) 36.00 33.00

Winged Shields and Cross of Lorraine
MAP1

1942 Litho. *Perf. 11½*

MC5 MAP1 6.50fr pale pink & rose car 5.00 4.00
MC6 MAP1 10fr lt bl & dl vio 5.50 4.50

Nos. MC5 and MC6 exist imperforate.
See Nos. MC7-MC8. For surcharges see Nos. MC9, MCB1-MCB2.

Souvenir Sheets

1942 Without Gum *Perf. 11*

MC7 Sheet of 2 40.00 *40.00*
a. MAP1 6.50fr pale pink & rose carmine 17.50 15.00
b. MAP1 10fr lt bl & dl violet 17.50 15.00

Imperf

MC8 Sheet of 2 40.00 *40.00*
a. MAP1 6.50fr pale pink & rose carmine 17.50 15.00
b. MAP1 10fr lt bl & dl violet 17.50 15.00

No. MC5 Srchd. in Rose Carmine

1942 *Perf. 11½*

MC9 MAP1 4fr on 6.50fr 4.00 4.00

Military Stamp of 1942 Srchd. in Black

1943

MC10 M1 4fr on 3fr Prus blue 3.50 2.50

MILITARY AIR POST SEMI-POSTAL STAMPS

Free French Administration

Military Air Post Stamps of 1942 Surcharged in Black

1943 Unwmk. *Perf. 11½*

MCB1 MAP1 6.50fr + 48.50fr 40.00 *37.50*
MCB2 MAP1 10fr + 100fr 40.00 *37.50*

POSTAL TAX STAMPS

Revenue Stamps Overprinted in Red or Black

R1

a

1945 Unwmk. *Perf. 10½x11½*

RA1 R1(a) 5p dark blue (R) *110.00 22.50*

On Stamps Overprinted — b

RA2 R1(a) 5p dk bl (Bk+Bk) *100.00 27.50*
RA3 R1(a) 5p dk bl (Bk+R) *115.00 27.50*
RA4 R1(a) 5p dk bl (R+R) *110.00 27.50*
RA5 R1(b) 5p dk bl (R+R) *105.00 24.00*

On Stamps Overprinted

RA6 R1(a) 5p dk bl (Bk+Bk) *100.00 30.00*
RA7 R1(a) 5p dk bl (Bk+R) *100.00 30.00*
RA8 R1(a) 5p dk bl (R+R) *100.00 30.00*
RA9 R1(b) 5p dk bl (R+R) *120.00 30.00*
Nos. RA1-RA9 (9) 960.00 249.00

The tax was for national defense.

Revenue Stamp Surcharged in Black

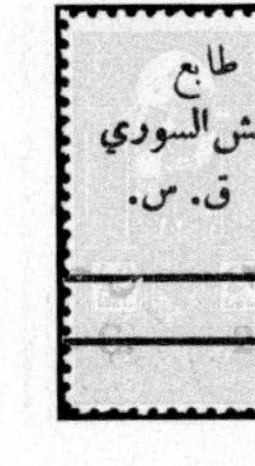
R2

1945 Unwmk. *Perf. 11*

RA10 R2 5p on 25c on 40c rose red *100.00* 32.50

The surcharge reads "Tax (postal) for Syrian Army."

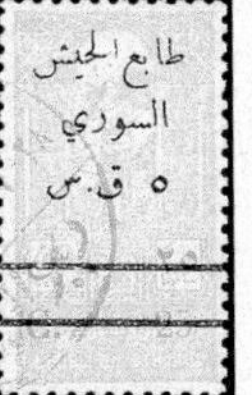
Revenue Stamp Surcharged in Black

1945

RA11 R2 5p on 25c on 40c rose red *110.00* 32.50

No. RA11 Overprinted in Black

RA12 R2 5p on 25c on 40c *90.00*

The tax on Nos. RA11-RA12 was for the army.

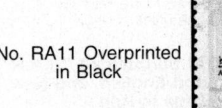

This overprint exists on No. RA10.

Revenue stamps without overprints occasionally were used as postage on covers through at least 1948.

ISSUES OF THE ARABIAN GOVERNMENT

The following issues replaced the British Military Occupation (E.E.F.) stamps (Palestine Nos. 2-14) which were used in central and eastern Syria from Nov. 1918 until Jan. 1920.

Turkish Stamps of 1913-18 Handstamped in Various Colors

Also Handstamp Surcharged with New Values as

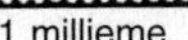
1 millieme

1 Egyptian piaster

The Seal reads: "Hakuma al Arabie" (The Arabian Government)

Perf. 11½, 12, 12½, 13½

1919-20 Unwmk.

1 A24 1m on 2pa red lil 1.00 1.00
2 A25 1m on 4pa dk brn 1.00 1.00
3 A26 2m on 5pa vio brn 1.75 1.75
4 A15 2m on 5pa on 10pa gray grn 1.25 1.25
5 A18 2m on 5pa ocher 25.00 25.00
6 A41 2m on 5pa grn *300.00 375.00*
7 A18 2m on 5pa ocher *50.00 50.00*
8 A28 4m on 10pa grn 7.00 7.00
9 A28 4m on 10pa grn 1.00 1.00
10 A22 4m on 10pa bl grn 2.00 2.00
11 A41 4m on 10pa car 40.00 40.00
12 A23 4m on 10pa grn 8.00 8.00
13 A44 4m on 10pa grn 2.00 2.00
14 A11 4m on 10pa on 20pa vio brn (B38) 2.25 2.25
15 A41 4m on 10pa car (B42) 1.10 1.10
16 SP1 4m on 10pa red vio (B46) 2.25 2.25
17 SP1 4m on 10pa on 20pa car rose (B47) 2.25 2.25
19 A21 5pa ocher
21 A21 20pa car rose *97.50 115.00*
22 A29 20pa red 2.00 2.00
23 A29 20pa red *300.00 300.00*
24 A17 20pa car 3.00 3.00
25 A21 20pa car rose 3.00 3.00
26 A22 20pa car rose 12.50 12.50
27 A21 20pa car rose 6.00 6.00
28 A41 20pa ultra 3.00 3.00
29 A16 20pa mag 12.50 12.50
30 A17 20pa car
31 A18 20pa car 8.50 8.50
32 A45 20pa dp rose 4.25 4.25
33 A21 20pa car rose (B8) 3.25 3.25
34 A22 20pa car rose (B33) 3.50 3.50
35 A22 20pa car rose (B36) 14.50 14.50
36 A41 20pa ultra (B43) .75 .75
37 A16 20pa mag (P140) 3.25 3.25
38 A17 20pa car (P144) *285.00 285.00*
39 A30 1pi bl 3.25 3.25
40 A31 1pi on 1½pi car & blk *425.00 425.00*
41 A30 1pi bl 100.00 100.00
42 A30 1pi on 1pi bl 150.00 150.00
43 A17 1pi blue 5.25 5.25
44 A18 1pi blue 60.00 60.00
45 A22 1pi ultra 6.25 6.25
46 A21 1pi ultra 11.00 11.00
47 A41 1pi vio & blk 2.25 2.25
48 A18 1pi brt bl 6.50 6.50
49 A46 1pi dl vio 2.25 2.25
50 A47 1pi on 50pa ultra 1.50 1.50
51 A21 1pi ultra (B9) 7.00 7.00
52 A22 1pi ultra (B15) 12.00 12.00
53 A18 1pi brt bl (B21) 7.00 7.00
54 A18 1pi blue (B23) 17.50 17.50
55 A22 1pi ultra (B34) 15.00 15.00
56 A41 1pi vio & blk (B44) 3.25 3.25
57 A33 2pi grn & blk 77.50 77.50
58 A13 2pi brn org 2.25 2.25
59 A18 2pi slate 30.00 30.00
60 A18 2pi slate 32.50 32.50
61 A21 2pi bl blk 5.75 5.75
62 A17 2pi org 4.75 4.75
63 A18 5pi brn 14.00 14.00
64 A22 5pi dl vio 25.00 25.00
65 A41 5pi yel brn & blk 5.50 5.50
66 A41 5pi yel brn & blk 5.50 5.50
67 A53 5pi on 2pa Prus bl 8.50 8.50
68 A21 5pi dk vio (B10) 300.00 300.00
69 A17 5pi lil rose (B20) 55.00 55.00
70 A41 5pi yel brn & blk (B45) 5.25 5.25
72 A50 10pi dk grn 145.00 145.00
73 A50 10pi dk vio 125.00 125.00
74 A50 10pi dk brn *425.00*
75 A18 10pi org brn (B2) 375.00 375.00
76 A37 25pi ol grn *375.00 375.00*
77 A40 25pi on 200pi grn & blk *550.00 550.00*
78 A17 25pi brn 400.00 400.00
79 A51 25pi car, *straw* 100.00 100.00
81 A52 50pi ind 225.00 225.00

The variety "surcharge omitted" exists on Nos. 1-5, 12-13, 16, 32, 49-50, 67.

A few examples of No. 377 (50pi) and No. 269 (100pi) were overprinted but not regularly issued.

Overprinted

The Inscription reads "Hakum Soria Arabie" (Syrian-Arabian Government)

On Stamp of 1913

83 A26 2m on 5pa vio brn 5.50 5.50

On Stamp of 1916-18

84 A45 20pa dp rose .75 .75

A1

Litho. *Perf. 11½*

85 A1 5m rose .75 .75
a. Tête bêche pair 22.50 10.00
b. Imperf.

Independence Issue

Arabic Overprint in Green "Souvenir of Syrian Independence March 8, 1920"

86 A1 5m rose 275.00 175.00
a. Tête bêche pair
b. Inverted overprint 400.00 400.00

A2

Litho.

Size: 22x18mm

87 A2 $\frac{1}{10}$pi lt brn .35 .35

Size: 28x22mm

88 A2 $\frac{2}{10}$pi yel grn .45 .25
a. $\frac{2}{10}$pi yellow (error) 10.00 10.00
89 A2 $\frac{3}{10}$pi yellow .50 .30
90 A2 1pi gray blue .45 .25
91 A2 2pi blue grn 2.25 1.00

Size: 31x25mm

92 A2 5pi vio brn 3.00 1.50
93 A2 10pi gray 3.25 2.00
Nos. 86-93 (8) 285.25 180.65

Nos. 86-93 exist imperf.
For overprint see No. J5.

PF1

PF2

Revenue Stamps Surcharged as on Postage Stamps, for Postal Use

1920 Unwmk. *Perf. 11½*

94	PF1	5m on 5pa red	.75	.35
95	PF2	1m on 5pa red	.75	.25
96	PF2	2m on 5pa red	.65	.25
97	PF2	1pi on 5pa red	1.25	.65

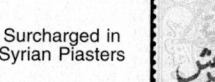

Surcharged in Syrian Piasters

98	PF2	2pi on 5pa red	.50	.25
99	PF2	3pi on 5pa red	.50	.25
		Nos. 94-99 (6)	4.40	2.00

ISSUES OF THE ARABIAN GOVERNMENT POSTAGE DUE STAMPS

Postage Due Stamps of Turkey, 1914, Handstamped and Surcharged

No. J1

No. J4

1920 Unwmk. *Perf. 12*

J1	D1	2m on 5pa claret	7.25	7.25
J2	D2	20pa red	7.25	7.25
J3	D3	1pi dark blue	7.25	7.25
J4	D4	2pi slate	7.25	7.25
		Nos. J1-J4 (4)	29.00	29.00

Type of Regular Issue

Litho. *Perf. 11½*

J5	A2	1pi black	1.75	1.75

UNITED ARAB REPUBLIC

Catalogue values for unused stamps in this section are for Never Hinged items.

See Egypt for stamps of types A1, A4, A7, A8, A14, A17, A19, A20, A24 with denomination in "M" (milliemes).

Issues for Syria

Linked Maps of Egypt and Syria — A1

Perf. 11½

1958, Feb. 1 Unwmk. Litho.

1	A1	12½p yellow & green	.25	.25

Establishment of UAR. See No. C1. See also Egypt No. 436.

Freedom Monument A2

1958, May

2	A2	5p yel & vio	.40	.25
3	A2	15p yel grn & brn red	.65	.35
		Nos. 2-3,C2-C3 (4)	3.00	1.35

British-French troop evacuation, 12th anniv.

Bronze Rattle — A3

Antique Art: 15p, Goddess. 20p, Lamgi Mari. 30p, Mithras fighting bull. 40p, Aspasia. 60p, Minerva. 75p, Flask. 100p, Enameled Vase. 150p, Mosaic from Omayyad Mosque, Damascus.

1958, Sept. 14 Litho. *Perf. 12*

4	A3	10p lt ol grn	.25	.25
5	A3	15p brown org	.25	.25
6	A3	20p rose lilac	.25	.25
7	A3	30p lt brown	.25	.25
8	A3	40p gray	.30	.25
9	A3	60p green	.50	.25
10	A3	75p blue	.80	.30
11	A3	100p brown car	1.20	.40
12	A3	150p dull purple	2.25	.60
		Nos. 4-12 (9)	6.05	2.80

Archaeological collections and museums.

Hand Holding Torch, Broken Chain and Flag — A4

1958, Oct. 14 *Perf. 11½*

13	A4	12.50p car rose	.25	.25

Establishment of Republic of Iraq. See Egypt No. 454.

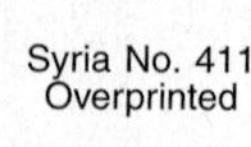

Syria No. 411 Overprinted

1958, Oct. 6 Wmk. 291 *Perf. 11½*

13A	A78	12½p olive	*55.00*	*55.00*
		Nos. 13A,C10-C11 (3)	*145.00*	*145.00*

Intl. Children's Day, 1958.

View of Damascus — A5

1958, Dec. 10 Unwmk.

14	A5	12½p green	.25	.25

4th Near East Regional Conference, Damascus, Dec. 10-20. See No. C14.

Secondary School, Damascus — A6

1959, Feb. 26 Litho. *Perf. 12*

15	A6	12½p dull green	.25	.25

See No. 26.

Flags of UAR and Yemen A7

Perf. 13x13½

1959, Mar. 8 Photo. Wmk. 318

16	A7	12½p grn, red & blk	.25	.25

1st anniversary of United Arab States. See Egypt No. 465.

Arms of UAR — A8

Perf. 12x11½

1959, Feb. 22 Litho. Wmk. 291

17	A8	12½p grn, blk & red	.25	.25

United Arab Republic, 1st anniv. See Egypt No. 462.

Mother and Children — A9

1959, Mar. 21 *Perf. 11½*

18	A9	15p carmine rose	.25	.25
19	A9	25p dk slate grn	.30	.25

Arab Mother's Day, Mar. 21. For overprints see Nos. 41-42.

Syria No. 378 Surcharged "U.A.R." in Arabic and English, and New Value in Red

1959, Apr. 6 Photo. Unwmk.

20	A68	2½p on 1p olive	.25	.25

Type of 1959 and

A10

Boys' School, Damascus — A11

Designs: 5p, 7½p, 10p, Various arabesques. 12½p, St. Simeon's Monastery. 17½p, Hittin school. 35p, Normal School for Girls, Damascus.

1959-61 Unwmk. Litho. *Perf. 11½*

21	A10	2½p violet	.25	.25
22	A10	5p olive bister	.25	.25
23	A10	7½p ultra	.25	.25
24	A10	10p bl grn	.25	.25
25	A11	12½p lt bl ('61)	.25	.25
26	A6	17½p brt lilac ('60)	.25	.25
27	A11	25p brt grnsh bl	.30	.25
28	A11	35p brown ('60)	.40	.25
		Nos. 21-28 (8)	2.20	2.00

Male Profile and Fair Emblem — A12

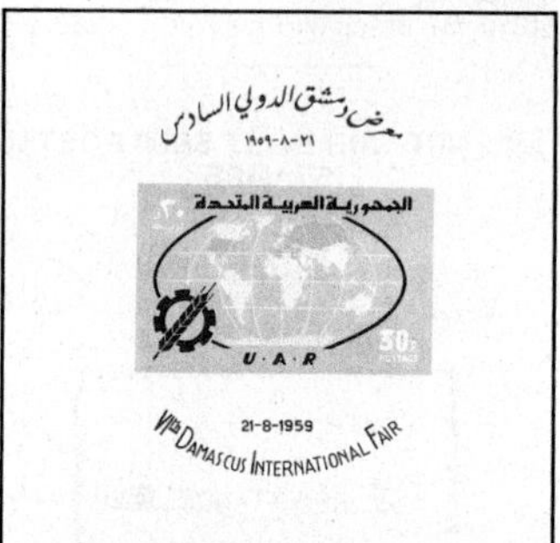

Fair Emblem and Globe — A13

1959, Aug. 30 Unwmk. *Perf. 11½*

30	A12	35p gray, grn & vio	.40	.25

Souvenir Sheet

Imperf

31	A13	30p dl yel & grn	1.50	1.50

6th International Damascus Fair.

Shield and Cogwheel — A14

Perf. 13½x13

1959, Oct. 20 Wmk. 328

32	A14	50p sepia	.60	.35

Issued for Army Day, 1959. See Egypt No. 491.

Syria Nos. 408 and 386 with Red Overprint Similar to

1959 Unwmk. Litho. *Perf. 11½*
33 A75 15p gray .25 .25

Photo.
34 A69 50p dk grn .60 .40

The overprints differ in size and lettering: No. 33 is 28x8½mm; No. 34 is 21x6mm. A period follows "R" on Nos. 33-34. The Arabic overprint means "United Arab Republic."
See Nos. C26-C28.

Cogwheel, Wheat and Cotton — A15

1959, Oct. 30 Litho.
35 A15 35p gray, bl & ocher .40 .25

Industrial and Agricultural Production Fair, Aleppo. For overprint see No. 46.

Type of Syria Air Post, 1956, Inscribed "U.A.R."

1959, Dec. 31 Unwmk. *Perf. 13½*
36 AP59 12½p gray ol & bister .25 .25

Day of the Tree. For overprint see No. 49.

A. R. Kawakbi — A16

1960, Jan. 11 *Perf. 12x11½*
37 A16 15p dark green .25 .25

Kawakbi, Arabic writer, 50th death anniv.

Arms and Flag — A17

Perf. 13½x13
1960, Feb. 22 Photo. Wmk. 328
38 A17 12½p red & dk sl grn .25 .25

United Arab Republic, 2nd anniversary.
See Egypt No. 499.

Diesel Train and Old Town — A18

Perf. 11½x11
1960, Mar. 15 Litho. Unwmk.
39 A18 12½p brn & brt bl .35 .25

Construction of the Latakia-Aleppo railroad.

Arab League Center, Cairo, and Arms of UAR A19

Perf. 13x13½
1960, Mar. 22 Photo. Wmk. 328
40 A19 12½p dl grn & blk .25 .25

Opening of the Arab League Center and the Arab Postal Museum in Cairo.
See Egypt No. 502.

Nos. 18-19 Overprinted in Black or Magenta

Wmk. 291
1960, Apr. 3 Litho. *Perf. 11½*
41 A9 15p car rose .25 .25
42 A9 25p dk slate grn (M) .35 .25

Issued for Arab Mother's Day.

Refugees Pointing to Map of Palestine A20

Perf. 13x13½
1960, Apr. 7 Photo. Wmk. 328
43 A20 12½p car rose .40 .25
44 A20 50p green .70 .30

World Refugee Year, 7/1/59-6/30/60.
See Egypt Nos. 503-504.

Evacuation Day, 1960 — A21

Perf. 11½
1960, May 12 Unwmk. Litho.
45 A21 12½p vio, rose & pale grn .25 .25

No. 35 Overprinted in Red

1960
46 A15 35p gray, bl & ocher .30 .25

1960 Industrial and Agricultural Production Fair, Aleppo.

Souvenir Sheet

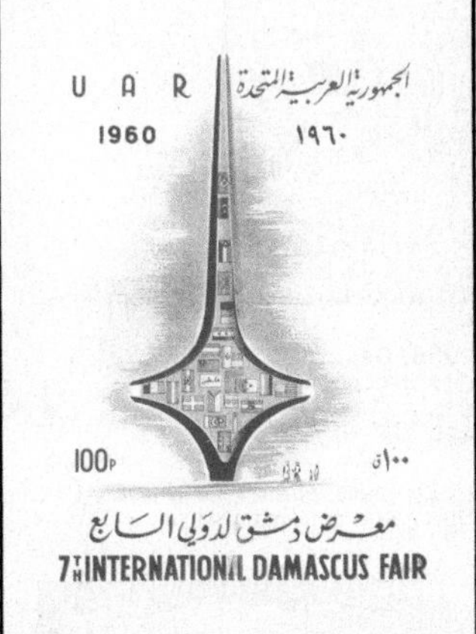

Flags in Symbolic Design — A22

1960 Unwmk. *Imperf.*
47 A22 100p gray, brn & lt bl 1.50 1.50

7th Intl. Damascus Fair.

Child — A23

1960 Litho. *Perf. 11½*
48 A23 35p dk grn & fawn .40 .25

Issued for Children's Day.

No. 36 Overprinted in Carmine

1960 Unwmk. *Perf. 11½*
49 AP59 12½p gray ol & bis .25 .25

Issued to publicize the Day of the Tree.

Coat of Arms and Victory Wreath — A24

Perf. 13½x13
1961, Feb. 22 Photo. Wmk. 328
50 A24 12½p lt vio .25 .25

United Arab Republic, 3rd anniversary.
See Egypt No. 517.

Cogwheel, Retort and Ear of Wheat — A25

Perf. 11½
1961, June 8 Unwmk. Litho.
51 A25 12½p multi .25 .25

Industrial and Agricultural Fair, Aleppo.

UAR SEMI-POSTAL STAMP

Catalogue values for unused stamp in this section is for a Never Hinged item.

Postal Emblem — SP1

Perf. 13½x13
1959, Jan. 2 Photo. Wmk. 318
B1 SP1 20p + 10p bl grn, red & blk .40 .40

Issued for Post Day. The surtax went to the social fund for postal employees.
See Egypt No. B18 for similar stamp with denomination in "M" (milliemes).

UAR AIR POST STAMPS

Catalogue values for unused stamps in this section are for Never Hinged items.

Map Type of Regular Issue
Perf. 11½
1958, Apr. 3 Unwmk. Litho.
C1 A1 17½p ultra & brn .35 .25

Broken Chain, Dove and Olive Branch AP1

1958, May 17
C2 AP1 35p rose & blk .70 .35
C3 AP1 45p bl & brn 1.25 .40

British-French troop evacuation, 12th anniv.

Scout Putting up Tent AP2

1958, Aug. 31 *Perf. 12*
C4 AP2 35p dk brn 3.00 1.50
C5 AP2 40p ultra 4.00 2.00

3rd Pan-Arab Boy Scout Jamboree.

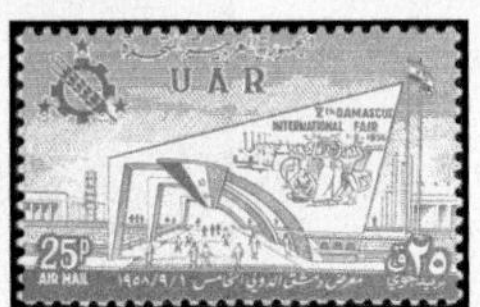

View of Damascus Fair — AP3

UAR Flag and Fair Emblem — AP4

Designs: 30p, Minaret, vase and emblem, vert. 45p, Mosque, chimneys and wheel, vert.

1958, Sept. 1 Litho. *Perf. 11½*
C6 AP3 25p vermilion .70 .60
C7 AP3 30p brt bl grn 1.00 .60
C8 AP3 45p violet .80 .55
Nos. C6-C8 (3) 2.50 1.75

Souvenir Sheet

Imperf

C9 AP4 100p brt grn, car & blk 50.00 50.00

Fifth Damascus International Fair.

Syria Nos. C244-C245 Overprinted

1958, Oct. 6 Wmk. 291 *Perf. 11½*
C10 A78 17½p ultra *45.00 45.00*
C11 A78 20p red brn *45.00 45.00*

International Children's Day.

Cotton and Cotton Material — AP5

1958, Oct. 10 Unwmk. *Perf. 12*
C12 AP5 25p brn & yel .40 .40
C13 AP5 35p brn & brick red .70 .50

Cotton Festival, Aleppo, Oct. 9-11.

Type of Regular Issue, 1958

1958, Dec. 10
C14 A5 17½p brt vio .25 .25

Children and Glider — AP6

1958, Dec. 1 Litho. *Perf. 12*
C15 AP6 7½p gray green .50 .30
C16 AP6 12½p olive 2.00 1.25

1958 glider festival.

UN Emblem — AP7

1958, Dec. 10
C17 AP7 25p dl pur .25 .25
C18 AP7 35p light blue .35 .25
C19 AP7 40p brn red .45 .30
Nos. C17-C19 (3) 1.05 .80

10th anniv. of the signing of the Universal Declaration of Human Rights.

Globe, Radio and Telegraph — AP8

1959, Mar. 1 *Perf. 12*
C20 AP8 40p grn & blk .50 .35

Arab Union of Telecommunications.
See Egypt No. 464 for similar stamp with denomination in "M" (milliemes).

Same Overprinted in Red

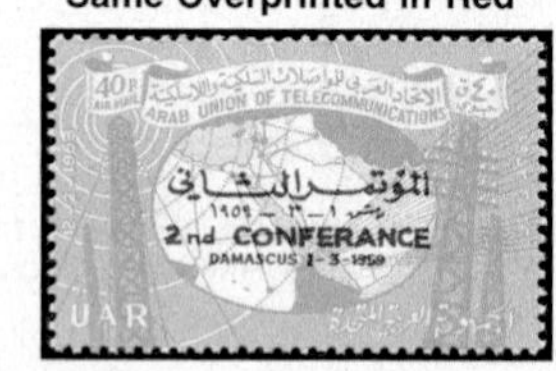

1959, Mar. 1
C21 AP8 40p grn & blk .40 .25

2nd Conference of the Arab Union of Telecommunications, Damascus.

Laurel and Map of Syria — AP9

Design: 35p, Torch and broken chain.

1959, Apr. 17 *Perf. 12x11½*
C22 AP9 15p ocher & green .25 .25
C23 AP9 35p gray & carmine .40 .25

British-French troop evacuation, 13th anniv.

"Emigration" — AP10

1959, Aug. 4 Unwmk. *Perf. 11½x12*
C24 AP10 80p brt grn, blk & red .70 .40

Convention of the Assoc. of Arab Emigrants in the US.

Refinery AP11

1959, Aug. 12 Litho.
C25 AP11 50p bl, blk & car .90 .40

Opening of first oil refinery in Syria.

Syria Nos. C246 and C181-C182 Overprinted like Nos. 33-34

1959 *Perf. 11½*
C26 AP64 5p bright green .25 .25
C27 AP44 50p deep plum .40 .25
C28 AP44 70p purple .70 .30
Nos. C26-C28 (3) 1.35 .80

The overprints differ in size and lettering: No. C26 is 25½x9½mm; Nos. C27-C28 are 27x8mm. A period follows "R" on Nos. C27-C28.

Cotton Boll and Thread — AP12

1959, Oct. 1 Litho. *Perf. 11½*
C29 AP12 45p gray blue .40 .25
C30 AP12 50p claret .40 .30

Cotton Festival, Aleppo.
For overprints see Nos. C33-C34.

Boy and Building Blocks — AP13

1959, Oct. 5
C31 AP13 25p dl lil, red & dk bl .25 .25

Issued for Children's Day.

Crane and Compass AP14

1960 Unwmk. *Perf. 11½*
C32 AP14 50p lt brn, crim & blk .40 .30

7th Damascus International Fair.

Nos. C29-C30 Overprinted in Claret or Gray Blue

1960 Litho. *Perf. 11½*
C33 AP12 45p gray blue (C) .40 .25
C34 AP12 50p claret (GB) .45 .30

1960 Cotton Festival, Aleppo.

17th Olympic Games, Rome — AP15

1960, Dec. 27 Unwmk. *Perf. 12*
C35 AP15 15p Basketball .25 .25
C36 AP15 20p Swimmer .35 .25
C37 AP15 25p Fencing .35 .25
C38 AP15 40p Horsemanship .60 .30
Nos. C35-C38 (4) 1.55 1.05

Globe, Laurel and "UN" — AP16

1960, Dec. 31
C39 AP16 35p multi .35 .25
C40 AP16 50p bl, red & yel .40 .25

United Nations, 15th anniversary.

Ibrahim Hanano — AP17

1961 Litho. *Perf. 12x11½*
C41 AP17 50p buff & slate grn .80 .25

Hanano, leader of liberation movement.

Soldier with Flag — AP18

1961, Apr. 17 Wmk. 291 *Perf. 11½*
C42 AP18 40p gray green 1.00 .25

Issued for Evacuation Day, 1961.

Arab and Map of Palestine — AP19

1961, May 15 ***Perf. 12***

C43	AP19 50p ultra & blk	2.00	.25

Issued for Palestine Day.

Abu-Tammam AP20

1961, July 20 Unwmk. ***Perf. 11½***

C44	AP20 50p brown	.50	.25

Abu-Tammam (807-845?), Arabian poet.

Discus Thrower and Lyre AP21

1961, Aug. 23 Litho. ***Perf. 11½***

C45	AP21 15p crimson & blk	.25	.25
C46	AP21 35p bl grn & vio	.50	.25

5th University Youth Festival.

A souvenir sheet contains one each of Nos. C45-C46 imperf.

Fair Emblem — AP22

UAR Pavilion — AP23

1961, Aug. 25

C47	AP22 17½p vio & grn	.25	.25
C48	AP23 50p brt lil & blk	.35	.25
a.	Black omitted		

8th International Damascus Fair.

St. Simeon's Monastery AP24

1961, Oct. Litho. ***Perf. 12***

C49	AP24 200p violet blue	1.50	.90

No. C49 was issued by the Syrian Arab Republic after dissolution of the UAR.

UAR AIR POST SEMI-POSTAL STAMP

Catalogue value for the unused stamp in this section is for a Never Hinged item.

Eye, Hand and UN Emblem SPAP1

Perf. 12x11½

1961, Apr. 29 Litho. Wmk. 291

CB1	SPAP1 40p + 10p sl grn & blk	.30	.30

UN welfare program for the blind.

TAHITI

tə-ˈhēt-ē

LOCATION — An island in the South Pacific Ocean, one of the Society group

GOVT. — A part of the French Oceania Colony

AREA — 600 sq. mi.

POP. — 19,029

CAPITAL — Papeete

The stamps of Tahiti were replaced by those of French Oceania (see French Polynesia in Vol. 2).

100 Centimes = 1 Franc

Counterfeits exist of surcharges and overprints on Nos. 1-31.

Stamps of French Colonies Surcharged in Black

a

b

c

d

1882 Unwmk. ***Imperf.***

1	A8(a)	25c on 35c dk vio, *org*	425.	350.
1A	A8(b)	25c on 35c dk vio, *org*	*4,500.*	*4,500.*
1B	A8(a)	25c on 40c ver, *straw*	*6,250.*	*6,750.*

Nos. 1-1B exist with surcharges inverted. Values for Nos. 1 and 1A are approximately the same as for normal stamps; No. 1B with surcharge inverted is worth about half the value of a normal stamp.

Surcharge exists reading either up or down on Nos. 1 and 1A, and double, one inverted on No. 1B. See *Scott Classic Specialized Catalogue of Stamps and Covers* for detailed listings of these and later Tahiti issues.

1884 ***Perf. 14x13½***

2	A9(c)	5c on 20c red, *yel grn*	300.	240.
3	A9(d)	10c on 20c red, *yel grn*	350.	300.
		Imperf		
4	A8(b)	25c on 1fr brnz grn, *straw*	750.	650.

Inverted and vertical surcharges on Nos. 2-4 are same value as normally placed surcharges.

Handstamped in Black

1893 ***Perf. 14x13½***

5	A9	1c blk, *lil bl*	950.00	875.00
6	A9	2c brown, *buff*	*3,200.*	*2,500.*
7	A9	4c claret, *lav*	1,500.	1,250.
8	A9	5c green, *grnsh*	55.00	47.50
9	A9	10c black, *lav*	60.00	52.50
10	A9	15c blue	60.00	47.50
11	A9	20c red, *green*	72.50	65.00
12	A9	25c yel, *straw*	*8,750.*	*7,250.*
13	A9	25c blk, *rose*	55.00	47.50
14	A9	35c violet, *org*	*2,600.*	*2,200.*
15	A9	75c carmine, *rose*	87.50	87.50
16	A9	1fr brnz grn, *straw*	92.50	92.50

Nearly all values of this set are known with overprint sloping up, sloping down and horizontal. Some occur double. Values the same as for the listed stamps.

For Nos. 6//16 with inverted overprint, see the *Scott Classic Specialized Catalogue of Stamps and Covers.*

Nos. 6, 12 and 14 are valued in the grade of Fine.

Overprinted in Black

1893

17	A9	1c blk, *lil bl*	925.00	800.00
18	A9	2c brn, *buff*	*3,750.*	*2,750.*
19	A9	4c claret, *lav*	1,850.	1,500.
20	A9	5c grn, *grnsh*	1,100.	950.00
21	A9	10c black, *lav*	350.00	350.00
22	A9	15c blue	55.00	50.00
23	A9	20c red, *grn*	60.00	55.00
24	A9	25c yel, *straw*	*50,000.*	*42,500.*
25	A9	25c black, *rose*	55.00	50.00
26	A9	35c violet, *org*	*2,600.*	*2,200.*
27	A9	75c carmine, *rose*	60.00	55.00
b.		Double overprint	*400.00*	
28	A9	1fr brnz grn, *straw*	75.00	60.00

Inverted Overprint

17a	A9	1c blk, *lil bl*	*1,350.*	1,200.
18a	A9	2c brn, *buff*	*4,000.*	3,900.
19a	A9	4c claret, *lav*	*2,000.*	1,900.
20a	A9	5c grn, *grnsh*	*1,600.*	*1,500.*
21a	A9	10c black, *lav*	*950.*	*900.*
22a	A9	15c blue	*250.*	*225.*
23a	A9	20c red, *grn*	*250.*	*225.*
25a	A9	25c black, *rose*	*250.*	*225.*
26a	A9	35c violet, *org*	*3,000.*	2,800.
27a	A9	75c carmine, *rose*	*300.*	*250.*
28a	A9	1fr brnz grn, *straw*	*300.*	*275.*

Stamps of French Polynesia Surcharged in Black or Carmine

g

h

1903

29	A1 (g)	10c on 15c bl (Bk)	11.00	11.00
a.		Double surcharge	67.50	67.50
b.		Inverted surcharge	72.50	72.50
30	A1 (h)	10c on 25c blk, *rose* (C)	11.00	11.00
a.		Double surcharge	67.50	67.50
b.		Inverted surcharge	80.00	80.00
31	A1 (h)	10c on 40c red, *straw* (Bk)	13.00	13.00
a.		Double surcharge	80.00	80.00
b.		Inverted surcharge	85.00	80.00
		Nos. 29-31 (3)	35.00	35.00

In the surcharges on Nos. 29-31 there are two varieties of the "1" in "10," i. e. with long and short serif.

SEMI-POSTAL STAMPS

Stamps of French Polynesia Overprinted in Red

1915 Unwmk. ***Perf. 14x13½***

B1	A1 15c blue	300.00	300.00
a.	Inverted overprint	1,100.	1,000.
B2	A1 15c gray	35.00	35.00
a.	Inverted overprint	425.00	425.00

Counterfeits exist.

POSTAGE DUE STAMPS

Counterfeits exist of overprints on Nos. J1-J26.

Inverted overprints exist on most, and double overprints on many, Tahiti postage due stamps. See the *Scott Classic Specialized Catalogue of Stamps and Covers* for detailed listings.

Postage Due Stamps of French Colonies Handstamped in Black like Nos. 5-16

1893 Unwmk. ***Imperf.***

J1	D1	1c black	*400.*	*400.*
J2	D1	2c black	*400.*	*400.*
J3	D1	3c black	*450.*	*450.*
J4	D1	4c black	*450.*	*450.*
J5	D1	5c black	*450.*	*450.*
J6	D1	10c black	*450.*	*450.*
J7	D1	15c black	*450.*	*450.*
J8	D1	20c black	*350.*	*350.*
J9	D1	30c black	*450.*	*450.*
J10	D1	40c black	*450.*	*450.*
J11	D1	60c black	*525.*	*525.*
J12	D1	1fr brown	*1,100.*	*1,100.*
J13	D1	2fr brown	*1,100.*	*1,100.*
		Nos. J1-J13 (13)	*7,025.*	*7,025.*

Overprinted in Black like Nos. 17-28

1893

J14	D1	1c black	*2,400.*	*2,400.*
J15	D1	2c black	*550.*	*550.*
J16	D1	3c black	*550.*	*550.*
J17	D1	4c black	*550.*	*550.*
J18	D1	5c black	*550.*	*550.*
J19	D1	10c black	*550.*	*550.*
J20	D1	15c black	*550.*	*550.*
J21	D1	20c black	*550.*	*550.*
J22	D1	30c black	*550.*	*550.*
J23	D1	40c black	*550.*	*550.*
J24	D1	60c black	*550.*	*550.*
J25	D1	1fr brown	*550.*	*550.*
J26	D1	2fr brown	*550.*	*550.*
		Nos. J14-J26 (13)	*9,000.*	*9,000.*

TAJIKISTAN

tä-jik-i-'stan

(Tadzhikistan)

LOCATION — Asia, bounded by Uzbekistan, Kyrgyzstan, People's Republic of China and Afghanistan
GOVT. — Republic
AREA — 55,240 sq. mi.
POP. — 6,102,854 (1999 est.)
CAPITAL — Dushanbe

With the breakup of the Soviet Union on Dec. 26, 1991, Tajikistan became independent.

100 Kopecks = 1 Ruble
100 Tanga = 1 Ruble
100 Dirams = 1 Somoni (2000)

Catalogue values for all unused stamps in this country are for Never Hinged items.

Gold Statue of Man on Horse — A1

1992, May 20 Litho. *Perf. 12x12½*
1 A1 50k multicolored .35 .35

For surcharge see No. 12.

Sheik Muslihiddin Mosque A2

1992, May 25 Photo. *Perf. 11½*
2 A2 50k multicolored .30 .30

For surcharges, see Nos. 13-14.

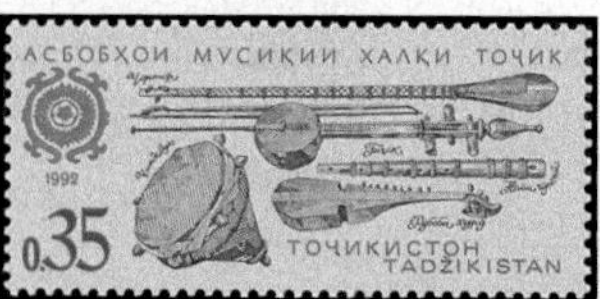

Musical Instruments of Tajikistan — A3

Photo. & Engr.
1992, Aug. 15 *Perf. 12x11½*
3 A3 35k multicolored .30 .30

For surcharges see Nos. 5-7.

Ram — A4

1992, Aug. 21 Photo. *Perf. 12x12½*
4 A4 30k multicolored .40 .40

No. 3 Surcharged in Black or Blue

Photo. & Engr.
1992, Nov. 12 *Perf. 12x11½*
5 A3 15r on 35k .85 .85
6 A3 15r on 35k (Bl) 2.25 2.25
7 A3 50r on 35k .85 .85
Nos. 5-7 (3) 3.95 3.95

Russia No. 5838 Surcharged

1992, Jan. 4 Litho. *Perf. 12x12½*
8 A2765 3r on 1k .35 .35
9 A2765 100r on 1k 2.10 2.10

Russia No. 5984 Surcharged in Violet Blue or Green

No. 1 Surcharged in Black

1992, May 7 Litho. *Perf. 12x12½*
10 A2765 10r on 2k (VB) .95 .95
11 A2765 15r on 2k (Gr) .95 .95
12 A1 60r on 50k 1.90 1.90
Nos. 10-12 (3) 3.80 3.80

Location and size of lettering on Nos. 10-11 varies.

No. 2 Surcharged

Methods and Perfs as Before
1992, Sept. 18
13 A2 5r on 50k multi .45 .45
14 A2 25r on 50k multi 1.10 1.10

Wild Animals A5

Designs: 3r, Ursus arctos. 10r, Cervas elaphus. 15r, Capra falconeri. 25r, Hystrix leucura. 100r, Uncia uncia.

1993, June 8 Litho. *Perf. 13½*
15 A5 3r multicolored .25 .25
16 A5 10r multicolored .35 .25
17 A5 15r multicolored .35 .25
18 A5 25r multicolored .70 .25
19 A5 100r multicolored 2.40 .40
Nos. 15-19 (5) 4.05 1.40

For surcharge, see No. 372.

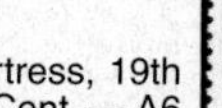

Fortress, 19th Cent. — A6

Academy — A6a

1r, Statue of Rudaki, poet, vert. 5r, Mountains, river. 10r, Statue with oriental inscription, vert. 15r, Mausoleum of Aini, poet, vert. 20r, Map, flag. 35r, Post office. 50r, Aini Opera House. #29, Theater. #30, Flag, map, diff. #31, Observatory. #32, Academy.

1993-94
20 A6 1r multicolored .25 .25
22 A6 5r multicolored .25 .25
23 A6 10r multicolored .25 .25
24 A6 15r multicolored .25 .25
25 A6 20r green & multi .25 .25
26 A6 25r multicolored .40 .40
27 A6 35r multicolored .25 .25
28 A6 50r multicolored .60 .60
29 A6 100r multicolored .55 .55
30 A6 100r blue & multi 1.10 1.10
31 A6 160r multicolored .65 .65
32 A6a 160r shown .65 .65
Nos. 20-32 (12) 5.45 5.45

Issued: 1r, 5r, 15r, 20r, 25r, 50r, No. 30, 6/8/93, others, 9/8/94.
For surcharges, see Nos. 169-171, 231-232, 301, 373.

Souvenir Sheet

1992 Summer Olympics, Barcelona — A7

1993, June 8
33 A7 50r multicolored 7.75 7.75

For surcharge see No. 52A.

Epic Poem "Book of Kings", by Ferdowsi, 1000th Anniv. A8

Designs: 5r, Combat with swords. 20r, Two men on horseback fighting with spears. 30r, Men in combat stopped by guide on giant bird, vert. 50r, Ferdowsi (c. 935-c. 1020), vert.

1993, June 8 Litho. *Perf. 13½*
34 A8 5r multicolored .50 .50
35 A8 20r multicolored 1.75 1.75
36 A8 30r multicolored 2.00 2.00
a. Sheet, 2 each # 34-36, + 4 labels 14.00 —
Nos. 34-36 (3) 4.25 4.25

Souvenir Sheet
37 A8 50r multicolored 3.25 3.25

No. 37 contains one 30x45mm stamp.

Traditional Art Pattern — A8a

1993, July 1 Litho. *Perf. 12x11½*
37A A8a 1.50r multicolored .70 .70

Dated 1992.
For surcharges see Nos. 62-65.

Ali Hamadani (1314-85), Persian Mystic — A9

1994, Feb. 22 Litho. *Perf. 13½*
38 A9 1000r multicolored 2.75 2.75
39 A9 1000r multicolored 2.75 2.75

Name in latin letters on No. 38 and in cyrillic letters on No. 39.

Natl. Arms — A10

1994, Feb. 22
40 A10 10r black brown & multi .25 .25
41 A10 15r purple & multi .25 .25
43 A10 35r olive & multi .25 .25
44 A10 50r red & multi .25 .25
46 A10 100r green & multi .30 .30
47 A10 160r blue & multi .50 .50

Size: 23x36mm
50 A10 500r blue & multi .75 .75
52 A10 1000r brown & multi 1.25 1.25
Nos. 40-52 (8) 3.80 3.80

No. 33 Overprinted

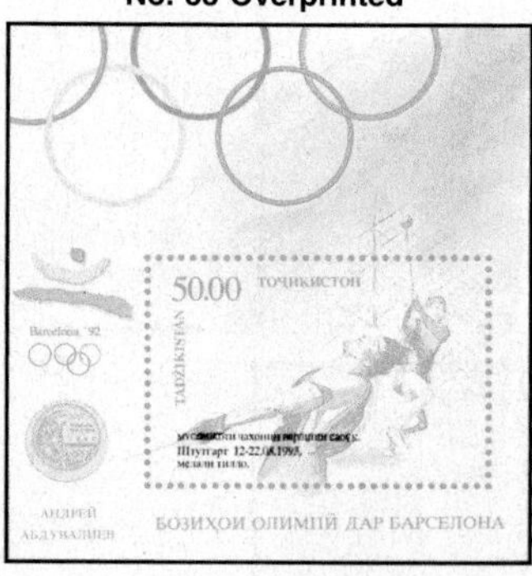

1994, Apr. 13 Litho. *Perf. 13½*
52A A7 50r multicolored 7.50 7.50

Prehistoric Animals A11

Designs: No. 53, Diatryma. No. 54, Triceratops. No. 55, Anatosaurus. No. 56, Tyrannosaurus. No. 57, Parasaurolophus. No. 58, Incorrectly inscribed "Tyrannosaurus," with horns, resembling an Ankalysaurus. No. 59, Spinosaurus. No. 60, Stegosaurus.

1994, Sept. 8 Litho. *Perf. 13½*

53-60	A11	500r Set of 8	7.25	2.50

Issued both in separate sheetlets of nine and together in a se-tenant sheetlet of nine, containing Nos. 53-60 and one label. Values: set of nine sheetlets, $60; se-tenant sheetlet, $40.

No. 37A Surcharged in Green

1995, Mar. 10 Litho. *Perf. 12x11½*

62	A8a	100r on 1.50r multi	.25	.25
63	A8a	600r on 1.50r multi	.50	.50
64	A8a	1000r on 1.50r multi	.90	.90
65	A8a	5000r on 1.50r multi	4.25	4.25
a.		Strip, #64-65, 2 ea #62-63	9.00	9.00
		Nos. 62-65 (4)	5.90	5.90

Issued in sheets of 36 stamps. Each vertical and horizontal strip has stamps in different order.

For surcharges see Nos. 111-114.

Membership Admissions — A13

Designs: No. 66, Member of UN. No. 67, Member of UPU, vert. No. 68, Member of OSCE (Organization of Security & Cooperation in Europe), vert.

1995, May 4 Litho. *Perf. 13½*

66	A13	1000r multicolored	1.00	.90
67	A13	1000r multicolored	1.00	.90
68	A13	1000r multicolored	1.00	.90
		Nos. 66-68 (3)	3.00	2.70

Lizards A14

#69, Alsophylax loricatus. #70, Varanus griseus. #71, Phrynocephalus mystaceus. #72, Phrynocephalus helioscopus. #73, Phrynocephalus sogdianus. #74, Teratoscincus scineus.

5000r, Eumeces schneideri.

1995, May 4 Litho. *Perf. 13½*

69	A14	500r multicolored	.60	.60
70	A14	500r multicolored	.60	.60
71	A14	500r multicolored	.60	.60
72	A14	500r multicolored	.60	.60
73	A14	500r multicolored	.60	.60
74	A14	500r multicolored	.60	.60
		Nos. 69-74 (6)	3.60	3.60

Souvenir Sheet

75	A14	5000r multicolored	6.25	3.75

For overprints see Nos. 77-78.

Souvenir Sheet

End of World War II, 50th Anniv. — A15

1995, May 8 Litho. *Perf. 13½*

76	A15	5000r multicolored	6.25	6.25
a.		As #76, color diff.	5.50	5.50

On No. 76 emblem in margin is bister, black & red. No. 76a emblem is yellow, black & red with missing letter "E" from second line of text.

No. 70 Ovptd.

No. 71 Ovptd.

1995, Dec. 1 Litho. *Perf. 13½*

77	A14	500r on #70	4.25	4.25
78	A14	500r on #71	4.25	4.25

Singapore '95 (#77), Beijing '95 (#78).

New Natl. Arms — A16

1995, Dec. 20

79	A16	1r olive & multi	.30	.30
80	A16	2r brown & multi	.30	.30
81	A16	5r green & multi	.30	.30
82	A16	12r red & multi	.50	.50
83	A16	40r green blue & multi	.90	.90
		Nos. 79-83 (5)	2.30	2.30

Birds A17

Designs: No. 84, Syrrhaptes tibetana. No. 85, Perdix daurica turcomana. No. 86, Tetraogallus tibetanus. No. 87, Otis undulata macqueeni. No. 88, Larus brunnicephalus. No. 89, Anser indicus.

600r, Phasianus colchicus.

1996, Feb. 1

84	A17	200r multicolored	1.40	1.40
85	A17	200r multicolored	1.40	1.40
86	A17	200r multicolored	1.40	1.40
87	A17	200r multicolored	1.40	1.40
88	A17	200r multicolored	1.40	1.40
89	A17	200r multicolored	1.40	1.40
		Nos. 84-89 (6)	8.40	8.40

Souvenir Sheet

90	A17	600r multicolored	6.50	6.50

Two each of Nos. 84-89 were issued in sheet of 12 + label.

UN, 50th Anniv. A18

Designs: 100r, UN headquarters, New York. 500r, Headquarters at night.

1996

90A	A18	100r multicolored	1.00	1.00

Souvenir Sheet

90B	A18	500r multicolored	4.00	4.00

Issued: 100r, 4/10; 500r, 2/1.

Souvenir Sheet

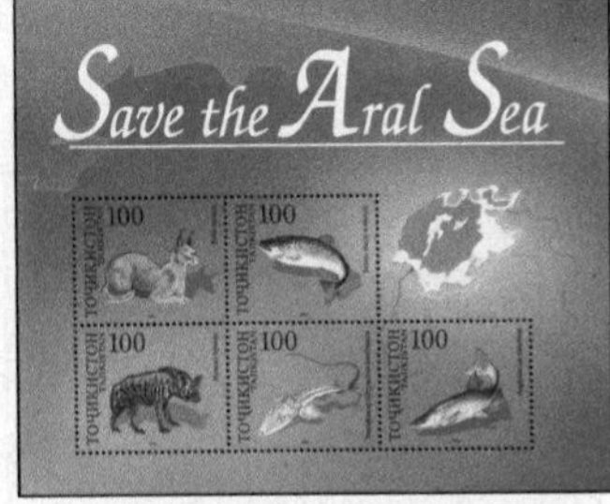

Save the Aral Sea — A19

Designs: a, Felis caracal. b, Salmo trutta aralensis. c, Hyaena hyaena. d, Pseudoscaphirhynchus kaufmanni. e, Aspiolucius esocinus.

1996, May 3 Litho. *Perf. 14*

91	A19	100r Sheet of 5, #a.-e.	5.75	5.75

See Kazakhstan No. 145, Kyrgyzstan No. 107, Turkmenistan No. 52, Uzbekistan No. 113.

A20

A20a

Designs: Nos. 92-95, 98, Otocolobus manul (different views). No. 96, Felis chaus oxiana. No. 97, Felix lynx isabellina.

1996, June 28 Litho. *Perf. 13½*

92	A20	100r brown & multi	2.00	2.00
93	A20	100r yellow & multi	2.00	2.00
94	A20	150r blue & multi	2.00	2.00
95	A20	150r lilac & multi	2.00	2.00
96	A20	200r multicolored	2.00	2.00
97	A20	200r multicolored	2.00	2.00
		Nos. 92-97 (6)	12.00	12.00

Souvenir Sheet

98	A20a	500r multicolored	8.00	8.00

World Wildlife Fund (#92-95).

1996 Summer Olympic Games, Atlanta A21

1996, July 12 Litho. *Perf. 13½*

99	A21	200r Judo	1.90	1.90
100	A21	200r Diving	1.90	1.90
101	A21	200r Hammer throw	1.90	1.90
102	A21	200r Soccer	1.90	1.90
103	A21	200r Pierre de Coubertin	1.90	1.90
		Nos. 99-103 (5)	9.50	9.50

Kamol Khujandi, Poet — A22

1996, Sept. 7 Litho. *Perf. 13½*

104	A22	500r Cyrillic name 14mm long	5.00	5.00
a.		Cyrillic name 13mm long	10.00	10.00
105	A22	500r English inscriptions	5.00	5.00

Central Asian Postal Union, 5th Anniv. A23

1996, Dec. 25 *Perf. 12¾*

106	A23	100r multicolored	5.50	5.50

Mountains A24

1997, July 16 *Perf. 13x12¾*

107	A24	100r Communism Peak	1.50	1.50
108	A24	100r Peak Korzhenevskoj	1.50	1.50
109	A24	100r Lenin Peak	1.50	1.50
a.		Strip of 3, #107-109	6.50	6.50

Souvenir Sheet

110	A24	500r Mountain climber	6.50	6.50

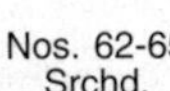

Nos. 62-65 Srchd.

1997, Oct. 27 Litho. *Perf. 12x11½*

111	A8a	(A) on 100r #62	1.00	1.00
112	A8a	(A) on 600r #63	1.00	1.00
113	A8a	(A) on 1000r #64	1.00	1.00
114	A8a	(A) on 5000r #65	1.00	1.00
a.		Strip, #113-114, 2 ea #111-112	6.00	6.00
		Nos. 111-114 (4)	4.00	4.00

A25

Traditional Costumes: #115, Woman with red shawl draped over head, carrying pitcher. #116, Woman in long formal dress, cape, tiara. #117, Man wearing long striped coat. #118, Man wearing long blue coat.

1998, Feb. 20 Litho. *Perf. 12½x13*

115	A25	100r multicolored	1.00	1.00
116	A25	100r multicolored	1.00	1.00
117	A25	150r multicolored	1.50	1.50
a.		Pair, #115, 117	2.50	2.50
118	A25	150r multicolored	1.50	1.50
a.		Pair, #116, 118	2.50	2.50
		Nos. 115-118 (4)	5.00	5.00

Dated 1997.

Handicrafts — A26

1998, Feb. 20 Litho. *Perf. 12¾*

119	A26	30r Urn	.50	.50
119A	A26	100r Cradles	1.50	1.50

Size: 64x64mm

Imperf

120 A26 300r Ceramic tile 3.75 3.75
Nos. 119-120 (3) 5.75 5.75

Dated 1997.

A27

Flowers: 12r, Tulipa greigii. 30r, Crocus korolkowii. 70r, Iris darwasica. 150r, Petilium eduardii. 300r, Juno nicolai.

1998, Apr. 3 Litho. ***Perf. 12½x13***

121 A27 12r multicolored .40 .40
122 A27 30r multicolored .60 .60
123 A27 70r multicolored 1.25 1.25
124 A27 150r multicolored 2.75 2.75
a. Sheet of 4, #121-124 5.50 5.50
Nos. 121-124 (4) 5.00 5.00

Souvenir Sheet

125 A27 300r multicolored 5.00 5.00

Stamps in No. 124a have margins continuing the background design of the sheet.

Butterflies A28

12r, Catocala timur. 30r, Celerio chamyla apocyni. 70r, Colias sieversi. 150r, Papilio alexanor.
300r, Anthocharis tomyris.

1998, Apr. 3 ***Perf. 13x12½***

126 A28 12r multicolored .75 .75
127 A28 30r multicolored .90 .90
128 A28 70r multicolored 1.25 1.25
129 A28 150r multicolored 2.50 2.50
a. Sheet of 4, #126-129 7.00 7.00
Nos. 126-129 (4) 5.40 5.40

Souvenir Sheet

130 A28 300r multicolored 6.50 6.50

Stamps of No. 129a have margins continuing the background design of the sheet.

Gems A29

1998, Aug. 21 Litho. ***Perf. 13x12¾***

131 A29 1r Sapphire .25 .25
132 A29 1r Ruby .25 .25
133 A29 12r Lapis lazuli .35 .35
134 A29 12r Tourmaline .35 .35
135 A29 150r Spinel 1.90 1.90
136 A29 150r Amethyst 1.90 1.90
a. Sheet of 6, #131-136, + 2 labels 5.00 5.00
Nos. 131-136 (6) 5.00 5.00

Souvenir Sheet

137 A29 350r Agate 5.00 5.00

Bobojon Ghafurov, Academician (1908-98) — A30

1998, Aug. 21 ***Perf. 12¾x13***

138 A30 12r blue & multi .30 .30
139 A30 150r red & multi 2.00 2.00

Each printed in sheets of 10.

Aleksander Pushkin (1799-1837), Russian Poet — A31

100r, Self-portrait drawing. 270r, Painting by Kiprensky.

1999, June Litho. ***Perf. 13¼x13½***

140 100r multicolored .75 .75
141 270r multicolored 2.25 2.25
a. A31 Pair, #140-141 3.00 3.00

For surcharges see Nos. 332-335.

"ILLEGAL" STAMPS

Tajikistan postal officials have declared as "illegal" the following items.

Sheets of nine stamps of various denominations depicting:

Elvis Presley, Barry White, Michael Douglas, Robert DeNiro, Grace Kelly, the television show "Ally McBeal," Harry Potter, Batman, Superman (two different sheets), Warner Brothers cartoon characters, U.S. Political Cartoons concerning the 2000 Presidential election, Mushrooms, Mushrooms in Art, Major League Baseball players, Sydney 2002 Olympic Games (two different sheets), Various golfers, U.S. Open Golf Championship, Golfer Eduardo Romero, Tiger Woods (two different sheets), Pope John Paul II, and Masonic emblems.

Sheet of 3 stamps of various denominations depicting Marilyn Monroe.

A32

A32a

A32b

1999, June 5 Litho. ***Perf. 13½***

142 A32 (40r) multi .30 .30
143 A32a (100r) multi .80 .80
144 A32b (270r) multi 1.90 1.90
Nos. 142-144 (3) 3.00 3.00

For surcharge see No. 358.

Samanid Dynasty — A33

1999, Aug. Litho. ***Perf. 12¾x13***

145 A33 30r Lion figurine .25 .25
146 A33 50r Round emblem .45 .45
147 A33 100r Handled figurine .90 .90
148 A33 270r Three figurines 2.50 2.50
Nos. 145-148 (4) 4.10 4.10

Souvenir Sheet

149 A33 500r King 5.50 5.50
a. Sheet, #149, 2 ea #145-148 10.00 10.00

Samanid Dynasty, 1100th Anniv. — A34

No. 150: a, 100r, King. b, 500r, Pres. Emomali Rakhmonov.

1999, Oct. Litho. ***Perf. 13½x13½***

150 A34 Sheet of 2, #a.-b. 9.75 9.75

Mushrooms A35

Designs: Nos. 151, 153a, 100r, Pleurotus eryngii. Nos. 152, 153b, 270r, Lepista nuda.
500r, Morchella steppicola.

1999, Nov. ***Perf. 13¼x13***

151 A35 100r multi 1.25 1.25
152 A35 270r multi 4.00 4.00

Miniature Sheet

153 A35 Sheet, 2 ea #153a-153b 3.75 3.75

Souvenir Sheet

154 A35 500r multi 3.00 3.00

Nos. 151-152 have white borders, while Nos. 153a-153b have borders which continue the sheet's central design.

In 2018, No. 153 was surcharged in blue with No. 153a revalued as a 20d stamp and No. 153b revalued as a 30d stamp. The sheet sold for 10s.

For surcharge see No. 229.

Fish — A36

Designs: 40r, Ophiocephalus argus. 100r, Barbus brachycephalus. 230r, Schizopygopsis stoliczkai. 270r, Pseudoscaphirhynchus fedtschenkoi.
500r, Pseudoscaphirhynchus kaufmanni.

2000 Litho. ***Perf. 13¼x13***

155-158 A36 Set of 4 4.25 4.25
158a Souvenir sheet, #155-158 5.00 5.00

Souvenir Sheet

159 A36 500r multi 5.00 5.00

On Nos. 158-159, Pseudoscaphirhynchus is misspelled "Pseudoscaphihynchus."

For surcharges see Nos. 218, 495.

UPU, 125th Anniv. (in 1999) — A37

2000

160 A37 270r multi 1.15 1.15

100 Dinars = 1 Somoni (2000)

Birds of Prey A38

Designs: 10d, Pandion haliaetus. 27d, Aquila chrysaetus, vert. 50d, Gyps himalayensis. 70d, Circaetus ferox, vert.
1s, Falco peregrinus, vert.

2001, Jan. 23 Litho. ***Perf. 14***

161-164 A38 Set of 4 6.75 6.75

Souvenir Sheet

165 A38 1s multi 4.25 4.25

No. 165 contains one 42x56mm stamp. Dated 2000.

For surcharge, see No. 468.

Chess — A39

Designs: 15d, Mikhail Botvinnik. 41d, Robert Fischer.

No. 168: a, 10d, Wilhelm Steinitz. b, 25d, Chess board, five people. c, 50d, José Raul Capablanca. d, 70d, Emanuel Lasker. e, 90d, Chess board, four people. f, 1s, Alexander Alekhine.

2001, May 29 ***Perf. 14¼x14***

166-167 A39 Set of 2 2.75 2.75

Souvenir Sheet

168 A39 Sheet of 6, #a-f 10.00 10.00

For overprints and surcharges, see Nos. 197, 445-446, 463-464.

No. 26 Surcharged in Green, Red or Black

a

b

c

2001, June 4 ***Perf. 13½***

169 A6(a) (6d) multi (G) .65 .65
170 A6(b) (15d) multi (R) 1.25 1.25
171 A6(c) (41d) multi (Bk) 3.75 3.75
Nos. 169-171 (3) 5.65 5.65

Souvenir Sheet

Satellite Communications — A40

2001, July 25 ***Perf. 13¼x13***

172 A40 1.50s multi 3.75 3.75

For overprint, see No. 408.

Souvenir Sheets

Nurec Hydroelectric Station — A41

Pres. Emomali Rakhmonov — A42

Independence, 10th Anniv. — A43

No. 175: a, 41d, Map, flag and arms (29x29mm). b, 54d, Emblem (29x29mm). c, 95d, Ratification of constitution (49x29mm).

2001, Sept. 7 ***Perf. 13¼x13¾***

173 A41 2.50s multi 30.00 30.00

Perf. 12¾x13¼

174 A42 3s multi 35.00 35.00

Perf. 14x13¾

175 A43 Sheet of 3, #a-c 25.00 25.00

Independence, 10th anniv.

Tajikistan postal officials have declared as "illegal" the following items:

Sheets of nine stamps of various denominations depicting Bruce Lee, Michael Jordan, Osama bin Laden, Captain America, Fantastic Four, Queen Mother's 100th Birthday, Formula 1 Racing, Motor Sports and the Netherlands Royal Wedding.

Sheets of six stamps of various denominations depicting Pope John Paul II and Motorcycle racers.

Sheet of three stamps of various denominations depicting Pope John Paul II.

Transportation — A44

Designs: 1s, Tu-154M Airplane.

No. 177: a, 41d, Vehicles on road. b, 90d, Locomotive.

2001, Dec. 12 Litho. ***Perf. 14x13¼***

176 A44 1s multi 2.75 2.75

Souvenir Sheet

177 A44 Sheet of 3, #176, 177a, 177b 6.50 6.50

Commonwealth of Independent States, 10th Anniv. — A45

2001, Dec. 17 ***Perf. 14¼x14***

178 A45 50d multi 2.00 2.00

Souvenir Sheet

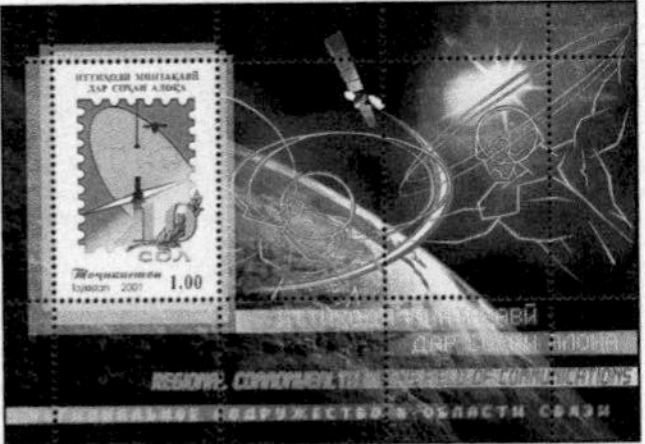

Regional Communications Accord — A46

2001, Dec. 17

179 A46 1s multi + 2 labels 3.50 3.50

For overprint, see No. 407.

Avesta, 2700th Anniv. — A47

Zoroastrian: 2d, Goddess Anahita. 3d, Priest.

No. 182: a, 70d, Goddess Haoma. b, 90d, God Farroh. c, 1s, God Surush. d, 2s, Goddess Din.

2002, Jan. 1 Litho. ***Perf. 10***

180-181 A47 Set of 2 2.00 2.00

Souvenir Sheet

182 A47 Sheet of 4, #a-d 13.00 13.00

No. 182 contains four 27x44mm stamps. Dated 2001.

Miniature Sheet

UN High Commissioner for Refugees, 50th Anniv. (in 2001) — A48

No. 183: a, Mothers holding children, refugees. b, Military helicopter, sun, refugees. c, Cloud, rainbow, moon, soldier, child.

2002, Jan. 1

183 A48 50d Sheet of 3, #a-c 5.00 5.00

Dated 2001.

Flora and Fauna of Central Asia — A49

No. 184: a, Bird facing right. b, Bird facing left. c, Mushrooms and snail. d, Rodent. e, Butterfly. f, Butterfly and tulip. g, Cat. h, Cat and tulip.

2002, Apr. 12 Litho. ***Perf. 13¾x13½***

184	Miniature sheet of 8	9.00	9.00
a.	A49 6d multi	.50	.50
b.	A49 15d multi	.50	.50
c.	A49 41d multi	.50	.50
d.	A49 50d multi	.60	.60
e.	A49 95d multi	1.10	1.10
f.-h.	A49 1.50s any single	1.75	1.75

No. 184 exists imperf. Value, $20.

Worldwide Fund for Nature (WWF) — A50

Reed cats: a, 1s, Two cats. b, 1.50s, One cat walking. c, 2s, One cat resting. d, 2s, Three kittens.

2002, Apr. 12 ***Perf. 14x14¼***

185 A50 Block of 4, #a-d 6.75 6.75
e. Sheet, 2 #185 15.00 15.00

For surcharges, see Nos. 465, 490.

Dushanbe Zoo, 40th Anniv. — A51

Designs: 2d, Pan troglodytes. 3d, Cervus nippon hortulorum. 10d, Panthera tigris altaice. 41d, Diceros bicornis michaeli. 50d, Giraffa camelopardis reticulata. 1s, Panthera leo.

2002, Aug. 29 Litho. ***Perf. 14¼x14***

186-191 A51 Set of 6 5.75 5.75

Souvenir Sheet

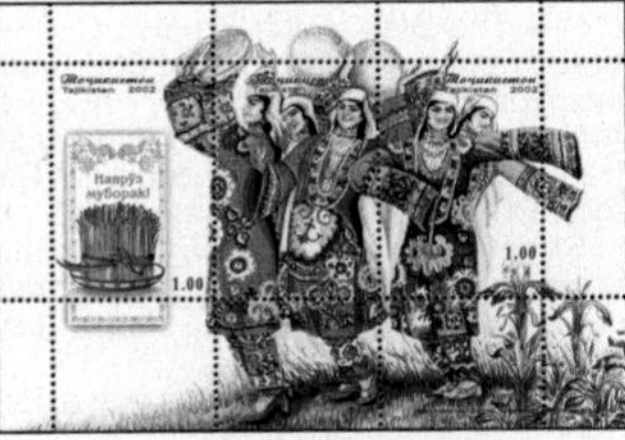

Navruz — A52

No. 192: a, 1s, Wheat bundle. b, 50d, Dancers in red costumes. c, 1s, Dancer in purple costume.

2002, Aug. 29

192 A52 Sheet of 3, #a-c 4.75 4.75

A53 A54

Istravashan, 2500th Anniv.

A55 A56

2002, Sept. 6

193	A53 50d brown & multi	1.00	1.00
194	A54 50d green & multi	1.00	1.00
195	A55 50d brown & multi	1.00	1.00
196	A56 50d green & multi	1.00	1.00
	Nos. 193-196 (4)	4.00	4.00

No. 168 Overprinted "2002" on Stamps and With Text in Margin

Souvenir Sheet

Designs as before.

2002, Sept. 20 Litho. ***Perf. 14¼x14***

197 A39 Sheet of 6, #a-f 11.00 11.00

No. 197 exists imperf. Value $300.

No. 197 also exists with violet overprint. Value: perf, $30; imperf $350.

Tajikistan postal officials have declared as "illegal" the following items.

Sheets of nine stamps of various denominations depicting: 20th Century Dreams (6 different sheets), Elephants and Rotary Intl. emblem, Owls, mushrooms and Rotary International emblem, Pandas, Chess, The Beatles, Locomotives, Princess Diana, the movie The Blair Witch Project, Defenders of Peace and Freedom, 2002 Brazilian World Cup Soccer Team, Harry Potter, Cartoon characters from South Park (Christmas), Warner Brothers Cartoon Characters (Christmas).

Sheets of six stamps of various denominations depicting Pokemon characters (eight sheets), Pope John Paul II, Dinosaurs.

Sheet of three stamps of various denominations depicting Elvis Presley.

Souvenir sheets of one stamp with 25.00 denomination depicting Harry Potter (2 different sheets), Penguins,

Souvenir sheet of one stamp with 20.00 denomination depicting Pope John Paul and New York fireman.

New Year 2002 (Year Of the Horse) — A57

No. 198: a, 2d, Thoroughbred racing. b, 3d, Harness racing. c, 95d, Troika. d, 95d, Polo.

No. 199: a, 50d, Dressage. b, 50d, Fox hunting. c, 1s, Steeplechase. d, 1s, Show jumping.

1.50s, Horses in circus act, vert.

2002, Oct. 15 Litho. *Perf. 14x14¼*

Blocks of 4, #a-d

198-199 A57 Set of 2 8.00 8.00

Souvenir Sheet

Perf. 14¼x14

200 A57 1.50s multi + 2 labels 4.25 4.25

For surcharges, see Nos. 484-485, 491.

Oriental Bazaar — A58

No. 201: a, Man in donkey cart. b, Man on donkey. c, Melon vendor. d, Man cooking shashliks.

2002, Dec. 25 Litho. *Perf. 14¼x14*

201 A58 65d Block of 4, #a-d 5.50 5.50

Traditional Sports A59

Designs: 1d, Archery. 20d, Horse racing. 53d, Polo. 65d, Stone throwing. 1s, Buzkashi. 1.24s, Wrestling.

2002, Dec. 25 *Perf. 14x14¼*

202-207 A59 Set of 6 6.00 6.00

Lunar Calendar — A60

Designs: 53d, Sun and zodiac animals. 65d, Zodiac animals and ram. 1s, Ram in circle. 1.50s, Ram.

2003, Mar. 11 *Perf. 14¼x14*

208-210 A60 Set of 3 5.50 5.50

Souvenir Sheet

211 A60 1.50s multi + 2 labels 4.50 4.50

Monument to Ismail Somoni — A61

2003, Mar. 11 *Perf. 13¼x14*

212	A61	1d	emerald	.80	.80
213	A61	2d	red violet	.80	.80
214	A61	3d	blue green	.80	.80
215	A61	4d	purple	.80	.80
216	A61	12d	brown	.80	.80
217	A61	20d	blue	.80	.80
			Nos. 212-217 (6)	4.80	4.80

No. 158a Surcharged in Purple

Souvenir Sheet

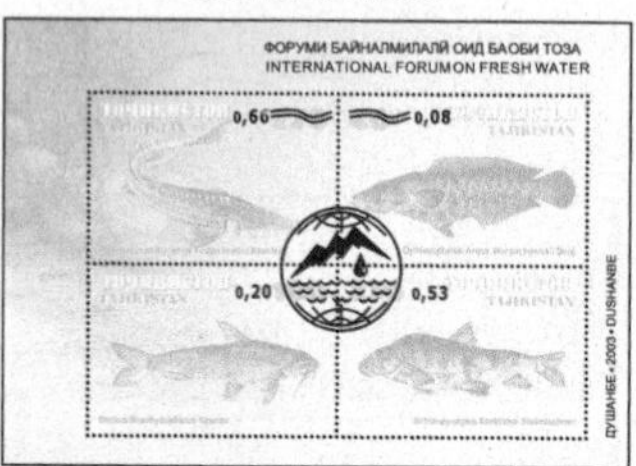

No. 218: a, 8d on 40r, Ophiocephalus argus. b, 20d on 100r, Barbus brachycephalus. c, 53d on 230r, Schizopygopsis stoliczkai. d, 66d on 270r, Pseudoscaphihynchus fedtschenkoi.

2003, May 12 Litho. *Perf. 13¼x13*

218 A36 Sheet of 4, #a-d 8.00 8.00

2004 Summer Olympics, Athens and 2008 Summer Olympics, Beijing — A62

No. 219: a, 53d, Archery. b, 1s, Track and field. c, 1.23s, Soccer. d, 2s, Gymnastics.

2003, May 20 *Perf. 14x13½*

219 A62 Sheet of 4, #a-d, + 2 labels 10.00 10.00

No. 219 exists imperf. with additional designs in margin. Value $32.50.

For overprint, see No. 389.

Philatelic Exhibitions and Fauna — A63

No. 220: a, 8d, 16th Asian Intl. Stamp Exhibition, China. b, 20d, Panthera tigris. c, 53d, Inachis io. d, 66d, Bangkok 2003 World Philatelic Exhibition. e, 1s, Rupicapra rupicapra. f, 1.50s, Ailuropoda melanoleuca. g, 1.50s, Leontopithecus rosalia. h, 2s, Elephas maximus.

2003, May 20

220 A63 Sheet of 8, #a-h 13.50 13.50

No. 220 exists imperf. Value $35.

For overprint see No. 341.

Intl. Forum on Fresh Water — A64

Designs: No. 221, 1.50s, Peak of Moskvin. No. 222, 1.50s, Iskanderkul.

2003, June 7 *Perf. 13½*

221-222 A64 Set of 2 5.25 5.25

Nos. 221-222 were printed setenant, both vertically and horiziontally, in one sheet.

Famous Men — A65

Designs: No. 223, 1.23s, Nosir Khusrav (1004-88), poet. No. 224, 1.23s, Sadridin Aini (1878-1954), writer.

2003, Sept. 1

223-224 A65 Set of 2 4.50 4.50

Intl. Association of Academies of Science, 10th Anniv. — A66

No. 225: a, Head, satellite dish, airplane, chemicals. b, Association emblem, cosmonaut, robotic hand, computer.

2003, Sept. 1

225 A66 1.23s Horiz. pair, #a-b 5.25 5.25

For overprint, see No. 418.

Intl. Year of Fresh Water — A67

Children's art: a, Fish above lake. b, Sun, river, tree and hills. c, River, hills and trees. d, Waterfalls.

2003, Oct. 20 *Perf. 14x14¼*

226 A67 66d Block of 4, #a-d 4.75 4.75

Racing Airplanes — A68

No. 227: a, Aero L-29A Delfin Akrobat. b, Yak-55. c, Cessna 172. d, SIAI-Marchetti SF-260. e, Europa XS. f, MBB BO 209 Monsun. g, Mudry Cap 10. h, Soko 2.

2003, Oct. 28 *Perf. 14x13½*

227 A68 1s Sheet of 8, #a-h 13.00 13.00

No. 227 exists imperf. Value $40.

Fauna of Central Asia — A69

No. 228: a, 8d, Mimas tiliae. 20d, Mustela erminea. 53d, Testudo horsfieldii. 64d, Mantis religiosa. 1.23s, Lanius collurio. 1.27s, Canis aureus. 1.76s, Capra falconeri. 2.29s, Alcedo atthis.

2003, Oct. 28

228 A69 Sheet of 8, #a-h 14.00 14.00

No. 228 exists imperf. Value $40.

No. 153 Surcharged in Red

2004, Jan. 4 Litho. *Perf. 13¼x13*

229 A35 Miniature sheet, 2 each #a-b 7.00 7.00

a. 20d on 100r #153a 1.75 1.75

b. 66d on 270r #153b 3.25 3.25

No. 229 exists surcharged in green. Value, $21.

National Dances — A70

No. 230 — Various dancers and frame color of: a, Brown. b, Purple. c, Green. d, Bright pink.

2004, Jan. 19 Litho. *Perf. 14¼x14*
230 A70 53d Block of 4, #a-d 4.25 4.25

Adjacent blocks in sheet are tete-beche. No. 230 exists with visible tagging that reads "Belarus."

No. 28 Surcharged in Black and Red

2004, Apr. 26 Litho. *Perf. 13½*
231 A6 A on 50r multi 1.10 1.10

Sold for 8d on day of issue.

No. 31 Surcharged in Black

2004, Apr. 26
232 A6 b on 160r multi 1.10 1.10

Sold for 20d on day of issue.

Miniature Sheet

New Year 2004 (Year of the Monkey) — A71

No. 233: a, 1s, Monkey covering eyes. b, 1.20s, Monkey covering ears. c, 1.50s, Monkey covering mouth.

2004, Aug. 13 *Perf. 13¾x13½*
233 A71 Sheet of 3, #a-c 6.25 6.25

Dushanbe Buildings — A72

Designs: 1d, National Circus. 2d, Ferdowsi National Library. 3d, National Bank. 8d, Finance Ministry. 20d, Communications Ministry. 50d, City Government Building.

2004, Aug. 13 *Perf. 13¾x13¼*

234	A72	1d multi	.60	.60
235	A72	2d multi	.60	.60
236	A72	3d multi	.60	.60
237	A72	8d multi	.60	.60
238	A72	20d multi	.60	.60
239	A72	50d multi	1.25	1.25
		Nos. 234-239 (6)	4.25	4.25

FIFA (Fédération Internationale de Football Association), Cent. — A73

Designs: 50d, Goalie, World Cup. 70d, FIFA General Secretariat Building, Zurich. 1s, Player with red shirt, vert. 2s, Player with yellow shirt, vert.

Perf. 13½x13¾, 13¾x13½
2004, Aug. 30
240-243 A73 Set of 4 8.00 8.00

Nos. 240-243 exist imperf. Value, set $35.

Miniature Sheet

2004 Summer Olympics, Athens — A74

No. 244: a, 30d, Wrestling. b, 45d, Track. c, 55d, Basketball. d, 60d, Shooting. e, 75d, Equestrian. f, 80d, Women's archery. g, 1.50s, Soccer. h, 2.50s, Rhythmic gymnastics.

2004, Sept. 6 *Perf. 14x13½*
244 A74 Sheet of 8, #a-h 12.50 12.50

No. 244 exists imperf. Value $35.

Miniature Sheet

Dushanbe Circus — A75

No. 245: a, 20d, Circus building. b, 50d, Tightrope walkers. c, 1s, Elephant and trainer. d, 1.10s, Genie, lamp and cat. e, 1.50s, Man riding donkey, dog. f, 1.70s, Bareback rider.

2004, Dec. 21 *Perf. 14x13½*
245 A75 Sheet of 6, #a-f 10.00 10.00

No. 245 exists imperf. Value $25.

Miniature Sheet

Vehicles — A76

No. 246: a, Fire engine. b, Ambulance and helicopter. c, Police cars. d, Postal van and train. e, Wrecker and damaged car. f, School bus.

2004, Dec. 21
246 A76 1s Sheet of 6, #a-f 9.25 9.25

No. 246 exists imperf. Value $25.

Miniature Sheet

Dushanbe as Capital City, 80th Anniv. — A77

No. 247: a, 20d, New apartment buildings on Rudaki Ave. b, 46d, Aini State Opera and Ballet Theater. c, 53d, National Bank. d, 62d, City Government Building. e, 1.27s, Parliament Building. f, 1.76s, Presidential Palace.

2004, Nov. 16 Litho. *Perf. 11½*
247 A77 Sheet of 6, #a-f 13.50 13.50

Musical Instruments — A78

No. 248: a, Gejak and bow. b, Adirna.

2004, Nov. 29 *Perf. 11½x11¾*
248 A78 2.50s Horiz. pair, #a-b 9.75 9.75

See Kazakhstan No. 470.

Fruit — A79

Designs: Nos. 249, 255, Apples. Nos. 250, 256, Apricots. Nos. 251, 257, Plums. Nos. 252, 258, Pears. Nos. 253, 259, Quince. Nos. 254, 260, Pomegranates.

2005, Mar. 19 *Perf. 14x14¼*

Panel Color

White Background

249	A79	6d lilac	.25	.25
250	A79	7d blue	.25	.25
251	A79	8d brn orange	.25	.25
252	A79	10d rose	.30	.25
253	A79	11d green	.30	.25
254	A79	12d yel orange	.30	.25

Pale Yellow Background

255	A79	20d purple	.50	.45
256	A79	50d violet	1.00	.90
257	A79	55d red	1.10	1.00
258	A79	75d red violet	1.50	1.25
259	A79	2s dk olive	4.00	3.50
260	A79	3s brown red	6.00	5.50
		Nos. 249-260 (12)	15.75	14.10

Lake Sarez — A80

No. 261: a, Katta Nardjonoi Bay (denomination in white). b, Iriht Bay (denomination in black).

2005, Apr. 4 *Perf. 13½*
261 A80 2s Horiz. pair, #a-b 6.75 6.75

Souvenir Sheet

End of World War II, 60th Anniv. — A81

No. 262: a, 18d. b, 75d.

2005, Apr. 15 *Perf. 14¼x14*
262 A81 Sheet of 2, #a-b, + central label 4.25 4.25

Souvenir Sheet

Hunting — A82

No. 263: a, 1s, Hunter facing left. b, 1.70s, Hunter facing right. c, 2.30s, Like 1s.

2005, July 27 *Perf. 13¾x13½*
263 A82 Sheet of 3, #a-c 10.00 10.00

Compare with Type A89.

Airbus A-380 — A83

No. 264 — Inset of airplane and: a, 1.50s, Left wing. b, 1.50s, Nose. c, 1.80s, Tail. d, 1.80s, Right wing.

2005, July 27 *Perf. 13½x14*
264 A83 Block of 4, #a-d 11.50 11.50

No. 264 exists imperf. Value $25.

Miniature Sheet

Mammals — A84

No. 265: a, 20d, Hyena on cliff. b, 20d, Turkestan lynx on tree branch. c, 75d, Badger. d, 75d, Fox. e, 80d, Snow leopard. f, 1s, Bear. g, 1.50s, Leopard. h, 1.80s, Tiger.

2005, Aug. 10 *Perf. 13½x14*
265 A84 Sheet of 8, #a-h 11.50 11.50

No. 265 exists imperf. Value $25.
For overprint, see No. 370.

Worldwide Fund for Nature (WWF) — A85

No. 266 — Various views of bharals: a, 1s. b, 1.45s. c, 1.70s. d, 2.25s.

2005, Aug. 26 ***Perf. 13½x14***

266 A85 Block of 4, #a-d 6.00 6.00

No. 266 exists imperf. Value $17.50.

Avicenna (980-1037), Scientist — A86

2005, Oct. 3 ***Perf. 13¼x13¾***

267	A86	6d Prus bl & blk	.25	.25
268	A86	8d brn & black	.25	.25
269	A86	10d purple & lilac	.25	.25
270	A86	12d blue	.45	.45
271	A86	50d blue green	1.40	1.40
272	A86	1s orange	3.00	3.00
		Nos. 267-272 (6)	5.60	5.60

World Post Day — A87

2005, Oct. 3 ***Perf. 13¼x13¾***

273	A87	5d blue & black	.30	.30
274	A87	7d brown	.30	.30
275	A87	11d green & lt grn	.30	.30
276	A87	20d purple	.50	.50
277	A87	55d gray blue	1.50	1.50
278	A87	75d orange	3.25	3.25
		Nos. 273-278 (6)	6.15	6.15

Mountains — A88

No. 279: a, 1s, Pendjikent. b, 1.50s, Muminabod. c, 2s, Pamir. d, 2.50s, Isfara.

2005, Dec. 6 ***Perf. 13½***

279 A88 Block of 4, #a-d 11.50 11.50

Souvenir Sheet

Hunting — A89

No. 280: a, Hunter holding falcon. b, Hunter killing leopard.

2005, Dec. 31 ***Perf. 13¾x13½***

280 A89 2.50s Sheet of 2, #a-b, + central label 9.25 9.25

Compare with type A82.
No. 280 exists imperf. Value $30.

Fairy Tales — A90

No. 281: a, 55d, The Peasant and the Bear. b, 75d, Three Brothers. c, 2s, Iradj-bogatyr. d, 3s, The Gold Fox.

2006, Mar. 20 ***Perf. 14¼x14***

281 A90 Block of 4, #a-d 9.75 9.75

Stamps in vertical columns are tete-beche.

Traditional Costumes — A91

No. 282: a, 75d, Man from Samarkand wearing red headdress. b, 75d, Man from Sugd wearing blue headdress. c, 1s, Woman from Bukhara with arms together. d, 1s, Woman from Kalayhum with arms apart.

2006, June 20 Litho. ***Perf. 14¼x14***

282 A91 Block or horiz. strip of 4, #a-d 6.00 6.00

Printed in sheets of eight containing two of each stamp.

Miniature Sheet

Fauna of Asia — A92

No. 283: a, 8d, Aquila chrysaetos. b, 20d, Panthera tigris longipilis. c, 55d, Hystrix hirsutirostris. d, 70d, Alluropoda melanoleuca. e, 75d, Meles meles. f, 1.60s, Ursus arctos. g, 1.92s, Mustela erminea. h, 2s, Bubo coromandus.

2006, June 29 ***Perf. 13¾x13½***

283 A92 Sheet of 8, #a-h 13.00 13.00

No. 283 exists imperf. Value $27.50.

2006 World Cup Soccer Championships, Germany — A93

No. 284: a, 1.50s, Five players. b, 1.50s, Three players and goalie. c, 1.50s, Four players. d, 2s, Three players and goalie, diff.

2006, June 29 ***Perf. 13½x13¾***

284 A93 Block of 4, #a-d 10.00 10.00
e. Miniature sheet, 2 each #284a-284d 20.00 20.00

For overprint, see No. 428.

Souvenir Sheet

Kulob, 2700th Anniv. — A94

No. 285: a, Anniversary emblem, flag of Tajikistan. b, Mausoleum of Mir Said Ali Hamadoni.

2006, Aug. 30

285 A94 2s Sheet of 2, #a-b 8.00 8.00

Miniature Sheet

Independence, 15th Anniv. — A95

No. 286: a, 1.50s, Presidential Palace. b, 2.50s, Arms of Tajikistan. c, 3s, Flag of Tajikistan, Pres. Emomali Rakhmonov.

2006, Aug. 30 ***Perf. 14x14¼***

286 A95 Sheet of 3, #a-c, + 3 labels 13.00 13.00

Souvenir Sheet

Commonwealth of Independent States, 15th Anniv. — A96

No. 287: a, Emblem of Commonwealth of Independent States, flags of member nations. b, Emblem of Regional Communications Commonwealth.

2006, Sept. 12 ***Perf. 14¼x14***

287 A96 1.50s Sheet of 2, #a-b, + central label 6.50 6.50

Cotton — A97

2006, Dec. 15 ***Perf. 13½x13¾***

Background Color

288	A97	5d olive green	.35	.35
289	A97	6d rose	.35	.35
290	A97	7d lilac	.35	.35
291	A97	8d light blue	.35	.35
292	A97	20d green	.55	.55
293	A97	75d blue	1.50	1.50
		Nos. 288-293 (6)	3.45	3.45

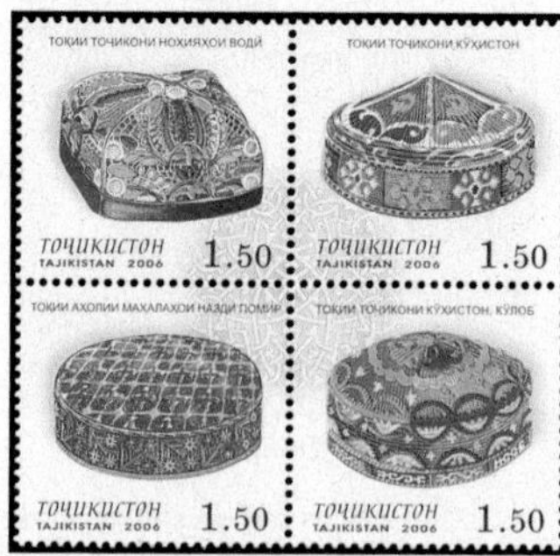

Headdresses — A98

No. 294 — Various headdresses with gray geometrical design at: a, LR. b, LL. c, UR. d, UL.

2006, Dec. 28 ***Perf. 14x14¼***

294 A98 1.50s Block of 4, #a-d 9.50 9.50

No. 294 exists imperf. Value $25.

Dogs — A99

Designs: 20d, West Siberian laika. 55d, Perdiguero de burgos. 75d, Afghan hound. 1s, Sredneasiatckaia ovtcharka. 2s, Saluki. 3s, Tosa.

2006, Dec. 28 ***Perf. 13¾x13½***

295-300 A99 Set of 6 11.75 11.75

Nos. 295-300 exist imperf. Value, set $25.

No. 32 Surcharged

Methods and Perfs As Before

2007, Mar. 31

301 A6a 75d on 160r #32 2.25 2.25

Souvenir Sheet

Snakes — A100

No. 302: a, Echis carinatus. b, Naja oxiana.

2007, Apr. 30 Litho. ***Perf. 14***

302 A100 2s Sheet of 2, #a-b 9.75 9.75

A101

A102

Mevlana (c. 1207-73), Poet — A103

2007, Aug. 30 ***Perf. 13¼x13¾***

303 A101	5d	red	.30	.30
304 A101	10d	bright blue	.30	.30
305 A101	20d	green	.30	.30
306 A101	(25d)	dark blue	.45	.45
307 A102	(1.35s)	brown violet	2.25	2.25
308 A103	(2.15s)	red violet	3.75	3.75
		Nos. 303-308 (6)	7.35	7.35

Jewelry — A104

No. 309: a, 50d, Earring. b, 2s, Necklace. c, 2.50s, Necklace, diff. d, 3s, Earring, diff.

2007, Dec. 18 ***Perf. 14¼x14***

309 A104 Block of 4, #a-d 11.00 11.00

Miniature Sheet

Transportation — A105

No. 310: a, 50d, Camels. b, 60d, Steam locomotive. c, 70d, Airplane and helicopter. d, 80d, Pickup truck. e, 90d, Donkey cart. f, 1.50s, Train. g, 1.70s, Bus. h, 2s, Dump truck.

2007, Dec. 27 ***Perf. 14x13½***

310 A105 Sheet of 8, #a-h 11.00 11.00

Birds — A106

Designs: Nos. 311, 317a, 1s, Aquila chrysaetos. Nos. 312, 317b, 1.10s, Phasianinae. Nos. 313, 317c, 1.20s, Aix galericulata. Nos. 314, 317d, 1.30s, Otididae. Nos. 315, 317e, 1.40s, Falco cherrug. Nos. 316, 317f, 1.60s Haliaeetus albicilla.

2007, Dec. 27 ***Perf. 14x13½***

Stamps With White Frames

311-316 A106 Set of 6 12.50 12.50

Stamps With Colored Frames

317 A106 Sheet of 6, #a-f 12.50 12.50

2008 Summer Olympics, Beijing A107

Designs: 1.50s, Soccer. No. 319, 2s, Hammer throw. No. 320, 2s, Judo. No. 321, 2s, Boxing.

2008, Feb. 28 Litho. ***Perf. 12½x13***

318-321 A107 Set of 4 8.25 8.25
321a Miniature sheet, 2 each #318-321 15.00 15.00

Cooking Pot — A108

Pitcher — A109

Pot With Lid — A110

Pitcher — A111

2008, Mar. 28 ***Perf. 14x14¼***

322 A108	20d	brown	.35	.35
323 A108	25d	dark blue	.45	.45
324 A109	50d	purple	.90	.90
325 A109	1s	indigo	1.75	1.75
326 A110	1.35s	dark green	2.40	2.40
327 A111	2s	brown	3.75	3.75
328 A110	2.15s	dark blue	4.00	4.00
329 A111	3s	dark red	5.50	5.50
		Nos. 322-329 (8)	19.10	19.10

Souvenir Sheet

Intl. Conference on Water Related Disaster Reduction, Dushanbe — A112

No. 330: a, Avalanche. b, Tornado.

2008, June 19 ***Perf. 14¼x14***

330 A112 2.50s Sheet of 2, #a-b, + label 9.50 9.50

Souvenir Sheet

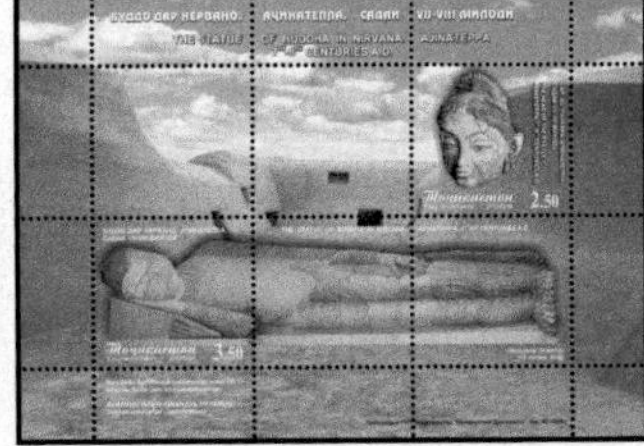

Buddha Statues, Ajinateppa — A113

No. 331: a, 2.50s, Head of Buddha. b, 3.50s, Buddha reclining.

2008, June 19 ***Perf. 14x14¼***

331 A113 Sheet of 2, #a-b, + 4 labels 10.00 10.00

Nos. 140-141 Surcharged in Black or Red

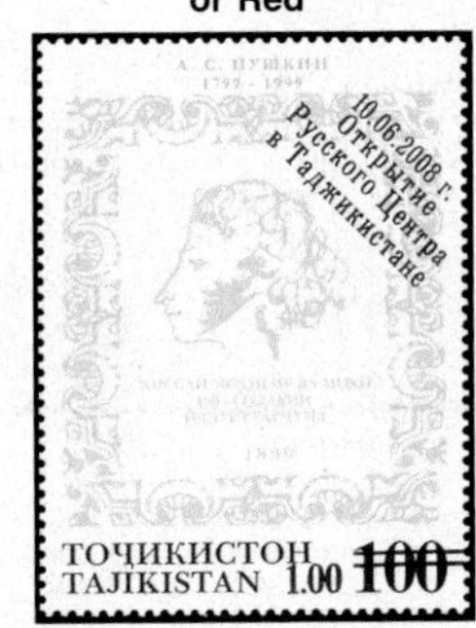

Methods and Perfs. As Before

2008, July 4 **Black Surcharge**

332	1s on 100r #140	3.25	3.25
333	1s on 100r #141	3.25	3.25
a.	A31 Pair, #332-333	6.50	6.50

Red Surcharge

334	1s on 100r #140	3.25	3.25
335	1s on 100r #141	3.25	3.25
a.	A31 Pair, #334-335	6.50	6.50
	Nos. 332-335 (4)	13.00	13.00

Souvenir Sheet

Rudaki (c. 859-940), Poet — A114

No. 336 — Rudaki facing: a, Right. b, Left.

2008, July 9 Litho. ***Perf. 14¼x14***

336 A114 2.50s Sheet of 2, #a-b, + label 8.25 8.25

Plants and Insects — A115

No. 337: a, 1.50s, Ribwort and grasshopper. b, 1.50s, Coltfoot and ladybug. c, 2s, Dandelion and beetle. d, 2s, Calendula and bee.

2008, Sept. 29 ***Perf. 14x14¼***

337 A115 Block of 4, #a-d 11.00 11.00

Souvenir Sheet

Snakes — A116

No. 338 — Snake facing: a, Right. b, Left.

2008, Sept. 29 ***Perf. 13½x14***

338 A116 2.50s Sheet of 2, #a-b 9.25 9.25

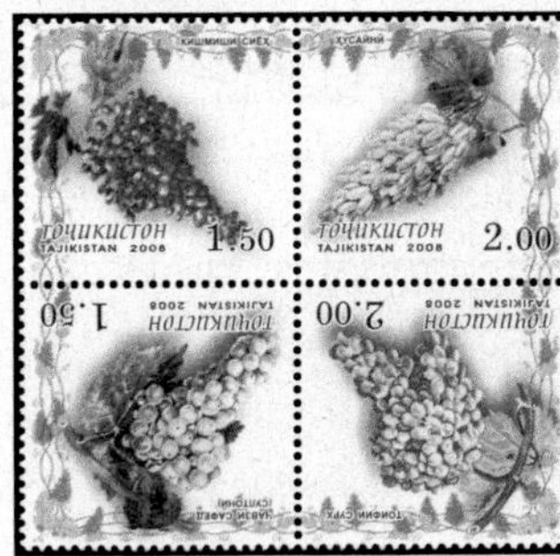

Grapes — A117

No. 339 — Color of grapes: a, 1.50s, Purple (Djaus). b, 1.50s, Pink (Black sultana). c, 2s, White (Ladies' fingers). d, 2s, Red (Red Taffi).

2008, Dec. 1 ***Perf. 14x14¼***

339 A117 Block of 4, #a-d 10.50 10.50

Musical Instruments — A118

No. 340: a, Gijak of Badahshon. b, Khoirasan local dotaar.

2008, Dec. 1 Litho. ***Perf. 14x14¼***

340 A118 Horiz. pair + central label 11.00 11.00
a.-b. 3s Either single 5.50 5.50

See Iran No. 2976.

No. 220 Overprinted

Designs as before.

Methods and Perfs As Before

2009, Feb. 1

341 A63 Sheet of 8, #a-h (#220) 13.50 13.50

Souvenir Sheet

Paintings — A119

No. 342: a, Flowering Indian Lilac — Luchob, by Zuhur Habibuloev. b, My Mother — My wings, by Sabzali Sharif.

2009, Mar. 31 Litho. *Perf. 13½*
342 A119 4s Sheet of 2, #a-b 11.50 11.50

Imam Azam's Celebration Year — A120

2009, July 28
343 A120 4s multi 4.75 4.75

Worldwide Fund for Nature (WWF) A121

Cervus elaphus bactrianus: 1.50s, Head of doe, bucks fighting. 2s, Buck. 2.50s, Buck, two does. 3s, Two does and fawn.

2009, July 28 *Perf. 13½x13¾*
344-347 A121 Set of 4 5.50 5.50
347a Sheet of 16, 4 each #344-347 20.00 20.00

Nos. 344-347, 347a exist imperf.

Animals — A122

Designs: No. 348, 1s, Equus przewalskii. No. 349, 1s, Panthera tigris tigris. No. 350, 1.50s, Camelus bactrianus. No. 351, 1.50s, Caracal caracal. No. 352, 2s, Ailuropoda melanoleuca. No. 353, 2s, Macaca fuscata. No. 354, 2.30s, Elephas maximus. No. 355, 2.30s, Ovis vignei.

2009, July 28 *Perf. 13¾x13½*
348-355 A122 Set of 8 11.00 11.00
355a Sheet of 8, #348-355 11.00 11.00

Nos. 348-355 were each printed in sheets of 9 + label.

Souvenir Sheet

Animal Circus Performers — A123

No. 356: a, Cat on ball. b, Dog balancing ball on nose.

2009, Sept. 14 *Perf. 14x14¼*
356 A123 3.50s Sheet of 2, #a-b 10.50 10.50

Souvenir Sheet

Tajikistan Glaciers — A124

No. 357 — Glaciers on mountain peaks: a, Abu ali ibn Sino. b, Ismoili Somoni.

2009, Sept. 14 *Perf. 13½*
357 A124 4s Sheet of 2, #a-b 11.00 11.00

No. 144 Surcharged

Method and Perf. As Before
2009, Dec. 1
358 A32b 15d on (270r) #144 .40 .40

Melons — A125

No. 359: a, 1.50s, Green melon (whole melon and quarter melon), and large green leaves. b, 1.50s, Yellow and brown melon (whole melon and ⅛ melon slice) and gray leaves. c, 2s, Yellow and brown melon (whole melon and half melon) and gray leaves. d, 2s, Yellow and brown melon (whole melon and quarter melon) and large green leaves.

2009, Dec. 3 Litho. *Perf. 14x14¼*
359 A125 Block of 4, #a-d 10.50 10.50

Stamps of same denomination are se-tenant within the block. No. 359 exists imperf. Value, $20.

Victory in World War II, 65th Anniv. — A126

No. 360: a, 1.35s, Soldiers and airplanes. b, 2.15s, Soviet Union soldiers holding Nazi flags near Kremlin in Moscow.

2010, Mar. 15 Litho. *Perf. 14¼x14*
360 A126 Pair, #a-b 3.75 3.75

Printed in sheets containing 3 #360a, 2 #360b + label.

Peonies — A127

No. 361 — Peony with butterfly at: a, 2s, Right. b, 3.20s, Left.

2010, Mar. 30 *Perf. 12½*
361 A127 Pair, #a-b 5.75 5.75
c. Souvenir sheet, #361b 3.75 3.75

Printed in sheets containing 3 each #361a-361b.

Rogun Hydroelectric Project — A128

Designs: 10d, Vakhsh River Dam. 15d, Transmission towers and lines. 20d, Turbines. 10s, Tunnel-boring machine.

2010, May 20 *Perf. 13¼x14*
362-365 A128 Set of 4 12.50 12.50

Khaje Abdullah Ansari (1006-88), Mystic A129

2010, July 25 *Perf. 13½*
366 A129 5s multi 5.75 5.75

See Afghanistan No. 1465, Iran No. 3016.

Miniature Sheet

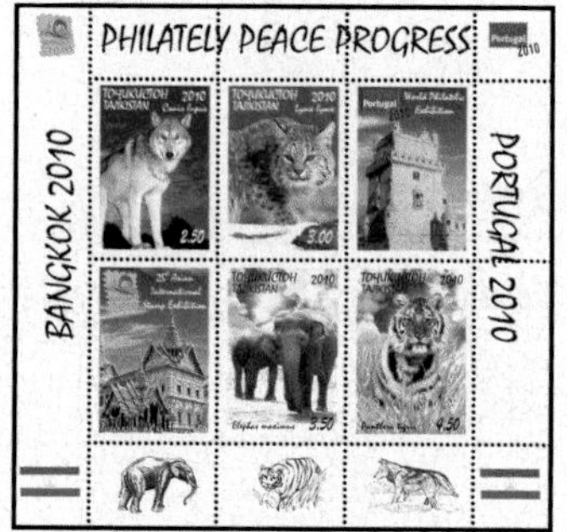

Mammals — A130

No. 367: a, 2.50s, Canis lupus. b, 3s, Lynx lynx. c, 3.50s, Elephas maximus. d, 4.50s, Panthera tigris.

2010, Aug. 2 *Perf. 14¼x14*
367 A130 Sheet of 4, #a-d, + 2 labels 11.50 11.50

Bangkok 2010 Intl. Stamp Exhibition, Portugal 2010 World Philatelic Exhibition.

Souvenir Sheet

Ancient Coins — A131

No. 368: a, 4s, Silver Sasani coin. b, 5s, Gold Shahanshoh Vasudeva coin.

2010, Nov. 19 *Perf. 13½x14*
368 A131 Sheet of 2, #a-b 11.00 11.00

Souvenir Sheet

Traditional Men's Dances — A132

No. 369: a, Man dancing, old man, boy, birds. b, Three men dancing.

2010, Nov. 19 *Perf. 14¼x14*
369 A132 4s Sheet of 2, #a-b 10.50 10.50

No. 265 Overprinted

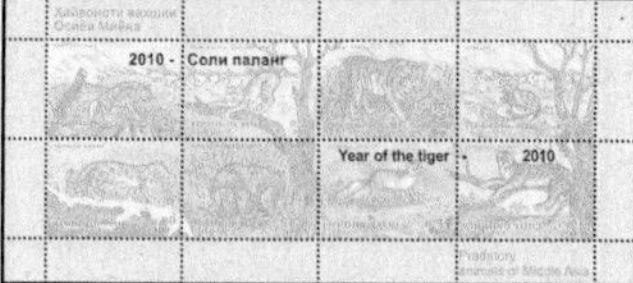

Methods and Perfs As Before
2010, Apr. 30
370 A84 Sheet of 8, #265c, 265e, 265f, 265h, 370a-370d 15.50 15.50
a. 20d "2010 -" on #265a .45 .45
b. 20d Cyrillic text overprinted on #265b .45 .45
c. 75d "Year of the tiger" overprinted on #265d 1.75 1.75
d. 1.50s "- 2010" overprinted on #265g 3.50 3.50

Souvenir Sheet

New Year 2011 (Year of the Rabbit) — A133

No. 371: a, Rabbit and carrots. b, Rabbit and cat.

2011, Apr. 1 Litho. *Perf. 14¼x14*
371 A133 2s Sheet of 2, #a-b 5.75 5.75

Nos. 18 and 27 Surcharged

Methods and Perfs As Before
2011, Apr. 27
372 A5 10d on 25r #18 .75 .75
373 A6 15d on 35r #27 1.10 1.10

Locomotives — A134

No. 374: a, 1-5-0, 1947. b, 1-4-0, 1912. c, 1-3-1, 1925. d, 2-3-1, 1925.

2011, June 3 Litho. *Perf. 14x14¼*
374 A134 1.50s Block of 4, #a-d 6.75 6.75

Apricot Blossoms — A135

No. 375 — Various blossoms: a, 3.50s. b, 4s.

2011, Aug. 10 *Perf. 13*
375 A135 Horiz. pair, #a-b 5.75 5.75

For overprint, see No. 456.

Miniature Sheet

Independence, 20th Anniv. — A136

No. 376: a, 2.50s, Norak Hydropower Plant (40x28mm). b, 2.50s, Sangtuda Hydropower Plant (40x28mm). c, 2.50s, Rogun Hydropower Plant (40x28mm). d, 3s, President Emomali Rakhmonov (40x84mm).

2011, Aug. 26 *Perf. 14x14¼*
376 A136 Sheet of 4, #a-d 12.00 12.00

Souvenir Sheet

Commonweath of Independent States, 20th Anniv. — A137

2011, Aug. 26 *Perf. 14¼x14*
377 A137 3.50s multi 9.25 9.25

Souvenir Sheet

Regional Communications Commonwealth, 20th Anniv. — A138

2011, Sept. 8
378 A138 2.50s multi 8.75 8.75

Sogdian Terra Cotta Heads — A139

Various terra cotta heads from 5th-8th cent.: 10d, Man with crown. 15d, Head of Rurel. 20d, Female figure in high relief. 25d, King.

2011, Dec. 23 Litho. *Perf. 14x14¼*
379-382 A139 Set of 4 1.40 1.40

Lunar Calendar Animals — A140

Designs: 2s, Dragon. 2.50s, Fish.

2012, Mar. 16
383-384 A140 Set of 2 5.25 5.25

A141

Native Costumes — A142

2012, June 19 *Perf. 14¼x14*
385 A141 1.35s multi 1.90 1.90
386 A142 2.15s multi 3.00 3.00

Miniature Sheet

2012 Summer Olympics, London — A143

No. 387: a, Judo. b, Taekwondo. c, Hammer throw. d, Boxing.

2012, June 19
387 A143 2s Sheet of 4, #a-d 8.75 8.75

Souvenir Sheet

Paintings — A144

No. 388: a, The Pomegranate, by Batyr Allabergenov, 2009. b, Wake Up!, by Rahim Safarov, 2004.

2012, June 19 *Perf. 13*
388 A144 4s Sheet of 2, #a-b 8.75 8.75

No. 219 Overprinted in Blue and Bluish Black

Methods and Perfs As Before

2012, July 26
389 A62 Sheet of 4, #219b, 219d, 389a, 389b, + 2 labels 13.00 13.00
a. 53d With Cyrillic text overprinted 1.50 1.50
b. 1.23s With Cyrillic text overprinted 3.50 3.50

2012 Summer Olympics, London.

A145

Flowers and Butterflies — A146

No. 390 — Stamps inscribed with flower names: a, 1.60s, Rose and grasshopper. b, 2.50s, Golden daisy and yellow, black and red butterfly. c, 3s, Golden daisy and orange, black and white butterfly. d, 3s, Rose and ladybug.

No. 391 — Stamps inscribed "Butterflies of Central Asia": a, 1.60s, Orange, black and white butterfly on flower. b, 2.50s, Red, black and white butterfly on flower. c, 3s, Blue butterfly on orange flower. d, 3s, Yellow, black and red butterfly on pink flower.

2012, Oct. 25 Litho. *Perf. 14x14¼*
390 A145 Block of 4, #a-d 9.25 9.25
391 A146 Block of 4, #a-d 9.25 9.25

Singers — A147

No. 392: a, Gurminj Zavqibekov (1929-2003). b, Khikmat Rizo.

2012, Dec. 30 Litho. *Perf. 14x13½*
392 A147 3s Pair, #a-b 5.00 5.00

Souvenir Sheet

New Year 2013 (Year of the Snake) — A148

No. 393: a, Snake with crown, denomination at UL. b, Snake wrapped around tree. c, Snake with crown, denomination at UR.

2013, Apr. 11 Litho. *Perf. 14x13½*
393 A148 2.50s Sheet of 3, #a-c 6.75 6.75

Cats — A149

Designs: No. 394, 2s, Maine Coon cat (maykun). No. 395, 2s, La Perm cat. No. 396, 2s, British shorthair cat.

2013, Apr. 11 Litho. *Perf. 14x13½*
394-396 A149 Set of 3 6.00 6.00

Nos. 394-396 each were printed in sheets of 9 + label.

Worldwide Fund for Nature (WWF) A150

Mustela altaica: No. 397, 4.50s, Head. No. 398, 4.50s, Standing on rock. No. 399, 5s, Carrying prey. No. 400, 5s, Two animals.

2013, Apr. 22 Litho. *Perf. 14x14¼*
397-400 A150 Set of 4 8.25 8.25
400a Sheet of 16, 4 each #397-400 33.00 33.00

Nos. 397-400 each were printed in sheets of 10.

Tajikistan Academy of Science, 20th Anniv. — A151

No. 401 — Emblems and: a, 1.60s, Flasks, books, molecular model, microscope, biological hazard emblem. b, 2.50s, Oil refinery, computer, telephone, satellite, satellite dish.

2013, July 16 Litho. *Perf. 13*
401 A151 Horiz. pair, #a-b 7.75 7.75

Trains — A152

No. 402: a, EU 733. b, TE 33 A emerging from tunnel, towers in background. c, TE 33 A emerging from tunnel, hill in background. d, TE 33 A on bridge over river.

2013, July 16 Litho. *Perf. 14x14¼*
402 A152 1.60s Block of 4, #a-d 6.75 6.75

Mobile Communications — A153

Emblems of telecommunications companies, satellite dish, and: 10d, Globe, denomination in blue. 15d, Like 10d, denomination in orange. 1.60s, Presidential palace.

2013, July 16 Litho. *Perf. 14x14¼*
403-405 A153 Set of 3 3.75 3.75

Transportation — A154

No. 406 — Emblem of Regional Communications Commonwealth and: a, Aiplane flying right, train. b, Airplane flying left, train. c, Yellow car with red, white and green stripes. d, Airplane and red Tajik Post car.

2013, July 16 Litho. *Perf. 14x14¼*
406 A154 2.50s Block of 4, #a-d 11.50 11.50

Nos. 172 and 179 Overprinted in Red

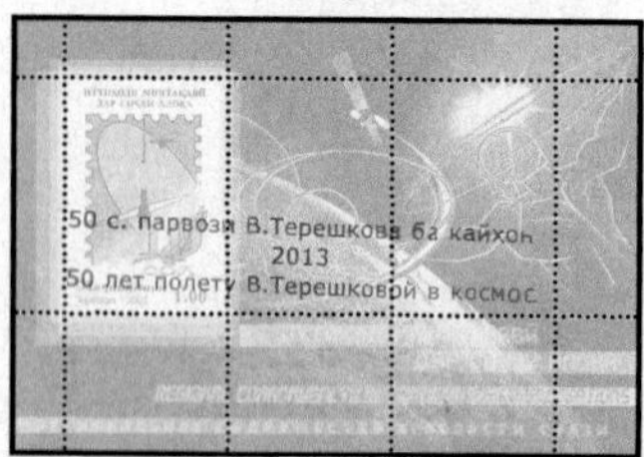

Methods and Perfs As Before

2013, July 26
407 A46 1s on #179 7.50 7.50
408 A40 1.50s on #172 11.50 11.50

Space flight of Valentina Tereshkova, first woman in space, 50th anniv.

Animals A155

Designs: No. 409, 1.60s, Tiger. No. 410, 1.60s, Bear. No. 411, 1.60s, Fox.

2013, Nov. 19 Litho. *Perf. 14x14¼*
409-411 A155 Set of 3 7.00 7.00
411a Souvenir sheet of 6, 2 each #409-411 14.00 14.00

Nos. 409-411 each were printed in sheets of 7 + label.

Birds — A156

No. 412: a, Partridges. b, Eagle and mountain. c, Eagle and rabbit. d, Owl (otus scops).

2013, Nov. 19 Litho. *Perf. 14x14¼*
412 A156 2s Block of 4, #a-d 8.75 8.75

Fish — A157

No. 413: a, Goldfish. b, Silurus. c, Salmo trutta. d, Sazan.

2013, Nov. 19 Litho. *Perf. 14x14¼*
413 A157 2s Block of 4, #a-d 8.75 8.75

Miniature Sheet

Architecture — A158

No. 414: a, Mausoleum of Mir Said Ali Hamadoni. b, Fortress of Hulbuk. c, New Mosque, Dushanbe. d, Fortress of Hisor.

2013, Nov. 19 Litho. *Perf. 14x14¼*
414 A158 3s Sheet of 4, #a-d 11.50 11.50

Horses — A159

No. 415: a, 1.60s, White horse running right. b, 1.60s, White horse running left. c, 2.50s, Brown horse running left. d, 2.50s, Brwon horse running right.

2014, Feb. 7 Litho. *Perf. 14x14¼*
415 A159 Block of 4, #a-d 7.50 7.50

2014 Winter Olympics, Sochi, Russia — A160

No. 416 — Emblem of Regional Communications Commonwealth and: a, 1.60s, Figure skating. b, 1.60s, Ice hockey. c, 2.50s, Skiing. d, 3s, Speed skating.

No. 417, 3s — Emblem of Regional Communication Commonwealth and design: a, Like #416a. b, Like #416b.

2014, Mar. 7 Litho. *Perf. 14x14¼*
416 A160 Block of 4, #a-d 10.50 10.50

Souvenir Sheet
Perf. 13½x14

417 A160 3s Sheet of 2, #a-b 12.50 12.50

No. 416 was printed in sheets of 10 containing 3 each Nos. 416a-416b and 2 each Nos. 416c-416d.

No. 225 Overprinted

Method and Perf. As Before

2014, Mar. 8
418 A66 1.23s on #225 8.75 8.75

Yuri Gagarin (1934-68), first man in space.

Dushanbe
A161 A162

Designs: 10d, Rudaki Garden. 30d, S. Ayni Opera and Ballet Theater. 50d, Civil registry office. 1s, Palace of Nations. 2.50s, Arms of Dushanbe.

2014, June 11 Litho. *Perf. 14x13½*
419 A161 10d multi .25 .25
420 A161 30d multi .35 .35
421 A161 50d multi .60 .60
422 A161 1s multi 1.25 1.25

Perf. 13½x14

423 A162 2.50s multi 3.00 3.00
Nos. 419-423 (5) 5.45 5.45

Khujand Intl. Airport — A163

No. 424: a, 2.50s, Airplanes on ground and in flight. b, 3s, Airplane over terminal.

2014, June 11 Litho. *Perf. 14x14¼*
424 A163 Horiz. pair, #a-b 5.50 5.50

Mammals A164

Designs: 1.60s, Arkhar ram. 2s, Wolf. 2.50s, Wild boar.

2014, June 11 Litho. *Perf. 14x14¼*
425-427 A164 Set of 3 7.50 7.50
427a Souvenir sheet of 6, 2 each #425-427 15.00 15.00

No. 284 Overprinted in Red

Method and Perf. As Before

2014, June 13
428 A93 on #284 11.50 11.50
a.-c. 1.50s Any single 2.60 2.60
d. 2s multi 3.50 3.50

2014 World Cup Soccer Championships, Brazil.

Mushrooms A165

Designs: 1.60s, Xerocomus rubellus, butterfly and ladybug. 2s, Cantharellus cibarius and butterfly. 2.50s, Cantharellula umbonata and hedgehog.

2014, Oct. 3 Litho. *Perf. 13½x14*
429-431 A165 Set of 3 7.00 7.00

Nos. 429-431 were each printed in sheets of 9 + label

Dogs A166

Designs: 2s, Polish ogar. 2.50s, Bulldogs. 3s, Shepherds.

2014, Oct. 3 Litho. *Perf. 14x14¼*
432-434 A166 Set of 3 7.25 7.25
434a Souvenir sheet of 6, 2 each #432-434 14.50 14.50

Nos. 432-434 were each printed in sheets of 7 + label.

New Year 2015 (Year of the Ram) — A167

No. 435: a, Ram. b, Ewe and lamb.

Perf. 13½x13¾

2015, Feb. 13 Litho.
435 A167 3s Pair, #a-b 5.25 5.25

Statue of Rumi — A168

2015, Feb. 13 Litho. ***Perf. 14¼x14***
436 A168 3s multi 4.00 4.00

Automobiles — A169

No. 437: a, 2s, ZIS 101. b, 2s, Moskvich 400 on road. c, 3s, 1938 Opel Admiral. d, 3s, Moskvich 400 on wooden bridge.

2015, Feb. 13 Litho. ***Perf. 14x14¼***
437 A169 Block of 4, #-d 9.50 9.50

Birds — A170

No. 438: a, Eagle. b, Sparrow.

2015, Apr. 18 Litho. ***Perf. 14x14¼***
438 A170 2s Pair, #a-b 5.00 5.00

Miniature Sheet

Flora and Fauna — A171

No. 439: a, 3s, Vanda Miss Joaquim orchid. b, 3s, Lotus flower. c, 3.50s, Elephant and leopard. d, 3.50s, Panda and leopard.

2015, Apr. 18 Litho. ***Perf. 12x12¼***
439 A171 Sheet of 6, #439c, 439d, 2 each #439a, 439b 15.00 15.00

Singapore 2015 Intl. Stamp Exhibition, Taipei 2015 Intl. Stamp Exhibition.

Souvenir Sheet

Space Exploration — A172

No. 440: a, Avicenna (c. 980-1037), astronomer and philosopher. b, Yuri Gagarin (1934-68), cosmonaut.

2015, June 13 Litho. ***Perf. 13½x13***
440 A172 5s Sheet of 2, #a-b 9.75 9.75

Miniature Sheet

Victory in World War II, 70th Anniv. — A173

No. 441: a, 2s, Statue of soldier with medals. b, 2s, Soldier wearing helmet. c, 2.50s, Military medal. d, 4.50s, Battle scene

2015, June 13 Litho. ***Perf. 12***
441 A173 Sheet of 9, #441a-441c, 6 #441d 22.00 22.00

See No. 447.

Tajikistan Railroads — A174

No. 442: a, 2.50s. Fountain and Dushanbe Station. b, 2.50s, Trains at Dushanbe Station. c, 3s, Steam locomotives at Dushanbe Station. d, 3s, Trains in repair barn.

2015, Aug. 20 Litho. ***Perf. 14x14¼***
442 A174 Block of 4, #a-d 10.00 10.00

Traditional Costumes — A175

No. 443: a, 2s. Musicians, man and woman near table. b, 2s, Woman, four musicians with horns. c, 3s, Two women. d, 3s, Musician and two women.

2015, Aug. 20 Litho. ***Perf. 14x14¼***
443 A175 Block of 4, #a-d 10.00 10.00

Souvenir Sheet

Silk Road — A176

No. 444: a, Market. b, Camel caravan.

2015, Aug. 20 Litho. ***Perf. 13½x14***
444 A176 5s Sheet of 2, #a-b 9.75 9.75

No. 168 Overprinted in Black or Blue

Methods and Perfs. As Before

2015, Oct. 26 Black Overprint
445 A39 Sheet of 6, #a-f 15.50 15.50

Blue Overprint

446 A39 Sheet of 6, #a-f 15.50 15.50

2015 Chess World Cup, Baku, Azerbaijan.

Victory in World War II, 70th Anniv. A177

2015, Dec. 27 Litho. ***Perf. 14x14¼***
447 A177 3.50s multi 3.75 3.75

No. 447 was printed in sheets of 5 + label.

New Year 2016 (Year of the Monkey) — A178

No. 448 — Adult and juvenile monkeys: a, On vine. b, On ground with bananas.

2016, Jan. 9 Litho. ***Perf. 13½x14***
448 A178 3s Pair, #a-b 5.00 5.00

Eagles — A179

No. 449: a, 2s, Two eagles in flight. b, 2s, Eagle and rabbit. c, 3s, Eagle and fox. d, 3s, Eagles at nest.

2016, Jan. 9 Litho. ***Perf. 14x14¼***
449 A179 Block or vert. strip of 4, #a-d 8.75 8.75

A180

Red Crescent Disaster Assistance — A181

Designs: 1s, Rescue workers, vehicle in background.

No. 451 — Tajikistan Red Crescent emblem, rescue workers and: a, Vehicle at left. b, Vehicle in background.

2016 Mar. 1 Litho. ***Perf. 13¾x13¼***
450 A180 1s multi .70 .70

Souvenir Sheet

Perf. 14¼x14

451 A181 5s Sheet of 2, #a-b 7.00 7.00

Dushanbe Sites — A182

Designs: 10d, Rudaki Garden. 15d, Poytakht Civil Registry Office. 30d, S. Ayni Opera and Ballet Theater. 75d, Palace of Nations.

2016, Mar. 1 Litho. ***Perf. 13¾x13¼***
452 A182 10d multi .25 .25
453 A182 15d multi .40 .40
454 A182 30d multi .75 .75
455 A182 75d multi 1.90 1.90
Nos. 452-455 (4) 3.30 3.30

No. 375 Overprinted in Red

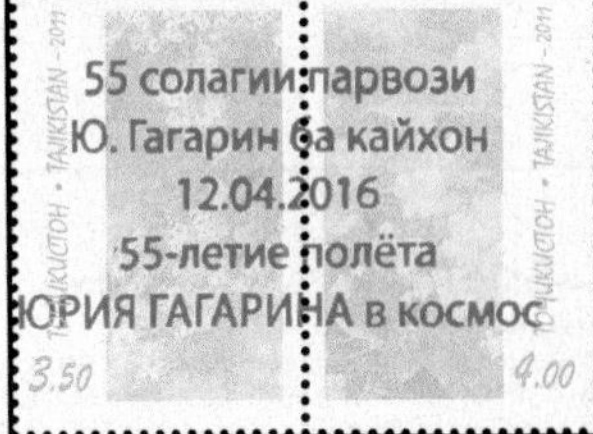

Method and Perf. As Before

2016, Apr. 12
456 A135 Horiz. pair on #375 6.50 6.50
a. 3.50s on #375a 3.00 3.00
b. 4s on #375b 3.50 3.50

Yuri Gagarin (1934-68), first man in space, 55th anniversary.

Regional Communications Commonwealth, 25th Anniv. — A183

Commonwealth of Independent States, 25th Anniv. — A184

2016, Apr. 13 Litho. ***Perf. 14¼x14***
457 A183 3.50s multi 3.25 3.25
458 A184 3.50s multi 3.25 3.25

National Cuisine A185

2016, May 23 Litho. ***Perf. 13½x14***
459 A185 3.50s multi 2.50 2.50

2016 Summer Olympics, Rio de Janeiro A186

Designs: No. 460, 2.50s, Soccer. No. 461, 2.50s, Taekwondo. No. 462, 2.50s, Cycling.

2016, May 23 Litho. *Perf. 14x14¼*

460-462 A186 Set of 3 6.50 6.50

462a Souvenir sheet of 6, 2 each #460-462 13.00 13.00

Nos. 460-462 were each printed in sheets of 5 + label.

Nos. 166, 167, 185 Surcharged

Methods and Perfs. As Before

2016, Aug. 15

463	A39	4s on 15d #166	1.90	1.90
464	A39	4s on 41d #167	1.90	1.90
465	A50	Block of 4	9.00	9.00
a.		4s on 1s #465a	2.25	2.25
b.		4s on 1.50s #465b	2.25	2.25
c.		4s on 2s #465c	2.25	2.25
d.		4s on 2s #465d	2.25	2.25

Turtles — A187

No. 466 — Turtle, two bees, and: a, Two dragonflies. b, One dragonfly.

2016, Sept. 1 Litho. *Perf. 14x14¼*

466 A187 3.50s Pair, #a-b 5.50 5.50

Souvenir Sheet

President Emomali Rahmon and Flag of Tajikistan — A188

2016, Sept. 1 Litho. *Perf. 14¼x14*

467 A188 10s multi 11.00 11.00

Independence, 25th Anniv.

No. 165 Surcharged in Blue

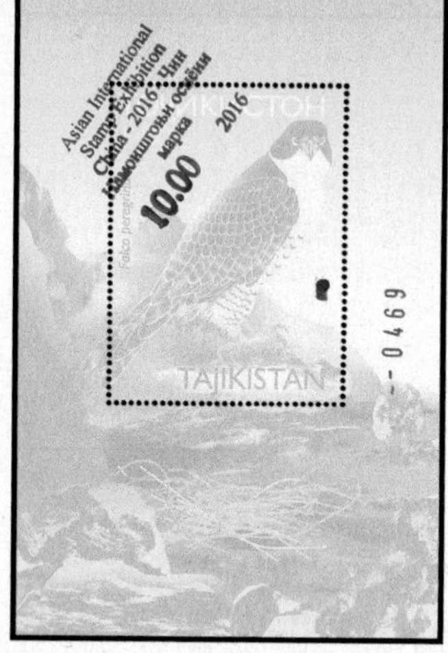

Method and Perf. As Before

2016, Dec. 13

468 A38 10s on 1s #165 9.75 9.75

2016 Asian International Stamp Exhibition, Nanning, People's Republic of China.

Wild Cats A189

Designs: 2.50s, Tiger and cubs laying down. 3.50s, Lion and tiger. 4s, Tiger and juvenile standing.

2016, Dec. 13 Litho. *Perf. 14x14¼*

469-471 A189 Set of 3 7.75 7.75

471a Souvenir sheet of 6, 2 each #469-471 15.50 15.50

Nos. 469-471 were each printed in sheets of 5 + label. The bottom row of stamps on No. 471a are tete-beche in relation to the top row.

New Year 2017 (Year of the Rooster) — A190

No. 472: a, 2.50s, Rooster, hen and chicks. b, 3s, Two roosters fighting.

2017, Jan. 20 Litho. *Perf. 14x14¼*

472 A190 Pair, #a-b 5.25 5.25

Worldwide Fund for Nature (WWF) — A191

Designs: 3.50s, Three Octocolobus manul manul. 4.50s, Octocolobus manul nigripecta with fish. 5.10s, Octocolobus manul ferruginea with bird. 8.70s, Octocolobus manul ferruginea on tree branch.

2017, Apr. 30 Litho. *Perf. 14x14½*

473-476 A191 Set of 4 11.50 11.50

476a Souvenir sheet of 8, 2 each #473-476 23.00 23.00

Nos. 473-476 were each printed in sheets of 9 + label.

Traditional Clothing — A192

No. 477: a, 1.85s, Socks. b, 4.20s, Gown.

2017, June 19 Litho. *Perf. 14½x14*

477 A192 Pair, #a-b 4.25 4.25

2018 World Cup Soccer Championships, Russia — A193

Designs: 3.50s, Three players. 4.20s, Two players. 5.80s, Four players.

2017, June 19 Litho. *Perf. 14x14½*

478-480 A193 Set of 3 8.00 8.00

Nos. 478-480 were each printed in sheets of 5 + label. Compare with Type A197.

For overprints. see Nos. 509-511.

Flowers A194

Designs: 3.50s, Rose and butterfly. 4.20s, Lotus flower. 5.80s, Orchids and butterfly.

2017, Aug. 2 Litho. *Perf. 14x14½*

481-483 A194 Set of 3 8.00 8.00

Nos. 481-483 were each printed in sheets of 5 + label.

Nos. 198-199 Surcharged in Blue

Methods and Perfs. As Before

2017, Aug. 6

484	A57	Block of 4	8.50	8.50
a.		3s on 2d #198a	1.90	1.90
b.		3s on 95d #198d	1.90	1.90
c.		3.50s on 3d #198b	2.25	2.25
d.		3.50s on 95d #198c	2.25	2.25
485	A57	Block of 4	8.50	8.50
a.		3s on 50d #199a	1.90	1.90
b.		3s on 1s #199d	1.90	1.90
c.		3.50s on 50d #199b	2.25	2.25
d.		3.50s on 1s #199c	2.25	2.25

City Transportation — A195

No. 486: a, 3s, Trolleybus. b, 3.50s, Bus.

2017, Oct. 27 Litho. *Perf. 14x14½*

486 A195 Pair, #a-b 5.50 5.50

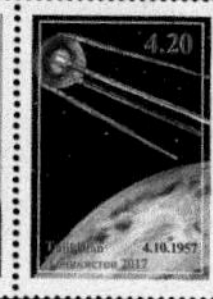

Space Exploration, 60th Anniv. — A196

No. 487: a, 1.85s, Al-Farabi (c. 872-c.950), astronomer. b. 4.20s, Sputnik 1 satellite. c, 5.80s, Yuri Gagarin (1934-68), first man in space.

2017, Oct. 27 Litho. *Perf. 14½x14*

487 A196 Horiz. strip of 3, #a-c 9.75 9.75

2018 World Cup Soccer Championships, Russia — A197

No. 488: a, 3.50s, Three players. b, 4.20s, Two players.

2017, Dec. 28 Litho. *Perf. 14x14¼*

Stamps With Black Frame Line

488 A197 Vert. pair, #a-b, + 2 labels *19.00 19.00*

Compare with Type A193.

New Year 2018 (Year of the Dog) — A198

No. 489: a, Dog and puppy. b, Dog and three puppies.

2018, Jan. 8 Litho. *Perf. 14x14¼*

489 A198 3.50s Pair, #a-b 5.50 5.50

No. 185e Overprinted and Surcharged in Blue

Methods and Perfs. As Before

2018, Feb. 18

490	A50	Sheet of 8	22.50	22.50
a.		2s Partial overprint at LR, #185c	2.10	2.10
b.		2s Partial overprint at LL, #185d	2.10	2.10
c.		2s Partial overprint at UR, #185d	2.10	2.10
d.		2s Partial overprint at UL, #185c	2.10	2.10
e.		3s on 1.50s, #185b, surcharge at LL	3.25	3.25
f.		3s on 1.50s, #185b, surcharge at UR	3.25	3.25
g.		3.50s on 1s #185a, surcharge at LR	3.75	3.75
h.		3.50s on 1s #185a, surcharge at UL	3.75	3.75

Year of Horse Type of 2002 Surcharged in Blue

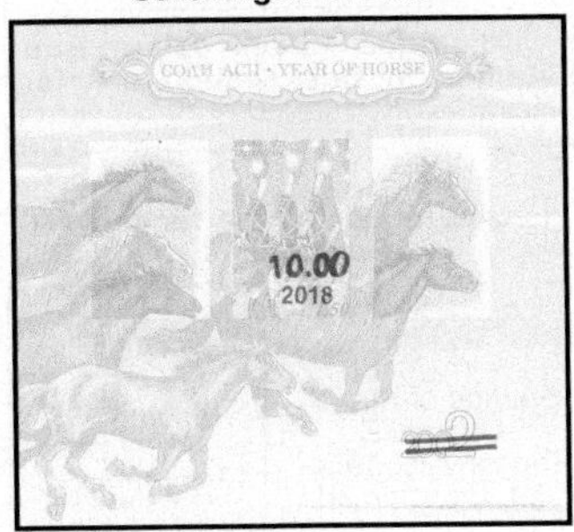

2018, Feb. 18 Litho. ***Imperf.***

491 A57 10s on 1.50s, #200 imperforate 16.00 16.00

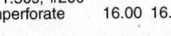

Cats — A199

No. 492: a, 3.50s, Persian cat with ball. b, 4.20s, Persian cat with butterfly. c, 5.80s, Tiger cat.

2018, Apr. 20 Litho. ***Perf. 14¼x14***

492 A199 Horiz. strip of 3, #a-c 7.00 7.00

Miniature Sheet

Sughd Region Buildings — A200

No. 493: a, 4.20s, Istiklol Independence Monument. b, 4.20s, Square in front of the central grand Masjidi Jami Mosque. c, 5.80s, Mosque, Istaravshan. d, 5.80s, Historical Museum, Khujand.

2018, Apr. 20 Litho. ***Perf. 14x14¼***

493 A200 Sheet of 4, #a-d 12.00 12.00

Miniature Sheet

Tourist Attractions of Gorno Badakhshan Autonomous Region — A201

No. 494: a, 4.20s, Building. b, 4.20s, Lake. c, 5.80s, Building and trees. d, 5.80s, Building and statue.

2018, Apr. 20 Litho. ***Perf. 14x14¼***

494 A201 Sheet of 4, #a-d 12.00 12.00

No. 159 Surcharged in Blue

Methods and Perfs. As Before

2018, Aug. 6

495 A36 10s on 500r #154 (Bl) 3.50 3.50

Landscapes — A202

Designs: 10d, Sharinav Lake. 20d, Seven Lake. 30d, Durum Lake. 40d, Alovidin Lake. 50d, Vakhsh River. 2s, Sarez Lake. 3s, Iskandar Lake. 20s, Nurek Lake.

2018, Nov. 1 Litho. ***Perf. 13¾x13¼***

496	A202	10d multi	.25	.25
497	A202	20d multi	.25	.25
498	A202	30d multi	.25	.25
499	A202	40d multi	.25	.25
500	A202	50d multi	.25	.25
501	A202	2s multi	.65	.65
502	A202	3s multi	1.00	1.00
503	A202	20s multi	6.75	6.75
		Nos. 496-503 (8)	9.65	9.65

A205

A206

Year of Tourism Development and Folk Crafts — A207

2018, Dec. 20 Litho. ***Perf. 14x©4¼***

506	Horiz. strip of 3	3.75	3.75
a.	A205 20d multi	.25	.25
b.	A206 30d multi	.25	.25
c.	A207 10s multi	3.25	3.25

No. 506 was printed in sheets containing two strips.

Nature Reserves — A208

No. 507 — Regional Communications Commonwealth emblem and: a, 1.60s, Leopard and bird. b, 3s, Partridges. c, 5s, Hedgehog, mushrooms and birds. d, 5.40s, Eagle and blackbird.

2018, Dec. 20 Litho. ***Perf. 14x14¼***

507 A208 Block of 4, #a-d 5.25 5.25

Cacti and Insects — A209

No. 508 — Cactus and: a, 1.60s, Butterflies. b, 2.50s, Butterfly, bee and ants (pink flower). c, 3.50s, Bees and ants. d, 5s, Butterfly, bee and ants (yellow flower).

2018, Dec. 20 Litho. ***Perf. 14x14¼***

508 A209 Block of 4, #a-d 4.25 4.25

Nos. 478-480 Handstamp Overprinted in Black, Red or Blue

Black Overprint in French

Red Overprint in Tajik

Blue Overprint in Russian

Methods and Perfs As Before

2018

509	A193	3.50s Black overprint (#478)	1.50	1.50
510	A193	4.20s Red overprint (#479)	1.75	1.75
511	A193	5.80s Blue overprint (#480)	2.50	2.50
		Nos. 509-511 (3)	5.75	5.75

The color of overprints used on each denomination appears to be consistent, but the languages of the overprints of at least Nos. 509 and 511 appear to not be consistent.

New Year 2019 (Year of the Pig) — A210

No. 512 — Pig with: a, 2s, Banner. b, 5.80s, Balloon.

2019, Apr. 1 Litho. ***Perf. 14¼x14***

512 A210 Pair, #a-b 2.75 2.75

Worldwide Fund for Nature (WWF) — A211

No. 513 — Worldwide Fund for Nature emblem and various depictions of snow leopards: a. 2s. b, 3.50s. c, 4.80s. d, 5s.

2019, Apr. 1 Litho. ***Perf. 14¼x14***

513 A211 Block or horiz. strip of 4, #a-d 5.25 5.25

Mushrooms A212

Various mushrooms and: 3.50s, Butterflies, grasshopper and snail. 4.20s, Butterflies and hedgehog. 5.80s, Butterflies, dragonfly and frog.

2019, July 2 Litho. ***Perf. 14x14¼***

514-516 A212 Set of 3 4.50 4.50

Nos. 514-516 were each printed in sheets of 9 + label.

Owls A213

Various owls: 3.50s, 4.50s, 5.80s, 6s.

2019, July 2 Litho. ***Perf. 14x14¼***

517-520 A213 Set of 4 6.75 6.75

Nos. 517-520 were each printed in sheets of 5 + label.

Handicrafts A214

No. 521 — Regional Communications Commonwealth emblem and: a, 2s, Pot, 20th cent. b, 5.80s, Pitcher, 19th cent.

2019, July 2 Litho. ***Perf. 14¼x14***

521 A214 Pair, #a-b 2.75 2.75

Miniature Sheet

Mohandas K. Gandhi (1869-1948), Indian Nationalist Leader — A215

No. 524 — Gandhi and: a, 2s, Flag of India. b, 2.50s, Building. c, 3.50, Crowd of people, Indian flags. d, 4.80s, Asoka Pillar, rocket and train.

2019, Oct. 1 Litho. *Perf. 14x14¼*

524 A215 Sheet of 4, #a-d 4.50 4.50

Transportation A216

Designs: Nos. 529, 537a, 10d, Taxi. Nos. 530, 537b, 15d, Bus. Nos. 531, 537c, 20d, Steamer. Nos. 532, 537d, 30d, Train. Nos. 533, 537e, 40d, Helicopter. Nos. 534, 537f, 50d, Airplane. Nos. 535, 537g, 1s, Bus station. Nos. 536, 537h, 15s, Trolley.

2019, Dec. 21 Litho. *Perf. 14x14¼*

529-536 A216 Set of 8 6.00 6.00

Miniature Sheet
Stamp Size: 40x28mm

537 A216 Sheet of 8, #a-h 6.00 6.00

Nos. 529-533, 536, have white backgrounds. Nos. 534-535 have colored backgrounds.

TANGANYIKA

ˌtan-gə-ˈnyē-kə

LOCATION — Southeastern Africa bordering on the Indian Ocean
GOVT. — Republic within British Commonwealth
AREA — 362,688 sq. mi.
POP. — 9,404,000 (est. 1961)
CAPITAL — Dar es Salaam

Before World War I, this area formed part of German East Africa. It was mandated to Britain after World War I and (in 1946) became a trust territory under the United Nations. In 1935, stamps of the mandate were replaced by those used jointly by Kenya, Uganda and Tanganyika (see Kenya, Uganda and Tanzania). On Dec. 9, 1961, Tanganyika became independent. On Dec. 9, 1962, it became a republic. April 26, 1964, it joined Zanzibar to form the United Republic of Tanganyika and Zanzibar (later renamed Tanzania). See Tanzania.

100 Cents = 1 Rupee
100 Cents = 1 Shilling (1922)
20 Shillings = 1 Pound

Catalogue values for unused stamps in this country are for Never Hinged items, beginning with Scott 45 in the regular postage section and Scott O1 in the officials section.

Stamps of East Africa & Uganda Protectorates Overprinted

1921 Wmk. 4 *Perf. 14*

1	A1	12c gray	12.00	*135.00*
2	A1	15c ultra	10.00	*19.00*
3	A1	50c dull violet & blk	18.00	*122.50*

Overprinted

4	A2	2r black & red, *blue*	57.50	*165.00*
5	A2	3r gray green & violet	135.00	*425.00*
7	A2	5r dull violet & ultra	175.00	*525.00*
		Nos. 1-7 (6)	407.50	*1,392.*

Overprinted in Red or Black

1922

8	A1	1c black (R)	2.25	*25.00*
9	A1	10c orange (Bk)	4.00	*15.00*

A3 Giraffe — A4

Perf. 14½x14

1922-25 Engr. Wmk. 4

10	A3	5c dk violet & blk	2.75	.25
11	A3	5c grn & blk ('25)	14.50	1.75
12	A3	10c green & blk	4.50	.95
13	A3	10c yel & blk ('25)	14.50	1.75
14	A3	15c carmine & blk	4.75	.25
15	A3	20c orange & blk	6.75	.25
16	A3	25c black	10.00	*7.50*
17	A3	25c blue & blk ('25)	5.00	*20.00*
18	A3	30c blue & blk	7.00	5.75
19	A3	30c dull vio & blk ('25)	9.75	*32.50*
20	A3	40c brown & black	7.50	5.25
21	A3	50c gray black	8.25	1.75
22	A3	75c bister & black	7.50	*25.00*

Perf. 14

23	A4	1sh green & black	8.25	*12.50*
a.		Wmk. sideways	14.00	*30.00*
24	A4	2sh brn vio & blk	9.50	*35.00*
a.		Wmk. sideways	12.50	*35.00*
25	A4	3sh blk, wmk. sideways	62.50	*62.50*
26	A4	5sh red & black	47.50	*115.00*
a.		Wmk. sideways	92.50	*140.00*
27	A4	10sh dp blue & blk	140.00	*250.00*
a.		Wmk. sideways	300.00	*525.00*
28	A4	£1 orange & black	450.00	*700.00*
a.		Wmk. sideways	500.00	*750.00*
		Nos. 10-28 (19)	820.50	*1,278.*

On No. 28 the words of value are in a curve between the circle and "POSTAGE & REVENUE."

King George V
A5 A6

1927-31 Typo.

29	A5	5c green & black	2.00	.25
30	A5	10c yellow & black	2.25	.25
31	A5	15c red & black	2.00	.25
32	A5	20c orange & black	3.00	.25
33	A5	25c ultra & black	4.25	2.25
34	A5	30c dull violet & blk	3.25	3.00
35	A5	30c ultra & blk ('31)	29.00	.35
36	A5	40c brown & black	2.25	*9.25*
37	A5	50c gray & black	2.75	1.10
38	A5	75c olive grn & blk	2.25	*26.00*
39	A6	1sh green & black	4.75	3.25
40	A6	2sh violet brn & blk	30.00	8.50
41	A6	3sh black	52.50	*115.00*
42	A6	5sh scarlet & blk	42.50	27.50
43	A6	10sh ultra & black	110.00	*160.00*
44	A6	£1 brown org & blk	275.00	*425.00*
		Nos. 29-44 (16)	567.75	*782.20*

Catalogue values for unused stamps in this section, from this point to the end of the section, are for Never Hinged items.

Independent State

A7 A8

Designs: 5c, Teacher instructing villagers, horiz. 10c, Nurse and infant. 15c, Coffee picker. 20c, Harvesting corn. 30c, Flag, horiz. 50c, Serengeti lions. 1sh, Nurse showing infant to mother, hospital horiz. 1sh30c, Torch and Mt. Kilimanjaro. 2sh, Dar es Salaam harbor, horiz. 5sh, Tractor & field workers, horiz. 10sh, Diamond mine & rose diamond, horiz. 20sh, Torch and Mt. Kilimanjaro, diff.

Perf. 14x14½, 14½x14

1961, Dec. 9 Photo. Unwmk.

45	A7	5c sepia & yel grn	.25	.25
46	A7	10c Prus grn	.25	.25
47	A7	15c sepia & blue	.25	.25
b.		Blue omitted	*1,750.*	
48	A7	20c orange brown	.25	.25
49	A7	30c dp grn, blk & yel	.30	.25
50	A7	50c sepia & yellow	.30	.25

Perf. 14½

51	A8	1sh cit brn & gray bl	.30	.25
52	A8	1sh30c multicolored	4.00	.25
53	A8	2sh multicolored	1.10	.25
54	A8	5sh Prus grn & dp org	1.10	.50
55	A8	10sh blk, bl & rose	15.50	4.75
a.		Rose (diamond) omitted	300.00	200.00
56	A8	20sh multicolored	4.25	*9.25*
		Nos. 45-56 (12)	27.85	16.75

Tanganyika's independence, Dec. 9, 1961.
For overprints see Nos. O21-O28.

Pres. Julius Nyerere with Pickax — A9

Designs: 50c, Flag hoisting on Mt. Kilimanjaro. 1sh30c, Presidential emblem. 2sh50c, Independence monument, Mnazi Moja.

1962, Dec. 9 *Perf. 14½x14*

57	A9	30c bright green	.25	.25
58	A9	50c multicolored	.25	.25
59	A9	1sh30c multicolored	.25	.25
60	A9	2sh50c dk blue, blk & red	.50	.40
		Nos. 57-60 (4)	1.25	1.15

Issued to commemorate the establishment of the Republic of Tanganyika, Dec. 9, 1962.

OFFICIAL STAMPS

Catalogue values for unused stamps in this section are for Never Hinged items.

Issued for use by the Tanganyika Government

Stamps of Kenya, Uganda & Tanganyika, 1954-59, Overprinted

Perf. 12½x13, 13x12½

1959 Engr. Wmk. 4

O1	A18a	5c choc & blk	.25	*1.25*
O2	A19	10c carmine	.25	*1.25*
O3	A20	15c lt bl & blk (on #106)	.35	*1.25*
O4	A19	20c org & blk	.25	.25
a.		Double overprint		*1,300.*
O5	A18a	30c ultra & black	.25	*.95*
O6	A19	50c dp red lilac	.75	.25
O7	A19	1sh dp mag & blk	.25	*.85*
O8	A20	1sh30c pur & red org	5.50	2.25
O9	A20	2sh dp grn & gray	1.40	1.10
O10	A20	5sh black & org	4.00	3.50
O11	A20	10sh ultra & blk	2.25	*4.00*
O12	A21	£1 black & ver	7.50	*17.50*
		Nos. O1-O12 (12)	23.00	34.40

Stamps of Kenya, Uganda & Tanganyika, 1960, Overprinted

Perf. 14½x14

1960, Oct. 1 Photo. Wmk. 314

O13	A23	5c dull blue	.25	*2.00*
O14	A23	10c lt olive green	.25	*2.00*
O15	A23	15c dull purple	.25	*2.00*
O16	A23	20c brt lilac rose	.25	*.55*
O17	A23	30c brt vermilion	.25	.25
O18	A23	50c dull violet	.35	*1.10*

Nos. 129 & 133 of Kenya, Uganda & Tanganyika Overprinted

Engr. *Perf. 14*

O19	A24	1sh violet & lilac red	.45	.30
O20	A24	5sh rose red & lilac	16.00	1.50
		Nos. O13-O20 (8)	18.05	9.70

Nos. 45-51 and 54 Overprinted "OFFICIAL" in Sans-serif Type of Various Sizes

Perf. 14x14½, 14½x14

1961, Dec. 9 Unwmk.

O21	A7	5c sepia & yellow grn	.25	.25
O22	A7	10c Prussian green	.25	.25
O23	A7	15c sepia & blue	.25	.25
O24	A7	20c orange brown	.25	.25
O25	A7	30c dp grn blk & yel	.25	.25
O26	A7	50c sepia & yellow	.25	.25
O27	A8	1sh citron brn & gray bl	.25	.25
O28	A8	5sh Prus grn & dp org	.75	.75
		Nos. O21-O28 (8)	2.50	2.50

TANNU TUVA

'tä-nə 'tü-və

(Tuva People's Republic)

LOCATION — Between Siberia and northwestern Mongolia at the sources of the Yenisei, in the basin formed by the Tannu-Ola and Sayan Mountains.
GOVT. — A former republic closely identified with Soviet Russia in Asia
AREA — 64,000 sq. mi. (approx.)
POP. — 95,000 (1941 est.)
CAPITAL — Kyzyl

This region, traditionally called Uriankhai, was ruled by the Mongols until the mid-18th century, when it became part of the Chinese Empire. Russia and China struggled for control of the country 1914-21, until it became independent as the Tannu Tuva People's Republic in 1921. In 1944 it was incorporated into the U.S.S.R. as an autonomous region of the Russian Soviet Federated Socialist Republic.

Russian, later Soviet, stamps were used in Tuva prior to 1926 and after 1944.

100 Mongo=1 Tugrik
100 Kopecks = 1 Ruble
100 Kopecks = 1 Tugrik (1934)
100 Kopecks = 1 Aksha (1936)

Watermarks

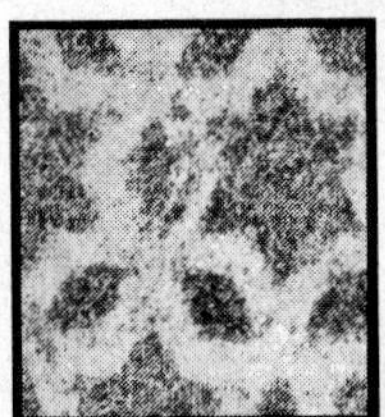

Wmk. 204 — Stars and Diamonds

Wmk. 170 — Greek Border and Rosettes

Most used examples of Nos. 1-38, 45-52a, 54-92 and C1-C18 on the market are cancelled to order, and the used values below are for such stamps.

Tuvan stamps, except for Nos. 117-123 and most of the overprints, were printed by the State Security Printers in Moscow.

Wheel of Truth — A1

1926 Litho. Wmk. 204 *Perf. 13½*

Size: 20x26mm

No.	Type	Value	Unused	Used
1	A1	1k red	1.50	1.50
2	A1	2k light blue	1.50	1.50
3	A1	5k orange	1.50	1.50
4	A1	8k yel green	2.00	1.75
5	A1	10k violet	2.00	1.75
6	A1	30k dark brown	2.00	1.75
7	A1	50k gray black	2.25	1.75

Size: 22½x30mm

Perf. 10½

No.	Type	Value	Unused	Used
8	A1	1r blue green	6.00	3.00
9	A1	3r red brown	8.00	5.75
10	A1	5r dark ultra	13.50	8.00
		Nos. 1-10 (10)	40.25	28.25
		Set, never hinged	77.50	

Nos. 1-10 have crackled white gum. Reprints can be distinguished by their smooth gum.

Nos. 1-10 in different colors are proofs.

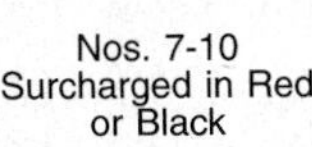

Nos. 7-10 Surcharged in Red or Black

Surcharged in Kyzyl.

1927 ***Perf. 13½***

No.	Type	Value	Unused	Used
11	A1	8k on 50k	25.00	12.50
a.		Inverted surcharge	65.00	
b.		Double surcharge	*100.00*	

Perf. 10½

No.	Type	Value	Unused	Used
12	A1	14k on 1r	25.00	12.50
a.		Inverted surcharge	75.00	
b.		Double surcharge	85.00	
13	A1	18k on 3r (Bk)	25.00	12.50
a.		Inverted surcharge	*90.00*	
b.		Double surcharge	75.00	
14	A1	28k on 5r (Bk)	25.00	12.50
a.		Inverted surcharge	*90.00*	
b.		Double surcharge	75.00	
		Nos. 11-14 (4)	100.00	50.00
		Set, never hinged	200.00	

Nos. 11-14 were surcharged with a shiny ink. Reprints are overprinted with a dull ink and are often smudged.

Tuvan Woman — A3

Map of Tannu Tuva A8

Sheep Herding — A11

Fording a Stream — A13

Tuvan Riding Reindeer — A16

Designs: 2k, Stag. 3k, Mountain goat. 4k, Tuvan and tent. 5k, Tuvan man. 10k, Archery competition. 14k, Camel caravan. 28k, Landscape. 50k, Weaving. 70k, Tuvan on horseback.

Printed in Moscow.

1927 Litho. *Perf. 12½*

No.	Type	Value	Unused	Used
15	A3	1k blk, lt brn & red	1.00	.60
16	A3	2k pur, dp brn & grn	1.20	.55
17	A3	3k blk, bl grn & yel	2.00	.60
18	A3	4k vio bl & choc	.90	.60
19	A3	5k org, blk & dk bl	.90	.65

Perf. 12½x12

No.	Type	Value	Unused	Used
20	A8	8k ol brn, pale bl & red brn	1.00	.65
21	A8	10k blk, grn & brn red	5.50	1.00
22	A8	14k vio bl & red org	10.00	3.50

Perf. 10½

No.	Type	Value	Unused	Used
23	A11	18k dk bl & red brn	10.00	5.00
24	A11	28k emer & blk brn	7.25	2.75
25	A13	40k rose & bl grn	5.00	2.50
26	A13	50k blk, grn & red brn	3.50	2.00
27	A13	70k dl red & bis	7.00	4.00
28	A16	1r yel brn & vio	16.00	6.75
		Nos. 15-28 (14)	71.25	31.15
		Set, never hinged	142.50	

Nos. 15-28 were issued with a crackled white gum. Reprints of the 1k-5k values exist and can be distinguished by their smooth gum.

Nos. 15-28 in different colors are proofs.

Nos. 25-27, 20-22 Surcharged in Various Colors

Surcharged in Moscow.

1932

No.	Type	Value	Unused	Used
29	A13	1k on 40k (Bk)	8.50	*11.00*
30	A13	2k on 50k (Br)	9.00	*11.00*
31	A13	3k on 70k (Bl)	9.00	*11.00*
a.		Inverted surcharge	*300.00*	
32	A8	5k on 8k (Bk)	9.00	*11.00*
33	A8	10k (Bk)	9.00	*11.00*
34	A8	15k on 14k (Bk)	14.00	*16.00*
		Nos. 29-34 (6)	58.50	71.00
		Set, never hinged	128.00	

Issued in connection with the Romanization of the alphabet.

No. 31 with black surcharge was prepared but not issued.

Nos. 20, 22-24 Surcharged in Black

No. 37

No. 38

Surcharged by numbering machine in Kyzyl.

1932-33 Wmk. 204

No.	Type	Value	Unused	Used
35	A8	10k on 8k	180.00	100.00
36	A8	15k on 14k	300.00	200.00
37	A11	35k on 18k (#23)	150.00	100.00
b.		Pair, one without surcharge	—	
c.		Inverted surcharge	*500.00*	
38	A11	35k on 28k	150.00	100.00
a.		Pair, one without surcharge	—	
		Nos. 35-38 (4)	780.00	500.00
		Set, never hinged	1,550.	

Revenue Stamps Surcharged — A19

Surcharged in Kyzyl.

Three types: type 1, figures of value 6.7mm high; type 2, figures of value 6.7mm high, letter "p" lengthened at bottom; type 3, figures of value 5.1mm high.

1933 ***Perf. 12x12½***

No.	Type	Value	Unused	Used
39	A19	15k on 6k org yel, type 1	300.00	150.00
40	A19	15k on 6k org yel, type 2	300.00	150.00
b.		Inverted surcharge	—	—
41	A19	15k on 6k org yel, type 3	500.00	300.00
42	A19	35k on 15k red brn, type 1	—	*4,000.*
43	A19	35k on 15k red brn, type 2	—	*4,000.*
44	A19	35k on 15k red brn, type 3	*1,500.*	800.00

Mounted Hunter — A20

Tuvan Inside of Yurt — A21

Tuvan Milking Yak — A22

Die I

Die II

Designs: 2k, Hunter stalking game. 4k, Tractor. 10k, Camel caravan. 15k, Herdsman lassoing reindeer. 20k, Hunter shooting fox with arrow.

Two dies on 10k: Die I, Crown at center top is light and matches the shade of the sky below; Die II, Crown at center top is bold, consistent with rest of design and darker than the sky.

Printed by State Security Printers, Moscow.

Wmk. 170

1934, Apr. Photo. *Perf. 12*

No.	Type	Value	Unused	Used
45	A20	1k red orange	1.50	1.00
46	A20	2k olive green	1.50	1.00
47	A21	3k rose red	1.50	1.00
48	A21	4k slate purple	3.50	1.75
49	A22	5k ultramarine	3.50	1.75
50	A22	10k brown, die II	3.50	1.75
51	A22	15k dark lilac	3.50	1.75
52	A22	20k gray black	4.75	2.75
		Nos. 45-52 (8)	23.25	12.75
		Set, never hinged	50.00	
		Set, imperf	50.00	32.50
		Set, imperf., never hinged	100.00	

Nos. 45-52 are inscribed "REGISTERED," but were used as regular postage stamps.

Nos. 46, 48 and 50 exist perf 11, and No. 50 also exists perf 11x10. No. 48 exists perf 11½, reportedly as a color trial proof.

No. 51 Surcharged in Black

Surcharged by numbering machine in Kyzyl.

1935

No.	Type	Description	Unused	Used
53	A22	20k on 15k	*175.00*	*325.00*
a.		Inverted surcharge		*400.00*

Map of Tuva — A23

Rocky Outcropping — A24

Designs: 3k, 5k, 10k, Different scenes of Yenisei River. 25k, Bei-kem rapids. 50k, Mounted hunters.

Printed by State Security Printers, Moscow.

Wmk. 170

1935, Mar. Photo. *Perf. 14*

No.	Type	Description	Unused	Used
54	A23	1k yellow orange	1.75	1.40
55	A23	3k deep green	1.75	1.40
56	A23	5k carmine red	2.40	1.60
57	A23	10k violet	2.60	1.60
b.		Pair, imperf between	—	
58	A24	15k olive green	2.75	2.00
59	A24	25k violet blue	3.25	2.00
60	A24	50k dark brown	4.75	2.25
		Nos. 54-60 (7)	19.25	12.25
		Set, never hinged	35.00	

Nos. 54-60 in different colors, perf and imperf, are proofs.

Badger A25

Squirrel — A26

Fox — A27

Elk — A28

Yak — A29

Designs: 5k, Ermine. 25k, Otter. 50k, Lynx. 3t, Bactrian camels. 5t, Bear.

Printed by State Security Printers, Moscow.

1935, Mar.

No.	Type	Description	Unused	Used
61	A25	1k orange	1.25	1.00
62	A26	3k emerald green	1.25	1.00
a.		Imperf, pair	*300.00*	
63	A25	5k rose red	1.25	1.10
64	A27	10k crimson red	1.25	1.10
65	A27	25k orange red	2.00	1.20
66	A27	50k deep blue	2.00	1.20
67	A28	1t violet	2.50	1.20
a.		Pair, imperf between	—	
68	A29	2t royal blue	3.75	1.20
69	A29	3t red brown	3.25	1.35
70	A28	5t indigo	4.00	1.75
a.		Imperf, pair	*300.00*	
b.		Pair, imperf between	—	
		Nos. 61-70 (10)	22.50	12.10
		Set, never hinged	42.50	

Nos. 61-70 in different colors are proofs.

Tuvan Arms — A30

Wrestlers — A31

Herdsman on Bull — A32

Athletic Competitions — A33

Soldiers A34

Designs: 2k, Pres. Chürmit-Dazhy. 3k, Tuvan with Bactrian camel. 5k, 8k, Archer. 10k, 15k, Spearfishing. 12k, 20k, Bear-hunting. 30k, Camel and train. 40k, 50k, Horse race. 80k, Partisans. 3t, Partisans confiscating cattle. 5t, 1921 battle scene.

Printed by State Security Printers, Moscow.

1936, July *Perf. 11, 14*

No.	Type	Description	Unused	Used
71	A30	1k bronze green	2.00	.70
72	A30	2k dark brown	2.50	1.50
73	A30	3k indigo blue	3.25	.75
74a	A31	4k orange red	3.50	.75
75	A31	5k brown purple	5.00	.70
76	A31	6k myrtle green	4.75	.70
77	A31	8k plum	4.75	.70
78a	A31	10k rose red	5.25	.75
79	A31	12k black brown	7.50	1.25
80	A31	15k bronze green	11.00	1.50
81	A31	20k deep blue	11.00	1.20
82	A32	25k orange red	6.00	1.20
83	A32	30k plum	30.00	1.25
84	A32	35k rose red	6.00	1.50
85a	A32	40k deep brown	7.00	1.50
86a	A32	50k indigo blue	13.00	1.50
87a	A33	70k plum	9.50	2.50
88a	A33	80k green	9.50	2.50
89b	A34	1a orange red	9.50	3.00
90	A34	2a rose red	11.00	3.00
91	A33	3a indigo blue	17.50	2.00
92	A33	5a black brown	15.00	2.50
		Nos. 71-92 (22)	194.50	32.95
		Set, never hinged	333.00	

15th anniversary of independence.

Values for Nos. 71-92 are for the most common varieties. For detailed listings, see the *Scott Classic Specialized Catalogue.*

Imperfs are remainders, later sold by the Soviet Postal Museum.

Values for Nos. 93-98 and 104-116 are for genuine examples. Expertization is essential for these issues.

Issues of 1934-36 Handstamped with Large Numerals and Old Values Obliterated with Bars or Blocks

1938, Aug.

No.	Type	Description	Unused	Used
93	A34	5k on 2a (#90a)		*400.00*
94	AP5	5k on 2a (#C17)		*375.00*
95	AP1	10k on 1t (#C8)		*350.00*
96	A24	20k on 50k (#60)		*350.00*
97	AP5	30k on 2a (#C17)		*350.00*
98	AP5	30k on 3a (#C18)		*325.00*

Types of 1935-36 with Modified Designs and New Colors

1938, Dec. Unwmk. *Perf. 12½*

No.	Type	Description	Unused	Used
99	A25	5k deep green	60.00	—
100	A31	10k indigo (dates removed)	60.00	—
101	AP3	15k red brown ("AIR MAIL," dates removed)	60.00	—
102	A31	20k orange red (dates removed)	85.00	—
103	A33	30k maroon (dates removed)	60.00	—
		Nos. 99-103 (5)	325.00	
		Set, never hinged	500.00	

Some experts believe that these stamps were issued in March 1941.

Stamps of 1934-35 Handstamp Surcharged with New Values in Black or Violet at Kyzyl

1939

No.	Type	Description	Unused	Used
104	AP1	10k on 1t (#C8)		225.00
105	AP1	10k on 1t (#B8) (V)		225.00
106	A24	20k on 50k (#60) (V)		200.00

Old values obliterated on Nos. 104-106.

Stamps of 1934-36 Handstamp Surcharged with New Values at Kyzyl

1940, Oct.-1941

No.	Type	Description	Unused	Used
107	AP1	10k on 1t (#C8)	—	125.00
a.		Double surcharge	—	—
108	A24	20k on 50k (#60)	—	150.00
109	A27	20k on 50k (#66)	—	350.00
110	A32	20k on 50k (#86a)	—	350.00
111	AP4	20k on 50k (#C14)	—	100.00
112	A33	20k on 70k (#87a)	—	*500.00*
113	AP4	20k on 75k (#C15)	—	110.00
114	A33	20k on 80k (#88)	—	*500.00*

The old values are not obliterated on Nos. 107 or 108.

Nos. 91, 92 Handstamp Surcharged with New Values at Kyzyl

1942

No.	Type	Description	Unused	Used
115	A33	25k on 3a (#91)	1,200.	—
116	A33	25k on 5a (#92)	—	—

Government House — A35

Exhibition Hall — A36

Tuvan Woman — A37

1942 Typo. Unwmk. *Imperf.*

No.	Type	Description	Unused	Used
117	A35	25k steel blue	950.00	100.00
118	A36	25k steel blue	950.00	100.00
119	A37	25k steel blue	950.00	150.00
		Nos. 117-119 (3)	2,850.	350.00

21st anniversary of independence.

Nos. 117-119 were hand-printed together in small sheetlets of five (117+119+118+117+119), so various se-tenant combinations are possible.

Two additional values, a 25k depicting a Tuvan man and a 50k depicting a soldier on a horse, were prepared, but not issued. A collective proof sheetlet of five, containing Nos. 117-119 and these two values, in the same color as the issued stamps, is also known.

Coat of Arms — A38

Government Building — A39

1943 *Perf. 11 (1 or 2 Sides)*

Buff Paper

No.	Type	Description	Unused	Used
120	A38	25k slate blue	100.00	—
121	A38	25k black	100.00	—
122	A38	25k blue green	90.00	—
123	A39	50k blue green	90.00	—
		Nos. 120-123 (4)	380.00	

White Paper

No.	Type	Description	Unused	Used
120a	A38	25k slate blue	90.00	—
b.		Strip of 3, imperf between		*250.00*

121a	A38 25k black	125.00	—
	Vertical strip of five	625.00	
122a	A38 25k blue green	95.00	—
123a	A39 50k blue green	95.00	—
	Nos. 120a-123a (4)	405.00	

22nd anniversary of independence.

Nos. 120 and 121 were each printed in vertical strips of five, perforated 11 between stamps and imperf on outside edges, so that these stamps may be perforated on top edge only, bottom edge only, or on both top and bottom edges. To make maximum use of limited wartime paper supplies, they were sometimes printed in strips of four. These smaller strips are rare.

Nos. 122 and 123 were printed together in blocks of four, containing a vertical pair of the 25k and a vertical pair of the 50k, perforated internally both vertically and horizontally and imperf on the outer edges. Setenant pairs, Value $225 (#122+123), $275 (#122a+123a).

Nos. 121 and 123a were issued with gum, No. 123a both with and without gum, and the balance of the set without gum.

Used examples and covers exist but are extremely rare.

AIR POST STAMPS

Airplane and Yaks — AP1

Airplane and Capercaillie — AP2

Designs, airplane over: 5k, 15k, Camels. 25k, Argali (wild sheep). 75k, Ox and cart. 2t, Roe deer.

Printed by State Security Printers, Moscow.

Wmk. 170

1934, Apr. 4 Photo. *Perf. 14*

C1	AP1	1k orange red	1.40	1.00
C2	AP1	5k emer green	1.40	1.00
C3	AP2	10k purple brown	4.50	2.75
C4	AP1	15k rose red	2.50	1.00
C5	AP2	25k slate purple	2.50	1.00
C6	AP1	50k dp bl green	2.50	1.00
C7	AP2	75k lake	2.50	1.00
C8	AP1	1t royal blue	3.25	1.75
a.		Perf 12½	77.50	*2,500.*
C9	AP2	2t ultra, 61x31mm	18.00	*21.00*
a.		54.5x29mm	40.00	—
		Nos. C1-C9 (9)	38.55	31.50
		Set, never hinged	55.00	

Nos. C1-C9 imperf or perf 11½ and stamps printed in different colors are proofs.

Tuvan Leading Laden Yak — AP3

Horseman and Zeppelin
AP4

Seaplane Above Dragon — AP5

Designs: 10k, Tuvan plowing. 50k, Villagers with biplane overhead.

Printed by State Security Printers, Moscow.

1936 Unwmk.

C10	AP3	5k indigo & beige	3.00	1.50
C11	AP3	10k pur & cinn	4.50	1.50
C12	AP3	15k blk brn & pale gray	4.50	1.75
C13	AP4	25k plum & cream	6.00	2.50
c.		Horiz. pair, perf 11, imperf between	—	—
C14	AP4	50k rose red & cream	6.50	2.50
C15	AP4	75k emer grn & pale yel	10.00	4.00
C16	AP5	1a bl grn & pale bl grn	12.00	5.00
C17	AP5	2a rose red & cream	9.50	3.75
C18	AP5	3a dk brn & beige	9.50	3.75
		Nos. C10-C18 (9)	65.50	26.25
		Set, never hinged	120.00	

15th anniversary of independence.

Nos. C10-C18 exist imperf.

TANZANIA

ˌtan-zə-ˈnē-ə

(Tanganyika and Zanzibar)

LOCATION — Southeastern Africa bordering on the Indian Ocean, and a group of islands about 20 miles off the coast

GOVT. — United republic in British Commonwealth

AREA — 364,886 sq. mi.

POP. — 31,270,820 (1999 est.)

CAPITAL — Dodoma

Tanganyika joined Zanzibar on April 26, 1964, to form the United Republic of Tanganyika and Zanzibar. In October 1965 the name was changed to United Republic of Tanzania.

Zanzibar stamps include two (Nos. 331, 334) inscribed "Tanzania."

100 Cents = 1 Shilling

Catalogue values for all unused stamps in this country are for Never Hinged items.

Watermark

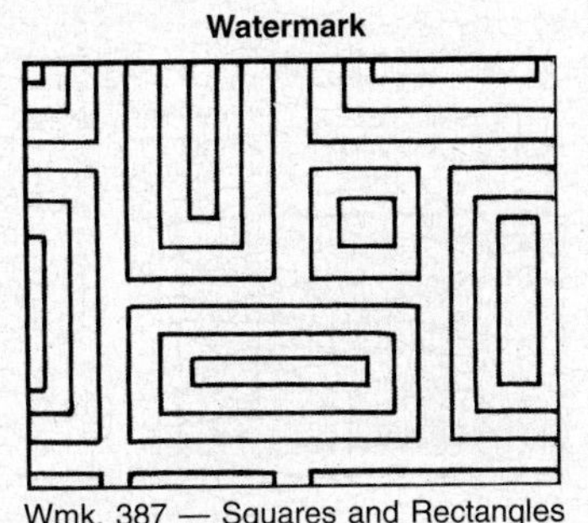

Wmk. 387 — Squares and Rectangles

Map — A1

Design: 30c, 1sh30c, Emblem (hands holding torch and spear).

Perf. 14x14½

1964, July 7 Photo. Unwmk.

1	A1	20c blue & emerald	.25	.25
2	A1	30c brn, dk & lt bl	.25	.25
3	A1	1.30sh ultra, blk & org	.30	.30
4	A1	2.50sh ultra & purple	.65	.65
		Nos. 1-4 (4)	1.45	1.45

Union of Tanganyika and Zanzibar. Not sold in Zanzibar, nor valid there.

Flag
A2

Native Handicraft
A3

Designs: 5c, Hale hydroelectric plant. 15c, Army squad. 20c, Road building. 40c, Giraffes. 50c, Zebras. 65c, Mt. Kilimanjaro. 1sh, Dar es Salaam harbor. 1.30sh, Zinjanthropus skull and Olduvai Gorge excavation. 2.50sh, Sailfish, dhow and map of Mafia Island. 5sh, Sisal industry. 10sh, State House, Dar es Salaam. 20sh, Tanzania coat of arms.

Perf. 14x14½, 14½x14

1965, Dec. 9 Photo. Unwmk.

Size: 21x17½mm, 17½x21mm

5	A2	5c orange & ultra	.40	.60
6	A2	10c ultra, grn, yel & blk	.40	.60
7	A3	15c grn, bl, brn & buff	.40	.60
8	A2	20c blue & brown	.40	.60
9	A3	30c black & red brn	.40	.60
10	A3	40c blue, yel grn & brn	.40	.60
11	A2	50c yellow grn & blue	.40	.60
12	A2	65c ultra, grn & red brn	.50	.75

Perf. 14½

Size: 41½x25, 25x41½mm

13	A2	1sh bl, grn, yel & brn	.60	.60
14	A2	1.30sh multicolored	.90	.60
15	A2	2.50sh blue & red brn	1.30	.95
16	A2	5sh bl, brt grn & red brn	2.60	1.40
17	A2	10sh blue & yellow	5.25	4.00
18	A3	20sh gray & multi	10.00	9.00
		Nos. 5-18 (14)	23.95	21.50

For overprints see Nos. O1-O8.

Turkeyfish — A4

Fish: 5c, Cardinalfish. 10c, Mudskipper. 15c, Toby puffer. 20c, Two sea horses. 30c, Batfish. 40c, Sweetlips. 50c, Birdfish. 65c, Butterflyfish. 70c, Grouper. 1.30sh, Surgeonfish. 1.50sh, Caesio xanthonotus. 2.50sh, Emperor snapper. 5sh, Moorish idol. 10sh, Striped triggerfish. 20sh, Squirrelfish.

1967-71 Photo. *Perf. 14x14½*

Size: 21x17½mm

Fish in Natural Colors

19	A4	5c black & citron	.30	*1.10*
20	A4	10c brown & olive	.30	*1.40*
21	A4	15c brown & blue	.30	.30
22	A4	20c brn & dk bl grn	.30	.30
23	A4	30c black & yel grn	.30	.30
24	A4	40c brown & emerald	.65	.60
25	A4	50c blk & dull bl grn	.30	.20
26	A4	65c blk & gray grn	2.40	*3.00*
27	A4	70c blk & olive ('69)	.95	*2.10*

Perf. 14½

Size: 41x25mm

28	A4	1sh brown & multi	.55	.25
29	A4	1.30sh black & olive	3.00	.25
30	A4	1.50sh black & ol ('69)	1.60	.25
31	A4	2.50sh brn yel & grn	2.40	.25
32	A4	5sh black & bl grn	3.50	.25
33	A4	10sh brn & gray grn	2.75	.60
34	A4	20sh blk & gray olive	5.50	1.75
		Nos. 19-34 (16)	25.10	12.90

Issued: #27, 30, 9/15/69; others, 12/9/67.

Values of Nos. 28-34 are for canceled-to-order stamps with printed cancellations. Postally used examples sell for higher prices.

For overprints see Nos. O9-O16.

Papilio Hornimani
A5

Euphaedra Neophron
A6

Butterflies: 10c, Colotis ione. 15c, Amauris makuyuensis. 20c, Libythea laius. 30c, Danaus chrysippus. 40c, Sallya rosa. 50c, Axiocerses styx. 60c, Eurema hecabe. 70c, Acraea insignis. 1.50sh, Precis octavia. 2.50sh, Charaxes eupale. 5sh, Charaxes pollux. 10sh, Salamis parhassus. 20sh, Papilio ophidicephalus.

1973, Dec. 3 Photo. *Perf. 14½x14*

35	A5	5c yellow grn & multi	.35	.35
a.		Booklet pane of 4	1.40	
36	A5	10c lt brown & multi	.35	.35
a.		Booklet pane of 4	1.40	
37	A5	15c ultra & multi	.35	.35
38	A5	20c fawn & multi	.35	.35
a.		Booklet pane of 4	1.40	
39	A5	30c yellow & multi	.35	.35
a.		Booklet pane of 4	1.50	
40	A5	40c multicolored	.35	.35
a.		Booklet pane of 4	1.60	
41	A5	50c citron & multi	.35	.35
a.		Booklet pane of 4	1.50	
42	A5	60c multicolored	.35	.35
43	A5	70c brt green & multi	.35	.35
a.		Booklet pane of 4	1.75	

Perf. 14½

44	A6	1sh green & multi	.60	.50
45	A6	1.50sh orange & multi	1.00	.80
46	A6	2.50sh multicolored	1.75	1.40
47	A6	5sh multicolored	4.00	3.25
48	A6	10sh lt green & multi	7.50	6.00
49	A6	20sh blue & multi	16.50	12.00
		Nos. 35-49 (15)	34.50	27.10

For surcharges and overprints see Nos. 50-53, 135-136, O17-O26.

Nos. 42, 45-46, 49 Surcharged with New Value and 2 Bars

Perf. 14½x14, 14½

1975, Nov. 17 Photo.

50	A5	80c on 60c multi	*4.00*	*3.75*
51	A6	2sh on 1.50sh multi	*8.00*	*7.50*
52	A6	3sh on 2.50sh multi	*24.00*	*29.00*
53	A6	40sh on 20sh multi	*12.00*	*14.00*
		Nos. 50-53 (4)	*48.00*	*54.25*

A6a

Designs: 50c, Microwave tower. 1sh, Cordless switchboard and operators, horiz. 2sh, Telephones of 1880, 1930 and 1976. 3sh, Message switching center, horiz.

1976, Apr. 15 Litho. *Perf. 14½*

54	A6a 50c blue & multi	.25	.25
55	A6a 1sh red & multi	.25	.25
56	A6a 2sh yellow & multi	.25	.30
57	A6a 3sh multicolored	.35	.40
a.	Souvenir sheet of 4	2.00	2.00
	Nos. 54-57 (4)	1.10	1.20

Telecommunications development in East Africa. No. 57a contains 4 stamps similar to Nos. 54-57 with simulated perforations.

Exist imperf. from Format International liquidation stock.

A6b

Designs: 50c, Akii Bua, Ugandan hurdler. 1sh, Filbert Bayi, Tanzanian runner. 2sh, Steve Muchoki, Kenyan boxer. 3sh, Olympic torch, flags of Kenya, Tanzania and Uganda.

1976, July 5 Litho. *Perf. 14½*

58	A6b 50c blue & multi	.25	.25
59	A6b 1sh red & multi	.25	.25
60	A6b 2sh yellow & multi	.25	.25
61	A6b 3sh blue & multi	.30	.35
a.	Souv. sheet of 4, #58-61, perf. 13	4.25	4.25
	Nos. 58-61 (4)	1.05	1.10

21st Olympic Games, Montreal, Canada, July 17-Aug. 1.

Exist imperf. from Format International liquidation stock.

A6c

Rail Transport in East Africa: 50c, Tanzania-Zambia Railway. 1sh, Nile Bridge, Uganda. 2sh, Nakuru Station, Kenya. 3sh, Class A locomotive, 1896.

1976, Oct. 4 Litho. *Perf. 14½*

62	A6c 50c lilac & multi	.25	.25
63	A6c 1sh emerald & multi	.30	.25
64	A6c 2sh brt rose & multi	.60	.35
65	A6c 3sh yellow & multi	.90	.60
a.	Souv. sheet of 4, #62-65, perf. 13	8.00	8.00
	Nos. 62-65 (4)	2.05	1.45

A6d

1977, Jan. 10 Litho. *Perf. 14½*

66	A6d 50c Nile perch	.25	.25
67	A6d 1sh Tilapia	.50	.45
68	A6d 3sh Sailfish	1.25	1.00
69	A6d 5sh Black marlin	2.25	2.25
a.	Souvenir sheet of 4, #66-69	4.25	3.50
	Nos. 66-69 (4)	4.25	3.95

A6e

50c, Masai tribesmen bleeding cow. 1sh, Dancers from Uganda. 2sh, Makonde sculpture. 3sh, Tribesmen skinning hippopotamus.

1977, Jan. 15 *Perf. 13½x14*

70	A6e 50c multicolored	.25	.25
71	A6e 1sh multicolored	.25	.25
72	A6e 2sh multicolored	.40	.30
73	A6e 3sh multicolored	.65	.45
a.	Souvenir sheet of 4, #70-73	2.25	2.25
	Nos. 70-73 (4)	1.55	1.25

2nd World Black and African Festival, Lagos, Nigeria, Jan. 15-Feb. 12.

A6f

50c, Automobile passing through village. 1sh, Winner at finish line. 2sh, Car going through washout. 5sh, Car, elephants and Mt. Kenya.

1977, Apr. 5 Litho. *Perf. 14*

74	A6f 50c multicolored	.25	.25
75	A6f 1sh multicolored	.25	.25
76	A6f 2sh multicolored	.55	.30
77	A6f 5sh multicolored	1.40	.85
a.	Souvenir sheet of 4, #74-77	3.25	3.25
	Nos. 74-77 (4)	2.45	1.65

25th Safari rally, Apr. 7-11.

A6g

Designs: 50c, Rev. Canon Apolo Kivebulaya. 1sh, Uganda Cathedral. 2sh, Early grass-topped Cathedral. 5sh, Early tent congregation, Kigezi.

1977, June 20 Litho. *Perf. 14*

78	A6g 50c multicolored	.25	.25
79	A6g 1sh multicolored	.25	.25
80	A6g 2sh multicolored	.25	.25
81	A6g 5sh multicolored	.65	.55
a.	Souvenir sheet of 4, #78-81	2.50	2.50
	Nos. 78-81 (4)	1.40	1.30

Church of Uganda, centenary.

A6h

Endangered species: 50c, Pancake tortoise. 1sh, Nile crocodile. 2sh, Hunter's hartebeest. 3sh, Red Colobus monkey. 5sh, Dugong.

1977, Sept. 26 Litho. *Perf. 14x13½*

82	A6h 50c multicolored	1.00	.35
83	A6h 1sh multicolored	2.40	.60
84	A6h 2sh multicolored	4.75	2.25
85	A6h 3sh multicolored	8.00	3.25
86	A6h 5sh multicolored	10.50	6.00
a.	Souvenir sheet of 4, #83-86	11.00	11.00
	Nos. 82-86 (5)	26.65	12.45

Prince Philip and Julius Nyerere, 1961 — A7

5sh, Queen Elizabeth II, Prince Philip, Prime Minister Nyerere in London, 1975. 10sh, Royal crown, flags of Tanzania and Commonwealth nations. 20sh, Coronation.

1977, Nov. 23 Litho. *Perf. 14x13½*

87	A7 50c multicolored	.25	.25
88	A7 5sh multicolored	.25	.25
89	A7 10sh multicolored	.25	.25
90	A7 20sh multicolored	.40	.40
a.	Souvenir sheet of 4, #87-90	1.25	1.25
	Nos. 87-90 (4)	1.15	1.15

25th anniv. of reign of Elizabeth II.

For overprints see Nos. 99-102, 179-180.

Women Fetching Water from Stream and Tap — A8

1sh, Flag raising. 3sh, Health care, laboratory and hospital. 5sh, Pres. Julius Nyerere.

1978, Feb. 5 Litho. *Perf. 13½x14*

91	A8 50c multicolored	.25	.25
92	A8 1sh multicolored	.25	.25
93	A8 3sh multicolored	.25	.25
94	A8 5sh multicolored	.35	.35
a.	Souvenir sheet of 4, #91-94	1.25	1.25
	Nos. 91-94 (4)	1.10	1.10

First anniversary of the New Revolutionary Party (Chama cha Mapinduzi).

A8a

50c, Soccer scene and Joe Kadenge. 1sh, Mohammed Chuma receiving trophy, and his portrait. 2sh, Shot on goal and Omari S. Kidevu. 3sh, Backfield defense and Polly Ouma.

1978, Apr. 17 Litho. *Perf. 14x13½*

95	A8a 50c green & multi	.25	.25
96	A8a 1sh lt brown & multi	.25	.25
97	A8a 2sh lilac & multi	.25	.25
98	A8a 3sh dk blue & multi	.35	.35
a.	Souvenir sheet of 4, #95-98	2.50	2.50
	Nos. 95-98 (4)	1.10	1.10

World Soccer Cup Championships, Argentina '78, June 1-25.

Nos. 87-90a Overprinted

Large Serifed Letters

Small Sans Serif Letters

1978, June 2

99	A7 50c multicolored	.25	.25
100	A7 5sh multicolored	.25	.25
101	A7 10sh multicolored	.25	.25
102	A7 20sh multicolored	.30	.30
a.	Souvenir sheet of 4, #99-102	1.00	1.00
	Nos. 99-102 (4)	1.05	1.05

25th anniv. of coronation of Elizabeth II.

Nos. 99-102a also exist overprinted with smaller, sans serif letters, perf. 12. Same values or less. The perf. 12 set does not exist without overprint.

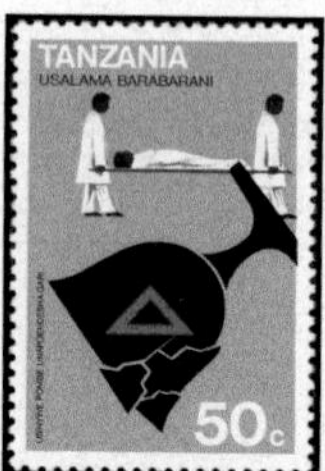

"Do not Drink when Driving" — A9

Designs: 1sh, "Courtesy to the young, old and handicapped." 3sh, "Observe highway code." 5sh, "Do not drive faulty vehicle."

1978, July 1 Litho. *Perf. 13½x13*

103	A9 50c multicolored	.25	.25
104	A9 1sh multicolored	.25	.25
105	A9 3sh multicolored	.40	.40
106	A9 5sh multicolored	1.60	1.60
a.	Souv. sheet, #103-106, perf. 14	2.75	2.75
	Nos. 103-106 (4)	2.50	2.50

Road Safety Campaign.

Lake Manyara Hotel — A10

Designs: 1sh, Lobo Wildlife Lodge. 3sh, Ngorongoro Crater Lodge. 5sh, Ngorongoro Wildlife Lodge. 10sh, Mafia Island Lodge. 20sh, Mikumi Wildlife Lodge.

1978, Sept. 11 Litho. *Perf. 13½*

107	A10 50c multicolored	.25	.25
108	A10 1sh multicolored	.25	.25
109	A10 3sh multicolored	.25	.25
110	A10 5sh multicolored	.40	.40
111	A10 10sh multicolored	.80	.80
112	A10 20sh multicolored	1.75	1.75
a.	Souvenir sheet of 6, #107-112	7.75	7.75
	Nos. 107-112 (6)	3.70	3.70

Game Lodges of Tanzania.

Chained African — A11

1sh, Division of races (black and white heads). 2.50sh, Racial harmony (black and white handshake and heads). 5sh, End of suppression and rise of freedom (hands breaking loose from chains).

1978, Oct. 24 Litho. *Perf. 14½x14*

113	A11 50c multicolored	.25	.25
114	A11 1sh multicolored	.25	.25
115	A11 2.50sh multicolored	.40	.40
116	A11 5sh multicolored	.80	.80
a.	Souvenir sheet of 4, #113-116	2.25	2.25
	Nos. 113-116 (4)	1.70	1.70

Anti-Apartheid Year.

Fokker Friendship at Dar Es Salaam Airport — A12

Designs: 1sh, Single-engine Dragon, 1930, Zanzibar. 2sh, British Airways Concorde. 5sh, Wright Brothers' Flyer 1, 1903.

1978, Dec. 28 Litho. *Perf. 13½*

117	A12 50c multicolored	.30	.30
118	A12 1sh multicolored	.45	.45
119	A12 2sh multicolored	.85	.85
120	A12 5sh multicolored	2.10	2.10
a.	Souvenir sheet of 4, #117-120	4.25	4.25
	Nos. 117-120 (4)	3.70	3.70

75th anniversary of 1st powered flight.

Emblem A13

Design: 5sh, Headquarters buildings.

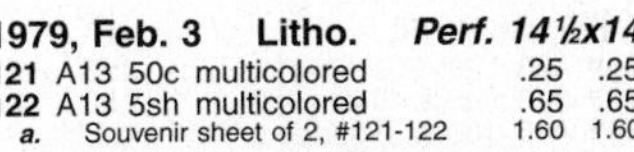

1979, Feb. 3 Litho. *Perf. 14½x14*

121	A13	50c multicolored	.25	.25
122	A13	5sh multicolored	.65	.65
a.		Souvenir sheet of 2, #121-122	1.60	1.60

Tanzania Post and Telecommunications Corporation, 1st anniversary.

Pres. Nyerere and Children — A14

Designs (UNICEF and Tanzanian IYC Emblems and): 1sh, Kindergarten. 2sh, Vaccination of infant. 5sh, Emblems.

1979, June 25 Litho. *Perf. 14½*

123	A14	50c multicolored	.25	.25
124	A14	1sh multicolored	.25	.25
125	A14	2sh multicolored	.25	.25
126	A14	5sh multicolored	.40	.40
a.		Souvenir sheet of 4, #123-126	2.10	2.10
		Nos. 123-126 (4)	1.15	1.15

International Year of the Child.

Tree Planting — A15

Forest Preservation and Expansion: 1sh, Seedling. 2sh, Rainfall. 5sh, Forest fire.

1979, Sept. 29 Litho. *Perf. 14½*

127	A15	50c multicolored	.25	.25
128	A15	1sh multicolored	.35	.35
129	A15	2sh multicolored	.60	.60
130	A15	5sh multicolored	1.60	1.60
		Nos. 127-130 (4)	2.80	2.80

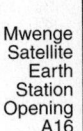

Mwenge Satellite Earth Station Opening A16

1979, Dec. 3 Litho. *Perf. 13½*

131	A16	10c multicolored	.25	.25
132	A16	40c multicolored	.25	.25
133	A16	50c multicolored	.25	.25
134	A16	1sh multicolored	.25	.25
		Nos. 131-134 (4)	1.00	1.00

Nos. 36, 43 Surcharged

1979 Litho. *Perf. 14½x14*

135	A5	40c (10 + 30) multi	4.00	4.00
136	A5	50c on 70c multi	6.00	6.00

Tabata Dispensary, Dar-es-Salaam, Rotary Emblem — A17

1sh, Ngomvu water project. 5sh, Flying doctor service. 20sh, Torch, anniversary emblem.

1980, Mar. 1 Litho. *Perf. 13x13½*

137	A17	50c shown	.25	.25
138	A17	1sh multicolored	.25	.25
139	A17	5sh multicolored	.45	.45
140	A17	20sh multicolored	2.00	2.00
a.		Souvenir sheet of 4, #137-140	2.75	2.75
		Nos. 137-140 (4)	2.95	2.95

Rotary International, 75th anniversary.
For overprints see Nos. 149-152.

Zanzibar Nos. 49 and 309, "Stamp History" Cancel A18

Cancel and: 50c, Tanganyika #58, postal worker, vert. 10sh, Tanganyika #16, 52. 20sh, Penny Black, Rowland Hill, vert.

1980, Apr. *Perf. 14*

141	A18	40c multicolored	.25	.25
142	A18	50c multicolored	.25	.25
143	A18	10sh multicolored	.50	.50
144	A18	20sh multicolored	1.00	1.00
a.		Souvenir sheet of 4, #141-144	2.75	2.75
		Nos. 141-144 (4)	2.00	2.00

Sir Rowland Hill (1795-1879), originator of penny postage; Tanzanian stamp history.

Overprinted: "LONDON 1980" / PHILATELIC EXHIBITION

1980, May 6 Litho. *Perf. 14*

145	A18	40c multicolored	.25	.25
146	A18	50c multicolored	.25	.25
147	A18	10sh multicolored	.50	.50
148	A18	20sh multicolored	1.00	1.00
a.		Souvenir sheet of 4, #145-148	2.75	2.75
		Nos. 145-148 (4)	2.00	2.00

London 80 Intl. Stamp Exhib., May 6-14.

Nos. 137-140a with Additional Inscription on 1 or 2 Lines: "District 920-55th Annual / Conference, Arusha, Tanzania"

1980, June 23 Litho. *Perf. 13x13½*

149	A17	50c multicolored	.25	.25
150	A17	1sh multicolored	.25	.25
151	A17	5sh multicolored	.65	.65
152	A17	20sh multicolored	2.75	2.75
a.		Souvenir sheet of 4, #149-152	4.00	4.00
		Nos. 149-152 (4)	3.90	3.90

District 920 Rotary Club, 55th Annual Conference, Arusha.

Pan African Postal Union and U.P.U. Emblems A19

1980, July 1 *Perf. 13x13½*

153	A19	50c purple & blk	.25	.25
154	A19	1sh ultra & blk	.25	.25
155	A19	5sh red orange & blk	.50	.50
156	A19	10sh green & blk	1.00	1.00
		Nos. 153-156 (4)	2.00	2.00

Pan African Postal Union Plenipotentiary Conference, Arusha, Jan. 8-18.

Gidamis Shahanga, Marathon — A20

Tanzanian Olympic Team: 1sh, Nzael Kyomo and sprinters. 10sh, Zakayo Malekwa and javelin. 20sh, William Lyimo and boxers.

1980, Aug. 18 Litho. *Perf. 13x13½*

157	A20	50c multicolored	.25	.25
158	A20	1sh multicolored	.25	.25
159	A20	10sh multicolored	.75	.75
160	A20	20sh multicolored	1.75	1.75
a.		Souvenir sheet of 4, #157-160	3.50	3.50
		Nos. 157-160 (4)	3.00	3.00

22nd Summer Olympic Games, Moscow, July 19-Aug. 3.
Issued also in sheets of 20 (5 of each value).

Spring Hare — A21

1980, Oct. 1 Litho. *Perf. 14*

161	A21	10c shown	.25	.25
162	A21	20c Genet	.25	.25
163	A21	40c Mongoose	.25	.25
164	A21	50c Ratel	.25	.25
165	A21	75c Rock hyrax	.25	.25
166	A21	80c Leopard	.25	.25

Perf. 14½
Size: 40x24mm

167	A21	1sh Impalas	.25	.25
168	A21	1.50sh Giraffes	.25	.25
169	A21	2sh Zebras	.25	.25
170	A21	3sh Buffalo	.25	.25
171	A21	5sh Lions	.30	.40
172	A21	10sh Rhinoceros	.65	.80
173	A21	20sh Elephants	1.30	1.60
174	A21	40sh Cheetahs	2.60	3.25
		Nos. 161-174 (14)	7.35	8.55

For overprints see Nos. O27-O36.

National Parks Emblem A22

50c, Ngorongoro Park. 5sh, Friends of Serengeti. 20sh, Friends of Ngorongoro.

1981, Jan. 26 Litho. *Perf. 13x13½*

175	A22	50c multicolored	.25	.25
176	A22	1sh shown	.25	.25
177	A22	5sh multicolored	.50	.50
178	A22	20sh multicolored	2.00	2.00
		Nos. 175-178 (4)	3.00	3.00

Ngorongoro & Serengeti Parks, 60th anniv.
For overprints see Nos. 299-302.

Nos. 89-90 Overprinted

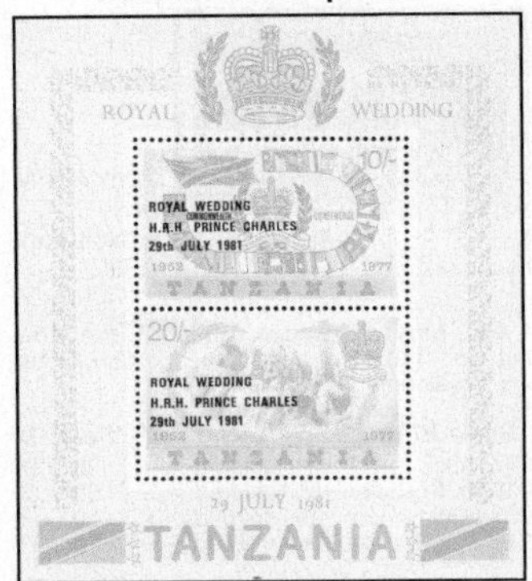

1981, July 29 Litho. *Perf. 14x13½*

179	A7	10sh multicolored	.35	.35
180	A7	20sh multicolored	.65	.65
a.		Souvenir sheet of 2, #179-180	5.50	5.50

Mail Runner A23

1sh, Letter sorting. 5sh, Post horn, carrier pigeon. 10sh, Commonwealth members' flags.

1981, Oct. 23 Litho. *Perf. 12½x12*

181	A23	50c shown	.25	.25
182	A23	1sh multicolored	.25	.25
183	A23	5sh multicolored	.55	.55
184	A23	10sh multicolored	1.20	1.20
a.		Souvenir sheet of 4, #181-184	2.75	2.75
		Nos. 181-184 (4)	2.25	2.25

Commonwealth Postal Administrations Conference, Arusha, June 29-July 10.

Intl. Year of the Disabled A24

1981, Nov. 30 Litho. *Perf. 14*

185	A24	50c Morris Nyunyusa, blind drummer	.30	.30
186	A24	1sh Sewing	.40	.40
187	A24	5sh Prostheses	1.40	1.40
188	A24	10sh Children	2.75	2.75
		Nos. 185-188 (4)	4.85	4.85

20th Anniv. of Independence — A25

1982, Jan. 13 Litho. *Perf. 13x13½*

189	A25	50c Pres. Nyerere, flag	.25	.25
190	A25	1sh Zanzibar Electricity Plant	.25	.25
191	A25	3sh Sisal plant, weaver	.50	.50
192	A25	10sh Pupils	1.75	1.75
a.		Souvenir sheet of 4, #189-192	3.00	3.00
		Nos. 189-192 (4)	2.75	2.75

Ostrich — A26

1982, Jan. 25 Litho. *Perf. 13½*

193	A26	50c shown	.65	.65
194	A26	1sh Secretary bird	1.00	1.00
195	A26	5sh Kori bustard	4.25	4.25
196	A26	10sh Saddle-bill stork	8.00	8.00
		Nos. 193-196 (4)	13.90	13.90

1982 World Cup A27

1982, June 2 Litho. *Perf. 14*

197	A27	50c Jella Mtagwa	.35	.35
198	A27	1sh Stadium	.35	.35
199	A27	10sh Diego Armando Maradona	3.00	3.00
200	A27	20sh Globe	6.50	6.50
a.		Souvenir sheet of 4, #197-200	10.50	10.50
		Nos. 197-200 (4)	10.20	10.20

Jade of Seronera and her Cubs A28

Animals Appearing in Movies or TV Shows: 1sh, Wild dog and puppies, Havoc. 5sh, Fifi and sons, Gombe. 10sh, Bahati and twins Rashidi and Ramadhani, Lake Manyara.

1982, July 15 Litho. *Perf. 14*

201	A28	50c multicolored	.30	.30
202	A28	1sh multicolored	.45	.45
203	A28	5sh multicolored	1.45	1.45
204	A28	10sh multicolored	3.00	3.00
a.		Souv. sheet, #201-204, perf. 14½	6.25	6.25
		Nos. 201-204 (4)	5.20	5.20

Scouting Year A29

1982, Aug. 25

205	A29	50c Brick laying	.25	.25
206	A29	1sh Camping	.25	.25
207	A29	10sh Tracing marks	1.75	1.75

208 A29 20sh Baden-Powell 3.75 3.75
a. Souvenir sheet of 4, #205-208 6.50 6.50
Nos. 205-208 (4) 6.00 6.00

For overprint see No. 303.

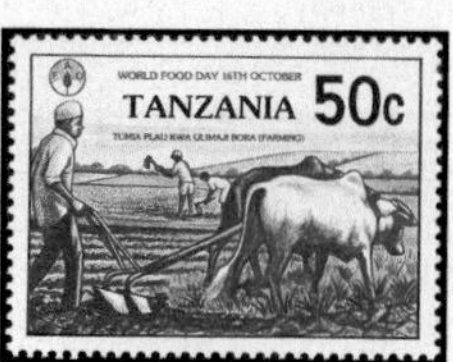

World Food Day — A30

1982, Oct. 16 Litho. *Perf. 14*
209 A30 50c Plowing .25 .25
210 A30 1sh Dairy cows .25 .25
211 A30 5sh Corn harvest .90 .90
212 A30 10sh Grain storage 1.75 1.75
a. Souvenir sheet of 4, #209-212 3.25 3.25
Nos. 209-212 (4) 3.15 3.15

TB Bacillus Centenary A31

1982, Dec. 5 *Perf. 12½x12*
213 A31 50c Child immunization .25 .25
214 A31 1sh Koch .25 .25
215 A31 5sh TB emblem .90 .90
216 A31 10sh WHO emblem 1.75 1.75
Nos. 213-216 (4) 3.15 3.15

A31a

1983, Mar. 14 Litho. *Perf. 14*
217 A31a 50c Pres. Nyerere .25 .25
218 A31a 1sh Running, boxing .25 .25
219 A31a 5sh Flags .75 .75
220 A31a 10sh Pres. Nyerere, Royal Family 1.50 1.50
a. Souvenir sheet of 4, #217-220 3.00 3.00
Nos. 217-220 (4) 2.75 2.75

Commonwealth Day. For overprint see #407.

5th Anniv. of Posts and Telecommunications Dept. — A32

1983, Feb. 3 Litho. *Perf. 12½x12*
221 A32 50c Letter post .25 .25
222 A32 1sh Training Institute .25 .25
223 A32 5sh Satellite communications .75 .75
224 A32 10sh Emblems 1.50 1.50
a. Souvenir sheet of 4, #221-224 2.75 2.75
Nos. 221-224 (4) 2.75 2.75

25th Anniv. of Economic Commission for Africa — A33

50c, Eastern & Southern African Management Institute, Arusha. 1sh, Emblems. 5sh, Mineral collections. 10sh, Emblems, diff.

1983, Sept. 12 Litho. *Perf. 12½x12*
225 A33 50c multicolored .45 .45
226 A33 1sh multicolored .60 .60
227 A33 5sh multicolored 2.40 2.40
228 A33 10sh multicolored 4.75 4.75
a. Souvenir sheet of 4, #225-228 8.25 8.25
Nos. 225-228 (4) 8.20 8.20

World Communications Year — A34

1983, Oct. 17 Litho. *Perf. 14*
229 A34 50c Rural telephone service .25 .25
230 A34 1sh Emblems .25 .25
231 A34 5sh Post Office 1.00 1.00
232 A34 10sh Microwave tower 2.00 2.00
a. Souvenir sheet of 4, #229-232 3.50 3.50
Nos. 229-232 (4) 3.50 3.50

Historical Buildings A35

1983, Dec. 12 Litho. *Perf. 12½x12*
233 A35 1sh Bagamoyo Boma .25 .25
234 A35 1.50sh Beit-El-Ajaib .30 .30
235 A35 5sh Anglican Church .70 .70
236 A35 10sh State House, old and new 1.25 1.25
a. Souvenir sheet of 4, #233-236 2.75 2.75
Nos. 233-236 (4) 2.50 2.50

20th Anniv. of Revolution A36

1sh, Muasisi Kwanza. 1.50sh, Clove farming. 5sh, Industrial development. 10sh, Housing developments. 15sh, Map, ship.

1984, June 18 Litho. *Perf. 14*
237 A36 1sh multicolored .25 .25
238 A36 1.50sh multicolored .30 .30
239 A36 5sh multicolored .90 .90
240 A36 10sh multicolored 1.75 1.75
Nos. 237-240 (4) 3.20 3.20

Souvenir Sheet
241 A36 15sh multicolored 3.25 3.25

1984 Summer Olympics A37

1984, Aug. 6 *Perf. 12½x12*
242 A37 1sh Boxing .25 .25
243 A37 1.50sh Running .25 .25
244 A37 5sh Basketball .70 .70
245 A37 20sh Soccer 2.00 2.00
a. Souvenir sheet of 4, #242-245 3.50 3.50
Nos. 242-245 (4) 3.20 3.20

For overprints see Nos. 275-278.

Intl. Civil Aviation Org. 40th Anniv. A38

1sh, Icarus. 1.50sh, Air Tanzania jets, traffic controller. 5sh, Aircraft maintenance. 10sh, ICAO emblem.

1984, Nov. 15 Litho. *Perf. 13*
246 A38 1sh multicolored .25 .25
247 A38 1.50sh multicolored .25 .25
248 A38 5sh multicolored .90 .90
249 A38 10sh multicolored 1.40 1.40
a. Souvenir sheet of 4, #246-249 3.25 3.25
Nos. 246-249 (4) 2.80 2.80

Traditional Houses A39

1984, Dec. 20 *Perf. 12½x12*
250 A39 1sh Sochi .25 .25
251 A39 1.50sh Isyenga .25 .25
252 A39 5sh Tembe .60 .60
253 A39 10sh Banda 1.10 1.10
a. Souvenir sheet of 4, #250-253 2.50 2.50
Nos. 250-253 (4) 2.20 2.20

Textile Industry A40

5th anniversary of the Southern Africa Development Coordination Conference — 4sh, Mining. 5sh, Transportation and communications. 20sh, Flags of member nations.

1985, Apr. 1 *Perf. 14*
254 A40 1.50sh shown .50 .50
255 A40 4sh multicolored 1.25 1.25
256 A40 5sh multicolored 1.40 1.40
257 A40 20sh multicolored 6.00 6.00
a. Souvenir sheet of 4, #254-257 10.00 10.00
Nos. 254-257 (4) 9.15 9.15

Rare Species of Zanzibar A41

Perf. 13½x13, 13x13½
1985, May 8 Litho.
258 A41 1sh Tortoise .50 .50
259 A41 4sh Leopard 1.50 1.50
260 A41 10sh Civet cat 3.00 3.00
261 A41 17.50sh Red colobus, vert. 4.75 4.75
Nos. 258-261 (4) 9.75 9.75

Souvenir Sheet
262 Sheet of 2 4.25 4.25
a. A41 15sh Black rhinoceros 1.75 1.75
b. A41 20sh Giant ground pangolin 2.50 2.50

For overprints see Nos. 408-409, 411.

Automobile Centenary — A42

Classic autos manufactured by Rolls-Royce.

1985, May 14 *Perf. 14½x14*
263 A42 1.50sh 1936 20/25 .25 .25
264 A42 5sh 1933 Phantom II .25 .25
265 A42 10sh 1926 Phantom I .25 .25
266 A42 30sh 1907 Silver Ghost .70 .70
a. Souvenir sheet of 4, #263-266 2.25 2.25
Nos. 263-266 (4) 1.45 1.45

Queen Mother, 85th Birthday — A43

1985, Sept. 30
267 A43 20sh Waving .25 .25
268 A43 20sh Facing left .25 .25
269 A43 100sh Wearing green hat .25 .25
a. Souvenir sheet, #267, 269 .75 .75
270 A43 100sh Facing right .25 .25
a. Souvenir sheet, #268, 270 .75 .75
Nos. 267-270 (4) 1.00 1.00

For overprints see Nos. 295-298.

Tanzania Railways Locomotives — A44

1985, Oct. 7 Litho. *Perf. 14½x14*
271 A44 5sh No. 3022 .25 .25
272 A44 10sh No. 3107 .25 .25
273 A44 20sh No. 6004 .35 .35
274 A44 30sh No. 3129 .55 .55
a. Souvenir sheet of 4, #271-274 1.25 1.25
Nos. 271-274 (4) 1.40 1.40

Nos. 242-245 Ovptd. with Winners and "GOLD MEDAL" in 2 or 3 Lines

1985, Oct. 22 *Perf. 12½x12*
275 A37 1sh Henry Tillman, USA .30 .30
276 A37 1.50sh USA .30 .30
277 A37 5sh USA .70 .70
278 A37 20sh France 2.10 2.10
a. Souvenir sheet of 4, #275-278 8.75 8.75
Nos. 275-278 (4) 3.40 3.40

Pottery A45

1.50sh, Water and cooking pots. 2sh, Frying pot and caldron. 5sh, Woman selling pots. 40sh, Beer pot.
30sh, Water pot.

1985, Nov. 4
279 A45 1.50sh multicolored .25 .25
280 A45 2sh multicolored .25 .25
281 A45 5sh multicolored .35 .35
282 A45 40sh multicolored 3.00 3.00
Nos. 279-282 (4) 3.85 3.85

Souvenir Sheet
283 A45 30sh multicolored 4.00 4.00

Locomotives — A46

1.50sh, Class 64. 2sh, Class 36. 5sh, Shunting DFH1013. 10sh, Diesel Electric DE1001. 30sh, Zanzibar, 1906.

1985, Nov. 25
284 A46 1.50sh multi .25 .25
285 A46 2sh multi .25 .25
286 A46 5sh multi .60 .60
287 A46 10sh multi 1.25 1.25
288 A46 30sh multi 3.50 3.50
Nos. 284-288 (5) 5.85 5.85

Souvenir Sheet
289 Sheet of 2 8.50 8.50
a. A46 15sh Class 30 steam 3.75 3.75
b. A46 20sh Class 11 steam 4.75 4.75

For overprints see Nos. 381A-381E.

Intl. Youth Year — A47

1986, Jan. 20 *Perf. 14*

290 A47 1.50sh Young Pioneers .25 .25
291 A47 4sh Health care .45 .45
292 A47 10sh Uhuru torch race .90 .90
293 A47 20sh World map 1.60 1.60
Nos. 290-293 (4) 3.20 3.20

Souvenir Sheet

294 A47 30sh Agriculture 3.50 3.50

Nos. 267-270 Ovptd. "CARIBBEAN/ ROYAL VISIT/ 1985" in Silver or Gold

1986, Feb. 10 *Perf. 14½x14*

295 A43 20sh on #267 *9.00 9.00*
296 A43 20sh on #268 *9.00 9.00*
297 A43 100sh on #269 *9.00 9.00*
a. Souvenir sheet, #295, 297 *20.00* —
298 A43 100sh on #270 *9.00 9.00*
a. Souvenir sheet, #296, 298 *20.00* —
Nos. 295-298 (4) 36.00 36.00

See footnote following No. 303.

Nos. 175-178, 208a Ovptd. "75th ANNIVERSARY GIRL GUIDES/ 1910-1985" in Silver or Black

1986, Feb. Litho. *Perf. 13x13½, 14*

299 A22 50c multicolored (S) *15.00 15.00*
300 A22 1sh multicolored *15.00 15.00*
301 A22 5sh multicolored *15.00 15.00*
302 A22 20sh multicolored *15.00 15.00*

Souvenir Sheet

303 Sheet of 4 *45.00 45.00*
a. A29 50c multicolored — —
b. A29 1sh multicolored — —
c. A29 10sh multicolored — —
d. A29 20sh multicolored — —

The status of this set, the Caribbean Royal Visit set and at least 12 stamps overprinted congratulating the Duke and Duchess of York on their marriage are in question.

Rotary Intl., World Chess Championships — A48

1986, Mar. 17 *Perf. 14*

304 A48 20sh shown .25 .25
305 A48 100sh Chess board 1.25 1.25
a. Souvenir sheet of 2, #304-305 1.75 1.75

Audubon Birth Bicent. — A49

Illustrations of American bird species by Audubon.

1986, May 22

306 A49 5sh Mallard .30 .30
307 A49 10sh American eider .30 .30
308 A49 20sh Scarlet ibis .55 .55
309 A49 30sh Roseate spoonbill .85 .85
a. Souvenir sheet of 4, #306-309 3.00 3.00
Nos. 306-309 (4) 2.00 2.00

Gemstones A50

1986, May 22

310 A50 1.50sh Pearls .60 .60
311 A50 2sh Sapphires .70 .70
312 A50 5sh Tanzanite 2.00 2.00
313 A50 40sh Diamonds 11.00 11.00
Nos. 310-313 (4) 14.30 14.30

Souvenir Sheet

314 A50 30sh Rubies 15.00 15.00

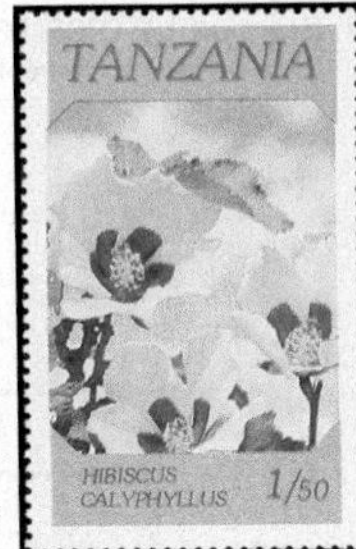

Indigenous Flowers — A51

1.50sh, Hibiscus calyphyllus. 5sh, Aloe graminicola. 10sh, Nersium oleander. 30sh, Nymphaea caerulea.

1986, June 2

315 A51 1.50sh multicolored .25 .25
316 A51 5sh multicolored .25 .25
317 A51 10sh multicolored .25 .25
318 A51 30sh multicolored .35 .35
a. Souvenir Sheet of 4, #315-318 1.00 1.00
Nos. 315-318 (4) 1.10 1.10

Endangered Wildlife — A52

1986, June 30 Litho. *Perf. 14x14½*

319 A52 5sh Oryx .25 .25
320 A52 10sh Giraffe .25 .25
321 A52 20sh Rhinoceros .30 .30
322 A52 30sh Cheetah .40 .40
a. Miniature sheet of 4, #319-322 1.25 1.25
Nos. 319-322 (4) 1.20 1.20

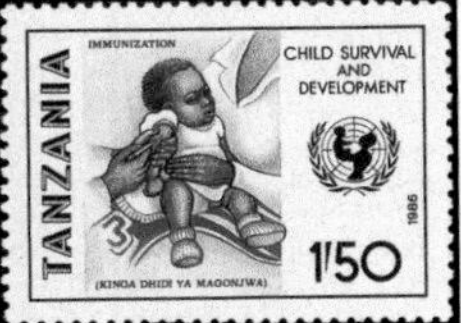

UN Child Survival Campaign A53

1.50sh, Immunization. 2sh, Growth monitoring. 5sh, Oral rehydration therapy. 40sh, Breast feeding.
30sh, Healthy child.

1986, July 29 *Perf. 12½x12*

323 A53 1.50sh multicolored .35 .35
324 A53 2sh multicolored .35 .35
325 A53 5sh multicolored .35 .35
326 A53 40sh multicolored 2.75 2.75
Nos. 323-326 (4) 3.80 3.80

Souvenir Sheet

327 A53 30sh multicolored 2.00 2.00

For overprints see Nos. 406, 410, 412.

Marine Life A54

1986, Aug. 20

328 A54 1.50sh Butterflyfish .80 .80
329 A54 4sh Parrotfish 1.75 1.75
330 A54 10sh Sea turtle 3.00 3.00
331 A54 20sh Octopus 4.50 4.50
Nos. 328-331 (4) 10.05 10.05

Souvenir Sheet

332 A54 30sh Coral 3.75 3.75

Queen Elizabeth II, 60th Birthday — A55

Photographs: 5sh, Royal family, Buckingham Palace balcony. 10sh, With princes in open carriage. 40sh, Elizabeth II. 60sh, Greeting crowd.

1987, Mar. 24 Litho. *Perf. 14*

333 A55 5sh multicolored *.20*
334 A55 10sh multicolored *.20*
335 A55 40sh multicolored *.60*
336 A55 60sh multicolored *1.00*
a. Souvenir sheet of 4, #333-336 *2.00*
Nos. 333-336 (4) *2.00*

1986 World Cup Soccer Championships, Mexico — A57

Designs: 1.50sh, Map, team captains, officials. 2sh, Foul. 10sh, Goal. 20sh, Goalie save. 30sh, Argentine natl. team.

1986, Oct. 30 Litho. *Perf. 14*

341 A57 1.50sh multicolored .30 .30
342 A57 2sh multicolored .30 .30
343 A57 10sh multicolored .60 .60
344 A57 20sh multicolored 1.10 1.10
Nos. 341-344 (4) 2.30 2.30

Souvenir Sheet

345 A57 30sh multicolored 1.50 1.50

Hair Styles — A58

1987, Mar. 16 *Perf. 14½*

346 A58 1.50sh Nungu Nungu .40 .40
347 A58 2sh Upanga wa Jogoo .60 .60
348 A58 10sh Morani 1.25 1.25
349 A58 20sh Twende Kilioni 1.75 1.75
Nos. 346-349 (4) 4.00 4.00

Souvenir Sheet

350 A58 30sh Kusuka Nywele 4.00 4.00

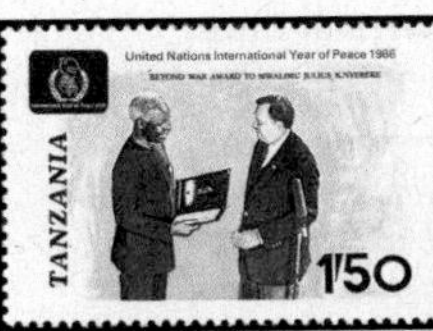

Intl. Peace Year A59

Designs: 1.50sh, Julius K. Nyerere, Beyond War Award winner. 2sh, Peace among nations. 10sh, Peaceful use of outer space. 20sh, Emblem, UN building. 30sh, Emblem, handshake.

1986, Dec. 22 Litho. *Perf. 14½*

351 A59 1.50sh multicolored .55 .55
352 A59 2sh multicolored .85 .85
353 A59 10sh multicolored 2.10 2.10
354 A59 20sh multicolored 3.00 3.00
Nos. 351-354 (4) 6.50 6.50

Souvenir Sheet

355 A59 30sh multicolored 2.75 2.75

Natl. Bank of Commerce, 20th Anniv. — A60

1.50sh, Mobile bank. 2sh, Headquarters. 5sh, Pres. Mwinyi laying foundation stone. 20sh, Cotton harvest.

1987, Feb. 6 Litho. *Perf. 14*

356 A60 1.50sh multicolored .45 .45
357 A60 2sh multicolored .75 .75
358 A60 5sh multicolored 1.25 1.25
359 A60 20sh multicolored 3.00 3.00
Nos. 356-359 (4) 5.45 5.45

New Revolutionary Party (CCM), 10th Anniv. — A61

2sh, Soldiers in formation . 3sh, Woman picking coffee beans. 10sh, Speaker at podium. 30sh, Nyerere, Mwinyi.

1987, Apr. 10 *Perf. 14½x14*

360 A61 2sh multicolored .25 .25
361 A61 3sh multicolored .25 .25
362 A61 10sh multicolored .35 .35
363 A61 30sh multicolored 1.00 1.00
Nos. 360-363 (4) 1.85 1.85

Arush Declaration, 20th anniv.

Insects A62

1987, Apr. 22 *Perf. 12½x12*

364 A62 1.50sh Bees .65 .65
365 A62 2sh Greater grain borer .85 .85
366 A62 10sh Tse-tse fly 1.90 1.90
367 A62 20sh Wasp 3.00 3.00
Nos. 364-367 (4) 6.40 6.40

Souvenir Sheet

368 A62 30sh Mosquito 5.25 5.25

Reptiles A63

1987, July 2

369 A63 2sh Crocodiles .70 .70
370 A63 3sh Black-striped grass snake .70 .70
371 A63 10sh Adder 1.40 1.40
372 A63 20sh Green mamba 2.75 2.75
Nos. 369-372 (4) 5.55 5.55

Souvenir Sheet

373 A63 30sh Tortoise 2.75 2.75

Posts and Telecommunications, Railways Emblems — A64

8sh, Air Tanzania, Port Authority.
20sh, Modes of communication and transportation.

1987, July 27 *Perf. 14*

374 A64 2sh shown .60 .60
375 A64 8sh multicolored 1.40 1.40

Souvenir Sheet

376 A64 20sh multicolored 5.00 5.00

Traditional Crafts A65

1987, Dec. 15 Litho. *Perf. 12½x12*

377 A65 2sh Baskets .30 .30
378 A65 3sh Gourds .30 .30
379 A65 10sh Stools .50 .50
380 A65 20sh Makonde carvings .90 .90
Nos. 377-380 (4) 2.00 2.00

Souvenir Sheet

381 A65 40sh Makonde carver at work 2.00 2.00

Nos. 284-288 Ovptd.

1987, Dec. 30 Litho. *Perf. 12½x12*

381A A46 1.50sh multicolored .70 .70
381B A46 2sh multicolored .70 .70
381C A46 5sh multicolored .85 .85
381D A46 10sh multicolored 1.75 1.75
381E A46 30sh multicolored 5.25 5.25
Nos. 381A-381E (5) 9.25 9.25

Plateosaurus — A66

1988, Apr. 22 *Perf. 12½*

382 A66 2sh shown .60 .60
383 A66 3sh Pteranodon .60 .60
384 A66 5sh Brontosaurus .60 .60
385 A66 7sh Lions .65 .65
386 A66 8sh Tiger .65 .65
387 A66 12sh Orangutans .75 .75
388 A66 20sh Elephants 1.00 1.00
389 A66 100sh Stegosaurus 2.50 2.50
Nos. 382-389 (8) 7.35 7.35

Traditional Games A67

1988, Feb. 15 Litho. *Perf. 12½x12*

390 A67 2sh Mdako (marbles) .50 .50
391 A67 3sh Mieleka (wrestling) .50 .50
392 A67 8sh Bull fight .50 .50
393 A67 20sh Bao (African chess) .80 .80
Nos. 390-393 (4) 2.30 2.30

Souvenir Sheet

394 A67 30sh Kulenga shabaha (archery) 2.00 2.00

Dated 1987.

Miniature Sheets

Statue of Liberty, Cent. (in 1986) — A68

No. 395: 1sh, Re-opening gala (evening), 1986. 2sh, Musicians performing. 3sh, Cheerleaders. 15sh, Statue holding tablet. 30sh, Tablet inscription. 40sh, Liberty Island. 50sh, Re-opening gala (afternoon), 1986. 60sh, Blimps over Liberty Island.

No. 396: 4sh, Statue, blimp. 5sh, Torch. 6sh, Torch and crown observatories lit at night, scaffolding. 7sh, Worker gilding torch. 8sh, Statue shrouded in scaffolding. 10sh, Two workers, torch. 12sh, Head, scaffolding. 18sh, Celebrant at re-opening (evening). 20sh, Goodyear blimp, skirt of Statue. 25sh, Boys' choir, statue. 35sh, Torch held aloft, full moon. 45sh, Worker cleaning tablet.

1988, June 15 Litho. *Perf. 14*

395 A68 Sheet of 8 + label 9.00 9.00
a. 1sh multicolored .25 .25
b. 2sh multicolored .25 .25
c. 3sh multicolored .25 .25
d. 15sh multicolored .60 .60
e. 30sh multicolored 1.25 1.25
f. 40sh multicolored 1.60 1.60
g. 50sh multicolored 2.00 2.00
h. 60sh multicolored 2.40 2.40
396 A68 Sheet of 12 9.00 9.00
a. 4sh multicolored .25 .25
b. 5sh multicolored .25 .25
c. 6sh multicolored .25 .25
d. 7sh multicolored .25 .25
e. 8sh multicolored .35 .35
f. 10sh multicolored .40 .40
g. 12sh multicolored .45 .45
h. 18sh multicolored .75 .75
i. 20sh multicolored .80 .80
j. 25sh multicolored 1.00 1.00
k. 35sh multicolored 1.40 1.40
l. 45sh multicolored 1.75 1.75

Natl. Monuments — A69

5sh, Independence Torch. 12sh, Arusha Declaration. 30sh, Askari. 60sh, Independence. 100sh, Soldier (Askari detail).

1988, June 15 **Litho.**

397 A69 5sh multicolored .25 .25
398 A69 12sh multicolored .25 .25
399 A69 30sh multicolored .25 .25
400 A69 60sh multicolored .45 .45
Nos. 397-400 (4) 1.20 1.20

Souvenir Sheet

401 A69 100sh multicolored 2.25 2.25

3rd Natl. Census, Aug. 28 — A70

3sh, Enumeration. 10sh, Health care. 20sh, Population figures.

40sh, Segments of economy and society.

1988, Aug. 8

402 A70 2sh shown .25 .25
403 A70 3sh multicolored .25 .25
404 A70 10sh multicolored .25 .25
405 A70 20sh multicolored .40 .40
Nos. 402-405 (4) 1.15 1.15

Souvenir Sheet

405A A70 40sh multicolored 1.10 1.10

Stamps of 1983-86 Overprinted

Nos. 406 & 410, 412 Overprinted

No. 407 Ovptd.

Nos. 408-409, 411 Overprinted

1988, Aug. 15 ***Perfs. as Before***

406 A53 5sh on #325 1.10 1.10
407 A31a 10sh on #220 15.00 15.00
a. Souv. sheet of 4, #218-220, 407 10.00 10.00
408 A41 10sh on #260 5.50 5.50
409 A41 17.50sh on #261 10.00 10.00
410 A53 40sh on #326 13.00 13.00
Nos. 406-410 (5) 44.60 44.60

Souvenir Sheets

411 Sheet of 2 6.75 6.75
a. A41 15sh on #262a 1.75 1.75
b. A41 20sh on #262b 3.75 3.75
412 A53 30sh on #327 6.75 6.75

1988 Olympics, Seoul and Calgary — A71

1988, Aug. 29 *Perf. 14*

414 A71 5sh Biathlon .50 .50
415 A71 10sh Soccer .25 .25
416 A71 20sh Cycling .80 .80
417 A71 25sh Pairs figuring skating .90 .90
418 A71 50sh Fencing .85 .85
419 A71 50sh Downhill skiing 1.60 1.60
420 A71 70sh Volleyball 1.00 1.00
421 A71 75sh Bobsled 1.90 1.90
Nos. 414-421 (8) 7.80 7.80

Souvenir Sheets

422 A71 100sh Flags, hockey sticks 4.00 4.00
423 A71 100sh Gymnastics 4.00 4.00

For overprint see No. 534A-534J.

1988 Summer Olympics, Seoul A71a

1988, Sept. 5 Litho. *Perf. 12½x12*

423A A71a 2sh Javelin .90 .90
423B A71a 3sh Hurdles .95 .95
423C A71a 7sh Long distance running 1.50 1.50
423D A71a 12sh Relay race 2.00 2.00
Nos. 423A-423D (4) 5.35 5.35

A souvenir sheet exists.

Disney Characters, Special Occasions — A72

1988, Sept. 9 *Perf. 14*

424 A72 4sh Love You, Dad .30 .30
425 A72 5sh Happy Birthday .30 .30
426 A72 10sh Trick or Treat .45 .45
427 A72 12sh Be Kind to Animals .45 .45
428 A72 15sh Love .55 .55
429 A72 20sh Let's Celebrate .80 .80
430 A72 30sh Keep In Touch 1.75 1.75
431 A72 50sh Love You, Mom 3.50 3.50
Nos. 424-431 (8) 8.10 8.10

Souvenir Sheets

432 A72 150sh Let's Work Together 4.50 4.50
433 A72 150sh Have a Super Sunday 4.50 4.50

Mickey Mouse, 60th anniv.

Domestic Animals A73

1988, Sept. 9

434 A73 4sh Goat, vert. .55 .55
435 A73 5sh Rabbit .55 .55
436 A73 8sh Cows .75 .75
437 A73 10sh Cat 1.00 1.00
438 A73 12sh Horse, vert. 1.25 1.25
439 A73 20sh Dog, vert. 2.00 2.00
Nos. 434-439 (6) 6.10 6.10

Souvenir Sheet

440 A73 100sh Chicken 4.50 4.50

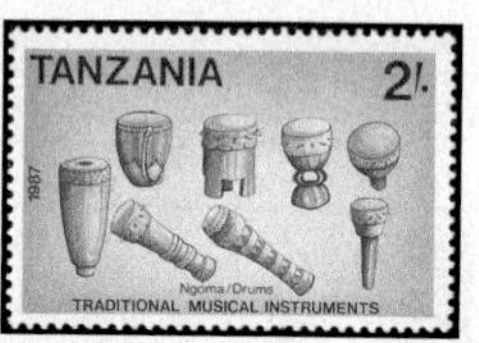

Traditional Musical Instruments — A74

1988, Sept. 30 Litho. *Perf. 14*

441 A74 2sh Drums .70 .70
442 A74 3sh Xylophones .70 .70
443 A74 10sh Thumb pianos 1.50 1.50
444 A74 20sh Fiddles 2.10 2.10
Nos. 441-444 (4) 5.00 5.00

Souvenir Sheet

445 A74 40sh Violins with calabash resonators 2.00 2.00

Dated 1987.

Butterflies A75

8sh, Charaxes varanes. 30sh, Neptis melicerta. 40sh, Mylothris chloris. 50sh, Charaxes bohemani. 60sh, Myrina ficedula. 75sh, Papilio phorcas. 90sh, Cyrestis camillus. 100sh, Salamis temora.

200sh, Asterope rosa. 250sh, Kallima rumia.

1988, Oct. 17 *Perf. 14½*

446 A75 8sh multicolored .75 .75
447 A75 30sh multicolored 1.40 1.40
448 A75 40sh multicolored 1.40 1.40
449 A75 50sh multicolored 1.75 1.75
450 A75 60sh multicolored 2.10 2.10
451 A75 75sh multicolored 2.75 2.75
452 A75 90sh multicolored 3.25 3.25
453 A75 100sh multicolored 3.25 3.25
Nos. 446-453 (8) 16.65 16.65

Souvenir Sheets

454 A75 200sh multicolored 7.50 7.50
455 A75 250sh multicolored 8.50 8.50

Intl. Lions Club at Dar es Salaam, 25th Anniv. A76

1988, Nov, 30 Litho. ***Perf. 14½***

456 A76 2sh Eye operation .40 .40
457 A76 3sh Shallow water well .40 .40
458 A76 7sh Map, rhinoceros 1.25 1.25
459 A76 12sh Donating school desks .50 .50
Nos. 456-459 (4) 2.55 2.55

Souvenir Sheet

460 A76 40sh Emblem 1.75 1.75

Community services: Matibabu Ya Macho Eye Camp (2sh); sanitary water supply in Dar es Salaam (3sh); wildlife conservation (7sh); aid to local schools (12sh).

Intl. Red Cross and Red Crescent Organizations, 125th Annivs. — A77

Design: 2sh, Assisting the wounded and sick. 3sh, Postnatal care clinic. 7sh, Red Cross flag. 12sh, Jean-Henry Dunant, founder. 40sh, Dunant, Thomas Maunier, Louis Appia, Gustave Moynier and Gen. Guillaume Henri Dufour, members of intl. committee that sponsored the conference in 1863 where the Red Cross was founded.

1988, Dec. 30 Litho. ***Perf. 12½x12***

461 A77 2sh multicolored .45 .45
462 A77 3sh multicolored .45 .45
463 A77 7sh multicolored .50 .50
464 A77 12sh multicolored .70 .70
Nos. 461-464 (4) 2.10 2.10

Souvenir Sheet

465 A77 40sh multicolored 1.75 1.75

Miniature Sheet

Paradise Whydah — A78

Birds: a, Paradise whydah. b, Black-collared barbet. c, Bataleur eagle. d, Openbill storks, lilac-breasted roller. e, Scarlet-tufted malachite sunbird. f, Dark chanting goshawk. g, White-fronted bee-eater, little bee-eater, carmine bee-eater. h, Marabou stork, Narina's trocon. i, African gray parrot. j, Hoopoe. k, Yellow-collared lovebird. l, Yellow-billed hornbill. m, Hammerkop. n, Flamingos, violet-crested turaco. o, Malachite kingfisher. p, Greater flamingo. q, Yellow-billed stork. r, Shoebill stork. s, Saddle-billed stork, blacksmith plover. t, Crowned crane.

1989, Jan. 10 ***Perf. 14***

466 Sheet of 20 30.00 30.00
a.-t. A78 20sh any single .75 .75

Souvenir Sheets

467 A78 350sh Helmeted guineafowl 8.00 8.00
467A A78 350sh Ostrich 8.00 8.00

No. 466 has a continuous design.

Endangered Species — A79

World Wildlife Fund: Various bushbabies, *Galago zanzibaricus.* 350sh, African palm civet.

1989, Jan. 24 ***Perf. 14***

468 A79 5sh shown .75 .75
469 A79 10sh multi, horiz. .95 .95
470 A79 20sh multi, diff. 1.20 1.20
471 A79 45sh multi, diff., horiz. 2.40 2.40
Nos. 468-471 (4) 5.30 5.30

Souvenir Sheet

472 A79 350sh multi, horiz. 8.75 8.75

Endangered Species — A80

30sh, Black cobra, umbrella acacia. 70sh, Red-tailed tropic bird, tree fern. 100sh, African tree frog, cocoa tree. 150sh, African black-necked heron, Egyptian papyrus. 350sh, Pink-backed pelicans, baobab tree.

1989, Jan. 24

473 A80 30sh shown 1.00 1.00
474 A80 70sh multicolored 4.50 4.50
475 A80 100sh multicolored 5.25 5.25
476 A80 150sh multicolored 8.00 8.00
Nos. 473-476 (4) 18.75 18.75

Souvenir Sheet

477 A80 350sh multicolored 9.25 9.25

Steam Locomotives — A81

10sh, Class P36, USSR. 25sh, Class 12, Belgium. 60sh, Class C62, Japan. 75sh, Class T1, Pennsylvania R.R. 80sh, Class WP, India. 90sh, Class 59, East African Railways. 150sh, People Class 4-6-2, China. 200sh, Southern Pacific Daylight Express, US.
No. 486, Stephenson's Planet, Britain. No. 487, Coronation Scot, Britain.

1989, Jan. 31

478 A81 10sh multicolored .80 .80
479 A81 25sh multicolored .85 .85
480 A81 60sh multicolored 1.25 1.25
481 A81 75sh multicolored 1.50 1.50
482 A81 80sh multicolored 1.60 1.60
483 A81 90sh multicolored 1.75 1.75
484 A81 150sh multicolored 2.75 2.75
485 A81 200sh multicolored 2.75 2.75
Nos. 478-485 (8) 13.25 13.25

Souvenir Sheets

486 A81 350sh multicolored 6.25 6.25
487 A81 350sh multicolored 6.25 6.25

Nos. 486-487 vert.

World-Class Athletes — A82

Designs: 4sh, Juma Ikangaa, Tanzania, marathon. 8.50sh, Steffi Graf, West Germany, tennis. 12sh, Yannick Noah, France, tennis. 40sh, Pele, Brazil, soccer. 100sh, Erhard Keller, West Germany, speed skater. 125sh, Sadanoyama, Japan, Sumo wrestler. 200sh, Taino, Japan, Sumo wrestler. 250sh, I. Aoki, Japan, golfer. No. 496, Joe Louis, US, world heavyweight boxing champion, 1937-1949. No. 497, T. Nakajima, Japan, golfer.

1989, Feb. 7

488 A82 4sh multicolored .40 .40
489 A82 8.50sh multicolored .40 .40
490 A82 12sh multicolored .40 .40
491 A82 40sh multicolored 1.25 1.25
492 A82 100sh multicolored 3.00 3.00
493 A82 125sh multicolored 3.50 3.50
494 A82 200sh multicolored 5.25 5.25
495 A82 250sh multicolored 6.75 6.75
Nos. 488-495 (8) 20.95 20.95

Souvenir Sheets

496 A82 350sh multicolored 8.50 8.50
497 A82 350sh multicolored 8.50 8.50

History of Space Exploration and 20th Anniv. of the 1st Moon Landing — A83

20sh, Luna 3. 30sh, Rendezvous of Gemini 6 & 7. 40sh, 1st US space walk. 60sh, First man on Moon. 70sh, Experiments on Moon. 100sh, Apollo 15 lunar rover. 150sh, Apollo-Soyuz. 200sh, Spacelab.
No. 506, Futuristic space station. No. 507, Eagle lunar module.

1989, July 20

498 A83 20sh multicolored .50 .50
499 A83 30sh multicolored .60 .60
500 A83 40sh multicolored .65 .65
501 A83 60sh multicolored .90 .90
502 A83 70sh multicolored 1.00 1.00
503 A83 100sh multicolored 1.35 1.35
504 A83 150sh multicolored 1.75 1.75
505 A83 200sh multicolored 2.25 2.25
Nos. 498-505 (8) 9.00 9.00

Souvenir Sheets

506 A83 250sh multicolored 3.75 3.75
507 A83 250sh multicolored 3.75 3.75

History of space exploration (Nos. 498-500, 503-506); others 20th anniv. of 1st Moon Landing.

St. Mary Magdalene in Penitence A84

Details from paintings by Titian: 10sh, Averoldi Polyptych. 15sh, St. Margaret. 50sh, Venus and Adonis. 75sh, Venus and the Lutenist. 100sh, Tarquin and Lucretia. 125sh, St. Jerome. 150sh, Madonna and Child with Saints. No. 516, St. Catherine of Alexandria at Prayer. No. 517, Adoration of the Holy Trinity. No. 517A, The Supper at Emmaus.

1989, Nov. 15 Litho. ***Perf. 13½x14***

508 A84 5sh multicolored .35 .35
509 A84 10sh multicolored .35 .35
510 A84 15sh multicolored .35 .35
511 A84 50sh multicolored .80 .80
512 A84 75sh multicolored 1.30 1.30
513 A84 100sh multicolored 1.50 1.50
514 A84 125sh multicolored 1.90 1.90
515 A84 150sh multicolored 2.25 2.25
Nos. 508-515 (8) 8.80 8.80

Souvenir Sheets

516 A84 300sh multicolored 4.00 4.00
517 A84 300sh multicolored 4.00 4.00
517A A84 300sh multicolored 4.00 4.00

500th birth anniv. of Titian.
No. 517A was not available until Jan. 8, 1991.

World Cup Soccer Championships, Italy — A85

1989, Nov. 15 ***Perf. 14***

Uniform colors

518 A85 25sh grn, red & yel 1.00 1.00
519 A85 60sh grn, yel & blue 2.10 2.10
520 A85 75sh orange & blue 2.75 2.75
521 A85 200sh blue & white 7.00 7.00
Nos. 518-521 (4) 12.85 12.85

Souvenir Sheets

522 A85 350sh org & bl, diff. 5.75 5.75
523 A85 350sh grn, yel & bl, diff. 5.75 5.75

Souvenir Sheet

Union Station, Washington, DC — A86

1989, Nov. 17

524 A86 500sh multicolored 9.50 9.50

World Stamp Expo '89.

Fish A87

9sh, Tiger tilapia. 13sh, Picasso fish. 20sh, Powder-blue surgeonfish. 40sh, Butterflyfish. 70sh, Guenther's notho. 100sh, Ansorge's noelebias. 150sh, Lyretail panchax. 200sh, Regal angelfish.
No. 533, Batfish. No. 534, Jewel cichlid.

1989, Dec. 14

525 A87 9sh multicolored .35 .35
526 A87 13sh multicolored .35 .35
527 A87 20sh multicolored .50 .50
528 A87 40sh multicolored .90 .90
529 A87 70sh multicolored 1.60 1.60
530 A87 100sh multicolored 2.40 2.40
531 A87 150sh multicolored 3.50 3.50
532 A87 200sh multicolored 5.00 5.00
Nos. 525-532 (8) 14.60 14.60

Souvenir Sheets

533 A87 350sh multicolored 6.75 6.75
534 A87 350sh multicolored 6.75 6.75

Nos. 533-534 each contain one 38x51mm stamp.

Nos. 414-423 Ovptd. and Similarly

No. 534B, "Gold - USSR / Silver - Brazil / Bronze - W. Germany". No. 534C, "Men's Match Sprint / Lutz Hesslich, DDR". No. 534D, "Pairs, Gordeeva & Grinkov, USSR". No. 534E, "Epee, Schmitt, W. Germany". No. 534F, "Zurbriggen, Switzerland". No. 534G, "Men's Team, USA". No. 534H, "Gold-USSR / Silver-DDR / Bronze-DDR".
No. 534I, "Ice Hockey: / Gold-USSR". No. 534J, "Women's Team, / Gold-USSR".

Perfs. as Before

1989, Dec. 19 **Litho.**

534A	A71	5sh shown	.55	.55
534B	A71	10sh multicolored	.75	.75
534C	A71	20sh multicolored	3.00	3.00
534D	A71	25sh multicolored	1.50	1.50
534E	A71	50sh multicolored	2.40	2.40
534F	A71	50sh multicolored	2.40	2.40
534G	A71	70sh multicolored	3.75	3.75
534H	A71	75sh multicolored	3.00	3.00
		Nos. 534A-534H (8)	17.35	17.35

Souvenir Sheets

534I	A71	100sh multicolored	11.00	11.00
534J	A71	100sh multicolored	4.00	4.00

Silver and Bronze medalists overprinted on margins of souvenir sheets.

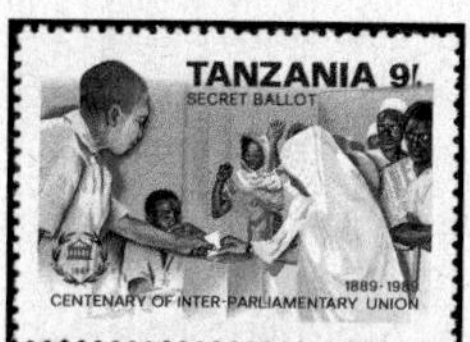

Inter-Parliamentary Union, Cent. — A88

Designs: 9sh, Secret ballot. 13sh, Parliament, Dar Es Salaam. 40sh, Sir William Randal Cremer, Frederic Passy. 80sh, Parliament in session. 100sh, IPU emblem.

1989, Dec. 22 ***Perf. 12½x12***

535	A88	9sh multicolored	.25	.25
536	A88	13sh multicolored	.25	.25
537	A88	80sh multicolored	.65	.65
538	A88	100sh lt bl, dp bl & blk	.75	.75
		Nos. 535-538 (4)	1.90	1.90

Souvenir Sheet

539	A88	40sh multicolored	1.25	1.25

Pan-African Postal Union, 10th Anniv. A89

9sh, PAPU emblem. 13sh, Post offices boxes. 70sh, Mail early, prompt delivery. 100sh, Modes of mail delivery.
40sh, Tanzania Post, PAPU, UPU emblems.

1990, Jan. 17 ***Perf. 13½***

540	A89	9sh multicolored	.30	.30
541	A89	13sh multicolored	.30	.30
542	A89	70sh multicolored	1.25	1.25
543	A89	100sh multicolored	2.10	2.10
		Nos. 540-543 (4)	3.95	3.95

Souvenir Sheet

544	A89	40sh multicolored	1.40	1.40

Extinct Animals A90

25sh, Tecopa pupfish. 40sh, Thylacine. 50sh, Quagga. 60sh, Passenger pigeon. 75sh, Rodriguez saddleback tortoise. 100sh, Toolache wallaby. 150sh, Texas red wolf. 200sh, Utah lake sculpin.

No. 553, Hawaiian O-O, vert. No. 554, South island whekau.

1990, Feb. 4 ***Perf. 14***

545	A90	25sh multicolored	.65	.65
546	A90	40sh multicolored	.95	.95
547	A90	50sh multicolored	1.30	1.30
548	A90	60sh multicolored	1.50	1.50
549	A90	75sh multicolored	1.90	1.90
550	A90	100sh multicolored	2.40	2.40
551	A90	150sh multicolored	3.50	3.50
552	A90	200sh multicolored	4.75	4.75
		Nos. 545-552 (8)	16.95	16.95

Souvenir Sheets

553	A90	350sh multicolored	6.75	6.75
554	A90	350sh multicolored	6.75	6.75

Nina, Admiral's Flag A91

60sh, Pinta, flag. 75sh, Santa Maria, flag. 200sh, Map of Columbus' first voyage.
350sh, Ships, bird's head.

1990, Feb. 20

555	A91	50sh shown	2.10	2.10
556	A91	60sh multicolored	2.50	2.50
557	A91	75sh multicolored	3.00	3.00
558	A91	200sh multicolored	8.25	8.25
		Nos. 555-558 (4)	15.85	15.85

Souvenir Sheet

559	A91	350sh multicolored	9.50	9.50

Discovery of America, 500th anniv. (in 1992).

Modern Discoveries — A92

Designs: 9sh, Bell X-1 breaking the sound barrier. 13sh, Bathyscaph Trieste reaches the deepest ocean bottom. 150sh, Transistor and computer chips. 250sh, Discovery of DNA structure. 350sh, Voyager 2 visits Neptune.

1990, Feb. 20

560	A92	9sh multicolored	.65	.65
561	A92	13sh multicolored	.65	.65
562	A92	150sh multicolored	1.50	1.50
563	A92	250sh multicolored	2.50	2.50
		Nos. 560-563 (4)	5.30	5.30

Souvenir Sheet

564	A92	350sh multicolored	5.75	5.75

Girl Guides, 60th Anniv. A93

1990, Feb. 22 ***Perf. 12½x12***

565	A93	9sh Hiking	.25	.25
566	A93	13sh Planting trees	.25	.25
567	A93	50sh Teaching writing	.60	.60
568	A93	100sh Teaching health care	1.20	1.20
		Nos. 565-568 (4)	2.30	2.30

Souvenir Sheet

Perf. 12x12½

569	A93	40sh Nursing school, vert.	1.40	1.40

Disney Characters, Automobiles — A94

20sh, Herbie, The Love Bug. 30sh, The Absent-Minded Professor's car. 45sh, Chitty-Chitty Bang-Bang. 60sh, Mr. Toad's wild ride. 75sh, Scrooge's limousine. 100sh, Shaggy dog's car. 150sh, Donald Duck's car. 200sh, Firetruck in "Dumbo".

No. 578, Cruella de Vil. No. 579, Mickeymobile.

1990, Mar. 20 ***Perf. 14x13½***

570	A94	20sh multicolored	.45	.45
571	A94	30sh multicolored	.50	.50
572	A94	45sh multicolored	.65	.65
573	A94	60sh multicolored	.90	.90
574	A94	75sh multicolored	1.10	1.10
575	A94	100sh multicolored	1.50	1.50
576	A94	150sh multicolored	2.40	2.40
577	A94	200sh multicolored	2.50	2.50
		Nos. 570-577 (8)	10.00	10.00

Souvenir Sheets

578	A94	350sh multicolored	6.00	6.00
579	A94	350sh multicolored	6.00	6.00

Black Entertainers A95

1990, Mar. 30 **Litho.** ***Perf. 14***

580	A95	9sh Miriam Makeba	.25	.25
581	A95	13sh Manu Dibango	.25	.25
582	A95	25sh Fela	.25	.25
583	A95	70sh Smokey Robinson	.90	.90
584	A95	100sh Gladys Knight	1.10	1.10
585	A95	150sh Eddie Murphy	2.00	2.00
586	A95	200sh Sammy Davis, Jr.	2.75	2.75
587	A95	250sh Stevie Wonder	2.75	2.75
		Nos. 580-587 (8)	10.25	10.25

Souvenir Sheets

Perf. 14½

588	A95	350sh Bill Cosby	3.75	3.75
589	A95	350sh Michael Jackson	3.75	3.75

Union of Tanganyika and Zanzibar, 25th Anniv. (in 1989) — A95a

Designs: 9sh, Fishing. 13sh, Grapes. 50sh, Cloves. 100sh, Presidents Nyerere and Karume exchanging Union instruments, vert.
40sh, Natl. arms, vert.

Perf. 12½x12, 12x12½

1990, Apr. 25 **Litho.**

589A	A95a	9sh multicolored	.55	.55
589B	A95a	13sh multicolored	.55	.55
589C	A95a	50sh multicolored	1.75	1.75
589D	A95a	100sh multicolored	3.50	3.50
		Nos. 589A-589D (4)	6.35	6.35

Souvenir Sheet

589E	A95a	40sh multicolored	2.75	2.75

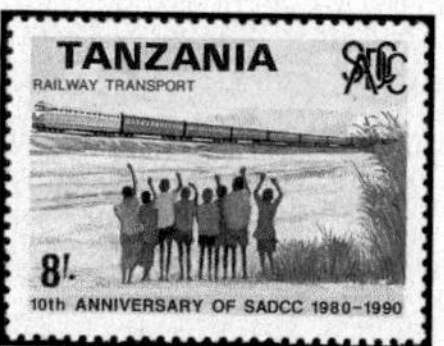

Southern Africa Development Coordinating Conf. (SADCC), 10th Anniv. — A96

8sh, Railway transport. 11.50sh, Paper industry. 25sh, Tractor production. 100sh, Flags, map.
50sh, Map.

1990, Aug. 8 ***Perf. 13½***

590	A96	8sh multicolored	.45	.45
591	A96	11.50sh multicolored	.45	.45
592	A96	25sh multicolored	.80	.80
593	A96	100sh multicolored	2.50	2.50
		Nos. 590-593 (4)	4.20	4.20

Souvenir Sheet

Perf. 12½

594	A96	50sh multicolored	2.50	2.50

A97

Pope John Paul II's Visit to Tanzania: 15sh, Wearing red vestments. 20sh, Wearing miter. 100sh, Papal arms. No. 599: a, Pope with arms outstretched. b, St. Joseph's Cathedral, Dar Es Salaam. c, Christ the King Cathedral, Moshi. d, Saint Theresa's Cathedral, Tabora. e, Cathedral of the Epiphany, Bugando Mwanza. f, St. Mathias Mulumba Kalemba Cathedral, Songea.

1990, Sept. 1 **Litho.** ***Perf. 14***

595	A97	10sh shown	.30	.30
596	A97	15sh multicolored	.45	.45
597	A97	20sh multicolored	.50	.50
598	A97	100sh multicolored	1.25	1.25
		Nos. 595-598 (4)	2.50	2.50

Souvenir Sheet

599		Sheet of 6	7.00	7.00
a.-f.		A97 50sh any single	.60	.60

A98

Players from participating countries.

1990, Sept. 28

600	A98	10sh West Germany	1.00	1.00
601	A98	60sh Italy	1.75	1.75
602	A98	100sh Scotland	3.00	3.00
603	A98	300sh Yugoslavia	5.25	5.25
		Nos. 600-603 (4)	11.00	11.00

Souvenir Sheets

604	A98	400sh Costa Rica	6.00	6.00
605	A98	400sh Belgium	6.00	6.00

World Cup Soccer Championships, Italy.

Birds — A99

5sh, Masked weaver. 9sh, Emerald cuckoo. 13sh, Little bee-eater. 15sh, Red bishop. 20sh, Bateleur. 25sh, Scarlet-chested sunbird. 30sh, Pigeons. 40sh, Lesser flamingo. 70sh, Helmeted guineafowl. 100sh, White pelican. 170sh, Saddle-billed stork. 200sh, Crowned crane. 300sh, Pied crow. 400sh, White-headed vulture. 500sh, Ostrich.

1990-91 **Litho.** ***Perf. 14***

606	A99	5sh multi	.45	.45
607	A99	9sh multi	.45	.45
608	A99	13sh multi	.80	.80
609	A99	15sh multi	.80	.80
610	A99	20sh multi	1.00	1.00
611	A99	25sh multi	1.00	1.00
a.		Bklt. pane, 2 ea #606-611	9.00	9.00
611B	A99	30sh multi	1.00	1.00

Size: 42x28mm

612	A99	40sh multi	1.00	1.00
613	A99	70sh multi	1.10	1.10
614	A99	100sh multi	1.25	1.25
615	A99	170sh multi	1.75	1.75
616	A99	200sh multi	2.00	2.00
616A	A99	300sh multi	2.25	2.25
616B	A99	400sh multi	2.50	2.50
617	A99	500sh multi	2.50	2.50
		Nos. 606-617 (15)	19.85	19.85

Souvenir Sheet

Stamp size: 42x28mm

617A		Sheet of 2	6.25	6.25
b.		A99 40sh Superb starling	1.10	1.10
c.		A99 60sh Lilac-breasted roller	1.60	1.60

Issued: 30sh, 300sh, 400sh, 1991; others, 10/1/90.

For surcharges, see Nos. 1723A, 1723B, 2157-2159C, 2267, 2627A-2627B.

Boats A100

1990, Oct. 10 Litho. *Perf. 12½x12*

618 A100 9sh Canoe .40 .40
619 A100 13sh Outrigger canoe .40 .40
620 A100 25sh Dhow .65 .65
621 A100 100sh Freighter 2.75 2.75
Nos. 618-621 (4) 4.20 4.20

Souvenir Sheet

622 A100 40sh Boat 3.25 3.25

Commonwealth Games, New Zealand — A101

1990, Oct. 22 *Perf. 14*

623 A101 9sh Sprinting .40 .40
624 A101 13sh Netball, vert. .65 .65
625 A101 25sh Pole vault .95 .95
626 A101 100sh Long jump, vert. 3.25 3.25
Nos. 623-626 (4) 5.25 5.25

Souvenir Sheet

627 A101 40sh Boxing 2.50 2.50

Orchids — A102

10sh, Phalaenopsis. 25sh, Lycaste. 30sh, Vuylstekeara, Cambria "Plush". 50sh, Vuylstekeara, Monica "Burnham". 90sh, Odontocidium. 100sh, Oncidioda. 250sh, Sophrolaeliocattleya. 300sh, Laeliocattleya.
No. 636, Cymbidium, Baldoyle "Melbury". No. 637, Cymbidium, Tapestry "Long Beach".

1990, Nov. 12

628 A102 10sh multicolored .40 .40
629 A102 25sh multicolored .40 .40
630 A102 30sh multicolored .45 .45
631 A102 50sh multicolored .70 .70
632 A102 90sh multicolored 1.25 1.25
633 A102 100sh multicolored 1.60 1.60
634 A102 250sh multicolored 4.00 4.00
635 A102 300sh multicolored 4.50 4.50
Nos. 628-635 (8) 13.30 13.30

Souvenir Sheets

636 A102 400sh multicolored 6.25 6.25
637 A102 400sh multicolored 6.25 6.25

Expo '90, the Intl. Garden and Greenery Exposition, Osaka, Japan.

1990 World Cup Soccer Championships, Italy — A102a

1990, Nov. 17 Litho. *Perf. 14*

637A A102a 9sh Long throw-in .75 .75
637B A102a 13sh Penalty kick .75 .75
637C A102a 25sh Dribbling 1.25 1.25
637D A102a 100sh Corner kick 4.25 4.25
Nos. 637A-637D (4) 7.00 7.00

Souvenir Sheet

637E A102a 50sh Trophy, map 4.50 4.50

Racing A103

5sh, Olympic Soling Class Yacht racing. 20sh, Olympic downhill ski racing. 30sh, Tour de France bicycle race. 40sh, Le Mans 24 hour endurance auto race. 75sh, Olympic 2-man bobsled. 100sh, Belgian Grand Prix motorcycle race. 250sh, Indianapolis 500 auto race. 300sh, Power boat gold cup racing. #646, Colorado 500 enduro motorcycle race. #647, Schneider Trophy air races.

1990, Nov. 19

638 A103 5sh multicolored .45 .45
639 A103 20sh multicolored .85 .85
640 A103 30sh multicolored 1.40 1.40
641 A103 40sh multicolored 1.40 1.40
642 A103 75sh multicolored 1.60 1.60
643 A103 100sh multicolored 2.40 2.40
644 A103 250sh multicolored 3.00 3.00
645 A103 300sh multicolored 3.25 3.25
Nos. 638-645 (8) 14.35 14.35

Souvenir Sheets

646 A103 400sh multicolored 7.00 7.00
647 A103 400sh multicolored 7.00 7.00

1992 Summer Olympics, Barcelona — A104

5sh, Archery. 10sh, Women's gymnastics. 25sh, Boxing. 50sh, Two-man kayak race. 100sh, Men's volleyball. 150sh, Mens' gymnastics. 200sh, 4x100 meter relay. 300sh, Judo.
No. 656, Men's 400 meter hurdles. No. 657, Men's cycling.

1990, Nov. 30

648 A104 5sh multicolored .30 .30
649 A104 10sh multicolored .30 .30
650 A104 25sh multicolored .30 .30
651 A104 50sh multicolored .55 .55
652 A104 100sh multicolored 1.10 1.10
653 A104 150sh multicolored 1.75 1.75
654 A104 200sh multicolored 2.25 2.25
655 A104 300sh multicolored 3.50 3.50
Nos. 648-655 (8) 10.05 10.05

Souvenir Sheets

656 A104 400sh multicolored 5.50 5.50
657 A104 400sh multicolored 5.50 5.50

Cog Railroads A105

Cog locomotives: 8sh, Petersberg Cog Railway, West Germany. 25sh, Engine *Waumbek* on Mt. Washington Cog Railway, US. 50sh, Doubleheaded cog engines on Dubrovnik-Sarajevo line, Yugoslavia. 100sh, Cog Railway, Budapest, Hungary 1874. 150sh, Vordenberg-Eisenerz line, Austria. 200sh, Rimutaka Incline, New Zealand, 1955. 250sh, John Stevens' cog engine, Hoboken, NJ, 1825. 300sh, Pilatusbahn Cog Railway, Switzerland, 1889. No. 666, Schneebergbahn of the OBB, Austria. No. 667, Sylvester Marsh, Mt. Washington Cog Railway, 1869.

1990, Dec. 8

658 A105 8sh multicolored .30 .30
659 A105 25sh multicolored .30 .30
660 A105 50sh multicolored .55 .55
661 A105 100sh multicolored 1.00 1.00
662 A105 150sh multicolored 1.60 1.60
663 A105 200sh multicolored 2.00 2.00
664 A105 250sh multicolored 3.00 3.00
665 A105 300sh multicolored 3.25 3.25
Nos. 658-665 (8) 12.00 12.00

Souvenir Sheets

666 A105 400sh multicolored 6.00 6.00
667 A105 400sh multicolored 6.00 6.00

First Postage Stamps, 150th Anniv. A106

Designs: No. 668, German Post Office at Dar Es Salaam, German East Africa No. 16. No. 669, Mailboat S.S. Reichstag, 1890, Germany No. 40 cancelled in Zanzibar. No. 670, Dhows used as mailboats, Zanzibar No. 1. No. 671, Mailplane Singapore I on Lake Victoria, 1928, Tanganyika No. 22. No. 672, Mailplane, Livingston's House, Zanzibar No. 316. No. 673, Passenger-mail train at Moshi Station, Tanganyika No. 52. No. 674, Royal mail coach, 1840. 150sh, Stephenson's *Rocket*, mail car, 1838. 200sh, Handley Page HP-42 mailplane. No. 677, Hand delivery of mail, Thurn & Taxis No. 44 on cover. No. 678, Sir Rowland Hill.

1990, Dec. 12

668 A106 50sh multicolored 1.00 1.00
669 A106 50sh multicolored 1.00 1.00
a. Pair, #668-669 2.00 2.00
670 A106 75sh multicolored 1.25 1.25
671 A106 75sh multicolored 1.25 1.25
a. Pair, #670-671 2.25 2.25
672 A106 100sh multicolored 1.75 1.75
673 A106 100sh multicolored 1.75 1.75
a. Pair, #672-673 3.50 3.50
674 A106 100sh multicolored 1.75 1.75
675 A106 150sh multicolored 2.60 2.60
676 A106 200sh multicolored 2.60 2.60
Nos. 668-676 (9) 14.95 14.95

Souvenir Sheets

677 A106 350sh multicolored 6.25 6.25
678 A106 350sh multicolored 6.25 6.25

500th anniv. of Thurn and Taxis Post (No. 677).
For overprints see Nos. 928-934.

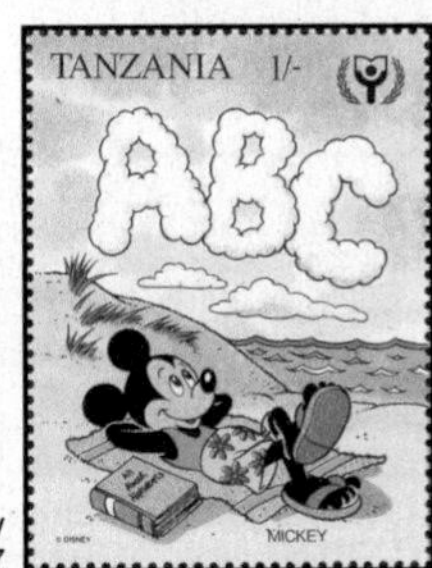

Intl. Literacy Year — A107

Nos. 679a-681i depict various Walt Disney characters and a letter of the alphabet.
No. 682, Mickey's train hauls Russian alphabet. No. 683, Children learning Hebrew.

1990, Dec. 27 *Perf. 13½x14*

Miniature Sheets

679 Sheet of 9 7.50 7.50
a. A107 1sh "ABC" .25 .25
b. A107 2sh "A" .25 .25
c. A107 3sh "B" .25 .25
d. A107 15sh "C" .25 .25
e. A107 55sh "D" .45 .45
f. A107 80sh "E" .65 .65
g. A107 120sh "F" .95 .95
h. A107 145sh "G" 1.10 1.10
i. A107 200sh "H" 1.60 1.60
680 Sheet of 9 7.25 7.25
a. A107 10sh "I" .25 .25
b. A107 20sh "J" .25 .25
c. A107 30sh "K" .25 .25
d. A107 40sh "L" .30 .30
e. A107 50sh "M" .40 .40
f. A107 60sh "N" .50 .50
g. A107 100sh "O" .80 .80
h. A107 125sh "P" 1.00 1.00
i. A107 150sh "Q" 1.25 1.25
681 Sheet of 9 7.50 7.50
a. A107 5sh "R" .25 .25
b. A107 18sh "S" .25 .25
c. A107 25sh "T" .25 .25
d. A107 35sh "U" .30 .30
e. A107 45sh "V" .35 .35
f. A107 75sh "W" .60 .60
g. A107 90sh "X" .70 .70
h. A107 160sh "Y" 1.25 1.25
i. A107 175sh "Z" 1.40 1.40

Souvenir Sheets

682 A107 600sh multicolored 8.50 8.50
683 A107 600sh multicolored 8.50 8.50

Intl. Literacy Year A108

9sh, Learning to read. 13sh, Learning to write. 25sh, Blackboard, books. 100sh, Reading newspapers.
50sh, Adult education.

1991, Mar. 15 Litho. *Perf. 14*

684 A108 9sh multicolored .25 .25
685 A108 13sh multicolored .35 .35
686 A108 25sh multicolored .45 .45
687 A108 100sh multicolored 2.50 2.50
Nos. 684-687 (4) 3.55 3.55

Souvenir Sheet

688 A108 50sh multicolored 2.25 2.25

For surcharge see No. 1431A.

Mickey Mouse — A109

Character roles: 5sh, Western cowboy. 10sh, Boxer. 15sh, Astronaut. 20sh, Romantic lead with Minnie. 100sh, Swashbuckling hero. 200sh, Detective with Donald Duck and Pistol Pete. 350sh, King with Donald as court jester. 450sh, Sailor with Donald and Goofy. No. 697, Minnie, Mickey as archaeologists in Egypt, Donald as a mummy. No. 698, Mickey as Canadian Mountie.

1991, Feb. 11 Litho. *Perf. 14x13½*

689 A109 5sh multicolored .45 .45
690 A109 10sh multicolored .50 .50
691 A109 15sh multicolored .50 .50
692 A109 20sh multicolored .50 .50
693 A109 100sh multicolored 2.00 2.00
694 A109 200sh multicolored 4.00 4.00
695 A109 350sh multicolored 4.50 4.50
696 A109 450sh multicolored 4.50 4.50
Nos. 689-696 (8) 16.95 16.95

Souvenir Sheets

697 A109 600sh multicolored 8.50 8.50
698 A109 600sh multicolored 8.50 8.50

Craters and Caves — A109a

Designs: 3sh, Ngorongoro Crater. 5sh, Kondoa Caves, prehistoric rock paintings. 9sh, Mount Kilimanjaro's inner crater. 12sh, Olduvai Gorge.
Amboni Caves: No. 698f, Open area of cave. g, People viewing cave, large stalactite. h, Woman seated beside welcome sign. i, Man climbing up to view cave.

1991, Mar. 28 Litho. *Perf. 14½*

698A A109a 3sh multi 3.25 3.25
698B A109a 5sh multi 3.25 3.25
698C A109a 9sh multi 4.25 4.25
698D A109a 12sh multi 6.25 6.25
Nos. 698A-698D (4) 17.00 17.00

Souvenir Sheet

698E A109a 10sh Sheet of 4, #f.-i. 8.00 8.00

Nos. 698A-698E were not available to the philatelic community until Mar. 1994.

Miniature Sheet

Peter Paul Rubens, 350th Death Anniv. — A110

Cycle of Decius Mus: No. 699a, Proclamation of the Vision. b, Divining of the Entrails. c, Dispatch of the Lictors. d, Dedication to Death. e, Victory and Death of Decius Mus. f, Funeral Rites. No. 700, Trophy of War, vert.

1991, Apr. 10 Litho. ***Perf. 14x13½***

699 A110 85sh Sheet of 6, #a.-f. 13.00 13.00

Souvenir Sheet

Perf. 13½x14

700 A110 500sh multicolored 11.00 11.00

Tanzania Investment Bank, 20th Anniv. — A111

Designs: 10sh, Dairy farming. 13sh, Industrial development. 25sh, Engineering. 100sh, Tea harvesting.

1991, June 7 ***Perf. 14***

701 A111 10sh multicolored .35 .35
702 A111 13sh multicolored .35 .35
703 A111 25sh multicolored .35 .35
704 A111 100sh multicolored 2.00 2.00
a. Souvenir sheet of 4, #701-704 3.00 3.00
Nos. 701-704 (4) 3.05 3.05

Phila Nippon '91 A112

Japanese locomotives: 10sh, First Japanese steam. 25sh, Series 4500 steam. 35sh, C 62 steam. 50sh, Mikado steam. 75sh, Series 6250 steam. 100sh, C 11 steam. 200sh, E 10 steam. 300sh, Series 8550 steam. No. 713, EF 58 electric. No. 714, DD 51 diesel. No. 715, Series 400 electric. No. 716, EH 10 electric.

1991, Aug. 15 Litho. ***Perf. 14***

705 A112 10sh multicolored .85 .85
706 A112 25sh multicolored 1.30 1.30
707 A112 35sh multicolored 1.50 1.50
708 A112 50sh multicolored 1.75 1.75
709 A112 75sh multicolored 2.10 2.10
710 A112 100sh multicolored 2.50 2.50
711 A112 200sh multicolored 3.00 3.00
712 A112 300sh multicolored 4.00 4.00
Nos. 705-712 (8) 17.00 17.00

Souvenir Sheets

713 A112 400sh multicolored 4.25 4.25
714 A112 400sh multicolored 4.25 4.25
715 A112 400sh multicolored 4.25 4.25
716 A112 400sh multicolored 4.25 4.25

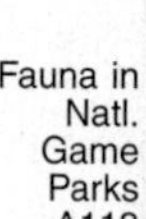

Fauna in Natl. Game Parks A113

Species and park: 10sh, Common zebra, golden-winged sunbird, Ngorongoro Crater Conservation Area. 25sh, Greater kudu, African elephant, Ruaha. 30sh, Sable antelope, red and yellow barbet, Mikumi. 50sh, Wildebeest, leopard, Serengeti. 90sh, Giraffe, white-starred bush robin, Ngurdoto Crater. 100sh, Eland, Abbot's duiker, Kilimanjaro. 250sh, Lion, impala, Lake Manyara. 300sh, Black rhinoceros, ostrich, Tarangire. No. 725, Paradise whydah, oryx, Mkomazi Game Reserve. No. 726, Blue-breasted kingfisher, defassa waterbuck, Selous Game Reserve.

1991, Aug. 22 Litho. ***Perf. 14***

717 A113 10sh multicolored .30 .30
718 A113 25sh multicolored .60 .60
719 A113 30sh multicolored .75 .75
720 A113 50sh multicolored 1.10 1.10
721 A113 90sh multicolored 1.90 1.90
722 A113 100sh multicolored 2.25 2.25
723 A113 250sh multicolored 5.50 5.50
724 A113 300sh multicolored 6.75 6.75
Nos. 717-724 (8) 19.15 19.15

Souvenir Sheets

725 A113 400sh multicolored 8.75 8.75
726 A113 400sh multicolored 8.75 8.75

Butterflies — A114

Designs: 10sh, Vine leaf vagrant. 15sh, Blue spot commodore. 35sh, Orange admiral. 75sh, Wanderer. 100sh, Jackson's leaf. 150sh, Painted empress. 200sh, Double-banded orange. 300sh, Crawshay's sapphire blue. No. 735, Noble swallowtail. No. 736, Club-tailed charaxes. No. 737, Satyr charaxes. No. 738, Green patch swallowtail.

1991, Aug. 28 Litho. ***Perf. 14***

727 A114 10sh multicolored .45 .45
728 A114 15sh multicolored .45 .45
729 A114 35sh multicolored .95 .95
730 A114 75sh multicolored 1.90 1.90
731 A114 100sh multicolored 2.50 2.50
732 A114 150sh multicolored 4.00 4.00
733 A114 200sh multicolored 5.00 5.00
734 A114 300sh multicolored 7.50 7.50
Nos. 727-734 (8) 22.75 22.75

Souvenir Sheets

735 A114 400sh multicolored 5.50 5.50
736 A114 400sh multicolored 5.50 5.50
737 A114 400sh multicolored 5.50 5.50
738 A114 400sh multicolored 5.50 5.50

While Nos. 727-736 have the same issue date as Nos. 737-738, the dollar value of Nos. 737-738 was lower when they were released.

Intelsat, 25th Anniv. A115

Designs: 10sh, Microwave link. 25sh, Earth. 100sh, Mwenge standard "B" Earth station. 500sh, Mwenge standard "A" Earth station. 50sh, World map.

1991, Sept. 5 Litho. ***Perf. 14***

739 A115 10sh multicolored .35 .35
740 A115 25sh multicolored .50 .50
741 A115 100sh multicolored 1.75 1.75
742 A115 500sh multicolored 7.00 7.00
Nos. 739-742 (4) 9.60 9.60

Souvenir Sheet

743 A115 50sh multicolored 3.50 3.50

UN Development Program, 40th Anniv. — A116

Designs: 10sh, Irrigated rice farming. 15sh, Vocational training. 100sh, Terrace farming. 500sh, Architectural renovations, vert. 40sh, Helping people to help themselves, vert.

1991, Sept. 16 ***Perf. 13½***

744 A116 10sh multicolored .30 .30
745 A116 15sh multicolored .30 .30
746 A116 100sh multicolored 1.25 1.25
747 A116 500sh multicolored 6.50 6.50
Nos. 744-747 (4) 8.35 8.35

Souvenir Sheet

Perf. 13x12½

748 A116 40sh black & blue 2.00 2.00

All Africa Games, Cairo — A117

Perf. 12x12½, 12½x12

1991, Sept. 20

749 A117 10sh Netball .45 .45
750 A117 15sh Soccer, horiz. .45 .45
751 A117 100sh Tennis 2.25 2.25
752 A117 200sh Running 3.00 3.00
753 A117 500sh Baseball, horiz. 6.75 6.75
Nos. 749-753 (5) 12.90 12.90

Souvenir Sheet

754 A117 500sh Basketball 9.50 9.50

Telecom '91 — A118

1991, Oct. 1 ***Perf. 13½x14, 14x13½***

755 A118 10sh shown .25 .25
756 A118 15sh Telecom '91, horiz. .25 .25
757 A118 35sh arrows .35 .35
758 A118 100sh like #757, horiz. .90 .90
Nos. 755-758 (4) 1.75 1.75

World Telecommunications Day (Nos. 757-758).

Dinosaurs A119

1991, Oct. 28 ***Perf. 12x12½***

759 A119 10sh Stegosaurus .25 .25
760 A119 15sh Triceratops .25 .25
761 A119 25sh Edmontosaurus .40 .40
762 A119 30sh Plateosaurus .55 .55
763 A119 35sh Diplodocus .65 .65
764 A119 100sh Iguanodon 1.75 1.75
765 A119 200sh Silviasaurus 3.25 3.25
Nos. 759-765 (7) 7.10 7.10

Souvenir Sheet

766 A119 150sh Rhamphorhynchus 4.25 4.25

Animals and Fish — A120

No. 767 — Horses: a, Shire. b, Thoroughbred. c, Kladruber. d, Appaloosa. e, Hanoverian. f, Arab. g, Breton. h, Exmoor. i, Connemara. j, Lipizzaner. k, Shetland. l, Percheron. m, Pinto. n, Orlov. o, Palomino. p, Welsh cob.

No. 768 — Cats: a, Japanese bobtail. b, Cornish rex. c, Malayan. d, Tonkinese. e, Abyssinian. f, Russian blue. g, Cymric. h, Somali. i, Siamese. j, Himalayan. k, Singapura. l, Manx. m, Oriental shorthair. n, Maine coon. o, Persian. p, Birman.

No. 769, vert. — African elephants: a, One walking left. b, Two with tusks entangled. c, One facing forward. d, One under tree. e, Adult and calf in water, zebra. f, Adult and calf walking into water. g, Two adults and calf in water. h, Adult and calf standing in water. i, One walking right. j, Two, one raising trunk in air. k, One raising trunk in air. l, One facing forward, trunk down, zebra. m, Adult, calf at edge of water, antelope. n, Adult and calf, two more in background. o, One walking toward water. p, Adult with trunk on calf.

No. 770 — Aquarium fish: a, Jewel tetra. b, Five-banded barb. c, Simpson platy. d, Guppy, e, Zebra danio. f, Neon tetra. g, Siamese fighting fish. h, Tiger barb. i, Red lyretail. j, Goldfish. k, Pearl gourami. l, Angelfish. m, Clown loach. n, Red swordtail. o, Brown discus. p, Rosy barb.

No. 771 — Birds: a, Budgerigar. b, Rainbow bunting. c, Golden-fronted leafbird. d, Black-headed caique. e, Java sparrow. f, Diamond sparrow. g, Peach-faced lovebird. h, Golden conure. i, Military macaw. j, Celestial parrotlet. k, Sulphur-crested cockatoo. l, Spectacled Amazon parrot. m, Paradise tanager. n, Gouldian finch. o, Masked lovebird. p, Hill mynah.

1991, Oct. 28 Litho. ***Perf. 14***

767 A120 50sh Sheet of 16, #a.-p. 17.00 17.00
768 A120 50sh Sheet of 16, #a.-p. 17.00 17.00
769 A120 75sh Sheet of 16, #a.-p. 17.00 17.00
770 A120 75sh Sheet of 16, #a.-p. 17.00 17.00
771 A120 75sh Sheet of 16, #a.-p. 17.00 17.00
Nos. 767-771 (5) 85.00 85.00

For overprints see Nos. 1529-1530.

Paintings by Vincent Van Gogh A121

Designs: 10sh, Peasant Woman Sewing. 15sh, Head of a Peasant Woman with Greenish Lace Cap. 35sh, Flowering Orchard. 75sh, Portrait of a Girl. 100sh, Portrait of a Woman with a Red Ribbon. 150sh, Vase with Flowers. 200sh, Houses in Antwerp. 400sh, Seated Peasant Woman with White Cap. No. 780, The Parsonage Garden at Nuenen in the Snow, horiz. No. 781, Bulb Fields, horiz.

1991, Nov. 20 Litho. ***Perf. 13½x14***

772 A121 10sh multicolored .30 .30
773 A121 15sh multicolored .30 .30
774 A121 35sh multicolored .70 .70
775 A121 75sh multicolored 1.40 1.40
776 A121 100sh multicolored 1.75 1.75
777 A121 150sh multicolored 2.75 2.75
778 A121 200sh multicolored 3.50 3.50
779 A121 400sh multicolored 7.25 7.25
Nos. 772-779 (8) 17.95 17.95

Size: 127x102mm

Imperf

780 A121 400sh multicolored 7.75 7.75
781 A121 400sh multicolored 7.75 7.75

Walt Disney Christmas Cards — A122

Design and date of card: 10sh, "Joy", 1968. 25sh, Mickey, Pluto and Goofy at fireplace, 1981. 35sh, Robin Hood and merry men celebrating, 1973. 75sh, Tree of greetings, Mickey, 1967. 100sh, Goofy, Mickey and Donald trying to catch Santa coming down chimney, 1969, vert. 150sh, Mickey on top of Christmas ornament, 1976, vert. 200sh, Clarabelle Cow with bells, 1935, vert. 300sh, Orphan mice reading book of tricks, 1935, vert. No. 790, Mickey wearing Santa hat and surrounded by Disney characters, 1968, vert. No. 791, Mickey with present for Donald, 1935, vert.

Perf. 13½x14, 14x13½

1991, Dec. **Litho.**

782 A122 10sh multicolored .30 .30
783 A122 25sh multicolored .55 .55
784 A122 35sh multicolored .70 .70
785 A122 75sh multicolored 1.40 1.40
786 A122 100sh multicolored 2.00 2.00
787 A122 150sh multicolored 2.50 2.50
788 A122 200sh multicolored 3.00 3.00
789 A122 300sh multicolored 4.00 4.00
Nos. 782-789 (8) 14.45 14.45

Souvenir Sheets

790 A122 500sh multicolored 8.50 8.50
791 A122 500sh multicolored 8.50 8.50

Elephants A123

Designs: 10sh, 15sh, 25sh, 100sh, Various pictures of elephas maximus. 30sh, 35sh, 200sh, Various pictures of loxodonta africana. 400sh, Mammut mammuthus.

Perf. 12x12½,12½x12

1991, Nov. 28 **Litho.**

792 A123 10sh multi, vert. .55 .55
793 A123 15sh multi, vert. .55 .55
794 A123 25sh multi, vert. .80 .80
795 A123 30sh multi, vert. 1.10 1.10
796 A123 35sh multicolored 1.35 1.35
797 A123 100sh multicolored 3.50 3.50
798 A123 200sh multicolored 6.75 6.75
Nos. 792-798 (7) 14.60 14.60

Souvenir Sheet

799 A123 400sh multicolored 6.50 6.50

Locomotives — A124

10sh, USSR 1930. 15sh, Japan 1964. 25sh, Russia 1834, vert. 35sh, France 1979. 60sh, France 1972. 100sh, United Kingdom 1972. 300sh, Russia 1837, vert.
No. 807, 100sh, France, 1952, vert.

1991, Dec. 10 *Perf. 12½x12, 12x12½*

800 A124 10sh multicolored .25 .25
801 A124 15sh multicolored .25 .25
802 A124 25sh multicolored .35 .35
803 A124 35sh multicolored .60 .60
804 A124 60sh multicolored 1.00 1.00
805 A124 100sh multicolored 1.40 1.40
806 A124 300sh multicolored 4.75 4.75
Nos. 800-806 (7) 8.60 8.60

Souvenir Sheet

807 A124 100sh multicolored 2.50 2.50

Entertainers — A125

Nos. 808a-808i, 812, Various portraits of Elvis Presley.
Nos. 809a-809i, 813, Various portraits of Marilyn Monroe.
Nos. 810a-810i, 814, Various portraits of Bruce Lee.
Black entertainers: No. 811: a, Scott Joplin. b, Sammy Davis, Jr. c, Joan Armatrading. d, Louis Armstrong. e, Miriam Makeba. f, Lionel Ritchie. g, Whitney Houston, h, Bob Marley. i, Tina Turner. No. 815, Kouyate family.

1992, Feb. 15 *Perf. 14*

808 A125 75sh Sheet of 9, #a.-i. 9.00 9.00
809 A125 75sh Sheet of 9, #a.-i. 10.50 10.50
810 A125 75sh Sheet of 9, #a.-i. 9.00 9.00
811 A125 75sh Sheet of 9, #a.-i. 9.00 9.00
Nos. 808-811 (4) 37.50 37.50

Souvenir Sheets

812 A125 500sh multicolored 8.00 8.00
813 A125 500sh multicolored 8.00 8.00
814 A125 500sh multicolored 8.00 8.00
815 A125 500sh multicolored 8.00 8.00
Nos. 812-815 (4) 32.00 32.00

Nos. 812-815 each contain one 29x43mm stamp.
See No. 949 for No. 808 inscribed "15th Anniversary."

Fish of Tanzania A126

Designs: 10sh, Malacanthus latovittatus. 15sh, Lamprologus tretocephalus. 25sh, Lamprologus calvus. 35sh, Hemichromis bimaculatusl. 60sh, Aphyosemion bivittatum. No. 821, Synanceia verrucosa. 300sh, Aphyosemion ahli. No. 823, Regalecus glesne.

1992, Mar. 8 *Perf. 12½x12*

816 A126 10sh multicolored .50 .50
817 A126 15sh multicolored .65 .65
818 A126 25sh multicolored .80 .80
819 A126 35sh multicolored 1.00 1.00
820 A126 60sh multicolored 1.35 1.35
821 A126 100sh multicolored 1.75 1.75
822 A126 300sh multicolored 4.75 4.75
Nos. 816-822 (7) 10.80 10.80

Souvenir Sheet

823 A126 100sh multicolored 2.75 2.75

World War II in the Pacific A127

Designs: No. 824a, British-designed radar at Pearl Harbor. b, Churchill declares war on Japan. c, Repulse destroyed. d, Prince of Wales sunk. e, Singapore falls to Japanese. f, Hermes is sunk off Ceylon. g, Airfields in Malaya attacked. h, Hong Kong falls to Japanese. i, Japanese Daihatsu landing craft. j, Japanese cruiser Haguro in Java Sea.

1992, Apr. 27 *Perf. 14½x15*

824 A127 75sh Sheet of 10, #a.-j. 20.00 20.00

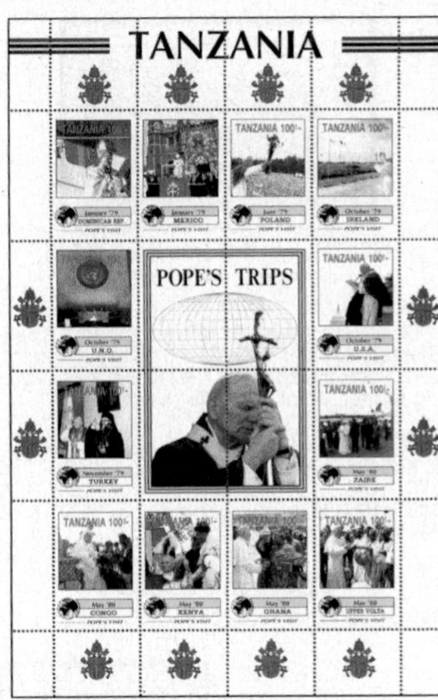

Visits of Pope John Paul II — A128

No. 825, 100sh: a, Dominican Republic, 1979. b, Mexico, 1979. c, Poland, 1979. d, Ireland, 1979. e, UN, New York, 1979. f, US, 1979. g, Turkey, 1979. h, Zaire, 1980. i, Congo, 1980. j, Kenya, 1980. k, Ghana, 1980. l, Upper Volta, 1980.
No. 826, 100sh: a, Ivory Coast, 1980. b, France, 1980. c, Brazil, 1980. d, West Germany, 1980. e, Pakistan, 1981. f, Philippines, 1981. g, Guam, 1981. h, Japan, 1981. h, Alaska, 1981. i, Nigeria, 1982. j, Benin, 1982. l. Gabon, 1982.
No. 827, 100sh: a, Equatorial Guinea, 1982. b, Portugal, 1982. c, Great Britain, 1982. d, Argentina, 1982. e, UN, Geneva, 1982. f, San Marino, 1982. g, Spain, 1982. h, Costa Rica, 1983. i, Panama, 1983. j, El Salvador, 1983. k, Nicaragua, 1983. l, Guatemala, 1983.
No. 828, 100sh: a, Honduras, 1983. b, Belize, 1983. c, Haiti, 1983. d, Poland, 1983. e, France, 1983. f, Austria, 1983. g, Alaska, 1984. h, South Korea, 1984. i, Papua New Guinea, 1984. j, Solomon Islands, 1984. k, Thailand, 1984. l, Switzerland, 1984.
No. 829, 100sh: a, Canada, 1984. b, Dominican Republic, 1984. c, Puerto Rico, 1984. d, Venezuela, 1985. e, Ecuador, 1985. f, Peru, 1985. g, Trinidad & Tobago, 1985. h, Netherlands, 1985. i, Luxembourg, 1985. j, Belgium, 1985. k, Togo, 1985. l, Ivory Coast, 1985.
No. 830, 100sh: a, Cameroun, 1985. b, Central African Republic, 1985. c, Zaire, 1985. d, Kenya, 1985. e, Morocco, 1985. f, Liechtenstein, 1985. g, India, 1986. h, Colombia, 1986. i, St. Lucia, 1986. j, France, 1986. k, Bangladesh, 1986. l, Singapore, 1986.
No. 831, 100sh: a, Fiji, 1986. b, New Zealand, 1986. c, Australia, 1986. d, Seychelles, 1986. e, Uruguay, 1987. f, Chile, 1987. g, Argentina, 1987. h, West Germany, 1987. i, Poland, 1987. j, US, 1987. k, Canada, 1987. l, Uruguay, 1988.
No. 832, 100sh: a, Bolivia, 1988. b, Peru, 1988. c, Paraguay, 1988. d, Austria, 1988. e, Zimbabwe, 1988. f, Botswana, 1988. g, Lesotho, 1988. h, Swaziland, 1988. i, Mozambique, 1988. j, France, 1988. k, Madagascar, 1989. l, Reunion, 1989.
No. 833, 100sh: a, Zambia, 1989. b, Malawi, 1989. c, Norway, 1989. d, Iceland, 1989. e, Finland, 1989. f, Denmark, 1989. g, Sweden, 1989. h, Spain, 1989. i, South Korea, 1989. j, Indonesia, 1989. k, Mauritius, 1989. l, Cape Verde, 1990.
No. 834, 100sh: a, Mali, 1990. b, Guinea-Bissau, 1990. c, Burkina Faso, 1990. d, Chad, 1990. e, Czechoslovakia, 1990. f, Mexico, 1990. g, Curacao, 1990. h, Malta, 1990. i, Tanzania, 1990. j, Burundi, 1990. k, Rwanda, 1990. l, Ivory Coast, 1990.

1992, Apr. 13 *Perf. 14*

Sheets of 12 + 4 Labels

825-834 A128 Set of 10 175.00 175.00

Zanzibar Stone Town A129

10sh, Balcony. 20sh, Bahlnara mosque. 30sh, High Court bldg. 200sh, Natl. museum.
No. 839a, 150sh, Old fort. b, 300sh, Maruhubi ruins.

1992, Apr. 15 *Perf. 12x12½, 12½x12*

835 A129 10sh multicolored .55 .55
836 A129 20sh multicolored 1.25 1.25
837 A129 30sh multicolored 1.75 1.75
838 A129 200sh multicolored 7.25 7.25
Nos. 835-838 (4) 10.80 10.80

Souvenir Sheet

839 A129 Sheet of 2, #a.-b. 9.00 9.00

Nos. 835-837 are vert.

Wolfgang Amadeus Mozart, Death Bicent. A130

Designs: 10sh, Marcella Sembrich as Zerlina in Don Giovanni. 50sh, Symphony Number 41, Jupiter. 300sh, Luciano Pavarotti as Idamente in Idomeneo. 500sh, Wolfgang Amadeus Mozart, vert.

1992, Aug. 1 *Perf. 14*

840 A130 10sh violet & blk 1.25 1.25
841 A130 50sh multicolored 3.00 3.00
842 A130 300sh violet & blk 7.00 7.00
Nos. 840-842 (3) 11.25 11.25

Souvenir Sheet

843 A130 500sh olive brn & blk 10.00 10.00

While No. 843 has the same issue date as Nos. 840-842, the dollar value was lower when it were released.
No. 843 contains one 38x50mm stamp.

1992, Aug. 1

Designs: 10sh, Insignia, giraffe and elephant. 15sh, Scouts in canoe. 400sh, John Glenn's Gemini space capsule orbiting Earth. 500sh, Boy scout, vert.

844 A130 10sh multicolored .40 .40
845 A130 15sh multicolored .40 .40
846 A130 400sh multicolored 9.25 9.25
Nos. 844-846 (3) 10.05 10.05

Souvenir Sheet

847 A130 500sh multicolored 7.75 7.75

Lord Robert Baden-Powell, Founder of Boy Scouts, 50th Death Anniv. (in 1991).
While No. 847 has the same issue date as Nos. 844-846, the dollar value was lower when it were released.
No. 847 contains one 38x50mm stamp.

1992, Aug. 1

Charles de Gaulle (1890-1970): 25sh, French Resistance Monument and medal. 30sh, First Free French tank at Omaha beach, Normandy. 150sh, Concorde at de Gaulle Airport. 500sh, France #439 with Cross of Lorraine overprint and Free French stamp, vert.

848 A130 25sh multicolored .80 .80
849 A130 30sh multicolored .90 .90
850 A130 150sh multicolored 9.00 9.00
Nos. 848-850 (3) 10.70 10.70

Souvenir Sheet

851 A130 500sh multicolored 11.50 11.50

While No. 851 has the same issue date as Nos. 848-850, the dollar value was lower when it was released.
No. 851 contains one 38x50mm stamp.

Common Chimpanzee A131

Various chimpanzees in natural habitat.
No. 860, Swinging from tree. No. 861, Eating termites.

1992

852 A131 10sh multicolored .35 .35
853 A131 15sh multicolored .35 .35
854 A131 35sh multicolored .75 .75
855 A131 75sh multicolored 1.60 1.60
856 A131 100sh multicolored 1.90 1.90
857 A131 150sh multicolored 3.00 3.00
858 A131 200sh multicolored 4.00 4.00
859 A131 300sh multicolored 6.25 6.25
Nos. 852-859 (8) 18.20 18.20

Souvenir Sheets

860 A131 400sh multicolored 5.75 5.75
861 A131 400sh multicolored 5.75 5.75

Spanish Art — A132

Drawings by Goya: 25sh, A Picador mounted on the shoulders of a Chulo, spears a Bull. 100sh, The Dream of Reason brings forth Monsters, vert. 150sh, Another Madness (of Martincho) in the Plaza de Zaragoza. 200sh, Recklessness of Martincho in the Plaza de Zaragoza.

No. 866, Seascape, by Mariano Salvador Maella.

1992 *Perf. 13*

862 A132 25sh blk & red brn .45 .45
863 A132 100sh black & brn 1.50 1.50
864 A132 150sh blk & red brn 2.50 2.50
865 A132 200sh blk & red brn 2.60 2.60

Size: 120x95mm

Imperf

866 A132 400sh multicolored 4.50 4.50
Nos. 862-866 (5) 11.55 11.55

Granada '92.

1992 *Perf. 13*

Drawings by Diego da Silva Velazquez: 35sh, Philip IV at Fraga. 50sh, The Head of the Stag. 75sh, The Cardinal Infante Don Fernando as a Hunter. 300sh, Pablo de Valladolid. No. 871, Two Men at Table.

867 A132 35sh multicolored .65 .65
868 A132 50sh multicolored .80 .80
869 A132 75sh multicolored 1.35 1.35
870 A132 300sh multicolored 3.25 3.25

Size: 120x95mm

Imperf

871 A132 400sh multicolored 4.50 4.50
Nos. 867-871 (5) 10.55 10.55

Granada '92.

A133

Chimpanzees of Gombe — A134

Designs: No. 872, Melisa and Mike. No. 873, Leakey and David Greybeard. No. 874, Fifi eating termites. No. 875 Galahad.

No. 876a, 10sh, Leakey. b, 15sh, Fifi. c, 20sh, Faben. d, 30sh, David Greybeard. e, 35sh, Mike. f, 50sh, Galahad. g, 100sh, Melisa. h, 200sh, Flo.

No. 877, Fifi, Flo, and Faben.

1992, May 29 **Litho.** *Perf. 14*

872 A133 10sh multicolored .90 .90
873 A133 15sh multicolored 1.10 1.10
874 A133 30sh multicolored 1.50 1.50
875 A133 35sh multicolored 1.75 1.75
Nos. 872-875 (4) 5.25 5.25

Miniature Sheet

876 A134 Sheet of 8, #a.-h. 10.50 10.50

Souvenir Sheet

877 A133 100sh multicolored 4.00 4.00

Natl. Bank of Commerce, 25th Anniv. — A135

Designs: 10sh, Sorghum plants. 15sh, Samora Avenue branch, computer operator, vert. 30sh, Head office. 35sh, Bankers Training Center. 40sh, Batik tie dyeing.

1992, June 22

878 A135 10sh multicolored .60 .60
879 A135 15sh multicolored .70 .70
880 A135 35sh multicolored 1.10 1.10
881 A135 40sh multicolored 1.10 1.10
Nos. 878-881 (4) 3.50 3.50

Souvenir Sheet

882 A135 30sh multicolored 2.25 2.25

Traditional Dress — A136

Designs: 3sh, Gogo, central area. 5sh, Swahili, coastal area. 9sh, Hehe, southern highlands and Makonde, southern area. 12sh, Maasai, northern area. 40sh, Mwarusha.

1992, Apr. 30 **Litho.** *Perf. 14½*

883 A136 3sh multicolored .60 .60
884 A136 5sh multicolored .70 .70
885 A136 9sh multicolored .80 .80
886 A136 12sh multicolored 1.00 1.00
Nos. 883-886 (4) 3.10 3.10

Souvenir Sheet

887 A136 40sh multicolored 4.00 4.00

Dated 1989.

1992 Summer Olympics, Barcelona A137

1992, July 23 *Perf. 12x12½*

888 A137 40sh Basketball .70 .70
889 A137 100sh Billiards 1.10 1.10
890 A137 200sh Table tennis 1.75 1.75
891 A137 400sh Darts 3.75 3.75
Nos. 888-891 (4) 7.30 7.30

Souvenir Sheet

892 A137 500sh Weight lifting 5.50 5.50

Fish A138

No. 893: a, Tilapia mariae. b, Capoeta hulstaerti. c, Tropheus moorii. d, Synodontis angelicus. e, Julidochromis dickfeldi. f, Tilapia nilotica. g, Nothobranchius rachovii. h, Pseudotropheus crabro. i, Lamprologus leleupi. j, Pseudotropheus zebra. k, Julidochromis marlieri. l, Chalinochromis brichardi.

Designs: No. 894, Haplochromis "electric blue." No. 895, Lamprologus brevis. No. 896, Nothobranchius palmqvisti.

1992, Oct. **Litho.** *Perf. 13½*

893 A138 100sh Sheet of 12, #a.-l. 17.50 17.50

Souvenir Sheets

894 A138 500sh multicolored 6.00 6.00
895 A138 500sh multicolored 6.00 6.00
896 A138 500sh multicolored 6.00 6.00

Discovery of America, 500th Anniv. A139

1992, Oct. **Litho.** *Perf. 14*

897 A139 70sh Sailing ship 1.50 1.50
898 A139 300sh Columbus 5.50 5.50

Souvenir Sheet

899 A139 500sh Columbus, diff. 4.50 4.50

Miniature Sheet

Flowers in Rio de Janeiro Botanical Garden — A140

No. 900: a, Couroupita guianensis. b, Jacaranda acutifolia. c, Psychopsis papilio. d, Nelumbo nucifera. e, Brownea grandiceps. f, Coffea arabica. g, Monodora myristica. h, Calaranthus rosea. i, Hibiscus schizopetalus. j, Carpobrotus edulis. k, Adenium obesum. l, Delonix regia. m, Agapanthus praecox. n, Zantedeschia aethiopica. o, Protea cynaroides. p, Cassia fistula. q, Aganisia cyanea. r, Heliconia rostrata. s, Cattelya luteola. t, Lagerstroemia speciosa.

500sh, Avenue of Royal Palms, Rio.

1992, Nov. 5 **Litho.** *Perf. 14½*

900 A140 70sh Sheet of 20, #a.-t. 21.50 21.50

Souvenir Sheet

901 A140 500sh multicolored 6.75 6.75

Dinosaurs — A141

No. 902: a, Iguanodon. b, Saltasaurus. c, Cetiosaurus. d, Camarasaurus. e, Spinosaurus. f, Stegosaurus. g, Allosaurus. h, Ceratosaurus. i, Lesothosaurus. j, Anchisaurus. k, Ornithomimus. l, Baronyx. m, Pachycephalosaurus. n, Heterodontosaurus. o, Dryosaurus. p, Coelophysis.

1992, Nov. 5 **Litho.** *Perf. 14*

902 A141 100sh Sheet of 16, #a.-p. 19.00 19.00

1992 Olympics, Albertville and Barcelona A142

Designs: 20sh, 4000-meter pursuit cycling, vert. 40sh, Double sculls. 50sh, Water polo. 70sh, Women's single luge. 100sh, Marathon. 150sh, Uneven parallel bars. 200sh, Ice hockey, vert, 400sh, Rings, vert.

No. 911, Tennis, vert. No. 912, Soccer, vert.

1992, Nov. 16 **Litho.** *Perf. 14*

903 A142 20sh multicolored .35 .35
904 A142 40sh multicolored .55 .55
905 A142 50sh multicolored .60 .60
906 A142 70sh multicolored .85 .85
907 A142 100sh multicolored 1.25 1.25
908 A142 150sh multicolored 1.75 1.75
909 A142 200sh multicolored 2.40 2.40
910 A142 400sh multicolored 4.75 4.75
Nos. 903-910 (8) 12.50 12.50

Souvenir Sheets

911 A142 500sh multicolored 6.00 6.00
912 A142 500sh multicolored 6.00 6.00

Mickey's Portrait Gallery A142a

Donald Duck in scenes from Disney movies: No. 915, Sea Scouts, 1939. 35sh, Fire Chief, 1940. 50sh, Truant Officer Donald, 1941. 500sh, With Daisy in Mr. Duck Steps Out, 1940.

No. 925, Daisy in Don Donald, 1937.

Disney characters in scenes from Disney movies: No. 913, Hawaiian Holiday, 1937. No. 914, Society Dog Show, 1939. 75sh, Clock Cleaners, 1937. No. 919, Magician Mickey, 1937. No. 920, Goofy and Wilbur, 1939. 200sh, The Nifty Nineties, 1941. 300sh, Society Dog Show, 1939. 400sh, Pluto's Quin-Puplets, 1937. No. 926, Brave Little Tailor, 1938, horiz. No. 927, Forever Goofy.

1992, Nov. 30 **Litho.** *Perf. 13½x14*

913 A142a 25sh multicolored .45 .45
914 A142a 25sh multicolored .45 .45
915 A142a 25sh multicolored .45 .45
916 A142a 35sh multicolored .55 .55
917 A142a 50sh multicolored .80 .80
918 A142a 75sh multicolored 1.00 1.00
919 A142a 100sh multicolored 1.10 1.10
920 A142a 100sh multicolored 1.10 1.10
921 A142a 200sh multicolored 1.75 1.75
922 A142a 300sh multicolored 2.50 2.50
923 A142a 400sh multicolored 2.75 2.75
924 A142a 500sh multicolored 2.75 2.75
Nos. 913-924 (12) 15.65 15.65

Souvenir Sheets

925 A142a 600sh multicolored 5.00 5.00

Perf. 14x13½

926 A142a 600sh multicolored 5.00 5.00

Perf. 13½x14

927 A142a 600sh multicolored 5.00 5.00

Nos. 668-673 & 678 Ovptd. in Black or Red

1992 **Litho.** *Perf. 14*

928 A106 50sh on #668 .35 .35
929 A106 50sh on #669 .35 .35
a. Pair, #928-929 .70 .70
930 A106 75sh on #670 .55 .55
931 A106 75sh on #671 .55 .55
a. Pair, #930-931 1.10 1.10
932 A106 100sh on #672 .75 .75
933 A106 100sh on #673 .75 .75
a. Pair, #932-933 1.50 1.50
Nos. 928-933 (6) 3.30 3.30

Souvenir Sheet

934 A106 350sh on #678 (R) 2.50 2.50

Overprint appears on one line in sheet margin of No. 934.

Traditional Hunting A143

Designs: 20sh, Slingshots used on birds. 40sh, Various weapons. 70sh, Bow and arrow used on gazelles. 100sh, Long knife, wooden club used on gazelles. 150sh, Spear and shield used on lion.

1992	Litho.		*Perf. 13½*	
935 A143	20sh multicolored		1.40	1.40
936 A143	70sh multicolored		1.75	1.75
937 A143	100sh multicolored		2.75	2.75
938 A143	150sh multicolored		4.00	4.00
	Nos. 935-938 (4)		9.90	9.90

Souvenir Sheet

Perf. 12½

939 A143	40sh multicolored	3.25	3.25

Shells — A144

Designs: 10sh, Lambis truncata Humphrey. 15sh, Cypraecassis rufa. 25sh, Vexillum rugosum. 30sh, Conus litteratus. 35sh, Corculum cardissa. 50sh, Murex ramosus. 250sh, Melo melo. 300sh, Tridacha gigas.

1992, June 30		*Perf. 12x12½*	
940 A144	10sh multicolored	.40	.40
941 A144	15sh multicolored	.55	.55
942 A144	25sh multicolored	.65	.65
943 A144	30sh multicolored	.65	.65
944 A144	35sh multicolored	.65	.65
945 A144	50sh multicolored	1.00	1.00
946 A144	250sh multicolored	4.00	4.00
	Nos. 940-946 (7)	7.90	7.90

Souvenir Sheet

947 A144	300sh multicolored	5.50	5.50

No. 808 Inscribed Vertically "15th Anniversary"

1992	Litho.	*Perf. 14*	
949 A125	75sh Sheet of 9, #a.-i.	11.00	11.00

Marine Life A145

1992	Litho.	*Perf. 14*	
950 A145	20sh Seal	1.25	1.25
951 A145	30sh Whale	3.00	3.00
952 A145	70sh Shark	1.75	1.75
953 A145	100sh Walrus	3.00	3.00
	Nos. 950-953 (4)	9.00	9.00

Souvenir Sheet

954 A145	500sh Sea turtle	10.00	10.00

A146

Anniversaries and Events — A147

Designs: 30sh, Count Ferdinand von Zeppelin. 70sh, Apollo-Soyuz. No. 957, Child being offered apple. No. 958, African elephant. No. 959, Lions Intl. emblem, man being given glasses. No. 960, Zebra. 300sh, Graf Zeppelin. No. 962, Space shuttle in Earth orbit. No. 963, Wolfgang Amadeus Mozart.

No. 964, Voyager 2. No. 965, Unidentified zeppelin. No. 966, African elephant, diff. No. 967, Scene from "The Magic Flute."

1992	Litho.	*Perf. 14*	
955 A146	30sh multicolored	3.25	3.25
956 A146	70sh multicolored	4.50	4.50
957 A146	150sh multicolored	2.00	2.00
958 A146	150sh multicolored	3.25	3.25
959 A146	200sh multicolored	2.40	2.40
960 A146	200sh multicolored	3.25	3.25
961 A146	300sh multicolored	3.25	3.25
962 A146	400sh multicolored	4.50	4.50
963 A147	400sh multicolored	3.25	3.25
	Nos. 955-963 (9)	29.65	29.65

Souvenir Sheets

964 A146	500sh multicolored	4.50	4.50
965 A146	500sh multicolored	4.50	4.50
966 A146	500sh multicolored	4.50	4.50
967 A147	800sh multicolored	6.50	6.50

Count Zeppelin, 75th death anniv. (#955, 961, 965). Intl. Space Year (#956, 962, 964). Intl. Conference on Nutrition (#957). Earth Summit, Rio de Janeiro (#958, 960, 966). Lions Intl., 75th anniv. (#959). Wolfgang Amadeus Mozart, bicent. of death (in 1991) (#963, 967).

Issued: Nos. 955-956, 961-962, 964-965, Nov.; Nos. 957-960, 966, Dec.

Cats — A147a

20sh, Abyssinian. 30sh, Havana. 50sh, Persian black. 70sh, Persian blue. 100sh, European silver tabby. 150sh, Persian silver tabby. 200sh, Maine.

300sh, European.

1992, Dec. 3	Litho.	*Perf. 12x12½*	
967A A147a	20sh multi	.65	.65
967B A147a	30sh multi	.65	.65
967C A147a	50sh multi	.80	.80
967D A147a	70sh multi	1.00	1.00
967E A147a	100sh multi	1.15	1.15
967F A147a	150sh multi	1.45	1.45
967G A147a	200sh multi	1.75	1.75
	Nos. 967A-967G (7)	7.45	7.45

Souvenir Sheet

967H A147a	300sh multi	4.50	4.50

Model Trains A148

Lionel models: 10sh, B & O Tunnel locomotive #5, 2⅞-inch gauge, 1904. 20sh, Liberty Bell #385E, standard gauge, 1930. 30sh, Armored motor car #203, standard gauge, 1917. 50sh, Open trolley #202, standard gauge, 1910-14. 70sh, Macy special #450, standrad gauge. 100sh, Milwaukee Road bipolar electric #381E, standard gauge, 1929. 200sh, New York Central "S" type, standard gauge, 1912. 300sh, 4-4-0 American #7 (thick rim), standard gauge, 1914.

No. 976, Wind-up hand car with Mickey and Minnie Mouse, O-27 gauge, 1936. No. 977, Clear plastic F-3 display model, O gauge, 1947.

1992, Dec. 10	Litho.	*Perf. 14*	
968 A148	10sh multicolored	.55	.55
969 A148	20sh multicolored	.65	.65
970 A148	30sh multicolored	.70	.70
971 A148	50sh multicolored	1.10	1.10
972 A148	70sh multicolored	1.35	1.35
973 A148	100sh multicolored	1.45	1.45
974 A148	200sh multicolored	2.10	2.10
975 A148	300sh multicolored	2.75	2.75
	Nos. 968-975 (8)	10.65	10.65

Souvenir Sheets

976 A148	500sh multicolored	4.50	4.50
977 A148	500sh multicolored	4.50	4.50

Genoa '92.

Birds — A149

5sh, Superb starling. 10sh, Canary. 15sh, Four-colored bush shrike. 25sh, Grey-headed kingfisher. 30sh, Common kingfisher. 35sh, Yellow-billed oxpecker. 150sh, Black throated honeyquide.

300sh, European cuckoo, horiz.

1992, Dec. 10	Litho.	*Perf. 12x12½*	
978 A149	5sh multicolored	.80	.80
979 A149	10sh multicolored	1.00	1.00
980 A149	15sh multicolored	1.00	1.00
981 A149	25sh multicolored	1.10	1.10
982 A149	30sh multicolored	1.10	1.10
983 A149	35sh multicolored	1.10	1.10
984 A149	150sh multicolored	2.75	2.75
	Nos. 978-984 (7)	8.85	8.85

Souvenir Sheet

Perf. 12½x12

985 A149	300sh multicolored	5.50	5.50

Makonde Art — A149a

Various carved faces.

1992, Dec. 24	Litho.	*Perf. 12x12½*	
985A A149a	20sh multicolored	.25	.25
985B A149a	30sh multicolored	.25	.25
985C A149a	50sh multicolored	.45	.45
985D A149a	70sh multicolored	.60	.60
985E A149a	100sh multicolored	.90	.90
985F A149a	150sh multicolored	1.35	1.35
985G A149a	200sh multicolored	1.75	1.75
	Nos. 985A-985G (7)	5.55	5.55

Souvenir Sheet

985H A149a	350sh multicolored	4.50	4.50

Bicycles A149b

20sh, Russia, 1813. 30sh, Germany, 1840. 50sh, Germany, 1818. 70sh, Germany, 1850. 100sh. Italy, 1988. 150sh, Sweden, 1982. 300sh, Italy, 1989.

350sh, Great Britain, 1887.

1992, Dec. 30	Litho.	*Perf. 12½x12*	
985I A149b	20sh multicolored	.40	.40
985J A149b	30sh multicolored	.40	.40
985K A149b	50sh multicolored	.55	.55
985L A149b	70sh multicolored	.55	.55
985M A149b	100sh multicolored	.60	.60
985N A149b	150sh multicolored	1.35	1.35
985O A149b	300sh multicolored	1.50	1.50
	Nos. 985I-985O (7)	5.35	5.35

Souvenir Sheet

985P A149b	350sh multicolored	4.50	4.50

Discovery of America, 500th Anniv. — A150

Designs: 10sh, Symbols of luck. 15sh, "Is this course right?," compass, chart. 25sh, "Earth!," first sight of land. 30sh, First meetings, horiz. 35sh, Nina, horiz. 75sh, Santa Maria, horiz. 250sh, Ship running aground, vert. 200sh, Columbus.

Perf. 12x12½, 12½x12

1992, Sept. 30		Litho.	
986 A150	10sh multicolored	.30	.30
987 A150	15sh multicolored	.35	.35
988 A150	25sh multicolored	.50	.50
989 A150	30sh multicolored	.55	.55
990 A150	35sh multicolored	.65	.65
991 A150	75sh multicolored	1.10	1.10
992 A150	250sh multicolored	2.00	2.00
	Nos. 986-992 (7)	5.45	5.45

Souvenir Sheet

993 A150	200sh multicolored	5.50	5.50

Louvre Museum, Bicent. — A151

No. 994 — Paintings by Jean-Baptiste-Simeon Chardin (1699-1779): a, Young Artist. b, The Buffet. c, The Provider. d, A Mother Working. e, Grace. f, The Copper Fountain. g, House of Cards. h, Child with Teetotum. 500sh, The Ray, horiz.

1993, Mar. 8	Litho.	*Perf. 12*	
994 A151	100sh Sheet of 8, #a.-h. + label	10.50	10.50

Souvenir Sheet

Perf. 14½

995 A151	500sh multicolored	6.00	6.00

No. 995 contains one 88x55mm stamp.

Coronation of Queen Elizabeth II, 40th Anniv. A152

No. 996: a, 100sh, Official coronation photograph. b, 150sh, Exeter salt. c, 200sh, Photograph of ceremony, 1953. d, 300sh, Queen, Prince Andrew.

500sh, Princess Elizabeth Opening the New Broadgate Coventry, by Dame Laura Knight, 1948.

1993, June 2	Litho.	*Perf. 13½x14*	
996 A152	Sheet of 2 ea, #a.-d.	12.50	12.50

Souvenir Sheet

Perf. 14

997 A152	500sh multicolored	5.50	5.50

No. 997 contains one 28x43mm stamp.

Famous Women — A153

Designs: a, 20sh, Valentina Tereshkova. b, 40sh, Marie Curie. c, 50sh, Indira Gandhi. d, 70sh, Wilma Rudolph. e, 100sh, Margaret Mead. f, 150sh, Golda Meir. g, 200sh, Dr. Elizabeth Blackwell. h, 400sh, Margaret Thatcher.
No. 999, Mother Teresa.

1993, July 15 ***Perf. 14***

998 A153 Sheet of 8, #a.-h. 13.50 13.50

Souvenir Sheet

999 A153 500sh multicolored 6.25 6.25

Wildlife — A154

No. 1000 — Wildlife at watering hole: No. 1000: a, Elephant. b, Gazelles. c, Hartebeest. d, Duiker. e, Genet. f, Civet. g, Pelicans. h, Waterbuck. i, Blacksmith plovers. j, Pied kingfisher. k, Black-winged stilts. l, Bush pig.
No. 1000M: n, Brown-hooded kingfisher. o, Sable antelope (n). p, Impala (q). q, Buffalo. r, Leopard. s, Aardvark (t). t, Hippopotamus. u, Spotted hyena. v, Crowned crane (w). w, Crocodile. x, Flamingo. y, Baboon.
No. 1001 — Wildlife on the plains: No. 1001: a, Potto. b, Flamingos. c, Grey-headed kingfisher. d, Red colobus monkey. e, Dik-dik. f, Aardwolf. g, Black-backed jackal. h, Tree pangolin. i, Serval. j, Yellow-billed hornbill. k, Pygmy mongoose. l, Bat-eared fox.
No. 1001M: n, Bushbaby. o, Egyptian vulture. p, Ostrich. q, Greater kudu. r, Diana monkey. s, Giraffe (w). t, Cheetah (s). u, Wildebeest (t). v, Chimpanzee. w, Warthog. x, Zebra. y, Rhinoceros.
No. 1002, Lions, horiz. No. 1003, African elephants, horiz.

1993, June 30

1000 A154 100sh Sheet of 12, #a.-l. 10.50 10.50
1000M A154 100sh Sheet of 12, #n.-y. 10.50 10.50
1001 A154 100sh Sheet of 12, #a.-l. 10.50 10.50
1001M A154 100sh Sheet of 12, #n.-y. 10.50 10.50
Nos. 1000-1001M (4) 42.00 42.00

Souvenir Sheets

1002 A154 500sh multi 6.00 6.00
1003 A154 500sh multi 6.00 6.00

For overprints see Nos. 1531, 1534.

Pancake Tortoise A155

1993, June 30

1004 A155 20sh On rock .50 .50
1005 A155 30sh Drinking .75 .75
1006 A155 50sh Crawling from under rocks .90 .90
1007 A155 70sh Hatchling 1.20 1.20
Nos. 1004-1007 (4) 3.35 3.35

World Wildlife Federation.

Mushrooms A156

Designs: 20sh, Macrolepiota rhacodes. 40sh, Mycena pura. 50sh, Chlorophyllum molybdites. 70sh, Agaricus campestris. 100sh, Volvariella volvacea. 150sh, Leucoagaricus naucinus. 200sh, Oudemansiella radicata. 300sh, Clitocybe nebularis.
No. 1016, Omphalotus olearius. No. 1017, Lepista nuda.

1993, June 18 **Litho.** ***Perf. 14***

1008 A156 20sh multicolored .30 .30
1009 A156 40sh multicolored .50 .50
1010 A156 50sh multicolored .55 .55
1011 A156 70sh multicolored .75 .75
1012 A156 100sh multicolored 1.25 1.25
1013 A156 150sh multicolored 1.60 1.60
1014 A156 200sh multicolored 2.10 2.10
1015 A156 300sh multicolored 3.50 3.50
Nos. 1008-1015 (8) 10.55 10.55

Souvenir Sheets

1016 A156 500sh multicolored 4.50 4.50
1017 A156 500sh multicolored 4.50 4.50

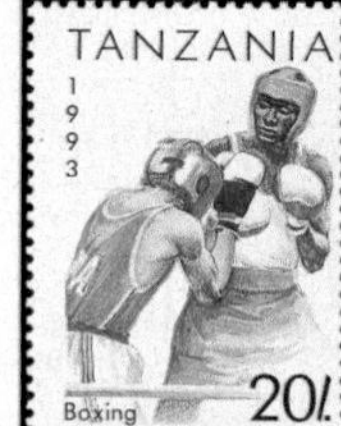

Sports — A157

1992, May 28 **Litho.** ***Perf. 12x12½***

1018 A157 20sh Boxing .30 .30
1019 A157 50sh Field hockey .70 .70
1020 A157 70sh Horse racing .60 .60
1021 A157 100sh Marathon .65 .65
1022 A157 150sh Soccer .85 .85
1023 A157 200sh Diving 1.10 1.10
1024 A157 400sh Basketball 2.10 2.10
Nos. 1018-1024 (7) 6.30 6.30

Souvenir Sheet

Perf. 12½x12

1025 A157 300sh High jump, horiz. 3.50 3.50

Animals A158

No. 1026: a, Female Grant's zebra, running. b, Male Grant's zebra, standing. c, Female Grant's gazelle. d, Male Grant's gazelle. e, Thompson's gazelle. f, White-bearded gnu, calf.
No. 1027: a, Female cheetah, cubs. b, Young cheetah. c, Lioness carrying her cub. d, Two hunting dogs. e, Three hunting dogs. f, Hunting dogs before an attack.
No. 1028, African rhinoceros. No. 1029, African elephant.

1993, June 30 **Litho.** ***Perf. 14***

1026 A158 100sh Sheet of 6, #a.-f. 9.00 9.00
1027 A158 100sh Sheet of 6, #a.-f. 9.00 9.00

Souvenir Sheets

1028 A158 500sh multicolored 10.00 10.00
1029 A158 500sh multicolored 10.00 10.00

For overprints see Nos. 1532-1533, 1535.

A159

1994 Winter Olympics, Lillehammer, Norway: 300sh, Matti Nykanen, ski jumping, 1988. 400sh, Stefan Krause, Jan Behrendt, double luge, 1992. 500sh, Downhill skiing, 1972.

1993, June 10 **Litho.** ***Perf. 14***

1030 A159 300sh multicolored 2.00 2.00
1031 A159 400sh multicolored 2.50 2.50

Souvenir Sheet

1032 A159 500sh multicolored 3.25 3.25

A160

100sh, Telescope. 300sh, Radio telescope. 500sh, Copernicus.

1993, June 10

1033 A160 100sh multicolored .70 .70
1034 A160 300sh multicolored 2.25 2.25

Souvenir Sheet

1035 A160 500sh multicolored 3.50 3.50

Copernicus, 450th anniv. of death.

Picasso (1881-1973) A160a

Various details of painting, Guernica, 1937.

1993, June 10 **Litho.** ***Perf. 14***

1035A A160a 30sh multi .25 .25
1035B A160a 200sh multi 1.25 1.25
1035C A160a 300sh multi 1.75 1.75
Nos. 1035A-1035C (3) 3.25 3.25

Souvenir Sheet

1035D A160a 500sh multi 3.00 3.00

Flowers — A161

Designs: 20sh, Leopard orchid. 30sh, African violet. 40sh, Stapelia semota lutea. 50sh, Busy Lizzie. 60sh, Senecio petraeus. 70sh, Kalanchoe velutina. 100sh, Dwarf ginger lily. 150sh, Nymphaea colorata. 200sh, Thunbergia battiscombei. 250sh, Crossandra nilotica. 300sh, African tulip tree. 350sh, Rutya fruticosa.
No. 1048, False African violet. No. 1049, Glory lily.

1993, Nov. 8 **Litho.** ***Perf. 13½***

1036 A161 20sh multicolored .45 .45
1037 A161 30sh multicolored .50 .50
1038 A161 40sh multicolored .50 .50
1039 A161 50sh multicolored .50 .50
1040 A161 60sh multicolored .70 .70
1041 A161 70sh multicolored .80 .80

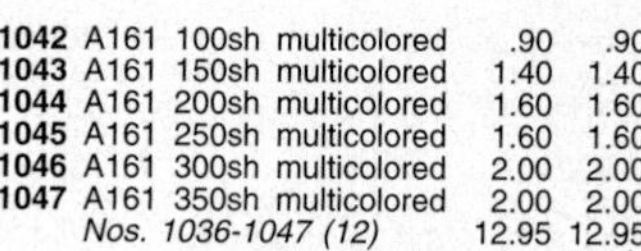
1042 A161 100sh multicolored .90 .90
1043 A161 150sh multicolored 1.40 1.40
1044 A161 200sh multicolored 1.60 1.60
1045 A161 250sh multicolored 1.60 1.60
1046 A161 300sh multicolored 2.00 2.00
1047 A161 350sh multicolored 2.00 2.00
Nos. 1036-1047 (12) 12.95 12.95

Souvenir Sheets

Perf. 13

1048 A161 500sh multicolored 3.75 3.75
1049 A161 500sh multicolored 3.75 3.75

Polska '93 — A162

Paintings: 200sh, Stone Masons, by Aleksander Kobzdej, 1952. 300sh, Child Wearing Plumed Helmut, by Z. Waliszewski, 1932.
500sh, In the Marketplace, by Stanislaw Osostowicz, 1939.

1993 **Litho.** ***Perf. 14***

1050 A162 200sh multicolored 1.60 1.60
1051 A162 300sh multicolored 2.25 2.25

Souvenir Sheet

1052 A162 500sh multicolored 3.50 3.50

Butterflies A163

No. 1053: a, Gold-banded forester. b, Twin dotted border. c, Aphnaeus flavescens. d, Orange-and-lemon. e, Club-tailed charaxes. f, Broad blue-banded swallowtail. g, African map. h, Buxton's hairstreak. i, Bush charaxes. j, Lilac nymph. k, Large striped swordtail. l, Charaxes acuminatus. m, African leaf. n, African wood white. o, Trimen's false acraea. p, Red line sapphire. q, Mother-of-pearl. r, Flame-bordered charaxes. s, Large blue charaxes. t, Emperor swallowtail.
No. 1054: a, Angled grass yellow. b, Figtree blue. c, Iolaus ismenias. d, Green-veined charaxes. e, Commodore. f, African monarch. g, Bush scarlet. h, Eyed pansy. i, Zebra white. j, Azure hairstreak. k, Yellow pansy. l, Regal purple tip.
No. 1054M: n, Iolaus aphnaeoides. o, Green charaxes. p, Beautiful monarch. q, Short-tailed admiral. r, Dusky dotted border. s, Charaxes anticlea. t, Blue salamis. u, Nepheronia argia. v, Acraea pseudolycia. w, Blue-banded diadem. x, Golden tip. y, Acraea bonasia.
No. 1055, Blood-red cymothoe. No. 1056, Precis octavia. No. 1056A, Noble swallowtail. No. 1056B, Violet-spotted charaxes.

1993, Nov. 8 **Litho.** ***Perf. 13***

1053 A163 100sh Sheet of 20, #a.-t. 25.00 25.00
1054 A163 100sh Sheet of 12, #a.-l. 15.00 15.00
1054M A163 100sh Sheet of 12, #n.-y. 15.00 15.00

Souvenir Sheets

1055 A163 500sh multi 6.00 6.00
1056 A163 500sh multi 6.00 6.00
1056A A163 500sh multi 6.00 6.00
1056B A163 500sh multi 6.00 6.00

A164

Players, country: 20sh, Gullit, Holland. 30sh, Sheehy, Ireland. 50sh, Giannini, Italy. 70sh, Cesar, Brazil. 250sh, Barnes, England; Grun, Belgium. 300sh, Chendo, Spain. 350sh,

Rijkaard, Holland. 400sh, Matthaeus, Germany.
No. 1065, 500sh, Berti, Italy; Caligiuri, US. No. 1066, 500sh, Walker, England; Gilhaus, Holland.

1993, Dec. ***Perf. 14***
1057-1064 A164 Set of 8 8.50 8.50

Souvenir Sheets

1065-1066 A164 Set of 2 8.50 8.50

1994 World Cup Soccer Championships, US.

A165

Hummel Figurines: 20sh, Boy with accordian. 40sh, Girl with guitar, boy with banjo. 50sh, Boy with tuba. 70sh, Boy with harmonica, bird. 100sh, Bird in tree, boy seated on fence. 150sh, Boy playing horn. 200sh, Boy with horn, bird. 300sh, Girl playing banjo. 350sh, Boy with cello on back. 400sh, Girls with banjo and sheet music.
No. 1077, 500sh, Four carolers. No. 1078, 500sh, Two figures in tower blowing horns at angel below.

1994, Feb. 10
1067-1076 A165 Set of 10 11.00 11.00

Souvenir Sheets

1077-1078 A165 Set of 2 10.00 10.00

Black Athletes — A166

No. 1079: a, 20sh, Arthur Ashe. b, 40sh, Michael Jordan. c, 50sh, Daley Thompson. d, 70sh, Jackie Robinson. e, 100sh, Kareem Abdul-Jabbar. f, 150sh, Florence Joyner. g, 200sh, Jesse Owens. h, 400sh, Jack Johnson.
500sh, Muhammad Ali, horiz.

1993, July 15
1079 A166 Sheet of 8, #a.-h. 8.00 8.00

Souvenir Sheet

1080 A166 500sh multicolored 5.00 5.00

First US Gas Balloon Flight, Bicent. A167

Designs: 200sh, Balloons filling with hot air. 400sh, Jean-Pierre Blanchard (1753-1809), balloon. 500sh, Hot air balloons in flight, vert.

1994, Apr. 25 **Litho.** ***Perf. 14***
1081 A167 200sh multicolored 2.00 2.00
1082 A167 400sh multicolored 3.75 3.75

Souvenir Sheet

1083 A167 500sh multicolored 6.00 6.00

Royal Air Force, 75th Anniv. A168

Designs: 200sh, Sopwith Camel. 400sh, BAE Harrier. 500sh, Supermarine Spitfire.

1993, Dec.
1084 A168 200sh multicolored 2.25 2.25
1085 A168 400sh multicolored 4.00 4.00

Souvenir Sheet

1086 A168 500sh multicolored 6.25 6.25

Automotive Anniversaries — A171

Designs: No. 1099, 200sh, 1893 Benz, 1993 500 SEL. No. 1100, 200sh, Henry Ford, 1922 Model T. No. 1101, 400sh, Karl Benz, emblem. No. 1102, 400sh, 1893 Ford, Mustang Cobra.
No. 1103, 500sh, Emblem, 1937 540 K. No. 1104, 500sh, Henry Ford, first Ford factory.

1994, Apr. 25 **Litho.** ***Perf. 14***
1099-1102 A171 Set of 4 9.50 9.50

Souvenir Sheets

1103-1104 A171 Set of 2 8.50 8.50

First Benz 4-wheel motor car, cent. (#1099, 1101, 1103). First Ford motor, cent. (#1100, 1102, 1104).

Birds A172

No. 1105, vert.: a, 20sh, African hawk eagle. b, 30sh, Shoe-bill stork. c, 50sh, Harrier eagle. d, 70sh, Casqued hornbill. e, 100sh, Crowned crane. f, 150sh, Greater flamingo.
No. 1106: a, 200sh, Pelican. b, 250sh, Jacana, black crake. c, 300sh, Ostrich. d, 350sh, Helmeted guinea fowl. e, 400sh, Malachite kingfisher. f, 500sh, Saddle-billed stork.

1994, May 11
1105 A172 Sheet of 6, #a.-f. 9.00 9.00
1106 A172 Sheet of 6, #a.-f. 11.00 11.00

Hong Kong '94 A173

Red-cap white pearl-scale goldfish and: No. 1107, Scarus ghobban. No. 1108, Regal angelfish.

1994, Feb. 18
1107 A173 350sh multicolored 2.00 2.00
1108 A173 350sh multicolored 2.00 2.00
a. Pair, #1107-1108 4.00 4.00

Nos. 1107-1108 issued in sheets of 5 pairs. No. 1108a is a continuous design.

Mickey Mouse, 65th Anniv. — A176

Disney characters on tour: 10sh, Boarding plane. 20sh, Dancing, Tonga. 30sh, Lawn bowling, Australia. 40sh, Building igloo, Arctic region. 50sh, Royal Palace Guard, London. 60sh, Esna bazaar, Egypt. 70sh, Zsambox cowboys, Hungary, vert. 100sh, Grand Canal, Venice, vert. 150sh, Dancing, Bali, Indonesia, vert. 200sh, Monks studying text, Bangkok, Thailand, vert. 300sh, Water skiing, Taj Mahal, India, vert. 400sh, Himalayas, Nepal.
No. 1125, Kilimanjaro Uhuru Peak, Kibo, Tanzania, vert. No. 1126, Kigoma railway station, Dar es Salaam, Tanzania, vert. No. 1127, Memorial to Dr. Livingstone, shores of Lake Tanganyika, Tanzania.

1994, Apr. 6 ***Perf. 14x13½, 13½x14***
1113 A176 10sh multicolored .30 .30
1114 A176 20sh multicolored .30 .30
1115 A176 30sh multicolored .30 .30
1116 A176 40sh multicolored .45 .45
1117 A177 50sh multicolored .50 .50
1118 A176 60sh multicolored .55 .55
1119 A176 70sh multicolored .75 .75
1120 A176 100sh multicolored 1.05 1.05
1121 A176 150sh multicolored 1.50 1.50
1122 A176 200sh multicolored 2.10 2.10
1123 A176 300sh multicolored 3.00 3.00
1124 A176 400sh multicolored 4.00 4.00
Nos. 1113-1124 (12) 14.80 14.80

Souvenir Sheets

1125 A176 500sh multicolored 4.25 4.25
1126 A176 500sh multicolored 4.25 4.25
1127 A176 500sh multicolored 4.25 4.25

Reptiles A177

Designs: 20sh, Geochelone elephantopus, vert. 50sh, Iguana iguana, vert. 70sh, Varanus salvator. 100sh, Naja oxiana, vert. 150sh, Chamaeleo jacksonii. 200sh, Eunectes murinus. 250sh, Alligator mississippensis.
500sh, Vipera berus, vert.

Perf. 12x12½, 12½x12

1993, June 28 **Litho.**
1128-1134 A177 Set of 7 6.00 6.00

Souvenir Sheet

1135 A177 500sh multicolored 4.75 4.75

Nos. 1128-1135 were were not available until July 1994.

Sharks A178

Designs: 20sh, Isurus oxyrinchus. 30sh, Etmopterus hillianus. 50sh, Galeocerdo cuvier. 70sh, Squatina africana. 100sh, Pristiophorus cirratus. 150sh, Triaenodon obesus. 200sh, Sphyrna lewini.
350sh, Hexanchus griseus, vert.

1993, July 27 ***Perf. 12½x12***
1136-1142 A178 Set of 7 4.75 4.75

Souvenir Sheet

Perf. 12x12½

1143 A178 350sh multicolored 3.00 3.00

Nos. 1136-1143 were not available until July 1994.

Dogs — A179

Designs: 20sh, Gordon setter. 30sh, Zwergschnauzer. 50sh, Labrador retriever. 70sh, Wire fox terrier. 100sh, English springer spaniel. 150sh, Newfoundlander. 200sh, Moscow toy terrier.
350sh, Doberman pinscher.

1993, Sept. 27 ***Perf. 12x12½***
1144-1150 A179 Set of 7 5.25 5.25

Souvenir Sheet

1151 A179 350sh multicolored 2.50 2.50

Nos. 1144-1151 were not available until July 1994.

Horses A180

Designs: 20sh, Norman-Arab. 40sh, Nonius. 50sh, Boulonnais. 70sh, Arab. 100sh, Anglo-Arab. 150sh, Tarpan. 200sh, Thorougbred.
No. 1159, Anglo-Norman.

1993, Nov. 30 ***Perf. 12½x12***
1152-1158 A180 Set of 7 5.25 5.25

Souvenir Sheet

Perf. 12x12½

1159 A180 400sh multicolored 2.50 2.50

Nos. 1152-1159 were not available until July 1994.

Military Aircraft A181

Designs: 20sh, ALFA jet. 30sh, Northrup F-5E. 50sh, Mirage 3NG. 70sh, MB-339C. 100sh, MIG-31. 150sh, C-101 AVIOJET. 200sh, F-16B.
500sh, EAP fighter, vert.

1994, Apr. 25 **Litho.** ***Perf. 12½x12***
1160-1166 A181 Set of 7 5.25 5.25

Souvenir Sheet

Perf. 12x12½

1167 A181 500sh multicolored 3.00 3.00

A182

Customs Co-operation Council Meeting, Arusha — A183

Designs: 20sh, Trans-border trade. 50sh, Customs-international trade by ship. 100sh, Customs-air transportation. 150sh, Postal service-customs co-operation, Customs and UPU emblems.
500sh, Emblem.

1994, Aug. 23 **Litho.** ***Perf. 13½***
1168-1171 A182 Set of 4 4.50 4.50

Souvenir Sheet

Perf. 12½

1172 A183 500sh multicolored 5.50 5.50

1994 World Cup Soccer Championships, US — A184

No. 1173: a, Giuseppe Signori. b, Ruud Gullit. c, Roberto Mancini. d, Marco Van Basten. e, Dennis Bergkamp. f, Oscar Ruggeri. g, Frank Rijkaard. h, Peter Schmeichel.
1000sh, World Cup trophy.

1994, Sept. 26 ***Perf. 14***

1173 A184 300sh Sheet of 8, #a.-h. 9.00 9.00

Souvenir Sheet

1174 A184 1000sh multi 5.00 5.00

1994 World Cup Soccer Championships, US — A184a

Letter in soccer ball: 40sh, B. 50sh, C. 70sh, D. 100sh, E. 170sh, A. 200sh, none. 250sh, F.
500sh, Two players and goalie.

1994, Sept. 30 Litho. ***Perf. 12½x12***

1174A-1174G A184a Set of 7 9.00 9.00
i. Souv. sheet of 6, #1174A-1174E, 1174G + 3 labels 7.25 7.25

Souvenir Sheet

1174H A184a 500sh multi 5.00 5.00

Dogs — A185

No. 1175, 120sh: a, Alsatian (German Shepherd). b, Japanese chin. c, Shetland sheepdog. d, Italian spinone. e, Great dane. f, English setter. g, Pembroke (welsh corgi). h, St. Bernard. i, Irish wolfhound.

No. 1176, 120sh: a, Afghan hound. b, Basenji (Congo dog). c, Siberian husky. d, Irish setter. e, Norwegian elkhound. f, Bracco Italiano (Italian hound). g, Australian cattle dog. h, German short haired pointer. i, Rhodesian ridgeback.

No. 1177, 120sh: a, Alaskan malamute. b, Scottish cairn terrier. c, American foxhound. d, British bulldog. e, Boston terrier. f, Borzoi (Russian wolfhound). g, Shar pei (Chinese fighting dog). h, Saluki (Persian greyhound). i, Bernese mountain dog.

No. 1178, 120sh: a, Doberman pinscher. b, Chihuahua. c, Bloodhound. d, Keeshond (Dutch barge dog). e, Tibetan spaniel. f, Japanese akita. g, Tervueren (Belgian shepherd dog). h, Chow chow (Chinese Spitz). i, Pharaoh hound.

No. 1179, 1000sh, Like #1175e. No. 1180, 1000sh, Like #1176b.

1994, Sept. 30 **Sheets of 9, #a-i**

1175-1178 A185 Set of 4 20.00 20.00

Souvenir Sheets

1179-1180 A185 Set of 2 12.00 12.00

Miniature Sheets of 8

Orchids — A186

No. 1181, 200sh: a, Rangaeris amaniensis. b, Eulophia macowanii. c, Cyrtorchis arcuata. d, Centrostigma occultans. e, Cirrhopetalum umbellatum. f, Ansellia gigantea. g, Angraecum ramosum. h, Disa englerana.

No. 1182, 200sh: a, Nervilia stolziana. b, Satyrium orbiculare. c, Schzochilus sulphureus. d, Disa stolzii. e, Platycoryne mediocris. f, Satyrium breve. g, Eulophia nuttii. h, Disa ornithantha.

No. 1183, 1000sh, Eulophia thomsonii, horiz. No. 1184, 1000sh, Phaius P. tankervilliae, horiz.

1994, Oct. 7 **Sheets of 8, #a-h**

1181-1182 A186 Set of 2 32.50 32.50

Souvenir Sheets

1183-1184 A186 Set of 2 18.00 18.00

Natl. Parks A187

Designs: 20sh, Ngorongoro Crater. 50sh, Ngurdoto Crater. 70sh, Kilimanjaro Natl. Park. 100sh, Gombe Natl. Park. 150sh, Selous Natl. Park. 200sh, Mikumi Natl. Park. 250sh, Serengeti Natl. Park.
500sh, Lake Manyara Natl. Park, vert.

1993, Oct. 29 **Litho.** ***Perf. 12***

1185-1191 A187 Set of 7 4.00 4.00

Souvenir Sheet

1192 A187 500sh multicolored 2.50 2.50

Nos. 1185-1192 are dated 1993 but were not available until Oct. 1994.

Historical African Costumes A188

Designs: 20sh, Berts style. 40sh, Galla style. 50sh, Guinean warrior. 70sh, Goloff style. 100sh, Peul style. 150sh, Abyssinian warrior. 200sh, Pahuin style.
350sh, Zulu style.

1993, Dec. 30

1193-1199 A188 Set of 7 2.75 2.75

Souvenir Sheet

1200 A189 350sh multicolored 1.75 1.75

Nos. 1193-1200 are dated 1993 but were not available until Oct. 1994.

1994 Winter Olympics, Lillehammer A189

Designs: 40sh, Downhill skiing. 50sh, Ice hockey. 70sh, Speed skating. 100sh, Bobsled. 120sh, Figure skating. 170sh, Free style skiing. 250sh, Biathlon.
500sh, Slalom skiing.

1994, Feb. 12

1201-1207 A189 Set of 7 4.00 4.00

Souvenir Sheet

1208 A189 500sh multicolored 2.25 2.25

Sailing Ships — A190

Designs: 40sh, Jahazi. 50sh, Caravel. 70sh, Carrack. 100sh, Galeas. 170sh, Line of battle ship. 200sh, Frigate. 250sh, Brig.
No. 1210, Bark.

1994, Apr. 20

1209-1215 A190 Set of 7 3.50 3.50

Souvenir Sheet

1216 A190 500sh multicolored 2.25 2.25

Prehistoric Animals — A191

Designs: 40sh, Diatruma. 50sh, Tyranosaurus. 100sh, Uintaterius. 120sh, Stiracosaurus. 170sh, Diplodocus. 250sh, Archaeopteryx. 300sh, Sordes.
500sh, Dimetrodon, vert.

1994, June 30

1217-1223 A191 Set of 7 7.25 7.25

Souvenir Sheet

1224 A191 500sh multicolored 3.00 3.00

Intl. Year of the Family — A192

Designs: 40sh, Family. 120sh, Father playing ball with children. 170sh, People at clinic, horiz. 250sh, Woman harvesting in field.
300sh, Emblem.

Perf. 12x12½, 12½x12

1994, Aug. 30 **Litho.**

1225-1228 A192 Set of 4 3.50 3.50

Souvenir Sheet

1229 A192 300sh multicolored 3.50 3.50

Zanzibar Revolution, 30th Anniv. — A193

Designs: 40sh, Pres. Salmin Amour. 70sh, Abeid Amani Karume, first president. 120sh, Processing cloves, horiz. 250sh, Zanzibar door.
500sh, Hands clasped over map.

1994, Aug. 1

1230-1233 A193 Set of 4 3.50 3.50

Souvenir Sheet

1234 A193 500sh multicolored 3.00 3.00

Arachnids A194

Designs: 40sh, Trombidium. 50sh, Eurypelma. 100sh, Salticus. 120sh, Micrommata rosea, vert. 170sh, Araneus, vert. 250sh, Micrathena, vert. 300sh, Araneus diadematus, vert.
500sh, Hadogenes, vert.

Perf. 12½x12, 12x12½

1994, Aug. 31

1235-1241 A194 Set of 7 5.00 5.00

Souvenir Sheet

1242 A194 500sh multicolored 2.25 2.25

Butterflies and Flowers A195

No. 1243, 120sh: a, Lunaria biennis, papilio glaucus. b, Phlox paniculata, danaus plexippus. c, Rudbeckia gloriosa, papilio troilus. d, Tithonia rotundifolia, hypolimnas antevorta. e, Osteospermum, cirrochroa imperatrix. f, Ursinia anethoides, vanessa atalanta. g, Wahlenbergia gloriosa, limenitis archippus. h, Mentzelia lindleyi, hypolimnas pandarus. i, Paeonia suffruticosa, anthocharis belia.

No. 1244, 120sh: a, Coreopsis laneolata, limenitis sydyi. b, Lantana camara, agraulis vanillae. c, Asclepias tuberosa, danaus chrysippus. d, Verbena canadensis, eurytides marcellus. e, Lonicera japonica, artopoetes pryeri. f, Pentas bussei, heliconius charitonius. g, Echinacea purpurea, limenitis weidemeyerii. h, Myosotis alpestris, phoebis sennae. i, Aster amellus, timelaea albescens.

No. 1245, 1000sh, Buddleia davidii, papilio polyxenes. No. 1246, 1000sh, Helianthus annuus, vanessa cardui.

1994, Nov. 19 ***Perf. 14***

Sheets of 9, #a-i

1243-1244 A195 Set of 2 16.00 16.00

Souvenir Sheets

1245-1246 A195 Set of 2 12.00 12.00

First Manned Moon Landing, 25th Anniv. A196

No. 1247, 150sh: a, Map of landing site. b, Location of Sea of Tranquility shown on Moon. c, Craters. d, Launch. e, Second stage separation. f, Separation of lunar modules. g, Command module, "Columbia," landing module, "Eagle." h, "Eagle" descending. i, Inside module.

No. 1248, 150sh: a, Michael Collins, Neil Armstrong, Edwin "Buzz" Aldrin. b, "Eagle" on lunar surface. c, Stepping foot on moon. d, Erecting solar wind devices. e, Gathering soil samples. f, Reflection in helmet. g, Astronaut, US flag. h, Carrying equipment. i, "Eagle" ascending from lunar surface.

No. 1249, 150sh: a, "Columbia" above lunar surface, Earth on horizon. b, "Eagle" above lunar surface. c, Release of S-4B rocket. d, Heading toward Earth. e, Re-entering atmosphere. f, Splashdown. g, Pickup at sea. h, Helicopter lifting men on board. i, Astronauts in quarantine.

1994, Nov. 30 **Sheets of 9, #a-i**

1247-1249 A196 Set of 3 27.00 27.00

A197

Dinosaurs — A198

No. 1250: a, Brontosaurus (e). b, Albertosaurus. c, Parasaurolophus. d, Pteranodon. e, Stegosaurus. f, Tyrannosaurus. g, Triceratops. h, Ornitholestes. i, Camarasaurus. j, Ankylosaurus. k, Trachodon. l, Allosaurus. m, Corythosaurus. n, Struthiomimus. o, Camptosaurus. p, Heterodontosaurus.

No. 1251: a, Deinonychus. b, Styracosaurus. c, Anatosaurus. d, Plateosaurus. e, Iguanodon. f, Oviraptor. g, Dimorphodon. h, Ornithomimus. i, Lambeosaurus. j, Megalosaurus. k, Cetiosaurus. l, Hypsilophodon. m, Rhamphorhynchus. n, Scelidosaurus. o, Antrodemus. p, Dimetrodon.

1000sh, Brachiosaurus, vert.

1994, Dec. 26

1250 A197 120sh Sheet of 16, #a.-p. 13.50 13.50
1251 A198 120sh Sheet of 16, #a.-p. 13.50 13.50

Souvenir Sheet

1252 A197 1000sh multi 7.50 7.50

No. 1250 is a continuous design.

Mickey Mouse, Safari Club — A199

Designs: No. 1253, 70sh, Donald, Mickey, lion cubs. No. 1254, 70sh, Goofy leaning on Donald. No, 1255, 100sh, Donald wearing tree disguise. No. 1256, 100sh, Donald under elephant. No. 1257, 120sh, Donald, hippopotamus. No. 1258, 120sh, Mickey writing in diary. No. 1259, 150sh, Goofy carrying gear, Donald, Mickey. No. 1260, 150sh, Mickey, elephant, Donald, Goofy in rain. No. 1261, 200sh, Donald, Goofy, Mickey reading book, lion. No. 1262, 200sh, Goofy, zebras. No. 1263, 250sh, Mickey, giraffe. No. 1264, 250sh, Donald filming picture.

No. 1265, 1000sh, Goofy hanging from tree, vert. No. 1266, 1000sh, Goofy holding camera, Donald, vert. No. 1267, 1000sh, Mickey holding camera, vert.

1994, Dec. 26 ***Perf. 14x13½***

1253-1264 A199 Set of 12 11.50 11.50

Souvenir Sheets

Perf. 13½x14

1265-1267 A199 Set of 3 14.50 14.50

A200

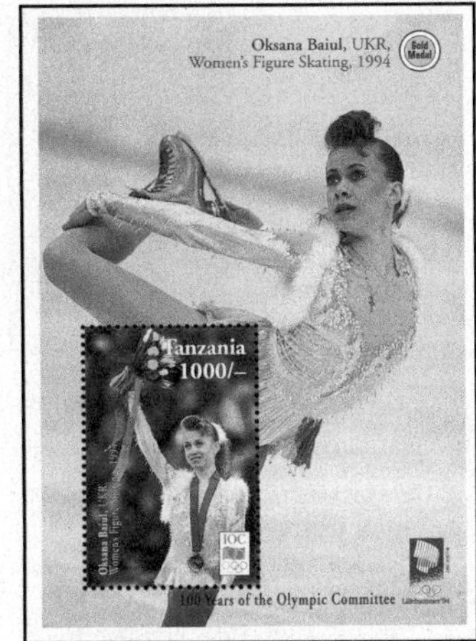

Olympic Gold Medalists — A201

Designs: 350sh, Kristin Otto, Germany, 50m free-style swimming, 1988. 500sh, Carl Lewis, US, track & field, 1984, 1988.

1000sh, Oksana Baiul, Ukraine, women's figure skating, 1994.

1994, Dec. 12 **Litho.** ***Perf. 14***

1268 A200 350sh multicolored 1.50 1.50
1269 A200 500sh multicolored 2.25 2.25

Souvenir Sheet

1270 A201 1000sh multicolored 4.50 4.50

Intl. Olympic Committee, cent. (No. 1270).

D-Day, 50th Anniv. A202

350sh, Combined forces attack Atlantic wall. 600sh, Waterproofed tanks support Marines at Omaha Beach.

No. 1273, 200sh: a, Gen. Eisenhower, US forces, Omaha Beach. b, P-51 Mustang, D-Day armada. c, US Coast Guard cutter, landing craft. d, US troops approaching Omaha Beach. e, US troops landing on Omaha Beach. f, US forces on Omaha Beach.

No. 1274, 200sh: a, Gen. Montgomery, White Ensign flies over Normandy beach. b, British forces with Churchill Avre tank, Gold Beach. c, USS Thompson refueled en route to Omaha Beach. d, HMS Warspite fires on German positions, Sword Beach. e, Royal Marine commandoes landing, Juno Beach. f, Sherman Crab flail tank landing on Normandy beach.

No. 1275, 200sh: a, Supermarine Spitfire over Normandy beaches. b, Bren gun carriers, Gold Beach. c, Le Regiment de la Chaudiere, Juno Beach. d, Canadian forces land on Juno Beach. e, Sherman tank on Normandy beach. f, German artillery fires on D-Day Armada.

No. 1276, 1000sh, US forces prepare to embark from England to Normandy beaches. No. 1277, 1000sh, US forces on Utah Beach. No. 1278, 1000sh, Beach obstacles.

1994, Dec. 12 **Litho.** ***Perf. 14***

1271 A202 350sh multicolored 1.60 1.60
1272 A202 600sh multicolored 3.00 3.00

Sheets of 6, #a-f

1273-1275 A202 Set of 3 18.00 18.00

Souvenir Sheets

1276-1278 A202 Set of 3 14.50 14.50

Raptors A203

Designs: 40sh, Terathopius ecaudatus, vert. 50sh, Spizaetus ornatus, vert. 100sh, Pandion haliaetus, vert. 120sh, Vultur gryphus, vert. 170sh, Haliaetus vocifer. 250sh, Sarcoramphus papa, vert. 400sh, Falco peregrinus.

500sh, Pseudogyps africanus, vert.

Perf. 12x12½, 12½x12

1994, Sept. 30

1279-1285 A203 Set of 7 8.00 8.00

Souvenir Sheet

1286 A203 500sh multicolored 3.25 3.25

Endangered Species — A204

Designs: 40sh, Phascolasctos cinereus. 70sh, Ailurus fulgens. 100sh, Aguila. 120sh, Loxodonta africana. 250sh, Monachus tropicalis. 400sh, Eschrichtius gibbosus. 500sh, Cetacea.

500sh, Panthera tigris, vert.

1994, July 29 ***Perf. 12½x12***

1287-1293 A204 Set of 7 7.75 7.75

Souvenir Sheet

Perf. 12x12½

1294 A204 500sh multicolored 3.50 3.50

No. 1288 shows a Giant Panda, and is incorrectly inscribed with the scientific name of the Lesser Panda.

Crabs — A205

Designs: 40sh, Astacus leptodactytus, horiz. 100sh, Eriocheir sinensis. 120sh, Caneer opillo. 170sh, Cardisoma quanhumi, horiz. 250sh, Birgus latro. 300sh, Menippe mercenaria, horiz. 400sh, Dromia vulgaris.

No. 1302, Callinectes sapidus, horiz.

Perf. 12½x12, 12x12½

1994, Nov. 30 **Litho.**

1295-1301 A205 Set of 7 6.00 6.00

Souvenir Sheet

1302 A205 500sh multicolored 1.75 1.75

Flowers — A206

Designs: 40sh, Dicentra spectabilis. 100sh, Thunbergia alata. 120sh, Cyrtanthus minimiflorus. 170sh, Nepenthes hybrida. 250sh, Allamanda cathartica. 300sh, Encyclia pentotis. 400sh, Protea lacticolor.

500sh, Tradescantia.

1995, Oct. 31 ***Perf. 12x12½***

1303-1309 A206 Set of 7 6.00 6.00

Souvenir Sheet

1310 A206 500sh multicolored 2.25 2.25

Dated 1994.

Woodstock Music Festival, 25th Anniv. — A207

No. 1311, Jimi Hendrix. No. 1312, Carlos Santana. No. 1313, John Lee Hooker.

1995 **Litho.** ***Imperf.***

Size: 124x84mm

1311 A207 2000sh multi 9.00 9.00

Souvenir Sheet

Self-Adhesive

1312 A207 2000sh multi 9.00 9.00

Size: 115x122mm

Imperf

Self-Adhesive

1313 A207 2000sh multi 10.00 10.00

Issued: No. 1311, 2/27; No. 1312, 5/15; No. 1313, 8/22.

Space Probes and Satellites A208

Designs: 40sh, Hubble telescope. 100sh, Mariner. 120sh, Voyager 2. 170sh, Work Package 03. 250sh, Orbiting solar observatory (OSO). 300sh, Magellan. 400sh, Galileo.

500sh, FOBOS.

1994, Dec. 30 **Litho.** ***Perf. 12½x12***

1319-1325 A208 Set of 7 6.25 6.25

Souvenir Sheet

1326 A208 500sh multicolored 3.25 3.25

Sierra Club, Cent. A209

No. 1327, 150sh, vert: a, Black rhinoceros. b, Aye-aye. c, Aye-aye, holding claw at mouth. d, Giraffes, Masai Mara Reserve. e, Red lechwe, group. f, Red lechwe running. g, White-handed gibbon, white coat. h, White-handed gibbon, dark coat. i, White-handed gibbon, ready to climb tree.

No. 1328, 150sh: a, Aye-aye. b, Black rhinoceros facing each other. c, Black rhinoceros. d, Red lechwe. e, Lions fighting, Masai Mara Reserve. f, Hyena, Masai Mara Reserve. g, Nile crocodile in water. h, Nile crocodile, mouth open. i, Nile crocodile in grass.

1995, July 6 **Litho.** ***Perf. 14***

Sheets of 9, #a-i

1327-1328 A209 Set of 2 16.00 16.00

Fruit A210

Designs: 70sh, Coconuts. 100sh, Pineapple. 150sh, Pawpaw. 200sh, Tomato.

500sh, Coconuts.

1995, June 30

1329-1332 A210 Set of 4 5.50 5.50

Souvenir Sheet

1333 A210 500sh multicolored 4.75 4.75

Miniature Sheets of 9

The Beatles — A211

No. 1334, 100sh: a, George Harrison. b, d, e, f, h, Various group portraits. c, Ringo Starr. g, Paul McCartney. i, John Lennon.

No. 1335, 100sh, vert.: a-i, Various portraits of John Lennon.

No. 1336, 500sh, John Lennon, vert. No. 1337, 500sh, Paul McCartney.

1995 Sheets of 9, #a-i ***Perf. 12½***

1334-1335 A211 Set of 2 11.50 11.50

Souvenir Sheets

1336-1337 A211 Set of 2 11.50 11.50

No. 1336 contains one 51x76mm stamp. No. 1337 contains one 57x51mm stamp.

Trains A212

No. 1338, 200sh: a, 0-6-0 Italy. b, 0-4-4-OT Mallet, Germany. c, 4-8-0 Tender Engine, Ghana. d, Mallet Tanks, Germany. e, 0-6-2T on the Zillertalbahn, Switzerland. f, Rack Lines, Austria. g, Sweden Jodemans Railway, Norway. h, 4-6-0 Portugal. i, 60CM gauge, Mine Railway, Spain.

No. 1339, 200sh: a, 640 Class 2-6-0s, Italy. b, Norway electric. c, Gordon Highlander 4-40s. d, High Line 9600 class 2-8-0 Japan. e, 4-6-0 Henschel, Portugal. f, Federal German State Railway 220 hydraulic. g, Caledonian 4-2-2, Scotland. h, M2 Locomotive, Denmark. i, Denver & Rio Grande, Western US.

No. 1340, 1000sh, Karl Golsdorf 2-6-0 tank engine, "Germany." No. 1341, 1000sh, High speed ET 403, Germany. No. 1342, 1000sh, AKO 1920, US. No. 1343 1000sh, Porter 2-4-OS, Hawaii.

1995, July 5 Litho. ***Perf. 14***

Sheets of 9, #a-i

1338-1339 A212 Set of 2 22.50 22.50

Souvenir Sheets

1340-1343 A212 Set of 4 25.00 25.00

Singapore '95.

FAO, 50th Anniv: — A213

No. 1344: a, Boy eating. b, Baby, mother eating. c, Two young people eating.

1000sh, Woman picking fruit, horiz.

1995, Aug. 14

1344 A213 250sh Strip of 3, #a.-c. 4.00 4.00

Souvenir Sheet

1345 A213 1000sh multicolored 4.75 4.75

No. 1344 is a continuous design.

Rotary International, 90th Anniv. — A214

Designs: 600sh, Paul Harris, Rotary emblem. 1000sh, Natl. flag, Rotary emblem.

1995, Aug. 14

1346 A214 600sh multicolored 3.00 3.00

Souvenir Sheet

1347 A214 1000sh multicolored 4.75 4.75

Queen Mother, 95th Birthday — A215

No. 1348: a, Drawing. b, With Queen Elizabeth II. c, Formal portrait. d, In black outfit.

1000sh, Blue dress with pearls.

1995, Aug. 14 ***Perf. 13½x14***

1348 A215 250sh Block or strip of 4, #a.-d. 4.50 4.50

Souvenir Sheet

1349 A215 1000sh multicolored 4.75 4.75

No. 1348 was issued in sheets of 8 stamps.

Sheets of Nos. 1348-1349 exist with black borders overprinted in sheet margins and text "In Memoriam 1900-2002."

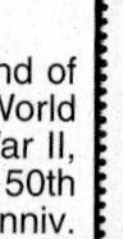

End of World War II, 50th Anniv. A216

No. 1350 — Flags of countries shaped as "VJ:" a, Singapore. b, Fiji. c, Malaysia. d, Marshall Islands. e, Philippines. f, Solomon Islands.

No. 1351: a, Pearl Harbor. b, North Africa. c, Battle of Atlantic. d, War in Soviet Union. e, "D" Day, June 6, 1944. f, Holocaust. g, War in Pacific. h, Hiroshima, Enola Gay, mushroom cloud.

No. 1352, 1000sh, Battle of Britain. No. 1353, 1000sh, British soldier, donkey with backpack.

1995, Aug. 14 Litho. ***Perf. 14***

1350 A216 250sh Sheet of 6, #a.-f. + label 7.75 7.75

1351 A216 250sh Sheet of 8, #a.-h. + label 7.75 7.75

Souvenir Sheets

1352-1353 A216 Set of 2 16.00 16.00

Reptiles A217

No. 1354: a, African rock python. b, Bell's hinged tortoise. c, Gaboon viper. d, Royal python. e, Savannah monitor. f, Nile monitor. g, Three-horned chameleon. h, Nile crocodile. i, Rough-scaled bush viper. j, Puff adder. k, Rhinocerous viper. l, Leopard tortoise.

No. 1355, 1000sh, Bush viper. No. 1356, 1000sh, Spitting cobra.

1995, Sept. 5

1354 A217 200sh Sheet of 12, #a.-l. 11.50 11.50

Souvenir Sheets

1355-1356 A217 Set of 2 11.00 11.00

UN, 50th Anniv. — A218

No. 1357 — Various races of people, within group: a, Woman holding baby on shoulders. b, Man holding child in arms. c, One child standing.

1000sh, UN soldier using binoculars.

1995, Aug. 14 Litho. ***Perf. 14***

1357 A218 250sh Strip of 3, #a.-c. 4.75 4.75

Souvenir Sheet

1358 A218 1000sh multicolored 4.75 4.75

No. 1357 is a continuous design.

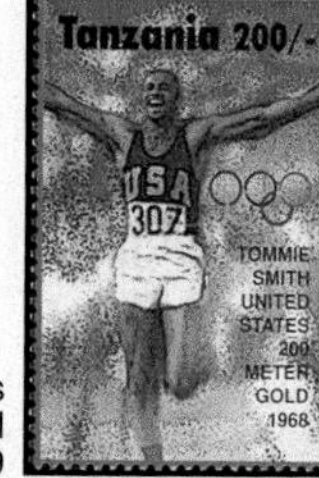

Summer Olympics Gold Medal Winners — A219

No. 1359 — 200sh, a, Tommie Smith, US, 1968. b, Jack Lovelock, New Zealand, 1936. c, Al Oerter, US, 1956-68. d, Daley Thompson, Great Britain, 1980. e, Greg Louganis, US, 1984-88. f, Sammy Lee, US, 1948. g, Dan Gable, US, 1972. h, Helen Meany, US, 1928. i, Sugar Ray Leonard, US, 1976.

No. 1360, 200sh: a, Robert Mathias, US, 1948-52 . b, Larissa Latynina, USSR, 1956. c, Martin Sheridan, US, 1904-08. d, Vera Caslavska, Czechoslovakia, 1968. e, Edwin Moses, US, 1984. f, Jesse Owens, US, 1936. g, Mary Lou Retton, US, 1984. h, Bobby Morrow, US, 1956. i, Joan Benoit, US, 1984.

No. 1361, 1000sh, Florence Griffith Joyner, Jackie Joyner-Kersee, US, 1988. No. 1362, 1000sh, Vasily Alexeyev USSR, 1972-76.

1995, Sept. 18 Sheets of 9, #a-i

1359-1360 A219 Set of 2 14.50 14.50

Souvenir Sheets

1361-1362 A219 Set of 2 9.00 9.00

Wild Animals A220

No. 1363: a, Snake, vulture. b, Vulture. c, Giraffe (d, g, h, k, l). d, African bateleur. e, Elephants (f). f, Kob, rhino (b, e, i, j, n). g, Rhinos. h, Baboon. i, Kob (m, n). j, Saddle billed stork, warthog (n). k, Cheetahs (g, j, n). l, African lion (h, k, o, p). m, Vulture. n, Dik-diks. o, Lion cubs. p, Lions (o).

No. 1364: a, Elands. b, Zebras. c, Lions. d, Baboons.

No. 1365, 1000sh, Rhinoceros. No. 1366, 1000sh, Leopard.

1995, Sept. 15

1363 A220 100sh Sheet of 16, #a.-p. 7.75 7.75

1364 A220 250sh Sheet of 4, #a.-d. 5.00 5.00

Souvenir Sheets

1365-1366 A220 Set of 2 9.00 9.00

UN, 50th Anniv. A221

Designs: 70sh, Corn farming, vert. 100sh, Cultivating land. 150sh, Women spinning cotton in factory. 200sh, Boy drawing at desk, vert.

500sh, UN emblem, "50."

Wmk. 387

1995, Oct. 24 Litho. ***Perf. 14***

1367-1370 A221 Set of 4 4.25 4.25

Souvenir Sheet

1371 A221 500sh multicolored 4.75 4.75

East African Treaty, 2nd Anniv. A222

Designs: 100sh, Heads of State. 150sh, Map, flags, vert. 180sh, Map, cotton, vert. 200sh, Fishing on Lake Victoria.

500sh, Heads of State.

1995, Oct. 24

1373-1376 A222 Set of 4 5.00 5.00

Souvenir Sheet

1377 A222 500sh multicolored 5.00 5.00

Hoofed Animals — A224

Designs: 70sh, Hippopotamus amphibius, horiz. 100sh, Litocranius walleri. 150sh, Sincerus caffer, horiz. 180sh, Antilocapridae, horiz. 200sh, Alcelphus buselaphus. 260sh, Taurotragus oryx. 380sh, Strepsiceros.

500sh, Giraffa camelopardalis.

Perf. 12½x12, 12x12½

1995, May 31 Litho.

1380-1386 A224 Set of 7 6.50 6.50

Souvenir Sheet

1387 A224 500sh multicolored 6.00 6.00

Cactus Flowers — A225

Designs: 70sh, Weingartia fidaiana. 100sh, Rebutia spegazziniana. 150sh, Caralluma lugarii. 180sh, Cerochlamys pachyphylla. 200sh, Schlumbergera orssighiana. 260sh, Epiphyllum darrahii. 380sh, Ceropegia nilotica.

500sh, Neoporteria nigrihorrida.

1995, Aug. 31 ***Perf. 12x12½***

1388-1394 A225 Set of 7 6.50 6.50

Souvenir Sheet

1395 A225 500sh multicolored 6.25 6.25

Bats A226

Designs: 70sh, Cheiromeles torquatus, vert. 100sh, Hypsignatus monstrosus, vert. 150sh, Rhinolophus, ferrum-equinum, vert. 180sh, Plecotus auritus. 200sh, Syconycteris australis, vert. 260sh, Plecotus auritus, vert. 380sh, Otomops martiensseni.

500sh, Pteropus.

1995, July 31 ***Perf. 12x12½, 12½x12***

1396-1402 A226 Set of 7 6.50 6.50

Souvenir Sheet

1403 A226 500sh multicolored 5.75 5.75

Marine Life of Coral Reefs A227

Designs: 70sh, Medusa. 100sh, Surgeonfish. 150sh, Angelfish. 180sh, Octopus. 200sh, Zebra fish. 260sh, Shark. 380sh, Ray.

500sh, Turtle.

1995, June 15 ***Perf. 12½x12***

1404-1410 A227 Set of 7 6.50 6.50

Souvenir Sheet

1411 A227 500sh multicolored 6.00 6.00

Jerry Garcia (d. 1995), Musician A228

Scenes of Grateful Dead performing on stage and: No. 1413A, Bears. No. 1413B, Skeletons.

1995 Litho. *Perf. 12½*

1412 A228 200sh multi 9.00 9.00

Souvenir Sheet

1413 A228 1000sh multi 8.50 8.50

Size: 140x92mm

Imperf

Self-Adhesive

1413A A228 2000sh multi 7.50 7.50
1413B A228 2000sh multi 7.50 7.50

No. 1412 was issued in sheets of 9. No. 1413 contains one 51x57mm stamp.

Issued: Nos. 1412-1413, 11/15/95; Nos. 1413A-1413B, 12/21/95.

Rock and Roll Stars A229

No. 1414: a, Chuck Berry. b, Bob Dylan. c, Aretha Franklin. d, The Supremes. e, Buddy Holly. f, Bruce Springsteen. g, Elton John. h, The Rolling Stones. i, Michael Jackson.

1000sh, The Beach Boys (Al Jardin, Mike Love, Brian Wilson, Carl Wilson, Dennis Wilson), horiz.

1995, Dec. 1 *Perf. 13½x14*

1414 A229 250sh Sheet of 9, #a.-i. 13.50 13.50

Souvenir Sheet

Perf. 14x13½

1415 A229 1000sh multi 7.75 7.75

Motion Pictures, Cent. A230

No. 1416: a, Noah's Ark, Dolores Costello. b, Ben-Hur, 1926, Ramon Novarro. c, Ben-Hur, 1926, Francis X. Bushman. d, Ben-Hur, 1959, Charlton Heston. e, Ben-Hur, 1959, Haya Harareet. f, Ben-Hur, 1959, Sam Jaffe. g, The Ten Commandments, 1923, Theodore Roberts. h, Samson and Delilah, Victor Mature. i, Samson and Delilah, Hedy Lamarr.

No. 1417, The Ten Commandments, Theodore Roberts.

1995, Dec. 1 *Perf. 13½x14*

1416 A230 250sh Sheet of 9, #a.-i. 17.00 17.00

Souvenir Sheet

1417 A230 1000sh multi 7.75 7.75

World Tourism Organization, 20th Anniv. — A231

Designs: 100sh, Olduvai Gorge, "Cradle of Mankind." 300sh, First State House, Bagamoyo. 400sh, Mount Kilimanjaro.

500sh, Rhinoceroses, Ngorongoro Crater.

1995, Dec. 18 Litho. *Perf. 14*

1418-1420 A231 Set of 3 6.00 6.00

Souvenir Sheet

1421 A231 500sh multicolored 5.75 5.75

Predatory Animals A232

Designs: 70sh, Acinonyx jubatus. 100sh, Felus serval. 150sh, Huaena buana. 200sh, Otocyon megalotis. 250sh, Lucaon pictus. 280sh, Pantera pardus. 300sh, Pantera leo.

500sh, Alligator.

1995, Sept. 30 Litho. *Perf. 12½x12*

1422-1428 A232 Set of 7 9.50 9.50

Souvenir Sheet

1429 A232 500sh multicolored 5.00 5.00

Horses — A233

No. 1430: a, True black Freisian. b, Appaloosa. c, Arab. d, Paint. e, Chestnut saddlebred. f, Standard thoroughbred. g, Belgian. h, Liver chestnut quarter. i, Hackney.

1000sh, Clydesdale.

1995 *Perf. 14*

1430 A233 250sh Sheet of 9, #a.-i. 17.00 17.00

Souvenir Sheet

1431 A233 1000sh multi 9.50 9.50

No. 685 Surcharged

1995, May 30 Litho. *Perf. 14*

1431A A108 70sh on 13sh #685 —

Paintings from the Metropolitan Museum of Art — A234

No. 1432, 200sh: a, La Orana Maria, by Gauguin. b, Young Herdsman with Cows, by Cuyp. c, Moses and the Burning Bush by, Domenichino. d, Path in the Île Saint-Martin, Vétheuil, by Monet. e, Dances, Pink and Green, by Degas. f, Terrace at Sainte-Adresse, by Monet. g, The Rehearsal Onstage, by Degas. h, Study for "A Sunday on La Grande Jatte," by Seurat.

No. 1433, 200sh: a, Madame Marsollier and Daughter, by Nattier. b, Christ and the Woman of Samaria, by Rembrandt. c, Rubens and His Wife and Son, by Rubens. d, Portrait of a Young Woman, by Vermeer. e, Portrait of a Man, by Van Dyck. f, Young Woman with a Water Jug, by Vermeer. g, Self Portrait, by Rembrandt. h, Young Man and Woman in an Inn, by Hals.

No. 1434, 1000sh, On the Beach at Trouville, by Boudin. No. 1435, 1000sh, A Dance in the Country, by G.D. Tiepolo.

1996, Mar. 7 *Perf. 13½x14*

Sheets of 8, #a-h, + Label

1432-1433 A234 Set of 2 29.50 29.50

Souvenir Sheets

Perf. 14

1434-1435 A234 Set of 2 18.00 18.00

Nos. 1434-1435 each contain one 81x53mm stamp.

Miniature Sheet

Cats and Dogs — A235

No. 1436 — Cats: a, Siberian. b, Classic silver tabby Persian. c, Brown Burmese. d, Norwegian forest. e, Tabby. f, Blue & white maine coon. g, Brown California spangled cat. h, Black & white bicolor Persian. i, Shaded silver American shorthair.

No. 1437 — Dogs: a, Red labrador. b, St. Bernard. c, Cocker spaniel. d, Black labrador. e, Bernese mountain dog. f, Beagle. g, Miniature pincher. h, Basset hound. i, German shepherd.

No. 1438, Silver tabby British shorthair. No. 1439, Alaskan malamute.

1996, Mar. 4 Litho. *Perf. 14*

1436 A235 250sh Sheet of 9, #a.-i. 13.50 13.50
1437 A235 250sh Sheet of 9, #a.-i. 13.50 13.50

Souvenir Sheets

1438 A235 1000sh multi 7.75 7.75
1439 A235 1000sh multi 7.75 7.75

Souvenir Sheets

Janis Joplin (1943-70), Rock Musician — A235a

Design: No. 1439B, Joplin seated atop a psychedelically-painted Porsche, horiz.

1996, Apr. 10 Litho. *Imperf.*

Self-Adhesive

1439A A235a 2000sh shown *22.50 22.50*
1439B A235a 2000sh multi *22.50 22.50*

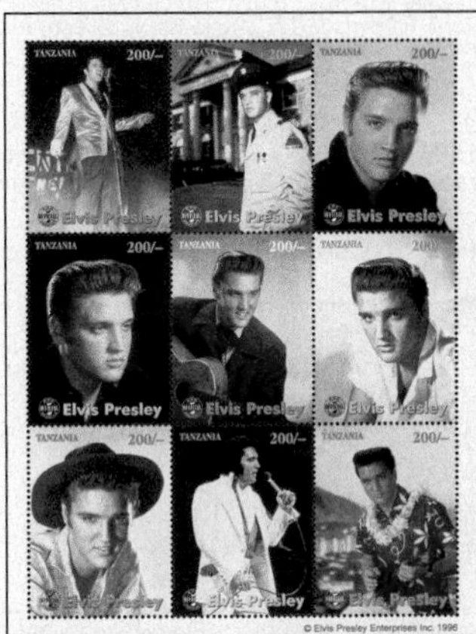

Elvis Presley (1935-77) — A235b

Various photographs with EPE (Elvis Presley Enterprises) official product emblem.

1996, Mar. 13 Litho. *Perf. 12½*

1439C A235b 200sh Sheet of 9, #d.-l. 11.50 11.50

New Year 1996 (Year of the Rat) A236

No. 1440: a, Arvicola oryzivora. b, Meriones hudsonicus. c, Mus missouriensis. d, Mus aureolus.

500sh, Fiber zibethicus.

1996, Apr. 12

1440 A236 200sh Block of 4, #a.-d. 4.00 4.00
e. Souvenir sheet of 1 #1440 4.00 4.00

Souvenir Sheet

1442 A236 500sh multicolored 4.00 4.00

No. 1440 was issued in sheets of 16 stamps.

Deng Xiaoping, Chinese Communist Leader A237

Various portraits.

1996, May 6 Litho. *Perf. 13*
1443 A237 250sh Sheet of 6, #a.-f. 11.50 11.50

Souvenir Sheet
1444 A237 500sh multicolored 5.00 5.00

CHINA '96, 9th Asian Intl. Philatelic Exhibition (No. 1443).

Butterflies A238

Designs: 70sh, Dirphia multicolor. 100sh, Inachis io, vert. 150sh, Automerisio. 200sh, Saturnia pyri. 250sh, Arctia villica. 260sh, Arctia caja. 300sh, Celerio euforbiae, vert.
500sh, Zygaena laeta.

Perf. 12½x12, 12x12½
1996, Jan. Litho.
1445-1451 A238 Set of 7 12.00 12.00

Souvenir Sheet
1452 A238 500sh multicolored 6.00 6.00

Frogs A239

Designs: 100sh, Bufo bufo laur. 140sh, Pyxicephalus adspersus. 180sh, Megalixalus laevis. 200sh, Xenopus laevis. 210sh, Hemisus marmoratus. 260sh, Rana beccarii. 300sh, Hyperolius cinctiventrus.
500sh, Rana goliaph.

1996, Jan. 31 *Perf. 12½x12*
1453-1459 A239 Set of 7 7.75 7.75

Souvenir Sheet
1460 A239 500sh multicolored 6.25 6.25

Souvenir Sheet

China 1996 Intl. Philatelic Exhibition — A239a

1996, June 5 Litho. *Perf. 12½*
1460A A239a 300sh multi 5.00 5.00

Souvenir Sheet

Shanghai Intl. Tea Culture Festival — A239b

1996 Litho. *Perf. 12½*
1460B A239b 300sh multi 4.50 4.50

Queen Elizabeth II, 70th Birthday — A240

No. 1461: a, Portrait. b, As young woman in evening dress. c, Wearing tiara, jewels.
1000sh, Portrait as young woman.

1996, July 3 Litho. *Perf. 13½x14*
1461 A240 300sh Strip of 3, #a.-c. 6.25 6.25

Souvenir Sheet
1462 A240 1000sh multicolored 7.25 7.25

No. 1461 was issued in sheets of 9 stamps.

Crocodiles, Alligators — A241

Designs: 100sh, Melanosuchus niger. 150sh, Caiman latirostris. 200sh, Alligator mississpiensis. 250sh, Gavialis gangeticus. 260sh, Crocodylus niloticus. 300sh, Crocodylus cataphractus. 380sh, Crocodylus rhombifer.
500sh, Crocodile.

1996 *Perf. 12½x12*
1463-1469 A241 Set of 7 8.50 8.50

Souvenir Sheet
1470 A241 500sh multicolored 6.75 6.75

Snakes A242

Designs: 100sh, Naja pallida. 140sh, Agkistrodon contortrix. 180sh, Bungarus fasciatus. 200sh, Micrurus frontalis, vert. 260sh, Bitis gabonica, vert. 300sh, Elaphe moellendorffi, vert. 400sh, Vipera ursini, vert.
700sh, Corallus caninus, vert.

1996 *Perf. 12½x12, 12x12½*
1471-1477 A242 Set of 7 8.00 8.00

Souvenir Sheet
1478 A242 700sh multicolored 6.75 6.75

Famous People, Events — A243

No. 1479, 250sh: a, Gandhi. b, Mao Tse-tung. c, Jonas Salk. d, John F. Kennedy. e, Neil Armstrong. f, Mikhail Gorbachev. g, Nelson Mandela. h, Gen. Colin Powell.
No. 1480, 250sh: a, Orville, Wilbur Wright. b, Battle of Verdun, 1916. c, Charles Lindbergh. d, Al Jolson. e, Alexander Fleming. f, Amelia Earhart. g, Franklin Roosevelt, Joseph Stalin, Winston Churchill, Yalta Conference, 1945. h, Atomic bomb blast, 1945, Enrico Fermi.
No. 1481, 1000sh, Deng Xiaoping.

1996, July 15 Litho. *Perf. 14*
Sheets of 8, #a-h
1479-1480 A243 Set of 2 19.00 19.00

Souvenir Sheet
1481 A243 multicolored 9.50 9.50

A244

Fruits of East Africa: 140sh, Pineapple. 180sh, Orange, lime. 200sh, Pear, apple. 300sh, Bananas.

1996, Sept. 4 Litho. *Perf. 13*
1482-1485 A244 Set of 4 6.75 6.75
1485a Souv. sheet of 1 #1485 4.00 4.00

Birds — A245

No. 1486, 300sh: a, Vidua macroura. b, Tockus erythrorynchus. c, Trachyphonus erythrocephalus. d, Bubo capensis. e, Gyps ruppellii. f, Sarkidiornis melanotus. g, Dendrocygna bicolor. h, Struthio camelus.
No. 1487, 300sh: a, Gypohierax angolensis. b, Aquila chrysaetos. c, Spilornis rufipectus. d, Eutriorchis astur. e, Haliaeetus albicilla. f, Ichthyophaga ichthyaetus. g, Spilornis holospilus. h, Dryotriorchis spectabilis.
No. 1488, 1000sh: African paradise flycatcher. No. 1489, 1000sh: Haliaeetus leucocephala, horiz.

1996, Sept. 16 *Perf. 14*
Sheets of 8, #a-h
1486-1487 A245 Set of 2 30.00 30.00

Souvenir Sheets
1488 A245 multicolored 8.50 8.50
1489 A245 multicolored 8.50 8.50

Reef Fish A246

Designs: 100sh, Yellowtail wrasse. 150sh, Jewel grouper. 250sh, Barred thick-lipped wrasse. 500sh, Bullethead parrotfish.
No. 1494: a, Golden cardinal fish. b, Yellowhead butterfly fish. c, Common banner fish (diver). d, Zanzibar butterfly fish. e, Lemon damsel. f, Blue and gold fusilier. g, Red firegoby. h, Threadfin fairy basslet. i, Rein rock basslet.
No. 1495, 1000sh, African pygmy angelfish. No. 1496, 1000sh, Blue green chromis.

1996, Sept. 23
1490-1493 A246 Set of 4 8.00 8.00
1494 A246 200sh Sheet of 9, #a.-i. 12.00 12.00

Souvenir Sheets
1495-1496 A246 Set of 2 8.00 8.00

Ferrari Cars A247

No. 1497: a, 1964 250LM. b, 1992 456 GT. c, 1995 F50. d, 1995 F512 M "Testarossa." e, 1984 BB 512. f, 1955 410 S coupe.
1000sh, 1964 250 GTO.

1996, Sept. 27 Litho. *Perf. 14*
1497 A247 250sh Sheet of 6, #a.-f. 11.00 11.00

Souvenir Sheet
1498 A247 1000sh multi 7.75 7.75

No. 1498 contains one 85x28mm stamp.

Radio, Cent. A248

Designs: 70sh, Franklin D. Roosevelt, 1st fireside chat, 1933. 100sh, Harry S. Truman

announces US use of atomic bomb, 1945. 150sh, Orson Welles, "Alien Invasion" broadcast, 1938. 200sh, Fiorello La Guardia reads newspaper comics via radio.
1000sh, Robin Williams as Adrian Cronauer, "Good Morning Viet Nam."

1996, July 15 Litho. *Perf. 13½x14*
1499-1502 A248 Set of 4 4.00 4.00

Souvenir Sheet
1503 A248 1000sh multicolored 7.75 7.75

Mercedes-Benz Automobiles — A249

No. 1504: a, 1952 300SL Coupè 1. b, 1932 680S. c, 1934 500K. d, 1934 Type 150. e, 1934 Type 150 Sport Roadster "Heck." f, 1937 W125.
1000sh, 1936 540K Roadster Class A.

1996, Sept. 27 *Perf. 14*
1504 A249 250sh Sheet of 6, #a.-f. 10.50 10.50

Souvenir Sheet
1505 A249 1000sh multi 7.75 7.75

UNICEF, 50th Anniv. — A250

Designs: 200sh, Child holding bowl. 250sh, Mother breastfeeding infant. 500sh, Tetsuko Kuroyanaga holding child.
1000sh, Girl.

1996, Oct. 4
1506-1508 A250 Set of 3 6.75 6.75

Souvenir Sheet
1509 A250 1000sh multicolored 7.00 7.00

UNESCO, 50th Anniv. — A251

Designs: 200sh, Ngorongoro Conservation Area, Tanzania. 250sh, Los Katios Natl. Park, Colombia. 600sh, Kilwa Kisiwani Makutani Complex, Tanzania.
1000sh, Kilimanjaro Natl. Park, Tanzania.

1996, Oct. 4
1510-1512 A251 Set of 3 10.00 10.00

Souvenir Sheet
1513 A251 1000sh multi 10.00 10.00

Flowers — A252

No. 1514, 300sh: a, Lily of the valley. b, Spanish iris. c, Spiderwort. d, Morning glory. e, Gazania. f, Pansy. g, Begonia. h, Madonna lily.
No. 1515, 300sh: a, Snowdrop. b, Treesia. c, Cosmos. d, Daffodil. e, Blue himalayan poppy. f, Blue daisy. g, Zinnia flore-pleno. h, Oriental poppy.
No. 1516, 1000sh, Fuchsia. No. 1517, 1000sh, Hanson's lily.

1996, Oct. 25
Sheets of 8, #1-h + Label
1514-1515 A252 Set of 2 32.50 32.50

Souvenir Sheets
1516-1517 A252 Set of 2 18.00 18.00

Domestic Cats A253

Designs: 100sh, Lilac point Siamese. 150sh, Somali. 200sh, British blue shorthair.
No. 1521: a, American shorthair silver tabby. b, Scottish fold. c, Persian blue. d, Ocicat.
1000sh, Ragdoll.

1996, Dec. 10 Litho. *Perf. 14*
1518-1520 A253 Set of 3 3.00 3.00
1521 A253 300sh Sheet of 4, #a.-d. 7.25 7.25

Souvenir Sheet
1522 A253 1000sh multicolored 7.75 7.75

Dogs A254

Designs: 70sh, Shar-pei. 250sh, Beagle. 600sh, Keeshond.
No. 1527: a, St. Bernard. b, Shetland sheepdog. c, Samoyed. d, Australian cattle dog.
1000sh, Collie.

1996, Dec. 10 Litho. *Perf. 14*
1524-1526 A254 Set of 3 6.00 6.00
1527 A254 300sh Sheet of 4, #a.-d. 8.50 8.50

Souvenir Sheet
1528 A254 1000sh multicolored 7.75 7.75

Nos. 767-768, 1001-1002, 1026-1028 Ovptd.

a

b

c

1996, Dec. 16
1529 A120(a-b) 50sh Sheet of 16, #a.-p. (#767) 9.75 9.75
1530 A120(c) 50sh Sheet of 16, #a.-p. (#768) 9.75 9.75
1531 A154(a-b) 100sh Sheet of 12, #a.-l. (#1001) 14.50 14.50
1532 A158(c) 100sh Sheet of 6, #a.-f. (#1026) 7.25 7.25
1533 A158(c) 100sh Sheet of 6, #a.-f. (#1027) 7.25 7.25

Souvenir Sheets
1534 A154(c) 500sh on #1002 6.00 6.00
1535 A158(a) 500sh on #1028 6.00 6.00

Size and location of overprint varies.
Overprints types a-b appear on alternating stamps of Nos. 1529, 1531.
Nos. 1529-1533 have additional overprints in sheet margin.

Mushrooms A255

No. 1536, 300sh: a, Amanita phalloides. b, Amanita muscaria. c, Morchella vulgaris. d, Tricholoma aurantium. e, Amanita caesarea. f, Psalliota haemorrhoidaria. g, Russula virescens. h, Boletus crocipodius.
No. 1537, 300sh: a, Coprinus comatus. b, Amanitopsis vaginata. c, Clitocybe geotropa. d, Cortinarius violaceus. e, Russula sardonia. f, Cortinarius collinitus. g, Boletus aereus. h, Lepiota procera.
No. 1538, 1000sh, Ganoderma lucidum. No. 1539, 1000sh, Collybia distorta.

1996, Dec. 17 Sheets of 8, #a-h
1536-1537 A255 Set of 2 29.50 29.50

Souvenir Sheets
1538-1539 A255 Set of 2 16.00 16.00

Souvenir Sheet

Watercolor Painting — A256

1996, May 6 Litho. *Perf. 13*
1540 A256 500sh multicolored 4.25 4.25

China '96. No. 1540 was not available until March 1997.

Sun Yat-Sen (1866-1925) A257

Various portraits.

1997 *Perf. 14*
1541 A257 300sh Sheet of 6, #a.-f. 11.50 11.50

Souvenir Sheet
1542 A257 1000sh multi 7.75 7.75

Hong Kong '97.

Horses A258

No. 1543: a, Blue Arabian horse. b, English thoroughbred. c, Tennessee walking horse. d, Anglo-Arab horse.
No. 1544: a, Trakehner. b, American saddlebred. c, Morgan. d, Frederiksborg. e, Mirror of #d. f, Mirror of #c. g, Mirror of #b. h, Mirror of #a.
No. 1545, 1000sh, Wielkopolski. No. 1546, 1000sh, Thiawari, vert.

1997, Mar. 20 Litho. *Perf. 14*
1543 A258 250sh Strip of 4, #a.-d. 7.75 7.75
1544 A258 250sh Sheet of 8, #a.-h. 13.50 13.50

Souvenir Sheets
1545-1546 A258 Set of 2 13.50 13.50

No. 1543 was issued in sheets of 8 stamps with second strip in reverse order.

COMESA A259

Designs: 140sh, Tourism. 180sh, Fishing. 200sh, Dar es Salaam Port. 300sh, TAZARA Railway.

1997 *Perf. 13*
1547-1550 A259 Set of 4 6.25 6.25

Souvenir Sheet
1551 A259 500sh Cotton 4.25 4.25

UN Volunteers, 25th Anniv. A260

Designs: 140sh, Health of mother and child. 200sh, Food distribution. 260sh, Clean water distribution. 300sh, Public education.
500sh, Refugee camp.

1997
1552-1555 A260 Set of 4 6.75 6.75

Souvenir Sheet
1556 A260 500sh multicolored 5.00 5.00

Birds A261

Designs: 150sh, Mockingbird. 200sh, House finch. 410sh, Bridled titmouse. 500sh, Cactus wren.
No. 1561: a, Sooty tern. b, Nunbird. c, Mottled wood owl. d, Turquoise-browed mot mot. e, Emerald toucanet. f, Dusky-headed conure.
No. 1562: a, Maguari stork. b, Spoonbills. c, Flamingo. d, Hammerkop. e, Limpkin. f, Pink-backed pelican.
No. 1563, 1000sh, Masked booby. No. 1564, 1000sh, Brown pelican.

1997, May 5 Litho. *Perf. 14*
1557-1560 A261 Set of 4 7.75 7.75
1561 A261 140sh Sheet of 6, #a.-f. 5.50 5.50
1562 A261 370sh Sheet of 6, #a.-f. 11.50 11.50

Souvenir Sheets
1563-1564 A261 Set of 2 14.50 14.50

A262

Flowers — A263

Designs: 100sh, Plumeria rubra acutifolia. 140sh, 150sh, Liliaceae. 180sh, Alamanda. 200sh, Lilaceae, diff. 210sh, 350sh, Zinnia. 260sh, Malvaviscus penduliflorus. 300sh, Carna. 380sh, Nerium oleander carneum. 400sh, Hibiscus rosa sinensis. 500sh, Catharanthus roseus. 600sh, Cartharanthus roseus. 700sh, Bougainvillea formosa. 750sh, Acalypha.

No. 1577: a, like #1571. b, like #1569. c, like #1572. d, like #1575.

1997-2004(?)			***Perf. 14½x15***	
1565	A262	100sh multi	.40	.40
1566	A262	140sh multi	.60	.60
1566A	A262	150sh multi	—	
1567	A262	180sh multi	.75	.75
1568	A262	200sh multi	.80	.80
1569	A262	210sh multi	.85	.85
1570	A262	260sh multi	1.00	1.00
1571	A262	300sh multi	1.25	1.25
1571A	A262	350sh multi	—	—
1572	A262	380sh multi	1.50	1.50
1573	A262	400sh multi	1.60	1.60
1573A	A262	500sh multi	—	—
1574	A262	600sh multi	2.50	2.50
1575	A262	700sh multi	3.00	3.00
1576	A262	750sh multi	3.50	3.50
	Nos. 1565-1566,1567-1576 (13)		17.75	17.75

Souvenir Sheet

Perf. 14½x14

1577	A263	125sh Sheet of 4, #a.-d.	2.50	2.50

Issued: #1566A, 1997; #1573A, 2004(?); others, 5/19.

For overprint see No. O49. For surcharges see Nos. 2268, 2335, 2337, 2337A.

Modern Olympic Games, Cent., 1996 Summer Olympic Games, Atlanta, — A264

1996	**Litho.**		***Perf. 11½***	
1578	A264	100sh Tennis	.80	.80
1579	A264	150sh Baseball	1.25	1.25
1580	A264	200sh Soccer	1.45	1.45
1581	A264	300sh Boxing	2.50	2.50
	Nos. 1578-1581 (4)		6.00	6.00

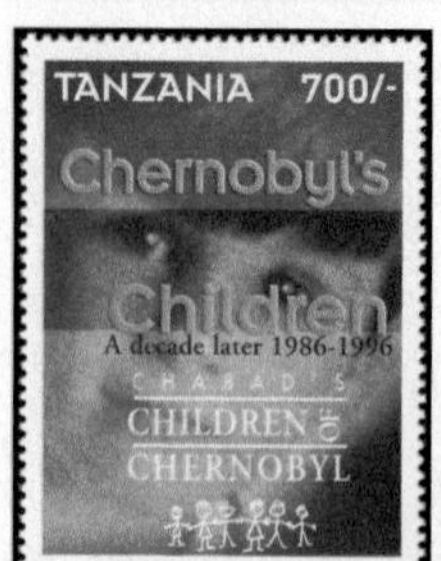

Chernobyl Disaster, 10th Anniv. A265

Designs: No. 1582, Chabad's Children of Chernobyl. No. 1583, UNESCO.

1997, Apr. 25	**Litho.**		***Perf. 13½x14***	
1582	A265	700sh multicolored	5.00	5.00
1583	A265	700sh multicolored	5.00	5.00

Flowers — A266

No. 1583A: b, Prunus dulcis. c, Spassky Clock tower. d, Crataegus monogyna. e, Amica montana. f, Campanula patula. g, Papaver orientalis.

No. 1584: a, Malus niedzwetzkayana. b, Golden domes of the Cathedral of the Annunciation, Moscow. c, Polygonatum multiflorum. d, Leucanthemum vulgare, e, Hypencum perforatum. f, Pulsatilla vulgaris.

No. 1585, 1000sh, Laburnum anagyroides, St. Basil's Cathedral, vert. No. 1585A, 1000sh, Rosa canina, Church of Christ Resurrection, Moscow.

1997			***Perf. 14x14½***	
1583A	A266	200sh Sheet of 6, #b.-g.	8.50	8.50
1584	A266	300sh Sheet of 6, #a.-f.	13.00	13.00

Souvenir Sheets

1585-1585A	A266	Set of 2	18.00	18.00

No. 1585 contains one 30x38mm stamp.

World AIDS Day A267

Designs: 140sh, Condom protects against AIDS, vert. 310sh, Caution, you may contract AIDS. 370sh, Control of AIDS is our responsibility. 410sh, Care and support AIDS orphans. 500sh, Like #1586.

1997	**Litho.**		***Perf. 13***	
1586-1589	A267	Set of 4	8.50	8.50

Souvenir Sheet

1590	A267	500sh multicolored	4.50	4.50

Paintings by Hiroshige (1797-1858) A268

No. 1591: a, Aoi Slope, Outside Toranomon Gate. b, Bikuni Bridge in Snow. c, Mount Atago, Shiba. d, Akasaka Kiribatake. e, Zojoji Pagoda & Akabane. f, Hibiya & Soto-Sakurada from Yamashita-cho.

No. 1592, 1000sh, Shiba Shinmei Shrine. No. 1593, 1000sh, Kanasugibashi Shibaura.

1997, July 21	**Litho.**		***Perf. 13½x14***	
1591	A268	250sh Sheet of 6, #a.-f.	9.50	9.50

Souvenir Sheets

1592-1593	A268	Set of 2	6.25	6.25

Queen Elizabeth II and Prince Philip, 50th Anniv. A269

No. 1594: a, Engagement picture of Queen. b, Royal arms. c, Queen, Prince in casual attire. d, Prince, Queen. e, Balmoral Castle. f, Prince Philip.

1500sh, Formal portrait.

1997, July 21	**Litho.**		***Perf. 14***	
1594	A269	370sh Sheet of 6, #a.-f.	9.50	9.50

Souvenir Sheet

1595	A269	1500sh multi	9.50	9.50

Return of Hong Kong to China — A270

No. 1596 — Split design comparing modern and early photographs of: a, Clock Tower, Tsim Sha Tsu, former terminal of Kowloon-Canton Railways. b, Legislative Council Building, previously Supreme Court.

No. 1597: a, Signing of Sino-British Joint Declaration on Question of Hong Kong, 1984. b, Deng Xiaoping, Chinese leaders, c, C.F. Tung, first Chinese chief executive of Hong Kong, 1996.

1997, July 21			***Perf. 14½***	
1596	A270	1000sh Sheet of 2, #a.-b.	10.00	10.00
1597	A270	1000sh Sheet of 3, #a.-c.	14.50	14.50

No. 1597 contains 3 59x28mm stamps.

Grimm's Fairy Tales A271

Mother Goose — A272

No. 1598 — Rumpelstiltskin: a, Woman at spinning wheel, Prince. b, Woman, Rumpelstiltskin at spinning wheel. c, Prince, woman playing mandolin.

No. 1599, Girl whistling. No. 1600, Rumpelstiltskin.

1997			***Perf. 13½x14***	
1598	A271	400sh Sheet of 3, #a.-c.	7.25	7.25

Souvenir Sheets

Perf. 14

1599	A272	1000sh multicolored	7.25	7.25

Perf. 13½x14

1600	A271	1500sh multicolored	7.25	7.25

1998 Winter Olympic Games, Nagano — A273

Designs: 100sh, Torvill & Dean, ice dancing. 200sh, Katarina Witt, figure skating. 500sh, First Olympic winter games, 1924, curling introduced. 600sh, Pirmin Zurbriggen, downhill skiing.

No. 1605: a, Dan Jansen, 1000m speed skating. b, Alberto Tomba, slalom & giant slalom skiing. c, Herma Plank-Szabo, figure skating. d, Donna Weinbrecht, mogul skiing.

No. 1606, 1000sh, Yukio Kasaya, ski jump. No. 1607, 1000sh, Barbara Ann Scott, figure skating.

1997, Oct. 6	**Litho.**		***Perf. 14***	
1601-1604	A273	Set of 4	8.00	8.00
1605	A273	250sh Block or strip of 4, #a.-d.	6.00	6.00

Souvenir Sheets

1606-1607	A273	Set of 2	11.00	11.00

Sinking of MV Bukoba A274

Designs: 140sh, Ship sinking. 350sh, Removing bodies. 370sh, Identification of the dead. 410sh, Mass funeral.

500sh, MV Bukoba.

1997, May 21	**Litho.**		***Perf. 14***	
1608-1611	A274	Set of 4	7.75	7.75

Souvenir Sheet

Perf. 14½

1612	A274	500sh multicolored	4.00	4.00

Tourist Attractions of East Africa — A275

Designs: 140sh, Mount Kilimanjaro. 310sh, Masai. 370sh, Zanzibar old stonetown. 410sh, Buffalo, plains of Ruaha.

500sh, Mount Kilimanjaro Kibo Peak.

1997, Oct. 9			***Perf. 13½***	
1613-1616	A275	Set of 4	7.75	7.75

Souvenir Sheet

1617	A275	500sh multicolored	4.25	4.25

1998 World Cup Soccer Championships, France — A276

Teams: 100sh, Italy, 1938. 150sh, Brazil, 1970. 200sh, Uruguay, 1930. 250sh, W. Germany, 1954. 500sh, Argentina, 1978. 600sh, England, 1966.

No. 1624, 250sh, vert. — Players: a, Muller, W. Germany. b, Kocsis, Hungary. c, Pele, Brazil. d, Schillaci, Italy. e, Fontaine, France. f, Nejedly, Czechoslovakia. g, Rahn, W. Germany. h, Lineker, England.

No. 1625, 250sh — Stadiums: a, The Rose Bowl, US, 1994. b, Torino Stadium, Italy, 1934. c, Olympia Stadium, Germany, 1974. d, Azteca Satdium, Mexico, 1970, 1986. e, Wembley, England, 1966. f, Maracana, Brazil,

1950. g, Centenary Stadium, Uruguay, 1930. h, Bernabeu Stadium, Spain, 1982.
No. 1626, 1000sh, Pele, Brazil. No. 1627, 1000sh, Eusebio, Portugal.

1997, Oct. 20 ***Perf. 14x13½, 13½x14***
1618-1623 A276 Set of 6 6.00 6.00

Sheets of 8, #a-h, + Label

1624-1625 A276 Set of 2 13.00 13.00

Souvenir Sheet

1626-1627 A276 Set of 2 7.75 7.75

Endangered Species — A277

Fauna A278

No. 1628, 250sh — Animals of Asia: a, Tiger. b, Japanese macaque. c, Slender loris. d, Musk deer. e, Przewalski's horse. f, Red panda.
No. 1629, 250sh — Animals of Latin America: a, Night monkey. b, Woolly opossum. c, Jaguar. d, Red uakaris. e, Ringtailed coati. f, Cotton-top tamarin.
No. 1630, 250sh — Animals of North America: a, Bobcat. b, Moose. c, American bison. d, Mountain goat. e, Walrus. f, Common racoon.
No. 1630G — Animals of Africa: h, Cheetah. i, Zebra. j, Gorilla. k, Brown lesser mouse lemur. l, Rhinoceros. m. Chimpanzee.
No. 1631, 250sh — Northern wilderness animals: a, Great horned owl. b, Bald eagle. c, Coyotes. d, Grizzly bear. e, Caribou (d). f, Walrus. g, Hooded seal. h, Humpback whale (g). i, Harp seal.
No. 1632, 250sh — African safari animals a, Barbary macaque. b, Turaco. c, Giraffe (f). d, Mountain gorilla, African elephant (a, b, e, g, h). e, Zebra. f, Grant's gazelle. g, Monarch butterfly, meerkat. h, African lion. i, Rhinoceros (f).
No. 1633, 1500sh, Maned wolf. No. 1634, 1500sh, Giant panda. No. 1635, 1500sh, Gray wolf. No. 1636, 1500sh, African elephant, diff.

1997, Oct. 30 ***Perf. 14***

Sheets of 6, #a-f

1628-1630 A277 Set of 3 50.00 50.00
1630G A277 250sh Sheet of 6, #h.-m. 16.00 16.00

Sheets of 9, #a-i

1631-1632 A278 250sh Set of 2 45.00 45.00

Souvenir Sheets

1633-1636 A277 1500sh Set of 4 55.00 55.00

A279

No. 1637 — Modern architecture: a, Sydney Opera House, Australia. b, Brasilia Cathedral, Brazil. c, Metropolitan Cathedral of Christ the King, Liverpool, England. d, Einstein Tower, Potsdam, Berlin, Germany. e, Solomon Guggenheim Museum, New York City, US. f, Palace of the Natl. Congress, Brasilla.
No. 1638 — Ancient wonders of the world, vert.: a, Temple of Artemis at Ephesus. b, Great Pyramid of Cheops. c, Mausoleum at Halicarnassus. d, Statue of Zeus at Olympia. e, Hanging Gardens of Babylon. f, Colossus of Rhodes.
No. 1639, 1000sh, Notre Dame Du Haut Chapel, Ronchamp, France. No. 1640, 1000sh, Lighthouse of Alexandria.

1997, Nov. 5 ***Perf. 14***
1637 A279 140sh Sheet of 6, #a.-f. 6.00 6.00
1638 A279 370sh Sheet of 6, #a.-f. 15.50 15.50

Souvenir Sheets

1639-1640 A279 Set of 2 16.00 16.00

Nos. 1639-1640 contain one 42x57mm or 57x42mm stamp, respectively.

A280

Coastal Birds: 140sh, Red hornbill. 350sh, Sacred ibis, horiz. 370sh, Sea gulls, horiz. 410sh, Ring-necked dove, horiz.
500sh, Hornbill, ibis, gulls, doves, horiz.

1997, Nov. 28 **Wmk. 233**
1641-1644 A280 Set of 4 8.00 8.00

Souvenir Sheet

1645 A280 500sh multicolored 3.25 3.25

Aircraft A281

Fighter Planes: 100sh, P-51D. 200sh, Lockheed P-38J Lightning. 300sh, B-29 Superfortress. 400sh, Lockheed P-80 Shooting Star P-80 A1. 500sh, Curtiss P-36A.
No. 1651, 150sh — Spitfires: a, MK IX providing altitude cover for bomber formations. b, MK Vc dog fighting. c, PRMK XIX, Photographic Reconnaissance Development Unit, RAF. d, MK Vb over North Africa. e, FR XIVE firing rockets. f, MK VIII (ZPZ), Japanese bomber. g, Supermarine Seafire being catapulted from HMS Indomitable. h, MK IX during D-Day landings. i, MK XII attacking V1 Flying Bomb.
No. 1652, 150sh — Spitfires: a, MK IXc, excorting crippled Lancaster Bomber. b, MK 1a dog fighting. c, PR MK XI, 14th Photo Sqdn., US 8th Air Force. d, MK Vb, North Africa. e, MK VIII with lightning bolt on nose. f, MK Vc with RAF, Yugoslav, American markings. g, Supermarine Seafire landing on British carrier. h, MK IXc D-Day. i, MK XII destroying V-1 Flying Bomb.
No. 1653: a, MKII in desert. b, Hurribomber dog fighting. c, MK 24, photo reconnaissance. d, Canadian MK 1 foreign squadron. e, Mark IXC convoy protection. f, Spitfire with clipped wings flanked by MK 22. g, Hurricanes MKII in desert. h, Hurribomber.
No. 1654, 1000sh, Boeing P-26. No. 1655, 1000sh, SR-71A. No. 1656, 1000sh, MK Vb. No. 1657, 1000sh,MK V Float plane. No. 1658, 1000sh, MK 1.

1997, Dec. 23 **Litho.** ***Perf. 14***
1646-1650 A281 Set of 5 10.00 10.00

Sheets of 9, #a-i

1651-1652 A281 Set of 2 13.50 13.50
1653 A281 250sh Sheet of 8, #a.-h. 22.50 22.50

Souvenir Sheets

1654-1658 A281 Set of 5 37.50 37.50

No. 1656 contains one 85x28mm stamp. Nos. 1657-1658 each contain one 57x42mm stamp.

Jackie Chan, Movie Star A282

Various portraits.

1997, Dec. 30
1659 A282 370sh Sheet of 6, #a.-f. 13.50 13.50

PAPU (Pan African Postal Union), 18th Anniv. A283

Designs: 150sh, Natl. flag of Tanzania, flag of PAPU. 250sh, PAPU emblem. 400sh, Delivery by EMS motorcycles. 500sh, Giraffes.

1998, Jan. 18 ***Perf. 13½***
1660-1663 A283 Set of 4 8.50 8.50

A284

1998 **Litho.** ***Perf. 14***
1664 A284 410sh Mt. Kilimanjaro 3.00 3.00

A285

Diana, Princess of Wales (1961-97): 150sh, In red jacket. 250sh, In lilac dress.
1000sh, In teal suit with Prince Harry (in sheet margin).

1998, Jan. 23
1665 A285 150sh multicolored 1.00 1.00
1666 A285 250sh multicolored 1.75 1.75

Souvenir Sheet

1667 A285 1000sh multicolored 6.50 6.50

Nos. 1665-1666 were each issued in sheets of 9.

Marine Life and Sea Birds A286

No. 1668: a, Black-browed albatross. b, Unidentified bird. c, Xantusi murrelet. d, Empress angelfish. e, Bottle nosed dolphins. f, Queen angelfish. g, Red sponge. h, Unidentified red and tan fish. i, Reef shark. j, Sea star. k, Unidentified white and black fish. l, Stingray.
No. 1669, 250sh: a, Black-saddled pufferfish. b, Harlequin tuskfish. c, Emperor angelfish. d, Foxface. e, Yellow tang. f, Catalina goby. g, Fifteen-spined stickleback. h, Banded pipefish. i, Weather loach.
No. 1670, 250sh, vert.: a, Octopus. b, Pantherfish. c, Hawksbill turtle. d, Skate. e, Jellyfish. f, White tip shark. g, Blue starfish. h, Brain coral. i, Anemone.
No. 1671, 1000sh, Clown fish. No. 1672, 1000sh, Shark. No. 1673, 1000sh, Yellow seahorse, vert.

1998, Jan. 30
1668 A286 200sh Sheet of 12, #a.-l. 16.00 16.00

Sheets of 9, #a-i

1669-1670 A286 Set of 2 35.00 35.00

Souvenir Sheets

1671-1673 A286 Set of 3 22.50 22.50

For overprints see #1697-1702.

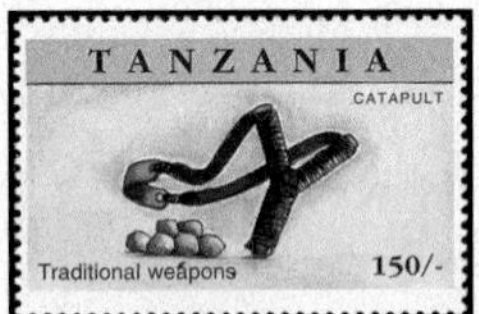

Traditional Weapons — A287

Designs: 150sh, Slingshot. 250sh, Cutlass and club. 400sh, Gun. 500sh, Bow, arrows.

1998, Mar. 16 **Litho.** ***Perf. 14***
1674-1677 A287 Set of 4 8.00 8.00

New Year 1998 (Year of the Tiger) — A288

No. 1678 — Stylized tiger: a, Walking right. b, Walking left. c, Lying down. d, Seated.
1500sh, Tiger standing.

1998, Mar. 30 **Litho.** ***Perf. 13½***
1678 A288 370sh Sheet of 4, #a.-d. 9.00 9.00

Souvenir Sheet

1679 A288 1500sh multi 9.00 9.00

John Denver (1943-97), Rock Musician — A288a

No. 1679A: c, Wearing green sweater. d, Wearing brown sweater (shoulders in middle of stamp). e, Wearing brown sweater (shoulder near corner of stamp). f, Wearing green sweater, hand at face.
1500sh, Wearing blue shirt.

1998, Apr. 30 **Litho.** ***Perf. 14***
1679A A288a 370sh Sheet of 4, #c-f 4.50 4.50

Souvenir Sheet

1679B A288a 1500sh multi 4.50 4.50

Most examples of Nos. 1679A-1679B were not available in the philatelic marketplace until Dec. 2002.

Antique Automobiles — A289

No. 1680, 370sh: a, 1901 Mercedes 35hp. b, 1903 Ford Model A. c, 1908 Legnano Type A. d, 1908-09 Rolls Royce 40-50hp Silver Ghost. e, 1910 Renault Petit Duc. f, 1913 Fischer Torpedo.

No. 1681, 370sh: a, 1923-24 Peugeot 18cv. b, 1926 Daimler 25-85hp. c, 1932 Bugatti Type 50T. d, 1933 Pierce-Arrow V12 "Silver Arrow." e, 1934 Tatra V8. f, 1937 Grosser Mercedes Benz.

No. 1682, 1000sh, 1900 Benz. No. 1683, 1000sh, 1893 Duryea.

1998, Aug. 4 Litho. *Perf. 14*

Sheets of 6, #a-f

1680-1681 A289 Set of 2 32.50 32.50

Souvenir Sheets

1682-1683 A289 Set of 2 16.00 16.00

Nos. 1682-1683 each contain one 64x48mm stamp.

Flowers and Insects — A290

No. 1684, vert: a, Euanthe sanderiana, teirataenia surinama. b, "Clown Mixed." c, Pansies, caterpiller of papilio polyxenes. d, "Prelude." e, Dendrobium primulinum, wasp beetle. f, Carrion beetle, clematis "Lasurstern." g, Sunflowers, "Autumn Beauty" & "Italian White," elder borer, painted daisy. h, Grape hyacinth.

No. 1685, 250sh: a, Platinum sun. b, Vespid wasp, oriental poppy. c, Anemone. d, Ipomoea alba, king's bee hawkmoth. e, Aussie delight, potter wasp. f, Colorado potato beetle, Japanese iris. g, Bomarea caldasii, azure damselfly. h, Hybrid macranthe, queen bumblebee. i, Love with lace iris, click beetle.

No. 1686, 250sh: a, Golden ray lily, South African longhorn beetle. b, Oncidium macianthum. c, Agelia petali, dendrobium. c, Cobaea scandens. d, Goldsmith beetle, paphiopedilum gilda. e, Iceland poppies, potter wasp. f, Pink beauty. g, Annual chrysanthemums. h, Little mal, m. femurrubrum.

No. 1687, 1500sh, Carolina Queen. No. 1688, 1500sh, Robert E. Lee daffodils. No. 1689, 1500sh, Orange scarlet hybrid "Tempo." No. 1690, 1500sh, Pansies.

1998, Aug. 18 Litho. *Perf. 14*

1684 A290 250sh Sheet of 8, #a.-h. 25.00 25.00

Sheets of 9, #a-i

1685-1686 A290 Set of 2 27.50 27.50

Souvenir Sheets

1687-1690 A290 Set of 4 42.50 42.50

A291

Endangered Species — A292

No. 1691: a, Hyacinth macaw. b, Gibbon. c, Bosman's potto. d, Scarlet crowned barbets. e, Giant anteater. f, Cacomistle. g, Tiger. h, Mara. i, Mandrill. j, Crocodile. k, Wood turtle. l, Baribusa.

No. 1692: a, Giant sable antelope. b, Cheetah. c, Giraffe. d, Black bear. e, African elephant. f, Giant panda.

No. 1693: a, Tiger. b, Bald eagle (a, c). c, Mountain gorilla. d, Sea lion. e, Green sea turtle. f, Hippopotamus.

No. 1694, Emerald tanager.

No. 1695, 1500sh, Florida manatee. No. 1696, 1500sh, Orangutan.

1998, Aug. 31 Litho. *Perf. 14*

1691 A291 200sh Sheet of 12, #a.-l. 17.00 17.00

1692 A292 370sh Sheet of 6, #a.-f. 15.00 15.00

1693 A292 370sh Sheet of 6, #a.-f. 15.00 15.00

Souvenir Sheets

1694 A291 1500sh multi 11.50 11.50

1695-1696 A292 Set of 2 23.50 23.50

Nos. 1692, 1695 each contain 51x38mm stamps. No. 1696 contains 43x28mm stamps.

Nos. 1668-1673 Ovptd.

1998, Sept. 2 Litho. *Perf. 14*

1697 A286 200sh Sheet of 12, #a.-l. (#1668) 22.50 22.50

1698 A286 250sh Sheet of 9 #a.-i. (#1669) 13.00 13.00

1699 A286 250sh Sheet of 9 #a.-i. (#1670) 13.00 13.00

Souvenir Sheets

1700 A286 1000sh multi (#1671) 10.00 10.00

1701 A286 1000sh multi (#1672) 10.00 10.00

1702 A286 1000sh multi (#1673) 10.00 10.00

The stamps of Nos. 1697-1699, 1701-1702 were ovptd. with Intl. Year of the Ocean emblem and the sheet margins contain one or two emblems with words "INTERNATIONAL YEAR OF THE OCEAN." No. 1700 has overprint only on sheet margin.

Aircraft A293

No. 1703, 300sh: a, Antoinette IV, 1908. b, Deperdussin Racer, 1912. c, Demoiselle, 1909. d, Bleriot XI, 1909. e, Avro FAV Roe, 1912. f, Breguet IV, 1910.

No. 1704, 300sh: a, Deperdussin. b, Ultralight, 1979-86. c, Amphibian, 1929-30. d, Pitts Special, 1930. e, BAC-221, 1960. f, Avro Tutor, 1931.

No. 1705, 300sh: a, KI-44 Tojo. b, Hawker Fury. c, Mustang. d, Zero. e, Travel Air Mystery Ship. f, F8F Bearcat.

No. 1706, 1000sh, USAAF Curtiss P-40M. No. 1707, 1000sh, Biplane. No. 1708, 1000sh, Balloon.

1998, Aug. 4 Litho. *Perf. 14*

Sheets of 6, #a-f

1703-1705 A293 Set of 3 40.00 40.00

Souvenir Sheets

1706-1708 A293 Set of 3 27.50 27.50

No. 1704a incorrectly inscribed 1900.

Eagles A294

No. 1709: a, Pallas's fish. b, Bateleur. c, Martial. d, Golden. e, Wedge-tailed. f, Java hawk.

1500sh, Wedge-tailed, diff.

1998, Aug. 31

1709 A294 370sh Sheet of 6, #a.-f. 14.00 14.00

Souvenir Sheet

1710 A294 1500sh multi 10.00 10.00

Fauna and Flora A295

Designs: 250sh, Takahe. 410sh, Lear's macaw. 500sh, Ring-tailed lemur. 600sh, Arabian oryx.

No. 1715, 370sh, : a, Japanese crested ibis. b, Kuai O'o. c, Bourke's hairstreak. d, Quokka. e, Tahitian lorikeet. f, Black-faced tamarin.

No. 1716, 370sh: a, Loggerhead turtle. b, Snow leopard. c, Gurney's pitta. d, Lowland gorilla. e, Echo parakeet. f, Orangutan.

No. 1717, 1500sh, Giant panda. No. 1718, 1500sh, Bengal tiger.

1998, Aug. 31 *Perf. 14x14½*

1711-1714 A295 Set of 4 12.50 12.50

Sheets of 6, #a-f

1715-1716 A295 Set of 2 21.00 21.00

Souvenir Sheets

1717-1718 A295 Set of 2 16.00 16.00

Children's Rights A296

Designs: 150sh, Equal rights for boys and girls. 250sh, Right to education. 400sh, Right not to be beaten, vert. No. 1722, 500sh, Right to be loved, vert.

No. 1723, Right to education.

1998 *Perf. 13*

1719-1722 A296 Set of 4 7.25 7.25

Souvenir Sheet

1723 A296 500sh multicolored 3.00 3.00

Nos. 608, 610 Surcharged

1998 Method and Perf. as Before

1723A A99 150sh on 13sh #608 —

1723B A99 150sh on 20sh #610 — —

Issued: No. 723A, 1/26; No. 1723B, 3/16.

World Stamp Day — A297

Designs: 150sh, UPU Emblem. 250sh, Letter facing and date stamping. 400sh, Trusted messenger. 500sh, Letter posting.

No. 1728, Trusted messenger, letter posting, UPU emblem.

1998, Oct. 9 Wmk. 387 *Perf. 14*

1724-1727 A297 Set of 4 7.25 7.25

Souvenir Sheet

1728 A297 500sh multicolored 3.00 3.00

A298

Marine Life, Sea Birds A299

Designs: 150sh, Equal sea star. 250sh, Mountain crab. 400sh, Wolffish. 500sh, Purple sea urchin.

No. 1733: a, Barred antshrike. b, Yellow-nosed albatross, common tern. c, Common tern, killer whale. d, Crimson-rumped toucanet. e, French angelfish. f, Grey shark (e). g, Manta ray (f, h). h, Yellow-backed damselfish. i, Green parrot wrasse. j, Silver badgerfish, pyjama wrasse. k, Skate, red-knobbed starfish (h). l, Striped snapper.

No. 1734: a, Common dolphin. b, Blue marlin. c, Arctic tern. d, Blackedge moray. e, Loggerhead turtle. f, Blacktip shark. g, Two-spotted octopus. h, Manta ray. i, Sailfin tang.

No. 1735, 1000sh, Aequipecten opercularis. No. 1736, 1000sh, Chrysaora quinquecirrha. 1500sh, Skate.

1998, Oct. 12

1729-1732 A298 Set of 4 8.25 8.25

1733 A299 200sh Sheet of 12, #a.-l. 16.50 16.50

1734 A298 300sh Sheet of 9, #a.-i. 20.00 20.00

Souvenir Sheets

1735-1736 A298 Set of 2 10.50 10.50

1737 A299 1500sh multi 8.25 8.25

Intl. Year of the Ocean (#1733-1737).

Mushrooms and Insects — A300

Designs: 140sh, Cardinal beetle, tricholoma batschii. 150sh, Tricholoma catigatum, painted lady. 200sh, Lyophylum decastes, speckled wood butterfly. 250sh, Tricholoma flavovfrens, speckled bush cricket. 370sh, Boletus chrysenteron, shieldbug. 410sh, Boletus zelleri, darter dragonfly. 500sh, Gyroporus castaneus, tortoise beetle. 600sh, Hissing cockroach, boletus satanas.

No. 1746, 250sh: a, Hygrocybe miniata, shieldbug. b, Peacock butterfly, cystolepiata adulterina. c, Collybia dryophila, bush cricket. d, Omphalotus olearius, halloween pennant butterfly. e, Macrolepiota rhacodes, helicon butterfly. f, Macrole piota puellaris, hornet. g, Carpenter bee. h, Mycena epipteryia, South African longhorn beetle. i, Amanita muscaria, skipper butterfly.

No. 1747 250sh, vert.: a, Leaf hopper cicadia, pleurotus ostreatus. b, Amanita muscaria, froghopper beetle. c, Wasp, amanita umbrinolutea. d, Butterfly, onnia tomentosa. e, Monarch butterfly, ganoderma lucidum. f, Broad-bodied libellua, macrolepiota procera. g, Butterfly anthocharis, suillus granulatus. h, Egyptian grasshopper, cortinarius praestans. i, Flying bush cricket, marasmius ramealis.

No. 1748, 1500sh, Coprinus silvaticus, thornbug. No. 1749, 1500sh, Black swallowtail, chroogomphus rutilus.

1998, Nov. 27

1738-1745 A300 Set of 8 15.50 15.50

Sheets of 9, #a-i

1746-1747 A300 Set of 2 32.50 32.50

Souvenir Sheets

1748-1749 A300 Set of 2 21.00 21.00

Rudolph the Red-Nosed Reindeer A301

No. 1752, 200sh: a, Milo. b, Rudolph (face). c, Leonard. d, Stormella. e, Ridley. f. Boone.

No. 1753, 200sh: a, Santa. b, Rudolph. c, Doggle. d, Edgar. e, Baby Rudolph. f, Toys.
No. 1754, 1000sh, Leonard, horiz. No. 1755, 1000sh, Rudolph. No. 1756, 1000sh, Baby Rudolph with ball on nose, diff. No. 1757, 1000sh, Santa with Rudolph.

Perf. 13½x14, 14x13½

1998, Dec. 15 Litho.

Sheets of 6, #a-f

1752-1753 A301 Set of 2 12.00 12.00

Souvenir Sheets

1754-1757 A301 Set of 4 22.50 22.50

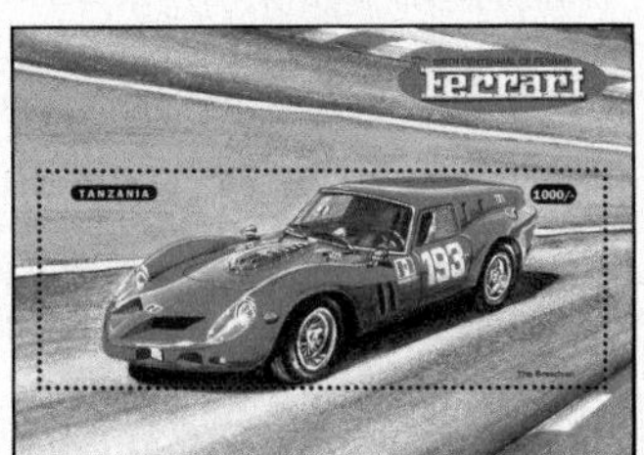

Ferrari Automobiles — A301a

No. 1757A: c, GTO. d, F40. e, 512S. 100sh, Breadvan.

1998, Dec. 16 Litho. *Perf. 14*

1757A A301a 500sh Sheet of 3, #c-e 12.00 12.00

Souvenir Sheet

Perf. 13¾x14¼

1757B A301a 1000sh multi 8.00 8.00

No. 1757A contains three 39x25mm stamps.

Diana, Princess of Wales (1961-97) — A302

No. 1758 — Denomination and country name at: a, Left. b, Right.

1998, Dec. 16 Litho. *Perf. 14*

1758 A302 600sh Horiz. pair, #a-b 6.25 6.25

Picasso — A303

Paintings: No. 1759, 400sh, Jacquelin with Crossedhand, 1954. No. 1760, 400sh, Straw Hat with Blue Foilage, 1936. 500sh, Reading the Letter, 1921.
1500sh, Woman Writing, 1934.

1998, Dec. 16 *Perf. 14½*

1759-1761 A303 Set of 3 6.75 6.75

Souvenir Sheet

1762 A303 1500sh multicolored 7.75 7.75

Mohandas Gandhi — A304

1998, Dec. 16 *Perf. 14*

1763 A304 370sh Portrait 3.25 3.25

Souvenir Sheet

1764 A304 1500sh Jawaharlal Nehru 11.00 11.00

No. 1763 was issued in sheets of 4.

1998 World Scout Jamboree, Chile A305

No. 1765: a, US Pres. William Howard Taft greets scouts during early years, 1908. b, Early Cub Scout pack enjoys musical camp break, 1930's. c, Dan Beard demonstrates tomahawk throw at Silver Bay, 1912.
1500sh, Ernest Thompson Seton (1860-1946), first Chief Scout.

1998, Dec. 16 Litho. *Perf. 14*

1765 A305 600sh Sheet of 3, #a.-c. 9.50 9.50

Souvenir Sheet

1766 A305 1500sh multi 8.50 8.50

Royal Air Force, 80th Anniv. A306

No. 1767: a, Panavia Tornado F3. b, Sepecat Jaguar GR1A. c, Jaguar GR1A. d, Jaguar GR1A, diff.
No. 1768, 1000sh, Harrier, Eurofighter. No. 1769, 1000sh, Biplane, hawk.

1998, Dec. 16 *Perf. 14*

1767 A306 500sh Sheet of 4, #a.-d. 11.50 11.50

Souvenir Sheets

1768-1769 A306 Set of 2 13.50 13.50

New Year 1999 (Year of the Rabbit) A307

No. 1770 — Color of rabbit : a, Red brown. b, Spotted. c, Yellow. d, Brown.
1500sh, White.

1999, Jan. 18 *Perf. 14*

1770 A307 250sh Sheet of 4, #a.-d. 6.25 6.25

Souvenir Sheet

1771 A307 1500sh multicolored 8.50 8.50

Tourism in Zanzibar A308

Designs: 100sh, Dhow Harbor, vert. 150sh, Girl on giant tortoise, vert. 250sh, Children with giant tortoise. 300sh, Street in Stone Town, vert. 400sh, Old fort. 500sh, Red colobus monkeys.
600sh, Girl on tortoise, street in Stone Town.

1998, Nov. 10 Litho. *Perf. 14*

1772-1777 A308 Set of 6 10.00 10.00

Souvenir Sheet

1778 A308 600sh multicolored 5.00 5.00

Tanzanian Posts Corp., 5th Anniv. A309

Designs: 150sh, Rural post office. 250sh, Overnight mail service. 350sh, Money fax service. 400sh, Post shop business.
500sh, Exterior view of high rise building, vert.

1999, Jan. 1

1779-1782 A309 Set of 4 6.25 6.25

Souvenir Sheet

1783 A309 500sh multicolored 3.25 3.25

Butterflies A310

200sh, Calycopis cecrops. 250sh, Heliconis melpomena, vert. 370sh, Citherias menander, vert. 410sh, Heliconis antiochus, vert.
No. 1788, 200sh: a, Acraea cerasa. b, Acraea semivitrea. c, Euchrysops scintilla. d, Papilio phorcas. e, Euphaedra eusemoides. f, Acraea masamba. g, Phyciodes emerantia. h, Hypothiris tricolor. i, Orimba jansoni.
No. 1789, 200sh: a, Papilio zagreus. b, Chlosyne narva. c, Phyciodes alsina. d, Pyronia bathseba. e, Eurema daira. f, Eurytides xanticles. g, Clossiana titania. h, Euphydryas cynthia. i, Polygonia c-album.
No. 1790, 1500sh, Ornithoptera priamus, vert. No. 1791, 1500sh, Phyciodes, vert.

1999, Feb. 18

1784-1787 A310 Set of 4 6.75 6.75

Sheets of 9, #a-i

1788-1789 A310 Set of 2 13.50 13.50

Souvenir Sheets

1790-1791 A310 Set of 2 17.00 17.00

Birds A311

No. 1792, 370sh: a, Yellow billed stork. b, Black egret. c, Crowned lapwing. d, Snowy plover. e, Crowned crane. f, Saddlebilled stork.
No. 1793, 370sh: a, Great blue heron. b, Chinese egret. c, Horned puffins. d, White faced ibis. e, Greater flamingo. f, Blue footed boobie.
No. 1794, 370sh: a, Blacksmith plover. b, Brolga crane. c, Green-backed heron. d, Straw-necked ibis. e, Little bittern. f, Marabou stork.
No. 1795, 370sh, vert.: a, Sandhill crane. b, Great egret. c, Spoonbill. d, Yellow-crowned night heron. e, Glossy ibis. f, Willet.
No. 1796, 1500sh, Purple heron. No. 1797, 1500sh, Kittliz's sandplover, vert. No. 1798, 1500sh, Black-crowned night heron. No. 1799, 1500sh, Black-headed heron.

1999, Feb. 18 Sheets of 6, #a-f

1792-1795 A311 Set of 4 35.00 35.00

Souvenir sheets

1796-1799 A311 Set of 4 32.50 32.50

A312

A313

Cats A314

Designs: No. 1800, 200sh, Bengal, horiz. No. 1801, 250sh, Seal lynx point birman. No. 1802, 370sh, Calico British shorthair, horiz. No. 1803, 420sh, Blue & white cornish rex.

Nos. 1804, 100sh, Burmese. No. 1805, 140sh, Burmilla. No. 1806, 150sh, Turkish van. No. 1807, 200sh, Snowshoe. No. 1808, 250sh, Bombay. No. 1809, 370sh, Seychellois longhair.
No. 1810: a, Silver classic tabby. b, Auburn Turkish van. c, Seal bicolor ragdoll. d, European shorthair. e, Black & white British shorthair. f, Gold California spangled. g, Chocolate tipped Burmilla. h, Red classic tabby manx.
No. 1811, 370sh: a, Pekeface Persian. b, American curl shorthair. c, Korat. d, Himalayan Persian. e, Exotic shorthair. f, Scottish fold.
No. 1812, 370sh: a, European shorthair. b, Chartreux. c, British shorthair. d, Maine coon. e, Japanese bobtail. f, Birman.
No. 1813 — Kittens chasing butterflies: a, Black & white kitten, butterfly UL. b, Black & white kitten, butterfly UR. c, Black & yellow kitten, butterfly UR. d, Yellow kitten, butterfly UL.
No. 1814, 1500sh, Black & white Persian, horiz. No. 1815, 1500sh, Cream tabby European shorthair.
No. 1816, 1500sh, American shorthair. No. 1817, 1500sh, American wirehair. No. 1818, Kitten, butterfly, vert.

1999, Feb. 23

1800-1803 A312 Set of 4 8.25 8.25

1804-1809 A313 Set of 6 8.25 8.25

1810 A312 250sh Sheet of 8, #a.-h. 10.00 10.00

Sheets of 6, #a-f

1811-1812 A313 Set of 2 22.00 22.00

1813 A314 500sh Sheet of 4, #a.-d. 10.00 10.00

Souvenir Sheets

1814-1815 A312 Set of 2 18.00 18.00

1816-1817 A313 Set of 2 18.00 18.00

1818 A314 1500sh multi 9.00 9.00

19th Century Ships A315

No. 1819, 370sh: a, Prince Consort (1). b, USS Kearsage (2). c, HMS Victoria (3). d, USS Brooklyn (4). e, Mount Stewart (5). f, Hougomont (6).
No. 1820, 370sh: a, Charles W. Morgan (1). b, RMS Britannia (2). c, Great Britain (3). d, Flying Cloud (4). e, HMS Warrior (5). f, Lightning (6).
No. 1821, 1500sh, Cutty Sark. No. 1822, 1500sh, Great Eastern.

1999, Feb. 9 Litho. *Perf. 14*

Sheets of 6, #a-f

1819-1820 A315 Set of 2 26.00 26.00

Souvenir Sheets

1821-1822 A315 Set of 2 17.00 17.00

Nos. 1821-1822 each contain one 57x43mm stamp.

Military Helicopters — A316

No. 1823: a, Germany DF 4. b, Germany. c, France. d, US, with rocket pods. e, US, with suspended lift sling. f, France, red on tail boom & stabilizers.

1999

1823 A316 370sh Sheet of 6, #a.-f. 13.50 13.50

Unidentified Flying Objects (UFOs) — A317

No. 1824, 370sh: a, US, 1968. b, Trinidad, 1958. c, Belgium, 1990. d, Finland, 1970. e, New Zealand, 1951. f, Australia, 1954.

No. 1825, 370sh: a, McMinnville, 1950. b, Albuquerque, 1963. c, Gulf Breeze, 1988. d, Madre de Dios, 1952. e, Merlin, 1964. f, Mexico City, 1991.

No. 1826, 1500sh, The Arnold Sighting, 1947. No. 1827, 1500sh, The Mantell case, 1948.

1999 Sheets of 6, #a-f

1824-1825 A317 Set of 2 15.50 15.50

Souvenir Sheets

1826-1827 A317 Set of 2 18.00 18.00

Dogs — A318

No. 1828: a, Boston terrier. b, Tyrolean hound. c, Rottweiler. d, Golden retriever. e, English bulldog. f, Spanish greyhound. g, Long-haired dachshund. h, Scottish terrier. i, Pekingese.

1500sh, English cocker spaniel.

1999

1828 A318 200sh Sheet of 9, #a.-i. 9.00 9.00

Souvenir Sheet

1829 A318 1500sh multi 8.50 8.50

Dinosaurs — A319

Designs: 200sh, Stegosaurus (inscribed Edmontonia). 250sh, Archaeopteryx. 370sh, Stegosaurus. 410sh, Lagosuchus.

No. 1834, 370sh: a, Dromiceiomimus. b, Saurolophus. c, Camarosaurus. d, Protoceratops. e, Psittacosaurus. f, Stegoceras.

No. 1835, 370sh: a, Gallimimus. b, Peteinosaurus. c, Lambeosaurus. d, Coelophysis. e, Parasaurolophus. f, Tyrannosaurus rex.

No. 1836, 1500sh, Quetzalcoatlus. No. 1837, 1500sh, Rhomaleosaurus.

1999, Apr. 30 Litho. *Perf. 14*

1830-1833 A319 Set of 4 6.75 6.75

Sheets of 6, #a-f

1834-1835 A319 Set of 2 26.00 26.00

Souvenir Sheets

1836-1837 A319 Set of 2 17.00 17.00

Tourism A320

No. 1838: a, Hoofed animals. b, Mount Kilimanjaro, crater. c, Animal life. d, Sacred ibis. e, Ngorongoro crater. f, Giraffe. g, Lions. h, Dik diks. i, Vulture. j, Lion cubs. k, Elephants. l, African lion. m, Stone Town, Zanzibar. n, National Museum. o, Carved door, Zanzibar. p, Map showing Zanzibar, Pemba, Indian Ocean. q, Herding animals. r, Fishing. s, Lion cub. t, Buildings, boats along shore. u, Masai. v, Birds wading in water. w, Buffalo stampede. x, Like #1838b, closer view.

1999 *Perf. 14½x14*

Booklet Stamps

1838	Souvenir Booklet	11.00	
a.-x.	A320 150sh any single	.45	.45
y.	Booklet pane, #1838a-1838f	2.75	
z.	Booklet pane, #1838g-1838l	2.75	
aa.	Bklt. pane, #1838m-1838r	2.75	
ab.	Bklt. pane, #1838s-1838x	2.75	

Space Exploration — A321

Designs: 70sh, Edward White. 100sh, Gemini 7. 150sh, Mir, Russian space station, vert. 200sh, Laika, Russian space dog. 250sh, Apollo Command & Service Modules. 370sh, Apollo Lunar Module.

1500sh, Saturn V Moon Rocket, vert.

1999 *Perf. 14*

1839-1844 A321 Set of 6 7.75 7.75

Souvenir Sheet

1845 A321 1500sh multi 9.00 9.00

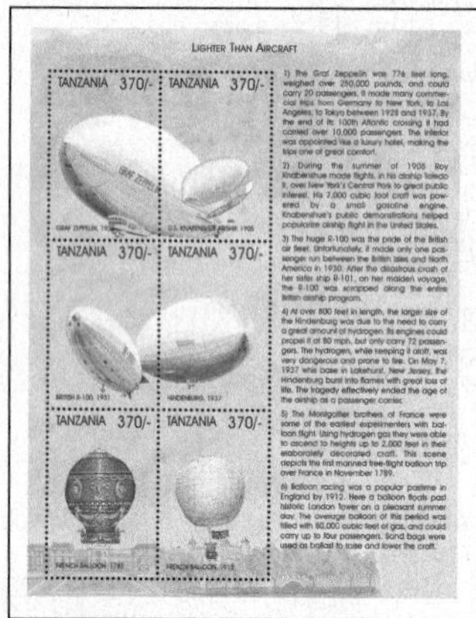

Airships, Balloons — A322

No. 1846: a, Graf Zeppelin, 1935 (b). b, Knabenshue Airship, 1905. c, British R-100, 1931. d, Hindenburg, 1937 (c). e, French Balloon, 1783. f, French Balloon, 1912.

1500sh, Sport ballooning.

1999

1846 A322 370sh Sheet of 6, #a.-f. 11.50 11.50

Souvenir Sheet

1847 A322 1500sh multi 7.75 7.75

Marine Life A323

Designs: 200sh, Powder blue surgeon. 250sh, Frilled anemone. 310sh, Red-finned batfish. 410sh, Red beard sponge.

No. 1852, 250sh: a, Right whale. b, Fin whale. c, Humpback whale. d. Tucuxi. e, Gray's beaked whale. f, Sperm whale. g, Bottlenose dolphin. h, Hector's dolphin. i, Hourglass dolphin.

No. 1853, 250sh: a, Horn shark. b, Nurse shark. c, Bonnethead. d, Tiger shark. e, Bull shark. f, Leopard shark. g, Blue shark. h, Zebra shark. i, Oceanic whitetip.

No. 1854, 1500sh, Pacific Electric ray, vert. No. 1855, 1500sh, Loggerhead turtle, vert.

1999, Feb. 9 Litho. *Perf. 14*

1848-1851 A323 Set of 4 5.00 5.00

Sheets of 9, #a.-i.

1852-1853 A323 Set of 2 26.00 26.00

Souvenir Sheets

1854-1855 A323 Set of 2 15.50 15.50

Airplanes A324

Designs: 20sh, Oiseau Bleu, 1929. 100sh, Beechcraft Model 17, 1934. No. 1858, 140sh, US Army Air Corps Beechcraft YC-43. No. 1859, 140sh, Deperdussin, 1913. 150sh, Beechcraft E17B, 1937. 200sh, Beechcraft B17L, 1936. 250sh, Beechcraft Model-G175, 1946. 370sh, Beechcraft Staggerwing Model-C17L.

No. 1864: a, Bird of Passage, Voisin Brothers, 1909. b, BS1, Geoffrey de Havilland, 1913. c, Taube-IGO Etrich, 1910. d, Curtiss Rheims Flyer, Glenn Curtiss, 1909. e, Wright Flyer III, Wright Brothers, 1905. f, Russky Vitvas, Igor Sikorsky, 1913.

No. 1865: a, Sikorsky S-38. b, EFA Eurofighter. c, F-16. d, Hawker Hurricane. e, Artiplast. f, Islander.

No. 1866, 1500sh, Piper Cherokee. No. 1867, 1500sh, MiG.

1999, Feb. 14

1856-1863 A324 Set of 8 7.75 7.75

Sheets of 6

1864 A324 370sh Sheet of 6, #a.-f. 9.50 9.50

1865 A324 370sh Sheet of 6, #a.-f. 9.50 9.50

Souvenir Sheets

1866-1867 A324 Set of 2 17.00 17.00

Nos. 1866-1867 contain one 56x42mm stamp.

Stamp inscriptions are incorrect on Nos. 1865b, 1865c, and perhaps others.

African Wildlife A325

Designs: 100sh, Black rhinoceros. 140sh, Zebra, vert. 150sh, Hippopotomus. 200sh, Nile crocodile. 250sh, African elephant, vert. 370sh, Cape buffalo.

No. 1874, 1500sh, Royal python. No. 1875, 1500sh, Giraffe.

1999, Feb. 18

1868-1873 A325 Set of 6 7.25 7.25

Souvenir Sheets

1874-1875 A325 Set of 2 16.50 16.50

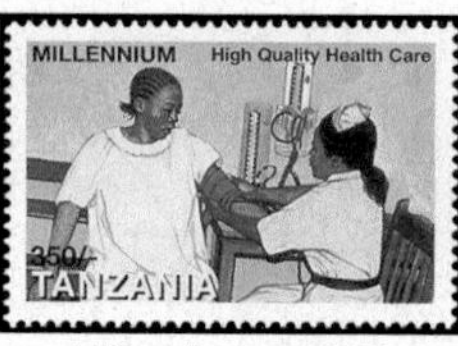

Millennium — A326

Designs: 350sh, High quality health care. 400sh, Good upbringing. 700sh, An abundance of food. 750sh, Clean water for all.

1500sh, Ostrich, "Enhancement of tourism promotion," vert.

1999, Mar. 29

1876-1879 A326 Set of 4 11.50 11.50

Souvenir Sheet

1880 A326 1500sh multi 8.50 8.50

Sharks A327

Designs: 200sh, Sand tiger. 250sh, Mako. 370sh, Great white. 410sh, Bull.

No. 1885: a, Basking. b, Whale. c, Tiger. d, Thresher. e, Caribbean reef. f, Nurse.

No. 1886, 1500sh, Scalloped hammerhead. No. 1887, 1500sh, Blue.

1999 Litho. *Perf. 14*

1881-1884 A327 Set of 4 7.00 7.00

1885 A327 370sh Sheet of 6, #a.-f. 14.00 14.00

Souvenir Sheets

1886-1887 A327 Set of 2 18.50 18.50

Rotary Club of Dar Es Salaam, 50th Anniv. A328

Designs: 150sh, Emblem. 250sh, Polio plus immunization, vert. 350sh, Paul P. Harris, founder of Rotary, Intl., vert. 400sh, Water supply.

500sh, Emblem, vert.

1999, June 30

1888-1891 A328 Set of 4 6.00 6.00

Souvenir Sheet

1892 A328 500sh multicolored 3.00 3.00

Endangered or Extinct Species — A330

No. 1898: a, Atitlan grebe. b, Cabot's tragopan. c, Spider monkey. d, Dibatag. e, Right whale. f, Imperial parrot. g, Cheetah. h, Brown-eared pheasant. i, Leatherback turtle. j, Imperial woodpecker. k, Andean condor. l, Barbary deer. m, Gray gentle lemur. n, Cuban parrot. o, Numbat. p, Short-tailed albatross. q, Green turtle. r, White rhinoceros. s, Diademed sifaka. t, Galapagos penguin.

No. 1899 — Tigers, horiz.: a, Caspian. b, Bengal. c, Javan. d, Indochinese. e, In white phase. f, Sumatran. g, Chinese. h, Bali. i, Siberian.

No. 1900, 1500sh, Rabbit-eared bandicoot. No. 1901, 1500sh, Grenada dove.

1999, Feb. 18

1898 A330 100sh Sheet of 20, #a.-t. 9.00 9.00

1899 A330 250sh Sheet of 9, #a.-i. 10.00 10.00

Souvenir Sheets

1900-1901 A330 Set of 2 13.50 13.50

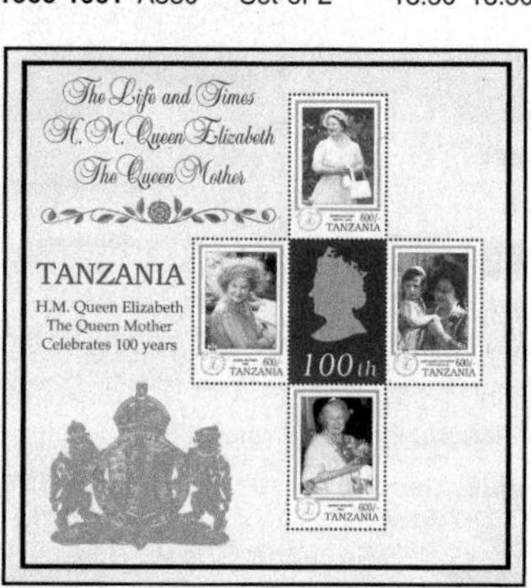

Queen Mother (b. 1900) — A331

No. 1902: a, In Kenya, 1959. b, In 1980. c, With Prince Charles, 1950. d, lin 1990.

1500sh, In Kenya, 1959, diff.

1999, Aug. 4 Litho. *Perf. 14*

1902 A331 600sh Sheet of 4, #a.-d. + label 9.00 9.00

Souvenir Sheet

Perf. 13¾

1903 A331 1500sh black 6.50 6.50

No. 1903 contains one 38x51mm stamp.

UPU, 125th Anniv. A332

Designs: 150sh, Mail conveyance. 300sh, Letter writing competition. 350sh, UPU committee meeting. 400sh, EMS Post net track and trace.
500sh, UPU emblem.

Wmk. 387

1999, Aug. 10 Litho. *Perf. 14*
1904-1907 A332 Set of 4 5.50 5.50

Souvenir Sheet

1908 A332 500sh multicolored 2.50 2.50

Souvenir Sheets

Philex France 99 — A333

Trains: No. 1909, 1500sh, 4-8-2 compound express locomotive. No. 1910, 1500sh, TGV.

1999, Aug. 20 Litho. *Perf. 13¾*
1909-1910 A333 Set of 2 12.50 12.50

Inscriptions are misspelled on Nos. 1909-1910.

Birds of Japan A334

No. 1911, 250sh: a, Steller's sea eagle. b, Japanese blue flycatcher. c, Great gray shrike. d, Kingfisher. e, Hen harrier. f, Siberian meadow bunting. g, Mandarin duck. h, Red-necked grebe. i, Fairy pitta.
No. 1912, 250sh: a, Black paradise flycatcher. b, Laysan albatross. c, Collared Scops owl. d, Ryukyu robin. e, Japanese green woodpecker. f, Lidth's jay. g, White-naped crane. h, Copper pheasant. i, Okinawa rail.
No. 1913, 1500sh, Gyrfalcon. No. 1914, 1500sh, Japanese yellow bunting.

1999, Aug. 20 Sheets of 9, #a.-i.
1911-1912 A334 Set of 2 21.00 21.00

Souvenir Sheets

1913-1914 A334 Set of 2 13.50 13.50

Inscription on No. 1912b, and perhaps others, is misspelled.
APS StampShow '99 (#1911-1912).

Hokusai Paintings — A335

No. 1915: a, A Ferry Boat at Onmayagashi. b, A Drum Bridge at Kameido. c, Sea Life (fish). d, Sea Life (Octopus). e, Measuring a Pine Tree at Mishima Pass. f, Mount Fuji Seen From the Banks of Minobu River.
1500sh, Mount Fuji and Edo Castle Seen From Nihonbashi, vert.

1999, Aug. 20
1915 A335 400sh Sheet of 6, #a.-f. 11.50 11.50

Souvenir Sheet

1916 A335 1500sh multi 6.75 6.75

Masks — A336

Various masks: 150sh, 250sh, 300sh, 350sh.

1999, Aug. 20 *Perf. 14*
1917-1920 A336 Set of 4 4.50 4.50

Souvenir Sheet

1921 A336 1500sh multicolored 6.25 6.25

Military Scenes — A337

150sh, British defeat Spanish Armada, 1588, horiz. No. 1923, 250sh, Battle of Waterloo. No. 1924, 250sh, Rorke's Drift, 24th Regiment, South Wales Borderers. No. 1925, 250sh, Special Air Services, Desert Storm. No. 1926, 300sh, Soldier on horseback. No. 1927, 300sh, World War I, horiz. No. 1928, 300sh, Bland's Dragoons, Battle of Dettingen. No. 1929, 350sh, Battle of Trafalgar, horiz. No. 1930, 350sh, Light Brigade. No. 1931, 350sh, Squadron 617, the "Dam Busters." No. 1932, 400sh, World War I tank, horiz. No. 1933, 400sh, Battle of Inkerman. No. 1934, 400sh, Battle of Salamanca, horiz. No. 1935, 500sh, Gen. James Wolfe, Battle of Quebec. No. 1936, 500sh, Parachute Regiment, Battle of Arnhem. No. 1937, 500sh, Battle of the Bulge.
No. 1938, 1500sh, Battle of the Nile. No. 1939, 1500sh, Battle of Albuhera.

1999, Sept. 30
1922-1937 A337 Set of 16 28.00 28.00

Souvenir Sheets

1938-1939 A337 Set of 2 12.50 12.50

Ships A338

No. 1940, 400sh: a, Bayan. b, Flying Cloud. c, Mayflower. d, Santa Maria. e, Morning Star. f, Ben Venue.
No. 1941, 400sh: a, Georg Stag. b, E. Starr Jones. c, Indiana. d, Brazilian coasting vessel. e, Nova Queen. f, Rainbow.
No. 1942, 1500sh, Dutch East Indiaman. No. 1943, 1500sh, Junk.

1999, Sept. 30 Sheets of 6, #a.-f.
1940-1941 A338 Set of 2 21.00 21.00

Souvenir Sheets

1942-1943 A338 Set of 2 13.50 13.50

Trains A339

No. 1944, 400sh: a, Adler 2-2-2, 1835. b, Beuth 2-2-2, 1843. c, Class 500 4-6-0, 1900. d, Northumbrian 0-2-2, 1830. e, Class 4-6-2, 1901. f, Claud Hamilton class 4-4-0.
No. 1945, 400sh: a, Firefly class 2-2-2, 1840. b, Single, 1854. c, 4-4-0, 1891. d, Medoc class 2-4-0, 1857. e, 4-4-0, 1893. f, Numar, 1846.
No. 1946, 1500sh, Planet class 2-2-0, 1830. No. 1947, 1500sh, Vauxhall 2-2-0, 1834. No. 1948, 1500sh, Class PB 4-6-0, 1906. No. 1949, 1500sh, 4-4-0, 1855.

1999, Sept. 30 Sheets of 6, #a.-f.
1944-1945 A339 Set of 2 21.00 21.00

Souvenir Sheets

1946-1949 A339 Set of 4 13.50 13.50

Airplanes A340

Designs: 200sh, Amref. No. 1951, 250sh, Westwind 2. 300sh, Morning Star. 400sh, Piper Warrior III.
No. 1954: a, Glasair Super II. b, Glastar. c, Cessna 120. d, Europa XS. e, Beechcraft Bonanza. f, Comache GTO. g, Lancir IV. h, Comanche 400.
No. 1955, 1500sh, Glastar, diff. No. 1956, 1500sh, Piper Archer III.

1999, Sept. 30 Litho. *Perf. 14*
1950-1953 A340 Set of 4 5.75 5.75
1954 A340 250sh Sheet of 8, #a.-h. 8.00 8.00

Souvenir Sheets

1955-1956 A340 Set of 2 13.50 13.50

Automobiles — A341

No. 1957, 400sh: a, Audi TT Coupe. b, Mitsubishi SST Spyder. c, Honda Dream. d, Renault 20. e, Renault Spider. f, Hyundai Euro I.
No. 1958, 400sh: a, Pininfarina Ethos. b, Jaguar XK120. c, Pininfarina Ethos II. d, Rinspeed E-GO Rocket. e, Volkswagen W12 Roadster. f, Chrysler Pronto Cruiser.
No. 1959, 1500sh, Ferrari Mythos. No. 1960, 1500sh, Hyundai Euro I, diff.

1999, Sept. 30 Sheets of 6, #a.-f.
1957-1958 A341 Set of 2 21.00 21.00

Souvenir Sheets

1959-1960 A341 Set of 2 12.50 12.50

Flowers A342

Designs; 150sh, Lilium longiflorum. 250sh, Strelitzia reginae. 400sh, Zantedeschia anim lily. 500sh, Iris.
600sh, Like 400sh.

1999, Oct. 6 Litho. *Perf. 14*
1961-1964 A342 Set of 4 5.75 5.75

Souvenir Sheet

1965 A342 600sh multicolored 2.75 2.75

Butterflies — A343

No. 1966: a, Basilarchia archippus. b, Eueides isabella. c, Colobura dirce. d, Papilio cresphontes. e, Agrias claudia. f, Callicore maimuna.
No. 1967, 1500sh, Anteos clorinade, horiz. No. 1968, 1500sh, Tithorea harmonia, horiz.

1999, Nov. 15
1966 A343 400sh Sheet of 6, #a.-f. 10.50 10.50

Souvenir Sheets

1967-1968 A343 Set of 2 14.50 14.50

Sea Birds A344

Designs: 150sh, Rockhopper penguin, vert. No. 1970, 250sh, Jackass penguin, vert. 300sh, Adelie penguin, vert. 350sh, White tern. 400sh, Great frigatebird. 500sh, Brown pelican.
No. 1975, 250sh: a, Manx shearwater. b, Ring-billed gull. c, Herring gull. d, Red-tailed tropic bird. e, Laysan albatross. f, Black-headed gull. g, Blue-footed booby. h, Parakeet auklet. i, Red-legged cormorant.
No. 1976, 250sh: a, Razorbill. b, Southern giant petrel. c, Atlantic puffin. d, Great cormorant. e, Northern gannet. f, Masked booby. g, Tufted puffin. h, Galapagos penguin. i, Macaroni penguin.
No. 1977, 1500sh, King penguin, vert. No. 1978, 1500sh, Emperor penguin, vert.

1999, Nov. 15
1969-1974 A344 Set of 6 9.00 9.00

Sheets of 9, #a.-i.

1975-1976 A344 Set of 2 21.00 21.00

Souvenir Sheets

1977-1978 A344 Set of 2 12.50 12.50

Dogs A345

No. 1979: a, Boxer. b, Mixed breed. c, Afghan hound. d, Chihuahua. e, Basset hound. f, Cavalier King Charles.
1500sh, Cocker spaniel.

1999, Nov. 15
1979 A345 400sh Sheet of 6, #a.-f. 9.00 9.00

Souvenir Sheet

1980 A345 1500sh multi 7.25 7.25

Paintings by Xu Beihong (1895-1953) A346

No. 1981: a, Chang K'uei. b, Fisherman. c, Orchid. d, Cock and Sunflower. e, Eagle. f, Sprite of the Mountain. g, Horse. h, Geese. i, Pigeon and Bamboo. j, Cat and Bamboo.
No. 1982: a, Spring Rain of Li River, horiz. b, The Himalayas, horiz.

1999 *Perf. 12½*
1981 A346 150sh Sheet of 10, #a.-j. 7.50 7.50

Perf. 13

1982 A346 600sh Sheet of 2, #a.-b. 6.00 6.00

China 1999 World Philatelic Exhibition.

Return of Macao to People's Republic of China — A347

No. 1983 — Nam Van: a, In 1850s. b, In 1930s. c, At present. d, View of lakes project.

1999 Litho. *Perf. 13¾*

1983 A347 300sh Sheet of 4, #a.-d. 6.50 6.50

China 1999 World Philatelic Exhibition.

Animals of the Central American Rain Forest — A348

No. 1984: a, Red howler monkey. b, Scarlet macaw. c, Rainbow boa, tree sloth. d, Iguana. e, Fruit bat. f, Rainbow boa. g, Crocodile. h, Manatee. i, Jaguar.
1500sh, Jaguar, diff.

1999, Nov. 15 Litho. *Perf. 14*

1984 A348 350sh Sheet of 9, #a.-i. 8.50 8.50

Souvenir Sheet

1985 A348 1500sh multi 4.00 4.00

Dinosaurs — A349

No. 1986: a, Tyrannosaurus. b, Coelurus. c, Stegosaurus. d, Corythosaurus. e, Thadeosaurus. f, Brachiosaurus.
1500sh, Ceratosaurus.

1999, Nov. 15

1986 A349 400sh Sheet of 6, #a.-f. 6.00 6.00

Souvenir Sheet

1987 A349 1500sh multi 4.25 4.25

Nos. 1986-1987 dated 1998. Inscription on No. 1986f is misspelled.

Cats A350

No. 1988: a, Si-Rex. b, Spotted Mist. c, Angora. d, Persian. e, Sphynx. f, Alaskan Snow.
1500sh, Ragdoll.

1999, Nov. 15

1988 A350 400sh Sheet of 6, #a.-f. 6.75 6.75

Souvenir Sheet

1989 A350 1500sh multi 4.50 4.50

Mushrooms A351

150sh, Tricholoma portentosum. 250sh, Tricholomopsis rutilans. 300sh, Russula foetens. 350sh, Russula aeruginea. #1994, 400sh, Cortinarius varius. 500sh, Hygrocybe coccineocrenata.

No. 1996, 400sh: a, Agaricus abruptibulbus. b, Anellaria semiovata. c, Cystoderma carcharias. d, Amanita rubescens. e, Amanita fulva. f, Tricholoma sulphureum.

No. 1997, 400sh: a, Xerocomus rubellus. b, Geastrum rufescens. c, Lactarius salmonicolor. d, Gomphus clavatus. e, Russula rhodopoda. f, Russula paludosa.

No. 1998, 1500sh, Owl. No. 1999, 1500sh, Chipmunk and Stropharia hornemanii, horiz.

1999, Nov. 15

1990-1995 A351 Set of 6 5.00 5.00

Sheets of 6, #a.-f.

1996-1997 A351 Set of 2 11.50 11.50

Souvenir Sheets

1998-1999 A351 Set of 2 7.00 7.00

Flora and Fauna A352

Designs: No. 2000, 150sh, Lion, vert. No. 2001, 150sh, Mountain gorilla, vert. No. 2002, 250sh, Pygmy hippopotamus, vert. No. 2003, 250sh, Japanese macaque, vert. No. 2004, 300sh, Cheetah. No. 2005, 300sh, Desert hare, vert. No. 2006, 350sh, Horned puffin. No. 2007, 350sh, Salvin's Amazon parrot. No. 2008, 400sh, Blueberries. No. 2009, 400sh, Bird's foot violet. No. 2010, 500sh, Orange groundsel. No. 2011, 500sh, Iguana.

No. 2012, 400sh: a, Polar bear. b, Woodland caribou. c, Snowy owl. d, Arctic fox. e, Willow ptarmigan. f, Arctic hare.

No. 2013, 400sh: a, White-tailed deer. b, Monarch butterfly. c, Yellow trumpet pitcher plants. d, Great blue heron. e, Yellow mud turtle. f, American alligator.

No. 2014, 400sh: a, Three-toed sloth. b, Emerald toucan. c, Praying mantis. d, Mouse opossum. e, Green palm viper. f, Phyllomedusa lemur.

No. 2015, 400sh: a, Ficus stupenda. b, Slow loris. c, Sambar deer. d, Thick-billed green pigeon. e, Bush cricket. f, Monitor lizard.

No. 2016, 1500sh, Three-toed jacamar. No. 2017, 1500sh, Chuckwallas. No. 2018, 1500sh, Swallowtail butterfly. No. 2019, 1500sh, Otter, vert.

1999, Nov. 15

2000-2011 A352 Set of 12 11.00 11.00

Sheets of 6, #a.-f.

2012-2015 A352 Set of 4 14.00 14.00

Souvenir Sheets

2016-2019 A352 Set of 4 15.00 15.00

Flowers — A353

Designs: 150sh, Foxglove. 250sh, Chrysanthemum. 400sh, Amaryllis. 500sh, Hidden lilies.

No. 2024, 350sh, horiz.: a, Gerbara daisies. b, Begonias. c, Clematis. d, Violas. e, Southern magnolia. f, Dwarf balloon flowers. g, Camellias. h, Day lilies. i, Roses.

No. 2025, 350sh, horiz.: a, Daffodils. b, Columbines. c, Nasturtiums. d, Gazanias. e, Rose. f, Crocuses. g, Trumpet vine. h, Dahlia. i, Oriental poppies.

No. 2026, 1500sh, Siberian iris. No. 2027, 1500sh, Water lily, horiz.

1999, Nov. 15 Litho. *Perf. 14*

2020-2023 A353 Set of 4 3.00 3.00

Sheets of 9, #a.-i.

2024-2025 A353 Set of 2 14.50 14.50

Souvenir Sheets

2026-2027 A353 Set of 2 6.75 6.75

Military Vehicles — A354

No. 2028, 400sh: a, French Hotchkiss H35 tank. b, German Panzer IV tank. c, US M4 tank. d, German Tiger tank. e, US Half track. f, British Cromwell tank.

No. 2029, 400sh: a, British MK IV tank. b, Japanese Type 95 tank. c, German Hunting Panther tank. d, French AMX30 tank. e, Israeli Merkava tank. f, US M1 tank.

No. 2030, 1500sh, AH-64A Apache helicopter. No. 2031, 1500sh, Austin armored car, vert.

1999, Sept. 30 Litho. *Perf. 14*

Sheets of 6, #a.-f.

2028-2029 A354 Set of 2 10.50 10.50

Souvenir Sheets

2030-2031 A354 Set of 2 7.25 7.25

African Flowers — A355

Designs: 150sh, Canarina abyssinica. 250sh, Diaphananthe kamerunensis. 350sh, Protea barbigera. 500sh, Angraecum scottianum.

No. 2036, 400sh: a, Bolusanthus speciosus. b, Cassia abbreviata. c, Erythrina lysistemon. d, Leucodendron discolor. e, Romulea fischeri. f, Lupinus princei.

No. 2037, 400sh: a, Ansellia africana. b, Kigelia africana. c, Aerangis brachycarpa. d, Brachcorythis kalbreyeri. e, Begonia meyeriijohannis. f, Saintpaulia ionantha.

No. 2038, 1500sh, Nymphaea caerulea. No. 2039, 1500sh, Aloe petricola.

1999, Nov. 15

2032-2035 A355 Set of 4 3.00 3.00

Sheets of 6, #a.-f.

2036-2037 A355 Set of 2 10.50 10.50

Souvenir Sheets

2038-2039 A355 Set of 2 6.75 6.75

African Wildlife — A356

No. 2040, horiz.: a, Mountain gorilla. b, Zebras. c, East African elephant. d, Crowned cranes. e, Cheetah. f, Tiger. g, Pygmy chimpanzee. h, Hippopotamus.

No. 2041, 1500sh, Giraffes. No. 2042, 1500sh, Rhinoceros.

1999, Nov. 15

2040 A356 300sh Sheet of 8, #a.-h. 11.00 11.00

Souvenir Sheets

2041-2042 A356 Set of 2 10.00 10.00

Marine Life A357

Designs: 350sh, Beluga whale. 400sh, Ghost crab. 500sh, Emperor penguin, vert.

No. 2046: a, Herring gulls. b, Dusky dolphin. c, Sandwich tern. d, Humpback whale. e, Right whale. f, Dusky dolphin, sergeant major. g, White-tipped shark. h, Manta ray, trunkfish. i, Purple moon angel. j, Scalloped hammerhead shark. k, Manatee. l, Striped fingerfish.

No. 2047, 1500sh, Humpback whales. No. 2048, 1500sh, Tiger shark.

1999, Nov. 15

2043-2045 A357 Set of 3 5.00 5.00

2046 A357 250sh Sheet of 12, #a.-l. 11.00 11.00

Souvenir Sheets

2047-2048 A357 Set of 2 10.00 10.00

Ballet A358

Designs: 300sh, Romeo and Juliet. 350sh, The Dying Swan. 400sh, Giselle, vert. 500sh, Spartacus, vert.

No. 2053, 1500sh, The Firebird, vert. No. 2054, 1500sh, Swan Lake, vert.

1999, Aug. 20 Litho. *Perf. 14*

2049-2052 A358 Set of 4 5.00 5.00

Souvenir Sheets

2053-2054 A358 Set of 2 9.00 9.00

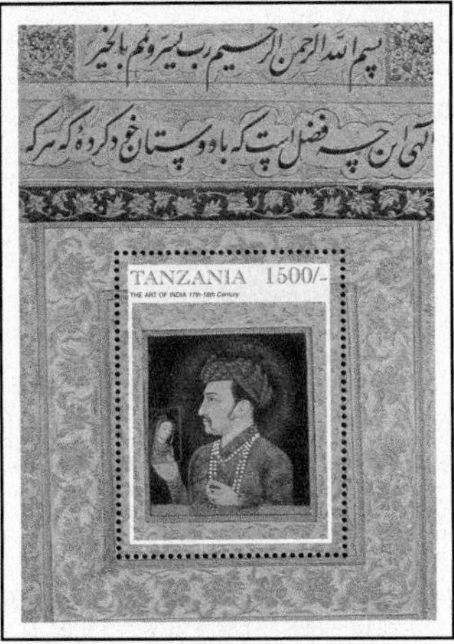

17th and 18th Century Indian Art — A359

No. 2055, 500sh: a, Krishna and the Gopis (large tree). b, Krishna Painting the Feet of Radha. c, Krishna Yearning for the Moon (woman with fan). d, Games of Krishna and Radha (boat).

No. 2056, 500sh: a, Balwant Singh Having His Beard Cut. b, Festival of Hou (women at right). c, Ragini Bialvali (woman with fan, woman on seat). d, Krishna Holding a Ball of Butter.

No. 2057, 1500sh, Portrait of Emperor Jahanoir (man with necklace), vert. No. 2058, 1500sh, Krishna and the Gopis, diff., vert.

Illustration reduced.

1999, Aug. 20 ***Perf. 13¾***

Sheets of 4, #a-d

2055-2056 A359 Set of 2 10.00 10.00

Souvenir Sheets

2057-2058 A359 Set of 2 8.00 8.00

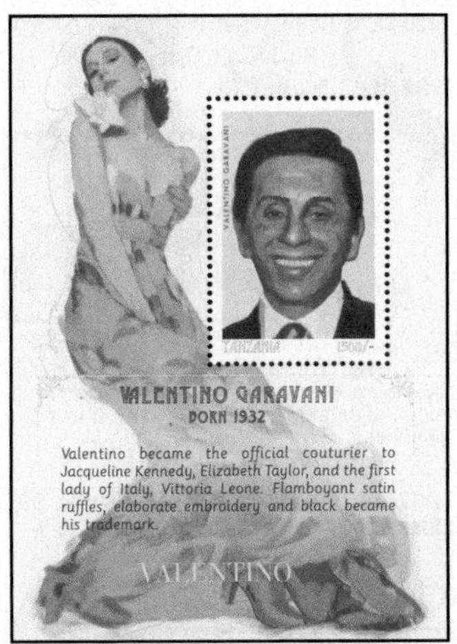

Fashion Designers — A360

No. 2059: a, Christian Dior. b, Model wearing Dior fashions. c, Bottle of Chanel No. 5, model wearing Chanel Fashions. d, Gabrielle "Coco" Chanel. e, Gianni Versace. f, Model wearing Versace fashions. g, Model wearing Yves Saint Laurent fashions. h, Yves Saint Laurent.

1500sh, Valentino Garavani.

1999, Aug. 20 ***Perf. 14***

2059 A360 300sh Sheet of 8, #a-h 6.00 6.00

Souvenir Sheet

2060 A360 1500sh multi 4.00 4.00

Nos. 2059b-2059c, 2059f-2059g are 53x39mm.

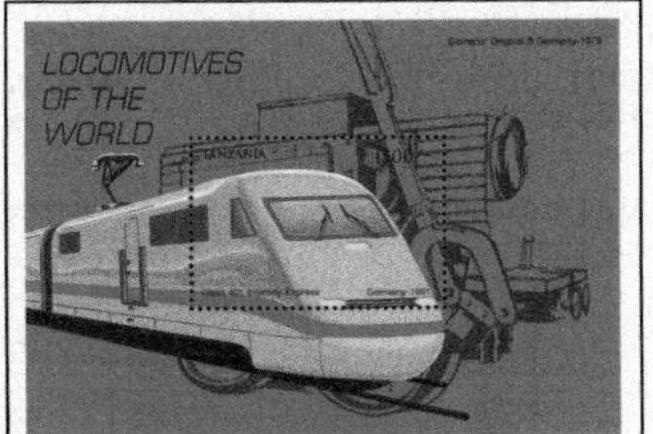

Locomotives — A361

No. 2061: a, Class EF 81 Bo-Bo, Japan. b, Class 120 Bo-Bo, West Germany. c, Shao Shan I Co-Co, China. d, TGV, France. e, F40 PH Bo-Bo, US. f, LRC Bo-Bo, Canada.

1500sh, Class 401 Intercity Express, Germany.

1999, Sept. 30

2061 A361 400sh Sheet of 6, #a-f 6.00 6.00

Souvenir Sheet

2062 A361 1500sh multi 3.75 3.75

Marine Life A362

Designs: 150sh, Great barracuda. 250sh, Common squid. No. 2065, 300sh, Atlantic salmon. 350sh, Ocean sunfish. 400sh, Lobster. 500sh, Yellowfin tuna.

No. 2069, 300sh: a, Flying fish. b, Sailfish. c, Common dolphin. d, Sperm whale. e, Spinner dolphin. f, Manta ray. g, Green turtle. h, Hammerhead shark. i, Marlin.

No. 2070, 300sh: a, Walrus. b, Killer whale. c, Arctic tern. d, White shark. e, Narwhal. f, Blue whale. g, Giant clam. h, Octopus. i, Conger eel.

No. 2071, 1500sh, Whale shark. No. 2072, 1500sh, Beluga, vert.

1999, Nov. 15

2063-2068 A362 Set of 6 6.00 6.00

Sheets of 9, #a-i

2069-2070 A362 Set of 2 14.00 14.00

Souvenir Sheets

2071-2072 A362 Set of 2 7.50 7.50

Pres. Julius K. Nyerere (1922-99) A363

Nyerere: 200sh, As young man and old man. 500sh, With Edward Moringe Sokoine. 600sh, The Compassionate leader, vert. 800sh, During the early days of independence, vert.

1000sh, Mausoleum.

2000, Apr. 13 ***Perf. 13***

2073-2076 A363 Set of 4 5.00 5.00

Souvenir Sheet

Perf. 13x13½

2077 A363 1000sh multi 2.50 2.50

No. 2077 contains one 35x28mm stamp.

Tourism A364

Designs: 400sh, Lion, Seronera Wildlife Lodge. No. 2079, 800sh, Hippopotami and hyenas, Selous Game Reserve. No. 2080, 800sh, Fish, Mafia Island. No. 2081, 800sh, Giraffes, Lobo Wildlife Lodge. No. 2082, 800sh, Rhinoceros, Ngorongoro Crater Wildlife Lodge. No. 2083, 800sh, Elephant, Mikumi Natl. Park. No. 2084, 800sh, Elephant, Lake Manyara Natl. Park. No. 2085, 800sh, Elephants, rhinoceros, Kibo Peak, Mt. Kilimanjaro.

1000sh, Lion, giraffes, elephant, rhinoceros, Lake Manyara Natl. Park, vert.

Perf. 13x13½, 13½x13

2000, June 10 **Litho.**

2078-2085 A364 Set of 8 20.00 20.00

Souvenir Sheet

2086 A364 1000sh multi 4.25 4.25

See Nos. 2102-2125.

Activities of World Vision A365

Designs: 200sh, Children with water pots on heads. 600sh, Family preparing food. 800sh, Nurse, family. 1000sh, Education of children.

2000, July 20 **Litho.** ***Perf. 13x13¼***

2087-2090 A365 Set of 4 6.00 6.00

Souvenir Sheet

2091 A365 500sh Two children 1.25 1.25

2000 Summer Olympics, Sydney A366

Designs: 150sh, Soccer. 350sh, Basketball, vert. 400sh, Women's 1500-meter race, vert. 800sh, Boxing.

500sh, Medal ceremony, vert.

2000, Sept. 15 ***Perf. 13¾***

2092-2095 A366 Set of 4 4.50 4.50

Souvenir Sheet

2096 A366 500sh multi 1.25 1.25

Universities of East Africa A367

Designs: 150sh, Medical students, Muhimbili University College of Health Sciences. 200sh, Zanzibar University. 600sh, Makerere University, Uganda, vert. 800sh, Egerton University, Kenya.

500sh, Emblem of Inter-university Council for East Africa.

2000 ***Perf. 13x13¼, 13¼x13***

2097-2100 A367 Set of 4 4.25 4.25

Perf. 14½

Size: 84x83mm

2101 A367 500sh multi 1.25 1.25

Tourism Type of 2000

No. 2102, 400sh, No. 2110, 500sh, No. 2118, 600sh, Like #2079. No. 2103, 400sh, No. 2111, 500sh, No. 2119, 600sh, Like #2080. No. 2104, 400sh, No. 2112, 500sh, No. 2120, 600sh, Like #2081. No. 2105, 400sh, No. 2113, 500sh, No. 2121, 600sh, Like #2082. No. 2106, 400sh, No. 2114, 500sh, No. 2122, 600sh, Like #2083. No. 2107, 400sh, No. 2115, 500sh, No. 2123, 600sh, Like #2084. No. 2108, 400sh, No. 2116, 500sh, No. 2124, 600sh, Like #2085. No. 2109, 500sh, No. 2117, 600sh, No. 2125, 800sh, Like #2078.

2000, June 1 **Litho.** ***Perf. 13x13½***

2102-2125 A364 Set of 24 50.00 50.00

Flowers A368

150sh, Bacciflava. 250sh, Hybridus pendulus. #2128, 300sh, Rhaphiolepis umbellata. 350sh, Magnoliaeflora. 400sh, Magnolia, vert. 500sh, Margot Koster, vert.

No. 2132, 300sh: a, Viola pedata. b, Magnolia. c, Felicia amelloides. d, Lythrum. e, Hemerocallis. f, Tithonia rotundifolia. g, Lilium. h, Iris. i, Stokesia laevis.

No. 2133, 300sh, vert.: a, Prunus subhirtella. b, Sanguinaria canadensis. c, Rosa palustris. d, Gordonia lasianthius. e, Aquilegia caerulea. f, Fremontodendron. g, Hypericum calycinum. h, Anemone vitifolia. i, Clematis.

No. 2134, 1500sh, Iris cristata, vert. No. 2134A, 1500sh, Aster prikartil.

2000 ***Perf. 14***

2126-2131 A368 Set of 6 5.00 5.00

Sheets of 9, #a-i

2132-2133 A368 Set of 2 13.00 13.00

Souvenir Sheet

2134-2134A A368 Set of 2 7.50 7.50

Social Security Fund A369

Designs: 200sh, Retirement. 350sh, Employment injury. 600sh, Invalidity. 800sh, Health insurance.

2000 **Wmk. 387** ***Perf. 13¾***

2135-2138 A369 Set of 4 5.00 5.00

Souvenir Sheet

2139 A369 500sh Maternity 1.25 1.25

Environmental Care — A370

Designs: 200sh, Tree planting campaign. 400sh, Water sources protection. 600sh, Cleaning sewage. 800sh, Protecting forests.

2000 **Wmk. 387** ***Perf. 13x13¼***

2140-2143 A370 Set of 4 5.00 5.00

Souvenir Sheet

2144 A370 1000sh Mountain 2.50 2.50

Zanzibar Millennium A371

Designs: 150sh, Fishing industry. 200sh, Trade and tourism. 400sh, Child and emblem, vert. 800sh, Right to higher learning, vert.

500sh, Peace and tranquility, vert.

2000 **Wmk. 387** ***Perf. 13¾***

2145-2148 A371 Set of 4 4.50 4.50

Souvenir Sheet

2149 A371 500sh multi 1.25 1.25

Orchids A372

Designs: 200sh, Vanilla planifolia. 250sh, Pleurothallus tuerckheimii. No. 2152, 370sh, Trichopilia fragrans.

No. 2153, 370sh: a, Cyrtopodium andersonii. b, Cochleanthes discolor. c, Catasetum barbatum. d, Caularthron bicornutum. e, Broughtonia sanguinea. f, Brassavola nodosa.

No. 2154, 370sh: a, Oeceoclades maculata. b, Isochilus linearis. c, Eulophia alta. d, Ionopsis utricularioides. e, Epidendrum ciliare. f, Dimerandra emarginata.

No. 2155, 1500sh, Brassavola cucullata. No. 2156, 1500sh, Epidendrum nocturnum.

2000 **Litho.** ***Perf. 14***

2150-2152 A372 Set of 3 3.50 3.50

Sheets of 6, #a-f

2153-2154 A372 Set of 2 14.00 14.00

Souvenir Sheets

2155-2156 A372 Set of 2 8.00 8.00

Nos. 607, 610, 612, 615, 617 Surcharged

Methods and perfs as before

1998-2001

2157 A99 100sh on 40sh multi
2158 A99 150sh on 9sh multi
2159 A99 200sh on 170sh multi
2159A A99 230sh on 20sh multi — —
2159B A99 230sh on 170sh multi
2159C A99 800sh on 500sh multi 2.00 2.00

Issued: No. 2158, 1/26/98; No. 2157, 8/6/98; No. 2159, 6/4/00; No. 2159C, 4/6/00; No. 2159B, 11/20/00; No. 2159A, 11/20/01.

Rare Birds A373

Designs: 150sh, Taita falcon. 300sh, Banded green. 400sh, Spotted ground thrush. 500sh, Fischer's turaco. 600sh, Blue swallow.

2000 Litho. *Perf. 14*

2160 A373 150sh multi .75 .75
2161 A373 300sh multi 1.25 1.25
2162 A373 400sh multi 1.75 1.75
2163 A373 500sh multi 2.00 2.00

Souvenir Sheet

2164 A373 600sh multi 3.00 3.00

Architecture — A374

Designs: 150sh, Ruins of Great Mosque, Kilwa Kisiwani. 200sh, German Boma, Mikindani. 250sh, German Boma, Bagamoyo. 300sh, Butiama Museum, Mara. 350sh, Chief Government Chemist Office. 400sh, Old Post Office, Dar es Salaam. 500sh, Dr. David Livingstone Lodge, Kwihara Tabora. 600sh, Original and present State Houses, vert. 700sh, Ngoni-Nyamwezi traditional houses. 800sh, The People's Palace Beit Elajaib, Zanzibar. 900sh, Tongoni Ruins, Tanga. 1000sh, Karimjee Hall, Dar es Salaam.
1500sh, Old Boma, Mikindani.

2000 (?) Litho. *Perf. 13*

2165 A374 150sh multi
2166 A374 200sh multi
2166A A374 250sh multi
2167 A374 300sh multi
2167A A374 350sh multi
2168 A374 400sh multi
2168A A374 500sh multi
2169 A374 600sh multi
2169A A374 700sh multi
2170 A374 800sh multi
2170A A374 900sh multi
2171 A374 1000sh multi

Souvenir Sheet

2172 A374 1500sh multi

For surcharge see No. 2336.

Flora and Fauna — A375

Designs: 100sh, Common babbler. 140sh, Eastern blue darner. 150sh, Cavalier mushroom. 200sh, Orange-barred sulphur. 250sh, Harlequin bug. No. 2179, 370sh, Brassolae liocattleya.

No. 2180, 370sh: a, Common yellowthroat. b, Great orange tip. c, Tiger lily. d, Shaggy mane. e, Sri Lanka grasshopper. f, Woodhouse's toad.

No. 2181, 370sh: a, Golden-crowned warbler. b, Fuchsia. c, Alfalfa butterfly. d, Lycaste aquila. e, Snail. f, Ground beetle.

No. 2182, 1500sh, Rufous-collared sparrow, horiz. No. 2183, 1500sh, Monarch butterfly, horiz.

2000 Litho. *Perf. 14*

2174-2179 A375 Set of 6 3.00 3.00

Sheets of 6, #a-f

2180-2181 A375 Set of 2 11.00 11.00

Souvenir Sheets

2182-2183 A375 Set of 2 8.00 8.00

Activities of World Vision — A375a

Design: 200sh, Children have a right to education, horiz. 600sh, Children have a right to happiness, horiz. 800sh, Children have a right not to be exploited. 1000sh, Children have a right to be heard.

2001, Apr. 30 Litho. *Perf. 13*

2183A A375a 200sh multi — —
2183B A375a 600sh multi — —
2183C A375a 800sh multi — —
2183D A375a 1000sh multi — —

Souvenir Sheet

2183E A375a 500sh multi — —

Endangered Animals A376

Designs: 200sh, Leopard. 400sh, Rhinoceros. No. 2186, 600sh, Crocodile. 800sh, Hunting wild dogs.

No. 2188, 600sh, Cheetah.

2001, June 15 Litho. *Perf. 13*

2184-2187 A376 Set of 4 5.00 5.00

Souvenir Sheet

2188 A376 600sh multi 1.75 1.75

UN High Commissioner for Refugees, 50th Anniv. — A377

Designs: 200sh, Refugee child being vaccinated. 400sh, Refugees crossing Lake Tanganyika. 600sh, Refugee woman, vert. 800sh, Fleeing refugees, vert.

2001, July 31

2189-2192 A377 Set of 4 5.00 5.00
2191a Souvenir sheet of 1 1.75 1.75

Landscapes A378

Designs: 200sh, Rufiji River, Selous Game Reserve. 400sh, Mangapwani Beach, Zanzibar. 600sh, Mountains, Mikumi Natl. Park. 800sh, Balancing Stones, Shore of Lake Victoria, Mwanza, vert.
700sh, Ruaha Natl. Park, vert.

2001, Nov. 30 Litho. *Perf. 13*

2193-2196 A378 Set of 4 5.00 5.00

Souvenir Sheet

2197 A378 700sh multi 1.75 1.75

Year of Dialogue Among Civilizations A379

Designs: 200sh, Talking with children. 400sh, Formal dress. 600sh, Exchanging ideas. 800sh, Letter writing.
700sh, Communication linkages, vert.

2001, Oct. 9 Litho.

2198-2201 A379 Set of 4 4.50 4.50

Souvenir Sheet

2202 A379 700sh multi 1.50 1.50

Conservation of Zanzibar Rare Species — A380

Designs: 250sh, Dolphins. 300sh, Coral reefs. 450sh, Coral reefs, diff. 800sh, Zanzibar red colobus, vert.
700sh, Zanzibar red colobus, diff.

2002, Aug. 30 Litho. *Perf. 13*

2203-2206 A380 Set of 4 4.50 4.50

Souvenir Sheet

2207 A380 700sh multi 2.00 2.00

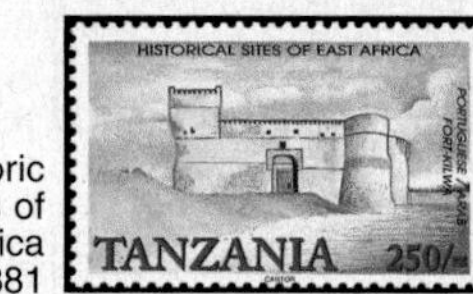

Historic Sites of East Africa A381

Designs: 250sh, Fort Kilwa. 300sh, Maruhubi Palace ruins, Zanzibar. 400sh, Old Provincial Office, Nairobi, 1913. 800sh, Mparu Tombs, Hoima, Uganda.
700sh, Map of East Africa, ship.

2001, Oct. 19

2208-2211 A381 Set of 4 3.75 3.75

Souvenir Sheet

2212 A381 700sh multi 1.50 1.50

Independence, 40th Anniv. — A382

Designs: 180sh, Tea estates. 230sh, Regional integration with Uganda and Kenya, vert. 350sh, University graduates, vert. 450sh, 1000sh, Lion, elephant, buffalo, cheetah, rhinoceros, Mt. Kilimanjaro. 650sh, Referral hospitals. 950sh, Mining industry.

2001, Dec. 30 Litho. *Perf. 14*

2213-2218 A382 Set of 6 6.00 6.00

Souvenir Sheet

2219 A382 1000sh multi 2.10 2.10

Ceremonial Costumes — A383

Designs: 250sh, Makonde mask dance. 350sh, Zanzibar Mwaka koga festival. 400sh, Lizombe dancer. 450sh, Zaramo bride's celebration.
500sh, Like 400sh.

Wmk. 387

2002, Mar. 30 Litho. *Perf. 13¾*

2220-2223 A383 Set of 4 4.00 4.00

Souvenir Sheet

2224 A383 500sh multi 1.50 1.50

Mountains A384

Designs: 250sh, Mt. Kilimanjaro. 350sh, Usambara Mountains. 400sh, Uluguru Mountains. 450sh, Mwanihana Peak, Udzungwa Mountains.
500sh, Like 250sh.

2002, June 30 Wmk. 387

2225-2228 A384 Set of 4 4.00 4.00

Souvenir Sheet

2229 A384 500sh multi 1.50 1.50

National Census A385

Census emblem and: 200sh, School children, vert. 250sh, Group of people. 350sh, Family. 600sh, Boy, census figures.
800sh, Group of people, vert.

Perf. 13x13¼ Sync., 13¼x13 Sync.

2002, Aug. 13 Unwmk.

2230-2233 A385 Set of 4 4.00 4.00

Souvenir Sheet

Perf. 13x13¼

2234 A385 800sh multi 1.75 1.75

Arts of Zanzibar A386

Designs: 200sh, Mat making. 250sh, Hand-sewn hats. 350sh, Chair making. 600sh, Hina painting.
800sh, Zanzibar door.

2002, Sept. 13 Unwmk. *Perf. 13¼*
2235-2238 A386 Set of 4 3.75 3.75

Souvenir Sheet
Perf. 13

2239 A386 800sh multi 1.75 1.75

Souvenir Sheet

Wildlife — A387

No. 2240: a, Leopard. b, Elephant. c, Rhinoceros. d, Lion. e, Buffalo.

Perf. 13x14
2002, Apr. 30 Wmk. 387
2240 A387 250sh Sheet of 5, #a-e 3.75 3.75

Compare No. 2240 with No. 2251.

Archaeology A388

Designs: 250sh, Ancient city of Kisimkazi, Zanzibar, vert. 400sh, Ruins of Kaole town, Bagamoyo. 450sh, Kondoa Irangi rock paintings, vert. 600sh, Great Mosque, Kilwa Kisiwani.
1000sh, Like 450sh.

Perf. 13¼
2002, Sept. 30 Unwmk. Litho.
2241-2244 A388 Set of 4 3.50 3.50

Souvenir Sheet
Perf. 13

2245 A388 1000sh multi 2.25 2.25

Wildlife A389

Designs: 400sh, Rhinoceroses. 500sh, Elephant. 600sh, Lion. 800sh, Leopard, vert. 1000sh, Buffalo.
1500sh, Rhinoceros, elephant, lion, leopard, buffalo, vert.

Perf. 13¼x12¾, 12¾x13¼
2003, Apr. 22 Litho. Wmk. 387
2246-2250 A389 Set of 5 8.00 8.00

Size: 85x115mm
Imperf

2251 A389 1500sh multi 4.00 4.00

Compare No. 2251 with No. 2240.

Cash Crops — A390

Designs: 250sh, Cotton. 300sh, Cashews. 600sh, Sisal. 800sh, Cloves.
1000sh, Tea, horiz.

Perf. 13x13¼ Syncopated
2003, June 10 Unwmk.
2252-2255 A390 Set of 4 3.75 3.75

Souvenir Sheet
Perf. 13¼x13 Syncopated

2256 A390 1000sh multi 2.25 2.25

Activities of World Vision A391

Designs: 300sh, Better nutrition with vitamin A. 600sh, Education opportunity for all children. 800sh, Clean and safe water for all, vert. 1000sh, Malaria prevention with treated mosquito nets.
500sh, Children have a right to be heard.

2003, July 3 *Perf. 13*
2257-2260 A391 Set of 4 5.25 5.25

Souvenir Sheet

2261 A391 500sh multi 1.25 1.25

Traditional Dances A392

Dances: 300sh, Nyamwezi. 500sh, Luo. 600sh, Pemba. 800sh, Baganda.
1000sh, Masai.

Perf. 13¼x13 Syncopated
2003, July 25
2262-2265 A392 Set of 4 4.25 4.25

Souvenir Sheet

2266 A392 1000sh multi 2.00 2.00

Nos. 612 and 1567 Surcharged

Methods and Perfs As Before

2002
2267 A99 250sh on 40sh #612 — —
2268 A262 250sh on 180sh #1567 — —

Issued: No. 2267, 7/23/02; No. 2268, 8/30/02.

Northern Circuit Tourist Attractions A393

Designs: 300sh, Lion, lioness, Mt. Kilimanjaro. 350sh, Kibo Peak, Mt. Kilimanjaro. 400sh, Zebras, Serengeti Natl. Park. 500sh, Elephants, Kilimanjaro Natl. Park. 600sh, Leopards, Serengeti Natl. Park. 800sh, Rhinoceros, Ngorongoro Crater.
1000sh, Buffalo, Arusha Natl. Park.

2003, Apr. 30 Litho. *Perf. 13¼x13*
2269-2274 A393 Set of 6 5.75 5.75

Souvenir Sheet

2275 A393 1000sh multi 2.00 2.00

Landscapes A394

Designs: 300sh, Rufiji Delta. 400sh, Zanzibar shore. 500sh, Lake Manyara, Rift Valley. 800sh, Kalambo Falls, vert.
1000sh, Coastal mangroves.

2003, July 22 Litho. *Perf. 13¼x13*
2276-2279 A394 Set of 4 4.00 4.00

Souvenir Sheet

2280 A394 1000sh multi 1.90 1.90

Zanzibar Tourist Attractions A395

Designs: 300sh, Old Fort. 500sh, Door, Beit al Ajaib, vert. 600sh, Coconut palm tree, Michamvi Beach, vert. 800sh, Dhow, Beit al Ajaib.

Perf. 13¼x13, 13x13¼
2003, Sept. 30 Litho.
2281-2284 A395 Set of 4 4.25 4.25
2284a Souvenir sheet, #2281, 2283, 2284 3.25 3.25

Marine Mammals A396

Designs: 300sh, Common dolphin. 350sh, Sperm whale. 400sh, Southern right whale. 600sh, Dugong.
500sh, Bottlenose dolphin.

2003, Oct. 11 Litho. *Perf. 13¼x13*
2285-2288 A396 Set of 4 4.25 4.25

Souvenir Sheet

2289 A396 500sh multi 1.75 1.75

Religious Festivals — A396a

Designs: 300sh, Muslims on pilgrimage to Mecca. 500sh, Choir at Christmas. 600sh, Prophet Mohammed's Birthday. 800sh, Church at Christmas.
1000sh, Crucifixion of Jesus.

Wmk. 387
2003, Nov. 4 Litho. *Perf. 14*
2289A-2289D A396a Set of 4 4.25 4.25

Souvenir Sheet

2289E A396a 1000sh multi 1.90 1.90

Tanzania Posts Corporation, 10th Anniv. — A397

Designs: 350sh, Counter automation. 400sh, Overnight mail delivery services. 600sh, Workers' participation. 800sh, Expedited mail services.
1000sh, Post Cargo.

Unwmk.
2004, Jan. 19 Litho. *Perf. 13*
2290-2293 A397 Set of 4 4.00 4.00
2293a Souvenir sheet, #2290-2293 4.00 4.00

Souvenir Sheet

2294 A397 1000sh multi 1.90 1.90

Western Union Money Transfer A398

Designs: 300sh, Exchange of American and Tanzanian currency. 400sh, Busalanga Primary School. 500sh, Woman, child, Tanzanian currency, vert. 600sh, World map.
800sh, Like 300sh, without Western Union emblem.

Perf. 13¼x13, 13x13¼
2004, Feb. 3 Litho.
2295-2298 A398 Set of 4 3.25 3.25

Souvenir Sheet

2299 A398 800sh multi 1.50 1.50

Girl Guides in Tanzania, 75th Anniv. A399

Designs: 300sh, Guides demonstrating solar cookers. 400sh, Camp training. 600sh, Bravery training. 800sh, Guides assisting at a mother and child clinic session.
1000sh, Like 800sh.

2004, May 15 *Perf. 13¼x13*
2300-2303 A399 Set of 4 3.75 3.75

Souvenir Sheet

2304 A399 1000sh multi 1.90 1.90

Tanganyika Christian Refugee Service, 40th Anniv. A400

Designs: 350sh, Truck carrying refugees and bicycles. 600sh, Public water source. 800sh, Students in classroom. 1000sh, Afforestation campaign.
1200sh, Four vignettes combined.

Unwmk.
2004, May 24 Litho. *Perf. 14*
2305-2308 A400 Set of 4 5.00 5.00

Souvenir Sheet
Perf. 14¼

2309 A400 1200sh multi 2.25 2.25

No. 2309 contains one 44x34mm stamp.

Zanzibar Watercraft Races A401

Designs: 350sh, Crowd cheering race winners. 400sh, Punt race. 600sh, Dhow race. 800sh, Sailboat race.
1000sh, Dhow, vert.

2004, June 25 *Perf. 13*

2310-2313 A401 Set of 4 4.00 4.00
2313a Souvenir sheet, #2310-2313 4.00 4.00

Souvenir Sheet

2314 A401 1000sh multi 1.90 1.90

Flora, Fauna and Mushrooms — A402

No. 2315, 550sh, horiz. — Animals: a, Red colobus monkey. b, Leopard. c, Giraffe. d, Eland. e, Zebra. f, African elephant.

No. 2316, 550sh, horiz. — Birds: a, European roller. b, Little swift. c, African gray parrot. d, Bateleur. e, European bee-eater. f, Hoopoe.

No. 2317, 550sh, horiz. — Butterflies: a, Gold-banded forester. b, Two-tailed pasha. c, Plain tiger. d, Common dotted border. e, African migrant. f, Forest queen.

No. 2318, 550sh, horiz. — Orchids: a, Cynorkis kassnerana. b, Habenaria rhodocheila. c, Vanilla planifola. d, Ansellia africana. e, Disa uniflora. f, Calathe rosea.

No. 2319, 550sh, horiz. — Mushrooms: a, Fly mushroom. b, Rosy-gill fairy helmet. c, Purple coincap. d, Velvet shank. e, Thick-footed morel. f, King bolete.

No. 2320, 2000sh, Olive baboon. No. 2321, 2000sh, Gray crowned crane. No. 2322, 2000sh, Blue diadem butterfly. No. 2323, 2000sh, Disa uniflora, diff. No. 2324, 2000sh, Sharp-scaled parasol mushroom.

2004, July 19 *Perf. 14*

Sheets of 6, #a-f

2315-2319 A402 Set of 5 30.00 30.00

Souvenir Sheets

2320-2324 A402 Set of 5 18.50 18.50

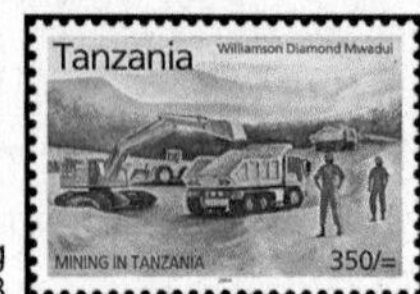

Mining A403

Designs: 350sh, Diamond mining at Williamson Diamond Mwadui. 500sh, Semi-processed jewels. No. 2327, 600sh, Drillers in deep mine. 800sh, Gold miners.
No. 2329, Unprocessed gemstones.

2004, July 30 *Perf. 13¼x12¾*

2325-2328 A403 Set of 4 4.25 4.25
2328a Souvenir sheet, #2325-2328 4.25 4.25

Souvenir Sheet

2329 A403 600sh multi 1.40 1.40

Southern African Development Community, 24th Anniv. A404

Designs: 350sh, Removal of water hyacinths from beach. 500sh, Irrigation ditch in corn field. 600sh, irrigation ditch at rice paddy. 800sh, Workers installing pipe in borehole, vert.
1000sh, Farm workers hoeing corn field irrigation ditches.

2004, Aug. 17 *Perf. 14x13, 13x14*

2330-2333 A404 Set of 4 4.25 4.25
2333a Souvenir sheet, #2330-2333, perf. 13½x13, 13x13½ 4.25 4.25

Souvenir Sheet

2334 A404 1000sh multi 1.90 1.90

Nos. 1565, 1569, 1571 and 2166 Surcharged

No. 2335

No. 2336

No. 2337A

Methods and Perfs As Before

2004, Nov. 13

2335 A262 350sh on 100sh #1565 — —
2336 A374 350sh on 200sh #2166 — —
2337 A262 350sh on 210sh #1569 — —
2337A A262 400sh on 300sh #1571 — —
b. Double surcharge —

Children's Rights A405

Inscriptions: No. 2338, 350sh, Involve children in school development. No. 2339, 350sh, Let's equip children with life skills. 400sh, Children need education before employment. 500sh, 1000sh, Disabled children need to be educated.

2004, Nov. 4 **Litho.** *Perf. 13¼x12¾*

2338-2341 A405 Set of 4 3.00 3.00

Souvenir Sheet

2342 A405 1000sh multi 1.90 1.90

Law and Peace in the Great Lakes Zone — A405a

Designs: 350sh, Julius K. Nyerere acting as facilitator in Burundi peace negotiations. 500sh, Burundi refugees at border. No. 2342C, 600sh, Nelson Mandela and Tanzania Pres. Banjamin W. Mkapa at Arusha peace talks. 800sh, Pres. Mkapa with Uganda Pres. Yoweri Musaveni and Burundi Pres. Domitien Ndayizeye at Dar es Salaam peace talks.
No. 2342E, 600sh, Arusha Intl. Conference Center.

2004, Oct. 15 **Litho.** *Perf. 14x13*

2342A-2342D A405a Set of 4 4.25 4.25
2342Df Souvenir sheet, #2342A-2342D 4.25 4.25

Souvenir Sheet

2342E A405a 600sh multi 1.10 1.10

Rotary International, Cent. — A406

Designs: 350sh, Rotary officials honor Tanzania Pres. Julius Nyerere. 500sh, Emblem of Dar es Salaam North Tanzania Club, vert. No. 2345 600sh, Eradication of polio. 800sh, Map and flags of District 9200 countries, Eritrea, Ethiopia, Uganda, Kenya and Tanzania, vert.

No. 2347: a, Environmental project. b, Self-reliance to the handicapped. c, Basic health care project, vert. d, Jaipur foot project. e, Malaria project. f, Eradication of river blindness project.
1000sh, Centenary emblem, vert.

2005, Feb. 23 **Litho.** *Perf. 13*

2343-2346 A406 Set of 4 4.25 4.25
2347 A406 600sh Sheet of 6, #a-f 6.50 6.50

Souvenir Sheet

2348 A406 1000sh multi 1.90 1.90

Safari Circuit Animals — A407

Designs: 350sh, Lionesses. 500sh, Cheetahs, horiz. No. 2351, 600sh, Red colobus monkey. 800sh, Zebras, horiz.

No. 2353, horiz.: a, Elephants. b, Rhinoceroses. c, Giraffes. d, Crocodile. e, Chimpanzees. f, Buffaloes.

No. 2354, horiz.: a, Leopard. b, Wild hunting dogs.

Perf. 12¾x13¼, 13¼x12¾

2005, Apr. 30

2349-2352 A407 Set of 4 4.25 4.25
2353 A407 600sh Sheet of 6, #a-f 6.50 6.50
2354 A407 1000sh Sheet of 2, #a-b 3.75 3.75

Zanzibar Heritage and Culture A408

Designs: 350sh, Bull fighting. 400sh, Narrow street in Stone Town, vert. No. 2357, 600sh, Women's traditional dress, vert. 800sh, Clove harvesting, vert.

No. 2359, 600sh: a, House of Wonders. b, Local Taarabu musicians. c, Man holding fish. d, Coconut palm. e, Women's indoor traditional dress. f, Old museum building.
500sh, Pemba-Zanzibar ferry boat.

Perf. 13½x13, 13x13½

2005, June 30 **Litho.**

2355-2358 A408 Set of 4 4.00 4.00
2359 A408 600sh Sheet of 6, #a-f 6.50 6.50

Souvenir Sheet

2360 A408 500sh multi 1.25 1.25

2004 Summer Olympics, Athens — A409

Designs: No. 2361, 350sh, Greco-Roman wrestlers. No. 2362, 350sh, Baron Godefroy de Blonay, vert. 500sh, Commemorative medal for 1928 Amsterdam Summer Olympics, vert. 1000sh, Greek javelin thrower sculpture, vert.

2005, May 2 **Litho.** *Perf. 13¼*

2361-2364 A409 Set of 4 4.00 4.00

Souvenir Sheet

Reign of Pope John Paul, 25th Anniv. (in 2003) — A410

No. 2365: a, Pope as boy, with mother, 1921. b, Visit to Poland, 1979. c, Meeting with Pres. George W. Bush, 2001. d, In Armenia, 2001.

2005, May 2 *Perf. 13½*

2365 A410 1000sh Sheet of 4, #a-d 8.00 8.00

Locomotives, Bicent. — A411

No. 2366: a, West Side Lumber 3-truck shay, Georgetown Loop Railroad. b, LK&P 0-4-0 Saddletanker. c, Double-headed C&T steam locomotive. d, Baldwin 4-6-0, Huckleberry Railroad.
2500sh, Heber Valley Railroad 2-8-0.

2005, May 2

2366 A411 1000sh Sheet of 4, #a-d 7.25 7.25

Souvenir Sheet

2367 A411 2500sh multi 4.50 4.50

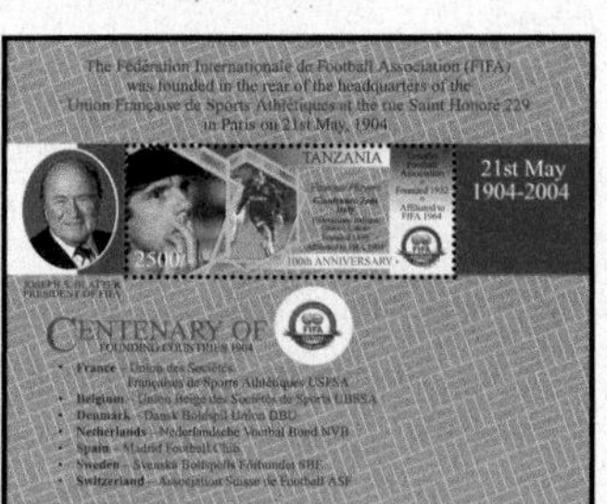

FIFA (Fédération Internationale de Football Association) Cent. (in 2004) — A412

No. 2368: a, Franco Baresi. b, Daniel Passarella. c, Miroslav Klose. d, Michel Platini.
2500sh, Gianfranco Zola.

2005, May 2 **Litho.** *Perf. 13½*

2368 A412 1000sh Sheet of 4, #a-d 7.25 7.25

Souvenir Sheet

2369 A412 2500sh multi 4.50 4.50

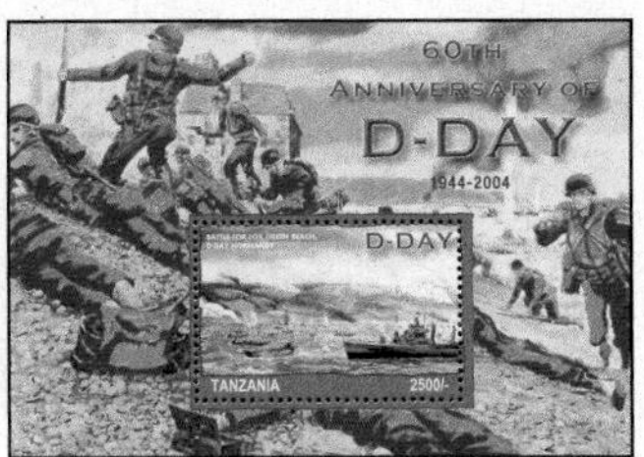

D-Day, 60th Anniv. (in 2004) — A413

No. 2370, vert.: a, Map of invasion. b, Gen. Dwight D. Eisenhower. c, American troops landing at Omaha Beach. d, British Mosquitos. e, Fleet Admiral Ernest J. King. f, Gen. George C. Marshall.
2500sh, Battle for Fox Green Beach.

2006, May 2
2370 A413 600sh Sheet of 6, #a-f 6.50 6.50

Souvenir Sheet

2371 A413 2500sh multi 4.50 4.50

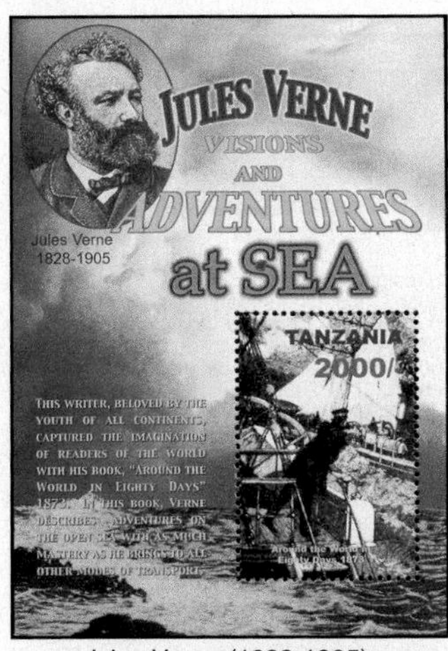

Jules Verne (1828-1905), Writer — A414

No. 2372, 800sh: a, Voyages Extraordinaires. b, Twenty Thousand Leagues Under the Sea. c, A Floating City (book cover). d, Adventures of Three Englishmen and Three Russians in South Africa.
No. 2373, 800sh: a, Mathias Sandorf. b, The Steam House, The Demon of Cawnpore. c, Hector Servadec on the Career of a Comet. d, An Antarctic Mystery.
No. 2374, 800sh: a, Around the World in Eighty Days. b, Dr. Ox's Experiment. c, The Purchase of the North Pole. d, Adrift in the Pacific.
No. 2375, 800sh: a, The Archipelago on Fire. b, The Vanished Diamond. c, Mistress Branican. d, The Castle of the Carpathians.
No. 2376, 800sh: a, The Invasion of the Sea. b, The Floating Island. c, A Floating City (men near ship railing). d, Dick Sands, Boy Captain.
No. 2377, 2000sh, Around the World in Eighty Days, diff. No. 2378, 2000sh, Five Weeks in a Balloon. No. 2379, 2000sh, The Mysterious Island. No. 2380, 2000sh, The Adventures of a Chinaman. No. 2381, 2000sh, The Invasion of the Sea, diff.

2005, May 16 ***Perf. 13½***

Sheets of 4, #a-d

2372-2376 A414 Set of 5 29.00 29.00

Souvenir Sheets

2377-2381 A414 Set of 5 18.00 18.00

Fish of Lake Victoria A415

Designs: No. 2382, 350sh, Labeo victorianus. 400sh, Lates niloticus. 600sh, Pundamilia nyererei. 800sh, Brycinus sadleri.
No. 2386, 350sh: a, Haplochromis sharpsnout. b, Haplochromis chilotes. c, Mormyrus kannume. d, Clarias gariepinus. e, Synodontis afrofischeri. f, Protopterus aethiopicus.
500sh, Oreochromis niloticus.

2005, Aug. 30 ***Perf. 13¼x13¾***
2382-2385 A415 Set of 4 3.75 3.75
2386 A415 350sh Sheet of 6, #a-f 3.75 3.75

Souvenir Sheet

2387 A415 500sh multi 1.25 1.25

Pope John Paul II (1920-2005), and Pres. Bill Clinton — A416

2005, Sept. 22 ***Perf. 12¾***
2388 A416 1500sh multi 3.25 3.25

Printed in sheets of 4, with each stamp having a slightly different background.

Rotary International, Cent. — A417

No. 2389: a, Child receiving polio vaccine. b, Dr. Jonas E. Salk, polio researcher. c, Hands, test tube.
2500sh, Salk and Rotary International centenary emblem.

2005, Sept. 22
2389 A417 1200sh Sheet of 3, #a-c 6.50 6.50

Souvenir Sheet

2390 A417 2500sh multi 4.50 4.50

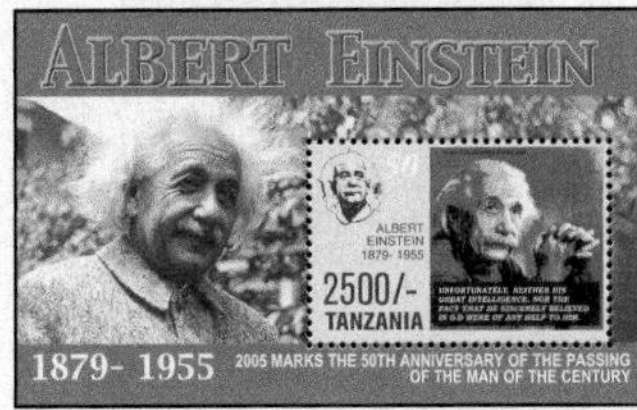

Albert Einstein (1879-1955), Physicist — A418

No. 2391 — Sketch of Einstein and: a, 1979 Swiss 5-franc coin. b, Time Magazine cover. c, Israel #117.
2500sh, Portrait of Einstein.

2005, Sept. 22
2391 A418 1300sh Sheet of 3, #a-c 7.00 7.00

Souvenir Sheet

2392 A418 2500sh multi 4.50 4.50

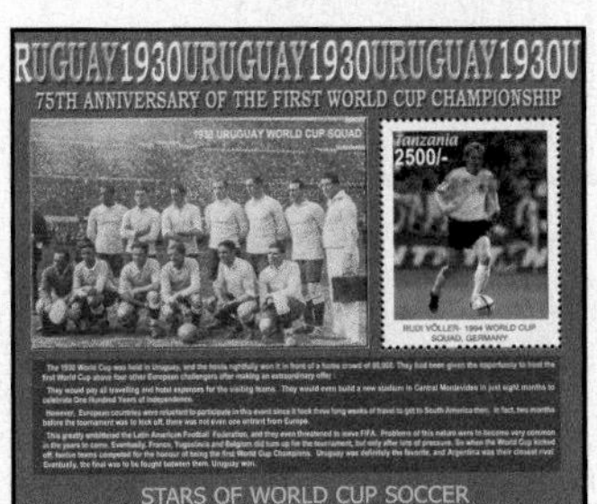

First World Cup Soccer Championships, 75th Anniv. — A419

No. 2393: a, Christian Ziege. b, Marko Rehmer. c, Jens Nowotny.
2500sh, Rudi Völler.

2005, Sept. 22 ***Perf. 13¼***
2393 A419 1200sh Sheet of 3, #a-c 6.50 6.50

Souvenir Sheet

2394 A419 2500sh multi 4.50 4.50

Butterflies A420

Designs: 350sh, Papilio ufipa. No. 2396, 500sh, Mylothris sagala mahale. No. 2397, 600sh, Amauris tartarea tukuyuensis. 800sh, Charaxes lucyae gabriellae.
No. 2399, 600sh: a, Like 350sh. b, Euphaedra neophron kiellandi. c, Like 800sh. d, Abisara zanzibarica. e, Acrae utengulensis.
No. 2400, 500sh, Charaxes usambarae maridadi.

2005, Oct. 27 ***Perf. 13¾x13½***
2395-2398 A420 Set of 4 4.50 4.50
2399 A420 600sh Sheet of 6, #2397, 2399a-2399e 6.50 6.50

Souvenir Sheet

2400 A420 500sh multi 1.50 1.50

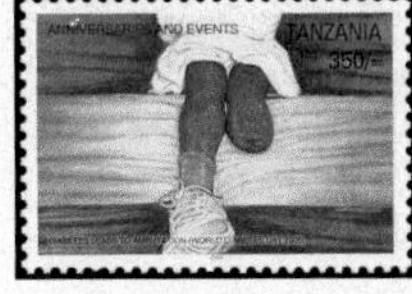

Anniversaries and Events A421

Designs: 350sh, Person with amputated leg. No. 2402, 500sh, Line of people at polling station. No. 2403, 600sh, Pope John Paul II, kneeling at airport. 800sh, Laurean Cardinal Rugambwa, Pope John Paul II and Pres. Alis Hassan Mwinyi.
No. 2405, 600sh: a, Pres. Julius Nyerere and Abeid Aman Karume signing Union Treaty. b, Woman holding child, casting ballot. c, Pope John Paul II, Pres. Mwinyi and Julius and Maria Nyerere. d, Pope John Paul II and Cardinal Rugambwa and car roof. e, Majimaji Museum, Songea. f, President B. W. Mkapa at fire.
No. 2406, 500sh, Majimaji Monument, vert.

2005, Dec. 9 ***Perf. 13¼x12¾***
2401-2404 A421 Set of 4 4.00 4.00
2405 A421 600sh Sheet of 6, #a-f 6.25 6.25

Souvenir Sheet

Perf. 12¾x13¼

2406 A421 500sh multi 1.25 1.25

World Diabetes Day (350sh); 2005 general elections (#2402, 2405b), Visit of Pope John Paul II, 15th anniv. (800sh, #2405c, 2405d).

Birds A422

Designs: 350sh, Rufous-winged sunbird. No. 2408, 500sh, Pemba white-eye. No. 2409, 600sh, Kilombero weaver. 800sh, Usambara eagle owl.
No. 2411, 600sh: a, Pemba scops owl. b, Spike-heeled lark. c, Pemba green pigeon. d, Uluguru bush shrike. e, Yellow-collared love birds. f, Usambara nightjar.
No. 2412, 500sh, Moreau's sunbird, vert.

2006, Mar. 25 ***Perf. 13***
2407-2410 A422 Set of 4 4.00 4.00
2411 A422 600sh Sheet of 6, #a-f 6.50 6.50

Souvenir Sheet

2412 A422 500sh multi 1.10 1.10

No. 2412 contains one 39x49mm stamp.

2006 World Cup Soccer Championships, Germany — A423

Designs: 350sh, New National Stadium, Dar es Salaam. 500sh, Map of Africa and flags of participating countries, vert. No. 2415, 600sh, Pres. Jakaya Kikwete holding World Cup trophy. 800sh, Mascot for 2006 World Cup, vert.
No. 2417, 600sh, World Cup Trophy and 2006 World Cup emblem.

Perf. 13¼x12¾, 12¾x13¼

2006, Mar. 25
2413-2416 A423 Set of 4 3.75 3.75
2416a Miniature sheet, #2413-2416 3.75 3.75

Souvenir Sheet

2417 A423 600sh multi 1.50 1.50

Miniature Sheet

Wolfgang Amadeus Mozart (1756-91), Composer — A424

No. 2418: a, Portrait of Mozart (blue panel). b, Mozart's birthplace, Salzburg. c, Poster for Don Giovanni. d, Portrait of Mozart (purple panel).

2006, June 13 ***Perf. 12¾***
2418 A424 1200sh Sheet of 4, #a-d 8.00 8.00

Queen Elizabeth II, 80th Birthday — A426

No. 2420 — Queen: a, Wearing blue robe. b, On reviewing stand. c, On horse. d, Wearing feathered hat.
2500sh, Wearing tiara.

Release of Elvis Presley Movie, *Jailhouse Rock,* 50th Anniv. — A425

No. 2419 — Presley with: a, Both arms at side. b, Arm raised above head. c, Arms outstretched and jacket pulled up behind head. d, Hand in front of chest.

2006, June 13 ***Perf. 13½***
2419 A425 1200sh Sheet of 4, #a-d 9.00 9.00

2006, June 13 *Perf. 14¼*

2420 A426 1200sh Sheet of 4, #a-d 9.50 9.50

Souvenir Sheet

2421 A426 2500sh multi 5.25 5.25

TANZANIA 3000/-
Rembrandt Harmensz van Rijn (1606 - 1669)

Rembrandt (1606-69), Painter — A427

No. 2422 — Painting details: a, Jan Pellicorne and His Son Caspar (Jan Pellicorne). b, Jan Pellicorne and His Son Caspar (Caspar). c, Susanna Van Collen, Wife of Jan Pellicorne, and Her Daughter, Eva Susanna (Susanna). d, Susanna Van Collen, Wife of Jan Pellicorne, and Her Daughter, Eva Susanna (Eva Susanna).
3000sh, A Turk.

2006, June 13 *Perf. 13¼*

2422 A427 1000sh Sheet of 4, #a-d 6.75 6.75

Imperf

Size: 70x100mm

2423 A427 3000sh multi 5.00 5.00

Beauty of Zanzibar A428

Designs: 350sh, Man and woman in traditional Zanzibar dress. No. 2425, 500sh, Zanzibar Museum. No. 2426, 600sh, Maruhubi Palace ruins. 800sh, Man climbing coconut tree.
No. 2428, 600sh: a, Green turtle at Mnemba Island. b, Red colobus monkey. c, Giant tortoise at Changuu Island. d, Dhow, Zanzibar sunset. e, Dhow sailing near Matemwe. f, Coconut crab, Chumbe Island.
No. 2429, 500sh, vert.: a, Clove foliage and enlargement of flower buds. b, Light Signal Tower.

2006, June 30 *Perf. 13½x13*

2424-2427 A428 Set of 4 4.00 4.00

2428 A428 600sh Sheet of 6, #a-f 6.00 6.00

Souvenir Sheet

Perf. 13x13½

2429 A428 500sh Sheet of 2, #a-b 1.75 1.75

Mountains — A429

Designs: 350sh, Mt. Kenya. 400sh, Udzungwa Mountain Range. 600sh, Sanje Falls, vert. 800sh, Ruwenzori Range.
No. 2434, 1000sh: a, Kiko Summit and Mawenzi, Mt. Kilimanjaro. b, Giraffe and Mt. Kilimanjaro.
No. 2435, 1000sh: a, Cattle, herder and Ol Doinyo Lengai. b, Ol Doinyo Lengai summit and crater, vert.

Perf. 13½x13¾, 13¾x13½

2006, Aug. 24

2430-2433 A429 Set of 4 3.50 3.50

Sheets of 2, #a-b

2434-2435 A429 Set of 2 6.50 6.50

Miniature Sheet

Tazara Railway, 30th Anniv. — A430

No. 2436: a, 350sh, Map of Tanzania and Zambia, waterfall, mountain, people waving, and men signing agreement. b, 350sh, Men and train, elephant and antelope. c, 600sh, Dar es Salaam Station, sign and wreaths with Chinese inscriptions. d, 600sh, New Kapiri Mposhi Station, people near train. e, 800sh, Train, bridge and tunnel, zebra and giraffe. f, 800sh, Train on bridge, lion and lioness.

2006, Oct. 25 *Perf. 12*

2436 A430 Sheet of 6, #a-f 6.00 6.00

Worldwide Fund for Nature (WWF) — A431

No. 2437 — Damaliscus lunatus jimela: a, Males butting heads. b, Close-up view of head. c, Adult and juvenile. d, Adult on mound.

2006, Nov. 24 *Perf. 13¼*

2437 A431 Horiz. or vert. strip 7.00 7.00

a.-d. 600sh Any single 1.25 1.25

e. Miniature sheet, 2 each #2437a-2437d 8.00 8.00

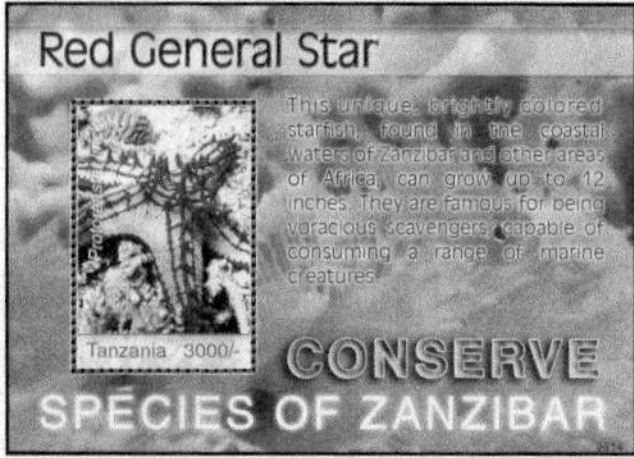

Zanzibar Flora and Fauna — A432

No. 2438, 1000sh: a, Coconut crab. b, Frangipane. c, Sykes monkey. d, Green sea turtle.
No. 2439, 1000sh: a, African civet. b, Four-toed elephant shrew. c, Lesser bushbaby. d, Pemba sunbird.
No. 2440, 3000sh, Protoreaster lincki. No. 2441, 3000sh, Tauraco fischeri.

2006, Nov. 24 *Perf. 13¼*

Sheets of 4, #a-d

2438-2439 A432 Set of 2 13.50 13.50

Souvenir Sheets

2440-2441 A432 Set of 2 10.00 10.00

Space Achievements — A433

No. 2442 — Intl. Space Station: a, Two rows of solar panels at top, part of Space Station at bottom. b, Connection point for arms holding solar panels. c, Main junction of Space Station. d, Space Station, denomination at UR. e, Space Shuttle with cargo door open. f, Space Station, "International Space Station" just above country name.
No. 2443 — Mars Reconnaissance Orbiter: a, Mars, launch of rocket. b, Orbiter, country name in white at UR. c, Orbiter, country name in red and black at LL. d, Orbiter, country name in white at UL.
No. 2444, 2500sh, Calipso and Cloudsat satellites. No. 2445, 2500sh, Muses-C probe.

2006, June 13 **Litho.** *Perf. 14*

2442 A433 800sh Sheet of 6, #a-f 7.75 7.75

2443 A433 1150sh Sheet of 4, #a-d 7.50 7.50

Souvenir Sheets

2444-2445 A433 Set of 2 8.00 8.00

Phila Africa 06 Stamp Exhibition, Dar es Salaam A434

2006, Aug. 24 *Perf. 13¾*

2446 A434 (700sh) multi 1.10 1.10

Souvenir Sheet

2447 A434 600sh multi .90 .90

No. 2447 contains one 47x32mm stamp.

Independence, 45th Anniv. — A435

Designs: 350sh, Pres. Julius K. Nyerere with torch. No. 2449, 400sh, University of Dar es Salaam, horiz. No. 2450, 600sh, Vice-president Abeid A. Karume, country name in green. 800sh, Nyerere.
No. 2452, 600sh: a, Prime Minister Rashidi Mfaume Kawawa. b, Nyerere, diff. c, Karume, country name in blue. d, Pres. Ali Hassan Mwinyi. e, Pres. Benjamin W. Mkapa. f, Pres. Jakaya Mrisho Kikwete.
No. 2453, National Uhuru Monument.

2006, Dec. 9 *Perf. 13½*

2448-2451 A435 Set of 4 3.50 3.50

2452 A435 600sh Sheet of 6, #a-f 5.75 5.75

Souvenir Sheet

2453 A435 400sh multi .65 .65

Safari Hunt Animals A436

Designs: 400sh, Wild dog. 600sh, Warthog. No. 2456, 700sh, Zebras. 800sh, Female monkeys and young.
No. 2458, 700sh: a, Elephant. b, Leopard in grass. c, Buffaloes. d, Lion and lioness. e, Leopard in foliage (66x46mm).
1000sh, Lionesses.

2007, Feb. 23 *Perf. 13¾*

2454-2457 A436 Set of 4 4.00 4.00

2458 A436 700sh Sheet of 5, #a-e 5.75 5.75

Souvenir Sheet

2459 A436 1000sh multi 1.60 1.60

No. 2459 contains one 47x32mm stamp.

Historical Zanzibar — A437

Designs: 400sh, Ruins. 600sh, Coral reef and fish west of Pemba, horiz. No. 2462, 700sh, Bet El Ajaib, cloves. 800sh, Coral reef and fish, diff.
No. 2464, 700sh, horiz.: a, Beach. b, Kizimbani Persian Bath. c, Maruhubi Ruins. d, Livingstone House. e, Old Dispensary. f, Cave.
No. 2465, 700sh, Colobus monkey, horiz.

2007, Apr. 26

2460-2463 A437 Set of 4 4.00 4.00

2464 A437 700sh Sheet of 6, #a-f 6.75 6.75

Souvenir Sheet

2465 A437 700sh multi 1.10 1.10

Activities of World Vision A438

Designs: No. 2466, 400sh, Food security. 600sh, Income generation and nutrition. No. 2468, 700sh, Advocating for children and rights. 800sh, Children's immunization. 1000sh, Education for development.
No. 2471, 700sh: a, Children's immunization. b, Education for development.
No. 2472, 400sh, Income generation and nutrition.

2007, May 31 **Litho.** *Perf. 13¾x13½*

2466-2470 A438 Set of 5 5.50 5.50

2471 A438 700sh Sheet of 3, #2468, 2471a, 2471b 3.50 3.50

Souvenir Sheet

2472 A438 400sh multi .65 .65

Environmental Care — A439

Designs: No. 2473, 400sh, Prof. Mark Mwandosya planting tree at Kiroka Secondary School, Morogoro. No. 2474, 500sh, Shinyanga. 700sh, Kihansi Waterfall, Nectophrynoides asperginis. 800sh, Natural regeneration of the land.
No. 2477, 400sh: a, Illegal mining. b, Tree planting, Morogoro. c, Planted trees in degraded areas. d, Traditional soil and moisture conservation method. e, Tree seedlings for rehabilitating degraded areas. f, Agriculture on steep mountains.
No. 2478, 500sh, Nguru Mountains catchment area.

2007, June 5 **Litho.** *Perf. 14*

2473-2476 A439 Set of 4 4.00 4.00

2477 A439 400sh Sheet of 6, #a-f 4.00 4.00

Souvenir Sheet

2478 A439 500sh multi .80 .80

Campaign Against AIDS — A440

Inscriptions: No. 2479, 400sh, Let us talk with our children about AIDS. 700sh, Be faithful in your marriage. 800sh, Fight against AIDS is our duty. 1000sh, Examine your health to be free.
No. 2483, 400sh: a, Let us get education about AIDS. b, Prevent yourself from new infection. c, Let us sing to stop AIDS. d, Let us not segregate the people with AIDS.

No. 2484, 400sh, Stop AIDS, keep the promise.

2007, July 14 Litho. ***Perf. 13¾x13½***
2479-2482 A440 Set of 4 4.50 4.50
2483 A440 400sh Sheet of 4, #a-d 2.50 2.50

Souvenir Sheet

2484 A440 400sh multi .65 .65

Reign of Aga Khan, 50th Anniv. A441

Designs: 400sh, Zanzibar Madrasa Resource Center. No. 2486, 600sh, Aga Khan Hospital, Dar es Salaam, gold frame. 700sh, Lake Manyara Serena Safari Lodge. 800sh, Zanzibar Serena Inn.
No. 2489, 600sh: a, Exterior of Stone Town Cultural Center, Zanzibar. b, View from balcony of Stone Town Cultural Center. c, Medical personnel treating patient at Aga Khan Hospital. d, Aga Khan Hospital, white frame.
1000sh, Women at Zanzibar Madrasa Resource Center, vert.

2007, Aug. 18 Litho. ***Perf. 14½***
2485-2488 A441 Set of 4 4.00 4.00
2489 A441 600sh Sheet of 4, #a-d 3.75 3.75

Souvenir Sheet

2490 A441 1000sh multi 1.60 1.60

Campaign Against Corruption A442

Emblem of Prevention of Corruption Bureau: No. 2491, 400sh, Group of people in map of Tanzania. 500sh, Police officer escorting arrested man. 700sh, Man with briefcase as marionette, vert. 800sh, Man initiating bribe.
No. 2495: a, 400sh, Emblem with bright yellow background. b, 600sh, Man, police officer, bus.
No. 2496, 400sh, Emblem with olive green background.

2007, Oct. 9 Litho. ***Perf. 13¼***
2491-2494 A442 Set of 4 4.25 4.25
2495 A442 Sheet of 5, #2492-2494, 2495a, 2495b 5.25 5.25

Souvenir Sheet

2496 A442 400sh multi .70 .70

Ceremonial Costumes — A443

Designs: No. 2497, 400sh, Iringa Hehe tribesman in traditional outfit. 600sh, Haya girls in bark cloth outfit. No. 2499, 700sh, Msewe dancers in Pemba, horiz. 800sh, Wabena tribesmen in traditional ceremony, horiz.
No. 2501, 700sh: a, Maasai girls. b, Maasai dancing. c, Singida Nyaturu girl. d, Sambaa tribesman in traditional outfit. e, Wabena woman grinding corn. f, Wairaq man and wife in leather outfit.
No. 2502, 400sh, Wanyaturu girls, horiz.

2007, Oct. 9 ***Perf. 14***
2497-2500 A443 Set of 4 4.50 4.50
2501 A443 700sh Sheet of 6, #a-f 7.50 7.50

Souvenir Sheet

2502 A443 400sh multi .70 .70

Pope Benedict XVI — A444

2007, Oct. 24 Litho. ***Perf. 13½***
2503 A444 600sh multi 1.50 1.50

Printed in sheets of 8.

Wedding of Queen Elizabeth II and Prince Philip, 60th Anniv. — A445

No. 2504: a, Queen and flowers. b, Couple.

2007, Oct. 24
2504 A445 750sh Pair, #a-b 2.60 2.60

Printed in sheets containing three of each stamp.

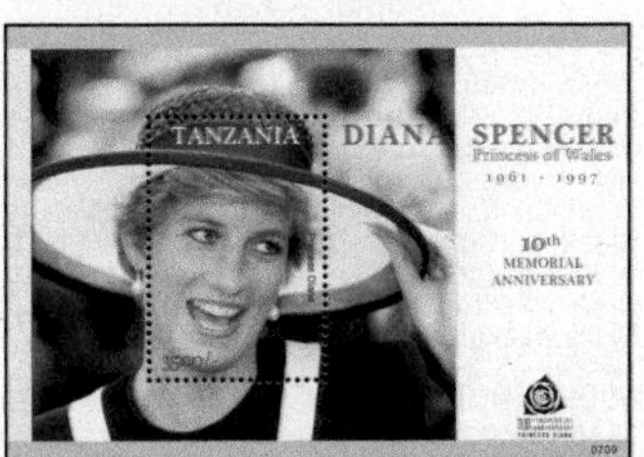

Princess Diana (1961-97) — A446

No. 2505 — Diana wearing: a, Purple and red hat, close-up. b, Blue and beige hat, close-up. c, Black and white hat. d, Blue and beige hat. e, Purple and red hat. f, Black and white hat, close-up.
3500sh, Blue and white hat.

2007, Oct. 24
2505 A446 750sh Sheet of 6, #a-f 7.75 7.75

Souvenir Sheet

2506 A446 3500sh multi 6.00 6.00

First Helicopter Flight, Cent. — A447

No. 2507: a, Hiller UH-12 Raven. b, Kamov Ka-25 Hormone. c, Cierva autogyro. d, Eurocopter Tiger.
3000sh, Bristol Sycamore.

2007, Oct. 24
2507 A447 1200sh Sheet of 4, #a-d 8.25 8.25

Souvenir Sheet

2508 A447 3000sh multi 5.25 5.25

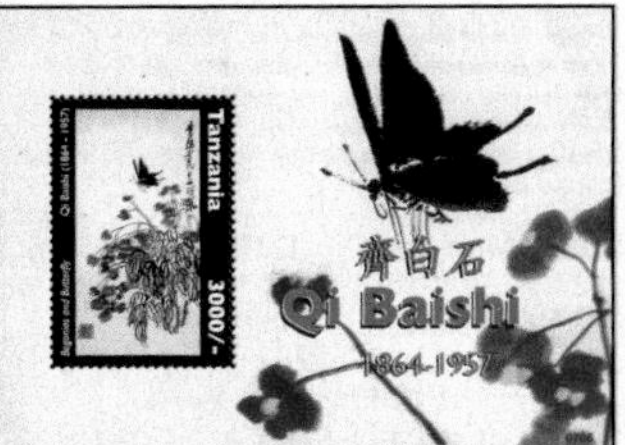

Paintings by Qi Baishi (1864-1957) — A448

No. 2509: a, Wisteria and Bees. b, Pine and Cicada. c, Narcissus, Rock and Quail. d, Pumpkins.
3000sh, Begonias and Butterfly.

2007, Oct. 24 ***Perf. 12½***
2509 A448 1000sh Sheet of 4, #a-d 7.00 7.00

Souvenir Sheet
Perf. 13½

2510 A448 3000sh multi 5.25 5.25

No. 2509 contains four 32x80mm stamps.

Animals A449

Designs: 400sh, Wildebeests and zebras grazing. No. 2512, 600sh, Lion and lioness, vert. 700sh, Lioness descending tree, vert. 800sh, Giraffes, vert.
No. 2515, 600sh: a, Leopard on tree, vert. b, Young chimpanzee, vert. c, Lioness resting on tree, vert. d, Adult male chimpanzee, vert. e, Cheetah with a kill. f, Baboons.
No. 2616, 600sh: a, Leopard and cubs. b, Impala.

Perf. 13¾x13½, 13½x13¼
2008, Jan. 30 Litho.
2511-2514 A449 Set of 4 4.25 4.25
2515 A449 600sh Sheet of 6, #a-f 6.25 6.25

Souvenir Sheet

2516 A449 600sh Sheet of 2, #a-b 2.10 2.10

For surcharge, see No. 2713.

Miniature Sheet

2008 Summer Olympics, Beijing — A450

No. 2517: a, Basketball. b, Marathon. c, Swimming. d, Javelin.

2008, Apr. 8 Litho. ***Perf. 12¾***
2517 A450 700sh Sheet of 4, #a-d 4.50 4.50

Spices of Zanzibar A451

Designs: 400sh, Nutmeg. No. 2519, 600sh, Man picking cloves. 700sh, Drying cloves, vert. 1000sh, Cardamom (iliki) seeds.
No. 2522, 600sh: a, Cardamom plants. b, Vanilla beans. c, Ginger. d, Cinnamon (mdalasini). e, Black pepper. f, Paprika peppers.
No. 2523, 600sh, Turmeric (binzari).

2008, Apr. 26 Litho. ***Perf. 13¼***
2518-2521 A451 Set of 4 4.50 4.50
2522 A451 600sh Sheet of 6, #a-f 6.00 6.00

Souvenir Sheet

2523 A451 600sh multi 1.00 1.00

For surcharge, see No. 2829.

Marine Life — A452

Designs: 400sh, Sea turtle. No. 2525, 600sh, Dugongs. 700sh, Octopus. 1000sh, Whale shark.
No. 2528, 600sh: a, Lizard fish. b, Eel. c, Sea turtle, diff. d, Lionfish. e, Anemone fish. f, Coelacanths.
No. 2529, 600sh, Seahorses, vert.

2008, Aug. 15 ***Perf. 13¾x13½***
2524-2527 A452 Set of 4 4.75 4.75

Perf. 13¾

2528 A452 600sh Sheet of 6, #a-f 6.25 6.25

Souvenir Sheet

2529 A452 600sh multi 1.10 1.10

No. 2528 contains six 42x32mm stamps. No. 2529 contains one 35x50mm stamp.

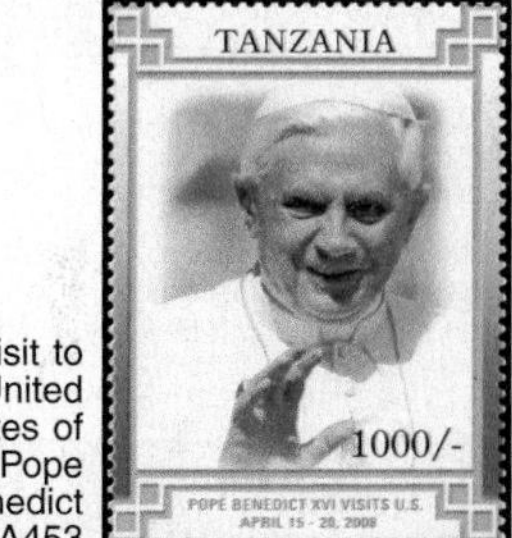

Visit to United States of Pope Benedict XVI — A453

2008, Sept. 3 Litho. ***Perf. 13¼***
2530 A453 1000sh multi 1.75 1.75

Printed in sheets of 4.

Miniature Sheet

Elvis Presley (1935-77) — A454

No. 2531 — Movies: a, Jailhouse Rock. b, Wild in the Country. c, Flaming Star. d, Roustabout.

2008, Sept. 3
2531 A454 1200sh Sheet of 4, #a-d 8.50 8.50

Botanical Gardens — A454a

Designs: 400sh, Flowers, Kitulo Natl. Park. No. 2531F, 600sh, Chameleon and butterfly, Amani Forest. 700sh, Monkey and waterfall, Udzungwa Mountains Forest. 1000sh, Trees, Saadani Natl. Park.
No. 2531I, 600sh: k, Flowers, Kitulo Natl. Park. l, Gazrden House, Vuga-Lushoto. m, Flowers, Udzungwa Mountains. n, Bird at Lake Rushwa, Kagera. o, Rufiji River, Selous Game Reserve. p, Rhinoceros, Ngorongoro Crater.
No. 2531J, 600sh, Bird, Kitulo Natl. Park.

Perf. 13¾x13½
2008, Nov. 15 Litho.
2531E-2531H A454a Set of 4 4.25 4.25
2531I A454a 600sh Sheet of 6, #k-p 5.75 5.75

Souvenir Sheet

Perf. 13¾

2531J A454a 600sh multi .95 .95

No. 2531J contains one 50x35mm stamp.

Tanzania Posts Corporation, 15th Anniv. — A455

Designs: 400sh, Window clerk. 600sh, Headquarters, vert.

Perf. 13¾x13½, 13½x13¾

2009, Jan. 20

2532-2533 A455 Set of 2 1.50 1.50

Miniature Sheet

Inauguration of US Pres. Barack Obama — A456

No. 2534 — Pres. Obama and: a, White background. b, Flag. c, Window. d, Wife, Michelle.

2009, Jan. 20 Litho. ***Perf. 11½x12***

2534 A456 1500sh Sheet of 4, #a-d 8.75 8.75

Souvenir Sheet

Signing of Millennium Challenge Compact Aid Package, 1st Anniv. — A457

No. 2535: a, US Pres. George W. Bush. b, Tanzania Pres. Jakaya Kikwete.

2009, Jan. 27 ***Perf. 13½***

2535 A457 1500sh Sheet of 2, #a-b 4.75 4.75

Space Exploration, 50th Anniv. (In 2007) — A458

No. 2536: a, 1200sh, Sputnik III. b, 1500sh, Sputnik III and clouds.

No. 2537: a, Huygens probe and technician. b, Cassini orbiter and Huygens probe in manufactuing facility. c, Titan IV-B/ Centaur launch vehicle. d, Cassini-Huygens in space. e, Saturn, Titan, Huygens probe. f, Huygens probe on Titan.

No. 2538, 1200sh: a, Sputnik II. b, Laika on Monument to the Conquerors of Space, Moscow. c, Statue of Laika. d, Laika the dog.

No. 2539, 1200sh: a, Vostok I. b, Yuri Gagarin. c, Vostok 8K72K. d, Statue of Gagarin.

No. 2540, 1200sh: a, Explorer I and technicians. b, Dr. James Van Allen, Explorer I. c, Explorer I atop Juno I. d, Explorer I in space.

No. 2541, 1200sh — Spitzer Space telescope: a, In space. b, In manufacturing facility, name in black at left. c, In manufacturing facility, name in white at right. d, In space, above Earth.

No. 2542, 3500sh, Sputnik III, horiz. No. 2543, 3500sh, Hubble Space Telescope, horiz.

2009, Mar. 13 Litho. ***Perf. 14***

2536 A458 Pair, #a-b 4.25 4.25

2537 A458 750sh Sheet of 6, #a-f 6.75 6.75

Sheets of 4, #a-d

2538-2541 A458 Set of 4 29.00 29.00

Souvenir Sheets

2542-2543 A458 Set of 2 10.50 10.50

No. 2536 was printed in sheets containing 2 pairs.

Nos. 2536-2543 exists imperf. Value, set $100.

Peonies A459

2009, Apr. 10 ***Perf. 13¼***

2544 A459 570sh multi .85 .85

Printed in sheets of 8.

Butterflies and Moths — A459a

Designs: 400sh, Mkuranga moth. No. 2544B, 600sh, Udzungwa butterfly, vert. 700sh, Acraea petraea. 800sh, Acraea petraea, diff.

No. 2544E, 600sh: f, Cymothoe alcimeda. g, Junonia octavia sesamus. h, Junonia oenone oenone. i, Hypolimnas misippus.

No. 2544J, 600sh, Vanessa cardui. No. 2544K, 600sh, Axiocerses tjoane, vert.

Perf. 13¼x13½, 13½x13¼

2009, June 30

Granite Paper

2544A-2544D A459a Set of 4 3.75 3.75

2544E A459a 600sh Sheet of 4, #f-i 3.75 3.75

Souvenir Sheets

2544J-2544K A459a Set of 2 1.90 1.90

Zanzibar Attractions — A459b

Designs: No. 2544L, 400sh, Red colobus monkey. No. 2544M, 600sh, House of Wonders, horiz. No. 2544N, 700sh, Carved door. No. 2544O, 1000sh, Coffee seller.

No. 2544P, 600sh: r, Man dragging outrigger canoe. s, Zanzibar seafront, horiz. t, Giant tortoise, horiz. u, Face of red colobus monkey. v, Chake Chake's Courthouse, horiz. w, Zumari, horiz.

No. 2544Q, 600sh, Zanzibar seafront and dhow, horiz.

2009, July 30 ***Perf. 14***

2544L-2544O A459b Set of 4 4.25 4.25

2544P A459b 600sh Sheet of 6, #r-w 5.50 5.50

Souvenir Sheet

2544Q A459b 600sh multi .95 .95

For surcharges, see Nos. 2831, 2834.

Miniature Sheets

A460

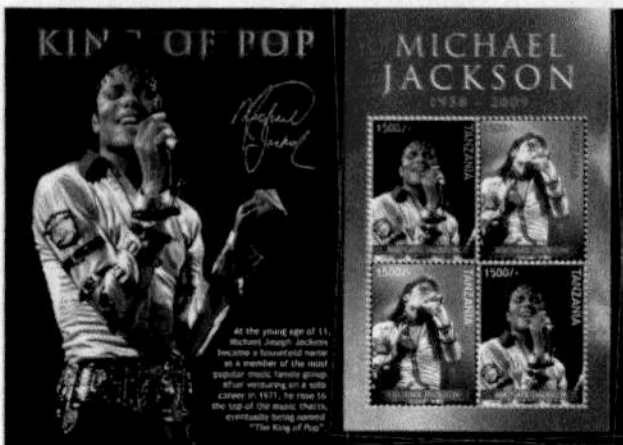

Michael Jackson (1958-2009), Singer — A461

No. 2545: a, Dull blue background, no frame. b, Yellow background, with gray frame. c, Orange background, with gray frame. d, Blue background, with gray frame.

No. 2546 — Various photographs with: a, Black background, purple denomination. b, Blue background, purple denomination. c, Blue background, white denomination. d, Black background, white denomination.

2009, Sept. 3 ***Perf. 11½x12***

2545 A460 1500sh Sheet of 4, #a-d 9.25 9.25

Perf. 12x11½

2546 A461 1500sh Sheet of 4, #a-d 9.25 9.25

Chinese Aviation, Cent. — A462

No. 2547 — Helicopters: a, Z-5. b, Z-6. c, Z-8. d, Z-11.

2700sh, Z-9 helicopter.

2009, Nov. 12 ***Perf. 14***

2547 A462 950sh Sheet of 4, #a-d 5.75 5.75

Souvenir Sheet

Perf. 14¼

2548 A462 2700sh multi 4.25 4.25

Aeropex 2009, Beijing. No. 2547 contains four 42x28mm stamps.

Youths at Play — A462a 2548A

Designs: 400sh, Girls playing Mdako game. No. 2548B, 600sh, Girls playing tennis. 700sh, Youths dancing. 1000sh, Boy on swing.

No. 2548E, 600sh: g, Boys playing Bao game. h, Boys playing basketball. i, Girls playing handball. j, Boys playing baseball. k, Boys running. l, Girls skipping rope.

No. 2548F, 600sh, Boys playing soccer.

2009, Dec. 30 ***Perf. 14***

2548A-2548D A462a Set of 4 4.00 4.00

2548E A462a 600sh Sheet of 6, #g-l 5.50 5.50

Souvenir Sheet

2548F A462a 600sh multi .90 .90

Miniature Sheet

Chinese Zodiac Animals — A463

No. 2549: a, Tiger. b, Ox. c, Rat. d, Horse. e, Rabbit. f, Dragon. g, Snake. h, Pig. i, Dog. j, Cock. k, Monkey. l, Goat.

2010, Jan. 4 Litho. ***Perf. 12¼***

2549 A463 300sh Sheet of 12, #a-l 5.50 5.50

Souvenir Sheet

New Year 2010 (Year of the Tiger) — A464

No. 2550 — Tiger facing: a, Right. b, Left.

2010, Jan. 4 ***Perf. 12***

2550 A464 2700sh Sheet of 2, #a-b 8.25 8.25

Miniature Sheets

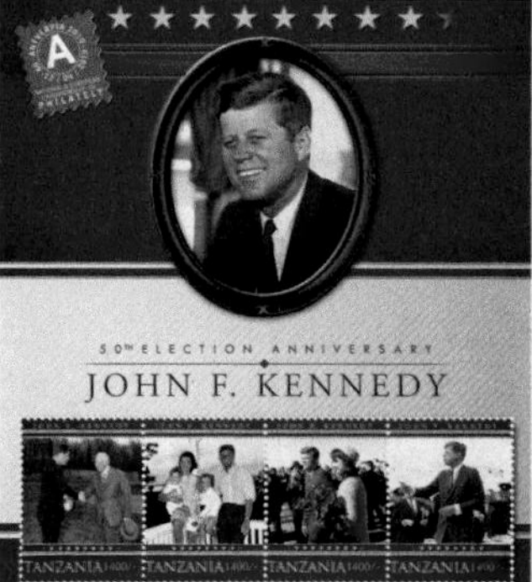

Election of Pres. John F. Kennedy, 50th Anniv. — A465

No. 2551, 1400sh — Pres. Kennedy (brown red panels) with: a, Pres. Dwight D. Eisenhower. b, Wife, Jacqueline, and children. c, Wife and crowd. d, Crowd.

No. 2552, 1400sh — Pres. Kennedy (violet blue panels): a, Shaking woman's hand. b, Leaving Air Force One with wife. c, With wife. d, Looking into space capsule.

2010, June 4 ***Perf. 11½***

Sheets of 4, #a-d

2551-2552 A465 Set of 2 15.50 15.50

Antverpia 2010 National and European Championship of Philately, Antwerp, Belgium (#2551).

Souvenir Sheet

Boy Scouts of America, Cent. — A466

No. 2553: a, Emblem of Charles L. Sommers National High Adventure Base, Scouts in canoe. b, Emblem of Northern Tier-Bissett National High Adventure Base, Scout skiing. c, Wmblem of Northern Tier-Roger's Atikokan National High Adventure Base, Scout fishing.

2010, July 15 *Perf. 13¼*
2553 A466 1900sh Sheet of 3, #a-c 7.50 7.50

Miniature Sheets

A467

Princess Diana (1961-97) — A468

No. 2554 — Diana wearing: a, Pink hat with brim with red edge. b, White gown and tiara, looking left. c, Hat with flower. d, Tiara, pink dress and necklace.

No. 2555 — Diana wearing: a, Black and white hat and dress. b, Pink hat. c, White gown and tiara, looking right. d, Tiara, red dress, touching face.

2010, Oct. 14 *Perf. 13¼x13*
2554 A467 1400sh Sheet of 4, #a-d 7.50 7.50
2555 A468 1400sh Sheet of 4, #a-d 7.50 7.50

Miniature Sheets

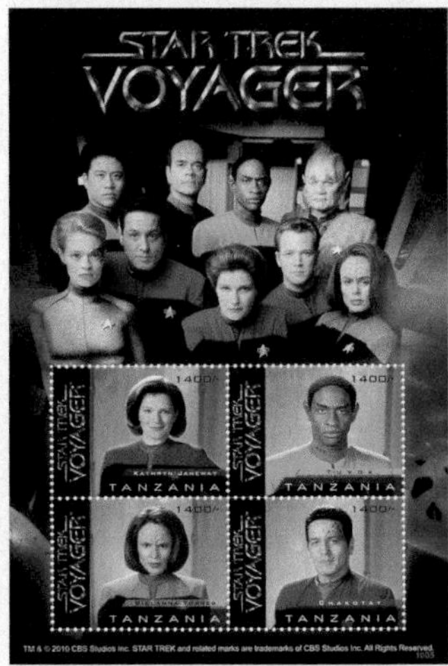

Characters From Star Trek Television Shows — A469

No. 2556, 1400sh — Characters from Star Trek Voyager: a, Capt. Kathryn Janeway. b, Tuvok. c, B'Elanna Torres. d, Chakotay.

No. 2557, 1400sh, vert. — Characters from Star Trek Deep Space Nine: a, Kira Nerys. b, Capt. Benjamin Sisko. c, Quark. d, Jadzia Dax.

2010, Oct. 14 *Perf. 11½x12, 12x11½*
Sheets of 4, #a-d
2556-2557 A469 Set of 2 15.00 15.00

A470

National Aeronautics and Space Administration, 50th Anniv. — A471

No. 2558: a, Earth, nose of Space Shuttle. b, Mars, fuselage of Space Shuttle. c, Jupiter. d, Neptune, astronaut.

No. 2559: a, Launch of Apollo 11, July 16, 1969. b, Launch of Space Shuttle Atlantis, May 14, 2010.

2010, Oct. 14
2558 A470 1400sh Sheet of 4, #a-d 7.50 7.50

Souvenir Sheet
Perf. 13¼x13
2559 A471 1400sh Sheet of 2, #a-b 3.75 3.75

Reign of Pope Benedict XVI, 5th Anniv. A472

Pope Benedict XVI: No. 2560, 1400sh, Holding censer. No. 2561, 1400sh, And St. Peter's Basilica.

2010, Dec. 23 *Perf. 12*
2560-2561 A472 Set of 2 3.75 3.75

Nos. 2560-2561 each were printed in sheets of 4.

Miniature Sheets

A473

Hu Jintao, President of People's Republic of China — A474

No. 2562 — Pres. Hu and: a, Chinese characters at left, English name in white, pale yellow area above first "0" in denomination. b, Chinese characters at right, English name in white, country name and denomination over pink area. c, Chinese characters at right, English name in black, denomination over pale yellow area. d, As "c," denomination over pink area. e, As "a," without pale yellow area above first "0" in denomination. f, As "b," hyphen at right over pale yellow area.

No. 2563 — Pres. Hu: a, Waving. b, Wearing red tie, with black door and knocker in background. c, Wearing blue tie, red and black background. d, Wearing red striped tie, gray background.

2010, Dec. 23
2562 A473 900sh Sheet of 6, #a-f 7.25 7.25
2563 A474 1100sh Sheet of 4, #a-d 6.00 6.00

Beijing 2010 Intl. Philatelic Exhibition.

Miniature Sheets

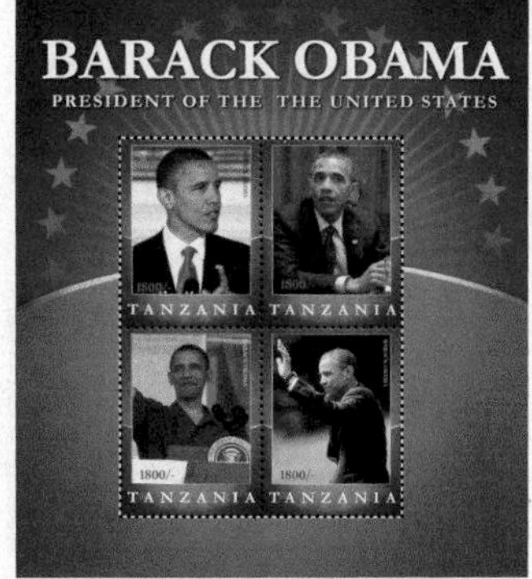

Pres. Barack Obama — A475

No. 2564, 1800sh — Pres. Obama (red and blue frames): a, With finger pointed up. b, Sitting, with arms on desk. c, Behind lectern, with arm raised. d, Waving.

No. 2565, 1800sh — Pres. Obama (purple panels at bottom): a, Writing. b, Standing, with shirt sleeves rolled up. c, Standing, wearing suit and red tie. d, Saluting.

2010, Dec. 23 **Litho.**
Sheets of 4, #a-d
2564-2565 A475 Set of 2 19.50 19.50

Start of Chimpanzee Research at Gombe by Jane Goodall, 50th Anniv. — A476

No. 2566, 2500sh: a, Black-and-white photograph of Goodall with chimpanzee. b, Goodall writing. c, Chimpanzees embracing.

No. 2567, 2500sh: a, Goodall shoveling dirt. b, Local people embracing. c, Goodall holding chimpanzee.

No. 2568, 4000sh, Goodall following chimpanzee in forest. No. 2569, 4000sh, Goodall holding camera, looking at chimpanzee. No. 2570, 4000sh, Goodall extending hand to three chimpanzees. No. 2571, 4000sh, Goodall in forest. No. 2572, 4000sh, Chimpanzee looking at ant-covered stick. No. 2573, 4000sh, Goodall holding binoculars, vert. No. 2574, 4000sh, Two chimpanzees, vert.

2010, Dec. 23 *Perf. 12*
Sheets of 3, #a-c
2566-2567 A476 Set of 2 20.50 20.50

Souvenir Sheets
2568-2574 A476 Set of 7 38.00 38.00

Souvenir Sheet

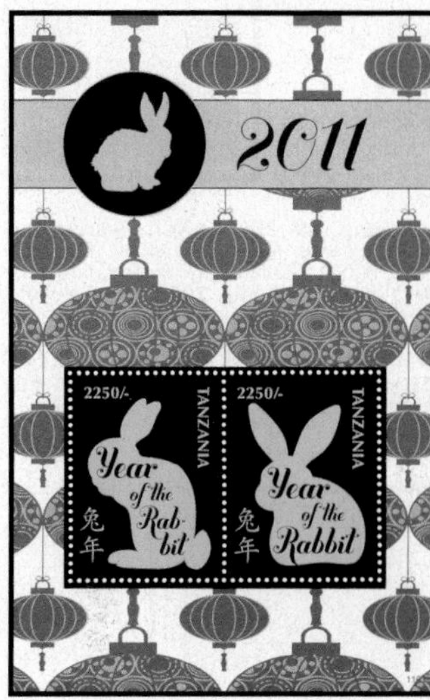

New Year 2011 (Year of the Rabbit) — A477

No. 2575: a, Rabbit standing on hind legs, word "Rabbit" hyphenated. b, Rabbit on all four legs, word "Rabbit" not hyphenated.

2010, Dec. 23
2575 A477 2250sh Sheet of 2, #a-b 6.25 6.25

Pan African Postal Union, 30th Anniv. A478

Emblem and: 400sh, Electronic money transfer. 500sh, Integrating physical mail into the digital world. 700sh, Track and trace of postal items.

600sh, Post office internet café service.

2010, Jan. 18 *Perf. 14½*
2576-2578 A478 Set of 3 2.40 2.40

Souvenir Sheet
2579 A478 600sh multi .90 .90

Wild Animals — A479

Designs: 400sh, Chimpanzees. 500sh, Lion and lioness, horiz. No. 2582, 600sh, Grant's red colobus monkeys, horiz. 700sh, Elephants. 800sh, Gnus, horiz. 1000sh, Waterbuck. 1800sh, Elephant looking for foliage. 2000sh, Zebras, horiz. 2500sh, Hunting dogs, horiz. 3000sh, Buffalo, horiz. 5000sh, Zebras and gazelles grazing, horiz.

No. 2591, 600sh, horiz.: a, Kirk's red colobus monkey. b, Lioness guarding her cubs. c, Udzungwa monkey. d, Female kongoni and juvenile. e, Female hippopotamus with juvenile. f, Leopard with cub.

No. 2592, 600sh, Male giraffe, horiz.

2010, Oct. 28 ***Perf. 14***

2580-2590 A479 Set of 11 25.00 25.00
2591 A479 600sh Sheet of 6, #a-f 5.00 5.00

Souvenir Sheet

2592 A479 600sh multi .80 .80

For surcharges, see Nos. 2714, 2832.

School of St. Jude, Arusha A480

Designs: No. 2593, 400sh, Teacher and three students. No. 2594, 400sh, Four students. 600sh, Students in cafeteria, three students with food bowls. 700sh, One student. 800sh, Students on bus.

2010, Oct. 28 ***Perf. 13x13¼***

2593-2597 A480 Set of 5 4.00 4.00
2597a Souvenir sheet of 4, #2594-2597 3.50 3.50

Wonders of Zanzibar A481

Designs: 400sh, Giant tortoise, Prison Island. 600sh, Red colobus monkey, Jozani Forest, vert. 700sh, Pemba flying fox. 800sh, Slave chambers, Manga Pwani.

No. 2602, 600sh: a, Ruins of Friday Mosque, Tumbatu Island. b, Beit el Mtoni. c, Anglican Cathedral. d, Beit el Jaib. e, Maruhubi Palace ruins. f, Old Fort.

No. 2603, 600sh, Chumbe Island Lighthouse, vert.

Perf. 14, 13¾x13½ (#2602)

2011, Feb. 22

2598-2601 A481 Set of 4 3.25 3.25
2602 A481 600sh Sheet of 6, #a-f 4.75 4.75

Souvenir Sheet

2603 A481 600sh multi .80 .80

No. 2602 contains six 35x25mm stamps. No. 2603 contains one 40x60mm stamp. For surcharge, see No. 2833.

Whales — A482

No. 2604: a, Orca (Killer whale). b, Sperm whale. c, Beluga whale. d, Humpback whale. e, Gray whale. f, Right whale.

3800sh, Blue whale.

2011, Mar. 31 ***Perf. 13 Syncopated***

2604 A482 1250sh Sheet of 6, #a-f, + label 10.00 10.00

Souvenir Sheet

Perf. 12

2605 A482 3800sh multi 5.00 5.00

Grasshoppers and Crickets — A483

Designs: No. 2606, 500sh, Truxalis species. No. 2607, 700sh, Common milkweed locust. No. 2608, 800sh, Common stick grasshopper. No. 2609, 900sh, Red locust.

No. 2610, 700sh: a, Migratory locust. b, Foam locust. c, Green milkweed locust. d, Edible grasshopper. e, Male cricket. f, Green bush cricket.

600sh, Elegant grasshopper.

2011, Apr. 15 ***Perf. 14***

2606-2609 A483 Set of 4 4.00 4.00
2610 A483 700sh Sheet of 6, #a-f 5.75 5.75

Souvenir Sheet

2611 A483 600sh multi .80 .80

Beatification of Pope John Paul II — A484

No. 2612 — Pope John Paul II: a, With children, country name at bottom. b, Greeting crowd, country name at bottom. c, As "b," country name at top. d, As "a," country name at top.

4000sh, Pope John Paul II, vert.

2011, May 16 ***Perf. 13 Syncopated***

2612 A484 1800sh Sheet of 4, #a-d 9.25 9.25

Souvenir Sheet

Perf. 12½

2613 A484 4000sh multi 5.25 5.25

No. 2613 contains one 38x51mm stamp.

Tourist Attractions A485

Designs: 500sh, Kibo Peak, Mt. Kilimanjaro. 700sh, Pemba Floating Island. 800sh, Giraffes in Serengeti National Park. 900sh, Lions in Serengeti National Park.

Serpentine Die Cut 14

2011, May 16 **Litho.**

Booklet Stamps
Self-Adhesive

2614 A485 500sh multi .65 .65
a. Booklet pane of 8 5.25
2615 A485 700sh multi .90 .90
a. Booklet pane of 8 7.25
2616 A485 800sh multi 1.00 1.00
a. Booklet pane of 8 8.00
2617 A485 900sh multi 1.25 1.25
a. Booklet pane of 8 10.00
Nos. 2614-2617 (4) 3.80 3.80

Traditional Grain Storage A486

Designs: No. 2618, 500sh, People and grain storage baskets. No. 2619, 700sh, Pole hanging grain storage. No. 2620, 800sh, Tree hanging grain storage. No. 2621, 900sh, Outdoor granary.

No. 2622: a, Covered granary on platform. b, Outdoor granaries, thatched roof. c, Corn (maize) granary. d, Granary container. e, Outdoor granary next to building. f, Indoor granary.

600sh, Outdoor grain storage (building on stilts).

2011, Aug. 25 **Litho.** ***Perf. 14***

2618-2621 A486 Set of 4 3.75 3.75
2622 A486 700sh Sheet of 6, 3a-f 5.25 5.25

Souvenir Sheet

2623 A486 600sh multi .75 .75

Flowers — A487

No. 2624: a, African foxglove. b, Bird of paradise. c, Water hyacinth. d, Torch lily.

3800sh, Fan aloe.

2011, Sept. 7 ***Perf. 12***

2624 A487 1500sh Sheet of 5, #2624a-2624c, 2 #2624d 9.25 9.25

Souvenir Sheet

Perf. 13¼

2625 A487 3800sh multi 4.75 4.75

No. 2625 contains one 44x44mm stamp.

Shells — A488

No. 2626: a, Telescopium telescopium. b, Tibia insulaechorab. c, Turbo sarmaticus. d, Bolinus cornutus.

3800sh, Oxymeris maculata, horiz.

2011, Sept. 7 ***Perf. 13¼x13***

2626 A488 1700sh Sheet of 4, #a-d 8.50 8.50

Souvenir Sheet

Perf. 13¼

2627 A488 3800sh multi 4.75 4.75

No. 2627 contains one 50x30mm stamp.

No. 611 Surcharged

No. 611B Surcharged

Methods and Perfs As Before

2011, Sept. 8

2627A A99 900sh on 25sh #611 — —
2627B A99 900sh on 30sh #611B — —

Sept. 11, 2001 Terrorist Attacks, 10th Anniv. — A489

No. 2628: a, American flag on Pentagon. b, Tribute in Light. c, World Trade Center.

4000sh, World Trade Center, diff.

2011, Sept. 11 ***Perf. 13 Syncopated***

2628 A489 2000sh Sheet of 3, #a-c 7.50 7.50

Souvenir Sheet

2629 A489 4000sh multi 5.00 5.00

Activities of World Vision A490

Inscriptions: 500sh, A child drawing safe and clean water. 800sh, Food security is one of our focus. 900sh, Children enjoy good health. 1000sh, Advocating for child's rights.

2011, Sept. 30 ***Perf. 14x13¼***

2630-2633 A490 Set of 4 3.75 3.75

Animals of Serengeti National Park — A491

No. 2634: a, Lion eating antelope. b, One hunting dog, horiz. c, Two hunting dogs, horiz. d, Two cheetahs.

1000sh, Zebras and gnus, horiz.

Perf. 13¼x13, 13x13¼x14x13 (#2634b, 2634c)

2011, Nov. 15

2634 A491 800sh Sheet of 4, #a-d 4.00 4.00

Souvenir Sheet

Perf. 13½x13

2635 A491 1000sh multi 1.25 1.25

No. 2635 contains one 45x35mm stamp.

Birds — A492

No. 2636, 1700sh: a, Senegal parrot. b, African gray parrot. c, Lilac-breasted roller. d, Southern masked weaver.

No. 2637, 1700sh: a, Pied crow. b, Ground woodpecker. c, Greater honeyguide. d, Bird with stripe above eye (misidentified as ground woodpecker).

No. 2638, 3800sh, Black-collared barbet. No. 2639, 3800sh, White-headed mousebird.

2011, Nov. 20 ***Perf. 13 Syncopated***

Sheets of 4, #a-d

2636-2637 A492 Set of 2 16.50 16.50

Souvenir Sheets

2638-2639 A492 Set of 2 9.25 9.25

Butterflies and Moths — A493

No. 2640, 1700sh: a, Fig eater butterfly. b, Green-veined emperor. c, Scarce forest emperor. d, Western blue charaxes.

No. 2641, 1700sh: a, Madagascar sunset moth. b, Angola white lady. c, Congo kuba cloth. d, Eggfly.

No. 2642, 3800sh, Mother of pearl. No. 2643, 3800sh, Monarch.

2011, Nov. 20 ***Perf. 12***

Sheets of 4, #a-d

2640-2641 A493 Set of 2 17.00 17.00

Souvenir Sheets

Perf. 12½

2642-2643 A493 Set of 2 9.50 9.50

Nos. 2642-2643 each contain one 51x38mm stamp.

Independence, 50th Anniv. — A494

No. 2644 — Tanzania flag and: a, Crowd celebrating complete independence. b, Students in Adult Education program. c, Presidents Julius K. Nyerere of Tanzania, Kenneth Kaunda of Zambia, Samora Machel of Mozambique. d, Pres. Nyerere and Edward Moringe Sokoine, 1982. e, Presidents Nyerere and Machel.

Tanzanian flag and: No. 2645, Pres. Nyerere and South African Pres. Nelson Mandela. No. 2646, Tanzania Pres. Jakaya Kikwete meeting with U. S. Pres. Barack Obama.

No. 2647, vert. — Tanzanian flag and: a, Pres. Nyerere, sepia-toned photograph. b, Pres. Al Haj Hassan Mwinyi. c, Pres. Mzee Benjamin William Mkapa. d, Pres. Kikwete. e, Vice-President Mzee Abeid Aman Karume. f, Prime Minister Mzee Rashid Mfaume Kawama. g, Prime Minister Edward Moringe Sokoine. h, Pres. Nyerere, color photograph.

No. 2648 — Tanzanian flag and: a, State House. b, Parliament of Tanzania, Dodoma. c, University of Dodoma. d, University of Dar es Salaam.

No. 2649 — Tanzanian flag and: a, 800sh, Pres. Nyerere and Cuban Pres. Fidel Castro. b, 800sh, Pres. Nyerere and Ghana Pres. Kwame Nkrumah. c, 900sh, Pres. Kikwete and Pres. Hu Jintao of People's Republic of China.

No. 2650, 900sh — Tanzanian flag and: a, Like #2645. b, Presidents Kikwete, Mwinyi and Mkapa.

2011, Dec. 9 ***Perf. 13x13¼***

2644 Horiz. strip of 5 3.25 3.25
a.-e. A494 500sh Any single .65 .65
2645 A494 800sh multi 1.00 1.00
2646 A494 900sh multi 1.25 1.25
a. Perf. 14x13¼x13x13¼ (#2649) 1.25 1.25
b. Perf. 13x13¼x14x13¼ (#2650) 1.25 1.25
Nos. 2644-2646 (3) 2.90 2.90

Perf. 13¼x13

2647 A494 700sh Sheet of 8, #a-h 7.25 7.25

Souvenir Sheets

Perf. 13x13¼

2648 A494 700sh Sheet of 4, #a-d 3.50 3.50
2649 A494 Sheet of 4, #2646a, 2649a-2649c 4.50 4.50
d. As "c," perf. 13x13¼x14x13¼ (#2650) 1.25 1.25

Perf. 13x13¼x14x13¼

2650 A494 900sh Sheet of 4, #2646b, 2649d, 2650a, 2650b 5.00 5.00
Nos. 2647-2650 (4) 20.25 20.25

Material Culture A495

Designs: No. 2651, 500sh, Beer pot with three mouths, cow-shaped water container. No. 2652, 700sh, Fiddle with calabash resonator. No. 2653, 800sh, Maasai beaded necklaces. No. 2654, 900sh, Container with lid, corn storage basket. No. 2655, 1000sh, Bamboo milk mugs, decorated calabash.

No. 2656, 800sh: a, Bao game. b, Grain storage. c, Cooking and storage pots. d, Drum on platform, wedding drums. e, Winnowing trays, drinking mug, storage basket. f, Fruit storage, dish cover.

2012, Mar. 15 ***Perf. 14x13½***

2651-2655 A495 Set of 5 5.00 5.00
2655a Souvenir sheet of 1 #2655 1.25 1.25

Miniature Sheet

2656 A495 800sh Sheet of 6, #a-f 6.25 6.25

Miniature Sheet

2012 Summer Olympics, London — A496

No. 2657: a, Basketball. b, Boxing. c, 3000-meter steeplechase. d, 5000-meter race.

2012, June 27 ***Perf. 14***

2657 A496 1300sh Sheet of 4, #a-d 6.50 6.50

Miniature Sheet

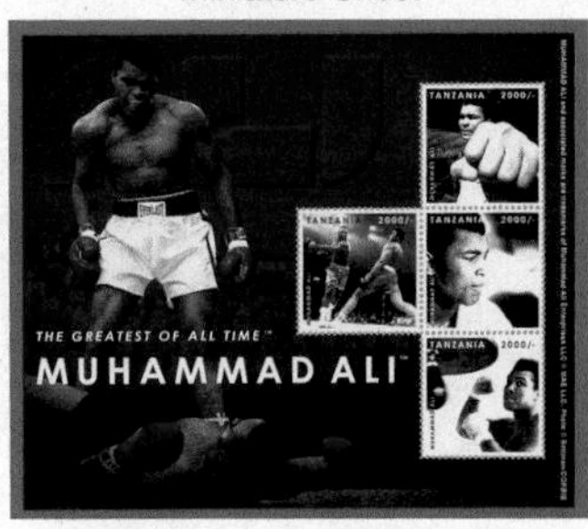

Muhammad Ali, Boxer — A497

No. 2658 — Ali: a, Showing fist. b, Dodging opponent's punch. c, In profile. d, Training with punching bag.

2012, Sept. 10 ***Perf. 12½***

2658 A497 2000sh Sheet of 4, #a-d 10.50 10.50

Miniature Sheet

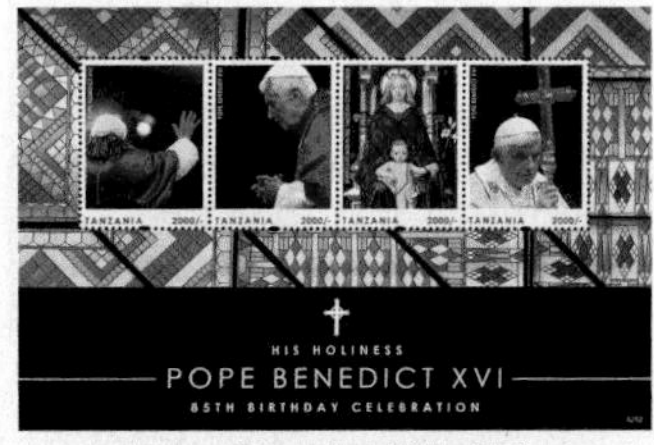

Pope Benedict XVI, 85th Birthday — A498

No. 2659: a, Pope Benedict XVI waving. b, Pope Benedict XVI praying. c, Madonna and Child stained-glass window, Vatican City Museum. d, Pope Benedict XVI with cross.

2012, Nov. 28 ***Perf. 13 Syncopated***

2659 A498 2000sh Sheet of 4, #a-d 10.00 10.00

Zanzibar Attractions A499

Designs: 500sh, New House of Representatives Building. 700sh, Four doors. No. 2662, 800sh, Ngalawa sailing off Jambian Coast, vert. 900sh, Huts.

No. 2664, 800sh: a, Zanzibar Pres. Ali Mohammed Shein harvesting cloves. b, Shein and First Vice-president Maalim Seif Sharif Hamad and others touring Zanzibar. c, Shein greeting students. d, Shein harvesting rice in paddy. e, Shein, Hamad and Second Vice-president Seif Ali Iddi. f, Shein and First Lady Mwanamwema Shein assisting in the separation of clove buds.

1000sh, Darajani Market.

Perf. 14x13¼, 13¼x14

2012, Apr. 26 **Litho.**

2660-2663 A499 Set of 4 3.75 3.75
2664 A499 800sh Sheet of 6, #a-f 6.25 6.25

Souvenir Sheet

2665 A499 1000sh multi 1.25 1.25

For surcharge, see No. 2830.

A500

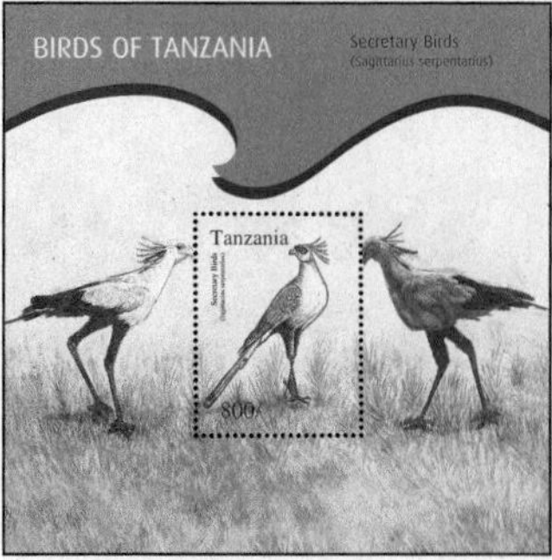

Birds — A501

No. 2666, 1000sh: a, Superb starling. b, Buffalo weaver. c, Quelea quelea. d, Bubalornis albirostris.

No. 2667, 1000sh: a, Malachite kingfisher. b, Gray-headed kingfisher. c, Woodland kingfisher. d, Pied kingfisher.

No. 2668, 1000sh: a, Verreaux's eagle owl. b, Augur buzzard. c, Red-tailed buzzard. d, Bateleur eagle. e, Adult Verreaux's eagle. f, Chanting goshawk. g, Immature Verreaux's eagle. h, Terathopius ecaudatus.

No. 2669, 800sh, Secretary bird. No. 2670, 800sh, Superb starling, horiz.

2012, July 10 **Litho.** ***Perf. 14***

Sheets of 4, #a-d

2666-2667 A500 Set of 2 10.50 10.50
2668 A500 1000sh Sheet of 8, #a-h 10.50 10.50

Souvenir Sheets

2669-2670 A501 Set of 2 2.00 2.00

Miniature Sheets

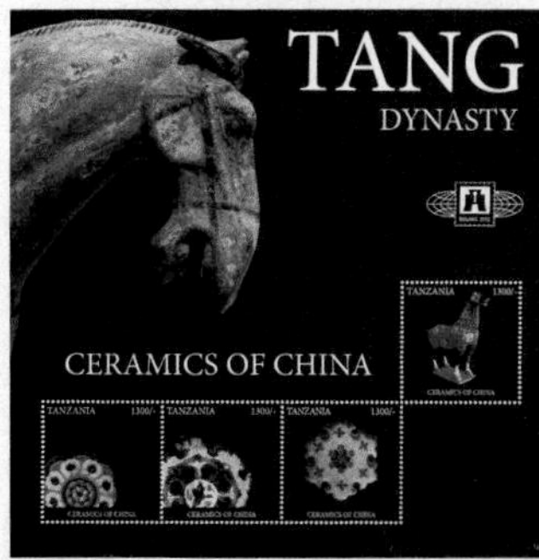

Tang Dynasty Ceramics — A502

Song Dynasty Ceramics — A503

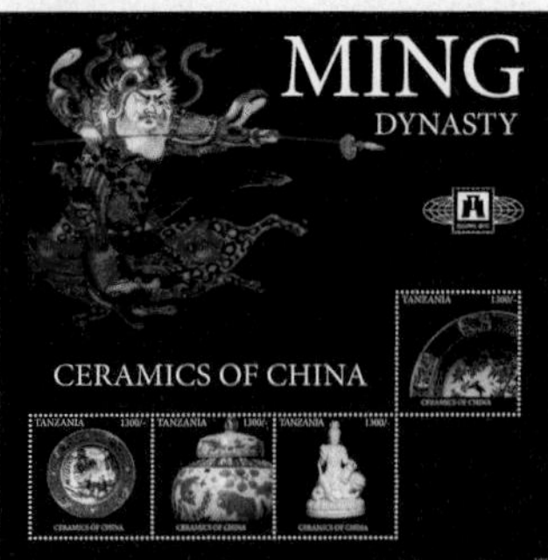

Ming Dynasty Ceramics — A504

Qing Dynasty Ceramics — A505

No. 2671: a, Plate with lotus flowers. b, Plate with bird. c, Hexagonal plate with upturned edges. d, Horse.

No. 2672: a, Pitcher with green glaze. b, Plate with bird, diff. c, Pitcher with gray glaze. d, Bowl.

No. 2673: a, Plate depicting building and people. b, Lidded bowl. c, Buddha. d, Plate with birds and flowers.

No. 2674: a, Plate with birds and flowers, diff. b, Plate with building and man on rock. c, Pitcher, diff. d, Round container.

2012, Oct. 10 Litho. *Perf. 13¾*

2671 A502 1300sh Sheet of 4, #a-d 6.50 6.50
2672 A503 1300sh Sheet of 4, #a-d 6.50 6.50
2673 A504 1300sh Sheet of 4, #a-d 6.50 6.50
2674 A505 1300sh Sheet of 4, #a-d 6.50 6.50
Nos. 2671-2674 (4) 26.00 26.00

2013 Beijing Intl. Stamp Exhibition.

Dragon — A506

Snake — A507

Snake A508

2012, Oct. 10 Litho. *Perf. 13¼x13*

2675 A506 350sh multi .45 .45
2676 A507 350sh multi .45 .45

Perf. 12

2677 A508 2000sh multi 2.50 2.50
Nos. 2675-2677 (3) 3.40 3.40

New Year 2013 (Year of the Snake). No. 2677 was printed in sheets of 4.

Chinese Character With Fish, Flowers and Butterfly A509

Chinese Character With Reindeer A510

Chinese Character With Cranes A511

Chinese Character With Birds and Flowers A512

Snake A513

2012, Oct. 10 Litho. *Perf. 13¼*

2678 Sheet of 20, #2678a-2678d, 16 #2678e 13.00 13.00
a. A509 500sh multi .65 .65
b. A510 500sh multi .65 .65
c. A511 500sh multi .65 .65
d. A512 500sh multi .65 .65
e. A513 500sh multi .65 .65

New Year 2013 (Year of the Snake).

Miniature Sheet

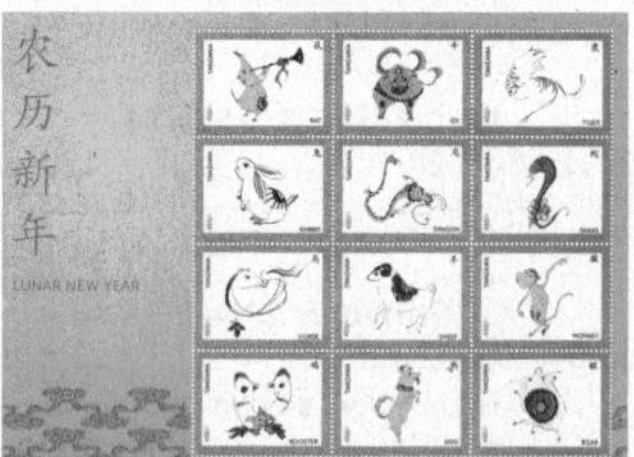

Chinese Zodiac Animals — A514

No. 2679: a, Rat. b, Ox. c, Tiger. d, Rabbit. e, Dragon. f, Snake. g, Horse. h, Sheep. i, Monkey. j, Rooster. k, Dog. l, Boar.

2012, Oct. 10 Litho. *Perf. 14*

2679 A514 450sh Sheet of 12, #a-l 6.75 6.75

Monkeys — A514a

No. 2679M: o, Iringa red colobus monkey eating. p, Black and white colobus in foliage. q, Iringa red colobus monkey on branch. r, Black and white colobus grasping tree. s, Iringa red colobus moneky in foliage facing left. t, Sanje crested mangabey monkey.

700sh, Zanzibar red colobus, vert.

2012, Oct. 15 Litho. *Perf. 14x13¾*

2679M A514a 800sh Sheet of 6, #o-t 6.00 6.00

Souvenir Sheet

2679N A514a 700sh multi .90 .90

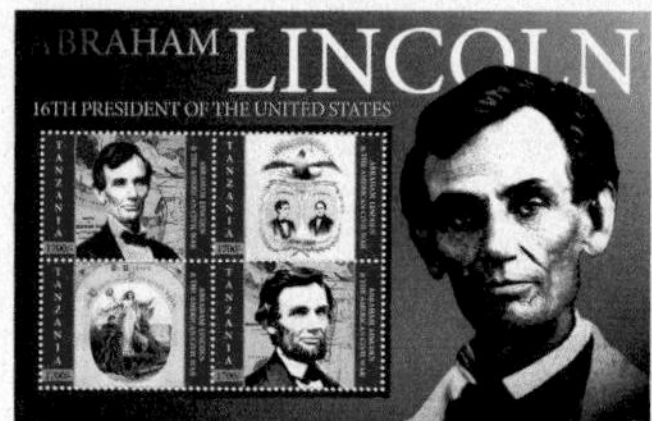

Pres. Abraham Lincoln (1809-65) — A515

No. 2680: a, Lincoln without beard. b, Presidential campaign poster of 1860 depicting Lincoln and Hannibal Hamlin. c, "In Defense of the Union and the Constitution" poster. d, Lincoln with beard.

5500sh, Lincoln with beard, diff.

2012, Nov. 28 Litho. *Perf. 12*

2680 A515 1700sh Sheet of 4, #a-d 8.50 8.50

Souvenir Sheet

Perf.

2681 A515 5500sh multi 7.00 7.00

No. 2681 contains one 43x33mm elliptical stamp.

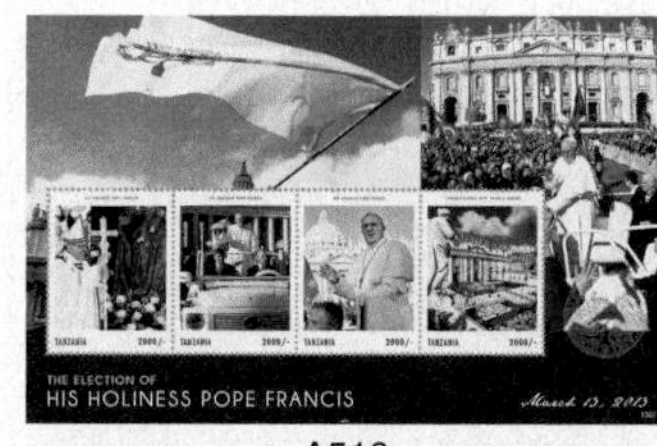

A516

Election of Pope Francis — A517

No. 2682: a, Pope Francis wearing miter, carrying crucifix. b, Pope Francis holding rail in Popemobile. c, Pope Francis with flag and St. Peter's Basilica in background. d, Crowd in St. Peter's Square.

2013, July 7 Litho. *Perf. 14*

2682 A516 2000sh Sheet of 4, #a-d 10.00 10.00

Litho., Margin Embossed With Foil Application

Souvenir Sheet

Imperf

2683 A517 13,000sh multi 16.50 16.50

Miniature Sheet

A518

Paintings of Flowers — A519

No. 2684: a, Roses, building, dragonfly, bird and nest. b, Begonias and butterfly at UL. c, Red flowers with long green leaves, mountain in background. d, White lilies. e, Passion flowers. f, Small pink flowers, mountains in background. g, Water lily, mosque in background. h, Hydrangea and butterfly at UR.

No. 2685: a, Hyacinths. b, Carnations. c, Four primrose plants, mountains in background. d, Tulips. e, Strelitzia. f, Two primrose plants. g, Lotuses. h, Pitcher plants and bird.

2013, July 7 Litho. *Perf. 12¾*

2684 A518 1200sh Sheet of 8, #a-h 12.00 12.00
2685 A519 1200sh Sheet of 8, #a-h 12.00 12.00

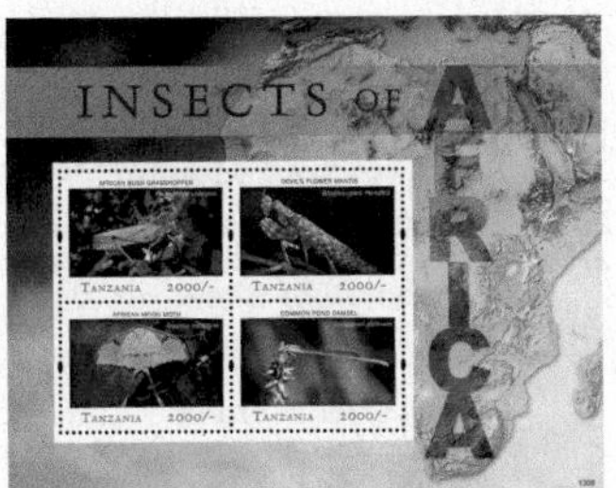

Insects — A520

No. 2686: a, African bush grasshopper. b, Devil's flower mantis. c, African moon moth. d, Common pond damsel.
5500sh, Giant African fruit beetle.

Perf. 13 Syncopated

2013, July 7 Litho.

2686 A520 2000sh Sheet of 4, #a-d 10.00 10.00

Souvenir Sheet

2687 A520 5500sh multi 7.00 7.00

African Animals — A521

No. 2688: a, Zebra. b, Rhinoceros. c, Hippopotami. d, African elephants.
5500sh, Giraffes.

2013, July 7 Litho. *Perf. 12*

2688 A521 2000sh Sheet of 4, #a-d 10.00 10.00

Souvenir Sheet

2689 A521 5500sh multi 7.00 7.00

No. 2689 contains one 30x50mm stamp.

Miniature Sheets

A522

Cats — A523

No. 2690: a, Gray tabby cat with gray green eyes looking up. b, Sleeping cat. c, Cat with brown eyes. d, Gray cat with gray green eyes looking down.
No. 2691: a, Cat in grass. b, Gray tabby sleeping. c, Brown tabby sleeping, black background. d, Two cats.

2013, Aug. 26 Litho. *Perf. 13¾*

2690 A522 2000sh Sheet of 4, #a-d 10.00 10.00

2691 A523 2000sh Sheet of 4, #a-d 10.00 10.00

Paintings by Dong Qichang (1555-1636) — A524

No. 2692: a, Valley with trees from *Eight Views of Autumn Moods* (leaf one). b, Trees and mountains from *Eight Views of Autumn Moods* (leaf four). c, Trees and body of water from *Eight Views of Autumn Moods* (leaf five). d, *Landscapes in the Manner of Old Masters.*
5500sh, *Wanluan Thatched Hall* (incorrectly inscribed *Eight Views of Autumn Moods.*), vert.

2013, Aug. 26 Litho. *Perf. 13¾*

2692 A524 2000sh Sheet of 4, #a-d 10.00 10.00

Souvenir Sheet

Perf. 12½

2693 A524 5500sh multi 7.00 7.00

China International Collection Expo 2013, Beijing. No. 2693 contains one 38x51mm stamp.

Fruit — A525

No. 2694: a, Watermelon. b, Calabashes. c, Passion fruit. d, Horned melons. e, Figs. f, Safous.
5500sh, Fig, safou, horned melon, passion fruit, calabash, watermelon, horiz.

2013, Aug. 26 Litho. *Perf. 13¾*

2694 A525 1500sh Sheet of 6, #a-f 11.50 11.50

Souvenir Sheet

Perf. 12

2695 A525 5500sh multi 7.00 7.00

No. 2695 contains one 80x30mm stamp.

Birth of Prince George of Cambridge — A526

No. 2696: a, Queen Elizabeth II holding Prince Charles. b, Princess Diana holding Prince William. c, Duchess of Cambridge holding Prince George. d, Duke and Duchess of Cambridge, Prince George.
8000sh, Prince George in arms of Duchess of Cambridge.

2013, Sept. 17 Litho. *Perf. 12½*

2696 A526 2000sh Sheet of 4, #a-d 10.00 10.00

Souvenir Sheet

Perf.

2697 A526 8000sh multi 10.00 10.00

No. 2697 contains one 38mm diameter stamp.

A527

Neslon Mandela (1918-2013), President of South Africa — A528

No. 2698 — Mandela: a, Wearing black and gray shirt. b, Wearing suit and tie, with arm raised. c, Wearing blue shirt with circular designs. d, In crowd, wearing blue shirt with circular designs. e, Wearing sports jersey, with arm raised. f, Holding dove.
No. 2699 — Mandela: a, Wearing blue shirt with circular designs, with arm raised. b, Wearing black and white shirt, with arm raised. c, Wearing green and black shirt. d, Wearing suit, vest and tie, fist clenched. e, Wearing suit and tie. f, Wearing jacket with Olympic rings.
No. 2700, 5500sh, Sepia-toned photograph of Mandela as young man, vert. No. 2701, 5500sh, Color photograph of Mandela wearing blue and white shirt, vert.

2013, Dec. 15 Litho. *Perf. 13¾*

2698 A527 1550sh Sheet of 6, #a-f 12.00 12.00

2699 A528 1550sh Sheet of 6, #a-f 12.00 12.00

Souvenir Sheets

Perf. 12½

2700-2701 A528 Set of 2 14.00 14.00

Nos. 2700-2701 each contain one 38x51mm stamp.

Zanzibar Tourism — A529

Designs: 600sh, Kizimkazi Mosque mihrab. No. 2703, 700sh, Bao game, horiz. 800sh, Wooden charpoys, horiz. 900sh, Giant tortoise, horiz.
No. 2706, 700sh: a, Tomb ruins, Mkumbuu. b, Stone pillars, Maruhubi Palace. c, Zanzibar red colobus monkey. d, Bao game, wooden chests, model boat. e, Crenellated walls of Palace Museum. f, Coconut crab on palm tree, Chumbe Island.
1600sh, Kibanda Beni, Forodhani Square, Stone Town, horiz.

Perf. 13¼x13, 13x13¼

2013, Apr. 26 Litho.

2702-2705 A529 Set of 4 3.75 3.75

Miniature Sheet

2706 A529 700sh Sheet of 6, #a-f 5.25 5.25

Souvenir Sheet

2707 A529 1600sh multi 2.00 2.00

Big Game Animals — A530

Designs: Nos. 2708a, 2709, Lioness. Nos. 2708b, 2709A, Elephants. Nos. 2708c, 2710, Buffalos. Nos. 2708d, 2710A, Leopard. Nos. 2708e, 2711, Rhinoceros.

2013, July 31 Litho. *Perf. 13x13¼*

2708 A530 1800sh Sheet of 5, #a-e 11.00 11.00

Souvenir Sheets

2709 A530 1600sh multi 2.00 2.00

2709A A530 1600sh multi 2.00 2.00

2710 A530 1600sh multi 2.00 2.00

2710A A530 1600sh multi 2.00 2.00

2711 A530 1600sh multi 2.00 2.00

Nos. 2709-2711 (5) 10.00 10.00

Miniature Sheet

Mao Zedong (1893-1976), Chinese Communist Leader — A531

Various photographs dated: a, 1949. b, 1952. c, 1954. d, 1959. e, 1961. f, 1965.

2013, Sept. 10 Litho. *Perf. 14*

2712 A531 350sh Sheet of 6, #a-f 2.60 2.60

No. 2511 Surcharged

No. 2580 Surcharged

Methods and Perfs As Before

2013, Aug. 1

2713 A449 500sh on 400sh #2511 — —

2714 A479 500sh on 400sh #2580 — —

Ceremonial Costumes A532

Designs: 600sh, Kuria lady from Mara. No. 2716, 700sh, Nyaturu woman. 800sh, Nyagatwa couple, vert. 900sh, Zarambo boy in Jando ceremony, vert.

No. 2719, 700sh, vert.: a, Mbunga woman. b, Makonde woman. c, Sukuma dancer. d, Haya Umwinyereko dancer. e, Kwele widow. f, Ngindo girl in Unyago ceremony.

1600sh, Manyema Kilua dancer.

Perf. 13x13¼, 13¼x13

2013, Nov. 30 Litho.

2715-2718 A532 Set of 4 3.75 3.75

Miniature Sheet

2719 A532 700sh Sheet of 6, #a-f 5.25 5.25

Souvenir Sheet

2720 A532 1600sh multi 2.00 2.00

Projects of World Vision — A533

Designs: 600sh, Child being weighed (Child's road to health). 800sh, Child tending farm animals (Child's well being, livelihood), horiz. 900sh, Mother breastfeeding child (Child's nutrition). 1000sh, Children at water pump (Water & sanitation), horiz.

2013, Dec. 20 Litho. *Perf. 14*

2721-2724 A533 Set of 4 4.25 4.25

2723a Souvenir sheet of 1 1.25 1.25

Reptiles — A534

No. 2725: a, Two-horned chameleon. b, Strange-nosed chameleon. c, Jackson's chameleon. d, Lined day gecko.

5500sh, Satanic leaf-tailed gecko.

2013, Dec. 31 Litho. *Perf. 12*

2725 A534 2000sh Sheet of 4, #a-d 10.00 10.00

Souvenir Sheet

Perf. 12¾

2726 A534 5500sh multi 7.00 7.00

No. 2726 contains one 51x38mm stamp.

Sunbirds — A535

No. 2727: a, Fraser's sunbird. b, Anchieta's sunbird. c, Collared sunbird. d, Olive sunbird.

5500sh, Nile Valley sunbird, horiz.

2013, Dec. 31 Litho. *Perf. 14*

2727 A535 2000sh Sheet of 4, #a-d 10.00 10.00

Souvenir Sheet

Perf. 12¾

2728 A535 5500sh multi 7.00 7.00

No. 2728 contains one 51x38mm stamp.

Dogs — A536

No. 2729, 2000sh: a, Scotch collie. b, Standard schnauzer. c, Sloughi. d, Saluki.

No. 2730, 2000sh: a, Taigan. b, Pyrenean mastiff. c, Thai ridgeback. d, Wirehaired pointing griffon.

No. 2731, 5500sh, Thai ridgeback, horiz. No. 2732, 5500sh, Siberian husky, horiz.

Perf. 14, 12 (#2730)

2013, Dec. 31 Litho.

Sheets of 4, #a-d

2729-2730 A536 Set of 2 20.00 20.00

Souvenir Sheets

Perf. 12¾

2731-2732 A536 Set of 2 14.00 14.00

Nos. 2731-2732 each contain one 51x38mm stamp.

Zanzibar Revolution, 50th Anniv. — A537

Designs: 500sh, Dr. Ali M. Shein, 7th President of Zanzibar. No. 2734, 700sh, Zanzibar Pres. Abeid A. Karume (1905-72) showing Tanzania Pres. Julius Nyerere model of development houses, horiz. 800sh, Pres. Karume with revolution commanders, 1964.

No. 2736 — Zanzibar Presidents: a, Aboud Jumbe Mwinyi (1920-2016). b, Ali Hassan Mwinyi. c, Idris A. Wakil (1925-2000). d, Dr. Salmin Amour Juma. e, Amani A. Karume. f, Shein.

No. 2737, 700sh — Zanzibar Vice-Presidents: a, Seif S. Hamad. b, Ambassador Seif Ali Iddi.

No. 2738, 1000sh, Zanzibar Mnazi Mmoja Hospital, horiz. No. 2738A, 1000sh, Zanzibar House of Representatives Building, horiz.

Perf. 13¼x14, 14x13¼

2014, Jan. 12 Litho.

2733-2735 A537 Set of 3 2.50 2.50

Miniature Sheet

2736 A537 600sh Sheet of 6, #a-f 4.50 4.50

Souvenir Sheets

2737 A537 700sh Sheet of 2, #a-b 1.75 1.75

2738 A537 1000sh multi 1.25 1.25

2738A A537 1000sh multi 1.25 1.25

Nos. 2736a-2736f, 2737a-2737b are not inscribed with the country name.

Orchids — A538

No. 2739, 2000sh: a, Anacamptis feinbruniae. b, Ophrys holosericea. c, Orchis boryi. d, Anacamptis caspia.

No. 2740, 2000sh: a, Bulbophyllum guttulatum. b, Orchis punctulata. c, Phaius wallichii. d, Vanilla phalaenopsis.

No. 2741, 6000sh, Dactylorhiza dinglensis. No. 2742, 6000sh, Orchis purpurea.

2014, Mar. 10 Litho. *Perf. 12x12½*

Sheets of 4, #a-d

2739-2740 A538 Set of 2 20.00 20.00

Souvenir Sheets

2741-2742 A538 Set of 2 15.00 15.00

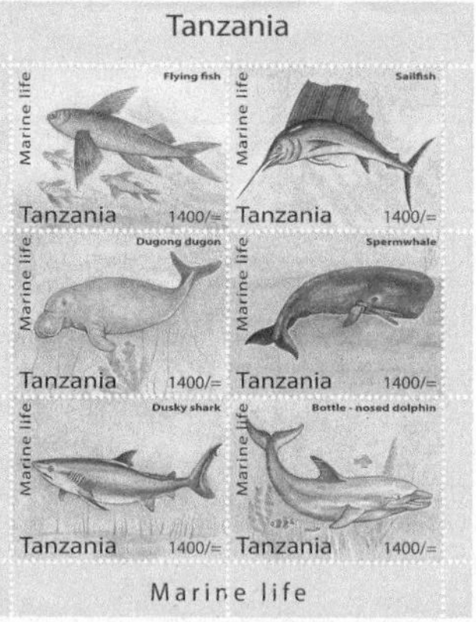

Marine Life — A539

No. 2743: a, Flying fish. b, Sailfish. c, Dugong dugon. d, Sperm whale. e, Dusky shark. f, Bottlenose dolphin.

No. 2744: a, Green sea turtle. b, Swimming crab. c, Smooth trunkfish. d, Sea star and sea whip. e, Lobster. f, Horse conch, lettered olives, chestnut cowries.

No. 2745: a, Swimming crab. b, Lined seahorse, c, Octopus. d, Lobster.

2014, Mar. 25 Litho. *Perf. 13¼*

Miniature Sheets

2743 A539 1400sh Sheet of 6, #a-f 10.50 10.50

2744 A539 1600sh Sheet of 6, #a-f 12.00 12.00

Perf. 14

2745 A539 1800sh Sheet of 4, #a-d 9.00 9.00

e. Souvenir sheet of 1 #2745c 2.25 2.25

Nos. 2743-2745 (3) 31.50 31.50

Farm Animals — A540

No. 2746, 2000sh: a, Cow. b, Pig. c, Duck. d, Dog.

No. 2747, 2000sh: a, Hen. b, Rooster. c, Chick. d, Turkey.

No. 2748, 3000sh: a, Goat. b, Sheep.

No. 2749, 3000sh: a, Donkey. b, Horse.

Perf. 13 Syncopated

2014, June 23 Litho.

Miniature Sheets of 4, #a-d

2746-2747 A540 Set of 2 19.50 19.50

Souvenir Sheets of 2, #a-b

2748-2749 A540 Set of 2 14.50 14.50

Tanzania Heritage Sites — A541

Designs: 600sh, Mbozi Iron Meteorite, Mbeya Region. No. 2751, 1400sh, No. 2754d, 1600sh, Palace Ruins, Songo Mnara and Kilwa Kisiwani, horiz. No. 2752, 1600sh, No. 2755, 1800sh, Old Laetoli Footprints, Ngorongoro Arusha, horiz. No. 2753, 1800sh, No. 2754f, 1600sh, Old Fort, Zanzibar Stone Town, horiz.

No. 2754, 1600sh, horiz.: a, Old Fort, Kilwa Kisiwani. b, Historic builiding, Bagamoyo. c, Tombs at Kaole Ruins, Bagamoyo. e, Isimila Stone Age Site, Iringa.

Perf. 14, 13¾ (#2754)

2014, Sept. 20 Litho.

2750-2753 A541 Set of 4 6.50 6.50

Miniature Sheet

2754 A541 1600sh Sheet of 6, #a-f 11.50 11.50

Souvenir Sheet

2755 A541 1800sh multi 2.25 2.25

Wildlife — A542

No. 2756: a, African elephant. b, Caracal. c, Cheetah. d, Zanzibar red colobus. e, Blue monkey. f, Gerenuk.

6000sh, Lions.

2015, June 15 Litho. *Perf. 13¾*

2756 A542 2000sh Sheet of 6, #a-f 11.00 11.00

Souvenir Sheet

2757 A542 6000sh multi 5.50 5.50

Ibises — A543

No. 2758: a, Glossy ibis in flight. b, Hadada ibis in flight. c, Olive ibis. d, Hadada ibis on ground. e, Glossy ibis in water.

No. 2759 — African sacred ibis: a, In flight. b, On ground.

2015, June 15 Litho. *Perf. 14*

2758 A543 2000sh Sheet of 5, #a-e 9.00 9.00

Souvenir Sheet

Perf. 12

2759 A543 3000sh Sheet of 2, 3a-b 5.50 5.50

Birds — A544

No. 2760: a, Fischer's lovebirds. b, Yellow-billed stork. c, Ruff. d, Secretary bird. e, African jacana. f, Black stork.

6000sh, Lilac-breasted roller.

2015, Sept. 2 Litho. *Perf. 11½x12*

2760 A544 2000sh Sheet of 6, #a-f 11.50 11.50

Souvenir Sheet

Perf. 12½

2761 A544 6000sh multi 5.50 5.50

No. 2761 contains one 31x31mm stamp.

Food and Agricultural Organization, 70th Anniv. — A545

No. 2762: a, Sugar cane field. b, Farmers herding buffalo. c, Corn. d, Ankole-Watusi cattle. e, Coffee beans. f, Tea field.
6000sh, Hand and seedling.

2015, Sept. 8 Litho. *Perf. 14*

2762 A545 2000sh Sheet of 6, #a-f 11.00 11.00

Souvenir Sheet

Perf. 12¾

2763 A545 6000sh multi 5.50 5.50

No. 2763 contains one 51x38mm stamp.

Christmas A546

Paintings by Titian: 2000sh, The Annunciation. 3000sh, Pesaro Madonna. 4000sh, Madonna of the Rabbit. 5000sh, The Annunciation, diff.

2015, Nov. 2 Litho. *Perf. 13¼*

2764-2767 A546 Set of 4 13.00 13.00

New Year 2016 (Year of the Monkey) — A547

No. 2768: a, Adult and juvenile monkeys. b, Man and monkey.

2016, Jan. 8 Litho. *Perf. 13¾*

2768 A547 800sh Horiz. pair, #a-b 1.50 1.50

Gray Crowned Crane — A548

No. 2769: a, Crane, black background. b, Head of crane. c, Crane facing right. d, Crane, water in background.
No. 2770 — Crane facing: a, Right. b, Left.

2016, Jan. 28 Litho. *Perf. 12*

2769 A548 2000sh Sheet of 4, #a-d 7.50 7.50

Souvenir Sheet

Perf. 12¾

2770 A548 3000sh Sheet of 2, #a-b 5.50 5.50

No. 2770 contains two 38x51mm stamps.

Birds — A549

No. 2771, 2000sh: a, Superb starling (35x35mm). b, Lilac-breasted roller (35x35mm). c, Crowned crane (35x70mm).
No. 2772, 2000sh: a, Lesser masked weaver (35x35mm). b, Southern yellow-billed hornbill (35x35mm). c, Saddle-billed stork (35x70mm).
No. 2773, 6000sh, Crowned lapwing. No. 2774, 6000sh, Lesser masked weaver, diff.

2016, Jan. 28 Litho. *Perf. 13¾*

Sheets of 3, #a-c

2771-2772 A549 Set of 2 11.00 11.00

Souvenir Sheets

Perf. 12½

2773-2774 A549 Set of 2 11.00 11.00

Nos. 2773-2774 each contain one 38x51mm stamp.

Frogs — A550

No. 2775, 2000sh: a, Argentine horned frog. b, Bumblebee poison frog. c, Blue poison dart frog. d, African bullfrog.
No. 2776, 2000sh: a, African bullfrog, diff. b, African dwarf bullfrog. c, Long-nosed horned frog. d, False tomato frog.
No. 2777, 6000sh, Red-eyed tree frog. No. 2778, 6000sh, Green-and-black poison dart frog.

2016, Jan. 28 Litho. *Perf. 13¾*

Miniature Sheets of 4, #a-d

2775-2776 A550 Set of 2 15.00 15.00

Souvenir Sheets

2777-2778 A550 Set of 2 11.00 11.00

Endangered Animals — A551

No. 2779, 2000sh: a, Greater bamboo lemur. b, Radiated tortoise. c, Dama gazelle. d, African wild dog.
No. 2780, 2000sh: a, Grévy's zebra. b, African penguin. c, Rothschild's giraffe. d, Western lowland gorilla.
No. 2781, 3000sh: a, Addax. b, Geometric tortoise.
No. 2782, 3000sh, a, Black rhinoceros. b, Mountain gorilla.

2016, Jan. 28 Litho. *Perf. 14*

Miniature Sheets of 4, #a-d

2779-2780 A551 Set of 2 15.00 15.00

Souvenir Sheets of 2, #a-b

2781-2782 A551 Set of 2 11.00 11.00

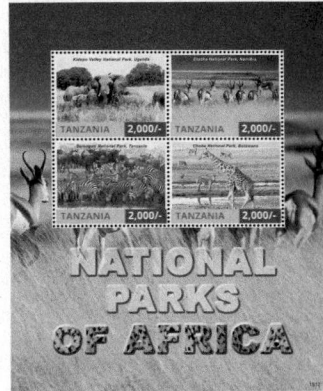

National Parks of Africa — A552

No. 2783, 2000sh — Wildlife in: a, Kidepo Valley National Park, Uganda. b, Etosha National Park, Namibia. c, Serengeti National Park, Tanzania. d, Chobe National Park, Botswana.
No. 2784, 2000sh — Landscapes from: a, Ahaggar National Park, Algeria. b, Lake Nakuru National Park, Kenya. c, Victoria Falls National Park, Zambia and Zimbabwe. d, Andringitra National Park, Madagascar.
No. 2785, 6000sh, Kruger National Park, South Africa. No. 2786, 6000sh, Queen Elizabeth National Park, Uganda.

2016, Jan. 28 Litho. *Perf. 14*

Miniature Sheets of 4, #a-d

2783-2784 A552 Set of 2 15.00 15.00

Souvenir Sheets

Perf. 12½

2785-2786 A552 Set of 2 11.00 11.00

Nos. 2785-2786 each contain one 51x38mm stamp.

Queen Elizabeth II, Longest-Reigning British Monarch — A553

No. 2787 — Queen Elizabeth II: a, Without hat. b, Wearing magenta hat. c, Wearing dark blue grey and white hat. d, Wearing lilac hat.
6000sh, Queen Elizabeth II and Duke of Cambridge, horiz.

2016, Feb. 20 Litho. *Perf. 14*

2787 A553 2000sh Sheet of 4, #a-d 7.50 7.50

Souvenir Sheet

Perf. 12

2788 A553 6000sh multi 5.50 5.50

No. 2788 contains one 50x30mm stamp.

Miniature Sheets

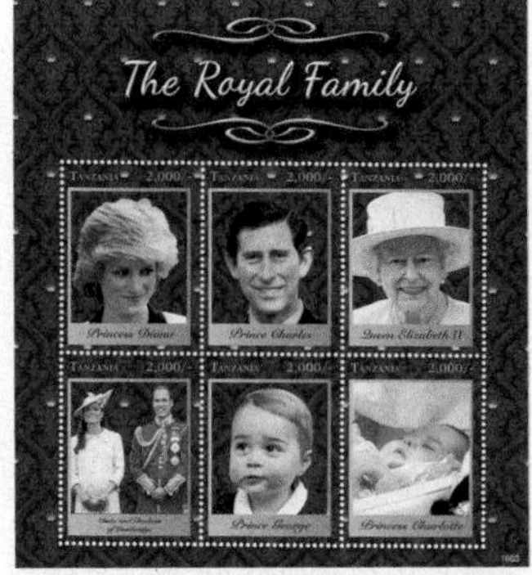

A554

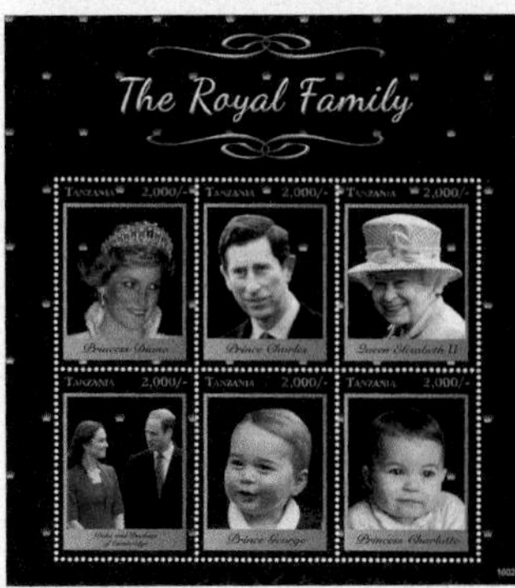

British Royal Family — A555

Nos. 2789 and 2790: a, Princess Diana (1961-97). b, Prince Charles. c, Queen Elizabeth II. d, Duke and Duchess of Cambridge. e, Prince George. f, Princess Charlotte.

2016, Feb. 20 Litho. *Perf. 14*

2789 A554 2000sh Sheet of 6, #a-f 11.00 11.00

2790 A555 2000sh Sheet of 6, #a-f 11.00 11.00

New York City Landmarks — A556

No. 2791: a, Grand Central Terminal. b, St. Patrick's Cathedral. c, Lion statue, New York City Public Library. d, Flatiron Building. e, Empire State Building. f, Statue of Liberty.
No. 2792, horiz. — Bow Bridge, Central Park, in: a, Spring (lamppost in foreground). b, Summer (building in background). c, Autumn (colored leaves in trees). d, Winter (snow scene).
10,000sh, Lower Manhattan skyline and Brooklyn Bridge, horiz.

2016, May 2 Litho. *Perf. 12x11½*

2791 A556 2150sh Sheet of 6, #a-f 12.00 12.00

Perf. 12½

2792 A556 2500sh Sheet of 4, #a-d 9.25 9.25

Souvenir Sheet

Perf. 12½x12

2793 A556 10,000sh multi 9.25 9.25

2016 World Stamp Show, New York. No. 2793 contains one 80x30mm stamp.

Queen Elizabeth II, 90th Birthday — A557

No. 2794: a, Prince Charles. b, Queen Elizabeth II. c, Prince George. d, Prince William.

No. 2795 — Queen Elizabeth II with: a, Prince Philip (30x40mm). b, Duke and Duchess of Cambridge, Prince George and Princess Charlotte (60x40mm).

2016, July 29 Litho. *Perf. 14*

2794 A557 2500sh Sheet of 4, #a-d 9.25 9.25

Souvenir Sheet

2795 A557 5000sh Sheet of 2, #a-b 9.25 9.25

A558

New Year 2017 (Year of the Rooster) A559

No. 2796 — Painted clay sculptures of rooster facing: a, Left. b, Right.

6500sh, Chick.

2017, Feb. 8 Litho. *Perf. 14*

2796 A558 4300sh Pair, #a-b 7.75 7.75

Perf.

2797 A559 6500sh multi 6.00 6.00

No. 2796 was printed in sheets containing two pairs. No. 2797 was printed in sheets of 2.

A560

Monkey King — A561

Various depictions of Chinese opera's Monkey King, as shown.

2017, Feb. 8 Litho. *Perf. 12½*

2798 A560 4300sh Sheet of 3, #a-c 11.50 11.50

2799 A561 4300sh Sheet of 4, #a-d 15.50 15.50

A562

Inauguration of Pres. Donald Trump — A563

No. 2800: a, Pres. Trump and Pres. Barack Obama (60x40mm). b, Donald Trump, Jr. (30x40mm). c, Ivanka Trump Kushner (30x40mm). d, Eric Trump (30x40mm). e, Tiffany Trump (30x40mm). f, Barron Trump (30x40mm). g, Melania Trump (30x40mm).

No. 2801: a, Pres. Trump, with wife, Melania, and son, Barron in Inaugural Parade. b, Trump family, Vice-President Mike Pence and wife, Karen, at Liberty Ball. c, Presidents Trump and Obama with wives.

2017, Apr. 14 Litho. *Perf. 14*

2800 A562 3000sh Sheet of 7, #a-g 19.00 19.00

Souvenir Sheet

2801 A563 4300sh Sheet of 3, #a-c 11.50 11.50

Miniature Sheets

A564

Pres. John F. Kennedy (1917-63) — A565

No. 2802 — Kennedy: a, Speaking at inauguration ceremony (60x40mm). b, As infant, bright blue panel (30x40mm). c, As child, white panel (30x40mm). d, Wearing naval uniform, scarlet panel (30x40mm). e, On wedding day, white panel (30x40mm). f, With wife, Jacqueline, and children, bright blue panel (30x40mm).

No. 2803 — Kennedy: a, Speaking on telephone, scarlet, white and bright blue panel. b, Signing document, scarlet panel. c, Speaking on telephone, white panel. d, At desk, bright blue panel.

2017, June 26 Litho. *Perf. 14*

2802 A564 3000sh Sheet of 6, #a-f 16.00 16.00

2803 A565 4000sh Sheet of 4, #a-d 14.50 14.50

A566

Princess Diana (1961-97) — A567

No. 2804 — Princess Diana: a, Holding child in Africa. b, With two boys in Asia. c, Holding head of girl in Asia. d, At Red Cross table in Asia. e, With children in South America. f, Holding girl in Australia.

No. 2805 — Princess Diana: a, Wearing maroon hat. b, Wearing headscarf. c, Wearing white hat.

2017, June 26 Litho. *Perf. 14*

2804 A566 3000sh Sheet of 6, #a-f 16.00 16.00

Souvenir Sheet

Perf. 12

2805 A567 4300sh Sheet of 3, #a-c 11.50 11.50

Lions Clubs International, Cent. — A568

No. 2806 — Lions Clubs International emblem and: a, 3000sh, Hands of adult and child. b, 3000sh, Leaf and raindrop. c, 4500sh, Wheat. d, 4500sh, Eye.

No. 2807, vert. — Lions Clubs International emblem, hands, leaf, wheat and eye with frame color of: a, 3000sh, Yellow. b, 6000sh, Deep Ultramarine.

2017, Dec. 17 Litho. *Perf. 13¾*

2806 A568 Sheet of 4, #a-d 13.50 13.50

Souvenir Sheet

Perf. 12½

2807 A568 Sheet of 2, #a-b 8.00 8.00

No. 2807 contains two 38x51mm stamps.

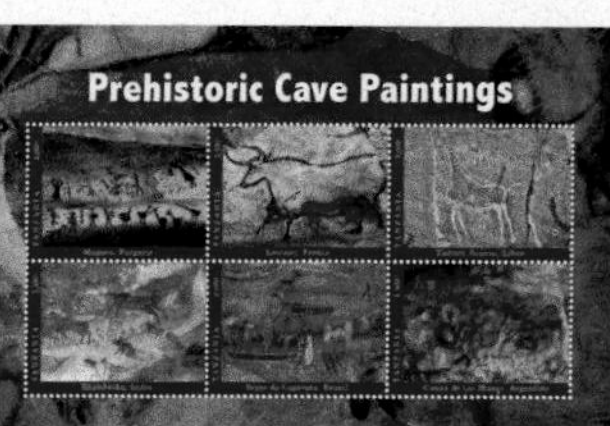

Prehistoric Cave Paintings — A569

No. 2808 — Cave painting from: a, 1500sh, Cueva de los Manos, Argentina. b, 2000sh, Serra da Capivara, Brazil. c, 2500sh, Bhimbetka, India. d, 3000sh, Tadrart Acacus, Libya. e, 3500sh, Lascaux, France. f, 4000sh, Magura, Bulgaria.

No. 2809, 3000sh, Kondoa Irangi, Tanzania, vert. 8500sh, Altamira, Spain.

2017, Dec. 17 Litho. *Perf. 14*

2808 A569 Sheet of 6, #a-f 15.00 15.00

Souvenir Sheets

Perf. 12½

2809 A569 3000sh multi 2.75 2.75

2810 A569 8500sh multi 7.75 7.75

No. 2809 contains one 38x51mm stamp. No. 2810 contains one 51x38mm stamp.

Giraffes — A570

No. 2811: a, 3000sh, Rothschild's giraffes. b, 4000sh, Reticulated giraffe, looking forwar. c, 4500sh, Reticulated giraffe, looking right. d, 5000sh, Masai giraffe.

No. 2812, horiz.: a, 3500sh, Masai giraffe, body facing left. b, 4000sh, Rothschild's giraffes. c, 4500sh, Masai giraffe, body facing forward.

2017, Dec. 17 Litho. *Perf. 14*

2811 A570 Sheet of 4, #a-d 15.00 15.00

Souvenir Sheet

Perf. 12

2812 A570 Sheet of 3, #a-c 11.00 11.00

Miniature Sheets

Cheetahs — A571

No. 2813 — Various photographs of cheetahs: a, 1000sh. b, 2000sh. c, 3000sh. d, 4000sh. e, 5000sh. f, 6000sh.

No. 2814 — Various photographs of cheetahs: a, 1500sh (40x30mm). b, 2500sh (40x30mm). c, 3500sh (40x30mm). d, 4500sh (40x30mm). e, 5500sh (40x60mm).

2017, Dec. 17 Litho. *Perf. 14*

2813 A571 Sheet of 6, #a-f 19.00 19.00

2814 A571 Sheet of 5, #a-e 15.50 15.50

African Wildlife — A572

No. 2815: a, 3000sh, Flamboyant, by Grant Wetherill (30x40mm). b, 3000sh, King of the World, by Wetherill (30x40mm). c, 3000sh, Elefante, by Wetherill (30x40mm). d, 3500sh, Lesser flamingos (60x40mm). e, 3500sh, Lion (60x40mm). f, 3500sh, African bush elephant (60x40mm).

No. 2816, vert.: a, 4500sh, Dottie, by Wetherill. b, 6500sh, Masai giraffe.

2017, Dec. 17 Litho. *Perf. 14*
2815 A572 Sheet of 6, #a-f 17.50 17.50

Souvenir Sheet
Perf. 12½

2816 A572 Sheet of 2, #a-b 9.75 9.75

No. 2816 contains two 38x51mm stamps.

Souvenir Sheets

Elvis Presley (1935-77) — A573

Inscriptions: No. 2817, 6500sh, First post-Army recording session. No. 2818, 6500sh, Earns first-degree black belt. No. 2819, 6500sh, Signs contract with Colonel Tom Parker, vert. No. 2820, 6500sh, Sells 100 millionth record, vert.

2017, Dec. 17 Litho. *Perf. 12½*
2817-2820 A573 Set of 4 23.00 23.00

New Year 2018 (Year of the Dog) — A574

No. 2821 — Wild canines: a, 2000sh, Dingo. b, 2000sh, Side-striped jackal. c, 3000sh, Gray wolf. d, 3000sh, Maned wolf.

No. 2822 — Wild canines: a, 2000sh, Western coyote. b, 2000sh, Black-backed jackal. c, 3000sh, African wild dog. d, 3000sh, Dhole.

2017, Dec. 17 Litho. *Perf. 14*
Sheets of 4, #a-d
2821-2822 A574 Set of 2 18.00 18.00

Reign of Aga Khan IV, 60th Anniv. A576

Inscriptions: No. 2826, 600sh, Coastal Rural Support Programme. No. 2826A, 600sh; No. 2826Ef, 1600sh, Early Childhood Development. No. 2826B, 600sh; No. 2826Eg, 1600sh, Graduates at Aga Khan University. No. 2826C, 600sh; No. 2826Eh, 1600sh, Restoration of Old Dispensary in Zanzibar. No. 2826D, 600sh; No. 2826Ei, 1600sh, Contributing to the Health Sector.

1400sh, Emblem, vert.

2017, Oct. 11 Litho. *Perf. 14½*
2826-2826D A576 Set of 5 2.75 2.75
2826E A576 1600sh Sheet of 4, #f-i 5.75 5.75

Souvenir Sheet

2827 A576 1400sh blue green 1.25 1.25

Miniature Sheet

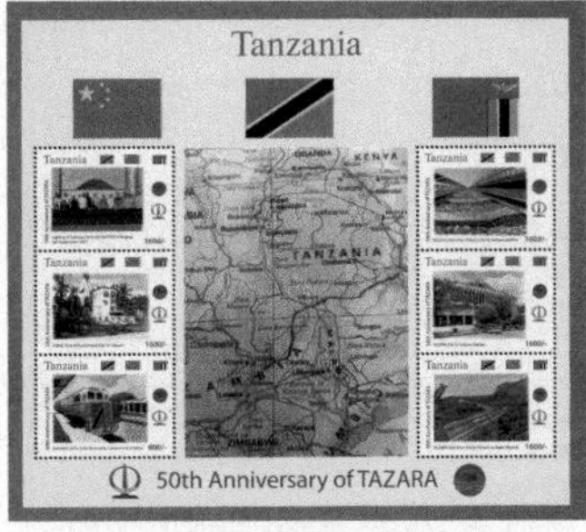

Tanzania-Zambia Railway Authority, 50th Anniv. — A577

No. 2828: a, 600sh, Handover of train donated by the government of China. b, 1600sh, Signing of contract to build TAZARA railway, Beijing, 1967. c, 1600sh, TAZARA train in Dar es Salaam Station, track tie with Chinese inscription. d, 1600sh, China Civil Engineering Construction Corporation, East African Limited Building, Dar es Salaam. e, 1600sh, TAZARA Station in Dar es Salaam. f, 1600sh, TAZARA train from Dar es Salaam to Kapiri Mposhi, Zambia.

2017, Dec. 31 Litho. *Perf. 14*
2828 A577 Sheet of 6, #a-f 7.75 7.75

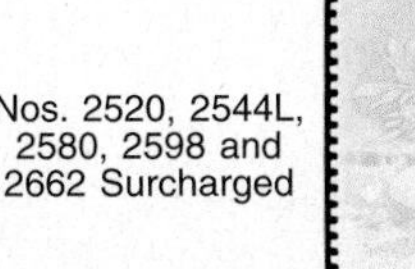

Nos. 2520, 2544L, 2580, 2598 and 2662 Surcharged

Methods and Perfs. As Before

2018 ?
2829 A451 1400sh on 700sh #2520 — —
2830 A499 1400sh on 800sh #2662 — —
2831 A459b 1400sh on 400sh #2544L — —
2832 A479 1600sh on 400sh #2580 — —
2833 A481 1600sh on 400sh #2598 — —

Location of surcharge varies.

No. 2544N Surcharged Like No. 2829

Methods and Perfs. As Before

2019 ?
2834 A459b 1400sh on 700sh #2544N — —

SEMI-POSTAL STAMPS

Natl. Solidarity Walk — SP1

1988, July 1 Litho. *Perf. 14½*
B1 SP1 2sh +1sh Flag, crowd .70 .70
B2 SP1 3sh +1sh Map, Pres. Mwinyi .70 .70

Souvenir Sheet

B3 SP1 50sh +1sh Flag, Pres. Mwinyi 1.75 1.75

Surtax for Chama Cha Mapinduzi party activities.

Natl. Solidarity Walk — SP2

1989, July 1 Litho. *Perf. 14½*
B4 SP2 5sh +1sh Party flag .45 .45
B5 SP2 10sh +1sh Pres. Mwinyi, walk .45 .45

Souvenir Sheet

B6 SP2 50sh +1sh Pres. Mwinyi 1.40 1.40

Natl. Solidarity Walk SP3

Designs: 4sh + 1sh, Pres. Mwinyi marching with crowd. 9sh + 1sh, Crowd around party flag. 13sh + 1sh, Pres. Mwinyi. 30sh + 1sh, Pres. Mwinyi planting tree. No. B11, Pres. Mwinyi sorting cloves. No. B12, Handshake across map, vert.

1991-92 Litho. *Perf. 13½*
B7 SP3 4sh +1sh multi ('92) .75 .75
B8 SP3 9sh +1sh multicolored 1.00 1.00
B9 SP3 13sh +1sh multicolored 1.00 1.00
B10 SP3 30sh +1sh multi ('92) 1.75 1.75
Nos. B7-B10 (4) 4.50 4.50

Souvenir Sheets
Perf. 12½

B11 SP3 50sh +1sh multicolored 3.00 3.00
B12 SP3 50sh +1sh multicolored 2.40 2.40

Issued: Nos. B8-B9, 7/6/90. Nos. B7, B10, 7/5/91.

POSTAGE DUE STAMPS

D1

Perf. 13¾x14
1978, July 31 Litho. Unwmk.
J1 D1 5c red .75 *1.00*
J2 D1 10c green .75 *1.00*
J3 D1 20c dark blue .75 *1.00*
J4 D1 30c reddish brown .75 *1.00*
J5 D1 40c bright rose lilac .75 *1.00*
J6 D1 1sh orange 1.25 *2.25*
Nos. J1-J6 (6) 5.00 7.25

1967, Jan. 3 *Perf. 14x13½*
J1a D1 5c red .35 *3.00*
J2a D1 10c green .35 *3.00*
J3a D1 20c dark blue .55 *5.25*
J4a D1 30c reddish brown .90 *7.50*
J5a D1 40c bright rose lilac 1.25 *10.50*
J6a D1 1sh orange 3.25 *22.50*
Nos. J1a-J6a (6) 6.65 51.75

1969-71 *Perf. 14x15*
J1b D1 5c red .70 *3.00*
J2b D1 10c green .70 *3.00*
J3b D1 20c dark blue 1.50 *5.25*
J4b D1 30c reddish brown 2.10 *7.50*
J5b D1 40c bright rose lilac 2.75 *10.50*
J6b D1 1sh orange ('71) 7.25 *22.50*
Nos. J1b-J6b (6) 15.00 51.75

1973, Dec. 12 *Perf. 15*
J1c D1 5c red .40 *3.25*
J2c D1 10c green .40 *3.25*
J3c D1 20c dark blue .60 *6.25*
J4c D1 30c reddish brown .90 *9.50*
J5c D1 40c bright rose lilac 1.25 *13.00*
J6c D1 1sh orange 3.00 *32.50*
Nos. J1c-J6c (6) 6.55 67.75

1984? *Perf. 14¾x14*
J1d D1 5c red brown — —
J2d D1 10c green — —
J4d D1 30c reddish brown — —

Additional stamps of this type with this perforation have been reported. The editors would like to examine any examples.

D2

1990 Litho. *Perf. 15x14*
J7 D2 50c dark green .85 .85
J8 D2 80c bright blue .85 .85
J9 D2 1sh orange brown .85 .85
J10 D2 2sh light olive green .85 .85
J11 D2 3sh purple .85 .85
J12 D2 5sh gray .85 .85
J13 D2 10sh brown .85 .85
J14 D2 20sh bister .85 .85
Nos. J7-J14 (8) 6.80 6.80

OFFICIAL STAMPS

Nos. 5-9, 11, 13 and 16 Overprinted: "OFFICIAL"
Perf. 14x14½, 14½x14
1965, Dec. 9 Photo. Unwmk.
Size: 21x17½mm, 17½x21mm

O1 A2 5c orange & ultra .25 .25
O2 A2 10c multicolored .25 .25
O3 A3 15c grn bl, brn & buff .25 .25
O4 A2 20c blue & brown .25 .25
O5 A3 30c black & red brn .25 .25
O6 A2 50c yellow grn & blk .25 .25

Perf. 14½
Size: 41½x25

O7 A2 1sh multicolored .30 .25
O8 A2 5sh bl, brt grn & red brn 1.50 1.00
Nos. O1-O8 (8) 3.30 2.75

Overprint size: 17mm on 5c, 10c, 20c, 50c. 14mm on 15c, 30c. 29x3½mm on 1sh, 5sh.

The overprint was also applied in 1967 in Dar es Salaam to 50c, 1sh and 5sh. Size: 29x3mm.

Nos. 19-23, 25, 27 and 30 Overprinted

Fish in Natural Colors
Size: 21x17½mm
Overprint Litho., 17mm Wide

1967, Dec. 9 Photo. *Perf. 14x14½*
O9 A4 5c black & citron .50 1.25
O10 A4 10c brown & olive .50 .60
O11 A4 15c brown & blue .50 .40
O12 A4 20c brown & dk blue grn .50 .40
O13 A4 30c black & yel grn .50 .40
O14 A4 50c black & dull bl grn .50 1.00

Perf. 14½
Size: 41x25mm
Overprint 29mm Wide

O15 A4 1sh brown & multi 1.00 *2.00*
O16 A4 5sh black & blue grn 4.00 *8.00*
Nos. O9-O16 (8) 8.00 14.05

Overprint Typo., 17½mm Wide

1970-73
O9a A4 5c black & citron .55 .55
O10a A4 10c brown & olive .55 .55
O12a A4 20c brn & dk bl grn .55 .55

No.	Type	Description	Unused	Used
O13a	A4	30c blk & yel grn	.80	.55
O13B	A4	40c multicolored ('73)		
		Nos. O9a-O13a (4)	2.45	2.20

The overprint was also applied in 1973 to 15c, 50c, 1sh (28mm wide), and 5sh.

Nos. 35-36, 38, 40-41, 43-47 Overprinted

a

b

1973, Dec. 10 Photo. *Perf. 14½x14*

No.	Type	Description	Unused	Used
O17	A5(a)	5c multicolored	1.10	*4.00*
O18	A5(a)	10c multicolored	1.40	.70
O19	A5(a)	20c multicolored	1.50	.70
O20	A5(a)	40c multicolored	2.25	.70
O21	A5(a)	50c multicolored	2.25	.70
O22	A5(a)	70c multicolored	2.25	.70
		Perf. 14½		
O23	A6(b)	1sh multicolored	3.25	.80
O24	A6(b)	1.50sh multicolored	3.75	*4.00*
O25	A6(b)	2.50sh multicolored	5.50	*6.00*
O26	A6(b)	5sh multicolored	7.50	*10.00*
		Nos. O17-O26 (10)	30.75	28.30

A larger overprint (17½mm wide instead of 14½mm) was applied locally to 10c, 20c, 40c, and 50c.

Provisional use of some values for regular postage is known.

Nos. 161-171 Overprinted

1980, Oct. 1 *Perf. 14*

No.	Type	Description	Unused	Used
O27	A21	10c multicolored	.70	.70
O28	A21	20c multicolored	.70	.70
O29	A21	40c multicolored	.70	.70
O30	A21	50c multicolored	.70	.70
O31	A21	75c multicolored	.70	.70
O32	A21	80c multicolored	.70	.70
		Perf. 14½		
O33	A21	1sh multicolored	.70	.70
O33A	A21	1.50sh multicolored		
O34	A21	2sh multicolored	1.40	1.40
O35	A21	3sh multicolored	1.90	1.90
O36	A21	5sh multicolored	3.25	3.25
		Nos. O27-O33,O34-O36 (10)	11.45	11.45

Overprint measures 13mm on Nos. O33-O36; reads up or down.

Nos. 606-614 Inscribed "OFFICIAL"

1990-91 Litho. *Perf. 14*

No.	Type	Description	Unused	Used
O37	A99	5sh multi	.60	.60
O38	A99	9sh multi	.60	.60
O39	A99	13sh multi	.60	.60
O40	A99	15sh multi	.60	.60
O41	A99	20sh multi	.90	.90
O42	A99	25sh multi	1.00	1.00
O42A	A99	30sh multi ('91)	1.40	1.40
O43	A99	40sh multi	1.75	1.75
O44	A99	70sh multi	3.00	3.00
O45	A99	100sh multi	4.50	4.50
		Nos. O37-O45 (10)	14.95	14.95

Inscription on Nos. O37-O42A is 15½mm long. Insription on Nos. O43-O45 is 19mm long.

Nos. 1565, 1566, 1568, 1570, 1571, and 1572 Overprinted

1997 (?) Litho. *Perf. 14½x15*

No.	Type	Description	Unused	Used
O47	A262	100sh multi	—	—
O48	A262	140sh multi	—	—
O49	A262	200sh multi	—	—
O50	A262	260sh multi	—	—
O51	A262	300sh multi	—	—
O52	A262	380sh multi	—	—

The editors suspect there are additional stamps in this set, and would like to examine any examples.

TETE

'tāt-ə

LOCATION — In southeastern Africa between Nyasaland and Southern Rhodesia

GOVT. — A district of the Portuguese East Africa Colony

AREA — 46,600 sq. mi. (approx.)

POP. — 367,000 (approx.)

CAPITAL — Tete

This district was formerly a part of Zambezia. Stamps of Mozambique replaced those of Tete. See Mozambique.

100 Centavos = 1 Escudo

Vasco da Gama Issue of Various Portuguese Colonies Surcharged

1913 Unwmk. *Perf. 12½, 16*

On Stamps of Macao

No.	Type	Description	Unused	Used
1	CD20	¼c on ½a bl grn	4.00	*5.00*
2	CD21	½c on 1a red	4.00	*2.10*
3	CD22	1c on 2a red vio	4.00	*2.10*
4	CD23	2½c on 4a yel grn	4.00	*2.10*
5	CD24	5c on 8a dk blue	4.00	*2.10*
6	CD25	7½c on 12a vio brn	5.50	*3.00*
7	CD26	10c on 16a bis brn	4.00	*2.25*
8	CD27	15c on 24a bister	4.00	*2.25*
		Nos. 1-8 (8)	33.50	*20.90*

On Stamps of Portuguese Africa

No.	Type	Description	Unused	Used
9	CD20	¼c on 2½r bl grn	4.00	*2.10*
10	CD21	½c on 5r red	4.00	*2.10*
11	CD22	1c on 10r red vio	4.00	*2.10*
12	CD23	2½c on 25r yel grn	4.00	*2.10*
13	CD24	5c on 50r dk blue	4.00	*2.10*
14	CD25	7½c on 75r vio brn	5.00	*3.00*
15	CD26	10c on 100r bis brn	4.00	*2.25*
16	CD27	15c on 150r bister	4.00	*2.25*
		Nos. 9-16 (8)	33.00	*18.00*

On Stamps of Timor

No.	Type	Description	Unused	Used
17	CD20	¼c on ½a bl grn	4.00	*2.10*
18	CD21	½c on 1a red	4.00	*2.10*
19	CD22	1c on 2a red vio	4.00	*2.10*
a.		Inverted overprint	60.00	60.00
20	CD23	2½c on 4a yel grn	4.00	*2.10*
21	CD24	5c on 8a dk blue	4.00	*2.10*
22	CD25	7½c on 12a vio brn	5.50	*3.00*
23	CD26	10c on 16a bis brn	4.00	*2.25*
24	CD27	15c on 24a bister	4.00	*2.25*
		Nos. 17-24 (8)	33.50	*18.00*
		Nos. 1-24 (24)	100.00	*56.90*

Common Design Types pictured following the introduction.

Ceres — A1

1914 Typo. *Perf. 15x14*

Name and Value in Black

No.	Type	Description	Unused	Used
25	A1	¼c olive brn	2.00	*2.25*
26	A1	½c black	2.00	*2.25*
27	A1	1c blue grn	2.00	*2.25*
28	A1	1½c lilac brn	2.00	*2.25*
29	A1	2c carmine	2.00	*2.25*
30	A1	2½c light vio	2.00	*2.25*
31	A1	5c deep blue	2.00	*2.25*
32	A1	7½c yel brn	4.00	*3.25*
33	A1	8c slate	4.00	*3.25*
34	A1	10c org brn	4.00	*6.00*
35	A1	15c plum	4.00	*6.00*
36	A1	20c yel green	6.00	*6.00*
37	A1	30c brn, *green*	6.00	*6.00*
38	A1	40c brn, *pink*	8.00	*9.00*
39	A1	50c org, *salmon*	10.00	*10.00*
40	A1	1e grn, *blue*	12.00	*15.00*
		Nos. 25-40 (16)	72.00	*80.25*

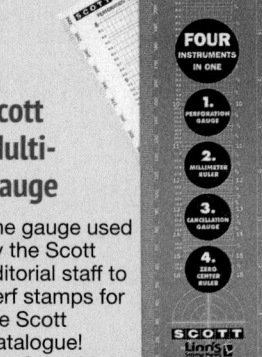

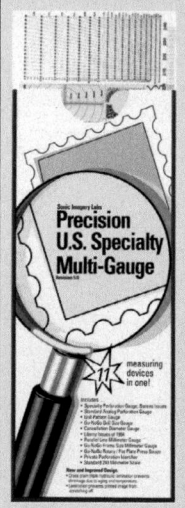

Vols. 6A-6B Number Additions, Deletions & Changes

Number in 2020 Catalogue	Number in 2021 Catalogue
Singapore	
deleted	1481a
new	1488b
new	1488c
new	1498e
new	1631j
new	1639h
new	1639i
Straits Settlements	
new	N13c
Switzerland	
new	232b
new	J4f
J6b	J6d
J8b	J8d
J9b	J9d
J22	J14Bc
new	J14Bd
new	J15b
new	J16b
new	J17b
new	J18b
new	J19b
new	J20b
new	J21a
new	J21h
new	J21k
new	J23a
new	J23b
new	J23c
new	J23d
new	J23e
new	J23h
new	J23k
new	J24a
new	J24b
new	J24c
new	J24d
new	J24e
new	J24h
new	J24k
new	J25a
new	J25b
new	J25c
new	J25d
new	J25e
new	J25h
new	J25k
new	J26a
new	J26b
new	J26c
new	J26e
new	J26h
new	J26k
new	J27a
new	J27b
new	J27c
new	J27e
new	J27h
new	J27k
new	J28j
new	J28k
new	J29a
new	J30a
new	J31a
new	J32a
new	J33a
new	J34a
Thailand	
new	19a-19d
new	40b-40e
new	50d
Timor	
new	1c
new	2c
new	7a
new	10a
new	21a
new	21b
new	44a
new	94a
new	103b
new	103c
new	122a
new	123a
new	185a
new	P3c
new	P4b
Uruguay	
new	1674a
new	1675b
new	1675c
new	1675d
new	1748Ab
Western Ukraine	
new	9a

Illustrated Identifier

This section pictures stamps or parts of stamp designs that will help identify postage stamps that do not have English words on them.

Many of the symbols that identify stamps of countries are shown here as well as typical examples of their stamps.

See the Index and Identifier for stamps with inscriptions such as "sen," "posta," "Baja Porto," "Helvetia," "K.S.A.", etc.

1. HEADS, PICTURES AND NUMERALS

GREAT BRITAIN

Great Britain stamps never show the country name, but, except for postage dues, show a picture of the reigning monarch.

Victoria

Edward VII George V Edward VIII

George VI

Elizabeth II

Some George VI and Elizabeth II stamps are surcharged in annas, new paisa or rupees. These are listed under Oman.

Silhouette (sometimes facing right, generally at the top of stamp)

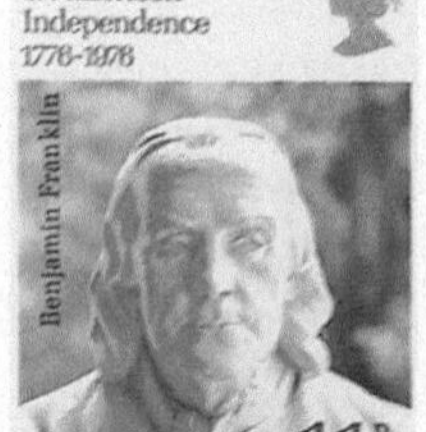

The silhouette indicates this is a British stamp. It is not a U.S. stamp.

VICTORIA

Queen Victoria

INDIA

Other stamps of India show this portrait of Queen Victoria and the words "Service" (or "Postage") and "Annas."

AUSTRIA

YUGOSLAVIA

(Also BOSNIA & HERZEGOVINA if imperf.)

BOSNIA & HERZEGOVINA

Denominations also appear in top corners instead of bottom corners.

HUNGARY

Another stamp has posthorn facing left

BRAZIL

AUSTRALIA

Kangaroo and Emu

GERMANY

Mecklenburg-Vorpommern

SWITZERLAND

PALAU

2. ORIENTAL INSCRIPTIONS

CHINA

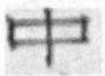

Any stamp with this one character is from China (Imperial, Republic or People's Republic). This character appears in a four-character overprint on stamps of Manchukuo. These stamps are local provisionals, which are unlisted. Other overprinted Manchukuo stamps show this character, but have more than four characters in the overprints. These are listed in People's Republic of China.

Some Chinese stamps show the Sun.

Most stamps of Republic of China show this series of characters.

Stamps with the China character and this character are from People's Republic of China. 人

中国人民邮政
T.34.(5-1)

Calligraphic form of People's Republic of China

(一)	(二)	(三)	(四)	(五)	(六)
1	2	3	4	5	6
(七)	(八)	(九)	(十)	(一十)	(二十)
7	8	9	10	11	12

Chinese stamps without China character

REPUBLIC OF CHINA

PEOPLE'S REPUBLIC OF CHINA

Mao Tse-tung

MANCHUKUO

Temple Emperor Pu-Yi

The first 3 characters are common to many Manchukuo stamps.

The last 3 characters are common to other Manchukuo stamps.

Orchid Crest

Manchukuo stamp without these elements

JAPAN

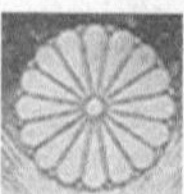

Chrysanthemum Crest Country Name

Japanese stamps without these elements

The number of characters in the center and the design of dragons on the sides will vary.

RYUKYU ISLANDS

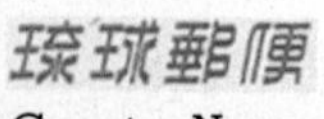

Country Name

PHILIPPINES (Japanese Occupation)

Country Name

NETHERLANDS INDIES (Japanese Occupation)

Indicates Japanese Occupation

Java / Sumatra

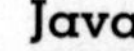

Country Name Country Name

Moluccas, Celebes and South Borneo

Country Name

NORTH BORNEO (Japanese Occupation)

Indicates Japanese Occupation Country Name

MALAYA (Japanese Occupation)

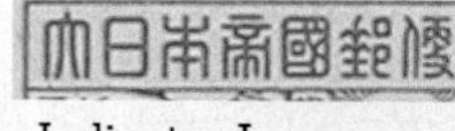

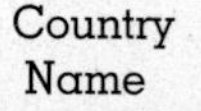

Indicates Japanese Occupation Country Name

BURMA

Union of Myanmar

Union of Myanmar

(Japanese Occupation)

Indicates Japanese Occupation

Country Name

Other Burma Japanese Occupation stamps without these elements

Burmese Script

KOREA

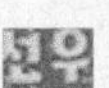

These two characters, in any order, are common to stamps from the Republic of Korea (South Korea) or of the People's Democratic Republic of Korea (North Korea).

This series of four characters can be found on the stamps of both Koreas. Most stamps of the Democratic People's Republic of Korea (North Korea) have just this inscription.

Indicates Republic of Korea (South Korea)

South Korean postage stamps issed after 1952 do not show currency expressed in Latin letters. Stamps wiith " HW," "HWAN," "WON," "WN," "W" or "W" with two lines through it, if not illustrated in listings of stamps before this date, are revenues. North Korean postage stamps do not have currency expressed in Latin letters.

Yin Yang appears on some stamps.

South Korean stamps show Yin Yang and starting in 1966, 'KOREA" in Latin letters

Example of South Korean stamps lacking Latin text, Yin Yang and standard Korean text of country name. North Korean stamps never show Yin Yang and starting in 1976 are inscribed "DPRK" or "DPR KOREA" in Latin letters.

THAILAND

Country Name

King Chulalongkorn

King Prajadhipok and Chao P'ya Chakri

3. CENTRAL AND EASTERN ASIAN INSCRIPTIONS

INDIA - FEUDATORY STATES

Alwar

Bhor

Bundi

Similar stamps come with different designs in corners and differently drawn daggers (at center of circle).

Dhar

Duttia

Faridkot

Hyderabad

Similar stamps exist with different central design which is inscribed "Postage" or "Post & Receipt."

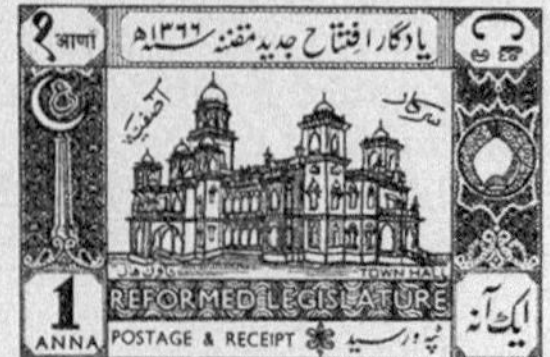

Indore

Jammu & Kashmir

Text varies.

Jasdan

Jhalawar

Kotah

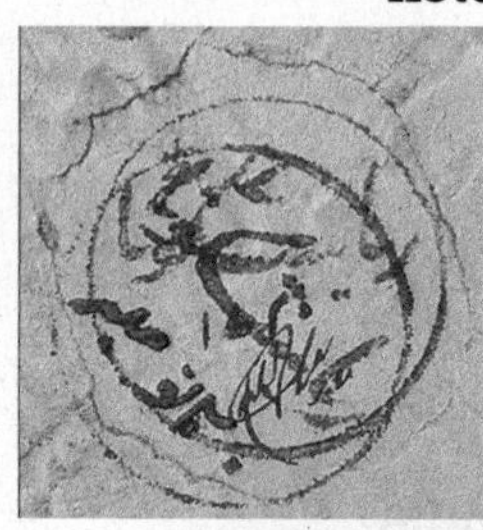

Size and text varies

Nandgaon

Nowanuggur

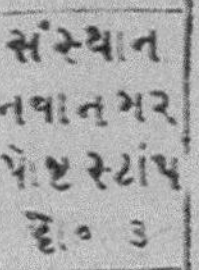

Poonch

Similar stamps exist in various sizes with different text

Rajasthan

Rajpeepla

Soruth

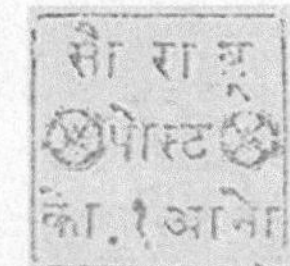

Tonk

BANGLADESH

Country Name

NEPAL

Similar stamps are smaller, have squares in upper corners and have five or nine characters in central bottom panel.

TANNU TUVA

ISRAEL

GEORGIA

This inscription is found on other pictorial stamps.

Country Name

ARMENIA

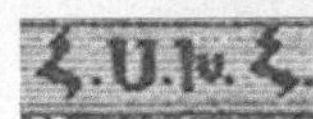

The four characters are found somewhere on pictorial stamps. On some stamps only the middle two are found.

4. AFRICAN INSCRIPTIONS

ETHIOPIA

5. ARABIC INSCRIPTIONS

١ ٢ ٣ ٤ ٥
1 2 3 4 5

٦ ٧ ٨ ٩ ٠
6 7 8 9 0

AFGHANISTAN

Many early Afghanistan stamps show Tiger's head, many of these have ornaments protruding from outer ring, others show inscriptions in black.

Arabic Script

Crest of King Amanullah

Mosque Gate & Crossed Cannons

The four characters are found somewhere on pictorial stamps. On some stamps only the middle two are found.

BAHRAIN

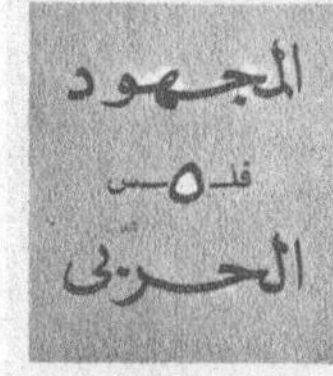

EGYPT

Postage

IRAN

Country Name

Royal Crown

Lion with Sword

Symbol

Emblem

IRAQ

JORDAN

LEBANON

Similar types have denominations at top and slightly different design.

LIBYA

Country Name in various styles

Other Libya stamps show Eagle and Shield (head facing either direction) or Red, White and Black Shield (with or without eagle in center).

Without Country Name

SAUDI ARABIA

Tughra (Central design)

Palm Tree and Swords

SYRIA

Arab Government Issues

THRACE

YEMEN

PAKISTAN

PAKISTAN - BAHAWALPUR

Country Name in top panel, star and crescent

TURKEY

Star & Crescent is a device found on many Turkish stamps, but is also found on stamps from other Arabic areas (see Pakistan-Bahawalpur)

Tughra (similar tughras can be found on stamps of Turkey in Asia, Afghanistan and Saudi Arabia)

Mohammed V

Mustafa Kemal

Plane, Star and Crescent

TURKEY IN ASIA

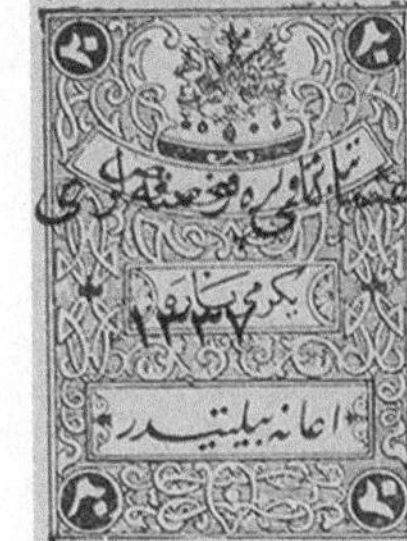

Other Turkey in Asia pictorials show star & crescent. Other stamps show tughra shown under Turkey.

6. GREEK INSCRIPTIONS

GREECE

Country Name in various styles (Some Crete stamps overprinted with the Greece country name are listed in Crete.)

Lepta

Drachma Drachmas Lepton

Abbreviated Country Name

Other forms of Country Name

No country name

CRETE

Country Name

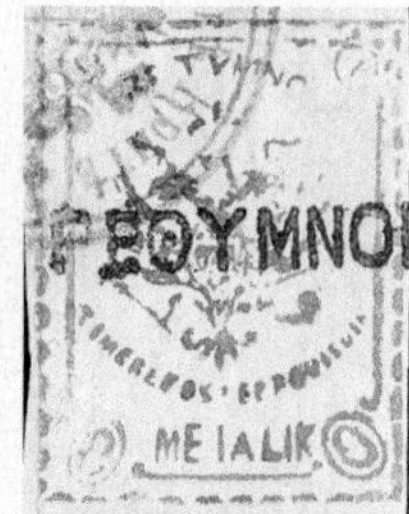

Crete stamps with a surcharge that have the year "1922" are listed under Greece.

EPIRUS

Similar stamps have text above the eagle.

IONIAN IS.

7. CYRILLIC INSCRIPTIONS

RUSSIA

Postage Stamp

Imperial Eagle

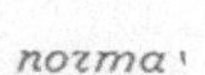
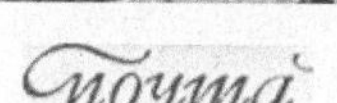

Postage in various styles

Abbreviation for Kopeck

Abbreviation for Ruble

Russia

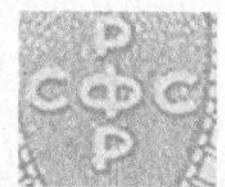

Abbreviation for Russian Soviet Federated Socialist Republic RSFSR stamps were overprinted (see below)

Abbreviation for Union of Soviet Socialist Republics

This item is footnoted in Latvia

RUSSIA - Army of the North

"OKCA"

RUSSIA - Wenden

RUSSIAN OFFICES IN THE TURKISH EMPIRE

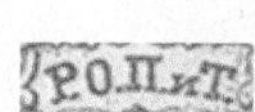

These letters appear on other stamps of the Russian offices.

The unoverprinted version of this stamp and a similar stamp were overprinted by various countries (see below).

ARMENIA

BELARUS

FAR EASTERN REPUBLIC

Country Name

FINLAND

Circles and Dots on stamps similar to Imperial Russia issues

SOUTH RUSSIA

Country Name

BATUM

Forms of Country Name

TRANSCAUCASIAN FEDERATED REPUBLICS

Abbreviation for Country Name

KAZAKHSTAN

ҚАЗАҚСТАН

KYRGYZSTAN

КЫРГЫЗСТАН

КЫРГЫЗСТАН Country Name

ROMANIA

TAJIKISTAN

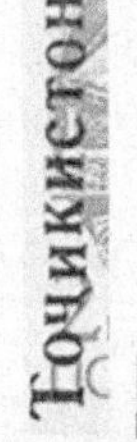

Country Name & Abbreviation

UKRAINE

Пошта України Україні Україні Україні

Country Name in various forms

The trident appears on many stamps, usually as an overprint.

УС РР

Abbreviation for Ukrainian Soviet Socialist Republic

WESTERN UKRAINE

Abbreviation for Country Name

AZERBAIJAN

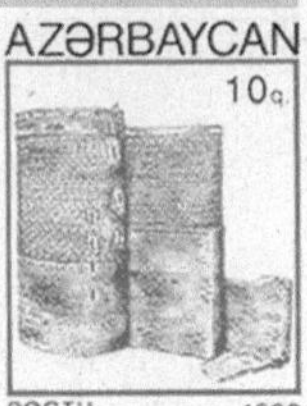

AZƏRBAYCAN

Country Name

А.С.С.Р. Abbreviation for Azerbaijan Soviet Socialist Republic

MONTENEGRO

ЦРНЕГОРЕ

ЦРНА ГОРА

Country Name in various forms

ЦРГОРЕ

Abbreviation for country name

No country name (A similar Montenegro stamp without country name has same vignette.)

SERBIA

СРПСКА СРБИЈА

Country Name in various forms

СРП. К.С.

Abbreviation for country name

No country name

MACEDONIA

МАКЕДОНИЈА

МАКЕДОНИЈА

Country Name

МАКЕДОНСКИ
11 Октомври 1997

Different form of Country Name

SERBIA & MONTENEGRO

YUGOSLAVIA

ЈУГОСЛАВИЈА

Showing country name

No Country Name

BOSNIA & HERZEGOVINA (Serb Administration)

РЕПУБЛИКА СРПСКА

Country Name

РЕПУБЛИКЕ СРПСКЕ

Different form of Country Name

No Country Name

BULGARIA

Country Name Postage

Stotinka

Stotinki (plural) Abbreviation for Stotinki

Country Name in various forms and styles

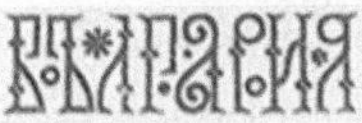

H P България

No country name

Abbreviation for Lev, leva

MONGOLIA

Country name in one word Tugrik in Cyrillic

Country name in two words Mung in Cyrillic

Mung in Mongolian

Tugrik in Mongolian

Arms

No Country Name

INDEX AND IDENTIFIER

All page numbers shown are those in this Volume 6A.

Postage stamps that do not have English words on them are shown in the Illustrated Identifier.

INDEX TO ADVERTISERS
2021 VOLUME 6A

2021
VOLUME 6A
DEALER DIRECTORY
YELLOW PAGE LISTINGS

This section of your Scott Catalogue contains advertisements to help you conveniently find what you need, when you need it...!

Appraisals

COLONIAL STAMP COMPANY
5757 Wilshire Blvd. PH #8
Los Angeles, CA 90036
PH: 323-933-9435
FAX: 323-939-9930
info@colonialstamps.com
www.colonialstamps.com

DR. ROBERT FRIEDMAN & SONS STAMP & COIN BUYING CENTER
2029 W. 75th St.
Woodridge, IL 60517
PH: 800-588-8100
FAX: 630-985-1588
stampcollections@drbobstamps.com
www.drbobfriedmanstamps.com

Auctions

COLONIAL STAMP COMPANY
5757 Wilshire Blvd. PH #8
Los Angeles, CA 90036
PH: 323-933-9435
FAX: 323-939-9930
info@colonialstamps.com
www.colonialstamps.com

DUTCH COUNTRY AUCTIONS
The Stamp Center
4115 Concord Pike
Wilmington, DE 19803
PH: 302-478-8740
FAX: 302-478-8779
auctions@dutchcountryauctions.com
www.dutchcountryauctions.com

British Commonwealth

COLLECTORS EXCHANGE ORLANDO STAMP SHOP
1814A Edgewater Drive
Orlando, FL 32804
PH: 407-620-0908
PH: 407-947-8603
FAX: 407-730-2131
jlatter@cfl.rr.com
www.OrlandoStampShop.com

ARON R. HALBERSTAM PHILATELISTS, LTD.
PO Box 150168
Van Brunt Station
Brooklyn, NY 11215-0168
PH: 718-788-3978
arh@arhstamps.com
www.arhstamps.com

ROY'S STAMPS
PO Box 28001
600 Ontario Street
St. Catharines, ON
CANADA L2N 7P8
Phone: 905-934-8377
Email: roystamp@cogeco.ca

THE STAMP ACT
PO Box 1136
Belmont, CA 94002
PH: 650-703-2342
thestampact@sbcglobal.net

British Commonwealth

British Empire
1840 - 1935

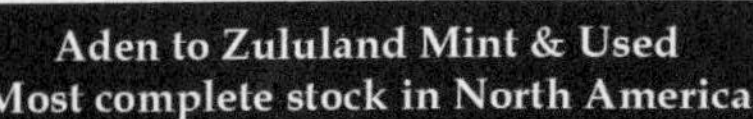

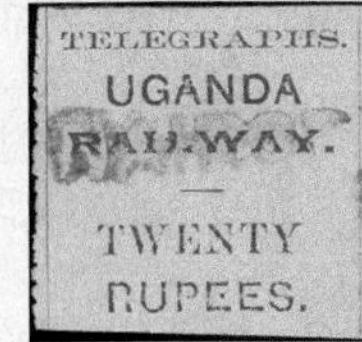

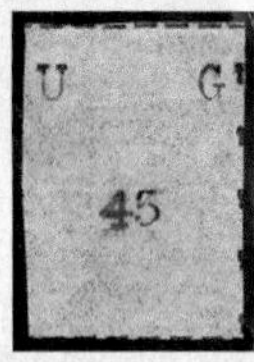

For over 40 years, we have built some of the world's finest collections. Our expert ***Want List Services*** can do the same for you. Over 50 volumes filled with singles, sets and rare stamps, we are sure we have what you need. We welcome your Want Lists in Scott or Stanley Gibbons numbers.

Put our expertise to work for you today!
You'll be glad you did!

Colonial Stamp Company

"Rarity and quality are remembered ...long after price is forgotten."

5757 Wilshire Blvd., Penthouse 8
Los Angeles, CA 90036 USA
Tel: +1 (323) 933-9435 Fax: +1 (323) 939-9930

Email: *Info@ColonialStamps.com*
www.ColonialStamps.com

Ask for your free Public Auction Catalogue today!

PayPal MasterCard VISA American Express DISCOVER

Buying

DR. ROBERT FRIEDMAN & SONS STAMP & COIN BUYING CENTER
2029 W. 75th St.
Woodridge, IL 60517
PH: 800-588-8100
FAX: 630-985-1588
stampcollections@drbobstamps.com
www.drbobfriedmanstamps.com

Canada

CANADA STAMP FINDER
PO Box 92591
Brampton, ON L6W 4R1
PH: 514-238-5751
Toll Free in North America:
877-412-3106
FAX: 323-315-2635
canadastampfinder@gmail.com
www.canadastampfinder.com

ROY'S STAMPS
PO Box 28001
600 Ontario Street
St. Catharines, ON
CANADA L2N 7P8
Phone: 905-934-8377
Email: roystamp@cogeco.ca

Collections

DR. ROBERT FRIEDMAN & SONS STAMP & COIN BUYING CENTER
2029 W. 75th St.
Woodridge, IL 60517
PH: 800-588-8100
FAX: 630-985-1588
stampcollections@drbobstamps.com
www.drbobfriedmanstamps.com

Ducks

MICHAEL JAFFE
PO Box 61484
Vancouver, WA 98666
PH: 360-695-6161
PH: 800-782-6770
FAX: 360-695-1616
mjaffe@brookmanstamps.com
www.brookmanstamps.com

German Colonies

COLONIAL STAMP COMPANY
5757 Wilshire Blvd. PH #8
Los Angeles, CA 90036
PH: 323-933-9435
FAX: 323-939-9930
info@colonialstamps.com
www.colonialstamps.com

Germany

HENRY GITNER PHILATELISTS, INC.
PO Box 3077-S
Middletown, NY 10940
PH: 845-343-5151
PH: 800-947-8267
FAX: 845-343-0068
hgitner@hgitner.com
www.hgitner.com

New Issues

DAVIDSON'S STAMP SERVICE
Personalized Service since 1970
PO Box 36355
Indianapolis, IN 46236-0355
PH: 317-826-2620
ed-davidson@earthlink.net
www.newstampissues.com

Sri Lanka

COLONIAL STAMP COMPANY
5757 Wilshire Blvd. PH #8
Los Angeles, CA 90036
PH: 323-933-9435
FAX: 323-939-9930
info@colonialstamps.com
www.colonialstamps.com

Stamp Stores

California

COLONIAL STAMP COMPANY
5757 Wilshire Blvd. PH #8
Los Angeles, CA 90036
PH: 323-933-9435
FAX: 323-939-9930
info@colonialstamps.com
www.colonialstamps.com

Delaware

DUTCH COUNTRY AUCTIONS
The Stamp Center
4115 Concord Pike
Wilmington, DE 19803
PH: 302-478-8740
FAX: 302-478-8779
auctions@dutchcountryauctions.com
www.dutchcountryauctions.com

Florida

DR. ROBERT FRIEDMAN & SONS STAMP & COIN BUYING CENTER
PH: 800-588-8100
FAX: 630-985-1588
stampcollections@drbobstamps.com
www.drbobfriedmanstamps.com

Illinois

DR. ROBERT FRIEDMAN & SONS STAMP & COIN BUYING CENTER
2029 W. 75th St.
Woodridge, IL 60517
PH: 800-588-8100
FAX: 630-985-1588
stampcollections@drbobstamps.com
www.drbobfriedmanstamps.com

Missouri

DAVID SEMSROTT STAMPS
11239 Manchester Rd.
St. Louis Kirkwood, MO 63122
PH: 314-984-8361
fixodine@sbcglobal.net
www.DavidSemsrott.com

New Jersey

BERGEN STAMPS & COLLECTIBLES
306 Queen Anne Rd.
Teaneck, NJ 07666
PH: 201-836-8987
bergenstamps@gmail.com

TRENTON STAMP & COIN
Thomas DeLuca
Store: Forest Glen Plaza
1800 Highway #33, Suite 103
Hamilton Square, NJ 08690
Mail: PO Box 8574
Trenton, NJ 08650
PH: 609-584-8100
FAX: 609-587-8664
TOMD4TSC@aol.com
www.trentonstampandcoin.com

Stamp Stores

New York

CK STAMPS
42-14 Union St. # 2A
Flushing, NY 11355
PH: 917-667-6641
ckstampsllc@yahoo.com

Ohio

HILLTOP STAMP SERVICE
Richard A. Peterson
PO Box 626
Wooster, OH 44691
PH: 330-262-8907 (0)
PH: 330-201-1377 (H)
hilltopstamps@sssnet.com
www.hilltopstamps.com

Straits Settlements

COLONIAL STAMP COMPANY
5757 Wilshire Blvd. PH #8
Los Angeles, CA 90036
PH: 323-933-9435
FAX: 323-939-9930
info@colonialstamps.com
www.colonialstamps.com

Supplies

BROOKLYN GALLERY COIN & STAMP, INC.
8725 4th Ave.
Brooklyn, NY 11209
PH: 718-745-5701
FAX: 718-745-2775
info@brooklyngallery.com
www.brooklyngallery.com

Thailand

THE STAMP ACT
PO Box 1136
Belmont, CA 94002
PH: 650-703-2342
thestampact@sbcglobal.net

Togo

COLONIAL STAMP COMPANY
5757 Wilshire Blvd. PH #8
Los Angeles, CA 90036
PH: 323-933-9435
FAX: 323-939-9930
info@colonialstamps.com
www.colonialstamps.com

Tonga

COLONIAL STAMP COMPANY
5757 Wilshire Blvd. PH #8
Los Angeles, CA 90036
PH: 323-933-9435
FAX: 323-939-9930
info@colonialstamps.com
www.colonialstamps.com

Topicals

HENRY GITNER PHILATELISTS, INC.
PO Box 3077-S
Middletown, NY 10940
PH: 845-343-5151
PH: 800-947-8267
FAX: 845-343-0068
hgitner@hgitner.com
www.hgitner.com

Topicals

E. JOSEPH McCONNELL, INC.
PO Box 683
Monroe, NY 10949
PH: 845-783-9791
FAX: 845-782-0347
ejstamps@gmail.com
www.EJMcConnell.com

Topicals - Columbus

MR. COLUMBUS
PO Box 1492
Fennville, MI 49408
PH: 269-543-4755
David@MrColumbus1492.com
www.MrColumbus1492.com

Transvaal

COLONIAL STAMP COMPANY
5757 Wilshire Blvd. PH #8
Los Angeles, CA 90036
PH: 323-933-9435
FAX: 323-939-9930
info@colonialstamps.com
www.colonialstamps.com

Uganda

COLONIAL STAMP COMPANY
5757 Wilshire Blvd. PH #8
Los Angeles, CA 90036
PH: 323-933-9435
FAX: 323-939-9930
info@colonialstamps.com
www.colonialstamps.com

United Nations

BRUCE M. MOYER
Box 12031
Charlotte, NC 28220
PH: 908-237-6967
moyer@unstamps.com
www.unstamps.com

United States

ACS STAMP COMPANY
2914 W 135th Ave
Broomfield, Colorado 80020
303-841-8666
www.ACSStamp.com

BROOKMAN STAMP CO.
PO Box 90
Vancouver, WA 98666
PH: 360-695-1391
PH: 800-545-4871
FAX: 360-695-1616
info@brookmanstamps.com
www.brookmanstamps.com

U.S. Classics/Moderns

BARDO STAMPS
PO Box 7437
Buffalo Grove, IL 60089
PH: 847-634-2676
jfb7437@aol.com
www.bardostamps.com

U.S.-Collections Wanted

DUTCH COUNTRY AUCTIONS
The Stamp Center
4115 Concord Pike
Wilmington, DE 19803
PH: 302-478-8740
FAX: 302-478-8779
auctions@dutchcountryauctions.com
www.dutchcountryauctions.com

U.S.-Collections Wanted

DR. ROBERT FRIEDMAN & SONS STAMP & COIN BUYING CENTER
2029 W. 75th St.
Woodridge, IL 60517
PH: 800-588-8100
FAX: 630-985-1588
stampcollections@drbobstamps.com
www.drbobfriedmanstamps.com

Want Lists - British Empire 1840-1935 German Cols./Offices

COLONIAL STAMP COMPANY
5757 Wilshire Blvd. PH #8
Los Angeles, CA 90036
PH: 323-933-9435
FAX: 323-939-9930
info@colonialstamps.com
www.colonialstamps.com

Wanted - Worldwide Collections

DUTCH COUNTRY AUCTIONS
The Stamp Center
4115 Concord Pike
Wilmington, DE 19803
PH: 302-478-8740
FAX: 302-478-8779
auctions@dutchcountryauctions.com
www.dutchcountryauctions.com

Websites

ACS STAMP COMPANY
2914 W 135th Ave
Broomfield, Colorado 80020
303-841-8666
www.ACSStamp.com

Worldwide

GUILLERMO JALIL
Maipu 466, local 4
1006 Buenos Aires
Argentina
guillermo@jalilstamps.com
philatino@philatino.com
www.philatino.com (worldwide stamp auctions)
www.jalilstamps.com (direct sale, worldwide stamps)

Worldwide-Collections

DR. ROBERT FRIEDMAN & SONS STAMP & COIN BUYING CENTER
2029 W. 75th St.
Woodridge, IL 60517
PH: 800-588-8100
FAX: 630-985-1588
stampcollections@drbobstamps.com
www.drbobfriedmanstamps.com

Worldwide